The National Hockey League

Official Guide & Record Book

2009

HOCKEY FIGHTS CANCER

THE NATIONAL HOCKEY LEAGUE
Official Guide & Record Book/2009

TERMS & CONDITIONS FOR USING THE DATA CONTAINED IN THIS BOOK

ATTENTION: PLEASE READ THIS DOCUMENT CAREFULLY BEFORE USING THIS BOOK (THE "BOOK") AND/OR THE DATA IT CONTAINS (THE "DATA"). INDIVIDUALS OR ENTITIES USING THE DATA ("END USERS") AGREE TO BE BOUND BY THE TERMS OF THIS LICENSE. IF YOU DO NOT AGREE TO THE TERMS OF THIS LICENSE, DO NOT USE THE DATA AND PROMPTLY RETURN THE UNUSED BOOK AND PROOF OF PAYMENT TO THE FOLLOWING ADDRESS FOR A REFUND:

Dan Diamond & Associates, Inc.
194 Dovercourt Road, Toronto, Ontario, M6J 3C8
dda.nhl@sympatico.ca.

Dan Diamond & Associates, Inc. (the "Publisher") owns, and retains ownership of, the Data. The Publisher reserves any right not expressly granted to End Users.

1. License. End-Users are granted a limited, non-exclusive license to do only the following, subject to the restrictions set out in Section 2 below:
   (a) End-Users may use the Data for personal, non-commercial purposes.
   (b) End-Users may reproduce individual player records, tables and data panels in connection with bona fide private study and research.
   (c) End-Users who are journalists may reproduce individual player records, tables and data panels for use by the broadcast and print media.
2. Restrictions. End-Users may NOT reproduce the Data, in whole or in part, in any form or by any means, electronic or mechanical, including photocopying, recording, or by any information storage and retrieval system now known or hereafter invented, without written permission from the Publisher. End-Users may NOT sublicense, assign, or distribute (via the World Wide Web or otherwise) copies of the Data, in whole or in part, to others. END-USERS MAY NOT MODIFY, ADAPT, TRANSLATE, RENT, LEASE, LOAN, RESELL FOR PROFIT, DISTRIBUTE, OR OTHERWISE ASSIGN OR TRANSFER THE DATA, OR CREATE DERIVATIVE WORKS BASED UPON THE DATA OR ANY PART THEREOF, EXCEPT AS PROVIDED ABOVE.
3. Commercial Users. Commercial users (such as sports reference and sports gaming websites) may obtain a license to use customized Data upon payment of a reasonable fee. Please contact the Publisher at the address provided above.
4. Termination. This License is effective until terminated. This License will terminate immediately without notice from the Publisher if the End User fails to comply with any of its provisions. Upon termination End Users must destroy the Data and all copies thereof.
5. General. This License will be governed by and construed in accordance with the laws of the province of Ontario and the laws of Canada applicable therein, and shall inure to the benefit of the Publisher and End-Users and their successors, assigns and legal representatives. If any provision of this License is held by a court of competent jurisdiction to be invalid or unenforceable to any extent under applicable law, that provision will be enforced to the maximum extent permissible and the remaining provisions of this License will remain in full force and effect. Any notices or other communications to be sent to the Publishers must be mailed first class, postage prepaid, to the address provided above. This Agreement constitutes the entire agreement between the parties with respect to the subject matter hereof, and all prior proposals, agreements, representations, statements and undertakings are hereby expressly cancelled and superseded. This Agreement may not be changed or amended except by a written instrument executed by a duly authorized officer of the Publisher.
6. Acknowledgment. BY USING THE DATA, THE END-USER ACKNOWLEDGES THAT IT HAS READ THIS LICENSE, UNDERSTANDS IT, AND AGREES TO BE BOUND BY ITS TERMS AND CONDITIONS. Should you have any questions concerning this License, contact the Publisher at the address provided above.

Compiled by the NHL Public Relations Department and the 30 NHL Club Public Relations Directors.

Published in Canada by: Dan Diamond and Associates, Inc., 194 Dovercourt Road, Toronto, Ontario M6J 3C8 Canada
ISBN in Canada 978-1-894801-14-0

Published in the United States by: Triumph Books, 542 South Dearborn Street, Chicago, Illinois 60605
ISBN in USA 978-1-60078-148-3

Staff

For the NHL: Dave McCarthy; Supervising Editor: Greg Inglis; Statistician: Benny Ercolani;
Editorial Staff: David Keon, Dave Baker, Mark Fischel, Jen Raimondi, Jackie Rinaldi, Kelley Rosset, Julie Young.

Senior Managing Editor: Ralph Dinger
Production Editors: John Pasternak, Alex Dubiel, Becky Gowing
Publisher: Dan Diamond
Associate Managing Editor: Paul Bontje
Photo Editor: Eric Zweig

Data Management and Typesetting: Caledon Data Management, Eden, Ontario
Film Output and Scanning: Embassy Graphics, Toronto, Ontario
Printing: Sunrise Consulting Inc., Port Perry, Ontario; Webcom, Toronto, Ontario
Production Management: Dan Diamond and Associates, Inc., Toronto, Ontario
Contributors and Photo Credits: see page 655

Distribution

Trade sales and distribution in Canada by:
North 49 Books, 35 Prince Andrew Drive, Toronto, Ontario M3C 2H2 416/449-4000; Fax 416/449-9924
Dan Diamond and Associates, Inc., Toronto 416/531-6535; Fax 416/531-3939 dda.nhl@sympatico.ca www.nhlofficialguide.com

Trade sales and distribution in the United States by:
Triumph Books, 542 South Dearborn Street, Chicago, Illinois 60605 312/939-3330; Fax 312/663-3557

International representatives:
Barkers Worldwide Publications, Unit 6/7 The Elms Centre, Glaziers Lane, Normandy, Guildford, Surrey GU3 2DF England
Tel 011/441/483/811-971; Fax 011/441/483/811-972 sales@bwpu.demon.co.uk www.bwpu.demon.co.uk

The National Hockey League
1185 Avenue of the Americas, 14th Floor, New York, New York 10036
1800 McGill College Ave., Suite 2600, Montreal, Quebec H3A 3J6
50 Bay Street, 11th Floor, Toronto, Ontario M5J 2X8

Table of Contents

Table of Contents *continued*

Introduction

WELCOME TO THE 77TH EDITION OF *THE NATIONAL HOCKEY LEAGUE OFFICIAL GUIDE & RECORD BOOK*, the definitive statistical record of the NHL. As always, if it has happened in this League, or if it's about to happen, it's in the *Guide*. The 2008 Stanley Cup-champion Detroit Red Wings are a case in point. Their success in the regular season and playoffs ripples through the pages of the *Guide & Record Book*. The club's careful defense and creative offense was built through every one of the player sources available to NHL general managers. Free agency was used to acquire Dallas Drake and Brian Rafalski in 2007 and, building for the upcoming season, Marian Hossa in 2008. (2008 Free Agent Signing Register is found on page 650; Drake's, Rafalski's and Hossa's career statistical panels are on pages 389, 509 and 425 respectively). A late-season trade brought defenseman Brad Stuart to the Red Wings for the last nine games of the regular season and the playoffs. (A 2007-08 Trade Register is found on page 652; Stuart's panel is on 545.) The core of the Red Wings has been built through the NHL Entry Draft. The *Guide & Record Book*'s comprehensive Entry Draft section, beginning on page 212, reveals that Detroit selected Pavel Datsyuk 171st overall in 1998; Henrik Zetterberg 210th in 1999; Niklas Kronwall 29th in 2000; Jiri Hudler 58th and Valterri Filppula 95th in 2002 and Johan Franzen 97th in 2004. The four-page Red Wings club section, beginning on page 55, lists every Detroit draft choice for the last 15 seasons, in addition to club records, all-time coaching, captains' and general managers' histories, retired numbers and all-time records vs. other clubs. Every NHL club has a similar section. Listed alphabetically, these begin with Anaheim Ducks on page 15 and conclude with the Washington Capitals on page 131. Key off-season signings and acquisitions are found in the top left corner of the first page of each club.

The Red Wings' success is also apparent in the *Guide & Record Book*'s listing of NHL trophies and awards beginning on page 204. Nicklas Lidstrom won the Norris Trophy as the NHL's top defenseman for the sixth time in seven seasons (page 204). Pavel Datsyuk won the Lady Byng Trophy for gentlemanly play and the Frank Selke Trophy as the NHL's top defensive foward, while Chris Osgood and Dominik Hasek shared the William Jennings Trophy as goaltenders for the team allowing the fewest goals-against and Henrik Zetterberg won the Conn Smythe Trophy as playoff MVP (all on page 205). The Red Wings' first-overall regular-season finish resulted in their winning the Presidents' Trophy (page 207). Detroit's magical year even extended to a double hall of fame induction for retired Red Wing forward Igor Larionov. This international superstar and double Olympic gold medalist became an honored member of the Hockey Hall of Fame (page 233) and the IIHF Hall of Fame (page 236) in 2008. All in all, a brilliant and well-played championship season. Congratulations, Red Wings.

New in this year's edition is an NHL Critical Dates Calendar for 2008-09 (page 6). Listed are special events like this season's Winter Classic on New Year's Day 2009 in Chicago as well as important dates such as the trade deadline on March 3. Other improvements throughout the *Guide* include a revamp of the list of NHL On-Ice Officials on page 8. Each referee's and linesman's age in now listed, matching the revised player personnel roster format that made its debut last year. In the Club section that begins on page 15, each club's list of drafted players from 2008 to 1994 now uses boldface to highlight those who have played in the NHL. In the Entry Draft section (pages 213 to 216), changes have been made to the tables that present junior, college, high school and international selections by club. To facilitate finding individual clubs, these tables are now presented alphabetically rather than in descending numerical order. As well, the three All-Star Team tables on page 225 have been reformatted for greater clarity. Totals are now easier to find and the Position Leaders in All-Star Selections table now includes the first and last seasons of each player's career.

For 2007-08, two players—Washington's Alex Ovechkin and Pittsburgh's Evgeni Malkin—reached the 100-point plateau. Three players—Ovechkin, Atlanta's Ilya Kovalchuk and Calgary's Jarome Iginla—scored 50-or-more goals. Ovechkin set a new single-season record for goals by a left winger with 65, eclipsing Luc Robitaille's mark of 63 in 1992-93. An all-time list of 50-goal and 100-point seasons begins on page 196. Detailed statistics for 2007-08 begin on page 135. Individual NHL Records begin on page 166, with special attention paid to the history of the League's all-time scoring marks on page 164.

This was also the third season of the shootout in the NHL, the result of which is that games can no longer end with the score tied. The shootout again proved popular with fans and created some surprising category leaders. Patrick Kane of the Chicago Blackhawks and Joe Pavelski of the St. Louis Blues led the NHL with seven shootout goals, while the Edmonton Oilers won 15 of 19 shootout games, led by goaltender Mathieu Garon who was 10-0 in shootout games, stopping 30 of 32 shots faced. Complete team and individual shootout statistics are found on page 143. Updated single-season and all-time shootout records are found in the Regular-Season Record Book. Team shootout records are found on page 163. Individual shootout scoring records are on page 169; goaltending shootout records are on page 176.

As always in the *NHL Guide & Record Book*, every one of the more than 6,000 players who have appeared in an NHL game, plus more than 1,000 prospects who have yet to do so, are in this book, either in the regular-season or playoff Record Books (pages 166 and 240), Hall of Fame section, Award Winners (209), All-Star Teams (226), Prospect Register (273), Active Player Register (344), Goaltender Register (579) or Retired Players Index (604). A special tribute to the 2008 inductees to the Hockey Hall of Fame is found on page 649.

A key to the abbreviations and symbols used in individual player and goaltender data panels, along with useful information on how to use the Registers, is found on page 272. Late additions are found on page 603 and each NHL club's minor-pro affiliates are found on page 14. A list of league abbreviations used in the Prospect, Player and Goaltender Registers is found on page 654 and a useful table on page 216 breaks down U.S. and Canadian-born draftees by state or province of birth. Players from 19 states and all 10 provinces were drafted in 2008.

As always, our thanks to readers, correspondents and members of the media who take the time to comment on the *Guide & Record Book*. Thanks as well to the people working in the communications departments of the NHL's member clubs and to their counterparts in minor pro, junior, college and European hockey. This edition is the 25th published in this large format and the 25th produced by the current editorial team. Your help has been appreciated since we put a young Wayne Gretzky on the cover, hoisting his first Stanley Cup in 1984.

Best wishes for an enjoyable 2008-09 season.

ACCURACY REMAINS THE *GUIDE & RECORD BOOK*'S TOP PRIORITY.

We appreciate comments and clarification from our readers. Please direct these to:

- Ralph Dinger — Senior Managing Editor, 194 Dovercourt Road, Toronto, Ontario M6J 3C8. e-mail: ralph.dda@sympatico.ca.
- Greg Inglis — 1185 Avenue of the Americas, New York, New York 10036 . . . or . . .
- David Keon — 50 Bay Street, 11th Floor, Toronto, Ontario, M5J 2X8

Your involvement makes a better book.

NATIONAL HOCKEY LEAGUE

New York, 1185 Avenue of the Americas, New York, NY 10036,
212/789-2000, Fax: 212/789-2020, PR Fax: 212/789-2080

Montréal, 1800 McGill College Avenue, Suite 2600, Montréal, Québec, H3A 3J6
514/841-9220, Fax: 514/841-1070

Toronto, 50 Bay Street, 11th Floor, Toronto, Ontario, M5J 2X8
416/359-7900, Fax: 416/981-2779

Executive

Commissioner .... Gary B. Bettman
Deputy Commissioner .... William Daly
Chief Operating Officer .... John Collins
Senior Executive Vice President of Hockey Operations .... Colin Campbell

NHL Critical Dates 2008-09

September

- 12 Opening Day of Rookie camp
- 16 Opening Day of NHL training camp for NYR, OTT, PIT, TB
- 19 Opening Day of NHL training camp
- 20 Pre-season schedule begins
- 23 Kraft Hockeyville Game, Roberval, QC (Buffalo Sabres vs. Montreal Canadiens)

October

- 1 Hockey Fights Cancer Awareness Month
- 4-5 NHL Premiere – Stockholm 2008 (Ottawa Senators vs. Pittsburgh Penguins)
- 4-5 NHL Premiere – Prague 2008 (New York Rangers, vs. Tampa Bay Lightning)
- 9 **91st NHL Regular Season begins** (North American games)
- 22 Lester Patrick Award luncheon (St. Paul, MN)

November

- 8 Hockey Hall of Fame Game (Montreal Canadiens at Toronto Maple Leafs)
- 10 Hockey Hall of Fame Induction Ceremony (Toronto, ON) Inductees: Glenn Anderson, Igor Larionov (Player category), Ed Chynoweth (Builder category), Ray Scapinello (Referee/Linesman category)

December

- 1 Signing deadline for Group 2 free agents
- 19-27 Holiday Roster Freeze in effect. For all players on an NHL active roster, injured reserve, or players with non-roster and injured non-roster status as of midnight, local time, December 19, a roster freeze shall apply through midnight local time December 27, with respect to waivers, trades and loans, subject to the exceptions provided for in CBA Article 16.10.
- 24-25 No scheduled practices (dressing rooms closed)
- 26 – Jan.5 IIHF World U20 Championship (Ottawa, ON)

January

- 1 NHL Winter Classic 2009, Wrigley Field, Chicago (Detroit Red Wings at Chicago Blackhawks)
- 14 Home Hardware CHL/NHL Top Prospects Game (Oshawa, ON)
- 18 NHL on NBC (game of the week coverage begins)
- 22-26 All-Star break (no games played)
- 24 NHL SuperSkills Competition (Bell Centre, Montreal, QC)
- 25 57th NHL All-Star Game (Bell Centre)

February

- 13-15 Hockey Weekend Across America (USA Hockey)
- 21 CBC's Hockey Day in Canada (hosted from Campbellton, NB)

March

- 3 Trade deadline (3:00 p.m. ET)

April

- 9-11 NCAA Frozen Four (Verizon Center, Washington, DC)
- 9-19 IIHF U18 World Championship (Fargo, ND & Moorhead, MN)
- 12 Last day of 2008-09 regular season
- 15 Stanley Cup Playoffs begin
- 24 – May 10 IIHF World Championship (Berne & Zurich-Kloten, Switzerland)

May

- 25-30 NHL Combine for Draft-eligible players (Toronto)

June

- 15 Last possible day for 2009 Stanley Cup Final
- TBA Deadline for first club-elected salary arbitration (the later of June 15 or 48 hours after the conclusion of the Stanley Cup Final, 5:00 p.m. ET)
- TBA NHL Awards show
- 17 Deadline for first club-elected salary arbitration (5:00 p.m. ET)
- 25 NHL Entry Draft Media Day – Top Prospects Media Lunch & Clinic (Montreal)
- 26 NHL Entry Draft (Bell Centre, Montreal) – first round
- 27 NHL Entry Draft (Bell Centre) – rounds 2-7

July

- 1 Free Agency period begins
- 5 Deadline for player-elected salary arbitration (5:00 p.m. ET)
- 6 Deadline for club-elected salary arbitration (5:00 p.m. ET)
- 10 Deadline for eligible players to elect Group 5 free agency (5:00 p.m. ET)
- 20 – Aug. 4 Salary arbitration hearings held

August

- 6 Deadline for salary arbitration decisions to be rendered

BOARD OF GOVERNORS

CHAIRMAN OF THE BOARD – JEREMY M. JACOBS

VICE CHAIR – TOM HICKS

Anaheim Ducks

Michael Schulman........Governor
Brian Burke........Alternate Governor
Tim Ryan........Alternate Governor

Atlanta Thrashers

Bruce Levenson........Governor
Don Waddell........Alternate Governor
J. Rutherford Seydel, II........Alternate Governor
Ed Peskowitz........Alternate Governor

Boston Bruins

Jeremy M. Jacobs........Governor
Charles Jacobs........Alternate Governor
Jeremy Jacobs, Jr........Alternate Governor
Louis Jacobs........Alternate Governor
Harry J. Sinden........Alternate Governor
Peter Chiarelli........Alternate Governor
Cam Neely........Alternate Governor

Buffalo Sabres

B. Thomas Golisano........Governor
Lawrence Quinn........Alternate Governor
Daniel J. DiPofi........Alternate Governor
Darcy Regier........Alternate Governor

Calgary Flames

Harley N. Hotchkiss........Governor
N. Murray Edwards........Alternate Governor
Ken King........Alternate Governor
Alvin Libin........Alternate Governor
Darryl Sutter........Alternate Governor

Carolina Hurricanes

Peter Karmanos, Jr........Governor
Jim Rutherford........Alternate Governor
Michael Amendola........Alternate Governor

Chicago Blackhawks

W. Rockwell Wirtz........Governor
Robert J. Pulford........Alternate Governor
John A. Ziegler, Jr........Alternate Governor
John McDonough........Alternate Governor

Colorado Avalanche

Stan Kroenke........Governor
Pierre Lacroix........Alternate Governor
Paul Andrews........Alternate Governor
Francois Giguere........Alternate Governor

Columbus Blue Jackets

John P. McConnell........Governor
Mike Priest........Alternate Governor
Scott Howson........Alternate Governor

Dallas Stars

Tom Hicks........Governor
Jeffrey Cogen........Alternate Governor
Tom Hicks, Jr........Alternate Governor

Detroit Red Wings

Michael Ilitch........Governor
Jim Devellano........Alternate Governor
Ken Holland........Alternate Governor
Christopher Ilitch........Alternate Governor
Steve Yzerman........Alternate Governor
Rob Carr........Alternate Governor

Edmonton Oilers

Daryl Katz........Governor
Cal Nichols........Alternate Governor
Patrick LaForge........Alternate Governor
Kevin Lowe........Alternate Governor

Florida Panthers

Alan Cohen........Governor
William A. Torrey........Alternate Governor
Michael Yormark........Alternate Governor
Jacques Martin........Alternate Governor
Cliff Viner........Alternate Governor

Los Angeles Kings

Timothy J. Leiweke........Governor
Philip F. Anschutz........Alternate Governor
Christian Anschutz........Alternate Governor
Luc Robitaille........Alternate Governor

Minnesota Wild

Craig Leopold........Governor
Phil Falcone........Alternate Governor
Doug Risebrough........Alternate Governor
Jac Sperling........Alternate Governor

Montréal Canadiens

George Gillett, Jr........Governor
Pierre Boivin........Alternate Governor
Jeff Joyce........Alternate Governor
Fred Steer........Alternate Governor
Foster Gillett........Alternate Governor
Bob Gainey........Alternate Governor

Nashville Predators

David Freeman........Governor
Herbert Fritch........Alternate Governor
Ed Lang........Alternate Governor
David Poile........Alternate Governor

New Jersey Devils

Lou Lamoriello........Governor
Jeff Vanderbeek........Alternate Governor
Michael Gilfillan........Alternate Governor

New York Islanders

Charles Wang........Governor
Roy Reichbach........Alternate Governor
Arthur J. McCarthy........Alternate Governor
Michael J. Picker........Alternate Governor
Garth Snow........Alternate Governor
Chris Dey........Alternate Governor

New York Rangers

James L. Dolan........Governor
Steve Mills........Alternate Governor
Glen Sather........Alternate Governor
Hank Ratner........Alternate Governor

Ottawa Senators

Eugene Melnyk........Governor
Roy Mlakar........Alternate Governor
Sheldon Plener........Alternate Governor

Philadelphia Flyers

Edward M. Snider........Governor
Philip I. Weinberg........Alternate Governor
Peter Luukko........Alternate Governor
Paul Holmgren........Alternate Governor

Phoenix Coyotes

Jeff Shumway........Governor
Wayne Gretzky........Alternate Governor
Doug Moss........Alternate Governor
Don Maloney........Alternate Governor

Pittsburgh Penguins

Ken Sawyer........Governor
Ronald Burkle........Alternate Governor
Anthony Liberati........Alternate Governor
Ray Shero........Alternate Governor
David Morehouse........Alternate Governor
Mario Lemieux........Alternate Governor

St. Louis Blues

Dave Checketts........Governor
Kenneth Munoz........Alternate Governor
John Davidson........Alternate Governor
Larry Pleau........Alternate Governor
Michael McCarthy........Alternate Governor

San Jose Sharks

Greg Jamison........Governor
Kevin Compton........Alternate Governor
Doug Wilson........Alternate Governor

Tampa Bay Lightning

Oren Koules........Governor
Len Barrie........Alternate Governor

Toronto Maple Leafs

Larry Tanenbaum........Governor
Richard A. Peddie........Alternate Governor
Dale Lastman........Alternate Governor
Dean Metcalf........Alternate Governor

Vancouver Canucks

Francesco Aquilini........Governor
Chris Zimmerman........Alternate Governor
Paolo Aquilini........Alternate Governor
Roberto Aquilini........Alternate Governor
Mike Gillis........Alternate Governor

Washington Capitals

Richard M. Patrick........Governor
Ted Leonsis........Alternate Governor
George McPhee........Alternate Governor

Commissioner and League Presidents

Gary B. Bettman

Gary B. Bettman took office as the NHL's first Commissioner on February 1, 1993. Since the League was formed in 1917, there have been five League Presidents.

NHL President	Years in Office
Frank Calder	1917-1943
Mervyn "Red" Dutton	1943-1946
Clarence Campbell	1946-1977
John A. Ziegler, Jr.	1977-1992
Gil Stein	1992-1993

Hockey Hall of Fame

Brookfield Place
30 Yonge Street
Toronto, Ontario M5E 1X8
Phone: 416/360-7735
Executive Fax: 416/360-1501
Resource Centre Fax: 416/360-1316
www.hhof.com

William C. Hay – Chairman and Chief Executive Officer
Jeff Denomme – President, C.O.O. and Treasurer
Craig Baines – Vice President, Operations
Peter Jagla – Vice President, Marketing
Phil Pritchard – Vice President, Resource Centre and Curator
Ron Ellis – Director, Public Affairs and Assistant to the President
Craig Campbell – Manager, Photography, Archives and Sales
Kelly Massé – Manager, Corporate & Media Relations
Steve Ozimec – Manager, Special Events & Hospitality
Jackie Schwartz – Manager, Marketing & Promotions
Matt Manor and Dave Sanford – Photographers

National Hockey League Players' Association

20 Bay Street, Suite 1700
Toronto, Ontario M5J 2N8
Phone: 416/313-2300
Fax: 416/313-2301
www.nhlpa.com

Paul Kelly – Executive Director
Ian Penny – General Counsel
Eric Lindros – Ombudsman
Mike Ouellet – Chief of Business Affairs
Glenn Healy – Director, Player Affairs
Roland Lee – Associate Counsel, Labour
Matt Nussbaum – Associate Counsel, Labour
Roman Stoykewych – Associate Counsel, Labour
Adam Larry – Associate Counsel, Licensing
Tyler Currie – Director, International Affairs
Kim Murdoch – Director, Player Insurance & Pensions
Richard Smit – Director, Finance & HRR
Devin Smith – Director, Marketing & Community Relations
Jonathan Weatherdon – Director, Communications

NHL On-Ice Officials

Total NHL Games and 2007-08 Games columns count regular-season games only.

Referees

#	Name	Birthplace	*Age	First NHL Game	Total NHL Games	2007-08 Games
15	Stephane Auger	Montreal, Que.	37	Apr. 1/00	456	72
44	David Banfield	Halifax, N.S.	29	Mar. 17/08	3	3
41	Chris Ciamaga	Cheektowaga, NY	31	Mar. 22/08	1	1
10	Paul Devorski	Guelph, Ont.	50	Oct. 14/89	1114	73
19	Gord Dwyer	Halifax, N.S.	31	Nov. 19/05	168	72
2	Kerry Fraser	Sarnia, Ont.	56	Apr. 6/75	1755	73
27	Eric Furlatt	Cap de la Madelaine, Que.	36	Oct. 8/01	386	73
30	Mike Hasenfratz	Regina, Sask.	42	Oct. 21/00	468	72
49	Ghislain Hebert	Dieppe, N.B.	37	...	...	...
8	Dave Jackson	Montreal, Que.	43	Dec. 23/90	973	73
25	Marc Joannette	Verdun, Que.	39	Oct. 27/99	509	74
18	Greg Kimmerly	Toronto, Ont.	43	Nov. 30/96	596	73
12	Don Koharski	Halifax, N.S.	52	Oct. 14/77	[1] 1653	73
32	Tom Kowal	Vernon, B.C.	40	Oct. 29/99	394	73
40	Steve Kozari	Penticton, B.C.	35	Oct. 15/05	120	74
14	Dennis LaRue	Savannah, GA	49	Mar. 26/91	788	73
48	Frederick L'Ecuyer	Trois-Rivieres, Que.	31	Oct. 11/07	12	12
28	Chris Lee	Saint John, N.B.	38	Apr. 2/00	368	74
3	Mike Leggo	North Bay, Ont.	43	Mar. 3/98	586	72
6	Dan Marouelli	Edmonton, Alta.	53	Nov. 2/84	1484	73
26	Rob Martell	Winnipeg, Man.	44	Mar. 14/84	[2] 482	73
4	Wes McCauley	Georgetown, Ont.	36	Jan. 20/03	243	73
7	Bill McCreary	Guelph, Ont.	52	Nov. 3/84	1524	73
34	Brad Meier	Dayton, OH	41	Oct. 23/99	510	73
36	Dean Morton	Peterborough, Ont.	40	Nov. 11/00	71	17
13	Dan O'Halloran	Essex, Ont.	44	Oct. 14/95	665	73
42	Dan O'Rourke	Calgary, Alta.	36	Oct. 2/99	[3] 242	71
20	Tim Peel	Toronto, Ont.	42	Oct. 21/99	519	73
43	Brian Pochmara	Detroit, MI	31	Dec. 23/05	50	18
33	Kevin Pollock	Kincardine, Ont.	38	Mar. 28/00	516	74
37	Kyle Rehman	Stettler, Alta.	40	Jan. 22/08	3	3
5	Chris Rooney	Boston, MA	44	Nov. 22/00	412	73
38	Francois St. Laurent	Greenfield Park, Que.	31	Nov. 10/05	48	20
45	Justin St. Pierre	Dolbeau, Que.	46	Nov. 9/05	172	73
16	Rob Shick	Port Alberni, B.C.	50	Apr. 6/86	1271	59
11	Kelly Sutherland	Victoria, B.C.	37	Dec. 19/00	452	73
21	Don Van Massenhoven	Parkhill, Ont.	48	Nov. 11/93	888	73
29	Ian Walsh	Philadelphia, PA	36	Oct. 14/00	354	74
23	Brad Watson	Regina, Sask.	47	Feb. 5/94	615	73

[1] plus 163 games as a linesman. [2] plus 1 game as a linesman. [3] plus 120 games as a linesman.

Linesmen

#	Name	Birthplace	*Age	First NHL Game	Total NHL Games	2007-08 Games
75	Derek Amell	Port Colborne, Ont.	40	Oct. 13/97	649	69
59	Steve Barton	Ottawa, Ont.	36	Nov. 1/00	431	73
96	David Brisebois	Sudbury, Ont.	32	Oct. 11/99	387	73
74	Lonnie Cameron	Victoria, B.C.	44	Oct. 5/96	769	72
67	Pierre Champoux	Ville St-Pierre, Que.	45	Oct. 8/88	1220	69
50	Scott Cherrey	Drayton, Ont.	32	Oct. 6/07	46	46
76	Michel Cormier	Trois-Rivieres, Que.	34	Oct. 10/03	292	73
88	Mike Cvik	Calgary, Alta.	46	Oct. 8/87	1351	72
54	Greg Devorski	Guelph, Ont.	39	Oct. 9/93	931	73
68	Scott Driscoll	Seaforth, Ont.	40	Oct. 10/92	1003	73
66	Darren Gibbs	Edmonton, Alta.	42	Oct. 1/97	621	74
82	Ryan Galloway	Winnipeg, Man.	36	Oct. 17/02	315	72
91	Don Henderson	Calgary, Alta.	40	Mar. 10/95	755	73
55	Shane Heyer	Summerland, B.C.	44	Oct. 1/99	[4] 932	73
71	Brad Kovachik	Woodstock, Ont.	37	Oct. 10/96	734	72
86	Brad Lazarowich	Vancouver, B.C.	46	Oct. 9/86	1445	71
78	Brian Mach	Little Falls, MN	34	Oct. 7/00	495	73
90	Andy McElman	Chicago Heights, IL	47	Oct. 7/93	937	72
89	Steve Miller	Stratford, Ont.	36	Oct. 11/00	482	72
97	Jean Morin	Sorel, Que.	45	Oct. 5/91	1046	73
93	Brian Murphy	Dover, NH	43	Oct. 7/88	[5] 1147	73
95	Jonny Murray	Beauport, Que.	34	Oct. 7/00	498	74
70	Derek Nansen	Ottawa, Ont.	36	Oct. 11/02	354	73
80	Thor Nelson	Westminster, CA	40	Feb. 16/95	653	73
77	Tim Nowak	Buffalo, NY	41	Oct. 8/93	938	74
79	Mark Paré	Windsor, Ont.	51	Oct. 11/79	2033	72
65	Pierre Racicot	Verdun, Que.	41	Oct. 12/93	966	73
73	Vaughan Rody	Winnipeg, Man.	39	Oct. 8/00	469	72
52	Dan Schachte	Madison, WI	50	Oct. 6/82	1753	71
61	Lyle Seitz	Brooks, Alta.	39	Oct. 6/92	[6] 593	66
84	Anthony Sericolo	Troy, NY	40	Oct. 21/98	590	74
57	Jay Sharrers	Jamaica, West Indies	41	Oct. 6/90	[7] 859	71
92	Mark Shewchyk	Hamilton, Ont.	33	Oct. 9/03	290	73
56	Mark Wheler	North Battleford, Sask.	43	Oct. 10/92	1031	72

[4] plus 386 games as a referee. [5] plus 88 games as a referee. [6] plus 10 games as a referee. [7] plus 136 games as a referee.

– Age at start of 2008-09 season

NHL History

1917 — National Hockey League organized November 26 in Montreal following suspension of operations by the National Hockey Association of Canada Limited (NHA). Montreal Canadiens, Montreal Wanderers, Ottawa Senators and Quebec Bulldogs attended founding meeting. Delegates decided to use NHA rules.

Toronto Arenas were later admitted as fifth team; Quebec decided not to operate during the first season. Quebec players allocated to remaining four teams.

Frank Calder elected president and secretary-treasurer.

First NHL games played December 19, with Toronto only arena with artificial ice. Clubs played 22-game split schedule.

1918 — Emergency meeting held January 3 due to destruction by fire of Montreal Arena which was home ice for both Canadiens and Wanderers.

Wanderers withdrew, reducing the NHL to three teams; Canadiens played remaining home games at 3,250-seat Jubilee rink.

Quebec franchise sold to P.J. Quinn of Toronto on October 18 on the condition that the team operate in Quebec City for 1918-19 season. Quinn did not attend the November League meeting and Quebec did not play in 1918-19.

1919-20 — NHL reactivated Quebec Bulldogs franchise. Former Quebec players returned to the club. New Mount Royal Arena became home of Canadiens. Toronto Arenas changed name to St. Patricks. Clubs played 24-game split schedule.

1920-21 — H.P. Thompson of Hamilton, Ontario made application for the purchase of an NHL franchise. Quebec franchise shifted to Hamilton with other NHL teams providing players to strengthen the club.

1921-22 — Split schedule abandoned. First and second place teams at the end of full schedule to play for championship.

1922-23 — Clubs agreed that players could not be sold or traded to clubs in any other league without first being offered to all other clubs in the NHL. In March, Foster Hewitt broadcasts radio's first hockey game.

1923-24 — Ottawa's new 10,000-seat arena opened. First U.S. franchise granted to Boston for following season.

Dr. Cecil Hart Trophy donated to NHL to be awarded to the player judged most useful to his team.

1924-25 — Canadian Arena Company of Montreal granted a franchise to operate Montreal Maroons. NHL now six team league with two clubs in Montreal. Inaugural game in new Montreal Forum played November 29, 1924 as Canadiens defeated Toronto 7-1. Forum was home rink for the Maroons, but no ice was available in the Canadiens arena November 29, resulting in a shift to the Forum.

Hamilton finished first in the standings, receiving a bye into the finals. But Hamilton players, demanding $200 each for additional games in the playoffs, went on strike. The NHL suspended all players, fining them $200 each. Stanley Cup finalist to be the winner of NHL semi-final between Toronto and Canadiens.

Prince of Wales and Lady Byng trophies donated to NHL.

Clubs played 30-game schedule.

1925-26 — Hamilton club dropped from NHL. Players signed by new New York Americans franchise. Pittsburgh Pirates granted franchise.

Clubs played 36-game schedule.

1926-27 — New York Rangers granted franchise May 15, 1926. Chicago Black Hawks and Detroit Cougars granted franchises September 25, 1926. NHL now ten-team league with an American and a Canadian Division.

Stanley Cup came under the control of NHL. In previous seasons, winners of the now-defunct Western or Pacific Coast leagues would play NHL champion in Cup finals.

Toronto franchise sold to a new company controlled by Hugh Aird and Conn Smythe. Name changed from St. Patricks to Maple Leafs.

Clubs played 44-game schedule.

The Montreal Canadiens donated the Vezina Trophy to be awarded to the team allowing the fewest goals-against in regular season play. The winning team would, in turn, present the trophy to the goaltender playing in the greatest number of games during the season.

1930-31 — Detroit franchise changed name from Cougars to Falcons. Pittsburgh transferred to Philadelphia for one season. Pirates changed name to Philadelphia Quakers. Trading deadline for teams set at February 15 of each year. NHL approved operation of farm teams by Rangers, Americans, Falcons and Bruins. Four-sided electric arena clock first demonstrated.

1931-32 — Philadelphia dropped out. Ottawa withdrew for one season. New Maple Leaf Gardens completed.

Clubs played 48-game schedule.

1932-33 — Detroit franchise changed name from Falcons to Red Wings. Franchise application received from St. Louis but refused because of additional travel costs. Ottawa team resumed play.

1933-34 — First All-Star Game played as a benefit for injured player Ace Bailey. Leafs defeated All-Stars 7-3 in Toronto.

1934-35 — Ottawa franchise transferred to St. Louis. Team called St. Louis Eagles and consisted largely of Ottawa's players.

1935-36 — Ottawa-St. Louis franchise terminated. Montreal Canadiens finished season with very poor record. To strengthen the club, NHL gave Canadiens first call on the services of all French-Canadian players for three seasons.

1937-38 — Second benefit All-Star game staged November 2 in Montreal in aid of the family of the late Canadiens star Howie Morenz.

Montreal Maroons withdrew from the NHL on June 22, 1938, leaving seven clubs in the League.

1938-39 — Expenses for each club regulated at $5 per man per day for meals and $2.50 per man per day for accommodation.

1939-40 — Benefit All-Star Game played October 29, 1939 in Montreal for the children of the late Albert (Babe) Siebert.

1940-41 — Ross-Tyer puck adopted as the official puck of the NHL. Early in the season it was apparent that this puck was too soft. The Spalding puck was adopted in its place.

On May 16, 1941, Arthur Ross, NHL governor from Boston, donated a perpetual trophy to be awarded annually to the player voted outstanding in the league. Due to wartime restrictions, the trophy was never awarded.

1941-42 — New York Americans changed name to Brooklyn Americans.

1942-43 — Brooklyn Americans withdrew from NHL, leaving six teams: Boston, Chicago, Detroit, Montreal, New York and Toronto. Playoff format saw first-place team play third-place team and second play fourth.

Clubs played 50-game schedule.

Frank Calder, president of the NHL since its inception, died in Montreal. Meryn "Red" Dutton, former manager of the New York Americans, became president. The NHL commissioned the Calder Memorial Trophy to be awarded to the League's outstanding rookie each year.

1945-46 — Philadelphia, Los Angeles and San Francisco applied for NHL franchises.

The Philadelphia Arena Company of the American Hockey League applied for an injunction to prevent the possible operation of an NHL franchise in that city.

1946-47 — Mervyn Dutton retired as president of the NHL prior to the start of the season. He was succeeded by Clarence S. Campbell.

Individual trophy winners and all-star team members to receive $1,000 awards.

Playoff guarantees for players introduced.

Clubs played 60-game schedule.

1947-48 — The first annual All-Star Game for the benefit of the players' pension fund was played when the All-Stars defeated the Stanley Cup Champion Toronto Maple Leafs 4-3 in Toronto on October 13, 1947.

Criteria for awarding Art Ross Trophy changed. Now awarded to top scorer. Elmer Lach was its first winner.

Philadelphia and Los Angeles franchise applications refused.

National Hockey League Pension Society formed.

1949-50 — Clubs played 70-game schedule.

First intra-league draft held April 30, 1950. Clubs allowed to protect 30 players. Remaining players available for $25,000 each.

1951-52 — Referees included in the League's pension plan.

1952-53 — In May of 1952, City of Cleveland applied for NHL franchise. Application denied. In March of 1953, the Cleveland Barons of the AHL challenged the NHL champions for the Stanley Cup. The NHL governors did not accept this challenge.

1953-54 — The James Norris Memorial Trophy presented to the NHL for annual presentation to the League's best defenseman.

Intra-league draft rules amended to allow teams to protect 18 skaters and two goaltenders, claiming price reduced to $15,000.

1954-55 — Each arena to operate an "out-of-town" scoreboard.

1956-57 — Referees and linesmen to wear shirts of black and white vertical stripes. Standardized signals for referees and linesmen introduced.

1960-61 — Canadian National Exhibition, City of Toronto and NHL reach agreement for the construction of a Hockey Hall of Fame on the CNE grounds. Hall opens on August 26, 1961.

1963-64 — Player development league established with clubs operated by NHL franchises located in Minneapolis, St. Paul, Indianapolis, Omaha and, beginning in 1964-65, Tulsa. First universal amateur draft took place. All players of qualifying age (17) unaffected by sponsorship of junior teams available to be drafted.

1964-65 — Conn Smythe Trophy presented to the NHL to be awarded annually to the outstanding player in the Stanley Cup playoffs.

Minimum age of players subject to amateur draft changed to 18.

1965-66 — NHL announced expansion plans for a second six-team division to begin play in 1967-68.

1966-67 — Fourteen applications for NHL franchises received.

Lester Patrick Trophy presented to the NHL to be awarded annually for outstanding service to hockey in the United States.

NHL sponsorship of junior teams ceased, making all players of qualifying age not already on NHL-sponsored lists eligible for the amateur draft.

1967-68 — Six new teams added: California Seals, Los Angeles Kings, Minnesota North Stars, Philadelphia Flyers, Pittsburgh Penguins, St. Louis Blues. New teams to play in West Division. Remaining six teams to play in East Division.

Minimum age of players subject to amateur draft changed to 20.

Clubs played 74-game schedule.

Clarence S. Campbell Trophy awarded to team finishing the regular season in first place in West Division.

California Seals change name to Oakland Seals on December 8, 1967.

1968-69 — Clubs played 76-game schedule.

Amateur draft expanded to cover any amateur player of qualifying age throughout the world.

1970-71 — Two new teams added: Buffalo Sabres and Vancouver Canucks. These teams joined East Division: Chicago switched to West Division. Oakland Seals change name to California Golden Seals prior to season.

Clubs played 78-game schedule.

1971-72 — Playoff format amended. In each division, first to play fourth; second to play third.

1972-73 — Soviet Nationals and Canadian NHL stars play eight-game pre-season series. Canadians win 4-3-1.

Two new teams added. Atlanta Flames join West Division; New York Islanders join East Division.

1974-75 — Two new teams added: Kansas City Scouts and Washington Capitals. Teams realigned into two nine-team conferences, the Prince of Wales made up of the Norris and Adams Divisions, and the Clarence Campbell made up of the Smythe and Patrick Divisions.

Clubs played 80-game schedule.

1976-77 — California franchise transferred to Cleveland. Team named Cleveland Barons. Kansas City franchise transferred to Denver. Team named Colorado Rockies.

1977-78 — Clarence S. Campbell retires as NHL president. Succeeded by John A. Ziegler, Jr.

1978-79 — Cleveland and Minnesota franchises merge, leaving NHL with 17 teams. Merged team placed in Adams Division, playing home games in Minnesota.

Minimum age of players subject to amateur draft changed to 19.

1979-80 — Four new teams added: Edmonton Oilers, Hartford Whalers, Quebec Nordiques and Winnipeg Jets.

Minimum age of players subject to entry draft changed to 18.

1980-81 — Atlanta franchise shifted to Calgary, retaining "Flames" name.

1981-82 — Teams realigned within existing divisions. New groupings based on geographical areas. Unbalanced schedule adopted.

1982-83 — Colorado Rockies franchise shifted to East Rutherford, New Jersey. Team named New Jersey Devils. Franchise moved to Patrick Division from Smythe; Winnipeg moved to Smythe Division from Norris.

NHL History — *continued*

1991-92 — San Jose Sharks added, making the NHL a 22-team league. NHL celebrates 75th Anniversary Season. The 1991-92 regular season suspended due to a players' strike on April 1, 1992. Play resumed April 12, 1992.

1992-93 — Gil Stein named NHL president (October, 1992). Gary Bettman named first NHL Commissioner (February, 1993). Ottawa Senators and Tampa Bay Lightning added, making the NHL a 24-team league. NHL celebrates Stanley Cup Centennial. Clubs played 84-game schedule.

1993-94 — Mighty Ducks of Anaheim and Florida Panthers added, making the NHL a 26-team league. Minnesota franchise shifted to Dallas, team named Dallas Stars. Prince of Wales and Clarence Campbell Conferences renamed Eastern and Western. Adams, Patrick, Norris and Smythe Divisions renamed Northeast, Atlantic, Central and Pacific. Winnipeg moved to Central Division from Pacific; Tampa Bay moved to Atlantic Division from Central; Pittsburgh moved to Northeast Division from Atlantic.

1994-95 — A lockout resulted in the cancellation of 468 games from October 1, 1994 to January 19, 1995. Clubs played a 48-game schedule that began January 20, 1995 and ended May 3, 1995. No inter-conference games were played.

1995-96 — Quebec franchise transferred to Denver. Team named Colorado Avalanche and placed in Pacific Division of Western Conference. Clubs to play 82-game schedule.

1996-97 — Winnipeg franchise transferred to Phoenix. Team named Phoenix Coyotes and placed in Central Division of Western Conference.

1997-98 — Hartford franchise transferred to Raleigh. Team named Carolina Hurricanes and remains in Northeast Division of Eastern Conference.

1998-99 — The addition of the Nashville Predators made the NHL a 27-team league and brought about the creation of two new divisions and a League-wide realignment in preparation for further expansion to 30 teams by 2000-2001. Nashville was added to the Central Division of the Western Conference, while Toronto moved into the Northeast Division of the Eastern Conference. Pittsburgh was shifted from the Northeast to the Atlantic, while Carolina left the Northeast for the newly created Southeast Division of the Eastern Conference. Florida, Tampa Bay and Washington also joined the Southeast. In the Western Conference, Calgary, Colorado, Edmonton and Vancouver make up the new Northwest Division. Dallas and Phoenix moved from the Central to the Pacific Division.

The NHL retired uniform number 99 in honor of all-time scoring leader Wayne Gretzky who retired at the end of the season.

1999-2000 — Atlanta Thrashers added, making the NHL a 28-team league.

2000-01 — Columbus Blue Jackets and Minnesota Wild added, making the NHL a 30-team league.

2003-04 — First outdoor NHL game. 57,167 attend Heritage Classic at Edmonton's Commonwealth Stadium. Montreal defeated Edmonton 4-3, November 22, 2003.

2004-05 — A lockout resulted in the cancellation of the season.

2007-08 — NHL-record crowd of 71,217 fills Buffalo's Ralph Wilson Stadium on New Year's Day for the 2008 Winter Classic, the first NHL outdoor game in the United States. Sidney Crosby's shootout goal gives the Pittsburgh Penguins a 2-1 win over the Buffalo Sabres.

NHL Attendance

Season	Regular Season Games	Regular Season Attendance	Playoffs Games	Playoffs Attendance	Total Attendance
1967-68	444	4,938,043	40	495,089	5,433,132
1968-69	456	5,550,613	33	431,739	5,982,352
1969-70	456	5,992,065	34	461,694	6,453,759
1970-71	546	7,257,677	43	707,633	7,965,310
1971-72	546	7,609,368	36	582,666	8,192,034
1972-73	624	8,575,651	38	624,637	9,200,288
1973-74	624	8,640,978	38	600,442	9,241,420
1974-75	720	9,521,536	51	784,181	10,305,717
1975-76	720	9,103,761	48	726,279	9,830,040
1976-77	720	8,563,890	44	646,279	9,210,169
1977-78	720	8,526,564	45	686,634	9,213,198
1978-79	680	7,758,053	45	694,521	8,452,574
1979-80	840	10,533,623	63	976,699	11,510,322
1980-81	840	10,726,198	68	966,390	11,692,588
1981-82	840	10,710,894	71	1,058,948	11,769,842
1982-83	840	11,020,610	66	1,088,222	12,028,832
1983-84	840	11,359,386	70	1,107,400	12,466,786
1984-85	840	11,633,730	70	1,107,500	12,741,230
1985-86	840	11,621,000	72	1,152,503	12,773,503
1986-87	840	11,855,880	87	1,383,967	13,239,847
1987-88	840	12,117,512	83	1,336,901	13,454,413
1988-89	840	12,417,969	83	1,327,214	13,745,183
1989-90	840	12,579,651	85	1,355,593	13,935,244
1990-91	840	12,343,897	92	1,442,203	13,786,100
1991-92	880	12,769,676	86	1,327,920	14,097,596
1992-93	1,008	14,158,177[1]	83	1,346,034	15,504,211
1993-94	1,092	16,105,604[2]	90	1,440,095	17,545,699
1994-95	624[3]	9,233,884	81	1,329,130	10,563,014
1995-96	1,066	17,041,614	86	1,540,140	18,581,754
1996-97	1,066	17,640,529	82	1,494,878	19,135,407
1997-98	1,066	17,264,678	82	1,507,416	18,772,094
1998-99	1,107	18,001,741	86	1,509,411	19,511,152
1999-2000	1,148	18,800,139	83	1,524,629	20,324,768
2000-01	1,230	20,373,379	86	1,584,011	21,957,390
2001-02	1,230	20,614,613	90	1,691,174	22,305,787
2002-03	1,230	20,408,704	89	1,636,120	22,044,824
2003-04	1,230	20,356,199	89	1,708,691	22,064,890
2004-05	....	....	....	....	....
2005-06	1,230	20,854,169	83	1,530,405	22,384,574
2006-07	1,230	20,861,787	81	1,496,501	22,358,288
2007-08	1,230	21,236,255	85	1,587,054	22,823,309

NHL Expansion: the NHL operated as a six-team league from 1942-43 to 1966-67. Six teams were added in 1967-68: California (later to move to Cleveland), Los Angeles, Minnesota (later to move to Dallas), Philadelphia, Pittsburgh and St. Louis. In 1970-71: Buffalo and Vancouver. In 1972-73: Atlanta (later to move to Calgary) and NYIslanders. In 1974-75: Kansas City (later to move to Colorado and then to New Jersey) and Washington. In 1979-80, Hartford (later to move to Carolina), Edmonton, Quebec (later to move to Colorado) and Winnipeg (later to move to Phoenix). In 1991-92, San Jose. In 1992-93, Ottawa and Tampa Bay. In 1993-94, Anaheim and Florida. In 1998-99, Nashville. In 1999-2000, Atlanta. In 2000-01, Columbus and Minnesota.

[1] Includes 24 neutral site games • [2] Includes 26 neutral site games
[3] Lockout resulted in the cancellation of 468 regular-season games.

Major Rule Changes

1910-11 — Game changed from two 30-minute periods to three 20-minute periods.

1911-12 — National Hockey Association (forerunner of the NHL) originated six-man hockey, replacing seven-man game.

1917-18 — Goalies permitted to fall to the ice to make saves. Previously a goaltender was penalized for dropping to the ice.

1918-19 — Penalty rules amended. For minor fouls, substitutes not allowed until penalized player had served three minutes. For major fouls, no substitutes for five minutes. For match fouls, no substitutes allowed for the remainder of the game.

With the addition of two lines painted on the ice twenty feet from center, three playing zones were created, producing a forty-foot neutral center ice area in which forward passing was permitted. Kicking the puck was permitted in this neutral zone.

Tabulation of assists began.

1921-22 — Goaltenders allowed to pass the puck forward up to their own blue line.

Overtime limited to twenty minutes.

Minor penalties changed from three minutes to two minutes.

1923-24 — Match foul defined as actions deliberately injuring or disabling an opponent. For such actions, a player was fined not less than $50 and ruled off the ice for the balance of the game. A player assessed a match penalty may be replaced by a substitute at the end of 20 minutes. Match penalty recipients must meet with the League president who can assess additional punishment.

1925-26 — Delayed penalty rules introduced. Each team must have a minimum of four players on the ice at all times.

Two rules were amended to encourage offense: No more than two defensemen permitted to remain inside a team's own blue line when the puck has left the defensive zone. A faceoff to be called for ragging the puck unless shorthanded.

Team captains only players allowed to talk to referees.

Goaltender's leg pads limited to 12-inch width.

Timekeeper's gong to mark end of periods rather than referee's whistle. Teams to dress a maximum of 12 players for each game from a roster of no more than 14 players.

1926-27 — Blue lines repositioned to sixty feet from each goal-line, thereby enlarging the neutral zone and standardizing distance from blue line to goal.

Uniform goal nets adopted throughout NHL with goal posts securely fastened to the ice.

1927-28 — To further encourage offense, forward passes allowed in defending and neutral zones and goaltender's pads reduced in width from 12 to 10 inches.

Game standardized at three twenty-minute periods of stop-time separated by ten-minute intermissions.

Teams to change ends after each period.

Ten minutes of sudden-death overtime to be played if the score is tied after regulation time.

Minor penalty to be assessed to any player other than a goaltender for deliberately picking up the puck while it is in play. Minor penalty to be assessed for deliberately shooting the puck out of play.

The Art Ross goal net adopted as the official net of the NHL.

Maximum length of hockey sticks limited to 53 inches measured from heel of blade to end of handle. No minimum length stipulated.

Home teams given choice of end to defend at start of game.

1928-29 — Forward passing permitted in defensive and neutral zones and into attacking zone if pass receiver is in neutral zone when pass is made. No forward passing allowed inside attacking zone.

Minor penalty to be assessed to any player who delays the game by passing the puck back into his defensive zone.

Ten-minute overtime without sudden-death provision to be played in games tied after regulation time. Games tied after this overtime period declared a draw.

Exclusive of goaltenders, team to dress at least 8 and no more than 12 skaters.

Major Rule Changes — *continued*

1929-30 — Forward passing permitted inside all three zones but not permitted across either blue line.

Kicking the puck allowed, but a goal cannot be scored by kicking the puck in.

No more than three players including the goaltender may remain in their defensive zone when the puck has gone up ice. Minor penalties to be assessed for the first two violations of this rule in a game; major penalties thereafter.

Goaltenders forbidden to hold the puck. Pucks caught must be cleared immediately. For infringement of this rule, a faceoff to be taken ten feet in front of the goal with no player except the goaltender standing between the faceoff spot and the goal-line.

Highsticking penalties introduced.

Maximum number of players in uniform increased from 12 to 15.

December 21, 1929 — Forward passing rules instituted at the beginning of the 1929-30 season more than doubled number of goals scored. Partway through the season, these rules were further amended to read, "No attacking player allowed to precede the play when entering the opposing defensive zone." This is similar to modern offside rule.

1930-31 — A player without a complete stick ruled out of play and forbidden from taking part in further action until a new stick is obtained. A player who has broken his stick must obtain a replacement at his bench.

A further refinement of the offside rule stated that the puck must first be propelled into the attacking zone before any player of the attacking side can enter that zone; for infringement of this rule a faceoff to take place at the spot where the infraction took place.

1931-32 — Though there is no record of a team attempting to play with two goaltenders on the ice, a rule was instituted which stated that each team was allowed only one goaltender on the ice at one time.

Attacking players forbidden to impede the movement or obstruct the vision of opposing goaltenders.

Defending players with the exception of the goaltender forbidden from falling on the puck within 10 feet of the net.

1932-33 — Each team to have captain on the ice at all times.

If the goaltender is removed from the ice to serve a penalty, the manager of the club to appoint a substitute.

Match penalty with substitution after five minutes instituted for kicking another player.

1933-34 — Number of players permitted to stand in defensive zone restricted to three including goaltender.

Visible time clocks required in each rink.

Two referees replace one referee and one linesman.

1934-35 — Penalty shot awarded when a player is tripped and thus prevented from having a clear shot on goal, having no player to pass to other than the offending player. Shot taken from inside a 10-foot circle located 38 feet from the goal. The goaltender must not advance more than one foot from his goal-line when the shot is taken.

1937-38 — Rules introduced governing icing the puck.

Penalty shot awarded when a player other than a goaltender falls on the puck within 10 feet of the goal.

1938-39 — Penalty shot modified to allow puck carrier to skate in before shooting.

One referee and one linesman replace two referee system.

Blue line widened to 12 inches.

Maximum number of players in uniform increased from 14 to 15.

1939-40 — A substitute replacing a goaltender removed from ice to serve a penalty may use a goaltender's stick and gloves but no other goaltending equipment.

1940-41 — Flooding ice surface between periods made obligatory.

1941-42 — Penalty shots classified as minor and major. Minor shot to be taken from a line 28 feet from the goal. Major shot, awarded when a player is tripped with only the goaltender to beat, permits the player taking the penalty shot to skate right into the goalkeeper and shoot from point-blank range.

One referee and two linesmen employed to officiate games.

For playoffs, standby minor league goaltenders employed by NHL as emergency substitutes.

1942-43 — Because of wartime restrictions on train scheduling, regular-season overtime was discontinued on November 21, 1942.

Player limit reduced from 15 to 14. Minimum of 12 men in uniform abolished.

1943-44 — Red line at center ice introduced to speed up the game and reduce offside calls. This rule is considered to mark the beginning of the modern era in the NHL.

1945-46 — Goal indicator lights synchronized with official time clock required at all rinks.

1946-47 — System of signals by officials to indicate infractions introduced.

Linesmen from neutral cities employed for all games.

1947-48 — Goal awarded when a player with the puck has an open net to shoot at and a thrown stick prevents the shot on goal. Major penalty to any player who throws his stick in any zone other than defending zone. If a stick is thrown by a player in his defending zone but the thrown stick is not considered to have prevented a goal, a penalty shot is awarded.

All playoff games played until a winner determined, with 20-minute sudden-death overtime periods separated by 10-minute intermissions.

1949-50 — Ice surface painted white.

Clubs allowed to dress 17 players exclusive of goaltenders.

Major penalties incurred by goaltenders served by a member of the goaltender's team instead of resulting in a penalty shot.

1950-51 — Each team required to provide an emergency goaltender in attendance with full equipment at each game for use by either team in the event of illness or injury to a regular goaltender.

1951-52 — Home teams to wear basic white uniforms; visiting teams basic colored uniforms.

Goal crease enlarged from 3 × 7 feet to 4 × 8 feet.

Number of players in uniform reduced to 15 plus goaltenders.

Faceoff circles enlarged from 10-foot to 15-foot radius.

1952-53 — Teams permitted to dress 15 skaters on the road and 16 at home.

1953-54 — Number of players in uniform set at 16 plus goaltenders.

1954-55 — Number of players in uniform set at 18 plus goaltenders up to December 1 and 16 plus goaltenders thereafter. Teams agree to wear colored uniforms at home and white uniforms on the road.

1956-57 — Player serving a minor penalty allowed to return to ice when a goal is scored by opposing team.

1959-60 — Players prevented from leaving their benches to enter into an altercation. Substitutions permitted providing substitutes do not enter into altercation.

1960-61 — Number of players in uniform set at 16 plus goaltenders.

1961-62 — Penalty shots to be taken by the player against whom the foul was committed. In the event of a penalty shot called in a situation where a particular player hasn't been fouled, the penalty shot to be taken by any player on the ice when the foul was committed.

1964-65 — No body contact on faceoffs.

In playoff games, each team to have its substitute goaltender dressed in his regular uniform except for leg pads and body protector. All previous rules governing standby goaltenders terminated.

1965-66 — Teams required to dress two goaltenders for each regular-season game. Maximum stick length increased to 55 inches.

1966-67 — Substitution allowed on coincidental major penalties.

Between-periods intermissions fixed at 15 minutes.

1967-68 — If a penalty incurred by a goaltender is a co-incident major, the penalty to be served by a player of the goaltender's team on the ice at the time the penalty was called. Limit of curvature of hockey stick blade set at 1$^1/_2$ inches.

1969-70 — Limit of curvature of hockey stick blade set at 1 inch.

1970-71 — Home teams to wear basic white uniforms; visiting teams to wear basic colored uniforms.

Limit of curvature of hockey stick blade set at $^1/_2$ inch.

Minor penalty for deliberately shooting the puck out of the playing area.

1971-72 — Number of players in uniform set at 17 plus 2 goaltenders.

Third man to enter an altercation assessed an automatic game misconduct penalty.

1972-73 — Minimum width of stick blade reduced to 2 inches from 2$^1/_2$ inches.

1974-75 — Bench minor penalty imposed if a penalized player does not proceed directly and immediately to the penalty box.

1976-77 — Rule dealing with fighting amended to provide a major and game misconduct penalty for any player who is clearly the instigator of a fight.

1977-78 — Teams requesting a stick measurement to be assessed a minor penalty in the event that the measured stick does not violate the rules.

1979-80 — Wearing of helmets made mandatory for players entering the NHL.

1980-81 — Maximum stick length increased to 58 inches.

1981-82 — If both of a team's listed goaltenders are incapacitated, the team can dress and play any eligible goaltender who is available.

1982-83 — Number of players in uniform set at 18 plus 2 goaltenders.

1983-84 — Five-minute sudden-death overtime to be played in regular-season games that are tied at the end of regulation time.

1985-86 — Substitutions allowed in the event of co-incidental minor penalties. Maximum stick length increased to 60 inches.

1986-87 — Delayed off-side is no longer in effect once the players of the offending team have cleared the opponents' defensive zone.

1990-91 — The goal lines, blue lines, defensive zone face-off circles and markings all moved one foot out from the end boards, creating 11 feet of room behind the nets and shrinking the neutral zone from 60 to 58 feet.

1991-92 — Video replays employed to assist referees in goal/no goal situations. Size of goal crease increased. Crease changed to semi-circular configuration. Time clock to record tenths of a second in last minute of each period and overtime. Major and game misconduct penalty for checking from behind into boards. Penalties added for crease infringement and unnecessary contact with goaltender. Goal disallowed if puck enters net while a player of the attacking team is standing on the goal crease line, is in the goal crease or places his stick in the goal crease.

1992-93 — No substitutions allowed in the event of coincidental minor penalties called when both teams are at full strength. Minor penalty for attempting to draw a penalty ("diving"). Major and game misconduct penalty for checking from behind into goal frame. Game misconduct penalty for instigating a fight. High sticking redefined to include any use of the stick above waist-height. Previous rule stipulated shoulder-height.

1993-94 — High sticking redefined to allow goals scored with a high stick below the height of the crossbar of the goal frame.

1996-97 — Maximum stick length increased to 63 inches. All players must be clear of the attacking zone prior to the puck being shot into that zone. The opportunity to "tag-up" and return into the zone has been removed.

1998-99 — The league instituted a two-referee system with each team to play 20 regular-season games with two referees and a pair of linesmen. Goal line moved to 13 feet from end boards. Goal crease altered to extend one foot beyond each goal post (eight feet across in total. Sides of crease squared off, extending 4'6". Only the top of the crease remains rounded. Only the top of the crease remains rounded.

1999-2000 — Each team to play 25 home and 25 road games using the two-referee system. Crease rule revised to implement a "no harm, no foul, no video review" standard. Teams to play with four skaters and a goaltender in regular-season overtime. If a goal is scored in regular-season overtime, the winner is awarded two points and the loser one point. In no goal is scored in overtime, both teams are awarded one point.

2000-01 — All games to be played using the two-referee system.

2002-03 — "Hurry-up" faceoff and line-change rules implemented.

2003-04 — Home teams to wear basic colored uniforms; visiting teams to wear basic white uniforms. Maximum length of goaltender's pads set at 38 inches.

2005-06 — The NHL adopted a comprehensive package of rule changes that included the following:

Goal line moved to 11 feet from end boards; blue lines moved to 75 feet from end boards, reducing neutral zone from 54 feet to 50 feet. Center red line eliminated for two-line passes. "Tag-up" off-side rule reinstituted. This rule was previously used from 1986-87 through 1995-96. Goaltender not permitted to play the puck outside a designated trapezoid-shaped area behind the net. A team that ices the puck will not be permitted to make any player substitutions prior to the ensuing faceoff. A player who instigates a fight in the final five minutes of regulation time or at any time of overtime will receive a minor, a major, a misconduct and an automatic one-game suspension. The size of goaltender equipment has been reduced by approximately 11 percent. If a game remains tied after five minutes of overtime, a shootout will be conducted to determine a winner.

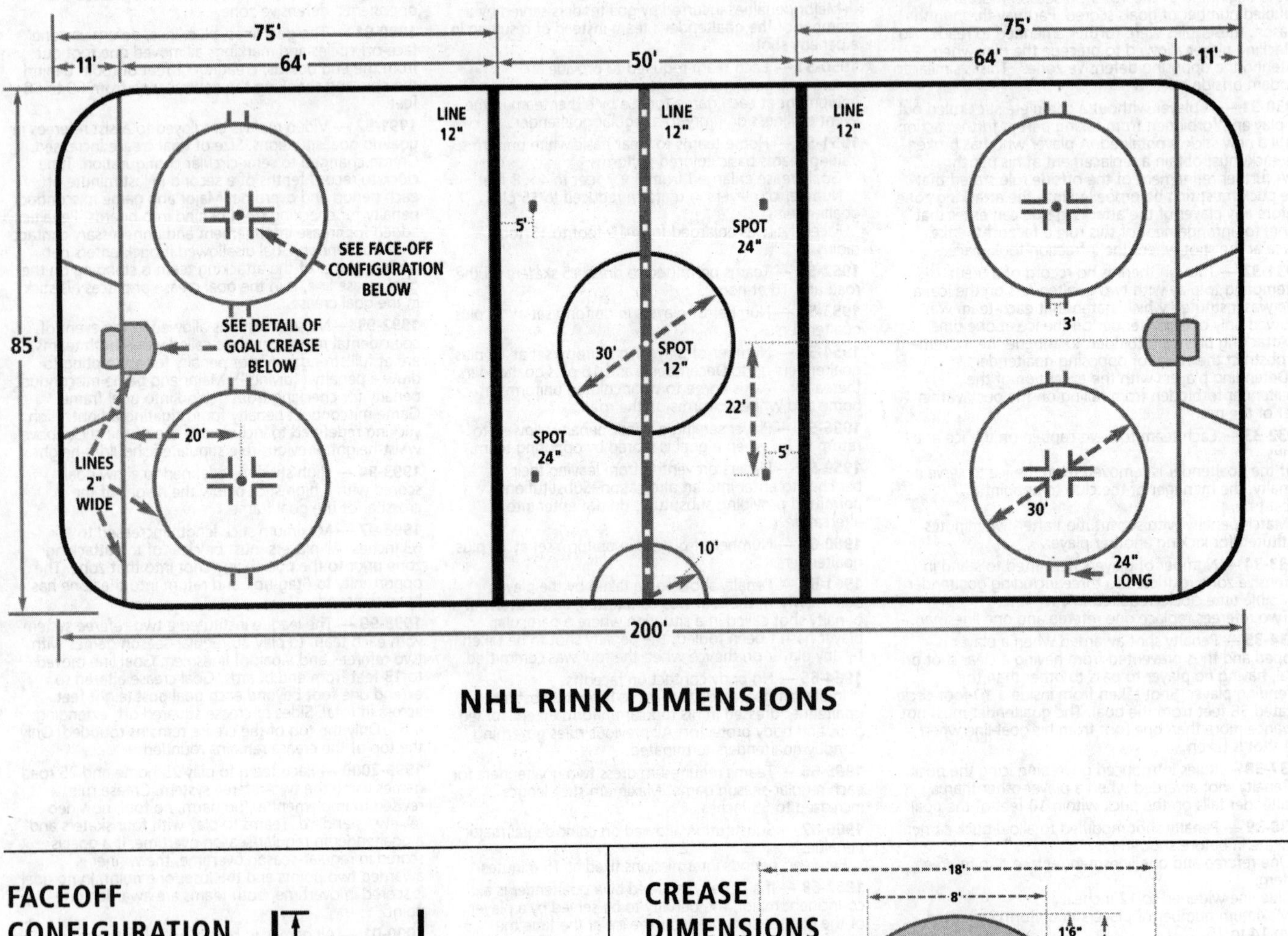

NHL RINK DIMENSIONS

FACEOFF CONFIGURATION

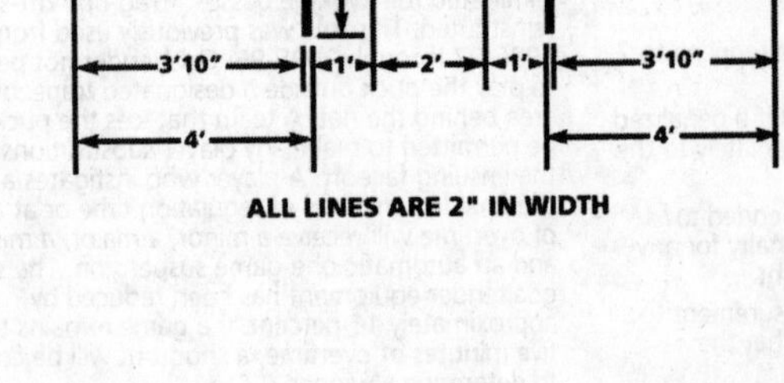

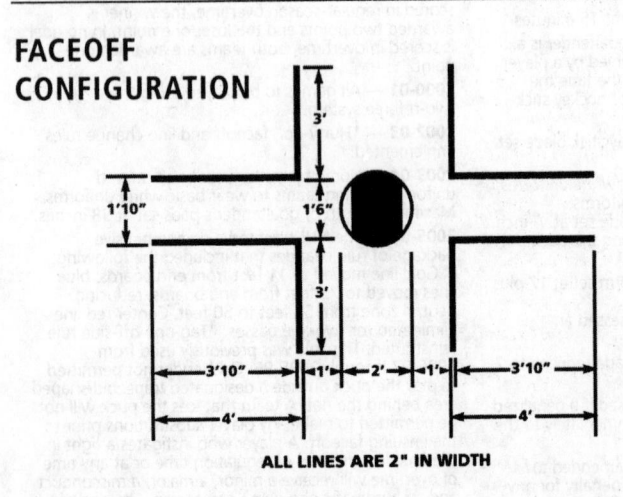

ALL LINES ARE 2" IN WIDTH

CREASE DIMENSIONS

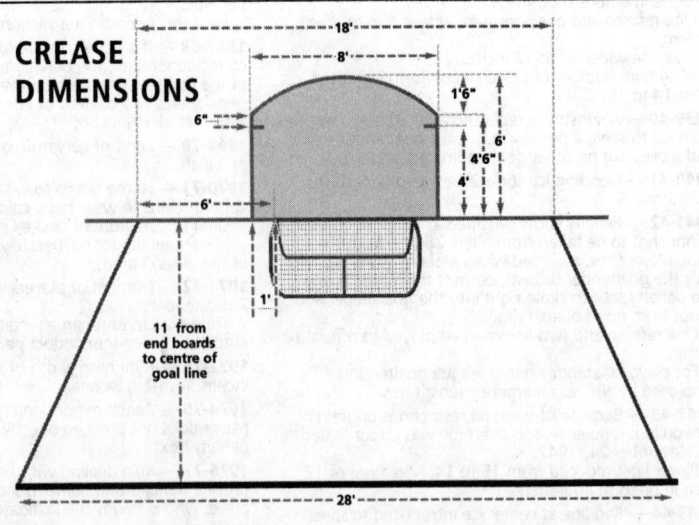

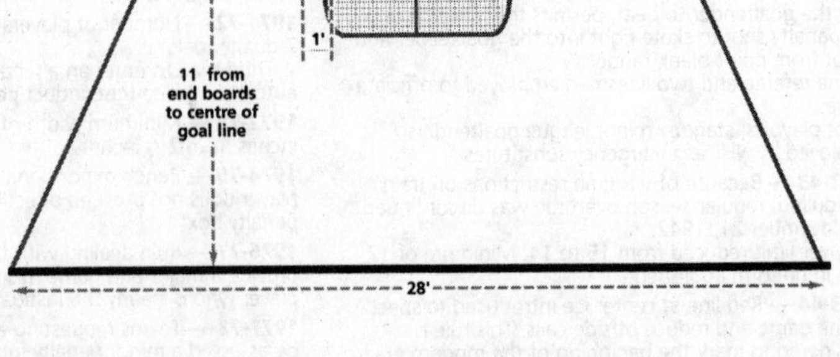

NHL League and Team Websites

National Hockey League ......www.nhl.com
NHL Site for Kids www2.nhl.com/kids
NHL Merchandise Shop ....shop.nhl.com
NHL Job Postings ....hockeyjobs.nhl.com
Hockey Fights Cancer ....www.nhl.com/nhlhq/hockeyfightscancer/index.html

Official NHL Team Websites:

Anaheim ....www.ducks.nhl.com
Atlanta ....www.thrashers.nhl.com
Boston................................www.bruins.nhl.com
Buffalo ....www.sabres.nhl.com
Calgary...............................www.flames.nhl.com
Carolina ....www.hurricanes.nhl.com
Chicago..............................www.blackhawks.nhl.com
Colorado ....www.avalanche.nhl.com
Columbus ....www.bluejackets.nhl.com
Dallas ....www.stars.nhl.com
Detroit...............................www.redwings.nhl.com
Edmonton ....www.oilers.nhl.com
Florida ....www.panthers.nhl.com
Los Angeles.......................www.kings.nhl.com
Minnesota ....www.wild.nhl.com
Montreal ....www.canadiens.nhl.com
Nashville ....www.predators.nhl.com
New Jersey ....www.devils.nhl.com
NY Islanders ....www.islanders.nhl.com
NY Rangers ....www.rangers.nhl.com
Ottawa ....www.senators.nhl.com
Philadelphia.......................www.flyers.nhl.com
Phoenix ....www.coyotes.nhl.com
Pittsburgh..........................www.penguins.nhl.com
St. Louis ....www.blues.nhl.com
San Jose ....www.sharks.nhl.com
Tampa Bay.........................www.lightning.nhl.com
Toronto ....www.mapleleafs.nhl.com
Vancouver ....www.canucks.nhl.com
Washington........................www.capitals.nhl.com

To order the *NHL Official Guide & Record Book* and other books about hockey:

www.nhlofficialguide.com

NHL Clubs' Minor-League Affiliations, 2008-09

NHL Club	Minor-League Affiliates
Anaheim	Iowa Chops (AHL) Bakersfield Condors (ECHL)
Atlanta	Chicago Wolves (AHL) Gwinnett Gladiators (ECHL)
Boston	Providence Bruins (AHL)
Buffalo	Portland Pirates (AHL)
Calgary	Quad Cities Flames (AHL) Las Vegas Wranglers (ECHL)
Carolina	Albany River Rats (AHL) Florida Everblades (ECHL)
Chicago	Rockford IceHogs (AHL) Fresno Falcons (ECHL)
Colorado	Lake Erie Monsters (AHL) Johnstown Chiefs (ECHL)
Columbus	Syracuse Crunch (AHL) Johnstown Chiefs (ECHL)
Dallas	Idaho Steelheads (ECHL)
Detroit	Grand Rapids Griffins (AHL)
Edmonton	Springfield Falcons (AHL) Stockton Thunder (ECHL)
Florida	Rochester Americans (AHL) Florida Everblades (ECHL)
Los Angeles	Manchester Monarchs (AHL) Ontario (CA) Reign (ECHL)
Minnesota	Houston Aeros (AHL)

NHL Club	Minor-League Affiliates
Montreal	Hamilton Bulldogs (AHL) Cincinnati Cyclones (ECHL)
Nashville	Milwaukee Admirals (AHL) Cincinnati Cyclones (ECHL)
New Jersey	Lowell Devils (AHL) Trenton Devils (ECHL)
NY Islanders	Bridgeport Sound Tigers (AHL) Utah Grizzlies (ECHL) Odessa Jackalopes (CHL)
NY Rangers	Hartford Wolf Pack (AHL) Charlotte Checkers (ECHL)
Ottawa	Binghamton Senators (AHL) Elmira Jackals (ECHL)
Philadelphia	Philadelphia Phantoms (AHL)
Phoenix	San Antonio Rampage (AHL) Arizona Sundogs (CHL)
Pittsburgh	Wilkes-Barre/Scranton Penguins (AHL) Wheeling Nailers (ECHL)
St. Louis	Peoria Rivermen (AHL) Alaska Aces (ECHL)
San Jose	Worcester Sharks (AHL) Phoenix RoadRunners (ECHL) China Sharks (Asian Hockey League)
Tampa Bay	Norfolk Admirals (AHL) Augusta Lynx (ECHL)
Toronto	Toronto Marlies (AHL) Reading Royals (ECHL)
Vancouver	Manitoba Moose (AHL) Victoria Salmon Kings (ECHL)
Washington	Hershey Bears (AHL) South Carolina Stingrays (ECHL)

Key Off-Season Signings/Acquisitions

2008

April 29 • Re-signed C **Ryan Carter**.
June 11 • Re-signed G **Jonas Hiller**.
25 • Re-signed C **Brian Sutherby**.
July 1 • Re-signed RW **Corey Perry**.
7 • Signed G **David LeNeveu**.
8 • Signed C **Brendan Morrison**.
11 • Signed D **Steve Montador**.

Anaheim Ducks

2007-08 Results: 47W-27L-1OTL-7SOL 102PTS.
Second, Pacific Division

Year-by-Year Record

		Home				Road				Overall								
Season	**GP**	**W**	**L**	**T**	**OL**	**W**	**L**	**T**	**OL**	**W**	**L**	**T**	**OL**	**GF**	**GA**	**Pts.**	**Finished**	**Playoff Result**
2007-08	82	28	9	....	4	19	18	....	4	47	27	....	8	205	191	102	2nd, Pacific Div.	Lost Conf. Quarter-Final
2006-07	**82**	**26**	**6**	....	**9**	**22**	**14**	....	**5**	**48**	**20**	....	**14**	**258**	**208**	**110**	**1st, Pacific Div.**	**Won Stanley Cup**
2005-06*	82	26	10	....	5	17	17	....	7	43	27	....	12	254	229	98	3rd, Pacific Div.	Lost Conf. Championship
2004-05*	....	....	....	....	....	....	....	....	....	....	....	....	....	....	....	....		
2003-04*	82	19	11	7	4	10	24	3	4	29	35	10	8	184	213	76	4th, Pacific Div.	Out of Playoffs
2002-03*	82	22	10	7	2	18	17	2	4	40	27	9	6	203	193	95	2nd, Pacific Div.	Lost Final
2001-02*	82	15	19	5	2	14	23	3	1	29	42	8	3	175	198	69	5th, Pacific Div.	Out of Playoffs
2000-01*	82	15	20	4	2	10	21	7	3	25	41	11	5	188	245	66	5th, Pacific Div.	Out of Playoffs
1999-2000*	82	19	13	7	2	15	20	5	1	34	33	12	3	217	227	83	5th, Pacific Div.	Out of Playoffs
1998-99*	82	21	14	6	....	14	20	7	....	35	34	13	....	215	206	83	3rd, Pacific Div.	Lost Conf. Quarter-Final
1997-98*	82	12	23	6	....	14	20	7	....	26	43	13	....	205	261	65	6th, Pacific Div.	Out of Playoffs
1996-97*	82	23	12	6	....	13	21	7	....	36	33	13	....	245	233	85	2nd, Pacific Div.	Lost Conf. Semi-Final
1995-96*	82	22	15	4	....	13	24	4	....	35	39	8	....	234	247	78	4th, Pacific Div.	Out of Playoffs
1994-95*	48	11	9	4	....	5	18	1	....	16	27	5	....	125	164	37	6th, Pacific Div.	Out of Playoffs
1993-94*	84	14	26	2	....	19	20	3	....	33	46	5	....	229	251	71	4th, Pacific Div.	Out of Playoffs

* Mighty Ducks of Anaheim

2008-09 Schedule

Oct.	Thu.	9	at San Jose
	Sun.	12	Phoenix*
	Tue.	14	at Los Angeles
	Wed.	15	Edmonton
	Fri.	17	San Jose
	Sun.	19	Carolina*
	Tue.	21	at Toronto
	Fri.	24	at Ottawa
	Sat.	25	at Montreal
	Mon.	27	at Columbus
	Wed.	29	Detroit
	Fri.	31	Vancouver
Nov.	Sun.	2	Calgary*
	Tue.	4	at Los Angeles
	Wed.	5	St. Louis
	Fri.	7	Dallas
	Sun.	9	Florida*
	Fri.	14	Nashville
	Sun.	16	Los Angeles*
	Wed.	19	Washington
	Fri.	21	at St. Louis
	Sat.	22	at Dallas
	Mon.	24	Colorado
	Fri.	28	Chicago*
	Sun.	30	at Carolina
Dec.	Mon.	1	at Detroit
	Wed.	3	at Chicago
	Sun.	7	Columbus*
	Wed.	10	St. Louis
	Thu.	11	at San Jose
	Sun.	14	Minnesota*
	Tue.	16	NY Rangers
	Fri.	19	at Edmonton
	Mon.	22	at Vancouver
	Tue.	23	at Calgary
	Sat.	27	at Dallas
	Sun.	28	at St. Louis*
	Wed.	31	Columbus
Jan.	Fri.	2	Philadelphia
	Sun.	4	Phoenix*
	Tue.	6	Los Angeles
	Thu.	8	at Los Angeles
	Fri.	9	Tampa Bay
	Sun.	11	New Jersey*
	Wed.	14	Detroit
	Fri.	16	at Pittsburgh
	Sat.	17	at Minnesota
	Tue.	20	at NY Rangers
	Wed.	21	at NY Islanders
	Tue.	27	at Phoenix
	Wed.	28	Chicago
	Sat.	31	at Colorado*
Feb.	Mon.	2	Buffalo
	Wed.	4	at Minnesota
	Thu.	5	at Nashville
	Sat.	7	at Calgary*
	Wed.	11	Calgary
	Sun.	15	Atlanta*
	Wed.	18	Los Angeles
	Fri.	20	at Detroit
	Sat.	21	at Columbus
	Tue.	24	at Buffalo
	Thu.	26	at Boston
	Sat.	28	at Dallas*
Mar.	Tue.	3	at Chicago
	Fri.	6	Dallas
	Sun.	8	Minnesota*
	Wed.	11	Vancouver
	Sun.	15	San Jose*
	Wed.	18	Nashville
	Thu.	19	at Phoenix
	Sun.	22	Phoenix*
	Tue.	24	at Nashville
	Wed.	25	at Colorado
	Fri.	27	Edmonton
	Sun.	29	Colorado*
	Tue.	31	at Edmonton
Apr.	Thu.	2	at Vancouver
	Sat.	4	at San Jose
	Sun.	5	San Jose*
	Fri.	10	Dallas
	Sat.	11	at Phoenix

* Denotes afternoon game.

Ryan Getzlaf matched the total he had put up in his first two NHL seasons when he led the Ducks with 58 assists in 2007-08. His 82 points and +32 ranking also led the team.

PACIFIC DIVISION
16th NHL Season

Franchise date: June 15, 1993

2008-09 Player Personnel

FORWARDS	HT	WT	S	Place of Birth	*Age	2007-08 Club
BELESKEY, Matt	6-0	206	L	Windsor, Ont.	20	Belleville
BODIE, Troy	6-4	196	R	Portage La Prairie, Man.	23	Springfield
BOGUNIECKI, Eric	5-8	192	R	New Haven, CT	33	Ingolstadt
CARTER, Ryan	6-2	203	L	White Bear Lake, MN	25	Anaheim-Portland (AHL)
DONALLY, Ryan	6-5	224	L	Tecumseh, Ont.	23	Quad City-Las Vegas
EBBETT, Andrew	5-10	174	L	Vernon, B.C.	25	Anaheim-Portland (AHL)
GETZLAF, Ryan	6-4	221	R	Regina, Sask.	23	Anaheim
GREEN, Josh	6-3	215	L	Camrose, Alta.	30	Salzburg
KUNITZ, Chris	5-11	195	L	Regina, Sask.	29	Anaheim
LINDSTROM, Joakim	6-0	187	L	Skelleftea, Sweden	24	Columbus-Syracuse
MARCHANT, Todd	5-10	180	L	Buffalo, NY	35	Anaheim
MAY, Brad	6-1	218	L	Toronto, Ont.	36	Anaheim
MILLER, Drew	6-2	174	L	Dover, NJ	24	Anaheim-Portland (AHL)
MOEN, Travis	6-2	215	L	Stewart Valley, Sask.	26	Anaheim
MORRISON, Brendan	5-11	181	L	Pitt Meadows, B.C.	33	Vancouver
NIEDERMAYER, Rob	6-2	200	L	Cassiar, B.C.	33	Anaheim
PAHLSSON, Samuel	6-0	203	L	Ange, Sweden	30	Anaheim
PARROS, George	6-5	229	R	Washington, PA	28	Anaheim
PERRY, Corey	6-3	209	R	Peterborough, Ont.	23	Anaheim
RYAN, Bobby	6-2	218	R	Cherry Hill, NJ	21	Anaheim-Portland (AHL)
SUTHERBY, Brian	6-3	210	L	Edmonton, Alta.	26	Washington-Anaheim
WIRTANEN, Petteri	6-2	207	L	Hyvinkaa, Finland	22	Anaheim-Portland (AHL)
DEFENSEMEN						
BEAUCHEMIN, Francois	6-0	213	L	Sorel, Que.	28	Anaheim
BICKEL, Stu	6-4	215	R	Chanhassen, MN	22	U. of Minnesota
EVANS, Brennan	6-3	220	L	North Battleford, Sask.	26	Worcester
FESTERLING, Brett	6-1	210	L	Quesnel, B.C.	22	Portland (AHL)
HUSKINS, Kent	6-3	209	L	Ottawa, Ont.	29	Anaheim
MIKKELSON, Brendan	6-3	202	L	Regina, Sask.	21	Portland (AHL)
MONTADOR, Steve	6-0	205	R	Vancouver, B.C.	28	Florida
NIEDERMAYER, Scott	6-1	200	L	Edmonton, Alta.	35	Anaheim
O'DONNELL, Sean	6-3	234	L	Ottawa, Ont.	36	Anaheim
PRONGER, Chris	6-6	213	L	Dryden, Ont.	33	Anaheim
SALCIDO, Brian	6-2	202	L	Los Angeles, CA	23	Portland (AHL)
SCHNEIDER, Mathieu	5-11	195	L	New York, NY	39	Anaheim

GOALTENDERS	HT	WT	C	Place of Birth	*Age	2007-08 Club
GIGUERE, Jean-Sebastien	6-1	201	L	Montreal, Que.	31	Anaheim
HILLER, Jonas	6-2	196	R	Felben Wellhausen, Switz.	26	Anaheim-Portland (AHL)
LeNEVEU, David	6-1	187	L	Fernie, B.C.	25	San Antonio-Hartford
LEVASSEUR, Jean-Philippe	6-1	205	R	Victoriaville, Que.	21	Portland (AHL)-Augusta

* – Age at start of 2008-09 season

Randy Carlyle

Head Coach

Born: Sudbury, Ont., April 19, 2008.

Randy Carlyle was hired as the head coach in Anaheim on August 1, 2005. In his first season behind the bench in 2005-06, he led the Ducks to the Western Conference Final. He led Anaheim to its first Stanley Cup championship in 2007.

Prior to joining the Ducks, Carlyle had served as the head coach of the Manitoba Moose, the Vancouver Canucks' primary development team. In all, Carlyle spent six seasons between 1996 and 2005 as head coach in Manitoba (both in the International and American Hockey Leagues) with his team posting an overall record of 222-159-52-7. He had the additional duties of general manager of the Moose from 1996 to 2000, and served as club president for the 2001-02 season. The Sudbury, Ontario, native helped the Moose to a 47-21-14 record for 108 points in 1998-99, for which he was named the IHL's general manager of the year.

Following the 2001-02 season, Carlyle joined the coaching staff of the Washington Capitals. He served as an assistant coach with Washington for two seasons (2002 to 2004), before rejoining Manitoba in 2004–05.

Carlyle played 17 seasons in the NHL with Toronto, Pittsburgh and Winnipeg. He appeared in 1,055 games and had 148 goals and 499 assists for 647 points. Known as a fiery, tough-nosed defenseman, he was selected to play in four NHL All-Star Games, winning the Norris Trophy as the league's top defenseman in 1981. At the conclusion of his playing career in 1993, Carlyle remained with the Winnipeg organization's hockey operations staff, eventually becoming an assistant coach for the 1995-96 season.

Coaching Record

			Regular Season				Playoffs			
Season	Team	League	GC	W	L	O/T	GC	W	L	T
1996-97	Manitoba	IHL	32	16	14	2	....	....	....	....
1997-98	Manitoba	IHL	82	39	36	7	3	0	3	....
1998-99	Manitoba	IHL	82	47	21	14	5	2	3	....
99-2000	Manitoba	IHL	82	37	31	14	2	0	2	....
2000-01	Manitoba	IHL	82	39	31	12	13	6	7	....
2004-05	Manitoba	AHL	80	44	26	10	14	6	8	....
2005-06	**Anaheim**	**NHL**	**82**	**43**	**27**	**12**	**16**	**9**	**7**	....
2006-07♦	**Anaheim**	**NHL**	**82**	**48**	**20**	**14**	**21**	**16**	**5**	....
2007-08	**Anaheim**	**NHL**	**82**	**47**	**27**	**8**	**6**	**2**	**4**	....
	NHL Totals		**246**	**138**	**74**	**34**	**43**	**27**	**16**	....

♦ Stanley Cup win.

2007-08 Scoring

* – rookie

Regular Season

Pos	#	Player	Team	GP	G	A	Pts	TOI	+/–	PIM	PP	SH	GW	S	%
C	15	Ryan Getzlaf	ANA	77	24	58	82	19:38	32	94	4	1	2	185	13.0
R	10	Corey Perry	ANA	70	29	25	54	17:57	12	108	11	0	4	200	14.5
L	14	Chris Kunitz	ANA	82	21	29	50	16:54	8	80	7	1	6	196	10.7
D	25	Chris Pronger	ANA	72	12	31	43	26:00	–1	128	8	0	4	182	6.6
R	4	Todd Bertuzzi	ANA	68	14	26	40	16:27	8	97	4	0	2	121	11.6
D	11	Mathieu Schneider	ANA	65	12	27	39	22:17	22	50	5	0	2	139	8.6
C	39	Doug Weight	STL	29	4	7	11	16:10	4	12	0	0	0	47	8.5
			ANA	38	6	8	14	13:25	0	20	2	0	1	49	12.2
			Total	67	10	15	25	14:36	4	32	2	0	1	96	10.4
D	27	Scott Niedermayer	ANA	48	8	17	25	23:54	–2	16	7	0	3	87	9.2
R	8	Teemu Selanne	ANA	26	12	11	23	18:07	5	8	7	0	2	87	13.8
D	23	Francois Beauchemin	ANA	82	2	19	21	25:31	–9	59	0	0	2	144	1.4
D	7	Marc-Andre Bergeron	NYI	46	9	9	18	18:17	–14	16	8	0	1	96	9.4
			ANA	9	0	1	1	12:50	–2	4	0	0	0	12	0.0
			Total	55	9	10	19	17:23	–16	20	8	0	1	108	8.3
D	40	Kent Huskins	ANA	76	4	15	19	16:04	23	59	1	0	2	46	8.7
C	22	Todd Marchant	ANA	75	9	7	16	14:49	–3	48	0	0	0	93	9.7
C	44	Rob Niedermayer	ANA	78	8	8	16	17:42	1	54	0	1	1	111	7.2
C	26	Samuel Pahlsson	ANA	56	6	9	15	18:46	–2	34	0	3	3	94	6.4
R	54 *	Bobby Ryan	ANA	23	5	5	10	11:15	–1	6	3	0	0	37	13.5
D	21	Sean O'Donnell	ANA	82	2	7	9	17:14	9	84	0	1	0	25	8.0
C	20 *	Ryan Carter	ANA	34	4	4	8	10:29	–2	36	0	0	1	56	7.1
L	32	Travis Moen	ANA	77	3	5	8	15:49	–10	81	0	1	1	98	3.1
L	18 *	Drew Miller	ANA	26	2	3	5	11:11	–1	6	0	0	0	30	6.7
D	33	Joe Dipenta	ANA	23	1	4	5	10:39	3	16	0	0	0	5	20.0
R	16	George Parros	ANA	69	1	4	5	05:56	3	183	0	0	0	30	3.3
L	24	Brad May	ANA	61	3	1	4	06:37	2	53	0	0	2	34	8.8
C	17	Brian Sutherby	WSH	5	1	0	1	06:49	–2	7	0	0	0	3	33.3
			ANA	45	0	1	1	08:47	–2	57	0	0	0	46	0.0
			Total	50	1	1	2	08:35	–4	64	0	0	0	49	2.0
C	56 *	Petteri Wirtanen	ANA	3	1	0	1	04:11	1	2	0	0	1	1	100.0
R	28	Mark Mowers	ANA	17	1	0	1	09:02	0	8	0	0	0	6	16.7
C	48 *	Andrew Ebbett	ANA	3	0	0	0	13:18	3	2	0	0	0	3	0.0
D	20	Maxim Kondratiev	ANA	4	0	0	0	07:30	–2	0	0	0	0	1	0.0
R	42	Jason King	ANA	4	0	0	0	10:56	–3	0	0	0	0	2	0.0
C	20	Geoff Platt	ANA	5	0	0	0	11:17	2	2	0	0	0	4	0.0

Goaltending

No.	Goaltender	GPI	Mins	Avg	W	L	OT	EN	SO	GA	SA	S%	G	A	PIM
1	* Jonas Hiller	23	1223	2.06	10	7	1	0	0	42	578	.927	0	1	0
35	Jean-Sebastien Giguere	58	3310	2.12	35	17	6	5	4	117	1508	.922	0	0	4
30	Ilja Bryzgalov	9	447	2.55	2	3	1	1	0	19	208	.909	0	0	0
	Totals	**82**	**5007**	**2.20**	**47**	**27**	**8**	**6**	**4**	**184**	**2300**	**.920**			

Playoffs

Pos	#	Player	Team	GP	G	A	Pts	TOI	+/–	PIM	PP	SH	GW	OT	S	%
D	25	Chris Pronger	ANA	6	2	3	5	24:13	–1	12	2	0	1	0	12	16.7
C	15	Ryan Getzlaf	ANA	6	2	3	5	20:29	–2	6	1	0	0	0	14	14.3
R	8	Teemu Selanne	ANA	6	2	2	4	19:34	–1	6	2	0	1	0	20	10.0
R	10	Corey Perry	ANA	3	2	1	3	14:54	1	8	0	0	0	0	7	28.6
C	22	Todd Marchant	ANA	6	2	0	2	17:39	1	0	0	0	0	0	8	25.0
D	21	Sean O'Donnell	ANA	6	1	1	2	15:31	3	2	0	0	0	0	3	33.3
L	32	Travis Moen	ANA	6	1	1	2	14:08	–1	2	0	0	0	0	4	25.0
D	27	Scott Niedermayer	ANA	6	0	2	2	24:24	–2	4	0	0	0	0	7	0.0
R	4	Todd Bertuzzi	ANA	6	0	2	2	14:14	–2	14	0	0	0	0	11	0.0
L	14	Chris Kunitz	ANA	6	0	2	2	18:30	–2	8	0	0	0	0	14	0.0
D	11	Mathieu Schneider	ANA	6	1	0	1	20:29	–3	8	0	0	0	0	7	14.3
C	39	Doug Weight	ANA	5	0	1	1	07:38	1	4	0	0	0	0	2	0.0
D	40	Kent Huskins	ANA	6	0	1	1	14:34	–3	2	0	0	0	0	2	0.0
R	16	George Parros	ANA	1	0	0	0	02:42	0	0	0	0	0	0	0	0.0
C	44	Rob Niedermayer	ANA	2	0	0	0	13:46	–1	0	0	0	0	0	1	0.0
C	17	Brian Sutherby	ANA	5	0	0	0	05:28	0	2	0	0	0	0	3	0.0
L	24	Brad May	ANA	6	0	0	0	06:55	1	4	0	0	0	0	6	0.0
C	26	Samuel Pahlsson	ANA	6	0	0	0	18:18	1	0	0	0	0	0	5	0.0
D	23	Francois Beauchemin	ANA	6	0	0	0	21:01	2	26	0	0	0	0	4	0.0
C	20 *	Ryan Carter	ANA	6	0	0	0	11:02	–2	6	0	0	0	0	6	0.0

Goaltending

No.	Goaltender	GPI	Mins	Avg	W	L	EN	SO	GA	SA	S%	G	A	PIM
35	Jean-Sebastien Giguere	6	358	3.18	2	4	1	0	19	187	.898	0	1	0
	Totals	**6**	**360**	**3.33**	**2**	**4**	**1**	**0**	**20**	**188**	**.894**			

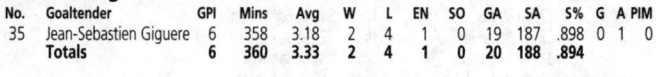

Club Records

Team

(Figures in brackets for season records are games played; records for fewest points, wins, ties, losses, goals, goals against are for 70 or more games)

Most Points	**110**	2006-07 (82)
Most Wins	**48**	2006-07 (82)
Most Ties	**13**	1996-97 (82), 1997-98 (82), 1998-99 (82)
Most Losses	**46**	1993-94 (84)
Most Goals	**258**	2006-07 (82)
Most Goals Against	**261**	1997-98 (82)
Fewest Points	**65**	1997-98 (82)
Fewest Wins	**25**	2000-01 (82)
Fewest Ties	**5**	1993-94 (84)
Fewest Losses	**20**	2006-07 (82)
Fewest Goals	**175**	2001-02 (82)
Fewest Goals Against	**191**	2007-08 (82)
Longest Winning Streak		
Overall	**7**	Feb. 20-Mar. 7/99
Home	**10**	Feb. 17-Mar. 26/08
Away	**7**	Nov. 28-Dec. 13/06
Longest Undefeated Streak		
Overall	**12**	Feb. 22-Mar. 19/97 (7 wins, 5 ties)
Home	**14**	Feb. 12-Apr. 9/97 (10 wins, 4 ties)
Away	**7**	Nov. 28-Dec. 13/06 (7 wins)
Longest Losing Streak		
Overall	**8**	Oct. 12-30/96, Nov. 3-20/05
Home	**8**	Jan. 10-Feb. 9/01
Away	**7**	Oct. 8-Nov. 12/05
Longest Winless Streak		
Overall	**9**	Three times
Home	**11**	Jan. 5-Feb. 14/01 (8 losses, 3 ties)
Away	**13**	Nov. 1-Dec. 27/03 (11 losses, 2 ties)
Most Shutouts, Season	**9**	2002-03 (82)
Most PIM, Season	**1,843**	1997-98 (82)
Most Goals, Game	**8**	Jan. 21/98 (Fla. 3 at Ana. 8), Mar. 21/04 (Det. 6 at Ana. 8)

Individual

Most Seasons	**10**	Steve Rucchin
Most Games	**616**	Steve Rucchin
Most Goals, Career	**325**	Teemu Selanne
Most Assists, Career	**369**	Paul Kariya
Most Points, Career	**689**	Teemu Selanne (325G, 364A)
Most PIM, Career	**788**	Dave Karpa
Most Shutouts, Career	**29**	Jean-Sebastien Giguere
Longest Consecutive Games Streak	**275**	Samuel Pahlsson (Feb. 7/03-Apr. 7/07)
Most Goals, Season	**52**	Teemu Selanne (1997-98)
Most Assists, Season	**62**	Paul Kariya (1998-99)
Most Points, Season	**109**	Teemu Selanne (1996-97; 51G, 58A)
Most PIM, Season	**285**	Todd Ewen (1995-96)
Most Points, Defenseman, Season	**69**	Scott Niedermayer (2006-07; 15G, 54A)
Most Points, Center, Season	**85**	Andy McDonald (2005-06; 34G, 51A)
Most Points, Right Wing, Season	**109**	Teemu Selanne (1996-97; 51G, 58A)
Most Points, Left Wing, Season	**108**	Paul Kariya (1995-96; 50G, 58A)
Most Points, Rookie, Season	**45**	Dustin Penner (2006-07; 29G, 16A)
Most Shutouts, Season	**8**	Jean-Sebastien Giguere (2002-03)
Most Goals, Game	**3**	Twenty-five times
Most Assists, Game	**5**	Dmitri Mironov (Dec. 12/97), Teemu Selanne (Nov. 19/06)
Most Points, Game	**5**	Ten times

General Managers' History

Jack Ferreira, 1993-94 to 1997-98; Pierre Gauthier, 1998-99 to 2001-02; Bryan Murray, 2002-03, 2003-04; Al Coates, 2004-05; Brian Burke, 2005-06 to date.

Coaching History

Ron Wilson, 1993-94 to 1996-97; Pierre Page, 1997-98; Craig Hartsburg, 1998-99, 1999-2000; Craig Hartsburg and Guy Charron, 2000-01; Bryan Murray, 2001-02; Mike Babcock, 2002-03 to 2004-05; Randy Carlyle, 2005-06 to date.

Captains' History

Troy Loney, 1993-94; Randy Ladouceur, 1994-95, 1995-96; Paul Kariya, 1996-97; Paul Kariya and Teemu Selanne, 1997-98; Paul Kariya, 1998-99 to 2002-03; Steve Rucchin, 2003-04; Scott Niedermayer, 2005-06, 2006-07; Chris Pronger, 2007-08 to date.

All-time Record vs. Other Clubs

Regular Season

	At Home								On Road								Total							
	GP	W	L	T	OL	GF	GA	PTS	GP	W	L	T	OL	GF	GA	PTS	GP	W	L	T	OL	GF	GA	PTS
Atlanta	5	3	2	0	0	14	10	6	5	4	1	0	0	18	11	8	10	7	3	0	0	32	21	14
Boston	10	3	3	2	2	20	25	10	9	4	4	0	1	27	27	9	19	7	7	2	3	47	52	19
Buffalo	10	3	7	0	0	19	31	6	10	2	4	3	1	22	28	8	20	5	11	3	1	41	59	14
Calgary	32	18	8	6	0	104	80	42	31	10	20	1	0	71	90	21	63	28	28	7	0	175	170	63
Carolina	10	5	4	1	0	31	32	11	10	3	6	1	0	21	27	7	20	8	10	2	0	52	59	18
Chicago	28	17	7	3	1	81	59	38	30	15	13	2	0	76	78	32	58	32	20	5	1	157	137	70
Colorado	27	11	11	3	2	67	69	27	27	7	14	4	2	63	80	20	54	18	25	7	4	130	149	47
Columbus	14	8	3	1	2	41	33	19	14	6	8	0	0	32	39	12	28	14	11	1	2	73	72	31
Dallas	39	17	18	3	1	95	103	38	39	8	26	2	3	72	130	21	78	25	44	5	4	167	233	59
Detroit	28	11	13	4	0	70	76	26	28	3	19	3	3	58	97	12	56	14	32	7	3	128	173	38
Edmonton	32	17	12	2	1	89	84	37	31	10	18	0	3	63	77	23	63	27	30	2	4	152	161	60
Florida	10	4	5	1	0	28	30	9	9	3	3	2	1	22	27	9	19	7	8	3	1	50	57	18
Los Angeles	42	21	8	7	6	144	113	55	42	16	20	4	2	110	123	38	84	37	28	11	8	254	236	93
Minnesota	14	8	4	0	2	33	33	18	14	4	7	2	1	26	35	11	28	12	11	2	3	59	68	29
Montreal	9	4	5	0	0	28	28	8	9	3	4	2	0	24	27	8	18	7	9	2	0	52	55	16
Nashville	18	15	1	0	2	58	29	32	18	7	7	2	2	42	42	18	36	22	8	2	4	100	71	50
New Jersey	11	5	5	1	0	30	28	11	9	2	6	0	1	16	32	5	20	7	11	1	1	46	60	16
NY Islanders	10	2	4	3	1	22	29	8	9	4	4	1	0	26	24	9	19	6	8	4	1	48	53	17
NY Rangers	9	6	1	0	2	35	29	14	10	6	2	1	1	30	24	14	19	12	3	1	3	65	53	28
Ottawa	10	5	3	2	0	24	19	12	9	4	4	1	0	23	27	9	19	9	7	3	0	47	46	21
Philadelphia	10	4	4	2	0	34	35	10	9	2	4	3	0	17	25	7	19	6	8	5	0	51	60	17
Phoenix	39	24	10	3	2	120	96	53	38	20	12	2	4	109	101	46	77	44	22	5	6	229	197	99
Pittsburgh	9	6	3	0	0	32	26	12	10	2	6	2	0	31	34	6	19	8	9	2	0	63	60	18
St. Louis	28	12	14	2	0	77	81	26	28	10	12	3	3	74	86	26	56	22	26	5	3	151	167	52
San Jose	42	17	20	2	3	113	131	39	42	22	17	2	1	116	112	47	84	39	37	4	4	229	243	86
Tampa Bay	9	5	3	1	0	28	22	11	10	6	4	0	0	27	20	12	19	11	7	1	0	55	42	23
Toronto	12	6	5	1	0	39	28	13	16	2	10	4	0	32	53	8	28	8	15	5	0	71	81	21
Vancouver	31	10	12	7	2	79	88	29	32	12	18	2	0	75	101	26	63	22	30	9	2	154	189	55
Washington	10	6	2	1	1	31	25	14	10	6	4	0	0	28	17	12	20	12	6	1	1	59	42	26
Totals	**558**	**273**	**197**	**58**	**30**	**1586**	**1472**	**634**	**558**	**203**	**277**	**49**	**29**	**1351**	**1594**	**484**	**1116**	**476**	**474**	**107**	**59**	**2937**	**3066**	**1118**

Playoffs

	Series	W	L	GP	W	L	T	GF	GA	Last Mtg.	Rnd.	Result
Calgary	1	1	0	7	4	3	0	17	16	2006	CQF	W 4-3
Colorado	1	1	0	4	4	0	0	16	4	2006	CSF	W 4-0
Dallas	2	1	1	12	6	6	0	27	34	2008	CQF	L 2-4
Detroit	4	2	2	18	8	10	0	40	53	2007	CF	W 4-2
Edmonton	1	0	1	5	1	4	0	13	16	2006	CF	L 1-4
Minnesota	2	2	0	9	8	1	0	21	10	2007	CQF	W 4-1
New Jersey	1	0	1	7	3	4	0	12	19	2003	F	L 3-4
Ottawa	1	1	0	5	4	1	0	16	11	2007	F	W 4-1
Phoenix	1	1	0	7	4	3	0	17	17	1997	CQF	W 4-3
Vancouver	1	1	0	5	4	1	0	14	8	2007	CSF	W 4-1
Totals	**15**	**10**	**5**	**79**	**46**	**33**	**0**	**193**	**188**			

Carolina totals include Hartford, 1993-94 to 1996-97.
Colorado totals include Quebec, 1993-94 to 1994-95.
Phoenix totals include Winnipeg, 1993-94 to 1995-96.

Playoff Results 2008-2003

Year	Round	Opponent	Result	GF	GA
2008	CQF	Dallas	L 2-4	13	20
2007	**F**	**Ottawa**	**W 4-1**	**16**	**11**
	CF	Detroit	W 4-2	16	17
	CSF	Vancouver	W 4-1	14	8
	CQF	Minnesota	W 4-1	12	9
2006	CF	Edmonton	L 1-4	13	16
	CSF	Colorado	W 4-0	16	4
	CQF	Calgary	W 4-3	17	16
2003	F	New Jersey	L 3-4	12	19
	CF	Minnesota	W 4-0	9	1
	CSF	Dallas	W 4-2	14	14
	CQF	Detroit	W 4-0	10	6

Abbreviations: Round: F - Final; **CF** – conference final; **CSF** – conference semi-final; **CQF** – conference quarter-final

2007-08 Results

Sep.	29	at Los Angeles	1-4	**Jan.**	2	Columbus	2-1
	30	Los Angeles	4-1		4	Chicago	2-1
Oct.	3	at Detroit	2-3†		5	at Phoenix	2-3†
	5	at Columbus	0-4		7	Nashville	5-2
	6	at Pittsburgh	4-5		9	Toronto	5-0
	10	Boston	2-1		13	San Jose	4-3*
	14	Minnesota	0-2		15	Dallas	4-2
	15	Detroit	6-3		17	at Nashville	2-1
	17	Nashville	3-1		18	at Minnesota	4-2
	20	at Dallas	1-3		20	at Dallas	2-5
	23	at St. Louis	2-4		23	Detroit	1-2
	25	Phoenix	0-1		24	at Los Angeles	1-3
	28	Edmonton	2-3†		30	at Minnesota	1-5
Nov.	1	Columbus	2-1†	**Feb.**	1	at St. Louis	0-1†
	3	at Phoenix	5-2		2	at Philadelphia	0-3
	5	Dallas	0-5		5	at NY Islanders	3-0
	7	Phoenix	5-6*		7	at NY Rangers	4-1
	9	San Jose	3-2†		8	at New Jersey	2-1
	13	Los Angeles	4-3†		10	at Detroit	3-2
	15	at Los Angeles	6-3		12	at Colorado	2-1
	17	at San Jose	2-1†		15	Dallas	2-4
	21	at Dallas	1-2		17	Calgary	4-2
	23	Phoenix	3-4†		20	Colorado	3-2†
	25	Los Angeles	3-2		22	St. Louis	2-1*
	27	at Vancouver	0-4		24	Chicago	6-3
	29	at Calgary	4-1		29	Calgary	3-1
	30	at Edmonton	1-5	**Mar.**	3	Ottawa	3-1
Dec.	2	Edmonton	0-4		5	at Chicago	0-3
	5	Buffalo	4-1		6	at Colorado	0-1
	7	at Chicago	5-3		9	Montreal	3-1
	8	at Nashville	2-4		11	at Phoenix	2-3†
	10	at Columbus	4-3*		12	Vancouver	4-1
	12	Vancouver	2-3		15	St. Louis	5-2
	14	Minnesota	2-5		19	at Dallas	2-1
	16	San Jose	1-2†		21	at San Jose	1-2
	18	at San Jose	2-0		22	at Phoenix	2-1
	19	Colorado	2-1*		26	Los Angeles	2-1†
	22	at San Jose	5-2		28	San Jose	1-3
	27	at Edmonton	2-1		30	Dallas	3-2†
	29	at Calgary	3-5	**Apr.**	5	at Los Angeles	4-3
	30	at Vancouver	1-2		6	Phoenix	3-2†

* – Overtime † – Shootout

Entry Draft Selections 2008-1994

Name in bold denotes played in NHL.

2008
Pick
17 Jake Gardiner
35 Nicolas Deschamps
39 Eric O'Dell
43 Justin Schultz
71 Josh Brittain
83 Marco Cousineau
85 Brandon McMillan
113 Ryan Hegarty
143 Stefan Warg
208 Nick Pryor

2007
Pick
19 Logan MacMillan
42 Eric Tangradi
63 Maxime Macenauer
92 Justin Vaive
93 Steven Kampfer
98 Sebastian Stefaniszin
121 Mattias Modig
151 Brett Morrison

2006
Pick
19 Mark Mitera
38 Bryce Swan
83 John Degray
112 Matt Beleskey
172 **Petteri Wirtanen**

2005
Pick
2 **Bobby Ryan**
31 Brendan Mikkelson
63 Jason Bailey
127 Bobby Bolt
141 Brian Salcido
197 Jean-Philippe Levasseur

2004
Pick
9 **Ladislav Smid**
39 Jordan Smith
74 Kyle Klubertanz
75 **Tim Brent**
172 Matt Auffrey
203 Gabriel Bouthillette
236 Matt Christie
269 Janne Pesonen

2003
Pick
19 **Ryan Getzlaf**
28 **Corey Perry**
86 Shane Hynes
90 Juha Alen
119 Nathan Saunders
186 **Drew Miller**
218 Dirk Southern
250 **Shane O'Brien**
280 Ville Mantymaa

2002
Pick
7 **Joffrey Lupul**
37 **Tim Brent**
71 Brian Lee
103 Joonas Vihko
140 George Davis
173 Luke Fritshaw
261 Francois Caron
267 Chris Petrow

2001
Pick
5 **Stanislav Chistov**
35 **Mark Popovic**
69 Joel Stepp
102 **Timo Parssinen**
105 Vladimir Korsunov
118 Brandon Rogers
137 **Joel Perrault**
170 Jan Tabacek
224 **Tony Martensson**
232 **Martin Gerber**
264 **Pierre Parenteau**

2000
Pick
12 **Alexei Smirnov**
44 **Ilya Bryzgalov**
98 **Jonas Ronnqvist**
134 Peter Podhradsky
153 Bill Cass

1999
Pick
44 **Jordan Leopold**
83 **Niclas Havelid**
105 Alexandr Chagodayev
141 Maxim Rybin
173 Jan Sandstrom
230 **Petr Tenkrat**
258 Brian Gornick

1998
Pick
5 **Vitaly Vishnevski**
32 **Stephen Peat**
112 Viktor Wallin
150 **Trent Hunter**
178 **Jesse Fibiger**
205 David Bernier
233 Pelle Prestberg
245 Andreas Andersson

1997
Pick
18 **Michael Holmqvist**
45 **Maxim Balmochnykh**
72 Jay Legault
125 Luc Vaillancourt
178 Tony Mohagen
181 Mat Snesrud
209 Rene Stussi
235 Tommi Degerman

1996
Pick
9 **Ruslan Salei**
35 **Matt Cullen**
117 Brendan Buckley
149 Blaine Russell
172 Timo Ahmaoja
198 Kevin Kellett
224 Tobias Johwelin

1995
Pick
4 **Chad Kilger**
29 **Brian Wesenberg**
55 **Mike Leclerc**
107 **Igor Nikulin**
133 **Peter LeBoutillier**
159 Mike LaPlante
185 Igor Karpenko

1994
Pick
2 **Oleg Tverdovsky**
28 **Johan Davidsson**
67 **Craig Reichert**
80 Byron Briske
106 **Pavel Trnka**
132 **Bates Battaglia**
158 Rocky Welsing
184 Brad Englehart
236 Tommi Miettinen
262 **Jeremy Stevenson**

Brian Burke

Vice President and General Manager

Born: Providence, RI, June 30, 1955.

Brian Burke was named Anaheim's new executive vice president and general manager on June 20, 2005. In his first year on the job in 2005-06, the Ducks reached the Western Conference Final. In 2007, Anaheim won the Stanley Cup.

Burke had served as the president and general manager of the Vancouver Canucks from 1998 to 2004. Under his leadership, the team increased its point total four consecutive years from 1999 to 2003. With 104 and 101 points respectively the last two NHL seasons (2002-03, 2003-04), the Canucks joined only Detroit, Ottawa and Philadelphia to record consecutive seasons with at least 100 points. The 2003–04 Canucks finished with a record of 43-24-10-5 for 101 points, winning the Northwest Division. Over his last four seasons with the team, Burke engineered four consecutive seasons of at least 90 points. In 2001, he was named NHL executive of the year by *The Sporting News*.

One of the most respected and experienced executives in the NHL, Burke originally joined the Canucks in June, 1987 as vice president and director of hockey operations. He left the Canucks in 1992 to become general manager of the Hartford Whalers, before being named NHL senior vice president and director of hockey operations (1993 to 1998). While working at the NHL league office, Burke worked closely with commissioner Gary Bettman on a wide variety of league issues and policies and was the NHL's chief disciplinarian.

Burke was born in New England and raised in Minnesota. He signed with the Philadelphia Flyers in 1977 as a player and was a member of the 1978 Calder Cup champion Maine Mariners. Burke then returned to Harvard Law School, where he graduated in 1981 before practicing law for six years in Boston. During his two stints in Vancouver, Burke was a valued and active member of the community, including his serving on the board of directors for Canuck Place.

Club Directory

Honda Center

Anaheim Ducks
Honda Center
2695 E. Katella Ave.
Anaheim, CA 92806
Phone **714/940-2900**
FAX 714/940-2953
Ticket Information 877/WILDWING
www.anaheimducks.com
Capacity: 17,174

Executive Management

Owners	Henry and Susan Samueli
Chief Executive Officer	Michael Schulman
Executive Vice President/General Manager	Brian P. Burke
Executive Vice President/Chief Operating Officer	Tim Ryan
Senior Vice President, Hockey Operations	Bob Murray
Assistant General Manager	David McNab
Senior Advisor of Hockey Operations	Dave Nonis
Senior Vice President/Chief Marketing Officer	Bob Wagner
Vice President of Sales & Marketing	Steve Obert
Vice President of Human Resources	Kim Kutcher
Vice President of Finance	Doug Heller
Vice President of Operations	Kevin Starkey
Exec. Asst. to the Executive V.P./G.M.	Maureen Nyeholt
Exec. Asst. to the Executive V.P./COO	Cheryl Gorman
Exec. Asst. to the Senior V.P./CMO	Janet Conley
Exec. Asst. to the V.P. of Sales & Marketing	Cindy Iwami
Administrative Assistant, Hockey Operations	Christina Morrow

Coaching Staff

Head Coach	Randy Carlyle
Assistant Coaches	Dave Farrish, Newell Brown
Goaltending Consultant	Francois Allaire
Video Coordinator	Joe Trotta
Strength & Conditioning Coach	Sean Skahan

Hockey Club Operations

Director of Professional Scouting	Rick Paterson
Director of Amateur Scouting	Martin Madden
Assistant Director of Amateur Scouting	Alain Chainey
Scouting Staff	Scott Carter, Glen Cochrane, Jeff Crisp, Jan-Åke Danielson, Joe Gibbs, Casey Hankinson, Konstantin Krylov, John McMorrow, Donald Marier, Pavel Routa, Jim Sandlak, Neil Smith, Daryl Stanley
Head Trainer	Tim Clark
Massage Therapist	James Partida
Equipment Manager	Doug Shearer
Assistant Equipment Manager	John Allaway
Visiting Team Equipment Attendant	Chris Kincaid
Manager of Hockey Operations	Ryan Lichtenfels
Iowa Chops (AHL) Head Coach	Gord Dineen
Iowa Assistant Coaches	Matt Laatsch, TBA
Team Physicians	Dr. Ronald Glousman, Dr. Craig Milhouse
Oral Surgeon	Dr. Jeff Pulver

Broadcasting

Director of Broadcasting	Aaron Teats
Associate Producer	Bob Sipowich
Television, Fox Sports Prime Ticket (Cable), KDOC-TV	John Ahlers & Brian Hayward
Radio, KLAA AM 830 & Ducks Radio Network	Steve Carroll & Brent Severyn

Communications

Director of Media & Communications	Alex Gilchrist
Media & Communications Managers	Steve Hoem, Lauren O'Gorman
Game Night Communications Staff	Jennifer Andrews, Lisa Parris, Courtney Strayer, Larry Woodard, Grant Young

Community Relations Department

Director of Community Relations & Public Affairs	Wendy Yamagishi
Community Relations Managers	Jesse Tyler, Jennifer Walker

Entertainment

Director of Entertainment/Multi-Media	Rod Murray
Entertainment Manager	Chris Brown
Editor/Producer	Rich Cooley
Arena Vision Editor/Producer	Davin Maske

Fan Development

Director of Fan Development	Matt Savant
Sr. Managers, School / Youth Hockey Programs	Joseph Hwang / Lynsie Estes
Fan Development Manager	Champ Baginski

Finance and Administration

Controller	Melody Martin
IT Manager	Mike Wing
Human Resources Managers	Wendy Mulhall, Donna Vass

Corporate Partnerships

Director of Corporate Partnerships	Wendy Grover
Director of Media Sales	Tanya Mitchell
Director of Corporate Relations & Research	Alex Evezich
Senior Manager of Media Sales	Jamal Spears
Senior Sales Manager	Bonner Paddock

Marketing Department

Director of Marketing	Tracie Jones
Senior Manager of Signature Programs & Events	Kris Loomis
Senior Media & Marketing Manager	Adam Mendelsohn

Publications & New Media

Director of Publications & New Media	Adam Brady

Premium Sales & Service Department

Director of Premium Sales & Service	Jim Panetta
Premium Account Executives	Geoff Matthews, Timothy Thompson
Premium Services Manager	Jana Cannavo

Ticketing Department

Manager of Ticket Operations	James Bakken
Assistant Ticketing Manager	Jonas Calicdan
Assistant Manager, Premium Ticketing	Gina Bulgheroni

Ticket Sales and Customer Service

Director of Ticket Sales & Service	Lisa Johnson
Senior Manager of Season & Group Sales	Mike Morrow
Inside Sales Manager	Zach Hollins

Atlanta Thrashers

Key Off-Season Signings/Acquisitions

2008

June 16 • Re-signed G **Johan Hedberg**.
20 • Named **John Anderson** head coach.
20 • Selected D **Zach Bogosian** (Peterborough, OHL) third overall in the 2008 Entry Draft.
July 2 • Signed D **Ron Hainsey**.
9 • Re-signed LW **Eric Boulton**.
15 • Signed C **Jason Williams**.

2007-08 Results: 34W-40L-2OTL-6SOL 76PTS.
Fourth, Southeast Division

Year-by-Year Record

		Home				Road				Overall								
Season	GP	W	L	T	OL	W	L	T	OL	W	L	T	OL	GF	GA	Pts.	Finished	Playoff Result
2007-08	82	19	19	....	3	15	21	....	5	34	40	....	8	216	272	76	4th, Southeast Div.	Out of Playoffs
2006-07	82	23	12	....	6	20	16	....	5	43	28	....	11	246	245	97	1st, Southeast Div.	Lost Conf. Quarter-Final
2005-06	82	24	13	....	4	17	20	....	4	41	33	....	8	281	275	90	3rd, Southeast Div.	Out of Playoffs
2004-05	....	....	....	....	....	....	....	....	....	....	....	....	....	....	....	....		
2003-04	82	18	17	4	2	15	20	4	2	33	37	8	4	214	243	78	2nd, Southeast Div.	Out of Playoffs
2002-03	82	15	19	4	3	16	20	3	2	31	39	7	5	226	284	74	3rd, Southeast Div.	Out of Playoffs
2001-02	82	11	21	9	0	8	26	2	5	19	47	11	5	187	288	54	5th, Southeast Div.	Out of Playoffs
2000-01	82	10	23	6	2	13	22	6	0	23	45	12	2	211	289	60	4th, Southeast Div.	Out of Playoffs
1999-2000	82	9	26	3	3	5	31	4	1	14	57	7	4	170	313	39	5th, Southeast Div.	Out of Playoffs

2008-09 Schedule

Oct.	Fri.	10	Washington		Thu.	8	at New Jersey
	Sat.	11	at Florida		Sat.	10	at Florida*
	Tue.	14	Minnesota		Wed.	14	Ottawa
	Thu.	16	New Jersey		Fri.	16	Toronto
	Sat.	18	Buffalo		Sat.	17	at Nashville
	Tue.	21	at Tampa Bay		Tue.	20	Montreal
	Fri.	24	at Detroit		Wed.	21	at Philadelphia
	Sat.	25	at Boston		Tue.	27	at Dallas
	Tue.	28	Philadelphia		Thu.	29	NY Islanders
	Thu.	30	at NY Rangers		Sat.	31	at Carolina
Nov.	Sat.	1	at New Jersey	**Feb.**	Tue.	3	at NY Rangers
	Sun.	2	Florida*		Fri.	6	New Jersey
	Thu.	6	NY Islanders		Sun.	8	Philadelphia*
	Fri.	7	at Buffalo		Tue.	10	at Tampa Bay
	Sun.	9	at Carolina*		Wed.	11	Chicago
	Fri.	14	Carolina		Sun.	15	at Anaheim*
	Sun.	16	at Philadelphia		Mon.	16	at Los Angeles
	Thu.	20	Pittsburgh		Thu.	19	at Phoenix
	Sat.	22	Columbus		Sat.	21	at San Jose*
	Tue.	25	at Toronto		Tue.	24	Colorado
	Wed.	26	at Washington		Thu.	26	at Washington
	Fri.	28	Nashville		Sat.	28	Carolina
	Sun.	30	St. Louis*	**Mar.**	Tue.	3	Florida
Dec.	Tue.	2	at Montreal		Fri.	6	Montreal
	Wed.	3	at Ottawa		Sun.	8	Calgary*
	Sat.	6	at NY Islanders		Tue.	10	at Colorado
	Wed.	10	NY Rangers		Thu.	12	at Edmonton
	Fri.	12	Boston		Sat.	14	at Buffalo
	Sat.	13	at Boston		Mon.	16	Washington
	Tue.	16	at Ottawa		Tue.	17	at Pittsburgh
	Thu.	18	Pittsburgh		Fri.	20	Detroit
	Sat.	20	Tampa Bay		Sat.	21	at Tampa Bay
	Mon.	22	Toronto		Tue.	24	at Montreal
	Tue.	23	at NY Islanders		Thu.	26	NY Rangers
	Fri.	26	Carolina		Sat.	28	Ottawa
	Sun.	28	Boston*	**Apr.**	Wed.	1	Buffalo
	Tue.	30	at Toronto		Fri.	3	at Florida
	Wed.	31	at Carolina		Sun.	5	at Washington*
Jan.	Fri.	2	Vancouver		Tue.	7	Washington
	Sun.	4	Tampa Bay*		Thu.	9	Florida
	Tue.	6	at Pittsburgh		Sat.	11	Tampa Bay

* Denotes afternoon game.

Ilya Kovalchuk scored 52 goals for the second time in the last three seasons. In 2005-06, that total tied him for third but was only four short of the league lead. His 52 goals in 2007-08 ranked him second to fellow Russian Alex Ovechkin, who led the NHL with 65.

SOUTHEAST DIVISION
10th NHL Season
Franchise date: June 25, 1997

2008-09 Player Personnel

FORWARDS	HT	WT	S	Place of Birth	*Age	2007-08 Club
ARMSTRONG, Colby	6-2	190	R	Lloydminster, Sask.	25	Pittsburgh-Atlanta
BOULTON, Eric	6-1	225	L	Halifax, N.S.	32	Atlanta
CHRISTENSEN, Erik	6-1	210	L	Edmonton, Alta.	24	Pittsburgh-Atlanta
CRABB, Joey	6-1	190	R	Anchorage, AK	25	Chicago (AHL)
ESPOSITO, Angelo	6-1	180	L	Montreal, Que.	19	Que (QMJHL)-Chi (AHL)
HOFFMAN, Mike	6-5	250	R	Weymouth, MA	28	Portland (AHL)
HOLZAPFEL, Riley	6-0	185	L	Regina, Sask.	20	Moose Jaw-Chicago (AHL)
KAIP, Rylan	6-1	185	L	Wilcox, Sask.	24	North Dakota
KOVALCHUK, Ilya	6-1	220	R	Tver, USSR	25	Atlanta
KOZLOV, Vyacheslav	5-10	190	L	Voskresensk, USSR	36	Atlanta
LARSEN, Brad	6-0	210	L	Nakusp, B.C.	31	Atlanta
LaVALLEE, Jordan	6-3	220	L	Corvallis, OR	22	Atlanta-Chicago (AHL)
LESSARD, Junior	5-11	200	R	St-Joseph-de-Beauce, Que.	28	Dal-Iowa-T.B.-Norfolk
LITTLE, Bryan	5-11	200	R	Edmonton, Alta.	20	Atlanta-Chicago (AHL)
MACHACEK, Spencer	6-1	195	R	Lethbridge, Alta.	19	Vancouver (WHL)
MOTZKO, Joe	6-0	185	R	Bemidji, MN	28	Wsh-Her-Chi (AHL)
PAINCHAUD, Chad	6-1	185	L	Mississauga, Ont.	22	Chicago (AHL)-Gwinnett
PERRIN, Eric	5-9	180	L	Laval, Que.	32	Atlanta
POSPISIL, Tomas	6-0	185	R	Sumperk, Czech.	21	Chicago (AHL)-Gwinnett
REASONER, Marty	6-1	202	L	Honeoye Falls, NY	31	Edmonton
SIDDALL, Matt	6-1	210	R	North Vancouver, B.C.	24	Northern Mich.
SLATER, Jim	6-0	195	L	Petoskey, MI	25	Atlanta-Chicago (AHL)
STERLING, Brett	5-8	180	L	Los Angeles, CA	24	Atlanta-Chicago (AHL)
STEVENSON, Grant	5-11	170	R	Spruce Grove, Alta.	26	Quad City
STOESZ, Myles	6-2	215	R	Steinbach, Man.	21	Gwinnett
STUART, Colin	6-2	205	L	Rochester, MN	26	Atlanta-Chicago (AHL)
THORBURN, Chris	6-3	225	R	Sault Ste. Marie, Ont.	25	Atlanta
WHITE, Todd	5-10	195	L	Kanata, Ont.	33	Atlanta
WILLIAMS, Jason	5-11	195	R	London, Ont.	28	Chicago
DEFENSEMEN						
BOGOSIAN, Zach	6-2	200	R	Massena, NY	18	Peterborough
DENNY, Chad	6-3	220	L	Sydney, N.S.	21	Chicago (AHL)-Gwinnett
ENSTROM, Tobias	5-10	175	L	Nordingra, Sweden	23	Atlanta
EXELBY, Garnet	6-1	210	L	Ste. Anne, Man.	27	Atlanta
HAINSEY, Ron	6-3	210	L	Bolton, CT	27	Columbus
HAVELID, Niclas	6-0	200	L	Stockholm, Sweden	35	Atlanta
KLEE, Ken	6-0	210	R	Indianapolis, IN	37	Atlanta
KULDA , Arturs	6-2	200	L	Riga, Latvia	20	Peterborough-Chicago (AHL)
LEHMAN, Scott	6-2	200	L	Fort McMurray, Alta.	22	Chicago (AHL)-Gwinnett
LEWIS, Grant	6-3	200	R	Pittsburgh, PA	23	Chicago (AHL)
OYSTRICK, Nathan	6-0	215	L	Regina, Sask.	25	Chicago (AHL)
VALABIK, Boris	6-7	240	L	Nitra, Czech.	22	Atlanta-Chicago (AHL)

GOALTENDERS	HT	WT	C	Place of Birth	*Age	2007-08 Club
HEDBERG, Johan	6-0	185	L	Leksand, Sweden	35	Atlanta
LEHTONEN, Kari	6-4	205	L	Helsinki, Finland	24	Atlanta-Chicago (AHL)
PAVELEC, Ondrej	6-2	200	L	Kladno, Czech.	21	Atlanta-Chicago (AHL)
TURPLE, Dan	6-6	210	L	Oakville, Ont.	23	Grand Rapids-Gwinnett

* – Age at start of 2008-09 season

Don Waddell

Vice President and General Manager

Born: Detroit, MI, August 19, 1958.

As the only general manager in the history of the Atlanta Thrashers, Don Waddell has established a foundation for long-term success in Atlanta by infusing the club with solid veterans to support a talented young line-up. Waddell built a team that set club records in wins (43) and points (97) in 2006-07, winning the Southeast Division and reaching the playoffs for the first time.

Waddell came to the franchise on June 23, 1998 – almost a year to the day after the NHL granted Atlanta a team. He has built the core of the franchise through the NHL Entry Draft and by stockpiling impressive prospects. He made Ilya Kovalchuk the first Russian player selected first overall in the history of the Entry Draft. In the 2002 Entry Draft, Waddell made Kari Lehtonen of Finland the highest-selected European goaltender in NHL draft history.

Waddell has a long-standing relationship with USA Hockey as a player and in management, and served as assistant general manager for the 2004 World Championship and World Cup teams. He was general manager of the 2005 World Championship team and the 2006 Olympic team. His extensive organizational experience also includes having previously built two professional hockey franchises: the San Diego Gulls and the Orlando Solar Bears of the now-defunct International Hockey League. He's also no stranger to winning through his role as assistant general manager for the Stanley Cup champion Detroit Red Wings during the 1997-98 season.

Waddell's playing experience includes more than nine seasons of professional hockey, mostly in the IHL. He was drafted by the NHL's Los Angeles Kings in 1978 and spent three years with the organization from 1980 to 1983. During a successful amateur career, Waddell helped the U.S. national team win the gold medal at the 1983 B-Pool World Championships. He played Division I hockey at Northern Michigan University from 1976 to 1980, where he majored in business management.

Coaching Record

			Regular Season				Playoffs			
Season	**Team**	**League**	**GC**	**W**	**L**	**O/T**	**GC**	**W**	**L**	**T**
2002-03	Atlanta	NHL	10	4	5	1	....	....	....	....
2007-08	Atlanta	NHL	76	34	34	8	....	....	....	....
	NHL Totals		**86**	**38**	**39**	**9**	....	....	....	....

2007-08 Scoring

* – rookie

Regular Season

Pos	#	Player	Team	GP	G	A	Pts	TOI	+/–	PIM	PP	SH	GW	S	%
L	17	Ilya Kovalchuk	ATL	79	52	35	87	21:30	–12	52	16	2	4	283	18.4
R	8	Mark Recchi	PIT	19	2	6	8	16:24	–2	12	2	0	0	36	5.6
			ATL	53	12	28	40	18:23	–16	20	5	0	0	85	14.1
			Total	72	14	34	48	17:52	–18	32	7	0	0	121	11.6
C	11	Eric Perrin	ATL	81	12	33	45	17:49	–5	26	2	2	0	121	9.9
L	13	Vyacheslav Kozlov	ATL	82	17	24	41	15:56	–10	26	5	0	4	161	10.6
D	39	* Tobias Enstrom	ATL	82	5	33	38	24:28	–5	42	4	0	0	105	4.8
C	12	Todd White	ATL	74	14	23	37	18:25	–12	36	6	1	4	111	12.6
R	19	Colby Armstrong	PIT	54	9	15	24	15:24	6	50	0	0	2	84	10.7
			ATL	18	4	7	11	18:01	–2	6	1	0	1	29	13.8
			Total	72	13	22	35	16:03	4	56	1	0	3	113	11.5
C	16	Bobby Holik	ATL	82	15	19	34	15:58	–14	90	3	0	3	140	10.7
C	9	Erik Christensen	PIT	49	9	11	20	12:36	–3	28	2	0	0	109	8.3
			ATL	10	2	2	4	16:57	–7	2	0	0	0	23	8.7
			Total	59	11	13	24	13:20	–10	30	2	0	0	132	8.3
R	27	Chris Thorburn	ATL	73	5	13	18	08:56	–4	92	0	0	1	72	6.9
C	10	* Bryan Little	ATL	48	6	10	16	15:36	–2	18	2	0	1	76	7.9
D	28	Niclas Havelid	ATL	81	1	13	14	20:30	2	42	0	0	0	54	1.9
C	23	Jim Slater	ATL	69	8	5	13	10:23	–10	41	0	2	0	95	8.4
D	22	Ken Klee	ATL	72	1	9	10	20:02	–5	60	0	0	0	56	1.8
L	36	Eric Boulton	ATL	74	4	5	9	07:26	–10	127	0	0	0	64	6.3
D	77	Alexei Zhitnik	ATL	65	3	5	8	19:01	–8	58	0	0	1	79	3.8
R	38	Darren Haydar	ATL	16	1	7	8	11:45	4	2	0	0	0	14	7.1
D	2	Garnet Exelby	ATL	79	2	5	7	18:53	–21	85	0	0	0	37	5.4
D	5	Steve McCarthy	ATL	55	1	6	7	15:47	–23	48	0	0	0	41	2.4
L	49	* Colin Stuart	ATL	18	3	2	5	12:19	2	6	0	1	1	19	15.8
D	3	Joel Kwiatkowski	ATL	18	0	5	5	16:44	–5	20	0	0	0	24	0.0
L	29	Brad Larsen	ATL	62	1	3	4	09:01	–17	12	0	0	0	35	2.9
L	21	* Brett Sterling	ATL	13	1	2	3	12:23	–2	14	0	0	0	14	7.1
L	50	* Jordan LaVallee	ATL	2	1	1	2	11:27	2	0	0	0	0	1	100.0
D	7	* Mark Popovic	ATL	33	0	2	2	14:28	–4	10	0	0	0	25	0.0
C	45	Kevin Doell	ATL	8	0	1	1	09:39	–2	4	0	0	0	6	0.0
D	48	* Boris Valabik	ATL	7	0	0	0	16:41	–2	42	0	0	0	5	0.0

Goaltending

No.	Goaltender	GPI	Mins	Avg	W	L	OT	EN	SO	GA	SA	S%	G	A	PIM
32	Kari Lehtonen	48	2707	2.90	17	22	5	2	4	131	1560	.916	0	2	4
33	* Ondrej Pavelec	7	347	3.11	3	3	0	1	0	18	190	.905	0	0	2
1	Johan Hedberg	36	1927	3.46	14	15	3	3	1	111	1026	.892	0	1	16
	Totals	**82**	**5012**	**3.18**	**34**	**40**	**8**	**6**	**5**	**266**	**2782**	**.904**			

After nearly five full seasons in the Swedish elite league, Tobias Enstrom made his NHL debut in 2007-08. He ranked fourth among rookies with 33 assists and led all rookie defensemen with 38 points.

General Managers' History

Don Waddell, 1999-2000 to date.

Captains' History

Kelly Buchberger, 1999-2000; Steve Staios, 2000-01; Ray Ferraro, 2001-02; no captain, 2002-03; Shawn McEachern, 2003-04; Scott Mellanby, 2005-06, 2006-07; Bobby Holik, 2007-08.

Coaching History

Curt Fraser, 1999-2000 to 2001-02; Curt Fraser, Don Waddell and Bob Hartley, 2002-03; Bob Hartley, 2003-04 to 2006-07; Bob Hartley and Don Waddell, 2007-08; John Anderson, 2008-09.

Club Records

Team

(Figures in brackets for season records are games played.)

Most Points	**97**	2006-07 (82)
Most Wins	**43**	2006-07 (82)
Most Ties	**12**	2000-01 (82)
Most Losses	**57**	1999-2000 (82)
Most Goals	**281**	2005-06 (82)
Most Goals Against	**313**	1999-2000 (82)
Fewest Points	**39**	1999-2000 (82)
Fewest Wins	**14**	1999-2000 (82)
Fewest Ties	**7**	1999-2000 (82), 2002-03 (82)
Fewest Losses	**33**	2005-06 (82)
Fewest Goals	**170**	1999-2000 (82)
Fewest Goals Against	**243**	2003-04 (82)
Longest Winning Streak		
Overall	**5**	Four times
Home	**7**	Mar. 2-18/07
Away	**4**	Jan. 13-Feb. 7/03, Nov. 3-21/07
Longest Undefeated Streak		
Overall	**5**	Five times
Home	**7**	Mar. 2-18/07 (7 wins)
Away	**7**	Oct. 21-Nov. 13/00 (3 wins, 4 ties)
Longest Losing Streak		
Overall	**12**	Jan. 24-Feb. 20/00
Home	***11**	Jan. 24-Mar. 16/00
Away	**10**	Oct. 6-Nov. 18/01
Longest Winless Streak		
Overall	**16**	Jan. 16-Feb. 20/00 (14 losses, 2 ties)
Home	***17**	Jan. 19-Mar. 29/00 (15 losses, 2 ties)
Away	**10**	Oct. 6-Nov. 18/01 (10 losses)
Most Shutouts, Season	**5**	2005-06 (82), 2007-08 (82)
Most PIM, Season	**1,505**	2003-04 (82)
Most Goals, Game	**9**	Nov. 12/05 (Atl. 9 at Car. 0)

Individual

Most Seasons	**6**	Patrik Stefan, Ilya Kovalchuk
Most Games	**466**	Ilya Kovalchuk
Most Goals, Career	**254**	Ilya Kovalchuk
Most Assists, Career	**212**	Ilya Kovalchuk
Most Points, Career	**466**	Ilya Kovalchuk (254G, 212A)
Most PIM, Career	**532**	Jeff Odgers
Most Shutouts, Career	**11**	Kari Lehtonen
Longest Consecutive Games Streak	**164**	Greg de Vries (Oct. 5/05-Apr. 7/07)
Most Goals, Season	**52**	Ilya Kovalchuk (2005-06, 2007-08)
Most Assists, Season	**69**	Marc Savard (2005-06)
Most Points, Season	**100**	Marian Hossa (2006-07; 43G, 57A)
Most PIM, Season	**226**	Jeff Odgers (2000-01)
Most Points, Defenseman, Season	**38**	Jaroslav Modry (2005-06; 7G, 31A), Alexei Zhitnik (2006-07; 7G, 31A), Tobias Enstrom (2007-08; 5G, 33A)
Most Points, Center, Season	**97**	Marc Savard (2005-06; 28G, 69A)
Most Points, Right Wing, Season	**100**	Marian Hossa (2006-07; 43G, 57A)
Most Points, Left Wing, Season	**98**	Ilya Kovalchuk (2005-06; 52G, 46A)
Most Points, Rookie, Season	**67**	Dany Heatley (2001-02; 26G, 41A)
Most Shutouts, Season	**4**	Kari Lehtonen (2006-07, 2007-08)
Most Goals, Game	**4**	Pascal Rheaume (Jan. 19/02), Ilya Kovalchuk (Nov. 11/05)
Most Assists, Game	**4**	Six times
Most Points, Game	**5**	Six times

* NHL Record.

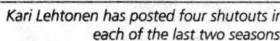

Kari Lehtonen has posted four shutouts in each of the last two seasons.

All-time Record vs. Other Clubs

Regular Season

	At Home								On Road								Total							
	GP	W	L	T	OL	GF	GA	PTS	GP	W	L	T	OL	GF	GA	PTS	GP	W	L	T	OL	GF	GA	PTS
Anaheim	5	1	4	0	0	11	18	2	5	2	3	0	0	10	14	4	10	3	7	0	0	21	32	6
Boston	16	8	8	0	0	51	45	16	16	6	5	2	3	55	55	17	32	14	13	2	3	106	100	33
Buffalo	16	10	3	1	2	55	49	23	16	6	10	0	0	41	73	12	32	16	13	1	2	96	122	35
Calgary	5	4	0	1	0	14	9	9	4	0	4	0	0	7	18	0	9	4	4	1	0	21	27	9
Carolina	25	5	14	3	3	65	85	16	25	9	12	1	3	76	83	22	50	14	26	4	6	141	168	38
Chicago	5	2	2	0	1	18	15	5	3	1	2	0	0	3	8	2	8	3	4	0	1	21	23	7
Colorado	5	1	2	1	1	9	13	4	5	3	2	0	0	16	20	6	10	4	4	1	1	25	33	10
Columbus	4	3	1	0	0	10	8	6	5	2	2	0	1	11	14	5	9	5	3	0	1	21	22	11
Dallas	5	0	4	0	1	12	21	1	5	1	4	0	0	9	11	2	10	1	8	0	1	21	32	3
Detroit	4	1	3	0	0	14	25	2	5	1	2	0	2	13	18	4	9	2	5	0	2	27	43	6
Edmonton	4	1	3	0	0	5	12	2	5	1	3	1	0	12	19	3	9	2	6	1	0	17	31	5
Florida	25	14	5	4	2	84	69	34	25	13	8	1	3	75	61	30	50	27	13	5	5	159	130	64
Los Angeles	5	2	3	0	0	13	18	4	5	1	4	0	0	15	26	2	10	3	7	0	0	28	44	6
Minnesota	3	1	2	0	0	9	12	2	4	0	3	1	0	6	13	1	7	1	5	1	0	15	25	3
Montreal	16	4	9	2	1	28	44	11	16	5	10	0	1	35	52	11	32	9	19	2	2	63	96	22
Nashville	5	3	0	1	1	16	13	8	4	1	3	0	0	6	15	2	9	4	3	1	1	22	28	10
New Jersey	16	5	9	2	0	38	59	12	16	7	7	1	1	35	46	16	32	12	16	3	1	73	105	28
NY Islanders	16	5	8	2	1	49	63	13	16	7	9	0	0	38	56	14	32	12	17	2	1	87	119	27
NY Rangers	16	7	9	0	0	47	53	14	16	9	5	1	1	47	46	20	32	16	14	1	1	94	99	34
Ottawa	16	6	9	1	0	53	62	13	16	5	10	1	0	45	74	11	32	11	19	2	0	98	136	24
Philadelphia	16	2	11	1	2	35	56	7	16	2	11	2	1	43	68	7	32	4	22	3	3	78	124	14
Phoenix	5	1	3	0	1	10	17	3	6	0	5	1	0	9	21	1	11	1	8	1	1	19	38	4
Pittsburgh	16	6	8	0	2	49	53	14	16	4	10	0	2	41	61	10	32	10	18	0	4	90	114	24
St. Louis	5	2	2	1	0	16	16	5	4	1	3	0	0	4	13	2	9	3	5	1	0	20	29	7
San Jose	5	1	3	1	0	8	16	3	5	0	4	1	0	10	21	1	10	1	7	2	0	18	37	4
Tampa Bay	25	15	5	3	2	82	65	35	25	8	13	1	3	64	93	20	50	23	18	4	5	146	158	55
Toronto	15	5	9	0	1	27	54	11	15	5	9	1	0	36	55	11	30	10	18	1	1	63	109	22
Vancouver	4	1	3	0	0	12	14	2	4	1	2	1	0	7	13	3	8	2	5	1	0	19	27	5
Washington	25	13	8	2	2	70	72	30	25	8	11	3	3	72	86	22	50	21	19	5	5	142	158	52
Totals	**328**	**129**	**150**	**26**	**23**	**910**	**1056**	**307**	**328**	**109**	**176**	**19**	**24**	**841**	**1153**	**261**	**656**	**238**	**326**	**45**	**47**	**1751**	**2209**	**568**

Playoffs

	Series	W	L	GP	W	L	T	GF	GA	Last Mtg.	Rnd.	Result
NY Rangers	1	0	1	4	0	4	0	6	17	2007	CQF	L 0-4
Totals	**1**	**0**	**1**	**4**	**0**	**4**	**0**	**6**	**17**			

Playoff Results 2008-2003

Year	Round	Opponent	Result	GF	GA
2007	CQF	NY Rangers	L 0-4	6	17

Abbreviations: Round: CQF – conference quarter-final.

2007-08 Results

Oct.	5	Washington	1-3		4	Carolina	3-4
	6	at Tampa Bay	2-5		6	Buffalo	5-2
	10	Ottawa	1-3		8	Philadelphia	1-4
	11	at Buffalo	0-6		10	Florida	2-3†
	13	New Jersey	5-6		12	Pittsburgh	3-2†
	16	at Philadelphia	0-4		15	at Detroit	5-1
	18	NY Rangers	5-3		17	Montreal	2-3†
	20	at Tampa Bay	2-6		18	at Buffalo	1-10
	23	at Toronto	5-4†		20	Edmonton	2-4
	25	at Nashville	0-3		22	at NY Rangers	0-4
	27	at Chicago	3-2		24	at NY Rangers	1-2†
	30	at Montreal	3-2†		30	Pittsburgh	4-1
Nov.	1	at Ottawa	4-6	**Feb.**	1	Buffalo	5-4†
	3	at Tampa Bay	6-4		2	at Washington	2-0
	6	Washington	2-1*		5	Philadelphia	2-3
	9	at Florida	4-1		7	Vancouver	1-2
	10	Carolina	3-5		9	Tampa Bay	2-1*
	13	Florida	3-2*		13	Washington	3-2†
	16	at Carolina	3-0		15	at New Jersey	4-3†
	19	Tampa Bay	4-3*		16	at NY Islanders	1-4
	21	at Washington	5-1		21	at Carolina	3-5
	23	New Jersey	0-3		23	at Toronto	1-3
	24	at Pittsburgh	0-5		26	at Montreal	1-5
	29	Toronto	2-4		28	NY Islanders	4-5*
Dec.	1	at NY Islanders	4-0	**Mar.**	1	at Boston	2-3†
	2	at New Jersey	2-3†		2	at Pittsburgh	2-3†
	5	NY Islanders	4-3†		5	Carolina	3-6
	7	NY Rangers	4-2		7	Minnesota	3-2†
	8	at Washington	3-6		8	at Florida	2-3*
	12	Boston	3-5		11	Colorado	2-5
	14	Toronto	0-4		13	Calgary	6-4
	15	at Ottawa	3-7		14	at Washington	1-4
	18	Tampa Bay	6-2		16	at Florida	1-3
	20	Ottawa	3-2		18	at Philadelphia	2-3
	22	Montreal	3-2†		19	Carolina	3-5
	23	at St. Louis	3-2*		21	Washington	3-5
	26	at Columbus	0-2		27	at Florida	3-2
	27	Florida	3-5		28	at Carolina	1-7
	29	Boston	5-0		31	at Tampa Bay	2-0
	31	at Boston	2-5	**Apr.**	1	Florida	2-3
Jan.	2	at Carolina	5-4*		5	Tampa Bay	4-1

* – Overtime † – Shootout

Entry Draft Selections 2008-1999

Name in bold denotes played in NHL.

2008
Pick
3 Zach Bogosian
29 Daultan Leveille
64 Danick Paquette
94 Vinny Saponari
124 Nicklas Lasu
154 Christopher Carrozzi
184 Zach Redmond

2007
Pick
67 Spencer Machacek
115 Niclas Lucenius
175 John Albert
205 Paul Postma

2006
Pick
12 **Bryan Little**
43 Riley Holzapfel
80 Michael Forney
135 Alex Kangas
165 Jonas Enlund
195 Jesse Martin
200 Arturs Kulda
210 Will O'Neill

2005
Pick
16 Alex Bourret
41 **Ondrej Pavelec**
49 Chad Denny
53 Andrew Kozek
116 **Jordan LaVallee**
135 Tomas Pospisil
187 Andrei Zubarev
207 Myles Stoesz

2004
Pick
10 **Boris Valabik**
40 Grant Lewis
76 Scott Lehman
106 Chad Painchaud
142 Juraj Gracik
186 Dan Turple
204 Miikka Tuomainen
237 Mitch Carefoot
270 Matt Siddall

2003
Pick
8 **Braydon Coburn**
110 Jim Sharrow
116 Guillaume Desbiens
136 Michael Vannelli
145 **Brett Sterling**
175 Mike Hamilton
203 Denis Loginov
239 **Tobias Enstrom**
269 Rylan Kaip

2002
Pick
2 **Kari Lehtonen**
30 **Jim Slater**
116 Patrick Dwyer
124 Lane Manson
144 Paul Flache
167 Brad Schell
198 Nathan Oystrick
230 Colton Fretter
236 Tyler Boldt
257 Pauli Levokari

2001
Pick
1 **Ilya Kovalchuk**
80 **Michael Garnett**
100 Brian Sipotz
112 Milan Gajic
135 **Colin Stuart**
189 **Pasi Nurminen**
199 Matt Suderman
201 Colin FitzRandolph
262 Mario Cartelli

2000
Pick
2 **Dany Heatley**
31 Ilja Nikulin
42 Libor Ustrnul
107 Carl Mallette
108 Blake Robson
147 Matt McRae
168 Zdenek Smid
178 Jeff Dwyer
180 **Darcy Hordichuk**
230 Samu Isosalo
242 Evan Nielsen
244 Eric Bowen
288 Mark McRae
290 **Simon Gamache**

1999
Pick
1 **Patrik Stefan**
30 **Luke Sellars**
68 **Zdenek Blatny**
98 David Kaczowka
99 Rob Zepp
128 **Derek MacKenzie**
159 Yuri Dobryshkin
188 Stephen Baby
217 **Garnet Exelby**
245 **Tommi Santala**
246 Raymond DiLauro

John Anderson

Head Coach

Born: Toronto, Ont., March 28, 1957.

The Atlanta Thrashers named John Anderson the fourth head coach in team history on June 20, 2008. Anderson led the Chicago Wolves, Atlanta's American Hockey League farm club, to the 2008 Calder Cup championship. It was his fifth championship in 13 seasons as a head coach in the minor leagues. Anderson spent 11 seasons as head coach of the Wolves, who have been the Thrashers' primary minor-league affiliate since 2001. During his tenure with Chicago, Anderson earned a 506-283-99 regular-season record, a 105-60 post-season record and captured two Calder Cup championships (2002, 2008,) and two Turner Cup titles (1998, 2000) when the team was a member of the International Hockey League. Anderson earned his first of five league titles as a head coach with the Quad City Mallards of the Colonial Hockey League in 1997.

Throughout his 13 seasons as a head coach in the minor leagues, Anderson's teams made the playoffs on 12 occasions, including 10 of his 11 seasons with the Wolves. Overall, he led his teams to the league finals eight times and advanced to the conference finals 10 times. He has won 40-or-more games in a season 10 times, including 50-or-more wins on four occasions, and has reached the 100-point mark seven times. He is also the Wolves all-time leader in regular-season wins (506) and playoff wins (105).

Under Anderson's leadership, the Wolves set several single-season team records, including 55 wins (1997-98); 114 points (1999-2000); 331 goals (2006-07); and 208 goals-against (2003-04). After the team joined the AHL in 2001, Anderson racked up 306 regular-season wins and led the squad to a 16-4 series record in the Calder Cup playoffs. Prior to joining the Wolves, Anderson led Quad City to the 1997 Colonial Cup championship. The previous season (1995-96), he began his coaching career with the Winston-Salem Mammoths, leading them to the Southern Hockey League finals. In July of 2007, Anderson made his international coaching debut when he led the United States squad to a gold medal at the World Jewish Cup in Metulla, Israel.

During his 12-year NHL playing career from 1977 to 1989, Anderson amassed 282 goals and 349 assists for 631 points in 814 games with the Toronto Maple Leafs (1977 to1985), Quebec Nordiques (1985-86) and Hartford Whalers (1986 to 1989). He also notched nine goals and 27 points in 37 career playoff games. Originally selected by the Maple Leafs in the first round, 11th overall, in the 1977 NHL Entry Draft, Anderson registered five 30-goal campaigns, including four straight from 1981 to 1985. His most productive season came in 1982-83, when he led Toronto with 80 points (31 goals, 49 assists) in 80 games.

After his NHL career, Anderson spent four full seasons in the minor leagues. With the New Haven Nighthawks in 1991-92, Anderson became the oldest player to win the AHL's MVP award at age 35. As a player/assistant coach with the San Diego Gulls of the IHL in 1992-93, he helped propel the club to an IHL-record 62 wins and a berth in the Turner Cup Finals.

Coaching Record

			Regular Season				Playoffs			
Season	Team	League	GC	W	L	O/T	GC	W	L	T
1995-96	Winston-Salem	SHL	60	30	23	7	9	4	5	....
1996-97	Quad City	CoHL	74	51	20	3	15	11	4	....
1997-98	Chicago	IHL	82	55	24	3	22	15	7	....
1998-99	Chicago	IHL	82	49	21	12	10	6	4	....
99-2000	Chicago	IHL	82	53	21	8	16	12	4	....
2000-01	Chicago	IHL	82	43	32	7	16	9	7	....
2001-02	Chicago	AHL	80	37	31	12	25	17	8	....
2002-03	Chicago	AHL	80	43	25	12	9	3	6	....
2003-04	Chicago	AHL	80	42	26	12	10	6	4	....
2004-05	Chicago	AHL	80	49	24	7	18	12	6	....
2005-06	Chicago	AHL	80	36	32	12	....	....	....	....
2006-07	Chicago	AHL	80	46	25	9	15	9	6	....
2007-08	Chicago	AHL	80	53	22	5	24	16	8	....

Club Directory

Philips Arena

Atlanta Thrashers
Centennial Tower
101 Marietta St.
Suite 1900
Atlanta, GA 30303
Phone **404/878-3800**
FAX 404/878-3765
www.atlantathrashers.com
Capacity: 18,545

Ownership . . . . Atlanta Spirit, LLC

Executive Management
Executive Vice President and General Manager . . . . Don Waddell
President of Philips Arena . . . . Bob Williams
General Manager, Hawks . . . . Rick Sund
Senior Vice President of Broadcast and Corporate Partnerships . . . . Tracy White
Chief Financial Officer . . . . Phil Ebinger
Vice President and Chief Legal Officer . . . . Scott Wilkinson

Hockey Operations
Vice President and Assistant General Manager . . . . Larry Simmons
Director of Amateur Scouting and Player Development . . . . Dan Marr
Director of Player Personnel . . . . Mark Dobson
Senior Director of Team Services . . . . Michele Zarzaca
Practice Facility Office Manager . . . . Leisa Ludwin

Coaching Staff
Head Coach . . . . John Anderson
Assistant Coaches . . . . Randy Cunneyworth, Todd Nelson, Steve Weeks
Video Coach . . . . Tony Borgford

Scouting Staff
Head Scout . . . . Marcel Comeau
Full-Time Scouts . . . . Evgeny Bogdanovich, Bernd Freimuller, Mark Hillier, Tavis MacMillan, Peter Mahovlich, Bob Owen, John Perpich, Normand Poisson
Part-Time Scouts . . . . Terry Brennan, Pat Carmichael

Training Staff
Strength and Conditioning Coach . . . . Ray Bear
Head Athletic Trainer . . . . Tommy Alva
Assistant Athletic Trainer . . . . Step Roberts
Massage Therapist . . . . Inar Treiguts

Equipment Staff
Head Equipment Manager . . . . Bobby Stewart
Assistant Equipment Managers . . . . Joe Guilmet, Jim Guilmet

Medical Staff
Team Physician and Orthopaedic Surgeon . . . . Dr. Scott Gillogly
Assistant Team Physician and Internist . . . . Dr. William Whaley
Oral and Maxillofacial Surgeon . . . . Dr. Glenn Maron
Team Dentists . . . . Dr. Lawrence Saltzman, Dr. Brett Silverman

Public Relations
Senior Director of Public Relations . . . . Rob Koch
Director of Media Relations . . . . Brian Potter
Media Relations Assistant . . . . Rob Tillotson

Miscellaneous
Television . . . . SportSouth
Television Broadcasters . . . . JP Dellacamera, Darren Eliot
Radio . . . . 680 the Fan
Radio Broadcaster . . . . Dan Kamal

Key Off-Season Signings/Acquisitions

2008

May 13 • Re-signed RW **Chuck Kobasew**.
20 • Re-signed D **Aaron Ward**.
June 24 • Re-signed D **Mark Stuart**.
July 1 • Signed RW **Michael Ryder** and RW **Blake Wheeler**.
2 • Re-signed C **Petteri Nokelainen**.

Boston Bruins

2007-08 Results: 41W-29L-5OTL-7SOL 94PTS.
Third, Northeast Division

Year-by-Year Record

Season	GP	Home W	Home L	Home T	Home OL	Road W	Road L	Road T	Road OL	Overall W	Overall L	Overall T	Overall OL	GF	GA	Pts.	Finished	Playoff Result
2007-08	82	21	16	....	4	20	13	....	8	41	29	....	12	212	222	94	3rd, Northeast Div.	Lost Conf. Quarter-Final
2006-07	82	18	19	....	4	17	22	....	2	35	41	....	6	219	289	76	5th, Northeast Div.	Out of Playoffs
2005-06	82	16	15	....	10	13	22	....	6	29	37	....	16	230	266	74	5th, Northeast Div.	Out of Playoffs
2004-05	....	....	....	....	....	....	....	....	....	....	....	....	....	....	....	....		
2003-04	82	18	12	9	2	23	7	6	5	41	19	15	7	209	188	104	1st, Northeast Div.	Lost Conf. Quarter-Final
2002-03	82	23	11	5	2	13	20	6	2	36	31	11	4	245	237	87	3rd, Northeast Div.	Lost Conf. Quarter-Final
2001-02	82	23	11	2	5	20	13	4	4	43	24	6	9	236	201	101	1st, Northeast Div.	Lost Conf. Quarter-Final
2000-01	82	21	12	5	3	15	18	3	5	36	30	8	8	227	249	88	4th, Northeast Div.	Out of Playoffs
1999-2000	82	12	17	11	1	12	16	8	5	24	33	19	6	210	248	73	5th, Northeast Div.	Out of Playoffs
1998-99	82	22	10	9	....	17	20	4	....	39	30	13	....	214	181	91	3rd, Northeast Div.	Lost Conf. Semi-Final
1997-98	82	19	16	6	....	20	14	7	....	39	30	13	....	221	194	91	2nd, Northeast Div.	Lost Conf. Quarter-Final
1996-97	82	14	20	7	....	12	27	2	....	26	47	9	....	234	300	61	6th, Northeast Div.	Out of Playoffs
1995-96	82	22	14	5	....	18	17	6	....	40	31	11	....	282	269	91	2nd, Northeast Div.	Lost Conf. Quarter-Final
1994-95	48	15	7	2	....	12	11	1	....	27	18	3	....	150	127	57	3rd, Northeast Div.	Lost Conf. Quarter-Final
1993-94	84	20	14	8	....	22	15	5	....	42	29	13	....	289	252	97	2nd, Northeast Div.	Lost Conf. Semi-Final
1992-93	84	29	10	3	....	22	16	4	....	51	26	7	....	332	268	109	1st, Adams Div.	Lost Div. Semi-Final
1991-92	80	23	11	6	....	13	21	6	....	36	32	12	....	270	275	84	2nd, Adams Div.	Lost Conf. Championship
1990-91	80	26	9	5	....	18	15	7	....	44	24	12	....	299	264	100	1st, Adams Div.	Lost Conf. Championship
1989-90	80	23	13	4	....	23	12	5	....	46	25	9	....	289	232	101	1st, Adams Div.	Lost Final
1988-89	80	17	15	8	....	20	14	6	....	37	29	14	....	289	256	88	2nd, Adams Div.	Lost Div. Final
1987-88	80	24	13	3	....	20	17	3	....	44	30	6	....	300	251	94	2nd, Adams Div.	Lost Final
1986-87	80	25	11	4	....	14	23	3	....	39	34	7	....	301	276	85	3rd, Adams Div.	Lost Div. Semi-Final
1985-86	80	24	9	7	....	13	22	5	....	37	31	12	....	311	288	86	3rd, Adams Div.	Lost Div. Semi-Final
1984-85	80	21	15	4	....	15	19	6	....	36	34	10	....	303	287	82	4th, Adams Div.	Lost Div. Semi-Final
1983-84	80	25	12	3	....	24	13	3	....	49	25	6	....	336	261	104	1st, Adams Div.	Lost Div. Semi-Final
1982-83	80	28	6	6	....	22	14	4	....	50	20	10	....	327	228	110	1st, Adams Div.	Lost Conf. Championship
1981-82	80	24	12	4	....	19	15	6	....	43	27	10	....	323	285	96	2nd, Adams Div.	Lost Div. Final
1980-81	80	26	10	4	....	11	20	9	....	37	30	13	....	316	272	87	2nd, Adams Div.	Lost Prelim. Round
1979-80	80	27	9	4	....	19	12	9	....	46	21	13	....	310	234	105	2nd, Adams Div.	Lost Quarter-Final
1978-79	80	25	10	5	....	18	13	9	....	43	23	14	....	316	270	100	1st, Adams Div.	Lost Semi-Final
1977-78	80	29	6	5	....	22	12	6	....	51	18	11	....	333	218	113	1st, Adams Div.	Lost Final
1976-77	80	27	7	6	....	22	16	2	....	49	23	8	....	312	240	106	1st, Adams Div.	Lost Final
1975-76	80	27	5	8	....	21	10	9	....	48	15	17	....	313	237	113	1st, Adams Div.	Lost Semi-Final
1974-75	80	29	5	6	....	11	21	8	....	40	26	14	....	345	245	94	2nd, Adams Div.	Lost Prelim. Round
1973-74	78	33	4	2	....	19	13	7	....	52	17	9	....	349	221	113	1st, East Div.	Lost Final
1972-73	78	27	10	2	....	24	12	3	....	51	22	5	....	330	235	107	2nd, East Div.	Lost Quarter-Final
1971-72	**78**	**28**	**4**	**7**	....	**26**	**9**	**4**	....	**54**	**13**	**11**	....	**330**	**204**	**119**	**1st, East Div.**	**Won Stanley Cup**
1970-71	78	33	4	2	....	24	10	5	....	57	14	7	....	399	207	121	1st, East Div.	Lost Quarter-Final
1969-70	**76**	**27**	**3**	**8**	....	**13**	**14**	**11**	....	**40**	**17**	**19**	....	**277**	**216**	**99**	**2nd, East Div.**	**Won Stanley Cup**
1968-69	76	29	3	6	....	13	15	10	....	42	18	16	....	303	221	100	2nd, East Div.	Lost Semi-Final
1967-68	74	22	9	6	....	15	18	4	....	37	27	10	....	259	216	84	3rd, East Div.	Lost Quarter-Final
1966-67	70	10	21	4	....	7	22	6	....	17	43	10	....	182	253	44	6th,	Out of Playoffs
1965-66	70	15	17	3	....	6	26	3	....	21	43	6	....	174	275	48	5th,	Out of Playoffs
1964-65	70	12	17	6	....	9	26	0	....	21	43	6	....	166	253	48	6th,	Out of Playoffs
1963-64	70	13	15	7	....	5	25	5	....	18	40	12	....	170	212	48	6th,	Out of Playoffs
1962-63	70	7	18	10	....	7	21	7	....	14	39	17	....	198	281	45	6th,	Out of Playoffs
1961-62	70	9	22	4	....	6	25	4	....	15	47	8	....	177	306	38	6th,	Out of Playoffs
1960-61	70	13	17	5	....	2	25	8	....	15	42	13	....	176	254	43	6th,	Out of Playoffs
1959-60	70	21	11	3	....	7	23	5	....	28	34	8	....	220	241	64	5th,	Out of Playoffs
1958-59	70	21	11	3	....	11	18	6	....	32	29	9	....	205	215	73	2nd,	Lost Semi-Final
1957-58	70	15	14	6	....	12	14	9	....	27	28	15	....	199	194	69	4th,	Lost Final
1956-57	70	20	9	6	....	14	15	6	....	34	24	12	....	195	174	80	3rd,	Lost Final
1955-56	70	14	14	7	....	9	20	6	....	23	34	13	....	147	185	59	5th,	Out of Playoffs
1954-55	70	16	10	9	....	7	16	12	....	23	26	21	....	169	188	67	4th,	Lost Semi-Final
1953-54	70	22	8	5	....	10	20	5	....	32	28	10	....	177	181	74	4th,	Lost Semi-Final
1952-53	70	19	10	6	....	9	19	7	....	28	29	13	....	152	172	69	3rd,	Lost Final
1951-52	70	15	12	8	....	10	17	8	....	25	29	16	....	162	176	66	4th,	Lost Semi-Final
1950-51	70	13	12	10	....	9	18	8	....	22	30	18	....	178	197	62	4th,	Lost Semi-Final
1949-50	70	15	12	8	....	7	20	8	....	22	32	16	....	198	228	60	5th,	Out of Playoffs
1948-49	60	18	10	2	....	11	13	6	....	29	23	8	....	178	163	66	2nd,	Lost Semi-Final
1947-48	60	12	8	10	....	11	16	3	....	23	24	13	....	167	168	59	3rd,	Lost Semi-Final
1946-47	60	18	7	5	....	8	16	6	....	26	23	11	....	190	175	63	3rd,	Lost Semi-Final
1945-46	50	11	5	4	....	13	13	4	....	24	18	8	....	167	156	56	2nd,	Lost Final
1944-45	50	11	12	2	....	5	18	2	....	16	30	4	....	179	219	36	4th,	Lost Semi-Final
1943-44	50	15	8	2	....	4	18	3	....	19	26	5	....	223	268	43	5th,	Out of Playoffs
1942-43	50	17	3	5	....	7	14	4	....	24	17	9	....	195	176	57	2nd,	Lost Final
1941-42	48	17	4	3	....	8	13	3	....	25	17	6	....	160	118	56	3rd,	Lost Semi-Final
1940-41	**48**	**15**	**4**	**5**	....	**12**	**4**	**8**	....	**27**	**8**	**13**	....	**168**	**102**	**67**	**1st,**	**Won Stanley Cup**
1939-40	48	20	3	1	....	11	9	4	....	31	12	5	....	170	98	67	1st,	Lost Semi-Final
1938-39	**48**	**20**	**2**	**2**	....	**16**	**8**	**0**	....	**36**	**10**	**2**	....	**156**	**76**	**74**	**1st,**	**Won Stanley Cup**
1937-38	48	18	3	3	....	12	8	4	....	30	11	7	....	142	89	67	1st, Amn. Div.	Lost Semi-Final
1936-37	48	9	11	4	....	14	7	3	....	23	18	7	....	120	110	53	2nd, Amn. Div.	Lost Quarter-Final
1935-36	48	15	8	1	....	7	12	5	....	22	20	6	....	92	83	50	2nd, Amn. Div.	Lost Quarter-Final
1934-35	48	17	7	0	....	9	9	6	....	26	16	6	....	129	112	58	1st, Amn. Div.	Lost Semi-Final
1933-34	48	11	11	2	....	7	14	3	....	18	25	5	....	111	130	41	4th, Amn. Div.	Out of Playoffs
1932-33	48	19	2	3	....	6	13	5	....	25	15	8	....	124	88	58	1st, Amn. Div.	Lost Semi-Final
1931-32	48	11	10	3	....	4	11	9	....	15	21	12	....	122	117	42	4th, Amn. Div.	Out of Playoffs
1930-31	44	16	1	5	....	12	9	1	....	28	10	6	....	143	90	62	1st, Amn. Div.	Lost Semi-Final
1929-30	44	21	1	0	....	17	4	1	....	38	5	1	....	179	98	77	1st, Amn. Div.	Lost Final
1928-29	**44**	**15**	**6**	**1**	....	**11**	**7**	**4**	....	**26**	**13**	**5**	....	**89**	**52**	**57**	**1st, Amn. Div.**	**Won Stanley Cup**
1927-28	44	13	4	5	....	7	9	6	....	20	13	11	....	77	70	51	1st, Amn. Div.	Lost Semi-Final
1926-27	44	15	7	0	....	6	13	3	....	21	20	3	....	97	89	45	2nd, Amn. Div.	Lost Final
1925-26	36	10	7	1	....	7	8	3	....	17	15	4	....	92	85	38	4th,	Out of Playoffs
1924-25	30	3	12	0	....	3	12	0	....	6	24	0	....	49	119	12	6th,	Out of Playoffs

2008-09 Schedule

Oct.	Thu.	9	at Colorado
	Sat.	11	at Minnesota
	Wed.	15	at Montreal
	Sat.	18	at Ottawa
	Mon.	20	Pittsburgh
	Tue.	21	at Buffalo
	Thu.	23	Toronto
	Sat.	25	Atlanta
	Mon.	27	at Edmonton
	Tue.	28	at Vancouver
	Thu.	30	at Calgary
Nov.	Sat.	1	Dallas
	Thu.	6	Toronto
	Sat.	8	Buffalo
	Wed.	12	at Chicago
	Thu.	13	Montreal
	Sat.	15	at NY Rangers
	Mon.	17	at Toronto
	Wed.	19	Buffalo
	Fri.	21	Florida
	Sat.	22	at Montreal
	Wed.	26	at Buffalo
	Fri.	28	NY Islanders*
	Sat.	29	Detroit
Dec.	Thu.	4	at Tampa Bay
	Sat.	6	at Florida
	Mon.	8	Tampa Bay
	Wed.	10	at Washington
	Fri.	12	at Atlanta
	Sat.	13	Atlanta
	Thu.	18	Toronto
	Sat.	20	Carolina*
	Sun.	21	at St. Louis*
	Tue.	23	at New Jersey
	Sat.	27	at Carolina
	Sun.	28	at Atlanta*
	Tue.	30	at Pittsburgh
Jan.	Thu.	1	Pittsburgh
	Sat.	3	Buffalo*
	Tue.	6	Minnesota
	Thu.	8	Ottawa
	Sat.	10	Carolina*
	Tue.	13	Montreal
	Thu.	15	at NY Islanders
	Sat.	17	at Washington
	Mon.	19	St. Louis*
	Wed.	21	at Toronto
	Tue.	27	Washington
	Thu.	29	New Jersey
	Sat.	31	NY Rangers*
Feb.	Sun.	1	at Montreal*
	Wed.	4	at Philadelphia
	Thu.	5	at Ottawa
	Sat.	7	Philadelphia*
	Tue.	10	San Jose
	Fri.	13	at New Jersey
	Sat.	14	at Nashville
	Tue.	17	at Carolina
	Sat.	21	at Florida
	Sun.	22	at Tampa Bay*
	Tue.	24	Florida
	Thu.	26	Anaheim
	Sat.	28	Washington*
Mar.	Tue.	3	Philadelphia
	Thu.	5	Phoenix
	Sat.	7	Chicago*
	Sun.	8	at NY Rangers*
	Tue.	10	at Columbus
	Thu.	12	Ottawa
	Sat.	14	NY Islanders*
	Sun.	15	at Pittsburgh*
	Thu.	19	Los Angeles
	Sun.	22	New Jersey*
	Sat.	28	at Toronto
	Sun.	29	at Philadelphia
	Tue.	31	Tampa Bay
Apr.	Thu.	2	Ottawa
	Sat.	4	NY Rangers*
	Tue.	7	at Ottawa
	Thu.	9	Montreal
	Sat.	11	at Buffalo*
	Sun.	12	at NY Islanders*

* Denotes afternoon game.

NORTHEAST DIVISION
85th NHL Season

Franchise date: November 1, 1924

2008-09 Player Personnel

FORWARDS	HT	WT	S	Place of Birth	*Age	2007-08 Club
AXELSSON, P.J.	6-1	188	L	Kungalv, Sweden	33	Boston
BERGERON, Patrice	6-2	194	R	Ancienne-Lorette, Que.	23	Boston
BITZ, Byron	6-5	215	R	Saskatoon, Sask.	24	Providence (AHL)
HAMILL, Zach	5-11	175	R	Vancouver, B.C.	20	Everett-Providence (AHL)
KARSUMS, Martins	5-10	198	R	Riga, Latvia	22	Providence (AHL)
KESSEL, Phil	5-11	180	R	Madison, WI	21	Boston
KOBASEW, Chuck	5-11	192	L	Vancouver, B.C.	26	Boston
KREJCI, David	6-0	177	R	Sternberk, Czech.	22	Boston-Providence (AHL)
LEHTONEN, Mikko	6-5	203	R	Espoo, Finland	21	Blues
LoVECCHIO, Jeff	6-2	194	L	Arlington Heights, IL	23	Western Mich.-Prov (AHL)
LUCIC, Milan	6-3	228	L	Vancouver, B.C.	20	Boston
MARCHAND, Brad	5-9	187	L	Halifax, N.S.	20	Val-d'Or-Halifax
MARQUARDT, Matt	6-3	216	L	North Bay, Ont.	21	Moncton-Baie-Comeau
NELSON, Levi	6-0	184	L	Calgary, Alta.	20	Swift Current
NOKELAINEN, Petteri	6-1	195	R	Imatra, Finland	22	Boston-Providence (AHL)
RABBIT, Wacey	5-10	171	L	Lethbridge, Alta.	21	Providence (AHL)
REICH, Jeremy	6-1	203	L	Craik, Sask.	29	Boston
RYDER, Michael	6-0	186	R	Bonavista, Nfld.	28	Montreal
ST. PIERRE, Martin	5-9	185	L	Ottawa, Ont.	25	Mytischi-Chi-Rockford
SAVARD, Marc	5-10	191	L	Ottawa, Ont.	31	Boston
SCHAEFER, Peter	6-1	200	L	Regina, Sask.	31	Boston
SOBOTKA, Vladimir	5-11	193	L	Trebic, Czech.	21	Boston-Providence (AHL)
STURM, Marco	6-0	194	L	Dingolfing, West Germany	30	Boston
THOMPSON, Nate	6-0	206	L	Anchorage, AK	23	Providence (AHL)
THORNTON, Shawn	6-2	217	R	Oshawa, Ont.	31	Boston
WHEELER, Blake	6-5	208	R	Robbinsdale, MN	22	U. of Minnesota

DEFENSEMEN	HT	WT	S	Place of Birth	*Age	2007-08 Club
ALBERTS, Andrew	6-5	218	L	Minneapolis, MN	27	Boston
BODNARCHUK, Andrew	5-11	185	L	Drumheller, Alta.	20	Halifax
BOYCHUK, Johnny	6-2	225	R	Edmonton, Alta.	24	Colorado-Lake Erie
CHARA, Zdeno	6-9	255	L	Trencin, Czech.	31	Boston
EGENER, Mike	6-4	216	L	Lahr, West Germany	24	Norfolk-Mississippi
FERENCE, Andrew	5-11	189	L	Edmonton, Alta.	29	Boston
HNIDY, Shane	6-2	204	R	Brandon, Man.	32	Anaheim-Boston
HUNWICK, Matt	5-11	193	L	Warren, MI	23	Boston-Providence (AHL)
LASHOFF, Matt	6-2	198	L	Albany, NY	22	Boston-Providence (AHL)
McQUAID, Adam	6-5	209	R	Charlottetown, PEI	21	Providence (AHL)
PENNER, Jeff	5-10	191	L	Steinbach, Man.	21	Alaska-Providence (AHL)
STOKES, Ryan	6-4	220	L	Sarnia, Ont.	25	Rockford
STUART, Mark	6-2	213	L	Rochester, MN	24	Boston
WARD, Aaron	6-2	209	R	Windsor, Ont.	35	Boston
WIDEMAN, Dennis	6-0	196	R	Kitchener, Ont.	25	Boston

GOALTENDERS	HT	WT	C	Place of Birth	*Age	2007-08 Club
COURCHAINE, Adam	6-2	181	L	Calgary, Alta.	19	Ottawa (OHL)-Providence (AHL)
FERNANDEZ, Manny	6-1	207	L	Etobicoke, Ont.	34	Boston
RASK, Tuukka	6-2	171	L	Savonlinna, Finland	21	Boston-Providence (AHL)
REGAN, Kevin	6-1	190	L	Boston, MA	24	New Hampshire-Providence (AHL)
THOMAS, Tim	5-11	208	L	Flint, MI	34	Boston

* – Age at start of 2008-09 season

Claude Julien

Head Coach

Born: Orleans, Ont., April 23, 1960.

The Boston Bruins named Claude Julien the 28th head coach in club history on June 21, 2007. In his first season behind the bench in 2007-08, he guided the Bruins back to the playoffs for the first time since 2003-04. Julien joined the Bruins with four years of NHL head coaching experience. In his lone season with New Jersey, he held a record of 47-24-8 before being replaced on April 2, 2007 with three games remaining in the 2006-07 regular season. At the time he was replaced by the Devils, Julien's club was in first place in the Atlantic Division.

Prior to being named head coach of the Devils, Julien spent three seasons as the head coach of the Montreal Canadiens, serving from January 2003 until January of 2006. During his tenure with Montreal, Julien led the Canadiens to a record of 72-71-16 in 159 games.

Before joining the NHL coaching ranks, Julien spent four seasons with Hull of the Quebec Major Junior Hockey League and three campaigns with Hamilton of the American Hockey League. While with Hamilton, Julien was co-awarded the Louis A. R. Pieri Award as the league's outstanding coach during the 2002-03 season.

Julien has also coached at the international level, having served as an assistant coach to Team Canada at the 2006 World Championship after he led Team Canada to a bronze medal as a head coach at the 2000 World Junior Championship.

A defenseman, Julien's professional playing career spanned 12 seasons from 1981 to 1992, highlighted by stints with the Quebec Nordiques between 1984 and 1986.

Coaching Record

			Regular Season				Playoffs			
Season	Team	League	GC	W	L	O/T	GC	W	L	T
1996-97	Hull	QMJHL	70	48	19	3	14	12	2	....
1997-98	Hull	QMJHL	70	32	37	1	11	6	5	....
1998-99	Hull	QMJHL	70	23	38	9	23	15	8	....
99-2000	Hull	QMJHL	72	42	24	6	15	9	6	....
2000-01	Hamilton	AHL	80	28	41	11	....	....	....	....
2001-02	Hamilton	AHL	80	37	30	13	15	10	5	....
2002-03	Hamilton	AHL	45	33	9	3	....	....	....	....
2002-03	**Montreal**	**NHL**	**36**	**12**	**16**	**8**	....	....	....	....
2003-04	**Montreal**	**NHL**	**82**	**41**	**30**	**11**	**11**	**4**	**7**	....
2004-05	**Montreal**				SEASON CANCELLED					
2005-06	**Montreal**	**NHL**	**41**	**19**	**16**	**6**	....	....	....	....
2006-07	**New Jersey**	**NHL**	**79**	**47**	**24**	**8**	....	....	....	....
2007-08	**Boston**	**NHL**	**82**	**41**	**29**	**12**	**7**	**3**	**4**	....
	NHL Totals		**320**	**160**	**115**	**45**	**18**	**7**	**11**	....

2007-08 Scoring

* – rookie

Regular Season

Pos	#	Player	Team	GP	G	A	Pts	TOI	+/–	PIM	PP	SH	GW	S	%
C	91	Marc Savard	BOS	74	15	63	78	20:31	3	66	4	0	2	196	7.7
L	16	Marco Sturm	BOS	80	27	29	56	17:59	11	40	10	1	5	229	11.8
D	33	Zdeno Chara	BOS	77	17	34	51	26:50	14	114	9	1	0	207	8.2
R	12	Chuck Kobasew	BOS	73	22	17	39	17:40	6	29	6	3	3	147	15.0
C	81	Phil Kessel	BOS	82	19	18	37	15:13	–6	28	5	0	3	213	8.9
D	6	Dennis Wideman	BOS	81	13	23	36	25:09	11	70	9	0	1	171	7.6
C	13	Glen Metropolit	BOS	82	11	22	33	16:25	–3	36	1	0	5	141	7.8
R	27	Glen Murray	BOS	63	17	13	30	18:12	–4	50	7	0	2	158	10.8
L	11	P.J. Axelsson	BOS	75	13	16	29	17:36	11	15	0	2	2	100	13.0
L	17 *	Milan Lucic	BOS	77	8	19	27	12:07	–2	89	1	0	4	88	9.1
C	46 *	David Krejci	BOS	56	6	21	27	14:55	–3	20	1	1	0	73	8.2
L	72	Peter Schaefer	BOS	63	9	17	26	14:57	4	18	0	0	0	91	9.9
D	21	Andrew Ference	BOS	59	1	14	15	22:14	–14	50	0	0	0	71	1.4
D	44	Aaron Ward	BOS	65	5	8	13	20:44	9	54	0	0	3	68	7.4
C	56 *	Petteri Nokelainen	BOS	57	7	3	10	08:16	0	19	0	0	1	40	17.5
D	45	Mark Stuart	BOS	82	4	4	8	15:22	2	81	0	0	1	60	6.7
D	34	Shane Hnidy	ANA	33	1	2	3	13:08	2	30	0	0	0	21	4.8
			BOS	43	1	4	5	14:42	–4	41	0	1	0	28	3.6
			Total	76	2	6	8	14:01	–2	71	0	1	0	49	4.1
L	22	Shawn Thornton	BOS	58	4	3	7	07:23	–1	74	0	0	1	65	6.2
C	37	Patrice Bergeron	BOS	10	3	4	7	18:10	2	2	2	0	0	24	12.5
C	60 *	Vladimir Sobotka	BOS	48	1	6	7	08:50	1	24	0	0	1	40	2.5
D	49 *	Matt Lashoff	BOS	18	1	4	5	13:34	–2	0	1	0	0	11	9.1
C	53	Jeremy Reich	BOS	58	2	2	4	08:15	–5	78	0	0	1	39	5.1
D	41	Andrew Alberts	BOS	35	0	2	2	20:37	4	39	0	0	0	25	0.0
D	48 *	Matt Hunwick	BOS	13	0	1	1	10:36	–1	4	0	0	0	6	0.0
R	32	Jeff Hoggan	BOS	1	0	0	0	07:57	0	0	0	0	0	0	0.0
L	42 *	Pascal Pelletier	BOS	6	0	0	0	11:03	–2	0	0	0	0	8	0.0
D	38	Bobby Allen	BOS	19	0	0	0	09:53	–2	2	0	0	0	10	0.0

Goaltending

No.	Goaltender	GPI	Mins	Avg	W	L	OT	EN	SO	GA	SA	S%	G	A	PIM
29	Alex Auld	23	1213	2.32	9	7	5	3	2	47	578	.919	0	0	0
30	Tim Thomas	57	3342	2.44	28	19	6	3	3	136	1731	.921	0	0	2
40	* Tuukka Rask	4	184	3.26	2	1	1	0	0	10	88	.886	0	0	0
35	Manny Fernandez	4	244	3.93	2	2	0	0	1	16	95	.832	0	0	0
	Totals	**82**	**5003**	**2.58**	**41**	**29**	**12**	**6**	**6**	**215**	**2498**	**.914**			

Playoffs

Pos	#	Player	Team	GP	G	A	Pts	TOI	+/–	PIM	PP	SH	GW	OT	S	%
C	91	Marc Savard	BOS	7	1	5	6	17:06	–1	6	0	0	1	1	14	7.1
C	46 *	David Krejci	BOS	7	1	4	5	19:09	1	2	1	0	0	0	15	6.7
C	81	Phil Kessel	BOS	4	3	1	4	14:30	1	2	1	0	0	0	13	23.1
L	16	Marco Sturm	BOS	7	2	2	4	18:19	–1	6	0	1	1	0	23	8.7
L	72	Peter Schaefer	BOS	7	1	3	4	12:49	2	0	0	0	0	0	6	16.7
D	21	Andrew Ference	BOS	7	0	4	4	21:38	1	6	0	0	0	0	10	0.0
D	6	Dennis Wideman	BOS	6	0	3	3	24:21	–2	0	0	0	0	0	8	0.0
C	60 *	Vladimir Sobotka	BOS	6	2	0	2	08:37	0	0	0	0	0	0	5	40.0
L	17 *	Milan Lucic	BOS	7	2	0	2	16:24	–1	4	0	0	0	0	12	16.7
D	34	Shane Hnidy	BOS	7	1	1	2	17:10	0	9	0	0	0	0	7	14.3
D	33	Zdeno Chara	BOS	7	1	1	2	25:51	–1	12	1	0	0	0	14	7.1
C	56 *	Petteri Nokelainen	BOS	7	0	2	2	12:38	1	4	0	0	0	0	6	0.0
C	13	Glen Metropolit	BOS	7	1	0	1	16:27	–3	4	0	0	1	0	11	9.1
D	44	Aaron Ward	BOS	6	0	1	1	22:20	–2	6	0	0	0	0	8	0.0
D	45	Mark Stuart	BOS	7	0	1	1	16:00	–5	8	0	0	0	0	4	0.0
D	41	Andrew Alberts	BOS	2	0	0	0	11:07	0	0	0	0	0	0	2	0.0
C	53	Jeremy Reich	BOS	4	0	0	0	10:27	–1	8	0	0	0	0	3	0.0
R	27	Glen Murray	BOS	7	0	0	0	14:16	–3	2	0	0	0	0	10	0.0
L	11	P.J. Axelsson	BOS	7	0	0	0	16:57	–4	2	0	0	0	0	14	0.0
L	22	Shawn Thornton	BOS	7	0	0	0	08:04	0	6	0	0	0	0	15	0.0

Goaltending

No.	Goaltender	GPI	Mins	Avg	W	L	EN	SO	GA	SA	S%	G	A	PIM
30	Tim Thomas	7	430	2.65	3	4	0	0	19	221	.914	0	0	0
	Totals	**7**	**432**	**2.64**	**3**	**4**	**0**	**0**	**19**	**221**	**.914**			

Coaching History

Art Ross, 1924-25 to 1927-28; Cy Denneny, 1928-29; Art Ross, 1929-30 to 1933-34; Frank Patrick, 1934-35, 1935-36; Art Ross, 1936-37 to 1938-39; Cooney Weiland, 1939-40, 1940-41; Art Ross, 1941-42 to 1944-45; Dit Clapper, 1945-46 to 1948-49; Georges Boucher, 1949-50; Lynn Patrick, 1950-51 to 1953-54; Lynn Patrick and Milt Schmidt, 1954-55; Milt Schmidt, 1955-56 to 1960-61; Phil Watson, 1961-62; Phil Watson and Milt Schmidt, 1962-63; Milt Schmidt, 1963-64 to 1965-66; Harry Sinden, 1966-67 to 1969-70; Tom Johnson, 1970-71, 1971-72; Tom Johnson and Bep Guidolin, 1972-73; Bep Guidolin, 1973-74; Don Cherry, 1974-75 to 1978-79; Fred Creighton and Harry Sinden, 1979-80; Gerry Cheevers, 1980-81 to 1983-84; Gerry Cheevers and Harry Sinden, 1984-85; Butch Goring, 1985-86; Butch Goring and Terry O'Reilly, 1986-87; Terry O'Reilly, 1987-88, 1988-89; Mike Milbury, 1989-90, 1990-91; Rick Bowness, 1991-92; Brian Sutter, 1992-93 to 1994-95; Steve Kasper, 1995-96, 1996-97; Pat Burns, 1997-98 to 1999-2000; Pat Burns and Mike Keenan, 2000-01; Robbie Ftorek, 2001-02; Robbie Ftorek and Mike O'Connell, 2002-03; Mike Sullivan, 2003-04 to 2005-06; Dave Lewis, 2006-07; Claude Julien, 2007-08 to date.

Club Records

Team

(Figures in brackets for season records are games played; records for fewest points, wins, ties, losses, goals, goals against are for 70 or more games)

Most Points 121 1970-71 (78)
Most Wins 57 1970-71 (78)
Most Ties 21 1954-55 (70)
Most Losses 47 1961-62 (70), 1996-97 (82)
Most Goals 399 1970-71 (78)
Most Goals Against 306 1961-62 (70)
Fewest Points 38 1961-62 (70)
Fewest Wins 14 1962-63 (70)
Fewest Ties 5 1972-73 (78)
Fewest Losses 13 1971-72 (78)
Fewest Goals 147 1955-56 (70)
Fewest Goals Against 172 1952-53 (70)
Longest Winning Streak
Overall .... 14 Dec. 3/29-Jan. 9/30
Home .... *20 Dec. 3/29-Mar. 18/30
Away .... 8 Feb. 17-Mar. 8/72, Mar. 15-Apr. 14/93
Longest Undefeated Streak
Overall .... 23 Dec. 22/40-Feb. 23/41 (15 wins, 8 ties)
Home .... 27 Nov. 22/70-Mar. 20/71 (26 wins, 1 tie)
Away .... 15 Dec. 22/40-Mar. 16/41 (9 wins, 6 ties)
Longest Losing Streak
Overall .... 11 Dec. 3/24-Jan. 5/25
Home .... *11 Dec. 8/24-Feb. 17/25
Away .... 14 Dec. 27/64-Feb. 21/65
Longest Winless Streak
Overall .... 20 Jan. 28-Mar. 11/62 (16 losses, 4 ties)
Home .... 11 Dec. 8/24-Feb. 17/25 (11 losses)
Away .... 14 Three times
Most Shutouts, Season 15 1927-28 (44)
Most PIM, Season 2,443 1987-88 (80)
Most Goals, Game .... 14 Jan. 21/45 (NYR 3 at Bos. 14)

Individual

Most Seasons .... 21 John Bucyk, Raymond Bourque
Most Games .... 1,518 Raymond Bourque
Most Goals, Career .... 545 John Bucyk
Most Assists, Career ...... 1,111 Raymond Bourque
Most Points, Career .... 1,506 Raymond Bourque (395G, 1,111A)
Most PIM, Career .... 2,095 Terry O'Reilly
Most Shutouts, Career ..... 74 Tiny Thompson
Longest Consecutive Games Streak ... 418 John Bucyk (Jan. 23/69-Mar. 2/75)
Most Goals, Season .... 76 Phil Esposito (1970-71)
Most Assists, Season ...... 102 Bobby Orr (1970-71)
Most Points, Season .... 152 Phil Esposito (1970-71; 76G, 76A)
Most PIM, Season .... 302 Jay Miller (1987-88)
Most Points, Defenseman, Season ... *139 Bobby Orr (1970-71; 37G, 102A)
Most Points, Center, Season ... 152 Phil Esposito (1970-71; 76G, 76A)
Most Points, Right Wing, Season ... 105 Ken Hodge (1970-71; 43G, 62A), (1973-74; 50G, 55A), Rick Middleton (1983-84; 47G, 58A)
Most Points, Left Wing, Season ... 116 John Bucyk (1970-71; 51G, 65A)
Most Points, Rookie, Season ... 102 Joe Juneau (1992-93; 32G, 70A)
Most Shutouts, Season ...... 15 Hal Winkler (1927-28)
Most Goals, Game .... 4 Twenty times
Most Assists, Game .... 6 Ken Hodge (Feb. 9/71), Bobby Orr (Jan. 1/73)
Most Points, Game .... 7 Bobby Orr (Nov. 15/73; 3G, 4A), Phil Esposito (Dec. 19/74; 3G, 4A), Barry Pederson (Apr. 4/82; 3G, 4A), Cam Neely (Oct. 16/88; 3G, 4A)

* NHL Record.

Retired Numbers

2	Eddie Shore	1926-1940
3	Lionel Hitchman	1925-1934
4	Bobby Orr	1966-1976
5	Dit Clapper	1927-1947
7	Phil Esposito	1967-1975
8	Cam Neely	1986-1996
9	John Bucyk	1957-1978
15	Milt Schmidt	1936-1955
24	Terry O'Reilly	1971-1985
77	Raymond Bourque	1979-2000

All-time Record vs. Other Clubs

Regular Season

	At Home								On Road								Total							
	GP	W	L	T	OL	GF	GA	PTS	GP	W	L	T	OL	GF	GA	PTS	GP	W	L	T	OL	GF	GA	PTS
Anaheim	9	5	4	0	0	27	27	10	10	5	3	2	0	25	20	12	19	10	7	2	0	52	47	22
Atlanta	16	8	4	2	2	55	55	20	16	8	7	0	1	45	51	17	32	16	11	2	3	100	106	37
Buffalo	119	65	39	14	1	430	352	145	120	43	59	15	3	349	430	104	239	108	98	29	4	779	782	249
Calgary	48	29	12	6	1	168	132	65	45	22	19	4	0	154	163	48	93	51	31	10	1	322	295	113
Carolina	84	47	29	7	1	286	227	102	82	38	34	9	1	281	274	86	166	85	63	16	2	567	501	188
Chicago	285	162	89	34	0	1026	809	358	287	95	145	45	2	772	929	237	572	257	234	79	2	1798	1738	595
Colorado	63	31	22	9	1	240	194	72	67	36	25	6	0	272	238	78	130	67	47	15	1	512	432	150
Columbus	3	2	1	0	0	10	7	4	4	2	0	0	2	18	8	6	7	4	1	0	2	28	15	10
Dallas	61	41	9	10	1	259	148	93	62	30	18	13	1	221	179	74	123	71	27	23	2	480	327	167
Detroit	288	154	90	43	1	1008	764	352	286	80	153	52	1	726	955	213	574	234	243	95	2	1734	1719	565
Edmonton	31	22	6	3	0	129	80	47	30	16	11	3	0	102	102	35	61	38	17	6	0	231	182	82
Florida	28	9	13	4	2	71	78	24	27	13	11	2	1	81	87	29	55	22	24	6	3	152	165	53
Los Angeles	62	44	12	6	0	287	175	94	62	34	21	7	0	232	216	75	124	78	33	13	0	519	391	169
Minnesota	4	0	4	0	0	5	15	0	3	1	2	0	0	5	9	2	7	1	6	0	0	10	24	2
Montreal	347	158	131	56	2	1016	941	374	346	99	199	47	1	814	1169	246	693	257	330	103	3	1830	2110	620
Nashville	6	3	2	1	0	17	10	7	7	4	2	0	1	16	18	9	13	7	4	1	1	33	28	16
New Jersey	62	33	17	8	4	235	193	78	59	28	16	11	4	186	157	71	121	61	33	19	8	421	350	149
NY Islanders	65	35	17	11	2	238	181	83	67	28	28	10	1	210	222	67	132	63	45	21	3	448	403	150
NY Rangers	304	162	96	42	4	1088	852	370	308	117	135	55	1	861	941	290	612	279	231	97	5	1949	1793	660
Ottawa	45	26	13	5	1	155	119	58	43	20	14	3	6	126	112	49	88	46	27	8	7	281	231	107
Philadelphia	82	48	21	11	2	297	228	109	79	35	33	10	1	236	260	81	161	83	54	21	3	533	488	190
Phoenix	31	22	4	4	1	137	94	49	31	15	13	3	0	105	102	33	62	37	17	7	1	242	196	82
Pittsburgh	84	60	17	6	1	371	238	127	86	37	33	15	1	304	293	90	170	97	50	21	2	675	531	217
St. Louis	60	35	15	9	1	248	165	80	60	23	24	9	4	200	191	59	120	58	39	18	5	448	356	139
San Jose	11	7	1	3	0	41	32	17	12	6	4	2	0	40	31	14	23	13	5	5	0	81	63	31
Tampa Bay	29	20	3	6	0	110	70	46	29	15	11	3	0	87	84	33	58	35	14	9	0	197	154	79
Toronto	310	168	93	47	2	1001	827	385	311	99	158	51	3	809	1034	252	621	267	251	98	5	1810	1861	637
Vancouver	53	39	7	7	0	219	124	85	52	27	17	8	0	211	171	62	105	66	24	15	0	430	295	147
Washington	62	37	15	9	1	224	161	84	61	30	17	12	2	207	176	74	123	67	32	21	3	431	337	158
Defunct Clubs	164	112	39	13	0	525	306	237	164	79	67	18	0	496	440	176	328	191	106	31	0	1021	746	413
Totals	**2816**	**1584**	**825**	**376**	**31**	**9923**	**7604**	**3575**	**2816**	**1085**	**1279**	**415**	**37**	**8191**	**9062**	**2622**	**5632**	**2669**	**2104**	**791**	**68**	**18114**	**16666**	**6197**

Playoffs

	Series	W	L	GP	W	L	T	GF	GA	Last Mtg.	Rnd.	Result
Buffalo	7	5	2	39	21	18	0	139	130	1999	CSF	L 2-4
Carolina	3	3	0	19	12	7	0	63	48	1999	CQF	W 4-2
Chicago	6	5	1	22	16	5	1	97	63	1978	QF	W 4-0
Colorado	2	1	1	11	6	5	0	37	36	1983	DSF	W 3-1
Dallas	1	0	1	3	0	3	0	13	20	1981	PRE	L 0-3
Detroit	7	4	3	33	19	14	0	96	98	1957	SF	W 4-1
Edmonton	2	0	2	9	1	8	0	20	41	1990	F	L 1-4
Florida	1	0	1	5	1	4	0	16	22	1996	CQF	L 1-4
Los Angeles	2	2	0	13	8	5	0	56	38	1977	QF	W 4-2
Montreal	31	7	24	159	60	99	0	386	488	2008	CQF	L 3-4
New Jersey	4	1	3	23	8	15	0	60	68	2003	CQF	L 1-4
NY Islanders	2	0	2	11	3	8	0	35	49	1983	CF	L 2-4
NY Rangers	9	6	3	42	22	18	2	114	104	1973	QF	L 1-4
Philadelphia	4	2	2	20	11	9	0	60	57	1978	SF	W 4-1
Pittsburgh	4	2	2	19	9	10	0	62	67	1992	CF	L 0-4
St. Louis	2	2	0	8	8	0	0	48	15	1972	SF	W 4-0
Toronto	13	5	8	62	30	31	1	153	150	1974	QF	W 4-0
Washington	2	1	1	10	6	4	0	28	21	1998	CQF	L 2-4
Defunct Clubs	3	1	2	11	4	5	2	20	20			
Totals	**105**	**47**	**58**	**519**	**245**	**268**	**6**	**1503**	**1535**			

Calgary totals include Atlanta Flames, 1972-73 to 1979-80. Carolina totals include Hartford, 1979-80 to 1996-97.
Colorado totals include Quebec, 1979-80 to 1994-95. Dallas totals include Minnesota North Stars, 1967-68 to 1992-93.
New Jersey totals include Kansas City, 1974-75, 1975-76, and Colorado Rockies, 1976-77 to 1981-82.
Phoenix totals include Winnipeg, 1979-80 to 1995-96.

Playoff Results 2008-2003

Year	Round	Opponent	Result	GF	GA
2008	CQF	Montreal	L 3-4	15	19
2004	CQF	Montreal	L 3-4	14	19
2003	CQF	New Jersey	L 1-4	8	13

Abbreviations: Round: F - Final; **CF** - conference final; **CSF** - conference semi-final; **CQF** - conference quarter-final; **DSF** - division semi-final; **SF** - semi-final; **QF** - quarter-final; **PRE** - preliminary round.

2007-08 Results

Oct.	5	at Dallas	1-4
	6	at Phoenix	3-1
	10	at Anaheim	1-2
	12	at Los Angeles	8-6
	13	at San Jose	2-1
	18	Tampa Bay	4-1
	20	NY Rangers	1-0†
	22	at Montreal	1-6
	25	Chicago	3-1
	27	Philadelphia	1-2
Nov.	1	Buffalo	4-3*
	3	at Ottawa	2-3
	4	Ottawa	1-2†
	7	at Buffalo	1-2*
	8	Montreal	1-2
	10	Buffalo	2-1
	15	Toronto	5-2
	17	at Montreal	4-7
	20	at Toronto	4-2
	23	NY Islanders	2-1
	24	at NY Islanders	1-2
	26	at Philadelphia	6-3
	29	at Florida	4-3
Dec.	1	at Tampa Bay	1-4
	3	at NY Islanders	3-1
	5	at New Jersey	3-4*
	6	Montreal	2-4
	8	at Toronto	2-1
	10	at Buffalo	4-1
	12	at Atlanta	5-3
	13	New Jersey	1-3
	15	Columbus	2-0
	18	Ottawa	2-3
	20	Pittsburgh	4-5†
	22	St. Louis	1-4
	23	at Pittsburgh	2-4
	28	at Carolina	3-4
	29	at Atlanta	0-5
	31	Atlanta	5-2
Jan.	3	Washington	2-0
	5	New Jersey	4-3
	8	Carolina	0-1
	10	Montreal	2-5
	12	at Philadelphia	4-3*
	17	Toronto	2-3†
	19	NY Rangers	4-3†
	20	at NY Rangers	3-1
	22	at Montreal	2-8
	24	NY Islanders	4-1
	29	Nashville	3-1
	31	at Ottawa	4-1
Feb.	2	Detroit	1-3
	5	Buffalo	2-4
	8	at Buffalo	3-2†
	9	Florida	3-6
	12	Carolina	2-3
	13	at Pittsburgh	2-1
	16	at Toronto	3-4*
	19	at Carolina	3-2†
	21	at Florida	5-4†
	23	at Tampa Bay	5-3
	26	Ottawa	4-0
	28	Pittsburgh	5-1
Mar.	1	Atlanta	3-2†
	3	at Washington	2-10
	4	Florida	0-1*
	6	Toronto	2-8
	8	Washington	2-1
	9	at NY Rangers	0-1†
	11	at Ottawa	1-4
	13	Tampa Bay	1-3
	15	Philadelphia	3-2*
	16	at Washington	1-2†
	20	Montreal	2-4
	22	at Montreal	2-3†
	25	at Toronto	6-2
	27	Toronto	4-2
	29	Ottawa	4-0
	30	at Buffalo	1-2*
Apr.	2	at New Jersey	2-3†
	4	at Ottawa	2-1
	5	Buffalo	0-3

* – Overtime † – Shootout

Entry Draft Selections 2008-1994

Name in bold denotes played in NHL.

2008

Pick	
16	Joe Colborne
47	Maxime Sauve
77	Michael Hutchinson
97	Jamie Arniel
173	Nick Tremblay
197	Mark Goggin

2007

Pick	
8	Zach Hamill
35	Tommy Cross
130	Denis Reul
159	Alain Goulet
169	Radim Ostrcil
189	Jordan Knackstedt

2006

Pick	
5	**Phil Kessel**
37	Yuri Alexandrov
50	**Milan Lucic**
71	Brad Marchand
128	Andrew Bodnarchuk
158	Levi Nelson

2005

Pick	
22	**Matt Lashoff**
39	**Petr Kalus**
83	Mikko Lehtonen
100	**Jonathan Sigalet**
106	**Vladimir Sobotka**
154	Wacey Rabbit
172	Lukas Vantuch
217	Brock Bradford

2004

Pick	
63	**David Krejci**
64	Martins Karsums
108	Ashton Rome
134	**Kris Versteeg**
160	**Ben Walter**
224	**Matt Hunwick**
255	Anton Hedman

2003

Pick	
21	**Mark Stuart**
45	**Patrice Bergeron**
66	**Masi Marjamaki**
107	Byron Bitz
118	Frank Rediker
129	Patrik Valcak
153	Mike Brown
183	**Nate Thompson**
247	Benoit Mondou
277	Kevin Regan

2002

Pick	
29	**Hannu Toivonen**
56	Vladislav Evseev
130	Jan Kubista
153	Peter Hamerlik
228	Dmitri Utkin
259	**Yan Stastny**
290	Pavel Frolov

2001

Pick	
19	**Shaone Morrisonn**
77	Darren McLachlan
111	Matti Kaltiainen
147	Jiri Jakes
179	**Andrew Alberts**
209	**Jordan Sigalet**
241	**Milan Jurcina**
282	Marcel Rodman

2000

Pick	
7	**Lars Jonsson**
27	**Martin Samuelsson**
37	**Andy Hilbert**
59	**Ivan Huml**
66	Tuukka Makela
73	**Sergei Zinovjev**
102	Brett Nowak
174	**Jarno Kultanen**
204	Chris Berti
237	**Zdenek Kutlak**
268	**Pavel Kolarik**
279	Andreas Lindstrom

1999

Pick	
21	**Nick Boynton**
56	Matt Zultek
89	**Kyle Wanvig**
118	Jaakko Harikkala
147	Seamus Kotyk
179	Donald Choukalos
207	Greg Barber
236	John Cronin
247	**Mikko Eloranta**
264	Georgy Pujacs

1998

Pick	
48	**Jonathan Girard**
52	**Bobby Allen**
78	**Peter Nordstrom**
135	**Andrew Raycroft**
165	Ryan Milanovic

1997

Pick	
1	**Joe Thornton**
8	**Sergei Samsonov**
27	**Ben Clymer**
54	Mattias Karlin
63	**Lee Goren**
81	Karol Bartanus
135	Denis Timofeev
162	Joel Trottier
180	Jim Baxter
191	**Antti Laaksonen**
218	Eric Van Acker
246	**Jay Henderson**

1996

Pick	
8	**Johnathan Aitken**
45	Henry Kuster
53	Eric Naud
80	Jason Doyle
100	**Trent Whitfield**
132	Elias Abrahamsson
155	Chris Lane
182	Thomas Brown
208	Bob Prier
234	Anders Soderberg

1995

Pick	
9	**Kyle McLaren**
21	**Sean Brown**
47	**Paxton Schafer**
73	Bill McCauley
99	**Cameron Mann**
151	**Yevgeny Shaldybin**
177	**P.J. Axelsson**
203	Sergei Zhukov
229	Jonathon Murphy

1994

Pick	
21	Evgeni Ryabchikov
47	**Daniel Goneau**
99	**Eric Nickulas**
125	Darren Wright
151	**Andre Roy**
177	Jeremy Schaefer
229	**John Grahame**
255	Neil Savary
281	Andrei Yakhanov

Captains' History

No captain, 1924-25 to 1926-27; Lionel Hitchman, 1927-28 to 1930-31; George Owen, 1931-32; Dit Clapper, 1932-33 to 1937-38; Cooney Weiland, 1938-39; Dit Clapper, 1939-40 to 1945-46; Dit Clapper and John Crawford, 1946-47; John Crawford 1947-48 to 1949-50; Milt Schmidt, 1950-51 to 1953-54; Milt Schmidt, Ed Sanford, 1954-55; Fern Flaman, 1955-56 to 1960-61; Don McKenney, 1961-62, 1962-63; Leo Boivin, 1963-64 to 1965-66; John Bucyk, 1966-67; no captain, 1967-68 to 1972-73; John Bucyk, 1973-74 to 1976-77; Wayne Cashman, 1977-78 to 1982-83; Terry O'Reilly, 1983-84, 1984-85; Raymond Bourque, Rick Middleton (co-captains) 1985-86 to 1987-88; Raymond Bourque, 1988-89 to 1999-2000; Jason Allison, 2000-01; no captain, 2001-02; Joe Thornton, 2002-03, 2003-04; Joe Thornton and no captain, 2005-06; Zdeno Chara, 2006-07 to date.

General Managers' History

Art Ross, 1924-25 to 1953-54; Lynn Patrick, 1954-55 to 1964-65; Hap Emms, 1965-66, 1966-67; Milt Schmidt, 1967-68 to 1971-72; Harry Sinden, 1972-73 to 1999-2000; Harry Sinden and Mike O'Connell, 2000-01; Mike O'Connell, 2001-02 to 2005-06; Peter Chiarelli, 2006-07 to date.

Peter Chiarelli

General Manager

Born: Nepean, Ont., August 5, 1964.

Peter Chiarelli became just the seventh man in club history to hold the position of general manager when he was named to the post on May 26, 2006. He is in charge of every aspect of the team's hockey operations. He officially began his position in Boston on July 10, 2006 as a result of a league-arbitrated compensation agreement that saw the Bruins surrender a third-round draft pick in the 2006 NHL Entry Draft (Eric Gryba, 68th overall) to the Ottawa Senators.

Chiarelli came to the Bruins after seven seasons with the Ottawa Senators, five as the director of legal relations and the last two as assistant general manager. He was involved in all aspects of that team's hockey operations, including contract research and negotiations, salary arbitration and all player personnel matters. He was also involved in overseeing Ottawa's top developmental affiliate, the Binghamtom Senators of the American Hockey League. The Senators had four 100+ point seasons during his tenure and never finished below 94 points, finished with the NHL's top record in 2002-03 (113 points) and the best record in the Eastern Conference in 2005-06 (113 points).

A native of the Ottawa area, Chiarelli played four seasons of college hockey at Harvard University where he served the team as captain and was a teammate of former Bruin Don Sweeney. He had 21 goals and 28 assists for 49 points with 70 penalty minutes in 109 career college games and earned his degree in Economics in 1987. He played professionally in Europe for one year before returning to school and obtaining his law degree from the University of Ottawa. He was admitted to the Ontario bar in 1993 and spent six years as a lawyer and player agent prior to joining the Senators front office in 1999.

Club Directory

TD Banknorth Garden

Boston Bruins
TD Banknorth Garden
100 Legends Way
Boston, MA 02114
Phone **617/624-2327**
FAX 617/523-7184
www.bostonbruins.com
Capacity: 17,565

Executive

Owner & Governor . . . Jeremy M. Jacobs
Alternate Governors . . . Charles Jacobs, Jeremy Jacobs Jr., Louis Jacobs, Harry Sinden, Peter Chiarelli
Senior Advisor to the Owner . . . Harry Sinden
Executive Vice President . . . Charlie Jacobs
Vice President . . . Cam Neely
Vice President, Business Operations . . . Dan Zimmer
Senior Vice President, Sales & Marketing . . . Amy Latimer
Vice President, Marketing . . . Jen Compton
Vice President, Finance . . . Jim Bednarek
Vice President of Corporate Partnerships . . . Chris Johnson
Vice President of Client Relations . . . Mary Clivio
Vice President of Technology and eBusiness . . . Lorraine Spadaro
Director of Administration . . . Dale Hamilton-Powers
Executive Assistant . . . Rita Brandano
Administrative Assistant . . . Karen Ondo

Hockey Operations

General Manager . . . Peter Chiarelli
Assistant General Manager . . . Jim Benning
Dir. of Hockey Operations and Player Development . . . Don Sweeney
Director of Player Personnel . . . Scott Bradley
Director of Amateur Scouting . . . Wayne Smith
Director of Collegiate Scouting . . . John Weisbrod
Scouting Staff . . . Adam Creighton, Alexei Dementiev, Scott Fitzgerald, Jukka Holtari, Denis LeBlanc, Dean Malkoc, Don Matheson, Mike McGraw, Tom McVie, Grant Sonier, Svenake Svensson
Manager of Hockey Administration . . . Ryan Nadeau
Assistant to Hockey Administration . . . Matt Falconer
Team Road Services Coordinator . . . John Bucyk

Coaching

Head Coach . . . Claude Julien
Assistant Coaches . . . Doug Houda, Craig Ramsay, Geoff Ward
Goaltending Coach . . . Bob Essensa
Skating Coach . . . Paul Vincent
Video Analyst . . . Brant Berglund

Medical & Training

Strength & Conditioning Coach . . . John Whitesides
Athletic Trainer . . . Don DelNegro
Physical Therapist . . . Scott Waugh
Assistant Athletic Therapist & Massage Therapist . . . Derek Repucci
Equipment Manager . . . Mark Dumas
Assistant Equipment Managers . . . Keith Robinson, TBA
Head Team Physician . . . Dr. Peter Asnis, Orthopedist
Team Psychologist . . . Dr. Frank Lodato

Communications & Community Relations

Director of Communications . . . Matthew Chmura
Director of Publications & Information . . . Heidi Holland
Director of Community Relations & Promotions . . . Kerry Collins
Director of Development, Boston Bruins Foundation . . . Bob Sweeney
Manager of Media Relations . . . Eric Tosi
Content Manager, BostonBruins.com . . . John Bishop
Community Relations Coordinator . . . Liz Serpico
Administrative Assistant, Alumni Office . . . Mal Viola

Sales & Marketing

Senior Director of Premium Sales . . . Leah Leahy
Senior Director, The Premium Club . . . Dana Petrie
Director of Ticket Sales . . . Leigh Castergine
Ticket Sales Manager . . . Mark Rodrigues
Marketing Manager . . . Liz d'Entremont
Promotions Manager . . . Brian Hayes
Graphics Designer . . . Jason Petrie
Promotions Coordinator . . . Beth Anthony
Marketing Coordinator . . . Rachael Markovitz

Finance, Legal & Box Office

Vice President of Business Operations . . . Dan Zimmer
Director of Human Resources . . . Joe Lawlor
Human Resources Generalist . . . Jamie Smith
Controller . . . Rick McGlinchey
Receipts & Disbursements Administrator . . . Linda Bartlett
Payroll & Benefits Manager . . . Botin Bou
Senior Staff Accountant . . . Dan Eccles
Director of Ticket Operations . . . Matthew Whelan
Assistant Director of Ticket Operations . . . Jim Foley
Senior Box Office Analyst . . . Allyson Leonard
Ticket Office Receptionist . . . Jo-Ann Connolly-White

Other

Retail Director . . . Lauma Cerlins

Television & Radio

Television . . . New England Sports Network (NESN)
Jack Edwards (play-by-play); Andy Brickley (color)
Radio . . . WBZ (1030 AM) & Bruins Radio Network
Dave Goucher (play-by-play); Bob Beers (color)

Key Off-Season Signings/Acquisitions

2008

June 30 • Re-signed C **Paul Gaustad**.
July 1 • Signed G **Patrick Lalime**.
4 • Traded RW **Steve Bernier** to Vancouver for a 3rd-round pick in 2009 and 2nd-round pick in 2010.
4 • Acquired D **Craig Rivet** and a 7th-round pick in 2010 from San Jose for 2nd-round picks in 2009 and 2010.

Buffalo Sabres

2007-08 Results: 39W-31L-3OTL-9SOL 90PTS.

Fourth, Northeast Division

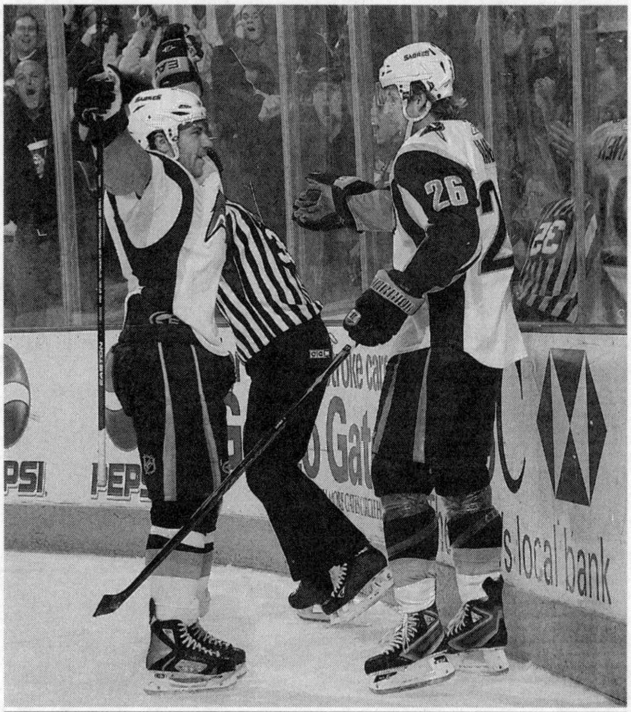

Derek Roy and Thomas Vanek celebrate a goal. They were the Sabres' two top goal-scorers in 2007-08. Vanek led the team with 36, while Roy had 32 and led the team with 81 points.

2008-09 Schedule

Oct.	Fri.	10	Montreal		Sat.	10	at Detroit
	Mon.	13	at NY Islanders*		Wed.	14	at Chicago
	Wed.	15	at NY Rangers		Thu.	15	at Dallas
	Fri.	17	Vancouver		Sat.	17	Carolina
	Sat.	18	at Atlanta		Mon.	19	at Florida
	Tue.	21	Boston		Wed.	21	at Tampa Bay
	Thu.	23	at Minnesota		Tue.	27	at Edmonton
	Sat.	25	at Colorado		Wed.	28	at Calgary
	Mon.	27	Ottawa		Sat.	31	at Phoenix
	Thu.	30	Tampa Bay	**Feb.**	Mon.	2	at Anaheim
Nov.	Sat.	1	Washington		Wed.	4	Toronto
	Mon.	3	at New Jersey		Fri.	6	Montreal
	Fri.	7	Atlanta		Sat.	7	at Ottawa
	Sat.	8	at Boston		Wed.	11	Ottawa
	Wed.	12	St. Louis		Fri.	13	San Jose
	Fri.	14	Columbus		Sun.	15	Carolina
	Sat.	15	at Pittsburgh		Tue.	17	at Toronto
	Wed.	19	at Boston		Thu.	19	at Philadelphia
	Fri.	21	Philadelphia		Sat.	21	NY Rangers
	Sat.	22	NY Islanders		Tue.	24	Anaheim
	Wed.	26	Boston		Thu.	26	at Carolina
	Fri.	28	Pittsburgh		Sat.	28	at NY Islanders
	Sat.	29	at Montreal	**Mar.**	Wed.	4	Montreal
Dec.	Mon.	1	Nashville		Fri.	6	Phoenix
	Thu.	4	at Florida		Sat.	7	at Ottawa
	Sat.	6	at Tampa Bay		Tue.	10	at Philadelphia
	Mon.	8	at Pittsburgh		Thu.	12	Florida
	Wed.	10	Tampa Bay		Sat.	14	Atlanta
	Fri.	12	Toronto		Tue.	17	at Ottawa
	Sat.	13	at New Jersey		Fri.	20	Philadelphia
	Wed.	17	New Jersey		Sat.	21	at NY Rangers
	Fri.	19	Los Angeles		Wed.	25	Florida
	Sat.	20	at Montreal		Fri.	27	Toronto
	Mon.	22	Pittsburgh		Sat.	28	at Montreal
	Fri.	26	at Washington	**Apr.**	Wed.	1	at Atlanta
	Sat.	27	NY Islanders		Fri.	3	at Washington
	Tue.	30	Washington		Sat.	4	New Jersey
Jan.	Thu.	1	at Toronto		Mon.	6	Detroit
	Sat.	3	at Boston*		Wed.	8	at Toronto
	Tue.	6	Ottawa		Thu.	9	at Carolina
	Fri.	9	NY Rangers		Sat.	11	Boston*

* Denotes afternoon game.

NORTHEAST DIVISION
39th NHL Season
Franchise date: May 22, 1970

Year-by-Year Record

		Home				Road				Overall								
Season	**GP**	**W**	**L**	**T**	**OL**	**W**	**L**	**T**	**OL**	**W**	**L**	**T**	**OL**	**GF**	**GA**	**Pts.**	**Finished**	**Playoff Result**
2007-08	82	20	15	....	6	19	16	....	6	39	31	....	12	255	242	90	4th, Northeast Div.	Out of Playoffs
2006-07	82	28	10	....	3	25	12	....	4	53	22	....	7	308	242	113	1st, Northeast Div.	Lost Conf. Championship
2005-06	82	27	11	....	3	25	13	....	3	52	24	....	6	281	239	110	2nd, Northeast Div.	Lost Conf. Championship
2004-05	....	....	....	....	....	....	....	....	....	....	....	....	....	....	....	....		
2003-04	82	21	13	4	3	16	21	3	1	37	34	7	4	220	221	85	5th, Northeast Div.	Out of Playoffs
2002-03	82	18	16	5	2	9	21	5	6	27	37	10	8	190	219	72	5th, Northeast Div.	Out of Playoffs
2001-02	82	20	16	5	0	15	19	6	1	35	35	11	1	213	200	82	5th, Northeast Div.	Out of Playoffs
2000-01	82	26	12	3	0	20	18	2	1	46	30	5	1	218	184	98	2nd, Northeast Div.	Lost Conf. Semi-Final
1999-2000	82	21	14	5	1	14	18	6	3	35	32	11	4	213	204	85	3rd, Northeast Div.	Lost Conf. Quarter-Final
1998-99	82	23	12	6	....	14	16	11	....	37	28	17	....	207	175	91	4th, Northeast Div.	Lost Final
1997-98	82	20	13	8	....	16	16	9	....	36	29	17	....	211	187	89	3rd, Northeast Div.	Lost Conf. Championship
1996-97	82	24	11	6	....	16	19	6	....	40	30	12	....	237	208	92	1st, Northeast Div.	Lost Conf. Semi-Final
1995-96	82	19	17	5	....	14	25	2	....	33	42	7	....	247	262	73	5th, Northeast Div.	Out of Playoffs
1994-95	48	15	8	1	....	7	11	6	....	22	19	7	....	130	119	51	4th, Northeast Div.	Lost Conf. Quarter-Final
1993-94	84	22	17	3	....	21	15	6	....	43	32	9	....	282	218	95	4th, Northeast Div.	Lost Conf. Quarter-Final
1992-93	84	25	15	2	....	13	21	8	....	38	36	10	....	335	297	86	4th, Adams Div.	Lost Div. Final
1991-92	80	22	13	5	....	9	24	7	....	31	37	12	....	289	299	74	3rd, Adams Div.	Lost Div. Semi-Final
1990-91	80	15	13	12	....	16	17	7	....	31	30	19	....	292	278	81	3rd, Adams Div.	Lost Div. Semi-Final
1989-90	80	27	11	2	....	18	16	6	....	45	27	8	....	286	248	98	2nd, Adams Div.	Lost Div. Semi-Final
1988-89	80	25	12	3	....	13	23	4	....	38	35	7	....	291	299	83	3rd, Adams Div.	Lost Div. Semi-Final
1987-88	80	19	14	7	....	18	18	4	....	37	32	11	....	283	305	85	3rd, Adams Div.	Lost Div. Semi-Final
1986-87	80	18	18	4	....	10	26	4	....	28	44	8	....	280	308	64	5th, Adams Div.	Out of Playoffs
1985-86	80	23	16	1	....	14	21	5	....	37	37	6	....	296	291	80	5th, Adams Div.	Out of Playoffs
1984-85	80	23	10	7	....	15	18	7	....	38	28	14	....	290	237	90	3rd, Adams Div.	Lost Div. Semi-Final
1983-84	80	25	9	6	....	23	16	1	....	48	25	7	....	315	257	103	2nd, Adams Div.	Lost Div. Semi-Final
1982-83	80	25	7	8	....	13	22	5	....	38	29	13	....	318	285	89	3rd, Adams Div.	Lost Div. Final
1981-82	80	23	8	9	....	16	18	6	....	39	26	15	....	307	273	93	3rd, Adams Div.	Lost Div. Semi-Final
1980-81	80	21	7	12	....	18	13	9	....	39	20	21	....	327	250	99	1st, Adams Div.	Lost Quarter-Final
1979-80	80	27	5	8	....	20	12	8	....	47	17	16	....	318	201	110	1st, Adams Div.	Lost Semi-Final
1978-79	80	19	13	8	....	17	15	8	....	36	28	16	....	280	263	88	2nd, Adams Div.	Lost Prelim. Round
1977-78	80	25	7	8	....	19	12	9	....	44	19	17	....	288	215	105	2nd, Adams Div.	Lost Quarter-Final
1976-77	80	27	8	5	....	21	16	3	....	48	24	8	....	301	220	104	2nd, Adams Div.	Lost Quarter-Final
1975-76	80	28	7	5	....	18	14	8	....	46	21	13	....	339	240	105	2nd, Adams Div.	Lost Quarter-Final
1974-75	80	28	6	6	....	21	10	9	....	49	16	15	....	354	240	113	1st, Adams Div.	Lost Final
1973-74	78	23	10	6	....	9	24	6	....	32	34	12	....	242	250	76	5th, East Div.	Out of Playoffs
1972-73	78	30	6	3	....	7	21	11	....	37	27	14	....	257	219	88	4th, East Div.	Lost Quarter-Final
1971-72	78	11	19	9	....	5	24	10	....	16	43	19	....	203	289	51	6th, East Div.	Out of Playoffs
1970-71	78	16	13	10	....	8	26	5	....	24	39	15	....	217	291	63	5th, East Div.	Out of Playoffs

2008-09 Player Personnel

FORWARDS	HT	WT	S	Place of Birth	*Age	2007-08 Club
AFINOGENOV, Maxim	6-0	192	L	Moscow, USSR	29	Buffalo
BOUCK, Tyler	6-0	196	L	Camrose, Alta.	28	Portland (AHL)
CONNOLLY, Tim	6-1	193	R	Syracuse, NY	27	Buffalo
DARCHE, Mathieu	6-1	220	L	St. Laurent, Que.	31	Tampa Bay-Norfolk
FRETTER, Colton	5-10	187	R	Harrow, Ont.	26	Chi (AHL)-Gwinnett-Bridgeport
GAUSTAD, Paul	6-5	214	L	Fargo, ND	26	Buffalo
HECHT, Jochen	6-1	196	L	Mannheim, West Germany	31	Buffalo
KALETA, Patrick	6-0	195	R	Buffalo, NY	22	Buffalo-Rochester
KOTALIK, Ales	6-2	227	R	Jindrichuv Hradec, Czech.	29	Buffalo
MacARTHUR, Clarke	6-0	195	L	Lloydminster, Alta.	23	Buffalo-Rochester
MAIR, Adam	6-1	208	R	Hamilton, Ont.	29	Buffalo
MURPHY, Colin	6-0	195	L	Fort McMurray, Alta.	28	Toronto (AHL)
PAILLE, Daniel	6-0	197	L	Welland, Ont.	24	Buffalo
PETERS, Andrew	6-4	226	L	St. Catharines, Ont.	28	Buffalo
POMINVILLE, Jason	6-0	186	R	Repentigny, Que.	25	Buffalo
ROY, Derek	5-9	188	L	Ottawa, Ont.	25	Buffalo
STAFFORD, Drew	6-2	213	R	Milwaukee, WI	22	Buffalo
VANEK, Thomas	6-2	208	R	Vienna, Austria	24	Buffalo
DEFENSEMEN						
LYDMAN, Toni	6-1	204	L	Lahti, Finland	31	Buffalo
NUMMINEN, Teppo	6-2	198	R	Tampere, Finland	40	Buffalo
PAETSCH, Nathan	6-1	198	L	Humboldt, Sask.	25	Buffalo
RIVET, Craig	6-2	210	R	North Bay, Ont.	34	San Jose
SEKERA, Andrej	6-0	199	L	Bojnice, Czech.	22	Buffalo-Rochester
SPACEK, Jaroslav	5-11	204	L	Rokycany, Czech.	34	Buffalo
TALLINDER, Henrik	6-3	214	L	Stockholm, Sweden	29	Buffalo
WEBER, Mike	6-2	214	L	Pittsburgh, PA	20	Buffalo-Rochester
GOALTENDERS	**HT**	**WT**	**C**	**Place of Birth**	***Age**	**2007-08 Club**
LALIME, Patrick	6-3	189	L	St-Bonaventure, Que.	34	Chicago
MILLER, Ryan	6-2	175	L	East Lansing, MI	28	Buffalo

* – Age at start of 2008-09 season

2007-08 Scoring

* – rookie

Regular Season

Pos	#	Player	Team	GP	G	A	Pts	TOI	+/–	PIM	PP	SH	GW	S	%
C	9	Derek Roy	BUF	78	32	49	81	20:58	13	46	6	3	4	218	14.7
R	29	Jason Pominville	BUF	82	27	53	80	19:58	16	20	2	1	1	232	11.6
L	26	Thomas Vanek	BUF	82	36	28	64	16:51	–5	64	19	0	9	240	15.0
C	55	Jochen Hecht	BUF	75	22	27	49	19:19	1	38	3	1	2	229	9.6
R	12	Ales Kotalik	BUF	79	23	20	43	15:20	–5	58	12	0	1	207	11.1
C	19	Tim Connolly	BUF	48	7	33	40	18:40	4	8	3	1	3	111	6.3
R	21	Drew Stafford	BUF	64	16	22	38	13:31	3	51	1	0	5	103	15.5
C	28	Paul Gaustad	BUF	82	10	26	36	17:09	–4	85	5	0	2	136	7.4
L	20	Daniel Paille	BUF	77	19	16	35	13:16	9	14	0	3	2	110	17.3
R	56	Steve Bernier	S.J.	59	13	10	23	13:07	–2	62	4	0	0	96	13.5
			BUF	17	3	6	9	14:05	1	2	0	0	0	35	8.6
			Total	76	16	16	32	13:20	–1	64	4	0	0	131	12.2
D	6	Jaroslav Spacek	BUF	60	9	23	32	22:58	7	42	7	0	1	95	9.5
R	61	Maxim Afinogenov	BUF	56	10	18	28	16:03	–16	42	1	0	1	114	8.8
D	5	Toni Lydman	BUF	82	4	22	26	21:39	1	74	3	0	0	86	4.7
D	10	Henrik Tallinder	BUF	71	1	17	18	21:02	5	48	0	0	0	70	1.4
C	22	Adam Mair	BUF	72	5	12	17	08:51	–2	66	0	0	2	62	8.1
L	41	* Clarke MacArthur	BUF	37	8	7	15	14:33	3	20	0	0	1	51	15.7
D	38	Nathan Paetsch	BUF	59	2	7	9	13:37	3	27	0	0	0	49	4.1
C	37	Michael Ryan	BUF	46	4	4	8	09:52	–4	30	0	0	0	60	6.7
D	44	* Andrej Sekera	BUF	37	2	6	8	19:37	5	16	0	0	1	28	7.1
D	45	Dmitri Kalinin	BUF	46	1	7	8	17:20	–7	32	1	0	0	60	1.7
D	4	Nolan Pratt	BUF	55	1	6	7	13:31	1	30	0	0	0	21	4.8
R	36	* Patrick Kaleta	BUF	40	3	2	5	06:19	1	41	0	0	0	26	11.5
D	34	* Mike Weber	BUF	16	0	3	3	16:40	12	14	0	0	0	12	0.0
L	76	Andrew Peters	BUF	44	1	1	2	03:08	–4	100	0	0	0	18	5.6
D	27	Teppo Numminen	BUF	1	0	0	0	16:03	0	0	0	0	0	1	0.0
L	17	* Marc-Andre Gragnani	BUF	2	0	0	0	06:17	–2	4	0	0	0	1	0.0
D	3	* Michael Funk	BUF	4	0	0	0	11:36	–3	0	0	0	0	1	0.0

Goaltending

No.	Goaltender	GPI	Mins	Avg	W	L	OT	EN	SO	GA	SA	S%	G	A	PIM
30	Ryan Miller	76	4474	2.64	36	27	10	8	3	197	2104	.906	0	1	6
35	Jocelyn Thibault	12	507	3.31	3	4	2	0	2	28	214	.869	0	0	0
	Totals	**82**	**5011**	**2.79**	**39**	**31**	**12**	**8**	**5**	**233**	**2326**	**.900**			

Jason Pominville established personal bests with 53 assists and 80 points in 2007-08.

Coaching History

Punch Imlach, 1970-71; Punch Imlach, Floyd Smith and Joe Crozier, 1971-72; Joe Crozier, 1972-73, 1973-74; Floyd Smith, 1974-75 to 1976-77; Marcel Pronovost, 1977-78; Marcel Pronovost and Billy Inglis, 1978-79; Scotty Bowman, 1979-80; Roger Neilson, 1980-81; Jim Roberts and Scotty Bowman, 1981-82; Scotty Bowman 1982-83 to 1984-85; Jim Schoenfeld and Scotty Bowman, 1985-86; Scotty Bowman, Craig Ramsay and Ted Sator, 1986-87; Ted Sator, 1987-88, 1988-89; Rick Dudley, 1989-90, 1990-91; Rick Dudley and John Muckler, 1991-92; John Muckler, 1992-93 to 1994-95; Ted Nolan, 1995-96, 1996-97; Lindy Ruff, 1997-98 to date.

Lindy Ruff

Head Coach

Born: Warburg, Alta., February 17, 1960.

A former captain of the Sabres, Lindy Ruff was appointed as the club's 15th head coach on July 21, 1997. In 1999, he led the Sabres to the Stanley Cup Finals for just the second time in club history and in 2006 he guided the Sabres to the Eastern Conference Final and was rewarded with the Jack Adams Award as coach of the year. The Sabres won the Presidents' Trophy for finishing first overall in the NHL standings in 2006-07, recording 113 points and a franchise-record 53 wins. Ruff is the winningest coach in club history. As a player, Ruff was drafted 32nd overall by the Sabres in the 1979 Entry Draft. He played both defense and left wing in an NHL career that spanned 12 seasons including 608 regular-season games with Buffalo. He became a playing assistant coach with Rochester of the AHL in 1991-92 and San Diego of the IHL in 1992-93. Ruff's San Diego club set a pro hockey record with 62 wins. In 1993-94 he became an NHL assistant coach with the Florida Panthers.

Coaching Record

			Regular Season				Playoffs			
Season	**Team**	**League**	**GC**	**W**	**L**	**O/T**	**GC**	**W**	**L**	**T**
1997-98	Buffalo	NHL	82	36	29	17	15	10	5	....
1998-99	Buffalo	NHL	82	37	28	17	21	14	7	....
99-2000	Buffalo	NHL	82	35	32	15	5	1	4	....
2000-01	Buffalo	NHL	82	46	30	6	13	7	6	....
2001-02	Buffalo	NHL	82	35	35	12	....	....	....	....
2002-03	Buffalo	NHL	82	27	37	18	....	....	....	....
2003-04	Buffalo	NHL	82	37	34	11	....	....	....	....
2004-05	Buffalo				SEASON CANCELLED					
2005-06	Buffalo	NHL	82	52	24	6	18	11	7	....
2006-07	Buffalo	NHL	82	53	22	7	16	9	7	....
2007-08	Buffalo	NHL	82	39	31	12	....	....	....	....
	NHL Totals		820	397	302	121	88	52	36	....

Captains' History

Floyd Smith, 1970-71; Gerry Meehan, 1971-72 to 1973-74; Gerry Meehan and Jim Schoenfeld, 1974-75; Jim Schoenfeld, 1975-76, 1976-77; Danny Gare, 1977-78 to 1980-81; Danny Gare and Gilbert Perreault, 1981-82; Gilbert Perreault, 1982-83 to 1985-86; Gilbert Perreault and Lindy Ruff, 1986-87; Lindy Ruff, 1987-88; Lindy Ruff and Mike Foligno, 1988-89; Mike Foligno, 1989-90; Mike Foligno and Mike Ramsey, 1990-91; Mike Ramsey, 1991-92; Mike Ramsey and Pat LaFontaine, 1992-93; Pat LaFontaine and Alexander Mogilny, 1993-94; Pat LaFontaine, 1994-95 to 1996-97; Donald Audette and Michael Peca, 1997-98; Michael Peca, 1998-99, 1999-2000; no captain, 2000-01; Stu Barnes. 2001-02, 2002-03; Miroslav Satan, Chris Drury, James Patrick, J.P. Dumont, Daniel Briere, 2003-04; Daniel Briere and Chris Drury, 2005-06, 2006-07; Jochen Hecht, Toni Lydman, Brian Campbell, Jaroslav Spacek, Jason Pominville, 2007-08.

Club Records

Team

(Figures in brackets for season records are games played; records for fewest points, wins, ties, losses, goals, goals against are for 70 or more games)

Most Points	**113**	1974-75 (80), 2006-07 (82)
Most Wins	**53**	2006-07 (82)
Most Ties	**21**	1980-81 (80)
Most Losses	**44**	1986-87 (80)
Most Goals	**354**	1974-75 (80)
Most Goals Against	**308**	1986-87 (80)
Fewest Points	**51**	1971-72 (78)
Fewest Wins	**16**	1971-72 (78)
Fewest Ties	**5**	2000-01 (82)
Fewest Losses	**16**	1974-75 (80)
Fewest Goals	**190**	2002-03 (82)
Fewest Goals Against	**175**	1998-99 (82)
Longest Winning Streak		
Overall	**10**	Jan. 4-23/84, Oct. 4-26/06
Home	**12**	Nov. 12/72-Jan. 7/73, Oct. 13-Dec. 10/89
Away	***10**	Dec. 10/83-Jan. 23/84, Oct. 4-Nov. 13/06
Longest Undefeated Streak		
Overall	**14**	Mar. 6-Apr. 6/80 (8 wins, 6 ties)
Home	**21**	Oct. 8/72-Jan. 7/73 (18 wins, 3 ties)
Away	**10**	Dec. 10/83-Jan. 23/84 (10 wins), Oct. 4-Nov. 13/06 (10 wins)
Longest Losing Streak		
Overall	**8**	Jan. 25-Feb. 13/03
Home	**6**	Oct. 10-Nov. 10/93, Mar. 3-Apr. 3/96
Away	**7**	Oct. 14-Nov. 7/70, Feb. 6-27/71, Jan. 10-Feb. 3/96
Longest Winless Streak		
Overall	**12**	Nov. 23-Dec. 20/91 (8 losses, 4 ties), Oct. 25-Nov. 19/02 (10 losses, 2 ties)
Home	**12**	Jan. 27-Mar. 10/91 (7 losses, 5 ties)
Away	**23**	Oct. 30/71-Feb. 19/72 (15 losses, 8 ties)
Most Shutouts, Season	**13**	1997-98 (82)
Most PIM, Season	***2,713**	1991-92 (80)
Most Goals, Game	**14**	Jan. 21/75 (Wsh. 2 at Buf. 14), Mar. 19/81 (Tor. 4 at Buf. 14)

Individual

Most Seasons	**17**	Gilbert Perreault
Most Games	**1,191**	Gilbert Perreault
Most Goals, Career	**512**	Gilbert Perreault
Most Assists, Career	**814**	Gilbert Perreault
Most Points, Career	**1,326**	Gilbert Perreault (512G, 814A)
Most PIM, Career	**3,189**	Rob Ray
Most Shutouts, Career	**55**	Dominik Hasek
Longest Consecutive Games Streak	**776**	Craig Ramsay (Mar. 27/73-Feb. 10/83)
Most Goals, Season	**76**	Alexander Mogilny (1992-93)
Most Assists, Season	**95**	Pat LaFontaine (1992-93)
Most Points, Season	**148**	Pat LaFontaine (1992-93; 53G, 95A)
Most PIM, Season	**354**	Rob Ray (1991-92)
Most Points, Defenseman, Season	**81**	Phil Housley (1989-90; 21G, 60A)
Most Points, Center, Season	**148**	Pat LaFontaine (1992-93; 53G, 95A)
Most Points, Right Wing, Season	**127**	Alexander Mogilny (1992-93; 76G, 51A)
Most Points, Left Wing, Season	**95**	Rick Martin (1974-75; 52G, 43A)
Most Points, Rookie, Season	**74**	Rick Martin (1971-72; 44G, 30A)
Most Shutouts, Season	**13**	Dominik Hasek (1997-98)
Most Goals, Game	**5**	Dave Andreychuk (Feb. 6/86)
Most Assists, Game	**5**	Gilbert Perreault (Feb. 1/76, Mar. 9/80, Jan. 4/84), Dale Hawerchuk (Jan. 15/92), Pat LaFontaine (Dec. 31/92, Feb. 10/93)
Most Points, Game	**7**	Gilbert Perreault (Feb. 1/76; 2G, 5A)

* NHL Record.

Retired Numbers

2	Tim Horton	1972-1974
7	Rick Martin	1971-1981
11	Gilbert Perreault	1970-1987
14	Rene Robert	1971-1979
16	Pat Lafontaine	1991-1996
18	Danny Gare	1974-1981

All-time Record vs. Other Clubs

Regular Season

	At Home								On Road								Total							
	GP	W	L	T	OL	GF	GA	PTS	GP	W	L	T	OL	GF	GA	PTS	GP	W	L	T	OL	GF	GA	PTS
Anaheim	10	5	2	3	0	28	22	13	10	7	3	0	0	31	19	14	20	12	5	3	0	59	41	27
Atlanta	16	10	5	0	1	73	41	21	16	5	7	1	3	49	55	14	32	15	12	1	4	122	96	35
Boston	120	62	40	15	3	430	349	142	119	40	62	14	3	352	430	97	239	102	102	29	6	782	779	239
Calgary	46	28	13	5	0	192	133	61	47	18	18	11	0	147	156	47	93	46	31	16	0	339	289	108
Carolina	83	50	25	7	1	339	242	108	84	38	33	11	2	252	247	89	167	88	58	18	3	591	489	197
Chicago	54	33	14	7	0	202	139	73	52	19	27	6	0	141	165	44	106	52	41	13	0	343	304	117
Colorado	64	36	19	9	0	249	207	81	65	23	31	11	0	203	231	57	129	59	50	20	0	452	438	138
Columbus	5	2	3	0	0	13	12	4	3	0	2	1	0	6	8	1	8	2	5	1	0	19	20	5
Dallas	53	29	13	11	0	192	142	69	55	22	27	6	0	158	174	50	108	51	40	17	0	350	316	119
Detroit	53	33	12	8	0	228	157	74	56	19	31	5	1	162	205	44	109	52	43	13	1	390	362	118
Edmonton	31	11	13	7	0	111	113	29	30	6	21	3	0	77	121	15	61	17	34	10	0	188	234	44
Florida	29	19	7	3	0	84	54	41	27	13	13	1	0	77	74	27	56	32	20	4	0	161	128	68
Los Angeles	54	29	16	9	0	227	158	67	55	23	23	9	0	189	193	55	109	52	39	18	0	416	351	122
Minnesota	4	1	3	0	0	8	13	2	4	3	1	0	0	10	6	6	8	4	4	0	0	18	19	8
Montreal	114	60	32	19	3	356	305	142	115	40	63	12	0	337	421	92	229	100	95	31	3	693	726	234
Nashville	5	1	3	1	0	17	20	3	6	4	2	0	0	16	12	8	11	5	5	1	0	33	32	11
New Jersey	60	34	17	8	1	230	180	77	60	27	21	9	3	187	177	66	120	61	38	17	4	417	357	143
NY Islanders	67	37	20	9	1	227	185	84	67	29	28	9	1	186	188	68	134	66	48	18	2	413	373	152
NY Rangers	74	42	20	10	2	300	230	96	72	26	29	15	2	195	232	69	146	68	49	25	4	495	462	165
Ottawa	43	26	14	3	0	136	98	55	45	20	16	7	2	121	122	49	88	46	30	10	2	257	220	104
Philadelphia	69	36	24	8	1	236	192	81	73	20	40	12	1	189	249	53	142	56	64	20	2	425	441	134
Phoenix	32	20	6	5	1	128	82	46	30	14	14	2	0	94	93	30	62	34	20	7	1	222	175	76
Pittsburgh	77	37	20	17	3	289	207	94	77	20	38	18	1	235	286	59	154	57	58	35	4	524	493	153
St. Louis	53	29	18	6	0	203	168	64	51	14	28	7	2	127	183	37	104	43	46	13	2	330	351	101
San Jose	12	11	1	0	0	52	32	22	11	2	4	4	1	40	37	9	23	13	5	4	1	92	69	31
Tampa Bay	29	18	9	2	0	94	81	38	29	20	6	3	0	93	61	43	58	38	15	5	0	187	142	81
Toronto	81	51	23	6	1	321	216	109	79	35	29	12	3	273	239	85	160	86	52	18	4	594	455	194
Vancouver	53	27	18	8	0	190	155	62	53	16	26	11	0	163	197	43	106	43	44	19	0	353	352	105
Washington	62	39	17	6	0	245	165	84	62	37	16	9	0	219	157	83	124	76	33	15	0	464	322	167
Defunct Clubs	23	13	5	5	0	94	63	31	23	12	8	3	0	97	76	27	46	25	13	8	0	191	139	58
Totals	**1476**	**829**	**432**	**197**	**18**	**5494**	**4161**	**1873**	**1476**	**572**	**667**	**212**	**25**	**4426**	**4814**	**1381**	**2952**	**1401**	**1099**	**409**	**43**	**9920**	**8975**	**3254**

Playoffs

	Series	W	L	GP	W	L	T	GF	GA	Last Mtg.	Rnd.	Result
Boston	7	2	5	39	18	21	0	130	139	1999	CSF	W 4-2
Carolina	1	0	1	7	3	4	0	17	22	2006	CF	L 3-4
Chicago	2	2	0	9	8	1	0	36	17	1980	QF	W 4-0
Colorado	2	0	2	8	2	6	0	27	35	1985	DSF	L 2-3
Dallas	3	1	2	13	5	8	0	37	39	1999	F	L 2-4
Montreal	7	3	4	35	17	18	0	111	124	1998	CSF	W 4-0
New Jersey	1	0	1	7	3	4	0	14	14	1994	CQF	L 3-4
NY Islanders	4	1	3	21	8	13	0	62	70	2007	CQF	W 4-1
NY Rangers	2	2	0	9	6	3	0	28	19	2007	CSF	W 4-2
Ottawa	4	3	1	21	13	8	0	52	47	2007	CF	L 1-4
Philadelphia	8	3	5	43	18	25	0	123	124	2006	CQF	W 4-2
Pittsburgh	2	0	2	10	4	6	0	26	26	2001	CSF	L 3-4
St. Louis	1	1	0	3	2	1	0	7	8	1976	PRE	W 2-1
Toronto	1	1	0	5	4	1	0	21	16	1999	CF	W 4-1
Vancouver	2	2	0	7	6	1	0	28	14	1981	PRE	W 3-0
Washington	1	0	1	6	2	4	0	11	13	1998	CF	L 2-4
Totals	**48**	**21**	**27**	**243**	**119**	**124**	**0**	**730**	**727**			

Calgary totals include Atlanta Flames, 1972-73 to 1979-80.
Colorado totals include Quebec, 1979-80 to 1994-95.
Carolina totals include Hartford, 1979-80 to 1996-97.
Dallas totals include Minnesota North Stars, 1970-71 to 1992-93.
New Jersey totals include Kansas City, 1974-75, 1975-76, and Colorado Rockies, 1976-77 to 1981-82.
Phoenix totals include Winnipeg, 1979-80 to 1995-96.

Playoff Results 2008-2003

Year	Round	Opponent	Result	GF	GA
2007	CF	Ottawa	L 1-4	10	15
	CSF	NY Rangers	W 4-2	17	13
	CQF	NY Islanders	W 4-1	17	11
2006	CF	Carolina	L 3-4	17	22
	CSF	Ottawa	W 4-1	16	13
	CQF	Philadelphia	W 4-2	27	14

Abbreviations: Round: F - Final; **CF** - conference final; **CSF** - conference semi-final; **CQF** - conference quarter-final; **DSF** - division semi-final; **QF** - quarter-final; **PRE** - preliminary round.

2007-08 Results

Month	Day	Opponent	Score	Month	Day	Opponent	Score
Oct.	5	NY Islanders	4-6		10	at Ottawa	2-3†
	6	at NY Islanders	2-3		12	New Jersey	2-3†
	11	Atlanta	6-0		16	at NY Rangers	1-2
	13	Washington	7-3		18	Atlanta	10-1
	15	Toronto	5-4*		19	at Toronto	2-4
	19	Columbus	0-3		21	at Phoenix	2-6
	20	at Montreal	2-4		24	at Dallas	2-1
	24	at Carolina	2-6		29	at Tampa Bay	4-2
	26	at Florida	4-2		30	at Florida	1-0
	27	at Tampa Bay	4-3*	**Feb.**	1	at Atlanta	4-5†
Nov.	1	at Boston	3-4*		5	at Boston	4-2
	2	Florida	2-4		6	New Jersey	3-2†
	5	at Montreal	0-2		8	Boston	2-3†
	7	Boston	2-1*		10	Florida	5-3
	9	Toronto	0-3		12	at Ottawa	5-1
	10	at Boston	1-2		13	Toronto	1-0
	15	at Ottawa	2-3		16	at NY Rangers	1-5
	16	Montreal	4-1		17	Pittsburgh	1-4
	21	Ottawa	4-2		20	Tampa Bay	4-3*
	23	Montreal	4-2		21	at Toronto	5-1
	24	at Montreal	3-0		23	NY Rangers	3-4
	26	at Washington	3-1		25	Philadelphia	3-4†
	28	St. Louis	3-4		27	Nashville	8-4
Dec.	1	Carolina	8-1		29	Montreal	2-6
	5	at Anaheim	1-4	**Mar.**	2	Detroit	2-4
	6	at Los Angeles	2-8		4	at Philadelphia	5-2
	8	at San Jose	7-1		5	Washington	1-3
	10	Boston	1-4		8	at Carolina	3-4*
	12	NY Islanders	5-3		10	NY Rangers	2-3†
	14	at Washington	5-3		12	at Pittsburgh	3-7
	15	Chicago	3-1		14	Carolina	7-1
	19	at NY Islanders	2-1		15	at Toronto	6-2
	21	Philadelphia	3-2		19	Tampa Bay	7-4
	22	at Philadelphia	6-5†		21	Toronto	1-4
	26	Ottawa	3-5		25	Ottawa	3-6
	28	at New Jersey	1-2†		27	at Ottawa	4-3†
	29	at Pittsburgh	0-2		28	Montreal	3-4*
Jan.	1	Pittsburgh	1-2†		30	Boston	2-1*
	4	Ottawa	3-5	**Apr.**	1	at Toronto	4-3†
	6	at Atlanta	2-5		3	at Montreal	1-3
	8	at New Jersey	1-2†		5	at Boston	3-0

* – Overtime † – Shootout

Entry Draft Selections 2008-1994

Name in bold denotes played in NHL.

2008
Pick
12 Tyler Myers
26 Tyler Ennis
44 Luke Adam
81 Corey Fienhage
101 Justin Jokinen
104 Jordon Southorn
134 Jacob Lagace
164 Nick Crawford

2007
Pick
31 T.J. Brennan
59 Drew Schiestel
89 Corey Tropp
139 Bradley Eidsness
147 Jean-Simon Allard
179 Paul Byron
187 Nick Eno
209 Drew Mackenzie

2006
Pick
24 Dennis Persson
46 Jhonas Enroth
57 **Mike Weber**
117 Felix Schutz
147 Alex Biega
207 Benjamin Breault

2005
Pick
13 Marek Zagrapan
48 Philip Gogulla
87 **Marc-Andre Gragnani**
96 Chris Butler
142 Nathan Gerbe
182 Adam Dennis
191 Vyacheslav Buravchikov
208 Matt Generous
227 Andrew Orpik

2004
Pick
13 **Drew Stafford**
43 **Michael Funk**
71 **Andrej Sekera**
145 Michal Valent
176 **Patrick Kaleta**
207 **Mark Mancari**
241 **Mike Card**
273 Dylan Hunter

2003
Pick
5 **Thomas Vanek**
65 Branislav Fabry
74 **Clarke MacArthur**
106 **Jan Hejda**
114 Denis Ezhov
150 Thomas Morrow
172 Pavel Voroshnin
202 **Nathan Paetsch**
235 Jeff Weber
266 Louis-Philippe Martin

2002
Pick
11 **Keith Ballard**
20 **Daniel Paille**
76 Michael Tessier
82 John Adams
108 Jakub Hulva
121 Marty Magers
178 Maxim Schevjev
208 **Radoslav Hecl**
241 **Dennis Wideman**
271 Martin Cizek

2001
Pick
22 **Jiri Novotny**
32 **Derek Roy**
50 **Chris Thorburn**
55 **Jason Pominville**
155 Michal Vondrka
234 Calle Aslund
247 Marek Dubec
279 Ryan Jorde

2000
Pick
15 Artem Kryukov
48 Gerard Dicaire
111 Ghyslain Rousseau
149 Denis Denisov
213 Vasily Bizyayev
220 **Paul Gaustad**
258 **Sean McMorrow**
277 Ryan Courtney

1999
Pick
20 **Barrett Heisten**
35 **Milan Bartovic**
55 **Doug Janik**
64 **Mike Zigomanis**
73 Tim Preston
117 Karel Mosovsky
138 **Ryan Miller**
146 Matt Kinch
178 Seneque Hyacinthe
206 Bret DeCecco
235 Brad Self
263 Craig Brunel

1998
Pick
18 **Dmitri Kalinin**
34 **Andrew Peters**
47 **Norm Milley**
50 **Jaroslav Kristek**
77 **Mike Pandolfo**
137 Aaron Goldade
164 **Ales Kotalik**
191 **Brad Moran**
218 **David Moravec**
249 Edo Terglav

1997
Pick
21 **Mika Noronen**
48 **Henrik Tallinder**
69 **Maxim Afinogenov**
75 Jeff Martin
101 Luc Theoret
128 Torrey DiRoberto
156 **Brian Campbell**
184 Jeremy Adduono
212 **Kamil Piros**
238 Dylan Kemp

1996
Pick
7 **Erik Rasmussen**
27 **Cory Sarich**
33 Darren Van Oene
54 Francois Methot
87 Kurt Walsh
106 Mike Martone
115 **Alexei Tezikov**
142 Ryan Davis
161 Darren Mortier
222 Scott Buhler

1995
Pick
14 **Jay McKee**
16 **Martin Biron**
42 Mark Dutiaume
68 Mathieu Sunderland
94 **Matt Davidson**
111 Marian Menhart
119 Kevin Popp
123 Daniel Bienvenue
172 Brian Scott
198 Mike Zanutto
224 **Rob Skrlac**

1994
Pick
17 **Wayne Primeau**
43 **Curtis Brown**
69 **Rumun Ndur**
121 Sergei Klimentiev
147 Cal Benazic
168 Steve Plouffe
173 **Shane Hnidy**
176 **Steve Webb**
199 Bob Westerby
225 **Craig Millar**
251 Mark Polak
277 Shayne Wright

General Managers' History

Punch Imlach, 1970-71 to 1977-78; John Anderson, 1978-79; Scotty Bowman, 1979-80 to 1985-86; Scotty Bowman and Gerry Meehan, 1986-87; Gerry Meehan, 1987-88 to 1992-93; John Muckler, 1993-94 to 1996-97; Darcy Regier, 1997-98 to date.

Darcy Regier

General Manager

Born: Swift Current, Sask., November 27, 1957.

Darcy Regier became the sixth general manager of the Buffalo Sabres on June 11, 1997 after a lengthy management apprenticeship in the New York Islanders organization. As a player, Regier played eight pro seasons, including part of the 1977-78 season with the Cleveland Barons and parts of the 1982-83 and 1983-84 campaigns with the New York Islanders.

He began his career as an administrator with the Islanders in 1984-85 and went on to serve in a variety of capacities including director of administration, assistant director of hockey operations, assistant coach and assistant general manager. He also served as an assistant coach with Hartford in 1991-92.

While with the Islanders, Regier benefited from working with talented managers and coaches including Bill Torrey and Al Arbour. As a minor pro player with Indianapolis of the CHL he became associated with another important influence on his hockey career, current Detroit Red Wing executive Jim Devellano.

Club Directory

HSBC Arena

Buffalo Sabres
HSBC Arena
One Seymour H. Knox III Plaza
Buffalo, NY 14203
Phone **716/855-4100**
Fax 716/855-4110
Tickets, U.S.: 888/GO-SABRES
Canada: 888/669-GOAL
www.sabres.com
Capacity: 18,690

Executive
Owner . . . B. Thomas Golisano
Managing Partner . . . Lawrence Quinn
Chief Operating Officer . . . Daniel DiPofi

Hockey Department
General Manager . . . Darcy Regier
Director of Amateur Scouting . . . Kevin Devine
Director of Pro Scouting . . . Jon Christiano
Pro Scout . . . Dennis Miller
Amateur Scouts . . . Bo Berglund, Nik Fattey, Iouri Khmylev, Al MacAdam, Paul Merritt, Craig Benning, Kim Gellert
Director of Amateur Scouting Operations . . . Scott Schranz
Hockey Department Analyst . . . Mark Jakubowski
Pro Scouting Coordinator . . . Ryan Vinz
Coordinator of Hockey Operations . . . Michael Bermingham
Amateur Scouting Coordinator . . . Eric Weissman

Coaching Staff
Head Coach . . . Lindy Ruff
Associate Coach . . . Brian McCutcheon
Assistant Coach . . . James Patrick
Strength & Conditioning Coach . . . Doug McKenney
Asst. Strength & Conditioning Coach . . . Kevin Collins
Goaltender Coach . . . Jim Corsi
Administrative Assistant Coach . . . Corey Smith
Athletic Trainer . . . Tim Macre
Equipment Managers . . . Rip Simonick, Dave Williams
Assistant Equipment Manager . . . George Babcock
Massage Therapist . . . Chuck Garlow

Medical
Medical Director . . . Les Bisson, M.D.
Team Physicians . . . Nicholas Aquino, M.D., William Hartrich, M.D.
Oral Surgeon . . . Steven Jenson, DDS
Team Dentist . . . Daniel Yustin, DDS, M.S.
Team Doctor Emeritus . . . John L. Butsch, M.D.

Legal
Director of Legal Affairs & Human Resources . . . Dave Zygaj

Finance and Administration
Director of Finance & Administration . . . Chuck LaMattina
Accounting Manager . . . Christine Ivansitz
Payroll & Human Resource Manager . . . Birgid Haensel
Accounts Payable Clerk . . . Kim Binkley
Executive Assistant . . . Nadine Lawicki
IT Systems Engineer . . . Dave Blaszak

Broadcast
Executive Producer . . . Matt Gould
Director of Broadcast Services . . . Chrisanne Bellas
Staff Producer . . . Joe Pinter
Broadcast Director . . . TBA
Feature Producer/Editor . . . Jeff Hill
Feature Editor . . . Drew Boeing
Photographer . . . Mark Blaszak
Broadcast Team . . . Rick Jeanneret (Play-by-Play), Harry Neale (Commentator), Kevin Sylvester (Studio Host), Mike Robitaille, Rob Ray (Analysts)

Merchandise
Director of Merchandise . . . Mike Kaminska
Merchandise Manager – Inventory Control . . . Glenn Barker
Merchandise Manager – Event Sales . . . Jeff Smith
Store Manager . . . Alec Moslow

Marketing
Director of Marketing . . . Rob Kopacz
Director of Game Presentation . . . Jenifer Dunford
Director of Creative Services . . . Frank Cravotta
Promotions Manager . . . Rich Wall
Database Marketing Manager . . . Tom Matheny
Website Manager . . . TBA

Public and Community Relations
Director of Public Relations . . . Michael Gilbert
Manager of Publications & Hockey Information . . . Kevin Snow
Manager of Community Development . . . Rich Jureller
Coordinator of Media Relations . . . Chris Bandura
Community Relations Coordinator . . . Teresa Belbas
Mascot Coordinator . . . Ed Grudzinski
Graduate Assistant . . . Chris Ostrander
Team Photographer . . . Bill Wippert
Director of Alumni Relations . . . Larry Playfair
Corporate & Community Relations Liaison . . . Gilbert Perreault

Sales and Business Development
V.P. Sales & Business Development . . . John Livsey
Senior Account Managers . . . Joe Foy, Chris Luterek
Director of Sales/Marketing – Rochester . . . Gary Muxworthy

Ticket Sales and Operations
Director of Ticket Operations & Services . . . John Sinclair
Account Services Manager . . . Michael Tout
Box Office Manager . . . Marty Maloney
Box Office Coordinators . . . Gretchen Knott, Ryan Handley
Account Services Representatives . . . Roxanne Anderson, Andrea Keane, Lisa Jacobs, Melissa Rugg
Account Executive . . . Sarah Kretz
Special Consultant . . . Joe Crozier

HSBC Arena
Director of Arena Operations . . . Stan Makowski, Jr.
Director of Arena Services . . . Thomas Ahern
Director of Event Booking . . . Jennifer Van Rysdam
Arena Marketing Manager . . . Christine Adamczyk
Director of Amateur Athletics . . . Kevin Sylvester
Event Managers . . . Matt Rabinowitz, Beth Guiliani Gatto
Technical Communications Mgrs. . . . Mike Queeno, Ray Riel
Chief Engineer . . . Barry Becker

Calgary Flames

2007-08 Results: 42W-30L-7OTL-3SOL 94PTS.
Third, Northwest Division

Key Off-Season Signings/Acquisitions

2008

- **June 20** • Acquired C **Mike Cammalleri** from Los Angeles for a 1st-round pick in 2008.
- **20** • Acquired a 1st-round pick in 2008 from Montreal for LW **Alex Tanguay**.
- **27** • Re-signed C **Craig Conroy**, C **Daymond Langkow**, LW **Eric Nystrom** and G **Curtis McElhinney**.
- **July 1** • Acquired LW **Rene Bourque** from Chicago for a conditional draft pick.
- **1** • Re-signed D **Mark Giordano**.
- **2** • Re-signed D **Jim Vandermeer** and signed LW **Peter Vandermeer**.
- **7** • Signed RW **Todd Bertuzzi**.

Jarome Iginla scored 50 goals for the second time in 2007-08. His 41st of the year on March 10th was the 365th of his career, breaking Theo Fleury's Flames franchise record.

2008-09 Schedule

Oct.	Thu.	9	at Vancouver
	Sat.	11	Vancouver
	Tue.	14	Colorado
	Fri.	17	Edmonton
	Sat.	18	at Edmonton
	Tue.	21	Washington
	Thu.	23	at Nashville
	Sat.	25	at Phoenix
	Tue.	28	Colorado
	Thu.	30	Boston
Nov.	Sat.	1	at Los Angeles
	Sun.	2	at Anaheim*
	Tue.	4	Phoenix
	Thu.	6	Nashville
	Sat.	8	at Columbus
	Sun.	9	at Chicago
	Tue.	11	Toronto
	Thu.	13	at San Jose
	Tue.	18	Colorado
	Thu.	20	at Colorado
	Sat.	22	Detroit
	Tue.	25	Los Angeles
	Thu.	27	at Vancouver
	Sat.	29	Vancouver
Dec.	Tue.	2	Dallas
	Fri.	5	at St. Louis
	Sun.	7	at NY Rangers
	Tue.	9	at Montreal
	Wed.	10	at Detroit
	Fri.	12	Florida
	Tue.	16	at St. Louis
	Wed.	17	at Minnesota
	Fri.	19	Chicago
	Tue.	23	Anaheim
	Sat.	27	Ottawa
	Mon.	29	Minnesota
	Wed.	31	Edmonton
Jan.	Sat.	3	at Nashville*
	Sun.	4	at Chicago
	Tue.	6	San Jose
	Thu.	8	NY Islanders
	Tue.	13	St. Louis
	Thu.	15	at San Jose
	Sat.	17	Phoenix
	Sun.	18	at Colorado
	Wed.	21	Columbus
	Wed.	28	Buffalo
	Fri.	30	Nashville
Feb.	Mon.	2	at Colorado
	Tue.	3	at Dallas
	Thu.	5	Chicago
	Sat.	7	Anaheim*
	Mon.	9	Montreal
	Wed.	11	at Anaheim
	Thu.	12	at Los Angeles
	Sat.	14	at Phoenix
	Tue.	17	Vancouver
	Thu.	19	at Minnesota
	Sat.	21	at Edmonton
	Tue.	24	Columbus
	Fri.	27	Minnesota
Mar.	Sun.	1	Tampa Bay
	Tue.	3	at Ottawa
	Thu.	5	at Philadelphia
	Fri.	6	at Carolina
	Sun.	8	at Atlanta*
	Tue.	10	at New Jersey
	Thu.	12	at Detroit
	Sat.	14	at Toronto
	Wed.	18	Dallas
	Fri.	20	St. Louis
	Mon.	23	Detroit
	Wed.	25	at Pittsburgh
	Thu.	26	at Columbus
	Sat.	28	Minnesota
	Mon.	30	San Jose
Apr.	Thu.	2	at Dallas
	Fri.	3	at Minnesota
	Mon.	6	Los Angeles
	Tue.	7	at Vancouver
	Fri.	10	at Edmonton
	Sat.	11	Edmonton

* Denotes afternoon game.

NORTHWEST DIVISION
37th NHL Season

Franchise date: June 6, 1972

Transferred from Atlanta to Calgary, June 24, 1980.

Year-by-Year Record

		Home				Road				Overall								
Season	**GP**	**W**	**L**	**T**	**OL**	**W**	**L**	**T**	**OL**	**W**	**L**	**T**	**OL**	**GF**	**GA**	**Pts.**	**Finished**	**Playoff Result**
2007-08	82	21	11	....	9	21	19	....	1	42	30	....	10	229	227	94	3rd, Northwest Div.	Lost Conf. Quarter-Final
2006-07	82	30	9	....	2	13	20	....	8	43	29	....	10	258	226	96	3rd, Northwest Div.	Lost Conf. Quarter-Final
2005-06	82	30	7	....	4	16	18	....	7	46	25	....	11	218	200	103	1st, Northwest Div.	Lost Conf. Quarter-Final
2004-05	....	....	....	....	....	....	....	....	....	....	....	....	....	....	....	....		
2003-04	82	21	14	5	1	21	16	2	2	42	30	7	3	200	176	94	3rd, Northwest Div.	Lost Final
2002-03	82	14	16	10	1	15	20	3	3	29	36	13	4	186	228	75	5th, Northwest Div.	Out of Playoffs
2001-02	82	20	14	5	2	12	21	7	1	32	35	12	3	201	220	79	4th, Northwest Div.	Out of Playoffs
2000-01	82	12	18	9	2	15	18	6	2	27	36	15	4	197	236	73	4th, Northwest Div.	Out of Playoffs
1999-2000	82	20	14	6	1	11	22	4	4	31	36	10	5	211	256	77	4th, Northwest Div.	Out of Playoffs
1998-99	82	15	20	6	....	15	20	6	....	30	40	12	....	211	234	72	3rd, Northwest Div.	Out of Playoffs
1997-98	82	18	17	6	....	8	24	9	....	26	41	15	....	217	252	67	5th, Pacific Div.	Out of Playoffs
1996-97	82	21	18	2	....	11	23	7	....	32	41	9	....	214	239	73	5th, Pacific Div.	Out of Playoffs
1995-96	82	18	18	5	....	16	19	6	....	34	37	11	....	241	240	79	2nd, Pacific Div.	Lost Conf. Quarter-Final
1994-95	48	15	7	2	....	9	10	5	....	24	17	7	....	163	135	55	1st, Pacific Div.	Lost Conf. Quarter-Final
1993-94	84	25	12	5	....	17	17	8	....	42	29	13	....	302	256	97	1st, Pacific Div.	Lost Conf. Quarter-Final
1992-93	84	23	14	5	....	20	16	6	....	43	30	11	....	322	282	97	2nd, Smythe Div.	Lost Div. Semi-Final
1991-92	80	19	14	7	....	12	23	5	....	31	37	12	....	296	305	74	5th, Smythe Div.	Out of Playoffs
1990-91	80	29	8	3	....	17	18	5	....	46	26	8	....	344	263	100	2nd, Smythe Div.	Lost Div. Semi-Final
1989-90	80	28	7	5	....	14	16	10	....	42	23	15	....	348	265	99	1st, Smythe Div.	Lost Div. Semi-Final
1988-89	**80**	**32**	**4**	**4**	....	**22**	**13**	**5**	....	**54**	**17**	**9**	....	**354**	**226**	**117**	**1st, Smythe Div.**	**Won Stanley Cup**
1987-88	80	26	11	3	....	22	12	6	....	48	23	9	....	397	305	105	1st, Smythe Div.	Lost Div. Final
1986-87	80	25	13	2	....	21	18	1	....	46	31	3	....	318	289	95	2nd, Smythe Div.	Lost Div. Semi-Final
1985-86	80	23	11	6	....	17	20	3	....	40	31	9	....	354	315	89	2nd, Smythe Div.	Lost Final
1984-85	80	23	11	6	....	18	16	6	....	41	27	12	....	363	302	94	3rd, Smythe Div.	Lost Div. Semi-Final
1983-84	80	22	11	7	....	12	21	7	....	34	32	14	....	311	314	82	2nd, Smythe Div.	Lost Div. Final
1982-83	80	21	12	7	....	11	22	7	....	32	34	14	....	321	317	78	2nd, Smythe Div.	Lost Div. Final
1981-82	80	20	11	9	....	9	23	8	....	29	34	17	....	334	345	75	3rd, Smythe Div.	Lost Div. Semi-Final
1980-81	80	25	5	10	....	14	22	4	....	39	27	14	....	329	298	92	3rd, Patrick Div.	Lost Semi-Final
1979-80*	80	18	15	7	....	17	17	6	....	35	32	13	....	282	269	83	4th, Patrick Div.	Lost Prelim. Round
1978-79*	80	25	11	4	....	16	20	4	....	41	31	8	....	327	280	90	4th, Patrick Div.	Lost Prelim. Round
1977-78*	80	20	13	7	....	14	14	12	....	34	27	19	....	274	252	87	3rd, Patrick Div.	Lost Prelim. Round
1976-77*	80	22	11	7	....	12	23	5	....	34	34	12	....	264	265	80	3rd, Patrick Div.	Lost Prelim. Round
1975-76*	80	19	14	7	....	16	19	5	....	35	33	12	....	262	237	82	3rd, Patrick Div.	Lost Prelim. Round
1974-75*	80	24	9	7	....	10	22	8	....	34	31	15	....	243	233	83	4th, Patrick Div.	Out of Playoffs
1973-74*	78	17	15	7	....	13	19	7	....	30	34	14	....	214	238	74	4th, West Div.	Lost Quarter-Final
1972-73*	78	16	16	7	....	9	22	8	....	25	38	15	....	191	239	65	7th, West Div.	Out of Playoffs

* Atlanta Flames

2008-09 Player Personnel

FORWARDS	HT	WT	S	Place of Birth	*Age	2007-08 Club
BERTUZZI, Todd	6-3	231	L	Sudbury, Ont.	33	Anaheim
BOURQUE, Rene	6-2	213	L	Lac La Biche, Alta.	26	Chicago
BOYD, Dustin	6-0	193	L	Winnipeg, Man.	22	Calgary-Quad City
CAMMALLERI, Michael	5-9	185	L	Richmond Hill, Ont.	26	Los Angeles
CONROY, Craig	6-2	193	R	Potsdam, NY	37	Calgary
GLENCROSS, Curtis	6-1	195	L	Kindersley, Sask.	25	Columbus-Edmonton
GREENTREE, Kyle	6-3	212	L	Victoria, B.C.	24	Phi-Phi (AHL)
IGINLA, Jarome	6-1	207	R	Edmonton, Alta.	31	Calgary
LANGKOW, Daymond	5-11	181	L	Edmonton, Alta.	32	Calgary
LOMBARDI, Matthew	6-0	198	L	Montreal, Que.	26	Calgary
LUNDMARK, Jamie	6-0	200	R	Edmonton, Alta.	27	Dynamo Moscow-Lake Erie
MOSS, Dave	6-3	200	L	Dearborn, MI	26	Calgary
NILSON, Marcus	6-2	189	R	Balsta, Sweden	30	Calgary
NYSTROM, Eric	6-1	197	L	Syosset, NY	25	Calgary-Quad City
PRIMEAU, Wayne	6-4	225	L	Scarborough, Ont.	32	Calgary
PRUST, Brandon	5-11	195	L	London, Ont.	24	Quad City
ROY, Andre	6-3	202	L	Port Chester, NY	33	Tampa Bay
VAN DER GULIK, David	5-11	183	L	Abbotsford, B.C.	25	Quad City
DEFENSEMEN						
AUCOIN, Adrian	6-2	212	R	Ottawa, Ont.	35	Calgary
ERIKSSON, Anders	6-3	224	L	Bollnas, Sweden	33	Calgary
GIORDANO, Mark	6-0	203	L	Toronto, Ont.	25	Dynamo Moscow
PHANEUF, Dion	6-3	214	L	Edmonton, Alta.	23	Calgary
REGEHR, Robyn	6-3	225	L	Recife, Brazil	28	Calgary
SARICH, Cory	6-4	207	R	Saskatoon, Sask.	30	Calgary
VANDERMEER, Jim	6-1	208	L	Caroline, Alta.	28	Chi-Phi-Cgy
WARRENER, Rhett	6-1	203	R	Shaunavon, Sask.	32	Calgary

GOALTENDERS	HT	WT	C	Place of Birth	*Age	2007-08 Club
KIPRUSOFF, Miikka	6-1	184	L	Turku, Finland	31	Calgary
McELHINNEY, Curtis	6-1	193	L	London, Ont.	25	Calgary-Quad City

* – Age at start of 2008-09 season

Mike Keenan

Head Coach

Born: Bowmanville, Ont., October 21, 1949.

Mike Keenan became the 13th head coach of the Calgary Flames on June 14, 2007, bringing an impressive coaching resume with him. He is fifth all-time in coaching wins with 626 and has reached the Stanley Cup Final on four occasions, winning in 1994 with the New York Rangers. He also coached teams to championships with Peterborough (OHL-1980), Rochester (AHL-1983) and the University of Toronto (CIAU-1984). He first coached in the NHL with Philadelphia and went on to coach seven NHL clubs: the Flyers, Blackhawks, Rangers, Blues, Canucks, Bruins and Panthers. He also served as general manager in Florida and coached Team Canada at the IIHF World Junior Championship in 1980 and the World Championship in 1993.

Coaching Record

			Regular Season				Playoffs			
Season	**Team**	**League**	**GC**	**W**	**L**	**O/T**	**GC**	**W**	**L**	**T**
1979-80	Peterborough	OHL	68	47	20	1	18	15	3	....
1980-81	Rochester	AHL	80	30	42	8	....	....	....	....
1981-82	Rochester	AHL	80	40	31	9	9	4	5	....
1982-83	Rochester	AHL	80	46	25	9	16	12	4	....
1983-84	U. of Toronto	CIAU	49	41	5	3	....	....	....	....
1984-85	**Philadelphia**	**NHL**	**80**	**53**	**20**	**7**	**19**	**12**	**7**	....
1985-86	**Philadelphia**	**NHL**	**80**	**53**	**23**	**4**	**5**	**2**	**3**	....
1986-87	**Philadelphia**	**NHL**	**80**	**46**	**26**	**8**	**26**	**15**	**11**	....
1987-88	**Philadelphia**	**NHL**	**80**	**38**	**33**	**9**	**7**	**3**	**4**	....
1988-89	**Chicago**	**NHL**	**80**	**27**	**41**	**12**	**16**	**9**	**7**	....
1989-90	**Chicago**	**NHL**	**80**	**41**	**33**	**6**	**20**	**10**	**10**	....
1990-91	**Chicago**	**NHL**	**80**	**49**	**23**	**8**	**6**	**2**	**4**	....
1991-92	**Chicago**	**NHL**	**80**	**36**	**29**	**15**	**18**	**12**	**6**	....
1993-94♦	**NY Rangers**	**NHL**	**84**	**52**	**24**	**8**	**23**	**16**	**7**	....
1994-95	**St. Louis**	**NHL**	**48**	**28**	**15**	**5**	**7**	**3**	**4**	....
1995-96	**St. Louis**	**NHL**	**82**	**32**	**34**	**16**	**13**	**7**	**6**	....
1996-97	**St. Louis**	**NHL**	**33**	**15**	**17**	**1**	....	....	....	....
1997-98	**Vancouver**	**NHL**	**63**	**21**	**30**	**12**	....	....	....	....
1998-99	**Vancouver**	**NHL**	**45**	**15**	**24**	**6**	....	....	....	....
2000-01	**Boston**	**NHL**	**74**	**33**	**26**	**15**	....	....	....	....
2001-02	**Florida**	**NHL**	**56**	**16**	**29**	**11**	....	....	....	....
2002-03	**Florida**	**NHL**	**82**	**24**	**36**	**22**	....	....	....	....
2003-04	**Florida**	**NHL**	**15**	**5**	**8**	**2**	....	....	....	....
2007-08	**Calgary**	**NHL**	**82**	**42**	**30**	**10**	**7**	**3**	**4**	....
	NHL Totals		**1304**	**626**	**501**	**177**	**167**	**94**	**73**	....

♦ Stanley Cup win.

2007-08 Scoring

* – rookie

Regular Season

Pos	#	Player	Team	GP	G	A	Pts	TOI	+/–	PIM	PP	SH	GW	S	%
R	12	Jarome Iginla	CGY	82	50	48	98	21:26	27	83	15	0	9	338	14.8
L	20	Kristian Huselius	CGY	81	25	41	66	17:41	10	40	6	0	5	202	12.4
C	22	Daymond Langkow	CGY	80	30	35	65	18:49	16	19	14	1	4	201	14.9
D	3	Dion Phaneuf	CGY	82	17	43	60	26:25	12	182	10	1	4	263	6.5
L	40	Alex Tanguay	CGY	78	18	40	58	18:45	11	48	3	2	3	121	14.9
C	18	Matthew Lombardi	CGY	82	14	22	36	17:18	–6	67	2	2	4	181	7.7
D	33	Adrian Aucoin	CGY	76	10	25	35	20:57	13	37	5	0	1	121	8.3
C	24	Craig Conroy	CGY	79	12	22	34	17:09	6	71	1	0	4	116	10.3
R	11	Owen Nolan	CGY	77	16	16	32	16:33	6	71	1	1	3	163	9.8
D	28	Robyn Regehr	CGY	82	5	15	20	21:20	11	79	1	1	0	93	5.4
D	8	Anders Eriksson	CGY	61	1	17	18	20:46	–5	36	1	0	0	50	2.0
D	4	Jim Vandermeer	CHI	26	2	7	9	19:37	3	44	1	0	0	23	8.7
			PHI	28	1	5	6	19:34	–1	27	1	0	0	26	3.8
			CGY	21	0	2	2	19:43	4	39	0	0	0	23	0.0
			Total	75	3	14	17	19:38	6	110	2	0	0	72	4.2
C	41	* Dustin Boyd	CGY	48	7	5	12	09:49	–11	6	0	0	1	46	15.2
C	7	Stephane Yelle	CGY	74	3	9	12	11:56	–4	20	0	1	0	62	4.8
L	25	Dave Moss	CGY	41	4	7	11	12:23	–4	10	0	0	0	60	6.7
C	19	Wayne Primeau	CGY	43	3	7	10	11:02	–3	26	0	0	0	39	7.7
L	23	* Eric Nystrom	CGY	44	3	7	10	11:29	–5	48	0	0	0	42	7.1
D	6	Cory Sarich	CGY	80	2	5	7	18:49	2	135	0	0	0	57	3.5
L	26	Marcus Nilson	CGY	47	3	2	5	09:48	2	4	0	0	0	47	6.4
D	44	Rhett Warrener	CGY	31	1	3	4	13:25	–2	21	0	0	0	15	6.7
C	16	Mark Smith	CGY	54	1	3	4	05:56	–6	59	0	0	0	27	3.7
R	17	Eric Godard	CGY	74	1	1	2	04:42	–8	171	0	0	1	14	7.1
D	21	David Hale	CGY	58	0	2	2	13:53	0	46	0	0	0	35	0.0
D	47	* Tim Ramholt	CGY	1	0	0	0	:45	–1	0	0	0	0	0	0.0

Goaltending

No.	Goaltender	GPI	Mins	Avg	W	L	OT	EN	SO	GA	SA	S%	G	A	PIM
36	* Matt Keetley	1	9	0.00	0	0	0	0	0	0	2	1.000	0	0	0
31	* Curtis McElhinney	5	150	2.00	0	2	0	1	0	5	51	.902	0	0	0
31	Curtis Joseph	9	400	2.55	3	2	0	1	0	17	181	.906	0	0	2
34	Miikka Kiprusoff	76	4398	2.69	39	26	10	3	2	197	2096	.906	0	2	8
	Totals	**82**	**4975**	**2.70**	**42**	**30**	**10**	**5**	**2**	**224**	**2335**	**.904**			

Playoffs

Pos	#	Player	Team	GP	G	A	Pts	TOI	+/–	PIM	PP	SH	GW	OT	S	%
R	12	Jarome Iginla	CGY	7	4	5	9	22:42	–1	2	3	0	0	0	27	14.8
D	3	Dion Phaneuf	CGY	7	3	4	7	27:06	–2	4	1	0	0	0	22	13.6
R	11	Owen Nolan	CGY	7	3	2	5	19:10	0	2	0	0	2	0	12	25.0
C	22	Daymond Langkow	CGY	7	3	2	5	18:21	0	0	2	0	0	0	16	18.8
L	20	Kristian Huselius	CGY	7	0	4	4	13:45	–1	6	0	0	0	0	5	0.0
L	40	Alex Tanguay	CGY	7	0	4	4	18:14	–1	4	0	0	0	0	6	0.0
D	33	Adrian Aucoin	CGY	7	0	3	3	18:13	3	4	0	0	0	0	6	0.0
C	7	Stephane Yelle	CGY	7	2	0	2	14:35	2	6	0	0	1	0	5	40.0
L	25	Dave Moss	CGY	5	1	1	2	10:20	2	4	0	0	0	0	6	16.7
C	24	Craig Conroy	CGY	7	0	2	2	16:42	0	8	0	0	0	0	12	0.0
D	28	Robyn Regehr	CGY	7	0	2	2	21:49	0	2	0	0	0	0	3	0.0
C	19	Wayne Primeau	CGY	7	1	0	1	10:35	0	4	0	0	0	0	6	16.7
D	8	Anders Eriksson	CGY	3	0	1	1	18:16	0	2	0	0	0	0	0	0.0
D	6	Cory Sarich	CGY	7	0	1	1	19:34	1	4	0	0	0	0	4	0.0
L	26	Marcus Nilson	CGY	2	0	0	0	04:49	0	0	0	0	0	0	0	0.0
R	17	Eric Godard	CGY	5	0	0	0	03:31	0	2	0	0	0	0	1	0.0
D	21	David Hale	CGY	6	0	0	0	12:47	–1	2	0	0	0	0	5	0.0
D	4	Jim Vandermeer	CGY	7	0	0	0	16:17	–6	4	0	0	0	0	6	0.0
C	18	Matthew Lombardi	CGY	7	0	0	0	17:14	–2	4	0	0	0	0	16	0.0
L	23	* Eric Nystrom	CGY	7	0	0	0	07:38	–2	2	0	0	0	0	4	0.0

Goaltending

No.	Goaltender	GPI	Mins	Avg	W	L	EN	SO	GA	SA	S%	G	A	PIM
31	Curtis Joseph	2	79	0.76	1	0	0	0	1	33	.970	0	0	0
34	Miikka Kiprusoff	7	336	3.21	2	4	0	1	18	196	.908	0	0	2
	Totals	**7**	**420**	**2.71**	**3**	**4**	**0**	**1**	**19**	**229**	**.917**			

Coaching History

Bernie Geoffrion, 1972-73, 1973-74; Bernie Geoffrion and Fred Creighton, 1974-75; Fred Creighton, 1975-76 to 1978-79; Al MacNeil, 1979-80 to 1981-82; Bob Johnson, 1982-83 to 1986-87; Terry Crisp, 1987-88 to 1989-90; Doug Risebrough, 1990-91; Doug Risebrough and Guy Charron, 1991-92; Dave King, 1992-93 to 1994-95; Pierre Page, 1995-96, 1996-97; Brian Sutter, 1997-98 to 1999-2000; Don Hay and Greg Gilbert, 2000-01; Greg Gilbert, 2001-02; Greg Gilbert, Al MacNeil and Darryl Sutter, 2002-03; Darryl Sutter, 2003-04 to 2005-06; Jim Playfair, 2006-07; Mike Keenan, 2007-08 to date.

Captains' History

Keith McCreary, 1972-73 to 1974-75; Pat Quinn, 1975-76, 1976-77; Tom Lysiak, 1977-78, 1978-79; Jean Pronovost, 1979-80; Brad Marsh, 1980-81; Phil Russell, 1981-82, 1982-83; Lanny McDonald, Doug Risebrough, 1983-84; Lanny McDonald, Doug Risebrough, Jim Peplinski, 1984-85 to 1986-87; Lanny McDonald, Jim Peplinski, 1987-88; Lanny McDonald, Jim Peplinski, Tim Hunter, 1988-89; Brad McCrimmon, 1989-90; alternating captains, 1990-91; Joe Nieuwendyk, 1991-92 to 1994-95; Theoren Fleury, 1995-96, 1996-97; Todd Simpson, 1997-98, 1998-99; Steve Smith, 1999-2000; Steve Smith and Dave Lowry, 2000-01; Dave Lowry; Bob Boughner and Craig Conroy, 2001-02; Bob Boughner and Craig Conroy, 2002-03; Jarome Iginla, 2003-04 to date.

Club Records

Team

(Figures in brackets for season records are games played; records for fewest points, wins, ties, losses, goals, goals against are for 70 or more games)

Most Points	**117**	1988-89 (80)
Most Wins	**54**	1988-89 (80)
Most Ties	**19**	1977-78 (80)
Most Losses	**41**	1996-97 (82), 1997-98 (82), 1999-2000 (82)
Most Goals	**397**	1987-88 (80)
Most Goals Against	**345**	1981-82 (80)
Fewest Points	**65**	1972-73 (78)
Fewest Wins	**25**	1972-73 (78)
Fewest Ties	**3**	1986-87 (80)
Fewest Losses	**17**	1988-89 (80)
Fewest Goals	**186**	2002-03 (82)
Fewest Goals Against	**176**	2003-04 (82)
Longest Winning Streak		
Overall	**10**	Oct. 14-Nov. 3/78
Home	**10**	Nov. 7-Dec. 12/06
Away	**7**	Nov. 10-Dec. 4/88
Longest Undefeated Streak		
Overall	**13**	Nov. 10-Dec. 8/88 (12 wins, 1 tie)
Home	**18**	Dec. 29/90-Mar. 14/91 (17 wins, 1 tie)
Away	**9**	Feb. 20-Mar. 21/88 (6 wins, 3 ties), Nov. 11-Dec. 16/90 (6 wins, 3 ties)
Longest Losing Streak		
Overall	**11**	Dec. 14/85-Jan. 7/86
Home	**6**	Dec. 5-31/98
Away	**9**	Dec. 1/85-Jan. 12/86
Longest Winless Streak		
Overall	**11**	Dec. 14/85-Jan. 7/86 (11 losses), Jan. 5-26/93 (9 losses, 2 ties)
Home	**10**	Oct. 21-Dec. 4/00 (6 losses, 4 ties)
Away	**13**	Feb. 3-Mar. 29/73 (10 losses, 3 ties)
Most Shutouts, Season	**11**	2003-04 (82)
Most PIM, Season	**2,643**	1991-92 (80)
Most Goals, Game	**13**	Feb. 10/93 (S.J. 1 at Cgy. 13)

Individual

Most Seasons	**13**	Al MacInnis
Most Games	**860**	Jarome Iginla
Most Goals, Career	**374**	Jarome Iginla
Most Assists, Career	**609**	Al MacInnis
Most Points, Career	**830**	Theoren Fleury (364G, 466A)
Most PIM, Career	**2,405**	Tim Hunter
Most Shutouts, Career	**23**	Miika Kiprusoff
Longest Consecutive Games Streak	**257**	Brad Marsh (Oct. 11/78-Nov. 10/81)
Most Goals, Season	**66**	Lanny McDonald (1982-83)
Most Assists, Season	**82**	Kent Nilsson (1980-81)
Most Points, Season	**131**	Kent Nilsson (1980-81; 49G, 82A)
Most PIM, Season	**375**	Tim Hunter (1988-89)
Most Points, Defenseman, Season	**103**	Al MacInnis (1990-91; 28G, 75A)
Most Points, Center, Season	**131**	Kent Nilsson (1980-81; 49G, 82A)
Most Points, Right Wing, Season	**110**	Joe Mullen (1988-89; 51G, 59A)
Most Points, Left Wing, Season	**90**	Gary Roberts (1991-92; 53G, 37A)
Most Points, Rookie, Season	**92**	Joe Nieuwendyk (1987-88; 51G, 41A)
Most Shutouts, Season	**10**	Miikka Kiprusoff (2005-06)
Most Goals, Game	**5**	Joe Nieuwendyk (Jan. 11/89)
Most Assists, Game	**6**	Guy Chouinard (Feb. 25/81), Gary Suter (Apr. 4/86)
Most Points, Game	**7**	Sergei Makarov (Feb. 25/90; 2G, 5A)

Records include Atlanta Flames, 1972-73 through 1979-80.

Retired Numbers

9	Lanny McDonald	1981-1989
30	Mike Vernon	1982-1994; 2000-02

All-time Record vs. Other Clubs

Regular Season

	At Home								On Road								Total							
	GP	W	L	T	OL	GF	GA	PTS	GP	W	L	T	OL	GF	GA	PTS	GP	W	L	T	OL	GF	GA	PTS
Anaheim	31	20	10	1	0	90	71	41	32	8	16	6	2	80	104	24	63	28	26	7	2	170	175	65
Atlanta	4	4	0	0	0	18	7	8	5	0	4	1	0	9	14	1	9	4	4	1	0	27	21	9
Boston	45	19	22	4	0	163	154	42	48	13	29	6	0	132	168	32	93	32	51	10	0	295	322	74
Buffalo	47	18	18	11	0	156	147	47	46	13	26	5	2	133	192	33	93	31	44	16	2	289	339	80
Carolina	30	22	6	2	0	143	92	46	29	14	10	5	0	107	94	33	59	36	16	7	0	250	186	79
Chicago	69	31	24	13	1	214	204	76	67	26	27	13	1	197	211	66	136	57	51	26	2	411	415	142
Colorado	59	28	19	9	3	205	173	68	59	21	25	11	2	189	213	55	118	49	44	20	5	394	386	123
Columbus	14	9	3	0	2	39	28	20	14	4	9	0	1	29	41	9	28	13	12	0	3	68	69	29
Dallas	68	36	16	14	2	221	166	88	68	23	33	11	1	209	245	58	136	59	49	25	3	430	411	146
Detroit	66	38	21	6	1	240	188	83	65	19	36	10	0	191	242	48	131	57	57	16	1	431	430	131
Edmonton	93	51	32	9	1	359	298	112	93	35	46	10	2	295	333	82	186	86	78	19	3	654	631	194
Florida	9	5	3	1	0	26	24	11	10	5	3	2	0	24	22	12	19	10	6	3	0	50	46	23
Los Angeles	100	60	28	12	0	437	325	132	97	39	47	9	2	335	358	89	197	99	75	21	2	772	683	221
Minnesota	22	16	2	3	1	62	43	36	23	11	8	1	3	46	53	26	45	27	10	4	4	108	96	62
Montreal	50	17	26	7	0	149	166	41	47	12	27	8	0	116	168	32	97	29	53	15	0	265	334	73
Nashville	18	8	5	3	2	51	41	21	19	5	13	1	0	42	68	11	37	13	18	4	2	93	109	32
New Jersey	43	28	6	8	1	184	112	65	46	28	15	3	0	166	129	59	89	56	21	11	1	350	241	124
NY Islanders	50	24	14	11	1	176	150	60	52	17	26	9	0	145	194	43	102	41	40	20	1	321	344	103
NY Rangers	50	28	11	10	1	220	151	67	53	23	23	5	2	186	182	53	103	51	34	15	3	406	333	120
Ottawa	12	7	4	1	0	40	26	15	11	3	5	3	0	25	27	9	23	10	9	4	0	65	53	24
Philadelphia	53	25	19	9	0	210	175	59	52	15	33	3	1	137	200	34	105	40	52	12	1	347	375	93
Phoenix	77	43	24	9	1	316	240	96	76	29	34	11	2	259	278	71	153	72	58	20	3	575	518	167
Pittsburgh	47	27	11	8	1	206	143	63	45	11	24	10	0	136	169	32	92	38	35	18	1	342	312	95
St. Louis	68	35	26	5	2	225	191	77	70	28	32	9	1	216	244	66	138	63	58	14	3	441	435	143
San Jose	38	22	12	4	0	135	105	48	40	20	15	4	1	119	119	45	78	42	27	8	1	254	224	93
Tampa Bay	11	6	4	0	1	34	27	13	11	5	5	1	0	41	37	11	22	11	9	1	1	75	64	24
Toronto	62	35	22	5	0	240	195	75	54	18	28	7	1	193	207	44	116	53	50	12	1	433	402	119
Vancouver	110	63	31	15	1	421	313	142	111	50	39	18	4	365	377	122	221	113	70	33	5	786	690	264
Washington	39	24	8	7	0	159	97	55	42	14	22	6	0	141	156	34	81	38	30	13	0	300	253	89
Defunct Clubs	13	8	4	1	0	51	34	17	13	7	3	3	0	43	33	17	26	15	7	4	0	94	67	34
Totals	**1398**	**757**	**431**	**188**	**22**	**5190**	**4086**	**1724**	**1398**	**516**	**663**	**191**	**28**	**4306**	**4878**	**1251**	**2796**	**1273**	**1094**	**379**	**50**	**9496**	**8964**	**2975**

Playoffs

	Series	W	L	GP	W	L	T	GF	GA	Last Mtg.	Rnd.	Result
Anaheim	1	0	1	7	3	4	0	16	17	2006	CQF	L 3-4
Chicago	3	2	1	12	7	5	0	37	33	1996	CQF	L 0-4
Dallas	1	0	1	6	2	4	0	18	25	1981	SF	L 2-4
Detroit	3	1	2	14	6	8	0	26	38	2007	CQF	L 2-4
Edmonton	5	1	4	30	11	19	0	96	132	1991	DSF	L 3-4
Los Angeles	6	2	4	26	13	13	0	112	105	1993	DSF	L 2-4
Montreal	2	1	1	11	5	6	0	32	31	1989	F	W 4-2
NY Rangers	1	0	1	4	1	3	0	8	14	1980	PRE	L 1-3
Philadelphia	2	1	1	11	4	7	0	28	43	1981	QF	W 4-3
Phoenix	3	1	2	13	6	7	0	43	45	1987	DSF	L 2-4
St. Louis	1	1	0	7	4	3	0	28	22	1986	CF	W 4-3
San Jose	3	1	2	20	10	10	0	68	57	2008	CQF	L 3-4
Tampa Bay	1	0	1	7	3	4	0	14	13	2004	F	L 3-4
Toronto	1	0	1	2	0	2	0	5	9	1979	PRE	L 0-2
Vancouver	6	4	2	32	17	15	0	101	96	2004	CQF	W 4-3
Totals	**39**	**15**	**24**	**202**	**92**	**110**	**0**	**632**	**680**			

Carolina totals include Hartford, 1979-80 to 1996-97.
Colorado totals include Quebec, 1979-80 to 1994-95.
Dallas totals include Minnesota North Stars, 1972-73 to 1992-93.
New Jersey totals include Kansas City, 1974-75, 1975-76, and Colorado Rockies, 1976-77 to 1981-82.
Phoenix totals include Winnipeg, 1979-80 to 1995-96.

Playoff Results 2008-2003

Year	Round	Opponent	Result	GF	GA
2008	CQF	San Jose	L 3-4	17	19
2007	CQF	Detroit	L 2-4	10	18
2006	CQF	Anaheim	L 3-4	16	17
2004	F	Tampa Bay	L 3-4	14	13
	CF	San Jose	W 4-2	16	12
	CSF	Detroit	W 4-2	11	12
	CQF	Vancouver	W 4-3	19	16

Abbreviations: Round: F - Final; **CF** - conference final; **CSF** - conference semi-final; **CQF** - conference quarter-final; **DSF** - division semi-final; **SF** - semi-final; **QF** - quarter-final; **PRE** - preliminary round.

2007-08 Results

Oct.	4	Philadelphia	2-3
	6	Vancouver	3-4*
	10	at Detroit	2-4
	12	at Dallas	3-2*
	13	at Nashville	7-4
	16	at Colorado	4-5†
	18	Los Angeles	4-3
	20	Edmonton	4-1
	22	San Jose	1-4
	24	Minnesota	5-3
	26	Colorado	2-3*
	30	Nashville	5-1
Nov.	1	Detroit	1-4
	3	at Minnesota	1-4
	5	at Colorado	1-4
	8	Vancouver	2-3
	10	Edmonton	2-4
	13	Minnesota	3-2
	17	at Edmonton	3-1
	18	at Vancouver	1-4
	20	Colorado	4-1
	22	Chicago	1-2
	24	at Colorado	5-2
	25	at St. Louis	0-3
	27	at Detroit	3-5
	29	Anaheim	1-4
Dec.	1	Columbus	3-4*
	4	St. Louis	3-1
	6	Pittsburgh	2-3†
	9	at Chicago	3-2
	11	at Florida	2-1†
	13	at Tampa Bay	9-6
	14	at Carolina	4-3
	16	at St. Louis	5-3
	18	at Columbus	3-1
	21	Dallas	2-3*
	23	New Jersey	0-1*
	27	at Vancouver	3-5
	29	Anaheim	5-3
	31	Vancouver	2-1
Jan.	2	NY Rangers	4-3
	3	at San Jose	3-2*
	5	at Los Angeles	6-4
	8	Phoenix	1-3
	11	NY Islanders	4-5†
	13	at Edmonton	1-2
	15	at Nashville	0-3
	16	at Minnesota	3-2†
	18	Los Angeles	6-1
	22	Minnesota	2-1
	30	San Jose	5-4
Feb.	2	Dallas	1-2
	4	at Edmonton	0-5
	5	Phoenix	4-3†
	7	Chicago	1-3
	9	Edmonton	4-1
	12	at San Jose	4-3*
	15	at Los Angeles	3-6
	17	at Anaheim	2-4
	19	at Phoenix	4-1
	20	at Dallas	3-2
	22	Detroit	1-0
	24	at Minnesota	2-1
	26	Colorado	2-3*
	29	at Anaheim	1-3
Mar.	1	at Phoenix	3-1
	4	Columbus	1-0
	7	Nashville	1-2*
	10	St. Louis	7-3
	12	at Washington	2-3
	13	at Atlanta	4-6
	16	at Chicago	4-2
	18	at Columbus	0-3
	20	Colorado	2-1
	22	Minnesota	5-4
	24	at Colorado	0-2
	25	Vancouver	3-2
	29	Edmonton	1-2
	30	at Vancouver	2-6
Apr.	1	at Edmonton	3-2
	3	at Minnesota	1-3
	5	at Vancouver	7-1

* – Overtime † – Shootout

Entry Draft Selections 2008-1994

Name in bold denotes played in NHL.

2008
Pick
25 Greg Nemisz
48 Mitch Wahl
78 Lance Bouma
108 Nick Larson
114 T.J. Brodie
168 Ryley Grantham
198 Alexander Deilert

2007
Pick
24 Mikael Backlund
70 John Negrin
116 Keith Aulie
143 Mickey Renaud
186 C.J. Severyn

2006
Pick
26 Leland Irving
87 John Armstrong
89 Aaron Marvin
118 Hugo Carpentier
149 Juuso Puustinen
179 Jordan Fulton
187 Devin Didiomete
209 Per Jonsson

2005
Pick
26 Matt Pelech
69 Gord Baldwin
74 Dan Ryder
111 J.D. Watt
128 Kevin Lalande
158 **Matt Keetley**
179 Brett Sutter
221 Myles Rumsey

2004
Pick
24 Kris Chucko
70 **Brandon Prust**
98 **Dustin Boyd**
118 Aki Seitsonen
121 Kris Hogg
173 Adam Pardy
182 Fred Wikner
200 Matt Schneider
213 James Spratt
279 Adam Cracknell

2003
Pick
9 **Dion Phaneuf**
39 **Tim Ramholt**
97 Ryan Donally
112 Jamie Tardif
143 **Greg Moore**
173 Tyler Johnson
206 Thomas Bellemare
240 Cam Cunning
270 Kevin Harvey

2002
Pick
10 **Eric Nystrom**
39 Brian McConnell
90 **Matthew Lombardi**
112 Yuri Artemenkov
141 Jiri Cetkovsky
142 Emanuel Peter
146 Viktor Bobrov
159 Kristofer Persson
176 **Curtis McElhinney**
206 David Van Der Gulik
207 Pierre Johnsson
238 Jyri Marttinen

2001
Pick
14 **Chuck Kobasew**
41 Andrei Taratukhin
56 Andrei Medvedev
108 **Tomi Maki**
124 Yegor Shastin
145 James Hakewill
164 Yuri Trubachev
207 Garrett Bembridge
220 **Dave Moss**
233 Joe Campbell
251 Ville Hamalainen

2000
Pick
9 Brent Krahn
40 **Kurtis Foster**
46 **Jarret Stoll**
116 Levente Szuper
141 Wade Davis
155 **Travis Moen**
176 **Jukka Hentunen**
239 David Hajek
270 **Micki DuPont**

1999
Pick
11 **Oleg Saprykin**
38 Dan Cavanaugh
77 **Craig Anderson**
106 Roman Rozakov
135 Matt Doman
153 Jesse Cook
166 Cory Pecker
170 **Matt Underhill**
190 Blair Stayzer
252 Dmitri Kirilenko

1998
Pick
6 **Rico Fata**
33 **Blair Betts**
62 **Paul Manning**
102 Shaun Sutter
108 **Dany Sabourin**
120 Brent Gauvreau
192 Radek Duda
206 Jonas Frogren
234 Kevin Mitchell

1997
Pick
6 **Daniel Tkaczuk**
32 Evan Lindsay
42 **John Tripp**
51 Dmitri Kokorev
60 Derek Schutz
70 **Erik Andersson**
92 Chris St. Croix
100 **Ryan Ready**
113 Martin Moise
140 Ilja Demidov
167 Jeremy Rondeau
223 Dustin Paul

1996
Pick
13 **Derek Morris**
39 **Travis Brigley**
40 **Steve Begin**
73 Dmitri Vlasenkov
89 **Toni Lydman**
94 Christian Lefebvre
122 Josef Straka
202 Ryan Wade
228 **Ronald Petrovicky**

1995
Pick
20 **Denis Gauthier**
46 Pavel Smirnov
72 **Rocky Thompson**
98 Jan Labraaten
150 **Clarke Wilm**
176 Ryan Gillis
233 Steve Shirreffs

1994
Pick
19 **Chris Dingman**
45 Dmitri Ryabykin
77 **Chris Clark**
91 Ryan Duthie
97 Johan Finnstrom
107 **Nils Ekman**
123 Frank Appel
149 Patrick Haltia
175 **Ladislav Kohn**
201 Keith McCambridge
227 **Jorgen Jonsson**
253 **Mike Peluso**
279 **Pavel Torgaev**

Darryl Sutter

General Manager

Born: Viking, Alta., August 19, 1958.

Darryl Sutter was named general manager of the Calgary Flames on April 11, 2003 after having joined the club as coach on December 28, 2002. In 2003-04, he led the team back to the playoffs after a seven-year absence and guided the club on a thrilling run to the seventh game of the Stanley Cup Finals. He stepped down as coach prior to the 2006-07 season.

Before joining the Flames, Sutter was the San Jose Sharks franchise leader in regular-season games coached (434) and wins (192). Prior to San Jose, Sutter coached Chicago for three years (1992 to 1995) and spent two seasons (1995 to 1997) with the Blackhawks as a consultant for special assignments. He spent the 1987-88 campaign as a Blackhawks assistant coach to Bob Murdoch and served as an associate coach for Mike Keenan during the 1990-91 and 1991-92 seasons. During his final season as associate coach, the Blackhawks advanced to the Stanley Cup Finals. Sutter spent two seasons coaching the Blackhawks' top development affiliate in the IHL, which played in Saginaw (1988-89) and in Indianapolis (1989-90). Under his leadership, the Indianapolis Ice won the Turner Cup championship. He was named IHL coach of the year.

As a player, Sutter was selected by Chicago in the ninth round, 179th overall, in the 1978 NHL Entry Draft. During his eight-year career with the Blackhawks from 1979 to 1987, he scored 279 points (161 goals, 118 assists) with 288 penalty minutes in 406 NHL career games. Sutter served as team captain with the Blackhawks for five seasons before he was forced to retire prematurely due to a series of injuries.

Darryl is a member of the famous Sutter hockey family that had six brothers who played in the NHL. Along with his brothers, Darryl is very involved in the Sutter Foundation, which raises money for non-profit organizations in Alberta.

Coaching Record

			Regular Season				Playoffs			
Season	Team	League	GC	W	L	O/T	GC	W	L	T
1992-93	Chicago	NHL	84	47	25	12	4	0	4	....
1993-94	Chicago	NHL	84	39	36	9	6	2	4	....
1994-95	Chicago	NHL	48	24	19	5	16	9	7	....
1997-98	San Jose	NHL	82	34	38	10	6	2	4	....
1998-99	San Jose	NHL	82	31	33	18	6	2	4	....
99-2000	San Jose	NHL	82	35	30	17	12	5	7	....
2000-01	San Jose	NHL	82	40	27	15	6	2	4	....
2001-02	San Jose	NHL	82	44	27	11	12	7	5	....
2002-03	San Jose	NHL	24	8	12	4	....	....	....	....
2002-03	Calgary	NHL	46	19	18	9	....	....	....	....
2003-04	Calgary	NHL	82	42	30	10	26	15	11	....
2004-05	Calgary				SEASON CANCELLED					
2005-06	Calgary	NHL	82	46	25	11	7	3	4	....
	NHL Totals		**860**	**409**	**320**	**131**	**101**	**47**	**54**	....

Club Directory

Pengrowth Saddledome

Calgary Flames
Pengrowth Saddledome
P.O. Box 1540 Station M
Calgary, Alberta T2P 3B9
Phone **403/777-2177**
FAX 403/777-2195
www.calgaryflames.com
Capacity: 19,289

Owners: N. Murray Edwards (Chairman), Harley N. Hotchkiss, Alvin G. Libin, Allan P. Markin, Jeff McCaig, Clayton H. Riddell, Byron J. Seaman, Daryl K. Seaman

Executive
President & Chief Executive Officer . . . . . Ken King
General Manager . . . . . Darryl Sutter
Vice-President, Hockey Administration/CFO . . . . . Michael Holditch
Vice-President, Building Operations . . . . . Libby Raines
Vice President, Advertising, Sponsorship & Marketing . Jim Bagshaw
Vice-President, Sales . . . . . Rollie Cyr
Vice-President, Communications . . . . . Peter Hanlon
Vice-President, Business Development . . . . . Jim Peplinski
Vice-President, Food and Beverage . . . . . Mark Vaillant

Hockey Club Personnel
General Manager . . . . . Darryl Sutter
Vice-President, Hockey Administration/CFO . . . . . Michael Holditch
Director, Hockey Administration . . . . . Mike Burke
Director, Player Personnel . . . . . Duane Sutter
Director, Goaltender Development/Pro Scout . . . . . Jamie McLennan
Head Coach . . . . . Mike Keenan
Associate Coach . . . . . Jim Playfair
Assistant Coaches . . . . . Rich Preston, Wayne Fleming, Rob Cookson
Goaltending Coach . . . . . David Marcoux
Team Services Manager . . . . . Sean O'Brien
Exec. Asst. to GM and Hockey Operations . . . . . Brenda Koyich
Director of Scouting . . . . . Tod Button
Director of Amateur Scouting . . . . . Mike Sands
Western Pro Scout . . . . . Ron Sutter
Eastern Pro Scout . . . . . Steve Leach
Scouts . . . . . Fred Devereaux, Bob MacMillan, Rob Pulford, Blair Reid, Greg Rejanen, Anders Steen, Rich Thibeau, Al Tuer, Tom Webster

Medical/Training Staff
Strength & Conditioning Coach . . . . . Rich Hesketh
Athletic Therapist . . . . . Morris Boyer
Assistant Athletic Therapist . . . . . Gerry Kurylowich
Equipment Manager . . . . . Gus Thorson
Assistant Equipment Manager . . . . . Mark De Pasquale
Massage Therapist . . . . . Bryan Lentz
Team Physician . . . . . Dr. Kelly Brett
Team Physician . . . . . Dr. Jim Thorne
Team Dentist . . . . . Dr. Bill Blair
Dressing Room Attendant . . . . . Jules Carriere

Quad City Flames
President, Quad City . . . . . Neil Bossola
Head Coach, Quad City . . . . . Ryan McGill
Assistant Coach, Quad City . . . . . Scott Allen
Director of Broadcasting & Media Relations . . . . . Aaron Roof

Communications
Vice-President, Communications . . . . . Peter Hanlon
Manager, Media Relations . . . . . Sean Kelso
Administrative Assistant, Communications . . . . . Bernie Hargrave

Administration
Exec. Asst. to President/CEO . . . . . Judy O'Brien
Exec. Asst. to V.P. Hockey Admin/CFO . . . . . Jill Stang
Director, Finance . . . . . Deniece Kennedy
Manager, Human Resources . . . . . Betty Mah

Marketing/Ticketing
V.P. Advertising, Sponsorship & Marketing . . . . . Jim Bagshaw
V.P. Sales . . . . . Rollie Cyr
V.P. Business Development . . . . . Jim Peplinski
Senior Director, Advertising . . . . . Pat Halls
Director, Corporate Sponsorship . . . . . Kevin Gross
Manager, Key Corporate Accounts . . . . . Mark Stiles
Manager, Promotions . . . . . Scott Matheson
Executive Assistant Marketing . . . . . Yvette Mutcheson
Executive Assistant to V.P. of Sales . . . . . Carolyn Huffman
Director, Executive Suites . . . . . Bob White
Sales Manager . . . . . Mike Franco
Customer Service Manager . . . . . Marc Leost
Director, Broadcast & Production . . . . . Carlo Petrini
Manager, Game Entertainment . . . . . Geordie Macleod
Director, Retail/FanAttic . . . . . Brent Gibbs
Publishing Manager . . . . . Laurie Wheeler
Website Manager . . . . . Mike Board

Pengrowth Saddledome
V.P. Building Operations . . . . . Libby Raines
V.P. Food and Beverage . . . . . Mark Vaillant
Operations Manager . . . . . George Greenwood
Director, Food Services . . . . . Art Hernandez
Senior Food Services Manager . . . . . Sheila Parisien
Security/Parking/Loss Prevention Manager . . . . . Bob Godun

Miscellaneous Data
Radio Affiliate . . . . . The FAN 960 (960 AM)
TV Affiliate . . . . . Rogers Sportsnet, CBC-TV, Flames PPV, TSN

General Managers' History

Cliff Fletcher, 1972-73 to 1990-91; Doug Risebrough, 1991-92 to 1994-95; Doug Risebrough and Al Coates, 1995-96; Al Coates, 1996-97 to 1999-2000; Craig Button, 2000-01 to 2002-03; Darryl Sutter, 2003-04 to date.

Carolina Hurricanes

2007-08 Results: 43W-33L-3OTL-3SOL 92PTS.
Second, Southeast Division

Key Off-Season Signings/Acquisitions

2008

- **April 16** • Re-signed RW **Sergei Samsonov**.
- **June 4** • Re-signed RW **Patrick Eaves**.
- **11** • Re-signed G **Michael Leighton**.
- **19** • Re-signed D **Tim Gleason**.
- **24** • Re-signed C **Tuomo Ruutu**.
- **July 1** • Re-signed D **Anton Babchuk**.
- **1** • Acquired D **Joni Pitkanen** from Edmonton for LW **Erik Cole**.
- **2** • Signed D **Josef Melichar**.
- **7** • Re-signed D **Dennis Seidenberg**.
- **9** • Re-signed C **Chad LaRose**.

Ray Whitney's totals of 25 goals and 61 points were topped only by Eric Staal (38 and 82) in Carolina in 2007-08. His 36 assists tied Matt Cullen for second on the team behind Staal's 44.

2008-09 Schedule

Oct.	Fri.	10	Florida
	Sat.	11	at Tampa Bay
	Mon.	13	Detroit
	Fri.	17	at Los Angeles
	Sun.	19	at Anaheim*
	Thu.	23	at Pittsburgh
	Sat.	25	at NY Islanders
	Tue.	28	at Montreal
	Thu.	30	at St. Louis
Nov.	Sat.	1	Edmonton*
	Sun.	2	Toronto*
	Tue.	4	at Toronto
	Thu.	6	at Washington
	Fri.	7	Ottawa
	Sun.	9	Atlanta*
	Wed.	12	Washington
	Fri.	14	at Atlanta
	Sun.	16	Tampa Bay*
	Tue.	18	Montreal
	Fri.	21	Phoenix
	Sun.	23	Nashville*
	Mon.	24	at Florida
	Wed.	26	Philadelphia
	Fri.	28	at Philadelphia*
	Sun.	30	Anaheim
Dec.	Thu.	4	Pittsburgh
	Sat.	6	Philadelphia
	Sun.	7	Washington*
	Thu.	11	at Philadelphia
	Sat.	13	at NY Rangers
	Tue.	16	Montreal
	Thu.	18	Florida
	Sat.	20	at Boston*
	Sun.	21	at Montreal
	Tue.	23	at Minnesota
	Fri.	26	at Atlanta
	Sat.	27	Boston
	Wed.	31	Atlanta
Jan.	Fri.	2	St. Louis
	Sat.	3	at Tampa Bay
	Tue.	6	New Jersey
	Thu.	8	at Florida
	Sat.	10	at Boston*
	Tue.	13	at Ottawa
	Thu.	15	Toronto
	Sat.	17	at Buffalo
	Mon.	19	at Toronto
	Tue.	20	at Pittsburgh
	Tue.	27	at NY Rangers
	Thu.	29	Tampa Bay
	Sat.	31	Atlanta
Feb.	Tue.	3	at Vancouver
	Thu.	5	at San Jose
	Sat.	7	at Phoenix
	Thu.	12	Florida
	Sat.	14	Columbus
	Sun.	15	at Buffalo
	Tue.	17	Boston
	Thu.	19	at NY Islanders
	Fri.	20	Tampa Bay
	Sun.	22	Colorado*
	Tue.	24	at Ottawa
	Thu.	26	Buffalo
	Sat.	28	at Atlanta
Mar.	Tue.	3	at Washington
	Fri.	6	Calgary
	Sat.	7	at Tampa Bay
	Mon.	9	NY Rangers
	Wed.	11	at Chicago
	Thu.	12	at Dallas
	Sat.	14	at Washington
	Wed.	18	New Jersey
	Fri.	20	NY Islanders
	Sat.	21	Washington
	Mon.	23	at Florida
	Wed.	25	Ottawa
	Sat.	28	at New Jersey
Apr.	Thu.	2	NY Rangers
	Sat.	4	Pittsburgh
	Tue.	7	NY Islanders
	Thu.	9	Buffalo
	Sat.	11	at New Jersey*

* Denotes afternoon game.

Year-by-Year Record

Season	GP	Home W	Home L	Home T	Home OL	Road W	Road L	Road T	Road OL	Overall W	Overall L	Overall T	Overall OL	GF	GA	Pts.	Finished	Playoff Result
2007-08	82	24	13	....	4	19	20	....	2	43	33	....	6	252	249	92	2nd, Southeast Div.	Out of Playoffs
2006-07	82	21	16	....	4	19	18	....	4	40	34	....	8	241	253	88	3rd, Southeast Div.	Out of Playoffs
2005-06	**82**	**31**	**8**	....	**2**	**21**	**14**	....	**6**	**52**	**22**	....	**8**	**294**	**260**	**112**	**1st, Southeast Div.**	**Won Stanley Cup**
2004-05	....	....	....	....	....	....	....	....	....	....	....	....	....	....	....	....		
2003-04	82	13	18	8	2	15	16	6	4	28	34	14	6	172	209	76	3rd, Southeast Div.	Out of Playoffs
2002-03	82	12	17	9	3	10	26	2	3	22	43	11	6	171	240	61	5th, Southeast Div.	Out of Playoffs
2001-02	82	15	13	11	2	20	13	5	3	35	26	16	5	217	217	91	1st, Southeast Div.	Lost Final
2000-01	82	23	15	3	0	15	17	6	3	38	32	9	3	212	225	88	2nd, Southeast Div.	Lost Conf. Quarter-Final
1999-2000	82	20	16	5	0	17	19	5	0	37	35	10	0	217	216	84	3rd, Southeast Div.	Out of Playoffs
1998-99	82	20	12	9	....	14	18	9	....	34	30	18	....	210	202	86	1st, Southeast Div.	Lost Conf. Quarter-Final
1997-98	82	16	18	7	....	17	23	1	....	33	41	8	....	200	219	74	6th, Northeast Div.	Out of Playoffs
1996-97*	82	23	15	3	....	9	24	8	....	32	39	11	....	226	256	75	5th, Northeast Div.	Out of Playoffs
1995-96*	82	22	15	4	....	12	24	5	....	34	39	9	....	237	259	77	4th, Northeast Div.	Out of Playoffs
1994-95*	48	12	10	2	....	7	14	3	....	19	24	5	....	127	141	43	5th, Northeast Div.	Out of Playoffs
1993-94*	84	14	22	6	....	13	26	3	....	27	48	9	....	227	288	63	6th, Northeast Div.	Out of Playoffs
1992-93*	84	12	25	5	....	14	27	1	....	26	52	6	....	284	369	58	5th, Adams Div.	Out of Playoffs
1991-92*	80	13	17	10	....	13	24	3	....	26	41	13	....	247	283	65	4th, Adams Div.	Lost Div. Semi-Final
1990-91*	80	18	16	6	....	13	22	5	....	31	38	11	....	238	276	73	4th, Adams Div.	Lost Div. Semi-Final
1989-90*	80	17	18	5	....	21	15	4	....	38	33	9	....	275	268	85	4th, Adams Div.	Lost Div. Semi-Final
1988-89*	80	21	17	2	....	16	21	3	....	37	38	5	....	299	290	79	4th, Adams Div.	Lost Div. Semi-Final
1987-88*	80	21	14	5	....	14	24	2	....	35	38	7	....	249	267	77	4th, Adams Div.	Lost Div. Semi-Final
1986-87*	80	26	9	5	....	17	21	2	....	43	30	7	....	287	270	93	1st, Adams Div.	Lost Div. Semi-Final
1985-86*	80	21	17	2	....	19	19	2	....	40	36	4	....	332	302	84	4th, Adams Div.	Lost Div. Final
1984-85*	80	17	18	5	....	13	23	4	....	30	41	9	....	268	318	69	5th, Adams Div.	Out of Playoffs
1983-84*	80	19	16	5	....	9	26	5	....	28	42	10	....	288	320	66	5th, Adams Div.	Out of Playoffs
1982-83*	80	13	22	5	....	6	32	2	....	19	54	7	....	261	403	45	5th, Adams Div.	Out of Playoffs
1981-82*	80	13	17	10	....	8	24	8	....	21	41	18	....	264	351	60	5th, Adams Div.	Out of Playoffs
1980-81*	80	14	17	9	....	7	24	9	....	21	41	18	....	292	372	60	4th, Norris Div.	Out of Playoffs
1979-80*	80	22	12	6	....	5	22	13	....	27	34	19	....	303	312	73	4th, Norris Div.	Lost Prelim. Round

* Hartford Whalers

SOUTHEAST DIVISION
30th NHL Season

Franchise date: June 22, 1979

Transferred from Hartford to Carolina, June 25, 1997.

2008-09 Player Personnel

FORWARDS	HT	WT	S	Place of Birth	*Age	2007-08 Club
ANGELIDIS, Mike	6-1	210	L	Woodbridge, Ont.	23	Albany
BAYDA, Ryan	5-11	185	L	Saskatoon, Sask.	27	Carolina-Albany
BLANCHARD, Nicolas	6-3	200	L	Granby, Que.	21	Albany
BOWMAN, Drayson	6-0	181	L	Grand Rapids, MI	19	Spokane
BRIND'AMOUR, Rod	6-1	205	L	Ottawa, Ont.	38	Carolina
BROOKBANK, Wade	6-4	225	L	Lanigan, Sask.	31	Carolina-Albany
CULLEN, Matt	6-1	200	L	Virginia, MN	31	Carolina
DWYER, Patrick	5-11	175	R	Spokane, WA	25	Albany
EAVES, Patrick	5-11	190	R	Calgary, Alta.	24	Ottawa-Carolina
GILLIES, Trevor	6-3	215	L	Cambridge, Ont.	29	Albany
HELMINEN, Dwight	5-10	191	L	Hancock, MI	25	JYP
HUGHES, Bobby	5-10	180	L	Richmond Hill, Ont.	20	Albany
JENSEN, Joe	5-11	180	L	Maple Grove, MN	25	Wilkes-Barre-Whlng-Car-Alb
LaROSE, Chad	5-10	181	R	Fraser, MI	26	Carolina
NOLAN, Brandon	5-10	185	L	Sault Ste. Marie, Ont.	25	Carolina-Albany
PETRUZALEK, Jakub	5-10	176	R	Most, Czech.	23	Albany
REED, Harrison	6-1	185	R	Newmarket, Ont.	20	Sarnia-Guelph
RUUTU, Tuomo	6-0	200	L	Vantaa, Finland	25	Chicago-Carolina
SAMSON, Jerome	5-11	175	R	Greenfield Park, Que.	21	Albany
SAMSONOV, Sergei	5-8	188	R	Moscow, USSR	29	Chi-Rockford-Car
STAAL, Eric	6-4	205	L	Thunder Bay, Ont.	23	Carolina
SUTTER, Brandon	6-3	183	R	Huntington, NY	19	Red Deer-Albany
WALKER, Scott	5-10	196	R	Cambridge, Ont.	35	Carolina
WHITNEY, Ray	5-10	180	R	Fort Saskatchewan, Alta.	36	Carolina
WILLIAMS, Justin	6-1	195	R	Cobourg, Ont.	27	Carolina
DEFENSEMEN						
BABCHUK, Anton	6-5	212	R	Kiev, USSR	24	Omsk
BABIN, Noah	6-0	200	R	Palm Beach Gardens, FL	24	Albany
BELLEMORE, Brett	6-4	205	R	Windsor, Ont.	20	Plymouth-Albany
BORER, Casey	6-2	205	L	Minneapolis, MN	23	Carolina-Albany
CARSON, Brett	6-5	220	R	Regina, Sask.	22	Albany
CONBOY, Tim	6-2	210	R	Farmington, MN	26	Carolina-Albany
CORVO, Joe	6-0	204	R	Oak Park, IL	31	Ottawa-Carolina
FLOOD, Mark	6-1	190	R	Charlottetown, PEI	24	Albany
GLEASON, Tim	6-0	217	L	Clawson, MI	25	Carolina
KABERLE, Frantisek	6-0	190	L	Kladno, Czech.	34	Carolina
MELICHAR, Josef	6-2	220	L	Ceske Budejovice, Czech.	29	C. Budejovice-Linkoping
PITKANEN, Joni	6-3	214	L	Oulu, Finland	25	Edmonton
RODNEY, Bryan	6-0	204	R	London, Ont.	24	Albany-Columbia-Elmira
SEIDENBERG, Dennis	6-1	210	L	Schwenningen, W. Ger.	27	Carolina
WALLIN, Niclas	6-3	220	L	Boden, Sweden	33	Carolina
GOALTENDERS	**HT**	**WT**	**C**	**Place of Birth**	***Age**	**2007-08 Club**
LEIGHTON, Michael	6-3	186	L	Petrolia, Ont.	27	Carolina-Albany
MANZATO, Daniel	6-0	178	L	Fribourg, Switz.	24	Albany-Charlotte-Las Vegas
PETERS, Justin	6-1	209	L	Blyth, Ont.	22	Albany-Florida (ECHL)
WARD, Cam	6-1	200	L	Saskatoon, Sask.	24	Carolina

* – Age at start of 2008-09 season

2007-08 Scoring

* – rookie

Regular Season

Pos	#	Player	Team	GP	G	A	Pts	TOI	+/–	PIM	PP	SH	GW	S	%
C	12	Eric Staal	CAR	82	38	44	82	21:38	–2	50	14	0	7	310	12.3
L	13	Ray Whitney	CAR	66	25	36	61	18:56	–6	30	6	0	4	204	12.3
L	26	Erik Cole	CAR	73	22	29	51	19:21	5	76	10	0	4	216	10.2
C	17	Rod Brind'Amour	CAR	59	19	32	51	22:27	0	38	6	0	4	151	12.6
C	8	Matt Cullen	CAR	59	13	36	49	16:52	2	32	8	0	1	137	9.5
D	77	Joe Corvo	OTT	51	6	21	27	17:41	13	18	1	0	1	111	5.4
			CAR	23	7	14	21	20:46	4	8	5	0	2	56	12.5
			Total	74	13	35	48	18:38	17	26	6	0	3	167	7.8
L	14	Sergei Samsonov	CHI	23	0	4	4	12:20	–7	6	0	0	0	38	0.0
			CAR	38	14	18	32	18:02	6	10	3	0	2	71	19.7
			Total	61	14	22	36	15:53	–1	16	3	0	2	109	12.8
R	24	Scott Walker	CAR	58	14	18	32	16:37	–3	115	4	2	4	122	11.5
C	15	Tuomo Ruutu	CHI	60	6	15	21	15:34	3	75	1	0	1	71	8.5
			CAR	17	4	7	11	17:01	1	16	3	0	0	29	13.8
			Total	77	10	22	32	15:53	4	91	4	0	1	100	10.0
R	11	Justin Williams	CAR	37	9	21	30	19:17	2	43	2	0	0	106	8.5
C	51	Jeff Hamilton	CAR	58	9	15	24	10:47	–8	10	7	0	1	116	7.8
C	59	Chad Larose	CAR	58	11	12	23	14:03	6	46	0	1	2	117	9.4
D	5	Frantisek Kaberle	CAR	80	0	22	22	17:08	–4	30	0	0	0	89	0.0
D	42	Tim Gleason	CAR	80	3	16	19	18:38	5	84	0	0	0	98	3.1
R	19	Trevor Letowski	CAR	75	9	9	18	10:16	–10	30	0	1	1	67	13.4
D	6	Bret Hedican	CAR	66	2	15	17	19:17	17	70	0	0	0	80	2.5
R	44	Patrick Eaves	OTT	26	4	6	10	12:44	0	6	1	0	1	59	6.8
			CAR	11	1	4	5	12:50	–2	4	1	0	0	22	4.5
			Total	37	5	10	15	12:46	–2	10	2	0	1	81	6.2
D	4	Dennis Seidenberg	CAR	47	0	15	15	18:50	6	18	0	0	0	80	0.0
R	37	Keith Aucoin	CAR	38	5	8	13	13:27	3	10	0	0	0	65	7.7
D	7	Niclas Wallin	CAR	66	2	6	8	18:07	–18	54	0	0	0	60	3.3
D	2	Glen Wesley	CAR	78	1	7	8	16:05	–3	52	0	0	1	63	1.6
L	18	Ryan Bayda	CAR	31	3	3	6	12:35	–2	28	0	0	0	58	5.2
D	38 *	Tim Conboy	CAR	19	0	5	5	06:58	1	60	0	0	0	16	0.0
D	53 *	Casey Borer	CAR	11	1	2	3	15:17	–3	4	0	0	0	5	20.0
D	45	David Tanabe	CAR	18	1	2	3	11:58	2	8	0	0	0	12	8.3
L	28	Wade Brookbank	CAR	32	1	1	2	03:48	4	76	0	0	0	12	8.3
C	34 *	Joe Jensen	CAR	6	1	0	1	06:30	1	2	0	0	1	6	16.7
C	36 *	Brandon Nolan	CAR	6	0	1	1	07:15	–2	0	0	0	0	2	0.0
D	29 *	Joey Mormina	CAR	1	0	0	0	07:45	0	0	0	0	0	1	0.0

Goaltending

No.	Goaltender	GPI	Mins	Avg	W	L	OT	EN	SO	GA	SA	S%	G	A	PIM
49	Michael Leighton	3	158	2.66	1	1	0	0	0	7	68	.897	0	0	0
30	Cam Ward	69	3930	2.75	37	25	5	3	4	180	1870	.904	0	1	4
47	John Grahame	17	848	3.75	5	7	1	3	0	53	424	.875	0	1	4
	Totals	**82**	**4964**	**2.97**	**43**	**33**	**6**	**6**	**4**	**246**	**2368**	**.896**			

Eric Staal was named Hurricanes MVP for 2007-08 by the Carolina chapter of the Professional Hockey Writers' Association.

Peter Laviolette

Head Coach

Born: Norwood, MA, December 7, 1964.

On December 15, 2003 the Carolina Hurricanes made Peter Laviolette the 11th head coach in team history. In 2006, he led Carolina to their first Stanley Cup victory.

Laviolette's career as an NHL head coach began with the New York Islanders in 2001-02. He led the team to the playoffs two years in a row after the club had failed to reach the postseason for seven straight seasons. Prior to joining the Islanders, Laviolette served as an assistant coach with the Boston Bruins after two years of guiding Boston's AHL affiliate, Providence. In 1998-99, Laviolette led the Providence Bruins to a 56-16-8 regular-season record, and a 15-4 playoff record that culminated with Providence hoisting the Calder Cup and Laviolette being named AHL coach of the year.

Laviolette played 11 seasons of professional hockey, mostly in the AHL and IHL, but did play 12 games with the New York Rangers during the 1988-89 season. He was a member of the 1988 and 1994 U.S. Olympic hockey teams, and captained the 1994 Olympic squad.

In the spring of 2004, Laviolette helped assure the United States a spot in the 2006 Olympic Games in Torino, Italy, when he guided Team USA to a bronze medal at the 2004 World Championship in the Czech Republic. He also served as an assistant to San Jose Sharks head coach Ron Wilson behind the bench for Team USA in the 2004 World Cup of Hockey and was head coach again at the 2005 World Championship and 2006 Olympics.

Coaching Record

			Regular Season				Playoffs			
Season	Team	League	GC	W	L	O/T	GC	W	L	T
1997-98	Wheeling	ECHL	70	37	24	9	15	8	7	....
1998-99	Providence	AHL	80	56	16	8	19	15	4	....
99-2000	Providence	AHL	80	33	38	9	14	10	4	....
2001-02	**NY Islanders**	**NHL**	**82**	**42**	**28**	**12**	**7**	**3**	**4**	....
2002-03	**NY Islanders**	**NHL**	**82**	**35**	**34**	**13**	**5**	**1**	**4**	....
2003-04	**Carolina**	**NHL**	**52**	**20**	**22**	**10**	....	....	....	....
2004-05	**Carolina**				SEASON CANCELLED					
2005-06♦	**Carolina**	**NHL**	**82**	**52**	**22**	**8**	**25**	**16**	**9**	....
2006-07	**Carolina**	**NHL**	**82**	**40**	**34**	**8**	....	....	....	....
2007-08	**Carolina**	**NHL**	**82**	**43**	**33**	**6**	....	....	....	....
	NHL Totals		**462**	**232**	**173**	**57**	**37**	**20**	**17**	....

♦ Stanley Cup win.

Coaching History

Don Blackburn, 1979-80; Don Blackburn and Larry Pleau, 1980-81; Larry Pleau, 1981-82; Larry Kish, Larry Pleau and John Cuniff, 1982- 83; Jack Evans, 1983-84 to 1986-87; Jack Evans and Larry Pleau, 1987-88; Larry Pleau, 1988-89; Rick Ley, 1989-90, 1990-91; Jim Roberts, 1991-92; Paul Holmgren, 1992-93; Paul Holmgren and Pierre Maguire, 1993-94; Paul Holmgren, 1994-95; Paul Holmgren and Paul Maurice, 1995-96; Paul Maurice, 1996-97 to 2002-03; Paul Maurice and Peter Laviolette, 2003-04; Peter Laviolette, 2004-05 to date.

Captains' History

Rick Ley, 1979-80; Rick Ley and Mike Rogers, 1980-81; Dave Keon, 1981-82; Russ Anderson, 1982-83; Mark Johnson, 1983-84; Mark Johnson and Ron Francis, 1984-85; Ron Francis, 1985-86 to 1990-91; Randy Ladouceur, 1991-92; Pat Verbeek, 1992-93 to 1994-95; Brendan Shanahan, 1995-96; Kevin Dineen, 1996-97, 1997-98; Keith Primeau, 1998-99; Keith Primeau and Ron Francis, 1999-2000; Ron Francis, 2000-01 to 2003-04; Rod Brind'Amour, 2005-06 to date.

Club Records

Team

(Figures in brackets for season records are games played; records for fewest points, wins, ties, losses, goals, goals against are for 70 or more games)

Most Points 112 2005-06 (82)
Most Wins 52 2005-06 (82)
Most Ties 19 1979-80 (80)
Most Losses 54 1982-83 (80)
Most Goals 332 1985-86 (80)
Most Goals Against 403 1982-83 (80)
Fewest Points 45 1982-83 (80)
Fewest Wins 19 1982-83 (80)
Fewest Ties 4 1985-86 (80)
Fewest Losses 22 2005-06 (82)
Fewest Goals 171 2002-03 (82)
Fewest Goals Against 202 1998-99 (82)

Longest Winning Streak
Overall .... 9 Oct. 22-Nov. 11/05, Dec. 31/05-Jan. 19/06
Home .... 9 Dec. 31/05-Jan. 28/06
Away .... 6 Nov. 10-Dec. 7/90

Longest Undefeated Streak
Overall .... 10 Jan. 20-Feb. 10/82 (6 wins, 4 ties)
Home .... 9 Dec. 15/00-Jan. 18/01 (8 wins, 1 tie), Dec. 31/05-Jan. 28/06 (9 wins)
Away .... 8 Nov. 11-Dec. 5/96 (4 wins, 4 ties)

Longest Losing Streak
Overall .... 9 Feb. 19-Mar. 8/83
Home .... 7 Dec. 27/02-Jan. 20/03
Away .... 13 Dec. 18/82-Feb. 5/83

Longest Winless Streak
Overall .... 14 Jan. 4-Feb. 9/92 (8 losses, 6 ties)
Home .... 13 Jan. 15-Mar. 10/85 (11 losses, 2 ties)
Away .... 15 Nov. 11/79-Jan. 9/80 (11 losses, 4 ties), Jan. 7-Mar. 2/03 (13 losses, 2 ties)

Most Shutouts, Season 8 1998-99 (82)
Most PIM, Season 2,354 1992-93 (84)
Most Goals, Game .... 11 Feb. 12/84 (Edm. 0 at Hfd. 11), Oct. 19/85 (Mtl. 6 at Hfd. 11), Jan. 17/86 (Que. 6 at Hfd. 11), Mar. 15/86 (Chi. 4 at Hfd. 11)

Individual

Most Seasons .... 16 Ron Francis
Most Games .... 1,186 Ron Francis
Most Goals, Career .... 382 Ron Francis
Most Assists, Career .... 793 Ron Francis
Most Points, Career .... 1,175 Ron Francis (382G, 793A)
Most PIM, Career .... 1,439 Kevin Dineen
Most Shutouts, Career .... 20 Arturs Irbe
Longest Consecutive Games Streak .... 419 Dave Tippett (Mar. 3/84-Oct. 7/89)
Most Goals, Season .... 56 Blaine Stoughton (1979-80)
Most Assists, Season .... 69 Ron Francis (1989-90)
Most Points, Season .... 105 Mike Rogers (1979-80; 44G, 61A), (1980-81; 40G, 65A)
Most PIM, Season .... 358 Torrie Robertson (1985-86)
Most Points, Defenseman, Season .... 69 Dave Babych (1985-86; 14G, 55A)
Most Points, Center, Season .... 105 Mike Rogers (1979-80; 44G, 61A), (1980-81; 40G, 65A)
Most Points, Right Wing, Season .... 100 Blaine Stoughton (1979-80; 56G, 44A)
Most Points, Left Wing, Season .... 89 Geoff Sanderson (1992-93; 46G, 43A)
Most Points, Rookie, Season .... 72 Sylvain Turgeon (1983-84; 40G, 32A)
Most Shutouts, Season .... 6 Arturs Irbe (1998-99, 2000-01), Kevin Weekes (2003-04)
Most Goals, Game .... 4 Jordy Douglas (Feb. 3/80), Ron Francis (Feb. 12/84)
Most Assists, Game .... 6 Ron Francis (Mar. 5/87)
Most Points, Game .... 6 Paul Lawless (Jan. 4/87; 2G, 4A), Ron Francis (Mar. 5/87; 6A) (Oct. 8/89; 3G, 3A)

Records include Hartford Whalers, 1979-80 through 1996-97.

All-time Record vs. Other Clubs

Regular Season

	At Home								On Road								Total							
	GP	W	L	T	OL	GF	GA	PTS	GP	W	L	T	OL	GF	GA	PTS	GP	W	L	T	OL	GF	GA	PTS
Anaheim	10	6	3	1	0	27	21	13	10	4	5	1	0	32	31	9	20	10	8	2	0	59	52	22
Atlanta	25	15	7	1	2	83	76	33	25	17	4	3	1	85	65	38	50	32	11	4	3	168	141	71
Boston	82	35	36	9	2	274	281	81	84	30	47	7	0	227	286	67	166	65	83	16	2	501	567	148
Buffalo	84	35	37	11	1	247	252	82	83	26	49	7	1	242	339	60	167	61	86	18	2	489	591	142
Calgary	29	10	14	5	0	94	107	25	30	6	22	2	0	92	143	14	59	16	36	7	0	186	250	39
Chicago	31	15	12	4	0	102	96	34	30	11	16	3	0	86	117	25	61	26	28	7	0	188	213	59
Colorado	63	24	26	12	1	207	219	61	66	17	40	9	0	193	279	43	129	41	66	21	1	400	498	104
Columbus	5	4	1	0	0	15	12	8	4	2	2	0	0	10	10	4	9	6	3	0	0	25	22	12
Dallas	33	14	15	4	0	106	114	32	30	10	16	2	2	90	120	24	63	24	31	6	2	196	234	56
Detroit	31	18	12	1	0	107	88	37	32	7	17	7	1	88	124	22	63	25	29	8	1	195	212	59
Edmonton	30	12	11	7	0	119	100	31	32	7	20	5	0	93	124	19	62	19	31	12	0	212	224	50
Florida	37	24	10	3	0	119	92	51	38	14	14	8	2	91	112	38	75	38	24	11	2	210	204	89
Los Angeles	32	16	11	5	0	116	116	37	31	11	17	3	0	116	131	25	63	27	28	8	0	232	247	62
Minnesota	3	3	0	0	0	6	2	6	5	1	2	2	0	16	14	4	8	4	2	2	0	22	16	10
Montreal	84	32	38	13	1	246	290	78	81	24	49	7	1	241	318	56	165	56	87	20	2	487	608	134
Nashville	6	3	1	1	1	19	17	8	5	1	4	0	0	7	10	2	11	4	5	1	1	26	27	10
New Jersey	50	20	21	8	1	149	149	49	51	18	27	4	2	157	178	42	101	38	48	12	3	306	327	91
NY Islanders	51	25	20	5	1	173	165	56	50	23	21	4	2	142	148	52	101	48	41	9	3	315	313	108
NY Rangers	49	28	18	3	0	163	151	59	51	16	30	4	1	127	187	37	100	44	48	7	1	290	338	96
Ottawa	33	18	11	4	0	95	87	40	35	16	15	4	0	91	100	36	68	34	26	8	0	186	187	76
Philadelphia	50	15	24	9	2	160	184	41	49	12	28	5	4	124	182	33	99	27	52	14	6	284	366	74
Phoenix	31	14	11	6	0	103	91	34	32	15	15	2	0	116	118	32	63	29	26	8	0	219	209	66
Pittsburgh	54	27	22	5	0	201	190	59	52	20	24	6	2	191	205	48	106	47	46	11	2	392	395	107
St. Louis	32	13	17	2	0	96	99	28	32	9	19	3	1	94	120	22	64	22	36	5	1	190	219	50
San Jose	12	7	5	0	0	40	27	14	12	4	8	0	0	34	54	8	24	11	13	0	0	74	81	22
Tampa Bay	39	22	8	7	2	125	108	53	38	12	21	3	2	96	113	29	77	34	29	10	4	221	221	82
Toronto	43	22	14	6	1	162	137	51	42	20	16	5	1	148	141	46	85	42	30	11	2	310	278	97
Vancouver	30	13	12	5	0	97	101	31	31	10	13	6	2	84	109	28	61	23	25	11	2	181	210	59
Washington	61	23	26	10	2	177	186	58	59	20	35	4	0	149	199	44	120	43	61	14	2	326	385	102
Totals	**1120**	**513**	**443**	**147**	**17**	**3628**	**3558**	**1190**	**1120**	**383**	**596**	**116**	**25**	**3262**	**4077**	**907**	**2240**	**896**	**1039**	**263**	**42**	**6890**	**7635**	**2097**

Playoffs

	Series	W	L	GP	W	L	T	GF	GA	Last Mtg.	Rnd.	Result
Boston	3	0	3	19	7	12	0	48	63	1999	CQF	L 2-4
Buffalo	1	1	0	7	4	3	0	22	17	2006	CF	W 4-3
Colorado	2	1	1	9	5	4	0	35	34	1987	DSF	L 2-4
Detroit	1	0	1	5	1	4	0	7	14	2002	F	L 1-4
Edmonton	1	1	0	7	4	3	0	19	16	2006	F	W 4-3
Montreal	7	2	5	39	16	23	0	106	125	2006	CQF	W 4-2
New Jersey	3	2	1	17	10	7	0	34	41	2006	CSF	W 4-1
Toronto	1	1	0	6	4	2	0	10	6	2002	CF	W 4-2
Totals	**19**	**8**	**11**	**109**	**51**	**58**	**0**	**281**	**316**			

Calgary totals include Atlanta Flames, 1979-80.
Dallas totals include Minnesota North Stars, 1979-80 to 1992-93.
Phoenix totals include Winnipeg, 1979-80 to 1995-96.

Playoff Results 2008-2003

Year	Round	Opponent	Result	GF	GA
2006	**F**	**Edmonton**	**W 4-3**	**19**	**16**
	CF	Buffalo	W 4-3	22	17
	CSF	New Jersey	W 4-1	17	10
	CQF	Montreal	W 4-2	15	17

Abbreviations: Round: F - Final; **CF** - conference final; **CSF** - conference semi-final; **CQF** - conference quarter-final; **DSF** - division semi-final.

Colorado totals include Quebec, 1979-80 to 1994-95.
New Jersey totals include Colorado Rockies, 1979-80 to 1981-82.

2007-08 Results

Oct.	3	Montreal	2-3*	**Jan.**	2	Atlanta	4-5*
	5	Pittsburgh	4-1		4	at Atlanta	4-3
	6	at Washington	0-2		5	at St. Louis	0-1
	9	at Toronto	7-1		8	at Boston	1-0
	11	at Ottawa	5-3		10	New Jersey	1-4
	13	at Montreal	3-1		12	Colorado	4-5
	19	at Pittsburgh	3-4†		15	at Toronto	4-5
	20	at Philadelphia	2-3*		17	at Ottawa	1-5
	22	Vancouver	3-1		18	Edmonton	7-2
	24	Buffalo	6-2		21	at NY Islanders	3-2*
	26	Montreal	4-7		22	NY Islanders	3-6
	27	at NY Islanders	8-3		29	NY Rangers	3-1
	31	at Florida	2-4		31	Toronto	3-2*
Nov.	3	Florida	4-2	**Feb.**	2	at Pittsburgh	1-4
	5	Washington	5-0		5	at Nashville	0-1
	8	Tampa Bay	1-5		8	at Washington	2-1
	10	at Atlanta	5-3		9	at New Jersey	1-6
	12	at Florida	4-3		12	at Boston	3-2
	14	at Tampa Bay	1-6		14	Pittsburgh	4-2
	16	Atlanta	0-3		16	Florida	5-4
	17	Florida	2-1		18	at New Jersey	1-5
	21	Philadelphia	3-6		19	Boston	2-3†
	23	Tampa Bay	4-3		21	Atlanta	5-3
	24	at Washington	2-5		23	Washington	6-3
	28	Philadelphia	1-3		26	New Jersey	2-1*
	30	Washington	4-3		28	NY Rangers	2-4
Dec.	1	at Buffalo	1-8	**Mar.**	1	Tampa Bay	5-1
	3	at NY Rangers	4-0		5	at Atlanta	6-3
	6	at Tampa Bay	1-2		6	Minnesota	3-2
	8	at Montreal	5-1		8	Buffalo	4-3*
	9	at Detroit	2-5		12	at Chicago	3-0
	12	Ottawa	0-6		14	at Buffalo	1-7
	14	Calgary	3-4		16	Ottawa	5-1
	15	at Philadelphia	6-5†		19	at Atlanta	5-3
	18	Toronto	3-2*		20	at Florida	2-1†
	20	at Florida	4-5		25	Washington	2-3†
	22	at Tampa Bay	4-1		28	Atlanta	7-1
	26	at NY Rangers	2-4		29	at Tampa Bay	1-2
	28	Boston	4-3	**Apr.**	1	at Washington	1-4
	29	at Columbus	1-4		2	Tampa Bay	6-2
	31	NY Islanders	1-4		4	Florida	3-4

* – Overtime † – Shootout

Entry Draft Selections 2008-1994

Name in bold denotes played in NHL.

2008
Pick
14 Zach Boychuk
45 Zac Dalpe
105 Michal Jordan
165 Mike Murphy
195 Samuel Morneau

2007
Pick
11 Brandon Sutter
72 Drayson Bowman
102 Justin McCrae
132 Chris Terry
162 Brett Bellemore

2006
Pick
63 Jamie McBain
93 Harrison Reed
123 Bobby Hughes
153 Stefan Chaput
183 Nick Dodge
213 Justin Krueger

2005
Pick
3 **Jack Johnson**
58 Nate Hagemo
64 Joe Barnes
94 Jakub Vojta
123 Ondrej Otcenas
145 Tim Kunes
159 Risto Korhonen
192 Nicolas Blanchard
198 Kyle Lawson

2004
Pick
4 **Andrew Ladd**
38 Justin Peters
69 **Casey Borer**
109 Brett Carson
137 Magnus Akerlund
202 Ryan Pottruff
235 Jonas Fiedler
268 Martin Vagner

2003
Pick
2 **Eric Staal**
31 **Danny Richmond**
102 Aaron Dawson
126 Kevin Nastiuk
130 Matej Trojovsky
137 Tyson Strachan
198 **Shay Stephenson**
230 Jamie Hoffmann
262 Ryan Rorabeck

2002
Pick
25 **Cam Ward**
91 Jesse Lane
160 Daniel Manzato
224 Adam Taylor

2001
Pick
15 Igor Knyazev
46 **Mike Zigomanis**
91 Kevin Estrada
110 Rob Zepp
181 Daniel Boisclair
211 Sean Curry
244 Carter Trevisani
274 Peter Reynolds

2000
Pick
32 **Tomas Kurka**
80 **Ryan Bayda**
97 **Niclas Wallin**
110 Jared Newman
181 J.D. Forrest
212 Magnus Kahnberg
235 Craig Kowalski
276 Troy Ferguson

1999
Pick
16 **David Tanabe**
49 **Brett Lysak**
84 **Brad Fast**
113 Ryan Murphy
174 **Damian Surma**
202 Jim Baxter
231 David Evans
237 Antti Jokela
259 Yevgeny Kurilin

1998
Pick
11 **Jeff Heerema**
70 Kevin Holdridge
71 **Erik Cole**
91 **Josef Vasicek**
93 **Tommy Westlund**
97 Chris Madden
184 Don Smith
208 **Jaroslav Svoboda**
211 Mark Kosick
239 Brent McDonald

1997
Pick
22 **Nikos Tselios**
28 **Brad DeFauw**
80 **Francis Lessard**
88 **Shane Willis**
142 Kyle Dafoe
169 Andrew Merrick
195 **Niklas Nordgren**
199 Randy Fitzgerald
225 **Kent McDonell**

1996
Pick
34 Trevor Wasyluk
61 Andrei Petrunin
88 **Craig MacDonald**
104 Steve Wasylko
116 Mark McMahon
143 Aaron Baker
171 **Greg Kuznik**
197 Kevin Marsh
223 **Craig Adams**
231 Ashkat Rakhmatullin

1995
Pick
13 **Jean-Sebastien Giguere**
35 Sergei Fedotov
85 **Ian MacNeil**
87 **Sami Kapanen**
113 Hugh Hamilton
165 **Byron Ritchie**
191 Milan Kostolny
217 **Mike Rucinski**

1994
Pick
5 **Jeff O'Neill**
83 **Hnat Domenichelli**
109 Ryan Risidore
187 Tom Buckley
213 Ashlin Halfnight
230 Matt Ball
239 Brian Regan
265 Steve Nimigon

General Managers' History

Jack Kelley, 1979-80, 1980-81; Larry Pleau, 1981-82, 1982-83; Emile Francis, 1983-84 to 1988-89; Eddie Johnston, 1989-90 to 1991-92; Brian Burke, 1992-93; Paul Holmgren, 1993-94; Jim Rutherford, 1994-95 to date.

Jim Rutherford

President and General Manager

Born: Beeton, Ont., February 17, 1949.

Jim Rutherford, a former NHL goaltender, is the franchise's seventh general manager and the only general manager of the Carolina Hurricanes. Named to his position on June 28, 1994, Rutherford has always taken an aggressive approach towards improving the fortunes of the franchise through trades and the NHL entry draft. In 2002, the team reached the Stanley Cup Finals for the first time in history. The Hurricanes won the Cup in 2006.

A veteran of 13 NHL seasons, Rutherford began his professional goaltending career in 1969 as a first-round selection of the Detroit Red Wings. While playing for Detroit, Pittsburgh, Toronto and Los Angeles, Rutherford collected 14 career shutouts. For five seasons he also served as the Red Wings' player representative. Rutherford also played for Team Canada at the World Championships in Vienna in 1977 and Moscow in 1979.

After his playing days with the Red Wings, Rutherford joined Compuware to serve as the director of hockey operations for Compuware Sports Corporation. Rutherford gained a wealth of experience in youth hockey and junior programs. As a former player, coach, and general manager, his ability to develop players and produce winning programs is widely respected throughout the hockey community.

He started his management career by guiding Compuware Sports Corporation's purchase of the Windsor Spitfires of the Ontario Hockey League in April of 1984. During the next four years, Rutherford acted as general manager of the Spitfires. After the Spitfires advanced to the 1988 Memorial Cup finals, Rutherford led Compuware's efforts to bring the first American-based OHL franchise to Detroit on December 11, 1989. Rutherford was voted the 1987 executive of the year in both the OHL and the Canadian Hockey League and won the OHL executive of the year award again in 1988.

Club Directory

RBC Center

Carolina Hurricanes
1400 Edwards Mill Rd.
Raleigh, NC 27607
Phone **919/467-7825**
FAX 919/462-0123
Tickets 1.866.NHL.CANES
www.carolinahurricanes.com
Capacity: 18,680

Executive Management	
Chief Executive Officer/Owner/Governor	Peter Karmanos, Jr.
President/General Manager	Jim Rutherford
General Partner	Thomas Thewes
Chief Financial Officer	Mike Amendola
Vice President and General Manager, RBC Center	Davin Olsen
Executive Director of Hockey Operations	Jason Karmanos
Hockey Operations	
Assistant G.M./Director of Player Development	Ron Francis
Head Coach	Peter Laviolette
Associate Head Coach	Kevin McCarthy
Assistant Coach	Tom Rowe
Goaltending Coach/Dir. of Goalie Development	Tom Barrasso
Director of Defensemen Development	Glen Wesley
Video Coach	Chris Huffine
Head Athletic Trainer/Strength Conditioning Coach	Peter Friesen
Assistant Athletic Trainer	Jason Bailey
Equipment Managers	Wally Tatomir, Skip Cunningham, Bob Gorman
Director of Team Operations	Brian Tatum
Executive Assistant to the President and G.M.	Mari Jeter
Motivational Consultant and Community Dev.	Doris E. Barksdale
Director of Amateur Scouting	Tony MacDonald
Amateur Scouts	Phil Horner, Bob Luccini, Mario Marois, Bert Marshall
Director of Pro Scouting/Pro Scouts	Marshall Johnston/Claude Larose, Ron Smith
European Scout	Robert Kron
Albany River Rats Head Coach/G.M.	Jeff Daniels
Albany River Rats Assistant Coach	Geordie Kinnear
Administration	
Receptionists	Mary Lou Ruetz, Janet Davis
General Office Assistant	Angela Dennis
Arena Operations	
Assistant General Manager, RBC Center	Larry Perkins
Marketing Manager	Crystal Pace
Security Manager	Clinton Peterson
Parking Manager	Mike Alexander
Event Services Manager	Steve Congress
Manager of Premium Services and Suite Sales	Suzanne Golden
Operations Manager	Dan McGowan
Assistant Operations Manager	Melvin Terrell
Facility Systems Manager	Rick Dunning
Box Office Manager	Joe Sousa
Assistant Box Office Manager	Erin Wallace
Assistant Ticket Operations Manager	Chris Jovino
Arena Office Manager	Hilman Huskey
Broadcasters	
Television Play-by-Play/Analyst	John Forslund/Tripp Tracy
Radio Play-by-Play	Chuck Kaiton
Communications	
Director, Media Relations	Mike Sundheim
Manager, Media Relations/Broadcast Coordinator	Kyle Hanlin
Director, Community Relations	Doug Warf
Community Relations Senior Coordinator	Anne Clinard Nelson
Community Relations Coordinator	Mike King
Team Photographers	Gregg Forwerck, Stan Gilliland
Finance/Information Technology	
General Counsel/Senior Director of Finance	William Traurig
Accounts Payable/Receivable	Michael Arrington/Patty Hilliard, Temika Smith-Harris
Director of Information Technology	Glenn Johnson
Food and Beverage	
Director of Food and Beverage	Chris Diamond
Concessions Manager	Rick Rhodes
Asst, Concessions Manager/Group Coordinator	Barbara Couch
Chefs	Dennis Atkinson, Michael Flood, Andrew Booger, Lecan Huynh, Kevin Heintz
Managers	Rick Rhodes, Katrina Ryan, Mary Williams, Skip Roach, Gary Berry, Lori Holtz, Jim O'Brien
Marketing	
Director of Marketing and Brand Development	Ben Aycock
Dir. of Advertising Production & In-Game Marketing	Pete Soto
Director of Promotions and Fan Development	Jon Chase
Website Producer	Paul Branecky
Graphic Designers	Lauren Baxter, Kara Kelly
Youth and Amateur Hockey Coordinator	Paul Strand
Promotions Coordinator	Ryan O'Quinn
Gale Force Media, CanesVision and Wolfpack TV	
Producers	Charles Graham, Don Sill
Web Producer	Eric Bridenstine
Graphics Producer	Stephen Rutherford
Merchandise	
Retail Operations Manager	James Blitch
Sales	
Director of Corporate Sales	Mike Hurley
Senior Account Executives, Corporate Sales	Rick Francis, Julia Zeigler
Sponsorship Account Executives	Pete Donahue, Joe Fontanetta, John Gill, Lindsey Moore
Director of Ticket Sales	Kyle Prairie
Sales & Client Services Executive	Peterson J. Avetta
Account Executives, Business Development	Rich Davis, Michael Miller
Client Relations Representatives	Brooke Baragona, Megan Berrio, Matthew Horton, Stephanie Zimmerman
Hurricanes Group Sales Manager	Brian Kapusta
RBC Center Group Sales Manager	Brian Slais
Team Information	
Cable Television Rightsholder	FSN South
Radio Flagship	WCMC 99.9 FM The Fan

Chicago Blackhawks

Key Off-Season Signings/Acquisitions

2008

May 21 • Re-signed RW **Adam Burish**, RW **Dustin Byfuglien** and D **James Wisniewski**.

June 23 • Re-signed LW **Andrew Ladd**.

July 1 • Signed D **Brian Campbell** and G **Cristobal Huet**.

7 • Signed D **Matt Walker**.

2008-09 Schedule

Oct.	Fri.	10	at NY Rangers
	Sat.	11	at Washington
	Mon.	13	Nashville
	Wed.	15	Phoenix
	Sat.	18	at St. Louis
	Sun.	19	Vancouver
	Wed.	22	Edmonton
	Sat.	25	Detroit
	Mon.	27	at Minnesota
	Fri.	31	Dallas
Nov.	Sat.	1	at Columbus
	Mon.	3	Colorado
	Sun.	9	Calgary
	Wed.	12	Boston
	Fri.	14	St. Louis
	Sun.	16	San Jose
	Tue.	18	at Phoenix
	Thu.	20	at Dallas
	Sat.	22	at Toronto
	Wed.	26	at San Jose
	Fri.	28	at Anaheim*
	Sat.	29	at Los Angeles*
Dec.	Wed.	3	Anaheim
	Sat.	6	at Detroit
	Sun.	7	Phoenix
	Wed.	10	Ottawa
	Fri.	12	at Colorado
	Sun.	14	Columbus
	Tue.	16	at Edmonton
	Fri.	19	at Calgary
	Sat.	20	at Vancouver
	Fri.	26	Philadelphia
	Sun.	28	at Minnesota*
	Tue.	30	at Detroit
Jan.	Thu.	1	Detroit*†
	Sun.	4	Calgary
	Tue.	6	at Phoenix
	Thu.	8	at Colorado
	Sat.	10	at Nashville
	Sun.	11	Nashville
	Wed.	14	Buffalo
	Fri.	16	NY Rangers
	Sat.	17	at St. Louis
	Mon.	19	Minnesota
	Wed.	21	St. Louis
	Wed.	28	at Anaheim
	Thu.	29	at Los Angeles
	Sat.	31	at San Jose
Feb.	Tue.	3	at Edmonton
	Thu.	5	at Calgary
	Sat.	7	at Vancouver
	Wed.	11	at Atlanta
	Fri.	13	at St. Louis
	Sat.	14	Dallas
	Tue.	17	at Tampa Bay
	Thu.	19	at Florida
	Sat.	21	at Dallas*
	Sun.	22	Minnesota
	Tue.	24	at Nashville
	Fri.	27	Pittsburgh
Mar.	Sun.	1	Los Angeles*
	Tue.	3	Anaheim
	Sat.	7	at Boston*
	Sun.	8	Colorado*
	Wed.	11	Carolina
	Fri.	13	Columbus
	Sun.	15	NY Islanders*
	Tue.	17	at New Jersey
	Wed.	18	at Columbus
	Fri.	20	Edmonton
	Sun.	22	Los Angeles*
	Wed.	25	San Jose
	Fri.	27	New Jersey
	Sun.	29	Vancouver
	Tue.	31	at Montreal
Apr.	Wed.	1	St. Louis
	Fri.	3	Nashville
	Sun.	5	at Columbus*
	Tue.	7	at Nashville
	Wed.	8	Columbus
	Sat.	11	at Detroit*
	Sun.	12	Detroit*

* Denotes afternoon game. † Game played at Wrigley Field.

CENTRAL DIVISION
83rd NHL Season

Franchise date: September 25, 1926

2007-08 Results: 40W-34L-4OTL-4SOL 88PTS.
Third, Central Division

Year-by-Year Record

Season	GP	Home W	Home L	Home T	Home OL	Road W	Road L	Road T	Road OL	Overall W	Overall L	Overall T	Overall OL	GF	GA	Pts.	Finished	Playoff Result
2007-08	82	23	16	....	2	17	18	....	6	40	34	....	8	239	235	88	3rd, Central Div.	Out of Playoffs
2006-07	82	17	20	....	4	14	22	....	5	31	42	....	9	201	258	71	5th, Central Div.	Out of Playoffs
2005-06	82	16	19	....	6	10	24	....	7	26	43	....	13	211	285	65	4th, Central Div.	Out of Playoffs
2004-05	....	....	....	....	....	....	....	....	....	....	....	....	....	....	....	....		
2003-04	82	13	17	6	5	7	26	5	3	20	43	11	8	188	259	59	5th, Central Div.	Out of Playoffs
2002-03	82	17	15	7	2	13	18	6	4	30	33	13	6	207	226	79	3rd, Central Div.	Out of Playoffs
2001-02	82	28	7	5	1	13	20	8	0	41	27	13	1	216	207	96	3rd, Central Div.	Lost Conf. Quarter-Final
2000-01	82	14	21	4	2	15	19	4	3	29	40	8	5	210	246	71	4th, Central Div.	Out of Playoffs
1999-2000	82	16	19	5	1	17	18	5	1	33	37	10	2	242	245	78	3rd, Central Div.	Out of Playoffs
1998-99	82	20	17	4	....	9	24	8	....	29	41	12	....	202	248	70	3rd, Central Div.	Out of Playoffs
1997-98	82	14	19	8	....	16	20	5	....	30	39	13	....	192	199	73	5th, Central Div.	Out of Playoffs
1996-97	82	16	21	4	....	18	14	9	....	34	35	13	....	223	210	81	5th, Central Div.	Lost Conf. Quarter-Final
1995-96	82	22	13	6	....	18	15	8	....	40	28	14	....	273	220	94	2nd, Central Div.	Lost Conf. Semi-Final
1994-95	48	11	10	3	....	13	9	2	....	24	19	5	....	156	115	53	3rd, Central Div.	Lost Conf. Championship
1993-94	84	21	16	5	....	18	20	4	....	39	36	9	....	254	240	87	5th, Central Div.	Lost Conf. Quarter-Final
1992-93	84	25	11	6	....	22	14	6	....	47	25	12	....	279	230	106	1st, Norris Div.	Lost Div. Semi-Final
1991-92	80	23	9	8	....	13	20	7	....	36	29	15	....	257	236	87	2nd, Norris Div.	Lost Final
1990-91	80	28	8	4	....	21	15	4	....	49	23	8	....	284	211	106	1st, Norris Div.	Lost Div. Semi-Final
1989-90	80	25	13	2	....	16	20	4	....	41	33	6	....	316	294	88	1st, Norris Div.	Lost Conf. Championship
1988-89	80	16	14	10	....	11	27	2	....	27	41	12	....	297	335	66	4th, Norris Div.	Lost Conf. Championship
1987-88	80	21	17	2	....	9	24	7	....	30	41	9	....	284	328	69	3rd, Norris Div.	Lost Div. Semi-Final
1986-87	80	18	13	9	....	11	24	5	....	29	37	14	....	290	310	72	3rd, Norris Div.	Lost Div. Semi-Final
1985-86	80	23	12	5	....	16	21	3	....	39	33	8	....	351	349	86	1st, Norris Div.	Lost Div. Semi-Final
1984-85	80	22	16	2	....	16	19	5	....	38	35	7	....	309	299	83	2nd, Norris Div.	Lost Conf. Championship
1983-84	80	25	13	2	....	5	29	6	....	30	42	8	....	277	311	68	4th, Norris Div.	Lost Div. Semi-Final
1982-83	80	29	8	3	....	18	15	7	....	47	23	10	....	338	268	104	1st, Norris Div.	Lost Conf. Championship
1981-82	80	20	13	7	....	10	25	5	....	30	38	12	....	332	363	72	4th, Norris Div.	Lost Conf. Championship
1980-81	80	21	11	8	....	10	22	8	....	31	33	16	....	304	315	78	2nd, Smythe Div.	Lost Prelim. Round
1979-80	80	21	12	7	....	13	15	12	....	34	27	19	....	241	250	87	1st, Smythe Div.	Lost Quarter-Final
1978-79	80	18	12	10	....	11	24	5	....	29	36	15	....	244	277	73	1st, Smythe Div.	Lost Quarter-Final
1977-78	80	20	9	11	....	12	20	8	....	32	29	19	....	230	220	83	1st, Smythe Div.	Lost Quarter-Final
1976-77	80	19	16	5	....	7	27	6	....	26	43	11	....	240	298	63	3rd, Smythe Div.	Lost Prelim. Round
1975-76	80	17	15	8	....	15	15	10	....	32	30	18	....	254	261	82	1st, Smythe Div.	Lost Quarter-Final
1974-75	80	24	12	4	....	13	23	4	....	37	35	8	....	268	241	82	3rd, Smythe Div.	Lost Quarter-Final
1973-74	78	20	6	13	....	21	8	10	....	41	14	23	....	272	164	105	2nd, West Div.	Lost Semi-Final
1972-73	78	26	9	4	....	16	18	5	....	42	27	9	....	284	225	93	1st, West Div.	Lost Final
1971-72	78	28	3	8	....	18	14	7	....	46	17	15	....	256	166	107	1st, West Div.	Lost Semi-Final
1970-71	78	30	6	3	....	19	14	6	....	49	20	9	....	277	184	107	1st, West Div.	Lost Final
1969-70	76	26	7	5	....	19	15	4	....	45	22	9	....	250	170	99	1st, East Div.	Lost Semi-Final
1968-69	76	20	14	4	....	14	19	5	....	34	33	9	....	280	246	77	6th, East Div.	Out of Playoffs
1967-68	74	20	13	4	....	12	13	12	....	32	26	16	....	212	222	80	4th, East Div.	Lost Semi-Final
1966-67	70	24	5	6	....	17	12	6	....	41	17	12	....	264	170	94	1st,	Lost Semi-Final
1965-66	70	21	8	6	....	16	17	2	....	37	25	8	....	240	187	82	2nd,	Lost Semi-Final
1964-65	70	20	13	2	....	14	15	6	....	34	28	8	....	224	176	76	3rd,	Lost Final
1963-64	70	26	4	5	....	10	18	7	....	36	22	12	....	218	169	84	2nd,	Lost Semi-Final
1962-63	70	17	9	9	....	15	12	8	....	32	21	17	....	194	178	81	2nd,	Lost Semi-Final
1961-62	70	20	10	5	....	11	16	8	....	31	26	13	....	217	186	75	3rd,	Lost Final
1960-61	**70**	**20**	**6**	**9**	....	**9**	**18**	**8**	....	**29**	**24**	**17**	....	**198**	**180**	**75**	**3rd,**	**Won Stanley Cup**
1959-60	70	18	11	6	....	10	18	7	....	28	29	13	....	191	180	69	3rd,	Lost Semi-Final
1958-59	70	14	12	9	....	14	17	4	....	28	29	13	....	197	208	69	3rd,	Lost Semi-Final
1957-58	70	15	17	3	....	9	22	4	....	24	39	7	....	163	202	55	5th,	Out of Playoffs
1956-57	70	12	15	8	....	4	24	7	....	16	39	15	....	169	225	47	6th,	Out of Playoffs
1955-56	70	9	19	7	....	10	20	5	....	19	39	12	....	155	216	50	6th,	Out of Playoffs
1954-55	70	6	21	8	....	7	19	9	....	13	40	17	....	161	235	43	6th,	Out of Playoffs
1953-54	70	8	21	6	....	4	30	1	....	12	51	7	....	133	242	31	6th,	Out of Playoffs
1952-53	70	14	11	10	....	13	17	5	....	27	28	15	....	169	175	69	4th,	Lost Semi-Final
1951-52	70	9	19	7	....	8	25	2	....	17	44	9	....	158	241	43	6th,	Out of Playoffs
1950-51	70	8	22	5	....	5	25	5	....	13	47	10	....	171	280	36	6th,	Out of Playoffs
1949-50	70	13	18	4	....	9	20	6	....	22	38	10	....	203	244	54	6th,	Out of Playoffs
1948-49	60	13	12	5	....	8	19	3	....	21	31	8	....	173	211	50	5th,	Out of Playoffs
1947-48	60	10	17	3	....	10	17	3	....	20	34	6	....	195	225	46	6th,	Out of Playoffs
1946-47	60	10	17	3	....	9	20	1	....	19	37	4	....	193	274	42	6th,	Out of Playoffs
1945-46	50	15	5	5	....	8	15	2	....	23	20	7	....	200	178	53	3rd,	Lost Semi-Final
1944-45	50	9	14	2	....	4	16	5	....	13	30	7	....	141	194	33	5th,	Out of Playoffs
1943-44	50	15	6	4	....	7	17	1	....	22	23	5	....	178	187	49	4th,	Lost Final
1942-43	50	14	3	8	....	3	15	7	....	17	18	15	....	179	180	49	5th,	Out of Playoffs
1941-42	48	15	8	1	....	7	15	2	....	22	23	3	....	145	155	47	4th,	Lost Quarter-Final
1940-41	48	11	10	3	....	5	15	4	....	16	25	7	....	112	139	39	5th,	Lost Semi-Final
1939-40	48	15	7	2	....	8	12	4	....	23	19	6	....	112	120	52	4th,	Lost Quarter-Final
1938-39	48	5	13	6	....	7	15	2	....	12	28	8	....	91	132	32	7th,	Out of Playoffs
1937-38	**48**	**10**	**10**	**4**	....	**4**	**15**	**5**	....	**14**	**25**	**9**	....	**97**	**139**	**37**	**3rd, Amn. Div.**	**Won Stanley Cup**
1936-37	48	8	13	3	....	6	14	4	....	14	27	7	....	99	131	35	4th, Amn. Div.	Out of Playoffs
1935-36	48	15	7	2	....	6	12	6	....	21	19	8	....	93	92	50	3rd, Amn. Div.	Lost Quarter-Final
1934-35	48	12	9	3	....	14	8	2	....	26	17	5	....	118	88	57	2nd, Amn. Div.	Lost Quarter-Final
1933-34	**48**	**13**	**4**	**7**	....	**7**	**13**	**4**	....	**20**	**17**	**11**	....	**88**	**83**	**51**	**2nd, Amn. Div.**	**Won Stanley Cup**
1932-33	48	12	7	5	....	4	13	7	....	16	20	12	....	88	101	44	4th, Amn. Div.	Out of Playoffs
1931-32	48	13	5	6	....	5	14	5	....	18	19	11	....	86	101	47	2nd, Amn. Div.	Lost Quarter-Final
1930-31	44	13	8	1	....	11	9	2	....	24	17	3	....	108	78	51	2nd, Amn. Div.	Lost Final
1929-30	44	12	9	1	....	9	9	4	....	21	18	5	....	117	111	47	2nd, Amn. Div.	Lost Quarter-Final
1928-29	44	3	13	6	....	4	16	2	....	7	29	8	....	33	85	22	5th, Amn. Div.	Out of Playoffs
1927-28	44	2	18	2	....	5	16	1	....	7	34	3	....	68	134	17	5th, Amn. Div.	Out of Playoffs
1926-27	44	12	8	2	....	7	14	1	....	19	22	3	....	115	116	41	3rd, Amn. Div.	Lost Quarter-Final

2008-09 Player Personnel

FORWARDS	HT	WT	S	Place of Birth	*Age	2007-08 Club
ADAMS, Craig	6-0	200	R	Seria, Brunei	31	Carolina-Chicago
BERTI, Adam	6-3	198	L	Scarborough, Ont.	22	Chi-Rockford-P'cola
BERTRAM, Dan	5-11	182	R	Calgary, Alta.	21	Boston College
BICKELL, Bryan	6-4	223	L	Bowmanville, Ont.	22	Chicago-Rockford
BLUNDEN, Michael	6-3	207	R	Toronto, Ont.	21	Chicago-Rockford
BOLLAND, Dave	6-0	176	R	Toronto, Ont.	22	Chicago-Rockford
BRENT, Tim	6-0	188	R	Cambridge, Ont.	24	Pittsburgh-Wilkes-Barre
BROPHEY, Evan	6-1	203	L	Kitchener, Ont.	21	Rockford
BROUWER, Troy	6-3	220	R	Vancouver, B.C.	23	Chicago-Rockford
BURISH, Adam	6-1	189	R	Madison, WI	25	Chicago
BYFUGLIEN, Dustin	6-3	246	R	Minneapolis, MN	23	Chicago-Rockford
DAVIS, Nathan	6-1	193	L	Cleveland, OH	22	Miami U.
DOWELL, Jake	6-0	202	L	Eau Claire, WI	23	Chicago-Rockford
EAGER, Ben	6-3	225	L	Ottawa, Ont.	24	Philadelphia-Chicago
FRASER, Colin	6-1	190	L	Surrey, B.C.	23	Chicago-Rockford
HAVLAT, Martin	6-1	204	L	Mlada Boleslav, Czech.	27	Chicago
HOBSON, Adam	6-0	210	L	Lund, Sweden	21	Rockford-Pensacola
KANE, Patrick	5-10	163	L	Buffalo, NY	19	Chicago
KONTIOLA, Petri	6-0	197	R	Seinajoki, Finland	24	Chicago-Rockford
LADD, Andrew	6-2	201	L	Maple Ridge, B.C.	22	Carolina-Albany-Chicago
LANG, Robert	6-3	216	R	Teplice, Czech.	37	Chicago
PELLETIER, Pascal	5-11	197	R	Labrador City, Nfld.	25	Boston-Providence (AHL)
SHARP, Patrick	6-1	197	R	Thunder Bay, Ont.	26	Chicago
SKILLE, Jack	6-1	198	R	Madison, WI	21	Chicago-Rockford
TOEWS, Jonathan	6-2	203	L	Winnipeg, Man.	20	Chicago
VERSTEEG, Kris	5-10	179	R	Lethbridge, Alta.	22	Chicago-Rockford
DEFENSEMEN						
BARKER, Cam	6-3	222	L	Winnipeg, Man.	22	Chicago-Rockford
BRENNAN, Mike	6-0	190	R	Smithtown, NY	22	Boston College
CAMPBELL, Brian	6-0	191	L	Strathroy, Ont.	29	Buffalo-San Jose
HAMBLY, Tim	6-0	185	L	White Bear Lake, MN	25	Quad City
HENDRY, Jordan	6-0	196	L	Nokomis, Sask.	24	Chicago-Rockford
HJALMARSSON, Niklas	6-3	196	L	Eksjo, Sweden	21	Chicago-Rockford
JANIK, Doug	6-2	209	L	Agawam, MA	28	Tampa Bay
JOHNSON, Aaron	6-2	211	L	Port Hawkesbury, N.S.	25	NY Islanders-Bridgeport
KEITH, Duncan	6-0	195	L	Winnipeg, Man.	25	Chicago
SAWYER, Jean-Claude	6-3	194	L	Saint John, N.B.	22	Rockford-Pensacola
SEABROOK, Brent	6-3	220	R	Richmond, B.C.	23	Chicago
SOPEL, Brent	6-2	205	R	Calgary, Alta.	31	Chicago
WALKER, Matt	6-3	213	R	Beaverlodge, Alta.	28	St. Louis
WISNIEWSKI, James	6-0	207	R	Canton, MI	24	Chicago
GOALTENDERS	**HT**	**WT**	**C**	**Place of Birth**	***Age**	**2007-08 Club**
CRAWFORD, Corey	6-2	183	L	Montreal, Que.	23	Chicago-Rockford
FALLON, Joseph	6-3	203	L	Bemidji, MN	23	U. of Vermont
HUET, Cristobal	6-1	204	L	St. Martin d'Heres, France	33	Montreal-Washington
KHABIBULIN, Nikolai	6-1	208	L	Sverdlovsk, USSR	35	Chicago
NIEMI, Antti	6-1	200	L	Vantaa, Finland	25	Pelicans

* – Age at start of 2008-09 season

2007-08 Scoring

* – rookie

Regular Season

Pos	#	Player	Team	GP	G	A	Pts	TOI	+/–	PIM	PP	SH	GW	S	%
R	88	* Patrick Kane	CHI	82	21	51	72	18:21	–5	52	7	0	4	191	11.0
R	10	Patrick Sharp	CHI	80	36	26	62	18:46	23	55	9	7	7	209	17.2
C	19	* Jonathan Toews	CHI	64	24	30	54	18:40	11	44	7	0	4	144	16.7
C	20	Robert Lang	CHI	76	21	33	54	18:25	9	50	7	0	3	172	12.2
R	52	Dustin Byfuglien	CHI	67	19	17	36	17:01	–7	59	7	0	4	163	11.7
C	29	Jason Williams	CHI	43	13	23	36	16:34	–2	22	6	0	4	101	12.9
D	2	Duncan Keith	CHI	82	12	20	32	25:33	30	56	1	1	0	148	8.1
D	7	Brent Seabrook	CHI	82	9	23	32	21:29	13	90	4	0	2	152	5.9
L	16	Andrew Ladd	CAR	43	9	9	18	11:44	9	31	0	0	1	76	11.8
			CHI	20	5	7	12	14:58	4	4	1	0	0	55	9.1
			Total	63	14	16	30	12:46	13	35	1	0	1	131	10.7
R	24	Martin Havlat	CHI	35	10	17	27	18:35	4	22	3	0	2	87	11.5
D	43	James Wisniewski	CHI	68	7	19	26	17:00	12	103	1	1	0	82	8.5
L	12	Rene Bourque	CHI	62	10	14	24	15:16	6	42	0	5	2	103	9.7
D	5	Brent Sopel	CHI	58	1	19	20	20:18	9	28	0	0	0	56	1.8
D	25	Cam Barker	CHI	45	6	12	18	17:11	–3	52	2	0	0	42	14.3
C	36	* Dave Bolland	CHI	39	4	13	17	13:43	6	28	0	0	0	49	8.2
C	94	Yanic Perreault	CHI	53	9	5	14	11:30	–1	24	0	0	0	58	15.5
R	28	Craig Adams	CAR	40	2	3	5	09:47	–8	34	0	0	0	31	6.5
			CHI	35	2	4	6	11:56	–8	24	0	1	1	32	6.3
			Total	75	4	7	11	10:47	–16	58	0	1	1	63	6.3
R	37	* Adam Burish	CHI	81	4	4	8	11:44	–13	214	0	1	1	69	5.8
R	11	* Jack Skille	CHI	16	3	2	5	11:58	1	0	0	0	0	23	13.0
D	27	Andrei Zyuzin	CHI	32	2	3	5	14:58	–11	38	1	0	0	34	5.9
C	34	* Petri Kontiola	CHI	12	0	5	5	14:33	5	6	0	0	0	13	0.0
R	32	* Kris Versteeg	CHI	13	2	2	4	15:52	–1	6	0	0	0	21	9.5
D	42	* Jordan Hendry	CHI	40	1	3	4	17:12	0	22	0	0	0	32	3.1
C	49	* Jacob Dowell	CHI	19	2	1	3	11:55	1	10	0	1	0	19	10.5
C	17	Kevyn Adams	CHI	27	0	2	2	10:56	–7	13	0	0	0	32	0.0
L	55	Ben Eager	PHI	23	0	0	0	05:29	–8	62	0	0	0	11	0.0
			CHI	9	0	2	2	06:37	–1	27	0	0	0	5	0.0
			Total	32	0	2	2	05:48	–9	89	0	0	0	16	0.0
R	26	* Troy Brouwer	CHI	2	0	1	1	11:56	1	0	0	0	0	0	0.0
D	41	* Niklas Hjalmarsson	CHI	13	0	1	1	13:37	–2	13	0	0	0	5	0.0
R	28	* Michael Blunden	CHI	1	0	0	0	07:51	–1	0	0	0	0	1	0.0
L	45	* Adam Berti	CHI	2	0	0	0	10:07	0	0	0	0	0	1	0.0
L	38	* Bryan Bickell	CHI	4	0	0	0	09:08	–1	2	0	0	0	3	0.0
C	16	* Martin St. Pierre	CHI	5	0	0	0	15:16	–3	0	0	0	0	2	0.0
C	46	* Colin Fraser	CHI	5	0	0	0	10:18	–2	7	0	0	0	4	0.0
D	44	Danny Richmond	CHI	7	0	0	0	09:24	–5	2	0	0	0	2	0.0
L	48	David Koci	CHI	18	0	0	0	03:38	–4	68	0	0	0	2	0.0

Goaltending

No.	Goaltender	GPI	Mins	Avg	W	L	OT	EN	SO	GA	SA	S%	G	A	PIM
50	* Corey Crawford	5	224	2.14	1	2	0	1	1	8	112	.929	0	0	0
39	Nikolai Khabibulin	50	2892	2.63	23	20	6	6	2	127	1389	.909	0	2	4
40	Patrick Lalime	32	1828	2.82	16	12	2	3	1	86	835	.897	0	0	8
	Totals	**82**	**4981**	**2.78**	**40**	**34**	**8**	**10**	**4**	**231**	**2346**	**.902**			

Denis Savard

Head Coach

Born: Pointe Gatineau, Que, February 4, 1961.

Denis Savard was named the 36th head coach in Chicago Blackhawks history on November 27, 2006. Savard first joined the Blackhawks coaching staff as an assistant coach on December 3, 1997 after beginning the 1997-98 season as the Blackhawks' developmental coach. He entered coaching after announcing his retirement from the National Hockey League in June of 1997.

A 17-year NHL veteran with Chicago, Montreal and Tampa Bay, Savard scored 473 goals and 865 assists (1,338 points) in 1,196 games played. As a Blackhawk, Savard recorded 377 goals and 719 assists (1,096 points) in 881 games played. In playoff competition, Savard scored 66 goals and 109 assists (175 points) in 169 games. As a Blackhawk, he tallied 61 goals and added 84 assists (145 points) in 131 playoff games.

Savard was originally the Blackhawks' first-round pick (third overall) in the 1980 NHL Entry Draft and recorded 75 points (28 goals, 47 assists) during his rookie season in 1980-81. He recorded 32 goals and 87 assists for 119 points the following season to become the second Blackhawk in history to record 100+ points in a single season. Savard was named to the NHL All-Star Second Team for the 1982-83 season when he compiled 35 goals and 86 assists for 121 points in 78 games. He appeared in seven NHL All-Star Games during his career (1982-84, 1986, 1988, 1991 and 1996). Savard tallied a career-high 47 goals during the 1985-86 campaign. He tallied career-highs in assists (87) and points (131) during the 1987-88 season. His 131-point season in 1987-88 is a Blackhawk record and his 87-assist seasons in 1981-82 and 1987-88 are also Blackhawk highs.

After 10 seasons with the Blackhawks, Savard was traded to the Montreal Canadiens in exchange for Chris Chelios and a second-round draft pick (Michael Pomichter) on June 29, 1990. Savard played three seasons for the Canadiens and won the Stanley Cup in 1993. He then played parts of two seasons with the Tampa Bay Lightning before being traded back to the Blackhawks on April 6, 1995.

Savard is one of only five players in Blackhawk history to have his number retired. His #18 was raised to the United Center rafters in a special pregame ceremony on March 19, 1998. He joined Blackhawk legends Glenn Hall (1), Bobby Hull (9), Stan Mikita (21) and Tony Esposito (35) as the only Blackhawks to be so honored. He was inducted into the Hockey Hall of Fame in 2000.

Coaching Record

			Regular Season				Playoffs			
Season	**Team**	**League**	**GC**	**W**	**L**	**O/T**	**GC**	**W**	**L**	**T**
2006-07	**Chicago**	**NHL**	**61**	**24**	**30**	**7**	....	....	....	....
2007-08	**Chicago**	**NHL**	**82**	**40**	**34**	**8**	....	....	....	....
	NHL Totals		**143**	**64**	**64**	**15**	....	....	....	....

General Managers' History

Major Frederic McLaughlin, 1926-27 to 1941-42; Bill Tobin, 1942-43 to 1953-54; Tommy Ivan, 1954-55 to 1976-77; Bob Pulford, 1977-78 to 1989-90; Mike Keenan, 1990-91, 1991-92; Mike Keenan and Bob Pulford, 1992-93; Bob Pulford, 1993-94 to 1996-97; Bob Murray, 1997-98, 1998-99; Bob Murray and Bob Pulford, 1999-2000; Mike Smith, 2000-01 to 2002-03; Mike Smith and Bob Pulford, 2003-04; Bob Pulford, 2004-05; Dale Tallon, 2005-06 to date.

Dale Tallon

Vice President and General Manager

Born: Noranda, Que., October 19, 1950.

The Chicago Blackhawks announced on June 21, 2005 that Dale Tallon had been named the eighth general manager in the team's storied history. Tallon, in his second stint with the Blackhawks front office, was named assistant general manager on November 5, 2003. He served four years (1998 to 2002) as the Blackhawks' director of player personnel before he returned to the radio and television booth prior to the 2002-03 season as color analyst for Blackhawk hockey.

Tallon was the Vancouver Canucks' first-round selection and the second player chosen overall (behind Gilbert Perreault, Buffalo) in the 1970 NHL Entry Draft. A defenseman, he immediately jumped into the NHL with the Canucks in the 1970–71 season. Tallon recorded a career-high 17 goals in 69 games with Vancouver during the 1971–72 season and appeared in the 1971 and 1972 NHL All-Star Games.

Tallon was traded to the Blackhawks for Jerry Korab and Gary Smith on May 14,1973. He had his best season as a professional with Chicago in 1975–76 with a career-high 47 assists and 62 points in 80 games. During his five-year Blackhawk career (1973 to 1978), Tallon scored 44 goals and added 112 assists for 156 points with 296 penalty minutes. He was dealt to Pittsburgh on October 9, 1978 and finished his playing career by playing two seasons with the Penguins. During his 10-year NHL career, Tallon scored 98 goals and added 238 assists for 336 points in 642 games. After retiring from the NHL following the 1979–80 season, he served as the Blackhawks color analyst for radio and television broadcasts for 16 seasons.

At the start of the 1998-99 season, Tallon joined the Blackhawk front office as director of player personnel. As he traveled the world, scouting hockey, Tallon's knowledge and expertise of the game were honed while aiding in selecting and developing the Blackhawks' young prospects.

Club Records

Team

(Figures in brackets for season records are games played; records for fewest points, wins, ties, losses, goals, goals against are for 70 or more games)

Most Points .... 107 — 1970-71 (78), 1971-72 (78)
Most Wins .... 49 — 1970-71 (78), 1990-91 (80)
Most Ties .... 23 — 1973-74 (78)
Most Losses .... 56 — 2005-06 (82)
Most Goals .... 351 — 1985-86 (80)
Most Goals Against .... 363 — 1981-82 (80)
Fewest Points .... 31 — 1953-54 (70)
Fewest Wins .... 12 — 1953-54 (70)
Fewest Ties .... 6 — 1989-90 (80)
Fewest Losses .... 14 — 1973-74 (78)
Fewest Goals .... *133 — 1953-54 (70)
Fewest Goals Against .... 164 — 1973-74 (78)
Longest Winning Streak
- **Overall** .... 8 — Dec. 9-26/71, Jan. 4-21/81
- **Home** .... 13 — Nov. 11-Dec. 20/70
- **Away** .... 7 — Dec. 9-29/64

Longest Undefeated Streak
- **Overall** .... 15 — Jan. 14-Feb. 16/67 (12 wins, 3 ties), Oct. 29-Dec. 3/75 (6 wins, 9 ties)
- **Home** .... 18 — Oct. 11-Dec. 20/70 (16 wins, 2 ties)
- **Away** .... 12 — Nov. 2-Dec. 16/67 (6 wins, 6 ties)

Longest Losing Streak
- **Overall** .... 12 — Feb. 25-Mar. 25/51
- **Home** .... 10 — Jan. 29-Mar. 21/28
- **Away** .... 19 — Nov. 10/03-Jan. 29/04

Longest Winless Streak
- **Overall** .... 21 — Dec. 17/50-Jan. 28/51 (18 losses, 3 ties)
- **Home** .... 15 — Dec. 16/28-Feb. 28/29 (11 losses, 4 ties)
- **Away** .... 22 — Dec. 19/50-Mar. 25/51 (20 losses, 2 ties)

Most Shutouts, Season .... 15 — 1969-70 (76)
Most PIM, Season .... 2,663 — 1991-92 (80)
Most Goals, Game .... 12 — Jan. 30/69 (Chi. 12 at Phi. 0)

Individual

Most Seasons .... 22 — Stan Mikita
Most Games .... 1,394 — Stan Mikita
Most Goals, Career .... 604 — Bobby Hull
Most Assists, Career .... 926 — Stan Mikita
Most Points, Career .... 1,467 — Stan Mikita (541G, 926A)
Most PIM, Career .... 1,495 — Chris Chelios
Most Shutouts, Career .... 74 — Tony Esposito
Longest Consecutive Games Streak .... 884 — Steve Larmer (Oct. 6/82-Apr. 15/93)
Most Goals, Season .... 58 — Bobby Hull (1968-69)
Most Assists, Season .... 87 — Denis Savard (1981-82, 1987-88)
Most Points, Season .... 131 — Denis Savard (1987-88; 44G, 87A)
Most PIM, Season .... 408 — Mike Peluso (1991-92)
Most Points, Defenseman, Season .... 85 — Doug Wilson (1981-82; 39G, 46A)
Most Points, Center, Season .... 131 — Denis Savard (1987-88; 44G, 87A)
Most Points, Right Wing, Season .... 101 — Steve Larmer (1990-91; 44G, 57A)
Most Points, Left Wing, Season .... 107 — Bobby Hull (1968-69; 58G, 49A)
Most Points, Rookie, Season .... 90 — Steve Larmer (1982-83; 43G, 47A)
Most Shutouts, Season .... 15 — Tony Esposito (1969-70)
Most Goals, Game .... 5 — Grant Mulvey (Feb. 3/82)
Most Assists, Game .... 6 — Pat Stapleton (Mar. 30/69)
Most Points, Game .... 7 — Max Bentley (Jan. 28/43; 4G, 3A), Grant Mulvey (Feb. 3/82; 5G, 2A)

* NHL Record.

Retired Numbers

1	Glenn Hall	1957-1967
9	Bobby Hull	1957-1972
18	Denis Savard	1980-1990, 1995-1997
21	Stan Mikita	1958-1980
35	Tony Esposito	1969-1984

All-time Record vs. Other Clubs

Regular Season

	At Home								On Road								Total							
	GP	W	L	T	OL	GF	GA	PTS	GP	W	L	T	OL	GF	GA	PTS	GP	W	L	T	OL	GF	GA	PTS
Anaheim	30	13	15	2	0	78	76	28	28	8	17	3	0	59	81	19	58	21	32	5	0	137	157	47
Atlanta	3	2	1	0	0	8	3	4	5	3	2	0	0	15	18	6	8	5	3	0	0	23	21	10
Boston	287	147	95	45	0	929	772	339	285	89	162	34	0	809	1026	212	572	236	257	79	0	1738	1798	551
Buffalo	52	27	18	6	1	165	141	61	54	14	33	7	0	139	202	35	106	41	51	13	1	304	343	96
Calgary	67	28	26	13	0	211	197	69	69	25	30	13	1	204	214	64	136	53	56	26	1	415	411	133
Carolina	30	16	10	3	1	117	86	36	31	12	15	4	0	96	102	28	61	28	25	7	1	213	188	64
Colorado	47	25	16	3	3	159	145	56	45	15	24	6	0	142	177	36	92	40	40	9	3	301	322	92
Columbus	22	13	7	1	1	67	51	28	23	9	11	1	2	73	76	21	45	22	18	2	3	140	127	49
Dallas	116	67	34	15	0	424	307	149	118	45	55	16	2	358	408	108	234	112	89	31	2	782	715	257
Detroit	350	159	137	51	3	1046	991	372	347	102	211	33	1	862	1196	238	697	261	348	84	4	1908	2187	610
Edmonton	50	25	15	7	3	187	167	60	51	19	26	5	1	156	187	44	101	44	41	12	4	343	354	104
Florida	11	5	4	2	0	35	33	12	9	5	2	1	1	33	22	12	20	10	6	3	1	68	55	24
Los Angeles	81	38	33	9	1	278	235	86	80	36	35	8	1	267	272	81	161	74	68	17	2	545	507	167
Minnesota	14	5	7	1	1	31	42	12	14	3	8	0	3	31	45	9	28	8	15	1	4	62	87	21
Montreal	274	94	125	55	0	733	762	243	277	54	173	48	2	656	1071	158	551	148	298	103	2	1389	1833	401
Nashville	29	16	11	1	1	81	77	34	28	11	10	3	4	82	93	29	57	27	21	4	5	163	170	63
New Jersey	47	24	12	10	1	178	130	59	48	16	20	11	1	143	149	44	95	40	32	21	2	321	279	103
NY Islanders	49	26	17	5	1	163	164	58	48	14	19	15	0	143	168	43	97	40	36	20	1	306	332	101
NY Rangers	287	129	115	43	0	872	793	301	286	113	118	55	0	808	843	281	573	242	233	98	0	1680	1636	582
Ottawa	9	5	2	2	0	22	21	12	11	7	4	0	0	34	34	14	20	12	6	2	0	56	55	26
Philadelphia	61	26	16	19	0	207	175	71	63	16	36	11	0	162	207	43	124	42	52	30	0	369	382	114
Phoenix	54	29	14	10	1	198	139	69	56	21	28	5	2	173	182	49	110	50	42	15	3	371	321	118
Pittsburgh	61	40	11	10	0	240	158	90	60	23	29	7	1	194	215	54	121	63	40	17	1	434	373	144
St. Louis	130	74	38	18	0	476	372	166	127	47	61	17	2	391	427	113	257	121	99	35	2	867	799	279
San Jose	31	14	13	2	2	90	96	32	32	10	17	3	2	81	95	25	63	24	30	5	4	171	191	57
Tampa Bay	15	9	4	2	0	50	36	20	12	4	4	3	1	30	29	12	27	13	8	5	1	80	65	32
Toronto	319	157	120	42	0	971	832	356	316	98	164	54	0	827	1075	250	635	255	284	96	0	1798	1907	606
Vancouver	77	48	19	7	3	280	183	106	78	23	38	15	2	219	234	63	155	71	57	22	5	499	417	169
Washington	41	23	12	6	0	156	120	52	42	16	21	5	0	131	148	37	83	39	33	11	0	287	268	89
Defunct Clubs	139	79	40	20	0	408	268	178	140	52	67	21	0	316	346	125	279	131	107	41	0	724	614	303
Totals	**2783**	**1363**	**987**	**410**	**23**	**8860**	**7572**	**3159**	**2783**	**910**	**1440**	**404**	**29**	**7634**	**9342**	**2253**	**5566**	**2273**	**2427**	**814**	**52**	**16494**	**16914**	**5412**

Playoffs

	Series	W	L	GP	W	L	T	GF	GA	Last Mtg.	Rnd.	Result
Boston	6	1	5	22	5	16	1	63	97	1978	QF	L 0-4
Buffalo	2	0	2	9	1	8	0	17	36	1980	QF	L 0-4
Calgary	3	1	2	12	5	7	0	33	37	1996	CQF	W 4-0
Colorado	2	0	2	12	4	8	0	28	49	1997	CQF	L 2-4
Dallas	6	4	2	33	19	14	0	120	118	1991	DSF	L 2-4
Detroit	14	8	6	69	38	31	0	210	190	1995	CF	L 1-4
Edmonton	4	1	3	20	8	12	0	77	102	1992	CF	W 4-0
Los Angeles	1	1	0	5	4	1	0	10	7	1974	QF	W 4-1
Montreal	17	5	12	81	29	50	2	185	261	1976	QF	L 0-4
NY Islanders	2	0	2	6	0	6	0	6	21	1979	QF	L 0-4
NY Rangers	5	4	1	24	14	10	0	66	54	1973	SF	W 4-1
Philadelphia	1	1	0	4	4	0	0	20	8	1971	QF	W 4-0
Pittsburgh	2	1	1	8	4	4	0	24	23	1992	F	L 0-4
St. Louis	10	7	3	50	28	22	0	171	142	2002	CQF	L 1-4
Toronto	9	3	6	38	15	22	1	89	111	1995	CQF	W 4-3
Vancouver	2	1	1	9	5	4	0	24	24	1995	CSF	W 4-0
Defunct Clubs	4	2	2	9	5	3	1	16	15			
Totals	**90**	**40**	**50**	**411**	**188**	**218**	**5**	**1159**	**1295**			

Calgary totals include Atlanta Flames, 1972-73 to 1979-80.
Carolina totals include Hartford, 1979-80 to 1996-97.
Colorado totals include Quebec, 1979-80 to 1994-95.
Dallas totals include Minnesota North Stars, 1967-68 to 1992-93.
New Jersey totals include Kansas City, 1974-75, 1975-76, and Colorado Rockies, 1976-77 to 1981-82.
Phoenix totals include Winnipeg, 1979-80 to 1995-96.

Playoff Results 2008-2003

(Last playoff appearance: 2002)

Abbreviations: Round: F - Final; **CF** - conference final; **CSF** - conference semi-final; **CQF** - conference quarter-final; **DSF** - division semi-final; **SF** - semi-final; **QF** - quarter-final.

2007-08 Results

Month	Date	Opponent	Score
Oct.	4	at Minnesota	0-1
	6	Detroit	4-3†
	10	San Jose	1-2
	12	at Detroit	3-2
	13	Dallas	2-1*
	17	St. Louis	1-3
	19	Colorado	5-3
	20	at Toronto	6-4
	23	Columbus	4-7
	25	at Boston	1-3
	27	Atlanta	2-3
	31	at Dallas	5-4
Nov.	3	at St. Louis	3-2
	4	Nashville	2-5
	7	Columbus	5-2
	9	St. Louis	4-2
	11	Detroit	3-2
	14	at Columbus	2-4
	15	at Nashville	4-5*
	17	at Detroit	5-3
	22	at Calgary	2-1
	24	at Edmonton	2-3†
	25	at Vancouver	0-2
	28	Tampa Bay	5-1
	30	Phoenix	6-1
Dec.	1	at St. Louis	1-3
	5	Vancouver	2-3
	7	Anaheim	3-5
	9	Calgary	2-3
	12	Los Angeles	6-3
	15	at Buffalo	1-3
	16	Florida	1-3
	19	Nashville	5-2
	22	at Ottawa	4-3*
	23	Edmonton	3-2
	26	Nashville	5-2
	30	Los Angeles	2-3*
Jan.	1	at Los Angeles	2-9
	3	at Phoenix	2-4
	4	at Anaheim	1-2
	6	Detroit	1-3
	8	at Montreal	3-4*
	9	Dallas	1-3
	11	Minnesota	2-5
	13	at Nashville	3-2†
	16	St. Louis	6-1
	18	at Colorado	2-1†
	19	at Phoenix	2-1†
	22	at San Jose	2-3
	24	Columbus	0-1
	30	at Colorado	3-6
Feb.	2	at San Jose	2-3†
	6	at Edmonton	1-4
	7	at Calgary	3-1
	10	at Vancouver	2-3†
	13	at Columbus	7-2
	14	at Nashville	6-1
	17	Colorado	2-1
	19	at St. Louis	1-5
	20	Minnesota	3-0
	23	at Los Angeles	6-5*
	24	at Anaheim	3-6
	27	Phoenix	1-0
	28	at Dallas	4-7
Mar.	2	Vancouver	4-1
	4	at Minnesota	4-2
	5	Anaheim	3-0
	7	San Jose	2-3
	9	Edmonton	5-6*
	11	at Detroit	1-3
	12	Carolina	0-3
	14	at Columbus	6-3
	16	Calgary	2-4
	19	Washington	5-0
	22	at Nashville	1-2†
	23	St. Louis	4-3*
	26	at Columbus	0-4
	29	at St. Louis	4-3
	30	Columbus	5-4†
Apr.	2	Detroit	6-2
	4	Nashville	3-1
	6	at Detroit	1-4

* – Overtime † – Shootout

Entry Draft Selections 2008-1994

Name in bold denotes played in NHL.

2008

Pick	
11	Kyle Beach
68	Shawn Lalonde
132	Teigan Zahn
162	Jonathan Carlsson
169	Ben Smith
179	Braden Birch
192	Joe Gleason

2007

Pick	
1	**Patrick Kane**
38	Bill Sweatt
56	Akim Aliu
69	Maxime Tanguay
86	Josh Unice
126	Joseph Lavin
156	Richard Greenop

2006

Pick	
3	**Jonathan Toews**
33	Igor Makarov
61	Simon Danis-Pepin
76	Tony Lagerstrom
95	Ben Shutron
96	Joe Palmer
156	Jan-Mikael Juutilainen
169	Chris Auger
186	Peter Leblanc

2005

Pick	
7	**Jack Skille**
43	**Michael Blunden**
54	Dan Bertram
68	Evan Brophey
108	**Niklas Hjalmarsson**
113	Nathan Davis
117	Denis Istomin
134	Brennan Turner
167	Joseph Fallon
188	Joe Charlebois
202	David Kuchejda
203	Adam Hobson

2004

Pick	
3	**Cam Barker**
32	**Dave Bolland**
41	**Bryan Bickell**
45	Ryan Garlock
54	Jakub Sindel
68	**Adam Berti**
120	Mitch Maunu
123	Karel Hromas
131	Trevor Kell
140	**Jake Dowell**
165	Scott McCulloch
196	**Petri Kontiola**
214	**Troy Brouwer**
223	Jared Walker
229	Eric Hunter
256	Matthew Ford
260	Marko Anttila

2003

Pick	
14	**Brent Seabrook**
52	**Corey Crawford**
59	**Michal Barinka**
151	**Lasse Kukkonen**
156	Alexei Ivanov
181	Johan Andersson
211	Mike Brodeur
245	**Dustin Byfuglien**
275	Michael Grenzy
282	Chris Porter

2002

Pick	
21	**Anton Babchuk**
54	**Duncan Keith**
93	Alexander Kojevnikov
128	**Matt Ellison**
156	**James Wisniewski**
188	Kevin Kantee
219	Tyson Kellerman
251	Jason Kostadine
282	**Adam Burish**

2001

Pick	
9	**Tuomo Ruutu**
29	**Adam Munro**
59	**Matt Keith**
73	**Craig Anderson**
104	Brent MacLellan
115	Vladimir Gusev
119	Alexei Zotkin
142	Tommi Jaminki
174	Alexander Golovin
186	Petr Puncochar
205	Teemu Jaaskelainen
216	Oleg Minakov
268	Jeff Miles

2000

Pick	
10	**Mikhail Yakubov**
11	**Pavel Vorobiev**
49	**Jonas Nordqvist**
74	**Igor Radulov**
106	Scott Balan
117	**Olli Malmivaara**
151	Alexander Barkunov
177	Michael Ayers
193	Joey Martin
207	Cliff Loya
225	Vladislav Luchkin
240	**Adam Berkhoel**
262	Peter Flache
271	**Reto Von Arx**
291	Arne Ramholt

1999

Pick	
23	**Steve McCarthy**
46	Dimitri Levinski
63	Stepan Mokhov
134	Michael Jacobsen
165	**Michael Leighton**
194	Mattias Wennerberg
195	Yorick Treille
223	Andrew Carver

1998

Pick	
8	**Mark Bell**
94	Matthias Trattnig
156	**Kent Huskins**
158	Jari Viuhkola
166	Jonathan Pelletier
183	**Tyler Arnason**
210	Sean Griffin
238	Alexandre Couture
240	Andrei Yershov

1997

Pick	
13	**Daniel Cleary**
16	**Ty Jones**
39	**Jeremy Reich**
67	Mike Souza
110	**Ben Simon**
120	Peter Gardiner
130	**Kyle Calder**
147	Heath Gordon
174	Jerad Smith
204	Sergei Shikhanov
230	Chris Feil

1996

Pick	
31	**Remi Royer**
42	**Jeff Paul**
46	Geoff Peters
130	Andy Johnson
184	Mike Vellinga
210	Chris Twerdun
236	Andrei Kozyrev

1995

Pick	
19	**Dmitri Nabokov**
45	**Christian Laflamme**
71	Kevin McKay
82	Chris Van Dyk
97	Pavel Kriz
146	Marc Magliarditi
149	Marty Wilford
175	Steve Tardif
201	**Casey Hankinson**
227	Mike Pittman

1994

Pick	
14	**Ethan Moreau**
40	**Jean-Yves Leroux**
85	**Steve McLaren**
118	Marc Dupuis
144	Jim Enson
170	Tyler Prosofsky
196	Mike Josephson
222	Lubomir Jandera
248	Lars Weibel
263	Rob Mara

Coaching History

Pete Muldoon, 1926-27; Barney Stanley and Hugh Lehman, 1927-28; Herb Gardiner and Dick Irvin, 1928-29; Tom Shaughnessy and Bill Tobin, 1929-30; Dick Irvin, 1930-31; Bill Tobin, 1931-32; Emil Iverson, Godfrey Matheson and Tommy Gorman, 1932-33; Tommy Gorman, 1933-34; Clem Loughlin, 1934-35 to 1936-37; Bill Stewart, 1937-38; Bill Stewart and Paul Thompson, 1938-39; Paul Thompson, 1939-40 to 1943-44; Paul Thompson and Johnny Gottselig, 1944-45; Johnny Gottselig, 1945-46, 1946-47; Johnny Gottselig and Charlie Conacher, 1947-48; Charlie Conacher, 1948-49, 1949-50; Ebbie Goodfellow, 1950-51, 1951-52; Sid Abel, 1952-53, 1953-54; Frank Eddolls, 1954-55; Dick Irvin, 1955-56; Tommy Ivan, 1956-57; Tommy Ivan and Rudy Pilous, 1957-58; Rudy Pilous, 1958-59 to 1962-63; Billy Reay, 1963-64 to 1975-76; Billy Reay and Bill White, 1976-77; Bob Pulford, 1977-78, 1978-79; Eddie Johnston, 1979-80; Keith Magnuson, 1980-81; Keith Magnuson and Bob Pulford, 1981-82; Orval Tessier, 1982-83, 1983-84; Orval Tessier and Bob Pulford, 1984-85; Bob Pulford, 1985-86, 1986-87; Bob Murdoch, 1987-88; Mike Keenan, 1988-89 to 1991-92; Darryl Sutter, 1992-93 to 1994-95; Craig Hartsburg, 1995-96 to 1997-98; Dirk Graham and Lorne Molleken, 1998-99; Lorne Molleken and Bob Pulford, 1999-2000; Alpo Suhonen, 2000-01; Brian Sutter, 2001-02 to 2004-05; Trent Yawney, 2005-06; Trent Yawney and Denis Savard, 2006-07; Denis Savard, 2007-08 to date.

Captains' History

Dick Irvin, 1926-27 to 1928-29; Duke Dukowski, 1929-30; Ty Arbour, 1930-31; Cy Wentworth, 1931-32; Helge Bostrom, 1932-33; Charlie Gardiner, 1933-34; no captain, 1934-35; Johnny Gottselig, 1935-36 to 1939-40; Earl Seibert, 1940-41, 1941-42; Doug Bentley, 1942-43, 1943-44; Clint Smith 1944-45; John Mariucci, 1945-46; Red Hamill, 1946-47; John Mariucci, 1947-48; Gaye Stewart, 1948-49; Doug Bentley, 1949-50; Jack Stewart, 1950-51, 1951-52; Bill Gadsby, 1952-53, 1953-54; Gus Mortson, 1954-55 to 1956-57; no captain, 1957-58; Ed Litzenberger, 1958-59 to 1960-61; Pierre Pilote, 1961-62 to 1967-68, no captain, 1968-69; Pat Stapleton, 1969-70; no captain, 1970-71 to 1974-75; Stan Mikita and Pit Martin, 1975-76; Stan Mikita, Pit Martin and Keith Magnuson, 1976-77; Keith Magnuson, 1977-78, 1978-79; Keith Magnuson and Terry Ruskowski, 1979-80; Terry Ruskowski, 1980-81, 1981-82; Darryl Sutter, 1982-83 to 1984-85; Darryl Sutter and Bob Murray, 1985-86; Darryl Sutter, 1986-87; no captain, 1987-88; Denis Savard and Dirk Graham, 1988-89; Dirk Graham, 1989-90 to 1994-95; Chris Chelios, 1995-96 to 1998-99; Doug Gilmour, 1999-2000; Tony Amonte, 2000-01, 2001-02; Alex Zhamnov, 2002-03, 2003-04; Adrian Aucoin and Martin Lapointe, 2005-06, 2006-07; no captain, 2007-08; Jonathan Toews, 2008-09.

Club Directory

United Center

Chicago Blackhawks
United Center
1901 W. Madison Street
Chicago, IL 60612
Phone **312/455-7000**
FAX 312/455-7041
www.chicagoblackhawks.com
Capacity: 20,500

Chairman	W. Rockwell "Rocky" Wirtz
President	John F. McDonough
Senior Vice President, Business Operations	Jay Blunk
General Manager	Dale Tallon
Assistant General Manager	Rick Dudley
Assistant General Manager, Hockey Operations	Stan Bowman
Director of Player Evaluation	Al MacIsaac
General Manager of Minor League Affiliations	Mark Bernard
Coaching Staff	
Head Coach	Denis Savard
Assistant Coaches	John Torchetti, Mike Haviland
Strength and Conditioning Coach	Paul Goodman
Goaltending Coach	Stephane Waite
Hockey Operations/Scouts	
Director of Pro Scouts	Marc Bergevin
Director of Amateur Scouting	Mark Kelley
Director of Amateur Scouting	Michel Dumas
Chief Amateur Scout	Ron Anderson
Amateur Scouts	Bruce Franklin, Tim Keon, Norm Maciver, Ryan Stewart
European Amateur Scouts	Karl Pavlik, Ruslan Shabanov
European Pro Scout	Mats Hallin
Senior Executive Assistant to GM	Julie Kavanaugh
Exec. Asst. to Pres. & Sr. V.P. of Bus. Operations	Janelle Miller
Director, Team Services	Tony Ommen
Training/Equipment Staff	
Head Athletic Trainer	Mike Gapski
Assistant Athletic Trainer	Jeff Thomas
Massage Therapist	Pawel Prylinski
Equipment Manager	Troy Parchman
Assistant Equipment Manager	Russ Holden
Equipment Assistant	Clinton Reif
Medical Staff	
Head Team Physician, Orthopedics	Michael Terry
Team Physician, Orthopedics	Sherwin Ho
Team Physicians, Internal Medicine	William Harper, Carl Meyer, Todd Stern
Team Dentists	Russ Baer, Anthony LaVacca, Martin Marcus
Eye Doctors	William Mieler, Louise Sclafani
Business Development	
Senior Director, Corporate Sponsorships	Steve Waight
Acct. Execs., Corporate Sponsorships	Sara Bailey, Steve McNelley, Rich Sommers, Bart Miller
Manager, Client Services	Kelly Smith
Administrative Assistant, Client Services	Kristin Ludden
Market Research Coordinator	Mark McGuire, Jr.
Finance and Human Resources	
Director of Finance	T.J. Skattum
Executive Director, Finance	John W. Kerr
Director, Human Resources	Marie Sutera
Human Resources Assistant	Kyleen M. King
Receptionist/Office Coordinator	Jillian Smith
Marketing and New Media	
Senior Director of Marketing and Advertising	Pete Hassen
Director of Promotions and Game Day Operations	Ben Broder
Director of New Media and Publications	Adam Kempenaar
New Media and Publications Assistant	John Sandberg
Graphic Designer	Chris Weibring
Marketing Assistant	Brian Howe
Media and Community Relations	
Director, Media Relations	Brandon Faber
Coordinator, Media Relations	Adam Rogowin
Assistant, Media Relations	Jordan Horst
Director, Youth Hockey	Annie Camins
Coordinator, Community Relations	Brooke Scheyer
Ticketing	
Sr. Exec. Dir., Ticket & Business Development	Chris Werner
Executive Director, Ticket Operations	James K. Bare
Director of Ticket Sales and Service	Dan Rozenblat
Manager, Group Sales	Steve DiLenardi
Manager, Database Marketing	Allison Ardolino
Manager, Customer Service	Trisha Ithal
Senior Customer Service Representative	Kathie Raimondi
Senior Account Executives	Matthew Powers, Chris Terwoord
Senior Account Executive, Group Sales	Eric Dumais
Account Executives, Ticket Sales	Jake Tuton, T.R. Johnson, Logan Schroeder
Account Executive, Group Sales	Nick Zombolas
Ticket Administrator	Allison Westfall
Inside Sales Representatives	Aaron Salsbury, Andrew Vardijan, Robert Russel, Greg Zinsmeister, Bradley Chase
Television and Radio	
TV Play-By-Play / Analyst	Pat Foley / Eddie Olczyk
Radio Play-By-Play / Analyst / Host	John Wiedeman / Troy Murray / Judd Sirott
Interns	
Community Relations	Ashley Hinton
Customer Service	Tracy Cunningham
Hockey Operations	Justin Murch
Human Resources	Ashley Redenius
Marketing	Matt Benjamin, Morgan Sharar-Stoppel
New Media and Publications	Brad Boron
Miscellaneous	
Team Photographer	Bill Smith
Assistant Photographer	Rudy Ayasse
Organist	Frank Pellico
Public Address Announcer	Gene Honda
Website Contributor	Harvey Wittenberg

Colorado Avalanche

2007-08 Results: 44W-31L-4OTL-3SOL 95PTS.
Second, Northwest Division

Key Off-Season Signings/Acquisitions

2008

May 22 • Named **Tony Granato** head coach.
June 24 • Re-signed RW **Scott Parker**.
30 • Re-signed D **Adam Foote** and D **John-Michael Liles**.
July 1 • Signed RW **Darcy Tucker** and G **Andrew Raycroft**.
2 • Re-signed LW **Wojtek Wolski**.
3 • Signed D **Daniel Tjarnqvist**.
9 • Named **Dave Barr** assistant coach.
14 • Re-signed LW **Cody McLeod**.
15 • Re-signed RW **Cody McCormick**.
15 • Signed RW **Brian Willsie**.

Milan Hejduk led the Avalanche with 29 goals in 2007-08. It was the fourth time he's led the team in goals scored. His 205 shots were also tops.

2008-09 Schedule

Oct.	Thu.	9	Boston
	Sun.	12	at Edmonton
	Tue.	14	at Calgary
	Thu.	16	Philadelphia
	Sat.	18	at Dallas*
	Mon.	20	at Los Angeles
	Thu.	23	Edmonton
	Sat.	25	Buffalo
	Tue.	28	at Calgary
	Thu.	30	Columbus
Nov.	Sun.	2	San Jose
	Mon.	3	at Chicago
	Thu.	6	Minnesota
	Sat.	8	Nashville
	Wed.	12	at Vancouver
	Sat.	15	at Edmonton
	Tue.	18	at Calgary
	Thu.	20	Calgary
	Sat.	22	at Los Angeles
	Mon.	24	at Anaheim
	Wed.	26	St. Louis
	Fri.	28	at Phoenix*
	Sat.	29	Tampa Bay
Dec.	Mon.	1	at Minnesota
	Thu.	4	at Nashville
	Fri.	5	at Dallas
	Sun.	7	Vancouver
	Tue.	9	Los Angeles
	Fri.	12	Chicago
	Mon.	15	at Detroit
	Tue.	16	at Philadelphia
	Thu.	18	at Tampa Bay
	Sun.	21	at Florida*
	Tue.	23	Phoenix
	Sat.	27	Detroit
	Mon.	29	Nashville
	Wed.	31	at Phoenix
Jan.	Fri.	2	Columbus
	Sun.	4	Minnesota
	Tue.	6	at Nashville
	Thu.	8	Chicago
	Sat.	10	Pittsburgh*
	Tue.	13	at Columbus
	Thu.	15	at St. Louis
	Fri.	16	Edmonton
	Sun.	18	Calgary
	Wed.	21	Los Angeles
	Tue.	27	San Jose
	Thu.	29	Toronto
	Sat.	31	Anaheim*
Feb.	Mon.	2	Calgary
	Thu.	5	Dallas
	Sat.	7	at St. Louis
	Tue.	10	at Columbus
	Wed.	11	at Minnesota
	Fri.	13	Montreal
	Sun.	15	at Detroit*
	Tue.	17	Ottawa
	Fri.	20	at Washington
	Sun.	22	at Carolina*
	Tue.	24	at Atlanta
	Thu.	26	at New Jersey
	Sat.	28	at NY Rangers
Mar.	Mon.	2	at NY Islanders
	Wed.	4	Detroit
	Sun.	8	at Chicago*
	Tue.	10	Atlanta
	Thu.	12	Minnesota
	Sat.	14	at Edmonton
	Sun.	15	at Vancouver
	Tue.	17	at Minnesota
	Thu.	19	Edmonton
	Sun.	22	at San Jose*
	Wed.	25	Anaheim
	Fri.	27	Vancouver
	Sun.	29	at Anaheim*
Apr.	Wed.	1	Phoenix
	Sun.	5	at Vancouver
	Tue.	7	at San Jose
	Thu.	9	Dallas
	Sat.	11	Vancouver*
	Sun.	12	St. Louis*

* Denotes afternoon game.

Year-by-Year Record

		Home				Road				Overall								
Season	**GP**	**W**	**L**	**T**	**OL**	**W**	**L**	**T**	**OL**	**W**	**L**	**T**	**OL**	**GF**	**GA**	**Pts.**	**Finished**	**Playoff Result**
2007-08	82	27	12	....	2	17	19	....	5	44	31	....	7	231	219	95	2nd, Northwest Div.	Lost Conf. Semi-Final
2006-07	82	22	16	....	3	22	15	....	4	44	31	....	7	272	251	95	4th, Northwest Div.	Out of Playoffs
2005-06	82	25	10	....	6	18	20	....	3	43	30	....	9	283	257	95	2nd, Northwest Div.	Lost Conf. Semi-Final
2004-05	....	....	....	....	....	....	....	....	....	....	....	....	....	....	....	....		
2003-04	82	19	14	6	2	21	8	7	5	40	22	13	7	236	198	100	2nd, Northwest Div.	Lost Conf. Semi-Final
2002-03	82	21	9	8	3	21	10	5	5	42	19	13	8	251	194	105	1st, Northwest Div.	Lost Conf. Quarter-Final
2001-02	82	24	12	4	1	21	16	4	0	45	28	8	1	212	169	99	1st, Northwest Div.	Lost Conf. Championship
2000-01	**82**	**28**	**6**	**5**	**2**	**24**	**10**	**5**	**2**	**52**	**16**	**10**	**4**	**270**	**192**	**118**	**1st, Northwest Div.**	**Won Stanley Cup**
1999-2000	82	25	12	4	0	17	16	7	1	42	28	11	1	233	201	96	1st, Northwest Div.	Lost Conf. Championship
1998-99	82	21	14	6	....	23	14	4	....	44	28	10	....	239	205	98	1st, Northwest Div.	Lost Conf. Championship
1997-98	82	21	10	10	....	18	16	7	....	39	26	17	....	231	205	95	1st, Pacific Div.	Lost Conf. Quarter-Final
1996-97	82	26	10	5	....	23	14	4	....	49	24	9	....	277	205	107	1st, Pacific Div.	Lost Conf. Championship
1995-96	**82**	**24**	**10**	**7**	....	**23**	**15**	**3**	....	**47**	**25**	**10**	....	**326**	**240**	**104**	**1st, Pacific Div.**	**Won Stanley Cup**
1994-95*	48	19	1	4	....	11	12	1	....	30	13	5	....	185	134	65	1st, Northeast Div.	Lost Conf. Quarter-Final
1993-94*	84	19	17	6	....	15	25	2	....	34	42	8	....	277	292	76	5th, Northeast Div.	Out of Playoffs
1992-93*	84	23	17	2	....	24	10	8	....	47	27	10	....	351	300	104	2nd, Adams Div.	Lost Div. Semi-Final
1991-92*	80	18	19	3	....	2	29	9	....	20	48	12	....	255	318	52	5th, Adams Div.	Out of Playoffs
1990-91*	80	9	23	8	....	7	27	6	....	16	50	14	....	236	354	46	5th, Adams Div.	Out of Playoffs
1989-90*	80	8	26	6	....	4	35	1	....	12	61	7	....	240	407	31	5th, Adams Div.	Out of Playoffs
1988-89*	80	16	20	4	....	11	26	3	....	27	46	7	....	269	342	61	5th, Adams Div.	Out of Playoffs
1987-88*	80	15	23	2	....	17	20	3	....	32	43	5	....	271	306	69	5th, Adams Div.	Out of Playoffs
1986-87*	80	20	13	7	....	11	26	3	....	31	39	10	....	267	276	72	4th, Adams Div.	Lost Div. Final
1985-86*	80	23	13	4	....	20	18	2	....	43	31	6	....	330	289	92	1st, Adams Div.	Lost Div. Semi-Final
1984-85*	80	24	12	4	....	17	18	5	....	41	30	9	....	323	275	91	2nd, Adams Div.	Lost Conf. Championship
1983-84*	80	24	11	5	....	18	17	5	....	42	28	10	....	360	278	94	3th, Adams Div.	Lost Div. Final
1982-83*	80	23	10	7	....	11	24	5	....	34	34	12	....	343	336	80	4th, Adams Div.	Lost Div. Semi-Final
1981-82*	80	24	13	3	....	9	18	13	....	33	31	16	....	356	345	82	4th, Adams Div.	Lost Conf. Championship
1980-81*	80	18	11	11	....	12	21	7	....	30	32	18	....	314	318	78	4th, Adams Div.	Lost Prelim. Round
1979-80*	80	17	16	7	....	8	28	4	....	25	44	11	....	248	313	61	5th, Adams Div.	Out of Playoffs

* Quebec Nordiques

NORTHWEST DIVISION
30th NHL Season

Franchise date: June 22, 1979

Transferred from Quebec to Denver, June 21, 1995.

2008-09 Player Personnel

FORWARDS	HT	WT	S	Place of Birth	*Age	2007-08 Club
ARNASON, Tyler	5-11	204	L	Oklahoma City, OK	29	Colorado
BURKI, Codey	6-0	190	L	Winnipeg, Man.	20	Lake Erie-Johnstown
DUPUIS, Philippe	6-0	196	R	Laval, Que.	23	Syracuse-Lake Erie
DURNO, Chris	6-4	205	L	Scarborough, Ont.	27	San Antonio
FRITSCHE, Tom	5-11	183	L	Parma, OH	22	Ohio State-Lake Erie
GALIARDI, T.J.	6-2	172	L	Calgary, Alta.	20	Calgary (WHL)
GUITE, Ben	6-1	211	R	Montreal, Que.	30	Colorado
HEJDUK, Milan	6-0	190	R	Usti nad Labem, Czech.	32	Colorado
HENDRICKS, Matt	6-0	215	L	Blaine, MN	27	Providence (AHL)
HENSICK, T.J.	5-10	185	R	Lansing, MI	22	Colorado-Lake Erie
JONES, David	6-2	220	R	Guelph, Ont.	24	Colorado-Lake Erie
LAPERRIERE, Ian	6-1	200	R	Montreal, Que.	34	Colorado
LEDIN, Per	6-0	194	L	Lulea, Sweden	30	HV 71
McCORMICK, Cody	6-3	215	R	London, Ont.	25	Colorado-Lake Erie
McLEOD, Cody	6-2	210	L	Binscarth, Man.	24	Colorado-Lake Erie
PARKER, Scott	6-5	240	R	Hanford, CA	30	Colorado
SAKIC, Joe	5-11	195	L	Burnaby, B.C.	39	Colorado
SERTICH, Marty	5-9	165	L	Roseville, MN	25	Iowa
SMITH, Nathan	6-2	206	L	Edmonton, Alta.	26	Pittsburgh-Wilkes-Barre
SMYTH, Ryan	6-1	190	L	Banff, Alta.	32	Colorado
STASTNY, Paul	6-0	205	L	Quebec City, Que.	22	Colorado
STEWART, Chris	6-2	228	R	Toronto, Ont.	20	Lake Erie
SVATOS, Marek	5-10	185	R	Kosice, Czech.	26	Colorado
TUCKER, Darcy	5-10	178	L	Castor, Alta.	33	Toronto
WILLSIE, Brian	6-1	202	R	London, Ont.	30	Los Angeles
WOLSKI, Wojtek	6-3	200	L	Zabrze, Poland	22	Colorado
DEFENSEMEN						
CAMPBELL, Darcy	6-1	180	L	Airdrie, Alta.	24	Syracuse-Lake Erie
CLARK, Brett	6-0	195	L	Wapella, Sask.	31	Colorado
CUMISKEY, Kyle	5-10	185	L	Abbotsford, B.C.	21	Colorado-Lake Erie
FOOTE, Adam	6-2	226	R	Toronto, Ont.	37	Columbus-Colorado
HANNAN, Scott	6-1	225	L	Richmond, B.C.	29	Colorado
LEOPOLD, Jordan	6-1	200	L	Golden Valley, MN	28	Colorado
LILES, John-Michael	5-10	185	L	Indianapolis, IN	27	Colorado
MACIAS, Ray	6-2	195	R	Long Beach, CA	22	Lake Erie-Johnstown
MacKENZIE, Aaron	6-0	193	L	Terrace Bay, Ont.	27	Peoria
O'NEILL, Wes	6-4	200	L	Windsor, Ont.	22	Lake Erie-Johnstown
PELTIER, Derek	5-11	190	L	Plymouth, MN	23	U. of Minnesota-Lake Erie
SALEI, Ruslan	6-1	212	L	Minsk, USSR	33	Florida-Colorado
TJARNQVIST, Daniel	6-2	200	L	Umea, Sweden	31	Yaroslavl
VERNACE, Michael	6-2	200	L	Toronto, Ont.	22	Lake Erie
WILLIAMS, Nigel	6-4	226	L	Aurora, IL	20	Saginaw-Belleville

GOALTENDERS	HT	WT	C	Place of Birth	*Age	2007-08 Club
BACASHIHUA, Jason	5-11	177	L	Garden City, MI	26	Peoria-Johnstown-Lake Erie
BUDAJ, Peter	6-1	200	L	Banska Bystrica, Czech.	26	Colorado
RAYCROFT, Andrew	6-0	185	L	Belleville, Ont.	28	Toronto
WEIMAN, Tyler	5-11	180	L	Saskatoon, Sask.	24	Colorado-Lake Erie

* – Age at start of 2008-09 season

2007-08 Scoring

* – rookie

Regular Season

Pos	#	Player	Team	GP	G	A	Pts	TOI	+/–	PIM	PP	SH	GW	S	%
C	26	Paul Stastny	COL	66	24	47	71	21:04	22	24	3	0	4	138	17.4
L	15	Andrew Brunette	COL	82	19	40	59	15:32	5	14	7	0	2	125	15.2
R	23	Milan Hejduk	COL	77	29	25	54	19:20	8	36	8	1	4	205	14.1
L	8	Wojtek Wolski	COL	77	18	30	48	15:55	10	14	4	0	6	158	11.4
C	19	Joe Sakic	COL	44	13	27	40	19:59	–4	20	5	0	1	124	10.5
R	40	Marek Svatos	COL	62	26	11	37	13:39	13	32	3	0	6	140	18.6
L	94	Ryan Smyth	COL	55	14	23	37	19:36	–4	50	2	0	3	168	8.3
D	4	John-Michael Liles	COL	81	6	26	32	19:40	2	26	5	0	1	163	3.7
C	39	Tyler Arnason	COL	70	10	21	31	15:15	–1	16	3	0	1	179	5.6
D	24	Ruslan Salei	FLA	65	3	20	23	23:16	–5	75	1	0	0	81	3.7
			COL	17	3	4	7	19:16	1	23	0	0	1	30	10.0
			Total	82	6	24	30	22:26	–4	98	1	0	1	111	5.4
C	17	Jaroslav Hlinka	COL	63	8	20	28	13:55	6	16	0	0	1	90	8.9
C	28	Ben Guite	COL	79	11	11	22	13:04	1	47	0	0	2	103	10.7
D	5	Brett Clark	COL	57	5	16	21	23:09	5	33	1	0	0	87	5.7
D	22	Scott Hannan	COL	82	2	19	21	22:40	–5	55	0	0	0	79	2.5
D	6	Jeff Finger	COL	72	8	11	19	19:57	12	40	1	1	1	93	8.6
R	14	Ian Laperriere	COL	70	4	15	19	13:39	–5	140	0	0	1	68	5.9
D	52	Adam Foote	CBJ	63	1	14	15	24:01	3	95	0	1	0	57	1.8
			COL	12	0	1	1	20:00	–1	12	0	0	0	9	0.0
			Total	75	1	15	16	23:23	2	107	0	1	0	66	1.5
C	21	Peter Forsberg	COL	9	1	13	14	19:14	7	8	0	0	0	15	6.7
D	44	Jordan Leopold	COL	43	5	8	13	15:59	5	20	2	0	1	35	14.3
C	37	* T.J. Hensick	COL	31	6	5	11	11:59	–4	2	4	0	1	52	11.5
L	55	* Cody McLeod	COL	49	4	5	9	10:07	–6	120	0	0	0	60	6.7
R	54	* David Jones	COL	27	2	4	6	11:21	–5	8	1	0	0	37	5.4
D	34	Kurt Sauer	COL	54	1	5	6	18:41	17	41	0	0	0	28	3.6
C	12	Brad Richardson	COL	22	2	3	5	13:28	–3	8	0	0	0	32	6.3
D	48	* Kyle Cumiskey	COL	38	0	5	5	12:07	–3	16	0	0	0	19	0.0
R	11	Cody McCormick	COL	40	2	2	4	10:58	5	50	0	0	1	45	4.4
C	10	Wyatt Smith	COL	25	0	3	3	11:38	–4	8	0	0	0	25	0.0
D	7	* Johnny Boychuk	COL	4	0	0	0	08:56	1	0	0	0	0	3	0.0
R	27	Scott Parker	COL	25	0	0	0	03:41	0	70	0	0	0	5	0.0

Goaltending

No.	Goaltender	GPI	Mins	Avg	W	L	OT	EN	SO	GA	SA	S%	G	A	PIM
35	* Tyler Weiman	1	16	0.00	0	0	0	0	0	0	10	1.000	0	0	0
60	Jose Theodore	53	3028	2.44	28	21	3	5	3	123	1367	.910	0	2	2
31	Peter Budaj	35	1912	2.57	16	10	4	6	0	82	849	.903	0	1	2
	Totals	**82**	**4988**	**2.60**	**44**	**31**	**7**	**11**	**3**	**216**	**2237**	**.903**			

Playoffs

Pos	#	Player	Team	GP	G	A	Pts	TOI	+/–	PIM	PP	SH	GW	OT	S	%
C	19	Joe Sakic	COL	10	2	8	10	19:07	–7	0	0	0	1	1	30	6.7
L	15	Andrew Brunette	COL	10	5	3	8	17:02	–5	2	3	0	0	0	18	27.8
R	23	Milan Hejduk	COL	10	3	3	6	19:04	–6	4	2	0	0	0	18	16.7
L	8	Wojtek Wolski	COL	7	2	3	5	13:15	–1	2	1	0	1	0	12	16.7
L	94	Ryan Smyth	COL	8	2	3	5	17:29	–1	2	1	0	1	0	22	9.1
C	39	Tyler Arnason	COL	10	2	3	5	14:12	–2	2	1	0	0	0	27	7.4
D	4	John-Michael Liles	COL	10	2	3	5	19:08	–1	2	1	0	0	0	21	9.5
C	21	Peter Forsberg	COL	7	1	4	5	18:16	3	14	0	0	0	0	13	7.7
D	24	Ruslan Salei	COL	10	1	4	5	20:51	0	4	1	0	0	0	10	10.0
C	26	Paul Stastny	COL	9	2	1	3	19:55	–1	6	0	0	1	0	16	12.5
D	44	Jordan Leopold	COL	7	0	3	3	16:59	0	0	0	0	0	0	5	0.0
R	14	Ian Laperriere	COL	10	1	1	2	12:53	0	19	0	0	0	0	12	8.3
L	55	* Cody McLeod	COL	10	1	1	2	12:22	–3	26	0	0	0	0	16	6.3
D	6	Jeff Finger	COL	5	0	2	2	22:05	–2	4	0	0	0	0	7	0.0
C	28	Ben Guite	COL	10	1	0	1	12:01	1	14	0	1	0	0	9	11.1
D	34	Kurt Sauer	COL	10	1	0	1	19:22	–3	8	0	0	0	0	5	20.0
C	37	* T.J. Hensick	COL	2	0	1	1	15:29	1	0	0	0	0	0	4	0.0
R	11	Cody McCormick	COL	4	0	1	1	11:52	–2	7	0	0	0	0	5	0.0
D	22	Scott Hannan	COL	9	0	1	1	19:15	0	4	0	0	0	0	10	0.0
R	54	* David Jones	COL	10	0	1	1	11:49	0	6	0	0	0	0	18	0.0
C	10	Wyatt Smith	COL	1	0	0	0	10:47	0	0	0	0	0	0	1	0.0
C	17	Jaroslav Hlinka	COL	1	0	0	0	15:15	–1	0	0	0	0	0	2	0.0
D	52	Adam Foote	COL	10	0	0	0	21:14	–6	6	0	0	0	0	5	0.0

Goaltending

No.	Goaltender	GPI	Mins	Avg	W	L	EN	SO	GA	SA	S%	G	A	PIM
60	Jose Theodore	10	514	3.15	4	6	0	0	27	286	.906	0	0	0
31	Peter Budaj	3	108	3.33	0	0	0	0	6	65	.908	0	0	0
	Totals	**10**	**624**	**3.17**	**4**	**6**	**0**	**0**	**33**	**351**				

Tony Granato

Head Coach

Born: Downers Grove, IL, July 25, 1964.

Tony Granato began his second tenure as head coach of the Colorado Avalanche on May 22, 2008. Granato previously served as the team's head coach from 2002 to 2004. After joining the club as an assistant coach on June 18, 2002, Granato was introduced as the 11th head coach in franchise history on December 18, 2002. The team posted a 32-11-4-4 stretch to close out the 2002-03 season with the franchise's NHL record ninth consecutive division title. Granato reached the 50-win mark in 87 games, the 11th fastest mark in NHL history. He returned to his position as assistant coach in 2005-06 and spent the next three years in that capacity.

Regarded as a feisty, two-way winger, Granato enjoyed a playing career that spanned 13 seasons in the National Hockey League. He skated in 773 regular season games with the New York Rangers, Los Angeles Kings and San Jose Sharks. During his tenure in the NHL, he posted 248 goals and 244 assists with 1,425 penalty minutes. Originally drafted by the New York Rangers 120th overall in the 1982 Entry Draft, Granato spent a season and a half with the Rangers before being dealt to the Los Angeles Kings, where he played six and a half seasons, cracking the 30-goal barrier three times. He played his final five seasons with San Jose after signing with the Sharks as a free agent in 1996.

Granato was named to the NHL All-Rookie Team in 1989, played in the NHL All-Star Game in 1997, and won the Bill Masterton Memorial Trophy, given for perseverance, sportsmanship and dedication to hockey, in 1997. Prior to joining the professional ranks, Granato played four years at the University of Wisconsin, where he was named to the WCHA Second All-Star Team for 1985 and 1987 and to the NCAA West Second All-Star Team in the same years. He was inducted into the University of Wisconsin's Hall of Fame. Granato was also a member of the 1988 U.S. National and Olympic hockey teams. His sister, Cammi, served as captain of the gold medal winning U.S. Women's National Hockey team at the 1998 Olympics and was a silver medalist in Salt Lake City in 2002.

Coaching Record

			Regular Season				Playoffs			
Season	Team	League	GC	W	L	O/T	GC	W	L	T
2002-03	Colorado	NHL	51	32	11	8	7	3	4	....
2003-04	Colorado	NHL	82	40	22	20	11	6	5	....
	NHL Totals		133	72	33	28	18	9	9	....

Coaching History

Jacques Demers, 1979-80; Maurice Filion and Michel Bergeron, 1980-81; Michel Bergeron, 1981-82 to 1986-87; Andre Savard and Ron Lapointe, 1987-88; Ron Lapointe and Jean Perron, 1988-89; Michel Bergeron, 1989-90; Dave Chambers, 1990-91; Dave Chambers and Pierre Page, 1991-92; Pierre Page, 1992-93, 1993-94; Marc Crawford, 1994-95 to 1997-98; Bob Hartley, 1998-99 to 2001-02; Bob Hartley and Tony Granato, 2002-03; Tony Granato, 2003-04; Joel Quenneville, 2004-05 to 2007-08; Tony Granato, 2008-09.

Captains' History

Marc Tardif, 1979-80, 1980-81; Robbie Ftorek and Andre Dupont, 1981-82; Mario Marois, 1982-83 to 1984-85; Mario Marois and Peter Stastny, 1985-86; Peter Stastny, 1986-87 to 1989-90; Joe Sakic and Steven Finn, 1990-91; Mike Hough, 1991-92; Joe Sakic, 1992-93 to date.

Club Records

Team

(Figures in brackets for season records are games played; records for fewest points, wins, ties, losses, goals, goals against are for 70 or more games)

Most Points **118** 2000-01 (82)
Most Wins **52** 2000-01 (82)
Most Ties **18** 1980-81 (80)
Most Losses **61** 1989-90 (80)
Most Goals **360** 1983-84 (80)
Most Goals Against **407** 1989-90 (80)
Fewest Points **31** 1989-90 (80)
Fewest Wins **12** 1989-90 (80)
Fewest Ties **5** 1987-88 (80)
Fewest Losses **16** 2000-01 (82)
Fewest Goals **212** 2001-02 (82)
Fewest Goals Against **169** 2001-02 (82)
Longest Winning Streak
Overall .... **12** Jan. 10-Feb. 7/99
Home .... **10** Nov. 26/83-Jan. 10/84, Mar. 6-Apr. 16/95
Away .... **7** Jan. 10-Feb. 7/99
Longest Undefeated Streak
Overall .... **12** Dec. 23/96-Jan. 20/97 (9 wins, 3 ties), Jan. 10-Feb. 7/99 (12 wins)
Home .... **14** Nov. 19/83-Jan. 21/84 (11 wins, 3 ties)
Away .... **10** Jan. 10-Mar. 3/99 (8 wins, 2 ties)
Longest Losing Streak
Overall .... **14** Oct. 21-Nov. 19/90
Home .... **8** Oct. 21-Nov. 24/90
Away .... **18** Jan. 18-Apr. 1/90
Longest Winless Streak
Overall .... **17** Oct. 21-Nov. 25/90 (15 losses, 2 ties)
Home .... **11** Nov. 14-Dec. 26/89 (7 losses, 4 ties)
Away .... **33** Oct. 8/91-Feb. 27/92 (25 losses, 8 ties)
Most Shutouts, Season **11** 2001-02 (82)
Most PIM, Season **2,104** 1989-90 (80)
Most Goals, Game .... **12** Feb. 1/83 (Hfd. 3 at Que. 12), Oct. 20/84 (Que. 12 at Tor. 3), Dec. 5/95 (S.J. 2 at Col. 12)

Individual

Most Seasons .... **19** Joe Sakic
Most Games .... **1,363** Joe Sakic
Most Goals, Career .... **623** Joe Sakic
Most Assists, Career ..... **1,006** Joe Sakic
Most Points, Career ...... **1,629** Joe Sakic (623G, 1,006A)
Most PIM, Career .... **1,562** Dale Hunter
Most Shutouts, Career .... **37** Patrick Roy
Longest Consecutive Games Streak .... **312** Dale Hunter (Oct. 9/80-Mar. 13/84)
Most Goals, Season .... **57** Michel Goulet (1982-83)
Most Assists, Season .... **93** Peter Stastny (1981-82)
Most Points, Season .... **139** Peter Stastny (1981-82; 46G, 93A)
Most PIM, Season .... **301** Gord Donnelly (1987-88)
Most Points, Defenseman, Season .... **82** Steve Duchesne (1992-93; 20G, 62A)
Most Points, Center, Season .... **139** Peter Stastny (1981-82; 46G, 93A)
Most Points, Right Wing, Season .... **103** Jacques Richard (1980-81; 52G, 51A)
Most Points, Left Wing, Season .... **121** Michel Goulet (1983-84; 56G, 65A)
Most Points, Rookie, Season .... **109** Peter Stastny (1980-81; 39G, 70A)
Most Shutouts, Season .... **9** Patrick Roy (2001-02)
Most Goals, Game .... **5** Mats Sundin (Mar. 5/92), Mike Ricci (Feb. 17/94)
Most Assists, Game .... **5** Eight times
Most Points, Game .... **8** Peter Stastny (Feb. 22/81; 4G, 4A), Anton Stastny (Feb. 22/81; 3G, 5A)

Records include Quebec Nordiques, 1979-80 through 1994-95.

Retired Numbers

3	J.C. Tremblay*	1972-1979
8	Marc Tardif*	1979-1983
16	Michel Goulet*	1979-1990
26	Peter Stastny*	1980-1990
33	Patrick Roy	1995-2003
77	Raymond Bourque	2000-2001

* Quebec Nordiques

All-time Record vs. Other Clubs

Regular Season

	At Home								On Road								Total							
	GP	W	L	T	OL	GF	GA	PTS	GP	W	L	T	OL	GF	GA	PTS	GP	W	L	T	OL	GF	GA	PTS
Anaheim	27	16	6	4	1	80	63	37	27	13	6	3	5	69	67	34	54	29	12	7	6	149	130	71
Atlanta	5	2	2	0	1	20	16	5	5	3	1	1	0	13	9	7	10	5	3	1	1	33	25	12
Boston	67	25	36	6	0	238	272	56	63	23	31	9	0	194	240	55	130	48	67	15	0	432	512	111
Buffalo	65	31	22	11	1	231	203	74	64	19	35	9	1	207	249	48	129	50	57	20	2	438	452	122
Calgary	59	27	20	11	1	213	189	66	59	22	28	9	0	173	205	53	118	49	48	20	1	386	394	119
Carolina	66	40	17	9	0	279	193	89	63	27	24	12	0	219	207	66	129	67	41	21	0	498	400	155
Chicago	45	24	13	6	2	177	142	56	47	19	25	3	0	145	159	41	92	43	38	9	2	322	301	97
Columbus	14	13	1	0	0	53	19	26	14	10	2	1	1	53	26	22	28	23	3	1	1	106	45	48
Dallas	47	25	12	7	3	167	121	60	47	16	25	5	1	131	159	38	94	41	37	12	4	298	280	98
Detroit	48	21	21	4	2	159	162	48	46	16	28	1	1	131	164	34	94	37	49	5	3	290	326	82
Edmonton	59	31	23	4	1	222	203	67	58	24	28	4	2	188	225	54	117	55	51	8	3	410	428	121
Florida	12	5	4	3	0	35	31	13	12	11	1	0	0	52	33	22	24	16	5	3	0	87	64	35
Los Angeles	48	25	20	3	0	193	162	53	49	16	27	5	1	163	195	38	97	41	47	8	1	356	357	91
Minnesota	23	16	5	2	0	74	54	34	22	10	6	1	5	62	55	26	45	26	11	3	5	136	109	60
Montreal	64	33	26	5	0	218	223	71	65	16	39	10	0	203	269	42	129	49	65	15	0	421	492	113
Nashville	18	9	6	2	1	48	41	21	18	8	5	3	2	57	52	21	36	17	11	5	3	105	93	42
New Jersey	36	18	14	4	0	126	102	40	37	14	19	4	0	125	150	32	73	32	33	8	0	251	252	72
NY Islanders	35	21	11	3	0	125	98	45	33	13	19	1	0	113	134	27	68	34	30	4	0	238	232	72
NY Rangers	36	20	13	3	0	147	133	43	35	12	19	4	0	101	135	28	71	32	32	7	0	248	268	71
Ottawa	16	12	3	1	0	72	47	25	19	8	8	3	0	66	54	19	35	20	11	4	0	138	101	44
Philadelphia	36	13	10	12	1	126	123	39	35	11	21	2	1	95	125	25	71	24	31	14	2	221	248	64
Phoenix	47	24	16	5	2	168	158	55	46	22	15	7	2	166	159	53	93	46	31	12	4	334	317	108
Pittsburgh	33	18	13	2	0	145	124	38	38	17	16	5	0	155	149	39	71	35	29	7	0	300	273	77
St. Louis	47	24	15	7	1	164	128	56	46	17	25	4	0	137	165	38	93	41	40	11	1	301	293	94
San Jose	29	17	7	4	1	103	58	39	30	18	11	1	0	107	85	37	59	35	18	5	1	210	143	76
Tampa Bay	14	9	3	2	0	54	30	20	13	4	8	1	0	35	39	9	27	13	11	3	0	89	69	29
Toronto	30	18	7	5	0	116	90	41	36	16	16	4	0	137	119	36	66	34	23	9	0	253	209	77
Vancouver	59	31	19	8	1	200	161	71	59	29	20	7	3	222	191	68	118	60	39	15	4	422	352	139
Washington	35	15	15	5	0	108	121	35	34	11	19	4	0	106	133	26	69	26	34	9	0	214	254	61
Totals	**1120**	**583**	**380**	**138**	**19**	**4061**	**3467**	**1323**	**1120**	**445**	**527**	**123**	**25**	**3625**	**3952**	**1038**	**2240**	**1028**	**907**	**261**	**44**	**7686**	**7419**	**2361**

Playoffs

	Series	W	L	GP	W	L	T	GF	GA	Last Mtg.	Rnd.	Result
Anaheim	1	0	1	4	0	4	0	4	16	2006	CSF	L 0-4
Boston	2	1	1	11	5	6	0	36	37	1983	DSF	L 1-3
Buffalo	2	2	0	8	6	2	0	35	27	1985	DSF	W 3-2
Carolina	2	1	1	9	4	5	0	34	35	1987	DSF	W 4-2
Chicago	2	2	0	12	8	4	0	49	28	1997	CQF	W 4-2
Dallas	4	2	2	24	14	10	0	66	62	2006	CQF	W 4-1
Detroit	6	3	3	34	17	17	0	88	97	2008	CSF	L 0-4
Edmonton	2	1	1	12	7	5	0	35	30	1998	CQF	L 3-4
Florida	1	1	0	4	4	0	0	15	4	1996	F	W 4-0
Los Angeles	2	2	0	14	8	6	0	33	23	2002	CQF	W 4-3
Minnesota	2	1	1	13	7	6	0	34	28	2008	CQF	W 4-2
Montreal	5	2	3	31	14	17	0	85	105	1993	DSF	L 2-4
New Jersey	1	1	0	7	4	3	0	19	11	2001	F	W 4-3
NY Islanders	1	0	1	4	0	4	0	9	18	1982	CF	L 0-4
NY Rangers	1	0	1	6	2	4	0	19	25	1995	CQF	L 2-4
Philadelphia	2	0	2	11	4	7	0	29	39	1985	CF	L 2-4
Phoenix	1	1	0	5	4	1	0	17	10	2000	CQF	W 4-1
St. Louis	1	1	0	5	4	1	0	17	11	2001	CF	W 4-1
San Jose	3	2	1	19	10	9	0	51	52	2004	CSF	L 2-4
Vancouver	2	2	0	10	8	2	0	40	26	2001	CQF	W 4-0
Totals	**43**	**25**	**18**	**243**	**130**	**113**	**0**	**715**	**684**			

Playoff Results 2008-2003

Year	Round	Opponent	Result	GF	GA
2008	CSF	Detroit	L 0-4	9	21
	CQF	Minnesota	W 4-2	17	12
2006	CSF	Anaheim	L 0-4	4	16
	CQF	Dallas	W 4-1	18	15
2004	CSF	San Jose	L 2-4	7	14
	CQF	Dallas	W 4-1	19	10
2003	CQF	Minnesota	L 3-4	17	16

Abbreviations: Round: F - Final; **CF** - conference final; **CSF** - conference semi-final; **CQF** - conference quarter-final; **DSF** - division semi-final.

Calgary totals include Atlanta Flames, 1979-80.
Dallas totals include Minnesota North Stars, 1979-80 to 1992-93.
Phoenix totals include Winnipeg, 1979-80 to 1995-96.
Carolina totals include Hartford, 1979-80 to 1996-97.
New Jersey totals include Colorado Rockies, 1979-80 to 1981-82.

2007-08 Results

Oct.	3	Dallas	4-3
	4	at Nashville	0-4
	7	San Jose	6-2
	12	at St. Louis	1-4
	13	Columbus	5-1
	16	Calgary	5-4†
	19	at Chicago	3-5
	21	at Minnesota	2-3
	23	at Edmonton	4-2
	26	at Calgary	3-2*
	28	Minnesota	3-1
Nov.	1	Pittsburgh	3-2
	3	Vancouver	3-4
	5	Calgary	4-1
	7	Edmonton	4-3†
	9	at Vancouver	1-2*
	11	Minnesota	4-2
	16	at Dallas	1-6
	18	at Minnesota	1-4
	20	at Calgary	1-4
	22	at Edmonton	3-2
	24	Calgary	2-5
	28	Edmonton	4-2
	30	at San Jose	2-3
Dec.	1	at Los Angeles	5-2
	3	San Jose	2-3
	5	at Columbus	4-5
	7	Philadelphia	2-1
	9	St. Louis	9-5
	12	at Columbus	1-4
	13	at Nashville	2-1
	15	Nashville	3-1
	17	at Los Angeles	4-2
	19	at Anaheim	1-2*
	21	NY Rangers	4-3*
	23	Vancouver	3-1
	27	Detroit	2-4
	29	Los Angeles	1-3
	31	at Phoenix	3-4†
Jan.	2	Phoenix	2-5
	5	NY Islanders	2-1*
	8	at Detroit	0-1
	9	at Washington	1-2
	12	at Carolina	5-4
	13	at Florida	4-3†
	15	at Tampa Bay	3-0
	18	Chicago	1-2†
	20	Columbus	3-1
	22	Nashville	0-4
	24	Minnesota	2-3
	30	Chicago	6-3
Feb.	1	at Detroit	0-2
	2	at St. Louis	6-4
	4	Phoenix	3-4*
	6	at San Jose	3-1
	9	at Vancouver	6-2
	12	Anaheim	1-2
	14	St. Louis	1-4
	17	at Chicago	1-2
	18	Detroit	0-4
	20	at Anaheim	2-3†
	22	at Phoenix	3-2†
	24	at Edmonton	2-3
	26	at Calgary	3-2*
	27	at Vancouver	3-2†
Mar.	1	Los Angeles	5-2
	4	Vancouver	2-1
	6	Anaheim	1-0
	8	Dallas	3-1
	9	at Dallas	0-3
	11	at Atlanta	5-2
	13	Edmonton	5-1
	15	New Jersey	2-4
	17	at Minnesota	1-3
	20	at Calgary	1-2
	22	at Edmonton	5-7
	24	Calgary	2-0
	26	Vancouver	6-3
	28	Edmonton	5-4†
	30	at Minnesota	2-3*
Apr.	1	at Vancouver	4-2
	6	Minnesota	4-3†

* – Overtime † – Shootout

Entry Draft Selections 2008-1994

Name in bold denotes played in NHL.

2008
Pick
50 Cameron Gaunce
61 Peter Delmas
110 Kelsey Tessier
140 Mark Olver
167 Joel Chouinard
170 Jonas Holos
200 Nathan Condon

2007
Pick
14 Kevin Shattenkirk
45 Colby Cohen
49 Trevor Cann
55 T.J. Galiardi
105 Brad Malone
113 Kent Patterson
135 Paul Carey
155 Jens Hellgren
195 Johan Alcen

2006
Pick
18 Chris Stewart
51 Nigel Williams
59 Codey Burki
81 Michael Carman
110 Kevin Montgomery
201 Billy Sauer

2005
Pick
34 Ryan Stoa
44 **Paul Stastny**
47 Tom Fritsche
52 Chris Durand
88 **T.J. Hensick**
124 Ray Macias
166 Jason Lynch
168 Justin Mercier
222 **Kyle Cumiskey**

2004
Pick
21 **Wojtek Wolski**
55 Victor Oreskovich
72 Denis Parshin
154 Richard Demen-Willaume
184 Derek Peltier
215 Ian Keserich
239 Brandon Yip
249 J.D. Corbin
281 Steve McClellan

2003
Pick
63 **David Liffiton**
131 David Svagrovsky
146 Mark McCutcheon
163 **Brad Richardson**
204 Linus Videll
225 Brett Hemingway
257 Darryl Yacboski
288 **David Jones**

2002
Pick
28 **Jonas Johansson**
61 **Johnny Boychuk**
94 Eric Lundberg
107 Mikko Kalteva
129 **Tom Gilbert**
164 **Tyler Weiman**
195 Taylor Christie
227 Ryan Steeves
258 Sergei Shemetov
289 Sean Collins

2001
Pick
63 **Peter Budaj**
97 **Danny Bois**
130 Colt King
143 Frantisek Skladany
144 **Cody McCormick**
149 Mikko Viitanen
165 Pierre-Luc Emond
184 Scott Horvath
196 **Charlie Stephens**
227 **Marek Svatos**

2000
Pick
14 **Vaclav Nedorost**
47 **Jared Aulin**
50 Sergei Soin
63 Agris Saviels
88 **Kurt Sauer**
92 Sergei Klyazmin
119 Brian Fahey
159 **John-Michael Liles**
189 Chris Bahen
221 Aaron Molnar
252 **Darryl Bootland**
266 Sean Kotary
285 Blake Ward

1999
Pick
25 **Mikhail Kuleshov**
45 **Martin Grenier**
93 **Branko Radivojevic**
112 Sanny Lindstrom
122 Kristian Kovac
142 Will Magnuson
152 **Jordan Krestanovich**
158 Anders Lovdahl
183 **Riku Hahl**
212 **Radim Vrbata**
240 **Jeff Finger**

1998
Pick
12 **Alex Tanguay**
17 **Martin Skoula**
19 **Robyn Regehr**
20 **Scott Parker**
28 **Ramzi Abid**
38 **Philippe Sauve**
53 **Steve Moore**
79 Evgeny Lazarev
141 K.C. Timmons
167 Alexander Ryazantsev

1997
Pick
26 Kevin Grimes
53 Graham Belak
55 **Rick Berry**
78 **Ville Nieminen**
87 **Brad Larsen**
133 Aaron Miskovich
161 **David Aebischer**
217 Doug Schmidt
243 Kyle Kidney
245 Stephen Lafleur

1996
Pick
25 **Peter Ratchuk**
51 **Yuri Babenko**
79 **Mark Parrish**
98 Ben Storey
107 Randy Petruk
134 Luke Curtin
146 **Brian Willsie**
160 Kai Fischer
167 **Dan Hinote**
176 **Samuel Pahlsson**
188 Roman Pylner
214 Matt Scorsune
240 Justin Clark

1995
Pick
25 **Marc Denis**
51 Nic Beaudoin
77 **John Tripp**
81 **Tomi Kallio**
129 **Brent Johnson**
155 John Cirjak
181 **Dan Smith**
207 Tomi Hirvonen
228 Chris George

1994
Pick
12 **Wade Belak**
22 Jeffrey Kealty
35 **Josef Marha**
61 Sebastien Bety
72 **Chris Drury**
87 **Milan Hejduk**
113 **Tony Tuzzolino**
139 Nicholas Windsor
165 Calvin Elfring
191 Jay Bertsch
217 **Tim Thomas**
243 Chris Pittman
285 Steven Low

General Managers' History

Maurice Filion, 1979-80 to 1987-88; Martin Madden, 1988-89; Martin Madden and Maurice Filion, 1989-90; Pierre Page, 1990-91 to 1993-94; Pierre Lacroix, 1994-95 to 2005-06; Francois Giguere, 2006-07 to date.

Francois Giguere

Executive Vice President and General Manager

Born: Ste-Foy, Que., June 24, 1963.

On May 24, 2006, the Colorado Avalanche announced the appointment of Francois Giguere as the club's executive vice president and general manager to lead the day-to-day operations of the club. Giguere returned to the franchise where he began his hockey tutelage over 16 years before. During that time, Giguere was involved with nearly every facet of an NHL hockey operation. Before spending five years with the Dallas Stars as assistant general manager, Giguere served as vice president of hockey operations for the Colorado Avalanche during the 2000-01 season. His roots with the organization date back to 1990 when he served as controller in the finance department with the Quebec Nordiques. In addition, he's held hockey administration (1992 to 1995), assistant GM (1995 to 2000) and VP hockey operations (2000-01) posts within the organization.

During his tenure with the Avalanche, Giguere was instrumental in developing and managing the hockey operations budget, and worked closely with Pierre Lacroix on contract negotiations, arbitration cases, player transactions and matters involving player personnel. He was also responsible for overseeing player development and player personnel staff and was the club's central liaison with its minor league hockey affiliates.

A 1985 graduate of Laval University where he obtained a degree in Administration, a license in accounting and a law certificate, Giguere worked for three years with a prominent Quebec accounting firm Caron Belanger Ernst and Young before being hired by the Nordiques as controller in 1990. His role with the Nordiques was expanded in 1992 to include hockey administration responsibilities by then general manager Pierre Page who needed additional support after Page assumed the head coaching role with the Nordiques in 1991. Pierre Lacroix named Giguere as assistant GM before the shortened 1994-95 season and he accompanied the franchise in its move to Colorado in May 1995.

Club Directory

Pepsi Center

Colorado Avalanche
Pepsi Center
1000 Chopper Circle
Denver, CO 80204
Phone **303/405-1100**
FAX 303/893-0614
Press Box 303/575-1926
www.coloradoavalanche.com
Capacity: 18,007

Owner & Governor	E. Stanley Kroenke
President & Alternate Governor	Pierre Lacroix
Exec. V.P., G.M. & Alternate Governor	Francois Giguere
Head Coach	Tony Granato
Assistant Coaches	Jacques Cloutier, Dave Barr
Goaltending Coach	Jeff Hackett
Assistant General Manager	Greg Sherman
Vice President of Hockey Operations	Craig Billington
Assistant to the Exec. V.P./General Manager	Michel Goulet
Director of Player Personnel	Brad Smith
Director of Amateur Scouting	Richard Pracey
Assistant Director of Amateur Scouting	Alan Hepple
Executive Director of Hockey Administration	Charlotte Grahame
Video Coordinator	PJ DeLuca
Team Services Coordinator	Erin DeGraff
Pro Scouts	Garth Joy, Terry Martin
Scouts	Anders Carlsson, Marc Fortier, Ted Hampson, Michal Krupa, Kirill Ladygin, Rick Lanz, Joni Lehto, Don Paarup, Guy Perron, Neil Shea
Strength and Conditioning Coach	Paul Goldberg
Head Athletic Trainer	Matthew Sokolowski
Assistant Athletic Trainer/Physical Therapist	Scott Woodward
Massage Therapist	Gregorio Pradera
Head Equipment Manager	Mark Miller
Inventory Manager	Wayne Flemming
Assistant Equipment Managers	Kurt Harvey, Cliff Halstead
Communications Department	
Sr. V.P., Communications & Business Operations	Jean Martineau
Director of Communications	Damen Zier
Director of Media Services/Internet	Brendan McNicholas
Website Coordinator	Craig Stancher
Lake Erie Monsters (AHL affiliate)	
General Manager	David Oliver
Head Coach	Joe Sacco
Assistant Coach	Sylvain Lefebvre
Head Athletic Trainer	Glenn Burke
Head Equipment Manager	Terry Geer
Team Information	
Practice Facility	South Suburban Family Sports Center
Television Outlet	Altitude Sports & Entertainment Network
Radio	Altitude Radio Network (flagship: AM 1510)

Picked 288th by Colorado among the 292 choices in the 2003 Entry Draft, David Jones made his NHL debut with the Avalanche in 2007-08. He had two goals and four assists in 27 games.

Columbus Blue Jackets

2007-08 Results: 34W-36L-4OTL-8SOL 80PTS.
Fourth, Central Division

Key Off-Season Signings/Acquisitions

2008

April 29 • Re-signed D **Jan Hejda**.
June 20 • Selected LW **Nikita Filatov** (CSKA, Russia) sixth overall in the 2008 Entry Draft.
20 • Acquired C **R.J. Umberger** and a 4th-round pick in 2008 from Philadelphia for a 1st-round pick and 3rd-round pick in 2008.
July 1 • Acquired LW **Raffi Torres** from Edmonton for C **Gilbert Brule**.
1 • Signed D **Mike Commodore**.
2 • Acquired D **Fedor Tyutin** and D **Christian Backman** from NY Rangers for RW **Nikolai Zherdev** and C **Dan Fritsche**
2 • Signed LW **Kristian Huselius**.
9 • Re-signed head coach **Ken Hitchcock**.
11 • Re-signed C **Michael Peca**.
14 • Signed LW **Craig MacDonald**.

Year-by-Year Record

		Home				Road				Overall								
Season	**GP**	**W**	**L**	**T**	**OL**	**W**	**L**	**T**	**OL**	**W**	**L**	**T**	**OL**	**GF**	**GA**	**Pts.**	**Finished**	**Playoff Result**
2007-08	82	20	14	....	7	14	22	....	5	34	36	....	12	193	218	80	4th, Central Div.	Out of Playoffs
2006-07	82	18	19	....	4	15	23	....	3	33	42	....	7	201	249	73	4th, Central Div.	Out of Playoffs
2005-06	82	23	18	....	0	12	25	....	4	35	43	....	4	223	279	74	3rd, Central Div.	Out of Playoffs
2004-05	....	....	....	....	....	....	....	....	....	....	....	....	....	....	....	....		
2003-04	82	17	18	4	2	8	27	4	2	25	45	8	4	177	238	62	4th, Central Div.	Out of Playoffs
2002-03	82	20	14	5	2	9	28	3	1	29	42	8	3	213	263	69	5th, Central Div.	Out of Playoffs
2001-02	82	14	18	5	4	8	29	3	1	22	47	8	5	164	255	57	5th, Central Div.	Out of Playoffs
2000-01	82	19	15	4	3	9	24	5	3	28	39	9	6	190	233	71	5th, Central Div.	Out of Playoffs

2008-09 Schedule

Oct.	Fri.	10	at Dallas
	Sat.	11	at Phoenix
	Tue.	14	at San Jose
	Fri.	17	Nashville
	Sat.	18	at Nashville
	Tue.	21	Vancouver
	Fri.	24	NY Rangers
	Sat.	25	at Minnesota
	Mon.	27	Anaheim
	Thu.	30	at Colorado
Nov.	Sat.	1	Chicago
	Mon.	3	at NY Islanders
	Wed.	5	Edmonton
	Fri.	7	Montreal
	Sat.	8	Calgary
	Wed.	12	Phoenix
	Fri.	14	at Buffalo
	Sat.	15	at Minnesota
	Tue.	18	Edmonton
	Sat.	22	at Atlanta
	Wed.	26	Phoenix
	Fri.	28	at Detroit
	Sat.	29	Washington
Dec.	Mon.	1	Vancouver
	Thu.	4	at San Jose
	Sat.	6	at Los Angeles
	Sun.	7	at Anaheim*
	Thu.	11	Nashville
	Sat.	13	NY Islanders
	Sun.	14	at Chicago
	Wed.	17	San Jose
	Thu.	18	at Dallas
	Sat.	20	at Phoenix
	Tue.	23	Los Angeles
	Sat.	27	Philadelphia
	Mon.	29	at Los Angeles
	Wed.	31	at Anaheim
Jan.	Fri.	2	at Colorado
	Sat.	3	at St. Louis
	Tue.	6	at Detroit
	Fri.	9	at Washington
	Sat.	10	Minnesota
	Tue.	13	Colorado
	Fri.	16	New Jersey
	Sun.	18	at Vancouver*
	Tue.	20	at Edmonton
	Wed.	21	at Calgary
	Tue.	27	Detroit
	Fri.	30	Ottawa
	Sat.	31	Dallas
Feb.	Tue.	3	St. Louis
	Fri.	6	at Pittsburgh
	Sat.	7	San Jose
	Tue.	10	Colorado
	Fri.	13	Detroit
	Sat.	14	at Carolina
	Mon.	16	Dallas
	Wed.	18	St. Louis
	Thu.	19	at Toronto
	Sat.	21	Anaheim
	Tue.	24	at Calgary
	Thu.	26	at Edmonton
Mar.	Sun.	1	at Vancouver*
	Tue.	3	Los Angeles
	Thu.	5	at Nashville
	Sat.	7	at Detroit
	Tue.	10	Boston
	Thu.	12	Pittsburgh
	Fri.	13	at Chicago
	Sun.	15	Detroit*
	Wed.	18	Chicago
	Sat.	21	at Florida
	Tue.	24	at Tampa Bay
	Thu.	26	Calgary
	Sat.	28	at St. Louis
	Sun.	29	St. Louis*
	Tue.	31	Nashville
Apr.	Sat.	4	at Nashville
	Sun.	5	Chicago*
	Wed.	8	at Chicago
	Fri.	10	at St. Louis
	Sat.	11	Minnesota

* Denotes afternoon game.

Rick Nash led the Blue Jackets in goals for the fourth straight season with 38 in 2007-08. He also established a career high with 31 assists to lead the team with 69 points.

CENTRAL DIVISION
9th NHL Season
Franchise date: June 25, 1997

2008-09 Player Personnel

FORWARDS	HT	WT	S	Place of Birth	*Age	2007-08 Club
BOLL, Jared	6-2	206	R	Crystal Lake, IL	22	Columbus
BRASSARD, Derick	6-0	188	L	Hull, Que.	21	Columbus-Syracuse
CHIMERA, Jason	6-2	216	L	Edmonton, Alta.	29	Columbus
DORSETT, Derek	5-11	187	R	Kindersley, Sask.	21	Syracuse
FILATOV, Nikita	6-0	172	R	Moscow, USSR	18	CSKA 2-CSKA
HUSELIUS, Kristian	6-1	179	L	Osterhaninge, Sweden	29	Calgary
KELLY, Steve	6-2	205	L	Vancouver, B.C.	31	Minnesota-Houston
MacDONALD, Craig	6-1	201	L	Antigonish, N.S.	31	Tampa Bay-Norfolk
MacKENZIE, Derek	5-10	178	L	Sudbury, Ont.	27	Columbus-Syracuse
MALHOTRA, Manny	6-2	217	L	Mississauga, Ont.	28	Columbus
MODIN, Fredrik	6-4	217	L	Sundsvall, Sweden	33	Columbus
MURRAY, Andrew	6-2	216	L	Selkirk, Man.	26	Columbus-Syracuse
NASH, Rick	6-4	218	L	Brampton, Ont.	24	Columbus
NOVOTNY, Jiri	6-3	209	R	Pelhrimov, Czech.	25	Columbus
PECA, Michael	5-11	183	R	Toronto, Ont.	34	Columbus
PICARD, Alexandre	6-2	194	L	Les Saules, Que.	22	Columbus-Syracuse
SESTITO, Tom	6-5	226	L	Utica, NY	21	Columbus-Syracuse
TORRES, Raffi	6-0	215	L	Toronto, Ont.	26	Edmonton
UMBERGER, R.J.	6-2	200	L	Pittsburgh, PA	26	Philadelphia
VIGILANTE, John	6-0	190	L	Dearborn, MI	23	Milwaukee
VORACEK, Jakub	6-1	205	L	Kladno, Czech.	19	Halifax
YORK, Mike	5-10	185	R	Waterford, MI	30	Phoenix
DEFENSEMEN						
BACKMAN, Christian	6-4	210	L	Alingsas, Alingsas	28	St. Louis-NY Rangers
COMMODORE, Mike	6-5	228	R	Fort Saskatchewan, Alta.	28	Carolina-Ottawa
HEJDA, Jan	6-3	229	L	Prague, Czech.	30	Columbus
KLESLA, Rostislav	6-3	220	L	Novy Jicin, Czech.	26	Columbus
METHOT, Marc	6-3	224	L	Ottawa, Ont.	23	Columbus-Syracuse
ROME, Aaron	6-1	204	L	Nesbitt, Man.	25	CBJ-Port (AHL)-Syr
RUSSELL, Kris	5-10	180	L	Caroline, Alta.	21	Columbus
SIGALET, Jonathan	6-1	185	L	Vancouver, B.C.	22	Providence (AHL)
TOLLEFSEN, Ole-Kristian	6-2	211	L	Oslo, Norway	24	Columbus
TYUTIN, Fedor	6-3	210	L	Izhevsk, USSR	25	NY Rangers
WILSON, Clay	6-0	195	L	Sturgeon Lake, MN	25	Port (AHL)-CBJ-Syr

GOALTENDERS	HT	WT	C	Place of Birth	*Age	2007-08 Club
LACOSTA, Dan	6-2	194	L	Labrador City, Nfld.	22	Columbus-Syracuse-Elmira
LECLAIRE, Pascal	6-2	200	L	Repentigny, Que.	25	Columbus
MASON, Steve	6-4	202	R	Oakville, Ont.	20	London-Kitchener
NORRENA, Fredrik	6-0	189	L	Pietarsaari, Finland	34	Columbus

* – Age at start of 2008-09 season

2007-08 Scoring

* – rookie

Regular Season

Pos	#	Player	Team	GP	G	A	Pts	TOI	+/-	PIM	PP	SH	GW	S	%
L	61	Rick Nash	CBJ	80	38	31	69	20:29	2	95	10	4	6	329	11.6
R	13	Nikolai Zherdev	CBJ	82	26	35	61	19:22	–9	34	7	0	3	254	10.2
C	19	Michael Peca	CBJ	65	8	26	34	18:34	–1	64	3	0	3	86	9.3
D	6	Ron Hainsey	CBJ	78	8	24	32	22:33	–7	25	8	0	0	161	5.0
L	25	Jason Chimera	CBJ	81	14	17	31	17:29	–5	98	1	1	3	198	7.1
C	27	Manny Malhotra	CBJ	71	11	18	29	16:27	–3	34	2	0	2	112	9.8
R	9	David Vyborny	CBJ	66	7	19	26	15:29	–8	34	2	0	0	106	6.6
C	49	Dan Fritsche	CBJ	69	10	12	22	12:20	2	22	1	1	4	109	9.2
C	12	Jiri Novotny	CBJ	65	8	14	22	17:43	–10	24	1	0	0	91	8.8
D	97	Rostislav Klesla	CBJ	82	6	12	18	23:12	7	60	3	0	1	130	4.6
D	23	Dick Tarnstrom	EDM	29	1	4	5	19:35	–6	40	0	0	0	22	4.5
			CBJ	19	2	7	9	19:03	–5	12	1	0	0	22	9.1
			Total	48	3	11	14	19:22	–11	52	1	0	0	44	6.8
D	8	Jan Hejda	CBJ	81	0	13	13	21:07	20	61	0	0	0	71	0.0
L	33	Fredrik Modin	CBJ	23	6	6	12	16:50	1	20	2	0	1	41	14.6
C	51	* Andrew Murray	CBJ	39	6	4	10	11:42	0	12	0	0	0	45	13.3
R	40	* Jared Boll	CBJ	75	5	5	10	08:00	–4	226	0	0	3	63	7.9
D	2	* Kris Russell	CBJ	67	2	8	10	14:47	–12	14	1	0	1	90	2.2
C	17	Gilbert Brule	CBJ	61	1	8	9	09:53	–4	24	0	0	1	74	1.4
C	38	* Joakim Lindstrom	CBJ	25	3	4	7	09:26	0	14	2	0	1	25	12.0
D	55	Ole-Kristian Tollefsen	CBJ	51	2	2	4	12:18	–3	111	0	1	0	21	9.5
D	10	Duvie Westcott	CBJ	23	1	3	4	16:25	–10	30	1	0	0	27	3.7
C	26	Derek MacKenzie	CBJ	17	2	0	2	07:46	–2	8	0	0	0	19	10.5
D	4	* Clay Wilson	CBJ	7	1	1	2	16:55	3	2	0	0	0	12	8.3
D	44	* Aaron Rome	CBJ	17	1	1	2	18:10	–4	33	0	0	0	15	6.7
C	16	* Derick Brassard	CBJ	17	1	1	2	09:03	–4	6	0	0	0	13	7.7
L	43	* Tommy Sestito	CBJ	1	0	0	0	04:36	0	17	0	0	0	0	0.0
C	28	Zenon Konopka	CBJ	3	0	0	0	07:54	0	15	0	0	0	4	0.0
L	21	Alexandre Picard	CBJ	3	0	0	0	06:46	0	2	0	0	0	1	0.0
R	41	* Adam Pineault	CBJ	3	0	0	0	11:02	–2	0	0	0	0	5	0.0
D	29	* Marc Methot	CBJ	9	0	0	0	14:13	–1	8	0	0	0	9	0.0

Goaltending

No.	Goaltender	GPI	Mins	Avg	W	L	OT	EN	SO	GA	SA	S%	G	A	PIM
34	* Dan Lacosta	1	13	0.00	0	0	0	0	0	0	5	1.000	0	0	0
31	Pascal Leclaire	54	2986	2.25	24	17	6	3	9	112	1379	.919	0	2	2
30	Fredrik Norrena	37	1960	2.72	10	19	6	6	2	89	856	.896	0	1	0
	Totals	**82**	**4988**	**2.53**	**34**	**36**	**12**	**9**	**11**	**210**	**2249**	**.907**			

Fellow goalie Fredrik Norrena congratulates Pascal Leclaire after a shutout in Buffalo. Leclaire posted four shutouts in his first six games and finished the 2007-08 season with nine.

Ken Hitchcock

Head Coach

Born: Edmonton, Alta., December 17, 1951.

Ken Hitchcock was named head coach of the Columbus Blue Jackets on November 22, 2006. In eight full seasons behind the bench before arriving in Columbus, Hitchcock led his teams to six division titles (Dallas, Central Division: 1996 to 2001; Philadelphia, Atlantic Division: 2003-04) and had a pair of second place finishes while recording at least 40 wins and 100 points in each of those campaigns. He also led his teams to a 66-51 record in the Stanley Cup playoffs, including a 16-7 mark in 1998-99 when he guided the Dallas Stars to the Stanley Cup championship.

Hitchcock began his professional coaching career as an assistant coach with the Flyers from 1990 to 1993 before spending two-plus seasons as the head coach of the Kalamazoo Wings/Michigan K-Wings, International Hockey League affiliate of the Dallas Stars. He took over as head coach of the Stars midway through the 1995-96 season and in his first full season at the helm led them to the Central Division title. That year, Dallas became just the ninth team in NHL history to go from last place to first place in one season. The club's 38-point improvement from 66 to 104 was tied for the fifth-best in league history. He holds Stars franchise records for career wins (277), playoff wins (47), regular-season winning percentage (.610) and playoff winning percentage (.588) and in 1998-99 led the club to franchise single season records for wins, points and highest winning percentage with a 51-19-12 record.

On May 14, 2002, Hitchcock was named Flyers head coach and led the club to three-straight 100-point seasons, capturing the Atlantic Division title in 2003-04 and also advanced to the Eastern Conference Finals that year. On March 21, 2006, Hitchcock guided the Flyers to a 2-1 win over New Jersey, becoming the fifth-fastest coach in NHL history to record 400 wins (736 games). The Edmonton, Alberta native has represented Canada at numerous international competitions, winning gold medals as an assistant/associate coach at the 2002 Salt Lake City Olympics, the 2004 World Cup of Hockey, the 2002 World Championship and the 1987 World Junior Championship. Prior to joining the professional ranks, Hitchcock was one of the winningest coaches in the history of the Western Hockey League with the Kamloops Blazers.

Coaching History

Dave King, 2000-01, 2001-02; Dave King and Doug MacLean, 2002-03; Doug MacLean and Gerard Gallant, 2003-04; Gerard Gallant, 2004-05, 2005-06; Gerard Gallant, Gary Agnew and Ken Hitchcock, 2006-07; Ken Hitchcock, 2007-08 to date.

Coaching Record

			Regular Season				Playoffs			
Season	Team	League	GC	W	L	O/T	GC	W	L	T
1984-85	Kamloops	WHL	71	52	17	2	15	10	5	....
1985-86	Kamloops	WHL	72	49	19	4	16	14	2	....
1986-87	Kamloops	WHL	72	55	14	3	13	8	5	....
1987-88	Kamloops	WHL	72	45	26	1	18	12	6	....
1988-89	Kamloops	WHL	72	34	33	5	16	8	8	....
1989-90	Kamloops	WHL	72	56	16	0	17	14	3	....
1993-94	Kalamazoo	IHL	81	48	26	7	5	1	4	....
1994-95	Kalamazoo	IHL	81	43	24	14	16	10	6	....
1995-96	Michigan	IHL	40	19	10	11	....	....	....	....
1995-96	**Dallas**	**NHL**	**43**	**15**	**23**	**5**	....	....	....	....
1996-97	**Dallas**	**NHL**	**82**	**48**	**26**	**8**	**7**	**3**	**4**	....
1997-98	**Dallas**	**NHL**	**82**	**49**	**22**	**11**	**17**	**10**	**7**	....
1998-99 ♦	**Dallas**	**NHL**	**82**	**51**	**19**	**12**	**23**	**16**	**7**	....
99-2000	**Dallas**	**NHL**	**82**	**43**	**23**	**16**	**23**	**14**	**9**	....
2000-01	**Dallas**	**NHL**	**82**	**48**	**24**	**10**	**10**	**4**	**6**	....
2001-02	**Dallas**	**NHL**	**50**	**23**	**17**	**10**	....	....	....	....
2002-03	**Philadelphia**	**NHL**	**82**	**45**	**20**	**17**	**13**	**6**	**7**	....
2003-04	**Philadelphia**	**NHL**	**82**	**40**	**21**	**21**	**18**	**11**	**7**	....
2004-05	**Philadelphia**				SEASON CANCELLED					
2005-06	**Philadelphia**	**NHL**	**82**	**45**	**26**	**11**	**6**	**2**	**4**	....
2006-07	**Philadelphia**	**NHL**	**8**	**1**	**6**	**1**	....	....	....	....
2006-07	**Columbus**	**NHL**	**62**	**28**	**29**	**5**	....	....	....	....
2007-08	**Columbus**	**NHL**	**82**	**34**	**36**	**12**	....	....	....	....
	NHL Totals		**901**	**470**	**292**	**139**	**117**	**66**	**51**	....

♦ Stanley Cup win.

Club Records

Team

(Figures in brackets for season records are games played.)

Most Points **80** 2007-08 (82)
Most Wins **35** 2005-06 (82)
Most Ties **9** 2000-01 (82)
Most Losses **47** 2001-02 (82)
Most Goals **223** 2005-06 (82)
Most Goals Against **279** 2005-06 (82)
Fewest Points **57** 2001-02 (82)
Fewest Wins **22** 2001-02 (82)
Fewest Ties **8** 2001-02 (82), 2002-03 (82), 2003-04 (82)
Fewest Losses **36** 2007-08 (82)
Fewest Goals **164** 2001-02 (82)
Fewest Goals Against **218** 2007-08 (82)

Longest Winning Streak
Overall .... **6** Mar. 24-Apr. 3/06
Home .... **6** Jan. 20-Feb. 8/06, Dec. 26/07-Jan. 15/08
Away .... **4** Dec. 2-12/06

Longest Undefeated Streak
Overall .... **6** Mar. 24-Apr. 3/06 (6 wins)
Home .... **6** Jan. 20-Feb. 12/03 (4 wins, 2 ties)
Away .... **4** Jan. 3-11/03 (3 wins, 1 tie), Dec. 2-12/06 (4 wins)

Longest Losing Streak
Overall .... **8** Nov. 17-Dec. 3/00, Mar. 3-18/04
Home .... **6** Oct. 12-Nov. 9/01
Away .... **11** Mar. 25-Oct. 29/02

Longest Winless Streak
Overall .... **9** Dec. 4-23/03 (8 losses, 1 tie)
Home .... **8** Oct. 4-Nov. 9/01 (6 losses, 2 ties), Dec. 4-31/03 (7 losses, 1 tie)
Away .... **14** Oct. 9-Dec. 23/03 (13 losses, 1 tie)

Most Shutouts, Season **11** 2007-08 (82)
Most PIM, Season **1,505** 2002-03 (82)
Most Goals, Game .... **7** Five times

Individual

Most Seasons .... **7** Rostislav Klesla, Jody Shelley, David Vyborny
Most Games .... **543** David Vyborny
Most Goals, Career .... **154** Rick Nash
Most Assists, Career .... **204** David Vyborny
Most Points, Career .... **317** David Vyborny (113G, 204A)
Most PIM, Career .... **1,025** Jody Shelley
Most Shutouts, Career .... **12** Marc Denis
Longest Consecutive Games Streak .... **243** Jason Chimera (Oct. 9/05-Apr. 5/08)
Most Goals, Season .... **41** Rick Nash (2003-04)
Most Assists, Season .... **52** Ray Whitney (2002-03)
Most Points, Season .... **76** Ray Whitney (2002-03; 24G, 52A)
Most PIM, Season .... **249** Jody Shelley (2002-03)
Most Points, Defenseman, Season .... **45** Jaroslav Spacek (2002-03; 9G, 36A)
Most Points, Center, Season .... **68** Andrew Cassels (2002-03; 20G, 48A)
Most Points, Right Wing, Season .... **65** David Vyborny (2005-06; 22G, 43A)
Most Points, Left Wing, Season .... **76** Ray Whitney (2002-03; 24G, 52A)
Most Points, Rookie, Season .... **39** Rick Nash (2002-03; 17G, 22A)
Most Shutouts, Season .... **9** Pascal Leclaire (2007-08)
Most Goals, Game .... **4** Geoff Sanderson (Mar. 29/03)
Most Assists, Game .... **5** Espen Knutsen (Mar. 24/01)
Most Points, Game .... **5** Espen Knutsen (Mar. 24/01; 5A), Geoff Sanderson (Mar. 29/03; 4G, 1A), Andrew Cassels (Mar. 29/03; 1G, 4A), David Vyborny (Feb. 28/04; 1G, 4A)

Captains' History

Lyle Odelein, 2000-01, 2001-02; Ray Whitney, 2002-03; Luke Richardson, 2003-04; Luke Richardson and Adam Foote, 2005-06; Adam Foote, 2006-07; Adam Foote and Rick Nash, 2007-08; Rick Nash, 2008-09.

All-time Record vs. Other Clubs

Regular Season

	At Home								On Road								Total							
	GP	W	L	T	OL	GF	GA	PTS	GP	W	L	T	OL	GF	GA	PTS	GP	W	L	T	OL	GF	GA	PTS
Anaheim	14	8	5	0	1	39	32	17	14	5	6	1	2	33	41	13	28	13	11	1	3	72	73	30
Atlanta	5	3	2	0	0	14	11	6	4	1	3	0	0	8	10	2	9	4	5	0	0	22	21	8
Boston	4	2	2	0	0	8	18	4	3	1	2	0	0	7	10	2	7	3	4	0	0	15	28	6
Buffalo	3	2	0	1	0	8	6	5	5	3	2	0	0	12	13	6	8	5	2	1	0	20	19	11
Calgary	14	10	3	0	1	41	29	21	14	5	9	0	0	28	39	10	28	15	12	0	1	69	68	31
Carolina	4	2	2	0	0	10	10	4	5	1	4	0	0	12	15	2	9	3	6	0	0	22	25	6
Chicago	23	13	9	1	0	76	73	27	22	8	12	1	1	51	67	18	45	21	21	2	1	127	140	45
Colorado	14	3	10	1	0	26	53	7	14	1	12	0	1	19	53	3	28	4	22	1	1	45	106	10
Dallas	14	4	8	0	2	32	44	10	14	3	10	0	1	25	43	7	28	7	18	0	3	57	87	17
Detroit	23	6	11	1	5	49	75	18	22	5	15	0	2	49	82	12	45	11	26	1	7	98	157	30
Edmonton	14	3	7	3	1	31	45	10	14	3	9	0	2	30	49	8	28	6	16	3	3	61	94	18
Florida	3	1	2	0	0	6	9	2	4	2	2	0	0	12	13	4	7	3	4	0	0	18	22	6
Los Angeles	14	9	4	0	1	39	44	19	14	5	8	1	0	30	36	11	28	14	12	1	1	69	80	30
Minnesota	13	9	3	1	0	35	22	19	14	4	8	0	2	29	42	10	27	13	11	1	2	64	64	29
Montreal	2	0	2	0	0	3	6	0	5	3	1	1	0	9	6	7	7	3	3	1	0	12	12	7
Nashville	22	8	12	0	2	49	67	18	23	4	17	1	1	45	76	10	45	12	29	1	3	94	143	28
New Jersey	5	3	2	0	0	16	15	6	3	0	2	1	0	4	6	1	8	3	4	1	0	20	21	7
NY Islanders	5	4	0	1	0	17	10	9	3	2	1	0	0	11	11	4	8	6	1	1	0	28	21	13
NY Rangers	5	4	1	0	0	20	10	8	3	1	1	1	0	8	9	3	8	5	2	1	0	28	19	11
Ottawa	3	1	1	1	0	13	11	3	4	1	2	1	0	9	14	3	7	2	3	2	0	22	25	6
Philadelphia	4	0	2	2	0	7	10	2	3	0	2	1	0	5	10	1	7	0	4	3	0	12	20	3
Phoenix	14	7	6	1	0	36	31	15	14	4	6	3	1	35	43	12	28	11	12	4	1	71	74	27
Pittsburgh	4	2	0	0	2	16	10	6	4	1	3	0	0	12	17	2	8	3	3	0	2	28	27	8
St. Louis	22	11	6	2	3	58	54	27	23	6	13	1	3	55	83	16	45	17	19	3	6	113	137	43
San Jose	14	7	6	0	1	36	30	15	14	1	11	0	2	21	55	4	28	8	17	0	3	57	85	19
Tampa Bay	4	2	1	1	0	10	7	5	4	1	3	0	0	5	9	2	8	3	4	1	0	15	16	7
Toronto	2	1	1	0	0	6	7	2	4	0	3	1	0	5	13	1	6	1	4	1	0	11	20	3
Vancouver	14	5	6	2	1	34	48	13	14	4	9	0	1	36	53	9	28	9	15	2	2	70	101	22
Washington	5	1	2	0	2	14	19	4	3	0	2	1	0	7	11	1	8	1	4	1	2	21	30	5
Totals	**287**	**131**	**116**	**18**	**22**	**749**	**806**	**302**	**287**	**75**	**178**	**15**	**19**	**612**	**929**	**184**	**574**	**206**	**294**	**33**	**41**	**1361**	**1735**	**486**

2007-08 Results

Oct.	5	Anaheim	4-0		5	at San Jose	2-3
	6	at Minnesota	2-3		8	at St. Louis	1-6
	10	Phoenix	3-0		11	St. Louis	6-4
	13	at Colorado	1-5		12	Nashville	2-1†
	17	Dallas	2-3†		15	Vancouver	3-2
	19	at Buffalo	3-0		17	at Phoenix	4-3
	21	Vancouver	1-4		19	at Dallas	1-3
	23	at Chicago	7-4		20	at Colorado	1-3
	25	St. Louis	3-0		22	at Dallas	4-2
	27	San Jose	2-1		24	at Chicago	1-0
	31	at Los Angeles	4-1		29	Phoenix	2-4
Nov.	1	at Anaheim	1-2†		31	at Nashville	2-4
	4	St. Louis	3-0	**Feb.**	2	Minnesota	1-4
	7	at Chicago	2-5		5	Washington	3-4*
	9	at Detroit	1-4		7	at Phoenix	2-1
	10	at Nashville	3-4†		8	at San Jose	1-2*
	12	Nashville	1-4		10	Los Angeles	2-3†
	14	Chicago	4-2		13	Chicago	2-7
	16	at St. Louis	2-3		15	at Detroit	5-1
	18	Detroit	4-5†		17	at St. Louis	1-5
	21	Florida	2-5		19	at Toronto	1-3
	23	at Minnesota	4-0		21	at Ottawa	3-2†
	24	Detroit	3-2†		23	at Montreal	3-0
	26	at Edmonton	1-3		27	San Jose	2-4
	29	at Vancouver	0-2		29	at Vancouver	3-2*
Dec.	1	at Calgary	4-3*	**Mar.**	2	at Edmonton	3-4†
	3	Dallas	1-2†		4	at Calgary	0-1
	5	Colorado	5-4		7	Edmonton	1-2*
	8	Minnesota	1-2		9	Tampa Bay	5-3
	10	Anaheim	3-4*		14	Chicago	3-6
	12	Colorado	4-1		16	Detroit	4-3
	15	at Boston	0-2		18	Calgary	3-0
	18	Calgary	1-3		19	at Detroit	1-3
	21	Los Angeles	2-1		22	Detroit	1-4
	23	Nashville	1-3		25	at Nashville	0-3
	26	Atlanta	2-0		26	Chicago	4-0
	27	at Nashville	3-4		28	Nashville	0-2
	29	Carolina	4-1		30	at Chicago	4-5†
	31	Edmonton	4-2	**Apr.**	3	at Detroit	2-3
Jan.	2	at Anaheim	1-2		5	at St. Louis	0-3
	3	at Los Angeles	4-3		6	St. Louis	1-4

* – Overtime † – Shootout

Entry Draft Selections 2008-2000

Name in bold denotes played in NHL.

2008

Pick	
6	Nikita Filatov
37	Cody Goloubef
107	Steven Delisle
118	Drew Olson
127	Matthew Calvert
135	Tomas Kubalik
137	Brent Regner
157	Cam Atkinson
187	Sean Collins

2007

Pick	
7	Jakub Voracek
37	Stefan Legein
53	Will Weber
68	Jake Hansen
94	Maxim Mayorov
158	Allen York
211	Trent Vogelhuber

2006

Pick	
6	**Derick Brassard**
69	Steve Mason
85	**Tommy Sestito**
113	Ben Wright
129	Robert Nyholm
136	Nick Sucharski
142	Maxime Frechette
159	Jesse Dudas
189	Derek Dorsett
194	Matt Marquardt

2005

Pick	
6	**Gilbert Brule**
55	Adam McQuaid
67	**Kris Russell**
101	**Jared Boll**
131	**Tomas Popperle**
177	Derek Reinhart
189	Kirill Starkov
201	Trevor Hendrikx

2004

Pick	
8	**Alexandre Picard**
46	**Adam Pineault**
59	Kyle Wharton
93	**Dan Lacosta**
96	Andrey Plekhanov
133	Petr Pohl
167	Rob Page
190	Lennart Petrell
198	Justin Vienneau
231	Brian McGuirk
233	Matt Greer
271	Grant Clitsome

2003

Pick	
4	**Nikolai Zherdev**
46	**Dan Fritsche**
71	Dmitry Kosmachev
103	Kevin Jarman
104	Philippe Dupuis
138	Arsi Piispanen
168	**Marc Methot**
200	Alexander Guskov
233	Mathieu Gravel
283	Trevor Hendrikx

2002

Pick	
1	**Rick Nash**
41	**Joakim Lindstrom**
65	**Ole-Kristian Tollefsen**
96	Jeff Genovy
98	Ivan Tkachenko
119	Jekabs Redlihs
133	**Lasse Pirjeta**
168	Tim Konsorada
184	**Jaroslav Balastik**
199	**Greg Mauldin**
225	**Steven Goertzen**
231	Jaroslav Kracik
263	Sergei Mozyakin

2001

Pick	
8	**Pascal Leclaire**
38	**Tim Jackman**
53	Kiel McLeod
85	**Aaron Johnson**
87	Per Mars
141	**Cole Jarrett**
173	Justin Aikins
187	Artem Vostrikov
204	Raffaele Sannitz
236	Ryan Bowness
242	**Andrew Murray**

2000

Pick	
4	**Rostislav Klesla**
69	Ben Knopp
133	**Petteri Nummelin**
138	Scott Heffernan
150	Tyler Kolarik
169	Shane Bendera
200	Janne Jokila
231	Peter Zingoni
278	Martin Paroulek
286	**Andrej Nedorost**
292	Louis Mandeville

General Managers' History

Doug MacLean, 2000-01 to 2006-07; Scott Howson, 2007-08 to date.

Scott Howson

General Manager

Born: Toronto, Ont., April 9, 1960.

The Columbus Blue Jackets announced the signing of Scott Howson as the second general manager in franchise history on June 15, 2007. Howson joined the Blue Jackets after spending seven years with the Edmonton Oilers. He joined the Oilers in June 2000 as assistant to the general manager and was named assistant general manager a year later. In that role, he was responsible for all aspects of the club's hockey administration, including player contracts, personnel decisions, the collective bargaining agreement, its American Hockey League affiliates and the salary cap.

During his six seasons with the Oilers, the club posted five-straight winning campaigns from 2000 to 2006, averaged 37 wins and 89 points per season, topped 90 points four times and advanced to the 2006 Stanley Cup Finals, where they were defeated in seven games by the Carolina Hurricanes.

Prior to his arrival in Edmonton, Howson spent six years with the club's AHL affiliates. As general manager of the Cape Breton Oilers from 1994 1o 1996, he oversaw the franchise's move to Hamilton in 1996 and was the Bulldogs' general manager from 1996 to 2000. During that time, he led Hamilton to a pair of berths in the Calder Cup Finals (1997, 2003) and a conference semifinals appearance in 2002.

Howson played three seasons in the Ontario Hockey League as a forward with the Kingston Canadiens from 1978 to 1981, serving as team captain and earning OHL All-Star honors. Following his junior career, he signed a free agent contract with the New York Islanders and spent the next five years playing at various levels throughout the organization.

During his rookie season in 1981-82, he was named the International Hockey League's rookie of the year after registering 55 goals and 65 assists for 120 points in 71 games with the Toledo Goaldiggers. He was the league's second-leading scorer that year and helped Toledo capture the league championship. Howson also won a Central Hockey League title with the Indianapolis Checkers in 1982-83. He made his NHL debut with the Islanders during the 1984-85 season and tallied 4 goals and one assist in eight games. He added a goal and two assists in 10 games the following season before retiring as a player at the end of the 1985-86 season. Howson received his bachelor's degree in 1987 from York University in Toronto and is a 1990 graduate of the university's Osgoode Hall Law School.

Club Directory

Nationwide Arena

Columbus Blue Jackets
Nationwide Arena
200 W. Nationwide Blvd.
Columbus, Ohio 43215
Phone **614/246-4625**
FAX 614/246-4007
www.BlueJackets.com
Capacity: 18,144

Ownership

Majority Owner/Governor	John P. McConnell

Executive Staff

President/Alternate Governor	Mike Priest
Sr. Vice President of Business Operations	Larry Hoepfner
Sr. Vice President and General Counsel	Greg Kirstein
Vice President of Premium Seating	Paul D'Aiuto
Vice President of Marketing	Marc Gregory
Vice President of Corporate Development	Cameron Scholvin
Vice President of Public Relations	Todd Sharrock
Chief Financial Officer	T.J. LaMendola

Hockey Operations

General Manager	Scott Howson
Assistant General Manager	Chris MacFarland
Director of Player Personnel	Don Boyd
Head Coach	Ken Hitchcock
Assistant Coaches	Gary Agnew, Gord Murphy, Claude Noel
Goaltending Coach	Clint Malarchuk
Strength & Conditioning Coach	Barry Brennan
Development Coach	Tyler Wright
Video Coordinator	Dan Singleton
Performance Psychologist	Dr. Kimberley Amirault
Director of Pro Scouting	Bob Strumm
Director of Amateur Scouting	Paul Castron
Assistant Director of Amateur Scouting	John Williams
Amateur Scouts	Brian Bates, Sam McMaster, Andrew Dickson
Pro Scout	Peter Dineen
Professional European Scout	Kjell Larsson
Regional Scouts	John McNamara, Bryan Raymond, Rob Riley, Andrew Shaw, Artem Telepin, Milan Tichy
Video Scout	Bryan Stewart
Video Scouting Assistant	Rob Froese
Manager of Hockey Administration	Josh Flynn
Manager of Team Services	Jim Rankin
Hockey Operations Coordinator	Julie Uhler
Head Athletic Trainer	Mike Vogt
Equipment Manager	Tim LeRoy
Assistant Equipment Manager	Jamie Healy
Equipment Assistant	Jason Stypinski
Administrative Assistant	April Lester

Business Operations

Director of Partnership Marketing	Cheri Wiles
Director of Communications	Karen Davis
Director of Event Presentation/Production	Kimberly Kershaw
Director of Marketing & Fan Development	J.D. Kershaw
Director of Community Development	Wendy Bradshaw
Director of Creative Services	Jason Rothwell
Director of Human Resources	Kelley Walton
Senior Graphic Designer	Will Bennett
Graphic Designer	James Korte
Manager of Communications	Ryan Holtmann
Manager of Multimedia	Ryan Mulcrone
Manager of Partnership Marketing	Erin Gibbons, Josh Hafer
Client Services Coordinator	Rachel Mayfield
Corporate Sales Analyst	Craig Smith
Corporate Development Account Executives	Jerry Angel, Jimmie Bryson, Mark Mead, A.J. Poole
Premium Sales Manager	Joe Jerele
Premium Seating Manager	Amanda Horning
Premium Seating Account Executive	Michelle Fogle
Managers of Production	David Bakalik, David Traube
Manager of Event Presentation	Lynn Truitt
Video Broadcast Engineer	Rick Shepherd
Graphics Coordinator	Andy Hookman
Payroll Coordinator	Christine Parthemore
Human Resources Assistant	Whitney Mitchell
Manager of Fan Development	Joel Siegman
Manager of Marketing	Nate Ferrall
Manager of Marketing, Youth & Amateur Hockey	Gordy Haggard
Partnership Activation Manager	Mike Kerrigan
Manager of Community Development	Kate Furman
Mascot Coordinator	Jason Zumpano
Legal Assistant	Rachel Phillips
Paralegal	Ken Erney

Finance

Controller	Jeremy Manly
Assistant Controller	Jason LaPlace
Staff Accountant	Nora Ludwig
Accounts Payable Coordinators	Beth Carpenter, Lindsay Wohlheter
Director of Information Technology	Jim Connolly
PC Specialist	Matthew DeStephen
Receptionis	Beth Carlisle

Ticket Operations

Director of Ticket Operations	Mark Morris
Director of Ticket Sales & Servivce	Joe Ondrejko
Manager of Ticket Sales & Service	Cory Rowe
Inside Sales Manager	Luke Burket
Manager of Group Sales	Andy Hire

Broadcasting

Director of Broadcasting	Russ Mollohan
FSN Ohio Play-by-Play/Color	Jeff Rimer/Danny Gare
Radio Play-by-Play/Color	George Matthews, Bill Davidge

Key Off-Season Signings/Acquisitions

2008

May 22 • Re-signed co-GMs **Les Jackson** and **Brett Hull**.
28 • Re-signed D **Trevor Daley**.
June 9 • Re-signed C **Toby Petersen**.
27 • Re-signed LW **Loui Eriksson**.
July 2 • Signed LW **Sean Avery**.
14 • Re-signed head coach **Dave Tippett**.

Dallas Stars

2007-08 Results: 45W-30L-4OTL-3SOL 97PTS.
Third, Pacific Division

With a pair of goals on November 7, 2007, Mike Modano became the all-time American-born points leader in NHL history. His 1,233rd point moved him past Phil Housley into top spot.

2008-09 Schedule

Month	Day	Date	Opponent
Oct.	Fri.	10	Columbus
	Sat.	11	at Nashville
	Wed.	15	Nashville
	Thu.	16	at St. Louis
	Sat.	18	Colorado*
	Mon.	20	at NY Rangers
	Wed.	22	at New Jersey
	Thu.	23	at NY Islanders
	Sat.	25	Washington
	Wed.	29	Minnesota
	Fri.	31	at Chicago
Nov.	Sat.	1	at Boston
	Fri.	7	at Anaheim
	Sat.	8	at San Jose
	Tue.	11	at Los Angeles
	Thu.	13	Los Angeles
	Sat.	15	at Phoenix
	Thu.	20	Chicago
	Sat.	22	Anaheim
	Mon.	24	at Philadelphia
	Wed.	26	at Minnesota
	Fri.	28	San Jose
	Sun.	30	Edmonton*
Dec.	Tue.	2	at Calgary
	Wed.	3	at Edmonton
	Fri.	5	Colorado
	Wed.	10	Phoenix
	Fri.	12	Detroit
	Sat.	13	at Nashville
	Tue.	16	Phoenix
	Thu.	18	Columbus
	Sat.	20	at Ottawa
	Tue.	23	at Toronto
	Sat.	27	Anaheim
	Mon.	29	San Jose
	Wed.	31	New Jersey
Jan.	Sat.	3	at Edmonton
	Sun.	4	at Vancouver
	Thu.	8	at Detroit
	Sat.	10	at Phoenix
	Mon.	12	Detroit
	Thu.	15	Buffalo
	Sat.	17	Los Angeles*
	Mon.	19	at Tampa Bay
	Wed.	21	at Florida
	Tue.	27	Atlanta
	Thu.	29	at Detroit
	Sat.	31	at Columbus
Feb.	Tue.	3	Calgary
	Thu.	5	at Colorado
	Fri.	6	NY Rangers
	Sun.	8	Nashville*
	Wed.	11	Phoenix
	Fri.	13	Vancouver
	Sat.	14	at Chicago
	Mon.	16	at Columbus
	Thu.	19	Edmonton
	Sat.	21	Chicago*
	Mon.	23	San Jose
	Thu.	26	St. Louis
	Sat.	28	Anaheim*
Mar.	Sun.	1	Pittsburgh*
	Tue.	3	at San Jose
	Thu.	5	at Los Angeles
	Fri.	6	at Anaheim
	Sun.	8	Montreal*
	Tue.	10	at St. Louis
	Thu.	12	Carolina
	Sat.	14	Minnesota
	Tue.	17	at Vancouver
	Wed.	18	at Calgary
	Sat.	21	at San Jose*
	Tue.	24	Vancouver
	Thu.	26	Los Angeles
	Sat.	28	Florida
	Mon.	30	at Phoenix
	Tue.	31	at Los Angeles
Apr.	Thu.	2	Calgary
	Sat.	4	St. Louis
	Tue.	7	at Minnesota
	Thu.	9	at Colorado
	Fri.	10	at Anaheim

* Denotes afternoon game.

Year-by-Year Record

		Home				Road				Overall								
Season	GP	W	L	T	OL	W	L	T	OL	W	L	T	OL	GF	GA	Pts.	Finished	Playoff Result
2007-08	82	23	16	....	2	22	14	....	5	45	30	....	7	242	207	97	3rd, Pacific Div.	Lost Conf. Championship
2006-07	82	28	11	....	2	22	14	....	5	50	25	....	7	226	197	107	3rd, Pacific Div.	Lost Conf. Quarter-Final
2005-06	82	28	11	....	2	25	12	....	4	53	23	....	6	265	218	112	1st, Pacific Div.	Lost Conf. Quarter-Final
2004-05	....	....	....	....	....	....	....	....	....	....	....	....	....	....	....	....		
2003-04	82	26	7	8	0	15	19	5	2	41	26	13	2	194	175	97	2nd, Pacific Div.	Lost Conf. Quarter-Final
2002-03	82	28	5	6	2	18	12	9	2	46	17	15	4	245	169	111	1st, Pacific Div.	Lost Conf. Semi-Final
2001-02	82	18	13	6	4	18	15	7	1	36	28	13	5	215	213	90	4th, Pacific Div.	Out of Playoffs
2000-01	82	26	10	5	0	22	14	3	2	48	24	8	2	241	187	106	1st, Pacific Div.	Lost Conf. Semi-Final
1999-2000	82	21	11	5	4	22	12	5	2	43	23	10	6	211	184	102	1st, Pacific Div.	Lost Final
1998-99	**82**	**29**	**8**	**4**	....	**22**	**11**	**8**	....	**51**	**19**	**12**	....	**236**	**168**	**114**	**1st, Pacific Div.**	**Won Stanley Cup**
1997-98	82	26	8	7	....	23	14	4	....	49	22	11	....	242	167	109	1st, Central Div.	Lost Conf. Championship
1996-97	82	25	13	3	....	23	13	5	....	48	26	8	....	252	198	104	1st, Central Div.	Lost Conf. Quarter-Final
1995-96	82	14	18	9	....	12	24	5	....	26	42	14	....	227	280	66	6th, Central Div.	Out of Playoffs
1994-95	48	9	10	5	....	8	13	3	....	17	23	8	....	136	135	42	5th, Central Div.	Lost Conf. Quarter-Final
1993-94	84	23	12	7	....	19	17	6	....	42	29	13	....	286	265	97	3rd, Central Div.	Lost Conf. Semi-Final
1992-93*	84	18	17	7	....	18	21	3	....	36	38	10	....	272	293	82	5th, Norris Div.	Out of Playoffs
1991-92*	80	20	16	4	....	12	26	2	....	32	42	6	....	246	278	70	4th, Norris Div.	Lost Div. Semi-Final
1990-91*	80	19	15	6	....	8	24	8	....	27	39	14	....	256	266	68	4th, Norris Div.	Lost Final
1989-90*	80	26	12	2	....	10	28	2	....	36	40	4	....	284	291	76	4th, Norris Div.	Lost Div. Semi-Final
1988-89*	80	17	15	8	....	10	22	8	....	27	37	16	....	258	278	70	3rd, Norris Div.	Lost Div. Semi-Final
1987-88*	80	10	24	6	....	9	24	7	....	19	48	13	....	242	349	51	5th, Norris Div.	Out of Playoffs
1986-87*	80	17	20	3	....	13	20	7	....	30	40	10	....	296	314	70	5th, Norris Div.	Out of Playoffs
1985-86*	80	21	15	4	....	17	18	5	....	38	33	9	....	327	305	85	2nd, Norris Div.	Lost Div. Semi-Final
1984-85*	80	14	19	7	....	11	24	5	....	25	43	12	....	268	321	62	4th, Norris Div.	Lost Div. Final
1983-84*	80	22	14	4	....	17	17	6	....	39	31	10	....	345	344	88	1st, Norris Div.	Lost Conf. Championship
1982-83*	80	23	6	11	....	17	18	5	....	40	24	16	....	321	290	96	2nd, Norris Div.	Lost Div. Final
1981-82*	80	21	7	12	....	16	16	8	....	37	23	20	....	346	288	94	1st, Norris Div.	Lost Div. Semi-Final
1980-81*	80	23	10	7	....	12	18	10	....	35	28	17	....	291	263	87	3rd, Adams Div.	Lost Final
1979-80*	80	25	8	7	....	11	20	9	....	36	28	16	....	311	253	88	3rd, Adams Div.	Lost Semi-Final
1978-79*	80	19	15	6	....	9	25	6	....	28	40	12	....	257	289	68	4th, Adams Div.	Out Of Playoffs
1977-78*	80	12	24	4	....	6	29	5	....	18	53	9	....	218	325	45	5th, Smythe Div.	Out of Playoffs
1976-77*	80	17	14	9	....	6	25	9	....	23	39	18	....	240	310	64	2nd, Smythe Div.	Lost Prelim. Round
1975-76*	80	15	22	3	....	5	31	4	....	20	53	7	....	195	303	47	4th, Smythe Div.	Out of Playoffs
1974-75*	80	17	20	3	....	6	30	4	....	23	50	7	....	221	341	53	4th, Smythe Div.	Out of Playoffs
1973-74*	78	18	15	6	....	5	23	11	....	23	38	17	....	235	275	63	7th, West Div.	Out of Playoffs
1972-73*	78	26	8	5	....	11	22	6	....	37	30	11	....	254	230	85	3rd, West Div.	Lost Quarter-Final
1971-72*	78	22	11	6	....	15	18	6	....	37	29	12	....	212	191	86	2nd, West Div.	Lost Quarter-Final
1970-71*	78	16	15	8	....	12	19	8	....	28	34	16	....	191	223	72	4th, West Div.	Lost Semi-Final
1969-70*	76	11	16	11	....	8	19	11	....	19	35	22	....	224	257	60	3rd, West Div.	Lost Quarter-Final
1968-69*	76	11	21	6	....	7	22	9	....	18	43	15	....	189	270	51	6th, West Div.	Out of Playoffs
1967-68*	74	17	12	8	....	10	20	7	....	27	32	15	....	191	226	69	4th, West Div.	Lost Semi-Final

* Minnesota North Stars

PACIFIC DIVISION
42nd NHL Season

Franchise date: June 5, 1967

Transferred from Minnesota to Dallas, June 9, 1993.

2008-09 Player Personnel

FORWARDS	HT	WT	S	Place of Birth	*Age	2007-08 Club
AVERY, Sean	5-10	195	L	Pickering, Ont.	28	NY Rangers
BARCH, Krys	6-2	220	L	Hamilton, Ont.	28	Dallas
BARNES, Stu	5-11	182	R	Spruce Grove, Alta.	37	Dallas
BRUNNSTROM, Fabian	6-1	202	L	Jonstorp, Sweden	23	Farjestad
CONNER, Chris	5-8	180	L	Westland, MI	24	Dallas-Iowa
CROMBEEN, B.J.	6-2	212	R	Denver, CO	23	Dallas-Iowa
ERIKSSON, Loui	6-1	183	L	Gothenburg, Sweden	23	Dallas-Iowa
LEHTINEN, Jere	6-0	192	R	Espoo, Finland	35	Dallas
LUNDQVIST, Joel	6-1	194	L	Are, Sweden	26	Dallas-Iowa
MODANO, Mike	6-3	210	L	Livonia, MI	38	Dallas
MORROW, Brenden	5-11	205	L	Carlyle, Sask.	29	Dallas
NEAL, James	6-2	185	L	Oshawa, Ont.	21	Iowa
OTT, Steve	6-0	193	L	Summerside, P.E.I.	26	Dallas
PETERSEN, Toby	5-10	197	L	Minneapolis, MN	29	Dallas-Iowa
RIBEIRO, Mike	6-0	175	L	Montreal, Que.	28	Dallas
RICHARDS, Brad	6-0	192	L	Murray Harbour, P.E.I.	28	Tampa Bay-Dallas
SAWADA, Raymond	6-2	195	R	Richmond, B.C.	23	Cornell-Iowa
TUKONEN, Lauri	6-2	200	R	Hyvinkaa, Finland	22	Los Angeles-Manchester
WATHIER, Francis	6-3	198	L	St Isidore, Ont.	23	Iowa

DEFENSEMEN	HT	WT	S	Place of Birth	*Age	2007-08 Club
BOUCHER, Philippe	6-3	218	R	Ste-Apollinaire, Que.	35	Dallas
DALEY, Trevor	5-11	207	L	Toronto, Ont.	24	Dallas
FISTRIC, Mark	6-2	232	L	Edmonton, Alta.	22	Dallas-Iowa
GROSSMAN, Nicklas	6-3	206	L	Stockholm, Sweden	23	Dallas-Iowa
JANCEVSKI, Dan	6-3	218	L	Windsor, Ont.	27	T.B.-Norfolk-Dal-Iowa
NISKANEN, Matt	6-0	194	R	Virginia, MN	21	Dallas
ROBIDAS, Stephane	5-11	190	R	Sherbrooke, Que.	31	Dallas
ZUBOV, Sergei	6-1	198	R	Moscow, USSR	38	Dallas

GOALTENDERS	HT	WT	C	Place of Birth	*Age	2007-08 Club
STEPHAN, Tobias	6-2	180	L	Zurich, Switz.	24	Dallas-Iowa
TURCO, Marty	5-11	185	L	Sault Ste. Marie, Ont.	33	Dallas

* – Age at start of 2008-09 season

Dave Tippett
Head Coach

Born: Moosomin, Sask., August 25, 1961.

The Dallas Stars announced the hiring of Dave Tippett as the club's head coach on May 16, 2002. In his first season behind the bench in 2002-03, he led the Stars to the best record in the Western Conference and the second best in the NHL. The Stars have never had less than 97 points in any of his five seasons behind the bench.

Before joining the Stars, Tippett had spent the previous three seasons as an assistant coach with the Los Angeles Kings. He served a five-game stint as interim head coach in 2002 while head coach Andy Murray recovered from an auto accident. In all three seasons Tippett was in Los Angeles the Kings qualified for the playoffs. They had reached the postseason just once out of the previous six seasons.

Under Tippett's direction, the Kings power-play led the NHL in 2001-02 with a 20.7 percent success rate. In 1998-99, the year before Tippett came aboard, the Kings power-play unit ranked 24th in the league. As a highly regarded minor league coach with tremendous work ethic, Tippett posted two 50-win seasons at Houston (International Hockey League) and led the Aeros to the 1999 Turner Cup championship while serving as general manager/head coach. He was also named IHL coach of the year.

Prior to becoming a coach, Tippett played 11 years as a forward in the National Hockey League with the Hartford Whalers, Washington Capitals, Pittsburgh Penguins and Philadelphia Flyers. He ended his playing career in 1995 as a player-assistant coach with the Houston Aeros (IHL). Internationally, he captained the 1984 Canadian Olympic team in Sarajevo, Yugoslavia, and he earned a silver medal as a member of the Canadian Olympic team in Albertville, France, in 1992. He was a member of the 1982 NCAA Division I championship squad at the University of North Dakota with former Stars defenseman Craig Ludwig.

Coaching Record

			Regular Season				Playoffs			
Season	Team	League	GC	W	L	O/T	GC	W	L	T
1995-96	Houston	IHL	42	17	18	7	....	....	....	....
1996-97	Houston	IHL	82	44	30	8	13	8	5	....
1997-98	Houston	IHL	82	50	22	10	4	1	3	....
1998-99	Houston	IHL	82	54	15	13	19	11	8	....
2002-03	**Dallas**	**NHL**	**82**	**46**	**17**	**19**	**12**	**6**	**6**	....
2003-04	**Dallas**	**NHL**	**82**	**41**	**26**	**15**	**5**	**1**	**4**	....
2004-05	**Dallas**				SEASON CANCELLED					
2005-06	**Dallas**	**NHL**	**82**	**53**	**23**	**6**	**5**	**1**	**4**	....
2006-07	**Dallas**	**NHL**	**82**	**50**	**25**	**7**	**7**	**3**	**4**	....
2007-08	**Dallas**	**NHL**	**82**	**45**	**30**	**7**	**18**	**10**	**8**	....
	NHL Totals		**410**	**235**	**121**	**54**	**47**	**21**	**26**	....

2007-08 Scoring

* – rookie

Regular Season

Pos	#	Player	Team	GP	G	A	Pts	TOI	+/-	PIM	PP	SH	GW	S	%
C	63	Mike Ribeiro	DAL	76	27	56	83	18:25	21	46	7	0	5	107	25.2
L	10	Brenden Morrow	DAL	82	32	42	74	19:59	23	105	12	2	7	207	15.5
C	91	Brad Richards	T.B.	62	18	33	51	24:16	–25	15	9	1	4	228	7.9
			DAL	12	2	9	11	19:14	–2	0	0	1	0	21	9.5
			Total	74	20	42	62	23:27	–27	15	9	2	4	249	8.0
C	9	Mike Modano	DAL	82	21	36	57	19:14	–11	48	5	1	4	200	10.5
L	15	Niklas Hagman	DAL	82	27	14	41	15:35	4	51	4	4	8	178	15.2
R	26	Jere Lehtinen	DAL	48	15	22	37	18:55	9	14	9	0	1	118	12.7
D	56	Sergei Zubov	DAL	46	4	31	35	25:41	6	12	2	0	0	84	4.8
R	20	Antti Miettinen	DAL	69	15	19	34	13:59	4	34	5	0	3	136	11.0
L	21	Loui Eriksson	DAL	69	14	17	31	14:01	5	28	4	0	0	120	11.7
D	3	Stephane Robidas	DAL	82	9	17	26	20:38	0	85	7	0	2	153	5.9
D	5 *	Matt Niskanen	DAL	78	7	19	26	20:29	22	36	2	0	0	99	7.1
D	6	Trevor Daley	DAL	82	5	19	24	19:48	–1	85	0	0	1	87	5.7
C	14	Stu Barnes	DAL	79	12	11	23	13:37	–3	26	0	2	4	71	16.9
C	29	Steve Ott	DAL	73	11	11	22	14:27	2	147	0	1	2	89	12.4
C	39	Joel Lundqvist	DAL	55	3	11	14	10:52	–3	22	0	0	0	48	6.3
D	43	Philippe Boucher	DAL	38	2	12	14	21:30	3	26	0	1	0	72	2.8
D	4	Mattias Norstrom	DAL	66	2	11	13	19:30	3	40	1	0	1	54	3.7
D	2 *	Nicklas Grossman	DAL	62	0	7	7	15:33	10	22	0	0	0	34	0.0
R	25 *	Chris Conner	DAL	22	3	2	5	11:59	0	6	0	0	0	27	11.1
L	16	Brad Winchester	DAL	41	1	2	3	07:34	–9	46	0	0	0	36	2.8
R	13	Krys Barch	DAL	48	1	2	3	06:30	–3	105	0	0	0	23	4.3
C	17	Toby Petersen	DAL	8	0	3	3	07:50	0	4	0	0	0	6	0.0
R	44 *	Brandon Crombeen	DAL	8	0	2	2	06:37	1	39	0	0	0	9	0.0
D	28 *	Mark Fistric	DAL	37	0	2	2	12:44	3	24	0	0	0	17	0.0
D	42	Dan Jancevski	T.B.	2	0	0	0	02:22	–1	2	0	0	0	0	0.0
			DAL	2	0	0	0	09:18	0	0	0	0	0	3	0.0
			Total	4	0	0	0	05:50	–1	2	0	0	0	3	0.0

Goaltending

No.	Goaltender	GPI	Mins	Avg	W	L	OT	EN	SO	GA	SA	S%	G	A	PIM
31	* Tobias Stephan	1	61	1.97	0	0	1	0	0	2	40	.950	0	0	0
35	Marty Turco	62	3629	2.31	32	21	6	5	3	140	1543	.909	0	3	16
41	* Mike Smith	21	1172	2.46	12	9	0	4	2	48	510	.906	0	0	6
40	Johan Holmqvist	2	80	3.75	1	0	0	0	0	5	35	.857	0	0	0
	Totals	**82**	**4975**	**2.46**	**45**	**30**	**7**	**9**	**5**	**204**	**2137**	**.905**			

Playoffs

Pos	#	Player	Team	GP	G	A	Pts	TOI	+/–	PIM	PP	SH	GW	OT	S	%
C	63	Mike Ribeiro	DAL	18	3	14	17	21:44	0	16	0	0	0	0	34	8.8
L	10	Brenden Morrow	DAL	18	9	6	15	23:16	0	22	4	0	2	2	43	20.9
C	91	Brad Richards	DAL	18	3	12	15	21:05	1	8	0	0	0	0	54	5.6
C	9	Mike Modano	DAL	18	5	7	12	19:42	–3	22	5	0	3	0	37	13.5
D	3	Stephane Robidas	DAL	18	3	8	11	25:31	0	12	3	0	0	0	41	7.3
R	26	Jere Lehtinen	DAL	14	4	4	8	20:34	2	2	3	0	0	0	31	12.9
L	21	Loui Eriksson	DAL	18	4	4	8	18:11	1	8	1	0	0	0	31	12.9
C	39	Joel Lundqvist	DAL	18	2	5	7	14:06	0	8	0	0	1	0	18	11.1
D	56	Sergei Zubov	DAL	11	1	5	6	26:01	–4	4	1	0	0	0	20	5.0
D	4	Mattias Norstrom	DAL	18	2	3	5	20:20	5	16	0	0	1	1	10	20.0
C	14	Stu Barnes	DAL	9	2	1	3	15:32	1	2	0	0	2	0	14	14.3
L	15	Niklas Hagman	DAL	18	2	1	3	13:24	3	14	0	0	0	0	33	6.1
C	29	Steve Ott	DAL	18	2	1	3	13:46	–2	22	1	0	1	0	15	13.3
D	5 *	Matt Niskanen	DAL	16	0	3	3	16:23	–2	10	0	0	0	0	17	0.0
R	20	Antti Miettinen	DAL	15	1	1	2	09:32	–2	0	0	0	0	0	16	6.3
D	2 *	Nicklas Grossman	DAL	18	1	1	2	18:37	3	6	0	0	0	0	14	7.1
D	6	Trevor Daley	DAL	18	1	0	1	18:51	0	20	0	0	0	0	25	4.0
R	25 *	Chris Conner	DAL	1	0	0	0	04:17	–1	0	0	0	0	0	0	0.0
D	43	Philippe Boucher	DAL	3	0	0	0	20:04	0	4	0	0	0	0	7	0.0
R	13	Krys Barch	DAL	3	0	0	0	02:21	0	2	0	0	0	0	0	0.0
R	44 *	Brandon Crombeen	DAL	5	0	0	0	04:16	0	0	0	0	0	0	3	0.0
L	16	Brad Winchester	DAL	6	0	0	0	06:49	–2	8	0	0	0	0	4	0.0
D	28 *	Mark Fistric	DAL	9	0	0	0	14:50	–1	6	0	0	0	0	3	0.0
C	17	Toby Petersen	DAL	16	0	0	0	09:45	–4	2	0	0	0	0	19	0.0

Goaltending

No.	Goaltender	GPI	Mins	Avg	W	L	EN	SO	GA	SA	S%	G	A	PIM
35	Marty Turco	18	1152	2.08	10	8	1	1	40	511	.922	0	2	4
	Totals	**18**	**1159**	**2.12**	**10**	**8**	**1**	**1**	**41**	**512**	**.920**			

Coaching History

Wren Blair, 1967-68; Wren Blair and John Muckler, 1968-69; Wren Blair and Charlie Burns, 1969-70; Jack Gordon, 1970-71 to 1972-73; Jack Gordon and Parker MacDonald, 1973-74; Jack Gordon and Charlie Burns, 1974-75; Ted Harris, 1975-76, 1976-77; Ted Harris, André Beaulieu and Lou Nanne, 1977-78; Harry Howell and Glen Sonmor, 1978-79; Glen Sonmor, 1979-80 to 1981-82; Glen Sonmor and Murray Oliver, 1982-83; Bill Mahoney, 1983-84, 1984-85; Lorne Henning, 1985-86; Lorne Henning and Glen Sonmor, 1986-87; Herb Brooks, 1987-88; Pierre Page, 1988-89, 1989-90; Bob Gainey, 1990-91 to 1994-95; Bob Gainey and Ken Hitchcock, 1995-96; Ken Hitchcock, 1996-97 to 2000-01; Ken Hitchcock and Rick Wilson, 2001-02; Dave Tippett, 2002-03 to date.

Club Records

Team

(Figures in brackets for season records are games played; records for fewest points, wins, ties, losses, goals, goals against are for 70 or more games)

Most Points **114** 1998-99 (82)
Most Wins **53** 2005-06 (82)
Most Ties **22** 1969-70 (76)
Most Losses **53** 1975-76 (80), 1977-78 (80)
Most Goals **346** 1981-82 (80)
Most Goals Against **349** 1987-88 (80)
Fewest Points **45** 1977-78 (80)
Fewest Wins **18** 1968-69 (76), 1977-78 (80)
Fewest Ties **4** 1989-90 (80)
Fewest Losses **19** 1998-99 (82)
Fewest Goals **189** 1968-69 (76)
Fewest Goals Against **167** 1997-98 (82)
Longest Winning Streak
Overall .... **7** Mar. 16-28/80, Mar. 16-Apr. 2/97, Nov. 22-Dec. 5/97, Jan. 29-Feb. 11/08
Home .... **11** Nov. 4-Dec. 27/72
Away .... **7** Four times
Longest Undefeated Streak
Overall .... **15** Dec. 6/98-Jan. 6/99 (12 wins, 3 ties)
Home .... **17** Jan. 23-Mar. 20/04 (13 wins, 4 ties)
Away .... **10** Jan. 12-Mar. 4/99 (8 wins, 2 ties), Dec. 27/02-Feb. 25/03 (7 wins, 3 ties)
Longest Losing Streak
Overall .... **10** Feb. 1-20/76
Home .... **6** Jan. 17-Feb. 4/70
Away .... **8** Oct. 19-Nov. 13/75, Jan. 28-Mar. 3/88
Longest Winless Streak
Overall .... **20** Jan. 15-Feb. 28/70 (15 losses, 5 ties)
Home .... **12** Jan. 17-Feb. 25/70 (8 losses, 4 ties)
Away .... **23** Oct. 25/74-Jan. 28/75 (19 losses, 4 ties)
Most Shutouts, Season **11** 2000-01 (82), 2002-03 (82)
Most PIM, Season **2,313** 1987-88 (80)
Most Goals, Game .... **15** Nov. 11/81 (Wpg. 2 at Min. 15)

Individual

Most Seasons .... **19** Mike Modano
Most Games .... **1,320** Mike Modano
Most Goals, Career .... **528** Mike Modano
Most Assists, Career .... **755** Mike Modano
Most Points, Career .... **1,283** Mike Modano (528G, 755A)
Most PIM, Career .... **1,883** Shane Churla
Most Shutouts, Career .... **33** Marty Turco
Longest Consecutive Games Streak .... **442** Danny Grant (Dec. 4/68-Apr. 7/74)
Most Goals, Season .... **55** Dino Ciccarelli (1981-82), Brian Bellows (1989-90)
Most Assists, Season .... **76** Neal Broten (1985-86)
Most Points, Season .... **114** Bobby Smith (1981-82; 43G, 71A)
Most PIM, Season .... **382** Basil McRae (1987-88)
Most Points, Defenseman, Season .... **77** Craig Hartsburg (1981-82; 17G, 60A)
Most Points, Center, Season .... **114** Bobby Smith (1981-82; 43G, 71A)
Most Points, Right Wing, Season .... **106** Dino Ciccarelli (1981-82; 55G, 51A)
Most Points, Left Wing, Season .... **99** Brian Bellows (1989-90; 55G, 44A)
Most Points, Rookie, Season .... **98** Neal Broten (1981-82; 38G, 60A)
Most Shutouts, Season .... **9** Ed Belfour (1997-98), Marty Turco (2003-04)
Most Goals, Game .... **5** Tim Young (Jan. 15/79)
Most Assists, Game .... **5** Murray Oliver (Oct. 24/71), Larry Murphy (Oct. 17/89), Brad Richards (Feb. 26/08)
Most Points, Game .... **7** Bobby Smith (Nov. 11/81; 4G, 3A)

Records include Minnesota North Stars, 1967-68 through 1992-93.

Retired Numbers

7	Neal Broten	1980-1995, 1996-1997
8	Bill Goldsworthy*	1967-1976
19	Bill Masterton*	1967-1968

* Minnesota North Stars

All-time Record vs. Other Clubs

Regular Season

	At Home								On Road								Total							
	GP	W	L	T	OL	GF	GA	PTS	GP	W	L	T	OL	GF	GA	PTS	GP	W	L	T	OL	GF	GA	PTS
Anaheim	39	29	8	2	0	130	72	60	39	19	14	3	3	103	95	44	78	48	22	5	3	233	167	104
Atlanta	5	4	1	0	0	11	9	8	5	5	0	0	0	21	12	10	10	9	1	0	0	32	21	18
Boston	62	19	30	13	0	179	221	51	61	10	41	10	0	148	259	30	123	29	71	23	0	327	480	81
Buffalo	55	27	22	6	0	174	158	60	53	13	29	11	0	142	192	37	108	40	51	17	0	316	350	97
Calgary	68	34	21	11	2	245	209	81	68	18	34	14	2	166	221	52	136	52	55	25	4	411	430	133
Carolina	30	18	10	2	0	120	90	38	33	15	14	4	0	114	106	34	63	33	24	6	0	234	196	72
Chicago	118	57	44	16	1	408	358	131	116	34	66	15	1	307	424	84	234	91	110	31	2	715	782	215
Colorado	47	26	14	5	2	159	131	59	47	15	24	7	1	121	167	38	94	41	38	12	3	280	298	97
Columbus	14	11	2	0	1	43	25	23	14	10	2	0	2	44	32	22	28	21	4	0	3	87	57	45
Detroit	112	53	40	18	1	378	334	125	112	39	57	16	0	353	426	94	224	92	97	34	1	731	760	219
Edmonton	51	28	16	7	0	183	141	63	50	21	20	8	1	167	190	51	101	49	36	15	1	350	331	114
Florida	9	4	2	2	1	29	25	11	11	5	4	1	1	29	24	12	20	9	6	3	2	58	49	23
Los Angeles	96	60	23	13	0	364	253	133	94	34	38	19	3	277	309	90	190	94	61	32	3	641	562	223
Minnesota	14	10	2	1	1	54	32	22	14	7	6	0	1	29	35	15	28	17	8	1	2	83	67	37
Montreal	60	18	30	12	0	157	204	48	59	12	38	9	0	146	254	33	119	30	68	21	0	303	458	81
Nashville	18	14	4	0	0	48	22	28	18	8	9	1	0	42	47	17	36	22	13	1	0	90	69	45
New Jersey	46	27	13	6	0	167	118	60	44	19	22	3	0	134	150	41	90	46	35	9	0	301	268	101
NY Islanders	48	18	21	8	1	139	173	45	49	15	25	8	1	137	178	39	97	33	46	16	2	276	351	84
NY Rangers	62	20	31	11	0	189	226	51	63	16	36	11	0	168	215	43	125	36	67	22	0	357	441	94
Ottawa	12	7	5	0	0	46	32	14	10	6	3	0	1	26	22	13	22	13	8	0	1	72	54	27
Philadelphia	67	28	23	16	0	219	214	72	68	10	42	16	0	154	256	36	135	38	65	32	0	373	470	108
Phoenix	67	33	25	9	0	230	197	75	66	36	26	4	0	223	203	76	133	69	51	13	0	453	400	151
Pittsburgh	65	37	21	6	1	249	217	81	64	19	39	6	0	179	240	44	129	56	60	12	1	428	457	125
St. Louis	121	58	40	22	1	407	348	139	123	34	66	21	2	347	441	91	244	92	106	43	3	754	789	230
San Jose	41	20	14	4	3	113	98	47	42	26	13	1	2	119	97	55	83	46	27	5	5	232	195	102
Tampa Bay	12	7	4	1	0	42	33	15	14	11	1	2	0	39	21	24	26	18	5	3	0	81	54	39
Toronto	98	51	36	11	0	368	307	113	102	36	49	17	0	321	357	89	200	87	85	28	0	689	664	202
Vancouver	77	42	23	12	0	276	222	96	77	32	33	10	2	230	268	76	154	74	56	22	2	506	490	172
Washington	42	22	11	8	1	156	111	53	41	17	16	8	0	132	124	42	83	39	27	16	1	288	235	95
Defunct Clubs	33	19	8	6	0	123	86	44	32	10	16	6	0	84	105	26	65	29	24	12	0	207	191	70
Totals	**1589**	**801**	**544**	**228**	**16**	**5406**	**4666**	**1846**	**1589**	**552**	**783**	**231**	**23**	**4502**	**5470**	**1358**	**3178**	**1353**	**1327**	**459**	**39**	**9908**	**10136**	**3204**

Playoffs

	Series	W	L	GP	W	L	T	GF	GA	Last Mtg.	Rnd.	Result
Anaheim	2	1	1	12	6	6	0	34	27	2008	CQF	W 4-2
Boston	1	1	0	3	3	0	0	20	13	1981	PRE	W 3-0
Buffalo	3	2	1	13	8	5	0	39	37	1999	F	W 4-2
Calgary	1	1	0	6	4	2	0	25	18	1981	SF	W 4-2
Chicago	6	2	4	33	14	19	0	118	120	1991	DSF	W 4-2
Colorado	4	2	2	24	10	14	0	62	66	2006	CQF	L 1-4
Detroit	4	0	4	24	8	16	0	50	72	2008	CF	L 2-4
Edmonton	8	6	2	42	27	15	0	118	104	2003	CQF	W 4-2
Los Angeles	1	1	0	7	4	3	0	26	21	1968	QF	W 4-3
Montreal	2	1	1	13	6	7	0	37	48	1980	QF	W 4-3
New Jersey	1	0	1	6	2	4	0	9	15	2000	F	L 2-4
NY Islanders	1	0	1	5	1	4	0	16	26	1981	F	L 1-4
Philadelphia	2	0	2	11	3	8	0	26	41	1980	SF	L 1-4
Pittsburgh	1	0	1	6	2	4	0	16	28	1991	F	L 2-4
St. Louis	12	6	6	66	34	32	0	197	187	2001	CSF	L 0-4
San Jose	3	3	0	15	12	3	0	46	19	2008	CSF	W 4-1
Toronto	2	2	0	7	6	1	0	35	26	1983	DSF	W 3-1
Vancouver	2	0	2	12	4	8	0	23	31	2007	CQF	L 3-4
Totals	**56**	**28**	**28**	**305**	**154**	**151**	**0**	**897**	**899**			

Calgary totals include Atlanta Flames, 1972-73 to 1979-80. Carolina totals include Hartford, 1979-80 to 1996-97.
Colorado totals include Quebec, 1979-80 to 1994-95.
New Jersey totals include Kansas City, 1974-75, 1975-76, and Colorado Rockies, 1976-77 to 1981-82.
Phoenix totals include Winnipeg, 1979-80 to 1995-96.

Playoff Results 2008-2003

Year	Round	Opponent	Result	GF	GA
2008	CF	Detroit	L 2-4	10	17
	CSF	San Jose	W 4-2	15	11
	CQF	Anaheim	W 4-2	20	13
2007	CQF	Vancouver	L 3-4	12	13
2006	CQF	Colorado	L 1-4	15	18
2004	CQF	Colorado	L 1-4	10	19
2003	CSF	Anaheim	L 2-4	14	14
	CQF	Edmonton	W 4-2	20	11

Abbreviations: Round: F - Final; **CF** - conference final; **CSF** - conference semi-final; **CQF** - conference quarter-final; **DSF** - division semi-final; **SF** - semi-final; **QF** - quarter-final; **PRE** - preliminary round.

2007-08 Results

Oct.	3	at Colorado	3-4
	5	Boston	4-1
	6	at Nashville	1-5
	10	Los Angeles	5-1
	12	Calgary	2-3*
	13	at Chicago	1-2*
	17	at Columbus	3-2†
	20	Anaheim	3-1
	25	at Los Angeles	1-2
	27	at Phoenix	5-3
	29	San Jose	2-4
	31	Chicago	4-5
Nov.	2	Phoenix	0-5
	5	at Anaheim	5-0
	7	at San Jose	3-1
	8	at Phoenix	2-5
	10	at Los Angeles	5-6*
	14	San Jose	3-4†
	16	Colorado	6-1
	19	Los Angeles	3-0
	21	Anaheim	2-1
	23	Toronto	3-1
	25	at NY Rangers	3-2
	26	at NY Islanders	3-2*
	28	at New Jersey	2-4
	30	at Pittsburgh	1-4
Dec.	1	at Philadelphia	4-1
	3	at Columbus	2-1†
	5	San Jose	2-3
	7	Ottawa	2-4
	10	Edmonton	5-4*
	13	Los Angeles	4-1
	15	at San Jose	4-2
	18	at Edmonton	2-1†
	20	at Vancouver	2-3
	21	at Calgary	3-2*
	23	Montreal	4-1
	26	Minnesota	8-3
	29	St. Louis	5-4†
	31	Nashville	0-1
Jan.	2	at Detroit	1-4
	3	at Minnesota	3-6
	5	Detroit	0-3
	7	Minnesota	3-1
	9	at Chicago	3-1
	10	at St. Louis	2-4
	12	at Los Angeles	3-4†
	15	at Anaheim	2-4
	17	at San Jose	4-2
	19	Columbus	3-1
	20	Anaheim	5-2
	22	Columbus	2-4
	24	Buffalo	1-2
	29	at Vancouver	4-3
Feb.	1	at Edmonton	4-1
	2	at Calgary	2-1
	5	Vancouver	3-2†
	7	at Minnesota	1-0
	9	St. Louis	6-2
	11	Phoenix	2-1
	14	at Phoenix	2-5
	15	at Anaheim	4-2
	17	Detroit	1-0
	20	Calgary	2-3
	22	Edmonton	5-2
	23	at Nashville	6-3
	26	at St. Louis	3-1
	28	Chicago	7-4
Mar.	1	Nashville	1-3
	5	Phoenix	1-2
	8	at Colorado	1-3
	9	Colorado	3-0
	13	at Detroit	3-5
	15	Vancouver	3-4
	19	Anaheim	1-2
	22	Los Angeles	2-4
	27	at San Jose	2-3*
	29	at Los Angeles	7-2
	30	at Anaheim	2-3†
Apr.	3	at Phoenix	4-2
	4	Phoenix	2-4
	6	San Jose	4-2

* – Overtime † – Shootout

Entry Draft Selections 2008-1994

Name in bold denotes played in NHL.

2008
Pick
59 Tyler Beskorowany
89 Scott Winkler
149 Philip Larsen
176 Matthew Tassone
209 Mike Bergin

2007
Pick
50 Nico Sacchetti
64 Sergei Korostin
112 Colton Sceviour
128 Austin Smith
129 Jamie Benn
136 Ondrej Roman
149 Michael Neal
172 Luke Gazdic

2006
Pick
27 Ivan Vishnevskiy
90 Aaron Snow
120 Richard Bachman
138 David McIntyre
150 Max Warn

2005
Pick
28 **Matt Niskanen**
33 James Neal
71 Richard Clune
75 Perttu Lindgren
146 Tom Wandell
160 Matt Watkins
223 Pat McGann

2004
Pick
28 **Mark Fistric**
34 Johan Fransson
52 Raymond Sawada
56 **Nicklas Grossman**
86 John Lammers
104 Fredrik Naslund
183 Trevor Ludwig
218 Sergei Kukushkin
248 Lukas Vomela
280 Matt McKnight

2003
Pick
33 **Loui Eriksson**
36 **Vojtech Polak**
54 **B.J. Crombeen**
99 Matt Nickerson
134 Alexander Naurov
144 Eero Kilpelainen
165 Gino Guyer
185 Francis Wathier
195 Drew Bagnall
196 Elias Granath
259 Niko Vainio

2002
Pick
26 Martin Vagner
32 Janos Vas
34 **Tobias Stephan**
42 Marius Holtet
43 **Trevor Daley**
78 Geoff Waugh
110 Jarkko A. Immonen
147 David Bararuk
180 Kirill Sidorenko
210 Bryan Hamm
243 Tuomas Mikkonen
273 Ned Havern

2001
Pick
26 **Jason Bacashihua**
70 Yared Hagos
92 Anthony Aquino
126 Daniel Volrab
161 **Mike Smith**
167 Michal Blazek
192 **Jussi Jokinen**
255 Marco Rosa
265 Dale Sullivan
285 Marek Tomica

2000
Pick
25 **Steve Ott**
60 **Dan Ellis**
68 **Joel Lundqvist**
91 Alexei Tereschenko
123 Vadim Khomitski
139 Ruslan Bernikov
162 Artem Chernov
192 Ladislav Vlcek
219 Marco Tuokko
224 **Antti Miettinen**

1999
Pick
32 **Michael Ryan**
66 **Dan Jancevski**
96 **Mathias Tjarnqvist**
126 Jeff Bateman
156 Gregor Baumgartner
184 Justin Cox
186 Brett Draney
215 **Jeff MacMillan**
243 Brian Sullivan
265 Jamie Chamberlain
272 Mikhail Donika

1998
Pick
39 **John Erskine**
57 **Tyler Bouck**
86 Gabriel Karlsson
153 **Pavel Patera**
173 **Niko Kapanen**
200 Scott Perry

1997
Pick
25 **Brenden Morrow**
52 **Roman Lyashenko**
77 **Steve Gainey**
105 Marcus Kristoffersson
132 Teemu Elomo
160 Alexei Timkin
189 Jeff McKercher
216 Alexei Komarov
242 **Brett McLean**

1996
Pick
5 **Ric Jackman**
70 **Jon Sim**
90 Mike Hurley
112 **Ryan Christie**
113 Yevgeny Tsybuk
166 Eoin McInerney
194 **Joel Kwiatkowski**
220 Nick Bootland

1995
Pick
11 **Jarome Iginla**
37 **Patrick Cote**
63 **Petr Buzek**
69 **Sergey Gusev**
115 Wade Strand
141 Dominic Marleau
173 Jeff Dewar
193 Anatoli Koveshnikov
202 Sergei Luchinkin
219 Stephen Lowe

1994
Pick
20 **Jason Botterill**
46 Lee Jinman
98 **Jamie Wright**
124 **Marty Turco**
150 Evgeny Petrochinin
228 Marty Flichel
254 Jimmy Roy
280 Chris Szysky

Club Directory

American Airlines Center

Dallas Stars
Office Address:
2601 Ave. of the Stars
Frisco, TX 75034
Phone **214/387-5500**
FAX 214/387-5564
Ticket Information 214/GO STARS
www.dallasstars.com
Capacity: 18,532

Co-General Manager	Brett Hull
Co-General Manager	Les Jackson
Assistant General Manager	Frank Provenzano
Director, Player Personnel	Dave Taylor
Head Coach	Dave Tippett
Associate Coach	Rick Wilson
Assistant Coach	Mark Lamb
Goaltending Consultant	Andy Moog
Video Coach	Derek MacKinnon
Strength and Conditioning Coach	J.J. McQueen
Director, Hockey Administration and Team Services	Lesa Moake
Director, Amateur Scouting	Tim Bernhardt
Director, Professional Scouting	Doug Overton
Director, European Scouting	Kari Takko
Scout	Bob Gernander
Professional Scouts	Paul McIntosh, Scott White
Regional Scouts	Shane Churla, Jack Foley, Dennis Holland, Jiri Hrdina, Jimmy Johnston, Alex LePore, Butch Ott, Jim Pederson, Borys Protsenko, Shane Turner, Bobby Vermette
Head Athletic Trainer	Dave Zeis
Head Equipment Manager	Steve Sumner
Assistant Athletic Trainer	Craig Lowry
Assistant Equipment Manager	Chris Davidson-Adams
Assistant Strength and Conditioning Coach	Manny Hernando
Equipment Assistant	Dennis Soetaert
Massage Therapist	Cleo Bates
Manager, Hockey Administration	Mark Janko
Administrative Assistant, Hockey Operations	Pam Wenzel

Captains' History

Bob Woytowich, 1967-68; Moose Vasko, 1968-69; Claude Larose, 1969-70; Ted Harris, 1970-71 to 1973-74; Bill Goldsworthy, 1974-75, 1975-76; Bill Hogaboam, 1976-77; Nick Beverley, 1977-78; J.P. Parise, 1978-79; Paul Shmyr, 1979-80, 1980-81; Tim Young, 1981-82; Craig Hartsburg, 1982-83; Craig Hartsburg and Brian Bellows, 1983-84; Craig Hartsburg, 1984-85 to 1987-88; Curt Fraser, Bob Rouse and Curt Giles, 1988-89; Curt Giles, 1989-90, 1990-91; Mark Tinordi, 1991-92 to 1993-94; Neal Broten and Derian Hatcher, 1994-95; Derian Hatcher, 1995-96 to 2002-03; Mike Modano, 2003-04 to 2005-06; Brenden Morrow, 2006-07 to date.

General Managers' History

Wren Blair, 1967-68 to 1973-74; Jack Gordon, 1974-75 to 1976-77; Lou Nanne, 1977-78 to 1987-88; Jack Ferreira, 1988-89, 1989-90; Bob Clarke 1990-91, 1991-92; Bob Gainey, 1992-93 to 2000-01; Bob Gainey and Doug Armstrong, 2001-02; Doug Armstrong, 2002-03 to 2006-07; Doug Armstrong and Brett Hull/Les Jackson, 2007-08; Brett Hull/Les Jackson, 2008-09.

Brett Hull

Co-General Manager

Born: Belleville, Ont., August 9, 1964.

Brett Hull was named interim co-general manager of the Dallas Stars along with Les Jackson on November 13, 2007. He and Jackson were both given the job on a permanent basis on May 22, 2008. Hull began the 2007-08 season as a special advisor to the hockey operations department. In 2006-07, he held various roles throughout the Stars organization. He also worked as the in-studio analyst on NBC's NHL Game of the Week.

Hull retired in 2005 after an illustrious 19-year NHL career spent with Calgary, St. Louis, Dallas, Detroit and Phoenix. In 1,269 career games, Hull netted 741 goals, which is good for third place in NHL history, trailing only Wayne Gretzky and Gordie Howe. His 24 career playoff game-winning goals are tied with Gretzky for the most in NHL history, while his 33 career hat tricks rank fourth all-time and his 265 power play goals trail only Dave Andreychuk in the league annals. Hull collected 1,391 career points (741 goals and 650 assists) and added 103 playoff goals (fourth-most all-time) and 87 assists for 190 points in 202 career playoff games.

Hull was a member of the Dallas Stars for three seasons from 1998-99 through 2000-01, and helped the club to its Stanley Cup championship in 1999. In 218 games as a Star, Hull posted 196 points (95 goals and 101 assists), and he added 46 points (21 goals and 25 assists) in 55 Stanley Cup Playoff games with Dallas. He also won the Stanley Cup in 2002 as a member of the Detroit Red Wings, appeared in eight NHL All-Star Games, and in 1991, won both the Hart Trophy and Lester B. Pearson Award as most outstanding player. He skated for Team USA at the 1998 and 2002 Winter Olympics, winning a silver medal in Salt Lake City in 2002, as well as at the 1996 and 2004 World Cup of Hockey.

Les Jackson

Co-General Manager

Born: Manning, Alta., December 21, 1952.

Les Jackson was named interim co-general manager of the Dallas Stars along with Brett Hull on November 13, 2007. He and Hull were both given the job on a permanent basis on May 22, 2008. Previously, Jackson had served as assistant general manager for the Stars for seven years.

Jackson began his career in the Stars organization as an assistant coach in Minnesota in 1985. As assistant general manager in Dallas, he oversaw the club's scouting program, including monitoring the development of all amateur and professional prospects. He also assisted in the evaluation of players as it related to movement within the organization including the entry draft, trades and free agent signings. Jackson was an assistant general manager with the Atlanta Thrashers for two seasons (1998 to 2000), and previous to that spent 13 years in the Dallas organization serving in a variety of roles.

Jackson was drafted by the Boston Bruins in 1972 and played three seasons in the minors before beginning his career as a hockey executive. His minor pro coaching career included stints in Billings, Montana; Tucson, Arizona.; New Westminster, British Columbia; Revelstoke, British Columbia; and Great Falls, Montana. He also spent five years as assistant coach and general manager of the Western Hockey League's Brandon Wheat Kings.

Detroit Red Wings

Key Off-Season Signings/Acquisitions

2008

June 11 • Re-signed head coach **Mike Babcock**.
30 • Re-signed D **Andreas Lilja**.
July 1 • Re-signed D **Brad Stuart**.
1 • Signed G **Ty Conklin**.
2 • Signed RW **Marian Hossa**.

2007-08 Results: 54W-21L-2OTL-5SOL 115PTS.

First, Central Division

Year-by-Year Record

		Home				Road				Overall								
Season	GP	W	L	T	OL	W	L	T	OL	W	L	T	OL	GF	GA	Pts.	Finished	Playoff Result
2007-08	**82**	**29**	**9**	**....**	**3**	**25**	**12**	**....**	**4**	**54**	**21**	**....**	**7**	**257**	**184**	**115**	**1st, Central Div.**	**Won Stanley Cup**
2006-07	82	29	4	....	8	21	15	....	5	50	19	....	13	254	199	113	1st, Central Div.	Lost Conf. Championship
2005-06	82	27	9	....	5	31	7	....	3	58	16	....	8	305	209	124	1st, Central Div.	Lost Conf. Quarter-Final
2004-05	....	....	....	....	....	....	....	....	....	....	....	....	....	....	....	....		
2003-04	82	30	7	4	0	18	14	7	2	48	21	11	2	255	189	109	1st, Central Div.	Lost Conf. Semi-Final
2002-03	82	28	6	5	2	20	14	5	2	48	20	10	4	269	203	110	1st, Central Div.	Lost Conf. Quarter-Final
2001-02	**82**	**28**	**7**	**5**	**1**	**23**	**10**	**5**	**3**	**51**	**17**	**10**	**4**	**251**	**187**	**116**	**1st, Central Div.**	**Won Stanley Cup**
2000-01	82	27	9	3	2	22	11	6	2	49	20	9	4	253	202	111	1st, Central Div.	Lost Conf. Quarter-Final
1999-2000	82	28	9	3	1	20	13	7	1	48	22	10	2	278	210	108	2nd, Central Div.	Lost Conf. Semi-Final
1998-99	82	27	12	2	....	16	20	5	....	43	32	7	....	245	202	93	1st, Central Div.	Lost Conf. Semi-Final
1997-98	**82**	**25**	**8**	**8**	**....**	**19**	**15**	**7**	**....**	**44**	**23**	**15**	**....**	**250**	**196**	**103**	**2nd, Central Div.**	**Won Stanley Cup**
1996-97	**82**	**20**	**12**	**9**	**....**	**18**	**14**	**9**	**....**	**38**	**26**	**18**	**....**	**253**	**197**	**94**	**2nd, Central Div.**	**Won Stanley Cup**
1995-96	82	36	3	2	....	26	10	5	....	62	13	7	....	325	181	131	1st, Central Div.	Lost Conf. Championship
1994-95	48	17	4	3	....	16	7	1	....	33	11	4	....	180	117	70	1st, Central Div.	Lost Final
1993-94	84	23	13	6	....	23	17	2	....	46	30	8	....	356	275	100	1st, Central Div.	Lost Conf. Quarter-Final
1992-93	84	25	14	3	....	22	14	6	....	47	28	9	....	369	280	103	2nd, Norris Div.	Lost Div. Semi-Final
1991-92	80	24	12	4	....	19	13	8	....	43	25	12	....	320	256	98	1st, Norris Div.	Lost Div. Final
1990-91	80	26	14	0	....	8	24	8	....	34	38	8	....	273	298	76	3rd, Norris Div.	Lost Div. Semi-Final
1989-90	80	20	14	6	....	8	24	8	....	28	38	14	....	288	323	70	5th, Norris Div.	Out of Playoffs
1988-89	80	20	14	6	....	14	20	6	....	34	34	12	....	313	316	80	1st, Norris Div.	Lost Div. Semi-Final
1987-88	80	24	10	6	....	17	18	5	....	41	28	11	....	322	269	93	1st, Norris Div.	Lost Conf. Championship
1986-87	80	20	14	6	....	14	22	4	....	34	36	10	....	260	274	78	2nd, Norris Div.	Lost Conf. Championship
1985-86	80	10	26	4	....	7	31	2	....	17	57	6	....	266	415	40	5th, Norris Div.	Out of Playoffs
1984-85	80	19	14	7	....	8	27	5	....	27	41	12	....	313	357	66	3rd, Norris Div.	Lost Div. Semi-Final
1983-84	80	18	20	2	....	13	22	5	....	31	42	7	....	298	323	69	3rd, Norris Div.	Lost Div. Semi-Final
1982-83	80	14	19	7	....	7	25	8	....	21	44	15	....	263	344	57	5th, Norris Div.	Out of Playoffs
1981-82	80	15	19	6	....	6	28	6	....	21	47	12	....	270	351	54	6th, Norris Div.	Out of Playoffs
1980-81	80	16	15	9	....	3	28	9	....	19	43	18	....	252	339	56	5th, Norris Div.	Out of Playoffs
1979-80	80	14	21	5	....	12	22	6	....	26	43	11	....	268	306	63	5th, Norris Div.	Out of Playoffs
1978-79	80	15	17	8	....	8	24	8	....	23	41	16	....	252	295	62	5th, Norris Div.	Out of Playoffs
1977-78	80	22	11	7	....	10	23	7	....	32	34	14	....	252	266	78	2nd, Norris Div.	Lost Quarter-Final
1976-77	80	12	22	6	....	4	33	3	....	16	55	9	....	183	309	41	5th, Norris Div.	Out of Playoffs
1975-76	80	17	15	8	....	9	29	2	....	26	44	10	....	226	300	62	4th, Norris Div.	Out of Playoffs
1974-75	80	17	17	6	....	6	28	6	....	23	45	12	....	259	335	58	4th, Norris Div.	Out of Playoffs
1973-74	78	21	12	6	....	8	27	4	....	29	39	10	....	255	319	68	6th, East Div.	Out of Playoffs
1972-73	78	22	12	5	....	15	17	7	....	37	29	12	....	265	243	86	5th, East Div.	Out of Playoffs
1971-72	78	25	11	3	....	8	24	7	....	33	35	10	....	261	262	76	5th, East Div.	Out of Playoffs
1970-71	78	17	15	7	....	5	30	4	....	22	45	11	....	209	308	55	7th, East Div.	Out of Playoffs
1969-70	76	20	11	7	....	20	10	8	....	40	21	15	....	246	199	95	3rd, East Div.	Lost Quarter-Final
1968-69	76	23	8	7	....	10	23	5	....	33	31	12	....	239	221	78	5th, East Div.	Out of Playoffs
1967-68	74	18	15	4	....	9	20	8	....	27	35	12	....	245	257	66	6th, East Div.	Out of Playoffs
1966-67	70	21	11	3	....	6	28	1	....	27	39	4	....	212	241	58	5th,	Out of Playoffs
1965-66	70	20	8	7	....	11	19	5	....	31	27	12	....	221	194	74	4th,	Lost Final
1964-65	70	25	7	3	....	15	16	4	....	40	23	7	....	224	175	87	1st,	Lost Semi-Final
1963-64	70	23	9	3	....	7	20	8	....	30	29	11	....	191	204	71	4th,	Lost Final
1962-63	70	19	10	6	....	13	15	7	....	32	25	13	....	200	194	77	4th,	Lost Final
1961-62	70	17	11	7	....	6	22	7	....	23	33	14	....	184	219	60	5th,	Out of Playoffs
1960-61	70	15	13	7	....	10	16	9	....	25	29	16	....	195	215	66	4th,	Lost Final
1959-60	70	18	14	3	....	8	15	12	....	26	29	15	....	186	197	67	4th,	Lost Semi-Final
1958-59	70	13	17	5	....	12	20	3	....	25	37	8	....	167	218	58	6th,	Out of Playoffs
1957-58	70	16	11	8	....	13	18	4	....	29	29	12	....	176	207	70	3rd,	Lost Semi-Final
1956-57	70	23	7	5	....	15	13	7	....	38	20	12	....	198	157	88	1st,	Lost Semi-Final
1955-56	70	21	6	8	....	9	18	8	....	30	24	16	....	183	148	76	2nd,	Lost Final
1954-55	**70**	**25**	**5**	**5**	**....**	**17**	**12**	**6**	**....**	**42**	**17**	**11**	**....**	**204**	**134**	**95**	**1st,**	**Won Stanley Cup**
1953-54	**70**	**24**	**4**	**7**	**....**	**13**	**15**	**7**	**....**	**37**	**19**	**14**	**....**	**191**	**132**	**88**	**1st,**	**Won Stanley Cup**
1952-53	70	20	5	10	....	16	11	8	....	36	16	18	....	222	133	90	1st,	Lost Semi-Final
1951-52	**70**	**24**	**7**	**4**	**....**	**20**	**7**	**8**	**....**	**44**	**14**	**12**	**....**	**215**	**133**	**100**	**1st,**	**Won Stanley Cup**
1950-51	70	25	3	7	....	19	10	6	....	44	13	13	....	236	139	101	1st,	Lost Semi-Final
1949-50	**70**	**19**	**9**	**7**	**....**	**18**	**10**	**7**	**....**	**37**	**19**	**14**	**....**	**229**	**164**	**88**	**1st,**	**Won Stanley Cup**
1948-49	60	21	6	3	....	13	13	4	....	34	19	7	....	195	145	75	1st,	Lost Final
1947-48	60	16	9	5	....	14	9	7	....	30	18	12	....	187	148	72	2nd,	Lost Final
1946-47	60	14	10	6	....	8	17	5	....	22	27	11	....	190	193	55	4th,	Lost Semi-Final
1945-46	50	16	5	4	....	4	15	6	....	20	20	10	....	146	159	50	4th,	Lost Semi-Final
1944-45	50	19	5	1	....	12	9	4	....	31	14	5	....	218	161	67	2nd,	Lost Final
1943-44	50	18	5	2	....	8	13	4	....	26	18	6	....	214	177	58	2nd,	Lost Semi-Final
1942-43	**50**	**16**	**4**	**5**	**....**	**9**	**10**	**6**	**....**	**25**	**14**	**11**	**....**	**169**	**124**	**61**	**1st,**	**Won Stanley Cup**
1941-42	48	14	7	3	....	5	18	1	....	19	25	4	....	140	147	42	5th,	Lost Final
1940-41	48	14	5	5	....	7	11	6	....	21	16	11	....	112	102	53	3rd,	Lost Final
1939-40	48	11	10	3	....	5	16	3	....	16	26	6	....	91	126	38	5th,	Lost Semi-Final
1938-39	48	14	8	2	....	4	16	4	....	18	24	6	....	107	128	42	5th,	Lost Semi-Final
1937-38	48	8	10	6	....	4	15	5	....	12	25	11	....	99	133	35	4th, Amn. Div.	Out of Playoffs
1936-37	**48**	**14**	**5**	**5**	**....**	**11**	**9**	**4**	**....**	**25**	**14**	**9**	**....**	**128**	**102**	**59**	**1st, Amn. Div.**	**Won Stanley Cup**
1935-36	**48**	**14**	**5**	**5**	**....**	**10**	**11**	**3**	**....**	**24**	**16**	**8**	**....**	**124**	**103**	**56**	**1st, Amn. Div.**	**Won Stanley Cup**
1934-35	48	11	8	5	....	8	14	2	....	19	22	7	....	127	114	45	4th, Amn. Div.	Out of Playoffs
1933-34	48	15	5	4	....	9	9	6	....	24	14	10	....	113	98	58	1st, Amn. Div.	Lost Final
1932-33*	48	17	3	4	....	8	12	4	....	25	15	8	....	111	93	58	2nd, Amn. Div.	Lost Semi-Final
1931-32	48	15	3	6	....	3	17	4	....	18	20	10	....	95	108	46	3rd, Amn. Div.	Lost Quarter-Final
1930-31**	44	10	7	5	....	6	14	2	....	16	21	7	....	102	105	39	4th, Amn. Div.	Out of Playoffs
1929-30	44	9	10	3	....	5	14	3	....	14	24	6	....	117	133	34	4th, Amn. Div.	Out of Playoffs
1928-29	44	11	6	5	....	8	10	4	....	19	16	9	....	72	63	47	3rd, Amn. Div.	Lost Quarter-Final
1927-28	44	9	10	3	....	10	9	3	....	19	19	6	....	88	79	44	4th, Amn. Div.	Out of Playoffs
1926-27***	44	5	16	0	....	7	12	4	....	12	28	4	....	76	105	28	5th, Amn. Div.	Out of Playoffs

* Team name changed to Red Wings. ** Team name changed to Falcons. *** Team named Cougars.

2008-09 Schedule

Oct.	Thu.	9	Toronto		Mon.	12	at Dallas
	Sat.	11	at Ottawa		Wed.	14	at Anaheim
	Mon.	13	at Carolina		Thu.	15	at Los Angeles
	Thu.	16	Vancouver		Sat.	17	at San Jose
	Sat.	18	NY Rangers		Tue.	20	at Phoenix
	Wed.	22	at St. Louis		Tue.	27	at Columbus
	Fri.	24	Atlanta		Thu.	29	Dallas
	Sat.	25	at Chicago		Sat.	31	at Washington*
	Mon.	27	at Los Angeles	**Feb.**	Mon.	2	St. Louis
	Wed.	29	at Anaheim		Wed.	4	Phoenix
	Thu.	30	at San Jose		Sat.	7	Edmonton*
Nov.	Sun.	2	at Vancouver		Sun.	8	at Pittsburgh*
	Sat.	8	New Jersey		Tue.	10	at Nashville
	Tue.	11	Pittsburgh		Thu.	12	Minnesota
	Thu.	13	at Tampa Bay		Fri.	13	at Columbus
	Fri.	14	at Florida		Sun.	15	Colorado*
	Mon.	17	Edmonton		Wed.	18	Nashville
	Thu.	20	at Edmonton		Fri.	20	Anaheim
	Sat.	22	at Calgary		Sat.	21	at Minnesota
	Mon.	24	at Vancouver		Wed.	25	San Jose
	Wed.	26	Montreal		Fri.	27	Los Angeles
	Fri.	28	Columbus		Sat.	28	at Nashville
	Sat.	29	at Boston	**Mar.**	Tue.	3	at St. Louis
Dec.	Mon.	1	Anaheim		Wed.	4	at Colorado
	Thu.	4	Vancouver		Sat.	7	Columbus
	Sat.	6	Chicago		Tue.	10	Phoenix
	Wed.	10	Calgary		Thu.	12	Calgary
	Fri.	12	at Dallas		Sat.	14	at St. Louis*
	Sat.	13	at Phoenix		Sun.	15	at Columbus*
	Mon.	15	Colorado		Tue.	17	Philadelphia
	Thu.	18	San Jose		Fri.	20	at Atlanta
	Sat.	20	Los Angeles		Mon.	23	at Calgary
	Tue.	23	St. Louis		Tue.	24	at Edmonton
	Fri.	26	at Nashville		Fri.	27	NY Islanders
	Sat.	27	at Colorado		Sun.	29	Nashville*
	Tue.	30	Chicago	**Apr.**	Thu.	2	St. Louis
Jan.	Thu.	1	at Chicago*†		Sun.	5	Minnesota*
	Sat.	3	at Minnesota		Mon.	6	at Buffalo
	Tue.	6	Columbus		Thu.	9	Nashville
	Thu.	8	Dallas		Sat.	11	Chicago*
	Sat.	10	Buffalo		Sun.	12	at Chicago*

* Denotes afternoon game. † Game played at Wrigley Field.

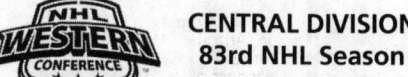

CENTRAL DIVISION
83rd NHL Season
Franchise date: September 25, 1926

2008-09 Player Personnel

FORWARDS	HT	WT	S	Place of Birth	*Age	2007-08 Club
ABDELKADER, Justin	6-1	195	L	Muskegon, MI	21	Michigan State-Detroit
CLEARY, Daniel	6-0	210	L	Carbonear, Nfld.	29	Detroit
DATSYUK, Pavel	5-11	197	L	Sverdlovsk, USSR	30	Detroit
DOWNEY, Aaron	6-1	215	R	Shelburne, Ont.	34	Detroit
DRAPER, Kris	5-10	188	L	Toronto, Ont.	37	Detroit
FILPPULA, Valtteri	6-0	193	L	Vantaa, Finland	24	Detroit
FRANZEN, Johan	6-3	220	L	Landsbro, Sweden	28	Detroit
HAYDAR, Darren	5-9	170	R	Toronto, Ont.	28	Atlanta-Chicago (AHL)
HELM, Darren	5-11	172	L	Winnipeg, Man.	21	Detroit-Grand Rapids
HOLMSTROM, Tomas	6-0	203	L	Pitea, Sweden	35	Detroit
HOSSA, Marian	6-1	210	L	Stara Lubovna, Czech.	29	Atlanta-Pittsburgh
HUDLER, Jiri	5-9	182	L	Olomouc, Czech.	24	Detroit
KOPECKY, Tomas	6-3	200	L	Ilava, Czech.	26	Detroit
LEINO, Ville	6-0	183	L	Savonlinna, Finland	24	Jokerit
MALTBY, Kirk	6-0	193	R	Guelph, Ont.	35	Detroit
SAMUELSSON, Mikael	6-2	213	R	Mariefred, Sweden	31	Detroit
ZETTERBERG, Henrik	5-11	195	L	Njurunda, Sweden	27	Detroit
DEFENSEMEN						
CHELIOS, Chris	6-0	191	R	Chicago, IL	46	Detroit
ERICSSON, Jonathan	6-4	206	L	Karlskrona, Sweden	24	Detroit-Grand Rapids
KINDL, Jakub	6-3	199	L	Sumperk, Czech.	21	Grand Rapids
KRONWALL, Niklas	6-0	189	L	Stockholm, Sweden	27	Detroit
LEBDA, Brett	5-9	195	L	Buffalo Grove, IL	26	Detroit
LIDSTROM, Nicklas	6-1	189	L	Vasteras, Sweden	38	Detroit
LILJA, Andreas	6-3	220	L	Helsingborg, Sweden	33	Detroit
MEECH, Derek	5-11	197	L	Winnipeg, Man.	24	Detroit-Grand Rapids
QUINCEY, Kyle	6-1	207	L	Kitchener, Ont.	23	Detroit-Grand Rapids
RAFALSKI, Brian	5-10	191	R	Dearborn, MI	35	Detroit
STUART, Brad	6-2	213	L	Rocky Mountain House, Alta.	28	Los Angeles-Detroit

GOALTENDERS	HT	WT	C	Place of Birth	*Age	2007-08 Club
CONKLIN, Ty	6-0	184	L	Anchorage, AK	32	Pittsburgh-Wilkes-Barre
HOWARD, James	6-0	218	L	Syracuse, NY	24	Detroit-Grand Rapids
OSGOOD, Chris	5-10	178	L	Peace River, Alta.	35	Detroit

* – Age at start of 2008-09 season

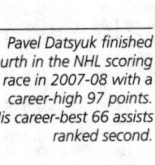

Pavel Datsyuk finished fourth in the NHL scoring race in 2007-08 with a career-high 97 points. His career-best 66 assists ranked second.

Mike Babcock

Head Coach

Born: Manitouwadge, Ont., April 29, 1963.

Mike Babcock became the 26th coach in Detroit Red Wings history on July 14, 2005. In 2008, he led the Red Wings to the Stanley Cup. In his first three seasons behind the bench, Detroit has topped the Western Conference standings each year, and won the Presidents' Trophy for finishing first in the NHL twice.

Babcock brought a winning track record to Detroit from all levels of play, including college and junior hockey, the American Hockey League, the NHL and international hockey. He is the only man to coach Team Canada to victories at both the World Junior Championship (1997) and the senior World Championship (2004.) Prior to joining the Red Wings, he had spent two seasons with Anaheim, leading the team to the Stanley Cup finals in his first season behind the bench in 2002-03. He became the first rookie coach to reach the Finals since Florida's Doug MacLean in 1996. With a four-game sweep over Detroit in the first round of the playoffs, the Ducks became the first team since the 1952 Red Wings (over Toronto) to sweep a defending Stanley Cup champion.

Before joining Anaheim, Babcock spent two seasons as head coach of the Cincinnati Mighty Ducks (2000 to 2002), the primary development affiliate for both Detroit and Anaheim in the American Hockey League. He led the club to a franchise-best 41 wins and 95 points in 2000-01. Babcock moved to Cincinnati after a successful six-year run as the head coach of the Spokane Chiefs of the Western Hockey League (1994 through 2000). He was twice named WHL coach of the year (1996 and 2000) after taking the Chiefs to the league finals in both seasons. He began his WHL coaching career with the Moose Jaw Warriors in 1991-92. In Canadian university play, Babcock won a national championship and was named the coach of the year with the Lethbridge Pronghorns in 1993-94. In 1988, he was named head coach at Red Deer College in Red Deer, Alberta. He spent three seasons at the school, winning the Alberta college championship and coach of the year award in 1989.

Babcock played in the WHL for Saskatoon (1980-81) and Kelowna (1982-83), where he was team captain. In between, he spent a year at the University of Saskatoon. Babcock also played four years at McGill University (1983 to 1987), twice being named an All-Star defenseman and team captain. He earned his bachelor's degree in physical education and attended graduate school in sports psychology at McGill.

2007-08 Scoring

* – rookie

Regular Season

Pos	#	Player	Team	GP	G	A	Pts	TOI	+/–	PIM	PP	SH	GW	S	%
C	13	Pavel Datsyuk	DET	82	31	66	97	21:23	41	20	10	1	6	264	11.7
L	40	Henrik Zetterberg	DET	75	43	49	92	22:04	30	34	16	1	7	358	12.0
D	5	Nicklas Lidstrom	DET	76	10	60	70	26:43	40	40	5	0	4	188	5.3
D	28	Brian Rafalski	DET	73	13	42	55	24:04	27	34	10	0	1	175	7.4
R	11	Daniel Cleary	DET	63	20	22	42	17:23	21	33	5	0	3	177	11.3
C	26	Jiri Hudler	DET	81	13	29	42	13:10	11	26	3	0	2	131	9.9
L	96	Tomas Holmstrom	DET	59	20	20	40	17:32	9	58	11	0	5	137	14.6
R	37	Mikael Samuelsson	DET	73	11	29	40	16:15	21	26	3	0	1	249	4.4
R	93	Johan Franzen	DET	72	27	11	38	17:43	12	51	14	0	8	199	13.6
C	51	Valtteri Filppula	DET	78	19	17	36	16:57	16	28	3	0	3	122	15.6
D	55	Niklas Kronvall	DET	65	7	28	35	21:06	25	44	0	0	0	108	6.5
D	23	Brad Stuart	L.A.	63	5	16	21	21:13	–16	67	2	0	1	111	4.5
			DET	9	1	1	2	20:45	6	2	0	0	0	21	4.8
			Total	72	6	17	23	21:09	–10	69	2	0	1	132	4.5
C	33	Kris Draper	DET	65	9	8	17	15:37	–2	68	0	2	2	97	9.3
D	22	Brett Lebda	DET	78	3	11	14	16:28	–1	48	0	0	1	110	2.7
C	82	Tomas Kopecky	DET	77	5	7	12	09:36	2	43	0	0	1	87	5.7
D	24	Chris Chelios	DET	69	3	9	12	16:57	11	36	0	0	1	60	5.0
D	3	Andreas Lilja	DET	79	2	10	12	18:13	–2	93	0	0	2	72	2.8
L	18	Kirk Maltby	DET	61	6	4	10	12:03	–8	32	0	0	1	70	8.6
R	17	Dallas Drake	DET	65	3	3	6	10:42	–12	41	0	1	0	46	6.5
C	44	Mark Hartigan	DET	23	3	1	4	07:09	–2	16	0	0	0	19	15.8
D	14 *	Derek Meech	DET	32	0	3	3	12:08	–5	6	0	0	0	44	0.0
R	20	Aaron Downey	DET	56	0	3	3	04:35	0	116	0	0	0	15	0.0
D	52 *	Jonathan Ericsson	DET	8	1	0	1	15:58	–3	4	1	0	0	19	5.3
C	42 *	Mattias Ritola	DET	2	0	1	1	05:46	0	0	0	0	0	2	0.0
R	25	Darren McCarty	DET	3	0	1	1	07:46	2	2	0	0	0	3	0.0
D	36	Garrett Stafford	DET	2	0	0	0	06:45	0	0	0	0	0	1	0.0
L	8 *	Justin Abdelkader	DET	2	0	0	0	12:13	0	2	0	0	0	6	0.0
D	4 *	Kyle Quincey	DET	6	0	0	0	13:58	–3	4	0	0	0	5	0.0
C	43 *	Darren Helm	DET	7	0	0	0	07:00	–2	2	0	0	0	7	0.0

Goaltending

No.	Goaltender	GPI	Mins	Avg	W	L	OT	EN	SO	GA	SA	S%	G	A	PIM
30	Chris Osgood	43	2409	2.09	27	9	4	1	4	84	976	.914	0	3	0
35	* James Howard	4	197	2.13	0	2	0	0	0	7	95	.926	0	0	0
39	Dominik Hasek	41	2350	2.14	27	10	3	3	5	84	855	.902	0	1	12
	Totals	**82**	**4979**	**2.16**	**54**	**21**	**7**	**4**	**9**	**179**	**1930**	**.907**			

Playoffs

Pos	#	Player	Team	GP	G	A	Pts	TOI	+/–	PIM	PP	SH	GW	OT	S	%
C	40	Henrik Zetterberg	DET	22	13	14	27	22:36	16	16	4	2	4	0	116	11.2
C	13	Pavel Datsyuk	DET	22	10	13	23	21:40	13	6	4	0	1	0	74	13.5
R	93	Johan Franzen	DET	16	13	5	18	18:49	13	14	6	2	5	1	70	18.6
D	55	Niklas Kronvall	DET	22	0	15	15	23:19	16	18	0	0	0	0	21	0.0
C	26	Jiri Hudler	DET	22	5	9	14	11:35	–1	14	2	0	2	0	46	10.9
D	28	Brian Rafalski	DET	22	4	10	14	24:53	6	12	2	0	0	0	58	6.9
R	37	Mikael Samuelsson	DET	22	5	8	13	15:55	8	8	0	0	1	0	79	6.3
D	5	Nicklas Lidstrom	DET	22	3	10	13	26:48	8	14	1	1	1	0	41	7.3
L	96	Tomas Holmstrom	DET	21	4	8	12	17:10	4	26	1	0	0	0	41	9.8
C	51	Valtteri Filppula	DET	22	5	6	11	16:39	7	2	0	0	0	0	39	12.8
D	23	Brad Stuart	DET	21	1	6	7	21:40	15	14	0	0	1	0	25	4.0
C	33	Kris Draper	DET	22	3	1	4	15:27	0	10	0	0	1	0	37	8.1
C	43 *	Darren Helm	DET	18	2	2	4	07:30	2	2	0	0	0	0	21	9.5
R	17	Dallas Drake	DET	22	1	3	4	11:22	2	12	0	0	0	0	27	3.7
R	11	Daniel Cleary	DET	22	2	1	3	17:49	1	4	0	1	0	0	54	3.7
R	25	Darren McCarty	DET	17	1	1	2	06:22	1	19	0	0	0	0	14	7.1
D	22	Brett Lebda	DET	19	0	2	2	12:33	0	6	0	0	0	0	12	0.0
C	44	Mark Hartigan	DET	4	0	1	1	05:21	0	4	0	0	0	0	0	0.0
L	18	Kirk Maltby	DET	12	0	1	1	09:47	0	10	0	0	0	0	10	0.0
D	3	Andreas Lilja	DET	12	0	1	1	14:05	3	16	0	0	0	0	7	0.0
D	24	Chris Chelios	DET	14	0	0	0	12:54	2	10	0	0	0	0	11	0.0

Goaltending

No.	Goaltender	GPI	Mins	Avg	W	L	EN	SO	GA	SA	S%	G	A	PIM
30	Chris Osgood	19	1160	1.55	14	4	0	3	30	430	.930	0	0	0
39	Dominik Hasek	4	206	2.91	2	2	1	0	10	89	.888	0	0	2
	Totals	**22**	**1372**	**1.79**	**16**	**6**	**1**	**3**	**41**	**520**	**.921**			

Coaching Record

			Regular Season				Playoffs			
Season	Team	League	GC	W	L	O/T	GC	W	L	T
1991-92	Moose Jaw	WHL	72	33	36	3	4	0	4	....
1992-93	Moose Jaw	WHL	72	27	42	3	....	....	....	....
1993-94	U of Lethbridge	CIAU	28	19	7	2	....	....	....	....
1994-95	Spokane	WHL	72	32	36	4	11	6	5	....
1995-96	Spokane	WHL	72	50	18	4	9	3	6	....
1996-97	Spokane	WHL	72	35	33	4	9	4	5	....
1997-98	Spokane	WHL	72	45	23	4	18	10	8	....
1998-99	Spokane	WHL	72	19	44	9	....	....	....	....
99-2000	Spokane	WHL	72	47	19	6	20	15	5	....
2000-01	Cincinnati	AHL	80	41	26	13	4	1	3	....
2001-02	Cincinnati	AHL	80	33	33	14	3	1	2	....
2002-03	**Anaheim**	**NHL**	**82**	**40**	**27**	**15**	**21**	**15**	**6**	....
2003-04	**Anaheim**	**NHL**	**82**	**29**	**35**	**18**	....	....	....	....
2004-05	**Anaheim**				SEASON CANCELLED					
2005-06	**Detroit**	**NHL**	**82**	**58**	**16**	**8**	**6**	**2**	**4**	....
2006-07	**Detroit**	**NHL**	**82**	**50**	**19**	**13**	**18**	**10**	**8**	....
2007-08♦	**Detroit**	**NHL**	**82**	**54**	**21**	**7**	**22**	**16**	**6**	....
	NHL Totals		**410**	**231**	**118**	**61**	**67**	**43**	**24**	....

♦ Stanley Cup win.

Club Records

Team

(Figures in brackets for season records are games played; records for fewest points, wins, ties, losses, goals, goals against are for 70 or more games)

Most Points	131	1995-96 (82)
Most Wins	*62	1995-96 (82)
Most Ties	18	1952-53 (70), 1980-81 (80), 1996-97 (82)
Most Losses	57	1985-86 (80)
Most Goals	369	1992-93 (84)
Most Goals Against	415	1985-86 (80)
Fewest Points	40	1985-86 (80)
Fewest Wins	16	1976-77 (80)
Fewest Ties	4	1966-67 (70)
Fewest Losses	13	1950-51 (70), 1995-96 (82)
Fewest Goals	167	1958-59 (70)
Fewest Goals Against	132	1953-54 (70)
Longest Winning Streak		
Overall	9	Seven times
Home	14	Jan. 21-Mar. 25/65
Away	12	Mar. 1-Apr. 15/06
Longest Undefeated Streak		
Overall	15	Nov. 27-Dec. 28/52 (8 wins, 7 ties)
Home	19	Dec. 31/00-Apr.7/01 (17 wins, 2 ties)
Away	15	Oct. 18-Dec. 20/51 (10 wins, 5 ties)
Longest Losing Streak		
Overall	14	Feb. 24-Mar. 25/82
Home	7	Feb. 20-Mar. 25/82
Away	14	Oct. 19-Dec. 21/66
Longest Winless Streak		
Overall	19	Feb. 26-Apr. 3/77 (18 losses, 1 tie)
Home	10	Dec. 11/85-Jan. 18/86 (9 losses, 1 tie)
Away	26	Dec. 15/76-Apr. 3/77 (23 losses, 3 ties)
Most Shutouts, Season	13	1953-54 (70)
Most. PIM, Season	2,393	1985-86 (80)
Most Goals, Game	15	Jan. 23/44 (NYR 0 at Det. 15)

Individual

Most Seasons	25	Gordie Howe
Most Games	1,687	Gordie Howe
Most Goals, Career	786	Gordie Howe
Most Assists, Career	1,063	Steve Yzerman
Most Points, Career	1,809	Gordie Howe (786G, 1,023A)
Most PIM, Career	2,090	Bob Probert
Most Shutouts, Career	85	Terry Sawchuk
Longest Consecutive Games Streak	548	Alex Delvecchio (Dec. 13/56-Nov. 11/64)
Most Goals, Season	65	Steve Yzerman (1988-89)
Most Assists, Season	90	Steve Yzerman (1988-89)
Most Points, Season	155	Steve Yzerman (1988-89; 65G, 90A)
Most PIM, Season	398	Bob Probert (1987-88)
Most Points, Defenseman, Season	80	Nicklas Lidstrom (2005-06; 16G, 64A)
Most Points, Center, Season	155	Steve Yzerman (1988-89; 65G, 90A)
Most Points, Right Wing, Season	103	Gordie Howe (1968-69; 44G, 59A)
Most Points, Left Wing, Season	105	John Ogrodnick (1984-85; 55G, 50A)
Most Points, Rookie, Season	87	Steve Yzerman (1983-84; 39G, 48A)
Most Shutouts, Season	12	Terry Sawchuk (1951-52, 1953-54, 1954-55), Glenn Hall (1955-56)
Most Goals, Game	6	Syd Howe (Feb. 3/44)
Most Assists, Game	*7	Billy Taylor (Mar. 16/47)
Most Points, Game	7	Carl Liscombe (Nov. 5/42; 3G, 4A), Don Grosso (Feb. 3/44; 1G, 6A), Billy Taylor (Mar. 16/47; 7A)

* NHL Record.

Retired Numbers

1	Terry Sawchuk	1949-55, 57-64, 68-69
7	Ted Lindsay	1944-57, 64-65
9	Gordie Howe	1946-1971
10	Alex Delvecchio	1951-1973
12	Sid Abel	1938-43, 45-52
19	Steve Yzerman	1983-2006

All-time Record vs. Other Clubs

Regular Season

	At Home								On Road								Total							
	GP	W	L	T	OL	GF	GA	PTS	GP	W	L	T	OL	GF	GA	PTS	GP	W	L	T	OL	GF	GA	PTS
Anaheim	28	22	3	3	0	97	58	47	28	13	11	4	0	76	70	30	56	35	14	7	0	173	128	77
Atlanta	5	4	1	0	0	18	13	8	4	3	1	0	0	25	14	6	9	7	2	0	0	43	27	14
Boston	286	154	80	52	0	955	726	360	288	91	153	43	1	764	1008	226	574	245	233	95	1	1719	1734	586
Buffalo	56	32	18	5	1	205	162	70	53	12	33	8	0	157	228	32	109	44	51	13	1	362	390	102
Calgary	65	36	19	10	0	242	191	82	66	22	38	6	0	188	240	50	131	58	57	16	0	430	431	132
Carolina	32	18	7	7	0	124	88	43	31	12	18	1	0	88	107	25	63	30	25	8	0	212	195	68
Chicago	347	212	100	33	2	1196	862	459	350	140	154	51	5	991	1046	336	697	352	254	84	7	2187	1908	795
Colorado	46	29	15	1	1	164	131	60	48	23	21	4	0	162	159	50	94	52	36	5	1	326	290	110
Columbus	22	17	3	0	2	82	49	36	23	16	5	1	1	75	49	34	45	33	8	1	3	157	98	70
Dallas	112	57	38	16	1	426	353	131	112	41	52	18	1	334	378	101	224	98	90	34	2	760	731	232
Edmonton	50	28	15	3	4	190	160	63	50	16	20	10	4	173	189	46	100	44	35	13	8	363	349	109
Florida	9	5	1	3	0	35	23	13	10	6	1	2	1	29	20	15	19	11	2	5	1	64	43	28
Los Angeles	85	41	31	13	0	330	289	95	86	29	42	14	1	268	331	73	171	70	73	27	1	598	620	168
Minnesota	14	9	3	1	1	53	33	20	14	9	1	2	2	41	30	22	28	18	4	3	3	94	63	42
Montreal	281	131	97	53	0	807	717	315	283	68	172	43	0	640	995	179	564	199	269	96	0	1447	1712	494
Nashville	29	21	3	2	3	105	62	47	28	14	10	2	2	82	75	32	57	35	13	4	5	187	137	79
New Jersey	41	26	13	2	0	169	131	54	41	11	21	9	0	105	139	31	82	37	34	11	0	274	270	85
NY Islanders	46	26	18	2	0	166	137	54	47	20	23	4	0	141	167	44	93	46	41	6	0	307	304	98
NY Rangers	286	165	76	45	0	1008	702	375	285	93	134	58	0	742	871	244	571	258	210	103	0	1750	1573	619
Ottawa	10	6	4	0	0	35	22	12	11	6	4	1	0	31	31	13	21	12	8	1	0	66	53	25
Philadelphia	60	32	18	10	0	216	185	74	59	13	35	11	0	169	236	37	119	45	53	21	0	385	421	111
Phoenix	57	29	20	8	0	222	187	66	55	24	17	14	0	180	158	62	112	53	37	22	0	402	345	128
Pittsburgh	66	41	13	12	0	256	179	94	66	18	44	4	0	197	281	40	132	59	57	16	0	453	460	134
St. Louis	122	59	43	17	3	440	361	138	122	42	57	20	3	344	396	107	244	101	100	37	6	784	757	245
San Jose	31	26	4	1	0	122	55	53	32	17	12	3	0	123	113	37	63	43	16	4	0	245	168	90
Tampa Bay	13	11	1	1	0	51	23	23	15	10	4	1	0	67	46	21	28	21	5	2	0	118	69	44
Toronto	323	169	106	46	2	973	793	386	317	105	164	47	1	848	1048	258	640	274	270	93	3	1821	1841	644
Vancouver	72	44	18	8	2	289	204	98	71	29	32	10	0	226	254	68	143	73	50	18	2	515	458	166
Washington	48	22	15	11	0	165	138	55	47	21	21	5	0	151	171	47	95	43	36	16	0	316	309	102
Defunct Clubs	141	76	40	25	0	430	307	177	141	49	63	29	0	364	375	127	282	125	103	54	0	794	682	304
Totals	**2783**	**1548**	**823**	**390**	**22**	**9571**	**7341**	**3508**	**2783**	**973**	**1363**	**425**	**22**	**7781**	**9225**	**2393**	**5566**	**2521**	**2186**	**815**	**44**	**17352**	**16566**	**5901**

Playoffs

	Series	W	L	GP	W	L	T	GF	GA	Last Mtg.	Rnd.	Result
Anaheim	4	2	2	18	10	8	0	53	40	2007	CF	L 2-4
Boston	7	3	4	33	14	19	0	98	96	1957	SF	L 1-4
Calgary	3	2	1	14	8	6	0	38	26	2007	CQF	W 4-2
Carolina	1	1	0	5	4	1	0	14	7	2002	F	W 4-1
Chicago	14	6	8	69	31	38	0	190	210	1995	CF	W 4-1
Colorado	6	3	3	34	17	17	0	97	88	2008	CSF	W 4-0
Dallas	4	4	0	24	16	8	0	72	50	2008	CF	W 4-2
Edmonton	3	0	3	16	4	12	0	43	58	2006	CQF	L 2-4
Los Angeles	2	1	1	10	6	4	0	32	21	2001	CQF	L 2-4
Montreal	12	7	5	62	29	33	0	149	161	1978	QF	L 1-4
Nashville	2	2	0	12	8	4	0	29	21	2008	CQF	W 4-2
New Jersey	1	0	1	4	0	4	0	7	16	1995	F	L 0-4
NY Rangers	5	4	1	23	13	10	0	57	49	1950	F	W 4-3
Philadelphia	1	1	0	4	4	0	0	16	6	1997	F	W 4-0
Phoenix	2	2	0	12	8	4	0	44	28	1998	CQF	W 4-2
Pittsburgh	1	1	0	6	4	2	0	17	10	2008	F	W 4-2
St. Louis	7	5	2	40	24	16	0	125	103	2002	CSF	W 4-1
San Jose	3	2	1	17	11	6	0	64	36	2007	CSF	W 4-2
Toronto	23	11	12	117	59	58	0	321	311	1993	DSF	L 3-4
Vancouver	1	1	0	6	4	2	0	22	16	2002	CQF	W 4-2
Washington	1	1	0	4	4	0	0	13	7	1998	F	W 4-0
Defunct Clubs	4	3	1	10	7	2	1	21	13			
Totals	**107**	**62**	**45**	**540**	**285**	**254**	**1**	**1522**	**1373**			

Calgary totals include Atlanta Flames, 1972-73 to 1979-80.
Colorado totals include Quebec, 1979-80 to 1994-95.
New Jersey totals include Kansas City, 1974-75, 1975-76, and Colorado Rockies, 1976-77 to 1981-82.
Phoenix totals include Winnipeg, 1979-80 to 1995-96.
Carolina totals include Hartford, 1979-80 to 1996-97.
Dallas totals include Minnesota North Stars, 1967-68 to 1992-93.

Playoff Results 2008-2003

Year	Round	Opponent	Result	GF	GA
2008	**F**	**Pittsburgh**	**W 4-2**	**17**	**10**
	CF	Dallas	W 4-2	17	10
	CSF	Colorado	W 4-0	21	9
	CQF	Nashville	W 4-2	17	12
2007	CF	Anaheim	L 2-4	17	16
	CSF	San Jose	W 4-2	13	9
	CQF	Calgary	W 4-2	18	10
2006	CQF	Edmonton	L 2-4	17	19
2004	CSF	Calgary	L 2-4	12	11
	CQF	Nashville	W 4-2	12	9
2003	CQF	Anaheim	L 0-4	6	10

Abbreviations: Round: F - Final; **CF** - conference final; **CSF** - conference semi-final; **CQF** - conference quarter-final; **DSF** - division semi-final; **SF** - semi-final; **QF** - quarter-final.

2007-08 Results

Oct.	3	Anaheim	3-2†		5	at Dallas	3-0
	6	at Chicago	3-4†		6	at Chicago	3-1
	8	Edmonton	4-2		8	Colorado	1-0
	10	Calgary	4-2		10	Minnesota	5-6†
	12	Chicago	2-3		12	at Ottawa	2-3
	14	at Los Angeles	4-1		15	Atlanta	1-5
	15	at Anaheim	3-6		17	Vancouver	3-2†
	18	at San Jose	4-2		19	at San Jose	6-3
	20	at Phoenix	5-2		22	at Los Angeles	3-0
	24	Vancouver	3-2		23	at Anaheim	2-1
	26	San Jose	5-1		30	Phoenix	3-2
	28	at Vancouver	3-2	Feb.	1	Colorado	2-0
	30	at Edmonton	2-1		2	at Boston	3-1
Nov.	1	at Calgary	4-1		5	at Minnesota	3-2*
	7	Nashville	3-2†		7	Los Angeles	3-5
	9	Columbus	4-1		9	at Toronto	2-3*
	11	at Chicago	2-3		10	Anaheim	2-3
	13	at St. Louis	3-4		12	at Nashville	2-4
	17	Chicago	3-5		15	Columbus	1-5
	18	at Columbus	5-4†		17	at Dallas	0-1
	21	St. Louis	3-0		18	at Colorado	4-0
	22	at Nashville	2-3		22	at Calgary	0-1
	24	at Columbus	2-3†		23	at Vancouver	1-4
	27	Calgary	5-3		26	at Edmonton	3-4†
	29	Tampa Bay	4-2		29	San Jose	2-3
Dec.	1	Phoenix	3-2	Mar.	2	at Buffalo	4-2
	4	at Montreal	4-1		5	St. Louis	4-1
	7	Minnesota	5-0		9	Nashville	4-3
	9	Carolina	5-2		11	Chicago	3-1
	10	at Nashville	2-1		13	Dallas	5-3
	13	Edmonton	3-4†		15	Nashville	1-3
	15	Florida	5-2		16	at Columbus	3-4
	17	Washington	4-3†		19	Columbus	3-1
	19	Los Angeles	6-2		20	at Nashville	6-3
	20	at St. Louis	2-3		22	at Columbus	4-1
	22	at Minnesota	4-1		25	at St. Louis	2-1
	26	at St. Louis	5-0		28	St. Louis	3-4*
	27	at Colorado	4-2		30	Nashville	1-0*
	29	at Phoenix	4-2	Apr.	2	at Chicago	2-6
	31	St. Louis	0-2		3	Columbus	3-2
Jan.	2	Dallas	4-1		6	Chicago	4-1

* – Overtime † – Shootout

Entry Draft Selections 2008-1994

Name in bold denotes played in NHL.

2008
Pick
30 Thomas McCollum
91 Max Nicastro
121 Gustav Nyquist
151 Julien Cayer
181 Stephen Johnston
211 Jesper Samuelsson

2007
Pick
27 Brendan Smith
88 Joakim Andersson
148 Randy Cameron
178 Zack Torquato
208 Bryan Rufenach

2006
Pick
41 Cory Emmerton
47 **Shawn Matthias**
62 Dick Axelsson
92 Daniel Larsson
182 Jan Mursak
191 Nick Oslund
212 Logan Pyett

2005
Pick
19 Jakub Kindl
42 **Justin Abdelkader**
80 Christofer Lofberg
103 **Mattias Ritola**
132 **Darren Helm**
137 Johan Ryno
151 Jeff May
175 Juho Mielonen
214 Bretton Stamler

2004
Pick
97 **Johan Franzen**
128 Evan McGrath
151 Sergei Kolosov
162 Tyler Haskins
192 Anton Axelsson
226 Steven Covington
257 Gennady Stolyarov
290 Nils Backstrom

2003
Pick
64 **James Howard**
132 **Kyle Quincey**
164 Ryan Oulahen
170 Andreas Sundin
194 Stefan Blom
226 Tomas Kollar
258 Vladimir Kutny
289 Mikael Johansson

2002
Pick
58 **Jiri Hudler**
63 **Tomas Fleischmann**
95 **Valtteri Filppula**
131 Johan Berggren
166 Logan Koopmans
197 Jimmy Cuddihy
229 **Derek Meech**
260 Pierre-Olivier Beaulieu
262 Christian Soderstrom
291 **Jonathan Ericsson**

2001
Pick
62 Igor Grigorenko
121 **Drew MacIntyre**
129 Miroslav Blatak
157 Andreas Jamtin
195 Nick Pannoni
258 **Dmitri Bykov**
288 Francois Senez

2000
Pick
29 **Niklas Kronwall**
38 **Tomas Kopecky**
102 Stefan Liv
127 Dmitri Semenov
128 Alexander Seluyanov
130 Aaron Van Leusen
187 Per Backer
196 Paul Ballantyne
228 Jimmie Svensson
251 Todd Jackson
260 Yevgeny Bumagin

1999
Pick
120 Jari Tolsa
149 Andrei Maximenko
181 **Kent McDonell**
210 **Henrik Zetterberg**
238 Anton Borodkin
266 Ken Davis

1998
Pick
25 **Jiri Fischer**
55 **Ryan Barnes**
56 Tomek Valtonen
84 Jake McCracken
111 Brent Hobday
142 Calle Steen
151 Adam DeLeeuw
171 **Pavel Datsyuk**
198 Jeremy Goetzinger
226 David Petrasek
256 Petja Pietilainen

1997
Pick
49 **Yuri Butsayev**
76 **Petr Sykora**
102 **Quintin Laing**
129 John Wikstrom
157 **B.J. Young**
186 Mike Laceby
213 Steve Willejto
239 Greg Willers

1996
Pick
26 **Jesse Wallin**
52 Aren Miller
108 Johan Forsander
135 Michal Podolka
144 Magnus Nilsson
162 Alexandre Jacques
189 Colin Beardsmore
215 Craig Stahl
241 Eugeny Afanasiev

1995
Pick
26 **Maxim Kuznetsov**
52 **Philippe Audet**
58 **Darryl Laplante**
104 Anatoli Ustyugov
125 Chad Wilchynski
126 David Arsenault
156 Tyler Perry
182 Per Eklund
208 Andrei Samokhvalov
234 David Engblom

1994
Pick
23 **Yan Golubovsky**
49 **Mathieu Dandenault**
75 Sean Gillam
114 Frederic Deschenes
127 Doug Battaglia
153 Pavel Agarkov
205 Jason Elliot
231 Jeff Mikesch
257 **Tomas Holmstrom**
283 Toivo Suursoo

Club Directory

Joe Louis Arena

Detroit Red Wings
Joe Louis Arena
19 Steve Yzerman Drive
Detroit, MI 48226
Phone **313/394-7000**
FAX PR: 313/567-0296
Media Hotline: 313/396-7599
www.detroitredwings.com
Capacity: 20,066

Owner/Governor . . . . . Mike Ilitch
Owner/Secretary-Treasurer . . . . . Marian Ilitch
President and CEO Ilitch Holdings/ Alternate Governor Red Wings . . . . . Christopher Ilitch
Vice-President Olympia Entertainment/ General Counsel Red Wings . . . . . Robert E. Carr
Senior Vice President. . . . . Jim Devellano
Exec. Vice President/General Manager. . . . . Ken Holland
Vice President/Hockey. . . . . Steve Yzerman
Vice President/Assistant General Manager. . . . . Jim Nill
Senior Vice President of Business Affairs . . . . . Steven Violetta
Director of Hockey Administration . . . . . Ryan Martin
Head Coach . . . . . Mike Babcock
Assistant Coaches. . . . . Paul MacLean, Brad McCrimmon
Video Coach. . . . . Keith McKittrick
Goaltending Coach. . . . . Jim Bedard
Director of Pro Scouting . . . . . Mark Howe
Pro Scouts . . . . . Pat Verbeek, Glenn Merkosky
Director of Amateur Scouting . . . . . Joe McDonnell
Amateur Scouts . . . . . Bruce Haralson, Mark Leach, Dave Kolb
Director of European Scouting . . . . . Hakan Andersson
European Scouts. . . . . Vladimir Havluj, Evgeni Erfilov
Part-Time Scout . . . . . Marty Stein
Vice-President of Finance . . . . . Paul MacDonald
Executive Assistant . . . . . Kathi Wyatt
Accounting Assistant . . . . . Bridget Merritt
Athletic Therapist . . . . . Piet Van Zant
Equipment Manager. . . . . Paul Boyer
Assistant Athletic Therapist. . . . . Russ Baumann
Assistant Equipment Manager. . . . . John Remejes
Team Masseur . . . . . Sergei Tchekmarev
Senior Director of Communications. . . . . John Hahn
Media Relations Manager. . . . . Todd Beam
Community Relations Manager. . . . . Anne Marie Krappmann
Public Relations Coordinator. . . . . Lisa Hickok
Community Relations Coordinator . . . . . Kelli Kearly
Medical Director. . . . . Dr. Donald Weaver
Team Physicians . . . . . Dr. Anthony Colucci, Dr. Doug Plagens
Team Dentist . . . . . Dr. C.J. Regula
Team Photographer . . . . . Dave Reginek
Radio Announcers, 97.1 FM The Ticket. . . . . Ken Kal, Paul Woods
Television Announcers, Fox Sports Net Detroit. . . . . Ken Daniels, Mickey Redmond

Coaching History

Art Duncan and Duke Keats, 1926-27; Jack Adams, 1927-28 to 1946-47; Tommy Ivan, 1947-48 to 1953-54; Jimmy Skinner, 1954-55 to 1956-57; Jimmy Skinner and Sid Abel, 1957-58; Sid Abel, 1958-59 to 1967-68; Bill Gadsby, 1968-69; Bill Gadsby and Sid Abel, 1969-70; Ned Harkness and Doug Barkley, 1970-71; Doug Barkley and Johnny Wilson, 1971-72; Johnny Wilson, 1972-73; Ted Garvin and Alex Delvecchio, 1973-74; Alex Delvecchio, 1974-75; Doug Barkley and Alex Delvecchio, 1975-76; Alex Delvecchio and Larry Wilson, 1976-77; Bobby Kromm, 1977-78, 1978-79; Bobby Kromm and Ted Lindsay, 1979-80; Ted Lindsay and Wayne Maxner, 1980-81; Wayne Maxner and Billy Dea, 1981-82; Nick Polano, 1982-83 to 1984-85; Harry Neale and Brad Park, 1985-86; Jacques Demers, 1986-87 to 1989-90; Bryan Murray, 1990-91 to 1992-93; Scotty Bowman, 1993-94 to 1997-98; Dave Lewis, Barry Smith (co-coaches) and Scotty Bowman, 1998-99; Scotty Bowman, 1999-2000 to 2001-02; Dave Lewis, 2002-03 to 2004-05; Mike Babcock, 2005-06 to date.

Ken Holland

General Manager

Born: Vernon, B.C., November 10, 1955.

Ken Holland has served in the Red Wings front office since 1985, and has been the club's general manager since July 18, 1997. He has established himself as one of the most innovative and aggressive GMs in the National Hockey League. Detroit's Stanley Cup victory in 2008 marked the team's third championship under his leadership. Holland began his tenure as the club's general manager after serving as assistant general manager for the previous three seasons.

Holland oversees all aspects of hockey operations including all matters relating to player personnel, development, contract negotiations and player movements, though he now takes a less prominent role in the NHL draft than he did during his seven years as the club's director of amateur scouting.

At the conclusion of his playing days as a goaltender, spending most of his pro career at the American Hockey League level, Holland began his off-ice career in 1985 as a western Canada scout followed by five years as an amateur scouting director before promotions led to his current position as general manager.

A native of Vernon, British Columbia, Holland played in the junior ranks for Medicine Hat (WHL) in 1974-75. He was Toronto's 13th pick (188th overall) in the 1975 draft but never saw action with the Maple Leafs. Holland twice signed with NHL teams as a free agent — in 1980 with Hartford and 1983 with Detroit. He spent most of his pro career with AHL clubs in Binghamton and Springfield, along with Adirondack, but did appear in four NHL games, making his debut with Hartford in 1980-81 and playing three contests for Detroit in 1983-84.

General Managers' History

Art Duncan and Duke Keats, 1926-27; Jack Adams, 1927-28 to 1961-62; Sid Abel, 1962-63 to 1969-70; Sid Abel and Ned Harkness, 1970-71; Ned Harkness, 1971-72 to 1973-74; Alex Delvecchio, 1974-75, 1975-76; Alex Delvecchio and Ted Lindsay, 1976-77; Ted Lindsay, 1977-78 to 1979-80; Jimmy Skinner, 1980-81, 1981-82; Jim Devellano, 1982-83 to 1989-90; Bryan Murray, 1990-91 to 1993-94; Jim Devellano (Senior Vice President), 1994-95 to 1996-97; Ken Holland, 1997-98 to date.

Captains' History

Art Duncan, 1926-27; Reg Noble, 1927-28 to 1929-30; George Hay, 1930-31; Carson Cooper, 1931-32; Larry Aurie, 1932-33; Herbie Lewis, 1933-34; Ebbie Goodfellow, 1934-35; Doug Young, 1935-36 to 1937-38; Ebbie Goodfellow, 1938-39 to 1940-41; Ebbie Goodfellow and Syd Howe, 1941-42; Sid Abel, 1942-43; Mud Bruneteau, Flash Hollett, 1943-44; Flash Hollett, 1944-45; Flash Hollett and Sid Abel, 1945-46; Sid Abel, 1946-47 to 1951-52; Ted Lindsay, 1952-53 to 1955-56; Red Kelly, 1956-57, 1957-58; Gordie Howe, 1958-59 to 1961-62; Alex Delvecchio, 1962-63 to 1972-73; Alex Delvecchio, Nick Libett, Red Berenson, Gary Bergman, Ted Harris, Mickey Redmond and Larry Johnston, 1973-74; Marcel Dionne, 1974-75; Danny Grant and Terry Harper, 1975-76; Danny Grant and Dennis Polonich, 1976-77; Dan Maloney and Dennis Hextall, 1977-78; Dennis Hextall, Nick Libett and Paul Woods, 1978-79; Dale McCourt, 1979-80; Errol Thompson and Reed Larson, 1980-81; Reed Larson, 1981-82; Danny Gare, 1982-83 to 1985-86; Steve Yzerman, 1986-87 to 2005-06; Nicklas Lidstrom, 2006-07 to date.

Edmonton Oilers

2007-08 Results: 41W-35L-2OTL-4SOL 88PTS.

Fourth, Northwest Division

Key Off-Season Signings/Acquisitions

2008

- **April 11** • Re-signed D **Tom Gilbert**.
- **12** • Re-signed RW **Robert Nilsson**.
- **14** • Re-signed D **Denis Grebeshkov**.
- **June 25** • Named **Kelly Buchberger** assistant coach.
- **30** • Acquired D **Lubomir Visnovsky** from Los Angeles for D **Matt Greene** and C **Jarret Stoll**.
- **July 1** • Acquired C **Gilbert Brule** from Columbus for LW **Raffi Torres**.
- **1** • Acquired LW **Erik Cole** from Carolina for D **Joni Pitkanen**.
- **9** • Re-signed C **Marc Pouliot** and LW **Jean-Francois Jacques**.
- **10** • Signed D **Jason Strudwick**.
- **15** • Re-signed RW **Zack Stortini**.

Year-by-Year Record

		Home				Road				Overall								
Season	GP	W	L	T	OL	W	L	T	OL	W	L	T	OL	GF	GA	Pts.	Finished	Playoff Result
2007-08	82	23	17	....	1	18	18	....	5	41	35	....	6	235	251	88	4th, Northwest Div.	Out of Playoffs
2006-07	82	19	19	....	3	13	24	....	4	32	43	....	7	195	248	71	5th, Northwest Div.	Out of Playoffs
2005-06	82	20	15	....	6	21	13	....	7	41	28	....	13	256	251	95	3rd, Northwest Div.	Lost Final
2004-05	....	....	....	....	....	....	....	....	....	....	....	....	....	....	....	....		
2003-04	82	22	12	4	3	14	17	8	2	36	29	12	5	221	208	89	4th, Northwest Div.	Out of Playoffs
2002-03	82	20	12	5	4	16	14	6	5	36	26	11	9	231	230	92	4th, Northwest Div.	Lost Conf. Quarter-Final
2001-02	82	23	14	4	0	15	14	8	4	38	28	12	4	205	182	92	3rd, Northwest Div.	Out of Playoffs
2000-01	82	23	9	7	2	16	19	5	1	39	28	12	3	243	222	93	2nd, Northwest Div.	Lost Conf. Quarter-Final
1999-2000	82	18	11	9	3	14	15	7	5	32	26	16	8	226	212	88	2nd, Northwest Div.	Lost Conf. Quarter-Final
1998-99	82	17	19	5	....	16	18	7	....	33	37	12	....	230	226	78	2nd, Northwest Div.	Lost Conf. Quarter-Final
1997-98	82	20	16	5	....	15	21	5	....	35	37	10	....	215	224	80	3rd, Pacific Div.	Lost Conf. Semi-Final
1996-97	82	21	16	4	....	15	21	5	....	36	37	9	....	252	247	81	3rd, Pacific Div.	Lost Conf. Semi-Final
1995-96	82	15	21	5	....	15	23	3	....	30	44	8	....	240	304	68	5th, Pacific Div.	Out of Playoffs
1994-95	48	11	12	1	....	6	15	3	....	17	27	4	....	136	183	38	5th, Pacific Div.	Out of Playoffs
1993-94	84	17	22	3	....	8	23	11	....	25	45	14	....	261	305	64	6th, Pacific Div.	Out of Playoffs
1992-93	84	16	21	5	....	10	29	3	....	26	50	8	....	242	337	60	5th, Smythe Div.	Out of Playoffs
1991-92	80	22	13	5	....	14	21	5	....	36	34	10	....	295	297	82	3rd, Smythe Div.	Lost Conf. Championship
1990-91	80	22	15	3	....	15	22	3	....	37	37	6	....	272	272	80	3rd, Smythe Div.	Lost Conf. Championship
1989-90	**80**	**23**	**11**	**6**	....	**15**	**17**	**8**	....	**38**	**28**	**14**	....	**315**	**283**	**90**	**2nd, Smythe Div.**	**Won Stanley Cup**
1988-89	80	21	16	3	....	17	18	5	....	38	34	8	....	325	306	84	3rd, Smythe Div.	Lost Div. Semi-Final
1987-88	**80**	**28**	**8**	**4**	....	**16**	**17**	**7**	....	**44**	**25**	**11**	....	**363**	**288**	**99**	**2nd, Smythe Div.**	**Won Stanley Cup**
1986-87	**80**	**29**	**6**	**5**	....	**21**	**18**	**1**	....	**50**	**24**	**6**	....	**372**	**284**	**106**	**1st, Smythe Div.**	**Won Stanley Cup**
1985-86	80	32	6	2	....	24	11	5	....	56	17	7	....	426	310	119	1st, Smythe Div.	Lost Div. Final
1984-85	**80**	**26**	**7**	**7**	....	**23**	**13**	**4**	....	**49**	**20**	**11**	....	**401**	**298**	**109**	**1st, Smythe Div.**	**Won Stanley Cup**
1983-84	**80**	**31**	**5**	**4**	....	**26**	**13**	**1**	....	**57**	**18**	**5**	....	**446**	**314**	**119**	**1st, Smythe Div.**	**Won Stanley Cup**
1982-83	80	25	9	6	....	22	12	6	....	47	21	12	....	424	315	106	1st, Smythe Div.	Lost Final
1981-82	80	31	5	4	....	17	12	11	....	48	17	15	....	417	295	111	1st, Smythe Div.	Lost Div. Semi-Final
1980-81	80	17	13	10	....	12	22	6	....	29	35	16	....	328	327	74	4th, Smythe Div.	Lost Quarter-Final
1979-80	80	17	14	9	....	11	25	4	....	28	39	13	....	301	322	69	4th, Smythe Div.	Lost Prelim. Round

2008-09 Schedule

Oct.	Sun.	12	Colorado
	Wed.	15	at Anaheim
	Fri.	17	at Calgary
	Sat.	18	Calgary
	Wed.	22	at Chicago
	Thu.	23	at Colorado
	Sat.	25	at Vancouver
	Mon.	27	Boston
	Thu.	30	at Nashville
Nov.	Sat.	1	at Carolina*
	Sun.	2	at Philadelphia*
	Wed.	5	at Columbus
	Thu.	6	at Pittsburgh
	Sun.	9	at New Jersey
	Mon.	10	at NY Rangers
	Thu.	13	Toronto
	Sat.	15	Colorado
	Mon.	17	at Detroit
	Tue.	18	at Columbus
	Thu.	20	Detroit
	Wed.	26	Los Angeles
	Sat.	29	at St. Louis*
	Sun.	30	at Dallas*
Dec.	Wed.	3	Dallas
	Fri.	5	at Los Angeles
	Sat.	6	at San Jose
	Thu.	11	Florida
	Sat.	13	Vancouver
	Tue.	16	Chicago
	Wed.	17	at Vancouver
	Fri.	19	Anaheim
	Mon.	22	Phoenix
	Fri.	26	at Vancouver
	Sun.	28	Nashville
	Tue.	30	Ottawa
	Wed.	31	at Calgary
Jan.	Sat.	3	Dallas
	Mon.	5	NY Islanders
	Wed.	7	Vancouver
	Fri.	9	San Jose
	Sun.	11	St. Louis
	Tue.	13	at Washington
	Thu.	15	at Minnesota
	Fri.	16	at Colorado
	Sun.	18	Phoenix
	Tue.	20	Columbus
	Tue.	27	Buffalo
	Fri.	30	Minnesota
Feb.	Sun.	1	Nashville*
	Tue.	3	Chicago
	Thu.	5	at St. Louis
	Sat.	7	at Detroit*
	Sun.	8	at Minnesota*
	Wed.	11	Montreal
	Sat.	14	at Los Angeles*
	Mon.	16	at Phoenix
	Tue.	17	at San Jose
	Thu.	19	at Dallas
	Sat.	21	Calgary
	Tue.	24	Tampa Bay
	Thu.	26	Columbus
	Sat.	28	Minnesota
Mar.	Tue.	3	at Nashville
	Thu.	5	at Ottawa
	Sat.	7	at Toronto
	Tue.	10	at Montreal
	Thu.	12	Atlanta
	Sat.	14	Colorado
	Tue.	17	St. Louis
	Thu.	19	at Colorado
	Fri.	20	at Chicago
	Sun.	22	at Minnesota*
	Tue.	24	Detroit
	Thu.	26	at Phoenix
	Fri.	27	at Anaheim
	Sun.	29	Minnesota
	Tue.	31	Anaheim
Apr.	Thu.	2	San Jose
	Sat.	4	Vancouver
	Tue.	7	Los Angeles
	Fri.	10	Calgary
	Sat.	11	at Calgary

* Denotes afternoon game.

Dustin Penner led the Oilers with 23 goals in 2007-08. His 13 power-play goals also led the team and tied him for 15th spot in the NHL.

NORTHWEST DIVISION

30th NHL Season

Franchise date: June 22, 1979

2008-09 Player Personnel

FORWARDS	HT	WT	S	Place of Birth	*Age	2007-08 Club
BRODZIAK, Kyle	6-2	209	R	St. Paul, Alta.	24	Edmonton
BRULE, Gilbert	5-10	180	R	Edmonton, Alta.	21	Columbus-Syracuse
COGLIANO, Andrew	5-10	184	L	Toronto, Ont.	21	Edmonton
COLE, Erik	6-2	205	L	Oswego, NY	29	Carolina
CORAZZINI, Carl	5-10	182	R	Framingham, MA	29	Grand Rapids
GAGNER, Sam	5-11	191	R	London, Ont.	19	Edmonton
GOULET, Stephane	6-3	185	L	Levis, Que.	22	Springfield-Stockton
HEMSKY, Ales	6-0	192	R	Pardubice, Czech.	25	Edmonton
HORCOFF, Shawn	6-1	208	L	Trail, B.C.	30	Edmonton
JACQUES, Jean-Francois	6-4	217	L	Montreal, Que.	23	Edmonton-Springfield
LERG, Bryan	5-10	175	L	Livonia, MI	22	Michigan State-Springfield
McDONALD, Colin	6-3	205	R	New Haven, CT	24	Springfield
MOREAU, Ethan	6-2	220	L	Huntsville, Ont.	33	Edmonton
NILSSON, Robert	5-11	185	L	Calgary, Alta.	23	Edmonton-Springfield
O'MARRA, Ryan	6-2	207	R	Tokyo, Japan	21	Springfield-Stockton
PAUKOVICH, Geoff	6-4	208	L	Englewood, CO	22	Stockton
PENNER, Dustin	6-4	245	L	Winkler, Man.	26	Edmonton
PISANI, Fernando	6-1	205	L	Edmonton, Alta.	31	Edmonton
POTULNY, Ryan	6-0	190	L	Grand Forks, ND	24	Phi-Phi (AHL)
POULIOT, Marc-Antoine	6-1	195	R	Quebec City, Que.	23	Edmonton-Springfield
REDDOX, Liam	5-10	180	L	East York, Ont.	22	Edmonton-Springfield
ROHLFS, David	6-3	225	R	Ann Arbor, MI	24	Springfield-Stockton
SCHREMP, Rob	5-11	200	L	Syracuse, NY	22	Edmonton-Springfield
SESTITO, Tim	6-0	195	L	Rome, NY	24	Springfield
SPURGEON, Tyler	5-11	188	L	Edmonton, Alta.	22	Springfield
STORTINI, Zack	6-4	220	R	Elliot Lake, Ont.	23	Edmonton-Springfield
TRUKHNO, Vyacheslav	6-1	197	L	Khimki, USSR	21	Springfield
DEFENSEMEN						
BISAILLON, Sebastien	6-0	205	R	Mont-Laurier, Que.	21	Springfield-Stockton
CHORNEY, Taylor	6-0	196	L	Thunder Bay, Ont.	21	North Dakota
GILBERT, Tom	6-3	206	R	Minneapolis, MN	25	Edmonton
GREBESHKOV, Denis	6-0	209	L	Yaroslavl, USSR	24	Edmonton
HRABAL, Josef	6-1	176	L	Prerov, Czech.	23	Cherepovets
PECKHAM, Theo	6-2	223	L	Richmond Hill, Ont.	20	Edmonton-Springfield
ROY, Mathieu	6-2	210	R	St-Georges, Que.	25	Edmonton-Springfield
SMID, Ladislav	6-3	226	L	Frydlant V Cechach, Czech.	22	Edmonton-Springfield
SOURAY, Sheldon	6-4	233	L	Elk Point, Alta.	32	Edmonton
STAIOS, Steve	6-1	200	R	Hamilton, Ont.	35	Edmonton
STRUDWICK, Jason	6-4	225	L	Edmonton, Alta.	33	NY Rangers
VISNOVSKY, Lubomir	5-10	188	L	Topolcany, Czech.	32	Los Angeles
WILD, Cody	6-1	185	L	Limestone, ME	21	Prov Coll-Springfield
YOUNG, Bryan	6-1	191	L	Kitchener, Ont.	22	Edmonton-Springfield

GOALTENDERS	HT	WT	C	Place of Birth	*Age	2007-08 Club
DROUIN-DESLAURIERS, Jeff	6-4	189	R	St-Jean-Richelieu, Que.	24	Springfield
DUBNYK, Devan	6-5	194	L	Regina, Sask.	22	Springfield
FISHER, Glenn	6-1	190	L	Edmonton, Alta.	25	Springfield-Stockton
GARON, Mathieu	6-2	207	R	Chandler, Que.	30	Edmonton
PITTON, Bryan	6-2	176	L	Mississauga, Ont.	20	Brampton-Springfield
ROLOSON, Dwayne	6-1	180	L	Simcoe, Ont.	38	Edmonton

* – Age at start of 2008-09 season

2007-08 Scoring

* – rookie

Regular Season

Pos	#	Player	Team	GP	G	A	Pts	TOI	+/–	PIM	PP	SH	GW	S	%
R	83	Ales Hemsky	EDM	74	20	51	71	18:34	–9	34	8	0	2	184	10.9
C	10	Shawn Horcoff	EDM	53	21	29	50	22:13	1	30	6	0	2	115	18.3
C	89 *	Sam Gagner	EDM	79	13	36	49	15:40	–21	23	4	0	1	135	9.6
L	27	Dustin Penner	EDM	82	23	24	47	17:12	–12	45	13	0	4	201	11.4
C	13 *	Andrew Cogliano	EDM	82	18	27	45	13:39	1	20	1	2	5	98	18.4
C	12	Robert Nilsson	EDM	71	10	31	41	13:55	8	22	3	0	0	102	9.8
C	16	Jarret Stoll	EDM	81	14	22	36	17:56	–23	74	8	3	1	187	7.5
D	77 *	Tom Gilbert	EDM	82	13	20	33	22:11	–6	20	3	0	1	98	13.3
C	51	Kyle Brodziak	EDM	80	14	17	31	12:55	–6	33	0	1	3	125	11.2
D	25	Joni Pitkanen	EDM	63	8	18	26	24:07	–5	56	1	1	1	101	7.9
L	20 *	Curtis Glencross	CBJ	36	6	6	12	12:07	3	25	1	0	1	63	9.5
			EDM	26	9	4	13	10:18	5	28	0	0	0	41	22.0
			Total	62	15	10	25	11:21	8	53	1	0	1	104	14.4
C	19	Marty Reasoner	EDM	82	11	14	25	14:57	–17	50	0	0	0	113	9.7
R	34	Fernando Pisani	EDM	56	13	9	22	16:31	–5	28	4	0	3	96	13.5
D	37	Denis Grebeshkov	EDM	71	3	15	18	16:52	2	22	1	0	0	34	8.8
D	24	Steve Staios	EDM	82	7	9	16	22:01	–14	121	1	0	0	73	9.6
L	8	Geoff Sanderson	EDM	41	3	10	13	10:09	–7	16	0	0	0	40	7.5
R	46	Zack Stortini	EDM	66	3	9	12	08:10	3	201	0	0	0	38	7.9
L	14	Raffi Torres	EDM	32	5	6	11	17:00	–4	36	1	0	2	87	5.7
D	44	Sheldon Souray	EDM	26	3	7	10	24:20	–7	36	2	0	1	71	4.2
L	18	Ethan Moreau	EDM	25	5	4	9	15:55	–4	39	1	0	0	54	9.3
C	78	Marc-Antoine Pouliot	EDM	24	1	6	7	10:20	–1	12	0	0	0	32	3.1
D	5	Ladislav Smid	EDM	65	0	4	4	17:51	–15	58	0	0	0	45	0.0
D	36 *	Mathieu Roy	EDM	13	0	1	1	10:23	0	27	0	0	0	8	0.0
D	2	Matt Greene	EDM	46	0	1	1	16:41	–3	53	0	0	0	28	0.0
L	85 *	Liam Reddox	EDM	1	0	0	0	05:55	–1	0	0	0	0	1	0.0
D	49 *	Theo Peckham	EDM	1	0	0	0	13:22	0	2	0	0	0	0	0.0
C	88 *	Rob Schremp	EDM	2	0	0	0	06:57	–1	0	0	0	0	3	0.0
D	76 *	Bryan Young	EDM	2	0	0	0	02:08	–1	0	0	0	0	0	0.0
L	22	J-F Jacques	EDM	9	0	0	0	06:09	–3	2	0	0	0	2	0.0
D	52	Allan Rourke	EDM	13	0	0	0	10:55	–1	5	0	0	0	4	0.0

Goaltending

No.	Goaltender	GPI	Mins	Avg	W	L	OT	EN	SO	GA	SA	S%	G	A	PIM
32	Mathieu Garon	47	2658	2.66	26	18	1	5	4	118	1359	.913	0	0	8
35	Dwayne Roloson	43	2340	3.05	15	17	5	5	0	119	1204	.901	0	1	2
	Totals	**82**	**5035**	**2.94**	**41**	**35**	**6**	**10**	**4**	**247**	**2573**	**.904**			

In his first full NHL season, Tom Gilbert played in all 82 games. He averaged better than 22 minutes of ice time per game and led all rookie defensemen with 13 goals.

Craig MacTavish

Head Coach

Born: London, Ont., August 15, 1958.

The Edmonton Oilers named Craig MacTavish as their head coach on June 22, 2000. He became the eighth person in the club's NHL history to hold the position. MacTavish joined Kevin Lowe and Glen Sather as head coaches who were former captains of the Oilers. In 2006, he led the Oilers to game seven of the Stanley Cup Final.

MacTavish played for 18 seasons in the NHL, including eight-and-three-quarter campaigns with the Oilers. He was instrumental in helping his teams win four Stanley Cup titles; three with Edmonton and one with the New York Rangers. Although he was the last player in the NHL to play without a helmet, MacTavish was known for his aggressive style, combined with above average skills.

MacTavish retired as a player in 1997 and was immediately named an assistant coach with the New York Rangers. He was with the Rangers for two seasons prior to joining the Oilers' coaching staff as an assistant under Kevin Lowe in 1999-2000. He also served as an assistant coach for Team Canada at the World Championship in 2005 and 2008.

Coaching Record

			Regular Season				Playoffs			
Season	**Team**	**League**	**GC**	**W**	**L**	**O/T**	**GC**	**W**	**L**	**T**
2000-01	Edmonton	NHL	82	39	28	15	....	....	....	....
2001-02	Edmonton	NHL	82	38	28	16	....	....	....	....
2002-03	Edmonton	NHL	82	36	26	20	6	2	4	....
2003-04	Edmonton	NHL	82	36	29	17	....	....	....	....
2004-05	Edmonton		SEASON CANCELLED							
2005-06	Edmonton	NHL	82	41	28	13	24	15	9	....
2006-07	Edmonton	NHL	82	32	43	7	....	....	....	....
2007-08	Edmonton	NHL	82	41	35	6	....	....	....	....
	NHL Totals		574	263	217	94	30	17	13	....

Coaching History

Glen Sather, 1979-80; Bryan Watson and Glen Sather, 1980-81; Glen Sather, 1981-82 to 1988-89; John Muckler, 1989-90, 1990-91; Ted Green, 1991-92, 1992-93; Ted Green and Glen Sather, 1993-94; George Burnett and Ron Low, 1994-95; Ron Low, 1995-96 to 1998-99; Kevin Lowe, 1999-2000; Craig MacTavish, 2000-01 to date.

Club Records

Team

(Figures in brackets for season records are games played; records for fewest points, wins, ties, losses, goals, goals against are for 70 or more games)

Most Points	119	1983-84 (80), 1985-86 (80)
Most Wins	57	1983-84 (80)
Most Ties	16	1980-81 (80), 1999-2000 (82)
Most Losses	50	1992-93 (84)
Most Goals	*446	1983-84 (80)
Most Goals Against	337	1992-93 (84)
Fewest Points	60	1992-93 (84)
Fewest Wins	25	1993-94 (84)
Fewest Ties	5	1983-84 (80)
Fewest Losses	17	1981-82 (80), 1985-86 (80)
Fewest Goals	195	2006-07 (82)
Fewest Goals Against	182	2001-02 (82)
Longest Winning Streak		
Overall	9	Feb. 20-Mar. 13/01
Home	8	Jan. 19-Feb. 22/85, Feb. 24-Apr. 2/86
Away	8	Dec. 9/86-Jan. 17/87
Longest Undefeated Streak		
Overall	15	Oct. 11-Nov. 9/84 (12 wins, 3 ties)
Home	14	Nov. 15/89-Jan. 6/90 (11 wins, 3 ties)
Away	9	Jan. 17-Mar. 2/82 (6 wins, 3 ties), Nov. 23/82-Jan. 18/83 (7 wins, 2 ties)
Longest Losing Streak		
Overall	11	Oct. 16-Nov. 7/93
Home	9	Oct. 16-Nov. 24/93
Away	9	Nov. 25-Dec. 30/80, Feb. 25-Apr. 5/07
Longest Winless Streak		
Overall	14	Oct. 11-Nov. 7/93 (13 losses, 1 tie)
Home	9	Oct. 16-Nov. 24/93 (9 losses)
Away	11	Dec. 18/01-Feb. 8/02 (7 losses, 4 ties)
Most Shutouts, Season	8	1997-98 (82); 2000-01 (82); 2001-02 (82)
Most PIM, Season	2,173	1987-88 (80)
Most Goals, Game	13	Nov. 19/83 (N.J. 4 at Edm. 13), Nov. 8/85 (Van. 0 at Edm. 13)

Individual

Most Seasons	15	Kevin Lowe
Most Games	1,037	Kevin Lowe
Most Goals, Career	583	Wayne Gretzky
Most Assists, Career	1,086	Wayne Gretzky
Most Points, Career	1,669	Wayne Gretzky (583G, 1,086A)
Most PIM, Career	1,747	Kelly Buchberger
Most Shutouts, Career	23	Tommy Salo
Longest Consecutive Games Streak	518	Craig MacTavish (Oct. 12/86-Jan. 2/93)
Most Goals, Season	*92	Wayne Gretzky (1981-82)
Most Assists, Season	*163	Wayne Gretzky (1985-86)
Most Points, Season	*215	Wayne Gretzky (1985-86; 52G, 163A)
Most PIM, Season	286	Steve Smith (1987-88)
Most Points, Defenseman, Season	138	Paul Coffey (1985-86; 48G, 90A)
Most Points, Center, Season	*215	Wayne Gretzky (1985-86; 52G, 163A)
Most Points, Right Wing, Season	135	Jari Kurri (1984-85; 71G, 64A)
Most Points, Left Wing, Season	106	Mark Messier (1982-83; 48G, 58A)
Most Points, Rookie, Season	75	Jari Kurri (1980-81; 32G, 43A)
Most Shutouts, Season	8	Curtis Joseph (1997-98), Tommy Salo (2000-01)
Most Goals, Game	5	Wayne Gretzky (Feb. 18/81, Dec. 30/81, Dec. 15/84, Dec. 6/87), Jari Kurri (Nov. 19/83), Pat Hughes (Feb. 3/84)
Most Assists, Game	*7	Wayne Gretzky (Feb. 15/80, Dec. 11/85, Feb. 14/86)
Most Points, Game	8	Wayne Gretzky (Nov. 19/83; 3G, 5A), (Jan. 4/84; 4G, 4A), Paul Coffey (Mar. 14/86; 2G, 6A)

* NHL Record.

Retired Numbers

3	Al Hamilton	1972-1980
7	Paul Coffey	1980-1987
9*	Glenn Anderson	1980-91, 1996
11	Mark Messier	1980-1991
17	Jari Kurri	1980-1990
31	Grant Fuhr	1981-1991
99	Wayne Gretzky	1979-1988

* - To be honored during 2008-09 season.

Captains' History

Ron Chipperfield, 1979-80; Blair MacDonald and Lee Fogolin, Jr., 1980-81; Lee Fogolin, Jr., 1981-82, 1982-83; Wayne Gretzky, 1983-84 to 1987-88; Mark Messier, 1988-89 to 1990-91; Kevin Lowe, 1991-92; Craig MacTavish, 1992-93, 1993-94; Shayne Corson, 1994-95; Kelly Buchberger, 1995-96 to 1998-99; Doug Weight, 1999-2000, 2000-01; Jason Smith, 2001-02 to 2006-07; Ethan Moreau, 2007-08 to date.

All-time Record vs. Other Clubs

Regular Season

	At Home								On Road								Total							
	GP	W	L	T	OL	GF	GA	PTS	GP	W	L	T	OL	GF	GA	PTS	GP	W	L	T	OL	GF	GA	PTS
Anaheim	31	21	9	0	1	77	63	43	32	13	17	2	0	84	89	28	63	34	26	2	1	161	152	71
Atlanta	5	3	1	1	0	19	12	7	4	3	1	0	0	12	5	6	9	6	2	1	0	31	17	13
Boston	30	11	15	3	1	102	102	26	31	6	21	3	1	80	129	16	61	17	36	6	2	182	231	42
Buffalo	30	21	6	3	0	121	77	45	31	13	10	7	1	113	111	34	61	34	16	10	1	234	188	79
Calgary	93	48	34	10	1	333	295	107	93	33	51	9	0	298	359	75	186	81	85	19	1	631	654	182
Carolina	32	20	7	5	0	124	93	45	30	11	12	7	0	100	119	29	62	31	19	12	0	224	212	74
Chicago	51	27	19	5	0	187	156	59	50	18	25	7	0	167	187	43	101	45	44	12	0	354	343	102
Colorado	58	30	23	4	1	225	188	65	59	24	29	4	2	203	222	54	117	54	52	8	3	428	410	119
Columbus	14	11	2	0	1	49	30	23	14	8	2	3	1	45	31	20	28	19	4	3	2	94	61	43
Dallas	50	21	16	8	5	190	167	55	51	16	26	7	2	141	183	41	101	37	42	15	7	331	350	96
Detroit	50	24	15	10	1	189	173	59	50	19	26	3	2	160	190	43	100	43	41	13	3	349	363	102
Florida	8	5	2	1	0	28	17	11	10	3	5	2	0	28	27	8	18	8	7	3	0	56	44	19
Los Angeles	83	43	25	15	0	370	295	101	83	37	30	15	1	332	317	90	166	80	55	30	1	702	612	191
Minnesota	23	10	9	3	1	54	56	24	22	10	8	1	3	49	58	24	45	20	17	4	4	103	114	48
Montreal	36	19	17	0	0	122	116	38	31	10	16	4	1	97	108	25	67	29	33	4	1	219	224	63
Nashville	18	8	8	0	2	48	56	18	19	7	9	3	0	55	53	17	37	15	17	3	2	103	109	35
New Jersey	32	14	11	6	1	137	117	35	34	16	13	3	2	113	113	37	66	30	24	9	3	250	230	72
NY Islanders	30	17	8	5	0	111	87	39	32	7	15	9	1	112	131	24	62	24	23	14	1	223	218	63
NY Rangers	29	13	13	3	0	104	96	29	31	14	9	6	2	117	117	36	60	27	22	9	2	221	213	65
Ottawa	12	7	3	2	0	42	30	16	11	5	3	2	1	29	23	13	23	12	6	4	1	71	53	29
Philadelphia	29	15	8	6	0	103	86	36	32	10	20	2	0	88	130	22	61	25	28	8	0	191	216	58
Phoenix	78	50	21	6	1	341	250	107	77	41	27	5	4	335	303	91	155	91	48	11	5	676	553	198
Pittsburgh	31	22	8	1	0	150	102	45	31	13	14	3	1	130	118	30	62	35	22	4	1	280	220	75
St. Louis	50	25	19	4	2	182	165	56	50	19	23	7	1	174	177	46	100	44	42	11	3	356	342	102
San Jose	39	23	9	7	0	127	88	53	38	15	16	5	2	113	127	37	77	38	25	12	2	240	215	90
Tampa Bay	11	7	4	0	0	27	24	14	12	6	4	2	0	38	35	14	23	13	8	2	0	65	59	28
Toronto	44	23	14	6	1	180	141	53	38	15	21	2	0	157	158	32	82	38	35	8	1	337	299	85
Vancouver	93	55	28	7	3	386	295	120	94	44	34	12	4	354	330	104	187	99	62	19	7	740	625	224
Washington	30	16	10	4	0	124	91	36	30	9	18	2	1	97	123	21	60	25	28	6	1	221	214	57
Totals	**1120**	**609**	**364**	**125**	**22**	**4252**	**3468**	**1365**	**1120**	**445**	**505**	**137**	**33**	**3821**	**4073**	**1060**	**2240**	**1054**	**869**	**262**	**55**	**8073**	**7541**	**2425**

Playoffs

	Series	W	L	GP	W	L	T	GF	GA	Last Mtg.	Rnd.	Result
Anaheim	1	1	0	5	4	1	0	16	13	2006	CF	W 4-1
Boston	2	2	0	9	8	1	0	41	20	1990	F	W 4-1
Calgary	5	4	1	30	19	11	0	132	96	1991	DSF	W 4-3
Carolina	1	0	1	7	3	4	0	16	19	2006	F	L 3-4
Chicago	4	3	1	20	12	8	0	102	77	1992	CF	L 0-4
Colorado	2	1	1	12	5	7	0	30	35	1998	CQF	W 4-3
Dallas	8	2	6	42	15	27	0	104	118	2003	CQF	L 2-4
Detroit	3	3	0	16	12	4	0	58	43	2006	CQF	W 4-2
Los Angeles	7	5	2	36	24	12	0	154	127	1992	DSF	W 4-2
Montreal	1	1	0	3	3	0	0	15	6	1981	PRE	W 3-0
NY Islanders	3	1	2	15	6	9	0	47	58	1984	F	W 4-1
Philadelphia	3	2	1	15	8	7	0	49	44	1987	F	W 4-3
Phoenix	6	6	0	26	22	4	0	120	75	1990	DSF	W 4-3
San Jose	1	1	0	6	4	2	0	19	12	2006	CSF	W 4-2
Vancouver	2	2	0	9	7	2	0	35	20	1992	DF	W 4-2
Totals	**49**	**34**	**15**	**251**	**152**	**99**	**0**	**938**	**763**			

Playoff Results 2008-2003

Year	Round	Opponent	Result	GF	GA
2006	F	Carolina	L 3-4	16	19
	CF	Anaheim	W 4-1	16	13
	CSF	San Jose	W 4-2	19	12
	CQF	Detroit	W 4-2	19	17
2003	CQF	Dallas	L 2-4	11	20

Abbreviations: Round: F - Final; **CF** - conference final; **CSF** - conference semi-final; **CQF** - conference quarter-final; **DF** - division final; **DSF** - division semi-final; **PRE** - preliminary round.

Calgary totals include Atlanta Flames, 1979-80.
Colorado totals include Quebec, 1979-80 to 1994-95.
New Jersey totals include Colorado Rockies, 1979-80 to 1981-82.

Carolina totals include Hartford, 1979-80 to 1996-97.
Dallas totals include Minnesota North Stars, 1979-80 to 1992-93.
Phoenix totals include Winnipeg, 1979-80 to 1995-96.

2007-08 Results

Month	Day	Opponent	Score
Oct.	4	San Jose	3-2†
	6	Philadelphia	5-3
	8	at Detroit	2-4
	10	at Minnesota	0-2
	12	Vancouver	2-5
	13	at Vancouver	1-4
	18	at Phoenix	4-2
	20	at Calgary	1-4
	23	Colorado	2-4
	25	Minnesota	5-4†
	27	at Los Angeles	1-4
	28	at Anaheim	3-2†
	30	Detroit	1-2
Nov.	2	Nashville	1-4
	5	at Minnesota	2-5
	7	at Colorado	3-4†
	10	at Calgary	4-2
	14	at Vancouver	1-0†
	15	Minnesota	2-4
	17	Calgary	1-3
	20	Vancouver	5-4†
	22	Colorado	2-3
	24	Chicago	3-2†
	26	Columbus	3-1
	28	at Colorado	2-4
	30	Anaheim	5-1
Dec.	2	at Anaheim	4-0
	3	at Los Angeles	4-3†
	5	Pittsburgh	2-4
	7	St. Louis	3-4
	10	at Dallas	4-5*
	11	at St. Louis	5-4†
	13	at Detroit	4-3†
	15	Vancouver	2-1†
	18	Dallas	1-2†
	21	New Jersey	1-3
	23	at Chicago	2-3
	27	Anaheim	1-2
	29	at Minnesota	4-5*
	31	at Columbus	2-4
Jan.	2	at St. Louis	3-2*
	3	at Nashville	2-5
	5	NY Rangers	3-2†
	7	NY Islanders	4-0
	10	Phoenix	5-2
	13	Calgary	2-1
	15	Los Angeles	1-3
	17	at Washington	4-5†
	18	at Carolina	2-7
	20	at Atlanta	4-2
	22	at Tampa Bay	3-4
	24	at Florida	4-3†
	29	San Jose	0-3
Feb.	1	Dallas	1-4
	4	Calgary	5-0
	6	Chicago	4-1
	9	at Calgary	1-4
	12	Minnesota	4-2
	14	at San Jose	3-2
	16	at Vancouver	2-4
	19	at Nashville	4-5
	22	at Dallas	2-5
	24	Colorado	3-2
	26	Detroit	4-3†
	28	Los Angeles	5-4
Mar.	2	Columbus	4-3†
	4	Nashville	1-5
	7	at Columbus	2-1*
	9	at Chicago	6-5*
	11	St. Louis	4-3*
	13	at Colorado	1-5
	15	at Phoenix	5-2
	16	at San Jose	2-1†
	18	Phoenix	8-4
	20	Vancouver	1-4
	22	Colorado	7-5
	24	Minnesota	5-3
	26	at Minnesota	1-3
	28	at Colorado	4-5†
	29	at Calgary	2-1
Apr.	1	Calgary	2-3
	3	at Vancouver	2-1

* – Overtime † – Shootout

Entry Draft Selections 2008-1994

Name in bold denotes played in NHL.

2008
Pick
22 Jordan Eberle
103 Johan Motin
133 Philippe Cornet
163 Teemu Hartikainen
193 Jordan Bendfeld

2007
Pick
6 **Sam Gagner**
15 Alex Plante
21 Riley Nash
97 Linus Omark
127 Milan Kytnar
157 William Quist

2006
Pick
45 Jeff Petry
75 **Theo Peckham**
133 Bryan Pitton
140 Cody Wild
170 Alexander Bumagin

2005
Pick
25 **Andrew Cogliano**
36 Taylor Chorney
81 **Danny Syvret**
86 Robby Dee
97 Chris Vande Velde
120 Vyacheslav Trukhno
157 Fredrik Pettersson
220 Matthew Glasser

2004
Pick
14 Devan Dubnyk
25 **Rob Schremp**
44 Roman Tesliuk
57 Geoff Paukovich
112 **Liam Reddox**
146 **Bryan Young**
177 Max Gordichuk
208 Stephane Goulet
242 Tyler Spurgeon
274 Bjorn Bjurling

2003
Pick
22 **Marc-Antoine Pouliot**
51 Colin McDonald
68 **Jean-Francois Jacques**
72 Mikhail Zhukov
94 **Zack Stortini**
147 Kalle Olsson
154 David Rohlfs
184 Dragan Umicevic
214 **Kyle Brodziak**
215 **Mathieu Roy**
248 Josef Hrabal
278 Troy Bodie

2002
Pick
15 Jesse Niinimaki
31 Jeff Drouin-Deslauriers
36 **Jarret Stoll**
44 **Matt Greene**
79 Brock Radunske
106 Ivan Koltsov
111 Jonas Almtorp
123 invalid pick
148 Glenn Fisher
181 **Mikko Luoma**
205 **J.F. Dufort**
211 Patrick Murphy
244 Dwight Helminen
245 Tomas Micka
274 Fredrik Johansson

2001
Pick
13 **Ales Hemsky**
43 **Doug Lynch**
52 Ed Caron
84 Kenny Smith
133 **Jussi Markkanen**
154 Jake Brenk
185 Mikael Svensk
215 Dan Baum
248 **Kari Haakana**
272 **Ales Pisa**
278 **Shay Stephenson**

2000
Pick
17 **Alexei Mikhnov**
35 **Brad Winchester**
83 Alexander Liubimov
113 Lou Dickenson
152 Paul Flache
184 Shaun Norrie
211 Joe Cullen
215 **Matthew Lombardi**
247 Jason Platt
274 Yevgeny Muratov

1999
Pick
13 **Jani Rita**
36 **Alexei Semenov**
41 **Tony Salmelainen**
81 **Adam Hauser**
91 **Mike Comrie**
139 Jonathan Fauteux
171 Chris Legg
199 Christian Chartier
256 Tamas Groschl

1998
Pick
13 Michael Henrich
67 **Alex Henry**
99 **Shawn Horcoff**
113 Kristian Antila
128 Paul Elliott
144 Oleg Smirnov
159 Trevor Ettinger
186 **Mike Morrison**
213 Christian Lefebvre
241 Maxim Spiridonov

1997
Pick
14 **Michel Riesen**
41 Patrick Dovigi
68 Sergei Yerkovich
94 Jonas Elofsson
121 **Jason Chimera**
141 **Peter Sarno**
176 Kevin Bolibruck
187 Chad Hinz
205 Chris Kerr
231 Alexander Fomichev

1996
Pick
6 **Boyd Devereaux**
19 **Matthieu Descoteaux**
32 **Chris Hajt**
59 **Tom Poti**
114 Brian Urick
141 Bryan Randall
168 David Bernier
170 Brandon Lafrance
195 **Fernando Pisani**
221 John Hultberg

1995
Pick
6 **Steve Kelly**
31 **Georges Laraque**
57 Lukas Zib
83 **Mike Minard**
109 Jan Snopek
161 Martin Cerven
187 Stephen Douglas
213 Jiri Antonin

1994
Pick
4 **Jason Bonsignore**
6 **Ryan Smyth**
32 **Mike Watt**
53 Corey Neilson
60 Brad Symes
79 Adam Copeland
95 Jussi Tarvainen
110 Jon Gaskins
136 Terry Marchant
160 Curtis Sheptak
162 Dmitri Shulga
179 Chris Wickenheiser
185 Rob Guinn
188 Jason Reid
214 Jeremy Jablonski
266 **Ladislav Benysek**

General Managers' History

Larry Gordon, 1979-80; Glen Sather, 1980-81 to 1999-2000; Kevin Lowe, 2000-01 to 2007-08; Steve Tambellini, 2008-09.

Steve Tambellini

General Manager

Born: Trail, B.C., May 14, 1958.

Steve Tambellini joined the Edmonton Oilers as general manager on July 31, 2008 after 17 seasons as a member of the Vancouver Canucks management team. During his tenure with Vancouver, which began in 1990-91, Tambellini served in several positions. During his last three years with the club, he was vice president and assistant general manager. In that role, he was involved in all aspects of the team's hockey operations, including contract negotiations, scouting and minor league affiliates.

Tambellini took over in Edmonton from Kevin Lowe, who was promoted to the position of President of Hockey Operations. Tambellini and Lowe have previously worked together as members of Team Canada's management team, helping lead Canada to success on the international stage. As director of player personnel, Tambellini helped put together the roster that won the gold medal at the 2002 Winter Olympics in Salt Lake City and he was also a member of the management team for Team Canada's gold medal triumph at the 2004 World Cup of Hockey. He also served as the general manager of Team Canada at the 2003 and 2005 World Championships, winning gold in 2003 and silver in 2005.

Inducted into the B.C. Hockey Hall of Fame in 2004, Tambellini played 10 seasons in the NHL after being selected 15th overall in the 1978 NHL Amateur Draft by the New York Islanders. A member of the Islanders' 1980 Stanley Cup championship team, he played 553 career NHL games with five NHL teams between 1978-79 and 1987-88. He had 160 goals and 150 assists for 310 career points with 105 penalty minutes with the Islanders, the Colorado Rockies, New Jersey Devils, Calgary Flames and Vancouver Canucks.

Besides his outstanding hockey resume, Tambellini has also been a contributor to the Canucks' off-ice activities. He served as the president of the Canucks for Kids Fund for 12 seasons and was awarded the B.C. Humanitarian of the Year Award by the B.C. Hockey Hall of Fame in 2006. He was also awarded the Jake Milford Plaque in 2004 for his significant and lasting contributions to hockey in his home province of British Columbia.

Club Directory

Rexall Place

Edmonton Oilers
11230 – 110 Street
Edmonton, Alberta T5G 3H7
Phone **780/414-4000**
Press Box 780/409-3780
Ticketing 780/414-4625
Media Lounge 780/409-3778
FAX 780/409-5848
www.edmontonoilers.com
Capacity: 16,839

Owner	Daryl A. Katz (Rexall Sports Corp)
Governor	Daryl A. Katz
Alternate Governors	Patrick LaForge, Kevin Lowe, Cal Nichols
President & Chief Executive Officer	Patrick LaForge
President of Hockey Operations	Kevin Lowe
Executive Vice President, Commercial Operations	Stew MacDonald
Vice-President of Finance and CFO	Darryl Boessenkool
Executive Assistant to the President/CFO	Connie Hadden/Sherry Smith
Hockey Operations	
General Manager	Steve Tambellini
Asst. G.M. & V.P., Hockey Operations	Kevin Prendergast
Asst. G.M. & Dir. of Hockey Ops./Legal Affairs	Ricky Olczyk
Head Coach	Craig MacTavish
Assistant Coaches	Charlie Huddy, Bill Moores, Kelly Buchberger
Goaltending Coach	Pete Peeters
Video Coach	Brian Ross
Director of Player Development	Bob Mancini
Skating & Skills Coach	Steve Serdachny
Fitness Consultant	Chad Moreau, D.C., C.S.C.S
Dir. of Research, Analysis & Software Development	Sean Draper
Coordinator of Hockey Operations	James McGregor
Scouting Staff	Michael Abbamont, Bob Brown, Bill Dandy, Rob Daum, Brad Davis, Morey Gare, Kent Hawley, Stu MacGregor, Chris McCarthy, Frank Musil, Kent Nilsson, Mike Peluso, Dave Semenko
Family Liaison	Jill Metz
Medical and Training Staff	
Head Medical Trainer	Ken Lowe
Head Equipment Manager	Barrie Stafford
Assistant Medical Trainer	Chris Davie
Equipment Managers	Lyle Kulchisky, Jeff Lang
Massage Therapist	Steve Lines
Team Medical Chief of Staff	Dr. David C. Reid
Medical Staff	Drs. John Clarke, Dhiren Naidu, Jeff Robinson, Don Groot, Ben Eastwood, Tony Sneazwell, Gordon Bell, Dave Magee, Brent Saik, John Dunn
Finance & Administration	
Director, New Business Development	Jason Quilley
Controller	Zeina Charara
Human Resource Manager	Tandy Kustiak
Legal Counsel	Keely Brown
Director, Facilities Operations	Craig Tkachuk
Payroll Manager	Shawna Quigley
Accounting	Christine Marceau, Yvonne Weleschuk, Jamie Schenknecht
Director/Manager, IT	Alfred Ng/Rod Pruden
Facilities Coordinator	Gilbert da Silva
Receptionists	Sandy Langley, Macy Beley
Communications & Broadcast	
Vice President, Communications & Broadcast	Allan Watt
Manager, Communications & Media Relations	J.J. Hebert
Information Coordinator	Steve Knowles
Team Services Coordinator	Patrick Garland
Director of Broadcast	Don Metz
Radio	Rod Phillips, Bob Stauffer
Corporate Partnerships	
Vice President, Corporate Partnerships	Brad MacGregor
Directors, Corporate Partnerships	Lisa Munro, Scott Murray, Daryl Zelinski
Manager, Executive Suites	Bob Haromy
Manager, Corporate Partnerships	Abe Hajar
Manager/Event Coordinator	Kathy Mendes/Jody Young
Partner Activation Specialists	Angie Zander, Matt McPhee, David Reyner, Janine Forsey, Sara Ripko, Greg Atkins
Business Analyst	Jason Lee
Ticket Sales & Customer Relations	
V.P., Ticket Sales and Customer Relationships	Sean Price
Manager, Ticket Operations – Edmonton Oilers	Corrine Carey
Manager, Ticket Operations – Edmonton Oil Kings	Sangeeta Chandra
Manager, Customer Relationships	Carmen Day
Ticket Sales Administrative Assistant	Kendra Morton
Group Ticket Account Executive	Tyler Frederick
Oilers Experience Representatives	Tabitha Lidgett, Shannon Werbicki, Dianne Kalita, Barbara Domet
Supervisor, Ticket Services	Paul Reid
Marketing	
Senior Director, Marketing	Pat McLaughlin
Senior Business Analyst	Sharon Lyseng
Manager, E-Marketing & Research	Christine Dmytryshyn
Manager, Retail & Licensing	Joyce LaBriola
Manager, Digital Media	Marc Ciampa
Digital Media Specialist/Producer	Jen Sharpe/Steve Taylor
Marketing Specialist	Debbie George
Game Night Supervisor/Producer	Kristi Van Binsbergen/Derek Dawley
Community	
Director, Community & Exec. Director, Oilers Community Foundation	Natalie Minckler
Manager, Community & Fan Development	Laurie Block
Community Partnership Coordinator	Amanda Penner
Grant & Fund Development Coordinator	Erin Barrett
ICE School Program Coordinator	Sandy VanRiper
Online Auction Coordinator	Dwain Tomkow

Florida Panthers

Key Off-Season Signings/Acquisitions

2008

May 5 • Re-signed RW **Wade Belak** and C **Kamil Kreps**.
8 • Signed 2007 1st-round pick (10th overall), D **Keaton Ellerby**.
16 • Re-signed GM **Jacques Martin**.
28 • Signed 2006 1st-round pick (10th overall), C **Michael Frolik**.
June 13 • Named **Peter DeBoer** head coach.
20 • Acquired D **Keith Ballard**, D **Nick Boynton** and a 2nd-round pick in 2008 from Phoenix for C **Olli Jokinen**.
26 • Re-signed C **Gregory Campbell**.
30 • Re-signed LW **Rostislav Olesz**.
July 1 • Signed LW **Cory Stillman**.
9 • Re-signed RW **Anthony Stewart**.
9 • Named **Jim Hulton** assistant coach.

2007-08 Results: 38W-35L-3OTL-6SOL 85PTS.
Third, Southeast Division

Year-by-Year Record

		Home				Road				Overall								
Season	GP	W	L	T	OL	W	L	T	OL	W	L	T	OL	GF	GA	Pts.	Finished	Playoff Result
2007-08	82	18	15	....	8	20	20	....	1	38	35	....	9	216	226	85	3rd, Southeast Div.	Out of Playoffs
2006-07	82	23	12	....	6	12	19	....	10	35	31	....	16	247	257	86	4th, Southeast Div.	Out of Playoffs
2005-06	82	25	11	....	5	12	23	....	6	37	34	....	11	240	257	85	4th, Southeast Div.	Out of Playoffs
2004-05	....	....	....	....	....	....	....	....	....	....	....	....	....	....	....	....		
2003-04	82	16	15	7	3	12	20	8	1	28	35	15	4	188	221	75	4th, Southeast Div.	Out of Playoffs
2002-03	82	8	21	7	5	16	15	6	4	24	36	13	9	176	237	70	4th, Southeast Div.	Out of Playoffs
2001-02	82	11	23	3	4	11	21	7	2	22	44	10	6	180	250	60	4th, Southeast Div.	Out of Playoffs
2000-01	82	12	18	7	4	10	20	6	5	22	38	13	9	200	246	66	3rd, Southeast Div.	Out of Playoffs
1999-2000	82	26	9	4	2	17	18	2	4	43	27	6	6	244	209	98	2nd, Southeast Div.	Lost Conf. Quarter-Final
1998-99	82	17	17	7	....	13	17	11	....	30	34	18	....	210	228	78	2nd, Southeast Div.	Out of Playoffs
1997-98	82	11	24	6	....	13	19	9	....	24	43	15	....	203	256	63	6th, Atlantic Div.	Out of Playoffs
1996-97	82	21	12	8	....	14	16	11	....	35	28	19	....	221	201	89	3rd, Atlantic Div.	Lost Conf. Quarter-Final
1995-96	82	25	12	4	....	16	19	6	....	41	31	10	....	254	234	92	3rd, Atlantic Div.	Lost Final
1994-95	48	9	12	3	....	11	10	3	....	20	22	6	....	115	127	46	5th, Atlantic Div.	Out of Playoffs
1993-94	84	15	18	9	....	18	16	8	....	33	34	17	....	233	233	83	5th, Atlantic Div.	Out of Playoffs

2008-09 Schedule

Oct.	Fri.	10	at Carolina
	Sat.	11	Atlanta
	Thu.	16	Minnesota
	Sat.	18	NY Islanders
	Mon.	20	at Montreal
	Wed.	22	at Ottawa
	Fri.	24	San Jose
	Sat.	25	at St. Louis
	Thu.	30	Ottawa
Nov.	Sat.	1	at Nashville
	Sun.	2	at Atlanta*
	Thu.	6	at Los Angeles
	Sat.	8	at Phoenix
	Sun.	9	at Anaheim*
	Wed.	12	Tampa Bay
	Fri.	14	Detroit
	Tue.	18	at Tampa Bay
	Thu.	20	at New Jersey
	Fri.	21	at Boston
	Mon.	24	Carolina
	Wed.	26	New Jersey
	Fri.	28	NY Rangers
	Sun.	30	at NY Rangers*
Dec.	Tue.	2	at Washington
	Thu.	4	Buffalo
	Sat.	6	Boston
	Mon.	8	at Ottawa
	Thu.	11	at Edmonton
	Fri.	12	at Calgary
	Sun.	14	at Vancouver
	Thu.	18	at Carolina
	Sun.	21	Colorado*
	Tue.	23	Nashville
	Fri.	26	Tampa Bay
	Sat.	27	at Tampa Bay
	Mon.	29	Montreal
	Wed.	31	at NY Islanders*
Jan.	Sat.	3	at Pittsburgh*
	Sun.	4	at Montreal*
	Tue.	6	at Toronto
	Thu.	8	Carolina
	Sat.	10	Atlanta*
	Fri.	16	Philadelphia
	Sat.	17	at Tampa Bay
	Mon.	19	Buffalo
	Wed.	21	Dallas
	Tue.	27	Philadelphia
	Thu.	29	Montreal
	Sat.	31	at NY Islanders
Feb.	Tue.	3	at Toronto
	Thu.	5	NY Islanders
	Sat.	7	at Washington
	Tue.	10	Toronto
	Thu.	12	at Carolina
	Fri.	13	NY Rangers
	Sun.	15	Washington*
	Tue.	17	New Jersey
	Thu.	19	Chicago
	Sat.	21	Boston
	Tue.	24	at Boston
	Thu.	26	at NY Rangers
	Sat.	28	at New Jersey*
Mar.	Sun.	1	at Washington*
	Tue.	3	at Atlanta
	Thu.	5	Pittsburgh
	Sat.	7	St. Louis
	Tue.	10	at Pittsburgh
	Thu.	12	at Buffalo
	Sat.	14	Tampa Bay
	Tue.	17	Washington
	Thu.	19	Toronto
	Sat.	21	Columbus
	Mon.	23	Carolina
	Wed.	25	at Buffalo
	Thu.	26	at Philadelphia
	Sat.	28	at Dallas
	Tue.	31	Ottawa
Apr.	Fri.	3	Atlanta
	Sun.	5	Pittsburgh*
	Tue.	7	at Philadelphia
	Thu.	9	at Atlanta
	Sat.	11	Washington

* Denotes afternoon game.

In his first season with Florida in 2007-08, Tomas Vokoun faced more shots (2,213) and made more saves (2,033) than any goalie in the NHL. His .919 save percentage ranked him 12th in the league.

SOUTHEAST DIVISION
16th NHL Season
Franchise date: June 14, 1993

2008-09 Player Personnel

FORWARDS	HT	WT	S	Place of Birth	*Age	2007-08 Club
BOOTH, David	6-0	212	L	Detroit, MI	23	Florida
BRINE, David	6-1	201	L	Truro, N.S.	23	Florida-Rochester
CALLA, Brady	6-0	190	R	North Vancouver, B.C.	20	M.Jaw-Kamlps-Roch
CAMPBELL, Gregory	6-0	194	L	London, Ont.	24	Florida
DUCO, Mike	5-10	200	L	Toronto, Ont.	21	Kitchener
DVORAK, Radek	6-2	200	R	Tabor, Czech.	31	Florida
FROLIK, Michael	6-1	185	L	Kladno, Czech.	20	Rimouski
GLASS, Tanner	6-0	196	L	Regina, Sask.	24	Florida-Rochester
GLOBKE, Rob	6-2	208	R	Farmington, MI	25	Florida-Rochester
HORTON, Nathan	6-2	229	R	Welland, Ont.	23	Florida
KILGER, Chad	6-4	224	L	Cornwall, Ont.	31	Toronto
KREPS, Kamil	6-2	194	R	Litomerice, Czech.	23	Florida-Rochester
LARMAN, Drew	6-3	195	R	Canton, MI	23	Florida-Rochester
MacINTYRE, Steve	6-6	265	L	Brock, Sask.	28	Providence (AHL)
MATTHIAS, Shawn	6-3	211	L	Mississauga, Ont.	20	Florida-Belleville
McARDLE, Kenndal	5-11	190	L	Toronto, Ont.	21	Rochester-Florida (ECHL)
McLEAN, Brett	5-11	185	L	Comox, B.C.	30	Florida
MEYER, Stefan	6-2	194	L	Medicine Hat, Alta.	23	Florida-Rochester
OLESZ, Rostislav	6-1	214	L	Bilovec, Czech.	22	Florida
PELTONEN, Ville	5-11	182	L	Vantaa, Finland	35	Florida
REPIK, Michal	5-10	180	R	Vlasim, Czech.	19	Vancouver (WHL)
SPRUKTS, Janis	6-3	235	L	Riga, Latvia	26	Lukko
STEWART, Anthony	6-2	239	R	LaSalle, Que.	23	Florida-Rochester
STILLMAN, Cory	6-0	200	L	Peterborough, Ont.	34	Carolina-Ottawa
WEISS, Stephen	5-11	185	L	Toronto, Ont.	25	Florida
ZEDNIK, Richard	6-0	200	L	Banska Bystrica, Czech.	32	Florida
DEFENSEMEN						
ALLEN, Bryan	6-4	220	L	Kingston, Ont.	28	Florida
BALLARD, Keith	5-11	208	L	Baudette, MN	25	Phoenix
BELAK, Wade	6-5	221	R	Saskatoon, Sask.	32	Toronto-Florida
BOUWMEESTER, Jay	6-4	212	L	Edmonton, Alta.	25	Florida
BOYNTON, Nick	6-2	210	R	Nobleton, Ont.	29	Phoenix
ELLERBY, Keaton	6-4	186	L	Strathmore, Alta.	19	Kamloops-Moose Jaw
FITZPATRICK, Rory	6-2	208	R	Rochester, NY	33	Phi-Phi (AHL)
MacDONALD, Franklin	6-0	198	L	Sydney, N.S.	23	Rochester-Florida (ECHL)
MURPHY, Cory	5-10	185	L	Kanata, Ont.	30	Florida
SKRASTINS, Karlis	6-1	210	L	Riga, Latvia	34	Colorado-Florida
VAN RYN, Mike	6-1	198	R	London, Ont.	29	Florida
WELCH, Noah	6-4	218	L	Brighton, MA	26	Florida
GOALTENDERS	**HT**	**WT**	**C**	**Place of Birth**	***Age**	**2007-08 Club**
ANDERSON, Craig	6-2	180	L	Park Ridge, IL	27	Florida
BECKFORD-TSEU, Chris	6-2	201	L	Toronto, Ont.	24	St. Louis-Peoria-Alaska
PLANTE, Tyler	6-3	191	L	Milwaukee, WI	21	Rochester-Florida (ECHL)
SHANTZ, David	6-1	202	L	Burlington, Ont.	22	Rochester-Florida (ECHL)
VOKOUN, Tomas	6-0	195	R	Karlovy Vary, Czech.	32	Florida

* – Age at start of 2008-09 season

Coaching History

Roger Neilson, 1993-94, 1994-95; Doug MacLean, 1995-96, 1996-97; Doug MacLean and Bryan Murray, 1997-98; Terry Murray, 1998-99, 1999-2000; Terry Murray and Duane Sutter, 2000-01; Duane Sutter and Mike Keenan, 2001-02; Mike Keenan, 2002-03; Mike Keenan, Rick Dudley and John Torchetti, 2003-04; Jacques Martin, 2004-05 to 2007-08; Peter DeBoer, 2008-09.

Peter DeBoer

Head Coach

Born: Dunnville, Ont., June 13, 1968.

The Florida Panthers named Peter DeBoer the 10th head coach in the club's history on June 13, 2008. DeBoer joined the Panthers from the Kitchener Rangers of the Ontario Hockey League, after guiding the team to the 2008 OHL championship before falling to the Spokane Chiefs in the Memorial Cup finals.

During his seven-year tenure as both coach and general manager in Kitchener, DeBoer earned 297 wins for a .676 winning percentage, while guiding his club to the 2003 Memorial Cup title. DeBoer earned his 500th OHL coaching victory in 2007-08, joining only five other coaches to have reached this milestone. He amassed a total of 539 OHL wins while coaching the Detroit Whalers (1995 to 1997), Plymouth Whalers (1997 to 2001) and the Kitchener Rangers (2001 to 2008), earning OHL coach of the year honors in 1999 and 2000. DeBoer was also named the 2000 Canadian Hockey League coach of the year, and was also a member of the coaching staff on Team Canada's 2005 gold medal-winning World Junior team.

As a player, DeBoer won the 1988 Memorial Cup as a member of the Windsor Spitfires. He was a 12th-round selection of the Toronto Maple Leafs in the 1988 NHL Entry Draft and played two full seasons professionally with the Milwaukee Admirals of the International Hockey League. He holds a law degree from the University of Windsor/University of Detroit.

Coaching Record

			Regular Season				Playoffs			
Season	Team	League	GC	W	L	O/T	GC	W	L	T
1995-96	Detroit	OHL	66	40	22	4	17	9	8	....
1996-97	Detroit	OHL	66	26	34	6	5	1	4	....
1997-98	Plymouth	OHL	66	37	22	7	15	8	7	....
1998-99	Plymouth	OHL	66	51	13	4	11	7	4	....
99-2000	Plymouth	OHL	68	45	18	5	23	15	8	....
2000-01	Plymouth	OHL	68	43	15	10	19	14	5	....
2001-02	Kitchener	OHL	68	35	22	11	4	0	4	....
2002-03	Kitchener	OHL	68	46	14	8	21	16	5	....
2003-04	Kitchener	OHL	68	34	26	8	5	1	4	....
2004-05	Kitchener	OHL	68	35	20	13	15	9	6	....
2005-06	Kitchener	OHL	68	47	19	2	5	1	4	....
2006-07	Kitchener	OHL	68	47	17	4	9	5	4	....
2007-08	Kitchener	OHL	68	53	11	4	20	16	4	....

2007-08 Scoring

* – rookie

Regular Season

Pos	#	Player	Team	GP	G	A	Pts	TOI	+/–	PIM	PP	SH	GW	S	%
C	12	Olli Jokinen	FLA	82	34	37	71	19:54	–19	67	18	0	5	341	10.0
R	16	Nathan Horton	FLA	82	27	35	62	18:44	15	85	9	0	3	212	12.7
C	9	Stephen Weiss	FLA	74	13	29	42	17:35	14	40	4	0	4	132	9.8
L	10	David Booth	FLA	73	22	18	40	16:10	13	26	1	0	6	228	9.6
D	4	Jay Bouwmeester	FLA	82	15	22	37	27:28	–5	72	4	0	0	182	8.2
C	53	Brett McLean	FLA	67	14	23	37	16:14	–5	34	3	1	1	140	10.0
R	20	Richard Zednik	FLA	54	15	11	26	17:35	–5	43	6	0	5	140	10.7
L	85	Rostislav Olesz	FLA	56	14	12	26	17:03	3	16	5	0	2	139	10.1
C	54 *	Kamil Kreps	FLA	76	8	17	25	12:58	10	29	1	0	2	99	8.1
D	7	Steve Montador	FLA	73	8	15	23	11:39	1	73	2	0	0	96	8.3
L	15	Jozef Stumpel	FLA	52	7	13	20	17:22	–11	10	3	0	1	64	10.9
L	18	Ville Peltonen	FLA	56	5	15	20	15:49	–2	20	1	0	0	108	4.6
C	11	Gregory Campbell	FLA	81	5	13	18	12:26	–12	72	0	2	1	113	4.4
R	14	Radek Dvorak	FLA	67	8	9	17	15:06	–1	16	0	1	1	146	5.5
D	21	Cory Murphy	FLA	47	2	15	17	15:23	0	22	1	0	0	65	3.1
D	5	Bryan Allen	FLA	73	2	14	16	21:17	5	67	0	0	0	67	3.0
D	6	Magnus Johansson	CHI	18	0	4	4	14:39	–5	4	0	0	0	15	0.0
			FLA	27	0	10	10	16:29	0	14	0	0	0	22	0.0
			Total	45	0	14	14	15:45	–5	18	0	0	0	37	0.0
D	22	Jassen Cullimore	FLA	65	3	10	13	18:04	21	38	0	0	1	55	5.5
D	3	Karlis Skrastins	COL	43	1	3	4	18:02	–2	20	0	0	0	34	2.9
			FLA	17	1	0	1	20:03	–9	12	0	0	1	11	9.1
			Total	60	2	3	5	18:36	–11	32	0	0	1	45	4.4
D	2	Branislav Mezei	FLA	57	2	2	4	14:27	–13	64	0	0	0	38	5.3
C	41 *	Shawn Matthias	FLA	4	2	0	2	13:07	–2	2	1	0	0	5	40.0
L	37 *	Tanner Glass	FLA	41	1	1	2	04:25	–5	39	0	0	0	11	9.1
D	26	Mike Van Ryn	FLA	20	0	2	2	17:48	–2	14	0	0	0	16	0.0
R	33	Wade Belak	TOR	30	1	0	1	04:01	–2	66	0	0	0	13	7.7
F			FLA	17	0	0	0	04:09	0	12	0	0	0	4	0.0
			Total	47	1	0	1	04:04	–2	78	0	0	0	17	5.9
C	50 *	Drew Larman	FLA	6	0	1	1	05:59	1	2	0	0	0	1	0.0
C	45 *	David Brine	FLA	9	0	1	1	06:02	–1	4	0	0	0	3	0.0
C	57	Anthony Stewart	FLA	26	0	1	1	06:08	–1	0	0	0	0	21	0.0
D	47 *	Martin Lojek	FLA	2	0	0	0	06:08	–1	0	0	0	0	2	0.0
D	27 *	Noah Welch	FLA	4	0	0	0	08:04	1	7	0	0	0	0	0.0
L	64 *	Stefan Meyer	FLA	4	0	0	0	02:25	–1	0	0	0	0	0	0.0
C	17	Garth Murray	MTL	1	0	0	0	12:46	0	0	0	0	0	0	0.0
			FLA	6	0	0	0	05:08	0	19	0	0	0	3	0.0
			Total	7	0	0	0	06:13	0	19	0	0	0	3	0.0
R	51	Rob Globke	FLA	9	0	0	0	07:43	–3	2	0	0	0	4	0.0

Goaltending

No.	Goaltender	GPI	Mins	Avg	W	L	OT	EN	SO	GA	SA	S%	G	A	PIM
31	Craig Anderson	17	935	2.25	8	6	1	0	2	35	535	.935	0	1	2
29	Tomas Vokoun	69	4031	2.68	30	29	8	5	4	180	2213	.919	0	6	4
	Totals	**82**	**4988**	**2.65**	**38**	**35**	**9**	**5**	**6**	**220**	**2753**	**.920**			

David Booth spent his first full season in the NHL in 2007-08. His 22 goals ranked him third on the team.

General Managers' History

Bob Clarke, 1993-94; Bryan Murray, 1994-95 to 1999-2000; Bryan Murray and Bill Torrey, 2000-01; Bill Torrey and Chuck Fletcher, 2001-02; Rick Dudley, 2002-03, 2003-04; Mike Keenan, 2004-05, 2005-06; Jacques Martin, 2006-07 to date.

Club Records

Team

(Figures in brackets for season records are games played; records for fewest points, wins, ties, losses, goals, goals against are for 70 or more games)

Most Points	**98**	1999-2000 (82)
Most Wins	**43**	1999-2000 (82)
Most Ties	**19**	1996-97 (82)
Most Losses	**44**	2001-02 (82)
Most Goals	**254**	1995-96 (82)
Most Goals Against	**257**	2005-06 (82), 2006-07 (82)
Fewest Points	**60**	2001-02 (82)
Fewest Wins	**22**	2000-01 (82), 2001-02 (82)
Fewest Ties	**6**	1999-2000 (82)
Fewest Losses	**27**	1999-2000 (82)
Fewest Goals	**176**	2002-03 (82)
Fewest Goals Against	**201**	1996-97 (82)
Longest Winning Streak		
Overall	**7**	Nov. 2-14/95, Mar. 17-29/06, Mar. 2-16/08
Home	**5**	Nov. 5-14/95, Mar. 17-Apr. 1/06, Mar. 6-16/08
Away	**4**	Five times
Longest Undefeated Streak		
Overall	**12**	Oct. 5-30/96 (8 wins, 4 ties)
Home	**8**	Nov. 5-26/95 (7 wins, 1 tie)
Away	**7**	Dec. 7-29/93 (5 wins, 2 ties), Oct. 5-29/96 (4 wins, 3 ties)
Longest Losing Streak		
Overall	**13**	Feb. 7-Mar. 23/98
Home	**6**	Feb. 25-Mar. 23/98
Away	**13**	Oct. 27-Dec. 17/05
Longest Winless Streak		
Overall	**15**	Feb. 1-Mar. 23/98 (14 losses, 1 tie)
Home	**13**	Feb. 5-Mar. 24/03 (11 losses, 2 ties)
Away	**16**	Jan. 2-Mar. 21/98 (12 losses, 4 ties)
Most Shutouts, Season	**7**	2002-03 (82), 2003-04 (82)
Most PIM, Season	**1,994**	2001-02 (82)
Most Goals, Game	**10**	Nov. 26/97 (Bos. 5 at Fla. 10)

Individual

Most Seasons	**9**	Paul Laus
Most Games	**573**	Robert Svehla
Most Goals, Career	**188**	Olli Jokinen
Most Assists, Career	**231**	Olli Jokinen
Most Points, Career	**419**	Olli Jokinen (188G, 231A)
Most PIM, Career	**1,702**	Paul Laus
Most Shutouts, Career	**22**	Roberto Luongo
Longest Consecutive Games Streak	**300**	Robert Svehla (Dec. 23/98-Apr. 14/02)
Most Goals, Season	**59**	Pavel Bure (2000-01)
Most Assists, Season	**53**	Viktor Kozlov (1999-2000)
Most Points, Season	**94**	Pavel Bure (1999-2000; 58G, 36A)
Most PIM, Season	**354**	Peter Worrell (2001-02)
Most Points, Defenseman, Season	**57**	Robert Svehla (1995-96; 8G, 49A)
Most Points, Center, Season	**91**	Olli Jokinen (2006-07; 39G, 52A)
Most Points, Right Wing, Season	**94**	Pavel Bure (1999-2000; 58G, 36A)
Most Points, Left Wing, Season	**71**	Ray Whitney (1999-2000; 29G, 42A)
Most Points, Rookie, Season	**50**	Jesse Belanger (1993-94; 17G, 33A)
Most Shutouts, Season	**7**	Roberto Luongo (2003-04)
Most Goals, Game	**4**	Mark Parrish (Oct. 30/98); Pavel Bure (Jan. 1/00, Feb. 10/01)
Most Assists, Game	**4**	Four times
Most Points, Game	**6**	Olli Jokinen (Mar. 17/07; 2G, 4A)

Captains' History

Brian Skrudland, 1993-94 to 1996-97; Scott Mellanby, 1997-98 to 2000-01; Pavel Bure, 2001-02; no captain, 2002-03; Olli Jokinen, 2003-04 to 2007-08.

All-time Record vs. Other Clubs

Regular Season

	At Home								On Road								Total							
	GP	W	L	T	OL	GF	GA	PTS	GP	W	L	T	OL	GF	GA	PTS	GP	W	L	T	OL	GF	GA	PTS
Anaheim	9	4	3	2	0	27	22	10	10	5	3	1	1	30	28	12	19	9	6	3	1	57	50	22
Atlanta	25	11	12	1	1	61	75	24	25	7	10	4	4	69	84	22	50	18	22	5	5	130	159	46
Boston	27	12	11	2	2	87	81	28	28	15	9	4	0	78	71	34	55	27	20	6	2	165	152	62
Buffalo	27	13	13	1	0	74	77	27	29	7	17	3	2	54	84	19	56	20	30	4	2	128	161	46
Calgary	10	3	3	2	2	22	24	10	9	3	4	1	1	24	26	8	19	6	7	3	3	46	50	18
Carolina	38	16	7	8	7	112	91	47	37	10	22	3	2	92	119	25	75	26	29	11	9	204	210	72
Chicago	9	3	5	1	0	22	33	7	11	4	5	2	0	33	35	10	20	7	10	3	0	55	68	17
Colorado	12	1	10	0	1	33	52	3	12	4	4	3	1	31	35	12	24	5	14	3	2	64	87	15
Columbus	4	2	0	0	2	13	12	6	3	2	1	0	0	9	6	4	7	4	1	0	2	22	18	10
Dallas	11	5	5	1	0	24	29	11	9	3	4	2	0	25	29	8	20	8	9	3	0	49	58	19
Detroit	10	2	4	2	2	20	29	8	9	1	5	3	0	23	35	5	19	3	9	5	2	43	64	13
Edmonton	10	5	2	2	1	27	28	13	8	2	5	1	0	17	28	5	18	7	7	3	1	44	56	18
Los Angeles	9	4	2	3	0	23	21	11	10	4	6	0	0	30	30	8	19	8	8	3	0	53	51	19
Minnesota	4	1	3	0	0	8	11	2	4	0	3	1	0	3	14	1	8	1	6	1	0	11	25	3
Montreal	28	14	10	3	1	80	72	32	27	13	7	3	4	62	67	33	55	27	17	6	5	142	139	65
Nashville	5	3	0	1	1	18	11	8	6	2	2	2	0	13	12	6	11	5	2	3	1	31	23	14
New Jersey	31	10	15	4	2	69	81	26	30	8	17	3	2	58	89	21	61	18	32	7	4	127	170	47
NY Islanders	31	15	10	6	0	99	92	36	31	14	11	2	4	83	81	34	62	29	21	8	4	182	173	70
NY Rangers	31	14	12	2	3	82	85	33	30	9	17	4	0	66	96	22	61	23	29	6	3	148	181	55
Ottawa	28	11	15	1	1	88	93	24	28	11	13	2	2	71	88	26	56	22	28	3	3	159	181	50
Philadelphia	30	8	19	1	2	69	102	19	31	12	12	6	1	79	83	31	61	20	31	7	3	148	185	50
Phoenix	9	4	5	0	0	28	23	8	11	4	3	3	1	34	31	12	20	8	8	3	1	62	54	20
Pittsburgh	28	16	10	1	1	83	67	34	29	11	13	3	2	82	89	27	57	27	23	4	3	165	156	61
St. Louis	10	3	4	2	1	20	21	9	10	2	7	1	0	13	25	5	20	5	11	3	1	33	46	14
San Jose	10	2	3	5	0	26	29	9	10	2	6	2	0	19	32	6	20	4	9	7	0	45	61	15
Tampa Bay	40	26	8	4	2	134	100	58	40	17	16	6	1	111	91	41	80	43	24	10	3	245	191	99
Toronto	23	6	10	5	2	61	68	19	21	6	11	2	2	58	69	16	44	12	21	7	4	119	137	35
Vancouver	9	4	3	1	1	25	30	10	10	1	3	5	1	22	29	8	19	5	6	6	2	47	59	18
Washington	40	19	15	4	2	104	99	44	40	16	17	5	2	99	118	39	80	35	32	9	4	203	217	83
Totals	**558**	**237**	**219**	**65**	**37**	**1539**	**1558**	**576**	**558**	**195**	**253**	**77**	**33**	**1388**	**1624**	**500**	**1116**	**432**	**472**	**142**	**70**	**2927**	**3182**	**1076**

Playoffs

	Series	W	L	GP	W	L	T	GF	GA	Last Mtg.	Rnd.	Result
Boston	1	1	0	5	4	1	0	22	16	1996	CQF	W 4-1
Colorado	1	0	1	4	0	4	0	4	15	1996	F	L 0-4
New Jersey	1	0	1	4	0	4	0	6	12	2000	CQF	L 0-4
NY Rangers	1	0	1	5	1	4	0	10	13	1997	CQF	L 1-4
Philadelphia	1	1	0	6	4	2	0	15	11	1996	CSF	W 4-2
Pittsburgh	1	1	0	7	4	3	0	20	15	1996	CF	W 4-3
Totals	**6**	**3**	**3**	**31**	**13**	**18**	**0**	**77**	**82**			

Colorado totals include Quebec, 1993-94 to 1994-95.
Phoenix totals include Winnipeg, 1993-94 to 1995-96.

Carolina totals include Hartford, 1993-94 to 1996-97.

Playoff Results 2008-2003

(Last playoff appearance: 2000)

Abbreviations: Round: F - Final; **CF** - conference final; **CSF** - conference semi-final; **CQF** - conference quarter-final.

2007-08 Results

Oct.	4	at NY Rangers	2-5
	6	New Jersey	1-4
	10	at Tampa Bay	1-2
	11	New Jersey	3-0
	13	Tampa Bay	6-4
	16	at Montreal	2-1†
	18	at Toronto	2-3
	20	at Ottawa	1-4
	24	Philadelphia	4-3
	26	Buffalo	2-4
	27	at Nashville	3-4
	31	Carolina	4-2
Nov.	2	at Buffalo	4-2
	3	at Carolina	2-4
	5	Tampa Bay	4-3
	7	at Tampa Bay	1-3
	9	Atlanta	1-4
	12	Carolina	3-4
	13	at Atlanta	2-3*
	15	Washington	2-1
	17	at Carolina	1-2
	19	at Washington	4-3
	21	at Columbus	5-2
	23	NY Rangers	3-2†
	28	at Washington	2-1†
	29	Boston	3-4
Dec.	1	Washington	1-2
	5	Ottawa	4-5
	7	NY Islanders	3-0
	11	Calgary	1-2†
	13	at St. Louis	1-0
	15	at Detroit	2-5
	16	at Chicago	3-1
	18	at Montreal	3-2
	20	Carolina	5-4
	22	Toronto	1-2*
	27	at Atlanta	5-3
	28	Montreal	1-5
	30	Philadelphia	0-1
Jan.	2	at New Jersey	2-3
	3	at NY Islanders	4-3*
	5	at Pittsburgh	0-3
	8	Pittsburgh	1-3
	10	at Atlanta	3-2†
	12	Tampa Bay	3-5
	13	Colorado	3-4†
	16	at Philadelphia	3-5
	18	at New Jersey	2-1
	19	at Washington	3-5
	22	Ottawa	5-3
	24	Edmonton	3-4†
	30	Buffalo	0-1
Feb.	1	Vancouver	4-3†
	2	at Tampa Bay	3-2
	5	at Toronto	8-0
	7	at Ottawa	4-5
	9	at Boston	6-3
	10	at Buffalo	3-5
	13	Montreal	1-2*
	15	Washington	4-2
	16	at Carolina	4-5
	19	at Pittsburgh	2-3
	21	Boston	4-5†
	23	at Philadelphia	2-1*
	24	at NY Rangers	0-5
	27	Toronto	3-4†
	29	Minnesota	2-3
Mar.	2	at NY Islanders	1-0
	4	at Boston	1-0*
	6	Pittsburgh	5-2
	8	Atlanta	3-2*
	12	NY Islanders	4-2
	14	NY Rangers	3-2
	16	Atlanta	3-1
	20	Carolina	1-2†
	22	Tampa Bay	4-2
	25	at Tampa Bay	1-3
	27	Atlanta	2-3
	29	Washington	0-3
Apr.	1	at Atlanta	3-2
	4	at Carolina	4-3
	5	at Washington	1-3

* – Overtime † – Shootout

Entry Draft Selections 2008-1994

Name in bold denotes played in NHL.

2008

Pick	
31	Jacob Markstrom
46	Colby Robak
80	Adam Comrie
100	A.J. Jenks
190	Matthew Bartkowski

2007

Pick	
10	Keaton Ellerby
40	Michal Repik
71	Evgeni Dadonov
101	Matt Rust
131	John Lee
181	Corey Syvret
191	Ryan Watson
202	Sergei Gaiduchenko

2006

Pick	
10	Michael Frolik
73	Brady Calla
103	Michael Caruso
116	Derrick Lapoint
155	Peter Aston
193	Marc Cheverie

2005

Pick	
20	Kenndal McArdle
32	Tyler Plante
90	Dan Collins
93	Olivier Legault
104	Matt Duffy
161	Brian Foster
164	Roman Derlyuk
224	Zach Bearson

2004

Pick	
7	**Rostislav Olesz**
37	David Shantz
53	**David Booth**
105	Evan Schafer
152	Bret Nasby
267	Spencer Dillon
283	Luke Beaverson

2003

Pick	
3	**Nathan Horton**
25	**Anthony Stewart**
38	**Kamil Kreps**
55	**Stefan Meyer**
105	**Martin Lojek**
124	James Pemberton
141	Dan Travis
162	Martin Tuma
171	Denis Stasyuk
223	Dany Roussin
234	Petr Kadlec
264	John Hecimovic
265	**Tanner Glass**

2002

Pick	
3	**Jay Bouwmeester**
9	**Petr Taticek**
40	**Rob Globke**
67	**Gregory Campbell**
134	Topi Jaakola
158	Vince Bellissimo
169	Jeremy Swanson
196	Mikael Vuorio
200	Denis Yachmenev
232	Peter Hafner

2001

Pick	
4	**Stephen Weiss**
24	**Lukas Krajicek**
34	Greg Watson
64	**Tomas Malec**
68	**Grant McNeill**
117	Mike Woodford
136	Billy Thompson
169	Dustin Johner
200	Toni Koivisto
231	Kyle Bruce
263	Jan Blanar
267	**Ivan Majesky**

2000

Pick	
58	Vladimir Sapozhnikov
77	Robert Fried
82	Sean O'Connor
115	Chris Eade
120	Davis Parley
190	**Josh Olson**
234	**Janis Sprukts**
253	Mathew Sommerfeld

1999

Pick	
12	**Denis Shvidki**
40	**Alex Auld**
70	**Niklas Hagman**
80	Jean-Francois Laniel
103	Morgan McCormick
109	Rod Sarich
169	Brad Woods
198	Travis Eagles
227	Jonathon Charron

1998

Pick	
30	**Kyle Rossiter**
61	**Joe DiPenta**
63	**Lance Ward**
89	**Ryan Jardine**
117	**Jaroslav Spacek**
148	Chris Ovington
176	B.J. Ketcheson
203	Ian Jacobs
231	Adrian Wichser

1997

Pick	
20	**Mike Brown**
47	**Kristian Huselius**
56	Vratislav Cech
74	**Nick Smith**
95	**Ivan Novoseltsev**
127	Pat Parthenais
155	Keith Delaney
183	Tyler Palmer
211	Doug Schueller
237	Benoit Cote

1996

Pick	
20	**Marcus Nilson**
60	**Chris Allen**
65	**Oleg Kvasha**
82	**Joey Tetarenko**
129	Andrew Long
156	Gaetan Poirier
183	Alexandre Couture
209	Denis Khloptonov
235	Russell Smith

1995

Pick	
10	**Radek Dvorak**
36	Aaron MacDonald
62	Mike O'Grady
80	**Dave Duerden**
88	**Daniel Tjarnqvist**
114	Francois Cloutier
166	**Peter Worrell**
192	**Filip Kuba**
218	David Lemanowicz

1994

Pick	
1	**Ed Jovanovski**
27	**Rhett Warrener**
31	**Jason Podollan**
36	**Ryan Johnson**
84	**David Nemirovsky**
105	Dave Geris
157	Matt O'Dette
183	Jason Boudrias
235	Tero Lehtera
261	**Per Gustafsson**

Jacques Martin

General Manager

Born: St. Pascal, Ont., October 1, 1952.

Jacques Martin was hired as coach of the Florida Panthers on May 6, 2004. He took over the role of general manager as well on September 3, 2006 and served in both capacities through the 2007-08 season before relinquishing the coach's job and agreeing to a new deal as general manager on May 16, 2008. Martin joined the Panthers after eight-and-a-half seasons with the Ottawa Senators. For his career with the Senators, he posted a 341-255-96 regular-season record and stands as the franchise's all-time leader in games coached (692), regular-season wins (341), playoff wins (31) and playoff games coached (69).

Under Martin's guidance, the Senators earned their first Presidents' Trophy and Eastern Conference title, posting a 52-22-8 mark in 2002-03. Martin has been nominated for the Jack Adams Award as coach of the year four times. He won the award in 1998-99 and was nominated in 1996-97, 2000-01 and 2002-03. Martin was named as an associate coach for Team Canada's men's hockey team that won gold at the 2002 Olympic Winter Games in Salt Lake City and served in the same capacity with Team Canada at the World Cup of Hockey in 2004 and at the Olympics again in 2006.

Martin joined Ottawa after spending the first half of the 1995-96 season with the Stanley Cup champion Colorado Avalanche, where he served as an assistant coach. Martin entered the NHL as head coach of the St. Louis Blues in 1986-87 and 1987-88, leading the Blues to the Norris Division championship in his rookie season. He joined the Blues after guiding the Ontario Hockey League's Guelph Platers to the 1986 Memorial Cup championship and winning OHL coach of the year honors.

Coaching Record

			Regular Season				Playoffs			
Season	Team	League	GC	W	L	O/T	GC	W	L	T
1986-87	St. Louis	NHL	80	32	33	15	6	2	4	....
1987-88	St. Louis	NHL	80	34	38	8	10	5	5	....
1995-96	Ottawa	NHL	38	10	24	4	....	....	....	....
1996-97	Ottawa	NHL	82	31	36	15	7	3	4	....
1997-98	Ottawa	NHL	82	34	33	15	11	5	6	....
1998-99	Ottawa	NHL	82	44	23	15	4	0	4	....
99-2000	Ottawa	NHL	82	41	28	13	6	2	4	....
2000-01	Ottawa	NHL	82	48	21	13	4	0	4	....
2001-02	Ottawa	NHL	80	38	26	16	12	7	5	....
2002-03	Ottawa	NHL	82	52	21	9	18	11	7	....
2003-04	Ottawa	NHL	82	43	23	16	7	3	4	....
2004-05	Florida				SEASON CANCELLED					
2005-06	Florida	NHL	82	37	34	11	....	....	....	....
2006-07	Florida	NHL	82	35	31	16	....	....	....	....
2007-08	Florida	NHL	82	38	35	9	....	....	....	....
	NHL Totals		**1098**	**517**	**406**	**175**	**85**	**38**	**47**	....

Club Directory

BankAtlantic Center

Florida Panthers
BankAtlantic Center
One Panther Parkway
Sunrise, FL 33323
Phone **954/835-7000**
FAX 954/835-7700
www.floridapanthers.com
Capacity: 19,250

Ownership
General Partner and Chairman of the Board/
Chief Executive Officer/Governor . . . . Alan Cohen (Panthers Hockey LC)
Vice Chairman/Alternate Governor/Limited Partner . . Cliff Viner (CGV Assets, LLC)
Managing Director/Limited Partner/
Chairman of Florida Panthers Foundation . . . . . . Stu Siegel (Siegent S&E, LLC)
Limited Partners . . . . Steve Cohen, David Epstein, Dr. Elliott Hahn (LABE Partners, LLC), H. Wayne Huizenga (HHI, LLC), Bernie Kosar (KHOC, LLC), Richard C. Lehman M.D. (RCL of Florida, LLC) Al E. Maroone, Michael E. Maroone, James L. Nederlander (Charley Dog, Inc.), Jordan Zimmerman (JRB Pelican Point, LLC)

Executive
President/Chief Operating Officer . . . . Michael R. Yormark
Sr. VP, Corporate Marketing &
New Business Development. . . . . Pedro Goncalves
Sr. VP, Sales & Marketing . . . . Chad Johnson
Chief Financial Officer, V.P. Finance . . . . Evelyn Lopez
General Manager, BankAtlantic Center/
VP, Operations . . . . Brett Stefansson
General Manager/V.P. incredibleICE . . . . Jeff Campol
Vice President, Human Resources/Payroll. . . . . Carol Duncanson
Vice President, Real Estate Development . . . . Uri Man
Vice President, Corporate Development . . . . RJ Martino
Vice President, Broadcasting & Panthers Alumni . . . Randy Moller
Vice President, Information Technology. . . . . Kelly Moyer
Vice President, Business Affairs . . . . Ed Wildermuth
Executive Assistant to the President/COO . . . . Heidi Leigh
Administrative Assistant to the President/COO . . . . . Jenna Desiderio
Executive Assistant to Chief Financial Officer. . . . . Cathy Stevenson

Hockey Operations
General Manager . . . . Jacques Martin
Assistant General Manager. . . . . Randy Sexton
Alternate Governor. . . . . William A. Torrey
Executive Assistant to the General Manager . . . . . . Giselle Seaone
Manager, Hockey Administration . . . . Murray Cawker
Manager, Team Services . . . . Mike Dixon
Director of Player Personnel/Pro Scout. . . . . Jack Birch
Director of Amateur Scouting . . . . Scott Luce
Director of Professional Scouting. . . . . Bill O'Flaherty
Amateur Scouts . . . . Fred Bandel, Paul Gallagher, Erin Ginnell, Luke Williams, Mike Yandle
Pro Scouts . . . . Phil Myre
European Scouts. . . . . Niklas Blomgren, Jari Kekalainen, Vadim Podrezov
Head Athletic Trainer . . . . David Zenobi
Assistant Athletic Trainer. Steve Dischiavi
Head Equipment Manager . . . . TBA
Assistant Equipment Managers . . . . Chris Moody, Frank Melendez

Coaching Staff
Head Coach . . . . Peter DeBoer
Assistant Coach . . . . Mike Kitchen
Assistant Coach . . . . Jim Hulton
Assistant Coach/Goaltending Coach . . . . Pierre Groulx
Strength & Conditioning Coach . . . . Andy O'Brien
Video Coach. . . . . Jamie Pringle

Communications
Manager, Communications. . . . . Justin Copertino
Manager, Public Relations/
Editor in Chief, UnRestricted . . . . Matthew F. Sacco
Coordinator, Communications . . . . Brian Goldman
Coordinator, Publications & Photography . . . . Tenille Lively
Editor, Publications . . . . Mason Kelley

Media Content
Director of Internet and Publication Content . . . . . . Dave Joseph
Website Coordinator . . . . Glenn Odebralski

Radio/TV Broadcasters
Television . . . . FSN Florida
Television Play-By-Play. . . . . Steve Goldstein
Television Analyst . . . . Denis Potvin
Panthers Review Host . . . . Craig Minervini
Radio . . . . Sports Talk 790 The Ticket
Radio Play-By-Play. . . . . Randy Moller
Radio Analyst . . . . Bill Lindsay

Los Angeles Kings

2007-08 Results: 32W-43L-4OTL-3SOL 71PTS.
Fifth, Pacific Division

Key Off-Season Signings/Acquisitions

2008

- **June 20** • Selected D **Drew Doughty** (Guelph, OHL) second overall in the 2008 Entry Draft.
- **21** • Acquired C **Brad Richardson** from Colorado for a 2nd-round pick in 2008.
- **30** • Acquired C **Jarret Stoll** and D **Matt Greene** from Edmonton for D **Lubomir Visnovsky**.
- **July 1** • Acquired D **Denis Gauthier** and a 2nd-round pick in 2010 from Philadelphia for D **Patrik Hersley** and LW **Ned Lukacevic**.
- **17** • Named **Terry Murray** head coach.

In just his second NHL season, Anze Kopitar led the Kings with 77 points (32 goals, 45 assists) and ranked among the league's top 25 scorers. At age 20, he became the second youngest player to be named Kings MVP behind 19-year-old Jimmy Carson who earned the honor back in 1987-88.

2008-09 Schedule

Oct.	Sat.	11	at San Jose		Mon.	12	Tampa Bay
	Sun.	12	San Jose		Thu.	15	Detroit
	Tue.	14	Anaheim		Sat.	17	at Dallas*
	Fri.	17	Carolina		Tue.	20	at Minnesota
	Mon.	20	Colorado		Wed.	21	at Colorado
	Fri.	24	at St. Louis		Thu.	29	Chicago
	Sat.	25	at Nashville		Sat.	31	at Montreal*
	Mon.	27	Detroit	**Feb.**	Tue.	3	at Ottawa
	Thu.	30	Vancouver		Thu.	5	at Washington
Nov.	Sat.	1	Calgary		Sat.	7	at New Jersey
	Tue.	4	Anaheim		Tue.	10	at NY Islanders
	Thu.	6	Florida		Thu.	12	Calgary
	Sat.	8	St. Louis		Sat.	14	Edmonton*
	Tue.	11	Dallas		Mon.	16	Atlanta
	Thu.	13	at Dallas		Wed.	18	at Anaheim
	Sat.	15	Nashville		Thu.	19	at San Jose
	Sun.	16	at Anaheim*		Sat.	21	Phoenix*
	Thu.	20	Washington		Tue.	24	at Minnesota
	Sat.	22	Colorado		Wed.	25	at Philadelphia
	Tue.	25	at Calgary		Fri.	27	at Detroit
	Wed.	26	at Edmonton	**Mar.**	Sun.	1	at Chicago*
	Sat.	29	Chicago*		Tue.	3	at Columbus
Dec.	Mon.	1	Toronto		Thu.	5	Dallas
	Tue.	2	at Phoenix		Sat.	7	Minnesota*
	Fri.	5	Edmonton		Mon.	9	Vancouver
	Sat.	6	Columbus		Fri.	13	at Vancouver
	Tue.	9	at Colorado		Sat.	14	at San Jose
	Thu.	11	St. Louis		Mon.	16	Nashville
	Sat.	13	Minnesota*		Thu.	19	at Boston
	Mon.	15	San Jose		Fri.	20	at Pittsburgh
	Wed.	17	NY Rangers		Sun.	22	at Chicago*
	Fri.	19	at Buffalo		Tue.	24	at St. Louis
	Sat.	20	at Detroit		Thu.	26	at Dallas
	Tue.	23	at Columbus		Sat.	28	at Nashville
	Fri.	26	Phoenix		Tue.	31	Dallas
	Sat.	27	at Phoenix	**Apr.**	Thu.	2	at Phoenix
	Mon.	29	Columbus		Sat.	4	Phoenix
Jan.	Sat.	3	Philadelphia		Mon.	6	at Calgary
	Tue.	6	at Anaheim		Tue.	7	at Edmonton
	Thu.	8	Anaheim		Thu.	9	at Vancouver
	Sat.	10	New Jersey		Sat.	11	San Jose*

* Denotes afternoon game.

Year-by-Year Record

		Home				Road				Overall								
Season	**GP**	**W**	**L**	**T**	**OL**	**W**	**L**	**T**	**OL**	**W**	**L**	**T**	**OL**	**GF**	**GA**	**Pts.**	**Finished**	**Playoff Result**
2007-08	82	17	21	....	3	15	22	....	4	32	43	....	7	231	266	71	5th, Pacific Div.	Out of Playoffs
2006-07	82	16	16	....	9	11	25	....	5	27	41	....	14	227	283	68	4th, Pacific Div.	Out of Playoffs
2005-06	82	26	14	....	1	16	21	....	4	42	35	....	5	249	270	89	4th, Pacific Div.	Out of Playoffs
2004-05	....	....	....	....	....	....	....	....	....	....	....	....	....	....	....	....		
2003-04	82	15	16	9	1	13	13	7	8	28	29	16	9	205	217	81	3rd, Pacific Div.	Out of Playoffs
2002-03	82	19	19	2	1	14	18	4	5	33	37	6	6	203	221	78	3rd, Pacific Div.	Out of Playoffs
2001-02	82	22	12	6	1	18	15	5	3	40	27	11	4	214	190	95	3rd, Pacific Div.	Lost Conf. Quarter-Final
2000-01	82	20	12	8	1	18	16	5	2	38	28	13	3	252	228	92	3rd, Pacific Div.	Lost Conf. Semi-Final
1999-2000	82	21	13	5	2	18	14	7	2	39	27	12	4	245	228	94	2nd, Pacific Div.	Lost Conf. Quater-Final
1998-99	82	18	20	3	....	14	25	2	....	32	45	5	....	189	222	69	5th, Pacific Div.	Out of Playoffs
1997-98	82	22	16	3	....	16	17	8	....	38	33	11	....	227	225	87	2nd, Pacific Div.	Lost Conf. Quater-Final
1996-97	82	18	16	7	....	10	27	4	....	28	43	11	....	214	268	67	6th, Pacific Div.	Out of Playoffs
1995-96	82	16	16	9	....	8	24	9	....	24	40	18	....	256	302	66	6th, Pacific Div.	Out of Playoffs
1994-95	48	7	11	6	....	9	12	3	....	16	23	9	....	142	174	41	4th, Pacific Div.	Out of Playoffs
1993-94	84	18	19	5	....	9	26	7	....	27	45	12	....	294	322	66	5th, Pacific Div.	Out of Playoffs
1992-93	84	22	15	5	....	17	20	5	....	39	35	10	....	338	340	88	3rd, Smythe Div.	Lost Final
1991-92	80	20	11	9	....	15	20	5	....	35	31	14	....	287	296	84	2nd, Smythe Div.	Lost Div. Semi-Final
1990-91	80	26	9	5	....	20	15	5	....	46	24	10	....	340	254	102	1st, Smythe Div.	Lost Div. Final
1989-90	80	21	16	3	....	13	23	4	....	34	39	7	....	338	337	75	4th, Smythe Div.	Lost Div. Final
1988-89	80	25	12	3	....	17	19	4	....	42	31	7	....	376	335	91	2nd, Smythe Div.	Lost Div. Final
1987-88	80	19	18	3	....	11	24	5	....	30	42	8	....	318	359	68	4th, Smythe Div.	Lost Div. Semi-Final
1986-87	80	20	17	3	....	11	24	5	....	31	41	8	....	318	341	70	4th, Smythe Div.	Lost Div. Semi-Final
1985-86	80	9	27	4	....	14	22	4	....	23	49	8	....	284	389	54	5th, Smythe Div.	Out of Playoffs
1984-85	80	20	14	6	....	14	18	8	....	34	32	14	....	339	326	82	4th, Smythe Div.	Lost Div. Semi-Final
1983-84	80	13	19	8	....	10	25	5	....	23	44	13	....	309	376	59	5th, Smythe Div.	Out of Playoffs
1982-83	80	20	13	7	....	7	28	5	....	27	41	12	....	308	365	66	5th, Smythe Div.	Out of Playoffs
1981-82	80	19	15	6	....	5	26	9	....	24	41	15	....	314	369	63	4th, Smythe Div.	Lost Div. Final
1980-81	80	22	11	7	....	21	13	6	....	43	24	13	....	337	290	99	2nd, Norris Div.	Lost Prelim. Round
1979-80	80	18	13	9	....	12	23	5	....	30	36	14	....	290	313	74	2nd, Norris Div.	Lost Prelim. Round
1978-79	80	20	13	7	....	14	21	5	....	34	34	12	....	292	286	80	3rd, Norris Div.	Lost Prelim. Round
1977-78	80	18	16	6	....	13	18	9	....	31	34	15	....	243	245	77	3rd, Norris Div.	Lost Prelim. Round
1976-77	80	20	13	7	....	14	18	8	....	34	31	15	....	271	241	83	2nd, Norris Div.	Lost Quarter-Final
1975-76	80	22	13	5	....	16	20	4	....	38	33	9	....	263	265	85	2nd, Norris Div.	Lost Quarter-Final
1974-75	80	22	7	11	....	20	10	10	....	42	17	21	....	269	185	105	2nd, Norris Div.	Lost Prelim. Round
1973-74	78	22	13	4	....	11	20	8	....	33	33	12	....	233	231	78	3rd, West Div.	Lost Quarter-Final
1972-73	78	21	11	7	....	10	25	4	....	31	36	11	....	232	245	73	6th, West Div.	Out of Playoffs
1971-72	78	14	23	2	....	6	26	7	....	20	49	9	....	206	305	49	7th, West Div.	Out of Playoffs
1970-71	78	17	14	8	....	8	26	5	....	25	40	13	....	239	303	63	5th, West Div.	Out of Playoffs
1969-70	76	12	22	4	....	2	30	6	....	14	52	10	....	168	290	38	6th, West Div.	Out of Playoffs
1968-69	76	19	14	5	....	5	28	5	....	24	42	10	....	185	260	58	4th, West Div.	Lost Semi-Final
1967-68	74	20	13	4	....	11	20	6	....	31	33	10	....	200	224	72	2nd, West Div.	Lost Quarter-Final

PACIFIC DIVISION
42nd NHL Season

Franchise date: June 5, 1967

2008-09 Player Personnel

FORWARDS	HT	WT	S	Place of Birth	*Age	2007-08 Club
ARMSTRONG, Derek	6-0	197	R	Ottawa, Ont.	35	Los Angeles
BOYLE, Brian	6-7	244	L	Hingham, MA	23	Los Angeles-Manchester
BROWN, Dustin	6-0	205	R	Ithaca, NY	23	Los Angeles
CALDER, Kyle	5-11	180	L	Mannville, Alta.	29	Los Angeles
ELLIS, Matt	6-0	207	L	Welland, Ont.	27	Detroit-Los Angeles
FROLOV, Alexander	6-2	216	R	Moscow, USSR	26	Los Angeles
HANDZUS, Michal	6-5	217	L	Banska Bystrica, Czech.	31	Los Angeles
IVANANS, Raitis	6-4	263	L	Riga, Latvia	29	Los Angeles
KOPITAR, Anze	6-4	221	L	Jesenice, Yugoslavia	21	Los Angeles
MOULSON, Matt	6-1	205	L	North York, Ont.	24	Los Angeles-Manchester
MURRAY, Brady	5-9	184	L	Brandon, Man.	24	Los Angeles-Manchester
O'SULLIVAN, Patrick	5-11	190	L	Winston Salem, NC	23	Los Angeles
PARSE, Scott	6-1	188	R	Portage, MI	24	Manchester-Reading
PURCELL, Teddy	6-3	197	R	St. Johns, Nfld.	23	Los Angeles-Manchester
RICHARDSON, Brad	5-11	185	L	Belleville, Ont.	23	Colorado-Lake Erie
STOLL, Jarret	6-1	210	R	Melville, Sask.	26	Edmonton
ZEILER, John	6-0	203	R	Jefferson Hills, PA	25	Los Angeles-Manchester
DEFENSEMEN						
BAGNALL, Drew	6-3	220	L	Oakbank, Man.	24	Manchester-Reading
DOUGHTY, Drew	6-1	219	R	London, Ont.	18	Guelph
DREWISKE, Davis	6-1	215	L	Hudson, WI	23	U. of Wisconsin-Manchester
GAUTHIER, Denis	6-3	224	L	Montreal, Que.	32	Philadelphia (AHL)
GREENE, Matt	6-3	233	R	Grand Ledge, MI	25	Edmonton
HARROLD, Peter	5-11	195	R	Kirtland Hills, OH	25	Los Angeles-Manchester
JOHNSON, Jack	6-1	212	L	Indianapolis, IN	21	Los Angeles
PREISSING, Tom	6-0	198	R	Arlington Heights, IL	29	Los Angeles

GOALTENDERS	HT	WT	C	Place of Birth	*Age	2007-08 Club
BERNIER, Jonathan	6-0	186	L	Laval, Que.	20	L.A.-Lewiston-Manchester
ERSBERG, Erik	6-0	182	L	Sala, Sweden	26	Los Angeles-Manchester
LaBARBERA, Jason	6-3	235	L	Burnaby, B.C.	28	Los Angeles
QUICK, Jonathan	6-1	206	L	Milford, CT	22	L.A.-Manchester-Reading

* – Age at start of 2008-09 season

Dustin Brown led the Kings with 33 goals in 2007-08, exceeding the total of 32 goals he had scored during the first three years of his career.

General Managers' History

Larry Regan, 1967-68 to 1972-73; Larry Regan and Jake Milford, 1973-74; Jake Milford, 1974-75 to 1976-77; George Maguire, 1977-78 to 1982-83; George Maguire and Rogie Vachon, 1983-84; Rogie Vachon, 1984-85 to 1991-92; Nick Beverley, 1992-93, 1993-94; Sam McMaster, 1994-95 to 1996-97; Dave Taylor, 1997-98 to 2005-06; Dean Lombardi, 2006-07 to date.

Captains' History

Bob Wall, 1967-68, 1968-69; Larry Cahan, 1969-70, 1970-71; Bob Pulford, 1971-72, 1972-73; Terry Harper, 1973-74, 1974-75; Mike Murphy, 1975-76 to 1980-81; Dave Lewis, 1981-82, 1982-83; Terry Ruskowski, 1983-84, 1984-85; Dave Taylor, 1985-86 to 1988-89; Wayne Gretzky, 1989-90 to 1991-92; Wayne Gretzky and Luc Robitaille, 1992-93; Wayne Gretzky, 1993-94, 1994-95; Wayne Gretzky and Rob Blake, 1995-96; Rob Blake, 1996-97 to 2000-01; Mattias Norstrom, 2001-02 to 2006-07; Rob Blake, 2007-08.

2007-08 Scoring

* – rookie

Regular Season

Pos	#	Player	Team	GP	G	A	Pts	TOI	+/–	PIM	PP	SH	GW	S	%
C	11	Anze Kopitar	L.A.	82	32	45	77	20:41	–15	22	12	2	3	201	15.9
L	24	Alexander Frolov	L.A.	71	23	44	67	18:47	1	22	5	0	7	160	14.4
L	23	Dustin Brown	L.A.	78	33	27	60	20:17	–13	55	12	2	4	219	15.1
C	12	Patrick O'Sullivan	L.A.	82	22	31	53	18:42	–8	36	3	3	2	220	10.0
C	13	Mike Cammalleri	L.A.	63	19	28	47	18:34	–16	30	10	0	1	210	9.0
D	17	Lubomir Visnovsky	L.A.	82	8	33	41	22:59	–18	34	3	0	1	153	5.2
C	7	Derek Armstrong	L.A.	77	8	27	35	13:16	4	63	1	0	2	118	6.8
D	4	Rob Blake	L.A.	71	9	22	31	22:44	–19	98	5	0	2	144	6.3
L	47	Ladislav Nagy	L.A.	38	9	17	26	13:47	–2	18	2	0	1	78	11.5
D	42	Tom Preissing	L.A.	77	8	16	24	17:52	–6	16	6	0	1	93	8.6
C	26	Michal Handzus	L.A.	82	7	14	21	15:14	–21	45	0	3	0	89	7.9
L	19	Kyle Calder	L.A.	65	7	13	20	12:59	–11	18	3	0	0	70	10.0
R	21	Brian Willsie	L.A.	53	4	8	12	10:37	–8	30	0	0	0	62	6.5
D	3 *	Jack Johnson	L.A.	74	3	8	11	21:41	–19	76	0	0	0	81	3.7
L	28 *	Matt Moulson	L.A.	22	5	4	9	12:04	2	4	0	0	0	35	14.3
L	41	Raitis Ivanans	L.A.	73	6	2	8	07:30	–10	134	0	0	0	48	12.5
L	27	Scott Thornton	L.A.	47	5	3	8	08:47	1	39	0	0	1	35	14.3
L	8	Matt Ellis	DET	35	2	4	6	05:22	1	12	0	0	1	28	7.1
			L.A.	19	1	1	2	12:40	2	14	0	1	0	38	2.6
			Total	54	3	5	8	07:56	3	26	0	1	1	66	4.5
D	38	Kevin Dallman	L.A.	34	3	4	7	12:53	4	4	0	0	1	41	7.3
L	29	Jeff Giuliano	L.A.	53	0	6	6	11:49	–9	14	0	0	0	30	0.0
C	22 *	Brian Boyle	L.A.	8	4	1	5	13:37	4	4	0	0	0	19	21.1
D	5 *	Peter Harrold	L.A.	25	2	3	5	16:23	3	2	0	0	0	16	12.5
C	54 *	Teddy Purcell	L.A.	10	1	2	3	11:59	2	0	0	0	0	10	10.0
L	15 *	Brady Murray	L.A.	4	1	0	1	11:18	–2	6	0	0	0	2	50.0
R	73 *	John Zeiler	L.A.	36	0	1	1	08:28	–6	23	0	0	0	18	0.0
R	34 *	Lauri Tukonen	L.A.	1	0	0	0	09:48	0	0	0	0	0	1	0.0
L	52 *	Gabe Gauthier	L.A.	3	0	0	0	07:07	0	0	0	0	0	2	0.0
D	25	Jon Klemm	L.A.	22	0	0	0	10:57	–5	10	0	0	0	6	0.0

Goaltending

No.	Goaltender	GPI	Mins	Avg	W	L	OT	EN	SO	GA	SA	S%	G	A	PIM
31	* Erik Ersberg	14	799	2.48	6	5	3	1	2	33	452	.927	0	0	0
35	Jason Labarbera	45	2421	3.00	17	23	2	3	1	121	1341	.910	0	0	2
30	J-Sebastien Aubin	19	828	3.19	5	6	1	3	0	44	385	.886	0	0	0
39	Dan Cloutier	9	489	3.44	2	4	1	1	0	28	247	.887	0	0	2
32	* Jonathan Quick	3	141	3.83	1	2	0	0	0	9	62	.855	0	0	0
45	* Jonathan Bernier	4	238	4.03	1	3	0	2	0	16	118	.864	0	0	0
46	* Daniel Taylor	1	20	6.00	0	0	0	0	0	2	10	.800	0	0	0
	Totals	**82**	**4977**	**3.17**	**32**	**43**	**7**	**10**	**3**	**263**	**2625**	**.900**			

Dean Lombardi

President and General Manager

Born: Holyoke, MA, March 5, 1958.

The Los Angeles Kings named Dean Lombardi president and general manager on April 21, 2006. Lombardi, formerly a member of the San Jose Sharks front office for 13 years, including seven seasons as general manager, followed by three years as a pro scout for the Philadelphia Flyers from 2003 to 2006, is the eighth general manager in Kings history.

An executive in the San Jose front office since 1990, Lombardi first served as assistant general manager (a post he held the previous two seasons with the Minnesota North Stars) for the expansion Sharks before being elevated to vice president, director of hockey operations in 1992. Four years later, he was promoted to executive vice president and general manager and given the responsibility of turning around the young franchise. During his tenure as general manager in San Jose from 1996 to 2003, Lombardi helped build the Sharks into one of the premier teams in the NHL. Under Lombardi, San Jose reached the playoffs five times – highlighted by two trips to the Western Conference Semifinals – and one Pacific Division title in 2002. The Lombardi-led Sharks in 2002 also tied an NHL-record with six consecutive seasons of improved point totals under one g.m. (Bill Torrey/New York Islanders) while building a roster that became progressively younger in age each season.

During his time as general manager in San Jose, Lombardi made many key personnel and player moves, stocking the Sharks organization with a good mix of veteran stars and up-and-coming youngsters that helped make the Sharks legitimate Stanley Cup contenders.

From the NHL Entry Draft, Lombardi brought to San Jose players Patrick Marleau, Vesa Toskala, Jonathan Cheechoo, Brad Stuart, Scott Hannan, Marco Sturm, Marcel Goc and Christian Ehrhoff. *The Hockey News* ranked the Sharks' prospects (age 22 and under) as the best in the NHL in 1999-2000 and second best in 2000-01. Lombardi's history in San Jose as it relates to trades and free agency is impressive as well, having brought in such players as Owen Nolan, Teemu Selanne, Adam Graves, Vincent Damphousse, Mike Ricci, Kyle McClaren, Mike Vernon, Todd Harvey, Bryan Marchment and Scott Thornton.

Prior to joining the North Stars, Lombardi spent three seasons as a player representative, including the representation of five members of the 1988 United States Olympic team, and at the time he joined Minnesota's front office Lombardi was only the second former player agent to be employed in an NHL front office (Brian Burke/Vancouver Canucks was the other).

Born in Holyoke, Massachusetts, and raised in nearby Ludlow, Lombardi received his undergraduate degree from the University of New Haven where he finished third in his class. On the ice he was the hockey team's captain his final two seasons, and he received a full athletic scholarship and the school's student-athlete of the year award. In 1985, Lombardi earned his Law degree (with honors) from Tulane Law School where he specialized in Labor Law.

Club Records

Team

(Figures in brackets for season records are games played; records for fewest points, wins, ties, losses, goals, goals against are for 70 or more games)

Most Points	**105**	1974-75 (80)
Most Wins	**46**	1990-91 (80)
Most Ties	**21**	1974-75 (80)
Most Losses	**52**	1969-70 (76)
Most Goals	**376**	1988-89 (80)
Most Goals Against	**389**	1985-86 (80)
Fewest Points	**38**	1969-70 (76)
Fewest Wins	**14**	1969-70 (76)
Fewest Ties	**5**	1998-99 (82)
Fewest Losses	**17**	1974-75 (80)
Fewest Goals	**168**	1969-70 (76)
Fewest Goals Against	**185**	1974-75 (80)
Longest Winning Streak		
Overall	**8**	Oct. 21-Nov. 7/72, Feb. 23-Mar. 9/92
Home	**12**	Oct. 10-Dec. 5/92
Away	**8**	Dec. 18/74-Jan. 16/75
Longest Undefeated Streak		
Overall	**11**	Feb. 28-Mar. 24/74 (9 wins, 2 ties)
Home	**13**	Oct. 10-Dec. 8/92 (12 wins, 1 tie)
Away	**11**	Oct. 10-Dec. 11/74 (6 wins, 5 ties)
Longest Losing Streak		
Overall	**11**	Mar. 16-Apr. 4/04
Home	**9**	Feb. 8-Mar. 12/86
Away	**11**	Jan. 11-Feb. 15/70
Longest Winless Streak		
Overall	**17**	Jan. 29-Mar. 5/70 (13 losses, 4 ties)
Home	**9**	Jan. 29-Mar. 5/70 (8 losses, 1 tie), Feb. 8-Mar. 12/86 (9 losses)
Away	**20**	Jan. 11-Apr. 3/70 (16 losses, 4 ties)
Most Shutouts, Season	**10**	2000-01 (82)
Most PIM, Season	**2,247**	1992-93 (84)
Most Goals, Game	**12**	Nov. 29/84 (Van. 1 at L.A. 12)

Individual

Most Seasons	**17**	Dave Taylor
Most Games	**1,111**	Dave Taylor
Most Goals, Career	**557**	Luc Robitaille
Most Assists, Career	**757**	Marcel Dionne
Most Points Career	**1,307**	Marcel Dionne (550G, 757A)
Most PIM, Career	**1,846**	Marty McSorley
Most Shutouts, Career	**32**	Rogie Vachon
Longest Consecutive Games Streak	**324**	Marcel Dionne (Jan. 7/78-Jan. 9/82)
Most Goals, Season	**70**	Bernie Nicholls (1988-89)
Most Assists, Season	**122**	Wayne Gretzky (1990-91)
Most Points, Season	**168**	Wayne Gretzky (1988-89; 54G, 114A)
Most PIM, Season	**399**	Marty McSorley (1992-93)
Most Points, Defenseman, Season	**76**	Larry Murphy (1980-81; 16G, 60A)
Most Points, Center, Season	**168**	Wayne Gretzky (1988-89; 54G, 114A)
Most Points, Right Wing, Season	**112**	Dave Taylor (1980-81; 47G, 65A)
Most Points, Left Wing, Season	***125**	Luc Robitaille (1992-93; 63G, 62A)
Most Points, Rookie, Season	**84**	Luc Robitaille (1986-87; 45G, 39A)
Most Shutouts, Season	**8**	Rogie Vachon (1976-77)
Most Goals, Game	**4**	Seventeen times
Most Assists, Game	**6**	Bernie Nicholls (Dec. 1/88), Tomas Sandstrom (Oct. 9/93)
Most Points, Game	**8**	Bernie Nicholls (Dec. 1/88; 2G, 6A)

* NHL Record.

Coaching History

Red Kelly, 1967-68, 1968-69; Hal Laycoe and Johnny Wilson, 1969-70; Larry Regan, 1970-71; Larry Regan and Fred Glover, 1971-72; Bob Pulford, 1972-73 to 1976-77; Ron Stewart, 1977-78; Bob Berry, 1978-79 to 1980-81; Parker MacDonald and Don Perry, 1981-82; Don Perry, 1982-83; Don Perry, Rogie Vachon and Roger Neilson, 1983-84; Pat Quinn, 1984-85, 1985-86; Pat Quinn and Mike Murphy 1986-87; Mike Murphy, Rogie Vachon and Robbie Ftorek, 1987-88; Robbie Ftorek, 1988-89; Tom Webster, 1989-90 to 1991-92; Barry Melrose, 1992-93, 1993-94; Barry Melrose and Rogie Vachon, 1994-95; Larry Robinson, 1995-96 to 1998-99; Andy Murray, 1999-2000 to 2004-05; Andy Murray and John Torchetti, 2005-06; Marc Crawford, 2006-07, 2007-08; Terry Murray, 2008-09.

Retired Numbers

16	Marcel Dionne	1975-1987
18	Dave Taylor	1977-1994
20	Luc Robitaille	1986-94, 97-01, 03-06
30	Rogie Vachon	1971-1978
99	Wayne Gretzky	1988-1996

All-time Record vs. Other Clubs

Regular Season

	At Home								On Road								Total							
	GP	W	L	T	OL	GF	GA	PTS	GP	W	L	T	OL	GF	GA	PTS	GP	W	L	T	OL	GF	GA	PTS
Anaheim	42	22	14	4	2	123	110	50	42	14	18	7	3	113	144	38	84	36	32	11	5	236	254	88
Atlanta	5	4	0	0	1	26	15	9	5	3	1	0	1	18	13	7	10	7	1	0	2	44	28	16
Boston	62	21	33	7	1	216	232	50	62	12	44	6	0	175	287	30	124	33	77	13	1	391	519	80
Buffalo	55	23	23	9	0	193	189	55	54	16	29	9	0	158	227	41	109	39	52	18	0	351	416	96
Calgary	97	49	39	9	0	358	335	107	100	28	57	12	3	325	437	71	197	77	96	21	3	683	772	178
Carolina	31	17	11	3	0	131	116	37	32	11	14	5	2	116	116	29	63	28	25	8	2	247	232	66
Chicago	80	36	33	8	3	272	267	83	81	34	37	9	1	235	278	78	161	70	70	17	4	507	545	161
Colorado	49	28	16	5	0	195	163	61	48	20	25	3	0	162	193	43	97	48	41	8	0	357	356	104
Columbus	14	8	5	1	0	36	30	17	14	5	6	0	3	44	39	13	28	13	11	1	3	80	69	30
Dallas	94	41	33	19	1	309	277	102	96	23	57	13	3	253	364	62	190	64	90	32	4	562	641	164
Detroit	86	43	29	14	0	331	268	100	85	31	38	13	3	289	330	78	171	74	67	27	3	620	598	178
Edmonton	83	31	35	15	2	317	332	79	83	25	43	15	0	295	370	65	166	56	78	30	2	612	702	144
Florida	10	6	4	0	0	30	30	12	9	2	4	3	0	21	23	7	19	8	8	3	0	51	53	19
Minnesota	14	5	5	2	2	30	34	14	14	5	5	3	1	28	31	14	28	10	10	5	3	58	65	28
Montreal	66	19	38	9	0	201	261	47	65	8	46	11	0	162	292	27	131	27	84	20	0	363	553	74
Nashville	18	10	7	0	1	55	51	21	18	10	5	3	0	47	36	23	36	20	12	3	1	102	87	44
New Jersey	43	29	8	6	0	204	132	64	44	19	19	5	1	151	148	44	87	48	27	11	1	355	280	108
NY Islanders	46	22	17	7	0	167	145	51	45	16	24	5	0	126	157	37	91	38	41	12	0	293	302	88
NY Rangers	61	24	26	10	1	203	217	59	59	18	35	6	0	176	235	42	120	42	61	16	1	379	452	101
Ottawa	11	9	1	1	0	48	21	19	10	4	5	1	0	29	35	9	21	13	6	2	0	77	56	28
Philadelphia	67	21	38	8	0	196	227	50	64	16	40	7	1	158	247	40	131	37	78	15	1	354	474	90
Phoenix	86	35	36	14	1	327	317	85	88	29	45	11	3	281	349	72	174	64	81	25	4	608	666	157
Pittsburgh	70	44	17	8	1	268	187	97	74	25	39	10	0	235	269	60	144	69	56	18	1	503	456	157
St. Louis	84	39	33	12	0	282	239	90	84	20	53	10	1	214	315	51	168	59	86	22	1	496	554	141
San Jose	49	26	18	4	1	145	132	57	49	17	26	3	3	134	166	40	98	43	44	7	4	279	298	97
Tampa Bay	12	1	9	2	0	25	40	4	11	5	5	0	1	24	26	11	23	6	14	2	1	49	66	15
Toronto	66	35	21	10	0	239	193	80	69	23	34	11	1	225	267	58	135	58	55	21	1	464	460	138
Vancouver	105	54	34	16	1	408	325	125	103	35	51	16	1	321	386	87	208	89	85	32	2	729	711	212
Washington	48	27	14	6	1	189	147	61	47	21	18	7	1	174	189	50	95	48	32	13	2	363	336	111
Defunct Clubs	35	27	6	2	0	141	76	56	34	11	14	9	0	91	109	31	69	38	20	11	0	232	185	87
Totals	**1589**	**756**	**603**	**211**	**19**	**5665**	**5108**	**1742**	**1589**	**506**	**837**	**213**	**33**	**4780**	**6078**	**1258**	**3178**	**1262**	**1440**	**424**	**52**	**10445**	**11186**	**3000**

Playoffs

	Series	W	L	GP	W	L	T	GF	GA	Last Mtg.	Rnd.	Result
Boston	2	0	2	13	5	8	0	38	56	1977	QF	L 2-4
Calgary	6	4	2	26	13	13	0	105	112	1993	DSF	W 4-2
Chicago	1	0	1	5	1	4	0	7	10	1974	QF	L 1-4
Colorado	2	0	2	14	6	8	0	23	33	2002	CQF	L 3-4
Dallas	1	0	1	7	3	4	0	21	26	1968	QF	L 3-4
Detroit	2	1	1	10	4	6	0	21	32	2001	CQF	W 4-2
Edmonton	7	2	5	36	12	24	0	127	154	1992	DSF	L 2-4
Montreal	1	0	1	5	1	4	0	12	15	1993	F	L 1-4
NY Islanders	1	0	1	4	1	3	0	10	21	1980	PRE	L 1-3
NY Rangers	2	0	2	6	1	5	0	14	32	1981	PRE	L 1-3
St. Louis	2	0	2	8	0	8	0	13	32	1998	CQF	L 0-4
Toronto	3	1	2	12	5	7	0	31	41	1993	CF	W 4-3
Vancouver	3	2	1	17	9	8	0	66	60	1993	DF	W 4-2
Defunct Clubs	1	1	0	7	4	3	0	23	25			
Totals	**34**	**11**	**23**	**170**	**65**	**105**	**0**	**511**	**649**			

Playoff Results 2008-2003

(Last playoff appearance: 2002)

Abbreviations: Round: F - Final;
CF - conference final; **CQF** - conference quarter-final;
DF - division final; **DSF** - division semi-final;
QF - quarter-final; **PRE** - preliminary round.

Calgary totals include Atlanta Flames, 1972-73 to 1979-80.
Carolina totals include Hartford, 1979-80 to 1996-97.
Colorado totals include Quebec, 1979-80 to 1994-95.
Dallas totals include Minnesota North Stars, 1967-68 to 1992-93.
New Jersey totals include Kansas City, 1974-75, 1975-76, and Colorado Rockies, 1976-77 to 1981-82.
Phoenix totals include Winnipeg, 1979-80 to 1995-96.

2007-08 Results

Sep.	29	Anaheim	4-1
	30	at Anaheim	1-4
Oct.	6	St. Louis	3-5
	10	at Dallas	1-5
	12	Boston	6-8
	14	Detroit	1-4
	16	Minnesota	4-3†
	18	at Calgary	3-4
	19	at Vancouver	4-2
	23	Nashville	6-0
	25	Dallas	2-1
	27	Edmonton	4-1
	31	Columbus	1-4
Nov.	2	at San Jose	5-2
	3	San Jose	1-3
	10	Dallas	6-5*
	13	at Anaheim	3-4†
	15	Anaheim	3-6
	17	Phoenix	0-1
	19	at Dallas	0-3
	21	at Phoenix	1-4
	24	at San Jose	2-1
	25	at Anaheim	2-3
	28	at San Jose	3-2†
Dec.	1	Colorado	2-5
	3	Edmonton	3-4†
	5	at Phoenix	1-4
	6	Buffalo	8-2
	8	Phoenix	2-4
	10	Vancouver	4-2
	12	at Chicago	3-6
	13	at Dallas	1-4
	15	Minnesota	1-2
	17	Colorado	2-4
	19	at Detroit	2-6
	21	at Columbus	1-2
	22	at Nashville	3-4
	26	San Jose	2-3
	29	at Colorado	3-1
	30	at Chicago	3-2*
Jan.	1	Chicago	9-2
	3	Columbus	3-4
	5	Calgary	4-6
	8	Nashville	0-7
	10	Toronto	5-2
	12	Dallas	4-3†
	15	at Edmonton	3-1
	18	at Calgary	1-6
	19	at Vancouver	4-3
	22	Detroit	0-3
	24	Anaheim	3-1
	29	at Philadelphia	2-3*
	31	at NY Islanders	3-1
Feb.	2	at New Jersey	3-6
	5	at NY Rangers	4-2
	7	at Detroit	5-3
	9	at Pittsburgh	2-4
	10	at Columbus	3-2†
	12	at St. Louis	2-4
	15	Calgary	6-3
	16	at Phoenix	3-4
	18	Phoenix	0-4
	21	St. Louis	5-1
	23	Chicago	5-6*
	28	at Edmonton	4-5
Mar.	1	at Colorado	2-5
	2	at Minnesota	1-2*
	4	at St. Louis	2-3
	6	Ottawa	2-0
	8	Montreal	2-5
	10	Vancouver	1-2*
	13	at Nashville	4-1
	15	at Minnesota	0-2
	18	San Jose	1-2
	20	at Phoenix	6-5†
	22	at Dallas	4-2
	26	at Anaheim	1-2†
	27	Phoenix	4-0
	29	Dallas	2-7
Apr.	1	at San Jose	2-5
	3	San Jose	4-2
	5	Anaheim	3-4

* – Overtime † – Shootout

Entry Draft Selections 2008-1994

Name in bold denotes played in NHL.

2008
Pick
2 Drew Doughty
13 Colten Teubert
32 Viatcheslav Voynov
63 Robert Czarnik
74 Andrew Campbell
88 Geordie Wudrick
123 Andrei Loktionov
153 Justin Azevedo
183 Garrett Roe

2007
Pick
4 Thomas Hickey
52 Oscar Moller
61 Wayne Simmonds
82 Bryan Cameron
95 Alec Martinez
109 Dwight King
124 Linden Rowat
137 Joshua Turnbull
184 Josh Kidd
188 Matt Fillier

2006
Pick
11 **Jonathan Bernier**
17 Trevor Lewis
48 Joe Ryan
74 Jeff Zatkoff
86 Bud Holloway
114 Niclas Andersen
134 David Meckler
144 Martin Nolet
164 Constantin Braun

2005
Pick
11 **Anze Kopitar**
50 Dany Roussin
60 T.J. Fast
72 **Jonathan Quick**
139 Patrik Hersley
184 Ryan McGinnis
206 Josh Meyers
226 John Seymour

2004
Pick
11 **Lauri Tukonen**
95 Paul Baier
110 Ned Lukacevic
143 Eric Neilson
174 Scott Parse
205 Mike Curry
221 **Daniel Taylor**
238 **Yutaka Fukufuji**
264 Valtteri Tenkanen

2003
Pick
13 **Dustin Brown**
26 **Brian Boyle**
27 **Jeff Tambellini**
44 **Konstantin Pushkarev**
82 Ryan Munce
152 **Brady Murray**
174 **Esa Pirnes**
231 Matt Zaba
244 Mike Sullivan
274 Marty Guerin

2002
Pick
18 **Denis Grebeshkov**
50 Sergei Anshakov
66 **Petr Kanko**
104 **Aaron Rome**
115 Mark Rooneem
152 Greg Hogeboom
157 Joel Andresen
185 Ryan Murphy
215 Mikhail Lyubushin
248 Tuukka Pulliainen
279 **Connor James**

2001
Pick
18 Jens Karlsson
30 **David Steckel**
49 **Michael Cammalleri**
51 **Jaroslav Bednar**
83 Henrik Juntunen
116 **Richard Petiot**
152 Terry Denike
153 Tuukka Mantyla
214 **Cristobal Huet**
237 Mike Gabinet
277 Sebastien Laplante

2000
Pick
20 **Alexander Frolov**
54 **Andreas Lilja**
86 **Yanick Lehoux**
118 **Lubomir Visnovsky**
165 Nathan Marsters
201 Yevgeny Fedorov
206 Tim Eriksson
218 Craig Olynick
245 Dan Welch
250 Flavien Conne
282 Carl Grahn

1999
Pick
43 Andrei Shefer
74 Jason Crain
76 **Frantisek Kaberle**
92 Cory Campbell
104 **Brian McGrattan**
125 Daniel Johansson
133 Jean-Francois Nogues
193 Kevin Baker
222 **George Parros**
250 **Noah Clarke**

1998
Pick
21 **Mathieu Biron**
46 **Justin Papineau**
76 Alexei Volkov
103 **Kip Brennan**
133 Joe Rullier
163 **Tomas Zizka**
190 Tommi Hannus
217 Jim Henkel
248 **Matthew Yeats**

1997
Pick
3 **Olli Jokinen**
15 Matt Zultek
29 **Scott Barney**
83 **Joe Corvo**
99 Sean Blanchard
137 Richard Seeley
150 Jeff Katcher
193 Jay Kopischke
220 Konrad Brand

1996
Pick
30 **Josh Green**
37 **Marian Cisar**
57 Greg Phillips
84 Mikael Simons
96 **Eric Belanger**
120 Jesse Black
123 Peter Hogan
190 **Steve Valiquette**
193 **Kai Nurminen**
219 Sebastien Simard

1995
Pick
3 **Aki Berg**
33 **Don MacLean**
50 **Pavel Rosa**
59 **Vladimir Tsyplakov**
118 **Jason Morgan**
137 Igor Melyakov
157 Benoit Larose
163 Juha Vuorivirta
215 Brian Stewart

1994
Pick
7 **Jamie Storr**
33 **Matt Johnson**
59 **Vitali Yachmenev**
111 **Chris Schmidt**
163 Luc Gagne
189 Andrew Dale
215 **Jan Nemecek**
241 Sergei Shalomai

Terry Murray

Head Coach

Born: Shawville, Que., July 20, 1950.

The Los Angeles Kings named Terry Murray their head coach on July 17, 2008. Murray – formerly the head coach of the Washington Capitals, Florida Panthers and the Philadelphia Flyers, where he led that club to the 1997 Stanley Cup Finals – is the 22nd head coach in Kings history.

Murray spent the four seasons prior to being hired by the Kings as an assistant coach with the Flyers, an organization he had worked for as a head coach, assistant coach, pro scout and player. In 2007-08, he helped the Flyers record 95 points and advance to Eastern Conference Finals after earning just 56 points in 2006-07. Murray compiled a 118-64-30 record as head coach of the Flyers for three seasons from 1994-95 through 1996-97. In addition to the 1997 Stanley Cup Finals / Eastern Conference Championship, Murray coached the team to two Atlantic Division Championships (1995 and 1996).

Murray's NHL head coaching career began with Washington for five seasons (1989-90 through 1993-94), where he compiled a 163-134-28 record. In his first season he helped lead the Capitals to the Eastern Conference Finals. Murray also coached Florida for three seasons (1998-99 through 2000-01), which included a franchise-record 98-point season and a team-record 43 wins in 1999-2000. He has also worked as an assistant coach with the Capitals (1983-84 through 1987-88); as head coach with the Baltimore Skipjacks of the American Hockey League; and as head coach with the Cincinnati Cyclones of the International Hockey League (1993-94).

As an NHL defenseman, Murray played in 302 career NHL regular season games over eight seasons with Washington, Philadelphia (two stints), the Detroit Red Wings and the California Golden Seals / California Seals, who originally drafted Murray in the seventh-round (88th overall) of the 1970 NHL Amateur Draft. He recorded 80 points (four goals, 76 assists) and 199 penalty minutes during his NHL career and he also played in 18 career NHL playoff games, recording two goals, two assists and 10 penalty minutes.

Club Directory

STAPLES Center

Los Angeles Kings
STAPLES Center
1111 South Figueroa Street
Los Angeles, CA 90015
Phone **213/742-7100**
GM FAX 310/535-4525
www.lakings.com
Capacity: 18,118

Ownership
Owner . . . . Philip F. Anschutz
Owner . . . . Edward P. Roski, Jr.
Governor . . . . Timothy J. Leiweke
Chief Operating Officer/Chief Financial Officer . . . . Dan Beckerman

Kings Executive
President/General Manager, Alternate Governor . . . Dean Lombardi
President, Business Operations, Alternate Governor . . Luc Robitaille
Chief Marketing Officer . . . . Chris McGowan
Executive Administrative Assistant to the Governor . . Carla Garcia
Executive Assistant to Chief Operating Officer/
Chief Financial Officer . . . . Karen Zamora
Executive Assistant to President/General Manager . . Tiffany Grommon
Executive Assistant to President, Business Operations . Kehly Sloane
Executive Assistant to Chief Marketing Officer . . . . Alicia Gonzalez

Hockey Operations
Vice President/Assistant General Manager . . . . Ron Hextall
Special Assistant to the G.M. . . . . Jack Ferreira
Vice President/Hockey Operations and Legal Affairs . . Jeff Solomon
Director of Pro Development . . . . Mike O'Connell
Director of Team Operations . . . . Marshall Dickerson

Coaches
Head Coach . . . . Terry Murray
Assistant Coaches . . . . Mark Hardy, Jamie Kompon
Assistant Coach/Development Coordinator . . . . . . Nelson Emerson
Goaltending Coach . . . . Bill Ranford

Training Staff — Medical
Head Athletic Trainer . . . . Chris Kingsley
Director of Rehabilitation/Assistant Athletic Trainer . Joe Caligiuri
Strength and Conditioning Coach . . . . Chad Smith
Assistant Athletic Trainer . . . . Myles Hirayama
Massage Therapist . . . . Mario Serban

Training Staff — Equipment
Head Equipment Manager . . . . Darren Granger
Assistant Equipment Manager . . . . Corey Osmak
Assistant Equipment Manager . . . . Dana Bryson

Medical
Team Physician . . . . Dr. Ronald Kvitne
Team Internist . . . . Dr. Michael Mellman
Team Dentist . . . . Dr. Jeffrey Hoy
Team Opthalmologist . . . . Dr. Howard Lazerson

Scouts/Hockey Operations
Scouting Operations Coordinator . . . . Lee Callans
Pro Scouts . . . . Rob Laird, Nickolai Bobrov, Bob Berry, Oto Hascak
Co-Director of Amateur Scouting . . . . Mark Yannetti
Co-Director of Amateur Scouting . . . . Michael Futa
Amateur Scout – Western Canada . . . . Brent McEwen
Amateur Scout – United States . . . . Tony Gasparini
Amateur Scout – Europe . . . . Pertti Hasanen
Amateur Scout – Quebec/Maritimes . . . . Denis Fugere
Amateur Scout – Northeastern United States . . . . . Bob Crocker
Amateur Scout – Russia . . . . Sergei Bobrov
Collegiate Scout – Western . . . . Mike Donnelly
Collegiate Scout – Eastern . . . . Steve Greeley
Video Technician . . . . Bob Friedlander
Video Technician . . . . Bill Gurney
Assistant Goaltending Consultant . . . . Kim Dillabaugh

Broadcasters
TV Play-by-Play Announcer . . . . Bob Miller
Radio Play-by-Play Announcer . . . . Nick Nickson
TV Color Commentator . . . . Jim Fox
Radio Color Commentator . . . . Daryl Evans

Communications
Vice President, Communications and Broadcasting . . Michael Altieri
Senior Director, Communications . . . . Jeff Moeller
Manager, Communications . . . . Mike Kalinowski
Supervisor, Communications and Broadcasting . . . . Jeremy Zager

Miscellaneous
Training Center . . . . Toyota Sports Center
Television . . . . FSN West
Radio Flagship . . . . KTLK AM 1150

Coaching Record

			Regular Season				Playoffs			
Season	Team	League	GC	W	L	O/T	GC	W	L	T
1988-89	Baltimore	AHL	80	30	46	4	....	....	....	....
1989-90	Baltimore	AHL	45	26	17	2	....	....	....	....
1989-90	**Washington**	**NHL**	**34**	**18**	**14**	**2**	**15**	**8**	**7**	....
1990-91	**Washington**	**NHL**	**80**	**37**	**36**	**7**	**11**	**5**	**6**	....
1991-92	**Washington**	**NHL**	**80**	**45**	**27**	**8**	**7**	**3**	**4**	....
1992-93	**Washington**	**NHL**	**84**	**43**	**34**	**7**	**6**	**2**	**4**	....
1993-94	Cincinnati	IHL	28	17	7	4	11	6	5	....
1993-94	**Washington**	**NHL**	**47**	**20**	**23**	**4**	....	....	....	....
1994-95	**Philadelphia**	**NHL**	**48**	**28**	**16**	**4**	**15**	**10**	**5**	....
1995-96	**Philadelphia**	**NHL**	**82**	**45**	**24**	**13**	**12**	**6**	**6**	....
1996-97	**Philadelphia**	**NHL**	**82**	**45**	**24**	**13**	**19**	**12**	**7**	....
1998-99	**Florida**	**NHL**	**82**	**30**	**34**	**18**	....	....	....	....
99-2000	**Florida**	**NHL**	**82**	**43**	**27**	**12**	**4**	**0**	**4**	....
2000-01	**Florida**	**NHL**	**36**	**6**	**18**	**12**	....	....	....	....
	NHL Totals		**737**	**360**	**277**	**100**	**89**	**46**	**43**	....

Minnesota Wild

2007-08 Results: 44W-28L-2OTL-8SOL 98PTS.
First, Northwest Division

Key Off-Season Signings/Acquisitions

2008

June 10 • Acquired D **Marc-Andre Bergeron** from Anaheim for a 3rd-round pick in 2008.

July 1 • Acquired D **Marek Zidlicky** from Nashville for RW **Ryan Jones** and a 2nd-round pick in 2009.

1 • Signed LW **Andrew Brunette**.

2 • Re-signed D **Kurtis Foster**.

3 • Signed RW **Antti Miettinen**.

6 • Signed RW **Owen Nolan**.

7 • Signed D **Tomas Mojzis**.

10 • Named **Matt Shaw** assistant coach.

11 • Acquired C **Corey Locke** from Montreal for D **Shawn Belle**.

11 • Signed C **Krys Kolanos**.

Year-by-Year Record

		Home				Road				Overall								
Season	**GP**	**W**	**L**	**T**	**OL**	**W**	**L**	**T**	**OL**	**W**	**L**	**T**	**OL**	**GF**	**GA**	**Pts.**	**Finished**	**Playoff Result**
2007-08	82	25	11	....	5	19	17	....	5	44	28	....	10	223	218	98	1st, Northwest Div.	Lost Conf. Quarter-Final
2006-07	82	29	7	....	5	19	19	....	3	48	26	....	8	235	191	104	2nd, Northwest Div.	Lost Conf. Quarter-Final
2005-06	82	23	16	....	2	15	20	....	6	38	36	....	8	231	215	84	5th, Northwest Div.	Out of Playoffs
2004-05	....	....	....	....	....	....	....	....	....	....	....	....	....	....	....	....		
2003-04	82	19	13	7	2	11	16	13	1	30	29	20	3	188	183	83	5th, Northwest Div.	Out of Playoffs
2002-03	82	25	13	3	0	17	16	7	1	42	29	10	1	198	178	95	3rd, Northwest Div.	Lost Conf. Championship
2001-02	82	14	14	8	5	12	21	4	4	26	35	12	9	195	238	73	5th, Northwest Div.	Out of Playoffs
2000-01	82	14	13	10	4	11	26	3	1	25	39	13	5	168	210	68	5th, Northwest Div.	Out of Playoffs

2008-09 Schedule

Oct.	Sat.	11	Boston
	Tue.	14	at Atlanta
	Thu.	16	at Florida
	Sat.	18	at Tampa Bay
	Thu.	23	Buffalo
	Sat.	25	Columbus
	Mon.	27	Chicago
	Wed.	29	at Dallas
	Thu.	30	Montreal
Nov.	Sat.	1	at Phoenix
	Tue.	4	at San Jose
	Thu.	6	at Colorado
	Sat.	8	at Vancouver
	Thu.	13	Phoenix
	Sat.	15	Columbus
	Tue.	18	at Pittsburgh
	Thu.	20	Vancouver
	Sat.	22	St. Louis
	Mon.	24	Washington
	Wed.	26	Dallas
	Fri.	28	Tampa Bay*
	Sat.	29	at Nashville
Dec.	Mon.	1	Colorado
	Wed.	3	St. Louis
	Fri.	5	Vancouver
	Sat.	6	at Nashville
	Thu.	11	at Phoenix
	Sat.	13	at Los Angeles*
	Sun.	14	at Anaheim*
	Wed.	17	Calgary
	Fri.	19	NY Islanders
	Sat.	20	at St. Louis
	Tue.	23	Carolina
	Sun.	28	Chicago*
	Mon.	29	at Calgary
	Wed.	31	San Jose*
Jan.	Sat.	3	Detroit
	Sun.	4	at Colorado
	Tue.	6	at Boston
	Thu.	8	at Philadelphia
	Sat.	10	at Columbus
	Tue.	13	Phoenix
	Thu.	15	Edmonton
	Sat.	17	Anaheim
	Mon.	19	at Chicago
	Tue.	20	Los Angeles
	Tue.	27	Toronto
	Fri.	30	at Edmonton
	Sat.	31	at Vancouver
Feb.	Wed.	4	Anaheim
	Fri.	6	Nashville
	Sun.	8	Edmonton*
	Wed.	11	Colorado
	Thu.	12	at Detroit
	Sat.	14	Ottawa
	Thu.	19	Calgary
	Sat.	21	Detroit
	Sun.	22	at Chicago
	Tue.	24	Los Angeles
	Fri.	27	at Calgary
	Sat.	28	at Edmonton
Mar.	Tue.	3	at Vancouver
	Thu.	5	at San Jose
	Sat.	7	at Los Angeles*
	Sun.	8	at Anaheim*
	Tue.	10	San Jose
	Thu.	12	at Colorado
	Sat.	14	at Dallas
	Sun.	15	at St. Louis*
	Tue.	17	Colorado
	Fri.	20	at New Jersey
	Sun.	22	Edmonton*
	Tue.	24	at NY Rangers
	Wed.	25	at NY Islanders
	Sat.	28	at Calgary
	Sun.	29	at Edmonton
	Tue.	31	Vancouver
Apr.	Fri.	3	Calgary
	Sun.	5	at Detroit*
	Tue.	7	Dallas
	Fri.	10	Nashville
	Sat.	11	at Columbus

* Denotes afternoon game.

Marian Gaborik established career highs in goals (42), assists (41) and points (83) in 2007-08. He led the team in both goals and points while ranking seventh and 12th in the NHL in those categories.

NORTHWEST DIVISION
9th NHL Season

Franchise date: June 25, 1997

2008-09 Player Personnel

FORWARDS	HT	WT	S	Place of Birth	*Age	2007-08 Club
BELANGER, Eric	6-0	185	L	Sherbrooke, Que.	30	Minnesota
BOOGAARD, Derek	6-7	258	R	Saskatoon, Sask.	26	Minnesota
BOUCHARD, Pierre-Marc	5-10	171	L	Sherbrooke, Que.	24	Minnesota
BRUNETTE, Andrew	6-1	212	L	Sudbury, Ont.	35	Colorado
CLUTTERBUCK, Cal	5-11	205	R	Welland, Ont.	20	Minnesota-Houston
EMMERSON, Riley	6-8	230	L	Burnaby, B.C.	22	Texas
GABORIK, Marian	6-1	199	L	Trencin, Czech.	26	Minnesota
GILLIES, Colton	6-4	194	L	White Rock, B.C.	19	Saskatoon-Houston
HAMILTON, Ryan	6-2	215	L	Oshawa, Ont.	23	Houston
IRMEN, Danny	6-0	190	R	Fargo, ND	24	Houston
KALUS, Petr	6-1	201	L	Ostrava, Czech.	21	Houston
KASSIAN, Matt	6-5	245	L	Edmonton, Alta.	21	Houston-Texas
KOIVU, Mikko	6-2	200	L	Turku, Finland	25	Minnesota
LOCKE, Corey	5-9	168	L	Toronto, Ont.	24	Montreal-Hamilton
LUNDBOHM, Bryan	5-10	185	R	Roseau, MN	31	KalPa-Vojens
MADSEN, Morten	6-2	205	L	Rodovre, Denmark	21	Houston
MIETTINEN, Antti	6-0	190	R	Hameenlinna, Finland	28	Dallas
NOLAN, Owen	6-1	214	R	Belfast, N.Ireland	36	Calgary
OLVECKY, Peter	6-2	214	L	Trencin, Czech.	22	Houston
POULIOT, Benoit	6-3	199	L	Alfred, Alfred	22	Minnesota-Houston
SCHULTZ, Jesse	6-1	195	R	Strasbourg, Sask.	26	Chicago (AHL)
SHEPPARD, James	6-2	210	L	Halifax, N.S.	20	Minnesota
VEILLEUX, Stephane	6-0	190	L	Beauceville, Que.	26	Minnesota
WELLER, Craig	6-4	220	R	Calgary, Alta.	27	Phoenix
DEFENSEMEN						
ALBERS, Paul	6-1	189	L	Melville, Sask.	22	Houston
BERGERON, Marc-Andre	5-10	197	L	St-Louis-de-France, Que.	27	NY Islanders-Anaheim
BURNS, Brent	6-5	219	R	Ajax, Ont.	23	Minnesota
FOSTER, Kurtis	6-5	220	R	Carp, Ont.	26	Minnesota
JOHNSSON, Kim	6-1	193	L	Malmo, Sweden	32	Minnesota
MOJZIS, Tomas	6-1	192	L	Kolin, Czech.	26	Novosibirsk
NOREAU, Maxim	5-11	190	R	Montreal, Que.	21	Houston-Texas
REITZ, Erik	6-1	215	R	Detroit, MI	26	Houston-Minnesota
ROGERS, Brandon	6-1	195	R	Rochester, NH	26	Houston
SCHULTZ, Nick	6-1	200	L	Strasbourg, Sask.	26	Minnesota
SCOTT, John	6-8	255	L	St. Catharines, Ont.	26	Houston
SKOULA, Martin	6-3	226	L	Litomerice, Czech.	28	Minnesota
STONER, Clayton	6-4	212	L	Port McNeill, B.C.	23	Houston
ZIDLICKY, Marek	5-11	190	R	Most, Czech.	31	Nashville

GOALTENDERS	HT	WT	C	Place of Birth	*Age	2007-08 Club
BACKSTROM, Niklas	6-1	196	L	Helsinki, Finland	30	Minnesota
BRUST, Barry	6-2	235	L	Swan River, Man.	25	Houston
HARDING, Josh	6-1	197	R	Regina, Sask.	24	Minnesota
KHUDOBIN, Anton	5-11	176	L	Ust-Kamenogorsk, USSR	22	Houston-Texas
SCHAEFER, Nolan	6-2	195	R	Yellow Grass, Sask.	28	Houston

* – Age at start of 2008-09 season

2007-08 Scoring

* – rookie

Regular Season

Pos	#	Player	Team	GP	G	A	Pts	TOI	+/–	PIM	PP	SH	GW	S	%
R	10	Marian Gaborik	MIN	77	42	41	83	19:35	17	63	11	1	8	278	15.1
C	96	Pierre-Marc Bouchard	MIN	81	13	50	63	16:50	11	34	6	0	4	129	10.1
R	12	Brian Rolston	MIN	81	31	28	59	20:04	–1	53	11	1	8	289	10.7
R	38	Pavol Demitra	MIN	68	15	39	54	19:42	9	24	2	0	1	126	11.9
D	8	Brent Burns	MIN	82	15	28	43	23:05	12	80	8	0	4	158	9.5
C	9	Mikko Koivu	MIN	57	11	31	42	20:53	13	42	2	0	2	144	7.6
C	25	Eric Belanger	MIN	75	13	24	37	17:13	–6	30	7	1	3	115	11.3
R	21	Mark Parrish	MIN	66	16	14	30	14:56	2	16	7	0	0	95	16.8
D	5	Kim Johnsson	MIN	80	4	23	27	23:26	–4	42	2	0	0	87	4.6
D	26	Kurtis Foster	MIN	56	7	12	19	16:24	0	37	3	0	2	118	5.9
C	15 *	James Sheppard	MIN	78	4	15	19	10:36	0	29	0	0	1	57	7.0
L	19	Stephane Veilleux	MIN	77	11	7	18	14:31	–13	61	0	0	0	136	8.1
R	92	Branko Radivojevic	MIN	73	7	10	17	14:54	–14	48	1	0	3	91	7.7
D	55	Nick Schultz	MIN	81	2	13	15	20:10	9	42	0	0	0	52	3.8
L	34	Aaron Voros	MIN	55	7	7	14	09:11	–7	141	0	0	1	52	13.5
L	17	Todd Fedoruk	DAL	11	0	2	2	06:49	2	33	0	0	0	6	0.0
			MIN	58	6	5	11	10:58	0	106	2	0	0	51	11.8
			Total	69	6	7	13	10:18	2	139	2	0	0	57	10.5
D	41	Martin Skoula	MIN	80	3	8	11	20:28	–16	26	0	0	1	63	4.8
D	3	Keith Carney	MIN	61	1	10	11	13:22	8	42	0	0	0	27	3.7
D	33	Petteri Nummelin	MIN	27	2	7	9	15:20	–2	2	1	0	1	31	6.5
D	6	Sean Hill	MIN	35	2	7	9	15:12	–16	32	1	0	1	18	11.1
R	83	Matt Foy	MIN	28	4	4	8	07:49	–1	28	0	0	1	38	10.5
C	37	Wes Walz	MIN	11	1	3	4	13:48	–5	6	0	0	0	9	11.1
L	67 *	Benoit Pouliot	MIN	11	2	1	3	08:49	–1	0	0	0	0	10	20.0
L	11	Chris Simon	NYI	28	1	2	3	06:58	–1	43	0	0	0	18	5.6
			MIN	10	0	0	0	07:43	–1	16	0	0	0	9	0.0
			Total	38	1	2	3	07:10	–2	59	0	0	0	27	3.7
C	16	Steve Kelly	MIN	2	0	0	0	03:43	0	0	0	0	0	1	0.0
R	22 *	Cal Clutterbuck	MIN	2	0	0	0	07:05	0	0	0	0	0	0	0.0
L	24	Derek Boogaard	MIN	34	0	0	0	03:55	–5	74	0	0	0	6	0.0

Goaltending

No.	Goaltender	GPI	Mins	Avg	W	L	OT	EN	SO	GA	SA	S%	G	A	PIM
32	Niklas Backstrom	58	3409	2.31	33	13	8	2	4	131	1629	.920	0	0	2
29	* Josh Harding	29	1571	2.94	11	15	2	0	1	77	838	.908	0	1	0
	Totals	**82**	**4999**	**2.52**	**44**	**28**	**10**	**2**	**5**	**210**	**2469**	**.915**			

Playoffs

Pos	#	Player	Team	GP	G	A	Pts	TOI	+/–	PIM	PP	SH	GW	OT	S	%
R	12	Brian Rolston	MIN	6	2	4	6	22:26	4	8	0	1	0	0	31	6.5
C	9	Mikko Koivu	MIN	6	4	1	5	21:56	0	4	0	1	0	0	20	20.0
C	96	Pierre-Marc Bouchard	MIN	6	2	2	4	17:46	1	2	1	0	1	1	18	11.1
R	38	Pavol Demitra	MIN	6	1	2	3	21:08	0	2	1	0	0	0	15	6.7
D	3	Keith Carney	MIN	6	1	1	2	15:12	2	0	0	0	1	1	2	50.0
L	17	Todd Fedoruk	MIN	6	1	1	2	13:37	–2	16	1	0	0	0	5	20.0
D	8	Brent Burns	MIN	6	0	2	2	27:34	0	6	0	0	0	0	17	0.0
L	34	Aaron Voros	MIN	5	1	0	1	10:39	–1	16	0	0	0	0	10	10.0
D	33	Petteri Nummelin	MIN	4	0	1	1	16:16	–1	0	0	0	0	0	10	0.0
D	5	Kim Johnsson	MIN	6	0	1	1	28:08	–1	18	0	0	0	0	12	0.0
R	10	Marian Gaborik	MIN	6	0	1	1	21:51	–3	4	0	0	0	0	25	0.0
C	15 *	James Sheppard	MIN	6	0	1	1	10:36	–1	4	0	0	0	0	4	0.0
R	21	Mark Parrish	MIN	1	0	0	0	05:04	0	0	0	0	0	0	1	0.0
D	55	Nick Schultz	MIN	1	0	0	0	16:11	0	0	0	0	0	0	0	0.0
R	83	Matt Foy	MIN	1	0	0	0	06:49	0	0	0	0	0	0	0	0.0
L	67 *	Benoit Pouliot	MIN	1	0	0	0	10:16	1	0	0	0	0	0	2	0.0
L	11	Chris Simon	MIN	2	0	0	0	06:54	–1	0	0	0	0	0	0	0.0
R	92	Branko Radivojevic	MIN	2	0	0	0	14:35	0	0	0	0	0	0	2	0.0
D	2 *	Erik Reitz	MIN	2	0	0	0	06:17	–1	0	0	0	0	0	0	0.0
D	6	Sean Hill	MIN	5	0	0	0	10:53	–2	4	0	0	0	0	1	0.0
C	25	Eric Belanger	MIN	6	0	0	0	18:34	–1	4	0	0	0	0	9	0.0
D	41	Martin Skoula	MIN	6	0	0	0	26:40	–1	0	0	0	0	0	3	0.0
L	19	Stephane Veilleux	MIN	6	0	0	0	15:42	–2	27	0	0	0	0	13	0.0
L	24	Derek Boogaard	MIN	6	0	0	0	04:48	–1	24	0	0	0	0	0	0.0

Goaltending

No.	Goaltender	GPI	Mins	Avg	W	L	EN	SO	GA	SA	S%	G	A	PIM
29	* Josh Harding	1	20	0.00	0	0	0	0	0	11	1.000	0	0	0
32	Niklas Backstrom	6	361	2.83	2	4	0	0	17	170	.900	0	0	0
	Totals	**6**	**384**	**2.66**	**2**	**4**	**0**	**0**	**17**	**181**	**.906**			

Jacques Lemaire

Head Coach

Born: LaSalle, Que., September 7, 1945.

The Minnesota Wild announced the signing of Jacques Lemaire as the club's first head coach on June 19, 2000. In 2002-03, he led Minnesota into the playoffs after just three seasons and went all the way to the Western Conference Final. He also won the Jack Adams Award as coach of the year. In 2007-08, Lemaire led the Wild to their first Northwest Division title. Prior to joining the Wild, Lemaire had spent parts of the previous two seasons as a senior consultant to the general manager for the Montreal Canadiens, the franchise with which he captured eight Stanley Cup championships as a player.

Lemaire spent five seasons behind the New Jersey Devils bench and compiled a 199-122-57 mark. In 1994-95, he coached the Devils to their first Stanley Cup championship. In his first season with the team (1993-94), he was awarded the Jack Adams Award for the first time.

Lemaire began his NHL coaching career with the Montreal Canadiens in 1983-84. He stepped aside as head coach following the 1984-85 campaign and moved to the front office where he held the position of assistant to the managing director. In that role, Lemaire played a part in Montreal's Stanley Cup championships of 1986 and 1993.

Lemaire spent his entire NHL playing career with Montreal from 1967 to 1979. He then began his coaching career in Switzerland where he served as player/coach of the Sierre club. He returned to North America in 1981 and was named the first head coach of the Quebec Major Junior Hockey League's expansion Longueuil Chevaliers. In his only season at the helm (1982-83), Lemaire guided the team to the QMJHL finals.

Coaching Record

			Regular Season				Playoffs			
Season	Team	League	GC	W	L	O/T	GC	W	L	T
1979-80	Sierre		STATISTICS UNAVAILABLE							
1980-81	Sierre		STATISTICS UNAVAILABLE							
1982-83	Longueuil	QMJHL	70	37	29	4	15	9	6	....
1983-84	**Montreal**	**NHL**	**17**	**7**	**10**	**0**	**15**	**9**	**6**	....
1984-85	**Montreal**	**NHL**	**80**	**41**	**27**	**12**	**12**	**6**	**6**	....
1993-94	**New Jersey**	**NHL**	**84**	**47**	**25**	**12**	**20**	**11**	**9**	....
1994-95♦	**New Jersey**	**NHL**	**48**	**22**	**18**	**8**	**20**	**16**	**4**	....
1995-96	**New Jersey**	**NHL**	**82**	**37**	**33**	**12**	....	....	....	....
1996-97	**New Jersey**	**NHL**	**82**	**45**	**23**	**14**	**10**	**5**	**5**	....
1997-98	**New Jersey**	**NHL**	**82**	**48**	**23**	**11**	**6**	**2**	**4**	....
2000-01	**Minnesota**	**NHL**	**82**	**25**	**39**	**18**	....	....	....	....
2001-02	**Minnesota**	**NHL**	**82**	**26**	**35**	**21**	....	....	....	....
2002-03	**Minnesota**	**NHL**	**82**	**42**	**29**	**11**	**18**	**8**	**10**	....
2003-04	**Minnesota**	**NHL**	**82**	**30**	**29**	**23**	....	....	....	....
2004-05	**Minnesota**		SEASON CANCELLED							
2005-06	**Minnesota**	**NHL**	**82**	**38**	**36**	**8**	....	....	....	....
2006-07	**Minnesota**	**NHL**	**82**	**48**	**26**	**8**	**5**	**1**	**4**	....
2007-08	**Minnesota**	**NHL**	**82**	**44**	**28**	**10**	**6**	**2**	**4**	....
	NHL Totals		**1049**	**500**	**381**	**168**	**112**	**60**	**52**	....

♦ Stanley Cup win.

Club Records

Team

(Figures in brackets for season records are games played.)

Most Points	**104**	2006-07 (82)
Most Wins	**48**	2006-07 (82)
Most Ties	**20**	2003-04 (82)
Most Losses	**39**	2000-01 (82)
Most Goals	**235**	2006-07 (82)
Most Goals Against	**238**	2001-02 (82)
Fewest Points	**68**	2000-01 (82)
Fewest Wins	**25**	2000-01 (82)
Fewest Ties	**10**	2002-03 (82)
Fewest Losses	**28**	2007-08 (82)
Fewest Goals	**168**	2000-01 (82)
Fewest Goals Against	**178**	2002-03 (82)
Longest Winning Streak		
Overall	**9**	Mar. 8-24/07
Home	**8**	Oct. 5-Nov. 2/06
Away	**5**	Mar. 8-17/07
Longest Undefeated Streak		
Overall	**9**	Dec. 13-30/03 (4 wins, 5 ties) Mar. 8-24/07 (9 wins)
Home	**9**	Dec. 13/00-Jan. 10/01 (5 wins, 4 ties)
Away	**7**	Dec. 6-30/03 (2 wins, 5 ties)
Longest Losing Streak		
Overall	**5**	Mar. 11-19/01, Jan. 28-Feb. 8/02, Mar. 29-Apr. 5/02
Home	**4**	Oct. 29-Nov. 15/00
Away	**6**	Feb. 12-Mar. 22/06
Longest Winless Streak		
Overall	**12**	Mar. 11-Apr. 4/01 (9 losses, 3 ties)
Home	**8**	Feb. 26-Mar. 28/01 (5 losses, 3 ties)
Away	**12**	Dec. 18/03-Jan. 31/04 (5 losses, 7 ties)
Most Shutouts, Season	**8**	2006-07 (82)
Most PIM, Season	**1,209**	2001-02 (82), 2005-06 (82)
Most Goals, Game	**8**	Mar. 25/04 (Min. 8 at Chi. 2)

Individual

Most Seasons	**7**	Marian Gaborik, Wes Walz
Most Games	**485**	Marian Gaborik
Most Goals, Career	**206**	Marian Gaborik
Most Assists, Career	**208**	Marian Gaborik
Most Points, Career	**414**	Marian Gaborik (206G, 208A)
Most PIM, Career	**698**	Matt Johnson
Most Shutouts, Career	**15**	Dwayne Roloson
Longest Consecutive Games Streak	**288**	Antti Laaksonen (Oct. 6/00-Dec. 29/03)
Most Goals, Season	**42**	Marian Gaborik (2007-08)
Most Assists, Season	**48**	Andrew Brunette (2001-02)
Most Points, Season	**83**	Marian Gaborik (2007-08; 42G, 41A)
Most PIM, Season	**201**	Matt Johnson (2002-03)
Most Points, Defenseman, Season	**43**	Brent Burns (2007-08; 15G, 28A)
Most Points, Center, Season	**79**	Brian Rolston (2005-06; 34G, 45A)
Most Points, Right Wing, Season	**83**	Marian Gaborik (2007-08; 42G, 41A)
Most Points, Left Wing, Season	**69**	Andrew Brunette (2001-02; 21G, 48A)
Most Points, Rookie, Season	**36**	Marian Gaborik (2000-01; 18G, 18A)
Most Shutouts, Season	**5**	Dwayne Roloson (2001-02, 2003-04), Nicklas Backstrom (2006-07)
Most Goals, Game	**5**	Marian Gaborik (Dec. 20/07)
Most Assists, Game	**4**	Andrew Brunette (Mar. 10/02), Marian Gaborik (Oct. 26/02) Pascal Dupuis (Mar. 25/04)
Most Points, Game	**6**	Marian Gaborik (Oct. 26/02; 2G, 4A, Dec. 20/07; 5G, 1A)

Captains' History

Sean O'Donnell, Scott Pellerin, Wes Walz, Brad Bombardir, Darby Hendrickson, 2000-01; Jim Dowd, Filip Kuba, Brad Brown, Andrew Brunette, 2001-02; Brad Bombardir, Matt Johnson, Sergei Zholtok, 2002-03; Brad Brown, Andrew Brunette, Richard Park, Brad Bombardir, Jim Dowd, 2003-04; Alex Henry, Filip Kuba, Willie Mitchell, Brian Rolston, Wes Walz, 2005-06; Brian Rolston, Keith Carney, Mark Parrish, 2006-07; Pavol Demitra, Brian Rolston, Mark Parrish, Nick Schultz, Marian Gaborik, 2007-08.

General Managers' History

Doug Risebrough, 2000-01 to date.

Coaching History

Jacques Lemaire, 2000-01 to date.

All-time Record vs. Other Clubs

Regular Season

	At Home								On Road								Total							
	GP	W	L	T	OL	GF	GA	PTS	GP	W	L	T	OL	GF	GA	PTS	GP	W	L	T	OL	GF	GA	PTS
Anaheim	14	8	3	2	1	35	26	19	14	6	7	0	1	33	33	13	28	14	10	2	2	68	59	32
Atlanta	4	3	0	1	0	13	6	7	3	2	0	0	1	12	9	5	7	5	0	1	1	25	15	12
Boston	3	2	1	0	0	9	5	4	4	4	0	0	0	15	5	8	7	6	1	0	0	24	10	12
Buffalo	4	1	3	0	0	6	10	2	4	3	1	0	0	13	8	6	8	4	4	0	0	19	18	8
Calgary	23	11	8	1	3	53	46	26	22	3	15	3	1	43	62	10	45	14	23	4	4	96	108	36
Carolina	5	2	1	2	0	14	16	6	3	0	3	0	0	2	6	0	8	2	4	2	0	16	22	6
Chicago	14	11	3	0	0	45	31	22	14	8	5	1	0	42	31	17	28	19	8	1	0	87	62	39
Colorado	22	11	7	1	3	55	62	26	23	5	15	2	1	54	74	13	45	16	22	3	4	109	136	39
Columbus	14	10	3	0	1	42	29	21	13	3	7	1	2	22	35	9	27	13	10	1	3	64	64	30
Dallas	14	7	6	0	1	35	29	15	14	3	8	1	2	32	54	9	28	10	14	1	3	67	83	24
Detroit	14	3	7	2	2	30	41	10	14	4	9	1	0	33	53	9	28	7	16	3	2	63	94	19
Edmonton	22	11	9	1	1	58	49	24	23	10	7	3	3	56	54	26	45	21	16	4	4	114	103	50
Florida	4	3	0	1	0	14	3	7	4	3	1	0	0	11	8	6	8	6	1	1	0	25	11	13
Los Angeles	14	6	4	3	1	31	28	16	14	7	3	2	2	34	30	18	28	13	7	5	3	65	58	34
Montreal	3	2	0	0	1	10	8	5	4	1	2	1	0	10	13	3	7	3	2	1	1	20	21	8
Nashville	14	8	3	3	0	46	36	19	14	4	8	2	0	30	41	10	28	12	11	5	0	76	77	29
New Jersey	4	1	1	1	1	10	12	4	4	0	2	1	1	10	16	2	8	1	3	2	2	20	28	6
NY Islanders	4	3	1	0	0	13	12	6	4	2	2	0	0	10	9	4	8	5	3	0	0	23	21	10
NY Rangers	5	2	2	0	1	17	16	5	4	1	3	0	0	8	13	2	9	3	5	0	1	25	29	7
Ottawa	4	1	1	1	1	11	14	4	3	1	2	0	0	7	9	2	7	2	3	1	1	18	23	6
Philadelphia	3	1	1	1	0	6	6	3	5	1	4	0	0	5	14	2	8	2	5	1	0	11	20	5
Phoenix	14	7	4	2	1	34	27	17	14	6	6	1	1	33	37	14	28	13	10	3	2	67	64	31
Pittsburgh	4	2	1	1	0	11	9	5	4	3	1	0	0	17	6	6	8	5	2	1	0	28	15	11
St. Louis	14	8	2	2	2	44	27	20	14	6	4	3	1	28	28	16	28	14	6	5	3	72	55	36
San Jose	14	5	7	1	1	31	34	12	14	6	6	1	1	29	36	14	28	11	13	2	2	60	70	26
Tampa Bay	4	3	1	0	0	15	11	6	4	2	1	1	0	12	10	5	8	5	2	1	0	27	21	11
Toronto	2	1	1	0	0	5	4	2	4	0	4	0	0	6	15	0	6	1	5	0	0	11	19	2
Vancouver	23	12	7	2	2	65	54	28	22	9	6	3	4	57	59	25	45	21	13	5	6	122	113	53
Washington	4	4	0	0	0	9	3	8	4	1	3	0	0	7	11	2	8	5	3	0	0	16	14	10
Totals	**287**	**149**	**87**	**28**	**23**	**767**	**654**	**349**	**287**	**104**	**135**	**27**	**21**	**671**	**779**	**256**	**574**	**253**	**222**	**55**	**44**	**1438**	**1433**	**605**

Playoffs

	Series	W	L	GP	W	L	T	GF	GA	Last Mtg.	Rnd.	Result
Anaheim	2	0	2	9	1	8	0	10	21	2007	CQF	L 1-4
Colorado	2	1	1	13	6	7	0	28	34	2008	CQF	L 2-4
Vancouver	1	1	0	7	4	3	0	26	17	2003	CSF	W 4-3
Totals	**5**	**2**	**3**	**29**	**11**	**18**	**0**	**64**	**72**			

Playoff Results 2008-2003

Year	Round	Opponent	Result	GF	GA
2008	CQF	Colorado	L 2-4	12	17
2007	CQF	Anaheim	L 1-4	9	12
2003	CF	Anaheim	L 0-4	1	9
	CSF	Vancouver	W 4-3	26	17
	CQF	Colorado	W 4-3	16	17

Abbreviations: Round: CF – conference final; **CSF** – conference semi-final; **CQF** – conference quarter-final.

2007-08 Results

Oct.	4	Chicago	1-0
	6	Columbus	3-2
	10	Edmonton	2-0
	13	at Phoenix	3-2
	14	at Anaheim	2-0
	16	at Los Angeles	3-4†
	20	at St. Louis	3-1
	21	Colorado	3-2
	24	at Calgary	3-5
	25	at Edmonton	4-5†
	28	at Colorado	1-3
	30	Pittsburgh	2-4
Nov.	1	St. Louis	2-3
	3	Calgary	4-1
	5	Edmonton	5-2
	11	at Colorado	2-4
	13	at Calgary	2-3
	15	at Edmonton	4-2
	16	at Vancouver	2-6
	18	Colorado	4-1
	21	Vancouver	2-4
	23	Columbus	0-4
	24	at Nashville	4-3
	28	Phoenix	3-1
	30	St. Louis	3-2*
Dec.	2	Vancouver	2-1
	5	Philadelphia	1-3
	7	at Detroit	0-5
	8	at Columbus	2-1
	11	at San Jose	1-4
	14	at Anaheim	5-2
	15	at Los Angeles	2-1
	18	Nashville	3-2
	20	NY Rangers	6-3
	22	Detroit	1-4
	26	at Dallas	3-8
	27	at Phoenix	3-2
	29	Edmonton	5-4*
	31	San Jose	2-3
Jan.	3	Dallas	6-3
	5	at Nashville	1-4
	7	at Dallas	1-3
	10	at Detroit	6-5†
	11	at Chicago	5-2
	13	Phoenix	4-1
	16	Calgary	2-3†
	18	Anaheim	2-4
	21	at Vancouver	4-2
	22	at Calgary	1-2
	24	at Colorado	3-2
	30	Anaheim	5-1
Feb.	2	at Columbus	4-1
	5	Detroit	2-3*
	7	Dallas	0-1
	9	NY Islanders	4-3*
	10	at St. Louis	2-1†
	12	at Edmonton	2-4
	14	at Vancouver	5-4†
	17	Nashville	5-4*
	19	Vancouver	2-3*
	20	at Chicago	0-3
	24	Calgary	1-2
	26	at Washington	1-4
	27	at Tampa Bay	3-2
	29	at Florida	3-2
Mar.	2	Los Angeles	2-1*
	4	Chicago	2-4
	6	at Carolina	2-3
	7	at Atlanta	2-3†
	9	San Jose	2-3†
	13	New Jersey	3-4†
	15	Los Angeles	2-0
	17	Colorado	3-1
	19	at San Jose	3-4†
	21	at Vancouver	2-1
	22	at Calgary	4-5
	24	at Edmonton	3-5
	26	Edmonton	3-1
	28	Vancouver	4-0
	30	Colorado	3-2*
Apr.	3	Calgary	3-1
	6	at Colorado	3-4†

* – Overtime † – Shootout

Entry Draft Selections 2008-2000

Name in bold denotes played in NHL.

2008
Pick
23 Tyler Cuma
55 Marco Scandella
115 Sean Lorenz
145 Eero Elo

2007
Pick
16 Colton Gillies
110 Justin Falk
140 Cody Almond
170 Harri Ilvonen
200 Carson McMillan

2006
Pick
9 **James Sheppard**
40 Ondrej Fiala
72 **Cal Clutterbuck**
102 Kyle Medvec
132 Niko Hovinen
162 Julian Walker
192 Chris Hickey

2005
Pick
4 **Benoit Pouliot**
57 Matt Kassian
65 Kristofer Westblom
110 Kyle Bailey
122 Morten Madsen
129 Anthony Aiello
199 Riley Emmerson

2004
Pick
12 A.J. Thelen
42 Roman Voloshenko
78 Peter Olvecky
79 Clayton Stoner
111 Ryan Jones
114 Patrick Bordeleau
117 Julien Sprunger
161 Jean-Claude Sawyer
175 Aaron Boogaard
195 Jean-Michel Rizk
206 Anton Khudobin
272 Kyle Wilson

2003
Pick
20 **Brent Burns**
56 **Patrick O'Sullivan**
78 Danny Irmen
157 Marcin Kolusz
187 Miroslav Kopriva
207 Georgy Misharin
219 Adam Courchaine
251 Mathieu Melanson
281 Jean-Michel Bolduc

2002
Pick
8 **Pierre-Marc Bouchard**
38 **Josh Harding**
72 Mike Erickson
73 **Barry Brust**
155 Armands Berzins
175 **Matt Foy**
204 Niklas Eckerblom
237 **Christoph Brandner**
268 Mikhail Tyulyapkin
269 Mika Hannula

2001
Pick
6 **Mikko Koivu**
36 **Kyle Wanvig**
74 Chris Heid
93 **Stephane Veilleux**
103 **Tony Virta**
202 **Derek Boogaard**
239 Jake Riddle

2000
Pick
3 **Marian Gaborik**
33 **Nick Schultz**
99 Marc Cavosie
132 **Maxim Sushinsky**
170 **Erik Reitz**
199 Brian Passmore
214 **Peter Bartos**
232 **Lubomir Sekeras**
255 Eric Johansson

The Wild's second pick (38th overall) in the 2002 draft, Josh Harding spent his first full season in the NHL in 2007-08.

Doug Risebrough

President and General Manager

Born: Guelph, Ont., January 29, 1954.

Doug Risebrough was hired as the first executive vice president and general manager of the Minnesota Wild on September 2, 1999. He is responsible for the club's overall hockey operations. His efforts to build a winner through the draft has been exemplified by the success of Marian Gaborik, the club's first-round choice in 2000. The Wild qualified for the playoffs after just three seasons, going all the way to the 2003 Western Conference Final. In 2007-08, the team won its first Northwest Division title.

After ending his 13-year NHL playing career with the Flames in 1987, Risebrough was named as assistant coach with Calgary and joined Terry Crisp behind the bench. Risebrough was appointed head coach of the Flames on May 18, 1990 and on May 16, 1991, he also assumed the role of general manager. Late in the 1991-92 campaign he directed his energies full-time to general manager duties, handing the coaching responsibilities over to Guy Charron for the balance of the season. Risebrough served as g.m. in Calgary through the start of the 1995-96 season. He was vice president of hockey operations for the Edmonton Oilers from 1996 to 1999.

Risebrough was Montreal's first selection, seventh overall, in the 1974 Amateur Draft. During his nine years with the Canadiens, he helped his club to four consecutive Stanley Cup championships between 1976 and 1979. He joined the Flames prior to the start of the club's 1982 training camp. During his NHL career, his clubs have won five Stanley Cup titles (1976-1979 as a player and 1989 as an assistant coach with Calgary) and two Presidents' Trophies (1987-88 and 1988-89 as an assistant coach).

Coaching Record

			Regular Season				Playoffs			
Season	Team	League	GC	W	L	O/T	GC	W	L	T
1990-91	Calgary	NHL	80	46	26	8	7	3	4	....
1991-92	Calgary	NHL	64	25	30	9	....	....	....	....
	NHL Totals		**144**	**71**	**56**	**17**	**7**	**3**	**4**	....

Club Directory

Xcel Energy Center

Minnesota Wild
317 Washington Street
St. Paul, MN 55102
Phone **651/602-6000**
FAX 651/222-1055
Tickets 651/222-9453
www.wild.com
Capacity: 18,064

Executive Management

Owner/Governor	Craig Leipold
Minority Owner	Phil Falcone
President/General Manager	Doug Risebrough
Executive Vice President, Chief Financial Officer	Pamela Wheelock
Executive Vice President	Matt Majka
Vice President, Sales and Service	Jamie Spencer
Vice President, Facility Administration/ General Manager, RiverCentre	Jim Ibister
Vice President/General Manager, Xcel Energy Center	Jack Larson
Vice President, Communications and Broadcasting	Bill Robertson
Vice President, Brand Marketing	John Maher
Executive Assistant	Stephanie Huseby
Executive Assistant, Hockey Operations	Laura Kinzel
Administrative Assistant, Sales and Service, Creative Services and Marketing	Tawnya Vidnovic
Administrative Assistant, Communications and Broadcasting, Corporate Sales & Service, Human Resources	Deb Hanson

Hockey Operations

Assistant General Manager/Hockey Operations	Tom Lynn
Assistant General Manager/Player Personnel	Tom Thompson
Head Coach	Jacques Lemaire
Assistant Coaches	Mike Ramsey, Matt Shaw, Mario Tremblay
Goaltending Coach	Bob Mason
Strength and Conditioning Coach	Kirk Olson
Coordinator of Amateur Scouting	Guy Lapointe
Director of Player Development	Barry MacKenzie
Director of Professional Scouting	Blair Mackasey
Amateur Scouts	Brian Hunter, Christopher Hamel, Ernie Vargas, Glen Sonmor, Marc Chamard, Paul Charles, Brian Foster, Ken Prost
European Scouts	Branislav Gaborik, Jiri Koluch, Ken Hoodikoff, Matti Vaisanen
Professional Scouts	Bill Berg, Jamie Hislop
Athletic Therapist	Don Fuller
Equipment Manager	Tony DaCosta
Assistant Equipment Managers	Brent Proulx, Matt Benz
Director of Hockey Operations	Chris Snow
Project Manager	Shep Harder
Hockey Operations Administrator	Cindy Sweiger
Medical Director	Dr. Sheldon Burns
Orthopedic Surgeon	Dr. Joel Boyd
Nutritionist	Carrie Peterson
Team Dentists	Kyle Edlund, Mike Nanne, Mike Pelke

Sales And Service

Director, Customer Sales	Matt Cords
Manager, Ticket Operations	Chris Turns
Sr. Account Exec., New Business Development	Michael Brinkman
Account Manager, Group and Event Suites	Cory Effertz
New Business Development	Emily Iversen, Mike McDonough, Todd Schneider, Britny Schultheis
Senior Manager, Customer Service	Maria Troje
Account Service Executives	Anna Johnson, Joshua Simonson, Natalie Kaess

Retail Operation

Director, Retail Operations	Nikki Braxmeier
Manager, Retail Operations	Scott Sarkis

Corporate Partnerships

Senior Director, Retail Management & Corporate Sales and Service	Carin Anderson
Account Executives	Bryan Bellows, Carl Levi, Michelle Radzik
Interactive Account Executive	Brandon Latack
Senior Manager, Corporate Services	Kathleen Borschke

Communications and Broadcasting

Manager, Media Relations and Team Services	Aaron Sickman
Coordinator, Media Relations and Team Services	Ryan Stanzel
Manager of Broadcasting	Maggie Kukar
Radio Operations Coordinator	Kevin Falness
Website Content	James MacDonald
Radio Play-By-Play / Analyst	Bob Kurtz / Tom Reid
Television Play-By-Play / Analyst	Dan Terhaar / Mike Greenlay
Intern	Robert Desimone

Marketing

Director, Events and Promotions	Wayne Petersen
Manager, Game Presentation	Paul Loomis
Manager, Production Services	Hank Dolan
Manager, Marketing	Emily Gausman
Team Curator	Roger Godin

Community Giving

Director, Community Partnerships	Brad Bombardir
Manager, Community Giving	Amy Woog-Patnode

Finance and Accounting

Director, Financial Systems & Internal Audit	Danette Kleinprintz
Director, Finance	Mitch Helgerson
Senior Manager, Accounting Services	Molly McArdle

Human Resources

Director, Human Resources	Delores Murphy

Information Technology

Director, Information Technology	David Weisbrod
Website Manager	Holly Doyle

Miscellaneous

Radio Network Flagship	WCCO (830 AM)
Television Networks	KSTC.TV Channel 45 (Over-the-Air), Fox Sports Net North (Cable)
Team Photographer	Bruce Kluckhohn
Public Address Announcer	Adam Abrams

Key Off-Season Signings/Acquisitions

2008

June 9 • Re-signed C **Maxim Lapierre**.
20 • Acquired LW **Alex Tanguay** and a 5th-round pick in 2008 from Calgary for a 1st-round pick in 2008 and 2nd-round pick in 2009.
July 1 • Re-signed LW **Andrei Kostitsyn**.
3 • Signed RW **Georges Laraque** and G **Marc Denis**.
8 • Re-signed G **Jaroslav Halak**.
9 • Re-signed D **Josh Gorges**.
11 • Acquired D **Shawn Belle** from Minnesota for C **Corey Locke**.

2008-09 Schedule

Month	Day	Date	Opponent	Month	Day	Date	Opponent
Oct.	Fri.	10	at Buffalo		Tue.	13	at Boston
	Sat.	11	at Toronto		Thu.	15	Nashville
	Mon.	13	at Philadelphia		Sat.	17	at Ottawa
	Wed.	15	Boston		Tue.	20	at Atlanta
	Sat.	18	Phoenix		Wed.	21	at New Jersey
	Mon.	20	Florida		Tue.	27	at Tampa Bay
	Sat.	25	Anaheim		Thu.	29	at Florida
	Tue.	28	Carolina		Sat.	31	Los Angeles*
	Thu.	30	at Minnesota	**Feb.**	Sun.	1	Boston*
Nov.	Sat.	1	at NY Islanders		Tue.	3	Pittsburgh
	Fri.	7	at Columbus		Fri.	6	at Buffalo
	Sat.	8	at Toronto		Sat.	7	Toronto
	Tue.	11	Ottawa		Mon.	9	at Calgary
	Thu.	13	at Boston		Wed.	11	at Edmonton
	Sat.	15	Philadelphia		Fri.	13	at Colorado
	Sun.	16	at St. Louis*		Sun.	15	at Vancouver
	Tue.	18	at Carolina		Wed.	18	at Washington
	Thu.	20	at Ottawa		Thu.	19	at Pittsburgh
	Sat.	22	Boston		Sat.	21	Ottawa*
	Mon.	24	NY Islanders		Tue.	24	Vancouver
	Wed.	26	at Detroit		Fri.	27	at Philadelphia
	Fri.	28	at Washington		Sat.	28	San Jose
	Sat.	29	Buffalo	**Mar.**	Wed.	4	at Buffalo
Dec.	Tue.	2	Atlanta		Fri.	6	at Atlanta
	Thu.	4	NY Rangers		Sun.	8	at Dallas*
	Sat.	6	New Jersey		Tue.	10	Edmonton
	Tue.	9	Calgary		Thu.	12	NY Islanders
	Thu.	11	Tampa Bay		Sat.	14	New Jersey
	Sat.	13	Washington		Tue.	17	NY Rangers
	Tue.	16	at Carolina		Thu.	19	at Ottawa
	Thu.	18	Philadelphia		Sat.	21	Toronto
	Sat.	20	Buffalo		Tue.	24	Atlanta
	Sun.	21	Carolina		Thu.	26	Tampa Bay
	Sat.	27	at Pittsburgh		Sat.	28	Buffalo
	Mon.	29	at Florida		Tue.	31	Chicago
	Tue.	30	at Tampa Bay	**Apr.**	Thu.	2	at NY Islanders
Jan.	Fri.	2	at New Jersey		Sat.	4	at Toronto
	Sun.	4	Florida*		Mon.	6	Ottawa
	Wed.	7	at NY Rangers		Tue.	7	at NY Rangers
	Thu.	8	Toronto		Thu.	9	at Boston
	Sat.	10	Washington		Sat.	11	Pittsburgh

* Denotes afternoon game.

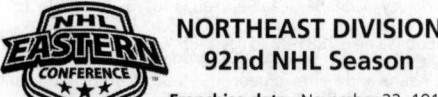

NORTHEAST DIVISION
92nd NHL Season
Franchise date: November 22, 1917

Montreal Canadiens

2007-08 Results: 47W-25L-4OTL-6SOL 104PTS.
First, Northeast Division

Year-by-Year Record

		Home				Road				Overall								
Season	GP	W	L	T	OL	W	L	T	OL	W	L	T	OL	GF	GA	Pts.	Finished	Playoff Result
2007-08	82	22	13	....	6	25	12	....	4	47	25	....	10	262	222	104	1st, Northeast Div.	Lost Conf. Semi-Final
2006-07	82	26	12	....	3	16	22	....	3	42	34	....	6	245	256	90	4th, Northeast Div.	Out of Playoffs
2005-06	82	24	13	....	4	18	18	....	5	42	31	....	9	243	247	93	3rd, Northeast Div.	Lost Conf. Quarter-Final
2004-05	....	....	....	....	....	....	....	....	....	....	....	....	....	....	....	....		
2003-04	82	23	13	4	1	18	17	3	3	41	30	7	4	208	192	93	4th, Northeast Div.	Lost Conf. Semi-Final
2002-03	82	16	16	5	4	14	19	3	5	30	35	8	9	206	234	77	4th, Northeast Div.	Out of Playoffs
2001-02	82	21	13	6	1	15	18	6	2	36	31	12	3	207	209	87	4th, Northeast Div.	Lost Conf. Semi-Final
2000-01	82	15	20	4	2	13	20	4	4	28	40	8	6	206	232	70	5th, Northeast Div.	Out of Playoffs
1999-2000	82	18	17	5	1	17	17	4	3	35	34	9	4	196	194	83	4th, Northeast Div.	Out of Playoffs
1998-99	82	21	15	5	....	11	24	6	....	32	39	11	....	184	209	75	5th, Northeast Div.	Out of Playoffs
1997-98	82	15	17	9	....	22	15	4	....	37	32	13	....	235	208	87	4th, Northeast Div.	Lost Conf. Semi-Final
1996-97	82	17	17	7	....	14	19	8	....	31	36	15	....	249	276	77	4th, Northeast Div.	Lost Conf. Quarter-Final
1995-96	82	23	12	6	....	17	20	4	....	40	32	10	....	265	248	90	3rd, Northeast Div.	Lost Conf. Quarter-Final
1994-95	48	15	5	4	....	3	18	3	....	18	23	7	....	125	148	43	6th, Northeast Div.	Out of Playoffs
1993-94	84	26	12	4	....	15	17	10	....	41	29	14	....	283	248	96	3rd, Northeast Div.	Lost Conf. Quarter-Final
1992-93	84	27	13	2	....	21	17	4	....	48	30	6	....	326	280	102	3rd, Adams Div.	Won Stanley Cup
1991-92	80	27	8	5	....	14	20	6	....	41	28	11	....	267	207	93	1st, Adams Div.	Lost Div. Final
1990-91	80	23	12	5	....	16	18	6	....	39	30	11	....	273	249	89	2nd, Adams Div.	Lost Div. Final
1989-90	80	26	8	6	....	15	20	5	....	41	28	11	....	288	234	93	3rd, Adams Div.	Lost Div. Final
1988-89	80	30	6	4	....	23	12	5	....	53	18	9	....	315	218	115	1st, Adams Div.	Lost Final
1987-88	80	26	8	6	....	19	14	7	....	45	22	13	....	298	238	103	1st, Adams Div.	Lost Div. Final
1986-87	80	27	9	4	....	14	20	6	....	41	29	10	....	277	241	92	2nd, Adams Div.	Lost Conf. Championship
1985-86	80	25	11	4	....	15	22	3	....	40	33	7	....	330	280	87	2nd, Adams Div.	Won Stanley Cup
1984-85	80	24	10	6	....	17	17	6	....	41	27	12	....	309	262	94	1st, Adams Div.	Lost Div. Final
1983-84	80	19	19	2	....	16	21	3	....	35	40	5	....	286	295	75	4th, Adams Div.	Lost Conf. Championship
1982-83	80	25	6	9	....	17	18	5	....	42	24	14	....	350	286	98	2nd, Adams Div.	Lost Div. Semi-Final
1981-82	80	25	6	9	....	21	11	8	....	46	17	17	....	360	223	109	1st, Adams Div.	Lost Div. Semi-Final
1980-81	80	31	7	2	....	14	15	11	....	45	22	13	....	332	232	103	1st, Norris Div.	Lost Prelim. Round
1979-80	80	30	7	3	....	17	13	10	....	47	20	13	....	328	240	107	1st, Norris Div.	Lost Quarter-Final
1978-79	80	29	6	5	....	23	11	6	....	52	17	11	....	337	204	115	1st, Norris Div.	Won Stanley Cup
1977-78	80	32	4	4	....	27	6	7	....	59	10	11	....	359	183	129	1st, Norris Div.	Won Stanley Cup
1976-77	80	33	1	6	....	27	7	6	....	60	8	12	....	387	171	132	1st, Norris Div.	Won Stanley Cup
1975-76	80	32	3	5	....	26	8	6	....	58	11	11	....	337	174	127	1st, Norris Div.	Won Stanley Cup
1974-75	80	27	8	5	....	20	6	14	....	47	14	19	....	374	225	113	1st, Norris Div.	Lost Semi-Final
1973-74	78	24	12	3	....	21	12	6	....	45	24	9	....	293	240	99	2nd, East Div.	Lost Quarter-inal
1972-73	78	29	4	6	....	23	6	10	....	52	10	16	....	329	184	120	1st, East Div.	Won Stanley Cup
1971-72	78	29	3	7	....	17	13	9	....	46	16	16	....	307	205	108	3rd, East Div.	Lost Quarter-Final
1970-71	78	29	7	3	....	13	16	10	....	42	23	13	....	291	216	97	3rd, East Div.	Won Stanley Cup
1969-70	76	21	9	8	....	17	13	8	....	38	22	16	....	244	201	92	5th, East Div.	Out of Playoffs
1968-69	76	26	7	5	....	20	12	6	....	46	19	11	....	271	202	103	1st, East Div.	Won Stanley Cup
1967-68	74	26	5	6	....	16	17	4	....	42	22	10	....	236	167	94	1st, East Div.	Won Stanley Cup
1966-67	70	19	9	7	....	13	16	6	....	32	25	13	....	202	188	77	2nd,	Lost Final
1965-66	70	23	11	1	....	18	10	7	....	41	21	8	....	239	173	90	1st,	Won Stanley Cup
1964-65	70	20	8	7	....	16	15	4	....	36	23	11	....	211	185	83	2nd,	Won Stanley Cup
1963-64	70	22	7	6	....	14	14	7	....	36	21	13	....	209	167	85	1st,	Lost Semi-Final
1962-63	70	15	10	10	....	13	9	13	....	28	19	23	....	225	183	79	3rd,	Lost Semi-Final
1961-62	70	26	2	7	....	16	12	7	....	42	14	14	....	259	166	98	1st,	Lost Semi-Final
1960-61	70	24	6	5	....	17	13	5	....	41	19	10	....	254	188	92	1st,	Lost Semi-Final
1959-60	70	23	4	8	....	17	14	4	....	40	18	12	....	255	178	92	1st,	Won Stanley Cup
1958-59	70	21	8	6	....	18	10	7	....	39	18	13	....	258	158	91	1st,	Won Stanley Cup
1957-58	70	23	8	4	....	20	9	6	....	43	17	10	....	250	158	96	1st,	Won Stanley Cup
1956-57	70	23	6	6	....	12	17	6	....	35	23	12	....	210	155	82	2nd,	Won Stanley Cup
1955-56	70	29	5	1	....	16	10	9	....	45	15	10	....	222	131	100	1st,	Won Stanley Cup
1954-55	70	26	5	4	....	15	13	7	....	41	18	11	....	228	157	93	2nd,	Lost Final
1953-54	70	27	5	3	....	8	19	8	....	35	24	11	....	195	141	81	2nd,	Lost Final
1952-53	70	18	12	5	....	10	11	14	....	28	23	19	....	155	148	75	2nd,	Won Stanley Cup
1951-52	70	22	8	5	....	12	18	5	....	34	26	10	....	195	164	78	2nd,	Lost Final
1950-51	70	17	10	8	....	8	20	7	....	25	30	15	....	173	184	65	3rd,	Lost Final
1949-50	70	17	8	10	....	12	14	9	....	29	22	19	....	172	150	77	2nd,	Lost Semi-Final
1948-49	60	19	8	3	....	9	15	6	....	28	23	9	....	152	126	65	3rd,	Lost Semi-Final
1947-48	60	13	13	4	....	7	16	7	....	20	29	11	....	147	169	51	5th,	Out of Playoffs
1946-47	60	19	6	5	....	15	10	5	....	34	16	10	....	189	138	78	1st,	Lost Final
1945-46	50	16	6	3	....	12	11	2	....	28	17	5	....	172	134	61	1st,	Won Stanley Cup
1944-45	50	21	2	2	....	17	6	2	....	38	8	4	....	228	121	80	1st,	Lost Semi-Final
1943-44	50	22	0	3	....	16	5	4	....	38	5	7	....	234	109	83	1st,	Won Stanley Cup
1942-43	50	14	4	7	....	5	15	5	....	19	19	12	....	181	191	50	4th,	Lost Semi-Final
1941-42	48	12	10	2	....	6	17	1	....	18	27	3	....	134	173	39	6th,	Lost Quarter-Final
1940-41	48	11	9	4	....	5	17	2	....	16	26	6	....	121	147	38	6th,	Lost Quarter-Final
1939-40	48	5	14	5	....	5	19	0	....	10	33	5	....	90	167	25	7th,	Out of Playoffs
1938-39	48	8	11	5	....	7	13	4	....	15	24	9	....	115	146	39	6th,	Lost Quarter-Final
1937-38	48	13	4	7	....	5	13	6	....	18	17	13	....	123	128	49	3rd, Cdn. Div.	Lost Quarter-Final
1936-37	48	16	8	0	....	8	10	6	....	24	18	6	....	115	111	54	1st, Cdn. Div.	Lost Semi-Final
1935-36	48	5	11	8	....	6	15	3	....	11	26	11	....	82	123	33	4th, Cdn. Div.	Out of Playoffs
1934-35	48	11	11	2	....	8	12	4	....	19	23	6	....	110	145	44	3rd, Cdn. Div.	Lost Quarter-Final
1933-34	48	16	6	2	....	6	14	4	....	22	20	6	....	99	101	50	2nd, Cdn. Div.	Lost Quarter-Final
1932-33	48	15	5	4	....	3	20	1	....	18	25	5	....	92	115	41	3rd, Cdn. Div.	Lost Quarter-Final
1931-32	48	18	3	3	....	7	13	4	....	25	16	7	....	128	111	57	1st, Cdn. Div.	Lost Semi-Final
1930-31	44	15	3	4	....	11	7	4	....	26	10	8	....	129	89	60	1st, Cdn. Div.	Won Stanley Cup
1929-30	44	13	5	4	....	8	9	5	....	21	14	9	....	142	114	51	2nd, Cdn. Div.	Won Stanley Cup
1928-29	44	12	4	6	....	10	3	9	....	22	7	15	....	71	43	59	1st, Cdn. Div.	Lost Semi-Final
1927-28	44	12	7	3	....	14	4	4	....	26	11	7	....	116	48	59	1st, Cdn. Div.	Lost Semi-Final
1926-27	44	15	5	2	....	13	9	0	....	28	14	2	....	99	67	58	2nd, Cdn. Div.	Lost Semi-Final
1925-26	36	5	12	1	....	6	12	0	....	11	24	1	....	79	108	23	7th,	Out of Playoffs
1924-25	30	10	5	0	....	7	6	2	....	17	11	2	....	93	56	36	3rd,	Lost Final
1923-24	24	10	2	0	....	3	9	0	....	13	11	0	....	59	48	26	2nd,	Won Stanley Cup
1922-23	24	10	2	0	....	3	7	2	....	13	9	2	....	73	61	28	2nd,	Lost NHL Final
1921-22	24	8	3	1	....	4	8	0	....	12	11	1	....	88	94	25	3rd,	Out of Playoffs
1920-21	24	9	3	0	....	4	8	0	....	13	11	0	....	112	99	26	3rd and 2nd*	Out of Playoffs
1919-20	24	8	4	0	....	5	7	0	....	13	11	0	....	129	113	26	2nd and 3rd*	Out of Playoffs
1918-19	18	7	2	0	....	3	6	0	....	10	8	0	....	88	78	20	1st and 2nd*	Cup Final but no Decision
1917-18	22	8	3	0	....	5	6	0	....	13	9	0	....	115	84	26	1st and 3rd*	Lost NHL Final

* Season played in two halves with no combined standing at end.
From 1917-18 through 1925-26, NHL champions played against PCHA/WCHL champions for Stanley Cup.

2008-09 Player Personnel

FORWARDS	HT	WT	S	Place of Birth	*Age	2007-08 Club
BEGIN, Steve	6-0	187	L	Trois-Rivieres, Que.	30	Montreal
CHIPCHURA, Kyle	6-2	204	L	Westlock, Alta.	22	Montreal-Hamilton
HIGGINS, Christopher	6-0	199	L	Smithtown, NY	25	Montreal
KOIVU, Saku	5-10	187	L	Turku, Finland	33	Montreal
KOSTITSYN, Andrei	6-0	201	L	Novopolotsk, USSR	23	Montreal
KOSTITSYN, Sergei	5-11	196	L	Novopolotsk, USSR	21	Montreal-Hamilton
KOSTOPOULOS, Tom	6-0	200	R	Mississauga, Ont.	29	Montreal
KOVALEV, Alex	6-1	224	L	Togliatti, USSR	35	Montreal
LAPIERRE, Maxim	6-2	200	R	St. Leonard, Que.	23	Montreal-Hamilton
LARAQUE, Georges	6-3	243	R	Montreal, Que.	31	Pittsburgh
LATENDRESSE, Guillaume	6-2	222	L	Ste-Catherine, Que.	21	Montreal
PLEKANEC, Tomas	5-10	194	L	Kladno, Czech.	25	Montreal
TANGUAY, Alex	6-1	189	L	Ste-Justine, Que.	28	Calgary
DEFENSEMEN						
BOUILLON, Francis	5-8	196	L	New York, NY	32	Montreal
DANDENAULT, Mathieu	6-0	204	R	Sherbrooke, Que.	32	Montreal
GORGES, Josh	6-1	195	L	Kelowna, B.C.	24	Montreal
HAMRLIK, Roman	6-2	215	L	Gottwaldov/Zlin, Czech.	34	Montreal
KOMISAREK, Mike	6-4	240	R	West Islip, NY	26	Montreal
MARKOV, Andrei	6-0	204	L	Voskresensk, USSR	29	Montreal
O'BYRNE, Ryan	6-6	228	R	Victoria, B.C.	24	Montreal-Hamilton

GOALTENDERS	HT	WT	C	Place of Birth	*Age	2007-08 Club
DENIS, Marc	6-1	193	L	Montreal, Que.	31	Tampa Bay-Norfolk
HALAK, Jaroslav	5-11	182	L	Bratislava, Czech.	23	Montreal-Hamilton
PRICE, Carey	6-3	226	L	Vancouver, B.C.	21	Montreal-Hamilton

* – Age at start of 2008-09 season

Coaching History

Jack Laviolette, 1909-10; Adolphe Lecours, 1910-11; Napoleon Dorval, 1911-12, 1912-13; Jimmy Gardner, 1913-14, 1914-15; Newsy Lalonde, 1915-16 to 1920-21; Newsy Lalonde and Léo Dandurand, 1921-22; Léo Dandurand, 1922-23 to 1925-26; Cecil Hart, 1926-27 to 1931-32; Newsy Lalonde, 1932-33, 1933-34; Newsy Lalonde and Léo Dandurand, 1934-35; Sylvio Mantha, 1935-36; Cecil Hart, 1936-37, 1937-38; Cecil Hart and Jules Dugal, 1938-39; Babe Siebert, 1939*; Pit Lepine, 1939-40; Dick Irvin 1940-41 to 1954-55; Toe Blake, 1955-56 to 1967-68; Claude Ruel, 1968-69, 1969-70; Claude Ruel and Al MacNeil, 1970-71; Scotty Bowman, 1971-72 to 1978-79; Bernie Geoffrion and Claude Ruel, 1979-80; Claude Ruel, 1980-81; Bob Berry, 1981-82, 1982-83; Bob Berry and Jacques Lemaire, 1983-84; Jacques Lemaire, 1984-85; Jean Perron, 1985-86 to 1987-88; Pat Burns, 1988-89 to 1991-92; Jacques Demers, 1992-93 to 1994-95; Jacques Demers, Jacques Laperriere, Mario Tremblay, 1995-96; Mario Tremblay, 1996-97; Alain Vigneault, 1997-98 to 1999-2000; Alain Vigneault and Michel Therrien, 2000-01; Michel Therrien, 2001-02; Michel Therrien and Claude Julien, 2002-03; Claude Julien, 2003-04, 2004-05; Claude Julien and Bob Gainey, 2005-06; Guy Carbonneau, 2006-07 to date.

* Named coach in summer but died before 1939-40 season began.

Bob Gainey

Vice President and General Manager

Born: Peterborough, Ont., December 13, 1953.

On June 2, 2003, the Montreal Canadiens announced the appointment of Bob Gainey as executive vice president and general manager, effective July 1, 2003. During the 2005-06 season, he also took over behind the bench and coached the Canadiens into the playoffs. Since then, Gainey has served only as general manager, assembling a team that finished first overall in the Eastern Conference in 2007-08.

As a player in Montreal, Gainey brought many elements to the Canadiens over his 16-year career. Described as the world's best all-around player by legendary Soviet national team coach Viktor Tikhonov, Gainey was a tenacious competitor, relentless checker and a respected team leader. His play helped the Canadiens win the Stanley Cup five times in the decade between 1976 and 1986. He won the Conn Smythe Trophy as playoff MVP in 1979 and was a four-time winner of the Selke Trophy as the NHL's best defensive forward. Gainey was captain of the Canadiens from 1981 until his retirement in 1989. He was elected to the Hockey Hall of Fame in 1992.

Gainey spent a year as a player-coach of the Epinal franchise in France before becoming head coach of the Minnesota North Stars in 1990-91. He was given the g.m.'s job in 1992 and was in the dual role when the Stars relocated to Dallas in 1993. Gainey stepped down as coach on January 8, 1996 to focus solely on the duties of general manager and built a powerhouse club that won five straight division titles from 1996-97 to 2000-01, the Presidents' Trophy in 1998 and 1999, and the Stanley Cup in 1999.

Coaching Record

			Regular Season				Playoffs			
Season	Team	League	GC	W	L	O/T	GC	W	L	T
1990-91	Minnesota	NHL	80	27	39	14	23	14	9	....
1991-92	Minnesota	NHL	80	32	42	6	7	3	4	....
1992-93	Minnesota	NHL	84	36	38	10	....	....	....	....
1993-94	Dallas	NHL	84	42	29	13	9	5	4	....
1994-95	Dallas	NHL	48	17	23	8	5	1	4	....
1995-96	Dallas	NHL	39	11	19	9	....	....	....	....
2005-06	Montreal	NHL	41	23	15	3	6	2	4	....
	NHL Totals		**456**	**188**	**205**	**63**	**50**	**25**	**25**	....

2007-08 Scoring

* – rookie

Regular Season

Pos	#	Player	Team	GP	G	A	Pts	TOI	+/–	PIM	PP	SH	GW	S	%
R	27	Alex Kovalev	MTL	82	35	49	84	19:33	18	70	17	0	5	230	15.2
C	14	Tomas Plekanec	MTL	81	29	40	69	18:04	15	42	12	2	6	186	15.6
D	32	Mark Streit	MTL	81	13	49	62	17:31	–6	28	7	0	3	165	7.9
D	79	Andrei Markov	MTL	82	16	42	58	24:58	1	63	10	1	2	145	11.0
C	11	Saku Koivu	MTL	77	16	40	56	18:07	–4	93	8	0	3	150	10.7
L	46	Andrei Kostitsyn	MTL	78	26	27	53	15:41	15	29	12	0	5	156	16.7
L	21	Chris Higgins	MTL	82	27	25	52	17:57	0	22	12	0	5	241	11.2
R	73	Michael Ryder	MTL	70	14	17	31	13:14	–4	30	1	0	2	134	10.4
R	84	Guillaume Latendresse	MTL	73	16	11	27	12:15	–2	41	2	0	3	116	13.8
L	74 *	Sergei Kostitsyn	MTL	52	9	18	27	14:21	9	51	3	1	0	49	18.4
D	44	Roman Hamrlik	MTL	77	5	21	26	23:08	7	38	3	0	3	129	3.9
C	20	Bryan Smolinski	MTL	64	8	17	25	13:07	–6	20	1	0	2	89	9.0
C	40	Maxim Lapierre	MTL	53	7	11	18	13:09	5	60	0	0	0	68	10.3
D	8	Mike Komisarek	MTL	75	4	13	17	21:09	9	101	0	0	1	75	5.3
R	25	Mathieu Dandenault	MTL	61	9	5	14	11:08	–11	34	0	1	0	69	13.0
R	6	Tom Kostopoulos	MTL	67	7	6	13	11:16	–3	113	0	3	1	98	7.1
C	28 *	Kyle Chipchura	MTL	36	4	7	11	11:22	–1	10	0	0	0	36	11.1
D	71	Patrice Brisebois	MTL	43	3	8	11	16:49	–2	26	2	0	0	42	7.1
C	54 *	Mikhail Grabovski	MTL	24	3	6	9	11:13	–4	8	0	0	1	23	13.0
D	26	Josh Gorges	MTL	62	0	9	9	16:20	0	32	0	0	0	41	0.0
L	22	Steve Begin	MTL	44	3	5	8	11:38	0	48	0	0	0	67	4.5
D	51	Francis Bouillon	MTL	74	2	6	8	17:21	9	61	0	0	0	60	3.3
D	3 *	Ryan O'Byrne	MTL	33	1	6	7	13:23	7	45	0	0	0	10	10.0
C	45 *	Corey Locke	MTL	1	0	0	0	05:59	–1	0	0	0	0	1	0.0
L	70 *	Greg Stewart	MTL	1	0	0	0	11:26	0	5	0	0	0	2	0.0
R	36 *	Matt D'Agostini	MTL	1	0	0	0	08:49	0	2	0	0	0	0	0.0

Goaltending

No.	Goaltender	GPI	Mins	Avg	W	L	OT	EN	SO	GA	SA	S%	G	A	PIM
41	* Jaroslav Halak	6	285	2.11	2	1	1	0	1	10	151	.934	0	0	0
38	Cristobal Huet	39	2278	2.55	21	12	6	4	2	97	1150	.916	0	1	0
31	* Carey Price	41	2413	2.56	24	12	3	2	3	103	1282	.920	0	2	0
	Totals	**82**	**4995**	**2.59**	**47**	**25**	**10**	**6**	**6**	**216**	**2589**	**.917**			

Playoffs

Pos	#	Player	Team	GP	G	A	Pts	TOI	+/–	PIM	PP	SH	GW	OT	S	%
R	27	Alex Kovalev	MTL	12	5	6	11	21:41	–4	8	2	1	1	1	39	12.8
C	14	Tomas Plekanec	MTL	12	4	5	9	18:02	–1	2	2	0	0	0	40	10.0
C	11	Saku Koivu	MTL	7	3	6	9	19:33	1	4	2	0	0	0	17	17.6
L	46	Andrei Kostitsyn	MTL	12	5	3	8	16:00	–4	2	1	0	1	0	25	20.0
L	74 *	Sergei Kostitsyn	MTL	12	3	5	8	15:08	5	14	0	0	0	0	22	13.6
D	71	Patrice Brisebois	MTL	10	1	5	6	16:33	–3	6	1	0	1	0	10	10.0
L	21	Chris Higgins	MTL	12	3	2	5	18:27	1	2	0	0	0	0	34	8.8
R	6	Tom Kostopoulos	MTL	12	3	1	4	13:34	–1	6	0	0	1	1	24	12.5
D	32	Mark Streit	MTL	11	1	3	4	14:47	–1	8	0	0	0	0	19	5.3
D	79	Andrei Markov	MTL	12	1	3	4	24:54	0	8	0	0	0	0	21	4.8
D	51	Francis Bouillon	MTL	7	1	2	3	15:54	0	4	0	0	0	0	10	10.0
C	20	Bryan Smolinski	MTL	12	1	2	3	14:32	1	2	0	0	0	0	17	5.9
D	44	Roman Hamrlik	MTL	12	1	2	3	22:54	–3	8	0	0	0	0	15	6.7
D	8	Mike Komisarek	MTL	12	1	2	3	20:02	3	18	0	0	1	0	18	5.6
L	22	Steve Begin	MTL	12	0	3	3	12:45	1	8	0	0	0	0	21	0.0
D	26	Josh Gorges	MTL	12	0	3	3	18:20	–2	0	0	0	0	0	7	0.0
C	40	Maxim Lapierre	MTL	12	0	3	3	11:37	–5	6	0	0	0	0	19	0.0
R	84	Guillaume Latendresse	MTL	8	0	1	1	10:42	–5	19	0	0	0	0	18	0.0
R	73	Michael Ryder	MTL	4	0	0	0	10:45	1	2	0	0	0	0	6	0.0
D	3 *	Ryan O'Byrne	MTL	4	0	0	0	10:46	–2	0	0	0	0	0	3	0.0
R	25	Mathieu Dandenault	MTL	9	0	0	0	08:45	–3	2	0	0	0	0	13	0.0

Goaltending

No.	Goaltender	GPI	Mins	Avg	W	L	EN	SO	GA	SA	S%	G	A	PIM
41	* Jaroslav Halak	2	77	2.34	0	1	1	0	3	27	.889	0	0	0
31	* Carey Price	11	648	2.78	5	6	1	2	30	304	.901	0	0	2
	Totals	**12**	**733**	**2.86**	**5**	**7**	**2**	**2**	**35**	**333**	**.895**			

General Managers' History

Jack Laviolette and Joseph Cattarinich, 1909-1910; George Kennedy, 1910-11 to 1920-21; Leo Dandurand, 1921-22 to 1934-35; Ernest Savard, 1935-36; Cecil Hart, 1936-37 to 1938-39; Jules Dugal, 1939-40; Tom P. Gorman, 1940-41 to 1945-46; Frank J. Selke, 1946-47 to 1963-64; Sam Pollock, 1964-65 to 1977-78; Irving Grundman, 1978-79 to 1982-83; Serge Savard, 1983-84 to 1994-95; Serge Savard and Réjean Houle, 1995-96; Réjean Houle, 1996-97 to 1999-2000; Réjean Houle and Andre Savard, 2000-01; Andre Savard, 2001-02, 2002-03; Bob Gainey, 2003-04 to date.

Captains' History

Jack Laviolette, 1909-10; Newsy Lalonde, 1910-11; Jack Laviolette, 1911-12; Newsy Lalonde, 1912-13; Jimmy Gardner, 1913-14, 1914-15; Howard McNamara, 1915-16; Newsy Lalonde, 1916-17 to 1921-22; Sprague Cleghorn, 1922-23 to 1924-25; Bill Coutu, 1925-26; Sylvio Mantha, 1926-27 to 1931-32; George Hainsworth, 1932-33; Sylvio Mantha, 1933-34 to 1935-36; Babe Siebert, 1936-37 to 1938-39; Walt Buswell, 1939-40; Toe Blake, 1940-41 to 1946-47; Toe Blake and Bill Durnan, 1947-48; Butch Bouchard, 1948-49 to 1955-56; Maurice Richard, 1956-57 to 1959-60; Doug Harvey, 1960-61; Jean Béliveau, 1961-62 to 1970-71; Henri Richard, 1971-72 to 1974-75; Yvan Cournoyer, 1975-76 to 1978-79; Serge Savard, 1979-80, 1980-81; Bob Gainey, 1981-82 to 1988-89; Guy Carbonneau and Chris Chelios, 1989-90; Guy Carbonneau, 1990-91 to 1993-94; Kirk Muller and Mike Keane, 1994-95; Mike Keane and Pierre Turgeon, 1995-96; Pierre Turgeon and Vincent Damphousse, 1996-97; Vincent Damphousse, 1997-98, 1998-99; Saku Koivu, 1999-2000 to date.

Club Records

Team

(Figures in brackets for season records are games played; records for fewest points, wins, ties, losses, goals, goals against are for 70 or more games)

Most Points	***132**	1976-77 (80)
Most Wins	**60**	1976-77 (80)
Most Ties	**23**	1962-63 (70)
Most Losses	**40**	1983-84 (80), 2000-01 (82)
Most Goals	**387**	1976-77 (80)
Most Goals Against	**295**	1983-84 (80)
Fewest Points	**65**	1950-51 (70)
Fewest Wins	**25**	1950-51 (70)
Fewest Ties	**5**	1983-84 (80)
Fewest Losses	***8**	1976-77 (80)
Fewest Goals	**155**	1952-53 (70)
Fewest Goals Against	***131**	1955-56 (70)
Longest Winning Streak		
Overall	**12**	Jan. 6-Feb. 3/68
Home	**13**	Nov. 2/43-Jan. 8/44, Jan. 30-Mar. 26/77
Away	**8**	Dec. 18/77-Jan. 18/78, Jan. 21-Feb. 21/82
Longest Undefeated Streak		
Overall	**28**	Dec. 18/77-Feb. 23/78 (23 wins, 5 ties)
Home	***34**	Nov. 1/76-Apr. 2/77 (28 wins, 6 ties)
Away	***23**	Nov. 27/74-Mar. 12/75 (14 wins, 9 ties)
Longest Losing Streak		
Overall	**12**	Feb. 13-Mar. 13/26
Home	**7**	Dec. 16/39-Jan. 18/40, Oct. 28-Nov. 25/00
Away	**10**	Jan. 16-Mar. 13/26
Longest Winless Streak		
Overall	**12**	Feb. 13-Mar. 13/26 (12 losses), Nov. 28-Dec. 29/35 (8 losses, 4 ties)
Home	**15**	Dec. 16/39-Mar. 7/40 (12 losses, 3 ties)
Away	**12**	Nov. 26/33-Jan. 28/34 (8 losses, 4 ties), Oct. 20-Dec. 13/51 (8 losses, 4 ties)
Most Shutouts, Season	***22**	1928-29 (44)
Most PIM, Season	**1,847**	1995-96 (82)
Most Goals, Game	***16**	Mar. 3/20 (Mtl. 16 at Que. 3)

Individual

Most Seasons	**20**	Henri Richard, Jean Béliveau
Most Games	**1,256**	Henri Richard
Most Goals, Career	**544**	Maurice Richard
Most Assists, Career	**728**	Guy Lafleur
Most Points, Career	**1,246**	Guy Lafleur (518G, 728A)
Most PIM, Career	**2,248**	Chris Nilan
Most Shutouts, Career	**75**	George Hainsworth
Longest Consecutive Games Streak	**560**	Doug Jarvis (Oct. 8/75-Apr. 4/82)
Most Goals, Season	**60**	Steve Shutt (1976-77), Guy Lafleur (1977-78)
Most Assists, Season	**82**	Pete Mahovlich (1974-75)
Most Points, Season	**136**	Guy Lafleur (1976-77; 56G, 80A)
Most PIM, Season	**358**	Chris Nilan (1984-85)
Most Points, Defenseman, Season	**85**	Larry Robinson (1976-77; 19G, 66A)
Most Points, Center, Season	**117**	Pete Mahovlich (1974-75; 35G, 82A)
Most Points, Right Wing, Season	**136**	Guy Lafleur (1976-77; 56G, 80A)
Most Points, Left Wing, Season	**110**	Mats Naslund (1985-86; 43G, 67A)
Most Points, Rookie, Season	**71**	Mats Naslund (1982-83; 26G, 45A), Kjell Dahlin (1985-86; 32G, 39A)
Most Shutouts, Season	***22**	George Hainsworth (1928-29)
Most Goals, Game	**6**	Newsy Lalonde (Jan. 10/20)
Most Assists, Game	**6**	Elmer Lach (Feb. 6/43)
Most Points, Game	**8**	Maurice Richard (Dec. 28/44; 5G, 3A), Bert Olmstead (Jan. 9/54; 4G, 4A)

* NHL Record.

Retired Numbers

1	Jacques Plante	1952-1963
2	Doug Harvey	1947-1961
4	Jean Béliveau	1950-1971
5	Bernard Geoffrion	1950-1964
7	Howie Morenz	1923-1937
9	Maurice Richard	1942-1960
10	Guy Lafleur	1971-1984
12	Dickie Moore	1951-1963
	Yvan Cournoyer	1963-1979
16	Henri Richard	1955-1975
18	Serge Savard	1966-1981
19	Larry Robinson	1972-1989
23	Bob Gainey	1973-1989
29	Ken Dryden	1970-1979

All-time Record vs. Other Clubs

Regular Season

	At Home								On Road								Total							
	GP	W	L	T	OL	GF	GA	PTS	GP	W	L	T	OL	GF	GA	PTS	GP	W	L	T	OL	GF	GA	PTS
Anaheim	9	4	3	2	0	27	24	10	9	5	4	0	0	28	28	10	18	9	7	2	0	55	52	20
Atlanta	16	11	3	0	2	52	35	24	16	10	3	2	1	44	28	23	32	21	6	2	3	96	63	47
Boston	346	200	98	47	1	1169	814	448	347	133	155	56	3	941	1016	325	693	333	253	103	4	2110	1830	773
Buffalo	115	63	37	12	3	421	337	141	114	35	58	19	2	305	356	91	229	98	95	31	5	726	693	232
Calgary	47	27	12	8	0	168	116	62	50	26	16	7	1	166	149	60	97	53	28	15	1	334	265	122
Carolina	81	50	23	7	1	318	241	108	84	39	30	13	2	290	246	93	165	89	53	20	3	608	487	201
Chicago	277	175	54	48	0	1071	656	398	274	125	94	55	0	762	733	305	551	300	148	103	0	1833	1389	703
Colorado	65	39	15	10	1	269	203	89	64	26	32	5	1	223	218	58	129	65	47	15	2	492	421	147
Columbus	5	1	2	1	1	6	9	4	2	2	0	0	0	6	3	4	7	3	2	1	1	12	12	8
Dallas	59	38	12	9	0	254	146	85	60	30	18	12	0	204	157	72	119	68	30	21	0	458	303	157
Detroit	283	172	68	43	0	995	640	387	281	97	130	53	1	717	807	248	564	269	198	96	1	1712	1447	635
Edmonton	31	17	9	4	1	108	97	39	36	17	17	0	2	116	122	36	67	34	26	4	3	224	219	75
Florida	27	11	11	3	2	67	62	27	28	11	14	3	0	72	80	25	55	22	25	6	2	139	142	52
Los Angeles	65	46	8	11	0	292	162	103	66	38	19	9	0	261	201	85	131	84	27	20	0	553	363	188
Minnesota	4	2	1	1	0	13	10	5	3	1	1	0	1	8	10	3	7	3	2	1	1	21	20	8
Nashville	5	4	0	0	1	19	14	9	5	2	2	1	0	13	19	5	10	6	2	1	1	32	33	14
New Jersey	60	35	19	6	0	194	147	76	60	26	29	4	1	204	184	57	120	61	48	10	1	398	331	133
NY Islanders	66	41	16	9	0	237	179	91	66	28	30	6	2	186	200	64	132	69	46	15	2	423	379	155
NY Rangers	296	193	63	40	0	1146	692	426	296	120	120	54	2	857	854	296	592	313	183	94	2	2003	1546	722
Ottawa	45	24	16	4	1	135	131	53	43	18	22	1	2	115	137	39	88	42	38	5	3	250	268	92
Philadelphia	80	39	26	14	1	274	239	93	79	33	29	16	1	240	238	83	159	72	55	30	2	514	477	176
Phoenix	30	25	3	2	0	147	68	52	30	14	9	7	0	116	96	35	60	39	12	9	0	263	164	87
Pittsburgh	88	64	14	10	0	405	227	138	88	44	29	13	2	312	262	103	176	108	43	23	2	717	489	241
St. Louis	60	41	11	7	1	258	165	90	58	29	14	15	0	199	150	73	118	70	25	22	1	457	315	163
San Jose	12	8	2	2	0	42	22	18	12	4	5	2	1	32	39	11	24	12	7	4	1	74	61	29
Tampa Bay	28	15	11	1	1	80	67	32	29	13	11	5	0	82	69	31	57	28	22	6	1	162	136	63
Toronto	345	205	94	43	3	1206	861	456	345	121	177	45	2	903	1054	289	690	326	271	88	5	2109	1915	745
Vancouver	54	38	11	5	0	244	139	81	56	33	14	8	1	204	152	75	110	71	25	13	1	448	291	156
Washington	66	39	17	8	2	250	143	88	65	27	28	9	1	197	182	64	131	66	45	17	3	447	325	152
Defunct Clubs	231	148	58	25	0	779	469	321	230	98	97	35	0	586	606	231	461	246	155	60	0	1365	1075	552
Totals	**2896**	**1775**	**717**	**382**	**22**	**10646**	**7115**	**3954**	**2896**	**1205**	**1207**	**455**	**29**	**8389**	**8396**	**2894**	**5792**	**2980**	**1924**	**837**	**51**	**19035**	**15511**	**6848**

Playoffs

	Series	W	L	GP	W	L	T	GF	GA	Last Mtg.	Rnd.	Result
Boston	31	24	7	159	99	60	0	488	386	2008	CQF	W 4-3
Buffalo	7	4	3	35	18	17	0	124	111	1998	CSF	L 0-4
Calgary	2	1	1	11	6	5	0	31	32	1989	F	L 2-4
Carolina	7	5	2	39	23	16	0	125	106	2006	CQF	L 2-4
Chicago	17	12	5	81	50	29	2	261	185	1976	QF	W 4-0
Colorado	5	3	2	31	17	14	0	105	85	1993	DSF	W 4-2
Dallas	2	1	1	13	7	6	0	48	37	1980	QF	L 3-4
Detroit	12	5	7	62	33	29	0	161	149	1978	QF	W 4-1
Edmonton	1	0	1	3	0	3	0	6	15	1981	PRE	L 0-3
Los Angeles	1	1	0	5	4	1	0	15	12	1993	F	W 4-1
New Jersey	1	0	1	5	1	4	0	11	22	1997	CQF	L 1-4
NY Islanders	4	3	1	22	14	8	0	64	55	1993	CF	W 4-1
NY Rangers	14	7	7	61	34	25	2	188	158	1996	CQF	L 2-4
Philadelphia	5	3	2	26	15	11	0	86	72	2008	CSF	L 1-4
Pittsburgh	1	1	0	6	4	2	0	18	15	1998	CQF	W 4-2
St. Louis	3	3	0	12	12	0	0	42	14	1977	QF	W 4-0
Tampa Bay	1	0	1	4	0	4	0	5	14	2004	CSF	L 0-4
Toronto	15	8	7	71	42	29	0	215	160	1979	QF	W 4-0
Vancouver	1	1	0	5	4	1	0	20	9	1975	QF	W 4-1
Defunct Clubs	10*	5	4	28	15	9	4	70	71			
Totals	**140***	**87**	**52**	**679**	**398**	**273**	**8**	**2083**	**1708**			

* 1919 Final incomplete due to influenza epidemic.

Playoff Results 2008-2003

Year	Round	Opponent	Result	GF	GA
2008	CSF	Philadelphia	L 1-4	14	20
	CQF	Boston	W 4-3	19	15
2006	CQF	Carolina	L 2-4	17	15
2004	CSF	Tampa Bay	L 0-4	5	14
	CQF	Boston	W 4-3	19	14

Abbreviations: Round: F - Final; **CF** - conference final; **CSF** - conference semi-final; **CQF** - conference quarter-final; **DSF** - division semi-final; **QF** - quarter-final; **PRE** - preliminary round.

Calgary totals include Atlanta Flames, 1972-73 to 1979-80.
Colorado totals include Quebec, 1979-80 to 1994-95.
New Jersey totals include Kansas City, 1974-75, 1975-76, and Colorado Rockies, 1976-77 to 1981-82.
Phoenix totals include Winnipeg, 1979-80 to 1995-96.
Carolina totals include Hartford, 1979-80 to 1996-97.
Dallas totals include Minnesota North Stars, 1967-68 to 1992-93.

2007-08 Results

Oct.	3	at Carolina	3-2*
	6	at Toronto	3-4*
	10	at Pittsburgh	3-2
	13	Carolina	1-3
	16	Florida	1-2†
	18	at Ottawa	3-4
	20	Buffalo	4-2
	22	Boston	6-1
	26	at Carolina	7-4
	27	at Pittsburgh	4-3†
	30	Atlanta	2-3†
Nov.	1	Philadelphia	5-2
	3	Toronto	2-3
	5	Buffalo	2-0
	8	at Boston	2-1
	10	at Ottawa	1-3
	13	at Toronto	4-3*
	16	at Buffalo	1-4
	17	Boston	7-4
	19	Ottawa	2-4
	21	at NY Islanders	4-1
	23	at Buffalo	2-4
	24	Buffalo	0-3
	27	at Toronto	4-3†
	30	at New Jersey	0-4
Dec.	1	Nashville	4-5†
	4	Detroit	1-4
	6	at Boston	4-2
	8	Carolina	1-5
	11	Tampa Bay	2-3†
	13	at Philadelphia	4-1
	15	Toronto	4-1
	18	Florida	2-3
	20	at Washington	5-2
	22	at Atlanta	2-3†
	23	at Dallas	1-4
	27	at Tampa Bay	5-2
	28	at Florida	5-1
	30	at NY Rangers	3-4*
Jan.	3	Tampa Bay	6-3
	5	Washington	4-5*
	8	Chicago	4-3*
	10	at Boston	5-2
	12	at NY Rangers	1-4
	15	at NY Islanders	3-1
	17	at Atlanta	3-2†
	19	Pittsburgh	0-2
	22	Boston	8-2
	24	at New Jersey	4-3
	29	Washington	4-0
	31	at Washington	4-5*
Feb.	2	NY Islanders	4-1
	3	NY Rangers	3-5
	5	Ottawa	4-3
	7	Toronto	2-4
	9	at Ottawa	1-6
	12	at Tampa Bay	2-3
	13	at Florida	2-1*
	16	Philadelphia	1-0
	17	at Philadelphia	5-3
	19	NY Rangers	6-5†
	21	Pittsburgh	4-5
	23	Columbus	0-3
	26	Atlanta	5-1
	29	at Buffalo	6-2
Mar.	1	New Jersey	2-1
	3	at San Jose	4-6
	6	at Phoenix	4-2
	8	at Los Angeles	5-2
	9	at Anaheim	1-3
	11	New Jersey	4-0
	13	Ottawa	0-3
	15	NY Islanders	3-0
	18	St. Louis	3-4†
	20	at Boston	4-2
	22	Boston	3-2†
	24	Ottawa	7-5
	28	at Buffalo	4-3*
	29	at Toronto	2-4
Apr.	1	at Ottawa	3-0
	3	Buffalo	3-1
	5	Toronto	3-1

* – Overtime † – Shootout

Entry Draft Selections 2008-1994

Name in bold denotes played in NHL.

2008
Pick
56 Danny Kristo
86 Steve Quailer
116 Jason Missiaen
138 Maxim Trunev
206 Patrick Johnson

2007
Pick
12 Ryan McDonagh
22 Max Pacioretty
43 P.K. Subban
65 Olivier Fortier
73 Yannick Weber
133 Joe Stejskal
142 Andrew Conboy
163 Nichlas Torp
192 Scott Kishel

2006
Pick
20 David Fischer
49 Ben Maxwell
53 Mathieu Carle
66 Ryan White
139 Pavel Valentenko
199 Cameron Cepek

2005
Pick
5 **Carey Price**
45 **Guillaume Latendresse**
121 Juraj Mikus
130 Mathieu Aubin
190 **Matt D'Agostini**
200 **Sergei Kostitsyn**
229 Philippe Paquet

2004
Pick
18 **Kyle Chipchura**
84 Alexei Yemelin
100 James Wyman
150 **Mikhail Grabovski**
181 Loic Lacasse
212 Jon Gleed
246 **Greg Stewart**
262 **Mark Streit**
278 Alex Dulac-Lemelin

2003
Pick
10 **Andrei Kostitsyn**
40 Cory Urquhart
61 **Maxim Lapierre**
79 **Ryan O'Byrne**
113 **Corey Locke**
123 Danny Stewart
177 Chris Heino-Lindberg
188 Mark Flood
217 Oskari Korpikari
241 Jimmy Bonneau
271 **Jaroslav Halak**

2002
Pick
14 **Christopher Higgins**
45 Tomas Linhart
99 Michael Lambert
182 Andre Deveaux
212 **Jonathan Ferland**
275 Konstantin Korneev

2001
Pick
7 **Mike Komisarek**
25 **Alexander Perezhogin**
37 **Duncan Milroy**
71 **Tomas Plekanec**
109 **Martti Jarventie**
171 Eric Himelfarb
203 Andrew Archer
266 Viktor Ujcik

2000
Pick
13 **Ron Hainsey**
16 **Marcel Hossa**
78 **Jozef Balej**
79 Tyler Hanchuck
109 Johan Eneqvist
114 Christian Larrivee
145 Ryan Glenn
172 Scott Selig
182 Petr Chvojka
243 Joni Puurula
275 Jonathan Gauthier

1999
Pick
39 Alexander Buturlin
58 **Matt Carkner**
97 Chris Dyment
107 Evan Lindsay
136 Dusty Jamieson
145 Marc-Andre Thinel
150 Matt Shasby
167 Sean Dixon
196 Vadim Tarasov
225 Mikko Hyytia
253 Jerome Marois

1998
Pick
16 **Eric Chouinard**
45 **Mike Ribeiro**
75 **Francois Beauchemin**
132 **Andrei Bashkirov**
152 **Gordie Dwyer**
162 **Andrei Markov**
189 Andrei Kruchinin
201 Craig Murray
216 **Michael Ryder**
247 Darcy Harris

1997
Pick
11 **Jason Ward**
37 Gregor Baumgartner
65 Ilkka Mikkola
91 Daniel Tetrault
118 Konstantin Sidulov
122 Gennady Razin
145 Jonathan Desroches
172 **Ben Guite**
197 Petr Kubos
202 Andrei Sidyakin
228 Jarl Espen Ygranes

1996
Pick
18 **Matt Higgins**
44 **Mathieu Garon**
71 **Arron Asham**
92 Kim Staal
99 Etienne Drapeau
127 Daniel Archambault
154 **Brett Clark**
181 Timo Vertala
207 Mattia Baldi
233 Michel Tremblay

1995
Pick
8 **Terry Ryan**
60 **Miloslav Guren**
74 Martin Hohenberger
86 **Jonathan Delisle**
112 Niklas Anger
138 Boyd Olson
164 **Stephane Robidas**
190 Greg Hart
216 **Eric Houde**

1994
Pick
18 **Brad Brown**
44 **Jose Theodore**
54 **Chris Murray**
70 **Marko Kiprusoff**
74 Martin Belanger
96 Arto Kuki
122 Jimmy Drolet
148 Joel Irving
174 Jessie Rezansoff
200 Peter Strom
226 **Tomas Vokoun**
252 Chris Aldous
278 Ross Parsons

Guy Carbonneau

Head Coach

Born: Sept-Iles, Que, March 18, 1960.

Guy Carbonneau was hired as an associate coach to Bob Gainey on January 14, 2006 and worked the last 41 games of the 2005-06 regular season. Almost five months later, on May 5, 2006, Carbonneau officially took over head coaching duties from Gainey. When going behind the bench himself and hiring Carbonneau as his assistant, Gainey had announced that Carbonneau would be the Canadiens' new head coach beginning with the 2006-07 season. In 2007-08, he guided the team to a first-place finish in the Eastern Conference standings and was a finalist for the Jack Adams Award as coach of the year.

Carbonneau began his coaching career as an assistant coach with the Canadiens from November 2000 until the end of the 2001-02 season (144 regular-season games and 12 playoff games). He held the position of supervisor of prospect development from August to November 2000. The 18-year NHL veteran had announced his retirement as a player in July 2000, following a brilliant career that saw him win three Stanley Cup championships and three Frank Selke trophies as the NHL's top defensive forward (1988, 1989 and 1992).

Carbonneau was a Canadiens' third round selection, 44th overall in 1979. He spent the first 12 seasons of his career in Montreal, winning the Stanley Cup in 1986 and 1993. Captain of the Canadiens for five seasons (1989 to 1994), he also donned a St. Louis Blues jersey in 1994-95, before joining the Dallas Stars where he played from 1995 to 2000 winning a third Stanley Cup in 1998-99. He made the Stanley Cup playoffs 17 out of 18 NHL seasons. Carbonneau also served as an assistant general manager in Dallas from 2002-03 until returning to Montreal during the 2005-06 season.

Coaching Record

			Regular Season				Playoffs			
Season	**Team**	**League**	**GC**	**W**	**L**	**O/T**	**GC**	**W**	**L**	**T**
2006-07	**Montreal**	**NHL**	**82**	**42**	**34**	**6**	....	....	....	....
2007-08	**Montreal**	**NHL**	**82**	**47**	**25**	**10**	**12**	**5**	**7**	....
	NHL Totals		**164**	**89**	**59**	**16**	**12**	**5**	**7**	....

Club Directory

Bell Centre

Club de Hockey Canadien
1260 de La Gauchetière Street W.
Montréal, QC H3B 5E8
Phone: **514/932-2582**
Media Hotline: 514/989-2835
Fax Lines (all area code 514):
Communications 932-8285
Hockey 989-2717
Press Lounge 932-5258
Marketing 925-2145
Community Relations 925-2144
www.canadiens.com
Capacity: 21,273

Executive Management
Owner, Chairman and Governor . . . . . George N. Gillett Jr.
Vice Chairman . . . . . Jeff Joyce
Managing Partner . . . . . Foster Gillett
President, Club de hockey Canadien & Centre Bell & Alternate Governor . . . . . Pierre Boivin
Executive Vice President Hockey and General Manager & Alternate Governor . . . . . Bob Gainey
Assistant General Manager . . . . . Pierre Gauthier
Vice President, Hockey Operations . . . . . Julien BriseBois
Chief Financial Officer & Alternate Governor . . . . . Fred Steer
Vice President, Marketing and Sales . . . . . Ray Lalonde
Vice President, Communications and Community Relations . . . . . Donald Beauchamp
Vice President, Building Operations . . . . . Alain Gauthier
Vice President & General Manager, Gillett Entertainment Group . . . . . Jacques Aubé
President, Effix – Advertising and Sponsorship Sales . . François Seigneur
Canadiens Alumni . . . . . Réjean Houle
Administrative Assistant to the President . . . . . Rolande Bernier

Hockey
Director of Player Recruitment and Development. . . Trevor Timmins
Head Coach . . . . . Guy Carbonneau
Associate Coach . . . . . Doug Jarvis
Assistant Coaches . . . . . Roland Melanson, Kirk Muller
Professional Scouts . . . . . Gordie Roberts, Doug Gibson
Scouting Staff . . . . . Elmer Benning, Bill Berglund, Michel Boucher, Pelle Eklund, Frank Jay, Vaughn Karpan, Hannu Laine, Dave Mayville, Mike McCann, Denis Morel, Antonin Routa, Nikolai Vakourov, Pat Westrum
Team Services & Hockey Administration Manager . . Claudine Crépin
Administrative Assistant to the General Manager . . Suzanne Charlebois
Team Services Coordinator . . . . . Alain Gagnon

Medical and Training Staff
Club Physician and Chief Surgeon . . . . . Dr. David Mulder
Consultant, Orthopedic Surgeon . . . . . Dr. Eric Lenczner
Dentist . . . . . Dr. Jean-François Desjardins
Consultant, Ophthalmologist . . . . . Dr. John Little
Consultant, Sports Medicine . . . . . Dr. Vincent Lacroix
Consultant, Ostheopathy . . . . . Dave Campbell
Head Athletic Therapist . . . . . Graham Rynbend
Athletic Therapist . . . . . Nick Addey-Jibb
Strength & Conditioning Coordinator . . . . . Scott Livingston
Video Coach . . . . . Mario Leblanc
Equipment Manager . . . . . Pierre Gervais
Assistants to the Equipment Manager . . . . . Patrick Langlois, Pierre Ouellette
Visiting team Coordinator . . . . . Richard Généreux

Communications
Director of Media Relations . . . . . Dominick Saillant
Administrative Assistant to the VP Communications . . Sylvie Lambert
Manager, History and Archives . . . . . Carl Lavigne
Communications Coordinator . . . . . Jasmin Pilon

Community Relations
Director of Community Relations . . . . . Geneviève Paquette
Coordinator, Canadiens Children's Foundation . . . . Marie-Christine Boucher
Community Relations Coordinator . . . . . Anne-Marie Bégin
Assistant, Community Relations . . . . . Sylvie Nadeau

Marketing And Sales
Director, Group Sales and Administration . . . . . Pierre Constant
Executive Director, Luxury Suites and Services . . . . . Richard Primeau
Director, Ticket Sales . . . . . Vincent Lucier
Director, Marketing, Media and Broadcast . . . . . Jon Trzcienski
Director, Consumer Products . . . . . Matt Zalkowitz
Group Manager, Broadcast and Advertising . . . . . Jonathan Prunier
Group Manager, Creative Services and Publications . . Jean Simard
Manager, Luxury Suites Services . . . . . Sabina D'Ascoli
Manager, Game Production . . . . . Paul Gallant
Manager, Group Sales . . . . . Stéphane Verret

Building Operations
Director of Ticket Office . . . . . Cathy D'Ascoli
Assistant Director of Ticket Office . . . . . Lucie Masse
Director of Building Operations . . . . . Xavier Luydlin
Director of Concessions . . . . . Alec Beaudry
Director of Customer Satisfaction . . . . . Caroline Hamel
Administrative Assistant to the VP Operations . . . . . Maryse Cartwright

Finance
Exec. Dir., Info. & Communication Technology . . . . Pierre-Éric Belzile
Controller . . . . . Dennis McKinley
Assistant Controller . . . . . Raymond Lamarche
Administrative, Human Ressources . . . . . Susan Cryans
Administrative Assistant, Chief Financial Officer. . . . Christine Ouellette

Broadcasting
Play-by-play – Radio/TV . . . . . Pierre Houde (RDS), Martin McGuire (CKAC), Rick Moffat (CJAD)
Colormen – Radio/TV . . . . . Benoit Brunet (RDS), Dany Dubé (CKAC), Murray Wilson (CJAD)
Radio/television Flagship Stations . . . . . RDS (Cable 33), CKAC (730 AM), CJAD (800 AM)

Key Off-Season Signings/Acquisitions

2008

May 12 • Re-signed RW **Martin Erat**.
June 16 • Re-signed D **Ryan Suter**.
23 • Re-signed G **Dan Ellis** and D **Shea Weber**.
July 9 • Signed LW **Josh Gratton**.

Nashville Predators

2007-08 Results: 41W-32L-4OTL-5SOL 91PTS.
Second, Central Division

Year-by-Year Record

		Home				Road				Overall								
Season	GP	W	L	T	OL	W	L	T	OL	W	L	T	OL	GF	GA	Pts.	Finished	Playoff Result
2007-08	82	23	14	....	4	18	18	....	5	41	32	....	9	230	229	91	2nd, Central Div.	Lost Conf. Quarter-Final
2006-07	82	28	8	....	5	23	15	....	3	51	23	....	8	272	212	110	2nd, Central Div.	Lost Conf. Quarter-Final
2005-06	82	32	8	....	1	17	17	....	7	49	25	....	8	259	227	106	2nd, Central Div.	Lost Conf. Quarter-Final
2004-05	....	....	....	....	....	....	....	....	....	....	....	....	....	....	....	....		
2003-04	82	22	10	7	2	16	19	4	2	38	29	11	4	216	217	91	3rd, Central Div.	Lost Conf. Quarter-Final
2002-03	82	18	17	5	1	9	18	8	6	27	35	13	7	183	206	74	4th, Central Div.	Out of Playoffs
2001-02	82	17	16	8	0	11	25	5	0	28	41	13	0	196	230	69	4th, Central Div.	Out of Playoffs
2000-01	82	16	18	7	0	18	18	2	3	34	36	9	3	186	200	80	3rd, Central Div.	Out of Playoffs
1999-2000	82	15	21	3	2	13	19	4	5	28	40	7	7	199	240	70	4th, Central Div.	Out of Playoffs
1998-99	82	15	22	4	....	13	25	3	....	28	47	7	....	190	261	63	4th, Central Div.	Out of Playoffs

2008-09 Schedule

Oct.	Fri.	10	at St. Louis		Sun.	11	at Chicago
	Sat.	11	Dallas		Tue.	13	at Toronto
	Mon.	13	at Chicago		Thu.	15	at Montreal
	Wed.	15	at Dallas		Sat.	17	Atlanta
	Fri.	17	at Columbus		Mon.	19	New Jersey
	Sat.	18	Columbus		Wed.	28	at Vancouver
	Thu.	23	Calgary		Fri.	30	at Calgary
	Sat.	25	Los Angeles	**Feb.**	Sun.	1	at Edmonton*
	Tue.	28	at Washington		Tue.	3	Phoenix
	Thu.	30	Edmonton		Thu.	5	Anaheim
Nov.	Sat.	1	Florida		Fri.	6	at Minnesota
	Tue.	4	at Vancouver		Sun.	8	at Dallas*
	Thu.	6	at Calgary		Tue.	10	Detroit
	Sat.	8	at Colorado		Thu.	12	St. Louis
	Tue.	11	at San Jose		Sat.	14	Boston
	Fri.	14	at Anaheim		Mon.	16	Ottawa
	Sat.	15	at Los Angeles		Wed.	18	at Detroit
	Mon.	17	San Jose		Thu.	19	St. Louis
	Fri.	21	at Tampa Bay		Sat.	21	at St. Louis
	Sun.	23	at Carolina*		Tue.	24	Chicago
	Tue.	25	St. Louis		Thu.	26	Phoenix
	Fri.	28	at Atlanta		Sat.	28	Detroit
	Sat.	29	Minnesota	**Mar.**	Tue.	3	Edmonton
Dec.	Mon.	1	at Buffalo		Thu.	5	Columbus
	Thu.	4	Colorado		Sat.	7	at Philadelphia
	Sat.	6	Minnesota		Tue.	10	Washington
	Mon.	8	at St. Louis		Thu.	12	NY Rangers
	Tue.	9	Vancouver		Sat.	14	at Phoenix
	Thu.	11	at Columbus		Mon.	16	at Los Angeles
	Sat.	13	Dallas		Wed.	18	at Anaheim
	Thu.	18	at Phoenix		Thu.	19	at San Jose
	Sat.	20	NY Islanders		Tue.	24	Anaheim
	Tue.	23	at Florida		Thu.	26	San Jose
	Fri.	26	Detroit		Sat.	28	Los Angeles
	Sun.	28	at Edmonton		Sun.	29	at Detroit*
	Mon.	29	at Colorado		Tue.	31	at Columbus
Jan.	Thu.	1	Vancouver	**Apr.**	Fri.	3	at Chicago
	Sat.	3	Calgary*		Sat.	4	Columbus
	Tue.	6	Colorado		Tue.	7	Chicago
	Thu.	8	Pittsburgh		Thu.	9	at Detroit
	Sat.	10	Chicago		Fri.	10	at Minnesota

* Denotes afternoon game.

Jason Arnott had one of the most productive seasons of his career in 2007-08. His 28 goals equaled the second best total of his career, his 44 assists matched a career high (and led the team) while his 72 points tied him for the team lead with J.P. Dumont.

CENTRAL DIVISION
11th NHL Season

Franchise date: June 25, 1997

2008-09 Player Personnel

FORWARDS	HT	WT	S	Place of Birth	*Age	2007-08 Club
ARNOTT, Jason	6-4	220	R	Collingwood, Ont.	33	Nashville
BONK, Radek	6-3	213	L	Krnov, Czech.	32	Nashville
DUMONT, J.P.	6-1	205	L	Montreal, Que.	30	Nashville
ERAT, Martin	6-0	195	L	Trebic, Czech.	27	Nashville
FIDDLER, Vernon	5-11	204	L	Edmonton, Alta.	28	Nashville
GRANT, Triston	6-1	215	L	Neepawa, Man.	24	Philadelphia (AHL)
GRATTON, Josh	6-2	214	L	Brantford, Ont.	26	Phx-San Antonio-Hart
HORNQVIST, Patric	5-11	194	L	Sollentuna, Sweden	21	Djurgarden
JONES, Ryan	6-1	207	L	Chatham, Ont.	24	Miami U.-Houston
LEGWAND, David	6-2	190	L	Detroit, MI	28	Nashville
MAKI, Ryan	6-2	207	R	Medford, NJ	23	Milwaukee-Cincinnati (ECHL)
NICHOL, Scott	5-9	175	R	Edmonton, Alta.	33	Nashville
O'REILLY, Cal	6-0	187	L	Toronto, Ont.	22	Milwaukee
ORTMEYER, Jed	6-0	197	R	Omaha, NE	30	Nashville
PEVERLEY, Rich	6-0	185	R	Guelph, Ont.	26	Milwaukee-Nashville
PIHLSTROM, Antti	5-10	181	L	Vanntaa, Finland	23	Nashville-Milwaukee
RADULOV, Alexander	6-1	188	L	Nizhny Tagil, USSR	22	Nashville
SANTORELLI, Mike	6-0	196	R	Vancouver, B.C.	22	Milwaukee
SMITHSON, Jerred	6-3	194	R	Vernon, B.C.	29	Nashville
SULLIVAN, Steve	5-8	165	R	Timmins, Ont.	34	Nashville
THURESSON, Andreas	6-1	208	R	Kristianstad, Sweden	20	Milwaukee
TOOTOO, Jordin	5-9	194	R	Churchill, Man.	25	Nashville
WARD, Joel	6-2	205	R	Toronto, Ont.	27	Houston
WILSON, Kelsey	6-1	218	L	Sault Ste. Marie, Ont.	22	Milwaukee
DEFENSEMEN						
BLUM, Jonathon	6-1	177	R	Long Beach, CA	19	Vancouver (WHL)
de VRIES, Greg	6-2	215	L	Sundridge, Ont.	35	Nashville
FRANSON, Cody	6-5	227	R	Salmon Arm, B.C.	21	Milwaukee
HAMHUIS, Dan	6-1	200	L	Smithers, B.C.	25	Nashville
KLEIN, Kevin	6-1	195	R	Kitchener, Ont.	23	Nashville-Milwaukee
KOISTINEN, Ville	5-11	190	L	Oulu, Finland	26	Nashville
SULZER, Alexander	6-1	207	L	Kaufbeuren, W. Ger.	24	Milwaukee
SUTER, Ryan	6-1	196	L	Madison, WI	23	Nashville
WEBER, Shea	6-3	213	R	Sicamous, B.C.	23	Nashville
ZANON, Greg	5-11	211	L	Burnaby, B.C.	28	Nashville

GOALTENDERS	HT	WT	C	Place of Birth	*Age	2007-08 Club
DEKANICH, Mark	6-2	196	L	N. Vancouver, B.C.	22	Colgate
ELLIS, Dan	6-0	185	L	Orangeville, Ont.	28	Nashville
MacINTYRE, Drew	6-2	185	L	Charlottetown, P.E.I.	25	Vancouver-Manitoba
RINNE, Pekka	6-5	207	L	Kempele, Finland	25	Nashville-Milwaukee

* – Age at start of 2008-09 season

David Poile

Vice President and General Manager

Born: Toronto, Ont., February 14, 1949.

Hired as the first general manager in franchise history on July 9, 1997, David Poile has been committed to building the team through the NHL Draft. In 2003-04, Nashville reached the playoffs for the first time in franchise history. During the 2006-07 season, the team was in contention for first overall in the NHL, setting club records with 51 wins and 110 points. Though forced to rebuild the roster for 2007-08, the Predators reached the playoffs for the fourth year in a row. Poile has an impressive reputation as an NHL leader and in 2001 he received the Lester Patrick Trophy for his contributions to hockey in the United States. His father, Norman "Bud" Poile, had won the honor in 1989.

Prior to joining Nashville, Poile spent 15 seasons as vice president/general manager of the Washington Capitals. During his tenure in Washington, the Capitals made 14 postseason appearances, winning their only Patrick Division title in 1989 and advancing to the Conference Finals in 1990. During Poile's 15 years in Washington, the Capitals compiled a record of 594-454-132, finished second in the Patrick Division seven times and recorded 90-or-more points seven different seasons.

Poile started his professional hockey career as an administrative assistant for the Atlanta Flames in 1972, shortly after graduating from Northeastern University in Boston. At Northeastern, he was hockey team captain, leading scorer and most valuable player for two years.

In 1977, he was named assistant general manager of the Atlanta Flames (who moved to Calgary in 1980), serving as the manager and coordinator of the Flames farm club.

Poile was instrumental in the NHL's adoption of the instant replay rule in 1991. He was awarded *Inside Hockey*'s man of the year for his leadership on the issue. He has also been honored three times as *The Sporting News* NHL executive of the year in 1982-83 1983-84 and 2006-07. Poile served as general manager of the 1998 and 1999 U.S. national teams for the World Championships.

2007-08 Scoring

* – rookie

Regular Season

Pos	#	Player	Team	GP	G	A	Pts	TOI	+/–	PIM	PP	SH	GW	S	%
R	71	J.P. Dumont	NSH	80	29	43	72	18:29	5	34	7	0	8	192	15.1
C	19	Jason Arnott	NSH	79	28	44	72	18:59	19	54	13	0	3	248	11.3
R	47	Alexander Radulov	NSH	81	26	32	58	16:23	7	44	4	0	2	183	14.2
R	10	Martin Erat	NSH	76	23	34	57	18:39	–3	40	4	0	6	163	14.1
C	11	David Legwand	NSH	65	15	29	44	18:00	–4	38	4	0	1	144	10.4
D	3	Marek Zidlicky	NSH	79	5	38	43	20:49	–5	63	4	0	0	122	4.1
L	17	Jan Hlavac	T.B.	62	9	13	22	14:45	–10	32	0	0	0	123	7.3
			NSH	18	3	10	13	16:28	9	8	0	0	2	29	10.3
			Total	80	12	23	35	15:08	–1	40	0	0	2	152	7.9
C	38	Vern Fiddler	NSH	79	11	21	32	13:56	–4	47	2	1	1	97	11.3
D	20	Ryan Suter	NSH	76	7	24	31	20:34	3	71	1	0	1	138	5.1
C	14	Radek Bonk	NSH	79	14	15	29	15:55	–31	40	6	0	1	138	10.1
D	2	Dan Hamhuis	NSH	80	4	23	27	22:43	–4	66	1	0	1	127	3.1
L	23	Martin Gelinas	NSH	57	9	11	20	14:06	5	20	0	1	1	110	8.2
D	6	Shea Weber	NSH	54	6	14	20	19:29	–6	49	5	0	2	152	3.9
R	22	Jordin Tootoo	NSH	63	11	7	18	09:53	–8	100	0	0	1	98	11.2
C	12	Scott Nichol	NSH	73	10	8	18	13:15	12	72	0	2	1	101	9.9
D	4 *	Ville Koistinen	NSH	48	4	13	17	16:47	13	18	2	0	1	60	6.7
C	25	Jerred Smithson	NSH	81	7	9	16	12:04	–9	50	0	2	2	61	11.5
D	7	Greg De Vries	NSH	77	4	11	15	18:51	7	71	0	0	1	66	6.1
R	24	Brandon Bochenski	BOS	20	0	6	6	12:47	2	6	0	0	0	30	0.0
			ANA	12	2	2	4	12:28	2	6	1	0	0	17	11.8
			NSH	8	1	2	3	09:00	2	0	0	0	0	9	11.1
			Total	40	3	10	13	11:56	6	12	1	0	0	56	5.4
C	37 *	Rich Peverley	NSH	33	5	5	10	10:19	4	8	0	0	2	43	11.6
R	41	Jed Ortmeyer	NSH	51	4	4	8	12:27	–8	32	0	1	0	68	5.9
D	5	Greg Zanon	NSH	78	0	5	5	18:27	–5	24	0	0	0	38	0.0
L	16	Darcy Hordichuk	NSH	45	1	2	3	05:09	–1	60	0	0	1	18	5.6
D	8 *	Kevin Klein	NSH	13	0	2	2	14:24	–3	6	0	0	0	14	0.0
L	42 *	Antti Pihlstrom	NSH	1	0	0	0	09:08	–1	0	0	0	0	1	0.0
R	15	Josh Langfeld	NSH	2	0	0	0	09:47	0	0	0	0	0	5	0.0

Goaltending

No.	Goaltender	GPI	Mins	Avg	W	L	OT	EN	SO	GA	SA	S%	G	A	PIM
35	* Pekka Rinne	1	29	0.00	0	0	0	0	0	0	8	1.000	0	0	0
39	Dan Ellis	44	2229	2.34	23	10	3	2	6	87	1147	.924	0	0	0
30	Chris Mason	51	2692	2.90	18	22	6	5	4	130	1278	.898	0	1	0
	Totals	**82**	**4983**	**2.70**	**41**	**32**	**9**	**7**	**10**	**224**	**2440**	**.908**			

Playoffs

Pos	#	Player	Team	GP	G	A	Pts	TOI	+/–	PIM	PP	SH	GW	OT	S	%
R	47	Alexander Radulov	NSH	6	2	2	4	15:59	0	6	1	0	0	0	14	14.3
R	10	Martin Erat	NSH	6	1	3	4	20:55	0	8	0	0	0	0	13	7.7
D	6	Shea Weber	NSH	6	1	3	4	19:29	0	6	0	0	0	0	4	25.0
D	3	Marek Zidlicky	NSH	6	0	3	3	19:04	–2	8	0	0	0	0	11	0.0
R	22	Jordin Tootoo	NSH	6	2	0	2	12:30	1	4	0	0	0	0	12	16.7
D	2	Dan Hamhuis	NSH	6	1	1	2	22:47	–4	6	1	0	0	0	8	12.5
D	20	Ryan Suter	NSH	6	1	1	2	21:12	–2	4	0	0	0	0	6	16.7
L	17	Jan Hlavac	NSH	6	0	2	2	18:12	–4	2	0	0	0	0	10	0.0
R	71	J.P. Dumont	NSH	6	0	2	2	17:23	–5	4	0	0	0	0	8	0.0
D	5	Greg Zanon	NSH	6	0	2	2	18:44	2	4	0	0	0	0	1	0.0
C	37 *	Rich Peverley	NSH	6	0	2	2	08:51	0	0	0	0	0	0	4	0.0
C	11	David Legwand	NSH	3	1	0	1	18:15	0	2	0	0	0	0	10	10.0
C	19	Jason Arnott	NSH	4	1	0	1	18:28	–1	4	0	0	1	0	6	16.7
C	14	Radek Bonk	NSH	6	1	0	1	17:56	–3	2	0	0	0	0	12	8.3
D	7	Greg De Vries	NSH	6	1	0	1	19:40	–2	2	0	0	1	0	3	33.3
C	12	Scott Nichol	NSH	2	0	0	0	07:30	0	0	0	0	0	0	1	0.0
R	24	Brandon Bochenski	NSH	3	0	0	0	06:36	–1	0	0	0	0	0	4	0.0
L	16	Darcy Hordichuk	NSH	5	0	0	0	03:31	0	2	0	0	0	0	1	0.0
C	25	Jerred Smithson	NSH	6	0	0	0	11:51	0	2	0	0	0	0	5	0.0
C	38	Vern Fiddler	NSH	6	0	0	0	16:47	0	0	0	0	0	0	11	0.0

Goaltending

No.	Goaltender	GPI	Mins	Avg	W	L	EN	SO	GA	SA	S%	G	A	PIM
39	Dan Ellis	6	357	2.52	2	4	2	0	15	240	.938	0	0	0
	Totals	**6**	**362**	**2.82**	**2**	**4**	**2**	**0**	**17**	**242**	**.930**			

General Managers' History

David Poile, 1998-99 to date.

Captains' History

Tom Fitzgerald, 1998-99 to 2001-02; Greg Johnson, 2002-03 to 2005-06; Kimmo Timonen, 2006-07; Jason Arnott, 2007-08 to date.

Club Records

Team

(Figures in brackets for season records are games played; records for fewest points, wins, ties, losses, goals, goals against are for 70 or more games)

Most Points **110** 2006-07 (82)
Most Wins **51** 2006-07 (82)
Most Ties **13** 2001-02 (82), 2002-03 (82)
Most Losses **47** 1998-99 (82)
Most Goals **272** 2006-07 (82)
Most Goals Against **261** 1998-99 (82)
Fewest Points **63** 1998-99 (82)
Fewest Wins **27** 2002-03 (82)
Fewest Ties **7** 1998-99 (82), 1999-2000 (82)
Fewest (Regulation) Losses **23** 2006-07 (82)
Fewest Goals **183** 2002-03 (82)
Fewest Goals Against **200** 2000-01 (82)

Longest Winning Streak
- **Overall** .... **8** Oct. 5-25/05
- **Home** .... **8** Jan. 6-Feb. 8/07
- **Away** .... **7** Oct. 16-Nov. 4/06

Longest Undefeated Streak
- **Overall** .... **8** Dec. 18/99-Jan. 1/00 (5 wins, 3 ties), Oct. 5-25/05 (8 wins)
- **Home** .... **11** Dec. 20/03-Jan. 31/04 (9 wins, 2 ties), Nov. 3-Dec. 23/01 (8 wins, 3 ties)
- **Away** .... **7** Oct. 16-Nov. 4/06 (7 wins)

Longest Losing Streak
- **Overall** .... **7** Nov. 20-Dec. 2/99
- **Home** .... **6** Jan. 21-Feb. 15/99, Feb. 26-Mar. 21/02, Feb. 21-Mar. 20/08
- **Away** .... **7** Jan. 26-Mar. 5/06

Longest Winless Streak
- **Overall** .... **15** Mar. 10-Apr. 6/03 (12 losses, 3 ties)
- **Home** .... **9** Jan. 21-Mar. 2/99 (8 losses, 1 tie)
- **Away** .... **9** Three times

Most Shutouts, Season **11** 2006-07 (82)
Most PIM, Season **1,533** 2005-06 (82)
Most Goals, Game .... **9** Mar. 4/04 (Nsh. 9 at Pit. 4), Mar. 18/06 (Cgy. 4 at Nsh. 9)

Individual

Most Seasons .... **9** David Legwand
Most Games .... **573** Kimmo Timonen
Most Goals, Career .... **121** David Legwand
Most Assists, Career .... **222** Kimmo Timonen
Most Points, Career .... **327** David Legwand (121G, 206A)
Most PIM, Career .... **544** Scott Hartnell
Most Shutouts, Career .... **21** Tomas Vokoun
Longest Consecutive Games Streak .... **269** Karlis Skrastins (Feb. 21/00-Apr. 6/03)
Most Goals, Season .... **31** Paul Kariya (2005-06), Steve Sullivan (2005-06)
Most Assists, Season .... **54** Paul Kariya (2005-06)
Most Points, Season .... **85** Paul Kariya (2005-06; 31G, 54A)
Most PIM, Season .... **242** Patrick Cote (1998-99)
Most Points, Defenseman, Season .... **55** Kimmo Timonen (2006-07; 13G, 42A)
Most Points, Center, Season .... **72** Jason Arnott (2007-08; 28G, 44A)
Most Points, Right Wing, Season .... **72** J.P. Dumont (2007-08; 29G, 43A)
Most Points, Left Wing, Season .... **85** Paul Kariya (2005-06; 31G, 54A)
Most Points, Rookie, Season .... **37** Alexander Radulov (2006-07; 18G, 19A)
Most Shutouts, Season .... **6** Dan Ellis (2007-08)
Most Goals, Game .... **3** 15 times
Most Assists, Game .... **5** Mark Zidlicky (Feb. 18/04)
Most Points, Game .... **5** Mark Zidlicky (Feb. 18/04; 5A), Dan Hamhuis (Mar. 4/04; 1G-4A)

All-time Record vs. Other Clubs

Regular Season

	At Home								On Road								Total							
	GP	W	L	T	OL	GF	GA	PTS	GP	W	L	T	OL	GF	GA	PTS	GP	W	L	T	OL	GF	GA	PTS
Anaheim	18	9	6	2	1	42	42	21	18	3	13	0	2	29	58	8	36	12	19	2	3	71	100	29
Atlanta	4	3	1	0	0	15	6	6	5	1	2	1	1	13	16	4	9	4	3	1	1	28	22	10
Boston	7	3	4	0	0	18	16	6	6	2	3	1	0	10	17	5	13	5	7	1	0	28	33	11
Buffalo	6	2	3	0	1	12	16	5	5	3	1	1	0	20	17	7	11	5	4	1	1	32	33	12
Calgary	19	13	5	1	0	68	42	27	18	7	5	3	3	41	51	20	37	20	10	4	3	109	93	47
Carolina	5	4	1	0	0	10	7	8	6	2	2	1	1	17	19	6	11	6	3	1	1	27	26	14
Chicago	28	14	8	3	3	93	82	34	29	12	16	1	0	77	81	25	57	26	24	4	3	170	163	59
Colorado	18	7	8	3	0	52	57	17	18	7	8	2	1	41	48	17	36	14	16	5	1	93	105	34
Columbus	23	18	3	1	1	76	45	38	22	14	6	0	2	67	49	30	45	32	9	1	3	143	94	68
Dallas	18	9	8	1	0	47	42	19	18	4	13	0	1	22	48	9	36	13	21	1	1	69	90	28
Detroit	28	12	14	2	0	75	82	26	29	6	16	2	5	62	105	19	57	18	30	4	5	137	187	45
Edmonton	19	9	7	3	0	53	55	21	18	10	6	0	2	56	48	22	37	19	13	3	2	109	103	43
Florida	6	2	2	2	0	12	13	6	5	1	3	1	0	11	18	3	11	3	5	3	0	23	31	9
Los Angeles	18	5	10	3	0	36	47	13	18	8	7	0	3	51	55	19	36	13	17	3	3	87	102	32
Minnesota	14	8	3	2	1	41	30	19	14	3	7	3	1	36	46	10	28	11	10	5	2	77	76	29
Montreal	5	2	1	1	1	19	13	6	5	1	3	0	1	14	19	3	10	3	4	1	2	33	32	9
New Jersey	6	1	4	0	1	12	18	3	6	4	1	0	1	18	18	9	12	5	5	0	2	30	36	12
NY Islanders	6	4	2	0	0	16	17	8	5	3	1	0	1	14	12	7	11	7	3	0	1	30	29	15
NY Rangers	5	2	3	0	0	14	19	4	7	4	2	1	0	18	18	9	12	6	5	1	0	32	37	13
Ottawa	5	3	2	0	0	14	11	6	6	2	4	0	0	13	20	4	11	5	6	0	0	27	31	10
Philadelphia	5	1	2	2	0	8	10	4	6	3	2	1	0	12	19	7	11	4	4	3	0	20	29	11
Phoenix	18	10	6	2	0	53	45	22	18	7	9	0	2	56	55	16	36	17	15	2	2	109	100	38
Pittsburgh	7	5	2	0	0	26	14	10	6	2	2	2	0	18	18	6	13	7	4	2	0	44	32	16
St. Louis	29	16	9	3	1	73	68	36	28	12	13	1	2	60	77	27	57	28	22	4	3	133	145	63
San Jose	18	9	8	1	0	46	47	19	18	6	9	1	2	43	49	15	36	15	17	2	2	89	96	34
Tampa Bay	7	2	4	0	1	13	18	5	5	1	2	2	0	13	15	4	12	3	6	2	1	26	33	9
Toronto	2	2	0	0	0	7	4	4	7	3	3	1	0	19	16	7	9	5	3	1	0	26	20	11
Vancouver	19	8	6	1	4	56	53	21	18	5	12	1	0	42	64	11	37	13	18	2	4	98	117	32
Washington	6	3	2	1	0	18	15	7	5	2	3	0	0	13	12	4	11	5	5	1	0	31	27	11
Totals	**369**	**186**	**134**	**34**	**15**	**1025**	**934**	**421**	**369**	**138**	**174**	**26**	**31**	**906**	**1088**	**333**	**738**	**324**	**308**	**60**	**46**	**1931**	**2022**	**754**

Playoffs

	Series	W	L	GP	W	L	T	GF	GA	Last Mtg.	Rnd.	Result
Detroit	2	0	2	12	4	8	0	21	29	2008	CQF	L 2-4
San Jose	2	0	2	10	2	8	0	24	33	2007	CQF	L 1-4
Totals	**4**	**0**	**4**	**22**	**6**	**16**	**0**	**45**	**62**			

Playoff Results 2008-2003

Year	Round	Opponent	Result	GF	GA
2008	CQF	Detroit	L 2-4	12	17
2007	CQF	San Jose	L 1-4	14	16
2006	CQF	San Jose	L 1-4	10	17
2004	CQF	Detroit	L 2-4	9	12

Abbreviations: Round: CQF - conference quarter-final.

2007-08 Results

Oct.	4	Colorado	4-0
	6	Dallas	5-1
	10	at St. Louis	1-4
	11	Phoenix	3-6
	13	Calgary	4-7
	17	at Anaheim	1-3
	20	at San Jose	0-3
	23	at Los Angeles	0-6
	25	Atlanta	3-0
	27	Florida	4-3
	30	at Calgary	1-5
Nov.	1	at Vancouver	3-0
	2	at Edmonton	4-1
	4	at Chicago	5-2
	7	at Detroit	2-3†
	10	Columbus	4-3†
	12	at Columbus	4-1
	15	Chicago	5-4*
	17	St. Louis	2-3†
	19	at St. Louis	1-2
	22	Detroit	3-2
	24	Minnesota	3-4
	29	at Ottawa	6-5
Dec.	1	at Montreal	5-4†
	4	at Toronto	1-3
	6	Vancouver	2-5
	8	Anaheim	4-2
	10	Detroit	1-2
	13	Colorado	1-2
	15	at Colorado	1-3
	18	at Minnesota	2-3
	19	at Chicago	2-5
	22	Los Angeles	4-3
	23	at Columbus	3-1
	26	at Chicago	2-5
	27	Columbus	4-3
	29	San Jose	2-5
	31	at Dallas	1-0
Jan.	3	Edmonton	5-2
	5	Minnesota	4-1
	7	at Anaheim	2-5
	8	at Los Angeles	7-0
	12	at Columbus	1-2†
	13	Chicago	2-3†
	15	Calgary	3-0
	17	Anaheim	1-2
	19	at St. Louis	5-2
	21	St. Louis	6-3
	22	at Colorado	4-0
	24	at Phoenix	3-4*
	29	at Boston	1-3
	31	Columbus	4-2
Feb.	2	Phoenix	3-2*
	5	Carolina	1-0
	7	Tampa Bay	1-2*
	9	at San Jose	3-4
	10	at Phoenix	6-3
	12	Detroit	4-2
	14	Chicago	1-6
	16	St. Louis	2-1*
	17	at Minnesota	4-5*
	19	Edmonton	5-4
	21	Vancouver	2-3†
	23	Dallas	3-6
	27	at Buffalo	4-8
Mar.	1	at Dallas	3-1
	4	at Edmonton	5-1
	6	at Vancouver	2-6
	7	at Calgary	2-1*
	9	at Detroit	3-4
	11	San Jose	1-2
	13	Los Angeles	1-4
	15	at Detroit	3-1
	18	Washington	2-4
	20	Detroit	3-6
	22	Chicago	2-1†
	25	Columbus	3-0
	28	at Columbus	2-0
	30	at Detroit	0-1*
Apr.	1	at St. Louis	4-3*
	3	St. Louis	3-2
	4	at Chicago	1-3

* – Overtime † – Shootout

Entry Draft Selections 2008-1998

Name in bold denotes played in NHL.

2008
Pick
7 Colin Wilson
18 Chet Pickard
38 Roman Josi
136 Taylor Stefishen
166 Jeffrey Foss
201 Jani Lajunen
207 Anders Lindback

2007
Pick
23 Jonathon Blum
54 Jeremy Smith
58 Nick Spaling
81 Ryan Thang
114 Ben Ryan
119 Mark Santorelli
144 Andreas Thuresson
174 Robert Dietrich
204 Atte Engren

2006
Pick
56 Blake Geoffrion
105 Niko Snellman
146 Mark Dekanich
176 Ryan Flynn
206 Viktor Sjodin

2005
Pick
18 **Ryan Parent**
78 Teemu Laakso
79 Cody Franson
150 Cal O'Reilly
176 Ryan Maki
213 Scott Todd
230 Patric Hornqvist

2004
Pick
15 **Alexander Radulov**
81 Vaclav Meidl
107 Nick Fugere
139 Kyle Moir
147 Janne Niskala
178 Mike Santorelli
193 Kevin Schaeffer
209 Stanislav Balan
243 Denis Kulyash
258 **Pekka Rinne**
275 Craig Switzer

2003
Pick
7 **Ryan Suter**
35 Konstantin Glazachev
37 **Kevin Klein**
49 **Shea Weber**
76 Richard Stehlik
89 Paul Brown
92 Alexander Sulzer
98 Grigory Shafigulin
117 Teemu Lassila
133 Rustam Sidikov
210 Andrei Mukhachev
213 Miroslav Hanuljak
268 Lauris Darzins

2002
Pick
6 **Scottie Upshall**
102 Brandon Segal
138 Patrick Jarrett
172 Mike McKenna
203 Josh Morrow
235 Kaleb Betts
264 Matt Davis
266 Steven Spencer

2001
Pick
12 **Dan Hamhuis**
33 **Timofei Shishkanov**
42 Tomas Slovak
75 Denis Platonov
76 Oliver Setzinger
98 **Jordin Tootoo**
178 Anton Lavrentiev
240 Gustav Grasberg
271 **Mikko Lehtonen**

2000
Pick
6 **Scott Hartnell**
36 Daniel Widing
72 Mattias Nilsson
89 **Libor Pivko**
131 Matt Hendricks
137 **Mike Stuart**
154 **Matt Koalska**
173 Tomas Harant
197 Zbynek Irgl
203 Jure Penko
236 Mats Christeen
284 Martin Hohener

1999
Pick
6 **Brian Finley**
33 **Jonas Andersson**
52 **Adam Hall**
54 **Andrew Hutchinson**
61 Ed Hill
65 **Jan Lasak**
72 Brett Angel
121 Yevgeny Pavlov
124 Alexandre Krevsun
131 Konstantin Panov
162 **Timo Helbling**
191 **Martin Erat**
205 Kyle Kettles
220 Miroslav Durak
248 **Darren Haydar**

1998
Pick
2 **David Legwand**
60 **Denis Arkhipov**
85 Geoff Koch
88 Kent Sauer
138 Martin Beauchesne
147 Craig Brunel
202 Martin Bartek
230 **Karlis Skrastins**

Coaching History

Barry Trotz, 1998-99 to date.

Barry Trotz

Head Coach

Born: Winnipeg, Man., July 15, 1962.

Barry Trotz became head coach of the Nashville Predators on August 6, 1997, after serving four seasons as head coach and director of hockey operations for the American Hockey League's Portland Pirates. He and assistant Paul Gardner spent the 1997-98 season scouting in preparation for the inaugural season of the Predators. In his sixth season behind the bench in 2003-04, Trotz led Nashville into the playoffs for the first time. During the 2006-07 season, Nashville was in contention for first overall in the NHL, setting club records with 51 wins and 110 points. In 2007-08, Trotz led a rebuilt Nashville roster back to the playoffs for the fourth consecutive season.

Trotz began his coaching career in 1984 as assistant coach with the University of Manitoba for one season, before serving two seasons as the head coach and general manager of the Dauphin Kings Junior Hockey Club from 1985 to 1987. He became head coach of the University of Manitoba during the 1987 season and also served as a scout for the Spokane Chiefs of the Western Hockey League that season. Trotz joined the Washington Capitals organization as their chief western scout during the 1988 season. The Winnipeg, Manitoba native was appointed an assistant coach of the Capitals' American Hockey League affiliate in Baltimore prior to the 1991 season before being named head coach prior to the 1992 season. When the franchise relocated to Portland, he guided the Pirates to two AHL Calder Cup Final appearances in the club's first four seasons. He led the Pirates to a league-best 43-27-10 record, captured the Calder Cup championship and was named the American Hockey League coach of the year following the 1994-95 season.

In 1995, Trotz guided Portland to a new North American professional hockey league record 17-game unbeaten streak (14-0-3) to start the season. He was named head coach for the U.S. team at the American Hockey League All-Star Game in 1996.

Prior to his coaching career, Trotz played junior hockey for the Western Hockey League's Regina Pats from 1979-83. During that time, he recorded 39 goals, 121 assists for 160 points, along with 490 penalty minutes in 204 games.

Coaching Record

			Regular Season				Playoffs			
Season	Team	League	GC	W	L	O/T	GC	W	L	T
1992-93	Baltimore	AHL	80	28	40	12	7	3	4	....
1993-94	Portland	AHL	80	43	27	10	8	6	2	....
1994-95	Portland	AHL	80	46	22	12	7	3	4	....
1995-96	Portland	AHL	80	32	34	14	24	14	10	....
1996-97	Portland	AHL	80	37	26	17	5	2	3	....
1998-99	**Nashville**	**NHL**	**82**	**28**	**47**	**7**	....	....	....	....
99-2000	**Nashville**	**NHL**	**82**	**28**	**40**	**14**	....	....	....	....
2000-01	**Nashville**	**NHL**	**82**	**34**	**36**	**12**	....	....	....	....
2001-02	**Nashville**	**NHL**	**82**	**28**	**41**	**13**	....	....	....	....
2002-03	**Nashville**	**NHL**	**82**	**27**	**35**	**20**	....	....	....	....
2003-04	**Nashville**	**NHL**	**82**	**38**	**29**	**15**	**6**	**2**	**4**	....
2004-05	**Nashville**				SEASON CANCELLED					
2005-06	**Nashville**	**NHL**	**82**	**49**	**25**	**8**	**5**	**1**	**4**	....
2006-07	**Nashville**	**NHL**	**82**	**51**	**23**	**8**	**5**	**1**	**4**	....
2007-08	**Nashville**	**NHL**	**82**	**41**	**32**	**9**	**6**	**2**	**4**	....
	NHL Totals		**738**	**324**	**308**	**106**	**22**	**6**	**16**	....

Club Directory

Sommet Center

Nashville Predators
Sommet Center
501 Broadway
Nashville, TN 37203
Phone **615/770-2300**
FAX 615/770-2309
Ticket Information 615/770-PUCK
www.nashvillepredators.com
Capacity: 17,113

Owner . . . . Predators Holdings LLC
Investor Group. . . . . Christopher Cigarran, Thomas Cigarran, Joel and Holly Dobberpuhl, David Freeman, Herbert Fritch, DeWitt Thompson V, John Thompson
Chairman and Governor . . . . David Freeman
Pres. of Hockey Ops./G.M./Alternate Gov. . . . . David Poile
Pres. of Business Ops. & Alternate Gov. . . . . Ed Lang
Exec. V.P. Finance & Administration . . . . Mark Floyd
Sr. V.P. Communications & Development . . . . Gerry Helper
Sr. V.P. of Corporate Development . . . . Chris Parker

Hockey Operations
Assistant General Manager . . . . Paul Fenton
Director of Hockey Operations . . . . Michael Santos
Head Coach . . . . Barry Trotz
Associate Coach . . . . Brent Peterson
Assistant Coach . . . . Peter Horachek
Goaltending Coach . . . . Mitch Korn
Video Coach . . . . Robert Bouchard
Strength and Conditioning Coach . . . . David Good
Chief Amateur Scout . . . . Jeff Kealty
Professional Scouts . . . . Nick Beverley, Shawn Dineen
North American Amateur Scouts . . . . Jason Bukala, Rick Knickle, Tom Nolan, Glen Sanders, David Westby
European Scouts . . . . Martin Bakula, Lucas Bergman, Janne Kekalainen
Head Athletic Trainer . . . . Dan Redmond
Assistant Athletic Trainer . . . . Andy Hosler
Equipment Manager . . . . Pete Rogers
Assistant Equipment Manager . . . . Jeff Camelio
Equipment Assistant . . . . Brad Peterson
Locker Room Attendant . . . . Craig "Partner" Baugh
Director of Team Services . . . . Gregory Harvey
Hockey Operations Manager . . . . Brandon Walker
Executive Assistant . . . . Connell Meekins

Team Doctors
Medical . . . . David R. Moore, MD; Blake Garside, MD; Cristin Wallace, DDS; Daniel Weikert, MD; Bryan D. Oslin, MD; Donald Griffin, MD; Gary S. Solomon, Ph. D.; Carl Hampf, MD; Richard W. Garman, MD

Communications/Development
Communications Manager . . . . Tim Darling
Communications Coordinator . . . . Kevin Wilson
Director of Community Relations . . . . Rebecca Ward
Youth and Amateur Hockey Manager . . . . Andee Boiman
Community Relations Coordinator . . . . Erich Wilhelm
Internet Development Manager . . . . Jay Levin
Team Photographer . . . . John Russell

Corporate Partnerships
Director of Corporate Partnerships . . . . Delmar Smith
Account Executives – Corporate Development . . . . . Bradford Hollingsworth, John McMillin
Account Service Managers – Corporate Partnerships . . Kathryn Cloud, Emily Cutler
Executive Assistant . . . . Gerry Pring

Marketing
Vice President of Marketing . . . . Randy Campbell
Director of Marketing . . . . Doug Aitken
Entertainment Manager . . . . Adam DeVault
Database Manager . . . . Joe Wiese
Game Operations Manager . . . . Brian Campbell
Promotions Manager . . . . Raquel Toombs

Premium Seating
Vice President of Premium Seat Sales . . . . Chris Junghans
Vice President of Premium Seating Service . . . . Susie Masotti
Director of Premium Seating Service . . . . Britt Kincheloe
Senior Manager of Premium Seat Sales . . . . Tim Wilson

Finance/Administration/Human Resources
Vice President of Finance . . . . Beth Snider
Director of Human Resources . . . . Allison Winters
Payroll Manager . . . . Susan Charnley

Technical Operations
Director of Technical Operations . . . . Blake Grant
Technical Operations Coordinator . . . . Patrick Abell

Broadcast
Broadcasting Director . . . . Bob Kohl
Play-by-Play Announcer . . . . Pete Weber
Color Analyst . . . . Terry Crisp
Manager, Video Production . . . . Mitch Jordan
Associate Producer . . . . David White
Videographer/Editor . . . . Brett Newkirk

Ticket Operations
Vice President of Ticket Sales . . . . Nat Harden
Director of Ticket Sales . . . . Marty Mulford
Senior Account Executives . . . . Brad Gillispie, Jenny Moss, Jason Mott
Account Executives . . . . Jack Burk, Chris Burton, Chris Harrington, Jason Rourke, Dan Shaefer, Tiffany Vanek
Ticket Operations Coordinators . . . . Sara Endwright, Mary Jane Rodgers
Fan Relations Supervisor . . . . Courtney Gray
Fan Relations Coordinators . . . . Paige Belew, Mac Maddox, Julia Potash
Ticket Sales Coordinator . . . . Mollie Roach
Radio . . . . WGFX 104.5-FM (flagship), WRQQ 97.1-FM
TV Flagship . . . . FSN South

New Jersey Devils

Key Off-Season Signings/Acquisitions

2008

May 22 • Re-signed D **Sheldon Brookbank** and D **Mike Mottau**.

July 1 • Re-signed LW **Jay Pandolfo**, D **Bryce Salvador** and RW **David Clarkson**.

1 • Signed C **Bobby Holik** and RW **Brian Rolston**

2007-08 Results: 46W-29L-3OTL-4SOL 99PTS.
Second, Atlantic Division

Martin Brodeur poses with the puck from his 500th career victory, November 17, 2007. Brodeur joined Patrick Roy as the only goalies in history to reach this milestone.

2008-09 Schedule

Oct.	Fri.	10	NY Islanders		Sun.	11	at Anaheim*
	Sat.	11	at Pittsburgh		Tue.	13	at Vancouver
	Mon.	13	at NY Rangers		Fri.	16	at Columbus
	Thu.	16	at Atlanta		Sat.	17	at NY Islanders
	Sat.	18	at Washington		Mon.	19	at Nashville
	Wed.	22	Dallas		Wed.	21	Montreal
	Fri.	24	Philadelphia		Tue.	27	at Ottawa
	Sat.	25	at Philadelphia		Thu.	29	at Boston
	Wed.	29	Toronto		Fri.	30	Pittsburgh
Nov.	Sat.	1	Atlanta	**Feb.**	Tue.	3	Washington
	Mon.	3	Buffalo		Fri.	6	at Atlanta
	Wed.	5	Tampa Bay		Sat.	7	Los Angeles
	Sat.	8	at Detroit		Mon.	9	NY Rangers
	Sun.	9	Edmonton		Wed.	11	NY Islanders
	Wed.	12	NY Rangers		Fri.	13	Boston
	Fri.	14	at Washington		Sun.	15	San Jose*
	Sat.	15	Washington		Tue.	17	at Florida
	Thu.	20	Florida		Thu.	19	at Tampa Bay
	Fri.	21	NY Islanders		Sat.	21	at NY Islanders
	Sun.	23	at Tampa Bay*		Thu.	26	Colorado
	Wed.	26	at Florida		Sat.	28	Florida*
	Sat.	29	at Pittsburgh	**Mar.**	Sun.	1	Philadelphia*
Dec.	Thu.	4	at Philadelphia		Tue.	3	at Toronto
	Sat.	6	at Montreal		Sat.	7	at NY Islanders*
	Wed.	10	Pittsburgh		Tue.	10	Calgary
	Fri.	12	NY Rangers		Thu.	12	Phoenix
	Sat.	13	Buffalo		Sat.	14	at Montreal
	Tue.	16	at Toronto		Tue.	17	Chicago
	Wed.	17	at Buffalo		Wed.	18	at Carolina
	Fri.	19	Ottawa		Fri.	20	Minnesota
	Sun.	21	Philadelphia*		Sun.	22	at Boston*
	Tue.	23	Boston		Mon.	23	at Philadelphia
	Fri.	26	Pittsburgh		Fri.	27	at Chicago
	Sat.	27	at NY Rangers		Sat.	28	Carolina
	Tue.	30	at St. Louis		Mon.	30	at NY Rangers
	Wed.	31	at Dallas	**Apr.**	Wed.	1	at Pittsburgh
Jan.	Fri.	2	Montreal		Fri.	3	Tampa Bay
	Sun.	4	Ottawa*		Sat.	4	at Buffalo
	Tue.	6	at Carolina		Tue.	7	Toronto
	Thu.	8	Atlanta		Thu.	9	at Ottawa
	Sat.	10	at Los Angeles		Sat.	11	Carolina*

* Denotes afternoon game.

Year-by-Year Record

		Home				Road				Overall								
Season	**GP**	**W**	**L**	**T**	**OL**	**W**	**L**	**T**	**OL**	**W**	**L**	**T**	**OL**	**GF**	**GA**	**Pts.**	**Finished**	**Playoff Result**
2007-08	82	25	14	....	2	21	15	....	5	46	29	....	7	206	197	99	2nd, Atlantic Div.	Lost Conf. Quarter-Final
2006-07	82	25	10	....	6	24	14	....	3	49	24	....	9	216	201	107	1st, Atlantic Div.	Lost Conf. Semi-Final
2005-06	82	27	11	....	3	19	16	....	6	46	27	....	9	242	229	101	1st, Atlantic Div.	Lost Conf. Semi-Final
2004-05	....	....	....	....	....	....	....	....	....	....	....	....	....	....	....	....		
2003-04	82	22	13	5	1	21	12	7	1	43	25	12	2	213	164	100	2nd, Atlantic Div.	Lost Conf. Quarter-Final
2002-03	**82**	**25**	**11**	**3**	**2**	**21**	**9**	**7**	**4**	**46**	**20**	**10**	**6**	**216**	**166**	**108**	**1st, Atlantic Div.**	**Won Stanley Cup**
2001-02	82	22	13	4	2	19	15	5	2	41	28	9	4	205	187	95	3rd, Atlantic Div.	Lost Conf. Quarter-Final
2000-01	82	24	11	6	0	24	8	6	3	48	19	12	3	295	195	111	1st, Atlantic Div.	Lost Final
1999-2000	**82**	**28**	**9**	**3**	**1**	**17**	**15**	**5**	**4**	**45**	**24**	**8**	**5**	**251**	**203**	**103**	**2nd, Atlantic Div.**	**Won Stanley Cup**
1998-99	82	19	14	8	....	28	10	3	....	47	24	11	....	248	196	105	1st, Atlantic Div.	Lost Conf. Quarter-Final
1997-98	82	29	10	2	....	19	13	9	....	48	23	11	....	225	166	107	1st, Atlantic Div.	Lost Conf. Quarter-Final
1996-97	82	23	9	9	....	22	14	5	....	45	23	14	....	231	182	104	1st, Atlantic Div.	Lost Conf. Semi-Final
1995-96	82	22	17	2	....	15	16	10	....	37	33	12	....	215	202	86	6th, Atlantic Div.	Out of Playoffs
1994-95	**48**	**14**	**4**	**6**	....	**8**	**14**	**2**	....	**22**	**18**	**8**	....	**136**	**121**	**52**	**2nd, Atlantic Div.**	**Won Stanley Cup**
1993-94	84	29	11	2	....	18	14	10	....	47	25	12	....	306	220	106	2nd, Atlantic Div.	Lost Conf. Championship
1992-93	84	24	14	4	....	16	23	3	....	40	37	7	....	308	299	87	4th, Patrick Div.	Lost Div. Semi-Final
1991-92	80	24	12	4	....	14	19	3	....	38	31	11	....	289	259	87	4th, Patrick Div.	Lost Div. Semi-Final
1990-91	80	23	10	7	....	9	23	8	....	32	33	15	....	272	264	79	4th, Patrick Div.	Lost Div. Semi-Final
1989-90	80	22	15	3	....	15	19	6	....	37	34	9	....	295	288	83	2nd, Patrick Div.	Lost Div. Semi-Final
1988-89	80	17	18	5	....	10	23	7	....	27	41	12	....	281	325	66	5th, Patrick Div.	Out of Playoffs
1987-88	80	23	16	1	....	15	20	5	....	38	36	6	....	295	296	82	4th, Patrick Div.	Lost Conf. Championship
1986-87	80	20	17	3	....	9	28	3	....	29	45	6	....	293	368	64	6th, Patrick Div.	Out of Playoffs
1985-86	80	17	21	2	....	11	28	1	....	28	49	3	....	300	374	59	6th, Patrick Div.	Out of Playoffs
1984-85	80	13	21	6	....	9	27	4	....	22	48	10	....	264	346	54	5th, Patrick Div.	Out of Playoffs
1983-84	80	10	28	2	....	7	28	5	....	17	56	7	....	231	350	41	5th, Patrick Div.	Out of Playoffs
1982-83	80	11	20	9	....	6	29	5	....	17	49	14	....	230	338	48	5th, Patrick Div.	Out of Playoffs
1981-82**	80	14	21	5	....	4	28	8	....	18	49	13	....	241	362	49	5th, Smythe Div.	Out of Playoffs
1980-81**	80	15	16	9	....	7	29	4	....	22	45	13	....	258	344	57	5th, Smythe Div.	Out of Playoffs
1979-80**	80	12	20	8	....	7	28	5	....	19	48	13	....	234	308	51	6th, Smythe Div.	Out of Playoffs
1978-79**	80	8	24	8	....	7	29	4	....	15	53	12	....	210	331	42	4th, Smythe Div.	Out of Playoffs
1977-78**	80	17	14	9	....	2	26	12	....	19	40	21	....	257	305	59	2nd, Smythe Div.	Lost Prelim. Round
1976-77**	80	12	20	8	....	8	26	6	....	20	46	14	....	226	307	54	5th, Smythe Div.	Out of Playoffs
1975-76*	80	8	24	8	....	4	32	4	....	12	56	12	....	190	351	36	5th, Smythe Div.	Out of Playoffs
1974-75*	80	12	20	8	....	3	34	3	....	15	54	11	....	184	328	41	5th, Smythe Div.	Out of Playoffs

* Kansas City Scouts. ** Colorado Rockies.

NHL EASTERN CONFERENCE

ATLANTIC DIVISION
35th NHL Season

Franchise date: June 11, 1974

Transferred from Denver to New Jersey, June 30, 1982.
Transferred from Kansas City to Denver, August 25, 1976.

2008-09 Player Personnel

FORWARDS	HT	WT	S	Place of Birth	*Age	2007-08 Club
BERGFORS, Nicklas	5-11	190	R	Sodertalje, Sweden	21	New Jersey-Lowell
BERUBE, Jean-Sebastien	6-3	185	L	Matane, Que.	18	Rouyn-Noranda
CLARKSON, David	6-1	200	R	Toronto, Ont.	24	New Jersey
CORMIER, Patrice	6-2	200	L	Moncton, N. B.	18	Rimouski
DAVIS, Patrick	6-3	210	R	Sterling, MI	21	Lowell
DiSALVATORE, Jon	6-1	200	R	Bangor, ME	27	San Antonio
ELIAS, Patrik	6-1	195	L	Trebic, Czech.	32	New Jersey
FEDOROV, Fedor	6-4	230	L	Appatity, USSR	27	Dynamo Moscow
GIONTA, Brian	5-7	175	R	Rochester, NY	29	New Jersey
GIONTA, Stephen	5-7	180	R	Rochester, NY	24	Lowell
HALISCHUK, Matt	5-11	175	R	Toronto, Ont.	20	Kitchener
HENRIQUE, Adam	5-11	185	L	Brantford, Ont.	18	Windsor
HOLIK, Bobby	6-4	230	R	Jihlava, Czech.	37	Atlanta
LANGENBRUNNER, Jamie	6-1	205	R	Cloquet, MN	33	New Jersey
LETOURNEAU-LEBLOND, Pierre-Luc	6-2	220	L	Levis, Que.	23	Lowell-Trenton
MADDEN, John	5-11	190	L	Barrie, Ont.	35	New Jersey
MURPHY, Ryan	6-1	205	L	Van Nuys, CA	29	Lowell
NAGY, Kory	5-11	195	L	London, Ont.	18	Oshawa
PALMIERI, Nick	6-3	215	R	Utica, NY	19	Erie (OHL)-Lowell
PANDOLFO, Jay	6-1	190	L	Winchester, MA	33	New Jersey
PARISE, Zach	5-11	190	L	Minneapolis, MN	24	New Jersey
PELLEY, Rod	6-0	200	L	Kitimat, B.C.	24	New Jersey-Lowell
ROLSTON, Brian	6-2	210	L	Flint, MI	35	Minnesota
ROMANO, Tony	5-11	175	R	Smithtown, NY	20	London
RUPP, Mike	6-5	230	L	Cleveland, OH	28	New Jersey
SNETSINGER, Brad	6-1	185	L	Ajax, Ont.	21	Windsor
TALLACKSON, Barry	6-5	215	R	Grafton, ND	25	New Jersey-Lowell
VRANA, Petr	5-10	190	L	Sternberk, Czech.	23	Lowell
WISEMAN, Chad	6-1	210	L	Burlington, Ont.	27	Wolfsburg
ZAJAC, Travis	6-2	200	R	Winnipeg, Man.	23	New Jersey
ZHARKOV, Vladimir	6-0	185	L	Elektrostal, USSR	20	CSKA-CSKA 2
ZUBRUS, Dainius	6-5	225	L	Elektrenai, USSR	30	New Jersey
DEFENSEMEN						
BROOKBANK, Sheldon	6-2	215	R	Lanigan, Sask.	28	New Jersey-Lowell
CORRENTE, Matthew	6-0	195	R	Mississauga, Ont.	20	Niagara
DELAHEY, Matt	6-3	215	L	Moose Jaw, Sask.	19	Regina
ECKFORD, Tyler	6-3	220	L	Vancouver, B.C.	23	Alaska
FRASER, Mark	6-3	220	L	Ottawa, Ont.	22	Lowell
GREENE, Andy	5-11	195	L	Trenton, MI	25	New Jersey
LEACH, Jay	6-4	220	L	Syracuse, NY	29	T.B.-Norfolk-Port (AHL)
MAGNAN-GRENIER, Olivier	6-2	200	L	Sherbrooke, Que.	22	Lowell
MARTIN, Paul	6-1	195	L	Minneapolis, MN	27	New Jersey
MOLLE, Ryan	6-3	195	R	Winnipeg, Man.	19	Swift Current
MOTTAU, Mike	6-0	190	L	Quincy, MA	30	New Jersey
ODUYA, Johnny	6-0	200	L	Stockholm, Sweden	27	New Jersey
SALMELA, Anssi	5-11	190	L	Tampere, Finland	24	Tappara
SALVADOR, Bryce	6-2	220	L	Brandon, Man.	32	St. Louis-New Jersey
SPILLER, Matthew	6-5	235	L	Daysland, Alta.	25	NY Islanders-Bridgeport
VISHNEVSKI, Vitaly	6-2	215	L	Kharkov, USSR	28	New Jersey
WHITE, Colin	6-4	220	L	New Glasgow, N.S.	30	New Jersey
YOUNG, Harry	6-4	205	L	Windsor, Ont.	18	Windsor
ZIMMERMAN, Sean	6-2	210	R	Denver, CO	21	Lowell-Trenton

GOALTENDERS	HT	WT	C	Place of Birth	*Age	2007-08 Club
BRODEUR, Martin	6-2	215	L	Montreal, Que.	36	New Jersey
CLEMMENSEN, Scott	6-3	205	L	Des Moines, IA	31	Toronto-Toronto (AHL)
FRAZEE, Jeff	6-0	195	L	Edina, MN	21	U. of Minnesota-Lowell
WEEKES, Kevin	6-2	215	L	Toronto, Ont.	33	New Jersey

* – Age at start of 2008-09 season

2007-08 Scoring

* – rookie

Regular Season

Pos	#	Player	Team	GP	G	A	Pts	TOI	+/–	PIM	PP	SH	GW	S	%
L	9	Zach Parise	N.J.	81	32	33	65	18:03	13	25	10	1	8	266	12.0
L	26	Patrik Elias	N.J.	74	20	35	55	18:28	10	38	7	0	8	263	7.6
R	14	Brian Gionta	N.J.	82	22	31	53	18:16	1	46	8	1	4	257	8.6
C	11	John Madden	N.J.	80	20	23	43	19:26	1	26	3	3	3	185	10.8
R	15	Jamie Langenbrunner	N.J.	64	13	28	41	18:17	–1	30	5	1	2	152	8.6
R	16	Dainius Zubrus	N.J.	82	13	25	38	15:41	2	38	4	0	2	128	10.2
C	19	Travis Zajac	N.J.	82	14	20	34	16:44	–11	31	5	0	1	155	9.0
D	7	Paul Martin	N.J.	73	5	27	32	23:53	20	22	2	0	2	93	5.4
D	29	John Oduya	N.J.	75	6	20	26	19:01	27	46	2	0	0	63	9.5
L	20	Jay Pandolfo	N.J.	54	12	12	24	17:16	10	22	0	0	1	78	15.4
R	23 *	David Clarkson	N.J.	81	9	13	22	12:01	1	183	0	0	1	151	6.0
D	27	Mike Mottau	N.J.	76	4	13	17	20:39	–11	48	1	0	1	68	5.9
L	18	Sergei Brylin	N.J.	82	6	10	16	13:32	–5	20	0	0	1	65	9.2
D	28	Karel Rachunek	N.J.	47	4	9	13	19:23	3	40	0	0	0	68	5.9
D	24	Bryce Salvador	STL	56	1	10	11	19:38	12	43	0	0	1	29	3.4
			N.J.	8	0	0	0	20:54	0	11	0	0	0	0	0.0
			Total	64	1	10	11	19:47	12	54	0	0	1	29	3.4
R	22	Arron Asham	N.J.	77	6	4	10	08:33	–6	84	0	0	2	68	8.8
D	5	Colin White	N.J.	57	2	8	10	19:40	–5	26	0	0	1	27	7.4
D	6 *	Andy Greene	N.J.	59	2	8	10	19:30	0	22	2	0	0	50	4.0
C	17	Mike Rupp	N.J.	64	3	6	9	08:03	–8	58	1	0	0	69	4.3
D	8	Sheldon Brookbank	N.J.	44	0	8	8	15:08	0	63	0	0	0	43	0.0
D	2	Vitaly Vishnevski	N.J.	69	2	5	7	15:32	–12	50	0	0	0	48	4.2
C	10 *	Rod Pelley	N.J.	58	2	4	6	09:18	–3	19	0	0	1	59	3.4
L	12	Noah Clarke	N.J.	1	1	0	1	10:39	0	0	0	0	0	3	33.3
R	12 *	Nicklas Bergfors	N.J.	1	0	0	0	11:17	–1	0	0	0	0	3	0.0
D	24 *	Olli Malmivaara	N.J.	2	0	0	0	08:48	2	0	0	0	0	0	0.0
R	21 *	Barry Tallackson	N.J.	3	0	0	0	07:03	0	0	0	0	0	0	0.0

Goaltending

No.	Goaltender	GPI	Mins	Avg	W	L	OT	EN	SO	GA	SA	S%	G	A	PIM
30	Martin Brodeur	77	4635	2.17	44	27	6	8	4	168	2089	.920	0	4	6
1	Kevin Weekes	9	343	2.97	2	2	1	0	0	17	160	.894	0	0	2
	Totals	**82**	**5002**	**2.32**	**46**	**29**	**7**	**8**	**4**	**193**	**2257**	**.914**			

Playoffs

Pos	#	Player	Team	GP	G	A	Pts	TOI	+/–	PIM	PP	SH	GW	OT	S	%
L	26	Patrik Elias	N.J.	5	4	2	6	20:30	–5	4	3	0	0	0	18	22.2
L	9	Zach Parise	N.J.	5	1	4	5	18:28	–5	2	1	0	0	0	20	5.0
R	15	Jamie Langenbrunner	N.J.	5	0	4	4	18:29	–5	4	0	0	0	0	18	0.0
C	11	John Madden	N.J.	5	2	1	3	21:17	–5	2	0	0	1	1	14	14.3
D	7	Paul Martin	N.J.	5	1	2	3	25:35	–8	2	1	0	0	0	13	7.7
L	18	Sergei Brylin	N.J.	5	1	0	1	11:39	0	0	0	0	0	0	4	25.0
D	24	Bryce Salvador	N.J.	5	1	0	1	17:55	1	2	0	0	0	0	1	100.0
D	27	Mike Mottau	N.J.	5	1	0	1	21:24	–3	0	0	0	0	0	4	25.0
R	14	Brian Gionta	N.J.	5	1	0	1	17:52	–2	2	0	0	0	0	14	7.1
R	16	Dainius Zubrus	N.J.	5	0	1	1	16:18	–3	8	0	0	0	0	5	0.0
R	22	Arron Asham	N.J.	5	0	1	1	05:04	1	2	0	0	0	0	3	0.0
C	17	Mike Rupp	N.J.	5	0	1	1	07:48	1	2	0	0	0	0	3	0.0
D	29	John Oduya	N.J.	5	0	1	1	20:40	–5	6	0	0	0	0	2	0.0
C	19	Travis Zajac	N.J.	5	0	1	1	13:35	0	4	0	0	0	0	3	0.0
D	6 *	Andy Greene	N.J.	2	0	0	0	15:11	–1	0	0	0	0	0	2	0.0
D	2	Vitaly Vishnevski	N.J.	3	0	0	0	13:29	3	2	0	0	0	0	1	0.0
L	20	Jay Pandolfo	N.J.	5	0	0	0	16:15	–2	2	0	0	0	0	13	0.0
D	5	Colin White	N.J.	5	0	0	0	20:27	–2	6	0	0	0	0	3	0.0
R	23 *	David Clarkson	N.J.	5	0	0	0	12:19	–2	4	0	0	0	0	3	0.0

Goaltending

No.	Goaltender	GPI	Mins	Avg	W	L	EN	SO	GA	SA	S%	G	A	PIM
30	Martin Brodeur	5	301	3.19	1	4	3	0	16	147	.891	0	0	2
	Totals	**5**	**306**	**3.73**	**1**	**4**	**3**	**0**	**19**	**150**	**.873**			

Lou Lamoriello

President and General Manager

Born: Providence, RI, October 21, 1942.

Lou Lamoriello has been president and general manager of the Devils since 1987-88 following more than 20 years with Providence College as a player, coach and administrator. His trades, signings and draft choices helped lead the Devils to their first Stanley Cup Championship in 1995 and were followed by victories again in 2000 and 2003. During his tenure, the Devils have had ten 100-point seasons, four Eastern Conference titles and seven Atlantic Division regular-season championships. In 2005-06, Lamoriello took over behind the bench and coached the Devils to first place in the Atlantic Division.

While at Providence, Lamoriello served as hockey coach for 15 seasons, compiling an impressive .578 winning percentage (248-179-13), while guiding the Friars to 12 post-season tournaments in a row. During his last five seasons (1978-83) of coaching, the school compiled a record of 107-58-4 and had more players drafted by the National Hockey League after entering college than any other college team during those years. Lamoriello helped propel numerous players and administrators toward NHL careers during his tenure at Providence. He was hired as president of the Devils on April 30, 1987, and assumed the responsibility of general manager on September 10, 1987. Lamoriello was G.M. of Team USA for the first World Cup of Hockey in 1996 as the U.S. captured the championship. He was also the G.M. for the 1998 U.S. Olympic Team.

Coaching Record

			Regular Season				Playoffs			
Season	Team	League	GC	W	L	O/T	GC	W	L	T
2005-06	New Jersey	NHL	50	32	14	4	9	5	4	....
2006-07	New Jersey	NHL	3	2	0	1	11	5	6	....
	NHL Totals		**53**	**34**	**14**	**5**	**20**	**10**	**10**	....

Captains' History

Simon Nolet, 1974-75 to 1976-77; Wilf Paiement, 1977-78; Gary Croteau, 1978-79; Mike Christie, Rene Robert and Lanny McDonald, 1979-80; Lanny McDonald, 1980-81; Lanny McDonald and Rob Ramage, 1981-82; Don Lever, 1982-83; Don Lever and Mel Bridgman, 1983-84; Mel Bridgman, 1984-85 to 1986-87; Kirk Muller, 1987-88 to 1990-91; Bruce Driver, 1991-92; Scott Stevens, 1992-93 to 2002-03; Scott Stevens and Scott Neidermayer, 2003-04; no captain, 2005-06; Patrik Elias, 2006-07; Patrik Elias and Jamie Langenbrunner, 2007-08; Jamie Langenbrunner, 2008-09.

Coaching History

Bep Guidolin, 1974-75; Bep Guidolin, Sid Abel and Eddie Bush, 1975-76; Johnny Wilson, 1976-77; Pat Kelly, 1977-78; Pat Kelly and Aldo Guidolin, 1978-79; Don Cherry, 1979-80; Bill MacMillan, 1980-81; Bert Marshall and Marshall Johnston, 1981-82; Bill MacMillan, 1982-83; Bill MacMillan and Tom McVie, 1983-84; Doug Carpenter, 1984-85 to 1986-87; Doug Carpenter and Jim Schoenfeld, 1987-88; Jim Schoenfeld, 1988-89; Jim Schoenfeld and John Cunniff, 1989-90; John Cunniff and Tom McVie, 1990-91; Tom McVie, 1991-92; Herb Brooks, 1992-93; Jacques Lemaire, 1993-94 to 1997-98; Robbie Ftorek, 1998-99; Robbie Ftorek and Larry Robinson, 1999-2000; Larry Robinson, 2000-01; Larry Robinson and Kevin Constantine, 2001-02; Pat Burns, 2002-03 to 2004-05; Larry Robinson and Lou Lamoriello, 2005-06; Claude Julien and Lou Lamoriello, 2006-07; Brent Sutter, 2007-08 to date.

Club Records

Team

(Figures in brackets for season records are games played; records for fewest points, wins, ties, losses, goals, goals against are for 70 or more games)

Most Points	**111**	2000-01 (82)
Most Wins	**49**	2006-07 (82)
Most Ties	**21**	1977-78 (80)
Most Losses	**56**	1975-76 (80), 1983-84 (80)
Most Goals	**308**	1992-93 (84)
Most Goals Against	**374**	1985-86 (80)
Fewest Points	***36**	1975-76 (80)
	41	1983-84 (80)
Fewest Wins	***12**	1975-76 (80)
	17	1982-83 (80), 1983-84 (80)
Fewest Ties	**3**	1985-86 (80)
Fewest Losses	**19**	2000-01 (82)
Fewest Goals	***184**	1974-75 (80)
	205	2001-02 (82)
Fewest Goals Against	**164**	2003-04 (82)
Longest Winning Streak		
Overall	**13**	Feb. 26-Mar. 23/01
Home	**8**	Oct. 9-Nov. 7/87, Jan. 3-Feb. 4/03, Jan. 3-Feb. 7/06
Away	****10**	Feb. 27-Apr. 7/01
Longest Undefeated Streak		
Overall	**13**	Four times
Home	**15**	Jan. 8-Mar. 15/97 (9 wins, 6 ties)
Away	**10**	Feb. 27-Apr. 7/01 (10 wins)
Longest Losing Streak		
Overall	***14**	Dec. 30/75-Jan. 29/76
	10	Oct. 14-Nov. 4/83
Home	**9**	Dec. 22/85-Feb. 6/86
Away	**12**	Oct. 19-Dec. 1/83
Longest Winless Streak		
Overall	***27**	Feb. 12-Apr. 4/76 (21 losses, 6 ties)
	18	Oct. 20-Nov. 26/82 (14 losses 4 ties)
Home	***14**	Feb. 12-Mar. 30/76 (10 losses, 4 ties), Feb. 4-Mar. 31/79 (12 losses, 2 ties)
	9	Dec. 22/85-Feb. 6/86 (9 losses)
Away	***32**	Nov. 12/77-Mar. 15/78 (22 losses, 10 ties)
	14	Dec. 26/82-Mar. 5/83 (13 losses, 1 tie)
Most Shutouts, Season	**14**	2003-04 (82)
Most PIM, Season	**2,494**	1988-89 (80)
Most Goals, Game	**9**	Nine times

Individual

Most Seasons	**20**	Ken Daneyko
Most Games	**1,283**	Ken Daneyko
Most Goals, Career	**347**	John MacLean
Most Assists, Career	**364**	Scott Niedermayer, Patrik Elias
Most Points, Career	**701**	John MacLean (347G, 354A)
Most PIM, Career	**2,519**	Ken Daneyko
Most Shutouts, Career	**96**	Martin Brodeur
Longest Consecutive Games Streak	**388**	Ken Daneyko (Nov. 4/89-Mar. 29/94)
Most Goals, Season	**48**	Brian Gionta (2005-06)
Most Assists, Season	**60**	Scott Stevens (1993-94)
Most Points, Season	**96**	Patrik Elias (2000-01; 40G, 56A)
Most PIM, Season	**295**	Krzysztof Oliwa (1997-98)
Most Points, Defenseman, Season	**78**	Scott Stevens (1993-94; 18G, 60A)
Most Points, Center, Season	**94**	Kirk Muller (1987-88; 37G, 57A)
Most Points, Right Wing, Season	**89**	Brian Gionta (2005-06; 48G, 41A)
Most Points, Left Wing, Season	**96**	Patrik Elias (2000-01; 40G, 56A)
Most Points, Rookie, Season	**70**	Scott Gomez (1999-2000; 19G, 51A)
Most Shutouts, Season	**12**	Martin Brodeur (2006-07)
Most Goals, Game	**4**	Five times
Most Assists, Game	**5**	Greg Adams (Oct. 10/85), Kirk Muller (Mar. 25/87), Tom Kurvers (Feb. 13/89), Scott Gomez (Mar. 30/03)
Most Points, Game	**6**	Kirk Muller (Nov. 29/86; 3G, 3A)

* Records include Kansas City Scouts and Colorado Rockies, 1974-75 through 1981-82.

** NHL Record.

General Managers' History

Sid Abel, 1974-75, 1975-76; Ray Miron, 1976-77 to 1980-81; Bill MacMillan, 1981-82, 1982-83; Bill MacMillan and Max McNab, 1983-84; Max McNab 1984-85 to 1986-87; Lou Lamoriello, 1987-88 to date.

Retired Numbers

3	Ken Daneyko	1982-2003
4	Scott Stevens	1991-2005

All-time Record vs. Other Clubs

Regular Season

	At Home								On Road								Total							
	GP	W	L	T	OL	GF	GA	PTS	GP	W	L	T	OL	GF	GA	PTS	GP	W	L	T	OL	GF	GA	PTS
Anaheim	9	7	2	0	0	32	16	14	11	5	5	1	0	28	30	11	20	12	7	1	0	60	46	25
Atlanta	16	8	4	1	3	46	35	20	16	9	3	2	2	59	38	22	32	17	7	3	5	105	73	42
Boston	59	20	28	11	0	157	186	51	62	21	31	8	2	193	235	52	121	41	59	19	2	350	421	103
Buffalo	60	24	27	9	0	177	187	57	60	18	33	8	1	180	230	45	120	42	60	17	1	357	417	102
Calgary	46	15	28	3	0	129	166	33	43	7	27	8	1	112	184	23	89	22	55	11	1	241	350	56
Carolina	51	29	18	4	0	178	157	62	50	22	18	8	2	149	149	54	101	51	36	12	2	327	306	116
Chicago	48	21	16	11	0	149	143	53	47	13	24	10	0	130	178	36	95	34	40	21	0	279	321	89
Colorado	37	19	13	4	1	150	125	43	36	14	18	4	0	102	126	32	73	33	31	8	1	252	251	75
Columbus	3	2	0	1	0	6	4	5	5	2	2	0	1	15	16	5	8	4	2	1	1	21	20	10
Dallas	44	22	19	3	0	150	134	47	46	13	26	6	1	118	167	33	90	35	45	9	1	268	301	80
Detroit	41	21	11	9	0	139	105	51	41	13	25	2	1	131	169	29	82	34	36	11	1	270	274	80
Edmonton	34	15	16	3	0	113	113	33	32	12	14	6	0	117	137	30	66	27	30	9	0	230	250	63
Florida	30	19	8	3	0	89	58	41	31	17	10	4	0	81	69	38	61	36	18	7	0	170	127	79
Los Angeles	44	20	19	5	0	148	151	45	43	8	27	6	2	132	204	24	87	28	46	11	2	280	355	69
Minnesota	4	3	0	1	0	16	10	7	4	2	1	1	0	12	10	5	8	5	1	2	0	28	20	12
Montreal	60	30	26	4	0	184	204	64	60	19	34	6	1	147	194	45	120	49	60	10	1	331	398	109
Nashville	6	2	3	0	1	18	18	5	6	5	1	0	0	18	12	10	12	7	4	0	1	36	30	15
NY Islanders	96	40	43	11	2	303	323	93	97	25	58	11	3	273	379	64	193	65	101	22	5	576	702	157
NY Rangers	98	52	37	7	2	326	306	113	96	27	45	20	4	278	352	78	194	79	82	27	6	604	658	191
Ottawa	29	17	10	2	0	80	70	36	30	18	8	3	1	76	70	40	59	35	18	5	1	156	140	76
Philadelphia	95	54	33	8	0	325	301	116	97	30	56	10	1	252	359	71	192	84	89	18	1	577	660	187
Phoenix	30	12	12	6	0	96	91	30	32	7	22	3	0	82	117	17	62	19	34	9	0	178	208	47
Pittsburgh	93	45	34	13	1	329	303	104	91	43	43	4	1	303	328	91	184	88	77	17	2	632	631	195
St. Louis	47	22	18	7	0	148	131	51	47	13	26	7	1	148	195	34	94	35	44	14	1	296	326	85
San Jose	13	8	4	1	0	47	26	17	11	6	3	1	1	32	26	14	24	14	7	2	1	79	52	31
Tampa Bay	32	21	7	2	2	114	63	46	31	15	9	5	2	90	70	37	63	36	16	7	4	204	133	83
Toronto	52	20	15	15	2	177	160	57	54	15	34	5	0	150	193	35	106	35	49	20	2	327	353	92
Vancouver	50	21	21	6	2	154	159	50	48	9	28	11	0	130	180	29	98	30	49	17	2	284	339	79
Washington	85	43	34	7	1	259	243	94	85	29	50	6	0	242	321	64	170	72	84	13	1	501	564	158
Defunct Clubs	8	4	2	2	0	25	19	10	8	2	3	3	0	19	27	7	16	6	5	5	0	44	46	17
Totals	**1320**	**636**	**508**	**159**	**17**	**4264**	**4007**	**1448**	**1320**	**439**	**684**	**169**	**28**	**3799**	**4765**	**1075**	**2640**	**1075**	**1192**	**328**	**45**	**8063**	**8772**	**2523**

Playoffs

	Series	W	L	GP	W	L	T	GF	GA	Last Mtg.	Rnd.	Result
Anaheim	1	1	0	7	4	3	0	19	12	2003	F	W 4-3
Boston	4	3	1	23	15	8	0	68	60	2003	CQF	W 4-1
Buffalo	1	1	0	7	4	3	0	14	14	1994	CQF	W 4-3
Carolina	3	1	2	17	7	10	0	41	34	2006	CSF	L 1-4
Colorado	1	0	1	7	3	4	0	11	19	2001	F	L 3-4
Dallas	1	1	0	6	4	2	0	15	9	2000	F	W 4-2
Detroit	1	1	0	4	4	0	0	16	7	1995	F	W 4-0
Florida	1	1	0	4	4	0	0	12	6	2000	CQF	W 4-0
Montreal	1	1	0	5	4	1	0	22	11	1997	CQF	W 4-1
NY Islanders	1	1	0	6	4	2	0	23	18	1988	DSF	W 4-2
NY Rangers	5	1	4	28	12	16	0	75	79	2008	CQF	L 1-4
Ottawa	3	1	2	18	7	11	0	40	41	2007	CSF	L 1-4
Philadelphia	4	2	2	20	9	11	0	50	49	2004	CQF	L 1-4
Pittsburgh	5	2	3	29	15	14	0	86	80	2001	CF	W 4-1
Tampa Bay	2	2	0	11	8	3	0	33	22	2007	CQF	W 4-2
Toronto	2	2	0	13	8	5	0	37	27	2001	CSF	W 4-3
Washington	2	1	1	13	6	7	0	43	44	1990	DSF	L 2-4
Totals	**38**	**22**	**16**	**218**	**118**	**100**	**0**	**605**	**532**			

Playoff Results 2008-2003

Year	Round	Opponent	Result	GF	GA
2008	CQF	NY Rangers	L 1-4	12	19
2007	CSF	Ottawa	L 1-4	11	15
	CQF	Tampa Bay	W 4-2	19	14
2006	CSF	Carolina	L 1-4	10	17
	CQF	NY Rangers	W 4-0	17	4
2004	CQF	Philadelphia	L 1-4	9	14
2003	**F**	**Anaheim**	**W 4-3**	**19**	**12**
	CF	Ottawa	W 4-3	17	13
	CSF	Tampa Bay	W 4-1	14	8
	CQF	Boston	W 4-1	13	8

Abbreviations: Round: F – Final; **CF** – conference final; **CSF** – conference semi-final; **CQF** – conference quarter-final; **DSF** – division semi-final.

Calgary totals include Atlanta Flames, 1974-75 to 1979-80.
Colorado totals include Quebec, 1979-80 to 1994-95.
Phoenix totals include Winnipeg, 1979-80 to 1995-96.

Carolina totals include Hartford, 1979-80 to 1996-97.
Dallas totals include Minnesota North Stars, 1974-75 to 1992-93.

2007-08 Results

Oct.	4	at Tampa Bay	1-3
	6	at Florida	4-1
	8	at Ottawa	2-4
	11	at Florida	0-3
	13	at Atlanta	6-5
	17	at Pittsburgh	5-4
	18	at Philadelphia	0-4
	20	at NY Islanders	3-4*
	25	at NY Rangers	0-2
	27	Ottawa	1-4
	31	Tampa Bay	6-1
Nov.	2	Toronto	3-2
	3	at NY Rangers	1-2†
	5	Pittsburgh	0-5
	8	Philadelphia	4-1
	10	at NY Islanders	1-2
	12	at Pittsburgh	3-2
	14	NY Rangers	2-4
	16	NY Islanders	0-1
	17	at Philadelphia	6-2
	21	at Pittsburgh	2-1
	23	at Atlanta	3-0
	24	at Tampa Bay	3-2
	28	Dallas	4-2
	30	Montreal	4-0
Dec.	2	Atlanta	3-2†
	5	Boston	4-3*
	7	Washington	3-2
	9	at NY Rangers	0-1*
	10	at Washington	2-3
	13	at Boston	3-1
	15	Phoenix	1-4
	16	Philadelphia	4-2
	18	at Vancouver	0-5
	21	at Edmonton	3-1
	23	at Calgary	1-0*
	28	Buffalo	2-1†
	29	at NY Islanders	2-5
Jan.	2	Florida	3-2
	4	Philadelphia	3-0
	5	at Boston	3-4
	8	Buffalo	2-1†
	10	at Carolina	4-1
	12	at Buffalo	3-2†
	16	NY Islanders	1-3
	18	Florida	1-2
	20	Toronto	3-2
	22	at Philadelphia	7-3
	24	Montreal	3-4
	29	Pittsburgh	2-4
Feb.	1	NY Rangers	1-3
	2	Los Angeles	6-3
	4	Pittsburgh	4-3*
	6	at Buffalo	2-3†
	8	Anaheim	1-2
	9	Carolina	6-1
	13	Ottawa	3-2*
	15	Atlanta	3-4†
	16	at Ottawa	3-2
	18	Carolina	5-1
	20	San Jose	3-2
	23	NY Islanders	4-2
	24	at Washington	2-1*
	26	at Carolina	1-2*
	29	Washington	0-4
Mar.	1	at Montreal	1-2
	4	at Toronto	4-1
	7	Tampa Bay	2-1*
	8	at Toronto	2-1
	11	at Montreal	0-4
	13	at Minnesota	4-3†
	15	at Colorado	4-2
	19	NY Rangers	1-2†
	21	NY Islanders	1-3
	22	at Pittsburgh	1-7
	25	Pittsburgh	0-2
	27	at NY Rangers	2-3
	28	Philadelphia	5-4†
Apr.	1	at NY Islanders	2-1*
	2	Boston	3-2†
	4	at Philadelphia	0-3
	6	NY Rangers	3-2†

* – Overtime † – Shootout

Entry Draft Selections 2008-1994

Name in bold denotes played in NHL.

2008
Pick
24 Mattias Tedenby
52 Brandon Burlon
54 Patrice Cormier
82 Adam Henrique
112 Matt Delahey
142 Kory Nagy
172 David Wohlberg
202 Harry Young
205 Jean-Sebastien Berube

2007
Pick
57 Mike Hoeffel
79 Nick Palmieri
87 Corbin McPherson
117 Matt Halischuk
177 Vili Sopanen
207 Ryan Molle

2006
Pick
30 Matthew Corrente
58 Alexander Vasyunov
67 Kirill Tulupov
77 Vladimir Zharkov
107 Tyler Miller
148 Olivier Magnan-Grenier
178 Tony Romano
208 Kyell Henegan

2005
Pick
23 **Nicklas Bergfors**
38 Jeff Frazee
84 **Mark Fraser**
99 Patrick Davis
155 Mark Fayne
170 Sean Zimmerman
218 Alexander Sundstrom

2004
Pick
20 **Travis Zajac**
155 Alexander Mikhailishin
185 Josh Disher
216 Pierre-Luc Letourneau-Leblond
217 Tyler Eckford
250 Nathan Perkovich
282 Valeri Klimov

2003
Pick
17 **Zach Parise**
42 Petr Vrana
93 Ivan Khomutov
167 Zach Tarkir
197 Jason Smith
261 **Joey Tenute**
292 Arseny Bondarev

2002
Pick
51 Anton Kadeykin
53 **Barry Tallackson**
64 **Jason Ryznar**
84 Marek Chvatal
85 Ahren Nittel
117 **Cam Janssen**
154 Krisjanis Redlihs
187 Eric Johansson
218 Ilkka Pikkarainen
250 Dan Glover
281 Bill Kinkel

2001
Pick
28 Adrian Foster
44 Igor Pohanka
48 **Tuomas Pihlman**
60 Victor Uchevatov
67 Robin Leblanc
72 **Brandon Nolan**
128 Andrei Posnov
163 **Andreas Salomonsson**
194 James Massen
229 **Aaron Voros**
257 Yevgeny Gamalei

2000
Pick
22 **David Hale**
39 Teemu Laine
56 **Alexander Suglobov**
57 Matt DeMarchi
62 **Paul Martin**
67 Max Birbraer
76 **Mike Rupp**
125 Phil Cole
135 **Mike Danton**
164 Matus Kostur
194 Deryk Engelland
198 Ken Magowan
257 Warren McCutcheon

1999
Pick
27 Ari Ahonen
42 **Mike Commodore**
50 Brett Clouthier
95 Andre Lakos
100 Teemu Kesa
185 Scott Cameron
214 Chris Hartsburg
242 Justin Dziama

1998
Pick
26 **Mike Van Ryn**
27 **Scott Gomez**
37 **Christian Berglund**
82 **Brian Gionta**
96 **Mikko Jokela**
105 **Pierre Dagenais**
119 Anton But
143 **Ryan Flinn**
172 Jacques Lariviere
199 Erik Jensen
227 Marko Ahosilta
257 Ryan Held

1997
Pick
24 **Jean-Francois Damphousse**
38 **Stanislav Gron**
104 Lucas Nehrling
131 **Jiri Bicek**
159 **Sascha Goc**
188 Mathieu Benoit
215 **Scott Clemmensen**
241 Jan Srdinko

1996
Pick
10 **Lance Ward**
38 Wes Mason
41 Josh DeWolf
47 **Pierre Dagenais**
49 **Colin White**
63 **Scott Parker**
91 **Josef Boumedienne**
101 Josh MacNevin
118 Glenn Crawford
145 Sean Ritchlin
173 Daryl Andrews
199 **Willie Mitchell**
205 Jay Bertsch
225 Pasi Petrilainen

1995
Pick
18 **Petr Sykora**
44 **Nathan Perrott**
70 **Sergei Vyshedkevich**
78 **David Gosselin**
79 **Alyn McCauley**
96 Henrik Rehnberg
122 **Chris Mason**
148 Adam Young
174 Richard Rochefort
200 Frederic Henry
226 Colin O'Hara

1994
Pick
25 **Vadim Sharifijanov**
51 **Patrik Elias**
71 **Sheldon Souray**
103 Zdenek Skorepa
129 Christian Gosselin
134 Ryan Smart
155 Luciano Caravaggio
181 Jeff Williams
207 **Eric Bertrand**
233 **Steve Sullivan**
259 Scott Swanjord
269 Mike Hanson

Brent Sutter

Head Coach

Born: Viking, Alta., June 10, 1962.

The New Jersey Devils named Brent Sutter to the position of head coach on July 13, 2007. He is the 14th coach since the club moved to New Jersey in 1982.

Sutter joined the Devils after spending the previous eight seasons as owner, president, general manager and coach of Red Deer of the Western Hockey League. Sutter guided Red Deer to its first league title and the Memorial Cup championship in 2001, and three consecutive WHL Eastern Conference championships from 2001 to 2003. He was the recipient of the 2001 Dunc McCallum Memorial Trophy as the league's top coach. Sutter has also coached internationally, guiding the Canadian national junior team to consecutive 6-0-0 marks and gold medals in 2005 and 2006, becoming the only individual to accomplish that feat.

Brent Sutter is the third youngest of seven Sutter brothers, six of whom played in the NHL. (His son Brandon was Carolina's first choice, 11th overall, in the 2007 NHL Entry Draft.) Brent's NHL playing career spanned 18 seasons with the New York Islanders and Chicago Blackhawks. A center, he recorded 363 goals and 466 assists for 829 points and 1,054 penalty minutes in 1,111 career regular-season games. Sutter added 30 goals and 44 assists for 74 points and 164 penalty minutes in 144 career playoff games.

Along with his brother Duane, he was a member of the Islanders' 1982 and 1983 Stanley Cup championship teams, and served as captain from 1987 through 1991. Sutter was traded to Chicago on October 25, 1991 and played seven more seasons, including three years for his brother Darryl. Sutter retired as a player on April 18, 1998. He was originally the Islanders' first choice, 17th overall, in the 1980 NHL Entry Draft.

Coaching Record

			Regular Season				Playoffs			
Season	**Team**	**League**	**GC**	**W**	**L**	**O/T**	**GC**	**W**	**L**	**T**
99-2000	Red Deer	WHL	72	32	31	9	4	0	4	....
2000-01	Red Deer	WHL	72	54	12	6	22	16	6	....
2001-02	Red Deer	WHL	72	46	18	8	23	14	9	....
2002-03	Red Deer	WHL	72	50	17	5	23	14	9	....
2003-04	Red Deer	WHL	72	35	22	15	19	10	9	....
2004-05	Red Deer	WHL	72	36	26	10	7	3	4	....
2005-06	Red Deer	WHL	72	26	40	6	....	....	....	....
2006-07	Red Deer	WHL	72	35	28	9	7	3	4	....
2007-08	**New Jersey**	**NHL**	**82**	**46**	**29**	**7**	**5**	**1**	**4**	....
	NHL Totals		**82**	**46**	**29**	**7**	**5**	**1**	**4**	....

Club Directory

Prudential Center

New Jersey Devils
Prudential Center
165 Mulberry Street
Newark, NJ 07102
Phone **973/757-6100**
FAX 973/757-6399
www.newjerseydevils.com
Capacity: 17,625

Owners . . . . . Jeff Vanderbeek, Michael Gilfillan, Peter Simon
Chairman/Managing Partner . . . . . Jeff Vanderbeek
President/CEO/General Manager . . . . . Lou Lamoriello
Sr. Executive Vice President/Chief Operating Officer . . . . Chris Modrzynski
Executive Vice President, Operations . . . . . Peter S. McMullen
Executive Vice President/Chief Financial Officer. . . . . Scott Struble
Executive Vice President, Administration. . . . . Gordon Lavalette
Senior Vice President, General Counsel . . . . . Joseph C. Benedetti
Senior Vice President, Ticket Operations. . . . . Terry Farmer
Senior Vice President, Corporate Partnerships. . . . . Kenneth F. Ferriter
Senior Vice President, Facilities. . . . . Mark Gheduzzi
Senior Vice President, Communications . . . . . Mike Levine
Vice President, Ticket Sales/Customer Service . . . . . David Beck
Vice President, Marketing/Community Development . . . Jeff Longo

Hockey Club Personnel
Exec. V.P., Hockey Operations/Director, Scouting . . . . . David Conte
Sr. V.P., Hockey Ops./GM, Lowell/Trenton & Scout. . . . . Chris Lamoriello
Vice President, Hockey Operations . . . . . Steve Pellegrini
Head Coach . . . . . Brent Sutter
Assistant Coaches . . . . . John MacLean, Tommy Albelin
Goaltending Coach . . . . . Jacques Caron
Special Assignment Coaches . . . . . Larry Robinson, Scott Stevens, Pat Burns, Jacques Laperriere, Chris Terreri
Assistant Director, Scouting . . . . . Claude Carrier
Scouting Staff . . . Glen Dirk, Milt Fisher, Ferny Flaman, Dan Labraaten, Scott Lachance, Pierre Mondou, Larry Perris, Marcel Pronovost, Lou Reycroft, Vaclav Slansky, Jr., Steve Smith, Geoff Stevens, Tim Taylor, Ed Thomlinson, Les Widdifield
Pro Scouting Staff. . . . . Bob Hoffmeyer, Jan Ludvig, Andre Boudrias, Gates Orlando
Hockey Ops. Video Coordinator . . . . . Taran Singleton
Hockey Ops. Video Assistant . . . . . Mike Ford
Scouting Staff Assistant . . . . . Callie A. Smith
Head Trainer . . . . . Richard Stinziano
Equipment Manager . . . . . Rich Matthews
Assistant Equipment Managers . . . . . Alex Abasto, Matthew Mitchell, Mike Thibault
Strength/Conditioning Coordinator . . . . . Michael Vasalani
Massage Therapist. . . . . Tommy Plasko
Team Orthopedists . . . . . Dr. Barry Fisher, Dr. Len Jaffe
Team Cardiologist . . . . . Dr. Joseph Niznik
Team Dentist. . . . . Dr. H. Hugh Gardy
Team Optometrist . . . . . Dr. Paul Berman
Fitness Consultant . . . . . Vladimir Bure
Exercise Physiologist . . . . . Dr. Garret Caffrey

President's Office
Hockey Ops. Exec. Asst. to the Pres./CEO/G.M. . . . . . Marie Carnevale
Corp. Exec. Asst. to Pres./CEO/G.M. & Dir., H.R. . . . . . Mary K. Morrison
Administrative Assistant. . . . . Christine DellaBarca
Senior Counsel . . . . . Christine Steinberg
Administrative Assistant, Legal. . . . . Lourdes Garcia

Operations
Receptionist . . . . . Jelsa Belotta
Staff Assistants . . . . . Pat Maione, Kyle Radzinski
Administrative Asst. to the Chief Operating Officer . . . . Alessandra Weingartner

Ticket Operations
Senior Director, Ticket Operations . . . . . Tom Bates
Director, Box Office Operations . . . . . Pat Shark
Ticket Service Managers . . . . . Frank Calandrillo, Kelly Baron
Senior Director, Group Sales . . . . . Neil Desormeaux
Group Sales Managers. . . . . John Tierney, Christine Myers

Sales
Assistant Director, Ticket Sales. . . . . Brooke Alper
Account Managers . . . . . Steve Banes, Robert Cornell, John Picciuto, Aaron Sanders, Isaac Satten, Glenn Sperber, Thomas Stocky
Manager, Inside Sales . . . . . David Krakower
Receptionist, Sales. . . . . Jessica Leschen

Corporate Partnerships
Senior Director, Corporate Partnerships . . . . . Michael DeMartino
Director, Corporate Partner Services. . . . . Matt Dugan
Account Manager, Corporate Partnerships. . . . . Greg Parassio

Marketing/Community Development
Sr. Director, Merchandising . . . . . David Perricone
Manager, Merchandising . . . . . Adam Manger
Sr. Dir., Premium Suites, Single Events/Grassroots. . . . . Michael Merolla
Coord., Premium Suites, Single Events/Grassroots . . . . . Jason Romano
Manager, Game Entertainment . . . . . David Schwinger
Game Entertainment Assistant. . . . . Rob Peters
Game Entertainment Graphics. . . . . Daniel de Graaf
Manager, Web Ops./Creative Services . . . . . Greg Orlando
Coordinator, Web Ops./Creative Services . . . . . Scott Modrzynski
Manager, Marketing . . . . . Heather Hall
Marketing Assistant. . . . . Bridgette Berra

Communications
Senior Director, Communications. . . . . Jeff Altstadter
Assistant Director, Communications. . . . . Pete Albietz
Staff Writer. . . . . Eric Marin
Coordinator, Communications. . . . . Daniel Beam

Finance
Contoller. . . . . Marc Weiss
Accounting Manager. . . . . Kristin Farina
Staff Accountants . . . . . Shanna Curlin, Skyler Daugherty, Shawn Santamaria, Michael Tonjes
Administrative Assistant. . . . . Kristen Gore

Computer Operations
Sr. Director, Programming/Computer Operations . . . . . Jack Skelley
Programmer/Analyst . . . . . Joseph Wyks
Systems Administrator . . . . . Mike Tukes
Technical Assistant . . . . . Antonio da Silva

Devils Arena Entertainment
Senior Vice President, Arena Operations. . . . . Jim Cima
Executive Asst. to the Chairman/Managing Partner . . . . Debbie Hildebrant
Director, Security. . . . . Les Wiser
Business Coordinator. . . . . Kim Rossi
Financial Analyst . . . . . David Steinfeld
Staff Attorney . . . . . Tim Lamoriello
Manager, Practice Ice Rink. . . . . Jon Sorg
Sales/Marketing Coordinator . . . . . Dana Fabrikant
Project Assistants. . . . . Amanda Brown, Javier Colon
Television . . . . . MSG Plus – Mike Emrick, play-by-play – Glenn Resch, color
Radio . . . . . SportsRadio 66 WFAN – Matt Loughlin, play-by-play – Sherry Ross, color

Key Off-Season Signings/Acquisitions

2008

July
- 1 • Signed D **Mark Streit**.
- 2 • Signed C **Doug Weight**.
- 8 • Re-signed D **Brendan Witt**.

New York Islanders

2007-08 Results: 35W-38L-6OTL-3SOL 79PTS.
Fifth, Atlantic Division

Named captain of the Islanders in 2007-08, Bill Guerin led the team with 23 goals and was second to Mike Comrie with 44 points.

2008-09 Schedule

Oct.	Fri.	10	at New Jersey
	Sat.	11	St. Louis
	Mon.	13	Buffalo*
	Thu.	16	at Tampa Bay
	Sat.	18	at Florida
	Thu.	23	Dallas
	Sat.	25	Carolina
	Mon.	27	NY Rangers
	Thu.	30	at Philadelphia
Nov.	Sat.	1	Montreal
	Mon.	3	Columbus
	Tue.	4	at NY Rangers
	Thu.	6	at Atlanta
	Sat.	8	Pittsburgh
	Tue.	11	Philadelphia*
	Thu.	13	at Ottawa
	Sat.	15	Ottawa
	Mon.	17	Vancouver
	Fri.	21	at New Jersey
	Sat.	22	at Buffalo
	Mon.	24	at Montreal
	Wed.	26	Pittsburgh
	Fri.	28	at Boston*
	Sat.	29	Ottawa
Dec.	Thu.	4	at Washington
	Sat.	6	Atlanta
	Mon.	8	at Toronto
	Tue.	9	at Philadelphia
	Thu.	11	at Pittsburgh
	Sat.	13	at Columbus
	Tue.	16	Washington
	Fri.	19	at Minnesota
	Sat.	20	at Nashville
	Tue.	23	Atlanta
	Fri.	26	Toronto
	Sat.	27	at Buffalo
	Mon.	29	at NY Rangers
	Wed.	31	Florida*
Jan.	Fri.	2	at Phoenix
	Sat.	3	at San Jose
	Mon.	5	at Edmonton
	Thu.	8	at Calgary
	Tue.	13	NY Rangers
	Thu.	15	Boston
	Sat.	17	New Jersey
	Mon.	19	Washington*
	Wed.	21	Anaheim
	Thu.	29	at Atlanta
	Sat.	31	Florida
Feb.	Tue.	3	Tampa Bay
	Thu.	5	at Florida
	Sat.	7	at Tampa Bay
	Tue.	10	Los Angeles
	Wed.	11	at New Jersey
	Sat.	14	at Philadelphia*
	Mon.	16	Pittsburgh*
	Wed.	18	at NY Rangers
	Thu.	19	Carolina
	Sat.	21	New Jersey
	Wed.	25	at Pittsburgh
	Thu.	26	Toronto
	Sat.	28	Buffalo
Mar.	Mon.	2	Colorado
	Thu.	5	NY Rangers
	Sat.	7	New Jersey*
	Sun.	8	Phoenix*
	Tue.	10	at Toronto
	Thu.	12	at Montreal
	Sat.	14	at Boston*
	Sun.	15	at Chicago*
	Fri.	20	at Carolina
	Sat.	21	at Ottawa
	Wed.	25	Minnesota
	Fri.	27	at Detroit
	Sat.	28	Philadelphia
Apr.	Wed.	1	at Washington
	Thu.	2	Montreal
	Sat.	4	Tampa Bay
	Tue.	7	at Carolina
	Thu.	9	at Pittsburgh
	Sat.	11	Philadelphia*
	Sun.	12	Boston*

* Denotes afternoon game.

Year-by-Year Record

		Home				Road				Overall								
Season	**GP**	**W**	**L**	**T**	**OL**	**W**	**L**	**T**	**OL**	**W**	**L**	**T**	**OL**	**GF**	**GA**	**Pts.**	**Finished**	**Playoff Result**
2007-08	82	18	18	....	5	17	20	....	4	35	38	....	9	194	243	79	5th, Atlantic Div.	Out of Playoffs
2006-07	82	22	13	....	6	18	17	....	6	40	30	....	12	248	240	92	4th, Atlantic Div.	Lost Conf. Quarter-Final
2005-06	82	20	18	....	3	16	22	....	3	36	40	....	6	230	278	78	4th, Atlantic Div.	Out of Playoffs
2004-05	....	....	....	....	....	....	....	....	....	....	....	....	....	....	....	....		
2003-04	82	25	11	4	1	13	18	7	3	38	29	11	4	237	210	91	3rd, Atlantic Div.	Lost Conf. Quarter-Final
2002-03	82	18	18	5	0	17	16	6	2	35	34	11	2	224	231	83	3rd, Atlantic Div.	Lost Conf. Quarter-Final
2001-02	82	21	13	5	2	21	15	3	2	42	28	8	4	239	220	96	2nd, Atlantic Div.	Lost Conf. Quarter-Final
2000-01	82	12	27	1	1	9	24	6	2	21	51	7	3	185	268	52	5th, Atlantic Div.	Out of Playoffs
1999-2000	82	10	25	5	1	14	23	4	0	24	48	9	1	194	275	58	5th, Atlantic Div.	Out of Playoffs
1998-99	82	11	23	7	....	13	25	3	....	24	48	10	....	194	244	58	5th, Atlantic Div.	Out of Playoffs
1997-98	82	17	20	4	....	13	21	7	....	30	41	11	....	212	225	71	4th, Atlantic Div.	Out of Playoffs
1996-97	82	19	18	4	....	10	23	8	....	29	41	12	....	240	250	70	7th, Atlantic Div.	Out of Playoffs
1995-96	82	14	21	6	....	8	29	4	....	22	50	10	....	229	315	54	7th, Atlantic Div.	Out of Playoffs
1994-95	48	10	11	3	....	5	17	2	....	15	28	5	....	126	158	35	7th, Atlantic Div.	Out of Playoffs
1993-94	84	23	15	4	....	13	21	8	....	36	36	12	....	282	264	84	4th, Atlantic Div.	Lost Conf. Quarter-Final
1992-93	84	20	19	3	....	20	18	4	....	40	37	7	....	335	297	87	3rd, Patrick Div.	Lost Conf. Championship
1991-92	80	20	15	5	....	14	20	6	....	34	35	11	....	291	299	79	5th, Patrick Div.	Out of Playoffs
1990-91	80	15	19	6	....	10	26	4	....	25	45	10	....	223	290	60	6th, Patrick Div.	Out of Playoffs
1989-90	80	15	17	8	....	16	21	3	....	31	38	11	....	281	288	73	4th, Patrick Div.	Lost Div. Semi-Final
1988-89	80	19	18	3	....	9	29	2	....	28	47	5	....	265	325	61	6th, Patrick Div.	Out of Playoffs
1987-88	80	24	10	6	....	15	21	4	....	39	31	10	....	308	267	88	1st, Patrick Div.	Lost Div. Semi-Final
1986-87	80	20	15	5	....	15	18	7	....	35	33	12	....	279	281	82	3rd, Patrick Div.	Lost Div. Final
1985-86	80	22	11	7	....	17	18	5	....	39	29	12	....	327	284	90	3rd, Patrick Div.	Lost Div. Semi-Final
1984-85	80	26	11	3	....	14	23	3	....	40	34	6	....	345	312	86	3rd, Patrick Div.	Lost Div. Final
1983-84	80	28	11	1	....	22	15	3	....	50	26	4	....	357	269	104	1st, Patrick Div.	Lost Final
1982-83	**80**	**26**	**11**	**3**	....	**16**	**15**	**9**	....	**42**	**26**	**12**	....	**302**	**226**	**96**	**2nd, Patrick Div.**	**Won Stanley Cup**
1981-82	**80**	**33**	**3**	**4**	....	**21**	**13**	**6**	....	**54**	**16**	**10**	....	**385**	**250**	**118**	**1st, Patrick Div.**	**Won Stanley Cup**
1980-81	**80**	**23**	**6**	**11**	....	**25**	**12**	**3**	....	**48**	**18**	**14**	....	**355**	**260**	**110**	**1st, Patrick Div.**	**Won Stanley Cup**
1979-80	**80**	**26**	**9**	**5**	....	**13**	**19**	**8**	....	**39**	**28**	**13**	....	**281**	**247**	**91**	**2nd, Patrick Div.**	**Won Stanley Cup**
1978-79	80	31	3	6	....	20	12	8	....	51	15	14	....	358	214	116	1st, Patrick Div.	Lost Semi-Final
1977-78	80	29	3	8	....	19	14	7	....	48	17	15	....	334	210	111	1st, Patrick Div.	Lost Quarter-Final
1976-77	80	24	11	5	....	23	10	7	....	47	21	12	....	288	193	106	2nd, Patrick Div.	Lost Semi-Final
1975-76	80	24	8	8	....	18	13	9	....	42	21	17	....	297	190	101	2nd, Patrick Div.	Lost Semi-Final
1974-75	80	22	6	12	....	11	19	10	....	33	25	22	....	264	221	88	3rd, Patrick Div.	Lost Semi-Final
1973-74	78	13	17	9	....	6	24	9	....	19	41	18	....	182	247	56	8th, East Div.	Out of Playoffs
1972-73	78	10	25	4	....	2	35	2	....	12	60	6	....	170	347	30	8th, East Div.	Out of Playoffs

ATLANTIC DIVISION
37th NHL Season

Franchise date: June 6, 1972

2008-09 Player Personnel

FORWARDS	HT	WT	S	Place of Birth	*Age	2007-08 Club
BAILEY, Joshua	6-1	188	L	Oshawa, Ont.	19	Windsor
BENTIVOGLIO, Sean	5-10	190	L	Thorold, Ont.	22	Bridgeport
BERGENHEIM, Sean	5-11	205	L	Helsinki, Finland	24	NY Islanders
COLLITON, Jeremy	6-2	195	R	Blackie, Alta.	23	NY Islanders-Bridgeport
COMEAU, Blake	6-1	207	R	Meadow Lake, Sask.	22	NY Islanders-Bridgeport
COMRIE, Mike	5-10	185	L	Edmonton, Alta.	28	NY Islanders
FRITZ, Mitch	6-8	258	L	Osoyoos, B.C.	27	Hartford
GUERIN, Bill	6-2	220	R	Worcester, MA	37	NY Islanders
HILBERT, Andy	5-11	194	L	Lansing, MI	27	NY Islanders
HUNTER, Trent	6-3	210	R	Red Deer, Alta.	28	NY Islanders
IGGULDEN, Mike	6-3	215	R	St. Catharines, Ont.	25	San Jose-Worcester
JACKMAN, Tim	6-4	210	R	Minot, ND	26	NY Islanders-Bridgeport
JOENSUU, Jesse	6-4	207	L	Pori, Finland	20	Assat-Bridgeport
MARCINKO, Tomas	6-4	187	R	Poprad, Czech.	20	Barrie
McLEAN, Kurtis	5-11	175	R	Kirkland Lake, Ont.	27	Wilkes-Barre
NIELSEN, Frans	5-11	172	L	Herning, Denmark	24	NY Islanders-Bridgeport
OKPOSO, Kyle	6-1	200	R	St. Paul, MN	20	U. of Minnesota-NYI-Bridgeport
PARK, Richard	5-11	190	R	Seoul, South Korea	32	NY Islanders
PITTON, Jason	6-3	216	L	Mississauga, Ont.	22	Bridgeport-Utah
RECHLICZ, Joel	6-4	220	R	Brookfield, WI	21	Albany-Kalamazoo
SILLINGER, Mike	5-11	198	R	Regina, Sask.	37	NY Islanders
SIM, Jon	5-10	195	L	New Glasgow, N.S.	31	NY Islanders
SMITH, Trevor	6-1	195	L	North Vancouver, B.C.	23	Bridgeport-Utah
TAMBELLINI, Jeff	5-11	186	L	Calgary, Alta.	24	NY Islanders-Bridgeport
WALTER, Ben	6-1	195	L	Beaconsfield, Que.	24	NY Islanders-Bridgeport
WEIGHT, Doug	5-11	196	L	Warren, MI	37	St. Louis-Anaheim
DEFENSEMEN						
CALLAHAN, Joe	6-3	221	R	Brockton, MA	25	Portland (AHL)
CAMPOLI, Chris	5-11	190	L	North York, Ont.	24	NY Islanders
FRASER, Jamie	6-1	200	L	Sarnia, Ont.	22	Bridgeport
GERVAIS, Bruno	6-0	188	R	Longueuil, Que.	24	NY Islanders
HILLEN, Jack	5-10	190	L	Portland, OR	22	Colorado College-NYI
KOHN, Dustin	6-2	182	L	Edmonton, Alta.	21	Bridgeport
LEE, Chris	6-0	185	L	MacTier, Ont.	28	Iowa
MacDONALD, Andrew	6-1	188	L	Judique, N.S.	22	Bridgeport-Utah
MARTINEK, Radek	5-11	200	R	Havlickuv Brod, Czech.	32	NY Islanders
MEYER, Freddy	5-10	192	L	Sanbornville, NH	27	Phx-San Antonio-NYI
SKINNER, Brett	6-1	195	L	Brandon, Man.	25	Providence (AHL)
STREIT, Mark	6-0	197	L	Englisberg, Switz.	30	Montreal
SUTTON, Andy	6-6	245	L	Kingston, Ont.	33	NY Islanders
WITT, Brendan	6-2	223	L	Humboldt, Sask.	33	NY Islanders

GOALTENDERS	HT	WT	C	Place of Birth	*Age	2007-08 Club
DANIS, Yann	6-0	181	L	Lafontaine, Que.	27	Hamilton
DiPIETRO, Rick	6-1	210	R	Winthrop, MA	27	NY Islanders
MacDONALD, Joey	6-0	197	L	Pictou, N.S.	28	NY Islanders-Bridgeport
MANNINO, Peter	6-0	200		Farmington Hills, MI	24	U. of Denver

* – Age at start of 2008-09 season

2007-08 Scoring

* – rookie

Regular Season

Pos	#	Player	Team	GP	G	A	Pts	TOI	+/–	PIM	PP	SH	GW	S	%
C	89	Mike Comrie	NYI	76	21	28	49	19:11	–21	87	4	0	3	194	10.8
R	13	Bill Guerin	NYI	81	23	21	44	17:22	–15	65	7	0	5	227	10.1
R	81	Miroslav Satan	NYI	80	16	25	41	18:19	–11	39	5	0	4	171	9.4
R	7	Trent Hunter	NYI	82	12	29	41	18:12	–17	43	2	0	1	222	5.4
C	63	Josef Vasicek	NYI	81	16	19	35	15:51	1	53	0	2	2	126	12.7
L	26	Ruslan Fedotenko	NYI	67	16	17	33	16:41	–9	40	8	0	2	121	13.2
R	10	Richard Park	NYI	82	12	20	32	15:13	–4	20	1	4	2	132	9.1
C	18	Mike Sillinger	NYI	52	14	12	26	18:36	–10	28	3	2	2	94	14.9
L	20	Sean Bergenheim	NYI	78	10	12	22	11:15	–3	62	1	0	1	155	6.5
D	4	Bryan Berard	NYI	54	5	17	22	17:38	–17	48	4	0	2	87	5.7
D	14	Chris Campoli	NYI	46	4	14	18	19:09	–1	16	2	1	0	68	5.9
L	11	Andy Hilbert	NYI	70	8	8	16	13:28	2	18	0	0	0	127	6.3
R	57 *	Blake Comeau	NYI	51	8	7	15	11:40	1	22	1	0	1	67	11.9
D	24	Radek Martinek	NYI	69	0	15	15	22:52	–9	40	0	0	0	98	0.0
D	8	Bruno Gervais	NYI	60	0	13	13	20:00	–5	34	0	0	0	59	0.0
D	44	Freddy Meyer	PHX	5	0	0	0	06:43	–4	0	0	0	0	2	0.0
			NYI	52	3	9	12	19:54	6	22	0	0	2	49	6.1
			Total	57	3	9	12	18:44	2	22	0	0	2	51	5.9
D	25	Andy Sutton	NYI	58	1	7	8	18:09	–6	86	0	0	1	57	1.8
D	32	Brendan Witt	NYI	59	2	5	7	21:46	–8	51	0	0	0	58	3.4
R	21 *	Kyle Okposo	NYI	9	2	3	5	16:27	3	2	1	0	1	15	13.3
L	15	Jeff Tambellini	NYI	31	1	3	4	10:25	–9	8	0	0	0	43	2.3
R	28	Tim Jackman	NYI	36	1	3	4	06:36	–3	57	0	0	0	36	2.8
C	51 *	Frans Nielsen	NYI	16	2	1	3	08:42	1	0	0	0	0	17	11.8
D	3	Rob Davison	S.J.	15	0	0	0	07:46	–3	21	0	0	0	10	0.0
			NYI	19	1	1	2	18:39	–3	32	0	1	0	22	4.5
			Total	34	1	1	2	13:51	–6	53	0	1	0	32	3.1
D	2	Aaron Johnson	NYI	30	0	2	2	13:51	2	30	0	0	0	16	0.0
C	29 *	Ben Walter	NYI	8	1	0	1	06:05	–1	0	1	0	0	6	16.7
L	16	Jon Sim	NYI	2	0	1	1	14:18	–1	2	0	0	0	8	0.0
D	38 *	Jack Hillen	NYI	2	0	1	1	15:32	1	4	0	0	0	3	0.0
R	27	Darryl Bootland	NYI	4	0	1	1	04:42	0	2	0	0	0	3	0.0
D	49 *	Drew Fata	NYI	5	0	1	1	17:30	–1	4	0	0	0	4	0.0
D	6	Matthew Spiller	NYI	9	0	1	1	19:47	–2	7	0	0	0	6	0.0
C	17	Shawn Bates	NYI	2	0	0	0	07:00	–2	0	0	0	0	0	0.0
L	37	Kip Brennan	NYI	3	0	0	0	04:21	0	12	0	0	0	0	0.0
R	27 *	Matt Keith	NYI	3	0	0	0	10:41	–1	0	0	0	0	3	0.0
L	48 *	Steve Regier	NYI	8	0	0	0	07:59	–1	4	0	0	0	7	0.0
C	72 *	Jeremy Colliton	NYI	16	0	0	0	08:46	–4	8	0	0	0	16	0.0

Goaltending

No.	Goaltender	GPI	Mins	Avg	W	L	OT	EN	SO	GA	SA	S%	G	A	PIM
34	Wade Dubielewicz	20	1132	2.70	9	9	1	3	0	51	627	.919	0	0	0
39	Rick DiPietro	63	3707	2.82	26	28	7	6	3	174	1779	.902	0	6	18
35	Joey MacDonald	2	120	3.00	0	1	1	0	0	6	73	.918	0	0	0
	Totals	**82**	**4987**	**2.89**	**35**	**38**	**9**	**9**	**3**	**240**	**2488**	**.904**			

Scott Gordon

Head Coach

Born: Brockton, MA, February 6, 1963.

The New York Islanders announced the hiring of Scott Gordon as their head coach on August 12, 2008. Gordon spent the previous eight seasons with the Providence Bruins, Boston's affiliate in the American Hockey League. He began as an assistant coach in Providence in 2000-01 and was hired as the head coach on July 25, 2003 after serving as interim head coach for part of the 2002-03 season. In 2007-08, he guided the Bruins to top spot in the AHL standings with a record of 55-18-7 and was named coach of the year.

Gordon began his coaching career with the International Hockey League's Atlanta Knights as an assistant coach in 1994-95. When he was named head coach on January 5, 1996, he became at age 32 the youngest head coach in the league's 53-year history. The team spent the next two seasons as the Quebec Rafales, with Gordon serving as an assistant. His next move came in 1998-99, when he was named head coach of the Roanoke Express of the East Coast Hockey League. He led the club to consecutive first-place finishes in the Northeast Division, setting franchise records for wins (44), points (94) and fewest goals against (181) in 1999-2000.

As a player, Gordon spent four years as a goaltender at Boston College from 1982 to 1986, posting a 64-35-3 record over that span. He backstopped the Eagles to a NCAA Final Four appearance in 1985 and was named a Hockey East First-Team All-Star in 1986. Following the completion of his collegiate career, Gordon began his professional playing career with the AHL's Frederiction Express in 1986-87. He made his NHL debut in 1989-90 playing 10 games with the Quebec Nordiques. He played 13 more games for Quebec in 1990-91. Gordon played on the 1992 United States Olympic team and was a member of the IHL's 1994 Turner Cup champions Atlanta Knights squad. Gordon played 150 AHL games with Fredericton, the Baltimore Skipjacks, the Halifax Citadels and the New Haven Nighthawks through 1993-94.

Coaching Record

			Regular Season				Playoffs			
Season	Team	League	GC	W	L	O/T	GC	W	L	T
1995-96	Atlanta	IHL	40	15	19	6	3	0	3	....
1998-99	Roanoke	ECHL	70	38	22	10	12	6	6	....
99-2000	Roanoke	ECHL	70	44	20	6	4	1	3	....
2002-03	Providence	AHL	9	3	3	3	1	0	1	....
2003-04	Providence	AHL	80	36	29	15	2	0	2	....
2004-05	Providence	AHL	80	40	30	10	17	10	7	....
2005-06	Providence	AHL	80	43	31	6	6	2	4	....
2006-07	Providence	AHL	80	44	30	6	13	6	7	....
2007-08	Providence	AHL	80	55	18	7	10	6	4	....

Kyle Okposo was the Islanders' first pick (seventh overall) in the 2006 Entry Draft. He made his NHL debut on March 18, 2008 against Toronto and picked up his first goal and first assist three nights later versus New Jersey.

Coaching History

Phil Goyette and Earl Ingarfield, 1972-73; Al Arbour, 1973-74 to 1985-86; Terry Simpson, 1986-87, 1987-88; Terry Simpson and Al Arbour, 1988-89; Al Arbour, 1989-90 to 1993-94; Lorne Henning, 1994-95; Mike Milbury, 1995-96; Mike Milbury and Rick Bowness, 1996-97; Rick Bowness and Mike Milbury, 1997-98; Mike Milbury and Bill Stewart, 1998-99; Butch Goring, 1999-2000; Butch Goring and Lorne Henning, 2000-01; Peter Laviolette, 2001-02, 2002-03; Steve Stirling, 2003-04, 2004-05; Steve Stirling and Brad Shaw, 2005-06; Ted Nolan, 2006-07, 2007-08; Scott Gordon, 2008-09.

Club Records

Team

(Figures in brackets for season records are games played; records for fewest points, wins, ties, losses, goals, goals against are for 70 or more games)

Most Points **118** 1981-82 (80)
Most Wins **54** 1981-82 (80)
Most Ties **22** 1974-75 (80)
Most Losses **60** 1972-73 (78)
Most Goals **385** 1981-82 (80)
Most Goals Against **347** 1972-73 (78)
Fewest Points **30** 1972-73 (78)
Fewest Wins **12** 1972-73 (78)
Fewest Ties **4** 1983-84 (80)
Fewest Losses **15** 1978-79 (80)
Fewest Goals **170** 1972-73 (78)
Fewest Goals Against **190** 1975-76 (80)

Longest Winning Streak
Overall .... **15** Jan. 21-Feb. 20/82
Home .... **14** Jan. 2-Feb. 25/82
Away .... **8** Feb. 27-Mar. 29/81

Longest Undefeated Streak
Overall .... **15** Three times
Home .... **23** Oct. 17/78-Jan. 20/79 (19 wins, 4 ties), Jan. 2-Apr. 3/82 (21 wins, 2 ties)
Away .... **8** Three times

Longest Losing Streak
Overall .... **12** Dec. 27/72-Jan. 16/73, Nov. 22-Dec. 15/88
Home .... **7** Nov. 13-Dec. 14/99
Away .... **15** Jan. 20-Mar. 31/73

Longest Winless Streak
Overall .... **15** Nov. 22-Dec. 21/72 (12 losses, 3 ties)
Home .... **9** Mar. 2-Apr. 6/99 (7 losses, 2 ties)
Away .... **20** Nov. 3/72-Jan. 13/73 (19 losses, 1 tie)

Most Shutouts, Season **10** 1975-76 (80)
Most PIM, Season **1,857** 1986-87 (80)
Most Goals, Game .... **11** Dec. 20/83 (Pit. 3 at NYI 11), Mar. 3/84 (NYI 11 at Tor. 6)

Individual

Most Seasons .... **17** Billy Smith
Most Games .... **1,123** Bryan Trottier
Most Goals, Career .... **573** Mike Bossy
Most Assists, Career .... **853** Bryan Trottier
Most Points, Career .... **1,353** Bryan Trottier (500G, 853A)
Most PIM, Career .... **1,879** Mick Vukota
Most Shutouts, Career .... **25** Glenn Resch
Longest Consecutive Games Streak .... **576** Billy Harris (Oct. 7/72-Nov. 30/79)
Most Goals, Season .... **69** Mike Bossy (1978-79)
Most Assists, Season .... **87** Bryan Trottier (1978-79)
Most Points, Season .... **147** Mike Bossy (1981-82; 64G, 83A)
Most PIM, Season .... **356** Brian Curran (1986-87)
Most Points, Defenseman, Season .... **101** Denis Potvin (1978-79; 31G, 70A)
Most Points, Center, Season .... **134** Bryan Trottier (1978-79; 47G, 87A)
Most Points, Right Wing, Season .... **147** Mike Bossy (1981-82; 64G, 83A)
Most Points, Left Wing, Season .... **100** John Tonelli (1984-85; 42G, 58A)
Most Points, Rookie, Season .... **95** Bryan Trottier (1975-76; 32G, 63A)
Most Shutouts, Season .... **7** Glenn Resch (1975-76)
Most Goals, Game .... **5** Bryan Trottier (Dec. 23/78, Feb. 13/82), John Tonelli (Jan. 6/81)
Most Assists, Game .... **6** Mike Bossy (Jan. 6/81)
Most Points, Game .... **8** Bryan Trottier (Dec. 23/78; 5G, 3A)

Captains' History

Ed Westfall, 1972-73 to 1975-76; Ed Westfall and Clark Gillies, 1976-77; Clark Gillies, 1977-78, 1978-79; Denis Potvin, 1979-80 to 1986-87; Brent Sutter, 1987-88 to 1990-91; Brent Sutter and Pat Flatley, 1991-92; Pat Flatley, 1992-93 to 1995-96; no captain, 1996-97; Bryan McCabe and Trevor Linden, 1997-98; Trevor Linden, 1998-99; Kenny Jonsson, 1999-2000, 2000-01; Michael Peca, 2001-02 to 2003-04; Alexei Yashin, 2005-06, 2006-07; Bill Guerin, 2007-08 to date.

Retired Numbers

5	Denis Potvin	1973-1988
9	Clark Gillies	1974-1986
19	Bryan Trottier	1975-1990
22	Mike Bossy	1977-1987
23	Bob Nystrom	1972-1986
31	Billy Smith	1972-1989

All-time Record vs. Other Clubs

Regular Season

	At Home								On Road								Total							
	GP	W	L	T	OL	GF	GA	PTS	GP	W	L	T	OL	GF	GA	PTS	GP	W	L	T	OL	GF	GA	PTS
Anaheim	9	4	4	1	0	24	26	9	10	5	2	3	0	29	22	13	19	9	6	4	0	53	48	22
Atlanta	16	9	7	0	0	56	38	18	16	9	3	2	2	63	49	22	32	18	10	2	2	119	87	40
Boston	67	29	28	10	0	222	210	68	65	19	33	11	2	181	238	51	132	48	61	21	2	403	448	119
Buffalo	67	29	28	9	1	188	186	68	67	21	36	9	1	185	227	52	134	50	64	18	2	373	413	120
Calgary	52	26	17	9	0	194	145	61	50	15	24	11	0	150	176	41	102	41	41	20	0	344	321	102
Carolina	50	23	22	4	1	148	142	51	51	21	25	5	0	165	173	47	101	44	47	9	1	313	315	98
Chicago	48	19	14	15	0	168	143	53	49	18	26	5	0	164	163	41	97	37	40	20	0	332	306	94
Colorado	33	19	13	1	0	134	113	39	35	11	20	3	1	98	125	26	68	30	33	4	1	232	238	65
Columbus	3	1	2	0	0	11	11	2	5	0	3	1	1	10	17	2	8	1	5	1	1	21	28	4
Dallas	49	26	14	8	1	178	137	61	48	22	18	8	0	173	139	52	97	48	32	16	1	351	276	113
Detroit	47	23	18	4	2	167	141	52	46	18	26	2	0	137	166	38	93	41	44	6	2	304	307	90
Edmonton	32	16	7	9	0	131	112	41	30	8	17	5	0	87	111	21	62	24	24	14	0	218	223	62
Florida	31	15	13	2	1	81	83	33	31	10	15	6	0	92	99	26	62	25	28	8	1	173	182	59
Los Angeles	45	24	16	5	0	157	126	53	46	17	22	7	0	145	167	41	91	41	38	12	0	302	293	94
Minnesota	4	2	2	0	0	9	10	4	4	1	2	0	1	12	13	3	8	3	4	0	1	21	23	7
Montreal	66	32	28	6	0	200	186	70	66	16	41	9	0	179	237	41	132	48	69	15	0	379	423	111
Nashville	5	2	2	0	1	12	14	5	6	2	4	0	0	17	16	4	11	4	6	0	1	29	30	9
New Jersey	97	61	23	11	2	379	273	135	96	45	37	11	3	323	303	104	193	106	60	22	5	702	576	239
NY Rangers	108	59	39	8	2	394	342	128	108	38	58	11	1	321	391	88	216	97	97	19	3	715	733	216
Ottawa	30	6	17	6	1	91	115	19	29	6	18	5	0	72	101	17	59	12	35	11	1	163	216	36
Philadelphia	110	54	40	15	1	388	330	124	107	34	62	11	0	297	377	79	217	88	102	26	1	685	707	203
Phoenix	31	14	9	8	0	116	93	36	31	15	12	4	0	108	102	34	62	29	21	12	0	224	195	70
Pittsburgh	98	53	34	8	3	384	322	117	100	38	46	14	2	345	375	92	198	91	80	22	5	729	697	209
St. Louis	50	25	13	11	1	185	134	62	48	21	17	9	1	159	169	52	98	46	30	20	2	344	303	114
San Jose	12	6	4	2	0	43	37	14	13	6	6	1	0	40	32	13	25	12	10	3	0	83	69	27
Tampa Bay	31	15	14	1	1	90	83	32	32	13	14	2	3	96	92	31	63	28	28	3	4	186	175	63
Toronto	59	34	21	3	1	226	170	72	61	25	31	4	1	203	219	55	120	59	52	7	2	429	389	127
Vancouver	48	26	12	10	0	175	137	62	48	21	23	3	1	155	158	46	96	47	35	13	1	330	295	108
Washington	87	47	38	2	0	321	265	96	87	34	40	11	2	273	283	81	174	81	78	13	2	594	548	177
Defunct Clubs	13	11	0	2	0	75	33	24	13	4	5	4	0	35	41	12	26	15	5	6	0	110	74	36
Totals	**1398**	**710**	**499**	**170**	**19**	**4947**	**4157**	**1609**	**1398**	**513**	**686**	**177**	**22**	**4314**	**4781**	**1225**	**2796**	**1223**	**1185**	**347**	**41**	**9261**	**8938**	**2834**

Playoffs

	Series	W	L	GP	W	L	T	GF	GA	Last Mtg.	Rnd.	Result
Boston	2	2	0	11	8	3	0	49	35	1983	CF	W 4-2
Buffalo	4	3	1	21	13	8	0	70	62	2007	CQF	L 1-4
Chicago	2	2	0	6	6	0	0	21	6	1979	QF	W 4-0
Colorado	1	1	0	4	4	0	0	18	9	1982	CF	W 4-0
Dallas	1	1	0	5	4	1	0	26	16	1981	F	W 4-1
Edmonton	3	2	1	15	9	6	0	58	47	1984	F	L 1-4
Los Angeles	1	1	0	4	3	1	0	21	10	1980	PRE	W 3-1
Montreal	4	1	3	22	8	14	0	55	64	1993	CF	L 1-4
New Jersey	1	0	1	6	2	4	0	18	23	1988	DSF	L 2-4
NY Rangers	8	5	3	39	20	19	0	129	132	1994	CQF	L 0-4
Ottawa	1	0	1	5	1	4	0	7	13	2003	CQF	L 1-4
Philadelphia	4	1	3	25	11	14	0	69	83	1987	DF	L 3-4
Pittsburgh	3	3	0	19	11	8	0	67	58	1993	DF	W 4-3
Tampa Bay	1	0	1	5	1	4	0	5	12	2004	CQF	L 1-4
Toronto	3	1	2	17	9	8	0	54	42	2002	CQF	L 3-4
Vancouver	2	2	0	6	6	0	0	26	14	1982	F	W 4-0
Washington	6	5	1	30	18	12	0	99	88	1993	DSF	W 4-2
Totals	**47**	**30**	**17**	**240**	**134**	**106**	**0**	**792**	**714**			

Calgary totals include Atlanta Flames, 1972-73 to 1979-80.
Colorado totals include Quebec, 1979-80 to 1994-95.
New Jersey totals include Kansas City, 1974-75, 1975-76, and Colorado Rockies, 1976-77 to 1981-82.
Phoenix totals include Winnipeg, 1979-80 to 1995-96.
Carolina totals include Hartford, 1979-80 to 1996-97.
Dallas totals include Minnesota North Stars, 1972-73 to 1992-93.

Playoff Results 2008-2003

Year	Round	Opponent	Result	GF	GA
2007	CQF	Buffalo	L 1-4	11	17
2004	CQF	Tampa Bay	L 1-4	5	12
2003	CQF	Ottawa	L 1-4	7	13

Abbreviations: Round: F – Final; **CF** – conference final; **CQF** – conference quarter-final; **DF** – division final; **DSF** – division semi-final; **QF** – quarter-final; **PRE** – preliminary round.

2007-08 Results

Oct.	5	at Buffalo	6-4
	6	Buffalo	3-2
	8	Washington	1-2
	10	NY Rangers	2-1
	11	at Toronto	1-8
	13	at Philadelphia	1-3
	18	at Washington	5-2
	20	New Jersey	4-3*
	27	Carolina	3-8
Nov.	1	Tampa Bay	4-0
	3	Pittsburgh	3-2
	6	NY Rangers	3-2
	10	New Jersey	2-1
	12	at Philadelphia	2-3
	15	at Pittsburgh	2-3
	16	at New Jersey	1-0
	19	at NY Rangers	2-1
	21	Montreal	1-4
	23	at Boston	1-2
	24	Boston	2-1
	26	Dallas	2-3*
	28	Ottawa	3-2†
	29	at NY Rangers	2-4
Dec.	1	Atlanta	0-4
	3	Boston	1-3
	5	at Atlanta	3-4†
	7	at Florida	0-3
	8	at Tampa Bay	3-2*
	12	at Buffalo	3-5
	13	Phoenix	3-2
	15	Pittsburgh	2-3
	19	Buffalo	1-2
	21	at Pittsburgh	4-2
	22	Washington	3-2*
	26	Toronto	4-3*
	27	at Ottawa	2-5
	29	New Jersey	5-2
	31	at Carolina	4-1
Jan.	3	Florida	3-4*
	5	at Colorado	1-2*
	7	at Edmonton	0-4
	8	at Vancouver	2-3†
	11	at Calgary	5-4†
	13	at Ottawa	3-1
	15	Montreal	1-3
	16	at New Jersey	3-1
	19	Philadelphia	3-5
	21	Carolina	2-3*
	22	at Carolina	6-3
	24	at Boston	1-4
	29	Ottawa	2-5
	31	Los Angeles	1-3
Feb.	2	at Montreal	1-4
	5	Anaheim	0-3
	7	at Pittsburgh	3-4
	9	at Minnesota	3-4*
	12	Philadelphia	4-3
	14	at Toronto	5-4
	16	Atlanta	4-1
	18	San Jose	3-2
	20	at Washington	3-2†
	21	Tampa Bay	1-0
	23	at New Jersey	2-4
	26	Pittsburgh	2-4
	28	at Atlanta	5-4*
Mar.	1	Philadelphia	1-4
	2	Florida	0-1
	4	at NY Rangers	4-3†
	6	NY Rangers	1-4
	8	at Philadelphia	1-4
	11	at Tampa Bay	4-8
	12	at Florida	2-4
	15	at Montreal	0-3
	18	Toronto	1-3
	21	at New Jersey	3-1
	23	at Philadelphia	1-4
	24	Pittsburgh	4-1
	27	at Pittsburgh	1-3
	29	Philadelphia	3-4†
Apr.	1	New Jersey	1-2*
	3	NY Rangers	0-3
	4	at NY Rangers	4-3†

* – Overtime † – Shootout

Entry Draft Selections 2008-1994

Name in bold denotes played in NHL.

2008

Pick	
9	Joshua Bailey
36	Corey Trivino
40	Aaron Ness
53	Travis Hamonic
66	David Toews
72	Jyri Niemi
73	Kirill Petrov
96	Matt Donovan
102	David Ullstrom
126	Kevin Poulin
148	Matt Martin
156	Jared Spurgeon
175	Justin Dibenedetto

2007

Pick	
62	Mark Katic
76	Jason Gregoire
106	Maxim Gratchev
166	Blake Kessel
196	Simon Lacroix

2006

Pick	
7	**Kyle Okposo**
60	Jesse Joensuu
70	Robin Figren
100	Rhett Rakhshani
108	Jase Weslosky
115	Tomas Marcinko
119	Doug Rogers
126	Shane Sims
141	Kim Johansson
160	Andrew Macdonald
171	Brian Day
173	Stefan Ridderwall
190	Troy Mattila

2005

Pick	
15	Ryan O'Marra
46	Dustin Kohn
76	Shea Guthrie
144	**Masi Marjamaki**
180	Tyrell Mason
196	Nicholas Tuzzolino
210	Luciano Aquino

2004

Pick	
16	**Petteri Nokelainen**
47	**Blake Comeau**
82	Sergei Ogorodnikov
115	Wes O'Neill
148	**Steve Regier**
179	Jaroslav Mrazek
210	Emil Axelsson
227	**Chris Campoli**
244	Jason Pitton
276	Sylvain Michaud

2003

Pick	
15	**Robert Nilsson**
48	Dmitri Chernykh
53	Evgeny Tunik
58	**Jeremy Colliton**
120	Stefan Blaho
182	**Bruno Gervais**
212	Denis Rehak
238	Cody Blanshan
246	Igor Volkov

2002

Pick	
22	**Sean Bergenheim**
87	**Frans Nielsen**
149	Marcus Paulsson
189	Alexei Stonkus
220	Brad Topping
252	Martin Chabada
283	Per Braxenholm

2001

Pick	
101	Cory Stillman
132	Dusan Salficky
166	**Andy Chiodo**
197	Jan Holub
228	Mike Bray
260	Bryan Perez
280	Roman Kuhtinov
287	Juha-Pekka Ketola

2000

Pick	
1	**Rick DiPietro**
5	**Raffi Torres**
101	Arto Tukio
105	Vladimir Gorbunov
136	Dmitri Upper
148	Kristofer Ottosson
202	**Ryan Caldwell**
264	Dmitri Altarev
267	**Tomi Pettinen**

1999

Pick	
5	**Tim Connolly**
8	**Taylor Pyatt**
10	**Branislav Mezei**
28	**Kristian Kudroc**
78	**Mattias Weinhandl**
87	Brian Collins
101	**Juraj Kolnik**
102	Johan Halvardsson
130	**Justin Mapletoft**
140	Adam Johnson
163	**Bjorn Melin**
228	**Radek Martinek**
255	Brett Henning
268	Tyler Scott

1998

Pick	
9	**Mike Rupp**
36	**Chris Nielsen**
95	Andy Burnham
123	**Jiri Dopita**
155	Kevin Clauson
182	**Evgeny Korolev**
209	Frederik Brindamour
237	Ben Blais
242	Jason Doyle
250	Radek Matejovsky

1997

Pick	
4	**Roberto Luongo**
5	**Eric Brewer**
31	**Jeff Zehr**
59	Jarrett Smith
79	**Robert Schnabel**
85	**Petr Mika**
115	Adam Edinger
139	Bobby Leavins
166	Kris Knoblauch
196	Jeremy Symington
222	Ryan Clark

1996

Pick	
3	**J.P. Dumont**
29	**Dan LaCouture**
56	**Zdeno Chara**
83	**Tyrone Garner**
109	**Bubba Berenzweig**
128	Petr Sachl
138	Todd Miller
165	J.R. Prestifilippo
192	**Evgeny Korolev**
218	Mike Muzechka

1995

Pick	
2	**Wade Redden**
28	**Jan Hlavac**
41	**D.J. Smith**
106	**Vladimir Orszagh**
158	Andrew Taylor
210	David MacDonald
211	Mike Broda

1994

Pick	
9	**Brett Lindros**
38	**Jason Holland**
63	**Jason Strudwick**
90	**Brad Lukowich**
112	Mark McArthur
116	Albert O'Connell
142	Jason Stewart
194	Mike Loach
203	Peter Hogardh
220	Gord Walsh
246	Kirk Dewaele
272	**Dick Tarnstrom**

General Managers' History

Bill Torrey, 1972-73 to 1991-92; Don Maloney, 1992-93 to 1994-95; Don Maloney and Mike Milbury, 1995-96; Mike Milbury, 1996-97 to 2005-06; Neil Smith and Garth Snow, 2006-07; Garth Snow, 2007-08 to date.

Garth Snow

General Manager

Born: Wrentham, MA, June 28, 1969.

Former Islanders' goaltender Garth Snow retired as a player on July 18, 2006 to become the fifth general manager of the New York Islanders. In his first season as general manager, Snow successfully bolstered the lineup with several key additions, the most notable being his deal with Edmonton for Ryan Smyth just minutes before the trade deadline. The moves helped to propel the Islanders into the postseason for the first time since the 2003–04 season and earned Snow the title of NHL Executive of the Year from *Sports Illustrated*.

Snow spent four seasons with the Islanders and 12 in the NHL. The goaltender was 135-147-44 with a 2.80 goals-against average and .901 save percentage over 368 games with Quebec, Philadelphia, Vancouver, Pittsburgh and the Islanders. Originally selected in the sixth round by Quebec in the 1987 NHL Entry Draft, the native of Wrentham, Massachusetts signed with the Islanders as a free agent on July 1, 2001.

Club Directory

Nassau Veterans' Memorial Coliseum

New York Islanders
Executive Office
1535 Old Country Rd.
Plainview, NY 11803
Phone **516/501-6700**
FAX 516/501-6850
www.newyorkislanders.com
Arena
Nassau Veterans' Memorial Coliseum
Uniondale, NY 11553
Capacity: 16,234

Owner & Governor	Charles B. Wang
President & Alternate Governor	Chris Dey
General Manager & Alternate Governor	Garth Snow
Alternate Governors	Art McCarthy, Roy Reichbach, Michael Picker

Hockey Operations

Executive Director of Player Development	Bryan Trottier
Assistant G.M./Director of Amateur Scouting	Ryan Jankowski
Director of Pro Scouting	Ken Morrow
Manager, Hockey Administration	Joanne Holewa
Assistant to the General Manager	Kerry Gwydir
Head Coach	Scott Gordon
Assistant Coaches	Gerard Gallant, John Chabot, Dan Lacroix
Goaltending Coach	Mike Dunham
Goaltending Consultant	Sudarshan Maharaj
Equipment Manager	Scott Boggs
Assistant Equipment Manager	Richard Krouse
Equipment Assistant	Tom Kitz
Head Athletic Trainer	Garrett Timms
Assistant Athletic Trainer	Nates Goto
Strength & Conditioning Coach	Chris Schwarz
Assistant Player Development	Eric Cairns
Head European Scout	Vellu-Pekka Kautonen
Pro Scouts	Rob Cowie, Anders Kallur, Toby O'Brien, Chris O'Sullivan, Mario Saraceno
Amateur Scouts	Brad Bowen, David Hymovitz, Tim Maclean, Denny Scanlon, Tim Schurman

Administration

Assistant to Charles B. Wang	Susie Schaefer
Executive Assistant to the President	Denise Zimmermann
Administrative Assistant	Devon Williams
Director of Legal Affairs	Jaimie Wolf
Human Resources Manager	John Lyons
Internship Coordinator	Michele Calabrese
IT Manager	Pawel Tauter
Receptionist	Bonnie Dreher

Corporate Partnerships & Islanders Business Club

V.P. of Sales, Corporate Partnerships	Dave Decina
Asst. to V.P. of Sales, Corp. Partnerships	Lori Ogden
Exec. Director of Islanders Business Club	Mike Bossy
G.M. Sales & Mktg., Corp. Partnerships	Dave Kotowski
Sr. Director of Sales, Corporate Partnerships	Sean Argaman
Director of Sales, Corporate Partnerships	Chris Lombardo
Sales Executive, Corporate Partnerships	Jen Meilan, Gary Park, Kevin Waters
Director of Partnership Marketing	Larry Goldman
Partnership Marketing Manager	Michelle Winter
Partnership Marketing Coordinator	Josh Kent, Lonnie Kussin, Mike Matranga

Retail & Merchandise Operations

Director of Retail Operations	Terry Goldstein
Merchandise Assistant	Colleen Carolan
Manager, Islanders Team Store	Monica Mantello

Ticket Sales, Marketing & Service

Vice President of Sales, Tickets	Ralph Sellitti
Director of Ticket Marketing & Service	Jessica Tuttle
Director of Sales, Group Tickets	Adam Jacobs
Senior Sales Executive, Group Tickets	Cliff Gault
Sales Executive, Group Tickets	Ariel Greenberg, J.J. Molesso, Rick McCarthy
Group Sales Coordinator	Dave DiLello
Sales Manager, Tickets	Anthony Noto
Senior Sales Executive, Tickets	Steve Beisel, Bryan Davis, Larry Fitzpatrick, Marc Gerstein, Jeff Guida
Sales Executives, Tickets	T.J. Carpenter, Joseph Cirillo, Theresa Coscia, Eddie Fisher, Rich Pascullo, Stan Pesner, Sam Romanella, Mike Surrey, Kevin Trotman
Director of Customer Service	Kerry Cornils
Customer Service Reps.	Rose Barre, Glenn Brewer, Sara Pesserillo, Nicholas Tullo, Adam Wertheimer
Ticket Manager	Adam Ortiz
Assistant Ticket Manager	Karen Stepnowski

Communications & Media Relations

Vice President of Communications	Josh Bernstein
Director of Communications	Seth Sylvan
Media Relations Manager	Corey Witt
Website & Publications Manager	Brett Topel
Website & Publications Coordinator	Jason Lockhart
Office Assistant	Todd Aronovich

Operations & Events

Vice President of Game Operations and Events	Tim Beach
Director of Operations, Events, Promotions	Ken Zore
Game Operations Manager	Mike Sciortino
Community Relations Manager	Ann Rina
Events Marketing Manager	Ann-Marie Dixon
Game Operations Video Producer	Brian Jones
Operations Coordinator	Andy Jacklin
Team Mascot Coordinator	Craig Rappaport
Game Operations and Events Assistant	Alexa Conforti
Director of Amateur Hockey Development	Dan Bedard
Amateur Hockey Development Coordinator	Adam Sherlip

Finance

Controller	Frank Romano
Senior Accountant	Chris Vardaro
Payroll Manager	Christine Bowler
Payroll Assistant	Michelle Finkelstein
Accounts Payable	Janet Nelson
Staff Accountant	Laura Ferretti, Sherrie Mayernik, Erica Palladino, Jennifer Penning

Marketing Services

Marketing Services Manager	JeanneMarie Borgia
Creative Services Manager	Thomas Rakoczy
Graphic Designer	John Tomaselli, Paul Dippolito
Web Designer	Tony Consalvo

New York Rangers

Key Off-Season Signings/Acquisitions

2008

July
- **1** • Re-signed D **Michal Rozsival** and G **Steve Valiquette**.
- **1** • Signed D **Wade Redden**, LW **Aaron Voros** and C **Patrick Rissmiller**.
- **2** • Acquired forwards RW **Nikolai Zherdev** and C **Dan Fritsche** from Columbus for D **Fedor Tyutin** and D **Christian Backman**.
- **3** • Signed LW **Markus Naslund** and D **Dmitri Kalinin**.
- **8** • Re-signed D **Paul Mara**.

2007-08 Results: 42W-27L-4OTL-9SOL 97PTS.
Third, Atlantic Division

Year-by-Year Record

		Home				Road				Overall								
Season	GP	W	L	T	OL	W	L	T	OL	W	L	T	OL	GF	GA	Pts.	Finished	Playoff Result
2007-08	82	25	13	....	3	17	14	....	10	42	27	....	13	213	199	97	3rd, Atlantic Div.	Lost Conf. Semi-Final
2006-07	82	21	15	....	5	21	15	....	5	42	30	....	10	242	216	94	3rd, Atlantic Div.	Lost Conf. Semi-Final
2005-06	82	25	10	....	6	19	16	....	6	44	26	....	12	257	215	100	3rd, Atlantic Div.	Lost Conf. Quarter-Final
2004-05	....	....	....	....	....	....	....	....	....	....	....	....	....	....	....	....		
2003-04	82	13	21	3	4	14	19	4	4	27	40	7	8	206	250	69	4th, Atlantic Div.	Out of Playoffs
2002-03	82	17	18	4	2	15	18	6	2	32	36	10	4	210	231	78	4th, Atlantic Div.	Out of Playoffs
2001-02	82	19	19	2	1	17	19	2	3	36	38	4	4	227	258	80	4th, Atlantic Div.	Out of Playoffs
2000-01	82	17	20	3	1	16	23	2	0	33	43	5	1	250	290	72	4th, Atlantic Div.	Out of Playoffs
1999-2000	82	15	20	5	1	14	18	7	2	29	38	12	3	218	246	73	4th, Atlantic Div.	Out of Playoffs
1998-99	82	17	19	5	....	16	19	6	....	33	38	11	....	217	227	77	4th, Atlantic Div.	Out of Playoffs
1997-98	82	14	18	9	....	11	21	9	....	25	39	18	....	197	231	68	5th, Atlantic Div.	Out of Playoffs
1996-97	82	21	14	6	....	17	20	4	....	38	34	10	....	258	231	86	4th, Atlantic Div.	Lost Conf. Championship
1995-96	82	22	10	9	....	19	17	5	....	41	27	14	....	272	237	96	2nd, Atlantic Div.	Lost Conf. Semi-Final
1994-95	48	11	10	3	....	11	13	0	....	22	23	3	....	139	134	47	4th, Atlantic Div.	Lost Conf. Semi-Final
1993-94	**84**	**28**	**8**	**6**	....	**24**	**16**	**2**	....	**52**	**24**	**8**	....	**299**	**231**	**112**	**1st, Atlantic Div.**	**Won Stanley Cup**
1992-93	84	20	17	5	....	14	22	6	....	34	39	11	....	304	308	79	6th, Patrick Div.	Out of Playoffs
1991-92	80	28	8	4	....	22	17	1	....	50	25	5	....	321	246	105	1st, Patrick Div.	Lost Div. Final
1990-91	80	22	11	7	....	14	20	6	....	36	31	13	....	297	265	85	2nd, Patrick Div.	Lost Div. Semi-Final
1989-90	80	20	11	9	....	16	20	4	....	36	31	13	....	279	267	85	1st, Patrick Div.	Lost Div. Final
1988-89	80	21	17	2	....	16	18	6	....	37	35	8	....	310	307	82	3rd, Patrick Div.	Lost Div. Semi-Final
1987-88	80	22	13	5	....	14	21	5	....	36	34	10	....	300	283	82	5th, Patrick Div.	Out of Playoffs
1986-87	80	18	18	4	....	16	20	4	....	34	38	8	....	307	323	76	4th, Patrick Div.	Lost Div. Semi-Final
1985-86	80	20	18	2	....	16	20	4	....	36	38	6	....	280	276	78	4th, Patick Div.	Lost Conf. Championship
1984-85	80	16	18	6	....	10	26	4	....	26	44	10	....	295	345	62	4th, Patrick Div.	Lost Div. Semi-Final
1983-84	80	27	12	1	....	15	17	8	....	42	29	9	....	314	304	93	4th, Patrick Div.	Lost Div. Semi-Final
1982-83	80	24	13	3	....	11	22	7	....	35	35	10	....	306	287	80	4th, Patrick Div.	Lost Div. Final
1981-82	80	19	15	6	....	20	12	8	....	39	27	14	....	316	306	92	2nd, Patrick Div.	Lost Div. Final
1980-81	80	17	13	10	....	13	23	4	....	30	36	14	....	312	317	74	4th, Patrick Div.	Lost Semi-Final
1979-80	80	22	10	8	....	16	22	2	....	38	32	10	....	308	284	86	3rd, Patrick Div.	Lost Quarter-Final
1978-79	80	19	13	8	....	21	16	3	....	40	29	11	....	316	292	91	3rd, Patrick Div.	Lost Final
1977-78	80	18	15	7	....	12	22	6	....	30	37	13	....	279	280	73	4th, Patrick Div.	Lost Prelim. Round
1976-77	80	17	18	5	....	12	19	9	....	29	37	14	....	272	310	72	4th, Patrick Div.	Out of Playoffs
1975-76	80	16	16	8	....	13	26	1	....	29	42	9	....	262	333	67	4th, Patrick Div.	Out of Playoffs
1974-75	80	21	11	8	....	16	18	6	....	37	29	14	....	319	276	88	2nd, Patrick Div.	Lost Prelim. Round
1973-74	78	26	7	6	....	14	17	8	....	40	24	14	....	300	251	94	3rd, East Div.	Lost Semi-Final
1972-73	78	26	8	5	....	21	15	3	....	47	23	8	....	297	208	102	3rd, East Div.	Lost Semi-Final
1971-72	78	26	6	7	....	22	11	6	....	48	17	13	....	317	192	109	2nd, East Div.	Lost Final
1970-71	78	30	2	7	....	19	16	4	....	49	18	11	....	259	177	109	2nd, East Div.	Lost Semi-Final
1969-70	76	22	8	8	....	16	14	8	....	38	22	16	....	246	189	92	4th, East Div.	Lost Quarter-Final
1968-69	76	27	7	4	....	14	19	5	....	41	26	9	....	231	196	91	3rd, East Div.	Lost Quarter-Final
1967-68	74	22	8	7	....	17	15	5	....	39	23	12	....	226	183	90	2nd, East Div.	Lost Quarter-Final
1966-67	70	18	12	5	....	12	16	7	....	30	28	12	....	188	189	72	4th,	Lost Semi-Final
1965-66	70	12	16	7	....	6	25	4	....	18	41	11	....	195	261	47	6th,	Out of Playoffs
1964-65	70	8	19	8	....	12	19	4	....	20	38	12	....	179	246	52	5th,	Out of Playoffs
1963-64	70	14	13	8	....	8	25	2	....	22	38	10	....	186	242	54	5th,	Out of Playoffs
1962-63	70	12	17	6	....	10	19	6	....	22	36	12	....	211	233	56	5th,	Out of Playoffs
1961-62	70	16	11	8	....	10	21	4	....	26	32	12	....	195	207	64	4th,	Lost Semi-Final
1960-61	70	15	15	5	....	7	23	5	....	22	38	10	....	204	248	54	5th,	Out of Playoffs
1959-60	70	10	15	10	....	7	23	5	....	17	38	15	....	187	247	49	6th,	Out of Playoffs
1958-59	70	14	16	5	....	12	16	7	....	26	32	12	....	201	217	64	5th,	Out of Playoffs
1957-58	70	14	15	6	....	18	10	7	....	32	25	13	....	195	188	77	2nd,	Lost Semi-Final
1956-57	70	15	12	8	....	11	18	6	....	26	30	14	....	184	227	66	4th,	Lost Semi-Final
1955-56	70	20	7	8	....	12	21	2	....	32	28	10	....	204	203	74	3rd,	Lost Semi-Final
1954-55	70	10	12	13	....	7	23	5	....	17	35	18	....	150	210	52	5th,	Out of Playoffs
1953-54	70	18	12	5	....	11	19	5	....	29	31	10	....	161	182	68	5th,	Out of Playoffs
1952-53	70	11	14	10	....	6	23	6	....	17	37	16	....	152	211	50	6th,	Out of Playoffs
1951-52	70	16	13	6	....	7	21	7	....	23	34	13	....	192	219	59	5th,	Out of Playoffs
1950-51	70	14	11	10	....	6	18	11	....	20	29	21	....	169	201	61	5th,	Out of Playoffs
1949-50	70	19	12	4	....	9	19	7	....	28	31	11	....	170	189	67	4th,	Lost Final
1948-49	60	13	12	5	....	5	19	6	....	18	31	11	....	133	172	47	6th,	Out of Playoffs
1947-48	60	11	12	7	....	10	14	6	....	21	26	13	....	176	201	55	4th,	Lost Semi-Final
1946-47	60	11	14	5	....	11	18	1	....	22	32	6	....	167	186	50	5th,	Out of Playoffs
1945-46	50	8	12	5	....	5	16	4	....	13	28	9	....	144	191	35	6th,	Out of Playoffs
1944-45	50	7	11	7	....	4	18	3	....	11	29	10	....	154	247	32	6th,	Out of Playoffs
1943-44	50	4	17	4	....	2	22	1	....	6	39	5	....	162	310	17	6th,	Out of Playoffs
1942-43	50	7	13	5	....	4	18	3	....	11	31	8	....	161	253	30	6th,	Out of Playoffs
1941-42	48	15	8	1	....	14	9	1	....	29	17	2	....	177	143	60	1st,	Lost Semi-Final
1940-41	48	13	7	4	....	8	12	4	....	21	19	8	....	143	125	50	4th,	Lost Quarter-Final
1939-40	**48**	**17**	**4**	**3**	....	**10**	**7**	**7**	....	**27**	**11**	**10**	....	**136**	**77**	**64**	**2nd,**	**Won Stanley Cup**
1938-39	48	13	8	3	....	13	8	3	....	26	16	6	....	149	105	58	2nd,	Lost Semi-Final
1937-38	48	15	5	4	....	12	10	2	....	27	15	6	....	149	96	60	2nd, Amn. Div.	Lost Quarter-Final
1936-37	48	9	7	8	....	10	13	1	....	19	20	9	....	117	106	47	3rd, Amn. Div.	Lost Final
1935-36	48	11	6	7	....	8	11	5	....	19	17	12	....	91	96	50	4th, Amn. Div.	Out of Playoffs
1934-35	48	11	8	5	....	11	12	1	....	22	20	6	....	137	139	50	3rd, Amn. Div.	Lost Semi-Final
1933-34	48	11	7	6	....	10	12	2	....	21	19	8	....	120	113	50	3rd, Amn. Div.	Lost Quarter-Final
1932-33	**48**	**12**	**7**	**5**	....	**11**	**10**	**3**	....	**23**	**17**	**8**	....	**135**	**107**	**54**	**3rd, Amn. Div.**	**Won Stanley Cup**
1931-32	48	13	7	4	....	10	10	4	....	23	17	8	....	134	112	54	1st, Amn. Div.	Lost Final
1930-31	44	10	9	3	....	9	7	6	....	19	16	9	....	106	87	47	3rd, Amn. Div.	Lost Semi-Final
1929-30	44	11	5	6	....	6	12	4	....	17	17	10	....	136	143	44	3rd, Amn. Div.	Lost Semi-Final
1928-29	44	12	6	4	....	9	7	6	....	21	13	10	....	72	65	52	2nd, Amn. Div.	Lost Final
1927-28	**44**	**10**	**8**	**4**	....	**9**	**8**	**5**	....	**19**	**16**	**9**	....	**94**	**79**	**47**	**2nd, Amn. Div.**	**Won Stanley Cup**
1926-27	44	13	5	4	....	12	8	2	....	25	13	6	....	95	72	56	1st, Amn. Div.	Lost Quarter-Final

2008-09 Schedule

Oct.	Sat.	4	at Tampa Bay†
	Sun.	5	Tampa Bay†
	Fri.	10	Chicago
	Sat.	11	at Philadelphia
	Mon.	13	New Jersey
	Wed.	15	Buffalo
	Fri.	17	Toronto
	Sat.	18	at Detroit
	Mon.	20	Dallas
	Fri.	24	at Columbus
	Sat.	25	Pittsburgh
	Mon.	27	at NY Islanders
	Thu.	30	Atlanta
Nov.	Sat.	1	at Toronto
	Tue.	4	NY Islanders
	Thu.	6	Tampa Bay
	Sat.	8	at Washington
	Mon.	10	Edmonton
	Wed.	12	at New Jersey
	Sat.	15	Boston
	Mon.	17	Ottawa
	Wed.	19	Vancouver
	Sat.	22	at Ottawa*
	Mon.	24	Phoenix
	Wed.	26	at Tampa Bay
	Fri.	28	at Florida
	Sun.	30	Florida*
Dec.	Wed.	3	Pittsburgh
	Thu.	4	at Montreal
	Sun.	7	Calgary
	Wed.	10	at Atlanta
	Fri.	12	at New Jersey
	Sat.	13	Carolina
	Tue.	16	at Anaheim
	Wed.	17	at Los Angeles
	Sat.	20	at San Jose
	Tue.	23	Washington
	Sat.	27	New Jersey
	Mon.	29	NY Islanders
Jan.	Sat.	3	at Washington
	Mon.	5	Pittsburgh
	Wed.	7	Montreal
	Fri.	9	at Buffalo
	Sat.	10	at Ottawa
	Tue.	13	at NY Islanders
	Fri.	16	at Chicago
	Sun.	18	at Pittsburgh*
	Tue.	20	Anaheim
	Tue.	27	Carolina
	Wed.	28	at Pittsburgh
	Sat.	31	at Boston*
Feb.	Tue.	3	Atlanta
	Fri.	6	at Dallas
	Mon.	9	at New Jersey
	Wed.	11	Washington
	Fri.	13	at Florida
	Sun.	15	Philadelphia
	Mon.	16	at St. Louis
	Wed.	18	NY Islanders
	Sat.	21	at Buffalo
	Sun.	22	Toronto
	Wed.	25	at Toronto
	Thu.	26	Florida
	Sat.	28	Colorado
Mar.	Thu.	5	at NY Islanders
	Sun.	8	Boston
	Mon.	9	at Carolina
	Thu.	12	at Nashville
	Sat.	14	at Philadelphia*
	Sun.	15	Philadelphia
	Tue.	17	at Montreal
	Sat.	21	Buffalo
	Sun.	22	Ottawa
	Tue.	24	Minnesota
	Thu.	26	at Atlanta
	Sat.	28	at Pittsburgh*
	Mon.	30	New Jersey
Apr.	Thu.	2	at Carolina
	Sat.	4	at Boston*
	Tue.	7	Montreal
	Thu.	9	Philadelphia
	Sun.	12	at Philadelphia*

* Denotes afternoon game. † Games played in Prague, CZ.

ATLANTIC DIVISION
83rd NHL Season

Franchise date: May 15, 1926

2008-09 Player Personnel

FORWARDS	HT	WT	S	Place of Birth	*Age	2007-08 Club
ANISIMOV, Artem	6-3	187	L	Yaroslavl, USSR	20	Hartford
BETTS, Blair	6-3	210	L	Edmonton, Alta.	28	NY Rangers
BYERS, Dane	6-3	195	L	Nipawin, Sask.	22	NY Rangers-Hartford
CALLAHAN, Ryan	5-11	190	R	Rochester, NY	23	NY Rangers-Hartford
DAWES, Nigel	5-9	190	L	Winnipeg, Man.	23	NY Rangers-Hartford
DRURY, Chris	5-10	190	R	Trumbull, CT	32	NY Rangers
DUBINSKY, Brandon	6-1	210	L	Anchorage, AK	22	NY Rangers
FRITSCHE, Dan	6-1	206	R	Parma, OH	23	Columbus
GOMEZ, Scott	5-11	200	L	Anchorage, AK	28	NY Rangers
KORPIKOSKI, Lauri	6-1	195	L	Turku, Finland	22	Hartford-NY Rangers
MOORE, Greg	6-1	210	R	Lisbon, ME	24	NY Rangers-Hartford
NASLUND, Markus	6-0	195	L	Ornskoldsvik, Sweden	35	Vancouver
ORR, Colton	6-3	222	R	Winnipeg, Man.	26	NY Rangers
PARENTEAU, Pierre	5-11	195	R	Hull, Que.	25	Hartford
PRUCHA, Petr	6-0	175	R	Chrudim, Czech.	26	NY Rangers
RISSMILLER, Patrick	6-4	220	L	Belmont, MA	29	San Jose
SJOSTROM, Fredrik	6-1	217	L	Fargelanda, Sweden	25	Phoenix-NY Rangers
VOROS, Aaron	6-3	202	L	Vancouver, B.C.	27	Minnesota-Houston
ZHERDEV, Nikolai	6-2	205	R	Kiev, USSR	23	Columbus
DEFENSEMEN						
GIRARDI, Dan	6-2	210	R	Welland, Ont.	24	NY Rangers
KALININ, Dmitri	6-3	215	L	Chelyabinsk, USSR	28	Buffalo
MARA, Paul	6-4	212	L	Ridgewood, NJ	29	NY Rangers
POCK, Thomas	6-1	210	L	Klagenfurt, Austria	26	NY Rangers-Hartford
REDDEN, Wade	6-2	209	L	Lloydminster, Sask.	31	Ottawa
ROZSIVAL, Michal	6-2	210	R	Vlasim, Czech.	30	NY Rangers
STAAL, Marc	6-4	210	L	Thunder Bay, Ont.	21	NY Rangers

GOALTENDERS	HT	WT	C	Place of Birth	*Age	2007-08 Club
LUNDQVIST, Henrik	6-1	195	L	Are, Sweden	26	NY Rangers
VALIQUETTE, Steve	6-6	210	L	Etobicoke, Ont.	31	NY Rangers

* – Age at start of 2008-09 season

Tom Renney

Head Coach

Born: Cranbrook, B.C., March 1, 1955.

Tom Renney took over as interim coach of the New York Rangers on February 25, 2004. He was officially named the 33rd head coach in franchise history on July 6. In 2005-06, Renney guided the Rangers to their first playoff berth since 1996-97. In the 2007 playoffs, the Rangers won a series for the first time since 1997.

Renney joined the Rangers on July 31, 2000 as director of player personnel and was promoted to vice president, player development on June 21, 2002. In that position, he oversaw all facets of the team's amateur scouting operations, while also assisting with the professional scouting process and player development within the organization. Renney joined the Rangers coaching staff as an assistant coach on July 21, 2003.

From June, 1996 through November, 1997, Renney served as head coach of the Vancouver Canucks. Prior to his return to the National Hockey League in New York, Renney held the position of vice president and head coach of the Canadian national team. Renney rejoined the Canadian Hockey Association in May, 1998. He began his affiliation with the Canadian national team in 1992 and coached Canada's Olympic hockey team to a silver medal at the 1994 Winter Games in Lillehammer, Norway. Later that year, he served as an assistant coach on Team Canada's gold medal-winning team at the World Championships. He won silver again as an assistant coach at the 2005 World Championship. Previously, he won the Memorial Cup with the Kamloops Blazers in 1992.

Coaching Record

			Regular Season				Playoffs			
Season	Team	League	GC	W	L	O/T	GC	W	L	T
1990-91	Kamloops	WHL	72	50	20	2	12	5	7	....
1991-92	Kamloops	WHL	72	51	17	4	16	11	5	....
1993-94*	Canada	Exhib	63	33	26	4	8	5	2	....
1994-95**	Canada	Exhib	57	37	17	3	8	3	2	2
1995-96***	Canada	Exhib	53	33	12	8	8	4	2	2
1996-97	**Vancouver**	**NHL**	**82**	**35**	**40**	**7**	....	....	....	....
1997-98	**Vancouver**	**NHL**	**19**	**4**	**13**	**2**	....	....	....	....
99-2000	Canada	Exhib	56	27	23	6	....	....	....	....
2003-04	**NY Rangers**	**NHL**	**20**	**5**	**11**	**4**	....	....	....	....
2004-05	**NY Rangers**				SEASON CANCELLED					
2005-06	**NY Rangers**	**NHL**	**82**	**44**	**26**	**12**	**4**	**0**	**4**	....
2006-07	**NY Rangers**	**NHL**	**82**	**42**	**30**	**10**	**10**	**6**	**4**	....
2007-08	**NY Rangers**	**NHL**	**82**	**42**	**27**	**13**	**10**	**5**	**5**	....
	NHL Totals		**367**	**172**	**147**	**48**	**24**	**11**	**13**	....

* Olympics (silver medal)
** World Championship (bronze)
*** World Championship (silver)

Coaching History

Lester Patrick, 1926-27 to 1938-39; Frank Boucher, 1939-40 to 1947-48; Frank Boucher and Lynn Patrick, 1948-49; Lynn Patrick, 1949-50; Neil Colville, 1950-51; Neil Colville and Bill Cook, 1951-52; Bill Cook, 1952-53; Frank Boucher and Muzz Patrick, 1953-54; Muzz Patrick, 1954-55; Phil Watson, 1955-56 to 1958-59; Phil Watson, Muzz Patrick and Alf Pike, 1959-60; Alf Pike, 1960-61; Doug Harvey, 1961-62; Muzz Patrick and Red Sullivan, 1962-63; Red Sullivan, 1963-64, 1964-65; Red Sullivan and Emile Francis, 1965-66; Emile Francis, 1966-67, 1967-68; Bernie Geoffrion and Emile Francis, 1968-69; Emile Francis, 1969-70 to 1972-73; Larry Popein and Emile Francis, 1973-74; Emile Francis, 1974-75; Ron Stewart and John Ferguson, 1975-76; John Ferguson, 1976-77; Jean-Guy Talbot, 1977-78; Fred Shero, 1978-79, 1979-80; Fred Shero and Craig Patrick, 1980-81; Herb Brooks, 1981-82 to 1983-84; Herb Brooks and Craig Patrick, 1984-85; Ted Sator, 1985-86; Ted Sator, Tom Webster and Phil Esposito, 1986-87; Michel Bergeron, 1987-88; Michel Bergeron and Phil Esposito, 1988-89; Roger Neilson, 1989-90 to 1991-92; Roger Neilson and Ron Smith, 1992-93; Mike Keenan, 1993-94; Colin Campbell, 1994-95 to 1996-97; Colin Campbell and John Muckler, 1997-98; John Muckler, 1998-99; John Muckler and John Tortorella, 1999-2000; Ron Low, 2000-01, 2001-02; Bryan Trottier and Glen Sather, 2002-03; Glen Sather and Tom Renney, 2003-04; Tom Renney, 2004-05 to date.

2007-08 Scoring

* – rookie

Regular Season

Pos	#	Player	Team	GP	G	A	Pts	TOI	+/–	PIM	PP	SH	GW	S	%
R	68	Jaromir Jagr	NYR	82	25	46	71	20:28	8	58	7	0	5	249	10.0
C	19	Scott Gomez	NYR	81	16	54	70	19:53	3	36	7	0	3	242	6.6
C	23	Chris Drury	NYR	82	25	33	58	19:47	–3	45	12	0	7	220	11.4
R	14	Brendan Shanahan	NYR	73	23	23	46	18:30	–2	35	11	0	3	265	8.7
C	82	Martin Straka	NYR	65	14	27	41	18:37	5	22	3	1	2	116	12.1
C	17 *	Brandon Dubinsky	NYR	82	14	26	40	14:29	8	79	1	0	0	157	8.9
D	3	Michal Rozsival	NYR	80	13	25	38	24:33	0	80	6	2	0	127	10.2
L	16	Sean Avery	NYR	57	15	18	33	15:50	6	154	2	0	4	125	12.0
L	10 *	Nigel Dawes	NYR	61	14	15	29	12:59	11	10	3	0	4	121	11.6
D	5	Dan Girardi	NYR	82	10	18	28	21:11	0	14	5	0	1	147	6.8
L	20	Fredrik Sjostrom	PHX	51	10	9	19	13:33	–2	14	2	2	1	84	11.9
			NYR	18	2	0	2	08:04	0	8	0	0	1	26	7.7
			Total	69	12	9	21	12:07	–2	22	2	2	2	110	10.9
D	51	Fedor Tyutin	NYR	82	5	15	20	20:26	5	43	1	0	0	131	3.8
D	55	Christian Backman	STL	45	1	9	10	19:22	–4	30	0	0	0	30	3.3
			NYR	18	2	6	8	18:48	2	20	1	0	0	21	9.5
			Total	63	3	15	18	19:12	–2	50	1	0	0	51	5.9
L	25	Petr Prucha	NYR	62	7	10	17	11:38	3	22	2	0	1	89	7.9
D	27	Paul Mara	NYR	61	1	16	17	17:53	1	52	0	0	0	80	1.3
R	24 *	Ryan Callahan	NYR	52	8	5	13	12:22	7	31	0	1	1	92	8.7
D	8	Marek Malik	NYR	42	2	8	10	19:14	7	48	0	0	0	34	5.9
D	18 *	Marc Staal	NYR	80	2	8	10	18:48	2	42	0	0	0	78	2.6
C	15	Blair Betts	NYR	75	2	5	7	11:51	–4	20	0	0	0	85	2.4
L	44	Ryan Hollweg	NYR	70	2	2	4	08:17	–12	96	0	0	0	59	3.4
D	34	Jason Strudwick	NYR	52	1	1	2	12:56	0	40	0	0	1	21	4.8
R	28	Colton Orr	NYR	74	1	1	2	07:49	–13	159	0	0	1	24	4.2
D	21 *	Ivan Baranka	NYR	1	0	1	1	12:44	1	0	0	0	0	1	0.0
D	22	Thomas Pock	NYR	1	0	0	0	18:53	–2	0	0	0	0	2	0.0
L	54 *	Dane Byers	NYR	1	0	0	0	05:05	–1	0	0	0	0	0	0.0
R	49 *	Greg Moore	NYR	6	0	0	0	11:49	–2	0	0	0	0	13	0.0

Goaltending

No.	Goaltender	GPI	Mins	Avg	W	L	OT	EN	SO	GA	SA	S%	G	A	PIM
40	Stephen Valiquette	13	686	2.19	5	3	3	1	2	25	296	.916	0	0	2
30	Henrik Lundqvist	72	4305	2.23	37	24	10	4	10	160	1823	.912	0	0	2
	Totals	**82**	**5018**	**2.27**	**42**	**27**	**13**	**5**	**12**	**190**	**2124**	**.911**			

Playoffs

Pos	#	Player	Team	GP	G	A	Pts	TOI	+/–	PIM	PP	SH	GW	OT	S	%
R	68	Jaromir Jagr	NYR	10	5	10	15	19:53	3	12	2	0	1	0	37	13.5
C	19	Scott Gomez	NYR	10	4	7	11	20:52	5	8	1	0	0	0	27	14.8
C	82	Martin Straka	NYR	10	3	7	10	19:56	2	16	1	0	0	0	13	23.1
C	17 *	Brandon Dubinsky	NYR	10	4	4	8	18:59	2	12	2	0	0	0	26	15.4
L	16	Sean Avery	NYR	8	4	3	7	14:14	3	6	1	0	1	0	13	30.8
C	23	Chris Drury	NYR	10	3	3	6	18:27	3	8	0	0	1	0	19	15.8
D	3	Michal Rozsival	NYR	10	1	5	6	25:04	4	10	0	0	0	0	13	7.7
R	14	Brendan Shanahan	NYR	10	1	4	5	17:04	0	8	0	0	0	0	30	3.3
L	10 *	Nigel Dawes	NYR	10	2	2	4	12:31	3	0	0	0	0	0	19	10.5
R	24 *	Ryan Callahan	NYR	10	2	2	4	15:55	3	10	0	1	1	0	25	8.0
D	18 *	Marc Staal	NYR	10	1	2	3	22:20	4	8	0	0	1	0	11	9.1
D	51	Fedor Tyutin	NYR	10	0	3	3	19:52	–1	4	0	0	0	0	9	0.0
D	5	Dan Girardi	NYR	10	0	3	3	20:41	1	6	0	0	0	0	14	0.0
L	22 *	Lauri Korpikoski	NYR	1	1	0	1	07:14	1	0	0	0	0	0	2	50.0
D	27	Paul Mara	NYR	10	0	1	1	17:47	3	20	0	0	0	0	12	0.0
L	20	Fredrik Sjostrom	NYR	10	0	1	1	06:28	0	2	0	0	0	0	2	0.0
D	34	Jason Strudwick	NYR	2	0	0	0	09:40	0	0	0	0	0	0	0	0.0
R	28	Colton Orr	NYR	2	0	0	0	04:26	0	0	0	0	0	0	1	0.0
L	25	Petr Prucha	NYR	3	0	0	0	08:13	0	0	0	0	0	0	3	0.0
D	55	Christian Backman	NYR	8	0	0	0	18:15	3	12	0	0	0	0	7	0.0
C	15	Blair Betts	NYR	8	0	0	0	07:16	–4	2	0	0	0	0	7	0.0
L	44	Ryan Hollweg	NYR	8	0	0	0	04:49	–2	2	0	0	0	0	5	0.0

Goaltending

No.	Goaltender	GPI	Mins	Avg	W	L	EN	SO	GA	SA	S%	G	A	PIM
30	Henrik Lundqvist	10	608	2.57	5	5	1	1	26	287	.909	0	0	0
	Totals	**10**	**613**	**2.64**	**5**	**5**	**1**	**1**	**27**	**288**	**.906**			

General Managers' History

Lester Patrick, 1926-27 to 1945-46; Frank Boucher, 1946-47 to 1954-55; Muzz Patrick, 1955-56 to 1963-64; Emile Francis, 1964-65 to 1974-75; Emile Francis and John Ferguson, 1975-76; John Ferguson, 1976-77, 1977-78; Fred Shero, 1978-79, 1979-80; Fred Shero and Craig Patrick, 1980-81; Craig Patrick, 1981-82 to 1985-86; Phil Esposito, 1986-87 to 1988-89; Neil Smith, 1989-90 to 1999-2000; Glen Sather, 2000-01 to date.

Captains' History

Bill Cook, 1926-27 to 1936-37; Art Coulter, 1937-38 to 1941-42; Ott Heller, 1942-43 to 1944-45; Neil Colville 1945-46 to 1948-49; Buddy O'Connor, 1949-50; Frank Eddolls, 1950-51; Frank Eddolls and Allan Stanley, 1951-52; Allan Stanley, 1952-53; Allan Stanley and Don Raleigh, 1953-54; Don Raleigh, 1954-55; Harry Howell, 1955-56, 1956-57; Red Sullivan, 1957-58 to 1960-61; Andy Bathgate, 1961-62, 1962-63; Andy Bathgate and Camille Henry, 1963-64; Camille Henry and Bob Nevin, 1964-65; Bob Nevin 1965-66 to 1970-71; Vic Hadfield, 1971-72 to 1973-74; Brad Park, 1974-75; Brad Park and Phil Esposito, 1975-76; Phil Esposito, 1976-77, 1977-78; Dave Maloney, 1978-79, 1979-80; Dave Maloney, Walt Tkaczuk and Barry Beck, 1980-81; Barry Beck, 1981-82 to 1985-86; Ron Greschner, 1986-87; Ron Greschner and Kelly Kisio, 1987-88; Kelly Kisio, 1988-89 to 1990-91; Mark Messier, 1991-92 to 1996-97; Brian Leetch, 1997-98 to 1999-2000; Mark Messier, 2000-01 to 2003-04; no captain, 2005-06; Jaromir Jagr, 2006-07, 2007-08.

Club Records

Team

(Figures in brackets for season records are games played; records for fewest points, wins, ties, losses, goals, goals against are for 70 or more games)

Most Points	112	1993-94 (84)
Most Wins	52	1993-94 (84)
Most Ties	21	1950-51 (70)
Most Losses	44	1984-85 (80)
Most Goals	321	1991-92 (80)
Most Goals Against	345	1984-85 (80)
Fewest Points	47	1965-66 (70)
Fewest Wins	17	1952-53 (70), 1954-55 (70), 1959-60 (70)
Fewest Ties	4	2001-02 (82)
Fewest Losses	17	1971-72 (78)
Fewest Goals	150	1954-55 (70)
Fewest Goals Against	177	1970-71 (78)
Longest Winning Streak		
Overall	10	Dec. 19/39-Jan. 13/40, Jan. 19-Feb. 10/73
Home	14	Dec. 19/39-Feb. 25/40
Away	7	Jan. 12-Feb. 12/35, Oct. 28-Nov. 29/78
Longest Undefeated Streak		
Overall	19	Nov. 23/39-Jan. 13/40 (14 wins, 5 ties)
Home	24	Oct. 14/70-Jan. 31/71 (18 wins, 6 ties), Oct. 24/95-Feb.15/96 (18 wins, 6 ties)
Away	11	Nov. 5/39-Jan. 13/40 (6 wins, 5 ties)
Longest Losing Streak		
Overall	11	Oct. 30-Nov. 27/43
Home	7	Oct. 20-Nov. 14/76, Mar. 24-Apr. 14/93
Away	10	Oct. 30-Dec. 23/43, Feb. 8-Mar. 15/61
Longest Winless Streak		
Overall	21	Jan. 23-Mar. 19/44 (17 losses, 4 ties)
Home	10	Jan. 30-Mar. 19/44 (7 losses, 3 ties)
Away	16	Oct. 9-Dec. 20/52 (12 losses, 4 ties)
Most Shutouts, Season	13	1928-29 (44)
Most PIM, Season	2,018	1989-90 (80)
Most Goals, Game	12	Nov. 21/71 (Cal. 1 at NYR 12)

Individual

Most Seasons	18	Rod Gilbert
Most Games	1,160	Harry Howell
Most Goals, Career	406	Rod Gilbert
Most Assists, Career	741	Brian Leetch
Most Points, Career	1,021	Rod Gilbert (406G, 615A)
Most PIM, Career	1,226	Ron Greschner
Most Shutouts, Career	96	Martin Brodeur
Longest Consecutive Games Streak	560	Andy Hebenton (Oct. 7/55-Mar. 24/63)
Most Goals, Season	54	Jaromir Jagr (2005-06)
Most Assists, Season	80	Brian Leetch (1991-92)
Most Points, Season	123	Jaromir Jagr (2005-06; 54G, 69A)
Most PIM, Season	305	Troy Mallette (1989-90)
Most Points, Defenseman, Season	102	Brian Leetch (1991-92; 22G, 80A)
Most Points, Center, Season	109	Jean Ratelle (1971-72; 46G, 63A)
Most Points, Right Wing, Season	123	Jaromir Jagr (2005-06; 54G, 69A)
Most Points, Left Wing, Season	106	Vic Hadfield (1971-72; 50G, 56A)
Most Points, Rookie, Season	76	Mark Pavelich (1981-82; 33G, 43A)
Most Shutouts, Season	13	John Ross Roach (1928-29)
Most Goals, Game	5	Don Murdoch (Oct. 12/76), Mark Pavelich (Feb. 23/83)
Most Assists, Game	5	Walt Tkaczuk (Feb. 12/72), Rod Gilbert (Mar. 2/75, Mar. 30/75, Oct. 8/76), Don Maloney (Jan. 3/87), Brian Leetch (Apr. 18/95), Wayne Gretzky (Feb. 15/99)
Most Points, Game	7	Steve Vickers (Feb. 18/76; 3G, 4A)

Retired Numbers

1	Ed Giacomin	1965-1975
2	Brian Leetch	1987-2004
7	Rod Gilbert	1960-1977
11	Mark Messier	1991-97; 2000-04
35	Mike Richter	1989-2003

All-time Record vs. Other Clubs

Regular Season

	At Home								On Road								Total							
	GP	W	L	T	OL	GF	GA	PTS	GP	W	L	T	OL	GF	GA	PTS	GP	W	L	T	OL	GF	GA	PTS
Anaheim	10	3	6	1	0	24	30	7	9	3	6	0	0	29	35	6	19	6	12	1	0	53	65	13
Atlanta	16	6	6	1	3	46	47	16	16	9	5	0	2	53	47	20	32	15	11	1	5	99	94	36
Boston	308	136	117	55	0	941	861	327	304	100	160	42	2	852	1088	244	612	236	277	97	2	1793	1949	571
Buffalo	72	31	24	15	2	232	195	79	74	22	41	10	1	230	300	55	146	53	65	25	3	462	495	134
Calgary	53	25	23	5	0	182	186	55	50	12	28	10	0	151	220	34	103	37	51	15	0	333	406	89
Carolina	51	31	15	4	1	187	127	67	49	18	28	3	0	151	163	39	100	49	43	7	1	338	290	106
Chicago	286	118	113	55	0	843	808	291	287	115	128	43	1	793	872	274	573	233	241	98	1	1636	1680	565
Colorado	35	19	10	4	2	135	101	44	36	13	18	3	2	133	147	31	71	32	28	7	4	268	248	75
Columbus	3	1	1	1	0	9	8	3	5	1	4	0	0	10	20	2	8	2	5	1	0	19	28	5
Dallas	63	36	16	11	0	215	168	83	62	31	19	11	1	226	189	74	125	67	35	22	1	441	357	157
Detroit	285	134	93	58	0	871	742	326	286	76	165	45	0	702	1008	197	571	210	258	103	0	1573	1750	523
Edmonton	31	11	14	6	0	117	117	28	29	13	12	3	1	96	104	30	60	24	26	9	1	213	221	58
Florida	30	17	9	4	0	96	66	38	31	15	11	2	3	85	82	35	61	32	20	6	3	181	148	73
Los Angeles	59	35	18	6	0	235	176	76	61	27	24	10	0	217	203	64	120	62	42	16	0	452	379	140
Minnesota	4	3	1	0	0	13	8	6	5	3	2	0	0	16	17	6	9	6	3	0	0	29	25	12
Montreal	296	122	119	54	1	854	857	299	296	63	192	40	1	692	1146	167	592	185	311	94	2	1546	2003	466
Nashville	7	2	3	1	1	18	18	6	5	3	1	0	1	19	14	7	12	5	4	1	2	37	32	13
New Jersey	96	49	26	20	1	352	278	119	98	39	49	7	3	306	326	88	194	88	75	27	4	658	604	207
NY Islanders	108	59	35	11	3	391	321	132	108	41	58	8	1	342	394	91	216	100	93	19	4	733	715	223
Ottawa	29	12	17	0	0	88	91	24	29	13	12	3	1	76	85	30	58	25	29	3	1	164	176	54
Philadelphia	122	52	43	23	4	387	359	131	121	49	56	14	2	342	383	114	243	101	99	37	6	729	742	245
Phoenix	30	18	10	2	0	129	107	38	32	15	13	4	0	108	110	34	62	33	23	6	0	237	217	72
Pittsburgh	113	60	43	9	1	435	370	130	112	47	46	14	5	393	391	113	225	107	89	23	6	828	761	243
St. Louis	61	45	10	6	0	248	145	96	64	29	25	10	0	207	192	68	125	74	35	16	0	455	337	164
San Jose	11	8	2	1	0	43	30	17	14	10	2	2	0	52	32	22	25	18	4	3	0	95	62	39
Tampa Bay	33	17	12	2	2	106	95	38	31	13	14	3	1	98	103	30	64	30	26	5	3	204	198	68
Toronto	289	123	109	56	1	893	854	303	288	88	160	39	1	762	994	216	577	211	269	95	2	1655	1848	519
Vancouver	55	38	12	5	0	239	142	81	52	33	16	3	0	204	166	69	107	71	28	8	0	443	308	150
Washington	88	44	34	9	1	326	291	98	90	34	44	9	3	288	336	80	178	78	78	18	4	614	627	178
Defunct Clubs	139	87	30	22	0	460	290	196	139	82	34	23	0	441	291	187	278	169	64	45	0	901	581	383
Totals	**2783**	**1342**	**971**	**447**	**23**	**9115**	**7888**	**3154**	**2783**	**1017**	**1373**	**361**	**32**	**8074**	**9458**	**2427**	**5566**	**2359**	**2344**	**808**	**55**	**17189**	**17346**	**5581**

Playoffs

	Series	W	L	GP	W	L	T	GF	GA	Last Mtg.	Rnd.	Result
Atlanta	1	1	0	4	4	0	0	17	6	2007	CQF	W 4-0
Boston	9	3	6	42	18	22	2	104	114	1973	QF	W 4-1
Buffalo	2	0	2	9	3	6	0	19	28	2007	CSF	L 2-4
Calgary	1	1	0	4	3	1	0	14	8	1980	PRE	W 3-1
Chicago	5	1	4	24	10	14	0	54	66	1973	SF	L 1-4
Colorado	1	1	0	6	4	2	0	25	19	1995	CQF	W 4-2
Detroit	5	1	4	23	10	13	0	49	57	1950	F	L 3-4
Florida	1	1	0	5	4	1	0	13	10	1997	CQF	W 4-1
Los Angeles	2	2	0	6	5	1	0	32	14	1981	PRE	W 3-1
Montreal	14	7	7	61	25	34	2	158	188	1996	CQF	W 4-2
New Jersey	5	4	1	28	16	12	0	79	75	2008	CQF	W 4-1
NY Islanders	8	3	5	39	19	20	0	132	129	1994	CQF	W 4-0
Philadelphia	10	4	6	47	20	27	0	153	157	1997	CF	L 1-4
Pittsburgh	4	0	4	20	4	16	0	56	79	2008	CSF	L 1-4
St. Louis	1	1	0	6	4	2	0	29	22	1981	QF	W 4-2
Toronto	8	5	3	35	19	16	0	86	86	1971	QF	W 4-2
Vancouver	1	1	0	7	4	3	0	21	19	1994	F	W 4-3
Washington	4	2	2	22	11	11	0	71	75	1994	CSF	W 4-1
Defunct Clubs	9	6	3	22	11	7	4	43	29			
Totals	**91**	**44**	**47**	**410**	**194**	**208**	**8**	**1155**	**1181**			

Calgary totals include Atlanta Flames, 1972-73 to 1979-80.
Colorado totals include Quebec, 1979-80 to 1994-95.
Carolina totals include Hartford, 1979-80 to 1996-97.
Dallas totals include Minnesota North Stars, 1967-68 to 1992-93.
New Jersey totals include Kansas City, 1974-75, 1975-76, and Colorado Rockies, 1976-77 to 1981-82.
Phoenix totals include Winnipeg, 1979-80 to 1995-96.

Playoff Results 2008-2003

Year	Round	Opponent	Result	GF	GA
2008	CSF	Pittsburgh	L 1-4	11	15
	CQF	New Jersey	W 4-1	19	12
2007	CSF	Buffalo	L 2-4	13	17
	CQF	Atlanta	W 4-0	17	6
2006	CQF	New Jersey	L 0-4	4	17

Abbreviations: Round: F – Final; **CF** – conference final; **CSF** – conference semi-final; **CQF** – conference quarter-final; **SF** – semi-final; **QF** – quarter-final; **PRE** – preliminary round.

2007-08 Results

Month	Day	Opponent	Score
Oct.	4	Florida	5-2
	6	at Ottawa	0-2
	10	at NY Islanders	1-2
	12	Washington	3-1
	13	Ottawa	1-3
	18	at Atlanta	3-5
	20	at Boston	0-1†
	23	at Pittsburgh	0-1
	25	New Jersey	2-0
	27	Toronto	1-4
	29	Tampa Bay	3-1
Nov.	1	Washington	2-0
	3	New Jersey	2-1†
	5	Philadelphia	2-0
	6	at NY Islanders	2-3
	8	Pittsburgh	4-2
	10	at Toronto	3-2†
	14	at New Jersey	4-2
	15	at Philadelphia	4-3†
	17	at Pittsburgh	4-3*
	19	NY Islanders	1-2
	21	at Tampa Bay	2-1
	23	at Florida	2-3†
	25	Dallas	2-3
	29	NY Islanders	4-2
Dec.	1	at Ottawa	5-2
	3	Carolina	0-4
	6	Toronto	2-6
	7	at Atlanta	2-4
	9	New Jersey	1-0*
	12	at Washington	4-5*
	16	Phoenix	1-5
	18	Pittsburgh	4-0
	20	at Minnesota	3-6
	21	at Colorado	3-4*
	23	Ottawa	1-3
	26	Carolina	4-2
	29	at Toronto	6-1
	30	Montreal	4-3*
Jan.	2	at Calgary	3-4
	3	at Vancouver	0-3
	5	at Edmonton	2-3†
	8	Tampa Bay	3-5
	10	Philadelphia	2-6
	12	Montreal	4-1
	14	at Pittsburgh	1-4
	16	Buffalo	2-1
	19	at Boston	3-4†
	20	Boston	1-3
	22	Atlanta	4-0
	24	Atlanta	2-1†
	29	at Carolina	1-3
	31	at Philadelphia	4-0
Feb.	1	at New Jersey	3-1
	3	at Montreal	5-3
	5	Los Angeles	2-4
	7	Anaheim	1-4
	9	at Philadelphia	2-0
	10	at Washington	2-3*
	16	Buffalo	5-1
	17	San Jose	3-1
	19	at Montreal	5-6†
	23	at Buffalo	4-3
	24	Florida	5-0
	28	at Carolina	4-2
Mar.	2	Philadelphia	5-4†
	4	NY Islanders	3-4†
	6	at NY Islanders	4-1
	9	Boston	1-0†
	10	at Buffalo	3-2†
	14	at Florida	2-3
	15	at Tampa Bay	0-3
	18	Pittsburgh	5-2
	19	at New Jersey	2-1†
	21	at Philadelphia	3-4†
	25	Philadelphia	1-2*
	27	New Jersey	3-2
	30	at Pittsburgh	1-3
	31	Pittsburgh	2-1*
Apr.	3	at NY Islanders	3-0
	4	NY Islanders	3-4†
	6	at New Jersey	2-3†

* – Overtime † – Shootout

Entry Draft Selections 2008-1994

Name in bold denotes played in NHL.

2008
Pick
20 Michael Del Zotto
51 Derek Stepan
75 Yevgeny Grachev
90 Tomas Kundratek
111 Dale Weise
141 Chris Doyle
171 Mitch Gaulton

2007
Pick
17 Alexei Cherepanov
48 Antoine Lafleur
138 Max Campbell
168 Carl Hagelin
193 David Skokan
198 Danny Hobbs

2006
Pick
21 Bobby Sanguinetti
54 Artem Anisimov
84 Ryan Hillier
104 David Kveton
137 Tomas Zaborsky
174 Eric Hunter
204 Lukas Zeliska

2005
Pick
12 **Marc Staal**
40 Michael Sauer
56 Marc-Andre Cliche
66 Brodie Dupont
77 Dalyn Flatt
107 Tom Pyatt
147 Trevor Koverko
178 Greg Beller
211 Ryan Russell

2004
Pick
6 Al Montoya
19 **Lauri Korpikoski**
36 Darin Olver
48 **Dane Byers**
51 Bruce Graham
60 **Brandon Dubinsky**
73 Zdenek Bahensky
80 Billy Ryan
127 **Ryan Callahan**
135 Roman Psurny
169 Jordan Foote
247 Jonathan Paiement
266 Jakub Petruzalek

2003
Pick
12 Hugh Jessiman
50 **Ivan Baranka**
75 Ken Roche
122 Corey Potter
149 **Nigel Dawes**
176 Ivan Dornic
179 Philippe Furrer
180 **Chris Holt**
209 Dylan Reese
243 Jan Marek

2002
Pick
33 Lee Falardeau
81 Marcus Jonasen
127 **Nate Guenin**
143 Mike Walsh
177 Jake Taylor
194 Kim Hirschovits
226 Joey Crabb
240 **Petr Prucha**
270 Rob Flynn

2001
Pick
10 **Dan Blackburn**
40 **Fedor Tyutin**
79 **Garth Murray**
113 **Bryce Lampman**
139 Shawn Collymore
176 **Marek Zidlicky**
206 Petr Preucil
226 Pontus Petterstrom
230 Leonid Zhvachkin
238 **Ryan Hollweg**
269 Juris Stals

2000
Pick
64 **Filip Novak**
95 **Dominic Moore**
112 Premysl Duben
140 Nathan Martz
143 Brandon Snee
175 Sven Helfenstein
205 **Henrik Lundqvist**
238 Danny Eberly
269 Martin Richter

1999
Pick
4 **Pavel Brendl**
9 **Jamie Lundmark**
59 David Inman
79 Johan Asplund
90 Patrick Aufiero
137 Garrett Bembridge
177 Jay Dardis
197 Arto Laatikainen
226 Yevgeny Gusakov
251 Petter Henning
254 Alexei Bulatov

1998
Pick
7 **Manny Malhotra**
40 Randy Copley
66 **Jason Labarbera**
114 **Boyd Kane**
122 **Patrick Leahy**
131 **Tomas Kloucek**
180 Stefan Lundqvist
207 **Johan Witehall**
235 **Jan Mertzig**

1997
Pick
19 Stefan Cherneski
46 Wes Jarvis
73 **Burke Henry**
93 Tomi Kallarsson
126 Jason McLean
134 **Johan Lindbom**
136 **Mike York**
154 Shawn Degagne
175 **Johan Holmqvist**
182 **Mike Mottau**
210 Andrew Proskurnicki
236 Richard Miller

1996
Pick
22 Jeff Brown
48 **Daniel Goneau**
76 Dmitri Subbotin
131 Colin Pepperall
158 Ola Sandberg
185 Jeff Dessner
211 Ryan McKie
237 **Ronnie Sundin**

1995
Pick
39 **Christian Dube**
65 Mike Martin
91 **Marc Savard**
110 **Alexei Vasiliev**
117 **Dale Purinton**
143 Peter Slamiar
169 Jeff Heil
195 Ilya Gorokhov
221 Bob Maudie

1994
Pick
26 **Dan Cloutier**
52 Rudolf Vercik
78 Adam Smith
100 Alexander Korobolin
104 **Sylvain Blouin**
130 Martin Ethier
135 Yuri Litvinov
156 David Brosseau
182 Alexei Lazarenko
208 Craig Anderson
209 **Vitali Yeremeyev**
234 **Eric Boulton**
260 Radoslav Kropac
267 Jamie Butt
286 **Kim Johnsson**

Glen Sather

President and General Manager

Born: High River, Alta., September 2, 1943.

Glen Sather, who spent parts of four seasons with the New York Rangers as a player from 1970 to 1974, became the franchise's 12th president and tenth general manager on June 2, 2000. He also served as coach of the team from January 30, 2003, to February 25, 2004.

Sather joined the Rangers following a 24-year career with the Edmonton Oilers, where he was the architect of five Stanley Cup championships between 1984 and 1990. One of the most respected executives in the National Hockey League, Sather was honored for his tremendous achievements in 1997 by becoming the first member of the Oilers organization to be selected to the Hockey Hall of Fame.

Named coach and vice president of hockey operations for the Oilers when the franchise joined the NHL in June of 1979, Sather became general manager and club president in May of 1980. He coached through the 1988-89 season and also returned for 60 games behind the bench in 1993-94. Sather-coached teams won the Stanley Cup four times in the 1980s. As general manager, Sather was instrumental in the Oilers' fifth Cup triumph in 1990.

He played for six different teams during a 10-year NHL career. He scored 80 goals in 658 games.

Coaching Record

			Regular Season				Playoffs			
Season	Team	League	GC	W	L	O/T	GC	W	L	T
1979-80	Edmonton	NHL	80	28	39	13	3	0	3	....
1980-81	Edmonton	NHL	62	25	26	11	9	5	4	....
1981-82	Edmonton	NHL	80	48	17	15	5	2	3	....
1982-83	Edmonton	NHL	80	47	21	12	16	11	5	....
1983-84♦	Edmonton	NHL	80	57	18	5	19	15	4	....
1984-85♦	Edmonton	NHL	80	49	20	11	18	15	3	....
1985-86	Edmonton	NHL	80	56	17	7	10	6	4	....
1986-87♦	Edmonton	NHL	80	50	24	6	21	16	5	....
1987-88♦*	Edmonton	NHL	80	44	25	11	19	16	2	1
1988-89	Edmonton	NHL	80	38	34	8	7	3	4	....
1993-94	Edmonton	NHL	60	22	27	11	....	....	....	....
2002-03	NY Rangers	NHL	28	11	10	7	....	....	....	....
2003-04	NY Rangers	NHL	62	22	29	11	....	....	....	....
	NHL Totals		**932**	**497**	**307**	**128**	**127**	**89**	**37**	**1**

♦ Stanley Cup win.
* Playoff game May 24, 1988 suspended due to power failure. Score tied.

Club Directory

Madison Square Garden

New York Rangers
14th Floor
2 Pennsylvania Plaza
New York, New York 10121
Phone **212/465-6486**
PR FAX 212/465-6494
www.newyorkrangers.com
Capacity: 18,200

Team Executive Management
President and Chief Executive Officer, Cablevision Systems Corporation;
Chairman, MSG & NHL Governor .... James L. Dolan
Vice Chairman, Cablevision Systems Corporation;
Vice Chairman, MSG & NHL Alternate Governor .. Hank J. Ratner
President, G.M. & NHL Alternate Governor .... Glen Sather
President, MSG Sports .... Scott O'Neil
President, Business Operations, MSG Sports Teams .. Steve Mills
Sr. V.P., Finance and Controller....... John Cudmore
Sr. V.P., Team Sales .... Brian Lafemina
Sr. V.P., Marketing – Teams .... Howard Jacobs
Sr. V.P., Sports Team Operations....... Mark Piazza
Sr. V.P. & Deputy General Counsel – Teams ...... Marc Schoenfeld
V.P., Public Relations and Player Recruitment...... John Rosasco
V.P., Marketing....... Jeanie Baumgartner
V.P., Marketing Services .... Janet Duch
V.P., Sports Team Publicity .... Sammy Steinlight
V.P., Team Sponsorships....... Robert Scolaro
V.P., Comm. Rels. and Fan Development – Teams .. Karin Buchholz
V.P., Community Relations – Teams .... Kerryann Tomlinson
V.P., Fan Development – Teams .... Dan Gladstone
V.P., Sports Team Operations .... Jason Vogel

Hockey Club Personnel
Head Coach .... Tom Renney
Asst. G.M., Player Personnel & G.M., Hartford Wolf Pack Jim Schoenfeld
Asst. G.M., Hockey Administration .... Cameron Hope
Assistant Coaches....... Benoit Allaire, Perry Pearn, Mike Pelino
Senior Advisor to the President & G.M.
Director of U.S. Amateur Scouting....... Mike Barnett
Director, Player Personnel .... Gordie Clark
Director, Player Personnel – Europe....... Christer Rockstrom
Assistant Director, Player Personnel....... Jeff Gorton
Amateur Scouting Staff....... Rich Brown, Ray Clearwater, Daniel Dore, Ernie Gare, Vladimir Lutchenko, Shanon Sather
Head Professional Scout, Europe....... Anders Hedberg
Professional Scouting Staff .... Rick Kehoe, Gilles Leger, Kevin Maxwell, Peter Stephan
European Scout .... Jan Gajdosik
Hockey and Business Operations....... Adam Graves
Head Athletic Trainer .... Jim Ramsay
Equipment Manager....... Acacio Marques
Assistant Equipment Manager....... James "Beets" Johnson
Massage Therapist/Assistant Trainer .... Bruce Lifrieri
Strength and Conditioning Coach....... Reg Grant
Strength and Conditioning Consultant – Europe ... Daniel Hedin
Video Analyst .... Jerry Dineen
Manager, Madison Square Garden Training Center. . Alex Case
Assistant, Madison Square Garden Training Center. . Myles Fee

Operations Department
Director, Accounting....... Jeanine McGrory
Manager of Scouting .... Victor Saljanin
Manager of Hockey Administration....... Sara Adamson
Executive Administrative Assistant....... Nicole Laszlo
Administrator, Sports Team Operations....... Tim Criscitelli
Administrative Assistant, Sports Team Operations . . Caroline Giglio

Public Relations Department
Director, Public Relations....... Brendan McIntyre
Manager, Public Relations....... Jody Sowa
Coordinator, Public Relations .... Dino Ticinelli

Marketing Department
Director, Event Presentation .... Ryan Halkett
Manager, Event Presentation .... Greg Kwizak
Music Director, MSG Sports .... Ray Castoldi
Design Director....... Joanecy Kagalingan
Art Director .... Anthony Spera
Manager, Marketing....... Leigh Anne Berte
Coordinator, Marketing .... Rachel Wohl
Administrative Assistant, Marketing .... Keely Respass

Sponsorships Department
Manager, Team Sponsorships .... Nathan Finkel
Coordinator, Team Sponsorships....... Erica Diesel

Community Relations and Fan Development Department
Dir., Special Projects & Comm. Relations Rep. ...... Rod Gilbert
Director, Fan Development .... Rick Nadeau
Coordinator, Field Marketing & Fan Development . . Bryan Girsch
Manager, Community Relations .... David Martella
Coordinator, Community Relations .... Anthony Zucconi

MSG Interactive
Manager, MSG Interactive Programming....... Dan David

Medical/Training Staff
Team Physician and Orthopedic Surgeon....... Dr. Andrew Feldman
Assistant Team Physician....... Dr. Anthony Maddalo
Medical Consultant....... Dr. Ron Preston and Dr. Ronald Weissman
Team Dentists....... Dr. Joe Esposito and Dr. Don Salomon

Additional Information
Television Network .... MSG Network
Radio Network .... MSG Radio

Ottawa Senators

Key Off-Season Signings/Acquisitions

2008

June 13 • Named **Craig Hartsburg** head coach.
21 • Re-signed C **Chris Kelly**.
July 1 • Signed G **Alex Auld**.
2 • Signed LW **Jarkko Ruutu**.
2 • Re-signed RW **Shean Donovan**.
8 • Signed D **Jason Smith**.
11 • Signed D **Brendan Bell**.
11 • Named **Curtis Hunt** assistant coach.

2007-08 Results: 43W-31L-3OTL-5SOL 94PTS.
Second, Northeast Division

Year-by-Year Record

		Home				Road				Overall								
Season	GP	W	L	T	OL	W	L	T	OL	W	L	T	OL	GF	GA	Pts.	Finished	Playoff Result
2007-08	82	22	15	....	4	21	16	....	4	43	31	....	8	261	247	94	2nd, Northeast Div.	Lost Conf. Quarter-Final
2006-07	82	25	13	....	3	23	12	....	6	48	25	....	9	288	222	105	2nd, Northeast Div.	Lost Final
2005-06	82	29	9	....	3	23	12	....	6	52	21	....	9	314	211	113	1st, Northeast Div.	Lost Conf. Semi-Final
2004-05	....	....	....	....	....	....	....	....	....	....	....	....	....	....	....	....		
2003-04	82	23	8	5	5	20	15	5	1	43	23	10	6	262	189	102	3rd, Northeast Div.	Lost Conf. Quarter-Final
2002-03	82	28	9	3	1	24	12	5	0	52	21	8	1	263	182	113	1st, Northeast Div.	Lost Conf. Championship
2001-02	82	21	13	3	4	18	14	6	3	39	27	9	7	243	208	94	3rd, Northeast Div.	Lost Conf. Semi-Final
2000-01	82	26	7	5	3	22	14	4	1	48	21	9	4	274	205	109	1st, Northeast Div.	Lost Conf. Quarter-Final
1999-2000	82	24	10	5	2	17	18	6	0	41	28	11	2	244	210	95	2nd, Northeast Div.	Lost Conf. Quarter-Final
1998-99	82	22	11	8	....	22	12	7	....	44	23	15	....	239	179	103	1st, Northeast Div.	Lost Conf. Quarter-Final
1997-98	82	18	16	7	....	16	17	8	....	34	33	15	....	193	200	83	5th, Northeast Div.	Lost Conf. Semi-Final
1996-97	82	16	17	8	....	15	19	7	....	31	36	15	....	226	234	77	3rd, Northeast Div.	Lost Conf. Quarter-Final
1995-96	82	8	28	5	....	10	31	0	....	18	59	5	....	191	291	41	6th, Northeast Div.	Out of Playoffs
1994-95	48	5	16	3	....	4	18	2	....	9	34	5	....	117	174	23	7th, Northeast Div.	Out of Playoffs
1993-94	84	8	30	4	....	6	31	5	....	14	61	9	....	201	397	37	7th, Northeast Div.	Out of Playoffs
1992-93	84	9	29	4	....	1	41	0	....	10	70	4	....	202	395	24	6th, Adams Div.	Out of Playoffs

2008-09 Schedule

Oct.	Sat.	4	Pittsburgh†
	Sun.	5	at Pittsburgh†
	Sat.	11	Detroit
	Fri.	17	Phoenix
	Sat.	18	Boston
	Wed.	22	Florida
	Fri.	24	Anaheim
	Sat.	25	at Toronto
	Mon.	27	at Buffalo
	Thu.	30	at Florida
Nov.	Sat.	1	at Tampa Bay
	Tue.	4	Washington
	Thu.	6	Philadelphia
	Fri.	7	at Carolina
	Tue.	11	at Montreal
	Thu.	13	NY Islanders
	Sat.	15	at NY Islanders
	Mon.	17	at NY Rangers
	Thu.	20	Montreal
	Sat.	22	NY Rangers*
	Thu.	27	Toronto
	Sat.	29	at NY Islanders
Dec.	Wed.	3	Atlanta
	Sat.	6	Pittsburgh*
	Mon.	8	Florida
	Wed.	10	at Chicago
	Fri.	12	at Washington
	Sat.	13	Tampa Bay
	Tue.	16	Atlanta
	Fri.	19	at New Jersey
	Sat.	20	Dallas
	Tue.	23	at Philadelphia
	Sat.	27	at Calgary
	Sun.	28	at Vancouver
	Tue.	30	at Edmonton
Jan.	Sat.	3	at Toronto
	Sun.	4	at New Jersey*
	Tue.	6	at Buffalo
	Thu.	8	at Boston
	Sat.	10	NY Rangers
	Tue.	13	Carolina
	Wed.	14	at Atlanta
	Sat.	17	Montreal
	Tue.	20	Washington
	Tue.	27	New Jersey
	Thu.	29	at St. Louis
	Fri.	30	at Columbus
Feb.	Sun.	1	at Washington*
	Tue.	3	Los Angeles
	Thu.	5	Boston
	Sat.	7	Buffalo
	Wed.	11	at Buffalo
	Thu.	12	at Philadelphia
	Sat.	14	at Minnesota
	Mon.	16	at Nashville
	Tue.	17	at Colorado
	Thu.	19	Vancouver
	Sat.	21	at Montreal*
	Tue.	24	Carolina
	Thu.	26	San Jose
	Sat.	28	Toronto
Mar.	Tue.	3	Calgary
	Thu.	5	Edmonton
	Sat.	7	Buffalo
	Mon.	9	Toronto
	Wed.	11	Tampa Bay
	Thu.	12	at Boston
	Sat.	14	at Pittsburgh*
	Tue.	17	Buffalo
	Thu.	19	Montreal
	Sat.	21	NY Islanders
	Sun.	22	at NY Rangers
	Wed.	25	at Carolina
	Sat.	28	at Atlanta
	Sun.	29	at Tampa Bay
	Tue.	31	at Florida
Apr.	Thu.	2	at Boston
	Sat.	4	Philadelphia
	Mon.	6	at Montreal
	Tue.	7	Boston
	Thu.	9	New Jersey
	Sat.	11	at Toronto

* Denotes afternoon game. † Games played in Stockholm, SE.

Jason Spezza led the Senators in scoring for the first time with a career-high 92 points (34 goals, 58 assists) in 2007-08. Spezza ranked eighth in the NHL in scoring and seventh in assists.

NORTHEAST DIVISION
17th NHL Season
Franchise date: December 16, 1991

2008-09 Player Personnel

FORWARDS	HT	WT	S	Place of Birth	*Age	2007-08 Club
ALFREDSSON, Daniel	5-11	205	R	Gothenburg, Sweden	35	Ottawa
BASS, Cody	6-0	212	R	Owen Sound, Ont.	21	Ottawa-Binghamton
BOIS, Danny	6-1	202	R	Thunder Bay, Ont.	25	Binghamton
DONOVAN, Shean	6-2	215	R	Timmins, Ont.	33	Ottawa
FISHER, Mike	6-1	209	R	Peterborough, Ont.	28	Ottawa
FOLIGNO, Nick	6-0	210	L	Buffalo, NY	20	Ottawa-Binghamton
HEATLEY, Dany	6-3	220	L	Freiburg, West Germany	27	Ottawa
HENNESSY, Josh	6-0	192	L	Brockton, MA	23	Ottawa-Binghamton
KELLY, Chris	6-0	195	L	Toronto, Ont.	27	Ottawa
MAULDIN, Greg	5-10	198	R	Boston, MA	26	Binghamton
McAMMOND, Dean	5-11	195	L	Grand Cache, Alta.	35	Ottawa
NEIL, Chris	6-1	214	R	Markdale, Ont.	29	Ottawa
NIKULIN, Alexander	6-1	205	L	Moscow, USSR	23	Ottawa-Binghamton
RUUTU, Jarkko	6-0	200	L	Vantaa, Finland	33	Pittsburgh
SPEZZA, Jason	6-3	214	R	Mississauga, Ont.	25	Ottawa
VERMETTE, Antoine	6-1	200	L	St-Agapit, Que.	26	Ottawa
WINCHESTER, Jesse	6-1	206	R	Long Sault, Ont.	25	Colgate-Ottawa
ZUBOV, Ilya	5-11	211	L	Chelyabinsk, USSR	21	Ottawa-Binghamton
DEFENSEMEN						
BELL, Brendan	6-1	205	L	Ottawa, Ont.	25	Phoenix-San Antonio
CARKNER, Matt	6-4	231	R	Winchester, Ont.	27	Binghamton
LEE, Brian	6-2	201	R	Fargo, ND	21	Ottawa-Binghamton
MESZAROS, Andrej	6-2	218	L	Povazska Bystrica, Czech.	22	Ottawa
NYCHOLAT, Lawrence	6-0	200	L	Calgary, Alta.	29	Ottawa-Binghamton
PHILLIPS, Chris	6-3	219	L	Calgary, Alta.	30	Ottawa
SCHUBERT, Christoph	6-3	229	L	Munich, West Germany	26	Ottawa
SMITH, Jason	6-3	215	R	Calgary, Alta.	34	Philadelphia
VOLCHENKOV, Anton	6-1	232	L	Moscow, USSR	26	Ottawa
WAUGH, Geoff	6-4	215	R	Winnipeg, Man.	25	Binghamton

GOALTENDERS	HT	WT	C	Place of Birth	*Age	2007-08 Club
AULD, Alex	6-5	221	L	Cold Lake, Alta.	27	Phoenix-San Antonio-Boston
ELLIOTT, Brian	6-2	200	L	Newmarket, Ont.	23	Ottawa-Binghamton
GERBER, Martin	5-11	201	L	Burgdorf, Switz.	34	Ottawa

* – Age at start of 2008-09 season

Craig Hartsburg

Head Coach

Born: Stratford, Ont., June 29, 1959.

Craig Hartsburg was introduced as head coach of the Ottawa Senators on June 13, 2008. Hartsburg had recently completed his fourth consecutive season with the Ontario Hockey League's Sault Ste. Marie Greyhounds, posting a 44-18-6 regular-season record before falling to the Kitchener Rangers in the OHL Western Conference final. The 2007-08 season marked Hartsburg's fifth in the Soo. He had completed his first season in 2001-02 before assuming an assistant coach's position with the Philadelphia Flyers for two campaigns.

Hartsburg was recognized as both the OHL and Canadian Hockey League coach of the year in 2001-02, marking the second such occasion he captured those honours. He first won the award in 1994-95 as bench boss of the Guelph Storm. Hartsburg also led Team Canada to gold-medal victories at the 2007 and 2008 world junior hockey championships and won gold as an assistant coach at the 2006 tourney.

Hartsburg has previously been an NHL coach with both the Chicago Blackhawks (1995 to 1998) and the then Mighty Ducks of Anaheim (1998 to 2000). His teams qualified for NHL post-season play on three of five occasions.

As a player, Hartsburg was drafted in the first round, sixth overall, by the Minnesota North Stars in the 1979 NHL draft. In 10 NHL seasons, all with Minnesota, he recorded 98 goals and 315 assists for 413 points in 570 career games. Hartsburg represented Canada internationally on six occasions: 1978 World Juniors (bronze), 1981 Canada Cup (silver), 1982, 1983, 1987 World Championships (bronze, bronze, fourth place) and the 1987 Canada Cup (gold).

Coaching Record

			Regular Season				Playoffs			
Season	Team	League	GC	W	L	O/T	GC	W	L	T
1994-95	Guelph	OHL	66	47	14	5	14	10	4	....
1995-96	**Chicago**	**NHL**	**82**	**40**	**28**	**14**	**10**	**6**	**4**	....
1996-97	**Chicago**	**NHL**	**82**	**34**	**35**	**13**	**6**	**2**	**4**	....
1997-98	**Chicago**	**NHL**	**82**	**30**	**39**	**13**	....	....	....	....
1998-99	**Anaheim**	**NHL**	**82**	**35**	**34**	**13**	**4**	**0**	**4**	....
99-2000	**Anaheim**	**NHL**	**82**	**34**	**33**	**15**	....	....	....	....
2000-01	**Anaheim**	**NHL**	**33**	**11**	**15**	**7**	....	....	....	....
2001-02	Sault Ste. Marie	OHL	68	38	20	10	6	2	4	....
2004-05	Sault Ste. Marie	OHL	68	33	25	10	7	3	4	....
2005-06	Sault Ste. Marie	OHL	68	29	31	8	4	0	4	....
2006-07	Sault Ste. Marie	OHL	68	37	23	8	13	7	6	....
2007-08	Sault Ste. Marie	OHL	68	44	18	6	14	9	5	....
	NHL Totals		**443**	**184**	**184**	**75**	**20**	**8**	**12**	....

2007-08 Scoring

* – rookie

Regular Season

Pos	#	Player	Team	GP	G	A	Pts	TOI	+/-	PIM	PP	SH	GW	S	%
C	19	Jason Spezza	OTT	76	34	58	92	20:40	26	66	11	0	6	210	16.2
R	11	Daniel Alfredsson	OTT	70	40	49	89	22:17	15	34	9	7	5	217	18.4
L	15	Dany Heatley	OTT	71	41	41	82	21:44	33	76	13	0	8	224	18.3
L	61	Cory Stillman	CAR	55	21	25	46	19:53	–7	14	10	0	6	124	16.9
			OTT	24	3	16	19	16:54	–8	10	1	0	0	42	7.1
			Total	79	24	41	65	18:58	–15	24	11	0	6	166	14.5
L	20	Antoine Vermette	OTT	81	24	29	53	17:34	3	51	4	3	3	175	13.7
C	12	Mike Fisher	OTT	79	23	24	47	19:45	–10	82	6	2	4	215	10.7
D	6	Wade Redden	OTT	80	6	32	38	22:12	11	60	4	0	1	136	4.4
D	14	Andrej Meszaros	OTT	82	9	27	36	21:02	5	50	6	1	1	160	5.6
C	22	Chris Kelly	OTT	75	11	19	30	16:36	3	30	0	1	1	124	8.9
C	27	Randy Robitaille	OTT	68	10	19	29	13:33	4	18	1	0	1	99	10.1
D	5	Christoph Schubert	OTT	82	8	16	24	13:34	7	64	1	0	0	137	5.8
C	37	Dean McAmmond	OTT	68	9	13	22	11:32	1	12	0	3	1	67	13.4
R	25	Chris Neil	OTT	68	6	14	20	12:45	–3	199	0	0	1	78	7.7
D	4	Chris Phillips	OTT	81	5	13	18	22:28	15	56	1	0	1	80	6.3
D	24	Anton Volchenkov	OTT	67	1	14	15	20:30	14	55	0	0	1	71	1.4
D	44	Mike Commodore	CAR	41	3	9	12	19:15	2	74	0	0	0	67	4.5
			OTT	26	0	2	2	16:33	–9	26	0	0	0	30	0.0
			Total	67	3	11	14	18:12	–7	100	0	0	0	97	3.1
R	28	Martin Lapointe	CHI	52	3	4	7	08:38	–3	47	0	0	0	39	7.7
			OTT	18	3	3	6	11:36	–2	23	1	0	0	24	12.5
			Total	70	6	7	13	09:24	–5	70	1	0	0	63	9.5
R	10	Shean Donovan	OTT	82	5	7	12	09:34	–3	73	0	0	3	91	5.5
L	71	* Nick Foligno	OTT	45	6	3	9	09:09	0	20	0	0	0	44	13.6
D	2	Luke Richardson	OTT	76	2	7	9	12:19	1	41	0	0	0	41	4.9
C	58	* Cody Bass	OTT	21	2	2	4	05:18	–1	19	0	1	1	12	16.7
R	16	Brian McGrattan	OTT	38	0	3	3	02:52	0	46	0	0	0	11	0.0
D	55	* Brian Lee	OTT	6	0	1	1	16:49	1	4	0	0	0	6	0.0
C	53	* Ilja Zubov	OTT	1	0	0	0	14:38	0	0	0	0	0	0	0.0
C	18	* Jesse Winchester	OTT	1	0	0	0	14:00	0	2	0	0	0	1	0.0
C	41	* Alexander Nikulin	OTT	2	0	0	0	04:55	–2	0	0	0	0	0	0.0
D	3	Lawrence Nycholat	OTT	3	0	0	0	11:56	1	0	0	0	0	4	0.0
C	36	* Josh Hennessy	OTT	5	0	0	0	03:45	–1	0	0	0	0	2	0.0

Goaltending

No.	Goaltender	GPI	Mins	Avg	W	L	OT	EN	SO	GA	SA	S%	G	A	PIM
30	* Brian Elliott	1	60	1.00	1	0	0	0	0	1	29	.966	0	0	0
29	Martin Gerber	57	3197	2.72	30	18	4	5	2	145	1619	.910	0	2	6
1	Ray Emery	31	1689	3.13	12	13	4	3	0	88	800	.890	0	0	6
	Totals	**82**	**4979**	**2.92**	**43**	**31**	**8**	**8**	**3**	**242**	**2456**	**.901**			

Playoffs

Pos	#	Player	Team	GP	G	A	Pts	TOI	+/-	PIM	PP	SH	GW	OT	S	%
L	61	Cory Stillman	OTT	4	2	0	2	18:26	–4	2	1	0	0	0	15	13.3
D	44	Mike Commodore	OTT	4	0	2	2	20:13	–1	0	0	0	0	0	6	0.0
R	10	Shean Donovan	OTT	4	1	0	1	13:59	–1	2	0	0	0	0	5	20.0
C	58	* Cody Bass	OTT	4	1	0	1	08:20	0	6	0	0	0	0	5	20.0
L	71	* Nick Foligno	OTT	4	1	0	1	12:49	0	2	0	0	0	0	6	16.7
C	27	Randy Robitaille	OTT	2	0	1	1	11:32	1	0	0	0	0	0	4	0.0
D	6	Wade Redden	OTT	4	0	1	1	19:20	–4	11	0	0	0	0	5	0.0
R	25	Chris Neil	OTT	4	0	1	1	11:16	0	22	0	0	0	0	3	0.0
L	15	Dany Heatley	OTT	4	0	1	1	21:41	–5	6	0	0	0	0	9	0.0
D	24	Anton Volchenkov	OTT	4	0	1	1	17:11	0	2	0	0	0	0	1	0.0
C	19	Jason Spezza	OTT	4	0	1	1	19:45	–4	0	0	0	0	0	10	0.0
D	14	Andrej Meszaros	OTT	4	0	1	1	18:59	–4	6	0	0	0	0	3	0.0
R	11	Daniel Alfredsson	OTT	2	0	0	0	19:20	–2	0	0	0	0	0	5	0.0
R	28	Martin Lapointe	OTT	4	0	0	0	08:14	–1	4	0	0	0	0	6	0.0
C	37	Dean McAmmond	OTT	4	0	0	0	13:29	0	4	0	0	0	0	4	0.0
D	4	Chris Phillips	OTT	4	0	0	0	21:59	–2	4	0	0	0	0	5	0.0
L	20	Antoine Vermette	OTT	4	0	0	0	20:32	–4	4	0	0	0	0	10	0.0
D	5	Christoph Schubert	OTT	4	0	0	0	11:57	0	8	0	0	0	0	7	0.0
D	55	* Brian Lee	OTT	4	0	0	0	14:30	–1	2	0	0	0	0	3	0.0

Goaltending

No.	Goaltender	GPI	Mins	Avg	W	L	EN	SO	GA	SA	S%	G	A	PIM
29	Martin Gerber	4	238	3.53	0	4	2	0	14	159	.912	0	0	0
	Totals	**4**	**240**	**4.00**	**0**	**4**	**2**	**0**	**16**	**161**	**.901**			

General Managers' History

Mel Bridgman, 1992-93; Randy Sexton, 1993-94, 1994-95; Randy Sexton and Pierre Gauthier, 1995-96; Pierre Gauthier, 1996-97, 1997-98; Rick Dudley, 1998-99; Marshall Johnston, 1999-2000 to 2001-02; John Muckler, 2002-03 to 2006-07; Bryan Murray, 2007-08 to date.

Club Records

Team

(Figures in brackets for season records are games played; records for fewest points, wins, ties, losses, goals, goals against are for 70 or more games)

Most Points	113	2002-03 (82), 2005-06 (82)
Most Wins	52	2002-03 (82), 2005-06 (82)
Most Ties	15	1996-97 (82), 1997-98 (82), 1998-99 (82)
Most Losses	70	1992-93 (84)
Most Goals	312	2005-06 (82)
Most Goals Against	397	1993-94 (84)
Fewest Points	24	1992-93 (84)
Fewest Wins	10	1992-93 (84)
Fewest Ties	4	1992-93 (84)
Fewest Losses	21	2000-01 (82), 2002-03 (82), 2005-06 (82)
Fewest Goals	191	1995-96 (82)
Fewest Goals Against	179	1998-99 (82)
Longest Winning Streak		
Overall	8	Oct. 13-Nov. 6/07
Home	8	Nov. 14-Dec. 14/02
Away	6	Mar. 18-Apr. 5/03
Longest Undefeated Streak		
Overall	11	Three times
Home	12	Dec. 18/03-Jan. 24/04 (10 wins, 2 ties)
Away	7	Three times
Longest Losing Streak		
Overall	14	Mar. 2-Apr. 7/93
Home	*11	Oct. 27-Dec. 8/93
Away	*38	Oct. 10/92-Apr. 3/93**
Longest Winless Streak		
Overall	21	Oct. 10-Nov. 23/92 (20 losses, 1 tie)
Home	*17	Oct. 28/95-Jan. 27/96 (15 losses, 2 ties)
Away	*38	Oct. 10/92-Apr. 3/93 (38 losses)
Most Shutouts, Season	10	2001-02 (82)
Most PIM, Season	1,716	1992-93 (84)
Most Goals, Game	11	Nov. 13/01 (Ott. 11 at Wsh. 5)

** NHL records do not include neutral site games

Individual

Most Seasons	12	Daniel Alfredsson
Most Games, Career	853	Daniel Alfredsson
Most Goals, Career	331	Daniel Alfredsson
Most Assists, Career	516	Daniel Alfredsson
Most Points, Career	847	Daniel Alfredsson (331G, 516A)
Most PIM, Career	1,152	Chris Neil
Most Shutouts, Career	30	Patrick Lalime
Longest Consecutive Games Streak	292	Alexei Yashin (Dec. 31/95-Apr. 17/99)
Most Goals, Season	50	Dany Heatley (2005-06; 2006-07)
Most Assists, Season	71	Jason Spezza (2005-06)
Most Points, Season	105	Dany Heatley (2006-07; 50G, 55A)
Most PIM, Season	318	Mike Peluso (1992-93)
Most Points, Defenseman, Season	63	Norm Maciver (1992-93; 17G, 46A)
Most Points, Center, Season	94	Alexei Yashin (1998-99; 44G, 50A)
Most Points, Right Wing, Season	103	Daniel Alfredsson (2005-06; 43G, 60A)
Most Points, Left Wing, Season	105	Dany Heatley (2006-07; 50G, 55A)
Most Points, Rookie, Season	79	Alexei Yashin (1993-94; 30G, 49A)
Most Shutouts, Season	8	Patrick Lalime (2002-03)
Most Goals, Game	4	Three times
Most Assists, Game	5	Marian Hossa (Jan. 4/01)
Most Points, Game	7	Daniel Alfredsson (Jan. 24/08; 3G, 4A)

* NHL Record.

Coaching History

Rick Bowness, 1992-93 to 1994-95; Rick Bowness, Dave Allison and Jacques Martin, 1995-96; Jacques Martin, 1996-97 to 2000-01; Jacques Martin and Roger Neilson, 2001-02; Jacques Martin, 2002-03, 2003-04; Bryan Murray, 2004-05 to 2006-07; John Paddock and Bryan Murray, 2007-08; Craig Hartsburg, 2008-09.

Captains' History

Laurie Boschman, 1992-93; Brad Shaw, Mark Lamb and Gord Dineen, 1993-94; Randy Cunneyworth, 1994-95 to 1997-98; Alexei Yashin, 1998-99; Daniel Alfredsson, 1999-2000 to date.

Retired Numbers

8 Frank Finnigan 1924-1934

All-time Record vs. Other Clubs

Regular Season

	At Home								On Road								Total							
	GP	W	L	T	OL	GF	GA	PTS	GP	W	L	T	OL	GF	GA	PTS	GP	W	L	T	OL	GF	GA	PTS
Anaheim	9	4	3	1	1	27	23	10	10	3	5	2	0	19	24	8	19	7	8	3	1	46	47	18
Atlanta	16	10	2	1	3	74	45	24	16	9	5	1	1	62	53	20	32	19	7	2	4	136	98	44
Boston	43	20	20	3	0	112	126	43	45	14	25	5	1	119	155	34	88	34	45	8	1	231	281	77
Buffalo	45	18	16	7	4	122	121	47	43	14	22	3	4	98	136	35	88	32	38	10	8	220	257	82
Calgary	11	5	2	3	1	27	25	14	12	4	6	1	1	26	40	10	23	9	8	4	2	53	65	24
Carolina	35	15	14	4	2	100	91	36	33	11	18	4	0	87	95	26	68	26	32	8	2	187	186	62
Chicago	11	4	5	0	2	34	34	10	9	2	4	2	1	21	22	7	20	6	9	2	3	55	56	17
Colorado	19	8	8	3	0	54	66	19	16	3	12	1	0	47	72	7	35	11	20	4	0	101	138	26
Columbus	4	2	0	1	1	14	9	6	3	1	1	1	0	11	13	3	7	3	1	2	1	25	22	9
Dallas	10	4	6	0	0	22	26	8	12	5	7	0	0	32	46	10	22	9	13	0	0	54	72	18
Detroit	11	4	5	1	1	31	31	10	10	4	5	0	1	22	35	9	21	8	10	1	2	53	66	19
Edmonton	11	4	5	2	0	23	29	10	12	3	7	2	0	30	42	8	23	7	12	4	0	53	71	18
Florida	28	15	10	2	1	88	71	33	28	16	11	1	0	93	88	33	56	31	21	3	1	181	159	66
Los Angeles	10	5	3	1	1	35	29	12	11	1	9	1	0	21	48	3	21	6	12	2	1	56	77	15
Minnesota	3	2	1	0	0	9	7	4	4	2	1	1	0	14	11	5	7	4	2	1	0	23	18	9
Montreal	43	24	18	1	0	137	115	49	45	17	23	4	1	131	135	39	88	41	41	5	1	268	250	88
Nashville	6	4	2	0	0	20	13	8	5	2	3	0	0	11	14	4	11	6	5	0	0	31	27	12
New Jersey	30	9	16	3	2	70	76	23	29	10	14	2	3	70	80	25	59	19	30	5	5	140	156	48
NY Islanders	29	18	6	5	0	101	72	41	30	18	5	6	1	115	91	43	59	36	11	11	1	216	163	84
NY Rangers	29	13	13	3	0	85	76	29	29	17	12	0	0	91	88	34	58	30	25	3	0	176	164	63
Philadelphia	30	12	12	6	0	86	88	30	29	10	17	2	0	80	97	22	59	22	29	8	0	166	185	52
Phoenix	12	5	6	1	0	36	36	11	11	6	4	1	0	42	36	13	23	11	10	2	0	78	72	24
Pittsburgh	33	11	15	5	2	96	109	29	33	11	16	4	2	92	113	28	66	22	31	9	4	188	222	57
St. Louis	11	5	6	0	0	26	38	10	10	4	4	2	0	29	29	10	21	9	10	2	0	55	67	20
San Jose	10	4	2	4	0	36	28	12	10	4	5	0	1	18	21	9	20	8	7	4	1	54	49	21
Tampa Bay	29	19	10	0	0	107	66	38	29	17	9	2	1	107	84	37	58	36	19	2	1	214	150	75
Toronto	32	20	9	1	2	107	88	43	34	18	13	2	1	106	89	39	66	38	22	3	3	213	177	82
Vancouver	11	5	4	1	1	25	26	12	12	5	5	1	1	28	36	12	23	10	9	2	2	53	62	24
Washington	29	15	12	1	1	106	88	32	30	11	14	4	1	86	99	27	59	26	26	5	2	192	187	59
Totals	**600**	**284**	**231**	**60**	**25**	**1810**	**1652**	**653**	**600**	**242**	**282**	**55**	**21**	**1708**	**1892**	**560**	**1200**	**526**	**513**	**115**	**46**	**3518**	**3544**	**1213**

Playoffs

	Series	W	L	GP	W	L	T	GF	GA	Last Mtg.	Rnd.	Result
Anaheim	1	0	1	5	1	4	0	11	16	2007	F	L 1-4
Buffalo	4	1	3	21	8	13	0	47	52	2007	CF	W 4-1
New Jersey	3	2	1	18	11	7	0	41	40	2007	CSF	W 4-1
NY Islanders	1	1	0	5	4	1	0	13	7	2003	CQF	W 4-1
Philadelphia	2	2	0	11	8	3	0	28	12	2003	CSF	W 4-2
Pittsburgh	2	1	1	9	4	5	0	23	26	2008	CQF	L 0-4
Tampa Bay	1	1	0	5	4	1	0	23	13	2006	CQF	W 4-1
Toronto	4	0	4	24	8	16	0	42	57	2004	CQF	L 3-4
Washington	1	0	1	5	1	4	0	7	18	1998	CSF	L 1-4
Totals	**19**	**8**	**11**	**103**	**49**	**54**	**0**	**235**	**241**			

Playoff Results 2008-2003

Year	Round	Opponent	Result	GF	GA
2008	CQF	Pittsburgh	L 0-4	5	16
2007	F	Anaheim	L 1-4	11	16
	CF	Buffalo	W 4-1	15	10
	CSF	New Jersey	W 4-1	15	11
	CQF	Pittsburgh	W 4-1	18	10
2006	CSF	Buffalo	L 1-4	13	16
	CQF	Tampa Bay	W 4-1	23	13
2004	CQF	Toronto	L 3-4	11	14
2003	CF	New Jersey	L 3-4	13	17
	CSF	Philadelphia	W 4-2	17	10
	CQF	NY Islanders	W 4-1	13	7

Abbreviations: Round: F - Final; **CF** – conference final; **CSF** – conference semi-final; **CQF** – conference quarter-final.

Colorado totals include Quebec, 1992-93 to 1994-95.
Dallas totals include Minnesota North Stars, 1992-93.

Carolina totals include Hartford, 1992-93 to 1996-97.
Phoenix totals include Winnipeg, 1992-93 to 1995-96.

2007-08 Results

Oct.	3	at Toronto	4-3*
	4	Toronto	3-2
	6	NY Rangers	2-0
	8	New Jersey	4-2
	10	at Atlanta	3-1
	11	Carolina	3-5
	13	at NY Rangers	3-1
	18	Montreal	4-3
	20	Florida	4-1
	27	at New Jersey	4-1
Nov.	1	Atlanta	6-4
	3	Boston	3-2
	4	at Boston	2-1†
	6	Toronto	5-1
	8	Washington	1-4
	10	Montreal	3-1
	15	Buffalo	3-2
	17	at Toronto	0-3
	19	at Montreal	4-2
	21	at Buffalo	2-4
	22	Pittsburgh	5-6†
	24	Philadelphia	3-4
	28	at NY Islanders	2-3†
	29	Nashville	5-6
Dec.	1	NY Rangers	2-5
	4	at Tampa Bay	3-4†
	5	at Florida	5-4
	7	at Dallas	4-2
	12	at Carolina	6-0
	13	at Pittsburgh	4-1
	15	Atlanta	7-3
	18	at Boston	3-2
	20	at Atlanta	2-3
	22	Chicago	3-4*
	23	at NY Rangers	3-1
	26	at Buffalo	5-3
	27	NY Islanders	5-2
	29	Washington	6-8
Jan.	1	at Washington	3-6
	4	at Buffalo	5-3
	5	Tampa Bay	4-3*
	10	Buffalo	3-2†
	12	Detroit	3-2
	13	NY Islanders	1-3
	15	at Washington	2-4
	17	Carolina	5-1
	19	Tampa Bay	0-2
	20	at Philadelphia	1-6
	22	at Florida	3-5
	24	at Tampa Bay	8-4
	29	at NY Islanders	5-2
	31	Boston	1-4
Feb.	2	at Toronto	2-4
	5	at Montreal	3-4
	7	Florida	5-4
	9	Montreal	6-1
	12	Buffalo	1-5
	13	at New Jersey	2-3*
	16	New Jersey	2-3
	19	Philadelphia	3-2†
	21	Columbus	2-3†
	23	at Pittsburgh	4-3*
	25	Toronto	0-5
	26	at Boston	0-4
	28	at Philadelphia	1-3
Mar.	1	Pittsburgh	5-4
	3	at Anaheim	1-3
	5	at San Jose	2-3*
	6	at Los Angeles	0-2
	8	at Phoenix	4-2
	11	Boston	4-1
	13	at Montreal	3-0
	16	at Carolina	1-5
	20	St. Louis	3-2
	22	Toronto	4-5
	24	at Montreal	5-7
	25	at Buffalo	6-3
	27	Buffalo	3-4†
	29	at Boston	0-4
Apr.	1	Montreal	0-3
	3	at Toronto	8-2
	4	Boston	1-2

* – Overtime † – Shootout

Entry Draft Selections 2008-1994

Name in bold denotes played in NHL.

2008
Pick
15 Erik Karlsson
42 Patrick Wiercioch
79 Zack Smith
109 Andre Petersson
119 Derek Grant
139 Mark Borowiecki
199 Emil Sandin

2007
Pick
29 James O'Brien
60 Ruslan Bashkirov
90 Louie Caporusso
120 Ben Blood

2006
Pick
28 **Nick Foligno**
68 Eric Gryba
91 Kaspars Daugavins
121 Pierre-Luc Lessard
151 Ryan Daniels
181 Kevin Koopman
211 Erik Condra

2005
Pick
9 **Brian Lee**
70 Vitali Anikeyenko
95 **Cody Bass**
98 **Ilja Zubov**
115 Janne Kolehmainen
136 Tomas Kudelka
186 Dmitri Megalinsky
204 Colin Greening

2004
Pick
23 **Andrej Meszaros**
58 Kirill Lyamin
77 Shawn Weller
87 Peter Regin
89 Jeff Glass
122 **Alexander Nikulin**
141 Jim McKenzie
156 Roman Wick
219 Joe Cooper
251 Matthew McIlvane
284 John Wikner

2003
Pick
29 **Patrick Eaves**
67 Igor Mirnov
100 Philippe Seydoux
135 Mattias Karlsson
142 Tim Cook
166 Sergei Gimayev
228 Will Colbert
260 Ossi Louhivaara
291 **Brian Elliott**

2002
Pick
16 **Jakub Klepis**
47 **Alexei Kaigorodov**
75 Arttu Luttinen
113 Scott Dobben
125 Johan Bjork
150 Brock Hooton
246 Josef Vavra
276 Vitali Atyushov

2001
Pick
2 **Jason Spezza**
23 **Tim Gleason**
81 Neil Komadoski
99 **Ray Emery**
127 **Christoph Schubert**
162 Stefan Schauer
193 **Brooks Laich**
218 Jan Platil
223 **Brandon Bochenski**
235 Neil Petruic
256 Gregg Johnson
286 **Toni Dahlman**

2000
Pick
21 **Anton Volchenkov**
45 **Mathieu Chouinard**
55 **Antoine Vermette**
87 Jan Bohac
122 Derrick Byfuglien
156 **Greg Zanon**
157 Grant Potulny
158 Sean Connolly
188 Jason Maleyko
283 James Demone

1999
Pick
26 **Martin Havlat**
48 **Simon Lajeunesse**
62 Teemu Sainomaa
94 **Chris Kelly**
154 Andrew Ianiero
164 **Martin Prusek**
201 Mikko Ruutu
209 **Layne Ulmer**
213 **Alexandre Giroux**
269 Konstantin Gorovikov

1998
Pick
15 **Mathieu Chouinard**
44 **Mike Fisher**
58 **Chris Bala**
74 **Julien Vauclair**
101 **Petr Schastlivy**
130 Gavin McLeod
161 **Chris Neil**
188 Michel Periard
223 Sergei Verenikin
246 Rastislav Pavlikovsky

1997
Pick
12 **Marian Hossa**
58 **Jani Hurme**
66 **Josh Langfeld**
119 **Magnus Arvedson**
146 Jeff Sullivan
173 Robin Bacul
203 Nick Gillis
229 **Karel Rachunek**

1996
Pick
1 **Chris Phillips**
81 **Antti-Jussi Niemi**
136 **Andreas Dackell**
163 Francois Hardy
212 **Erich Goldmann**
216 **Ivan Ciernik**
239 **Sami Salo**

1995
Pick
1 **Bryan Berard**
27 **Marc Moro**
53 **Brad Larsen**
89 Kevin Bolibruck
103 Kevin Boyd
131 David Hruska
183 Kaj Linna
184 **Ray Schultz**
231 Erik Kaminski

1994
Pick
3 **Radek Bonk**
29 **Stan Neckar**
81 Bryan Masotta
131 Mike Gaffney
133 **Daniel Alfredsson**
159 Doug Sproule
210 **Frederic Cassivi**
211 Danny Dupont
237 Stephen MacKinnon
274 **Antti Tormanen**

Bryan Murray

General Manager

Born: Shawville, Que., December 5, 1942.

On June 18, 2007, Bryan Murray was appointed as the seventh general manager of the Ottawa Senators. Murray had joined the organization on June 8, 2004, when he was named the club's head coach. Murray resigned as senior vice president and general manager of Anaheim to take the coaching position in Ottawa. As coach in Ottawa in 2006–07, Murray led the Senators to the Stanley Cup Finals for the first time in franchise history, only to lose to his former Anaheim team. He also has previous front office experience as vice president and general manager of the Florida Panthers from 1994 to 2001, assembling a team that reached the Stanley Cup Finals in just its third year of existence in 1996.

Murray, who was back behind the bench in Ottawa briefly in 2007-08, began his NHL career as head coach of the Washington Capials in 1981. He has served 16+ years behind the bench, coaching more than 1,300 regular-season and playoff games, including 672 wins. He earned the Jack Adams Award as coach of the year in 1983-84. Murray's regular-season coaching record in Ottawa is 107-55-20 and includes winning the 2007 Prince of Wales Trophy as the NHL's Eastern Conference champions.

Coaching Record

			Regular Season				Playoffs			
Season	**Team**	**League**	**GC**	**W**	**L**	**O/T**	**GC**	**W**	**L**	**T**
1981-82	Washington	NHL	66	25	28	13	....	....	....	....
1982-83	Washington	NHL	80	39	25	16	4	1	3	....
1983-84	Washington	NHL	80	48	27	5	8	4	4	....
1984-85	Washington	NHL	80	46	25	9	5	2	3	....
1985-86	Washington	NHL	80	50	23	7	9	5	4	....
1986-87	Washington	NHL	80	38	32	10	7	3	4	....
1987-88	Washington	NHL	80	38	33	9	14	7	7	....
1988-89	Washington	NHL	80	41	29	10	6	2	4	....
1989-90	Washington	NHL	46	18	24	4	....	....	....	....
1990-91	Detroit	NHL	80	34	38	8	7	3	4	....
1991-92	Detroit	NHL	80	43	25	12	11	4	7	....
1992-93	Detroit	NHL	84	47	28	9	7	3	4	....
1997-98	Florida	NHL	59	17	31	11	....	....	....	....
2001-02	Anaheim	NHL	82	29	42	11	....	....	....	....
2004-05	Ottawa				SEASON CANCELLED					
2005-06	Ottawa	NHL	82	52	21	9	10	5	5	....
2006-07	Ottawa	NHL	82	48	25	9	20	13	7	....
2007-08	Ottawa	NHL	18	7	9	2	4	0	4	....
	NHL Totals		**1239**	**620**	**465**	**154**	**112**	**52**	**60**	....

Club Directory

Scotiabank Place

Ottawa Senators
Scotiabank Place
1000 Palladium Drive
Ottawa, Ontario
K2V 1A5
Phone **613/599-0250**
FAX 613/599-0358
www.ottawasenators.com
Capacity: 19,153

Executive
Owner, Governor and Chairman . . . Eugene Melnyk
President, CEO and Alternate Governor . . . Roy Mlakar
Chief Operating Officer. . . . Cyril Leeder
Chief Financial officer . . . Erin Crowe
General Manager . . . Bryan Murray
V.P. and Executive Director, Scotiabank Place . . . Tom Conroy
Executive Assistant to the President and CEO . . . Cheryl Blake
Executive Assistant to the COO . . . Gail Martineau

Hockey Operations
Assistant General Manager . . . Tim Murray
Director of Hockey Operations . . . Brent Flahr
Assistant to the General Manager . . . Allison Vaughan
Head Coach . . . Craig Hartsburg
Assistant Coaches . . . Greg Carvel,Curtis Hunt
Goaltender Coach . . . Eli Wilson
Director of Player Development . . . Randy Lee
Video Coach . . . Tim Pattyson
Conditioning Coach . . . Adam Douglas
Director of Player Services . . . Chad Schella
Manager of Team Travel . . . Jordan Silmser
Hockey Administrator . . . Kevin Billet
Head Athletic Therapist . . . Gerry Townend
Assistant Athletic Therapist . . . Andy Playter
Equipment Manager . . . Scott Allegrino
Assistant Equipment Manager . . . Chris Cook
Massage Therapist . . . Shawn Markwick

Scouts
Scouts . . . Pierre Dorion, George Fargher, Bob Janecyk, Bob Lowes, Bill McCarthy, Lew Mongelluzzo, Greg Royce, Vaclav Burda, Anders Forsberg, Mikko Ruutu, Boris Shagas
Pro Scouts . . . Archie Henderson, Nick Polano

Legal
General Counsel . . . Rhonda Wing

Communications and Publications
Vice-President, Communications . . . Phil Legault
Director, Publications . . . Karen Ruttan
Manager, Communications . . . Brian Morris
Communications Co-ordinator . . . Chris Moore
Writer/Ediorial Manager . . . Rob Brodie
Translator . . . Eric Tremblay
Communications & Publications Assistant . . . Deborah Wilson

Broadcasting
Vice-President, Broadcast . . . Jim Steel

Corporate & Ticket Sales and Service
Senior Vice-President, Corporate & Ticketing Sales . Mark Bonneau
Exec. Ass't. To Sr. V.P., Corporate & Ticketing Sales . Brooke Brown
Director, Corporate Sales . . . Bill Courchaine
Senior Corporate Account Managers . . . Steve Chestnut, Mark Clatney, Francois Robert
Director, Business Development . . . Gina Hillcoat
Director, Ticket Sales . . . Jim Orban
Manager, Sales . . . Chris Atack
Manager, Group Sales . . . Devon Hogan
Senior Account Manager, Group Sales . . . Jim Armstrong
Director, Premium Services . . . Christine Clancy
Manager, Premium Client Services . . . Tracey Bonner

Finance
Executive Assistant to the CFO . . . Collette Hiscott
Controller . . . Derek Winch
Accounting Manager, Ottawa Senators . . . Morgan Cranley

Information Technology
Director, Information Technology . . . Sean Shrubsole
Co-ordinator, Information Technology . . . Robin Zanichkowsky
Help Desk Supervisor . . . Don Morin

Marketing
Vice-President, Marketing . . . Jeff Kyle
Executive Assistant, Marketing . . . Kathy Downs
Director, Marketing . . . Isabelle Perrault-Lachapelle
Director, Merchandise . . . Kevin Lawton
Director, Game Entertainment . . . Glen Gower
Director, Fan and Community Development . . . Aaron Robinson
Art Director . . . Wendy Moenig
Manager, Marketing . . . Lisa Trevisanutto

Operations and Events
Assistant to the V.P. & Executive Director . . . Linda Julian
Director, Engineering & Operations . . . Ed Healy
Director, Scotiabank Place Marketing . . . Krista Galbraith

People Department
Director, People Department . . . Sandi Horner

Sens Foundation
President . . . Danielle Robinson

Miscellaneous
Radio . . . Team 1200 (English), 104,7 FM (French)
Television . . . Rogers Sportsnet and RDS
Team Photographer . . . Freestyle Photography (André Ringuette)
Anthem singer . . . Lyndon Slewidge
Mascot . . . Spartacat

Philadelphia Flyers

2007-08 Results: 42W-29L-5OTL-6SOL 95PTS.
Fourth, Atlantic Division

Key Off-Season Signings/Acquisitions

2008

June 20 • Traded C **R.J. Umberger** and a 4th-round pick in 2008 to Columbus for a 1st-round and 3rd-round pick in 2008.

20 • Acquired D **Steve Eminger** and a 3rd-round pick in 2008 from Washington for a 1st-round pick in 2008.

27 • Re-signed C **Jeff Carter**.

July 1 • Signed D **Ossi Vaananen** and C **Glen Metropolit**.

2 • Re-signed D **Randy Jones** and LW **Riley Cote**.

7 • Signed RW **Arron Asham**.

Year-by-Year Record

		Home				Road				Overall								
Season	GP	W	L	T	OL	W	L	T	OL	W	L	T	OL	GF	GA	Pts.	Finished	Playoff Result
2007-08	82	21	14	....	6	21	15	....	5	42	29	....	11	248	233	95	4th, Atlantic Div.	Lost Conf. Championship
2006-07	82	10	24	....	7	12	24	....	5	22	48	....	12	214	303	56	5th, Atlantic Div.	Out of Playoffs
2005-06	82	22	13	....	6	23	13	....	5	45	26	....	11	267	259	101	2nd, Atlantic Div.	Lost Conf. Quarter-Final
2004-05	....	....	....	....	....	....	....	....	....	....	....	....	....	....	....	....		
2003-04	82	24	11	3	3	16	10	12	3	40	21	15	6	229	186	101	1st, Atlantic Div.	Lost Conf. Championship
2002-03	82	21	10	8	2	24	10	5	2	45	20	13	4	211	166	107	2nd, Atlantic Div.	Lost Conf. Semi-Final
2001-02	82	20	13	5	3	22	14	5	0	42	27	10	3	234	192	97	1st, Atlantic Div.	Lost Conf. Quarter-Final
2000-01	82	26	11	4	0	17	14	7	3	43	25	11	3	240	207	100	2nd, Atlantic Div.	Lost Conf. Quarter-Final
1999-2000	82	25	6	7	3	20	16	5	0	45	22	12	3	237	179	105	1st, Atlantic Div.	Lost Conf. Championship
1998-99	82	21	9	11	....	16	17	8	....	37	26	19	....	231	196	93	2nd, Atlantic Div.	Lost Conf. Quarter-Final
1997-98	82	24	11	6	....	18	18	5	....	42	29	11	....	242	193	95	2nd, Atlantic Div.	Lost Conf. Quarter-Final
1996-97	82	23	12	6	....	22	12	7	....	45	24	13	....	274	217	103	2nd, Atlantic Div.	Lost Final
1995-96	82	27	9	5	....	18	15	8	....	45	24	13	....	282	208	103	1st, Atlantic Div.	Lost Conf. Semi-Final
1994-95	48	16	7	1	....	12	9	3	....	28	16	4	....	150	132	60	1st, Atlantic Div.	Lost Conf. Championship
1993-94	84	19	20	3	....	16	19	7	....	35	39	10	....	294	314	80	6th, Atlantic Div.	Out of Playoffs
1992-93	84	23	14	5	....	13	23	6	....	36	37	11	....	319	319	83	5th, Patrick Div.	Out of Playoffs
1991-92	80	22	11	7	....	10	26	4	....	32	37	11	....	252	273	75	6th, Patrick Div.	Out of Playoffs
1990-91	80	18	16	6	....	15	21	4	....	33	37	10	....	252	267	76	5th, Patrick Div.	Out of Playoffs
1989-90	80	17	19	4	....	13	20	7	....	30	39	11	....	290	297	71	6th, Patrick Div.	Out of Playoffs
1988-89	80	22	15	3	....	14	21	5	....	36	36	8	....	307	285	80	4th, Patrick Div.	Lost Conf. Championship
1987-88	80	20	14	6	....	18	19	3	....	38	33	9	....	292	292	85	3rd, Patrick Div.	Lost Div. Semi-Final
1986-87	80	29	9	2	....	17	17	6	....	46	26	8	....	310	245	100	1st, Patrick Div.	Lost Final
1985-86	80	33	6	1	....	20	17	3	....	53	23	4	....	335	241	110	1st, Patrick Div.	Lost Div. Semi-Final
1984-85	80	32	4	4	....	21	16	3	....	53	20	7	....	348	241	113	1st, Patrick Div.	Lost Final
1983-84	80	25	10	5	....	19	16	5	....	44	26	10	....	350	290	98	3rd, Patrick Div.	Lost Div. Semi-Final
1982-83	80	29	8	3	....	20	15	5	....	49	23	8	....	326	240	106	1st, Patrick Div.	Lost Div. Semi-Final
1981-82	80	25	10	5	....	13	21	6	....	38	31	11	....	325	313	87	3rd. Patrick Div.	Lost Div. Semi-Final
1980-81	80	23	9	8	....	18	15	7	....	41	24	15	....	313	249	97	2nd, Patrick Div.	Lost Quarter-Final
1979-80	80	27	5	8	....	21	7	12	....	48	12	20	....	327	254	116	1st, Patrick Div.	Lost Final
1978-79	80	26	10	4	....	14	15	11	....	40	25	15	....	281	248	95	2nd, Patrick Div.	Lost Quarter-Final
1977-78	80	29	6	5	....	16	14	10	....	45	20	15	....	296	200	105	2nd, Patrick Div.	Lost Semi-Final
1976-77	80	33	6	1	....	15	10	15	....	48	16	16	....	323	213	112	1st, Patrick Div.	Lost Semi-Final
1975-76	80	36	2	2	....	15	11	14	....	51	13	16	....	348	209	118	1st, Patrick Div.	Lost Final
1974-75	**80**	**32**	**6**	**2**	....	**19**	**12**	**9**	....	**51**	**18**	**11**	....	**293**	**181**	**113**	**1st, Patrick Div.**	**Won Stanley Cup**
1973-74	**78**	**28**	**6**	**5**	....	**22**	**10**	**7**	....	**50**	**16**	**12**	....	**273**	**164**	**112**	**1st, West Div.**	**Won Stanley Cup**
1972-73	78	27	8	4	....	10	22	7	....	37	30	11	....	296	256	85	2nd, West Div.	Lost Semi-Final
1971-72	78	19	13	7	....	7	25	7	....	26	38	14	....	200	236	66	5th, West Div.	Out of Playoffs
1970-71	78	20	10	9	....	8	23	8	....	28	33	17	....	207	225	73	3rd, West Div.	Lost Quarter-Final
1969-70	76	11	14	13	....	6	21	11	....	17	35	24	....	197	225	58	5th, West Div.	Out of Playoffs
1968-69	76	14	16	8	....	6	19	13	....	20	35	21	....	174	225	61	3rd, West Div.	Lost Quarter-Final
1967-68	74	17	13	7	....	14	19	4	....	31	32	11	....	173	179	73	1st, West Div.	Lost Quarter-Final

2008-09 Schedule

Oct.	Sat.	11	NY Rangers
	Mon.	13	Montreal
	Tue.	14	at Pittsburgh
	Thu.	16	at Colorado
	Sat.	18	at San Jose
	Wed.	22	San Jose
	Fri.	24	at New Jersey
	Sat.	25	New Jersey
	Tue.	28	at Atlanta
	Thu.	30	NY Islanders
Nov.	Sun.	2	Edmonton*
	Thu.	6	at Ottawa
	Sat.	8	Tampa Bay
	Tue.	11	at NY Islanders*
	Thu.	13	at Pittsburgh
	Sat.	15	at Montreal
	Sun.	16	Atlanta
	Fri.	21	at Buffalo
	Sat.	22	Phoenix
	Mon.	24	Dallas
	Wed.	26	at Carolina
	Fri.	28	Carolina*
	Sat.	29	at Toronto
Dec.	Tue.	2	Tampa Bay
	Thu.	4	New Jersey
	Sat.	6	at Carolina
	Tue.	9	NY Islanders
	Thu.	11	Carolina
	Sat.	13	Pittsburgh*
	Tue.	16	Colorado
	Thu.	18	at Montreal
	Sat.	20	Washington*
	Sun.	21	at New Jersey*
	Tue.	23	Ottawa
	Fri.	26	at Chicago
	Sat.	27	at Columbus
	Tue.	30	at Vancouver
Jan.	Fri.	2	at Anaheim
	Sat.	3	at Los Angeles
	Tue.	6	at Washington
	Thu.	8	Minnesota
	Sat.	10	Toronto
	Tue.	13	Pittsburgh
	Thu.	15	at Tampa Bay
	Fri.	16	at Florida
	Wed.	21	Atlanta
	Tue.	27	at Florida
	Fri.	30	at Tampa Bay
	Sat.	31	at St. Louis
Feb.	Wed.	4	Boston
	Sat.	7	at Boston*
	Sun.	8	at Atlanta*
	Thu.	12	Ottawa
	Sat.	14	NY Islanders*
	Sun.	15	at NY Rangers
	Thu.	19	Buffalo
	Sat.	21	Pittsburgh*
	Tue.	24	at Washington
	Wed.	25	Los Angeles
	Fri.	27	Montreal
Mar.	Sun.	1	at New Jersey*
	Tue.	3	at Boston
	Thu.	5	Calgary
	Sat.	7	Nashville
	Tue.	10	Buffalo
	Thu.	12	Washington
	Sat.	14	NY Rangers*
	Sun.	15	at NY Rangers *
	Tue.	17	at Detroit
	Fri.	20	at Buffalo
	Sun.	22	at Pittsburgh*
	Mon.	23	New Jersey
	Thu.	26	Florida
	Sat.	28	at NY Islanders
	Sun.	29	Boston
Apr.	Wed.	1	at Toronto
	Fri.	3	Toronto
	Sat.	4	at Ottawa
	Tue.	7	Florida
	Thu.	9	at NY Rangers
	Sat.	11	at NY Islanders*
	Sun.	12	NY Rangers*

* Denotes afternoon game.

A key free-agent acquisition in the summer of 2007, Daniel Briere helped the Flyers rebound into a playoff spot after finishing last overall in 2006-07. Briere was second on the team in goals (31) and points (72) in 2007-08.

ATLANTIC DIVISION
42nd NHL Season

Franchise date: June 5, 1967

2008-09 Player Personnel

FORWARDS	HT	WT	S	Place of Birth	*Age	2007-08 Club
ASHAM, Arron	5-11	205	R	Portage La Prairie, Man.	30	New Jersey
BRIERE, Daniel	5-10	179	R	Gatineau, Que.	30	Philadelphia
CARTER, Jeff	6-3	200	R	London, Ont.	23	Philadelphia
COTE, Riley	6-1	210	L	Winnipeg, Man.	26	Philadelphia
DOWNIE, Steve	5-11	200	R	Newmarket, Ont.	21	Phi-Phi (AHL)
GAGNE, Simon	6-0	195	L	Ste-Foy, Que.	28	Philadelphia
GIROUX, Claude	5-11	180	R	Hearst, Ont.	20	Philadelphia-Gatineau
HARTNELL, Scott	6-2	210	L	Regina, Sask.	26	Philadelphia
KNUBLE, Mike	6-3	230	R	Toronto, Ont.	36	Philadelphia
LUPUL, Joffrey	6-1	205	R	Fort Saskatchewan, Alta.	25	Philadelphia
METROPOLIT, Glen	5-10	193	R	Toronto, Ont.	34	Boston
RICHARDS, Mike	5-11	195	L	Kenora, Ont.	23	Philadelphia
UPSHALL, Scottie	6-0	197	L	Fort McMurray, Alta.	24	Philadelphia
DEFENSEMEN						
COBURN, Braydon	6-5	220	L	Calgary, Alta.	23	Philadelphia
EMINGER, Steve	6-2	212	R	Woodbridge, Ont.	24	Washington
GUENIN, Nate	6-2	210	R	Sewickley, PA	25	Phi-Phi (AHL)
HATCHER, Derian	6-5	235	L	Sterling Hts., MI	36	Philadelphia
JONES, Randy	6-2	200	L	Quispamsis, N.B.	27	Philadelphia
KUKKONEN, Lasse	6-1	190	L	Oulu, Finland	27	Philadelphia
PARENT, Ryan	6-2	205	L	Prince Albert, Sask.	21	Phi-Phi (AHL)
RAMHOLT, Tim	6-1	194	L	Zurich, Switz.	23	Calgary-Quad City
SYVRET, Danny	5-11	203	L	Millgrove, Ont.	23	Springfield-Hershey
TIMONEN, Kimmo	5-10	194	L	Kuopio, Finland	33	Philadelphia
VAANANEN, Ossi	6-4	215	L	Vantaa, Finland	28	Djurgarden
GOALTENDERS	**HT**	**WT**	**C**	**Place of Birth**	***Age**	**2007-08 Club**
BIRON, Martin	6-3	163	L	Lac-St-Charles, Que.	31	Philadelphia
NIITTYMAKI, Antero	6-1	215	L	Turku, Finland	28	Philadelphia

* – Age at start of 2008-09 season

Coaching History

Keith Allen, 1967-68, 1968-69; Vic Stasiuk, 1969-70, 1970-71; Fred Shero, 1971-72 to 1977-78; Bob McCammon and Pat Quinn, 1978-79; Pat Quinn, 1979-80, 1980-81; Pat Quinn and Bob McCammon, 1981-82; Bob McCammon, 1982-83, 1983-84; Mike Keenan, 1984-85 to 1987-88; Paul Holmgren, 1988-89 to 1990-91; Paul Holmgren and Bill Dineen, 1991-92; Bill Dineen, 1992-93; Terry Simpson, 1993-94; Terry Murray, 1994-95 to 1996-97; Wayne Cashman and Roger Neilson, 1997-98; Roger Neilson, 1998-99, 1999-2000; Craig Ramsay and Bill Barber, 2000-01; Bill Barber, 2001-02; Ken Hitchcock, 2002-03 to 2005-06; Ken Hitchcock and John Stevens, 2006-07; John Stevens, 2007-08 to date.

John Stevens

Head Coach

Born: Campbellton, N.B., December 30, 1965.

John Stevens took over as head coach of the Philadelphia Flyers on October 22, 2006. In his first full season behind the bench in 2007-08, he led the Flyers back to the playoffs after finishing last overall in the NHL the year before. Stevens had been the head coach of the Flyers' American Hockey League affiliate, the Philadelphia Phantoms, for six seasons (2000-01 through 2005-06) and led the team to the Calder Cup championship in 2005. He was named assistant coach of the Flyers on June 5, 2006. Stevens joined the Phantoms coaching staff as an assistant on February 10, 1999 after announcing his retirement from hockey due to an eye injury. He became the second head coach in Phantoms history on June 8, 2000.

Stevens played 15 seasons of professional hockey as a defenseman (1984-85 to 1998-99), including 53 career NHL games with the Flyers and Hartford Whalers. Over parts of five seasons (1986-87 and 1987-88 with the Flyers and 1990-91, 1991-92 and 1993-94 with Hartford), Stevens recorded 10 assists and 48 penalty minutes in 53 games. He was a member of three Calder Cup championship teams as a player (Hershey,1988; Springfield, 1991; and Philadelphia, 1998) and won the Barry Ashbee Award as the Phantoms' top defenseman for the 1996-97 season. He was named the Phantoms' first captain on October 1, 1996. Stevens was originally drafted by the Flyers in the third round (47th overall) of the 1984 NHL Entry Draft.

Coaching Record

			Regular Season				Playoffs			
Season	Team	League	GC	W	L	O/T	GC	W	L	T
2000-01	Philadelphia	AHL	80	36	34	10	10	5	5	....
2001-02	Philadelphia	AHL	80	33	27	20	5	2	3	....
2002-03	Philadelphia	AHL	80	33	33	14	....	....	....	....
2003-04	Philadelphia	AHL	80	46	25	9	12	6	6	....
2004-05	Philadelphia	AHL	80	48	25	7	21	16	5	....
2006-07	**Philadelphia**	**NHL**	**74**	**21**	**42**	**11**	....	....	....	....
2007-08	**Philadelphia**	**NHL**	**82**	**42**	**29**	**11**	**17**	**9**	**8**	....
	NHL Totals		**156**	**63**	**71**	**22**	**17**	**9**	**8**	....

2007-08 Scoring

* – rookie

Regular Season

Pos	#	Player	Team	GP	G	A	Pts	TOI	+/–	PIM	PP	SH	GW	S	%
C	18	Mike Richards	PHI	73	28	47	75	21:30	14	76	8	5	6	212	13.2
C	48	Daniel Briere	PHI	79	31	41	72	18:51	–22	68	14	0	3	182	17.0
L	40	Vaclav Prospal	T.B.	62	29	28	57	19:59	–7	39	9	0	4	175	16.6
			PHI	18	4	10	14	17:14	7	6	1	0	1	40	10.0
			Total	80	33	38	71	19:22	0	45	10	0	5	215	15.3
R	22	Mike Knuble	PHI	82	29	26	55	18:54	–3	72	15	1	3	177	16.4
C	17	Jeff Carter	PHI	82	29	24	53	18:50	6	55	7	2	5	260	11.2
C	20	R.J. Umberger	PHI	74	13	37	50	17:52	0	19	4	0	3	173	7.5
R	15	Joffrey Lupul	PHI	56	20	26	46	18:12	2	35	7	0	3	176	11.4
D	44	Kimmo Timonen	PHI	80	8	36	44	23:34	0	50	3	1	1	125	6.4
L	19	Scott Hartnell	PHI	80	24	19	43	16:10	2	159	10	1	6	176	13.6
D	5	Braydon Coburn	PHI	78	9	27	36	21:14	17	74	5	0	2	113	8.0
D	6	Randy Jones	PHI	71	5	26	31	19:23	8	58	1	0	0	103	4.9
R	9	Scottie Upshall	PHI	61	14	16	30	13:20	2	74	3	0	1	128	10.9
L	12	Simon Gagne	PHI	25	7	11	18	18:08	–8	4	5	0	2	76	9.2
R	27 *	Steve Downie	PHI	32	6	6	12	09:50	2	73	0	1	1	25	24.0
C	34	Jim Dowd	PHI	73	5	5	10	08:26	0	41	0	1	0	41	12.2
D	21	Jason Smith	PHI	77	1	9	10	17:56	–4	86	0	0	0	58	1.7
D	26	Jaroslav Modry	L.A.	61	1	5	6	18:34	2	42	0	0	0	39	2.6
			PHI	19	0	3	3	20:37	–11	8	0	0	0	17	0.0
			Total	80	1	8	9	19:03	–9	50	0	0	0	56	1.8
R	24	Sami Kapanen	PHI	74	5	3	8	13:19	–12	16	0	1	1	76	6.6
L	25	Patrick Thoresen	EDM	17	2	1	3	10:42	–4	6	0	0	0	18	11.1
			PHI	21	0	5	5	12:35	–6	8	0	0	0	21	0.0
			Total	38	2	6	8	11:45	–10	14	0	0	0	39	5.1
D	2	Derian Hatcher	PHI	44	2	5	7	21:05	4	33	0	0	1	27	7.4
R	53 *	Denis Tolpeko	PHI	26	1	5	6	08:16	–4	24	0	0	0	24	4.2
D	28	Lasse Kukkonen	PHI	53	1	4	5	15:44	3	38	0	0	0	31	3.2
R	14	Stefan Ruzicka	PHI	14	1	3	4	08:39	5	27	0	0	0	10	10.0
L	32 *	Riley Cote	PHI	70	1	3	4	04:16	2	202	0	0	0	17	5.9
C	11	Ryan Potulny	PHI	7	0	1	1	06:30	0	4	0	0	0	5	0.0
D	8	Rory Fitzpatrick	PHI	19	0	1	1	12:43	–12	11	0	0	0	10	0.0
D	29 *	Nathan Guenin	PHI	2	0	0	0	09:56	2	2	0	0	0	0	0.0
R	56 *	Claude Giroux	PHI	2	0	0	0	09:34	–2	0	0	0	0	2	0.0
L	65 *	Kyle Greentree	PHI	2	0	0	0	09:11	–1	0	0	0	0	3	0.0
R	36	Jesse Boulerice	PHI	5	0	0	0	03:52	–2	29	0	0	0	1	0.0
D	77 *	Ryan Parent	PHI	22	0	0	0	14:58	–4	6	0	0	0	9	0.0

Goaltending

No.	Goaltender	GPI	Mins	Avg	W	L	OT	EN	SO	GA	SA	S%	G	A	PIM
43	Martin Biron	62	3539	2.59	30	20	9	1	5	153	1865	.918	0	1	8
30	Antero Niittymaki	28	1424	2.91	12	9	2	4	1	69	739	.907	0	0	0
	Totals	**82**	**4985**	**2.73**	**42**	**29**	**11**	**5**	**6**	**227**	**2609**	**.913**			

Playoffs

Pos	#	Player	Team	GP	G	A	Pts	TOI	+/–	PIM	PP	SH	GW	OT	S	%
C	48	Daniel Briere	PHI	17	9	7	16	18:26	–3	20	6	0	3	0	45	20.0
C	20	R.J. Umberger	PHI	17	10	5	15	16:51	7	10	1	0	2	0	40	25.0
C	18	Mike Richards	PHI	17	7	7	14	20:55	0	10	1	2	0	0	53	13.2
L	40	Vaclav Prospal	PHI	17	3	10	13	16:48	–3	6	1	0	0	0	34	8.8
C	17	Jeff Carter	PHI	17	6	5	11	20:07	0	12	3	0	1	0	72	8.3
R	15	Joffrey Lupul	PHI	17	4	6	10	16:12	1	2	2	0	1	1	46	8.7
R	22	Mike Knuble	PHI	12	3	4	7	18:34	–1	6	0	0	1	1	25	12.0
L	19	Scott Hartnell	PHI	17	3	4	7	15:28	–2	20	0	0	0	0	23	13.0
R	9	Scottie Upshall	PHI	17	3	4	7	13:56	1	44	1	0	1	0	37	8.1
D	44	Kimmo Timonen	PHI	13	0	6	6	24:40	3	8	0	0	0	0	24	0.0
D	5	Braydon Coburn	PHI	14	0	6	6	22:25	4	14	0	0	0	0	24	0.0
D	2	Derian Hatcher	PHI	15	1	2	3	21:14	2	40	0	0	0	0	7	14.3
C	34	Jim Dowd	PHI	17	1	2	3	08:54	0	4	0	0	0	0	11	9.1
D	26	Jaroslav Modry	PHI	9	0	3	3	19:49	–6	0	0	0	0	0	6	0.0
R	24	Sami Kapanen	PHI	16	2	0	2	10:46	–4	2	0	0	0	0	19	10.5
L	25	Patrick Thoresen	PHI	14	0	2	2	09:22	1	4	0	0	0	0	10	0.0
D	28	Lasse Kukkonen	PHI	14	0	2	2	15:21	–1	6	0	0	0	0	6	0.0
D	6	Randy Jones	PHI	16	0	2	2	21:24	6	4	0	0	0	0	21	0.0
D	21	Jason Smith	PHI	17	0	2	2	16:42	–4	4	0	0	0	0	2	0.0
D	77 *	Ryan Parent	PHI	4	0	1	1	16:35	–1	0	0	0	0	0	2	0.0
R	27 *	Steve Downie	PHI	6	0	1	1	06:03	–2	10	0	0	0	0	2	0.0
L	32 *	Riley Cote	PHI	3	0	0	0	04:08	0	0	0	0	0	0	0	0.0

Goaltending

No.	Goaltender	GPI	Mins	Avg	W	L	EN	SO	GA	SA	S%	G	A	PIM
43	Martin Biron	17	1049	2.97	9	8	2	1	52	540	.904	0	1	2
	Totals	**17**	**1054**	**3.07**	**9**	**8**	**2**	**1**	**54**	**542**	**.900**			

Captains' History

Lou Angotti, 1967-68; Ed Van Impe, 1968-69 to 1971-72; Ed Van Impe and Bobby Clarke, 1972-73; Bobby Clarke, 1973-74 to 1978-79; Mel Bridgman, 1979-80, 1980-81; Bill Barber, 1981-82; Bill Barber and Bobby Clarke, 1982-83; Bobby Clarke, 1983-84; Dave Poulin, 1984-85 to 1988-89; Dave Poulin and Ron Sutter, 1989-90; Ron Sutter, 1990-91; Rick Tocchet, 1991-92; no captain, 1992-93; Kevin Dineen, 1993-94; Eric Lindros, 1994-95 to 1998-99; Eric Lindros and Eric Desjardins, 1999-2000; Eric Desjardins, 2000-01; Eric Desjardins and Keith Primeau, 2001-02; Keith Primeau, 2002-03, 2003-04; Keith Primeau and Derian Hatcher, 2005-06; Peter Forsberg, 2006-07; Jason Smith, 2007-08.

Club Records

Team

(Figures in brackets for season records are games played; records for fewest points, wins, ties, losses, goals, goals against are for 70 or more games)

Most Points	118	1975-76 (80)
Most Wins	53	1984-85 (80), 1985-86 (80)
Most Ties	*24	1969-70 (76)
Most Losses	48	2006-07 (82)
Most Goals	350	1983-84 (80)
Most Goals Against	319	1992-93 (84)
Fewest Points	56	2006-07 (82)
Fewest Wins	17	1969-70 (76)
Fewest Ties	4	1985-86 (80)
Fewest Losses	12	1979-80 (80)
Fewest Goals	173	1967-68 (74)
Fewest Goals Against	164	1973-74 (78)
Longest Winning Streak		
Overall	13	Oct. 19-Nov. 17/85
Home	*20	Jan. 4-Apr. 3/76
Away	8	Dec. 22/82-Jan. 16/83
Longest Undefeated Streak		
Overall	*35	Oct. 14/79-Jan. 6/80 (25 wins, 10 ties)
Home	26	Oct. 11/79-Feb. 3/80 (19 wins, 7 ties)
Away	16	Oct. 20/79-Jan. 6/80 (11 wins, 5 ties)
Longest Losing Streak		
Overall	9	Dec. 8-27/06
Home	13	Nov. 29/06-Feb. 8/07
Away	8	Oct. 25-Nov. 26/72, Mar. 3-29/88
Longest Winless Streak		
Overall	12	Feb. 24-Mar. 16/99 (8 losses, 4 ties)
Home	13	Nov. 29/06-Feb. 8/07 (13 losses)
Away	19	Oct. 23/71-Jan. 27/72 (15 losses, 4 ties)
Most Shutouts, Season	13	1974-75 (80)
Most PIM, Season	2,621	1980-81 (80)
Most Goals, Game	13	Mar. 22/84 (Pit. 4 at Phi. 13), Oct. 18/84 (Van. 2 at Phi. 13)

Individual

Most Seasons	15	Bobby Clarke
Most Games	1,144	Bobby Clarke
Most Goals, Career	420	Bill Barber
Most Assists, Career	852	Bobby Clarke
Most Points, Career	1,210	Bobby Clarke (358G, 852A)
Most PIM, Career	1,817	Rick Tocchet
Most Shutouts, Career	50	Bernie Parent
Longest Consecutive Game Streak	484	Rod Brind'Amour (Feb. 24/93-Apr. 18/99)
Most Goals, Season	61	Reggie Leach (1975-76)
Most Assists, Season	89	Bobby Clarke (1974-75, 1975-76)
Most Points, Season	123	Mark Recchi (1992-93; 53G, 70A)
Most PIM, Season	*472	Dave Schultz (1974-75)
Most Points, Defenseman, Season	82	Mark Howe (1985-86; 24G, 58A)
Most Points, Center, Season	119	Bobby Clarke (1975-76; 30G, 89A)
Most Points, Right Wing, Season	123	Mark Recchi (1992-93; 53G, 70A)
Most Points, Left Wing, Season	112	Bill Barber (1975-76; 50G, 62A)
Most Points, Rookie, Season	82	Mikael Renberg (1993-94; 38G, 44A)
Most Shutouts, Season	12	Bernie Parent (1973-74, 1974-75)
Most Goals, Game	4	Sixteen times
Most Assists, Game	6	Eric Lindros (Feb. 26/97)
Most Points, Game	8	Tom Bladon (Dec. 11/77; 4G, 4A)

* NHL Record.

Retired Numbers

1	Bernie Parent	1967-1971, 1973-1979
4	Barry Ashbee	1970-1974
7	Bill Barber	1972-1985
16	Bobby Clarke	1969-1984

All-time Record vs. Other Clubs

Regular Season

	At Home								On Road								Total							
	GP	W	L	T	OL	GF	GA	PTS	GP	W	L	T	OL	GF	GA	PTS	GP	W	L	T	OL	GF	GA	PTS
Anaheim	9	4	2	3	0	25	17	11	10	4	3	2	1	35	34	11	19	8	5	5	1	60	51	22
Atlanta	16	12	1	2	1	68	43	27	16	13	2	1	0	56	35	27	32	25	3	3	1	124	78	54
Boston	79	34	33	10	2	260	236	80	82	23	45	11	3	228	297	60	161	57	78	21	5	488	533	140
Buffalo	73	41	17	12	3	249	189	97	69	25	36	8	0	192	236	58	142	66	53	20	3	441	425	155
Calgary	52	34	14	3	1	200	137	72	53	19	25	9	0	175	210	47	105	53	39	12	1	375	347	119
Carolina	49	32	10	5	2	182	124	71	50	26	14	9	1	184	160	62	99	58	24	14	3	366	284	133
Chicago	63	36	16	11	0	207	162	83	61	16	26	19	0	175	207	51	124	52	42	30	0	382	369	134
Colorado	35	22	9	2	2	125	95	48	36	11	12	12	1	123	126	35	71	33	21	14	3	248	221	83
Columbus	3	2	0	1	0	10	5	5	4	2	0	2	0	10	7	6	7	4	0	3	0	20	12	11
Dallas	68	42	10	16	0	256	154	100	67	23	28	16	0	214	219	62	135	65	38	32	0	470	373	162
Detroit	59	35	13	11	0	236	169	81	60	18	32	10	0	185	216	46	119	53	45	21	0	421	385	127
Edmonton	32	20	10	2	0	130	88	42	29	8	15	6	0	86	103	22	61	28	25	8	0	216	191	64
Florida	31	13	10	6	2	83	79	34	30	21	8	1	0	102	69	43	61	34	18	7	2	185	148	77
Los Angeles	64	41	15	7	1	247	158	90	67	38	21	8	0	227	196	84	131	79	36	15	1	474	354	174
Minnesota	5	4	1	0	0	14	5	8	3	1	1	1	0	6	6	3	8	5	2	1	0	20	11	11
Montreal	79	30	32	16	1	238	240	77	80	27	37	14	2	239	274	70	159	57	69	30	3	477	514	147
Nashville	6	2	2	1	1	19	12	6	5	2	0	2	1	10	8	7	11	4	2	3	2	29	20	13
New Jersey	97	57	27	10	3	359	252	127	95	33	51	8	3	301	325	77	192	90	78	18	6	660	577	204
NY Islanders	107	62	32	11	2	377	297	137	110	41	52	15	2	330	388	99	217	103	84	26	4	707	685	236
NY Rangers	121	58	46	14	3	383	342	133	122	47	49	23	3	359	387	120	243	105	95	37	6	742	729	253
Ottawa	29	17	9	2	1	97	80	37	30	12	11	6	1	88	86	31	59	29	20	8	2	185	166	68
Phoenix	32	23	9	0	0	136	86	46	32	16	14	2	0	106	103	34	64	39	23	2	0	242	189	80
Pittsburgh	118	88	20	8	2	493	300	186	118	42	53	22	1	377	418	107	236	130	73	30	3	870	718	293
St. Louis	68	46	12	10	0	268	156	102	69	36	26	7	0	224	196	79	137	82	38	17	0	492	352	181
San Jose	12	6	4	2	0	37	30	14	13	7	4	2	0	32	28	16	25	13	8	4	0	69	58	30
Tampa Bay	31	15	7	7	2	92	72	39	32	18	13	1	0	94	96	37	63	33	20	8	2	186	168	76
Toronto	73	44	21	8	0	268	175	96	73	32	25	14	2	241	229	80	146	76	46	22	2	509	404	176
Vancouver	55	37	17	1	0	238	164	75	52	30	10	12	0	211	146	72	107	67	27	13	0	449	310	147
Washington	89	55	27	6	1	337	242	117	86	37	34	13	2	277	282	89	175	92	61	19	3	614	524	206
Defunct Clubs	34	24	4	6	0	137	67	54	35	13	14	8	0	102	89	34	69	37	18	14	0	239	156	88
Totals	**1589**	**936**	**430**	**193**	**30**	**5771**	**4176**	**2095**	**1589**	**641**	**661**	**264**	**23**	**4989**	**5176**	**1569**	**3178**	**1577**	**1091**	**457**	**53**	**10760**	**9352**	**3664**

Playoffs

	Series	W	L	GP	W	L	T	GF	GA	Last Mtg.	Rnd.	Result
Boston	4	2	2	20	9	11	0	57	60	1978	SF	L 1-4
Buffalo	8	5	3	43	25	18	0	124	123	2006	CQF	L 2-4
Calgary	2	1	1	11	7	4	0	43	28	1981	QF	L 3-4
Chicago	1	0	1	4	0	4	0	8	20	1971	QF	L 0-4
Colorado	2	2	0	11	7	4	0	39	29	1985	CF	W 4-2
Dallas	2	2	0	11	8	3	0	41	26	1980	SF	W 4-1
Detroit	1	0	1	4	0	4	0	6	16	1997	F	L 0-4
Edmonton	3	1	2	15	7	8	0	44	49	1987	F	L 3-4
Florida	1	0	1	6	2	4	0	11	15	1996	CSF	L 2-4
Montreal	5	2	3	26	11	15	0	72	86	2008	CSF	W 4-1
New Jersey	4	2	2	20	11	9	0	49	50	2004	CQF	W 4-1
NY Islanders	4	3	1	25	14	11	0	83	69	1987	DF	W 4-3
NY Rangers	10	6	4	47	27	20	0	157	153	1997	CF	W 4-1
Ottawa	2	0	2	11	3	8	0	12	28	2003	CSF	L 2-4
Pittsburgh	4	3	1	23	13	10	0	75	71	2008	CF	L 1-4
St. Louis	2	0	2	11	3	8	0	20	34	1969	QF	L 0-4
Tampa Bay	2	1	1	13	7	6	0	45	34	2004	CF	L 3-4
Toronto	6	5	1	36	22	14	0	119	85	2004	CSF	W 4-2
Vancouver	1	1	0	3	2	1	0	15	9	1979	PRE	W 2-1
Washington	4	2	2	23	11	12	0	78	85	2008	CQF	W 4-3
Totals	**68**	**38**	**30**	**363**	**189**	**174**	**0**	**1098**	**1070**			

Calgary totals include Atlanta Flames, 1972-73 to 1979-80.
Carolina totals include Hartford, 1979-80 to 1996-97.
Colorado totals include Quebec, 1979-80 to 1994-95.
Dallas totals include Minnesota North Stars, 1967-68 to 1992-93.
New Jersey totals include Kansas City, 1974-75, 1975-76, and Colorado Rockies, 1976-77 to 1981-82.
Phoenix totals include Winnipeg, 1979-80 to 1995-96.

Playoff Results 2008-2003

Year	Round	Opponent	Result	GF	GA
2008	CF	Pittsburgh	L 1-4	9	20
	CSF	Montreal	W 4-1	20	14
	CQF	Washington	W 4-3	23	20
2006	CQF	Buffalo	L 2-4	14	27
2004	CF	Tampa Bay	L 3-4	19	21
	CSF	Toronto	W 4-2	17	13
	CQF	New Jersey	W 4-1	14	9
2003	CSF	Ottawa	L 2-4	10	17
	CQF	Toronto	W 4-3	24	16

Abbreviations: Round: F – Final; **CF** – conference final; **CSF** – conference semi-final; **CQF** – conference quarter-final; **DF** – division final; **SF** – semi-final; **QF** – quarter-final; **PRE** – preliminary round.

2007-08 Results

Month	Day	Opponent	Score
Oct.	4	at Calgary	3-2
	6	at Edmonton	3-5
	10	at Vancouver	8-2
	13	NY Islanders	3-1
	16	Atlanta	4-0
	18	New Jersey	4-0
	20	Carolina	3-2*
	24	at Florida	3-4
	25	at Tampa Bay	2-5
	27	at Boston	2-1
Nov.	1	at Montreal	2-5
	2	at Washington	3-2
	5	at NY Rangers	0-2
	7	at Pittsburgh	3-1
	8	at New Jersey	1-4
	10	Pittsburgh	5-2
	12	NY Islanders	3-2
	15	NY Rangers	3-4†
	17	New Jersey	2-6
	21	at Carolina	6-3
	23	Washington	3-4*
	24	at Ottawa	4-3
	26	Boston	3-6
	28	at Carolina	3-1
Dec.	1	Dallas	1-4
	5	at Minnesota	3-1
	7	at Colorado	1-2
	11	Pittsburgh	8-2
	13	Montreal	1-4
	15	Carolina	5-6†
	16	at New Jersey	2-4
	18	Phoenix	2-3
	21	at Buffalo	2-3
	22	Buffalo	5-6†
	27	Toronto	4-1
	29	at Tampa Bay	4-2
	30	at Florida	1-0
Jan.	4	at New Jersey	0-3
	5	at Toronto	3-2
	8	at Atlanta	4-1
	10	at NY Rangers	6-2
	12	Boston	3-4*
	13	at Washington	6-4
	16	Florida	5-3
	19	at NY Islanders	5-3
	20	Ottawa	6-1
	22	New Jersey	3-7
	24	Pittsburgh	4-3
	29	Los Angeles	3-2*
	31	NY Rangers	0-4
Feb.	2	Anaheim	3-0
	5	at Atlanta	3-2
	6	Washington	3-4
	9	NY Rangers	0-2
	10	at Pittsburgh	3-4
	12	at NY Islanders	3-4
	14	Tampa Bay	3-5
	16	at Montreal	0-1
	17	Montreal	3-5
	19	at Ottawa	2-3†
	21	San Jose	1-3
	23	Florida	1-2*
	25	at Buffalo	4-3†
	28	Ottawa	3-1
Mar.	1	at NY Islanders	4-1
	2	at NY Rangers	4-5†
	4	Buffalo	2-5
	6	Tampa Bay	3-2
	8	NY Islanders	4-1
	11	at Toronto	3-4*
	12	Toronto	2-3
	15	at Boston	2-3*
	16	at Pittsburgh	1-7
	18	Atlanta	3-2
	21	NY Rangers	4-3†
	23	NY Islanders	4-1
	25	at NY Rangers	2-1*
	28	at New Jersey	4-5†
	29	at NY Islanders	4-3†
Apr.	2	at Pittsburgh	2-4
	4	New Jersey	3-0
	6	Pittsburgh	2-0

* – Overtime † – Shootout

Entry Draft Selections 2008-1994

Name in bold denotes played in NHL.

2008
Pick
19 Luca Sbisa
67 Marc-Andre Bourdon
84 Jacob Deserres
178 Zac Rinaldo
196 Joacim Eriksson

2007
Pick
2 James vanRiemsdyk
41 Kevin Marshall
66 Garrett Klotz
122 Mario Kempe
152 Jonathon Kalinski
161 Patrick Maroon
182 Brad Phillips

2006
Pick
22 **Claude Giroux**
39 Andreas Nodl
42 Michael Ratchuk
55 Denis Bodrov
79 Jonathan Matsumoto
101 Joonas Lehtivuori
109 Jakub Kovar
145 Jonathan Rheault
175 Michael Dupont
205 Andrei Popov

2005
Pick
29 **Steve Downie**
91 Oskars Bartulis
119 Jeremy Duchesne
152 Josh Beaulieu
174 John Flatters
215 Matt Clackson

2004
Pick
92 Rob Bellamy
101 R.J. Anderson
124 David Laliberte
144 Chris Zarb
149 Gino Pisellini
170 Ladislav Scurko
171 Frederik Cabana
232 **Martin Houle**
253 Travis Gawryletz
286 **Triston Grant**
291 John Carter

2003
Pick
11 **Jeff Carter**
24 **Mike Richards**
69 **Colin Fraser**
81 **Stefan Ruzicka**
85 **Alexandre Picard**
87 **Ryan Potulny**
95 Rick Kozak
108 Kevin Romy
140 David Tremblay
191 Rejean Beauchemin
193 Ville Hostikka

2002
Pick
4 **Joni Pitkanen**
105 Rosario Ruggeri
126 Konstantin Baranov
161 Dov Grumet-Morris
192 Nikita Korovkin
193 **Joey Mormina**
201 Mathieu Brunelle

2001
Pick
27 **Jeff Woywitka**
95 **Patrick Sharp**
146 **Jussi Timonen**
150 Bernd Bruckler
158 Roman Malek
172 **Dennis Seidenberg**
177 Andrei Razin
208 Thierry Douville
225 **David Printz**

2000
Pick
28 **Justin Williams**
94 Alexander Drozdetsky
171 **Roman Cechmanek**
195 Colin Shields
210 John Eichelberger
227 **Guillaume Lefebvre**
259 Regan Kelly
287 Milan Kopecky

1999
Pick
22 **Maxime Ouellet**
119 Jeff Feniak
160 Konstantin Rudenko
200 Pavel Kasparik
208 **Vaclav Pletka**
224 David Nystrom

1998
Pick
22 **Simon Gagne**
42 Jason Beckett
51 Ian Forbes
109 Jean-Philippe Morin
124 **Francis Belanger**
139 Garrett Prosofsky
168 **Antero Niittymaki**
175 Cam Ondrik
195 **Tomas Divisek**
222 Lubomir Pistek
243 **Petr Hubacek**
253 **Bruno St. Jacques**
258 Sergei Skrobot

1997
Pick
30 **Jean-Marc Pelletier**
50 **Pat Kavanagh**
62 Kris Mallette
103 Mikhail Chernov
158 Jordon Flodell
164 **Todd Fedoruk**
214 Marko Kauppinen
240 Par Styf

1996
Pick
15 **Dainius Zubrus**
64 Chester Gallant
124 Per-Ragna Bergqvist
133 **Jesse Boulerice**
187 Roman Malov
213 Jeff Milleker

1995
Pick
22 **Brian Boucher**
48 Shane Kenny
100 **Radovan Somik**
132 **Dmitri Tertyshny**
135 Jamie Sokolsky
152 **Martin Spanhel**
178 Martin Streit
204 Ruslan Shafikov
230 **Jeff Lank**

1994
Pick
62 Artem Anisimov
88 Adam Magarrell
101 Sebastien Vallee
140 **Alex Selivanov**
166 **Colin Forbes**
192 Derek Diener
202 **Raymond Giroux**
218 **Johan Hedberg**
244 Andre Payette
270 Jan Lipiansky

General Managers' History

Bud Poile, 1967-68, 1968-69; Bud Poile and Keith Allen, 1969-70; Keith Allen, 1970-71 to 1982-83; Bob McCammon, 1983-84; Bob Clarke, 1984-85 to 1989-90; Russ Farwell, 1990-91 to 1993-94; Bob Clarke, 1994-95 to 2005-06; Bob Clarke and Paul Holmgren, 2006-07; Paul Holmgren, 2007-08 to date.

Paul Holmgren

General Manager

Born: St. Paul, MN, December 2, 1955.

Paul Holmgren was named interim general manager of the Philadelphia Flyers on November 11, 2006, replacing Bob Clarke who resigned on October 22. On March 14, 2007, Holmgren was officially announced as the club's new g.m. In his first full season on the job in 2007-08, the Flyers returned to the playoffs after finishing last overall in the NHL the year before. Prior to his promotion, Holmgren had served the previous seven seasons as the team's assistant general manager. He rejoined the Flyers organization as a scout after being replaced as the Hartford Whalers' head coach on November 6, 1995. He had served as a head coach with both the Whalers and the Flyers and also served as general manager in Hartford during the 1993–94 season.

Holmgren retired from playing after the 1984-85 season, having recorded 144 goals and 179 assists for 323 points and 1,684 penalty minutes in 527 career regular season NHL games with the Flyers and the Minnesota North Stars. He recorded 138 goals and 171 assists for 309 points and 1,600 penalty minutes in 500 games over parts of nine seasons with the Flyers (1975-76 to 1983-84). His 1,600 penalty minutes with the Flyers are second all-time in club history. Holmgren was drafted from the University of Minnesota by the Flyers in the sixth round (108th overall) of the 1975 NHL Entry Draft.

Coaching Record

			Regular Season				Playoffs			
Season	Team	League	GC	W	L	O/T	GC	W	L	T
1988-89	Philadelphia	NHL	80	36	36	8	19	10	9	....
1989-90	Philadelphia	NHL	80	30	39	11	....	....	....	....
1990-91	Philadelphia	NHL	80	33	37	10	....	....	....	....
1991-92	Philadelphia	NHL	24	8	14	2	....	....	....	....
1992-93	Hartford	NHL	84	26	52	6	....	....	....	....
1993-94	Hartford	NHL	17	4	11	2	....	....	....	....
1994-95	Hartford	NHL	48	19	24	5	....	....	....	....
1995-96	Hartford	NHL	12	5	6	1	....	....	....	....
	NHL Totals		**425**	**161**	**219**	**45**	**19**	**10**	**9**	....

Club Directory

Wachovia Center

Philadelphia Flyers
Wachovia Center
3601 South Broad Street
Philadelphia, PA 19148-5290
Phone **215/465-4500**
PR FAX 215/389-9403
www.philadelphiaflyers.com
Capacity: 19,537

Executive Management
Chairman . . . . . Ed Snider
President and COO of Comcast-Spectacor. . . . . Peter A. Luukko
General Manager . . . . . Paul Holmgren
Senior Vice President. . . . . Bob Clarke
Executive Vice President . . . . . Keith Allen
Governor . . . . . Ed Snider
Alternate Governors . . . . . Paul Holmgren, Peter A. Luukko, Phil Weinberg
Senior Vice President, Business Operations . . . . . Shawn Tilger

Hockey Club Personnel
Assistant General Manager. . . . . Barry Hanrahan
Director of Hockey Operations . . . . . Chris Pryor
Director of Player Development. . . . . Don Luce
Director of Player Personnel . . . . . Dave Brown
Head Coach . . . . . John Stevens
Assistant Coaches. . . . . Jack McIlhargey, Joe Mullen, Craig Berube
Goaltending Coach. . . . . Reggie Lemelin
Player Development Coach . . . . . Eric Desjardins
Pro Scouts . . . . . John Chapman, Ross Fitzpatrick, Al Hill
Scouting Staff . . . . . Andre Beaulieu, Patrick Burke, Wade Clarke, Mark Greig, Todd Hearty, Matti Kautto, Simon Nolet, Dennis Patterson, John Riley, Ilkka Sinisalo, Vaclav Slansky, Evgeny Zimin
Video Coordinator . . . . . Adam Patterson
Director of Team Services . . . . . Bryan Hardenbergh
Executive Assistant . . . . . Dianna Taylor
Administrative Assistant . . . . . Jody Clarke

Medical/Training Staff
Team Physicians . . . . . Bill DeLong, M.D.; Gary Dorshimer, M.D.; Tom Graham, M.D.; Guy Lanzi, D.M.D.; Emanuel Sanfilippo, D.C.
Athletic Trainer/Strength and Conditioning Coach. . Jim McCrossin
Assistant Athletic Trainer. . . . . Sal Raffa
Massage Therapist . . . . . Brad Smith
Head Equipment Manager . . . . . Derek Settlemyre
Equipment Managers . . . . . Harry Bricker, Anthony Oratorio, Luke Clarke
Training Center Maintenance . . . . . Mike Craytor

Communications Department
Senior Director of Communications. . . . . Zack Hill
Director of Media Services and Publications. . . . . Joe Klueg
Manager, Communications and New Media . . . . . Kevin Kurz
Communications Office Manager . . . . . Jill Lipson
Media Services and Publications Coordinator. . . . . Joe Siville

Community Relations Department
Director of Community Relations and Special Events . . Linda Mantai
Manager of Community Relations. . . . . Jason Tempesta
Manager of Fan Development. . . . . Rob Baer
Hockey Coordinator . . . . . Francis Walmsley
Ambassador of Hockey . . . . . Bob Kelly
Fan Relations Assistant . . . . . Jerry Callahan
Ambassadors . . . . . Gary Dornhoefer, Joe Kadlec, Bernie Parent

Customer Service Department
Vice President of Customer Solutions . . . . . Cindy Stutman
Director of Customer Service. . . . . Melissa Keeler
Customer Service Account Managers . . . . . Dan Fuchs, Nadine Heeger, Lauren Pawlowski, Courtney Sams, Andrew Shanks

Game Presentation Department
Director of Game Presentation . . . . . Anthony Gioia
Producer/Director . . . . . Artie Halstead
Public Address Announcer . . . . . Lou Nolan
Anthem Singer . . . . . Lauren Hart

Marketing Department
Director of Marketing . . . . . Lindsey Domers
Business Development Manager . . . . . Jeremy Bland
New Media Manager . . . . . Lauren Cochran
Publicist . . . . . Shauna Adams

Ticket Sales Department
Vice President of Sales . . . . . Jim Willits
Director of Ticket Sales . . . . . Shawn Anderson
Ticket Sales Coordinator . . . . . Angela Prendergast
Senior Account Executive . . . . . Bryan Anton
Account Executives. . . . . Warren Avart, James Darlington, Erin Dunn, Chris Engart, Tim Gobs, Lindsay Heck, Travis Kraus, Scott Riese, J.T. Stewart
Sales Associates . . . . . Ryan Ciavaglia, Billy Gilman, Stephanie Hanlin, Steve Remillard, Joe Rossi, Daniel Ryan

Ticketing Department
Vice President, Ticket Operations . . . . . Cecilia Baker
Ticket Office Manager. . . . . Linda Fleischer
Assistant Ticket Office Manager . . . . . Lisa Albertson
Ticket Operations and Processing Manager . . . . . Michelle Diago
Ticket Office Administration . . . . . Joan Kadlec

Finance Department
Director of Finance . . . . . Dave Jablonski
Controller. . . . . Marisa Spear
Staff Accountants. . . . . Kim Chuba, Doreen Holmgren
Payroll Accountant . . . . . Renee Eiler
Accounting Clerk . . . . . Michele Dominic

Team Consultant . . . . . Ron Ryan
Executive Assistants . . . . . Sharon Allison, Cheri Arnao, Ann Marie Nasuti
Receptionist . . . . . Ann Bachich, Dana Hanratty

Phoenix Coyotes

2007-08 Results: 38W-37L-1OTL-6SOL 83PTS.
Fourth, Pacific Division

Key Off-Season Signings/Acquisitions

2008

April 14 • Signed 2008 Hobey Baker Award winner LW **Kevin Porter**.

June 20 • Acquired C **Olli Jokinen** from Florida for D **Keith Ballard**, D **Nick Boynton** and a 2nd-round pick in 2008.

25 • Acquired RW **Brian McGrattan** from Ottawa for a 5th-round pick in 2009.

July 1 • Signed D **Kurt Sauer** and LW **Todd Fedoruk**.

3 • Signed D **David Hale**.

3 • Re-signed D **Matt Jones**.

10 • Named **Doug Sulliman** assistant coach.

Year-by-Year Record

		Home				Road				Overall								
Season	GP	W	L	T	OL	W	L	T	OL	W	L	T	OL	GF	GA	Pts.	Finished	Playoff Result
2007-08	82	17	20	....	4	21	17	....	3	38	37	....	7	214	231	83	4th, Pacific Div.	Out of Playoffs
2006-07	82	18	20	....	3	13	26	....	2	31	46	....	5	216	284	67	5th, Pacific Div.	Out of Playoffs
2005-06	82	19	18	....	4	19	21	....	1	38	39	....	5	246	271	81	5th, Pacific Div.	Out of Playoffs
2004-05	....	....	....	....	....	....	....	....	....	....	....	....	....	....	....	....		
2003-04	82	11	19	7	4	11	17	11	2	22	36	18	6	188	245	68	5th, Pacific Div.	Out of Playoffs
2002-03	82	17	16	6	2	14	19	5	3	31	35	11	5	204	230	78	4th, Pacific Div.	Out of Playoffs
2001-02	82	27	8	3	3	13	19	6	3	40	27	9	6	228	210	95	2nd, Pacific Div.	Lost Conf. Quarter-Final
2000-01	82	21	11	7	2	14	16	10	1	35	27	17	3	214	212	90	4th, Pacific Div.	Out of Playoffs
1999-2000	82	22	16	2	1	17	15	6	3	39	31	8	4	232	228	90	3rd, Pacific Div.	Lost Conf. Quarter-Final
1998-99	82	23	13	5	....	16	18	7	....	39	31	12	....	205	197	90	2nd, Pacific Div.	Lost Conf. Quarter-Final
1997-98	82	19	16	6	....	16	19	6	....	35	35	12	....	224	227	82	4th, Central Div.	Lost Conf. Quarter-Final
1996-97	82	15	19	7	....	23	18	0	....	38	37	7	....	240	243	83	3rd, Central Div.	Lost Conf. Quarter-Final
1995-96*	82	22	16	3	....	14	24	3	....	36	40	6	....	275	291	78	5th, Central Div.	Lost Conf. Quarter-Final
1994-95*	48	10	10	4	....	6	15	3	....	16	25	7	....	157	177	39	6th, Central Div.	Out of Playoffs
1993-94*	84	15	23	4	....	9	28	5	....	24	51	9	....	245	344	57	6th, Central Div.	Out of Playoffs
1992-93*	84	23	16	3	....	17	21	4	....	40	37	7	....	322	320	87	4th, Smythe Div.	Lost Div. Semi-Final
1991-92*	80	20	14	6	....	13	18	9	....	33	32	15	....	251	244	81	4th, Smythe Div.	Lost Div. Semi-Final
1990-91*	80	17	18	5	....	9	25	6	....	26	43	11	....	260	288	63	5th, Smythe Div.	Out of Playoffs
1989-90*	80	22	13	5	....	15	19	6	....	37	32	11	....	298	290	85	3rd, Smythe Div.	Lost Div. Semi-Final
1988-89*	80	17	18	5	....	9	24	7	....	26	42	12	....	300	355	64	5th, Smythe Div.	Out of Playoffs
1987-88*	80	20	14	6	....	13	22	5	....	33	36	11	....	292	310	77	3rd, Smythe Div.	Lost Div. Semi-Final
1986-87*	80	25	12	3	....	15	20	5	....	40	32	8	....	279	271	88	3rd, Smythe Div.	Lost Div. Final
1985-86*	80	18	19	3	....	8	28	4	....	26	47	7	....	295	372	59	3rd, Smythe Div.	Lost Div. Semi-Final
1984-85*	80	21	13	6	....	22	14	4	....	43	27	10	....	358	332	96	2nd, Smythe Div.	Lost Div. Final
1983-84*	80	17	15	8	....	14	23	3	....	31	38	11	....	340	374	73	4th, Smythe Div.	Lost Div. Semi-Final
1982-83*	80	22	16	2	....	11	23	6	....	33	39	8	....	311	333	74	4th, Smythe Div.	Lost Div. Semi-Final
1981-82*	80	18	13	9	....	15	20	5	....	33	33	14	....	319	332	80	2nd, Norris Div.	Lost Div. Semi-Final
1980-81*	80	7	25	8	....	2	32	6	....	9	57	14	....	246	400	32	6th, Smythe Div.	Out of Playoffs
1979-80*	80	13	19	8	....	7	30	3	....	20	49	11	....	214	314	51	5th, Smythe Div.	Out of Playoffs

* Winnipeg Jets

2008-09 Schedule

Oct.	Sat.	11	Columbus		Thu.	8	Tampa Bay
	Sun.	12	at Anaheim*		Sat.	10	Dallas
	Wed.	15	at Chicago		Tue.	13	at Minnesota
	Fri.	17	at Ottawa		Thu.	15	at Vancouver
	Sat.	18	at Montreal		Sat.	17	at Calgary
	Thu.	23	Washington		Sun.	18	at Edmonton
	Sat.	25	Calgary		Tue.	20	Detroit
	Thu.	30	Pittsburgh		Tue.	27	Anaheim
Nov.	Sat.	1	Minnesota		Thu.	29	at San Jose
	Tue.	4	at Calgary		Sat.	31	Buffalo
	Thu.	6	at Vancouver	**Feb.**	Tue.	3	at Nashville
	Sat.	8	Florida		Wed.	4	at Detroit
	Sun.	9	San Jose		Sat.	7	Carolina
	Wed.	12	at Columbus		Wed.	11	at Dallas
	Thu.	13	at Minnesota		Thu.	12	Vancouver
	Sat.	15	Dallas		Sat.	14	Calgary
	Tue.	18	Chicago		Mon.	16	Edmonton
	Fri.	21	at Carolina		Thu.	19	Atlanta
	Sat.	22	at Philadelphia		Sat.	21	at Los Angeles*
	Mon.	24	at NY Rangers		Tue.	24	at St. Louis
	Wed.	26	at Columbus		Thu.	26	at Nashville
	Fri.	28	Colorado*		Sat.	28	St. Louis
	Sat.	29	San Jose	**Mar.**	Thu.	5	at Boston
Dec.	Tue.	2	Los Angeles		Fri.	6	at Buffalo
	Thu.	4	Toronto		Sun.	8	at NY Islanders*
	Sat.	6	at St. Louis		Tue.	10	at Detroit
	Sun.	7	at Chicago		Thu.	12	at New Jersey
	Wed.	10	at Dallas		Sat.	14	Nashville
	Thu.	11	Minnesota		Tue.	17	San Jose
	Sat.	13	Detroit		Thu.	19	Anaheim
	Tue.	16	at Dallas		Sat.	21	Vancouver
	Thu.	18	Nashville		Sun.	22	at Anaheim*
	Sat.	20	Columbus		Thu.	26	Edmonton
	Mon.	22	at Edmonton		Sat.	28	at San Jose
	Tue.	23	at Colorado		Mon.	30	Dallas
	Fri.	26	at Los Angeles	**Apr.**	Wed.	1	at Colorado
	Sat.	27	Los Angeles		Thu.	2	Los Angeles
	Wed.	31	Colorado		Sat.	4	at Los Angeles
Jan.	Fri.	2	NY Islanders		Tue.	7	St. Louis
	Sun.	4	at Anaheim*		Thu.	9	at San Jose
	Tue.	6	Chicago		Sat.	11	Anaheim

* Denotes afternoon game.

Drafted eighth overall by the Coyotes in 2006, Peter Mueller played 81 games in his debut season of 2007-08 and ranked among the rookie leaders in most offensive categories. His 22 goals, 32 assists and 54 points all ranked third among Phoenix scorers.

PACIFIC DIVISION
30th NHL Season

Franchise date: June 22, 1979

Transferred from Winnipeg to Phoenix, July 1, 1996.

2008-09 Player Personnel

FORWARDS	HT	WT	S	Place of Birth	*Age	2007-08 Club
BOEDKER, Mikkel	5-11	195	L	Brondby, Denmark	18	Kitchener
BOURRET, Alex	5-11	205	L	Drummondville, Que.	21	Hartford
CARCILLO, Daniel	5-11	203	L	King City, Ont.	23	Phoenix-San Antonio
DOAN, Shane	6-2	216	R	Halkirk, Alta.	31	Phoenix
FEDORUK, Todd	6-2	240	L	Redwater, Alta.	29	Dallas-Minnesota
GOERTZEN, Steven	6-2	216	R	Stony Plain, Alta.	24	Syracuse-San Antonio
HANZAL, Martin	6-5	208	L	Pisek, Czech.	21	Phoenix
HOGGAN, Jeff	6-1	188	L	Hope, B.C.	30	Boston-Providence (AHL)
JOKINEN, Olli	6-3	214	L	Kuopio, Finland	29	Florida
KOLARIK, Chad	5-10	175	R	Abington, PA	22	U. of Michigan-San Antonio
LESSARD, Francis	6-3	225	R	Montreal, Que.	29	Hartford
LISIN, Enver	6-2	190	L	Moscow, USSR	22	Phoenix-San Antonio
MACLEAN, Brett	6-2	197	R	Port Elgin, Ont.	19	Oshawa
McGRATTAN, Brian	6-4	234	R	Hamilton, Ont.	27	Ottawa
MUELLER, Peter	6-2	205	R	Bloomington, MN	20	Phoenix
MURRAY, Garth	6-2	209	L	Regina, Sask.	26	Montreal-Florida
NESBITT, Derek	6-0	185	L	Egmondville, Ont.	26	Rockford-Gwinnett
PERRAULT, Joel	6-1	197	R	Montreal, Que.	25	Phoenix-San Antonio
PORTER, Kevin	5-11	194	L	Detroit, MI	22	U. of Michigan-San Antonio
REINPRECHT, Steve	6-0	191	L	Edmonton, Alta.	32	Phoenix
TIKHONOV, Viktor	6-2	187	R	Riga, Latvia	20	Cherepovets
TURRIS, Kyle	6-1	180	R	New Westminster, B.C.	19	U. of Wisconsin-Phoenix
WINNIK, Daniel	6-2	210	R	Toronto, Ont.	23	Phoenix
ZIGOMANIS, Mike	6-1	200	R	Toronto, Ont.	27	Phoenix-San Antonio
DEFENSEMEN						
AHNELOV, Jonas	6-3	205	L	Huddinge, Sweden	20	Boras-Frolunda
FATA, Drew	6-1	220	L	Sault Ste. Marie, Ont.	25	NY Islanders-Bridgeport
HALE, David	6-2	213	L	Colorado Springs, CO	27	Calgary
JONES, Matt	6-0	215	L	Downers Grove, IL	25	Phoenix-San Antonio
JOVANOVSKI, Ed	6-2	210	L	Windsor, Ont.	32	Phoenix
LANNON, Ryan	6-1	198	L	Worcester, MA	25	Wilkes-Barre
MICHALEK, Zbynek	6-1	200	R	Jindrichuv Hradec, Czech.	25	Phoenix
MORRIS, Derek	6-0	220	R	Edmonton, Alta.	30	Phoenix
ROSS, Nick	6-1	188	L	Edmonton, Alta.	19	Regn-Kamlps-San Antonio
SAUER, Kurt	6-4	220	L	St. Cloud, MN	27	Colorado
STEPHENSON, Logan	6-3	197	L	Saskatoon, Sask.	22	San Antonio
YANDLE, Keith	6-2	195	L	Boston, MA	22	Phoenix-San Antonio

GOALTENDERS	HT	WT	C	Place of Birth	*Age	2007-08 Club
BRYZGALOV, Ilya	6-3	210	L	Togliatti, USSR	28	Anaheim-Phoenix
MONTOYA, Al	6-2	193	L	Chicago, IL	23	Hartford-San Antonio
TELLQVIST, Mikael	5-11	185	L	Sundbyberg, Sweden	29	Phoenix
TORDJMAN, Josh	6-1	155	L	Montreal, Que.	23	San Antonio

* – Age at start of 2008-09 season

2007-08 Scoring

* – rookie

Regular Season

Pos	#	Player	Team	GP	G	A	Pts	TOI	+/–	PIM	PP	SH	GW	S	%
R	19	Shane Doan	PHX	80	28	50	78	20:45	4	59	9	2	5	243	11.5
R	17	Radim Vrbata	PHX	76	27	29	56	18:12	6	14	7	3	5	246	11.0
C	88 *	Peter Mueller	PHX	81	22	32	54	17:15	–13	32	7	0	3	201	10.9
D	55	Ed Jovanovski	PHX	80	12	39	51	22:32	–13	73	8	0	2	240	5.0
C	28	Steve Reinprecht	PHX	81	16	30	46	15:42	–3	26	5	1	0	105	15.2
C	11 *	Martin Hanzal	PHX	72	8	27	35	16:44	–7	28	1	1	3	111	7.2
C	39	Niko Kapanen	PHX	79	10	18	28	13:48	–1	34	5	0	5	85	11.8
L	34 *	Daniel Winnik	PHX	79	11	15	26	14:06	–3	25	0	0	1	122	9.0
D	53	Derek Morris	PHX	82	8	17	25	21:42	8	83	2	0	0	135	5.9
L	13 *	Daniel Carcillo	PHX	57	13	11	24	12:43	1	324	3	0	1	106	12.3
D	2	Keith Ballard	PHX	82	6	15	21	21:15	7	85	2	1	1	105	5.7
C	26	Joel Perrault	PHX	49	7	10	17	14:26	–11	48	3	0	2	87	8.0
D	4	Zbynek Michalek	PHX	75	4	13	17	21:35	9	34	0	0	2	92	4.3
L	16	Mike York	PHX	63	6	8	14	11:59	–8	4	4	0	1	85	7.1
D	3 *	Keith Yandle	PHX	43	5	7	12	14:04	–12	14	4	0	0	72	6.9
D	44	Nick Boynton	PHX	79	3	9	12	17:00	–9	125	0	1	0	94	3.2
L	22	Mathias Tjarnqvist	PHX	78	4	7	11	13:38	–1	34	0	0	0	90	4.4
R	12	Craig Weller	PHX	59	3	8	11	10:22	–7	80	0	0	1	72	4.2
L	81	Marcel Hossa	NYR	36	1	7	8	14:35	8	24	0	0	0	54	1.9
			PHX	14	0	0	0	11:39	–6	4	0	0	0	12	0.0
			Total	50	1	7	8	13:46	2	28	0	0	0	66	1.5
R	18 *	Enver Lisin	PHX	13	4	1	5	14:27	–5	6	1	0	0	27	14.8
C	15	Mike Zigomanis	PHX	33	2	1	3	12:24	–7	6	0	0	0	35	5.7
D	5	Matt Jones	PHX	45	0	2	2	14:33	–13	10	0	0	0	25	0.0
L	18	Matt Murley	PHX	3	0	1	1	11:43	1	0	0	0	0	3	0.0
C	91 *	Kyle Turris	PHX	3	0	1	1	19:45	–5	2	0	0	0	11	0.0
L	24	Josh Gratton	PHX	1	0	0	0	09:40	1	5	0	0	0	0	0.0
L	75	Peter Vandermeer	PHX	2	0	0	0	07:33	0	0	0	0	0	0	0.0
D	29	Ryan Caldwell	PHX	2	0	0	0	06:07	0	2	0	0	0	1	0.0
D	6	Brendan Bell	PHX	2	0	0	0	14:49	–2	0	0	0	0	0	0.0
R	21	Bill Thomas	PHX	7	0	0	0	13:08	–2	0	0	0	0	9	0.0

Goaltending

No.	Goaltender	GPI	Mins	Avg	W	L	OT	EN	SO	GA	SA	S%	G	A	PIM
30	Ilja Bryzgalov	55	3167	2.43	26	22	5	4	3	128	1621	.921	0	0	2
32	Mikael Tellqvist	22	1224	2.75	9	8	2	2	2	56	607	.908	0	1	2
1	David Aebischer	1	60	3.00	0	1	0	0	0	3	33	.909	0	0	0
29	Alex Auld	9	509	3.54	3	6	0	2	1	30	249	.880	0	0	0
	Totals	**82**	**4995**	**2.70**	**38**	**37**	**7**	**8**	**6**	**225**	**2518**	**.911**			

Wayne Gretzky

Head Coach

Born: Brantford, Ont., January 26, 1961.

Phoenix Coyotes chairman and governor Steve Ellman announced on August 8, 2005 that Wayne Gretzky had agreed to a multiyear contract to serve as head coach of the Phoenix Coyotes. In addition to serving as the Coyotes' head coach, Gretzky also continues as managing partner and alternate governor for the Coyotes, a role that he had performed for the previous four seasons. Gretzky officially joined the franchise on February 15, 2001, when the Ellman and Moyes ownership group completed the purchase of the Coyotes.

Gretzky played 20 seasons in the National Hockey League with Edmonton, Los Angeles, St. Louis and the New York Rangers, dominating the game unlike any player in history. Gretzky helped win four Stanley Cup championships and three Canada Cup tournament titles during his illustrious playing career. He became the NHL's all-time leading goal, assist and point producer for a single season and career (both regular season and playoffs). Gretzky won the Art Ross Trophy as the NHL's leading scorer 10 times, the Hart Trophy as the League's MVP nine times (including eight consecutive seasons) and the Conn Smythe Trophy as playoff MVP twice. He earned the Lady Byng Trophy as the NHL's most gentlemanly player five times and made 18 consecutive All-Star Game appearances, securing three All-Star MVP Awards. Gretzky is an eight-time First All-Star Team member and seven-time Second All-Star Team member. He holds virtually every offensive record in the NHL and his tireless support of the game has contributed significantly to the popularity it enjoys today.

On November 22, 1999 – seven months after his retirement – Gretzky was inducted into the Hockey Hall of Fame in Toronto, becoming the tenth and final player in Hockey Hall of Fame history to have the mandatory three-year waiting period for enshrinement waived by the Hall's board of directors.

Gretzky's incredible success in hockey has continued past his playing career. In a managerial role with Team Canada, Gretzky served as executive director for Team Canada, responsible for assembling Canada's best hockey players at the 2002 Olympic Winter Games in Salt Lake City and again in 2004 at the World Cup of Hockey. Under Gretzky's leadership, Team Canada won the gold medal for the first time in 50 years at the 2002 Olympics. Two years later, Team Canada repeated the feat by winning the 2004 World Cup of Hockey championship. Gretzky also served as executive director again at the 2006 Olympics.

Coaching Record

			Regular Season				Playoffs			
Season	Team	League	GC	W	L	O/T	GC	W	L	T
2005-06	Phoenix	NHL	82	38	39	5	....	....	....	....
2006-07	Phoenix	NHL	82	31	46	5	....	....	....	....
2007-08	Phoenix	NHL	82	38	37	7	....	....	....	....
	NHL Totals		246	107	122	17	....	....	....	....

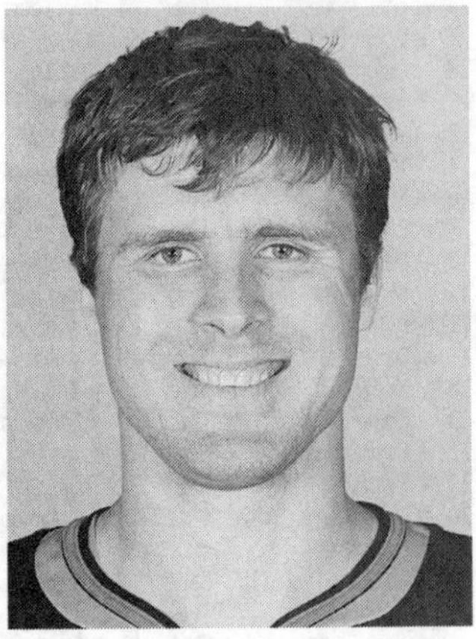

Acquired by the Coyotes early in the 2007-08 season, Ilja Bryzgalov earned a shutout in his Phoenix debut on November 17. Overall, his .920 save percentage ranked among the league leaders.

Coaching History

Tom McVie and Bill Sutherland, 1979-80; Tom McVie, Bill Sutherland and Mike Smith, 1980-81; Tom Watt, 1981-82, 1982-83; Tom Watt and Barry Long, 1983-84; Barry Long, 1984-85; Barry Long and John Ferguson, 1985-86; Dan Maloney, 1986-87, 1987-88; Dan Maloney and Rick Bowness, 1988-89; Bob Murdoch, 1989-90, 1990-91; John Paddock, 1991-92 to 1993-94; John Paddock and Terry Simpson, 1994-95; Terry Simpson, 1995-96; Don Hay, 1996-97; Jim Schoenfeld, 1997-98, 1998-99; Bob Francis, 1999-2000 to 2002-03; Bob Francis and Rick Bowness, 2003-04; Rick Bowness, 2004-05; Wayne Gretzky, 2005-06 to date.

Club Records

Team

(Figures in brackets for season records are games played; records for fewest points, wins, ties, losses, goals, goals against are for 70 or more games)

Most Points 96 1984-85 (80)
Most Wins 43 1984-85 (80)
Most Ties 18 2003-04 (82)
Most Losses 57 1980-81 (80)
Most Goals 358 1984-85 (80)
Most Goals Against 400 1980-81 (80)
Fewest Points 32 1980-81 (80)
Fewest Wins 9 1980-81 (80)
Fewest Ties 6 1995-96 (82)
Fewest Losses 27 1984-85 (80), 2000-01 (82), 2001-02 (82)
Fewest Goals 188 2003-04 (82)
Fewest Goals Against 197 1998-99 (82)

Longest Winning Streak
Overall .... 9 Mar. 8-27/85
Home .... 9 Dec. 27/92-Jan. 23/93
Away .... 8 Feb. 25-Apr. 6/85

Longest Undefeated Streak
Overall .... 14 Oct. 25-Nov. 28/98 (12 wins, 2 ties)
Home .... 11 Dec. 23/83-Feb. 5/84 (6 wins, 5 ties), Oct. 15-Dec. 20/98 (10 wins, 1 tie)
Away .... 9 Feb. 25-Apr. 7/85 (8 wins, 1 tie), Dec. 7/03-Jan. 9/04 (5 wins, 4 ties)

Longest Losing Streak
Overall .... 10 Nov. 30-Dec. 20/80, Feb. 6-25/94
Home .... 6 Oct. 6-Nov. 3/07
Away .... 13 Jan. 26-Apr. 14/94

Longest Winless Streak
Overall .... *30 Oct. 19-Dec. 20/80 (23 losses, 7 ties)
Home .... 14 Oct. 19-Dec. 14/80 (9 losses, 5 ties)
Away .... 18 Oct. 10-Dec. 20/80 (16 losses, 2 ties)

Most Shutouts, Season 9 1998-99 (82)
Most PIM, Season 2,278 1987-88 (80)
Most Goals, Game .... 12 Feb. 25/85 (Wpg. 12 at NYR 5)

Individual

Most Seasons .... 15 Teppo Numminen
Most Games .... 1,098 Teppo Numminen
Most Goals, Career .... 379 Dale Hawerchuk
Most Assists, Career .... 553 Thomas Steen
Most Points, Career .... 929 Dale Hawerchuk (379G, 550A)
Most PIM, Career .... 1,508 Keith Tkachuk
Most Shutouts, Career .... 21 Nikolai Khabibulin
Longest Consecutive Games Streak .... 475 Dale Hawerchuk (Dec. 19/82-Dec. 10/88)
Most Goals, Season .... 76 Teemu Selanne (1992-93)
Most Assists, Season .... 79 Phil Housley (1992-93)
Most Points, Season .... 132 Teemu Selanne (1992-93; 76G, 56A)
Most PIM, Season .... 347 Tie Domi (1993-94)
Most Points, Defenseman, Season .... 97 Phil Housley (1992-93; 18G, 79A)
Most Points, Center, Season .... 130 Dale Hawerchuk (1984-85; 53G, 77A)
Most Points, Right Wing, Season .... 132 Teemu Selanne (1992-93; 76G, 56A)
Most Points, Left Wing, Season .... 98 Keith Tkachuk (1995-96; 50G, 48A)
Most Points, Rookie, Season .... *132 Teemu Selanne (1992-93; 76G, 56A)
Most Shutouts, Season .... 8 Nikolai Khabibulin (1998-99)
Most Goals, Game .... 5 Willy Lindstrom (Mar. 2/82), Alexei Zhamnov (Apr. 1/95)
Most Assists, Game .... 5 Dale Hawerchuk (Mar. 6/84, Mar. 18/89, Mar. 4/90), Phil Housley (Jan. 18/93), Keith Tkachuk (Feb. 23/01)
Most Points, Game .... 6 Willy Lindstrom (Mar. 2/82; 5G, 1A), Dale Hawerchuk (Dec. 14/83; 3G, 3A, Mar. 5/88; 2G, 4A, Mar. 18/89; 1G, 5A), Thomas Steen (Oct. 24/84; 2G, 4A), Ed Olczyk (Dec. 21/91; 2G, 4A)

* NHL Record.
Records include Winnipeg Jets, 1979-80 through 1995-96.

Winnipeg Jets Retired Numbers

9	Bobby Hull	1972-1980
10	Dale Hawerchuk	1981-1990
25	Thomas Steen	1981-1995

Captains' History

Lars-Erik Sjoberg, 1979-80; Morris Lukowich, 1980-81; Dave Christian, 1981-82; Dave Christian and Lucien DeBlois, 1982-83; Lucien DeBlois, 1983-84; Dale Hawerchuk, 1984-85 to 1988-89; Randy Carlyle, Dale Hawerchuk and Thomas Steen (tri-captains), 1989-90; Randy Carlyle and Thomas Steen (co-captains), 1990-91; Troy Murray, 1991-92; Troy Murray and Dean Kennedy, 1992-93; Dean Kennedy and Keith Tkachuk, 1993-94; Keith Tkachuk, 1994-95; Kris King, 1995-96; Keith Tkachuk, 1996-97 to 2000-01; Teppo Numminen, 2001-02, 2002-03; Shane Doan, 2003-04 to date.

All-time Record vs. Other Clubs

Regular Season

	At Home								On Road								Total							
	GP	W	L	T	OL	GF	GA	PTS	GP	W	L	T	OL	GF	GA	PTS	GP	W	L	T	OL	GF	GA	PTS
Anaheim	38	16	16	2	4	101	109	38	39	12	21	3	3	96	120	30	77	28	37	5	7	197	229	68
Atlanta	6	5	0	1	0	21	9	11	5	4	1	0	0	17	10	8	11	9	1	1	0	38	19	19
Boston	31	13	15	3	0	102	105	29	31	5	22	4	0	94	137	14	62	18	37	7	0	196	242	43
Buffalo	30	14	14	2	0	93	94	30	32	7	20	5	0	82	128	19	62	21	34	7	0	175	222	49
Calgary	76	36	29	11	0	278	259	83	77	25	42	9	1	240	316	60	153	61	71	20	1	518	575	143
Carolina	32	15	14	2	1	118	116	33	31	11	13	6	1	91	103	29	63	26	27	8	2	209	219	62
Chicago	56	30	20	5	1	182	173	66	54	15	28	10	1	139	198	41	110	45	48	15	2	321	371	107
Colorado	46	17	21	7	1	159	166	42	47	18	22	5	2	158	168	43	93	35	43	12	3	317	334	85
Columbus	14	7	4	3	0	43	35	17	14	6	7	1	0	31	36	13	28	13	11	4	0	74	71	30
Dallas	66	26	33	4	3	203	223	59	67	25	32	9	1	197	230	60	133	51	65	13	4	400	453	119
Detroit	55	17	24	14	0	158	180	48	57	20	29	8	0	187	222	48	112	37	53	22	0	345	402	96
Edmonton	77	31	39	5	2	303	335	69	78	22	48	6	2	250	341	52	155	53	87	11	4	553	676	121
Florida	11	4	3	3	1	31	34	12	9	5	4	0	0	23	28	10	20	9	7	3	1	54	62	22
Los Angeles	88	48	27	11	2	349	281	109	86	37	33	14	2	317	327	90	174	85	60	25	4	666	608	199
Minnesota	14	7	6	1	0	37	33	15	14	5	7	2	0	27	34	12	28	12	13	3	0	64	67	27
Montreal	30	9	14	7	0	96	116	25	30	3	25	2	0	68	147	8	60	12	39	9	0	164	263	33
Nashville	18	11	5	0	2	55	56	24	18	6	7	2	3	45	53	17	36	17	12	2	5	100	109	41
New Jersey	32	22	7	3	0	117	82	47	30	12	12	6	0	91	96	30	62	34	19	9	0	208	178	77
NY Islanders	31	12	15	4	0	102	108	28	31	9	14	8	0	93	116	26	62	21	29	12	0	195	224	54
NY Rangers	32	13	14	4	1	110	108	31	30	10	17	2	1	107	129	23	62	23	31	6	2	217	237	54
Ottawa	11	4	6	1	0	36	42	9	12	6	5	1	0	36	36	13	23	10	11	2	0	72	78	22
Philadelphia	32	14	16	2	0	103	106	30	32	9	23	0	0	86	136	18	64	23	39	2	0	189	242	48
Pittsburgh	32	14	14	3	1	118	114	32	31	10	21	0	0	87	123	20	63	24	35	3	1	205	237	52
St. Louis	57	30	20	7	0	187	176	67	56	19	26	11	0	155	190	49	113	49	46	18	0	342	366	116
San Jose	47	23	18	3	3	143	135	52	44	19	21	4	0	129	151	42	91	42	39	7	3	272	286	94
Tampa Bay	12	6	6	0	0	29	29	12	11	5	6	0	0	36	38	10	23	11	12	0	0	65	67	22
Toronto	40	21	13	6	0	166	143	48	44	22	20	2	0	165	160	46	84	43	33	8	0	331	303	94
Vancouver	75	36	28	10	1	270	260	83	78	20	48	10	0	215	293	50	153	56	76	20	1	485	553	133
Washington	31	15	9	7	0	113	111	37	32	9	17	5	1	88	121	24	63	24	26	12	1	201	232	61
Totals	**1120**	**516**	**450**	**131**	**23**	**3823**	**3738**	**1186**	**1120**	**376**	**591**	**135**	**18**	**3350**	**4187**	**905**	**2240**	**892**	**1041**	**266**	**41**	**7173**	**7925**	**2091**

Playoffs

	Series	W	L	GP	W	L	T	GF	GA	Last Mtg.	Rnd.	Result
Anaheim	1	0	1	7	3	4	0	17	17	1997	CQF	L 3-4
Calgary	3	2	1	13	7	6	0	45	43	1987	DSF	W 4-2
Colorado	1	0	1	5	1	4	0	10	17	2000	CQF	L 1-4
Detroit	2	0	2	12	4	8	0	28	44	1998	CQF	L 2-4
Edmonton	6	0	6	26	4	22	0	75	120	1990	DSF	L 3-4
St. Louis	2	0	2	11	4	7	0	29	39	1999	CQF	L 3-4
San Jose	1	0	1	5	1	4	0	7	13	2002	CQF	L 1-4
Vancouver	2	0	2	13	5	8	0	34	50	1993	DSF	L 2-4
Totals	**18**	**2**	**16**	**92**	**29**	**63**	**0**	**245**	**343**			

Calgary totals include Atlanta Flames, 1979-80.
Colorado totals include Quebec, 1979-80 to 1994-95.
New Jersey totals include Colorado Rockies, 1979-80 to 1981-82.
Carolina totals include Hartford, 1979-80 to 1996-97.
Dallas totals include Minnesota North Stars, 1979-80 to 1992-93.

Playoff Results 2008-2003

(Last playoff appearance: 2002)

Abbreviations: Round: CQF – conference quarter-final; **DSF** – division semi-final.

2007-08 Results

Oct.	4	St. Louis	3-2
	6	Boston	1-3
	10	at Columbus	0-3
	11	at Nashville	6-3
	13	Minnesota	2-3
	18	Edmonton	2-4
	20	Detroit	2-5
	25	at Anaheim	1-0
	27	Dallas	3-5
	30	at St. Louis	2-1
Nov.	2	at Dallas	5-0
	3	Anaheim	2-5
	7	at Anaheim	6-5*
	8	Dallas	5-2
	10	at San Jose	1-4
	12	at San Jose	0-5
	15	San Jose	0-6
	17	at Los Angeles	1-0
	21	Los Angeles	4-1
	23	at Anaheim	4-3†
	24	Toronto	5-1
	28	at Minnesota	1-3
	30	at Chicago	1-6
Dec.	1	at Detroit	2-3
	3	at Pittsburgh	1-3
	5	Los Angeles	4-1
	7	San Jose	0-1
	8	at Los Angeles	4-2
	13	at NY Islanders	2-3
	15	at New Jersey	4-1
	16	at NY Rangers	5-1
	18	at Philadelphia	3-2
	20	at San Jose	3-2†
	22	Vancouver	1-2†
	27	Minnesota	2-3
	29	Detroit	2-4
	31	Colorado	4-3†
Jan.	2	at Colorado	5-2
	3	Chicago	4-2
	5	Anaheim	3-2†
	8	at Calgary	3-1
	10	at Edmonton	2-5
	11	at Vancouver	4-3
	13	at Minnesota	1-4
	15	San Jose	5-3
	17	Columbus	3-4
	19	Chicago	1-2†
	21	Buffalo	6-2
	24	Nashville	4-3*
	29	at Columbus	4-2
	30	at Detroit	2-3
Feb.	2	at Nashville	2-3*
	4	at Colorado	4-3*
	5	at Calgary	3-4†
	7	Columbus	1-2
	10	Nashville	3-6
	11	at Dallas	1-2
	14	Dallas	5-2
	16	Los Angeles	4-3
	18	at Los Angeles	4-0
	19	Calgary	1-4
	22	Colorado	2-3†
	24	St. Louis	2-0
	27	at Chicago	0-1
	28	at St. Louis	2-1
Mar.	1	Calgary	1-3
	5	at Dallas	2-1
	6	Montreal	2-4
	8	Ottawa	2-4
	11	Anaheim	3-2†
	13	Vancouver	2-0
	15	Edmonton	2-5
	17	at Vancouver	1-3
	18	at Edmonton	4-8
	20	Los Angeles	5-6†
	22	Anaheim	1-2
	25	San Jose	5-4*
	27	at Los Angeles	0-4
	30	at San Jose	1-3
Apr.	3	Dallas	2-4
	4	at Dallas	4-2
	6	at Anaheim	2-3†

* – Overtime † – Shootout

Entry Draft Selections 2008-1994

Name in bold denotes played in NHL.

2008

Pick	
8	Mikkel Boedker
28	Viktor Tikhonov
49	Jared Staal
69	Michael Stone
76	Mathieu Brodeur
99	Colin Long
159	Brett Hextall
189	Tim Billingsley

2007

Pick	
3	**Kyle Turris**
30	Nick Ross
32	Brett Maclean
36	Joel Gistedt
103	Vladimir Ruzicka
123	Maxim Goncharov
153	Scott Darling

2006

Pick	
8	**Peter Mueller**
29	Chris Summers
88	Jonas Ahnelov
130	Brett Bennett
131	Martin Latal
152	Jordan Bendfeld
188	Chris Frank
196	Benn Ferriero

2005

Pick	
17	**Martin Hanzal**
59	Pier-Olivier Pelletier
105	**Keith Yandle**
148	Anton Krysanov
212	Pat Brosnihan

2004

Pick	
5	Blake Wheeler
35	Logan Stephenson
50	**Enver Lisin**
103	Roman Tomanek
119	Kevin Porter
168	Kevin Cormier
199	Chad Kolarik
240	Aaron Gagnon
261	Will Engasser
265	**Daniel Winnik**

2003

Pick	
77	Tyler Redenbach
80	Dmitri Pestunov
115	Liam Lindstrom
178	Ryan Gibbons
208	Randall Gelech
242	Eduard Lewandowski
272	Sean Sullivan
290	Loic Burkhalter

2002

Pick	
19	Jakub Koreis
23	**Ben Eager**
46	**David LeNeveu**
70	Joe Callahan
80	**Matt Jones**
97	Lance Monych
132	**John Zeiler**
186	Jeff Pietrasiak
216	Ladislav Kouba
249	Marcus Smith
280	Russell Spence

2001

Pick	
11	**Fredrik Sjostrom**
31	**Matthew Spiller**
45	Martin Podlesak
78	Beat Forster
148	David Klema
180	Scott Polaski
210	Steve Belanger
243	Frantisek Lukes
273	Severin Blindenbacher

2000

Pick	
19	**Krys Kolanos**
53	Alexander Tatarinov
85	**Ramzi Abid**
160	Nate Kiser
186	Brent Gauvreau
217	Igor Samoilov
249	Sami Venalainen
281	Peter Fabus

1999

Pick	
15	Scott Kelman
19	**Kirill Safronov**
53	**Brad Ralph**
71	**Jason Jaspers**
116	Ryan Lauzon
123	Preston Mizzi
168	Erik Lewerstrom
234	**Goran Bezina**
262	Alexei Litvinenko

1998

Pick	
14	**Patrick DesRochers**
43	**Ossi Vaananen**
73	Pat O'Leary
100	Ryan Vanbuskirk
115	**Jay Leach**
116	Josh Blackburn
129	**Robert Schnabel**
160	**Rickard Wallin**
187	**Erik Westrum**
214	Justin Hansen

1997

Pick	
43	Juha Gustafsson
96	Scott McCallum
123	Curtis Suter
151	Robert Francz
207	Alexander Andreyev
233	**Wyatt Smith**

1996

Pick	
11	**Dan Focht**
24	**Daniel Briere**
62	Per-Anton Lundstrom
119	**Richard Lintner**
139	**Robert Esche**
174	**Trevor Letowski**
200	Nicholas Lent
226	Marc-Etienne Hubert

1995

Pick	
7	**Shane Doan**
32	**Marc Chouinard**
34	**Jason Doig**
67	**Brad Isbister**
84	**Justin Kurtz**
121	Brian Elder
136	Sylvain Daigle
162	Paul Traynor
188	**Jaroslav Obsut**
189	Fredrik Loven
214	Rob Deciantis

1994

Pick	
30	**Deron Quint**
56	Dorian Anneck
58	**Tavis Hansen**
82	Steve Cheredaryk
108	**Craig Mills**
143	Steve Vezina
146	Chris Kibermanis
186	Ramil Saifullin
212	Henrik Smangs
238	Mike Mader
264	Jason Issel

General Managers' History

John Ferguson, 1979-80 to 1987-88; John Ferguson and Mike Smith, 1988-89; Mike Smith, 1989-90 to 1992-93; Mike Smith and John Paddock, 1993-94; John Paddock, 1994-95, 1995-96; John Paddock and Bobby Smith, 1996-97; Bobby Smith, 1997-98 to 1999-2000; Bobby Smith and Cliff Fletcher, 2000-01; Cliff Fletcher and Michael Barnett, 2001-02; Michael Barnett, 2002-03 to 2006-07; Don Maloney, 2007-08 to date.

Don Maloney

General Manager

Born: Lindsay, Ont., September 5, 1958.

Don Maloney was signed as general manager of the Phoenix Coyotes on May 30, 2007, joining the team from the New York Rangers for whom he served as vice president of player personnel and assistant general manager. He assisted Rangers' president and g.m. Glen Sather in all player transactions and contract negotiations and was involved with the team's professional and amateur scouting operations. Maloney spent 10 seasons in the Rangers' front office. He played a key role in the Rangers' development of several prospects into productive NHL players, including Henrik Lundqvist and Peter Prucha. Maloney also served as assistant general manager for Team Canada squads that won gold medals at the 2003 and 2004 World Championships.

Maloney's first front office position in the NHL was as assistant general manager of the New York Islanders following his retirement as a player with the club on January 17, 1991. Maloney later served as Islanders' general manager from August 17, 1992 to December 2, 1995. Among the players drafted by the Islanders during Maloney's tenure with the club were Todd Bertuzzi, Bryan McCabe, Ziggy Palffy, Tommy Salo and Darius Kasparaitis. Maloney then served as Eastern professional scout for the San Jose Sharks during the 1996-97 season prior to joining the Rangers' front office.

As a player, Maloney registered 214 goals, 350 assists, and 564 points as well as 815 penalty minutes in 765 regular-season games over 13 NHL campaigns with the Rangers, Hartford Whalers and Islanders. He also collected 22 goals, 35 assists, and 57 points in 94 career playoff games. Maloney spent 11 seasons with the Rangers after being selected by the club in the second round (26th overall) of the 1978 NHL Entry Draft. He helped lead the Rangers to the 1980 Stanley Cup Final by posting 20 points (7 goals, 13 assists) that postseason, a playoff record for rookies at the time. Maloney played in the NHL All-Star Game in 1983 and 1984. He was named MVP of the 1984 game.

Club Directory

Jobing.com Arena

Phoenix Coyotes
6751 N. Sunset Blvd. #200
Glendale, AZ 85305
Phone **623/772-3200**
FAX 623/872-2000
Tickets 480/563-PUCK

Jobing.com Arena
9400 W. Maryland Avenue
Glendale, AZ 85305
Phone 623/772-3200
FAX 623/772-3201
Capacity: 17,125
www.PhoenixCoyotes.com

Club Officers and Executives

Majority Investor	Jerry Moyes
Chief Executive Officer & Governor	Jeff A. Shumway
Managing Partner, Alt. Gov. & Head Coach	Wayne Gretzky
President, Chief Operating Officer & Alt. Gov.	Douglas Moss
Executive V.P., G.M. & Alt. Gov.	Don Maloney
Assistant G.M./G.M. San Antonio	Brad Treliving
Executive V.P., Chief Marketing Officer	Michael Bucek
Executive V.P., Chief Financial Officer	Michael Nealy
Executive V.P., Chief Communications Officer	Jeff Holbrook
Executive Assistant to the President	Cheryl Taylor
Executive Assistant to Hockey Operations	Kimberly Trichel
Administrative Assistant to the CMO	Pamela Mann

Hockey Operations

Head Coach	Wayne Gretzky
Associate Coach	Ulf Samuelsson
Assistant Coach	Doug Sulliman
Goaltending Coach	Grant Fuhr
Video Coach	Steve Peters
Power Skating Coach	Mark Ciaccio
Director of Hockey Administration	Chris O'Hearn
Head Athletic Trainer	Jason Serbus
Assistant Athletic Trainer	John Bernal
Strength & Conditioning Coordinator	Mike Bahn
Massage Therapist	Jukka Nieminen
Head Equipment Manager	Stan Wilson
Equipment Manager	Tony Silva
Assistant Equipment Manager	Jason Rudee
Team Travel Coordinator	Rick Braunstein
Manager of Team Services	Lesa Guth
Professional Scouts	Frank Effinger, Thomas Steen, Eric Lacroix
Director of Amateur Scouting	Keith Gretzky
Assistant Director of Amateur Scouting	Steve Lyons
Head European Scout	Christian Ruuttu
European & Amateur Scouts	Rob Murphy, Robert Nordmark, Barclay Parneta, Gord Pell, Keith Sullivan
Director of Team Security	Jim O'Neal
Team Internist	Robert Luberto, D.O.
Team Orthopedic Surgeons	Dr. Lawrence Emmott, Dr. Doug Freedberg, Dr. Gary Waslewski
Team Dentists	Dr. Ron Foeldi
San Antonio (AHL) Head Coach	Greg Ireland
San Antonio (AHL) Assistant Coach	Ray Edwards
San Antonio (AHL) Athletic Trainer	Mike Ermantinger
San Antonio (AHL) Equipment Manager	John Krouse

Broadcasting

TV Play-by-Play / Analyst	Dave Strader / Darren Pang
TV/Radio Host	Todd Walsh
Radio Play-by-Play / Analyst	Bob Heethuis / Louie DeBrusk
Director of Broadcasting	Doug Cannon

Communications

Vice President of News Content	Dave Vest
Director of Media Relations	Sergey Kocharov
Director of Publicity	Ryan Narramore
Manager of Communications	Rob Crean

Community Relations

Director of Community Relations & Fan Development	Sarah Finecey
Manager of Hockey Development	Scott Storkan
Community Relations Manager	Don Schwartz

Marketing

Director of Promotions	Stacey Cohen
Director of Advertising & Media	Ted Santiago
Director of Event Presentation	Matt Coy

Corporate Sales & Service

Vice President of Client Services	Thea Crum
Senior Director of Corporate Partnerships	Judd Norris
Corporate Partnerships Director	Michael Whalen

Suite Sales

Director of Suite Sales	Mike Briody

Ticket Operations

Director of Ticket Operations	Douglas Vanderheyden

Ticket Sales & Services

Vice President of Ticket Sales	Flavil Hampsten
Sr. Director of Ticket Sales	David Burke

Finance & Accounting

Vice President of Finance and Controller	Joe Leibfried
Assistant Controller	Burlenti Shaban

Legal

Vice President, General Counsel	Steve Weinreich

Human Resources

Vice President of Human Resources	Julie Atherton

Technology

Senior Director of IT	Jay Gaskin

Team Information

Broadcast Television Station	KAZT-TV
Regional Sports Network	FSN Arizona
Radio Station	XTRA Sports 910
Team Photographer	Norm Hall

Pittsburgh Penguins

Key Off-Season Signings/Acquisitions

2008

July

- **1** • Re-signed RW **Pascal Dupuis** and D **Mark Eaton**.
- **1** • Signed RW **Eric Godard**.
- **2** • Re-signed C **Evgeni Malkin** and D **Brooks Orpik**.
- **3** • Signed RW **Miroslav Satan** and LW **Ruslan Fedotenko**.
- **3** • Re-signed G **Marc-Andre Fleury**.
- **5** • Signed LW **Matt Cooke**.
- **7** • Signed 2008 Finnish league scoring champion LW **Janne Pesonen**.

2007-08 Results: 47W-27L-4OTL-4SOL 102PTS.
First, Atlantic Division

Evgeni Malkin put the Penguins on his back in 2007-08 when Sidney Crosby missed 29 games due to injuries. Malkin finished the season second in the NHL with 106 points and fourth in goals with 47.

2008-09 Schedule

Oct.	Sat.	4	at Ottawa†		Thu.	8	at Nashville
	Sun.	5	Ottawa†		Sat.	10	at Colorado*
	Sat.	11	New Jersey		Tue.	13	at Philadelphia
	Tue.	14	Philadelphia		Wed.	14	Washington
	Thu.	16	Washington		Fri.	16	Anaheim
	Sat.	18	Toronto		Sun.	18	NY Rangers*
	Mon.	20	at Boston		Tue.	20	Carolina
	Thu.	23	Carolina		Wed.	28	NY Rangers
	Sat.	25	at NY Rangers		Fri.	30	at New Jersey
	Tue.	28	at San Jose		Sat.	31	at Toronto
	Thu.	30	at Phoenix	**Feb.**	Tue.	3	at Montreal
Nov.	Sat.	1	at St. Louis		Wed.	4	Tampa Bay
	Thu.	6	Edmonton		Fri.	6	Columbus
	Sat.	8	at NY Islanders		Sun.	8	Detroit*
	Tue.	11	at Detroit		Wed.	11	San Jose
	Thu.	13	Philadelphia		Sat.	14	at Toronto
	Sat.	15	Buffalo		Mon.	16	at NY Islanders*
	Tue.	18	Minnesota		Thu.	19	Montreal
	Thu.	20	at Atlanta		Sat.	21	at Philadelphia*
	Sat.	22	Vancouver*		Sun.	22	at Washington*
	Wed.	26	at NY Islanders		Wed.	25	NY Islanders
	Fri.	28	at Buffalo		Fri.	27	at Chicago
	Sat.	29	New Jersey	**Mar.**	Sun.	1	at Dallas*
Dec.	Wed.	3	at NY Rangers		Tue.	3	at Tampa Bay
	Thu.	4	at Carolina		Thu.	5	at Florida
	Sat.	6	at Ottawa*		Sun.	8	at Washington*
	Mon.	8	Buffalo		Tue.	10	Florida
	Wed.	10	at New Jersey		Thu.	12	at Columbus
	Thu.	11	NY Islanders		Sat.	14	Ottawa*
	Sat.	13	at Philadelphia*		Sun.	15	Boston*
	Thu.	18	at Atlanta		Tue.	17	Atlanta
	Sat.	20	Toronto		Fri.	20	Los Angeles
	Mon.	22	at Buffalo		Sun.	22	Philadelphia*
	Tue.	23	Tampa Bay		Wed.	25	Calgary
	Fri.	26	at New Jersey		Sat.	28	NY Rangers*
	Sat.	27	Montreal	**Apr.**	Wed.	1	New Jersey
	Tue.	30	Boston		Sat.	4	at Carolina
Jan.	Thu.	1	at Boston		Sun.	5	at Florida*
	Sat.	3	Florida*		Tue.	7	at Tampa Bay
	Mon.	5	at NY Rangers		Thu.	9	NY Islanders
	Tue.	6	Atlanta		Sat.	11	at Montreal

* Denotes afternoon game. † Games played in Stockholm, SE.

Year-by-Year Record

Season	GP	Home W	Home L	Home T	Home OL	Road W	Road L	Road T	Road OL	Overall W	Overall L	Overall T	Overall OL	GF	GA	Pts.	Finished	Playoff Result
2007-08	82	26	10	....	5	21	17	....	3	47	27	....	8	247	216	102	1st, Atlantic Div.	Lost Final
2006-07	82	26	10	....	5	21	14	....	6	47	24	....	11	277	246	105	2nd, Atlantic Div.	Lost Conf. Quarter-Final
2005-06	82	12	21	....	8	10	25	....	6	22	46	....	14	244	316	58	5th, Atlantic Div.	Out of Playoffs
2004-05	....	....	....	....	....	....	....	....	....	....	....	....	....	....	....	....		
2003-04	82	13	22	6	0	10	25	2	4	23	47	8	4	190	303	58	5th, Atlantic Div.	Out of Playoffs
2002-03	82	15	22	2	2	12	22	4	3	27	44	6	5	189	255	65	5th, Atlantic Div.	Out of Playoffs
2001-02	82	16	20	4	1	12	21	4	4	28	41	8	5	198	249	69	5th, Atlantic Div.	Out of Playoffs
2000-01	82	24	15	2	0	18	13	7	3	42	28	9	3	281	256	96	3rd, Atlantic Div.	Lost Conf. Championship
1999-2000	82	23	11	7	0	14	20	1	6	37	31	8	6	241	236	88	3rd, Atlantic Div.	Lost Conf. Semi-Final
1998-99	82	21	10	10	....	17	20	4	....	38	30	14	....	242	225	90	3rd, Atlantic Div.	Lost Conf. Semi-Final
1997-98	82	21	10	10	....	19	14	8	....	40	24	18	....	228	188	98	1st, Northeast Div.	Lost Conf. Quarter-Final
1996-97	82	25	11	5	....	13	25	3	....	38	36	8	....	285	280	84	2nd, Northeast Div.	Lost Conf. Quarter-Final
1995-96	82	32	9	0	....	17	20	4	....	49	29	4	....	362	284	102	1st, Northeast Div.	Lost Conf. Championship
1994-95	48	18	5	1	....	11	11	2	....	29	16	3	....	181	158	61	2nd, Northeast Div.	Lost Conf. Semi-Final
1993-94	84	25	9	8	....	19	18	5	....	44	27	13	....	299	285	101	1st, Northeast Div.	Lost Conf. Quarter-Final
1992-93	84	32	6	4	....	24	15	3	....	56	21	7	....	367	268	119	1st, Patrick Div.	Lost Div. Final
1991-92	**80**	**21**	**13**	**6**	....	**18**	**19**	**3**	....	**39**	**32**	**9**	....	**343**	**308**	**87**	**3rd, Patrick Div.**	**Won Stanley Cup**
1990-91	**80**	**25**	**12**	**3**	....	**16**	**21**	**3**	....	**41**	**33**	**6**	....	**342**	**305**	**88**	**1st, Patrick Div.**	**Won Stanley Cup**
1989-90	80	22	15	3	....	10	25	5	....	32	40	8	....	318	359	72	5th, Patrick Div.	Out of Playoffs
1988-89	80	24	13	3	....	16	20	4	....	40	33	7	....	347	349	87	2nd, Patrick Div.	Lost Div. Final
1987-88	80	22	12	6	....	14	23	3	....	36	35	9	....	319	316	81	6th, Patrick Div.	Out of Playoffs
1986-87	80	19	15	6	....	11	23	6	....	30	38	12	....	297	290	72	5th, Patrick Div.	Out of Playoffs
1985-86	80	20	15	5	....	14	23	3	....	34	38	8	....	313	305	76	5th, Patrick Div.	Out of Playoffs
1984-85	80	17	20	3	....	7	31	2	....	24	51	5	....	276	385	53	6th, Patrick Div.	Out of Playoffs
1983-84	80	7	29	4	....	9	29	2	....	16	58	6	....	254	390	38	6th, Patrick Div.	Out of Playoffs
1982-83	80	14	22	4	....	4	31	5	....	18	53	9	....	257	394	45	6th, Patrick Div.	Out of Playoffs
1981-82	80	21	11	8	....	10	25	5	....	31	36	13	....	310	337	75	4th, Patrick Div.	Lost Div. Semi-Final
1980-81	80	21	16	3	....	9	21	10	....	30	37	13	....	302	345	73	3rd, Norris Div.	Lost Prelim. Round
1979-80	80	20	13	7	....	10	24	6	....	30	37	13	....	251	303	73	3rd, Norris Div.	Lost Prelim. Round
1978-79	80	23	12	5	....	13	19	8	....	36	31	13	....	281	279	85	2nd, Norris Div.	Lost Quarter-Final
1977-78	80	16	15	9	....	9	22	9	....	25	37	18	....	254	321	68	4th, Norris Div.	Out of Playoffs
1976-77	80	22	12	6	....	12	21	7	....	34	33	13	....	240	252	81	3rd, Norris Div.	Lost Prelim. Round
1975-76	80	23	11	6	....	12	22	6	....	35	33	12	....	339	303	82	3rd, Norris Div.	Lost Prelim. Round
1974-75	80	25	5	10	....	12	23	5	....	37	28	15	....	326	289	89	3rd, Norris Div.	Lost Quarter-Final
1973-74	78	15	18	6	....	13	23	3	....	28	41	9	....	242	273	65	5th, West Div.	Out of Playoffs
1972-73	78	24	11	4	....	8	26	5	....	32	37	9	....	257	265	73	5th, West Div.	Out of Playoffs
1971-72	78	18	15	6	....	8	23	8	....	26	38	14	....	220	258	66	4th, West Div.	Lost Quarter-Final
1970-71	78	18	12	9	....	3	25	11	....	21	37	20	....	221	240	62	6th, West Div.	Out of Playoffs
1969-70	76	17	13	8	....	9	25	4	....	26	38	12	....	182	238	64	2nd, West Div.	Lost Semi-Final
1968-69	76	12	20	6	....	8	25	5	....	20	45	11	....	189	252	51	5th, West Div.	Out of Playoffs
1967-68	74	15	12	10	....	12	22	3	....	27	34	13	....	195	216	67	5th, West Div.	Out of Playoffs

ATLANTIC DIVISION

42nd NHL Season

Franchise date: June 5, 1967

2008-09 Player Personnel

FORWARDS	HT	WT	S	Place of Birth	*Age	2007-08 Club
BEECH, Kris	6-3	211	L	Salmon Arm, B.C.	27	CBJ-Syr-Van-Pit
BOOGAARD, Aaron	6-3	220	R	Newmarket, Ont.	22	Wilkes-Barre-Wheeling
CAPUTI, Luca	6-2	184	L	Toronto, Ont.	20	Niagara-Wilkes-Barre
COOKE, Matt	5-11	205	L	Belleville, Ont.	30	Vancouver-Washington
CROSBY, Sidney	5-11	200	L	Cole Harbour, N.S.	21	Pittsburgh
DUPUIS, Pascal	6-1	205	L	Laval, Que.	29	Atlanta-Pittsburgh
FEDOTENKO, Ruslan	6-2	195	L	Kiev, USSR	29	NY Islanders
FILEWICH, Jonathan	6-2	208	R	Kelowna, B.C.	24	Pittsburgh-Wilkes-Barre
GODARD, Eric	6-4	214	R	Vernon, B.C.	28	Calgary
GOVE, David	5-9	190	L	Centerville, MA	30	Albany-Wilkes-Barre
HENRICH, Adam	6-4	231	L	Thornhill, Ont.	24	Norfolk-Wheeling
JAMES, Connor	5-10	180	R	Calgary, Alta.	26	Pittsburgh-Wilkes-Barre
JEFFREY, Dustin	6-1	205	L	Sarnia, Ont.	20	Sault Ste. Marie-Wilkes-Barre
JOHNSON, Nick	6-1	183	R	Calgary, Alta.	22	Dartmouth-Wilkes-Barre
KENNEDY, Tyler	5-11	183	R	Sault Ste. Marie, Ont.	22	Pittsburgh-Wilkes-Barre
LETESTU, Mark	5-11	195	R	Elk Point, Alta.	23	Wilkes-Barre-Wheeling
MALKIN, Evgeni	6-3	195	L	Magnitogorsk, USSR	22	Pittsburgh
MINARD, Chris	6-1	190	L	Thompson, Man.	26	Pittsburgh-Wilkes-Barre
PESONEN, Janne	5-11	180	L	Suomussalmi, Finland	26	Karpat
SATAN, Miroslav	6-3	191	L	Topolcany, Czech.	33	NY Islanders
STAAL, Jordan	6-4	220	L	Thunder Bay, Ont.	20	Pittsburgh
STONE, Ryan	6-2	207	L	Calgary, Alta.	23	Pittsburgh-Wilkes-Barre
SYKORA, Petr	6-0	190	L	Plzen, Czech.	31	Pittsburgh
TAFFE, Jeff	6-3	207	L	Hastings, MN	27	Pittsburgh-Wilkes-Barre
TALBOT, Maxime	5-11	190	L	Lemoyne, Que.	24	Pittsburgh
THOMAS, Bill	6-1	191	R	Pittsburgh, PA	25	Phoenix-San Antonio
WALLACE, Tim	6-1	207	R	Anchorage, AK	24	Wilkes-Barre
DEFENSEMEN						
BISSONNETTE, Paul	6-2	211	L	Welland, Ont.	23	Wilkes-Barre-Wheeling
D'AVERSA, Jonathan	6-2	200	R	Richmond Hill, Ont.	22	Wilkes-Barre-Wheeling
EATON, Mark	6-2	204	L	Wilmington, DE	31	Pittsburgh
ENGELLAND, Deryk	6-2	202	R	Edmonton, Alta.	26	Wilkes-Barre
FERNHOLM, Daniel	6-4	218	L	Stockholm, Sweden	24	Linkoping
GILL, Hal	6-7	250	L	Concord, MA	33	Toronto-Pittsburgh
GOLIGOSKI, Alex	5-11	180	R	Grand Rapids, MN	23	Pittsburgh-Wilkes-Barre
GONCHAR, Sergei	6-2	211	L	Chelyabinsk, USSR	34	Pittsburgh
KEMP, T.J.	5-11	197	L	Pickering, Ont.	27	Springfield
LETANG, Kris	6-0	201	R	Montreal, Que.	21	Pittsburgh-Wilkes-Barre
LOVEJOY, Ben	6-2	214	R	Concord, NH	24	Wilkes-Barre
MORMINA, Joey	6-6	220	L	Montreal, Que.	26	Carolina-Albany
ORPIK, Brooks	6-2	219	L	San Francisco, CA	28	Pittsburgh
RICHMOND, Danny	6-0	192	L	Chicago, IL	24	Chicago-Rockford
SCUDERI, Rob	6-0	218	L	Syosset, NY	29	Pittsburgh
SYDOR, Darryl	6-1	211	L	Edmonton, Alta.	36	Pittsburgh
WHITNEY, Ryan	6-4	219	L	Boston, MA	25	Pittsburgh

GOALTENDERS	HT	WT	C	Place of Birth	*Age	2007-08 Club
BROWN, David	6-0	185	L	Stoney Creek, Ont.	23	Wilkes-Barre-Wheeling
CURRY, John	5-11	185	L	Shorewood, MN	24	Wilkes-Barre-Las Vegas-Whlng
FLEURY, Marc-Andre	6-2	180	L	Sorel, Que.	23	Pittsburgh-Wilkes-Barre
SABOURIN, Dany	6-4	200	L	Val-d'Or, Que.	28	Pittsburgh

* – Age at start of 2008-09 season

Coaching History

Red Sullivan, 1967-68, 1968-69; Red Kelly, 1969-70 to 1971-72; Red Kelly and Ken Schinkel, 1972-73; Ken Schinkel and Marc Boileau, 1973-74; Marc Boileau, 1974-75; Marc Boileau and Ken Schinkel, 1975-76; Ken Schinkel, 1976-77; Johnny Wilson, 1977-78 to 1979-80; Eddie Johnston, 1980-81 to 1982-83; Lou Angotti, 1983-84; Bob Berry, 1984-85 to 1986-87; Pierre Creamer, 1987-88; Gene Ubriaco, 1988-89; Gene Ubriaco and Craig Patrick, 1989-90; Bob Johnson, 1990-91, 1991-92; Scotty Bowman, 1991-92, 1992-93; Eddie Johnston, 1993-94 to 1995-96; Eddie Johnston and Craig Patrick, 1996-97; Kevin Constantine, 1997-98, 1998-99; Kevin Constantine and Herb Brooks, 1999-2000; Ivan Hlinka, 2000-01; Ivan Hlinka and Rick Kehoe, 2001-02; Rick Kehoe, 2002-03; Ed Olczyk, 2003-04, 2004-05; Ed Olczyk and Michel Therrien, 2005-06; Michel Therrien, 2006-07 to date.

Michel Therrien

Head Coach

Born: Montreal, Que., November 4, 1963.

Michel Therrien took over as head coach of the Pittsburgh Penguins on December 15, 2005. He was promoted from Pittsburgh's top minor-league affiliate in Wilkes-Barre/Scranton, where he guided the AHL Penguins for two and a half seasons. In the NHL in 2006-07, he guided Pittsburgh back into the playoffs for the first time since 2000-01 and was a finalist for coach of the year. In 2007-08, the Penguins advanced to the Stanley Cup Final.

Prior to joining Wilkes-Barre and Pittsburgh, Therrien spent six seasons in the Montreal Canadiens organization, including a stint as the team's head coach. In 2001-02, Therrien led the Canadiens to their first postseason appearance in four seasons. He spent four seasons as a head coach in the American Hockey League with the Canadiens' AHL affiliates, the Fredericton Canadiens and Quebec Citadelles, winning a division championship in 1999-00.

Prior to joining the Canadiens, Therrien coached Laval and Granby in the Quebec Major Junior Hockey League. He posted a .720 winning percentage in four seasons as a head coach in the QMJHL and was the head coach of a Memorial Cup-winning team in Granby in 1995-96. Beginning in 1993-94, Therrien's teams led the QMJHL in points for three straight seasons. He also played three seasons in the AHL (1983 to 1985 and 1986-87) for Nova Scotia, Sherbrooke and Baltimore, recording 89 points (16 goals, 73 assists).

2007-08 Scoring

* – rookie

Regular Season

Pos	#	Player	Team	GP	G	A	Pts	TOI	+/–	PIM	PP	SH	GW	S	%
C	71	Evgeni Malkin	PIT	82	47	59	106	21:19	16	78	17	0	5	272	17.3
C	87	Sidney Crosby	PIT	53	24	48	72	20:50	18	39	6	0	4	173	13.9
R	18	Marian Hossa	ATL	60	26	30	56	21:55	–14	30	8	2	4	229	11.4
			PIT	12	3	7	10	18:34	0	6	0	0	0	35	8.6
			Total	72	29	37	66	21:21	–14	36	8	2	4	264	11.0
D	55	Sergei Gonchar	PIT	78	12	53	65	25:54	13	66	8	0	2	173	6.9
R	17	Petr Sykora	PIT	81	28	35	63	16:50	1	41	15	0	4	201	13.9
L	12	Ryan Malone	PIT	77	27	24	51	19:04	14	103	11	2	6	159	17.0
D	19	Ryan Whitney	PIT	76	12	28	40	22:26	–2	45	7	1	1	119	10.1
C	11	Jordan Staal	PIT	82	12	16	28	18:16	–5	55	3	0	4	183	6.6
R	9	Pascal Dupuis	ATL	62	10	5	15	14:46	–4	24	0	3	1	111	9.0
			PIT	16	2	10	12	16:49	4	8	0	0	0	32	6.3
			Total	78	12	15	27	15:11	0	32	0	3	1	143	8.4
C	25	Maxime Talbot	PIT	63	12	14	26	15:27	8	53	0	2	1	80	15.0
D	2	Hal Gill	TOR	63	2	18	20	20:42	0	52	0	0	0	69	2.9
			PIT	18	1	3	4	17:31	6	16	0	0	0	17	5.9
			Total	81	3	21	24	19:59	6	68	0	0	0	86	3.5
C	48	* Tyler Kennedy	PIT	55	10	9	19	12:13	2	35	1	0	4	104	9.6
D	58	* Kris Letang	PIT	63	6	11	17	18:09	–1	23	1	0	3	68	8.8
L	37	Jarkko Ruutu	PIT	71	6	10	16	10:12	3	138	0	1	1	55	10.9
L	10	Gary Roberts	PIT	38	3	12	15	13:20	–3	40	1	0	0	41	7.3
R	27	Georges Laraque	PIT	71	4	9	13	07:42	0	141	0	0	2	29	13.8
D	5	Darryl Sydor	PIT	74	1	12	13	17:33	1	26	1	0	0	59	1.7
L	38	Jeff Taffe	PIT	45	5	7	12	09:35	2	8	1	0	1	56	8.9
C	24	Kris Beech	CBJ	16	5	4	9	12:59	3	2	2	0	0	24	20.8
			VAN	4	1	1	2	09:36	1	0	0	0	0	6	16.7
			PIT	5	0	0	0	08:14	–1	2	0	0	0	6	0.0
			Total	25	6	5	11	11:30	3	4	2	0	0	36	16.7
D	44	Brooks Orpik	PIT	78	1	10	11	16:57	11	57	0	0	0	50	2.0
R	28	Adam Hall	PIT	46	2	4	6	11:52	–2	24	0	0	0	39	5.1
D	4	Rob Scuderi	PIT	71	0	5	5	18:44	3	26	0	0	0	28	0.0
D	3	Mark Eaton	PIT	36	0	3	3	19:40	6	4	0	0	0	28	0.0
L	39	* Chris Minard	PIT	15	1	1	2	03:52	–1	10	0	0	0	9	11.1
D	67	* Alex Goligoski	PIT	3	0	2	2	13:56	2	2	0	0	0	2	0.0
L	36	* Connor James	PIT	13	1	0	1	07:25	–2	2	1	0	0	9	11.1
C	33	* Ryan Stone	PIT	6	0	1	1	06:25	–1	5	0	0	0	3	0.0
C	47	* Tim Brent	PIT	1	0	0	0	04:34	–1	0	0	0	0	0	0.0
R	34	* Jonathan Filewich	PIT	5	0	0	0	08:41	–2	0	0	0	0	3	0.0
D	32	Alain Nasreddine	PIT	6	0	0	0	12:53	–4	4	0	0	0	3	0.0
C	41	* Nathan Smith	PIT	13	0	0	0	07:40	0	2	0	0	0	3	0.0

Goaltending

No.	Goaltender	GPI	Mins	Avg	W	L	OT	EN	SO	GA	SA	S%	G	A	PIM
29	Marc-Andre Fleury	35	1857	2.33	19	10	2	2	4	72	909	.921	0	1	0
35	Ty Conklin	33	1866	2.51	18	8	5	1	2	78	1013	.923	0	1	4
30	Dany Sabourin	24	1242	2.75	10	9	1	2	2	57	596	.904	0	0	2
	Totals	**82**	**4986**	**2.55**	**47**	**27**	**8**	**5**	**8**	**212**	**2523**	**.916**			

Playoffs

Pos	#	Player	Team	GP	G	A	Pts	TOI	+/–	PIM	PP	SH	GW	OT	S	%
C	87	Sidney Crosby	PIT	20	6	21	27	20:41	7	12	2	0	1	0	59	10.2
R	18	Marian Hossa	PIT	20	12	14	26	20:59	8	12	5	0	2	1	76	15.8
C	71	Evgeni Malkin	PIT	20	10	12	22	20:47	3	24	5	1	3	0	75	13.3
L	12	Ryan Malone	PIT	20	6	10	16	18:42	4	25	3	0	2	0	43	14.0
D	55	Sergei Gonchar	PIT	20	1	13	14	25:12	0	8	1	0	0	0	40	2.5
R	17	Petr Sykora	PIT	20	6	3	9	14:56	2	16	2	0	1	1	42	14.3
C	25	Maxime Talbot	PIT	17	3	6	9	14:27	4	36	0	0	1	0	16	18.8
C	11	Jordan Staal	PIT	20	6	1	7	18:15	–4	14	1	0	1	0	34	17.6
R	9	Pascal Dupuis	PIT	20	2	5	7	16:13	5	18	0	0	0	0	38	5.3
D	19	Ryan Whitney	PIT	20	1	5	6	20:46	8	25	1	0	0	0	37	2.7
R	28	Adam Hall	PIT	17	3	1	4	10:58	–1	8	0	0	1	0	14	21.4
L	10	Gary Roberts	PIT	11	2	2	4	10:15	–4	32	1	0	1	0	9	22.2
C	48	* Tyler Kennedy	PIT	20	0	4	4	10:17	0	13	0	0	0	0	34	0.0
L	37	Jarkko Ruutu	PIT	20	2	1	3	10:37	–1	26	0	0	1	0	23	8.7
R	27	Georges Laraque	PIT	15	1	2	3	06:01	–1	4	0	0	0	0	4	25.0
D	4	Rob Scuderi	PIT	20	0	3	3	19:02	5	2	0	0	0	0	4	0.0
D	58	* Kris Letang	PIT	16	0	2	2	17:06	5	12	0	0	0	0	14	0.0
D	44	Brooks Orpik	PIT	20	0	2	2	20:47	–3	18	0	0	0	0	14	0.0
D	2	Hal Gill	PIT	20	0	1	1	19:17	2	12	0	0	0	0	16	0.0
D	5	Darryl Sydor	PIT	4	0	0	0	16:20	1	2	0	0	0	0	2	0.0

Goaltending

No.	Goaltender	GPI	Mins	Avg	W	L	EN	SO	GA	SA	S%	G	A	PIM
29	Marc-Andre Fleury	20	1251	1.97	14	6	2	3	41	610	.933	0	0	2
	Totals	**20**	**1257**	**2.05**	**14**	**6**	**2**	**3**	**43**	**612**	**.930**			

Coaching Record

			Regular Season				Playoffs			
Season	Team	League	GC	W	L	O/T	GC	W	L	T
1993-94	Laval	QMJHL	72	49	22	1	21	14	7	....
1994-95	Laval	QMJHL	72	48	22	2	20	14	6	....
1995-96	Granby	QMJHL	70	56	12	2	21	17	4	....
1996-97	Granby	QMJHL	70	44	20	6	5	1	4	....
1997-98	Fredericton	AHL	80	33	32	15	4	1	3	....
1998-99	Fredericton	AHL	80	33	36	11	15	9	6	....
99-2000	Quebec	AHL	80	37	34	9	3	0	3	....
2000-01	**Montreal**	**NHL**	**62**	**23**	**27**	**12**	....	....	....	....
2000-01	Quebec	AHL	19	12	6	1	....	....	....	....
2001-02	**Montreal**	**NHL**	**82**	**36**	**31**	**15**	**12**	**6**	**6**	....
2002-03	**Montreal**	**NHL**	**46**	**18**	**19**	**9**	....	....	....	....
2003-04	Wilkes-Barre	AHL	80	34	28	18	24	12	12	....
2004-05	Wilkes-Barre	AHL	80	39	27	14	11	5	6	....
2005-06	**Pittsburgh**	**NHL**	**51**	**14**	**29**	**8**	....	....	....	....
2005-06	Wilkes-Barre	AHL	25	21	1	3	....	....	....	....
2006-07	**Pittsburgh**	**NHL**	**82**	**47**	**24**	**11**	**5**	**1**	**4**	....
2007-08	**Pittsburgh**	**NHL**	**82**	**47**	**27**	**8**	**20**	**14**	**6**	....
	NHL Totals		**405**	**185**	**157**	**63**	**37**	**21**	**16**	....

Club Records

Team

(Figures in brackets for season records are games played; records for fewest points, wins, ties, losses, goals, goals against are for 70 or more games)

Most Points **119** 1992-93 (84)
Most Wins **56** 1992-93 (84)
Most Ties **20** 1970-71 (78)
Most Losses **58** 1983-84 (80)
Most Goals **367** 1992-93 (84)
Most Goals Against **394** 1982-83 (80)
Fewest Points **38** 1983-84 (80)
Fewest Wins **16** 1983-84 (80)
Fewest Ties **4** 1995-96 (82)
Fewest Losses **21** 1992-93 (84)
Fewest Goals **182** 1969-70 (76)
Fewest Goals Against **188** 1997-98 (82)
Longest Winning Streak
Overall .... ***17** Mar. 9-Apr. 10/93
Home .... **11** Jan. 5-Mar. 7/91
Away .... **7** Mar. 14-Apr. 9/93
Longest Undefeated Streak
Overall .... **18** Mar. 9-Apr. 14/93 (17 wins, 1 tie)
Home .... **20** Nov. 30/74-Feb. 22/75 (12 wins, 8 ties)
Away .... **8** Mar. 14-Apr. 14/93 (7 wins, 1 tie)
Longest Losing Streak
Overall .... **18** Jan. 13-Feb. 22/04
Home .... **14** Dec. 31/03-Feb. 22/04
Away .... **18** Dec. 23/82-Mar. 4/83
Longest Winless Streak
Overall .... **18** Jan. 2-Feb. 10/83 (17 losses, 1 tie), Jan. 13-Feb. 22/04 (18 losses)
Home .... **16** Dec. 31/03-Mar. 4/04 (15 losses, 1 tie)
Away .... **18** Oct. 25/70-Jan. 14/71 (11 losses, 7 ties), Dec. 23/82-Mar. 4/83 (18 losses)
Most Shutouts, Season **9** 1998-99 (82)
Most PIM, Season **2,670** 1988-89 (80)
Most Goals, Game .... **12** Mar. 15/75 (Wsh. 1 at Pit. 12), Dec. 26/91 (Tor. 1 at Pit. 12)

Individual

Most Seasons .... **17** Mario Lemieux
Most Games .... **915** Mario Lemieux
Most Goals, Career .... **690** Mario Lemieux
Most Assists, Career .... **1,033** Mario Lemieux
Most Points, Career .... **1,723** Mario Lemieux (690G, 1,033A)
Most PIM, Career .... **1,048** Kevin Stevens
Most Shutouts, Career .... **22** Tom Barrasso
Longest Consecutive Games Streak .... **320** Ron Schock (Oct. 24/73-Apr. 3/77)
Most Goals, Season .... **85** Mario Lemieux (1988-89)
Most Assists, Season .... **114** Mario Lemieux (1988-89)
Most Points, Season .... **199** Mario Lemieux (1988-89; 85G, 114A)
Most PIM, Season .... **409** Paul Baxter (1981-82)
Most Points, Defenseman, Season .... **113** Paul Coffey (1988-89; 30G, 83A)
Most Points, Center, Season .... **199** Mario Lemieux (1988-89; 85G, 114A)
Most Points, Right Wing, Season .... ***149** Jaromir Jagr (1995-96; 62G, 87A)
Most Points, Left Wing, Season .... **123** Kevin Stevens (1991-92; 54G, 69A)
Most Points, Rookie, Season .... **102** Sidney Crosby (2005-06; 39G, 63A)
Most Shutouts, Season .... **7** Tom Barrasso (1997-98)
Most Goals, Game .... **5** Mario Lemieux (Dec. 31/88, Apr. 9/93, Mar. 26/96)
Most Assists, Game .... **6** Ron Stackhouse (Mar. 8/75), Greg Malone (Nov. 28/79), Mario Lemieux (Oct. 15/88, Dec. 5/92, Nov. 1/95)
Most Points, Game .... **8** Mario Lemieux (Oct. 15/88; 2G, 6A, Dec. 31/88; 5G, 3A)

* NHL Record.

Captains' History

Ab McDonald, 1967-68; Earl Ingarfield, 1968-69; no captain, 1968-69 to 1972-73; Ron Schock, 1973-74 to 1976-77; Jean Pronovost, 1977-78; Orest Kindrachuk, 1978-79 to 1980-81; Randy Carlyle, 1981-82 to 1983-84; Mike Bullard, 1984-85, 1985-86; Mike Bullard and Terry Ruskowski, 1986-87; Dan Frawley and Mario Lemieux, 1987-88; Mario Lemieux, 1988-89 to 1993-94; Ron Francis, 1994-95; Mario Lemieux, 1995-96, 1996-97; Ron Francis, 1997-98; Jaromir Jagr, 1998-99 to 2000-01; Mario Lemieux, 2001-02 to 2003-04; Mario Lemieux and no captain, 2005-06; no captain, 2006-07; Sidney Crosby, 2007-08 to date.

Retired Numbers

21	Michel Brière	1969-1970
66	Mario Lemieux	1984-2006

All-time Record vs. Other Clubs

Regular Season

	At Home								On Road								Total							
	GP	W	L	T	OL	GF	GA	PTS	GP	W	L	T	OL	GF	GA	PTS	GP	W	L	T	OL	GF	GA	PTS
Anaheim	10	6	2	2	0	34	31	14	9	3	4	0	2	26	32	8	19	9	6	2	2	60	63	22
Atlanta	16	12	3	0	1	61	41	25	16	10	4	0	2	53	49	22	32	22	7	0	3	114	90	47
Boston	86	34	35	15	2	293	304	85	84	18	59	6	1	238	371	43	170	52	94	21	3	531	675	128
Buffalo	77	39	19	18	1	286	235	97	77	23	36	17	1	207	289	64	154	62	55	35	2	493	524	161
Calgary	45	24	11	10	0	169	136	58	47	12	27	8	0	143	206	32	92	36	38	18	0	312	342	90
Carolina	52	26	20	6	0	205	191	58	54	22	25	5	2	190	201	51	106	48	45	11	2	395	392	109
Chicago	60	30	23	7	0	215	194	67	61	11	40	10	0	158	240	32	121	41	63	17	0	373	434	99
Colorado	38	16	17	5	0	149	155	37	33	13	17	2	1	124	145	29	71	29	34	7	1	273	300	66
Columbus	4	3	1	0	0	17	12	6	4	2	2	0	0	10	16	4	8	5	3	0	0	27	28	10
Dallas	64	39	19	6	0	240	179	84	65	22	36	6	1	217	249	51	129	61	55	12	1	457	428	135
Detroit	66	44	18	4	0	281	197	92	66	13	40	12	1	179	256	39	132	57	58	16	1	460	453	131
Edmonton	31	15	13	3	0	118	130	33	31	8	22	1	0	102	150	17	62	23	35	4	0	220	280	50
Florida	29	15	10	3	1	89	82	34	28	11	14	1	2	67	83	25	57	26	24	4	3	156	165	59
Los Angeles	74	39	25	10	0	269	235	88	70	18	43	8	1	187	268	45	144	57	68	18	1	456	503	133
Minnesota	4	1	3	0	0	6	17	2	4	1	2	1	0	9	11	3	8	2	5	1	0	15	28	5
Montreal	88	31	42	13	2	262	312	77	88	14	61	10	3	227	405	41	176	45	103	23	5	489	717	118
Nashville	6	2	2	2	0	18	18	6	7	2	5	0	0	14	26	4	13	4	7	2	0	32	44	10
New Jersey	91	44	40	4	3	328	303	95	93	35	43	13	2	303	329	85	184	79	83	17	5	631	632	180
NY Islanders	100	48	36	14	2	375	345	112	98	37	51	8	2	322	384	84	198	85	87	22	4	697	729	196
NY Rangers	112	51	45	14	2	391	393	118	113	44	58	9	2	370	435	99	225	95	103	23	4	761	828	217
Ottawa	33	18	10	4	1	113	92	41	33	17	11	5	0	109	96	39	66	35	21	9	1	222	188	80
Philadelphia	118	54	42	22	0	418	377	130	118	22	84	8	4	300	493	56	236	76	126	30	4	718	870	186
Phoenix	31	21	10	0	0	123	87	42	32	15	14	3	0	114	118	33	63	36	24	3	0	237	205	75
St. Louis	65	32	21	12	0	239	194	76	65	15	42	6	2	171	250	38	130	47	63	18	2	410	444	114
San Jose	10	4	4	1	1	42	34	10	14	6	6	2	0	56	37	14	24	10	10	3	1	98	71	24
Tampa Bay	29	16	7	3	3	104	79	38	29	11	15	2	1	70	89	25	58	27	22	5	4	174	168	63
Toronto	75	39	29	6	1	300	242	85	73	26	33	11	3	236	290	66	148	65	62	17	4	536	532	151
Vancouver	51	33	11	7	0	229	175	73	51	24	22	4	1	189	181	53	102	57	33	11	1	418	356	126
Washington	89	52	29	7	1	349	277	112	92	37	45	9	1	336	377	84	181	89	74	16	2	685	654	196
Defunct Clubs	35	22	6	7	0	148	93	51	34	13	10	11	0	108	101	37	69	35	16	18	0	256	194	88
Totals	**1589**	**810**	**553**	**205**	**21**	**5871**	**5160**	**1846**	**1589**	**505**	**871**	**178**	**35**	**4835**	**6177**	**1223**	**3178**	**1315**	**1424**	**383**	**56**	**10706**	**11337**	**3069**

Playoffs

	Series	W	L	GP	W	L	T	GF	GA	Last Mtg.	Rnd.	Result
Boston	4	2	2	19	10	9	0	67	62	1992	CF	W 4-0
Buffalo	2	2	0	10	6	4	0	26	26	2001	CSF	W 4-3
Chicago	2	1	1	8	4	4	0	23	24	1992	F	W 4-0
Dallas	1	1	0	6	4	2	0	28	16	1991	F	W 4-2
Detroit	1	0	1	6	2	4	0	10	17	2008	F	L 2-4
Florida	1	0	1	7	3	4	0	15	20	1996	CF	L 3-4
Montreal	1	0	1	6	2	4	0	15	18	1998	CQF	L 2-4
New Jersey	5	3	2	29	14	15	0	80	86	2001	CF	L 1-4
NY Islanders	3	0	3	19	8	11	0	58	67	1993	DF	L 3-4
NY Rangers	4	4	0	20	16	4	0	79	56	2008	CSF	W 4-1
Ottawa	2	1	1	9	5	4	0	26	23	2008	CQF	W 4-0
Philadelphia	4	1	3	23	10	13	0	71	75	2008	CF	W 4-1
St. Louis	3	1	2	13	6	7	0	40	45	1981	PRE	L 2-3
Toronto	3	0	3	12	4	8	0	27	39	1999	CSF	L 2-4
Washington	7	6	1	42	26	16	0	137	121	2001	CQF	W 4-2
Defunct Clubs	1	1	0	4	4	0	0	13	6			
Totals	**44**	**23**	**21**	**233**	**124**	**109**	**0**	**715**	**701**			

Playoff Results 2008-2003

Year	Round	Opponent	Result	GF	GA
2008	F	Detroit	L 2-4	10	17
	CF	Philadelphia	W 4-1	20	9
	CSF	NY Rangers	W 4-1	15	11
	CQF	Ottawa	W 4-0	16	5
2007	CQF	Ottawa	L 1-4	10	18

Abbreviations: Round: F – Final; **CF** – conference final; **CSF** – conference semi-final; **CQF** – conference quarter-final; **DF** – division final; **PRE** – preliminary round.

Calgary totals include Atlanta Flames, 1972-73 to 1979-80. Carolina totals include Hartford, 1979-80 to 1996-97.
Colorado totals include Quebec, 1979-80 to 1994-95. Dallas totals include Minnesota North Stars, 1967-68 to 1992-93.
New Jersey totals include Kansas City, 1974-75, 1975-76, and Colorado Rockies, 1976-77 to 1981-82.
Phoenix totals include Winnipeg, 1979-80 to 1995-96.

2007-08 Results

Oct.	5	at Carolina	1-4		8	at Florida	3-1
	6	Anaheim	5-4		10	at Tampa Bay	4-1
	10	Montreal	2-3		12	at Atlanta	2-3†
	13	at Toronto	6-4		14	NY Rangers	4-1
	17	New Jersey	4-5		18	Tampa Bay	0-3
	19	Carolina	4-3†		19	at Montreal	2-0
	20	at Washington	2-1		21	Washington	5-6†
	23	NY Rangers	1-0		24	at Philadelphia	3-4
	25	Toronto	2-5		29	at New Jersey	4-2
	27	Montreal	3-4†		30	at Atlanta	1-4
	30	at Minnesota	4-2	**Feb.**	2	Carolina	4-1
Nov.	1	at Colorado	2-3		4	at New Jersey	3-4*
	3	at NY Islanders	2-3		7	NY Islanders	4-3
	5	at New Jersey	5-0		9	Los Angeles	4-2
	7	Philadelphia	1-3		10	Philadelphia	4-3
	8	at NY Rangers	2-4		13	Boston	1-2
	10	at Philadelphia	2-5		14	at Carolina	2-4
	12	New Jersey	2-3		17	at Buffalo	4-1
	15	NY Islanders	3-2		19	Florida	3-2
	17	NY Rangers	3-4*		21	at Montreal	5-4
	21	New Jersey	1-2		23	Ottawa	3-4*
	22	at Ottawa	6-5†		24	San Jose	1-2†
	24	Atlanta	5-0		26	at NY Islanders	4-2
	30	Dallas	4-1		28	at Boston	1-5
Dec.	1	at Toronto	2-4	**Mar.**	1	at Ottawa	4-5
	3	Phoenix	3-1		2	Atlanta	3-2†
	5	at Edmonton	4-2		4	at Tampa Bay	2-0
	6	at Calgary	3-2†		6	at Florida	2-5
	8	at Vancouver	2-1†		9	at Washington	4-2
	11	at Philadelphia	2-8		12	Buffalo	7-3
	13	Ottawa	1-4		16	Philadelphia	7-1
	15	at NY Islanders	3-2		18	at NY Rangers	2-5
	18	at NY Rangers	0-4		20	Tampa Bay	4-2
	20	at Boston	5-4†		22	New Jersey	7-1
	21	NY Islanders	2-4		24	at NY Islanders	1-4
	23	Boston	4-2		25	at New Jersey	2-0
	27	Washington	4-3*		27	NY Islanders	3-1
	29	Buffalo	2-0		30	NY Rangers	3-1
Jan.	1	at Buffalo	2-1†		31	at NY Rangers	1-2*
	3	Toronto	6-2	**Apr.**	2	Philadelphia	4-2
	5	Florida	3-0		6	at Philadelphia	0-2

* – Overtime † – Shootout

Entry Draft Selections 2008-1994

Name in bold denotes played in NHL.

2008

Pick	
120	Nathan Moon
150	Alexander Pechursky
180	Patrick Killeen
210	Nicholas D'Agostino

2007

Pick	
20	Angelo Esposito
51	Keven Veilleux
78	Robert Bortuzzo
80	Casey Pierro-Zabotel
111	Luca Caputi
118	Alex Grant
141	Jake Muzzin
171	Dustin Jeffrey

2006

Pick	
2	**Jordan Staal**
32	Carl Sneep
65	Brian Strait
125	Chad Johnson
185	Timo Seppanen

2005

Pick	
1	**Sidney Crosby**
61	Michael Gergen
62	**Kris Letang**
125	Tommi Leinonen
126	Tim Crowder
194	Jean-Philippe Paquet
195	Joe Vitale

2004

Pick	
2	**Evgeni Malkin**
31	Johannes Salmonsson
61	**Alex Goligoski**
67	Nick Johnson
85	Brian Gifford
99	**Tyler Kennedy**
130	Michal Sersen
164	Moises Gutierrez
194	Chris Peluso
222	Jordan Morrison
228	David Brown
259	Brian Ihnacak

2003

Pick	
1	**Marc-Andre Fleury**
32	**Ryan Stone**
70	**Jonathan Filewich**
73	**Daniel Carcillo**
121	Paul Bissonnette
161	Evgeni Isakov
169	Lukas Bolf
199	**Andy Chiodo**
229	Stephen Dixon
232	**Joe Jensen**
263	**Matt Moulson**

2002

Pick	
5	**Ryan Whitney**
35	Ondrej Nemec
69	**Erik Christensen**
101	Daniel Fernholm
136	Andrew Sertich
137	Cam Paddock
171	Robert Goepfert
202	Patrik Bartschi
234	**Maxime Talbot**
239	Ryan Lannon
265	Dwight Labrosse

2001

Pick	
21	**Colby Armstrong**
54	**Noah Welch**
86	**Drew Fata**
96	Alexandre Rouleau
120	**Tomas Surovy**
131	Ben Eaves
156	Andy Schneider
217	Tomas Duba
250	Brandon Crawford-West

2000

Pick	
18	**Brooks Orpik**
52	**Shane Endicott**
84	Peter Hamerlik
124	**Michel Ouellet**
146	**David Koci**
185	Patrick Foley
216	Jim Abbott
248	Steve Crampton
273	**Roman Simicek**
280	Nick Boucher

1999

Pick	
18	**Konstantin Koltsov**
51	**Matt Murley**
57	Jeremy Van Hoof
86	**Sebastien Caron**
115	**Ryan Malone**
144	Tomas Skvaridlo
157	Vladimir Malenkykh
176	Doug Meyer
204	**Tom Kostopoulos**
233	Darcy Robinson
261	Andrew McPherson

1998

Pick	
23	**Milan Kraft**
54	Alexander Zevakhin
80	David Cameron
110	Scott Myers
134	**Rob Scuderi**
169	Jan Fadrny
196	Joel Scherban
224	Mika Lehto
244	**Toby Petersen**
254	**Matt Hussey**

1997

Pick	
17	**Robert Dome**
44	Brian Gaffaney
71	**Josef Melichar**
97	Alexandre Mathieu
124	Harlan Pratt
152	Petr Havelka
179	Mark Moore
208	**Andrew Ference**
234	Eric Lind

1996

Pick	
23	Craig Hillier
28	**Pavel Skrbek**
72	**Boyd Kane**
77	Boris Protsenko
105	**Michal Rozsival**
150	Peter Bergman
186	**Eric Meloche**
238	Timo Seikkula

1995

Pick	
24	**Aleksey Morozov**
76	**Jean-Sebastien Aubin**
102	Oleg Belov
128	**Jan Hrdina**
154	Alexei Kolkunov
180	Derrick Pyke
206	Sergei Voronov
232	Frank Ivankovic

1994

Pick	
24	**Chris Wells**
50	**Richard Park**
57	**Sven Butenschon**
73	**Greg Crozier**
76	Alexei Krivchenkov
102	Tom O'Connor
128	Clint Johnson
154	Valentin Morozov
161	**Serge Aubin**
180	Drew Palmer
206	Boris Zelenko
232	Jason Godbout
258	Mikhail Kazakevich
284	Brian Leitza

General Managers' History

Jack Riley, 1967-68 to 1969-70; Red Kelly, 1970-71; Red Kelly and Jack Riley, 1971-72; Jack Riley, 1972-73; Jack Riley and Jack Button, 1973-74; Jack Button, 1974-75; Wren Blair, 1975-76; Wren Blair and Baz Bastien, 1976-77; Baz Bastien, 1977-78 to 1982-83; Eddie Johnston, 1983-84 to 1987-88; Tony Esposito, 1988-89; Tony Esposito and Craig Patrick, 1989-90; Craig Patrick, 1990-91 to 2005-06; Ray Shero, 2006-07 to date.

Ray Shero

General Manager

Born: Hartsdale, NY, July 28, 1962.

The Pittsburgh Penguins signed Ray Shero to a five-year contract as their new general manager on May 25, 2006. His fresh ideas and calm but firm management style helped transform the Penguins organization in his first year on the job as the team made the playoffs in 2006-07 for the first time since 2000-01. In 2007-08 the team posted the second-best record in the Eastern Conference and advanced to the Stanley Cup Final. Shero is the son of the late Fred Shero, who coached the Philadelphia Flyers for seven years and led them to back-to-back Stanley Cup championships in 1973-74 and 1974-75. Fred Shero also was g.m. and coach of the New York Rangers from 1978 to 1980. Ray Shero played college hockey at St. Lawrence University, serving twice as team captain, and was drafted by the Los Angeles Kings in 1982. He worked as a player agent for seven years before entering NHL management.

Before joining the Penguins, Shero had been assistant general manager of the Nashville Predators for eight seasons, working closely with Predators g.m. David Poile on all aspects of the club's hockey operations. His specific responsibilities included scouting at the amateur and professional levels, contract negotiations, and personnel matters such as arbitration, in addition to overseeing operations of the Predators top minor-league affiliate, the Milwaukee Admirals of the American Hockey League. Before joining the Predators organization, Shero spent six seasons as assistant general manager of the Ottawa Senators – joining the club in its second year of existence as an expansion team.

Both Ottawa and Nashville made significant improvement during Shero's tenure as assistant g.m., building with youth while adhering to a budget and business plan. The Predators went 49-25-8 and established a club record with 106 points in 2005-06, qualifying for the Stanley Cup playoffs for the second straight season. They had the third-best record in the Western Conference and fifth-best in the NHL.

Shero also played an important role in the success of the Milwaukee Admirals, Nashville's top affiliate in the American Hockey League. In 2003-04, the Admirals led the AHL in wins (43) and points (102) and won the Calder Cup by defeating the Wilkes-Barre/Scranton Penguins in the league final. Milwaukee reached the Calder Cup Final again in 2005-06.

Club Directory

Mellon Arena

Pittsburgh Penguins
Mellon Arena
66 Mario Lemieux Place
Pittsburgh, PA 15219
Phone **412/642-1300**
FAX 412/642-1859
Media Relations FAX 412/642-1322
www.pittsburghpenguins.com
Capacity: 16,940

Ownership	Lemieux Group LP
Executive Operations	
Co-owner/Chairman	Mario Lemieux
Co-owner	Ron Burkle
CEO	Ken Sawyer
President	David Morehouse
Executive VP/General Manager	Ray Shero
Vice President, Business & Legal Affairs	Travis Williams
Vice President & Controller	Kevin Hart
Sr. Vice President, Sales	David Soltesz
Vice President, Marketing	James Santilli
Vice President, Communications	Tom McMillan
Senior Consultant	Ron Porter
Executive Assistants	Fay McNamara, Kim Wood
Receptionist	Kelly Hart
Mailroom Supervisor	Brett Hart
Hockey Operations	
Assistant General Manager	Chuck Fletcher
Senior Advisor/Hockey Operations	Ed Johnston
Director of Player Development	Tom Fitzgerald
Director of Hockey Administration	Jason Botterill
Head Coach	Michel Therrien
Assistant Coaches	Andre Savard, Mike Yeo
Goaltending Coach	Gilles Meloche
Strength & Conditioning Coach	Mike Kadar
Senior Director of Team Services and Communications	Frank Buonomo
Executive Assistant	Kristen Yunn
Video Coordinator	Travis Ramsay
Scouts	
Director of Professional Scouting	Dan MacKinnon
Professional Scouts	Derek Clancey, Kevin Stevens
Director of Amateur Scouting	Jay Heinbuck
Amateur Scouts	Brian Fitzgerald, Chuck Grillo, Jim Madigan, David McNamara, Wayne Meier
European Scouts	Patrik Allvin, Robert Neuhauser
Training Staff	
Equipment Manager	Dana Heinze
Assistant Equipment Managers	Paul DeFazio, Danny Kroll
Team Physician	Dr. Charles Burke
Head Athletic Trainer	Chris Stewart
Assistant Athletic Trainer	Scott Adams
Physical Therapist	Mark Mortland
Wilkes-Barre/Scranton Coaching Staff	
Head Coach, Wilkes-Barre/Scranton (AHL)	Dan Bylsma
Assistant Coach, Wilkes-Barre/Scranton (AHL)	
Communications	
Director of Communications	Jennifer Bullano
Communications Coordinator	Erik Heasley
Director of Content/Publications	Joe Sager
Executive Producer, Penguins Radio Network	Ray Walker
Radio Broadcasters	Mike Lange, Phil Bourque
Marketing	
Director of Marketing	Ross Miller
Marketing Coordinator	Sarah Swartz
Director of Game Operations/Video Production	Chris DeVivo
Creative Director	Barb Pilarski
Graphic Designer	Erin Halley
Director of Amateur Hockey	Mark Shuttleworth
Director of Fan Development & Special Events	Jill Shipley
Director of Community/Alumni Relations	Cindy Himes
Director of New Media	Jeremy Zimmer
New Media Assistant	Jonathan Meck
Game Night Producer	Billy Wareham
Manager of Arts & Graphics	Dori Minnis
Editors	James Archer, Mike Davenport, Steve Finerty, Aaron Spiegel
Corporate Sales	
Senior Director of Corporate Sales	Kimberly Bogesdorfer
Managers of Corporate Sales	David Schleter, Danny Smith
Senior Account Service Manager	Lori Wineland
Account Service Manager	Jamie Greenwald
Account Service Coordinator	Ronald Hay
Corporate Sales Liason	Pierre Larouche
Finance	
Assistant Controller	Mark R. Kuczinski
Senior Accountant	Troy Ussack
Payroll Manager	Andrea Winschel
Accounts Payable	Tawni Love
Ticketing	
Senior Director of Ticketing	Chad Slencak
Director of Premium Seating/Group Sales	Mike Guiffre
Manager of Premium Sales	Brian Magness
Box Office Manager	Carol Coulson
Manager of Box Office Operations	Jason Onufer
Manager of Customer Service	Kathy Davis
Customer Service Representatives	Cori Shrader, Amanda Rameas, Kathleen Unger, Dana Cammer
Director of Database Marketing	Erin Exley
General Information	
TV Station	FSN Pittsburgh
TV Announcers	Paul Steigerwald, Bob Errey
Radio Announcers	Mike Lange, Phil Bourque
Flagship Radio Station	The X (105.9 FM)

St. Louis Blues

2007-08 Results: 33W-36L-8OTL-5SOL 79PTS.
Fifth, Central Division

Key Off-Season Signings/Acquisitions

2008

May 13 • Signed 2005 1st-round pick (24th overall), C **T.J. Oshie** and 2007 1st-round pick (13th overall), C **Lars Eller**.

28 • Named **Doug Armstrong** vice president of player personnel.

June 20 • Acquired G **Chris Mason** from Nashville for a 4th-round pick in 2008.

20 • Selected D **Alex Pietrangelo** (Niagara, OHL) fourth overall in the 2008 Entry Draft.

July 1 • Matched the Vancouver Canucks offer sheet to C **David Backes**.

3 • Re-signed C **Yan Stastny**.

10 • Signed D **Mike Weaver**.

14 • Signed RW **Matt Foy**.

14 • Re-signed C **Jay McClement**.

16 • Signed LW **Brad Winchester**.

Brad Boyes and Paul Kariya celebrate a goal. Boyes had a breakout season with the Blues in 2007-08, finishing among the league leaders with 43 goals. He and Kariya tied for the team lead with 65 points.

2008-09 Schedule

Oct.	Fri.	10	Nashville		Tue.	13	at Calgary
	Sat.	11	at NY Islanders		Thu.	15	Colorado
	Mon.	13	at Toronto*		Sat.	17	Chicago
	Thu.	16	Dallas		Mon.	19	at Boston*
	Sat.	18	Chicago		Wed.	21	at Chicago
	Wed.	22	Detroit		Thu.	29	Ottawa
	Fri.	24	Los Angeles		Sat.	31	Philadelphia
	Sat.	25	Florida	**Feb.**	Mon.	2	at Detroit
	Thu.	30	Carolina		Tue.	3	at Columbus
Nov.	Sat.	1	Pittsburgh		Thu.	5	Edmonton
	Wed.	5	at Anaheim		Sat.	7	Colorado
	Thu.	6	at San Jose		Tue.	10	Vancouver
	Sat.	8	at Los Angeles		Thu.	12	at Nashville
	Wed.	12	at Buffalo		Fri.	13	Chicago
	Fri.	14	at Chicago		Mon.	16	NY Rangers
	Sun.	16	Montreal*		Wed.	18	at Columbus
	Fri.	21	Anaheim		Thu.	19	at Nashville
	Sat.	22	at Minnesota		Sat.	21	Nashville
	Tue.	25	at Nashville		Tue.	24	Phoenix
	Wed.	26	at Colorado		Thu.	26	at Dallas
	Sat.	29	Edmonton*		Sat.	28	at Phoenix
	Sun.	30	at Atlanta*	**Mar.**	Tue.	3	Detroit
Dec.	Wed.	3	at Minnesota		Fri.	6	at Tampa Bay
	Fri.	5	Calgary		Sat.	7	at Florida
	Sat.	6	Phoenix		Tue.	10	Dallas
	Mon.	8	Nashville		Thu.	12	San Jose
	Wed.	10	at Anaheim		Sat.	14	Detroit*
	Thu.	11	at Los Angeles		Sun.	15	Minnesota*
	Sat.	13	at San Jose		Tue.	17	at Edmonton
	Tue.	16	Calgary		Thu.	19	at Vancouver
	Thu.	18	at Washington		Fri.	20	at Calgary
	Sat.	20	Minnesota		Tue.	24	Los Angeles
	Sun.	21	Boston*		Thu.	26	Vancouver
	Tue.	23	at Detroit		Sat.	28	Columbus
	Sat.	27	San Jose		Sun.	29	at Columbus*
	Sun.	28	Anaheim*	**Apr.**	Wed.	1	at Chicago
	Tue.	30	New Jersey		Thu.	2	at Detroit
Jan.	Fri.	2	at Carolina		Sat.	4	at Dallas
	Sat.	3	Columbus		Tue.	7	at Phoenix
	Fri.	9	at Vancouver		Fri.	10	Columbus
	Sun.	11	at Edmonton		Sun.	12	at Colorado*

* Denotes afternoon game.

CENTRAL DIVISION
42nd NHL Season

Franchise date: June 5, 1967

Year-by-Year Record

Season	GP	Home W	L	T	OL	Road W	L	T	OL	Overall W	L	T	OL	GF	GA	Pts.	Finished	Playoff Result
2007-08	82	20	15	....	6	13	21	....	7	33	36	....	13	205	237	79	5th, Central Div.	Out of Playoffs
2006-07	82	18	19	....	4	16	16	....	9	34	35	....	13	214	254	81	3rd, Central Div.	Out of Playoffs
2005-06	82	12	23	....	6	9	23	....	9	21	46	....	15	197	292	57	5th, Central Div.	Out of Playoffs
2004-05	....	....	....	....	....	....	....	....	....	....	....	....	....	....	....	....		
2003-04	82	23	11	7	0	16	19	4	2	39	30	11	2	191	198	91	2nd, Central Div.	Lost Conf. Quarter-Final
2002-03	82	23	11	4	3	18	13	7	3	41	24	11	6	253	222	99	2nd, Central Div.	Lost Conf. Quarter-Final
2001-02	82	27	12	1	1	16	15	7	3	43	27	8	4	227	188	98	2nd, Central Div.	Lost Conf. Semi-Final
2000-01	82	28	5	5	3	15	17	7	2	43	22	12	5	249	195	103	2nd, Central Div.	Lost Conf. Championship
1999-2000	82	24	9	7	1	27	10	4	0	51	19	11	1	248	165	114	1st, Central Div.	Lost Conf. Quarter-Final
1998-99	82	18	17	6	....	19	15	7	....	37	32	13	....	237	209	87	2nd, Central Div.	Lost Conf. Semi-Final
1997-98	82	26	10	5	....	19	19	3	....	45	29	8	....	256	204	98	3rd, Central Div.	Lost Conf. Semi-Final
1996-97	82	17	20	4	....	19	15	7	....	36	35	11	....	236	239	83	4th, Central Div.	Lost Conf. Quarter-Final
1995-96	82	15	17	9	....	17	17	7	....	32	34	16	....	219	248	80	4th, Central Div.	Lost Conf. Semi-Final
1994-95	48	16	6	2	....	12	9	3	....	28	15	5	....	178	135	61	2nd, Central Div.	Lost Conf. Quarter-Final
1993-94	84	23	11	8	....	17	22	3	....	40	33	11	....	270	283	91	4th, Central Div.	Lost Conf. Quarter-Final
1992-93	84	22	13	7	....	15	23	4	....	37	36	11	....	282	278	85	4th, Norris Div.	Lost Div. Final
1991-92	80	25	12	3	....	11	21	8	....	36	33	11	....	279	266	83	3rd, Norris Div.	Lost Div. Semi-Final
1990-91	80	24	9	7	....	23	13	4	....	47	22	11	....	310	250	105	2nd, Norris Div.	Lost Div. Final
1989-90	80	20	15	5	....	17	19	4	....	37	34	9	....	295	279	83	2nd, Norris Div.	Lost Div. Final
1988-89	80	22	11	7	....	11	24	5	....	33	35	12	....	275	285	78	2nd, Norris Div.	Lost Div. Final
1987-88	80	18	17	5	....	16	21	3	....	34	38	8	....	278	294	76	2nd, Norris Div.	Lost Div. Final
1986-87	80	21	12	7	....	11	21	8	....	32	33	15	....	281	293	79	1st, Norris Div.	Lost Div. Semi-Final
1985-86	80	23	11	6	....	14	23	3	....	37	34	9	....	302	291	83	3rd, Norris Div.	Lost Conf. Championship
1984-85	80	21	12	7	....	16	19	5	....	37	31	12	....	299	288	86	1st, Norris Div.	Lost Div. Semi-Final
1983-84	80	23	14	3	....	9	27	4	....	32	41	7	....	293	316	71	2nd, Norris Div.	Lost Div. Final
1982-83	80	16	16	8	....	9	24	7	....	25	40	15	....	285	316	65	4th, Norris Div.	Lost Div. Semi-Final
1981-82	80	22	14	4	....	10	26	4	....	32	40	8	....	315	349	72	3rd Norris Div.	Lost Div. Final
1980-81	80	29	7	4	....	16	11	13	....	45	18	17	....	352	281	107	1st, Smythe Div.	Lost Quarter-Final
1979-80	80	20	13	7	....	14	21	5	....	34	34	12	....	266	278	80	2nd, Smythe Div.	Lost Prelim. Round
1978-79	80	14	20	6	....	4	30	6	....	18	50	12	....	249	348	48	3rd, Smythe Div.	Out of Playoffs
1977-78	80	12	20	8	....	8	27	5	....	20	47	13	....	195	304	53	4th, Smythe Div.	Out of Playoffs
1976-77	80	22	13	5	....	10	26	4	....	32	39	9	....	239	276	73	1st, Smythe Div.	Lost Quarter-Final
1975-76	80	20	12	8	....	9	25	6	....	29	37	14	....	249	290	72	3rd, Smythe Div.	Lost Prelim. Round
1974-75	80	23	13	4	....	12	18	10	....	35	31	14	....	269	267	84	2nd, Smythe Div.	Lost Prelim. Round
1973-74	78	16	16	7	....	10	24	5	....	26	40	12	....	206	248	64	6th, West Div.	Out of Playoffs
1972-73	78	21	11	7	....	11	23	5	....	32	34	12	....	233	251	76	4th, West Div.	Lost Quarter-Final
1971-72	78	17	17	5	....	11	22	6	....	28	39	11	....	208	247	67	3rd, West Div.	Lost Semi-Final
1970-71	78	23	7	9	....	11	18	10	....	34	25	19	....	223	208	87	2nd, West Div.	Lost Quarter-Final
1969-70	76	24	9	5	....	13	18	7	....	37	27	12	....	224	179	86	1st, West Div.	Lost Final
1968-69	76	21	8	9	....	16	17	5	....	37	25	14	....	204	157	88	1st, West Div.	Lost Final
1967-68	74	18	12	7	....	9	19	9	....	27	31	16	....	177	191	70	3rd, West Div.	Lost Final

2008-09 Player Personnel

FORWARDS	HT	WT	S	Place of Birth	*Age	2007-08 Club
BACKES, David	6-3	216	R	Blaine, MN	24	St. Louis
BERGLUND, Patrik	6-4	187	L	Vasteras, Sweden	20	Vasteras
BOYES, Brad	6-0	195	R	Mississauga, Ont.	26	St. Louis
DRAZENOVIC, Nicholas	6-0	172	L	Prince George, B.C.	21	Peoria
ELLER, Lars	6-0	198	L	Herlev, Denmark	19	Boras-Frolunda Jr.-Frolunda
FOY, Matt	6-2	228	R	Oakville, Ont.	25	Minnesota
HINOTE, Dan	6-0	187	R	Leesburg, FL	31	St. Louis
JANSSEN, Cam	6-0	210	R	St. Louis, MO	24	St. Louis-Lowell
KANA, Tomas	6-0	202	R	Opava, Czech.	20	Alaska-Ostrava-Vitkovice-Usti n. L.
KARIYA, Paul	5-10	180	L	Vancouver, B.C.	33	St. Louis
KING, D.J.	6-3	228	L	Meadow Lake, Sask.	24	St. Louis
LEMTYUGOV, Nikolai	6-0	183	L	Miass, USSR	22	Peoria
LINGLET, Charles	6-2	205	L	Montreal, Que.	26	Peoria
McCLEMENT, Jay	6-1	201	L	Kingston, Ont.	25	St. Louis
McDONALD, Andy	5-11	183	L	Strathroy, Ont.	31	Anaheim-St. Louis
OSHIE, T.J.	5-10	170	R	Mt. Vernon, WA	21	North Dakota
PADDOCK, Cam	6-1	191	R	Vancouver, B.C.	25	San Antonio
PERRON, David	6-0	180	R	Sherbrooke, Que.	20	St. Louis
PORTER, Chris	6-1	203	L	Toronto, Ont.	24	Peoria
REAVES, Ryan	6-1	193	R	Winnipeg, Man.	21	Peoria-Alaska
REGIER, Steve	6-4	194	L	Edmonton, Alta.	24	NY Islanders-Bridgeport
STASTNY, Yan	5-10	191	L	Quebec City, Que.	26	St. Louis-Peoria
STEMPNIAK, Lee	6-0	195	R	Buffalo, NY	25	St. Louis
TALBOT, Julian	5-11	181	L	Wahnapitae, Ont.	23	Peoria
TKACHUK, Keith	6-2	232	L	Melrose, MA	36	St. Louis
WHITFIELD, Trent	5-11	209	L	Estevan, Sask.	31	Peoria
WINCHESTER, Brad	6-5	228	L	Madison, WI	27	Dallas-Iowa
DEFENSEMEN						
BREWER, Eric	6-3	222	L	Vernon, B.C.	29	St. Louis
FAST, T.J.	6-1	190	L	Calgary, Alta.	21	Tri-City
HELLSTROM, Alexander	6-2	207	L	Falun, Sweden	21	Peoria
JACKMAN, Barret	6-0	203	L	Trail, B.C.	27	St. Louis
JOHNSON, Erik	6-4	219	R	Bloomington, MN	20	St. Louis-Peoria
JUNLAND, Jonas	6-2	198	L	Linkoping, Sweden	20	Linkoping
McKEE, Jay	6-4	203	L	Kingston, Ont.	31	St. Louis
POLAK, Roman	6-1	198	R	Ostrava, Czech.	22	St. Louis-Peoria
WAGNER, Steve	6-2	190	L	Grand Rapids, MN	24	St. Louis-Peoria
WEAVER, Mike	5-9	182	R	Bramalea, Ont.	30	Vancouver
WOYWITKA, Jeff	6-2	217	L	Vermilion, Alta.	25	St. Louis-Peoria
WOZNIEWSKI, Andy	6-5	225	L	Buffalo Grove, IL	28	Toronto-Toronto (AHL)

GOALTENDERS	HT	WT	C	Place of Birth	*Age	2007-08 Club
BISHOP, Ben	6-5	205	L	Denver, CO	21	U. of Maine-Peoria
LEGACE, Manny	5-10	200	L	Toronto, Ont.	35	St. Louis
MASON, Chris	6-0	195	L	Red Deer, Alta.	32	Nashville
SCHWARZ, Marek	6-0	180	R	Mlada Boleslav, Czech.	22	St. Louis-Peoria-Alaska

* – Age at start of 2008-09 season

2007-08 Scoring

* – rookie

Regular Season

Pos	#	Player	Team	GP	G	A	Pts	TOI	+/–	PIM	PP	SH	GW	S	%
R	22	Brad Boyes	STL	82	43	22	65	17:56	1	20	11	0	9	207	20.8
L	9	Paul Kariya	STL	82	16	49	65	18:43	–10	50	5	0	1	223	7.2
C	7	Keith Tkachuk	STL	79	27	31	58	16:51	–2	69	12	1	1	177	15.3
C	10	Andy McDonald	ANA	33	4	12	16	16:41	–4	30	0	0	0	79	5.1
			STL	49	14	22	36	18:40	–17	32	3	0	1	103	13.6
			Total	82	18	34	52	17:52	–21	62	3	0	1	182	9.9
R	12	Lee Stempniak	STL	80	13	25	38	15:53	0	40	3	0	2	162	8.0
D	6	* Erik Johnson	STL	69	5	28	33	18:11	–9	28	4	0	3	105	4.8
C	42	David Backes	STL	72	13	18	31	14:40	–11	99	3	0	2	129	10.1
L	57	* David Perron	STL	62	13	14	27	12:33	16	38	3	0	1	68	19.1
R	21	Jamal Mayers	STL	80	12	15	27	15:55	–19	91	0	1	3	153	7.8
C	18	Jay McClement	STL	81	9	13	22	13:55	–17	26	0	0	2	110	8.2
D	4	Eric Brewer	STL	77	1	21	22	24:37	–18	91	0	0	0	101	1.0
C	17	Ryan Johnson	STL	79	5	13	18	14:21	–2	22	0	1	1	85	5.9
L	26	Martin Rucinsky	STL	40	5	11	16	15:00	–9	40	1	0	0	67	7.5
D	5	Barret Jackman	STL	78	2	14	16	22:24	–12	93	1	0	0	80	2.5
R	13	Dan Hinote	STL	58	5	5	10	10:30	–3	42	0	0	0	42	11.9
D	77	Jay McKee	STL	66	2	7	9	17:53	2	42	0	0	2	42	4.8
D	49	* Steve Wagner	STL	24	2	6	8	18:28	–4	8	1	0	0	25	8.0
D	29	Jeff Woywitka	STL	27	2	6	8	16:04	2	12	0	0	0	25	8.0
L	19	Dwayne King	STL	61	3	3	6	05:36	–4	100	0	0	1	36	8.3
R	20	Mike Johnson	STL	21	2	3	5	13:01	–4	8	0	0	0	21	9.5
C	25	Yan Stastny	STL	12	1	1	2	10:59	0	9	0	0	0	10	10.0
D	28	Matt Walker	STL	43	1	1	2	15:53	–3	61	0	0	0	47	2.1
D	46	* Roman Polak	STL	6	0	1	1	11:32	1	0	0	0	0	2	0.0
R	55	Cam Janssen	STL	12	0	1	1	07:07	–1	18	0	0	0	9	0.0
D	36	Micki Dupont	STL	2	0	0	0	12:34	1	2	0	0	0	3	0.0
R	15	Mike Glumac	STL	4	0	0	0	10:08	–1	5	0	0	0	3	0.0

Goaltending

No.	Goaltender	GPI	Mins	Avg	W	L	OT	EN	SO	GA	SA	S%	G	A	PIM
45	* Chris Beckford-Tseu	1	27	2.22	0	0	0	0	0	1	9	.889	0	0	0
34	Manny Legace	66	3666	2.41	27	25	8	6	5	147	1648	.911	0	2	4
35	Hannu Toivonen	23	1202	3.44	6	10	5	2	0	69	566	.878	0	0	2
40	* Marek Schwarz	2	50	7.20	0	1	0	1	0	6	17	.647	0	0	0
	Totals	**82**	**4979**	**2.80**	**33**	**36**	**13**	**9**	**5**	**232**	**2249**	**.897**			

Manny Legace made his first appearance in the All-Star Game in 2008. He was named the NHL's First Star of the Week twice during the season.

Andy Murray

Head Coach

Born: Gladstone, Man., March 3, 1951.

Andy Murray was named the head coach of the St. Louis Blues on December 11, 2006. Previously, Murray coached the Los Angeles Kings from 1999 to 2006 and is the all-time franchise leader in wins (215) and games coached (480). Prior to joining the Kings, Murray was the head coach of the Canadian national team from 1996 to 1998. During the 1998-99 season, Murray coached Shattuck-St. Mary's in Faribault, Minnesota, where he led the prep school to a 70-9-2 record and the Midget Triple A USA Hockey national championship.

Murray's coaching career began in 1976 with the Brandon Travelers of the Manitoba Junior A Hockey League. He moved on to become head coach for Brandon University from 1978 to 1981 and led the Bobcats to a league championship and the number-one ranking in Canadian University hockey during his final year. His lengthy coaching experience also includes seven seasons as an NHL assistant or associate coach with the Winnipeg Jets (1993 to 1995), Minnesota North Stars (1990 to 1992) and Philadelphia Flyers (1988 to 1990). He has also coached in Europe and guided Canada to gold medals at the World Championship in 1997, 2003 and 2007.

Coaching Record

			Regular Season				Playoffs			
Season	**Team**	**League**	**GC**	**W**	**L**	**O/T**	**GC**	**W**	**L**	**T**
99-2000	Los Angeles	NHL	82	39	27	16	4	0	4	....
2000-01	Los Angeles	NHL	82	38	28	16	13	7	6	....
2001-02	Los Angeles	NHL	82	40	27	15	7	3	4	....
2002-03	Los Angeles	NHL	82	33	37	12	....	....	....	....
2003-04	Los Angeles	NHL	82	28	29	25	....	....	....	....
2004-05	Los Angeles				SEASON CANCELLED					
2005-06	Los Angeles	NHL	70	37	28	5	....	....	....	....
2006-07	St. Louis	NHL	56	27	18	11	....	....	....	....
2007-08	St. Louis	NHL	82	33	36	13	....	....	....	....
	NHL Totals		618	275	230	113	24	10	14	....

Coaching History

Lynn Patrick and Scotty Bowman, 1967-68; Scotty Bowman, 1968-69, 1969-70; Al Arbour and Scotty Bowman, 1970-71; Sid Abel, Bill McCreary and Al Arbour, 1971-72; Al Arbour and Jean-Guy Talbot, 1972-73; Jean-Guy Talbot and Lou Angotti, 1973-74; Lou Angotti, Lynn Patrick and Garry Young, 1974-75; Garry Young, Lynn Patrick and Leo Boivin, 1975-76; Emile Francis, 1976-77; Leo Boivin and Barclay Plager, 1977-78; Barclay Plager, 1978-79; Barclay Plager and Red Berenson, 1979-80; Red Berenson, 1980-81; Red Berenson and Emile Francis, 1981-82; Emile Francis and Barclay Plager, 1982-83; Jacques Demers, 1983-84 to 1985-86; Jacques Martin, 1986-87, 1987-88; Brian Sutter, 1988-89 to 1991-92; Bob Plager and Bob Berry, 1992-93; Bob Berry, 1993-94; Mike Keenan, 1994-95, 1995-96; Mike Keenan, Jim Roberts and Joel Quenneville, 1996-97; Joel Quenneville, 1997-98 to 2002-03; Joel Quenneville and Mike Kitchen, 2003-04; Mike Kitchen, 2004-05, 2005-06; Mike Kitchen and Andy Murray, 2006-07; Andy Murray, 2007-08 to date.

Captains' History

Al Arbour, 1967-68 to 1969-70; Red Berenson and Barclay Plager, 1970-71; Barclay Plager, 1971-72 to 1975-76; no captain, 1976-77; Red Berenson, 1977-78; Barry Gibbs, 1978-79; Brian Sutter, 1979-80 to 1987-88; Bernie Federko, 1988-89; Rick Meagher, 1989-90; Scott Stevens, 1990-91; Garth Butcher, 1991-92; Brett Hull, 1992-93 to 1994-95; Brett Hull, Shayne Corson and Wayne Gretzky, 1995-96; no captain, 1996-97; Chris Pronger, 1997-98 to 2001-02; Al MacInnis, 2002-03, 2003-04; Dallas Drake, 2005-06, 2006-07; Eric Brewer, 2007-08 to date.

Club Records

Team

(Figures in brackets for season records are games played; records for fewest points, wins, ties, losses, goals, goals against are for 70 or more games)

Most Points	114	1999-2000 (82)
Most Wins	51	1999-2000 (82)
Most Ties	19	1970-71 (78)
Most Losses	50	1978-79 (80)
Most Goals	352	1980-81 (80)
Most Goals Against	349	1981-82 (80)
Fewest Points	48	1978-79 (80)
Fewest Wins	18	1978-79 (80)
Fewest Ties	7	1983-84 (80)
Fewest Losses	18	1980-81 (80)
Fewest Goals	177	1967-68 (74)
Fewest Goals Against	157	1968-69 (76)
Longest Winning Streak		
Overall	10	Jan. 3-23/02
Home	9	Jan. 26-Feb. 26/91
Away	*10	Jan. 21-Mar. 2/00
Longest Undefeated Streak		
Overall	12	Nov. 10-Dec. 8/68 (5 wins, 7 ties), Nov. 24-Dec. 26/00 (11 wins, 1 tie)
Home	11	Four times
Away	11	Jan. 21-Mar. 4/00 (10 wins, 1 tie)
Longest Losing Streak		
Overall	13	Mar. 16-Apr. 8/06
Home	7	Oct. 22-Nov. 26/05, Nov. 25-Dec. 17/06
Away	10	Jan. 20-Mar. 8/82, Dec. 29/05-Feb. 1/06
Longest Winless Streak		
Overall	13	Mar. 16-Apr. 8/06 (13 losses)
Home	7	Dec. 28/82-Jan. 25/83 (5 losses, 2 ties), Oct. 22-Nov. 26/05 (7 losses)
Away	17	Jan. 23-Apr. 7/74 (14 losses, 3 ties)
Most Shutouts, Season	13	1968-69 (76)
Most PIM, Season	2,041	1990-91 (80)
Most Goals, Game	11	Feb. 26/94 (St.L. 11 at Ott. 1)

Individual

Most Seasons	13	Bernie Federko
Most Games	927	Bernie Federko
Most Goals, Career	527	Brett Hull
Most Assists, Career	721	Bernie Federko
Most Points, Career	1,073	Bernie Federko (352G, 721A)
Most PIM, Career	1,786	Brian Sutter
Most Shutouts, Career	16	Glenn Hall
Longest Consecutive Games Streak	662	Garry Unger (Feb. 7/71-Apr. 8/79)
Most Goals, Season	86	Brett Hull (1990-91)
Most Assists, Season	90	Adam Oates (1990-91)
Most Points, Season	131	Brett Hull (1990-91; 86G, 45A)
Most PIM, Season	306	Bob Gassoff (1975-76)
Most Points, Defenseman, Season	78	Jeff Brown (1992-93; 25G, 53A)
Most Points, Center, Season	115	Adam Oates (1990-91; 25G, 90A)
Most Points, Right Wing, Season	131	Brett Hull (1990-91; 86G, 45A)
Most Points, Left Wing, Season	102	Brendan Shanahan (1993-94; 52G, 50A)
Most Points, Rookie, Season	73	Jorgen Pettersson (1980-81; 37G, 36A)
Most Shutouts, Season	8	Glenn Hall (1968-69)
Most Goals, Game	6	Red Berenson (Nov. 7/68)
Most Assists, Game	5	Brian Sutter (Nov. 22/83), Bernie Federko (Feb. 27/88), Adam Oates (Jan. 26/91), Dallas Drake (Oct. 29/03)
Most Points, Game	7	Red Berenson (Nov. 7/68; 6G, 1A), Garry Unger (Mar. 13/71; 3G, 4A)

* NHL Record.

Retired Numbers

2	Al MacInnis	1994-2004
3	Bob Gassoff	1973-1977
8	Barclay Plager	1967-1977
11	Brian Sutter	1976-1988
16	Brett Hull	1987-1998
24	Bernie Federko	1976-1989

All-time Record vs. Other Clubs

Regular Season

	At Home								On Road								Total							
	GP	W	L	T	OL	GF	GA	PTS	GP	W	L	T	OL	GF	GA	PTS	GP	W	L	T	OL	GF	GA	PTS
Anaheim	28	15	7	3	3	86	74	36	28	14	11	2	1	81	77	31	56	29	18	5	4	167	151	67
Atlanta	4	3	0	0	1	13	4	7	5	2	2	1	0	16	16	5	9	5	2	1	1	29	20	12
Boston	60	28	23	9	0	191	200	65	60	16	35	9	0	165	248	41	120	44	58	18	0	356	448	106
Buffalo	51	30	14	7	0	183	127	67	53	18	29	6	0	168	203	42	104	48	43	13	0	351	330	109
Calgary	70	33	28	9	0	244	216	75	68	28	32	5	3	191	225	64	138	61	60	14	3	435	441	139
Carolina	32	20	9	3	0	120	94	43	32	17	13	2	0	99	96	36	64	37	22	5	0	219	190	79
Chicago	127	63	45	17	2	427	391	145	130	38	69	18	5	372	476	99	257	101	114	35	7	799	867	244
Colorado	46	25	15	4	2	165	137	56	47	16	24	7	0	128	164	39	93	41	39	11	2	293	301	95
Columbus	23	16	6	1	0	83	55	33	22	9	9	2	2	54	58	22	45	25	15	3	2	137	113	55
Dallas	123	68	34	21	0	441	347	157	121	41	56	22	2	348	407	106	244	109	90	43	2	789	754	263
Detroit	122	60	42	20	0	396	344	140	122	46	57	17	2	361	440	111	244	106	99	37	2	757	784	251
Edmonton	50	24	17	7	2	177	174	57	50	21	24	4	1	165	182	47	100	45	41	11	3	342	356	104
Florida	10	7	2	1	0	25	13	15	10	5	3	2	0	21	20	12	20	12	5	3	0	46	33	27
Los Angeles	84	54	19	10	1	315	214	119	84	33	39	12	0	239	282	78	168	87	58	22	1	554	496	197
Minnesota	14	5	5	3	1	28	28	14	14	4	6	2	2	27	44	12	28	9	11	5	3	55	72	26
Montreal	58	14	29	15	0	150	199	43	60	12	41	7	0	165	258	31	118	26	70	22	0	315	457	74
Nashville	28	15	10	1	2	77	60	33	29	10	11	3	5	68	73	28	57	25	21	4	7	145	133	61
New Jersey	47	27	12	7	1	195	148	62	47	18	22	7	0	131	148	43	94	45	34	14	1	326	296	105
NY Islanders	48	18	19	9	2	169	159	47	50	14	25	11	0	134	185	39	98	32	44	20	2	303	344	86
NY Rangers	64	25	28	10	1	192	207	61	61	10	44	6	1	145	248	27	125	35	72	16	2	337	455	88
Ottawa	10	4	4	2	0	29	29	10	11	6	5	0	0	38	26	12	21	10	9	2	0	67	55	22
Philadelphia	69	26	34	7	2	196	224	61	68	12	45	10	1	156	268	35	137	38	79	17	3	352	492	96
Phoenix	56	26	19	11	0	190	155	63	57	20	27	7	3	176	187	50	113	46	46	18	3	366	342	113
Pittsburgh	65	44	15	6	0	250	171	94	65	21	31	12	1	194	239	55	130	65	46	18	1	444	410	149
San Jose	34	18	14	1	1	104	89	38	30	21	7	1	1	96	70	44	64	39	21	2	2	200	159	82
Tampa Bay	12	10	2	0	0	48	29	20	14	5	5	3	1	46	43	14	26	15	7	3	1	94	72	34
Toronto	103	58	30	14	1	349	285	131	100	31	58	11	0	295	371	73	203	89	88	25	1	644	656	204
Vancouver	77	45	21	9	2	284	215	101	78	35	31	9	3	246	231	82	155	80	52	18	5	530	446	183
Washington	42	21	13	8	0	169	130	50	40	15	20	4	1	121	141	35	82	36	33	12	1	290	271	85
Defunct Clubs	32	25	4	3	0	131	55	53	33	11	10	12	0	95	100	34	65	36	14	15	0	226	155	87
Totals	**1589**	**827**	**520**	**218**	**24**	**5427**	**4573**	**1896**	**1589**	**549**	**791**	**214**	**35**	**4541**	**5526**	**1347**	**3178**	**1376**	**1311**	**432**	**59**	**9968**	**10099**	**3243**

Playoffs

	Series	W	L	GP	W	L	T	GF	GA	Last Mtg.	Rnd.	Result
Boston	2	0	2	8	0	8	0	15	48	1972	SF	L 0-4
Buffalo	1	0	1	3	1	2	0	8	7	1976	PRE	L 1-2
Calgary	1	0	1	7	3	4	0	22	28	1986	CF	L 3-4
Chicago	10	3	7	50	22	28	0	142	171	2002	CQF	W 4-1
Colorado	1	0	1	5	1	4	0	11	17	2001	CF	L 1-4
Dallas	12	6	6	66	32	34	0	187	197	2001	CSF	W 4-0
Detroit	7	2	5	40	16	24	0	103	125	2002	CSF	L 1-4
Los Angeles	2	2	0	8	8	0	0	32	13	1998	CQF	W 4-0
Montreal	3	0	3	12	0	12	0	14	42	1977	QF	L 0-4
NY Rangers	1	0	1	6	2	4	0	22	29	1981	QF	L 2-4
Philadelphia	2	2	0	11	8	3	0	34	20	1969	QF	W 4-0
Phoenix	2	2	0	11	7	4	0	39	29	1999	CQF	W 4-3
Pittsburgh	3	2	1	13	7	6	0	45	40	1981	PRE	W 3-2
San Jose	3	1	2	18	8	10	0	47	43	2004	CQF	L 1-4
Toronto	5	3	2	31	17	14	0	88	90	1996	CQF	W 4-2
Vancouver	2	0	2	14	6	8	0	48	44	2003	CQF	L 3-4
Totals	**57**	**23**	**34**	**303**	**138**	**165**	**0**	**857**	**943**			

Calgary totals include Atlanta Flames, 1972-73 to 1979-80.
Carolina totals include Hartford, 1979-80 to 1996-97.
Colorado totals include Quebec, 1979-80 to 1994-95.
Dallas totals include Minnesota North Stars, 1967-68 to 1992-93.
New Jersey totals include Kansas City, 1974-75, 1975-76, and Colorado Rockies, 1976-77 to 1981-82.
Phoenix totals include Winnipeg, 1979-80 to 1995-96.

Playoff Results 2008-2003

Year	Round	Opponent	Result	GF	GA
2004	CQF	San Jose	L 1-4	9	12
2003	CQF	Vancouver	L 3-4	21	17

Abbreviations: Round: CF – conference final; **CSF** – conference semi-final; **CQF** – conference quarter-final; **SF** – semi-final; **QF** – quarter-final; **PRE** – preliminary round.

2007-08 Results

Oct.	4	at Phoenix	2-3
	6	at Los Angeles	5-3
	10	Nashville	4-1
	12	Colorado	4-1
	17	at Chicago	3-1
	20	Minnesota	1-3
	23	Anaheim	4-2
	25	at Columbus	0-3
	27	Washington	4-3
	30	Phoenix	1-2
Nov.	1	at Minnesota	3-2
	3	Chicago	2-3
	4	at Columbus	0-3
	9	at Chicago	2-4
	13	Detroit	4-3
	16	Columbus	3-2
	17	at Nashville	3-2†
	19	Nashville	2-1
	21	at Detroit	0-3
	23	Vancouver	3-1
	25	Calgary	3-0
	28	at Buffalo	4-3
	30	at Minnesota	2-3*
Dec.	1	Chicago	3-1
	4	at Calgary	1-3
	7	at Edmonton	4-3
	9	at Colorado	5-9
	11	Edmonton	4-5†
	13	Florida	0-1
	16	Calgary	3-5
	20	Detroit	3-2
	22	at Boston	4-1
	23	Atlanta	2-3*
	26	Detroit	0-5
	28	San Jose	0-1
	29	at Dallas	4-5†
	31	at Detroit	2-0
Jan.	2	Edmonton	2-3*
	5	Carolina	1-0
	8	Columbus	6-1
	10	Dallas	4-2
	11	at Columbus	4-6
	13	Vancouver	3-4†
	16	at Chicago	1-6
	19	Nashville	2-5
	21	at Nashville	3-6
	23	at Vancouver	2-3†
	24	at San Jose	1-4
	29	at Toronto	3-2
Feb.	1	Anaheim	1-0†
	2	Colorado	4-6
	5	Tampa Bay	4-5
	9	at Dallas	2-6
	10	Minnesota	1-2†
	12	Los Angeles	4-2
	14	at Colorado	4-1
	16	at Nashville	1-2*
	17	Columbus	5-1
	19	Chicago	5-1
	21	at Los Angeles	1-5
	22	at Anaheim	1-2*
	24	at Phoenix	0-2
	26	Dallas	1-3
	28	Phoenix	1-2
Mar.	1	San Jose	0-2
	4	Los Angeles	3-2
	5	at Detroit	1-4
	8	at Vancouver	2-4
	10	at Calgary	3-7
	11	at Edmonton	3-4*
	14	at San Jose	1-4
	15	at Anaheim	2-5
	18	at Montreal	4-3†
	20	at Ottawa	2-3
	23	at Chicago	3-4*
	25	Detroit	1-2
	28	at Detroit	4-3*
	29	Chicago	3-4
Apr.	1	Nashville	3-4*
	3	at Nashville	2-3
	5	Columbus	3-0
	6	at Columbus	4-1

* – Overtime † – Shootout

Entry Draft Selections 2008-1994

Name in bold denotes played in NHL.

2008
Pick
- 4 Alex Pietrangelo
- 33 Philip McRae
- 34 Jake Allen
- 65 Jori Lehtera
- 70 James Livingston
- 87 Ian Schultz
- 95 David Warsofsky
- 125 Kristofer Berglund
- 155 Anthony Nigro
- 185 Paul Karpowich

2007
Pick
- 13 Lars Eller
- 18 Ian Cole
- 26 **David Perron**
- 39 Simon Hjalmarsson
- 44 Aaron Palushaj
- 85 Brett Sonne
- 96 Cade Fairchild
- 100 Travis Erstad
- 160 Anthony Peluso
- 190 Trevor Nill

2006
Pick
- 1 **Erik Johnson**
- 25 Patrik Berglund
- 31 Tomas Kana
- 64 Jonas Junland
- 94 Ryan Turek
- 106 Reto Berra
- 124 Andy Sackrison
- 154 Matthew McCollem
- 184 Alexander Hellstrom

2005
Pick
- 24 T.J. Oshie
- 37 Scott Jackson
- 85 Ben Bishop
- 156 Ryan Reaves
- 169 Mike Gauthier
- 171 Nicholas Drazenovic
- 219 Nikolai Lemtyugov

2004
Pick
- 17 **Marek Schwarz**
- 49 Carl Soderberg
- 83 Viktor Alexandrov
- 116 Michal Birner
- 136 Nikita Nikitin
- 180 **Roman Polak**
- 211 David Fredriksson
- 277 Jonathan Michel Boutin

2003
Pick
- 30 **Shawn Belle**
- 62 **David Backes**
- 84 Konstantin Barulin
- 88 **Zach Fitzgerald**
- 101 Konstantin Zakharov
- 127 Alexandre Bolduc
- 148 **Lee Stempniak**
- 159 **Chris Beckford-Tseu**
- 189 Jonathan Lehun
- 221 Evgeny Skachkov
- 253 Andrei Pervyshin
- 284 Juhamatti Aaltonen

2002
Pick
- 48 Alexei Shkotov
- 62 Andrei Mikhnov
- 89 Tomas Troliga
- 120 Robin Jonsson
- 165 Justin Maiser
- 191 **D.J. King**
- 221 Jonas Johnson
- 253 **Tom Koivisto**
- 284 Ryan MacMurchy

2001
Pick
- 57 **Jay McClement**
- 89 Tuomas Nissinen
- 122 Igor Valeev
- 159 Dmitri Semin
- 190 Brett Scheffelmaier
- 253 **Petr Cajanek**
- 270 Grant Jacobsen
- 283 Simon Skoog

2000
Pick
- 30 **Jeff Taffe**
- 65 **Dave Morisset**
- 75 **Justin Papineau**
- 96 Antoine Bergeron
- 129 Troy Riddle
- 167 **Craig Weller**
- 229 Brett Lutes
- 261 **Reinhard Divis**
- 293 Lauri Kinos

1999
Pick
- 17 **Barret Jackman**
- 85 **Peter Smrek**
- 114 Chad Starling
- 143 Trevor Byrne
- 180 Tore Vikingstad
- 203 Phil Osaer
- 221 **Colin Hemingway**
- 232 **Alexander Khavanov**
- 260 Brian McMeekin
- 270 James Desmarais

1998
Pick
- 24 **Christian Backman**
- 41 Maxim Linnik
- 83 **Matt Walker**
- 157 Brad Voth
- 170 Andrei Troschinsky
- 197 Brad Twordik
- 225 Yevgeny Pastukh
- 255 **John Pohl**

1997
Pick
- 40 Tyler Rennette
- 86 Didier Tremblay
- 98 Jan Horacek
- 106 **Jame Pollock**
- 149 Nicholas Bilotto
- 177 **Ladislav Nagy**
- 206 Bobby Haglund
- 232 Dmitri Plekhanov
- 244 Marek Ivan

1996
Pick
- 14 **Marty Reasoner**
- 67 **Gordie Dwyer**
- 95 Jonathan Zukiwsky
- 97 Andrei Petrakov
- 159 Stephen Wagner
- 169 **Daniel Corso**
- 177 **Reed Low**
- 196 **Andrej Podkonicky**
- 203 Tony Hutchins
- 229 **Konstantin Shafranov**

1995
Pick
- 49 **Jochen Hecht**
- 75 Scott Roche
- 101 **Michal Handzus**
- 127 Jeff Ambrosio
- 153 **Denis Hamel**
- 179 **Jean-Luc Grand-Pierre**
- 205 **Derek Bekar**
- 209 **Libor Zabransky**

1994
Pick
- 68 Stephane Roy
- 94 Tyler Harlton
- 120 Edvin Frylen
- 172 **Roman Vopat**
- 198 Steve Noble
- 224 Marc Stephan
- 250 Kevin Harper
- 276 **Scott Fankhouser**

General Managers' History

Lynn Patrick, 1967-68; Scotty Bowman, 1968-69 to 1970-71; Lynn Patrick, 1971-72; Sid Abel, 1972-73; Charles Catto, 1973-74; Gerry Ehman, 1974-75; Dennis Ball, 1975-76; Emile Francis, 1976-77 to 1982-83; Ron Caron, 1983-84 to 1993-94; Mike Keenan, 1994-95, 1995-96; Mike Keenan and Ron Caron, 1996-97; Larry Pleau, 1997-98 to date.

Larry Pleau

Senior Vice President and General Manager

Born: Lynn, MA, June 29, 1947.

Larry Pleau was named general manager on June 9, 1997, becoming the tenth person to hold that position in team history. Under his leadership the Blues won the President's Trophy in 1999-2000 and reached the Western Conference Finals in 2000-01. In international hockey, he served as associate general manager of the silver medal-winning 2002 U.S. Olympic team and as general manager of Team USA at the World Championships in 2003 and 2004 (bronze medal) and at the 2004 World Cup.

Pleau joined the Blues after spending eight seasons with the New York Rangers organization, reaching the position of vice president of player personnel. He joined the Rangers in 1989 as assistant general manager of player development. During Pleau's tenure in New York, the Rangers drafted NHL stars Sergei Zubov, Doug Weight, Alex Kovalev and Niklas Sundstrom. Prior to joining the Rangers, Pleau spent 17 seasons with the Hartford Whalers organization as a player, assistant coach, head coach, general manager and minor league general manager and head coach. He was also instrumental in drafting Ray Ferraro, Ron Francis, Kevin Dineen and Ulf Samuelsson while a member of the Whalers organization.

Pleau played three seasons with the Montreal Canadiens (1969-1972) in the National Hockey League before being the first player signed by the Hartford Whalers of the World Hockey Association. He was a center/left wing for the Whalers from 1972 until his retirement in 1979. He played in 468 regular season games for Hartford, accumulating 157 goals and 215 assists for 372 points. He also played for the 1968 United States Olympic team, the 1969 U.S. national team and went to training camp with Team USA for the 1976 Canada Cup tournament.

Coaching Record

			Regular Season				Playoffs			
Season	Team	League	GC	W	L	O/T	GC	W	L	T
1980-81	Hartford	NHL	20	6	12	2	....	....	....	....
1981-82	Hartford	NHL	80	21	41	18	....	....	....	....
1982-83	Hartford	NHL	18	4	13	1	....	....	....	....
1987-88	Hartford	NHL	26	13	13	0	6	2	4	....
1988-89	Hartford	NHL	80	37	38	5	4	0	4	....
	NHL Totals		**224**	**81**	**117**	**26**	**10**	**2**	**8**	....

Club Directory

Scottrade Center

St. Louis Blues
Scottrade Center
1401 Clark Avenue
St. Louis, MO 63103
Phone **314/622-2500**
FAX 314/622-2582
www.stlouisblues.com
Capacity: 19,150

SCP Worldwide

Chairman/Governor	David W. Checketts
Partner/Vice Chairman/Alternate Governor	Michael McCarthy
Partner/Alternate Governor	Kenneth W. Munoz
Partner	Steven Potter

Executive

President of Hockey Operations/Alt. Gov.	John Davidson
CEO of St. Louis Blues Enterprises/Alt. Gov.	Peter McLoughlin
Sr. V.P. and General Manager	Larry Pleau
Vice President, Player Personnel	Doug Armstrong
Vice President, Hockey Operations	Al MacInnis
Executive V.P., CMO	David Bullock
Executive V.P., Corporate Sponsorship and Sales	Mark Toffolo
Executive V.P., GM, Scottrade Center	Martin Brooks
Sr. V.P., Business Development, SCP Worldwide	Dennis Petrullo
Sr. V.P., Business Development	Eric Stisser
Sr. V.P., Finance and Administration	Phil Siddle
Sr. V.P., Marketing	Karrie Yager
Vice President, Public Relations	Mike Caruso
Vice President, Sponsorship Sales	Jim Goessling
Vice President, Sales	Todd Lambert
Vice President, Entertainment and Event Marketing	Mark Tamar
Vice President, Food and Beverage	Joe Dennehy
Exec. Asst. to the President and G.M.	Donna Lembke
Exec. Asst. to the CEO, St. Louis Blues Ent.	Amber Daniels
Exec. Asst. to the G.M., Scottrade Center	Cherri Kraenzle

Hockey Operations

Asst. G.M./Dir. of Amateur Scouting	Jarmo Kekalainen
Dir. of Pro Scouting and Peoria G.M.	Kevin McDonald
Head Coach	Andy Murray
Assistant Coach/Goaltending Coach	Rick Wamsley
Assistant Coaches	Ray Bennett, Brad Shaw
Strength and Conditioning Coach	Nelson Ayotte
Video Coach	Scott Masters
Asst. Dirs. of Public Relations/Team Services	Scott Bonanni, Rich Jankowski

Training

Athletic Trainer	Ray Barile
Equipment Manager	Bert Godin
Assistant Equipment Manager	Steve Wissman
Equipment Assistant	Ray Halle
Massage Therapist	Jeff Wright

Scouting

Professional Scouts	Rob DiMaio, Tony Feltrin, Wayne Mundey, Jan Vopat
Amateur Scouts	Mike Antonovich, Bill Armstrong, Craig Channell, Dan Ginnell, Ville Siren
Part-Time Amateur Scouts	Thomas Carlsson, Vladimir Havluj, Jr., Basil McRae, Rick Meagher, Barclay Parneta, Georgi Zhuravlev

Medical

Orthopedic Surgeons	Drs. Rick Wright, Matt Matava, Jerome Gilden
Internists	Drs. William Birenbaum, Aaron Birenbaum
Neurosurgeon	Dr. Ralph Dacey
General Surgery	Dr. Michael Brunt
Plastic Surgery	Dr. Tom Francel
Dentist	Dr. Glenn Edwards
Ophthalmologist	Dr. Gill Grand
Optometrist	Dr. Rex Ghormley
Oral Surgeon	Dr. Ken Kram

Marketing

Sr. Director, Advertising and Promotions	Lisa Kampeter
Sr. Director, Digital Media	Beth Schwartz
Director, Community Relations, 14 Fund	Renah Jones
KMOX Radio/Community Relations	Bob Plager
Director, Event Presentation	Chris Frome
Team Photographer	Mark Buckner

Sponsorship

Sr. Director, Corporate Sales	Bryan Lucas
Director, Sponsorship Sales	Deni Allen
Director, Corporate Sponsorship Services	Julie Drochelman

Sales

Senior Director Suite Sales, Premium Seating	Chris Diiorio
Director of Ticket Sales and Service	Theo Hodges
Suite Sales Manager	Nick Wierciak
Inside Sales Manager	Yancey Jones
Sales Data Manager	Jason Penning

Group Sales

Senior Director of Group Ticket Sales	Jennifer Nevins

Box Office

Senior Director, Ticket Operations	Rob Fasoldt
Director, Box Office	Carol Chilton

Finance

Finance Controller	Keith Hegger
Managers, Accounting	Craig Bryant, Mike Clark, Kristy Horner
Payroll Manager	Pam Di Rie

Retail

Retail Director	George Pavlik

Team Broadcasters

Executive Director, Broadcasting and Blues Alumni	Bruce Affleck
Radio Station	KMOX 1120 AM
Radio Broadcasters	Chris Kerber, Kelly Chase
Television Station	KPLR-TV, CW11
Regional Sports Network	FSN Midwest
Television Broadcasters	John Kelly, Bernie Federko, Dan McLaughlin

San Jose Sharks

Key Off-Season Signings/Acquisitions

2008

June 12 • Named **Todd McLellan** head coach.
25 • Re-signed C **Jeremy Roenick**, C **Joe Pavelski** and G **Brian Boucher**.
30 • Re-signed LW **Jody Shelley**.
July 3 • Signed D **Rob Blake**.
4 • Acquired D **Dan Boyle** and D **Brad Lukowich** from Tampa Bay for D **Matt Carle**, D **Ty Wishart**, a 1st-round pick in 2009 and 4th-round pick in 2010.
9 • Re-signed D **Christian Ehrhoff**.
11 • Re-signed C **Marcel Goc**.

2007-08 Results: 49W-23L-4OTL-6SOL 108PTS.
First, Pacific Division

Year-by-Year Record

		Home				Road				Overall								
Season	**GP**	**W**	**L**	**T**	**OL**	**W**	**L**	**T**	**OL**	**W**	**L**	**T**	**OL**	**GF**	**GA**	**Pts.**	**Finished**	**Playoff Result**
2007-08	82	22	13	....	6	27	10	....	4	49	23	....	10	222	193	108	1st, Pacific Div.	Lost Conf. Semi-Final
2006-07	82	25	12	....	4	26	14	....	1	51	26	....	5	258	199	107	2nd, Pacific Div.	Lost Conf. Semi-Final
2005-06	82	25	9	....	7	19	18	....	4	44	27	....	11	266	242	99	2nd, Pacific Div.	Lost Conf. Semi-Final
2004-05	....	....	....	....	....	....	....	....	....	....	....	....	....	....	....	....		
2003-04	82	24	8	7	2	19	13	5	4	43	21	12	6	219	183	104	1st, Pacific Div.	Lost Conf. Championship
2002-03	82	17	16	5	3	11	21	4	5	28	37	9	8	214	239	73	5th, Pacific Div.	Out of Playoffs
2001-02	82	25	11	3	2	19	16	5	1	44	27	8	3	248	199	99	1st, Pacific Div.	Lost Conf. Semi-Final
2000-01	82	22	14	4	1	18	13	8	2	40	27	12	3	217	192	95	2nd, Pacific Div.	Lost Conf. Quarter-Final
1999-2000	82	21	14	3	3	14	16	7	4	35	30	10	7	225	214	87	4th, Pacific Div.	Lost Conf. Semi-Final
1998-99	82	17	15	9	....	14	18	9	....	31	33	18	....	196	191	80	4th, Pacific Div.	Lost Conf. Quarter-Final
1997-98	82	17	19	5	....	17	19	5	....	34	38	10	....	210	216	78	4th, Pacific Div.	Lost Conf. Quarter-Final
1996-97	82	14	23	4	....	13	24	4	....	27	47	8	....	211	278	62	7th, Pacific Div.	Out of Playoffs
1995-96	82	12	26	3	....	8	29	4	....	20	55	7	....	252	357	47	7th, Pacific Div.	Out of Playoffs
1994-95	48	10	13	1	....	9	12	3	....	19	25	4	....	129	161	42	3rd, Pacific Div.	Lost Conf. Semi-Final
1993-94	84	19	13	10	....	14	22	6	....	33	35	16	....	252	265	82	3rd, Pacific Div.	Lost Conf. Semi-Final
1992-93	84	8	33	1	....	3	38	1	....	11	71	2	....	218	414	24	6th, Smythe Div.	Out of Playoffs
1991-92	80	14	23	3	....	3	35	2	....	17	58	5	....	219	359	39	6th, Smythe Div.	Out of Playoffs

2008-09 Schedule

Oct.	Thu.	9	Anaheim
	Sat.	11	Los Angeles
	Sun.	12	at Los Angeles
	Tue.	14	Columbus
	Fri.	17	at Anaheim
	Sat.	18	Philadelphia
	Wed.	22	at Philadelphia
	Fri.	24	at Florida
	Sat.	25	at Tampa Bay
	Tue.	28	Pittsburgh
	Thu.	30	Detroit
Nov.	Sun.	2	at Colorado
	Tue.	4	Minnesota
	Thu.	6	St. Louis
	Sat.	8	Dallas
	Sun.	9	at Phoenix
	Tue.	11	Nashville
	Thu.	13	Calgary
	Sun.	16	at Chicago
	Mon.	17	at Nashville
	Sat.	22	Washington
	Wed.	26	Chicago
	Fri.	28	at Dallas
	Sat.	29	at Phoenix
Dec.	Tue.	2	Toronto
	Thu.	4	Columbus
	Sat.	6	Edmonton
	Thu.	11	Anaheim
	Sat.	13	St. Louis
	Mon.	15	at Los Angeles
	Wed.	17	at Columbus
	Thu.	18	at Detroit
	Sat.	20	NY Rangers
	Tue.	23	Vancouver
	Sat.	27	at St. Louis
	Mon.	29	at Dallas
	Wed.	31	at Minnesota*
Jan.	Sat.	3	NY Islanders
	Tue.	6	at Calgary
	Fri.	9	at Edmonton
	Sat.	10	at Vancouver
	Tue.	13	Tampa Bay
	Thu.	15	Calgary
	Sat.	17	Detroit
	Tue.	20	Vancouver
	Tue.	27	at Colorado
	Thu.	29	Phoenix
	Sat.	31	Chicago
Feb.	Thu.	5	Carolina
	Sat.	7	at Columbus
	Tue.	10	at Boston
	Wed.	11	at Pittsburgh
	Fri.	13	at Buffalo
	Sun.	15	at New Jersey*
	Tue.	17	Edmonton
	Thu.	19	Los Angeles
	Sat.	21	Atlanta*
	Mon.	23	at Dallas
	Wed.	25	at Detroit
	Thu.	26	at Ottawa
	Sat.	28	at Montreal
Mar.	Tue.	3	Dallas
	Thu.	5	Minnesota
	Sat.	7	at Vancouver
	Tue.	10	at Minnesota
	Thu.	12	at St. Louis
	Sat.	14	Los Angeles
	Sun.	15	at Anaheim*
	Tue.	17	at Phoenix
	Thu.	19	Nashville
	Sat.	21	Dallas*
	Sun.	22	Colorado*
	Wed.	25	at Chicago
	Thu.	26	at Nashville
	Sat.	28	Phoenix
	Mon.	30	at Calgary
Apr.	Thu.	2	at Edmonton
	Sat.	4	Anaheim
	Sun.	5	at Anaheim*
	Tue.	7	Colorado
	Thu.	9	Phoenix
	Sat.	11	at Los Angeles*

* Denotes afternoon game.

Usually used to a heavy workload, Evgeni Nabokov appeared in a career-high 77 games in 2007-08. His 46 wins were the fourth-highest single-season total in NHL history. His 2.14 average ranked third in the league.

PACIFIC DIVISION
18th NHL Season
Franchise date: May 9, 1990

2008-09 Player Personnel

FORWARDS	HT	WT	S	Place of Birth	*Age	2007-08 Club
ARMSTRONG, Riley	5-11	190	R	Saskatoon, Sask.	23	Worcester
CAVANAGH, Tom	6-0	200	L	Warwick, RI	26	San Jose-Worcester
CHEECHOO, Jonathan	6-1	205	R	Moose Factory, Ont.	28	San Jose
CLOWE, Ryane	6-2	225	R	St. John's, Nfld.	26	San Jose
COUTURE, Logan	6-0	195	L	Guelph, Ont.	19	Ottawa (OHL)
FOX, T.J.	6-1	200	L	Oswego, NY	24	Worcester
GOC, Marcel	6-0	205	L	Calw, West Germany	25	San Jose
GRIER, Mike	6-1	225	R	Detroit, MI	33	San Jose
JONES, Matt	6-4	205	R	Kentwood, MI	22	Merrimack-Worcester
KASPAR, Lukas	6-2	220	L	Most, Czech.	23	San Jose-Worcester
MARLEAU, Patrick	6-2	220	L	Aneroid, Sask.	29	San Jose
McGINN, Jamie	6-0	185	L	Fergus, Ont.	20	Ottawa (OHL)-Worcester
McLAREN, Frazer	6-5	230	L	Winnipeg, Man.	20	Port (WHL)-M.Jaw-Wor
MICHALEK, Milan	6-2	225	L	Jindrichuv Hradec, Czech.	23	San Jose
MITCHELL, Torrey	5-11	190	R	Montreal, Que.	23	San Jose
MORRIS, Mike	6-1	185	R	Dorchester, MA	25	Worcester
PAVELSKI, Joe	5-11	195	L	Plover, WI	24	San Jose
PLIHAL, Tomas	6-1	200	L	Frydlant, Czech.	25	San Jose-Worcester
ROENICK, Jeremy	6-1	205	R	Boston, MA	38	San Jose
SETOGUCHI, Devin	6-0	205	R	Taber, Alta.	21	San Jose-Worcester
SHELLEY, Jody	6-4	230	L	Thompson, Man.	32	Columbus-San Jose
STAUBITZ, Brad	6-1	215	R	Bright's Grove, Ont.	24	Worcester
THORNTON, Joe	6-4	235	L	London, Ont.	29	San Jose
VESCE, Ryan	5-8	165	R	Lloyd Harbor, NY	26	HIFK
ZALEWSKI, Steven	6-0	190	L	Utica, NY	22	Clarkson-Worcester
DEFENSEMEN						
BLAKE, Rob	6-4	225	R	Simcoe, Ont.	38	Los Angeles
BOYLE, Dan	5-11	190	R	Ottawa, Ont.	32	Tampa Bay
EHRHOFF, Christian	6-2	205	L	Moers, West Germany	26	San Jose
JOSLIN, Derek	6-1	210	L	Richmond Hill, Ont.	21	Worcester
LUKOWICH, Brad	6-1	201	L	Cranbrook, B.C.	32	Tampa Bay
McLAREN, Kyle	6-4	235	L	Humboldt, Sask.	31	San Jose
MOORE, Mike	6-1	200	L	Calgary, Alta.	23	Princeton-Worcester
MURRAY, Douglas	6-3	240	L	Bromma, Sweden	28	San Jose
PETRECKI, Nicholas	6-3	215	L	Schenectady, NY	19	Boston College
SEMENOV, Alexei	6-6	235	L	Murmansk, USSR	27	San Jose
VLASIC, Marc-Edouard	6-1	200	L	Montreal, Que.	21	San Jose-Worcester

GOALTENDERS	HT	WT	C	Place of Birth	*Age	2007-08 Club
BOUCHER, Brian	6-2	198	L	Woonsocket, RI	31	Philadelphia (AHL)-San Jose
DAKERS, Taylor	6-1	175	L	Richmond, B.C.	22	Worcester-Phoenix
GREISS, Thomas	6-1	200	L	Straubing, West Germany	22	San Jose-Worcester
NABOKOV, Evgeni	6-0	200	L	Ust-Kamenogorsk, USSR	33	San Jose
PIELMEIER, Timo	5-11	175	L	Deggendorf, West Germany	19	St. John's
SEXSMITH, Tyson	6-0	204	L	Calgary, Alta.	19	Vancouver (WHL)

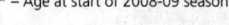

* – Age at start of 2008-09 season

Doug Wilson

Vice President and General Manager

Born: Ottawa, Ont., July 5, 1957.

Hired as executive vice president and general manager on May 13, 2003, Doug Wilson has led the San Jose Sharks to its most successful era since the team's inception. In 2003-04, the Sharks rebounded from missing the playoffs to capture the Pacific Division title and advance to the Western Conference Final. Since then, the Sharks have set new team records with 51 wins in 2006-07 and 108 points in 2007-08 when the team again won the Pacific Division and finished second overall in the NHL standings.

In his role with the Sharks, Wilson has overall authority regarding all hockey-related operations. He oversees all player personnel decisions, negotiates player contracts, coordinates the efforts of the team's scouting department, leads the team in its draft-day preparations and administers the club's player evaluation process at all professional, minor and junior levels.

In his previous role as the team's director of pro development (1997 to 2003), the 16-year NHL veteran's primary responsibilities included evaluating talent at all professional and minor league levels and continuous assessment of the Sharks roster and reserve list. In addition, he provided valuable input assisting the club's player development programs and consulting with the hockey department on all major personnel issues, special assignments and contract negotiations.

A first-round choice (sixth overall) of the Blackhawks in 1977 after a stellar junior career with the Ottawa 67s, Wilson played 14 seasons in Chicago and still ranks as the club's highest scoring defenseman in goals (225), assists (554) and points (779). In addition, he led all Blackhawks defensemen in scoring for 10 consecutive seasons (1980-81 through 1990-91) and captured the 1982 Norris Trophy, symbolic of the NHL's top defenseman, when he tallied 39 goals and 85 points – still Blackhawks single-season records for goals and points by a defenseman.

2007-08 Scoring

* – rookie

Regular Season

Pos	#	Player	Team	GP	G	A	Pts	TOI	+/–	PIM	PP	SH	GW	S	%
C	19	Joe Thornton	S.J.	82	29	67	96	21:23	18	59	11	0	5	178	16.3
D	51	Brian Campbell	BUF	63	5	38	43	25:06	–1	12	3	0	0	102	4.9
			S.J.	20	3	16	19	25:06	9	8	2	0	0	40	7.5
			Total	83	8	54	62	25:06	8	20	5	0	0	142	5.6
L	9	Milan Michalek	S.J.	79	24	31	55	18:04	19	47	5	1	8	233	10.3
C	12	Patrick Marleau	S.J.	78	19	29	48	18:13	–19	33	7	0	2	185	10.3
C	8	Joe Pavelski	S.J.	82	19	21	40	14:06	1	28	8	1	4	207	9.2
R	14	Jonathan Cheechoo	S.J.	69	23	14	37	16:35	11	46	10	0	4	220	10.5
D	52	Craig Rivet	S.J.	74	5	30	35	21:11	3	104	2	0	0	105	4.8
C	27	Jeremy Roenick	S.J.	69	14	19	33	13:44	–8	26	7	0	10	89	15.7
R	25	Mike Grier	S.J.	78	9	13	22	16:12	–8	24	1	3	4	132	6.8
D	10	Christian Ehrhoff	S.J.	77	1	21	22	21:43	9	72	1	0	1	97	1.0
C	17 *	Torrey Mitchell	S.J.	82	10	10	20	14:18	–3	50	1	2	0	110	9.1
R	16 *	Devin Setoguchi	S.J.	44	11	6	17	14:14	6	8	3	0	2	105	10.5
L	34	Patrick Rissmiller	S.J.	79	8	9	17	13:09	–8	30	0	0	2	119	6.7
D	24	Sandis Ozolinsh	S.J.	39	3	13	16	16:58	–11	24	2	0	0	39	7.7
D	18	Matt Carle	S.J.	62	2	13	15	16:32	–8	26	2	0	1	63	3.2
D	44	Marc-Edouard Vlasic	S.J.	82	2	12	14	21:36	–12	24	1	0	0	72	2.8
D	4	Kyle McLaren	S.J.	61	3	8	11	18:21	3	84	0	0	0	39	7.7
D	3	Doug Murray	S.J.	66	1	9	10	17:28	20	98	0	0	0	48	2.1
C	37	Curtis Brown	S.J.	33	5	4	9	10:48	4	10	0	0	0	38	13.2
C	11	Marcel Goc	S.J.	51	5	3	8	10:41	–15	12	0	0	0	87	5.7
L	29	Ryane Clowe	S.J.	15	3	5	8	14:17	–1	22	2	0	0	22	13.6
L	45	Jody Shelley	CBJ	31	0	0	0	04:20	–2	44	0	0	0	10	0.0
			S.J.	31	1	6	7	07:23	–2	91	0	0	0	31	3.2
			Total	62	1	6	7	05:51	–4	135	0	0	0	41	2.4
D	21	Alexei Semenov	S.J.	22	1	3	4	15:14	–8	36	1	0	0	23	4.3
C	39 *	Tomas Plihal	S.J.	22	2	1	3	10:49	4	4	0	0	0	34	5.9
R	47 *	Tom Cavanagh	S.J.	1	0	1	1	13:54	1	0	0	0	0	0	0.0
C	46 *	Mike Iggulden	S.J.	1	0	0	0	06:40	–1	0	0	0	0	1	0.0
L	43 *	Lukas Kaspar	S.J.	3	0	0	0	12:14	–2	0	0	0	0	5	0.0

Goaltending

No.	Goaltender	GPI	Mins	Avg	W	L	OT	EN	SO	GA	SA	S%	G	A	PIM
33	Brian Boucher	5	238	1.76	3	1	1	0	1	7	103	.932	0	0	0
20	Evgeni Nabokov	77	4561	2.14	46	21	8	6	6	163	1802	.910	0	2	12
1	* Thomas Greiss	3	129	3.26	0	1	1	0	0	7	50	.860	0	0	0
30	* Dimitri Patzold	3	44	5.45	0	0	0	0	0	4	20	.800	0	0	0
	Totals	**82**	**5000**	**2.24**	**49**	**23**	**10**	**6**	**7**	**187**	**1981**	**.906**			

Playoffs

Pos	#	Player	Team	GP	G	A	Pts	TOI	+/–	PIM	PP	SH	GW	OT	S	%
C	19	Joe Thornton	S.J.	13	2	8	10	24:41	3	2	1	0	1	0	29	6.9
L	29	Ryane Clowe	S.J.	13	5	4	9	18:59	–2	12	2	0	0	0	41	12.2
C	8	Joe Pavelski	S.J.	13	5	4	9	22:02	3	0	2	0	3	1	44	11.4
C	12	Patrick Marleau	S.J.	13	4	4	8	23:04	–2	2	0	2	0	0	45	8.9
R	14	Jonathan Cheechoo	S.J.	13	4	4	8	18:21	3	4	0	0	1	0	34	11.8
D	51	Brian Campbell	S.J.	13	1	6	7	29:19	3	4	0	0	0	0	22	4.5
D	52	Craig Rivet	S.J.	13	0	6	6	23:01	2	16	0	0	0	0	17	0.0
C	27	Jeremy Roenick	S.J.	12	2	3	5	14:30	0	2	1	0	0	0	20	10.0
D	10	Christian Ehrhoff	S.J.	10	0	5	5	23:03	1	14	0	0	0	0	9	0.0
L	9	Milan Michalek	S.J.	13	4	0	4	17:33	5	4	1	0	1	0	23	17.4
C	17 *	Torrey Mitchell	S.J.	13	1	2	3	14:00	–2	10	1	0	0	0	20	5.0
R	16 *	Devin Setoguchi	S.J.	9	1	1	2	10:25	–2	2	0	0	0	0	12	8.3
D	3	Doug Murray	S.J.	13	1	1	2	18:08	0	2	0	0	0	0	19	5.3
D	18	Matt Carle	S.J.	11	0	1	1	13:56	0	4	0	0	0	0	7	0.0
R	25	Mike Grier	S.J.	13	0	1	1	15:20	–2	2	0	0	0	0	22	0.0
D	44	Marc-Edouard Vlasic	S.J.	13	0	1	1	24:39	–2	0	0	0	0	0	15	0.0
D	21	Alexei Semenov	S.J.	2	0	0	0	11:15	0	2	0	0	0	0	3	0.0
C	11	Marcel Goc	S.J.	4	0	0	0	08:02	1	2	0	0	0	0	5	0.0
C	39 *	Tomas Plihal	S.J.	4	0	0	0	13:16	1	0	0	0	0	0	9	0.0
D	4	Kyle McLaren	S.J.	5	0	0	0	09:45	–2	6	0	0	0	0	0	0.0
L	45	Jody Shelley	S.J.	6	0	0	0	03:15	–1	2	0	0	0	0	1	0.0
C	37	Curtis Brown	S.J.	7	0	0	0	09:10	–2	4	0	0	0	0	5	0.0
L	34	Patrick Rissmiller	S.J.	8	0	0	0	11:25	–3	4	0	0	0	0	13	0.0

Goaltending

No.	Goaltender	GPI	Mins	Avg	W	L	EN	SO	GA	SA	S%	G	A	PIM
33	Brian Boucher	1	2	0.00	0	0	1	0	0	0	.000	0	0	0
20	Evgeni Nabokov	13	853	2.18	6	7	0	1	31	333	.907	0	0	0
	Totals	**13**	**859**	**2.24**	**6**	**7**	**1**	**1**	**32**	**334**	**.904**			

General Managers' History

Jack Ferreira, 1991-92; Chuck Grillo (V.P. Director of Player Personnel), 1992-93 to 1995-96; Dean Lombardi, 1996-97 to 2002-03; Doug Wilson, 2003-04 to date.

Coaching History

George Kingston, 1991-92, 1992-93; Kevin Constantine, 1993-94, 1994-95; Kevin Constantine and Jim Wiley, 1995-96; Al Sims, 1996-97; Darryl Sutter, 1997-98 to 2001-02; Darryl Sutter, Cap Raeder and Ron Wilson, 2002-03; Ron Wilson, 2003-04 to 2007-08; Todd McLellan, 2008-09.

Club Records

Team

(Figures in brackets for season records are games played; records for fewest points, wins, ties, losses, goals, goals against are for 70 or more games)

Most Points	**108**	2007-08 (82)
Most Wins	**51**	2006-07 (82)
Most Ties	**18**	1998-99 (82)
Most Losses	***71**	1992-93 (84)
Most Goals	**266**	2005-06 (82)
Most Goals Against	**414**	1992-93 (84)
Fewest Points	**24**	1992-93 (84)
Fewest Wins	**11**	1992-93 (84)
Fewest Ties	***2**	1992-93 (84)
Fewest Losses	**23**	2007-08 (82)
Fewest Goals	**196**	1998-99 (82)
Fewest Goals Against	**183**	2003-04 (82)
Longest Winning Streak		
Overall	**11**	Feb. 21-Mar. 14/08
Home	**8**	Jan. 24-Mar. 3/04
Away	**10**	Nov. 14-Dec. 31/07
Longest Undefeated Streak		
Overall	**10**	Nov. 27-Dec. 19/01 (9 wins, 1 tie)
Home	**11**	Nov. 15-Dec. 29/03 (8 wins, 3 ties)
Away	**10**	Dec. 26/00-Feb. 16/01 (6 wins, 4 ties)
Longest Losing Streak		
Overall	***17**	Jan. 4-Feb. 12/93
Home	**9**	Nov. 19-Dec. 19/92
Away	**19**	Nov. 27/92-Feb. 12/93
Longest Winless Streak		
Overall	**20**	Dec. 29/92-Feb. 12/93 (19 losses, 1 tie)
Home	**9**	Nov. 19-Dec. 19/92 (9 losses), Oct. 16-Nov. 18/03 (4 losses, 5 ties)
Away	**19**	Nov. 27/92-Feb. 12/93 (19 losses)
Most Shutouts, Season	**11**	2003-04 (82), 2006-07 (82)
Most PIM, Season	**2,134**	1992-93 (84)
Most Goals, Game	**10**	Jan. 13/96 (S.J. 10 at Pit. 8), Mar. 30/02 (CBJ 2 at S.J. 10)

Individual

Most Seasons	**11**	Mike Rathje
Most Games, Career	**795**	Patrick Marleau
Most Goals, Career	**238**	Patrick Marleau
Most Assists, Career	**301**	Patrick Marleau
Most Points, Career	**539**	Patrick Marleau (238G, 301A)
Most PIM, Career	**1,001**	Jeff Odgers
Most Shutouts, Career	**40**	Evgeni Nabokov
Longest Consecutive Games Streak	**228**	Mike Ricci (Nov. 22/97-Oct. 20/00)
Most Goals, Season	**56**	Jonathan Cheechoo (2005-06)
Most Assists, Season	**92**	Joe Thornton (2006-07)
Most Points, Season	**114**	Joe Thornton (2006-07; 22G, 92A)
Most PIM, Season	**326**	Link Gaetz (1991-92)
Most Points, Defenseman, Season	**64**	Sandis Ozolinsh (1993-94; 26G, 38A)
Most Points, Center, Season	**114**	Joe Thornton (2006-07; 22G, 92A)
Most Points, Right Wing, Season	**93**	Jonathan Cheechoo (2005-06; 56G, 37A)
Most Points, Left Wing, Season	**66**	Johan Garpenlov (1992-93; 22G, 44A); Milan Michalek (2006-07; 26G, 40A)
Most Points, Rookie, Season	**59**	Pat Falloon (1991-92; 25G, 34A)
Most Shutouts, Season	**9**	Evgeni Nabokov (2003-04)
Most Goals, Game	**4**	Owen Nolan (Dec. 19/95)
Most Assists, Game	**4**	Thirteen times
Most Points, Game	**6**	Owen Nolan (Oct. 4/99; 3G, 3A)

* NHL Record.

Captains' History

Doug Wilson, 1991-92, 1992-93; Bob Errey, 1993-94; Bob Errey and Jeff Odgers, 1994-95; Jeff Odgers, 1995-96; Todd Gill, 1996-97, 1997-98; Owen Nolan, 1998-99 to 2002-03; Mike Ricci, Vincent Damphousse, Alyn McCauley, Patrick Marleau, 2003-04; Patrick Marleau, 2005-06 to date.

All-time Record vs. Other Clubs

Regular Season

	At Home								On Road								Total							
	GP	W	L	T	OL	GF	GA	PTS	GP	W	L	T	OL	GF	GA	PTS	GP	W	L	T	OL	GF	GA	PTS
Anaheim	42	18	20	2	2	112	116	40	42	23	13	2	4	131	113	52	84	41	33	4	6	243	229	92
Atlanta	5	4	0	1	0	21	10	9	5	3	0	1	1	16	8	8	10	7	0	2	1	37	18	17
Boston	12	4	6	2	0	31	40	10	11	1	7	3	0	32	41	5	23	5	13	5	0	63	81	15
Buffalo	11	5	2	4	0	37	40	14	12	1	11	0	0	32	52	2	23	6	13	4	0	69	92	16
Calgary	40	16	18	4	2	119	119	38	38	12	21	4	1	105	135	29	78	28	39	8	3	224	254	67
Carolina	12	8	4	0	0	54	34	16	12	5	7	0	0	27	40	10	24	13	11	0	0	81	74	26
Chicago	32	19	9	3	1	95	81	42	31	15	12	2	2	96	90	34	63	34	21	5	3	191	171	76
Colorado	30	11	18	1	0	85	107	23	29	8	16	4	1	58	103	21	59	19	34	5	1	143	210	44
Columbus	14	13	0	0	1	55	21	27	14	7	7	0	0	30	36	14	28	20	7	0	1	85	57	41
Dallas	42	15	21	1	5	97	119	36	41	17	19	4	1	98	113	39	83	32	40	5	6	195	232	75
Detroit	32	12	16	3	1	113	123	28	31	4	24	1	2	55	122	11	63	16	40	4	3	168	245	39
Edmonton	38	18	13	5	2	127	113	43	39	9	21	7	2	88	127	27	77	27	34	12	4	215	240	70
Florida	10	6	2	2	0	32	19	14	10	3	2	5	0	29	26	11	20	9	4	7	0	61	45	25
Los Angeles	49	29	16	3	1	166	134	62	49	19	24	4	2	132	145	44	98	48	40	7	3	298	279	106
Minnesota	14	7	5	1	1	36	29	16	14	8	4	1	1	34	31	18	28	15	9	2	2	70	60	34
Montreal	12	6	3	2	1	39	32	15	12	2	8	2	0	22	42	6	24	8	11	4	1	61	74	21
Nashville	18	11	5	1	1	49	43	24	18	8	8	1	1	47	46	18	36	19	13	2	2	96	89	42
New Jersey	11	4	5	1	1	26	32	10	13	4	7	1	1	26	47	10	24	8	12	2	2	52	79	20
NY Islanders	13	6	5	1	1	32	40	14	12	4	6	2	0	37	43	10	25	10	11	3	1	69	83	24
NY Rangers	14	2	10	2	0	32	52	6	11	2	7	1	1	30	43	6	25	4	17	3	1	62	95	12
Ottawa	10	6	4	0	0	21	18	12	10	2	4	4	0	28	36	8	20	8	8	4	0	49	54	20
Philadelphia	13	4	7	2	0	28	32	10	12	4	6	2	0	30	37	10	25	8	13	4	0	58	69	20
Phoenix	44	21	15	4	4	151	129	50	47	21	21	3	2	135	143	47	91	42	36	7	6	286	272	97
Pittsburgh	14	6	6	2	0	37	56	14	10	5	4	1	0	34	42	11	24	11	10	3	0	71	98	25
St. Louis	30	8	19	1	2	70	96	19	34	15	17	1	1	89	104	32	64	23	36	2	3	159	200	51
Tampa Bay	11	4	6	1	0	35	37	9	13	5	6	1	1	35	34	12	24	9	12	2	1	70	71	21
Toronto	16	6	7	3	0	35	42	15	19	5	12	2	0	52	73	12	35	11	19	5	0	87	115	27
Vancouver	40	16	17	5	2	116	121	39	38	14	19	4	1	105	132	33	78	30	36	9	3	221	253	72
Washington	11	7	3	1	0	33	27	15	13	8	5	0	0	39	36	16	24	15	8	1	0	72	63	31
Totals	**640**	**292**	**262**	**58**	**28**	**1884**	**1862**	**670**	**640**	**234**	**318**	**63**	**25**	**1672**	**2040**	**556**	**1280**	**526**	**580**	**121**	**53**	**3556**	**3902**	**1226**

Playoffs

	Series	W	L	GP	W	L	T	GF	GA	Last Mtg.	Rnd.	Result
Calgary	3	2	1	20	10	10	0	57	68	2008	CQF	W 4-3
Colorado	3	1	2	19	9	10	0	52	51	2004	CSF	W 4-2
Dallas	3	0	3	15	3	12	0	19	46	2008	CSF	L 1-4
Detroit	3	1	2	17	6	11	0	36	64	2007	CSF	L 2-4
Edmonton	1	0	1	6	2	4	0	12	19	2006	CSF	L 2-4
Nashville	2	2	0	10	8	2	0	33	24	2007	CQF	W 4-1
Phoenix	1	1	0	5	4	1	0	13	7	2002	CQF	W 4-1
St. Louis	3	2	1	18	10	8	0	43	47	2004	CQF	W 4-1
Toronto	1	0	1	7	3	4	0	21	26	1994	CSF	L 3-4
Totals	**20**	**9**	**11**	**117**	**55**	**62**	**0**	**286**	**352**			

Playoff Results 2008-2003

Year	Round	Opponent	Result	GF	GA
2008	CSF	Dallas	L 2-4	11	15
	CQF	Calgary	W 4-3	19	17
2007	CSF	Detroit	L 2-4	9	13
	CQF	Nashville	W 4-1	16	14
2006	CSF	Edmonton	L 2-4	12	19
	CQF	Nashville	W 4-1	17	10
2004	CF	Calgary	L 2-4	12	16
	CSF	Colorado	W 4-2	14	7
	CQF	St. Louis	W 4-1	12	9

Abbreviations: Round: CF – conference final; **CSF** – conference semi-final; **CQF** – conference quarter-final.

Carolina totals include Hartford, 1991-92 to 1996-97.
Dallas totals include Minnesota North Stars, 1991-92 to 1992-93.
Colorado totals include Quebec, 1991-92 to 1994-95.
Phoenix totals include Winnipeg, 1991-92 to 1995-96.

2007-08 Results

Month	Day	Opponent	Score
Oct.	4	at Edmonton	2-3†
	5	at Vancouver	3-1
	7	at Colorado	2-6
	10	at Chicago	2-1
	13	Boston	1-2
	15	at Vancouver	4-2
	18	Detroit	2-4
	20	Nashville	3-0
	22	at Calgary	4-1
	26	at Detroit	1-5
	27	at Columbus	1-2
	29	at Dallas	4-2
Nov.	2	Los Angeles	2-5
	3	at Los Angeles	3-1
	7	Dallas	1-3
	9	at Anaheim	2-3†
	10	Phoenix	4-1
	12	Phoenix	5-0
	14	at Dallas	4-3†
	15	at Phoenix	6-0
	17	Anaheim	1-2†
	24	Los Angeles	1-2
	28	Los Angeles	2-3†
	30	Colorado	3-2
Dec.	3	at Colorado	3-2
	5	at Dallas	3-2
	7	at Phoenix	1-0
	8	Buffalo	1-7
	11	Minnesota	4-1
	13	Vancouver	5-2
	15	Dallas	2-4
	16	at Anaheim	2-1†
	18	Anaheim	0-2
	20	Phoenix	2-3†
	22	Anaheim	2-5
	26	at Los Angeles	3-2
	28	at St. Louis	1-0
	29	at Nashville	5-2
	31	at Minnesota	3-2
Jan.	3	Calgary	2-3*
	5	Columbus	3-2
	10	Vancouver	3-1
	12	Toronto	3-2
	13	at Anaheim	3-4*
	15	at Phoenix	3-5
	17	Dallas	2-4
	19	Detroit	3-6
	22	Chicago	3-2
	24	St. Louis	4-1
	29	at Edmonton	3-0
	30	at Calgary	4-5
Feb.	2	Chicago	3-2†
	6	Colorado	1-3
	8	Columbus	2-1*
	9	Nashville	4-3
	12	Calgary	3-4*
	14	Edmonton	2-3
	17	at NY Rangers	1-3
	18	at NY Islanders	2-3
	20	at New Jersey	2-3
	21	at Philadelphia	3-1
	24	at Pittsburgh	2-1†
	27	at Columbus	4-2
	29	at Detroit	3-2
Mar.	1	at St. Louis	2-0
	3	Montreal	6-4
	5	Ottawa	3-2*
	7	at Chicago	3-2
	9	at Minnesota	3-2†
	11	at Nashville	2-1
	14	St. Louis	4-1
	16	Edmonton	1-2†
	18	at Los Angeles	2-1
	19	Minnesota	4-3†
	21	Anaheim	2-1
	25	at Phoenix	4-5*
	27	Dallas	3-2*
	28	at Anaheim	3-1
	30	Phoenix	3-1
Apr.	1	Los Angeles	5-2
	3	at Los Angeles	2-4
	6	at Dallas	2-4

* – Overtime † – Shootout

Entry Draft Selections 2008-1994

Name in bold denotes played in NHL.

2008
Pick
62 Justin Daniels
92 Samuel Groulx
106 Harri Sateri
146 Julien Demers
177 Tommy Wingels
186 Jason Demers
194 Drew Daniels

2007
Pick
9 Logan Couture
28 Nicholas Petrecki
83 Timo Pielmeier
91 Tyson Sexsmith
165 Patrik Zackrisson
173 Nick Bonino
201 Justin Braun
203 Frazer McLaren

2006
Pick
16 Ty Wishart
36 Jamie McGinn
98 James Delory
143 Ashton Rome
202 John McCarthy
203 Jay Barriball

2005
Pick
8 **Devin Setoguchi**
35 **Marc-Edouard Vlasic**
112 Alex Stalock
140 Taylor Dakers
149 Derek Joslin
162 P.J. Fenton
183 Will Colbert
193 Tony Lucia

2004
Pick
22 **Lukas Kaspar**
94 **Thomas Greiss**
126 **Torrey Mitchell**
129 Jason Churchill
153 Steven Zalewski
201 Michael Vernace
225 David MacDonald
234 Derek MacIntyre
288 Brian Mahoney-Wilson
289 Christian Jensen

2003
Pick
6 **Milan Michalek**
16 **Steve Bernier**
43 **Josh Hennessy**
47 **Matt Carle**
139 Patrick Ehelechner
201 Jonathan Tremblay
205 **Joe Pavelski**
216 Kai Hospelt
236 Alexander Hult
267 Brian O'Hanley
276 Carter Lee

2002
Pick
27 Mike Morris
52 Dan Spang
86 Jonas Fiedler
139 **Kris Newbury**
163 Tom Walsh
217 **Tim Conboy**
288 Michael Hutchins

2001
Pick
20 **Marcel Goc**
106 **Christian Ehrhoff**
107 **Dimitri Patzold**
140 **Tomas Plihal**
175 **Ryane Clowe**
182 **Tom Cavanagh**

2000
Pick
41 Tero Maatta
104 **Jon Disalvatore**
142 Michal Pinc
166 **Nolan Schaefer**
183 Michal Macho
246 **Chad Wiseman**
256 Pasi Saarinen

1999
Pick
14 **Jeff Jillson**
82 Mark Concannon
111 Willie Levesque
155 **Niko Dimitrakos**
229 Eric Betournay
241 **Douglas Murray**
257 **Hannes Hyvonen**

1998
Pick
3 **Brad Stuart**
29 **Jonathan Cheechoo**
65 Eric Laplante
98 **Rob Davison**
104 **Miroslav Zalesak**
127 Brandon Coalter
145 **Mikael Samuelsson**
185 Robert Mulick
212 **Jim Fahey**

1997
Pick
2 **Patrick Marleau**
23 **Scott Hannan**
82 Adam Colagiacomo
107 Adam Nittel
163 Joe Dusbabek
192 **Cam Severson**
219 **Mark Smith**

1996
Pick
2 **Andrei Zyuzin**
21 **Marco Sturm**
55 Terry Friesen
102 **Matt Bradley**
137 **Michel Larocque**
164 Jake Deadmarsh
191 Cory Cyrenne
217 David Thibeault

1995
Pick
12 Teemu Riihijarvi
38 Peter Roed
64 Marko Makinen
90 **Vesa Toskala**
116 **Miikka Kiprusoff**
130 Michal Bros
140 Timo Hakanen
142 Jaroslav Kudrna
167 Brad Mehalko
168 Robert Jindrich
194 **Ryan Kraft**
220 Mikko Markkanen

1994
Pick
11 **Jeff Friesen**
37 Angel Nikolov
66 **Alexei Yegorov**
89 **Vaclav Varada**
115 **Brian Swanson**
141 **Alexander Korolyuk**
167 Sergei Gorbachev
193 Eric Landry
219 **Evgeni Nabokov**
240 Tomas Pisa
245 Aniket Dhadphale
271 David Beauregard

Todd McLellan

Head Coach

Born: Melville, Sask., October 3, 1967.

The San Jose Sharks introduced Todd McLellan as their new head coach on June 12, 2008. Most recently, McLellan had captured the 2008 Stanley Cup in his third season as an assistant coach under Mike Babcock with the Detroit Red Wings. Over the course of those three seasons, the Red Wings won the Presidents' Trophy as the NHL's top regular season team twice (2007-08 and 2005-06) and finished second in 2006-07, tying the Buffalo Sabres for first in points (113) but having three fewer wins. One of McLellan's key responsibilities was working with the Detroit power play, which finished third in the NHL in 2007-08 (20.7%) and first in 2005-06 (22.1%).

Prior to being hired in Detroit, McLellan spent four seasons as head coach of the Houston Aeros in the American Hockey League, including capturing the 2003 AHL Calder Cup championship. He also was selected to coach in two AHL All-Star Games during his tenure with Houston. In 2000-01, he served as the head coach of the Cleveland Lumberjacks of the International Hockey League.

From 1994-95 through 1999-2000, McLellan coached the Swift Current Broncos of the Western Hockey League, where he also served as general manager in his final four WHL seasons. He was named WHL coach of the year in 2000 and WHL executive of the year in 1997. In his 14 years of serving as a head and assistant coach prior to arriving in San Jose, McLellan's teams never missed the postseason.

McLellan played his junior hockey with Saskatoon (WHL) and was drafted by the New York Islanders in the fifth round (104th overall) in the 1986 NHL Entry Draft. He played parts of two seasons with Springfield in the American Hockey League and played in five games with the Islanders in 1987-88, posting two points (one goal, one assist) before a shoulder injury ended his NHL career.

Coaching Record

			Regular Season				Playoffs			
Season	Team	League	GC	W	L	O/T	GC	W	L	T
1994-95	Swift Current	WHL	72	31	34	7	6	2	4	....
1995-96	Swift Current	WHL	72	36	31	5	6	2	4	....
1996-97	Swift Current	WHL	72	44	23	5	10	4	4	....
1997-98	Swift Current	WHL	72	44	19	9	12	7	5	....
1998-99	Swift Current	WHL	72	34	32	6	6	2	4	....
99-2000	Swift Current	WHL	72	47	18	7	12	6	6	....
2000-01	Cleveland	IHL	82	43	32	7	4	0	4	....
2001-02	Houston	AHL	80	39	26	15	14	8	6	....
2002-03	Houston	AHL	80	47	23	10	23	15	8	....
2003-04	Houston	AHL	80	28	34	18	2	0	2	....
2004-05	Houston	AHL	80	40	28	12	5	1	4	....

Club Directory

HP Pavilion at San Jose

San Jose Sharks
HP Pavilion at San Jose
525 West Santa Clara Street
San Jose, CA 95113
Phone **408/287-7070**
FAX 408/999-5797
www.sjsharks.com
Capacity: 17,496

San Jose Sports & Entertainment Enterprises Ownership Group
Kevin Compton, Hasso Plattner, Greg Reyes, Stratton Sclavos, Gary Valenzuela, Gordon Russell, Rudy Staedler, Floyd Kvamme, Greg Jamison, Harvey Armstrong, Tom McEnery, George Gund III

Executive Staff
President, CEO & NHL Governor . . . . Greg Jamison
Executive V.P. of Business Operations . . . . Malcolm Bordelon
Executive V.P. & G.M. (HP Pavilion at San Jose) . . . . Jim Goddard
Executive V.P. & General Counsel . . . . Don Gralnek
Executive V.P. & G.M. (Sharks) . . . . Doug Wilson
Executive V.P. & Chief Financial Officer . . . . Charlie Faas
President, Sharks Minor Holdings . . . . Michael T. Lehr
Vice President of Finance . . . . Ken Caveney
Vice President of Corporate Partnerships . . . . Eric Mastalir
Vice President of Sales & Marketing . . . . Kent Russell
Vice President of Building Operations . . . . Rich Sotelo
Vice President and Assistant G.M. (Sharks) . . . . Wayne Thomas
Executive Assistants . . . . Tricia Sullivan, Michelle Simmons, Misty Macias

Hockey Operations
Director of Hockey Operations . . . . Joe Will
Head Coach . . . . Todd McLellan
Assistant Coach . . . . Trent Yawney
Assistant Coach . . . . Todd Richards
Assistant Coach . . . . Jay Woodcroft
Goaltending Development Coach . . . . Corey Schwab
Development Coach . . . . Mike Ricci
Director of Scouting . . . . Tim Burke
Scouts . . . . Gilles Cote, Pat Funk, Jack Gardiner, Rob Grillo, Brian Gross, Karel Masopust, Graeme Townshend
Scout/Player Development . . . . Bryan Marchment
Director of Hockey Administration . . . . Rosemary Tebaldi
Manager of Hockey Technology . . . . Paul Fink
Head Athletic Trainer . . . . Ray Tufts, ATC
Assistant Athletic Trainer . . . . Wes Howard, ATC
Strength & Conditioning Coordinator . . . . Mike Potenza
Massage Therapist . . . . Arnulfo Aguirre, CMT
Equipment Manager . . . . Mike Aldrich
Assistant Equipment Manager . . . . Rick Bronwell
Equipment Assistant & Equipment Transportation . . . . Roy Sneesby
Cleaning Specialist . . . . Norma Hernandez
Team Physician . . . . Arthur J. Ting, M.D.
Team Internists . . . . Greg Whitley M.D., John Chiu, M.D.
Team Dentists . . . . Don Goudy, D.D.S., Robert Bonahoom, D.D.S.
Team Vision Specialists . . . . Vincent S. Zuccaro, O.D., F.A.A.O.
Medical Staff . . . . Steve Franzino, M.D., Robert Millard, M.D., Mark Sontag, M.D.
Chiropractic Consultant . . . . Mike McMurray, D. C.
Manual Therapy Consultant . . . . Tobe Hanson

SVS&E/Business Operations
Senior Director of Communications . . . . Ken Arnold
Director of Broadcasting . . . . Frank Albin
Director of Marketing . . . . Doug Bentz
Director of Ticket Sales . . . . John Castro
Director of Media Relations . . . . Scott Emmert
Director of Fan Development/The Sharks Foundation . . Rob Jaynes
Director of Event Presentation . . . . Steve Maroni
Director of Suite Sales & Service . . . . Bruce Ross
Director of Communications & Internet Services . . . . Roger Ross
Director of Public Relations . . . . Jim Sparaco
Senior Sales Manager, Corporate Partnerships . . . . . Jennifer Birmingham, Bryan Deierling
Senior Ticket Operations Manager . . . . Scott Fitzsimmons
Senior Service Manager, Corporate Partnerships . . . . Heather Hunter
Sales Managers, Corporate Partnerships . . . . Justin Piper, Tarrah Pollaro
Account Sales Managers . . . . Ted Chuba, Patrick Frost, Adam King, Adam Requarth
Account Service Managers . . . . Sharon Holman, Sarah Bauerle, Julie Kennedy
Marketing Manager . . . . TBD
Creative Services Manager . . . . Derik Green
Media Relations Manager . . . . Tom Holy
Suite Sales Manager . . . . Chris Hutchins
Sharks Foundation Manager . . . . Laura Johnston
Mascot Operations Manager . . . . Tim Patnode
Suite Service Manager . . . . Kathy Payne-Tovar
Operations Manager, National Match Play . . . . Tyson Durm
Event Presentation Coordinator . . . . Marissa Zankich
Service Managers, Corporate Partnerships . . . . Ryan Hilgers, Jennifer De Carlo
Media Relations and Team Services Coordinator . . . . Ryan Stenn

Finance
Director of Human Resources . . . . Cathy Chandler
Director of Information Technology . . . . Uy Ut
Controller . . . . Stephanie Reitz

Building Operations
Director of Ticket Operations . . . . Daniel DeBoer
Director of Booking & Events . . . . Steve Kirsner, James Hamnett
Director of Guest Services . . . . David Cahill
Director of Building Services . . . . Monte Chavez
Facilities Technical Director . . . . Greg Carrolan

Miscellaneous
Television Station . . . . Comcast SportsNet Bay Area
Radio Network Flagship . . . . 98.5 K-FOX (KUFX FM)
Television Play-By-Play/Color/In-Game Host . . . . . . Randy Hahn/Drew Remenda/TBD
Radio Play-By-Play/Color/Reporter . . . . Dan Rusanowsky, Jamie Baker/David Maley
Production Associate . . . . Elisabeth Farkas
Team Photographers . . . . Don Smith, Rocky Widner
P.A. Announcer . . . . Joe Ike
In Game Host . . . . Danny Miller
Mascot . . . . S.J. Sharkie

Tampa Bay Lightning

Key Off-Season Signings/Acquisitions

2008

June
- **2** • Re-signed D **Alexandre Picard**.
- **20** • Selected C **Steve Stamkos** (Sarnia, OHL) first overall in the 2008 Entry Draft.
- **24** • Named **Barry Melrose** head coach.
- **25** • Named **Brian Lawton** vice president of hockey operations.
- **30** • Signed LW **Gary Roberts**, C/LW **Vaclav Prospal** and LW **Ryan Malone**.

July
- **1** • Signed G **Olaf Kolzig**, RW **Radim Vrbata** and RW **Adam Hall**.
- **2** • Re-signed C **Ryan Craig**.
- **4** • Acquired D **Matt Carle**, D **Ty Wishart**, a 1st-round pick in 2009 and 4th-round pick in 2010 from San Jose for D **Dan Boyle** and D **Brad Lukowich**.
- **8** • Re-signed RW **Evgeni Artyukhin**.
- **8** • Signed RW **Mark Recchi** and RW **Brandon Bochenski**.
- **9** • Signed D **Andrew Hutchinson**.
- **9** • Named **Rick Tocchet** and **Cap Raeder** assistant coaches.
- **11** • Re-signed D **Chris Gratton**.
- **13** • Re-signed C **Vincent Lecavalier**.
- **14** • Re-signed G **Mike Smith**.

2008-09 Schedule

Oct.	Sat.	4	NY Rangers†
	Sun.	5	at NY Rangers†
	Sat.	11	Carolina
	Thu.	16	NY Islanders
	Sat.	18	Minnesota
	Tue.	21	Atlanta
	Sat.	25	San Jose
	Tue.	28	at Toronto
	Thu.	30	at Buffalo
Nov.	Sat.	1	Ottawa
	Wed.	5	at New Jersey
	Thu.	6	at NY Rangers
	Sat.	8	at Philadelphia
	Mon.	10	at Washington
	Wed.	12	at Florida
	Thu.	13	Detroit
	Sun.	16	at Carolina*
	Tue.	18	Florida
	Fri.	21	Nashville
	Sun.	23	New Jersey*
	Wed.	26	NY Rangers
	Fri.	28	at Minnesota*
	Sat.	29	at Colorado
Dec.	Tue.	2	at Philadelphia
	Thu.	4	Boston
	Sat.	6	Buffalo
	Mon.	8	at Boston
	Wed.	10	at Buffalo
	Thu.	11	at Montreal
	Sat.	13	at Ottawa
	Thu.	18	Colorado
	Sat.	20	at Atlanta
	Tue.	23	at Pittsburgh
	Fri.	26	at Florida
	Sat.	27	Florida
	Tue.	30	Montreal
Jan.	Thu.	1	at Washington
	Sat.	3	Carolina
	Sun.	4	at Atlanta*
	Thu.	8	at Phoenix
	Fri.	9	at Anaheim
	Mon.	12	at Los Angeles
	Tue.	13	at San Jose
	Thu.	15	Philadelphia
	Sat.	17	Florida
	Mon.	19	Dallas
	Wed.	21	Buffalo
	Tue.	27	Montreal
	Thu.	29	at Carolina
	Fri.	30	Philadelphia
Feb.	Tue.	3	at NY Islanders
	Wed.	4	at Pittsburgh
	Sat.	7	NY Islanders
	Tue.	10	Atlanta
	Thu.	12	Toronto
	Sat.	14	Washington
	Tue.	17	Chicago
	Thu.	19	New Jersey
	Fri.	20	at Carolina
	Sun.	22	Boston*
	Tue.	24	at Edmonton
	Fri.	27	at Vancouver
Mar.	Sun.	1	at Calgary
	Tue.	3	Pittsburgh
	Fri.	6	St. Louis
	Sat.	7	Carolina
	Wed.	11	at Ottawa
	Thu.	12	at Toronto
	Sat.	14	at Florida
	Tue.	17	Toronto
	Thu.	19	Washington
	Sat.	21	Atlanta
	Tue.	24	Columbus
	Thu.	26	at Montreal
	Fri.	27	at Washington
	Sun.	29	Ottawa
	Tue.	31	at Boston
Apr.	Fri.	3	at New Jersey
	Sat.	4	at NY Islanders
	Tue.	7	Pittsburgh
	Thu.	9	Washington
	Sat.	11	at Atlanta

* Denotes afternoon game. † Games played in Prague, CZ.

SOUTHEAST DIVISION
17th NHL Season

Franchise date: December 16, 1991

2007-08 Results: 31W-42L-8OTL-1SOL 71PTS.
Fifth, Southeast Division

Year-by-Year Record

		Home				Road				Overall								
Season	**GP**	**W**	**L**	**T**	**OL**	**W**	**L**	**T**	**OL**	**W**	**L**	**T**	**OL**	**GF**	**GA**	**Pts.**	**Finished**	**Playoff Result**
2007-08	82	20	18	....	3	11	24	....	6	31	42	....	9	223	267	71	5th, Southeast Div.	Out of Playoffs
2006-07	82	22	18	....	1	22	15	....	4	44	33	....	5	253	261	93	2nd, Southeast Div.	Lost Conf. Quarter-Final
2005-06	82	25	14	....	2	18	19	....	4	43	33	....	6	252	260	92	2nd, Southeast Div.	Lost Conf. Quarter-Final
2004-05	....	....	....	....	....	....	....	....	....	....	....	....	....	....	....	....		
2003-04	**82**	**24**	**10**	**4**	**3**	**22**	**12**	**4**	**3**	**46**	**22**	**8**	**6**	**245**	**192**	**106**	**1st, Southeast Div.**	**Won Stanley Cup**
2002-03	82	22	9	7	3	14	16	9	2	36	25	16	5	219	210	93	1st, Southeast Div.	Lost Conf. Semi-Final
2001-02	82	16	17	5	3	11	23	6	1	27	40	11	4	178	219	69	3rd, Southeast Div.	Out of Playoffs
2000-01	82	17	19	3	2	7	28	3	3	24	47	6	5	201	280	59	5th, Southeast Div.	Out of Playoffs
1999-2000	82	13	20	4	4	6	27	5	3	19	47	9	7	204	310	54	4th, Southeast Div.	Out of Playoffs
1998-99	82	12	25	4	....	7	29	5	....	19	54	9	....	179	292	47	4th, Southeast Div.	Out of Playoffs
1997-98	82	11	23	7	....	6	32	3	....	17	55	10	....	151	269	44	7th, Atlantic Div.	Out of Playoffs
1996-97	82	15	18	8	....	17	22	2	....	32	40	10	....	217	247	74	6th, Atlantic Div.	Out of Playoffs
1995-96	82	22	14	5	....	16	18	7	....	38	32	12	....	238	248	88	5th, Atlantic Div.	Lost Conf. Quarter-Final
1994-95	48	10	14	0	....	7	14	3	....	17	28	3	....	120	144	37	6th, Atlantic Div.	Out of Playoffs
1993-94	84	14	22	6	....	16	21	5	....	30	43	11	....	224	251	71	7th, Atlantic Div.	Out of Playoffs
1992-93	84	12	27	3	....	11	27	4	....	23	54	7	....	245	332	53	6th, Norris Div.	Out of Playoffs

Dealt to Tampa Bay from Dallas as part of the deal for Brad Richards, Jeff Halpern wound up playing 83 games in 2007-08. The 20 goals he scored were his most since the 2000-01 season.

2008-09 Player Personnel

FORWARDS	HT	WT	S	Place of Birth	*Age	2007-08 Club
ARTYUKHIN, Evgeny	6-5	254	L	Moscow, USSR	25	Omsk-CSKA
BOCHENSKI, Brandon	6-1	187	R	Blaine, MN	26	Bos-Prov (AHL)-Ana-Nsh
CRAIG, Ryan	6-2	212	L	Abbotsford, B.C.	26	Tampa Bay-Norfolk
GRATTON, Chris	6-4	226	L	Brantford, Ont.	33	Tampa Bay
HALL, Adam	6-3	206	R	Kalamazoo, MI	28	Pittsburgh
HALPERN, Jeff	6-0	203	R	Potomac, MD	32	Dallas-Tampa Bay
JOKINEN, Jussi	5-11	190	L	Kalajoki, Finland	25	Dallas-Tampa Bay
JONES, Blair	6-3	210	R	Central Butte, Sask.	22	Norfolk-Tampa Bay
KOCI, David	6-6	238	L	Prague, Czech.	27	Chicago-Rockford-Norfolk
KONOPKA, Zenon	6-1	213	L	Niagara Falls, Ont.	27	Columbus-Syracuse
LECAVALIER, Vincent	6-4	219	L	Ile Bizard, Que.	28	Tampa Bay
MALONE, Ryan	6-4	224	L	Pittsburgh, PA	28	Pittsburgh
OUELLET, Michel	6-1	193	R	Rimouski, Que.	26	Tampa Bay
PROSPAL, Vaclav	6-2	198	L	Ceske Budejovice, Czech.	33	Tampa Bay-Philadelphia
RECCHI, Mark	5-10	195	L	Kamloops, B.C.	40	Pittsburgh-Atlanta
ROBERTS, Gary	6-2	215	L	North York, Ont.	42	Pittsburgh
ST. LOUIS, Martin	5-9	177	L	Laval, Que.	33	Tampa Bay
SMITH, Wyatt	5-11	205	L	Thief River Falls, MN	31	Colorado-Lake Erie
STAMKOS, Steven	6-0	176	R	Markham, Ont.	18	Sarnia
SZCZECHURA, Paul	5-11	175	R	Brantford, Ont.	22	Iowa-Norfolk
TARNASKY, Nick	6-2	224	L	Rocky Mtn. House, Alta.	23	Tampa Bay
VRBATA, Radim	6-1	190	R	Mlada Boleslav, Czech.	27	Phoenix
WARD, Jason	6-2	208	R	Chapleau, Ont.	29	Tampa Bay
DEFENSEMEN						
CARLE, Matt	6-0	205	L	Anchorage, AK	24	San Jose
HUTCHINSON, Andrew	6-2	206	R	Evanston, IL	28	Hartford
KUBA, Filip	6-5	225	L	Ostrava, Czech.	31	Tampa Bay
LUNDIN, Mike	6-2	188	L	Burnsville, MN	24	Tampa Bay
NISKALA, Janne	5-11	199	L	Vasteras, Sweden	27	Milwaukee
O'BRIEN, Shane	6-3	224	L	Port Hope, Ont.	25	Tampa Bay
PICARD, Alexandre	6-2	220	L	Gatineau, Que.	23	Phi-Phi (AHL)-T.B.-Norfolk
RANGER, Paul	6-3	208	L	Whitby, Ont.	24	Tampa Bay
SMABY, Matt	6-5	222	L	Minneapolis, MN	23	Tampa Bay-Norfolk

GOALTENDERS	HT	WT	C	Place of Birth	*Age	2007-08 Club
KOLZIG, Olaf	6-3	224	L	Johannesburg, S. Africa	38	Washington
RAMO, Karri	6-2	201	L	Asikkala, Finland	22	Tampa Bay-Norfolk
SMITH, Mike	6-3	211	L	Kingston, Ont.	26	Dallas-Tampa Bay

* – Age at start of 2008-09 season

Martin St. Louis and Vincent Lecavalier were the top two scorers in Tampa Bay for the second straight season.

Coaching History

Terry Crisp, 1992-93 to 1996-97; Terry Crisp, Rick Paterson and Jacques Demers, 1997-98; Jacques Demers, 1998-99; Steve Ludzik, 1999-2000; Steve Ludzik and John Tortorella, 2000-01; John Tortorella, 2001-02 to 2007-08; Barry Melrose, 2008-09.

2007-08 Scoring

* – rookie

Regular Season

Pos	#	Player	Team	GP	G	A	Pts	TOI	+/-	PIM	PP	SH	GW	S	%
C	4	Vincent Lecavalier	T.B.	81	40	52	92	22:57	–17	89	10	1	7	318	12.6
R	26	Martin St. Louis	T.B.	82	25	58	83	24:17	–23	26	10	2	5	241	10.4
C	11	Jeff Halpern	DAL	64	10	14	24	16:21	–2	40	1	1	0	86	11.6
			T.B.	19	10	8	18	18:12	2	14	3	0	2	46	21.7
			Total	83	20	22	42	16:46	0	54	4	1	2	132	15.2
L	10	Jussi Jokinen	DAL	52	14	14	28	12:43	2	14	5	0	2	93	15.1
			T.B.	20	2	12	14	18:56	–16	4	1	0	0	38	5.3
			Total	72	16	26	42	14:27	–14	18	6	0	2	131	12.2
R	7	Michel Ouellet	T.B.	64	17	19	36	13:37	11	12	5	0	0	132	12.9
D	54	Paul Ranger	T.B.	72	10	21	31	25:13	–13	56	0	1	0	105	9.5
D	71	Filip Kuba	T.B.	75	6	25	31	24:57	–8	40	2	0	0	113	5.3
D	22	Dan Boyle	T.B.	37	4	21	25	27:24	–29	57	2	0	1	74	5.4
L	21	Mathieu Darche	T.B.	73	7	15	22	14:25	–14	20	1	1	0	120	5.8
C	77	Chris Gratton	T.B.	60	10	11	21	12:42	–7	77	1	0	1	92	10.9
D	55	Shane O'Brien	T.B.	77	4	17	21	21:13	–2	154	0	0	1	69	5.8
R	16	Jason Ward	T.B.	79	8	6	14	12:32	–18	42	1	1	0	85	9.4
C	29	Craig MacDonald	T.B.	65	2	9	11	10:52	–10	16	0	0	0	84	2.4
C	74	Nick Tarnasky	T.B.	80	6	4	10	08:14	–15	78	1	0	1	91	6.6
R	36	Andre Roy	T.B.	63	4	3	7	05:27	–1	108	0	0	0	38	10.5
D	37	Brad Lukowich	T.B.	59	1	6	7	16:36	–15	20	0	0	0	28	3.6
D	2	Alexandre Picard	PHI	4	0	0	0	13:01	–3	2	0	0	0	3	0.0
			T.B.	20	3	3	6	21:53	–9	8	1	0	1	21	14.3
			Total	24	3	3	6	20:25	–12	10	1	0	1	24	12.5
D	39	* Mike Lundin	T.B.	81	0	6	6	13:47	3	16	0	0	0	33	0.0
C	24	Andreas Karlsson	T.B.	58	2	2	4	09:39	–7	10	0	0	1	31	6.5
D	3	Doug Janik	T.B.	61	1	3	4	09:19	–3	45	0	0	0	23	4.3
C	34	Ryan Craig	T.B.	7	1	1	2	13:03	–1	0	1	0	0	8	12.5
R	42	Junior Lessard	DAL	2	0	0	0	12:05	–1	2	0	0	0	3	0.0
			T.B.	19	1	1	2	09:38	–5	9	0	0	0	18	5.6
			Total	21	1	1	2	09:52	–6	11	0	0	0	21	4.8
R	46	Kyle Wanvig	T.B.	7	1	0	1	10:09	–1	7	0	0	1	10	10.0
D	38	Jay Leach	T.B.	2	0	0	0	04:37	–1	0	0	0	0	0	0.0
C	49	* Blair Jones	T.B.	4	0	0	0	01:55	0	0	0	0	0	1	0.0
L	61	Karl Stewart	T.B.	9	0	0	0	04:06	–2	2	0	0	0	2	0.0
D	32	* Matt Smaby	T.B.	14	0	0	0	12:08	–6	12	0	0	0	7	0.0

Goaltending

No.	Goaltender	GPI	Mins	Avg	W	L	OT	EN	SO	GA	SA	S%	G	A	PIM
41	* Mike Smith	13	774	2.79	3	10	0	5	1	36	338	.893	0	1	6
40	Johan Holmqvist	45	2469	3.01	20	16	6	1	2	124	1129	.890	0	1	0
31	* Karri Ramo	22	1269	3.03	7	11	3	6	0	64	632	.899	0	1	4
30	Marc Denis	10	415	4.05	1	5	0	2	0	28	199	.859	0	0	2
	Totals	**82**	**4963**	**3.22**	**31**	**42**	**9**	**14**	**3**	**266**	**2312**	**.885**			

Barry Melrose

Head Coach

Born: Kelvington, Sask., July 15, 1956.

New club owners Oren Koules and Len Barrie named Barry Melrose the sixth head coach of the Tampa Bay Lightning by on June 24, 2008. A winner at every level he has coached, Melrose spent three seasons (1992 to 1995) as the head coach in Los Angeles, leading the Kings to the Stanley Cup Finals for the first time in 1993. Melrose began his coaching career in 1987 when he led the Western Hockey League's Medicine Hat Tigers to a 44-22-6 record and the Memorial Cup title.

Known for his no-nonsense approach and ability to develop young players, Melrose also coached the Seattle Thunderbirds for the 1988-89 season and the Adirondack Red Wings of the American Hockey League for three seasons (1989 to 1992). Melrose guided the Red Wings to the Calder Cup championship in 1991. He also served as the team's general manager during his final two seasons.

During his 11 years as a player, Melrose played 300 career games as a defenseman in the NHL with Winnipeg, Toronto and Detroit (1979 to 1986), recording 10 goals, 23 assists and 728 penalty minutes. He skated in seven Stanley Cup playoff games with the Toronto Maple Leafs, assisting on two goals and recording 38 penalty minutes. He also played three seasons with Cincinnati in the World Hockey Association (1976 to 1979).

Melrose most recently served as NHL studio analyst for ESPN and ESPN2. Melrose appeared regularly on ESPN2's NHL 2Night, the network's NHL news and highlights program. He also provided reports for SportsCenter, appeared on ESPN Radio and was a regular contributor to ESPN The Magazine. From 1996 to 2002, Melrose also called regular-season and playoff games for ESPN and ABC Sports (2000 to 2002). From 2003 to 2004, he provided studio analysis for ABC Sports' NHL telecasts.

In January 2004, Melrose became part owner of the Adirondack club in the United Hockey League.

Coaching Record

			Regular Season				Playoffs			
Season	Team	League	GC	W	L	O/T	GC	W	L	T
1987-88	Medicine Hat	WHL	72	44	22	6	16	12	4	....
1988-89	Seattle	WHL	72	33	35	4	....	....	....	....
1989-90	Adirondack	AHL	80	42	27	11	6	2	4	....
1990-91	Adirondack	AHL	80	33	37	10	2	0	2	....
1991-92	Adirondack	AHL	80	40	36	4	19	14	5	....
1992-93	**Los Angeles**	**NHL**	**84**	**39**	**35**	**10**	**24**	**13**	**11**	....
1993-94	**Los Angeles**	**NHL**	**84**	**27**	**45**	**12**	....	....	....	....
1994-95	**Los Angeles**	**NHL**	**41**	**13**	**21**	**7**	....	....	....	....
2003-04	Adirondack	UHL	1	0	0	1	....	....	....	....
2005-06	Adirondack	UHL	1	0	0	1	....	....	....	....
	NHL Totals		**209**	**79**	**101**	**29**	**24**	**13**	**11**	....

Club Records

Team

(Figures in brackets for season records are games played; records for fewest points, wins, ties, losses, goals, goals against are for 70 or more games)

Most Points	**106**	2003-04 (82)
Most Wins	**46**	2003-04 (82)
Most Ties	**16**	2002-03 (82)
Most Losses	**55**	1997-98 (82)
Most Goals	**253**	2006-07 (82)
Most Goals Against	**332**	1992-93 (84)
Fewest Points	**44**	1997-98 (82)
Fewest Wins	**17**	1997-98 (82)
Fewest Ties	**6**	2000-01 (82)
Fewest Losses	**22**	2003-04 (82)
Fewest Goals	**151**	1997-98 (82)
Fewest Goals Against	**192**	2003-04 (82)
Longest Winning Streak		
Overall	**8**	Feb. 23-Mar. 6/04
Home	**8**	Mar. 17-Apr. 8/06
Away	**7**	Jan. 7-Feb. 1/07
Longest Undefeated Streak		
Overall	**13**	Mar. 7-Apr. 2/03 (7 wins, 6 ties)
Home	**10**	Jan. 29-Mar. 12/04 (9 wins, 1 tie)
Away	**7**	Feb. 23-Mar. 10/04 (6 wins, 1 tie), Jan. 7-Feb. 1/07 (7 wins)
Longest Losing Streak		
Overall	**13**	Jan. 3-Feb. 2/98
Home	**10**	Jan. 3-Feb. 26/98
Away	**11**	Oct. 24-Dec. 10/97
Longest Winless Streak		
Overall	**16**	Oct. 10-Nov. 17/97 (15 losses, 1 tie), Jan. 2-Feb. 5/98 (14 losses, 2 ties)
Home	**11**	Jan. 2-Feb. 26/98 (10 losses, 1 tie)
Away	**17**	Dec. 2/99-Feb. 19/00 (14 losses, 3 ties)
Most Shutouts, Season	**9**	2001-02 (82)
Most PIM, Season	**1,823**	1997-98 (82)
Most Goals, Game	**9**	Nov. 8/03 (Pit. 0 at T.B. 9)

Individual

Most Seasons	**9**	Vincent Lecavalier
Most Games, Career	**710**	Vincent Lecavalier
Most Goals, Career	**273**	Vincent Lecavalier
Most Assists, Career	**339**	Brad Richards
Most Points, Career	**602**	Vincent Lecavalier (273G, 329A)
Most PIM, Career	**818**	Chris Gratton
Most Shutouts, Career	**14**	Nikolai Khabibulin
Longest Consecutive Games Streak	**388**	Cory Sarich (Nov. 27/01-Apr. 7/07)
Most Goals, Season	**52**	Vincent Lecavalier (2006-07)
Most Assists, Season	**68**	Brad Richards (2005-06)
Most Points, Season	**108**	Vincent Lecavalier (2006-07; 52G, 56A)
Most PIM, Season	**258**	Enrico Ciccone (1995-96)
Most Points, Defenseman, Season	**65**	Roman Hamrlik (1995-96; 16G, 49A)
Most Points, Center, Season	**108**	Vincent Lecavalier (2006-07; 52G, 56A)
Most Points, Right Wing, Season	**102**	Martin St. Louis (2006-07; 43G, 59A)
Most Points, Left Wing, Season	**80**	Cory Stillman (2003-04; 25G, 55A), Vaclav Prospal (2005-06; 25G, 55A)
Most Points, Rookie, Season	**62**	Brad Richards (2000-01; 21G, 41A)
Most Shutouts, Season	**7**	Nikolai Khabibulin (2001-02)
Most Goals, Game	**4**	Chris Kontos (Oct. 7/92)
Most Assists, Game	**4**	Six times
Most Points, Game	**6**	Doug Crossman (Nov. 7/92; 3G, 3A)

Captains' History

No captain, 1992-93 to 1994-95; Paul Ysebaert, 1995-96, 1996-97; Paul Ysebaert and Mikael Renberg, 1997-98; Rob Zamuner, 1998-99; Bill Houlder, Chris Gratton and Vincent Lecavalier, 1999-2000; Vincent Lecavalier, 2000-01; no captain, 2001-02; Dave Andreychuk, 2002-03, 2003-04; Dave Andreychuk and no captain, 2005-06; Tim Taylor, 2006-07, 2007-08.

All-time Record vs. Other Clubs

Regular Season

	At Home								On Road								Total							
	GP	W	L	T	OL	GF	GA	PTS	GP	W	L	T	OL	GF	GA	PTS	GP	W	L	T	OL	GF	GA	PTS
Anaheim	10	4	6	0	0	20	27	8	9	3	5	1	0	22	28	7	19	7	11	1	0	42	55	15
Atlanta	25	16	7	1	1	93	64	34	25	7	12	3	3	65	82	20	50	23	19	4	4	158	146	54
Boston	29	11	13	3	2	84	87	27	29	3	17	6	3	70	110	15	58	14	30	9	5	154	197	42
Buffalo	29	6	17	3	3	61	93	18	29	9	16	2	2	81	94	22	58	15	33	5	5	142	187	40
Calgary	11	5	5	1	0	37	41	11	11	5	5	0	1	27	34	11	22	10	10	1	1	64	75	22
Carolina	38	23	12	3	0	113	96	49	39	10	20	7	2	108	125	29	77	33	32	10	2	221	221	78
Chicago	12	5	3	3	1	29	30	14	15	4	9	2	0	36	50	10	27	9	12	5	1	65	80	24
Colorado	13	8	3	1	1	39	35	18	14	3	9	2	0	30	54	8	27	11	12	3	1	69	89	26
Columbus	4	3	1	0	0	9	5	6	4	1	2	1	0	7	10	3	8	4	3	1	0	16	15	9
Dallas	14	1	10	2	1	21	39	5	12	4	7	1	0	33	42	9	26	5	17	3	1	54	81	14
Detroit	15	4	9	1	1	46	67	10	13	1	11	1	0	23	51	3	28	5	20	2	1	69	118	13
Edmonton	12	4	5	2	1	35	38	11	11	4	7	0	0	24	27	8	23	8	12	2	1	59	65	19
Florida	40	17	16	6	1	91	111	41	40	10	22	4	4	100	134	28	80	27	38	10	5	191	245	69
Los Angeles	11	6	4	0	1	26	24	13	12	9	1	2	0	40	25	20	23	15	5	2	1	66	49	33
Minnesota	4	1	2	1	0	10	12	3	4	1	3	0	0	11	15	2	8	2	5	1	0	21	27	5
Montreal	29	11	12	5	1	69	82	28	28	12	15	1	0	67	80	25	57	23	27	6	1	136	162	53
Nashville	5	2	1	2	0	15	13	6	7	5	2	0	0	18	13	10	12	7	3	2	0	33	26	16
New Jersey	31	11	15	5	0	70	90	27	32	9	20	2	1	63	114	21	63	20	35	7	1	133	204	48
NY Islanders	32	17	12	2	1	92	96	37	31	15	14	1	1	83	90	32	63	32	26	3	2	175	186	69
NY Rangers	31	15	12	3	1	103	98	34	33	14	16	2	1	95	106	31	64	29	28	5	2	198	204	65
Ottawa	29	10	16	2	1	84	107	23	29	10	18	0	1	66	107	21	58	20	34	2	2	150	214	44
Philadelphia	32	13	17	1	1	96	94	28	31	9	15	7	0	72	92	25	63	22	32	8	1	168	186	53
Phoenix	11	6	5	0	0	38	36	12	12	6	6	0	0	29	29	12	23	12	11	0	0	67	65	24
Pittsburgh	29	16	11	2	0	89	70	34	29	10	15	3	1	79	104	24	58	26	26	5	1	168	174	58
St. Louis	14	6	5	3	0	43	46	15	12	2	9	0	1	29	48	5	26	8	14	3	1	72	94	20
San Jose	13	7	5	1	0	34	35	15	11	6	4	1	0	37	35	13	24	13	9	2	0	71	70	28
Toronto	26	7	17	1	1	56	85	16	27	7	17	1	2	69	104	17	53	14	34	2	3	125	189	33
Vancouver	10	4	5	0	1	35	40	9	10	0	7	2	1	18	45	3	20	4	12	2	2	53	85	12
Washington	41	16	22	2	1	106	127	35	41	12	23	4	2	103	146	30	82	28	45	6	3	209	273	65
Totals	**600**	**255**	**268**	**56**	**21**	**1644**	**1788**	**587**	**600**	**191**	**327**	**56**	**26**	**1505**	**1994**	**464**	**1200**	**446**	**595**	**112**	**47**	**3149**	**3782**	**1051**

Playoffs

	Series	W	L	GP	W	L	T	GF	GA	Last Mtg.	Rnd.	Result
Calgary	1	1	0	7	4	3	0	13	14	2004	F	W 4-3
Montreal	1	1	0	4	4	0	0	14	5	2004	CSF	W 4-0
New Jersey	2	0	2	11	3	8	0	22	33	2007	CQF	L 2-4
NY Islanders	1	1	0	5	4	1	0	12	5	2004	CQF	W 4-1
Ottawa	1	0	1	5	1	4	0	13	23	2006	CQF	L 1-4
Philadelphia	2	1	1	13	6	7	0	34	45	2004	CF	W 4-3
Washington	1	1	0	6	4	2	0	14	15	2003	CQF	W 4-2
Totals	**9**	**5**	**4**	**51**	**26**	**25**	**0**	**122**	**140**			

Playoff Results 2008-2003

Year	Round	Opponent	Result	GF	GA
2007	CQF	New Jersey	L 2-4	14	19
2006	CQF	Ottawa	L 1-4	13	23
2004	**F**	**Calgary**	**W 4-3**	**13**	**14**
	CF	Philadelphia	W 4-3	21	19
	CSF	Montreal	W 4-0	14	5
	CQF	NY Islanders	W 4-1	12	5
2003	CSF	New Jersey	L 1-4	8	14
	CQF	Washington	W 4-2	14	15

Abbreviations: Round: F – Final; **CF** – conference final; **CSF** – conference semi-final; **CQF** – conference quarter-final.

Carolina totals include Hartford, 1992-93 to 1996-97.
Dallas totals include Minnesota North Stars, 1992-93.

Colorado totals include Quebec, 1992-93 to 1994-95.
Phoenix totals include Winnipeg, 1992-93 to 1995-96.

2007-08 Results

Oct.	4	New Jersey	3-1		5	at Ottawa	3-4*
	6	Atlanta	5-2		8	at NY Rangers	5-3
	10	Florida	2-1		10	Pittsburgh	1-4
	13	at Florida	4-6		12	at Florida	5-3
	18	at Boston	1-4		15	Colorado	0-3
	20	Atlanta	6-2		18	at Pittsburgh	3-0
	24	at Washington	3-5		19	at Ottawa	2-0
	25	Philadelphia	5-2		22	Edmonton	4-3
	27	Buffalo	3-4*		24	Ottawa	4-8
	29	at NY Rangers	1-3		29	Buffalo	2-4
	31	at New Jersey	1-6		31	Vancouver	4-3
Nov.	1	at NY Islanders	0-4	**Feb.**	2	Florida	2-3
	3	Atlanta	4-6		5	at St. Louis	5-4
	5	at Florida	3-4		7	at Nashville	2-1*
	7	Florida	3-1		9	at Atlanta	1-2*
	8	at Carolina	5-1		12	Montreal	3-2
	10	at Washington	5-2		14	at Philadelphia	5-3
	14	Carolina	6-1		16	Washington	2-3
	16	Washington	5-2		20	at Buffalo	3-4*
	19	at Atlanta	3-4*		21	at NY Islanders	0-1
	21	NY Rangers	1-2		23	Boston	3-5
	23	at Carolina	3-4		27	Minnesota	2-3
	24	New Jersey	2-3		29	Toronto	3-2*
	28	at Chicago	1-5	**Mar.**	1	at Carolina	1-5
	29	at Detroit	2-4		4	Pittsburgh	0-2
Dec.	1	Boston	4-1		6	at Philadelphia	2-3
	4	Ottawa	4-3†		7	at New Jersey	1-2*
	6	Carolina	2-1		9	at Columbus	3-5
	8	NY Islanders	2-3*		11	NY Islanders	8-4
	10	at Toronto	1-6		13	at Boston	3-1
	11	at Montreal	3-2†		15	NY Rangers	3-0
	13	Calgary	6-9		19	at Buffalo	4-7
	15	Washington	2-3		20	at Pittsburgh	2-4
	18	at Atlanta	2-6		22	at Florida	2-4
	20	Toronto	2-1		25	Florida	3-1
	22	Carolina	1-4		27	Washington	3-4*
	26	at Washington	2-3		29	Carolina	2-1
	27	Montreal	2-5		31	Atlanta	0-2
	29	Philadelphia	2-4	**Apr.**	2	at Carolina	2-6
Jan.	1	at Toronto	3-4†		3	at Washington	1-4
	3	at Montreal	3-6		5	at Atlanta	1-4

* – Overtime † – Shootout

Entry Draft Selections 2008-1994

Name in bold denotes played in NHL.

2008
Pick
1 Steven Stamkos
117 James Wright
122 Dustin Tokarski
147 Kyle De Coste
152 Mark Barberio
160 Luke Witkowski
182 Matias Sointu
203 David Carle

2007
Pick
47 Dana Tyrell
75 Luca Cunti
77 Alexander Killorn
107 Mitch Fadden
150 Matt Marshall
167 Johan Harju
183 Torrie Jung
197 Michael Ward
210 Justin Courtnall

2006
Pick
15 Riku Helenius
78 Kevin Quick
168 Dane Crowley
198 Denis Kazionov

2005
Pick
30 Vladimir Mihalik
73 Radek Smolenak
89 Chris Lawrence
92 Marek Bartanus
102 **Blair Jones**
133 Stanislav Lascek
163 Marek Kvapil
165 Kevin Beech
225 John Wessbecker

2004
Pick
30 Andy Rogers
65 Mark Tobin
102 **Mike Lundin**
158 Brandon Elliott
163 Dusty Collins
188 Jan Zapletal
191 **Karri Ramo**
245 Justin Keller

2003
Pick
34 Mike Egener
41 **Matt Smaby**
96 Jonathan Boutin
192 **Doug O'Brien**
224 **Gerald Coleman**
227 Jay Rosehill
255 Raimonds Danilics
256 Brady Greco
273 Albert Vishnyakov
286 Zbynek Hrdel
287 **Nick Tarnasky**

2002
Pick
60 Adam Henrich
100 Dmitri Kazionov
135 Joe Pearce
162 Gerard Dicaire
170 P.J. Atherton
174 Karri Akkanen
183 **Paul Ranger**
213 **Fredrik Norrena**
233 Vasily Koshechkin
255 **Ryan Craig**
256 **Darren Reid**
286 Alexei Glukhov
287 John Toffey

2001
Pick
3 **Alexander Svitov**
47 Alexander Polushin
61 Andreas Holmqvist
94 **Evgeny Artyukhin**
123 Aaron Lobb
138 Paul Lynch
188 Art Femenella
219 Dennis Packard
222 Jeremy Van Hoof
252 J.F. Soucy
259 Dmitri Bezrukov
261 Vitali Smolyaninov
281 Ilja Solarev
289 Henrik Bergfors

2000
Pick
8 **Nikita Alexeev**
34 Ruslan Zainullin
81 **Alexander Kharitonov**
126 Johan Hagglund
161 Pavel Sedov
191 Aaron Gionet
222 Marek Priechodsky
226 **Brian Eklund**
233 Alexander Polukeyev
263 **Thomas Ziegler**

1999
Pick
47 **Sheldon Keefe**
67 **Evgeny Konstantinov**
75 Brett Scheffelmaier
88 **Jimmie Olvestad**
127 **Kaspars Astashenko**
148 Michal Lanicek
182 **Fedor Fedorov**
187 Ivan Rachunek
216 Erkki Rajamaki
244 Mikko Kuparinen

1998
Pick
1 **Vincent Lecavalier**
64 **Brad Richards**
72 **Dmitry Afanasenkov**
92 **Eric Beaudoin**
121 Curtis Rich
146 Sergei Kuznetsov
174 Brett Allan
194 Oak Hewer
221 Daniel Hulak
229 Chris Lyness
252 **Martin Cibak**

1997
Pick
7 **Paul Mara**
33 Kyle Kos
61 **Matt Elich**
108 Mark Thompson
109 Jan Sulc
112 **Karel Betik**
153 **Andrei Skopintsev**
168 Justin Jack
170 Eero Somervuori
185 Samuel St-Pierre
198 Shawn Skolney
224 **Paul Comrie**

1996
Pick
16 **Mario Larocque**
69 Curtis Tipler
125 Jason Robinson
152 Nikolai Ignatov
157 **Xavier Delisle**
179 **Pavel Kubina**

1995
Pick
5 **Daymond Langkow**
30 **Mike McBain**
56 **Shane Willis**
108 Konstantin Golokhvastov
134 Eduard Pershin
160 Cory Murphy
186 Joe Cardarelli
212 **Zac Bierk**

1994
Pick
8 **Jason Wiemer**
34 Colin Cloutier
55 Vadim Epanchintsev
86 Dmitri Klevakin
137 Daniel Juden
138 **Bryce Salvador**
164 Chris Maillet
190 Alexei Baranov
216 Yuri Smirnov
242 Shawn Gervais
268 **Brian White**

General Managers' History

Phil Esposito, 1992-93 to 1997-98; Jacques Demers, 1998-99; Rick Dudley, 1999-2000, 2000-01; Rick Dudley and Jay Feaster, 2001-02; Jay Feaster, 2002-03 to 2007-08.

Brian Lawton

Vice President of Hockey Operations

Born: New Brunswick, NJ, June 29, 1965.

Brian Lawton was named Vice President of Hockey Operations for the Tampa Bay Lightning on June 25, 2008. Lawton spent the previous 14 years as a player agent, representing prominent NHLers such as Mike Modano, Mark Parrish and the Lightning's Jeff Halpern, to name a few. A native of New Jersey who grew up in Rhode Island, Lawton was drafted first overall by the Minnesota North Stars in 1983, becoming the first player ever selected first overall directly out of a U.S. high school. He went on to play 483 NHL games for Minnesota, the New York Rangers, Hartford, Quebec, Boston and San Jose between 1983-84 and 1992-93.

Having served four seasons as his team's player representative for the NHL Players Association, Lawton put that knowledge to use when he retired by becoming a player agent. He started his own firm, Lawton Sport and Financial, in 1994, and became a prominent agent, negotiating more than $300 million in player contracts.

Named three times to The Hockey News' list of the "100 Most Powerful People in Hockey," Lawton eventually sold his business in 1998 to Octagon Athlete Representation, one of the largest sports agencies in the United States. Based out of Minneapolis, Lawton became Managing Director of Octagon's Hockey Division. With Octagon Lawton built the second largest hockey agency in the NHL, with clients that included Bret Hedican, Keith Carney, Ryan Miller, Ryan Malone and Kari Lehtonen.

A graduate of Mount Saint Charles Academy in Woonsocket, Rhode Island, Lawton represented the U.S. on several occasions, including the 1982 World Junior Championship, the 1983 World Championship, the 1984 Canada Cup, the 1987 World Championship and the 1988 Canada Cup.

Club Directory

St. Pete Times Forum

Tampa Bay Lightning
St. Pete Times Forum
401 Channelside Drive
Tampa, FL 33602
Phone **813/301-6500**
FAX 813/301-1480
Ticket Info. 813/301-6600
www.tampabaylightning.com
Capacity: 19,758

Executive

Ownership Group . . . OK Hockey
Owner, Governor . . . Oren Koules
Owner, Alternate Governor . . . Len Barrie
Owners . . . Mark Burg, Russell Belinsky, Dr. Richard C. Lehman, Irwin Novack, Craig Sher, Jordan Zimmerman
Vice President of Hockey Operations . . . Brian Lawton
Executive Vice President/Chief Operating Officer . . . Sean Henry
Executive VP of Corporate Sales & Marketing . . . Harry Hutt
Executive VP, Business Operations . . . Brian Rogers
Vice President of Sponsorship Sales . . . Rob Keith
Director of Govt. Relations/Community Affairs . . . Ron Pierce
Vice President of Sales and Marketing . . . Brad Lott
Vice President of Corporate Partnerships . . . Arden Robbins
Vice President of Corporate Sales . . . Kyle Draper
Executive Assistants . . . Michele Rooney, Julie Stein
Executive Vice President, Communications . . . Bill Wickett
Vice President, General Counsel . . . Paul Davis
Executive Vice President of Finance/CFO . . . Joe Fada
Executive Director of Lightning Foundation . . . Nancy Crane
Sr. Vice President of Administration . . . David Everett

Hockey Operations

Assistant General Managers . . . Claude Loiselle, Tom Kurvers
Director of Player Personnel . . . Jim Hammett
Assistant to the General Manager . . . Ryan Belec
Hockey Ops Executive Assistant . . . Liz Sylvia
Special Asst. to the VP of Hockey Ops . . . Mike Vernon
Head Professional Scout . . . Greg Malone
Head Coach . . . Barry Melrose
Assistant Coaches . . . Rick Tocchet, Wes Walz, Cap Raeder
Strength & Conditioning Coach . . . Kevin Ziegler
Video Coach . . . Nigel Kirwan
Scouting Staff . . . Angelo Bumbacco, Charlie Hodge, Gerry O'Flaherty, Mikael Andersson, Stephen Baker, Dave Heitz, Kari Kettunen, Miroslav Prihoda, Billy Coupland, Jim Hammett, Darryl Plandowski, Brad Stepan
Director of Team Services . . . Phil Thibodeau
Medical Director . . . Dr. Ira Guttentag
Head Athletic Trainer . . . Tom Mulligan
Assistant Athletic Trainer . . . Michael Poirier
Massage Therapist . . . Mike Griebel
Equipment Manager . . . Ray Thill
Assistant Equipment Managers . . . Rob Kennedy, Clay Roffer
General Manager, Norfolk Admirals . . . Mike Butters
Head Coach, Norfolk Admirals . . . Darren Rumble
Assistant Coach, Norfolk Admirals . . . Alan May
Head Athletic Trainer, Norfolk Admirals . . . Brad Chavis
Head Equipment Mgr, Norfolk Admirals . . . Peter Henderson
Team Physician . . . Dr. Ira Guttentag

Premium Services

Director of Premium Services . . . Amanda Graul
Premium Services Ticket Manager . . . Missy Davis
Premium Services Suite Manager . . . Lakisha Sharpe

Finance

Director of Accounting . . . Doug Riefler
Accounts Payable . . . Donna Clark
Staff Accountants . . . Kathleen Cook, Krystal Mihopulos

Internal Support Staff

Sr. Vice President of Administration . . . David Everett
Assistant Information Services Manager . . . Rosie Chhuor
Web Administrator . . . Jamie Williams

Box Office

Vice President of Ticket Operations . . . Jim Mannino
Asst. Box Office Manager . . . Helen Junker
Box Office Coordinators . . . Bobby Loman, Chrissy Hitchman, Chris Lau, Liz Mulhearn

Ticket Sales

Vice President of Sales . . . Patrick Duffy
Director of Suite Sales . . . Matt Hill
Director of Corporate Sales . . . Mike Clough
Director of Group Sales . . . Courtney Simons
Director of Outside Sales . . . Ryan West

Sponsorship Sales and Marketing

Sr. Director of Marketing and Promotions . . . Mark Gullett
Marketing Coordinator . . . Bobby Lanza
Marketing Coordinator/Plaza Host . . . Greg Wolf
Director of Corporate Partnerships . . . Giles Dowden
Sr. Director of Marketing . . . Holly Brown
Director of Broadcast Production & Game Ops . . . Jim Ciotoli
Entertainment Manager . . . Hope Donnelly
Director of Fan Development . . . David Cole

Communications

Director of Public Relations . . . Jay Preble
Media Relations Manager . . . Brian Breseman
Community Relations/Lightning Foundation Mngr. . . Arlynn Haarer
Public Relations Coordinator . . . Dana O'Shea

Broadcast Information

Television . . . SunSports Network
Television Broadcasters . . . Rick Peckham, Bobby "the Chief" Taylor, Paul Kennedy
Radio . . . WDAE 620 AM, WHOO 1080 AM (Orlando)
Radio Broadcasters . . . David Mishkin, Phil Esposito, Matt Sammon

Toronto Maple Leafs

2007-08 Results: 36W-35L-7OTL-4SOL 83PTS.

Fifth, Northeast Division

Key Off-Season Signings/Acquisitions

2008

June 10 • Named **Ron Wilson** head coach.

20 • Acquired RW **Jamal Mayers** from St. Louis for a 3rd-round pick in 2008.

20 • Selected D **Luke Schenn** (Kelowna, WHL) fifth overall in 2008 Entry Draft.

July 1 • Signed D **Jeff Finger**, LW **Niklas Hagman** and G **Curtis Joseph**.

3 • Acquired C **Mikhail Grabovski** from Montreal for the rights to D **Greg Pateryn** and a 2nd-round pick in 2010.

3 • Re-signed C **Dominic Moore**.

7 • Re-signed C **Matt Stajan**.

8 • Named **Joe Nieuwendyk** special assistant to the general manager.

14 • Acquired LW **Ryan Hollweg** from NY Rangers for a 5th-round pick in 2009.

15 • Re-signed RW **Ben Ondrus**.

2008-09 Schedule

Oct.	Thu.	9	at Detroit		Sat.	10	at Philadelphia
	Sat.	11	Montreal		Tue.	13	Nashville
	Mon.	13	St. Louis*		Thu.	15	at Carolina
	Fri.	17	at NY Rangers		Fri.	16	at Atlanta
	Sat.	18	at Pittsburgh		Mon.	19	Carolina
	Tue.	21	Anaheim		Wed.	21	Boston
	Thu.	23	at Boston		Tue.	27	at Minnesota
	Sat.	25	Ottawa		Thu.	29	at Colorado
	Tue.	28	Tampa Bay		Sat.	31	Pittsburgh
	Wed.	29	at New Jersey	**Feb.**	Tue.	3	Florida
Nov.	Sat.	1	NY Rangers		Wed.	4	at Buffalo
	Sun.	2	at Carolina*		Sat.	7	at Montreal
	Tue.	4	Carolina		Tue.	10	at Florida
	Thu.	6	at Boston		Thu.	12	at Tampa Bay
	Sat.	8	Montreal		Sat.	14	Pittsburgh
	Tue.	11	at Calgary		Tue.	17	Buffalo
	Thu.	13	at Edmonton		Thu.	19	Columbus
	Sat.	15	at Vancouver*		Sat.	21	Vancouver
	Mon.	17	Boston		Sun.	22	at NY Rangers
	Sat.	22	Chicago		Wed.	25	NY Rangers
	Tue.	25	Atlanta		Thu.	26	at NY Islanders
	Thu.	27	at Ottawa		Sat.	28	at Ottawa
	Sat.	29	Philadelphia	**Mar.**	Tue.	3	New Jersey
Dec.	Mon.	1	at Los Angeles		Thu.	5	at Washington
	Tue.	2	at San Jose		Sat.	7	Edmonton
	Thu.	4	at Phoenix		Mon.	9	at Ottawa
	Sat.	6	Washington		Tue.	10	NY Islanders
	Mon.	8	NY Islanders		Thu.	12	Tampa Bay
	Fri.	12	at Buffalo		Sat.	14	Calgary
	Tue.	16	New Jersey		Tue.	17	at Tampa Bay
	Thu.	18	at Boston		Thu.	19	at Florida
	Sat.	20	at Pittsburgh		Sat.	21	at Montreal
	Mon.	22	at Atlanta		Tue.	24	Washington
	Tue.	23	Dallas		Fri.	27	at Buffalo
	Fri.	26	at NY Islanders		Sat.	28	Boston
	Sun.	28	at Washington	**Apr.**	Wed.	1	Philadelphia
	Tue.	30	Atlanta		Fri.	3	at Philadelphia
Jan.	Thu.	1	Buffalo		Sat.	4	Montreal
	Sat.	3	Ottawa		Tue.	7	at New Jersey
	Tue.	6	Florida		Wed.	8	Buffalo
	Thu.	8	at Montreal		Sat.	11	Ottawa

* Denotes afternoon game.

Year-by-Year Record

Season	GP	Home W	L	T	OL	Road W	L	T	OL	Overall W	L	T	OL	GF	GA	Pts.	Finished	Playoff Result
2007-08	82	18	17	....	6	18	18	....	5	36	35	....	11	231	260	83	5th, Northeast Div.	Out of Playoffs
2006-07	82	21	15	....	5	19	16	....	6	40	31	....	11	258	269	91	3rd, Northeast Div.	Out of Playoffs
2005-06	82	26	12	....	3	15	21	....	5	41	33	....	8	257	270	90	4th, Northeast Div.	Out of Playoffs
2004-05	....	....	....	....	....	....	....	....	....	....	....	....	....	....	....	....		
2003-04	82	22	14	3	2	23	10	7	1	45	24	10	3	242	204	103	2nd, Northeast Div.	Lost Conf. Semi-Final
2002-03	82	24	13	4	0	20	15	3	3	44	28	7	3	236	208	98	2nd, Northeast Div.	Lost Conf. Quarter-Final
2001-02	82	24	11	6	0	19	14	4	4	43	25	10	4	249	207	100	2nd, Northeast Div.	Lost Conf. Championship
2000-01	82	19	11	7	4	18	18	4	1	37	29	11	5	232	207	90	3rd, Northeast Div.	Lost Conf. Semi-Final
1999-2000	82	24	12	5	0	21	15	2	3	45	27	7	3	246	222	100	1st, Northeast Div.	Lost Conf. Semi-Final
1998-99	82	23	13	5	....	22	17	2	....	45	30	7	....	268	231	97	2nd, Northeast Div.	Lost Conf. Championship
1997-98	82	16	20	5	....	14	23	4	....	30	43	9	....	194	237	69	6th, Central Div.	Out of Playoffs
1996-97	82	18	20	3	....	12	24	5	....	30	44	8	....	230	273	68	6th, Central Div.	Out of Playoffs
1995-96	82	19	15	7	....	15	21	5	....	34	36	12	....	247	252	80	3rd, Central Div.	Lost Conf. Quarter-Final
1994-95	48	15	7	2	....	6	12	6	....	21	19	8	....	135	146	50	4th, Central Div.	Lost Conf. Quarter-Final
1993-94	84	23	15	4	....	20	14	8	....	43	29	12	....	280	243	98	2nd, Central Div.	Lost Conf. Championship
1992-93	84	25	11	6	....	19	18	5	....	44	29	11	....	288	241	99	3rd, Norris Div.	Lost Conf. Championship
1991-92	80	21	16	3	....	9	27	4	....	30	43	7	....	234	294	67	5th, Norris Div.	Out of Playoffs
1990-91	80	15	21	4	....	8	25	7	....	23	46	11	....	241	318	57	5th, Norris Div.	Out of Playoffs
1989-90	80	24	14	2	....	14	24	2	....	38	38	4	....	337	358	80	3rd, Norris Div.	Lost Div. Semi-Final
1988-89	80	15	20	5	....	13	26	1	....	28	46	6	....	259	342	62	5th, Norris Div.	Out of Playoffs
1987-88	80	14	20	6	....	7	29	4	....	21	49	10	....	273	345	52	4th, Norris Div.	Lost Div. Semi-Final
1986-87	80	22	14	4	....	10	28	2	....	32	42	6	....	286	319	70	4th, Norris Div.	Lost Div. Final
1985-86	80	16	21	3	....	9	27	4	....	25	48	7	....	311	386	57	4th, Norris Div.	Lost Div. Final
1984-85	80	10	28	2	....	10	24	6	....	20	52	8	....	253	358	48	5th, Norris Div.	Out of Playoffs
1983-84	80	17	16	7	....	9	29	2	....	26	45	9	....	303	387	61	5th, Norris Div.	Out of Playoffs
1982-83	80	20	15	5	....	8	25	7	....	28	40	12	....	293	330	68	3rd, Norris Div.	Lost Div. Semi-Final
1981-82	80	12	20	8	....	8	24	8	....	20	44	16	....	298	380	56	5th, Norris Div.	Out of Playoffs
1980-81	80	14	21	5	....	14	16	10	....	28	37	15	....	322	367	71	5th, Adams Div.	Lost Prelim. Round
1979-80	80	17	19	4	....	18	21	1	....	35	40	5	....	304	327	75	4th, Adams Div.	Lost Prelim. Round
1978-79	80	20	12	8	....	14	21	5	....	34	33	13	....	267	252	81	3rd, Adams Div.	Lost Quarter-Final
1977-78	80	21	13	6	....	20	16	4	....	41	29	10	....	271	237	92	3rd, Adams Div.	Lost Semi-Final
1976-77	80	18	13	9	....	15	19	6	....	33	32	15	....	301	285	81	3rd, Adams Div.	Lost Quarter-Final
1975-76	80	23	12	5	....	11	19	10	....	34	31	15	....	294	276	83	3rd, Adams Div.	Lost Quarter-Final
1974-75	80	19	12	9	....	12	21	7	....	31	33	16	....	280	309	78	3rd, Adams Div.	Lost Quarter-Final
1973-74	78	21	11	7	....	14	16	9	....	35	27	16	....	274	230	86	4th, East Div.	Lost Quarter-Final
1972-73	78	20	12	7	....	7	29	3	....	27	41	10	....	247	279	64	6th, East Div.	Out of Playoffs
1971-72	78	21	11	7	....	12	20	7	....	33	31	14	....	209	208	80	4th, East Div.	Lost Quarter-Final
1970-71	78	24	9	6	....	13	24	2	....	37	33	8	....	248	211	82	4th, East Div.	Lost Quarter-Final
1969-70	76	18	13	7	....	11	21	6	....	29	34	13	....	222	242	71	6th, East Div.	Out of Playoffs
1968-69	76	20	8	10	....	15	18	5	....	35	26	15	....	234	217	85	4th, East Div.	Lost Quarter-Final
1967-68	74	24	9	4	....	9	22	6	....	33	31	10	....	209	176	76	5th, East Div.	Out of Playoffs
1966-67	**70**	**21**	**8**	**6**	....	**11**	**19**	**5**	....	**32**	**27**	**11**	....	**204**	**211**	**75**	**3rd,**	**Won Stanley Cup**
1965-66	70	22	9	4	....	12	16	7	....	34	25	11	....	208	187	79	3rd,	Lost Semi-Final
1964-65	70	17	15	3	....	13	11	11	....	30	26	14	....	204	173	74	4th,	Lost Semi-Final
1963-64	**70**	**22**	**7**	**6**	....	**11**	**18**	**6**	....	**33**	**25**	**12**	....	**192**	**172**	**78**	**3rd,**	**Won Stanley Cup**
1962-63	**70**	**21**	**8**	**6**	....	**14**	**15**	**6**	....	**35**	**23**	**12**	....	**221**	**180**	**82**	**1st,**	**Won Stanley Cup**
1961-62	**70**	**25**	**5**	**5**	....	**12**	**17**	**6**	....	**37**	**22**	**11**	....	**232**	**180**	**85**	**2nd,**	**Won Stanley Cup**
1960-61	70	21	6	8	....	18	13	4	....	39	19	12	....	234	176	90	2nd,	Lost Semi-Final
1959-60	70	20	9	6	....	15	17	3	....	35	26	9	....	199	195	79	2nd,	Lost Final
1958-59	70	17	13	5	....	10	19	6	....	27	32	11	....	189	201	65	4th,	Lost Final
1957-58	70	12	16	7	....	9	22	4	....	21	38	11	....	192	226	53	6th,	Out of Playoffs
1956-57	70	12	16	7	....	9	18	8	....	21	34	15	....	174	192	57	5th,	Out of Playoffs
1955-56	70	19	10	6	....	5	23	7	....	24	33	13	....	153	181	61	4th,	Lost Semi-Final
1954-55	70	14	10	11	....	10	14	11	....	24	24	22	....	147	135	70	3rd,	Lost Semi-Final
1953-54	70	22	6	7	....	10	18	7	....	32	24	14	....	152	131	78	3rd,	Lost Semi-Final
1952-53	70	17	12	6	....	10	18	7	....	27	30	13	....	156	167	67	5th,	Out of Playoffs
1951-52	70	17	10	8	....	12	15	8	....	29	25	16	....	168	157	74	3rd,	Lost Semi-Final
1950-51	**70**	**22**	**8**	**5**	....	**19**	**8**	**8**	....	**41**	**16**	**13**	....	**212**	**138**	**95**	**2nd,**	**Won Stanley Cup**
1949-50	70	18	9	8	....	13	18	4	....	31	27	12	....	176	173	74	3rd,	Lost Semi-Final
1948-49	**60**	**12**	**8**	**10**	....	**10**	**17**	**3**	....	**22**	**25**	**13**	....	**147**	**161**	**57**	**4th,**	**Won Stanley Cup**
1947-48	**60**	**22**	**3**	**5**	....	**10**	**12**	**8**	....	**32**	**15**	**13**	....	**182**	**143**	**77**	**1st,**	**Won Stanley Cup**
1946-47	**60**	**20**	**8**	**2**	....	**11**	**11**	**8**	....	**31**	**19**	**10**	....	**209**	**172**	**72**	**2nd,**	**Won Stanley Cup**
1945-46	50	10	13	2	....	9	11	5	....	19	24	7	....	174	185	45	5th,	Out of Playoffs
1944-45	**50**	**13**	**9**	**3**	....	**11**	**13**	**1**	....	**24**	**22**	**4**	....	**183**	**161**	**52**	**3rd,**	**Won Stanley Cup**
1943-44	50	13	11	1	....	10	12	3	....	23	23	4	....	214	174	50	3rd,	Lost Semi-Final
1942-43	50	17	6	2	....	5	13	7	....	22	19	9	....	198	159	53	3rd,	Lost Semi-Final
1941-42	**48**	**18**	**6**	**0**	....	**9**	**12**	**3**	....	**27**	**18**	**3**	....	**158**	**136**	**57**	**2nd,**	**Won Stanley Cup**
1940-41	48	16	5	3	....	12	9	3	....	28	14	6	....	145	99	62	2nd,	Lost Semi-Final
1939-40	48	15	3	6	....	10	14	0	....	25	17	6	....	134	110	56	3rd,	Lost Final
1938-39	48	13	8	3	....	6	12	6	....	19	20	9	....	114	107	47	3rd,	Lost Final
1937-38	48	13	6	5	....	11	9	4	....	24	15	9	....	151	127	57	1st, Cdn. Div.	Lost Final
1936-37	48	14	9	1	....	8	12	4	....	22	21	5	....	119	115	49	3rd, Cdn. Div.	Lost Quarter-Final
1935-36	48	15	4	5	....	8	15	1	....	23	19	6	....	126	106	52	2nd, Cdn. Div.	Lost Final
1934-35	48	16	6	2	....	14	8	2	....	30	14	4	....	157	111	64	1st, Cdn. Div.	Lost Final
1933-34	48	19	2	3	....	7	11	6	....	26	13	9	....	174	119	61	1st, Cdn. Div.	Lost Semi-Final
1932-33	48	16	4	4	....	8	14	2	....	24	18	6	....	119	111	54	1st, Cdn. Div.	Lost Final
1931-32	**48**	**17**	**4**	**3**	....	**6**	**14**	**4**	....	**23**	**18**	**7**	....	**155**	**127**	**53**	**2nd, Cdn. Div.**	**Won Stanley Cup**
1930-31	44	15	4	3	....	7	9	6	....	22	13	9	....	118	99	53	2nd, Cdn. Div.	Lost Quarter-Final
1929-30	44	10	8	4	....	7	13	2	....	17	21	6	....	116	124	40	4th, Cdn. Div.	Out of Playoffs
1928-29	44	15	5	2	....	6	13	3	....	21	18	5	....	85	69	47	3rd, Cdn. Div.	Lost Semi-Final
1927-28	44	9	8	5	....	9	10	3	....	18	18	8	....	89	88	44	4th, Cdn. Div.	Out of Playoffs
1926-27*	44	10	10	2	....	5	14	3	....	15	24	5	....	79	94	35	5th, Cdn. Div.	Out of Playoffs
1925-26	36	11	5	2	....	1	16	1	....	12	21	3	....	92	114	27	6th,	Out of Playoffs
1924-25	30	10	5	0	....	9	6	0	....	19	11	0	....	90	84	38	2nd,	Lost NHL S-Final
1923-24	24	7	5	0	....	3	9	0	....	10	14	0	....	59	85	20	3rd,	Out of Playoffs
1922-23	24	10	1	1	....	3	9	0	....	13	10	1	....	82	88	27	3rd,	Out of Playoffs
1921-22	**24**	**8**	**4**	**0**	....	**5**	**6**	**1**	....	**13**	**10**	**1**	....	**98**	**97**	**27**	**2nd,**	**Won Stanley Cup**
1920-21	24	9	3	0	....	6	6	0	....	15	9	0	....	105	100	30	2nd and 1st***	Lost NHL Final
1919-20**	24	8	4	0	....	4	8	0	....	12	12	0	....	119	106	24	3rd and 2nd***	Out of Playoffs
1918-19	18	5	4	0	....	0	9	0	....	5	13	0	....	64	92	10	3rd and 3rd***	Out of Playoffs
1917-18	**22**	**10**	**1**	**0**	....	**3**	**8**	**0**	....	**13**	**9**	**0**	....	**108**	**109**	**26**	**2nd and 1st*****	**Won Stanley Cup**

* Name changed from St. Patricks to Maple Leafs (February, 1927). ** Name changed from Arenas to St. Patricks.

*** Season played in two halves with no combined standing at end.

From 1917-18 through 1925-26, NHL champions played against PCHA/WCHL champions for Stanley Cup.

NORTHEAST DIVISION

92nd NHL Season

Franchise date: November 22, 1917

2008-09 Player Personnel

FORWARDS	HT	WT	S	Place of Birth	*Age	2007-08 Club
ANTROPOV, Nik	6-6	230	L	Ust-Kamenogorsk, USSR	28	Toronto
BELL, Mark	6-4	220	L	St. Pauls, Ont.	28	Toronto
BLAKE, Jason	5-10	180	L	Moorhead, MN	35	Toronto
DEVEREAUX, Boyd	6-2	195	L	Seaforth, Ont.	30	Toronto
GRABOVSKI, Mikhail	5-11	179	L	Potsdam, East Germany	24	Montreal-Hamilton
HAGMAN, Niklas	6-0	205	L	Espoo, Finland	28	Dallas
HOLLWEG, Ryan	5-11	210	L	Downey, CA	25	NY Rangers
KULEMIN, Nikolai	6-1	183	L	Magnitogorsk, USSR	22	Magnitogorsk
MAYERS, Jamal	6-1	214	R	Toronto, Ont.	33	St. Louis
MITCHELL, John	6-2	205	L	Waterloo, Ont.	23	Toronto (AHL)
MOORE, Dominic	6-0	190	L	Sarnia, Ont.	28	Minnesota-Toronto
NEWBURY, Kris	5-10	200	L	Brampton, Ont.	26	Toronto-Toronto (AHL)
PONIKAROVSKY, Alexei	6-4	220	L	Kiev, USSR	28	Toronto
STAJAN, Matt	6-1	200	L	Mississauga, Ont.	24	Toronto
STEEN, Alex	6-1	205	L	Winnipeg, Man.	24	Toronto
TLUSTY, Jiri	6-0	209	L	Slany, Czech.	20	Toronto-Toronto (AHL)
DEFENSEMEN						
COLAIACOVO, Carlo	6-1	200	L	Toronto, Ont.	25	Toronto-Toronto (AHL)
FINGER, Jeff	6-1	205	R	Hancock, MI	28	Colorado
FROGREN, Jonas	6-2	194	L	Falun, Sweden	28	Farjestad
KABERLE, Tomas	6-1	198	L	Rakovnik, Czech.	30	Toronto
KRONWALL, Staffan	6-3	209	L	Jarfalla, Sweden	26	Toronto-Toronto (AHL)
KUBINA, Pavel	6-4	244	R	Celadna, Czech.	31	Toronto
McCABE, Bryan	6-2	220	L	St. Catharines, Ont.	33	Toronto
STRALMAN, Anton	6-1	200	R	Tibro, Sweden	22	Toronto-Toronto (AHL)
WHITE, Ian	5-10	185	R	Steinbach, Man.	24	Toronto

GOALTENDERS	HT	WT	C	Place of Birth	*Age	2007-08 Club
JOSEPH, Curtis	5-11	193	L	Keswick, Ont.	41	Calgary
TOSKALA, Vesa	5-10	195	L	Tampere, Finland	31	Toronto

* – Age at start of 2008-09 season

Coaching History

Dick Carroll, 1917-18, 1918-19; Frank Heffernan and Harry Sproule, 1919-20; Frank Carroll, 1920-21; George O'Donohue, 1921-22; George O'Donohue and Charles Querrie, 1922-23; Charles Querrie, 1923-24; Eddie Powers, 1924-25, 1925-26; Charles Querrie, Mike Rodden and Alex Romeril, 1926-27; Conn Smythe, 1927-28 to 1929-30; Conn Smythe and Art Duncan, 1930-31; Art Duncan and Dick Irvin, 1931-32; Dick Irvin, 1932-33 to 1939-40; Hap Day, 1940-41 to 1949-50; Joe Primeau, 1950-51 to 1952-53; King Clancy, 1953-54 to 1955-56; Howie Meeker, 1956-57; Billy Reay, 1957-58; Billy Reay and Punch Imlach, 1958-59; Punch Imlach, 1959-60 to 1968-69; John McLellan, 1969-70 to 1972-73; Red Kelly, 1973-74 to 1976-77; Roger Neilson, 1977-78, 1978-79; Floyd Smith, Dick Duff and Punch Imlach, 1979-80; Joe Crozier and Mike Nykoluk, 1980-81; Mike Nykoluk, 1981-82 to 1983-84; Dan Maloney, 1984-85, 1985-86; John Brophy, 1986-87, 1987-88; John Brophy and George Armstrong, 1988-89; Doug Carpenter, 1989-90; Doug Carpenter and Tom Watt, 1990-91; Tom Watt, 1991-92; Pat Burns, 1992-93 to 1994-95; Pat Burns and Nick Beverley, 1995-96; Mike Murphy, 1996-97, 1997-98; Pat Quinn, 1998-99 to 2005-06; Paul Maurice, 2006-07, 2007-08; Ron Wilson, 2008-09.

Captains' History

Hap Day, 1927-28 to 1936-37; Charlie Conacher, 1937-38; Red Horner, 1938-39, 1939-40; Syl Apps, 1940-41 to 1942-43; Bob Davidson, 1943-44, 1944-45; Syl Apps, 1945-46 to 1947-48; Ted Kennedy, 1948-49 to 1954-55; Sid Smith, 1955-56; Jimmy Thomson, Ted Kennedy, 1956-57; George Armstrong, 1957-58 to 1968-69; Dave Keon, 1969-70 to 1974-75; Darryl Sittler, 1975-76 to 1980-81; Rick Vaive, 1981-82 to 1985-86; no captain, 1986-87 to 1988-89; Rob Ramage, 1989-90, 1990-91; Wendel Clark, 1991-92 to 1993-94; Doug Gilmour, 1994-95 to 1996-97; Mats Sundin, 1997-98 to date.

2007-08 Scoring

* – rookie

Regular Season

Pos	#	Player	Team	GP	G	A	Pts	TOI	+/–	PIM	PP	SH	GW	S	%
C	13	Mats Sundin	TOR	74	32	46	78	20:04	17	76	10	1	4	259	12.4
R	80	Nik Antropov	TOR	72	26	30	56	20:06	10	92	12	0	5	165	15.8
D	15	Tomas Kaberle	TOR	82	8	45	53	24:52	–8	22	6	0	1	155	5.2
L	55	Jason Blake	TOR	82	15	37	52	17:49	–4	28	2	0	0	332	4.5
L	10	Alex Steen	TOR	76	15	27	42	18:05	0	32	2	1	2	169	8.9
D	31	Pavel Kubina	TOR	72	11	29	40	23:55	5	116	6	0	4	136	8.1
L	23	Alexei Ponikarovsky	TOR	66	18	17	35	15:57	3	36	1	0	1	150	12.0
R	16	Darcy Tucker	TOR	74	18	16	34	16:26	–8	100	7	0	3	152	11.8
C	14	Matt Stajan.	TOR	82	16	17	33	18:54	–11	47	2	1	3	127	12.6
D	24	Bryan McCabe	TOR	54	5	18	23	25:55	–2	81	4	0	2	107	4.7
C	42	Kyle Wellwood	TOR	59	8	13	21	12:38	–12	0	5	0	1	57	14.0
D	7	Ian White	TOR	81	5	16	21	18:48	–9	44	0	0	2	116	4.3
C	22	Boyd Devereaux	TOR	62	7	11	18	13:58	–6	24	0	1	1	81	8.6
L	18	Chad Kilger	TOR	53	10	7	17	11:38	1	18	0	0	0	74	13.5
C	19	Dominic Moore	MIN	30	1	2	3	11:57	–11	10	0	0	0	28	3.6
			TOR	38	4	10	14	14:21	7	14	1	0	0	72	5.6
			Total	68	5	12	17	13:17	–4	24	1	0	0	100	5.0
C	11 *	Jiri Tlusty	TOR	58	10	6	16	10:55	–12	14	2	0	2	69	14.5
L	9	Mark Bell	TOR	35	4	6	10	09:44	–2	60	0	0	0	42	9.5
D	36 *	Anton Stralman	TOR	50	3	6	9	12:48	–10	18	0	0	0	40	7.5
D	56	Andy Wozniewski	TOR	48	2	7	9	14:10	5	54	0	0	0	34	5.9
D	8	Carlo Colaiacovo	TOR	28	2	4	6	17:26	–4	10	0	0	1	30	6.7
C	21	John Pohl	TOR	33	1	4	5	07:05	–4	10	0	0	1	23	4.3
L	39	Simon Gamache	TOR	11	2	2	4	09:35	–1	6	1	0	0	11	18.2
R	48 *	Jeremy Williams	TOR	18	2	0	2	07:20	–3	4	0	0	0	16	12.5
C	54 *	Kris Newbury	TOR	28	1	1	2	04:22	–7	32	0	0	0	14	7.1
L	52 *	Robbie Earl	TOR	9	0	1	1	09:14	–2	0	0	0	0	9	0.0
C	50	Darryl Boyce	TOR	1	0	0	0	03:20	0	0	0	0	0	0	0.0
R	26	Ben Ondrus	TOR	3	0	0	0	05:07	–1	5	0	0	0	4	0.0
C	32 *	Alex Foster	TOR	3	0	0	0	03:32	0	0	0	0	0	1	0.0
L	33	Bates Battaglia	TOR	13	0	0	0	04:45	–6	7	0	0	0	6	0.0
D	44	Staffan Kronvall	TOR	18	0	0	0	11:07	–2	7	0	0	0	9	0.0

Goaltending

No.	Goaltender	GPI	Mins	Avg	W	L	OT	EN	SO	GA	SA	S%	G	A	PIM
35	Vesa Toskala	66	3837	2.74	33	25	6	7	3	175	1824	.904	0	5	4
30	Scott Clemmensen	3	154	3.90	1	1	0	0	0	10	62	.839	0	0	0
1	Andrew Raycroft	19	965	3.92	2	9	5	1	1	63	509	.876	0	0	0
	Totals	**82**	**4991**	**3.08**	**36**	**35**	**11**	**8**	**4**	**256**	**2403**	**.893**			

Ron Wilson

Head Coach

Born: Windsor, Ont., May 28, 1955.

The Toronto Maple Leafs announced on June 10, 2008 that Ron Wilson had been named the 27th head coach in the club's history. Wilson previously held NHL head coaching duties with Anaheim, Washington, and the San Jose Sharks.

Under Wilson's guidance the Sharks were the only NHL team to have won at least one playoff round in each season from 2003-04 through 2007-08. In his four full seasons behind the Sharks bench, the team advanced to the Western Conference Final for the first time ever in 2004, and reached the Conference semifinals in 2006, 2007 and 2008. His Sharks teams garnered two Pacific Division championships (2004 and 2008); twice finished second in their division, and twice posted the second-best point total in the conference. With 206 victories in San Jose, Wilson surpassed Darryl Sutter as the Sharks' all-time wins leader on March 1, 2008.

Wilson coached the Washington Capitals from 1997 until 2002, with his tenure in the United State's capital highlighted by the team's only trip to the Stanley Cup Final in 1998. Prior to spending five seasons with the Capitals, Wilson had served as the first head coach of the expansion Mighty Ducks of Anaheim in 1993, and he led the team to the postseason for the very first time in 1996-97.

Throughout his professional and amateur career, Wilson has enjoyed a long-standing relationship with USA Hockey. He led Team USA to the gold medal in 1996 at the inaugural World Cup of Hockey and he coached the team again at the 2004 tournament. Wilson also coached the U.S. national team at the 1994 and 1996 World Championships where his teams finished fourth and third respectively. Wilson also served as head coach for Team USA at the 1998 Nagano Winter Olympics.

Wilson was a seventh-round selection of the Toronto Maple Leafs (132nd overall) in the 1975 NHL Amateur Draft. He made his NHL debut by playing in 13 games for Toronto in 1977-78, followed by 46 games in 1978-79 and five games in 1979-80. In 177 career NHL games as a player with Toronto and Minnesota, Wilson recorded 26 goals and 67 assists for 93 points. He is one of 15 individuals that have both played for the Maple Leafs and then went on to coach at least one game for the Original Six franchise. He is the son of Larry Wilson and the nephew of Johnny Wilson, both former players on Stanley Cup winning teams from Detroit.

Coaching Record

			Regular Season				Playoffs			
Season	**Team**	**League**	**GC**	**W**	**L**	**O/T**	**GC**	**W**	**L**	**T**
1993-94	**Anaheim**	**NHL**	**84**	**33**	**46**	**5**	....	....	....	....
1994-95	**Anaheim**	**NHL**	**48**	**16**	**27**	**5**	....	....	....	....
1995-96	**Anaheim**	**NHL**	**82**	**35**	**39**	**8**	....	....	....	....
1996-97	**Anaheim**	**NHL**	**82**	**36**	**33**	**13**	**11**	**4**	**7**	....
1997-98	**Washington**	**NHL**	**82**	**40**	**30**	**12**	**21**	**12**	**9**	....
1998-99	**Washington**	**NHL**	**82**	**31**	**45**	**6**	....	....	....	....
99-2000	**Washington**	**NHL**	**82**	**44**	**24**	**14**	**5**	**1**	**4**	....
2000-01	**Washington**	**NHL**	**82**	**41**	**27**	**14**	**6**	**2**	**4**	....
2001-02	**Washington**	**NHL**	**82**	**36**	**33**	**13**	....	....	....	....
2002-03	**San Jose**	**NHL**	**57**	**19**	**25**	**13**	....	....	....	....
2003-04	**San Jose**	**NHL**	**82**	**43**	**21**	**18**	**17**	**10**	**7**	....
2004-05	**San Jose**				SEASON CANCELLED					
2005-06	**San Jose**	**NHL**	**82**	**44**	**27**	**11**	**11**	**6**	**5**	....
2006-07	**San Jose**	**NHL**	**82**	**51**	**26**	**5**	**11**	**6**	**5**	....
2007-08	**San Jose**	**NHL**	**82**	**49**	**23**	**10**	**13**	**6**	**7**	....
	NHL Totals		**1091**	**518**	**426**	**147**	**95**	**47**	**48**	....

Club Records

Team

(Figures in brackets for season records are games played; records for fewest points, wins, ties, losses, goals, goals against are for 70 or more games)

Most Points **103** 2003-04 (82)
Most Wins **45** 1998-99 (82), 1999-2000 (82), 2003-04 (82)
Most Ties **22** 1954-55 (70)
Most Losses **52** 1984-85 (80)
Most Goals **337** 1989-90 (80)
Most Goals Against **387** 1983-84 (80)
Fewest Points **48** 1984-85 (80)
Fewest Wins **20** 1981-82 (80), 1984-85 (80)
Fewest Ties **4** 1989-90 (80)
Fewest Losses **16** 1950-51 (70)
Fewest Goals **147** 1954-55 (70)
Fewest Goals Against ***131** 1953-54 (70)
Longest Winning Streak
Overall .... **10** Oct. 7-28/93
Home .... **9** Nov. 11-Dec. 26/53, Mar. 6-Apr. 7/07
Away .... **7** Three times
Longest Undefeated Streak
Overall .... **11** Oct. 15-Nov. 8/50 (8 wins, 3 ties), Jan. 6-Feb. 1/94 (7 wins, 4 ties)
Home .... **18** Nov. 28/33-Mar. 10/34 (15 wins, 3 ties), Oct. 31/53-Jan. 23/54 (16 wins, 2 ties)
Away .... **9** Nov. 30/47-Jan. 11/48 (4 wins, 5 ties)
Longest Losing Streak
Overall .... **10** Jan. 15-Feb. 8/67
Home .... **7** Nov. 11-Dec. 5/84
Away .... **11** Feb. 20-Apr. 1/88
Longest Winless Streak
Overall .... **15** Dec. 26/87-Jan. 25/88 (11 losses, 4 ties)
Home .... **11** Dec. 19/87-Jan. 25/88 (7 losses, 4 ties)
Away .... **18** Oct. 6/82-Jan. 5/83 (13 losses, 5 ties)
Most Shutouts, Season **13** 1953-54 (70)
Most PIM, Season **2,419** 1989-90 (80)
Most Goals, Game .... **14** Mar. 16/57 (NYR 1 at Tor. 14)

Individual

Most Seasons .... **21** George Armstrong
Most Games .... **1,187** George Armstrong
Most Goals, Career .... **420** Mats Sundin
Most Assists, Career .... **620** Borje Salming
Most Points, Career .... **987** Mats Sundin (420G, 567A)
Most PIM, Career .... **2,265** Tie Domi
Most Shutouts, Career .... **62** Turk Broda
Longest Consecutive Games Streak .... **486** Tim Horton (Feb. 11/61-Feb. 4/68)
Most Goals, Season .... **54** Rick Vaive (1981-82)
Most Assists, Season .... **95** Doug Gilmour (1992-93)
Most Points, Season .... **127** Doug Gilmour (1992-93; 32G, 95A)
Most PIM, Season .... **365** Tie Domi (1997-98)
Most Points, Defenseman, Season .... **79** Ian Turnbull (1976-77; 22G, 57A)
Most Points, Center, Season .... **127** Doug Gilmour (1992-93; 32G, 95A)
Most Points, Right Wing, Season .... **97** Wilf Paiement (1980-81; 40G, 57A)
Most Points, Left Wing, Season .... **99** Dave Andreychuk (1993-94; 53G, 46A)
Most Points, Rookie, Season .... **66** Peter Ihnacak (1982-83; 28G, 38A)
Most Shutouts, Season .... **13** Harry Lumley (1953-54)
Most Goals, Game .... **6** Corb Denneny (Jan. 26/21), Darryl Sittler (Feb. 7/76)
Most Assists, Game .... **6** Babe Pratt (Jan. 8/44), Doug Gilmour (Feb. 13/93)
Most Points, Game .... ***10** Darryl Sittler (Feb. 7/76; 6G, 4A)

* NHL Record.

Retired Numbers

5	Bill Barilko	1946-1951
6	Ace Bailey	1926-1934

Honored Numbers

1	Turk Broda	1936-43, 45-52
	Johnny Bower	1958-1970
4	Hap Day	1926-1937
	Red Kelly	1959-1967
7	King Clancy	1930-1937
	Tim Horton	1949-50, 51-70
9	Charlie Conacher	1929-1938
	Ted Kennedy	1942-55, 56-57
10	Syl Apps	1936-43, 45-48
	George Armstrong	1949-50, 51-71
17*	Wendel Clark	1985-94, 96-98, 2000
21	Borje Salming	1973-1989
27	Frank Mahovlich	1956-1968
	Darryl Sittler	1970-1982
93*	Doug Gilmour	1992-97, 2003

* – To be honored during 2008-09 season.

All-time Record vs. Other Clubs

Regular Season

	At Home								On Road								Total							
	GP	W	L	T	OL	GF	GA	PTS	GP	W	L	T	OL	GF	GA	PTS	GP	W	L	T	OL	GF	GA	PTS
Anaheim	16	10	2	4	0	53	32	24	12	5	6	1	0	28	39	11	28	15	8	5	0	81	71	35
Atlanta	15	9	3	1	2	55	36	21	15	10	4	0	1	54	27	21	30	19	7	1	3	109	63	42
Boston	311	161	99	51	0	1034	809	373	310	95	164	47	4	827	1001	241	621	256	263	98	4	1861	1810	614
Buffalo	79	32	33	12	2	239	273	78	81	24	50	6	1	216	321	55	160	56	83	18	3	455	594	133
Calgary	54	29	17	7	1	207	193	66	62	22	33	5	2	195	240	51	116	51	50	12	3	402	433	117
Carolina	42	17	20	5	0	141	148	39	43	15	19	6	3	137	162	39	85	32	39	11	3	278	310	78
Chicago	316	164	98	54	0	1075	827	382	319	120	157	42	0	832	971	282	635	284	255	96	0	1907	1798	664
Colorado	36	16	16	4	0	119	137	36	30	7	18	5	0	90	116	19	66	23	34	9	0	209	253	55
Columbus	4	3	0	1	0	13	5	7	2	1	0	0	1	7	6	3	6	4	0	1	1	20	11	10
Dallas	102	49	36	17	0	357	321	115	98	36	51	11	0	307	368	83	200	85	87	28	0	664	689	198
Detroit	317	165	105	47	0	1048	848	377	323	108	169	46	0	793	973	262	640	273	274	93	0	1841	1821	639
Edmonton	38	21	15	2	0	158	157	44	44	15	22	6	1	141	180	37	82	36	37	8	1	299	337	81
Florida	21	13	6	2	0	69	58	28	23	12	6	5	0	68	61	29	44	25	12	7	0	137	119	57
Los Angeles	69	35	23	11	0	267	225	81	66	21	35	10	0	193	239	52	135	56	58	21	0	460	464	133
Minnesota	4	4	0	0	0	15	6	8	2	1	1	0	0	4	5	2	6	5	1	0	0	19	11	10
Montreal	345	179	117	45	4	1054	903	407	345	97	203	43	2	861	1206	239	690	276	320	88	6	1915	2109	646
Nashville	7	3	3	1	0	16	19	7	2	0	1	0	1	4	7	1	9	3	4	1	1	20	26	8
New Jersey	54	34	15	5	0	193	150	73	52	17	18	15	2	160	177	51	106	51	33	20	2	353	327	124
NY Islanders	61	32	24	4	1	219	203	69	59	22	31	3	3	170	226	50	120	54	55	7	4	389	429	119
NY Rangers	288	161	86	39	2	994	762	363	289	110	121	56	2	854	893	278	577	271	207	95	4	1848	1655	641
Ottawa	34	14	14	2	4	89	106	34	32	11	18	1	2	88	107	25	66	25	32	3	6	177	213	59
Philadelphia	73	27	31	14	1	229	241	69	73	21	43	8	1	175	268	51	146	48	74	22	2	404	509	120
Phoenix	44	20	22	2	0	160	165	42	40	13	21	6	0	143	166	32	84	33	43	8	0	303	331	74
Pittsburgh	73	36	25	11	1	290	236	84	75	30	39	6	0	242	300	66	148	66	64	17	1	532	536	150
St. Louis	100	58	29	11	2	371	295	129	103	31	58	14	0	285	349	76	203	89	87	25	2	656	644	205
San Jose	19	12	5	2	0	73	52	26	16	7	6	3	0	42	35	17	35	19	11	5	0	115	87	43
Tampa Bay	27	19	7	1	0	104	69	39	26	18	5	1	2	85	56	39	53	37	12	2	2	189	125	78
Vancouver	61	28	22	11	0	220	201	67	65	24	30	11	0	219	229	59	126	52	52	22	0	439	430	126
Washington	54	29	19	6	0	229	184	64	56	20	32	4	0	161	201	44	110	49	51	10	0	390	385	108
Defunct Clubs	232	158	53	21	0	860	515	337	233	84	120	29	0	607	745	197	465	242	173	50	0	1467	1260	534
Totals	**2896**	**1538**	**945**	**393**	**20**	**9951**	**8176**	**3489**	**2896**	**997**	**1481**	**390**	**28**	**7988**	**9674**	**2412**	**5792**	**2535**	**2426**	**783**	**48**	**17939**	**17850**	**5901**

Playoffs

	Series	W	L	GP	W	L	T	GF	GA	Last Mtg.	Rnd.	Result
Boston	13	8	5	62	31	30	1	150	153	1974	QF	L 0-4
Buffalo	1	0	1	5	1	4	0	16	21	1999	CF	L 1-4
Calgary	1	1	0	2	2	0	0	9	5	1979	PRE	W 2-0
Carolina	1	0	1	6	2	4	0	6	10	2002	CF	L 2-4
Chicago	9	6	3	38	22	15	1	111	89	1995	CQF	L 3-4
Dallas	2	0	2	7	1	6	0	26	35	1983	DSF	L 1-3
Detroit	23	12	11	117	58	59	0	311	321	1993	DSF	W 4-3
Los Angeles	3	2	1	12	7	5	0	41	31	1993	CF	L 3-4
Montreal	15	7	8	71	29	42	0	160	215	1979	QF	L 0-4
New Jersey	2	0	2	13	5	8	0	27	37	2001	CSF	L 3-4
NY Islanders	3	2	1	17	8	9	0	42	54	2002	CQF	W 4-3
NY Rangers	8	3	5	35	16	19	0	86	86	1971	QF	L 2-4
Ottawa	4	4	0	24	16	8	0	57	42	2004	CQF	W 4-3
Philadelphia	6	1	5	36	14	22	0	85	119	2004	CSF	L 2-4
Pittsburgh	3	3	0	12	8	4	0	39	27	1999	CSF	W 4-2
St. Louis	5	2	3	31	14	17	0	90	88	1996	CQF	L 2-4
San Jose	1	1	0	7	4	3	0	26	21	1994	CSF	W 4-3
Vancouver	1	0	1	5	1	4	0	9	16	1994	CF	L 1-4
Defunct Clubs	8	6	2	24	12	10	2	59	57			
Totals	**109**	**58**	**51**	**524**	**251**	**269**	**4**	**1350**	**1427**			

Calgary totals include Atlanta Flames, 1972-73 to 1979-80. Carolina totals include Hartford, 1979-80 to 1996-97.
Colorado totals include Quebec, 1979-80 to 1994-95. Dallas totals include Minnesota North Stars, 1967-68 to 1992-93.
New Jersey totals include Kansas City, 1974-75, 1975-76, and Colorado Rockies, 1976-77 to 1981-82.
Phoenix totals include Winnipeg, 1979-80 to 1995-96.

Playoff Results 2008-2003

Year	Round	Opponent	Result	GF	GA
2004	CSF	Philadelphia	L 2-4	13	17
	CQF	Ottawa	W 4-3	14	11
2003	CQF	Philadelphia	L 3-4	16	24

Abbreviations: Round: CF – conference final; **CSF** – conference semi-final; **CQF** – conference quarter-final; **DSF** – division semi-final; **QF** – quarter-final; **PRE** – preliminary round.

2007-08 Results

Oct.	3	Ottawa	3-4*
	4	at Ottawa	2-3
	6	Montreal	4-3*
	9	Carolina	1-7
	11	NY Islanders	8-1
	13	Pittsburgh	4-6
	15	at Buffalo	4-5*
	18	Florida	3-2
	20	Chicago	4-6
	23	Atlanta	4-5†
	25	at Pittsburgh	5-2
	27	at NY Rangers	4-1
	29	Washington	1-7
Nov.	2	at New Jersey	2-3
	3	at Montreal	3-2
	6	at Ottawa	1-5
	9	at Buffalo	3-0
	10	NY Rangers	2-3†
	13	Montreal	3-4*
	15	at Boston	2-5
	17	Ottawa	3-0
	20	Boston	2-4
	23	at Dallas	1-3
	24	at Phoenix	1-5
	27	Montreal	3-4†
	29	at Atlanta	4-2
Dec.	1	Pittsburgh	4-2
	4	Nashville	3-1
	6	at NY Rangers	6-2
	8	Boston	1-2
	10	Tampa Bay	6-1
	14	at Atlanta	4-0
	15	at Montreal	1-4
	18	at Carolina	2-3*
	20	at Tampa Bay	1-2
	22	at Florida	2-1*
	26	at NY Islanders	3-4*
	27	at Philadelphia	1-4
	29	NY Rangers	1-6
Jan.	1	Tampa Bay	4-3†
	3	at Pittsburgh	2-6
	5	Philadelphia	2-3
	9	at Anaheim	0-5
	10	at Los Angeles	2-5
	12	at San Jose	2-3
	15	Carolina	5-4
	17	at Boston	3-2†
	19	Buffalo	4-2
	20	at New Jersey	2-3
	23	Washington	3-2
	24	at Washington	1-2
	29	St. Louis	2-3
	31	at Carolina	2-3*
Feb.	2	Ottawa	4-2
	5	Florida	0-8
	7	at Montreal	4-2
	9	Detroit	3-2*
	13	at Buffalo	0-1
	14	NY Islanders	4-5
	16	Boston	4-3*
	19	Columbus	3-1
	21	Buffalo	1-5
	23	Atlanta	3-1
	25	at Ottawa	5-0
	27	at Florida	4-3†
	29	at Tampa Bay	2-3*
Mar.	1	at Washington	3-2
	4	New Jersey	1-4
	6	at Boston	8-2
	8	New Jersey	1-2
	11	Philadelphia	4-3*
	12	at Philadelphia	3-2
	15	Buffalo	2-6
	18	at NY Islanders	3-1
	21	at Buffalo	4-1
	22	at Ottawa	5-4
	25	Boston	2-6
	27	at Boston	2-4
	29	Montreal	4-2
Apr.	1	Buffalo	3-4†
	3	Ottawa	2-8
	5	at Montreal	1-3

* – Overtime † – Shootout

Entry Draft Selections 2008-1994

Name in bold denotes played in NHL.

2008

Pick	
5	Luke Schenn
60	Jimmy Hayes
98	Mikhail Stefanovich
128	Greg Pateryn
129	Joel Champagne
130	Jerome Flaake
158	Grant Rollheiser
188	Andrew MacWilliam

2007

Pick	
74	Dale Mitchell
99	Matt Frattin
104	Ben Winnett
134	Juraj Mikus
164	Christopher Didomenico
194	Carl Gunnarsson

2006

Pick	
13	**Jiri Tlusty**
44	Nikolai Kulemin
99	James Reimer
111	Korbinian Holzer
161	Viktor Stahlberg
166	Tyler Ruegsegger
180	Leo Komarov

2005

Pick	
21	**Tuukka Rask**
82	Phil Oreskovic
153	Alex Berry
173	Johan Dahlberg
216	**Anton Stralman**
228	Chad Rau

2004

Pick	
90	Justin Pogge
113	Roman Kukumberg
157	Dmitri Vorobiev
187	**Robbie Earl**
220	Maxim Semenov
252	Jan Steber
285	Pierce Norton

2003

Pick	
57	John Doherty
91	Martin Sagat
125	Konstantin Volkov
158	John Mitchell
220	**Jeremy Williams**
237	Shaun Landolt

2002

Pick	
24	**Alex Steen**
57	**Matt Stajan**
74	Todd Ford
88	Dominic D'Amour
122	David Turon
191	**Ian White**
222	Scott May
254	**Jarkko Immonen**
285	**Staffan Kronwall**

2001

Pick	
17	**Carlo Colaiacovo**
39	**Karel Pilar**
65	**Brendan Bell**
82	**Jay Harrison**
88	Nicolas Corbeil
134	**Kyle Wellwood**
168	**Maxim Kondratiev**
183	Jaroslav Sklenar
198	Ivan Kolozvary
213	Jan Chovan
246	**Tomas Mojzis**
276	Mike Knoepfli

2000

Pick	
24	**Brad Boyes**
51	**Kris Vernarsky**
70	**Mikael Tellqvist**
90	Jean-Francois Racine
100	Miguel Delisle
179	Vadim Sozinov
209	Markus Seikola
223	Lubos Velebny
254	Alexander Shinkar
265	**Jean-Philippe Cote**

1999

Pick	
24	Luca Cereda
60	Peter Reynolds
108	Mirko Murovic
110	Jon Zion
151	Vaclav Zavoral
161	Jan Sochor
211	Vladimir Kulikov
239	**Pierre Hedin**
267	Peter Metcalf

1998

Pick	
10	**Nik Antropov**
35	**Petr Svoboda**
69	Jamie Hodson
87	**Alexei Ponikarovsky**
126	Morgan Warren
154	**Allan Rourke**
181	Jonathan Gagnon
215	Dwight Wolfe
228	Michal Travnicek
236	Sergei Rostov

1997

Pick	
57	**Jeff Farkas**
84	**Adam Mair**
111	Frantisek Mrazek
138	Eric Gooldy
165	Hugo Marchand
190	**Shawn Thornton**
194	Russ Bartlett
221	**Jonathan Hedstrom**

1996

Pick	
36	**Marek Posmyk**
50	Francis Larivee
66	Mike Lankshear
68	Konstantin Kalmikov
86	Jason Sessa
103	Vladimir Antipov
110	Peter Cava
111	Brandon Sugden
140	**Dmitri Yakushin**
148	Chris Bogas
151	Lucio DeMartinis
178	Reggie Berg
204	**Tomas Kaberle**
230	Jared Hope

1995

Pick	
15	**Jeff Ware**
54	Ryan Pepperall
139	Doug Bonner
145	**Yannick Tremblay**
171	Marek Melenovsky
197	Mark Murphy
223	**Danny Markov**

1994

Pick	
16	**Eric Fichaud**
48	**Sean Haggerty**
64	**Fredrik Modin**
126	Mark Deyell
152	Kam White
178	Tommi Rajamaki
204	Rob Butler
256	**Sergei Berezin**
282	Doug Nolan

General Managers' History

Charles Querrie, 1917-18 to 1926-27; Conn Smythe, 1927-28 to 1956-57; Hap Day, 1957-58; Punch Imlach, 1958-59 to 1968-69; Jim Gregory, 1969-70 to 1978-79; Punch Imlach, 1979-80, 1980-81; Punch Imlach and Gerry McNamara, 1981-82; Gerry McNamara, 1982-83 to 1987-88; Gord Stellick, 1988-89; Floyd Smith, 1989-90, 1990-91; Cliff Fletcher, 1991-92 to 1996-97; Ken Dryden, 1997-98, 1998-99; Pat Quinn, 1999-2000 to 2002-03; John Ferguson, 2003-04 to 2006-07; John Ferguson and Cliff Fletcher, 2007-08; Cliff Fletcher, 2008-09.

Cliff Fletcher

General Manager

Born: Montreal, Que., August 16, 1935.

Cliff Fletcher, who was inducted into the Hockey Hall of Fame in the Builder category in 2004, brings more than 50 years of experience in his return to the Toronto Maple Leafs, including more than 25 years as an NHL general manager. He rejoined the Maple Leafs on January 22, 2008. Fletcher originally took over an underachieving Maple Leafs franchise on July 1, 1991 as chief operating officer, president and general manager and presided over a turnaround that saw the team advance to the conference finals (in 1993 and 1994) for the first time since 1978. In 1993, *The Hockey News* chose him "Man of the Year" and "Executive of the Year".

A native of Montreal, Fletcher was a scout with the Montreal Canadiens for 10 years beginning in 1956 under the legendary Sam Pollock. He later became the general manager of the Verdun Blues junior hockey team. Fletcher served as a scout and assistant general manager with the St. Louis Blues from 1966 to 1972 before being named general manager of the expansion Atlanta Flames in 1972. He was the Flames' general manager during the team's first 19 years of existence. He oversaw the beginning of the Atlanta Flames franchise in 1972 and the move to Calgary in 1980. In 11 seasons with Calgary, the team won the Presidents' Trophy twice, two Campbell Conference crowns, two Smythe Division titles and the Stanley Cup in 1989.

Beginning in 1999 Fletcher served as senior advisor to the general manager of the Tampa Bay Lightning for two seasons. He joined the Phoenix Coyotes in February 2001 as general manager and executive vice president, moving up to senior executive vice president of hockey operations the following year. Fletcher worked in Phoenix until 2007.

Club Directory

Air Canada Centre

Toronto Maple Leafs
Air Canada Centre
40 Bay St., Suite 400
Toronto, Ontario M5J 2X2
Phone **416/815-5700**
FAX 416/359-9331
www.mapleleafs.com
Capacity: 18,819

Board of Directors

Lawrence M. Tanenbaum (Chairman of the Board), James W. Leech, Robert G. Bertram, Erol Uzumeri, Dean Metcalf, Ivan Fecan, Robert MacLellan, Dale H. Lastman, Richard Peddie

Maple Leaf Sports & Entertainment

Chairman, NHL Governor	Lawrence M. Tanenbaum
President, Chief Executive Officer and Alternate NHL Governor	Richard Peddie
Alternate NHL Governor	Dale H. Lastman
Alternate NHL Governor	Dean Metcalf
Executive Vice-President, Chief Operating Officer	Tom Anselmi
Executive V.P., CFO & Business Development	Ian Clarke
Executive Vice-President, Venues and Entertainment	Bob Hunter
Sr. V.P., General Counsel & Corp. Secretary	Robin Brudner
Senior Vice-President, Communications	John Lashway
Senior Vice-President, People	Mardi Walker
Senior Vice-President, Broadcast and Content	Chris Hebb
V.P., Corporate & Community Partnerships	Dave Hopkinson
Vice-President, Finance	Kevin Nonomura
Vice-President, Ticket Sales and Service	Beth Robertson
Vice-President, Live Entertainment	Patti-Anne Tarlton
President, General Manager, Toronto Raptors	Bryan Colangelo

Management

General Manager	Cliff Fletcher
Assistant G.M. & Dir. of Hockey Operations	Jeff Jackson
Director of Player Personnel	Al Coates
Special Assistant to the General Manager	Joe Nieuwendyk
Head Coach	Ron Wilson
Assistant Coaches	Keith Acton, Tim Hunter, Rob Zettler
Director of Player Development	Dallas Eakins
Player Development Coach	Paul Dennis
Manager, Hockey Admin. & Scouting Coordinator	Reid Mitchell
Strength and Conditioning Coordinator	Matt Nichol
Manager, Team Services	Dave Griffiths
Video Analyst	Chris Dennis
Director of Pro Scouting	Mike Penny
Director of Amateur Scouting	Dave Morrison
Pro Scouts	Pat Conacher, Dennis Bonvie
Amateur Scouts	Gary Harker, John Lilley, Garth Malarchuk, Mike Palmateer, Clint McConnachie, Allan Power, George Armstrong
European Scouts	Thommie Bergman, Peter Ihnacak, Jan Kovac, Nikolai Ladygin, Jari Gronstrand
Community Representatives	Wendel Clark, Darryl Sittler
Assistant to the General Manager's Office	Brad Lynn
Travel Coordinator	Mary Speck

Medical and Training Staff

Head Athletic Therapist	Rudy Cantu
Assistant Athletic Therapist	Steve Dias
Equipment Manager	Brian Papineau
Assistant Equipment Managers	Tom Blatchford, Bobby Hastings
Medical Director, Maple Leafs and Marlies	Dr. Noah Forman
Orthopedic Consultant	Dr. John Theodoropoulos
Team Dentists	Dr. Marvin Lean, Dr. Charles Goldberg

Communications, Community Development and Game Operations

Senior Vice-President, Communications	John Lashway
Director, Media Relations	Pat Park
Coordinator, Media Relations	Craig Downey
Director, Corporate Communications	Rajani Kamath
Manager, Leafs Fund, Community Relations	Nancy Gilks
Manager, Youth Hockey Development	Dave De Freitas
Manager, Game Presentation	Mike Ferriman

Television and Radio Broadcast Information

Senior Vice-President, Broadcast and Content	Chris Hebb
Director, Broadcast and Networks	Liana Bristol
Director, Content and Networks General Manager	Frank Hayward
Director, Creative Production and Venue Services	Dean Bender
Director, Broadcast and Content Operations	Duncan Blair
Director, Business Development	Aaron Lafontaine
Director, Interactive Services	John McCauley
Director, Finance	Wayne Zronik
Senior Networks Producer	Mark Askin
Game Director	Jacques Primeau
Manager, Broadcast and Networks	Dale Taylor
Supervisor, Networks Production and Programming	Peter Papulkas
Associate Producer, Broadcast	Matt Runge
Supervising Producer, Leafs TV	Dan Gladman
Creative Producer, Production and Content	Marnie Starkman
Producer, Leafs TV	Jamie Arnold
Associate Producers, Leafs TV	Amanda DaPonte, Rebecca Virgin
Coordinator, Networks and Creative Service	Ashley Boland
Supervisor, Broadcast Engineering	Drew Kikauka
Talent, Leafs TV	Joe Bowen, Paul Hendrick, Bob McGill, Greg Millen, Andi Petrillo, Jody Vance
AM 640 Toronto Radio, Play-By-Play	Joe Bowen, Dennis Beyak (mid-week)
AM 640 Toronto Radio, Analyst	Jim Ralph
Television Play-By-Play	Joe Bowen (mid-week)
Television Analysts	Bob McGill, Greg Millen
Interactive Production and Content	Mike Ball, Chris Clarke, Mike Ulmer, Mike Brock, Latham Bromwich, Matthew Iaboni, Scott Clark

Vancouver Canucks

2007-08 Results: 39W-33L-1OTL-9SOL 88PTS.
Fifth, Northwest Division

Key Off-Season Signings/Acquisitions

2008

April 23 • Named **Mike Gillis** general manager.
May 21 • Re-signed head coach **Alain Vigneault**.
June 17 • Named **Ryan Walter** assistant coach.
25 • Claimed C **Kyle Wellwood** on waivers from Toronto.
July 1 • Signed LW **Darcy Hordichuk**.
2 • Signed C **Ryan Johnson**.
2 • Re-signed G **Curtis Sanford**.
4 • Acquired RW **Steve Bernier** from Buffalo for a 2nd-round pick in 2010 and 3rd-round pick in 2009.
10 • Signed RW **Pavol Demitra** and D **Rob Davison**.
14 • Signed C **Jason Krog**.

Daniel (22) and Henrik (33) Sedin battle on the boards with Calgary's Dion Phaneuf. Daniel led the Canucks with 29 goals in 2007-08 while Henrik was among the league leaders with 61 assists. The twins finished 1–2 in team scoring for the second year in a row.

2008-09 Schedule

Oct.	Thu.	9	Calgary
	Sat.	11	at Calgary
	Mon.	13	at Washington
	Thu.	16	at Detroit
	Fri.	17	at Buffalo
	Sun.	19	at Chicago
	Tue.	21	at Columbus
	Sat.	25	Edmonton
	Tue.	28	Boston
	Thu.	30	at Los Angeles
	Fri.	31	at Anaheim
Nov.	Sun.	2	Detroit
	Tue.	4	Nashville
	Thu.	6	Phoenix
	Sat.	8	Minnesota
	Wed.	12	Colorado
	Sat.	15	Toronto*
	Mon.	17	at NY Islanders
	Wed.	19	at NY Rangers
	Thu.	20	at Minnesota
	Sat.	22	at Pittsburgh*
	Mon.	24	Detroit
	Thu.	27	Calgary
	Sat.	29	at Calgary
Dec.	Mon.	1	at Columbus
	Thu.	4	at Detroit
	Fri.	5	at Minnesota
	Sun.	7	at Colorado
	Tue.	9	at Nashville
	Sat.	13	at Edmonton
	Sun.	14	Florida
	Wed.	17	Edmonton
	Sat.	20	Chicago
	Mon.	22	Anaheim
	Tue.	23	at San Jose
	Fri.	26	Edmonton
	Sun.	28	Ottawa
	Tue.	30	Philadelphia
Jan.	Thu.	1	at Nashville
	Fri.	2	at Atlanta
	Sun.	4	Dallas
	Wed.	7	at Edmonton
	Fri.	9	St. Louis
	Sat.	10	San Jose
	Tue.	13	New Jersey
	Thu.	15	Phoenix
	Sun.	18	Columbus*
	Tue.	20	at San Jose
	Wed.	28	Nashville
	Sat.	31	Minnesota
Feb.	Tue.	3	Carolina
	Sat.	7	Chicago
	Tue.	10	at St. Louis
	Thu.	12	at Phoenix
	Fri.	13	at Dallas
	Sun.	15	Montreal
	Tue.	17	at Calgary
	Thu.	19	at Ottawa
	Sat.	21	at Toronto
	Tue.	24	at Montreal
	Fri.	27	Tampa Bay
Mar.	Sun.	1	Columbus*
	Tue.	3	Minnesota
	Sat.	7	San Jose
	Mon.	9	at Los Angeles
	Wed.	11	at Anaheim
	Fri.	13	Los Angeles
	Sun.	15	Colorado
	Tue.	17	Dallas
	Thu.	19	St. Louis
	Sat.	21	at Phoenix
	Tue.	24	at Dallas
	Thu.	26	at St. Louis
	Fri.	27	at Colorado
	Sun.	29	at Chicago
	Tue.	31	at Minnesota
Apr.	Thu.	2	Anaheim
	Sat.	4	at Edmonton
	Sun.	5	Colorado
	Tue.	7	Calgary
	Thu.	9	Los Angeles
	Sat.	11	at Colorado*

* Denotes afternoon game.

Year-by-Year Record

		Home				Road				Overall								
Season	**GP**	**W**	**L**	**T**	**OL**	**W**	**L**	**T**	**OL**	**W**	**L**	**T**	**OL**	**GF**	**GA**	**Pts.**	**Finished**	**Playoff Result**
2007-08	82	21	15	....	5	18	18	....	5	39	33	....	10	213	215	88	5th, Northwest Div.	Out of Playoffs
2006-07	82	26	11	....	4	23	15	....	3	49	26	....	7	222	201	105	1st, Northwest Div.	Lost Conf. Semi-Final
2005-06	82	25	10	....	6	17	22	....	2	42	32	....	8	256	255	92	4th, Northwest Div.	Out of Playoffs
2004-05	....	....	....	....	....	....	....	....	....	....	....	....	....	....	....	....		
2003-04	82	21	13	7	0	22	11	3	5	43	24	10	5	235	194	101	1st, Northwest Div.	Lost Conf. Quarter-Final
2002-03	82	22	13	6	0	23	10	7	1	45	23	13	1	264	208	104	2nd, Northwest Div.	Lost Conf. Semi-Final
2001-02	82	23	11	5	2	19	19	2	1	42	30	7	3	254	211	94	2nd, Northwest Div.	Lost Conf. Quarter-Final
2000-01	82	21	12	5	3	15	16	6	4	36	28	11	7	239	238	90	3rd, Northwest Div.	Lost Conf. Quarter-Final
1999-2000	82	16	14	5	6	14	15	10	2	30	29	15	8	227	237	83	3rd, Northwest Div.	Out of Playoffs
1998-99	82	14	21	6	....	9	26	6	....	23	47	12	....	192	258	58	4th, Northwest Div.	Out of Playoffs
1997-98	82	15	22	4	....	10	21	10	....	25	43	14	....	224	273	64	7th, Pacific Div.	Out of Playoffs
1996-97	82	20	17	4	....	15	23	3	....	35	40	7	....	257	273	77	4th, Pacific Div.	Out of Playoffs
1995-96	82	15	19	7	....	17	16	8	....	32	35	15	....	278	278	79	3rd, Pacific Div.	Lost Conf. Quarter-Final
1994-95	48	10	8	6	....	8	10	6	....	18	18	12	....	153	148	48	2nd, Pacific Div.	Lost Conf. Semi-Final
1993-94	84	20	19	3	....	21	21	0	....	41	40	3	....	279	276	85	2nd, Pacific Div.	Lost Final
1992-93	84	27	11	4	....	19	18	5	....	46	29	9	....	346	278	101	1st, Smythe Div.	Lost Div. Final
1991-92	80	23	10	7	....	19	16	5	....	42	26	12	....	285	250	96	1st, Smythe Div.	Lost Div. Final
1990-91	80	18	17	5	....	10	26	4	....	28	43	9	....	243	315	65	4th, Smythe Div.	Lost Div. Semi-Final
1989-90	80	13	16	11	....	12	25	3	....	25	41	14	....	245	306	64	5th, Smythe Div.	Out of Playoffs
1988-89	80	19	15	6	....	14	24	2	....	33	39	8	....	251	253	74	4th, Smythe Div.	Lost Div. Semi-Final
1987-88	80	15	20	5	....	10	26	4	....	25	46	9	....	272	320	59	5th, Smythe Div.	Out of Playoffs
1986-87	80	17	19	4	....	12	24	4	....	29	43	8	....	282	314	66	5th, Smythe Div.	Out of Playoffs
1985-86	80	17	18	5	....	6	26	8	....	23	44	13	....	282	333	59	4th, Smythe Div.	Lost Div. Semi-Final
1984-85	80	15	21	4	....	10	25	5	....	25	46	9	....	284	401	59	5th, Smythe Div.	Out of Playoffs
1983-84	80	20	16	4	....	12	23	5	....	32	39	9	....	306	328	73	3rd, Smythe Div.	Lost Div. Semi-Final
1982-83	80	20	12	8	....	10	23	7	....	30	35	15	....	303	309	75	3rd, Smythe Div.	Lost Div. Semi-Final
1981-82	80	20	8	12	....	10	25	5	....	30	33	17	....	290	286	77	2nd, Smythe Div.	Lost Final
1980-81	80	17	12	11	....	11	20	9	....	28	32	20	....	289	301	76	3rd, Smythe Div.	Lost Prelim. Round
1979-80	80	14	17	9	....	13	20	7	....	27	37	16	....	256	281	70	3rd, Smythe Div.	Lost Prelim. Round
1978-79	80	15	18	7	....	10	24	6	....	25	42	13	....	217	291	63	2nd, Smythe Div.	Lost Prelim. Round
1977-78	80	13	15	12	....	7	28	5	....	20	43	17	....	239	320	57	3rd, Smythe Div.	Out of Playoffs
1976-77	80	13	21	6	....	12	21	7	....	25	42	13	....	235	294	63	4th, Smythe Div.	Out of Playoffs
1975-76	80	22	11	7	....	11	21	8	....	33	32	15	....	271	272	81	2nd, Smythe Div.	Lost Prelim. Round
1974-75	80	23	12	5	....	15	20	5	....	38	32	10	....	271	254	86	1st, Smythe Div.	Lost Quarter-Final
1973-74	78	14	18	7	....	10	25	4	....	24	43	11	....	224	296	59	7th, East Div.	Out of Playoffs
1972-73	78	17	18	4	....	5	29	5	....	22	47	9	....	233	339	53	7th, East Div.	Out of Playoffs
1971-72	78	14	20	5	....	6	30	3	....	20	50	8	....	203	297	48	7th, East Div.	Out of Playoffs
1970-71	78	17	18	4	....	7	28	4	....	24	46	8	....	229	296	56	6th, East Div.	Out of Playoffs

NORTHWEST DIVISION
39th NHL Season
Franchise date: May 22, 1970

2008-09 Player Personnel

FORWARDS	HT	WT	S	Place of Birth	*Age	2007-08 Club
BERNIER, Steve	6-2	225	R	Quebec City, Que.	23	San Jose-Buffalo
BROWN, Mike	6-0	210	R	Northbrook, IL	23	Vancouver-Manitoba
BURROWS, Alexandre	6-1	190	L	Pincourt, Que.	27	Vancouver
COWAN, Jeff	6-2	205	L	Scarborough, Ont.	32	Vancouver
CULLEN, Mark	5-11	190	L	Moorhead, MN	29	Grand Rapids
DEMITRA, Pavol	6-0	200	L	Dubnica, Czech.	33	Minnesota
GRABNER, Michael	6-0	187	L	Villach, Austria	20	Manitoba
HANSEN, Jannik	6-1	194	R	Herlev, Denmark	22	Vancouver-Manitoba
HORDICHUK, Darcy	6-1	215	L	Kamsack, Sask.	28	Nashville
JAFFRAY, Jason	6-1	205	L	Rimbey, Alta.	27	Vancouver-Manitoba
JOHNSON, Ryan	6-1	202	L	Thunder Bay, Ont.	32	St. Louis
KESLER, Ryan	6-2	205	R	Livonia, MI	24	Vancouver
KROG, Jason	5-11	185	R	Fernie, B.C.	32	Chicago (AHL)
PETTINGER, Matt	6-1	205	L	Edmonton, Alta.	27	Washington-Vancouver
PYATT, Taylor	6-4	230	L	Thunder Bay, Ont.	27	Vancouver
RAYMOND, Mason	6-0	182	L	Cochrane, Alta.	23	Vancouver-Manitoba
RYPIEN, Rick	5-11	184	R	Coleman, Alta	24	Vancouver-Manitoba
SEDIN, Daniel	6-1	185	L	Ornskoldsvik, Sweden	28	Vancouver
SEDIN, Henrik	6-2	190	L	Ornskoldsvik, Sweden	28	Vancouver
SHANNON, Ryan	5-9	173	R	Darien, CT	25	Vancouver-Manitoba
WELLWOOD, Kyle	5-10	180	R	Windsor, Ont.	25	Toronto
DEFENSEMEN						
BAUMGARTNER, Nolan	6-2	205	R	Calgary, Alta.	32	Iowa-Manitoba
BIEKSA, Kevin	6-1	205	R	Grimsby, Ont.	27	Vancouver-Manitoba
DAVISON, Rob	6-3	220	L	St. Catharines, Ont.	28	San Jose-NY Islanders
EDLER, Alexander	6-3	220	L	Ostersund, Sweden	22	Vancouver-Manitoba
KRAJICEK, Lukas	6-2	200	L	Prostejov, Czech.	25	Vancouver
McIVER, Nathan	6-2	206	L	Kinkora, P.E.I.	23	Vancouver-Manitoba
MITCHELL, Willie	6-3	210	L	Port McNeill, B.C.	31	Vancouver
OHLUND, Mattias	6-2	220	L	Pitea, Sweden	32	Vancouver
SALO, Sami	6-3	215	R	Turku, Finland	34	Vancouver

GOALTENDERS	HT	WT	C	Place of Birth	*Age	2007-08 Club
LUONGO, Roberto	6-3	205	L	Montreal, Que.	29	Vancouver
SANFORD, Curtis	5-10	187	L	Owen Sound, Ont.	28	Vancouver

* – Age at start of 2008-09 season

2007-08 Scoring

* – rookie

Regular Season

Pos	#	Player	Team	GP	G	A	Pts	TOI	+/–	PIM	PP	SH	GW	S	%
C	33	Henrik Sedin	VAN	82	15	61	76	19:30	6	56	4	1	2	141	10.6
L	22	Daniel Sedin	VAN	82	29	45	74	19:03	6	50	12	0	7	247	11.7
L	19	Markus Naslund	VAN	82	25	30	55	17:23	–7	46	9	0	2	237	10.5
C	17	Ryan Kesler	VAN	80	21	16	37	19:03	1	79	4	2	2	177	11.9
L	9	Taylor Pyatt	VAN	79	16	21	37	15:47	9	60	7	0	2	167	9.6
L	14	Alex Burrows	VAN	82	12	19	31	15:05	11	179	1	3	3	126	9.5
C	7	Brendan Morrison	VAN	39	9	16	25	15:22	–3	18	3	0	3	54	16.7
D	6	Sami Salo	VAN	63	8	17	25	23:38	8	38	6	0	1	122	6.6
D	2	Mattias Ohlund	VAN	53	9	15	24	23:46	–1	79	4	0	2	128	7.0
L	21	* Mason Raymond	VAN	49	9	12	21	12:31	1	2	1	0	0	80	11.3
D	23	* Alexander Edler	VAN	75	8	12	20	21:20	6	42	4	0	0	124	6.5
L	25	Matt Pettinger	WSH	56	2	5	7	14:42	–11	25	1	0	1	98	2.0
			VAN	20	4	2	6	13:10	0	11	0	0	2	29	13.8
			Total	76	6	7	13	14:18	–11	36	1	0	3	127	4.7
R	26	Ryan Shannon	VAN	27	5	8	13	12:53	–1	24	4	0	0	34	14.7
C	16	Trevor Linden	VAN	59	7	5	12	11:18	0	15	0	2	1	45	15.6
D	3	Kevin Bieksa	VAN	34	2	10	12	23:23	–11	90	1	0	1	64	3.1
D	8	Willie Mitchell	VAN	72	2	10	12	23:11	6	81	0	0	1	65	3.1
L	27	Brad Isbister	VAN	55	6	5	11	10:49	–4	38	0	0	1	71	8.5
C	15	Byron Ritchie	VAN	71	3	8	11	12:19	–10	80	0	0	0	73	4.1
D	5	Lukas Krajicek	VAN	39	2	9	11	18:10	–3	36	1	0	0	28	7.1
D	4	Aaron Miller	VAN	57	1	8	9	17:20	–1	32	0	0	1	27	3.7
L	29	Jason Jaffray	VAN	19	2	4	6	12:35	4	19	1	0	1	15	13.3
C	37	* Rick Rypien	VAN	22	1	2	3	08:06	–5	41	0	0	0	8	12.5
D	28	* Luc Bourdon	VAN	27	2	0	2	12:52	7	20	1	0	0	26	7.7
R	13	* Mike Brown	VAN	19	1	0	1	06:18	–2	55	0	0	0	9	11.1
L	20	Jeff Cowan	VAN	46	0	1	1	08:44	–5	110	0	0	0	35	0.0
D	18	Mike Weaver	VAN	55	0	1	1	14:01	1	33	0	0	0	33	0.0
D	49	* Zach Fitzgerald	VAN	1	0	0	0	13:20	0	0	0	0	0	1	0.0
R	36	* Jannik Hansen	VAN	5	0	0	0	11:33	0	2	0	0	0	3	0.0
D	45	* Nathan McIver	VAN	17	0	0	0	10:27	–8	52	0	0	0	9	0.0

Goaltending

No.	Goaltender	GPI	Mins	Avg	W	L	OT	EN	SO	GA	SA	S%	G	A	PIM
1	Roberto Luongo	73	4233	2.38	35	29	9	3	6	168	2029	.917	0	3	4
41	Curtis Sanford	16	679	2.83	4	3	1	0	0	32	313	.898	0	1	2
31	* Drew MacIntyre	2	61	2.95	0	1	0	0	0	3	22	.864	0	0	0
	Totals	**82**	**5006**	**2.47**	**39**	**33**	**10**	**3**	**6**	**206**	**2367**	**.913**			

Roberto Luongo had another busy season in 2007-08, playing in 73 games and ranking among the league leaders in goals-against average (2.38) and shutouts (6).

Alain Vigneault

Head Coach

Born: Quebec City, Que., May 14, 1961.

On June 20, 2006, Alain Vigneault became the 16th head coach in Vancouver Canucks history. He previously served in the NHL as head coach of the Montreal Canadiens from 1997 to 2001, becoming the second youngest coach in club history at the age of 36. Vigneault was nominated for the Jack Adams Award as NHL coach of the year following the 1999-2000 season. In 2006-07, he led the Canucks to first place in the Northwest Division by setting new club records with 49 wins and 105 points after the club had missed the playoffs the previous season. Vigneault was rewarded with the Jack Adams Award as NHL coach of the year.

Vigneault joined the Canucks from the club's AHL affiliate, the Manitoba Moose, where he led the team to within one game of the conference finals in 2005-06. Prior to joining the Moose, Vigneault spent many years as a head coach in the QMJHL with Trois-Rivieres, Hull, Beauport and PEI. In 1988, Vigneault led the Hull Olympiques into the Memorial Cup and was subsequently named CHL coach of the year. He has also been honoured as coach of the QMJHL's Second All-Star team on three separate occasions. Vigneault has also achieved success on the international stage. He served as an assistant coach with Canada's national junior team in 1989 and 1991, winning a gold medal at the 1991 World Junior Championships in Saskatoon.

As a player, Vigneault was a member of the St. Louis Blues from 1981 to 1983. Drafted by the Blues in the eighth round, 167th overall, in the 1981 Entry Draft, the defenceman recorded two goals, five assists and 82 penalty minutes in his NHL career. Vigneault went on to serve as a scout for the Blues for two seasons and as an assistant coach for the Ottawa Senators from 1992 to 1996.

Coaching Record

			Regular Season				Playoffs			
Season	Team	League	GC	W	L	O/T	GC	W	L	T
1986-87	Trois-Rivieres	QMJHL	70	28	40	2	....	....	....	....
1987-88	Hull	QMJHL	70	43	23	4	19	12	7	....
1988-89	Hull	QMJHL	70	40	25	5	9	5	4	....
1989-90	Hull	QMJHL	70	36	29	5	11	4	7	....
1990-91	Hull	QMJHL	70	36	27	7	6	2	4	....
1991-92	Hull	QMJHL	70	41	24	5	6	2	4	....
1995-96	Beauport	QMJHL	31	19	7	5	20	13	7	....
1996-97	Beauport	QMJHL	70	24	44	2	4	1	3	....
1997-98	**Montreal**	**NHL**	**82**	**37**	**32**	**13**	**10**	**4**	**6**	....
1998-99	**Montreal**	**NHL**	**82**	**32**	**39**	**11**	....	....	....	....
99-2000	**Montreal**	**NHL**	**82**	**35**	**34**	**13**	....	....	....	....
2000-01	**Montreal**	**NHL**	**20**	**5**	**13**	**2**	....	....	....	....
2003-04	PEI	QMJHL	70	40	19	11	11	6	5	....
2004-05	PEI	QMJHL	70	24	39	7	....	....	....	....
2005-06	Manitoba	AHL	80	44	24	12	13	7	6	....
2006-07	**Vancouver**	**NHL**	**82**	**49**	**26**	**7**	**12**	**5**	**7**	....
2007-08	**Vancouver**	**NHL**	**82**	**39**	**33**	**10**	....	....	....	....
	NHL Totals		**430**	**197**	**177**	**56**	**22**	**9**	**13**	....

Coaching History

Hal Laycoe, 1970-71, 1971-72; Vic Stasiuk, 1972-73; Bill McCreary and Phil Maloney, 1973-74; Phil Maloney, 1974-75, 1975-76; Phil Maloney and Orland Kurtenbach, 1976-77; Orland Kurtenbach, 1977-78; Harry Neale, 1978-79 to 1980-81; Harry Neale and Roger Neilson, 1981-82; Roger Neilson, 1982-83; Roger Neilson and Harry Neale, 1983-84; Bill Laforge and Harry Neale, 1984-85; Tom Watt, 1985-86, 1986-87; Bob McCammon, 1987-88 to 1989-90; Bob McCammon and Pat Quinn, 1990-91; Pat Quinn, 1991-92 to 1993-94; Rick Ley, 1994-95; Rick Ley and Pat Quinn, 1995-96; Tom Renney, 1996-97; Tom Renney and Mike Keenan, 1997-98; Mike Keenan and Marc Crawford, 1998-99; Marc Crawford, 1999-2000 to 2005-06; Alain Vigneault, 2006-07 to date.

Club Records

Team

(Figures in brackets for season records are games played; records for fewest points, wins, ties, losses, goals, goals against are for 70 or more games)

Most Points	**105**	2006-07 (82)
Most Wins	**49**	2006-07 (82)
Most Ties	**20**	1980-81 (80)
Most Losses	**50**	1971-72 (78)
Most Goals	**346**	1992-93 (84)
Most Goals Against	**401**	1984-85 (80)
Fewest Points	**48**	1971-72 (78)
Fewest Wins	**20**	1971-72 (78), 1977-78 (80)
Fewest Ties	**3**	1993-94 (84)
Fewest Losses	**24**	2002-03 (82)
Fewest Goals	**192**	1998-99 (82)
Fewest Goals Against	**194**	2003-04 (82)
Longest Winning Streak		
Overall	**10**	Nov. 9-30/02
Home	**9**	Nov. 6-Dec. 9/92
Away	**8**	Dec. 20/03-Jan. 13/04
Longest Undefeated Streak		
Overall	**14**	Jan.26-Feb. 25/03 (10 wins, 4 ties)
Home	**18**	Nov. 4/92-Jan. 16/93 (16 wins, 2 ties)
Away	**9**	Feb. 4-Mar. 3/03 (6 wins, 3 ties)
Longest Losing Streak		
Overall	**10**	Oct. 23-Nov. 11/97
Home	**6**	Dec. 18/70-Jan. 20/71
Away	**12**	Nov. 28/81-Feb. 6/82
Longest Winless Streak		
Overall	**13**	Nov. 9-Dec. 7/73 (10 losses, 3 ties)
Home	**11**	Dec. 18/70-Feb. 6/71 (10 losses, 1 tie)
Away	**20**	Jan. 2-Apr. 2/86 (14 losses, 6 ties)
Most Shutouts, Season	**8**	1974-75 (80), 2001-02 (82)
Most PIM, Season	**2,326**	1992-93 (84)
Most Goals, Game	**11**	Mar. 28/71 (Cal. 5 at Van. 11), Nov. 25/86 (L.A. 5 at Van. 11), Mar. 1/92 (Cgy. 0 at Van. 11)

Individual

Most Seasons	**16**	Trevor Linden
Most Games	**1,140**	Trevor Linden
Most Goals, Career	**346**	Markus Naslund
Most Assists, Career	**415**	Trevor Linden
Most Points, Career	**756**	Markus Naslund (346G, 410A)
Most PIM, Career	**2,127**	Gino Odjick
Most Shutouts, Career	**20**	Kirk McLean
Longest Consecutive Games Streak	**534**	Brendan Morrison (Mar. 16/00-Dec. 10/07)
Most Goals, Season	**60**	Pavel Bure (1992-93, 1993-94)
Most Assists, Season	**71**	Henrik Sedin (2006-07)
Most Points, Season	**110**	Pavel Bure (1992-93; 60G, 50A)
Most PIM, Season	**372**	Donald Brashear (1997-98)
Most Points, Defenseman, Season	**63**	Doug Lidster (1986-87; 12G, 51A)
Most Points, Center, Season	**91**	Patrik Sundstrom (1983-84; 38G, 53A)
Most Points, Right Wing, Season	**110**	Pavel Bure (1992-93; 60G, 50A)
Most Points, Left Wing, Season	**104**	Markus Naslund (2002-03; 48G, 56A)
Most Points, Rookie, Season	**60**	Ivan Hlinka (1981-82; 23G, 37A), Pavel Bure (1991-92; 34G, 26A)
Most Shutouts, Season	**7**	Dan Cloutier (2001-02)
Most Goals, Game	**4**	Twelve times
Most Assists, Game	**6**	Patrik Sundstrom (Feb. 29/84)
Most Points, Game	**7**	Patrik Sundstrom (Feb. 29/84; 1G, 6A)

Retired Numbers

12	Stan Smyl	1978-1991

General Managers' History

Bud Poile, 1970-71 to 1972-73; Hal Laycoe, 1973-74; Phil Maloney, 1974-75 to 1976-77; Jake Milford, 1977-78 to 1981-82; Harry Neale, 1982-83 to 1984-85; Jack Gordon, 1985-86, 1986-87; Pat Quinn, 1987-88 to 1997-98; Brian Burke, 1998-99 to 2003-04; David Nonis, 2004-05 to 2007-08; Mike Gillis, 2008-09.

Captains' History

Orland Kurtenbach, 1970-71 to 1973-74; no captain, 1974-75; Andre Boudrias, 1975-76; Chris Oddleifson, 1976-77; Don Lever, 1977-78; Don Lever and Kevin McCarthy, 1978-79; Kevin McCarthy, 1979-80 to 1981-82; Stan Smyl, 1982-83 to 1989-90; Dan Quinn, Doug Lidster and Trevor Linden, 1990-91; Trevor Linden, 1991-92 to 1996-97; Mark Messier, 1997-98 to 1999-2000; Markus Naslund, 2000-01 to 2007-08.

All-time Record vs. Other Clubs

Regular Season

	At Home								On Road								Total							
	GP	W	L	T	OL	GF	GA	PTS	GP	W	L	T	OL	GF	GA	PTS	GP	W	L	T	OL	GF	GA	PTS
Anaheim	32	18	12	2	0	101	75	38	31	14	10	7	0	88	79	35	63	32	22	9	0	189	154	73
Atlanta	4	2	1	1	0	13	7	5	4	3	1	0	0	14	12	6	8	5	2	1	0	27	19	11
Boston	52	17	26	8	1	171	211	43	53	7	38	7	1	124	219	22	105	24	64	15	2	295	430	65
Buffalo	53	26	16	11	0	197	163	63	53	18	26	8	1	155	190	45	106	44	42	19	1	352	353	108
Calgary	111	43	48	18	2	377	365	106	110	32	63	15	0	313	421	79	221	75	111	33	2	690	786	185
Carolina	31	15	10	6	0	109	84	36	30	12	13	5	0	101	97	29	61	27	23	11	0	210	181	65
Chicago	78	40	23	15	0	234	219	95	77	22	46	7	2	183	280	53	155	62	69	22	2	417	499	148
Colorado	59	23	26	7	3	191	222	56	59	20	29	8	2	161	200	50	118	43	55	15	5	352	422	106
Columbus	14	10	2	0	2	53	36	22	14	7	4	2	1	48	34	17	28	17	6	2	3	101	70	39
Dallas	77	35	31	10	1	268	230	81	77	23	40	12	2	222	276	60	154	58	71	22	3	490	506	141
Detroit	71	32	29	10	0	254	226	74	72	20	42	8	2	204	289	50	143	52	71	18	2	458	515	124
Edmonton	94	38	41	12	3	330	354	91	93	31	50	7	5	295	386	74	187	69	91	19	8	625	740	165
Florida	10	4	1	5	0	29	22	13	9	4	3	1	1	30	25	10	19	8	4	6	1	59	47	23
Los Angeles	103	52	33	16	2	386	321	122	105	35	53	16	1	325	408	87	208	87	86	32	3	711	729	209
Minnesota	22	10	5	3	4	59	57	27	23	9	11	2	1	54	65	21	45	19	16	5	5	113	122	48
Montreal	56	15	33	8	0	152	204	38	54	11	38	5	0	139	244	27	110	26	71	13	0	291	448	65
Nashville	18	12	4	1	1	64	42	26	19	10	8	1	0	53	56	21	37	22	12	2	1	117	98	47
New Jersey	48	28	9	11	0	180	130	67	50	23	21	6	0	159	154	52	98	51	30	17	0	339	284	119
NY Islanders	48	24	21	3	0	158	155	51	48	12	25	10	1	137	175	35	96	36	46	13	1	295	330	86
NY Rangers	52	16	33	3	0	166	204	35	55	12	38	5	0	142	239	29	107	28	71	8	0	308	443	64
Ottawa	12	6	5	1	0	36	28	13	11	5	5	1	0	26	25	11	23	11	10	2	0	62	53	24
Philadelphia	52	10	29	12	1	146	211	33	55	17	36	1	1	164	238	36	107	27	65	13	2	310	449	69
Phoenix	78	48	19	10	1	293	215	107	75	29	35	10	1	260	270	69	153	77	54	20	2	553	485	176
Pittsburgh	51	23	23	4	1	181	189	51	51	11	33	7	0	175	229	29	102	34	56	11	1	356	418	80
St. Louis	78	34	35	9	0	231	246	77	77	23	45	9	0	215	284	55	155	57	80	18	0	446	530	132
San Jose	38	20	13	4	1	132	105	45	40	19	16	5	0	121	116	43	78	39	29	9	1	253	221	88
Tampa Bay	10	8	0	2	0	45	18	18	10	6	4	0	0	40	35	12	20	14	4	2	0	85	53	30
Toronto	65	30	22	11	2	229	219	73	61	22	28	11	0	201	220	55	126	52	50	22	2	430	439	128
Washington	40	19	15	5	1	139	125	44	41	15	21	4	1	123	134	35	81	34	36	9	2	262	259	79
Defunct Clubs	19	14	3	2	0	82	48	30	19	10	8	1	0	71	68	21	38	24	11	3	0	153	116	51
Totals	**1476**	**672**	**568**	**210**	**26**	**5006**	**4731**	**1580**	**1476**	**482**	**790**	**181**	**23**	**4343**	**5468**	**1168**	**2952**	**1154**	**1358**	**391**	**49**	**9349**	**10199**	**2748**

Playoffs

	Series	W	L	GP	W	L	T	GF	GA	Last Mtg.	Rnd.	Result
Anaheim	1	0	1	5	1	4	0	8	14	2007	CSF	L 1-4
Buffalo	2	0	2	7	1	6	0	14	28	1981	PRE	L 0-3
Calgary	6	2	4	32	15	17	0	96	101	2004	CQF	L 3-4
Chicago	2	1	1	9	4	5	0	24	24	1995	CSF	L 0-4
Colorado	2	0	2	10	2	8	0	26	40	2001	CQF	L 0-4
Dallas	2	2	0	12	8	4	0	31	23	2007	CQF	W 4-3
Detroit	1	0	1	6	2	4	0	16	22	2002	CQF	L 2-4
Edmonton	2	0	2	9	2	7	0	20	35	1992	DF	L 2-4
Los Angeles	3	1	2	17	8	9	0	60	66	1993	DF	L 2-4
Minnesota	1	0	1	7	3	4	0	17	26	2003	CSF	L 3-4
Montreal	1	0	1	5	1	4	0	9	20	1975	QF	L 1-4
NY Islanders	2	0	2	6	0	6	0	14	26	1982	F	L 0-4
NY Rangers	1	0	1	7	3	4	0	19	21	1994	F	L 3-4
Philadelphia	1	0	1	3	1	2	0	9	15	1979	PRE	L 1-2
Phoenix	2	2	0	13	8	5	0	50	34	1993	DSF	W 4-2
St. Louis	2	2	0	14	8	6	0	44	48	2003	CQF	W 4-3
Toronto	1	1	0	5	4	1	0	16	9	1994	CF	W 4-1
Totals	**32**	**11**	**21**	**167**	**71**	**96**	**0**	**473**	**552**			

Calgary totals include Atlanta Flames, 1972-73 to 1979-80.
Colorado totals include Quebec, 1979-80 to 1994-95.
New Jersey totals include Kansas City, 1974-75, 1975-76, and Colorado Rockies, 1976-77 to 1981-82.
Phoenix totals include Winnipeg, 1979-80 to 1995-96.
Carolina totals include Hartford, 1979-80 to 1996-97.
Dallas totals include Minnesota North Stars, 1970-71 to 1992-93.

Playoff Results 2008-2003

Year	Round	Opponent	Result	GF	GA
2007	CSF	Anaheim	L 1-4	8	14
	CQF	Dallas	W 4-3	13	12
2004	CQF	Calgary	L 3-4	16	19
2003	CSF	Minnesota	L 3-4	17	26
	CQF	St. Louis	W 4-3	17	21

Abbreviations: Round: F – Final;
CF – conference final; **CSF** – conference semi-final;
CQF – conference quarter-final; **DF** – division final;
DSF – division semi-final; **QF** – quarter-final;
PRE – preliminary round.

2007-08 Results

Oct.	5	San Jose	1-3
	6	at Calgary	4-3*
	10	Philadelphia	2-8
	12	at Edmonton	5-2
	13	Edmonton	4-1
	15	San Jose	2-4
	19	Los Angeles	2-4
	21	at Columbus	4-1
	22	at Carolina	1-3
	24	at Detroit	2-3
	26	at Washington	3-2
	28	Detroit	2-3
Nov.	1	Nashville	0-3
	3	at Colorado	4-3
	8	at Calgary	3-2
	9	Colorado	2-1*
	14	Edmonton	0-1†
	16	Minnesota	6-2
	18	Calgary	4-1
	20	at Edmonton	4-5†
	21	at Minnesota	4-2
	23	at St. Louis	1-3
	25	Chicago	2-0
	27	Anaheim	4-0
	29	Columbus	2-0
Dec.	2	at Minnesota	1-2
	5	at Chicago	3-2
	6	at Nashville	5-2
	8	Pittsburgh	1-2†
	10	at Los Angeles	2-4
	12	at Anaheim	3-2
	13	at San Jose	2-5
	15	at Edmonton	1-2†
	18	New Jersey	5-0
	20	Dallas	3-2
	22	at Phoenix	2-1†
	23	at Colorado	1-3
	27	Calgary	5-3
	30	Anaheim	2-1
	31	at Calgary	1-2
Jan.	3	NY Rangers	3-0
	8	NY Islanders	3-2†
	10	at San Jose	1-3
	11	Phoenix	3-4
	13	at St. Louis	4-3†
	15	at Columbus	2-3
	17	at Detroit	2-3†
	19	Los Angeles	3-4
	21	Minnesota	2-4
	23	St. Louis	3-2†
	29	Dallas	3-4
	31	at Tampa Bay	3-4
Feb.	1	at Florida	3-4†
	5	at Dallas	2-3†
	7	at Atlanta	2-1
	9	Colorado	2-6
	10	Chicago	3-2†
	14	Minnesota	4-5†
	16	Edmonton	4-2
	19	at Minnesota	3-2*
	21	at Nashville	3-2†
	23	Detroit	4-1
	27	Colorado	2-3†
	29	Columbus	2-3*
Mar.	2	at Chicago	1-4
	4	at Colorado	1-2
	6	Nashville	6-2
	8	St. Louis	4-2
	10	at Los Angeles	2-1*
	12	at Anaheim	1-4
	13	at Phoenix	0-2
	15	at Dallas	4-3
	17	Phoenix	3-1
	20	at Edmonton	4-1
	21	Minnesota	1-2
	25	at Calgary	2-3
	26	at Colorado	3-6
	28	at Minnesota	0-4
	30	Calgary	6-2
Apr.	1	Colorado	2-4
	3	Edmonton	1-2
	5	Calgary	1-7

* – Overtime † – Shootout

Entry Draft Selections 2008-1994

Name in bold denotes played in NHL.

2008
Pick
10 Cody Hodgson
41 Yann Sauve
131 Prab Rai
161 Mats Froshaug
191 Morgan Clark

2007
Pick
25 Patrick White
33 Taylor Ellington
145 Charles-Antoine Messier
146 Ilja Kablukov
176 Taylor Matson
206 Dan Gendur

2006
Pick
14 Michael Grabner
82 Daniel Rahimi
163 Sergei Shirokov
167 Juraj Simek
197 Evan Fuller

2005
Pick
10 **Luc Bourdon**
51 **Mason Raymond**
114 Alexandre Vincent
138 Matt Butcher
185 Kris Fredheim
205 Mario Bliznak

2004
Pick
26 Cory Schneider
91 **Alexander Edler**
125 Andrew Sarauer
159 **Mike Brown**
189 Julien Ellis
254 David Schulz
287 **Jannik Hansen**

2003
Pick
23 **Ryan Kesler**
60 Marc-Andre Bernier
111 **Brandon Nolan**
128 Ty Morris
160 Nicklas Danielsson
190 Chad Brownlee
222 Francois-Pierre Guenette
252 Sergei Topol
254 **Nathan McIver**
285 Matthew Hansen

2002
Pick
49 Kirill Koltsov
55 Denis Grot
68 Brett Skinner
83 Lukas Mensator
114 John Laliberte
151 **Rob McVicar**
214 Marc-Andre Roy
223 Ilia Krikunov
247 Matt Violin
277 Thomas Nussli
278 Matt Gens

2001
Pick
16 **R.J. Umberger**
66 **Fedor Fedorov**
114 Evgeny Gladskikh
151 **Kevin Bieksa**
212 **Jason King**
245 Konstantin Mikhailov

2000
Pick
23 **Nathan Smith**
71 Thatcher Bell
93 Tim Branham
144 Pavel Duma
208 **Brandon Reid**
241 Nathan Barrett
272 Tim Smith

1999
Pick
2 **Daniel Sedin**
3 **Henrik Sedin**
69 Rene Vydareny
129 Ryan Thorpe
172 Josh Reed
189 Kevin Swanson
218 Markus Kankaanpera
271 Darrell Hay

1998
Pick
4 **Bryan Allen**
31 **Artem Chubarov**
68 **Jarkko Ruutu**
81 Justin Morrison
90 Regan Darby
136 David Ytfeldt
140 Rick Bertran
149 Paul Cabana
177 Vincent Malts
204 Greg Mischler
219 Curtis Valentine
232 Jason Metcalfe

1997
Pick
10 **Brad Ference**
34 **Ryan Bonni**
36 **Harold Druken**
64 **Kyle Freadrich**
90 Chris Stanley
114 David Darguzas
117 Matt Cockell
144 **Matt Cooke**
148 Larry Shapley
171 Rod Leroux
201 Denis Martynyuk
227 Peter Brady

1996
Pick
12 **Josh Holden**
75 **Zenith Komarniski**
93 Jonas Soling
121 Tyler Prosofsky
147 Nolan McDonald
175 Clint Cabana
201 Jeff Scissons
227 **Lubomir Vaic**

1995
Pick
40 **Chris McAllister**
61 **Larry Courville**
66 **Peter Schaefer**
92 Lloyd Shaw
120 Todd Norman
144 **Brent Sopel**
170 Stewart Bodtker
196 Tyler Willis
222 Jason Cugnet

1994
Pick
13 **Mattias Ohlund**
39 **Robb Gordon**
42 **Dave Scatchard**
65 Chad Allan
92 Mike Dubinsky
117 Yanick Dube
169 Yuri Kuznetsov
195 Rob Trumbley
221 **Bill Muckalt**
247 **Tyson Nash**
273 Robert Longpre

Mike Gillis

General Manager

Born: Sudbury, Ont., December 1, 1958.

The Vancouver Canucks announced on April 23, 2008, that Mike Gillis had been named the tenth general manager in club history. Gillis joined the Canucks organization after spending the previous 16 years as a player representative.

Gillis began his NHL career in 1978 as a member of the Colorado Rockies. In 246 NHL regular season games, Gillis recorded 76 points (33 goals, 43 assists) and 186 penalty minutes with Colorado and Boston before a leg injury forced him to retire in 1985. He then returned to Kingston, Ontario, where he had grown up, to obtain his law degree from Queen's University in 1990. Gillis began his career as a NHL player representative in 1992 and became one of the most successful in his industry. His ability to evaluate players, negotiate contracts and his extensive knowledge of the Collective Bargaining Agreement, provided him the opportunity to work with a number of the NHL's most elite players.

Club Directory

General Motors Place

Vancouver Canucks
General Motors Place
800 Griffiths Way
Vancouver, B.C. V6B 6G1
Phone **604/899-4600**
FAX 604/899-4640
www.canucks.com
Capacity: 18,630

Executive Directory

Chairman & Governor, NHL	Francesco Aquilini
Alternate Governor, NHL	Paolo Aquilini
Alternate Governor, NHL	Roberto Aquilini
President & CEO & Alt. Gov., NHL	Chris Zimmerman
Executive Assistant	Erin Lewyk
General Manager & Alternate Governor, NHL	Mike Gillis
Chief Operating Officer	Victor de Bonis
Legal Counsel	James Conrad
Exec. Vice President, Business & General Counsel	Jon Festinger
Vice President, Business Development	Gord Forbes
Vice President, People Development	Susanne Haine
Vice President & G.M., Arena Operations	Harvey Jones
Vice President, Finance & Chief Financial Officer	Todd Kobus

Hockey Operations

General Manager & Alternate Governor	Mike Gillis
Executive Assistant	Michelle Di Tomaso
Director, Hockey Administration	Laurence Gilman
Executive Assistant	Lori Meehan
Head Coach	Alain Vigneault
Associate Coach	Rick Bowness
Assistant Coaches	Ryan Walter, Darryl Williams
Goaltending Consultant	Ian Clark
Strength & Conditioning Coach	Roger Takahashi
Director, Player Personnel	Lorne Henning
Director, Player Development	Dave Gagner
Director, Collegiate Scouting	Stan Smyl
Chairman, True North & Gov., Manitoba Moose	Mark Chipman
President & CEO, Manitoba Moose	Jim Ludlow
Head Coach, Manitoba Moose	Scott Arniel
Assistant Coach, Manitoba Moose	Brad Berry
Director, Media Relations & Team Operations	T.C. Carling
Manager, Media Relations & Team Operations	Ben Brown
Coordinator, Media Relations & Publications	Stephanie Maniago
Assistant, Media Relations	Jen Herrington
Director, Community Partnerships	Debbie Butt
Manager, Community Partnership & Events	Karen Christiansen
Coordinator, Community Partnerships	Tara Clarke
Coordinator, Community Partnerships & Education	Jessica Danylchuk
Manager, Hockey Development & Alumni Liaison	Rod Brathwaite
Coordinator, Comm. Partnerships & Mascot Liaison	Paul Buckley

Scouting Staff

Chief Scout	Ron Delorme
Amateur Scouts	Brian Chapman, Sergei Chibisov, Jim Eagle, Thomas Gradin, Frank Kollar, Raymond Payne, Harold Snepsts
Professional Scouts	Eric Crawford, Lucien DeBlois, Lars Lindgren
Manager, Scouting & Player Information	Jonathan Wall

Medical & Training Staff

Medical Trainer	Mike Burnstein
Assistant Medical Trainer	Marty Dudgeon
Assistant Medical Trainer	Jon Sanderson
Equipment Manager	Pat O'Neill
Assistant Equipment Manager	Jamie Hendricks
Trainer's Assistant	Brian Hamilton
Game Dressing Room Attendants	John Jukich, Ron Shute, Brian Brumwell
Team Physicians	Dr. Rui Avelar, Dr. Bill Regan, Dr. Mike Wilkinson
Team Dentist	Dr. Jeffrey Norden
Team Chiropractor	Dr. Sid Sheard
Team Optometrist	Dr. Alan R. Boyco

Broadcast

Director, Facilities & In-House Productions	Paul Brettell
Director, Production Services	Mike Hall
Senior Broadcast Technician	Greg Story
Senior Multimedia Producer	Jason Steensma
Multimedia Producer	Gayla Anderson
Broadcast Business Manager	Shannon Baker

Business Development

Directors	David Altman, Sharon Butler, James Douglas, Darren Moscovitch

Canucks Team Store

Director, Retail & Consumer Product Marketing	Janeil Mackay

Customer Sales & Ticket Operations

Director, Client Service & Ticket Operations	Mary Nagy

Engineering

Director, Engineering	Al Hutchings

Event Services

Director, Event Services	Indira Fisher

Finance & Administration

Director, Finance	Aaron Wilson
Controller, Hockey Operations	Patricia Bigonzi

Marketing, Creative Services

Director, Brand Management	Paul Dal Monte

People Development

Manager, People Development	Dana Clark

Travel

Travel Manager	Cathie Moroney

Website

Director, Website & New Media	Kevin Kinghorn

Washington Capitals

Key Off-Season Signings/Acquisitions

2008

May 22 • Signed 2007 1st-round pick (5th overall), D **Karl Alzner**.
27 • Re-signed RW **Matt Bradley**.
July 1 • Re-signed D **Mike Green**.
1 • Signed G **Jose Theodore**.
3 • Signed C **Keith Aucoin**.
9 • Re-signed C **Brooks Laich**.
10 • Re-signed RW **Eric Fehr**.
11 • Re-signed C/RW **Boyd Gordon**.
14 • Re-signed C **Sergei Fedorov**.

2007-08 Results: 43W-31L-4OTL-4SOL 94PTS.
First, Southeast Division

The face of the franchise. Alex Ovechkin celebrated a new 13-year contract extension in style in 2007-08. His 65 goals established a new team record and was the highest total in the NHL since Mario Lemieux scored 69 in 1995-96. His 112 points also led the league.

2008-09 Schedule

Oct.	Fri.	10	at Atlanta		Fri.	9	Columbus
	Sat.	11	Chicago		Sat.	10	at Montreal
	Mon.	13	Vancouver		Tue.	13	Edmonton
	Thu.	16	at Pittsburgh		Wed.	14	at Pittsburgh
	Sat.	18	New Jersey		Sat.	17	Boston
	Tue.	21	at Calgary		Mon.	19	at NY Islanders*
	Thu.	23	at Phoenix		Tue.	20	at Ottawa
	Sat.	25	at Dallas		Tue.	27	at Boston
	Tue.	28	Nashville		Sat.	31	Detroit*
Nov.	Sat.	1	at Buffalo	**Feb.**	Sun.	1	Ottawa*
	Tue.	4	at Ottawa		Tue.	3	at New Jersey
	Thu.	6	Carolina		Thu.	5	Los Angeles
	Sat.	8	NY Rangers		Sat.	7	Florida
	Mon.	10	Tampa Bay		Wed.	11	at NY Rangers
	Wed.	12	at Carolina		Sat.	14	at Tampa Bay
	Fri.	14	New Jersey		Sun.	15	at Florida*
	Sat.	15	at New Jersey		Wed.	18	Montreal
	Wed.	19	at Anaheim		Fri.	20	Colorado
	Thu.	20	at Los Angeles		Sun.	22	Pittsburgh*
	Sat.	22	at San Jose		Tue.	24	Philadelphia
	Mon.	24	at Minnesota		Thu.	26	Atlanta
	Wed.	26	Atlanta		Sat.	28	at Boston*
	Fri.	28	Montreal	**Mar.**	Sun.	1	Florida*
	Sat.	29	at Columbus		Tue.	3	Carolina
Dec.	Tue.	2	Florida		Thu.	5	Toronto
	Thu.	4	NY Islanders		Sun.	8	Pittsburgh*
	Sat.	6	at Toronto		Tue.	10	at Nashville
	Sun.	7	at Carolina*		Thu.	12	at Philadelphia
	Wed.	10	Boston		Sat.	14	Carolina
	Fri.	12	Ottawa		Mon.	16	at Atlanta
	Sat.	13	at Montreal		Tue.	17	at Florida
	Tue.	16	at NY Islanders		Thu.	19	at Tampa Bay
	Thu.	18	St. Louis		Sat.	21	at Carolina
	Sat.	20	at Philadelphia*		Tue.	24	at Toronto
	Tue.	23	at NY Rangers		Fri.	27	Tampa Bay
	Fri.	26	Buffalo	**Apr.**	Wed.	1	NY Islanders
	Sun.	28	Toronto		Fri.	3	Buffalo
	Tue.	30	at Buffalo		Sun.	5	Atlanta*
Jan.	Thu.	1	Tampa Bay		Tue.	7	at Atlanta
	Sat.	3	NY Rangers		Thu.	9	at Tampa Bay
	Tue.	6	Philadelphia		Sat.	11	at Florida

* Denotes afternoon game.

Year-by-Year Record

		Home				Road				Overall								
Season	**GP**	**W**	**L**	**T**	**OL**	**W**	**L**	**T**	**OL**	**W**	**L**	**T**	**OL**	**GF**	**GA**	**Pts.**	**Finished**	**Playoff Result**
2007-08	82	23	15	....	3	20	16	....	5	43	31	....	8	242	231	94	1st, Southeast Div.	Lost Conf. Quarter-Final
2006-07	82	17	17	....	7	11	23	....	7	28	40	....	14	235	286	70	5th, Southeast Div.	Out of Playoffs
2005-06	82	16	18	....	7	13	23	....	5	29	41	....	12	237	306	70	5th, Southeast Div.	Out of Playoffs
2004-05	....	....	....	....	....	....	....	....	....	....	....	....	....	....	....	....		
2003-04	82	13	20	6	2	10	26	4	1	23	46	10	3	186	253	59	5th, Southeast Div.	Out of Playoffs
2002-03	82	24	13	2	2	15	16	6	4	39	29	8	6	224	220	92	2nd, Southeast Div.	Lost Conf. Quarter-Final
2001-02	82	21	12	6	2	15	21	5	0	36	33	11	2	228	240	85	2nd, Southeast Div.	Out of Playoffs
2000-01	82	24	9	6	2	17	18	4	2	41	27	10	4	233	211	96	1st, Southeast Div.	Lost Conf. Quarter-Final
1999-2000	82	26	5	8	2	18	19	4	0	44	24	12	2	227	194	102	1st, Southeast Div.	Lost Conf. Quarter-Final
1998-99	82	16	23	2	....	15	22	4	....	31	45	6	....	200	218	68	3rd, Southeast Div.	Out of Playoffs
1997-98	82	23	12	6	....	17	18	6	....	40	30	12	....	219	202	92	3rd, Atlantic Div.	Lost Final
1996-97	82	19	17	5	....	14	23	4	....	33	40	9	....	214	231	75	5th, Atlantic Div.	Out of Playoffs
1995-96	82	21	15	5	....	18	17	6	....	39	32	11	....	234	204	89	4th, Atlantic Div.	Lost Conf. Quarter-Final
1994-95	48	15	6	3	....	7	12	5	....	22	18	8	....	136	120	52	3rd, Atlantic Div.	Lost Conf. Quarter-Final
1993-94	84	17	16	9	....	22	19	1	....	39	35	10	....	277	263	88	3rd, Atlantic Div.	Lost Conf. Semi-Final
1992-93	84	21	15	6	....	22	19	1	....	43	34	7	....	325	286	93	2nd, Patrick Div.	Lost Div. Semi-Final
1991-92	80	25	12	3	....	20	15	5	....	45	27	8	....	330	275	98	2nd, Patrick Div.	Lost Div. Semi-Final
1990-91	80	21	14	5	....	16	22	2	....	37	36	7	....	258	258	81	3rd, Patrick Div.	Lost Div. Final
1989-90	80	19	18	3	....	17	20	3	....	36	38	6	....	284	275	78	3rd, Patrick Div.	Lost Conf. Championship
1988-89	80	25	12	3	....	16	17	7	....	41	29	10	....	305	259	92	1st, Patrick Div.	Lost Div. Semi-Final
1987-88	80	22	14	4	....	16	19	5	....	38	33	9	....	281	249	85	2nd, Patrick Div.	Lost Div. Final
1986-87	80	22	15	3	....	16	17	7	....	38	32	10	....	285	278	86	2nd, Patrick Div.	Lost Div. Semi-Final
1985-86	80	30	8	2	....	20	15	5	....	50	23	7	....	315	272	107	2nd, Patrick Div.	Lost Div. Final
1984-85	80	27	11	2	....	19	14	7	....	46	25	9	....	322	240	101	2nd, Patrick Div.	Lost Div. Semi-Final
1983-84	80	26	11	3	....	22	16	2	....	48	27	5	....	308	226	101	2nd, Patrick Div.	Lost Div. Final
1982-83	80	22	12	6	....	17	13	10	....	39	25	16	....	306	283	94	3rd, Patrick Div.	Lost Div. Semi-Final
1981-82	80	16	16	8	....	10	25	5	....	26	41	13	....	319	338	65	5th, Patrick Div.	Out of Playoffs
1980-81	80	16	17	7	....	10	19	11	....	26	36	18	....	286	317	70	5th, Patrick Div.	Out of Playoffs
1979-80	80	20	14	6	....	7	26	7	....	27	40	13	....	261	293	67	5th, Patrick Div.	Out of Playoffs
1978-79	80	15	19	6	....	9	22	9	....	24	41	15	....	273	338	63	4th, Norris Div.	Out of Playoffs
1977-78	80	10	23	7	....	7	26	7	....	17	49	14	....	195	321	48	5th, Norris Div.	Out of Playoffs
1976-77	80	17	15	8	....	7	27	6	....	24	42	14	....	221	307	62	4th, Norris Div.	Out of Playoffs
1975-76	80	6	26	8	....	5	33	2	....	11	59	10	....	224	394	32	5th, Norris Div.	Out of Playoffs
1974-75	80	7	28	5	....	1	39	0	....	8	67	5	....	181	446	21	5th, Norris Div.	Out of Playoffs

SOUTHEAST DIVISION
35th NHL Season
Franchise date: June 11, 1974

2008-09 Player Personnel

FORWARDS	HT	WT	S	Place of Birth	*Age	2007-08 Club
AUCOIN, Keith	5-9	187	R	Waltham, MA	29	Carolina-Albany
BACKSTROM, Nicklas	6-0	183	L	Gavle, Sweden	20	Washington
BEAGLE, Jay	6-3	207	R	Calgary, Alta.	22	Hershey
BOUCHARD, Francois	6-1	193	L	Sherbrooke, Que.	20	Baie-Comeau-Hershey
BOURQUE, Chris	5-9	173	L	Boston, MA	22	Washington-Hershey
BRADLEY, Matt	6-3	210	R	Stittsville, Ont.	30	Washington
BRASHEAR, Donald	6-3	239	L	Bedford, IN	36	Washington
CLARK, Chris	6-0	202	R	South Windsor, CT	32	Washington
FEDOROV, Sergei	6-2	207	L	Pskov, USSR	38	Columbus-Washington
FEHR, Eric	6-4	212	R	Winkler, Man.	23	Washington-Hershey
FLEISCHMANN, Tomas	6-1	192	L	Koprivnice, Czech.	24	Washington
GIROUX, Alexandre	6-3	190	L	Quebec City, Que.	27	Chicago (AHL)-Hershey
GORDON, Andrew	6-0	198	R	Halifax, N.S.	22	Hershey-South Carolina
GORDON, Boyd	6-2	201	R	Unity, Sask.	24	Washington
JOUDREY, Andrew	5-11	191	L	Halifax, N.S.	24	Hershey
KOZLOV, Viktor	6-4	224	R	Togliatti, USSR	33	Washington
LAICH, Brooks	6-2	205	L	Wawota, Sask.	25	Washington
LAING, Quintin	6-2	200	L	Rosetown, Sask.	29	Washington-Hershey
MINK, Graham	6-3	220	R	Stowe, VT	29	Worcester
MORIN, Travis	6-2	195	L	Minneapolis, MN	24	Hershey-South Carolina
NYLANDER, Michael	6-1	195	L	Stockholm, Sweden	36	Washington
OSALA, Oskar	6-4	225	L	Vaasa, Finland	20	Blues
OVECHKIN, Alex	6-2	217	R	Moscow, USSR	23	Washington
PERREAULT, Mathieu	5-10	165	L	Drummondville, Que.	20	Acadie-Bathurst-Hershey
PINIZZOTTO, Steve	6-1	196	R	Mississauga, Ont.	24	Hershey-South Carolina
SEMIN, Alexander	6-2	205	L	Krasnoyarsk, USSR	24	Washington
STECKEL, David	6-5	218	L	Westbend, WI	26	Washington
WILSON, Kyle	6-0	200	R	Oakville, Ont.	23	Hershey
DEFENSEMEN						
ALZNER, Karl	6-2	205	L	Burnaby, B.C.	20	Calgary (WHL)
COLLINS, Sean	6-1	212	R	Troy, MI	24	Hershey-South Carolina
DOVGAN, Viktor	6-1	205	L	Moscow, USSR	21	CSKA
ERSKINE, John	6-4	218	L	Kingston, Ont.	28	Washington
GODFREY, Josh	6-0	202	R	Collingwood, Ont.	20	Sault Ste. Marie-Hershey
GREEN, Mike	6-2	201	R	Calgary, Alta.	22	Washington
JURCINA, Milan	6-4	237	R	Liptovsky Mikulas, Czech.	25	Washington
LEPISTO, Sami	6-1	195	L	Espoo, Finland	23	Washington-Hershey
McNEILL, Patrick	6-0	198	L	Strathroy, Ont.	21	Hershey-South Carolina
MORRISONN, Shaone	6-4	212	L	Vancouver, B.C.	25	Washington
POKULOK, Sasha	6-6	220	L	Montreal, Que.	22	Hershey-South Carolina
POTHIER, Brian	6-0	200	R	New Bedford, MA	31	Washington
POTI, Tom	6-3	210	L	Worcester, MA	31	Washington
SCHULTZ, Jeff	6-6	221	L	Calgary, Alta.	22	Washington-Hershey
SLOAN, Tyler	6-4	190	L	Calgary, Alta.	27	Hershey

GOALTENDERS	HT	WT	C	Place of Birth	*Age	2007-08 Club
JOHNSON, Brent	6-3	210	L	Farmington, MI	31	Washington-Hershey
MACHESNEY, Daren	6-0	182	L	Hamilton, Ont.	21	Hershey
NEUVIRTH, Michal	6-1	190	L	Usti nad Labem, Czech.	20	Plymouth-Windsor-Oshawa
THEODORE, Jose	5-11	182	R	Laval, Que.	32	Colorado-Lake Erie
VARLAMOV, Simeon	6-1	200	L	Kuybyshev, USSR	20	Yaroslavl

* – Age at start of 2008-09 season

General Managers' History

Milt Schmidt, 1974-75; Milt Schmidt and Max McNab, 1975-76; Max McNab, 1976-77 to 1980-81; Max McNab and Roger Crozier, 1981-82; David Poile, 1982-83 to 1996-97; George McPhee, 1997-98 to date.

George McPhee

Vice President and General Manager

Born: Wallaceburg, Ont., July 2, 1958.

On June 9, 1997, George McPhee became the fifth general manager of the Washington Capitals. In his first year on the job, McPhee led the Caps to the Stanley Cup Finals for the first time in franchise history. He has begun rebuilding the Capitals with younger players and used the first overall choice at the 2004 NHL Entry Draft to select Alex Ovechkin.

Prior to joining the Capitals, McPhee spent five years in the front office of the Vancouver Canucks where he served as vice president of hockey operations and alternate governor. He has earned degrees in both law and business and, while attending law school at Rutgers University, interned at the United States Court of International Trade in 1991.

A back injury forced McPhee to retire as an active player at the conclusion of the 1988-89 season, after a seven year playing career with the New York Rangers and New Jersey Devils. McPhee originally signed as a free agent with the Rangers in July, 1982, after graduating from Bowling Green State University with a business degree. McPhee did not waste any time in college, tallying 40 goals and 48 assists in his freshman season and easily winning CCHA rookie of the year honors. His outstanding collegiate hockey career was capped off when he was named the recipient of the Hobey Baker Award as the top U.S. collegiate player in his senior season. McPhee also earned All-America honors as a senior and finished his career at Bowling Green as the CCHA's all-time leading scorer with 114-153-267. He was the first player in CCHA history to make the Conference's all-academic team three straight seasons.

2007-08 Scoring

* – rookie

Regular Season

Pos	#	Player	Team	GP	G	A	Pts	TOI	+/–	PIM	PP	SH	GW	S	%
L	8	Alex Ovechkin	WSH	82	65	47	112	23:06	28	40	22	0	11	446	14.6
C	19 *	Nicklas Backstrom	WSH	82	14	55	69	18:59	13	24	3	0	4	153	9.2
D	52	Mike Green	WSH	82	18	38	56	23:38	6	62	8	0	4	234	7.7
C	25	Viktor Kozlov	WSH	81	16	38	54	17:34	28	18	2	0	2	219	7.3
L	28	Alexander Semin	WSH	63	26	16	42	16:54	–18	54	10	0	2	185	14.1
C	91	Sergei Fedorov	CBJ	50	9	19	28	17:27	–3	30	5	0	1	94	9.6
			WSH	18	2	11	13	18:15	–2	8	1	0	1	34	5.9
			Total	68	11	30	41	17:40	–5	38	6	0	2	128	8.6
C	21	Brooks Laich	WSH	82	21	16	37	14:02	–3	35	8	2	4	122	17.2
C	92	Michael Nylander	WSH	40	11	26	37	19:09	–19	24	5	0	1	77	14.3
L	43	Tomas Fleischmann	WSH	75	10	20	30	12:37	–7	18	1	0	1	107	9.3
D	3	Tom Poti	WSH	71	2	27	29	23:28	9	46	0	0	0	99	2.0
L	24	Matt Cooke	VAN	61	7	9	16	13:23	–4	64	0	0	1	68	10.3
			WSH	17	3	4	7	12:19	5	27	0	1	0	18	16.7
			Total	78	10	13	23	13:09	1	91	0	1	1	86	11.6
R	10	Matt Bradley	WSH	77	7	11	18	09:59	1	74	1	1	2	111	6.3
D	55	Jeff Schultz	WSH	72	5	13	18	18:05	12	28	0	0	0	36	13.9
C	15	Boyd Gordon	WSH	67	7	9	16	15:44	5	12	0	1	0	100	7.0
D	2	Brian Pothier	WSH	38	5	9	14	18:41	5	20	1	0	1	65	7.7
C	39 *	David Steckel	WSH	67	5	7	12	13:33	1	34	0	0	1	66	7.6
D	26	Shaone Morrisonn	WSH	76	1	9	10	20:16	4	63	0	0	1	47	2.1
R	17	Chris Clark	WSH	18	5	4	9	16:54	0	43	1	0	1	29	17.2
D	4	John Erskine	WSH	51	2	7	9	15:42	1	96	0	0	1	48	4.2
D	23	Milan Jurcina	WSH	75	1	8	9	16:38	4	30	1	0	0	58	1.7
L	87	Donald Brashear	WSH	80	5	3	8	07:51	–7	119	0	0	0	59	8.5
R	14	Eric Fehr	WSH	23	1	5	6	10:30	4	6	0	0	0	40	2.5
L	53	Quintin Laing	WSH	39	1	5	6	11:33	4	10	0	0	1	48	2.1
R	50	Joe Motzko	WSH	8	2	2	4	12:27	1	0	0	0	0	10	20.0
D	44	Steve Eminger	WSH	20	0	2	2	11:08	–4	8	0	0	0	14	0.0
D	42 *	Sami Lepisto	WSH	7	0	1	1	13:17	–1	12	0	0	0	8	0.0
L	56 *	Chris Bourque	WSH	4	0	0	0	08:41	0	2	0	0	0	4	0.0

Goaltending

No.	Goaltender	GPI	Mins	Avg	W	L	OT	EN	SO	GA	SA	S%	G	A	PIM
38	Cristobal Huet	13	771	1.63	11	2	0	1	2	21	329	.936	0	1	0
1	Brent Johnson	19	1032	2.67	7	8	2	3	0	46	500	.908	0	0	0
37	Olaf Kolzig	54	3154	2.91	25	21	6	3	1	153	1423	.892	0	2	8
	Totals	**82**	**4987**	**2.73**	**43**	**31**	**8**	**7**	**3**	**227**	**2259**	**.900**			

Playoffs

Pos	#	Player	Team	GP	G	A	Pts	TOI	+/–	PIM	PP	SH	GW	OT	S	%
L	8	Alex Ovechkin	WSH	7	4	5	9	24:03	–1	0	1	0	2	0	37	10.8
L	28	Alexander Semin	WSH	7	3	5	8	19:45	2	8	2	0	1	0	28	10.7
D	52	Mike Green	WSH	7	3	4	7	26:58	–2	15	2	0	0	0	19	15.8
C	19 *	Nicklas Backstrom	WSH	7	4	2	6	20:26	3	2	3	0	0	0	19	21.1
C	21	Brooks Laich	WSH	7	1	5	6	18:36	2	4	0	0	0	0	20	5.0
C	91	Sergei Fedorov	WSH	7	1	4	5	21:38	–1	8	0	0	0	0	18	5.6
C	25	Viktor Kozlov	WSH	7	0	3	3	17:57	–4	2	0	0	0	0	13	0.0
L	87	Donald Brashear	WSH	7	1	1	2	07:30	1	0	0	0	0	0	5	20.0
C	39 *	David Steckel	WSH	7	1	1	2	14:23	–2	4	0	0	0	0	9	11.1
R	10	Matt Bradley	WSH	7	0	2	2	11:40	–3	2	0	0	0	0	8	0.0
D	4	John Erskine	WSH	7	0	2	2	17:06	1	6	0	0	0	0	8	0.0
D	44	Steve Eminger	WSH	5	1	0	1	16:06	2	2	0	0	0	0	1	100.0
R	14	Eric Fehr	WSH	5	1	0	1	09:41	1	0	0	0	0	0	5	20.0
D	3	Tom Poti	WSH	7	0	1	1	24:00	–1	8	0	0	0	0	9	0.0
D	26	Shaone Morrisonn	WSH	7	0	1	1	21:17	–3	6	0	0	0	0	2	0.0
L	43	Tomas Fleischmann	WSH	2	0	0	0	09:49	–2	0	0	0	0	0	1	0.0
D	55	Jeff Schultz	WSH	2	0	0	0	10:24	–2	2	0	0	0	0	0	0.0
L	24	Matt Cooke	WSH	7	0	0	0	13:54	–1	4	0	0	0	0	8	0.0
D	23	Milan Jurcina	WSH	7	0	0	0	16:26	1	6	0	0	0	0	3	0.0
C	15	Boyd Gordon	WSH	7	0	0	0	13:22	–2	0	0	0	0	0	5	0.0

Goaltending

No.	Goaltender	GPI	Mins	Avg	W	L	EN	SO	GA	SA	S%	G	A	PIM
38	Cristobal Huet	7	451	2.93	3	4	1	0	22	242	.909	0	0	2
	Totals	**7**	**453**	**3.05**	**3**	**4**	**1**	**0**	**23**	**243**	**.905**			

Coaching History

Jim Anderson, Red Sullivan and Milt Schmidt, 1974-75; Milt Schmidt and Tom McVie, 1975-76; Tom McVie, 1976-77, 1977-78; Danny Belisle, 1978-79; Danny Belisle and Gary Green, 1979-80; Gary Green, 1980-81; Gary Green, Roger Crozier and Bryan Murray, 1981-82; Bryan Murray, 1982-83 to 1988-89; Bryan Murray and Terry Murray, 1989-90; Terry Murray, 1990-91 to 1992-93; Terry Murray and Jim Schoenfeld, 1993-94; Jim Schoenfeld, 1994-95 to 1996-97; Ron Wilson, 1997-98 to 2001-02; Bruce Cassidy, 2002-03; Bruce Cassidy and Glen Hanlon, 2003-04; Glen Hanlon, 2004-05 to 2006-07; Glen Hanlon and Bruce Boudreau, 2007-08; Bruce Boudreau, 2008-09.

Club Records

Team

(Figures in brackets for season records are games played; records for fewest points, wins, ties, losses, goals, goals against are for 70 or more games)

Most Points	107	1985-86 (80)
Most Wins	50	1985-86 (80)
Most Ties	18	1980-81 (80)
Most Losses	67	1974-75 (80)
Most Goals	330	1991-92 (80)
Most Goals Against	*446	1974-75 (80)
Fewest Points	*21	1974-75 (80)
Fewest Wins	*8	1974-75 (80)
Fewest Ties	5	1974-75 (80), 1983-84 (80)
Fewest Losses	23	1985-86 (80)
Fewest Goals	181	1974-75 (80)
Fewest Goals Against	194	1999-00 (82)
Longest Winning Streak		
Overall	10	Jan. 27-Feb. 18/84
Home	10	Jan. 4-Feb. 23/00
Away	6	Feb. 26-Apr. 1/84
Longest Undefeated Streak		
Overall	14	Nov. 24-Dec. 23/82 (9 wins, 5 ties), Jan. 17-Feb. 18/84 (13 wins, 1 tie)
Home	13	Nov. 25/92-Jan. 31/93 (9 wins, 4 ties), Dec. 27/99-Feb. 23/00 (11 wins, 2 ties)
Away	10	Nov. 24/82-Jan. 8/83 (6 wins, 4 ties)
Longest Losing Streak		
Overall	*17	Feb. 18-Mar. 26/75
Home	*11	Feb. 18-Mar. 30/75
Away	37	Oct. 9/74-Mar. 26/75
Longest Winless Streak		
Overall	25	Nov. 29/75-Jan. 21/76 (22 losses, 3 ties)
Home	14	Dec. 3/75-Jan. 21/76 (11 losses, 3 ties)
Away	37	Oct. 9/74-Mar. 26/75 (37 losses)
Most Shutouts, Season	9	1995-96 (82)
Most PIM, Season	2,204	1989-90 (80)
Most Goals, Game	12	Feb. 6/90 (Que. 2 at Wsh. 12), Jan. 11/03 (Fla. 2 at Wsh. 12)

Individual

Most Seasons	16	Olaf Kolzig
Most Games	983	Calle Johansson
Most Goals, Career	472	Peter Bondra
Most Assists, Career	418	Michal Pivonka
Most Points, Career	825	Peter Bondra (472G, 353A)
Most PIM, Career	2,003	Dale Hunter
Most Shutouts, Career	35	Olaf Kolzig
Longest Consecutive Games Streak	422	Bob Carpenter (Oct. 7/81-Nov. 22/86)
Most Goals, Season	65	Alex Ovechkin (2007-08)
Most Assists, Season	76	Dennis Maruk (1981-82)
Most Points, Season	136	Dennis Maruk (1981-82; 60G, 76A)
Most PIM, Season	339	Alan May (1989-90)
Most Points, Defenseman, Season	81	Larry Murphy (1986-87; 23G, 58A)
Most Points, Center, Season	136	Dennis Maruk (1981-82; 60G, 76A)
Most Points, Right Wing, Season	102	Mike Gartner (1984-85; 50G, 52A)
Most Points, Left Wing, Season	112	Alex Ovechkin (2007-08; 65G, 47A)
Most Points, Rookie, Season	106	Alex Ovechkin (2005-06; 52G, 54A)
Most Shutouts, Season	9	Jim Carey (1995-96)
Most Goals, Game	5	Bengt Gustafsson (Jan. 8/84), Peter Bondra (Feb. 5/94)
Most Assists, Game	6	Mike Ridley (Jan. 7/89)
Most Points, Game	7	Dino Ciccarelli (Mar. 18/89; 4G, 3A), Jaromir Jagr (Jan. 11/03; 3G, 4A)

* NHL Record.

Retired Numbers

5	Rod Langway	1982-1993
7	Yvon Labre	1974-1981
32	Dale Hunter	1987-1999

Captains' History

Doug Mohns, 1974-75; Bill Clement and Yvon Labre, 1975-76; Yvon Labre, 1976-77, 1977-78; Guy Charron, 1978-79; Ryan Walter, 1979-80 to 1981-82; Rod Langway, 1982-83 to 1991-92; Rod Langway and Kevin Hatcher, 1992-93; Kevin Hatcher, 1993-94; Dale Hunter, 1994-95 to 1998-99; Adam Oates, 1999-2000, 2000-01; Brendan Witt and Steve Konowalchuk, 2001-02; Steve Konowalchuk, 2002-03, 2003-04; Jeff Halpern, 2005-06; Chris Clark, 2006-07 to date.

All-time Record vs. Other Clubs

Regular Season

	At Home								On Road								Total							
	GP	W	L	T	OL	GF	GA	PTS	GP	W	L	T	OL	GF	GA	PTS	GP	W	L	T	OL	GF	GA	PTS
Anaheim	10	4	6	0	0	17	28	8	10	3	6	1	0	25	31	7	20	7	12	1	0	42	59	15
Atlanta	25	14	7	3	1	86	72	32	25	10	9	2	4	72	70	26	50	24	16	5	5	158	142	58
Boston	61	19	27	12	3	176	207	53	62	16	34	9	3	161	224	44	123	35	61	21	6	337	431	97
Buffalo	62	16	36	9	1	157	219	42	62	17	39	6	0	165	245	40	124	33	75	15	1	322	464	82
Calgary	42	22	14	6	0	156	141	50	39	8	24	7	0	97	159	23	81	30	38	13	0	253	300	73
Carolina	59	35	19	4	1	199	149	75	61	28	21	10	2	186	177	68	120	63	40	14	3	385	326	143
Chicago	42	21	15	5	1	148	131	48	41	12	23	6	0	120	156	30	83	33	38	11	1	268	287	78
Colorado	34	19	10	4	1	133	106	43	35	15	15	5	0	121	108	35	69	34	25	9	1	254	214	78
Columbus	3	2	0	1	0	11	7	5	5	4	1	0	0	19	14	8	8	6	1	1	0	30	21	13
Dallas	41	16	17	8	0	124	132	40	42	12	22	8	0	111	156	32	83	28	39	16	0	235	288	72
Detroit	47	21	21	5	0	171	151	47	48	15	20	11	2	138	165	43	95	36	41	16	2	309	316	90
Edmonton	30	19	9	2	0	123	97	40	30	10	16	4	0	91	124	24	60	29	25	6	0	214	221	64
Florida	40	19	11	5	5	118	99	48	40	17	18	4	1	99	104	39	80	36	29	9	6	217	203	87
Los Angeles	47	19	21	7	0	189	174	45	48	15	27	6	0	147	189	36	95	34	48	13	0	336	363	81
Minnesota	4	3	1	0	0	11	7	6	4	0	3	0	1	3	9	1	8	3	4	0	1	14	16	7
Montreal	65	29	27	9	0	182	197	67	66	19	38	8	1	143	250	47	131	48	65	17	1	325	447	114
Nashville	5	3	2	0	0	12	13	6	6	2	3	1	0	15	18	5	11	5	5	1	0	27	31	11
New Jersey	85	50	26	6	3	321	242	109	85	35	40	7	3	243	259	80	170	85	66	13	6	564	501	189
NY Islanders	87	42	33	11	1	283	273	96	87	38	46	2	1	265	321	79	174	80	79	13	2	548	594	175
NY Rangers	90	47	31	9	3	336	288	106	88	35	43	9	1	291	326	80	178	82	74	18	4	627	614	186
Ottawa	30	15	11	4	0	99	86	34	29	13	15	1	0	88	106	27	59	28	26	5	0	187	192	61
Philadelphia	86	36	37	13	0	282	277	85	89	28	55	6	0	242	337	62	175	64	92	19	0	524	614	147
Phoenix	32	18	8	5	1	121	88	42	31	9	15	7	0	111	113	25	63	27	23	12	1	232	201	67
Pittsburgh	92	46	35	9	2	377	336	103	89	30	51	7	1	277	349	68	181	76	86	16	3	654	685	171
St. Louis	40	21	15	4	0	141	121	46	42	13	21	8	0	130	169	34	82	34	36	12	0	271	290	80
San Jose	13	5	7	0	1	36	39	11	11	3	7	1	0	27	33	7	24	8	14	1	1	63	72	18
Tampa Bay	41	25	10	4	2	146	103	56	41	23	14	2	2	127	106	50	82	48	24	6	4	273	209	106
Toronto	56	32	19	4	1	201	161	69	54	19	28	6	1	184	229	45	110	51	47	10	2	385	390	114
Vancouver	41	22	15	4	0	134	123	48	40	16	18	5	1	125	139	38	81	38	33	9	1	259	262	86
Defunct Clubs	10	2	8	0	0	28	42	4	10	4	5	1	0	30	39	9	20	6	13	1	0	58	81	13
Totals	**1320**	**642**	**498**	**153**	**27**	**4518**	**4109**	**1464**	**1320**	**469**	**677**	**150**	**24**	**3853**	**4725**	**1112**	**2640**	**1111**	**1175**	**303**	**51**	**8371**	**8834**	**2576**

Playoffs

	Series	W	L	GP	W	L	T	GF	GA	Last Mtg.	Rnd.	Result
Boston	2	1	1	10	4	6	0	21	28	1998	CQF	W 4-2
Buffalo	1	1	0	6	4	2	0	13	11	1998	CF	W 4-2
Detroit	1	0	1	4	0	4	0	7	13	1998	F	L 0-4
New Jersey	2	1	1	13	7	6	0	44	43	1990	DSF	W 4-2
NY Islanders	6	1	5	30	12	18	0	88	99	1993	DSF	L 2-4
NY Rangers	4	2	2	22	11	11	0	75	71	1994	CSF	L 1-4
Ottawa	1	1	0	5	4	1	0	18	7	1998	CSF	W 4-1
Philadelphia	4	2	2	23	12	11	0	85	78	2008	CQF	L 3-4
Pittsburgh	7	1	6	42	16	26	0	121	137	2001	CQF	L 2-4
Tampa Bay	1	0	1	6	2	4	0	15	14	2003	CQF	L 2-4
Totals	**29**	**10**	**19**	**161**	**72**	**89**	**0**	**487**	**501**			

Playoff Results 2008-2003

Year	Round	Opponent	Result	GF	GA
2008	CQF	Philadelphia	L 3-4	20	23
2003	CQF	Tampa Bay	L 2-4	15	14

Abbreviations: Round: F – Final; **CF** – conference final; **CSF** – conference semi-final; **CQF** – conference quarter-final; **DSF** – division semi-final.

Calgary totals include Atlanta Flames, 1974-75 to 1979-80. Carolina totals include Hartford, 1979-80 to 1996-97.
Colorado totals include Quebec, 1979-80 to 1994-95. Dallas totals include Minnesota North Stars, 1974-75 to 1992-93.
New Jersey totals include Kansas City, 1974-75, 1975-76, and Colorado Rockies, 1976-77 to 1981-82.
Phoenix totals include Winnipeg, 1979-80 to 1995-96.

2007-08 Results

Oct.	5	at Atlanta	3-1
	6	Carolina	2-0
	8	at NY Islanders	2-1
	12	at NY Rangers	1-3
	13	at Buffalo	3-7
	18	NY Islanders	2-5
	20	Pittsburgh	1-2
	24	Tampa Bay	5-3
	26	Vancouver	2-3
	27	at St. Louis	3-4
	29	at Toronto	7-1
Nov.	1	at NY Rangers	0-2
	2	Philadelphia	2-3
	5	at Carolina	0-5
	6	at Atlanta	1-2*
	8	at Ottawa	4-1
	10	Tampa Bay	2-5
	15	at Florida	1-2
	16	at Tampa Bay	2-5
	19	Florida	3-4
	21	Atlanta	1-5
	23	at Philadelphia	4-3*
	24	Carolina	5-2
	26	Buffalo	1-3
	28	Florida	1-2†
	30	at Carolina	3-4
Dec.	1	at Florida	2-1
	7	at New Jersey	2-3
	8	Atlanta	6-3
	10	New Jersey	3-2
	12	NY Rangers	5-4*
	14	Buffalo	3-5
	15	at Tampa Bay	3-2
	17	at Detroit	3-4†
	20	Montreal	2-5
	22	at NY Islanders	2-3*
	26	Tampa Bay	3-2
	27	at Pittsburgh	3-4*
	29	at Ottawa	8-6
Jan.	1	Ottawa	6-3
	3	at Boston	0-2
	5	at Montreal	5-4*
	9	Colorado	2-1
	13	Philadelphia	4-6
	15	Ottawa	4-2
	17	Edmonton	5-4†
	19	Florida	5-3
	21	at Pittsburgh	6-5†
	23	at Toronto	2-3
	24	Toronto	2-1
	29	at Montreal	0-4
	31	Montreal	5-4*
Feb.	2	Atlanta	0-2
	5	at Columbus	4-3*
	6	at Philadelphia	4-3
	8	Carolina	1-2
	10	NY Rangers	3-2*
	13	at Atlanta	2-3†
	15	at Florida	2-4
	16	at Tampa Bay	3-2
	20	NY Islanders	2-3†
	23	at Carolina	3-6
	24	New Jersey	1-2*
	26	Minnesota	4-1
	29	at New Jersey	4-0
Mar.	1	Toronto	2-3
	3	Boston	10-2
	5	at Buffalo	3-1
	8	at Boston	1-2
	9	Pittsburgh	2-4
	12	Calgary	3-2
	14	Atlanta	4-1
	16	Boston	2-1†
	18	at Nashville	4-2
	19	at Chicago	0-5
	21	at Atlanta	5-3
	25	at Carolina	3-2†
	27	at Tampa Bay	4-3*
	29	at Florida	3-0
Apr.	1	Carolina	4-1
	3	Tampa Bay	4-1
	5	Florida	3-1

* – Overtime † – Shootout

Entry Draft Selections 2008-1994

Name in bold denotes played in NHL.

2008

Pick	
21	Anton Gustafsson
27	John Carlson
57	Eric Mestery
58	Dmitry Kugryshev
93	Braden Holtby
144	Joel Broda
174	Greg Burke
204	Stefan Della Rovere

2007

Pick	
5	Karl Alzner
34	Josh Godfrey
46	Theo Ruth
84	Phil Desimone
108	Brett Bruneteau
125	Brett Leffler
154	Dan Dunn
180	Justin Taylor
185	Nick Larson
199	Andrew Glass

2006

Pick	
4	**Nicklas Backstrom**
23	Simeon Varlamov
34	Michal Neuvirth
35	Francois Bouchard
52	Keith Seabrook
97	Oskar Osala
122	Luke Lynes
127	Maxime Lacroix
157	Brent Gwidt
177	Mathieu Perreault

2005

Pick	
14	Sasha Pokulok
27	Joe Finley
109	Andrew Thomas
118	Patrick McNeill
143	Daren Machesney
181	Tim Kennedy
209	Viktor Dovgan
209	Ineligible Claim

2004

Pick	
1	**Alex Ovechkin**
27	**Jeff Schultz**
29	**Mike Green**
33	**Chris Bourque**
62	Mikhail Yunkov
66	**Sami Lepisto**
88	Clayton Barthel
132	Oscar Hedman
138	Pasi Salonen
166	Peter Guggisberg
197	Andrew Gordon
230	Justin Mrazek
263	Travis Morin

2003

Pick	
18	**Eric Fehr**
83	Steve Werner
109	Andreas Valdix
155	Josh Robertson
249	Andrew Joudrey
279	Mark Olafson

2002

Pick	
12	**Steve Eminger**
13	**Alexander Semin**
17	**Boyd Gordon**
59	Maxime Daigneault
77	Patrick Wellar
92	Derek Krestanovich
109	Jevon Desautels
118	Petr Dvorak
145	Rob Gherson
179	Marian Havel
209	Joni Lindlof
242	Igor Ignatushkin
272	Patric Blomdahl

2001

Pick	
58	**Nathan Paetsch**
90	**Owen Fussey**
125	Jeff Lucky
160	Artem Ternavsky
191	Zbynek Novak
221	**Johnny Oduya**
249	Matt Maglione
254	Peter Polcik
275	Robert Muller
284	Viktor Hubl

2000

Pick	
26	**Brian Sutherby**
43	**Matt Pettinger**
61	**Jakub Cutta**
121	Ryan Vanbuskirk
163	Ivan Nepryayev
289	Bjorn Nord

1999

Pick	
7	**Kris Beech**
29	**Michal Sivek**
31	**Charlie Stephens**
34	**Ross Lupaschuk**
37	**Nolan Yonkman**
132	**Roman Tvrdon**
175	Kyle Clark
192	David Bornhammar
219	Maxim Orlov
249	Igor Shadilov

1998

Pick	
49	Jomar Cruz
59	Todd Hornung
106	**Krys Barch**
107	**Chris Corrinet**
118	**Mike Siklenka**
125	Erik Wendell
179	Nate Forster
193	**Rastislav Stana**
220	**Mike Farrell**
251	Blake Evans

1997

Pick	
9	**Nick Boynton**
35	**Jean-Francois Fortin**
89	Curtis Cruickshank
116	Kevin Caulfield
143	Henrik Petre
200	Pierre-Luc Therrien
226	Matt Oikawa

1996

Pick	
4	**Alexandre Volchkov**
17	**Jaroslav Svejkovsky**
43	**Jan Bulis**
58	Sergei Zimakov
74	Dave Weninger
78	Shawn McNeil
85	Justin Davis
126	Matthew Lahey
153	Andrew Van Bruggen
180	Michael Anderson
206	Oleg Orekhovsky
232	Chad Cavanagh

1995

Pick	
17	**Brad Church**
23	**Miika Elomo**
43	**Dwayne Hay**
93	**Sebastien Charpentier**
95	Joel Theriault
105	**Benoit Gratton**
124	Joel Cort
147	Frederick Jobin
199	Vasili Turkovsky
225	Scott Swanson

1994

Pick	
10	**Nolan Baumgartner**
15	Alexander Kharlamov
41	Scott Cherrey
93	**Matt Herr**
119	Yanick Jean
145	Dmitri Mekeshkin
171	Daniel Reja
197	Chris Patrick
223	John Tuohy
249	**Richard Zednik**
275	Sergei Tertyshny

Bruce Boudreau

Head Coach

Born: Toronto, Ont., January 9, 1955.

Bruce Boudreau became the 14th head coach in Washington Capitals history when he was named to the position on an interim basis on November 22, 2007. He had the interim tag removed on December 26. His tremendously successful first season behind the bench in Washington landed the Capitals a playoff berth and earned Boudreau the Jack Adams Award as the NHL's coach of the year. Boudreau led the Capitals on a remarkable comeback from 30th in the NHL when he took over the team to the Southeast Division championship. He was the first coach in NHL history to lead his team from 14th place at midseason to a playoff berth.

Boudreau spent nine seasons as a head coach in the American Hockey League, compiling a record of 340-216-99. He won the Calder Cup with the Hershey Bears in 2006 and won the Kelly Cup as head coach and director of hockey operations for the Mississippi Sea Wolves (ECHL) in 1999. He was named coach of the year in the International Hockey League in 1994 after leading the Fort Wayne Komets to the Turner Cup finals.

Boudreau played parts of eight seasons in the NHL with the Toronto Maple Leafs and Chicago Blackhawks, recording 70 points in 141 games. He enjoyed one of the best seasons ever by a Canadian junior player during 1974-75, collecting 165 points for the Toronto Marlboros, a Canadian Hockey League record until Wayne Gretzky surpassed the mark during the 1977-78 season. An outstanding minor league scorer, no AHL player in the 1980s notched more points than Boudreau.

Coaching Record

			Regular Season				Playoffs			
Season	Team	League	GC	W	L	O/T	GC	W	L	T
1992-93	Muskegon	CoHL	60	28	27	5	7	3	4	....
1993-94	Fort Wayne	IHL	81	41	29	11	18	10	8	....
1994-95	Fort Wayne	IHL	39	15	21	3	....	....	....	....
1996-97	Mississippi	ECHL	70	34	26	10	3	0	3	....
1997-98	Mississippi	ECHL	70	34	27	9	....	....	....	....
1998-99	Mississippi	ECHL	70	41	22	7	18	14	4	....
99-2000	Lowell	AHL	80	33	36	11	7	3	4	....
2000-01	Lowell	AHL	80	35	35	10	4	1	3	....
2001-02	Manchester	AHL	80	38	28	14	5	2	3	....
2002-03	Manchester	AHL	80	40	23	17	3	0	3	....
2003-04	Manchester	AHL	80	40	28	12	6	2	4	....
2004-05	Manchester	AHL	80	51	21	8	6	2	4	....
2005-06	Hershey	AHL	80	44	21	15	21	16	5	....
2006-07	Hershey	AHL	80	51	17	12	19	13	6	....
2007-08	Hershey	AHL	15	8	7	0	....	....	....	....
2007-08	**Washington**	**NHL**	**61**	**37**	**17**	**7**	**7**	**3**	**4**	....
	NHL Totals		**61**	**37**	**17**	**7**	**7**	**3**	**4**	....

Club Directory

Verizon Center

Washington Capitals
627 N. Glebe Road, Suite 850
Arlington, VA 22203
Phone **202/266-2200**
PR FAX 202/266-2360
www.washingtoncaps.com
Capacity: 18,277

Ownership (Lincoln Holdings LLC)
Chairman & Majority Owner . . . Ted Leonsis
President & Owner . . . Dick Patrick
Owner . . . Jack Davies, Richard Fairbank, Raul Fernandez, Michelle D. Freeman, Sheila Johnson, Richard Kay, Jeong Kim, Mark D. Lerner, George Stamas
CFO, Lincoln Holdings LLC . . . Ellen Folts
Director of Office Admin./Exec. Asst. . . . Michelle Trostle

Hockey Operations
Vice President & General Manager . . . George McPhee
Assistant General Manager, Dir. of Legal Affairs . . . Don Fishman
Head Coach . . . Bruce Boudreau
Assistant Coaches . . . Jay Leach, Dean Evason
Goaltending Coach . . . Dave Prior
Video Coach . . . Jonas Plumb
Strength and Conditioning Coach . . . Mark Nemish
Physiologist . . . Jack Blatherwick
Director, Team Operations . . . Katy Headman
Hockey Operations Assistants . . . Eric Garvey, Evan Gold
Manager, Team Services . . . Ian Anderson

Scouting Staff
Assistant General Manager, Player Personnel . . . Brian MacLellan
Pro Scouts . . . Larry Carriere, Jason Fitzsimmons
Player Development . . . Steve Richmond
Director, Amateur Scouting . . . Ross Mahoney
Amateur Scouts . . . Blaine Forsythe, Darroll Baumgartner, Steve Bowman, Ed McColgan, Martin Pouliot, Tony Richardson
European Scouts . . . Gleb Chistyakov, Vojtech Kucera, Petri Skriko, Mats Weiderstal
Director, Scouting Operations . . . Kris Wagner

Medical Staff
Team Physician . . . Ben Shaffer, MD
Team Internist . . . Chris Walsh, MD
Team Ophthalmologist . . . Thomas Clinch, MD
Team Dentist . . . Thomas Lenz, DDS, PC

Training Staff
Head Athletic Trainer . . . Greg Smith
Assistant Athletic Trainer . . . Ben Reisz
Massage Therapist . . . Shawn Reid
Head Equipment Manager . . . Brock Myles
Assistant Equipment Manager . . . Craig Leydig
Equipment Assistant . . . Brian Metzger

Business Operations
Information Technology Manager . . . Brian McPartland
Office Assistant . . . Valerie Garrett
Receptionist . . . Chuquita Pettus
Building Engineer . . . Edwin Hernandez

Marketing and Communications
Senior Vice President, Chief Marketing Officer . . . Tim McDermott
Vice President, Communications, CCO . . . Kurt Kehl
Director, Media Relations . . . Nate Ewell
Manager, Media Relations . . . Paul Rovnak
Director, Community Relations . . . Elizabeth Wodatch
Community Relations Coordinator . . . Jennifer Vassil
Director, New Media . . . Sean Parker
Senior Writer . . . Mike Vogel
Graphic Designer . . . Andrew Mattice
Director, Marketing . . . Joe Dupriest
Director, Game Production . . . Scott Brooks
Senior Manager, Fan Development & Promotions . . . Kim Frank
Marketing Manager . . . Mike Chan
Amateur Hockey & Fan Development Coordinator . . . Peter Robinson
Promotions Coordinator . . . Lauren Gilmore
Mascot Coordinator . . . Kevin Giambi

Finance
Vice President, Finance . . . Keith Burrows
Accounting Manager . . . Jill Ruehle
Accounts Payable Manager . . . Adam Porcelli
Staff Accountant . . . Marta Sokol

Sales
Vice President, Ticket Sales . . . Jim Van Stone
Director, Group Sales . . . Darren Montgomery
Director, Season Ticket Sales . . . Anthony Aspaas
Director, Inside Sales . . . Bill Hanni
Senior Regional Sales Manager, Groups . . . Tim Bronaugh
Senior Regional Sales Manager . . . David Boettinger
Regional Sales Managers . . . Nova Ackerman, Jaclyn Benjamin, Wes Delancey, Travis Gendron, Sean Goodman, Joseph O'Neill, Sara Plietz, Jason Rocco, Harry Schroeder
Regional Sales Manager, Groups . . . Jimm Bonk, Pat Jeffries, Jeff Keeney, Pete Sekulow
Account Executives . . . Julie Bohling, Christi Carson, Anthony Cirillo, Joshua Gains, Bill Lempenski, Kirk Madsen, Rachael Malenich, Ryan Michaels, Jim Minichiello, Whitney Palmer, Allie Swanson, Rob Van Der Eijk, Paige Winebrenner

Corporate Partnerships
Senior Director, Corporate Partnerships . . . John Greeley
Assistant Director, Corporate Partnerships . . . Marco Gentile, Letitia Petrillo

Ticket Operations
Director, Ticket Operations . . . Chris Sheap
Manager, Ticket Operations . . . Jordan Cookler
Assistant Manager, Ticket Operations . . . Stephen Kaufman
Coordinator, Ticket Operations . . . Jill Salisbury

Guest Services
Director, Guest Services . . . Greg Monares
Specialists, Guest Services . . . Justin Fenlon, Ryan Kronebusch, Rick Olivieri

Broadcasting
Radio Rightsholder . . . Talk Radio 3WT
Radio Play-by-Play/Analyst/Host . . . Steve Kolbe/Ken Sabourin/Jonathan Warner
Television Rightsholder . . . Comcast SportsNet
Television Play-by-Play/Analyst . . . Joe Beninati/Craig Laughlin
Television Reporters . . . Al Koken, Lisa Hillary

2007-2008 Final Statistics

Standings

Abbreviations: GP – games played; **W** – wins; **L** – losses; **OT** – overtime and shootout losses; **GF** – goals for; **GA** – goals against; **PTS** – points.

EASTERN CONFERENCE

Northeast Division

	GP	W	L	OT	GF	GA	PTS
Montreal	82	47	25	10	262	222	104
Ottawa	82	43	31	8	261	247	94
Boston	82	41	29	12	212	222	94
Buffalo	82	39	31	12	255	242	90
Toronto	82	36	35	11	231	260	83

Atlantic Division

	GP	W	L	OT	GF	GA	PTS
Pittsburgh	82	47	27	8	247	216	102
New Jersey	82	46	29	7	206	197	99
NY Rangers	82	42	27	13	213	199	97
Philadelphia	82	42	29	11	248	233	95
NY Islanders	82	35	38	9	194	243	79

Southeast Division

	GP	W	L	OT	GF	GA	PTS
Washington	82	43	31	8	242	231	94
Carolina	82	43	33	6	252	249	92
Florida	82	38	35	9	216	226	85
Atlanta	82	34	40	8	216	272	76
Tampa Bay	82	31	42	9	223	267	71

WESTERN CONFERENCE

Central Division

	GP	W	L	OT	GF	GA	PTS
Detroit	82	54	21	7	257	184	115
Nashville	82	41	32	9	230	229	91
Chicago	82	40	34	8	239	235	88
Columbus	82	34	36	12	193	218	80
St. Louis	82	33	36	13	205	237	79

Pacific Division

	GP	W	L	OT	GF	GA	PTS
San Jose	82	49	23	10	222	193	108
Anaheim	82	47	27	8	205	191	102
Dallas	82	45	30	7	242	207	97
Phoenix	82	38	37	7	214	231	83
Los Angeles	82	32	43	7	231	266	71

Northwest Division

	GP	W	L	OT	GF	GA	PTS
Minnesota	82	44	28	10	223	218	98
Colorado	82	44	31	7	231	219	95
Calgary	82	42	30	10	229	227	94
Edmonton	82	41	35	6	235	251	88
Vancouver	82	39	33	10	213	215	88

Russian stars Ilya Kovalchuk, Sergei Gonchar, Evgeni Malkin, Andrei Markov and Alex Ovechkin pose prior to the SuperSkills Competition at the 2008 All-Star Game. Ovechkin and Malkin finished 1-2 in scoring in 2007-08. Ovechkin and Kovalchuk were 1-2 in goals.

INDIVIDUAL LEADERS

Goal Scoring

Player	Team	GP	G
Alex Ovechkin	Washington	82	65
Ilya Kovalchuk	Atlanta	79	52
Jarome Iginla	Calgary	82	50
Evgeni Malkin	Pittsburgh	82	47
Henrik Zetterberg	Detroit	75	43
Brad Boyes	St. Louis	82	43
Marian Gaborik	Minnesota	77	42
Dany Heatley	Ottawa	71	41
Daniel Alfredsson	Ottawa	70	40
Vincent Lecavalier	Tampa Bay	81	40

Assists

Player	Team	GP	A
Joe Thornton	San Jose	82	67
Pavel Datsyuk	Detroit	82	66
Marc Savard	Boston	74	63
Henrik Sedin	Vancouver	82	61
Nicklas Lidstrom	Detroit	76	60
Evgeni Malkin	Pittsburgh	82	59
Jason Spezza	Ottawa	76	58
Ryan Getzlaf	Anaheim	77	58
Martin St. Louis	Tampa Bay	82	58

Power-play Goals

Player	Team	GP	PP
Alex Ovechkin	Washington	82	22
Thomas Vanek	Buffalo	82	19
Olli Jokinen	Florida	82	18
Alex Kovalev	Montreal	82	17
Evgeni Malkin	Pittsburgh	82	17
Henrik Zetterberg	Detroit	75	16
Ilya Kovalchuk	Atlanta	79	16
Petr Sykora	Pittsburgh	81	15
Mike Knuble	Philadelphia	82	15
Jarome Iginla	Calgary	82	15

Shorthand Goals

Player	Team	GP	SH
Daniel Alfredsson	Ottawa	70	7
Patrick Sharp	Chicago	80	7
Rene Bourque	Chicago	62	5
Mike Richards	Philadelphia	73	5
Rick Nash	Columbus	80	4
Richard Park	NY Islanders	82	4
Niklas Hagman	Dallas	82	4

Game-winning Goals

Player	Team	GP	GW
Alex Ovechkin	Washington	82	11
Jeremy Roenick	San Jose	69	10
Jarome Iginla	Calgary	82	9
Brad Boyes	St. Louis	82	9
Thomas Vanek	Buffalo	82	9

Shots

Player	Team	GP	S
Alex Ovechkin	Washington	82	446
Henrik Zetterberg	Detroit	75	358
Olli Jokinen	Florida	82	341
Jarome Iginla	Calgary	82	338
Jason Blake	Toronto	82	332
Rick Nash	Columbus	80	329
Vincent Lecavalier	Tampa Bay	81	318

Shooting Percentage

(minimum 82 shots)

Player	Team	GP	G	S	%
Mike Ribeiro	Dallas	76	27	107	25.2
Brad Boyes	St. Louis	82	43	207	20.8
Marek Svatos	Colorado	62	26	140	18.6
Ilya Kovalchuk	Atlanta	79	52	283	18.4
Daniel Alfredsson	Ottawa	70	40	217	18.4
*Andrew Cogliano	Edmonton	82	18	98	18.4

Penalty Minutes

Player	Team	GP	PIM
*Daniel Carcillo	Phoenix	57	324
*Jared Boll	Columbus	75	226
*Adam Burish	Chicago	81	214
*Riley Cote	Philadelphia	70	202
Zack Stortini	Edmonton	66	201
Chris Neil	Ottawa	68	199

Plus/Minus

Player	Team	GP	+/–
Pavel Datsyuk	Detroit	82	41
Nicklas Lidstrom	Detroit	76	40
Dany Heatley	Ottawa	71	33
Ryan Getzlaf	Anaheim	77	32
Henrik Zetterberg	Detroit	75	30
Duncan Keith	Chicago	82	30
Viktor Kozlov	Washington	81	28
Alex Ovechkin	Washington	82	28

* rookie

Individual Leaders

Abbreviations: GP – games played; **G** – goals; **A** – assists; **Pts** – points; **+/–** – difference between Goals For (**GF**) scored when a player is on the ice with his team at even strength or shorthanded and Goals Against (**GA**) scored when the same player is on the ice with his team at even strength or on a power play; **PIM** – penalties in minutes; **PP** – power play goals; **SH** – shorthanded goals; **GW** – game-winning goals; **S** – shots on goal; **%** – percentage of shots on goal resulting in goals.

Individual Scoring Leaders for Art Ross Trophy

Player	Team	GP	G	A	Pts	+/–	PIM	PP	SH	GW	S	%
Alex Ovechkin	Washington	82	65	47	112	28	40	22	0	11	446	14.6
Evgeni Malkin	Pittsburgh	82	47	59	106	16	78	17	0	5	272	17.3
Jarome Iginla	Calgary	82	50	48	98	27	83	15	0	9	338	14.8
Pavel Datsyuk	Detroit	82	31	66	97	41	20	10	1	6	264	11.7
Joe Thornton	San Jose	82	29	67	96	18	59	11	0	5	178	16.3
Henrik Zetterberg	Detroit	75	43	49	92	30	34	16	1	7	358	12.0
Vincent Lecavalier	Tampa Bay	81	40	52	92	-17	89	10	1	7	318	12.6
Jason Spezza	Ottawa	76	34	58	92	26	66	11	0	6	210	16.2
Daniel Alfredsson	Ottawa	70	40	49	89	15	34	9	7	5	217	18.4
Ilya Kovalchuk	Atlanta	79	52	35	87	-12	52	16	2	4	283	18.4
Alex Kovalev	Montreal	82	35	49	84	18	70	17	0	5	230	15.2
Marian Gaborik	Minnesota	77	42	41	83	17	63	11	1	8	278	15.1
Mike Ribeiro	Dallas	76	27	56	83	21	46	7	0	5	107	25.2
Martin St. Louis	Tampa Bay	82	25	58	83	-23	26	10	2	5	241	10.4
Dany Heatley	Ottawa	71	41	41	82	33	76	13	0	8	224	18.3
Eric Staal	Carolina	82	38	44	82	-2	50	14	0	7	310	12.3
Ryan Getzlaf	Anaheim	77	24	58	82	32	94	4	1	2	185	13.0
Derek Roy	Buffalo	78	32	49	81	13	46	6	3	4	218	14.7
Jason Pominville	Buffalo	82	27	53	80	16	20	2	1	1	232	11.6
Mats Sundin	Toronto	74	32	46	78	17	76	10	1	4	259	12.4
Shane Doan	Phoenix	80	28	50	78	4	59	9	2	5	243	11.5
Marc Savard	Boston	74	15	63	78	3	66	4	0	2	196	7.7
Anze Kopitar	Los Angeles	82	32	45	77	-15	22	12	2	3	201	15.9
Henrik Sedin	Vancouver	82	15	61	76	6	56	4	1	2	141	10.6
Mike Richards	Philadelphia	73	28	47	75	14	76	8	5	6	212	13.2
Brenden Morrow	Dallas	82	32	42	74	23	105	12	2	7	207	15.5

Defencemen Scoring Leaders

Player	Team	GP	G	A	Pts	+/–	PIM	PP	SH	GW	S	%
Nicklas Lidstrom	Detroit	76	10	60	70	40	40	5	0	4	188	5.3
Sergei Gonchar	Pittsburgh	78	12	53	65	13	66	8	0	2	173	6.9
Mark Streit	Montreal	81	13	49	62	-6	28	7	0	3	165	7.9
Brian Campbell	Buf-S.J.	83	8	54	62	8	20	5	0	0	142	5.6
Dion Phaneuf	Calgary	82	17	43	60	12	182	10	1	4	263	6.5
Andrei Markov	Montreal	82	16	42	58	1	63	10	1	2	145	11.0
Mike Green	Washington	82	18	38	56	6	62	8	0	4	234	7.7
Brian Rafalski	Detroit	73	13	42	55	27	34	10	0	1	175	7.4
Tomas Kaberle	Toronto	82	8	45	53	-8	22	6	0	1	155	5.2
Zdeno Chara	Boston	77	17	34	51	14	114	9	1	0	207	8.2
Ed Jovanovski	Phoenix	80	12	39	51	-13	73	8	0	2	240	5.0
Joe Corvo	Ott-Car	74	13	35	48	17	26	6	0	3	167	7.8
Kimmo Timonen	Philadelphia	80	8	36	44	0	50	3	1	1	125	6.4
Brent Burns	Minnesota	82	15	28	43	12	80	8	0	4	158	9.5
Chris Pronger	Anaheim	72	12	31	43	-1	128	8	0	4	182	6.6
Marek Zidlicky	Nashville	79	5	38	43	-5	63	4	0	0	122	4.1
Lubomir Visnovsky	Los Angeles	82	8	33	41	-18	34	3	0	1	153	5.2
Ryan Whitney	Pittsburgh	76	12	28	40	-2	45	7	1	1	119	10.1
Pavel Kubina	Toronto	72	11	29	40	5	116	6	0	4	136	8.1
Mathieu Schneider	Anaheim	65	12	27	39	22	50	5	0	2	139	8.6
Michal Rozsival	NY Rangers	80	13	25	38	0	80	6	2	0	127	10.2
Wade Redden	Ottawa	80	6	32	38	11	60	4	0	1	136	4.4
*Tobias Enstrom	Atlanta	82	5	33	38	-5	42	4	0	0	105	4.8
Jay Bouwmeester	Florida	82	15	22	37	-5	72	4	0	0	182	8.2
Dennis Wideman	Boston	81	13	23	36	11	70	9	0	1	171	7.6

CONSECUTIVE SCORING STREAKS

Goals

Games	Player	Team	G
6	Alex Ovechkin	Washington	7
6	Alexander Radulov	Nashville	7
6	Brian Rolston	Minnesota	6
6	J.P. Dumont	Nashville	6
6	Henrik Zetterberg	Detroit	6

Assists

Games	Player	Team	A
12	Marc Savard	Boston	17
9	Sidney Crosby	Pittsburgh	13
9	Marc Savard	Boston	12
9	Jason Spezza	Ottawa	12
9	Evgeni Malkin	Pittsburgh	12
9	Daniel Alfredsson	Ottawa	11
8	Vincent Lecavalier	Tampa Bay	14
8	Marc Savard	Boston	11
8	Matt Cullen	Carolina	11
8	Joe Sakic	Colorado	10
8	*Sam Gagner	Edmonton	9
8	Todd White	Atlanta	8
7	Jason Spezza	Ottawa	11
7	Scott Gomez	NY Rangers	9
7	Dustin Brown	Los Angeles	7

Points

Games	Player	Team	G	A	PTS
19	Sidney Crosby	Pittsburgh	11	19	30
17	Henrik Zetterberg	Detroit	13	14	27
16	J.P. Dumont	Nashville	8	14	22
15	Ryan Getzlaf	Anaheim	6	16	22
15	Evgeni Malkin	Pittsburgh	7	15	22
13	Scott Gomez	NY Rangers	4	15	19
12	Derek Roy	Buffalo	5	15	20
12	Marc Savard	Boston	2	17	19
11	Daniel Alfredsson	Ottawa	9	6	15
11	Shane Doan	Phoenix	6	9	15
10	Evgeni Malkin	Pittsburgh	8	16	24
10	Jason Spezza	Ottawa	9	11	20
10	Ray Whitney	Carolina	7	10	17
10	Ilya Kovalchuk	Atlanta	8	8	16
10	Daniel Alfredsson	Ottawa	4	11	15
10	Jason Pominville	Buffalo	6	6	12
10	*Jonathan Toews	Chicago	5	5	10

* rookie

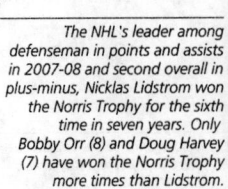

Washington's Mike Green led all NHL defensemen with 18 goals in 2007-08. One of three first-round picks Washington made at the 2004 Entry Draft, Green had scored just three goals in 92 games over two NHL seasons before his big breakthrough.

The NHL's leader among defenseman in points and assists in 2007-08 and second overall in plus-minus, Nicklas Lidstrom won the Norris Trophy for the sixth time in seven years. Only Bobby Orr (8) and Doug Harvey (7) have won the Norris Trophy more times than Lidstrom.

Individual Rookie Scoring Leaders

Rookie	Team	GP	G	A	Pts	+/–	PIM	PP	SH	GW	S	%
Patrick Kane	Chicago	82	21	51	72	–5	52	7	0	4	191	11.0
Nicklas Backstrom	Washington	82	14	55	69	13	24	3	0	4	153	9.2
Jonathan Toews	Chicago	64	24	30	54	11	44	7	0	4	144	16.7
Peter Mueller	Phoenix	81	22	32	54	–13	32	7	0	3	201	10.9
Sam Gagner	Edmonton	79	13	36	49	–21	23	4	0	1	135	9.6
Andrew Cogliano	Edmonton	82	18	27	45	1	20	1	2	5	98	18.4
Brandon Dubinsky	NY Rangers	82	14	26	40	8	79	1	0	0	157	8.9
Tobias Enstrom	Atlanta	82	5	33	38	–5	42	4	0	0	105	4.8
Martin Hanzal	Phoenix	72	8	27	35	–7	28	1	1	3	111	7.2
Tom Gilbert	Edmonton	82	13	20	33	–6	20	3	0	1	98	13.3
Erik Johnson	St. Louis	69	5	28	33	–9	28	4	0	3	105	4.8
Nigel Dawes	NY Rangers	61	14	15	29	11	10	3	0	4	121	11.6
David Perron	St. Louis	62	13	14	27	16	38	3	0	1	68	19.1
Sergei Kostitsyn	Montreal	52	9	18	27	9	51	3	1	0	49	18.4
Milan Lucic	Boston	77	8	19	27	–2	89	1	0	4	88	9.1
David Krejci	Boston	56	6	21	27	–3	20	1	1	0	73	8.2
Daniel Winnik	Phoenix	79	11	15	26	–3	25	0	0	1	122	9.0
Matt Niskanen	Dallas	78	7	19	26	22	36	2	0	0	99	7.1
Curtis Glencross	CBJ-Edm	62	15	10	25	8	53	1	0	1	104	14.4
Kamil Kreps	Florida	76	8	17	25	10	29	1	0	2	99	8.1
Daniel Carcillo	Phoenix	57	13	11	24	1	324	3	0	1	106	12.3
David Clarkson	New Jersey	81	9	13	22	1	183	0	0	1	151	6.0
Mason Raymond	Vancouver	49	9	12	21	1	2	1	0	0	80	11.3
Torrey Mitchell	San Jose	82	10	10	20	–3	50	1	2	0	110	9.1
Alexander Edler	Vancouver	75	8	12	20	6	42	4	0	0	124	6.5
Tyler Kennedy	Pittsburgh	55	10	9	19	2	35	1	0	4	104	9.6

Goal Scoring

Name	Team	GP	G
Jonathan Toews	Chicago	64	24
Peter Mueller	Phoenix	81	22
Patrick Kane	Chicago	82	21
Andrew Cogliano	Edmonton	82	18
Curtis Glencross	CBJ-Edm	62	15
Nigel Dawes	NY Rangers	61	14
Brandon Dubinsky	NY Rangers	82	14
Nicklas Backstrom	Washington	82	14

Assists

Name	Team	GP	A
Nicklas Backstrom	Washington	82	55
Patrick Kane	Chicago	82	51
Sam Gagner	Edmonton	79	36
Tobias Enstrom	Atlanta	82	33
Peter Mueller	Phoenix	81	32
Jonathan Toews	Chicago	64	30
Erik Johnson	St. Louis	69	28
Martin Hanzal	Phoenix	72	27
Andrew Cogliano	Edmonton	82	27
Brandon Dubinsky	NY Rangers	82	26

Power-play Goals

Name	Team	GP	PP
Jonathan Toews	Chicago	64	7
Peter Mueller	Phoenix	81	7
Patrick Kane	Chicago	82	7
T.J. Hensick	Colorado	31	4
Keith Yandle	Phoenix	43	4
Erik Johnson	St. Louis	69	4
Alexander Edler	Vancouver	75	4
Sam Gagner	Edmonton	79	4
Tobias Enstrom	Atlanta	82	4

Shorthand Goals

Name	Team	GP	SH
Torrey Mitchell	San Jose	82	2
Andrew Cogliano	Edmonton	82	2
Colin Stuart	Atlanta	18	1
Jacob Dowell	Chicago	19	1
Cody Bass	Ottawa	21	1
Steve Downie	Philadelphia	32	1
Ryan Callahan	NY Rangers	52	1
Sergei Kostitsyn	Montreal	52	1
David Krejci	Boston	56	1
Martin Hanzal	Phoenix	72	1
Adam Burish	Chicago	81	1

Game-winning Goals

Name	Team	GP	GW
Andrew Cogliano	Edmonton	82	5
Tyler Kennedy	Pittsburgh	55	4
Nigel Dawes	NY Rangers	61	4
Jonathan Toews	Chicago	64	4
Milan Lucic	Boston	77	4
Nicklas Backstrom	Washington	82	4
Patrick Kane	Chicago	82	4

Shots

Name	Team	GP	S
Peter Mueller	Phoenix	81	201
Patrick Kane	Chicago	82	191
Brandon Dubinsky	NY Rangers	82	157
Nicklas Backstrom	Washington	82	153
David Clarkson	New Jersey	81	151
Jonathan Toews	Chicago	64	144
Sam Gagner	Edmonton	79	135
Alexander Edler	Vancouver	75	124
Daniel Winnik	Phoenix	79	122
Nigel Dawes	NY Rangers	61	121

Shooting Percentage

(minimum 82 shots)

Name	Team	GP	G	S	%
Andrew Cogliano	Edmonton	82	18	98	18.4
Jonathan Toews	Chicago	64	24	144	16.7
Curtis Glencross	CBJ-Edm	62	15	104	14.4
Tom Gilbert	Edmonton	82	13	98	13.3
Daniel Carcillo	Phoenix	57	13	106	12.3
Nigel Dawes	NY Rangers	61	14	121	11.6
Patrick Kane	Chicago	82	21	191	11.0
Peter Mueller	Phoenix	81	22	201	10.9
Devin Setoguchi	San Jose	44	11	105	10.5

Penalty Minutes

Name	Team	GP	PIM
Daniel Carcillo	Phoenix	57	324
Jared Boll	Columbus	75	226
Adam Burish	Chicago	81	214
Riley Cote	Philadelphia	70	202
David Clarkson	New Jersey	81	183
Cody Mcleod	Colorado	49	120
Milan Lucic	Boston	77	89
Brandon Dubinsky	NY Rangers	82	79
Jack Johnson	Los Angeles	74	76
Steve Downie	Philadelphia	32	73

Plus/Minus

Name	Team	GP	+/–
Matt Niskanen	Dallas	78	22
David Perron	St. Louis	62	16
Ville Koistinen	Nashville	48	13
Nicklas Backstrom	Washington	82	13
Mike Weber	Buffalo	16	12
Nigel Dawes	NY Rangers	61	11
Jonathan Toews	Chicago	64	11
Nicklas Grossman	Dallas	62	10
Kamil Kreps	Florida	76	10

Three-or-More-Goal Games

Player	Team	Date	Final Score	G
Daniel Alfredsson	Ottawa	Jan. 24	Ott 8 T.B. 4	3
Nik Antropov	Toronto	Dec. 6	Tor 6 NYR 2	3
Jason Arnott	Nashville	Dec. 22	L.A. 3 Nsh 4	3
Daniel Briere	Philadelphia	Nov. 21	Phi 6 Car 3	3
Rod Brind'Amour	Carolina	Oct. 27	Car 8 NYI 3	3
Dustin Byfuglien	Chicago	Nov. 30	Phx 1 Chi 6	3
*Daniel Carcillo	Phoenix	Apr. 4	Phx 4 Dal 2	3
Jonathan Cheechoo	San Jose	Feb. 9	Nsh 3 S.J. 4	3
Joe Corvo	Carolina	Mar. 16	Ott 1 Car 5	3
Martin Erat	Nashville	Mar. 4	Nsh 5 Edm 1	3
Mike Fisher	Ottawa	Dec. 29	Wsh 8 Ott 6	3
Alexander Frolov	Los Angeles	Feb. 21	St.L. 1 L.A. 5	3
Marian Gaborik	Minnesota	Dec. 20	NYR 3 Min 6	5
Bill Guerin	NY Islanders	Oct. 18	NYI 5 Wsh 2	3
Niklas Hagman	Dallas	Feb. 28	Chi 4 Dal 7	3
Scott Hartnell	Philadelphia	Jan. 10	Phi 6 NYR 2	3
Scott Hartnell	Philadelphia	Jan. 19	Phi 5 NYI 3	3
Dany Heatley	Ottawa	Mar. 11	Bos 1 Ott 4	3
Milan Hejduk	Colorado	Dec. 9	St.L. 5 Col 9	3
Marian Hossa	Atlanta	Jan. 15	Atl 5 Det 1	3
Kristian Huselius	Calgary	Dec. 13	Cgy 9 T.B. 6	3
Jarome Iginla	Calgary	Dec. 13	Cgy 9 T.B. 6	3
Jarome Iginla	Calgary	Mar. 22	Min 4 Cgy 5	3
Jussi Jokinen	Dallas	Nov. 16	Col 1 Dal 6	4
Paul Kariya	St. Louis	Dec. 29	St.L. 4 Dal 5	3
Phil Kessel	Boston	Oct. 12	Bos 8 L.A. 6	3
Mike Knuble	Philadelphia	Feb. 2	Ana 0 Phi 3	3
Ilya Kovalchuk	Atlanta	Nov. 1	Atl 4 Ott 6	3
Ilya Kovalchuk	Atlanta	Nov. 3	Atl 6 T.B. 4	3
Ilya Kovalchuk	Atlanta	Mar. 13	Cgy 4 Atl 6	3
Daymond Langkow	Calgary	Jan. 18	L.A. 1 Cgy 6	3
Chad Larose	Carolina	Apr. 2	T.B. 2 Car 6	3
Vincent Lecavalier	Tampa Bay	Nov. 14	Car 1 T.B. 6	3
Vincent Lecavalier	Tampa Bay	Mar. 11	NYI 4 T.B. 8	3
David Legwand	Nashville	Oct. 6	Dal 1 Nsh 5	3
Joffrey Lupul	Philadelphia	Dec. 11	Pit 2 Phi 8	3
Joffrey Lupul	Philadelphia	Dec. 15	Car 6 Phi 5	3
Evgeni Malkin	Pittsburgh	Jan. 3	Tor 2 Pit 6	3
Evgeni Malkin	Pittsburgh	Jan. 14	NYR 1 Pit 4	3
*Peter Mueller	Phoenix	Nov. 7	Phx 6 Ana 5	3
*Peter Mueller	Phoenix	Feb. 5	Phx 3 Cgy 4	3
Ladislav Nagy	Los Angeles	Jan. 1	Chi 2 L.A. 9	3
Rick Nash	Columbus	Dec. 31	Edm 2 CBJ 4	3
Markus Naslund	Vancouver	Nov. 21	Van 4 Min 2	3
Owen Nolan	Calgary	Jan. 30	S.J. 4 Cgy 5	3
Alex Ovechkin	Washington	Dec. 29	Wsh 8 Ott 6	4
Alex Ovechkin	Washington	Jan. 31	Mtl 4 Wsh 5	4
Alex Ovechkin	Washington	Mar. 3	Bos 2 Wsh10	3
Jay Pandolfo	New Jersey	Oct. 31	T.B. 1 N.J. 6	3
Zach Parise	New Jersey	Nov. 30	Mtl 0 N.J. 4	3
Tomas Plekanec	Montreal	Feb. 29	Mtl 6 Buf 2	3
Steve Reinprecht	Phoenix	Jan. 2	Phx 5 Col 2	3
Derek Roy	Buffalo	Jan. 18	Atl 1 Buf 10	3
Joe Sakic	Colorado	Oct. 13	CBJ 1 Col 5	3
Teemu Selanne	Anaheim	Feb. 24	Chi 3 Ana 6	3
Patrick Sharp	Chicago	Nov. 17	Chi 5 Det 3	3
Fredrik Sjostrom	Phoenix	Oct. 11	Phx 6 Nsh 3	3
Jason Spezza	Ottawa	Feb. 9	Mtl 1 Ott 6	3
Eric Staal	Carolina	Jan. 18	Edm 2 Car 7	3
Drew Stafford	Buffalo	Jan. 18	Atl 1 Buf 10	3
Paul Stastny	Colorado	Oct. 3	Dal 3 Col 4	3
Cory Stillman	Carolina	Nov. 5	Wsh 0 Car 5	3
Joe Thornton	San Jose	Mar. 5	S.J. 4 Phx 5	3
R.J. Umberger	Philadelphia	Dec. 11	Pit 2 Phi 8	3
Thomas Vanek	Buffalo	Feb. 12	Buf 5 Ott 1	3
Thomas Vanek	Buffalo	Feb. 20	T.B. 3 Buf 4	3
Thomas Vanek	Buffalo	Mar. 19	T.B. 4 Buf 7	3
Thomas Vanek	Buffalo	Apr. 5	Buf 3 Bos 0	3
Antoine Vermette	Ottawa	Apr. 3	Ott 8 Tor 2	3
Radim Vrbata	Phoenix	Jan. 24	Nsh 3 Phx 4	3
Richard Zednik	Phoenix	Feb. 5	Fla 8 Tor 0	3
Henrik Zetterberg	Detroit	Dec. 7	Min 0 Det 5	3
Henrik Zetterberg	Detroit	Mar. 19	CBJ 1 Det 3	3

2007-08 Penalty Shots

(For shootout statistics, see page 143.)

Scored

Eric Staal (Carolina) scored against Cristobal Huet (Montreal) October 26, 2007. Final Score: Montreal 7 at Carolina 4

Jozef Stumpel (Florida) scored against Dan Ellis (Nashville) October 27, 2007. Final Score: Florida 3 at Nashville 4

Vincent Lecavalier (Tampa Bay) scored against Henrik Lundqvist (NY Rangers) October 29, 2007. Final Score: Tampa Bay 1 at NY Rangers 3

Jay McClement (St. Louis) scored against Jose Theodore (Colorado) December 9, 2007. Final Score: St. Louis 5 at Colorado 9

Samuel Pahlsson (Anaheim) scored against Pascal Leclaire (Columbus) December 10, 2007. Final Score: Anaheim 4 at Columbus 3

Valtteri Filppula (Detroit) scored against Dan Ellis (Nashville) December 10, 2007. Final Score: Detroit 2 at Nashville 1

Valtteri Filppula (Detroit) scored against Tomas Vokoun (Florida) December 15, 2007. Final Score: Florida 2 at Detroit 5

Chad Larose (Carolina) scored against Tim Thomas (Boston) December 28, 2007. Final Score: Boston 3 at Carolina 4

Radim Vrbata (Phoenix) scored against Chris Osgood (Detroit) December 29, 2007. Final Score: Detroit 4 at Phoenix 2

Daniel Alfredsson (Ottawa) scored against Olaf Kolzig (Washington) December 29, 2007. Final Score: Washington 8 at Ottawa 6

Joffrey Lupul (Philadelphia) scored against Karri Ramo (Tampa Bay) December 29, 2007. Final Score: Philadelphia 4 at Tampa Bay 2

Eric Staal (Carolina) scored against Mathieu Garon (Edmonton) January 18, 2008. Final Score: Edmonton 2 at Carolina 7

Sergei Kostitsyn (Montreal) scored against Henrik Lundqvist (NY Rangers) February 3, 2008. Final Score: NY Rangers 5 at Montreal 3

Nathan Horton (Florida) scored against John Grahame (Carolina) February 16, 2008. Final Score: Florida 4 at Carolina 5

Eric Perrin (Atlanta) scored against Rick DiPietro (NY Islanders) February 28, 2008. Final Score: NY Islanders 5 at Atlanta 4

Ilya Kovalchuk (Atlanta) scored against Tim Thomas (Boston) March 1, 2008. Final Score: Atlanta 2 at Boston 3

Vincent Lecavalier (Tampa Bay) scored against Pascal Leclaire (Columbus) March 9, 2008. Final Score: Tampa Bay 3 at Columbus 5

Tomas Plihal (San Jose) scored against Niklas Backstrom (Minnesota) March 9, 2008. Final Score: San Jose 3 at Minnesota 2

Patrick Marleau (San Jose) scored against Hannu Toivonen (St. Louis) March 14, 2008. Final Score: St. Louis 1 at San Jose 4

Detroit's Valterri Filppula accepts congratulations from the Red Wings bench after his penalty shot goal against Florida on December 15, 2007. It was the second time in three games that Filppula had scored on a penalty shot.

Stopped

Ryan Miller (Buffalo) stopped Rick Nash (Columbus) October 19, 2007. Final Score: Columbus 3 at Buffalo 0

Henrik Lundqvist (NY Rangers) stopped Jordan Staal (Pittsburgh) October 23, 2007. Final Score: NY Rangers 0 at Pittsburgh 1

John Grahame (Carolina) stopped Richard Park (NY Islanders) October 27, 2007. Final Score: Carolina 8 at NY Islanders 3

Martin Biron (Philadelphia) stopped Phil Kessel (Boston) October 27, 2007. Final Score: Philadelphia 2 at Boston 1

Mikael Tellqvist (Phoenix) stopped Lee Stempniak (St. Louis) October 30, 2007. Final Score: Phoenix 2 at St. Louis 1

Martin Biron (Philadelphia) stopped Roman Hamrlik (Montreal) November 1, 2007. Final Score: Philadelphia 2 at Montreal 5

Evgeni Nabokov (San Jose) stopped Sergei Zubov (Dallas) November 7, 2007. Final Score: Dallas 3 at San Jose 1

Cam Ward (Carolina) stopped Vincent Lecavalier (Tampa Bay) November 8, 2007. Final Score: Tampa Bay 5 at Carolina 1

Cristobal Huet (Montreal) stopped Daniel Alfredsson (Ottawa) November 10, 2007. Final Score: Montreal 1 at Ottawa 3

Mikael Tellqvist (Phoenix) stopped Joe Pavelski (San Jose) November 12, 2007. Final Score: Phoenix 0 at San Jose 5

Cam Ward (Carolina) stopped Mike Richards (Philadelphia) November 21, 2007. Final Score: Philadelphia 6 at Carolina 3

Evgeni Nabokov (San Jose) stopped Ladislav Nagy (Los Angeles) November 24, 2007. Final Score: Los Angeles 2 at San Jose 1

Dwayne Roloson (Edmonton) stopped Rick Nash (Columbus) November 26, 2007. Final Score: Columbus 1 at Edmonton 3

Jonas Hiller (Anaheim) stopped Henrik Sedin (Vancouver) November 27, 2007. Final Score: Anaheim 0 at Vancouver 4

Olaf Kolzig (Washington) stopped Chad Larose (Carolina) November 30, 2007. Final Score: Washington 3 at Carolina 4

John Grahame (Carolina) stopped Drew Stafford (Buffalo) December 1, 2007. Final Score: Carolina 1 at Buffalo 8

Ray Emery (Ottawa) stopped Kamil Kreps (Florida) December 5, 2007. Final Score: Ottawa 5 at Florida 4

Rick DiPietro (NY Islanders) stopped Stephen Weiss (Florida) December 7, 2007. Final Score: NY Islanders 0 at Florida 3

Roberto Luongo (Vancouver) stopped Sidney Crosby (Pittsburgh) December 8, 2007. Final Score: Pittsburgh 2 at Vancouver 1

Tomas Vokoun (Florida) stopped Pavel Datsyuk (Detroit) December 15, 2007. Final Score: Florida 2 at Detroit 5

Jean-Sebastien Giguere (Anaheim) stopped Milan Michalek (San Jose) December 16, 2007. Final Score: San Jose 2 at Anaheim 1

Martin Brodeur (New Jersey) stopped Daniel Briere (Philadelphia) December 16, 2007. Final Score: Philadelphia 2 at New Jersey 4

Ray Emery (Ottawa) stopped Patrick Sharp (Chicago) December 22, 2007. Final Score: Chicago 4 at Ottawa 3

Evgeni Nabokov (San Jose) stopped Todd Bertuzzi (Anaheim) December 22, 2007. Final Score: Anaheim 5 at San Jose 2

Ryan Miller (Buffalo) stopped Aaron Asham (New Jersey) December 28, 2007. Final Score: Buffalo 1 at New Jersey 2

Manny Legace (St. Louis) stopped Christian Erhoff (San Jose) December 28. Final Score: San Jose 1 at St. Louis 0

Anterro Niittymaki (Philadelphia) stopped Radek Dvorak (Florida) December 30, 2007. Final Score: Philadelphia 1 at Florida 0

Marty Turco (Dallas) stopped Scott Nichol (Nashville) December 31, 2007. Final Score: Nashville 1 at Dallas 0

Dan Ellis (Nashville) stopped Kyle Brodziak (Edmonton) January 3, 2008. Final Score: Edmonton 2 at Nashville 5

Niklas Backstrom (Minnesota) stopped Mike Ribeiro (Dallas) January 7, 2008. Final Score: Minnesota 1 at Dallas 3

Patrick Lalime (Chicago) stopped Mark Streit (Montreal) January 8, 2008. Final Score: Chicago 3 at Montreal 4

Marty Turco (Dallas) stopped Patrick Kane (Chicago) January 9, 2008. Final Score: Dallas 3 at Chicago 1

Mathieu Garon (Edmonton) stopped Shane Doan (Phoenix) January 10, 2008. Final Score: Phoenix 2 at Edmonton 5

Marty Turco (Dallas) stopped Chris Kunitz (Anaheim) January 15, 2008. Final Score: Dallas 2 at Anaheim 4

Ilya Bryzgalov (Phoenix) stopped Rene Bourque (Chicago) January 19, 2008. Final Score: Chicago 2 at Phoenix 1

Tomas Vokoun (Florida) stopped Markus Naslund (Vancouver) February 1, 2008. Final Score: Vancouver 3 at Florida 4

Evgeni Nabokov (San Jose) stopped Rick Nash (Columbus) February 8, 2008. Final Score: Columbus 1 at San Jose 2

Nikolai Khabibulin (Chicago) stopped Daniel Sedin (Vancouver) February 10, 2008. Final Score: Chicago 2 at Vancouver 3

Dan Ellis (Nashville) stopped Keith Yandle (Phoenix) February 10, 2008. Final Score: Nashville 6 at Phoenix 3

Miikka Kiprusoff (Calgary) stopped Jeff Giuliano (Los Angeles) February 15, 2008. Final Score: Calgary 3 at Los Angeles 6

Ryan Miller (Buffalo) stopped Scott Nichol (Nashville) February 27, 2008. Final Score: Nashville 4 at Buffalo 8

Mike Smith (Tampa Bay) stopped Petr Sykora (Pittsburgh) March 4, 2008. Final Score: Pittsburgh 2 at Tampa Bay 0

Chris Osgood (Detroit) stopped Robert Lang (Chicago) March 11, 2008. Final Score: Chicago 1 at Detroit 3

Marty Turco (Dallas) stopped Markus Naslund (Vancouver) March 15, 2008. Final Score: Vancouver 4 at Dallas 3

Vesa Toskala (Toronto) stopped Christopher Higgins (Montreal) March 29, 2008. Final Score: Montreal 2 at Toronto 4

Summary

64 penalty shots resulted in 19 goals.

Goaltending Leaders

Minimum 25 games

Goals Against Average

Goaltender	Team	GPI	MINS	GA	Avg
Chris Osgood	Detroit	43	2409	84	2.09
Jean-Sebastien Giguere	Anaheim	58	3310	117	2.12
Evgeni Nabokov	San Jose	77	4561	163	2.14
Dominik Hasek	Detroit	41	2350	84	2.14
Martin Brodeur	New Jersey	77	4635	168	2.17
Henrik Lundqvist	NY Rangers	72	4305	160	2.23
Pascal Leclaire	Columbus	54	2986	112	2.25

Wins

Goaltender	Team	GPI	MINS	W	L	OT
Evgeni Nabokov	San Jose	77	4561	46	21	8
Martin Brodeur	New Jersey	77	4635	44	27	6
Miikka Kiprusoff	Calgary	76	4398	39	26	10
Cam Ward	Carolina	69	3930	37	25	5
Henrik Lundqvist	NY Rangers	72	4305	37	24	10
Ryan Miller	Buffalo	76	4474	36	27	10
Jean-Sebastien Giguere	Anaheim	58	3310	35	17	6

Save Percentage

Goaltender	Team	GPI	MINS	GA	SA	S%	W	L
Dan Ellis	Nashville	44	2229	87	1147	.924	23	10
Ty Conklin	Pittsburgh	33	1866	78	1013	.923	18	8
Jean-Sebastien Giguere	Anaheim	58	3310	117	1508	.922	35	17
Tim Thomas	Boston	57	3342	136	1731	.921	28	19
Marc-Andre Fleury	Pittsburgh	35	1857	72	909	.921	19	10
Martin Brodeur	New Jersey	77	4635	168	2089	.920	44	27
Ilya Bryzgalov	Ana-Phx	64	3614	147	1829	.920	28	25

Shutouts

Goaltender	Team	GPI	MINS	SO	W	L	OT
Henrik Lundqvist	NY Rangers	72	4305	10	37	24	10
Pascal Leclaire	Columbus	54	2986	9	24	17	6
Dan Ellis	Nashville	44	2229	6	23	10	3
Roberto Luongo	Vancouver	73	4233	6	35	29	9
Evgeni Nabokov	San Jose	77	4561	6	46	21	8
Dominik Hasek	Detroit	41	2350	5	27	10	3
Martin Biron	Philadelphia	62	3539	5	30	20	9

Team-by-Team Point Totals

2002-03 to 2007-08

(Ranked by five-year point %)

Team	07-08	06-07	05-06	03-04	02-03	Pts%
Detroit	115	113	124	109	110	.696
Ottawa	94	105	113	102	113	.643
Dallas	97	107	112	97	111	.639
New Jersey	99	107	101	100	108	.628
San Jose	108	107	99	104	73	.599
Colorado	95	95	95	100	105	.598
Vancouver	88	105	92	101	104	.598
Anaheim	102	110	98	76	95	.587
Nashville	91	110	106	91	74	.576
Buffalo	90	113	110	85	72	.573
Toronto	83	91	90	103	98	.567
Minnesota	98	104	84	83	95	.566
Calgary	94	96	103	94	75	.563
Philadelphia	95	56	101	101	107	.561
Montreal	104	90	93	93	77	.557
Tampa Bay	71	93	92	106	93	.555
NY Rangers	97	94	100	69	78	.534
Boston	94	76	74	104	87	.530
Edmonton	88	71	95	89	92	.530
Carolina	92	88	112	76	61	.523
NY Islanders	79	92	78	91	83	.516
Atlanta	76	97	90	78	74	.506
St. Louis	79	81	57	91	99	.496
Florida	85	86	85	75	70	.489
Pittsburgh	102	105	58	58	65	.473
Los Angeles	71	68	89	81	78	.472
Washington	94	70	70	60	92	.471
Phoenix	83	67	81	68	78	.460
Chicago	88	71	65	59	79	.441
Columbus	80	73	74	62	69	.437

Team Record When Scoring First Goal of a Game

Team	FG	W	L	OT
Anaheim	33	26	4	3
Atlanta	34	20	9	5
Boston	42	30	7	5
Buffalo	37	25	6	6
Calgary	44	29	11	4
Carolina	35	26	6	3
Chicago	45	29	13	3
Colorado	37	30	4	3
Columbus	37	25	6	6
Dallas	40	25	10	5
Detroit	50	43	5	2
Edmonton	36	27	6	3
Florida	39	25	8	6
Los Angeles	33	17	11	5
Minnesota	45	36	4	5
Montreal	49	38	5	6
Nashville	44	34	6	4
New Jersey	40	29	7	4
NY Islanders	38	26	6	6
NY Rangers	47	32	9	6
Ottawa	47	34	7	6
Philadelphia	43	29	7	7
Phoenix	35	27	4	4
Pittsburgh	40	29	6	5
San Jose	56	38	13	5
St. Louis	40	23	8	9
Tampa Bay	38	22	11	5
Toronto	37	22	8	7
Vancouver	42	30	8	4
Washington	43	30	11	2

Team Plus/Minus Differential

Team	GF	PPGF	Net GF	GA	PPGA	Net GA	Goal Differential
Detroit	257	81	176	184	57	127	+49
Ottawa	261	60	201	247	72	175	+26
Anaheim	205	60	145	191	69	122	+23
Dallas	242	64	178	207	51	156	+22
Pittsburgh	247	77	170	216	68	148	+22
Colorado	231	49	182	219	56	163	+19
Chicago	239	58	181	235	69	166	+15
Calgary	229	59	170	227	72	155	+15
Washington	242	65	177	231	68	163	+14
New Jersey	206	50	156	197	54	143	+13
Montreal	262	90	172	222	60	162	+10
NY Rangers	213	61	152	199	53	146	+6
Boston	212	56	156	222	71	151	+5
Buffalo	255	66	189	242	56	186	+3
San Jose	222	70	152	193	44	149	+3
Carolina	252	79	173	249	75	174	–1
Vancouver	213	63	150	215	64	151	–1
Nashville	230	53	177	229	49	180	–3
Philadelphia	248	84	164	233	65	168	–4
Florida	216	60	156	226	66	160	–4
Minnesota	223	64	159	218	49	169	–10
Toronto	231	61	170	260	77	183	–13
Columbus	193	53	140	218	63	155	–15
Phoenix	214	63	151	231	64	167	–16
Edmonton	235	57	178	251	56	195	–17
St. Louis	205	47	158	237	56	181	–23
NY Islanders	194	48	146	243	68	175	–29
Los Angeles	231	64	167	266	68	198	–31
Atlanta	216	52	164	272	75	197	–33
Tampa Bay	223	57	166	267	56	211	–45

The Rangers' Henrik Lundqvist ranked among the NHL leaders in goals-against average and wins in 2007-08, as well as leading all goalies with 10 shutouts.

Team Record When Leading, Trailing, Tied

Team	Leading after 1 period			Leading after 2 periods			Trailing after 1 period			Trailing after 2 periods			Tied after 1 period			Tied after 2 periods		
	W	L	OT	W	L	OT	W	L	OT	W	L	OT	W	L	OT	W	L	OT
Anaheim	23	2	3	30	1	2	11	14	2	6	24	1	13	11	3	11	2	5
Atlanta	14	4	2	16	3	3	8	26	2	7	30	2	12	10	4	11	7	3
Boston	21	4	4	31	0	4	6	14	4	6	25	1	14	11	4	4	4	7
Buffalo	19	2	3	24	1	5	10	16	4	6	25	4	10	13	5	9	5	3
Calgary	17	2	3	24	1	5	9	14	3	4	24	1	16	14	4	14	5	4
Carolina	23	5	1	32	4	1	5	17	2	4	25	2	15	11	3	7	4	3
Chicago	20	4	1	27	0	2	7	16	2	5	29	1	13	14	5	8	5	5
Colorado	14	3	1	28	2	2	11	21	2	8	22	2	19	7	4	8	7	3
Columbus	21	2	4	24	3	1	4	20	2	5	27	4	9	14	6	5	6	7
Dallas	19	5	3	31	5	4	8	16	2	5	18	3	18	9	2	9	7	0
Detroit	35	3	1	36	3	1	5	11	5	6	13	3	14	7	1	12	5	3
Edmonton	16	4	3	24	2	3	6	18	1	1	25	2	19	13	2	16	8	1
Florida	20	6	5	21	4	4	6	18	2	6	23	1	12	11	2	11	8	4
Los Angeles	13	7	3	22	2	0	9	22	1	5	35	3	10	14	3	5	6	4
Minnesota	23	3	4	32	0	4	4	18	3	4	22	3	17	7	3	8	6	3
Montreal	28	2	3	32	1	4	4	14	2	3	20	6	15	9	5	12	4	0
Nashville	24	4	2	26	1	1	4	17	4	5	24	4	13	11	3	10	7	4
New Jersey	25	3	3	29	3	1	7	14	1	8	22	2	14	12	3	9	4	4
NY Islanders	16	3	4	22	1	2	5	21	2	4	31	3	14	14	3	9	6	4
NY Rangers	25	3	5	27	1	3	3	12	4	6	23	6	14	12	4	9	3	4
Ottawa	22	3	3	30	1	4	5	20	3	5	26	2	16	8	2	8	4	2
Philadelphia	17	3	2	30	1	3	9	18	5	4	22	6	16	8	4	8	6	2
Phoenix	14	5	1	27	4	2	7	23	2	2	29	3	17	9	4	9	4	2
Pittsburgh	21	3	2	36	1	3	10	14	1	6	20	3	16	10	5	5	6	2
San Jose	24	8	4	35	1	2	6	8	2	4	20	3	19	7	4	10	2	5
St. Louis	16	2	3	22	1	4	6	16	4	3	27	2	11	18	6	8	8	7
Tampa Bay	15	2	3	23	4	4	5	22	2	0	25	2	11	18	4	8	13	3
Toronto	13	6	4	22	3	4	10	24	4	6	26	2	13	5	3	8	6	5
Vancouver	18	6	2	27	1	1	3	18	4	2	29	2	18	9	4	10	3	7
Washington	21	6	2	27	1	2	6	16	2	1	25	2	16	9	4	15	5	4

Team Statistics

TEAMS' HOME AND ROAD RECORD

Eastern Conference

	Home							Road						
Team	GP	W	L	OT	GF	GA	PTS	GP	W	L	OT	GF	GA	PTS
MTL	41	22	13	6	129	107	50	41	25	12	4	133	115	54
PIT	41	26	10	5	136	97	57	41	21	17	3	111	119	45
N.J.	41	25	14	2	110	95	52	41	21	15	5	96	102	47
NYR	41	25	13	3	106	90	53	41	17	14	10	107	109	44
PHI	41	21	14	6	127	116	48	41	21	15	5	121	117	47
WSH	41	23	15	3	127	110	49	41	20	16	5	115	121	45
OTT	41	22	15	4	133	126	48	41	21	16	4	128	121	46
BOS	41	21	16	4	100	96	46	41	20	13	8	112	126	48
CAR	41	24	13	4	140	121	52	41	19	20	2	112	128	40
BUF	41	20	15	6	140	123	46	41	19	16	6	115	119	44
FLA	41	18	15	8	110	114	44	41	20	20	1	106	112	41
TOR	41	18	17	6	121	147	42	41	18	18	5	110	113	41
NYI	41	18	18	5	89	110	41	41	17	20	4	105	133	38
ATL	41	19	19	3	122	129	41	41	15	21	5	94	143	35
T.B.	41	20	18	3	121	118	43	41	11	24	6	102	149	28
Total	**615**	**322**	**225**	**68**	**1811**	**1699**	**712**	**615**	**285**	**257**	**73**	**1667**	**1827**	**643**

Western Conference

Team	GP	W	L	OT	GF	GA	PTS	GP	W	L	OT	GF	GA	PTS
DET	41	29	9	3	132	93	61	41	25	12	4	125	91	54
S.J.	41	22	13	6	110	103	50	41	27	10	4	112	90	58
ANA	41	28	9	4	115	88	60	41	19	18	4	90	103	42
MIN	41	25	11	5	114	91	55	41	19	17	5	109	127	43
DAL	41	23	16	2	124	96	48	41	22	14	5	118	111	49
COL	41	27	12	2	129	103	56	41	17	19	5	102	116	39
CGY	41	21	11	9	112	101	51	41	21	19	1	117	126	43
NSH	41	23	14	4	120	113	50	41	18	18	5	110	116	41
EDM	41	23	17	1	123	115	47	41	18	18	5	112	136	41
CHI	41	23	16	2	128	102	48	41	17	18	6	111	133	40
VAN	41	21	15	5	114	103	47	41	18	18	5	99	112	41
PHX	41	17	20	4	111	123	38	41	21	17	3	103	108	45
CBJ	41	20	14	7	105	106	47	41	14	22	5	88	112	33
ST.L	41	20	15	6	107	96	46	41	13	21	7	98	141	33
L.A.	41	17	21	3	128	132	37	41	15	22	4	103	134	34
Total	**615**	**322**	**225**	**68**	**1811**	**1699**	**712**	**615**	**284**	**263**	**68**	**1597**	**1756**	**636**
	1230	**661**	**438**	**131**	**3583**	**3264**	**1453**	**1230**	**569**	**520**	**141**	**3264**	**3583**	**1279**

The Senators led all NHL teams with 18 shorthand goals in 2007-08. Daniel Alfredsson's seven shorthand goals tied Chicago's Patrick Sharp for the NHL lead.

TEAMS' DIVISIONAL RECORD

Northeast Division

	Against Own Division							Against Other Divisions						
	GP	W	L	OT	GF	GA	PTS	GP	W	L	OT	GF	GA	PTS
MTL	32	20	11	1	106	86	41	50	27	14	9	156	136	63
OTT	32	18	13	1	96	92	37	50	25	18	7	165	155	57
BOS	32	13	13	6	81	95	32	50	28	16	6	131	127	62
BUF	32	15	13	4	87	88	34	50	24	18	8	168	154	56
TOR	32	14	13	5	93	102	33	50	22	22	6	138	158	50
Total	**160**	**80**	**63**	**17**	**463**	**463**	**177**	**250**	**126**	**88**	**36**	**758**	**730**	**288**

Atlantic Division

	GP	W	L	OT	GF	GA	PTS	GP	W	L	OT	GF	GA	PTS
PIT	32	15	14	3	89	87	33	50	32	13	5	158	129	69
N.J.	32	13	15	4	70	87	30	50	33	14	3	136	110	69
NYR	32	20	7	5	84	63	45	50	22	20	8	129	136	52
PHI	32	17	12	3	96	91	37	50	25	17	8	152	142	58
NYI	32	15	15	2	76	87	32	50	20	23	7	118	156	47
Total	**160**	**80**	**63**	**17**	**415**	**415**	**177**	**250**	**132**	**87**	**31**	**693**	**673**	**295**

Southeast Division

	GP	W	L	OT	GF	GA	PTS	GP	W	L	OT	GF	GA	PTS
WSH	32	18	11	3	89	82	39	50	25	20	5	153	149	55
CAR	32	19	11	2	107	91	40	50	24	22	4	145	158	52
FLA	32	16	14	2	86	90	34	50	22	21	7	130	136	51
ATL	32	15	15	2	92	102	32	50	19	25	6	124	170	44
T.B.	32	12	17	3	91	100	27	50	19	25	6	132	167	44
Total	**160**	**80**	**68**	**12**	**465**	**465**	**172**	**250**	**109**	**113**	**28**	**684**	**780**	**246**

Central Division

	GP	W	L	OT	GF	GA	PTS	GP	W	L	OT	GF	GA	PTS
DET	32	17	12	3	90	79	37	50	37	9	4	167	105	78
NSH	32	18	9	5	88	82	41	50	23	23	4	142	147	50
CHI	32	19	11	2	106	91	40	50	21	23	6	133	144	48
CBJ	32	11	18	3	77	104	25	50	23	18	9	116	114	55
ST.L.	32	15	14	3	82	87	33	50	18	22	10	123	150	46
Total	**160**	**80**	**64**	**16**	**443**	**443**	**176**	**250**	**122**	**95**	**33**	**681**	**660**	**277**

Pacific Division

	GP	W	L	OT	GF	GA	PTS	GP	W	L	OT	GF	GA	PTS
S.J.	32	16	10	6	84	78	38	50	33	13	4	138	115	70
ANA	32	17	10	5	81	81	39	50	30	17	3	124	110	63
DAL	32	16	11	5	96	83	37	50	29	19	2	146	124	60
PHX	32	19	11	2	90	85	40	50	19	26	5	124	146	43
L.A.	32	12	18	2	77	101	26	50	20	25	5	154	165	45
Total	**160**	**80**	**60**	**20**	**428**	**428**	**180**	**250**	**131**	**100**	**19**	**686**	**660**	**281**

Northwest Division

	GP	W	L	OT	GF	GA	PTS	GP	W	L	OT	GF	GA	PTS
MIN	32	17	11	4	93	85	38	50	27	17	6	130	133	60
COL	32	20	10	2	100	83	42	50	24	21	5	131	136	53
CGY	32	16	12	4	83	85	36	50	26	18	6	146	142	58
EDM	32	13	16	3	81	101	29	50	28	19	3	154	150	59
VAN	32	14	13	5	87	90	33	50	25	20	5	126	125	55
Total	**160**	**80**	**62**	**18**	**444**	**444**	**178**	**250**	**130**	**95**	**25**	**687**	**686**	**285**

TEAM STREAKS

Consecutive Wins

Games	Team	From	To
11	San Jose	Feb. 21	Mar. 14
9	Detroit	Oct. 18	Nov. 9
9	New Jersey	Nov. 17	Dec. 7
8	Ottawa	Oct. 13	Nov. 6
8	Pittsburgh	Dec. 23	Jan. 10
8	Detroit	Jan. 17	Feb. 5
7	Detroit	Nov. 27	Dec. 10
7	Dallas	Jan. 29	Feb. 11
7	Florida	Mar. 2	Mar. 16
7	Washington	Mar. 21	Apr. 5

Consecutive Home Wins

Games	Team	From	To
10	Anaheim	Feb. 17	Mar. 26
8	Pittsburgh	Mar. 2	Apr. 2
7	Anaheim	Dec. 19	Jan. 15
7	Edmonton	Feb. 4	Mar. 2
6	Colorado	Oct. 3	Nov. 1
6	Philadelphia	Oct. 13	Nov. 12
6	St. Louis	Nov. 13	Dec. 1
6	Detroit	Nov. 21	Dec. 9
6	Vancouver	Dec. 18	Jan. 8
6	Pittsburgh	Dec. 23	Jan. 14
6	Columbus	Dec. 26	Jan. 15
6	Washington	Mar. 12	Apr. 5
6	Minnesota	Mar. 15	Apr.3

Consecutive Road Wins

Games	Team	From	To
10	San Jose	Nov. 14	Dec. 31
9	San Jose	Feb. 21	Mar. 18
6	Calgary	Dec. 9	Dec. 18
6	Phoenix	Dec. 15	Jan. 8
6	Detroit	Dec. 22	Jan. 6
6	Philadelphia	Jan. 5	Feb. 5
6	Tampa Bay	Jan. 8	Feb. 7
6	Toronto	Mar. 1	Mar. 22

TEAM PENALTIES

Abbreviations: GP – games played; **PEN** – total penalty minutes including bench minutes; **BMI** – total bench minor minutes; **AVG** – average penalty minutes/game calculated by dividing total penalty minutes by games played

Team	GP	PEN	BMI	AVG	Team	GP	PEN	BMI	AVG
DET	82	937	4	11.4	MIN	82	1098	12	13.4
L.A.	82	954	24	11.6	NYR	82	1154	12	14.1
N.J.	82	974	18	11.9	ST.L.	82	1153	16	14.1
WSH	82	975	22	11.9	DAL	82	1176	14	14.3
COL	82	995	22	12.1	EDM	82	1175	26	14.3
BUF	82	1004	14	12.2	OTT	82	1175	22	14.3
FLA	82	1026	24	12.5	CAR	82	1183	18	14.4
NSH	82	1027	12	12.5	PIT	82	1179	24	14.4
NYI	82	1041	18	12.7	PHX	82	1193	18	14.5
T.B.	82	1040	16	12.7	CBJ	82	1325	22	16.2
BOS	82	1069	18	13.0	CGY	82	1342	14	16.4
ATL	82	1077	20	13.1	CHI	82	1383	12	16.9
S.J.	82	1075	14	13.1	PHI	82	1471	14	17.9
MTL	82	1090	18	13.3	VAN	82	1474	16	18.0
TOR	82	1087	8	13.3	ANA	82	1481	16	18.1
					Total	**1230**	**34333**	**508**	**27.9**

Twelve of Thomas Plekanec's career-high 29 goals in 2007-08 came on the power-play. The Canadiens led the NHL in power-play goals (90) and percentage (24.1).

TEAMS' POWER-PLAY RECORD

Abbreviations: ADV – total advantages; **PPGF** – power-play goals for; **%** – calculated by dividing number of power-play goals by total advantages.

	Home					Road					Overall				
	Team	GP	ADV	PPGF	%	Team	GP	ADV	PPGF	%	Team	GP	ADV	PPGF	%
1	Mtl	41	184	45	24.5	Mtl	41	190	45	23.7	Mtl	82	374	90	24.1
2	Pit	41	199	46	23.1	Det	41	188	39	20.7	Phi	82	385	84	21.8
3	Phi	41	200	46	23.0	Phi	41	185	38	20.5	Det	82	391	81	20.7
4	T.B.	41	163	35	21.5	Dal	41	175	35	20.0	Pit	82	378	77	20.4
5	L.A.	41	193	41	21.2	Cgy	41	154	30	19.5	T.B.	82	296	57	19.3
6	Det	41	203	42	20.7	Bos	41	156	30	19.2	Fla	82	313	60	19.2
7	Wsh	41	180	37	20.6	Van	41	157	30	19.1	Min	82	338	64	18.9
8	Car	41	236	48	20.3	Tor	41	158	30	19.0	Car	82	420	79	18.8
9	Fla	41	163	33	20.2	Min	41	170	32	18.8	Wsh	82	346	65	18.8
10	Buf	41	191	37	19.4	S.J.	41	168	31	18.5	S.J.	82	374	70	18.7
11	Min	41	168	32	19.0	Phx	41	152	28	18.4	Phx	82	339	63	18.6
12	S.J.	41	206	39	18.9	Ott	41	148	27	18.2	Ott	82	328	60	18.3
13	Phx	41	187	35	18.7	Fla	41	150	27	18.0	Dal	82	354	64	18.1
14	Ana	41	189	35	18.5	Atl	41	168	30	17.9	Buf	82	366	66	18.0
15	Ott	41	180	33	18.3	Edm	41	174	31	17.8	Tor	82	343	61	17.8
16	Col	41	171	30	17.5	NYR	41	187	33	17.6	Bos	82	319	56	17.6
17	Chi	41	200	34	17.0	Pit	41	179	31	17.3	L.A.	82	366	64	17.5
18	Tor	41	185	31	16.8	Wsh	41	166	28	16.9	Van	82	369	63	17.1
19	CBJ	41	176	29	16.5	Car	41	184	31	16.8	Cgy	82	352	59	16.8
20	Dal	41	179	29	16.2	N.J.	41	162	27	16.7	Ana	82	361	60	16.6
21	Bos	41	163	26	16.0	Buf	41	175	29	16.6	Edm	82	344	57	16.6
22	Nsh	41	198	31	15.7	NYI	41	170	28	16.5	NYR	82	370	61	16.5
23	Van	41	212	33	15.6	T.B.	41	133	22	16.5	Atl	82	316	52	16.5
24	NYR	41	183	28	15.3	Ana	41	172	25	14.5	Chi	82	365	58	15.9
25	Edm	41	170	26	15.3	Chi	41	165	24	14.5	N.J.	82	320	50	15.6
26	Atl	41	148	22	14.9	Nsh	41	160	22	13.8	CBJ	82	356	53	14.9
27	St.L.	41	183	27	14.8	L.A.	41	173	23	13.3	Nsh	82	358	53	14.8
28	Cgy	41	198	29	14.6	CBJ	41	180	24	13.3	Col	82	335	49	14.6
29	N.J.	41	158	23	14.6	St.L.	41	151	20	13.2	NYI	82	330	48	14.5
30	NYI	41	160	20	12.5	Col	41	164	19	11.6	St.L.	82	334	47	14.1
TOTAL		**1230**	**5526**	**1002**	**18.1**		**1230**	**5014**	**869**	**17.3**		**1230**	**10540**	**1871**	**17.8**

TEAMS' PENALTY KILLING RECORD

Abbreviations: TSH – total times shorthanded; **PPGA** – power-play goals against; **%** – calculated by dividing times short minus power-play goals against by times short.

	Home					Road					Overall				
	Team	GP	TSH	PPGA	%	Team	GP	TSH	PPGA	%	Team	GP	TSH	PPGA	%
1	St.L.	41	167	20	88.0	S.J.	41	161	17	89.4	S.J.	82	310	44	85.8
2	Edm	41	173	21	87.9	Nsh	41	172	22	87.2	Dal	82	354	51	85.6
3	Van	41	172	22	87.2	Dal	41	191	28	85.3	Nsh	82	335	49	85.4
4	Min	41	154	21	86.4	Det	41	191	29	84.8	Min	82	330	49	85.2
5	Dal	41	163	23	85.9	CBJ	41	208	32	84.6	Edm	82	366	56	84.7
6	NYR	41	151	22	85.4	Mtl	41	181	28	84.5	NYR	82	343	53	84.5
7	Pit	41	170	26	84.7	Min	41	176	28	84.1	St.L.	82	359	56	84.4
8	Buf	41	145	23	84.1	NYR	41	192	31	83.9	Det	82	357	57	84.0
9	Ana	41	185	30	83.8	Phi	41	204	35	82.8	CBJ	82	378	63	83.3
10	Cgy	41	185	30	83.8	Fla	41	196	34	82.7	Phi	82	388	65	83.2
11	Phi	41	184	30	83.7	Col	41	149	26	82.6	Buf	82	333	56	83.2
12	Nsh	41	163	27	83.4	Ana	41	223	39	82.5	Ana	82	408	69	83.1
13	N.J.	41	156	26	83.3	Ott	41	188	33	82.4	N.J.	82	314	54	82.8
14	Det	41	166	28	83.1	Buf	41	188	33	82.4	Van	82	368	64	82.6
15	Bos	41	154	26	83.1	N.J.	41	158	28	82.3	Mtl	82	342	60	82.5
16	NYI	41	179	31	82.7	T.B.	41	156	28	82.1	Fla	82	374	66	82.4
17	Chi	41	183	32	82.5	Edm	41	193	35	81.9	T.B.	82	312	56	82.1
18	Wsh	41	159	28	82.4	Chi	41	202	37	81.7	Chi	82	385	69	82.1
19	T.B.	41	156	28	82.1	Phx	41	164	30	81.7	NYI	82	375	68	81.9
20	Fla	41	178	32	82.0	Tor	41	167	31	81.4	Col	82	301	56	81.4
21	S.J.	41	149	27	81.9	St.L.	41	192	36	81.3	Cgy	82	388	72	81.4
22	CBJ	41	170	31	81.8	NYI	41	196	37	81.1	Ott	82	380	72	81.1
23	Atl	41	162	30	81.5	Car	41	184	35	81.0	Pit	82	357	68	81.0
24	Col	41	152	30	80.3	Cgy	41	203	42	79.3	Phx	82	332	64	80.7
25	Mtl	41	161	32	80.1	Wsh	41	190	40	78.9	Wsh	82	349	68	80.5
26	Phx	41	168	34	79.8	Van	41	196	42	78.6	Car	82	355	75	78.9
27	Ott	41	192	39	79.7	Pit	41	187	42	77.5	Atl	82	354	75	78.8
28	L.A.	41	161	34	78.9	L.A.	41	148	34	77.0	Bos	82	332	71	78.6
29	Car	41	171	40	76.6	Atl	41	192	45	76.6	Tor	82	352	77	78.1
30	Tor	41	185	46	75.1	Bos	41	178	45	74.7	L.A.	82	309	68	78.0
TOTAL		**1230**	**5014**	**869**	**82.7**		**1230**	**5526**	**1002**	**81.9**		**1230**	**10540**	**1871**	**82.2**

SHORTHAND GOALS FOR

	Home			Road			Overall		
	Team	GP	SHGF	Team	GP	SHGF	Team	GP	SHGF
1	Ott	41	10	Chi	41	11	Ott	82	18
2	Atl	41	10	Ott	41	8	Chi	82	17
3	Dal	41	8	Phx	41	8	Dal	82	13
4	Cgy	41	6	Phi	41	7	Phi	82	13
5	Chi	41	6	L.A.	41	6	Atl	82	13
6	Phi	41	6	NYI	41	6	L.A.	82	11
7	L.A.	41	5	CBJ	41	6	Phx	82	11
8	T.B.	41	5	Dal	41	5	NYI	82	10
9	Mtl	41	5	Bos	41	5	Cgy	82	9
10	N.J.	41	5	Buf	41	5	Buf	82	9
11	Ana	41	4	Van	41	5	Bos	82	9
12	Buf	41	4	Ana	41	4	Ana	82	8
13	NYI	41	4	S.J.	41	4	Mtl	82	8
14	Bos	41	4	Edm	41	4	CBJ	82	8
15	NYR	41	3	Nsh	41	4	Van	82	8
16	Nsh	41	3	Mtl	41	3	T.B.	82	7
17	Edm	41	3	Pit	41	3	Nsh	82	7
18	Phx	41	3	Atl	41	3	Edm	82	7
19	Van	41	3	Det	41	3	S.J.	82	7
20	Wsh	41	3	Cgy	41	3	N.J.	82	6
21	Pit	41	3	Fla	41	2	Pit	82	6
22	S.J.	41	3	Tor	41	2	Det	82	5
23	Car	41	2	St.L.	41	2	Wsh	82	5
24	Det	41	2	Wsh	41	2	Car	82	4
25	Tor	41	2	Car	41	2	Tor	82	4
26	Min	41	2	T.B.	41	2	NYR	82	4
27	CBJ	41	2	N.J.	41	1	Fla	82	4
28	Fla	41	2	Col	41	1	Min	82	3
29	Col	41	1	NYR	41	1	St.L.	82	3
30	St.L.	41	1	Min	41	1	Col	82	2
TOTAL		**1230**	**120**		**1230**	**119**		**1230**	**239**

SHORTHAND GOALS AGAINST

	Home			Road			Overall		
	Team	GP	SHGA	Team	GP	SHGA	Team	GP	SHGA
1	Ott	41	1	CBJ	41	1	Mtl	82	3
2	Fla	41	1	L.A.	41	2	Fla	82	3
3	Mtl	41	1	Mtl	41	2	L.A.	82	4
4	L.A.	41	2	Fla	41	2	Col	82	5
5	Chi	41	2	Col	41	2	CBJ	82	5
6	Ana	41	3	S.J.	41	2	Ott	82	6
7	Det	41	3	Tor	41	3	NYR	82	6
8	Col	41	3	N.J.	41	3	Chi	82	6
9	NYR	41	3	Phi	41	3	Phi	82	6
10	Wsh	41	3	Bos	41	3	Bos	82	6
11	Phi	41	3	NYR	41	3	Ana	82	7
12	Bos	41	3	Van	41	3	Det	82	7
13	T.B.	41	4	Cgy	41	3	T.B.	82	7
14	Min	41	4	T.B.	41	3	N.J.	82	7
15	Edm	41	4	Ana	41	4	Van	82	7
16	CBJ	41	4	Dal	41	4	Dal	82	8
17	Buf	41	4	Chi	41	4	Cgy	82	8
18	Atl	41	4	Buf	41	4	Buf	82	8
19	Dal	41	4	Det	41	4	Wsh	82	8
20	Van	41	4	Nsh	41	4	S.J.	82	9
21	NYI	41	4	Ott	41	5	Tor	82	10
22	N.J.	41	4	St.L.	41	5	Nsh	82	10
23	Cgy	41	5	Pit	41	5	Min	82	10
24	Pit	41	5	Wsh	41	5	Edm	82	10
25	Nsh	41	6	Car	41	6	Pit	82	10
26	Phx	41	6	Atl	41	6	Atl	82	10
27	Car	41	7	Edm	41	6	Phx	82	12
28	Tor	41	7	Phx	41	6	Car	82	13
29	S.J.	41	7	Min	41	6	St.L.	82	13
30	St.L.	41	8	NYI	41	11	NYI	82	15
TOTAL		**1230**	**119**		**1230**	**120**		**1230**	**239**

Regular-Season Overtime Results

2007-08 to 1987-88

	2007-08				2006-07				2005-06				2003-04				2002-03			
Team	GP	W	L	SO	GP	W	L	SO	GP	W	L	SO	GP	W	L	T	GP	W	L	T
ANA	20	4	1	15	23	5	4	14	18	3	5	10	22	4	8	10	21	6	6	9
ATL	23	6	2	15	25	7	7	11	18	5	3	10	18	6	4	8	19	7	5	7
BOS	21	3	5	13	19	4	2	13	22	4	8	10	30	8	7	15	21	6	4	11
BUF	21	5	3	13	22	5	3	14	17	6	1	10	13	2	4	7	21	3	8	10
CGY	16	3	7	6	15	2	5	8	15	2	4	9	13	3	3	7	19	2	6	11
CAR/HFD	13	5	3	5	14	6	3	5	20	4	6	10	25	5	6	14	15	4	3	8
CHI	17	4	4	9	18	3	2	13	22	7	7	8	23	4	8	11	23	6	4	13
COL/QUE	18	4	4	10	15	3	3	9	15	3	3	9	28	8	7	13	23	4	6	13
CBJ	17	2	4	11	16	4	2	10	18	6	1	11	18	6	4	8	28	7	8	13
DAL/MIN	15	3	4	8	22	6	3	13	21	3	5	13	18	3	2	13	24	5	4	15
DET	14	2	2	10	18	3	5	10	15	3	5	7	20	7	2	11	21	7	4	10
EDM	25	4	2	19	11	1	4	6	26	6	4	16	23	6	5	12	27	7	9	11
FLA	18	4	3	11	21	3	8	10	23	8	6	9	24	5	4	15	26	4	9	13
L.A.	14	2	4	8	20	2	8	10	15	4	4	7	27	2	9	16	19	6	7	6
MIN	19	6	2	11	25	7	1	17	14	1	5	8	24	1	3	20	19	8	1	10
MTL	20	5	4	11	14	2	1	11	18	7	6	5	16	5	4	7	19	2	9	8
NSH	17	5	4	8	17	3	3	11	17	3	5	9	22	7	4	11	24	8	6	10
N.J.	22	7	3	12	22	3	1	18	22	4	5	13	21	7	2	12	25	5	7	13
NYI	19	5	6	8	22	2	7	13	18	3	3	12	17	2	4	11	18	5	2	11
NYR	25	4	4	17	22	3	5	14	23	4	8	11	18	3	8	7	20	6	4	10
OTT	14	3	3	8	13	2	3	8	13	2	3	8	19	3	6	10	16	7	1	8
PHI	17	3	5	9	16	3	6	7	22	7	5	10	23	2	6	15	23	6	4	13
PHX/WPG	16	4	1	11	12	2	3	7	15	6	2	7	29	5	6	18	20	4	5	11
PIT	16	1	4	11	27	6	5	16	19	4	8	7	19	7	4	8	14	3	5	6
ST.L.	17	1	8	8	23	4	7	12	22	3	7	12	24	11	2	11	19	2	8	9
S.J.	19	3	4	12	8	1	3	4	21	9	4	8	21	3	6	12	23	6	6	11
T.B.	13	2	8	3	20	5	3	12	18	6	2	10	18	4	6	8	23	2	5	16
TOR	19	5	7	7	19	4	4	11	18	7	1	10	17	4	3	10	17	7	3	7
VAN	20	4	1	15	24	12	3	9	16	4	4	8	26	11	5	10	19	5	1	13
WSH	19	7	4	8	19	4	3	12	21	2	6	13	14	1	3	10	20	6	6	8
Totals	**272**	**116**		**156**	**281**	**117**		**164**	**281**	**136**		**145**	**315**	**145**		**170**	**313**	**156**		**157**

	2001-02				2000-01				1999-2000				1998-99				1997-98			
Team	GP	W	L	T	GP	W	L	T	GP	W	L	T	GP	W	L	T	GP	W	L	T
ANA	14	3	3	8	20	4	5	11	18	3	3	12	17	1	3	13	20	3	4	13
ATL	19	3	5	11	16	2	2	12	11	0	4	7	...	...	...	...	...	...	...	...
BOS	24	9	9	6	20	4	8	8	26	1	6	19	17	2	2	13	17	3	1	13
BUF	16	4	1	11	10	4	1	5	20	5	4	11	23	3	3	17	21	3	1	17
CGY	17	2	3	12	22	3	4	15	26	11	5	10	16	3	1	12	22	4	3	15
CAR/HFD	27	6	5	16	18	6	3	9	14	4	0	10	24	1	5	18	12	2	2	8
CHI	17	3	1	13	15	2	5	8	17	5	2	10	15	1	2	12	18	1	4	13
COL/QUE	13	4	1	8	20	6	4	10	17	5	1	11	12	2	0	10	22	2	3	17
CBJ	15	2	5	8	18	3	6	9	...	...	...	...	...	...	...	...	...	...	...	...
DAL/MIN	21	3	5	13	16	6	2	8	19	3	6	10	16	3	1	12	17	5	1	11
DET	24	10	4	10	23	10	4	9	16	4	2	10	10	2	1	7	15	0	0	15
EDM	19	3	4	12	20	5	3	12	27	3	8	16	20	3	5	12	15	3	2	10
FLA	16	0	6	10	24	2	9	13	15	3	6	6	21	1	2	18	20	3	2	15
L.A.	18	3	4	11	19	3	3	13	21	5	4	12	12	5	2	5	16	3	2	11
MIN	21	0	9	12	22	4	5	13	...	...	...	...	...	...	...	...	...	...	...	...
MTL	17	2	3	12	16	2	6	8	17	4	4	9	15	0	4	11	20	3	4	13
NSH	18	5	0	13	17	5	3	9	18	4	7	7	10	1	2	7	...	...	...	...
N.J.	19	6	4	9	20	5	3	12	16	3	5	8	15	3	1	11	16	2	3	11
NYI	18	6	4	8	12	2	3	7	15	5	1	9	17	1	6	10	13	0	2	11
NYR	13	5	4	4	11	5	1	5	21	6	3	12	19	5	3	11	24	2	4	18
OTT	19	3	7	9	16	3	4	9	15	2	2	11	18	1	2	15	17	2	0	15
PHI	16	3	3	10	19	5	3	11	21	6	3	12	24	2	3	19	15	3	1	11
PHX/WPG	19	4	6	9	23	3	3	17	16	4	4	8	15	2	1	12	14	0	2	12
PIT	20	7	5	8	15	3	3	9	17	3	6	8	22	7	1	14	23	3	2	18
ST.L.	18	6	4	8	23	6	5	12	17	5	1	11	15	1	1	13	12	2	2	8
S.J.	13	2	3	8	22	7	3	12	21	4	7	10	21	1	2	18	12	0	2	10
T.B.	19	4	4	11	13	2	5	6	16	0	7	9	12	1	2	9	13	0	3	10
TOR	17	3	4	10	19	3	5	11	17	7	3	7	14	6	1	7	10	1	0	9
VAN	14	4	3	7	23	5	7	11	27	4	8	15	13	0	1	12	17	0	3	14
WSH	19	6	2	11	16	2	4	10	19	5	2	12	11	2	3	6	17	4	1	12
Totals	**270**	**121**		**149**	**274**	**122**		**152**	**260**	**114**		**146**	**222**	**60**		**162**	**219**	**54**		**165**

	1996-97				1995-96				1994-95				1993-94				1992-93			
Team	GP	W	L	T	GP	W	L	T	GP	W	L	T	GP	W	L	T	GP	W	L	T
ANA	16	3	0	13	16	6	2	8	7	2	0	5	12	2	5	5	...	...	...	...
ATL	...	...	...	...	...	...	...	...	...	...	...	...	...	...	...	...	...	...	...	...
BOS	15	3	3	9	19	2	6	11	8	2	3	3	17	2	2	13	15	5	3	7
BUF	21	5	4	12	15	2	6	7	9	1	1	7	13	0	4	9	18	4	4	10
CGY	16	3	4	9	16	2	3	11	9	1	1	7	18	3	2	13	19	4	4	11
CAR/HFD	18	3	4	11	14	2	3	9	9	1	1	7	14	4	1	9	18	3	9	6
CHI	19	1	5	13	19	1	4	14	7	2	0	5	16	2	5	9	16	1	3	12
COL/QUE	15	2	3	10	6	1	0	5	8	0	0	8	15	3	3	9	15	4	1	10
CBJ	...	...	...	...	...	...	...	...	...	...	...	...	...	...	...	...	...	...	...	...
DAL/MIN	15	4	3	8	15	1	0	14	9	0	1	8	22	6	3	13	10	0	0	10
DET	27	7	2	18	11	3	1	7	4	0	0	4	15	5	2	8	11	2	0	9
EDM	16	1	6	9	14	4	2	8	7	1	2	4	21	1	6	14	17	5	4	8
FLA	26	3	4	19	13	0	3	10	9	0	3	6	24	2	5	17	...	...	...	...
L.A.	14	0	3	11	23	3	2	18	9	0	0	9	18	3	3	12	13	2	1	10
MIN	...	...	...	...	...	...	...	...	...	...	...	...	...	...	...	...	...	...	...	...
MTL	21	2	4	15	15	2	3	10	10	1	2	7	19	3	2	14	14	5	3	6
NSH	...	...	...	...	...	...	...	...	...	...	...	...	...	...	...	...	...	...	...	...
N.J.	17	1	2	14	19	7	0	12	11	1	2	8	14	1	1	12	11	4	0	7
NYI	17	3	2	12	17	2	5	10	7	1	1	5	19	5	2	12	13	3	3	7
NYR	13	3	0	10	17	2	1	14	3	0	0	3	12	3	1	8	17	2	4	11
OTT	17	0	2	15	8	0	3	5	7	1	1	5	17	4	4	9	10	0	6	4
PHI	18	3	2	13	20	4	3	13	8	3	1	4	18	3	5	10	17	4	2	11
PHX/WPG	16	5	4	7	8	2	0	6	9	0	2	7	15	1	5	9	11	2	2	7
PIT	13	1	4	8	9	3	2	4	5	1	1	3	19	4	2	13	10	3	0	7
ST.L.	13	1	1	11	18	1	1	16	7	1	1	5	17	4	2	11	17	2	4	11
S.J.	12	3	1	8	9	1	1	7	5	1	0	4	19	2	1	16	10	3	5	2
T.B.	16	4	2	10	18	3	3	12	7	2	2	3	18	3	4	11	14	3	4	7
TOR	10	1	1	8	18	4	2	12	8	0	0	8	17	4	1	12	13	1	1	11
VAN	14	5	2	7	20	1	4	15	13	0	1	12	12	5	4	3	10	1	0	9
WSH	13	2	2	9	16	4	1	11	9	0	1	8	14	2	2	10	11	2	2	7
Totals	**214**	**70**		**144**	**201**	**64**		**137**	**101**	**26**		**75**	**214**	**74**		**140**	**165**	**65**		**100**

	1991-92				1990-91				1989-90				1988-89				1987-88			
Team	GP	W	L	T	GP	W	L	T	GP	W	L	T	GP	W	L	T	GP	W	L	T
ANA	...	...	...	...	...	...	...	...	...	...	...	...	...	...	...	...	...	...	...	...
ATL	...	...	...	...	...	...	...	...	...	...	...	...	...	...	...	...	...	...	...	...
BOS	20	6	2	12	17	5	0	12	14	3	2	9	19	3	2	14	14	4	4	6
BUF	16	2	2	12	24	3	2	19	15	4	3	8	13	2	4	7	12	0	1	11
CGY	19	2	5	12	15	3	4	8	21	3	3	15	17	5	3	9	15	2	4	9
CAR/HFD	18	2	3	13	9	1	1	7	9	0	0	9	10	1	4	5	12	3	2	7
CHI	19	2	2	15	12	3	1	8	10	2	2	6	17	2	3	12	15	4	2	9
COL/QUE	17	0	5	12	18	1	3	14	8	0	1	7	10	2	1	7	9	2	2	5
CBJ	...	...	...	...	...	...	...	...	...	...	...	...	...	...	...	...	...	...	...	...
DAL/MIN	8	0	2	6	17	0	3	14	11	3	4	4	17	0	1	16	16	1	2	13
DET	16	3	1	12	14	2	4	8	17	2	1	14	16	3	1	12	16	2	3	11
EDM	12	0	2	10	15	4	5	6	20	5	1	14	15	4	3	8	16	3	2	11
FLA	...	...	...	...	...	...	...	...	...	...	...	...	...	...	...	...	...	...	...	...
L.A.	16	1	1	14	16	4	2	10	12	3	2	7	14	6	1	7	12	1	3	8
MIN	...	...	...	...	...	...	...	...	...	...	...	...	...	...	...	...	...	...	...	...
MTL	20	6	3	11	17	3	3	11	17	4	2	11	11	2	0	9	16	1	2	13
NSH	...	...	...	...	...	...	...	...	...	...	...	...	...	...	...	...	...	...	...	...
N.J.	17	2	4	11	17	1	1	15	16	3	4	9	17	1	4	12	12	4	2	6
NYI	16	3	2	11	15	2	3	10	16	3	2	11	11	3	3	5	13	3	0	10
NYR	11	5	1	5	16	1	2	13	17	2	2	13	10	1	1	8	11	0	1	10
OTT	...	...	...	...	...	...	...	...	...	...	...	...	...	...	...	...	...	...	...	...
PHI	17	2	4	11	11	1	0	10	18	2	5	11	14	1	5	8	13	1	3	9
PHX/WPG	20	1	4	15	14	1	2	11	19	4	4	11	20	6	2	12	21	8	2	11
PIT	12	2	1	9	12	4	2	6	14	3	3	8	10	2	1	7	16	5	2	9
ST.L.	15	2	2	11	18	3	4	11	15	2	4	9	16	3	1	12	14	2	4	8
S.J.	9	1	3	5	...	...	...	...	...	...	...	...	...	...	...	...	...	...	...	...
T.B.	...	...	...	...	...	...	...	...	...	...	...	...	...	...	...	...	...	...	...	...
TOR	11	4	0	7	17	4	2	11	11	3	4	4	11	1	4	6	13	1	2	10
VAN	17	4	1	12	15	3	3	9	21	2	5	14	14	2	4	8	11	0	2	9
WSH	12	2	2	8	14	4	3	7	9	2	1	6	16	2	4	10	15	2	4	9
Totals	**169**	**52**		**117**	**166**	**54**		**112**	**155**	**55**		**100**	**149**	**52**		**97**	**146**	**49**		**97**

Abbreviations: GP – games played; **W** – overtime win; **L** – overtime loss;
SO – game tied after overtime. Game decided in shootout. (2005-06 to date); See page 143.
T – game tied after overtime. (Up to and including 2003-04.)

2007-08 Shootout Summary

Team Shootout Statistics

	OVERALL								HOME								ROAD							
Team	GP	W	L	G	S	S%	SA	GA	Sv%	W	L	G	S	S%	SA	GA	Sv%	W	L	G	S	S%	SA	GA	Sv%
ANA	15	8	7	16	48	.333	45	16	.644	7	3	15	35	.429	33	11	.667	1	4	1	13	.077	12	5	.583
ATL	15	9	6	17	51	.333	49	12	.755	6	2	10	23	.435	22	4	.818	3	4	7	28	.250	27	8	.704
BOS	13	6	7	8	35	.229	36	11	.694	3	3	4	15	.267	15	6	.600	3	4	4	20	.200	21	5	.762
BUF	13	4	9	12	43	.279	43	17	.605	1	5	5	16	.312	16	9	.438	3	4	7	27	.259	27	8	.704
CAR	5	2	3	7	14	.500	14	8	.429	0	2	0	5	.000	6	3	.500	2	1	7	9	.778	8	5	.375
CBJ	11	3	8	11	37	.297	33	14	.576	2	4	9	23	.391	22	10	.545	1	4	2	14	.143	11	4	.636
CGY	6	3	3	7	18	.389	17	6	.647	1	2	3	10	.300	9	4	.556	2	1	4	8	.500	8	2	.750
CHI	9	5	4	10	26	.385	28	9	.679	2	0	2	4	.500	6	0	1.000	3	4	8	22	.364	22	9	.591
COL	10	7	3	16	39	.410	37	10	.730	4	1	10	16	.625	15	5	.667	3	2	6	23	.261	22	5	.773
DAL	8	5	3	10	28	.357	29	9	.690	2	1	3	11	.273	11	3	.727	3	2	7	17	.412	18	6	.667
DET	10	5	5	12	30	.400	28	11	.607	4	2	8	17	.471	15	4	.733	1	3	4	13	.308	13	7	.462
EDM	19	15	4	24	65	.369	69	12	.826	8	1	13	29	.448	29	5	.828	7	3	11	36	.306	40	7	.825
FLA	11	5	6	9	41	.220	41	11	.732	2	6	2	24	.083	24	7	.708	3	0	7	17	.412	17	4	.765
L.A.	8	5	3	12	29	.414	28	10	.643	2	1	5	10	.500	8	3	.625	3	2	7	19	.368	20	7	.650
MIN	11	3	8	10	33	.303	35	18	.486	0	3	1	8	.125	9	5	.444	3	5	9	25	.360	26	13	.500
MTL	11	5	6	9	37	.243	38	10	.737	2	5	4	20	.200	21	7	.667	3	1	5	17	.294	17	3	.824
N.J.	12	8	4	15	42	.357	43	11	.744	6	2	12	31	.387	33	8	.758	2	2	3	11	.273	10	3	.700
NSH	8	3	5	6	21	.286	22	9	.591	2	3	4	13	.308	14	5	.643	1	2	2	8	.250	8	4	.500
NYI	8	5	3	11	32	.344	34	10	.706	1	1	2	9	.222	9	2	.778	4	2	9	23	.391	25	8	.680
NYR	17	8	9	15	53	.283	53	16	.698	4	2	8	21	.381	21	5	.762	4	7	7	32	.219	32	11	.656
OTT	8	3	5	10	31	.323	31	12	.613	2	3	6	19	.316	19	8	.579	1	2	4	12	.333	12	4	.667
PHI	9	3	6	10	25	.400	23	13	.435	1	3	4	11	.364	9	5	.444	2	3	6	14	.429	14	8	.429
PHX	11	5	6	12	39	.308	42	12	.714	3	4	7	28	.250	30	8	.733	2	2	5	11	.454	12	4	.667
PIT	11	7	4	17	44	.386	44	13	.705	2	3	7	20	.350	20	8	.600	5	1	10	24	.417	24	5	.792
S.J.	12	6	6	18	41	.439	40	18	.550	2	4	7	21	.333	19	9	.526	4	2	11	20	.550	21	9	.571
STL	8	3	5	5	27	.185	26	6	.769	1	3	3	14	.214	13	4	.692	2	2	2	13	.154	13	2	.846
T.B.	3	2	1	4	10	.400	9	3	.667	1	0	2	4	.500	4	1	.750	1	1	2	6	.333	5	2	.600
TOR	7	3	4	8	24	.333	24	9	.625	1	4	5	18	.278	19	9	.526	2	0	3	6	.500	5	0	1.000
VAN	15	6	9	13	56	.232	58	17	.707	3	4	6	27	.222	28	8	.714	3	5	7	29	.241	30	9	.700
WSH	8	4	4	10	39	.256	39	11	.718	2	2	6	29	.207	28	5	.821	2	2	4	10	.400	11	6	.455

Team Shootout Leaders

Wins

	W	L	Win%
EDM	**15**	4	.789
ATL	**9**	6	.600
N.J.	**8**	4	.667
ANA	**8**	7	.533
NYR	**8**	9	.471
COL	**7**	3	.700
PIT	**7**	4	.636
S.J.	**6**	6	.500
BOS	**6**	7	.462
VAN	**6**	9	.400

Goals Scored

	G	S	S%
EDM	**24**	65	.369
S.J.	**18**	41	.439
PIT	**17**	44	.386
ATL	**17**	51	.333
ANA	**16**	48	.333
N.J.	**15**	42	.357
NYR	**15**	53	.283
VAN	**13**	56	.232
BUF	**12**	43	.279
FLA	**9**	41	.220

Fewest Goals Against

	GA	SA	Sv%
T.B.	**3**	9	.667
STL	**6**	26	.769
CGY	**6**	17	.647
CAR	**8**	14	.429
DAL	**9**	29	.690
CHI	**9**	28	.679
TOR	**9**	24	.625
NSH	**9**	22	.591
MTL	**10**	38	.737
COL	**10**	37	.730
NYI	**10**	34	.706
L.A.	**10**	28	.643

Save Percentage

	Sv%	SA	GA
EDM	**.826**	69	12
STL	**.769**	26	6
ATL	**.755**	49	12
N.J.	**.744**	43	11
MTL	**.737**	38	10
FLA	**.732**	41	11
COL	**.730**	37	10
WSH	**.718**	39	11
PHX	**.714**	42	12
VAN	**.707**	58	17

Shootout Abbreviations

G........Goals Scored
GA......Goals Against
GDG ...Game Deciding Goal
S.........Shots Taken
SA ......Shots Against
S% ....Goal Scoring %
Sv%....Save %

Individual Shootout Leaders – Goaltenders

Goaltender Shootout Wins

	Team	W	L
Mathieu Garon	EDM	**10**	0
Martin Brodeur	N.J.	**8**	4
Jose Theodore	COL	**6**	1
J-S Giguere	ANA	**6**	5
Evgeni Nabokov	S.J.	**6**	6
Henrik Lundqvist	NYR	**6**	7
Roberto Luongo	VAN	**6**	8
4 Goaltenders with ...		**5**	

Goaltender Shootout Shots Against

	Team	SA	GA	Sv%
Roberto Luongo	VAN	**54**	15	.722
Martin Brodeur	N.J.	**43**	11	.744
Henrik Lundqvist	NYR	**42**	13	.690
Tomas Vokoun	FLA	**41**	11	.732
Evgeni Nabokov	S.J.	**40**	18	.550
Dwayne Roloson	EDM	**37**	10	.730
Olaf Kolzig	WSH	**34**	11	.676
Ryan Miller	BUF	**33**	14	.576
Mathieu Garon	EDM	**32**	2	.938
Johan Hedberg	ATL	**31**	7	.774
J-S Giguere	ANA	**30**	10	.667

Goaltender Shootout Save Percentage

(min. 10 shots faced)	Team	Sv%	SA	GA
Mathieu Garon	EDM	**.938**	32	2
Carey Price	MTL	**.818**	22	4
Jose Theodore	COL	**.786**	28	6
Patrick Lalime	CHI	**.778**	9	2
Hannu Toivonen	STL	**.778**	9	2
Erik Ersberg	L.A.	**.778**	9	2
Johan Hedberg	ATL	**.774**	31	7
Dany Sabourin	PIT	**.769**	26	6
Manny Legace	STL	**.765**	17	4
Mikael Tellqvist	PHX	**.750**	16	4
Dominik Hasek	DET	**.750**	12	3
Dan Cloutier	L.A.	**.750**	4	1
Johan Holmqvist	DAL	**.750**	4	1

Sometimes its better to be lucky than good. Edmonton's Mathieu Garon was beaten by the Kings' Mike Cammalleri on this shot, but it clanged off the crossbar. Garon surrendered only two goals on 32 shootout shots in posting a 10-0 record in 2007-08.

Individual Shootout Leaders – Skaters

Shootout Goals Scored

	Team	G	S	S%
Patrick Kane	CHI	**7**	9	.778
Joe Pavelski	S.J.	**7**	11	.636
Erik Christensen	ATL	**6**	11	.546
Ales Hemsky	EDM	**6**	16	.375
13 players with		**5**		

Shootout Shots Taken

	Team	S	G	S%
Sam Gagner	EDM	**17**	5	.294
Ales Hemsky	EDM	**16**	6	.375
Brendan Shanahan	NYR	**15**	5	.333
Vyacheslav Kozlov	ATL	**14**	5	.357
Phil Kessel	BOS	**13**	5	.385
Ales Kotalik	BUF	**12**	5	.417
Brian Gionta	N.J.	**12**	3	.250
Ryan Getzlaf	ANA	**12**	2	.167
4 Players with		**11**		

Shootout Scoring Percentage

(min. 5 shots taken)	Team	S%	S	G
Patrik Elias	N.J.	**.833**	6	5
Jeremy Roenick	S.J.	**.800**	5	4
Kristian Huselius	CGY	**.800**	5	4
Patrick O'Sullivan	L.A.	**.800**	5	4
Patrick Kane	CHI	**.778**	9	7
Shawn Horcoff	EDM	**.714**	7	5
Jason Spezza	OTT	**.667**	6	4
Joe Pavelski	S.J.	**.636**	11	7
Nikolai Zherdev	CBJ	**.625**	8	5
Kristopher Letang	PIT	**.625**	8	5
Radim Vrbata	PHX	**.625**	8	5

Shootout Game-Deciding Goals

	Team	GDG	S	G
Phil Kessel	BOS	**5**	13	5
Ales Hemsky	EDM	**4**	16	6
Sam Gagner	EDM	**4**	17	5
Brendan Shanahan	NYR	**4**	15	5
Patrick Kane	CHI	**3**	9	7
Kristopher Letang	PIT	**3**	8	5
Shawn Horcoff	EDM	**3**	7	5
Patrick O'Sullivan	L.A.	**3**	5	4
Jeremy Roenick	S.J.	**3**	5	4
Corey Perry	ANA	**3**	7	4
Zach Parise	N.J.	**3**	11	4

Shootout Register, 2007-08

Skaters

Player	Team	S	G	S%	GDG
Afinogenov, Maxim	BUF	3	1	.333	1
Alfredsson, Daniel	OTT	7	2	.286	1
Antropov, Nik	TOR	3	1	.333	0
Arnason, Tyler	COL	1	1	1.000	0
Asham, Arron	N.J.	1	0	.000	0
Avery, Sean	NYR	1	0	.000	0
Backstrom, Nicklas	WSH	2	1	.500	0
Ballard, Keith	PHX	2	0	.000	0
Barker, Cameron	CHI	1	0	.000	0
Belanger, Eric	MIN	1	0	.000	0
Bergenheim, Sean	NYI	1	0	.000	0
Bergeron, Patrice	BOS	1	0	.000	0
Bernier, Steve	S.J.	1	0	.000	0
Bertuzzi, Todd	ANA	6	1	.167	0
Blake, Jason	TOR	2	0	.000	0
Bochenski, Brandon	ANA	1	0	.000	0
Bonk, Radek	NSH	2	2	1.000	0
Booth, David	FLA	1	0	.000	0
Bouchard, Pierre-Marc	MIN	3	1	.333	0
Bouwmeester, Jay	FLA	1	0	.000	0
Boyes, Brad	STL	8	4	.500	2
Bradley, Matt	WSH	1	1	1.000	1
Brashear, Donald	WSH	1	0	.000	0
Briere, Daniel	PHI	7	3	.429	2
Brind'Amour, Rod	CAR	1	1	1.000	1
Brown, Dustin	L.A.	8	4	.500	1
Brule, Gilbert	CBJ	3	0	.000	0
Brunette, Andrew	COL	1	0	.000	0
Brylin, Sergei	N.J.	1	0	.000	0
Burns, Brent	MIN	5	3	.600	1
Burrows, Alex	VAN	1	0	.000	0
Callahan, Ryan	NYR	1	0	.000	0
Cammalleri, Mike	L.A.	5	1	.200	1
Carcillo, Daniel	PHX	3	0	.000	0
Carter, Jeff	PHI	6	3	.500	0
Chara, Zdeno	BOS	2	1	.500	0
Cheechoo, Jonathan	S.J.	6	1	.167	0
Chimera, Jason	CBJ	2	0	.000	0
Christensen, Erik	PIT-ATL	11	6	.546	2
Cleary, Daniel	DET	1	0	.000	0
Clowe, Ryane	S.J.	1	0	.000	0
Cogliano, Andrew	EDM	1	0	.000	0
Comeau, Blake	NYI	2	1	.500	0
Comrie, Mike	NYI	4	1	.250	1
Connolly, Tim	BUF	3	0	.000	0
Crosby, Sidney	PIT	7	2	.286	2
Cullen, Matt	CAR	3	2	.667	0
Datsyuk, Pavel	DET	10	4	.400	1
Dawes, Nigel	NYR	9	5	.556	2
Demitra, Pavol	MIN	4	1	.250	0
Doan, Shane	PHX	4	1	.250	0
Drury, Chris	NYR	5	0	.000	0
Dubinsky, Brandon	NYR	1	0	.000	0
Dumont, J.P.	NSH	4	0	.000	0
Dupuis, Pascal	ATL	1	1	1.000	0
Edler, Alexander	VAN	7	2	.286	2
Elias, Patrik	N.J.	6	5	.833	2
Enstrom, Tobias	ATL	1	0	.000	0
Erat, Martin	NSH	5	2	.400	2
Erskine, John	WSH	1	0	.000	0
Fedorov, Sergei	CBJ	2	0	.000	0
Fisher, Mike	OTT	2	1	.500	0
Fleischmann, Tomas	WSH	1	0	.000	0
Foote, Adam	CBJ	1	0	.000	0
Franzen, Johan	DET	1	1	1.000	1
Frolov, Alexander	L.A.	2	0	.000	0
Gaborik, Marian	MIN	5	1	.200	1
Gagner, Sam	EDM	17	5	.294	4
Getzlaf, Ryan	ANA	12	2	.167	2
Gilbert, Tom	EDM	1	0	.000	0
Gionta, Brian	N.J.	12	3	.250	1
Giroux, Claude	PHI	1	0	.000	0
Glencross, Curtis	CBJ	1	1	1.000	0
Gomez, Scott	NYR	4	2	.500	1
Gonchar, Sergei	PIT	1	0	.000	0
Gordon, Boyd	WSH	3	1	.333	0
Green, Mike	WSH	2	0	.000	0
Guerin, Bill	NYI	4	2	.500	0
Guite, Ben	COL	1	0	.000	0
Hagman, Niklas	DAL	3	1	.333	1
Hamilton, Jeff	CAR	4	2	.500	0
Hanzal, Martin	PHX	1	0	.000	0
Havlat, Martin	CHI	4	1	.250	0
Heatley, Dany	OTT	4	0	.000	0
Hecht, Jochen	BUF	1	0	.000	0
Hejduk, Milan	COL	6	3	.500	1
Hemsky, Ales	EDM	16	6	.375	4
Hensick, T.J.	COL	2	0	.000	0
Higgins, Christopher	MTL	3	0	.000	0
Holik, Bobby	ATL	1	0	.000	0
Horcoff, Shawn	EDM	7	5	.714	3
Horton, Nathan	FLA	10	3	.300	0
Hossa, Marcel	PHX	4	1	.250	0
Hossa, Marian	PIT	10	2	.200	1
Hudler, Jiri	DET	8	4	.500	1
Hunter, Trent	NYI	3	0	.000	0
Huselius, Kristian	CGY	5	4	.800	2
Iginla, Jarome	CGY	5	3	.600	1
Isbister, Brad	VAN	1	0	.000	0
Jagr, Jaromir	NYR	5	0	.000	0
Jokinen, Jussi	DAL	4	2	.500	1
Jokinen, Olli	FLA	8	3	.375	2
Jones, David	COL	1	0	.000	0
Jovanovski, Ed	PHX	1	0	.000	0
Kaberle, Tomas	TOR	4	3	.750	1
Kane, Patrick	CHI	9	7	.778	3
Kapanen, Niko	PHX	1	0	.000	0
Kariya, Paul	STL	6	0	.000	0
Kesler, Ryan	VAN	9	1	.111	0
Kessel, Phil	BOS	13	5	.385	5
Kobasew, Chuck	BOS	3	0	.000	0
Koivu, Mikko	MIN	7	1	.143	1
Koivu, Saku	MTL	11	5	.454	2
Kopitar, Anze	L.A.	8	3	.375	0
Kostitsyn, Andrei	MTL	6	2	.333	2
Kostitsyn, Sergei	MTL	1	0	.000	0
Kotalik, Ales	BUF	12	5	.417	1
Kovalchuk, Ilya	ATL	10	4	.400	2
Kovalev, Alex	MTL	7	1	.143	0
Kozlov, Viktor	WSH	7	3	.429	1
Kozlov, Vyacheslav	ATL	14	5	.357	1
Krejci, David	BOS	5	1	.200	0
Kreps, Kamil	FLA	2	1	.500	0
Kubina, Pavel	TOR	1	0	.000	0
Kunitz, Chris	ANA	5	2	.400	1
Laich, Brooks	WSH	2	0	.000	0
Lang, Robert	CHI	2	1	.500	1
Langenbrunner, Jamie	N.J.	6	3	.500	2
Laperriere, Ian	COL	1	0	.000	0
Lecavalier, Vincent	T.B.	3	1	.333	0
Legwand, David	NSH	1	0	.000	0
Lehtinen, Jere	DAL	2	0	.000	0
Letang, Kris	PIT	8	5	.625	3
Liles, John-Michael	COL	1	1	1.000	0
Linden, Trevor	VAN	9	5	.556	0
Lindstrom, Joakim	CBJ	1	0	.000	0
Little, Bryan	ATL	1	1	1.000	0
Lombardi, Matthew	CGY	1	0	.000	0
Lupul, Joffrey	PHI	1	1	1.000	0
MacArthur, Clarke	BUF	3	0	.000	0
Madden, John	N.J.	2	0	.000	0
Malkin, Evgeni	PIT	5	0	.000	0
Marchant, Todd	ANA	1	0	.000	0
Markov, Andrei	MTL	2	1	.500	1
Marleau, Patrick	S.J.	8	4	.500	1
McAmmond, Dean	OTT	3	1	.333	1
McDonald, Andy	ANA-STL	5	3	.600	1
McLeod, Cody	COL	1	1	1.000	1
Metropolit, Glen	BOS	1	0	.000	0
Michalek, Milan	S.J.	1	0	.000	0
Miettinen, Antti	DAL	1	1	1.000	0
Mitchell, Torrey	S.J.	2	0	.000	0
Modano, Mike	DAL	6	2	.333	1
Montador, Steve	FLA	2	0	.000	0
Moreau, Ethan	EDM	1	0	.000	0
Morrison, Brendan	VAN	3	0	.000	0
Morrow, Brenden	DAL	1	1	1.000	1
Mueller, Peter	PHX	10	3	.300	3
Nash, Rick	CBJ	10	4	.400	2
Naslund, Markus	VAN	5	1	.200	0
Nielsen, Frans	NYI	1	0	.000	0
Nilsson, Robert	EDM	7	4	.571	1
Nolan, Owen	CGY	2	0	.000	0
Novotny, Jiri	CBJ	2	0	.000	0
Nummelin, Petteri	MIN	3	2	.667	0
Nylander, Michael	WSH	1	0	.000	0
O'Sullivan, Patrick	L.A.	5	4	.800	3
Okposo, Kyle	NYI	2	1	.500	0
Olesz, Rostislav	FLA	3	0	.000	0
Ovechkin, Alex	WSH	6	1	.167	0
Parise, Zach	N.J.	11	4	.364	3
Park, Richard	NYI	5	2	.400	2
Pavelski, Joe	S.J.	11	7	.636	0
Peca, Michael	CBJ	4	1	.250	0
Peltonen, Ville	FLA	4	0	.000	0
Penner, Dustin	EDM	1	0	.000	0
Perrault, Joel	PHX	4	1	.250	0
Perreault, Yanic	CHI	2	0	.000	0
Perrin, Eric	ATL	4	2	.500	2
Perron, David	STL	5	0	.000	0
Perry, Corey	ANA	7	4	.571	3
Pettinger, Matt	WSH	2	0	.000	0
Peverley, Rich	NSH	1	1	1.000	0
Phaneuf, Dion	CGY	3	0	.000	0
Pisani, Fernando	EDM	3	2	.667	2
Plekanec, Tomas	MTL	4	0	.000	0
Plihal, Tomas	S.J.	1	0	.000	0
Pohl, John	TOR	1	0	.000	0
Pominville, Jason	BUF	4	2	.500	0
Pothier, Brian	WSH	1	0	.000	0
Poti, Tom	WSH	1	0	.000	0
Pronger, Chris	ANA	1	0	.000	0
Prospal, Vaclav	T.B.	1	1	1.000	1
Prucha, Petr	NYR	4	1	.250	1
Pyatt, Taylor	VAN	8	1	.125	1
Rachunek, Karel	N.J.	1	0	.000	0
Radulov, Alexander	NSH	8	1	.125	1
Raymond, Mason	VAN	3	1	.333	1
Reasoner, Marty	EDM	3	0	.000	0
Recchi, Mark	PIT-ATL	5	1	.200	1
Reinprecht, Steve	PHX	2	0	.000	0
Ribeiro, Mike	DAL	5	1	.200	0
Richards, Brad	T.B.-DAL	4	3	.750	1
Richards, Mike	PHI	6	2	.333	1
Rissmiller, Patrick	S.J.	1	0	.000	0
Ritchie, Byron	VAN	1	0	.000	0
Robitaille, Randy	OTT	1	0	.000	0
Roenick, Jeremy	S.J.	5	4	.800	3
Rolston, Brian	MIN	5	1	.200	0
Roy, Derek	BUF	5	1	.200	1
Rozsival, Michal	NYR	1	0	.000	0
Rucinsky, Martin	STL	1	0	.000	0
Ruutu, Jarkko	PIT	6	3	.500	1
Ryan, Bobby	ANA	3	0	.000	0
Ryder, Michael	MTL	1	0	.000	0
Sakic, Joe	COL	5	3	.600	2
Samsonov, Sergei	CAR	3	1	.333	1
Sanderson, Geoff	EDM	1	0	.000	0
Satan, Miroslav	NYI	5	1	.200	0
Savard, Marc	BOS	1	0	.000	0
Schneider, Mathieu	ANA	3	2	.667	2
Sedin, Daniel	VAN	5	1	.200	1
Selanne, Teemu	ANA	4	3	.750	0
Semin, Alexander	WSH	7	3	.429	2
Setoguchi, Devin	S.J.	3	1	.333	1
Shanahan, Brendan	NYR	15	5	.333	4
Shannon, Ryan	VAN	4	1	.250	1
Sharp, Patrick	CHI	5	1	.200	1
Sillinger, Mike	NYI	3	2	.667	1
Sjostrom, Fredrik	NYR	2	1	.500	0
Smyth, Ryan	COL	3	1	.333	1
Souray, Sheldon	EDM	1	0	.000	0
Spezza, Jason	OTT	6	4	.667	1
St. Louis, Martin	T.B.	1	0	.000	0
Staal, Eric	CAR	2	1	.500	0
Stafford, Drew	BUF	4	1	.250	1
Stastny, Paul	COL	1	0	.000	0
Steckel, David	WSH	1	0	.000	0
Steen, Alexander	TOR	3	1	.333	0
Stempniak, Lee	STL	2	0	.000	0
Stoll, Jarret	EDM	3	1	.333	1
Straka, Martin	NYR	1	0	.000	0
Streit, Mark	MTL	2	0	.000	0
Stumpel, Jozef	FLA	3	1	.333	1
Sturm, Marco	BOS	8	1	.125	1
Sundin, Mats	TOR	6	3	.500	2
Svatos, Marek	COL	7	2	.286	1
Sykora, Petr	PIT	7	2	.286	0
Tallinder, Henrik	BUF	2	1	.500	0
Tambellini, Jeff	NYI	1	1	1.000	1
Tanguay, Alex	CGY	2	0	.000	0
Thorburn, Chris	ATL	1	0	.000	0
Thornton, Joe	S.J.	1	1	1.000	0
Timonen, Kimmo	PHI	3	1	.333	0
Tkachuk, Keith	STL	1	0	.000	0
Tlusty, Jiri	TOR	1	0	.000	0
Toews, Jonathan	CHI	2	0	.000	0
Torres, Raffi	EDM	3	1	.333	0
Tucker, Darcy	TOR	1	0	.000	0
Turris, Kyle	PHX	1	1	1.000	0
Upshall, Scottie	PHI	1	0	.000	0
Vanek, Thomas	BUF	6	1	.167	0
Vasicek, Josef	NYI	1	0	.000	0
Vermette, Antoine	OTT	8	2	.250	0
Vrbata, Radim	PHX	8	5	.625	1
Vyborny, David	CBJ	3	0	.000	0
Weight, Doug	STL-ANA	3	0	.000	0
Weiss, Stephen	FLA	6	1	.167	1
Wellwood, Kyle	TOR	1	0	.000	0
White, Todd	ATL	1	0	.000	0
Whitney, Ryan	PIT	1	0	.000	0
Whitney, Ray	CAR	1	0	.000	0
Wideman, Dennis	BOS	1	0	.000	0
Williams, Jeremy	TOR	1	0	.000	0
Williams, Jason	CHI	1	0	.000	0
Willsie, Brian	L.A.	1	0	.000	0
Wolski, Wojtek	COL	8	4	.500	1
Yandle, Keith	PHX	1	0	.000	0
York, Michael	PHX	1	1	1.000	0
Zajac, Travis	N.J.	1	0	.000	0
Zednik, Richard	FLA	1	0	.000	0
Zetterberg, Henrik	DET	10	3	.300	2
Zherdev, Nikolai	CBJ	8	5	.625	1
Zubov, Sergei	DAL	5	1	.200	1
Zubrus, Dainius	N.J.	1	0	.000	0

Goaltenders

Goaltender	Team	W	L	SA	GA	Sv %
Aubin, J-Sebastien	L.A.	1	1	4	2	.500
Auld, Alex	BOS	2	3	15	5	.667
Backstrom, Niklas	MIN	1	6	21	12	.429
Biron, Martin	PHI	2	6	20	13	.350
Brodeur, Martin	N.J.	8	4	43	11	.744
Bryzgalov, Ilja	ANA-PHX	5	5	29	9	.690
Budaj, Peter	COL	1	2	9	4	.556
Clemmensen, Scott	TOR	1	0	3	1	.667
Cloutier, Dan	L.A.	1	0	4	1	.750
Conklin, Ty	PIT	2	3	15	7	.533
Denis, Marc	T.B.	1	0	3	0	1.000
DiPietro, Rick	NYI	3	2	21	6	.714
Dubielewicz, Wade	NYI	2	1	13	4	.692
Ellis, Dan	NSH	2	1	9	4	.556
Emery, Ray	OTT	1	3	15	7	.533
Ersberg, Erik	L.A.	1	1	9	2	.778
Fernandez, Manny	BOS	1	0	3	0	1.000
Fleury, Marc-Andre	PIT	1	0	3	0	1.000
Garon, Mathieu	EDM	10	0	32	2	.938
Gerber, Martin	OTT	2	2	16	5	.688
Giguere, J-S	ANA	6	5	30	10	.667
Grahame, John	CAR	1	0	3	2	.333
Halak, Jaroslav	MTL	0	1	3	1	.667
Harding, Josh	MIN	2	2	14	6	.571
Hasek, Dominik	DET	3	2	12	3	.750
Hedberg, Johan	ATL	5	3	31	7	.774
Hiller, Jonas	ANA	2	1	12	5	.583
Holmqvist, Johan	T.B.	1	0	4	1	.750
Huet, Cristobal	MTL-WSH	4	3	18	5	.722
Khabibulin, Nikolai	CHI	2	4	19	7	.632
Kiprusoff, Miikka	CGY	3	3	17	6	.647
Kolzig, Olaf	WSH	2	4	34	11	.676
LaBarbera, Jason	L.A.	2	1	10	5	.500
Lalime, Patrick	CHI	3	0	9	2	.778
Leclaire, Pascal	CBJ	3	4	23	10	.565
Legace, Manny	STL	2	3	17	4	.765
Lehtonen, Kari	ATL	4	3	18	5	.722
Lundqvist, Henrik	NYR	6	7	42	13	.690
Luongo, Roberto	VAN	6	8	54	15	.722
Mason, Chris	NSH	1	4	13	5	.615
Miller, Ryan	BUF	4	7	33	14	.576
Nabokov, Evgeni	S.J.	6	6	40	18	.550
Niittymaki, Antero	PHI	1	0	3	0	1.000
Norrena, Fredrik	CBJ	0	4	10	4	.600
Osgood, Chris	DET	2	3	16	8	.500
Price, Carey	MTL	3	2	22	4	.818
Ramo, Karri	T.B.	0	1	2	2	.000
Raycroft, Andrew	TOR	0	1	6	2	.667
Roloson, Dwayne	EDM	5	4	37	10	.730
Sabourin, Dany	PIT	4	1	26	6	.769
Sanford, Curtis	VAN	0	1	4	2	.500
Smith, Mike	T.B.	2	0	6	0	1.000
Tellqvist, Mikael	PHX	0	2	16	4	.750
Theodore, Jose	COL	6	1	28	6	.786
Thibault, Jocelyn	BUF	0	2	10	3	.700
Thomas, Tim	BOS	3	4	18	6	.667
Toivonen, Hannu	STL	1	2	9	2	.778
Toskala, Vesa	TOR	2	3	15	6	.600
Turco, Marty	DAL	3	3	23	9	.609
Valiquette, Stephen	NYR	2	2	11	3	.727
Vokoun, Tomas	FLA	5	6	41	11	.732
Ward, Cam	CAR	1	3	11	6	.454

NHL Record Book

All-Time Standings of NHL Teams

(ranked by percentage)

Active Teams

Team	Games	Wins	Losses	Ties	OT Losses	SO Losses	Goals For	Goals Against	Points	Pts %	First Season
Montreal	5792	2980	1924	837	37	14	19035	15511	6848	.591	1917-18
Philadelphia	3178	1577	1091	457	35	18	10760	9352	3664	.576	1967-68
Buffalo	2952	1401	1099	409	25	18	9920	8975	3254	.551	1970-71
Boston	5632	2669	2104	791	49	19	18114	16666	6197	.550	1924-25
Edmonton	2240	1054	869	262	39	16	8073	7541	2425	.541	1979-80
Calgary	2796	1273	1094	379	35	15	9496	8964	2975	.532	1972-73
Detroit	5566	2521	2186	815	28	16	17352	16566	5901	.530	1926-27
Colorado	2240	1028	907	261	31	13	7686	7419	2361	.527	1979-80
Minnesota	574	253	222	55	26	18	1438	1433	605	.527	2000-01
Nashville	738	324	308	60	33	13	1931	2022	754	.511	1998-99
St. Louis	3178	1376	1311	432	40	19	9968	10099	3243	.510	1967-68
Toronto	5792	2535	2426	783	30	18	17939	17850	5901	.509	1917-18
NY Islanders	2796	1223	1185	347	30	11	9261	8938	2834	.507	1972-73
Ottawa	1200	526	513	115	29	17	3518	3544	1213	.505	1992-93
Dallas	3178	1353	1327	459	31	8	9908	10136	3204	.504	1967-68
NY Rangers	5566	2359	2344	808	37	18	17189	17346	5581	.501	1926-27
Anaheim	1116	476	474	107	35	24	2937	3066	1118	.501	1993-94
Washington	2640	1111	1175	303	30	21	8371	8834	2576	.488	1974-75
Chicago	5566	2273	2427	814	35	17	16494	16914	5412	.486	1926-27
Pittsburgh	3178	1315	1424	383	40	16	10706	11337	3069	.483	1967-68
Florida	1116	432	472	142	51	19	2927	3182	1076	.482	1993-94
San Jose	1280	526	580	121	38	15	3556	3902	1226	.479	1991-92
New Jersey	2640	1075	1192	328	29	16	8063	8772	2523	.478	1974-75
Los Angeles	3178	1262	1440	424	42	10	10445	11186	3000	.472	1967-68
Carolina	2240	896	1039	263	32	10	6890	7635	2097	.468	1979-80
Phoenix	2240	892	1041	266	30	11	7173	7925	2091	.467	1979-80
Vancouver	2952	1154	1358	391	32	17	9349	10199	2748	.465	1970-71
Tampa Bay	1200	446	595	112	40	7	3149	3782	1051	.438	1992-93
Atlanta	656	238	326	45	32	15	1751	2209	568	.433	1999-2000
Columbus	574	206	294	33	25	16	1361	1735	486	.423	2000-01

Defunct Teams

Team	Games	Wins	Losses	Ties	Goals For	Goals Against	Points	Pts %	First Season	Last Season
Ottawa Senators	542	258	221	63	1458	1333	579	.534	1917-18	1933-34
Montreal Maroons	622	271	260	91	1474	1405	633	.509	1924-25	1937-38
NY/Brooklyn Americans	784	255	402	127	1643	2182	637	.406	1925-26	1941-42
Hamilton Tigers	126	47	78	1	414	475	95	.377	1920-21	1924-25
Cleveland Barons	160	47	87	26	470	617	120	.375	1976-77	1977-78
Pittsburgh Pirates	212	67	122	23	376	519	157	.370	1925-26	1929-30
Calif./Oakland Seals	698	182	401	115	1826	2580	479	.343	1967-68	1975-76
St. Louis Eagles	48	11	31	6	86	144	28	.292	1934-35	1934-35
Quebec Bulldogs	24	4	20	0	91	177	8	.167	1919-20	1919-20
Montreal Wanderers	6	1	5	0	17	35	2	.167	1917-18	1917-18
Philadelphia Quakers	44	4	36	4	76	184	12	.136	1930-31	1930-31

Calgary totals include Atlanta Flames, 1972-73 to 1979-80.
Carolina totals include Hartford, 1979-80 to 1996-97.
Colorado totals include Quebec, 1979-80 to 1994-95.
Dallas totals include Minnesota North Stars, 1967-68 to 1992-93.
Detroit totals include Cougars, 1926-27 to 1929-30, and Falcons, 1930-31 to 1931-32.
New Jersey totals include Kansas City, 1974-75 to 1975-76, and Colorado Rockies, 1976-77 to 1981-82.
Phoenix totals include Winnipeg, 1979-80 to 1995-96.
Toronto totals include Arenas, 1917-18 to 1918-19, and St. Patricks, 1919-20 to 1925-26.

Year-By-Year Final Standings & Leading Scorers

*Stanley Cup winner

1917-18

First Half

Team	GP	W	L	T	GF	GA	PTS
Montreal	14	10	4	0	81	47	20
Toronto	14	8	6	0	71	75	16
Ottawa	14	5	9	0	67	79	10
**Mtl. Wanderers	6	1	5	0	17	35	2

**Montreal Arena burned down and Wanderers forced to withdraw from League. Montreal Canadiens and Toronto each counted a win for defaulted games with Wanderers.

Second Half

Team	GP	W	L	T	GF	GA	PTS
*Toronto	8	5	3	0	37	34	10
Ottawa	8	4	4	0	35	35	8
Montreal	8	3	5	0	34	37	6

Leading Scorers

Player	Team	GP	G	A	PTS	PIM
Joe Malone	Montreal	20	44	4	48	30
Cy Denneny	Ottawa	20	36	10	46	80
Reg Noble	Toronto	20	30	10	40	35
Newsy Lalonde	Montreal	14	23	7	30	51
Corb Denneny	Toronto	21	20	9	29	14
Harry Cameron	Toronto	21	17	10	27	28
Didier Pitre	Montreal	20	17	6	23	29
Eddie Gerard	Ottawa	20	13	7	20	26
Jack Darragh	Ottawa	18	14	5	19	26
Frank Nighbor	Ottawa	10	11	8	19	6
Harry Meeking	Toronto	21	10	9	19	28

1918-19

First Half

Team	GP	W	L	T	GF	GA	PTS
• Montreal	10	7	3	0	57	50	14
Ottawa	10	5	5	0	39	39	10
Toronto	10	3	7	0	42	49	6

Second Half

Team	GP	W	L	T	GF	GA	PTS
Ottawa	8	7	1	0	32	14	14
Montreal	8	3	5	0	31	28	6
Toronto	8	2	6	0	22	43	4

• NHL Champion. Stanley Cup not awarded due to influenza epidemic.

Leading Scorers

Player	Team	GP	G	A	PTS	PIM
Newsy Lalonde	Montreal	17	22	10	32	40
Odie Cleghorn	Montreal	17	22	6	28	22
Frank Nighbor	Ottawa	18	19	9	28	27
Cy Denneny	Ottawa	18	18	4	22	58
Didier Pitre	Montreal	17	14	5	19	12
Alf Skinner	Toronto	17	12	4	16	26
Harry Cameron	Tor., Ott.	14	11	3	14	35
Jack Darragh	Ottawa	14	11	3	14	33
Ken Randall	Toronto	15	8	6	14	27
Sprague Cleghorn	Ottawa	18	7	6	13	27

1919-20

First Half

Team	GP	W	L	T	GF	GA	PTS
Ottawa	12	9	3	0	59	23	18
Montreal	12	8	4	0	62	51	16
Toronto	12	5	7	0	52	62	10
Quebec	12	2	10	0	44	81	4

Second Half

Team	GP	W	L	T	GF	GA	PTS
*Ottawa	12	10	2	0	62	41	20
Toronto	12	7	5	0	67	44	14
Montreal	12	5	7	0	67	62	10
Quebec	12	2	10	0	47	96	4

Leading Scorers

Player	Team	GP	G	A	PTS	PIM
Joe Malone	Quebec	24	39	10	49	12
Newsy Lalonde	Montreal	23	37	9	46	34
Frank Nighbor	Ottawa	23	26	15	41	18
Corb Denneny	Toronto	24	24	12	36	20
Jack Darragh	Ottawa	23	22	14	36	22
Reg Noble	Toronto	24	24	9	33	52
Amos Arbour	Montreal	22	21	5	26	13
Cully Wilson	Toronto	23	20	6	26	86
Didier Pitre	Montreal	22	14	12	26	6
Punch Broadbent	Ottawa	21	19	6	25	40

1920-21

First Half

Team	GP	W	L	T	GF	GA	PTS
*Ottawa	10	8	2	0	49	23	16
Toronto	10	5	5	0	39	47	10
Montreal	10	4	6	0	37	51	8
Hamilton	10	3	7	0	34	38	6

Second Half

Team	GP	W	L	T	GF	GA	PTS
Toronto	14	10	4	0	66	53	20
Montreal	14	9	5	0	75	48	18
Ottawa	14	6	8	0	48	52	12
Hamilton	14	3	11	0	58	94	6

Leading Scorers

Player	Team	GP	G	A	PTS	PIM
Newsy Lalonde	Montreal	24	33	10	43	36
Babe Dye	Ham., Tor.	24	35	5	40	32
Cy Denneny	Ottawa	24	34	5	39	10
Joe Malone	Hamilton	20	28	9	37	6
Frank Nighbor	Ottawa	24	19	10	29	10
Reg Noble	Toronto	24	19	8	27	54
Harry Cameron	Toronto	24	18	9	27	35
Goldie Prodgers	Hamilton	24	18	9	27	8
Corb Denneny	Toronto	20	19	7	26	29
Jack Darragh	Ottawa	24	11	15	26	20

1921-22

Team	GP	W	L	T	GF	GA	PTS
Ottawa	24	14	8	2	106	84	30
*Toronto	24	13	10	1	98	97	27
Montreal	24	12	11	1	88	94	25
Hamilton	24	7	17	0	88	105	14

Leading Scorers

Player	Team	GP	G	A	PTS	PIM
Punch Broadbent	Ottawa	24	32	14	46	28
Cy Denneny	Ottawa	22	27	12	39	20
Babe Dye	Toronto	24	31	7	38	39
Harry Cameron	Toronto	24	18	17	35	22
Joe Malone	Hamilton	24	24	7	31	4
Corb Denneny	Toronto	24	19	9	28	28
Reg Noble	Toronto	24	17	11	28	19
Sprague Cleghorn	Montreal	24	17	9	26	80
Georges Boucher	Ottawa	23	13	12	25	12
Odie Cleghorn	Montreal	23	21	3	24	26

1922-23

Team	GP	W	L	T	GF	GA	PTS
*Ottawa	24	14	9	1	77	54	29
Montreal	24	13	9	2	73	61	28
Toronto	24	13	10	1	82	88	27
Hamilton	24	6	18	0	81	110	12

Leading Scorers

Player	Team	GP	G	A	PTS	PIM
Babe Dye	Toronto	22	26	11	37	19
Cy Denneny	Ottawa	24	23	11	34	28
Billy Boucher	Montreal	24	24	7	31	55
Jack Adams	Toronto	23	19	9	28	42
Mickey Roach	Hamilton	24	17	10	27	8
Odie Cleghorn	Montreal	24	19	6	25	18
Georges Boucher	Ottawa	24	14	9	23	58
Reg Noble	Toronto	24	12	11	23	47
Cully Wilson	Hamilton	23	16	5	21	46
Aurel Joliat	Montreal	24	12	9	21	37

1923-24

Team	GP	W	L	T	GF	GA	PTS
Ottawa	24	16	8	0	74	54	32
*Montreal	24	13	11	0	59	48	26
Toronto	24	10	14	0	59	85	20
Hamilton	24	9	15	0	63	68	18

Leading Scorers

Player	Team	GP	G	A	PTS	PIM
Cy Denneny	Ottawa	22	22	2	24	10
Georges Boucher	Ottawa	21	13	10	23	38
Billy Boucher	Montreal	23	16	6	22	48
Billy Burch	Hamilton	24	16	6	22	6
Aurel Joliat	Montreal	24	15	5	20	27
Babe Dye	Toronto	19	16	3	19	23
Jack Adams	Toronto	22	14	4	18	51
Reg Noble	Toronto	23	12	5	17	79
Howie Morenz	Montreal	24	13	3	16	20
King Clancy	Ottawa	24	8	8	16	26

1924-25

Team	GP	W	L	T	GF	GA	PTS
Hamilton	30	19	10	1	90	60	39
Toronto	30	19	11	0	90	84	38
• Montreal	30	17	11	2	93	56	36
Ottawa	30	17	12	1	83	66	35
Mtl. Maroons	30	9	19	2	45	65	20
Boston	30	6	24	0	49	119	12

• NHL Champion (Stanley Cup won by Victoria Cougars, WCHL)

Leading Scorers

Player	Team	GP	G	A	PTS	PIM
Babe Dye	Toronto	29	38	8	46	41
Cy Denneny	Ottawa	29	27	15	42	16
Aurel Joliat	Montreal	25	30	11	41	85
Howie Morenz	Montreal	30	28	11	39	46
Red Green	Hamilton	30	19	15	34	81
Jack Adams	Toronto	27	21	10	31	67
Billy Boucher	Montreal	30	17	13	30	92
Billy Burch	Hamilton	27	20	7	27	10
Jimmy Herberts	Boston	30	17	7	24	55
Hooley Smith	Ottawa	30	10	13	23	81

1925-26

Team	GP	W	L	T	GF	GA	PTS
Ottawa	36	24	8	4	77	42	52
*Mtl. Maroons	36	20	11	5	91	73	45
Pittsburgh	36	19	16	1	82	70	39
Boston	36	17	15	4	92	85	38
NY Americans	36	12	20	4	68	89	28
Toronto	36	12	21	3	92	114	27
Montreal	36	11	24	1	79	108	23

Leading Scorers

Player	Team	GP	G	A	PTS	PIM
Nels Stewart	Mtl. Maroons	36	34	8	42	119
Cy Denneny	Ottawa	36	24	12	36	18
Carson Cooper	Boston	36	28	3	31	10
Jimmy Herberts	Boston	36	26	5	31	47
Howie Morenz	Montreal	31	23	3	26	39
Jack Adams	Toronto	36	21	5	26	52
Aurel Joliat	Montreal	35	17	9	26	52
Billy Burch	NY Americans	36	22	3	25	33
Hooley Smith	Ottawa	28	16	9	25	53
Frank Nighbor	Ottawa	35	12	13	25	40

1926-27

Canadian Division

Team	GP	W	L	T	GF	GA	PTS
*Ottawa	44	30	10	4	86	69	64
Montreal	44	28	14	2	99	67	58
Mtl. Maroons	44	20	20	4	71	68	44
NY Americans	44	17	25	2	82	91	36
Toronto	44	15	24	5	79	94	35

American Division

Team	GP	W	L	T	GF	GA	PTS
NY Rangers	44	25	13	6	95	72	56
Boston	44	21	20	3	97	89	45
Chicago	44	19	22	3	115	116	41
Pittsburgh	44	15	26	3	79	108	33
Detroit	44	12	28	4	76	105	28

Leading Scorers

Player	Team	GP	G	A	PTS	PIM
Bill Cook	NY Rangers	44	33	4	37	58
Dick Irvin	Chicago	43	18	18	36	34
Howie Morenz	Montreal	44	25	7	32	49
Frank Fredrickson	Det., Bos.	41	18	13	31	46
Babe Dye	Chicago	41	25	5	30	14
Ace Bailey	Toronto	42	15	13	28	82
Frank Boucher	NY Rangers	44	13	15	28	17
Billy Burch	NY Americans	43	19	8	27	40
Harry Oliver	Boston	42	18	6	24	17
Duke Keats	Bos., Det.	42	16	8	24	52

1927-28

Canadian Division

Team	GP	W	L	T	GF	GA	PTS
Montreal	44	26	11	7	116	48	59
Mtl. Maroons	44	24	14	6	96	77	54
Ottawa	44	20	14	10	78	57	50
Toronto	44	18	18	8	89	88	44
NY Americans	44	11	27	6	63	128	28

American Division

Team	GP	W	L	T	GF	GA	PTS
Boston	44	20	13	11	77	70	51
*NY Rangers	44	19	16	9	94	79	47
Pittsburgh	44	19	17	8	67	76	46
Detroit	44	19	19	6	88	79	44
Chicago	44	7	34	3	68	134	17

Leading Scorers

Player	Team	GP	G	A	PTS	PIM
Howie Morenz	Montreal	43	33	18	51	66
Aurel Joliat	Montreal	44	28	11	39	105
Frank Boucher	NY Rangers	44	23	12	35	15
George Hay	Detroit	42	22	13	35	20
Nels Stewart	Mtl. Maroons	41	27	7	34	104
Art Gagne	Montreal	44	20	10	30	75
Bun Cook	NY Rangers	44	14	14	28	45
Bill Carson	Toronto	32	20	6	26	36
Frank Finnigan	Ottawa	38	20	5	25	34
Bill Cook	NY Rangers	43	18	6	24	42
Duke Keats	Det., Chi.	38	14	10	24	60

1928-29

Canadian Division

Team	GP	W	L	T	GF	GA	PTS
Montreal	44	22	7	15	71	43	59
NY Americans	44	19	13	12	53	53	50
Toronto	44	21	18	5	85	69	47
Ottawa	44	14	17	13	54	67	41
Mtl. Maroons	44	15	20	9	67	65	39

American Division

Team	GP	W	L	T	GF	GA	PTS
*Boston	44	26	13	5	89	52	57
NY Rangers	44	21	13	10	72	65	52
Detroit	44	19	16	9	72	63	47
Pittsburgh	44	9	27	8	46	80	26
Chicago	44	7	29	8	33	85	22

Leading Scorers

Player	Team	GP	G	A	PTS	PIM
Ace Bailey	Toronto	44	22	10	32	78
Nels Stewart	Mtl. Maroons	44	21	8	29	74
Carson Cooper	Detroit	43	18	9	27	14
Howie Morenz	Montreal	42	17	10	27	47
Andy Blair	Toronto	44	12	15	27	41
Frank Boucher	NY Rangers	44	10	16	26	8
Harry Oliver	Boston	43	17	6	23	24
Bill Cook	NY Rangers	43	15	8	23	41
Jimmy Ward	Mtl. Maroons	43	14	8	22	46

Seven players tied with 19 points

1929-30

Canadian Division

Team	GP	W	L	T	GF	GA	PTS
Mtl. Maroons	44	23	16	5	141	114	51
*Montreal	44	21	14	9	142	114	51
Ottawa	44	21	15	8	138	118	50
Toronto	44	17	21	6	116	124	40
NY Americans	44	14	25	5	113	161	33

American Division

Team	GP	W	L	T	GF	GA	PTS
Boston	44	38	5	1	179	98	77
Chicago	44	21	18	5	117	111	47
NY Rangers	44	17	17	10	136	143	44
Detroit	44	14	24	6	117	133	34
Pittsburgh	44	5	36	3	102	185	13

Leading Scorers

Player	Team	GP	G	A	PTS	PIM
Cooney Weiland	Boston	44	43	30	73	27
Frank Boucher	NY Rangers	42	26	36	62	16
Dit Clapper	Boston	44	41	20	61	48
Bill Cook	NY Rangers	44	29	30	59	56
Hec Kilrea	Ottawa	44	36	22	58	72
Nels Stewart	Mtl. Maroons	44	39	16	55	81
Howie Morenz	Montreal	44	40	10	50	72
Normie Himes	NY Americans	44	28	22	50	15
Joe Lamb	Ottawa	44	29	20	49	119
Dutch Gainor	Boston	42	18	31	49	39

1930-31

Canadian Division

Team	GP	W	L	T	GF	GA	PTS
*Montreal	44	26	10	8	129	89	60
Toronto	44	22	13	9	118	99	53
Mtl. Maroons	44	20	18	6	105	106	46
NY Americans	44	18	16	10	76	74	46
Ottawa	44	10	30	4	91	142	24

American Division

Team	GP	W	L	T	GF	GA	PTS
Boston	44	28	10	6	143	90	62
Chicago	44	24	17	3	108	78	51
NY Rangers	44	19	16	9	106	87	47
Detroit	44	16	21	7	102	105	39
Philadelphia	44	4	36	4	76	184	12

Leading Scorers

Player	Team	GP	G	A	PTS	PIM
Howie Morenz	Montreal	39	28	23	51	49
Ebbie Goodfellow	Detroit	44	25	23	48	32
Charlie Conacher	Toronto	37	31	12	43	78
Bill Cook	NY Rangers	43	30	12	42	39
Ace Bailey	Toronto	40	23	19	42	46
Joe Primeau	Toronto	38	9	32	41	18
Nels Stewart	Mtl. Maroons	42	25	14	39	75
Frank Boucher	NY Rangers	44	12	27	39	20
Cooney Weiland	Boston	44	25	13	38	14
Bun Cook	NY Rangers	44	18	17	35	72
Aurel Joliat	Montreal	43	13	22	35	73

1931-32

Canadian Division

Team	GP	W	L	T	GF	GA	PTS
Montreal	48	25	16	7	128	111	57
*Toronto	48	23	18	7	155	127	53
Mtl. Maroons	48	19	22	7	142	139	45
NY Americans	48	16	24	8	95	142	40

American Division

Team	GP	W	L	T	GF	GA	PTS
NY Rangers	48	23	17	8	134	112	54
Chicago	48	18	19	11	86	101	47
Detroit	48	18	20	10	95	108	46
Boston	48	15	21	12	122	117	42

Leading Scorers

Player	Team	GP	G	A	PTS	PIM
Busher Jackson	Toronto	48	28	25	53	63
Joe Primeau	Toronto	46	13	37	50	25
Howie Morenz	Montreal	48	24	25	49	46
Charlie Conacher	Toronto	44	34	14	48	66
Bill Cook	NY Rangers	48	34	14	48	33
Dave Trottier	Mtl. Maroons	48	26	18	44	94
Hooley Smith	Mtl. Maroons	43	11	33	44	49
Babe Siebert	Mtl. Maroons	48	21	18	39	64
Dit Clapper	Boston	48	17	22	39	21
Aurel Joliat	Montreal	48	15	24	39	46

1932-33

Canadian Division

Team	GP	W	L	T	GF	GA	PTS
Toronto	48	24	18	6	119	111	54
Mtl. Maroons	48	22	20	6	135	119	50
Montreal	48	18	25	5	92	115	41
NY Americans	48	15	22	11	91	118	41
Ottawa	48	11	27	10	88	131	32

American Division

Team	GP	W	L	T	GF	GA	PTS
Boston	48	25	15	8	124	88	58
Detroit	48	25	15	8	111	93	58
*NY Rangers	48	23	17	8	135	107	54
Chicago	48	16	20	12	88	101	44

Leading Scorers

Player	Team	GP	G	A	PTS	PIM
Bill Cook	NY Rangers	48	28	22	50	51
Busher Jackson	Toronto	48	27	17	44	43
Baldy Northcott	Mtl. Maroons	48	22	21	43	30
Hooley Smith	Mtl. Maroons	48	20	21	41	66
Paul Haynes	Mtl. Maroons	48	16	25	41	18
Aurel Joliat	Montreal	48	18	21	39	53
Marty Barry	Boston	48	24	13	37	40
Bun Cook	NY Rangers	48	22	15	37	35
Nels Stewart	Boston	47	18	18	36	62
Howie Morenz	Montreal	46	14	21	35	32
Johnny Gagnon	Montreal	48	12	23	35	64
Eddie Shore	Boston	48	8	27	35	102
Frank Boucher	NY Rangers	46	7	28	35	4

1933-34

Canadian Division

Team	GP	W	L	T	GF	GA	PTS
Toronto	48	26	13	9	174	119	61
Montreal	48	22	20	6	99	101	50
Mtl. Maroons	48	19	18	11	117	122	49
NY Americans	48	15	23	10	104	132	40
Ottawa	48	13	29	6	115	143	32

American Division

Team	GP	W	L	T	GF	GA	PTS
Detroit	48	24	14	10	113	98	58
*Chicago	48	20	17	11	88	83	51
NY Rangers	48	21	19	8	120	113	50
Boston	48	18	25	5	111	130	41

Leading Scorers

Player	Team	GP	G	A	PTS	PIM
Charlie Conacher	Toronto	42	32	20	52	38
Joe Primeau	Toronto	45	14	32	46	8
Frank Boucher	NY Rangers	48	14	30	44	4
Marty Barry	Boston	48	27	12	39	12
Cecil Dillon	NY Rangers	48	13	26	39	10
Nels Stewart	Boston	48	21	17	38	68
Busher Jackson	Toronto	38	20	18	38	38
Aurel Joliat	Montreal	48	22	15	37	27
Hooley Smith	Mtl. Maroons	47	18	19	37	58
Paul Thompson	Chicago	48	20	16	36	17

1934-35

Canadian Division

Team	GP	W	L	T	GF	GA	PTS
Toronto	48	30	14	4	157	111	64
*Mtl. Maroons	48	24	19	5	123	92	53
Montreal	48	19	23	6	110	145	44
NY Americans	48	12	27	9	100	142	33
St. Louis	48	11	31	6	86	144	28

American Division

Team	GP	W	L	T	GF	GA	PTS
Boston	48	26	16	6	129	112	58
Chicago	48	26	17	5	118	88	57
NY Rangers	48	22	20	6	137	139	50
Detroit	48	19	22	7	127	114	45

Leading Scorers

Player	Team	GP	G	A	PTS	PIM
Charlie Conacher	Toronto	47	36	21	57	24
Syd Howe	St.L., Det.	50	22	25	47	34
Larry Aurie	Detroit	48	17	29	46	24
Frank Boucher	NY Rangers	48	13	32	45	2
Busher Jackson	Toronto	42	22	22	44	27
Herbie Lewis	Detroit	47	16	27	43	26
Art Chapman	NY Americans	47	9	34	43	4
Marty Barry	Boston	48	20	20	40	33
Sweeney Schriner	NY Americans	48	18	22	40	6
Nels Stewart	Boston	47	21	18	39	45
Paul Thompson	Chicago	48	16	23	39	20

1935-36

Canadian Division

Team	GP	W	L	T	GF	GA	PTS
Mtl. Maroons	48	22	16	10	114	106	54
Toronto	48	23	19	6	126	106	52
NY Americans	48	16	25	7	109	122	39
Montreal	48	11	26	11	82	123	33

American Division

Team	GP	W	L	T	GF	GA	PTS
*Detroit	48	24	16	8	124	103	56
Boston	48	22	20	6	92	83	50
Chicago	48	21	19	8	93	92	50
NY Rangers	48	19	17	12	91	96	50

Leading Scorers

Player	Team	GP	G	A	PTS	PIM
Sweeney Schriner	NY Americans	48	19	26	45	8
Marty Barry	Detroit	48	21	19	40	16
Paul Thompson	Chicago	45	17	23	40	19
Bill Thoms	Toronto	48	23	15	38	29
Charlie Conacher	Toronto	44	23	15	38	74
Hooley Smith	Mtl. Maroons	47	19	19	38	75
Doc Romnes	Chicago	48	13	25	38	6
Art Chapman	NY Americans	47	10	28	38	14
Herbie Lewis	Detroit	45	14	23	37	25
Baldy Northcott	Mtl. Maroons	48	15	21	36	41

1936-37

Canadian Division

Team	GP	W	L	T	GF	GA	PTS
Montreal	48	24	18	6	115	111	54
Mtl. Maroons	48	22	17	9	126	110	53
Toronto	48	22	21	5	119	115	49
NY Americans	48	15	29	4	122	161	34

American Division

Team	GP	W	L	T	GF	GA	PTS
*Detroit	48	25	14	9	128	102	59
Boston	48	23	18	7	120	110	53
NY Rangers	48	19	20	9	117	106	47
Chicago	48	14	27	7	99	131	35

Leading Scorers

Player	Team	GP	G	A	PTS	PIM
Sweeney Schriner	NY Americans	48	21	25	46	17
Syl Apps	Toronto	48	16	29	45	10
Marty Barry	Detroit	48	17	27	44	6
Larry Aurie	Detroit	45	23	20	43	20
Busher Jackson	Toronto	46	21	19	40	12
Johnny Gagnon	Montreal	48	20	16	36	38
Bob Gracie	Mtl. Maroons	47	11	25	36	18
Nels Stewart	Bos., NYA	43	23	12	35	37
Paul Thompson	Chicago	47	17	18	35	28
Bill Cowley	Boston	46	13	22	35	4

1937-38

Canadian Division

Team	GP	W	L	T	GF	GA	PTS
Toronto	48	24	15	9	151	127	57
NY Americans	48	19	18	11	110	111	49
Montreal	48	18	17	13	123	128	49
Mtl. Maroons	48	12	30	6	101	149	30

American Division

Team	GP	W	L	T	GF	GA	PTS
Boston	48	30	11	7	142	89	67
NY Rangers	48	27	15	6	149	96	60
*Chicago	48	14	25	9	97	139	37
Detroit	48	12	25	11	99	133	35

Leading Scorers

Player	Team	GP	G	A	PTS	PIM
Gordie Drillon	Toronto	48	26	26	52	4
Syl Apps	Toronto	47	21	29	50	9
Paul Thompson	Chicago	48	22	22	44	14
Georges Mantha	Montreal	47	23	19	42	12
Cecil Dillon	NY Rangers	48	21	18	39	6
Bill Cowley	Boston	48	17	22	39	8
Sweeney Schriner	NY Americans	49	21	17	38	22
Bill Thoms	Toronto	48	14	24	38	14
Clint Smith	NY Rangers	48	14	23	37	0
Nels Stewart	NY Americans	48	19	17	36	29
Neil Colville	NY Rangers	45	17	19	36	11

1938-39

Team	GP	W	L	T	GF	GA	PTS
*Boston	48	36	10	2	156	76	74
NY Rangers	48	26	16	6	149	105	58
Toronto	48	19	20	9	114	107	47
NY Americans	48	17	21	10	119	157	44
Detroit	48	18	24	6	107	128	42
Montreal	48	15	24	9	115	146	39
Chicago	48	12	28	8	91	132	32

Leading Scorers

Player	Team	GP	G	A	PTS	PIM
Toe Blake	Montreal	48	24	23	47	10
Sweeney Schriner	NY Americans	48	13	31	44	20
Bill Cowley	Boston	34	8	34	42	2
Clint Smith	NY Rangers	48	21	20	41	2
Marty Barry	Detroit	48	13	28	41	4
Syl Apps	Toronto	44	15	25	40	4
Tom Anderson	NY Americans	48	13	27	40	14
Johnny Gottselig	Chicago	48	16	23	39	15
Paul Haynes	Montreal	47	5	33	38	27
Roy Conacher	Boston	47	26	11	37	12
Lorne Carr	NY Americans	46	19	18	37	16
Neil Colville	NY Rangers	48	18	19	37	12
Phil Watson	NY Rangers	48	15	22	37	42

1939-40

Team	GP	W	L	T	GF	GA	PTS
Boston	48	31	12	5	170	98	67
*NY Rangers	48	27	11	10	136	77	64
Toronto	48	25	17	6	134	110	56
Chicago	48	23	19	6	112	120	52
Detroit	48	16	26	6	91	126	38
NY Americans	48	15	29	4	106	140	34
Montreal	48	10	33	5	90	168	25

Leading Scorers

Player	Team	GP	G	A	PTS	PIM
Milt Schmidt	Boston	48	22	30	52	37
Woody Dumart	Boston	48	22	21	43	16
Bobby Bauer	Boston	48	17	26	43	2
Gordie Drillon	Toronto	43	21	19	40	13
Bill Cowley	Boston	48	13	27	40	24
Bryan Hextall	NY Rangers	48	24	15	39	52
Neil Colville	NY Rangers	48	19	19	38	22
Syd Howe	Detroit	46	14	23	37	17
Toe Blake	Montreal	48	17	19	36	48
Murray Armstrong	NY Americans	48	16	20	36	12

1940-41

Team	GP	W	L	T	GF	GA	PTS
*Boston	48	27	8	13	168	102	67
Toronto	48	28	14	6	145	99	62
Detroit	48	21	16	11	112	102	53
NY Rangers	48	21	19	8	143	125	50
Chicago	48	16	25	7	112	139	39
Montreal	48	16	26	6	121	147	38
NY Americans	48	8	29	11	99	186	27

Leading Scorers

Player	Team	GP	G	A	PTS	PIM
Bill Cowley	Boston	46	17	45	62	16
Bryan Hextall	NY Rangers	48	26	18	44	16
Gordie Drillon	Toronto	42	23	21	44	2
Syl Apps	Toronto	41	20	24	44	6
Lynn Patrick	NY Rangers	48	20	24	44	12
Syd Howe	Detroit	48	20	24	44	8
Neil Colville	NY Rangers	48	14	28	42	28
Eddie Wiseman	Boston	48	16	24	40	10
Bobby Bauer	Boston	48	17	22	39	2
Sweeney Schriner	Toronto	48	24	14	38	6
Roy Conacher	Boston	40	24	14	38	7
Milt Schmidt	Boston	44	13	25	38	23

1941-42

Team	GP	W	L	T	GF	GA	PTS
NY Rangers	48	29	17	2	177	143	60
*Toronto	48	27	18	3	158	136	57
Boston	48	25	17	6	160	118	56
Chicago	48	22	23	3	145	155	47
Detroit	48	19	25	4	140	147	42
Montreal	48	18	27	3	134	173	39
Brooklyn	48	16	29	3	133	175	35

Leading Scorers

Player	Team	GP	G	A	PTS	PIM
Bryan Hextall	NY Rangers	48	24	32	56	30
Lynn Patrick	NY Rangers	47	32	22	54	18
Don Grosso	Detroit	48	23	30	53	13
Phil Watson	NY Rangers	48	15	37	52	48
Sid Abel	Detroit	48	18	31	49	45
Toe Blake	Montreal	47	17	28	45	19
Bill Thoms	Chicago	47	15	30	45	8
Gordie Drillon	Toronto	48	23	18	41	6
Syl Apps	Toronto	38	18	23	41	0
Tom Anderson	Brooklyn	48	12	29	41	54

1942-43

Team	GP	W	L	T	GF	GA	PTS
*Detroit	50	25	14	11	169	124	61
Boston	50	24	17	9	195	176	57
Toronto	50	22	19	9	198	159	53
Montreal	50	19	19	12	181	191	50
Chicago	50	17	18	15	179	180	49
NY Rangers	50	11	31	8	161	253	30

Leading Scorers

Player	Team	GP	G	A	PTS	PIM
Doug Bentley	Chicago	50	33	40	73	18
Bill Cowley	Boston	48	27	45	72	10
Max Bentley	Chicago	47	26	44	70	2
Lynn Patrick	NY Rangers	50	22	39	61	28
Lorne Carr	Toronto	50	27	33	60	15
Billy Taylor	Toronto	50	18	42	60	2
Bryan Hextall	NY Rangers	50	27	32	59	28
Toe Blake	Montreal	48	23	36	59	28
Elmer Lach	Montreal	45	18	40	58	14
Buddy O'Connor	Montreal	50	15	43	58	2

1943-44

Team	GP	W	L	T	GF	GA	PTS
*Montreal	50	38	5	7	234	109	83
Detroit	50	26	18	6	214	177	58
Toronto	50	23	23	4	214	174	50
Chicago	50	22	23	5	178	187	49
Boston	50	19	26	5	223	268	43
NY Rangers	50	6	39	5	162	310	17

Leading Scorers

Player	Team	GP	G	A	PTS	PIM
Herb Cain	Boston	48	36	46	82	4
Doug Bentley	Chicago	50	38	39	77	22
Lorne Carr	Toronto	50	36	38	74	9
Carl Liscombe	Detroit	50	36	37	73	17
Elmer Lach	Montreal	48	24	48	72	23
Clint Smith	Chicago	50	23	49	72	4
Bill Cowley	Boston	36	30	41	71	12
Bill Mosienko	Chicago	50	32	38	70	10
Art Jackson	Boston	49	28	41	69	8
Gus Bodnar	Toronto	50	22	40	62	18

1944-45

Team	GP	W	L	T	GF	GA	PTS
Montreal	50	38	8	4	228	121	80
Detroit	50	31	14	5	218	161	67
*Toronto	50	24	22	4	183	161	52
Boston	50	16	30	4	179	219	36
Chicago	50	13	30	7	141	194	33
NY Rangers	50	11	29	10	154	247	32

Leading Scorers

Player	Team	GP	G	A	PTS	PIM
Elmer Lach	Montreal	50	26	54	80	37
Maurice Richard	Montreal	50	50	23	73	36
Toe Blake	Montreal	49	29	38	67	15
Bill Cowley	Boston	49	25	40	65	2
Ted Kennedy	Toronto	49	29	25	54	14
Bill Mosienko	Chicago	50	28	26	54	0
Joe Carveth	Detroit	50	26	28	54	6
Ab DeMarco	NY Rangers	50	24	30	54	10
Clint Smith	Chicago	50	23	31	54	0
Syd Howe	Detroit	46	17	36	53	6

1945-46

Team	GP	W	L	T	GF	GA	PTS
*Montreal	50	28	17	5	172	134	61
Boston	50	24	18	8	167	156	56
Chicago	50	23	20	7	200	178	53
Detroit	50	20	20	10	146	159	50
Toronto	50	19	24	7	174	185	45
NY Rangers	50	13	28	9	144	191	35

Leading Scorers

Player	Team	GP	G	A	PTS	PIM
Max Bentley	Chicago	47	31	30	61	6
Gaye Stewart	Toronto	50	37	15	52	8
Toe Blake	Montreal	50	29	21	50	2
Clint Smith	Chicago	50	26	24	50	2
Maurice Richard	Montreal	50	27	21	48	50
Bill Mosienko	Chicago	40	18	30	48	12
Ab DeMarco	NY Rangers	50	20	27	47	20
Elmer Lach	Montreal	50	13	34	47	34
Alex Kaleta	Chicago	49	19	27	46	17
Billy Taylor	Toronto	48	23	18	41	14
Pete Horeck	Chicago	50	20	21	41	34

1946-47

Team	GP	W	L	T	GF	GA	PTS
Montreal	60	34	16	10	189	138	78
*Toronto	60	31	19	10	209	172	72
Boston	60	26	23	11	190	175	63
Detroit	60	22	27	11	190	193	55
NY Rangers	60	22	32	6	167	186	50
Chicago	60	19	37	4	193	274	42

Leading Scorers

Player	Team	GP	G	A	PTS	PIM
Max Bentley	Chicago	60	29	43	72	12
Maurice Richard	Montreal	60	45	26	71	69
Billy Taylor	Detroit	60	17	46	63	35
Milt Schmidt	Boston	59	27	35	62	40
Ted Kennedy	Toronto	60	28	32	60	27
Doug Bentley	Chicago	52	21	34	55	18
Bobby Bauer	Boston	58	30	24	54	4
Roy Conacher	Detroit	60	30	24	54	6
Bill Mosienko	Chicago	59	25	27	52	2
Woody Dumart	Boston	60	24	28	52	12

1947-48

Team	GP	W	L	T	GF	GA	PTS
*Toronto	60	32	15	13	182	143	77
Detroit	60	30	18	12	187	148	72
Boston	60	23	24	13	167	168	59
NY Rangers	60	21	26	13	176	201	55
Montreal	60	20	29	11	147	169	51
Chicago	60	20	34	6	195	225	46

Leading Scorers

Player	Team	GP	G	A	PTS	PIM
Elmer Lach	Montreal	60	30	31	61	72
Buddy O'Connor	NY Rangers	60	24	36	60	8
Doug Bentley	Chicago	60	20	37	57	16
Gaye Stewart	Tor., Chi.	61	27	29	56	83
Max Bentley	Chi., Tor.	59	26	28	54	14
Bud Poile	Tor., Chi.	58	25	29	54	17
Maurice Richard	Montreal	53	28	25	53	89
Syl Apps	Toronto	55	26	27	53	12
Ted Lindsay	Detroit	60	33	19	52	95
Roy Conacher	Chicago	52	22	27	49	4

1948-49

Team	GP	W	L	T	GF	GA	PTS
Detroit	60	34	19	7	195	145	75
Boston	60	29	23	8	178	163	66
Montreal	60	28	23	9	152	126	65
*Toronto	60	22	25	13	147	161	57
Chicago	60	21	31	8	173	211	50
NY Rangers	60	18	31	11	133	172	47

Leading Scorers

Player	Team	GP	G	A	PTS	PIM
Roy Conacher	Chicago	60	26	42	68	8
Doug Bentley	Chicago	58	23	43	66	38
Sid Abel	Detroit	60	28	26	54	49
Ted Lindsay	Detroit	50	26	28	54	97
Jim Conacher	Det., Chi.	59	26	23	49	43
Paul Ronty	Boston	60	20	29	49	11
Harry Watson	Toronto	60	26	19	45	0
Billy Reay	Montreal	60	22	23	45	33
Gus Bodnar	Chicago	59	19	26	45	14
Johnny Peirson	Boston	59	22	21	43	45

1949-50

Team	GP	W	L	T	GF	GA	PTS
*Detroit	70	37	19	14	229	164	88
Montreal	70	29	22	19	172	150	77
Toronto	70	31	27	12	176	173	74
NY Rangers	70	28	31	11	170	189	67
Boston	70	22	32	16	198	228	60
Chicago	70	22	38	10	203	244	54

Leading Scorers

Player	Team	GP	G	A	PTS	PIM
Ted Lindsay	Detroit	69	23	55	78	141
Sid Abel	Detroit	69	34	35	69	46
Gordie Howe	Detroit	70	35	33	68	69
Maurice Richard	Montreal	70	43	22	65	114
Paul Ronty	Boston	70	23	36	59	8
Roy Conacher	Chicago	70	25	31	56	16
Doug Bentley	Chicago	64	20	33	53	28
Johnny Peirson	Boston	57	27	25	52	49
Metro Prystai	Chicago	65	29	22	51	31
Bep Guidolin	Chicago	70	17	34	51	42

1950-51

Team	GP	W	L	T	GF	GA	PTS
Detroit	70	44	13	13	236	139	101
*Toronto	70	41	16	13	212	138	95
Montreal	70	25	30	15	173	184	65
Boston	70	22	30	18	178	197	62
NY Rangers	70	20	29	21	169	201	61
Chicago	70	13	47	10	171	280	36

Leading Scorers

Player	Team	GP	G	A	PTS	PIM
Gordie Howe	Detroit	70	43	43	86	74
Maurice Richard	Montreal	65	42	24	66	97
Max Bentley	Toronto	67	21	41	62	34
Sid Abel	Detroit	69	23	38	61	30
Milt Schmidt	Boston	62	22	39	61	33
Ted Kennedy	Toronto	63	18	43	61	32
Ted Lindsay	Detroit	67	24	35	59	110
Tod Sloan	Toronto	70	31	25	56	105
Red Kelly	Detroit	70	17	37	54	24
Sid Smith	Toronto	70	30	21	51	10
Cal Gardner	Toronto	66	23	28	51	42

1951-52

Team	GP	W	L	T	GF	GA	PTS
*Detroit	70	44	14	12	215	133	100
Montreal	70	34	26	10	195	164	78
Toronto	70	29	25	16	168	157	74
Boston	70	25	29	16	162	176	66
NY Rangers	70	23	34	13	192	219	59
Chicago	70	17	44	9	158	241	43

Leading Scorers

Player	Team	GP	G	A	PTS	PIM
Gordie Howe	Detroit	70	47	39	86	78
Ted Lindsay	Detroit	70	30	39	69	123
Elmer Lach	Montreal	70	15	50	65	36
Don Raleigh	NY Rangers	70	19	42	61	14
Sid Smith	Toronto	70	27	30	57	6
Bernie Geoffrion	Montreal	67	30	24	54	66
Bill Mosienko	Chicago	70	31	22	53	10
Sid Abel	Detroit	62	17	36	53	32
Ted Kennedy	Toronto	70	19	33	52	33
Milt Schmidt	Boston	69	21	29	50	57
Johnny Peirson	Boston	68	20	30	50	30

1952-53

Team	GP	W	L	T	GF	GA	PTS
Detroit	70	36	16	18	222	133	90
*Montreal	70	28	23	19	155	148	75
Boston	70	28	29	13	152	172	69
Chicago	70	27	28	15	169	175	69
Toronto	70	27	30	13	156	167	67
NY Rangers	70	17	37	16	152	211	50

Leading Scorers

Player	Team	GP	G	A	PTS	PIM
Gordie Howe	Detroit	70	49	46	95	57
Ted Lindsay	Detroit	70	32	39	71	111
Maurice Richard	Montreal	70	28	33	61	112
Wally Hergesheimer	NY Rangers	70	30	29	59	10
Alex Delvecchio	Detroit	70	16	43	59	28
Paul Ronty	NY Rangers	70	16	38	54	20
Metro Prystai	Detroit	70	16	34	50	12
Red Kelly	Detroit	70	19	27	46	8
Bert Olmstead	Montreal	69	17	28	45	83
Fleming Mackell	Boston	65	27	17	44	63
Jim McFadden	Chicago	70	23	21	44	29

1953-54

Team	GP	W	L	T	GF	GA	PTS
*Detroit	70	37	19	14	191	132	88
Montreal	70	35	24	11	195	141	81
Toronto	70	32	24	14	152	131	78
Boston	70	32	28	10	177	181	74
NY Rangers	70	29	31	10	161	182	68
Chicago	70	12	51	7	133	242	31

Leading Scorers

Player	Team	GP	G	A	PTS	PIM
Gordie Howe	Detroit	70	33	48	81	109
Maurice Richard	Montreal	70	37	30	67	112
Ted Lindsay	Detroit	70	26	36	62	110
Bernie Geoffrion	Montreal	54	29	25	54	87
Bert Olmstead	Montreal	70	15	37	52	85
Red Kelly	Detroit	62	16	33	49	18
Dutch Reibel	Detroit	69	15	33	48	18
Ed Sandford	Boston	70	16	31	47	42
Fleming Mackell	Boston	67	15	32	47	60
Ken Mosdell	Montreal	67	22	24	46	64
Paul Ronty	NY Rangers	70	13	33	46	18

1954-55

Team	GP	W	L	T	GF	GA	PTS
*Detroit	70	42	17	11	204	134	95
Montreal	70	41	18	11	228	157	93
Toronto	70	24	24	22	147	135	70
Boston	70	23	26	21	169	188	67
NY Rangers	70	17	35	18	150	210	52
Chicago	70	13	40	17	161	235	43

Leading Scorers

Player	Team	GP	G	A	PTS	PIM
Bernie Geoffrion	Montreal	70	38	37	75	57
Maurice Richard	Montreal	67	38	36	74	125
Jean Béliveau	Montreal	70	37	36	73	58
Dutch Reibel	Detroit	70	25	41	66	15
Gordie Howe	Detroit	64	29	33	62	68
Red Sullivan	Chicago	69	19	42	61	51
Bert Olmstead	Montreal	70	10	48	58	103
Sid Smith	Toronto	70	33	21	54	14
Ken Mosdell	Montreal	70	22	32	54	82
Danny Lewicki	NY Rangers	70	29	24	53	8

1955-56

Team	GP	W	L	T	GF	GA	PTS
*Montreal	70	45	15	10	222	131	100
Detroit	70	30	24	16	183	148	76
NY Rangers	70	32	28	10	204	203	74
Toronto	70	24	33	13	153	181	61
Boston	70	23	34	13	147	185	59
Chicago	70	19	39	12	155	216	50

Leading Scorers

Player	Team	GP	G	A	PTS	PIM
Jean Béliveau	Montreal	70	47	41	88	143
Gordie Howe	Detroit	70	38	41	79	100
Maurice Richard	Montreal	70	38	33	71	89
Bert Olmstead	Montreal	70	14	56	70	94
Tod Sloan	Toronto	70	37	29	66	100
Andy Bathgate	NY Rangers	70	19	47	66	59
Bernie Geoffrion	Montreal	59	29	33	62	66
Dutch Reibel	Detroit	68	17	39	56	10
Alex Delvecchio	Detroit	70	25	26	51	24
Dave Creighton	NY Rangers	70	20	31	51	43
Bill Gadsby	NY Rangers	70	9	42	51	84

1956-57

Team	GP	W	L	T	GF	GA	PTS
Detroit	70	38	20	12	198	157	88
*Montreal	70	35	23	12	210	155	82
Boston	70	34	24	12	195	174	80
NY Rangers	70	26	30	14	184	227	66
Toronto	70	21	34	15	174	192	57
Chicago	70	16	39	15	169	225	47

Leading Scorers

Player	Team	GP	G	A	PTS	PIM
Gordie Howe	Detroit	70	44	45	89	72
Ted Lindsay	Detroit	70	30	55	85	103
Jean Béliveau	Montreal	69	33	51	84	105
Andy Bathgate	NY Rangers	70	27	50	77	60
Ed Litzenberger	Chicago	70	32	32	64	48
Maurice Richard	Montreal	63	33	29	62	74
Don McKenney	Boston	69	21	39	60	31
Dickie Moore	Montreal	70	29	29	58	56
Henri Richard	Montreal	63	18	36	54	71
Norm Ullman	Detroit	64	16	36	52	47

1957-58

Team	GP	W	L	T	GF	GA	PTS
*Montreal	70	43	17	10	250	158	96
NY Rangers	70	32	25	13	195	188	77
Detroit	70	29	29	12	176	207	70
Boston	70	27	28	15	199	194	69
Chicago	70	24	39	7	163	202	55
Toronto	70	21	38	11	192	226	53

Leading Scorers

Player	Team	GP	G	A	PTS	PIM
Dickie Moore	Montreal	70	36	48	84	65
Henri Richard	Montreal	67	28	52	80	56
Andy Bathgate	NY Rangers	65	30	48	78	42
Gordie Howe	Detroit	64	33	44	77	40
Bronco Horvath	Boston	67	30	36	66	71
Ed Litzenberger	Chicago	70	32	30	62	63
Fleming Mackell	Boston	70	20	40	60	72
Jean Béliveau	Montreal	55	27	32	59	93
Alex Delvecchio	Detroit	70	21	38	59	22
Don McKenney	Boston	70	28	30	58	22

1958-59

Team	GP	W	L	T	GF	GA	PTS
*Montreal	70	39	18	13	258	158	91
Boston	70	32	29	9	205	215	73
Chicago	70	28	29	13	197	208	69
Toronto	70	27	32	11	189	201	65
NY Rangers	70	26	32	12	201	217	64
Detroit	70	25	37	8	167	218	58

Leading Scorers

Player	Team	GP	G	A	PTS	PIM
Dickie Moore	Montreal	70	41	55	96	61
Jean Béliveau	Montreal	64	45	46	91	67
Andy Bathgate	NY Rangers	70	40	48	88	48
Gordie Howe	Detroit	70	32	46	78	57
Ed Litzenberger	Chicago	70	33	44	77	37
Bernie Geoffrion	Montreal	59	22	44	66	30
Red Sullivan	NY Rangers	70	21	42	63	56
Andy Hebenton	NY Rangers	70	33	29	62	8
Don McKenney	Boston	70	32	30	62	20
Tod Sloan	Chicago	59	27	35	62	79

1959-60

Team	GP	W	L	T	GF	GA	PTS
*Montreal	70	40	18	12	255	178	92
Toronto	70	35	26	9	199	195	79
Chicago	70	28	29	13	191	180	69
Detroit	70	26	29	15	186	197	67
Boston	70	28	34	8	220	241	64
NY Rangers	70	17	38	15	187	247	49

Leading Scorers

Player	Team	GP	G	A	PTS	PIM
Bobby Hull	Chicago	70	39	42	81	68
Bronco Horvath	Boston	68	39	41	80	60
Jean Béliveau	Montreal	60	34	40	74	57
Andy Bathgate	NY Rangers	70	26	48	74	28
Henri Richard	Montreal	70	30	43	73	66
Gordie Howe	Detroit	70	28	45	73	46
Bernie Geoffrion	Montreal	59	30	41	71	36
Don McKenney	Boston	70	20	49	69	28
Vic Stasiuk	Boston	69	29	39	68	121
Dean Prentice	NY Rangers	70	32	34	66	43

1960-61

Team	GP	W	L	T	GF	GA	PTS
Montreal	70	41	19	10	254	188	92
Toronto	70	39	19	12	234	176	90
*Chicago	70	29	24	17	198	180	75
Detroit	70	25	29	16	195	215	66
NY Rangers	70	22	38	10	204	248	54
Boston	70	15	42	13	176	254	43

Leading Scorers

Player	Team	GP	G	A	PTS	PIM
Bernie Geoffrion	Montreal	64	50	45	95	29
Jean Béliveau	Montreal	69	32	58	90	57
Frank Mahovlich	Toronto	70	48	36	84	131
Andy Bathgate	NY Rangers	70	29	48	77	22
Gordie Howe	Detroit	64	23	49	72	30
Norm Ullman	Detroit	70	28	42	70	34
Red Kelly	Toronto	64	20	50	70	12
Dickie Moore	Montreal	57	35	34	69	62
Henri Richard	Montreal	70	24	44	68	91
Alex Delvecchio	Detroit	70	27	35	62	26

1961-62

Team	GP	W	L	T	GF	GA	PTS
Montreal	70	42	14	14	259	166	98
*Toronto	70	37	22	11	232	180	85
Chicago	70	31	26	13	217	186	75
NY Rangers	70	26	32	12	195	207	64
Detroit	70	23	33	14	184	219	60
Boston	70	15	47	8	177	306	38

Leading Scorers

Player	Team	GP	G	A	PTS	PIM
Bobby Hull	Chicago	70	50	34	84	35
Andy Bathgate	NY Rangers	70	28	56	84	44
Gordie Howe	Detroit	70	33	44	77	54
Stan Mikita	Chicago	70	25	52	77	97
Frank Mahovlich	Toronto	70	33	38	71	87
Alex Delvecchio	Detroit	70	26	43	69	18
Ralph Backstrom	Montreal	66	27	38	65	29
Norm Ullman	Detroit	70	26	38	64	54
Bill Hay	Chicago	60	11	52	63	34
Claude Provost	Montreal	70	33	29	62	22

1962-63

Team	GP	W	L	T	GF	GA	PTS
*Toronto	70	35	23	12	221	180	82
Chicago	70	32	21	17	194	178	81
Montreal	70	28	19	23	225	183	79
Detroit	70	32	25	13	200	194	77
NY Rangers	70	22	36	12	211	233	56
Boston	70	14	39	17	198	281	45

Leading Scorers

Player	Team	GP	G	A	PTS	PIM
Gordie Howe	Detroit	70	38	48	86	100
Andy Bathgate	NY Rangers	70	35	46	81	54
Stan Mikita	Chicago	65	31	45	76	69
Frank Mahovlich	Toronto	67	36	37	73	56
Henri Richard	Montreal	67	23	50	73	57
Jean Béliveau	Montreal	69	18	49	67	68
John Bucyk	Boston	69	27	39	66	36
Alex Delvecchio	Detroit	70	20	44	64	8
Bobby Hull	Chicago	65	31	31	62	27
Murray Oliver	Boston	65	22	40	62	38

1963-64

Team	GP	W	L	T	GF	GA	PTS
Montreal	70	36	21	13	209	167	85
Chicago	70	36	22	12	218	169	84
*Toronto	70	33	25	12	192	172	78
Detroit	70	30	29	11	191	204	71
NY Rangers	70	22	38	10	186	242	54
Boston	70	18	40	12	170	212	48

Leading Scorers

Player	Team	GP	G	A	PTS	PIM
Stan Mikita	Chicago	70	39	50	89	146
Bobby Hull	Chicago	70	43	44	87	50
Jean Béliveau	Montreal	68	28	50	78	42
Andy Bathgate	NYR, Tor.	71	19	58	77	34
Gordie Howe	Detroit	69	26	47	73	70
Kenny Wharram	Chicago	70	39	32	71	18
Murray Oliver	Boston	70	24	44	68	41
Phil Goyette	NY Rangers	67	24	41	65	15
Rod Gilbert	NY Rangers	70	24	40	64	62
Dave Keon	Toronto	70	23	37	60	6

1964-65

Team	GP	W	L	T	GF	GA	PTS
Detroit	70	40	23	7	224	175	87
*Montreal	70	36	23	11	211	185	83
Chicago	70	34	28	8	224	176	76
Toronto	70	30	26	14	204	173	74
NY Rangers	70	20	38	12	179	246	52
Boston	70	21	43	6	166	253	48

Leading Scorers

Player	Team	GP	G	A	PTS	PIM
Stan Mikita	Chicago	70	28	59	87	154
Norm Ullman	Detroit	70	42	41	83	70
Gordie Howe	Detroit	70	29	47	76	104
Bobby Hull	Chicago	61	39	32	71	32
Alex Delvecchio	Detroit	68	25	42	67	16
Claude Provost	Montreal	70	27	37	64	28
Rod Gilbert	NY Rangers	70	25	36	61	52
Pierre Pilote	Chicago	68	14	45	59	162
John Bucyk	Boston	68	26	29	55	24
Ralph Backstrom	Montreal	70	25	30	55	41
Phil Esposito	Chicago	70	23	32	55	44

1965-66

Team	GP	W	L	T	GF	GA	PTS
*Montreal	70	41	21	8	239	173	90
Chicago	70	37	25	8	240	187	82
Toronto	70	34	25	11	208	187	79
Detroit	70	31	27	12	221	194	74
Boston	70	21	43	6	174	275	48
NY Rangers	70	18	41	11	195	261	47

Leading Scorers

Player	Team	GP	G	A	PTS	PIM
Bobby Hull	Chicago	65	54	43	97	70
Stan Mikita	Chicago	68	30	48	78	58
Bobby Rousseau	Montreal	70	30	48	78	20
Jean Béliveau	Montreal	67	29	48	77	50
Gordie Howe	Detroit	70	29	46	75	83
Norm Ullman	Detroit	70	31	41	72	35
Alex Delvecchio	Detroit	70	31	38	69	16
Bob Nevin	NY Rangers	69	29	33	62	10
Henri Richard	Montreal	62	22	39	61	47
Murray Oliver	Boston	70	18	42	60	30

1966-67

Team	GP	W	L	T	GF	GA	PTS
Chicago	70	41	17	12	264	170	94
Montreal	70	32	25	13	202	188	77
*Toronto	70	32	27	11	204	211	75
NY Rangers	70	30	28	12	188	189	72
Detroit	70	27	39	4	212	241	58
Boston	70	17	43	10	182	253	44

Leading Scorers

Player	Team	GP	G	A	PTS	PIM
Stan Mikita	Chicago	70	35	62	97	12
Bobby Hull	Chicago	66	52	28	80	52
Norm Ullman	Detroit	68	26	44	70	26
Kenny Wharram	Chicago	70	31	34	65	21
Gordie Howe	Detroit	69	25	40	65	53
Bobby Rousseau	Montreal	68	19	44	63	58
Phil Esposito	Chicago	69	21	40	61	40
Phil Goyette	NY Rangers	70	12	49	61	6
Doug Mohns	Chicago	61	25	35	60	58
Henri Richard	Montreal	65	21	34	55	28
Alex Delvecchio	Detroit	70	17	38	55	10

1967-68

East Division

Team	GP	W	L	T	GF	GA	PTS
*Montreal	74	42	22	10	236	167	94
NY Rangers	74	39	23	12	226	183	90
Boston	74	37	27	10	259	216	84
Chicago	74	32	26	16	212	222	80
Toronto	74	33	31	10	209	176	76
Detroit	74	27	35	12	245	257	66

West Division

Team	GP	W	L	T	GF	GA	PTS
Philadelphia	74	31	32	11	173	179	73
Los Angeles	74	31	33	10	200	224	72
St. Louis	74	27	31	16	177	191	70
Minnesota	74	27	32	15	191	226	69
Pittsburgh	74	27	34	13	195	216	67
Oakland	74	15	42	17	153	219	47

Leading Scorers

Player	Team	GP	G	A	PTS	PIM
Stan Mikita	Chicago	72	40	47	87	14
Phil Esposito	Boston	74	35	49	84	21
Gordie Howe	Detroit	74	39	43	82	53
Jean Ratelle	NY Rangers	74	32	46	78	18
Rod Gilbert	NY Rangers	73	29	48	77	12
Bobby Hull	Chicago	71	44	31	75	39
Norm Ullman	Det., Tor.	71	35	37	72	28
Alex Delvecchio	Detroit	74	22	48	70	14
John Bucyk	Boston	72	30	39	69	8
Kenny Wharram	Chicago	74	27	42	69	18

1968-69

East Division

Team	GP	W	L	T	GF	GA	PTS
*Montreal	76	46	19	11	271	202	103
Boston	76	42	18	16	303	221	100
NY Rangers	76	41	26	9	231	196	91
Toronto	76	35	26	15	234	217	85
Detroit	76	33	31	12	239	221	78
Chicago	76	34	33	9	280	246	77

West Division

Team	GP	W	L	T	GF	GA	PTS
St. Louis	76	37	25	14	204	157	88
Oakland	76	29	36	11	219	251	69
Philadelphia	76	20	35	21	174	225	61
Los Angeles	76	24	42	10	185	260	58
Pittsburgh	76	20	45	11	189	252	51
Minnesota	76	18	43	15	189	270	51

Leading Scorers

Player	Team	GP	G	A	PTS	PIM
Phil Esposito	Boston	74	49	77	126	79
Bobby Hull	Chicago	74	58	49	107	48
Gordie Howe	Detroit	76	44	59	103	58
Stan Mikita	Chicago	74	30	67	97	52
Ken Hodge	Boston	75	45	45	90	75
Yvan Cournoyer	Montreal	76	43	44	87	31
Alex Delvecchio	Detroit	72	25	58	83	8
Red Berenson	St. Louis	76	35	47	82	43
Jean Béliveau	Montreal	69	33	49	82	55
Frank Mahovlich	Detroit	76	49	29	78	38
Jean Ratelle	NY Rangers	75	32	46	78	26

1969-70

East Division

Team	GP	W	L	T	GF	GA	PTS
Chicago	76	45	22	9	250	170	99
*Boston	76	40	17	19	277	216	99
Detroit	76	40	21	15	246	199	95
NY Rangers	76	38	22	16	246	189	92
Montreal	76	38	22	16	244	201	92
Toronto	76	29	34	13	222	242	71

West Division

Team	GP	W	L	T	GF	GA	PTS
St. Louis	76	37	27	12	224	179	86
Pittsburgh	76	26	38	12	182	238	64
Minnesota	76	19	35	22	224	257	60
Oakland	76	22	40	14	169	243	58
Philadelphia	76	17	35	24	197	225	58
Los Angeles	76	14	52	10	168	290	38

Leading Scorers

Player	Team	GP	G	A	PTS	PIM
Bobby Orr	Boston	76	33	87	120	125
Phil Esposito	Boston	76	43	56	99	50
Stan Mikita	Chicago	76	39	47	86	50
Phil Goyette	St. Louis	72	29	49	78	16
Walt Tkaczuk	NY Rangers	76	27	50	77	38
Jean Ratelle	NY Rangers	75	32	42	74	28
Red Berenson	St. Louis	67	33	39	72	38
Jean-Paul Parise	Minnesota	74	24	48	72	72
Gordie Howe	Detroit	76	31	40	71	58
Frank Mahovlich	Detroit	74	38	32	70	59
Dave Balon	NY Rangers	76	33	37	70	100
John McKenzie	Boston	72	29	41	70	114

1970-71

East Division

Team	GP	W	L	T	GF	GA	PTS
Boston	78	57	14	7	399	207	121
NY Rangers	78	49	18	11	259	177	109
*Montreal	78	42	23	13	291	216	97
Toronto	78	37	33	8	248	211	82
Buffalo	78	24	39	15	217	291	63
Vancouver	78	24	46	8	229	296	56
Detroit	78	22	45	11	209	308	55

West Division

Team	GP	W	L	T	GF	GA	PTS
Chicago	78	49	20	9	277	184	107
St. Louis	78	34	25	19	223	208	87
Philadelphia	78	28	33	17	207	225	73
Minnesota	78	28	34	16	191	223	72
Los Angeles	78	25	40	13	239	303	63
Pittsburgh	78	21	37	20	221	240	62
California	78	20	53	5	199	320	45

Leading Scorers

Player	Team	GP	G	A	PTS	PIM
Phil Esposito	Boston	78	76	76	152	71
Bobby Orr	Boston	78	37	102	139	91
John Bucyk	Boston	78	51	65	116	8
Ken Hodge	Boston	78	43	62	105	113
Bobby Hull	Chicago	78	44	52	96	32
Norm Ullman	Toronto	73	34	51	85	24
Wayne Cashman	Boston	77	21	58	79	100
John McKenzie	Boston	65	31	46	77	120
Dave Keon	Toronto	76	38	38	76	4
Jean Béliveau	Montreal	70	25	51	76	40
Fred Stanfield	Boston	75	24	52	76	12

1971-72

East Division

Team	GP	W	L	T	GF	GA	PTS
*Boston	78	54	13	11	330	204	119
NY Rangers	78	48	17	13	317	192	109
Montreal	78	46	16	16	307	205	108
Toronto	78	33	31	14	209	208	80
Detroit	78	33	35	10	261	262	76
Buffalo	78	16	43	19	203	289	51
Vancouver	78	20	50	8	203	297	48

West Division

Team	GP	W	L	T	GF	GA	PTS
Chicago	78	46	17	15	256	166	107
Minnesota	78	37	29	12	212	191	86
St. Louis	78	28	39	11	208	247	67
Pittsburgh	78	26	38	14	220	258	66
Philadelphia	78	26	38	14	200	236	66
California	78	21	39	18	216	288	60
Los Angeles	78	20	49	9	206	305	49

Leading Scorers

Player	Team	GP	G	A	PTS	PIM
Phil Esposito	Boston	76	66	67	133	76
Bobby Orr	Boston	76	37	80	117	106
Jean Ratelle	NY Rangers	63	46	63	109	4
Vic Hadfield	NY Rangers	78	50	56	106	142
Rod Gilbert	NY Rangers	73	43	54	97	64
Frank Mahovlich	Montreal	76	43	53	96	36
Bobby Hull	Chicago	78	50	43	93	24
Yvan Cournoyer	Montreal	73	47	36	83	15
John Bucyk	Boston	78	32	51	83	4
Bobby Clarke	Philadelphia	78	35	46	81	87
Jacques Lemaire	Montreal	77	32	49	81	26

1972-73

East Division

Team	GP	W	L	T	GF	GA	PTS
*Montreal	78	52	10	16	329	184	120
Boston	78	51	22	5	330	235	107
NY Rangers	78	47	23	8	297	208	102
Buffalo	78	37	27	14	257	219	88
Detroit	78	37	29	12	265	243	86
Toronto	78	27	41	10	247	279	64
Vancouver	78	22	47	9	233	339	53
NY Islanders	78	12	60	6	170	347	30

West Division

Team	GP	W	L	T	GF	GA	PTS
Chicago	78	42	27	9	284	225	93
Philadelphia	78	37	30	11	296	256	85
Minnesota	78	37	30	11	254	230	85
St. Louis	78	32	34	12	233	251	76
Pittsburgh	78	32	37	9	257	265	73
Los Angeles	78	31	36	11	232	245	73
Atlanta	78	25	38	15	191	239	65
California	78	16	46	16	213	323	48

Leading Scorers

Player	Team	GP	G	A	PTS	PIM
Phil Esposito	Boston	78	55	75	130	87
Bobby Clarke	Philadelphia	78	37	67	104	80
Bobby Orr	Boston	63	29	72	101	99
Rick MacLeish	Philadelphia	78	50	50	100	69
Jacques Lemaire	Montreal	77	44	51	95	16
Jean Ratelle	NY Rangers	78	41	53	94	12
Mickey Redmond	Detroit	76	52	41	93	24
John Bucyk	Boston	78	40	53	93	12
Frank Mahovlich	Montreal	78	38	55	93	51
Jim Pappin	Chicago	76	41	51	92	82

Bobby Clarke cracked the top 10 in scoring seven times during the 1970s. The Flyers star finished as high as second in 1972-73 and 1975-76.

1973-74

East Division

Team	GP	W	L	T	GF	GA	PTS
Boston	78	52	17	9	349	221	113
Montreal	78	45	24	9	293	240	99
NY Rangers	78	40	24	14	300	251	94
Toronto	78	35	27	16	274	230	86
Buffalo	78	32	34	12	242	250	76
Detroit	78	29	39	10	255	319	68
Vancouver	78	24	43	11	224	296	59
NY Islanders	78	19	41	18	182	247	56

West Division

Team	GP	W	L	T	GF	GA	PTS
*Philadelphia	78	50	16	12	273	164	112
Chicago	78	41	14	23	272	164	105
Los Angeles	78	33	33	12	233	231	78
Atlanta	78	30	34	14	214	238	74
Pittsburgh	78	28	41	9	242	273	65
St. Louis	78	26	40	12	206	248	64
Minnesota	78	23	38	17	235	275	63
California	78	13	55	10	195	342	36

Leading Scorers

Player	Team	GP	G	A	PTS	PIM
Phil Esposito	Boston	78	68	77	145	58
Bobby Orr	Boston	74	32	90	122	82
Ken Hodge	Boston	76	50	55	105	43
Wayne Cashman	Boston	78	30	59	89	111
Bobby Clarke	Philadelphia	77	35	52	87	113
Rick Martin	Buffalo	78	52	34	86	38
Syl Apps Jr.	Pittsburgh	75	24	61	85	37
Darryl Sittler	Toronto	78	38	46	84	55
Lowell MacDonald	Pittsburgh	78	43	39	82	14
Brad Park	NY Rangers	78	25	57	82	148
Dennis Hextall	Minnesota	78	20	62	82	138

1974-75

PRINCE OF WALES CONFERENCE

Norris Division

Team	GP	W	L	T	GF	GA	PTS
Montreal	80	47	14	19	374	225	113
Los Angeles	80	42	17	21	269	185	105
Pittsburgh	80	37	28	15	326	289	89
Detroit	80	23	45	12	259	335	58
Washington	80	8	67	5	181	446	21

Adams Division

Team	GP	W	L	T	GF	GA	PTS
Buffalo	80	49	16	15	354	240	113
Boston	80	40	26	14	345	245	94
Toronto	80	31	33	16	280	309	78
California	80	19	48	13	212	316	51

CLARENCE CAMPBELL CONFERENCE

Patrick Division

Team	GP	W	L	T	GF	GA	PTS
*Philadelphia	80	51	18	11	293	181	113
NY Rangers	80	37	29	14	319	276	88
NY Islanders	80	33	25	22	264	221	88
Atlanta	80	34	31	15	243	233	83

Smythe Division

Team	GP	W	L	T	GF	GA	PTS
Vancouver	80	38	32	10	271	254	86
St. Louis	80	35	31	14	269	267	84
Chicago	80	37	35	8	268	241	82
Minnesota	80	23	50	7	221	341	53
Kansas City	80	15	54	11	184	328	41

Leading Scorers

Player	Team	GP	G	A	PTS	PIM
Bobby Orr	Boston	80	46	89	135	101
Phil Esposito	Boston	79	61	66	127	62
Marcel Dionne	Detroit	80	47	74	121	14
Guy Lafleur	Montreal	70	53	66	119	37
Pete Mahovlich	Montreal	80	35	82	117	64
Bobby Clarke	Philadelphia	80	27	89	116	125
Rene Robert	Buffalo	74	40	60	100	75
Rod Gilbert	NY Rangers	76	36	61	97	22
Gilbert Perreault	Buffalo	68	39	57	96	36
Rick Martin	Buffalo	68	52	43	95	72

1975-76

PRINCE OF WALES CONFERENCE

Norris Division

Team	GP	W	L	T	GF	GA	PTS
*Montreal	80	58	11	11	337	174	127
Los Angeles	80	38	33	9	263	265	85
Pittsburgh	80	35	33	12	339	303	82
Detroit	80	26	44	10	226	300	62
Washington	80	11	59	10	224	394	32

Adams Division

Team	GP	W	L	T	GF	GA	PTS
Boston	80	48	15	17	313	237	113
Buffalo	80	46	21	13	339	240	105
Toronto	80	34	31	15	294	276	83
California	80	27	42	11	250	278	65

CLARENCE CAMPBELL CONFERENCE

Patrick Division

Team	GP	W	L	T	GF	GA	PTS
Philadelphia	80	51	13	16	348	209	118
NY Islanders	80	42	21	17	297	190	101
Atlanta	80	35	33	12	262	237	82
NY Rangers	80	29	42	9	262	333	67

Smythe Division

Team	GP	W	L	T	GF	GA	PTS
Chicago	80	32	30	18	254	261	82
Vancouver	80	33	32	15	271	272	81
St. Louis	80	29	37	14	249	290	72
Minnesota	80	20	53	7	195	303	47
Kansas City	80	12	56	12	190	351	36

Leading Scorers

Player	Team	GP	G	A	PTS	PIM
Guy Lafleur	Montreal	80	56	69	125	36
Bobby Clarke	Philadelphia	76	30	89	119	136
Gilbert Perreault	Buffalo	80	44	69	113	36
Bill Barber	Philadelphia	80	50	62	112	104
Pierre Larouche	Pittsburgh	76	53	58	111	33
Jean Ratelle	Bos., NYR	80	36	69	105	18
Pete Mahovlich	Montreal	80	34	71	105	76
Jean Pronovost	Pittsburgh	80	52	52	104	24
Darryl Sittler	Toronto	79	41	59	100	90
Syl Apps Jr.	Pittsburgh	80	32	67	99	24

1976-77

PRINCE OF WALES CONFERENCE

Norris Division

Team	GP	W	L	T	GF	GA	PTS
*Montreal	80	60	8	12	387	171	132
Los Angeles	80	34	31	15	271	241	83
Pittsburgh	80	34	33	13	240	252	81
Washington	80	24	42	14	221	307	62
Detroit	80	16	55	9	183	309	41

Adams Division

Team	GP	W	L	T	GF	GA	PTS
Boston	80	49	23	8	312	240	106
Buffalo	80	48	24	8	301	220	104
Toronto	80	33	32	15	301	285	81
Cleveland	80	25	42	13	240	292	63

CLARENCE CAMPBELL CONFERENCE

Patrick Division

Team	GP	W	L	T	GF	GA	PTS
Philadelphia	80	48	16	16	323	213	112
NY Islanders	80	47	21	12	288	193	106
Atlanta	80	34	34	12	264	265	80
NY Rangers	80	29	37	14	272	310	72

Smythe Division

Team	GP	W	L	T	GF	GA	PTS
St. Louis	80	32	39	9	239	276	73
Minnesota	80	23	39	18	240	310	64
Chicago	80	26	43	11	240	298	63
Vancouver	80	25	42	13	235	294	63
Colorado	80	20	46	14	226	307	54

Leading Scorers

Player	Team	GP	G	A	PTS	PIM
Guy Lafleur	Montreal	80	56	80	136	20
Marcel Dionne	Los Angeles	80	53	69	122	12
Steve Shutt	Montreal	80	60	45	105	28
Rick MacLeish	Philadelphia	79	49	48	97	42
Gilbert Perreault	Buffalo	80	39	56	95	30
Tim Young	Minnesota	80	29	66	95	58
Jean Ratelle	Boston	78	33	61	94	22
Lanny McDonald	Toronto	80	46	44	90	77
Darryl Sittler	Toronto	73	38	52	90	89
Bobby Clarke	Philadelphia	80	27	63	90	71

1977-78

PRINCE OF WALES CONFERENCE

Norris Division

Team	GP	W	L	T	GF	GA	PTS
*Montreal	80	59	10	11	359	183	129
Detroit	80	32	34	14	252	266	78
Los Angeles	80	31	34	15	243	245	77
Pittsburgh	80	25	37	18	254	321	68
Washington	80	17	49	14	195	321	48

Adams Division

Team	GP	W	L	T	GF	GA	PTS
Boston	80	51	18	11	333	218	113
Buffalo	80	44	19	17	288	215	105
Toronto	80	41	29	10	271	237	92
Cleveland	80	22	45	13	230	325	57

CLARENCE CAMPBELL CONFERENCE

Patrick Division

Team	GP	W	L	T	GF	GA	PTS
NY Islanders	80	48	17	15	334	210	111
Philadelphia	80	45	20	15	296	200	105
Atlanta	80	34	27	19	274	252	87
NY Rangers	80	30	37	13	279	280	73

Smythe Division

Team	GP	W	L	T	GF	GA	PTS
Chicago	80	32	29	19	230	220	83
Colorado	80	19	40	21	257	305	59
Vancouver	80	20	43	17	239	320	57
St. Louis	80	20	47	13	195	304	53
Minnesota	80	18	53	9	218	325	45

Leading Scorers

Player	Team	GP	G	A	PTS	PIM
Guy Lafleur	Montreal	78	60	72	132	26
Bryan Trottier	NY Islanders	77	46	77	123	46
Darryl Sittler	Toronto	80	45	72	117	100
Jacques Lemaire	Montreal	76	36	61	97	14
Denis Potvin	NY Islanders	80	30	64	94	81
Mike Bossy	NY Islanders	73	53	38	91	6
Terry O'Reilly	Boston	77	29	61	90	211
Gilbert Perreault	Buffalo	79	41	48	89	20
Bobby Clarke	Philadelphia	71	21	68	89	83
Lanny McDonald	Toronto	74	47	40	87	54
Wilf Paiement	Colorado	80	31	56	87	114

1978-79

PRINCE OF WALES CONFERENCE

Norris Division

Team	GP	W	L	T	GF	GA	PTS
*Montreal	80	52	17	11	337	204	115
Pittsburgh	80	36	31	13	281	279	85
Los Angeles	80	34	34	12	292	286	80
Washington	80	24	41	15	273	338	63
Detroit	80	23	41	16	252	295	62

Adams Division

Team	GP	W	L	T	GF	GA	PTS
Boston	80	43	23	14	316	270	100
Buffalo	80	36	28	16	280	263	88
Toronto	80	34	33	13	267	252	81
Minnesota	80	28	40	12	257	289	68

CLARENCE CAMPBELL CONFERENCE

Patrick Division

Team	GP	W	L	T	GF	GA	PTS
NY Islanders	80	51	15	14	358	214	116
Philadelphia	80	40	25	15	281	248	95
NY Rangers	80	40	29	11	316	292	91
Atlanta	80	41	31	8	327	280	90

Smythe Division

Team	GP	W	L	T	GF	GA	PTS
Chicago	80	29	36	15	244	277	73
Vancouver	80	25	42	13	217	291	63
St. Louis	80	18	50	12	249	348	48
Colorado	80	15	53	12	210	331	42

Leading Scorers

Player	Team	GP	G	A	PTS	PIM
Bryan Trottier	NY Islanders	76	47	87	134	50
Marcel Dionne	Los Angeles	80	59	71	130	30
Guy Lafleur	Montreal	80	52	77	129	28
Mike Bossy	NY Islanders	80	69	57	126	25
Bob MacMillan	Atlanta	79	37	71	108	14
Guy Chouinard	Atlanta	80	50	57	107	14
Denis Potvin	NY Islanders	73	31	70	101	58
Bernie Federko	St. Louis	74	31	64	95	14
Dave Taylor	Los Angeles	78	43	48	91	124
Clark Gillies	NY Islanders	75	35	56	91	68

1979-80

PRINCE OF WALES CONFERENCE

Norris Division

Team	GP	W	L	T	GF	GA	PTS
Montreal	80	47	20	13	328	240	107
Los Angeles	80	30	36	14	290	313	74
Pittsburgh	80	30	37	13	251	303	73
Hartford	80	27	34	19	303	312	73
Detroit	80	26	43	11	268	306	63

Adams Division

Team	GP	W	L	T	GF	GA	PTS
Buffalo	80	47	17	16	318	201	110
Boston	80	46	21	13	310	234	105
Minnesota	80	36	28	16	311	253	88
Toronto	80	35	40	5	304	327	75
Quebec	80	25	44	11	248	313	61

CLARENCE CAMPBELL CONFERENCE

Patrick Division

Team	GP	W	L	T	GF	GA	PTS
Philadelphia	80	48	12	20	327	254	116
*NY Islanders	80	39	28	13	281	247	91
NY Rangers	80	38	32	10	308	284	86
Atlanta	80	35	32	13	282	269	83
Washington	80	27	40	13	261	293	67

Smythe Division

Team	GP	W	L	T	GF	GA	PTS
Chicago	80	34	27	19	241	250	87
St. Louis	80	34	34	12	266	278	80
Vancouver	80	27	37	16	256	281	70
Edmonton	80	28	39	13	301	322	69
Winnipeg	80	20	49	11	214	314	51
Colorado	80	19	48	13	234	308	51

Leading Scorers

Player	Team	GP	G	A	PTS	PIM
Marcel Dionne	Los Angeles	80	53	84	137	32
Wayne Gretzky	Edmonton	79	51	86	137	21
Guy Lafleur	Montreal	74	50	75	125	12
Gilbert Perreault	Buffalo	80	40	66	106	57
Mike Rogers	Hartford	80	44	61	105	10
Bryan Trottier	NY Islanders	78	42	62	104	68
Charlie Simmer	Los Angeles	64	56	45	101	65
Blaine Stoughton	Hartford	80	56	44	100	16
Darryl Sittler	Toronto	73	40	57	97	62
Blair MacDonald	Edmonton	80	46	48	94	6
Bernie Federko	St. Louis	79	38	56	94	24

1980-81

PRINCE OF WALES CONFERENCE

Norris Division

Team	GP	W	L	T	GF	GA	PTS
Montreal	80	45	22	13	332	232	103
Los Angeles	80	43	24	13	337	290	99
Pittsburgh	80	30	37	13	302	345	73
Hartford	80	21	41	18	292	372	60
Detroit	80	19	43	18	252	339	56

Adams Division

Team	GP	W	L	T	GF	GA	PTS
Buffalo	80	39	20	21	327	250	99
Boston	80	37	30	13	316	272	87
Minnesota	80	35	28	17	291	263	87
Quebec	80	30	32	18	314	318	78
Toronto	80	28	37	15	322	367	71

CLARENCE CAMPBELL CONFERENCE

Patrick Division

Team	GP	W	L	T	GF	GA	PTS
*NY Islanders	80	48	18	14	355	260	110
Philadelphia	80	41	24	15	313	249	97
Calgary	80	39	27	14	329	298	92
NY Rangers	80	30	36	14	312	317	74
Washington	80	26	36	18	286	317	70

Smythe Division

Team	GP	W	L	T	GF	GA	PTS
St. Louis	80	45	18	17	352	281	107
Chicago	80	31	33	16	304	315	78
Vancouver	80	28	32	20	289	301	76
Edmonton	80	29	35	16	328	327	74
Colorado	80	22	45	13	258	344	57
Winnipeg	80	9	57	14	246	400	32

Leading Scorers

Player	Team	GP	G	A	PTS	PIM
Wayne Gretzky	Edmonton	80	55	109	164	28
Marcel Dionne	Los Angeles	80	58	77	135	70
Kent Nilsson	Calgary	80	49	82	131	26
Mike Bossy	NY Islanders	79	68	51	119	32
Dave Taylor	Los Angeles	72	47	65	112	130
Peter Stastny	Quebec	77	39	70	109	37
Charlie Simmer	Los Angeles	65	56	49	105	62
Mike Rogers	Hartford	80	40	65	105	32
Bernie Federko	St. Louis	78	31	73	104	47
Jacques Richard	Quebec	78	52	51	103	39
Rick Middleton	Boston	80	44	59	103	16
Bryan Trottier	NY Islanders	73	31	72	103	74

1981-82

CLARENCE CAMPBELL CONFERENCE

Norris Division

Team	GP	W	L	T	GF	GA	PTS
Minnesota	80	37	23	20	346	288	94
Winnipeg	80	33	33	14	319	332	80
St. Louis	80	32	40	8	315	349	72
Chicago	80	30	38	12	332	363	72
Toronto	80	20	44	16	298	380	56
Detroit	80	21	47	12	270	351	54

Smythe Division

Team	GP	W	L	T	GF	GA	PTS
Edmonton	80	48	17	15	417	295	111
Vancouver	80	30	33	17	290	286	77
Calgary	80	29	34	17	334	345	75
Los Angeles	80	24	41	15	314	369	63
Colorado	80	18	49	13	241	362	49

PRINCE OF WALES CONFERENCE

Adams Division

Team	GP	W	L	T	GF	GA	PTS
Montreal	80	46	17	17	360	223	109
Boston	80	43	27	10	323	285	96
Buffalo	80	39	26	15	307	273	93
Quebec	80	33	31	16	356	345	82
Hartford	80	21	41	18	264	351	60

Patrick Division

Team	GP	W	L	T	GF	GA	PTS
*NY Islanders	80	54	16	10	385	250	118
NY Rangers	80	39	27	14	316	306	92
Philadelphia	80	38	31	11	325	313	87
Pittsburgh	80	31	36	13	310	337	75
Washington	80	26	41	13	319	338	65

Leading Scorers

Player	Team	GP	G	A	PTS	PIM
Wayne Gretzky	Edmonton	80	92	120	212	26
Mike Bossy	NY Islanders	80	64	83	147	22
Peter Stastny	Quebec	80	46	93	139	91
Dennis Maruk	Washington	80	60	76	136	128
Bryan Trottier	NY Islanders	80	50	79	129	88
Denis Savard	Chicago	80	32	87	119	82
Marcel Dionne	Los Angeles	78	50	67	117	50
Bobby Smith	Minnesota	80	43	71	114	82
Dino Ciccarelli	Minnesota	76	55	51	106	138
Dave Taylor	Los Angeles	78	39	67	106	130

1982-83

CLARENCE CAMPBELL CONFERENCE

Norris Division

Team	GP	W	L	T	GF	GA	PTS
Chicago	80	47	23	10	338	268	104
Minnesota	80	40	24	16	321	290	96
Toronto	80	28	40	12	293	330	68
St. Louis	80	25	40	15	285	316	65
Detroit	80	21	44	15	263	344	57

Smythe Division

Team	GP	W	L	T	GF	GA	PTS
Edmonton	80	47	21	12	424	315	106
Calgary	80	32	34	14	321	317	78
Vancouver	80	30	35	15	303	309	75
Winnipeg	80	33	39	8	311	333	74
Los Angeles	80	27	41	12	308	365	66

PRINCE OF WALES CONFERENCE

Adams Division

Team	GP	W	L	T	GF	GA	PTS
Boston	80	50	20	10	327	228	110
Montreal	80	42	24	14	350	286	98
Buffalo	80	38	29	13	318	285	89
Quebec	80	34	34	12	343	336	80
Hartford	80	19	54	7	261	403	45

Patrick Division

Team	GP	W	L	T	GF	GA	PTS
Philadelphia	80	49	23	8	326	240	106
*NY Islanders	80	42	26	12	302	226	96
Washington	80	39	25	16	306	283	94
NY Rangers	80	35	35	10	306	287	80
New Jersey	80	17	49	14	230	338	48
Pittsburgh	80	18	53	9	257	394	45

Leading Scorers

Player	Team	GP	G	A	PTS	PIM
Wayne Gretzky	Edmonton	80	71	125	196	59
Peter Stastny	Quebec	75	47	77	124	78
Denis Savard	Chicago	78	35	86	121	99
Mike Bossy	NY Islanders	79	60	58	118	20
Marcel Dionne	Los Angeles	80	56	51	107	22
Barry Pederson	Boston	77	46	61	107	47
Mark Messier	Edmonton	77	48	58	106	72
Michel Goulet	Quebec	80	57	48	105	51
Glenn Anderson	Edmonton	72	48	56	104	70
Kent Nilsson	Calgary	80	46	58	104	10
Jari Kurri	Edmonton	80	45	59	104	22

1983-84

CLARENCE CAMPBELL CONFERENCE

Norris Division

Team	GP	W	L	T	GF	GA	PTS
Minnesota	80	39	31	10	345	344	88
St. Louis	80	32	41	7	293	316	71
Detroit	80	31	42	7	298	323	69
Chicago	80	30	42	8	277	311	68
Toronto	80	26	45	9	303	387	61

Smythe Division

Team	GP	W	L	T	GF	GA	PTS
*Edmonton	80	57	18	5	446	314	119
Calgary	80	34	32	14	311	314	82
Vancouver	80	32	39	9	306	328	73
Winnipeg	80	31	38	11	340	374	73
Los Angeles	80	23	44	13	309	376	59

PRINCE OF WALES CONFERENCE

Adams Division

Team	GP	W	L	T	GF	GA	PTS
Boston	80	49	25	6	336	261	104
Buffalo	80	48	25	7	315	257	103
Quebec	80	42	28	10	360	278	94
Montreal	80	35	40	5	286	295	75
Hartford	80	28	42	10	288	320	66

Patrick Division

Team	GP	W	L	T	GF	GA	PTS
NY Islanders	80	50	26	4	357	269	104
Washington	80	48	27	5	308	226	101
Philadelphia	80	44	26	10	350	290	98
NY Rangers	80	42	29	9	314	304	93
New Jersey	80	17	56	7	231	350	41
Pittsburgh	80	16	58	6	254	390	38

Leading Scorers

Player	Team	GP	G	A	PTS	PIM
Wayne Gretzky	Edmonton	74	87	118	205	39
Paul Coffey	Edmonton	80	40	86	126	104
Michel Goulet	Quebec	75	56	65	121	76
Peter Stastny	Quebec	80	46	73	119	73
Mike Bossy	NY Islanders	67	51	67	118	8
Barry Pederson	Boston	80	39	77	116	64
Jari Kurri	Edmonton	64	52	61	113	14
Bryan Trottier	NY Islanders	68	40	71	111	59
Bernie Federko	St. Louis	79	41	66	107	43
Rick Middleton	Boston	80	47	58	105	14

1984-85

CLARENCE CAMPBELL CONFERENCE

Norris Division

Team	GP	W	L	T	GF	GA	PTS
St. Louis	80	37	31	12	299	288	86
Chicago	80	38	35	7	309	299	83
Detroit	80	27	41	12	313	357	66
Minnesota	80	25	43	12	268	321	62
Toronto	80	20	52	8	253	358	48

Smythe Division

Team	GP	W	L	T	GF	GA	PTS
*Edmonton	80	49	20	11	401	298	109
Winnipeg	80	43	27	10	358	332	96
Calgary	80	41	27	12	363	302	94
Los Angeles	80	34	32	14	339	326	82
Vancouver	80	25	46	9	284	401	59

PRINCE OF WALES CONFERENCE

Adams Division

Team	GP	W	L	T	GF	GA	PTS
Montreal	80	41	27	12	309	262	94
Quebec	80	41	30	9	323	275	91
Buffalo	80	38	28	14	290	237	90
Boston	80	36	34	10	303	287	82
Hartford	80	30	41	9	268	318	69

Patrick Division

Team	GP	W	L	T	GF	GA	PTS
Philadelphia	80	53	20	7	348	241	113
Washington	80	46	25	9	322	240	101
NY Islanders	80	40	34	6	345	312	86
NY Rangers	80	26	44	10	295	345	62
New Jersey	80	22	48	10	264	346	54
Pittsburgh	80	24	51	5	276	385	53

Leading Scorers

Player	Team	GP	G	A	PTS	PIM
Wayne Gretzky	Edmonton	80	73	135	208	52
Jari Kurri	Edmonton	73	71	64	135	30
Dale Hawerchuk	Winnipeg	80	53	77	130	74
Marcel Dionne	Los Angeles	80	46	80	126	46
Paul Coffey	Edmonton	80	37	84	121	97
Mike Bossy	NY Islanders	76	58	59	117	38
John Ogrodnick	Detroit	79	55	50	105	30
Denis Savard	Chicago	79	38	67	105	56
Bernie Federko	St. Louis	76	30	73	103	27
Mike Gartner	Washington	80	50	52	102	71

1985-86

CLARENCE CAMPBELL CONFERENCE

Norris Division

Team	GP	W	L	T	GF	GA	PTS
Chicago	80	39	33	8	351	349	86
Minnesota	80	38	33	9	327	305	85
St. Louis	80	37	34	9	302	291	83
Toronto	80	25	48	7	311	386	57
Detroit	80	17	57	6	266	415	40

Smythe Division

Team	GP	W	L	T	GF	GA	PTS
Edmonton	80	56	17	7	426	310	119
Calgary	80	40	31	9	354	315	89
Winnipeg	80	26	47	7	295	372	59
Vancouver	80	23	44	13	282	333	59
Los Angeles	80	23	49	8	284	389	54

PRINCE OF WALES CONFERENCE

Adams Division

Team	GP	W	L	T	GF	GA	PTS
Quebec	80	43	31	6	330	289	92
*Montreal	80	40	33	7	330	280	87
Boston	80	37	31	12	311	288	86
Hartford	80	40	36	4	332	302	84
Buffalo	80	37	37	6	296	291	80

Patrick Division

Team	GP	W	L	T	GF	GA	PTS
Philadelphia	80	53	23	4	335	241	110
Washington	80	50	23	7	315	272	107
NY Islanders	80	39	29	12	327	284	90
NY Rangers	80	36	38	6	280	276	78
Pittsburgh	80	34	38	8	313	305	76
New Jersey	80	28	49	3	300	374	59

Leading Scorers

Player	Team	GP	G	A	PTS	PIM
Wayne Gretzky	Edmonton	80	52	163	215	52
Mario Lemieux	Pittsburgh	79	48	93	141	43
Paul Coffey	Edmonton	79	48	90	138	120
Jari Kurri	Edmonton	78	68	63	131	22
Mike Bossy	NY Islanders	80	61	62	123	14
Peter Stastny	Quebec	76	41	81	122	60
Denis Savard	Chicago	80	47	69	116	111
Mats Naslund	Montreal	80	43	67	110	16
Dale Hawerchuk	Winnipeg	80	46	59	105	44
Neal Broten	Minnesota	80	29	76	105	47

1986-87

CLARENCE CAMPBELL CONFERENCE

Norris Division

Team	GP	W	L	T	GF	GA	PTS
St. Louis	80	32	33	15	281	293	79
Detroit	80	34	36	10	260	274	78
Chicago	80	29	37	14	290	310	72
Toronto	80	32	42	6	286	319	70
Minnesota	80	30	40	10	296	314	70

Smythe Division

Team	GP	W	L	T	GF	GA	PTS
*Edmonton	80	50	24	6	372	284	106
Calgary	80	46	31	3	318	289	95
Winnipeg	80	40	32	8	279	271	88
Los Angeles	80	31	41	8	318	341	70
Vancouver	80	29	43	8	282	314	66

PRINCE OF WALES CONFERENCE

Adams Division

Team	GP	W	L	T	GF	GA	PTS
Hartford	80	43	30	7	287	270	93
Montreal	80	41	29	10	277	241	92
Boston	80	39	34	7	301	276	85
Quebec	80	31	39	10	267	276	72
Buffalo	80	28	44	8	280	308	64

Patrick Division

Team	GP	W	L	T	GF	GA	PTS
Philadelphia	80	46	26	8	310	245	100
Washington	80	38	32	10	285	278	86
NY Islanders	80	35	33	12	279	281	82
NY Rangers	80	34	38	8	307	323	76
Pittsburgh	80	30	38	12	297	290	72
New Jersey	80	29	45	6	293	368	64

Leading Scorers

Player	Team	GP	G	A	PTS	PIM
Wayne Gretzky	Edmonton	79	62	121	183	28
Jari Kurri	Edmonton	79	54	54	108	41
Mario Lemieux	Pittsburgh	63	54	53	107	57
Mark Messier	Edmonton	77	37	70	107	73
Doug Gilmour	St. Louis	80	42	63	105	58
Dino Ciccarelli	Minnesota	80	52	51	103	92
Dale Hawerchuk	Winnipeg	80	47	53	100	54
Michel Goulet	Quebec	75	49	47	96	61
Tim Kerr	Philadelphia	75	58	37	95	57
Raymond Bourque	Boston	78	23	72	95	36

1987-88

CLARENCE CAMPBELL CONFERENCE

Norris Division

Team	GP	W	L	T	GF	GA	PTS
Detroit	80	41	28	11	322	269	93
St. Louis	80	34	38	8	278	294	76
Chicago	80	30	41	9	284	328	69
Toronto	80	21	49	10	273	345	52
Minnesota	80	19	48	13	242	349	51

Smythe Division

Team	GP	W	L	T	GF	GA	PTS
Calgary	80	48	23	9	397	305	105
*Edmonton	80	44	25	11	363	288	99
Winnipeg	80	33	36	11	292	310	77
Los Angeles	80	30	42	8	318	359	68
Vancouver	80	25	46	9	272	320	59

PRINCE OF WALES CONFERENCE

Adams Division

Team	GP	W	L	T	GF	GA	PTS
Montreal	80	45	22	13	298	238	103
Boston	80	44	30	6	300	251	94
Buffalo	80	37	32	11	283	305	85
Hartford	80	35	38	7	249	267	77
Quebec	80	32	43	5	271	306	69

Patrick Division

Team	GP	W	L	T	GF	GA	PTS
NY Islanders	80	39	31	10	308	267	88
Washington	80	38	33	9	281	249	85
Philadelphia	80	38	33	9	292	292	85
New Jersey	80	38	36	6	295	296	82
NY Rangers	80	36	34	10	300	283	82
Pittsburgh	80	36	35	9	319	316	81

Leading Scorers

Player	Team	GP	G	A	PTS	PIM
Mario Lemieux	Pittsburgh	77	70	98	168	92
Wayne Gretzky	Edmonton	64	40	109	149	24
Denis Savard	Chicago	80	44	87	131	95
Dale Hawerchuk	Winnipeg	80	44	77	121	59
Luc Robitaille	Los Angeles	80	53	58	111	82
Peter Stastny	Quebec	76	46	65	111	69
Mark Messier	Edmonton	77	37	74	111	103
Jimmy Carson	Los Angeles	80	55	52	107	45
Hakan Loob	Calgary	80	50	56	106	47
Michel Goulet	Quebec	80	48	58	106	56

1988-89

CLARENCE CAMPBELL CONFERENCE

Norris Division

Team	GP	W	L	T	GF	GA	PTS
Detroit	80	34	34	12	313	316	80
St. Louis	80	33	35	12	275	285	78
Minnesota	80	27	37	16	258	278	70
Chicago	80	27	41	12	297	335	66
Toronto	80	28	46	6	259	342	62

Smythe Division

Team	GP	W	L	T	GF	GA	PTS
*Calgary	80	54	17	9	354	226	117
Los Angeles	80	42	31	7	376	335	91
Edmonton	80	38	34	8	325	306	84
Vancouver	80	33	39	8	251	253	74
Winnipeg	80	26	42	12	300	355	64

PRINCE OF WALES CONFERENCE

Adams Division

Team	GP	W	L	T	GF	GA	PTS
Montreal	80	53	18	9	315	218	115
Boston	80	37	29	14	289	256	88
Buffalo	80	38	35	7	291	299	83
Hartford	80	37	38	5	299	290	79
Quebec	80	27	46	7	269	342	61

Patrick Division

Team	GP	W	L	T	GF	GA	PTS
Washington	80	41	29	10	305	259	92
Pittsburgh	80	40	33	7	347	349	87
NY Rangers	80	37	35	8	310	307	82
Philadelphia	80	36	36	8	307	285	80
New Jersey	80	27	41	12	281	325	66
NY Islanders	80	28	47	5	265	325	61

Leading Scorers

Player	Team	GP	G	A	PTS	PIM
Mario Lemieux	Pittsburgh	76	85	114	199	100
Wayne Gretzky	Los Angeles	78	54	114	168	26
Steve Yzerman	Detroit	80	65	90	155	61
Bernie Nicholls	Los Angeles	79	70	80	150	96
Rob Brown	Pittsburgh	68	49	66	115	118
Paul Coffey	Pittsburgh	75	30	83	113	193
Joe Mullen	Calgary	79	51	59	110	16
Jari Kurri	Edmonton	76	44	58	102	69
Jimmy Carson	Edmonton	80	49	51	100	36
Luc Robitaille	Los Angeles	78	46	52	98	65

1989-90

CLARENCE CAMPBELL CONFERENCE

Norris Division

Team	GP	W	L	T	GF	GA	PTS
Chicago	80	41	33	6	316	294	88
St. Louis	80	37	34	9	295	279	83
Toronto	80	38	38	4	337	358	80
Minnesota	80	36	40	4	284	291	76
Detroit	80	28	38	14	288	323	70

Smythe Division

Team	GP	W	L	T	GF	GA	PTS
Calgary	80	42	23	15	348	265	99
*Edmonton	80	38	28	14	315	283	90
Winnipeg	80	37	32	11	298	290	85
Los Angeles	80	34	39	7	338	337	75
Vancouver	80	25	41	14	245	306	64

PRINCE OF WALES CONFERENCE

Adams Division

Team	GP	W	L	T	GF	GA	PTS
Boston	80	46	25	9	289	232	101
Buffalo	80	45	27	8	286	248	98
Montreal	80	41	28	11	288	234	93
Hartford	80	38	33	9	275	268	85
Quebec	80	12	61	7	240	407	31

Patrick Division

Team	GP	W	L	T	GF	GA	PTS
NY Rangers	80	36	31	13	279	267	85
New Jersey	80	37	34	9	295	288	83
Washington	80	36	38	6	284	275	78
NY Islanders	80	31	38	11	281	288	73
Pittsburgh	80	32	40	8	318	359	72
Philadelphia	80	30	39	11	290	297	71

Leading Scorers

Player	Team	GP	G	A	PTS	PIM
Wayne Gretzky	Los Angeles	73	40	102	142	42
Mark Messier	Edmonton	79	45	84	129	79
Steve Yzerman	Detroit	79	62	65	127	79
Mario Lemieux	Pittsburgh	59	45	78	123	78
Brett Hull	St. Louis	80	72	41	113	24
Bernie Nicholls	L.A., NYR	79	39	73	112	86
Pierre Turgeon	Buffalo	80	40	66	106	29
Pat LaFontaine	NY Islanders	74	54	51	105	38
Paul Coffey	Pittsburgh	80	29	74	103	95
Joe Sakic	Quebec	80	39	63	102	27
Adam Oates	St. Louis	80	23	79	102	30

1990-91

CLARENCE CAMPBELL CONFERENCE

Norris Division

Team	GP	W	L	T	GF	GA	PTS
Chicago	80	49	23	8	284	211	106
St. Louis	80	47	22	11	310	250	105
Detroit	80	34	38	8	273	298	76
Minnesota	80	27	39	14	256	266	68
Toronto	80	23	46	11	241	318	57

Smythe Division

Team	GP	W	L	T	GF	GA	PTS
Los Angeles	80	46	24	10	340	254	102
Calgary	80	46	26	8	344	263	100
Edmonton	80	37	37	6	272	272	80
Vancouver	80	28	43	9	243	315	65
Winnipeg	80	26	43	11	260	288	63

PRINCE OF WALES CONFERENCE

Adams Division

Team	GP	W	L	T	GF	GA	PTS
Boston	80	44	24	12	299	264	100
Montreal	80	39	30	11	273	249	89
Buffalo	80	31	30	19	292	278	81
Hartford	80	31	38	11	238	276	73
Quebec	80	16	50	14	236	354	46

Patrick Division

Team	GP	W	L	T	GF	GA	PTS
*Pittsburgh	80	41	33	6	342	305	88
NY Rangers	80	36	31	13	297	265	85
Washington	80	37	36	7	258	258	81
New Jersey	80	32	33	15	272	264	79
Philadelphia	80	33	37	10	252	267	76
NY Islanders	80	25	45	10	223	290	60

Leading Scorers

Player	Team	GP	G	A	PTS	PIM
Wayne Gretzky	Los Angeles	78	41	122	163	16
Brett Hull	St. Louis	78	86	45	131	22
Adam Oates	St. Louis	61	25	90	115	29
Mark Recchi	Pittsburgh	78	40	73	113	48
John Cullen	Pit., Hfd.	78	39	71	110	101
Joe Sakic	Quebec	80	48	61	109	24
Steve Yzerman	Detroit	80	51	57	108	34
Theoren Fleury	Calgary	79	51	53	104	136
Al MacInnis	Calgary	78	28	75	103	90
Steve Larmer	Chicago	80	44	57	101	79

1991-92

CLARENCE CAMPBELL CONFERENCE

Norris Division

Team	GP	W	L	T	GF	GA	PTS
Detroit	80	43	25	12	320	256	98
Chicago	80	36	29	15	257	236	87
St. Louis	80	36	33	11	279	266	83
Minnesota	80	32	42	6	246	278	70
Toronto	80	30	43	7	234	294	67

Smythe Division

Team	GP	W	L	T	GF	GA	PTS
Vancouver	80	42	26	12	285	250	96
Los Angeles	80	35	31	14	287	296	84
Edmonton	80	36	34	10	295	297	82
Winnipeg	80	33	32	15	251	244	81
Calgary	80	31	37	12	296	305	74
San Jose	80	17	58	5	219	359	39

PRINCE OF WALES CONFERENCE

Adams Division

Team	GP	W	L	T	GF	GA	PTS
Montreal	80	41	28	11	267	207	93
Boston	80	36	32	12	270	275	84
Buffalo	80	31	37	12	289	299	74
Hartford	80	26	41	13	247	283	65
Quebec	80	20	48	12	255	318	52

Patrick Division

Team	GP	W	L	T	GF	GA	PTS
NY Rangers	80	50	25	5	321	246	105
Washington	80	45	27	8	330	275	98
*Pittsburgh	80	39	32	9	343	308	87
New Jersey	80	38	31	11	289	259	87
NY Islanders	80	34	35	11	291	299	79
Philadelphia	80	32	37	11	252	273	75

Leading Scorers

Player	Team	GP	G	A	PTS	PIM
Mario Lemieux	Pittsburgh	64	44	87	131	94
Kevin Stevens	Pittsburgh	80	54	69	123	254
Wayne Gretzky	Los Angeles	74	31	90	121	34
Brett Hull	St. Louis	73	70	39	109	48
Luc Robitaille	Los Angeles	80	44	63	107	95
Mark Messier	NY Rangers	79	35	72	107	76
Jeremy Roenick	Chicago	80	53	50	103	23
Steve Yzerman	Detroit	79	45	58	103	64
Brian Leetch	NY Rangers	80	22	80	102	26
Adam Oates	St.L., Bos.	80	20	79	99	22

1992-93

CLARENCE CAMPBELL CONFERENCE

Norris Division

Team	GP	W	L	T	GF	GA	PTS
Chicago	84	47	25	12	279	230	106
Detroit	84	47	28	9	369	280	103
Toronto	84	44	29	11	288	241	99
St. Louis	84	37	36	11	282	278	85
Minnesota	84	36	38	10	272	293	82
Tampa Bay	84	23	54	7	245	332	53

Smythe Division

Team	GP	W	L	T	GF	GA	PTS
Vancouver	84	46	29	9	346	278	101
Calgary	84	43	30	11	322	282	97
Los Angeles	84	39	35	10	338	340	88
Winnipeg	84	40	37	7	322	320	87
Edmonton	84	26	50	8	242	337	60
San Jose	84	11	71	2	218	414	24

PRINCE OF WALES CONFERENCE

Adams Division

Team	GP	W	L	T	GF	GA	PTS
Boston	84	51	26	7	332	268	109
Quebec	84	47	27	10	351	300	104
*Montreal	84	48	30	6	326	280	102
Buffalo	84	38	36	10	335	297	86
Hartford	84	26	52	6	284	369	58
Ottawa	84	10	70	4	202	395	24

Patrick Division

Team	GP	W	L	T	GF	GA	PTS
Pittsburgh	84	56	21	7	367	268	119
Washington	84	43	34	7	325	286	93
NY Islanders	84	40	37	7	335	297	87
New Jersey	84	40	37	7	308	299	87
Philadelphia	84	36	37	11	319	319	83
NY Rangers	84	34	39	11	304	308	79

Leading Scorers

Player	Team	GP	G	A	PTS	PIM
Mario Lemieux	Pittsburgh	60	69	91	160	38
Pat LaFontaine	Buffalo	84	53	95	148	63
Adam Oates	Boston	84	45	97	142	32
Steve Yzerman	Detroit	84	58	79	137	44
Teemu Selanne	Winnipeg	84	76	56	132	45
Pierre Turgeon	NY Islanders	83	58	74	132	26
Alexander Mogilny	Buffalo	77	76	51	127	40
Doug Gilmour	Toronto	83	32	95	127	100
Luc Robitaille	Los Angeles	84	63	62	125	100
Mark Recchi	Philadelphia	84	53	70	123	95

1993-94

EASTERN CONFERENCE

Northeast Division

Team	GP	W	L	T	GF	GA	PTS
Pittsburgh	84	44	27	13	299	285	101
Boston	84	42	29	13	289	252	97
Montreal	84	41	29	14	283	248	96
Buffalo	84	43	32	9	282	218	95
Quebec	84	34	42	8	277	292	76
Hartford	84	27	48	9	227	288	63
Ottawa	84	14	61	9	201	397	37

Atlantic Division

Team	GP	W	L	T	GF	GA	PTS
*NY Rangers	84	52	24	8	299	231	112
New Jersey	84	47	25	12	306	220	106
Washington	84	39	35	10	277	263	88
NY Islanders	84	36	36	12	282	264	84
Florida	84	33	34	17	233	233	83
Philadelphia	84	35	39	10	294	314	80
Tampa Bay	84	30	43	11	224	251	71

WESTERN CONFERENCE

Central Division

Team	GP	W	L	T	GF	GA	PTS
Detroit	84	46	30	8	356	275	100
Toronto	84	43	29	12	280	243	98
Dallas	84	42	29	13	286	265	97
St. Louis	84	40	33	11	270	283	91
Chicago	84	39	36	9	254	240	87
Winnipeg	84	24	51	9	245	344	57

Pacific Division

Team	GP	W	L	T	GF	GA	PTS
Calgary	84	42	29	13	302	256	97
Vancouver	84	41	40	3	279	276	85
San Jose	84	33	35	16	252	265	82
Anaheim	84	33	46	5	229	251	71
Los Angeles	84	27	45	12	294	322	66
Edmonton	84	25	45	14	261	305	64

Leading Scorers

Player	Team	GP	G	A	PTS	PIM
Wayne Gretzky	Los Angeles	81	38	92	130	20
Sergei Fedorov	Detroit	82	56	64	120	34
Adam Oates	Boston	77	32	80	112	45
Doug Gilmour	Toronto	83	27	84	111	105
Pavel Bure	Vancouver	76	60	47	107	86
Jeremy Roenick	Chicago	84	46	61	107	125
Mark Recchi	Philadelphia	84	40	67	107	46
Brendan Shanahan	St. Louis	81	52	50	102	211
Dave Andreychuk	Toronto	83	53	46	99	98
Jaromir Jagr	Pittsburgh	80	32	67	99	61

1994-95

EASTERN CONFERENCE

Northeast Division

Team	GP	W	L	T	GF	GA	PTS
Quebec	48	30	13	5	185	134	65
Pittsburgh	48	29	16	3	181	158	61
Boston	48	27	18	3	150	127	57
Buffalo	48	22	19	7	130	119	51
Hartford	48	19	24	5	127	141	43
Montreal	48	18	23	7	125	148	43
Ottawa	48	9	34	5	117	174	23

Atlantic Division

Team	GP	W	L	T	GF	GA	PTS
Philadelphia	48	28	16	4	150	132	60
*New Jersey	48	22	18	8	136	121	52
Washington	48	22	18	8	136	120	52
NY Rangers	48	22	23	3	139	134	47
Florida	48	20	22	6	115	127	46
Tampa Bay	48	17	28	3	120	144	37
NY Islanders	48	15	28	5	126	158	35

WESTERN CONFERENCE

Central Division

Team	GP	W	L	T	GF	GA	PTS
Detroit	48	33	11	4	180	117	70
St. Louis	48	28	15	5	178	135	61
Chicago	48	24	19	5	156	115	53
Toronto	48	21	19	8	135	146	50
Dallas	48	17	23	8	136	135	42
Winnipeg	48	16	25	7	157	177	39

Pacific Division

Team	GP	W	L	T	GF	GA	PTS
Calgary	48	24	17	7	163	135	55
Vancouver	48	18	18	12	153	148	48
San Jose	48	19	25	4	129	161	42
Los Angeles	48	16	23	9	142	174	41
Edmonton	48	17	27	4	136	183	38
Anaheim	48	16	27	5	125	164	37

Leading Scorers

Player	Team	GP	G	A	PTS	PIM
Jaromir Jagr	Pittsburgh	48	32	38	70	37
Eric Lindros	Philadelphia	46	29	41	70	60
Alex Zhamnov	Winnipeg	48	30	35	65	20
Joe Sakic	Quebec	47	19	43	62	30
Ron Francis	Pittsburgh	44	11	48	59	18
Theoren Fleury	Calgary	47	29	29	58	112
Paul Coffey	Detroit	45	14	44	58	72
Mikael Renberg	Philadelphia	47	26	31	57	20
John LeClair	Mtl., Phi.	46	26	28	54	30
Mark Messier	NY Rangers	46	14	39	53	40
Adam Oates	Boston	48	12	41	53	8

1995-96

EASTERN CONFERENCE

Northeast Division

Team	GP	W	L	T	GF	GA	PTS
Pittsburgh	82	49	29	4	362	284	102
Boston	82	40	31	11	282	269	91
Montreal	82	40	32	10	265	248	90
Hartford	82	34	39	9	237	259	77
Buffalo	82	33	42	7	247	262	73
Ottawa	82	18	59	5	191	291	41

Atlantic Division

Team	GP	W	L	T	GF	GA	PTS
Philadelphia	82	45	24	13	282	208	103
NY Rangers	82	41	27	14	272	237	96
Florida	82	41	31	10	254	234	92
Washington	82	39	32	11	234	204	89
Tampa Bay	82	38	32	12	238	248	88
New Jersey	82	37	33	12	215	202	86
NY Islanders	82	22	50	10	229	315	54

WESTERN CONFERENCE

Central Division

Team	GP	W	L	T	GF	GA	PTS
Detroit	82	62	13	7	325	181	131
Chicago	82	40	28	14	273	220	94
Toronto	82	34	36	12	247	252	80
St. Louis	82	32	34	16	219	248	80
Winnipeg	82	36	40	6	275	291	78
Dallas	82	26	42	14	227	280	66

Pacific Division

Team	GP	W	L	T	GF	GA	PTS
*Colorado	82	47	25	10	326	240	104
Calgary	82	34	37	11	241	240	79
Vancouver	82	32	35	15	278	278	79
Anaheim	82	35	39	8	234	247	78
Edmonton	82	30	44	8	240	304	68
Los Angeles	82	24	40	18	256	302	66
San Jose	82	20	55	7	252	357	47

Leading Scorers

Player	Team	GP	G	A	PTS	PIM
Mario Lemieux	Pittsburgh	70	69	92	161	54
Jaromir Jagr	Pittsburgh	82	62	87	149	96
Joe Sakic	Colorado	82	51	69	120	44
Ron Francis	Pittsburgh	77	27	92	119	56
Peter Forsberg	Colorado	82	30	86	116	47
Eric Lindros	Philadelphia	73	47	68	115	163
Paul Kariya	Anaheim	82	50	58	108	20
Teemu Selanne	Wpg., Ana.	79	40	68	108	22
Alexander Mogilny	Vancouver	79	55	52	107	16
Sergei Fedorov	Detroit	78	39	68	107	48

1996-97

EASTERN CONFERENCE

Northeast Division

Team	GP	W	L	T	GF	GA	PTS
Buffalo	82	40	30	12	237	208	92
Pittsburgh	82	38	36	8	285	280	84
Ottawa	82	31	36	15	226	234	77
Montreal	82	31	36	15	249	276	77
Hartford	82	32	39	11	226	256	75
Boston	82	26	47	9	234	300	61

Atlantic Division

Team	GP	W	L	T	GF	GA	PTS
New Jersey	82	45	23	14	231	182	104
Philadelphia	82	45	24	13	274	217	103
Florida	82	35	28	19	221	201	89
NY Rangers	82	38	34	10	258	231	86
Washington	82	33	40	9	214	231	75
Tampa Bay	82	32	40	10	217	247	74
NY Islanders	82	29	41	12	240	250	70

WESTERN CONFERENCE

Central Division

Team	GP	W	L	T	GF	GA	PTS
Dallas	82	48	26	8	252	198	104
*Detroit	82	38	26	18	253	197	94
Phoenix	82	38	37	7	240	243	83
St. Louis	82	36	35	11	236	239	83
Chicago	82	34	35	13	223	210	81
Toronto	82	30	44	8	230	273	68

Pacific Division

Team	GP	W	L	T	GF	GA	PTS
Colorado	82	49	24	9	277	205	107
Anaheim	82	36	33	13	245	233	85
Edmonton	82	36	37	9	252	247	81
Vancouver	82	35	40	7	257	273	77
Calgary	82	32	41	9	214	239	73
Los Angeles	82	28	43	11	214	268	67
San Jose	82	27	47	8	211	278	62

Leading Scorers

Player	Team	GP	G	A	PTS	PIM
Mario Lemieux	Pittsburgh	76	50	72	122	65
Teemu Selanne	Anaheim	78	51	58	109	34
Paul Kariya	Anaheim	69	44	55	99	6
John LeClair	Philadelphia	82	50	47	97	58
Wayne Gretzky	NY Rangers	82	25	72	97	28
Jaromir Jagr	Pittsburgh	63	47	48	95	40
Mats Sundin	Toronto	82	41	53	94	59
Ziggy Palffy	NY Islanders	80	48	42	90	43
Ron Francis	Pittsburgh	81	27	63	90	20
Brendan Shanahan	Hfd., Det.	81	47	41	88	131

1997-98

EASTERN CONFERENCE

Northeast Division

Team	GP	W	L	T	GF	GA	PTS
Pittsburgh	82	40	24	18	228	188	98
Boston	82	39	30	13	221	194	91
Buffalo	82	36	29	17	211	187	89
Montreal	82	37	32	13	235	208	87
Ottawa	82	34	33	15	193	200	83
Carolina	82	33	41	8	200	219	74

Atlantic Division

Team	GP	W	L	T	GF	GA	PTS
New Jersey	82	48	23	11	225	166	107
Philadelphia	82	42	29	11	242	193	95
Washington	82	40	30	12	219	202	92
NY Islanders	82	30	41	11	212	225	71
NY Rangers	82	25	39	18	197	231	68
Florida	82	24	43	15	203	256	63
Tampa Bay	82	17	55	10	151	269	44

WESTERN CONFERENCE

Central Division

Team	GP	W	L	T	GF	GA	PTS
Dallas	82	49	22	11	242	167	109
*Detroit	82	44	23	15	250	196	103
St. Louis	82	45	29	8	256	204	98
Phoenix	82	35	35	12	224	227	82
Chicago	82	30	39	13	192	199	73
Toronto	82	30	43	9	194	237	69

Pacific Division

Team	GP	W	L	T	GF	GA	PTS
Colorado	82	39	26	17	231	205	95
Los Angeles	82	38	33	11	227	225	87
Edmonton	82	35	37	10	215	224	80
San Jose	82	34	38	10	210	216	78
Calgary	82	26	41	15	217	252	67
Anaheim	82	26	43	13	205	261	65
Vancouver	82	25	43	14	224	273	64

Leading Scorers

Player	Team	GP	G	A	PTS	PIM
Jaromir Jagr	Pittsburgh	77	35	67	102	64
Peter Forsberg	Colorado	72	25	66	91	94
Pavel Bure	Vancouver	82	51	39	90	48
Wayne Gretzky	NY Rangers	82	23	67	90	28
John LeClair	Philadelphia	82	51	36	87	32
Ziggy Palffy	NY Islanders	82	45	42	87	34
Ron Francis	Pittsburgh	81	25	62	87	20
Teemu Selanne	Anaheim	73	52	34	86	30
Jason Allison	Boston	81	33	50	83	60
Jozef Stumpel	Los Angeles	77	21	58	79	53

1998-99

EASTERN CONFERENCE

Northeast Division

Team	GP	W	L	T	GF	GA	PTS
Ottawa	82	44	23	15	239	179	103
Toronto	82	45	30	7	268	231	97
Boston	82	39	30	13	214	181	91
Buffalo	82	37	28	17	207	175	91
Montreal	82	32	39	11	184	209	75

Atlantic Division

Team	GP	W	L	T	GF	GA	PTS
New Jersey	82	47	24	11	248	196	105
Philadelphia	82	37	26	19	231	196	93
Pittsburgh	82	38	30	14	242	225	90
NY Rangers	82	33	38	11	217	227	77
NY Islanders	82	24	48	10	194	244	58

Southeast Division

Team	GP	W	L	T	GF	GA	PTS
Carolina	82	34	30	18	210	202	86
Florida	82	30	34	18	210	228	78
Washington	82	31	45	6	200	218	68
Tampa Bay	82	19	54	9	179	292	47

WESTERN CONFERENCE

Central Division

Team	GP	W	L	T	GF	GA	PTS
Detroit	82	43	32	7	245	202	93
St Louis	82	37	32	13	237	209	87
Chicago	82	29	41	12	202	248	70
Nashville	82	28	47	7	190	261	63

Pacific Division

Team	GP	W	L	T	GF	GA	PTS
*Dallas	82	51	19	12	236	168	114
Phoenix	82	39	31	12	205	197	90
Anaheim	82	35	34	13	215	206	83
San Jose	82	31	33	18	196	191	80
Los Angeles	82	32	45	5	189	222	69

Northwest Division

Team	GP	W	L	T	GF	GA	PTS
Colorado	82	44	28	10	239	205	98
Edmonton	82	33	37	12	230	226	78
Calgary	82	30	40	12	211	234	72
Vancouver	82	23	47	12	192	258	58

Leading Scorers

Player	Team	GP	G	A	PTS	PIM
Jaromir Jagr	Pittsburgh	81	44	83	127	66
Teemu Selanne	Anaheim	75	47	60	107	30
Paul Kariya	Anaheim	82	39	62	101	40
Peter Forsberg	Colorado	78	30	67	97	108
Joe Sakic	Colorado	73	41	55	96	29
Alexei Yashin	Ottawa	82	44	50	94	54
Eric Lindros	Philadelphia	71	40	53	93	120
Theoren Fleury	Cgy., Col.	75	40	53	93	86
John LeClair	Philadelphia	76	43	47	90	30
Pavol Demitra	St Louis	82	37	52	89	16

1999-2000

EASTERN CONFERENCE

Northeast Division

Team	GP	W	L	T	OTL	GF	GA	PTS
Toronto	82	45	27	7	3	246	222	100
Ottawa	82	41	28	11	2	244	210	95
Buffalo	82	35	32	11	4	213	204	85
Montreal	82	35	34	9	4	196	194	83
Boston	82	24	33	19	6	210	248	73

Atlantic Division

Team	GP	W	L	T	OTL	GF	GA	PTS
Philadelphia	82	45	22	12	3	237	179	105
*New Jersey	82	45	24	8	5	251	203	103
Pittsburgh	82	37	31	8	6	241	236	88
NY Rangers	82	29	38	12	3	218	246	73
NY Islanders	82	24	48	9	1	194	275	58

Southeast Division

Team	GP	W	L	T	OTL	GF	GA	PTS
Washington	82	44	24	12	2	227	194	102
Florida	82	43	27	6	6	244	209	98
Carolina	82	37	35	10	0	217	216	84
Tampa Bay	82	19	47	9	7	204	310	54
Atlanta	82	14	57	7	4	170	313	39

WESTERN CONFERENCE

Central Division

Team	GP	W	L	T	OTL	GF	GA	PTS
St. Louis	82	51	19	11	1	248	165	114
Detroit	82	48	22	10	2	278	210	108
Chicago	82	33	37	10	2	242	245	78
Nashville	82	28	40	7	7	199	240	70

Pacific Division

Team	GP	W	L	T	OTL	GF	GA	PTS
Dallas	82	43	23	10	6	211	184	102
Los Angeles	82	39	27	12	4	245	228	94
Phoenix	82	39	31	8	4	232	228	90
San Jose	82	35	30	10	7	225	214	87
Anaheim	82	34	33	12	3	217	227	83

Northwest Division

Team	GP	W	L	T	OTL	GF	GA	PTS
Colorado	82	42	28	11	1	233	201	96
Edmonton	82	32	26	16	8	226	212	88
Vancouver	82	30	29	15	8	227	237	83
Calgary	82	31	36	10	5	211	256	77

Leading Scorers

Player	Team	GP	G	A	PTS	PIM
Jaromir Jagr	Pittsburgh	63	42	54	96	50
Pavel Bure	Florida	74	58	36	94	16
Mark Recchi	Philadelphia	82	28	63	91	50
Paul Kariya	Anaheim	74	42	44	86	24
Teemu Selanne	Anaheim	79	33	52	85	12
Owen Nolan	San Jose	78	44	40	84	110
Tony Amonte	Chicago	82	43	41	84	48
Mike Modano	Dallas	77	38	43	81	48
Joe Sakic	Colorado	60	28	53	81	28
Steve Yzerman	Detroit	78	35	44	79	34

Steve Yzerman (left) was one of the NHL's most prolific scorers throughout his career, topping 100 points six times and finishing in the top 10 in scoring six times. Sergei Fedorov finished second in scoring with 120 points in 1993-94 and was tenth in the NHL with 107 points in 1995-96.

Pavel Bure was a top-10 scorer twice with the Vancouver Canucks and twice with the Florida Panthers. He led the NHL with 60 goals for the Canucks in 1993-94, and with 58 and 59 goals for the Panthers in 1999-2000 and 2000-01.

2000-01

EASTERN CONFERENCE

Northeast Division

Team	GP	W	L	T	OTL	GF	GA	PTS
Ottawa	82	48	21	9	4	274	205	109
Buffalo	82	46	30	5	1	218	184	98
Toronto	82	37	29	11	5	232	207	90
Boston	82	36	30	8	8	227	249	88
Montreal	82	28	40	8	6	206	232	70

Atlantic Division

Team	GP	W	L	T	OTL	GF	GA	PTS
New Jersey	82	48	19	12	3	295	195	111
Philadelphia	82	43	25	11	3	240	207	100
Pittsburgh	82	42	28	9	3	281	256	96
NY Rangers	82	33	43	5	1	250	290	72
NY Islanders	82	21	51	7	3	185	268	52

Southeast Division

Team	GP	W	L	T	OTL	GF	GA	PTS
Washington	82	41	27	10	4	233	211	96
Carolina	82	38	32	9	3	212	225	88
Florida	82	22	38	13	9	200	246	66
Atlanta	82	23	45	12	2	211	289	60
Tampa Bay	82	24	47	6	5	201	280	59

WESTERN CONFERENCE

Central Division

Team	GP	W	L	T	OTL	GF	GA	PTS
Detroit	82	49	20	9	4	253	202	111
St. Louis	82	43	22	12	5	249	195	103
Nashville	82	34	36	9	3	186	200	80
Chicago	82	29	40	8	5	210	246	71
Columbus	82	28	39	9	6	190	233	71

Pacific Division

Team	GP	W	L	T	OTL	GF	GA	PTS
Dallas	82	48	24	8	2	241	187	106
San Jose	82	40	27	12	3	217	192	95
Los Angeles	82	38	28	13	3	252	228	92
Phoenix	82	35	27	17	3	214	212	90
Anaheim	82	25	41	11	5	188	245	66

Northwest Division

Team	GP	W	L	T	OTL	GF	GA	PTS
*Colorado	82	52	16	10	4	270	192	118
Edmonton	82	39	28	12	3	243	222	93
Vancouver	82	36	28	11	7	239	238	90
Calgary	82	27	36	15	4	197	236	73
Minnesota	82	25	39	13	5	168	210	68

Leading Scorers

Player	Team	GP	G	A	PTS	PIM
Jaromir Jagr	Pittsburgh	81	52	69	121	42
Joe Sakic	Colorado	82	54	64	118	30
Patrik Elias	New Jersey	82	40	56	96	51
Alex Kovalev	Pittsburgh	79	44	51	95	96
Jason Allison	Boston	82	36	59	95	85
Martin Straka	Pittsburgh	82	27	68	95	38
Pavel Bure	Florida	82	59	33	92	58
Doug Weight	Edmonton	82	25	65	90	91
Ziggy Palffy	Los Angeles	73	38	51	89	20
Peter Forsberg	Colorado	73	27	62	89	54

2001-02

EASTERN CONFERENCE

Northeast Division

Team	GP	W	L	T	OTL	GF	GA	PTS
Boston	82	43	24	6	9	236	201	101
Toronto	82	43	25	10	4	249	207	100
Ottawa	82	39	27	9	7	243	208	94
Montreal	82	36	31	12	3	207	209	87
Buffalo	82	35	35	11	1	213	200	82

Atlantic Division

Team	GP	W	L	T	OTL	GF	GA	PTS
Philadelphia	82	42	27	10	3	234	192	97
NY Islanders	82	42	28	8	4	239	220	96
New Jersey	82	41	28	9	4	205	187	95
NY Rangers	82	36	38	4	4	227	258	80
Pittsburgh	82	28	41	8	5	198	249	69

Southeast Division

Team	GP	W	L	T	OTL	GF	GA	PTS
Carolina	82	35	26	16	5	217	217	91
Washington	82	36	33	11	2	228	240	85
Tampa Bay	82	27	40	11	4	178	219	69
Florida	82	22	44	10	6	180	250	60
Atlanta	82	19	47	11	5	187	288	54

WESTERN CONFERENCE

Central Division

Team	GP	W	L	T	OTL	GF	GA	PTS
*Detroit	82	51	17	10	4	251	187	116
St. Louis	82	43	27	8	4	227	188	98
Chicago	82	41	27	13	1	216	207	96
Nashville	82	28	41	13	0	196	230	69
Columbus	82	22	47	8	5	164	255	57

Pacific Division

Team	GP	W	L	T	OTL	GF	GA	PTS
San Jose	82	44	27	8	3	248	199	99
Phoenix	82	40	27	9	6	228	210	95
Los Angeles	82	40	27	11	4	214	190	95
Dallas	82	36	28	13	5	215	213	90
Anaheim	82	29	42	8	3	175	198	69

Northwest Division

Team	GP	W	L	T	OTL	GF	GA	PTS
Colorado	82	45	28	8	1	212	169	99
Vancouver	82	42	30	7	3	254	211	94
Edmonton	82	38	28	12	4	205	182	92
Calgary	82	32	35	12	3	201	220	79
Minnesota	82	26	35	12	9	195	238	73

Leading Scorers

Player	Team	GP	G	A	PTS	PIM
Jarome Iginla	Calgary	82	52	44	96	77
Markus Naslund	Vancouver	81	40	50	90	50
Todd Bertuzzi	Vancouver	72	36	49	85	110
Mats Sundin	Toronto	82	41	39	80	94
Jaromir Jagr	Washington	69	31	48	79	30
Joe Sakic	Colorado	82	26	53	79	18
Pavol Demitra	St. Louis	82	35	43	78	46
Adam Oates	Wsh., Phi.	80	14	64	78	28
Mike Modano	Dallas	78	34	43	77	38
Ron Francis	Carolina	80	27	50	77	18

2002-03

EASTERN CONFERENCE

Northeast Division

Team	GP	W	L	T	OTL	GF	GA	PTS
Ottawa	82	52	21	8	1	263	182	113
Toronto	82	44	28	7	3	236	208	98
Boston	82	36	31	11	4	245	237	87
Montreal	82	30	35	8	9	206	234	77
Buffalo	82	27	37	10	8	190	219	72

Atlantic Division

Team	GP	W	L	T	OTL	GF	GA	PTS
*New Jersey	82	46	20	10	6	216	166	108
Philadelphia	82	45	20	13	4	211	166	107
NY Islanders	82	35	34	11	2	224	231	83
NY Rangers	82	32	36	10	4	210	231	78
Pittsburgh	82	27	44	6	5	189	255	65

Southeast Division

Team	GP	W	L	T	OTL	GF	GA	PTS
Tampa Bay	82	36	25	16	5	219	210	93
Washington	82	39	29	8	6	224	220	92
Atlanta	82	31	39	7	5	226	284	74
Florida	82	24	36	13	9	176	237	70
Carolina	82	22	43	11	6	171	240	61

WESTERN CONFERENCE

Central Division

Team	GP	W	L	T	OTL	GF	GA	PTS
Detroit	82	48	20	10	4	269	203	110
St. Louis	82	41	24	11	6	253	222	99
Chicago	82	30	33	13	6	207	226	79
Nashville	82	27	35	13	7	183	206	74
Columbus	82	29	42	8	3	213	263	69

Pacific Division

Team	GP	W	L	T	OTL	GF	GA	PTS
Dallas	82	46	17	15	4	245	169	111
Anaheim	82	40	27	9	6	203	193	95
Los Angeles	82	33	37	6	6	203	221	78
Phoenix	82	31	35	11	5	204	230	78
San Jose	82	28	37	9	8	214	239	73

Northwest Division

Team	GP	W	L	T	OTL	GF	GA	PTS
Colorado	82	42	19	13	8	251	194	105
Vancouver	82	45	23	13	1	264	208	104
Minnesota	82	42	29	10	1	198	178	95
Edmonton	82	36	26	11	9	231	230	92
Calgary	82	29	36	13	4	186	228	75

Leading Scorers

Player	Team	GP	G	A	PTS	PIM
Peter Forsberg	Colorado	75	29	77	106	70
Markus Naslund	Vancouver	82	48	56	104	52
Joe Thornton	Boston	77	36	65	101	109
Milan Hejduk	Colorado	82	50	48	98	52
Todd Bertuzzi	Vancouver	82	46	51	97	144
Pavol Demitra	St. Louis	78	36	57	93	32
Glen Murray	Boston	82	44	48	92	64
Mario Lemieux	Pittsburgh	67	28	63	91	43
Dany Heatley	Atlanta	77	41	48	89	58
Ziggy Palffy	Los Angeles	76	37	48	85	47
Mike Modano	Dallas	79	28	57	85	30

Ziggy Palffy reached the top 10 in scoring four times from 1996-97 to 2002-03. He did it twice with the New York Islanders and twice with the Los Angeles Kings. After retiring midway through the 2005-06 season, Palffy returned to action in his native Slovakia in 2007-08.

2003-04

EASTERN CONFERENCE

Northeast Division

Team	GP	W	L	T	OTL	GF	GA	PTS
Boston	82	41	19	15	7	209	188	104
Toronto	82	45	24	10	3	242	204	103
Ottawa	82	43	23	10	6	262	189	102
Montreal	82	41	30	7	4	208	192	93
Buffalo	82	37	34	7	4	220	221	85

Atlantic Division

Team	GP	W	L	T	OTL	GF	GA	PTS
Philadelphia	82	40	21	15	6	229	186	101
New Jersey	82	43	25	12	2	213	164	100
NY Islanders	82	38	29	11	4	237	210	91
NY Rangers	82	27	40	7	8	206	250	69
Pittsburgh	82	23	47	8	4	190	303	58

Southeast Division

Team	GP	W	L	T	OTL	GF	GA	PTS
*Tampa Bay	82	46	22	8	6	245	192	106
Atlanta	82	33	37	8	4	214	243	78
Carolina	82	28	34	14	6	172	209	76
Florida	82	28	35	15	4	188	221	75
Washington	82	23	46	10	3	186	253	59

WESTERN CONFERENCE

Central Division

Team	GP	W	L	T	OTL	GF	GA	PTS
Detroit	82	48	21	11	2	255	189	109
St. Louis	82	39	30	11	2	191	198	91
Nashville	82	38	29	11	4	216	217	91
Columbus	82	25	45	8	4	177	238	62
Chicago	82	20	43	11	8	188	259	59

Pacific Division

Team	GP	W	L	T	OTL	GF	GA	PTS
San Jose	82	43	21	12	6	219	183	104
Dallas	82	41	26	13	2	194	175	97
Los Angeles	82	28	29	16	9	205	217	81
Anaheim	82	29	35	10	8	184	213	76
Phoenix	82	22	36	18	6	188	245	68

Northwest Division

Team	GP	W	L	T	OTL	GF	GA	PTS
Vancouver	82	43	24	10	5	235	194	101
Colorado	82	40	22	13	7	236	198	100
Calgary	82	42	30	7	3	200	176	94
Edmonton	82	36	29	12	5	221	208	89
Minnesota	82	30	29	20	3	188	183	83

Leading Scorers

Player	Team	GP	G	A	PTS	PIM
Martin St. Louis	Tampa Bay	82	38	56	94	24
Ilya Kovalchuk	Atlanta	81	41	46	87	63
Joe Sakic	Colorado	81	33	54	87	42
Markus Naslund	Vancouver	78	35	49	84	58
Marian Hossa	Ottawa	81	36	46	82	46
Patrik Elias	New Jersey	82	38	43	81	44
Daniel Alfredsson	Ottawa	77	32	48	80	24
Cory Stillman	Tampa Bay	81	25	55	80	36
Robert Lang	Wsh., Det.	69	30	49	79	24
Brad Richards	Tampa Bay	82	26	53	79	12
Alex Tanguay	Colorado	69	25	54	79	42

2004-05

SEASON CANCELLED

2005-06

EASTERN CONFERENCE

Northeast Division

Team	GP	W	L	OL	GF	GA	PTS
Ottawa	82	52	21	9	314	211	113
Buffalo	82	52	24	6	281	239	110
Montreal	82	42	31	9	243	247	93
Toronto	82	41	33	8	257	270	90
Boston	82	29	37	16	230	266	74

Atlantic Division

Team	GP	W	L	OL	GF	GA	PTS
New Jersey	82	46	27	9	242	229	101
Philadelphia	82	45	26	11	267	259	101
NY Rangers	82	44	26	12	257	215	100
NY Islanders	82	36	40	6	230	278	78
Pittsburgh	82	22	46	14	244	316	58

Southeast Division

Team	GP	W	L	OL	GF	GA	PTS
*Carolina	82	52	22	8	294	260	112
Tampa Bay	82	43	33	6	252	260	92
Atlanta	82	41	33	8	281	275	90
Florida	82	37	34	11	240	257	85
Washington	82	29	41	12	237	306	70

2005-06 *(continued)*

WESTERN CONFERENCE

Central Division

Team	GP	W	L	OL	GF	GA	PTS
Detroit	82	58	16	8	305	209	124
Nashville	82	49	25	8	259	227	106
Columbus	82	35	43	4	223	279	74
Chicago	82	26	43	13	211	285	65
St. Louis	82	21	46	15	197	292	57

Pacific Division

Team	GP	W	L	OL	GF	GA	PTS
Dallas	82	53	23	6	265	218	112
San Jose	82	44	27	11	266	242	99
Anaheim	82	43	27	12	254	229	98
Los Angeles	82	42	35	5	249	270	89
Phoenix	82	38	39	5	246	271	81

Northwest Division

Team	GP	W	L	OL	GF	GA	PTS
Calgary	82	46	25	11	218	200	103
Colorado	82	43	30	9	283	257	95
Edmonton	82	41	28	13	256	251	95
Vancouver	82	42	32	8	256	255	92
Minnesota	82	38	36	8	231	215	84

Leading Scorers

Player	Team	GP	G	A	PTS	PIM
Joe Thornton	Bos., S.J.	81	29	96	125	61
Jaromir Jagr	NY Rangers	82	54	69	123	72
Alex Ovechkin	Washington	81	52	54	106	52
Dany Heatley	Ottawa	82	50	53	103	86
Daniel Alfredsson	Ottawa	77	43	60	103	50
Sidney Crosby	Pittsburgh	81	39	63	102	110
Eric Staal	Carolina	82	45	55	100	81
Ilya Kovalchuk	Atlanta	78	52	46	98	68
Marc Savard	Atlanta	82	28	69	97	100
Jonathan Cheechoo	San Jose	82	56	37	93	58

2006-07

EASTERN CONFERENCE

Northeast Division

Team	GP	W	L	OL	GF	GA	PTS
Buffalo	82	53	22	7	308	242	113
Ottawa	82	48	25	9	288	222	105
Toronto	82	40	31	11	258	269	91
Montreal	82	42	34	6	245	256	90
Boston	82	35	41	6	219	289	76

Atlantic Division

Team	GP	W	L	OL	GF	GA	PTS
New Jersey	82	49	24	9	216	201	107
Pittsburgh	82	47	24	11	277	246	105
NY Rangers	82	42	30	10	242	216	94
NY Islanders	82	40	30	12	248	240	92
Philadelphia	82	22	48	12	214	303	56

Southeast Division

Team	GP	W	L	OL	GF	GA	PTS
Atlanta	82	43	28	11	246	245	97
Tampa Bay	82	44	33	5	253	261	93
Carolina	82	40	34	8	241	253	88
Florida	82	35	31	16	247	257	86
Washington	82	28	40	14	235	286	70

WESTERN CONFERENCE

Central Division

Team	GP	W	L	OL	GF	GA	PTS
Detroit	82	50	19	13	254	199	113
Nashville	82	51	23	8	272	212	110
St. Louis	82	34	35	13	214	254	81
Columbus	82	33	42	7	201	249	73
Chicago	82	31	42	9	201	258	71

Pacific Division

Team	GP	W	L	OL	GF	GA	PTS
*Anaheim	82	48	20	14	258	208	110
San Jose	82	51	26	5	258	199	107
Dallas	82	50	25	7	226	197	107
Los Angeles	82	27	41	14	227	283	68
Phoenix	82	31	46	5	216	284	67

Northwest Division

Team	GP	W	L	OL	GF	GA	PTS
Vancouver	82	49	26	7	222	201	105
Minnesota	82	48	26	8	235	191	104
Calgary	82	43	29	10	258	226	96
Colorado	82	44	31	7	272	251	95
Edmonton	82	32	43	7	195	248	71

Leading Scorers

Player	Team	GP	G	A	PTS	PIM
Sidney Crosby	Pittsburgh	79	36	84	120	60
Joe Thornton	San Jose	82	22	92	114	44
Vincent Lecavalier	Tampa Bay	82	52	56	108	44
Dany Heatley	Ottawa	82	50	55	105	74
Martin St. Louis	Tampa Bay	82	43	59	102	28
Marian Hossa	Atlanta	82	43	57	100	49
Joe Sakic	Colorado	82	36	64	100	46
Jaromir Jagr	NY Rangers	82	30	66	96	78
Marc Savard	Boston	82	22	74	96	96
Daniel Briere	Buffalo	81	32	63	95	89

2007-08

EASTERN CONFERENCE

Northeast Division

Team	GP	W	L	OL	GF	GA	PTS
Montreal	82	47	25	10	262	222	104
Ottawa	82	43	31	8	261	247	94
Boston	82	41	29	12	212	222	94
Buffalo	82	39	31	12	255	242	90
Toronto	82	36	35	11	231	260	83

Atlantic Division

Team	GP	W	L	OL	GF	GA	PTS
Pittsburgh	82	47	27	8	247	216	102
New Jersey	82	46	29	7	206	197	99
NY Rangers	82	42	27	13	213	199	97
Philadelphia	82	42	29	11	248	233	95
NY Islanders	82	35	38	9	194	243	79

Southeast Division

Team	GP	W	L	OL	GF	GA	PTS
Washington	82	43	31	8	242	231	94
Carolina	82	43	33	6	252	249	92
Florida	82	38	35	9	216	226	85
Atlanta	82	34	40	8	216	272	76
Tampa Bay	82	31	42	9	223	267	71

WESTERN CONFERENCE

Central Division

Team	GP	W	L	OL	GF	GA	PTS
*Detroit	82	54	21	7	257	184	115
Nashville	82	41	32	9	230	229	91
Chicago	82	40	34	8	239	235	88
Columbus	82	34	36	12	193	218	80
St. Louis	82	33	36	13	205	237	79

Pacific Division

Team	GP	W	L	OL	GF	GA	PTS
San Jose	82	49	23	10	222	193	108
Anaheim	82	47	27	8	205	191	102
Dallas	82	45	30	7	242	207	97
Phoenix	82	38	37	7	214	231	83
Los Angeles	82	32	43	7	231	266	71

Northwest Division

Team	GP	W	L	OL	GF	GA	PTS
Minnesota	82	44	28	10	223	218	98
Colorado	82	44	31	7	231	219	95
Calgary	82	42	30	10	229	227	94
Edmonton	82	41	35	6	235	251	88
Vancouver	82	39	33	10	213	215	88

Leading Scorers

Player	Team	GP	G	A	PTS	PIM
Alex Ovechkin	Washington	82	65	47	112	40
Evgeni Malkin	Pittsburgh	82	47	59	106	78
Jarome Iginla	Calgary	82	50	48	98	83
Pavel Datsyuk	Detroit	82	31	66	97	20
Joe Thornton	San Jose	82	29	67	96	59
Henrik Zetterberg	Detroit	75	43	49	92	34
Vincent Lecavalier	Tampa Bay	81	40	52	92	89
Jason Spezza	Ottawa	76	34	58	92	66
Daniel Alfredsson	Ottawa	70	40	49	89	34
Ilya Kovalchuk	Atlanta	79	52	35	87	52

Note: Detailed statistics for 2007-08 are listed in the Final Statistics, 2007-08 section of the *NHL Guide & Record Book*. **See page 135.**

Team Records

Regular Season

FINAL STANDINGS

MOST POINTS, ONE SEASON:
132 – Montreal Canadiens, 1976-77. 60W-8L-12T. 80GP
131 – Detroit Red Wings, 1995-96. 62W-13L-7T. 82GP
129 – Montreal Canadiens, 1977-78. 59W-10L-11T. 80GP

BEST POINTS PERCENTAGE, ONE SEASON:
.875 – Boston Bruins, 1929-30. 38W-5L-1T. 77PTS in 44GP
.830 – Montreal Canadiens, 1943-44. 38W-5L-7T. 83PTS in 50GP
.825 – Montreal Canadiens, 1976-77. 60W-8L-12T. 132PTS in 80GP
.806 – Montreal Canadiens, 1977-78. 59W-10L-11T. 129PTS in 80GP
.800 – Montreal Canadiens, 1944-45. 38W-8L-4T. 80PTS in 50GP

FEWEST POINTS, ONE SEASON:
8 – Quebec Bulldogs, 1919-20. 4W-20L-0T. 24GP
10 – Toronto Arenas, 1918-19. 5W-13L-0T. 18GP
12 – Hamilton Tigers, 1920-21. 6W-18L-0T. 24GP
– Hamilton Tigers, 1922-23. 6W-18L-0T. 24GP
– Boston Bruins, 1924-25. 6W-24L-0T. 30GP
– Philadelphia Quakers, 1930-31. 4W-36L-4T. 44GP

FEWEST POINTS, ONE SEASON (MINIMUM 70-GAME SCHEDULE):
21 – Washington Capitals, 1974-75. 8W-67L-5T. 80GP
24 – Ottawa Senators, 1992-93. 10W-70L-4T. 84GP
– San Jose Sharks, 1992-93. 11W-71L-2T. 84GP
30 – New York Islanders, 1972-73. 12W-60L-6T. 78GP

WORST POINTS PERCENTAGE, ONE SEASON:
.131 – Washington Capitals, 1974-75. 8W-67L-5T. 21PTS in 80GP
.136 – Philadelphia Quakers, 1930-31. 4W-36L-4T. 12PTS in 44GP
.143 – Ottawa Senators, 1992-93. 10W-70L-4T. 24PTS in 84GP
– San Jose Sharks, 1992-93. 11W-71L-2T. 24PTS in 84GP
.148 – Pittsburgh Pirates, 1929-30. 5W-36L-3T. 13PTS in 44GP

TEAM WINS

Most Wins

MOST WINS, ONE SEASON:
62 – Detroit Red Wings, 1995-96. 82GP
60 – Montreal Canadiens, 1976-77. 80GP
59 – Montreal Canadiens, 1977-78. 80GP

MOST HOME WINS, ONE SEASON:
36 – Philadelphia Flyers, 1975-76. 40GP
– Detroit Red Wings, 1995-96. 41GP
33 – Boston Bruins, 1970-71. 39GP
– Boston Bruins, 1973-74. 39GP
– Montreal Canadiens, 1976-77. 40GP
– Philadelphia Flyers, 1976-77. 40GP
– New York Islanders, 1981-82. 40GP
– Philadelphia Flyers, 1985-86. 40GP

MOST ROAD WINS, ONE SEASON:
31 – Detroit Red Wings, 2005-06. 41GP
28 – New Jersey Devils, 1998-99. 41GP
27 – Montreal Canadiens, 1976-77. 40GP
– Montreal Canadiens, 1977-78. 40GP
– St. Louis Blues, 1999-2000. 41GP
– San Jose Sharks, 2007-08. 41GP
26 – Boston Bruins, 1971-72. 39GP
– Montreal Canadiens, 1975-76. 40GP
– Edmonton Oilers, 1983-84. 40GP
– Detroit Red Wings, 1995-96. 41GP
– San Jose Sharks, 2006-07. 41GP

Fewest Wins

FEWEST WINS, ONE SEASON:
4 – Quebec Bulldogs, 1919-20. 24GP
– Philadelphia Quakers, 1930-31. 44GP
5 – Toronto Arenas, 1918-19. 18GP
Pittsburgh Pirates, 1929-30. 44GP

FEWEST WINS, ONE SEASON (MINIMUM 70-GAME SCHEDULE):
8 – Washington Capitals, 1974-75. 80GP
9 – Winnipeg Jets, 1980-81. 80GP
10 – Ottawa Senators, 1992-93. 84GP

FEWEST HOME WINS, ONE SEASON:
2 – Chicago Blackhawks, 1927-28. 22GP
3 – Boston Bruins, 1924-25. 15GP
– Chicago Blackhawks, 1928-29. 22GP
– Philadelphia Quakers, 1930-31. 22GP

FEWEST HOME WINS, ONE SEASON (MINIMUM 70-GAME SCHEDULE):
6 – Chicago Blackhawks, 1954-55. 35GP
– Washington Capitals, 1975-76. 40GP
7 – Boston Bruins, 1962-63. 35GP
– Washington Capitals, 1974-75. 40GP
– Winnipeg Jets, 1980-81. 40GP
– Pittsburgh Penguins, 1983-84. 40GP

FEWEST ROAD WINS, ONE SEASON:
0 – Toronto Arenas, 1918-19. 9GP
– Quebec Bulldogs, 1919-20. 12GP
– Pittsburgh Pirates, 1929-30. 22GP
1 – Hamilton Tigers, 1921-22. 12GP
– Toronto St. Patricks, 1925-26. 18GP
– Philadelphia Quakers, 1930-31. 22GP
– New York Americans, 1940-41. 24GP
– Washington Capitals, 1974-75. 40GP
* – Ottawa Senators, 1992-93. 41GP

FEWEST ROAD WINS, ONE SEASON (MINIMUM 70-GAME SCHEDULE):
1 – Washington Capitals, 1974-75. 40GP
*** – Ottawa Senators**, 1992-93. 41GP
2 – Boston Bruins, 1960-61. 35GP
– Los Angeles Kings, 1969-70. 38GP
– New York Islanders, 1972-73. 39GP
– California Golden Seals, 1973-74. 39GP
– Colorado Rockies, 1977-78. 40GP
– Winnipeg Jets, 1980-81. 40GP
– Quebec Nordiques, 1991-92. 40GP

TEAM LOSSES

Fewest Losses

FEWEST LOSSES, ONE SEASON:
5 – Ottawa Senators, 1919-20. 24GP
– Boston Bruins, 1929-30. 44GP
– Montreal Canadiens, 1943-44. 50GP

FEWEST HOME LOSSES, ONE SEASON:
0 – Ottawa Senators, 1922-23. 12GP
– Montreal Canadiens, 1943-44. 25GP
1 – Toronto Arenas, 1917-18. 11GP
– Ottawa Senators, 1918-19. 9GP
– Ottawa Senators, 1919-20. 12GP
– Toronto St. Patricks, 1922-23. 12GP
– Boston Bruins, 1929-30. 22GP
– Boston Bruins, 1930-31. 22GP
– Montreal Canadiens, 1976-77. 40GP
– Quebec Nordiques, 1994-95. 24GP

FEWEST ROAD LOSSES, ONE SEASON:
3 – Montreal Canadiens, 1928-29. 22GP
4 – Ottawa Senators, 1919-20. 12GP
– Montreal Canadiens, 1927-28. 22GP
– Boston Bruins, 1929-30. 20GP
– Boston Bruins, 1940-41. 24GP

FEWEST LOSSES, ONE SEASON (MINIMUM 70-GAME SCHEDULE):
8 – Montreal Canadiens, 1976-77. 80GP
10 – Montreal Canadiens, 1972-73. 78GP
– Montreal Canadiens, 1977-78. 80GP
11 – Montreal Canadiens, 1975-76. 80GP

FEWEST HOME LOSSES, ONE SEASON (MINIMUM 70-GAME SCHEDULE):
1 – Montreal Canadiens, 1976-77. 40GP
2 – Montreal Canadiens, 1961-62. 35GP
– New York Rangers, 1970-71. 39GP
– Philadelphia Flyers, 1975-76. 40GP

FEWEST ROAD LOSSES, ONE SEASON (MINIMUM 70-GAME SCHEDULE):
6 – Montreal Canadiens, 1972-73. 39GP
– Montreal Canadiens, 1974-75. 40GP
– Montreal Canadiens, 1977-78. 40GP
7 – Detroit Red Wings, 1951-52. 35GP
– Montreal Canadiens, 1976-77. 40GP
– Philadelphia Flyers, 1979-80. 40GP
– Boston Bruins, 2003-04. 41GP
– Detroit Red Wings, 2005-06. 41GP

Most Losses

MOST LOSSES, ONE SEASON:
71 – San Jose Sharks, 1992-93. 84GP
70 – Ottawa Senators, 1992-93. 84GP
67 – Washington Capitals, 1974-75. 80GP
61 – Quebec Nordiques, 1989-90. 80GP
– Ottawa Senators, 1993-94. 84GP

MOST HOME LOSSES, ONE SEASON:
***32 – San Jose Sharks**, 1992-93. 41GP
29 – Pittsburgh Penguins, 1983-84. 40GP
* – Ottawa Senators, 1993-94. 41GP

MOST ROAD LOSSES, ONE SEASON:
***40 – Ottawa Senators**, 1992-93. 41GP
39 – Washington Capitals, 1974-75. 40GP
37 – California Golden Seals, 1973-74. 39GP
* – San Jose Sharks, 1992-93. 41GP

* – Does not include neutral site games

TEAM TIES

Most Ties

MOST TIES, ONE SEASON:
24 – Philadelphia Flyers, 1969-70. 76GP
23 – Montreal Canadiens, 1962-63. 70GP
– Chicago Blackhawks, 1973-74. 78GP

MOST HOME TIES, ONE SEASON:
13 – New York Rangers, 1954-55. 35GP
– Philadelphia Flyers, 1969-70. 38GP
– California Golden Seals, 1971-72. 39GP
– California Golden Seals, 1972-73. 39GP
– Chicago Blackhawks, 1973-74. 39GP

MOST ROAD TIES, ONE SEASON:
15 – Philadelphia Flyers, 1976-77. 40GP
14 – Montreal Canadiens, 1952-53. 35GP
– Montreal Canadiens, 1974-75. 40GP
– Philadelphia Flyers, 1975-76. 40GP

Fewest Ties

FEWEST TIES, ONE SEASON (Since 1926-27):
1 – Boston Bruins, 1929-30. 44GP
2 – Montreal Canadiens, 1926-27. 44GP
– New York Americans, 1926-27. 44GP
– Boston Bruins, 1938-39. 48GP
– New York Rangers, 1941-42. 48GP
– San Jose Sharks, 1992-93. 84GP

FEWEST TIES, ONE SEASON (MINIMUM 70-GAME SCHEDULE):
2 – San Jose Sharks, 1992-93. 84GP
3 – New Jersey Devils, 1985-86. 80GP
– Calgary Flames, 1986-87. 80GP
– Vancouver Canucks, 1993-94. 84GP

WINNING STREAKS

LONGEST WINNING STREAK, ONE SEASON:
17 Games – Pittsburgh Penguins, Mar. 9 – Apr. 10, 1993.
15 Games – New York Islanders, Jan. 21 – Feb. 20, 1982.
14 Games – Boston Bruins, Dec. 3, 1929 – Jan. 9, 1930.

LONGEST HOME WINNING STREAK, ONE SEASON:
20 Games – Boston Bruins, Dec. 3, 1929 – Mar. 18, 1930.
– Philadelphia Flyers, Jan. 4 – Apr. 3, 1976.

LONGEST ROAD WINNING STREAK, ONE SEASON:
12 Games – Detroit Red Wings, Mar. 1 – Apr. 15, 2006.
10 Games – Buffalo Sabres, Dec. 10, 1983 – Jan. 23, 1984.
– St. Louis Blues, Jan. 21 – Mar. 2, 2000.
– New Jersey Devils, Feb. 27 – Apr. 7, 2001.
– Buffalo Sabres, Oct. 4 – Nov. 13, 2006.
– San Jose Sharks, Nov. 14 – Dec. 31, 2007.

LONGEST WINNING STREAK FROM START OF SEASON:
10 Games – Toronto Maple Leafs, 1993-94.
– Buffalo Sabres, 2006-07.
8 Games – Toronto Maple Leafs, 1934-35.
– Buffalo Sabres, 1975-76.
– Nashville Predators, 2005-06.
7 Games – Edmonton Oilers, 1983-84.
– Quebec Nordiques, 1985-86.
– Pittsburgh Penguins, 1986-87.
– Pittsburgh Penguins, 1994-95.

LONGEST HOME WINNING STREAK FROM START OF SEASON:
11 Games – Chicago Blackhawks, 1963-64.
10 Games – Ottawa Senators, 1925-26.
9 Games – Montreal Canadiens, 1953-54.
– Chicago Blackhawks, 1971-72.

LONGEST ROAD WINNING STREAK FROM START OF SEASON:
7 Games – Toronto Maple Leafs, Nov. 14 – Dec. 15, 1940.
– Philadelphia Flyers, Oct. 12 – Nov. 16, 1985.
– Detroit Red Wings, Oct. 6 – Nov. 6, 2005.

LONGEST WINNING STREAK, INCLUDING PLAYOFFS:
15 Games – Detroit Red Wings, Feb. 27 – Apr. 5, 1955.
(9 regular-season games, 6 playoff games)
– New Jersey Devils, Mar. 28 – Apr. 29, 2006.
(11 regular-season games, 4 playoff games)

LONGEST HOME WINNING STREAK, INCLUDING PLAYOFFS:
24 Games – Philadelphia Flyers, Jan. 4 – Apr. 25, 1976.
(20 regular-season games, 4 playoff games)

LONGEST ROAD WINNING STREAK, INCLUDING PLAYOFFS:
11 Games – New Jersey Devils, Feb. 27 – Apr. 17, 2001.
(10 regular-season games, 1 playoff game)

UNDEFEATED STREAKS

LONGEST UNDEFEATED STREAK, ONE SEASON:
35 Games – Philadelphia Flyers, Oct. 14, 1979 – Jan. 6, 1980. 25W-10T
28 Games – Montreal Canadiens, Dec. 18, 1977 – Feb. 23, 1978. 23W-5T

LONGEST HOME UNDEFEATED STREAK, ONE SEASON:
34 Games – Montreal Canadiens, Nov. 1, 1976 – Apr. 2, 1977. 28W-6T
27 Games – Boston Bruins, Nov. 22, 1970 – Mar. 20, 1971. 26W-1T

LONGEST ROAD UNDEFEATED STREAK, ONE SEASON:
23 Games – Montreal Canadiens, Nov. 27, 1974 – Mar. 12, 1975. 14W-9T
17 Games – Montreal Canadiens, Dec. 18, 1977 – Mar. 1, 1978. 14W-3T

LONGEST UNDEFEATED STREAK FROM START OF SEASON:
15 Games – Edmonton Oilers, 1984-85. 12W-3T
14 Games – Montreal Canadiens, 1943-44. 11W-3T

LONGEST HOME UNDEFEATED STREAK FROM START OF SEASON:
26 Games – Philadelphia Flyers, Oct. 11, 1979 – Feb. 3, 1980. 19W-7T

LONGEST ROAD UNDEFEATED STREAK FROM START OF SEASON:
15 Games – Detroit Red Wings, Oct. 18 – Dec. 20, 1951. 10W-5T

LONGEST UNDEFEATED STREAK, INCLUDING PLAYOFFS:
24 Games – Montreal Canadiens, Feb. 21 – Apr. 11, 1980.
15W-6T in regular season and 3W in playoffs.
21 Games – Pittsburgh Penguins, Mar. 9 – Apr. 22, 1993.
17W-1T in regular season and 3W in playoffs.

LONGEST HOME UNDEFEATED STREAK, INCLUDING PLAYOFFS:
38 Games – Montreal Canadiens, Nov. 1, 1976 – Apr. 26, 1977.
28W-6T in regular season and 4W in playoffs.

LONGEST ROAD UNDEFEATED STREAK, INCLUDING PLAYOFFS:
13 Games – Philadelphia Flyers, Feb. 26 – Apr. 21, 1977. 6W-4T in regular season and 3W in playoffs.
– Montreal Canadiens, Feb. 26 – Apr. 20, 1980. 6W-4T in regular season and 3W in playoffs.
– New York Islanders, Mar. 16 – May 1, 1980. 3W-3T in regular season and 7W in playoffs.

LOSING STREAKS

LONGEST LOSING STREAK, ONE SEASON:
17 Games – Washington Capitals, Feb. 18 – Mar. 26, 1975.
– San Jose Sharks, Jan. 4 – Feb. 12, 1993.
15 Games – Philadelphia Quakers, Nov. 29, 1930 – Jan. 8, 1931.

LONGEST HOME LOSING STREAK, ONE SEASON:
14 Games – Pittsburgh Penguins, Dec. 31, 2003 – Feb. 22, 2004.
11 Games – Boston Bruins, Dec. 8, 1924 – Feb. 17, 1925.
– Washington Capitals, Feb. 18 – Mar. 30, 1975.
– Ottawa Senators, Oct. 27 – Dec. 8, 1993.
– Atlanta Thrashers, Jan. 24 – Mar. 16, 2000.

LONGEST ROAD LOSING STREAK, ONE SEASON:
***38 Games – Ottawa Senators**, Oct. 10, 1992 – Apr. 3, 1993.
37 Games – Washington Capitals, Oct. 9, 1974 – Mar. 26, 1975.

LONGEST LOSING STREAK FROM START OF SEASON:
11 Games – New York Rangers, 1943-44.
7 Games – Montreal Canadiens, 1938-39.
– Chicago Blackhawks, 1947-48.
– Washington Capitals, 1983-84.
– Chicago Blackhawks, 1997-98.

LONGEST HOME LOSING STREAK FROM START OF SEASON:
8 Games – Los Angeles Kings, Oct. 13 – Nov. 6, 1971.

LONGEST ROAD LOSING STREAK FROM START OF SEASON:
***38 Games – Ottawa Senators**, Oct. 10, 1992 – Apr. 3, 1993.

WINLESS STREAKS

LONGEST WINLESS STREAK, ONE SEASON:
30 Games – Winnipeg Jets, Oct. 19 – Dec. 20, 1980. 23L-7T
27 Games – Kansas City Scouts, Feb. 12 – Apr. 4, 1976. 21L-6T
25 Games – Washington Capitals, Nov. 29, 1975 – Jan. 21, 1976. 22L-3T

LONGEST HOME WINLESS STREAK, ONE SEASON:
17 Games – Ottawa Senators, Oct. 28, 1995 – Jan. 27, 1996. 15L-2T
– Atlanta Thrashers, Jan. 19 – Mar. 29, 2000. 15L-2T
16 Games – Pittsburgh Penguins, Dec. 31, 2003 – Mar. 4, 2004. 15L-1T

LONGEST ROAD WINLESS STREAK, ONE SEASON:
***38 Games – Ottawa Senators**, Oct. 10, 1992 – Apr. 3, 1993. 38L
37 Games – Washington Capitals, Oct. 9, 1974 – Mar. 26, 1975. 37L

LONGEST WINLESS STREAK FROM START OF SEASON:
15 Games – New York Rangers, 1943-44. 14L-1T
11 Games – Pittsburgh Pirates, 1927-28. 8L-3T
– Minnesota North Stars, 1973-74. 5L-6T
– San Jose Sharks, 1995-96. 7L-4T

LONGEST HOME WINLESS STREAK FROM START OF SEASON:
11 Games – Pittsburgh Penguins, Oct. 8 – Nov. 19, 1983. 9L-2T

LONGEST ROAD WINLESS STREAK FROM START OF SEASON:
***38 Games – Ottawa Senators**, Oct. 10, 1992 – Apr. 3, 1993. 38L

NON-SHUTOUT STREAKS

LONGEST NON-SHUTOUT STREAK:
264 Games – Calgary Flames, Nov. 12, 1981 – Jan. 9, 1985.
261 Games – Los Angeles Kings, Mar. 15, 1986 – Oct. 22, 1989.
244 Games – Washington Capitals, Oct. 31, 1989 – Nov. 11, 1993.
236 Games – New York Rangers, Dec. 20, 1989 – Dec. 13, 1992.
230 Games – Quebec Nordiques, Feb. 10, 1980 – Jan. 12, 1983.

LONGEST NON-SHUTOUT STREAK, INCLUDING PLAYOFFS:
264 Games – Los Angeles Kings, Mar. 15, 1986 – Apr. 6, 1989.
(5 playoff games in 1987; 5 in 1988; 2 in 1989).
262 Games – Chicago Blackhawks, Mar. 14, 1970 – Feb. 21, 1973.
(8 playoff games in 1970; 18 in 1971; 8 in 1972).
251 Games – Quebec Nordiques, Feb. 10, 1980 – Jan. 12, 1983.
(5 playoff games in 1981; 16 in 1982).
246 Games – Pittsburgh Penguins, Jan. 7, 1989 – Oct. 26, 1991.
(11 playoff games in 1989; 24 in 1991).

* – Does not include neutral site games

TEAM GOALS

Most Goals

MOST GOALS, ONE SEASON:
446 – Edmonton Oilers, 1983-84. 80GP
426 – Edmonton Oilers, 1985-86. 80GP
424 – Edmonton Oilers, 1982-83. 80GP
417 – Edmonton Oilers, 1981-82. 80GP
401 – Edmonton Oilers, 1984-85. 80GP

MOST GOALS, ONE TEAM, ONE GAME:
16 – Montreal Canadiens, Mar. 3, 1920, at Quebec. Montreal won 16-3.

MOST GOALS, BOTH TEAMS, ONE GAME:
21 – Montreal Canadiens (14), Toronto St. Patricks (7), Jan. 10, 1920, at Montreal.
– Edmonton Oilers (12), Chicago Blackhawks (9), Dec. 11, 1985, at Chicago.
20 – Edmonton Oilers (12), Minnesota North Stars (8), Jan. 4, 1984, at Edmonton.
– Toronto Maple Leafs (11), Edmonton Oilers (9), Jan. 8, 1986, at Toronto.
19 – Montreal Wanderers (10), Toronto Arenas (9), Dec. 19, 1917, at Montreal.
– Montreal Canadiens (16), Quebec Bulldogs (3), Mar. 3, 1920, at Quebec.
– Montreal Canadiens (13), Hamilton Tigers (6), Feb. 26, 1921, at Montreal.
– Boston Bruins (10), New York Rangers (9), Mar. 4, 1944, at Boston.
– Detroit Red Wings (10), Boston Bruins (9), Mar. 16, 1944, at Detroit.
– Vancouver Canucks (10), Minnesota North Stars (9), Oct. 7, 1983, at Vancouver.

MOST GOALS, ONE TEAM, ONE PERIOD:
9 – Buffalo Sabres, Mar. 19, 1981, at Buffalo, second period during 14-4 win over Toronto.
8 – Detroit Red Wings, Jan. 23, 1944, at Detroit, third period during 15-0 win over NY Rangers.
– Boston Bruins, Mar. 16, 1969, at Boston, second period during 11-3 win over Toronto.
– New York Rangers, Nov. 21, 1971, at NY Rangers, third period during 12-1 win over California.
– Philadelphia Flyers, Mar. 31, 1973, at Philadelphia, second period during 10-2 win over NY Islanders.
– Buffalo Sabres, Dec. 21, 1975, at Buffalo, third period during 14-2 win over Washington.
– Minnesota North Stars, Nov. 11, 1981, at Minnesota, second period during 15-2 win over Winnipeg.
– Pittsburgh Penguins, Dec. 17, 1991, at Pittsburgh, second period during 10-2 win over San Jose.
– Washington Capitals, Feb. 3, 1999, at Washington, second period during 10-1 win over Tampa Bay.

MOST GOALS, BOTH TEAMS, ONE PERIOD:
12 – Buffalo Sabres (9), Toronto Maple Leafs (3), Mar. 19, 1981, at Buffalo, second period. Buffalo won 14-4.
– Edmonton Oilers (6), Chicago Blackhawks (6), Dec. 11, 1985, at Chicago, second period. Edmonton won 12-9.
10 – New York Rangers (7), New York Americans (3), Mar. 16, 1939, at NY Americans, third period. NY Rangers won 11-5.
– Toronto Maple Leafs (6), Detroit Red Wings (4), Mar. 17, 1946, at Detroit, third period. Toronto won 11-7.
– Buffalo Sabres (6), Vancouver Canucks (4), Jan. 8, 1976, at Buffalo, third period. Buffalo won 8-5.
– Buffalo Sabres (5), Montreal Canadiens (5), Oct. 26, 1982, at Montreal, first period. Teams tied 7-7.
– Quebec Nordiques (6), Boston Bruins (4), Dec. 7, 1982, at Quebec, second period. Quebec won 10-5.
– Vancouver Canucks (6), Calgary Flames (4), Jan. 16, 1987, at Vancouver, first period. Vancouver won 9-5.
– Detroit Red Wings (7), Winnipeg Jets (3), Nov. 25, 1987, at Detroit, third period. Detroit won 10-8.
– Chicago Blackhawks (5), St. Louis Blues (5), Mar. 15, 1988, at St. Louis, third period. Teams tied 7-7.

MOST CONSECUTIVE GOALS, ONE TEAM, ONE GAME:
15 – Detroit Red Wings, Jan. 23, 1944, at Detroit during 15-0 win over NY Rangers.

Fewest Goals

FEWEST GOALS, ONE SEASON:
33 – Chicago Blackhawks, 1928-29. 44GP
45 – Montreal Maroons, 1924-25. 30GP
46 – Pittsburgh Pirates, 1928-29. 44GP

FEWEST GOALS, ONE SEASON (MINIMUM 70-GAME SCHEDULE):
133 – Chicago Blackhawks, 1953-54. 70GP
147 – Toronto Maple Leafs, 1954-55. 70GP
– Boston Bruins, 1955-56. 70GP
150 – New York Rangers, 1954-55. 70GP

TEAM POWER-PLAY GOALS

MOST POWER-PLAY GOALS, ONE SEASON:
119 – Pittsburgh Penguins, 1988-89. 80GP
113 – Detroit Red Wings, 1992-93. 84GP
111 – New York Rangers, 1987-88. 80GP
110 – Pittsburgh Penguins, 1987-88. 80GP
– Winnipeg Jets, 1987-88. 80GP

TEAM SHORTHAND GOALS

MOST SHORTHAND GOALS, ONE SEASON:
36 – Edmonton Oilers, 1983-84. 80GP
28 – Edmonton Oilers, 1986-87. 80GP
27 – Edmonton Oilers, 1985-86. 80GP
– Edmonton Oilers, 1988-89. 80GP

TEAM GOALS-PER-GAME

HIGHEST GOALS-PER-GAME AVERAGE, ONE SEASON:
5.58 – Edmonton Oilers, 1983-84. 446G in 80GP.
5.38 – Montreal Canadiens, 1919-20. 129G in 24GP.
5.33 – Edmonton Oilers, 1985-86. 426G in 80GP.
5.30 – Edmonton Oilers, 1982-83. 424G in 80GP.
5.23 – Montreal Canadiens, 1917-18. 115G in 22GP.

LOWEST GOALS-PER-GAME AVERAGE, ONE SEASON:
0.75 – Chicago Blackhawks, 1928-29. 33G in 44GP.
1.05 – Pittsburgh Pirates, 1928-29. 46G in 44GP.
1.20 – New York Americans, 1928-29. 53G in 44GP.

TEAM ASSISTS

MOST ASSISTS, ONE SEASON:
737 – Edmonton Oilers, 1985-86. 80GP
736 – Edmonton Oilers, 1983-84. 80GP
706 – Edmonton Oilers, 1981-82. 80GP

FEWEST ASSISTS, ONE SEASON (Since 1926-27):
45 – New York Rangers, 1926-27. 44GP

FEWEST ASSISTS, ONE SEASON (MINIMUM 70-GAME SCHEDULE):
206 – Chicago Blackhawks, 1953-54. 70GP

TEAM TOTAL POINTS

MOST SCORING POINTS, ONE SEASON:
1,182 – Edmonton Oilers, 1983-84. (446G-736A) 80GP
1,163 – Edmonton Oilers, 1985-86. (426G-737A) 80GP
1,123 – Edmonton Oilers, 1981-82. (417G-706A) 80GP

MOST SCORING POINTS, ONE TEAM, ONE GAME:
40 – Buffalo Sabres, Dec. 21, 1975, at Buffalo. Buffalo defeated Washington 14-2, and had 26A.
39 – Minnesota North Stars, Nov. 11, 1981, at Minnesota. Minnesota defeated Winnipeg 15-2, and had 24A.
37 – Detroit Red Wings, Jan. 23, 1944, at Detroit. Detroit defeated NY Rangers 15-0, and had 22A.
– Toronto Maple Leafs, Mar. 16, 1957, at Toronto. Toronto defeated NY Rangers 14-1, and had 23A.
– Buffalo Sabres, Feb. 25, 1978, at Cleveland. Buffalo defeated Cleveland 13-3, and had 24A.
– Calgary Flames, Feb. 10, 1993, at Calgary. Calgary defeated San Jose 13-1, and had 24A.

MOST SCORING POINTS, BOTH TEAMS, ONE GAME:
62 – Edmonton Oilers, Chicago Blackhawks, Dec. 11, 1985, at Chicago. Edmonton won 12-9. Edmonton had 24A, Chicago, 17A.
53 – Quebec Nordiques, Washington Capitals, Feb. 22, 1981, at Washington. Quebec won 11-7. Quebec had 22A, Washington, 13A.
– Edmonton Oilers, Minnesota North Stars, Jan. 4, 1984, at Edmonton. Edmonton won 12-8. Edmonton had 20A, Minnesota, 13A.
– Minnesota North Stars, St. Louis Blues, Jan. 27, 1984, at St. Louis. Minnesota won 10-8. Minnesota had 19A, St. Louis, 16A.
– Toronto Maple Leafs, Edmonton Oilers, Jan. 8, 1986, at Toronto. Toronto won 11-9. Toronto had 17A, Edmonton, 16A.
52 – Montreal Maroons, New York Americans, Feb. 18, 1936, at NY Americans. Teams tied 8-8. NY Americans had 20A, Montreal, 16A. (3A allowed for each goal.)
– Vancouver Canucks, Minnesota North Stars, Oct. 7, 1983, at Vancouver. Vancouver won 10-9. Vancouver had 16A, Minnesota, 17A.

MOST SCORING POINTS, ONE TEAM, ONE PERIOD:
23 – New York Rangers, Nov. 21, 1971, at NY Rangers, third period during 12-1 win over California. NY Rangers had 8G, 15A.
– Buffalo Sabres, Dec. 21, 1975, at Buffalo, third period during 14-2 win over Washington. Buffalo had 8G, 15A.
– Buffalo Sabres, Mar. 19, 1981, at Buffalo, second period during 14-4 win over Toronto. Buffalo had 9G, 14A.
22 – Detroit Red Wings, Jan. 23, 1944, at Detroit, third period during 15-0 win over NY Rangers. Detroit had 8G, 14A.
– Boston Bruins, Mar. 16, 1969, at Boston, second period during 11-3 win over Toronto. Boston had 8G, 14A.
– Minnesota North Stars, Nov. 11, 1981, at Minnesota, second period during 15-2 win over Winnipeg. Minnesota had 8G, 14A.
– Pittsburgh Penguins, Dec. 17, 1991, at Pittsburgh, second period during 10-2 win over San Jose. Pittsburgh had 8G, 14A.
– Washington Capitals, Feb. 3, 1999, at Washington, second period during 10-1 win over Tampa Bay. Washington had 8G, 14A.

MOST SCORING POINTS, BOTH TEAMS, ONE PERIOD:
35 – Edmonton, Oilers, Chicago Blackhawks, Dec. 11, 1985, at Chicago, second period. Edmonton won 12-9. Edmonton had 6G, 12A; Chicago, 6G, 11A.
31 – Buffalo Sabres, Toronto Maple Leafs, Mar. 19, 1981, at Buffalo, second period. Buffalo won 14-4. Buffalo had 9G, 14A; Toronto, 3G, 5A.
29 – Winnipeg Jets, Detroit Red Wings, Nov. 25, 1987, at Detroit, third period. Detroit won 10-8. Detroit had 7G, 13A; Winnipeg, 3G, 6A.
– Chicago Blackhawks, St. Louis Blues, Mar. 15, 1988, at St. Louis, third period. Teams tied 7-7. St. Louis had 5G, 10A; Chicago, 5G, 9A.

FASTEST GOALS

FASTEST SIX GOALS, BOTH TEAMS:

3:00 – Quebec Nordiques, Washington Capitals, Feb. 22, 1981, at Washington. Scorers: Peter Stastny, Quebec, 18:51; Pierre Lacroix, Quebec, 19:57 (first period); Anton Stastny, Quebec, 0:34; Jacques Richard, Quebec, 1:07 and 1:37; Rick Green, Washington, 1:51 (second period). Quebec won 11-7.

3:15 – Montreal Canadiens, Toronto Maple Leafs, Jan. 4, 1944, at Montreal, first period. Scorers: Maurice Richard, Montreal, 14:10; Don Webster, Toronto, 15:13; Fern Majeau, Montreal, 15:41; Phil Watson, Montreal, 15:52; Lorne Carr, Toronto, 16:55; Butch Bouchard, Montreal, 17:25. Montreal won 6-3.

FASTEST FIVE GOALS, BOTH TEAMS:

1:24 – Chicago Blackhawks, Toronto Maple Leafs, Oct. 15, 1983, at Toronto, second period. Scorers: Gaston Gingras, Toronto, 16:49; Denis Savard, Chicago, 17:12; Steve Larmer, Chicago, 17:27; Denis Savard, Chicago, 17:42; John Anderson, Toronto, 18:13. Toronto won 10-8.

1:39 – Detroit Red Wings, Toronto Maple Leafs, Nov. 15, 1944, at Toronto, third period. Scorers: Ted Kennedy, Toronto, 10:36 and 10:55; Harold Jackson, Detroit, 11:48; Steve Wojciechowski, Detroit, 12:02; Don Grosso, Detroit, 12:15. Detroit won 8-4.

FASTEST FIVE GOALS, ONE TEAM:

2:07 – Pittsburgh Penguins, Nov. 22, 1972, at Pittsburgh, third period. Scorers: Bryan Hextall, Jr., 12:00; Jean Pronovost, 12:18; Al McDonough, 13:40; Ken Schinkel, 13:49; Ron Schock, 14:07. Pittsburgh defeated St. Louis 10-4.

2:37 – New York Islanders, Jan. 26, 1982, at NY Islanders, first period. Scorers: Duane Sutter, 1:31; John Tonelli, 2:30; Bryan Trottier, 2:46 and 3:31; Duane Sutter, 4:08. NY Islanders defeated Pittsburgh 9-2.

2:55 – Boston Bruins, Dec. 19, 1974, at Boston. Scorers: Bobby Schmautz, 19:13 (first period); Ken Hodge, 0:18; Phil Esposito, 0:43; Don Marcotte, 0:58; John Bucyk, 2:08 (second period). Boston defeated NY Rangers 11-3.

FASTEST FOUR GOALS, BOTH TEAMS:

0:53 – Chicago Blackhawks, Toronto Maple Leafs, Oct. 15, 1983, at Toronto, second period. Scorers: Gaston Gingras, Toronto, 16:49; Denis Savard, Chicago, 17:12; Steve Larmer, Chicago, 17:27; Denis Savard, Chicago, 17:42. Toronto won 10-8.

0:57 – Quebec Nordiques, Detroit Red Wings, Jan. 27, 1990, at Quebec, first period. Scorers: Paul Gillis, Quebec, 18:01; Claude Loiselle, Quebec, 18:12; Joe Sakic, Quebec, 18:27; Jimmy Carson, Detroit, 18:58. Detroit won 8-6.

1:01 – Colorado Rockies, New York Rangers, Jan. 15, 1980, at NY Rangers, first period. Scorers: Doug Sulliman, NY Rangers, 7:52; Eddie Johnstone, NY Rangers, 7:57; Warren Miller, NY Rangers, 8:20; Rob Ramage, Colorado, 8:53. Teams tied 6-6.

– Chicago Blackhawks, Toronto Maple Leafs, Oct. 15, 1983, at Toronto, second period. Scorers: Denis Savard, Chicago, 17:12; Steve Larmer, Chicago, 17:27; Denis Savard, Chicago, 17:42; John Anderson, Toronto, 18:13. Toronto won 10-8.

FASTEST FOUR GOALS, ONE TEAM:

1:20 – Boston Bruins, Jan. 21, 1945, at Boston, second period. Scorers: Bill Thoms, 6:34; Frank Mario, 7:08 and 7:27; Ken Smith, 7:54. Boston defeated NY Rangers 14-3.

FASTEST THREE GOALS, BOTH TEAMS:

0:15 – Minnesota North Stars, New York Rangers, Feb. 10, 1983, at Minnesota, second period. Scorers: Mark Pavelich, NY Rangers, 19:18; Ron Greschner, NY Rangers, 19:27; Willi Plett, Minnesota, 19:33. Minnesota won 7-5.

0:18 – Montreal Canadiens, New York Rangers, Dec. 12, 1963, at Montreal, first period. Scorers: Dave Balon, Montreal, 0:58; Gilles Tremblay, Montreal, 1:04; Camille Henry, NY Rangers, 1:16. Montreal won 6-4.

– California Golden Seals, Buffalo Sabres, Feb. 1, 1976, at California, third period. Scorers: Jim Moxey, California, 19:38; Wayne Merrick, California, 19:45; Danny Gare, Buffalo, 19:56. Buffalo won 9-5.

FASTEST THREE GOALS, ONE TEAM:

0:20 – Boston Bruins, Feb. 25, 1971, at Boston, third period. Scorers: John Bucyk, 4:50; Ed Westfall, 5:02; Ted Green, 5:10. Boston defeated Vancouver 8-3.

0:21 – Chicago Blackhawks, Mar. 23, 1952, at NY Rangers, third period. Bill Mosienko scored all three goals, at 6:09, 6:20 and 6:30. Chicago defeated NY Rangers 7-6.

– Washington Capitals, Nov. 23, 1990, at Washington, first period. Scorers: Michal Pivonka, 16:18; Stephen Leach, 16:29 and 16:39. Washington defeated Pittsburgh 7-3.

FASTEST THREE GOALS FROM START OF PERIOD, BOTH TEAMS:

1:05 – Hartford Whalers, Montreal Canadiens, Mar. 11, 1989, at Montreal, second period. Scorers: Kevin Dineen, Hartford, 0:11; Guy Carbonneau, Montreal, 0:36; Petr Svoboda, Montreal, 1:05. Montreal won 5-3.

FASTEST THREE GOALS FROM START OF PERIOD, ONE TEAM:

0:53 – Calgary Flames, Feb. 10, 1993, at Calgary, third period. Scorers: Gary Suter, 0:17; Chris Lindberg, 0:40; Ron Stern, 0:53. Calgary defeated San Jose 13-1.

FASTEST TWO GOALS, BOTH TEAMS:

0:02 – St. Louis Blues, Boston Bruins, Dec. 19, 1987, at Boston, third period. Scorers: Ken Linseman, Boston, 19:50; Doug Gilmour, St. Louis, 19:52. St. Louis won 7-5.

0:03 – Chicago Blackhawks, Minnesota North Stars, Nov. 5, 1988, at Minnesota, third period. Scorers: Steve Thomas, Chicago, 6:03; Dave Gagner, Minnesota, 6:06. Teams tied 5-5.

FASTEST TWO GOALS, ONE TEAM:

0:03 – Minnesota Wild, Jan. 21, 2004, at Minnesota, third period. Scorers: Jim Dowd, 19:44; Richard Park, 19:47. Minnesota defeated Chicago 4-2.

0:04 – Montreal Maroons, Jan. 3, 1931, at Montreal, third period. Nels Stewart scored both goals, at 8:24 and 8:28. Mtl. Maroons defeated Boston 5-3.

– Buffalo Sabres, Oct. 17, 1974, at Buffalo, third period. Scorers: Lee Fogolin, Jr., 14:55; Don Luce, 14:59. Buffalo defeated California 6-1.

– Toronto Maple Leafs, Dec. 29, 1988, at Quebec, third period. Scorers: Ed Olczyk, 5:24; Gary Leeman, 5:28. Toronto defeated Quebec 6-5.

– Calgary Flames, Oct. 17, 1989, at Quebec, third period. Scorers: Doug Gilmour, 19:45; Paul Ranheim, 19:49. Teams tied 8-8.

– Winnipeg Jets, Dec. 15, 1995, at Winnipeg, second period. Deron Quint scored both goals, at 7:51 and 7:55. Winnipeg defeated Edmonton 9-4.

FASTEST TWO GOALS FROM START OF GAME, ONE TEAM:

0:24 – Edmonton Oilers, Mar. 28, 1982, at Los Angeles. Scorers: Mark Messier, 0:14; Dave Lumley, 0:24. Edmonton defeated Los Angeles 6-2.

0:27 – Boston Bruins, Feb. 14, 2003, at Florida. Mike Knuble scored both goals, at 0:10 and 0:27. Boston defeated Florida 6-5.

0:29 – Pittsburgh Penguins, Dec. 6, 1980, at Pittsburgh. Scorers: George Ferguson, 0:17; Greg Malone, 0:29. Pittsburgh defeated Chicago 6-4.

FASTEST TWO GOALS FROM START OF PERIOD, BOTH TEAMS:

0:14 – New York Rangers, Quebec Nordiques, Nov. 5, 1983, at Quebec, third period. Scorers: Andre Savard, Quebec, 0:08; Pierre Larouche, NY Rangers, 0:14. Teams tied 4-4.

0:25 – St. Louis Blues, Chicago Blackhawks, Feb. 2, 2006, at St. Louis, second period. Scorers: Peter Cajanek, St. Louis, 0:10; Tyler Arnason, Chicago, 0:25. St. Louis won 6-5.

0:28 – Boston Bruins, Montreal Canadiens, Oct. 11, 1989, at Montreal, third period. Scorers: Jim Wiemer, Boston 0:10; Tom Chorske, Montreal 0:28. Montreal won 4-2.

FASTEST TWO GOALS FROM START OF PERIOD, ONE TEAM:

0:21 – Chicago Blackhawks, Nov. 5, 1983, at Minnesota, second period. Scorers: Ken Yaremchuk, 0:12; Darryl Sutter, 0:21. Minnesota defeated Chicago 10-5.

0:24 – Edmonton Oilers, Mar. 28, 1982, at Los Angeles, first period. Scorers: Mark Messier, 0:14; Dave Lumley, 0:24. Edmonton defeated Los Angeles 6-2.

0:27 – Boston Bruins, Feb. 14, 2003, at Florida. Mike Knuble scored both goals, at 0:10 and 0:27. Boston defeated Florida 6-5.

50, 40, 30, 20-GOAL SCORERS

MOST 50-OR-MORE GOAL SCORERS, ONE SEASON:

3 – Edmonton Oilers, 1983-84. 80GP. Wayne Gretzky, 87; Glenn Anderson, 54; Jari Kurri, 52.

– Edmonton Oilers, 1985-86. 80GP. Jari Kurri, 68; Glenn Anderson, 54; Wayne Gretzky, 52.

2 – Boston Bruins, 1970-71. 78GP. Phil Esposito, 76; John Bucyk, 51.
– Boston Bruins, 1973-74. 78GP. Phil Esposito, 68; Ken Hodge, 50.
– Philadelphia Flyers, 1975-76. 80GP. Reggie Leach, 61; Bill Barber, 50.
– Pittsburgh Penguins, 1975-76. 80GP. Pierre Larouche, 53; Jean Pronovost, 52.
– Montreal Canadiens, 1976-77. 80GP. Steve Shutt, 60; Guy Lafleur, 56.
– Los Angeles Kings, 1979-80. 80GP. Charlie Simmer, 56; Marcel Dionne, 53.
– Montreal Canadiens, 1979-80. 80GP. Pierre Larouche, 50; Guy Lafleur, 50.
– Los Angeles Kings, 1980-81. 80GP. Marcel Dionne, 58; Charlie Simmer, 56.
– Edmonton Oilers, 1981-82. 80GP. Wayne Gretzky, 92; Mark Messier, 50.
– New York Islanders, 1981-82. 80GP. Mike Bossy, 64; Bryan Trottier, 50.
– Edmonton Oilers, 1984-85. 80GP. Wayne Gretzky, 73; Jari Kurri, 71.
– Washington Capitals, 1984-85. 80GP. Bob Carpenter, 53; Mike Gartner, 50.
– Edmonton Oilers, 1986-87. 80GP. Wayne Gretzky, 62; Jari Kurri, 54.
– Calgary Flames, 1987-88. 80GP. Joe Nieuwendyk, 51; Hakan Loob, 50.
– Los Angeles Kings, 1987-88. 80GP. Jimmy Carson, 55; Luc Robitaille, 53.
– Calgary Flames, 1988-89. 80GP. Joe Nieuwendyk, 51; Joe Mullen, 51.
– Los Angeles Kings, 1988-89. 80GP. Bernie Nicholls, 70; Wayne Gretzky, 54.
– Buffalo Sabres, 1992-93. 84GP. Alexander Mogilny, 76; Pat LaFontaine, 53.
– Pittsburgh Penguins, 1992-93. 84GP. Mario Lemieux, 69; Kevin Stevens, 55.
– St. Louis Blues, 1992-93. 84GP. Brett Hull, 54; Brendan Shanahan, 51.
– Detroit Red Wings, 1993-94. 84GP. Sergei Fedorov, 56; Ray Sheppard, 52.
– St. Louis Blues, 1993-94. 84GP. Brett Hull, 57; Brendan Shanahan, 52.
– Pittsburgh Penguins, 1995-96. 82GP. Mario Lemieux, 69; Jaromir Jagr, 62.

MOST 40-OR-MORE GOAL SCORERS, ONE SEASON:

4 – Edmonton Oilers, 1982-83. 80GP. Wayne Gretzky, 71; Glenn Anderson, 48; Mark Messier, 48; Jari Kurri, 45.

– Edmonton Oilers, 1983-84. 80GP. Wayne Gretzky, 87; Glenn Anderson, 54; Jari Kurri, 52; Paul Coffey, 40.

– Edmonton Oilers, 1984-85. 80GP. Wayne Gretzky, 73; Jari Kurri, 71; Mike Krushelnyski, 43; Glenn Anderson, 42.

– Edmonton Oilers, 1985-86. 80GP. Jari Kurri, 68; Glenn Anderson, 54; Wayne Gretzky, 52; Paul Coffey, 48.

– Calgary Flames, 1987-88. 80GP. Joe Nieuwendyk, 51; Hakan Loob, 50; Mike Bullard, 48; Joe Mullen, 40.

3 – Boston Bruins, 1970-71. 78GP. Phil Esposito, 76; John Bucyk, 51; Ken Hodge, 43.
– New York Rangers, 1971-72. 78GP. Vic Hadfield, 50; Jean Ratelle, 46; Rod Gilbert, 43.
– Buffalo Sabres, 1975-76. 80GP. Danny Gare, 50; Rick Martin, 49; Gilbert Perreault, 44.
– Montreal Canadiens, 1979-80. 80GP. Guy Lafleur, 50; Pierre Larouche, 50; Steve Shutt, 47.
– Buffalo Sabres, 1979-80. 80GP. Danny Gare, 56; Rick Martin, 45; Gilbert Perreault, 40.
– Los Angeles Kings, 1980-81. 80GP. Marcel Dionne, 58; Charlie Simmer, 56; Dave Taylor, 47.
– Los Angeles Kings, 1984-85. 80GP. Marcel Dionne, 46; Bernie Nicholls, 46; Dave Taylor, 41.
– New York Islanders, 1984-85. 80GP. Mike Bossy, 58; Brent Sutter, 42; John Tonelli, 42.
– Chicago Blackhawks, 1985-86. 80GP. Denis Savard, 47; Troy Murray, 45; Al Secord, 40.

– Chicago Blackhawks, 1987-88. 80GP. Denis Savard, 44; Rick Vaive, 43; Steve Larmer, 41.
– Edmonton Oilers, 1987-88. 80GP. Craig Simpson, 43; Jari Kurri, 43; Wayne Gretzky, 40.
– Los Angeles Kings, 1988-89. 80GP. Bernie Nicholls, 70; Wayne Gretzky, 54; Luc Robitaille, 46.
– Los Angeles Kings, 1990-91. 80GP. Luc Robitaille, 45; Tomas Sandstrom, 45; Wayne Gretzky, 41.
– Pittsburgh Penguins, 1991-92. 80GP. Kevin Stevens, 54; Mario Lemieux, 44; Joe Mullen, 42.
– Pittsburgh Penguins, 1992-93. 84GP. Mario Lemieux, 69; Kevin Stevens, 55; Rick Tocchet, 48.
– Calgary Flames, 1993-94. 84GP. Gary Roberts, 41; Robert Reichel, 40; Theoren Fleury, 40.
– Pittsburgh Penguins, 1995-96. 82GP. Mario Lemieux, 69; Jaromir Jagr, 62; Petr Nedved, 45.

MOST 30-OR-MORE GOAL SCORERS, ONE SEASON:
6 – Buffalo Sabres, 1974-75. 80GP. Rick Martin, 52; Rene Robert, 40; Gilbert Perreault, 39; Don Luce, 33; Rick Dudley, 31; Danny Gare, 31.
– New York Islanders, 1977-78. 80GP. Mike Bossy, 53; Bryan Trottier, 46; Clark Gillies, 35; Denis Potvin, 30; Bob Nystrom, 30; Bob Bourne, 30.
– Winnipeg Jets, 1984-85. 80GP. Dale Hawerchuk, 53; Paul MacLean, 41; Laurie Boschman, 32; Brian Mullen, 32; Doug Smail, 31; Thomas Steen, 30.
5 – Chicago Blackhawks, 1968-69. 76GP
– Boston Bruins, 1970-71. 78GP
– Montreal Canadiens, 1971-72. 78GP
– Philadelphia Flyers, 1972-73. 78GP
– Boston Bruins, 1973-74. 78GP
– Montreal Canadiens, 1974-75. 80GP
– Montreal Canadiens, 1975-76. 80GP
– Pittsburgh Penguins, 1975-76. 80GP
– New York Islanders, 1978-79. 80GP
– Detroit Red Wings, 1979-80. 80GP
– Philadelphia Flyers, 1979-80. 80GP
– New York Islanders, 1980-81. 80GP
– St. Louis Blues, 1980-81. 80GP
– Chicago Blackhawks, 1981-82. 80GP
– Edmonton Oilers, 1981-82. 80GP
– Montreal Canadiens, 1981-82. 80GP
– Quebec Nordiques, 1981-82. 80GP
– Washington Capitals, 1981-82. 80GP
– Edmonton Oilers, 1982-83. 80GP
– Edmonton Oilers, 1983-84. 80GP
– Edmonton Oilers, 1984-85. 80GP
– Los Angeles Kings, 1984-85. 80GP
– Edmonton Oilers, 1985-86. 80GP
– Edmonton Oilers, 1986-87. 80GP
– Edmonton Oilers, 1987-88. 80GP
– Edmonton Oilers, 1988-89. 80GP
– Detroit Red Wings, 1991-92. 80GP
– New York Rangers, 1991-92. 80GP
– Pittsburgh Penguins, 1991-92. 80GP
– Detroit Red Wings, 1992-93. 84GP
– Pittsburgh Penguins, 1992-93. 84GP

MOST 20-OR-MORE GOAL SCORERS, ONE SEASON:
11 – Boston Bruins, 1977-78. 80GP. Peter McNab, 41; Terry O'Reilly, 29; Bobby Schmautz, 27; Stan Jonathan, 27; Jean Ratelle, 25; Rick Middleton, 25; Wayne Cashman, 24; Gregg Sheppard, 23; Brad Park, 22; Don Marcotte, 20; Bob Miller, 20.
10 – Boston Bruins, 1970-71. 78GP
– Montreal Canadiens, 1974-75. 80GP
– St. Louis Blues, 1980-81. 80GP

100-POINT SCORERS

MOST 100 OR-MORE-POINT SCORERS, ONE SEASON:
4 – Boston Bruins, 1970-71. 78GP. Phil Esposito, 76G-76A-152PTS; Bobby Orr, 37G-102A-139PTS; John Bucyk, 51G-65A-116PTS; Ken Hodge, 43G-62A-105PTS.
– Edmonton Oilers, 1982-83. 80GP. Wayne Gretzky, 71G-125A-196PTS; Mark Messier, 48G-58A-106PTS; Glenn Anderson, 48G-56A-104PTS; Jari Kurri, 45G-59A-104PTS.
– Edmonton Oilers, 1983-84. 80GP. Wayne Gretzky, 87G-118A-205PTS; Paul Coffey, 40G-86A-126PTS; Jari Kurri, 52G-61A-113PTS; Mark Messier, 37G-64A-101PTS.
– Edmonton Oilers, 1985-86. 80GP. Wayne Gretzky, 52G-163A-215PTS; Paul Coffey, 48G-90A-138PTS; Jari Kurri, 68G-63A-131PTS; Glenn Anderson, 54G-48A-102PTS.
– Pittsburgh Penguins, 1992-93. 84GP. Mario Lemieux, 69G-91A-160PTS; Kevin Stevens, 55G-56A-111PTS; Rick Tocchet, 48G-61A-109PTS; Ron Francis, 24G-76A-100PTS.
3 – Boston Bruins, 1973-74. 78GP. Phil Esposito, 68G-77A-145PTS; Bobby Orr, 32G-90A-122PTS; Ken Hodge, 50G-55A-105PTS.
– New York Islanders, 1978-79. 80GP. Bryan Trottier, 47G-87A-134PTS; Mike Bossy, 69G-57A-126PTS; Denis Potvin, 31G-70A-101PTS.
– Los Angeles Kings, 1980-81. 80GP. Marcel Dionne, 58G-77A-135PTS; Dave Taylor, 47G-65A-112PTS; Charlie Simmer, 56G-49A-105PTS.
– Edmonton Oilers, 1984-85. 80GP. Wayne Gretzky, 73G-135A-208PTS; Jari Kurri, 71G-64A-135PTS; Paul Coffey, 37G-84A-121PTS.
– New York Islanders, 1984-85. 80GP. Mike Bossy, 58G-59A-117PTS; Brent Sutter, 42G-60A-102PTS; John Tonelli, 42G-58A-100PTS.
– Edmonton Oilers, 1986-87. 80GP. Wayne Gretzky, 62G-121A-183PTS; Jari Kurri, 54G-54A-108PTS; Mark Messier, 37G-70A-107PTS.
– Pittsburgh Penguins, 1988-89. 80GP. Mario Lemieux, 85G-114A-199PTS; Rob Brown, 49G-66A-115PTS; Paul Coffey, 30G-83A-113PTS.
– Pittsburgh Penguins, 1995-96. 82GP. Mario Lemieux, 69G-92A-161PTS; Jaromir Jagr, 62G-87A-149PTS; Ron Francis, 27G-92A-119PTS.

SHOTS ON GOAL

MOST SHOTS, BOTH TEAMS, ONE GAME:
141 – New York Americans, Pittsburgh Pirates, Dec. 26, 1925, at NY Americans. NY Americans won 3-1 with 73 shots; Pittsburgh had 68 shots.

MOST SHOTS, ONE TEAM, ONE GAME:
83 – Boston Bruins, Mar. 4, 1941, at Boston. Boston defeated Chicago 3-2.
73 – New York Americans, Dec. 26, 1925, at NY Americans. NY Americans defeated Pittsburgh 3-1.
– Boston Bruins, Mar. 21, 1991, at Boston. Boston tied Quebec 3-3.
72 – Boston Bruins, Dec. 10, 1970, at Boston. Boston defeated Buffalo 8-2.

MOST SHOTS, ONE TEAM, ONE PERIOD:
33 – Boston Bruins, Mar. 4, 1941, at Boston, second period. Boston defeated Chicago 3-2.

TEAM GOALS AGAINST

Fewest Goals Against

FEWEST GOALS AGAINST, ONE SEASON:
42 – Ottawa Senators, 1925-26. 36GP
43 – Montreal Canadiens, 1928-29. 44GP
48 – Montreal Canadiens, 1923-24. 24GP
– Montreal Canadiens, 1927-28. 44GP

FEWEST GOALS AGAINST, ONE SEASON (MINIMUM 70-GAME SCHEDULE):
131 – Toronto Maple Leafs, 1953-54. 70GP
– Montreal Canadiens, 1955-56. 70GP
132 – Detroit Red Wings, 1953-54. 70GP
133 – Detroit Red Wings, 1951-52. 70GP
– Detroit Red Wings, 1952-53. 70GP

LOWEST GOALS-AGAINST-PER-GAME AVERAGE, ONE SEASON:
0.98 – Montreal Canadiens, 1928-29. 43GA in 44GP.
1.09 – Montreal Canadiens, 1927-28. 48GA in 44GP.
1.17 – Ottawa Senators, 1925-26. 42GA in 36GP.

Most Goals Against

MOST GOALS AGAINST, ONE SEASON:
446 – Washington Capitals, 1974-75. 80GP
415 – Detroit Red Wings, 1985-86. 80GP
414 – San Jose Sharks, 1992-93. 84GP
407 – Quebec Nordiques, 1989-90. 80GP
403 – Hartford Whalers, 1982-83. 80GP

HIGHEST GOALS-AGAINST-PER-GAME AVERAGE, ONE SEASON:
7.38 – Quebec Bulldogs, 1919-20. 177GA in 24GP.
6.20 – New York Rangers, 1943-44. 310GA in 50GP.
5.58 – Washington Capitals, 1974-75. 446GA in 80GP.

MOST POWER-PLAY GOALS AGAINST, ONE SEASON:
122 – Chicago Blackhawks, 1988-89. 80GP
120 – Pittsburgh Penguins, 1987-88. 80GP
116 – Washington Capitals, 2005-06. 82GP
115 – New Jersey Devils, 1988-89. 80GP
– Ottawa Senators, 1992-93. 84GP
114 – Los Angeles Kings, 1992-93. 84GP

MOST SHORTHAND GOALS AGAINST, ONE SEASON:
22 – Pittsburgh Penguins, 1984-85. 80GP
– Minnesota North Stars, 1991-92. 80GP
– Colorado Avalanche, 1995-96. 82GP
21 – Calgary Flames, 1984-85. 80GP
– Pittsburgh Penguins, 1989-90. 80GP

SHUTOUTS

MOST SHUTOUTS, ONE SEASON:
22 – Montreal Canadiens, 1928-29. All by George Hainsworth. 44GP
16 – New York Americans, 1928-29. Roy Worters 13, Flat Walsh 3. 44GP
15 – Ottawa Senators, 1925-26. All by Alex Connell. 36GP
– Ottawa Senators, 1927-28. All by Alex Connell. 44GP
– Boston Bruins, 1927-28. All by Hal Winkler. 44GP
– Chicago Blackhawks, 1969-70. All by Tony Esposito. 76GP

MOST CONSECUTIVE SHUTOUTS, ONE SEASON:
6 – Ottawa Senators, Jan. 31 – Feb. 18, 1928. All by Alex Connell.

MOST CONSECUTIVE SHUTOUTS TO START SEASON:
5 – Toronto Maple Leafs, Nov. 13 – 22, 1930. Lorne Chabot 3, Benny Grant 2.

MOST GAMES SHUTOUT, ONE SEASON:
20 – Chicago Blackhawks, 1928-29. 44GP

MOST CONSECUTIVE GAMES SHUTOUT:
8 – Chicago Blackhawks, Feb. 7 – 28, 1929.

MOST CONSECUTIVE GAMES SHUTOUT TO START SEASON:
3 – Montreal Maroons, Nov. 11 – 18, 1930.

TEAM SHOOTOUT RECORDS

MOST SHOOTOUT GAMES, ONE SEASON:
19 – Edmonton, 2007-08
18 – New Jersey, 2006-07
17 – Minnesota, 2006-07
– NY Rangers, 2007-08

MOST SHOOTOUT GAMES, ALL-TIME:
42 – NY Rangers
41 – Edmonton
39 – Anaheim

MOST SHOOTOUT WINS, ONE SEASON:
15 – Edmonton, 2007-08, 20GP
12 – Dallas, 2005-06, 13GP
10 – Tampa Bay, 2006-07, 12GP
– Buffalo, 2006-07, 14GP
– Pittsburgh, 2006-07, 16GP
– Minnesota, 2006-07, 17GP
– New Jersey, 2006-07, 18GP

MOST SHOOTOUT WINS, ALL-TIME:
26 – Dallas, 34GP
25 – Edmonton, 41GP
24 – NY Rangers, 42GP

MOST SHOOTOUT HOME WINS, ONE SEASON:
8 – Edmonton, 2007-08, 9GP
7 – Anaheim, 2007-08, 10GP
– Minnesota, 2006-07, 11GP

MOST SHOOTOUT HOME WINS, ALL-TIME:
13 – Atlanta, 19GP
– Edmonton, 19GP
12 – NY Rangers, 17GP
– Nashville, 18GP
– New Jersey, 18GP

MOST SHOOTOUT ROAD WINS, ONE SEASON:
7 – Dallas, 2005-06, 8GP
– Dallas, 2006-07, 9GP
– Edmonton, 2007-08, 10GP

MOST SHOOTOUT ROAD WINS, ALL-TIME:
17 – Dallas, 22GP
12 – Buffalo, 21GP
– Edmonton, 22GP
– NY Rangers, 25GP

MOST SHOOTOUT SHOTS TAKEN, ONE SEASON:
65 – Edmonton, 2007-08, 19GP
62 – Minnesota, 2006-07, 17GP
– New Jersey, 2006-07, 18GP

MOST SHOOTOUT SHOTS TAKEN, ALL-TIME:
159 – NY Rangers, 42GP
140 – Edmonton, 41GP
134 – Anaheim, 39GP

MOST SHOOTOUT GOALS SCORED, ONE SEASON:
27 – Minnesota, 2006-07, 17GP
25 – New Jersey, 2006-07, 18GP
24 – Dallas, 2005-06, 13GP
– Edmonton, 2007-08, 19GP

MOST SHOOTOUT GOALS SCORED, ALL-TIME:
52 – Dallas, 34GP
50 – NY Rangers, 42GP
49 – Edmonton, 41GP

BEST SHOOTOUT SCORING PERCENTAGE, ONE SEASON:
.583 – San Jose, 2006-07, 4GP (7G, 12S)
.571 – Dallas, 2005-06, 13GP (24G, 42S)
.517 – Atlanta, 2006-07, 11GP (15G, 29S)

BEST SHOOTOUT SCORING PERCENTAGE, ALL-TIME:
.431 – New Jersey, 35GP (47G, 109S)
.430 – Dallas, 34GP (52G, 121S)
.421 – Los Angeles, 25GP (40G, 85S)

FEWEST SHOOTOUT GOALS AGAINST, ONE SEASON:
3 – Tampa Bay, 2007-08, 3GP (9SA)
– Los Angeles, 2005-06, 7GP (21SA)
4 – Montreal, 2005-06, 5GP (15SA)

FEWEST SHOOTOUT GOALS AGAINST, ALL-TIME:
18 – Tampa Bay, 25GP (89SA)
24 – San Jose, 21GP (66SA)
25 – Phoenix, 25GP (96SA)

BEST SHOOTOUT WINNING PERCENTAGE, ONE SEASON:
.923 – Dallas, 2005-06, 13GP (12W)
.857 – Los Angeles, 2005-06, 7GP (6W)
.833 – Tampa Bay, 2006-07, 12GP (10W)

BEST SHOOTOUT WINNING PERCENTAGE, ALL-TIME:
.765 – Dallas, 34GP (26W)
.720 – Tampa Bay, 25GP (18W)
.667 – NY Islanders, 33GP (22W)

TEAM PENALTIES

MOST PENALTY MINUTES, ONE SEASON:
2,713 – Buffalo Sabres, 1991-92. 80GP
2,670 – Pittsburgh Penguins, 1988-89. 80GP
2,663 – Chicago Blackhawks, 1991-92. 80GP
2,643 – Calgary Flames, 1991-92. 80GP
2,621 – Philadelphia Flyers, 1980-81. 80GP

MOST PENALTIES, BOTH TEAMS, ONE GAME:
85 – Edmonton Oilers (44), Los Angeles Kings (41), Feb. 28, 1990, at Los Angeles. Edmonton received 26 minors, 7 majors, 6 10-minute misconducts, 4 game misconducts and 1 match penalty; Los Angeles received 26 minors, 9 majors, 3 10-minute misconducts and 3 game misconducts.

MOST PENALTY MINUTES, BOTH TEAMS, ONE GAME:
419 – Ottawa Senators (206), Philadelphia Flyers (213), Mar. 5, 2004, at Philadelphia. Ottawa received 8 minors, 10 majors, 4 10-minute misconducts and 10 game misconducts. Philadelphia received 9 minors, 11 majors, 4 10-minute misconducts and 10 game misconducts.

MOST PENALTIES, ONE TEAM, ONE GAME:
44 – Edmonton Oilers, Feb. 28, 1990, at Los Angeles. Edmonton received 26 minors, 7 majors, 6 10-minute misconducts, 4 game misconducts and 1 match penalty.
42 – Minnesota North Stars, Feb. 26, 1981, at Boston. Minnesota received 18 minors, 13 majors, 4 10-minute misconducts and 7 game misconducts.
– Boston Bruins, Feb. 26, 1981, at Boston vs. Minnesota. Boston received 20 minors, 13 majors, 3 10-minute misconducts and 6 game misconducts.

MOST PENALTY MINUTES, ONE TEAM, ONE GAME:
213 – Philadelphia Flyers, Mar. 5, 2004, at Philadelphia. Philadelphia received 9 minors, 11 majors, 4 10-minute misconducts and 10 game misconducts.

MOST PENALTIES, BOTH TEAMS, ONE PERIOD:
67 – Minnesota North Stars (34), Boston Bruins (33), Feb. 26, 1981, at Boston, first period. Minnesota received 15 minors, 8 majors, 4 10-minute misconducts and 7 game misconducts. Boston had 16 minors, 8 majors, 3 10-minute misconducts and 6 game misconducts.

MOST PENALTY MINUTES, BOTH TEAMS, ONE PERIOD:
409 – Ottawa Senators (200), Philadelphia Flyers (209), Mar. 5, 2004, at Philadelphia, third period. Ottawa received 5 minors, 10 majors, 4 10-minute misconducts and 10 game misconducts. Philadelphia received 7 minors, 11 majors, 4 10-minute misconducts and 10 game misconducts.

MOST PENALTIES, ONE TEAM, ONE PERIOD:
34 – Minnesota North Stars, Feb. 26, 1981, at Boston, first period. Minnesota received 15 minors, 8 majors, 4 10-minute misconducts and 7 game misconducts.

MOST PENALTY MINUTES, ONE TEAM, ONE PERIOD:
209 – Philadelphia Flyers, Mar. 5, 2004, at Philadelphia vs. Ottawa, third period. Philadelphia received 7 minors, 11 majors, 4 10-minute misconducts and 10 game misconducts.
200 – Ottawa Senators, Mar. 5, 2004, at Philadelphia, third period. Ottawa received 5 minors, 10 majors, 4 10-minute misconducts and 10 game misconducts.

NHL Individual Scoring Records – History

Six individual scoring records stand as benchmarks in the history of the game: most goals, single-season and career; most assists, single-season and career; and most points, single-season and career. The evolution of these six records is traced here, beginning with 1917-18, the NHL's first season. New research has resulted in changes to scoring records in the NHL's first nine seasons.

MOST GOALS, ONE SEASON

44 —Joe Malone, Montreal, 1917-18.
Scored goal #44 against Toronto's Harry Holmes on March 2, 1918 and finished the season with 44 goals.
50 —Maurice Richard, Montreal, 1944-45.
Scored goal #45 against Toronto's Frank McCool on February 25, 1945 and finished the season with 50 goals.
50 —Bernie Geoffrion, Montreal, 1960-61.
Scored goal #50 against Toronto's Cesare Maniago on March 16, 1961 and finished the season with 50 goals.
50 —Bobby Hull, Chicago, 1961-62.
Scored goal #50 against NY Rangers' Gump Worsley on March 25, 1962 and finished the season with 50 goals.
54 —Bobby Hull, Chicago, 1965-66.
Scored goal #51 against NY Rangers' Cesare Maniago on March 12, 1966 and finished the season with 54 goals.
58 —Bobby Hull, Chicago, 1968-69.
Scored goal #55 against Boston's Gerry Cheevers on March 20, 1969 and finished the season with 58 goals.
76 —Phil Esposito, Boston, 1970-71.
Scored goal #59 against Los Angeles' Denis DeJordy on March 11, 1971 and finished the season with 76 goals.
92 —Wayne Gretzky, Edmonton, 1981-82.
Scored goal #77 against Buffalo's Don Edwards on February 24, 1982 and finished the season with 92 goals.

MOST ASSISTS, ONE SEASON

10 —Cy Denneny, Ottawa, 1917-18.
—Reg Noble, Toronto, 1917-18.
—Harry Cameron, Toronto, 1917-18.
—Newsy Lalonde, Montreal, 1918-19.
15 —Frank Nighbor, Ottawa, 1919-20.
—Jack Darragh, Ottawa, 1920-21.
17 —Harry Cameron, Toronto, 1921-22.
18 —Dick Irvin, Chicago, 1926-27.
—Howie Morenz, Montreal, 1927-28.
36 —Frank Boucher, NY Rangers, 1929-30.
37 —Joe Primeau, Toronto, 1931-32.
45 —Bill Cowley, Boston, 1940-41.
—Bill Cowley, Boston, 1942-43.
49 —Clint Smith, Chicago, 1943-44.
54 —Elmer Lach, Montreal, 1944-45.
55 —Ted Lindsay, Detroit, 1949-50.
56 —Bert Olmstead, Montreal, 1955-56.
58 —Jean Beliveau, Montreal, 1960-61.
—Andy Bathgate, NY Rangers/Toronto, 1963-64.
59 —Stan Mikita, Chicago, 1964-65.
62 —Stan Mikita, Chicago, 1966-67.
77 —Phil Esposito, Boston, 1968-69.
87 —Bobby Orr, Boston, 1969-70.
102 —Bobby Orr, Boston, 1970-71.
109 —Wayne Gretzky, Edmonton, 1980-81.
120 —Wayne Gretzky, Edmonton, 1981-82.
125 —Wayne Gretzky, Edmonton, 1982-83.
135 —Wayne Gretzky, Edmonton, 1984-85.
163 —Wayne Gretzky, Edmonton, 1985-86.

MOST POINTS, ONE SEASON

48 —Joe Malone, Montreal, 1917-18.
49 —Joe Malone, Montreal, 1919-20.
51 —Howie Morenz, Montreal, 1927-28.
73 —Cooney Weiland, Boston, 1929-30.
—Doug Bentley, Chicago, 1942-43.
82 —Herb Cain, Boston, 1943-44.
86 —Gordie Howe, Detroit, 1950-51.
95 —Gordie Howe, Detroit, 1952-53.
96 —Dickie Moore, Montreal, 1958-59.
97 —Bobby Hull, Chicago, 1965-66.
—Stan Mikita, Chicago, 1966-67.
126 —Phil Esposito, Boston, 1968-69.
152 —Phil Esposito, Boston, 1970-71.
164 —Wayne Gretzky, Edmonton, 1980-81.
212 —Wayne Gretzky, Edmonton, 1981-82.
215 —Wayne Gretzky, Edmonton, 1985-86.

MOST REGULAR-SEASON GOALS, CAREER

44 —Joe Malone, Montreal.
Malone led the NHL in goals in the league's first season with 44 goals in 20 games in 1917-18.
54 —Cy Denneny, Ottawa.
Denneny passed Malone during the 1918-19 season, and led the NHL in goals with 54 after two seasons.
143 —Joe Malone, Montreal, Quebec Bulldogs, Hamilton.
Malone passed Denneny during the 1919-20 season and finished his career with 143 goals.
248 —Cy Denneny, Ottawa, Boston.
Denneny passed Malone with goal #144 during the 1922-23 season and finished his career with 248 goals.
271 —Howie Morenz, Montreal, Chicago, NY Rangers.
Morenz passed Denneny with goal #249 during the 1933-34 season and finished his career with 271 goals.
324 —Nels Stewart, Montreal Maroons, Boston, NY Americans.
Stewart passed Morenz with goal #272 during the 1936-37 season and finished his career with 324 goals.
544 —Maurice Richard, Montreal.
Richard passed Stewart with goal #325 on Nov. 8, 1952 and finished his career with 544 goals.
801 —Gordie Howe, Detroit, Hartford.
Howe passed Richard with goal #545 on Nov. 10, 1963 and finished his career with 801 goals.
894 —Wayne Gretzky, Edmonton, Los Angeles, St. Louis, NY Rangers.
Gretzky passed Howe with goal #802 on March 23, 1994 and finished his career with 894 goals.

Before he became one of the greatest coaches in NHL history, Dick Irvin had already been one of the game's top players. A high-scoring star as an amateur in Winnipeg in the 1910s and then in the pro leagues out west in the 1920s, Irvin entered the NHL in 1926-27 and finished second in scoring with 18 goals and a league record 18 assists that year. Like Irvin, Joe Malone (right) was a scoring star long before reaching the NHL. He twice topped 40 goals during 20-game seasons in the National Hockey Association before scoring 44 in 20 games during the NHL's inaugural 1917-18 campaign. Malone went on to become the first NHL player to top 100 career points, totaling 143 goals and 175 points in just 126 career NHL games.

MOST REGULAR-SEASON ASSISTS, CAREER

(minimum 100 assists)

100 —Frank Boucher, Ottawa, NY Rangers.
In 1930-31, Boucher became the first NHL player to reach the 100-assist milestone.

263 —Frank Boucher, Ottawa, NY Rangers.
Boucher retired as the NHL's career assist leader in 1938 with 253. He returned to the NHL in 1943-44 and remained the NHL's career assist leader until he was overtaken by Bill Cowley in 1943-44. He finished his career with 263 assists.

353 —Bill Cowley, St. Louis Eagles, Boston.
Cowley passed Boucher with assist #264 in 1943-44. He retired as the NHL's career assist leader in 1947 with 353.

408 —Elmer Lach, Montreal.
Lach passed Cowley with assist #354 in 1951-52. He retired as the NHL's career assist leader in 1954 with 408.

1,049 —Gordie Howe, Detroit, Hartford.
Howe passed Lach with assist #409 in 1957-58. He retired as the NHL's career assist leader in 1980 with 1,049.

1,963 —Wayne Gretzky, Edmonton, Los Angeles, St. Louis, NY Rangers.
Gretzky passed Howe with assist #1,050 in 1988-89. He retired as the NHL's current career assist leader with 1,963.

MOST REGULAR-SEASON POINTS, CAREER

(minimum 100 points)

100 —Joe Malone, Montreal, Quebec Bulldogs, Hamilton.
In 1919-20, Malone became the first player in NHL history to record 100 points.

200 —Cy Denneny, Ottawa.
In 1923-24, Denneny became the first player in NHL history to record 200 points.

300 —Cy Denneny, Ottawa.
In 1926-27, Denneny became the first player in NHL history to record 300 points.

333 —Cy Denneny, Ottawa, Boston.
Denneny retired as the NHL's career point-scoring leader in 1929 with 333 points.

472 —Howie Morenz, Montreal, Chicago, NY Rangers.
Morenz passed Cy Denneny with point #334 in 1931-32. At the time his career ended in 1937, he was the NHL's career point- scoring leader with 472 points.

515 —Nels Stewart, Montreal Maroons, Boston, NY Americans.
Stewart passed Morenz with point #473 in 1938-39. He retired as the NHL's career point-scoring leader in 1940 with 515 points.

528 —Syd Howe, Ottawa, Philadelphia Quakers, Toronto, St. Louis Eagles, Detroit.
Howe passed Nels Stewart with point #516 on March 8, 1945. He retired as the NHL's career point-scoring leader in 1946 with 528 points.

548 —Bill Cowley, St. Louis Eagles, Boston.
Cowley passed Syd Howe with point #529 on Feb. 12, 1947. He retired as the NHL's career point-scoring leader in 1947 with 548 points.

610 —Elmer Lach, Montreal.
Lach passed Bill Cowley with point #549 on Feb. 23, 1952. He remained the NHL's career point-scoring leader until he was overtaken by Maurice Richard in 1953-54. He finished his career with 623 points.

946 —Maurice Richard, Montreal.
Richard passed teammate Elmer Lach with point #611 on Dec. 12, 1953. He remained the NHL's career point-scoring leader until he was overtaken by Gordie Howe in 1959-60. He finished his career with 965 points.

1,850 —Gordie Howe, Detroit, Hartford.
Howe passed Richard with point #947 on Jan. 16, 1960. He retired as the NHL's career point-scoring leader in 1980 with 1,850 points.

2,857 —Wayne Gretzky, Edmonton, Los Angeles, St. Louis, NY Rangers.
Gretzky passed Howe with point #1,851 on Oct. 15, 1989. He retired as the NHL's current career points leader with 2,857.

Individual Records

Regular Season

SEASONS

MOST SEASONS:
26 – Gordie Howe, Detroit, 1946-47 – 1970-71; Hartford, 1979-80.
25 – Mark Messier, Edmonton, NY Rangers, Vancouver, 1979-80 – 2003-04.
24 – Alex Delvecchio, Detroit, 1950-51 – 1973-74.
– Tim Horton, Toronto, NY Rangers, Pittsburgh, Buffalo, 1949-50, 1951-52 – 1973-74.
– Chris Chelios, Montreal, Chicago, Detroit, 1983-84 – 2003-04, 2005-06 – 2007-08.
23 – John Bucyk, Detroit, Boston, 1955-56 – 1977-78.
– Ron Francis, Hartford, Pittsburgh, Carolina, Toronto, 1981-82 – 2003-04.
– Al MacInnis, Calgary, St. Louis, 1981-82 – 2003-04.
– Dave Andreychuk, Buffalo, Toronto, New Jersey, Boston, Colorado, Tampa Bay, 1982-83 – 2003-04, 2005-06.

GAMES

MOST GAMES:
1,767 – Gordie Howe, Detroit, 1946-47 – 1970-71; Hartford, 1979-80.
1,756 – Mark Messier, Edmonton, NY Rangers, Vancouver, 1979-80 – 2003-04.
1,731 – Ron Francis, Hartford, Pittsburgh, Carolina, Toronto, 1981-82 – 2003-04.
1,639 – Dave Andreychuk, Buffalo, Toronto, New Jersey, Boston, Colorado, Tampa Bay, 1982-83 – 2003-04, 2005-06.
1,635 – Scott Stevens, Washington, St. Louis, New Jersey, 1982-83 – 2003-04.
1,616 – Chris Chelios, Montreal, Chicago, Detroit, 1983-84 – 2003-04, 2005-06 – 2007-08.

MOST GAMES, INCLUDING PLAYOFFS:
1,992 – Mark Messier, Edmonton, NY Rangers, Vancouver, 1,756 regular-season games, 236 playoff games.
1,924 – Gordie Howe, Detroit, Hartford, 1,767 regular-season games, 157 playoff games.
1,902 – Ron Francis, Hartford, Pittsburgh, Carolina, Toronto, 1,731 regular-season games, 171 playoff games.
1,876 – Chris Chelios, Montreal, Chicago, Detroit, 1,616 regular-season games, 260 playoff games.
1,868 – Scott Stevens, Washington, St. Louis, New Jersey, 1,635 regular-season games, 233 playoff games.

MOST CONSECUTIVE GAMES:
964 – Doug Jarvis, Montreal, Washington, Hartford, Oct. 8, 1975 – Oct. 10, 1987.
914 – Garry Unger, Toronto, Detroit, St. Louis, Atlanta, Feb. 24, 1968 – Dec. 21, 1979.
884 – Steve Larmer, Chicago, Oct. 6, 1982 – Apr. 15, 1993.
776 – Craig Ramsay, Buffalo, Mar. 27, 1973 – Feb. 10, 1983.
630 – Andy Hebenton, NY Rangers, Boston, Oct. 7, 1955 – Mar. 22, 1964.

GOALS

MOST GOALS:
894 – Wayne Gretzky, Edmonton, Los Angeles, St. Louis, NY Rangers, in 20 seasons. 1,487GP
801 – Gordie Howe, Detroit, Hartford, in 26 seasons. 1,767GP
741 – Brett Hull, Calgary, St. Louis, Dallas, Detroit, Phoenix, in 19 seasons. 1,269GP
731 – Marcel Dionne, Detroit, Los Angeles, NY Rangers, in 18 seasons. 1,348GP
717 – Phil Esposito, Chicago, Boston, NY Rangers, in 18 seasons. 1,282GP

MOST GOALS, INCLUDING PLAYOFFS:
1,016 – Wayne Gretzky, Edmonton, Los Angeles, St. Louis, NY Rangers, 894G in 1,487 regular-season games, 122G in 208 playoff games.
869 – Gordie Howe, Detroit, Hartford, 801G in 1,767 regular-season games, 68G in 157 playoff games.
844 – Brett Hull, Calgary, St. Louis, Dallas, Detroit, Phoenix, 741G in 1,269 regular-season games, 103G in 202 playoff games.
803 – Mark Messier, Edmonton, NY Rangers, Vancouver, 694G in 1,756 regular-season games, 109G in 236 playoff games.
778 – Phil Esposito, Chicago, Boston, NY Rangers, 717G in 1,282 regular-season games, 61G in 130 playoff games.

MOST GOALS, ONE SEASON:
92 – Wayne Gretzky, Edmonton, 1981-82. 80GP – 80 game schedule.
87 – Wayne Gretzky, Edmonton, 1983-84. 74GP – 80 game schedule.
86 – Brett Hull, St. Louis, 1990-91. 78GP – 80 game schedule.
85 – Mario Lemieux, Pittsburgh, 1988-89. 76GP – 80 game schedule.
76 – Phil Esposito, Boston, 1970-71. 78GP – 78 game schedule.
– Alexander Mogilny, Buffalo, 1992-93. 77GP – 84 game schedule.
– Teemu Selanne, Winnipeg, 1992-93. 84GP – 84 game schedule.
73 – Wayne Gretzky, Edmonton, 1984-85. 80GP – 80 game schedule.
72 – Brett Hull, St. Louis, 1989-90. 80GP – 80 game schedule.
71 – Wayne Gretzky, Edmonton, 1982-83. 80GP – 80 game schedule.
– Jari Kurri, Edmonton, 1984-85. 73GP – 80 game schedule.
70 – Mario Lemieux, Pittsburgh, 1987-88. 77GP – 80 game schedule.
– Bernie Nicholls, Los Angeles, 1988-89. 79GP – 80 game schedule.
– Brett Hull, St. Louis, 1991-92. 73GP – 80 game schedule.

MOST GOALS, ONE SEASON, INCLUDING PLAYOFFS:
100 – Wayne Gretzky, Edmonton, 1983-84, 87G in 74 regular-season games, 13G in 19 playoff games.
97 – Wayne Gretzky, Edmonton, 1981-82, 92G in 80 regular-season games, 5G in 5 playoff games.
– Mario Lemieux, Pittsburgh, 1988-89, 85G in 76 regular-season games, 12G in 11 playoff games.
– Brett Hull, St. Louis, 1990-91, 86G in 78 regular-season games, 11G in 13 playoff games.
90 – Wayne Gretzky, Edmonton, 1984-85, 73G in 80 regular-season games, 17G in 18 playoff games.
– Jari Kurri, Edmonton, 1984-85, 71G in 80 regular-season games, 19G in 18 playoff games.
85 – Mike Bossy, NY Islanders, 1980-81, 68G in 79 regular-season games, 17G in 18 playoff games.
– Brett Hull, St. Louis, 1989-90, 72G in 80 regular-season games, 13G in 12 playoff games.
83 – Wayne Gretzky, Edmonton, 1982-83, 71G in 73 regular-season games, 12G in 16 playoff games.
– Alexander Mogilny, Buffalo, 1992-93, 76G in 77 regular-season games, 7G in 7 playoff games.

MOST GOALS, 50 GAMES FROM START OF SEASON:
61 – Wayne Gretzky, Edmonton, 1981-82. Oct. 7, 1981 – Jan. 22, 1982. (80-game schedule)
– Wayne Gretzky, Edmonton, 1983-84. Oct. 5, 1983 – Jan. 25, 1984. (80-game schedule)
54 – Mario Lemieux, Pittsburgh, 1988-89. Oct. 7, 1988 – Jan. 31, 1989. (80-game schedule)
53 – Wayne Gretzky, Edmonton, 1984-85. Oct. 11, 1984 – Jan. 28, 1985. (80-game schedule)
52 – Brett Hull, St. Louis, 1990-91. Oct. 4, 1990 – Jan. 26, 1991. (80-game schedule)
50 – Maurice Richard, Montreal, 1944-45. Oct. 28, 1944 – Mar. 18, 1945. (50-game schedule)
– Mike Bossy, NY Islanders, 1980-81. Oct. 11, 1980 – Jan. 24, 1981. (80-game schedule)
– Brett Hull, St. Louis, 1991-92. Oct. 5, 1991 – Jan. 28, 1992. (80-game schedule)

MOST GOALS, ONE GAME:
7 – Joe Malone, Quebec, Jan. 31, 1920, at Quebec. Quebec 10, Toronto 6.
6 – Newsy Lalonde, Montreal, Jan. 10, 1920, at Montreal. Montreal 14, Toronto 7.
– Joe Malone, Quebec, Mar. 10, 1920, at Quebec. Quebec 10, Ottawa 4.
– Corb Denneny, Toronto, Jan. 26, 1921, at Toronto. Toronto 10, Hamilton 3.
– Cy Denneny, Ottawa, Mar. 7, 1921, at Ottawa. Ottawa 12, Hamilton 5.
– Syd Howe, Detroit, Feb. 3, 1944, at Detroit. Detroit 12, NY Rangers 2.
– Red Berenson, St. Louis, Nov. 7, 1968, at Philadelphia. St. Louis 8, Philadelphia 0.
– Darryl Sittler, Toronto, Feb. 7, 1976, at Toronto. Toronto 11, Boston 4.

Early era hockey star Newsy Lalonde was the first player in NHL history to score six goals in a game, accomplishing the feat exactly three weeks before Joe Malone scored a record seven in one game.

Maurice Richard, Elmer Lach and Toe Blake formed the Montreal Canadiens' famed Punch Line of the mid 1940s. Lach set what was then an NHL record with 54 assists in 1944-45 when Richard scored 50 goals in 50 games. Lach, Richard and Blake finished 1-2-3 in the scoring race that season.

MOST GOALS, ONE ROAD GAME:

6 – Red Berenson, St. Louis, Nov. 7, 1968, at Philadelphia. St. Louis 8, Philadelphia 0.
5 – Joe Malone, Montreal, Dec. 19, 1917, at Ottawa. Montreal 7, Ottawa 4.
– Red Green, Hamilton, Dec. 5, 1924, at Toronto. Hamilton 10, Toronto 3.
– Babe Dye, Toronto, Dec. 22, 1924, at Boston. Toronto 10, Boston 1.
– Punch Broadbent, Mtl. Maroons, Jan. 7, 1925, at Hamilton. Mtl. Maroons 6, Hamilton 2.
– Don Murdoch, NY Rangers, Oct. 12, 1976, at Minnesota. NY Rangers 10, Minnesota 4.
– Tim Young, Minnesota, Jan. 15, 1979, at NY Rangers. Minnesota 8, NY Rangers 1.
– Willy Lindstrom, Winnipeg, Mar. 2, 1982, at Philadelphia. Winnipeg 7, Philadelphia 6.
– Bengt Gustafsson, Washington, Jan. 8, 1984, at Philadelphia. Washington 7, Philadelphia 1.
– Wayne Gretzky, Edmonton, Dec. 15, 1984, at St. Louis. Edmonton 8, St. Louis 2.
– Dave Andreychuk, Buffalo, Feb. 6, 1986, at Boston. Buffalo 8, Boston 6.
– Mats Sundin, Quebec, Mar. 5, 1992, at Hartford. Quebec 10, Hartford 4.
– Mario Lemieux, Pittsburgh, Apr. 9, 1993, at NY Rangers. Pittsburgh 10, NY Rangers 4.
– Mike Ricci, Quebec, Feb. 17, 1994, at San Jose. Quebec 8, San Jose 2.
– Alex Zhamnov, Winnipeg, Apr. 1, 1995, at Los Angeles. Winnipeg 7, Los Angeles 7.

MOST GOALS, ONE PERIOD:

4 – Busher Jackson, Toronto, Nov. 20, 1934, at St. Louis, third period. Toronto 5, St. Louis 2.
– Max Bentley, Chicago, Jan. 28, 1943, at Chicago, third period. Chicago 10, NY Rangers 1.
– Clint Smith, Chicago, Mar. 4, 1945, at Chicago, third period. Chicago 6, Montreal 4.
– Red Berenson, St. Louis, Nov. 7, 1968, at Philadelphia, second period. St. Louis 8, Philadelphia 0.
– Wayne Gretzky, Edmonton, Feb. 18, 1981, at Edmonton, third period. Edmonton 9, St. Louis 2.
– Grant Mulvey, Chicago, Feb. 3, 1982, at Chicago, first period. Chicago 9, St. Louis 5.
– Bryan Trottier, NY Islanders, Feb. 13, 1982, at NY Islanders, second period. NY Islanders 8, Philadelphia 2.
– Al Secord, Chicago, Jan. 7, 1987, at Chicago, second period. Chicago 6, Toronto 4.
– Joe Nieuwendyk, Calgary, Jan. 11, 1989, at Calgary, second period. Calgary 8, Winnipeg 3.
– Peter Bondra, Washington, Feb. 5, 1994, at Washington, first period. Washington 6, Tampa Bay 3.
– Mario Lemieux, Pittsburgh, Jan. 26, 1997, at Montreal, third period. Pittsburgh 5, Montreal 2.

ASSISTS

MOST ASSISTS:

1,963 – Wayne Gretzky, Edmonton, Los Angeles, St. Louis, NY Rangers, in 20 seasons. 1,487GP
1,249 – Ron Francis, Hartford, Pittsburgh, Carolina, Toronto, in 23 seasons. 1,731GP
1,193 – Mark Messier, Edmonton, NY Rangers, Vancouver, in 25 seasons. 1,756GP
1,169 – Raymond Bourque, Boston, Colorado, in 22 seasons. 1,612GP
1,135 – Paul Coffey, Edmonton, Pittsburgh, Los Angeles, Detroit, Hartford, Philadelphia, Chicago, Carolina, Boston, in 21 seasons. 1,409GP

MOST ASSISTS, INCLUDING PLAYOFFS:

2,223 – Wayne Gretzky, Edmonton, Los Angeles, St. Louis, NY Rangers, 1,963A in 1,487 regular-season games, 260A in 208 playoff games.
1,379 – Mark Messier, Edmonton, NY Rangers, Vancouver, 1,193A in 1,756 regular-season games, 186A in 236 playoff games.
1,346 – Ron Francis, Hartford, Pittsburgh, Carolina, Toronto, 1,249A in 1,731 regular-season games, 97A in 171 playoff games.
1,308 – Raymond Bourque, Boston, Colorado, 1,169A in 1,612 regular-season games, 139A in 214 playoff games.
1,272 – Paul Coffey, Edmonton, Pittsburgh, Los Angeles, Detroit, Hartford, Philadelphia, Chicago, Carolina, Boston, 1,135A in 1,409 regular-season games, 137A in 194 playoff games.

MOST ASSISTS, ONE SEASON:

163 – Wayne Gretzky, Edmonton, 1985-86. 80GP – 80 game schedule.
135 – Wayne Gretzky, Edmonton, 1984-85. 80GP – 80 game schedule.
125 – Wayne Gretzky, Edmonton, 1982-83. 80GP – 80 game schedule.
122 – Wayne Gretzky, Los Angeles, 1990-91. 78GP – 80 game schedule.
121 – Wayne Gretzky, Edmonton, 1986-87. 79GP – 80 game schedule.
120 – Wayne Gretzky, Edmonton, 1981-82. 80GP – 80 game schedule.
118 – Wayne Gretzky, Edmonton, 1983-84. 74GP – 80 game schedule.
114 – Mario Lemieux, Pittsburgh, 1988-89. 76GP – 80 game schedule.
– Wayne Gretzky, Los Angeles, 1988-89. 78GP – 80 game schedule.
109 – Wayne Gretzky, Edmonton, 1980-81. 80GP – 80 game schedule.
– Wayne Gretzky, Edmonton, 1987-88. 64GP – 80 game schedule.
102 – Bobby Orr, Boston, 1970-71. 78GP – 78 game schedule.
– Wayne Gretzky, Los Angeles, 1989-90. 73GP – 80 game schedule.

MOST ASSISTS, ONE SEASON, INCLUDING PLAYOFFS:
174 – Wayne Gretzky, Edmonton, 1985-86,
163A in 80 regular-season games, 11A in 10 playoff games.
165 – Wayne Gretzky, Edmonton, 1984-85,
135A in 80 regular-season games, 30A in 18 playoff games.
151 – Wayne Gretzky, Edmonton, 1982-83,
125A in 80 regular-season games, 26A in 16 playoff games.
150 – Wayne Gretzky, Edmonton, 1986-87,
121A in 79 regular-season games, 29A in 21 playoff games.
140 – Wayne Gretzky, Edmonton, 1983-84,
118A in 74 regular-season games, 22A in 19 playoff games.
– Wayne Gretzky, Edmonton, 1987-88,
109A in 64 regular-season games, 31A in 19 playoff games.
133 – Wayne Gretzky, Los Angeles, 1990-91,
122A in 78 regular-season games, 11A in 12 playoff games.
131 – Wayne Gretzky, Los Angeles, 1988-89,
114A in 78 regular-season games, 17A in 11 playoff games.
127 – Wayne Gretzky, Edmonton, 1981-82,
120A in 80 regular-season games, 7A in 5 playoff games.
123 – Wayne Gretzky, Edmonton, 1980-81,
109A in 80 regular-season games, 14A in 9 playoff games.
121 – Mario Lemieux, Pittsburgh, 1988-89,
114A in 76 regular-season games, 7A in 11 playoff games.

MOST ASSISTS, ONE GAME:
7 – Billy Taylor, Detroit, Mar. 16, 1947, at Chicago. Detroit 10, Chicago 6.
– Wayne Gretzky, Edmonton, Feb. 15, 1980, at Edmonton.
Edmonton 8, Washington 2.
– Wayne Gretzky, Edmonton, Dec. 11, 1985, at Chicago.
Edmonton 12, Chicago 9.
– Wayne Gretzky, Edmonton, Feb. 14, 1986, at Edmonton.
Edmonton 8, Quebec 2.
6 – Six assists have been recorded in one game on 24 occasions since Elmer Lach of Montreal first accomplished the feat vs. Boston on Feb. 6, 1943. The most recent player is Eric Lindros of Philadelphia on Feb. 26, 1997 at Ottawa.

MOST ASSISTS, ONE ROAD GAME:
7 – Billy Taylor, Detroit, Mar. 16, 1947, at Chicago. Detroit 10, Chicago 6.
– Wayne Gretzky, Edmonton, Dec. 11, 1985, at Chicago.
Edmonton 12, Chicago 9.
6 – Bobby Orr, Boston, Jan. 1, 1973, at Vancouver. Boston 8, Vancouver 2.
– Patrik Sundstrom, Vancouver, Feb. 29, 1984, at Pittsburgh.
Vancouver 9, Pittsburgh 5.
– Mario Lemieux, Pittsburgh, Dec. 5, 1992, at San Jose.
Pittsburgh 9, San Jose 4.
– Eric Lindros, Philadelphia, Feb. 26, 1997, at Ottawa.
Philadelphia 8, Ottawa 5.

MOST ASSISTS, ONE PERIOD:
5 – Dale Hawerchuk, Winnipeg, Mar. 6, 1984, at Los Angeles, second period. Winnipeg 7, Los Angeles 3.
4 – Four assists have been recorded in one period on 67 occasions since Mickey Roach of Hamilton first accomplished the feat vs. Toronto on Feb. 23, 1921. The most recent player is Joe Thornton of San Jose on Apr. 1, 2007 vs. Los Angeles.

POINTS

MOST POINTS:
2,857 – Wayne Gretzky, Edmonton, Los Angeles, St. Louis, NY Rangers, in 20 seasons. 1,487GP (894G-1,963A)
1,887 – Mark Messier, Edmonton, NY Rangers, Vancouver, in 25 seasons. 1,756GP (694G-1,193A)
1,850 – Gordie Howe, Detroit, Hartford, in 26 seasons. 1,767GP (801G-1,049A)
1,798 – Ron Francis, Hartford, Pittsburgh, Carolina, Toronto, in 23 seasons. 1,731GP (549G-1,249A)
1,771 – Marcel Dionne, Detroit, Los Angeles, NY Rangers, in 18 seasons. 1,348GP (731G-1,040A)

MOST POINTS, INCLUDING PLAYOFFS:
3,239 – Wayne Gretzky, Edmonton, Los Angeles, St. Louis, NY Rangers,
2,857PTS in 1,487 regular-season games, 382PTS in 208 playoff games.
2,182 – Mark Messier, Edmonton, NY Rangers, Vancouver,
1,887PTS in 1,756 regular-season games, 295PTS in 236 playoff games.
2,010 – Gordie Howe, Detroit, Hartford,
1,850PTS in 1,767 regular-season games, 160PTS in 157 playoff games.
1,941 – Ron Francis, Hartford, Pittsburgh, Carolina, Toronto,
1,798PTS in 1,731 regular-season games, 143PTS in 171 playoff games
1,940 – Steve Yzerman, Detroit,
1,755PTS in 1,514 regular-season games, 185PTS in 196 playoff games.

MOST POINTS, ONE SEASON:
215 – Wayne Gretzky, Edmonton, 1985-86. 80GP – 80 game schedule.
212 – Wayne Gretzky, Edmonton, 1981-82. 80GP – 80 game schedule.
208 – Wayne Gretzky, Edmonton, 1984-85. 80GP – 80 game schedule.
205 – Wayne Gretzky, Edmonton, 1983-84. 74GP – 80 game schedule.
199 – Mario Lemieux, Pittsburgh, 1988-89. 76GP – 80 game schedule.
196 – Wayne Gretzky, Edmonton, 1982-83. 80GP – 80 game schedule.
183 – Wayne Gretzky, Edmonton, 1986-87. 79GP – 80 game schedule.
168 – Mario Lemieux, Pittsburgh, 1987-88, 77GP – 80 game schedule.
– Wayne Gretzky, Los Angeles, 1988-89. 78GP – 80 game schedule.
164 – Wayne Gretzky, Edmonton, 1980-81. 80GP – 80 game schedule.
163 – Wayne Gretzky, Los Angeles, 1990-91. 78GP – 80 game schedule.
161 – Mario Lemieux, Pittsburgh, 1995-96. 70GP – 82 game schedule.
160 – Mario Lemieux, Pittsburgh, 1992-93. 60GP – 84 game schedule.

MOST POINTS, ONE SEASON, INCLUDING PLAYOFFS:
255 – Wayne Gretzky, Edmonton, 1984-85,
208PTS in 80 regular-season games, 47PTS in 18 playoff games.
240 – Wayne Gretzky, Edmonton, 1983-84,
205PTS in 74 regular-season games, 35PTS in 19 playoff games.
234 – Wayne Gretzky, Edmonton, 1982-83,
196PTS in 80 regular-season games, 38PTS in 16 playoff games.
– Wayne Gretzky, Edmonton, 1985-86,
215PTS in 80 regular-season games, 19PTS in 10 playoff games.
224 – Wayne Gretzky, Edmonton, 1981-82,
212PTS in 80 regular-season games, 12PTS in 5 playoff games.
218 – Mario Lemieux, Pittsburgh, 1988-89,
199PTS in 76 regular-season games, 19PTS in 11 playoff games.
217 – Wayne Gretzky, Edmonton, 1986-87,
183PTS in 79 regular-season games, 34PTS in 21 playoff games.
192 – Wayne Gretzky, Edmonton, 1987-88,
149PTS in 64 regular-season games, 43PTS in 19 playoff games.
190 – Wayne Gretzky, Los Angeles, 1988-89,
168PTS in 78 regular-season games, 22PTS in 11 playoff games.
188 – Mario Lemieux, Pittsburgh, 1995-96,
161PTS in 70 regular-season games, 27PTS in 18 playoff games.
185 – Wayne Gretzky, Edmonton, 1980-81,
164PTS in 80 regular-season games, 21PTS in 9 playoff games.

MOST POINTS, ONE GAME:
10 – Darryl Sittler, Toronto, Feb. 7, 1976, at Toronto, 6G-4A.
Toronto 11, Boston 4.
8 – Maurice Richard, Montreal, Dec. 28, 1944, at Montreal, 5G-3A.
Montreal 9, Detroit 1.
– Bert Olmstead, Montreal, Jan. 9, 1954, at Montreal, 4G-4A.
Montreal 12, Chicago 1.
– Tom Bladon, Philadelphia, Dec. 11, 1977, at Philadelphia, 4G-4A.
Philadelphia 11, Cleveland 1.
– Bryan Trottier, NY Islanders, Dec. 23, 1978, at NY Islanders, 5G-3A.
NY Islanders 9, NY Rangers 4.
– Peter Stastny, Quebec, Feb. 22, 1981, at Washington, 4G-4A.
Quebec 11, Washington 7.
– Anton Stastny, Quebec, Feb. 22, 1981, at Washington, 3G-5A.
Quebec 11, Washington 7.
– Wayne Gretzky, Edmonton, Nov. 19, 1983, at Edmonton, 3G-5A.
Edmonton 13, New Jersey 4.
– Wayne Gretzky, Edmonton, Jan. 4, 1984, at Edmonton, 4G-4A.
Edmonton 12, Minnesota 8.
– Paul Coffey, Edmonton, Mar. 14, 1986, at Edmonton, 2G-6A.
Edmonton 12, Detroit 3.
– Mario Lemieux, Pittsburgh, Oct. 15, 1988, at Pittsburgh, 2G-6A.
Pittsburgh 9, St. Louis 2.
– Bernie Nicholls, Los Angeles, Dec. 1, 1988, at Los Angeles, 2G-6A.
Los Angeles 9, Toronto 3.
– Mario Lemieux, Pittsburgh, Dec. 31, 1988, at Pittsburgh, 5G-3A.
Pittsburgh 8, New Jersey 6.

MOST POINTS, ONE ROAD GAME:
8 – Peter Stastny, Quebec, Feb. 22, 1981, at Washington. 4G-4A.
Quebec 11, Washington 7.
– Anton Stastny, Quebec, Feb. 22, 1981, at Washington. 3G-5A.
Quebec 11, Washington 7.
7 – Red Green, Hamilton, Dec. 5, 1924, at Toronto. 5G-2A.
Hamilton 10, Toronto 3.
– Billy Taylor, Detroit, Mar. 16, 1947, at Chicago. 7A. Detroit 10, Chicago 6.
– Red Berenson, St. Louis, Nov. 7, 1968, at Philadelphia. 6G-1A.
St. Louis 8, Philadelphia 0.
– Gilbert Perreault, Buffalo, Feb. 1, 1976, at California. 2G-5A.
Buffalo 9, California 5.
– Peter Stastny, Quebec, Apr. 1, 1982, at Boston. 3G-4A. Quebec 8, Boston 5.
– Wayne Gretzky, Edmonton, Nov. 6, 1983, at Winnipeg. 4G-3A.
Edmonton 8, Winnipeg 5.
– Patrik Sundstrom, Vancouver, Feb. 29, 1984, at Pittsburgh. 1G-6A.
Vancouver 9, Pittsburgh 5.
– Wayne Gretzky, Edmonton, Dec. 11, 1985, at Chicago. 7A.
Edmonton 12, Chicago 9.
– Cam Neely, Boston, Oct. 16, 1988, at Chicago. 3G-4A.
Boston 10, Chicago 3.
– Mario Lemieux, Pittsburgh, Jan. 21, 1989, at Edmonton. 2G-5A.
Pittsburgh 7, Edmonton 4.
– Dino Ciccarelli, Washington, Mar. 18, 1989, at Hartford. 4G-3A.
Washington 8, Hartford 2.
– Mats Sundin, Quebec, Mar. 5, 1992, at Hartford. 5G-2A.
Quebec 10, Hartford 4.
– Mario Lemieux, Pittsburgh, Dec. 5, 1992, at San Jose. 1G-6A.
Pittsburgh 9, San Jose 4.
– Eric Lindros, Philadelphia, Feb. 26, 1997, at Ottawa. 1G-6A.
Philadelphia 8, Ottawa 5.
– Daniel Alfredsson, Ottawa, Jan. 24, 2008, at Tampa Bay. 3G-4A.
Ottawa 8, Tampa Bay 4.

With 10 shorthand goals in 1988-89, Dirk Graham put himself on the list with future Hall of Famers Mario Lemieux, Wayne Gretzky and Marcel Dionne for the most shorthand goals in a single season.

MOST POINTS, ONE PERIOD:
6 – Bryan Trottier, NY Islanders, Dec. 23, 1978, at NY Islanders, second period. 3G-3A. NY Islanders 9, NY Rangers 4.
5 – Bill Cook, NY Rangers, Mar. 12, 1933, at NY Americans, third period. 3G-2A. NY Rangers 8, NY Americans 2.
– Les Cunningham, Chicago, Jan. 28, 1940, at Chicago, third period. 2G-3A. Chicago 8, Montreal 1.
– Max Bentley, Chicago, Jan. 28, 1943, at Chicago, third period. 4G-1A. Chicago 10, NY Rangers 1.
– Leo Labine, Boston, Nov. 28, 1954, at Boston, second period. 3G-2A. Boston 6, Detroit 2.
– Darryl Sittler, Toronto, Feb. 7, 1976, at Toronto, second period. 3G-2A. Toronto 11, Boston 4.
– Grant Mulvey, Chicago, Feb. 3, 1982, at Chicago, first period. 4G-1A. Chicago 9, St. Louis 5.
– Dale Hawerchuk, Winnipeg, Mar. 6, 1984, at Los Angeles, second period. 5A. Winnipeg 7, Los Angeles 3.
– Jari Kurri, Edmonton, Oct. 26, 1984, at Edmonton, second period. 2G-3A. Edmonton 8, Los Angeles 2.
– Pat Elynuik, Winnipeg, Jan. 20, 1989, at Winnipeg, second period. 2G-3A. Winnipeg 7, Pittsburgh 3.
– Ray Ferraro, Hartford, Dec. 9, 1989, at Hartford, first period. 3G-2A. Hartford 7, New Jersey 3.
– Stephane Richer, Montreal, Feb. 14, 1990, at Montreal, first period. 2G-3A. Montreal 10, Vancouver 1.
– Cliff Ronning, Vancouver, Apr. 15, 1993, at Los Angeles, third period. 3G-2A. Vancouver 8, Los Angeles 6.
– Peter Forsberg, Colorado, Mar. 3, 1999, at Florida, third period. 2G-3A. Colorado 7, Florida 5.

POWER-PLAY AND SHORTHAND GOALS

MOST POWER-PLAY GOALS, CAREER:
274 – Dave Andreychuk, Buffalo, Toronto, New Jersey, Boston, Colorado, Tampa Bay, in 23 seasons. 1,639GP
265 – Brett Hull, Calgary, St. Louis, Dallas, Detroit, Phoenix, in 19 seasons. 1,269GP
249 – Phil Esposito, Chicago, Boston, NY Rangers, in 18 seasons. 1,282GP

MOST POWER-PLAY GOALS, ONE SEASON:
34 – Tim Kerr, Philadelphia, 1985-86. 76GP – 80 game schedule.
32 – Dave Andreychuk, Buffalo, Toronto, 1992-93. 83GP – 84 game schedule.
31 – Joe Nieuwendyk, Calgary, 1987-88. 75GP – 80 game schedule.
– Mario Lemieux, Pittsburgh, 1988-89. 76GP – 80 game schedule.
– Mario Lemieux, Pittsburgh, 1995-96. 70GP – 82 game schedule.
29 – Michel Goulet, Quebec, 1987-88. 80GP – 80 game schedule.
– Brett Hull, St. Louis, 1990-91. 78GP – 80 game schedule.
– Brett Hull, St. Louis, 1992-93. 80GP – 84 game schedule.

MOST SHORTHAND GOALS, ONE SEASON:
13 – Mario Lemieux, Pittsburgh, 1988-89. 76GP – 80 game schedule.
12 – Wayne Gretzky, Edmonton, 1983-84. 74GP – 80 game schedule.
11 – Wayne Gretzky, Edmonton, 1984-85. 80GP – 80 game schedule.
10 – Marcel Dionne, Detroit, 1974-75. 80GP – 80 game schedule.
– Mario Lemieux, Pittsburgh, 1987-88. 77GP – 80 game schedule.
– Dirk Graham, Chicago, 1988-89. 80GP – 80 game schedule.

MOST SHORTHAND GOALS, ONE GAME:
3 – Theoren Fleury, Calgary, Mar. 9, 1991, at St. Louis. Calgary 8, St. Louis 4.

OVERTIME SCORING

MOST OVERTIME GOALS, CAREER:
15 – Mats Sundin, Quebec, Toronto.
– Jaromir Jagr, Pittsburgh, Washington, NY Rangers.
14 – Sergei Fedorov, Detroit, Anaheim, Columbus, Washington.
– Patrik Elias, New Jersey.
13 – Steve Thomas, Toronto, Chicago, NY Islanders, New Jersey, Anaheim.
12 – Nels Stewart, Mtl. Maroons, Boston, NY Americans.
– Brett Hull, Calgary, St. Louis, Dallas, Detroit, Phoenix.
– Brendan Shanahan, New Jersey, St. Louis, Hartford, Detroit, NY Rangers.
– Olli Jokinen, Los Angeles, NY Islanders, Florida.

MOST OVERTIME ASSISTS, CAREER:
18 – Mark Messier, Edmonton, NY Rangers, Vancouver.
– Nicklas Lidstrom, Detroit.
17 – Adam Oates, Detroit, St. Louis, Boston, Washington, Philadelphia, Anaheim.
– Pavol Demitra, Ottawa, St. Louis, Los Angeles, Minnesota.
15 – Wayne Gretzky, Edmonton, Los Angeles, St. Louis, NY Rangers.
– Doug Gilmour, St. Louis, Calgary, Toronto, New Jersey, Chicago, Buffalo, Montreal.
– Sergei Fedorov, Detroit, Anaheim, Columbus, Washington.
– Tomas Kaberle, Toronto.

MOST OVERTIME POINTS, CAREER:
29 – Sergei Fedorov, Detroit, Anaheim, Columbus, Washington. 14G-15A
28 – Mats Sundin, Quebec, Toronto. 15G-13A
27 – Jaromir Jagr, Pittsburgh, Washington, NY Rangers. 15G-12A
26 – Mark Messier, Edmonton, NY Rangers, Vancouver. 8G-18A
– Jaromir Jagr, Pittsburgh, Washington, NY Rangers. 15G-11A
25 – Patrik Elias, New Jersey. 14G-11A
– Pavol Demitra, Ottawa, St. Louis, Los Angeles, Minnesota. 8G-17A
23 – Steve Thomas, Toronto, Chicago, NY Islanders, New Jersey, Anaheim. 13G-10A

MOST OVERTIME GOALS, ONE SEASON:
4 – Howie Morenz, Montreal, 1929-30.
– Frank Finnigan, Ottawa, 1929-30.
– Johnny Gagnon, Montreal 1936-37.
– Mats Sundin, Toronto, 1999-2000.
– Scott Niedermayer, New Jersey, 2001-02.
– Patrik Elias, New Jersey, 2003-04.
– Markus Naslund, Vancouver, 2003-04.
– Olli Jokinen, Florida, 2005-06.
– Daniel Sedin, Vancouver 2006-07.

SHOOTOUT GOALS

MOST SHOOTOUT GOALS, ONE SEASON:
10 – Jussi Jokinen, Dallas, 2005-06, (13s)
8 – Viktor Kozlov, New Jersey, 2005-06, (12s)
– Erik Christensen, Pittsburgh, 2006-07, (14s)
– Mikko Koivu, Minnesota, 2006-07, (15s)

MOST SHOOTOUT GOALS, ALL-TIME:
17 – Jussi Jokinen, Dallas, Tampa Bay (29s)
– Vyacheslav Kozlov, Atlanta (32s)
16 – Viktor Kozlov, New Jersey, NY Islanders, Washington (32s)
15 – Erik Christensen, Pittsburgh, Atlanta (26s)
14 – Brad Richards, Tampa Bay, Dallas (25s)
– Brian Gionta, New Jersey (35s)

MOST SHOOTOUT SHOTS TAKEN, ONE SEASON:
17 – Sam Gagner, Edmonton, 2007-08 (5G)
16 – Ales Hemsky, Edmonton, 2007-08 (6G)
15 – Mikko Koivu, Minnesota, 2006-07 (8G)
– Sidney Crosby, Pittsburgh, 2006-07 (5G)
– Brendan Shanahan, NY Rangers, 2007-08 (5G)

MOST SHOOTOUT SHOTS TAKEN, ALL-TIME:
36 – Ales Hemsky, Edmonton, (12G)
35 – Brian Gionta, New Jersey, (14G)
32 – Vyacheslav Kozlov, Atlanta, (17G)
– Viktor Kozlov, New Jersey, NY Islanders, Washington, (16G)
31 – Alex Ovechkin, Washington, (9G)

BEST SHOOTOUT SCORING PERCENTAGE, ONE SEASON: *(minimum 5 shots)*
.857 – Petteri Nummelin, Minnesota, 2006-07 (6G, 7s)
.833 – Patrik Elias, New Jersey, 2007-08 (5G, 6s)
.800 – Ray Whitney, Carolina, 2005-06 (4G, 5s)
– Kristian Huselius, Calgary, 2007-08 (4G, 5s)
– Patrick O'Sullivan, Los Angeles, 2007-08 (4G, 5s)
– Jeremy Roenick, San Jose, 2007-08 (4G, 5s)

BEST SHOOTOUT SCORING PERCENTAGE, ALL-TIME: *(minimum 10 shots)*
.800 – Petteri Nummelin, Minnesota (8G, 10s)
.714 – Joe Pavelski, San Jose (10G, 14s)
.586 – Jussi Jokinen, Dallas, Tampa Bay (17G, 29s)
.583 – Trevor Linden, Vancouver (7G, 12s)
.577 – Erik Christensen, Pittsburgh, Atlanta (15G, 26s)

GAME DECIDING SHOOTOUT GOALS, ONE SEASON:
5 – Miroslav Satan, NY Islanders, 2005-06, (10s)
– Viktor Kozlov, New Jersey, 2005-06, (12s)
– Vyacheslav Kozlov, Atlanta, 2006-07, (11s)
– Phil Kessel, Boston, 2007-08, (11s)

GAME DECIDING SHOOTOUT GOALS, ALL-TIME:
9 – Phil Kessel, Boston (20s)
8 – Viktor Kozlov, New Jersey, NY Islanders, Washington (32s)
– Vyacheslav Kozlov, Atlanta (32s)
7 – Brad Richards, Tampa Bay, Dallas (25s)
– Sidney Crosby, Pittsburgh (28s)
– Miroslav Satan, NY Islanders (23s)
– Sergei Zubov, Dallas (29s)

SCORING BY A CENTER

MOST GOALS BY A CENTER, CAREER:

894 – Wayne Gretzky, Edmonton, Los Angeles, St. Louis, NY Rangers, in 20 seasons. 1,487GP
731 – Marcel Dionne, Detroit, Los Angeles, NY Rangers, in 18 seasons. 1,348GP
717 – Phil Esposito, Chicago, Boston, NY Rangers, in 18 seasons. 1,282GP
694 – Mark Messier, Edmonton, NY Rangers, Vancouver, in 25 seasons. 1,756GP
692 – Steve Yzerman, Detroit, in 22 seasons. 1,514GP

MOST GOALS BY A CENTER, ONE SEASON:

92 – Wayne Gretzky, Edmonton, 1981-82. 80GP – 80 game schedule.
87 – Wayne Gretzky, Edmonton, 1983-84. 74GP – 80 game schedule.
85 – Mario Lemieux, Pittsburgh, 1988-89. 76GP – 80 game schedule.
76 – Phil Esposito, Boston, 1970-71. 78GP – 78 game schedule.
73 – Wayne Gretzky, Edmonton, 1984-85. 80GP – 80 game schedule.

MOST ASSISTS BY A CENTER, CAREER:

1,963 – Wayne Gretzky, Edmonton, Los Angeles, St. Louis, NY Rangers, in 20 seasons. 1,487GP
1,249 – Ron Francis, Hartford, Pittsburgh, Carolina, Toronto, in 23 seasons. 1,731GP
1,193 – Mark Messier, Edmonton, NY Rangers, Vancouver, in 25 seasons. 1,756GP
1,079 – Adam Oates, Detroit, St. Louis, Boston, Washington, Philadelphia, Anaheim, Edmonton, in 19 seasons. 1,337GP
1,063 – Steve Yzerman, Detroit, in 22 seasons. 1,514GP

MOST ASSISTS BY A CENTER, ONE SEASON:

163 – Wayne Gretzky, Edmonton, 1985-86. 80GP – 80 game schedule.
135 – Wayne Gretzky, Edmonton, 1984-85. 80GP – 80 game schedule.
125 – Wayne Gretzky, Edmonton, 1982-83. 80GP – 80 game schedule.
122 – Wayne Gretzky, Los Angeles, 1990-91. 78GP – 80 game schedule.
121 – Wayne Gretzky, Edmonton, 1986-87. 79GP – 80 game schedule.

MOST POINTS BY A CENTER, CAREER:

2,857 – Wayne Gretzky, Edmonton, Los Angeles, St. Louis, NY Rangers, in 20 seasons. 1,487GP (894G-1,963A)
1,887 – Mark Messier, Edmonton, NY Rangers, Vancouver, in 25 seasons. 1,756GP (694G-1,193A)
1,798 – Ron Francis, Hartford, Pittsburgh, Carolina, Toronto, in 23 seasons. 1,731GP (549G-1,249A)
1,771 – Marcel Dionne, Detroit, Los Angeles, NY Rangers, in 18 seasons. 1,348GP (731G-1,040A)
1,755 – Steve Yzerman, Detroit, in 22 seasons. 1,514GP (682G-1,063A)

MOST POINTS BY A CENTER, ONE SEASON:

215 – Wayne Gretzky, Edmonton, 1985-86. 80GP – 80 game schedule.
212 – Wayne Gretzky, Edmonton, 1981-82. 80GP – 80 game schedule.
208 – Wayne Gretzky, Edmonton, 1984-85. 80GP – 80 game schedule.
205 – Wayne Gretzky, Edmonton, 1983-84. 74GP – 80 game schedule.
199 – Mario Lemieux, Pittsburgh, 1988-89. 76GP – 80 game schedule.

SCORING BY A LEFT WING

MOST GOALS BY A LEFT WING, CAREER:

668 – Luc Robitaille, Los Angeles, Pittsburgh, NY Rangers, Detroit, in 19 seasons. 1,431GP
650 – Brendan Shanahan, New Jersey, St. Louis, Hartford, Detroit, NY Rangers, in 20 seasons. 1,490GP
640 – Dave Andreychuk, Buffalo, Toronto, New Jersey, Boston, Colorado, Tampa Bay, in 23 seasons. 1,639GP
610 – Bobby Hull, Chicago, Winnipeg, Hartford, in 16 seasons. 1,063GP
556 – John Bucyk, Detroit, Boston, in 23 seasons. 1,540GP

With his league-leading 65 goals in 2007-08, Alex Ovechkin set a new single-season goal-scoring record for left wingers. His total of 112 points is the fifth-leading single-season mark at his position.

MOST GOALS BY A LEFT WING, ONE SEASON:

65 – Alex Ovechkin, Washington, 2007-08. 82GP – 82 game schedule.
63 – Luc Robitaille, Los Angeles, 1991-93. 84GP – 84 game schedule.
60 – Steve Shutt, Montreal, 1976-77. 80GP – 80 game schedule.
58 – Bobby Hull, Chicago, 1968-69. 74GP – 76 game schedule.
57 – Michel Goulet, Quebec, 1982-83. 80GP – 80 game schedule.

MOST ASSISTS BY A LEFT WING, CAREER:

813 – John Bucyk, Detroit, Boston, in 23 seasons. 1,540GP
726 – Luc Robitaille, Los Angeles, Pittsburgh, NY Rangers, Detroit, in 19 seasons. 1,431GP
698 – Dave Andreychuk, Buffalo, Toronto, New Jersey, Boston, Colorado, Tampa Bay, in 23 seasons. 1,639GP
690 – Brendan Shanahan, New Jersey, St. Louis, Hartford, Detroit, NY Rangers, in 20 seasons. 1,490GP
604 – Michel Goulet, Quebec, Chicago, in 15 seasons. 1,089GP

MOST ASSISTS BY A LEFT WING, ONE SEASON:

70 – Joe Juneau, Boston, 1992-93. 84GP – 84 game schedule.
69 – Kevin Stevens, Pittsburgh, 1991-92. 80GP – 80 game schedule.
67 – Mats Naslund, Montreal, 1985-86. 80GP – 80 game schedule.
65 – John Bucyk, Boston, 1970-71. 78GP – 78 game schedule.
– Michel Goulet, Quebec, 1983-84. 75GP – 80 game schedule.
64 – Mark Messier, Edmonton, 1983-84. 73GP – 80 game schedule.

MOST POINTS BY A LEFT WING, CAREER:

1,394 – Luc Robitaille, Los Angeles, Pittsburgh, NY Rangers, Detroit, in 19 seasons. 1,431GP (668G-726A)
1,340 – Brendan Shanahan, New Jersey, St. Louis, Hartford, Detroit, NY Rangers, in 20 seasons. 1,490GP (650G-690A)
1,369 – John Bucyk, Detroit, Boston, in 23 seasons. 1,540GP (556G-813A)
1,338 – Dave Andreychuk, Buffalo, Toronto, New Jersey, Boston, Colorado, Tampa Bay, in 23 seasons. 1,639GP (640G-698A)
1,170 – Bobby Hull, Chicago, Winnipeg, Hartford, in 16 seasons. 1,063GP (610G-560A)

MOST POINTS BY A LEFT WING, ONE SEASON:

125 – Luc Robitaille, Los Angeles, 1992-93. 84GP – 84 game schedule.
123 – Kevin Stevens, Pittsburgh, 1991-92. 80GP – 80 game schedule.
121 – Michel Goulet, Quebec, 1983-84. 75GP – 80 game schedule.
116 – John Bucyk, Boston, 1970-71. 78GP – 78 game schedule.
112 – Bill Barber, Philadelphia, 1975-76. 80GP – 80 game schedule.
– Alex Ovechkin, Washington, 2007-08. 82GP – 82 game schedule.

SCORING BY A RIGHT WING

MOST GOALS BY A RIGHT WING, CAREER:

801 – Gordie Howe, Detroit, Hartford, in 26 seasons. 1,767GP
741 – Brett Hull, Calgary, St. Louis, Dallas, Detroit, Phoenix, in 19 seasons. 1,269GP
708 – Mike Gartner, Washington, Minnesota, NY Rangers, Toronto, Phoenix, in 19 seasons. 1,432GP
646 – Jaromir Jagr, Pittsburgh, Washington, NY Rangers, in 17 seasons. 1,273GP
608 – Dino Ciccarelli, Minnesota, Washington, Detroit, Tampa Bay, Florida, in 19 seasons. 1,232GP

MOST GOALS BY A RIGHT WING, ONE SEASON:

86 – Brett Hull, St. Louis, 1990-91. 78GP – 80 game schedule.
76 – Alexander Mogilny, Buffalo, 1992-93. 77GP – 84 game schedule.
– Teemu Selanne, Winnipeg, 1992-93. 84GP – 84 game schedule.
72 – Brett Hull, St. Louis, 1989-90. 80GP – 80 game schedule.
71 – Jari Kurri, Edmonton, 1984-85. 73GP – 80 game schedule.
70 – Brett Hull, St. Louis, 1991-92. 73GP – 80 game schedule.

MOST ASSISTS BY A RIGHT WING, CAREER:

1,049 – Gordie Howe, Detroit, Hartford, in 26 seasons. 1,767GP
953 – Jaromir Jagr, Pittsburgh, Washington, NY Rangers, in 17 seasons. 1,273GP
859 – Mark Recchi, Pittsburgh, Philadelphia, Montreal, Carolina, Atlanta, in 19 seasons. 1,410GP
797 – Jari Kurri, Edmonton, Los Angeles, NY Rangers, Anaheim, Colorado, in 17 seasons. 1,251GP
793 – Guy Lafleur, Montreal, NY Rangers, Quebec, in 17 seasons. 1,126GP

MOST ASSISTS BY A RIGHT WING, ONE SEASON:

87 – Jaromir Jagr, Pittsburgh, 1995-96. 82GP – 82 game schedule.
83 – Mike Bossy, NY Islanders, 1981-82. 80GP – 80 game schedule.
– Jaromir Jagr, Pittsburgh, 1998-99. 81GP – 82 game schedule.
80 – Guy Lafleur, Montreal, 1976-77. 80GP – 80 game schedule.
77 – Guy Lafleur, Montreal, 1978-79. 80GP – 80 game schedule.

MOST POINTS BY A RIGHT WING, CAREER:
1,850 – Gordie Howe, Detroit, Hartford, in 26 seasons. 1,767GP (801G-1,049A)
1,599 – Jaromir Jagr, Pittsburgh, Washington, NY Rangers, in 17 seasons. 1,273GP (646G-953A)
1,398 – Jari Kurri, Edmonton, Los Angeles, NY Rangers, Anaheim, Colorado, in 17 seasons. 1,251GP (601G-797A)
1,390 – Brett Hull, Calgary, St. Louis, Dallas, Detroit, Phoenix, in 19 seasons. 1,269GP (741G-649A)
1,381 – Mark Recchi, Pittsburgh, Philadelphia, Montreal, Carolina, Atlanta, in 19 seasons. 1,410GP (522G-859A)

MOST POINTS BY A RIGHT WING, ONE SEASON:
149 – Jaromir Jagr, Pittsburgh, 1995-96. 82GP – 82 game schedule.
147 – Mike Bossy, NY Islanders, 1981-82. 80GP – 80 game schedule.
136 – Guy Lafleur, Montreal, 1976-77. 80GP – 80 game schedule.
135 – Jari Kurri, Edmonton, 1984-85. 73GP – 80 game schedule.
132 – Guy Lafleur, Montreal, 1977-78. 78GP – 80 game schedule.
– Teemu Selanne, Winnipeg, 1992-93. 84GP – 84 game schedule.

SCORING BY A DEFENSEMAN

MOST GOALS BY A DEFENSEMAN, CAREER:
410 – Raymond Bourque, Boston, Colorado, in 22 seasons. 1,612GP
396 – Paul Coffey, Edmonton, Pittsburgh, Los Angeles, Detroit, Hartford, Philadelphia, Chicago, Carolina, Boston, in 21 seasons. 1,409GP
340 – Al MacInnis, Calgary, St. Louis, in 23 seasons. 1,416GP
338 – Phil Housley, Buffalo, Winnipeg, St. Louis, Calgary, New Jersey, Washington, Chicago, Toronto, in 21 seasons. 1,495GP
310 – Denis Potvin, NY Islanders, in 15 seasons. 1,060GP

MOST GOALS BY A DEFENSEMAN, ONE SEASON:
48 – Paul Coffey, Edmonton, 1985-86. 79GP – 80 game schedule.
46 – Bobby Orr, Boston, 1974-75. 80GP – 80 game schedule.
40 – Paul Coffey, Edmonton, 1983-84. 80GP – 80 game schedule.
39 – Doug Wilson, Chicago, 1981-82. 76GP – 80 game schedule.
37 – Bobby Orr, Boston, 1970-71. 78GP – 78 game schedule.
– Bobby Orr, Boston, 1971-72. 76GP – 78 game schedule.
– Paul Coffey, Edmonton, 1984-85. 80GP – 80 game schedule.

MOST GOALS BY A DEFENSEMAN, ONE GAME:
5 – Ian Turnbull, Toronto, Feb. 2, 1977, at Toronto. Toronto 9, Detroit 1.
4 – Harry Cameron, Toronto, Dec. 26, 1917, at Toronto. Toronto 7, Montreal 5.
– Harry Cameron, Montreal, Mar. 3, 1920, at Quebec. Montreal 16, Quebec 3.
– Sprague Cleghorn, Montreal, Jan. 14, 1922, at Montreal. Montreal 10, Hamilton 6.
– John McKinnon, Pittsburgh, Nov. 19, 1929, at Pittsburgh. Pittsburgh 10, Toronto 5.
– Hap Day, Toronto, Nov. 19, 1929, at Pittsburgh. Pittsburgh 10, Toronto 5.
– Tom Bladon, Philadelphia, Dec. 11, 1977, at Philadelphia. Philadelphia 11, Cleveland 1.
– Ian Turnbull, Los Angeles, Dec. 12, 1981, at Los Angeles. Los Angeles 7, Vancouver 5.
– Paul Coffey, Edmonton, Oct. 26, 1984, at Calgary. Edmonton 6, Calgary 5.

MOST ASSISTS BY A DEFENSEMAN, CAREER:
1,169 – Raymond Bourque, Boston, Colorado, in 22 seasons. 1,612GP
1,135 – Paul Coffey, Edmonton, Pittsburgh, Los Angeles, Detroit, Hartford, Philadelphia, Chicago, Carolina, Boston, in 21 seasons. 1,409GP
934 – Al MacInnis, Calgary, St. Louis, in 23 seasons. 1,416GP
929 – Larry Murphy, Los Angeles, Washington, Minnesota, Pittsburgh, Toronto, Detroit, in 21 seasons. 1,615GP
894 – Phil Housley, Buffalo, Winnipeg, St. Louis, Calgary, New Jersey, Washington, Chicago, Toronto, in 21 seasons. 1,495GP

MOST ASSISTS BY A DEFENSEMAN, ONE SEASON:
102 – Bobby Orr, Boston, 1970-71. 78GP – 78 game schedule.
90 – Bobby Orr, Boston, 1973-74. 74GP – 78 game schedule.
– Paul Coffey, Edmonton, 1985-86. 79GP – 80 game schedule.
89 – Bobby Orr, Boston, 1974-75. 80GP – 80 game schedule.
87 – Bobby Orr, Boston, 1969-70. 76GP – 78 game schedule.

MOST ASSISTS BY A DEFENSEMAN, ONE GAME:
6 – Babe Pratt, Toronto, Jan. 8, 1944, at Toronto. Toronto 12, Boston 3.
– **Pat Stapleton**, Chicago, Mar. 30, 1969, at Chicago. Chicago 9, Detroit 5.
– **Bobby Orr**, Boston, Jan. 1, 1973, at Vancouver. Boston 8, Vancouver 2.
– **Ron Stackhouse**, Pittsburgh, Mar. 8, 1975, at Pittsburgh. Pittsburgh 8, Philadelphia 2.
– **Paul Coffey**, Edmonton, Mar. 14, 1986, at Edmonton. Edmonton 12, Detroit 3.
– **Gary Suter**, Calgary, Apr. 4, 1986, at Calgary. Calgary 9, Edmonton 3.

MOST POINTS BY A DEFENSEMAN, CAREER:
1,579 – Raymond Bourque, Boston, Colorado, in 22 seasons. 1,612GP (410G-1,169A)
1,531 – Paul Coffey, Edmonton, Pittsburgh, Los Angeles, Detroit, Hartford, Philadelphia, Chicago, Carolina, Boston, in 21 seasons. 1,409GP (396G-1,135A)
1,274 – Al MacInnis, Calgary, St. Louis, in 23 seasons. 1,416GP (340G-934A)
1,232 – Phil Housley, Buffalo, Winnipeg, St. Louis, Calgary, New Jersey, Washington, Chicago, Toronto, in 21 seasons. 1,495GP (338G-894A)
1,216 – Larry Murphy, Los Angeles, Washington, Minnesota, Pittsburgh, Toronto, Detroit, in 21 seasons. 1,615GP (287G-929A)

MOST POINTS BY A DEFENSEMAN, ONE SEASON:
139 – Bobby Orr, Boston, 1970-71. 78GP – 78 game schedule.
138 – Paul Coffey, Edmonton, 1985-86. 79GP – 80 game schedule.
135 – Bobby Orr, Boston, 1974-75. 80GP – 80 game schedule.
126 – Paul Coffey, Edmonton, 1983-84. 80GP – 80 game schedule.
122 – Bobby Orr, Boston, 1973-74. 74GP – 78 game schedule.

MOST POINTS BY A DEFENSEMAN, ONE GAME:
8 – Tom Bladon, Philadelphia, Dec. 11, 1977, at Philadelphia. 4G-4A. Philadelphia 11, Cleveland 1.
– **Paul Coffey**, Edmonton, Mar. 14, 1986, at Edmonton. 2G-6A. Edmonton 12, Detroit 3.
7 – Bobby Orr, Boston, Nov. 15, 1973, at Boston. 3G-4A. Boston 10, NY Rangers 2.

SCORING BY A GOALTENDER

MOST POINTS BY A GOALTENDER, CAREER:
48 – Tom Barrasso, Buffalo, Pittsburgh, Ottawa, Carolina, Toronto, St. Louis, in 19 seasons. 777GP
46 – Grant Fuhr, Edmonton, Toronto, Buffalo, Los Angeles, St. Louis, Calgary, in 19 seasons. 868GP

MOST POINTS BY A GOALTENDER, ONE SEASON:
14 – Grant Fuhr, Edmonton, 1983-84. 45GP – 80 game schedule.
9 – Curtis Joseph, St. Louis, 1991-92. 60GP – 80 game schedule.
8 – Mike Palmateer, Washington, 1980-81. 49GP – 80 game schedule.
– Grant Fuhr, Edmonton, 1987-88. 75GP – 80 game schedule.
– Ron Hextall, Philadelphia, 1988-89. 64GP – 80 game schedule.
– Tom Barrasso, Pittsburgh, 1992-93. 63GP – 84 game schedule.

MOST POINTS BY A GOALTENDER, ONE GAME:
3 – Jeff Reese, Calgary, Feb. 10, 1993, at Calgary. Calgary 13, San Jose 1.

New York Islanders star Denis Potvin (seen battling Philadelphia's Reg Leach) was the first defenseman in NHL history to top 300 goals and 1,000 points. He had a career-high 101 points (31 goals, 70 assists) in 1978-79.

SCORING BY A ROOKIE

MOST GOALS BY A ROOKIE, ONE SEASON:
76 – Teemu Selanne, Winnipeg, 1992-93. 84GP – 84 game schedule.
53 – Mike Bossy, NY Islanders, 1977-78. 73GP – 80 game schedule.
52 – Alex Ovechkin, Washington, 2005-06. 81GP – 82 game schedule.
51 – Joe Nieuwendyk, Calgary, 1987-88. 75GP – 80 game schedule.
45 – Dale Hawerchuk, Winnipeg, 1981-82. 80GP – 80 game schedule.
– Luc Robitaille, Los Angeles, 1986-87. 79GP – 80 game schedule.

MOST GOALS BY A PLAYER IN HIS FIRST NHL SEASON, ONE GAME:
5 – Howie Meeker, Toronto, Jan. 8, 1947, at Toronto. Toronto 10, Chicago 4.
– Don Murdoch, NY Rangers, Oct. 12, 1976, at Minnesota. NY Rangers 10, Minnesota 4.

MOST GOALS BY A PLAYER IN HIS FIRST NHL GAME:
3 – Alex Smart, Montreal, Jan. 14, 1943, at Montreal. Montreal 5, Chicago 1.
– Real Cloutier, Quebec, Oct. 10, 1979, at Quebec. Atlanta 5, Quebec 3.

MOST ASSISTS BY A ROOKIE, ONE SEASON:
70 – Peter Stastny, Quebec, 1980-81. 77GP – 80 game schedule.
– Joe Juneau, Boston, 1992-93. 84GP – 84 game schedule.
63 – Bryan Trottier, NY Islanders, 1975-76. 80GP – 80 game schedule.
– Sidney Crosby, Pittsburgh, 2005–06. 81GP – 82 game schedule.
62 – Sergei Makarov, Calgary, 1989-90. 80GP – 80 game schedule.
60 – Larry Murphy, Los Angeles, 1980-81. 80GP – 80 game schedule.

MOST ASSISTS BY A PLAYER IN HIS FIRST NHL SEASON, ONE GAME:
7 – Wayne Gretzky, Edmonton, Feb. 15, 1980, at Edmonton. Edmonton 8, Washington 2.
6 – Gary Suter, Calgary, Apr. 4, 1986, at Calgary. Calgary 9, Edmonton 3.

MOST ASSISTS BY A PLAYER IN HIS FIRST NHL GAME:
4 – Dutch Reibel, Detroit, Oct. 8, 1953, at Detroit. Detroit 4, NY Rangers 1.
– Roland Eriksson, Minnesota, Oct. 6, 1976, at NY Rangers. NY Rangers 6, Minnesota 5.
3 – Al Hill, Philadelphia, Feb. 14, 1977, at Philadelphia. Philadelphia 6, St. Louis 4.
– Jarno Kultanen, Boston, Oct. 5, 2000, at Boston. Boston 4, Ottawa 4.
– Stanislav Chistov, Anaheim, Oct. 10, 2002, at St. Louis. Anaheim 4, St. Louis 3.
– Dominic Moore, NY Rangers, Nov. 1, 2003, at Montreal. NY Rangers 5, Montreal 1.

MOST POINTS BY A ROOKIE, ONE SEASON:
132 – Teemu Selanne, Winnipeg, 1992-93. 84GP – 84 game schedule.
109 – Peter Stastny, Quebec, 1980-81. 77GP – 80 game schedule.
106 – Alex Ovechkin, Washington, 2005-06. 81GP – 82 game schedule.
103 – Dale Hawerchuk, Winnipeg, 1981-82. 80GP – 80 game schedule.
102 – Joe Juneau, Boston, 1992-93. 84GP – 84 game schedule.
– Sidney Crosby, Pittsburgh, 2005–06. 81GP – 82 game schedule.
100 – Mario Lemieux, Pittsburgh, 1984-85. 73GP – 80 game schedule.

MOST POINTS BY A PLAYER IN HIS FIRST NHL SEASON, ONE GAME:
8 – Peter Stastny, Quebec, Feb. 22, 1981, at Washington. 4G-4A. Quebec 11, Washington 7.
– Anton Stastny, Quebec, Feb. 22, 1981, at Washington. 3G-5A. Quebec 11, Washington 7.
7 – Wayne Gretzky, Edmonton, Feb. 15, 1980, at Edmonton. 7A. Edmonton 8, Washington 2.
– Sergei Makarov, Calgary, Feb. 25, 1990, at Calgary. 2G-5A. Calgary 10, Edmonton 4.
6 – Wayne Gretzky, Edmonton, Mar. 29, 1980, at Toronto. 2G-4A. Edmonton 8, Toronto 5.
– Gary Suter, Calgary, Apr. 4, 1986, at Calgary. 6A. Calgary 9, Edmonton 3.

MOST POINTS BY A PLAYER IN HIS FIRST NHL GAME:
5 – Al Hill, Philadelphia, Feb. 14, 1977, at Philadelphia. 2G-3A. Philadelphia 6, St. Louis 4.
4 – Alex Smart, Montreal, Jan. 14, 1943, at Montreal. 3G-1A. Montreal 5, Chicago 1.
– Dutch Reibel, Detroit, Oct. 8, 1953, at Detroit. 4A. Detroit 4, NY Rangers 1.
– Roland Eriksson, Minnesota, Oct. 6, 1976, at NY Rangers. 4A. NY Rangers 6, Minnesota 5.
– Stanislav Chistov, Anaheim, Oct. 10, 2002, at St. Louis. 1G-3A. Anaheim 4, St. Louis 3.

SCORING BY A ROOKIE DEFENSEMAN

MOST GOALS BY A ROOKIE DEFENSEMAN, ONE SEASON:
23 – Brian Leetch, NY Rangers, 1988-89. 68GP – 80 game schedule.
22 – Barry Beck, Colorado, 1977-78. 75GP – 80 game schedule.
20 – Dion Phaneuf, 2005-06. 82GP – 82 game schedule.

MOST ASSISTS BY A ROOKIE DEFENSEMAN, ONE SEASON:
60 – Larry Murphy, Los Angeles, 1980-81. 80GP – 80 game schedule.
55 – Chris Chelios, Montreal, 1984-85. 74GP – 80 game schedule.
50 – Stefan Persson, NY Islanders, 1977-78. 66GP – 80 game schedule.
– Gary Suter, Calgary, 1985-86. 80GP – 80 game schedule.
49 – Nicklas Lidstrom, Detroit, 1991-92. 80GP – 80 game schedule.

MOST POINTS BY A ROOKIE DEFENSEMAN, ONE SEASON:
76 – Larry Murphy, Los Angeles, 1980-81. 80GP – 80 game schedule.
71 – Brian Leetch, NY Rangers, 1988-89. 68GP – 80 game schedule.
68 – Gary Suter, Calgary, 1985-86. 80GP – 80 game schedule.
66 – Phil Housley, Buffalo, 1982-83. 77GP – 80 game schedule.
65 – Raymond Bourque, Boston, 1979-80. 80GP – 80 game schedule.

Larry Murphy set records for a rookie defenseman with 60 assists and 76 points with the Los Angeles Kings in 1980-81. He went on to accumulate 287 goals, 929 assists and 1,216 points in a 21-year career that landed him in the Hall of Fame.

PER-GAME SCORING AVERAGES

HIGHEST GOALS-PER-GAME AVERAGE, CAREER (AMONG PLAYERS WITH 200-OR-MORE GOALS):
- **.762 – Mike Bossy**, NY Islanders, 1977-78 – 1986-87, with 573G in 752GP.
- .756 – Cy Denneny, Ottawa, Boston, 1917-18 – 1928-29, with 248G in 328GP.
- .754 – Mario Lemieux, Pittsburgh, 1984-85 – 1996-97, 2000-01 – 2003-04, 2005-06, with 690G in 915GP.
- .742 – Babe Dye, Toronto, Hamilton, Chicago, NY Americans, 1919-20 – 1930-31, with 201G in 271GP.
- .623 – Pavel Bure, Vancouver, Florida, NY Rangers, 1991-92 – 2002-03, with 437G in 702GP.

HIGHEST GOALS-PER-GAME AVERAGE, ONE SEASON (AMONG PLAYERS WITH 20-OR-MORE GOALS):
- **2.20 – Joe Malone**, Montreal, 1917-18, with 44G in 20GP.
- 1.80 – Cy Denneny, Ottawa, 1917-18, with 36G in 20GP.
- 1.64 – Newsy Lalonde, Montreal, 1917-18, with 23G in 14GP.
- 1.63 – Joe Malone, Quebec, 1919-20, with 39G in 24GP.
- 1.61 – Newsy Lalonde, Montreal, 1919-20, with 37G in 23GP.

HIGHEST GOALS-PER-GAME AVERAGE, ONE SEASON (AMONG PLAYERS WITH 50-OR-MORE GOALS):
- **1.18 – Wayne Gretzky**, Edmonton, 1983-84, with 87G in 74GP.
- 1.15 – Wayne Gretzky, Edmonton, 1981-82, with 92G in 80GP.
- – Mario Lemieux, Pittsburgh, 1992-93, with 69G in 60GP.
- 1.12 – Mario Lemieux, Pittsburgh, 1988-89, with 85G in 76GP.
- 1.10 – Brett Hull, St. Louis, 1990-91, with 86G in 78GP.
- 1.02 – Cam Neely, Boston, 1993-94, with 50G in 49GP.
- 1.00 – Maurice Richard, Montreal, 1944-45, with 50G in 50GP.

HIGHEST ASSISTS-PER-GAME AVERAGE, CAREER (AMONG PLAYERS WITH 300-OR-MORE ASSISTS):
- **1.320 – Wayne Gretzky**, Edmonton, Los Angeles, St. Louis, NY Rangers, 1979-80 – 1998-99, with 1,963A in 1,487GP.
- 1.129 – Mario Lemieux, Pittsburgh, 1984-85 – 1996-97, 2000-01 – 2003-04, 2005-06, with 1,033A in 915GP.
- .982 – Bobby Orr, Boston, Chicago, 1966-67 – 1978-79, with 645A in 657GP.
- .901 – Peter Forsberg, Quebec, Colorado, Philadelphia, Nashville, 1994-95 – 2000-01, 2002-03, 2003-04, 2005-06 – 2007-08 with 636A in 706GP.
- .808 – Peter Stastny, Quebec, New Jersey, St. Louis, 1980-81 – 1994-95, with 789A in 977GP.

HIGHEST ASSISTS-PER-GAME AVERAGE, ONE SEASON (AMONG PLAYERS WITH 35-OR-MORE ASSISTS):
- **2.04 – Wayne Gretzky, Edmonton**, 1985-86, with 163A in 80GP.
- 1.70 – Wayne Gretzky, Edmonton, 1987-88, with 109A in 64GP.
- 1.69 – Wayne Gretzky, Edmonton, 1984-85, with 135A in 80GP.
- 1.59 – Wayne Gretzky, Edmonton, 1983-84, with 118A in 74GP.
- 1.56 – Wayne Gretzky, Edmonton, 1982-83, with 125A in 80GP.
- – Wayne Gretzky, Los Angeles, 1990-91, with 122A in 78GP.
- 1.53 – Wayne Gretzky, Edmonton, 1986-87, with 121A in 79GP.
- 1.52 – Mario Lemieux, Pittsburgh, 1992-93, with 91A in 60GP.
- 1.50 – Wayne Gretzky, Edmonton, 1981-82, with 120A in 80GP.
- – Mario Lemieux, Pittsburgh, 1988-89, with 114A in 76GP.

HIGHEST POINTS-PER-GAME AVERAGE, CAREER (AMONG PLAYERS WITH 500-OR-MORE POINTS):
- **1.921 – Wayne Gretzky**, Edmonton, Los Angeles, St. Louis, NY Rangers, 1979-80 – 1998-99, with 2,857PTS (894G-1,963A) in 1,487GP.
- 1.883 – Mario Lemieux, Pittsburgh, 1984-85 – 1996-97, 2000-01 – 2003-04, 2005-06, with 1,723PTS (690G-1,033A) in 915GP.
- 1.497 – Mike Bossy, NY Islanders, 1977-78 – 1986-87, with 1,126PTS (573G-553A) in 752GP.
- 1.393 – Bobby Orr, Boston, Chicago, 1966-67 – 1978-79, with 915PTS (270G-645A) in 657GP.
- 1.314 – Marcel Dionne, Detroit, Los Angeles, NY Rangers, 1971-72 – 1988-89, with 1,771PTS (731G-1,040A) in 1,348GP.

HIGHEST POINTS-PER-GAME AVERAGE, ONE SEASON (AMONG PLAYERS WITH 50-OR-MORE POINTS):
- **2.77 – Wayne Gretzky**, Edmonton, 1983-84, with 205PTS in 74GP.
- 2.69 – Wayne Gretzky, Edmonton, 1985-86, with 215PTS in 80GP.
- 2.67 – Mario Lemieux, Pittsburgh, 1992-93, with 160PTS in 60GP.
- 2.65 – Wayne Gretzky, Edmonton, 1981-82, with 212PTS in 80GP.
- 2.62 – Mario Lemieux, Pittsburgh, 1988-89, with 199PTS in 76GP.
- 2.60 – Wayne Gretzky, Edmonton, 1984-85, with 208PTS in 80GP.
- 2.45 – Wayne Gretzky, Edmonton, 1982-83, with 196PTS in 80GP.
- 2.33 – Wayne Gretzky, Edmonton, 1987-88, with 149PTS in 64GP.
- 2.32 – Wayne Gretzky, Edmonton, 1986-87, with 183PTS in 79GP.
- 2.30 – Mario Lemieux, Pittsburgh, 1995-96, with 161PTS in 70GP.
- 2.18 – Mario Lemieux, Pittsburgh, 1987-88, with 168PTS in 77GP.
- 2.15 – Wayne Gretzky, Los Angeles, 1988-89, with 168PTS in 78GP.
- 2.09 – Wayne Gretzky, Los Angeles, 1990-91, with 163PTS in 78GP.
- 2.08 – Mario Lemieux, Pittsburgh, 1989-90, with 123PTS in 59GP.

SCORING PLATEAUS

MOST 20-OR-MORE GOAL SEASONS:
- **22 – Gordie Howe**, Detroit, Hartford, in 26 seasons.
- 20 – Ron Francis, Hartford, Pittsburgh, Carolina, Toronto, in 23 seasons.
- 19 – Dave Andreychuk, Buffalo, Toronto, New Jersey, Boston, Colorado, Tampa Bay, in 23 seasons.
- – Brendan Shanahan, New Jersey, St. Louis, Hartford, Detroit, NY Rangers, in 20 seasons.
- 17 – Marcel Dionne, Detroit, Los Angeles, NY Rangers, in 18 seasons.
- – Mike Gartner, Washington, Minnesota, NY Rangers, Toronto, Phoenix, in 18 seasons.
- – Wayne Gretzky, Edmonton, Los Angeles, St. Louis, NY Rangers, in 20 seasons.
- – Mark Messier, Edmonton, NY Rangers, Vancouver, in 25 seasons.
- – Brett Hull, Calgary, St. Louis, Dallas, Detroit, Phoenix, in 19 seasons.
- – Joe Sakic, Quebec, Colorado, in 19 seasons.
- – Mats Sundin, Quebec, Toronto, in 17 seasons.
- – Jaromir Jagr, Pittsburgh, Washington, NY Rangers, in 17 seasons.

MOST CONSECUTIVE 20-OR-MORE GOAL SEASONS:
- **22 – Gordie Howe**, Detroit, 1949-50 – 1970-71.
- 19 – Brendan Shanahan, New Jersey, St. Louis, Hartford, Detroit, NY Rangers, 1988-89 – 2007-08.
- 17 – Marcel Dionne, Detroit, Los Angeles, NY Rangers, 1971-72 – 1987-88.
- – Brett Hull, Calgary, St. Louis, Dallas, Detroit, 1987-88 – 2003-04.
- – Jaromir Jagr, Pittsburgh, Washington, NY Rangers, 1990-91 – 2007-08.
- – Mats Sundin, Quebec, Toronto, 1990-91 – 2007-08.

In a season limited by injuries to just 49 games, Cam Neely still managed to score 50 goals in 1993-94, rating him among the highest goals-per-game averages in NHL history for players with 50 goals or more.

MOST 30-OR-MORE GOAL SEASONS:
17 – Mike Gartner, Washington, Minnesota, NY Rangers, Toronto, Phoenix, in 19 seasons.
15 – Jaromir Jagr, Pittsburgh, Washington, NY Rangers, in 17 seasons.
14 – Gordie Howe, Detroit, Hartford, in 26 seasons.
– Marcel Dionne, Detroit, Los Angeles, NY Rangers, in 18 seasons.
– Wayne Gretzky, Edmonton, Los Angeles, St. Louis, NY Rangers, in 20 seasons.
13 – Bobby Hull, Chicago, Winnipeg, Hartford, in 16 seasons.
– Phil Esposito, Chicago, Boston, NY Rangers, in 18 seasons.
– Brett Hull, Calgary, St. Louis, Dallas, Detroit, Phoenix, in 19 seasons.
– Mats Sundin, Quebec, Toronto, in 17 seasons.

MOST CONSECUTIVE 30-OR-MORE GOAL SEASONS:
15 – Mike Gartner, Washington, Minnesota, NY Rangers, Toronto, 1979-80 – 1993-94.
– Jaromir Jagr, Pittsburgh, Washington, NY Rangers, 1991-92 – 2006-07.
13 – Bobby Hull, Chicago, 1959-60 – 1971-72.
– Phil Esposito, Boston, NY Rangers, 1967-68 – 1979-80.
– Wayne Gretzky, Edmonton, Los Angeles, 1979-80 – 1991-92.

MOST 40-OR-MORE GOAL SEASONS:
12 – Wayne Gretzky, Edmonton, Los Angeles, St. Louis, NY Rangers, in 20 seasons.
10 – Marcel Dionne, Detroit, Los Angeles, NY Rangers, in 18 seasons.
– Mario Lemieux, Pittsburgh, in 17 seasons.
9 – Mike Bossy, NY Islanders, in 10 seasons.
– Mike Gartner, Washington, Minnesota, NY Rangers, Toronto, Phoenix, in 19 seasons.

MOST CONSECUTIVE 40-OR-MORE GOAL SEASONS:
12 – Wayne Gretzky, Edmonton, Los Angeles, 1979-80 – 1990-91.
9 – Mike Bossy, NY Islanders, 1977-78 – 1985-86.
8 – Luc Robitaille, Los Angeles, 1986-87 – 1993-94.
7 – Phil Esposito, Boston, 1968-69 – 1974-75.
– Michel Goulet, Quebec, 1981-82 – 1987-88.
– Jari Kurri, Edmonton, 1982-83 – 1988-89.

MOST 50-OR-MORE GOAL SEASONS:
9 – Mike Bossy, NY Islanders, in 10 seasons.
– Wayne Gretzky, Edmonton, Los Angeles, St. Louis, NY Rangers, in 20 seasons.
6 – Guy Lafleur, Montreal, NY Rangers, Quebec, in 17 seasons.
– Marcel Dionne, Detroit, Los Angeles, NY Rangers, in 18 seasons.
– Mario Lemieux, Pittsburgh, in 17 seasons.
5 – Bobby Hull, Chicago, Winnipeg, Hartford, in 16 seasons.
– Phil Esposito, Chicago, Boston, NY Rangers, in 18 seasons.
– Brett Hull, Calgary, St. Louis, Dallas, Detroit, Phoenix, in 19 seasons.
– Steve Yzerman, Detroit, in 22 seasons.
– Pavel Bure, Vancouver, Florida, NY Rangers, in 12 seasons.

MOST CONSECUTIVE 50-OR-MORE GOAL SEASONS:
9 – Mike Bossy, NY Islanders, 1977-78 – 1985-86.
8 – Wayne Gretzky, Edmonton, 1979-80 – 1986-87.
6 – Guy Lafleur, Montreal, 1974-75 – 1979-80.
5 – Phil Esposito, Boston, 1970-71 – 1974-75.
– Marcel Dionne, Los Angeles, 1978-79 – 1982-83.
– Brett Hull, St. Louis, 1989-90 – 1993-94.

MOST 60-OR-MORE GOAL SEASONS:
5 – Mike Bossy, NY Islanders, in 10 seasons.
– Wayne Gretzky, Edmonton, Los Angeles, St. Louis, NY Rangers, in 20 seasons.
4 – Phil Esposito, Chicago, Boston, NY Rangers, in 18 seasons.
– Mario Lemieux, Pittsburgh, in 17 seasons.

MOST CONSECUTIVE 60-OR-MORE GOAL SEASONS:
4 – Wayne Gretzky, Edmonton, 1981-82 – 1984-85.
3 – Mike Bossy, NY Islanders, 1980-81 – 1982-83.
– Brett Hull, St. Louis, 1989-90 – 1991-92.
2 – Phil Esposito, Boston, 1970-71 – 1971-72, 1973-74 – 1974-75.
– Jari Kurri, Edmonton, 1984-85 – 1985-86.
– Mario Lemieux, Pittsburgh, 1987-88 – 1988-89.
– Steve Yzerman, Detroit, 1988-89 – 1989-90.
– Pavel Bure, Vancouver, 1992-93 – 1993-94.

MOST 100-OR-MORE POINT SEASONS:
15 – Wayne Gretzky, Edmonton, Los Angeles, St. Louis, NY Rangers, in 20 seasons.
10 – Mario Lemieux, Pittsburgh, in 17 seasons.
8 – Marcel Dionne, Detroit, Los Angeles, NY Rangers, in 18 seasons.
7 – Mike Bossy, NY Islanders, in 10 seasons.
– Peter Stastny, Quebec, New Jersey, St. Louis, in 15 seasons.

MOST CONSECUTIVE 100-OR-MORE POINT SEASONS:
13 – Wayne Gretzky, Edmonton, Los Angeles, 1979-80 – 1991-92.
6 – Bobby Orr, Boston, 1969-70 – 1974-75.
– Guy Lafleur, Montreal, 1974-75 – 1979-80.
– Mike Bossy, NY Islanders,1980-81 – 1985-86.
– Peter Stastny, Quebec, 1980-81 – 1985-86.
– Mario Lemieux, Pittsburgh, 1984-85 – 1989-90.
– Steve Yzerman, Detroit, 1987-88 – 1992-93.

THREE-OR-MORE-GOAL GAMES

MOST THREE-OR-MORE GOAL GAMES, CAREER:
50 – Wayne Gretzky, Edmonton, Los Angeles, St. Louis, NY Rangers, in 20 seasons, 37 three-goal games, 9 four-goal games, 4 five-goal games.
40 – Mario Lemieux, Pittsburgh, in 17 seasons, 27 three-goal games, 10 four-goal games, 3 five-goal games.
39 – Mike Bossy, NY Islanders, in 10 seasons, 30 three-goal games, 9 four-goal games.
33 – Brett Hull, Calgary, St. Louis, Dallas, Detroit, Phoenix, in 19 seasons, 30 three-goal games, 3 four-goal games.
32 – Phil Esposito, Chicago, Boston, NY Rangers, in 18 seasons, 27 three-goal games, 5 four-goal games.

MOST THREE-OR-MORE GOAL GAMES, ONE SEASON:
10 – Wayne Gretzky, Edmonton, 1981-82. 6 three-goal games, 3 four-goal games, 1 five-goal game.
– Wayne Gretzky, Edmonton, 1983-84. 6 three-goal games, 4 four-goal games.
9 – Mike Bossy, NY Islanders, 1980-81. 6 three-goal games, 3 four-goal games.
– Mario Lemieux, Pittsburgh, 1988-89. 7 three-goal games, 1 four-goal game, 1 five-goal game.
8 – Brett Hull, St. Louis, 1991-92. 8 three-goal games.
7 – Joe Malone, Montreal, 1917-18. 2 three-goal games, 2 four-goal games, 3 five-goal games.
– Phil Esposito, Boston, 1970-71. 7 three-goal games.
– Rick Martin, Buffalo, 1975-76. 6 three-goal games, 1 four-goal game.
– Alexander Mogilny, Buffalo, 1992-93. 5 three-goal games, 2 four-goal games.

SCORING STREAKS

LONGEST CONSECUTIVE GOAL-SCORING STREAK:
16 Games – Punch Broadbent, Ottawa, 1921-22. 27G
14 Games – Joe Malone, Montreal, 1917-18. 35G
13 Games – Newsy Lalonde, Montreal, 1920-21. 24G
– Charlie Simmer, Los Angeles, 1979-80. 17G
12 Games – Cy Denneny, Ottawa, 1917-18. 23G
– Dave Lumley, Edmonton, 1981-82. 15G
– Mario Lemieux, Pittsburgh, 1992-93. 18G

LONGEST CONSECUTIVE ASSIST-SCORING STREAK:
23 Games – Wayne Gretzky, Los Angeles, 1990-91. 48A
18 Games – Adam Oates, Boston, 1992-93. 28A
17 Games – Wayne Gretzky, Edmonton, 1983-84. 38A
– Paul Coffey, Edmonton, 1985-86. 27A
– Wayne Gretzky, Los Angeles, 1989-90. 35A
16 Games – Jaromir Jagr, Pittsburgh, 2000-01. 24A

LONGEST CONSECUTIVE POINT-SCORING STREAK:
51 Games – Wayne Gretzky, Edmonton, 1983-84. 61G-92A-153PTS
46 Games – Mario Lemieux, Pittsburgh, 1989-90. 39G-64A-103PTS
39 Games – Wayne Gretzky, Edmonton, 1985-86. 33G-75A-108PTS
30 Games – Wayne Gretzky, Edmonton, 1982-83. 24G-52A-76PTS
– Mats Sundin, Quebec, 1992-93. 21G-25A-46PTS

Though he always considered himself a playmaker first (and set plenty of assist records to prove it!), Wayne Gretzky was also the NHL's greatest goal scorer. He topped 60 in a season four times and recorded 50 hat tricks, including 10 in each of two seasons.

LONGEST CONSECUTIVE POINT-SCORING STREAK FROM START OF SEASON:
51 Games – Wayne Gretzky, Edmonton, 1983-84. 61G-92A-153PTS. Streak ended by Los Angeles and goaltender Markus Mattsson on Jan. 28, 1984.

LONGEST CONSECUTIVE POINT-SCORING STREAK BY A DEFENSEMAN:
28 Games – Paul Coffey, Edmonton, 1985-86. 16G-39A-55PTS
19 Games – Raymond Bourque, Boston, 1987-88. 6G-21A-27PTS
17 Games – Raymond Bourque, Boston, 1984-85. 4G-24A-28PTS
– Brian Leetch, NY Rangers, 1991-92. 5G-24A-29PTS
16 Games – Gary Suter, Calgary, 1987-88. 8G-17A-25PTS
15 Games – Bobby Orr, Boston, 1970-71. 10G-23A-33PTS
– Bobby Orr, Boston, 1973-74. 8G-15A-23PTS
– Steve Duchesne, Quebec, 1992-93. 4G-17A-21PTS
– Chris Chelios, Chicago, 1995-96. 4G-16A-20PTS

LONGEST CONSECUTIVE POINT-SCORING STREAK BY A ROOKIE:
20 Games – Paul Stastny, Colorado, 2006-07. 11G-18A-29PTS
17 Games – Teemu Selanne, Winnipeg, 1992-93. 20G-14A-34PTS
16 Games – Peter Stastny, Quebec, 1980-81
15 Games – Jude Drouin, Minnesota North Stars, 1970-71

FASTEST GOALS AND ASSISTS

FASTEST GOAL FROM START OF A GAME:
0:05 – Doug Smail, Winnipeg, Dec. 20, 1981, at Winnipeg. Winnipeg 5, St. Louis 4.
– Bryan Trottier, NY Islanders, Mar. 22, 1984, at Boston. NY Islanders 3, Boston 3.
– Alexander Mogilny, Buffalo, Dec. 21, 1991, at Toronto. Buffalo 4, Toronto 1.
0:06 – Henry Boucha, Detroit, Jan. 28, 1973, at Montreal. Detroit 4, Montreal 2.
– Jean Pronovost, Pittsburgh, Mar. 25, 1976, at St. Louis. St. Louis 5, Pittsburgh 2.
0:07 – Charlie Conacher, Toronto, Feb. 6, 1932, at Toronto. Toronto 6, Boston 0.
– Danny Gare, Buffalo, Dec. 17, 1978, at Buffalo. Buffalo 6, Vancouver 3.
– Tiger Williams, Los Angeles, Feb. 14, 1987, at Los Angeles. Los Angeles 5, Harford 2.
0:08 – Ron Martin, NY Americans, Dec. 4, 1932, at NY Americans. NY Americans 4, Montreal 2.
– Chuck Arnason, Colorado, Jan. 28, 1977, at Atlanta. Colorado 3, Atlanta 3.
– Wayne Gretzky, Edmonton, Dec. 14, 1983, at NY Rangers. Edmonton 9, NY Rangers 4.
– Gaetan Duchesne, Washington, Mar. 14, 1987, at St. Louis. Washington 3, St. Louis 3.
– Tim Kerr, Philadelphia, Mar. 7, 1989, at Philadelphia. Philadelphia 4, Edmonton 4.
– Grant Ledyard, Buffalo, Dec. 4, 1991, at Winnipeg. Buffalo 4, Winnipeg 4.
– Brent Sutter, Chicago, Feb. 5, 1995, at Vancouver. Chicago 9, Vancouver 4.
– Paul Kariya, Anaheim, Mar. 9, 1997, at Colorado. Anaheim 2, Colorado 2.
– Tony Hrkac, Dallas, Nov. 7, 1998, at Los Angeles. Dallas 4, Los Angeles 3.
– Sergei Fedorov, Detroit, Nov. 21, 1998, at Vancouver. Detroit 4, Vancouver 2.
– Ronald Petrovicky, Atlanta, Dec. 20, 2003, at Pittsburgh. Atlanta 7, Pittsburgh 4.
– Mike Modano, Dallas, Dec. 27, 2003, at Columbus. Dallas 4, Columbus 3.
– Antti Laaksonen, Colorado, Feb. 10, 2006, at Columbus. Colorado 4, Columbus 1.

FASTEST GOAL FROM START OF A PERIOD:
0:04 – Claude Provost, Montreal, Nov. 9, 1957, at Montreal, second period. Montreal 4, Boston 2.
– Denis Savard, Chicago, Jan. 12, 1986, at Chicago, third period. Chicago 4, Hartford 2.

FASTEST GOAL BY A PLAYER IN HIS FIRST NHL GAME:
0:15 – Gus Bodnar, Toronto, Oct. 30, 1943, at Toronto. Toronto 5, NY Rangers 2.
0:18 – Danny Gare, Buffalo, Oct. 10, 1974, at Buffalo. Buffalo 9, Boston 5.
0:20 – Alexander Mogilny, Buffalo, Oct. 5, 1989, at Buffalo. Buffalo 4, Quebec 3.

FASTEST TWO GOALS FROM START OF A GAME:
0:27 – Mike Knuble, Boston, Feb. 14, 2003, at Florida. 0:10 and 0:27. Boston 6, Florida 5.

FASTEST TWO GOALS:
0:04 – Nels Stewart, Mtl. Maroons, Jan. 3, 1931, at Mtl. Maroons. 8:24 and 8:28, third period. Mtl. Maroons 5, Boston 3.
– Deron Quint, Winnipeg, Dec. 15, 1995, at Winnipeg. 7:51 and 7:55, second period. Winnipeg 9, Edmonton 4.
0:05 – Pete Mahovlich, Montreal, Feb. 20, 1971, at Montreal. 12:16 and 12:21, third period. Montreal 7, Chicago 1.
0:06 – Jim Pappin, Chicago, Feb. 16, 1972, at Chicago. 2:57 and 3:03, third period. Chicago 3, Philadelphia 3.
– Ralph Backstrom, Los Angeles, Nov. 2, 1972, at Los Angeles. 8:30 and 8:36, third period. Los Angeles 5, Boston 2.
– Lanny McDonald, Calgary, Mar. 22, 1984, at Calgary. 16:23 and 16:29, first period. Detroit 6, Calgary 4.
– Sylvain Turgeon, Hartford, Mar. 28, 1987, at Hartford. 13:59 and 14:05, second period. Hartford 5, Pittsburgh 4.

FASTEST THREE GOALS:
0:21 – Bill Mosienko, Chicago, Mar. 23, 1952, at NY Rangers, against goaltender Lorne Anderson. Mosienko scored at 6:09, 6:20 and 6:30 of third period, all with both teams at full strength. Chicago 7, NY Rangers 6.
0:44 – Jean Béliveau, Montreal, Nov. 5, 1955, at Montreal, against goaltender Terry Sawchuk. Béliveau scored at 0:42, 1:08 and 1:26 of second period, all with Montreal holding a 6-4 man advantage. Montreal 4, Boston 2.

FASTEST THREE ASSISTS:
0:21 – Gus Bodnar, Chicago, Mar. 23, 1952, at NY Rangers, Bodnar assisted on Bill Mosienko's three goals at 6:09, 6:20 and 6:30 of third period. Chicago 7, NY Rangers 6.
0:44 – Bert Olmstead, Montreal, Nov. 5, 1955, at Montreal, Olmstead assisted on Jean Béliveau's three goals at 0:42, 1:08 and 1:26 of second period. Montreal 4, Boston 2.

SHOTS ON GOAL

MOST SHOTS ON GOAL, ONE SEASON:
550 – Phil Esposito, Boston, 1970-71. 78GP – 78 game schedule.
446 – Alex Ovechkin, Washington, 2007-08. 82GP – 82 game schedule.
429 – Paul Kariya, Anaheim, 1998-99. 82GP – 82 game schedule.
426 – Phil Esposito, Boston, 1971-72. 76GP – 78 game schedule.
425 – Alex Ovechkin, Washington, 2005-06. 81GP – 82 game schedule.

PENALTIES

MOST PENALTY MINUTES, CAREER:
3,966 – Tiger Williams, Toronto, Vancouver, Detroit, Los Angeles, Hartford, in 14 seasons. 962GP
3,565 – Dale Hunter, Quebec, Washington, Colorado, in 19 seasons. 1,407GP
3,515 – Tie Domi, Toronto, NY Rangers, Winnipeg, in 16 seasons. 1,020GP
3,381 – Marty McSorley, Pittsburgh, Edmonton, Los Angeles, NY Rangers, San Jose, Boston, in 17 seasons. 961GP
3,300 – Bob Probert, Detroit, Chicago, in 17 seasons. 935GP

MOST PENALTY MINUTES, CAREER, INCLUDING PLAYOFFS:
4,421 – Tiger Williams, Toronto, Vancouver, Detroit, Los Angeles, Hartford, 3,966 in 962 regular-season games; 455 in 83 playoff games.
4,294 – Dale Hunter, Quebec, Washington, Colorado, 3,565 in 1,407 regular-season games; 729 in 186 playoff games.
3,755 – Marty McSorley, Pittsburgh, Edmonton, Los Angeles, NY Rangers, San Jose, Boston, 3,381 in 961 regular-season games; 374 in 115 playoff games.
3,753 – Tie Domi, Toronto, NY Rangers, Winnipeg, 3,515 in 1,020 regular-season games; 238 in 98 playoff games.
3,584 – Chris Nilan, Montreal, NY Rangers, Boston, 3,043 in 688 regular-season games; 541 in 111 playoff games.

MOST PENALTY MINUTES, ONE SEASON:
472 – Dave Schultz, Philadelphia, 1974-75.
409 – Paul Baxter, Pittsburgh, 1981-82.
408 – Mike Peluso, Chicago, 1991-92.
405 – Dave Schultz, Los Angeles, Pittsburgh, 1977-78.

MOST PENALTIES, ONE GAME:
10 – Chris Nilan, Boston, Mar. 31, 1991, at Boston vs. Hartford. 6 minors, 2 majors, 1 10-minute misconduct, 1 game misconduct.
9 – Jim Dorey, Toronto, Oct. 16, 1968, at Toronto vs. Pittsburgh. 4 minors, 2 majors, 2 10-minute misconducts, 1 game misconduct.
– Dave Schultz, Pittsburgh, Apr. 6, 1978, at Detroit. 5 minors, 2 majors, 2 10-minute misconducts.
– Randy Holt, Los Angeles, Mar. 11, 1979, at Philadelphia. 1 minor, 3 majors, 2 10-minute misconducts, 3 game misconducts.
– Russ Anderson, Pittsburgh, Jan. 19, 1980, at Pittsburgh vs. Edmonton. 3 minors, 3 majors, 3 game misconducts.
– Kim Clackson, Quebec, Mar. 8, 1981, at Quebec vs. Chicago. 4 minors, 3 majors, 2 game misconducts.
– Terry O'Reilly, Boston, Dec. 19, 1984, at Hartford. 5 minors, 3 majors, 1 game misconduct.
– Larry Playfair, Los Angeles, Dec. 9, 1986, at NY Islanders. 6 minors, 2 majors, 1 10-minute misconduct.
– Marty McSorley, Los Angeles, Apr. 14, 1992, at Vancouver. 5 minors, 2 majors, 1 10-minute misconduct, 1 game misconduct.
– Reed Low, St. Louis, Dec. 31, 2002, at Detroit. 4 minors, 1 major, 1 10-minute misconduct, 3 game misconducts.

MOST PENALTY MINUTES, ONE GAME:
67 – Randy Holt, Los Angeles, Mar. 11, 1979, at Philadelphia. 1 minor, 3 majors, 2 10-minute misconducts, 3 game misconducts.
57 – Brad Smith, Toronto, Nov. 15, 1986, at Toronto vs. Detroit. 1 minor, 3 majors, 2 10-minute misconducts, 2 game misconducts.
– Reed Low, St. Louis, Feb. 28, 2002, at St. Louis vs. Calgary. 1 minor, 3 majors, 1 10-minute misconduct, 3 game misconducts.

MOST PENALTIES, ONE PERIOD:
9 – Randy Holt, Los Angeles, Mar. 11, 1979, at Philadelphia, first period. 1 minor, 3 majors, 2 10-minute misconducts, 3 game misconducts.

MOST PENALTY MINUTES, ONE PERIOD:
67 – Randy Holt, Los Angeles, Mar. 11, 1979, at Philadelphia, first period. 1 minor, 3 majors, 2 10-minute misconducts, 3 game misconducts.

GOALTENDING

MOST GAMES APPEARED IN BY A GOALTENDER, CAREER:
1,029 – Patrick Roy, Montreal, Colorado,1984-85 – 2002-03.
971 – Terry Sawchuk, Detroit, Boston, Toronto, Los Angeles, NY Rangers, 1949-50 – 1969-70.
968 – Martin Brodeur, New Jersey, 1991-92 – 2003-04, 2005-06 – 2007-08.
963 – Ed Belfour, Chicago, San Jose, Dallas, Toronto, Florida, 1988-89 – 2003-04, 2005-06, 2006-07.
922 – Curtis Joseph, St. Louis, Edmonton, Toronto, Detroit, Phoenix, Calgary, 1989-90 – 2003-04, 2005-06 – 2007-08.

MOST CONSECUTIVE COMPLETE GAMES BY A GOALTENDER:
502 – Glenn Hall, Detroit, Chicago. Played 502 games from beginning of 1955-56 season through first 12 games of 1962-63 season. In his 503rd straight game, Nov. 7, 1962, at Chicago, Hall was removed from the game against Boston with a back injury in the first period.

MOST GAMES APPEARED IN BY A GOALTENDER, ONE SEASON:
79 – Grant Fuhr, St. Louis, 1995-96.
78 – Martin Brodeur, New Jersey, 2006-07.
77 – Martin Brodeur, New Jersey, 1995-96.
– Bill Ranford, Edmonton, Boston, 1995-96.
– Arturs Irbe, Carolina, 2000-01.
– Marc Denis, Columbus, 2002-03.
– Martin Brodeur, New Jersey, 2007-08
– Evgeni Nabokov, San Jose, 2007-08.

MOST MINUTES PLAYED BY A GOALTENDER, CAREER:
60,235 – Patrick Roy, Montreal, Colorado, 1984-85 – 2002-03.
57,208 – Martin Brodeur, New Jersey, 1991-92 – 2003-04, 2005-06 – 2007-08.
57,194 – Terry Sawchuk, Detroit, Boston, Toronto, Los Angeles, NY Rangers, 1949-50 – 1969-70.

MOST MINUTES PLAYED BY A GOALTENDER, ONE SEASON:
4,697 – Martin Brodeur, New Jersey, 2006-07.
4,635 – Martin Brodeur, New Jersey, 2007-08.
4,561 – Evgeni Nabokov, San Jose, 2007-08.
4,555 – Martin Brodeur, New Jersey, 2003-04.
4,511 – Marc Denis, Columbus, 2002-03.

MOST SHUTOUTS, CAREER:
103 – Terry Sawchuk, Detroit, Boston, Toronto, Los Angeles, NY Rangers, in 21 seasons. (1949-50 – 1969-70)
96 – Martin Brodeur, New Jersey, in 15 seasons. (1991-92, 1993-94 – 2003-04, 2005-06 – 2007-08)
94 – George Hainsworth, Montreal, Toronto, in 11 seasons. (1926-27 – 1936-37)

MOST SHUTOUTS, ONE SEASON:
22 – George Hainsworth, Montreal, 1928-29. 44GP
15 – Alec Connell, Ottawa, 1925-26. 36GP
– Alec Connell, Ottawa, 1927-28. 44GP
– Hal Winkler, Boston, 1927-28. 44GP
– Tony Esposito, Chicago, 1969-70. 63GP
14 – George Hainsworth, Montreal, 1926-27. 44GP

LONGEST SHUTOUT SEQUENCE BY A GOALTENDER:
461:29 – Alec Connell, Ottawa, 1927-28, six consecutive shutouts.
(Forward passing not permitted in attacking zones in 1927-28.)
343:05 – George Hainsworth, Montreal, 1928-29, four consecutive shutouts.
(Forward passing not permitted in attacking zones in 1928-29.)
332:01 – Brian Boucher, Phoenix, 2003-04, five consecutive shutouts.
324:40 – Roy Worters, NY Americans, 1930-31, four consecutive shutouts.
309:21 – Bill Durnan, Montreal, 1948-49, four consecutive shutouts.

MOST WINS BY A GOALTENDER, CAREER:
551 – Patrick Roy, Montreal, Colorado, in 19 seasons. 1,029GP
538 – Martin Brodeur, New Jersey, in 15 seasons. 968GP
484 – Ed Belfour, Chicago, San Jose, Dallas, Toronto, Florida, in 17 seasons. 963GP
449 – Curtis Joseph, St. Louis, Edmonton, Toronto, Detroit, Phoenix, Calgary, in 18 seasons. 922GP
447 – Terry Sawchuk, Detroit, Boston, Toronto, Los Angeles, NY Rangers, in 21 seasons. 971GP

MOST WINS BY A GOALTENDER, ONE SEASON:
48 – Martin Brodeur, New Jersey, 2006-07. 78GP
47 – Bernie Parent, Philadelphia, 1973-74. 73GP
– Roberto Luongo, Vancouver, 2006-07. 76GP
46 – Evgeni Nabokov, San Jose, 2007-08. 77GP
44 – Terry Sawchuk, Detroit, 1950-51. 70GP
– Terry Sawchuk, Detroit, 1951-52. 70GP
– Bernie Parent, Philadelphia, 1974-75. 68GP
– Martin Brodeur, New Jersey, 2007-08. 77GP

LONGEST WINNING STREAK BY A GOALTENDER, ONE SEASON:
17 – Gilles Gilbert, Boston, 1975-76.
14 – Tiny Thompson, Boston, 1929-30.
– Ross Brooks, Boston, 1973-74.
– Don Beaupre, Minnesota, 1985-86.
– Tom Barrasso, Pittsburgh, 1992-93.

LONGEST UNDEFEATED STREAK BY A GOALTENDER, ONE SEASON:
32 Games – Gerry Cheevers, Boston, 1971-72. 24W-8T
31 Games – Pete Peeters, Boston, 1982-83. 26W-5T
27 Games – Pete Peeters, Philadelphia, 1979-80. 22W-5T

LONGEST UNDEFEATED STREAK BY A GOALTENDER IN HIS FIRST NHL SEASON:
23 Games – Grant Fuhr, Edmonton, 1981-82. 15W-8T

LONGEST UNDEFEATED STREAK BY A GOALTENDER FROM START OF CAREER:
16 Games – Patrick Lalime, Pittsburgh, 1996-97. 14W-2T

MOST 30-OR-MORE WIN SEASONS BY A GOALTENDER:
13 – Patrick Roy, Montreal, Colorado, in 19 seasons.
12 – Martin Brodeur, New Jersey, in 15 seasons.
9 – Ed Belfour, Chicago, San Jose, Dallas, Toronto, Florida, in 17 seasons.
8 – Tony Esposito, Montreal, Chicago, in 16 seasons.
7 – Jacques Plante, Montreal, NY Rangers, St. Louis, Toronto, Boston, in 18 seasons.
– Ken Dryden, Montreal, in 8 seasons.
– Curtis Joseph, St. Louis, Edmonton, Toronto, Detroit, Phoenix, Calgary, in 18 seasons.
– Dominik Hasek, Chicago, Buffalo, Detroit, Ottawa, in 16 seasons.

MOST CONSECUTIVE 30-OR-MORE WIN SEASONS BY A GOALTENDER:
12 – Martin Brodeur, New Jersey, 1995-96 – 2003-04, 2005-06 – 2007-08.
8 – Patrick Roy, Montreal, Colorado, 1995-96 – 2002-03.
7 – Tony Esposito, Chicago, 1969-70 – 1975-76.
6 – Jacques Plante, Montreal, 1954-55 – 1959-60.
5 – Terry Sawchuk, Detroit, 1950-51 – 1954-55.
– Ken Dryden, Montreal, 1974-75 – 1978-79.
– Marty Turco, Dallas, 2002-03, 2003-04, 2005-06 – 2007-08.

MOST 40-OR-MORE WIN SEASONS BY A GOALTENDER:
7 – Martin Brodeur, New Jersey, in 15 seasons.
3 – Terry Sawchuk, Detroit, Boston, Toronto, Los Angeles, NY Rangers, in 21 seasons.
– Jacques Plante, Montreal, NY Rangers, St. Louis, Toronto, Boston, in 18 seasons.
2 – Bernie Parent, Boston, Philadelphia, Toronto, in 13 seasons.
– Ken Dryden, Montreal, in 8 seasons.
– Ed Belfour, Chicago, San Jose, Dallas, Toronto, Florida, in 17 seasons.
– Miikka Kiprusoff, San Jose, Calgary, in 6 seasons.

MOST CONSECUTIVE 40-OR-MORE WIN SEASONS BY A GOALTENDER:
3 – Martin Brodeur, New Jersey, 2005-06 – 2007-08.
2 – Terry Sawchuk, Detroit, 1950-51 – 1951-52.
– Bernie Parent, Philadelphia, 1973-74 – 1974-75.
– Ken Dryden, Montreal, 1975-76 – 1976-77.
– Martin Brodeur, New Jersey, 1999-2000 – 2000-01.
– Miikka Kiprusoff, Calgary, 2005-06 – 2006-07.

MOST LOSSES BY A GOALTENDER, CAREER:
352 – Gump Worsley, NY Rangers, Montreal, Minnesota, in 21 seasons. 861GP
351 – Gilles Meloche, Chicago, California, Cleveland, Minnesota, Pittsburgh, in 18 seasons. 788GP
346 – John Vanbiesbrouck, NY Rangers, Florida, Philadelphia, NY Islanders, New Jersey, in 20 seasons. 882GP
343 – Curtis Joseph, St. Louis, Edmonton, Toronto, Detroit, Phoenix, in 18 seasons. 922GP
341 – Sean Burke, New Jersey, Hartford, Carolina, Vancouver, Philadelphia, Florida, Phoenix, Tampa Bay, Los Angeles, in 18 seasons. 820GP

MOST LOSSES BY A GOALTENDER, ONE SEASON:
48 – Gary Smith, California, 1970-71. 71GP
47 – Al Rollins, Chicago, 1953-54. 66GP
46 – Peter Sidorkiewicz, Ottawa, 1992-93. 64GP

GOALTENDER SHOOTOUT RECORDS

MOST SHOOTOUT WINS, ONE SEASON:
10 – Mathieu Garon, Edmonton, 2007-08, (10GP)
– Ryan Miller, Buffalo, 2006-07, (14GP)
– Martin Brodeur, New Jersey, 2006-07, (16GP)
9 – Marc-Andre Fleury, Pittsburgh, 2006-07, (14GP)

MOST SHOOTOUT WINS, ALL-TIME:
26 – Martin Brodeur, New Jersey, (35GP)
19 – Marty Turco, Dallas, (24GP)
18 – Henrik Lundqvist, NY Rangers (25GP)

MOST SHOOTOUT SHOTS AGAINST, ONE SEASON:
60 – Martin Brodeur, New Jersey, 2006-07, (20GA)
54 – Roberto Luongo, Vancouver, 2007-08 (15GA)
50 – Henrik Lundqvist, NY Rangers, 2006-07, (9GA)
46 – Tim Thomas, Boston, 2006-07, (8GA)
– Ryan Miller, Buffalo, 2006-07, (9GA)
– Marty Turco, Dallas, 2006-07, (11GA)

MOST SHOOTOUT SHOTS AGAINST, ALL-TIME:
141 – Martin Brodeur, New Jersey, (40GA)
129 – Henrik Lundqvist, NY Rangers, (31GA)
112 – Roberto Luongo, Vancouver, (32GA)

BEST SHOOTOUT SAVE PERCENTAGE, ONE SEASON: *(minimum 20 shots)*
.938 – Mathieu Garon, Edmonton, 2007-08, (32S, 2GA)
.900 – Marc Denis, Tampa Bay, 2006-07, (20S, 2GA)
.879 – Johan Holmqvist, Tampa Bay, 2006-07, (33S, 4GA)
.850 – Kari Lehtonen, Atlanta, 2005-06, (20S, 3GA)

BEST SHOOTOUT SAVE PERCENTAGE, ALL-TIME: *(minimum 40 shots)*
.854 – Marc Denis, Tampa Bay, (41S, 6GA)
.825 – Jose Theodore, Colorado, (40S, 7GA)
.818 – Mathieu Garon, Edmonton, (66S, 12GA)

Active NHL Players' Three-or-More-Goal Games

Regular Season

Teams named are the ones the players were with at the time of their multiple-scoring games. Players listed alphabetically.

Boston's Phil Kessel recorded his first career hat trick in an 8-6 win over the Los Angeles Kings on October 12, 2007.

Player	Team(s)	3-Goals	4-Goals	5-Goals
Adams, Kevyn	Carolina	2	—	—
Alfredsson, Daniel	Ottawa	5	1	—
Antropov, Nik	Toronto	2	—	—
Armstrong, Derek	Los Angeles	1	—	—
Arnason, Tyler	Chicago	1	—	—
Arnott, Jason	Edm., N.J., Dal., Nsh.	7	—	—
Barnes, Stu	Wpg., Pit., Dal.	4	—	—
Battaglia, Bates	Carolina	1	—	—
Belanger, Eric	Los Angeles	1	—	—
Berard, Bryan	Columbus	1	—	—
Bergeron, Marc-Andre	Edmonton	1	—	—
Bertuzzi, Todd	Vancouver	5	—	—
Blake, Jason	NY Islanders	5	—	—
Blake, Rob	Los Angeles	1	—	—
Bochenski, Brandon	Ottawa	1	—	—
Bonk, Radek	Ottawa	1	—	—
Boucher, Philippe	Dallas	1	—	—
Boyes, Brad	Boston	1	—	—
Boyle, Dan	Tampa Bay	1	—	—
Briere, Daniel	Buf., Phi.	3	—	—
Brind'Amour, Rod	Phi., Car.	3	—	—
Brown, Curtis	Buffalo	1	—	—
Brunette, Andrew	Colorado	1	—	—
Bulis, Jan	Montreal	—	1	—
Burrows, Alexandre	Vancouver	1	—	—
Byfuglien, Dustin	Chicago	1	—	—
Carcillo, Daniel	Phoenix	1	—	—
Cheechoo, Jonathan	San Jose	9	—	—
Chouinard, Marc	Minnesota	1	—	—
Clark, Chris	Washington	2	—	—
Cleary, Daniel	Detroit	1	—	—
Clowe, Ryane	San Jose	1	—	—
Cole, Erik	Carolina	4	—	—
Conroy, Craig	St.L., L.A.	2	—	—
Corvo, Joe	Carolina	1	—	—
Crosby, Sidney	Pittsburgh	1	—	—
Demitra, Pavol	St.L., L.A.	4	—	—
Devereaux, Boyd	Edmonton	1	—	—
Donovan, Shean	Atlanta	1	—	—
Drury, Chris	Buffalo	1	—	—
Dumont, J.P.	Chi., Buf.	3	—	—
Dvorak, Radek	NY Rangers	1	1	—
Ekman, Nils	Pittsburgh	1	—	—
Elias, Patrik	New Jersey	6	1	—
Erat, Martin	Nashville	1	—	—
Fedorov, Sergei	Detroit	4	1	1
Fisher, Mike	Ottawa	1	—	—
Forsberg, Peter	Colorado	6	—	—
Frolov, Alexander	Los Angeles	3	—	—
Gaborik, Marian	Minnesota	6	—	1
Gagne, Simon	Philadelphia	2	—	—
Gelinas, Martin	Edm., Van.	2	1	—
Gionta, Brian	New Jersey	1	—	—
Gomez, Scott	New Jersey	2	—	—
Gonchar, Sergei	Washington	1	—	—
Gratton, Chris	Tampa Bay	1	—	—
Grier, Mike	Edmonton	1	—	—
Guerin, Bill	N.J., Bos., Dal., St.L., S.J., NYI	9	—	—
Hagman, Niklas	Dallas	1	—	—
Hamilton, Jeff	Chicago	2	—	—
Handzus, Michal	St. Louis	1	—	—
Hartnell, Scott	Nsh., Phi.	3	—	—
Havlat, Martin	Ottawa	3	1	—
Heatley, Dany	Atl., Ott.	6	1	—
Hecht, Jochen	Buffalo	1	—	—
Hejduk, Milan	Colorado	4	—	—
Holik, Bobby	New Jersey	3	—	—
Holmstrom, Tomas	Detroit	3	—	—
Horcoff, Shawn	Edmonton	1	—	—
Horton, Nathan	Florida	1	—	—
Hossa, Marian	Ott., Atl.	6	1	—
Huselius, Kristian	Calgary	1	—	—
Iginla, Jarome	Calgary	6	1	—
Jagr, Jaromir	Pit., NYR	13	1	—
Jokinen, Jussi	Dallas	—	1	—
Jokinen, Olli	Florida	4	—	—
Kaberle, Tomas	Toronto	1	—	—
Kapanen, Niko	Dallas	1	—	—
Kariya, Paul	Ana., Nsh., St.L.	10	—	—
Kessel, Phil	Boston	1	—	—
Knuble, Mike	Philadelphia	1	—	—
Kobasew, Chuck	Calgary	1	—	—
Koivu, Saku	Montreal	1	—	—
Kovalchuk, Ilya	Atlanta	9	1	—
Kovalev, Alex	NYR, Pit.	10	—	—
Kozlov, Viktor	Fla., NYI	1	1	—
Kozlov, Vyacheslav	Det., Atl.	4	1	—
Kunitz, Chris	Anaheim	1	—	—
Laaksonen, Antti	Minnesota	1	—	—
Lang, Robert	Washington	1	—	—
Langkow, Daymond	Phx., Cgy.	3	—	—
Laperriere, Ian	Los Angeles	1	—	—
Lapointe, Martin	Det., Bos.	2	—	—
Laraque, Georges	Edmonton	1	—	—
Larose, Chad	Carolina	1	—	—
Lecavalier, Vincent	Tampa Bay	6	—	—
Legwand, David	Nashville	2	—	—
Lehtinen, Jere	Dallas	2	—	—
Lombardi, Matthew	Calgary	1	—	—
Lupul, Joffrey	Philadelphia	2	—	—
Madden, John	New Jersey	1	1	—
Malkin, Evgeni	Pittsburgh	2	—	—
Malone, Ryan	Pittsburgh	2	—	—
Maltby, Kirk	Detroit	1	—	—
Marleau, Patrick	San Jose	2	—	—
Modano, Mike	Min., Dal.	6	1	—
Modin, Fredrik	Tampa Bay	3	—	—
Morrison, Brendan	Vancouver	1	—	—
Morrow, Brenden	Dallas	1	—	—
Mueller, Peter	Phoenix	2	—	—
Murray, Glen	L.A., Bos.	5	—	—
Nagy, Ladislav	Phx., L.A.	3	—	—
Nash, Rick	Columbus	2	—	—
Naslund, Markus	Pit., Van.	9	2	—
Nolan, Owen	Que., S.J., Cgy.	10	1	—
Nylander, Michael	Hfd., Chi.	1	1	—
O'Neill, Jeff	Hfd. Car., Tor.	3	—	—
Orszagh, Vladimir	Nashville	1	—	—
Ovechkin, Alex	Washington	3	2	—
Pandolfo, Jay	New Jersey	1	—	—
Parise, Zach	New Jersey	1	—	—
Parrish, Mark	Fla., NYI, Min.	4	1	—
Peca, Michael	Buffalo	1	—	—
Perreault, Yanic	L.A., Tor., Mtl.	3	1	—
Petersen, Toby	Pittsburgh	1	—	—
Petrovicky, Ronald	Atlanta	1	—	—
Pisani, Fernando	Edmonton	1	—	—
Plekanec, Thomas	Montreal	1	—	—
Pominville, Jason	Buffalo	1	—	—
Prospal, Vaclav	Ana., T.B.	2	—	—
Pyatt, Taylor	Buffalo	2	—	—
Quint, Deron	Columbus	1	—	—
Recchi, Mark	Pit., Mtl., Phi.	7	—	—
Reinprecht, Steve	Col., Phx.	3	—	—
Richards, Mike	Philadelphia	1	—	—
Roberts, Gary	Cgy., Car., Tor.	12	1	—
Roenick, Jeremy	Chi., Phx.	7	2	—
Rolston, Brian	N.J., Min.	2	—	—
Roy, Derek	Buffalo	3	—	—
Rucinsky, Martin	Montreal	2	—	—
Ryder, Michael	Montreal	2	—	—
Sakic, Joe	Que., Col.	14	1	—
Salo, Sami	Ottawa	1	—	—
Samsonov, Sergei	Boston	1	—	—
Sanderson, Geoff	Har., Buf., CBJ	7	1	—
Satan, Miroslav	Buf., NYI	6	1	—
Savard, Marc	Calgary	1	1	—
Scatchard, Dave	NY Islanders	2	—	—
Schneider, Mathieu	Detroit	2	—	—
Sedin, Daniel	Vancouver	1	1	—
Selanne, Teemu	Wpg., Ana., S.J.	18	2	—
Semin, Alexander	Washington	2	—	—
Shanahan, Brendan	N.J., St.L., Hfd., Det., NYR	17	1	—
Sharp, Patrick	Chicago	1	—	—
Sim, Jon	Florida	1	—	—
Sjostrom, Fredrik	Phoenix	1	—	—
Smolinski, Bryan	Bos., L.A.	3	—	—
Smyth, Ryan	Edmonton	5	—	—
Souray, Sheldon	Montreal	1	—	—
Spezza, Jason	Ottawa	1	—	—
St. Louis, Martin	Tampa Bay	4	—	—
Staal, Eric	Carolina	4	—	—
Staal, Jordan	Pittsburgh	1	—	—
Stafford, Drew	Buffalo	1	—	—
Stastny, Paul	Colorado	1	—	—
Steen, Alex	Toronto	1	—	—
Stillman, Cory	Cgy., St.L., Car.	4	—	—
Straka, Martin	Pit., NYR	6	—	—
Stumpel, Jozef	Bos., L.A.	2	—	—
Sturm, Marco	S.J., Bos.	2	—	—
Sullivan, Steve	Tor., Chi., Nsh.	5	1	—
Sundin, Mats	Que., Tor.	6	1	1
Svatos, Marek	Colorado	2	—	—
Sydor, Darryl	Dallas	1	—	—
Tanguay, Alex	Colorado	2	—	—
Tenkrat, Petr	Nashville	1	—	—
Thornton, Joe	Bos., S.J.	3	—	—
Thornton, Scott	San Jose	1	—	—
Tkachuk, Keith	Phoenix	7	2	—
Umberger, R.J.	Philadelphia	1	—	—
Vanek, Thomas	Buffalo	4	—	—
Vasicek, Josef	Carolina	1	—	—
Vermette, Antoine	Ottawa	1	—	—
Visnovsky, Lubomir	Los Angeles	1	—	—
Vrbata, Radim	Col., Car., Phx.	3	—	—
Vyborny, David	Columbus	1	—	—
Walker, Scott	Nashville	2	—	—
Weight, Doug	Edm., St.L.	2	—	—
Weiss, Stephen	Florida	1	—	—
Wellwood, Kyle	Toronto	1	—	—
Whitney, Ray	CBJ, Car.	2	—	—
Williams, Jason	Detroit	1	—	—
Williams, Justin	Carolina	1	—	—
Zednik, Richard	Wsh., Fla.	2	—	—
Zetterberg, Henrik	Detroit	3	—	—

Top 100 All-Time Goal-Scoring Leaders

* active player

	Player	Seasons	Games	Goals	Goals per game
1.	**Wayne Gretzky**, Edm., L.A., St.L., NYR	20	1487	**894**	.601
2.	**Gordie Howe**, Det., Hfd.	26	1767	**801**	.453
3.	**Brett Hull**, Cgy., St.L., Dal., Det., Phx.	20	1269	**741**	.584
4.	**Marcel Dionne**, Det., L.A., NYR	18	1348	**731**	.542
5.	**Phil Esposito**, Chi., Bos., NYR	18	1282	**717**	.559
6.	**Mike Gartner**, Wsh., Min., NYR, Tor., Phx.	19	1432	**708**	.494
7.	**Mark Messier**, Edm., NYR, Van.	25	1756	**694**	.395
8.	**Steve Yzerman**, Det.	22	1514	**692**	.457
9.	**Mario Lemieux**, Pit.	18	915	**690**	.754
10.	**Luc Robitaille**, L.A., Pit., NYR, Det.	19	1431	**668**	.467
* 11.	**Brendan Shanahan**, N.J., St.L., Hfd., Det., NYR	20	1490	**650**	.436
* 12.	**Jaromir Jagr**, Pit., Wsh., NYR	17	1273	**646**	.507
13.	**Dave Andreychuk**, Buf., Tor., N.J., Bos., Col., T.B.	23	1639	**640**	.390
* 14.	**Joe Sakic**, Que., Col.	19	1363	**623**	.457
15.	**Bobby Hull**, Chi., Wpg., Hfd.	16	1063	**610**	.574
16.	**Dino Ciccarelli**, Min., Wsh., Det., T.B., Fla.	19	1232	**608**	.494
17.	**Jari Kurri**, Edm., L.A., NYR, Ana., Col.	17	1251	**601**	.480
18.	**Mike Bossy**, NYI	10	752	**573**	.762
19.	**Joe Nieuwendyk**, Cgy., Dal., N.J., Tor., Fla.	20	1257	**564**	.449
20.	**Guy Lafleur**, Mtl., NYR, Que.	17	1126	**560**	.497
21.	**John Bucyk**, Det., Bos.	23	1540	**556**	.361
* 22.	**Mats Sundin**, Que., Tor.	17	1305	**555**	.425
* 23.	**Teemu Selanne**, Wpg., Ana., S.J., Col.	15	1067	**552**	.517
24.	**Ron Francis**, Hfd., Pit., Car., Tor.	23	1731	**549**	.317
25.	**Michel Goulet**, Que., Chi.	15	1089	**548**	.503
26.	**Maurice Richard**, Mtl.	18	978	**544**	.556
27.	**Stan Mikita**, Chi.	22	1394	**541**	.388
28.	**Frank Mahovlich**, Tor., Det., Mtl.	18	1181	**533**	.451
* 29.	**Mike Modano**, Min., Dal.	19	1320	**528**	.400
30.	**Bryan Trottier**, NYI, Pit.	18	1279	**524**	.410
31.	**Pat Verbeek**, N.J., Hfd., NYR, Dal., Det.	20	1424	**522**	.367
* 32.	**Mark Recchi**, Pit., Phi., Mtl., Car., Atl.	19	1410	**522**	.370
33.	**Dale Hawerchuk**, Wpg., Buf., St.L., Phi.	16	1188	**518**	.436
34.	**Pierre Turgeon**, Buf., NYI, Mtl., St.L., Dal., Col.	19	1294	**515**	.398
35.	**Gilbert Perreault**, Buf.	17	1191	**512**	.430
* 36.	**Jeremy Roenick**, Chi., Phx., Phi., L.A., S.J.	19	1321	**509**	.385
37.	**Jean Beliveau**, Mtl.	20	1125	**507**	.451
38.	**Peter Bondra**, Wsh., Ott., Atl., Chi.	16	1081	**503**	.465
39.	**Joe Mullen**, St.L., Cgy., Pit., Bos.	17	1062	**502**	.473
* 40.	**Keith Tkachuk**, Wpg., Phx., St.L., Atl.	16	1055	**500**	.474
41.	**Lanny McDonald**, Tor., Col., Cgy.	16	1111	**500**	.450
42.	**Glenn Anderson**, Edm., Tor., NYR, St.L.	16	1129	**498**	.441
43.	**Jean Ratelle**, NYR, Bos.	21	1281	**491**	.383
44.	**Norm Ullman**, Det., Tor.	20	1410	**490**	.348
45.	**Brian Bellows**, Min., Mtl., T.B., Ana., Wsh.	17	1188	**485**	.408
46.	**Darryl Sittler**, Tor., Phi., Det.	15	1096	**484**	.442
47.	**Bernie Nicholls**, L.A., NYR, Edm., N.J., Chi., S.J.	18	1127	**475**	.421
48.	**Denis Savard**, Chi., Mtl., T.B.	17	1196	**473**	.395
49.	**Alexander Mogilny**, Buf., Van., N.J., Tor.	16	990	**473**	.478
* 50.	**Sergei Fedorov**, Det., Ana., CBJ, Wsh.	17	1196	**472**	.395
51.	**Pat LaFontaine**, NYI, Buf., NYR	15	865	**468**	.541
52.	**Alex Delvecchio**, Det.	24	1549	**456**	.294
53.	**Theoren Fleury**, Cgy., Col., NYR, Chi.	15	1084	**455**	.420
54.	**Peter Stastny**, Que., N.J., St.L.	15	977	**450**	.461
55.	**Doug Gilmour**, St.L., Cgy., Tor., N.J., Chi., Buf., Mtl.	20	1474	**450**	.305
56.	**Rick Middleton**, NYR, Bos.	14	1005	**448**	.446
57.	**Steve Larmer**, Chi., NYR	15	1006	**441**	.438
58.	**Rick Vaive**, Van., Tor., Chi., Buf.	13	876	**441**	.503
59.	**Rick Tocchet**, Phi., Pit., L.A., Bos., Wsh., Phx.	18	1144	**440**	.385
60.	**Pavel Bure**, Van., Fla., NYR	12	702	**437**	.623
* 61.	**Gary Roberts**, Cgy., Car., Tor., Fla., Pit.	21	1194	**434**	.363
62.	**Vincent Damphousse**, Tor., Edm., Mtl., S.J.	18	1378	**432**	.313
63.	**Dave Taylor**, L.A.	17	1111	**431**	.388
64.	**Yvan Cournoyer**, Mtl.	16	968	**428**	.442
* 65.	**Rod Brind'Amour**, St.L., Phi., Car.	19	1324	**427**	.323
66.	**Brian Propp**, Phi., Bos., Min., Hfd.	15	1016	**425**	.418
67.	**Steve Shutt**, Mtl., L.A.	13	930	**424**	.456
68.	**Steve Thomas**, Tor., Chi., NYI, N.J., Ana., Det.	20	1235	**421**	.341
69.	**Stephane Richer**, Mtl., N.J., T.B., St.L., Pit.	17	1054	**421**	.399
70.	**Bill Barber**, Phi.	14	903	**420**	.465
71.	**Tony Amonte**, NYR, Chi., Phx., Phi., Cgy.	16	1174	**416**	.354
72.	**Garry Unger**, Tor., Det., St.L., Atl., L.A., Edm.	16	1105	**413**	.374
73.	**John MacLean**, N.J., S.J., NYR, Dal.	18	1194	**413**	.346
74.	**Raymond Bourque**, Bos., Col.	22	1612	**410**	.254
75.	**Ray Ferraro**, Hfd., NYI, NYR, L.A., Atl., St.L.	18	1258	**408**	.324
76.	**Rod Gilbert**, NYR	18	1065	**406**	.381
77.	**John LeClair**, Mtl., Phi., Pit.	16	967	**406**	.420
78.	**John Ogrodnick**, Det., Que., NYR	14	928	**402**	.433
79.	**Paul Coffey**, Edm., Pit., L.A., Det., Hfd., Phi., Chi., Car., Bos.	21	1409	**396**	.281
80.	**Dave Keon**, Tor., Hfd.	18	1296	**396**	.306
81.	**Cam Neely**, Van., Bos.	13	726	**395**	.544
82.	**Pierre Larouche**, Pit., Mtl., Hfd., NYR	14	812	**395**	.486
83.	**Tomas Sandstrom**, NYR, L.A., Pit., Det., Ana.	15	983	**394**	.401
84.	**Bernie Geoffrion**, Mtl., NYR	16	883	**393**	.445
85.	**Jean Pronovost**, Pit., Atl., Wsh.	14	998	**391**	.392
86.	**Dean Prentice**, NYR, Bos., Det., Pit., Min.	22	1378	**391**	.284
* 87.	**Bill Guerin**, N.J., Edm., Bos., Dal., St.L., S.J., NYI	16	1107	**387**	.350
88.	**Rick Martin**, Buf., L.A.	11	685	**384**	.561
* 89.	**Paul Kariya**, Ana., Col., Nsh., St.L.	13	903	**382**	.423
90.	**Reggie Leach**, Bos., Cal., Phi., Det.	13	934	**381**	.408
* 91.	**Owen Nolan**, Que., Col., S.J., Tor., Phx., Cgy.	16	1068	**381**	.357
92.	**Claude Lemieux**, Mtl., N.J., Col., Phx., Dal.	20	1197	**379**	.317
93.	**Ted Lindsay**, Det., Chi.	17	1068	**379**	.355
94.	**Trevor Linden**, Van., NYI, Mtl., Wsh.	19	1382	**375**	.271
95.	**Butch Goring**, L.A., NYI, Bos.	16	1107	**375**	.339
* 96.	**Jarome Iginla**, Cgy.	12	860	**374**	.435
97.	**Eric Lindros**, Phi., NYR, Tor., Dal.	14	760	**372**	.489
98.	**Rick Kehoe**, Tor., Pit.	14	906	**371**	.409
* 99.	**Markus Naslund**, Pit., Van.	14	1035	**371**	.358
100.	**Tim Kerr**, Phi., NYR, Hfd.	13	655	**370**	.565

Keith Tkachuk's 27th and final goal of the 2007-08 season was the 500th of his career. He also played in his 1,000th career game on December 1, 2007.

Top 100 Active Goal-Scoring Leaders

	Player	Seasons	Games	Goals	Goals per game
1.	**Brendan Shanahan**, N.J., St.L., Hfd., Det., NYR	20	1490	**650**	.436
2.	**Jaromir Jagr**, Pit., Wsh., NYR	17	1273	**646**	.507
3.	**Joe Sakic**, Que., Col.	19	1363	**623**	.457
4.	**Mats Sundin**, Que., Tor.	17	1305	**555**	.425
5.	**Teemu Selanne**, Wpg., Ana., S.J., Col.	15	1067	**552**	.517
6.	**Mike Modano**, Min., Dal.	19	1320	**528**	.400
7.	**Mark Recchi**, Pit., Phi., Mtl., Car., Atl.	19	1410	**522**	.370
8.	**Jeremy Roenick**, Chi., Phx., Phi., L.A., S.J.	19	1321	**509**	.385
9.	**Keith Tkachuk**, Wpg., Phx., St.L., Atl.	16	1055	**500**	.474
10.	**Sergei Fedorov**, Det., Ana., CBJ, Wsh.	17	1196	**472**	.395
11.	**Gary Roberts**, Cgy., Car., Tor., Fla., Pit.	21	1194	**434**	.363
12.	**Rod Brind'Amour**, St.L., Phi., Car.	19	1324	**427**	.323
13.	**Bill Guerin**, N.J., Edm., Bos., Dal., St.L., S.J., NYI	16	1107	**387**	.350
14.	**Paul Kariya**, Ana., Col., Nsh., St.L.	13	903	**382**	.423
15.	**Owen Nolan**, Que., Col., S.J., Tor., Phx., Cgy.	16	1068	**381**	.357
16.	**Jarome Iginla**, Cgy.	12	860	**374**	.435
17.	**Markus Naslund**, Pit., Van.	14	1035	**371**	.358
18.	**Alex Kovalev**, NYR, Pit., Mtl.	15	1073	**368**	.343
19.	**Geoff Sanderson**, Hfd., Car., Van., Buf., CBJ, Phx., Phi., Edm.	17	1104	**355**	.322
20.	**Glen Murray**, Bos., Pit., L.A.	16	1009	**337**	.334
21.	**Miroslav Satan**, Edm., Buf., NYI	12	947	**337**	.356
22.	**Alexei Yashin**, Ott., NYI	12	850	**337**	.396
23.	**Daniel Alfredsson**, Ott.	12	853	**331**	.388
24.	**Jason Arnott**, Edm., N.J., Dal., Nsh.	14	971	**331**	.341
25.	**Bobby Holik**, Hfd., N.J., NYR, Atl.	17	1252	**322**	.257
26.	**Vyacheslav Kozlov**, Det., Buf., Atl.	16	1045	**322**	.308
27.	**Martin Gelinas**, Edm., Que., Van., Car., Cgy., Fla., Nsh.	19	1273	**309**	.243
28.	**Marian Hossa**, Ott., Atl., Pit.	10	701	**299**	.427
29.	**Brian Rolston**, N.J., Col., Bos., Min.	13	977	**286**	.293
30.	**Milan Hejduk**, Col.	9	701	**285**	.407
31.	**Ryan Smyth**, Edm., NYI, Col.	13	843	**284**	.337
32.	**Pavol Demitra**, Ott., St.L., L.A., Min.	14	750	**281**	.375
33.	**Ray Whitney**, S.J., Edm., Fla., CBJ, Det., Car.	16	910	**279**	.307
34.	**Petr Sykora**, N.J., Ana., NYR, Edm., Pit.	10	845	**275**	.325
35.	**Bryan Smolinski**, Bos., Pit., NYI, L.A., Ott., Chi., Van., Mtl.	15	1056	**274**	.259
36.	**Vincent Lecavalier**, T.B.	9	710	**273**	.385
37.	**Doug Weight**, NYR, Edm., St.L., Car., Ana.	17	1131	**265**	.234
38.	**Patrik Elias**, N.J.	12	745	**264**	.354
39.	**Stu Barnes**, Wpg., Fla., Pit., Buf., Dal.	16	1136	**261**	.230
40.	**Martin Straka**, Pit., Ott., NYI, Fla., L.A., NYR	15	954	**257**	.269
41.	**Ilya Kovalchuk**, Atl.	6	466	**254**	.545
42.	**Peter Forsberg**, Que., Col., Phi., Nsh.	13	706	**249**	.353
43.	**Yanic Perreault**, Tor., L.A., Mtl., Nsh., Phx., Chi.	14	859	**247**	.288
44.	**Martin Rucinsky**, Edm., Que., Col., Mtl., Dal., NYR, St.L., Van.	16	961	**241**	.251
45.	**Todd Bertuzzi**, NYI, Van., Fla., Det., Ana.	12	793	**240**	.303
46.	**Joe Thornton**, Bos., S.J.	10	754	**240**	.318
47.	**Patrick Marleau**, S.J.	10	795	**238**	.299
48.	**Mike Sillinger**, Det., Ana., Van., Phi., T.B., Fla., Ott., CBJ, Phx., St.L.	17	1042	**238**	.228
49.	**Cory Stillman**, Cgy., St.L., T.B., Car., Ott.	9	839	**234**	.279
50.	**Robert Lang**, L.A., Bos., Pit., Wsh., Det., Chi.	14	875	**234**	.267
51.	**Jere Lehtinen**, Dal.	12	769	**231**	.300
52.	**Steve Sullivan**, N.J., Tor., Chi., Nsh.	11	723	**228**	.315
53.	**Shane Doan**, Wpg., Phx.	12	883	**227**	.257
54.	**Daymond Langkow**, T.B., Phi., Phx., Cgy.	12	868	**224**	.258
55.	**Rob Blake**, L.A., Col.	18	1127	**223**	.198
56.	**Dany Heatley**, Atl., Ott.	6	425	**221**	.520
57.	**Chris Drury**, Col., Cgy., Buf., NYR	9	710	**218**	.307
58.	**Chris Gratton**, T.B., Phi., Buf., Phx., Col., Fla.	14	1068	**214**	.200
59.	**Nicklas Lidstrom**, Det.	16	1252	**212**	.169
60.	**Mathieu Schneider**, Mtl., NYI, Tor., NYR, L.A., Det., Ana.	19	1197	**212**	.177
61.	**Fredrik Modin**, Tor., T.B., CBJ	11	764	**211**	.276
62.	**Olli Jokinen**, L.A., NYI, Fla.	10	723	**208**	.288
63.	**Martin St. Louis**, Cgy., T.B.	9	608	**208**	.342
64.	**Mark Parrish**, Fla., NYI, L.A., Min.	9	660	**208**	.315
65.	**Simon Gagne**, Phi.	7	527	**208**	.395
66.	**Marian Gaborik**, Min.	7	485	**206**	.425
67.	**Marco Sturm**, S.J., Bos.	10	760	**205**	.270
68.	**Michael Nylander**, Hfd., Cgy., T.B., Chi., Wsh., Bos., NYR	14	848	**200**	.236

Shane Doan's first goal of the 2007-08 season was the 200th of his career. He also recorded his 300th career assist and 500th career point during the season.

	Player	Seasons	Games	Goals	Goals per game
69.	**Darcy Tucker**, Mtl., T.B., Tor.	12	813	**197**	.242
70.	**Jozef Stumpel**, Bos., L.A., Fla.	16	957	**196**	.205
71.	**Daniel Briere**, Phx., Buf., Phi.	10	562	**193**	.343
72.	**Sergei Samsonov**, Bos., Edm., Mtl., Chi., Car.	10	657	**192**	.292
73.	**Andrew Brunette**, Wsh., Nsh., Atl., Min., Col.	12	788	**191**	.242
74.	**Mike Knuble**, Det., NYR, Bos., Phi.	11	738	**188**	.255
75.	**Sergei Gonchar**, Wsh., Bos., Pit.	13	904	**185**	.205
76.	**Radek Bonk**, Ott., Mtl., Nsh.	13	903	**185**	.205
77.	**Chris Chelios**, Mtl., Chi., Det.	24	1616	**185**	.114
78.	**Viktor Kozlov**, S.J., Fla., N.J., NYI, Wsh.	13	830	**185**	.223
79.	**Richard Zednik**, Wsh., Mtl., NYI, Fla.	12	675	**183**	.271
80.	**Martin Lapointe**, Det., Bos., Chi., Ott.	16	991	**181**	.183
81.	**Jamie Langenbrunner**, Dal., N.J.	13	803	**180**	.224
82.	**Radek Dvorak**, Fla., NYR, Edm., St.L.	12	895	**179**	.200
83.	**Vaclav Prospal**, Phi., Ott., Fla., T.B., Ana.	11	792	**179**	.226
84.	**Alex Tanguay**, Col., Cgy.	8	609	**177**	.291
85.	**Tomas Holmstrom**, Det.	11	758	**175**	.231
86.	**Saku Koivu**, Mtl.	12	727	**175**	.241
87.	**Dean McAmmond**, Chi., Edm., Phi., Cgy., Col., St.L., Ott.	15	872	**173**	.198
88.	**Michael Peca**, Van., Buf., NYI, Edm., Tor., CBJ	13	793	**172**	.217
89.	**J.P. Dumont**, Chi., Buf., Nsh.	9	596	**171**	.287
90.	**Todd Marchant**, NYR, Edm., CBJ, Ana.	14	966	**171**	.177
91.	**Marc Savard**, NYR, Cgy., Atl., Bos.	10	659	**170**	.258
92.	**Brenden Morrow**, Dal.	8	573	**168**	.293
93.	**Sandis Ozolinsh**, S.J., Col., Car., Fla., Ana., NYR	15	875	**167**	.191
94.	**Craig Conroy**, Mtl., St.L., Cgy., L.A.	13	846	**165**	.195
95.	**Alex Ovechkin**, Wsh.	3	245	**163**	.665
96.	**Brendan Morrison**, N.J., Van.	10	674	**159**	.236
97.	**Rob Niedermayer**, Fla., Cgy., Ana.	14	932	**157**	.168
98.	**Rick Nash**, CBJ	5	363	**154**	.424
99.	**Jonathan Cheechoo**, S.J.	5	374	**153**	.409
100.	**Henrik Zetterberg**, Det.	5	355	**152**	.428

Top 100 All-Time Assist Leaders

* active player

	Player	Seasons	Games	Assists	Assists per game
1.	**Wayne Gretzky**, Edm., L.A., St.L., NYR	20	1487	**1963**	1.320
2.	**Ron Francis**, Hfd., Pit., Car., Tor.	23	1731	**1249**	.722
3.	**Mark Messier**, Edm., NYR, Van.	25	1756	**1193**	.679
4.	**Raymond Bourque**, Bos., Col.	22	1612	**1169**	.725
5.	**Paul Coffey**, Edm., Pit., L.A., Det., Hfd., Phi., Chi., Car., Bos.	21	1409	**1135**	.806
6.	**Adam Oates**, Det., St.L., Bos., Wsh., Phi., Ana., Edm.	19	1337	**1079**	.807
7.	**Steve Yzerman**, Det.	22	1514	**1063**	.702
8.	**Gordie Howe**, Det., Hfd.	26	1767	**1049**	.594
9.	**Marcel Dionne**, Det., L.A., NYR	18	1348	**1040**	.772
10.	**Mario Lemieux**, Pit.	18	915	**1033**	1.129
* 11.	**Joe Sakic**, Que., Col.	19	1363	**1006**	.738
12.	**Doug Gilmour**, St.L., Cgy., Tor., N.J., Chi., Buf., Mtl.	20	1474	**964**	.654
* 13.	**Jaromir Jagr**, Pit., Wsh., NYR	17	1273	**953**	.749
14.	**Al MacInnis**, Cgy., St.L.	23	1416	**934**	.660
15.	**Larry Murphy**, L.A., Wsh., Min., Pit., Tor., Det.	21	1615	**929**	.575
16.	**Stan Mikita**, Chi.	22	1394	**926**	.664
17.	**Bryan Trottier**, NYI, Pit.	18	1279	**901**	.704
18.	**Phil Housley**, Buf., Wpg., St.L., Cgy., N.J., Wsh., Chi., Tor.	21	1495	**894**	.598
19.	**Dale Hawerchuk**, Wpg., Buf., St.L., Phi.	16	1188	**891**	.750
20.	**Phil Esposito**, Chi., Bos., NYR	18	1282	**873**	.681
21.	**Denis Savard**, Chi., Mtl., T.B.	17	1196	**865**	.723
* 22.	**Mark Recchi**, Pit., Phi., Mtl., Car., Atl.	19	1410	**859**	.609
23.	**Bobby Clarke**, Phi.	15	1144	**852**	.745
24.	**Alex Delvecchio**, Det.	24	1549	**825**	.533
25.	**Gilbert Perreault**, Buf.	17	1191	**814**	.683
26.	**John Bucyk**, Det., Bos.	23	1540	**813**	.528
27.	**Pierre Turgeon**, Buf., NYI, Mtl., St.L., Dal., Col.	19	1294	**812**	.628
28.	**Jari Kurri**, Edm., L.A., NYR, Ana., Col.	17	1251	**797**	.637
29.	**Guy Lafleur**, Mtl., NYR, Que.	17	1126	**793**	.704
30.	**Peter Stastny**, Que., N.J., St.L.	15	977	**789**	.808
31.	**Brian Leetch**, NYR, Tor., Bos.	18	1205	**781**	.648
32.	**Jean Ratelle**, NYR, Bos.	21	1281	**776**	.606
33.	**Vincent Damphousse**, Tor., Edm., Mtl., S.J.	18	1378	**773**	.561
* 34.	**Mats Sundin**, Que., Tor.	17	1305	**766**	.587
* 35.	**Chris Chelios**, Mtl., Chi., Det.	24	1616	**763**	.472
36.	**Bernie Federko**, St.L., Det.	14	1000	**761**	.761
* 37.	**Mike Modano**, Min., Dal.	19	1320	**755**	.572
38.	**Larry Robinson**, Mtl., L.A.	20	1384	**750**	.542
39.	**Denis Potvin**, NYI	15	1060	**742**	.700
40.	**Norm Ullman**, Det., Tor.	20	1410	**739**	.524
41.	**Bernie Nicholls**, L.A., NYR, Edm., N.J., Chi., S.J.	18	1127	**734**	.651
42.	**Luc Robitaille**, L.A., Pit., NYR, Det.	19	1431	**726**	.507
* 43.	**Nicklas Lidstrom**, Det.	16	1252	**726**	.580
44.	**Scott Stevens**, Wsh., St.L., N.J.	22	1635	**712**	.435
45.	**Jean Beliveau**, Mtl.	20	1125	**712**	.633
* 46.	**Doug Weight**, NYR, Edm., St.L., Car., Ana.	17	1131	**704**	.622
47.	**Dave Andreychuk**, Buf., Tor., N.J., Bos., Col., T.B.	23	1639	**698**	.426
48.	**Dale Hunter**, Que., Wsh., Col.	19	1407	**697**	.495
* 49.	**Jeremy Roenick**, Chi., Phx., Phi., L.A., S.J.	19	1321	**694**	.525
* 50.	**Brendan Shanahan**, N.J., St.L., Hfd., Det., NYR	20	1490	**690**	.463
51.	**Henri Richard**, Mtl.	20	1256	**688**	.548
* 52.	**Rod Brind'Amour**, St.L., Phi., Car.	19	1324	**687**	.519
53.	**Brad Park**, NYR, Bos., Det.	17	1113	**683**	.614
54.	**Bobby Smith**, Min., Mtl.	15	1077	**679**	.630
* 55.	**Sergei Fedorov**, Det., Ana., CBJ, Wsh.	17	1196	**674**	.564
56.	**Brett Hull**, Cgy., St.L., Dal., Det., Phx.	20	1269	**650**	.512
57.	**Bobby Orr**, Bos., Chi.	12	657	**645**	.982
58.	**Gary Suter**, Cgy., Chi., S.J.	17	1145	**641**	.560
59.	**Dave Taylor**, L.A.	17	1111	**638**	.574
60.	**Darryl Sittler**, Tor., Phi., Det.	15	1096	**637**	.581
61.	**Borje Salming**, Tor., Det.	17	1148	**637**	.555
* 62.	**Peter Forsberg**, Que., Col., Phi., Nsh.	13	706	**636**	.901
63.	**Neal Broten**, Min., Dal., N.J., L.A.	17	1099	**634**	.577
64.	**Theoren Fleury**, Cgy., Col., NYR, Chi.	15	1084	**633**	.584
65.	**Mike Gartner**, Wsh., Min., NYR, Tor., Phx.	19	1432	**627**	.438
66.	**Andy Bathgate**, NYR, Tor., Det., Pit.	17	1069	**624**	.584
67.	**Rod Gilbert**, NYR	18	1065	**615**	.577
* 68.	**Sergei Zubov**, NYR, Pit., Dal.	15	1058	**615**	.581
* 69.	**Teemu Selanne**, Wpg., Ana., S.J., Col.	15	1067	**606**	.568
70.	**Michel Goulet**, Que., Chi.	15	1089	**604**	.555
71.	**Kirk Muller**, N.J., Mtl., NYI, Tor., Fla., Dal.	19	1349	**602**	.446
72.	**Glenn Anderson**, Edm., Tor., NYR, St.L.	16	1129	**601**	.532

Colorado's Joe Sakic moved past Phil Esposito into eighth place on the NHL career points list and also became the 11th player in NHL history to tally 1,000 career assists.

	Player	Seasons	Games	Assists	Assists per game
73.	**Dino Ciccarelli**, Min., Wsh., Det., T.B., Fla.	19	1232	**592**	.481
74.	**Dave Keon**, Tor., Hfd.	18	1296	**590**	.455
75.	**Doug Wilson**, Chi., S.J.	16	1024	**590**	.576
76.	**Dave Babych**, Wpg., Hfd., Van., Phi., L.A.	19	1195	**581**	.486
77.	**Brian Propp**, Phi., Bos., Min., Hfd.	15	1016	**579**	.570
78.	**Steve Larmer**, Chi., NYR	15	1006	**571**	.568
79.	**Frank Mahovlich**, Tor., Det., Mtl.	18	1181	**570**	.483
80.	**Craig Janney**, Bos., St.L., S.J., Wpg., Phx., T.B., NYI	12	760	**563**	.741
81.	**Cliff Ronning**, St.L., Van., Phx., Nsh., L.A., Min., NYI	18	1137	**563**	.495
82.	**Joe Nieuwendyk**, Cgy., Dal., N.J., Tor., Fla.	20	1257	**562**	.447
83.	**Joe Mullen**, St.L., Cgy., Pit., Bos.	17	1062	**561**	.528
84.	**Bobby Hull**, Chi., Wpg., Hfd.	16	1063	**560**	.527
85.	**Alexander Mogilny**, Buf., Van., N.J., Tor.	16	990	**559**	.565
86.	**Mike Bossy**, NYI	10	752	**553**	.735
87.	**Thomas Steen**, Wpg.	14	950	**553**	.582
88.	**Ken Linseman**, Phi., Edm., Bos., Tor.	14	860	**551**	.641
89.	**Tom Lysiak**, Atl., Chi.	13	919	**551**	.600
* 90.	**Paul Kariya**, Ana., Col., Nsh., St.L.	13	903	**549**	.608
91.	**Mark Howe**, Hfd., Phi., Det.	16	929	**545**	.587
92.	**Pat LaFontaine**, NYI, Buf., NYR	15	865	**545**	.630
93.	**Red Kelly**, Det., Tor.	20	1316	**542**	.412
94.	**Pat Verbeek**, N.J., Hfd., NYR, Dal., Det.	20	1424	**541**	.380
95.	**Rick Middleton**, NYR, Bos.	14	1005	**540**	.537
96.	**Brian Bellows**, Min., Mtl., T.B., Ana., Wsh.	17	1188	**537**	.452
97.	**Andrew Cassels**, Mtl., Hfd., Cgy., Van., CBJ, Wsh.	16	1015	**528**	.520
98.	**Steve Duchesne**, L.A., Phi., Que., St.L., Ott., Det.	16	1113	**525**	.472
99.	**Dennis Maruk**, Cal., Cle., Min., Wsh.	14	888	**522**	.588
*100.	**Joe Thornton**, Bos., S.J.	10	754	**516**	.684

Top 100 Active Assist Leaders

San Jose's Joe Thornton recorded his 500th career assist on February 17, 2008. He also joined Wayne Gretzky, Bobby Orr and Stan Mikita as just the fourth player to lead the NHL in assists for three straight seasons.

	Player	Seasons	Games	Assists	Assists per game
1.	**Joe Sakic**, Que., Col.	19	1363	**1006**	.738
2.	**Jaromir Jagr**, Pit., Wsh., NYR	17	1273	**953**	.749
3.	**Mark Recchi**, Pit., Phi., Mtl., Car., Atl.	19	1410	**859**	.609
4.	**Mats Sundin**, Que., Tor.	17	1305	**766**	.587
5.	**Chris Chelios**, Mtl., Chi., Det.	24	1616	**763**	.472
6.	**Mike Modano**, Min., Dal.	19	1320	**755**	.572
7.	**Nicklas Lidstrom**, Det.	16	1252	**726**	.580
8.	**Doug Weight**, NYR, Edm., St.L., Car., Ana.	17	1131	**704**	.622
9.	**Jeremy Roenick**, Chi., Phx., Phi., L.A., S.J.	19	1321	**694**	.525
10.	**Brendan Shanahan**, N.J., St.L., Hfd., Det., NYR	20	1490	**690**	.463
11.	**Rod Brind'Amour**, St.L., Phi., Car.	19	1324	**687**	.519
12.	**Sergei Fedorov**, Det., Ana., CBJ, Wsh.	17	1196	**674**	.564
13.	**Peter Forsberg**, Que., Col., Phi., Nsh.	13	706	**636**	.901
14.	**Sergei Zubov**, NYR, Pit., Dal.	15	1058	**615**	.581
15.	**Teemu Selanne**, Wpg., Ana., S.J., Col.	15	1067	**606**	.568
16.	**Paul Kariya**, Ana., Col., Nsh., St.L.	13	903	**549**	.608
17.	**Joe Thornton**, Bos., S.J.	10	754	**516**	.684
18.	**Daniel Alfredsson**, Ott.	12	853	**516**	.605
19.	**Alex Kovalev**, NYR, Pit., Mtl.	15	1073	**508**	.473
20.	**Teppo Numminen**, Wpg., Phx., Dal., Buf.	19	1315	**505**	.384
21.	**Mathieu Schneider**, Mtl., NYI, Tor., NYR, L.A., Det., Ana.	19	1197	**490**	.409
22.	**Scott Niedermayer**, N.J., Ana.	16	1101	**485**	.441
23.	**Keith Tkachuk**, Wpg., Phx., St.L., Atl.	16	1055	**484**	.459
24.	**Jozef Stumpel**, Bos., L.A., Fla.	16	957	**481**	.503
25.	**Rob Blake**, L.A., Col.	18	1127	**479**	.425
26.	**Gary Roberts**, Cgy., Car., Tor., Fla., Pit.	21	1194	**469**	.393
27.	**Martin Straka**, Pit., Ott., NYI, Fla., L.A., NYR	15	954	**460**	.482
28.	**Ray Whitney**, S.J., Edm., Fla., CBJ, Det., Car.	16	910	**455**	.500
29.	**Markus Naslund**, Pit., Van.	14	1035	**452**	.437
30.	**Michael Nylander**, Hfd., Cgy., T.B., Chi., Wsh., Bos., NYR	14	848	**446**	.526
31.	**Alexei Yashin**, Ott., NYI	12	850	**444**	.522
32.	**Jason Arnott**, Edm., N.J., Dal., Nsh.	14	971	**439**	.452
33.	**Sergei Gonchar**, Wsh., Bos., Pit.	13	904	**430**	.476
34.	**Vyacheslav Kozlov**, Det., Buf., Atl.	16	1045	**429**	.411
35.	**Chris Pronger**, Hfd., St.L., Edm., Ana.	14	940	**427**	.454
36.	**Owen Nolan**, Que., Col., S.J., Tor., Phx., Cgy.	16	1068	**426**	.399
37.	**Pavol Demitra**, Ott., St.L., L.A., Min.	14	750	**418**	.557
38.	**Bobby Holik**, Hfd., N.J., NYR, Atl.	17	1252	**416**	.332
39.	**Saku Koivu**, Mtl.	12	727	**416**	.572
40.	**Marc Savard**, NYR, Cgy., Atl., Bos.	10	659	**405**	.615
41.	**Robert Lang**, L.A., Bos., Pit., Wsh., Det., Chi.	14	875	**401**	.458
42.	**Sandis Ozolinsh**, S.J., Col., Car., Fla., Ana., NYR	15	875	**397**	.454
43.	**Roman Hamrlik**, T.B., Edm., NYI, Cgy., Mtl.	15	1076	**395**	.367
44.	**Darryl Sydor**, L.A., Dal., CBJ, T.B., Pit.	16	1171	**389**	.332
45.	**Scott Gomez**, N.J., NYR	8	629	**388**	.617
46.	**Jarome Iginla**, Cgy.	12	860	**388**	.451
47.	**Bryan Smolinski**, Bos., Pit., NYI, L.A., Ott., Chi., Van., Mtl.	15	1056	**377**	.357
48.	**Bill Guerin**, N.J., Edm., Bos., Dal., St.L., S.J., NYI	16	1107	**376**	.340
49.	**Vaclav Prospal**, Phi., Ott., Fla., T.B., Ana.	11	792	**375**	.473
50.	**Alexei Zhitnik**, L.A., Buf., NYI, Phi., Atl.	15	1085	**375**	.346
51.	**Martin Rucinsky**, Edm., Que., Col., Mtl., Dal., NYR, St.L., Van.	16	961	**371**	.386
52.	**Cory Stillman**, Cgy., St.L., T.B., Car., Ott.	9	839	**368**	.439
53.	**Patrik Elias**, N.J.	12	745	**364**	.489
54.	**Alex Tanguay**, Col., Cgy.	8	609	**362**	.594
55.	**Andrew Brunette**, Wsh., Nsh., Atl., Min., Col.	12	788	**358**	.454
56.	**Petr Sykora**, N.J., Ana., NYR, Edm., Pit.	10	845	**353**	.418
57.	**Martin Gelinas**, Edm., Que., Van., Car., Cgy., Fla., Nsh.	19	1273	**351**	.276
58.	**Chris Gratton**, T.B., Phi., Buf., Phx., Col., Fla.	14	1068	**351**	.329
59.	**Marian Hossa**, Ott., Atl., Pit.	10	701	**349**	.498
60.	**Steve Sullivan**, N.J., Tor., Chi., Nsh.	11	723	**349**	.483
61.	**Brian Rolston**, N.J., Col., Bos., Min.	13	977	**348**	.356
62.	**Miroslav Satan**, Edm., Buf., NYI	12	947	**348**	.367
63.	**Brad Richards**, T.B., Dal.	7	564	**348**	.617
64.	**Geoff Sanderson**, Hfd., Car., Van., Buf., CBJ, Phx., Phi., Edm.	17	1104	**345**	.313
65.	**Todd Bertuzzi**, NYI, Van., Fla., Det., Ana.	12	793	**340**	.429
66.	**Stu Barnes**, Wpg., Fla., Pit., Buf., Dal.	16	1136	**336**	.296
67.	**Tomas Kaberle**, Tor.	9	681	**333**	.489
68.	**Daymond Langkow**, T.B., Phi., Phx., Cgy.	12	868	**331**	.381
69.	**Vincent Lecavalier**, T.B.	9	710	**329**	.463
70.	**Shane Doan**, Wpg., Phx.	12	883	**323**	.366
71.	**Ryan Smyth**, Edm., NYI, Col.	13	843	**317**	.376
72.	**Brendan Morrison**, N.J., Van.	10	674	**315**	.467
73.	**Glen Murray**, Bos., Pit., L.A.	16	1009	**314**	.311
74.	**Milan Hejduk**, Col.	9	701	**313**	.447
75.	**Craig Conroy**, Mtl., St.L., Cgy., L.A.	13	846	**312**	.369
76.	**Viktor Kozlov**, S.J., Fla., N.J., NYI, Wsh.	13	830	**311**	.375
77.	**Brian Rafalski**, N.J., Det.	8	614	**309**	.503
78.	**Wade Redden**, Ott.	11	838	**309**	.369
79.	**Patrice Brisebois**, Mtl., Col.	17	947	**309**	.326
80.	**Mike Sillinger**, Det., Ana., Van., Phi., T.B., Fla., Ott., CBJ, Phx., St.L.	17	1042	**308**	.296
81.	**Chris Drury**, Col., Cgy., Buf., NYR	9	710	**304**	.428
82.	**Bryan McCabe**, NYI, Van., Chi., Tor.	12	917	**303**	.330
83.	**Patrick Marleau**, S.J.	10	795	**301**	.379
84.	**Martin St. Louis**, Cgy., T.B.	9	608	**297**	.488
85.	**Jamie Langenbrunner**, Dal., N.J.	13	803	**296**	.369
86.	**Henrik Sedin**, Van.	7	564	**291**	.516
87.	**Ed Jovanovski**, Fla., Van., Phx.	12	821	**288**	.351
88.	**Radek Dvorak**, Fla., NYR, Edm., St.L.	12	895	**287**	.321
89.	**Radek Bonk**, Ott., Mtl., Nsh.	13	903	**287**	.318
90.	**Pavel Datsyuk**, Det.	6	445	**286**	.643
91.	**Todd Marchant**, NYR, Edm., CBJ, Ana.	14	966	**279**	.289
92.	**Michael Peca**, Van., Buf., NYI, Edm., Tor., CBJ	13	793	**271**	.342
93.	**Yanic Perreault**, Tor., L.A., Mtl., Nsh., Phx., Chi.	14	859	**269**	.313
94.	**Sergei Samsonov**, Bos., Edm., Mtl., Chi., Car.	10	657	**262**	.399
95.	**Kimmo Timonen**, Nsh., Phi.	9	653	**258**	.395
96.	**Daniel Briere**, Phx., Buf., Phi.	10	562	**255**	.454
97.	**Olli Jokinen**, L.A., NYI, Fla.	10	723	**253**	.350
98.	**Derian Hatcher**, Min., Dal., Det., Phi.	16	1045	**251**	.240
99.	**Rob Niedermayer**, Fla., Cgy., Ana.	14	932	**250**	.268
100.	**Dany Heatley**, Atl., Ott.	6	425	**250**	.588

Top 100 All-Time Point Leaders

* active player

	Player	Seasons	Games	Goals	Assists	Points	Points per game
1.	**Wayne Gretzky**, Edm., L.A., St.L., NYR	20	1487	894	1963	**2857**	1.921
2.	**Mark Messier**, Edm., NYR, Van.	25	1756	694	1193	**1887**	1.075
3.	**Gordie Howe**, Det., Hfd.	26	1767	801	1049	**1850**	1.047
4.	**Ron Francis**, Hfd., Pit., Car., Tor.	23	1731	549	1249	**1798**	1.039
5.	**Marcel Dionne**, Det., L.A., NYR	18	1348	731	1040	**1771**	1.314
6.	**Steve Yzerman**, Det.	22	1514	692	1063	**1755**	1.159
7.	**Mario Lemieux**, Pit.	18	915	690	1033	**1723**	1.883
* 8.	**Joe Sakic**, Que., Col.	19	1363	623	1006	**1629**	1.195
* 9.	**Jaromir Jagr**, Pit., Wsh., NYR	17	1273	646	953	**1599**	1.256
10.	**Phil Esposito**, Chi., Bos., NYR	18	1282	717	873	**1590**	1.240
11.	**Raymond Bourque**, Bos., Col.	22	1612	410	1169	**1579**	.980
12.	**Paul Coffey**, Edm., Pit., L.A., Det., Hfd., Phi., Chi., Car., Bos.	21	1409	396	1135	**1531**	1.087
13.	**Stan Mikita**, Chi.	22	1394	541	926	**1467**	1.052
14.	**Bryan Trottier**, NYI, Pit.	18	1279	524	901	**1425**	1.114
15.	**Adam Oates**, Det., St.L., Bos., Wsh., Phi., Ana., Edm.	19	1337	341	1079	**1420**	1.062
16.	**Doug Gilmour**, St.L., Cgy., Tor., N.J., Chi., Buf., Mtl.	20	1474	450	964	**1414**	.959
17.	**Dale Hawerchuk**, Wpg., Buf., St.L., Phi.	16	1188	518	891	**1409**	1.186
18.	**Jari Kurri**, Edm., L.A., NYR, Ana., Col.	17	1251	601	797	**1398**	1.118
19.	**Luc Robitaille**, L.A., Pit., NYR, Det.	19	1431	668	726	**1394**	.974
20.	**Brett Hull**, Cgy., St.L., Dal., Det., Phx.	20	1269	741	650	**1391**	1.096
* 21.	**Mark Recchi**, Pit., Phi., Mtl., Car., Atl.	19	1410	522	859	**1381**	.979
22.	**John Bucyk**, Det., Bos.	23	1540	556	813	**1369**	.889
23.	**Guy Lafleur**, Mtl., NYR, Que.	17	1126	560	793	**1353**	1.202
* 24.	**Brendan Shanahan**, N.J., St.L., Hfd., Det., NYR	20	1490	650	690	**1340**	.899
25.	**Dave Andreychuk**, Buf., Tor., N.J., Bos., Col., T.B.	23	1639	640	698	**1338**	.816
26.	**Denis Savard**, Chi., Mtl., T.B.	17	1196	473	865	**1338**	1.119
27.	**Mike Gartner**, Wsh., Min., NYR, Tor., Phx.	19	1432	708	627	**1335**	.932
28.	**Pierre Turgeon**, Buf., NYI, Mtl., St.L., Dal., Col.	19	1294	515	812	**1327**	1.026
29.	**Gilbert Perreault**, Buf.	17	1191	512	814	**1326**	1.113
* 30.	**Mats Sundin**, Que., Tor.	17	1305	555	766	**1321**	1.012
* 31.	**Mike Modano**, Min., Dal.	19	1320	528	755	**1283**	.972
32.	**Alex Delvecchio**, Det.	24	1549	456	825	**1281**	.827
33.	**Al MacInnis**, Cgy., St.L.	23	1416	340	934	**1274**	.900
34.	**Jean Ratelle**, NYR, Bos.	21	1281	491	776	**1267**	.989
35.	**Peter Stastny**, Que., N.J., St.L.	15	977	450	789	**1239**	1.268
36.	**Phil Housley**, Buf., Wpg., St.L., Cgy., N.J., Wsh., Chi., Tor.	21	1495	338	894	**1232**	.824
37.	**Norm Ullman**, Det., Tor.	20	1410	490	739	**1229**	.872
38.	**Jean Beliveau**, Mtl.	20	1125	507	712	**1219**	1.084
39.	**Larry Murphy**, L.A., Wsh., Min., Pit., Tor., Det.	21	1615	287	929	**1216**	.753
40.	**Bobby Clarke**, Phi.	15	1144	358	852	**1210**	1.058
41.	**Bernie Nicholls**, L.A., NYR, Edm., N.J., Chi., S.J.	18	1127	475	734	**1209**	1.073
42.	**Vincent Damphousse**, Tor., Edm., Mtl., S.J.	18	1378	432	773	**1205**	.874
* 43.	**Jeremy Roenick**, Chi., Phx., Phi., L.A., S.J.	19	1321	509	694	**1203**	.911
44.	**Dino Ciccarelli**, Min., Wsh., Det., T.B., Fla.	19	1232	608	592	**1200**	.974
45.	**Bobby Hull**, Chi., Wpg., Hfd.	16	1063	610	560	**1170**	1.101
* 46.	**Teemu Selanne**, Wpg., Ana., S.J., Col.	15	1067	552	606	**1158**	1.085
47.	**Michel Goulet**, Que., Chi.	15	1089	548	604	**1152**	1.058
* 48.	**Sergei Fedorov**, Det., Ana., CBJ, Wsh.	17	1196	472	674	**1146**	.958
49.	**Bernie Federko**, St.L., Det.	14	1000	369	761	**1130**	1.130
50.	**Joe Nieuwendyk**, Cgy., Dal., N.J., Tor., Fla.	20	1257	564	562	**1126**	.896
51.	**Mike Bossy**, NYI	10	752	573	553	**1126**	1.497
52.	**Darryl Sittler**, Tor., Phi., Det.	15	1096	484	637	**1121**	1.023
* 53.	**Rod Brind'Amour**, St.L., Phi., Car.	19	1324	427	687	**1114**	.841
54.	**Frank Mahovlich**, Tor., Det., Mtl.	18	1181	533	570	**1103**	.934
55.	**Glenn Anderson**, Edm., Tor., NYR, St.L.	16	1129	498	601	**1099**	.973
56.	**Theoren Fleury**, Cgy., Col., NYR, Chi.	15	1084	455	633	**1088**	1.004
57.	**Dave Taylor**, L.A.	17	1111	431	638	**1069**	.962
58.	**Joe Mullen**, St.L., Cgy., Pit., Bos.	17	1062	502	561	**1063**	1.001

Mats Sundin broke Darryl Sitter's team records for most goals and most points by a Maple Leaf in 2007-08, upping his totals in Toronto to 420 and 987.

	Player	Seasons	Games	Goals	Assists	Points	Points per game
59.	**Pat Verbeek**, N.J., Hfd., NYR, Dal., Det.	20	1424	522	541	**1063**	.746
60.	**Denis Potvin**, NYI	15	1060	310	742	**1052**	.992
61.	**Henri Richard**, Mtl.	20	1256	358	688	**1046**	.833
62.	**Bobby Smith**, Min., Mtl.	15	1077	357	679	**1036**	.962
63.	**Alexander Mogilny**, Buf., Van., N.J., Tor.	16	990	473	559	**1032**	1.042
64.	**Brian Leetch**, NYR, Tor., Bos.	18	1205	247	781	**1028**	.853
65.	**Brian Bellows**, Min., Mtl., T.B., Ana., Wsh.	17	1188	485	537	**1022**	.860
66.	**Rod Gilbert**, NYR	18	1065	406	615	**1021**	.959
67.	**Dale Hunter**, Que., Wsh., Col.	19	1407	323	697	**1020**	.725
68.	**Pat LaFontaine**, NYI, Buf., NYR	15	865	468	545	**1013**	1.171
69.	**Steve Larmer**, Chi., NYR	15	1006	441	571	**1012**	1.006
70.	**Lanny McDonald**, Tor., Col., Cgy.	16	1111	500	506	**1006**	.905
71.	**Brian Propp**, Phi., Bos., Min., Hfd.	15	1016	425	579	**1004**	.988
72.	**Rick Middleton**, NYR, Bos.	14	1005	448	540	**988**	.983
73.	**Dave Keon**, Tor., Hfd.	18	1296	396	590	**986**	.761
* 74.	**Keith Tkachuk**, Wpg., Phx., St.L., Atl.	16	1055	500	484	**984**	.933
75.	**Andy Bathgate**, NYR, Tor., Det., Pit.	17	1069	349	624	**973**	.910
* 76.	**Doug Weight**, NYR, Edm., St.L., Car., Ana.	17	1131	265	704	**969**	.857
77.	**Maurice Richard**, Mtl.	18	978	544	421	**965**	.987
78.	**Kirk Muller**, N.J., Mtl., NYI, Tor., Fla., Dal.	19	1349	357	602	**959**	.711
79.	**Larry Robinson**, Mtl., L.A.	20	1384	208	750	**958**	.692
80.	**Rick Tocchet**, Phi., Pit., L.A., Bos., Wsh., Phx.	18	1144	440	512	**952**	.832
* 81.	**Chris Chelios**, Mtl., Chi., Det.	24	1616	185	763	**948**	.587
* 82.	**Nicklas Lidstrom**, Det.	16	1252	212	726	**938**	.749
83.	**Steve Thomas**, Tor., Chi., NYI, N.J., Ana., Det.	20	1235	421	512	**933**	.755
* 84.	**Paul Kariya**, Ana., Col., Nsh., St.L.	13	903	382	549	**931**	1.031
85.	**Neal Broten**, Min., Dal., N.J., L.A.	17	1099	289	634	**923**	.840
86.	**Bobby Orr**, Bos., Chi.	12	657	270	645	**915**	1.393
87.	**Scott Stevens**, Wsh., St.L., N.J.	22	1635	196	712	**908**	.555
* 88.	**Gary Roberts**, Cgy., Car., Tor., Fla., Pit.	21	1194	434	469	**903**	.756
89.	**Tony Amonte**, NYR, Chi., Phx., Phi., Cgy.	16	1174	416	484	**900**	.767
90.	**Ray Ferraro**, Hfd., NYI, NYR, L.A., Atl., St.L.	18	1258	408	490	**898**	.714
91.	**Brad Park**, NYR, Bos., Det.	17	1113	213	683	**896**	.805
92.	**Peter Bondra**, Wsh., Ott., Atl., Chi.	16	1081	503	389	**892**	.825
93.	**Butch Goring**, L.A., NYI, Bos.	16	1107	375	513	**888**	.802
* 94.	**Peter Forsberg**, Que., Col., Phi., Nsh.	13	706	249	636	**885**	1.254
95.	**Bill Barber**, Phi.	14	903	420	463	**883**	.978
96.	**Dennis Maruk**, Cal., Cle., Min., Wsh.	14	888	356	522	**878**	.989
* 97.	**Alex Kovalev**, NYR, Pit., Mtl.	15	1073	368	508	**876**	.816
98.	**Cliff Ronning**, St.L., Van., Phx., Nsh., L.A., Min., NYI	18	1137	306	563	**869**	.764
99.	**Trevor Linden**, Van., NYI, Mtl., Wsh.	19	1382	375	492	**867**	.627
100.	**Ivan Boldirev**, Bos., Cal., Chi., Atl., Van., Det.	15	1052	361	505	**866**	.823

Top 100 Active Points Leaders

	Player	Seasons	Games	Goals	Assists	Points	Points per game
1.	**Joe Sakic**, Que., Col.	19	1363	623	1006	**1629**	1.195
2.	**Jaromir Jagr**, Pit., Wsh., NYR	17	1273	646	953	**1599**	1.256
3.	**Mark Recchi**, Pit., Phi., Mtl., Car., Atl.	19	1410	522	859	**1381**	.979
4.	**Brendan Shanahan**, N.J., St.L., Hfd., Det., NYR	20	1490	650	690	**1340**	.899
5.	**Mats Sundin**, Que., Tor.	17	1305	555	766	**1321**	1.012
6.	**Mike Modano**, Min., Dal.	19	1320	528	755	**1283**	.972
7.	**Jeremy Roenick**, Chi., Phx., Phi., L.A., S.J.	19	1321	509	694	**1203**	.911
8.	**Teemu Selanne**, Wpg., Ana., S.J., Col.	15	1067	552	606	**1158**	1.085
9.	**Sergei Fedorov**, Det., Ana., CBJ, Wsh.	17	1196	472	674	**1146**	.958
10.	**Rod Brind'Amour**, St.L., Phi., Car.	19	1324	427	687	**1114**	.841
11.	**Keith Tkachuk**, Wpg., Phx., St.L., Atl.	16	1055	500	484	**984**	.933
12.	**Doug Weight**, NYR, Edm., St.L., Car., Ana.	17	1131	265	704	**969**	.857
13.	**Chris Chelios**, Mtl., Chi., Det.	24	1616	185	763	**948**	.587
14.	**Nicklas Lidstrom**, Det.	16	1252	212	726	**938**	.749
15.	**Paul Kariya**, Ana., Col., Nsh., St.L.	13	903	382	549	**931**	1.031
16.	**Gary Roberts**, Cgy., Car., Tor., Fla., Pit.	21	1194	434	469	**903**	.756
17.	**Peter Forsberg**, Que., Col., Phi., Nsh.	13	706	249	636	**885**	1.254
18.	**Alex Kovalev**, NYR, Pit., Mtl.	15	1073	368	508	**876**	.816
19.	**Daniel Alfredsson**, Ott.	12	853	331	516	**847**	.993
20.	**Markus Naslund**, Pit., Van.	14	1035	371	452	**823**	.795
21.	**Owen Nolan**, Que., Col., S.J., Tor., Phx., Cgy.	16	1068	381	426	**807**	.756
22.	**Alexei Yashin**, Ott., NYI	12	850	337	444	**781**	.919
23.	**Jason Arnott**, Edm., N.J., Dal., Nsh.	14	971	331	439	**770**	.793
24.	**Sergei Zubov**, NYR, Pit., Dal.	15	1058	152	615	**767**	.725
25.	**Bill Guerin**, N.J., Edm., Bos., Dal., St.L., S.J., NYI	16	1107	387	376	**763**	.689
26.	**Jarome Iginla**, Cgy.	12	860	374	388	**762**	.886
27.	**Joe Thornton**, Bos., S.J.	10	754	240	516	**756**	1.003
28.	**Vyacheslav Kozlov**, Det., Buf., Atl.	16	1045	322	429	**751**	.719
29.	**Bobby Holik**, Hfd., N.J., NYR, Atl.	17	1252	322	416	**738**	.589
30.	**Ray Whitney**, S.J., Edm., Fla., CBJ, Det., Car.	16	910	279	455	**734**	.807
31.	**Martin Straka**, Pit., Ott., NYI, Fla., L.A., NYR	15	954	257	460	**717**	.752
32.	**Rob Blake**, L.A., Col.	18	1127	223	479	**702**	.623
33.	**Mathieu Schneider**, Mtl., NYI, Tor., NYR, L.A., Det., Ana.	19	1197	212	490	**702**	.586
34.	**Geoff Sanderson**, Hfd., Car., Van., Buf., CBJ, Phx., Phi., Edm.	17	1104	355	345	**700**	.634
35.	**Pavol Demitra**, Ott., St.L., L.A., Min.	14	750	281	418	**699**	.932
36.	**Miroslav Satan**, Edm., Buf., NYI	12	947	337	348	**685**	.723
37.	**Jozef Stumpel**, Bos., L.A., Fla.	16	957	196	481	**677**	.707
38.	**Martin Gelinas**, Edm., Que., Van., Car., Cgy., Fla., Nsh.	19	1273	309	351	**660**	.518
39.	**Glen Murray**, Bos., Pit., L.A.	16	1009	337	314	**651**	.645
40.	**Bryan Smolinski**, Bos., Pit., NYI, L.A., Ott., Chi., Van., Mtl.	15	1056	274	377	**651**	.616
41.	**Marian Hossa**, Ott., Atl., Pit.	10	701	299	349	**648**	.924
42.	**Michael Nylander**, Hfd., Cgy., T.B., Chi., Wsh., Bos., NYR	14	848	200	446	**646**	.762
43.	**Robert Lang**, L.A., Bos., Pit., Wsh., Det., Chi.	14	875	234	401	**635**	.726
44.	**Brian Rolston**, N.J., Col., Bos., Min.	13	977	286	348	**634**	.649
45.	**Scott Niedermayer**, N.J., Ana.	16	1101	148	485	**633**	.575
46.	**Petr Sykora**, N.J., Ana., NYR, Edm., Pit.	10	845	275	353	**628**	.743
47.	**Patrik Elias**, N.J.	12	745	264	364	**628**	.843
48.	**Teppo Numminen**, Wpg., Phx., Dal., Buf.	19	1315	115	505	**620**	.471
49.	**Sergei Gonchar**, Wsh., Bos., Pit.	13	904	185	430	**615**	.680
50.	**Martin Rucinsky**, Edm., Que., Col., Mtl., Dal., NYR, St.L., Van.	16	961	241	371	**612**	.637
51.	**Vincent Lecavalier**, T.B.	9	710	273	329	**602**	.848
52.	**Cory Stillman**, Cgy., St.L., T.B., Car., Ott.	9	839	234	368	**602**	.718
53.	**Ryan Smyth**, Edm., NYI, Col.	13	843	284	317	**601**	.713
54.	**Milan Hejduk**, Col.	9	701	285	313	**598**	.853
55.	**Stu Barnes**, Wpg., Fla., Pit., Buf., Dal.	16	1136	261	336	**597**	.526
56.	**Saku Koivu**, Mtl.	12	727	175	416	**591**	.813

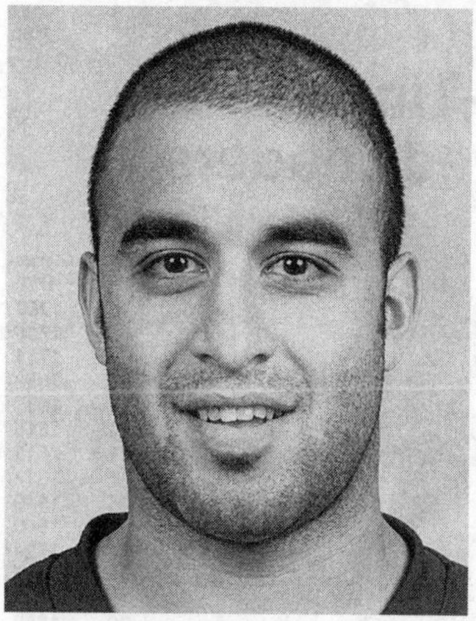

Scott Gomez ranked among the league leaders in assists in 2007-08, his first season with the New York Rangers. Both Gomez and teammate Chris Drury picked up their 500th career points on February 1, 2008.

	Player	Seasons	Games	Goals	Assists	Points	Points per game
57.	**Todd Bertuzzi**, NYI, Van., Fla., Det., Ana.	12	793	240	340	**580**	.731
58.	**Steve Sullivan**, N.J., Tor., Chi., Nsh.	11	723	228	349	**577**	.798
59.	**Marc Savard**, NYR, Cgy., Atl., Bos.	10	659	170	405	**575**	.873
60.	**Chris Gratton**, T.B., Phi., Buf., Phx., Col., Fla.	14	1068	214	351	**565**	.529
61.	**Sandis Ozolinsh**, S.J., Col., Car., Fla., Ana., NYR	15	875	167	397	**564**	.645
62.	**Chris Pronger**, Hfd., St.L., Edm., Ana.	14	940	131	427	**558**	.594
63.	**Daymond Langkow**, T.B., Phi., Phx., Cgy.	12	868	224	331	**555**	.639
64.	**Vaclav Prospal**, Phi., Ott., Fla., T.B., Ana.	11	792	179	375	**554**	.699
65.	**Shane Doan**, Wpg., Phx.	12	883	227	323	**550**	.623
66.	**Andrew Brunette**, Wsh., Nsh., Atl., Min., Col.	12	788	191	358	**549**	.697
67.	**Mike Sillinger**, Det., Ana., Van., Phi., T.B., Fla., Ott., CBJ, Phx., St.L.	17	1042	238	308	**546**	.524
68.	**Alex Tanguay**, Col., Cgy.	8	609	177	362	**539**	.885
69.	**Patrick Marleau**, S.J.	10	795	238	301	**539**	.678
70.	**Roman Hamrlik**, T.B., Edm., NYI, Cgy., Mtl.	15	1076	136	395	**531**	.493
71.	**Chris Drury**, Col., Cgy., Buf., NYR	9	710	218	304	**522**	.735
72.	**Scott Gomez**, N.J., NYR	8	629	132	388	**520**	.827
73.	**Yanic Perreault**, Tor., L.A., Mtl., Nsh., Phx., Chi.	14	859	247	269	**516**	.601
74.	**Martin St. Louis**, Cgy., T.B.	9	608	208	297	**505**	.831
75.	**Brad Richards**, T.B., Dal.	7	564	152	348	**500**	.887
76.	**Viktor Kozlov**, S.J., Fla., N.J., NYI, Wsh.	13	830	185	311	**496**	.598
77.	**Darryl Sydor**, L.A., Dal., CBJ, T.B., Pit.	16	1171	95	389	**484**	.413
78.	**Craig Conroy**, Mtl., St.L., Cgy., L.A.	13	846	165	312	**477**	.564
79.	**Jamie Langenbrunner**, Dal., N.J.	13	803	180	296	**476**	.593
80.	**Brendan Morrison**, N.J., Van.	10	674	159	315	**474**	.703
81.	**Jere Lehtinen**, Dal.	12	769	231	242	**473**	.615
82.	**Radek Bonk**, Ott., Mtl., Nsh.	13	903	185	287	**472**	.523
83.	**Dany Heatley**, Atl., Ott.	6	425	221	250	**471**	1.108
84.	**Alexei Zhitnik**, L.A., Buf., NYI, Phi., Atl.	15	1085	96	375	**471**	.434
85.	**Radek Dvorak**, Fla., NYR, Edm., St.L.	12	895	179	287	**466**	.521
86.	**Ilya Kovalchuk**, Atl.	6	466	254	212	**466**	1.000
87.	**Olli Jokinen**, L.A., NYI, Fla.	10	723	208	253	**461**	.638
88.	**Sergei Samsonov**, Bos., Edm., Mtl., Chi., Car.	10	657	192	262	**454**	.691
89.	**Todd Marchant**, NYR, Edm., CBJ, Ana.	14	966	171	279	**450**	.466
90.	**Daniel Briere**, Phx., Buf., Phi.	10	562	193	255	**448**	.797
91.	**Michael Peca**, Van., Buf., NYI, Edm., Tor., CBJ	13	793	172	271	**443**	.559
92.	**Darcy Tucker**, Mtl., T.B., Tor.	12	813	197	239	**436**	.536
93.	**Pavel Datsyuk**, Det.	6	445	139	286	**425**	.955
94.	**Bryan McCabe**, NYI, Van., Chi., Tor.	12	917	115	303	**418**	.456
95.	**Fredrik Modin**, Tor., T.B., CBJ	11	764	211	205	**416**	.545
96.	**Marco Sturm**, S.J., Bos.	10	760	205	211	**416**	.547
97.	**Dean McAmmond**, Chi., Edm., Phi., Cgy., Col., St.L., Ott.	15	872	173	242	**415**	.476
98.	**Marian Gaborik**, Min.	7	485	206	208	**414**	.854
99.	**Wade Redden**, Ott.	11	838	101	309	**410**	.489
100.	**Simon Gagne**, Phi.	7	527	208	202	**410**	.778

Top 100 All-Time Games Played Leaders

* active player

	Player	Seasons	Games Played
	1. **Gordie Howe**, Det., Hfd.	26	**1767**
	2. **Mark Messier**, Edm., NYR, Van.	25	**1756**
	3. **Ron Francis**, Hfd., Pit., Car., Tor.	23	**1731**
	4. **Dave Andreychuk**, Buf., Tor., N.J., Bos., Col., T.B.	23	**1639**
	5. **Scott Stevens**, Wsh., St.L., N.J.	22	**1635**
*	6. **Chris Chelios**, Mtl., Chi., Det.	24	**1616**
	7. **Larry Murphy**, L.A., Wsh., Min., Pit., Tor., Det.	21	**1615**
	8. **Raymond Bourque**, Bos., Col.	22	**1612**
	9. **Alex Delvecchio**, Det.	24	**1549**
	10. **John Bucyk**, Det., Bos.	23	**1540**
	11. **Steve Yzerman**, Det.	22	**1514**
	12. **Phil Housley**, Buf., Wpg., St.L., Cgy., N.J., Wsh., Chi., Tor.	21	**1495**
*	13. **Brendan Shanahan**, N.J., St.L., Hfd., Det., NYR	20	**1490**
	14. **Wayne Gretzky**, Edm., L.A., St.L., NYR	20	**1487**
	15. **Doug Gilmour**, St.L., Cgy., Tor., N.J., Chi., Buf., Mtl.	20	**1474**
	16. **Glen Wesley**, Bos., Hfd., Car., Tor.	20	**1457**
	17. **Tim Horton**, Tor., NYR, Pit., Buf.	24	**1446**
	18. **Mike Gartner**, Wsh., Min., NYR, Tor., Phx.	19	**1432**
	19. **Luc Robitaille**, L.A., Pit., NYR, Det.	19	**1431**
	20. **Scott Mellanby**, Phi., Edm., Fla., St.L., Atl.	21	**1431**
	21. **Pat Verbeek**, N.J., Hfd., NYR, Dal., Det.	20	**1424**
	22. **Al MacInnis**, Cgy., St.L.	23	**1416**
*	23. **Luke Richardson**, Tor., Edm., Phi., CBJ, T.B., Ott.	20	**1415**
	24. **Harry Howell**, NYR, Oak., Cal., L.A.	21	**1411**
*	25. **Mark Recchi**, Pit., Phi., Mtl., Car., Atl.	19	**1410**
	26. **Norm Ullman**, Det., Tor.	20	**1410**
	27. **Paul Coffey**, Edm., Pit., L.A., Det., Hfd., Phi., Chi., Car., Bos.	21	**1409**
	28. **Dale Hunter**, Que., Wsh., Col.	19	**1407**
	29. **Stan Mikita**, Chi.	22	**1394**
	30. **Doug Mohns**, Bos., Chi., Min., Atl., Wsh.	22	**1390**
	31. **Larry Robinson**, Mtl., L.A.	20	**1384**
	32. **Trevor Linden**, Van., NYI, Mtl., Wsh.	19	**1382**
	33. **Vincent Damphousse**, Tor., Edm., Mtl., S.J.	18	**1378**
	34. **Dean Prentice**, NYR, Bos., Det., Pit., Min.	22	**1378**
*	35. **Joe Sakic**, Que., Col.	19	**1363**
	36. **Ron Stewart**, Tor., Bos., St.L., NYR, Van., NYI	21	**1353**
	37. **Kirk Muller**, N.J., Mtl., NYI, Tor., Fla., Dal.	19	**1349**
	38. **Marcel Dionne**, Det., L.A., NYR	18	**1348**
	39. **Adam Oates**, Det., St.L., Bos., Wsh., Phi., Ana., Edm.	19	**1337**
*	40. **Rod Brind'Amour**, St.L., Phi., Car.	19	**1324**
*	41. **Jeremy Roenick**, Chi., Phx., Phi., L.A., S.J.	19	**1321**
*	42. **Mike Modano**, Min., Dal.	19	**1320**
	43. **Guy Carbonneau**, Mtl., St.L., Dal.	19	**1318**
	44. **Red Kelly**, Det., Tor.	20	**1316**
*	45. **Teppo Numminen**, Wpg., Phx., Dal., Buf.	19	**1315**
*	46. **Mats Sundin**, Que., Tor.	17	**1305**
	47. **Dave Keon**, Tor., Hfd.	18	**1296**
	48. **Pierre Turgeon**, Buf., NYI, Mtl., St.L., Dal., Col.	19	**1294**
	49. **Ken Daneyko**, N.J.	20	**1283**
	50. **Phil Esposito**, Chi., Bos., NYR	18	**1282**
	51. **Jean Ratelle**, NYR, Bos.	21	**1281**
	52. **James Patrick**, NYR, Hfd., Cgy., Buf.	21	**1280**
	53. **Bryan Trottier**, NYI, Pit.	18	**1279**
*	54. **Jaromir Jagr**, Pit., Wsh., NYR	17	**1273**
*	55. **Martin Gelinas**, Edm., Que., Van., Car., Cgy., Fla., Nsh.	19	**1273**
	56. **Brett Hull**, Cgy., St.L., Dal., Det., Phx.	20	**1269**
	57. **Ray Ferraro**, Hfd., NYI, NYR, L.A., Atl., St.L.	18	**1258**
	58. **Joe Nieuwendyk**, Cgy., Dal., N.J., Tor., Fla.	20	**1257**
	59. **Craig Ludwig**, Mtl., NYI, Min., Dal.	17	**1256**
	60. **Henri Richard**, Mtl.	20	**1256**
	61. **Kevin Lowe**, Edm., NYR.	19	**1254**
*	62. **Nicklas Lidstrom**, Det.	16	**1252**
*	63. **Bobby Holik**, Hfd., N.J., NYR, Atl.	17	**1252**
	64. **Jari Kurri**, Edm., L.A., NYR, Ana., Col.	17	**1251**
	65. **Bill Gadsby**, Chi., NYR, Det.	20	**1248**
	66. **Allan Stanley**, NYR, Chi., Bos., Tor., Phi.	21	**1244**
	67. **Steve Thomas**, Tor., Chi., NYI, N.J., Ana., Det.	20	**1235**
	68. **Dino Ciccarelli**, Min., Wsh., Det., T.B., Fla.	19	**1232**
	69. **Ed Westfall**, Bos., NYI	18	**1226**
	70. **Brad McCrimmon**, Bos., Phi., Cgy., Det., Hfd., Phx.	18	**1222**
	71. **Eric Nesterenko**, Tor., Chi.	21	**1219**
	72. **Marcel Pronovost**, Det., Tor.	21	**1206**
	73. **Brian Leetch**, NYR, Tor., Bos.	18	**1205**
*	74. **Mathieu Schneider**, Mtl., NYI, Tor., NYR, L.A., Det., Ana.	19	**1197**
	75. **Claude Lemieux**, Mtl., N.J., Col., Phx., Dal.	20	**1197**
	76. **Denis Savard**, Chi., Mtl., T.B.	17	**1196**
*	77. **Sergei Fedorov**, Det., Ana., CBJ, Wsh.	17	**1196**
	78. **Dave Babych**, Wpg., Hfd., Van., Phi., L.A.	19	**1195**
	79. **John MacLean**, N.J., S.J., NYR, Dal.	18	**1194**
*	80. **Gary Roberts**, Cgy., Car., Tor., Fla., Pit.	21	**1194**
	81. **Gilbert Perreault**, Buf.	17	**1191**
	82. **Marc Bergevin**, Chi., NYI, Hfd., T.B., Det., St.L., Pit., Van.	20	**1191**
	83. **Dale Hawerchuk**, Wpg., Buf., St.L., Phi.	16	**1188**
	84. **Brian Bellows**, Min., Mtl., T.B., Ana., Wsh.	17	**1188**
	85. **Kevin Dineen**, Hfd., Phi., Car., Ott., CBJ	19	**1188**
	86. **George Armstrong**, Tor.	21	**1187**
	87. **Kelly Buchberger**, Edm., Atl., L.A., Phx., Pit.	18	**1182**
	88. **Scott Young**, Hfd., Pit., Que., Col., Ana., St.L., Dal.	17	**1181**
	89. **Frank Mahovlich**, Tor., Det., Mtl.	18	**1181**
	90. **Bob Carpenter**, Wsh., NYR, L.A., Bos., N.J.	19	**1178**
	91. **Don Marshall**, Mtl., NYR, Buf., Tor.	19	**1176**
	92. **Tony Amonte**, NYR, Chi., Phx., Phi., Cgy.	16	**1174**
*	93. **Darryl Sydor**, L.A., Dal., CBJ, T.B., Pit.	16	**1171**
	94. **Sylvain Cote**, Hfd., Wsh., Tor., Chi., Dal.	19	**1171**
	95. **Mike Keane**, Mtl., Col., NYR, Dal., St.L., Van.	16	**1161**
	96. **Bob Gainey**, Mtl.	16	**1160**
	97. **Kevin Hatcher**, Wsh., Dal., Pit., NYR, Car.	17	**1157**
	98. **Eric Weinrich**, N.J., Hfd., Chi., Mtl., Bos., Phi., St.L., Van.	17	**1157**
	99. **Shayne Corson**, Mtl., Edm., St.L., Tor., Dal.	19	**1156**
	100. **Adam Graves**, Det., Edm., NYR, S.J.	16	**1152**

Detroit's Chris Chelios, who turned 46 on January 25, 2008, became the second-oldest player in NHL history, trailing only Gordie Howe. His 24 seasons tie him for third place, and his 1,616 games rank sixth.

Top 100 Active Games Played Leaders

	Player	Seasons	Games Played
1.	**Chris Chelios**, Mtl., Chi., Det.	24	**1616**
2.	**Brendan Shanahan**, N.J., St.L., Hfd., Det., NYR	20	**1490**
3.	**Luke Richardson**, Tor., Edm., Phi., CBJ, T.B., Ott.	20	**1415**
4.	**Mark Recchi**, Pit., Phi., Mtl., Car., Atl.	19	**1410**
5.	**Joe Sakic**, Que., Col.	19	**1363**
6.	**Rod Brind'Amour**, St.L., Phi., Car.	19	**1324**
7.	**Jeremy Roenick**, Chi., Phx., Phi., L.A., S.J.	19	**1321**
8.	**Mike Modano**, Min., Dal.	19	**1320**
9.	**Teppo Numminen**, Wpg., Phx., Dal., Buf.	19	**1315**
10.	**Mats Sundin**, Que., Tor.	17	**1305**
11.	**Jaromir Jagr**, Pit., Wsh., NYR	17	**1273**
12.	**Martin Gelinas**, Edm., Que., Van., Car., Cgy., Fla., Nsh.	19	**1273**
13.	**Nicklas Lidstrom**, Det.	16	**1252**
14.	**Bobby Holik**, Hfd., N.J., NYR, Atl.	17	**1252**
15.	**Mathieu Schneider**, Mtl., NYI, Tor., NYR, L.A., Det., Ana.	19	**1197**
16.	**Sergei Fedorov**, Det., Ana., CBJ, Wsh.	17	**1196**
17.	**Gary Roberts**, Cgy., Car., Tor., Fla., Pit.	21	**1194**
18.	**Darryl Sydor**, L.A., Dal., CBJ, T.B., Pit.	16	**1171**
19.	**Stu Barnes**, Wpg., Fla., Pit., Buf., Dal.	16	**1136**
20.	**Doug Weight**, NYR, Edm., St.L., Car., Ana.	17	**1131**
21.	**Rob Blake**, L.A., Col.	18	**1127**
22.	**Bill Guerin**, N.J., Edm., Bos., Dal., St.L., S.J., NYI	16	**1107**
23.	**Geoff Sanderson**, Hfd., Car., Van., Buf., CBJ, Phx., Phi., Edm.	17	**1104**
24.	**Scott Niedermayer**, N.J., Ana.	16	**1101**
25.	**Alexei Zhitnik**, L.A., Buf., NYI, Phi., Atl.	15	**1085**
26.	**Roman Hamrlik**, T.B., Edm., NYI, Cgy., Mtl.	15	**1076**
27.	**Alex Kovalev**, NYR, Pit., Mtl.	15	**1073**
28.	**Chris Gratton**, T.B., Phi., Buf., Phx., Col., Fla.	14	**1068**
29.	**Owen Nolan**, Que., Col., S.J., Tor., Phx., Cgy.	16	**1068**
30.	**Teemu Selanne**, Wpg., Ana., S.J., Col.	15	**1067**
31.	**Sergei Zubov**, NYR, Pit., Dal.	15	**1058**
32.	**Bryan Smolinski**, Bos., Pit., NYI, L.A., Ott., Chi., Van., Mtl.	15	**1056**
33.	**Keith Tkachuk**, Wpg., Phx., St.L., Atl.	16	**1055**
34.	**Vyacheslav Kozlov**, Det., Buf., Atl.	16	**1045**
35.	**Derian Hatcher**, Min., Dal., Det., Phi.	16	**1045**
36.	**Mike Sillinger**, Det., Ana., Van., Phi., T.B., Fla., Ott., CBJ, Phx., St.L.	17	**1042**
37.	**Markus Naslund**, Pit., Van.	14	**1035**
38.	**Keith Carney**, Buf., Chi., Phx., Ana., Van., Min.	14	**1018**
39.	**Glen Murray**, Bos., Pit., L.A.	16	**1009**
40.	**Adam Foote**, Que., Col., CBJ	16	**998**
41.	**Martin Lapointe**, Det., Bos., Chi., Ott.	16	**991**
42.	**Bret Hedican**, St.L., Van., Fla., Car.	16	**988**
43.	**Brian Rolston**, N.J., Col., Bos., Min.	13	**977**
44.	**Jason Arnott**, Edm., N.J., Dal., Nsh.	14	**971**
45.	**Martin Brodeur**, N.J.	15	**968**
46.	**Todd Marchant**, NYR, Edm., CBJ, Ana.	14	**966**
47.	**Martin Rucinsky**, Edm., Que., Col., Mtl., Dal., NYR, St.L., Van.	16	**961**
48.	**Jozef Stumpel**, Bos., L.A., Fla.	16	**957**
49.	**Martin Straka**, Pit., Ott., NYI, Fla., L.A., NYR	15	**954**
50.	**Kris Draper**, Wpg., Det.	17	**950**
51.	**Miroslav Satan**, Edm., Buf., NYI	12	**947**
52.	**Patrice Brisebois**, Mtl., Col.	17	**947**
53.	**Jason Smith**, N.J., Tor., Edm., Phi.	13	**945**
54.	**Brad May**, Buf., Van., Phx., Col., Ana.	16	**943**
55.	**Kirk Maltby**, Edm., Det.	14	**942**
56.	**Scott Thornton**, Tor., Edm., Mtl., Dal., S.J., L.A.	17	**941**
57.	**Chris Pronger**, Hfd., St.L., Edm., Ana.	14	**940**
58.	**Sean O'Donnell**, L.A., Min., N.J., Bos., Phx., Ana.	13	**932**
59.	**Rob Niedermayer**, Fla., Cgy., Ana.	14	**932**
60.	**Ian Laperriere**, St.L., NYR, L.A., Col.	14	**927**
61.	**Donald Brashear**, Mtl., Van., Phi., Wsh.	14	**926**
62.	**Curtis Joseph**, Edm., Tor., Det., Phx., Cgy.	18	**922**
63.	**Bryan McCabe**, NYI, Van., Chi., Tor.	12	**917**
64.	**Ray Whitney**, S.J., Edm., Fla., CBJ, Det., Car.	16	**910**
65.	**Sergei Gonchar**, Wsh., Bos., Pit.	13	**904**
66.	**Radek Bonk**, Ott., Mtl., Nsh.	13	**903**
67.	**Paul Kariya**, Ana., Col., Nsh., St.L.	13	**903**
68.	**Mattias Norstrom**, NYR, L.A., Dal.	14	**903**
69.	**Radek Dvorak**, Fla., NYR, Edm., St.L.	12	**895**
70.	**Shane Doan**, Wpg., Phx.	12	**883**
71.	**Sean Hill**, Mtl., Ana., Ott., Car., St.L., Fla., NYI, Min.	17	**876**
72.	**Robert Lang**, L.A., Bos., Pit., Wsh., Det., Chi.	14	**875**
73.	**Sandis Ozolinsh**, S.J., Col., Car., Fla., Ana., NYR	15	**875**
74.	**Dean McAmmond**, Chi., Edm., Phi., Cgy., Col., St.L., Ott.	15	**872**
75.	**Daymond Langkow**, T.B., Phi., Phx., Cgy.	12	**868**
76.	**Ken Klee**, Wsh., Tor., N.J., Col., Atl.	13	**863**
77.	**Jarome Iginla**, Cgy.	12	**860**
78.	**Yanic Perreault**, Tor., L.A., Mtl., Nsh., Phx., Chi.	14	**859**
79.	**Shean Donovan**, S.J., Col., Atl., Pit., Cgy., Bos., Ott.	13	**856**

Alex Kovalev topped 1,000 games played in 2007-08, suiting up in all 82 for the Montreal Canadiens. His 35 goals and 84 points last year were among the best totals of his career.

	Player	Seasons	Games Played
80.	**Daniel Alfredsson**, Ott.	12	**853**
81.	**Mike Grier**, Edm., Wsh., Buf., S.J.	11	**852**
82.	**Michael Nylander**, Hfd., Cgy., T.B., Chi., Wsh., Bos., NYR	14	**848**
83.	**Craig Conroy**, Mtl., St.L., Cgy., L.A.	13	**846**
84.	**Petr Sykora**, N.J., Ana., NYR, Edm., Pit.	10	**845**
85.	**Stephane Yelle**, Col., Cgy.	12	**844**
86.	**Ryan Smyth**, Edm., NYI, Col.	13	**843**
87.	**Cory Stillman**, Cgy., St.L., T.B., Car., Ott.	9	**839**
88.	**Wade Redden**, Ott.	11	**838**
89.	**Sami Kapanen**, Hfd., Car., Phi.	12	**831**
90.	**Viktor Kozlov**, S.J., Fla., N.J., NYI, Wsh.	13	**830**
91.	**Mathieu Dandenault**, Det., Mtl.	12	**827**
92.	**Ed Jovanovski**, Fla., Van., Phx.	12	**821**
93.	**Darcy Tucker**, Mtl., T.B., Tor.	12	**813**
94.	**Greg de Vries**, Edm., Nsh., Col., NYR, Ott., Atl.	12	**807**
95.	**Jamie Langenbrunner**, Dal., N.J.	13	**803**
96.	**Richard Matvichuk**, Min., Dal., N.J.	14	**796**
97.	**Patrick Marleau**, S.J.	10	**795**
98.	**Todd Bertuzzi**, NYI, Van., Fla., Det., Ana.	12	**793**
99.	**Michael Peca**, Van., Buf., NYI, Edm., Tor., CBJ	13	**793**
100.	**Vaclav Prospal**, Phi., Ott., Fla., T.B., Ana.	11	**792**

Goaltending Records

All-Time Shutout Leaders (Minimum 50 Shutouts)

	Goaltender	Team	Shutouts	Games	Seasons
1.	**Terry Sawchuk**	Detroit	85	734	14
	(1949-1970)	Boston	11	102	2
		Toronto	4	91	3
		Los Angeles	2	36	1
		NY Rangers	1	8	1
		Total	**103**	971	21
2.	***Martin Brodeur**	New Jersey	**96**	968	15
	(1991-2008)				
3.	**George Hainsworth**	Montreal	75	318	7½
	(1926-1937)	Toronto	19	147	3½
		Total	**94**	465	11
4.	**Glenn Hall**	Detroit	17	148	4
	(1952-1971)	Chicago	51	618	10
		St. Louis	16	140	4
		Total	**84**	906	18
5.	**Jacques Plante**	Montreal	58	556	11
	(1952-1973)	NY Rangers	5	98	2
		St. Louis	10	69	2
		Toronto	7	106	2¾
		Boston	2	8	¼
		Total	**82**	837	18
6.	**Alex Connell**	Ottawa	64	293	8
	(1924-1937)	Detroit	6	48	1
		NY Americans	0	1	1
		Mtl. Maroons	11	75	2
		Total	**81**	417	12
7.	**Tiny Thompson**	Boston	74	468	10¼
	(1928-1940)	Detroit	7	85	1¾
		Total	**81**	553	12
8.	**Dominik Hasek**	Chicago	1	25	2
	(1990-2008)	Buffalo	55	491	9
		Detroit	20	176	4
		Ottawa	5	43	1
		Total	**81**	735	16
9.	**Tony Esposito**	Montreal	2	13	1
	(1968-1984)	Chicago	74	873	15
		Total	**76**	886	16
10.	**Ed Belfour**	Chicago	30	415	7⅔
	(1988-2007)	San Jose	1	13	⅓
		Dallas	27	307	5
		Toronto	17	170	3
		Florida	1	58	1
		Total	**76**	963	17
11.	**Lorne Chabot**	NY Rangers	21	80	2
	(1926-1937)	Toronto	31	214	5
		Montreal	8	47	1
		Chicago	8	48	1
		Mtl. Maroons	2	16	1
		NY Americans	1	6	1
		Total	**71**	411	11
12.	**Harry Lumley**	Detroit	26	324	6½
	(1943-1960)	NY Rangers	0	1	½
		Chicago	5	134	2
		Toronto	34	267	4
		Boston	6	78	3
		Total	**71**	804	16
13.	**Roy Worters**	Pittsburgh Pirates	22	123	3
	(1925-1937)	NY Americans	45	360	9
		**Montreal	0	1	
		Total	**67**	484	12
14.	**Patrick Roy**	Montreal	29	551	11½
	(1984-2003)	Colorado	37	478	7½
		Total	**66**	1,029	19
15.	**Turk Broda**	Toronto	**62**	629	14
	(1936-1952)				
16.	**John Ross Roach**	Toronto	13	222	7
	(1921-1935)	NY Rangers	30	89	4
		Detroit	15	180	3
		Total	**58**	491	14
17.	**Clint Benedict**	Ottawa	19	158	7
	(1917-1930)	Mtl. Maroons	38	204	6
		Total	**57**	362	13
18.	**Bernie Parent**	Boston	1	57	2
	(1965-1979)	Philadelphia	50	486	9½
		Toronto	3	65	1½
		Total	**54**	608	13
19.	**Ed Giacomin**	NY Rangers	49	539	10¼
	(1965-1978)	Detroit	5	71	2¾
		Total	**54**	610	13
20.	**Dave Kerr**	Mtl. Maroons	11	101	3
	(1930-1941)	NY Americans	0	1	1
		NY Rangers	40	324	7
		Total	**51**	426	11
21.	**Rogie Vachon**	Montreal	13	206	5¼
	(1966-1982)	Los Angeles	32	389	6¾
		Detroit	4	109	2
		Boston	2	91	2
		Total	**51**	795	16
22.	***Curtis Joseph**	St. Louis	5	280	6
	(1989-2008)	Edmonton	14	177	3
		Toronto	17	249	4
		Detroit	7	92	2
		Phoenix	8	115	2
		Calgary	0	9	1
		Total	**51**	922	18

* Active goalie
** Played 1 game for Montreal in 1929-30.

Ten or More Shutouts, One Season

Number of Shutouts	Goaltender	Team	Season	Length of Schedule
22	George Hainsworth	Montreal	1928-29	44
15	Alex Connell	Ottawa	1925-26	36
	Alex Connell	Ottawa	1927-28	44
	Hal Winkler	Boston	1927-28	44
	Tony Esposito	Chicago	1969-70	76
14	George Hainsworth	Montreal	1926-27	44
13	Clint Benedict	Mtl. Maroons	1926-27	44
	Alex Connell	Ottawa	1926-27	44
	George Hainsworth	Montreal	1927-28	44
	John Ross Roach	NY Rangers	1928-29	44
	Roy Worters	NY Americans	1928-29	44
	Harry Lumley	Toronto	1953-54	70
	Dominik Hasek	Buffalo	1997-98	82
12	Tiny Thompson	Boston	1928-29	44
	Charlie Gardiner	Chicago	1930-31	44
	Terry Sawchuk	Detroit	1951-52	70
	Terry Sawchuk	Detroit	1953-54	70
	Terry Sawchuk	Detroit	1954-55	70
	Glenn Hall	Detroit	1955-56	70
	Bernie Parent	Philadelphia	1973-74	78
	Bernie Parent	Philadelphia	1974-75	80
	Martin Brodeur	New Jersey	2006-07	82
11	Lorne Chabot	NY Rangers	1927-28	44
	Hap Holmes	Detroit	1927-28	44
	Roy Worters	Pittsburgh Pirates	1927-28	44
	Clint Benedict	Mtl. Maroons	1928-29	44
	Joe Miller	Pittsburgh Pirates	1928-29	44
	Tiny Thompson	Boston	1932-33	48
	Terry Sawchuk	Detroit	1950-51	70
	Dominik Hasek	Buffalo	2000-01	82
	Martin Brodeur	New Jersey	2003-04	82
10	Lorne Chabot	NY Rangers	1926-27	44
	Lorne Chabot	Toronto	1928-29	44
	Dolly Dolson	Detroit	1928-29	44
	John Ross Roach	Detroit	1932-33	48
	Charlie Gardiner	Chicago	1933-34	48
	Tiny Thompson	Boston	1935-36	48
	Frank Brimsek	Boston	1938-39	48
	Bill Durnan	Montreal	1948-49	60
	Harry Lumley	Toronto	1952-53	70
	Gerry McNeil	Montreal	1952-53	70
	Tony Esposito	Chicago	1973-74	78
	Ken Dryden	Montreal	1976-77	80
	Martin Brodeur	New Jersey	1996-97	82
	Martin Brodeur	New Jersey	1997-98	82
	Byron Dafoe	Boston	1998-99	82
	Roman Cechmanek	Philadelphia	2000-01	82
	Ed Belfour	Toronto	2003-04	82
	Miikka Kiprusoff	Calgary	2005-06	82
	Henrik Lundqvist	NY Rangers	**2007-08**	82

All-Time Win Leaders

(Minimum 250 Wins)

Goaltender	Wins	GP	Dec.	Losses	OT/Ties
1. Patrick Roy	**551**	1029	997	315	131
2. * Martin Brodeur	**538**	968	953	290	125
3. Ed Belfour	**484**	963	929	320	125
4. * Curtis Joseph	**449**	922	887	343	95
5. Terry Sawchuk	**447**	971	949	330	172
6. Jacques Plante	**437**	837	829	247	145
7. Tony Esposito	**423**	886	880	306	151
8. Glenn Hall	**407**	906	896	326	163
9. Grant Fuhr	**403**	868	812	295	114
10. Dominik Hasek	**389**	735	707	223	95
11. Mike Vernon	**385**	781	750	273	92
12. John Vanbiesbrouck	**374**	882	839	346	119
13. Andy Moog	**372**	713	669	209	88
14. Tom Barrasso	**369**	777	732	277	86
15. * Chris Osgood	**363**	664	639	195	81
16. Rogie Vachon	**355**	795	773	291	127
17. Gump Worsley	**335**	861	837	352	150
18. Harry Lumley	**330**	803	801	329	142
19. Sean Burke	**324**	820	775	341	110
20. Billy Smith	**305**	680	643	233	105
21. Turk Broda	**302**	629	627	224	101
22. Mike Richter	**301**	666	632	258	73
23. * Olaf Kolzig	**301**	711	680	293	86
24. Ron Hextall	**296**	608	579	214	69
25. Mike Liut	**294**	663	639	271	74
26. Ed Giacomin	**289**	610	594	208	97
27. Dan Bouchard	**286**	655	631	232	113
28. Tiny Thompson	**284**	553	553	194	75
29. * Nikolai Khabibulin	**274**	636	608	259	75
30. Bernie Parent	**271**	608	590	198	121
31. Kelly Hrudey	**271**	677	624	265	88
32. Gilles Meloche	**270**	788	752	351	131
33. Don Beaupre	**268**	667	620	277	75
34. Felix Potvin	**266**	635	611	260	85
35. Ken Dryden	**258**	397	389	57	74
36. Frank Brimsek	**252**	514	514	182	80
37. Johnny Bower	**250**	552	535	195	90

* active player

Active Shutout Leaders

(Minimum 25 Shutouts)

Goaltender	Teams	Shutouts	Games	Seasons
1. Martin Brodeur	New Jersey	**96**	968	15
2. Curtis Joseph	St.L., Edm., Tor., Det., Phx., Cgy.	**51**	922	18
3. Chris Osgood	Det., NYI, St.L.	**47**	664	14
4. Evgeni Nabokov	San Jose	**40**	430	8
5. Jocelyn Thibault	Que., Col., Mtl., Chi., Pit., Buf.	**39**	586	14
6. Roberto Luongo	NYI, Fla., Van.	**38**	490	8
7. Nikolai Khabibulin	Wpg., Phx., T.B., Chi.	**38**	636	12
8. Patrick Lalime	Pit., Ott., St.L., Chi.	**35**	397	9
9. Olaf Kolzig	Washington	**35**	711	16
10. Marty Turco	Dallas	**33**	382	7
11. Jean-Sebastien Giguere	Hfd., Cgy., Ana.	**29**	411	10
12. Miikka Kiprusoff	San Jose, Calgary	**26**	309	7
13. Jose Theodore	Montreal, Colorado	**26**	444	11
14. Tomas Vokoun	Mtl., Nsh., Fla.	**25**	453	10

All-Time Penalty-Minute Leaders

* active player

Player	Seasons	Games	Penalty Minutes	Mins. per game
1. **Tiger Williams**, Tor., Van., Det., L.A., Hfd.	14	962	**3966**	4.12
2. **Dale Hunter**, Que., Wsh., Col.	19	1407	**3565**	2.53
3. **Tie Domi**, Tor., NYR, Wpg.	16	1020	**3515**	3.45
4. **Marty McSorley**, Pit., Edm., L.A., NYR, S.J., Bos.	17	961	**3381**	3.52
5. **Bob Probert**, Det., Chi.	16	935	**3300**	3.53
6. **Rob Ray**, Buf., Ott.	15	900	**3207**	3.56
7. **Craig Berube**, Phi., Tor., Cgy., Wsh., NYI	17	1054	**3149**	2.99
8. **Tim Hunter**, Cgy., Que., Van., S.J.	16	815	**3146**	3.86
9. **Chris Nilan**, Mtl., NYR, Bos.	13	688	**3043**	4.42
10. **Rick Tocchet**, Phi., Pit., L.A., Bos., Wsh., Phx.	18	1144	**2972**	2.60
11. **Pat Verbeek**, N.J., Hfd., NYR, Dal., Det.	20	1424	**2905**	2.04
* 12. **Chris Chelios**, Mtl., Chi., Det.	24	1616	**2873**	1.78
13. **Dave Manson**, Chi., Edm., Wpg., Phx., Mtl., Dal., Tor.	16	1103	**2792**	2.53
14. **Scott Stevens**, Wsh., St.L., N.J.	22	1635	**2785**	1.70
15. **Willi Plett**, Atl., Cgy., Min., Bos.	13	834	**2572**	3.08

Goals-Against Average Leaders (Minimum 25 games played)

(Exceptions: Minimum 13 games played, 1994-95; minimum 26 games played, 1992-93 to 1993-94; minimum 15 games played, 1917-18 to 1925-26)

Season	Goaltender, Team	GP	Mins.	GA	SO	AVG.
2007-08	Chris Osgood, Detroit	43	2,409	84	4	2.09
2006-07	Niklas Backstrom, Minnesota	41	2,227	73	5	1.97
2005-06	Miikka Kiprusoff, Calgary	74	4,380	151	10	2.07
2003-04	Miikka Kiprusoff, Calgary	38	2,301	65	4	1.69
2002-03	Marty Turco, Dallas	55	3,203	92	7	1.72
2001-02	Patrick Roy, Colorado	63	3,773	122	9	1.94
2000-01	Marty Turco, Dallas	26	1,266	40	3	1.90
99-2000	Brian Boucher, Philadelphia	35	2,038	65	4	1.91
1998-99	Ron Tugnutt, Ottawa	43	2,508	75	3	1.79
1997-98	Ed Belfour, Dallas	61	3,581	112	9	1.88
1996-97	Martin Brodeur, New Jersey	67	3,838	120	10	1.88
1995-96	Ron Hextall, Philadelphia	53	3,102	112	4	2.17
1994-95	Dominik Hasek, Buffalo	41	2,416	85	5	2.11
1993-94	Dominik Hasek, Buffalo	58	3,358	109	7	1.95
1992-93	Felix Potvin, Toronto	48	2,781	116	2	2.50
1991-92	Patrick Roy, Montreal	67	3,935	155	5	2.36
1990-91	Ed Belfour, Chicago	74	4,127	170	4	2.47
1989-90	Mike Liut, Hartford, Washington	37	2,161	91	4	2.53
1988-89	Patrick Roy, Montreal	48	2,744	113	4	2.47
1987-88	Pete Peeters, Washington	35	1,896	88	2	2.78
1986-87	Brian Hayward, Montreal	37	2,178	102	1	2.81
1985-86	Bob Froese, Philadelphia	51	2,728	116	5	2.55
1984-85	Tom Barrasso, Buffalo	54	3,248	144	5	2.66
1983-84	Pat Riggin, Washington	41	2,299	102	4	2.66
1982-83	Pete Peeters, Boston	62	3,611	142	8	2.36
1981-82	Denis Herron, Montreal	27	1,547	68	3	2.64
1980-81	Richard Sevigny, Montreal	33	1,777	71	2	2.40
1979-80	Bob Sauve, Buffalo	32	1,880	74	4	2.36
1978-79	Ken Dryden, Montreal	47	2,814	108	5	2.30
1977-78	Ken Dryden, Montreal	52	3,071	105	5	2.05
1976-77	Michel Larocque, Montreal	26	1,525	53	4	2.09
1975-76	Ken Dryden, Montreal	62	3,580	121	8	2.03
1974-75	Bernie Parent, Philadelphia	68	4,041	137	12	2.03
1973-74	Bernie Parent, Philadelphia	73	4,314	136	12	1.89
1972-73	Ken Dryden, Montreal	54	3,165	119	6	2.26
1971-72	Tony Esposito, Chicago	48	2,780	82	9	1.77
1970-71	Jacques Plante, Toronto	40	2,329	73	4	1.88
1969-70	Ernie Wakely, St. Louis	30	1,651	58	4	2.11
1968-69	Jacques Plante, St. Louis	37	2,139	70	5	1.96
1967-68	Gump Worsley, Montreal	40	2,213	73	6	1.98
1966-67	Glenn Hall, Chicago	32	1,664	66	2	2.38
1965-66	Johnny Bower, Toronto	35	1,998	75	3	2.25
1964-65	Johnny Bower, Toronto	34	2,040	81	3	2.38
1963-64	Johnny Bower, Toronto	51	3,009	106	5	2.11
1962-63	Don Simmons, Toronto	28	1,680	69	1	2.46
1961-62	Jacques Plante, Montreal	70	4,200	166	4	2.37
1960-61	Charlie Hodge, Montreal	30	1,800	74	4	2.47
1959-60	Jacques Plante, Montreal	69	4,140	175	3	2.54
1958-59	Jacques Plante, Montreal	67	4,000	144	9	2.16
1957-58	Jacques Plante, Montreal	57	3,386	119	9	2.11
1956-57	Jacques Plante, Montreal	61	3,660	122	9	2.00
1955-56	Jacques Plante, Montreal	64	3,840	119	7	1.86
1954-55	Harry Lumley, Toronto	69	4,140	134	8	1.94
1953-54	Harry Lumley, Toronto	69	4,140	128	13	1.86
1952-53	Terry Sawchuk, Detroit	63	3,780	120	9	1.90
1951-52	Terry Sawchuk, Detroit	70	4,200	133	12	1.90
1950-51	Al Rollins, Toronto	40	2,367	70	5	1.77
1949-50	Bill Durnan, Montreal	64	3,840	141	8	2.20
1948-49	Bill Durnan, Montreal	60	3,600	126	10	2.10
1947-48	Turk Broda, Toronto	60	3,600	143	5	2.38
1946-47	Bill Durnan, Montreal	60	3,600	138	4	2.30
1945-46	Bill Durnan, Montreal	40	2,400	104	4	2.60
1944-45	Bill Durnan, Montreal	50	3,000	121	1	2.42
1943-44	Bill Durnan, Montreal	50	3,000	109	2	2.18
1942-43	Johnny Mowers, Detroit	50	3,010	124	6	2.47
1941-42	Frank Brimsek, Boston	47	2,930	115	3	2.35
1940-41	Turk Broda, Toronto	48	2,970	99	5	2.00
1939-40	Dave Kerr, NY Rangers	48	3,000	77	8	1.54
1938-39	Frank Brimsek, Boston	43	2,610	68	10	1.56
1937-38	Tiny Thompson, Boston	48	2,970	89	7	1.80
1936-37	Normie Smith, Detroit	48	2,980	102	6	2.05
1935-36	Tiny Thompson, Boston	48	2,930	82	10	1.68
1934-35	Lorne Chabot, Chicago	48	2,940	88	8	1.80
1933-34	Wilf Cude, Detroit, Montreal	30	1,920	47	5	1.47
1932-33	Tiny Thompson, Boston	48	3,000	88	11	1.76
1931-32	Charlie Gardiner, Chicago	48	2,989	92	4	1.85
1930-31	Roy Worters, NY Americans	44	2,760	74	8	1.61
1929-30	Tiny Thompson, Boston	44	2,680	98	3	2.19
1928-29	George Hainsworth, Montreal	44	2,800	43	22	0.92
1927-28	George Hainsworth, Montreal	44	2,730	48	13	1.05
1926-27	Clint Benedict, Mtl. Maroons	43	2,748	65	13	1.42
1925-26	Alex Connell, Ottawa	36	2,251	42	15	1.12
1924-25	Georges Vezina, Montreal	30	1,860	56	5	1.81
1923-24	Georges Vezina, Montreal	24	1,459	48	3	1.97
1922-23	Clint Benedict, Ottawa	24	1,478	54	4	2.18
1921-22	Clint Benedict, Ottawa	24	1,508	84	2	3.34
1920-21	Clint Benedict, Ottawa	24	1,457	75	2	3.09
1919-20	Clint Benedict, Ottawa	24	1,444	64	5	2.66
1918-19	Clint Benedict, Ottawa	18	1,113	53	2	2.86
1917-18	Georges Vezina, Montreal	21	1,282	84	1	3.93

All-Time Regular-Season NHL Coaching Register

Regular Season, 1917-2008

Coach	Team	Games Coached	Wins	Losses	O/T	Years	Cup Wins	Career
Abel, Sid	Chicago	140	39	79	22	2		
	Detroit	811	340	339	132	12		
	St. Louis	10	3	6	1	1		
	Kansas City	3	0	3	0	1		
	Totals	964	382	427	155	16		1952-76
Adams, Jack	Detroit	964	413	390	161	20	3	1927-47
Agnew, Gary	Columbus	5	0	4	1	1		2006-07
Allen, Keith	Philadelphia	150	51	67	32	2		1967-69
Allison, Dave	Ottawa	25	2	22	1	1		1995-96
Anderson, Jim	Washington	54	4	45	5	1		1974-75
Angotti, Lou	St. Louis	32	6	20	6	2		
	Pittsburgh	80	16	58	6	1		
	Totals	112	22	78	12	3		1973-84
Arbour, Al	St. Louis	107	42	40	25	3		
	NY Islanders	1500	740	537	223	20	4	
	Totals	1607	782	577	248	23	4	1970-08
Armstrong, George	Toronto	47	17	26	4	1		1988-89
Babcock, Mike	Anaheim	164	69	62	33	3		
	Detroit	246	162	56	28	3	1	
	Totals	410	231	118	61	17	1	2002-08
Barber, Bill	Philadelphia	136	73	40	23	2		2000-02
Barkley, Doug	Detroit	77	20	46	11	3		1970-76
Beaulieu, Andre	Minnesota	32	6	23	3	1		1977-78
Belisle, Danny	Washington	96	28	51	17	2		1978-80
Berenson, Red	St. Louis	204	100	72	32	3		1979-82
Bergeron, Michel	Quebec	634	265	283	86	8		
	NY Rangers	158	73	67	18	2		
	Totals	792	338	350	104	10		1980-90
Berry, Bob	Los Angeles	240	107	94	39	3		
	Montreal	223	116	71	36	3		
	Pittsburgh	240	88	127	25	3		
	St. Louis	157	73	63	21	2		
	Totals	860	384	355	121	11		1978-94
Beverley, Nick	Toronto	17	9	6	2	1		1995-96
Blackburn, Don	Hartford	140	42	63	35	2		1979-81
Blair, Wren	Minnesota	147	48	65	34	3		1967-70
Blake, Toe	Montreal	914	500	255	159	13	8	1955-68
Boileau, Marc	Pittsburgh	151	66	61	24	3		1973-76
Boivin, Leo	St. Louis	97	28	53	16	2		1975-78
Boucher, Frank	NY Rangers	527	181	263	83	11	1	1939-54
Boucher, Georges	Mtl. Maroons	12	6	5	1	1		
	Ottawa	48	13	29	6	1		
	St. Louis	35	9	20	6	1		
	Boston	70	22	32	16	1		
	Totals	165	50	86	29	4		1930-50
Boudreau, Bruce	Washington	61	37	17	7	1		2007-08
Bowman, Scotty	St. Louis	238	110	83	45	4		
	Montreal	634	419	110	105	8	5	
	Buffalo	404	210	134	60	7		
	Pittsburgh	164	95	53	16	2	1	
	Detroit	701	410	194	97	9	3	
	Totals	2141	1244	574	323	30	9	1967-02
Bowness, Rick	Winnipeg	28	8	17	3	1		
	Boston	80	36	32	12	1		
	Ottawa	235	39	178	18	4		
	NY Islanders	100	38	50	12	2		
	Phoenix	20	2	12	6	2		
	Totals	463	123	289	51	10		1988-05
Brooks, Herb	NY Rangers	285	131	113	41	4		
	Minnesota	80	19	48	13	1		
	New Jersey	84	40	37	7	1		
	Pittsburgh	57	29	21	7	1		
	Totals	506	219	219	68	7		1981-00
Brophy, John	Toronto	193	64	111	18	3		1986-89
Burnett, George	Edmonton	35	12	20	3	1		1994-95
Burns, Charlie	Minnesota	86	22	50	14	2		1969-75
Burns, Pat	Montreal	320	174	104	42	4		
	Toronto	281	133	107	41	4		
	Boston	254	105	97	52	4		
	New Jersey	164	89	45	30	3	1	
	Totals	1019	501	353	165	15	1	1988-05
Bush, Eddie	Kansas City	32	1	23	8	1		1975-76
Campbell, Colin	NY Rangers	269	118	108	43	4		1994-98
Carbonneau, Guy	Montreal	164	89	59	16	2		2006-08
Carlyle, Randy	Anaheim	246	138	74	34	3	1	2005-08
Carpenter, Doug	New Jersey	290	100	166	24	4		
	Toronto	91	39	47	5	2		
	Totals	381	139	213	29	6		1984-91
Carroll, Dick	Toronto	40	18	22	0	2	1	1917-19
Carroll, Frank	Toronto	24	15	9	0	1		1920-21
Cashman, Wayne	Philadelphia	61	32	20	9	1		1997-98
Cassidy, Bruce	Washington	110	47	47	16	2		2002-04
Chambers, Dave	Quebec	98	19	64	15	2		1990-92
Charron, Guy	Calgary	16	6	7	3	1		
	Anaheim	49	14	26	9	1		
	Totals	65	20	33	12	2		1991-01
Cheevers, Gerry	Boston	376	204	126	46	5		1980-85
Cherry, Don	Boston	400	231	105	64	5		
	Colorado	80	19	48	13	1		
	Totals	480	250	153	77	6		1974-80
Clancy, King	Mtl. Maroons	18	6	11	1	1		
	Toronto	210	80	81	49	3		
	Totals	228	86	92	50	4		1937-56
Clapper, Dit	Boston	230	102	88	40	4		1945-49
Cleghorn, Odie	Pittsburgh	168	62	86	20	4		1925-29
Cleghorn, Sprague	Mtl. Maroons	48	19	22	7	1		1931-32
Colville, Neil	NY Rangers	93	26	41	26	2		1950-52
Conacher, Charlie	Chicago	162	56	84	22	3		1947-50
Conacher, Lionel	NY Americans	44	14	25	5	1		1929-30
Constantine, Kevin	San Jose	157	55	78	24	3		
	Pittsburgh	189	86	64	39	3		
	New Jersey	31	20	8	3	1		
	Totals	377	161	150	66	7		1993-02
Cook, Bill	NY Rangers	117	34	59	24	2		1951-53
Crawford, Marc	Quebec	48	30	13	5	1		
	Colorado	246	135	75	36	3	1	
	Vancouver	529	246	189	94	8		
	Los Angeles	164	59	84	21	2		
	Totals	987	470	361	156	14	1	1994-08
Creamer, Pierre	Pittsburgh	80	36	35	9	1		1987-88
Creighton, Fred	Atlanta	348	156	136	56	5		
	Boston	73	40	20	13	1		
	Totals	421	196	156	69	6		1974-80
Crisp, Terry	Calgary	240	144	63	33	3	1	
	Tampa Bay	391	142	204	45	6		
	Totals	631	286	267	78	9	1	1987-98
Crozier, Joe	Buffalo	192	77	80	35	3		
	Toronto	40	13	22	5	1		
	Totals	232	90	102	40	4		1971-81
Crozier, Roger	Washington	1	0	1	0	1		1981-82
Cunniff, John	Hartford	13	3	9	1	1		
	New Jersey	133	59	56	18	2		
	Totals	146	62	65	19	3		1982-91
Curry, Alex	Ottawa	36	24	8	4	1		1925-26
Dandurand, Leo	Montreal	163	78	76	9	6	1	1921-35
Day, Hap	Toronto	546	259	206	81	10	5	1940-50
Dea, Billy	Detroit	11	3	8	0	1		1981-82
Delvecchio, Alex	Detroit	245	82	131	32	4		1973-77
Demers, Jacques	Quebec	80	25	44	11	1		
	St. Louis	240	106	106	28	3		
	Detroit	320	137	136	47	4		
	Montreal	220	107	86	27	4	1	
	Tampa Bay	147	34	96	17	2		
	Totals	1007	409	468	130	14	1	1979-99
Denneny, Cy	Boston	44	26	13	5	1	1	
	Ottawa	48	11	27	10	1		
	Totals	92	37	40	15	2	1	1928-33
Dineen, Bill	Philadelphia	140	60	60	20	2		1991-93
Dudley, Rick	Buffalo	188	85	72	31	3		
	Florida	40	13	15	12	1		
	Totals	228	98	87	43	4		1989-04
Duff, Dick	Toronto	2	0	2	0	1		1979-80
Dugal, Jules	Montreal	18	9	6	3	1		1938-39
Duncan, Art	Detroit	33	10	21	2	1		
	Toronto	47	21	16	10	2		
	Totals	80	31	37	12	3		1926-32
Dutton, Red	NY Americans	288	90	151	47	6		
	Brooklyn	48	16	29	3	1		
	Totals	336	106	180	50	7		1935-42
Eddolls, Frank	Chicago	70	13	40	17	1		1954-55
Esposito, Phil	NY Rangers	45	24	21	0	2		1986-89
Evans, Jack	California	80	27	42	11	1		
	Cleveland	160	47	87	26	2		
	Hartford	374	163	174	37	5		
	Totals	614	237	303	74	8		1975-88
Fashoway, Gordie	Oakland	10	4	5	1	1		1967-68
Ferguson, John	NY Rangers	121	43	59	19	2		
	Winnipeg	14	7	6	1	1		
	Totals	135	50	65	20	3		1975-86
Filion, Maurice	Quebec	6	1	3	2	1		1980-81
Francis, Bob	Phoenix	390	165	144	81	5		1999-04
Francis, Emile	NY Rangers	654	342	209	103	10		
	St. Louis	124	46	64	14	3		
	Totals	778	388	273	117	13		1965-83
Fraser, Curt	Atlanta	279	64	169	46	4		1999-03
Fredrickson, Frank	Pittsburgh	44	5	36	3	1		1929-30
Ftorek, Robbie	Los Angeles	132	65	56	11	2		
	New Jersey	156	88	44	24	2		
	Boston	155	76	52	27	2		
	Totals	443	229	152	62	6		1987-03
Gadsby, Bill	Detroit	78	35	31	12	2		1968-70
Gainey, Bob	Minnesota	244	95	119	30	3		
	Dallas	171	70	71	30	3		
	Montreal	41	23	15	3	1		
	Totals	456	188	205	63	7		1990-06
Gallant, Gerard	Columbus	142	56	76	10	4		2003-07
Gardiner, Herb	Chicago	32	5	23	4	1		1928-29
Gardner, Jimmy	Hamilton	30	19	10	1	1		1924-25
Garvin, Ted	Detroit	11	2	8	1	1		1973-74

Coach	Team	Games Coached	Wins	Losses	O/T	Years	Cup Wins	Career
Geoffrion, Bernie	NY Rangers	43	22	18	3	1		
	Atlanta	208	77	92	39	3		
	Montreal	30	15	9	6	1		
	Totals	281	114	119	48	5		1968-80
Gerard, Eddie	Ottawa	22	9	13	0	1		
	Mtl. Maroons	294	129	122	43	7	1	
	NY Americans	92	34	40	18	2		
	St. Louis	13	2	11	0	1		
	Totals	421	174	186	61	11	1	1917-35
Gilbert, Greg	Calgary	121	42	56	23	3		2000-03
Gill, David	Ottawa	132	64	41	27	3	1	1926-29
Glover, Fred	Oakland	152	51	76	25	2		
	California	204	45	131	28	4		
	Los Angeles	68	18	42	8	1		
	Totals	424	114	249	61	6		1968-74
Goodfellow, Ebbie	Chicago	140	30	91	19	2		1950-52
Gordon, Jackie	Minnesota	289	116	123	50	5		1970-75
Goring, Butch	Boston	93	42	38	13	2		
	NY Islanders	147	41	88	18	2		
	Totals	240	83	126	31	4		1985-01
Gorman, Tommy	NY Americans	80	31	33	16	2		
	Chicago	73	28	28	17	2	1	
	Mtl. Maroons	174	74	71	29	4	1	
	Totals	327	133	132	62	8	2	1925-38
Gottselig, Johnny	Chicago	187	62	105	20	4		1944-48
Goyette, Phil	NY Islanders	48	6	38	4	1		1972-73
Graham, Dirk	Chicago	59	16	35	8	1		1998-99
Granato, Tony	Colorado	133	72	33	28	2		2002-04
Green, Gary	Washington	157	50	78	29	3		1979-82
Green, Pete	Ottawa	150	94	52	4	6	3	1919-25
Green, Shorty	NY Americans	44	11	27	6	1		1927-28
Green, Ted	Edmonton	188	65	102	21	3		1991-94
Gretzky, Wayne	Phoenix	246	107	122	17	3		2005-08
Guidolin, Aldo	Colorado	59	12	39	8	1		1978-79
Guidolin, Bep	Boston	104	72	23	9	2		
	Kansas City	125	26	84	15	2		
	Totals	229	98	107	24	4		1972-76
Hanlon, Glen	Washington	239	78	122	39	5		2003-08
Harkness, Ned	Detroit	38	12	22	4	1		1970-71
Harris, Ted	Minnesota	179	48	104	27	3		1975-78
Hart, Cecil	Montreal	394	196	125	73	9	2	1926-39
Hartley, Bob	Colorado	359	193	108	58	5	1	
	Atlanta	291	136	118	37	6		
	Totals	650	329	226	95	10	1	1998-08
Hartsburg, Craig	Chicago	246	104	102	40	3		
	Anaheim	197	80	82	35	3		
	Totals	443	184	184	75	12		1995-01
Harvey, Doug	NY Rangers	70	26	32	12	1		1961-62
Hay, Don	Phoenix	82	38	37	7	1		
	Calgary	68	23	28	17	1		
	Totals	150	61	65	24	2		1996-01
Heffernan, Frank	Toronto	12	5	7	0	1		1919-20
Henning, Lorne	Minnesota	158	68	72	18	2		
	NY Islanders	65	19	39	7	2		
	Totals	223	87	111	25	4		1985-01
Hitchcock, Ken	Dallas	503	277	154	72	7	1	
	Philadelphia	254	131	73	50	5		
	Columbus	144	62	65	17	2		
	Totals	901	470	292	139	21	1	1995-08
Hlinka, Ivan	Pittsburgh	86	42	32	12	2		2000-02
Holmgren, Paul	Philadelphia	264	107	126	31	4		
	Hartford	161	54	93	14	4		
	Totals	425	161	219	45	8		1988-96
Howell, Harry	Minnesota	11	3	6	2	1		1978-79
Imlach, Punch	Toronto	770	370	275	125	12	4	
	Buffalo	119	32	62	25	2		
	Totals	889	402	337	150	14	4	1958-80
Ingarfield, Earl	NY Islanders	30	6	22	2	1		1972-73
Inglis, Bill	Buffalo	56	28	18	10	1		1978-79
Irvin, Dick	Chicago	126	45	62	19	3		
	Toronto	427	216	152	59	9	1	
	Montreal	896	431	313	152	15	3	
	Totals	1449	692	527	230	27	4	1928-56
Ivan, Tommy	Detroit	470	262	118	90	7	3	
	Chicago	103	26	56	21	2		
	Totals	573	288	174	111	9	3	1947-58
Iverson, Emil	Chicago	21	8	7	6	1		1932-33
Johnson, Bob	Calgary	400	193	155	52	5		
	Pittsburgh	80	41	33	6	1	1	
	Totals	480	234	188	58	6	1	1982-91
Johnson, Tom	Boston	208	142	43	23	3	1	1970-73
Johnston, Eddie	Chicago	80	34	27	19	1		
	Pittsburgh	516	232	224	60	7		
	Totals	596	266	251	79	8		1979-97
Johnston, Marshall	California	69	13	45	11	2		
	Colorado	56	15	32	9	1		
	Totals	125	28	77	20	3		1973-82
Julien, Claude	Montreal	159	72	62	25	4		
	New Jersey	79	47	24	8	1		
	Boston	82	41	29	12	1		
	Totals	320	160	115	45	12		2002-08
Kasper, Steve	Boston	164	66	78	20	2		1995-97
Keats, Duke	Detroit	11	2	7	2	1		1926-27

Coach	Team	Games Coached	Wins	Losses	O/T	Years	Cup Wins	Career
Keenan, Mike	Philadelphia	320	190	102	28	4		
	Chicago	320	153	126	41	4		
	NY Rangers	84	52	24	8	1	1	
	St. Louis	163	75	66	22	3		
	Vancouver	108	36	54	18	2		
	Boston	74	33	26	15	1		
	Florida	153	45	73	35	3		
	Calgary	82	42	30	10	1		
	Totals	1304	626	501	177	24	1	1984-08
Kehoe, Rick	Pittsburgh	160	55	81	22	2		2001-03
Kelly, Pat	Colorado	101	22	54	25	2		1977-79
Kelly, Red	Los Angeles	150	55	75	20	2		
	Pittsburgh	274	90	132	52	4		
	Toronto	318	133	123	62	4		
	Totals	742	278	330	134	10		1967-77
King, Dave	Calgary	216	109	76	31	3		
	Columbus	204	64	106	34	3		
	Totals	420	173	182	65	6		1992-03
Kingston, George	San Jose	164	28	129	7	2		1991-93
Kish, Larry	Hartford	49	12	32	5	1		1982-83
Kitchen, Mike	St. Louis	129	38	70	21	4		2003-07
Kromm, Bobby	Detroit	231	79	111	41	3		1977-80
Kurtenbach, Orland	Vancouver	125	36	62	27	2		1976-78
LaForge, Bill	Vancouver	20	4	14	2	1		1984-85
Lalonde, Newsy	Montreal	207	96	97	14	8		
	NY Americans	44	17	25	2	1		
	Ottawa	88	31	45	12	2		
	Totals	339	144	167	28	11		1917-35
Lamoriello, Lou	New Jersey	53	34	14	5	2		2005-07
Laperriere, Jacques	Montreal	1	0	1	0	1		1995-96
Lapointe, Ron	Quebec	89	33	50	6	2		1987-89
Laviolette, Peter	NY Islanders	164	77	62	25	2		
	Carolina	298	155	111	32	5	1	
	Totals	462	232	173	57	10	1	2001-08
Laycoe, Hal	Los Angeles	24	5	18	1	1		
	Vancouver	156	44	96	16	2		
	Totals	180	49	114	17	3		1969-72
Lehman, Hugh	Chicago	21	3	17	1	1		1927-28
Lemaire, Jacques	Montreal	97	48	37	12	2		
	New Jersey	378	199	122	57	5	1	
	Minnesota	574	253	222	99	8		
	Totals	1049	500	381	168	18	1	1983-08
Lepine, Pit	Montreal	48	10	33	5	1		1939-40
LeSueur, Percy	Hamilton	10	3	7	0	1		1923-24
Lewis, Dave	Detroit *	169	100	42	27	4		
	Boston	82	35	41	6	1		
	Totals	251	135	83	33	5		1998-07

* Shared a record of 4-1-0 with co-coach Barry Smith in 1998-99

Coach	Team	Games Coached	Wins	Losses	O/T	Years	Cup Wins	Career
Ley, Rick	Hartford	160	69	71	20	2		
	Vancouver	124	47	50	27	2		
	Totals	284	116	121	47	4		1989-96
Lindsay, Ted	Detroit	29	5	21	3	2		1979-81
Long, Barry	Winnipeg	205	87	93	25	3		1983-86
Loughlin, Clem	Chicago	144	61	63	20	3		1934-37
Low, Ron	Edmonton	341	139	162	40	5		
	NY Rangers	164	69	81	14	2		
	Totals	505	208	243	54	7		1994-02
Lowe, Kevin	Edmonton	82	32	26	24	1		1999-00
Ludzik, Steve	Tampa Bay	121	31	67	23	2		1999-01
MacDonald, Parker	Minnesota	61	20	30	11	1		
	Los Angeles	42	13	24	5	1		
	Totals	103	33	54	16	2		1973-82
MacLean, Doug	Florida	187	83	71	33	3		
	Columbus	79	24	43	12	2		
	Totals	266	107	114	45	5		1995-04
MacMillan, Bill	Colorado	80	22	45	13	1		
	New Jersey	100	19	67	14	2		
	Totals	180	41	112	27	3		1980-84
MacNeil, Al	Montreal	55	31	15	9	1	1	
	Atlanta	80	35	32	13	1		
	Calgary	171	72	66	33	3		
	Totals	306	138	113	55	5	1	1970-03
MacTavish, Craig	Edmonton	574	263	217	94	8		2000-08
Magnuson, Keith	Chicago	132	49	57	26	2		1980-82
Mahoney, Bill	Minnesota	93	42	39	12	2		1983-85
Maloney, Dan	Toronto	160	45	100	15	2		
	Winnipeg	212	91	93	28	3		
	Totals	372	136	193	43	5		1984-89
Maloney, Phil	Vancouver	232	95	105	32	4		1973-77
Mantha, Sylvio	Montreal	48	11	26	11	1		1935-36
Marshall, Bert	Colorado	24	3	17	4	1		1981-82
Martin, Jacques	St. Louis	160	66	71	23	2		
	Ottawa	692	341	235	116	9		
	Florida	246	110	100	36	4		
	Totals	1098	517	406	175	15		1986-08
Matheson, Godfrey	Chicago	2	0	2	0	1		1932-33
Maurice, Paul	Hartford	152	61	72	19	2		
	Carolina	522	207	219	96	7		
	Toronto	164	76	66	22	2		
	Totals	838	344	357	137	11		1995-08
Maxner, Wayne	Detroit	129	34	68	27	2		1980-82
McCammon, Bob	Philadelphia	218	119	68	31	4		
	Vancouver	294	102	156	36	4		
	Totals	512	221	224	67	8		1978-91

Coach	Team	Games Coached	Wins	Losses	O/T	Years	Cup Wins	Career
McCreary, Bill	St. Louis	24	6	14	4	1		
	Vancouver	41	9	25	7	1		
	California	32	8	20	4	1		
	Totals	97	23	59	15	3		1971-75
McGuire, Pierre	Hartford	67	23	37	7	1		1993-94
McLellan, John	Toronto	310	126	139	45	4		1969-73
McVie, Tom	Washington	204	49	122	33	3		
	Winnipeg	105	20	67	18	2		
	New Jersey	153	57	74	22	3		
	Totals	462	126	263	73	8		1975-92
Meeker, Howie	Toronto	70	21	34	15	1		1956-57
Melrose, Barry	Los Angeles	209	79	101	29	3		1992-95
Milbury, Mike	Boston	160	90	49	21	2		
	NY Islanders	191	56	111	24	4		
	Totals	351	146	160	45	6		1989-99
Molleken, Lorne	Chicago	47	18	19	10	2		1998-00
Muckler, John	Minnesota	35	6	23	6	1		
	Edmonton	160	75	65	20	2	1	
	Buffalo	268	125	109	34	4		
	NY Rangers	185	70	88	27	3		
	Totals	648	276	285	87	10	1	1968-00
Muldoon, Pete	Chicago	44	19	22	3	1		1926-27
Munro, Dunc	Mtl. Maroons	76	37	29	10	2		1929-31
Murdoch, Bob	Chicago	80	30	41	9	1		
	Winnipeg	160	63	75	22	2		
	Totals	240	93	116	31	3		1987-91
Murphy, Mike	Los Angeles	65	20	37	8	2		
	Toronto	164	60	87	17	2		
	Totals	229	80	124	25	4		1986-98
Murray, Andy	Los Angeles	480	215	176	89	7		
	St. Louis	138	60	54	24	2		
	Totals	618	275	230	113	9		1999-08
Murray, Bryan	Washington	672	343	246	83	9		
	Detroit	244	124	91	29	3		
	Florida	59	17	31	11	1		
	Anaheim	82	29	42	11	1		
	Ottawa	182	107	55	20	4		
	Totals	1239	620	465	154	18		1981-08
Murray, Terry	Washington	325	163	134	28	5		
	Philadelphia	212	118	64	30	3		
	Florida	200	79	79	42	3		
	Totals	737	360	277	100	12		1989-01
Nanne, Lou	Minnesota	29	7	18	4	1		1977-78
Neale, Harry	Vancouver	407	142	189	76	6		
	Detroit	35	8	23	4	1		
	Totals	442	150	212	80	7		1978-86
Neilson, Roger	Toronto	160	75	62	23	2		
	Buffalo	80	39	20	21	1		
	Vancouver	133	51	61	21	3		
	Los Angeles	28	8	17	3	1		
	NY Rangers	280	141	104	35	4		
	Florida	132	53	56	23	2		
	Philadelphia	185	92	57	36	3		
	Ottawa	2	1	1	0	1		
	Totals	1000	460	378	162	16		1977-02
Nolan, Ted	Buffalo	164	73	72	19	2		
	NY Islanders	163	74	68	21	2		
	Totals	327	147	140	40	4		1995-08
Nykoluk, Mike	Toronto	280	89	144	47	4		1980-84
O'Connell, Mike	Boston	9	3	3	3	1		2002-03
O'Donoghue, George	Toronto	29	15	13	1	2	1	1921-23
Olczyk, Ed	Pittsburgh	113	31	64	18	3		2003-06
Oliver, Murray	Minnesota	41	21	12	8	2		1981-83
Olmstead, Bert	Oakland	64	11	37	16	1		1967-68
O'Reilly, Terry	Oakland	227	115	86	26	3		1986-89
Paddock, John	Winnipeg	281	106	138	37	4		
	Ottawa	64	36	22	6	1		
	Totals	345	142	160	43	5		1991-08
Page, Pierre	Minnesota	160	63	77	20	2		
	Quebec	230	98	103	29	3		
	Calgary	164	66	78	20	2		
	Anaheim	82	26	43	13	1		
	Totals	636	253	301	82	8		1988-98
Park, Brad	Detroit	45	9	34	2	1		1985-86
Paterson, Rick	Tampa Bay	6	0	6	0	1		1997-98
Patrick, Craig	NY Rangers	95	37	45	13	2		
	Pittsburgh	74	29	36	9	2		
	Totals	169	66	81	22	4		1980-97
Patrick, Frank	Boston	96	48	36	12	2		1934-36
Patrick, Lester	NY Rangers	604	281	216	107	13	2	1926-39
Patrick, Lynn	NY Rangers	107	40	51	16	2		
	NY Rangers	310	117	130	63	5		
	St. Louis	26	8	15	3	3		
	Totals	443	165	196	82	10		1948-76
Patrick, Muzz	NY Rangers	136	43	66	27	4		1953-63
Perron, Jean	Montreal	240	126	84	30	3	1	
	Quebec	47	16	26	5	1		
	Totals	287	142	110	35	4	1	1985-89
Perry, Don	Los Angeles	168	52	85	31	3		1981-84
Pike, Alf	NY Rangers	123	36	66	21	2		1959-61
Pilous, Rudy	Chicago	387	162	151	74	6	1	1957-63
Plager, Barclay	St. Louis	178	49	96	33	4		1977-83
Plager, Bob	St. Louis	11	4	6	1	1		1992-93
Playfair, Jim	Calgary	82	43	29	10	1		2006-07
Pleau, Larry	Hartford	224	81	117	26	5		1980-89

Coach	Team	Games Coached	Wins	Losses	O/T	Years	Cup Wins	Career
Polano, Nick	Detroit	240	79	127	34	3		1982-85
Popein, Larry	NY Rangers	41	18	14	9	1		1973-74
Powers, Eddie	Toronto	66	31	32	3	2		1924-26
Primeau, Joe	Toronto	210	97	71	42	3	1	1950-53
Pronovost, Marcel	Buffalo	104	52	29	23	2		1977-79
Pulford, Bob	Los Angeles	396	178	150	68	5		
	Chicago	433	185	180	68	7		
	Totals	829	363	330	136	12		1972-00
Quenneville, Joel	St. Louis	593	307	191	95	8		
	Colorado	246	131	92	23	4		
	Totals	839	438	283	118	12		1996-08
Querrie, Charles	Toronto	72	29	38	5	3		1922-27
Quinn, Mike	Quebec	24	4	20	0	1		1919-20
Quinn, Pat	Philadelphia	262	141	73	48	4		
	Los Angeles	202	75	101	26	3		
	Vancouver	280	141	111	28	5		
	Toronto	574	300	196	78	8		
	Totals	1318	657	481	180	20		1978-06
Raeder, Cap	San Jose	1	1	0	0	1		2002-03
Ramsay, Craig	Buffalo	21	4	15	2	1		
	Philadelphia	28	12	12	4	1		
	Totals	49	16	27	6	2		1986-01
Randall, Ken	Hamilton	14	6	8	0	1		1923-24
Reay, Billy	Toronto	90	26	50	14	2		
	Chicago	1012	516	335	161	14		
	Totals	1102	542	385	175	16		1957-77
Regan, Larry	Los Angeles	88	27	47	14	2		1970-72
Renney, Tom	Vancouver	101	39	53	9	2		
	NY Rangers	266	133	94	39	5		
	Totals	367	172	147	48	13		1996-08
Risebrough, Doug	Calgary	144	71	56	17	2		1990-92
Roberts, Jim	Buffalo	45	21	16	8	1		
	Hartford	80	26	41	13	1		
	St. Louis	9	3	3	3	1		
	Totals	134	50	60	24	3		1981-97
Robinson, Larry	Los Angeles	328	122	161	45	4		
	New Jersey	173	87	56	30	4	1	
	Totals	501	209	217	75	8	1	1995-06
Rodden, Mike	Toronto	2	0	2	0	1		1926-27
Romeril, Alex	Toronto	13	7	5	1	1		1926-27
Ross, Art	Mtl. Wanderers	6	1	5	0	1		
	Hamilton	24	6	18	0	1		
	Boston	728	361	277	90	16	1	
	Totals	758	368	300	90	18	1	1917-45
Ruel, Claude	Montreal	305	172	82	51	5	1	1968-81
Ruff, Lindy	Buffalo	820	397	302	121	11		1997-08
Sather, Glen	Buffalo	842	464	268	110	11	4	
	NY Rangers	90	33	39	18	2		
	Totals	932	497	307	128	13	4	1979-04
Sator, Ted	NY Rangers	99	41	48	10	2		
	Buffalo	207	96	89	22	3		
	Totals	306	137	137	32	4		1985-89
Savard, Andre	Quebec	24	10	13	1	1		1987-88
Savard, Denis	Chicago	143	64	64	15	2		2006-08
Schinkel, Ken	Pittsburgh	203	83	92	28	4		1972-77
Schmidt, Milt	Boston	726	245	360	121	11		
	Washington	44	5	34	5	2		
	Totals	770	250	394	126	13		1954-76
Schoenfeld, Jim	Buffalo	43	19	19	5	1		
	New Jersey	124	50	59	15	3		
	Washington	249	113	102	34	4		
	Phoenix	164	74	66	24	2		
	Totals	580	256	246	78	10		1985-99
Shaughnessy, Tom	Chicago	21	10	8	3	1		1929-30
Shaw, Brad	NY Islanders	40	18	18	4	1		2005-06
Shero, Fred	Philadelphia	554	308	151	95	7	2	
	NY Rangers	180	82	74	24	3		
	Totals	734	390	225	119	10	2	1971-81
Simpson, Joe	NY Americans	144	42	72	30	3		1932-35
Simpson, Terry	NY Islanders	187	81	82	24	3		
	Philadelphia	84	35	39	10	1		
	Winnipeg	97	43	47	7	2		
	Totals	368	159	168	41	6		1986-96
Sims, Al	San Jose	82	27	47	8	1		1996-97
Sinden, Harry	Boston	327	153	116	58	6	1	1966-85
Skinner, Jimmy	Detroit	247	123	78	46	4	1	1954-58
Smeaton, Cooper	Philadelphia	44	4	36	4	1		1930-31
Smith, Alf	Ottawa	18	12	6	0	1		1918-19
Smith, Barry	Detroit *	5	4	1	0	1		1998-99

* Results Shared with co-coach Dave Lewis

Coach	Team	Games Coached	Wins	Losses	O/T	Years	Cup Wins	Career
Smith, Floyd	Buffalo	241	143	62	36	4		
	Toronto	68	30	33	5	1		
	Totals	309	173	95	41	5		1971-80
Smith, Mike	Winnipeg	23	2	17	4	1		1980-81
Smith, Ron	NY Rangers	44	15	22	7	1		1992-93
Smythe, Conn	Toronto	134	57	57	20	4		1927-31
Sonmor, Glen	Minnesota	417	174	161	82	7		1978-87
Sproule, Harvey	Toronto	12	7	5	0	1		1919-20
Stanley, Barney	Chicago	23	4	17	2	1		1927-28
Stasiuk, Vic	Philadelphia	154	45	68	41	2		
	California	75	21	38	16	1		
	Vancouver	78	22	47	9	1		
	Totals	307	88	153	66	4		1969-73
Stevens, John	Philadelphia	156	63	71	22	2		2006-08

Coach	Team	Games Coached	Wins	Losses	O/T	Years	Cup Wins	Career
Stewart, Bill	Chicago	69	22	35	12	2	1	1937-39
Stewart, Bill	NY Islanders	37	11	19	7	1		1998-99
Stewart, Ron	NY Rangers	39	15	20	4	1		
	Los Angeles	80	31	34	15	1		
	Totals	119	46	54	19	2		1975-78
Stirling, Steve	NY Islanders	124	56	51	17	3		2003-06
Suhonen, Alpo	Chicago	82	29	41	12	1		2000-01
Sullivan, Mike	Boston	164	70	56	38	3		2003-06
Sullivan, Red	NY Rangers	196	58	103	35	4		
	Pittsburgh	150	47	79	24	2		
	Washington	18	2	16	0	1		
	Totals	364	107	198	59	7		1962-75
Sutherland, Bill	Winnipeg	32	7	22	3	2		1979-81
Sutter, Brent	New Jersey	82	46	29	7	1		2007-08
Sutter, Brian	St. Louis	320	153	124	43	4		
	Boston	216	120	73	23	3		
	Calgary	246	87	117	42	3		
	Chicago	246	91	103	52	4		
	Totals	1028	451	417	160	14		1988-05
Sutter, Darryl	Chicago	216	110	80	26	3		
	San Jose	434	192	167	75	6		
	Calgary	210	107	73	30	4		
	Totals	860	409	320	131	12		1992-06
Sutter, Duane	Florida	72	22	35	15	2		2000-02
Talbot, Jean-Guy	St. Louis	120	52	53	15	2		
	NY Rangers	80	30	37	13	1		
	Totals	200	82	90	28	3		1972-78
Tessier, Orval	Chicago	213	99	93	21	3		1982-85
Therrien, Michel	Montreal	190	77	77	36	3		
	Pittsburgh	215	108	80	27	3		
	Totals	405	185	157	63	15		2000-08
Thompson, Paul	Chicago	272	104	127	41	7		1938-45
Thompson, Percy	Hamilton	48	13	35	0	2		1920-22
Tippett, Dave	Dallas	410	235	121	54	6		2002-08
Tobin, Bill	Chicago	71	29	29	13	2		1929-32
Torchetti, John	Florida	27	10	12	5	1		
	Los Angeles	12	5	7	0	1		
	Totals	39	15	19	5	2		2003-06
Tortorella, John	NY Rangers	4	0	3	1	1		
	Tampa Bay	535	239	222	74	8	1	
	Totals	539	239	225	75	9	1	1999-08
Tremblay, Mario	Montreal	159	71	63	25	2		1995-97
Trottier, Bryan	NY Rangers	54	21	26	7	1		2002-03
Trotz, Barry	Nashville	738	324	308	106	10		1998-08
Ubriaco, Gene	Pittsburgh	106	50	47	9	2		1988-90
Vachon, Rogie	Los Angeles	10	4	3	3	3		1983-95
Vigneault, Alain	Montreal	266	109	118	39	4		
	Vancouver	164	88	59	17	2		
	Totals	430	197	177	56	17		1997-08
Waddell, Don	Atlanta	86	38	39	9	2		2002-08
Watson, Bryan	Edmonton	18	4	9	5	1		1980-81
Watson, Phil	NY Rangers	295	119	124	52	5		
	Boston	84	16	55	13	2		
	Totals	379	135	179	65	7		1955-63
Watt, Tom	Winnipeg	181	72	85	24	3		
	Vancouver	160	52	87	21	2		
	Toronto	149	52	80	17	2		
	Totals	490	176	252	62	7		1981-92
Webster, Tom	NY Rangers	18	5	9	4	1		
	Los Angeles	240	115	94	31	3		
	Totals	258	120	103	35	4		1986-92
Weiland, Cooney	Boston	96	58	20	18	2	1	1939-41
White, Bill	Chicago	46	16	24	6	1		1976-77
Wiley, Jim	San Jose	57	17	37	3	1		1995-96
Wilson, Johnny	Los Angeles	52	9	34	9	1		
	Detroit	145	67	56	22	2		
	Colorado	80	20	46	14	1		
	Pittsburgh	240	91	105	44	3		
	Totals	517	187	241	89	7		1969-80
Wilson, Larry	Detroit	36	3	29	4	1		1976-77
Wilson, Rick	Dallas	32	13	11	8	1		2001-02
Wilson, Ron	Anaheim	296	120	145	31	4		
	Washington	410	192	159	59	5		
	San Jose	385	206	122	57	6		
	Totals	1091	518	426	147	15		1993-08
Yawney, Trent	Chicago	103	33	55	15	2		2005-07
Young, Garry	California	12	2	7	3	1		
	St. Louis	98	41	41	16	2		
	Totals	110	43	48	19	3		1972-76

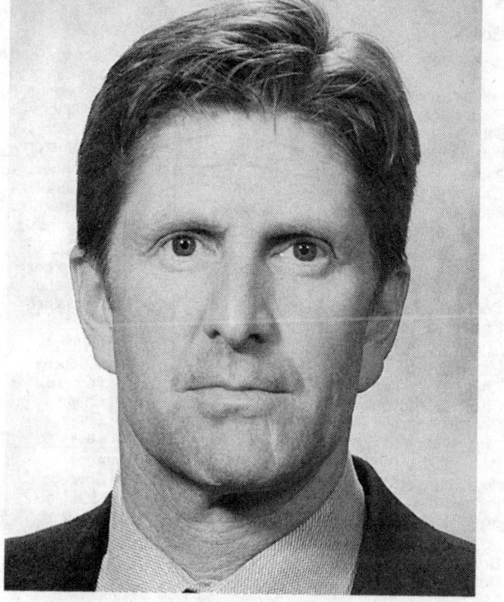

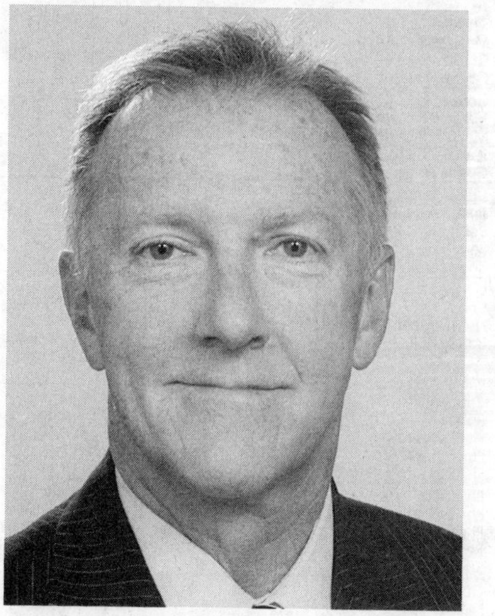

Mike Babcock (top) led the 2007-08 Detroit Red Wings to the NHL's best record during the regular season, then to the Stanley Cup. He joins Scotty Bowman (Montreal), Tom Johnson (Boston), Mike Keenan (Philadelphia), Glen Sather (Edmonton) and Fred Shero (Philadelphia) as the only coaches to lead their clubs to back-to-back 50-win seasons. Ron Wilson (middle) led the San Jose Sharks to a club-record 108 points in 2007-08 and takes over as the new head coach of the Toronto Maple Leafs in 2008-09. Guy Carbonneau (bottom) led the Canadiens to 47 wins last year, their best total since the 1992-93 season.

Year-by-Year Individual Regular-Season Leaders

Season	Goals	G	Assists	A	Points	Pts.	Penalty Minutes	PIM
1917-18	Joe Malone	44	Cy Denneny, Reg Noble, Harry Cameron	10	Joe Malone	48	Joe Hall	100
1918-19	Newsy Lalonde	22	Newsy Lalonde, Eddie Gerard	10	Newsy Lalonde	32	Joe Hall	135
1919-20	Joe Malone	39	Frank Nighbor	15	Joe Malone	49	Cully Wilson	86
1920-21	Babe Dye	35	Jack Darragh	15	Newsy Lalonde	43	Bert Corbeau	86
1921-22	Punch Broadbent	32	Harry Cameron	17	Punch Broadbent	46	Sprague Cleghorn	63
1922-23	Babe Dye	26	Edmond Bouchard	12	Babe Dye	37	Georges Boucher	58
1923-24	Cy Denneny	22	Georges Boucher	10	Cy Denneny	24	Bert Corbeau	55
1924-25	Babe Dye	38	Cy Denneny, Red Green	15	Babe Dye	46	Georges Boucher	95
1925-26	Nels Stewart	34	Frank Nighbor	13	Nels Stewart	42	Bert Corbeau	121
1926-27	Bill Cook	33	Dick Irvin	18	Bill Cook	37	Nels Stewart	133
1927-28	Howie Morenz	33	Howie Morenz	18	Howie Morenz	51	Eddie Shore	165
1928-29	Ace Bailey	22	Frank Boucher	16	Ace Bailey	32	Red Dutton	139
1929-30	Cooney Weiland	43	Frank Boucher	36	Cooney Weiland	73	Joe Lamb	119
1930-31	Charlie Conacher	31	Joe Primeau	32	Howie Morenz	51	Harvey Rockburn	118
1931-32	Charlie Conacher, Bill Cook	34	Joe Primeau	37	Busher Jackson	53	Red Dutton	107
1932-33	Bill Cook	28	Frank Boucher	28	Bill Cook	50	Red Horner	144
1933-34	Charlie Conacher	32	Joe Primeau	32	Charlie Conacher	52	Red Horner	126 *
1934-35	Charlie Conacher	36	Art Chapman	34	Charlie Conacher	57	Red Horner	125
1935-36	Charlie Conacher, Bill Thoms	23	Art Chapman	28	Sweeney Schriner	45	Red Horner	167
1936-37	Larry Aurie, Nels Stewart	23	Syl Apps	29	Sweeney Schriner	46	Red Horner	124
1937-38	Gordie Drillon	26	Syl Apps	29	Gordie Drillon	52	Red Horner	82 *
1938-39	Roy Conacher	26	Bill Cowley	34	Toe Blake	47	Red Horner	85
1939-40	Bryan Hextall	24	Milt Schmidt	30	Milt Schmidt	52	Red Horner	87
1940-41	Bryan Hextall	26	Bill Cowley	45	Bill Cowley	62	Jimmy Orlando	99
1941-42	Lynn Patrick	32	Phil Watson	37	Bryan Hextall	56	Pat Egan	124
1942-43	Doug Bentley	33	Bill Cowley	45	Doug Bentley	73	Jimmy Orlando	89 *
1943-44	Doug Bentley	38	Clint Smith	49	Herb Cain	82	Mike McMahon	98
1944-45	Maurice Richard	50	Elmer Lach	54	Elmer Lach	80	Pat Egan	86
1945-46	Gaye Stewart	37	Elmer Lach	34	Max Bentley	61	Jack Stewart	73
1946-47	Maurice Richard	45	Billy Taylor	46	Max Bentley	72	Gus Mortson	133
1947-48	Ted Lindsay	33	Doug Bentley	37	Elmer Lach	61	Bill Barilko	147
1948-49	Sid Abel	28	Doug Bentley	43	Roy Conacher	68	Bill Ezinicki	145
1949-50	Maurice Richard	43	Ted Lindsay	55	Ted Lindsay	78	Bill Ezinicki	144
1950-51	Gordie Howe	43	Gordie Howe, Ted Kennedy	43	Gordie Howe	86	Gus Mortson	142
1951-52	Gordie Howe	47	Elmer Lach	50	Gordie Howe	86	Gus Kyle	127
1952-53	Gordie Howe	49	Gordie Howe	46	Gordie Howe	95	Maurice Richard	112
1953-54	Maurice Richard	37	Gordie Howe	48	Gordie Howe	81	Gus Mortson	132
1954-55	Maurice Richard, Bernie Geoffrion	38	Bert Olmstead	48	Bernie Geoffrion	75	Fern Flaman	150
1955-56	Jean Beliveau	47	Bert Olmstead	56	Jean Beliveau	88	Lou Fontinato	202
1956-57	Gordie Howe	44	Ted Lindsay	55	Gordie Howe	89	Gus Mortson	147
1957-58	Dickie Moore	36	Henri Richard	52	Dickie Moore	84	Lou Fontinato	152
1958-59	Jean Beliveau	45	Dickie Moore	55	Dickie Moore	96	Ted Lindsay	184
1959-60	Bobby Hull, Bronco Horvath	39	Don McKenney	49	Bobby Hull	81	Carl Brewer	150
1960-61	Bernie Geoffrion	50	Jean Beliveau	58	Bernie Geoffrion	95	Pierre Pilote	165
1961-62	Bobby Hull	50	Andy Bathgate	56	Bobby Hull, Andy Bathgate	84	Lou Fontinato	167
1962-63	Gordie Howe	38	Henri Richard	50	Gordie Howe	86	Howie Young	273
1963-64	Bobby Hull	43	Andy Bathgate	58	Stan Mikita	89	Vic Hadfield	151
1964-65	Norm Ullman	42	Stan Mikita	59	Stan Mikita	87	Carl Brewer	177
1965-66	Bobby Hull	54	Stan Mikita, Bobby Rousseau, Jean Beliveau	48	Bobby Hull	97	Reggie Fleming	166
1966-67	Bobby Hull	52	Stan Mikita	62	Stan Mikita	97	John Ferguson	177
1967-68	Bobby Hull	44	Phil Esposito	49	Stan Mikita	87	Barclay Plager	153
1968-69	Bobby Hull	58	Phil Esposito	77	Phil Esposito	126	Forbes Kennedy	219
1969-70	Phil Esposito	43	Bobby Orr	87	Bobby Orr	120	Keith Magnuson	213
1970-71	Phil Esposito	76	Bobby Orr	102	Phil Esposito	152	Keith Magnuson	291
1971-72	Phil Esposito	66	Bobby Orr	80	Phil Esposito	133	Bryan Watson	212
1972-73	Phil Esposito	55	Phil Esposito	75	Phil Esposito	130	Dave Schultz	259
1973-74	Phil Esposito	68	Bobby Orr	90	Phil Esposito	145	Dave Schultz	348
1974-75	Phil Esposito	61	Bobby Orr, Bobby Clarke	89	Bobby Orr	135	Dave Schultz	472
1975-76	Reggie Leach	61	Bobby Clarke	89	Guy Lafleur	125	Steve Durbano	370
1976-77	Steve Shutt	60	Guy Lafleur	80	Guy Lafleur	136	Tiger Williams	338
1977-78	Guy Lafleur	60	Bryan Trottier	77	Guy Lafleur	132	Dave Schultz	405
1978-79	Mike Bossy	69	Bryan Trottier	87	Bryan Trottier	134	Tiger Williams	298
1979-80	Charlie Simmer, Danny Gare, Blaine Stoughton	56	Wayne Gretzky	86	Marcel Dionne, Wayne Gretzky	137	Jimmy Mann	287
1980-81	Mike Bossy	68	Wayne Gretzky	109	Wayne Gretzky	164	Tiger Williams	343
1981-82	Wayne Gretzky	92	Wayne Gretzky	120	Wayne Gretzky	212	Paul Baxter	409
1982-83	Wayne Gretzky	71	Wayne Gretzky	125	Wayne Gretzky	196	Randy Holt	275
1983-84	Wayne Gretzky	87	Wayne Gretzky	118	Wayne Gretzky	205	Chris Nilan	338
1984-85	Wayne Gretzky	73	Wayne Gretzky	135	Wayne Gretzky	208	Chris Nilan	358
1985-86	Jari Kurri	68	Wayne Gretzky	163	Wayne Gretzky	215	Joe Kocur	377
1986-87	Wayne Gretzky	62	Wayne Gretzky	121	Wayne Gretzky	183	Tim Hunter	361
1987-88	Mario Lemieux	70	Wayne Gretzky	109	Mario Lemieux	168	Bob Probert	398
1988-89	Mario Lemieux	85	Mario Lemieux, Wayne Gretzky	114	Mario Lemieux	199	Tim Hunter	375
1989-90	Brett Hull	72	Wayne Gretzky	102	Wayne Gretzky	142	Basil McRae	351
1990-91	Brett Hull	86	Wayne Gretzky	122	Wayne Gretzky	163	Rob Ray	350
1991-92	Brett Hull	70	Wayne Gretzky	90	Mario Lemieux	131	Mike Peluso	408
1992-93	Teemu Selanne, Alexander Mogilny	76	Adam Oates	97	Mario Lemieux	160	Marty McSorley	399
1993-94	Pavel Bure	60	Wayne Gretzky	92	Wayne Gretzky	130	Tie Domi	347
1994-95	Peter Bondra	34	Ron Francis	48	Jaromir Jagr, Eric Lindros	70	Enrico Ciccone	225
1995-96	Mario Lemieux	69	Mario Lemieux, Ron Francis	92	Mario Lemieux	161	Matthew Barnaby	335
1996-97	Keith Tkachuk	52	Mario Lemieux, Wayne Gretzky	72	Mario Lemieux	122	Gino Odjick	371
1997-98	Teemu Selanne, Peter Bondra	52	Jaromir Jagr, Wayne Gretzky	67	Jaromir Jagr	102	Donald Brashear	372
1998-99	Teemu Selanne	47	Jaromir Jagr	83	Jaromir Jagr	127	Rob Ray	261
99-2000	Pavel Bure	58	Mark Recchi	63	Jaromir Jagr	96	Denny Lambert	219
2000-01	Pavel Bure	59	Jaromir Jagr, Adam Oates	69	Jaromir Jagr	121	Matthew Barnaby	265
2001-02	Jarome Iginla	52	Adam Oates	64	Jarome Iginla	96	Peter Worell	354
2002-03	Milan Hejduk	50	Peter Forsberg	77	Peter Forsberg	106	Jody Shelley	249
2003-04	Rick Nash, Jarome Iginla, Ilya Kovalchuk	41	Scott Gomez, Martin St. Louis	56	Martin St. Louis	94	Sean Avery	261
2004-05	....	....	....	....	....	....	....	....
2005-06	Jonathan Cheechoo	56	Joe Thornton	96	Joe Thornton	125	Sean Avery	257
2006-07	Vincent Lecavalier	52	Joe Thornton	92	Sidney Crosby	120	Ben Eager	233
2007-08	Alex Ovechkin	65	Joe Thornton	67	Alex Ovechkin	112	Daniel Carcillo	324

* Match Misconduct penalty not included in total penalty minutes.
1946-47 was the first season that a Match penalty was automaticaly written into the player's total penalty minutes as 20 minutes.
Beginning in 1947-48 all penalties, Match, Game Misconduct, and Misconduct, are written as 10 minutes.

One Season Scoring Records

Goals-Per-Game Leaders, One Season

(Among players with 20 goals or more in one season)

Player	Team	Season	Games	Goals	Goals per game average
Joe Malone	Montreal	1917-18	20	44	2.20
Cy Denneny	Ottawa	1917-18	20	36	1.80
Newsy Lalonde	Montreal	1917-18	14	23	1.64
Joe Malone	Quebec	1919-20	24	39	1.63
Newsy Lalonde	Montreal	1919-20	23	37	1.61
Reg Noble	Toronto	1917-18	20	30	1.50
Babe Dye	Ham., Tor.	1920-21	24	35	1.46
Cy Denneny	Ottawa	1920-21	24	34	1.42
Joe Malone	Hamilton	1920-21	20	28	1.40
Newsy Lalonde	Montreal	1920-21	24	33	1.38
Punch Broadbent	Ottawa	1921-22	24	32	1.33
Babe Dye	Toronto	1924-25	29	38	1.31
Babe Dye	Toronto	1921-22	24	31	1.29
Newsy Lalonde	Montreal	1918-19	17	22	1.29
Odie Cleghorn	Montreal	1918-19	17	22	1.29
Cy Denneny	Ottawa	1921-22	22	27	1.23
Aurel Joliat	Montreal	1924-25	25	30	1.20
Wayne Gretzky	Edmonton	1983-84	74	87	1.18
Babe Dye	Toronto	1922-23	22	26	1.18
Wayne Gretzky	Edmonton	1981-82	80	92	1.15
Mario Lemieux	Pittsburgh	1992-93	60	69	1.15
Frank Nighbor	Ottawa	1919-20	23	26	1.13
Mario Lemieux	Pittsburgh	1988-89	76	85	1.12
Brett Hull	St. Louis	1990-91	78	86	1.10
Cam Neely	Boston	1993-94	49	50	1.02
Maurice Richard	Montreal	1944-45	50	50	1.00
Reg Noble	Toronto	1919-20	24	24	1.00
Corb Denneny	Toronto	1919-20	24	24	1.00
Joe Malone	Hamilton	1921-22	24	24	1.00
Billy Boucher	Montreal	1922-23	24	24	1.00
Cy Denneny	Ottawa	1923-24	22	22	1.00
Alexander Mogilny	Buffalo	1992-93	77	76	0.99
Mario Lemieux	Pittsburgh	1995-96	70	69	0.99
Cooney Weiland	Boston	1929-30	44	43	0.98
Phil Esposito	Boston	1970-71	78	76	0.97
Jari Kurri	Edmonton	1984-85	73	71	0.97

Traded to Phoenix by Pittsburgh for tough guy Georges Laraque, Daniel Carcillo proved more than willing to mix it up for the Coyotes in 2007-08 with a league-leading 324 penalty minutes. He also scored 13 goals in just 57 games in his first full NHL season, including a hat trick on April 4.

Assists-Per-Game Leaders, One Season

(Among players with 35 assists or more in one season)

Player	Team	Season	Games	Assists	Assists per game average
Wayne Gretzky	Edmonton	1985-86	80	163	2.04
Wayne Gretzky	Edmonton	1987-88	64	109	1.70
Wayne Gretzky	Edmonton	1984-85	80	135	1.69
Wayne Gretzky	Edmonton	1983-84	74	118	1.59
Wayne Gretzky	Edmonton	1982-83	80	125	1.56
Wayne Gretzky	Los Angeles	1990-91	78	122	1.56
Wayne Gretzky	Edmonton	1986-87	79	121	1.53
Mario Lemieux	Pittsburgh	1992-93	60	91	1.52
Wayne Gretzky	Edmonton	1981-82	80	120	1.50
Mario Lemieux	Pittsburgh	1988-89	76	114	1.50
Adam Oates	St. Louis	1990-91	61	90	1.48
Wayne Gretzky	Los Angeles	1988-89	78	114	1.46
Wayne Gretzky	Los Angeles	1989-90	73	102	1.40
Wayne Gretzky	Edmonton	1980-81	80	109	1.36
Mario Lemieux	Pittsburgh	1991-92	64	87	1.36
Mario Lemieux	Pittsburgh	1989-90	59	78	1.32
Bobby Orr	Boston	1970-71	78	102	1.31
Mario Lemieux	Pittsburgh	1995-96	70	92	1.31
Mario Lemieux	Pittsburgh	1987-88	77	98	1.27
Bobby Orr	Boston	1973-74	74	90	1.22
Wayne Gretzky	Los Angeles	1991-92	74	90	1.22
Joe Thornton	Bos., S.J.	2005-06	81	96	1.19
Ron Francis	Pittsburgh	1995-96	77	92	1.19
Mario Lemieux	Pittsburgh	1985-86	79	93	1.18
Bobby Clarke	Philadelphia	1975-76	76	89	1.17
Peter Stastny	Quebec	1981-82	80	93	1.16
Adam Oates	Boston	1992-93	84	97	1.15
Doug Gilmour	Toronto	1992-93	83	95	1.14
Wayne Gretzky	Los Angeles	1993-94	81	92	1.14
Paul Coffey	Edmonton	1985-86	79	90	1.14
Bobby Orr	Boston	1969-70	76	87	1.14
Bryan Trottier	NY Islanders	1978-79	76	87	1.14
Bobby Orr	Boston	1972-73	63	72	1.14
Bill Cowley	Boston	1943-44	36	41	1.14
Pat LaFontaine	Buffalo	1992-93	84	95	1.13
Steve Yzerman	Detroit	1988-89	80	90	1.13
Paul Coffey	Pittsburgh	1987-88	46	52	1.13
Joe Thornton	San Jose	2006-07	82	92	1.12
Bobby Orr	Boston	1974-75	80	89	1.11
Bobby Clarke	Philadelphia	1974-75	80	89	1.11
Paul Coffey	Pittsburgh	1988-89	75	83	1.11
Wayne Gretzky	Los Angeles	1992-93	45	49	1.11
Denis Savard	Chicago	1982-83	78	86	1.10
Denis Savard	Chicago	1981-82	80	87	1.09
Denis Savard	Chicago	1987-88	80	87	1.09
Wayne Gretzky	Edmonton	1979-80	79	86	1.09
Ron Francis	Pittsburgh	1994-95	44	48	1.09
Paul Coffey	Edmonton	1983-84	80	86	1.08
Elmer Lach	Montreal	1944-45	50	54	1.08
Peter Stastny	Quebec	1985-86	76	81	1.07
Jaromir Jagr	Pittsburgh	1995-96	82	87	1.06
Mark Messier	Edmonton	1989-90	79	84	1.06
Sidney Crosby	Pittsburgh	2006-07	79	84	1.06
Peter Forsberg	Colorado	1995-96	82	86	1.05
Paul Coffey	Edmonton	1984-85	80	84	1.05
Marcel Dionne	Los Angeles	1979-80	80	84	1.05
Bobby Orr	Boston	1971-72	76	80	1.05
Mike Bossy	NY Islanders	1981-82	80	83	1.04
Adam Oates	Boston	1993-94	77	80	1.04
Phil Esposito	Boston	1968-69	74	77	1.04
Bryan Trottier	NY Islanders	1983-84	68	71	1.04
Jason Spezza	Ottawa	2005-06	68	71	1.04
Pete Mahovlich	Montreal	1974-75	80	82	1.03
Kent Nilsson	Calgary	1980-81	80	82	1.03
Peter Stastny	Quebec	1982-83	75	77	1.03
Peter Forsberg	Colorado	2002-03	75	77	1.03
Denis Savard	Chicago	1988-89	58	59	1.02
Jaromir Jagr	Pittsburgh	1998-99	81	83	1.02
Doug Gilmour	Toronto	1993-94	83	84	1.01
Bernie Nicholls	Los Angeles	1988-89	79	80	1.01
Guy Lafleur	Montreal	1979-80	74	75	1.01
Guy Lafleur	Montreal	1976-77	80	80	1.00
Marcel Dionne	Los Angeles	1984-85	80	80	1.00
Brian Leetch	NY Rangers	1991-92	80	80	1.00
Bryan Trottier	NY Islanders	1977-78	77	77	1.00
Mike Bossy	NY Islanders	1983-84	67	67	1.00
Jean Ratelle	NY Rangers	1971-72	63	63	1.00
Steve Yzerman	Detroit	1993-94	58	58	1.00
Ron Francis	Hartford	1985-86	53	53	1.00
Guy Chouinard	Calgary	1980-81	52	52	1.00
Elmer Lach	Montreal	1943-44	48	48	1.00

Points-Per-Game Leaders, One Season

(Among players with 50 points or more in one season)

Player	Team	Season	Games	Points	Points per game average
Wayne Gretzky	Edmonton	1983-84	74	205	2.77
Wayne Gretzky	Edmonton	1985-86	80	215	2.69
Mario Lemieux	Pittsburgh	1992-93	60	160	2.67
Wayne Gretzky	Edmonton	1981-82	80	212	2.65
Mario Lemieux	Pittsburgh	1988-89	76	199	2.62
Wayne Gretzky	Edmonton	1984-85	80	208	2.60
Wayne Gretzky	Edmonton	1982-83	80	196	2.45
Wayne Gretzky	Edmonton	1987-88	64	149	2.33
Wayne Gretzky	Edmonton	1986-87	79	183	2.32
Mario Lemieux	Pittsburgh	1995-96	70	161	2.30
Mario Lemieux	Pittsburgh	1987-88	77	168	2.18
Wayne Gretzky	Los Angeles	1988-89	78	168	2.15
Wayne Gretzky	Los Angeles	1990-91	78	163	2.09
Mario Lemieux	Pittsburgh	1989-90	59	123	2.08
Wayne Gretzky	Edmonton	1980-81	80	164	2.05
Mario Lemieux	Pittsburgh	1991-92	64	131	2.05
Bill Cowley	Boston	1943-44	36	71	1.97
Phil Esposito	Boston	1970-71	78	152	1.95
Wayne Gretzky	Los Angeles	1989-90	73	142	1.95
Steve Yzerman	Detroit	1988-89	80	155	1.94
Bernie Nicholls	Los Angeles	1988-89	79	150	1.90
Adam Oates	St. Louis	1990-91	61	115	1.89
Phil Esposito	Boston	1973-74	78	145	1.86
Jari Kurri	Edmonton	1984-85	73	135	1.85
Mike Bossy	NY Islanders	1981-82	80	147	1.84
Jaromir Jagr	Pittsburgh	1995-96	82	149	1.82
Mario Lemieux	Pittsburgh	1985-86	79	141	1.78
Bobby Orr	Boston	1970-71	78	139	1.78
Jari Kurri	Edmonton	1983-84	64	113	1.77
Mario Lemieux	Pittsburgh	2000-01	43	76	1.77
Pat LaFontaine	Buffalo	1992-93	84	148	1.76
Bryan Trottier	NY Islanders	1978-79	76	134	1.76
Mike Bossy	NY Islanders	1983-84	67	118	1.76
Paul Coffey	Edmonton	1985-86	79	138	1.75
Phil Esposito	Boston	1971-72	76	133	1.75
Peter Stastny	Quebec	1981-82	80	139	1.74
Wayne Gretzky	Edmonton	1979-80	79	137	1.73
Jean Ratelle	NY Rangers	1971-72	63	109	1.73
Marcel Dionne	Los Angeles	1979-80	80	137	1.71
Herb Cain	Boston	1943-44	48	82	1.71
Guy Lafleur	Montreal	1976-77	80	136	1.70
Dennis Maruk	Washington	1981-82	80	136	1.70
Phil Esposito	Boston	1968-69	74	126	1.70
Guy Lafleur	Montreal	1974-75	70	119	1.70
Mario Lemieux	Pittsburgh	1986-87	63	107	1.70
Adam Oates	Boston	1992-93	84	142	1.69
Bobby Orr	Boston	1974-75	80	135	1.69
Marcel Dionne	Los Angeles	1980-81	80	135	1.69
Guy Lafleur	Montreal	1977-78	78	132	1.69
Guy Lafleur	Montreal	1979-80	74	125	1.69
Rob Brown	Pittsburgh	1988-89	68	115	1.69
Jari Kurri	Edmonton	1985-86	78	131	1.68
Brett Hull	St. Louis	1990-91	78	131	1.68
Phil Esposito	Boston	1972-73	78	130	1.67
Cooney Weiland	Boston	1929-30	44	73	1.66
Alexander Mogilny	Buffalo	1992-93	77	127	1.65
Peter Stastny	Quebec	1982-83	75	124	1.65
Bobby Orr	Boston	1973-74	74	122	1.65
Kent Nilsson	Calgary	1980-81	80	131	1.64
Denis Savard	Chicago	1987-88	80	131	1.64
Wayne Gretzky	Los Angeles	1991-92	74	121	1.64
Steve Yzerman	Detroit	1992-93	84	137	1.63
Marcel Dionne	Los Angeles	1978-79	80	130	1.63
Dale Hawerchuk	Winnipeg	1984-85	80	130	1.63
Mark Messier	Edmonton	1989-90	79	129	1.63
Bryan Trottier	NY Islanders	1983-84	68	111	1.63
Pat LaFontaine	Buffalo	1991-92	57	93	1.63
Charlie Simmer	Los Angeles	1980-81	65	105	1.62
Guy Lafleur	Montreal	1978-79	80	129	1.61
Bryan Trottier	NY Islanders	1981-82	80	129	1.61
Phil Esposito	Boston	1974-75	79	127	1.61
Steve Yzerman	Detroit	1989-90	79	127	1.61
Peter Stastny	Quebec	1985-86	76	122	1.61
Mario Lemieux	Pittsburgh	1996-97	76	122	1.61
Michel Goulet	Quebec	1983-84	75	121	1.61
Wayne Gretzky	Los Angeles	1993-94	81	130	1.60
Bryan Trottier	NY Islanders	1977-78	77	123	1.60
Bobby Orr	Boston	1972-73	63	101	1.60
Guy Chouinard	Calgary	1980-81	52	83	1.60
Elmer Lach	Montreal	1944-45	50	80	1.60
Pierre Turgeon	NY Islanders	1992-93	83	132	1.59
Steve Yzerman	Detroit	1987-88	64	102	1.59
Mike Bossy	NY Islanders	1978-79	80	126	1.58
Paul Coffey	Edmonton	1983-84	80	126	1.58
Marcel Dionne	Los Angeles	1984-85	80	126	1.58
Bobby Orr	Boston	1969-70	76	120	1.58
Eric Lindros	Philadelphia	1995-96	73	115	1.58
Charlie Simmer	Los Angeles	1979-80	64	101	1.58
Teemu Selanne	Winnipeg	1992-93	84	132	1.57
Jaromir Jagr	Pittsburgh	1998-99	81	127	1.57
Bobby Clarke	Philadelphia	1975-76	76	119	1.57
Guy Lafleur	Montreal	1975-76	80	125	1.56
Dave Taylor	Los Angeles	1980-81	72	112	1.56
Denis Savard	Chicago	1982-83	78	121	1.55
Ron Francis	Pittsburgh	1995-96	77	119	1.55
Joe Thornton	Bos., S.J.	2005-06	81	125	1.54
Mike Bossy	NY Islanders	1985-86	80	123	1.54
Kevin Stevens	Pittsburgh	1991-92	80	123	1.54
Bobby Orr	Boston	1971-72	76	117	1.54
Mike Bossy	NY Islanders	1984-85	76	117	1.54
Kevin Stevens	Pittsburgh	1992-93	72	111	1.54
Doug Bentley	Chicago	1943-44	50	77	1.54
Doug Gilmour	Toronto	1992-93	83	127	1.53
Marcel Dionne	Los Angeles	1976-77	80	122	1.53
Sidney Crosby	Pittsburgh	2006-07	79	120	1.52
Jaromir Jagr	Pittsburgh	99-2000	63	96	1.52
Eric Lindros	Philadelphia	1996-97	52	79	1.52
Eric Lindros	Philadelphia	1994-95	46	70	1.52
Marcel Dionne	Detroit	1974-75	80	121	1.51
Mike Bossy	NY Islanders	1980-81	79	119	1.51
Paul Coffey	Edmonton	1984-85	80	121	1.51
Dale Hawerchuk	Winnipeg	1987-88	80	121	1.51
Paul Coffey	Pittsburgh	1988-89	75	113	1.51
Jaromir Jagr	Pittsburgh	1996-97	63	95	1.51
Cam Neely	Boston	1993-94	49	74	1.51

Dit Clapper, Cooney Weiland and Dutch Gainor were a Boston trio dubbed the Dynamite Line when they exploded onto the scoring scene under more modern forward passing rules in 1929-30. Weiland led the NHL with 43 goals and 73 points in just 44 games that season, an average of 1.66 points per game.

The Blackhawks unveiled a pair of promising rookies in 2007-08. Jonathan Toews (left) was picked third overall in the 2006 Entry Draft. He led all NHL rookies with 24 goals in just 64 games last season. Patrick Kane (right) jumped directly to the NHL after being picked first overall in the 2007 Draft. He played in all 82 games and led all rookies with 72 points on 21 goals and 51 assists.

Rookie Scoring Records

All-Time Top 50 Goal-Scoring Rookies

	Rookie	Team	Position	Season	GP	G	A	PTS
1.	* Teemu Selanne	Winnipeg	Right wing	1992-93	84	**76**	56	132
2.	* Mike Bossy	NY Islanders	Right wing	1977-78	73	**53**	38	91
3.	* Alex Ovechkin	Washington	Left wing	2005-06	81	**52**	54	106
4.	* Joe Nieuwendyk	Calgary	Center	1987-88	75	**51**	41	92
5.	* Dale Hawerchuk	Winnipeg	Center	1981-82	80	**45**	58	103
	* Luc Robitaille	Los Angeles	Left wing	1986-87	79	**45**	39	84
7.	Rick Martin	Buffalo	Left wing	1971-72	73	**44**	30	74
	Barry Pederson	Boston	Center	1981-82	80	**44**	48	92
9.	* Steve Larmer	Chicago	Right wing	1982-83	80	**43**	47	90
	* Mario Lemieux	Pittsburgh	Center	1984-85	73	**43**	57	100
11.	Eric Lindros	Philadelphia	Center	1992-93	61	**41**	34	75
12.	Darryl Sutter	Chicago	Left wing	1980-81	76	**40**	22	62
	Sylvain Turgeon	Hartford	Left wing	1983-84	76	**40**	32	72
	Warren Young	Pittsburgh	Left wing	1984-85	80	**40**	32	72
15.	* Eric Vail	Atlanta	Left wing	1974-75	72	**39**	21	60
	* Peter Stastny	Quebec	Center	1980-81	77	**39**	70	109
	Anton Stastny	Quebec	Left wing	1980-81	80	**39**	46	85
	Steve Yzerman	Detroit	Center	1983-84	80	**39**	48	87
	Sidney Crosby	Pittsburgh	Center	2005-06	81	**39**	63	102
20.	* Gilbert Perreault	Buffalo	Center	1970-71	78	**38**	34	72
	Neal Broten	Minnesota	Center	1981-82	73	**38**	60	98
	Ray Sheppard	Buffalo	Right wing	1987-88	74	**38**	27	65
	Mikael Renberg	Philadelphia	Left wing	1993-94	83	**38**	44	82
24.	Jorgen Pettersson	St. Louis	Left wing	1980-81	62	**37**	36	73
	Jimmy Carson	Los Angeles	Center	1986-87	80	**37**	42	79
26.	Mike Foligno	Detroit	Right wing	1979-80	80	**36**	35	71
	Paul MacLean	Winnipeg	Right wing	1981-82	74	**36**	25	61
	Mike Bullard	Pittsburgh	Center	1981-82	75	**36**	27	63
	Tony Granato	NY Rangers	Right wing	1988-89	78	**36**	27	63
30.	Marian Stastny	Quebec	Right wing	1981-82	74	**35**	54	89
	Brian Bellows	Minnesota	Right wing	1982-83	78	**35**	30	65
	Tony Amonte	NY Rangers	Right wing	1991-92	79	**35**	34	69
33.	Nels Stewart	Mtl. Maroons	Center	1925-26	36	**34**	8	42
	* Danny Grant	Minnesota	Left wing	1968-69	75	**34**	31	65
	Norm Ferguson	Oakland	Right wing	1968-69	76	**34**	20	54
	Brian Propp	Philadelphia	Left wing	1979-80	80	**34**	41	75
	Wendel Clark	Toronto	Left wing	1985-86	66	**34**	11	45
	* Pavel Bure	Vancouver	Right wing	1991-92	65	**34**	26	60
39.	* Willi Plett	Atlanta	Right wing	1976-77	64	**33**	23	56
	Dale McCourt	Detroit	Center	1977-78	76	**33**	39	72
	Steve Bozek	Los Angeles	Center	1981-82	71	**33**	23	56
	Ron Flockhart	Philadelphia	Center	1981-82	72	**33**	39	72
	Mark Pavelich	NY Rangers	Center	1981-82	79	**33**	43	76
	Jason Arnott	Edmonton	Center	1993-94	78	**33**	35	68
	* Evgeni Malkin	Pittsburgh	Center	2006-07	78	**33**	52	85
46.	Bill Mosienko	Chicago	Right wing	1943-44	50	**32**	38	70
	Michel Bergeron	Detroit	Right wing	1975-76	72	**32**	27	59
	* Bryan Trottier	NY Islanders	Center	1975-76	80	**32**	63	95
	Don Murdoch	NY Rangers	Right wing	1976-77	59	**32**	24	56
	Jari Kurri	Edmonton	Left wing	1980-81	75	**32**	43	75
	Bobby Carpenter	Washington	Center	1981-82	80	**32**	35	67
	Petr Klima	Detroit	Left wing	1985-86	74	**32**	24	56
	Kjell Dahlin	Montreal	Right wing	1985-86	77	**32**	39	71
	Darren Turcotte	NY Rangers	Right wing	1989-90	76	**32**	34	66
	Joe Juneau	Boston	Center	1992-93	84	**32**	70	102
	Marek Svatos	Colorado	Right wing	2005-06	61	**32**	18	50

* Calder Trophy Winner

All-Time Top 50 Point-Scoring Rookies

	Rookie	Team	Position	Season	GP	G	A	PTS
1.	* Teemu Selanne	Winnipeg	Right wing	1992-93	84	76	56	**132**
2.	* Peter Stastny	Quebec	Center	1980-81	77	39	70	**109**
3.	* Alex Ovechkin	Washington	Left wing	2005-06	81	52	54	**106**
4.	* Dale Hawerchuk	Winnipeg	Center	1981-82	80	45	58	**103**
5.	Joe Juneau	Boston	Center	1992-93	84	32	70	**102**
	Sidney Crosby	Pittsburgh	Center	2005-06	81	39	63	**102**
7.	* Mario Lemieux	Pittsburgh	Center	1984-85	73	43	57	**100**
8.	Neal Broten	Minnesota	Center	1981-82	73	38	60	**98**
9.	* Bryan Trottier	NY Islanders	Center	1975-76	80	32	63	**95**
10.	Barry Pederson	Boston	Center	1981-82	80	44	48	**92**
	* Joe Nieuwendyk	Calgary	Center	1987-88	75	51	41	**92**
12.	* Mike Bossy	NY Islanders	Right wing	1977-78	73	53	38	**91**
13.	* Steve Larmer	Chicago	Right wing	1982-83	80	43	47	**90**
14.	Marian Stastny	Quebec	Right wing	1981-82	74	35	54	**89**
15.	Steve Yzerman	Detroit	Center	1983-84	80	39	48	**87**
16.	* Sergei Makarov	Calgary	Right wing	1989-90	80	24	62	**86**
17.	Anton Stastny	Quebec	Left wing	1980-81	80	39	46	**85**
18.	* Evgeni Malkin	Pittsburgh	Center	2006-07	78	33	52	**85**
19.	* Luc Robitaille	Los Angeles	Left wing	1986-87	79	45	39	**84**
20.	Mikael Renberg	Philadelphia	Left wing	1993-94	83	38	44	**82**
21.	Jimmy Carson	Los Angeles	Center	1986-87	80	37	42	**79**
	Sergei Fedorov	Detroit	Center	1990-91	77	31	48	**79**
	Alexei Yashin	Ottawa	Center	1993-94	83	30	49	**79**
24.	Paul Stastny	Colorado	Center	2006-07	82	28	50	**78**
25.	Marcel Dionne	Detroit	Center	1971-72	78	28	49	**77**
26.	Larry Murphy	Los Angeles	Defense	1980-81	80	16	60	**76**
	Mark Pavelich	NY Rangers	Center	1981-82	79	33	43	**76**
	Dave Poulin	Philadelphia	Center	1983-84	73	31	45	**76**
29.	Brian Propp	Philadelphia	Left wing	1979-80	80	34	41	**75**
	Jari Kurri	Edmonton	Left wing	1980-81	75	32	43	**75**
	Denis Savard	Chicago	Center	1980-81	76	28	47	**75**
	Mike Modano	Minnesota	Center	1989-90	80	29	46	**75**
	Eric Lindros	Philadelphia	Center	1992-93	61	41	34	**75**
34.	Rick Martin	Buffalo	Left wing	1971-72	73	44	30	**74**
	* Bobby Smith	Minnesota	Center	1978-79	80	30	44	**74**
36.	Jorgen Pettersson	St. Louis	Left wing	1980-81	62	37	36	**73**
37.	* Gilbert Perreault	Buffalo	Center	1970-71	78	38	34	**72**
	Dale McCourt	Detroit	Center	1977-78	76	33	39	**72**
	Ron Flockhart	Philadelphia	Center	1981-82	72	33	39	**72**
	Sylvain Turgeon	Hartford	Left wing	1983-84	76	40	32	**72**
	Carey Wilson	Calgary	Center	1984-85	74	24	48	**72**
	Warren Young	Pittsburgh	Left wing	1984-85	80	40	32	**72**
	Alex Zhamnov	Winnipeg	Center	1992-93	68	25	47	**72**
	* Patrick Kane	Chicago	Right Wing	**2007-08**	82	21	51	**72**
45.	Mike Foligno	Detroit	Right wing	1979-80	80	36	35	**71**
	Dave Christian	Winnipeg	Center	1980-81	80	28	43	**71**
	Mats Naslund	Montreal	Left wing	1982-83	74	26	45	**71**
	Kjell Dahlin	Montreal	Right wing	1985-86	77	32	39	**71**
	* Brian Leetch	NY Rangers	Defense	1988-89	68	23	48	**71**
50.	Bill Mosienko	Chicago	Right wing	1943-44	50	32	38	**70**
	* Scott Gomez	New Jersey	Center	99-2000	82	19	51	**70**

* Calder Trophy Winner

50-Goal Seasons

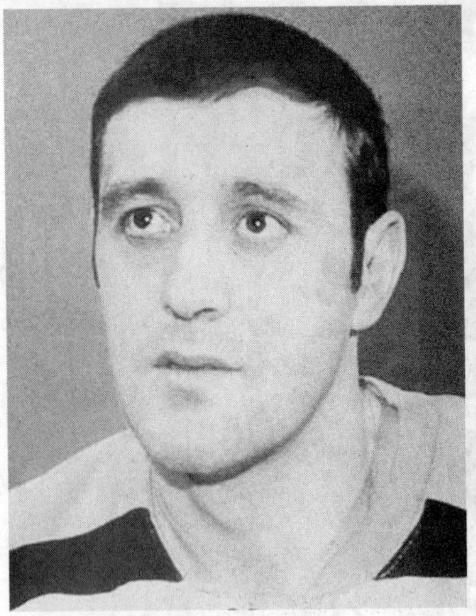

Phil Esposito

Steve Shutt

Charlie Simmer

Player	Team	Date of 50th Goal	Score	Goaltender	Player's Game No.	Team Game No.	Total Goals	Total Games	Age When First 50th Scored (Yrs. & Mos.)
Maurice Richard	Mtl.	Mar. 18/45	Mtl. 4 at Bos. 2	Harvey Bennett	50	50	50	50	23.7
Bernie Geoffrion	Mtl.	Mar. 16/61	Tor. 2 at Mtl. 5	Cesare Maniago	62	68	50	64	30.1
Bobby Hull	Chi.	Mar. 25/62	Chi. 1 at NYR 4	Gump Worsley	70	70	50	70	23.2
Bobby Hull	Chi.	Mar. 2/66	Det. 4 at Chi. 5	Hank Bassen	52	57	54	65	
Bobby Hull	Chi.	Mar. 18/67	Chi. 5 at Tor. 9	Bruce Gamble	63	66	52	66	
Bobby Hull	Chi.	Mar. 5/69	NYR 4 at Chi. 4	Ed Giacomin	64	66	58	74	
Phil Esposito	Bos.	Feb. 20/71	Bos. 4 at L.A. 5	Denis DeJordy	58	58	76	78	29.0
John Bucyk	Bos.	Mar. 16/71	Bos. 11 at Det. 4	Roy Edwards	69	69	51	78	35.10
Phil Esposito	Bos.	Feb. 20/72	Bos. 3 at Chi. 1	Tony Esposito	60	60	66	76	
Bobby Hull	Chi.	Apr. 2/72	Det. 1 at Chi. 6	Andy Brown	78	78	50	78	
Vic Hadfield	NYR	Apr. 2/72	Mtl. 6 at NYR 5	Denis DeJordy	78	78	50	78	31.6
Phil Esposito	Bos.	Mar. 25/73	Buf. 1 at Bos. 6	Roger Crozier	75	75	55	78	
Mickey Redmond	Det.	Mar. 27/73	Det. 8 at Tor. 1	Ron Low	73	75	52	76	25.3
Rick MacLeish	Phi.	Apr. 1/73	Phi. 4 at Pit. 5	Cam Newton	78	78	50	78	23.2
Phil Esposito	Bos.	Feb. 20/74	Bos. 5 at Min. 5	Cesare Maniago	56	56	68	78	
Mickey Redmond	Det.	Mar. 23/74	NYR 3 at Det. 5	Ed Giacomin	69	71	51	76	
Ken Hodge	Bos.	Apr. 6/74	Bos. 2 at Mtl. 6	Michel Larocque	75	77	50	76	29.10
Rick Martin	Buf.	Apr. 7/74	St.L. 2 at Buf. 5	Wayne Stephenson	78	78	52	78	22.9
Phil Esposito	Bos.	Feb. 8/75	Bos. 8 at Det. 5	Jim Rutherford	54	54	61	79	
Guy Lafleur	Mtl.	Mar. 29/75	K.C. 1 at Mtl. 4	Denis Herron	66	76	53	70	23.6
Danny Grant	Det.	Apr. 2/75	Wsh. 3 at Det. 8	John Adams	78	78	50	80	29.2
Rick Martin	Buf.	Apr. 3/75	Bos. 2 at Buf. 4	Ken Broderick	67	79	52	68	
Reggie Leach	Phi.	Mar. 14/76	Atl. 1 at Phi. 6	Dan Bouchard	69	69	61	80	25.11
Jean Pronovost	Pit.	Mar. 24/76	Bos. 5 at Pit. 5	Gilles Gilbert	74	74	52	80	30.3
Guy Lafleur	Mtl.	Mar. 27/76	K.C. 2 at Mtl. 8	Denis Herron	76	76	56	80	
Bill Barber	Phi.	Apr. 3/76	Buf. 2 at Phi. 5	Al Smith	79	79	50	80	23.9
Pierre Larouche	Pit.	Apr. 3/76	Wsh. 5 at Pit. 4	Ron Low	75	79	53	76	20.5
Danny Gare	Buf.	Apr. 4/76	Tor. 2 at Buf. 5	Gord McRae	79	80	50	79	21.11
Steve Shutt	Mtl.	Mar. 1/77	Mtl. 5 at NYI 4	Glenn Resch	65	65	60	80	24.8
Guy Lafleur	Mtl.	Mar. 6/77	Mtl. 1 at Buf. 4	Don Edwards	68	68	56	80	
Marcel Dionne	L.A.	Apr. 2/77	Min. 2 at L.A. 7	Pete LoPresti	79	79	53	80	25.8
Guy Lafleur	Mtl.	Mar. 8/78	Wsh. 3 at Mtl. 4	Jim Bedard	63	65	60	78	
Mike Bossy	NYI	Apr. 1/78	Wsh. 2 at NYI 3	Bernie Wolfe	69	76	53	73	21.2
Mike Bossy	NYI	Feb. 24/79	Det. 1 at NYI 3	Rogie Vachon	58	58	69	80	
Marcel Dionne	L.A.	Mar. 11/79	L.A. 3 at Phi. 6	Wayne Stephenson	68	68	59	80	
Guy Lafleur	Mtl.	Mar. 31/79	Pit. 3 at Mtl. 5	Denis Herron	76	76	52	80	
Guy Chouinard	Atl.	Apr. 6/79	NYR 2 at Atl. 9	John Davidson	79	79	50	80	22.5
Marcel Dionne	L.A.	Mar. 12/80	L.A. 2 at Pit. 4	Nick Ricci	70	70	53	80	
Mike Bossy	NYI	Mar. 16/80	NYI 6 at Chi. 1	Tony Esposito	68	71	51	75	
Charlie Simmer	L.A.	Mar. 19/80	Det. 3 at L.A. 4	Jim Rutherford	57	73	56	64	26.0
Pierre Larouche	Mtl.	Mar. 25/80	Chi. 4 at Mtl. 8	Tony Esposito	72	75	50	73	
Danny Gare	Buf.	Mar. 27/80	Det. 1 at Buf. 10	Jim Rutherford	71	75	56	76	
Blaine Stoughton	Hfd.	Mar. 28/80	Hfd. 4 at Van. 4	Glen Hanlon	75	75	56	80	27.0
Guy Lafleur	Mtl.	Apr. 2/80	Mtl. 7 at Det. 2	Rogie Vachon	72	78	50	74	
Wayne Gretzky	Edm.	Apr. 2/80	Min. 1 at Edm. 1	Gary Edwards	78	79	51	79	19.2
Reggie Leach	Phi.	Apr. 3/80	Wsh. 2 at Phi. 4	empty net	75	79	50	76	
Mike Bossy	NYI	Jan. 24/81	Que. 3 at NYI 7	Ron Grahame	50	50	68	79	
Charlie Simmer	L.A.	Jan. 26/81	L.A. 7 at Que. 5	Michel Dion	51	51	56	65	
Marcel Dionne	L.A.	Mar. 8/81	L.A. 4 at Wpg. 1	Markus Mattsson	68	68	58	80	
Wayne Babych	St.L.	Mar. 12/81	St.L. 3 at Mtl. 4	Richard Sevigny	70	68	54	78	22.9
Wayne Gretzky	Edm.	Mar. 15/81	Edm. 3 at Cgy. 3	Pat Riggin	69	69	55	80	
Rick Kehoe	Pit.	Mar. 16/81	Pit. 7 at Edm. 6	Eddie Mio	70	70	55	80	29.7
Jacques Richard	Que.	Mar. 29/81	Mtl. 0 at Que. 4	Richard Sevigny	76	75	52	78	28.6
Dennis Maruk	Wsh.	Apr. 5/81	Det. 2 at Wsh. 7	Larry Lozinski	80	80	50	80	25.3
Wayne Gretzky	Edm.	Dec. 30/81	Phi. 5 at Edm. 7	empty net	39	39	92	80	
Dennis Maruk	Wsh.	Feb. 21/82	Wpg. 3 at Wsh. 6	Doug Soetaert	61	61	60	80	
Mike Bossy	NYI	Mar. 4/82	Tor. 1 at NYI 10	Michel Larocque	66	66	64	80	
Dino Ciccarelli	Min.	Mar. 8/82	St.L. 1 at Min. 8	Mike Liut	67	68	55	76	22.1
Rick Vaive	Tor.	Mar. 24/82	St.L. 3 at Tor. 4	Mike Liut	72	75	54	77	22.10
Blaine Stoughton	Hfd.	Mar. 28/82	Min. 5 at Hfd. 2	Gilles Meloche	76	76	52	80	
Rick Middleton	Bos.	Mar. 28/82	Bos. 5 at Buf. 9	Paul Harrison	72	77	51	75	28.11
Marcel Dionne	L.A.	Mar. 30/82	Cgy. 7 at L.A. 5	Pat Riggin	75	77	50	78	
Mark Messier	Edm.	Mar. 31/82	L.A. 3 at Edm. 7	Mario Lessard	78	79	50	78	21.3
Bryan Trottier	NYI	Apr. 3/82	Phi. 3 at NYI 6	Pete Peeters	79	79	50	80	25.9
Lanny McDonald	Cgy.	Feb. 18/83	Cgy. 1 at Buf. 5	Bob Sauve	60	60	66	80	30.0
Wayne Gretzky	Edm.	Feb. 19/83	Edm. 10 at Pit. 7	Nick Ricci	60	60	71	80	
Michel Goulet	Que.	Mar. 5/83	Hfd. 3 at Que. 10	Mike Veisor	67	67	57	80	22.11
Mike Bossy	NYI	Mar. 12/83	Wsh. 2 at NYI 6	Al Jensen	70	71	60	79	
Marcel Dionne	L.A.	Mar. 17/83	Que. 3 at L.A. 4	Dan Bouchard	71	71	56	80	
Al Secord	Chi.	Mar. 20/83	Tor. 3 at Chi. 7	Mike Palmateer	73	73	54	80	25.0
Rick Vaive	Tor.	Mar. 30/83	Tor. 4 at Det. 2	Gilles Gilbert	76	78	51	78	
Wayne Gretzky	Edm.	Jan. 7/84	Hfd. 3 at Edm. 5	Greg Millen	42	42	87	74	
Michel Goulet	Que.	Mar. 8/84	Que. 8 at Pit. 6	Denis Herron	63	69	56	75	
Rick Vaive	Tor.	Mar. 14/84	Min. 3 at Tor. 3	Gilles Meloche	69	72	52	76	
Mike Bullard	Pit.	Mar. 14/84	Pit. 6 at L.A. 7	Markus Mattsson	71	72	51	76	23.0
Jari Kurri	Edm.	Mar. 15/84	Edm. 2 at Mtl. 3	Rick Wamsley	57	73	52	64	23.10
Glenn Anderson	Edm.	Mar. 21/84	Hfd. 3 at Edm. 5	Greg Millen	76	76	54	80	23.6
Tim Kerr	Phi.	Mar. 22/84	Pit. 4 at Phi. 13	Denis Herron	74	75	54	79	24.3

Player	Team	Date of 50th Goal	Score	Goaltender	Player's Game No.	Team Game No.	Total Goals	Total Games	Age When First 50th Scored (Yrs. & Mos.)
Mike Bossy	NYI	Mar. 31/84	NYI 3 at Wsh. 1	Pat Riggin	67	79	51	67	
Wayne Gretzky	Edm.	Jan. 26/85	Pit. 3 at Edm. 6	Denis Herron	49	49	73	80	
Jari Kurri	Edm.	Feb. 3/85	Hfd. 3 at Edm. 6	Greg Millen	50	53	71	73	
Mike Bossy	NYI	Mar. 5/85	Phi. 5 at NYI 4	Bob Froese	61	65	58	76	
Michel Goulet	Que.	Mar. 6/85	Buf. 3 at Que. 4	Tom Barrasso	62	73	55	69	
Tim Kerr	Phi.	Mar. 7/85	Wsh. 6 at Phi. 9	Pat Riggin	63	65	54	74	
John Ogrodnick	Det.	Mar. 13/85	Det. 6 at Edm. 7	Grant Fuhr	69	69	55	79	25.9
Bob Carpenter	Wsh.	Mar. 21/85	Wsh. 2 at Mtl. 3	Steve Penney	72	72	53	80	21.9
Dale Hawerchuk	Wpg.	Mar. 29/85	Chi. 5 at Wpg. 5	W. Skorodenski	77	77	53	80	21.11
Mike Gartner	Wsh.	Apr. 7/85	Pit. 3 at Wsh. 7	Brian Ford	80	80	50	80	25.5
Jari Kurri	Edm.	Mar. 4/86	Edm. 6 at Van. 2	Richard Brodeur	63	65	68	78	
Mike Bossy	NYI	Mar. 11/86	Cgy. 4 at NYI 8	Reggie Lemelin	67	67	61	80	
Glenn Anderson	Edm.	Mar. 14/86	Det. 3 at Edm. 12	Greg Stefan	63	71	54	72	
Michel Goulet	Que.	Mar. 17/86	Que. 8 at Mtl. 6	Patrick Roy	67	72	53	75	
Wayne Gretzky	Edm.	Mar. 18/86	Wpg. 2 at Edm. 6	Brian Hayward	72	72	52	80	
Tim Kerr	Phi.	Mar. 20/86	Pit. 1 at Phi. 5	Roberto Romano	68	72	58	76	
Wayne Gretzky	Edm.	Feb. 4/87	Edm. 6 at Min. 5	Don Beaupre	55	55	62	79	
Dino Ciccarelli	Min.	Mar. 7/87	Pit. 7 at Min. 3	Gilles Meloche	66	66	52	80	
Mario Lemieux	Pit.	Mar. 12/87	Que. 3 at Pit. 6	Mario Gosselin	53	70	54	63	21.5
Tim Kerr	Phi.	Mar. 17/87	NYR 1 at Phi. 4	J. Vanbiesbrouck	67	71	58	75	
Jari Kurri	Edm.	Mar. 17/87	N.J. 4 at Edm. 7	Craig Billington	69	70	54	79	
Mario Lemieux	Pit.	Feb. 2/88	Wsh. 2 at Pit. 3	Pete Peeters	51	54	70	77	
Steve Yzerman	Det.	Mar. 1/88	Buf. 0 at Det. 4	Tom Barrasso	64	64	50	64	22.10
Joe Nieuwendyk	Cgy.	Mar. 12/88	Buf. 4 at Cgy. 10	Tom Barrasso	66	70	51	75	21.5
Craig Simpson	Edm.	Mar. 15/88	Buf. 4 at Edm. 6	Jacques Cloutier	71	71	56	80	21.1
Jimmy Carson	L.A.	Mar. 26/88	Chi. 5 at L.A. 9	Darren Pang	77	77	55	88	19.8
Luc Robitaille	L.A.	Apr. 1/88	L.A. 6 at Cgy. 3	Mike Vernon	79	79	53	80	21.10
Hakan Loob	Cgy.	Apr. 3/88	Min. 1 at Cgy. 4	Don Beaupre	80	80	50	80	27.9
Stephane Richer	Mtl.	Apr. 3/88	Mtl. 4 at Buf. 4	Tom Barrasso	72	80	50	72	21.10
Mario Lemieux	Pit.	Jan. 20/89	Pit. 3 at Wpg. 7	Pokey Reddick	44	46	85	76	
Bernie Nicholls	L.A.	Jan. 28/89	Edm. 7 at L.A. 6	Grant Fuhr	51	51	70	79	27.7
Steve Yzerman	Det.	Feb. 5/89	Det. 6 at Wpg. 2	Pokey Reddick	55	55	65	80	
Wayne Gretzky	L.A.	Mar. 4/89	Phi. 2 at L.A. 6	Ron Hextall	66	67	54	78	
Joe Nieuwendyk	Cgy.	Mar. 21/89	NYI 1 at Cgy. 4	Mark Fitzpatrick	72	74	51	77	
Joe Mullen	Cgy.	Mar. 31/89	Wpg. 1 at Cgy. 4	Bob Essensa	78	79	51	79	32.1
Brett Hull	St.L.	Feb. 6/90	Tor. 4 at St.L. 6	Jeff Reese	54	54	72	80	25.6
Steve Yzerman	Det.	Feb. 24/90	Det. 3 at NYI 3	Glenn Healy	63	63	62	79	
Cam Neely	Bos.	Mar. 10/90	Bos. 3 at NYI 3	Mark Fitzpatrick	69	71	55	76	24.9
Brian Bellows	Min.	Mar. 22/90	Min. 5 at Det. 1	Tim Cheveldae	75	75	55	80	25.6
Pat LaFontaine	NYI	Mar. 24/90	NYI 5 at Edm. 5	Bill Ranford	71	77	54	74	25.1
Stephane Richer	Mtl.	Mar. 24/90	Mtl. 4 at Hfd. 7	Peter Sidorkiewicz	75	77	51	75	
Gary Leeman	Tor.	Mar. 28/90	NYI 6 at Tor. 3	Mark Fitzpatrick	78	78	51	80	26.1
Luc Robitaille	L.A.	Mar. 31/90	L.A. 3 at Van. 6	Kirk McLean	79	79	52	80	
Brett Hull	St.L.	Jan. 25/91	St.L. 9 at Det. 4	David Gagnon	49	49	86	78	
Cam Neely	Bos.	Mar. 26/91	Bos. 7 at Que. 4	empty net	67	78	51	69	
Theoren Fleury	Cgy.	Mar. 26/91	Van. 2 at Cgy. 7	Bob Mason	77	77	51	79	22.9
Steve Yzerman	Det.	Mar. 30/91	NYR 5 at Det. 6	Mike Richter	79	79	51	80	
Brett Hull	St.L.	Jan. 28/92	St.L. 3 at L.A. 3	Kelly Hrudey	50	50	70	73	
Jeremy Roenick	Chi.	Mar. 7/92	Chi. 2 at Bos. 1	Daniel Berthiaume	67	67	53	80	22.2
Kevin Stevens	Pit.	Mar. 24/92	Pit. 3 at Det. 4	Tim Cheveldae	74	74	54	80	26.11
Gary Roberts	Cgy.	Mar. 31/92	Edm. 2 at Cgy. 5	Bill Ranford	73	77	53	76	25.10
Alexander Mogilny	Buf.	Feb. 3/93	Hfd. 2 at Buf. 3	Sean Burke	46	53	76	77	23.11
Teemu Selanne	Wpg.	Feb. 28/93	Min. 6 at Wpg. 7	Darcy Wakaluk	63	63	76	84	22.6
Pavel Bure	Van.	Mar. 1/93	Van. 5 at Buf. 2*	Grant Fuhr	63	63	60	83	21.11
Steve Yzerman	Det.	Mar. 10/93	Det. 6 at Edm. 3	Bill Ranford	70	70	58	84	
Luc Robitaille	L.A.	Mar. 15/93	L.A. 4 at Buf. 2	Grant Fuhr	69	69	63	84	
Brett Hull	St.L.	Mar. 20/93	St.L. 2 at L.A. 3	Robb Stauber	73	73	54	80	
Mario Lemieux	Pit.	Mar. 21/93	Pit. 6 at Edm. 4**	Ron Tugnutt	48	72	69	60	
Kevin Stevens	Pit.	Mar. 21/93	Pit. 6 at Edm. 4**	Ron Tugnutt	62	72	55	72	
Dave Andreychuk	Tor.	Mar. 23/93	Tor. 5 at Wpg. 4	Bob Essensa	72	73	54	83	29.6
Pat LaFontaine	Buf.	Mar. 28/93	Ott. 1 at Buf. 3	Peter Sidorkiewicz	75	75	53	84	
Pierre Turgeon	NYI	Apr. 2/93	NYI 3 at NYR 2	Mike Richter	75	76	58	83	23.8
Mark Recchi	Phi.	Apr. 3/93	T.B. 2 at Phi. 6	J-C Bergeron	77	77	53	84	25.2
Brendan Shanahan	St.L.	Apr. 15/93	T.B. 5 at St.L. 6	Pat Jablonski	71	84	51	71	24.3
Jeremy Roenick	Chi.	Apr. 15/93	Tor. 2 at Chi. 3	Felix Potvin	84	84	50	84	
Cam Neely	Bos.	Mar. 7/94	Wsh. 3 at Bos. 6	Don Beaupre	44	66	50	49	
Sergei Fedorov	Det.	Mar. 15/94	Van. 2 at Det. 5	Kirk McLean	67	69	56	82	24.3
Pavel Bure	Van.	Mar. 23/94	Van. 6 at L.A. 3	empty net	65	73	60	76	
Adam Graves	NYR	Mar. 23/94	NYR 5 at Edm. 3	Bill Ranford	74	74	51	84	25.11
Dave Andreychuk	Tor.	Mar. 24/94	S.J. 2 at Tor. 1	Arturs Irbe	73	74	53	83	
Brett Hull	St.L.	Mar. 25/94	Dal. 3 at St.L. 5	Andy Moog	71	74	57	81	
Ray Sheppard	Det.	Mar. 29/94	Hfd. 2 at Det. 6	Sean Burke	74	76	52	82	27.10
Brendan Shanahan	St.L.	Apr. 12/94	St.L. 5 at Dal. 9	Andy Moog	80	83	52	81	
Mike Modano	Dal.	Apr. 12/94	St.L. 5 at Dal. 9	Curtis Joseph	75	83	50	76	23.11
Mario Lemieux	Pit.	Feb. 23/96	Hfd. 4 at Pit. 5	Sean Burke	50	59	69	70	
Jaromir Jagr	Pit.	Feb. 23/96	Hfd. 4 at Pit. 5	Sean Burke	59	59	62	82	24.0
Alexander Mogilny	Van.	Feb. 29/96	St.L. 2 at Van. 2	Grant Fuhr	60	63	55	79	
Peter Bondra	Wsh.	Apr. 3/96	Wsh. 5 at Buf. 1	Andrei Trefilov	62	77	52	67	28.1
Joe Sakic	Col.	Apr. 7/96	Col. 4 at Dal. 1	empty net	79	79	51	82	26.7
John LeClair	Phi.	Apr. 10/96	Phi. 5 at N.J. 1	Corey Schwab	80	80	51	82	26.7
Keith Tkachuk	Wpg.	Apr. 12/96	L.A. 3 at Wpg. 5	empty net	75	81	50	76	24.0
Paul Kariya	Ana.	Apr. 14/96	Wpg. 2 at Ana. 5	N. Khabibulin	82	82	50	82	21.5
Keith Tkachuk	Phx.	Apr. 6/97	Phx. 1 at Col. 2	Patrick Roy	78	79	52	81	
Teemu Selanne	Ana.	Apr. 9/97	L.A. 1 at Ana. 4	empty net	77	81	51	78	
Mario Lemieux	Pit.	Apr. 11/97	Pit. 2 at Fla. 4	J. Vanbiesbrouck	75	81	50	76	

Joe Nieuwendyk

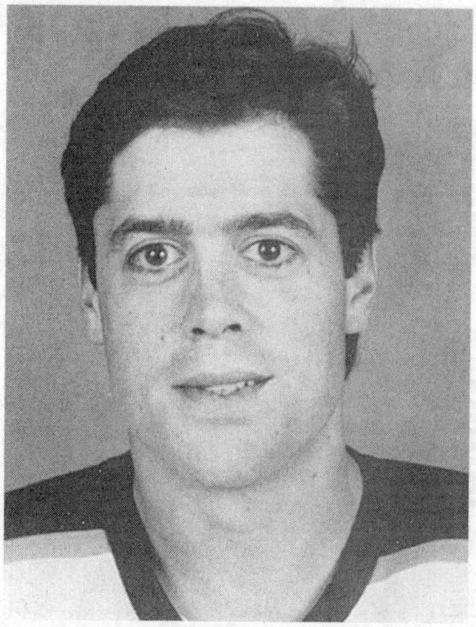
Pat LaFontaine

Jarome Iginla

Ilya Kovalchuk

Player	Team	Date of 50th Goal	Score	Goaltender	Player's Game No.	Team Game No.	Total Goals	Total Games	Age When First 50th Scored (Yrs. & Mos.)
John LeClair	Phi.	Apr. 13/97	N.J. 4 at Phi. 5	Mike Dunham	82	82	50	82	
Teemu Selanne	Ana.	Mar. 25/98	Ana. 3 at Chi. 2	Jeff Hackett	66	71	52	73	
John LeClair	Phi.	Apr. 13/98	Phi. 1 at Buf. 2	Dominik Hasek	79	79	51	82	
Pavel Bure	Van.	Apr. 17/98	Cgy. 4 at Van. 2	Dwayne Roloson	81	81	51	82	
Peter Bondra	Wsh.	Apr. 18/98	Wsh. 4 at Car. 3	Mike Fountain	75	80	52	76	
Pavel Bure	Fla.	Mar. 18/00	Fla. 4 at NYI 2	empty net	63	71	58	74	
Pavel Bure	Fla.	Mar. 16/01	Pit. 6 at Fla. 3	Johan Hedberg	72	72	59	82	
Joe Sakic	Col.	Apr. 4/01	Ana. 1 at Col. 1	J-S Giguere	80	80	54	82	
Jaromir Jagr	Pit.	Apr. 4/01	T.B. 2 at Pit. 4	Kevin Weekes	80	80	52	81	
Jarome Iginla	Cgy.	Apr. 7/02	Cgy. 2 at Chi. 3	Jocelyn Thibault	79	79	52	82	24.9
Milan Hejduk	Col.	Apr. 6/03	St. L. 2 at Col. 5	Brent Johnson	82	82	50	82	27.1
Jaromir Jagr	NYR	Mar. 24/06	NYR 2 at Fla. 3	Roberto Luongo	70	70	54	82	
Ilya Kovalchuk	Atl.	Apr. 6/06	Atl. 2 at T.B. 3	Sean Burke	72	76	52	78	22.11
Jonathan Cheechoo	S.J.	Apr. 10/06	S.J. 3 at Phx. 2	David LeNeveu	78	78	56	82	25.8
Alex Ovechkin	Wsh.	Apr. 13/06	Wsh. 3 at Atl. 5	Mike Dunham	78	79	52	81	20.6
Dany Heatley	Ott.	Apr. 18/06	Ott. 5 at NYR 1	Henrik Lundqvist	82	82	50	82	25.2
Vincent Lecavalier	T.B.	Mar. 30/07	T.B. 4 at Car. 2	Cam Ward	78	78	52	82	26.11
Dany Heatley	Ott.	Apr. 7/07	Ott. 6 at Bos. 3	Tim Thomas	82	82	50	82	
Alex Ovechkin	Wsh.	Mar. 3/08	Bos. 2 at Wsh. 10	Tim Thomas	67	67	65	82	
Ilya Kovalchuk	Atl.	Mar. 18/08	Atl. 2 at Phi. 3	Antero Niittymaki	72	75	52	79	
Jarome Iginla	Cgy.	Apr. 5/08	Cgy. 7 at Van. 1	Curtis Sanford	82	82	50	82	

* neutral site game played at Hamilton; ** neutral site game played at Cleveland

100-Point Seasons

Guy Lafleur

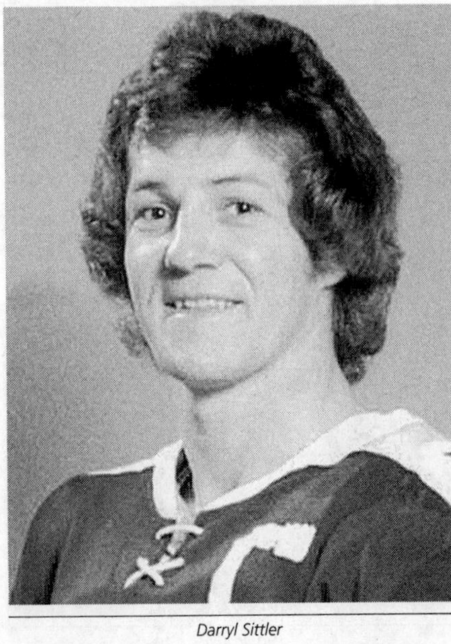

Darryl Sittler

Player	Team	Date of 100th Point	G or A	Score	Player's Game No.	Team Game No.	G - A PTS	Total Games	Age when first 100th point scored (Yrs. & Mos.)
Phil Esposito	Bos.	Mar. 2/69	(G)	Pit. 0 at Bos. 4	60	62	49-77 — 126	74	27.1
Bobby Hull	Chi.	Mar. 20/69	(G)	Chi. 5 at Bos. 5	71	71	58-49 — 107	76	30.2
Gordie Howe	Det.	Mar. 30/69	(G)	Det. 5 at Chi. 9	76	76	44-59 — 103	76	41.0
Bobby Orr	Bos.	Mar. 15/70	(G)	Det. 5 at Bos. 5	67	67	33-87 — 120	76	22.11
Phil Esposito	Bos.	Feb. 6/71	(A)	Buf. 3 at Bos. 4	51	51	76-76 — 152	78	
Bobby Orr	Bos.	Feb. 20/71	(A)	Bos. 4 at L.A. 5	58	58	37-102 — 139	78	
John Bucyk	Bos.	Mar. 13/71	(G)	Bos. 6 at Van. 3	68	68	51-65 — 116	78	35.10
Ken Hodge	Bos.	Mar. 21/71	(A)	Buf. 7 at Bos. 5	72	72	43-62 — 105	78	26.9
Jean Ratelle	NYR	Feb. 18/72	(A)	NYR 2 at Cal. 2	58	58	46-63 — 109	63	31.4
Phil Esposito	Bos.	Feb. 19/72	(A)	Bos. 6 at Min. 4	59	59	66-67 — 133	76	
Bobby Orr	Bos.	Mar. 2/72	(A)	Van. 3 at Bos. 7	64	64	37-80 — 117	76	
Vic Hadfield	NYR	Mar. 25/72	(A)	NYR 3 at Mtl. 3	74	74	50-56 — 106	78	31.5
Phil Esposito	Bos.	Mar. 3/73	(A)	Bos. 1 at Mtl. 5	64	64	55-75 — 130	78	
Bobby Clarke	Phi.	Mar. 29/73	(G)	Atl. 2 at Phi. 4	76	76	37-67 — 104	78	23.7
Bobby Orr	Bos.	Mar. 31/73	(G)	Bos. 3 at Tor. 7	62	77	29-72 — 101	63	
Rick MacLeish	Phi.	Apr. 1/73	(G)	Phi. 4 at Pit. 5	78	78	50-50 — 100	78	23.3
Phil Esposito	Bos.	Feb. 13/74	(A)	Bos. 9 at Cal. 6	53	53	68-77 — 145	78	
Bobby Orr	Bos.	Mar. 12/74	(A)	Buf. 0 at Bos. 4	62	66	32-90 — 122	74	
Ken Hodge	Bos.	Mar. 24/74	(A)	Mtl. 3 at Bos. 6	72	72	50-55 — 105	76	
Phil Esposito	Bos.	Feb. 8/75	(A)	Bos. 8 at Det. 5	54	54	61-66 — 127	79	
Bobby Orr	Bos.	Feb. 13/75	(A)	Bos. 1 at Buf. 3	57	57	46-89 — 135	80	
Guy Lafleur	Mtl.	Mar. 7/75	(G)	Wsh. 4 at Mtl. 8	56	66	53-66 — 119	70	24.6
Marcel Dionne	Det.	Mar. 9/75	(A)	Det. 5 at Phi. 8	67	67	47-74 — 121	80	23.7
Pete Mahovlich	Mtl.	Mar. 9/75	(G)	Mtl. 5 at NYR 3	67	67	35-82 — 117	80	29.5
Bobby Clarke	Phi.	Mar. 22/75	(A)	Min. 0 at Phi. 4	72	72	27-89 — 116	80	
Rene Robert	Buf.	Apr. 5/75	(A)	Buf. 4 at Tor. 2	74	80	40-60 — 100	74	26.4
Guy Lafleur	Mtl.	Mar. 10/76	(G)	Mtl. 5 at Chi. 1	69	69	56-69 — 125	80	
Bobby Clarke	Phi.	Mar. 11/76	(A)	Buf. 1 at Phi. 6	64	68	30-89 — 119	76	
Bill Barber	Phi.	Mar. 18/76	(A)	Van. 2 at Phi. 3	71	71	50-62 — 112	80	23.8
Gilbert Perreault	Buf.	Mar. 21/76	(A)	K.C. 1 at Buf. 3	73	73	44-69 — 113	80	25.4
Pierre Larouche	Pit.	Mar. 24/76	(G)	Bos. 5 at Pit. 5	70	74	53-58 — 111	76	20.4
Pete Mahovlich	Mtl.	Mar. 28/76	(A)	Mtl. 2 at Bos. 2	77	77	34-71 — 105	80	
Jean Ratelle	Bos.	Mar. 30/76	(G)	Buf. 4 at Bos. 4	77	77	36-69 — 105	80	
Jean Pronovost	Pit.	Apr. 3/76	(A)	Wsh. 5 at Pit. 4	79	79	52-52 — 104	80	30.4
Darryl Sittler	Tor.	Apr. 3/76	(A)	Bos. 4 at Tor. 2	78	79	41-59 — 100	79	25.7
Guy Lafleur	Mtl.	Feb. 26/77	(A)	Cle. 3 at Mtl. 5	63	63	56-80 — 136	80	
Marcel Dionne	L.A.	Mar. 5/77	(G)	Pit. 3 at L.A. 3	67	67	53-69 — 122	80	
Steve Shutt	Mtl.	Mar. 27/77	(A)	Mtl. 6 at Det. 0	77	77	60-45 — 105	80	24.9
Bryan Trottier	NYI	Feb. 25/78	(A)	Chi. 1 at NYI 7	59	60	46-77 — 123	77	21.7
Guy Lafleur	Mtl.	Feb. 28/78	(G)	Det. 3 at Mtl. 9	69	61	60-72 — 132	78	
Darryl Sittler	Tor.	Mar. 12/78	(A)	Tor. 7 at Pit. 1	67	67	45-72 — 117	80	
Guy Lafleur	Mtl.	Feb. 27/79	(A)	Mtl. 3 at NYI 7	61	61	52-77 — 129	80	
Bryan Trottier	NYI	Mar. 6/79	(A)	Buf. 3 at NYI 2	59	63	47-87 — 134	76	
Marcel Dionne	L.A.	Mar. 8/79	(G)	L.A. 4 at Buf. 6	66	66	59-71 — 130	80	
Mike Bossy	NYI	Mar. 11/79	(G)	NYI 4 at Bos. 4	66	66	69-57 — 126	80	22.2
Bob MacMillan	Atl.	Mar. 15/79	(A)	Atl. 4 at Phi. 5	68	69	37-71 — 108	79	26.6
Guy Chouinard	Atl.	Mar. 30/79	(G)	L.A. 3 at Atl. 5	75	75	50-57 — 107	80	22.5
Denis Potvin	NYI	Apr. 8/79	(A)	NYI 5 at NYR 2	73	80	31-70 — 101	73	25.5

Player	Team	Date of 100th Point	G or A	Score	Player's Game No.	Team Game No.	G - A PTS	Total Games	Age when first 100th point scored (Yrs. & Mos.)
Marcel Dionne	L.A.	Feb. 6/80	(A)	L.A. 3 at Hfd. 7	53	53	53-84 — 137	80	
Guy Lafleur	Mtl.	Feb. 10/80	(A)	Mtl. 3 at Bos. 2	55	55	50-75 — 125	74	
Wayne Gretzky	Edm.	Feb. 24/80	(A)	Bos. 4 at Edm. 2	61	62	51-86 — 137	79	19.2
Bryan Trottier	NYI	Mar. 30/80	(A)	NYI 9 at Que. 6	75	77	42-62 — 104	78	
Gilbert Perreault	Buf.	Apr. 1/80	(A)	Buf. 5 at Atl. 2	77	77	40-66 — 106	80	
Mike Rogers	Hfd.	Apr. 4/80	(A)	Que. 2 at Hfd. 9	79	79	44-61 — 105	80	25.5
Charlie Simmer	L.A.	Apr. 5/80	(G)	Van. 5 at L.A. 3	64	80	56-45 — 101	64	26.0
Blaine Stoughton	Hfd.	Apr. 6/80	(A)	Det. 3 at Hfd. 5	80	80	56-44 — 100	80	27.0
Wayne Gretzky	Edm.	Feb. 6/81	(G)	Wpg. 4 at Edm. 10	53	53	55-109 — 164	80	
Marcel Dionne	L.A.	Feb. 12/81	(A)	L.A. 5 at Chi. 5	58	58	58-77 — 135	80	
Charlie Simmer	L.A.	Feb. 14/81	(A)	Bos. 5 at L.A. 4	59	59	56-49 — 105	65	
Kent Nilsson	Cgy.	Feb. 27/81	(G)	Hfd. 1 at Cgy. 5	64	64	49-82 — 131	80	24.6
Mike Bossy	NYI	Mar. 3/81	(G)	Edm. 8 at NYI 8	65	66	68-51 — 119	79	
Dave Taylor	L.A.	Mar. 14/81	(G)	Min. 4 at L.A. 10	63	70	47-65 — 112	72	25.3
Mike Rogers	Hfd.	Mar. 22/81	(G)	Tor. 3 at Hfd. 3	74	74	40-65 — 105	80	
Bernie Federko	St.L.	Mar. 28/81	(A)	Buf. 4 at St.L. 7	74	76	31-73 — 104	78	24.10
Rick Middleton	Bos.	Mar. 28/81	(A)	Chi. 2 at Bos. 5	76	76	44-59 — 103	80	27.4
Bryan Trottier	NYI	Mar. 29/81	(G)	NYI 5 at Wsh. 4	69	76	31-72 — 103	73	
Jacques Richard	Que.	Mar. 29/81	(G)	Mtl. 0 at Que. 4	75	76	52-51 — 103	78	28.6
Peter Stastny	Que.	Mar. 29/81	(A)	Mtl. 0 at Que. 4	73	76	39-70 — 109	77	24.6
Wayne Gretzky	Edm.	Dec. 27/81	(G)	L.A. 3 at Edm. 10	38	38	92-120 — 212	80	
Mike Bossy	NYI	Feb. 13/82	(A)	Phi. 2 at NYI 8	55	55	64-83 — 147	80	
Peter Stastny	Que.	Feb. 16/82	(A)	Wpg. 3 at Que. 7	60	60	46-93 — 139	80	
Dennis Maruk	Wsh.	Feb. 20/82	(G)	Wsh. 3 at Min. 7	60	60	60-76 — 136	80	26.3
Bryan Trottier	NYI	Feb. 23/82	(G)	Chi. 1 at NYI 5	61	61	50-79 — 129	80	
Denis Savard	Chi.	Feb. 27/82	(A)	Chi. 5 at L.A. 3	64	64	32-87 — 119	80	21.1
Bobby Smith	Min.	Mar. 3/82	(A)	Det. 4 at Min. 6	66	66	43-71 — 114	80	24.1
Marcel Dionne	L.A.	Mar. 6/82	(G)	L.A. 6 at Hfd. 7	64	66	50-67 — 117	78	
Dave Taylor	L.A.	Mar. 20/82	(A)	Pit. 5 at L.A. 7	71	72	39-67 — 106	78	
Dale Hawerchuk	Wpg.	Mar. 24/82	(G)	L.A. 3 at Wpg. 5	74	74	45-58 — 103	80	18.11
Dino Ciccarelli	Min.	Mar. 27/82	(A)	Min. 6 at Bos. 5	72	76	55-52 — 107	76	21.8
Glenn Anderson	Edm.	Mar. 28/82	(G)	Edm. 6 at L.A. 2	78	78	38-67 — 105	80	21.7
Mike Rogers	NYR	Apr. 2/82	(G)	Pit. 7 at NYR 5	79	79	38-65 — 103	80	
Wayne Gretzky	Edm.	Jan. 5/83	(A)	Edm. 8 at Wpg. 3	42	42	71-125 — 196	80	
Mike Bossy	NYI	Mar. 3/83	(A)	Tor. 1 at NYI 5	66	67	60-58 — 118	79	
Peter Stastny	Que.	Mar. 5/83	(A)	Hfd. 3 at Que. 10	62	67	47-77 — 124	75	
Denis Savard	Chi.	Mar. 6/83	(G)	Mtl. 4 at Chi. 5	65	67	35-86 — 121	78	
Mark Messier	Edm.	Mar. 23/83	(G)	Edm. 4 at Wpg. 7	73	76	48-58 — 106	77	22.2
Barry Pederson	Bos.	Mar. 26/83	(A)	Hfd. 4 at Bos. 7	73	76	46-61 — 107	77	22.0
Marcel Dionne	L.A.	Mar. 26/83	(A)	Edm. 9 at L.A. 3	75	75	56-51 — 107	80	
Michel Goulet	Que.	Mar. 27/83	(A)	Que. 6 at Buf. 6	77	77	57-48 — 105	80	22.11
Glenn Anderson	Edm.	Mar. 29/83	(A)	Edm. 7 at Van. 4	70	78	48-56 — 104	72	
Jari Kurri	Edm.	Mar. 29/83	(A)	Edm. 7 at Van. 4	78	78	45-59 — 104	80	22.10
Kent Nilsson	Cgy.	Mar. 29/83	(G)	L.A. 3 at Cgy. 5	78	78	46-58 — 104	80	
Wayne Gretzky	Edm.	Dec. 18/83	(G)	Edm. 7 at Wpg. 5	34	34	87-118 — 205	74	
Paul Coffey	Edm.	Mar. 4/84	(A)	Mtl. 1 at Edm. 6	68	68	40-86 — 126	80	22.9
Michel Goulet	Que.	Mar. 4/84	(A)	Que. 1 at Buf. 1	62	67	56-65 — 121	75	
Jari Kurri	Edm.	Mar. 7/84	(G)	Chi. 4 at Edm. 7	53	69	52-61 — 113	64	
Peter Stastny	Que.	Mar. 8/84	(A)	Que. 8 at Pit. 6	69	69	46-73 — 119	80	
Mike Bossy	NYI	Mar. 8/84	(G)	Tor. 5 at NYI 9	56	68	51-67 — 118	67	
Barry Pederson	Bos.	Mar. 14/84	(A)	Bos. 4 at Det. 2	71	71	39-77 — 116	80	
Bryan Trottier	NYI	Mar. 18/84	(G)	NYI 4 at Hfd. 5	62	73	40-71 — 111	68	
Bernie Federko	St.L.	Mar. 20/84	(A)	Wpg. 3 at St.L. 9	75	76	41-66 — 107	79	
Rick Middleton	Bos.	Mar. 27/84	(G)	Bos. 6 at Que. 4	77	77	47-58 — 105	80	
Dale Hawerchuk	Wpg.	Mar. 27/84	(G)	Wpg. 3 at L.A. 3	77	77	37-65 — 102	80	
Mark Messier	Edm.	Mar. 27/84	(G)	Edm. 9 at Cgy. 2	72	79	37-64 — 101	73	
Wayne Gretzky	Edm.	Dec. 29/84	(A)	Det. 3 at Edm. 6	35	35	73-135 — 208	80	
Jari Kurri	Edm.	Jan. 29/85	(G)	Edm. 4 at Cgy. 2	48	51	71-64 — 135	73	
Mike Bossy	NYI	Feb. 23/85	(G)	Bos. 1 at NYI 7	56	60	58-59 — 117	76	
Dale Hawerchuk	Wpg.	Feb. 25/85	(A)	Wpg. 12 at NYR 5	64	64	53-77 — 130	80	
Marcel Dionne	L.A.	Mar. 5/85	(A)	Pit. 0 at L.A. 6	66	66	46-80 — 126	80	
Brent Sutter	NYI	Mar. 12/85	(A)	NYI 6 at St.L. 5	68	68	42-60 — 102	72	22.10
John Ogrodnick	Det.	Mar. 22/85	(A)	NYR 3 at Det. 5	73	73	55-50 — 105	79	25.9
Paul Coffey	Edm.	Mar. 26/85	(G)	Edm. 7 at NYI 5	74	74	37-84 — 121	80	
Denis Savard	Chi.	Mar. 29/85	(A)	Chi. 5 at Wpg. 5	75	76	38-67 — 105	79	
Peter Stastny	Que.	Apr. 2/85	(A)	Bos. 4 at Que. 6	74	77	32-68 — 100	75	
Bernie Federko	St.L.	Apr. 4/85	(A)	NYR 5 at St.L. 4	74	78	30-73 — 103	76	
Paul MacLean	Wpg.	Apr. 6/85	(A)	Wpg. 6 at Edm. 5	78	79	41-60 — 101	79	27.1
Bernie Nicholls	L.A.	Apr. 6/85	(A)	Van. 4 at L.A. 4	80	80	46-54 — 100	80	22.9
John Tonelli	NYI	Apr. 6/85	(G)	N.J. 5 at NYI 5	80	80	42-58 — 100	80	28.1
Mike Gartner	Wsh.	Apr. 7/85	(G)	Pit. 3 at Wsh. 7	80	80	50-52 — 102	80	25.6
Mario Lemieux	Pit.	Apr. 7/85	(G)	Pit. 3 at Wsh. 7	73	80	43-57 — 100	73	19.6
Wayne Gretzky	Edm.	Jan. 4/86	(A)	Hfd. 3 at Edm. 4	39	39	52-163 — 215	80	
Mario Lemieux	Pit.	Feb. 15/86	(G)	Van. 4 at Pit. 9	55	56	48-93 — 141	79	
Paul Coffey	Edm.	Feb. 19/86	(A)	Tor. 5 at Edm. 9	59	60	48-90 — 138	79	
Peter Stastny	Que.	Mar. 1/86	(A)	Buf. 8 at Que. 4	66	68	41-81 — 122	76	
Jari Kurri	Edm.	Mar. 2/86	(G)	Phi. 1 at Edm. 2	62	64	68-63 — 131	78	
Mike Bossy	NYI	Mar. 8/86	(G)	Wsh. 6 at NYI 2	65	65	61-62 — 123	80	
Denis Savard	Chi.	Mar. 12/86	(A)	Buf. 7 at Chi. 6	69	69	47-69 — 116	80	
Mats Naslund	Mtl.	Mar. 13/86	(A)	Mtl. 2 at Bos. 3	70	70	43-67 — 110	80	26.4
Michel Goulet	Que.	Mar. 24/86	(A)	Que. 1 at Min. 0	70	75	53-50 — 103	75	
Glenn Anderson	Edm.	Mar. 25/86	(G)	Edm. 7 at Det. 2	66	74	54-48 — 102	72	
Neal Broten	Min.	Mar. 26/86	(A)	Min. 6 at Tor. 1	76	76	29-76 — 105	80	26.4
Dale Hawerchuk	Wpg.	Mar. 31/86	(A)	Wpg. 5 at L.A. 2	78	78	46-59 — 105	80	
Bernie Federko	St.L.	Apr. 5/86	(G)	Chi. 5 at St.L. 7	79	79	34-68 — 102	80	

Gilbert Perreault

Michel Goulet

John Ogrodnick

Dino Ciccarelli

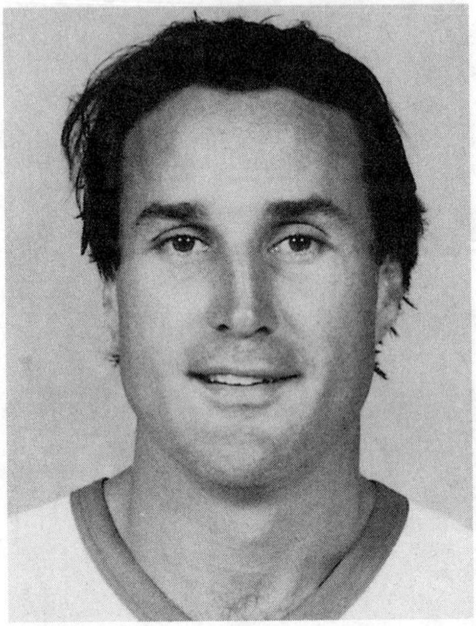

Paul Coffey

John Cullen

Player	Team	Date of 100th Point	G or A	Score		Player's Game No.	Team Game No.	G - A	PTS	Total Games	Age when first 100th point scored (Yrs. & Mos.)
Wayne Gretzky	Edm.	Jan. 11/87	(A)	Cgy. 3	at Edm. 5	42	42	62-121	— 183	79	
Jari Kurri	Edm.	Mar. 14/87	(A)	Buf. 3	at Edm. 5	67	68	54-54	— 108	79	
Mario Lemieux	Pit.	Mar. 18/87	(A)	St.L. 4	at Pit. 5	55	72	54-53	— 107	63	
Mark Messier	Edm.	Mar. 19/87	(A)	Edm. 4	at Cgy. 5	71	71	37-70	— 107	77	
Dino Ciccarelli	Min.	Mar. 30/87	(A)	NYR 6	at Min. 5	78	78	52-51	— 103	80	
Doug Gilmour	St.L.	Apr. 2/87	(A)	Buf. 3	at St.L. 5	78	78	42-63	— 105	80	23.10
Dale Hawerchuk	Wpg.	Apr. 5/87	(A)	Wpg. 3	at Cgy. 1	80	80	47-53	— 100	80	
Mario Lemieux	Pit.	Jan. 20/88	(G)	Pit. 8	at Chi. 3	45	48	70-98	— 168	77	
Wayne Gretzky	Edm.	Feb. 11/88	(A)	Edm. 7	at Van. 2	43	56	40-109	— 149	64	
Denis Savard	Chi.	Feb. 12/88	(A)	St.L. 3	at Chi. 4	57	57	44-87	— 131	80	
Dale Hawerchuk	Wpg.	Feb. 23/88	(G)	Wpg. 4	at Pit. 3	61	61	44-77	— 121	80	
Steve Yzerman	Det.	Feb. 27/88	(A)	Det. 4	at Que. 5	63	63	50-52	— 102	64	22.10
Peter Stastny	Que.	Mar. 8/88	(A)	Hfd. 4	at Que. 6	63	67	46-65	— 111	76	
Mark Messier	Edm.	Mar. 15/88	(A)	Buf. 4	at Edm. 6	68	71	37-74	— 111	77	
Jimmy Carson	L.A.	Mar. 26/88	(A)	Chi. 5	at L.A. 9	77	77	55-52	— 107	80	19.8
Hakan Loob	Cgy.	Mar. 26/88	(A)	Van. 1	at Cgy. 6	76	76	50-56	— 106	80	27.9
Mike Bullard	Cgy.	Mar. 26/88	(A)	Van. 1	at Cgy. 6	76	76	48-55	— 103	79	27.1
Michel Goulet	Que.	Mar. 27/88	(A)	Pit. 6	at Que. 3	76	76	48-58	— 106	80	
Luc Robitaille	L.A.	Mar. 30/88	(G)	Cgy. 7	at L.A. 9	78	78	53-58	— 111	80	22.1
Mario Lemieux	Pit.	Dec. 31/88	(A)	N.J. 6	at Pit. 8	36	38	85-114	— 199	76	
Wayne Gretzky	L.A.	Jan. 21/89	(A)	L.A. 4	at Hfd. 5	47	48	54-114	— 168	78	
Bernie Nicholls	L.A.	Jan. 21/89	(A)	L.A. 4	at Hfd. 5	48	48	70-80	— 150	79	
Steve Yzerman	Det.	Jan. 27/89	(G)	Tor. 1	at Det. 8	50	50	65-90	— 155	80	
Rob Brown	Pit.	Mar. 16/89	(A)	Pit. 2	at N.J. 1	60	72	49-66	— 115	68	20.11
Paul Coffey	Pit.	Mar. 20/89	(A)	Pit. 2	at Min. 7	69	74	30-83	— 113	75	
Joe Mullen	Cgy.	Mar. 23/89	(A)	L.A. 2	at Cgy. 4	74	75	51-59	— 110	79	32.1
Jari Kurri	Edm.	Mar. 29/89	(A)	Edm. 5	at Van. 2	75	79	44-58	— 102	76	
Jimmy Carson	Edm.	Apr. 2/89	(A)	Edm. 2	at Cgy. 4	80	80	49-51	— 100	80	
Mario Lemieux	Pit.	Jan. 28/90	(G)	Pit. 2	at Buf. 7	50	50	45-78	— 123	59	
Wayne Gretzky	L.A.	Jan. 30/90	(A)	N.J. 2	at L.A. 5	51	51	40-102	— 142	73	
Steve Yzerman	Det.	Feb. 19/90	(A)	Mtl. 5	at Det. 5	61	61	62-65	— 127	79	
Mark Messier	Edm.	Feb. 20/90	(A)	Edm. 4	at Van. 2	62	62	45-84	— 129	79	
Brett Hull	St.L.	Mar. 3/90	(A)	NYI 4	at St.L. 5	67	67	72-41	— 113	80	25.7
Bernie Nicholls	NYR	Mar. 12/90	(A)	L.A. 6	at NYR 2	70	71	39-73	— 112	79	
Pierre Turgeon	Buf.	Mar. 25/90	(G)	N.J. 4	at Buf. 3	76	76	40-66	— 106	80	20.7
Paul Coffey	Pit.	Mar. 25/90	(A)	Pit. 2	at Hfd. 4	77	77	29-74	— 103	80	
Pat LaFontaine	NYI	Mar. 27/90	(G)	Cgy. 4	at NYI 2	72	78	54-51	— 105	74	25.1
Adam Oates	St.L.	Mar. 29/90	(G)	Pit. 4	at St.L. 5	79	79	23-79	— 102	80	27.7
Joe Sakic	Que.	Mar. 31/90	(G)	Hfd. 3	at Que. 2	79	79	39-63	— 102	80	20.8
Ron Francis	Hfd.	Mar. 31/90	(G)	Hfd. 3	at Que. 2	79	79	32-69	— 101	80	27.0
Luc Robitaille	L.A.	Apr. 1/90	(A)	L.A. 4	at Cgy. 8	80	80	52-49	— 101	80	
Wayne Gretzky	L.A.	Jan. 30/91	(A)	N.J. 4	at L.A. 2	50	51	41-122	— 163	78	
Brett Hull	St.L.	Feb. 23/91	(G)	Bos. 2	at St.L. 9	60	62	86-45	— 131	78	
Mark Recchi	Pit.	Mar. 5/91	(G)	Van. 1	at Pit. 4	66	67	40-73	— 113	78	23.1
Steve Yzerman	Det.	Mar. 10/91	(G)	Det. 4	at St.L. 1	72	72	51-57	— 108	80	
John Cullen	Hfd.	Mar. 16/91	(G)	N.J. 2	at Hfd. 6	71	71	39-71	— 110	78	26.7
Adam Oates	St.L.	Mar. 17/91	(A)	St.L. 4	at Chi. 6	54	73	25-90	— 115	61	
Joe Sakic	Que.	Mar. 19/91	(G)	Edm. 7	at Que. 6	74	74	48-61	— 109	80	
Steve Larmer	Chi.	Mar. 24/91	(A)	Min. 4	at Chi. 5	76	76	44-57	— 101	80	29.9
Theoren Fleury	Cgy.	Mar. 26/91	(G)	Van. 2	at Cgy. 7	77	77	51-53	— 104	79	22.9
Al MacInnis	Cgy.	Mar. 28/91	(A)	Edm. 4	at Cgy. 4	78	78	28-75	— 103	78	27.8
Brett Hull	St.L.	Mar. 2/92	(G)	St.L. 5	at Van. 3	66	66	70-39	— 109	73	
Wayne Gretzky	L.A.	Mar. 3/92	(A)	Phi. 1	at L.A. 4	60	66	31-90	— 121	74	
Kevin Stevens	Pit.	Mar. 7/92	(A)	Pit. 3	at L.A. 5	66	66	54-69	— 123	80	26.11
Mario Lemieux	Pit.	Mar. 10/92	(A)	Cgy. 2	at Pit. 5	53	67	44-87	— 131	64	
Luc Robitaille	L.A.	Mar. 17/92	(A)	Wpg. 4	at L.A. 5	73	73	44-63	— 107	80	
Mark Messier	NYR	Mar. 22/92	(G)	N.J. 3	at NYR 6	74	75	35-72	— 107	79	
Jeremy Roenick	Chi.	Mar. 29/92	(A)	Tor. 1	at Chi. 5	77	77	53-50	— 103	80	22.2
Steve Yzerman	Det.	Apr. 14/92	(G)	Det. 7	at Min. 4	79	80	45-58	— 103	79	
Brian Leetch	NYR	Apr. 16/92	(G)	Pit. 1	at NYR 7	80	80	22-80	— 102	80	24.1
Mario Lemieux	Pit.	Dec. 31/92	(G)	Tor. 3	at Pit. 3	38	39	69-91	— 160	60	
Pat LaFontaine	Buf.	Feb. 10/93	(A)	Buf. 6	at Wpg. 2	55	55	53-95	— 148	84	
Adam Oates	Bos.	Feb. 14/93	(A)	Bos. 3	at T.B. 3	58	58	45-97	— 142	84	
Steve Yzerman	Det.	Feb. 24/93	(A)	Det. 7	at Buf. 10	64	64	58-79	— 137	84	
Pierre Turgeon	NYI	Feb. 28/93	(G)	NYI 7	at Hfd. 6	62	63	58-74	— 132	83	
Doug Gilmour	Tor.	Mar. 3/93	(A)	Min. 1	at Tor. 3	64	64	32-95	— 127	83	
Alexander Mogilny	Buf.	Mar. 5/93	(A)	Hfd. 4	at Buf. 2	58	65	76-51	— 127	77	24.1
Mark Recchi	Phi.	Mar. 7/93	(G)	Phi. 3	at N.J. 7	66	66	53-70	— 123	84	
Teemu Selanne	Wpg.	Mar. 9/93	(G)	Wpg. 4	at T.B. 2	68	68	76-56	— 132	84	22.7
Luc Robitaille	L.A.	Mar. 15/93	(A)	L.A. 4	at Buf. 2	69	69	63-62	— 125	84	
Kevin Stevens	Pit.	Mar. 23/93	(A)	S.J. 2	at Pit. 7	63	73	55-56	— 111	72	
Mats Sundin	Que.	Mar. 27/93	(G)	Phi. 3	at Que. 8	71	75	47-67	— 114	80	22.1
Pavel Bure	Van.	Apr. 1/93	(G)	Van. 5	at T.B. 3	77	77	60-50	— 110	83	22.0
Jeremy Roenick	Chi.	Apr. 4/93	(G)	St.L. 4	at Chi. 5	79	79	50-57	— 107	84	
Craig Janney	St.L.	Apr. 4/93	(G)	St.L. 4	at Chi. 5	79	79	24-82	— 106	84	25.7
Rick Tocchet	Pit.	Apr. 7/93	(G)	Mtl. 3	at Pit. 4	77	81	48-61	— 109	80	28.11
Joe Sakic	Que.	Apr. 8/93	(A)	Que. 2	at Bos. 6	75	81	48-57	— 105	78	
Ron Francis	Pit.	Apr. 9/93	(A)	Pit. 10	at NYR 4	82	82	24-76	— 100	84	
Brett Hull	St.L.	Apr. 11/93	(G)	Min. 1	at St.L. 5	78	82	54-47	— 101	80	
Theoren Fleury	Cgy.	Apr. 11/93	(G)	Cgy. 3	at Van. 6	82	82	34-66	— 100	83	
Joe Juneau	Bos.	Apr. 14/93	(A)	Bos. 4	at Ott. 2	84	84	32-70	— 102	84	25.3
Wayne Gretzky	L.A.	Feb. 14/94	(A)	Bos. 3	at L.A. 2	56	56	38-92	— 130	81	

Player	Team	Date of 100th Point	G or A	Score		Player's Game No.	Team Game No.	G - A	PTS	Total Games	Age when first 100th point scored (Yrs. & Mos.)
Sergei Fedorov	Det.	Mar. 1/94	(A)	Cgy. 2	at Det. 5	63	63	56-64	— 120	82	24.2
Doug Gilmour	Tor.	Mar. 23/94	(G)	Tor. 1	at Fla. 1	74	74	27-84	— 111	83	
Adam Oates	Bos.	Mar. 26/94	(A)	Mtl. 3	at Bos. 6	68	75	32-80	— 112	77	
Mark Recchi	Phi.	Mar. 27/94	(A)	Ana. 3	at Phi. 2	76	76	40-67	— 107	84	
Pavel Bure	Van.	Mar. 28/94	(A)	Tor. 2	at Van. 3	68	76	60-47	— 107	76	
Jeremy Roenick	Chi.	Mar. 31/94	(G)	Chi. 3	at Wsh. 6	78	78	46-61	— 107	84	
Brendan Shanahan	St.L.	Apr. 12/94	(G)	St.L. 5	at Dal. 9	80	83	52-50	— 102	81	25.2
Mario Lemieux	Pit.	Jan. 16/96	(G)	Col. 5	at Pit. 2	38	44	69-92	— 161	70	
Jaromir Jagr	Pit.	Feb. 6/96	(G)	Bos. 5	at Pit. 6	52	52	62-87	— 149	82	23.11
Ron Francis	Pit.	Mar. 9/96	(A)	N.J. 4	at Pit. 3	61	66	27-92	— 119	77	
Peter Forsberg	Col.	Mar. 9/96	(A)	Col. 7	at Van. 5	68	68	30-86	— 116	82	22.7
Joe Sakic	Col.	Mar. 17/96	(A)	Edm. 1	at Col. 8	70	70	51-69	— 120	82	
Eric Lindros	Phi.	Mar. 25/96	(A)	Hfd. 0	at Phi. 3	65	73	47-68	— 115	73	23
Teemu Selanne	Ana.	Mar. 25/96	(A)	Ana. 1	at Det. 5	70	73	40-68	— 108	79	
Alexander Mogilny	Van.	Mar. 25/96	(A)	L.A. 1	at Van. 4	72	75	55-52	— 107	79	
Wayne Gretzky	St.L.	Mar. 28/96	(A)	N.J. 4	at St.L. 4	76	75	23-79	— 102	80	
Doug Weight	Edm.	Mar. 30/96	(G)	Tor. 4	at Edm. 3	76	76	25-79	— 104	82	25.3
Sergei Fedorov	Det.	Apr. 2/96	(A)	Det. 3	at S.J. 6	72	76	39-68	— 107	78	
Paul Kariya	Ana.	Apr. 7/96	(G)	Ana. 5	at S.J. 3	78	78	50-58	— 108	82	21.5
Mario Lemieux	Pit.	Mar. 8/97	(A)	Phi. 2	at Pit. 3	61	65	50-72	— 122	76	
Teemu Selanne	Ana.	Apr. 1/97	(A)	Chi. 3	at Ana. 3	74	78	51-58	— 109	78	
Jaromir Jagr	Pit.	Apr. 15/98	(G)	T.B. 1	at Pit. 5	76	80	35-67	— 102	77	
Jaromir Jagr	Pit.	Mar. 13/99	(G)	Phi. 0	at Pit. 4	65	65	44-83	— 127	81	
Teemu Selanne	Ana.	Apr. 5/99	(A)	Ana. 2	at Det. 3	69	76	47-60	— 107	75	
Paul Kariya	Ana.	Apr. 17/99	(G)	Ana. 3	at S.J. 3	82	82	39-62	— 101	82	
Jaromir Jagr	Pit.	Mar. 10/01	(G)	Cgy. 3	at Pit. 6	68	68	52-69	— 121	81	
Joe Sakic	Col.	Mar. 18/01	(G)	Min. 3	at Col. 4	72	72	54-64	— 118	82	
Markus Naslund	Van.	Mar. 27/03	(A)	Phx. 1	at Van. 5	78	78	48-56	— 104	82	29.8
Peter Forsberg	Col.	Mar. 31/03	(A)	S.J. 1	at Col. 3	72	79	29-77	— 106	79	
Joe Thornton	Bos.	Apr. 4/03	(A)	Buf. 5	at Bos. 8	77	82	36-65	— 101	77	23.9
Jaromir Jagr	NYR	Mar. 18/06	A	Tor. 2	at NYR 5	67	67	54-69	— 123	82	
Joe Thornton	S.J.	Mar. 21/06	A	S.J. 6	at St.L. 0	66	67	29-96	— 125	81	
Alex Ovechkin	Wsh.	Apr. 10/06	G	Wsh. 2	at Bos. 1	77	78	52-54	— 106	81	20.6
Dany Heatley	Ott.	Apr. 13/06	A	Fla. 5	at Ott. 4	80	80	50-53	— 103	82	25.2
Daniel Alfredsson	Ott.	Apr. 15/06	A	Fla. 5	at Ott. 4	76	81	43-60	— 103	77	33.4
Eric Staal	Car.	Apr. 15/06	A	Car. 2	at T.B. 3	81	81	45-55	— 100	82	21.5
Sidney Crosby	Pit.	Apr. 17/06	A	NYI 1	at Pit. 6	80	81	39-63	— 102	81	18.8
Sidney Crosby	Pit.	Mar. 10/07	G	NYR 2	at Pit. 3	65	68	36-84	— 120	79	
Joe Thornton	S.J.	Mar. 22/07	A	S.J. 5	at Atl. 1	75	75	22-92	— 114	82	
Vincent Lecavalier	T.B.	Mar. 24/07	A	Ott. 7	at T.B. 2	76	76	52-56	— 108	82	26.11
Dany Heatley	Ott.	Mar. 31/07	G	Ott. 5	at NYI 2	79	79	50-55	— 105	82	
Martin St. Louis	T.B.	Mar. 31/07	A	Wsh. 2	at T.B. 5	79	79	43-59	— 102	82	31.10
Marian Hossa	Atl.	Apr. 7/07	A	T.B. 2	at Atl. 3	82	82	43-57	— 100	82	28.3
Joe Sakic	Col.	Apr. 8/07	G	Cgy. 3	at Col. 6	82	82	36-64	— 100	82	
Alex Ovechkin	Wsh.	Mar. 18/08	A	Wsh. 4	at Nsh. 2	74	74	65-47	— 112	82	
Evgeni Malkin	Pit.	Mar. 22/08	G	N.J. 1	at Pit. 7	75	75	47-59	— 106	82	21.8

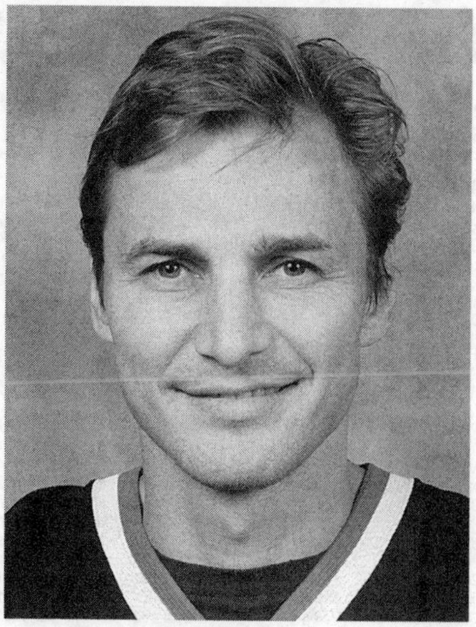

Sergei Fedorov

Jaromir Jagr

Alex Ovechkin

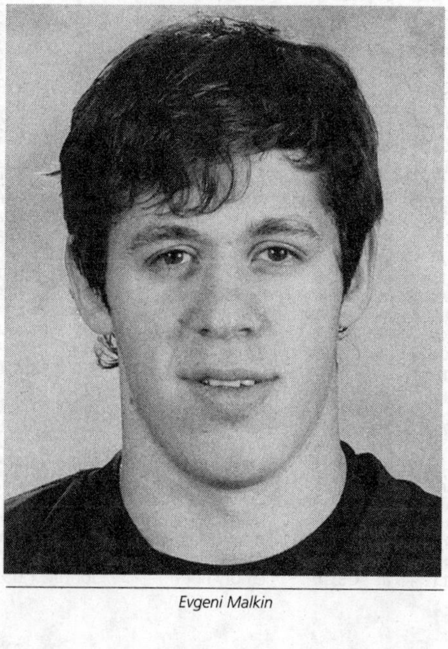

Evgeni Malkin

Vincent Lecavalier

Five-or-more-Goal Games

Player	Team	Date	Score			Opposing Goaltender
SEVEN GOALS						
Joe Malone	Quebec Bulldogs	Jan. 31/20	Tor. 6	at	Que. 10	Ivan Mitchell
SIX GOALS						
Newsy Lalonde	Montreal	Jan. 10/20	Tor. 7	at	Mtl. 14	Ivan Mitchell
Joe Malone	Quebec Bulldogs	Mar. 10/20	Ott. 4	at	Que. 10	Clint Benedict
Corb Denneny	Toronto St. Pats	Jan. 26/21	Ham. 3	at	Tor. 10	Howard Lockhart
Cy Denneny	Ottawa Senators	Mar. 7/21	Ham. 5	at	Ott. 12	Howard Lockhart
Syd Howe	Detroit	Feb. 3/44	NYR 2	at	Det. 12	Ken McAuley
Red Berenson	St. Louis	Nov. 7/68	St.L. 8	at	Phi. 0	Doug Favell
Darryl Sittler	Toronto	Feb. 7/76	Bos. 4	at	Tor. 11	Dave Reece
FIVE GOALS						
Joe Malone	Montreal	Dec. 19/17	Mtl. 7	at	Ott. 4	Clint Benedict
Harry Hyland	Mtl. Wanderers	Dec. 19/17	Tor. 9	at	Mtl. W. 10	Art Brooks, Sammy Hebert
Joe Malone	Montreal	Jan. 12/18	Ott. 4	at	Mtl. 9	Clint Benedict
Joe Malone	Montreal	Feb. 2/18	Tor. 2	at	Mtl. 11	Hap Holmes
Mickey Roach	Toronto St. Pats	Mar. 6/20	Que. 2	at	Tor. 11	Howard Lockhart
Newsy Lalonde	Montreal	Feb. 16/21	Ham. 5	at	Mtl. 10	Howard Lockhart
Babe Dye	Toronto St. Pats	Dec. 16/22	Mtl. 2	at	Tor. 7	Georges Vezina
Red Green	Hamilton Tigers	Dec. 5/24	Ham. 10	at	Tor. 3	John Ross Roach
Babe Dye	Toronto St. Pats	Dec. 22/24	Tor. 10	at	Bos. 1	Hec Fowler
Punch Broadbent	Mtl. Maroons	Jan. 7/25	Mtl. 6	at	Ham. 2	Jake Forbes
Pit Lepine	Montreal	Dec. 14/29	Ott. 4	at	Mtl. 6	Alex Connell
Howie Morenz	Montreal	Mar. 18/30	NYA 3	at	Mtl. 8	Roy Worters
Charlie Conacher	Toronto	Jan. 19/32	NYA 3	at	Tor. 11	Roy Worters (3) Al Shields (2)
Ray Getliffe	Montreal	Feb. 6/43	Bos. 3	at	Mtl. 8	Frank Brimsek
Maurice Richard	Montreal	Dec. 28/44	Det. 1	at	Mtl. 9	Harry Lumley
Howie Meeker	Toronto	Jan. 8/47	Chi. 4	at	Tor. 10	Paul Bibeault
Bernie Geoffrion	Montreal	Feb. 19/55	NYR 2	at	Mtl. 10	Gump Worsley
Bobby Rousseau	Montreal	Feb. 1/64	Det. 3	at	Mtl. 9	Roger Crozier
Yvan Cournoyer	Montreal	Feb. 15/75	Chi. 3	at	Mtl. 12	Mike Veisor
Don Murdoch	NY Rangers	Oct. 12/76	NYR 10	at	Min. 4	Gary Smith
Ian Turnbull	Toronto	Feb. 2/77	Det. 1	at	Tor. 9	Ed Giacomin (2) Jim Rutherford (3)
Bryan Trottier	NY Islanders	Dec. 23/78	NYR 4	at	NYI 9	Wayne Thomas (4) John Davidson (1)
Tim Young	Minnesota	Jan. 15/79	Min. 8	at	NYR 1	Doug Soetaert (3) Wayne Thomas (2)
John Tonelli	NY Islanders	Jan. 6/81	Tor. 3	at	NYI 6	Jiri Crha (4) empty net (1)
Wayne Gretzky	Edmonton	Feb. 18/81	St.L. 2	at	Edm. 9	Mike Liut (3) Ed Staniowski (2)
Wayne Gretzky	Edmonton	Dec. 30/81	Phi. 5	at	Edm. 7	Pete Peeters (4) empty net (1)
Grant Mulvey	Chicago	Feb. 3/82	St.L. 5	at	Chi. 9	Mike Liut (4) Gary Edwards (1)
Bryan Trottier	NY Islanders	Feb. 13/82	Phi. 2	at	NYI 8	Pete Peeters
Willy Lindstrom	Winnipeg	Mar. 2/82	Wpg. 7	at	Phi. 6	Pete Peeters
Mark Pavelich	NY Rangers	Feb. 23/83	Hfd. 3	at	NYR 11	Greg Millen
Jari Kurri	Edmonton	Nov. 19/83	N.J. 4	at	Edm. 13	Glenn Resch (3) Ron Low (2)
Bengt Gustafsson	Washington	Jan. 8/84	Wsh. 7	at	Phi. 1	Pelle Lindbergh
Pat Hughes	Edmonton	Feb. 3/84	Cgy. 5	at	Edm. 10	Don Edwards (3) Reggie Lemelin (2)
Wayne Gretzky	Edmonton	Dec. 15/84	Edm. 8	at	St.L. 2	Rick Wamsley (4) Mike Liut(1)
Dave Andreychuk	Buffalo	Feb. 6/86	Buf. 8	at	Bos. 6	Pat Riggin (1) Doug Keans (4)
Wayne Gretzky	Edmonton	Dec. 6/87	Min. 4	at	Edm. 10	Don Beaupre (4) Kari Takko (1)
Mario Lemieux	Pittsburgh	Dec. 31/88	N.J. 6	at	Pit. 8	Bob Sauve (3) Chris Terreri (2)
Joe Nieuwendyk	Calgary	Jan. 11/89	Wpg. 3	at	Cgy. 8	Daniel Berthiaume
Mats Sundin	Quebec	Mar. 5/92	Que. 10	at	Hfd. 4	Peter Sidorkiewicz (3) Kay Whitmore (2)
Mario Lemieux	Pittsburgh	Apr. 9/93	Pit. 10	at	NYR 4	Corey Hirsch (3) Mike Richter (2)
Peter Bondra	Washington	Feb. 5/94	T.B. 3	at	Wsh. 6	Daren Puppa (4) Pat Jablonski (1)
Mike Ricci	Quebec	Feb. 17/94	Que. 8	at	S.J. 2	Arturs Irbe (3) Jimmy Waite (2)
Alex Zhamnov	Winnipeg	Apr. 1/95	Wpg. 7	at	L.A. 7	Kelly Hrudey (3) Grant Fuhr (2)
Mario Lemieux	Pittsburgh	Mar. 26/96	St.L. 4	at	Pit. 8	Grant Fuhr (1) Jon Casey (4)
Sergei Fedorov	Detroit	Dec. 26/96	Wsh. 4	at	Det. 5	Jim Carey
Marian Gaborik	Minnesota	Dec. 20/07	NYR 3	at	Min. 6	Henrik Lundqvist

Players' 500th Goals

Regular Season

Player	Team	Date	Game No.	Score			Opposing Goaltender	Total Goals	Total Games
Maurice Richard	Montreal	Oct. 19/57	863	Chi. 1	at	Mtl. 3	Glenn Hall	544	978
Gordie Howe	Detroit	Mar. 14/62	1,045	Det. 2	at	NYR 3	Gump Worsley	801	1,767
Bobby Hull	Chicago	Feb. 21/70	861	NYR. 2	at	Chi. 4	Ed Giacomin	610	1,063
Jean Béliveau	Montreal	Feb. 11/71	1,101	Min. 2	at	Mtl. 6	Gilles Gilbert	507	1,125
Frank Mahovlich	Montreal	Mar. 21/73	1,105	Van. 2	at	Mtl. 3	Dunc Wilson	533	1,181
Phil Esposito	Boston	Dec. 22/74	803	Det. 4	at	Bos. 5	Jim Rutherford	717	1,282
John Bucyk	Boston	Oct. 30/75	1,370	St.L. 2	at	Bos. 3	Yves Bélanger	556	1,540
Stan Mikita	Chicago	Feb. 27/77	1,221	Van. 4	at	Chi. 3	Cesare Maniago	541	1,394
Marcel Dionne	Los Angeles	Dec. 14/82	887	L.A. 2	at	Wsh. 7	Al Jensen	731	1,348
Guy Lafleur	Montreal	Dec. 20/83	918	Mtl. 6	at	N.J. 0	Glenn Resch	560	1,126
Mike Bossy	NY Islanders	Jan. 2/86	647	Bos. 5	at	NYI 7	empty net	573	752
Gilbert Perreault	Buffalo	Mar. 9/86	1,159	N.J. 3	at	Buf. 4	Alain Chevrier	512	1,191
Wayne Gretzky	Edmonton	Nov. 22/86	575	Van. 2	at	Edm. 5	empty net	894	1,487
Lanny McDonald	Calgary	Mar. 21/89	1,107	NYI 1	at	Cgy. 4	Mark Fitzpatrick	500	1,111
Bryan Trottier	NY Islanders	Feb. 13/90	1,104	Cgy. 4	at	NYI 2	Rick Wamsley	524	1,279
Mike Gartner	NY Rangers	Oct. 14/91	936	Wsh. 5	at	NYR 3	Mike Liut	708	1,432
Michel Goulet	Chicago	Feb. 16/92	951	Cgy. 5	at	Chi. 5	Jeff Reese	548	1,089
Jari Kurri	Los Angeles	Oct. 17/92	833	Bos. 6	at	L.A. 8	empty net	601	1,251
Dino Ciccarelli	Detroit	Jan. 8/94	946	Det. 6	at	L.A. 3	Kelly Hrudey	608	1,232
Mario Lemieux	Pittsburgh	Oct. 26/95	605	Pit. 7	at	NYI 5	Tommy Soderstrom	690	915
Mark Messier	NY Rangers	Nov. 6/95	1,141	Cgy. 2	at	NYR 4	Rick Tabaracci	694	1,756
Steve Yzerman	Detroit	Jan. 17/96	906	Col. 2	at	Det. 3	Patrick Roy	692	1,514
Dale Hawerchuk	St. Louis	Jan. 31/96	1,103	St.L. 4	at	Tor. 0	Felix Potvin	518	1,188
Brett Hull	St. Louis	Dec. 22/96	693	L.A. 4	at	St.L. 7	Stephane Fiset	741	1,269
Joe Mullen	Pittsburgh	Mar. 14/97	1,052	Pit. 3	at	Col. 6	Patrick Roy	502	1,062
Dave Andreychuk	New Jersey	Mar. 15/97	1,070	Wsh. 2	at	N.J. 3	Bill Ranford	640	1,639
Luc Robitaille	Los Angeles	Jan. 7/99	928	Buf. 2	at	L.A. 4	Dwayne Roloson	668	1,431
Pat Verbeek	Detroit	Mar. 22/00	1,285	Cgy. 2	at	Det. 2	Fred Brathwaite	522	1,424
Ron Francis	Carolina	Jan. 2/02	1,533	Bos. 6	at	Car. 3	Byron Dafoe	549	1,731
*Brendan Shanahan	Detroit	Mar. 23/02	1,100	Det. 2	at	Col. 0	Patrick Roy	650	1,490
*Joe Sakic	Colorado	Dec. 11/02	1,044	Col. 1	at	Van. 3	Dan Cloutier	623	1,363
Joe Nieuwendyk	New Jersey	Jan. 17/03	1,094	N.J. 2	at	Car. 1	Kevin Weekes	564	1,257
*Jaromir Jagr	Washington	Feb. 4/03	928	Wsh. 5	at	T.B. 1	John Grahame	646	1,273
Pierre Turgeon	Colorado	Nov. 8/05	1,229	S.J. 2	at	Col. 5	Vesa Toskala	515	1,294
*Mats Sundin	Toronto	Oct. 14/06	1,162	Cgy. 4	at	Tor. 5	Miikka Kiprusoff	555	1,305
*Teemu Selanne	Anaheim	Nov. 22/06	982	Ana. 2	at	Col. 3	Jose Theodore	552	1,067
Peter Bondra	Chicago	Dec. 22/06	1,050	Tor. 1	at	Chi. 3	J.S. Aubin	503	1,081
*Mark Recchi	Pittsburgh	Jan. 26/07	1,303	Pit. 4	at	Dal. 3	Marty Turco	522	1,410
*Mike Modano	Dallas	Mar. 13/07	1,225	Phi. 2	at	Dal. 3	Antero Niittymaki	528	1,320
*Jeremy Roenick	San Jose	Nov. 10/07	1,267	Phx. 1	at	S.J. 4	Alex Auld	509	1,321
*Keith Tkachuk	St. Louis	Apr. 6/08	1,055	St.L. 4	at	CBJ 1	empty net	500	1,055

*Active

Right winger Marian Gaborik of the Minnesota Wild became the first player in nearly 11 years to score five goals in a single game. He also picked up an assist in a 6-3 victory over the Rangers on December 20, 2007.

Players' 1,000th Points

Regular Season

Player	Team	Date	Game No.	G or A	Score	Total Points G A PTS	Total Games
Gordie Howe	Detroit	Nov. 27/60	938	(A)	Tor. 0 at Det. 2	801-1,049–1,850	1,767
Jean Béliveau	Montreal	Mar. 3/68	911	(G)	Mtl. 2 at Det. 5	507-712–1,219	1,125
Alex Delvecchio	Detroit	Feb. 16/69	1,143	(A)	L.A. 3 at Det. 6	456-825–1,281	1,549
Bobby Hull	Chicago	Dec. 13/70	909	(A)	Min. 2 at Chi. 5	610-560–1,170	1,063
Norm Ullman	Toronto	Oct. 16/71	1,113	(A)	NYR 5 at Tor. 3	490-739–1,229	1,410
Stan Mikita	Chicago	Oct. 15/72	924	(A)	St.L. 3 at Chi. 1	541-926–1,467	1,394
John Bucyk	Boston	Nov. 9/72	1,144	(G)	Det. 3 at Bos. 8	556-813–1,369	1,540
Frank Mahovlich	Montreal	Feb. 17/73	1,090	(A)	Phi. 7 at Mtl. 6	533-570–1,103	1,181
Henri Richard	Montreal	Dec. 20/73	1,194	(A)	Mtl. 2 at Buf. 2	358-688–1,046	1,256
Phil Esposito	Boston	Feb. 15/74	745	(A)	Bos. 4 at Van. 2	717-873–1,590	1,282
Rod Gilbert	NY Rangers	Feb. 19/77	1,027	(G)	NYR 2 at NYI 5	406-615–1,021	1,065
Jean Ratelle	Boston	Apr. 3/77	1,007	(A)	Tor. 4 at Bos. 7	491-776–1,267	1,281
Marcel Dionne	Los Angeles	Jan. 7/81	740	(G)	L.A. 5 at Hfd. 3	731-1,040–1,771	1,348
Guy Lafleur	Montreal	Mar. 4/81	720	(G)	Mtl. 9 at Wpg. 3	560-793–1,353	1,126
Bobby Clarke	Philadelphia	Mar. 19/81	922	(G)	Bos. 3 at Phi. 5	358-852–1,210	1,144
Gilbert Perreault	Buffalo	Apr. 3/82	871	(A)	Buf. 5 at Mtl. 4	512-814–1,326	1,191
Darryl Sittler	Philadelphia	Jan. 20/83	927	(G)	Cgy. 2 at Phi. 5	484-637–1,121	1,096
Wayne Gretzky	Edmonton	Dec. 19/84	424	(A)	L.A. 3 at Edm. 7	894-1,963–2,875	1,487
Bryan Trottier	NY Islanders	Jan. 29/85	726	(G)	Min. 4 at NYI 4	524-901–1,425	1,279
Mike Bossy	NY Islanders	Jan. 24/86	656	(A)	NYI 7 at Wsh. 5	573-553–1,126	752
Denis Potvin	NY Islanders	Apr. 4/87	987	(G)	Buf. 6 at NYI 6	310-742–1,052	1,060
Bernie Federko	St. Louis	Mar. 19/88	855	(A)	Hfd. 5 at St.L. 3	369-761–1,130	1,000
Lanny McDonald	Calgary	Mar. 7/89	1,101	(G)	Wpg. 5 at Cgy. 9	500-506–1,006	1,111
Peter Stastny	Quebec	Oct. 19/89	682	(G)	Que. 5 at Chi. 3	450-789–1,239	977
Jari Kurri	Edmonton	Jan. 2/90	716	(A)	Edm. 6 at St.L. 4	601-797–1,398	1,251
Denis Savard	Chicago	Mar. 11/90	727	(A)	St.L. 6 at Chi. 4	473-865–1,338	1,196
Paul Coffey	Pittsburgh	Dec. 22/90	770	(A)	Pit. 4 at NYI 3	396-1,135–1,531	1,409
Mark Messier	Edmonton	Jan. 13/91	822	(A)	Edm. 5 at Phi. 3	694-1,193–1,887	1,756
Dave Taylor	Los Angeles	Feb. 5/91	930	(A)	L.A. 3 at Phi. 2	431-638–1,069	1,111
Michel Goulet	Chicago	Feb. 23/91	878	(G)	Chi. 3 at Min. 3	548-604–1,152	1,089
Dale Hawerchuk	Buffalo	Mar. 8/91	781	(G)	Chi. 5 at Buf. 3	518-891–1,409	1,188
Bobby Smith	Minnesota	Nov. 30/91	986	(A)	Min. 4 at Tor. 3	357-679–1,036	1,077
Mike Gartner	NY Rangers	Jan. 4/92	971	(G)	NYR 4 at N.J. 6	708-627–1,335	1,432
Raymond Bourque	Boston	Feb. 29/92	933	(A)	Wsh. 5 at Bos. 5	410-1,169–1,579	1,612
Mario Lemieux	Pittsburgh	Mar. 24/92	513	(A)	Pit. 3 at Det. 4	690-1,033–1,723	915
Glenn Anderson	Toronto	Feb. 22/93	954	(G)	Tor. 8 at Van. 1	498-601–1,099	1,129
Steve Yzerman	Detroit	Feb. 24/93	737	(A)	Det. 7 at Buf. 10	692-1,063–1,755	1,514
Ron Francis	Pittsburgh	Oct. 28/93	893	(G)	Que. 7 at Pit. 3	549-1,249–1,798	1,731
Bernie Nicholls	New Jersey	Feb. 13/94	858	(G)	N.J. 3 at T.B. 3	475-734–1,209	1,127
Dino Ciccarelli	Detroit	Mar. 9/94	957	(G)	Det. 5 at Cgy. 1	608-592–1,200	1,232
Brian Propp	Hartford	Mar. 19/94	1,008	(G)	Hfd. 5 at Phi. 3	425-579–1,004	1,016
Joe Mullen	Pittsburgh	Feb. 7/95	935	(A)	Fla. 3 at Pit. 7	502-561–1,063	1,062
Steve Larmer	NY Rangers	Mar. 8/95	983	(A)	N.J. 4 at NYR 6	441-571–1,012	1,006
Doug Gilmour	Toronto	Dec. 23/95	935	(A)	Edm. 1 at Tor. 6	450-964–1,414	1,474
Larry Murphy	Toronto	Mar. 27/96	1,228	(G)	Tor. 6 at Van. 2	287-929–1,216	1,615
Dave Andreychuk	New Jersey	Apr. 7/96	998	(G)	NYR 2 at N.J. 4	640-698–1,338	1,639
Adam Oates	Washington	Oct. 8/97	830	(G)	Wsh. 6 at NYI 3	341-1,079–1,420	1,337
Phil Housley	Washington	Nov. 8/97	1,081	(A)	Edm. 1 at Wsh. 2	338-894–1,232	1,495
Dale Hunter	Washington	Jan. 9/98	1,308	(A)	Phi. 1 at Wsh. 4	323-697–1,020	1,407
Pat LaFontaine	NY Rangers	Jan. 22/98	847	(G)	Phi. 4 at NYR 3	468-545–1,013	865
Luc Robitaille	Los Angeles	Jan. 29/98	882	(G)	Cgy. 3 at L.A. 5	668-726–1,394	1,431
Al MacInnis	St. Louis	Apr. 7/98	1,056	(A)	St.L. 3 at Det. 5	340-934–1,274	1,416
Brett Hull	Dallas	Nov. 14/98	815	(A)	Dal. 3 at Bos. 1	741-650–1,391	1,269
Brian Bellows	Washington	Jan. 2/99	1,147	(A)	Tor. 2 at Wsh. 5	485-537–1,022	1,188
Pierre Turgeon	St. Louis	Oct. 9/99	881	(G)	St.L. 4 at Edm. 3	515-812–1,327	1,294
*Joe Sakic	Colorado	Dec. 27/99	810	(A)	St.L. 1 at Col. 5	623-1,006–1,629	1,363
Pat Verbeek	Detroit	Feb. 27/00	1,275	(A)	T.B. 1 at Det. 3	522-541–1,063	1,424
V. Damphousse	San Jose	Oct. 14/00	1,090	(A)	Bos. 2 at S.J. 5	432-773–1,205	1,378
*Jaromir Jagr	Pittsburgh	Dec. 30/00	763	(G)	Ott. 3 at Pit. 5	646-953–1,599	1,273
*Mark Recchi	Philadelphia	Mar. 13/01	920	(A)	St.L. 2 at Phi. 5	522-859–1,381	1,410
Theoren Fleury	NY Rangers	Oct. 29/01	960	(A)	Dal. 2 at NYR 4	455-633–1,088	1,084
*B. Shanahan	Detroit	Jan. 12/02	1,073	(G)	Dal. 2 at Det. 5	650-690–1,340	1,490
*Jeremy Roenick	Philadelphia	Jan. 30/02	961	(G)	Phi. 1 at Ott. 3	509-694–1,203	1,321
*Mike Modano	Dallas	Nov. 15/02	965	(A)	Col. 2 at Dal. 4	528-755–1,283	1,320
Joe Nieuwendyk	New Jersey	Feb. 23/03	1,094	(G)	N.J. 4 at Pit. 3	564-562–1,126	1,257
*Mats Sundin	Toronto	Mar. 10/03	994	(G)	Tor. 3 at Edm. 2	555-766–1,321	1,305
*Sergei Fedorov	Anaheim	Feb. 14/04	965	(A)	Ana. 2 at Van. 1	472-674–1,146	1,196
Alexander Mogilny	Toronto	Mar. 15/04	946	(A)	Tor. 6 at Buf. 5	473-559–1,032	990
Brian Leetch	Boston	Oct. 18/05	1,151	(A)	Bos. 3 at Mtl. 4	247-781–1,028	1,205
*Teemu Selanne	Anaheim	Jan. 30/06	928	(G)	L.A. 3 at Ana. 4	552-606–1,158	1,067
*Rod Brind'Amour	Carolina	Nov. 4/06	1,202	(A)	Car. 3 at Ott. 2	427-687–1,114	1,324

*Active

Joe Mullen was the first American-born player to register 500 goals and 1,000 points in the NHL.

Jeremey Roenick, who reached 1,000 points back in 2001-02, poses with his son and the puck from his 500th career goal scored on November 10, 2007. Roenick had just 14 goals for San Jose in 2007-08, but 10 of them were game winners.

Individual Awards

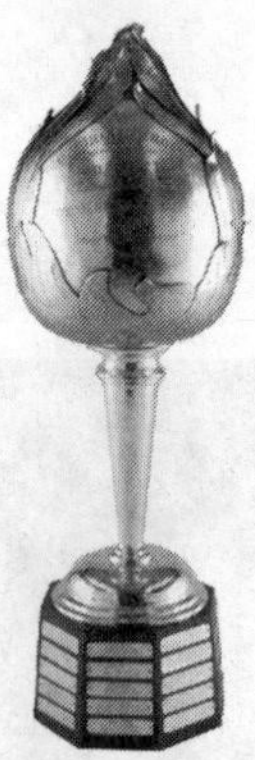

Hart Memorial Trophy

Art Ross Trophy

Calder Memorial Trophy

James Norris Memorial Trophy

HART MEMORIAL TROPHY

An annual award "to the player adjudged to be the most valuable to his team." Winner selected in a poll by the Professional Hockey Writers' Association in the 30 NHL cities at the end of the regular schedule.

History: The Hart Memorial Trophy was presented by the National Hockey League in 1960 after the original Hart Trophy was retired to the Hockey Hall of Fame. The original Hart Trophy was donated to the NHL in 1923 by Dr. David A. Hart, father of Cecil Hart, former manager-coach of the Montreal Canadiens.

2007-08 Winner: **Alex Ovechkin, Washington Capitals**
Runners-up: **Evgeni Malkin, Pittsburgh Penguins**
Jarome Iginla, Calgary Flames

Alex Ovechkin of the Washington Capitals captured the Hart Memorial Trophy in a near-unanimous selection. Ovechkin received 128 of 134 first-place votes for 1,313 points, besting Evgeni Malkin of the Pittsburgh Penguins, who tallied just one first-place vote and 659 points. Jarome Iginla of the Calgary Flames received two first place votes and a total of 565 points. Other players to receive first-place votes were Nicklas Lidstrom of the Detroit Red Wings, who received two first-place nods and finished fourth in the voting with 246 points, and Martin Brodeur of the New Jersey Devils, who received one first-place vote and finished fifth with 239 points. Ovechkin, a first-time Hart nominee, tallied 112 points (65 goals, 47 assists) in 82 games, capturing the Art Ross Trophy as NHL scoring leader and Maurice Richard Trophy as the Leagues top goal scorer. He also led all players in power-play goals (22) and game-winning goals (11). Ovechkin set a new single-season NHL record for goals by a left winger, surpassing Luc Robitaille's 63 with Los Angeles in 1992-93. His 65 goals were the most by an NHL player since Mario Lemieux had 69 in 1995-96.

CALDER MEMORIAL TROPHY

An annual award "to the player selected as the most proficient in his first year of competition in the National Hockey League." Winner selected in a poll by the Professional Hockey Writers' Association at the end of the regular schedule.

History: From 1936-37 until his death in 1943, Frank Calder, NHL President, bought a trophy each year to be given permanently to the outstanding rookie. After Calder's death, the NHL presented the Calder Memorial Trophy in his memory and the trophy is to be kept in perpetuity. To be eligible for the award, a player cannot have played more than 25 games in any single preceding season nor in six or more games in each of any two preceding seasons in any major professional league. Beginning in 1990-91, to be eligible for this award a player must not have attained his twenty-sixth birthday by September 15th of the season in which he is eligible.

2007-08 Winner: **Patrick Kane, Chicago Blackhawks**
Runners-up: **Nicklas Backstrom, Washington Capitals**
Jonathan Toews, Chicago Blackhawks

Right winger Patrick Kane of the Chicago Blackhawks won the Calder Memorial Trophy. Kane received 71 of 133 first-place votes and a total of 1,078 points, outdistancing Washington Capitals center Nicklas Backstrom, who polled 30 first-place votes and 872 points. Kane's teammate Jonathan Toews received 19 first-place votes and 647 points. Montreal Canadiens goalie Carey Price was named first on 11 ballots and finished fourth in voting with 461 points. Peter Mueller of Phoenix was fifth in the voting with 195 points. Tobias Enstrom of Atlanta received the final two first-place votes and finished sixth with 79 points.

The first player selected in the 2007 Entry Draft, Kane tallied 16 points in October as an 18-year-old, the most by an NHL rookie in the season's opening month since 1992-93. In his second NHL game his shootout goal against Buffalo childhood hero Dominik Hasek gave the Blackhawks their first victory of the season, a 4-3 decision over Detroit on October 6. Kane finished the season as the NHL's rookie scoring leader and was tops on the Blackhawks with 72 points (21 goals, 51 assists) in 82 games.

ART ROSS TROPHY

An annual award "to the player who leads the league in scoring points at the end of the regular season."

History: Arthur Howey Ross, former manager-coach of the Boston Bruins, presented the trophy to the National Hockey League in 1947. If two players finish the schedule with the same number of points, the trophy is awarded in the following manner: 1. Player with most goals. 2. Player with fewer games played. 3. Player scoring first goal of the season.

2007-08 Winner: **Alex Ovechkin, Washington Capitals**
Runners-up: **Evgeni Malkin, Pittsburgh Penguins**
Jarome Iginla, Calgary Flames

In just his third season in the NHL in 2007-08, Alex Ovechkin became the first player born and trained in Russia to win the Art Ross Trophy. He also joined an elite group of players who have led the NHL in both goals and points in the same year. Ovechkin tallied 65 goals and 47 assists for 112 points, six more than fellow Russian Evgeni Malkin of the Pittsburgh Penguins. Ovechkin is just the sixth player in the past 37 years to lead the NHL in goals and points in the same season, joining a group that includes Phil Esposito (1970-71 through 1973-74), Guy Lafleur (1977-78), Wayne Gretzky (1981-82 through 1984-85, plus 1986-87), Mario Lemieux (1987-88, 1988-89) and Jarome Iginla (2001-02).

JAMES NORRIS MEMORIAL TROPHY

An annual award "to the defense player who demonstrates throughout the season the greatest all-round ability in the position." Winner selected in a poll by the Professional Hockey Writers' Association at the end of the regular schedule.

History: The James Norris Memorial Trophy was presented in 1953 by the four children of the late James Norris in memory of the former owner-president of the Detroit Red Wings.

2007-08 Winner: **Nicklas Lidstrom, Detroit Red Wings**
Runners-up: **Dion Phaneuf, Calgary Flames**
Zdeno Chara, Boston Bruins

For the sixth time in seven seasons, Nicklas Lidstrom of the Detroit Red Wings won the James Norris Memorial Trophy. Lidstrom received 127 of 134 first-place votes and 1,313 points. Dion Phaneuf of the Calgary Flames finished second in the balloting, receiving two first-place votes and 561 points. Zdeno Chara of the Boston Bruins received three first-place votes, but finished third with 486 points. The Pittsburgh Penguins Sergei Gonchar and Brian Campbell, who was traded from the Buffalo Sabres to the San Jose Sharks, each reach received one first-place vote. Gonchar finished fourth in the balloting with 370 points, while Campbell was fifth with 333.

Lidstrom helped the Red Wings post the NHLs best defensive record in 2007-08 while also leading all NHL defensemen in scoring with 70 points (10 goals, 60 assists) in 76 games. He ranked second in the NHL to teammate Pavel Datsyuk in plus-minus (+40) and was fourth among all players in average ice time per game (26:43). The 38-year-old native of Vasteras, Sweden is the third defenseman in NHL history with as many as six Norris Trophy wins, joining Hockey Hall of Fame members Bobby Orr (eight) and Doug Harvey (seven).

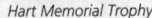

Vezina Trophy

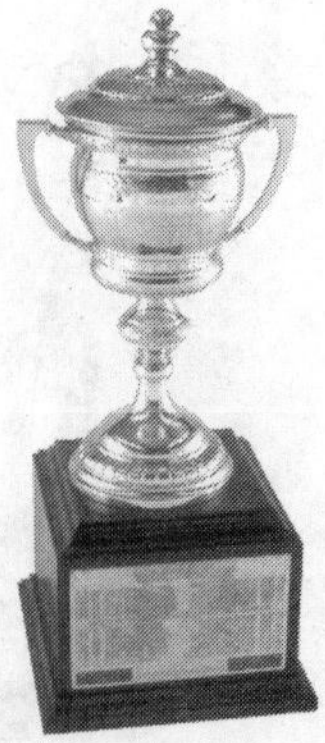

Lady Byng Memorial Trophy

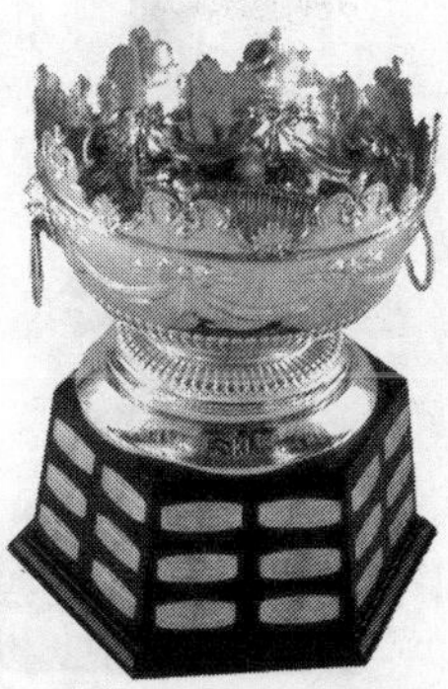

Frank J. Selke Trophy

Conn Smythe Trophy

VEZINA TROPHY

An annual award "to the goalkeeper adjudged to be the best at his position" as voted by the general managers of each of the 30 clubs.

History: Leo Dandurand, Louis Letourneau and Joe Cattarinich, former owners of the Montreal Canadiens, presented the trophy to the National Hockey League in 1926-27 in memory of Georges Vezina, outstanding goalkeeper of the Canadiens who collapsed during an NHL game on November 28, 1925, and died of tuberculosis a few months later. Until the 1981-82 season, the goalkeeper(s) of the team allowing the fewest number of goals during the regular season were awarded the Vezina Trophy.

2007-08 Winner: **Martin Brodeur, New Jersey Devils**
Runners-up: **Evgeni Nabokov, San Jose Sharks**
Henrik Lundqvist, New York Rangers

Martin Brodeur of the New Jersey Devils captured the Vezina Trophy for the fourth time in the past five seasons. Brodeur was named on 29 of 30 ballots, including 15 first-place selections, and collected 113 points. San Jose Sharks goaltender Evgeni Nabokov finished a close second, garnering 13 first-place votes and 106 points. Henrik Lundqvist of the New York Rangers received one first-place vote and 13 points. Miikka Kiprusoff of the Calgary Flames also received one first-place vote, but finished fifth in the balloting behind Jean-Sebastien Giguere of the Anaheim Ducks.

Brodeur posted a 44-27-6 record with a 2.17 goals-against average, a .920 save percentage and four shutouts, ranking among NHL leaders in minutes played (first, 4,635), wins (second) and goals-against average (fifth). He became just the second goaltender in NHL history to reach the 500-win mark, following Patrick Roy, and ended the season with 96 career shutouts, seven shy of all-time leader Terry Sawchuk. He extended NHL records by registering his third consecutive and seventh career 40-win season, and tenth consecutive campaign with 70-or-more games played.

LADY BYNG MEMORIAL TROPHY

An annual award "to the player adjudged to have exhibited the best type of sportsmanship and gentlemanly conduct combined with a high standard of playing ability." Winner selected in a poll by the Professional Hockey Writers' Association at the end of the regular schedule.

History: Lady Byng, wife of Canada's Governor-General at the time, presented the Lady Byng Trophy in the 1924-25 season. After Frank Boucher of the New York Rangers won the award seven times in eight seasons, he was given the trophy to keep and Lady Byng donated another trophy in 1936. After Lady Byng's death in 1949, the National Hockey League presented a new trophy, changing the name to Lady Byng Memorial Trophy.

2007-08 Winner: **Pavel Datsyuk, Detroit Red Wings**
Runners-up: **Martin St. Louis, Tampa Bay Lightning**
Jason Pominville, Buffalo Sabres

Detroit Red Wings center Pavel Datsyuk won his third consecutive Lady Byng Memorial Trophy. Datsyuk received 75 first-place votes and 984 points to finish ahead of Martin St. Louis of the Tampa Bay Lightning, who repeated his second-place finish of 2006-07 with 261 points, including two first-place votes. Jason Pominville of the Buffalo Sabres had three-first-place votes, and finished third with 253 points. A total of 18 players received at least one first-place vote, including Detroit teammates Nicklas Lidstrom (who had nine and finished fourth with 211 points) and Henrik Zetterberg (six and 185).

Datsyuk becomes the first player in more than 70 years to capture the award three consecutive times. The New York Rangers Frank Boucher won the Lady Byng Trophy from 1933 through 1935, capping a run of seven Byng trophies in eight seasons. Datsyuk finished fourth in the NHL scoring race with a career-high 97 points (31 goals, 66 assists) in 82 games and led all NHL players with a +41 rating while recording only 20 penalty minutes. He led the Red Wings in scoring for a third consecutive season, matching the feat of franchise greats Ted Lindsay, Gordie Howe and Steve Yzerman.

FRANK J. SELKE TROPHY

An annual award "to the forward who best excels in the defensive aspects of the game." Winner selected in a poll by the Professional Hockey Writers' Association at the end of the regular schedule.

History: Presented to the National Hockey League in 1977 by the Board of Governors of the NHL in honor of Frank J. Selke, one of the great architects of Montreal and Toronto championship teams.

2007-08 Winner: **Pavel Datsyuk, Detroit Red Wings**
Runners-up: **John Madden, New Jersey Devils**
Henrik Zetterberg, Detroit Red Wings

Detroit Red Wings center Pavel Datsyuk captured the Frank Selke Trophy for the first time. Datsyuk was named on 62 of 134 ballots, including 43 first-place votes and posted a 90-point victory over New Jersey Devils center John Madden, 537-447. Madden received 18 first-place votes. Henrik Zetterberg of the Red Wings placed first on 22 ballots, but finished third overall with 425 points.

Datsyuk led all NHL players in plus-minus with a career-best +41 rating, topped all NHL forwards with 144 takeaways, 67 percent more than his nearest rival (Mike Modano of the Dallas Stars, 86) and ranked first among Red Wings forwards in blocked shots (42). The Red Wings posted the top defensive record in the NHL with 184 goals-against.

WILLIAM M. JENNINGS TROPHY

An annual award "to the goalkeeper(s) having played a minimum of 25 games for the team with the fewest goals scored against it." Winners selected on regular-season play.

History: The Jennings Trophy was presented in 1981-82 by the National Hockey League's Board of Governors to honor the late William M. Jennings, longtime governor and president of the New York Rangers and one of the great builders of hockey in the United States.

2007-08 Winners: **Chris Osgood/Dominik Hasek, Detroit Red Wings**
Runners-up: **Jean-Sebastien Giguere, Anaheim Ducks**
Evgeni Nabokov, San Jose Sharks

Chris Osgood and Dominik Hasek, who split time in the Detroit Red Wings net with 43 and 41 appearances, respectively, backstopped the club to the NHLs top defensive record with 179 team goals against. Both Osgood and Hasek posted 27 wins and allowed 84 goals. Osgood led the league with a 2.09 goals-against average, while Hasek finished tied for third at 2.14. Jean-Sebastien Giguere saw the bulk of the action in Anaheim for a Ducks team that allowed just 184 team goals. He had a .922 save percentage that ranked third in the NHL. Evgeni Nabokov carried the load in San Jose, leading the league with 46 wins and posting a 2.14 average for a team that allowed 187 goals.

CONN SMYTHE TROPHY

An annual award "to the most valuable player for his team in the playoffs." Winner selected by the Professional Hockey Writers' Association at the conclusion of the final game in the Stanley Cup Finals.

History: Presented by Maple Leaf Gardens Limited in 1964 to honor Conn Smythe, the former coach, manager, president and owner-governor of the Toronto Maple Leafs.

2007-08 Winner: **Henrik Zetterberg, Detroit Red Wings**

Detroit Red Wings left winger Henrik Zetterberg won the Conn Smythe Trophy after helping his team win the Stanley Cup. Zetterberg, a 27-year-old native of Njurunda, Sweden, was the 210th player selected in the 1999 Entry Draft and played his fifth season with the Red Wings in 2007-08. He finished the 2008 Stanley Cup playoffs at or near the top of several categories, tying teammate Johan Franzen for most goals (13) and tying Sidney Crosby of the Pittsburgh Penguins for most points (27). In addition, Zetterberg's work on the Red Wings' penalty-killing unit was a key reason why Detroit defeated Pittsburgh in the Finals. During the regular season, Zetterberg reached career highs in goals (43), assists (49) and points (92).

William M. Jennings Trophy

Jack Adams Award

Bill Masterton Trophy

Lester Patrick Trophy

JACK ADAMS AWARD

An annual award presented by the National Hockey League Broadcasters' Association to "the NHL coach adjudged to have contributed the most to his team's success." Winner selected by a poll among members of the NHL Broadcasters' Association at the end of the regular season.

History: The award was presented by the NHL Broadcasters' Association in 1974 to commemorate the late Jack Adams, coach and general manager of the Detroit Red Wings, whose lifetime dedication to hockey serves as an inspiration to all who aspire to further the game.

2007-08 Winner: **Bruce Boudreau, Washington Capitals**
Runners-up: **Guy Carbonneau, Montreal Canadiens**
Mike Babcock, Detroit Red Wings

Washington Capitals head coach Bruce Boudreau captured the Jack Adams Award. Boudreau received 31 of 74 first-place votes and 208 points to edge Guy Carbonneau of the Montreal Canadiens, who polled 24 first-place votes and 196 points. Mike Babcock of the Detroit Red Wings finished third in the balloting with 65 points, including eight first-place votes. Seven other coaches received at least one first-place vote, including Barry Trotz of the Nashville Predators (four), Ron Wilson of the San Jose Sharks (two) and Michel Therrien of the Pittsburgh Penguins (two).

Boudreau brought more than 1,000 games of minor-league coaching experience to his first NHL assignment behind the bench and led the Capitals to one of the most dramatic turnarounds in league history. Named head coach November 22, 2007 with the 6-14-1 Capitals at the bottom of the Eastern Conference standings, Boudreau led his club to a 37-17-7 mark the rest of the way capped by seven consecutive victories to close the season and captured the Southeast Division title in the seasons final game. He became the fastest Capitals coach to 20 victories (34 games) and 30 victories (53 games) in franchise history. Boudreau joins Bill Barber (Philadelphia Flyers, 2000-01) as the only men to be named coach of the year after taking over a team in midseason.

BILL MASTERTON MEMORIAL TROPHY

An annual award under the trusteeship of the Professional Hockey Writers' Association to "the National Hockey League player who best exemplifies the qualities of perseverance, sportsmanship and dedication to hockey." Winner selected by a poll among the 30 chapters of the PHWA at the end of the regular season. A $2,500 grant from the PHWA is awarded annually to the Bill Masterton Scholarship Fund, based in Bloomington, MN, in the name of the Masterton Trophy winner.

History: The trophy was presented by the NHL Writers' Association in 1968 to commemorate the late Bill Masterton, a player with the Minnesota North Stars, who exhibited to a high degree the qualities of perseverance, sportsmanship and dedication to hockey, and who died January 15, 1968.

2007-08 Winner: **Jason Blake, Toronto Maple Leafs**
Runners-up: **Chris Chelios, Detroit Red Wings**
Fernando Pisani, Edmonton Oilers

Toronto Maple Leafs left winger Jason Blake is the 2007-08 recipient of the Bill Masterton Memorial Trophy. In October, Blake was diagnosed with chronic myelogenous leukemia (CML), a rare but treatable form of cancer. Nonetheless, the native of Moorhead, Minnesota, completed the season as one of only three players to appear in all 82 Maple Leafs games. Blake hosted a leukemia awareness night at Air Canada Centre in January and donated $1,000 per goal and $500 per assist during the month to the Leukemia and Lymphoma Society of Canada.

LESTER PATRICK TROPHY

An annual award "for outstanding service to hockey in the United States." Eligible recipients are players, officials, coaches, executives and referees. Winners are selected by an award committee consisting of the commissioner of the NHL, an NHL governor, a representative of the New York Rangers, a member of the Hockey Hall of Fame builder's section, a member of the Hockey Hall of Fame player's section, a member of the U.S. Hockey Hall of Fame, a member of the NHL Broadcasters' Association and a member of the Professional Hockey Writers' Association. Each except the League Commissioner is rotated annually. The winner receives a miniature of the trophy.

History: Presented by the New York Rangers in 1966 to honor the late Lester Patrick, longtime general manager and coach of the New York Rangers, whose teams finished out of the playoffs only once in his first 16 years with the club.

2007 Winners: **Brian Leetch**
Cammi Granato
Stan Fischler
John Halligan

2008 Winners: **Bob Naegele, Jr.**
Brian Burke
Phil Housley
Ted Lindsay

Brian Leetch was one of the top defensemen of his generation. In an 18-year pro career from 1988 to 2006, Leetch captured the Calder Trophy as the NHL's top rookie in 1988-89 and won the Norris Trophy as best defenseman in 1992 and 1997. In 1994, he became the first U.S.-born player to win the Conn Smythe Trophy as playoff MVP.

Cammi Granato's career has played a key role in the growth of women's hockey. After playing with boys while growing up, she went on to star at Providence College. A member of the U.S. women's national team beginning in 1990, Granato is the program's all-time scoring leader and captained the team to an historic Olympic gold medal in 1998.

Stan Fischler has worked as a writer, broadcaster and historian for more than half a century. With the help of his wife Shirley, Fischler has authored or co-authored more than 90 books. Fischler has worked for numerous newspapers and magazines since 1950. He has appeared on hockey broadcasts involving the New York area's NHL clubs since March of 1975.

John Halligan has worked as a public relations executive, author, historian and archivist with the New York Rangers and the NHL since 1963. Halligan worked for the Rangers for 24 years. He worked for the NHL from 1983 to 1986 and then from 1990 to 2006 as director of communications and special projects. He has earned many honors in his career.

Bob Naegele, Jr. was the lead investor of an informal association of hockey enthusiasts whose dream was to see the return of NHL hockey to Minnesota. The Wild were admitted to the league on June 25, 1997, and began playing in 2000-01. With Naegele as majority owner, the Wild became one of the most successful expansion franchises in pro sports.

Brian Burke obtained a degree from Harvard Law School in 1981. After six years as a player representative, the former college and AHL player launched his NHL career with the Vancouver Canucks in 1987. He later served in the NHL front office from 1993 to 1998. Burke won the Stanley Cup as GM of the Anaheim Ducks in 2007.

Phil Housley was a high school hockey star in Minnesota who became a rookie sensation in the NHL when the Buffalo Sabres selected him sixth overall in the 1982 Entry Draft. Housley went on to play 21 NHL seasons with eight clubs and ranked as the NHL's all-time leader among U.S.-born players in games (1,495) and points (1,232) at the time of his retirement.

Ted Lindsay is an icon in Detroit sports history. He played 14 of his 17 NHL seasons with the Red Wings and was a key member of the Detroit dynasty that captured seven consecutive regular-season titles and the Stanley Cup four times from 1948-49 through 1954-55. He was the left winger on Detroit's famed Production Line with Gordie Howe and Sid Abel.

King Clancy Memorial Trophy

Presidents' Trophy

Maurice "Rocket" Richard Trophy

Lester B. Pearson Award

KING CLANCY MEMORIAL TROPHY

An annual award "to the player who best exemplifies leadership qualities on and off the ice and has made a noteworthy humanitarian contribution in his community."

History: The King Clancy Memorial Trophy was presented to the National Hockey League by the Board of Governors in 1988 to honor the late Frank "King" Clancy.

2007-08 Winner: Vincent Lecavalier, Tampa Bay Lightning

Tampa Bay Lightning center Vincent Lecavalier has made community giving and charitable work a part of his daily life since joining the Tampa Bay Lightning a decade ago. In 2003, Lecavalier formalized his charitable efforts through the creation of the Vincent Lecavalier Foundation, dedicated to the development of youth and families in the Tampa Bay and Rimouski, Quebec communities through charitable outreach programs.

On October 16, 2007, Lecavalier made his largest commitment yet to the Tampa Bay community, announcing a $3-million pledge to construct the Vincent Lecavalier Pediatric Cancer and Blood Disorders Center at All Children's Hospital in St. Petersburg, Florida. The 26,500 square-foot wing on the seventh floor of All-Children's Hospital will include 28 individual patient rooms with accommodations to allow parents to stay overnight with their children. The entire Center will be designed with a special airflow system that will allow patients with weakened immune systems the chance to move freely throughout the wing instead of being confined to their rooms. The Center is currently under construction and set to open in 2009.

MAURICE "ROCKET" RICHARD TROPHY

An annual award "presented to the player finishing the regular season as the League's goal-scoring leader."

History: A gift to the NHL from the Montreal Canadiens in 1999, the Maurice "Rocket" Richard Trophy honors one of the game's greatest stars. During his 18-year career with the Canadiens from 1942-43 through 1959-60, Richard was the first player in NHL history to score 50 goals in a season and 500 in his career. He played on eight Stanley Cup champions and led the League in goal scoring five times.

2007-08 Winner: Alex Ovechkin, Washington Capitals
Runners-up: Ilya Kovalchuk, Atlanta Thrashers
Jarome Iginla, Calgary Flames

Left winger Alex Ovechkin of the Washington Capitals is the 2007-08 winner of the Maurice Rocket Richard Trophy. Ovechkin set the single-season NHL record for goals by a left winger with 65, surpassing Luc Robitaille's 63 with Los Angeles in 1992-93, and his goal tally was the most by NHL player since Mario Lemieux scored 69 in 1995-96. He also led all players in power-play goals (22) and game-winning goals (11), and his 446 shots on goal were the second-highest total in NHL history behind Phil Espositos 550 shots in 1970-71. Ovechkin scored 51 of his goals in the 61 games after Bruce Boudreau was named head coach on November 22, pacing the 37-17-7 run that carried the Capitals into the playoffs. Ovechkin led fellow Russian Ilya Kovalchuk (52 goals) of the Atlanta Thrashers by 13 goals, while Jarome Iginla of the Calgary Flames was third with 50 goals.

PRESIDENTS' TROPHY

An annual award to the club finishing the regular-season with the best overall record.

History: Presented to the National Hockey League in 1985-86 by the NHL Board of Governors to recognize the team compiling the top regular-season record.

2007-08 Winner: Detroit Red Wings
Runners-up: San Jose Sharks
Montreal Canadiens

The Detroit Red Wings captured the Presidents Trophy for the sixth time since the 1994-95 season, leading the NHL with 54 wins (54-21-7) and 115 points. Detroit won the Central Division title for the sixth year in a row and the tenth time in total dating back to 1994-95. The Red Wings were the NHL's best defensive team, allowing just 179 goals, and were third best offensively with 252 goals scored. The San Jose Sharks posted a record of 49-23-10 and set a club record with 108 points to win the Pacific Division for the third time. The Montreal Canadiens scored 257 goals (to trail only the Ottawa Senators, who scored 258) en route to a 47-25-10 season and 104 points, which saw the team, finish with the best record in the Eastern Conference.

LESTER B. PEARSON AWARD

The Lester B. Pearson Award is presented annually to the "most outstanding player" in the NHL as voted by fellow members of the National Hockey League Players' Association. The winner receives $20,000, and the two finalists receive $10,000 each to donate to the grassroots hockey program of their choice, through the NHLPA's Goals & Dreams Fund.

History: The award was first presented in 1970-71 by the NHLPA in honor of the late Lester B. Pearson, former Prime Minister of Canada.

2007-08 Winner: Alex Ovechkin, Washington Capitals
Runners-up: Evgeni Malkin, Pittsburgh Penguins
Jarome Iginla, Calgary Flames

Alex Ovechkin of the Washington Capitals was the recipient of the 2007-08 Lester B. Pearson Award. Ovechkin appeared in all 82 games for the Washington Capitals, securing the NHL's top spot for goals (65) and points (112). A finalist for the 2005-06 Lester B. Pearson Award, Ovechkin has taken the NHL by storm with his extraordinary ability to score goals and his exuberant enthusiasm for the game of hockey. In just his third season, the 22-year-old led the Capitals to the playoffs, after an incredible run that saw the club clinch the Southeast Division crown. Ovechkin becomes just the second Russian born player to receive the honor, following Sergei Fedorov (1993-94). Ovechkin also represents the first time a member of the Washington Capitals has won the prestigious award.

In honor of the outstanding seasons of the Lester B. Pearson nominees, the NHLPA Goals & Dreams fund will be allocating a total of $40,000 dollars to the grassroots hockey programs of the Pearson Finalists choice. Ovechkin will designate a Russian orphanage as the beneficiary of the $20,000 that accompanies the Pearson Award. Jarome Iginla of the Calgary Flames allocated $10,000 between the St. Albert Minor Hockey Association and the Calgary Minor Hockey Association, while Evgeni Malkin of the Pittsburgh Penguins designated $10,000 to a local Pittsburgh childrens charity.

2007-08 NHL Player of the Week/Month Award Winners

Player of the Week/Month

Period Ending	First Star	Second Star	Third Star
Oct. 7	Paul Stastny, COL	Mike Comrie, NYI	Chris Mason, NSH
Oct. 14	Cam Ward, CAR	Brian Campbell, BUF	Henrik Zetterberg, DET
Oct. 21	Martin Biron, PHI	Jarome Iginla, CGY	Jason Williams, CHI
Oct. 28	Jason Labarbera, LA	Rod Brind'Amour, CAR	Alex Ovechkin, WSH
October	Henrik Zetterberg, DET	Pascal Leclaire, CBJ	Jarome Iginla, CGY
Nov. 4	Ilya Kovalchuk, ATL	Henrik Lundqvist, NYR	Marian Gaborik, MIN
Nov. 11	Vincent Lecavalier, TB	Steve Reinprecht, PHX	Jeremy Roenick, S.J.
Nov. 18	Vincent Lecavalier, TB	Evgeni Nabokov, S.J.	Martin Erat, NSH
Nov. 25	Daniel Briere, PHI	Ilya Bryzgalov, PHX	Mike Smith, DAL
November	Ilya Kovalchuk, ATL	Roberto Luongo, VAN	Vincent Lecavalier, TB
Dec. 2	Roberto Luongo, VAN	Martin Brodeur, N.J.	Niklas Backstrom, MIN
Dec. 9	Milan Hejduk, COL	Dominik Hasek, DET	Anze Kopitar, L.A.
Dec. 16	Jarome Iginla, CGY	Sergei Zubov, DAL	Joffrey Lupul, PHI
Dec. 23	Marian Gaborik, MIN	Kari Lehtonen. ATL	Jason Arnott, NSH
Dec. 30	Alex Ovechkin, WSH	Jaromir Jagr, NYR	Evgeni Nabokov, S.J.
December	Jason Spezza, OTT	Pavel Datsyuk, DET	Evgeni Nabokov, S.J.
Jan. 6	Manny Legace, STL	Kristian Huselius, CGY	Ty Conklin, PIT
Jan. 13	Marian Gaborik, MIN	Mathieu Garon, EDM	Scott Hartnell, PHI
Jan. 20	Ryan Getzlaf, ANA	Johan Holmqvist, T.B.	Scott Hartnell, PHI
Jan. 27	Daniel Alfredsson, OTT	Alex Ovechkin, WSH	Pascal Leclaire, CBJ
January	Alex Ovechkin, WSH	J.P. Dumont, NSH	Cristobal Huet, MTL
Feb. 3	Pavel Datsyuk, DET	Marty Turco, DAL	Chris Drury, NYR
Feb. 10	Jason Spezza, OTT	Evgeni Malkin, PIT	Jean-Sebastien Giguere, ANA
Feb. 17	Manny Legace, STL	Ruslan Fedotenko, NYI	Carey Price, MTL
Feb. 24	Teemu Selanne, ANA	Miikka Kiprusoff, CGY	Martin Brodeur, N.J.
February	Evgeni Malkin, PIT	Marty Turco, DAL	Thomas Vanek, BUF
Mar. 2	Mats Sundin, TOR	Tim Thomas, BOS	Mike Knuble, PHI
Mar. 9	Alex Ovechkin, WSH	Martin Brodeur, N.J.	Joe Thornton, S.J.
Mar. 16	Jarome Iginla, CGY	Petr Sykora, PIT	Tomas Vokoun, FLA
Mar. 23	Alex Ovechkin, WSH	Vesa Toskala, TOR	Daniel Briere, PHI
Mar. 30	Joe Thornton, S.J.	Dan Ellis, NSH	David Krejci, BOS
March	Alex Ovechkin, WSH	Marc-Andre Fleury, PIT	Johan Franzen, DET
Apr. 6	Carey Price, MTL	Jaromir Jagr, NYR	Cristobal Huet, WSH

Rookie of the Month

Month	Player
October	Patrick Kane, Chicago
November	Tobias Enstrom, Atlanta
December	Nicklas Backstrom, Washington
January	Peter Mueller, Phoenix
February	Sam Gagner, Edmonton
March	Carey Price, Montreal

Paul Stastny (above) of the Colorado Avalanche was the NHL's first star of the week for the first week of the 2007-08 season. Stastny had a hat trick on October 3 and a goal and four assists on October 7 to finish the week with eight points in three games. Calgary's Kristian Huselius (right) had nine points (four goals, five assists) in four games to earn second star honors for the week ending January 6. Cristobal Huet (far right) posted a 3-0-0 record with a 1.00 goals-against average and a .955 save percentage as the Capitals rallied to win the Southwest Division during the final week of the NHL season.

NATIONAL HOCKEY LEAGUE INDIVIDUAL AWARD WINNERS

ART ROSS TROPHY

	Winner	Runner-up
2008	Alex Ovechkin, Wsh.	Evgeni Malkin, Pit.
2007	Sidney Crosby, Pit.	Joe Thornton, S.J.
2006	Joe Thornton, Bos., S.J.	Jaromir Jagr, NYR
2005	....	....
2004	Martin St. Louis, T.B.	Ilya Kovalchuk, Atl.
2003	Peter Forsberg, Col.	Markus Naslund, Van.
2002	Jarome Iginla, Cgy.	Markus Naslund, Van.
2001	Jaromir Jagr, Pit.	Joe Sakic, Col.
2000	Jaromir Jagr, Pit.	Pavel Bure, Fla.
1999	Jaromir Jagr, Pit.	Teemu Selanne, Ana.
1998	Jaromir Jagr, Pit.	Peter Forsberg, Col.
1997	Mario Lemieux, Pit.	Teemu Selanne, Ana.
1996	Mario Lemieux, Pit.	Jaromir Jagr, Pit.
1995	Jaromir Jagr, Pit.	Eric Lindros, Phi.
1994	Wayne Gretzky, L.A.	Sergei Fedorov, Det.
1993	Mario Lemieux, Pit.	Pat LaFontaine, Buf.
1992	Mario Lemieux, Pit.	Kevin Stevens, Pit.
1991	Wayne Gretzky, L.A.	Brett Hull, St.L.
1990	Wayne Gretzky, L.A.	Mark Messier, Edm.
1989	Mario Lemieux, Pit.	Wayne Gretzky, L.A.
1988	Mario Lemieux, Pit.	Wayne Gretzky, Edm.
1987	Wayne Gretzky, Edm.	Jari Kurri, Edm.
1986	Wayne Gretzky, Edm.	Mario Lemieux, Pit.
1985	Wayne Gretzky, Edm.	Jari Kurri, Edm.
1984	Wayne Gretzky, Edm.	Paul Coffey, Edm.
1983	Wayne Gretzky, Edm.	Peter Stastny, Que.
1982	Wayne Gretzky, Edm.	Mike Bossy, NYI
1981	Wayne Gretzky, Edm.	Marcel Dionne, L.A.
1980	Marcel Dionne, L.A.	Wayne Gretzky, Edm.
1979	Bryan Trottier, NYI	Marcel Dionne, L.A.
1978	Guy Lafleur, Mtl.	Bryan Trottier, NYI
1977	Guy Lafleur, Mtl.	Marcel Dionne, L.A.
1976	Guy Lafleur, Mtl.	Bobby Clarke, Phi.
1975	Bobby Orr, Bos.	Phil Esposito, Bos.
1974	Phil Esposito, Bos.	Bobby Orr, Bos.
1973	Phil Esposito, Bos.	Bobby Clarke, Phi.
1972	Phil Esposito, Bos.	Bobby Orr, Bos.
1971	Phil Esposito, Bos.	Bobby Orr, Bos.
1970	Bobby Orr, Bos.	Phil Esposito, Bos.
1969	Phil Esposito, Bos.	Bobby Hull, Chi.
1968	Stan Mikita, Chi.	Phil Esposito, Bos.
1967	Stan Mikita, Chi.	Bobby Hull, Chi.
1966	Bobby Hull, Chi.	Stan Mikita, Chi.
1965	Stan Mikita, Chi.	Norm Ullman, Det.
1964	Stan Mikita, Chi.	Bobby Hull, Chi.
1963	Gordie Howe, Det.	Andy Bathgate, NYR
1962	Bobby Hull, Chi.	Andy Bathgate, NYR
1961	Bernie Geoffrion, Mtl.	Jean Beliveau, Mtl.
1960	Bobby Hull, Chi.	Bronco Horvath, Bos.
1959	Dickie Moore, Mtl.	Jean Beliveau, Mtl.
1958	Dickie Moore, Mtl.	Henri Richard, Mtl.
1957	Gordie Howe, Det.	Ted Lindsay, Det.
1956	Jean Beliveau, Mtl.	Gordie Howe, Det.
1955	Bernie Geoffrion, Mtl.	Maurice Richard, Mtl.
1954	Gordie Howe, Det.	Maurice Richard, Mtl.
1953	Gordie Howe, Det.	Ted Lindsay, Det.
1952	Gordie Howe, Det.	Ted Lindsay, Det.
1951	Gordie Howe, Det.	Maurice Richard, Mtl.
1950	Ted Lindsay, Det.	Sid Abel, Det.
1949	Roy Conacher, Chi.	Doug Bentley, Chi.
1948*	Elmer Lach, Mtl.	Buddy O'Connor, NYR
1947	Max Bentley, Chi.	Maurice Richard, Mtl.
1946	Max Bentley, Chi.	Gaye Stewart, Tor.
1945	Elmer Lach, Mtl.	Maurice Richard, Mtl.
1944	Herb Cain, Bos.	Doug Bentley, Chi.
1943	Doug Bentley, Chi.	Bill Cowley, Bos.
1942	Bryan Hextall, NYR	Lynn Patrick, NYR
1941	Bill Cowley, Bos.	Bryan Hextall, NYR
1940	Milt Schmidt, Bos.	Woody Dumart, Bos.
1939	Toe Blake, Mtl.	Sweeney Schriner, NYA
1938	Gordie Drillon, Tor.	Syl Apps, Tor.
1937	Sweeney Schriner, NYA	Syl Apps, Tor.
1936	Sweeney Schriner, NYA	Marty Barry, Det.
1935	Charlie Conacher, Tor.	Syd Howe, St.L., Det.
1934	Charlie Conacher, Tor.	Joe Primeau, Tor
1933	Bill Cook, NYR	Busher Jackson, Tor.
1932	Busher Jackson, Tor.	Joe Primeau, Tor.
1931	Howie Morenz, Mtl.	Ebbie Goodfellow, Det.
1930	Cooney Weiland, Bos.	Frank Boucher, NYR
1929	Ace Bailey, Tor.	Nels Stewart, Mtl.M
1928	Howie Morenz, Mtl.	Aurel Joliat, Mtl.
1927	Bill Cook, NYR	Dick Irvin, Chi.
1926	Nels Stewart, Mtl.M.	Cy Denneny, Ott.
1925	Babe Dye, Tor.	Cy Denneny, Ott.
1924	Cy Denneny, Ott.	Billy Boucher, Mtl.
1923	Babe Dye, Tor.	Cy Denneny, Ott.
1922	Punch Broadbent, Ott.	Cy Denneny, Ott.
1921	Newsy Lalonde, Mtl.	Babe Dye, Ham., Tor.
1920	Joe Malone, Que.	Newsy Lalonde, Mtl.
1919	Newsy Lalonde, Mtl.	Odie Cleghorn, Mtl.
1918	Joe Malone, Mtl.	Cy Denneny, Ott.

* Trophy first awarded in 1948.
Scoring leaders listed from 1918 to 1947.

HART MEMORIAL TROPHY

	Winner	Runner-up
2008	Alex Ovechkin, Wsh.	Evgeni Malkin, Pit.
2007	Sidney Crosby, Pit.	Roberto Luongo, Van.
2006	Joe Thornton, Bos., S.J.	Jaromir Jagr, NYR
2005	....	....
2004	Martin St. Louis, T.B.	Jarome Iginla, Cgy.
2003	Peter Forsberg, Col.	Markus Naslund, Van.
2002	Jose Theodore, Mtl.	Jarome Iginla, Cgy.
2001	Joe Sakic, Col.	Mario Lemieux, Pit.
2000	Chris Pronger, St.L.	Jaromir Jagr, Pit.
1999	Jaromir Jagr, Pit.	Alexei Yashin, Ott.
1998	Dominik Hasek, Buf.	Jaromir Jagr, Pit.
1997	Dominik Hasek, Buf.	Paul Kariya, Ana.
1996	Mario Lemieux, Pit.	Mark Messier, NYR
1995	Eric Lindros, Phi.	Jaromir Jagr, Pit.
1994	Sergei Fedorov, Det.	Dominik Hasek, Buf.
1993	Mario Lemieux, Pit.	Doug Gilmour, Tor.
1992	Mark Messier, NYR	Patrick Roy, Mtl.
1991	Brett Hull, St.L.	Wayne Gretzky, L.A.
1990	Mark Messier, Edm.	Raymond Bourque, Bos.
1989	Wayne Gretzky, L.A.	Mario Lemieux, Pit.
1988	Mario Lemieux, Pit.	Grant Fuhr, Edm.
1987	Wayne Gretzky, Edm.	Raymond Bourque, Bos.
1986	Wayne Gretzky, Edm.	Mario Lemieux, Pit.
1985	Wayne Gretzky, Edm.	Dale Hawerchuk, Wpg.
1984	Wayne Gretzky, Edm.	Rod Langway, Wsh.
1983	Wayne Gretzky, Edm.	Pete Peeters, Bos.
1982	Wayne Gretzky, Edm.	Bryan Trottier, NYI
1981	Wayne Gretzky, Edm.	Mike Liut, St.L.
1980	Wayne Gretzky, Edm.	Marcel Dionne, L.A.
1979	Bryan Trottier, NYI	Guy Lafleur, Mtl
1978	Guy Lafleur, Mtl.	Bryan Trottier, NYI
1977	Guy Lafleur, Mtl.	Bobby Clarke, Phi.
1976	Bobby Clarke, Phi.	Denis Potvin, NYI
1975	Bobby Clarke, Phi.	Rogie Vachon, L.A.
1974	Phil Esposito, Bos.	Bernie Parent, Phi.
1973	Bobby Clarke, Phi.	Phil Esposito, Bos.
1972	Bobby Orr, Bos.	Ken Dryden, Mtl.
1971	Bobby Orr, Bos.	Phil Esposito, Bos.
1970	Bobby Orr, Bos.	Tony Esposito, Chi.
1969	Phil Esposito, Bos.	Jean Beliveau, Mtl.
1968	Stan Mikita, Chi.	Jean Beliveau, Mtl.
1967	Stan Mikita, Chi.	Ed Giacomin, NYR
1966	Bobby Hull, Chi.	Jean Beliveau, Mtl.
1965	Bobby Hull, Chi.	Norm Ullman, Det.
1964	Jean Beliveau, Mtl.	Bobby Hull, Chi.
1963	Gordie Howe, Det.	Stan Mikita, Chi.
1962	Jacques Plante, Mtl.	Doug Harvey, NYR
1961	Bernie Geoffrion, Mtl.	Johnny Bower, Tor.
1960	Gordie Howe, Det.	Bobby Hull, Chi.
1959	Andy Bathgate, NYR	Gordie Howe, Det.
1958	Gordie Howe, Det.	Andy Bathgate, NYR
1957	Gordie Howe, Det.	Jean Beliveau, Mtl.
1956	Jean Beliveau, Mtl.	Tod Sloan, Tor.
1955	Ted Kennedy, Tor.	Harry Lumley, Tor.
1954	Al Rollins, Chi.	Red Kelly, Det.
1953	Gordie Howe, Det.	Al Rollins, Chi.
1952	Gordie Howe, Det.	Elmer Lach, Mtl.
1951	Milt Schmidt, Bos.	Maurice Richard, Mtl.
1950	Chuck Rayner, NYR	Ted Kennedy, Tor.
1949	Sid Abel, Det.	Bill Durnan, Mtl.
1948	Buddy O'Connor, NYR	Frank Brimsek, Bos.
1947	Maurice Richard, Mtl.	Milt Schmidt, Bos.
1946	Max Bentley, Chi.	Gaye Stewart, Tor.
1945	Elmer Lach, Mtl.	Maurice Richard, Mtl.
1944	Babe Pratt, Tor.	Bill Cowley, Bos.
1943	Bill Cowley, Bos.	Doug Bentley, Chi.
1942	Tom Anderson, Bro.	Syl Apps, Tor.
1941	Bill Cowley, Bos.	Dit Clapper, Bos.
1940	Ebbie Goodfellow, Det.	Syl Apps, Tor.
1939	Toe Blake, Mtl.	Syl Apps, Tor.
1938	Eddie Shore, Bos.	Paul Thompson, Chi.
1937	Babe Siebert, Mtl.	Lionel Conacher, Mtl.M
1936	Eddie Shore, Bos.	Hooley Smith, Mtl.M
1935	Eddie Shore, Bos.	Charlie Conacher, Tor.
1934	Aurel Joliat, Mtl.	Lionel Conacher, Chi.
1933	Eddie Shore, Bos.	Bill Cook, NYR
1932	Howie Morenz, Mtl.	Ching Johnson, NYR
1931	Howie Morenz, Mtl.	Eddie Shore, Bos.
1930	Nels Stewart, Mtl.M.	Lionel Hitchman, Bos.
1929	Roy Worters, NYA	Ace Bailey, Tor.
1928	Howie Morenz, Mtl.	Roy Worters, Pit.
1927	Herb Gardiner, Mtl.	Bill Cook, NYR
1926	Nels Stewart, Mtl.M.	Sprague Cleghorn, Bos.
1925	Billy Burch, Ham.	Howie Morenz, Mtl.
1924	Frank Nighbor, Ott.	Sprague Cleghorn, Mtl.

MAURICE "ROCKET" RICHARD TROPHY

2008	Alex Ovechkin	Washington
2007	Vincent Lecavalier	Tampa Bay
2006	Jonathan Cheechoo	San Jose
2005	....	....
2004	Rick Nash	Columbus
	Jarome Iginla	Calgary
	Ilya Kovalchuk	Atlanta
2003	Milan Hejduk	Colorado
2002	Jarome Iginla	Calgary
2001	Pavel Bure	Florida
2000	Pavel Bure	Florida
1999	Teemu Selanne	Anaheim

WILLIAM M. JENNINGS TROPHY

	Winner	Runner-up
2008	Chris Osgood, Det.	Jean-Sebastien Giguere, Ana.
	Dominik Hasek, Det.	
2007	Niklas Backstrom, Min.	Dominik Hasek, Det.
		Manny Fernandez, Min.
2006	Miikka Kiprusoff, Cgy.	Manny Legace, Det.
		Chris Osgood, Det.
2005	....	....
2004	Martin Brodeur, N.J.	Marty Turco, Dal.
2003	Martin Brodeur, N.J.	Marty Turco, Dal.
	Roman Cechmanek, Phi.	Ron Tugnutt, Dal.
	Robert Esche, Phi.	
2002	Patrick Roy, Col.	Tommy Salo, Edm.
2001	Dominik Hasek, Buf.	Ed Belfour, Dal.
		Marty Turco, Dal.
2000	Roman Turek, St.L.	John Vanbiesbrouck, Phi.
		Brian Boucher, Phi.
1999	Ed Belfour, Dal.	Dominik Hasek, Buf.
	Roman Turek, Dal.	
1998	Martin Brodeur, N.J.	Ed Belfour, Dal.
1997	Martin Brodeur, N.J.	Chris Osgood, Det.
	Mike Dunham, N.J.	Mike Vernon, Det.
1996	Chris Osgood, Det.	Martin Brodeur, N.J.
	Mike Vernon, Det.	
1995	Ed Belfour, Chi.	Mike Vernon, Det.
		Chris Osgood, Det.
1994	Dominik Hasek, Buf.	Martin Brodeur, N.J.
	Grant Fuhr, Buf.	Chris Terreri, N.J.
1993	Ed Belfour, Chi.	Felix Potvin, Tor.
		Grant Fuhr, Tor.
1992	Patrick Roy, Mtl.	Ed Belfour, Chi.
1991	Ed Belfour, Chi.	Patrick Roy, Mtl.
1990	Andy Moog, Bos.	Patrick Roy, Mtl.
	Reggie Lemelin, Bos.	Brian Hayward, Mtl.
1989	Patrick Roy, Mtl.	Mike Vernon, Cgy.
	Brian Hayward, Mtl.	Rick Wamsley, Cgy.
1988	Patrick Roy, Mtl.	Clint Malarchuk, Wsh.
	Brian Hayward, Mtl.	Pete Peeters, Wsh.
1987	Patrick Roy, Mtl.	Ron Hextall, Phi.
	Brian Hayward, Mtl.	
1986	Bob Froese, Phi.	Al Jensen, Wsh.
	Darren Jensen, Phi.	Pete Peeters, Wsh.
1985	Tom Barrasso, Buf.	Pat Riggin, Wsh.
	Bob Sauve, Buf.	
1984	Al Jensen, Wsh.	Tom Barrasso, Buf.
	Pat Riggin, Wsh.	Bob Sauve, Buf.
1983	Roland Melanson, NYI	Pete Peeters, Bos.
	Billy Smith, NYI	
1982	Rick Wamsley, Mtl.	Billy Smith, NYI
	Denis Herron, Mtl.	Roland Melanson, NYI

BILL MASTERTON MEMORIAL TROPHY

2008	Jason Blake	Toronto
2007	Phil Kessel	Boston
2006	Teemu Selanne	Anaheim
2005	....	....
2004	Bryan Berard	Chicago
2003	Steve Yzerman	Detroit
2002	Saku Koivu	Montreal
2001	Adam Graves	NY Rangers
2000	Ken Daneyko	New Jersey
1999	John Cullen	Tampa Bay
1998	Jamie McLennan	St. Louis
1997	Tony Granato	San Jose
1996	Gary Roberts	Calgary
1995	Pat LaFontaine	Buffalo
1994	Cam Neely	Boston
1993	Mario Lemieux	Pittsburgh
1992	Mark Fitzpatrick	NY Islanders
1991	Dave Taylor	Los Angeles
1990	Gord Kluzak	Boston
1989	Tim Kerr	Philadelphia
1988	Bob Bourne	Los Angeles
1987	Doug Jarvis	Hartford
1986	Charlie Simmer	Boston
1985	Anders Hedberg	NY Rangers
1984	Brad Park	Detroit
1983	Lanny McDonald	Calgary
1982	Glenn Resch	Colorado
1981	Blake Dunlop	St. Louis
1980	Al MacAdam	Minnesota
1979	Serge Savard	Montreal
1978	Butch Goring	Los Angeles
1977	Ed Westfall	NY Islanders
1976	Rod Gilbert	NY Rangers
1975	Don Luce	Buffalo
1974	Henri Richard	Montreal
1973	Lowell MacDonald	Pittsburgh
1972	Bobby Clarke	Philadelphia
1971	Jean Ratelle	NY Rangers
1970	Pit Martin	Chicago
1969	Ted Hampson	Oakland
1968	Claude Provost	Montreal

LADY BYNG MEMORIAL TROPHY

	Winner	Runner-up
2008	Pavel Datsyuk, Det.	Martin St. Louis, T.B.
2007	Pavel Datsyuk, Det.	Martin St. Louis, T.B.
2006	Pavel Datsyuk, Det.	Brad Richards, T.B.
2005	....	....
2004	Brad Richards, T.B.	Daniel Alfredsson, Ott.
2003	Alexander Mogilny, Tor.	Nicklas Lidstrom, Det.
2002	Ron Francis, Car.	Joe Sakic, Col.
2001	Joe Sakic, Col.	Nicklas Lidstrom, Det.
2000	Pavol Demitra, St.L.	Nicklas Lidstrom, Det.
1999	Wayne Gretzky, NYR.	Nicklas Lidstrom, Det.
1998	Ron Francis, Pit.	Teemu Selanne, Ana.
1997	Paul Kariya, Ana.	Teemu Selanne, Ana.
1996	Paul Kariya, Ana.	Adam Oates, Bos.
1995	Ron Francis, Pit.	Adam Oates, Bos.
1994	Wayne Gretzky, L.A.	Adam Oates, Bos.
1993	Pierre Turgeon, NYI	Adam Oates, Bos.
1992	Wayne Gretzky, L.A.	Joe Sakic, Que.
1991	Wayne Gretzky, L.A.	Brett Hull, St.L.
1990	Brett Hull, St.L.	Wayne Gretzky, L.A.
1989	Joe Mullen, Cgy.	Wayne Gretzky, L.A.
1988	Mats Naslund, Mtl.	Wayne Gretzky, Edm.
1987	Joe Mullen, Cgy.	Wayne Gretzky, Edm.
1986	Mike Bossy, NYI	Jari Kurri, Edm.
1985	Jari Kurri, Edm.	Joe Mullen, St.L.
1984	Mike Bossy, NYI	Rick Middleton, Bos.
1983	Mike Bossy, NYI	Rick Middleton, Bos.
1982	Rick Middleton, Bos.	Mike Bossy, NYI
1981	Rick Kehoe, Pit.	Wayne Gretzky, Edm.
1980	Wayne Gretzky, Edm.	Marcel Dionne, L.A.
1979	Bob MacMillan, Atl.	Marcel Dionne, L.A.
1978	Butch Goring, L.A.	Peter McNab, Bos.
1977	Marcel Dionne, L.A.	Jean Ratelle, Bos.
1976	Jean Ratelle, NYR-Bos.	Jean Pronovost, Pit.
1975	Marcel Dionne, Det.	John Bucyk, Bos.
1974	John Bucyk, Bos.	Lowell MacDonald, Pit.
1973	Gilbert Perreault, Buf.	Jean Ratelle, NYR
1972	Jean Ratelle, NYR	John Bucyk, Bos.
1971	John Bucyk, Bos.	Dave Keon, Tor.
1970	Phil Goyette, St.L.	John Bucyk, Bos.
1969	Alex Delvecchio, Det.	Ted Hampson, Oak.
1968	Stan Mikita, Chi.	John Bucyk, Bos.
1967	Stan Mikita, Chi.	Dave Keon, Tor.
1966	Alex Delvecchio, Det.	Bobby Rousseau, Mtl.
1965	Bobby Hull, Chi.	Alex Delvecchio, Det.
1964	Kenny Wharram, Chi.	Dave Keon, Tor.
1963	Dave Keon, Tor.	Camille Henry, NYR
1962	Dave Keon, Tor.	Claude Provost, Mtl.
1961	Red Kelly, Tor.	Norm Ullman, Det.
1960	Don McKenney, Bos.	Andy Hebenton, NYR
1959	Alex Delvecchio, Det.	Andy Hebenton, NYR
1958	Camille Henry, NYR	Don Marshall, Mtl.
1957	Andy Hebenton, NYR	Dutch Reibel, Det.
1956	Dutch Reibel, Det.	Floyd Curry, Mtl.
1955	Sid Smith, Tor.	Danny Lewicki, NYR
1954	Red Kelly, Det.	Don Raleigh, NYR
1953	Red Kelly, Det.	Wally Hergesheimer, NYR
1952	Sid Smith, Tor.	Red Kelly, Det.
1951	Red Kelly, Det.	Woody Dumart, Bos.
1950	Edgar Laprade, NYR	Red Kelly, Det.
1949	Bill Quackenbush, Det.	Harry Watson, Tor.
1948	Buddy O'Connor, NYR	Syl Apps, Tor.
1947	Bobby Bauer, Bos.	Syl Apps, Tor.
1946	Toe Blake, Mtl.	Clint Smith, Chi.
1945	Bill Mosienko, Chi.	Syd Howe, Det.
1944	Clint Smith, Chi.	Herb Cain, Bos.
1943	Max Bentley, Chi.	Buddy O'Connor, Mtl.
1942	Syl Apps, Tor.	Gordie Drillon, Tor.
1941	Bobby Bauer, Bos.	Gordie Drillon, Tor.
1940	Bobby Bauer, Bos.	Clint Smith, NYR
1939	Clint Smith, NYR	Marty Barry, Det.
1938	Gordie Drillon, Tor.	Clint Smith, NYR
1937	Marty Barry, Det.	Gordie Drillon, Tor.
1936	Doc Romnes, Chi.	Sweeney Schriner, NYA
1935	Frank Boucher, NYR	Russ Blinco, Mtl.M
1934	Frank Boucher, NYR	Joe Primeau, Tor.
1933	Frank Boucher, NYR	Joe Primeau, Tor.
1932	Joe Primeau, Tor.	Frank Boucher, NYR
1931	Frank Boucher, NYR	Normie Himes, NYA
1930	Frank Boucher, NYR	Normie Himes, NYA
1929	Frank Boucher, NYR	Harold Darragh, Pit.
1928	Frank Boucher, NYR	George Hay, Det.
1927	Billy Burch, NYA	Dick Irvin, Chi.
1926	Frank Nighbor, Ott.	Billy Burch, NYA
1925	Frank Nighbor, Ott.	none

KING CLANCY MEMORIAL TROPHY

2008	Vincent Lecavalier	Tampa Bay
2007	Saku Koivu	Montreal
2006	Olaf Kolzig	Washington
2005	....	....
2004	Jarome Iginla	Calgary
2003	Brendan Shanahan	Detroit
2002	Ron Francis	Carolina
2001	Shjon Podein	Colorado
2000	Curtis Joseph	Toronto
1999	Rob Ray	Buffalo
1998	Kelly Chase	St. Louis
1997	Trevor Linden	Vancouver
1996	Kris King	Winnipeg
1995	Joe Nieuwendyk	Calgary
1994	Adam Graves	NY Rangers
1993	Dave Poulin	Boston
1992	Raymond Bourque	Boston
1991	Dave Taylor	Los Angeles
1990	Kevin Lowe	Edmonton
1989	Bryan Trottier	NY Islanders
1988	Lanny McDonald	Calgary

VEZINA TROPHY

	Winner	Runner-up
2008	Martin Brodeur, N.J.	Evgeni Nabokov, S.J.
2007	Martin Brodeur, N.J.	Roberto Luongo, Van.
2006	Miikka Kiprusoff, Cgy.	Martin Brodeur, N.J.
2005	....	....
2004	Martin Brodeur, N.J.	Miikka Kiprusoff, Cgy.
2003	Martin Brodeur, N.J.	Marty Turco, Dal.
2002	Jose Theodore, Mtl.	Patrick Roy, Col.
2001	Dominik Hasek, Buf.	Roman Cechmanek, Phi.
2000	Olaf Kolzig, Wsh.	Roman Turek, St.L.
1999	Dominik Hasek, Buf.	Curtis Joseph, Tor.
1998	Dominik Hasek, Buf.	Martin Brodeur, N.J.
1997	Dominik Hasek, Buf.	Martin Brodeur, N.J.
1996	Jim Carey, Wsh.	Chris Osgood, Det.
1995	Dominik Hasek, Buf.	Ed Belfour, Chi.
1994	Dominik Hasek, Buf.	John Vanbiesbrouck, Fla.
1993	Ed Belfour, Chi.	Tom Barrasso, Pit.
1992	Patrick Roy, Mtl.	Kirk McLean, Van.
1991	Ed Belfour, Chi.	Patrick Roy, Mtl.
1990	Patrick Roy, Mtl.	Daren Puppa, Buf.
1989	Patrick Roy, Mtl.	Mike Vernon, Cgy.
1988	Grant Fuhr, Edm.	Tom Barrasso, Buf.
1987	Ron Hextall, Phi.	Mike Liut, Hfd.
1986	John Vanbiesbrouck, NYR	Bob Froese, Phi.
1985	Pelle Lindbergh, Phi.	Tom Barrasso, Buf.
1984	Tom Barrasso, Buf.	Reggie Lemelin, Cgy.
1983	Pete Peeters, Bos.	Roland Melanson, NYI
1982	Billy Smith, NYI	Grant Fuhr, Edm.
1981	Richard Sevigny, Mtl.	Pete Peeters, Phi.
	Denis Herron, Mtl.	Rick St. Croix, Phi.
	Michel Larocque, Mtl.	
1980	Bob Sauve, Buf.	Gerry Cheevers, Bos.
	Don Edwards, Buf.	Gilles Gilbert, Bos.
1979	Ken Dryden, Mtl.	Glenn Resch, NYI
	Michel Larocque, Mtl.	Billy Smith, NYI
1978	Ken Dryden, Mtl.	Bernie Parent, Phi.
	Michel Larocque, Mtl.	Wayne Stephenson, Phi.
1977	Ken Dryden, Mtl.	Glenn Resch, NYI
	Michel Larocque, Mtl.	Billy Smith, NYI
1976	Ken Dryden, Mtl.	Glenn Resch, NYI
		Billy Smith, NYI
1975	Bernie Parent, Phi.	Rogie Vachon, L.A.
		Gary Edwards, L.A.
1974	Bernie Parent, Phi. (tie)	Gilles Gilbert, Bos.
	Tony Esposito, Chi. (tie)	
1973	Ken Dryden, Mtl.	Ed Giacomin, NYR
		Gilles Villemure, NYR
1972	Tony Esposito, Chi.	Cesare Maniago, Min.
	Gary Smith, Chi.	Gump Worsley, Min.
1971	Ed Giacomin, NYR	Tony Esposito, Chi.
	Gilles Villemure, NYR	
1970	Tony Esposito, Chi.	Jacques Plante, St.L.
		Ernie Wakely, St.L.
1969	Jacques Plante, St.L.	Ed Giacomin, NYR
	Glenn Hall, St.L.	
1968	Gump Worsley, Mtl.	Johnny Bower, Tor.
	Rogie Vachon, Mtl.	Bruce Gamble, Tor.
1967	Glenn Hall, Chi.	Charlie Hodge, Mtl.
	Denis DeJordy, Chi.	
1966	Gump Worsley, Mtl.	Glenn Hall, Chi.
	Charlie Hodge, Mtl.	
1965	Terry Sawchuk, Tor.	Roger Crozier, Det.
	Johnny Bower, Tor.	
1964	Charlie Hodge, Mtl.	Glenn Hall, Chi.
1963	Glenn Hall, Chi.	Johnny Bower, Tor.
		Don Simmons, Tor.
1962	Jacques Plante, Mtl.	Johnny Bower, Tor.
1961	Johnny Bower, Tor.	Glenn Hall, Chi.
1960	Jacques Plante, Mtl.	Glenn Hall, Chi.
1959	Jacques Plante, Mtl.	Johnny Bower, Tor.
		Ed Chadwick, Tor.
1958	Jacques Plante, Mtl.	Gump Worsley, NYR
		Marcel Paille, NYR
1957	Jacques Plante, Mtl.	Glenn Hall, Det.
1956	Jacques Plante, Mtl.	Glenn Hall, Det.
1955	Terry Sawchuk, Det.	Harry Lumley, Tor.
1954	Harry Lumley, Tor.	Terry Sawchuk, Det.
1953	Terry Sawchuk, Det.	Gerry McNeil, Mtl.
1952	Terry Sawchuk, Det.	Al Rollins, Tor.
1951	Al Rollins, Tor.	Terry Sawchuk, Det.
1950	Bill Durnan, Mtl.	Harry Lumley, Det.
1949	Bill Durnan, Mtl.	Harry Lumley, Det.
1948	Turk Broda, Tor.	Harry Lumley, Det.
1947	Bill Durnan, Mtl.	Turk Broda, Tor.
1946	Bill Durnan, Mtl.	Frank Brimsek, Bos.
1945	Bill Durnan, Mtl.	Frank McCool, Tor. (tie)
		Harry Lumley, Det. (tie)
1944	Bill Durnan, Mtl.	Paul Bibeault, Tor.
1943	Johnny Mowers, Det.	Turk Broda, Tor.
1942	Frank Brimsek, Bos.	Turk Broda, Tor.
1941	Turk Broda, Tor.	Frank Brimsek, Bos. (tie)
		Johnny Mowers, Det. (tie)
1940	Dave Kerr, NYR	Frank Brimsek, Bos.
1939	Frank Brimsek, Bos.	Dave Kerr, NYR
1938	Tiny Thompson, Bos.	Dave Kerr, NYR
1937	Normie Smith, Det.	Dave Kerr, NYR
1936	Tiny Thompson, Bos.	Mike Karakas, Chi.
1935	Lorne Chabot, Chi.	Alex Connell, Mtl.M
1934	Charlie Gardiner, Chi.	Wilf Cude, Det.
1933	Tiny Thompson, Bos.	John Ross Roach, Det.
1932	Charlie Gardiner, Chi.	Alex Connell, Det.
1931	Roy Worters, NYA	Charlie Gardiner, Chi.
1930	Tiny Thompson, Bos.	Charlie Gardiner, Chi.
1929	George Hainsworth, Mtl.	Tiny Thompson, Bos.
1928	George Hainsworth, Mtl.	Alex Connell, Ott.
1927	George Hainsworth, Mtl.	Clint Benedict, Mtl.M

CALDER MEMORIAL TROPHY

	Winner	Runner-up
2008	Patrick Kane, Chi.	Nicklas Backstrom, Wsh.
2007	Evgeni Malkin, Pit.	Paul Stastny, Col.
2006	Alex Ovechkin, Wsh.	Sidney Crosby, Pit.
2005	....	....
2004	Andrew Raycroft, Bos.	Michael Ryder, Mtl.
2003	Barret Jackman, St.L.	Henrik Zetterberg, Det.
2002	Dany Heatley, Atl.	Ilya Kovalchuk, Atl.
2001	Evgeni Nabokov, S.J.	Brad Richards, T.B.
2000	Scott Gomez, N.J.	Brad Stuart, S.J.
1999	Chris Drury, Col.	Marian Hossa, Ott.
1998	Sergei Samsonov, Bos.	Mattias Ohlund, Van.
1997	Bryan Berard, NYI	Jarome Iginla, Cgy.
1996	Daniel Alfredsson, Ott.	Eric Daze, Chi.
1995	Peter Forsberg, Que.	Jim Carey, Wsh.
1994	Martin Brodeur, N.J.	Jason Arnott, Edm.
1993	Teemu Selanne, Wpg.	Joe Juneau, Bos.
1992	Pavel Bure, Van.	Nicklas Lidstrom, Det
1991	Ed Belfour, Chi.	Sergei Fedorov, Det.
1990	Sergei Makarov, Cgy.	Mike Modano, Min.
1989	Brian Leetch, NYR	Trevor Linden, Van.
1988	Joe Nieuwendyk, Cgy.	Ray Sheppard, Buf.
1987	Luc Robitaille, L.A.	Ron Hextall, Phi.
1986	Gary Suter, Cgy.	Wendel Clark, Tor.
1985	Mario Lemieux, Pit.	Chris Chelios, Mtl.
1984	Tom Barrasso, Buf.	Steve Yzerman, Det.
1983	Steve Larmer, Chi.	Phil Housley, Buf.
1982	Dale Hawerchuk, Wpg.	Barry Pederson, Bos.
1981	Peter Stastny, Que.	Larry Murphy, L.A.
1980	Raymond Bourque, Bos.	Mike Foligno, Det.
1979	Bobby Smith, Min	Ryan Walter, Wsh.
1978	Mike Bossy, NYI	Barry Beck, Col.
1977	Willi Plett, Atl.	Don Murdoch, NYR
1976	Bryan Trottier, NYI	Glenn Resch, NYI
1975	Eric Vail, Atl.	Pierre Larouche, Pit.
1974	Denis Potvin, NYI	Tom Lysiak, Atl.
1973	Steve Vickers, NYR	Bill Barber, Phi.
1972	Ken Dryden, Mtl.	Rick Martin, Buf.
1971	Gilbert Perreault, Buf.	Jude Drouin, Min.
1970	Tony Esposito, Chi.	Bill Fairbairn, NYR
1969	Danny Grant, Min.	Norm Ferguson, Oak.
1968	Derek Sanderson, Bos.	Jacques Lemaire, Mtl.
1967	Bobby Orr, Bos.	Ed Van Impe, Chi.
1966	Brit Selby, Tor.	Bert Marshall, Det.
1965	Roger Crozier, Det.	Ron Ellis, Tor.
1964	Jacques Laperriere, Mtl.	John Ferguson, Mtl.
1963	Kent Douglas, Tor.	Doug Barkley, Det.
1962	Bobby Rousseau, Mtl.	Cliff Pennington, Bos.
1961	Dave Keon, Tor.	Bob Nevin, Tor.
1960	Bill Hay, Chi.	Murray Oliver, Det.
1959	Ralph Backstrom, Mtl.	Carl Brewer, Tor.
1958	Frank Mahovlich, Tor.	Bobby Hull, Chi.
1957	Larry Regan, Bos.	Ed Chadwick, Tor.
1956	Glenn Hall, Det.	Andy Hebenton, NYR
1955	Ed Litzenberger, Chi.	Don McKenney, Bos.
1954	Camille Henry, NYR	Dutch Reibel, Det.
1953	Gump Worsley, NYR	Gord Hannigan, Tor.
1952	Bernie Geoffrion, Mtl.	Hy Buller, NYR
1951	Terry Sawchuk, Det.	Al Rollins, Tor.
1950	Jack Gelineau, Bos.	Phil Maloney, Bos.
1949	Pentti Lund, NYR	Allan Stanley, NYR
1948	Jim McFadden, Det.	Pete Babando, Bos.
1947	Howie Meeker, Tor.	Jim Conacher, Det.
1946	Edgar Laprade, NYR	George Gee, Chi.
1945	Frank McCool, Tor.	Ken Smith, Bos.
1944	Gus Bodnar, Tor.	Bill Durnan, Mtl.
1943	Gaye Stewart, Tor.	Glen Harmon, Mtl.
1942	Grant Warwick, NYR	Buddy O'Connor, Mtl.
1941	John Quilty, Mtl.	Johnny Mowers, Det.
1940	Kilby MacDonald, NYR	Wally Stanowski, Tor.
1939	Frank Brimsek, Bos.	Roy Conacher, Bos.
1938	Cully Dahlstrom, Chi.	Murph Chamberlain, Tor.
1937	Syl Apps, Tor.	Gordie Drillon, Tor.
1936	Mike Karakas, Chi.	Bucko McDonald, Det.
1935	Sweeney Schriner, NYA	Bert Connelly, NYR
1934	Russ Blinco, Mtl.M.	none
1933	Carl Voss, Det.	none

FRANK J. SELKE TROPHY

	Winner	Runner-up
2008	Pavel Datsyuk, Det.	John Madden, N.J.
2007	Rod Brind'Amour, Car.	Samuel Pahlsson, Ana.
2006	Rod Brind'Amour, Car.	Jere Lehtinen, Dal.
2005	....	....
2004	Kris Draper, Det.	John Madden, N.J.
2003	Jere Lehtinen, Dal.	John Madden, N.J.
2002	Michael Peca, NYI	Craig Conroy, Cgy.
2001	John Madden, N.J.	Joe Sakic, Col.
2000	Steve Yzerman, Det.	Michal Handzus, St.L.
1999	Jere Lehtinen, Dal.	Magnus Arvedson, Ott.
1998	Jere Lehtinen, Dal.	Michael Peca, Buf.
1997	Michael Peca, Buf.	Peter Forsberg, Col.
1996	Sergei Fedorov, Det.	Ron Francis, Pit.
1995	Ron Francis, Pit.	Esa Tikkanen, St.L.
1994	Sergei Fedorov, Det.	Doug Gilmour, Tor.
1993	Doug Gilmour, Tor.	Dave Poulin, Bos.
1992	Guy Carbonneau, Mtl.	Sergei Fedorov, Det.
1991	Dirk Graham, Chi.	Esa Tikkanen, Edm.
1990	Rick Meagher, St.L.	Guy Carbonneau, Mtl.
1989	Guy Carbonneau, Mtl.	Esa Tikkanen, Edm.
1988	Guy Carbonneau, Mtl.	Steve Kasper, Bos.
1987	Dave Poulin, Phi.	Guy Carbonneau, Mtl.
1986	Troy Murray, Chi.	Ron Sutter, Phi.
1985	Craig Ramsay, Buf.	Doug Jarvis, Wsh.
1984	Doug Jarvis, Wsh.	Bryan Trottier, NYI
1983	Bobby Clarke, Phi.	Jari Kurri, Edm.
1982	Steve Kasper, Bos.	Bob Gainey, Mtl.
1981	Bob Gainey, Mtl.	Craig Ramsay, Buf.
1980	Bob Gainey, Mtl.	Craig Ramsay, Buf.
1979	Bob Gainey, Mtl.	Don Marcotte, Bos.
1978	Bob Gainey, Mtl.	Craig Ramsay, Buf.

CONN SMYTHE TROPHY

2008	Henrik Zetterberg	Detroit
2007	Scott Niedermayer	Anaheim
2006	Cam Ward	Carolina
2005	....	
2004	Brad Richards	Tampa Bay
2003	Jean-Sebastien Giguere	Anaheim
2002	Nicklas Lidstrom	Detroit
2001	Patrick Roy	Colorado
2000	Scott Stevens	New Jersey
1999	Joe Nieuwendyk	Dallas
1998	Steve Yzerman	Detroit
1997	Mike Vernon	Detroit
1996	Joe Sakic	Colorado
1995	Claude Lemieux	New Jersey
1994	Brian Leetch	NY Rangers
1993	Patrick Roy	Montreal
1992	Mario Lemieux	Pittsburgh
1991	Mario Lemieux	Pittsburgh
1990	Bill Ranford	Edmonton
1989	Al MacInnis	Calgary
1988	Wayne Gretzky	Edmonton
1987	Ron Hextall	Philadelphia
1986	Patrick Roy	Montreal
1985	Wayne Gretzky	Edmonton
1984	Mark Messier	Edmonton
1983	Billy Smith	NY Islanders
1982	Mike Bossy	NY Islanders
1981	Butch Goring	NY Islanders
1980	Bryan Trottier	NY Islanders
1979	Bob Gainey	Montreal
1978	Larry Robinson	Montreal
1977	Guy Lafleur	Montreal
1976	Reggie Leach	Philadelphia
1975	Bernie Parent	Philadelphia
1974	Bernie Parent	Philadelphia
1973	Yvan Cournoyer	Montreal
1972	Bobby Orr	Boston
1971	Ken Dryden	Montreal
1970	Bobby Orr	Boston
1969	Serge Savard	Montreal
1968	Glenn Hall	St. Louis
1967	Dave Keon	Toronto
1966	Roger Crozier	Detroit

JAMES NORRIS MEMORIAL TROPHY

	Winner	Runner-up
2008	Nicklas Lidstrom, Det.	Dion Phaneuf, Cgy.
2007	Nicklas Lidstrom, Det.	Scott Niedermayer, Ana.
2006	Nicklas Lidstrom, Det.	Scott Niedermayer, Ana.
2005	....	....
2004	Scott Niedermayer, N.J.	Zdeno Chara, Ott.
2003	Nicklas Lidstrom, Det.	Al MacInnis, St.L.
2002	Nicklas Lidstrom, Det.	Chris Chelios, Det.
2001	Nicklas Lidstrom, Det.	Raymond Bourque, Col.
2000	Chris Pronger, St.L.	Nicklas Lidstrom, Det.
1999	Al MacInnis, St.L.	Nicklas Lidstrom, Det.
1998	Rob Blake, L.A.	Nicklas Lidstrom, Det.
1997	Brian Leetch, NYR	V. Konstantinov, Det.
1996	Chris Chelios, Chi.	Raymond Bourque, Bos.
1995	Paul Coffey, Det.	Chris Chelios, Chi.
1994	Raymond Bourque, Bos.	Scott Stevens, N.J.
1993	Chris Chelios, Chi.	Raymond Bourque, Bos.
1992	Brian Leetch, NYR	Raymond Bourque, Bos.
1991	Raymond Bourque, Bos.	Al MacInnis, Cgy.
1990	Raymond Bourque, Bos.	Al MacInnis, Cgy.
1989	Chris Chelios, Mtl	Paul Coffey, Pit.
1988	Raymond Bourque, Bos.	Scott Stevens, Wsh.
1987	Raymond Bourque, Bos.	Mark Howe, Phi.
1986	Paul Coffey, Edm.	Mark Howe, Phi.
1985	Paul Coffey, Edm.	Raymond Bourque, Bos.
1984	Rod Langway, Wsh.	Paul Coffey, Edm.
1983	Rod Langway, Wsh.	Mark Howe, Phi.
1982	Doug Wilson, Chi.	Raymond Bourque, Bos.
1981	Randy Carlyle, Pit.	Denis Potvin, NYI
1980	Larry Robinson, Mtl.	Borje Salming, Tor.
1979	Denis Potvin, NYI	Larry Robinson, Mtl.
1978	Denis Potvin, NYI	Brad Park, Bos.
1977	Larry Robinson, Mtl.	Borje Salming, Tor.
1976	Denis Potvin, NYI	Brad Park, NYR-Bos.
1975	Bobby Orr, Bos.	Denis Potvin, NYI
1974	Bobby Orr, Bos.	Brad Park, NYR
1973	Bobby Orr, Bos.	Guy Lapointe, Mtl.
1972	Bobby Orr, Bos.	Brad Park, NYR
1971	Bobby Orr, Bos.	Brad Park, NYR
1970	Bobby Orr, Bos.	Brad Park, NYR
1969	Bobby Orr, Bos.	Tim Horton, Tor.
1968	Bobby Orr, Bos.	J.C. Tremblay, Mtl
1967	Harry Howell, NYR	Pierre Pilote, Chi.
1966	Jacques Laperriere, Mtl.	Pierre Pilote, Chi.
1965	Pierre Pilote, Chi.	Jacques Laperriere, Mtl.
1964	Pierre Pilote, Chi.	Tim Horton, Tor.
1963	Pierre Pilote, Chi.	Carl Brewer, Tor.
1962	Doug Harvey, NYR	Pierre Pilote, Chi.
1961	Doug Harvey, Mtl.	Marcel Pronovost, Det.
1960	Doug Harvey, Mtl.	Allan Stanley, Tor.
1959	Tom Johnson, Mtl.	Bill Gadsby, NYR
1958	Doug Harvey, Mtl.	Bill Gadsby, NYR
1957	Doug Harvey, Mtl.	Red Kelly, Det.
1956	Doug Harvey, Mtl.	Bill Gadsby, NYR
1955	Doug Harvey, Mtl.	Red Kelly, Det.
1954	Red Kelly, Det.	Doug Harvey, Mtl.

LESTER PATRICK TROPHY

2008	Brian Burke	Phil Housley
	Ted Lindsay	Bob Naegele, Jr.
2007	Brian Leetch	Cammi Granato
	Stan Fischler	John Halligan
2006	Red Berenson	Marcel Dionne
	Reed Larson	Glen Sonmor
	Steve Yzerman	
2005	....	
2004	John Davidson	Mike Emrick
	Ray Miron	
2003	Raymond Bourque	Ron DeGregorio
	Willie O'Ree	
2002	Herb Brooks	Larry Pleau
	1960 U.S. Olympic Team	
2001	Gary Bettman	Scotty Bowman
	David Poile	
2000	Mario Lemieux	Craig Patrick
	Lou Vairo	
1999	Harry Sinden	
	1998 U.S. Olympic Women's Team	
1998	Neal Broten	Peter Karmanos
	John Mayasich	Max McNab
1997	Bill Cleary	* Seymour H. Knox III
	Pat LaFontaine	
1996	George Gund	Ken Morrow
	Milt Schmidt	
1995	Bob Fleming	Brian Mullen
	Joe Mullen	
1994	Wayne Gretzky	Robert Ridder
1993	*Frank Boucher	* Mervyn "Red" Dutton
	Bruce McNall	Gil Stein
1992	Al Arbour	Art Berglund
	Lou Lamoriello	
1991	Rod Gilbert	Mike Ilitch
1990	Len Ceglarski	
1989	Dan Kelly	Lou Nanne
	*Lynn Patrick	Bud Poile
1988	Keith Allen	Fred Cusick
	Bob Johnson	
1987	*Hobey Baker	Frank Mathers
1986	John MacInnes	Jack Riley
1985	Jack Butterfield	Arthur M. Wirtz
1984	*Arthur Howey Ross	John A. Ziegler, Jr.
1983	Bill Torrey	
1982	Emile P. Francis	
1981	Charles M. Schulz	
1980	Bobby Clarke	Frederick A. Shero
	Edward M. Snider	1980 U.S. Olympic Team
1979	Bobby Orr	
1978	Phil Esposito	Tom Fitzgerald
	William T. Tutt	William W. Wirtz
1977	Murray A. Armstrong	John P. Bucyk
	John Mariucci	
1976	George A. Leader	Stanley Mikita
	Bruce A. Norris	
1975	William L. Chadwick	Donald M. Clark
	Thomas N. Ivan	
1974	*Weston W. Adams, Sr.	* Charles L. Crovat
	Alex Delvecchio	Murray Murdoch
1973	Walter L. Bush, Jr.	
1972	Clarence S. Campbell	John A. "Snooks" Kelly
	*James D. Norris	Ralph "Cooney" Weiland
1971	William M. Jennings	* Terrance G. Sawchuk
	*John B. Sollenberger	
1970	*James C. V. Hendy	Edward W. Shore
1969	Robert M. Hull	* Edward J. Jeremiah
1968	*Walter A. Brown	* Gen. John R. Kilpatrick
	Thomas F. Lockhart	
1967	*Charles F. Adams	Gordon Howe
	*James Norris, Sr.	
1966	J.J. "Jack" Adams	

* awarded posthumously

PRESIDENTS' TROPHY

	Winner	Runner-up
2008	Detroit Red Wings	San Jose Sharks
2007	Buffalo Sabres	Detroit Red Wings
2006	Detroit Red Wings	Ottawa Senators
2005	....	....
2004	Detroit Red Wings	Tampa Bay Lightning
2003	Ottawa Senators	Dallas Stars
2002	Detroit Red Wings	Boston Bruins
2001	Colorado Avalanche	Detroit Red Wings
2000	St. Louis Blues	Detroit Red Wings
1999	Dallas Stars	New Jersey Devils
1998	Dallas Stars	New Jersey Devils
1997	Colorado Avalanche	Dallas Stars
1996	Detroit Red Wings	Colorado Avalanche
1995	Detroit Red Wings	Quebec Nordiques
1994	New York Rangers	New Jersey Devils
1993	Pittsburgh Penguins	Boston Bruins
1992	New York Rangers	Washington Capitals
1991	Chicago Blackhawks	St. Louis Blues
1990	Boston Bruins	Calgary Flames
1989	Calgary Flames	Montreal Canadiens
1988	Calgary Flames	Montreal Canadiens
1987	Edmonton Oilers	Philadelphia Flyers
1986	Edmonton Oilers	Philadelphia Flyers

LESTER B. PEARSON AWARD

2008	Alex Ovechkin	Washington
2007	Sidney Crosby	Pittsburgh
2006	Jaromir Jagr	NY Rangers
2005	....	
2004	Martin St. Louis	Tampa Bay
2003	Markus Naslund	Vancouver
2002	Jarome Iginla	Calgary
2001	Joe Sakic	Colorado
2000	Jaromir Jagr	Pittsburgh
1999	Jaromir Jagr	Pittsburgh
1998	Dominik Hasek	Buffalo
1997	Dominik Hasek	Buffalo
1996	Mario Lemieux	Pittsburgh
1995	Eric Lindros	Philadelphia
1994	Sergei Fedorov	Detroit
1993	Mario Lemieux	Pittsburgh
1992	Mark Messier	NY Rangers
1991	Brett Hull	St. Louis
1990	Mark Messier	Edmonton
1989	Steve Yzerman	Detroit
1988	Mario Lemieux	Pittsburgh
1987	Wayne Gretzky	Edmonton
1986	Mario Lemieux	Pittsburgh
1985	Wayne Gretzky	Edmonton
1984	Wayne Gretzky	Edmonton
1983	Wayne Gretzky	Edmonton
1982	Wayne Gretzky	Edmonton
1981	Mike Liut	St. Louis
1980	Marcel Dionne	Los Angeles
1979	Marcel Dionne	Los Angeles
1978	Guy Lafleur	Montreal
1977	Guy Lafleur	Montreal
1976	Guy Lafleur	Montreal
1975	Bobby Orr	Boston
1974	Phil Esposito	Boston
1973	Bobby Clarke	Philadelphia
1972	Jean Ratelle	NY Rangers
1971	Phil Esposito	Boston

JACK ADAMS AWARD

	Winner	Runner-up
2008	Bruce Boudreau, Wsh.	Guy Carbonneau, Mtl.
2007	Alain Vigneault, Van.	Lindy Ruff, Buf.
2006	Lindy Ruff, Buf.	Peter Laviolette, Car.
2005	....	....
2004	John Tortorella, T.B.	Ron Wilson, S.J.
2003	Jacques Lemaire, Min.	John Tortorella, T.B.
2002	Bob Francis, Phx.	Brian Sutter, Chi.
2001	Bill Barber, Phi.	Scotty Bowman, Det.
2000	Joel Quenneville, St.L.	Alain Vigneault, Mtl.
1999	Jacques Martin, Ott.	Pat Quinn, Tor.
1998	Pat Burns, Bos.	Larry Robinson, L.A.
1997	Ted Nolan, Buf.	Ken Hitchcock, Dal.
1996	Scotty Bowman, Det.	Doug MacLean, Fla.
1995	Marc Crawford, Que.	Scotty Bowman, Det.
1994	Jacques Lemaire, N.J.	Kevin Constantine, S.J.
1993	Pat Burns, Tor.	Brian Sutter, Bos.
1992	Pat Quinn, Van.	Roger Neilson, NYR
1991	Brian Sutter, St.L.	Tom Webster, L.A.
1990	Bob Murdoch, Wpg.	Mike Milbury, Bos.
1989	Pat Burns, Mtl.	Bob McCammon, Van.
1988	Jacques Demers, Det.	Terry Crisp, Cgy.
1987	Jacques Demers, Det.	Jack Evans, Hfd.
1986	Glen Sather, Edm.	Jacques Demers, St.L.
1985	Mike Keenan, Phi.	Barry Long, Wpg.
1984	Bryan Murray, Wsh.	Scotty Bowman, Buf.
1983	Orval Tessier, Chi.	
1982	Tom Watt, Wpg.	
1981	Red Berenson, St.L.	Bob Berry, L.A.
1980	Pat Quinn, Phi.	
1979	Al Arbour, NYI	Fred Shero, NYR
1978	Bobby Kromm, Det.	Don Cherry, Bos.
1977	Scotty Bowman, Mtl.	Tom McVie, Wsh.
1976	Don Cherry, Bos.	
1975	Bob Pulford, L.A.	
1974	Fred Shero, Phi.	

TM

NHL Entry Draft

History

Year	Location	Date	Players Drafted
1963–1968	Montreal	—	122
1969	Queen Elizabeth Hotel, Montreal	June 12	84
1970	Queen Elizabeth Hotel, Montreal	June 11	115
1971	Queen Elizabeth Hotel, Montreal	June 10	117
1972	Queen Elizabeth Hotel, Montreal	June 8	152
1973	Mount Royal Hotel, Montreal	May 15	168
1974	NHL Montreal Office	May 28	247
1975	NHL Montreal Office	June 3	217
1976	NHL Montreal Office	June 1	135
1977	NHL Montreal Office	June 14	185
1978	Queen Elizabeth Hotel, Montreal	June 15	234
1979	Queen Elizabeth Hotel, Montreal	August 9	126
1980	Montreal Forum	June 11	210
1981	Montreal Forum	June 10	211
1982	Montreal Forum	June 9	252
1983	Montreal Forum	June 8	242
1984	Montreal Forum	June 9	250
1985	Toronto Convention Centre	June 15	252
1986	Montreal Forum	June 21	252
1987	Joe Louis Arena, Detroit	June 13	252
1988	Montreal Forum	June 11	252
1989	Met Sports Center, Minnesota	June 17	252
1990	B.C. Place, Vancouver	June 16	250
1991	Memorial Auditorium, Buffalo	June 22	264
1992	Montreal Forum	June 20	264
1993	Le Colisée, Quebec	June 26	286
1994	Hartford Civic Center	June 28-29	286
1995	Edmonton Coliseum	July 8	234
1996	Kiel Center, St. Louis	June 22	241
1997	Civic Arena, Pittsburgh	June 21	246
1998	Marine Midland Arena, Buffalo	June 27	258
1999	FleetCenter, Boston	June 26	272
2000	Saddledome, Calgary	June 24-25	293
2001	National Car Rental Center, Florida	June 23-24	289
2002	Air Canada Centre, Toronto	June 22-23	290
2003	Gaylord Entertainment Center, Nashville	June 21-22	292
2004	RBC Center, Carolina	June 26-27	291
2005	Sheraton Hotel and Towers, Ottawa	July 30	230
2006	General Motors Place, Vancouver	June 24	213
2007	Nationwide Arena, Columbus	June 22-23	211
2008	Scotiabank Place, Ottawa	June 20-21	211

First Selections

Year	Player	Pos	Team	Drafted From	Age
1963	Garry Monahan	LW	Montreal	St. Michael's Juveniles	16.7
1964	Claude Gauthier		Detroit	Comite des jeunes (Rosemont)	
1965	Andre Veilleux	RW	NY Rangers	Montreal Ranger Jr. B	
1966	Barry Gibbs	D	Boston	Estevan Bruins	17.7
1967	Rick Pagnutti	D	Los Angeles	Garson Native Sons	20.6
1968	Michel Plasse	G	Montreal	Drummondville Rangers	20.0
1969	Rejean Houle	LW	Montreal	Montreal Jr. Canadiens	19.8
1970	Gilbert Perreault	C	Buffalo	Montreal Jr. Canadiens	19.7
1971	Guy Lafleur	RW	Montreal	Quebec Remparts	19.9
1972	Billy Harris	RW	NY Islanders	Toronto Marlboros	20.4
1973	Denis Potvin	D	NY Islanders	Ottawa 67's	19.7
1974	Greg Joly	D	Washington	Regina Pats	20.0
1975	Mel Bridgman	C	Philadelphia	Victoria Cougars	20.1
1976	Rick Green	D	Washington	London Knights	20.3
1977	Dale McCourt	C	Detroit	St. Catharines Fincups	20.4
1978	Bobby Smith	C	Minnesota	Ottawa 67's	20.4
1979	Rob Ramage	D	Colorado	London Knights	20.5
1980	Doug Wickenheiser	C	Montreal	Regina Pats	19.2
1981	Dale Hawerchuk	C	Winnipeg	Cornwall Royals	18.2
1982	Gord Kluzak	D	Boston	Nanaimo Islanders	18.3
1983	Brian Lawton	C	Minnesota	Mount St. Charles HS	18.11
1984	Mario Lemieux	C	Pittsburgh	Laval Voisins	18.8
1985	Wendel Clark	LW/D	Toronto	Saskatoon Blades	18.7
1986	Joe Murphy	C	Detroit	Michigan State Spartans	18.8
1987	Pierre Turgeon	C	Buffalo	Granby Bisons .	17.10
1988	Mike Modano	C	Minnesota	Prince Albert Raiders	18.0
1989	Mats Sundin	RW	Quebec	Nacka (Sweden)	18.4
1990	Owen Nolan	RW	Quebec	Cornwall Royals	18.4
1991	Eric Lindros	C	Quebec	Oshawa Generals	18.3
1992	Roman Hamrlik	D	Tampa Bay	ZPS Zlin (Czech.)	18.2
1993	Alexandre Daigle	C	Ottawa	Victoriaville Tigres	18.5
1994	Ed Jovanovski	D	Florida	Windsor Spitfires	18.0
1995	Bryan Berard	D	Ottawa	Detroit Jr. Red Wings	18.4
1996	Chris Phillips	D	Ottawa	Prince Albert Raiders	18.3
1997	Joe Thornton	C	Boston	Sault Ste. Marie Greyhounds	17.11
1998	Vincent Lecavalier	C	Tampa Bay	Rimouski Oceanic	18.2
1999	Patrik Stefan	C	Atlanta	Long Beach Ice Dogs (IHL)	18.9
2000	Rick DiPietro	G	NY Islanders	Boston University Terriers	18.9
2001	Ilya Kovalchuk	LW	Atlanta	Spartak (Russia)	18.2
2002	Rick Nash	LW	Columbus	London Knights	18.0
2003	Marc-Andre Fleury	G	Pittsburgh	Cape Breton Screaming Eagles	18.0
2004	Alex Ovechkin	LW	Washington	Dynamo Moscow (Russia)	18.9
2005	Sidney Crosby	C	Pittsburgh	Rimouski Oceanic	17.11
2006	Erik Johnson	D	St. Louis	U.S. National U-18	18.3
2007	Patrick Kane	RW	Chicago	London Knights	18.7
2008	Steven Stamkos	C	Tampa Bay	Sarnia Sting	18.4

Draft Summary

Following is a summary of the players drafted from the Ontario Hockey League (OHL), Quebec Major Junior Hockey League (QMJHL), Western Hockey League (WHL), United States colleges, United States high schools, European leagues and other North American leagues since 1969. "Other" may include Canadian and U.S. Jr. A and Jr. B, minor professional leagues (AHL, IHL), midget and other teams playing in leagues not listed above.

Year	Total	OHL		QMJHL		WHL		College		Hi School		Int'l		Other	
	Picks	Picks	%	Picks	%	Picks	%	Picks	%	Picks	%	Picks	%	Picks	%
1969	84	36	42.9	11	13.1	20	23.8	7	8.3	-	-	1	1.2	9	10.7
1970	115	51	44.3	13	11.3	22	19.1	16	13.9	-	-	-	-	13	11.3
1971	117	41	35.0	13	11.1	28	23.9	22	18.8	-	-	-	-	13	11.1
1972	152	46	30.3	30	19.7	44	28.9	21	13.8	-	-	-	-	11	7.2
1973	168	56	33.3	24	14.3	49	29.2	25	14.9	-	-	-	-	14	8.3
1974	247	69	27.9	40	16.2	66	26.7	41	16.6	-	-	6	2.4	25	10.1
1975	217	55	25.3	28	12.9	57	26.3	59	27.2	-	-	6	2.8	12	5.5
1976	135	47	34.8	18	13.3	33	24.4	26	19.3	-	-	8	5.9	3	2.2
1977	185	42	22.7	40	21.6	44	23.8	49	26.5	-	-	5	2.7	5	2.7
1978	234	59	25.2	22	9.4	48	20.5	73	31.2	-	-	16	6.8	16	6.8
1979	126	48	38.1	19	15.1	37	29.4	15	11.9	-	-	6	4.8	1	0.8
1980	210	73	34.8	24	11.4	41	19.5	42	20.0	7	3.3	13	6.2	10	4.8
1981	211	59	28.0	28	13.3	37	17.5	21	10.0	17	8.1	32	15.2	17	8.1
1982	252	60	23.8	17	6.7	55	21.8	20	7.9	47	18.7	35	13.9	18	7.1
1983	242	57	23.6	24	9.9	41	16.9	14	5.8	35	14.5	34	14.0	37	15.3
1984	250	55	22.0	16	6.4	37	14.8	22	8.8	44	17.6	40	16.0	36	14.4
1985	252	59	23.4	15	6.0	48	19.0	20	7.9	48	19.0	31	12.3	31	12.3
1986	252	66	26.2	22	8.7	32	12.7	22	8.7	40	15.9	28	11.1	42	16.7
1987	252	32	12.7	17	6.7	36	14.3	40	15.9	69	27.4	38	15.1	20	7.9
1988	252	32	12.7	22	8.7	30	11.9	48	19.0	56	22.2	39	15.5	25	9.9
1989	252	39	15.5	16	6.3	44	17.5	48	19.0	47	18.7	38	15.1	20	7.9
1990	250	39	15.6	14	5.6	33	13.2	38	15.2	57	22.8	53	21.2	16	6.4
1991	264	43	16.3	25	9.5	40	15.2	43	16.3	37	14.0	55	20.8	21	8.0
1992	264	57	21.6	22	8.3	45	17.0	9	3.4	25	9.5	84	31.8	22	8.3
1993	286	60	21.0	23	8.0	44	15.4	17	5.9	33	11.5	78	27.3	31	10.8
1994	286	45	15.7	28	9.8	66	23.1	6	2.1	28	9.8	80	28.0	33	11.5
1995	234	54	23.1	35	15.0	55	23.5	5	2.1	2	0.9	69	29.5	14	6.0
1996	241	51	21.2	31	12.9	54	22.4	25	10.4	6	2.5	58	24.1	16	6.6
1997	246	52	21.1	19	7.7	63	25.6	26	10.6	4	1.6	63	25.6	19	7.7
1998	258	50	19.4	41	15.9	44	17.1	27	10.5	7	2.7	75	29.1	14	5.4
1999	272	52	19.1	20	7.4	40	14.7	36	13.2	9	3.3	94	34.6	21	7.7
2000	293	39	13.3	21	7.2	41	14.0	35	11.9	7	2.4	123	42.0	27	9.2
2001	289	41	14.2	26	9.0	45	15.6	24	8.3	8	2.8	119	41.2	26	9.0
2002	290	35	12.1	23	7.9	43	14.8	41	14.1	6	2.1	110	37.9	32	11.0
2003	292	44	15.1	38	13.0	41	14.0	23	7.9	10	3.4	93	31.8	43	14.7
2004	291	42	14.4	27	9.3	44	15.1	28	9.6	18	6.2	88	30.2	44	15.1
2005	230	43	18.7	23	10.0	43	18.7	13	5.6	18	7.8	50	21.7	40	17.4
2006	213	29	13.6	25	11.7	24	11.2	18	8.4	19	8.9	63	29.5	35	16.4
2007	211	35	16.6	25	11.8	37	17.5	8	3.8	14	6.6	36	17.0	56	56.5
2008	211	46	21.8	27	12.8	37	17.5	9	4.2	15	7.1	39	18.5	38	18.0
Total		**1939**	**21.2**	**952**	**10.4**	**1688**	**18.5**	**1082**	**11.9**	**733**	**8.0**	**1806**	**19.8**	**926**	**10.1**

Total Players Drafted (1969-2008): 9,126

Alex Pietrangelo, Tyler Myers, Steven Stamkos, Drew Doughty and Zach Bogosian pose for a picture while participating in the NHL Top Prospects Clinic prior to the 2008 NHL Entry Draft. Stamkos (Tampa Bay), Doughty (Los Angeles), Bogosian (Atlanta) and Pietrangelo (St. Louis) were the first four picks in the draft. Myers was selected 12th by Buffalo.

Ontario Hockey League Draft Selections by Club

Total	Club	'08	'07	'06	'05	'04	'03	'02	'01	'00	'99	'98	'97	'96	'95	'94	'93	'92	'91	'90	'89	'88	'87	'86	'85	'84	'83	'82	'81	'80	'79	'78	'69 to '77
24	Barrie	2	–	1	–	–	1	1	1	3	6	3	4	2	–	–	–	–	–	–	–	–	–	–	–	–	–	–	–	–	–	–	0
64	Belleville	3	4	2	2	–	–	2	3	1	5	2	5	–	3	3	–	4	1	2	4	–	2	5	4	4	3	–	–	–	–	–	0
31	Brampton	3	–	4	4	2	4	3	3	6	2	–	–	–	–	–	–	–	–	–	–	–	–	–	–	–	–	–	–	–	–	–	0
23	Erie	1	5	–	2	2	–	2	2	3	2	1	3	–	–	–	–	–	–	–	–	–	–	–	–	–	–	–	–	–	–	–	0
71	Guelph	3	1	1	2	2	1	2	4	1	3	5	1	6	5	7	2	2	–	–	4	–	2	8	3	5	1	–	–	–	–	–	0
99	Kingston	2	–	4	2	–	1	1	2	–	4	1	4	4	3	2	5	3	2	2	–	1	1	4	3	3	1	2	5	8	2	9	18
142	Kitchener	2	4	–	4	2	1	4	1	1	–	5	3	2	4	2	4	1	3	5	7	1	2	3	6	4	8	5	5	4	4	4	41
142	London	1	3	1	3	6	4	2	2	1	4	8	1	4	1	1	4	3	1	3	3	6	2	3	1	7	3	5	5	2	6	3	43
13	Niagara/Mississauga	1	3	1	1	3	2	–	–	2	–	–	–	–	–	–	–	–	–	–	–	–	–	–	–	–	–	–	–	–	–	–	0
150	Oshawa	2	2	2	–	3	3	3	1	2	3	4	3	1	10	1	4	4	4	2	4	2	3	6	6	6	5	5	9	2	3	3	42
135	Ottawa	2	1	1	2	3	2	–	3	2	6	2	5	2	1	1	4	6	5	5	–	1	2	3	3	2	2	9	4	8	3	5	40
29	Owen Sound	1	1	2	2	1	1	1	–	1	–	1	2	3	2	3	4	2	1	1	–	–	–	–	–	–	–	–	–	–	–	–	0
164	Peterborough	2	1	1	2	5	5	1	2	1	4	1	5	4	5	2	4	4	3	4	2	2	5	2	9	3	7	5	3	10	9	6	45
56	Plymouth	2	3	2	3	3	3	3	3	6	2	2	4	3	6	2	7	2	2	–	–	–	–	–	–	–	–	–	–	–	–	–	0
67	Saginaw/North Bay	3	–	2	3	1	2	2	3	2	2	2	1	1	2	7	2	5	2	4	1	3	3	3	3	4	4	–	–	–	–	–	0
34	Sarnia	4	1	1	3	–	5	2	1	3	1	3	2	7	1	–	–	–	–	–	–	–	–	–	–	–	–	–	–	–	–	–	0
109	Sault Ste. Marie	2	3	–	1	3	1	2	1	1	1	4	1	4	3	4	3	7	2	1	3	2	1	7	5	4	6	1	8	3	3	5	17
20	St. Michael's	4	–	–	–	4	5	1	5	1	–	–	–	–	–	–	–	–	–	–	–	–	–	–	–	–	–	–	–	–	–	–	0
110	Sudbury	2	1	2	4	–	1	1	2	–	5	5	3	1	2	2	10	2	8	2	1	–	1	3	5	2	–	4	2	7	3	4	25
82	Windsor	4	2	2	3	2	2	2	2	2	2	1	5	1	4	3	–	3	–	1	2	5	–	7	3	2	2	3	5	3	2	4	3
	Teams no longer operating																																
27	Brantford	–	–	–	–	–	–	–	–	–	–	–	–	–	–	–	–	–	–	–	–	–	–	–	–	2	7	2	5	8	3	–	0
37	Cornwall	–	–	–	–	–	–	–	–	–	–	–	–	–	–	–	–	5	3	3	2	3	3	2	2	3	4	7	–	–	–	–	0
62	Hamilton	–	–	–	–	–	–	–	–	–	–	–	–	–	–	–	–	–	2	–	–	4	4	6	3	–	–	–	–	–	1	8	34
20	Montreal	–	–	–	–	–	–	–	–	–	–	–	–	–	–	–	–	–	–	–	–	–	–	–	–	–	–	–	–	–	–	–	20
5	Newmarket	–	–	–	–	–	–	–	–	–	–	–	–	–	–	2	3	–	–	–	–	–	–	–	–	–	–	–	–	–	–	–	0
72	Niagara Falls	–	–	–	–	–	–	–	–	–	–	–	–	6	2	3	4	4	4	4	4	–	–	–	–	–	–	6	6	8	5	3	13
52	St. Catharines	–	–	–	–	–	–	–	–	–	–	–	–	–	–	–	–	–	–	–	–	–	–	–	–	–	–	–	–	–	–	–	52
97	Toronto	–	–	–	–	–	–	–	–	–	–	–	–	–	–	–	–	–	–	–	2	2	1	4	3	4	4	6	2	10	4	5	50

Quebec Major Junior Hockey League Draft Selections by Club

Total	Club	'08	'07	'06	'05	'04	'03	'02	'01	'00	'99	'98	'97	'96	'95	'94	'93	'92	'91	'90	'89	'88	'87	'86	'85	'84	'83	'82	'81	'80	'79	'78	'69 to '77
9	Acadie-Bathurst	–	–	2	–	–	3	2	–	–	2	–	–	–	–	–	–	–	–	–	–	–	–	–	–	–	–	–	–	–	–	–	–
20	Baie-Comeau	2	1	3	–	3	2	1	3	2	–	3	–	–	–	–	–	–	–	–	–	–	–	–	–	–	–	–	–	–	–	–	–
14	Cape Breton	1	–	1	–	3	2	2	1	1	–	3	–	–	–	–	–	–	–	–	–	–	–	–	–	–	–	–	–	–	–	–	–
54	Chicoutimi	3	–	–	4	–	1	3	1	1	–	1	2	–	2	3	1	1	–	1	1	2	2	1	3	–	3	1	6	3	1	1	6
54	Drummondville	–	–	2	2	1	1	–	1	1	–	2	2	3	4	1	2	2	4	–	1	4	2	2	2	1	–	–	–	–	–	–	14
74	Gatineau/Hull	1	1	2	–	4	4	5	2	–	4	3	–	3	3	1	3	3	3	3	2	2	3	4	–	1	3	–	1	3	–	3	7
30	Halifax	–	2	3	1	3	6	–	3	2	–	3	3	1	3	–	–	–	–	–	–	–	–	–	–	–	–	–	–	–	–	–	–
77	Lewiston/Sher.	2	3	2	5	2	1	–	3	–	–	5	1	–	4	2	3	–	–	–	–	–	–	–	–	–	–	2	5	1	4	3	29
19	Moncton	1	1	3	1	2	3	2	–	–	2	2	1	1	–	–	–	–	–	–	–	–	–	–	–	–	–	–	–	–	–	–	–
22	PEI/Mtl. Rocket	2	2	–	2	8	1	3	1	1	2	–	–	–	–	–	–	–	–	–	–	–	–	–	–	–	–	–	–	–	–	–	–
24	Quebec	3	2	2	2	1	3	1	3	–	3	4	–	–	–	–	–	–	–	–	–	–	–	–	–	–	–	–	–	–	–	–	–
28	Rimouski	2	4	–	2	3	4	–	4	2	2	5	–	–	–	–	–	–	–	–	–	–	–	–	–	–	–	–	–	–	–	–	–
17	Rouyn-Noranda	2	1	3	1	–	2	–	–	4	1	3	–	–	–	–	–	–	–	–	–	–	–	–	–	–	–	–	–	–	–	–	–
4	Saint John	1	2	1	–	–	–	–	–	–	–	–	–	–	–	–	–	–	–	–	–	–	–	–	–	–	–	–	–	–	–	–	–
6	St. John's	2	4	–	–	–	–	–	–	–	–	–	–	–	–	–	–	–	–	–	–	–	–	–	–	–	–	–	–	–	–	–	–
75	Shawinigan	–	1	1	1	3	2	2	1	1	1	3	1	4	2	1	1	3	2	–	2	–	1	2	–	2	5	5	2	2	–	–	24
23	Val-d'Or	2	–	–	2	1	1	1	2	2	3	–	2	4	2	1	–	–	–	–	–	–	–	–	–	–	–	–	–	–	–	–	–
34	Victoriaville	3	1	–	–	–	–	3	1	3	2	1	2	3	1	1	6	2	–	1	–	4	–	–	–	–	–	–	–	–	–	–	–
	Teams no longer operating																																
21	Beauport	–	–	–	–	–	–	–	–	–	–	–	3	3	7	3	1	3	1	–	–	–	–	–	–	–	–	–	–	–	–	–	–
45	Cornwall	–	–	–	–	–	–	–	–	–	–	–	–	–	–	–	–	–	–	–	–	–	–	–	–	–	–	–	5	5	1	6	28
30	Granby	–	–	–	–	–	–	–	–	–	–	–	1	3	2	5	1	–	2	–	2	–	4	2	2	3	1	2	–	–	–	–	–
54	Laval	–	–	–	–	–	–	–	–	–	–	3	1	2	4	5	2	1	4	3	3	1	3	5	–	2	1	2	–	–	1	2	9
12	Longueuil	–	–	–	–	–	–	–	–	–	–	–	–	–	–	–	–	–	3	2	–	–	1	2	1	2	1	–	–	–	–	–	–
32	Montreal	–	–	–	–	–	–	–	–	–	–	–	–	–	–	–	–	–	–	–	–	–	–	–	–	–	–	3	–	3	4	2	20
47	Quebec	–	–	–	–	–	–	–	–	–	–	–	–	–	–	–	–	–	–	–	–	–	–	–	3	2	2	1	2	2	3	1	31
15	St. Hyacinthe	–	–	–	–	–	–	–	–	–	–	–	–	4	–	4	1	2	1	3	–	–	–	–	–	–	–	–	–	–	–	–	–
16	St. Jean	–	–	–	–	–	–	–	–	–	–	–	–	–	1	1	2	1	3	–	1	3	0	1	1	–	2	–	–	–	–	–	–
2	St. Jerome	–	–	–	–	–	–	–	–	–	–	–	–	–	–	–	–	–	–	–	–	–	–	–	–	–	–	–	–	–	–	–	2
28	Sorel	–	–	–	–	–	–	–	–	–	–	–	–	–	–	–	–	–	–	–	–	–	–	–	–	–	–	–	5	–	–	–	23
47	Trois Rivieres	–	–	–	–	–	–	–	–	–	–	–	–	–	–	–	–	1	2	1	3	3	1	–	3	–	3	1	2	2	2	3	20
27	Verdun	–	–	–	–	–	–	–	–	–	–	–	–	–	–	–	–	3	–	–	1	3	0	3	–	3	3	–	–	3	3	1	4

Edmonton Sam Gagner (top) was selected sixth overall in 2007 from the London Knights of the OHL and jumped directly into the NHL in 2007-08. Dave Perron made a similar jump to the St. Louis Blues after being selected 26th overall from Lewiston in the "Q".

2008 NHL Entry Draft Order of Selection

The first 14 picks of the 2008 Entry Draft were determined by the NHL's annual Draft Drawing, a weighted lottery system used to determine the order of selection.

The 14 teams that did not qualify for the 2008 Stanley Cup Playoffs, or clubs that acquired those clubs' 2008 first-round draft picks, participated in the drawing.

The club selected in the drawing may not move up more than four positions in the draft order, thus only the five clubs with the fewest regular-season points have the opportunity to select first overall.
No club can move down more than one position as a result of the Draft Drawing.
For 2008, the Tampa Bay Lightning won the right to the first overall pick.

In the first round of the 2008 Entry Draft, the order of selection was as follows:

a) The winner of the Draft Drawing followed by the remaining non-playoff teams, in inverse order of points. (Note that the original holder of each selection is listed followed by the club that acquired and used that selection in the first round of the 2008 Entry Draft.);

1. Tampa Bay.	8. Phoenix
2. Los Angeles	9. Florida [NYI]
3. Atlanta	10. Vancouver
4. St. Louis	11. Chicago
5. NY Islanders [TOR]	12. Edmonton [BUF]
6. Columbus	13. Buffalo [L.A.]
7. Toronto [NSH]	14. Carolina

b) Clubs eliminated in the first two rounds of the 2008 Stanley Cup Playoffs, regular-season division winners excluded, in inverse order of points;

15. Nashville [OTT]	20. NY Rangers
16. Boston	21. New Jersey [WSH]
17. Calgary [ANA]	22. Anaheim [EDM]
18. Ottawa [NSH]	23. Washington [MIN]
19. Colorado [PHI]	

c) Regular-season division winning clubs eliminated in the first two rounds of the 2008 Stanley Cup Playoffs, in inverse order of points;

24. Minnesota [N.J.] 26. San Jose [BUF]
25. Montreal [CGY]

d) Clubs eliminated in the 2008 Conference Finals, in inverse order of points;

27. Philadelphia [WSH] 28. Dallas [PHX]

e) Loser of Stanley Cup Final

29. Pittsburgh [ATL]

f) Stanley Cup champion

30. Detroit

Because Tampa Bay was both the winner of the Draft Drawing and the Club with the fewest regular-season points, the order of selection in the second and subsequent rounds was identical to that used in the first round.

Western Hockey League Draft Selections by Club

Total	Club	'08	'07	'06	'05	'04	'03	'02	'01	'00	'99	'98	'97	'96	'95	'94	'93	'92	'91	'90	'89	'88	'87	'86	'85	'84	'83	'82	'81	'80	'79	'78	'69 to '77
100	Brandon	2	1	1	2	–	3	4	2	–	–	4	5	2	6	5	2	1	1	1	–	3	3	1	2	3	1	2	2	5	10	1	25
36	Calgary	2	4	1	2	5	3	2	1	4	6	3	–	3	–	–	–	–	–	–	–	–	–	–	–	–	–	–	–	–	–	–	–
2	Chilliwack	–	2	–	–	–	–	–	–	–	–	–	–	–	–	–	–	–	–	–	–	–	–	–	–	–	–	–	–	–	–	–	–
8	Everett	1	3	4	–	–	–	–	–	–	–	–	–	–	–	–	–	–	–	–	–	–	–	–	–	–	–	–	–	–	–	–	–
106	Kamloops	–	1	1	2	5	2	5	2	4	4	1	3	4	5	9	2	3	6	4	5	1	3	4	4	4	4	2	–	–	–	–	16
34	Kelowna	4	2	–	2	4	4	1	1	1	2	2	7	4	–	–	–	–	–	–	–	–	–	–	–	–	–	–	–	–	–	–	–
16	Kootenay	–	1	1	3	2	1	3	2	1	2	–	–	–	–	–	–	–	–	–	–	–	–	–	–	–	–	–	–	–	–	–	–
90	Lethbridge	2	2	1	–	2	2	2	1	3	–	1	5	1	3	3	4	3	7	4	3	3	–	1	5	1	2	7	4	1	4	5	8
107	Medicine Hat	2	–	2	4	2	3	3	2	–	1	4	2	7	2	6	1	3	3	1	4	1	5	2	6	1	2	1	2	4	–	4	27
62	Moose Jaw	3	1	1	3	3	3	3	3	5	1	2	4	4	4	3	2	3	2	1	3	–	3	1	4	–	–	–	–	–	–	–	–
106	Portland	–	2	1	3	2	1	2	–	6	1	3	3	1	2	3	4	4	1	1	4	1	3	4	2	5	7	7	6	8	7	8	4
80	Prince Albert	–	–	–	2	4	2	1	4	2	3	3	5	3	4	3	5	2	6	4	3	3	1	6	6	2	2	4	–	–	–	–	–
26	Prince George	–	1	4	1	2	2	–	4	–	2	4	2	2	2	–	–	–	–	–	–	–	–	–	–	–	–	–	–	–	–	–	–
43	Red Deer	1	1	1	1	1	4	4	6	1	1	5	3	4	2	5	3	–	–	–	–	–	–	–	–	–	–	–	–	–	–	–	–
111	Regina	3	3	1	1	–	2	1	2	2	4	2	3	4	2	3	–	4	–	1	5	–	2	3	4	4	8	6	5	3	1	4	28
108	Saskatoon	3	3	–	4	1	–	–	4	1	4	2	2	2	2	4	2	3	2	2	3	4	4	5	1	3	5	5	3	2	2	1	29
94	Seattle	2	1	1	3	2	5	1	5	4	6	2	8	1	5	5	4	2	3	6	2	4	2	1	3	1	–	6	–	3	2	4	–
63	Spokane	3	3	1	4	1	–	3	3	2	1	1	4	5	4	4	4	7	5	1	2	3	1	–	–	–	–	–	1	–	–	–	–
64	Swift Current	4	2	2	1	2	2	4	1	3	1	2	2	1	4	4	5	1	1	2	2	2	5	–	–	–	–	–	–	–	–	–	11
53	Tri-City	2	–	–	2	4	1	3	2	2	1	4	1	6	6	2	2	5	3	3	4	–	–	–	–	–	–	–	–	–	–	–	–
15	Vancouver	3	4	1	3	2	1	1	–	–	–	–	–	–	–	–	–	–	–	–	–	–	–	–	–	–	–	–	–	–	–	–	–
Teams no longer operating																																	
13	Billings	–	–	–	–	–	–	–	–	–	–	–	–	–	–	–	–	–	–	–	–	–	–	–	–	–	–	–	2	4	3	4	–
66	Calgary	–	–	–	–	–	–	–	–	–	–	–	–	–	–	–	–	–	–	–	–	–	–	2	3	3	3	4	5	2	–	3	41
38	Edmonton	–	–	–	–	–	–	–	–	–	–	–	4	–	–	–	–	–	–	–	–	–	–	–	–	–	–	–	–	–	2	–	32
12	Estevan	–	–	–	–	–	–	–	–	–	–	–	–	–	–	–	–	–	–	–	–	–	–	–	–	–	–	–	–	–	–	–	12
39	Flin Flon	–	–	–	–	–	–	–	–	–	–	–	–	–	–	–	–	–	–	–	–	–	–	–	–	–	–	–	–	–	–	5	34
11	Kelowna	–	–	–	–	–	–	–	–	–	–	–	–	–	–	–	–	–	–	–	–	–	–	–	5	4	2	–	–	–	–	–	–
6	Nanaimo	–	–	–	–	–	–	–	–	–	–	–	–	–	–	–	–	–	–	–	–	–	–	–	–	–	1	5	–	–	–	–	–
62	New Westm'r	–	–	–	–	–	–	–	–	–	–	–	–	–	–	–	–	–	–	–	–	1	2	1	1	2	–	–	–	1	5	6	43
12	Tacoma	–	–	–	–	–	–	–	–	–	–	–	–	–	2	5	2	3	–	–	–	–	–	–	–	–	–	–	–	–	–	–	–
2	Vancouver	–	–	–	–	–	–	–	–	–	–	–	–	–	–	–	–	–	–	–	–	–	–	–	–	–	–	–	–	–	–	–	2
70	Victoria	–	–	–	–	–	–	–	–	–	–	–	–	–	–	2	2	1	–	2	4	4	2	1	2	4	3	2	6	8	1	3	32
34	Winnipeg	–	–	–	–	–	–	–	–	–	–	–	–	–	–	–	–	–	–	–	–	–	–	–	–	–	1	4	1	–	–	–	28

U.S. College Hockey Draft Selections by School

Total	Club	'08	'07	'06	'05	'04	'03	'02	'01	'00	'99	'98	'97	'96	'95	'94	'93	'92	'91	'90	'89	'88	'87	'86	'85	'84	'83	'82	'81	'80	'79	'78	'69 to '77
38	Boston College	1	–	1	1	1	1	3	2	3	–	3	3	2	–	–	–	–	–	–	2	–	2	1	–	–	–	1	1	2	–	5	3
52	Boston U.	1	–	1	–	1	–	3	2	1	3	2	1	1	1	–	1	1	2	2	1	3	2	2	1	1	–	–	1	–	1	5	12
28	Bowling Green	–	–	1	1	–	–	1	1	–	1	1	1	–	–	–	–	1	3	1	2	3	–	–	–	–	1	–	–	1	1	1	7
13	Brown	–	–	–	–	1	–	–	–	1	–	–	–	–	–	–	–	–	1	–	–	–	–	–	–	–	–	1	–	–	–	2	7
33	Clarkson	–	–	1	–	–	–	–	–	1	1	3	–	–	–	–	1	1	2	3	1	1	1	–	–	1	1	1	1	1	1	2	9
13	Colgate	–	–	1	–	1	–	1	–	–	–	–	–	–	–	–	–	–	2	2	1	1	–	–	–	–	–	–	–	–	1	2	1
33	Colorado	–	1	–	1	–	2	1	1	2	1	3	–	–	1	–	–	–	–	2	–	1	–	1	–	3	–	–	–	1	–	2	10
34	Cornell	–	–	–	1	2	2	1	–	2	2	–	1	–	–	–	–	–	–	2	5	2	1	–	2	1	–	1	1	1	–	1	6
10	Dartmouth	–	1	–	–	1	2	–	–	1	–	–	–	–	–	–	–	–	1	–	–	–	1	–	–	–	–	–	–	1	–	1	1
43	Denver	–	–	–	2	1	–	1	–	–	1	–	3	–	–	–	–	–	–	–	1	1	4	2	1	–	–	1	–	1	2	2	20
34	Harvard	–	–	–	1	–	–	3	2	2	1	2	1	3	–	1	2	–	–	–	2	1	1	–	2	–	1	1	–	–	–	2	6
24	Lake Superior	–	–	–	–	–	–	1	–	–	1	–	1	1	–	–	1	–	1	3	2	3	–	3	–	1	–	–	–	–	–	3	3
22	Maine	–	–	1	–	1	2	–	–	1	4	1	1	1	–	–	1	–	–	1	2	3	–	1	–	–	1	1	–	–	–	–	–
22	Miami U.	1	1	1	1	2	–	1	1	–	–	1	–	–	–	–	1	1	2	–	2	4	2	–	1	–	–	–	–	–	–	–	–
67	Michigan	–	1	2	1	3	2	3	2	1	2	3	1	3	–	1	1	2	4	5	3	2	1	–	1	1	–	–	–	4	–	6	12
48	Michigan State	–	–	1	–	2	1	4	–	2	2	1	1	1	–	1	1	1	4	5	4	4	1	1	–	2	–	2	–	2	–	–	5
46	Michigan Tech	–	–	–	–	–	–	–	1	–	–	–	–	1	–	2	1	–	2	1	2	1	1	2	2	2	–	1	–	4	1	2	20
68	Minnesota	–	1	1	1	–	2	3	–	3	3	1	2	3	2	–	–	–	–	–	1	1	1	2	–	–	1	1	1	3	2	5	28
13	Minn.-Duluth	–	–	–	–	–	–	–	–	–	–	1	–	–	–	–	–	–	1	2	1	2	–	–	–	–	–	–	1	–	–	1	4
31	New Hampshire	–	–	–	–	1	–	1	–	2	1	–	1	–	–	–	–	–	–	–	–	1	–	–	–	2	1	1	1	2	1	1	15
39	North Dakota	–	–	1	–	1	1	1	–	1	1	–	2	–	–	–	–	–	1	1	2	–	–	–	–	1	–	–	1	3	3	2	17
10	Northeastern	–	–	–	–	–	–	–	–	–	1	1	–	–	–	–	–	–	–	1	1	–	–	1	1	–	1	–	–	1	–	1	1
23	Northern Mich.	1	–	–	–	2	2	–	–	1	–	–	–	1	–	–	–	–	1	–	2	1	4	–	–	–	–	1	2	1	–	4	–
32	Notre Dame	–	1	1	–	2	–	2	1	1	2	–	2	1	–	–	–	–	–	–	–	–	–	–	–	–	–	–	–	1	1	3	14
21	Ohio State	–	–	–	1	–	1	2	2	–	1	–	1	1	–	–	1	1	1	1	–	2	2	–	–	1	–	–	–	–	–	1	2
10	Princeton	–	–	–	–	–	–	–	1	–	–	1	–	–	–	–	1	–	–	–	1	–	1	–	–	–	1	–	1	1	–	1	1
36	Providence	–	–	2	–	–	1	1	–	2	–	2	1	–	–	–	–	–	–	1	–	–	–	1	1	–	2	1	4	5	–	4	8
26	RPI	1	–	–	–	–	–	–	1	2	2	–	1	–	–	–	–	1	3	–	–	2	2	–	1	–	1	1	2	1	–	3	2
23	St. Lawrence	–	–	–	–	–	–	1	–	–	1	–	1	1	–	–	1	–	2	1	1	1	1	1	1	1	–	3	–	–	–	4	2
20	Vermont	–	–	–	1	–	–	–	2	–	–	–	–	1	–	1	–	–	1	–	–	1	–	–	2	1	1	–	1	1	–	1	6
24	W. Michigan	–	–	1	–	–	–	1	–	–	–	1	1	–	–	–	2	–	4	1	1	1	1	2	–	2	2	–	–	2	–	–	2
45	Wisconsin	2	–	–	–	2	–	–	–	3	2	–	–	–	–	–	–	–	1	–	1	–	1	–	1	1	–	2	3	–	1	–	25
16	Yale	–	–	1	–	2	–	3	–	–	–	–	–	–	–	–	1	–	–	–	1	–	2	1	–	–	–	–	–	1	–	2	2

Colleges with fewer than 10 players selected: 9 - Ferris State; 8 - Merrimack, St.Cloud State; 7 - Mass.-Lowell; 6 - Illinois-Chicago, St. Louis; 5 - Pennsylvania, Union College, Mass.-Amherst; 4 - Alaska-Anchorage, Nebraska-Omaha; 3 - Babson College, Alaska (Fairbanks), Minnesota State (Mankato); 1 - Air Force, American International College, Army, Bemidji State, Greenway, Hamilton, St. Anselm College, St. Thomas, Salem State, San Diego U., Wisconsin-River Falls.

U.S. High and Prep Schools Draft Selections by School (10 or more players drafted)

Total	School (State)	'08	'07	'06	'05	'04	'03	'02	'01	'00	'99	'98	'97	'96	'95	'94	'93	'92	'91	'90	'89	'88	'87	'86	'85	'84	'83	'82	'81	'80
11	Avon Old Farms (CT)	–	1	–	–	–	–	–	–	–	–	1	1	–	–	–	–	–	–	3	3	–	–	1	1	–	–	–	–	–
17	Belmont Hill (MA)	–	–	1	–	–	–	–	–	–	–	–	–	–	–	1	–	2	1	2	3	1	2	1	2	–	1	–	–	–
11	Canterbury (CT)	–	–	–	–	–	1	–	–	–	–	–	–	–	–	–	1	2	–	2	–	3	–	2	–	–	–	–	–	–
14	Catholic Memorial (MA)	–	–	–	–	2	–	–	–	–	–	1	–	–	–	2	1	2	–	–	2	1	1	–	2	–	–	–	–	–
10	Choate-Rosemary (CT)	–	–	–	–	–	–	–	–	1	–	–	–	–	–	–	–	1	1	1	–	3	2	–	1	–	–	–	–	–
12	Culver Mil. Acad. (IN)	–	–	–	–	–	–	–	–	–	–	–	–	–	–	–	2	2	1	2	2	1	2	–	–	–	–	–	–	–
21	Cushing Acad. (MA)	–	–	1	1	2	–	–	1	–	–	–	1	1	–	2	2	–	1	3	2	3	–	–	–	1	–	–	–	–
14	Deerfield (IL)	–	1	–	–	1	1	1	–	2	1	–	–	–	–	–	–	–	1	–	2	1	1	–	1	1	–	–	–	–
15	Edina (MN)	–	–	–	–	–	–	–	–	–	–	–	–	–	–	–	–	1	–	1	2	2	1	–	–	2	2	4	–	–
15	Hill-Murray (MN)	–	–	–	–	–	–	–	–	–	–	–	–	–	–	1	–	–	–	3	2	–	3	3	–	3	–	–	–	–
11	Hotchkiss (CT)	–	–	–	–	1	–	–	1	–	–	–	–	2	1	3	–	–	–	1	–	1	–	–	1	–	–	–	–	–
10	Lawrence Acad. (MA)	–	–	–	–	–	–	–	–	–	–	–	–	1	–	1	1	–	1	1	–	2	–	–	2	–	1	–	–	–
10	Matignon (MA)	–	–	–	–	–	–	–	–	–	–	–	–	–	–	–	–	–	1	–	–	–	3	–	–	3	–	1	1	1
13	Mount St. Charles (RI)	–	–	–	–	–	–	–	–	–	–	–	–	–	–	–	–	–	–	1	1	3	1	2	–	1	3	–	1	–
20	Northwood Prep (NY)	1	–	–	–	1	–	–	–	1	–	–	–	–	–	1	1	–	–	3	1	1	3	2	2	–	1	2	–	–
10	Roseau (MN)	–	–	–	–	–	–	–	–	–	–	–	–	–	–	–	–	–	1	3	1	–	–	1	–	1	1	1	–	1
13	St. Sebastian's (MA)	–	–	1	–	–	4	1	1	–	–	1	–	–	–	1	2	2	–	–	–	–	–	–	–	–	–	–	–	–
10	Thayer Acad. (MA)	–	–	–	2	1	–	–	–	–	2	–	–	–	–	–	–	2	–	–	–	2	–	1	–	–	–	–	–	–

U.S. College and High School Firsts

1967 – First U.S. College Player Drafted • Michigan Tech center Al Karlander was selected 17th overall by the Detroit Red Wings.

1979 – First U.S. College First- Round Selection • Minnesota-born defenseman Mike Ramsey (currently an assistant coach with the Minnesota Wild) was selected 11th overall by the Buffalo Sabres.

1980 – First U.S. High School Player Drafted • Center Jay North of Bloomington-Jefferson H.S. was taken 62nd overall by the Buffalo Sabres in 1980.

1981 – First U.S. High School First- Round Selection • Center Bob Carpenter of St. John's prep school was selected third overall by Washington in 1981.

Minnesota G.M. Lou Nanne drafted high-schooler Brian Lawton first overall in 1983.

1983 – First U.S. High School Player Drafted First Overall • Minnesota North Stars selected left winger Brian Lawton from Mount St. Charles H.S. first overall in 1983.

1986 – First U.S. College Player Drafted First Overall • Detroit selected right winger Joe Murphy from Michigan State first overall in 1986.

2005 – Most U.S. College Players Selected in the First Round • The 2005 draft saw eight U.S. college players selected in the first round, the most in Entry Draft history. Seven were selected in the first round in 2003 and 1986, six in 2000, five in 2002, four in 2001 and three in each of the 1986 and 1999 Entry Drafts.

International

Ranked by total number of players drafted

Total	Club	'08	'07	'06	'05	'04	'03	'02	'01	'00	'99	'98	'97	'96	'95	'94	'93	'92	'91	'90	'89	'88	'87	'86	'85	'84	'83	'82	'81	'80	'79	'78	'69 to '77
519	Russia/CIS/USSR	9	7	16	11	24	32	33	36	44	29	22	16	17	27	35	31	45	25	14	18	11	2	1	2	1	5	3	–	–	–	2	1
444	Sweden	19	16	18	15	18	19	24	14	24	24	19	14	16	8	17	18	11	11	7	9	14	15	9	16	14	10	14	14	9	5	8	14
405	CzRep/Slovakia	2	4	11	15	24	20	21	28	28	20	20	17	14	21	18	15	17	9	21	8	5	11	6	8	13	9	13	4	–	1	2	–
312	Finland	6	4	13	8	14	12	26	29	19	17	12	11	7	12	8	9	8	6	9	3	7	6	10	4	10	9	5	12	4	–	2	10
45	Germany	1	4	2	1	1	4	1	7	1	–	–	1	3	1	1	3	2	1	–	–	2	1	–	1	2	1	–	2	–	–	2	–
44	Switzerland	1	1	3	–	4	5	4	5	7	3	2	3	1	–	1	2	–	1	–	–	–	–	–	–	–	–	–	–	–	–	–	1
8	Norway	1	–	–	–	–	–	1	–	–	–	–	1	–	–	–	–	–	1	2	–	–	2	–	–	–	–	–	–	–	–	–	–
4	Denmark	–	–	–	–	2	–	–	–	–	–	–	–	–	–	–	–	–	–	–	–	–	1	1	–	–	–	–	–	–	–	–	–
2	Japan	–	–	–	–	1	–	–	–	–	–	–	–	–	–	–	–	1	–	–	–	–	–	–	–	–	–	–	–	–	–	–	–
2	Poland	–	–	–	–	–	1	–	–	–	–	–	–	–	–	–	–	–	1	–	–	–	–	–	–	–	–	–	–	–	–	–	–
1	Hungary	–	–	–	–	–	–	–	–	–	1	–	–	–	–	–	–	–	–	–	–	–	–	–	–	–	–	–	–	–	–	–	–
1	Scotland	–	–	–	–	–	–	–	–	–	–	–	–	–	–	–	–	–	–	–	–	–	–	1	–	–	–	–	–	–	–	–	–

Czech Republic and Slovakia

Total	Club	'08	'07	'06	'05	'04	'03	'02	'01	'00	'99	'98	'97	'96	'95	'94	'93	'92	'91	'90	'89	'88	'87	'86	'85	'84	'83	'82	'81	'80	'79	'78	'69 to '77
8	Brno	–	–	–	–	–	–	–	–	–	–	1	–	–	–	–	–	1	–	2	–	–	3	–	1	–	–	–	–	–	–	–	–
31	Ceske Budejovice	–	–	2	2	1	2	–	2	3	1	1	2	1	3	2	1	–	–	2	1	–	1	–	–	1	1	2	–	–	–	–	–
3	Havirov	–	–	–	–	–	–	2	–	1	–	–	–	–	–	–	–	–	–	–	–	–	–	–	–	–	–	–	–	–	–	–	–
28	Jihlava	–	–	–	–	–	–	–	–	1	–	–	–	2	2	1	1	1	2	3	1	1	3	–	1	3	4	2	–	–	–	–	–
4	Karlovy Vary	–	–	–	–	–	1	1	1	1	–	–	–	–	–	–	–	–	–	–	–	–	–	–	–	–	–	–	–	–	–	–	–
23	Kladno	–	–	3	1	1	1	–	1	1	2	–	–	2	–	2	1	–	2	1	–	–	–	1	–	1	–	1	2	–	–	–	–
15	Kosice	–	–	1	1	–	–	–	1	–	1	1	1	1	–	–	–	–	–	2	–	–	–	1	–	2	–	2	1	–	–	–	–
4	Liberec	–	–	–	1	1	–	–	2	–	–	–	–	–	–	–	–	–	–	–	–	–	–	–	–	–	–	–	–	–	–	–	–
34	Litvinov	–	–	–	–	3	2	–	1	–	1	1	2	2	2	4	2	3	1	2	2	–	–	–	–	2	1	3	–	–	–	–	–
6	Martin	–	–	–	–	1	–	–	1	1	–	–	–	–	2	–	–	–	–	–	–	1	–	–	–	–	–	–	–	–	–	–	–
7	Nitra	–	–	–	–	–	1	–	1	–	–	1	–	1	–	–	1	–	2	–	–	–	–	–	–	–	–	–	–	–	–	–	–
7	Olomouc	–	–	–	–	–	–	–	–	–	–	1	–	–	2	1	–	2	–	–	1	–	–	–	–	–	–	–	–	–	–	–	–
13	Pardubice	–	–	–	–	–	–	3	1	–	–	–	1	–	1	2	–	–	–	–	–	–	1	–	2	–	2	–	–	–	–	–	–
14	Plzen	1	–	–	–	–	–	2	1	1	–	1	–	–	1	1	–	3	–	1	1	–	–	1	–	–	–	–	–	–	–	–	–
3	Presov	–	–	–	1	–	–	–	–	–	–	–	1	–	–	–	1	–	–	–	–	–	–	–	–	–	–	–	–	–	–	–	–
28	Slavia Praha	–	1	–	1	1	2	2	5	3	2	5	4	–	–	–	1	–	–	–	–	–	–	–	–	1	–	–	–	–	–	–	–
22	Slovan Bratis.	–	–	–	–	–	3	1	–	2	2	1	1	1	–	3	–	–	–	1	–	–	1	1	1	–	–	2	–	–	1	1	–
28	Sparta Praha	–	–	1	2	4	1	1	2	1	–	1	1	–	1	–	1	1	–	2	1	2	1	1	1	2	–	1	–	–	–	–	–
30	Trencin	–	1	1	1	4	3	–	2	3	2	–	1	2	1	–	2	2	–	2	1	1	–	–	–	1	–	–	–	–	–	–	–
9	Trinec	1	–	1	1	–	1	1	1	1	2	–	–	–	–	–	–	–	–	–	–	–	–	–	–	–	–	–	–	–	–	–	–
19	Vitkovice	–	–	1	1	2	–	2	–	1	1	1	–	1	1	1	3	1	–	1	–	–	–	–	–	–	–	–	1	–	–	1	–
14	Vsetin	–	1	1	–	1	1	3	2	2	–	1	2	–	–	–	–	–	–	–	–	–	–	–	–	–	–	–	–	–	–	–	–
21	Zlin[1]	–	–	–	1	2	–	–	2	–	2	2	1	–	2	–	1	2	2	–	–	–	1	1	1	–	1	–	–	–	–	–	–
7	Zvolen	–	–	–	–	–	–	–	–	2	2	–	–	1	1	–	–	1	–	–	–	–	–	–	–	–	–	–	–	–	–	–	–

Former club names: [1]–Gottwaldov. **Teams with two players selected:** Ingstav Brno, IS Banska Bystrica, Dubnica, Michalovce, Partizan Liptovsky Mikulas, VTJ Pisek, Skalica, Spisska Nova Ves, Topolcany. **Teams with one player selected:** Banik Sokolov, KLH Chomutov, Havlickuv Brod, Ostrava, KC SKP Poprad, Povazska Bystrica, HK Trnava, KHM Zvolen.

Finland

Total	Club	'08	'07	'06	'05	'04	'03	'02	'01	'00	'99	'98	'97	'96	'95	'94	'93	'92	'91	'90	'89	'88	'87	'86	'85	'84	'83	'82	'81	'80	'79	'78	'69 to '77
16	Assat	–	–	2	–	–	–	1	–	–	–	1	–	–	1	1	1	–	–	1	–	1	–	–	–	2	2	–	1	–	–	–	2
17	Blues Espoo	1	–	–	1	1	–	1	2	–	2	–	1	–	1	2	–	2	1	1	–	1	–	–	–	–	–	–	–	–	–	–	–
39	HIFK Helsinki	–	–	4	1	2	–	5	2	2	4	2	1	–	1	–	2	–	–	–	1	2	–	–	1	2	2	1	1	–	–	–	3
12	HPK	–	–	1	–	–	–	1	1	3	1	1	1	–	–	–	–	2	–	–	1	–	–	–	–	–	–	–	–	–	–	–	–
34	Ilves	1	–	3	3	–	–	2	4	3	1	2	–	–	2	–	–	–	1	1	–	1	–	1	–	2	2	–	2	–	–	2	1
36	Jokerit	–	–	2	–	1	2	6	4	3	3	1	1	1	–	1	–	3	–	2	–	1	1	–	–	1	–	–	1	2	–	–	–
11	JyP Jyvaskyla	–	–	–	–	1	–	2	1	–	3	–	1	2	–	–	–	–	–	–	–	–	1	–	–	–	–	–	–	–	–	–	–
11	KalPa	1	–	1	–	–	1	–	2	1	–	1	–	–	–	2	1	–	–	–	–	–	1	–	–	–	–	–	–	–	–	–	–
24	Karpat	–	–	–	2	2	3	3	3	–	–	1	1	–	–	–	1	–	1	–	–	–	2	2	–	1	–	1	–	1	–	–	–
3	Kiekoo-67	–	–	–	–	–	–	–	–	–	–	–	–	–	3	–	–	–	–	–	–	–	–	–	–	–	–	–	–	–	–	–	–
20	Lukko	1	1	–	–	1	1	1	3	1	2	–	–	–	–	–	–	1	–	1	–	–	1	–	1	–	2	–	–	–	–	–	3
9	Pelicans	–	1	–	–	1	–	–	–	–	–	–	–	1	–	–	1	–	2	–	–	–	–	–	–	1	1	1	–	–	–	–	–
7	SaiPa	–	–	–	1	1	1	–	1	1	–	–	–	–	–	–	–	–	–	1	–	–	–	–	–	–	–	–	1	–	–	–	–
24	Tappara	2	2	–	–	1	2	2	2	1	–	–	2	1	1	–	–	–	–	1	–	1	–	4	–	–	–	2	–	–	–	–	1
34	TPS Turku	–	–	–	–	1	1	1	3	3	1	3	3	1	3	2	3	–	–	–	–	–	–	1	1	–	–	–	6	1	–	–	–

Teams with two players selected: KooKoo Kouvola, Sapko Savonlinna, Sport Vaasa, TuTo.
Teams with one player selected: Ahmat Hyvinkaa, Hermes Kokkola, Junkkarit Kalajoki, GrIFK Kauniainen, LeKi, S-Kiekko Seinajoki.

Martin Hanzel (top) of the Czech Republic made his NHL debut with Phoenix last year after being the Coyotes top pick (17th overall) in the 2005 Entry Draft. Sweden's Nicklas Backstrom was one of the NHL's top scoring rookies in 2007-08 after being selected fourth overall by the Washington Capitals in 2006.

Note: International draft selections played outside North America in their draft year.

European-born players drafted from the OHL, QMJHL, WHL, U.S. colleges or other North American leagues are not counted as International players.

For analysis by birthplace, see the following page.

Russia/CIS/USSR

Total	Club	'08	'07	'06	'05	'04	'03	'02	'01	'00	'99	'98	'97	'96	'95	'94	'93	'92	'91	'90	'89	'88	'87	'86	'85	'84	'83	'82	'81	'80	'79	'78	'69 to '77
6	Ak Bars Kazan	1	–	–	–	–	1	–	1	1	–	1	–	–	–	1	–	–	–	–	–	–	–	–	–	–	–	–	–	–	–	–	–
3	Ak Bars Kazan 2	–	–	–	–	–	1	–	1	–	1	–	–	–	–	–	–	–	–	–	–	–	–	–	–	–	–	–	–	–	–	–	–
9	Avangard Omsk	–	–	–	–	–	–	1	3	1	–	–	–	1	–	3	–	–	–	–	–	–	–	–	–	–	–	–	–	–	–	–	–
5	Avangard Omsk 2	–	–	–	–	1	1	–	3	–	–	–	–	–	–	–	–	–	–	–	–	–	–	–	–	–	–	–	–	–	–	–	–
5	CSK VVS Samara	–	–	–	–	1	1	–	1	–	1	–	–	–	1	–	–	–	–	–	–	–	–	–	–	–	–	–	–	–	–	–	–
63	CSKA Moscow	–	2	1	1	3	3	–	–	–	3	1	–	3	2	5	3	7	4	3	8	5	1	1	1	–	4	1	–	–	–	1	1
13	CSKA Moscow 2	2	–	2	1	1	2	–	–	–	–	–	2	2	–	1	–	–	–	–	–	–	–	–	–	–	–	–	–	–	–	–	–
46	Dynamo Moscow	–	1	–	–	1	1	–	–	2	2	1	1	1	7	1	2	10	7	4	3	2	–	–	–	–	–	–	–	–	–	–	–
16	Dynamo Moscow 2	–	–	–	–	–	1	–	–	4	–	3	3	–	–	2	1	2	–	–	–	–	–	–	–	–	–	–	–	–	–	–	–
4	Dyn-Energ. Yekat.[1]	–	–	–	–	–	1	–	–	–	1	1	–	1	–	–	–	–	–	–	–	–	–	–	–	–	–	–	–	–	–	–	–
16	Elektrostal	–	–	–	–	–	2	9	1	–	–	–	1	–	–	–	–	3	–	–	–	–	–	–	–	–	–	–	–	–	–	–	–
11	HC CSKA	–	–	–	–	–	–	4	–	5	2	–	–	–	–	–	–	–	–	–	–	–	–	–	–	–	–	–	–	–	–	–	–
3	Kristall Saratov	–	–	–	–	1	–	–	1	–	–	–	–	–	–	–	1	–	–	–	–	–	–	–	–	–	–	–	–	–	–	–	–
33	Krylja Sovetov	–	–	1	1	2	–	1	1	1	2	1	1	2	3	5	1	3	4	2	1	1	–	–	–	–	–	–	–	–	–	–	–
4	Krylja Sovetov 2	–	–	–	–	–	–	3	–	–	–	–	–	–	–	–	1	–	–	–	–	–	–	–	–	–	–	–	–	–	–	–	–
18	Lada Togliatti	–	–	2	–	2	–	2	–	2	2	1	3	1	–	–	2	1	–	–	–	–	–	–	–	–	–	–	–	–	–	–	–
6	Lada Togliatti 2	–	–	–	1	–	–	–	2	2	1	–	–	–	–	–	–	–	–	–	–	–	–	–	–	–	–	–	–	–	–	–	–
22	Lokomotiv Yaro.[2]	–	–	–	–	–	4	2	–	1	1	3	1	1	5	1	–	–	2	1	–	–	–	–	–	–	–	–	–	–	–	–	–
31	Lokomotiv Yaro.2	2	1	3	2	–	3	1	1	9	–	4	2	2	1	–	–	–	–	–	–	–	–	–	–	–	–	–	–	–	–	–	–
7	Magnitogorsk	–	–	1	–	1	1	1	3	–	–	–	–	–	–	–	–	–	–	–	–	–	–	–	–	–	–	–	–	–	–	–	–
6	Nizhnekamsk	–	–	–	–	1	–	–	2	2	–	–	1	–	–	–	–	–	–	–	–	–	–	–	–	–	–	–	–	–	–	–	–
4	Nizhny Novgorod[3]	–	–	–	–	–	–	–	–	1	–	–	–	–	–	–	–	2	–	1	–	–	–	–	–	–	–	–	–	–	–	–	–
7	Novokuznetsk	–	–	–	–	1	1	–	1	2	2	–	–	–	–	–	–	–	–	–	–	–	–	–	–	–	–	–	–	–	–	–	–
10	Pardaugava Riga[4]	–	–	–	–	–	–	–	–	–	–	–	–	–	–	–	1	4	1	–	2	1	–	–	–	–	–	–	–	–	–	–	–
5	Perm	–	–	–	–	–	–	1	1	1	–	–	–	–	1	1	–	–	–	–	–	–	–	–	–	–	–	–	–	–	–	–	–
14	Severstal Cher.[5]	1	–	1	–	–	2	–	–	1	5	–	–	1	1	–	1	1	–	–	–	–	–	–	–	–	–	–	–	–	–	–	–
4	Severstal Cher. 2	1	–	–	–	–	–	1	–	1	1	–	–	–	–	–	–	–	–	–	–	–	–	–	–	–	–	–	–	–	–	–	–
11	SKA St. Pete.[6]	–	–	–	–	–	–	–	2	1	2	–	–	–	–	1	–	1	2	–	–	–	–	–	–	–	–	1	–	–	–	1	1
11	Sokol Kiev	–	–	–	–	–	–	–	–	–	–	–	–	–	2	–	1	3	2	1	–	1	–	–	–	1	–	–	–	–	–	–	–
22	Spartak Moscow	–	–	–	–	–	–	6	–	1	–	–	–	–	1	6	–	4	1	–	–	–	1	–	1	–	–	1	–	–	–	–	–
9	THC Tver	–	–	–	–	3	3	–	1	2	–	–	–	–	–	–	–	–	–	–	–	–	–	–	–	–	–	–	–	–	–	–	–
5	Tivali Minsk[7]	–	–	–	–	1	–	–	–	–	–	–	–	–	–	1	2	–	–	–	–	1	–	–	–	–	–	–	–	–	–	–	–
21	Traktor Chelyabinsk	1	1	1	2	–	–	1	–	–	–	1	1	–	1	1	7	2	–	–	2	–	–	–	–	–	–	–	–	–	–	–	–
9	Ufa	–	–	–	–	–	1	–	–	1	–	–	1	1	1	2	2	–	–	–	–	–	–	–	–	–	–	–	–	–	–	–	–
9	Ust-Kamenogorsk	–	–	–	–	–	1	–	–	–	1	2	–	–	1	2	1	1	–	–	–	–	–	–	–	–	–	–	–	–	–	–	–
14	Voskresensk	–	–	–	–	–	1	–	1	1	–	2	–	–	–	1	–	2	1	3	1	–	–	–	–	–	1	–	–	–	–	–	–

Former club names: 1–Avtomobilist Yekaterinburg, 2–Torpedo Yaroslavl, 3–Torpedo Gorky, 4–Dynamo Riga,HC Riga, 5–Metallurg Cherepovets, 6–SKA Leningrad, 7–Dynamo Minsk.
Teams with two players selected: Dizelist Penza, Metallurg Magnitogorsk 2, Metallurg Novokuznetsk 2, Salavat Yulayev Ufa 2, Spartak Moscow 2, Torpedo Nizhny Novgorod 2, Yunost Minsk. **Teams with one player selected:** Amur Khabarovsk, Argus Moscow, Avangard Omsk, HC CSKA Moscow 2, Dynamo Khazov, Dynamo-81 Riga, Gazovik Tyumen, HK Gomel, Izohets St. Petersburg, Kapitan Stupino, Khimik Novopolotsk, Khimik Voskresensk 2, Mechel Chelyabinsk, Metalurgs Liepaja, Mostovik Kurgan, Neftekhimik Nizhnekamsk 2, Neftyanik Almetjevsk, SKA St. Petersburg 2, Spartak St. Petersburg, Sibir Novosibirsk 2, Stalkers-Juniors, Torpedo Nizhny Novgorod 2, THC Tver, Vityaz Podolsk, Vityaz Podolsk 2.

Sweden

Total	Club	'08	'07	'06	'05	'04	'03	'02	'01	'00	'99	'98	'97	'96	'95	'94	'93	'92	'91	'90	'89	'88	'87	'86	'85	'84	'83	'82	'81	'80	'79	'78	'69 to '77
24	AIK Solna	–	–	–	–	–	–	1	1	–	3	1	1	–	–	1	–	1	1	1	–	–	–	–	4	–	1	3	2	–	1	1	1
9	Bjorkloven	1	–	2	1	–	–	–	–	–	–	–	–	–	–	–	–	–	–	–	–	1	–	–	1	–	–	–	1	2	–	–	–
3	Boden	–	–	–	–	–	–	–	–	–	–	–	–	–	–	1	–	–	–	–	–	–	–	1	–	–	–	–	–	–	–	–	1
29	Brynas Gavle	4	1	1	–	–	2	–	2	1	1	2	1	1	–	–	1	–	–	–	–	–	4	–	–	2	1	–	1	1	1	1	1
39	Djurgarden	1	–	1	1	2	–	2	1	4	1	–	2	2	3	–	1	1	2	1	1	–	2	1	–	1	2	1	–	2	1	–	3
3	Falun	–	–	–	–	–	–	–	–	–	–	–	–	–	–	–	–	–	1	–	–	1	–	–	–	–	–	–	1	–	–	–	–
33	Farjestad	–	–	1	–	–	–	2	1	–	1	6	3	–	2	–	1	2	1	–	1	–	–	–	2	1	1	1	2	1	–	2	2
46	Frolunda	4	5	3	3	4	2	3	3	4	2	1	–	1	1	3	–	1	–	–	1	1	1	–	1	2	–	–	–	–	–	–	–
3	Grums	–	–	–	–	–	–	–	–	1	1	–	–	–	–	1	–	–	–	–	–	–	–	–	–	–	–	–	–	–	–	–	–
10	Hammarby	–	–	1	–	–	–	3	–	1	–	–	1	–	–	–	1	1	–	–	–	–	–	–	–	–	–	–	–	1	1	–	–
7	Huddinge	–	–	1	–	–	–	1	1	–	1	–	–	2	–	–	–	–	1	–	–	–	–	–	–	–	–	–	–	–	–	–	–
26	HV 71	3	1	–	1	2	1	1	–	1	3	4	1	2	–	2	–	–	–	1	–	1	1	–	–	–	–	–	1	–	–	–	–
30	Leksand	–	–	1	1	–	2	–	–	5	–	2	–	1	–	2	2	–	2	–	1	2	1	1	2	2	–	1	–	–	1	–	1
5	Linkoping	1	1	1	1	1	–	–	–	–	–	–	–	–	–	–	–	–	–	–	–	–	–	–	–	–	–	–	–	–	–	–	–
14	Lulea	–	3	–	–	1	–	–	–	2	–	1	1	–	–	–	–	1	–	–	–	1	1	1	–	–	–	–	1	1	–	–	–
18	Malmo	1	1	1	1	1	1	4	–	1	1	–	–	2	–	1	1	1	–	–	–	1	–	–	–	–	–	–	–	–	–	–	–
36	MODO	–	–	–	1	1	–	3	–	3	7	–	3	3	–	–	5	2	2	–	–	–	1	–	–	2	–	1	–	–	1	–	1
6	Mora	–	–	–	–	–	1	–	1	–	–	–	1	1	–	–	–	–	–	–	–	–	–	1	–	–	1	–	–	–	–	–	–
3	Morrum	–	–	–	–	–	–	2	1	–	–	–	–	–	–	–	–	–	–	–	–	–	–	–	–	–	–	–	–	–	–	–	–
4	Nacka	–	–	–	–	–	–	–	–	–	–	–	–	–	–	–	–	2	–	–	1	–	–	1	–	–	–	–	–	–	–	–	–
6	Orebro	–	–	–	–	1	–	–	–	–	–	–	–	–	–	–	–	–	–	–	–	–	1	–	1	–	1	–	–	–	–	1	1
3	Pitea	–	–	–	–	–	–	–	–	–	–	–	–	–	–	1	–	–	–	1	–	–	–	–	–	–	–	1	–	–	–	–	–
10	Rogle	–	1	–	–	–	–	–	–	–	1	–	–	–	1	2	2	–	–	–	–	2	1	–	–	–	–	–	–	–	–	–	–
10	Skelleftea	–	–	–	–	–	–	–	–	–	–	–	1	–	–	–	1	–	–	–	–	1	–	–	–	1	2	1	1	–	–	–	2
25	Sodertalje	–	1	2	3	1	2	–	1	1	–	1	–	–	–	–	1	–	–	–	2	–	–	2	2	2	1	1	1	–	–	1	–
3	Stocksund	–	–	–	–	2	–	–	–	–	–	–	–	–	–	–	–	–	–	–	–	–	–	–	–	–	–	1	–	–	–	–	–
3	Team Kiruna	–	–	–	–	–	–	–	–	–	–	–	–	–	–	–	1	–	–	–	–	–	–	–	–	–	–	1	–	–	–	1	–
8	Timra	–	–	–	–	–	–	1	–	–	1	–	–	–	–	1	–	–	–	–	–	–	–	1	1	–	–	–	2	1	–	–	–
4	Troja/Ljungby	–	–	–	–	–	1	–	–	–	1	–	–	–	–	–	–	–	–	–	–	1	–	–	1	–	–	–	–	–	–	–	–
16	Vasteras	1	1	3	–	1	–	1	–	1	–	–	–	–	–	1	1	–	1	1	2	2	–	–	–	–	–	–	–	–	–	–	–
3	Vita Hasten	1	–	–	–	–	–	–	1	–	–	–	–	1	–	–	–	–	–	–	–	–	–	–	–	–	–	–	–	–	–	–	–

Teams with two players selected: Almtuna, Bofors, Ostersund, Tingsryd. **Teams with one player selected:** Arboga, Arvika, Danderyd Hockey, Fagersta, Jamtland, Karskoga, Kumla, Stocksund, S/G Hockey 83 Gavle, Skovde, Sunne, Talje, Tunabro, Uppsala, Vallentuna, Vasby. Karskoga, Kumla, Stocksund, S/G Hockey 83 Gavle, Skovde, Sunne, Talje, Tunabro, Uppsala, Vallentuna, Vasby.

European Draft Firsts

1969 – First European (and Finn) • LW Tommi Salmelainen, 66th overall by St. Louis.

1974 – First Swede • C Per Alexandersson, 49th overall by Toronto. Four other Swedish-born players were selected that year, including defenseman Stefan Persson, 214th overall by the NY Islanders, who became the first European-trained player to be part of a Stanley Cup winner with the Islanders in 1980.

1975 – First Russian • C Viktor Khatulev, 160th overall by Philadelphia.

1976 – First European Taken in the First Round • Swedish D Bjorn Johansson, 5th overall by the California Seals.

1976 – First Swiss • C Jacques Soguel, 121st overall by St. Louis.

1978 – First Czechoslovak • LW Ladislav Svozil, 194th overall by Detroit.

1978 – First Germans • G Bernard Englbrecht, 196th overall by Atlanta and F Gerd Truntschka, 200th overall by St. Louis.

1989 – First European Taken First Overall • Swedish C Mats Sundin, first overall by Quebec in 1989.

2008 Entry Draft Analysis

BY BIRTHPLACE

Country of Origin

Country	Players Drafted
Canada	120
USA	45
Sweden	17
Russia	8
Finland	7
Czech Republic	3
Norway	3
Denmark	2
Belarus	1
France	1
Germany	1
Italy	1
Latvia	1
Switzerland	1
Total	**211**

Canadian-Born Players

Province	Players Drafted
Ontario	52
Quebec	22
Alberta	13
British Columbia	10
Saskatchewan	9
Manitoba	7
New Brunswick	4
Newfoundland`	1
Nova Scotia	1
Prince Edward Island	1
Total	**120**

U.S.-Born Players

State	Players Drafted
Minnesota	10
Michigan	5
Illinois	4
Massachusetts	4
California	3
Colorado	2
Connecticut	2
Pennsylvania	2
Texas	2
Wisconsin	2
Alaska	1
Georgia	1
Kansas	1
New Hampshire	1
New York	1
North Carolina	1
North Dakota	1
Oklahoma	1
Virginia	1
Total	**45**

BY BIRTH YEAR

Year	Players Drafted
1990	131
1989	51
1988	27
1987	2

BY POSITION

Position	Players Drafted
Defense	25
Center	64
Right Wing	78
Left Wing	21
Goaltender	23

Notes on 2008 First-Round Selections

1. TAMPA BAY • **STEVEN STAMKOS** • C • One of the fastest players available in the draft, Steven Stamkos uses his speed to go to the net fearlessly. He is a point producer that plays with an edge to his game and an aggressive attitude. His skill level, awareness on the ice and hockey sense are all highly advanced. Stamkos ranked second in the OHL with 58 goals and fifth with 105 points in 61 games during the 2007-08 season. He also helped Team Canada win gold at the 2008 World Junior Championship.

2. LOS ANGELES • **DREW DOUGHTY** • D • A highly skilled defenseman with intelligence and enthusiasm, Drew Doughty has the ability to lead the rush and the knowledge to know when to stay back. He is highly patient with the puck and usually makes good decisions. Doughty was named best offensive defenseman in the OHL coaches poll in both 2007 and 2008. He was named best defenseman at the 2008 World Junior Championship and won gold with Team Canada.

3. ATLANTA • **ZACH BOGOSIAN** • D • At 6'2" and 200 pounds, Zach Bogosian combines good size with strong skating ability. He is solid defensively and can carry the puck. Bogosian was the only defenseman in the OHL to lead his team (Peterborough Petes) in scoring in 2007-08 (11-50-61) and was nominated for the league's MVP award. He played high school hockey at Cushing Academy, where former NHL great Raymond Bourque was an assistant coach.

4. ST. LOUIS • **ALEX PIETRANGELO** • D • A defenseman with plenty of potential, Alex Pietrangelo is poised with the puck and remains unflustered in the face of a hard forecheck. He knows when to carry the puck out of his zone and when to pass it. Pietrangelo has the ability to dictate the flow and the pace of the game. He finished seventh in scoring among OHL defenseman (13-40-53) in 2007-08. Former NHL goaltender Frank Pietrangelo is his father's second cousin.

5. TORONTO • **LUKE SCHENN** • D • A stay-at-home defenseman with a tough edge to him, Luke Schenn makes opposing forwards pay a physical price. He likes to keep things simple and play a sound defensive game, patterning his style after NHL defenseman Adam Foote. Though his style is not always suited to the international game, he won gold medals with Team Canada at the 2006 World Under-18 Championship and at the 2008 World Junior Championship.

6. COLUMBUS • **NIKITA FILATOV** • LW • A team leader with a great attitude and excellent work ethic, Nikita Filatov also has a lot of talent. He is an excellent skater who can change pace, even at top speed. He is 6' but weighs just 172 pounds, yet still plays an aggressive game. Filatov was the top scorer for the Russian team at the 2008 World Junior Championship and captained the World Under-18 team.

7. NASHVILLE • **COLIN WILSON** • C • Physically strong with excellent hands, Colin Wilson is a very good passer. He anticipates the play at both ends of the ice and is very reliable defensively. Wilson won a gold medal with Team USA at the 2006 World Under-18 Championship and was tied for the lead with six goals at the 2008 World Junior Championship. Father Carey and grandfather Jerry both played in the NHL.

8. PHOENIX • **MIKKEL BOEDKER** • LW • A strong skater with breakaway speed, Mikkel Boedker has a good shot and excels as a playmaker. He uses great body position to protect the puck and is strong along the boards. A native of Denmark, Boedker left home to play junior hockey in Sweden at age 15. He helped Vastra Frolunda win the Swedish junior championship in 2006-07 before joining the OHL's Kitchener Rangers.

9. NY ISLANDERS • **JOSHUA BAILEY** • C • A playmaking center who can feed his linemates or shoot himself, Josh Bailey is a hard worker who can play the game at both ends of the ice. Bailey led the Windsor Spitfires in scoring in 2007-08 (29-67-96), ranking tenth in the OHL in points and third in assists. He was selected to play in the 2008 OHL All-Star Game and scored two goals in the Top Prospects Game.

10. VANCOUVER • **CODY HODGSON** • C • A skilled center with good hockey sense, Cody Hodgson knows when to pass and went to shoot. He's also strong on face-offs. He led the Brampton Battalion with 40 goals in 2007-08 and ranked among the top 20 in the OHL with 85 points. He was voted smartest player in the Eastern Conference in the OHL coaches poll. Hodgson played minor hockey with Steven Stamkos

11. CHICAGO • **KYLE BEACH** • C • A feisty forward with a reputation for being physical, Kyle Beach has good scoring skills and a very accurate shot. Known as an agitator, Beach sometimes lets his temper get the better of him. He was the only player in the WHL to average a point per game while also averaging over three penalty minutes per game. He was named rookie of the year in the WHL in 2006-07 after scoring 29 goals and adding 32 assists.

12. BUFFALO • **TYLER MYERS** • D • At a towering 6'7", Tyler Myers was the tallest player available in the 2008 NHL Entry Draft but skates very well for a player his size. Myers has a strong shot from the point and his long reach gives him an excellent poke check. Myers grew up in Houston, Texas and was a fan of the Dallas Stars. When he was 10, his family moved to Alberta to further his hockey career. He won gold for Canada at the 2008 World Under-18 Championship.

13. LOS ANGELES • **COLTEN TEUBERT** • D • A big (6'4"), strong defenseman, Colten Teubert can take charge in his own end. He is a smooth skater who can carry the puck out of trouble. Teubert was the first player selected in the 2005 WHL bantam draft and made his debut in the league at age 16. He played for Team Canada at the 2007 Under-18 Ivan Hlinka Memorial tournament and again at the 2008 World Under-18 Championship, where he won a gold medal.

14. CAROLINA • **ZACH BOYCHUK** • C • An all-around offensive player who sees the ice well, Zach Boychuk has above average speed and great hockey sense. He can reach top speed in just two steps and he can handle the puck well at high speed. In a span of 18 months, Boychuk represented Canada at the 2007 World Under-18 Championship, the Canada-Russia Summit Series and the 2008 World Junior Championship. He led the WHL with 13 playoff goals in 2008.

15. OTTAWA • **ERIK KARLSSON** • D • At 5'11" and 165 pounds, Erik Karlsson compensates for his lack of size with his mobility, vision and passing skill. His natural hockey sense makes him an offensive threat. His 24 assists in 38 games led all defenseman (and all players under age 18) in the Swedish junior league in 2007-08. His seven assists in six games at the 2008 World Under-18 Championship ranked him third at the tournament, where he was named best defenseman.

16. BOSTON • **JOE COLBORNE** • C • Standing 6'6", Joe Colborne is rangy with his stick, has good on-ice awareness and is a good playmaker. He skates well and has soft hands. Colborne tied for the lead in assists (57) in the Alberta Junior Hockey League in 2007-08 and finished second in points (90). He tied for the playoff lead with 16 points (8 goals, 8 assists) to lead Camrose to the title and starred in the Canadian Junior A championship, where Camrose reached the finals.

17. ANAHEIM • **JAKE GARDINER** • D • A forward until his junior year in high school, Jake Gardiner was moved to defense full time in 2007-08 and blossomed into a top-rated prospect. Gardiner is a pure skater who is smart with the puck and has a quick, dangerous wrist shot. He was a finalist for Minnesota's "Mr. Hockey" award in 2007-08 after ranking third in scoring (20-28-48) among high school defensemen.

18. NASHVILLE • **CHET PICKARD** • G • A goaltender with very good instincts, Chet Pickard's net coverage is very good and he reads the play well. He is strong in his crease and very consistent. Pickard led WHL goalies with 46 wins in 2007-08 and was fourth in save percentage (.916) to win the league's goaltender of the year award, which former teammate Carey Price won the season before.

19. PHILADELPHIA • **LUCA SBISA** • D • A smart player who handles the puck with poise, Luca Sbisa adapted well to the North American game while playing in the WHL in 2007-08. Born in Italy but raised in Switzerland, he was named rookie of the year with the Lethbridge Hurricanes. Sbisa played for the Swiss team at the 2007 Under-18 Ivan Hlinka Memorial tournament and at the 2008 World Junior Championship.

20. NY RANGERS • **MICHAEL DEL ZOTTO** • D • An offensive defenseman who jumps into the rush effectively, Michael Del Zotto is effective with the puck and can be a physical presence. He ranked third among OHL defensemen in scoring (16-47-63) in 2007-08. As a rookie in 2006-07, he was the first 16-year-old defenseman to play in the OHL All-Star Game. He played with Steven Stamkos in minor hockey.

21. WASHINGTON • **ANTON GUSTAFSSON** • C • The son of former NHLer and current Swedish national team coach Bengt Gustafsson, Anton Gustafsson is s a highly skilled player with strong puckhandling skills and playmaking ability. He is an effective passer through traffic who also has a good selection of shots. Gustafsson is a strong and talented two-way center with good vision and a fine understanding of the game. His team has won two straight Swedish junior titles.

22. EDMONTON • **JORDAN LBERLE** • C • A good skater with great hands, Jordan Eberle is a very gifted puck handler with great finish around the net. At 5'10" and 174 pounds, he is small but deceptive. Eberle scored 42 goals in 2007-08, ranking him fifth in the WHL and accounting for 19 percent of the goals scored by the Regina Pats. He was also the team's scholastic player of the year. Eberle won gold with Canada at the 2008 World Under-18 Championship.

23. MINNESOTA • **TYLER CUMA** • D • A defenseman who plays well at both ends of the ice, Tyler Cuma is a versatile performer who is dedicated to the game. Cuma is a strong skater. He did not become a defenseman until his last year of minor hockey, but regularly plays against opponents' top forwards in the OHL. He was the Ottawa 67's rookie of the year in 2006-07 and won a gold medal with Team Canada at the 2008 World Under-18 Championship.

24. NEW JERSEY • **MATTIAS TEDENBY** • LW • Small but fearless, Mattias Tedenby is 5'10" and 175 pounds but has outstanding speed and stick work. He creates scoring chances with his outstanding skating and is very difficult to stop when he is at full speed. He has excellent balance and quick, smooth hands, but needs to improve his defensive awareness. Tedenby made his debut in the Swedish elite league in 2007-08 and starred at the World Under-18 Championship.

25. CALGARY • **GREG NEMISZ** • C • At 6'3" and 200 pounds, Greg Nemisz is not overly physical but he goes to the net well and is hard to move from in front. He has a good shot and possesses great hands. Nemisz improved from 34 points as an OHL rookie in 2006-07 to 34 goals in 2007-08 and went from a -22 to a +28. Nemisz won gold with Canada at the 2008 Under-18 World Championship

26. BUFFALO • **TYLER ENNIS** • C • Standing only 5'9" and weighing in the range of 160 pounds, Tyler Ennis has tremendous speed and can turn on a dime. He can drive wide on a defenseman who is unaware or a little slow. Ennis is also hard to contain in the corners because of his speed. He is a pure offensive talent. His 43 goals ranked second in the WHL in 2007-08 and his 91 points were fourth.

27. WASHINGTON • **JOHN CARLSON** • D • A big defenseman at 6'2" and 218 pounds, John Carlson is a strong skater with a heavy shot who can run the power-play. He is good on his feet and agile for his size. Carlson was third in scoring (9-28-37 in 53 games) as a rookie in the USHL in 2007-08 and played in the All-Star Game. He was an assistant captain for the U.S. team at the 2007 Ivan Hlinka Memorial tournament.

28. PHOENIX • **VIKTOR TIKHONOV** • LW/RW • Grandson of the former Soviet national team coach, Viktor Tikhonov was raised in Northern California where his father worked for the San Jose Sharks. Tikhonov was one of the most improved young players in the Russian league in 2007-08. He shows a high level of competitiveness and is a dedicated team player with a keen ability to read and react to the play. Tikhonov won a bronze medal with Russia at the 2008 World Junior Championship and was named best forward.

29. ATLANTA • **DAULTAN LEVEILLE** • C • Among the fastest players available in the draft, Daultan Leveille is a technically skilled skater who can run the power-play. He is also effective at killing penalties. Leveille played Junior B hockey for the St. Catharines Falcons, a program that has never before produced an NHL draft pick. He had 14 goals in 16 playoff games to lead his team to the league final.

30. DETROIT • **THOMAS McCOLLUM** • G • Displaying strong net position and a great butterfly, Thomas McCollum has good net coverage and is very competitive. He is good at challenging shooters and handles the puck well. McCollum was the only three-time winner of the CHL goaltender of the week honor in 2007-08. In 2007 he won a silver medal with Team USA at the World Under-18 Championship.

1: Steven Stamkos
C – Tampa Bay

2: Drew Doughty
D – Los Angeles

3: Zach Bogosian
D – Atlanta

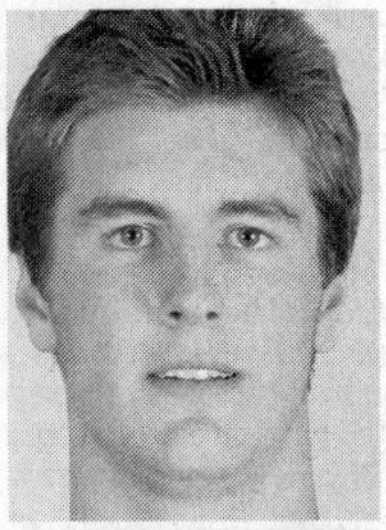

4: Alex Petrangelo
D – St. Louis

5: Luke Schenn
D – Toronto

6: Nikita Filatov
LW – Columbus

7: Colin Wilson
C – Nashville

8: Mikkel Boedker
LW – Phoenix

9: Joshua Bailey
C – NY Islanders

10: Cody Hodgson
C – Vancouver

Players selected first through tenth in the 2008 NHL Entry Draft.

2008 NHL ENTRY DRAFT

FIRST ROUND

Pick	Claimed by		Amateur Club	Position
1	T.B.	Steven Stamkos	Sarnia	C
2	L.A.	Drew Doughty	Guelph	D
3	ATL	Zach Bogosian	Peterborough	D
4	STL	Alex Pietrangelo	Niagara	D
5	TOR	Luke Schenn	Kelowna	D
6	CBJ	Nikita Filatov	CSKA 2	LW
7	NSH	Colin Wilson	Boston University	C
8	PHX	Mikkel Boedker	Kitchener	LW
9	NYI	Joshua Bailey	Windsor	C
10	VAN	Cody Hodgson	Brampton	C
11	CHI	Kyle Beach	Everett	C
12	BUF	Tyler Myers	Kelowna	D
13	L.A.	Colten Teubert	Regina	D
14	CAR	Zach Boychuk	Lethbridge	C
15	OTT	Erik Karlsson	Frolunda Jr.	D
16	BOS	Joe Colborne	Camrose	C
17	ANA	Jake Gardiner	Minnetonka	D
18	NSH	Chet Pickard	Tri-City	G
19	PHI	Luca Sbisa	Lethbridge	D
20	NYR	Michael Del Zotto	Oshawa	D
21	WSH	Anton Gustafsson	Frolunda Jr.	C
22	EDM	Jordan Eberle	Regina	C
23	MIN	Tyler Cuma	Ottawa	D
24	N.J.	Mattias Tedenby	HV 71	LW
25	CGY	Greg Nemisz	Windsor	C
26	BUF	Tyler Ennis	Medicine Hat	C
27	WSH	John Carlson	Indiana	D
28	PHX	Viktor Tikhonov	Cherepovets	W
29	ATL	Daultan Leveille	St. Catharines	C
30	DET	Thomas McCollum	Guelph	G

SECOND ROUND

Pick	Claimed by		Amateur Club	Position
31	FLA	Jacob Markstrom	Brynas Jr.	G
32	L.A.	Vjateslav Voinov	Chelyabinsk	D
33	STL	Philip McRae	London	C
34	STL	Jake Allen	St. John's	G
35	ANA	Nicolas Deschamps	Chicoutimi	C
36	NYI	Corey Trivino	Stouffville	C
37	CBJ	Cody Goloubef	U. of Wisconsin	D
38	NSH	Roman Josi	Bern	D
39	ANA	Eric O'Dell	Sudbury	C
40	NYI	Aaron Ness	Roseau High	D
41	VAN	Yann Sauve	Saint John	D
42	OTT	Patrick Wiercioch	Omaha	D
43	ANA	Justin Schultz	Westside	D
44	BUF	Luke Adam	St. John's	C
45	CAR	Zac Dalpe	Penticton	C/RW
46	FLA	Colby Robak	Brandon	D
47	BOS	Maxime Sauve	Val d'Or	C
48	CGY	Mitch Wahl	Spokane	C
49	PHX	Jared Staal	Sudbury	RW
50	COL	Cameron Gaunce	St. Michael's	D
51	NYR	Derek Stepan	Shattuck St.Mary's	C
52	N.J.	Brandon Burlon	St. Michael's	D
53	NYI	Travis Hamonic	Moose Jaw	D
54	N.J.	Patrice Cormier	Rimouski	C
55	MIN	Marco Scandella	Val d'Or	D
56	MTL	Danny Kristo	U-18	RW
57	WSH	Eric Mestery	Tri-City	D
58	WSH	Dmitri Kugryshev	CSKA 2	RW
59	DAL	Tyler Beskorowany	Owen Sound	G
60	TOR	Jimmy Hayes	Lincoln	RW
61	COL	Peter Delmas	Lewiston	G

THIRD ROUND

Pick	Claimed by		Amateur Club	Position
62	S.J.	Justin Daniels	Kent School	C
63	L.A.	Robert Czarnik	USA U-18	C/RW
64	ATL	Danick Paquette	Lewiston	RW
65	STL	Jori Lehtera	Tappara	C
66	NYI	David Toews	Shattuck St.Mary's	C
67	PHI	Marc-Andre Bourdon	Rouyn-Noranda	D
68	CHI	Shawn Lalonde	Belleville	D
69	PHX	Michael Stone	Calgary	D
70	STL	James Livingston	Sault Ste. Marie	RW
71	ANA	Josh Brittain	Kingston	LW
72	NYI	Jyri Niemi	Saskatoon	D
73	NYI	Kirill Petrov	Kazan	RW
74	L.A.	Andrew Campbell	Sault Ste. Marie	D
75	NYR	Evgeny Grachev	Yaroslavl 2	C
76	PHX	Mathieu Brodeur	Cape Breton	D
77	BOS	Michael Hutchinson	Barrie	G
78	CGY	Lance Bouma	Vancouver	C
79	OTT	Zack Smith	Swift Current	C
80	FLA	Adam Comrie	Saginaw	D
81	BUF	Corey Fienhage	Eastview High	D
82	N.J.	Adam Henrique	Windsor	C
83	ANA	Marco Cousineau	Baie-Comeau	G
84	PHI	Jacob Deserres	Seattle	G
85	ANA	Brandon McMillan	Kelowna	C
86	MTL	Steve Quailer	Sioux City	RW
87	STL	Ian Schultz	Calgary	RW
88	L.A.	Geordie Wudrick	Swift Current	LW
89	DAL	Scott Winkler	Russell Stover	C
90	NYR	Tomas Kundratek	Trinec	D
91	DET	Max Nicastro	Chicago	D

FOURTH ROUND

Pick	Claimed by		Amateur Club	Position
92	S.J.	Samuel Groulx	Quebec	D
93	WSH	Braden Holtby	Saskatoon	G
94	ATL	Vinny Saponari	USA U-18	RW
95	STL	David Warsofsky	USA U-18	D
96	NYI	Matt Donovan	Cedar Rapids	D
97	BOS	Jamie Arniel	Sarnia	C
98	TOR	Mikhail Stefanovich	Quebec	C
99	PHX	Colin Long	Kelowna	C
100	FLA	Aj Jenks	Plymouth	LW
101	BUF	Justin Jokinen	Cloquet	RW
102	NYI	David Ullstrom	HV71 Jr.	W
103	EDM	Johan Motin	Bofors	D
104	BUF	Jordon Southorn	PEI	D
105	CAR	Michal Jordan	Plymouth	D
106	S.J.	Harri Sateri	Tappara	G
107	CBJ	Steven Delisle	Gatineau	D
108	CGY	Nicholas Larson	Waterloo	LW
109	OTT	Andre Petersson	HV71 Jr.	W
110	COL	Kelsey Tessier	Quebec	C
111	NYR	Dale Weise	Swift Current	RW
112	N.J.	Matt Delahey	Regina	D
113	ANA	Ryan Hegarty	USA U-18	D
114	CGY	T.J. Brodie	Saginaw	D
115	MIN	Sean Lorenz	USA U-18	D
116	MTL	Jason Missiaen	Peterborough	G
117	T.B.	James Wright	Vancouver	C
118	CBJ	Drew Olson	Brainerd High	D
119	OTT	Derek Grant	Langley	C
120	PIT	Nathan Moon	Kingston	C
121	DET	Gustav Nyquist	Malmo Jr.	C

FIFTH ROUND

Pick	Claimed by		Amateur Club	Position
122	T.B.	Dustin Tokarski	Spokane	G
123	L.A.	Andrei Loktionov	Yaroslavl 2	C
124	ATL	Nicklas Lasu	Frolunda Jr.	LW
125	STL	Kristoffer Berglund	Bjorkloven	D
126	NYI	Kevin Poulin	Victoriaville	G
127	CBJ	Matthew Calvert	Brandon	LW
128	TOR	Greg Pateryn	Ohio	D
129	TOR	Joel Champagne	Chicoutimi	C
130	TOR	Jerome Flaake	Koln	LW
131	VAN	Prab Rai	Seattle	C
132	CHI	Teigan Zahn	Saskatoon	D
133	EDM	Philippe Cornet	Rimouski	LW
134	BUF	Jacob Lagace	Chicoutimi	LW
135	CBJ	Tomas Kubalik	Plzen	RW
136	NSH	Taylor Stefishen	Langley	LW
137	CBJ	Brent Regner	Vancouver	D
138	MTL	Maxim Trunev	Cherepovets 2	F
139	OTT	Mark Borowiecki	Smiths Falls	D
140	COL	Mark Olver	Northern Mich.	C
141	NYR	Chris Doyle	PEI	C
142	N.J.	Kory Nagy	Oshawa	C
143	ANA	Stefan Warg	Vasteras Jr.	D
144	WSH	Joel Broda	Moose Jaw	C
145	MIN	Eero Elo	Lukko Jr.	LW
146	S.J.	Julien Demers	Ottawa	D
147	T.B.	Kyle De Coste	Brampton	RW
148	NYI	Matthew Martin	Sarnia	LW
149	DAL	Philip Larsen	Frolunda	D
150	PIT	Alexander Pechurski	Magnitogorsk 2	G
151	DET	Julien Cayer	Northwood School	C

SIXTH ROUND

Pick	Claimed by		Amateur Club	Position
152	T.B.	Mark Barberio	Moncton	D
153	L.A.	Justin Azevedo	Kitchener	C
154	ATL	Christopher Carrozzi	St. Michael's	G
155	STL	Anthony Nigro	Guelph	C
156	NYI	Jared Spurgeon	Spokane	D
157	CBJ	Cameron Atkinson	Avon Old Farms	RW
158	TOR	Grant Rollheiser	Trail	G
159	PHX	Brett Hextall	Penticton	C
160	T.B.	Luke Witkowski	Ohio	D
161	VAN	Mats Froshaug	Linkoping Jr.	C
162	CHI	Jonathan Carlsson	Brynas	D
163	EDM	Teemu Hartikainen	Kalpa Jr.	C
164	BUF	Nick Crawford	Saginaw	D
165	CAR	Mike Murphy	Belleville	G
166	NSH	Jeffrey Foss	RPI	D
167	COL	Joel Chouinard	Victoriaville	D
168	CGY	Ryley Grantham	Moose Jaw	C
169	CHI	Ben Smith	Boston College	RW
170	COL	Jonas Holos	Sarpsborg	D
171	NYR	Mitch Gaulton	Erie	D
172	N.J.	David Wohlberg	USA U-18	C
173	BOS	Nicholas Tremblay	Smiths Falls	C
174	WSH	Greg Burke	Jr. Monarchs	LW
175	NYI	Justin Dibenedetto	Sarnia	C
176	DAL	Matthew Tassone	Swift Current	C
177	S.J.	Tommy Wingels	Miami U.	C
178	PHI	Zac Rinaldo	St. Michael's	C
179	CHI	Braden Birch	Oakville	D
180	PIT	Patrick Killeen	Brampton	G
181	DET	Stephen Johnston	Belleville	LW

SEVENTH ROUND

Pick		Claimed by	Amateur Club	Position
182	T.B.	Matias Sointu	Ilves Jr.	RW
183	L.A.	Garrett Roe	St. Cloud State	LW
184	ATL	Zach Redmond	Ferris State	D
185	STL	Paul Karpowich	Wellington	G
186	S.J.	Jason Demers	Victoriaville	D
187	CBJ	Sean Collins	Waywayseecappo	C
188	TOR	Andrew MacWilliam	Camrose	D
189	PHX	Tim Billingsley	St. Michael's	D
190	FLA	Matthew Bartkowski	Lincoln	D
191	VAN	Morgan Clark	Red Deer	G
192	CHI	Joe Gleason	Edina High	D
193	EDM	Jordan Bendfeld	Medicine Hat	D
194	S.J.	Drew Daniels	Kent School	RW
195	CAR	Samuel Morneau	Baie-Comeau	LW
196	PHI	Joacim Eriksson	Brynas Jr.	G
197	BOS	Mark Goggin	Choate-Rosemary	C
198	CGY	Alexander Deilert	Djurgarden Jr.	D
199	OTT	Emil Sandin	Brynas	LW
200	COL	Nathan Condon	Wausau	C
201	NSH	Jani Lajunen	Blues Jr.	C
202	N.J.	Harry Young	Windsor	D
203	T.B.	David Carle	Shattuck St.Mary's	D
204	WSH	Stefan Della Rovere	Barrie	LW
205	N.J.	Jean-Sebastien Berube	Rouyn-Noranda	LW
206	MTL	Patrick Johnson	U. of Wisconsin	C
207	NSH	Anders Lindback	Brynas	G
208	ANA	Nick Pryor	USA U-18	D
209	DAL	Mike Bergin	Smiths Falls	D
210	PIT	Nicholas D'Agostino	St. Michael's	D
211	DET	Jesper Samuelsson	Timra	C

First Two Rounds 2007–2005

2007

FIRST ROUND

Pick		Claimed by	Amateur Club	Position
1	CHI	Patrick Kane	London	RW
2	PHI	James vanRiemsdyk	USA U-18	LW
3	PHX	Kyle Turris	Burnaby	C
4	LA	Thomas Hickey	Seattle	D
5	WSH	Karl Alzner	Calgary	D
6	EDM	Sam Gagner	London	C/W
7	CBJ	Jakub Voracek	Halifax	RW
8	BOS	Zach Hamill	Everett	C
9	SJ	Logan Couture	Ottawa	C
10	FLA	Keaton Ellerby	Kamloops	D
11	CAR	Brandon Sutter	Red Deer	C/RW
12	MTL	Ryan McDonagh	Cretin-Derham	D
13	STL	Lars Eller	Frolunda Jr.	C
14	COL	Kevin Shattenkirk	USA U-18	D
15	EDM	Alex Plante	Calgary	D
16	MIN	Colton Gillies	Saskatoon	C
17	NYR	Alexei Cherepanov	Omsk	RW
18	STL	Ian Cole	USA U-18	D
19	ANA	Logan MacMillan	Halifax	C
20	PIT	Angelo Esposito	Quebec	C
21	EDM	Riley Nash	Salmon Arm	C
22	MTL	Max Pacioretty	Sioux City	LW
23	NSH	Jonathon Blum	Vancouver	D
24	CGY	Mikael Backlund	Vasteras	C
25	VAN	Patrick White	Tri-City	C
26	STL	David Perron	Lewiston	LW
27	DET	Brendan Smith	St. Michael's	D
28	SJ	Nicholas Petrecki	Omaha	D
29	OTT	James O'Brien	U of Minnesota	C
30	PHX	Nick Ross	Regina	D

SECOND ROUND

Pick		Claimed by	Amateur Club	Position
31	BUF	T.J. Brennan	St. John's	D
32	PHX	Brett MacLean	Oshawa	LW
33	VAN	Taylor Ellington	Everett	D
34	WSH	Josh Godfrey	Sault Ste. Marie	D
35	BOS	Tommy Cross	Westminster	D
36	PHX	Joel Gistedt	Frolunda	G
37	CBJ	Stefan Legein	Mississauga	RW
38	CHI	William Sweatt	Colorado College	LW
39	STL	Simon Hjalmarsson	Frolunda Jr.	RW
40	FLA	Michal Repik	Vancouver	RW
41	PHI	Kevin Marshall	Lewiston	D
42	ANA	Eric Tangradi	Belleville	C
43	MTL	P.K. Subban	Belleville	D
44	STL	Aaron Palushaj	Des Moines	RW
45	COL	Colby Cohen	Lincoln	D
46	WSH	Theo Ruth	USA U-18	D
47	TB	Dana Tyrell	Prince George	C/RW
48	NYR	Antoine Lafleur	PEI	G
49	COL	Trevor Cann	Peterborough	G
50	LA	Nico Sacchetti	Virginia High	C
51	PIT	Keven Veilleux	Victoriaville	C
52	L.A	Oscar Moller	Chilliwack	RW
53	CBJ	Will Weber	Gaylord High	D
54	NSH	Jeremy Smith	Plymouth	G
55	COL	T.J. Galiardi	Dartmouth	W
56	CHI	Akim Aliu	Sudbury	C/RW
57	NJ	Mike Hoeffel	USA U-18	W
58	NSH	Nick Spaling	Kitchener	C
59	BUF	Drew Schiestel	Mississauga	D
60	OTT	Ruslan Bashkirov	Quebec	LW
61	LA	Wayne Simmonds	Owen Sound	RW

2006

FIRST ROUND

Pick		Claimed by	Amateur Club	Position
1	STL	Erik Johnson	USA U-18	D
2	PIT	Jordan Staal	Peterborough	C
3	CHI	Jonathan Toews	U. of North Dakota	C
4	WSH	Nicklas Backstrom	Brynas	C
5	BOS	Phil Kessel	U. of Minnesota	C
6	CBJ	Derick Brassard	Drummondville	C
7	NYI	Kyle Okposo	Des Moines	RW
8	PHX	Peter Mueller	Everett	C
9	MIN	James Sheppard	Cape Breton	C
10	FLA	Michael Frolik	Kladno	C
11	L.A.	Jonathan Bernier	Lewiston	G
12	ATL	Bryan Little	Barrie	C
13	TOR	Jiri Tlusty	Kladno	C
14	VAN	Michael Grabner	Spokane	RW
15	T.B.	Riku Helenius	Ilves	G
16	S.J.	Ty Wishart	Prince George	D
17	L.A.	Trevor Lewis	Des Moines	C
18	COL	Chris Stewart	Kingston	RW
19	ANA	Mark Mitera	U. of Michigan	D
20	MTL	David Fischer	Apple Valley	D
21	NYR	Bobby Sanguinetti	Owen Sound	D
22	PHI	Claude Giroux	Gatineau	RW
23	WSH	Simeon Varlamov	Yaroslavl 2	G
24	BUF	Dennis Persson	Vasteras	D
25	STL	Patrik Berglund	Vasteras	C
26	CGY	Leland Irving	Everett	G
27	DAL	Ivan Vishnevskiy	Rouyn Noranda	D
28	OTT	Nick Foligno	Sudbury	LW
29	PHX	Chris Summers	USA U-18	D
30	N.J.	Matthew Corrente	Saginaw	D

SECOND ROUND

Pick		Claimed by	Amateur Club	Position
31	STL	Tomas Kana	Vitkovice	C
32	PIT	Carl Sneep	Brainerd	D
33	CHI	Igor Makarov	Krylja	RW
34	WSH	Michal Neuvirth	Sparta Jr.	G
35	WSH	Francois Bouchard	Baie Comeau	RW
36	S.J.	Jamie Mcginn	Ottawa	LW
37	BOS	Yuri Alexandrov	Cherepovets	D
38	ANA	Bryce Swan	Halifax	RW
39	PHI	Andreas Nodl	Sioux Falls	RW
40	MIN	Ondrej Fiala	Everett	C
41	DET	Cory Emmerton	Kingston	C
42	PHI	Michael Ratchuk	USA U-18	D
43	ATL	Riley Holzapfel	Moose Jaw	C
44	TOR	Nikolai Kulemin	Magnitogorsk	W
45	EDM	Jeff Petry	Des Moines	D
46	BUF	Jhonas Enroth	Sodertalje	G
47	DET	Shawn Matthias	Belleville	C
48	L.A.	Joe Ryan	Quebec	D
49	MTL	Ben Maxwell	Kootenay	C
50	BOS	Milan Lucic	Vancouver	LW
51	COL	Nigel Williams	USA U-18	D
52	WSH	Keith Seabrook	Burnaby	D
53	MTL	Mathieu Carle	Acadie-Bathurst	D
54	NYR	Artem Anisimov	Yaroslavl	C
55	PHI	Denis Bodrov	Togliatti	D
56	NSH	Blake Geoffrion	USA U-18	LW
57	BUF	Mike Weber	Windsor	D
58	N.J.	Alexander Vasyunov	Yaroslavl 2	LW
59	COL	Codey Burki	Brandon	C
60	NYI	Jesse Joensuu	Assat	W
61	CHI	Simon Danis-Pepin	U. of Maine	D
62	DET	Dick Axelsson	Huddinge	W
63	CAR	Jamie Mcbain	USA U-18	D

2005

FIRST ROUND

Pick		Claimed by	Amateur Club	Position
1	PIT	Sidney Crosby	Rimouski	C
2	ANA	Bobby Ryan	Owen Sound	RW
3	CAR	Jack Johnson	USA U-18	D
4	MIN	Benoit Pouliot	Sudbury	LW
5	MTL	Carey Price	Tri-City	G
6	CBJ	Gilbert Brule	Vancouver	C
7	CHI	Jack Skille	USA U-18	RW
8	S.J.	Devin Setoguchi	Saskatoon	RW
9	OTT	Brian Lee	Moorhead	D
10	VAN	Luc Bourdon	Val D'or	D
11	L.A.	Anze Kopitar	Sodertalje Jr.	C
12	NYR	Marc Staal	Sudbury	D
13	BUF	Marek Zagrapan	Chicoutimi	C
14	WSH	Sasha Pokulok	Cornell	D
15	NYI	Ryan O'Marra	Erie	C
16	ATL	Alex Bourret	Lewiston	RW
17	PHX	Martin Hanzal	C. Budejovice	C
18	NSH	Ryan Parent	Guelph	D
19	DET	Jakub Kindl	Kitchener	D
20	FLA	Kenndal McArdle	Moose Jaw	LW
21	TOR	Tuukka Rask	Ilves Jr.	G
22	BOS	Matt Lashoff	Kitchener	D
23	N.J.	Nicklas Bergfors	Sodertalje	RW
24	STL	T.J. Oshie	Warroad	C
25	EDM	Andrew Cogliano	St. Mike's B's	C
26	CGY	Matt Pelech	Sarnia	D
27	WSH	Joe Finley	Sioux Falls	D
28	DAL	Matt Niskanen	Virginia	D
29	PHI	Steve Downie	Windsor	RW
30	T.B.	Vladimir Mihalik	Presov	D

SECOND ROUND

Pick		Claimed by	Amateur Club	Position
31	ANA	Brendan Mikkelson	Portland	D
32	FLA	Tyler Plante	Brandon	G
33	DAL	James Neal	Plymouth	LW
34	COL	Ryan Stoa	USA U-18	C
35	S.J.	Marc-Edouard Vlasic	Quebec	D
36	EDM	Taylor Chorney	Shat.-St. Mary's	D
37	STL	Scott Jackson	Seattle	D
38	N.J.	Jeff Frazee	USA U-18	G
39	BOS	Petr Kalus	Vitkovice Jr.	LW
40	NYR	Michael Sauer	Portland	D
41	ATL	Ondrej Pavelec	Kladno Jr.	G
42	DET	Justin Abdelkader	Cedar Rapids	LW
43	CHI	Michael Blunden	Erie	RW
44	COL	Paul Stastny	U. of Denver	C
45	MTL	Guillaume Latendresse	Drummondville	RW
46	NYI	Dustin Kohn	Calgary	D
47	COL	Tom Fritsche	Ohio State	LW
48	BUF	Philip Gogulla	Koln	RW
49	ATL	Chad Denny	Lewiston	D
50	L.A.	Dany Roussin	Rimouski	LW
51	VAN	Mason Raymond	Camrose	LW
52	COL	Chris Durand	Seattle	C
53	ATL	Andrew Kozek	South Surrey	W
54	CHI	Dan Bertram	Boston College	RW
55	CBJ	Adam McQuaid	Sudbury	D
56	NYR	Marc-Andre Cliche	Lewiston	RW
57	MIN	Matt Kassian	Kamloops	LW
58	CAR	Nathan Hagemo	U. of Minnesota	D
59	PHX	Pier-Olivier Pelletier	Drummondville	G
60	L.A.	T.J. Fast	Camrose	D
61	PIT	Michael Gergen	Shat.-St. Mary's	W

First Round and Other Notable Selections 2004–1969

2004

FIRST ROUND

Pick		Claimed by	Amateur Club	Position
1	WSH	Alex Ovechkin	Dynamo	LW
2	PIT	Evgeni Malkin	Magnitogorsk	C
3	CHI	Cam Barker	Medicine Hat	D
4	CAR	Andrew Ladd	Calgary	LW
5	PHX	Blake Wheeler	Breck	RW
6	NYR	Al Montoya	U. of Michigan	G
7	FLA	Rostislav Olesz	Vitkovice	C
8	CBJ	Alexandre Picard	Lewiston	LW
9	ANA	Ladislav Smid	Liberec	D
10	ATL	Boris Valabik	Kitchener	D
11	L.A.	Lauri Tukonen	Blues Espoo	RW
12	MIN	A.J. Thelen	Michigan State	D
13	BUF	Drew Stafford	U. of North Dakota	RW
14	EDM	Devan Dubnyk	Kamloops	G
15	NSH	Alexander Radulov	Tver	LW
16	NYI	Petteri Nokelainen	SaiPa	C
17	STL	Marek Schwarz	Sparta Praha	G
18	MTL	Kyle Chipchura	Prince Albert	C
19	NYR	Lauri Korpikoski	TPS Turku Jr.	LW
20	N.J.	Travis Zajac	Salmon Arm	C
21	COL	Wojtek Wolski	Brampton	LW
22	S.J.	Lukas Kaspar	Litvinov	RW
23	OTT	Andrej Meszaros	Trencin	D
24	CGY	Kris Chucko	Salmon Arm	LW
25	EDM	Rob Schremp	London	C
26	VAN	Cory Schneider	Phillips-Andover	G
27	WSH	Jeff Schultz	Calgary	D
28	DAL	Mark Fistric	Vancouver	D
29	WSH	Mike Green	Saskatoon	D
30	T.B.	Andy Rogers	Calgary	D

OTHER NOTABLE SELECTIONS

Pick		Claimed by	Amateur Club	Position
91	VAN	Alexander Edler	Jamtland	D
97	DET	Johan Franzen	Linkoping	C
98	CGY	Dustin Boyd	Moose Jaw	C
126	S.J.	Torrey Mitchell	Hotchkiss	C
127	NYR	Ryan Callahan	Guelph	RW
191	T.B.	Karri Ramo	Pelicans Jr.	G
227	NYI	Chris Campoli	Erie	D
262	MTL	Mark Streit	Zurich	D
265	PHX	Daniel Winnik	U. of New Hampshire	C/LW

2003

FIRST ROUND

Pick	Claimed by		Amateur Club	Position
1	PIT	Marc-Andre Fleury	Cape Breton	G
2	CAR	Eric Staal	Peterborough	C
3	FLA	Nathan Horton	Oshawa	C
4	CBJ	Nikolai Zherdev	CSKA Moscow	W
5	BUF	Thomas Vanek	U. of Minnesota	LW
6	S.J.	Milan Michalek	Budejovice	RW
7	NSH	Ryan Suter	U.S. National U-18	D
8	ATL	Braydon Coburn	Portland	D
9	CGY	Dion Phaneuf	Red Deer	D
10	MTL	Andrei Kostitsyn	CSKA Moscow 2	RW
11	PHI	Jeff Carter	Sault Ste. Marie	C
12	NYR	Hugh Jessiman	Dartmouth	RW
13	L.A.	Dustin Brown	Guelph	RW
14	CHI	Brent Seabrook	Lethbridge	D
15	NYI	Robert Nilsson	Leksand	RW
16	S.J.	Steve Bernier	Moncton	RW
17	N.J.	Zach Parise	North Dakota	C
18	WSH	Eric Fehr	Brandon	RW
19	ANA	Ryan Getzlaf	Calgary	C
20	MIN	Brent Burns	Brampton	RW
21	BOS	Mark Stuart	Colorado College	D
22	EDM	Marc-Antoine Pouliot	Rimouski	C
23	VAN	Ryan Kesler	Ohio State	C
24	PHI	Mike Richards	Kitchener	C
25	FLA	Anthony Stewart	Kingston	C
26	L.A.	Brian Boyle	St. Sebastian's H.S.	C
27	L.A.	Jeff Tambellini	U. of Michigan	LW
28	ANA	Corey Perry	London	RW
29	OTT	Patrick Eaves	Boston College	RW
30	STL	Shawn Belle	Tri-City	D

OTHER NOTABLE SELECTIONS

Pick	Claimed by		Amateur Club	Position
45	BOS	Patrice Bergeron	Acadie-Bathurst	C
47	S.J.	Matt Carle	River City	D
49	NSH	Shea Weber	Kelowna	D
61	MTL	Maxim Lapierre	Montreal	C
148	STL	Lee Stempniak	Dartmouth	RW
271	MTL	Jaroslav Halak	Bratislava Jr.	G

2002

FIRST ROUND

Pick	Claimed by		Amateur Club	Position
1	CBJ	Rick Nash	London	LW
2	ATL	Kari Lehtonen	Jokerit	G
3	FLA	Jay Bouwmeester	Medicine Hat	D
4	PHI	Joni Pitkanen	Karpat	D
5	PIT	Ryan Whitney	Boston U.	D
6	NSH	Scottie Upshall	Kamloops	RW
7	ANA	Joffrey Lupul	Medicine Hat	C
8	MIN	Pierre-Marc Bouchard	Chicoutimi	C
9	FLA	Petr Taticek	Sault Ste. Marie	C
10	CGY	Eric Nystrom	U. of Michigan	LW
11	BUF	Keith Ballard	U. of Minnesota	D
12	WSH	Steve Eminger	Kitchener	D
13	WSH	Alexander Semin	Chelyabinsk	LW
14	MTL	Christopher Higgins	Yale	C
15	EDM	Jesse Niinimaki	Ilves Tampere	C
16	OTT	Jakub Klepis	Portland	C
17	WSH	Boyd Gordon	Red Deer	RW
18	L.A.	Denis Grebeshkov	Yaroslavl	D
19	PHX	Jakub Koreis	Plzen	C
20	BUF	Dan Paille	Guelph	LW
21	CHI	Anton Babchuk	Elektrostal	D
22	NYI	Sean Bergenheim	Jokerit	C
23	PHX	Ben Eager	Oshawa	LW
24	TOR	Alexander Steen	Vastra Frolunda	C
25	CAR	Cam Ward	Red Deer	G
26	DAL	Martin Vagner	Hull	D
27	S.J.	Mike Morris	St. Sebastian's H.S.	RW
28	COL	Jonas Johansson	HV 71 Jonkoping Jr.	RW
29	BOS	Hannu Toivonen	HPK Jr.	G
30	ATL	Jim Slater	Michigan State	C

OTHER NOTABLE SELECTIONS

Pick	Claimed by		Amateur Club	Position
36	EDM	Jarret Stoll	Kootenay	C
43	DAL	Trevor Daley	Sault Ste. Marie	D
44	EDM	Matt Greene	Green Bay	D
46	PHX	David Leneveu	Cornell	G
57	TOR	Matt Stajan	Belleville	C
58	DET	Jiri Hudler	Vsetin	C
90	CGY	Matthew Lomardi	Victoriaville	C
117	N.J.	Cam Janssen	Windsor	RW
133	CBJ	Lasse Pirjeta	Karpat	C
191	TOR	Ian White	Swift Current	D
240	NYR	Petr Prucha	Pardubice	RW
254	TOR	Jarkko Immonen	Assat	C
259	BOS	Jan Stastny	U. of Notre Dame	C

2001

FIRST ROUND

Pick	Claimed by		Amateur Club	Position
1	ATL	Ilya Kovalchuk	Spartak	LW
2	OTT	Jason Spezza	Windsor	C
3	T.B.	Alexander Svitov	Avangard Omsk	C
4	FLA	Stephen Weiss	Plymouth	C
5	ANA	Stanislav Chistov	Avangard Omsk	LW
6	MIN	Mikko Koivu	TPS Turku	C
7	MTL	Mike Komisarek	U. of Michigan	D
8	CBJ	Pascal Leclaire	Halifax	G
9	CHI	Tuomo Ruutu	Jokerit	C/LW
10	NYR	Dan Blackburn	Kootenay	G
11	PHX	Fredrik Sjostrom	Vastra Frolunda	RW
12	NSH	Dan Hamhuis	Prince George	D
13	EDM	Ales Hemsky	Hull	RW
14	CGY	Chuck Kobasew	Boston College	C
15	CAR	Igor Knyazev	Spartak	D
16	VAN	R.J. Umberger	Ohio State	C
17	TOR	Carlo Colaiacovo	Erie	D
18	L.A.	Jens Karlsson	Vastra Frolunda	RW
19	BOS	Shaone Morrisonn	Kamloops	D
20	S.J.	Marcel Goc	Schwenningen	C
21	PIT	Colby Armstrong	Red Deer	RW
22	BUF	Jiri Novotny	Budejovice	C
23	OTT	Tim Gleason	Windsor	D
24	FLA	Lukas Krajicek	Peterborough	D
25	MTL	Alexander Perezhogin	Avangard Omsk	C
26	DAL	Jason Bacashihua	Chicago (NAHL)	G
27	PHI	Jeff Woywitka	Red Deer	D
28	N.J.	Adrian Foster	Saskatoon	C
29	CHI	Adam Munro	Erie	G
30	L.A.	Dave Steckel	Ohio State	C

OTHER NOTABLE SELECTIONS

Pick	Claimed by		Amateur Club	Position
32	BUF	Derek Roy	Kitchener	C
49	L.A.	Mike Cammalleri	U. of Michigan	C
98	NSH	Jordin Tootoo	Brandon	RW
99	OTT	Ray Emery	S.S. Marie	G
106	S.J.	Christoph Ehrhoff	Krefeld	D
132	NYI	Dusan Salficky	Plzen	G
134	TOR	Kyle Wellwood	Belleville	C
172	PHI	Dennis Seidenberg	Mannheim	D
176	NSH	Marek Zidlicky	HIFK	D
189	ATL	Pasi Nurminen	Jokerit	G
214	L.A.	Cristobal Huet	Lugano	G
232	ANA	Martin Gerber	Langnau	G
253	STL	Petr Cajanek	Zlin	RW

2000

FIRST ROUND

Pick	Claimed by		Amateur Club	Position
1	NYI	Rick DiPietro	Boston U.	G
2	ATL	Dany Heatley	U. of Wisconsin	RW
3	MIN	Marian Gaborik	Dukla Trencin	RW
4	CBJ	Rostislav Klesla	Brampton	D
5	NYI	Raffi Torres	Brampton	LW
6	NSH	Scott Hartnell	Prince Albert	LW
7	BOS	Lars Jonsson	Leksand	D
8	T.B.	Nikita Alexeev	Erie	RW
9	CGY	Brent Krahn	Calgary	G
10	CHI	Mikhail Yakubov	Lada Togliatti	C
11	CHI	Pavel Vorobiev	Yaroslavl	RW
12	ANA	Alexei Smirnov	Tver	LW
13	MTL	Ron Hainsey	U. of Mass-Lowell	D
14	COL	Vaclav Nedorost	Budejovice	C
15	BUF	Artem Kryukov	Yaroslavl	C
16	MTL	Marcel Hossa	Portland	LW
17	EDM	Alexei Mikhnov	Yaroslavl	LW
18	PIT	Brooks Orpik	Boston College	D
19	PHX	Krys Kolanos	Boston College	C
20	L.A.	Alexander Frolov	Yaroslavl 2	LW
21	OTT	Anton Volchenkov	HC Moscow	D
22	N.J.	David Hale	Sioux City	D
23	VAN	Nathan Smith	Swift Current	C
24	TOR	Brad Boyes	Erie	C
25	DAL	Steve Ott	Windsor	C
26	WSH	Brian Sutherby	Moose Jaw	C
27	BOS	Martin Samuelsson	MoDo Ornskoldsvik	RW
28	PHI	Justin Williams	Plymouth	RW
29	DET	Niklas Kronwall	Djurgarden	D
30	STL	Jeff Taffe	U. of Minnesota	C

OTHER NOTABLE SELECTIONS

Pick	Claimed by		Amateur Club	Position
33	MIN	Nick Schultz	Prince Albert	D
43	WSH	Matt Pettinger	Calgary	LW
44	ANA	Ilya Bryzgalov	Lada Togliatti	G
46	CGY	Jarret Stoll	Kootenay	C
54	L.A.	Andreas Lilja	Malmo	D
76	N.J.	Michael Rupp	Erie	LW
97	CAR	Niclas Wallin	Brynas	D
118	L.A.	Lubomir Visnovsky	Bratislava	D
155	CGY	Travis Moen	Kelowna	LW
159	COL	John-Michael Liles	Michigan State	D
171	PHI	Roman Cechmanek	Vsetin	G
220	BUF	Paul Gaustad	Portland	C

1999

FIRST ROUND

Pick	Claimed by		Amateur Club	Position
1	ATL	Patrik Stefan	Long Beach	C
2	VAN	Daniel Sedin	MoDo Ornskoldsvik	LW
3	VAN	Henrik Sedin	MoDo Ornskoldsvik	C
4	NYR	Pavel Brendl	Calgary	RW
5	NYI	Tim Connolly	Erie	C
6	NSH	Brian Finley	Barrie	G
7	WSH	Kris Beech	Calgary	C
8	NYI	Taylor Pyatt	Sudbury	LW
9	NYR	Jamie Lundmark	Moose Jaw	C
10	NYI	Branislav Mezei	Belleville	D
11	CGY	Oleg Saprykin	Seattle	LW
12	FLA	Denis Shvidki	Barrie	RW
13	EDM	Jani Rita	Jokerit	LW
14	S.J.	Jeff Jillson	U. of Michigan	D
15	PHX	Scott Kelman	Seattle	C
16	CAR	David Tanabe	U. of Wisconsin	D
17	STL	Barret Jackman	Regina	D
18	PIT	Konstantin Koltsov	Cherepovets	RW
19	PHX	Kirill Safronov	St. Petersburg	D
20	BUF	Barrett Heisten	U. of Maine	LW
21	BOS	Nick Boynton	Ottawa	D
22	PHI	Maxime Ouellet	Quebec	G
23	CHI	Steve McCarthy	Kootenay	D
24	TOR	Luca Cereda	Ambri	C
25	COL	Mikhail Kuleshov	Cherepovets	LW
26	OTT	Martin Havlat	Trinec	LW
27	N.J.	Ari Ahonen	JyP HT Jr.	G
28	NYI	Kristian Kudroc	Michalovce	D

OTHER NOTABLE SELECTIONS

Pick	Claimed by		Amateur Club	Position
42	N.J.	Mike Commodore	North Dakota	D
70	FLA	Niklas Hagman	HIFK Helsinki	LW
76	L.A.	Frantisek Kaberle	MoDo Ornskoldsvik	D
83	ANA	Niclas Havelid	Malmo	D
91	EDM	Mike Comrie	U. of Michigan	C
115	PIT	Ryan Malone	Omaha	LW
191	NSH	Martin Erat	ZPS Zlin Jr.	LW
210	DET	Henrik Zetterberg	Timra	LW
212	COL	Radim Vrbata	Hull	RW
232	STL	Alexander Khavanov	Dynamo	D
247	BOS	Mikko Eloranta	TPS Turku	LW

1998

FIRST ROUND

Pick	Claimed by		Amateur Club	Position
1	T.B.	Vincent Lecavalier	Rimouski	C
2	NSH	David Legwand	Plymouth	C
3	S.J.	Brad Stuart	Regina	D
4	VAN	Bryan Allen	Oshawa	D
5	ANA	Vitaly Vishnevski	Yaroslavl 2	D
6	CGY	Rico Fata	London	RW
7	NYR	Manny Malhotra	Guelph	C
8	CHI	Mark Bell	Ottawa	C
9	NYI	Mike Rupp	Erie	RW
10	TOR	Nik Antropov	Ust-Kamenogorsk	C
11	CAR	Jeff Heerema	Sarnia	RW
12	COL	Alex Tanguay	Halifax	LW
13	EDM	Michael Henrich	Barrie	RW
14	PHX	Patrick DesRochers	Sarnia	G
15	OTT	Mathieu Chouinard	Shawinigan	G
16	MTL	Eric Chouinard	Quebec	LW
17	COL	Martin Skoula	Barrie	D
18	BUF	Dmitri Kalinin	Chelyabinsk	D
19	COL	Robyn Regehr	Kamloops	D
20	COL	Scott Parker	Kelowna	RW
21	L.A.	Mathieu Biron	Shawinigan	D
22	PHI	Simon Gagne	Quebec	LW
23	PIT	Milan Kraft	Keramika Plzen Jr.	C
24	STL	Christian Backman	Vastra Frolunda Jr.	D
25	DET	Jiri Fischer	Hull	D
26	N.J.	Mike Van Ryn	U. of Michigan	D
27	N.J.	Scott Gomez	Tri-City	C

OTHER NOTABLE SELECTIONS

Pick	Claimed by		Amateur Club	Position
29	S.J.	Jonathan Cheechoo	Belleville	RW
43	PHX	Ossi Vaananen	Jokerit Jr.	D
44	OTT	Mike Fisher	Sudbury	C
64	T.B.	Brad Richards	Rimouski	C
71	CAR	Erik Cole	Clarkson	LW
87	TOR	Alexei Ponikarovsky	Dyn-2 Moscow	LW
91	CAR	Josef Vasicek	Slavia Praha Jr.	C
99	EDM	Shawn Horcoff	Michigan State	C
117	FLA	Jaroslav Spacek	Farjestad Karlstad	D
135	BOS	Andrew Raycroft	Sudbury	G
150	ANA	Trent Hunter	Prince George	RW
162	MTL	Andrei Markov	Khimik	D
171	DET	Pavel Datsyuk	Yekateringburg	C
216	MTL	Michael Ryder	Hull	RW
230	NSH	Karlis Skrastins	TPS Turku	D

1997

FIRST ROUND

Pick	Claimed by	Amateur Club	Position
1	BOS Joe Thornton	Sault Ste. Marie	C
2	S.J. Patrick Marleau	Seattle	C
3	L.A. Olli Jokinen	HIFK Helsinki	C
4	NYI Roberto Luongo	Val-d'Or	G
5	NYI Eric Brewer	Prince George	D
6	CGY Daniel Tkaczuk	Barrie	C
7	T.B. Paul Mara	Sudbury	D
8	BOS Sergei Samsonov	Detroit	LW
9	WSH Nick Boynton	Ottawa	D
10	VAN Brad Ference	Spokane	D
11	MTL Jason Ward	Erie	RW
12	OTT Marian Hossa	Dukla Trencin	RW
13	CHI Daniel Cleary	Belleville	RW
14	EDM Michel Riesen	Biel-Bienne	RW
15	L.A. Matt Zultek	Ottawa	LW
16	CHI Ty Jones	Spokane	RW
17	PIT Robert Dome	Las Vegas (IHL)	RW
18	ANA Mikael Holmqvist	Djurgarden	C
19	NYR Stefan Cherneski	Brandon	RW
20	FLA Mike Brown	Red Deer	LW
21	BUF Mika Noronen	Tappara Tampere	G
22	CAR Nikos Tselios	Belleville	D
23	S.J. Scott Hannan	Kelowna	D
24	N.J. J-F Damphousse	Moncton	G
25	DAL Brenden Morrow	Portland	LW
26	COL Kevin Grimes	Kingston	D

OTHER NOTABLE SELECTIONS

Pick	Claimed by	Amateur Club	Position
27	BOS Ben Clymer	Minnesota-Duluth	LW
48	BUF Henrik Tallinder	AIK Solna	D
69	BUF Maxim Afinogenov	Dynamo Moscow	RW
119	OTT Magnus Arvedson	Farjestad Karlstad	LW
130	CHI Kyle Calder	Regina	LW
136	NYR Mike York	Michigan State	LW
144	VAN Matt Cooke	Windsor	C
156	BUF Brian Campbell	Ottawa	D
161	COL David Aebischer	Fribourg-Gotteron	G
177	STL Ladislav Nagy	Dragon Presov	C
191	BOS Antti Laaksonen	U. of Denver	LW
208	PIT Andrew Ference	Portland	D
242	CHI Brett McLean	Kelowna	C

1996

FIRST ROUND

Pick	Claimed by	Amateur Club	Position
1	OTT Chris Phillips	Prince Albert	D
2	S.J. Andrei Zyuzin	Salavat Yulayev Ufa	D
3	NYI J.P. Dumont	Val-d'Or	RW
4	WSH Alexandre Volchkov	Barrie	C
5	DAL Ric Jackman	Sault Ste. Marie	D
6	EDM Boyd Devereaux	Kitchener	C
7	BUF Erik Rasmussen	U. of Minnesota	LW/C
8	BOS Johnathan Aitken	Medicine Hat	D
9	ANA Ruslan Salei	Las Vegas (IHL)	D
10	N.J. Lance Ward	Red Deer	D
11	PHX Dan Focht	Tri-City	D
12	VAN Josh Holden	Regina	C
13	CGY Derek Morris	Regina	D
14	STL Marty Reasoner	Boston College	C
15	PHI Dainius Zubrus	Pembroke Jr. A	RW
16	T.B. Mario Larocque	Hull	D
17	WSH Jaroslav Svejkovsky	Tri-City	RW
18	MTL Matt Higgins	Moose Jaw	C
19	EDM Matthieu Descoteaux	Shawinigan	D
20	FLA Marcus Nilson	Djurgarden	LW
21	S.J. Marco Sturm	Landshut	LW
22	NYR Jeff Brown	Sarnia	D
23	PIT Craig Hillier	Ottawa	G
24	PHX Daniel Briere	Drummondville	C
25	COL Peter Ratchuk	Shattuck St. Mary's H.S.	D
26	DET Jesse Wallin	Red Deer	D

OTHER NOTABLE SELECTIONS

Pick	Claimed by	Amateur Club	Position
35	ANA Matt Cullen	St. Cloud State	C
49	N.J. Colin White	Hull	D
56	NYI Zdeno Chara	Dukla Trencin	D
59	EDM Tom Poti	Cushing Academy	D
65	FLA Oleg Kvasha	CSKA Moscow	LW/C
79	COL Mark Parrish	St. Cloud State	RW
105	PIT Michal Rozsival	Dukla Jihlava	D
136	OTT Andreas Dackell	Brynas Gavle	RW
139	PHX Robert Esche	Detroit	G
174	PHX Trevor Letowski	Sarnia	RW
176	COL Samuel Pahlsson	MoDo	C
179	T.B. Pavel Kubina	Vitkovice	D
204	TOR Tomas Kaberle	Kladno	D

1995

FIRST ROUND

Pick	Claimed by	Amateur Club	Position
1	OTT Bryan Berard	Detroit	D
2	NYI Wade Redden	Brandon	D
3	L.A. Aki Berg	Kiekko-67 Turku	D
4	ANA Chad Kilger	Kingston	C
5	T.B. Daymond Langkow	Tri-City	C
6	EDM Steve Kelly	Prince Albert	C
7	WPG Shane Doan	Kamloops	RW
8	MTL Terry Ryan	Tri-City	LW
9	BOS Kyle McLaren	Tacoma	D
10	FLA Radek Dvorak	HC Ceske Budejovice	RW
11	DAL Jarome Iginla	Kamloops	RW
12	S.J. Teemu Riihijarvi	Kiekko-Espoo	LW
13	HFD Jean-Sebastien Giguere	Halifax	G
14	BUF Jay McKee	Niagara Falls	D
15	TOR Jeff Ware	Oshawa	D
16	BUF Martin Biron	Beauport	G
17	WSH Brad Church	Prince Albert	LW
18	N.J. Petr Sykora	Detroit	RW
19	CHI Dmitri Nabokov	Krylja Sovetov	C/LW
20	CGY Denis Gauthier	Drummondville	D
21	BOS Sean Brown	Belleville	D
22	PHI Brian Boucher	Tri-City	G
23	WSH Miika Elomo	Kiekko-67 Turku	LW
24	PIT Aleksey Morozov	Krylja Sovetov	RW
25	COL Marc Denis	Chicoutimi	G
26	DET Maxim Kuznetsov	Dynamo	D

OTHER NOTABLE SELECTIONS

Pick	Claimed by	Amateur Club	Position
31	EDM Georges Laraque	St-Jean	RW
45	CHI Christian Laflamme	Beauport	D
49	STL Jochen Hecht	Mannheim	C
66	VAN Peter Schaefer	Brandon	LW
67	WPG Brad Isbister	Portland	LW
79	N.J. Alyn McCauley	Ottawa	C
87	HFD Sami Kapanen	HIFK Helsinki	RW
91	NYR Marc Savard	Oshawa	C
101	STL Michal Handzus	IS Banska Bystrica	C
116	S.J. Miikka Kiprusoff	TPS Turku Jr.	G
128	PIT Jan Hrdina	Seattle	C
144	VAN Brent Sopel	Swift Current	D
166	FLA Peter Worrell	Hull	LW
177	BOS P.J. Axelsson	Vastra Frolunda	LW
223	TOR Danny Markov	Spartak	D

1994

FIRST ROUND

Pick	Claimed by	Amateur Club	Position
1	FLA Ed Jovanovski	Windsor	D
2	ANA Oleg Tverdovsky	Krylja Sovetov	D
3	OTT Radek Bonk	Las Vegas (IHL)	C
4	EDM Jason Bonsignore	Niagara Falls	C
5	HFD Jeff O'Neill	Guelph	RW
6	EDM Ryan Smyth	Moose Jaw	LW
7	L.A. Jamie Storr	Owen Sound	G
8	T.B. Jason Wiemer	Portland	C
9	NYI Brett Lindros	Kingston	RW
10	WSH Nolan Baumgartner	Kamloops	D
11	S.J. Jeff Friesen	Regina	LW
12	QUE Wade Belak	Saskatoon	D/RW
13	VAN Mattias Ohlund	Pitea	D
14	CHI Ethan Moreau	Niagara Falls	LW
15	WSH Alexander Kharlamov	CSKA Moscow	C
16	TOR Eric Fichaud	Chictoutimi	G
17	BUF Wayne Primeau	Owen Sound	C
18	MTL Brad Brown	North Bay	D
19	CGY Chris Dingman	Brandon	LW
20	DAL Jason Botterill	U. of Michigan	LW
21	BOS Evgeni Ryabchikov	Molot Perm	G
22	QUE Jeffrey Kealty	Catholic Memorial H.S.	D
23	DET Yan Golubovsky	Dynamo 2	D
24	PIT Chris Wells	Seattle	C
25	N.J. Vadim Sharifijanov	Salavat Yulayev Ufa	LW
26	NYR Dan Cloutier	Sault Ste. Marie	G

OTHER NOTABLE SELECTIONS

Pick	Claimed by	Amateur Club	Position
27	FLA Rhett Warrener	Saskatoon	D
43	BUF Curtis Brown	Moose Jaw	C/LW
49	DET Mathieu Dandenault	Sherbrooke	RW/D
51	N.J. Patrik Elias	Kladno	C
64	TOR Fredrik Modin	Timra	LW
72	QUE Chris Drury	Fairfield Prep	C
87	QUE Milan Hejduk	Pardubice	RW
124	DAL Marty Turco	Cambridge Jr. A	G
132	ANA Bates Battaglia	Caledon Jr. A	LW
133	OTT Daniel Alfredsson	Vastra Frolunda	RW
210	N.J. Steve Sullivan	Sault Ste. Marie	RW
219	S.J. Evgeni Nabokov	Ust-Kamengorsk	G
272	NYI Dick Tarnstrom	AIK Solna	D

1993

FIRST ROUND

Pick	Claimed by	Amateur Club	Position
1	OTT Alexandre Daigle	Victoriaville	C
2	HFD Chris Pronger	Peterborough	D
3	T.B. Chris Gratton	Kingston	C
4	ANA Paul Kariya	U. of Maine	LW
5	FLA Rob Niedermayer	Medicine Hat	C
6	S.J. Viktor Kozlov	Dynamo	C
7	EDM Jason Arnott	Oshawa	C
8	NYR Niklas Sundstrom	MoDo Ornskoldsvik	RW
9	DAL Todd Harvey	Detroit	RW/C
10	QUE Jocelyn Thibault	Sherbrooke	G
11	WSH Brendan Witt	Seattle	D
12	TOR Kenny Jonsson	Rogle Angelholm	D
13	N.J. Denis Pederson	Prince Albert	C/RW
14	QUE Adam Deadmarsh	Portland	RW
15	WPG Mats Lindgren	Skelleftea	C/LW
16	EDM Nick Stajduhar	London	D
17	WSH Jason Allison	London	C
18	CGY Jesper Mattsson	Malmo	C
19	TOR Landon Wilson	Dubuque Jr. A	RW
20	VAN Mike Wilson	Sudbury	D
21	MTL Saku Koivu	TPS Turku	C
22	DET Anders Eriksson	MoDo Ornskoldsvik	D
23	NYI Todd Bertuzzi	Guelph	RW
24	CHI Eric Lecompte	Hull	LW
25	BOS Kevyn Adams	Miami of Ohio	C
26	PIT Stefan Bergkvist	Leksand	D

OTHER NOTABLE SELECTIONS

Pick	Claimed by	Amateur Club	Position
28	S.J. Shean Donovan	Ottawa	RW
71	PHI Vaclav Prospal	Motor Ceske Budejovice	C
72	HFD Marek Malik	Vitkovice	D
90	CHI Eric Daze	Beauport	RW
111	EDM Miroslav Satan	Dukla Trencin	LW
118	NYI Tommy Salo	Vasteras	G
124	VAN Scott Walker	Owen Sound	RW
151	MTL Darcy Tucker	Kamloops	RW
164	NYR Todd Marchant	Clarkson	C
207	BOS Hal Gill	Nashoba H.S.	D
219	STL Mike Grier	St. Sebastian's H.S.	RW
227	OTT Pavol Demitra	Dukla Trencin	LW
252	CGY German Titov	TPS Turku	LW

1992

FIRST ROUND

Pick	Claimed by	Amateur Club	Position
1	T.B. Roman Hamrlik	ZPS Zlin	D
2	OTT Alexei Yashin	Dynamo	C
3	S.J. Mike Rathje	Medicine Hat	D
4	QUE Todd Warriner	Windsor	LW
5	NYI Darius Kasparaitis	Dynamo	D
6	CGY Cory Stillman	Windsor	LW
7	PHI Ryan Sittler	Nichols H.S.	LW
8	TOR Brandon Convery	Sudbury	C
9	HFD Robert Petrovicky	Dukla Trencin	C
10	S.J. Andrei Nazarov	Dynamo	LW
11	BUF David Cooper	Medicine Hat	D
12	CHI Sergei Krivokrasov	CSKA Moscow	RW
13	EDM Joe Hulbig	St. Sebastian's H.S.	LW
14	WSH Sergei Gonchar	Chelyabinsk	D
15	PHI Jason Bowen	Tri-City	D
16	BOS Dmitri Kvartalnov	San Diego (IHL)	LW
17	WPG Sergei Bautin	Dynamo	D
18	N.J. Jason Smith	Regina	D
19	PIT Martin Straka	HC Skoda Plzen	C
20	MTL David Wilkie	Kamloops	D
21	VAN Libor Polasek	Vitkovice	C
22	DET Curtis Bowen	Ottawa	LW
23	TOR Grant Marshall	Ottawa	RW
24	NYR Peter Ferraro	Waterloo Jr. A	LW

OTHER NOTABLE SELECTIONS

Pick	Claimed by	Amateur Club	Position
27	WPG Boris Mironov	CSKA Moscow	D
33	MTL Valeri Bure	Spokane	RW
36	CHI Jeff Shantz	Regina	C
38	STL Igor Korolev	Dynamo	C
40	VAN Michael Peca	Ottawa	C
42	N.J. Sergei Brylin	CSKA Moscow	C
46	DET Darren McCarty	Bellevile	RW
48	NYR Mattias Norstrom	AIK Solna	D
65	EDM Kirk Maltby	Owen Sound	RW
78	CGY Robert Svehla	Dukla Trencin	D
83	BUF Matthew Barnaby	Beauport	RW
158	STL Ian Laperriere	Drummondville	C/RW
186	N.J. Stephane Yelle	Oshawa	C
204	WPG Nikolai Khabibulin	CSKA Moscow	G

1991

FIRST ROUND

Pick	Claimed by		Amateur Club	Position
1	QUE	Eric Lindros	Oshawa	C
2	S.J.	Pat Falloon	Spokane	RW
3	N.J.	Scott Niedermayer	Kamloops	D
4	NYI	Scott Lachance	Boston U.	D
5	WPG	Aaron Ward	U. of Michigan	D
6	PHI	Peter Forsberg	MoDo Ornskoldsvik	C
7	VAN	Alek Stojanov	Hamilton	RW
8	MIN	Richard Matvichuk	Saskatoon	D
9	HFD	Patrick Poulin	St-Hyacinthe	C
10	DET	Martin Lapointe	Laval	RW
11	N.J.	Brian Rolston	Detroit Compuware Jr. A	C/RW
12	EDM	Tyler Wright	Swift Current	C
13	BUF	Philippe Boucher	Granby	D
14	WSH	Pat Peake	Detroit	C
15	NYR	Alex Kovalev	Dynamo	RW
16	PIT	Markus Naslund	MoDo Ornskoldsvik	LW
17	MTL	Brent Bilodeau	Seattle	D
18	BOS	Glen Murray	Sudbury	RW
19	CGY	Niklas Sundblad	AIK Solna	RW
20	EDM	Martin Rucinsky	CHZ Litvinov	LW
21	WSH	Trevor Halverson	North Bay	LW
22	CHI	Dean McAmmond	Prince Albert	LW

OTHER NOTABLE SELECTIONS

Pick	Claimed by		Amateur Club	Position
23	S.J.	Ray Whitney	Spokane	LW
26	NYI	Ziggy Palffy	AC Nitra	RW
30	S.J.	Sandis Ozolinsh	Dynamo Riga	D
40	BOS	Jozef Stumpel	AC Nitra	C
52	CGY	Sandy McCarthy	Laval	RW
58	WSH	Steve Konowalchuk	Portland	LW
59	HFD	Michael Nylander	Huddinge	C
71	CHI	Igor Kravchuk	CSKA Moscow	D
81	L.A.	Alexei Zhitnik	Sokol Kiev	D
103	QUE	Bill Lindsay	Tri-City	RW
106	BOS	Mariusz Czerkawski	GKS Tychy	RW
122	PHI	Dmitry Yushkevich	Yaroslavl	D
203	WPG	Igor Ulanov	Khimik Voskresensk	D

1990

FIRST ROUND

Pick	Claimed by		Amateur Club	Position
1	QUE	Owen Nolan	Cornwall	RW
2	VAN	Petr Nedved	Seattle	C
3	DET	Keith Primeau	Niagara Falls	C
4	PHI	Mike Ricci	Peterborough	C
5	PIT	Jaromir Jagr	Kladno	RW
6	NYI	Scott Scissons	Saskatoon	C
7	L.A.	Darryl Sydor	Kamloops	D
8	MIN	Derian Hatcher	North Bay	D
9	WSH	John Slaney	Cornwall	D
10	TOR	Drake Berehowsky	Kingston	D
11	CGY	Trevor Kidd	Brandon	G
12	MTL	Turner Stevenson	Seattle	RW
13	NYR	Michael Stewart	Michigan State	D
14	BUF	Brad May	Niagara Falls	LW
15	HFD	Mark Greig	Lethbridge	RW
16	CHI	Karl Dykhuis	Hull	D
17	EDM	Scott Allison	Prince Albert	C
18	VAN	Shawn Antoski	North Bay	LW
19	WPG	Keith Tkachuk	Malden Catholic H.S.	LW
20	N.J.	Martin Brodeur	St-Hyacinthe	G
21	BOS	Bryan Smolinski	Michigan State	C

OTHER NOTABLE SELECTIONS

Pick	Claimed by		Amateur Club	Position
23	VAN	Jiri Slegr	CHZ Litvinov	D
31	TOR	Felix Potvin	Chicoutimi	G
34	NYR	Doug Weight	Lake Superior State	C
36	HFD	Geoff Sanderson	Swift Current	LW
45	DET	Vyacheslav Kozlov	Khimik Voskresensk	RW
85	NYR	Sergei Zubov	CSKA Moscow	D
86	VAN	Gino Odjick	Laval	RW
97	BUF	Richard Smehlik	Vitkovice	D
133	L.A.	Robert Lang	CHZ Litvinov	C
156	WSH	Peter Bondra	Kosice	RW
177	WSH	Ken Klee	Bowling Green	D
244	NYR	Sergei Nemchinov	Krylja Sovetov	LW

1989

FIRST ROUND

Pick	Claimed by		Amateur Club	Position
1	QUE	Mats Sundin	Nacka	C
2	NYI	Dave Chyzowski	Kamloops	LW
3	TOR	Scott Thornton	Belleville	C
4	WPG	Stu Barnes	Tri-City	C
5	N.J.	Bill Guerin	Springfield Jr. B	RW
6	CHI	Adam Bennett	Sudbury	D
7	MIN	Doug Zmolek	John Marshall H.S.	D
8	VAN	Jason Herter	North Dakota	D
9	STL	Jason Marshall	Vernon Jr. A	D
10	HFD	Bobby Holik	Dukla Jihlava	C
11	DET	Mike Sillinger	Regina	C
12	TOR	Rob Pearson	Belleville	RW
13	MTL	Lindsay Vallis	Seattle	D
14	BUF	Kevin Haller	Regina	D
15	EDM	Jason Soules	Niagara Falls	D
16	PIT	Jamie Heward	Regina	D
17	BOS	Shayne Stevenson	Kitchener	RW
18	N.J.	Jason Miller	Medicine Hat	LW
19	WSH	Olaf Kolzig	Tri-City	G
20	NYR	Steven Rice	Kitchener	RW
21	TOR	Steve Bancroft	Belleville	D

OTHER NOTABLE SELECTIONS

Pick	Claimed by		Amateur Club	Position
22	QUE	Adam Foote	Sault Ste. Marie	D
23	NYI	Travis Green	Spokane	C
53	DET	Nicklas Lidstrom	Vasteras	D
62	WPG	Kris Draper	Canadian National	C
73	HFD	Jim McKenzie	Victoria	LW
74	DET	Sergei Fedorov	CSKA Moscow	C
82	WSH	Trent Klatt	Osseo H.S.	RW
113	VAN	Pavel Bure	CSKA Moscow	RW
116	DET	Dallas Drake	Northern Michigan	RW
183	BUF	Donald Audette	Laval	RW
196	MIN	Arturs Irbe	Dynamo Riga	G
221	DET	Vladimir Konstantinov	CSKA Moscow	D

1988

FIRST ROUND

Pick	Claimed by		Amateur Club	Position
1	MIN	Mike Modano	Prince Albert	C
2	VAN	Trevor Linden	Medicine Hat	RW
3	QUE	Curtis Leschyshyn	Saskatoon	D
4	PIT	Darrin Shannon	Windsor	LW
5	QUE	Daniel Dore	Drummondville	RW
6	TOR	Scott Pearson	Kingston	LW
7	L.A.	Martin Gelinas	Hull	LW
8	CHI	Jeremy Roenick	Thayer Academy	C
9	STL	Rod Brind'Amour	Notre Dame Jr. A	C
10	WPG	Teemu Selanne	Jokerit	RW
11	HFD	Chris Govedaris	Toronto	LW
12	N.J.	Corey Foster	Peterborough	D
13	BUF	Joel Savage	Victoria	RW
14	PHI	Claude Boivin	Drummondville	LW
15	WSH	Reggie Savage	Victoriaville	C
16	NYI	Kevin Cheveldayoff	Brandon	D
17	DET	Kory Kocur	Saskatoon	RW
18	BOS	Rob Cimetta	Toronto	W
19	EDM	Francois Leroux	St-Jean	D
20	MTL	Eric Charron	Trois-Rivieres	D
21	CGY	Jason Muzzatti	Michigan State	G

OTHER NOTABLE SELECTIONS

Pick	Claimed by		Amateur Club	Position
27	TOR	Tie Domi	Peterborough	RW
60	BOS	Steve Heinze	Lawrence Academy	RW
67	PIT	Mark Recchi	Kamloops	RW
68	NYR	Tony Amonte	Thayer Academy	RW
89	BUF	Alexander Mogilny	CSKA Moscow	RW
97	BUF	Rob Ray	Cornwall	RW
120	WSH	Dmitri Khristich	Sokol Kiev	LW/C
163	NYI	Marty McInnis	Milton Academy	RW
198	STL	Bret Hedican	North St. Paul H.S.	D
234	QUE	Claude Lapointe	Laval	LW/C

1987

FIRST ROUND

Pick	Claimed by		Amateur Club	Position
1	BUF	Pierre Turgeon	Granby	C
2	N.J.	Brendan Shanahan	London	LW
3	BOS	Glen Wesley	Portland	D
4	L.A.	Wayne McBean	Medicine Hat	D
5	PIT	Chris Joseph	Seattle	D
6	MIN	Dave Archibald	Portland	C/LW
7	TOR	Luke Richardson	Peterborough	D
8	CHI	Jimmy Waite	Chicoutimi	G
9	QUE	Bryan Fogarty	Kingston	D
10	NYR	Jay More	New Westminster	D
11	DET	Yves Racine	Longueuil	D
12	STL	Keith Osborne	North Bay	RW
13	NYI	Dean Chynoweth	Medicine Hat	D
14	BOS	Stephane Quintal	Granby	D
15	QUE	Joe Sakic	Swift Current	C
16	WPG	Bryan Marchment	Belleville	D
17	MTL	Andrew Cassels	Ottawa	C
18	HFD	Jody Hull	Peterborough	RW
19	CGY	Bryan Deasley	U. of Michigan	LW
20	PHI	Darren Rumble	Kitchener	D
21	EDM	Peter Soberlak	Swift Current	LW

OTHER NOTABLE SELECTIONS

Pick	Claimed by		Amateur Club	Position
25	CGY	Stephane Matteau	Hull	LW
33	MTL	John LeClair	Bellows Academy	LW
38	MTL	Eric Desjardins	Granby	D
44	MTL	Mathieu Schneider	Cornwall	D
71	TOR	Joe Sacco	Medford H.S.	RW
108	VAN	Garry Valk	Sherwood Park Jr. A	RW
110	PIT	Shawn McEachern	Matignon H.S.	RW
159	STL	Guy Hebert	Hamilton College	G
166	CGY	Theoren Fleury	Moose Jaw	RW

1986

FIRST ROUND

Pick	Claimed by		Amateur Club	Position
1	DET	Joe Murphy	Michigan State	RW
2	L.A.	Jimmy Carson	Verdun	C
3	N.J.	Neil Brady	Medicine Hat	C
4	PIT	Zarley Zalapski	Canadian National	D
5	BUF	Shawn Anderson	Canadian National	D
6	TOR	Vincent Damphousse	Laval	C
7	VAN	Dan Woodley	Portland	RW
8	WPG	Pat Elynuik	Prince Albert	RW
9	NYR	Brian Leetch	Avon Old Farms H.S.	D
10	STL	Jocelyn Lemieux	Laval	RW
11	HFD	Scott Young	Boston U.	RW
12	MIN	Warren Babe	Lethbridge	LW
13	BOS	Craig Janney	Boston College	C
14	CHI	Everett Sanipass	Verdun	LW
15	MTL	Mark Pederson	Medicine Hat	LW
16	CGY	George Pelawa	Bemidji H.S.	RW
17	NYI	Tom Fitzgerald	Austin Prep	RW
18	QUE	Ken McRae	Sudbury	C
19	WSH	Jeff Greenlaw	Canadian National	LW
20	PHI	Kerry Huffman	Guelph	D
21	EDM	Kim Issel	Prince Albert	RW

OTHER NOTABLE SELECTIONS

Pick	Claimed by		Amateur Club	Position
22	DET	Adam Graves	Windsor	LW
27	MTL	Benoit Brunet	Hull	LW
29	WPG	Teppo Numminen	Tappara Tampere	D
47	BUF	Bob Corkum	U. of Maine	C
57	MTL	Jyrki Lumme	Ilves Tampere	D
67	PIT	Rob Brown	Kamloops	RW
72	NYR	Mark Janssens	Regina	C
85	DET	Johan Garpenlov	Nacka	LW
114	NYR	Darren Turcotte	North Bay	C
141	MTL	Lyle Odelein	Moose Jaw	D
143	NYI	Rich Pilon	Prince Albert AAA	D
167	PHI	Murray Baron	Vernon Jr. A	D

1985

FIRST ROUND

Pick	Claimed by		Amateur Club	Position
1	TOR	Wendel Clark	Saskatoon	LW/D
2	PIT	Craig Simpson	Michigan State	LW
3	N.J.	Craig Wolanin	Kitchener	D
4	VAN	Jim Sandlak	London	RW
5	HFD	Dana Murzyn	Calgary	D
6	NYI	Brad Dalgarno	Hamilton	RW
7	NYR	Ulf Dahlen	Ostersund	LW
8	DET	Brent Fedyk	Regina	LW
9	L.A.	Craig Duncanson	Sudbury	LW
10	L.A.	Dan Gratton	Oshawa	C
11	CHI	Dave Manson	Prince Albert	D
12	MTL	Jose Charbonneau	Drummondville	RW
13	NYI	Derek King	Sault Ste. Marie	LW
14	BUF	Calle Johansson	Vastra Frolunda	D
15	QUE	David Latta	Kitchener	LW
16	MTL	Tom Chorske	Minneapolis SW H.S.	LW
17	CGY	Chris Biotti	Belmont Hill H.S.	D
18	WPG	Ryan Stewart	Kamloops	C
19	WSH	Yvon Corriveau	Toronto	LW
20	EDM	Scott Metcalfe	Kingston	LW
21	PHI	Glen Seabrooke	Peterborough	C

OTHER NOTABLE SELECTIONS

Pick	Claimed by		Amateur Club	Position
24	N.J.	Sean Burke	Toronto	G
27	CGY	Joe Nieuwendyk	Cornell	C
28	NYR	Mike Richter	Northwood Prep	G
32	N.J.	Eric Weinrich	North Yarmouth Academy	D
35	BUF	Benoit Hogue	St-Jean	C
44	STL	Nelson Emerson	Stratford Jr. A	RW
52	BOS	Bill Ranford	New Westminster	G
81	WPG	Fredrik Olausson	Farjestad Karlstad	D
113	DET	Randy McKay	Michigan Tech	RW
119	BUF	Joe Reekie	Cornwall	D
188	EDM	Kelly Buchberger	Moose Jaw	RW
214	VAN	Igor Larionov	CSKA Moscow	C

1984

FIRST ROUND

Pick	Claimed by		Amateur Club	Position
1	PIT	Mario Lemieux	Laval	C
2	N.J.	Kirk Muller	Guelph	LW
3	CHI	Eddie Olczyk	Team USA	C
4	TOR	Al Iafrate	Belleville	D
5	MTL	Petr Svoboda	CHZ Litvinov	D
6	L.A.	Craig Redmond	U. of Denver	D
7	DET	Shawn Burr	Kitchener	LW/C
8	MTL	Shayne Corson	Brantford	LW
9	PIT	Doug Bodger	Kamloops	D
10	VAN	J.J. Daigneault	Longueuil	D
11	HFD	Sylvain Cote	Quebec	D
12	CGY	Gary Roberts	Ottawa	LW
13	MIN	David Quinn	Kent H.S.	D
14	NYR	Terry Carkner	Peterborough	D

Pick	Claimed by	Amateur Club	Position
15	QUE Trevor Stienburg	Guelph	RW
16	PIT Roger Belanger	Kingston	C
17	WSH Kevin Hatcher	North Bay	D
18	BUF Mikael Andersson	Vastra Frolunda	LW
19	BOS Dave Pasin	Prince Albert	RW
20	NYI Duncan MacPherson	Saskatoon	D
21	EDM Selmar Odelein	Regina	D

OTHER NOTABLE SELECTIONS

Pick	Claimed by	Amateur Club	Position
25	TOR Todd Gill	Windsor	D
27	PHI Scott Mellanby	Henry Carr Jr. B	RW
29	MTL Stephane Richer	Granby	RW
38	CGY Paul Ranheim	Edina H.S.	LW
51	MTL Patrick Roy	Granby	G
59	WSH Michal Pivonka	Kladno	C
60	BUF Ray Sheppard	Cornwall	RW
117	CGY Brett Hull	Penticton Jr. A	RW
119	NYR Kjell Samuelsson	Leksand	D
134	STL Cliff Ronning	New Westminster	C
166	BOS Don Sweeney	St. Paul's H.S.	D
171	L.A. Luc Robitaille	Hull	LW
180	CGY Gary Suter	U. of Wisconsin	D

1983

FIRST ROUND

Pick	Claimed by	Amateur Club	Position
1	MIN Brian Lawton	Mount St. Charles H.S.	LW
2	HFD Sylvain Turgeon	Hull	LW
3	NYI Pat LaFontaine	Verdun	C
4	DET Steve Yzerman	Peterborough	C
5	BUF Tom Barrasso	Acton-Boxborough	G
6	N.J. John MacLean	Oshawa	RW
7	TOR Russ Courtnall	Victoria	RW
8	WPG Andrew McBain	North Bay	RW
9	VAN Cam Neely	Portland	RW
10	BUF Normand Lacombe	New Hampshire	RW
11	BUF Adam Creighton	Ottawa	C
12	NYR Dave Gagner	Brantford	C
13	CGY Dan Quinn	Belleville	C
14	WPG Bobby Dollas	Laval	D
15	PIT Bob Errey	Peterborough	LW
16	NYI Gerald Diduck	Lethbridge	D
17	MTL Alfie Turcotte	Portland	C
18	CHI Bruce Cassidy	Ottawa	D
19	EDM Jeff Beukeboom	Sault Ste. Marie	D
20	HFD David Jensen	Lawrence Academy	C
21	BOS Nevin Markwart	Regina	LW

OTHER NOTABLE SELECTIONS

Pick	Claimed by	Amateur Club	Position
26	MTL Claude Lemieux	Trois-Rivieres	RW
46	DET Bob Probert	Brantford	LW
60	CHI Marc Bergevin	Chicoutimi	D
82	EDM Esa Tikkanen	HIFK Helsinki	LW
88	DET Petr Klima	Dukla Jihlava	W
91	DET Joe Kocur	Saskatoon	RW
103	L.A. Garry Galley	Bowling Green	D
114	VAN Dave Lowry	London	LW
125	PHI Rick Tocchet	Sault Ste. Marie	RW
150	N.J. Viacheslav Fetisov	CSKA Moscow	D
207	CHI Dominik Hasek	Pardubice	G
223	BUF Uwe Krupp	Koln	D
241	CGY Sergei Makarov	CSKA Moscow	RW

1982

FIRST ROUND

Pick	Claimed by	Amateur Club	Position
1	BOS Gord Kluzak	Billings	D
2	MIN Brian Bellows	Kitchener	LW
3	TOR Gary Nylund	Portland	D
4	PHI Ron Sutter	Lethbridge	C
5	WSH Scott Stevens	Kitchener	D
6	BUF Phil Housley	South St. Paul H.S.	D
7	CHI Ken Yaremchuk	Portland	C
8	N.J. Rocky Trottier	Nanaimo	RW
9	BUF Paul Cyr	Victoria	LW
10	PIT Rich Sutter	Lethbridge	RW
11	VAN Michel Petit	Sherbrooke	D
12	WPG Jim Kyte	Cornwall	D
13	QUE David Shaw	Kitchener	D
14	HFD Paul Lawless	Windsor	LW
15	NYR Chris Kontos	Toronto	LW/C
16	BUF Dave Andreychuk	Oshawa	LW
17	DET Murray Craven	Medicine Hat	LW
18	N.J. Ken Daneyko	Seattle	D
19	MTL Alain Heroux	Chicoutimi	LW
20	EDM Jim Playfair	Portland	D
21	NYI Pat Flatley	U. of Wisconsin	RW

OTHER NOTABLE SELECTIONS

Pick	Claimed by	Amateur Club	Position
36	NYR Tomas Sandstrom	Farjestad Karlstad	RW
43	N.J. Pat Verbeek	Sudbury	RW
45	TOR Ken Wregget	Lethbridge	G
56	HFD Kevin Dineen	U. of Denver	RW
60	BOS Dave Reid	Peterborough	LW
67	HFD Ulf Samuelsson	Leksand	D
75	WPG Dave Ellett	Ottawa Jr. A	D
80	MIN Bob Rouse	Nanaimo	D
88	HFD Ray Ferraro	Penticton Jr. A	C
119	PHI Ron Hextall	Brandon	G
120	NYR Tony Granato	Northwood Prep	RW
134	STL Doug Gilmour	Cornwall	C
140	PHI Dave Brown	Saskatoon	RW
181	QUE Mike Hough	Kitchener	LW
183	NYR Kelly Miller	Michigan State	LW

1981

FIRST ROUND

Pick	Claimed by	Amateur Club	Position
1	WPG Dale Hawerchuk	Cornwall	C
2	L.A. Doug Smith	Ottawa	C
3	WSH Bob Carpenter	St. John's Prep	C
4	HFD Ron Francis	Sault Ste. Marie	C
5	COL Joe Cirella	Oshawa	D
6	TOR Jim Benning	Portland	D
7	MTL Mark Hunter	Brantford	RW
8	EDM Grant Fuhr	Victoria	G
9	NYR James Patrick	Prince Albert	D
10	VAN Garth Butcher	Regina	D
11	QUE Randy Moller	Lethbridge	D
12	CHI Tony Tanti	Oshawa	RW
13	MIN Ron Meighan	Niagara Falls	D
14	BOS Normand Leveille	Chicoutimi	LW
15	CGY Al MacInnis	Kitchener	D
16	PHI Steve Smith	Sault Ste. Marie	D
17	BUF Jiri Dudacek	Kladno	RW
18	MTL Gilbert Delorme	Chicoutimi	D
19	MTL Jan Ingman	Farjestad Karlstad	LW
20	STL Marty Ruff	Lethbridge	D
21	NYI Paul Boutilier	Sherbrooke	D

OTHER NOTABLE SELECTIONS

Pick	Claimed by	Amateur Club	Position
40	MTL Chris Chelios	Moose Jaw	D
56	CGY Mike Vernon	Calgary	G
72	NYR John Vanbiesbrouck	Sault Ste. Marie	G
108	COL Bruce Driver	U. of Wisconsin	D
111	EDM Steve Smith	London	D
116	QUE Mike Eagles	Kitchener	C/LW
145	MTL Tom Kurvers	Minnesota-Duluth	D
152	WSH Gaetan Duchesne	Quebec	LW

1980

FIRST ROUND

Pick	Claimed by	Amateur Club	Position
1	MTL Doug Wickenheiser	Regina	C
2	WPG Dave Babych	Portland	D
3	CHI Denis Savard	Montreal	C
4	L.A. Larry Murphy	Peterborough	D
5	WSH Darren Veitch	Regina	D
6	EDM Paul Coffey	Kitchener	D
7	VAN Rick Lanz	Oshawa	D
8	HFD Fred Arthur	Cornwall	D
9	PIT Mike Bullard	Brantford	C
10	L.A. Jim Fox	Ottawa	RW
11	DET Mike Blaisdell	Regina	RW
12	STL Rik Wilson	Kingston	D
13	CGY Denis Cyr	Montreal	RW
14	NYR Jim Malone	Toronto	C
15	CHI Jerome Dupont	Toronto	D
16	MIN Brad Palmer	Victoria	LW
17	NYI Brent Sutter	Red Deer Jr. A	C
18	BOS Barry Pederson	Victoria	C
19	COL Paul Gagne	Windsor	LW
20	BUF Steve Patrick	Brandon	RW
21	PHI Mike Stothers	Kingston	D

OTHER NOTABLE SELECTIONS

Pick	Claimed by	Amateur Club	Position
37	MIN Don Beaupre	Sudbury	G
38	NYI Kelly Hrudey	Medicine Hat	G
39	CGY Steve Konroyd	Oshawa	D
46	DET Mark Osborne	Niagara Falls	LW
61	MTL Craig Ludwig	North Dakota	D
69	EDM Jari Kurri	Jokerit	RW
73	L.A. Bernie Nicholls	Kingston	C
80	NYI Greg Gilbert	Toronto	LW
81	BOS Steve Kasper	Verdun	C
106	COL Aaron Broten	Minnesota-Duluth	LW/C
120	CHI Steve Larmer	Niagara Falls	RW
124	MTL Mike McPhee	RPI	LW
128	WPG Brian Mullen	U.S. Jr. National	RW
132	EDM Andy Moog	Billings	G
133	VAN Doug Lidster	Colorado College	D
167	BUF Randy Cunneyworth	Ottawa	LW

1979

FIRST ROUND

Pick	Claimed by	Amateur Club	Position
1	COL Rob Ramage	London	D
2	STL Perry Turnbull	Portland	C
3	DET Mike Foligno	Sudbury	RW
4	WSH Mike Gartner	Niagara Falls	RW
5	VAN Rick Vaive	Sherbrooke	RW
6	MIN Craig Hartsburg	Sault Ste. Marie	D
7	CHI Keith Brown	Portland	D
8	BOS Raymond Bourque	Verdun	D
9	TOR Laurie Boschman	Brandon	C
10	MIN Tom McCarthy	Oshawa	LW
11	BUF Mike Ramsey	U. of Minnesota	D
12	ATL Paul Reinhart	Kitchener	D
13	NYR Doug Sulliman	Kitchener	RW
14	PHI Brian Propp	Brandon	LW
15	BOS Brad McCrimmon	Brandon	D
16	L.A. Jay Wells	Kingston	D
17	NYI Duane Sutter	Lethbridge	RW
18	HFD Ray Allison	Brandon	RW
19	WPG Jimmy Mann	Sherbrooke	RW
20	QUE Michel Goulet	Quebec	LW
21	EDM Kevin Lowe	Quebec	D

OTHER NOTABLE SELECTIONS

Pick	Claimed by	Amateur Club	Position
26	VAN Brent Ashton	Saskatoon	LW
30	L.A. Mark Hardy	Montreal	D
32	BUF Lindy Ruff	Lethbridge	D/LW
37	MTL Mats Naslund	Brynas Gavle	LW
40	WPG Dave Christian	North Dakota	RW
41	QUE Dale Hunter	Sudbury	C
42	MIN Neal Broten	Minnesota-Duluth	C
44	MTL Guy Carbonneau	Chicoutimi	C
48	EDM Mark Messier	St. Albert Jr. A	C
54	ATL Tim Hunter	Seattle	RW
66	DET John Ogrodnick	New Westminster	LW
69	EDM Glenn Anderson	U. of Denver	RW
75	ATL Jim Peplinski	Toronto	RW
83	QUE Anton Stastny	Slovan Bratislava	LW
89	VAN Dirk Graham	Regina	RW/LW
103	WPG Thomas Steen	Leksand	C
120	BOS Mike Krushelnyski	Montreal	LW/C

1978

FIRST ROUND

Pick	Claimed by	Amateur Club	Position
1	MIN Bobby Smith	Ottawa	C
2	WSH Ryan Walter	Seattle	C/LW
3	STL Wayne Babych	Portland	RW
4	VAN Bill Derlago	Brandon	C
5	COL Mike Gillis	Kingston	LW
6	PHI Behn Wilson	Kingston	D
7	PHI Ken Linseman	Kingston	C
8	MTL Danny Geoffrion	Cornwall	RW
9	DET Willie Huber	Hamilton	D
10	CHI Tim Higgins	Ottawa	RW
11	ATL Brad Marsh	London	D
12	DET Brent Peterson	Portland	C
13	BUF Larry Playfair	Portland	D
14	PHI Danny Lucas	Sault Ste. Marie	RW
15	NYI Steve Tambellini	Lethbridge	C
16	BOS Al Secord	Hamilton	LW
17	MTL Dave Hunter	Sudbury	LW
18	WSH Tim Coulis	Hamilton	LW

OTHER NOTABLE SELECTIONS

Pick	Claimed by	Amateur Club	Position
19	MIN Steve Payne	Ottawa	LW
21	TOR Joel Quenneville	Windsor	D
26	NYR Don Maloney	Kitchener	LW
32	BUF Tony McKegney	Kingston	LW
40	VAN Stan Smyl	New Westminster	RW
54	MIN Curt Giles	Minnesota-Duluth	D
55	WSH Bengt-Ake Gustafsson	Farjestad Karlstad	RW
93	NYR Tom Laidlaw	Northern Michigan	D
103	MTL Keith Acton	Peterborough	C
109	STL Paul MacLean	Hull	RW
153	BOS Craig MacTavish	University of Lowell	C
173	STL Risto Siltanen	Ilves Tampere	D
179	CHI Darryl Sutter	Lethbridge	LW
231	MTL Chris Nilan	Northeastern	RW

1977

FIRST ROUND

Pick	Claimed by	Player	Amateur Club	Position
1	DET	Dale McCourt	St. Catharines	C
2	COL	Barry Beck	New Westminster	D
3	WSH	Robert Picard	Montreal	D
4	VAN	Jere Gillis	Sherbrooke	LW
5	Cle.	Mike Crombeen	Kingston	RW
6	CHI	Doug Wilson	Ottawa	D
7	MIN	Brad Maxwell	New Westminster	D
8	NYR	Lucien DeBlois	Sorel	C
9	STL	Scott Campbell	London	D
10	MTL	Mark Napier	Toronto	RW
11	TOR	John Anderson	Toronto	RW
12	TOR	Trevor Johansen	Toronto	D
13	NYR	Ron Duguay	Sudbury	C/RW
14	BUF	Ric Seiling	St. Catharines	RW/C
15	NYI	Mike Bossy	Laval	RW
16	BOS	Dwight Foster	Kitchener	RW
17	PHI	Kevin McCarthy	Winnipeg	D
18	MTL	Norm Dupont	Montreal	LW

OTHER NOTABLE SELECTIONS

Pick	Claimed by	Player	Amateur Club	Position
25	MIN	Dave Semenko	Brandon	LW
33	NYI	John Tonelli	Toronto	LW
36	MTL	Rod Langway	New Hampshire	D
43	MTL	Alain Cote	Chicoutimi	LW
54	MTL	Gordie Roberts	Victoria	D
62	NYR	Mario Marois	Quebec	D
66	PIT	Mark Johnson	U. of Wisconsin	C
102	PIT	Greg Millen	Peterborough	G
118	ATL	Bobby Gould	New Hampshire	RW
135	PHI	Pete Peeters	Medicine Hat	G
162	MTL	Craig Laughlin	Clarkson	RW

1976

FIRST ROUND

Pick	Claimed by	Player	Amateur Club	Position
1	WSH	Rick Green	London	D
2	PIT	Blair Chapman	Saskatoon	RW
3	MIN	Glen Sharpley	Hull	C
4	DET	Fred Williams	Saskatoon	C
5	CAL	Bjorn Johansson	Orebro	D
6	NYR	Don Murdoch	Medicine Hat	RW
7	STL	Bernie Federko	Saskatoon	C
8	ATL	Dave Shand	Peterborough	D
9	CHI	Real Cloutier	Quebec	RW
10	ATL	Harold Phillipoff	New Westminster	LW
11	K.C.	Paul Gardner	Oshawa	C
12	MTL	Peter Lee	Ottawa	RW
13	MTL	Rod Schutt	Sudbury	LW
14	NYI	Alex McKendry	Sudbury	W
15	WSH	Greg Carroll	Medicine Hat	C
16	BOS	Clayton Pachal	New Westminster	C/LW
17	PHI	Mark Suzor	Kingston	D
18	MTL	Bruce Baker	Ottawa	RW

OTHER NOTABLE SELECTIONS

Pick	Claimed by	Player	Amateur Club	Position
20	STL	Brian Sutter	Lethbridge	LW
22	DET	Reed Larson	Minnesota-Duluth	D
30	TOR	Randy Carlyle	Sudbury	D
42	NYR	Mike McEwen	Toronto	D
45	CHI	Thomas Gradin	MoDo Ornskoldsvik	C
47	PIT	Morris Lukowich	Medicine Hat	LW
56	STL	Mike Liut	Bowling Green	G
64	ATL	Kent Nilsson	Djurgarden	C
68	NYI	Ken Morrow	Bowling Green	D
133	MTL	Ron Wilson	St. Catharines	C

1975

FIRST ROUND

Pick	Claimed by	Player	Amateur Club	Position
1	PHI	Mel Bridgman	Victoria	C
2	K.C.	Barry Dean	Medicine Hat	LW
3	CAL	Ralph Klassen	Saskatoon	C
4	MIN	Bryan Maxwell	Medicine Hat	D
5	DET	Rick Lapointe	Victoria	D
6	TOR	Don Ashby	Calgary	C
7	CHI	Greg Vaydik	Medicine Hat	C
8	ATL	Richard Mulhern	Sherbrooke	D
9	MTL	Robin Sadler	Edmonton	D
10	VAN	Rick Blight	Brandon	RW
11	NYI	Pat Price	Saskatoon	D
12	NYR	Wayne Dillon	Toronto	C
13	PIT	Gord Laxton	New Westminster	G
14	BOS	Doug Halward	Peterborough	D
15	MTL	Pierre Mondou	Montreal	C
16	L.A.	Tim Young	Ottawa	C

OTHER NOTABLE SELECTIONS

Pick	Claimed by	Player	Amateur Club	Position
17	BUF	Bob Sauve	Laval	G
21	CAL	Dennis Maruk	London	C
24	TOR	Doug Jarvis	Peterborough	C
43	CHI	Mike O'Connell	Kingston	D
57	CAL	Greg Smith	Colorado College	D
80	ATL	Willi Plett	St. Catharines	RW
108	PHI	Paul Holmgren	U. of Minnesota	RW
210	L.A.	Dave Taylor	Clarkson	RW

1974

FIRST ROUND

Pick	Claimed by	Player	Amateur Club	Position
1	WSH	Greg Joly	Regina	D
2	K.C.	Wilf Paiement	St. Catharines	RW
3	CAL	Rick Hampton	St. Catharines	LW/D
4	NYI	Clark Gillies	Regina	LW
5	MTL	Cam Connor	Flin Flon	RW
6	MIN	Doug Hicks	Flin Flon	D
7	MTL	Doug Risebrough	Kitchener	C
8	PIT	Pierre Larouche	Sorel	C
9	DET	Bill Lochead	Oshawa	LW
10	MTL	Rick Chartraw	Kitchener	D/RW
11	BUF	Lee Fogolin Jr.	Oshawa	D
12	MTL	Mario Tremblay	Montreal	RW
13	TOR	Jack Valiquette	Sault Ste. Marie	C
14	NYR	Dave Maloney	Kitchener	D
15	MTL	Gord McTavish	Sudbury	C
16	CHI	Grant Mulvey	Calgary	RW
17	CAL	Ron Chipperfield	Brandon	C
18	BOS	Don Larway	Swift Current	RW

OTHER NOTABLE SELECTIONS

Pick	Claimed by	Player	Amateur Club	Position
22	NYI	Bryan Trottier	Swift Current	C
25	BOS	Mark Howe	Toronto	D
29	BUF	Danny Gare	Calgary	RW
31	TOR	Tiger Williams	Swift Current	LW
32	NYR	Ron Greschner	New Westminster	D
38	K.C.	Bob Bourne	Saskatoon	C
39	CAL	Charlie Simmer	Sault Ste. Marie	LW
52	CHI	Bob Murray	Cornwall	D
59	VAN	Harold Snepsts	Edmonton	D
70	CHI	Terry Ruskowski	Swift Current	C
125	PHI	Reggie Lemelin	Sherbrooke	G
199	MTL	Dave Lumley	New Hampshire	RW
214	NYI	Stefan Persson	Brynas Gavle	D

1973

FIRST ROUND

Pick	Claimed by	Player	Amateur Club	Position
1	NYI	Denis Potvin	Ottawa	D
2	ATL	Tom Lysiak	Medicine Hat	C
3	VAN	Dennis Ververgaert	London	RW
4	TOR	Lanny McDonald	Medicine Hat	RW
5	STL	John Davidson	Calgary	G
6	BOS	Andre Savard	Quebec	C
7	PIT	Blaine Stoughton	Flin Flon	RW
8	MTL	Bob Gainey	Peterborough	LW
9	VAN	Bob Dailey	Toronto	D
10	TOR	Bob Neely	Peterborough	LW
11	DET	Terry Richardson	New Westminster	G
12	BUF	Morris Titanic	Sudbury	LW
13	CHI	Darcy Rota	Edmonton	LW
14	NYR	Rick Middleton	Oshawa	RW
15	TOR	Ian Turnbull	Ottawa	D
16	ATL	Vic Mercredi	New Westminster	C

OTHER NOTABLE SELECTIONS

Pick	Claimed by	Player	Amateur Club	Position
21	ATL	Eric Vail	Sudbury	LW
27	PIT	Colin Campbell	Peterborough	D
30	NYR	Pat Hickey	Hamilton	LW
33	NYI	Dave Lewis	Saskatoon	D
49	NYI	Andre St. Laurent	Montreal	C
85	ATL	Ken Houston	Chatham Jr. B.	RW
130	CAL	Larry Patey	Braintree H.S.	C
134	PIT	Gord Lane	New Westminster	D
162	ATL	Greg Fox	U. of Michigan	D

1972

FIRST ROUND

Pick	Claimed by	Player	Amateur Club	Position
1	NYI	Billy Harris	Toronto	RW
2	ATL	Jacques Richard	Quebec	LW
3	VAN	Don Lever	Niagara Falls	LW
4	MTL	Steve Shutt	Toronto	LW
5	BUF	Jim Schoenfeld	Niagara Falls	D
6	MTL	Michel Larocque	Ottawa	G
7	PHI	Bill Barber	Kitchener	LW
8	MTL	Dave Gardner	Toronto	C
9	STL	Wayne Merrick	Ottawa	C
10	NYR	Al Blanchard	Kitchener	LW
11	TOR	George Ferguson	Toronto	C
12	MIN	Jerry Byers	Kitchener	LW
13	CHI	Phil Russell	Edmonton	D
14	MTL	John Van Boxmeer	Guelph	D
15	NYR	Bob MacMillan	St. Catharines	RW
16	BOS	Mike Bloom	St. Catharines	LW

OTHER NOTABLE SELECTIONS

Pick	Claimed by	Player	Amateur Club	Position
17	NYI	Lorne Henning	New Westminster	C
23	PHI	Tom Bladon	Edmonton	D
33	NYI	Bob Nystrom	Calgary	RW
39	PHI	Jimmy Watson	Calgary	D
55	PHI	Al MacAdam	University of PEI	RW
85	BUF	Peter McNab	U. of Denver	C
97	NYI	Richard Brodeur	Cornwall	G
139	TOR	Pat Boutette	Minnesota-Duluth	C/RW
144	NYI	Garry Howatt	Flin Flon	LW

1971

FIRST ROUND

Pick	Claimed by	Player	Amateur Club	Position
1	MTL	Guy Lafleur	Quebec	RW
2	DET	Marcel Dionne	St. Catharines	C
3	VAN	Jocelyn Guevremont	Montreal	D
4	STL	Gene Carr	Flin Flon	C
5	BUF	Rick Martin	Montreal	LW
6	BOS	Ron Jones	Edmonton	D
7	MTL	Chuck Arnason	Flin Flon	RW
8	PHI	Larry Wright	Regina	C
9	PHI	Pierre Plante	Drummondville	RW
10	NYR	Steve Vickers	Toronto	LW
11	MTL	Murray Wilson	Ottawa	LW
12	CHI	Dan Spring	Edmonton	C
13	NYR	Steve Durbano	Toronto	D
14	BOS	Terry O'Reilly	Oshawa	RW

OTHER NOTABLE SELECTIONS

Pick	Claimed by	Player	Amateur Club	Position
17	VAN	Bobby Lalonde	Montreal	C
19	BUF	Craig Ramsay	Peterborough	LW
20	MTL	Larry Robinson	Kitchener	D
22	TOR	Rick Kehoe	Hamilton	RW
33	BUF	Bill Hajt	Saskatoon	D
48	L.A.	Neil Komadoski	Winnipeg	D
55	NYR	Jerry Butler	Hamilton	RW

1970

FIRST ROUND

Pick	Claimed by	Player	Amateur Club	Position
1	BUF	Gilbert Perreault	Montreal	C
2	VAN	Dale Tallon	Toronto	D
3	BOS	Reggie Leach	Flin Flon	RW
4	BOS	Rick MacLeish	Peterborough	C
5	MTL	Ray Martyniuk	Flin Flon	G
6	MTL	Chuck Lefley	Canadian National	LW
7	PIT	Greg Polis	Estevan	LW
8	TOR	Darryl Sittler	London	C
9	BOS	Ron Plumb	Peterborough	D
10	CAL	Chris Oddleifson	Winnipeg	C
11	NYR	Norm Gratton	Montreal	LW
12	DET	Serge Lajeunesse	Montreal	D/RW
13	BOS	Bob Stewart	Oshawa	D
14	CHI	Dan Maloney	London	LW

OTHER NOTABLE SELECTIONS

Pick	Claimed by	Player	Amateur Club	Position
18	PHI	Bill Clement	Ottawa	C
22	TOR	Errol Thompson	Charlottetown Sr.	LW
25	NYR	Mike Murphy	Toronto	RW
27	BOS	Dan Bouchard	London	G
32	PHI	Bob Kelly	Oshawa	LW
40	DET	Yvon Lambert	Drummondville	LW
59	L.A.	Billy Smith	Cornwall	G
70	CHI	Gilles Meloche	Verdun	G
88	OAK	Terry Murray	Ottawa	D
103	TOR	Ron Low	Dauphin Jr. A.	G

1969

FIRST ROUND

Pick	Claimed by	Player	Amateur Club	Position
1	MTL	Rejean Houle	Montreal	W
2	MTL	Marc Tardif	Montreal	LW
3	BOS	Don Tannahill	Niagara Falls	LW
4	BOS	Frank Spring	Edmonton	RW
5	MIN	Dick Redmond	St. Catharines	D
6	PHI	Bob Currier	Cornwall	C
7	OAK	Tony Featherstone	Peterborough	RW
8	NYR	Andre Dupont	Montreal	D
9	TOR	Ernie Moser	Estevan	RW
10	DET	Jim Rutherford	Hamilton	G
11	BOS	Ivan Boldirev	Oshawa	C
12	NYR	Pierre Jarry	Ottawa	LW

OTHER NOTABLE SELECTIONS

Pick	Claimed by	Player	Amateur Club	Position
17	PHI	Bobby Clarke	Flin Flon	C
18	OAK	Ron Stackhouse	Peterborough	D
25	MIN	Gilles Gilbert	London	G
26	PIT	Michel Briere	Shawinigan	C
51	L.A.	Butch Goring	Dauphin Jr. A.	C
52	PHI	Dave Schultz	Sorel	LW
55	TOR	Brian Spencer	Swift Current	LW
64	PHI	Don Saleski	Regina	RW

NHL All-Stars

Active Players' All-Star Selection Records

Player	Total		First Team Selections		Second Team Selections
GOALTENDER					
Martin Brodeur	**7**	(3)	2002-03; 2003-04; 2006-07	(4)	1996-97; 1997-98; 2005-06;2007-08.
Roberto Luongo	**2**	(0)		(2)	2003-04; 2006-07.
Olaf Kolzig	**1**	(1)	99-2000.	(0)	
Miikka Kiprusoff	**1**	(1)	2005-06.	(0)	
Evgeni Nabokov	**1**	(1)	2007-08.	(0)	
Chris Osgood	**1**	(0)		(1)	1995-96.
Jose Theodore	**1**	(0)		(1)	2001-02.
Marty Turco	**1**	(0)		(1)	2002-03.
DEFENSE					
Nicklas Lidstrom	**9**	(9)	1997-98; 1998-99; 99-2000; 2000-01; 2001-02; 2002-03; 2005-06; 2006-07; 2007-08	(0)	
Chris Chelios	**7**	(5)	1988-89; 1992-93; 1994-95;	(2)	1990-91; 1996-97. 1995-96; 2001-02.
Scott Niedermayer	**4**	(3)	2003-04; 2005-06; 2006-07	(1)	2002-03.
Rob Blake	**4**	(1)	1997-98.	(3)	99-2000; 2000-01; 2001-02.
Chris Pronger	**4**	(1)	99-2000.	(3)	1997-98; 2003-04; 2006-07.
Zdeno Chara	**3**	(1)	2003-04.	(2)	2005-06; 2007-08.
Sergei Gonchar	**2**	(0)		(2)	2001-02; 2002-03.
Dion Phaneuf	**1**	(1)	2007-08.	(0)	
Derian Hatcher	**1**	(0)		(1)	2002-03.
Bryan McCabe	**1**	(0)		(1)	2003-04.
Sergei Zubov	**1**	(0)		(1)	2005-06.
Dan Boyle	**1**	(0)		(1)	2006-07.
Brian Campbell	**1**	(0)		(1)	2007-08.
CENTER					
Peter Forsberg	**3**	(3)	1997-98; 1998-99; 2002-03.	(0)	
Joe Sakic	**3**	(3)	2000-01; 2001-02; 2003-04.	(0)	
Joe Thornton	**3**	(1)	2005-06.	(2)	2002-03; 2007-08.
Mats Sundin	**2**	(0)		(2)	2001-02; 2003-04.
Sergei Fedorov	**1**	(1)	1993-94.	(0)	
Sidney Crosby	**1**	(1)	2006-07.	(0)	
Evgeni Malkin	**1**	(1)	2007-08.	(0)	
Mike Modano	**1**	(0)		(1)	99-2000.
Eric Staal	**1**	(0)		(1)	2005-06.
Vincent Lecavalier	**1**	(0)		(1)	2006-07.
RIGHT WING					
Jaromir Jagr	**8**	(7)	1994-95; 1995-96; 1997-98; 1998-99; 99-2000; 2000-01; 2005-06.	(1)	1996-97.
Teemu Selanne	**4**	(2)	1992-93; 1996-97.	(2)	1997-98; 1998-99.
Jarome Iginla	**3**	(2)	2001-02; 2007-08.	(1)	2003-04.
Martin St. Louis	**2**	(1)	2003-04.	(1)	2006-07.
Todd Bertuzzi	**1**	(1)	2002-03.	(0)	
Dany Heatley	**1**	(1)	2006-07.	(0)	
Mark Recchi	**1**	(0)		(1)	1991-92.
Bill Guerin	**1**	(0)		(1)	2001-02.
Milan Hejduk	**1**	(0)		(1)	2002-03.
Daniel Alfredsson	**1**	(0)		(1)	2005-06.
Alex Kovalev	**1**	(0)		(1)	2007-08.
LEFT WING					
Paul Kariya	**5**	(3)	1995-96; 1996-97; 1998-99.	(2)	99-2000; 2002-03.
Markus Naslund	**3**	(3)	2001-02; 2002-03; 2003-04.	(0)	
Alex Ovechkin	**3**	(3)	2005-06; 2006-07; 2007-08.	(0)	
Brendan Shanahan	**3**	(2)	1993-94; 99-2000.	(1)	2001-02.
Keith Tkachuk	**2**	(0)		(2)	1994-95; 1997-98.
Patrik Elias	**1**	(1)	2000-01.	(0)	
Ilya Kovalchuk	**1**	(0)		(1)	2003-04.
Dany Heatley	**1**	(0)		(1)	2005-06.
Thomas Vanek	**1**	(0)		(1)	2006-07.
Henrik Zetterberg	**1**	(0)		(1)	2007-08.

Leading NHL All-Stars 1930-31 to 2007-08

Player	Pos	Team(s)	Total Selections	First Team Selections	Second Team Selections	NHL Seasons
Gordie Howe	RW	Detroit	**21**	12	9	26
Raymond Bourque	D	Bos., Col.	**19**	13	6	22
Wayne Gretzky	C	Edm., L.A., NYR	**15**	8	7	20
Maurice Richard	RW	Montreal	**14**	8	6	18
Bobby Hull	LW	Chicago	**12**	10	2	16
Doug Harvey	D	Mtl., NYR	**11**	10	1	19
Glenn Hall	G	Det., Chi., St.L.	**11**	7	4	18
Jean Beliveau	C	Montreal	**10**	6	4	20
Earl Seibert	D	NYR, Chi.	**10**	4	6	15
* Nicklas Lidstrom	D	Detroit	**9**	9	0	16
Bobby Orr	D	Boston	**9**	8	1	12
Ted Lindsay	LW	Detroit	**9**	8	1	17
Mario Lemieux	C	Pittsburgh	**9**	5	4	17
Frank Mahovlich	LW	Tor., Det., Mtl.	**9**	3	6	18
Eddie Shore	D	Boston	**8**	7	1	14
* Jaromir Jagr	RW	Pit., NYR	**8**	7	1	17
Phil Esposito	C	Boston	**8**	6	2	18
Red Kelly	D	Detroit	**8**	6	2	20
Stan Mikita	C	Chicago	**8**	6	2	22
Mike Bossy	RW	NY Islanders	**8**	5	3	10
Pierre Pilote	D	Chicago	**8**	5	3	14
Luc Robitaille	LW	Los Angeles	**8**	5	3	19
Paul Coffey	D	Edm., Pit., Det.	**8**	4	4	21
Frank Brimsek	G	Boston	**8**	2	6	10
Denis Potvin	D	NY Islanders	**7**	5	2	15
Brad Park	D	NYR, Bos.	**7**	5	2	17
* Chris Chelios	D	Mtl., Chi.	**7**	5	2	24
Al MacInnis	D	Cgy., St.L.	**7**	4	3	23
Jacques Plante	G	Mtl., Tor.	**7**	3	4	18
Bill Gadsby	D	Chi., NYR, Det.	**7**	3	4	20
Terry Sawchuk	G	Detroit	**7**	3	4	21
* Martin Brodeur	G	New Jersey	**7**	3	4	15
Bill Durnan	G	Montreal	**6**	6	0	7
Dominik Hasek	G	Buffalo	**6**	6	0	15
Guy Lafleur	RW	Montreal	**6**	6	0	17
Ken Dryden	G	Montreal	**6**	5	1	8
Patrick Roy	G	Montreal	**6**	4	2	19
Dit Clapper	RW/D	Boston	**6**	3	3	20
Larry Robinson	D	Montreal	**6**	3	3	20
Tim Horton	D	Toronto	**6**	3	3	24
Borje Salming	D	Toronto	**6**	1	5	17
Bill Cowley	C	Boston	**5**	4	1	13
Busher Jackson	LW	Toronto	**5**	4	1	15
Mark Messier	LW/C	Edm., NYR	**5**	4	1	25
* Paul Kariya	LW	Anaheim	**5**	3	2	13
Charlie Conacher	RW	Toronto	**5**	3	2	12
Jack Stewart	D	Detroit	**5**	3	2	12
Toe Blake	LW	Montreal	**5**	3	2	14
Elmer Lach	C	Montreal	**5**	3	2	14
Bill Quackenbush	D	Det., Bos.	**5**	3	2	14
Michel Goulet	LW	Quebec	**5**	3	2	15
Tony Esposito	G	Chicago	**5**	3	2	16
Ken Reardon	D	Montreal	**5**	2	3	7
Syl Apps	C	Toronto	**5**	2	3	10
John LeClair	LW	Mtl., Phi.	**5**	2	3	16
Ed Giacomin	G	NY Rangers	**5**	2	3	13
Brian Leetch	D	NY Rangers	**5**	2	3	17
Jari Kurri	RW	Edmonton	**5**	2	3	17
Scott Stevens	D	Wsh., N.J.	**5**	2	3	21

* Active

Position Leaders in All-Star Selections

Position	Player	Total	First Team	Second Team	NHL Seasons	Career
GOALTENDER	Glenn Hall	**11**	7	4	18	1952-53 to 1970-71
	Frank Brimsek	**8**	2	6	10	1938-39 to 1949-50
	* Martin Brodeur	**7**	3	4	15	1991-92 to 2007-08
	Jacques Plante	**7**	3	4	18	1952-53 to 1972-73
	Terry Sawchuk	**7**	3	4	21	1949-50 to 1969-70
	Bill Durnan	**6**	6	0	7	1943-44 to 1949-50
	Dominik Hasek	**6**	6	0	15	1990-91 to 2007-08
	Ken Dryden	**6**	5	1	8	1970-71 to 1978-79
	Patrick Roy	**6**	4	2	19	1984-85 to 2002-03
DEFENSE	Raymond Bourque	**19**	13	6	22	1979-80 to 2000-01
	Doug Harvey	**11**	10	1	20	1947-48 to 1968-69
	Earl Seibert	**10**	4	6	15	1931-32 to 1945-46
	* Nicklas Lidstrom	**9**	9	0	16	1991-92 to 2007-08
	Bobby Orr	**9**	8	1	12	1966-67 to 1978-79
	Eddie Shore	**8**	7	1	14	1926-27 to 1939-40
	Red Kelly	**8**	6	2	20	1947-48 to 1966-67
	Pierre Pilote	**8**	5	3	14	1955-56 to 1968-69
	Paul Coffey	**8**	4	4	21	1980-81 to 2000-01

Position	Player	Total	First Team	Second Team	NHL Seasons	Career
CENTER	Wayne Gretzky	**15**	8	7	20	1979-80 to 1998-99
	Jean Beliveau	**10**	6	4	20	1950-51 to 1970-71
	Mario Lemieux	**9**	5	4	18	1984-85 to 2005-06
	Phil Esposito	**8**	6	2	18	1963-64 to 1980-81
	Stan Mikita	**8**	6	2	22	1958-59 to 1979-80
RIGHT WING	Gordie Howe	**21**	12	9	26	1946-47 to 1979-80
	Maurice Richard	**14**	8	6	18	1942-43 to 1959-60
	* Jaromir Jagr	**8**	7	1	17	1990-91 to 2007-08
	Mike Bossy	**8**	5	3	10	1977-78 to 1986-87
	Guy Lafleur	**6**	6	0	17	1971-72 to 1990-91
LEFT WING	Bobby Hull	**12**	10	2	16	1957-58 to 1979-80
	Ted Lindsay	**9**	8	1	17	1944-45 to 1964-65
	Frank Mahovlich	**9**	3	6	18	1956-57 to 1973-74
	Luc Robitaille	**8**	5	3	19	1986-87 to 2005-06

* active player

All-Star Teams

1930-2008

Voting for the NHL All-Star Team is conducted among the representatives of the Professional Hockey Writers' Association at the end of the season.

Following is a list of the First and Second All-Star Teams since their inception in 1930-31.

2007-08

First Team		Second Team
Evgeni Nabokov, S.J.	G	Martin Brodeur, N.J.
Nicklas Lidstrom, Det.	D	Brian Campbell, Buf., S.J.
Dion Phaneuf, Cgy.	D	Zdeno Chara, Bos.
Evgeni Malkin, Pit.	C	Joe Thornton, S.J.
Jarome Iginla, Cgy.	RW	Alex Kovalev, Mtl.
Alex Ovechkin, Wsh.	LW	Henrik Zetterberg, Det.

2006-07

First Team		Second Team
Martin Brodeur, N.J.	G	Roberto Luongo, Van.
Nicklas Lidstrom, Det.	D	Chris Pronger, Ana.
Scott Niedermayer, Ana.	D	Dan Boyle, T.B.
Sidney Crosby, Pit.	C	Vincent Lecavalier, T.B.
Dany Heatley, Ott.	RW	Martin St. Louis, T.B.
Alex Ovechkin, Wsh.	LW	Thomas Vanek, Buf.

2005-06

First Team		Second Team
Miikka Kiprusoff, Cgy.	G	Martin Brodeur, N.J.
Nicklas Lidstrom, Det.	D	Zdeno Chara, Ott.
Scott Niedermayer, Ana.	D	Sergei Zubov, Dal.
Joe Thornton, Bos., S.J.	C	Eric Staal, Car.
Jaromir Jagr, NYR	RW	Daniel Alfredsson, Ott.
Alex Ovechkin, Wsh.	LW	Dany Heatley, Ott.

2004-05

Season Cancelled

2003-04

First Team		Second Team
Martin Brodeur, N.J.	G	Roberto Luongo, Fla.
Scott Niedermayer, N.J.	D	Chris Pronger, St.L.
Zdeno Chara, Ott.	D	Bryan McCabe, Tor.
Joe Sakic, Col.	C	Mats Sundin, Tor.
Martin St. Louis, T.B.	RW	Jarome Iginla, Cgy.
Markus Naslund, Van.	LW	Ilya Kovalchuk, Atl.

2002-03

First Team		Second Team
Martin Brodeur, N.J.	G	Marty Turco, Dal.
Al MacInnis, St.L.	D	Sergei Gonchar, Wsh.
Nicklas Lidstrom, Det.	D	Derian Hatcher, Dal.
Peter Forsberg, Col.	C	Joe Thornton, Bos.
Todd Bertuzzi, Van.	RW	Milan Hejduk, Col.
Markus Naslund, Van.	LW	Paul Kariya, Ana.

2001-02

First Team		Second Team
Patrick Roy, Col.	G	Jose Theodore, Mtl.
Nicklas Lidstrom, Det.	D	Rob Blake, Col.
Chris Chelios, Det.	D	Sergei Gonchar, Wsh.
Joe Sakic, Col.	C	Mats Sundin, Tor.
Jarome Iginla, Cgy.	RW	Bill Guerin, Bos.
Markus Naslund, Van.	LW	Brendan Shanahan, Det.

2000-01

First Team		Second Team
Dominik Hasek, Buf.	G	Roman Cechmanek, Phi.
Nicklas Lidstrom, Det.	D	Rob Blake, L.A., Col.
Raymond Bourque, Col.	D	Scott Stevens, N.J.
Joe Sakic, Col.	C	Mario Lemieux, Pit.
Jaromir Jagr, Pit.	RW	Pavel Bure, Fla.
Patrik Elias, N.J.	LW	Luc Robitaille, L.A.

1999-2000

First Team		Second Team
Olaf Kolzig, Wsh.	G	Roman Turek, St.L.
Chris Pronger, St.L.	D	Rob Blake, L.A.
Nicklas Lidstrom, Det.	D	Eric Desjardins, Phi.
Steve Yzerman, Det.	C	Mike Modano, Dal.
Jaromir Jagr, Pit.	RW	Pavel Bure, Fla.
Brendan Shanahan, Det.	LW	Paul Kariya, Ana.

1998-99

First Team		Second Team
Dominik Hasek, Buf.	G	Byron Dafoe, Bos.
Al MacInnis, St.L.	D	Raymond Bourque, Bos.
Nicklas Lidstrom, Det.	D	Eric Desjardins, Phi.
Peter Forsberg, Col.	C	Alexei Yashin, Ott.
Jaromir Jagr, Pit.	RW	Teemu Selanne, Ana.
Paul Kariya, Ana.	LW	John LeClair, Phi.

1997-98

First Team		Second Team
Dominik Hasek, Buf.	G	Martin Brodeur, N.J.
Nicklas Lidstrom, Det.	D	Chris Pronger, St.L.
Rob Blake, L.A.	D	Scott Niedermayer, N.J.
Peter Forsberg, Col.	C	Wayne Gretzky, NYR
Jaromir Jagr, Pit.	RW	Teemu Selanne, Ana.
John LeClair, Phi.	LW	Keith Tkachuk, Phx.

1996-97

First Team		Second Team
Dominik Hasek, Buf.	G	Martin Brodeur, N.J.
Brian Leetch, NYR	D	Chris Chelios, Chi.
Sandis Ozolinsh, Col.	D	Scott Stevens, N.J.
Mario Lemieux, Pit.	C	Wayne Gretzky, NYR
Teemu Selanne, Ana.	RW	Jaromir Jagr, Pit.
Paul Kariya, Ana.	LW	John LeClair, Phi.

1995-96

First Team		Second Team
Jim Carey, Wsh.	G	Chris Osgood, Det.
Chris Chelios, Chi.	D	V. Konstantinov, Det.
Raymond Bourque, Bos.	D	Brian Leetch, NYR
Mario Lemieux, Pit.	C	Eric Lindros, Phi.
Jaromir Jagr, Pit.	RW	Alexander Mogilny, Van.
Paul Kariya, Ana.	LW	John LeClair, Phi.

1994-95

First Team		Second Team
Dominik Hasek, Buf.	G	Ed Belfour, Chi.
Paul Coffey, Det.	D	Raymond Bourque, Bos.
Chris Chelios, Chi.	D	Larry Murphy, Pit.
Eric Lindros, Phi.	C	Alexei Zhamnov, Wpg.
Jaromir Jagr, Pit.	RW	Theoren Fleury, Cgy.
John LeClair, Mtl., Phi.	LW	Keith Tkachuk, Wpg.

1993-94

First Team		Second Team
Dominik Hasek, Buf.	G	John Vanbiesbrouck, Fla.
Raymond Bourque, Bos.	D	Al MacInnis, Cgy.
Scott Stevens, N.J.	D	Brian Leetch, NYR
Sergei Fedorov, Det.	C	Wayne Gretzky, L.A.
Pavel Bure, Van.	RW	Cam Neely, Bos.
Brendan Shanahan, St.L.	LW	Adam Graves, NYR

1992-93

First Team		Second Team
Ed Belfour, Chi.	G	Tom Barrasso, Pit.
Chris Chelios, Chi.	D	Larry Murphy, Pit.
Raymond Bourque, Bos.	D	Al Iafrate, Wsh.
Mario Lemieux, Pit.	C	Pat LaFontaine, Buf.
Teemu Selanne, Wpg.	RW	Alexander Mogilny, Buf.
Luc Robitaille, L.A.	LW	Kevin Stevens, Pit.

1991-92

First Team		Second Team
Patrick Roy, Mtl.	G	Kirk McLean, Van.
Brian Leetch, NYR	D	Phil Housley, Wpg.
Raymond Bourque, Bos.	D	Scott Stevens, N.J.
Mark Messier, NYR	C	Mario Lemieux, Pit.
Brett Hull, St.L.	RW	Mark Recchi, Pit., Phi.
Kevin Stevens, Pit.	LW	Luc Robitaille, L.A.

1990-91

First Team		Second Team
Ed Belfour, Chi.	G	Patrick Roy, Mtl.
Raymond Bourque, Bos.	D	Chris Chelios, Chi.
Al MacInnis, Cgy.	D	Brian Leetch, NYR
Wayne Gretzky, L.A.	C	Adam Oates, St.L.
Brett Hull, St.L.	RW	Cam Neely, Bos.
Luc Robitaille, L.A.	LW	Kevin Stevens, Pit.

1989-90

First Team		Second Team
Patrick Roy, Mtl.	G	Daren Puppa, Buf.
Raymond Bourque, Bos.	D	Paul Coffey, Pit.
Al MacInnis, Cgy.	D	Doug Wilson, Chi.
Mark Messier, Edm.	C	Wayne Gretzky, L.A.
Brett Hull, St.L.	RW	Cam Neely, Bos.
Luc Robitaille, L.A.	LW	Brian Bellows, Min.

1988-89

First Team		Second Team
Patrick Roy, Mtl.	G	Mike Vernon, Cgy.
Chris Chelios, Mtl.	D	Al MacInnis, Cgy.
Paul Coffey, Pit.	D	Raymond Bourque, Bos.
Mario Lemieux, Pit.	C	Wayne Gretzky, L.A.
Joe Mullen, Cgy.	RW	Jari Kurri, Edm.
Luc Robitaille, L.A.	LW	Gerard Gallant, Det.

1987-88

First Team		Second Team
Grant Fuhr, Edm.	G	Patrick Roy, Mtl.
Raymond Bourque, Bos.	D	Gary Suter, Cgy.
Scott Stevens, Wsh.	D	Brad McCrimmon, Cgy.
Mario Lemieux, Pit.	C	Wayne Gretzky, Edm.
Hakan Loob, Cgy.	RW	Cam Neely, Bos.
Luc Robitaille, L.A.	LW	Michel Goulet, Que.

1986-87

First Team		Second Team
Ron Hextall, Phi.	G	Mike Liut, Hfd.
Raymond Bourque, Bos.	D	Larry Murphy, Wsh.
Mark Howe, Phi.	D	Al MacInnis, Cgy.
Wayne Gretzky, Edm.	C	Mario Lemieux, Pit.
Jari Kurri, Edm.	RW	Tim Kerr, Phi.
Michel Goulet, Que.	LW	Luc Robitaille, L.A.

1985-86

First Team		Second Team
John Vanbiesbrouck, NYR	G	Bob Froese, Phi.
Paul Coffey, Edm.	D	Larry Robinson, Mtl.
Mark Howe, Phi.	D	Raymond Bourque, Bos.
Wayne Gretzky, Edm.	C	Mario Lemieux, Pit.
Mike Bossy, NYI	RW	Jari Kurri, Edm.
Michel Goulet, Que.	LW	Mats Naslund, Mtl.

1984-85

First Team		Second Team
Pelle Lindbergh, Phi.	G	Tom Barrasso, Buf.
Paul Coffey, Edm.	D	Rod Langway, Wsh.
Raymond Bourque, Bos.	D	Doug Wilson, Chi.
Wayne Gretzky, Edm.	C	Dale Hawerchuk, Wpg.
Jari Kurri, Edm.	RW	Mike Bossy, NYI
John Ogrodnick, Det.	LW	John Tonelli, NYI

1983-84

First Team		Second Team
Tom Barrasso, Buf.	*G*	Pat Riggin, Wsh.
Rod Langway, Wsh.	*D*	Paul Coffey, Edm.
Raymond Bourque, Bos.	*D*	Denis Potvin, NYI
Wayne Gretzky, Edm.	*C*	Bryan Trottier, NYI
Mike Bossy, NYI	*RW*	Jari Kurri, Edm.
Michel Goulet, Que.	*LW*	Mark Messier, Edm.

1982-83

First Team		Second Team
Pete Peeters, Bos.	*G*	Roland Melanson, NYI
Mark Howe, Phi.	*D*	Raymond Bourque, Bos.
Rod Langway, Wsh.	*D*	Paul Coffey, Edm.
Wayne Gretzky, Edm.	*C*	Denis Savard, Chi.
Mike Bossy, NYI	*RW*	Lanny McDonald, Cgy.
Mark Messier, Edm.	*LW*	Michel Goulet, Que.

1981-82

First Team		Second Team
Billy Smith, NYI	*G*	Grant Fuhr, Edm.
Doug Wilson, Chi.	*D*	Paul Coffey, Edm.
Raymond Bourque, Bos.	*D*	Brian Engblom, Mtl.
Wayne Gretzky, Edm.	*C*	Bryan Trottier, NYI
Mike Bossy, NYI	*RW*	Rick Middleton, Bos.
Mark Messier, Edm.	*LW*	John Tonelli, NYI

1980-81

First Team		Second Team
Mike Liut, St.L.	*G*	Mario Lessard, L.A.
Denis Potvin, NYI	*D*	Larry Robinson, Mtl.
Randy Carlyle, Pit.	*D*	Raymond Bourque, Bos.
Wayne Gretzky, Edm.	*C*	Marcel Dionne, L.A.
Mike Bossy, NYI	*RW*	Dave Taylor, L.A.
Charlie Simmer, L.A.	*LW*	Bill Barber, Phi.

1979-80

First Team		Second Team
Tony Esposito, Chi.	*G*	Don Edwards, Buf.
Larry Robinson, Mtl.	*D*	Borje Salming, Tor.
Raymond Bourque, Bos.	*D*	Jim Schoenfeld, Buf.
Marcel Dionne, L.A.	*C*	Wayne Gretzky, Edm.
Guy Lafleur, Mtl.	*RW*	Danny Gare, Buf.
Charlie Simmer, L.A.	*LW*	Steve Shutt, Mtl.

1978-79

First Team		Second Team
Ken Dryden, Mtl.	*G*	Glenn Resch, NYI
Denis Potvin, NYI	*D*	Borje Salming, Tor.
Larry Robinson, Mtl.	*D*	Serge Savard, Mtl.
Bryan Trottier, NYI	*C*	Marcel Dionne, L.A.
Guy Lafleur, Mtl.	*RW*	Mike Bossy, NYI
Clark Gillies, NYI	*LW*	Bill Barber, Phi.

1977-78

First Team		Second Team
Ken Dryden, Mtl.	*G*	Don Edwards, Buf.
Denis Potvin, NYI	*D*	Larry Robinson, Mtl.
Brad Park, Bos.	*D*	Borje Salming, Tor.
Bryan Trottier, NYI	*C*	Darryl Sittler, Tor.
Guy Lafleur, Mtl.	*RW*	Mike Bossy, NYI
Clark Gillies, NYI	*LW*	Steve Shutt, Mtl.

1976-77

First Team		Second Team
Ken Dryden, Mtl.	*G*	Rogie Vachon, L.A.
Larry Robinson, Mtl.	*D*	Denis Potvin, NYI
Borje Salming, Tor.	*D*	Guy Lapointe, Mtl.
Marcel Dionne, L.A.	*C*	Gilbert Perreault, Buf.
Guy Lafleur, Mtl.	*RW*	Lanny McDonald, Tor.
Steve Shutt, Mtl.	*LW*	Rick Martin, Buf.

1975-76

First Team		Second Team
Ken Dryden, Mtl.	*G*	Glenn Resch, NYI
Denis Potvin, NYI	*D*	Borje Salming, Tor.
Brad Park, Bos.	*D*	Guy Lapointe, Mtl.
Bobby Clarke, Phi.	*C*	Gilbert Perreault, Buf.
Guy Lafleur, Mtl.	*RW*	Reggie Leach, Phi.
Bill Barber, Phi.	*LW*	Rick Martin, Buf.

1974-75

First Team		Second Team
Bernie Parent, Phi.	*G*	Rogie Vachon, L.A.
Bobby Orr, Bos.	*D*	Guy Lapointe, Mtl.
Denis Potvin, NYI	*D*	Borje Salming, Tor.
Bobby Clarke, Phi.	*C*	Phil Esposito, Bos.
Guy Lafleur, Mtl.	*RW*	René Robert, Buf.
Rick Martin, Buf.	*LW*	Steve Vickers, NYR

1973-74

First Team		Second Team
Bernie Parent, Phi.	*G*	Tony Esposito, Chi.
Bobby Orr, Bos.	*D*	Bill White, Chi.
Brad Park, NYR	*D*	Barry Ashbee, Phi.
Phil Esposito, Bos.	*C*	Bobby Clarke, Phi.
Ken Hodge, Bos.	*RW*	Mickey Redmond, Det.
Rick Martin, Buf.	*LW*	Wayne Cashman, Bos.

1972-73

First Team		Second Team
Ken Dryden, Mtl.	*G*	Tony Esposito, Chi.
Bobby Orr, Bos.	*D*	Brad Park, NYR
Guy Lapointe, Mtl.	*D*	Bill White, Chi.
Phil Esposito, Bos.	*C*	Bobby Clarke, Phi.
Mickey Redmond, Det.	*RW*	Yvan Cournoyer, Mtl.
Frank Mahovlich, Mtl.	*LW*	Dennis Hull, Chi.

1971-72

First Team		Second Team
Tony Esposito, Chi.	*G*	Ken Dryden, Mtl.
Bobby Orr, Bos.	*D*	Bill White, Chi.
Brad Park, NYR	*D*	Pat Stapleton, Chi.
Phil Esposito, Bos.	*C*	Jean Ratelle, NYR
Rod Gilbert, NYR	*RW*	Yvan Cournoyer, Mtl.
Bobby Hull, Chi.	*LW*	Vic Hadfield, NYR

1970-71

First Team		Second Team
Ed Giacomin, NYR	*G*	Jacques Plante, Tor.
Bobby Orr, Bos.	*D*	Brad Park, NYR
J.C. Tremblay, Mtl.	*D*	Pat Stapleton, Chi.
Phil Esposito, Bos.	*C*	Dave Keon, Tor.
Ken Hodge, Bos.	*RW*	Yvan Cournoyer, Mtl.
John Bucyk, Bos.	*LW*	Bobby Hull, Chi.

1969-70

First Team		Second Team
Tony Esposito, Chi.	*G*	Ed Giacomin, NYR
Bobby Orr, Bos.	*D*	Carl Brewer, Det.
Brad Park, NYR	*D*	Jacques Laperriere, Mtl.
Phil Esposito, Bos.	*C*	Stan Mikita, Chi.
Gordie Howe, Det.	*RW*	John McKenzie, Bos.
Bobby Hull, Chi.	*LW*	Frank Mahovlich, Det.

1968-69

First Team		Second Team
Glenn Hall, St.L.	*G*	Ed Giacomin, NYR
Bobby Orr, Bos.	*D*	Ted Green, Bos.
Tim Horton, Tor.	*D*	Ted Harris, Mtl.
Phil Esposito, Bos.	*C*	Jean Béliveau, Mtl.
Gordie Howe, Det.	*RW*	Yvan Cournoyer, Mtl.
Bobby Hull, Chi.	*LW*	Frank Mahovlich, Det.

1967-68

First Team		Second Team
Gump Worsley, Mtl.	*G*	Ed Giacomin, NYR
Bobby Orr, Bos.	*D*	J.C. Tremblay, Mtl.
Tim Horton, Tor.	*D*	Jim Neilson, NYR
Stan Mikita, Chi.	*C*	Phil Esposito, Bos.
Gordie Howe, Det.	*RW*	Rod Gilbert, NYR
Bobby Hull, Chi.	*LW*	John Bucyk, Bos.

1966-67

First Team		Second Team
Ed Giacomin, NYR	*G*	Glenn Hall, Chi.
Pierre Pilote, Chi.	*D*	Tim Horton, Tor.
Harry Howell, NYR	*D*	Bobby Orr, Bos.
Stan Mikita, Chi.	*C*	Norm Ullman, Det.
Kenny Wharram, Chi.	*RW*	Gordie Howe, Det.
Bobby Hull, Chi.	*LW*	Don Marshall, NYR

1965-66

First Team		Second Team
Glenn Hall, Chi.	*G*	Gump Worsley, Mtl.
Jacques Laperriere, Mtl.	*D*	Allan Stanley, Tor.
Pierre Pilote, Chi.	*D*	Pat Stapleton, Chi.
Stan Mikita, Chi.	*C*	Jean Béliveau, Mtl.
Gordie Howe, Det.	*RW*	Bobby Rousseau, Mtl.
Bobby Hull, Chi.	*LW*	Frank Mahovlich, Tor.

1964-65

First Team		Second Team
Roger Crozier, Det.	*G*	Charlie Hodge, Mtl.
Pierre Pilote, Chi.	*D*	Bill Gadsby, Det.
Jacques Laperriere, Mtl.	*D*	Carl Brewer, Tor.
Norm Ullman, Det.	*C*	Stan Mikita, Chi.
Claude Provost, Mtl.	*RW*	Gordie Howe, Det.
Bobby Hull, Chi.	*LW*	Frank Mahovlich, Tor.

1963-64

First Team		Second Team
Glenn Hall, Chi.	*G*	Charlie Hodge, Mtl.
Pierre Pilote, Chi.	*D*	Moose Vasko, Chi.
Tim Horton, Tor.	*D*	Jacques Laperriere, Mtl.
Stan Mikita, Chi.	*C*	Jean Béliveau, Mtl.
Kenny Wharram, Chi.	*RW*	Gordie Howe, Det.
Bobby Hull, Chi.	*LW*	Frank Mahovlich, Tor.

1962-63

First Team		Second Team
Glenn Hall, Chi.	*G*	Terry Sawchuk, Det.
Pierre Pilote, Chi.	*D*	Tim Horton, Tor.
Carl Brewer, Tor.	*D*	Moose Vasko, Chi.
Stan Mikita, Chi.	*C*	Henri Richard, Mtl.
Gordie Howe, Det.	*RW*	Andy Bathgate, NYR
Frank Mahovlich, Tor.	*LW*	Bobby Hull, Chi.

1961-62

First Team		Second Team
Jacques Plante, Mtl.	*G*	Glenn Hall, Chi.
Doug Harvey, NYR	*D*	Carl Brewer, Tor.
Jean-Guy Talbot, Mtl.	*D*	Pierre Pilote, Chi.
Stan Mikita, Chi.	*C*	Dave Keon, Tor.
Andy Bathgate, NYR	*RW*	Gordie Howe, Det.
Bobby Hull, Chi.	*LW*	Frank Mahovlich, Tor.

1960-61

First Team		Second Team
Johnny Bower, Tor.	*G*	Glenn Hall, Chi.
Doug Harvey, Mtl.	*D*	Allan Stanley, Tor.
Marcel Pronovost, Det.	*D*	Pierre Pilote, Chi.
Jean Béliveau, Mtl.	*C*	Henri Richard, Mtl.
Bernie Geoffrion, Mtl.	*RW*	Gordie Howe, Det.
Frank Mahovlich, Tor.	*LW*	Dickie Moore, Mtl.

1959-60

First Team		Second Team
Glenn Hall, Chi.	*G*	Jacques Plante, Mtl.
Doug Harvey, Mtl.	*D*	Allan Stanley, Tor.
Marcel Pronovost, Det.	*D*	Pierre Pilote, Chi.
Jean Béliveau, Mtl.	*C*	Bronco Horvath, Bos.
Gordie Howe, Det.	*RW*	Bernie Geoffrion, Mtl.
Bobby Hull, Chi.	*LW*	Dean Prentice, NYR

1958-59

First Team		Second Team
Jacques Plante, Mtl.	*G*	Terry Sawchuk, Det.
Tom Johnson, Mtl.	*D*	Marcel Pronovost, Det.
Bill Gadsby, NYR	*D*	Doug Harvey, Mtl.
Jean Béliveau, Mtl.	*C*	Henri Richard, Mtl.
Andy Bathgate, NYR	*RW*	Gordie Howe, Det.
Dickie Moore, Mtl.	*LW*	Alex Delvecchio, Det.

1957-58

First Team		Second Team
Glenn Hall, Chi.	*G*	Jacques Plante, Mtl.
Doug Harvey, Mtl.	*D*	Fern Flaman, Bos.
Bill Gadsby, NYR	*D*	Marcel Pronovost, Det.
Henri Richard, Mtl.	*C*	Jean Béliveau, Mtl.
Gordie Howe, Det.	*RW*	Andy Bathgate, NYR
Dickie Moore, Mtl.	*LW*	Camille Henry, NYR

1956-57

First Team		Second Team
Glenn Hall, Det.	G	Jacques Plante, Mtl.
Doug Harvey, Mtl.	D	Fern Flaman, Bos.
Red Kelly, Det.	D	Bill Gadsby, NYR
Jean Béliveau, Mtl.	C	Ed Litzenberger, Chi.
Gordie Howe, Det.	RW	Maurice Richard, Mtl.
Ted Lindsay, Det.	LW	Real Chevrefils, Bos.

1955-56

First Team		Second Team
Jacques Plante, Mtl.	G	Glenn Hall, Det.
Doug Harvey, Mtl.	D	Red Kelly, Det.
Bill Gadsby, NYR	D	Tom Johnson, Mtl.
Jean Béliveau, Mtl.	C	Tod Sloan, Tor.
Maurice Richard, Mtl.	RW	Gordie Howe, Det.
Ted Lindsay, Det.	LW	Bert Olmstead, Mtl.

1954-55

First Team		Second Team
Harry Lumley, Tor.	G	Terry Sawchuk, Det.
Doug Harvey, Mtl.	D	Bob Goldham, Det.
Red Kelly, Det.	D	Fern Flaman, Bos.
Jean Béliveau, Mtl.	C	Ken Mosdell, Mtl.
Maurice Richard, Mtl.	RW	Bernie Geoffrion, Mtl.
Sid Smith, Tor.	LW	Danny Lewicki, NYR

1953-54

First Team		Second Team
Harry Lumley, Tor.	G	Terry Sawchuk, Det.
Red Kelly, Det.	D	Bill Gadsby, Chi.
Doug Harvey, Mtl.	D	Tim Horton, Tor.
Ken Mosdell, Mtl.	C	Ted Kennedy, Tor.
Gordie Howe, Det.	RW	Maurice Richard, Mtl.
Ted Lindsay, Det.	LW	Ed Sandford, Bos.

1952-53

First Team		Second Team
Terry Sawchuk, Det.	G	Gerry McNeil, Mtl.
Red Kelly, Det.	D	Bill Quackenbush, Bos.
Doug Harvey, Mtl.	D	Bill Gadsby, Chi.
Fleming MacKell, Bos.	C	Alex Delvecchio, Det.
Gordie Howe, Det.	RW	Maurice Richard, Mtl.
Ted Lindsay, Det.	LW	Bert Olmstead, Mtl.

1951-52

First Team		Second Team
Terry Sawchuk, Det.	G	Jim Henry, Bos.
Red Kelly, Det.	D	Hy Buller, NYR
Doug Harvey, Mtl.	D	Jimmy Thomson, Tor.
Elmer Lach, Mtl.	C	Milt Schmidt, Bos.
Gordie Howe, Det.	RW	Maurice Richard, Mtl.
Ted Lindsay, Det.	LW	Sid Smith, Tor.

1950-51

First Team		Second Team
Terry Sawchuk, Det.	G	Chuck Rayner, NYR
Red Kelly, Det.	D	Jimmy Thomson, Tor.
Bill Quackenbush, Bos.	D	Leo Reise Jr., Det.
Milt Schmidt, Bos.	C	Sid Abel, Det.
		Ted Kennedy, Tor. (tied)
Gordie Howe, Det.	RW	Maurice Richard, Mtl.
Ted Lindsay, Det.	LW	Sid Smith, Tor.

1949-50

First Team		Second Team
Bill Durnan, Mtl.	G	Chuck Rayner, NYR
Gus Mortson, Tor.	D	Leo Reise Jr., Det.
Ken Reardon, Mtl.	D	Red Kelly, Det.
Sid Abel, Det.	C	Ted Kennedy, Tor.
Maurice Richard, Mtl.	RW	Gordie Howe, Det.
Ted Lindsay, Det.	LW	Tony Leswick, NYR

1948-49

First Team		Second Team
Bill Durnan, Mtl.	G	Chuck Rayner, NYR
Bill Quackenbush, Det.	D	Glen Harmon, Mtl.
Jack Stewart, Det.	D	Ken Reardon, Mtl.
Sid Abel, Det.	C	Doug Bentley, Chi.
Maurice Richard, Mtl.	RW	Gordie Howe, Det.
Roy Conacher, Chi.	LW	Ted Lindsay, Det.

1947-48

First Team		Second Team
Turk Broda, Tor.	G	Frank Brimsek, Bos.
Bill Quackenbush, Det.	D	Ken Reardon, Mtl.
Jack Stewart, Det.	D	Neil Colville, NYR
Elmer Lach, Mtl.	C	Buddy O'Connor, NYR
Maurice Richard, Mtl.	RW	Bud Poile, Chi.
Ted Lindsay, Det.	LW	Gaye Stewart, Chi.

1946-47

First Team		Second Team
Bill Durnan, Mtl.	G	Frank Brimsek, Bos.
Ken Reardon, Mtl.	D	Jack Stewart, Det.
Butch Bouchard, Mtl.	D	Bill Quackenbush, Det.
Milt Schmidt, Bos.	C	Max Bentley, Chi.
Maurice Richard, Mtl.	RW	Bobby Bauer, Bos.
Doug Bentley, Chi.	LW	Woody Dumart, Bos.

1945-46

First Team		Second Team
Bill Durnan, Mtl.	G	Frank Brimsek, Bos.
Jack Crawford, Bos.	D	Ken Reardon, Mtl.
Butch Bouchard, Mtl.	D	Jack Stewart, Det.
Max Bentley, Chi.	C	Elmer Lach, Mtl.
Maurice Richard, Mtl.	RW	Bill Mosienko, Chi.
Gaye Stewart, Tor.	LW	Toe Blake, Mtl.
Dick Irvin, Mtl.	Coach	Johnny Gottselig, Chi.

1944-45

First Team		Second Team
Bill Durnan, Mtl.	G	Mike Karakas, Chi.
Butch Bouchard, Mtl.	D	Glen Harmon, Mtl.
Flash Hollett, Det.	D	Babe Pratt, Tor.
Elmer Lach, Mtl.	C	Bill Cowley, Bos.
Maurice Richard, Mtl.	RW	Bill Mosienko, Chi.
Toe Blake, Mtl.	LW	Syd Howe, Det.
Dick Irvin, Mtl.	Coach	Jack Adams, Det.

1943-44

First Team		Second Team
Bill Durnan, Mtl.	G	Paul Bibeault, Tor.
Earl Seibert, Chi.	D	Butch Bouchard, Mtl.
Babe Pratt, Tor.	D	Dit Clapper, Bos.
Bill Cowley, Bos.	C	Elmer Lach, Mtl.
Lorne Carr, Tor.	RW	Maurice Richard, Mtl.
Doug Bentley, Chi.	LW	Herb Cain, Bos.
Dick Irvin, Mtl.	Coach	Hap Day, Tor.

1942-43

First Team		Second Team
Johnny Mowers, Det.	G	Frank Brimsek, Bos.
Earl Seibert, Chi.	D	Jack Crawford, Bos.
Jack Stewart, Det.	D	Flash Hollett, Bos.
Bill Cowley, Bos.	C	Syl Apps, Tor.
Lorne Carr, Tor.	RW	Bryan Hextall, NYR
Doug Bentley, Chi.	LW	Lynn Patrick, NYR
Jack Adams, Det.	Coach	Art Ross, Bos.

1941-42

First Team		Second Team
Frank Brimsek, Bos.	G	Turk Broda, Tor.
Earl Seibert, Chi.	D	Pat Egan, Bro.
Tom Anderson, Bro.	D	Bucko McDonald, Tor.
Syl Apps, Tor.	C	Phil Watson, NYR
Bryan Hextall, NYR	RW	Gordie Drillon, Tor.
Lynn Patrick, NYR	LW	Sid Abel, Det.
Frank Boucher, NYR	Coach	Paul Thompson, Chi.

1940-41

First Team		Second Team
Turk Broda, Tor.	G	Frank Brimsek, Bos.
Dit Clapper, Bos.	D	Earl Seibert, Chi.
Wally Stanowski, Tor.	D	Ott Heller, NYR
Bill Cowley, Bos.	C	Syl Apps, Tor.
Bryan Hextall, NYR	RW	Bobby Bauer, Bos.
Sweeney Schriner, Tor.	LW	Woody Dumart, Bos.
Cooney Weiland, Bos.	Coach	Dick Irvin, Mtl.

1939-40

First Team		Second Team
Dave Kerr, NYR	G	Frank Brimsek, Bos.
Dit Clapper, Bos.	D	Art Coulter, NYR
Ebbie Goodfellow, Det.	D	Earl Seibert, Chi.
Milt Schmidt, Bos.	C	Neil Colville, NYR
Bryan Hextall, NYR	RW	Bobby Bauer, Bos.
Toe Blake, Mtl.	LW	Woody Dumart, Bos.
Paul Thompson, Chi.	Coach	Frank Boucher, NYR

1938-39

First Team		Second Team
Frank Brimsek, Bos.	G	Earl Robertson, NYA
Eddie Shore, Bos.	D	Earl Seibert, Chi.
Dit Clapper, Bos.	D	Art Coulter, NYR
Syl Apps, Tor.	C	Neil Colville, NYR
Gordie Drillon, Tor.	RW	Bobby Bauer, Bos.
Toe Blake, Mtl.	LW	Johnny Gottselig, Chi.
Art Ross, Bos.	Coach	Red Dutton, NYA

1937-38

First Team		Second Team
Tiny Thompson, Bos.	G	Dave Kerr, NYR
Eddie Shore, Bos.	D	Art Coulter, NYR
Babe Siebert, Mtl.	D	Earl Seibert, Chi.
Bill Cowley, Bos.	C	Syl Apps, Tor.
Cecil Dillon, NYR	RW	
Gordie Drillon, Tor. *(tied)*		
Paul Thompson, Chi.	LW	Toe Blake, Mtl.
Lester Patrick, NYR	Coach	Art Ross, Bos.

1936-37

First Team		Second Team
Normie Smith, Det.	G	Wilf Cude, Mtl.
Babe Siebert, Mtl.	D	Earl Seibert, Chi.
Ebbie Goodfellow, Det.	D	Lionel Conacher, Mtl. M.
Marty Barry, Det.	C	Art Chapman, NYA
Larry Aurie, Det.	RW	Cecil Dillon, NYR
Busher Jackson, Tor.	LW	Sweeney Schriner, NYA
Jack Adams, Det.	Coach	Cecil Hart, Mtl.

1935-36

First Team		Second Team
Tiny Thompson, Bos.	G	Wilf Cude, Mtl.
Eddie Shore, Bos.	D	Earl Seibert, Chi.
Babe Siebert, Bos.	D	Ebbie Goodfellow, Det.
Hooley Smith, Mtl. M.	C	Bill Thoms, Tor.
Charlie Conacher, Tor.	RW	Cecil Dillon, NYR
Sweeney Schriner, NYA	LW	Paul Thompson, Chi.
Lester Patrick, NYR	Coach	Tommy Gorman, Mtl. M.

1934-35

First Team		Second Team
Lorne Chabot, Chi.	G	Tiny Thompson, Bos.
Eddie Shore, Bos.	D	Cy Wentworth, Mtl. M.
Earl Seibert, NYR	D	Art Coulter, Chi.
Frank Boucher, NYR	C	Cooney Weiland, Det.
Charlie Conacher, Tor.	RW	Dit Clapper, Bos.
Busher Jackson, Tor.	LW	Aurel Joliat, Mtl.
Lester Patrick, NYR	Coach	Dick Irvin, Tor.

1933-34

First Team		Second Team
Charlie Gardiner, Chi.	G	Roy Worters, NYA
King Clancy, Tor.	D	Eddie Shore, Bos.
Lionel Conacher, Chi.	D	Ching Johnson, NYR
Frank Boucher, NYR	C	Joe Primeau, Tor.
Charlie Conacher, Tor.	RW	Bill Cook, NYR
Busher Jackson, Tor.	LW	Aurel Joliat, Mtl.
Lester Patrick, NYR	Coach	Dick Irvin, Tor.

1932-33

First Team		Second Team
John Ross Roach, Det.	G	Charlie Gardiner, Chi.
Eddie Shore, Bos.	D	King Clancy, Tor.
Ching Johnson, NYR	D	Lionel Conacher, Mtl. M.
Frank Boucher, NYR	C	Howie Morenz, Mtl.
Bill Cook, NYR	RW	Charlie Conacher, Tor.
Baldy Northcott, Mtl. M.	LW	Busher Jackson, Tor.
Lester Patrick, NYR	Coach	Dick Irvin, Tor.

1931-32

First Team		Second Team
Charlie Gardiner, Chi.	G	Roy Worters, NYA
Eddie Shore, Bos.	D	Sylvio Mantha, Mtl.
Ching Johnson, NYR	D	King Clancy, Tor.
Howie Morenz, Mtl.	C	Hooley Smith, Mtl. M.
Bill Cook, NYR	RW	Charlie Conacher, Tor.
Busher Jackson, Tor.	LW	Aurel Joliat, Mtl.
Lester Patrick, NYR	Coach	Dick Irvin, Tor.

1930-31

First Team		Second Team
Charlie Gardiner, Chi.	G	Tiny Thompson, Bos.
Eddie Shore, Bos.	D	Sylvio Mantha, Mtl.
King Clancy, Tor.	D	Ching Johnson, NYR
Howie Morenz, Mtl.	C	Frank Boucher, NYR
Bill Cook, NYR	RW	Dit Clapper, Bos.
Aurel Joliat, Mtl.	LW	Bun Cook, NYR
Lester Patrick, NYR	Coach	Dick Irvin, Chi.

NHL ALL-ROOKIE TEAM

Voting for the NHL All-Rookie Team is conducted among the representatives of the Professional Hockey Writers' Association at the end of the season. The rookie all-star team was first selected for the 1982-83 season.

	2007-08
Goal	Carey Price, Montreal
Defense	Tobias Enstrom, Atlanta
Defense	Tom Gilbert, Edmonton
Forward	Nicklas Backstrom, Washington
Forward	Patrick Kane, Chicago
Forward	Jonathan Toews, Chicago

	2006-07
Goal	Mike Smith, Dallas
Defense	Matt Carle, San Jose
Defense	Marc-Edouard Vlasic, San Jose
Forward	Evgeni Malkin, Pittsburgh
Forward	Jordan Staal, Pittsburgh
Forward	Paul Stastny, Colorado

	2005-06
Goal	Henrik Lundqvist, NY Rangers
Defense	Andrej Meszaros, Ottawa
Defense	Dion Phaneuf, Calgary
Forward	Brad Boyes, Boston
Forward	Sidney Crosby, Pittsburgh
Forward	Alex Ovechkin, Washington

	2004-05
Goal	
Defense	
Defense	*Season Cancelled*
Forward	
Forward	
Forward	

	2003-04
Goal	Andrew Raycroft, Boston
Defense	John-Michael Liles, Colorado
Defense	Joni Pitkanen, Philadelphia
Forward	Trent Hunter, NY Islanders
Forward	Ryan Malone, Pittsburgh
Forward	Michael Ryder, Montreal

	2002-03
Goal	Sebastien Caron, Pittsburgh
Defense	Jay Bouwmeester, Florida
Defense	Barret Jackman, St. Louis
Forward	Tyler Arnason, Chicago
Forward	Rick Nash, Columbus
Forward	Henrik Zetterberg, Detroit

2001-02
Dan Blackburn, NY Rangers
Nick Boynton, Boston
Rostislav Klesla, Columbus
Dany Heatley, Atlanta
Ilya Kovalchuk, Atlanta
Kristian Huselius, Florida

2000-01
Evgeni Nabokov, San Jose
Lubomir Visnovsky, Los Angeles
Colin White, New Jersey
Martin Havlat, Ottawa
Brad Richards, Tampa Bay
Shane Willis, Carolina

1999-2000
Brian Boucher, Philadelphia
Brian Rafalski, New Jersey
Brad Stuart, San Jose
Simon Gagne, Philadelphia
Scott Gomez, New Jersey
Michael York, NY Rangers

1998-99
Jamie Storr, Los Angeles
Tom Poti, Edmonton
Sami Salo, Ottawa
Chris Drury, Colorado
Milan Hejduk, Colorado
Marian Hossa, Ottawa

1997-98
Jamie Storr, Los Angeles
Mattias Ohlund, Vancouver
Derek Morris, Calgary
Sergei Samsonov, Boston
Patrick Elias, New Jersey
Mike Johnson, Toronto

1996-97
Patrick Lalime, Pittsburgh
Bryan Berard, NY Islanders
Janne Niinimaa, Philadelphia
Jarome Iginla, Calgary
Jim Campbell, St. Louis
Sergei Berezin, Toronto

1995-96
Corey Hirsch, Vancouver
Ed Jovanovski, Florida
Kyle McLaren, Boston
Daniel Alfredsson, Ottawa
Eric Daze, Chicago
Petr Sykora, New Jersey

1994-95
Jim Carey, Washington
Chris Therien, Philadelphia
Kenny Jonsson, Toronto
Peter Forsberg, Quebec
Jeff Friesen, San Jose
Paul Kariya, Anaheim

1993-94
Martin Brodeur, New Jersey
Chris Pronger, Hartford
Boris Mironov, Wpg./Edm.
Jason Arnott, Edmonton
Mikael Renberg, Philadelphia
Oleg Petrov, Montreal

1992-93
Felix Potvin, Toronto
Vladimir Malakhov, NY Islanders
Scott Niedermayer, New Jersey
Eric Lindros, Philadelphia
Teemu Selanne, Winnipeg
Joe Juneau, Boston

1991-92
Dominik Hasek, Chicago
Nicklas Lidstrom, Detroit
Vladimir Konstantinov, Detroit
Kevin Todd, New Jersey
Tony Amonte, NY Rangers
Gilbert Dionne, Montreal

1990-91
Ed Belfour, Chicago
Eric Weinrich, New Jersey
Rob Blake, Los Angeles
Sergei Fedorov, Detroit
Ken Hodge, Boston
Jaromir Jagr, Pittsburgh

1989-90
Bob Essensa, Winnipeg
Brad Shaw, Hartford
Geoff Smith, Edmonton
Mike Modano, Minnesota
Sergei Makarov, Calgary
Rod Brind'Amour, St. Louis

1988-89
Peter Sidorkiewicz, Hartford
Brian Leetch, NY Rangers
Zarley Zalapski, Pittsburgh
Trevor Linden, Vancouver
Tony Granato, NY Rangers
David Volek, NY Islanders

1987-88
Darren Pang, Chicago
Glen Wesley, Boston
Calle Johansson, Buffalo
Joe Nieuwendyk, Calgary
Ray Sheppard, Buffalo
Iain Duncan, Winnipeg

1986-87
Ron Hextall, Philadelphia
Steve Duchesne, Los Angeles
Brian Benning, St. Louis
Jimmy Carson, Los Angeles
Jim Sandlak, Vancouver
Luc Robitaille, Los Angeles

1985-86
Patrick Roy, Montreal
Gary Suter, Calgary
Dana Murzyn, Hartford
Mike Ridley, NY Rangers
Kjell Dahlin, Montreal
Wendel Clark, Toronto

1984-85
Steve Penney, Montreal
Chris Chelios, Montreal
Bruce Bell, Quebec
Mario Lemieux, Pittsburgh
Tomas Sandstrom, NY Rangers
Warren Young, Pittsburgh

1983-84
Tom Barrasso, Buffalo
Thomas Eriksson, Philadelphia
Jamie Macoun, Calgary
Steve Yzerman, Detroit
Hakan Loob, Calgary
Sylvain Turgeon, Hartford

1982-83
Pelle Lindbergh, Philadelphia
Scott Stevens, Washington
Phil Housley, Buffalo
Dan Daoust, Mtl./Tor.
Steve Larmer, Chicago
Mats Naslund, Montreal

2008 All-Star Game Summary

JANUARY 27, 2008 at Atlanta, GA East 8, West 7

PLAYERS ON ICE: **East** — DiPietro, Vokoun, T. Thomas, A. Markov, Chara, B. Campbell, Gonchar, T. Kaberle, K. Timonen, Lecavalier, Alfredsson, Gomez, Malkin, Savard, Marian Hossa, Kovalchuk, Ovechkin, M. Richards, Spezza, E. Staal, St. Louis.

West — Osgood, Nabokov, Legace, Lidstrom, Phaneuf, Jovanovski, D. Keith, Pronger, S. Niedermayer, Iginla, Datsyuk, Arnott, Gaborik, Getzlaf, Horcoff, Kopitar, R. Nash, H. Sedin, Perry, J. Thornton, Ribeiro.

SUMMARY

First Period

1.	West	Nash	(unassisted)	0:12
2.	East	Staal	(Campbell, Malkin)	1:20
3.	East	Markov	(Richards, Hossa)	9:43
4.	East	Ovechkin	(Spezza, St. Louis)	13:35
5.	East	Campbell	(Malkin, Lecavalier)	15:10
6.	East	Ovechkin	(St. Louis, Spezza)	17:49

PENALTIES: None

Second Period

7.	West	Nash	(Datsyuk)	9:34
8.	West	Niedermayer	(Thornton, Sedin)	15:08

PENALTIES: None

Third Period

9.	West	Getzlaf	(Jovanovski)	0:41
10.	West	Nash	(Iginla)	1:56
11.	East	Hossa	(Gomez, Chara)	4:08
12.	West	Phaneuf	(Getzlaf, Arnott)	5:07
13.	West	Gaborik	(Sedin)	10:57
14.	East	Staal	(Kovalchuk, Savard)	12:35
15.	East	Savard	(Campbell, Staal)	19:39

PENALTIES: None

SHOTS ON GOAL BY:

East	16	8	9	**33**
West	13	20	18	**51**

	Goaltenders:	Time	SA	GA	ENG	Dec
East	DiPietro	20:00	13	1	0	
East	Vokoun	20:00	20	2	0	
East	Thomas	20:00	18	4	0	W
West	Osgood	20:00	16	5	0	
West	Nabokov	20:00	8	0	0	
West	Legace	19:42	9	3	0	L

PP Conversions: East 0/0; West 0/0.
Referees: Rob Martell, Brad Watson
Linesmen: Pat Dapuzzo, Lyle Seitz

Attendance: 18,644

A 20-year-old with just a few months of professional experience, Montreal's Carey Price led NHL rookie netminders with 24 wins, 1,179 saves, a .920 save percentage and three shutouts in 2007-08 to earn a spot on the All-Rookie Team.

All-Star Game Results

Year	Venue	Score	Coaches	Attendance
2008	Atlanta	East 8, West 7	John Paddock, Mike Babcock	18,644
2007	Dallas	West 12, East 9	Lindy Ruff, Randy Carlyle	18,532
2004	Minnesota	East 6, West 4	Pat Quinn, Dave Lewis	19,434
2003	Florida	West 6, East 5	Marc Crawford, Jacques Martin	19,250
2002	Los Angeles	World 8, North America 5	Scotty Bowman, Pat Quinn	18,118
2001	Colorado	North America 14, World 12	Joel Quenneville, Jacques Martin	18,646
2000	Toronto	World 9, North America 4	Scotty Bowman, Pat Quinn	19,300
1999	Tampa Bay	North America 8, World 6	Lindy Ruff, Ken Hitchcock	19,758
1998	Vancouver	North America 8, World 7	Jacques Lemaire, Ken Hitchcock	18,422
1997	San Jose	East 11, West 7	Doug MacLean, Ken Hitchcock	17,422
1996	Boston	East 5, West 4	Doug MacLean, Scotty Bowman	17,565
1994	NY Rangers	East 9, West 8	Jacques Demers, Barry Melrose	18,200
1993	Montreal	Wales 16, Campbell 6	Scotty Bowman, Mike Keenan	17,137
1992	Philadelphia	Campbell 10, Wales 6	Bob Gainey, Scotty Bowman	17,380
1991	Chicago	Campbell 11, Wales 5	John Muckler, Mike Milbury	18,472
1990	Pittsburgh	Wales 12, Campbell 7	Pat Burns, Terry Crisp	16,236
1989	Edmonton	Campbell 9, Wales 5	Glen Sather, Terry O'Reilly	17,503
1988	St. Louis	Wales 6, Campbell 5 OT	Mike Keenan, Glen Sather	17,878
1986	Hartford	Wales 4, Campbell 3 OT	Mike Keenan, Glen Sather	15,100
1985	Calgary	Wales 6, Campbell 4	Al Arbour, Glen Sather	16,825
1984	New Jersey	Wales 7, Campbell 6	Al Arbour, Glen Sather	18,939
1983	NY Islanders	Campbell 9, Wales 3	Roger Neilson, Al Arbour	15,230
1982	Washington	Wales 4, Campbell 2	Al Arbour, Glen Sonmor	18,130
1981	Los Angeles	Campbell 4, Wales 1	Pat Quinn, Scotty Bowman	15,761
1980	Detroit	Wales 6, Campbell 3	Scotty Bowman, Al Arbour	21,002
1978	Buffalo	Wales 3, Campbell 2 OT	Scotty Bowman, Fred Shero	16,433
1977	Vancouver	Wales 4, Campbell 3	Scotty Bowman, Fred Shero	15,607
1976	Philadelphia	Wales 7, Campbell 5	Floyd Smith, Fred Shero	16,436
1975	Montreal	Wales 7, Campbell 1	Bep Guidolin, Fred Shero	16,080
1974	Chicago	West 6, East 4	Billy Reay, Scotty Bowman	16,426
1973	NY Rangers	East 5, West 4	Tom Johnson, Billy Reay	16,986
1972	Minnesota	East 3, West 2	Al MacNeil, Billy Reay	15,423
1971	Boston	West 2, East 1	Scotty Bowman, Harry Sinden	14,790
1970	St. Louis	East 4, West 1	Claude Ruel, Scotty Bowman	16,587
1969	Montreal	East 3, West 3	Toe Blake, Scotty Bowman	16,260
1968	Toronto	Toronto 4, All-Stars 3	Punch Imlach, Toe Blake	15,753
1967	Montreal	Montreal 3, All-Stars 0	Toe Blake, Sid Abel	14,284
1965	Montreal	All-Stars 5, Montreal 2	Billy Reay, Toe Blake	13,529
1964	Toronto	All-Stars 3, Toronto 2	Sid Abel, Punch Imlach	14,232
1963	Toronto	All-Stars 3, Toronto 3	Sid Abel, Punch Imlach	14,034
1962	Toronto	Toronto 4, All-Stars 1	Punch Imlach, Rudy Pilous	14,236
1961	Chicago	All-Stars 3, Chicago 1	Sid Abel, Rudy Pilous	14,534
1960	Montreal	All-Stars 2, Montreal 1	Punch Imlach, Toe Blake	13,949
1959	Montreal	Montreal 6, All-Stars 1	Toe Blake, Punch Imlach	13,818
1958	Montreal	Montreal 6, All-Stars 3	Toe Blake, Milt Schmidt	13,989
1957	Montreal	All-Stars 5, Montreal 3	Milt Schmidt, Toe Blake	13,003
1956	Montreal	All-Stars 1, Montreal 1	Jim Skinner, Toe Blake	13,095
1955	Detroit	Detroit 3, All-Stars 1	Jim Skinner, Dick Irvin	10,111
1954	Detroit	All-Stars 2, Detroit 2	King Clancy, Jim Skinner	10,689
1953	Montreal	All-Stars 3, Montreal 1	Lynn Patrick, Dick Irvin	14,153
1952	Detroit	1st Team 1, 2nd Team 1	Tommy Ivan, Dick Irvin	10,680
1951	Toronto	1st Team 2, 2nd Team 2	Joe Primeau, Dick Irvin	11,469
1950	Detroit	Detroit 7, All-Stars 1	Tommy Ivan, Lynn Patrick	9,166
1949	Toronto	All-Stars 3, Toronto 1	Tommy Ivan, Hap Day	13,541
1948	Chicago	All-Stars 3, Toronto 1	Tommy Ivan, Hap Day	12,794
1947	Toronto	All-Stars 4, Toronto 3	Dick Irvin, Hap Day	14,169

There was no All-Star contest during the calendar year of 1966 because the game was moved from the start of season to mid-season. In 1979, the Challenge Cup series between the Soviet Union and Team NHL replaced the All-Star Game. In 1987, Rendez-Vous '87, two games between the Soviet Union and Team NHL replaced the All-Star Game.

NHL ALL-STAR GAME MVP

2008	Eric Staal, Car.	1991	Vincent Damphousse, Tor.	1975	Syl Apps Jr., Pit.
2007	Daniel Briere, Buf.	1990	Mario Lemieux, Pit.	1974	Garry Unger, St.L.
2004	Joe Sakic, Col..	1989	Wayne Gretzky, L.A.	1973	Greg Polis, Pit.
2003	Dany Heatley, Atl.	1988	Mario Lemieux, Pit.	1972	Bobby Orr, Bos.
2002	Eric Daze, Chi.	1986	Grant Fuhr, Edm.	1971	Bobby Hull, Chi.
2001	Bill Guerin, Bos.	1985	Mario Lemieux, Pit.	1970	Bobby Hull, Chi.
2000	Pavel Bure, Fla.	1984	Don Maloney, NYR	1969	Frank Mahovlich, Det.
1999	Wayne Gretzky, NYR	1983	Wayne Gretzky, Edm.	1968	Bruce Gamble, Tor.
1998	Teemu Selanne, Ana.	1982	Mike Bossy, NYI	1967	Henri Richard, Mtl.
1997	Mark Recchi, Mtl.	1981	Mike Liut, St.L.	1965	Gordie Howe, Det.
1996	Raymond Bourque, Bos.	1980	Reggie Leach, Phi.	1964	Jean Beliveau, Mtl.
1994	Mike Richter, NYR	1978	Billy Smith, NYI	1963	Frank Mahovlich, Tor.
1993	Mike Gartner, NYR	1977	Rick Martin, Buf.	1962	Eddie Shack, Tor.
1992	Brett Hull, St.L.	1976	Pete Mahovlich, Mtl.		

All-Star Game Records 1947 through 2008

TEAM RECORDS

MOST GOALS, BOTH TEAMS, ONE GAME:
26 — North America 14, World 12, 2001 at Colorado
22 — Wales 16, Campbell 6, 1993 at Montreal
21 — West 12, East 9, 2007 at Dallas
19 — Wales 12, Campbell 7, 1990 at Pittsburgh
18 — East 11, West 7, 1997 at San Jose
17 — East 9, West 8, 1994 at NY Rangers
16 — Campbell 11, Wales 5, 1991 at Chicago
— Campbell 10, Wales 6, 1992 at Philadelphia

FEWEST GOALS, BOTH TEAMS, ONE GAME:
2 — First Team All-Stars 1, Second Team All-Stars 1, 1952 at Detroit
— NHL All-Stars 1, Montreal Canadiens 1, 1956 at Montreal
3 — NHL All-Stars 2, Montreal Canadiens 1, 1960 at Montreal
— Montreal Canadiens 3, NHL All-Stars 0, 1967 at Montreal
— West 2, East 1, 1971 at Boston

MOST GOALS, ONE TEAM, ONE GAME:
16 — Wales 16, Campbell 6, 1993 at Montreal
14 — North America 14, World 12, 2001 at Colorado
12 — Wales 12, Campbell 7, 1990 at Pittsburgh
— World 12, North America 14, 2001 at Colorado
— West 12, East 9, 2007 at Dallas

FEWEST GOALS, ONE TEAM, ONE GAME:
0 — NHL All-Stars 0, Montreal Canadiens 3, 1967 at Montreal
1 — 17 times (1981, 1975, 1971, 1970, 1962, 1961, 1960, 1959, both teams 1956, 1955, 1953, both teams 1952, 1950, 1949, 1948)

MOST SHOTS, BOTH TEAMS, ONE GAME (SINCE 1955):
102 — 1994 at NY Rangers — East 9 (56 shots), West 8 (46 shots)
98 — 2001 at Colorado — North America 14 (53 shots), World 12 (45 shots)
90 — 1993 at Montreal — Wales 16 (49 shots), Campbell 6 (41 shots)
89 — 2002 at Los Angeles — World 8 (39 shots), North America 5 (50 shots)

FEWEST SHOTS, BOTH TEAMS, ONE GAME (SINCE 1955):
52 — 1978 at Buffalo — Campbell 2 (12 shots) Wales 3 (40 shots)
53 — 1960 at Montreal — NHL All-Stars 2 (27 shots) Montreal Canadiens 1 (26 shots)
55 — 1956 at Montreal — NHL All-Stars 1 (28 shots) Montreal Canadiens 1 (27 shots)
— 1971 at Boston — West 2 (28 shots) East 1 (27 shots)

MOST SHOTS, ONE TEAM, ONE GAME (SINCE 1955):
56 — 1994 at NY Rangers — East (9-8 vs. West)
53 — 2001 at Colorado — North America (14-12 vs. World)
51 — 2008 at Atlanta — West (7-8 vs. East)
50 — 2002 at Los Angeles — North America (5-8 vs. World)

FEWEST SHOTS, ONE TEAM, ONE GAME (SINCE 1955):
12 — 1978 at Buffalo — Campbell (2-3 vs. Wales)
17 — 1970 at St. Louis — West (1-4 vs. East)
23 — 1961 at Chicago — Chicago Black Hawks (1-3 vs. NHL All-Stars)
24 — 1976 at Philadelphia — Campbell (5-7 vs. Wales)

MOST POWER-PLAY GOALS, BOTH TEAMS, ONE GAME (SINCE 1950):
3 — 1953 at Montreal — NHL All-Stars 3 (2 power-play goals), Montreal Canadiens 1 (1 power-play goal)
— 1954 at Detroit — NHL All-Stars 2 (1 power-play goal) Detroit Red Wings 2 (2 power-play goals)
— 1958 at Montreal — NHL All-Stars 3 (1 power-play goal) Montreal Canadiens 6 (2 power-play goals)

FEWEST POWER-PLAY GOALS, BOTH TEAMS, ONE GAME (SINCE 1950):
0 — 24 times (1952, 1959, 1960, 1967, 1968, 1969, 1972, 1973, 1976, 1980, 1981, 1984, 1985, 1992, 1994, 1996, 1999, 2000, 2001, 2002, 2003, 2004, 2007, 2008)

FASTEST TWO GOALS, BOTH TEAMS, FROM START OF GAME:
0:37 — 1970 at St. Louis — Jacques Laperriere of East scored at 0:20 and Dean Prentice of West scored at 0:37. Final score: East 4, West 1.

1:20 — 2008 at Atlanta — Rick Nash of West scored at 0:12 and Eric Staal of East scored at 1:20. Final score: East 8, West 7.

2:15 — 1998 at Vancouver — Teemu Selanne scored at 0:53 and Jaromir Jagr scored at 2:15 for World. Final score: North America 8, World 7.

FASTEST TWO GOALS, BOTH TEAMS:
0:08 — 1997 at San Jose — Owen Nolan scored at 18:54 and 19:02 of second period for West. Final Score: East 11, West 7.

0:10 — 1976 at Philadelphia — Dennis Ververgaert scored at 4:33 and at 4:43 of third period for Campbell. Final score: Wales 7, Campbell 5.

0:13 — 1998 at Vancouver — Teemu Selanne scored at 4:00 of first period for World and John LeClair scored at 4:13 for North America. Final score: North America 8, World 7.

FASTEST THREE GOALS, BOTH TEAMS:
0:48 — 2007 at Dallas — Martin Havlat scored at 19:00 of third period for West; Sheldon Souray scored at 19:25 for East; Dion Phaneuf scored at 19:48 for West. Final score: West 12, East 9.

1:08 — 1993 at Montreal — all by Wales — Mike Gartner scored at 3:15 and at 3:37 of first period; Peter Bondra scored at 4:23. Final score: Wales 16, Campbell 6.

1:14 — 1994 at NY Rangers — Bob Kudelski scored at 9:46 of first period for East; Sergei Fedorov scored at 10:20 for West; Eric Lindros scored at 11:00 for East. Final score: East 9, West 8.

FASTEST FOUR GOALS, BOTH TEAMS:
2:24 — 1997 at San Jose — Brendan Shanahan scored at 16:38 of second period for West; Dale Hawerchuk scored at 17:28 for East; Owen Nolan scored at 18:54 and 19:02 for West. Final score: East 11, West 7.

2:52 — 2007 at Dallas — Rick Nash scored at 10:40 of second period for West; Martin Havlat scored at 11:34 for West; Yanic Perreault scored at 12:47 for West; Alex Ovechkin scored at 13:32 for East. Final score: West 12, East 9.

2:57 — 2002 at Los Angeles — Sergei Fedorov scored at 16:59 of third period for World; Markus Naslund scored at 18:17 for World; Alex Zhamnov scored at 19:12 for World; Sami Kapanen scored at 19:56 for World. Final score: World 8, North America 5.

FASTEST TWO GOALS, ONE TEAM, FROM START OF GAME:
2:15 — 1998 at Vancouver — World — Teemu Selanne scored at 0:53 and Jaromir Jagr scored at 2:15. Final score: North America 8, World 7.

3:37 — 1993 at Montreal — Wales — Mike Gartner scored at 3:15 and at 3:37. Final score: Wales 16, Campbell 6.

4:19 — 1980 at Detroit — Wales — Larry Robinson scored at 3:58 and Steve Payne scored at 4:19. Final score: Wales 6, Campbell 3.

FASTEST TWO GOALS, ONE TEAM:
0:08 — 1997 at San Jose — West — Owen Nolan scored at 18:54 and at 19:02 of second period. Final score: East 11, West 7.

0:10 — 1976 at Philadelphia — Campbell — Dennis Ververgaert scored at 4:33 and at 4:43 of third period. Final score: Wales 7, Campbell 5.

0:14 — 1989 at Edmonton — Campbell — Steve Yzerman and Gary Leeman scored at 17:21 and 17:35 of second period. Final score: Campbell 9, Wales 5.

FASTEST THREE GOALS, ONE TEAM:
1:08 — 1993 at Montreal — Wales — Mike Gartner scored at 3:15 and 3:37 of first period; Peter Bondra scored at 4:23. Final score: Wales 16, Campbell 6.

1:32 — 1980 at Detroit — Wales — Ron Stackhouse scored at 11:40 of third period; Craig Hartsburg scored at 12:40; Reed Larson scored at 13:12. Final score: Wales 6, Campbell 3.

1:39 — 2002 at Los Angeles — Markus Naslund scored at 18:17 of third period; Alex Zhamnov scored at 19:12; Sami Kapanen scored at 19:56. Final score: World 8, North America 5.

FASTEST FOUR GOALS, ONE TEAM:
2:57 — 2002 at Los Angeles — World — Sergei Fedorov scored at 16:59 of third period; Markus Naslund scored at 18:17; Alex Zhamnov scored at 19:12; Sami Kapanen scored at 19:56. Final score: World 8, North America 5.

4:17 — 2007 at Dallas — Brian Rolston scored at 8:30 of second period; Rick Nash scored at 10:40; Martin Havlat scored at 11:34; Yanic Perreault scored at 12:47. Final score: West 12, East 9.

4:19 — 1992 at Philadelphia — Campbell — Brian Bellows scored at 7:40 of second period; Jeremy Roenick scored at 8:13; Theoren Fleury scored at 11:06, Brett Hull scored at 11:59. Final score: Campbell 10, Wales 6.

MOST GOALS, BOTH TEAMS, ONE PERIOD:
10 — 1997 at San Jose — Second period — East (6), West (4).
Final score: East 11, West 7.

— 2001 at Colorado — Second period — North America (6), World (4).
Final score: North America 14, World 12.

— 2001 at Colorado — Third period — North America (5), World (5).
Final score: North America 14, World 12.

9 — 1990 at Pittsburgh — First period — Wales (7), Campbell (2).
Final score: Wales 12, Campbell 7.

— 2007 at Dallas — Second period — West (6), East (3).
Final score: West 12, East 9.

MOST GOALS, ONE TEAM, ONE PERIOD:
7 — 1990 at Pittsburgh — First period — Wales. Final score: Wales 12, Campbell 7.

6 — 1983 at NY Islanders — Third period — Campbell.
Final score: Campbell 9, Wales 3.

— 1992 at Philadelphia — Second period — Campbell.
Final score: Campbell 10, Wales 6.

— 1993 at Montreal — First period — Wales.
Final score: Wales 16, Campbell 6.

— 1993 at Montreal — Second period — Wales.
Final score: Wales 16, Campbell 6.

— 1997 at San Jose — Second period — East.
Final score: East 11, West 7.

— 2001 at Colorado — Second period — North America.
Final score: North America 14, World 12.

— 2007 at Dallas — Second period — West.
Final score: West 12, East 9.

MOST SHOTS, BOTH TEAMS, ONE PERIOD:
39 — 1994 at NY Rangers — Second period — West (21), East (18).
Final score: East 9, West 8.

— 2001 at Colorado — Third period — World (23), North America (16).
Final score: North America 14, World 12.

36 — 1990 at Pittsburgh — Third period — Campbell (22), Wales (14).
Final score: Wales 12, Campbell 7.

— 1994 at NY Rangers — First period — East (19), West (17).
Final score: East 9, West 8.

— 2002 at Los Angeles — Third period — North America (20), World (16).
Final score: World 8, North America 5.

MOST SHOTS, ONE TEAM, ONE PERIOD:
23 — 2001 at Colorado — Third period — World.
Final score: North America 14, World 12.

22 — 1990 at Pittsburgh — Third period — Campbell.
Final score: Wales 12, Campbell 7.

— 1991 at Chicago — Third period — Wales.
Final score: Campbell 11, Wales 5.

— 1993 at Montreal — First period — Wales.
Final score: Wales 16, Campbell 6.

FEWEST SHOTS, BOTH TEAMS, ONE PERIOD:
9 — 1971 at Boston — Third period — East (2), West (7).
Final score: West 2, East 1.

— 1980 at Detroit — Second period — Campbell (4), Wales (5).
Final score: Wales 6, Campbell 3.

13 — 1982 at Washington — Third period — Campbell (6), Wales (7).
Final score: Wales 4, Campbell 2.

14 — 1978 at Buffalo — First period — Campbell (7), Wales (7).
Final score: Wales 3, Campbell 2.

— 1986 at Hartford — First period — Campbell (6), Wales (8).
Final score: Wales 4, Campbell 3.

FEWEST SHOTS, ONE TEAM, ONE PERIOD:
2 — 1971 at Boston — Third period — East.
Final score: West 2, East 1.

— 1978 at Buffalo — Second period — Campbell.
Final score: Wales 3, Campbell 2.

3 — 1978 at Buffalo — Third period — Campbell.
Final score: Wales 3, Campbell 2.

4 — 1955 at Detroit — First period — NHL All-Stars.
Final score: Detroit Red Wings 3, NHL All-Stars 1.

— 1980 at Detroit — Second period — Campbell.
Final score: Wales 6, Campbell 3.

Carolina's Eric Staal scores on Chris Osgood for his first of two goals in the 2008 NHL All-Star Game. Staal's two goals and one assist helped offset a hat trick by Rick Nash of Columbus and lead the Eastern Conference to an 8-7 victory. Staal was named the game's MVP.

INDIVIDUAL RECORDS

Games

MOST GAMES PLAYED:
23 — Gordie Howe, 1948 through 1980
19 — Raymond Bourque, 1981 through 2001
18 — Wayne Gretzky, 1980 through 1999
15 — Frank Mahovlich, 1959 through 1974
— Mark Messier, 1982 through 2004

Goals

MOST GOALS (CAREER):
13 — Wayne Gretzky in 18GP
— Mario Lemieux in 10GP
10 — Gordie Howe in 23GP
9 — Teemu Selanne in 10GP
8 — Frank Mahovlich in 15GP
— Luc Robitaille in 8GP

MOST GOALS, ONE GAME:
4 — Wayne Gretzky, Campbell, 1983
— Mario Lemieux, Wales, 1990
— Vince Damphousse, Campbell, 1991
— Mike Gartner, Wales, 1993
— Dany Heatley, East, 2003
3 — Ted Lindsay, Detroit, 1950
— Mario Lemieux, Wales, 1988
— Pierre Turgeon, Wales, 1993
— Mark Recchi, East, 1997
— Owen Nolan, West, 1997
— Teemu Selanne, World, 1998
— Pavel Bure, World, 2000
— Bill Guerin, North America, 2001
— Joe Sakic, West, 2004
— Rick Nash, West, 2008

MOST GOALS, ONE PERIOD:
4 — Wayne Gretzky, Campbell, Third period, 1983
3 — Mario Lemieux, Wales, First period, 1990
— Vincent Damphousse, Campbell, Third period, 1991
— Mike Gartner, Wales, First period, 1993

Assists

MOST ASSISTS (CAREER):
16 — Joe Sakic in 12GP
14 — Mark Messier in 15GP
13 — Raymond Bourque in 19GP
12 — Adam Oates in 5GP
— Mats Sundin in 8GP
— Wayne Gretzky in 18GP

MOST ASSISTS, ONE GAME:
5 — Mats Naslund, Wales, 1988
4 — Raymond Bourque, Wales, 1985
— Adam Oates, Campbell, 1991
— Adam Oates, Wales, 1993
— Mark Recchi, Wales, 1993
— Pierre Turgeon, East, 1994
— Fredrik Modin, World, 2001
— Joe Sakic, West, 2007
— Daniel Briere, East, 2007
— Marian Hossa, East, 2007

MOST ASSISTS, ONE PERIOD:
4 — Adam Oates, Wales, First period, 1993
3 — Mark Messier, Campbell, Third period, 1983
3 — Marian Hossa, East, Third period, 2007

Points

MOST POINTS, CAREER:
25 — Wayne Gretzky (13G-12A in 18GP)
23 — Mario Lemieux (13G-10A in 10GP)
22 — Joe Sakic (6G-16A in 12GP)
20 — Mark Messier (6G-14A in 15GP)
19 — Gordie Howe (10G-9A in 23GP)

MOST POINTS, ONE GAME:
6 — Mario Lemieux, Wales, 1988 (3G-3A)
5 — Mats Naslund, Wales, 1988 (5A)
— Adam Oates, Campbell, 1991 (1G-4A)
— Mike Gartner, Wales, 1993 (4G-1A)
— Mark Recchi, Wales, 1993 (1G-4A)
— Pierre Turgeon, Wales, 1993 (3G-2A)
— Bill Guerin, North America, 2001 (3G-2A)
— Dany Heatley, East, 2003 (4G-1A)
— Daniel Briere, East, 2007 (1G-4A)

MOST POINTS, ONE PERIOD:
4 — Wayne Gretzky, Campbell, Third period, 1983 (4G)
— Mike Gartner, Wales, First period, 1993 (3G-1A)
— Adam Oates, Wales, First period, 1993 (4A)
3 — Gordie Howe, NHL All-Stars, Second period, 1965 (1G-2A)
— Pete Mahovlich, Wales, First period, 1976 (1G-2A)
— Mark Messier, Campbell, Third period, 1983 (3A)
— Mario Lemieux, Wales, Second period, 1988 (1G-2A)
— Mario Lemieux, Wales, First period, 1990 (3G)
— Vince Damphousse, Campbell, Third period, 1991 (3G)
— Mark Recchi, Wales, Second period, 1993 (1G-2A)
— Tony Amonte, North America, Second period, 2001 (2G-1A)
— Daniel Alfredsson, East, Second period, 2004 (2G-1A)
— Marian Hossa, East, Third period, 2007 (3A)

Power-Play Goals

MOST POWER-PLAY GOALS, CAREER:
6 — Gordie Howe in 23GP
3 — Bobby Hull in 12GP
— Maurice Richard in 13GP

Fastest Goals

FASTEST GOAL FROM START OF GAME:
0:12 — Rick Nash, West, 2008
0:19 — Ted Lindsay, Detroit, 1950
0:20 — Jacques Laperriere, East, 1970
0:21 — Mario Lemieux, Wales, 1990
0:35 — Vincent Damphousse, North America, 2002

FASTEST GOAL FROM START OF A PERIOD:
0:12 — Rick Nash, West, 2008 (first period)
0:17 — Raymond Bourque, North America, 1999 (second period)
0:19 — Ted Lindsay, Detroit, 1950 (first period)
— Rick Tocchet, Wales, 1993 (second period)
0:20 — Jacques Laperriere, East, 1970 (first period)

FASTEST TWO GOALS (ONE PLAYER) FROM START OF GAME:
3:37 — Mike Gartner, Wales, 1993, at 3:15 and 3:37.
4:00 — Teemu Selanne, World, 1998, at 0:53 and 4:00
5:25 — Wally Hergesheimer, NHL All-Stars, 1953, at 4:06 and 5:25.

FASTEST TWO GOALS (ONE PLAYER) FROM START OF A PERIOD:
3:37 — Mike Gartner, Wales, 1993, at 3:15 and 3:37 of first period.
4:00 — Teemu Selanne, World, 1998, at 0:53 and 4:00 of first period.
4:43 — Dennis Ververgaert, Campbell, 1976, at 4:33 and 4:43 of third period.

FASTEST TWO GOALS (ONE PLAYER):
0:08 — Owen Nolan, West, 1997. Scored at 18:54 and 19:02 of second period.
0:10 — Dennis Ververgaert, Campbell, 1976. Scored at 4:33 and 4:43 of third period.
0:22 — Mike Gartner, Wales, 1993. Scored at 3:15 and 3:37 of first period.

Penalties

MOST PENALTY MINUTES:
25 — Gordie Howe in 23GP
21 — Gus Mortson in 9GP
16 — Harry Howell in 7GP

Goaltenders

MOST GAMES PLAYED:
13 — Glenn Hall from 1955 through 1969
11 — Terry Sawchuk from 1950 through 1968
— Patrick Roy from 1988 through 2003
9 — Martin Brodeur from 1996 through 2007
8 — Jacques Plante from 1956 through 1970

MOST MINUTES PLAYED:
540 — Glenn Hall in 13GP
467 — Terry Sawchuk in 11GP
370 — Jacques Plante in 8GP
250 — Patrick Roy in 11GP
209 — Turk Broda in 4GP

MOST GOALS AGAINST:
31 — Patrick Roy in 11GP
22 — Glenn Hall in 13GP
21 — Mike Vernon in 5GP
19 — Terry Sawchuk in 11GP
18 — Jacques Plante in 8GP
— Andy Moog in 4GP

BEST GOALS-AGAINST-AVERAGE AMONG THOSE WITH AT LEAST TWO GAMES PLAYED:
0.68 — Gilles Villemure in 3GP
1.49 — Gerry McNeil in 3GP
1.50 — Johnny Bower in 4GP
1.51 — Frank Brimsek in 3GP
1.64 — Gump Worsley in 4GP

Hockey Hall of Fame

(Year of induction is listed after each Honoured Members name)

Location: Brookfield Place, at the corner of Front and Yonge Streets in the heart of downtown Toronto. Easy access from all major highways running into Toronto. Close to TTC subway and Union Station.

Telephone: administration (416) 360-7735; information (416) 360-7765.

Public Hours of Operation: Open every day except Christmas Day, New Year's Day and Induction Day (November 10, 2008). Please call our information number (above) or visit our website (below) for times.

The Hockey Hall of Fame can be booked for private functions after hours.

Website address: www.hhof.com

History: The Hockey Hall of Fame was established in 1943. Members were first honoured in 1945. On August 26, 1961, the Hockey Hall of Fame opened its doors to the public in a building located on the grounds of the Canadian National Exhibition in Toronto. The Hockey Hall of Fame relocated to its current location and welcomed the hockey world on June 18, 1993.

Honour Roll: There are 352 Honoured Members in the Hockey Hall of Fame. 240 have been inducted as players, 97 as builders and 15 as Referees/Linesmen. In addition, there are 80 media honourees.

Founding/Premiere Sponsors: Imperial Oil, International Ice Hockey Federation, MCI Canada, Molson Canada, National Hockey League, National Hockey League Players' Association, Panasonic Canada, Pepsi-Cola Canada, The Toronto Sun, The Sports Network (TSN/RDS).

Glenn Anderson celebrated five Stanley Cup victories in 11 seasons with the Edmonton Oilers. He added a sixth championship with the New York Rangers in 1994. Anderson scored 498 goals in his career. He added 93 more in the playoffs, which ranks him fifth all time.

PLAYERS

* Abel, Sidney Gerald 1969
* Adams, John James "Jack" 1959
Anderson, Glenn 2008
* Apps, Charles Joseph Sylvanus "Syl" 1961
Armstrong, George Edward 1975
* Bailey, Irvine Wallace "Ace" 1975
* Bain, Donald H. "Dan" 1949
* Baker, Hobart "Hobey" 1945
Barber, William Charles "Bill" 1990
* Barry, Martin J. "Marty" 1965
Bathgate, Andrew James "Andy" 1978
* Bauer, Robert Theodore "Bobby" 1996
Béliveau, Jean Arthur 1972
* Benedict, Clinton S. 1965
* Bentley, Douglas Wagner 1964
* Bentley, Maxwell H. L. 1966
* Blake, Hector "Toe" 1966
Boivin, Leo Joseph 1986
* Boon, Richard R. "Dickie" 1952
Bossy, Michael 1991
Bouchard, Emile Joseph "Butch" 1966
* Boucher, Frank 1958
* Boucher, Georges "Buck" 1960
Bourque, Raymond 2004
Bower, John William 1976
* Bowie, Russell 1947
* Brimsek, Francis Charles 1966
* Broadbent, Harry L. "Punch" 1962
* Broda, Walter Edward "Turk" 1967
Bucyk, John Paul 1981
* Burch, Billy 1974
* Cameron, Harold Hugh "Harry" 1962
Cheevers, Gerald Michael "Gerry" 1985
* Clancy, Francis Michael "King" 1958
* Clapper, Aubrey "Dit" 1947
Clarke, Robert "Bobby" 1987
* Cleghorn, Sprague 1958
Coffey, Paul 2004
* Colville, Neil MacNeil 1967
* Conacher, Charles W. 1961
* Conacher, Lionel Pretoria 1994
* Conacher, Roy Gordon 1998
* Connell, Alex 1958
* Cook, Fred "Bun" 1995
* Cook, William Osser 1952
* Coulter, Arthur Edmund 1974
Cournoyer, Yvan Serge 1982
* Cowley, William Mailes 1968
* Crawford, Samuel Russell "Rusty" 1962
* Darragh, John Proctor "Jack" 1962
* Davidson, Allan M. "Scotty" 1950
* Day, Clarence Henry "Hap" 1961
Delvecchio, Alex 1977
* Denneny, Cyril "Cy" 1959
Dionne, Marcel 1992
* Drillon, Gordon Arthur 1975
* Drinkwater, Charles Graham 1950
Dryden, Kenneth Wayne 1983
Duff, Dick 2006
* Dumart, Woodrow "Woody" 1992
* Dunderdale, Thomas 1974
* Durnan, William Ronald 1964
* Dutton, Mervyn A. "Red" 1958
* Dye, Cecil Henry "Babe" 1970
Esposito, Anthony James "Tony" 1988
Esposito, Philip Anthony 1984
* Farrell, Arthur F. 1965
Federko, Bernie 2002
Fetisov, Viacheslav 2001
Flaman, Ferdinand Charles "Fern" 1990
* Foyston, Frank 1958
Francis, Ron 2007
* Fredrickson, Frank 1958
Fuhr, Grant 2003
Gadsby, William Alexander 1970
Gainey, Bob 1992
* Gardiner, Charles Robert "Chuck" 1945
* Gardiner, Herbert Martin "Herb" 1958
* Gardner, James Henry "Jimmy" 1962
Gartner, Michael Alfred 2001
* Geoffrion, Jos. A. Bernard "Boom Boom" 1972
* Gerard, Eddie 1945
Giacomin, Edward "Eddie" 1987
Gilbert, Rodrigue Gabriel "Rod" 1982
Gillies, Clark 2002
* Gilmour, Hamilton Livingstone "Billy" 1962
* Goheen, Frank Xavier "Moose" 1952
* Goodfellow, Ebenezer R. "Ebbie" 1963
Goulet, Michel 1998
* Grant, Michael "Mike" 1950
* Green, Wilfred "Shorty" 1962
Gretzky, Wayne Douglas 1999
* Griffis, Silas Seth "Si" 1950
* Hainsworth, George 1961
Hall, Glenn Henry 1975
* Hall, Joseph Henry 1961
* Harvey, Douglas Norman 1973
Hawerchuk, Dale Martin 2001
* Hay, George 1958
* Hern, William Milton "Riley" 1962
* Hextall, Bryan Aldwyn 1969
* Holmes, Harry "Hap" 1972
* Hooper, Charles Thomas "Tom" 1962
* Horner, George Reginald "Red" 1965
* Horton, Miles Gilbert "Tim" 1977
Howe, Gordon 1972
* Howe, Sydney Harris 1965
Howell, Henry Vernon "Harry" 1979
Hull, Robert Marvin 1983
* Hutton, John Bower "Bouse" 1962
* Hyland, Harry M. 1962
* Irvin, James Dickenson "Dick" 1958
* Jackson, Harvey "Busher" 1971
* Johnson, Ernest "Moose" 1952
* Johnson, Ivan "Ching" 1958
* Johnson, Thomas Christian 1970
* Joliat, Aurel 1947
* Keats, Gordon "Duke" 1958
Kelly, Leonard Patrick "Red" 1969
Kennedy, Theodore Samuel "Teeder" 1966
Keon, David Michael 1986
* Kharlamov, Valeri 2005
Kurri, Jari 2001
Lach, Elmer James 1966
Lafleur, Guy Damien 1988
LaFontaine, Pat 2003
* Lalonde, Edouard Charles "Newsy" 1950
Langway, Rod Corry 2002
Laperriere, Jacques 1987
Lapointe, Guy 1993
Laprade, Edgar 1993
Larionov, Igor 2008
* Laviolette, Jean Baptiste "Jack" 1962
* Lehman, Hugh 1958
Lemaire, Jacques Gerard 1984
Lemieux, Mario 1997
* LeSueur, Percy 1961
* Lewis, Herbert A. 1989
Lindsay, Robert Blake Theodore "Ted" 1966
* Lumley, Harry 1980
MacInnis, Al 2007
* MacKay, Duncan "Mickey" 1952
Mahovlich, Frank William 1981
* Malone, Joseph "Joe" 1950
* Mantha, Sylvio 1960
* Marshall, John "Jack" 1965
* Maxwell, Fred G. "Steamer" 1962
McDonald, Lanny 1992
* McGee, Frank 1945
* McGimsie, William George "Billy" 1962
* McNamara, George 1958
Messier, Mark 2007
Mikita, Stanley 1983
Moore, Richard Winston "Dickie" 1974
* Moran, Patrick Joseph "Paddy" 1958
* Morenz, Howie 1945
* Mosienko, William "Billy" 1965
Mullen, Joseph P. 2000
Murphy, Larry 2004
Neely, Cam 2005
* Nighbor, Frank 1947
* Noble, Edward Reginald "Reg" 1962
* O'Connor, Herbert William "Buddy" 1988
* Oliver, Harry 1967
Olmstead, Murray Bert "Bert" 1985

Orr, Robert Gordon 1979
Parent, Bernard Marcel 1984
Park, Douglas Bradford "Brad" 1988
* Patrick, Joseph Lynn 1980
* Patrick, Lester 1947
Perreault, Gilbert 1990
* Phillips, Tommy 1945
Pilote, Joseph Albert Pierre Paul 1975
* Pitre, Didier "Pit" 1962
* Plante, Joseph Jacques Omer 1978
Potvin, Denis 1991
* Pratt, Walter "Babe" 1966
* Primeau, A. Joseph 1963
Pronovost, Joseph René Marcel 1978
Pulford, Bob 1991
* Pulford, Harvey 1945
* Quackenbush, Hubert George "Bill" 1976
* Rankin, Frank 1961
Ratelle, Joseph Gilbert Yvan Jean "Jean" 1985
* Rayner, Claude Earl "Chuck" 1973
* Reardon, Kenneth Joseph 1966
Richard, Joseph Henri 1979
* Richard, Joseph Henri Maurice "Rocket" 1961
* Richardson, George Taylor 1950
* Roberts, Gordon 1971
Robinson, Larry 1995
* Ross, Arthur Howey 1949
Roy, Patrick 2006
* Russel, Blair 1965
* Russell, Ernest 1965
* Ruttan, J.D. "Jack" 1962
Salming, Borje Anders 1996
Savard, Denis Joseph 2000
Savard, Serge 1986
* Sawchuk, Terrance Gordon "Terry" 1971
* Scanlan, Fred 1965
Schmidt, Milton Conrad "Milt" 1961
* Schriner, David "Sweeney" 1962
* Seibert, Earl Walter 1963
* Seibert, Oliver Levi 1961
* Shore, Edward W. "Eddie" 1947
Shutt, Stephen 1993
* Siebert, Albert C. "Babe" 1964
* Simpson, Harold Edward "Bullet Joe" 1962
Sittler, Darryl Glen 1989
* Smith, Alfred E. 1962
Smith, Clint 1991
* Smith, Reginald "Hooley" 1972
* Smith, Thomas James 1973
Smith, William John "Billy" 1993
Stanley, Allan Herbert 1981
* Stanley, Russell "Barney" 1962
Stastny, Peter 1998
Stevens, Scott 2007
* Stewart, John Sherratt "Black Jack" 1964
* Stewart, Nelson "Nels" 1952
* Stuart, Bruce 1961
* Stuart, Hod 1945
* Taylor, Frederick "Cyclone" (O.B.E.) 1947
* Thompson, Cecil R. "Tiny" 1959
Tretiak, Vladislav 1989
* Trihey, Col. Harry J. 1950
Trottier, Bryan 1997
Ullman, Norman V. Alexander "Norm" 1982
* Vezina, Georges 1945
* Walker, John Phillip "Jack" 1960
* Walsh, Martin "Marty" 1962
* Watson, Harry E. 1962
* Watson, Harry 1994
* Weiland, Ralph "Cooney" 1971
* Westwick, Harry 1962
* Whitcroft, Fred 1962
* Wilson, Gordon Allan "Phat" 1962
* Worsley, Lorne John "Gump" 1980
* Worters, Roy 1969

BUILDERS

* Adams, Charles 1960
* Adams, Weston W. 1972
* Ahearn, Thomas Franklin "Frank" 1962
* Ahearne, John Francis "Bunny" 1977
* Allan, Sir Montagu (C.V.O.) 1945
Allen, Keith 1992
Arbour, Alger Joseph "Al" 1996
* Ballard, Harold Edwin 1977
* Bauer, Father David 1989
* Bickell, John Paris 1978
Bowman, Scotty 1991
* Brooks, Herb 2006
* Brown, George V. 1961
* Brown, Walter A. 1962
* Buckland, Frank 1975
Bush, Walter 2000
Butterfield, Jack Arlington 1980
* Calder, Frank 1947
* Campbell, Angus D. 1964
* Campbell, Clarence Sutherland 1966
* Cattarinich, Joseph 1977
* **Chynoweth, Ed 2008**
Costello, Murray 2005
* Dandurand, Joseph Viateur "Leo" 1963
* Dilio, Francis Paul 1964
* Dudley, George S. 1958
* Dunn, James A. 1968
Fletcher, Cliff 2004
Francis, Emile 1982
* Gibson, Dr. John L. "Jack" 1976
* Gorman, Thomas Patrick "Tommy" 1963
Gregory, Jim 2007
* Griffiths, Frank A. 1993
* Hanley, William 1986
* Hay, Charles 1974
* Hendy, James C. 1968
* Hewitt, Foster 1965
* Hewitt, William Abraham 1947
Hotchkiss, Harley 2006
* Hume, Fred J. 1962
Illitch, Mike 2003
* Imlach, George "Punch" 1984
* Ivan, Thomas N. 1974
* Jennings, William M. 1975
* Johnson, Bob 1992
* Juckes, Gordon W. 1979
* Kilpatrick, Gen. John Reed 1960
Kilrea, Brian Blair 2003
* Knox, Seymour H. III 1993
* Leader, George Alfred 1969
* LeBel, Robert 1970
* Lockhart, Thomas F. 1965
* Loicq, Paul 1961
* Mariucci, John 1985
* Mathers, Frank 1992
* McLaughlin, Major Frederic 1963
* Milford, John "Jake" 1984
* Molson, Hon. Hartland de Montarville 1973
Morrison, Ian "Scotty" 1999
* Murray, Monsignor Athol 1998
* Neilson, Roger 2002
* Nelson, Francis 1947
* Norris, Bruce A. 1969
* Norris, Sr., James 1958
* Norris, James Dougan 1962
* Northey, William M. 1947
* O'Brien, John Ambrose 1962
O'Neill, Brian 1994
* Page, Fred 1993
Patrick, Craig 2001
* Patrick, Frank 1950
* Pickard, Allan W. 1958
* Pilous, Rudy 1985
* Poile, Norman "Bud" 1990
* Pollock, Samuel Patterson Smyth 1978
* Raymond, Sen. Donat 1958
* Robertson, John Ross 1947
* Robinson, Claude C. 1947
* Ross, Philip D. 1976
* Sabetzki, Dr. Gunther 1995
Sather, Glen 1997
* Selke, Frank J. 1960
Sinden, Harry James 1983
* Smith, Frank D. 1962
* Smythe, Conn 1958
Snider, Edward M. 1988
* Stanley of Preston, Lord (G.C.B.) 1945
* Sutherland, Cap. James T. 1947
* Tarasov, Anatoli V. 1974
Torrey, Bill 1995
* Turner, Lloyd 1958
* Tutt, William Thayer 1978
* Voss, Carl Potter 1974
* Waghorne, Fred 1961
* Wirtz, Arthur Michael 1971
* Wirtz, William W. "Bill" 1976
Ziegler, John A. Jr. 1987

REFEREES/LINESMEN

Armstrong, Neil 1991
* Ashley, John George 1981
Chadwick, William L. 1964
* D'Amico, John 1993
* Elliott, Chaucer 1961
* Hayes, George William 1988
* Hewitson, Robert W. 1963
* Ion, Fred J. "Mickey" 1961
Pavelich, Matt 1987
* Rodden, Michael J. "Mike" 1962
Scapinello, Ray 2008
* Smeaton, J. Cooper 1961
* Storey, Roy Alvin "Red" 1967
Udvari, Frank Joseph 1973
Van Hellemond, Andy 1999

Igor Larionov was named to both the Hockey Hall of Fame and the International Ice Hockey Federation's Hall of Fame in 2008. A longtime star in the Soviet Union, he entered the NHL with Vancouver in 1989-90 and later won the Stanley Cup three times with Detroit.

Foster Hewitt Memorial Award Winners

In recognition of members of the radio and television industry who made outstanding contributions to their profession and the game during their career in hockey broadcasting. Selected by the NHL Broadcasters' Association.

Cole, Bob, Hockey Night in Canada 1996
Cusick, Fred, Boston 1984
* Darling, Ted, Buffalo 1994
Emrick, Mike, New Jersey, U.S. networks, 2008
* Gallivan, Danny, Montreal 1984
Garneau, Richard, Montreal 1999
* Hart, Gene, Philadelphia 1997
* Hewitt, Bill, Hockey Night in Canada 2007
* Hewitt, Foster, Toronto 1984
Irvin, Dick, Montreal 1988
Kaiton, Chuck, Hartford/Carolina 2004
* Kelly, Dan, St. Louis 1989
Lange, Mike, Pittsburgh 2001
* Lecavelier, René, Montreal 1984
Lynch, Budd, Detroit 1985
Maher, Peter, Calgary 2006
Martyn, Bruce, Detroit 1991
McDonald, Jiggs, Los Angeles, Atlanta, NY Islanders 1990
McFarlane, Brian, Hockey Night in Canada 1995
* McKnight, Wes, Toronto 1986
Meeker, Howie, Hockey Night in Canada 1998
Messina, Sal, New York 2005
Miller, Bob, Los Angeles 2000
Pettit, Lloyd, Chicago 1986
Phillips, Rod, Edmonton 2003
Robson, Jim, Vancouver 1992
Shaver, Al, Minnesota 1993
* Smith, Doug, Montreal 1985
Tremblay, Gilles, La Soirée du Hockey 2002
Wilson, Bob, Boston 1987

* Deceased

United States Hockey Hall of Fame

On May 11, 2007, the U.S. Hockey Hall of Fame and USA Hockey came to a historic agreement that transferred rights to the selection process and induction event associated with the Hall, including the Wayne Gretzky International Award, to USA Hockey. As part of the agreement, the U.S. Hockey Hall of Fame Museum, located in Eveleth, Minn., formed a separate Board of Directors to govern the national shrine for American Hockey.

There are 138 enshrined members in the U.S. Hockey Hall of Fame (www.ushockeyhalloffame.com). New members are inducted annually and must have made a significant contribution to hockey in the United States during the course of their career. A special Wayne Gretzky International Award pays tribute to international individuals who have made major contributions to hockey in the USA.

The United States Hockey Hall of Fame Museum was opened on June 21, 1973. It is dedicated to honoring the sport of ice hockey in the United States by preserving those previous memories and legends of the game. It is located in Eveleth, Minn., 60 miles north of Duluth on Highway 53. The facility is open Memorial Day through Labor Day, Monday to Saturday, 9 a.m. to 5 p.m. and Sundays from 10 a.m. to 3 p.m. After Labor Day, it is open Friday through Sunday. Admission is $8.00 for adults, $7.00 for seniors and youths (13-17) and $6.00 for children (6-12). Children under 6 are free. For further information, call 800-443-7825 or 218-744-5167, or visit www.ushockeyhall.com.

Elmer Ferguson Memorial Award Winners

In recognition of distinguished members of the newspaper profession whose words have brought honor to journalism and to hockey. Selected by the Professional Hockey Writers' Association.

* Barton, Charlie, Buffalo-Courier Express 1985
* Beauchamp, Jacques, Montreal Matin/Journal de Montréal 1984
* Brennan, Bill, Detroit News 1987
* Burchard, Jim, New York World Telegram 1984
* Burnett, Red, Toronto Star 1984
* Carroll, Dink, Montreal Gazette 1984
* Coleman, Jim, Southam Newspapers 1984

Conway, Russ, Eagle-Tribune 1999
* Damata, Ted, Chicago Tribune 1984

Delano, Hugh, New York Post 1991
Desjardins, Marcel, Montréal La Presse 1984
Duhatschek, Eric, Calgary Herald/Globe and Mail 2001
* Dulmage, Jack, Windsor Star 1984
* Dunnell, Milt, Toronto Star 1984

Dupont, Kevin Paul, Boston Globe 2002
Elliott, Helene, Los Angeles Times 2005
Farber, Michael, Montreal Gazette/Sports Illustrated 2003
Fay, Dave, Washington Times 2007
* Ferguson, Elmer, Montreal Herald/Star 1984
* Fitzgerald, Tom, Boston Globe 1984

Frayne, Trent, Toronto Telegram/Globe and Mail/Sun 1984
Gatecliff, Jack, St. Catharines Standard 1995
Gross, George, Toronto Telegram/Sun 1985
Johnston, Dick, Buffalo News 1986
Kelley, Jim, Buffalo News 2004
* Laney, Al, New York Herald-Tribune 1984
* Larochelle, Claude, Le Soleil 1989

L'Esperance, Zotique, Journal de Montréal/ le Petit Journal 1985
* MacLeod, Rex, Toronto Globe and Mail/Star 1987

Matheson, Jim, Edmonton Journal 2000
* Mayer, Charles, Journal de Montréal/la Patrie 1985
* McKenzie, Ken, The Hockey News 1997

Monahan, Leo, Boston Daily Record/Record-American/Herald American 1986
Moriarty, Tim, UPI/Newsday 1986
Morrison, Scott, Toronto Sun/Rogers Sportsnet 2006
* Nichols, Joe, New York Times 1984
* O'Brien, Andy, Weekend Magazine 1985

Orr, Frank, Toronto Star 1989
Olan, Ben, New York Associated Press 1987
* O'Meara, Basil, Montreal Star 1984

Pedneault, Yvon, La Presse/Journal de Montréal 1998
* Proudfoot, Jim, Toronto Star 1988

Raymond, Bertrand, Journal de Montréal 1990
Rosa, Fran, Boston Globe 1987
Stevens, Neil, Canadian Press 2008
Strachan, Al, Globe and Mail/Toronto Sun 1993
* Vipond, Jim, Toronto Globe and Mail 1984

Walter, Lewis, Detroit Times 1984
* Young, Scott, Toronto Globe and Mail/Telegram 1988

INDIVIDUALS

* Abel, Clarence "Taffy" 1973
* Almquist, Oscar 1983
* Baker, Hobart "Hobey" 1973
* Bartholome, Earl 1977

Bessone, Amo 1992
* Bessone, Peter 1978

Blake, Robert 1985
Boucha, Henry 1995
* Brimsek, Frank 1973

Brink, Milton "Curly" 2006
* Brooks, Herb 1990

Broten, Aaron 2007
Broten, Neal 2000
Brown, George V. 1973
Brown, Walter A. 1973
Bush, Walter 1980
Carpenter, Bobby 2007
Cavanagh, Joe 1994
Ceglarski, Len 1992
Chadwick, William 1974
* Chaisson, Ray 1974
* Chase, John P. 1973

Christian, Dave 2001
Christian, Roger 1989
Christian, William "Bill" 1984
Christiansen, Keith 2005
* Clark, Donald 1978

Claypool, James 1995
Cleary, Robert 1981
Cleary, William 1976
* Conroy, Anthony 1975

Coppo, Paul 2004
* Cunniff, John 2003

Curran, Mike 1998
* Dahlstrom, Carl "Cully" 1973
* Desjardins, Victor 1974
* Desmond, Richard 1988
* Dill, Robert 1979

Dougherty, Richard "Dick" 2003
* Everett, Doug 1974

Ftorek, Robbie 1991
* Fullerton, James 1992

Fusco, Mark 2002
Fusco, Scott 2002
Gambucci, Gary 2006
Gambucci, Sergio 1996
* Garrison, John B. 1973

Garrity, Jack 1986
* Gibson, J.C. "Doc" 1973
* Goheen, Frank "Moose" 1973
* Gordon, Malcolm K. 1973

Granato, Cammi 2008
Grant, Wally 1994
* Harding, Francis "Austie" 1975

Harkness, Nevin D. "Ned" 1994
* Heyliger, Victor 1974
* Holt, Jr. Charles E. 1997

Housley, Phil 2004
Howe, Mark 2003
Hull, Brett 2008
* Iglehart, Stewart 1975

Ikola, Willard 1990
Ilitch, Mike 2004
* Jennings, William M. 1981
* Jeremiah, Edward J. 1973
* Johnson, Bob 1991

Johnson, Mark 2004
Johnson, Paul 2001
* Johnson, Virgil 1974
* Kahler, Nick 1980
* Karakas, Mike 1973
* Kelley, John "Snooks" 1974

Kelley, John H. "Jack" 1993
Kirrane, Jack 1987
LaFontaine, Pat 2003
* Lane, Myles J. 1973

Langevin, David R. 1993
Langway, Rod 1999
Larson, Reed 1996
Leetch, Brian 2008
* Linder, Joseph 1975
* Lockhart, Thomas F. 1973
* LoPresti, Sam L. 1973

MacDonald, Lane 2005
MacInnes, John 2007
* Mariucci, John 1973
* Marvin, Cal 1982

Matchefts, John 1991
* Mather, Bruce 1998

Mayasich, John 1976
McCartan, Jack 1983
Milbury, Mike 2006
* Moe, William 1974

Morrow, Ken 1995
* Moseley, Fred 1975

Mullen, Joe 1998
* Murray, Sr. Hugh "Muzz" 1987

Nanne, Lou 1998
* Nelson, Hubert "Hub" 1978
* Nyrop, William D. 1997
* Olson, Eddie 1977
* Owen, Jr. George 1973

Palazzari, Doug 2000
* Palmer, Winthrop 1973

Paradise, Robert 1989
Patrick, Craig 1996
Pleau, Larry 2000
* Pleban, Jon "Connie" 1990
* Purpur, Clifford "Fido" 1974

Ramsey, Mike 2001
Richter, Mike 2008
* Ridder, Robert 1976

Riley, Jack 1979
* Riley, Joe 2002
* Riley, William 1977

Roberts, Gordie 1999
* Roberts, Moe 2005
* Romnes, Elwin "Doc" 1973
* Rondeau, Richard 1985
* Ross, Larry 1988
* Schulz, Charles M. 1993

Sheehy, Timothy K. 1997
* Stewart, William 1982
* Thompson, Clifford R. 1973

Trumble, Harold 1985
* Tutt, William Thayer 1973

Vanbiesbrouck, John 2007
* Watson, Sid 1999
* Williams, Thomas 1981

Williamson, Murray 2005
Winsor, Alfred "Ralph" 1973
* Winters, Frank "Coddy" 1973

Wirtz, William W. "Bill" 1984
Woog, Doug 2002
* Wright, Lyle Z. 1973
* Yackel, Ken 1986

TEAMS

1960 Olympic Team 2000
1980 Olympic Team 2003

WAYNE GRETZKY AWARD

Wayne Gretzky 1999
The Howe family 2000
Scotty Morrison 2001
Scotty Bowman 2002
Bobby Hull 2003
* Herb Brooks 2004

* Deceased

International Ice Hockey Federation Hall of Fame

The IIHF Hall of Fame was founded in 1997.

Candidates for election as Honoured Members in the player category shall be chosen on the basis of their playing ability, sportsmanship, character and their contribution to their team or teams and to the game of ice hockey in general.

Candidates for election as Honoured Members in the builder category shall be chosen on the basis of their coaching, managerial or executive ability, where applicable, their sportsmanship and character, and their contribution to their organization or organizations and to the game of ice hockey in general.

Candidates for election as Honoured Members in the referee or linesman category shall be chosen on the basis of their officiating ability, sportsmanship, character and their contribution to the game of ice hockey in general. The Paul Loicq Award, named for the longtime former IIHF president, is presented to honor a person for his service to the international hockey community.

Inductees' names are followed by their country and year of induction.

PLAYERS

Alexandrov, Veniamin, RUS, 2007
Balderis, Helmut, LAT, 1998
Ball, Rudi, GER, 2004
Bergqvist, Sven, SWE, 1999
Bjorn, Lars, SWE, 1998
Bobrov, Vsevolod, RUS, 1997
Bourbonnais, Roger, CAN, 1999
Bouzek, Vladimir, CzRep, 2007
Bozon, Phillippe, FRA 2008
Bubnik, Vlastimil, CzRep, 1997
Cattini, Ferdinand, SUI, 1998
Cattini, Hans, SUI, 1998
Cerny, Josef, CzRep, 2007
Christian, Bill, USA, 1998
Cleary, Bill, USA, 1997
Cosby, Gerry, USA, 1997
Craig, Jim, USA, 1999
Curran, Mike, USA, 1999
Davydov, Vitaly, RUS, 2004
Drobny, Jaroslav, CzRep, 1997
Dzurilla, Vladimir, SVK, 1998
Erhardt, Carl, G.B., 1998
Fetisov, Vyacheslav, RUS, 2005
Firsov, Anatoli, RUS, 1998
Golonka, Josef, SVK, 1998
Granato, Cammi, USA 2008
Gretzky, Wayne, CAN, 2000
Gruth, Henryk, POL, 2006
Gustafsson, Bengt-Ake, SWE, 2003
Gut, Karel, CzRep, 1998
Heaney, Geraldine, CAN 2008
Hedberg, Anders, SWE, 1997
Hlinka, Ivan, CzRep, 2002
Holecek, Jiri, CzRep, 1998
Holik, Jiri, CzRep, 1999
Holmqvist, Leif, SWE, 1999
Huck, Fran, CAN, 1999
Jaenecke, Gustav, GER, 1998
James, Angela, CAN 2008
Johnson, Mark, USA, 1999
Johnston, Marshall, CAN, 1998
Jonsson, Tomas, SWE, 2000
Jutila, Timo, FIN, 2003
Keinonen, Matti, FIN, 2002
Kharlamov, Valeri, RUS, 1998
Kiessling, Udo, GER, 2000
Kolliker, Jakob, SUI, 2007
Konovalenko, Viktor, RUS, 2007
Kuhnhackl, Erich, GER, 1997
Kurri, Jari, FIN, 2000
Kuzkin, Viktor, RUS, 2005
Lacarriere, Jacques, FRA, 1998
Larionov, Igor RUS 2008
Lemieux, Mario CAN 2008
Loktev, Konstantin, RUS, 2007
Loob, Hakan, SWE, 1998
Lundquist, Vic, CAN, 1997
Machac, Oldrich, CzRep, 1999
MacKenzie, Barry, CAN, 1999
Makarov, Sergei, RUS, 2001
Malecek, Josef, CzRep, 2003
Maltsev, Alexander, RUS, 1999
Marjamaki, Pekka, FIN, 1998
Martin, Seth, CAN, 1997
Martinec, Vladimir, CzRep, 2001
Mayasich, John, USA, 1997
Mayorov, Boris, RUS, 1999
McCartan, Jack, USA, 1998
McLeod, Jackie, CAN, 1999
Mikhailov, Boris, RUS, 2000
Nanne, Lou, USA, 2004
Naslund, Mats, SWE, 2005
Nedomansky, Vaclav, CzRep, 1997
Nilsson, Kent, SWE, 2006
Nilsson, Nisse, SWE, 2002
O'Malley, Terry, CAN, 1998
Oksanen, Lasse, FIN, 1999
Pana, Eduard, ROM, 1998
Patton, Peter, G.B., 2002
Peltonen, Esa, FIN, 2007
Petrov, Vladimir, RUS, 2006
Pettersson, Ronald, SWE, 2004
Pospisil, Frantisek, CzRep, 1999
Puschnig, Josef, AUT, 1999
Ragulin, Alexander, RUS, 1997
Rampf, Hans, GER, 2001
Rundqvist, Thomas, SWE, 2007
Salming, Borje, SWE, 1998
Schloder, Alois, GER, 2005
Sinden, Harry, CAN, 1997
Sologubov, Nikolai, RUS, 2004
Starshinov, Vyacheslav, RUS, 2007
Stastny, Peter, SVK, 2000
Sterner, Ulf, SWE, 2001
Stoltz, Roland, SWE, 1999
Tikal, Frantisek, CzRep, 2004
Torriani, Bibi, SUI, 1997
Tretiak, Vladislav, RUS, 1997
Tumba, Sven, SWE, 1997
Valtonen, Jorma, FIN, 1999
Vasiliev, Valeri, RUS, 1998
Wahlsten, Vladimir, FIN, 2006
Watson, Harry, CAN, 1998
Yakushev, Alexander, RUS, 2003
Ylonen, Urpo, FIN, 1997
Zabrodsky, Vladimir, CzRep, 1997
Ziesche, Joachim, GER, 1999

BUILDERS

Ahearne, Bunny, G.B., 1997
Aljancic Sr., Ernest, SLO, 2002
Bauer, Father David, CAN, 1997
Berglund, Art USA 2008
Berglund, Curt, SWE, 2003
Bokac, Ludek, CzRep, 2007
Brooks, Herb, USA, 1999
Brown, Walter, USA, 1997
Buckna, Mike, CAN, 2004
Calcaterra, Enrico, ITA, 1999
Chernyshev, Arkady, RUS, 1999
Dimitriev, Igor, RUS, 2007
Dobida, Hans, AUT, 2007
Eklow, Rudolf, SWE, 1999
Grunander, Arne, SWE, 1997
Henschel, Heinz, GER, 2003
Hewitt, William, CAN, 1998
Holmes, Derek, CAN, 1999
Horsky, Ladislav, SVK, 2004
Hviid, Jorgen, DEN, 2005
Johannessen, Tore, NOR, 1999
Juckes, Gordon, CAN, 1997
Kawabuchi, Tsutomu, JPN, 2004
Khorozov, Anatoli, UKR, 2006
King, Dave, CAN, 2001
Kostka, Vladimir, CzRep, 1997
LeBel, Bob, CAN, 1997
Lindblad, Harry, FIN, 1999
Loicq, Paul, BEL, 1997
Luhti, Cesar W., SUI, 1998
Magnus, Louis, FRA, 1997
Pasztor, Gyorgy, HUN, 2001
Renwick, Gordon, CAN, 2002
Ridder, Bob, USA, 1998
Riley, Jack, USA, 1998
Sabetzki, Dr. Gunther, GER, 1997
Starovoitov, Andrei, RUS, 1997
Starsi, Jan, SVK, 1999
Stromberg, Arne, SWE, 1998
Stubb, Goran, FIN, 2000
Subrt, Miroslav, CzRep, 2004
Tarasov, Anatoli, RUS, 1997
Tikhonov, Viktor, RUS, 1998
Tomita, Shoichi, JPN, 2006
Trumble, Hal, USA, 1999
Tsutsumi, Yoshiaki, JPN, 1999
Tutt, Thayer, USA, 2002
Unsinn, Xaver, GER, 1998
Wasservogel, Walter, AUT, 1997
Yurzinov, Vladimir, RUS, 2002

REFEREES

Adamec, Quido, CzRep, 2005
Dahlberg, Ove, SWE, 2004
Karandin, Yuri, RUS, 2004
Kompalla, Josef, GER, 2003
Wiitala, Unto, FIN, 2003

PAUL LOICQ AWARD

Montag, Wolf-Dieter, GER, 1998
Neumayer, Roman, GER, 1999
Kukushkin, Vsevolod, RUS, 2000
Kataoka, Isao, JPN, 2001
Marsh, Pat, G.B., 2002
Nagobads, George, USA, 2003
Kukulowicz, Aggie, CAN, 2004
Hrabcek, Rita, AUS, 2005
Tovland, Bo, SWE, 2006
Nadin, Bob, CAN, 2007
Okolicany, Juraj, SVK 2008

CENTENNIAL ALL-STAR TEAM (1908-2008)

Goaltender: Vladislav Tretiak, RUS
Defenseman: Vyacheslav Fetisov, RUS
Defenseman: Borje Salming, SWE
Winger: Valeri Kharlamov, RUS
Winger: Sergei Makarov, RUS
Center: Wayne Gretzky, CAN

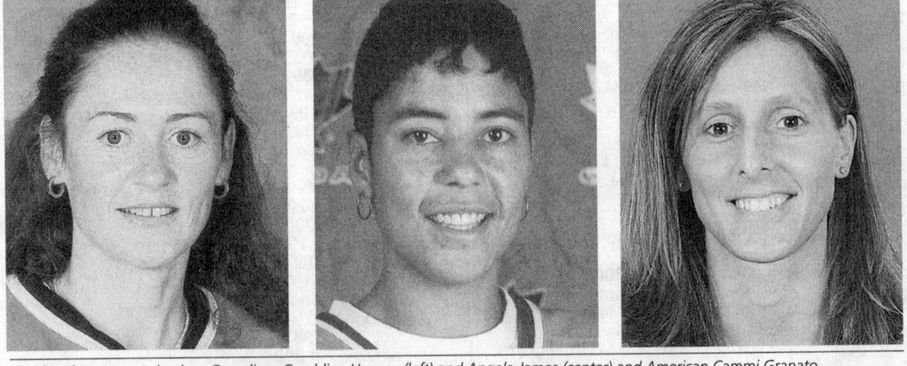

In a first for women's hockey, Canadians Geraldine Heaney (left) and Angela James (center) and American Cammi Granato were named to the IIHF Hall of Fame in 2008. Granato was also named to the U.S. Hockey Hall of Fame.

2008 Stanley Cup Playoffs

Results

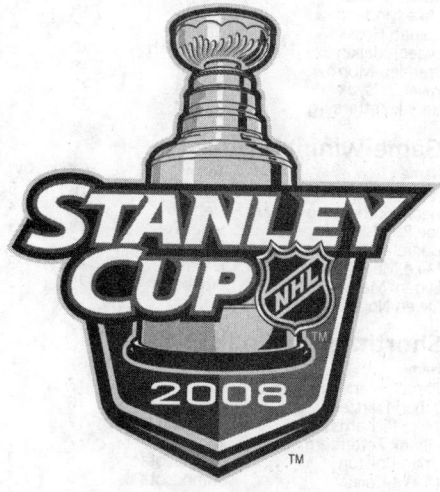

CONFERENCE QUARTER-FINALS

(Best-of-seven series)

Eastern Conference

Series 'A'

Thu. Apr. 10	Boston 1	at	Montreal 4
Sat. Apr. 12	Boston 2	at	Montreal 3*
Sun. Apr. 13	Montreal 1	at	Boston 2**
Tue. Apr. 15	Montreal 1	at	Boston 0
Thu. Apr. 17	Boston 5	at	Montreal 1
Sat. Apr. 19	Montreal 4	at	Boston 5
Mon. Apr. 21	Boston 0	at	Montreal 5

*Alex Kovalev scored at 2:30 of overtime
**Marc Savard scored at 9:25 of overtime
(Montreal won series 4-3)

Series 'B'

Wed. Apr. 9	Ottawa 0	at	Pittsburgh 4
Fri. Apr. 11	Ottawa 3	at	Pittsburgh 5
Mon. Apr. 14	Pittsburgh 4	at	Ottawa 1
Wed. Apr. 16	Pittsburgh 3	at	Ottawa 1

(Pittsburgh won series 4-0)

Series 'C'

Fri. Apr. 11	Philadelphia 4	at	Washington 5
Sun. Apr. 13	Philadelphia 2	at	Washington 0
Tue. Apr. 15	Washington 3	at	Philadelphia 6
Thu. Apr. 17	Washington 3	at	Philadelphia 4*
Sat. Apr. 19	Philadelphia 2	at	Washington 3
Mon. Apr. 21	Washington 4	at	Philadelphia 2
Tue. Apr. 22	Philadelphia 3	at	Washington 2**

*Mike Knuble scored at 26:40 of overtime
**Joffrey Lupul scored at 6:06 of overtime
(Philadelphia won series 4-3)

Series 'D'

Wed. Apr. 9	NY Rangers 4	at	New Jersey 1
Fri. Apr. 11	NY Rangers 2	at	New Jersey 1
Sun. Apr. 13	New Jersey 4	at	NY Rangers 3*
Wed. Apr. 16	New Jersey 3	at	NY Rangers 5
Fri. Apr. 18	NY Rangers 5	at	New Jersey 3

*John Madden scored at 6:01 of overtime
(NY Rangers won series 4-1)

Western Conference

Series 'E'

Thu. Apr. 10	Nashville 1	at	Detroit 3
Sat. Apr. 12	Nashville 2	at	Detroit 4
Mon. Apr. 14	Detroit 3	at	Nashville 5
Wed. Apr. 16	Detroit 2	at	Nashville 3
Fri. Apr. 18	Nashville 1	at	Detroit 2*
Sun. Apr. 20	Detroit 3	at	Nashville 0

*Johan Franzen scored at 1:48 of overtime
(Detroit won series 4-2)

Series 'F'

Wed. Apr. 9	Calgary 3	at	San Jose 2
Thu. Apr. 10	Calgary 0	at	San Jose 2
Sun. Apr. 13	San Jose 3	at	Calgary 4
Tue. Apr. 15	San Jose 3	at	Calgary 2
Thu. Apr. 17	Calgary 3	at	San Jose 4
Sun. Apr. 20	San Jose 0	at	Calgary 2
Tue. Apr. 22	Calgary 3	at	San Jose 5

(San Jose won series 4-3)

Series 'G'

Wed. Apr. 9	Colorado 3	at	Minnesota 2*
Fri. Apr. 11	Colorado 2	at	Minnesota 3**
Mon. Apr. 14	Minnesota 3	at	Colorado 2***
Tue. Apr. 15	Minnesota 1	at	Colorado 5
Thu. Apr. 17	Colorado 3	at	Minnesota 2
Sat. Apr. 19	Minnesota 1	at	Colorado 2

*Joe Sakic scored at 11:11 of overtime
**Keith Carney scored at 1:14 of overtime
***Pierre-Marc Bouchard scored at 11:58 of overtime
(Colorado won series 4-2)

Series 'H'

Thu. Apr. 10	Dallas 4	at	Anaheim 0
Sat. Apr. 12	Dallas 5	at	Anaheim 2
Tue. Apr. 15	Anaheim 4	at	Dallas 2
Thu. Apr. 17	Anaheim 1	at	Dallas 3
Fri. Apr. 18	Dallas 2	at	Anaheim 5
Sun. Apr. 20	Anaheim 1	at	Dallas 4

(Dallas won series 4-2)

CONFERENCE SEMI-FINALS

(Best-of-seven series)

Eastern Conference

Series 'I'

Thu. Apr. 24	Philadelphia 3	at	Montreal 4*
Sat. Apr. 26	Philadelphia 4	at	Montreal 2
Mon. Apr. 28	Montreal 2	at	Philadelphia 3
Wed. Apr. 30	Montreal 2	at	Philadelphia 4
Sat. May 3	Philadelphia 6	at	Montreal 4

*Tom Kostopoulos scored at 0:48 of overtime
(Philadelphia won series 4-1)

Series 'J'

Fri. Apr. 25	NY Rangers 4	at	Pittsburgh 5
Sun. Apr. 27	NY Rangers 0	at	Pittsburgh 2
Tue. Apr. 29	Pittsburgh 5	at	NY Rangers 3
Thu. May 1	Pittsburgh 0	at	NY Rangers 3
Sun. May 4	NY Rangers 2	at	Pittsburgh 3*

*Marian Hossa scored at 7:10 of overtime
(Pittsburgh won series 4-1)

Western Conference

Series 'K'

Thu. Apr. 24	Colorado 3	at	Detroit 4
Sat. Apr. 26	Colorado 1	at	Detroit 5
Tue. Apr. 29	Detroit 4	at	Colorado 3
Thu. May 1	Detroit 8	at	Colorado 2

(Detroit won series 4-0)

Series 'L'

Fri. Apr. 25	Dallas 3	at	San Jose 2*
Sun. Apr. 27	Dallas 5	at	San Jose 2
Tue. Apr. 29	San Jose 1	at	Dallas 2**
Wed. Apr. 30	San Jose 2	at	Dallas 1
Fri. May 2	Dallas 2	at	San Jose 3***
Sun. May 4	San Jose 1	at	Dallas 2****

*Brenden Morrow scored at 4:39 of overtime
**Mattias Norstrom scored at 4:37 of overtime
***Joe Pavelski scored at 1:05 of overtime
****Brenden Morrow scored at 69:03 of overtime
(Dallas won series 4-2)

CONFERENCE FINALS

(Best-of-seven series)

Eastern Conference

Series 'M'

Fri. May 9	Philadelphia 2	at	Pittsburgh 4
Sun. May 11	Philadelphia 2	at	Pittsburgh 4
Tue. May 13	Pittsburgh 4	at	Philadelphia 1
Thu. May 15	Pittsburgh 2	at	Philadelphia 4
Sun. May 18	Philadelphia 0	at	Pittsburgh 6

(Pittsburgh won series 4-1)

Western Conference

Series 'N'

Thu. May 8	Dallas 1	at	Detroit 4
Sat. May 10	Dallas 1	at	Detroit 2
Mon. May 12	Detroit 5	at	Dallas 2
Wed. May 14	Detroit 1	at	Dallas 3
Sat. May 17	Dallas 2	at	Detroit 1
Mon. May 19	Detroit 4	at	Dallas 1

(Detroit won series 4-2)

STANLEY CUP FINAL

(Best-of-seven series)

Series 'O'

Sat. May 24	Pittsburgh 0	at	Detroit 4
Mon. May 26	Pittsburgh 0	at	Detroit 3
Wed. May 28	Detroit 2	at	Pittsburgh 3
Sat. May 31	Detroit 2	at	Pittsburgh 1
Mon. June 2	Pittsburgh 4	at	Detroit 3*
Wed. June 4	Detroit 3	at	Pittsburgh 2

*Petr Sykora scored at 49:57 of overtime
(Detroit won series 4-2)

Team Playoff Records

	GP	W	L	GF	GA	%
Detroit	22	16	6	72	41	.727
Pittsburgh	20	14	6	61	43	.700
Dallas	18	10	8	45	41	.556
Philadelphia	17	9	8	52	54	.529
San Jose	13	6	7	30	32	.462
NY Rangers	10	5	5	31	27	.500
Montreal	12	5	7	33	35	.417
Colorado	10	4	6	26	33	.400
Calgary	7	3	4	17	19	.429
Washington	7	3	4	20	23	.429
Boston	7	3	4	15	19	.429
Nashville	6	2	4	12	17	.333
Minnesota	6	2	4	12	17	.333
Anaheim	6	2	4	13	20	.333
New Jersey	5	1	4	12	19	.200
Ottawa	4	0	4	5	16	.000

Individual Leaders

Abbreviations: GP – games played; **G** – goals; **A** – assists; **PTS** – points; **+/–** – difference between Goals For (**GF**) scored when a player is on the ice with his team at even strength or shorthanded and Goals Against (**GA**) scored when the same player is on the ice with his team at even strength or on a power play; **PIM** – penalties in minutes; **PP** – power play goals; **SH** – shorthanded goals; **GW** – game-winning goals; **OT** – overtime goals; **S** – shots on goal; **%** – percentage of shots resulting in goals.

Playoff Scoring Leaders

Player	Team	GP	G	A	PTS	+/–	PIM	PP	SH	GW	OT	S	%
Henrik Zetterberg	Detroit	22	13	14	27	16	16	4	2	4	0	116	11.2
Sidney Crosby	Pittsburgh	20	6	21	27	7	12	2	0	1	0	59	10.2
Marian Hossa	Pittsburgh	20	12	14	26	8	12	5	0	2	1	76	15.8
Pavel Datsyuk	Detroit	22	10	13	23	13	6	4	0	1	0	74	13.5
Evgeni Malkin	Pittsburgh	20	10	12	22	3	24	5	1	3	0	75	13.3
Johan Franzen	Detroit	16	13	5	18	13	14	6	2	5	1	70	18.6
Mike Ribeiro	Dallas	18	3	14	17	0	16	0	0	0	0	34	8.8
Daniel Briere	Philadelphia	17	9	7	16	-3	20	6	0	3	0	45	20.0
Ryan Malone	Pittsburgh	20	6	10	16	4	25	3	0	2	0	43	14.0
R.J. Umberger	Philadelphia	17	10	5	15	7	10	1	0	2	0	40	25.0
Brenden Morrow	Dallas	18	9	6	15	0	22	4	0	2	2	43	20.9
Jaromir Jagr	NY Rangers	10	5	10	15	3	12	2	0	1	0	37	13.5
Brad Richards	Dallas	18	3	12	15	1	8	0	0	0	0	54	5.6
Niklas Kronvall	Detroit	22	0	15	15	16	18	0	0	0	0	21	0.0
Mike Richards	Philadelphia	17	7	7	14	0	10	1	2	0	0	53	13.2
Jiri Hudler	Detroit	22	5	9	14	-1	14	2	0	2	0	46	10.9
Brian Rafalski	Detroit	22	4	10	14	6	12	2	0	0	0	58	6.9
Sergei Gonchar	Pittsburgh	20	1	13	14	0	8	1	0	0	0	40	2.5
Mikael Samuelsson	Detroit	22	5	8	13	8	8	0	0	1	0	79	6.3
Vaclav Prospal	Philadelphia	17	3	10	13	-3	6	1	0	0	0	34	8.8
Nicklas Lidstrom	Detroit	22	3	10	13	8	14	1	1	1	0	41	7.3
Mike Modano	Dallas	18	5	7	12	-3	22	5	0	3	0	37	13.5
Tomas Holmstrom	Detroit	21	4	8	12	4	26	1	0	0	0	41	9.8
Jeff Carter	Philadelphia	17	6	5	11	0	12	3	0	1	0	72	8.3
Alex Kovalev	Montreal	12	5	6	11	-4	8	2	1	1	1	39	12.8
Valtteri Filppula	Detroit	22	5	6	11	7	2	0	0	0	0	39	12.8

Playoff Defencemen Scoring Leaders

Player	Team	GP	G	A	PTS	+/–	PIM	PP	SH	GW	OT	S	%
Niklas Kronvall	Detroit	22	0	15	15	16	18	0	0	0	0	21	0.0
Brian Rafalski	Detroit	22	4	10	14	6	12	2	0	0	0	58	6.9
Sergei Gonchar	Pittsburgh	20	1	13	14	0	8	1	0	0	0	40	2.5
Nicklas Lidstrom	Detroit	22	3	10	13	8	14	1	1	1	0	41	7.3
Stephane Robidas	Dallas	18	3	8	11	0	12	3	0	0	0	41	7.3
Dion Phaneuf	Calgary	7	3	4	7	-2	4	1	0	0	0	22	13.6
Mike Green	Washington	7	3	4	7	-2	15	2	0	0	0	19	15.8
Brian Campbell	San Jose	13	1	6	7	3	4	0	0	0	0	22	4.5
Brad Stuart	Detroit	21	1	6	7	15	14	0	0	1	0	25	4.0
Patrice Brisebois	Montreal	10	1	5	6	-3	6	1	0	1	0	10	10.0
Michal Rozsival	NY Rangers	10	1	5	6	4	10	0	0	0	0	13	7.7
Sergei Zubov	Dallas	11	1	5	6	-4	4	1	0	0	0	20	5.0
Ryan Whitney	Pittsburgh	20	1	5	6	8	25	1	0	0	0	37	2.7
Craig Rivet	San Jose	13	0	6	6	2	16	0	0	0	0	17	0.0

GOALTENDING LEADERS

Goals Against Average

Goaltender	Team	GP	Mins	GA	Avg.
Chris Osgood	Detroit	19	1160	30	1.55
Marc-Andre Fleury	Pittsburgh	20	1251	41	1.97
Marty Turco	Dallas	18	1152	40	2.08
Evgeni Nabokov	San Jose	13	853	31	2.18
Henrik Lundqvist	NY Rangers	10	608	26	2.57

Wins

Goaltender	Team	GP	Mins	W	L
Chris Osgood	Detroit	19	1160	14	4
Marc-Andre Fleury	Pittsburgh	20	1251	14	6
Marty Turco	Dallas	18	1152	10	8
Martin Biron	Philadelphia	17	1049	9	8
Evgeni Nabokov	San Jose	13	853	6	7

Save Percentage

Goaltender	Team	GP	Mins	GA	SA	S%	W	L
Marc-Andre Fleury	Pittsburgh	20	1251	41	610	.933	14	6
Chris Osgood	Detroit	19	1160	30	430	.930	14	4
Marty Turco	Dallas	18	1152	40	511	.922	10	8
Tim Thomas	Boston	7	430	19	221	.914	3	4
Henrik Lundqvist	NY Rangers	10	608	26	287	.909	5	5
Cristobal Huet	Washington	7	451	22	242	.909	3	4

Shutouts

Goaltender	Team	GP	Mins	SO
Chris Osgood	Detroit	19	1160	3
Marc-Andre Fleury	Pittsburgh	20	1251	3
*Carey Price	Montreal	11	648	2
Miikka Kiprusoff	Calgary	7	336	1
Henrik Lundqvist	NY Rangers	10	608	1
Evgeni Nabokov	San Jose	13	853	1
Martin Biron	Philadelphia	17	1049	1
Marty Turco	Dallas	18	1152	1

* rookie

Goals

Name	Team	GP	G
Johan Franzen	Detroit	16	13
Henrik Zetterberg	Detroit	22	13
Marian Hossa	Pittsburgh	20	12
R.J. Umberger	Philadelphia	17	10
Evgeni Malkin	Pittsburgh	20	10
Pavel Datsyuk	Detroit	22	10
Daniel Briere	Philadelphia	17	9
Brenden Morrow	Dallas	18	9
Mike Richards	Philadelphia	17	7
Jeff Carter	Philadelphia	17	6
Petr Sykora	Pittsburgh	20	6
Ryan Malone	Pittsburgh	20	6
Sidney Crosby	Pittsburgh	20	6
Jordan Staal	Pittsburgh	20	6
Jaromir Jagr	NY Rangers	10	5

Assists

Name	Team	GP	A
Sidney Crosby	Pittsburgh	20	21
Niklas Kronvall	Detroit	22	15
Mike Ribeiro	Dallas	18	14
Marian Hossa	Pittsburgh	20	14
Henrik Zetterberg	Detroit	22	14
Sergei Gonchar	Pittsburgh	20	13
Pavel Datsyuk	Detroit	22	13
Brad Richards	Dallas	18	12
Evgeni Malkin	Pittsburgh	20	12
Jaromir Jagr	NY Rangers	10	10
Vaclav Prospal	Philadelphia	17	10
Ryan Malone	Pittsburgh	20	10
Nicklas Lidstrom	Detroit	22	10
Brian Rafalski	Detroit	22	10
Jiri Hudler	Detroit	22	9

Power-play Goals

Name	Team	GP	PP
Johan Franzen	Detroit	16	6
Daniel Briere	Philadelphia	17	6
Mike Modano	Dallas	18	5
Marian Hossa	Pittsburgh	20	5
Evgeni Malkin	Pittsburgh	20	5
Brenden Morrow	Dallas	18	4
Pavel Datsyuk	Detroit	22	4
Henrik Zetterberg	Detroit	22	4

Game-winning Goals

Name	Team	GP	GW
Johan Franzen	Detroit	16	5
Henrik Zetterberg	Detroit	22	4
Joe Pavelski	San Jose	13	3
Daniel Briere	Philadelphia	17	3
Mike Modano	Dallas	18	3
Evgeni Malkin	Pittsburgh	20	3
Owen Nolan	Calgary	7	2

Shorthanded Goals

Name	Team	GP	SH
Patrick Marleau	San Jose	13	2
Johan Franzen	Detroit	16	2
Mike Richards	Philadelphia	17	2
Henrik Zetterberg	Detroit	22	2
Brian Rolston	Minnesota	6	1
Mikko Koivu	Minnesota	6	1
Marco Sturm	Boston	7	1
Ben Guite	Colorado	10	1
*Ryan Callahan	NY Rangers	10	1
Alex Kovalev	Montreal	12	1
Evgeni Malkin	Pittsburgh	20	1
Nicklas Lidstrom	Detroit	22	1
Daniel Cleary	Detroit	22	1

Overtime Goals

Name	Team	GP	OT
Brenden Morrow	Dallas	18	2
John Madden	New Jersey	5	1
Keith Carney	Minnesota	6	1
Pierre-Marc Bouchard	Minnesota	6	1

Shots

Name	Team	GP	S
Henrik Zetterberg	Detroit	22	116
Mikael Samuelsson	Detroit	22	79
Marian Hossa	Pittsburgh	20	76
Evgeni Malkin	Pittsburgh	20	75
Pavel Datsyuk	Detroit	22	74
Jeff Carter	Philadelphia	17	72
Johan Franzen	Detroit	16	70

Plus/Minus

Name	Team	GP	+/–
Henrik Zetterberg	Detroit	22	16
Niklas Kronvall	Detroit	22	16
Brad Stuart	Detroit	21	15
Johan Franzen	Detroit	16	13
Pavel Datsyuk	Detroit	22	13

TEAMS' PLAYOFF HOME/ROAD RECORD

	HOME					Win	ROAD					Win
	GP	W	L	GF	GA	%	GP	W	L	GF	GA	%
DET	11	9	2	35	16	.818	11	7	4	37	25	.636
PIT	11	9	2	39	20	.818	9	5	4	22	23	.556
DAL	9	5	4	20	20	.556	9	5	4	25	21	.556
PHI	7	5	2	24	20	.714	10	4	6	28	34	.400
S.J.	7	4	3	20	19	.571	6	2	4	10	13	.333
NYR	4	2	2	14	12	.500	6	3	3	17	15	.500
MTL	7	4	3	23	21	.571	5	1	4	10	14	.200
COL	5	2	3	14	17	.400	5	2	3	12	16	.400
CGY	3	2	1	8	6	.667	4	1	3	9	13	.250
WSH	4	2	2	10	11	.500	3	1	2	10	12	.333
BOS	3	2	1	7	6	.667	4	1	3	8	13	.250
NSH	3	2	1	8	8	.667	3	0	3	4	9	.000
MIN	3	1	2	7	8	.333	3	1	2	5	9	.333
ANA	3	1	2	7	11	.333	3	1	2	6	9	.333
N.J.	3	0	3	5	11	.000	2	1	1	7	8	.500
OTT	2	0	2	2	7	.000	0	2	3	9	.000	
Total	**85**	**50**	**35**	**243**	**213**	**.588**	**85**	**35**	**50**	**213**	**243**	**.412**

TEAMS' POWER-PLAY RECORD

Abbreviations: ADV-total advantages; **PPGF**-power play goals for; **%** arrived by dividing number of power-play goals by total advantages.

HOME					ROAD					OVERALL				
Team	GP	ADV	PPGF	%	Team	GP	ADV	PPGF	%	Team	GP	ADV	PPGF	%
1 Min	3	11	3	27.3	Cgy	4	14	4	28.6	Cgy	7	22	6	27.3
2 Pit	11	55	15	27.3	N.J.	2	11	3	27.3	Wsh	7	35	8	22.9
3 Cgy	3	8	2	25	Wsh	3	16	4	25	Pit	20	92	21	22.8
4 Ana	3	12	3	25	Col	5	16	4	25	Phi	17	67	15	22.4
5 Phi	7	33	8	24.2	Dal	9	45	10	22.2	N.J.	5	24	5	20.8
6 NYR	4	21	5	23.8	Phi	10	34	7	20.6	Ana	6	24	5	20.8
7 Wsh	4	19	4	21.1	Det	11	46	9	19.6	Col	10	48	10	20.8
8 Col	5	32	6	18.8	Ana	3	12	2	16.7	Dal	18	90	18	20
9 Det	11	60	11	18.3	Pit	9	37	6	16.2	Det	22	106	20	18.9
10 Dal	9	45	8	17.8	Bos	4	20	3	15	NYR	10	42	7	16.7
11 S.J.	7	31	5	16.1	Mtl	5	23	3	13	Mtl	12	55	8	14.5
12 Mtl	7	32	5	15.6	S.J.	6	25	3	12	Min	6	21	3	14.3
13 N.J.	3	13	2	15.4	Ott	2	9	1	11.1	S.J.	13	56	8	14.3
14 Nsh	3	11	1	9.1	NYR	6	21	2	9.5	Bos	7	30	3	10
15 Ott	2	4	0	0	Nsh	3	12	1	8.3	Nsh	6	23	2	8.7
16 Bos	3	10	0	0	Min	3	10	0	0	Ott	4	13	1	7.7
Total	**85**	**397**	**78**	**19.6**		**85**	**351**	**62**	**17.7**		**85**	**748**	**140**	**18.7**

TEAMS' PENALTY KILLING RECORD

Abbreviations: TSH – Total times shorthanded; **PPGA** – power-play goals against; **%** arrived by dividing times shorthanded minus power-play goals against by times short.

HOME					ROAD					OVERALL				
Team	GP	TSH	PPGA	%	Team	GP	TSH	PPGA	%	Team	GP	TSH	PPGA	%
1 Det.	11	46	3	93.5	Nsh.	3	13	1	92.3	Bos.	7	33	3	90.9
2 Bos.	3	11	1	90.9	Min.	3	22	2	90.9	Nsh.	6	26	3	88.5
3 Dal.	9	36	4	88.9	Bos.	4	22	2	90.9	Pit.	20	85	11	87.1
4 Pit.	11	43	5	88.4	Mtl.	5	17	2	88.2	Det.	22	98	14	85.7
5 N.J.	3	8	1	87.5	Pit.	9	42	6	85.7	Mtl.	12	44	7	84.1
6 Nsh.	3	13	2	84.6	NYR	6	30	5	83.3	Dal.	18	76	13	82.9
7 Ott.	2	12	2	83.3	Wsh.	3	19	4	78.9	Cgy.	7	31	6	80.6
8 Cgy.	3	12	2	83.3	Cgy.	4	19	4	78.9	Min.	6	30	6	80
9 Mtl.	7	27	5	81.5	Det.	11	52	11	78.8	NYR	10	48	10	79.2
10 Col.	5	21	4	81	Ana.	3	18	4	77.8	Wsh.	7	36	8	77.8
11 Phi.	7	33	7	78.8	S.J.	6	18	4	77.8	Col.	10	44	10	77.3
12 Wsh.	4	17	4	76.5	Dal.	9	40	9	77.5	N.J.	5	17	4	76.5
13 S.J.	7	26	7	73.1	Col.	5	23	6	73.9	Phi.	17	75	18	76
14 NYR	4	18	5	72.2	Phi.	10	42	11	73.8	S.J.	13	44	11	75
15 Ana.	3	20	6	70	N.J.	2	9	3	66.7	Ott.	4	23	6	73.9
16 Min.	3	8	4	50	Ott.	2	11	4	63.6	Ana.	6	38	10	73.7
Total	**85**	**351**	**62**	**82.3**		**85**	**397**	**78**	**80.4**		**85**	**748**	**140**	**81.3**

SHORTHAND GOALS

GOALS FOR			GOALS AGAINST		
Team	GP	GF	Team	GP	GA
DET.	22	6	DET.	22	0
MIN.	6	2	S.J.	13	0
S.J.	13	2	NYR	10	0
PHI.	17	2	BOS.	7	0
BOS.	7	1	WSH.	7	0
NYR	10	1	CGY.	7	0
COL.	10	1	ANA.	6	0
MTL.	12	1	OTT.	4	0
PIT.	20	1	NSH.	6	1
OTT.	4	0	MIN.	6	1
N.J.	5	0	N.J.	5	1
NSH.	6	0	PIT.	20	2
ANA.	6	0	PHI.	17	2
WSH.	7	0	MTL.	12	2
CGY.	7	0	DAL.	18	4
DAL.	18	0	COL.	10	4
Total	**85**	**17**		**85**	**17**

TEAM PENALTIES

Abbreviations: GP – games played; **PEN** – total penalty minutes, including bench penalties; **BMI** – total bench minor minutes; **AVG** – average penalty minutes/game arrived by dividing total penalty minutes by games played

Team	GP	PEN	BMI	AVG
Det	82	937	4	11.4
L.A.	82	954	24	11.6
N.J.	82	974	18	11.9
Wsh	82	975	22	11.9
Col	82	995	22	12.1
Buf	82	1004	14	12.2
Fla	82	1026	24	12.5
Nsh	82	1027	12	12.5
NYI	82	1041	18	12.7
T.B.	82	1040	16	12.7
Bos	82	1069	18	13.0
Atl	82	1077	20	13.1
S.J.	82	1075	14	13.1
Mtl	82	1090	18	13.3
Tor	82	1087	8	13.3
Min	82	1098	12	13.4
NYR	82	1154	12	14.1
St.L.	82	1153	16	14.1
Dal	82	1176	14	14.3
Edm	82	1175	26	14.3
Ott	82	1175	22	14.3
Car	82	1183	18	14.4
Pit	82	1179	24	14.4
Phx	82	1193	18	14.5
CBJ	82	1325	22	16.2
Cgy	82	1342	14	16.4
Chi	82	1383	12	16.9
Phi	82	1471	14	17.9
Van	82	1474	16	18.0
Ana	82	1481	16	18.1
Total	**1230**	**34333**	**508**	**27.9**

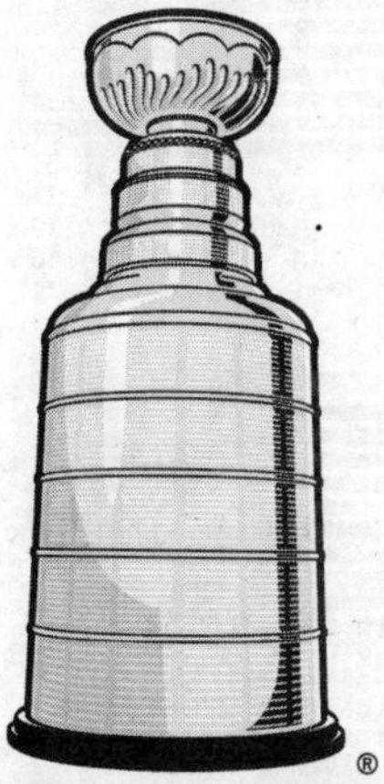

Detroit's Henrik Zetterberg, who tied for the postseason lead with 13 goals and 27 points while also providing stellar defensive work, was rewarded with the Conn Smythe Trophy as playoff MVP.

Stanley Cup Record Book

History: The Stanley Cup, the oldest trophy competed for by professional athletes in North America, was donated by Frederick Arthur, Lord Stanley of Preston and son of the Earl of Derby, in 1893. Lord Stanley purchased the trophy for 10 guineas ($50 at that time) for presentation to the amateur hockey champions of Canada. Since 1906, when Canadian teams began to pay their players openly, the Stanley Cup has been the symbol of professional hockey supremacy. It has been competed for only by NHL teams since 1926-27 and has been under the exclusive control of the NHL since 1947.

Stanley Cup Standings

1918-2008

(ranked by Cup wins)

Teams	Cup Wins	Yrs.	Series	Wins	Losses	Games	Wins	Losses	Ties	Goals For	Goals Against	Winning %
Montreal[1,2]	23	76	141	88	52	679	398	273	8	2083	1708	.592
Toronto[3]	13	64	109	58	51	524	251	269	4	1350	1427	.483
Detroit	11	56	107	62	45	540	285	254	1	1522	1373	.529
Boston	5	63	105	47	58	519	245	268	6	1503	1535	.478
Edmonton	5	20	49	34	15	251	152	99	0	938	763	.606
NY Rangers	4	51	91	44	47	410	194	208	8	1155	1181	.483
NY Islanders	4	21	47	30	17	240	134	106	0	792	714	.558
Chicago	3	53	90	40	50	411	188	218	5	1176	1311	.464
New Jersey[4]	3	19	38	22	16	218	118	100	0	605	532	.541
Philadelphia	2	32	68	38	30	363	189	174	0	1098	1070	.521
Pittsburgh	2	23	44	23	21	233	124	109	0	715	701	.532
Colorado[5]	2	20	43	25	18	243	130	113	0	715	684	.535
Dallas[6]	1	29	56	28	28	305	154	151	0	897	899	.505
Calgary[7]	1	25	39	15	24	202	92	110	0	632	680	.455
Carolina[8]	1	12	19	8	11	109	51	58	0	277	314	.469
Anaheim	1	6	15	10	5	79	46	33	0	193	188	.582
Tampa Bay	1	5	9	5	4	51	26	25	0	122	140	.510
St. Louis	0	34	57	23	34	303	138	165	0	857	943	.455
Buffalo	0	27	48	21	27	243	119	124	0	730	727	.490
Los Angeles	0	23	34	11	23	170	65	105	0	511	649	.382
Vancouver	0	21	32	11	21	167	71	96	0	473	552	.425
Washington	0	19	29	10	19	161	72	89	0	487	501	.447
Phoenix[9]	0	16	18	2	16	92	29	63	0	245	343	.315
San Jose	0	11	20	9	11	117	55	62	0	286	352	.470
Ottawa[10]	0	11	19	8	11	103	49	54	0	235	241	.476
Nashville	0	4	4	0	4	22	6	16	0	45	62	.273
Florida	0	3	6	3	3	31	13	18	0	77	82	.419
Minnesota	0	3	5	2	3	29	11	18	0	64	72	.379
Atlanta	0	1	1	0	1	4	0	4	0	6	17	.000
Columbus	0	0	0	0	0	0	0	0	0	0	0	.000

1 Montreal also won the Stanley Cup in 1916.
2 1919 final incomplete due to influenza epidemic.
3 Toronto Blueshirts also won the Stanley Cup in 1914.
4 Includes totals of Colorado Rockies 1976-82.
5 Includes totals of Quebec Nordiques 1979-95.
6 Includes totals of Minnesota North Stars 1967-93.
7 Includes totals of Atlanta Flames 1972-80.
8 Includes totals of Hartford Whalers 1979-97.
9 Includes totals of Winnipeg Jets 1979-96.
10 Modern Ottawa Senators franchise only, 1992 to date.

Stanley Cup Winners Prior to Formation of NHL in 1917

Season	Champions	Manager	Coach
1916-17	Seattle Metropolitans	Pete Muldoon	Pete Muldoon
1915-16	Montreal Canadiens	George Kennedy	George Kennedy
1914-15	Vancouver Millionaires	Frank Patrick	Frank Patrick
1913-14	Toronto Blueshirts	Jack Marshall	Scotty Davidson*
1912-13**	Quebec Bulldogs	M.J. Quinn	Joe Malone*
1911-12	Quebec Bulldogs	M.J. Quinn	Charley Nolan
1910-11	Ottawa Senators		Percy LeSueur
1909-10	Montreal Wanderers (Mar. 1910)	Dickie Boon	Pud Glass*
1909-10	Ottawa Senators (Jan. 1910)		Bruce Stuart*
1908-09	Ottawa Senators		Bruce Stuart*
1907-08	Montreal Wanderers	Dickie Boon	Cecil Blachford
1906-07	Montreal Wanderers (Mar. 25, 1907)	Dickie Boon	Cecil Blachford
1906-07	Kenora Thistles (Jan./Mar. 18, 1907)	F.A. Hudson	Tom Phillips*
1905-06	Montreal Wanderers (Mar. 1906)	Cecil Blachford*	
1905-06	Ottawa Silver Seven (Feb. 1906)		Alf Smith
1904-05	Ottawa Silver Seven		Alf Smith
1903-04	Ottawa Silver Seven		Alf Smith
1902-03	Ottawa Silver Seven (Mar. 1903)		Alf Smith
1902-03	Montreal A.A.A. (Feb. 1903)		C. McKerrow
1901-02	Montreal A.A.A. (Mar. 1902)		C. McKerrow
1901-02	Winnipeg Victorias (Jan. 1902)		
1900-01	Winnipeg Victorias		Dan Bain*
1899-1900	Montreal Shamrocks		Harry Trihey*
1898-99	Montreal Shamrocks (Mar. 1899)		Harry Trihey*
1898-99	Montreal Victorias (Feb. 1899)		Mike Grant*
1897-98	Montreal Victorias		Frank Richardson
1896-97	Montreal Victorias		Mike Grant*
1895-96	Montreal Victorias (Dec. 1896)		Mike Grant*
1895-96	Winnipeg Victorias (Feb. 1896)		Jack Armitage
1894-95	Montreal Victorias		Mike Grant*
1893-94	Montreal A.A.A.		
1892-93	Montreal A.A.A.		

* In the early years the teams were frequently run by the Captain. *Indicates Captain
** Victoria defeated Quebec in challenge series. No official recognition.

Stanley Cup Winners

Year	W-L-T in Finals	Winner	Coach	Finalist	Coach
2008	4-2	Detroit	Mike Babcock	Pittsburgh	Michel Therrien
2007	4-1	Anaheim	Randy Carlyle	Ottawa	Bryan Murray
2006	4-3	Carolina	Peter Laviolette	Edmonton	Craig MacTavish
2005	....	....	....	....	....
2004	4-3	Tampa Bay	John Tortorella	Calgary	Darryl Sutter
2003	4-3	New Jersey	Pat Burns	Anaheim	Mike Babcock
2002	4-1	Detroit	Scotty Bowman	Carolina	Paul Maurice
2001	4-3	Colorado	Bob Hartley	New Jersey	Larry Robinson
2000	4-2	New Jersey	Larry Robinson	Dallas	Ken Hitchcock
1999	4-2	Dallas	Ken Hitchcock	Buffalo	Lindy Ruff
1998	4-0	Detroit	Scotty Bowman	Washington	Ron Wilson
1997	4-0	Detroit	Scotty Bowman	Philadelphia	Terry Murray
1996	4-0	Colorado	Marc Crawford	Florida	Doug MacLean
1995	4-0	New Jersey	Jacques Lemaire	Detroit	Scotty Bowman
1994	4-3	NY Rangers	Mike Keenan	Vancouver	Pat Quinn
1993	4-1	Montreal	Jacques Demers	Los Angeles	Barry Melrose
1992	4-0	Pittsburgh	Scotty Bowman	Chicago	Mike Keenan
1991	4-2	Pittsburgh	Bob Johnson	Minnesota	Bob Gainey
1990	4-1	Edmonton	John Muckler	Boston	Mike Milbury
1989	4-2	Calgary	Terry Crisp	Montreal	Pat Burns
1988	4-0	Edmonton	Glen Sather	Boston	Terry O'Reilly
1987	4-3	Edmonton	Glen Sather	Philadelphia	Mike Keenan
1986	4-1	Montreal	Jean Perron	Calgary	Bob Johnson
1985	4-1	Edmonton	Glen Sather	Philadelphia	Mike Keenan
1984	4-1	Edmonton	Glen Sather	NY Islanders	Al Arbour
1983	4-0	NY Islanders	Al Arbour	Edmonton	Glen Sather
1982	4-0	NY Islanders	Al Arbour	Vancouver	Roger Neilson
1981	4-1	NY Islanders	Al Arbour	Minnesota	Glen Sonmor
1980	4-2	NY Islanders	Al Arbour	Philadelphia	Pat Quinn
1979	4-1	Montreal	Scotty Bowman	NY Rangers	Fred Shero
1978	4-2	Montreal	Scotty Bowman	Boston	Don Cherry
1977	4-0	Montreal	Scotty Bowman	Boston	Don Cherry
1976	4-0	Montreal	Scotty Bowman	Philadelphia	Fred Shero
1975	4-2	Philadelphia	Fred Shero	Buffalo	Floyd Smith
1974	4-2	Philadelphia	Fred Shero	Boston	Bep Guidolin
1973	4-2	Montreal	Scotty Bowman	Chicago	Billy Reay
1972	4-2	Boston	Tom Johnson	NY Rangers	Emile Francis
1971	4-3	Montreal	Al MacNeil	Chicago	Billy Reay
1970	4-0	Boston	Harry Sinden	St. Louis	Scotty Bowman
1969	4-0	Montreal	Claude Ruel	St. Louis	Scotty Bowman
1968	4-0	Montreal	Toe Blake	St. Louis	Scotty Bowman
1967	4-2	Toronto	Punch Imlach	Montreal	Toe Blake
1966	4-2	Montreal	Toe Blake	Detroit	Sid Abel
1965	4-3	Montreal	Toe Blake	Chicago	Billy Reay
1964	4-3	Toronto	Punch Imlach	Detroit	Sid Abel
1963	4-1	Toronto	Punch Imlach	Detroit	Sid Abel
1962	4-2	Toronto	Punch Imlach	Chicago	Rudy Pilous
1961	4-2	Chicago	Rudy Pilous	Detroit	Sid Abel
1960	4-0	Montreal	Toe Blake	Toronto	Punch Imlach
1959	4-1	Montreal	Toe Blake	Toronto	Punch Imlach
1958	4-2	Montreal	Toe Blake	Boston	Milt Schmidt
1957	4-1	Montreal	Toe Blake	Boston	Milt Schmidt
1956	4-1	Montreal	Toe Blake	Detroit	Jimmy Skinner
1955	4-3	Detroit	Jimmy Skinner	Montreal	Dick Irvin
1954	4-3	Detroit	Tommy Ivan	Montreal	Dick Irvin
1953	4-1	Montreal	Dick Irvin	Boston	Lynn Patrick
1952	4-0	Detroit	Tommy Ivan	Montreal	Dick Irvin
1951	4-1	Toronto	Joe Primeau	Montreal	Dick Irvin
1950	4-3	Detroit	Tommy Ivan	NY Rangers	Lynn Patrick
1949	4-0	Toronto	Hap Day	Detroit	Tommy Ivan
1948	4-0	Toronto	Hap Day	Detroit	Tommy Ivan
1947	4-2	Toronto	Hap Day	Montreal	Dick Irvin
1946	4-1	Montreal	Dick Irvin	Boston	Dit Clapper
1945	4-3	Toronto	Hap Day	Detroit	Jack Adams
1944	4-0	Montreal	Dick Irvin	Chicago	Paul Thompson
1943	4-0	Detroit	Jack Adams	Boston	Art Ross
1942	4-3	Toronto	Hap Day	Detroit	Jack Adams
1941	4-0	Boston	Cooney Weiland	Detroit	Ebbie Goodfellow
1940	4-2	NY Rangers	Frank Boucher	Toronto	Dick Irvin
1939	4-1	Boston	Art Ross	Toronto	Dick Irvin
1938	3-1	Chicago	Bill Stewart	Toronto	Dick Irvin
1937	3-2	Detroit	Jack Adams	NY Rangers	Lester Patrick
1936	3-1	Detroit	Jack Adams	Toronto	Dick Irvin
1935	3-0	Mtl. Maroons	Tommy Gorman	Toronto	Dick Irvin
1934	3-1	Chicago	Tommy Gorman	Detroit	Herbie Lewis
1933	3-1	NY Rangers	Lester Patrick	Toronto	Dick Irvin
1932	3-0	Toronto	Dick Irvin	NY Rangers	Lester Patrick
1931	3-2	Montreal	Cecil Hart	Chicago	Dick Irvin
1930	2-0	Montreal	Cecil Hart	Boston	Art Ross
1929	2-0	Boston	Cy Denneny	NY Rangers	Lester Patrick
1928	3-2	NY Rangers	Lester Patrick	Mtl. Maroons	Eddie Gerard
1927	2-0-2	Ottawa	Dave Gill	Boston	Art Ross
		The National Hockey League assumed control of Stanley Cup competition after 1926			
1926	3-1	Mtl. Maroons	Eddie Gerard	Victoria	Lester Patrick
1925	3-1	Victoria	Lester Patrick	Montreal	Leo Dandurand
1924	2-0	Montreal	Leo Dandurand	Cgy. Tigers	Eddie Oatman
1923	2-0	Ottawa	Pete Green	Edm. Eskimos	Ken McKenzie
1922	3-2	Tor. St. Pats	George O'Donoghue	Van. Millionaires	Lloyd Cook/Frank Patrick
1921	3-2	Ottawa	Pete Green	Van. Millionaires	Lloyd Cook/Frank Patrick
1920	3-2	Ottawa	Pete Green	Seattle	Pete Muldoon
1919	2-2-1	No decision - series between Montreal and Seattle cancelled due to influenza epidemic			
1918	3-2	Tor. Arenas	Dick Carroll	Van. Millionaires	Frank Patrick

Championship Trophies

PRINCE OF WALES TROPHY

Beginning with the 1993-94 season, the club which advances to the Stanley Cup Finals as the winner of the Eastern Conference Championship is presented with the Prince of Wales Trophy.

History: His Royal Highness, the Prince of Wales, donated the trophy to the National Hockey League in 1925. It was originally awarded to the winner of the first game played in Madison Square Garden, December 15, 1925 (Montreal Canadiens 3 at NY Americans 1). It was then awarded to the NHL playoff champion in 1925-26 and 1926-27. From 1927-28 through 1937-38, the award was presented to the regular-season champion of the American Division of the NHL. (The team finishing first in the Canadian Division received the O'Brien Trophy during these years.) From 1938-39, when the NHL reverted to one section, to 1966-67, it was presented to the team winning the NHL regular-season championship. With expansion in 1967-68, it again became a divisional trophy, awarded to the regular-season champions of the East Division through to the end of the 1973-74 season. Beginning in 1974-75, it was awarded to the regular-season winner of the conference bearing the name of the trophy. From 1981-82 to 1992-93 the trophy was presented to the playoff champion in the Wales Conference. Since 1993-94, the trophy has been presented to the playoff champion in the Eastern Conference.

2007-08 Winner: Pittsburgh Penguins

The Pittsburgh Penguins won the Prince of Wales Trophy on May 18, 2008 after defeating the Philadelphia Flyers 6-0 in game 5 of the Eastern Conference Finals. Before defeating the Flyers, the Penguins had series wins over the Ottawa Senators and New York Rangers.

PRINCE OF WALES TROPHY WINNERS

2007-08	Pittsburgh	1978-79	Montreal	1950-51	Detroit
2006-07	Ottawa	1977-78	Montreal	1949-50	Detroit
2005-06	Carolina	1976-77	Montreal	1948-49	Detroit
2003-04	Tampa Bay	1975-76	Montreal	1947-48	Toronto
2002-03	New Jersey	1974-75	Buffalo	1946-47	Montreal
2001-02	Carolina	1973-74	Boston	1945-46	Montreal
2000-01	New Jersey	1972-73	Montreal	1944-45	Montreal
99-2000	New Jersey	1971-72	Boston	1943-44	Montreal
1998-99	Buffalo	1970-71	Boston	1942-43	Detroit
1997-98	Washington	1969-70	Chicago	1941-42	NY Rangers
1996-97	Philadelphia	1968-69	Montreal	1940-41	Boston
1995-96	Florida	1967-68	Montreal	1939-40	Boston
1994-95	New Jersey	1966-67	Chicago	1938-39	Boston
1993-94	NY Rangers	1965-66	Montreal	1937-38	Boston
1992-93	Montreal	1964-65	Detroit	1936-37	Detroit
1991-92	Pittsburgh	1963-64	Montreal	1935-36	Detroit
1990-91	Pittsburgh	1962-63	Toronto	1934-35	Boston
1989-90	Boston	1961-62	Montreal	1933-34	Detroit
1988-89	Montreal	1960-61	Montreal	1932-33	Boston
1987-88	Boston	1959-60	Montreal	1931-32	NY Rangers
1986-87	Philadelphia	1958-59	Montreal	1930-31	Boston
1985-86	Montreal	1957-58	Montreal	1929-30	Boston
1984-85	Philadelphia	1956-57	Detroit	1928-29	Boston
1983-84	NY Islanders	1955-56	Montreal	1927-28	Boston
1982-83	NY Islanders	1954-55	Detroit	1926-27	Ottawa
1981-82	NY Islanders	1953-54	Detroit	1925-26	Mtl. Maroons
1980-81	Montreal	1952-53	Detroit	Dec. 15/25	Montreal
1979-80	Buffalo	1951-52	Detroit	1923-24	Montreal*

* Engraved by Montreal Canadiens in 1925-26.

CLARENCE S. CAMPBELL BOWL

Beginning with the 1993-94 season, the club which advances to the Stanley Cup Finals as the winner of the Western Conference Championship is presented with the Clarence S. Campbell Bowl.

History: Presented by the member clubs in 1968 for perpetual competition by the National Hockey League in recognition of the services of Clarence S. Campbell, President of the NHL from 1946 to 1977. From 1967-68 through 1973-74, the trophy was awarded to the regular-season champions of the West Division. Beginning in 1974-75, it was awarded to the regular-season winner of the conference bearing the name of the trophy. From 1981-82 to 1992-93 the trophy was presented to the playoff champion in the Campbell Conference. Since 1993-94, the trophy has been presented to the playoff champion in the Western Conference. The trophy itself is a hallmark piece made of sterling silver and was crafted by a British silversmith in 1878.

2007-08 Winner: Detroit Red Wings

The Detroit Red Wings won the Clarence Campbell Bowl on May 19, 2008 after defeating the Dallas Stars 4-1 in game 6 of the Western Conference Finals. Before defeating the Stars, the Red Wings had series wins over the Nashville Predators and Colorado Avalanche.

CLARENCE S. CAMPBELL BOWL WINNERS

2007-08	Detroit	1992-93	Los Angeles	1978-79	NY Islanders
2006-07	Anaheim	1991-92	Chicago	1977-78	NY Islanders
2005-06	Edmonton	1990-91	Minnesota	1976-77	Philadelphia
2003-04	Calgary	1989-90	Edmonton	1975-76	Philadelphia
2002-03	Anaheim	1988-89	Calgary	1974-75	Philadelphia
2001-02	Detroit	1987-88	Edmonton	1973-74	Philadelphia
2000-01	Colorado	1986-87	Edmonton	1972-73	Chicago
99-2000	Dallas	1985-86	Calgary	1971-72	Chicago
1998-99	Dallas	1984-85	Edmonton	1970-71	Chicago
1997-98	Detroit	1983-84	Edmonton	1969-70	St. Louis
1996-97	Detroit	1982-83	Edmonton	1968-69	St. Louis
1995-96	Colorado	1981-82	Vancouver	1967-68	Philadelphia
1994-95	Detroit	1980-81	NY Islanders		
1993-94	Vancouver	1979-80	Philadelphia		

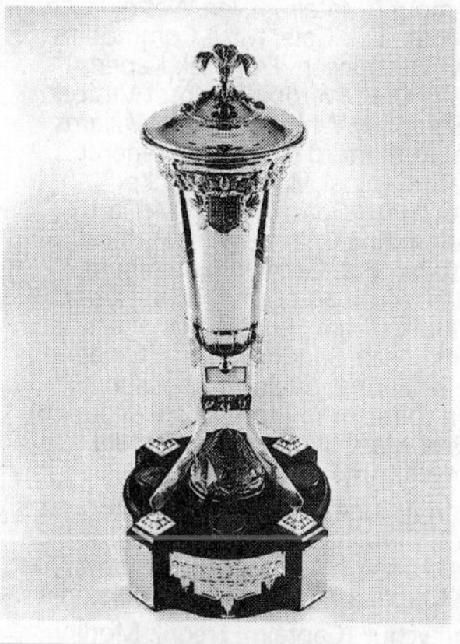

Prince of Wales Trophy

Clarence S. Campbell Bowl

Stanley Cup

Stanley Cup Winners

Rosters and Final Series Scores

2007-08 — Detroit Red Wings — Nicklas Lidstrom (Captain), Chris Chelios, Daniel Clearly, Pavel Datsyuk, Aaron Downey, Dallas Drake, Kris Draper, Valtteri Filppula, Johan Franzen, Dominik Hasek, Darren Helm, Tomas Holmstrom, Jiri Hudler, Tomas Kopecky, Niklas Kronwall, Brett Lebda, Andreas Lilja, Kirk Maltby, Darren McCarty, Derek Meech, Chris Osgood, Brian Rafalski, Mikael Samuelsson, Brad Stuart, Henrik Zetterberg, Michael Ilitch (Owner/Governor), Marian Ilitch (Owner/Secretary-Treasurer), Christopher Ilitch (Vice President/Alternate Governor), Denise Ilitch, Ronald Ilitch, Machael Ilitch Jr., Lisa Ilitch Murray, Atanas Ilitch, Carole Ilitch. Jim Devellano (Senior Vice President/Alternate Governor), Ken Holland (General Manager/Alternate Governor), Steve Yzerman (Vice President/Alternate Governor), Jim Nill (Assistant General Manager), Ryan Martin (Director, Hockey Operations), Scotty Bowman (Consultant), Mike Babcock (Head Coach), Todd McLellan (Associate Coach), Paul MacLean (Assistant Coach), Jim Bedard (Goaltending Consultant), Jay Woodcroft (Video Coordinator), Mark Howe (Director, Pro Scouting), Joe McDonnell (Director, Amateur Scouting), Hakan Andersson (Director, Amateur Scouting Europe), Piet Van Zant (Athletic Trainer), Paul Boyer (Equipment Manager), Russ Baumann, Christopher Scoppetto (Assistant Athletic Trainers).

Scores: May 24, at Detroit — Detroit 4, Pittsburgh 0; May 26, at Detroit — Detroit 3, Pittsburgh 0; May 28, at Pittsburgh — Pittsburgh 3, Detroit 2; May 31, at Pittsburgh — Detroit 2, Pittsburgh 1; June 2, at Detroit — Pittsburgh 4, Detroit 3; June 4, at Pittsburgh — Detroit 3, Pittsburgh 2.

2006-07 — Anaheim Ducks — Scott Niedermayer (Captain), Rob Niedermayer, Chris Pronger, Teemu Selanne, Sean O'Donnell, Brad May, Todd Marchant, Jean-Sebastien Giguere, Andy McDonald, Samuel Pahlsson, Shawn Thornton, Ric Jackman, Joe DiPenta, Kent Huskins, Chris Kunitz, George Parros, Joe Motzko, Ilya Bryzgalov, Francois Beauchemin, Travis Moen, Ryan Carter, Drew Miller, Ryan Shannon, Dustin Penner, Ryan Getzlaf, Corey Perry; Henry Samueli, Susan Samueli (Owners), Michael Schulman (CEO), Brian Burke (Executive Vice President/General Manager), Tim Ryan (Executive Vice President/COO), Bob Wagner (Senior Vice President/Chief Marketing Officer), Bob Murray (Senior Vice President-Hockey Operations), David McNab (Assistant General Manager), Al Coates (Senior Advisor to GM), Randy Carlyle (Head Coach), Dave Farrish, Newell Brown (Assistant Coaches), Francois Allaire (Goaltending Consultant), Sean Skahan (Strength and Conditioning Coach), Joe Trotta (Video Coordinator), Tim Clark (Head Trainer), Mark O'Neill (Equipment Manager), John Allaway (Assistant Equipment Manager), James Partida (Massage Therapist), Rick Paterson (Director of Professional Scouting), Alain Chainey (Director of Amateur Scouting).

Scores: May 28, at Anaheim - Anaheim 3, Ottawa 2; May 30, at Anaheim - Anaheim 1, Ottawa 0; June 2, at Ottawa - Ottawa 5, Anaheim 3; June 4, at Ottawa - Anaheim 3, Ottawa 2; June 6, at Anaheim - Anaheim 6, Ottawa 2.

2005-06 — Carolina Hurricanes — Rod Brind'Amour (Captain), Glen Wesley, Cory Stillman, Kevyn Adams, Craig Adams, Anton Babchuk, Erik Cole, Mike Commodore, Matt Cullen, Martin Gerber, Bret Hedican, Andrew Hutchinson, Frantisek Kaberle, Andrew Ladd, Chad LaRose, Mark Recchi, Eric Staal, Oleg Tverdovsky, Josef Vasicek, Niclas Wallin, Aaron Ward, Cam Ward, Doug Weight, Ray Whitney, Justin Williams; Peter Karmanos Jr., Thomas Thewes (Owners), Jim Rutherford (President/General Manager), Jason Karmanos (Vice President/Assistant General Manager), Mike Amendola (Chief Financial Officer), Peter Laviolette (Head Coach), Kevin McCarthy, Jeff Daniels (Assistant Coaches), Greg Stefan (Goaltending Coach), Chris Huffine (Video Coordinator), Skip Cunningham, Wally Tatomir, Bob Gorman (Equipment Managers), Peter Friesen (Head Athletic Therapist/Strength and Conditioning Coach), Chris Stewart (Associate Athletic Trainer), Brian Tatum (Team Services Manager), Kelly Kirwin (Event Coordinator-Hockey Operations), Mike Sundheim (Director of Media Relations), Kyle Hanlin (Manager of Media Relations), Sheldon Ferguson (Director of Amateur Scouting), Marshall Johnston (Director of Professional Scouting), Claude Larose, Ron Smith (Professional Scouts), Bert Marshall, Tony MacDonald, Martin Madden (Amateur Scouts), Tom Rowe (Lowell (AHL) - Coach).

Scores: June 5, at Carolina - Carolina 5, Edmonton 4; June 7, at Carolina - Carolina 5, Edmonton 0; June 10, at Edmonton - Edmonton 2, Carolina 1; June 12, at Edmonton - Carolina 2, Edmonton 1; June 14, at Carolina - Edmonton 4, Carolina 3; June 17, at Edmonton - Edmonton 4, Carolina 0; June 19, at Carolina - Carolina 3, Edmonton 1.

2003-04 — Tampa Bay Lightning — Dave Andreychuk (Captain), Fredrik Modin, Vincent Lecavalier, Martin St. Louis, Brad Richards, Nikolai Khabibulin, Pavel Kubina, Dan Boyle, Ruslan Fedotenko, Darryl Sydor, Cory Sarich, Tim Taylor, Cory Stillman, Jassen Cullimore, John Grahame, Chris Dingman, Nolan Pratt, Brad Lukowich, Andre Roy, Dmitry Afanasenkov, Martin Cibak, Ben Clymer, Darren Rumble, Stan Neckar, Eric Perrin; William Davidson (Owner), Tom Wilson (Governor), Ron Campbell (President), Jay Feaster (General Manager), John Tortorella (Head Coach), Craig Ramsay (Associate Coach), Jeff Reese (Assistant Coach), Nigel Kirwan (Video Coach), Eric Lawson (Strength and Conditioning Coach), Tom Mulligan (Trainer), Adam Rambo (Assistant Trainer), Ray Thill (Equipment Manager), Dana Heinze, Jim Pickard (Assistant Equipment Managers), Mike Griebel (Massage Therapist), Bill Barber (Director of Player Personnel), Jake Goertzen (Head Scout), Phil Thibodeau (Director of Team Services), Ryan Belec (Assistant to the GM), Rick Paterson (Chief Pro Scout), Kari Kettunen, Glen Zacharias, Steve Baker, Dave Heitz, Yuri Yanchenkov, (Scouts), Bill Wickett (Senior Vice President - Communications), Sean Henry (Executive Vice President/COO).

Scores: May 25, at Tampa Bay - Calgary 4, Tampa Bay 1; May 27, at Tampa Bay - Tampa Bay 4, Calgary 1; May 29, at Calgary - Calgary 3, Tampa Bay 0; May 31, at Calgary - Tampa Bay 1, Calgary 0; June 3, at Tampa Bay - Calgary 3, Tampa Bay 2; June 5, at Calgary - Tampa Bay 3, Calgary 2; June 7, at Tampa Bay - Tampa Bay 2, Calgary 1.

2002-03 — New Jersey Devils — Tommy Albelin, Jiri Bicek, Martin Brodeur, Sergei Brylin, Ken Daneyko, Patrik Elias, Jeff Friesen, Brian Gionta, Scott Gomez, Jamie Langenbrunner, John Madden, Grant Marshall, Jim McKenzie, Scott Niedermayer, Joe Nieuwendyk, Jay Pandolfo, Brian Rafalski, Pascal Rheaume, Mike Rupp, Corey Schwab, Richard Smehlik, Scott Stevens (Captain), Turner Stevenson, Oleg Tverdovsky, Colin White; Raymond Chambers, Lewis Catz (Owners), Peter Simon (Chairman), Lou Lamoriello (CEO/President/General Manager), Pat Burns (Head Coach), Bob Carpenter, John MacLean (Assistant Coaches), Jacques Caron (Goaltending Coach), Larry Robinson (Special Assignment Coach), David Conte (Director - Scouting), Claude Carrier (Assistant Director - Scouting), Chris Lamoriello (Scout/Albany (AHL) - General Manager), Milt Fisher, Dan Labraaten, Marcel Pronovost (Scouts), Bob Hoffmeyer, Jan Ludvig (Pro Scouts), Dr. Barry Fisher (Orthopedist), Chris Modrzynski (Executive Vice President), Terry Farmer (Vice President - Ticket Operations), Vladimir Bure (Fitness Consultant), Taran Singleton (Hockey Operations), Bill Murray (Medical Trainer), Michael Vasalani (Strength and Conditioning Coordinator), Rick Matthews (Equipment Manager), Juergen Merz (Massage Therapist), Alex Abasto (Assistant Equipment Manager).

Scores: May 27, at New Jersey - New Jersey 3, Anaheim 0; May 29, at New Jersey - New Jersey 3, Anaheim 0; May 31, at Anaheim - Anaheim 3, New Jersey 2; June 2, at Anaheim - Anaheim 1, New Jersey 0; June 5, at New Jersey - New Jersey 6, Anaheim 3; June 7, at Anaheim - Anaheim 5, New Jersey 2; June 9, at New Jersey - New Jersey 3, Anaheim 0.

2001-02 — Detroit Red Wings — Steve Yzerman (Captain), Dominik Hasek, Manny Legace, Chris Chelios, Mathieu Dandenault, Steve Duchesne, Jiri Fischer, Nicklas Lidstrom, Fredrik Olausson, Jiri Slegr, Pavel Datsyuk, Boyd Devereaux, Kris Draper, Sergei Fedorov, Tomas Holmstrom, Brett Hull, Igor Larionov, Kirk Maltby, Darren McCarty, Luc Robitaille, Brendan Shanahan, Jason Williams; Michael Ilitch (Owner/Governor), Marian Ilitch (Owner/Secretary Treasurer), Christoper Ilitch (Vice President), Denise Ilitch (Alternate Governor), Ronald Ilitch, Michael Ilitch Jr., Lisa Ilitch Murray, Atanas Ilitch, Carole Ilitch, Jim Devellano (Senior Vice President), Ken Holland (General Manager), Jim Nill (Assistant General Manager), Scotty Bowman (Head Coach), Dave Lewis, Barry Smith (Associate Coaches), Jim Bedard (Goaltending Consultant), Joe Kocur (Video Coordinator), John Wharton (Athletic Trainer), Piet Van Zant (Assistant Athletic Trainer), Paul Boyer (Equipment Manager), Paul MacDonald (Senior Director of Finance), Nancy Beard (Executive Assistant), Dan Belisle, Mark Howe, Bob McCammon (Pro Scouts), Hakan Andersson (Director of European Scouting), Bruce Haralson, Mark Leach, Joe McDonnell, Glenn Merkosky (Scouts).

Scores: June 4, at Detroit - Carolina 3, Detroit 2; June 6, at Detroit - Detroit 3, Carolina 1; June 8, at Carolina - Detroit 3, Carolina 2; June 10, at Carolina - Detroit 3, Carolina 0; June 13, at Detroit - Detroit 3, Carolina 1.

2000-01 — Colorado Avalanche — David Aebischer, Rob Blake, Raymond Bourque, Greg de Vries, Chris Dingman, Chris Drury, Adam Foote, Peter Forsberg, Milan Hejduk, Dan Hinote, Jon Klemm, Eric Messier, Bryan Muir, Ville Nieminen, Scott Parker, Shjon Podein, Nolan Pratt, Dave Reid, Steve Reinprecht, Patrick Roy, Joe Sakic (Captain), Martin Skoula, Alex Tanguay, Stephane Yelle; E. Stanley Kroenke (Owner/Governor), Pierre Lacroix (President/ General Manager), Bob Hartley (Head Coach), Jacques Cloutier, Bryan Trottier (Assistant Coaches), Paul Fixter (Video Coach), Francois Giguere (Vice President - Hockey Operations), Brian MacDonald (Assistant General Manager), Michel Goulet (Vice President - Player Personnel), Jean Martineau (Vice President - Communications and Team Services), Pat Karns (Head Athletic Trainer), Matthew Sokolowski (Assistant Athletic Trainer), Wayne Flemming, Mark Miller (Equipment Managers), Dave Randolph (Assistant Equipment Manager), Paul Goldberg (Strength and Conditioning Coach), Gregorio Pradera (Massage Therapist), Brad Smith (Pro Scout), Jim Hammett (Chief Scout), Garth Joy, Steve Lyons, Joni Lehto, Orval Tessier (Scouts), Charlotte Grahame (Director of Hockey Administration).

Scores: May 26, at Colorado - Colorado 5, New Jersey 0; May 29, at Colorado - New Jersey 2, Colorado 1; May 31, at New Jersey - Colorado 3, New Jersey 1; June 2, at New Jersey - New Jersey 3, Colorado 2; June 4, at Colorado - New Jersey 4, Colorado 1; June 7, at New Jersey - Colorado 4, New Jersey 0; June 9, at Colorado - Colorado 3, New Jersey 1.

1999-2000 — New Jersey Devils — Jason Arnott, Brad Bombardir, Martin Brodeur, Steve Brule, Sergei Brylin, Ken Daneyko, Patrik Elias, Scott Gomez, Bobby Holik, Steve Kelly, Claude Lemieux, John Madden, Vladimir Malakhov, Randy McKay, Alexander Mogilny, Sergei Nemchinov, Scott Niedermayer, Krzysztof Oliwa, Jay Pandolfo, Brian Rafalski, Ken Sutton, Scott Stevens (Captain), Petr Sykora, Chris Terreri, Colin White; Dr. John J. McMullen (Owner/Chairman), Peter S. McMullen (Owner), Lou Lamoriello (President/General Manager), Larry Robinson (Head Coach), Viacheslav Fetisov (Assistant Coach), Jacques Caron (Goaltending Coach), Bob Carpenter (Assistant Coach), John Cuniff (Albany (AHL) - Coach), David Conte (Director of Scouting), Claude Carrier (Assistant Director of Scouting), Milt Fisher, Dan Labraaten, Marcel Pronovost (Scouts), Bob Hoffmeyer (Pro Scout), Dr. Barry Fisher (Orthopedist), Dennis Gendron (Albany (AHL) - Assistant Coach), Robbie Ftorek (Coach), Vladimir Bure (Consultant), Taran Singleton, Marie Carnevale, Callie Smith (Hockey Operations), Bill Murray (Medical Trainer), Michael Vasalani (Strength and Conditioning Coordinator), Dana McGuane (Equipment Manager), Juergen Merz (Massage Therapist), Harry Bricker, Lou Centanni Jr. (Assistant Equipment Managers).

Scores: May 30, at New Jersey - New Jersey 7, Dallas 3; June 1, at New Jersey - Dallas 2, New Jersey 1; June 3, at Dallas - New Jersey 2, Dallas 1; June 5, at Dallas - New Jersey 3, Dallas 1; June 8, at New Jersey - Dallas 1 - New Jersey 0; June 10, at Dallas, New Jersey 2 - Dallas 1.

1998-99 — Dallas Stars — Derian Hatcher (Captain), Mike Modano, Joe Nieuwendyk, Craig Ludwig, Sergei Zubov, Ed Belfour, Guy Carbonneau, Shawn Chambers, Benoit Hogue, Tony Hrkac, Brett Hull, Mike Keane, Jamie Langenbrunner, Jere Lehtinen, Grant Marshall, Richard Matvichuk, Derek Plante, Dave Reid, Brent Severyn, Jon Sim, Brian Skrudland, Blake Sloan, Darryl Sydor, Roman Turek, Pat Verbeek; Thomas Hicks (Chairman/Owner), Jim Lites (President), Bob Gainey (Vice President - Hockey Operations/General Manager), Doug Armstrong (Assistant General Manager), Craig Button (Director of Player Personnel), Ken Hitchcock (Head Coach), Doug Jarvis, Rick Wilson (Assistant Coaches), Rick McLaughlin (Vice President/Chief Financial Officer), Jeff Cogen (Vice President - Marketing and Promotion), Bill Strong (Vice President - Marketing and Broadcasting), Tim Bernhardt (Director of Amateur Scouting), Doug Overton (Director of Pro Scouting), Bob Gernander (Chief Scout), Stu MacGregor (Western Scout), Dave Suprenant (Medical Trainer), Dave Smith, Rich Matthews (Equipment Managers), J.J. McQueen (Strength and Conditioning Coach), Rick St. Croix (Goaltending Consultant), Dan Stuchal (Director of Team Services), Larry Kelly (Director of Public Relations).

Scores: June 8, at Dallas - Buffalo 3, Dallas 2; June 10, at Dallas - Dallas 4, Buffalo 2; June 12, at Buffalo - Dallas 2, Buffalo 1; June 15, at Buffalo - Buffalo 2, Dallas 1; June 17, at Dallas - Dallas 2, Buffalo 0; June 19, at Buffalo - Dallas 2, Buffalo 1.

1997-98 — Detroit Red Wings — Steve Yzerman (Captain), Doug Brown, Mathieu Dandenault, Kris Draper, Anders Eriksson, Sergei Fedorov, Viacheslav Fetisov, Brent Gilchrist, Kevin Hodson, Tomas Holmstrom, Mike Knuble, Joe Kocur, Vladimir Konstantinov, Vyacheslav Kozlov, Martin Lapointe, Igor Larionov, Nicklas Lidstrom, Jamie Macoun, Kirk Maltby, Darren McCarty, Dmitri Mironov, Larry Murphy, Chris Osgood, Bob Rouse, Brendan Shanahan, Aaron Ward; Mike Ilitch, (Owner/Chairman), Marian Ilitch (Owner), Atanas Ilitch, Christopher Ilitch (Vice Presidents), Denise Ilitch, Ronald Ilitch, Michael Ilitch Jr., Lisa Ilitch Murray, Carole Ilitch Trepeck, Jim Devellano (Senior Vice President), Ken Holland (General Manager), Don Waddell (Assistant General Manager), Scotty Bowman (Head Coach), Barry Smith, Dave Lewis (Associate Coaches), Jim Nill (Director of Player Development), Dan Belisle, Mark Howe (Pro Scouts), Jim Bedard (Goaltending Consultant), Hakan Andersson (Director of European Scouting), Mark Leach (USA Scout), Joe McDonnell (Eastern Scout), Bruce Haralson (Western Scout), John Wharton (Athletic Trainer), Paul Boyer (Equipment Manager), Tim Abbott (Assistant Equipment Manager), Bob Huddleston (Masseur), Sergei Mnatsakanov, Wally Crossman (Dressing Room Assistant).

Scores: June 9, at Detroit — Detroit 2, Washington 1; June 11, at Detroit — Detroit 5, Washington 4; June 13, at Washington — Detroit 2, Washington 1; June 16, at Washington — Detroit 4, Washington 1.

1996-97 — Detroit Red Wings — Steve Yzerman (Captain), Doug Brown, Mathieu Dandenault, Kris Draper, Sergei Fedorov, Viacheslav Fetisov, Kevin Hodson, Tomas Holmstrom, Joe Kocur, Vladimir Konstantinov, Vyacheslav Kozlov, Martin Lapointe, Igor Larionov, Nicklas Lidstrom, Kirk Maltby, Darren McCarty, Larry Murphy, Chris Osgood, Jamie Pushor, Bob Rouse, Tomas Sandstrom, Brendan Shanahan, Tim Taylor, Mike Vernon, Aaron Ward; Mike Ilitch (Owner/Chairman), Marian Ilitch (Owner), Atanas Ilitch, Christopher Ilitch (Vice Presidents), Denise Ilitch Lites, Ronald Ilitch, Michael Ilitch Jr., Lisa Ilitch Murray, Carole Ilitch Trepeck, Jim Devellano (Senior Vice President), Scotty Bowman (Head Coach/Director of Player Personnel), Ken Holland (Assistant General Manager), Barry Smith, Dave Lewis (Associate Coaches), Mike Krushelnyski (Assistant Coach), Jim Nill (Director of Player Development), Dan Belisle, Bruce Haralson, Mark Howe (Scouts), Hakan Andersson (Director of European Scouting), John Wharton (Athletic Trainer), Wally Crossman (Dressing Room Assistant), Mark Leach (Scout), Paul Boyer (Equipment Manager), Tim Abbott (Assistant Equipment Manager), Sergei Mnatsakanov (Masseur), Joe McDonnell (Scout).

Scores: May 31, at Philadelphia — Detroit 4, Philadelphia 2; June 3, at Philadelphia — Detroit 4, Philadelphia 2; June 5, at Detroit — Detroit 6, Philadelphia 1; June 7, at Detroit — Detroit 2, Philadelphia 1.

1995-96 — Colorado Avalanche — Rene Corbet, Adam Deadmarsh, Stephane Fiset, Adam Foote, Peter Forsberg, Alexei Gusarov, Dave Hannan, Valeri Kamensky, Mike Keane, Jon Klemm, Uwe Krupp, Sylvain Lefebvre, Claude Lemieux, Curtis Leschyshyn, Troy Murray, Sandis Ozolinsh, Mike Ricci, Patrick Roy, Warren Rychel, Joe Sakic (Captain), Chris Simon, Craig Wolanin, Stephane Yelle, Scott Young; Charlie Lyons (Chairman/CEO), Pierre Lacroix (Executive Vice President/General Manager), Marc Crawford (Head Coach), Joel Quenneville, Jacques Cloutier (Assistant Coaches), Francois Giguere (Assistant General Manager), Michel Goulet (Director of Player Personnel), Dave Draper (Chief Scout), Jean Martineau (Director of Public Relations), Pat Karns (Trainer), Matthew Sokolowski (Assistant Trainer), Rob McLean (Equipment Manager), Mike Kramer, Brock Gibbins (Assistant Equipment Managers), Skip Allen (Strength and Conditioning Coach), Paul Fixter (Video Coordinator), Leo Vyssokov (Massage Therapist).

Scores: June 4, at Colorado — Colorado 3, Florida 1; June 6, at Colorado — Colorado 8, Florida 1; June 8, at Florida — Colorado 3, Florida 2; June 10, at Florida — Colorado 1, Florida 0.

1994-95 — New Jersey Devils — Tommy Albelin, Martin Brodeur, Neal Broten, Sergei Brylin, Bob Carpenter, Shawn Chambers, Tom Chorske, Danton Cole, Ken Daneyko, Kevin Dean, Jim Dowd, Bruce Driver, Bill Guerin, Bobby Holik, Claude Lemieux, John MacLean, Chris McAlpine, Randy McKay, Scott Niedermayer, Mike Peluso, Stephane Richer, Brian Rolston, Scott Stevens (Captain), Chris Terreri, Valeri Zelepukin; Dr. John J. McMullen (Owner/Chairman), Peter S. McMullen (Owner), Lou Lamoriello (President/General Manager), Jacques Lemaire (Head Coach), Jacques Caron (Goaltender Coach), Dennis Gendron, Larry Robinson (Assistant Coaches), Robbie Ftorek (Albany (AHL) - Coach), Alex Abasto (Assistant Equipment Manager), Bob Huddleston (Massage Therapist), David Nichols (Equipment Manager), Ted Schuch (Medical Trainer), Michael Vasalani (Strength and Conditioning Coach), David Conte (Director of Scouting), Milt Fisher, Claude Carrier, Dan Labraaten, Marcel Pronovost (Scouts).
Scores: June 17, at Detroit — New Jersey 2, Detroit 1; June 20, at Detroit — New Jersey 4, Detroit 2; June 22, at New Jersey — New Jersey 5, Detroit 2; June 24, at New Jersey — New Jersey 5, Detroit 2.

1993-94 — New York Rangers — Mark Messier (Captain), Brian Leetch, Kevin Lowe, Adam Graves, Steve Larmer, Glenn Anderson, Jeff Beukeboom, Greg Gilbert, Glenn Healy, Mike Hudson, Alexander Karpovtsev, Joe Kocur, Alex Kovalev, Nick Kypreos, Doug Lidster, Stephane Matteau, Craig MacTavish, Sergei Nemchinov, Brian Noonan, Esa Tikkanen, Mike Richter, Jay Wells, Sergei Zubov, Ed Olczyk, Mike Hartman; Neil Smith (President/General Manager/Governor), Robert Gutkowski, Stanley Jaffe, Kenneth Munoz (Governors), Larry Pleau (Assistant General Manager), Mike Keenan (Head Coach), Colin Campbell (Associate Coach), Dick Todd (Assistant Coach), Matthew Loughren (Manager - Team Operations), Barry Watkins (Director - Communications), Christer Rockstrom, Tony Feltrin, Martin Madden, Herb Hammond, Darwin Bennett (Scouts), Dave Smith, Joe Murphy, Mike Folga, Bruce Lifrieri (Trainers).
Scores: May 31, at New York — Vancouver 3, NY Rangers 2; June 2, at New York — NY Rangers 3, Vancouver 1; June 4, at Vancouver — NY Rangers 5, Vancouver 1; June 7, at Vancouver — NY Rangers 4, Vancouver 2; June 9, at New York — Vancouver 6, at NY Rangers 3; June 11, at Vancouver — Vancouver 4, NY Rangers 1; June 14, at New York — NY Rangers 3, Vancouver 2.

1992-93 — Montreal Canadiens — Guy Carbonneau (Captain), Patrick Roy, Andre Racicot, Rob Ramage, Kirk Muller, Mike Keane, Kevin Haller, Paul DiPietro, John LeClair, Denis Savard, Benoit Brunet, Brian Bellows, Lyle Odelein, Vincent Damphousse, Gary Leeman, Mathieu Schneider, Eric Desjardins, Jesse Belanger, Ed Ronan, Mario Roberge, Donald Dufresne, Todd Ewen, Sean Hill, Patrice Brisebois, Gilbert Dionne, Stephan Lebeau, J.J. Daigneault; Ronald Corey (President), Serge Savard (Managing Director/Vice President - Hockey), Jacques Demers (Head Coach), Jacques Laperriere, Charles Thiffault (Assistant Coaches), Francois Allaire (Goaltending Instructor), Jean Béliveau (Senior Vice President - Corporate Affairs), Jacques Lemaire (Assistant to the Managing Director), André Boudrias (Assistant to the Managing Director/Director of Scouting), Gaeten Lefebvre (Athletic Trainer), John Shipman (Assistant to the Athletic Trainer), Eddy Palchak (Equipment Manager), Pierre Gervais, Robert Boulanger (Assistants to the Equipment Manager).
Scores: June 1, at Montreal — Los Angeles 4, Montreal 1; June 2, at Montreal — Montreal 3, Los Angeles 2; June 5, at Los Angeles — Montreal 4, Los Angeles 3; June 7, at Los Angeles — Montreal 3, Los Angeles 2; June 9, at Montreal — Montreal 4, Los Angeles 1.

1991-92 — Pittsburgh Penguins — Mario Lemieux (Captain), Ron Francis, Bryan Trottier, Kevin Stevens, Bob Errey, Phil Bourque, Troy Loney, Rick Tocchet, Joe Mullen, Jaromir Jagr, Jiri Hrdina, Shawn McEachern, Ulf Samuelsson, Kjell Samuelsson, Larry Murphy, Gordie Roberts, Jim Paek, Paul Stanton, Tom Barrasso, Ken Wregget, Jay Caufield, Jamie Leach, Wendell Young, Grant Jennings, Peter Taglianetti, Jock Callander, Dave Michayluk, Mike Needham, Jeff Chychrun, Ken Priestlay, Jeff Daniels; Morris Belzberg, Howard Baldwin, Thomas Ruta (Owners), Donn Patton (Executive Vice President/Chief Financial Officer), Paul Martha (Executive Vice President/General Counsel), Craig Patrick (Executive Vice President/General Manager), Bob Johnson (Head Coach), Scotty Bowman (Director of Player Development/Coach), Barry Smith, Rick Kehoe, Pierre McGuire, Gilles Meloche, Rick Paterson (Assistant Coaches), Steve Latin (Equipment Manager), Skip Thayer (Trainer), John Welday (Strength and Conditioning Coach), Greg Malone, Les Binkley, Charlie Hodge, John Gill, Ralph Cox (Scouts).
Scores: May 26, at Pittsburgh — Pittsburgh 5, Chicago 4; May 28, at Pittsburgh — Pittsburgh 3, Chicago 1; May 30, at Chicago — Pittsburgh 1, Chicago 0; June 1, at Chicago — Pittsburgh 6, Chicago 5.

1990-91 — Pittsburgh Penguins — Mario Lemieux (Captain), Paul Coffey, Randy Hillier, Bob Errey, Tom Barrasso, Phil Bourque, Jay Caufield, Ron Francis, Randy Gilhen, Jiri Hrdina, Jaromir Jagr, Grant Jennings, Troy Loney, Joe Mullen, Larry Murphy, Jim Paek, Frank Pietrangelo, Barry Pederson, Mark Recchi, Gordie Roberts, Ulf Samuelsson, Paul Stanton, Kevin Stevens, Peter Taglianetti, Bryan Trottier, Scott Young, Wendell Young; Edward J. DeBartolo Sr. (Owner), Marie D. DeBartolo York (President), Paul Martha (Vice President/General Counsel), Craig Patrick (General Manager), Scotty Bowman (Director of Player Development and Recruitment), Bob Johnson (Head Coach), Rick Kehoe, Rick Paterson, Barry Smith (Assistant Coaches), Gilles Meloche (Goaltending Coach/Scout), Steve Latin (Equipment Manager), Skip Thayer (Trainer), John Welday (Strength and Conditioning Coach), Greg Malone (Scout).
Scores: May 15, at Pittsburgh — Minnesota 5, Pittsburgh 4; May 17, at Pittsburgh — Pittsburgh 4, Minnesota 1; May 19, at Minnesota — Minnesota 3, Pittsburgh 1; May 21, at Minnesota — Pittsburgh 5, Minnesota 3; May 23, at Pittsburgh — Pittsburgh 6, Minnesota 4; May 25, at Minnesota — Pittsburgh 8, Minnesota 0.

1989-90 — Edmonton Oilers — Mark Messier (Captain), Jari Kurri, Kevin Lowe, Steve Smith, Jeff Beukeboom, Mark Lamb, Joe Murphy, Glenn Anderson, Adam Graves, Craig MacTavish, Kelly Buchberger, Craig Simpson, Martin Gelinas, Randy Gregg, Charlie Huddy, Geoff Smith, Reijo Ruotsalainen, Craig Muni, Bill Ranford, Dave Brown, Pokey Reddick, Petr Klima, Esa Tikkanen, Grant Fuhr; Peter Pocklington (Owner), Glen Sather (President/General Manager), John Muckler (Head Coach), Ted Green (Co-Coach), Ron Low (Assistant Coach), Bruce MacGregor (Assistant General Manager), Barry Fraser (Director of Player Personnel), Bill Tuele (Director of Public Relations), Werner Baum (Vice President), Dr. Gordon Cameron (Medical Chief of Staff), Dr. David Reid (Team Physician), Ken Lowe (Athletic Therapist), Barrie Stafford (Athletic Trainer), Stuart Poirier (Massage Therapist), Lyle Kulchisky (Assistant Trainer), John Blackwell (Cape Breton (AHL) - Director of Operations), Ace Bailey, Ed Chadwick, Lorne Davis, Harry Howell, Albert Reeves, Matti Vaisanen (Scouts).
Scores: May 15, at Boston — Edmonton 3, Boston 2; May 18, at Boston — Edmonton 7, Boston 2; May 20, at Edmonton — Boston 2, Edmonton 1; May 22, at Edmonton — Edmonton 5, Boston 1; May 24, at Boston — Edmonton 4, Boston 1.

1988-89 — Calgary Flames — Lanny McDonald (Co- Captain), Jim Peplinski (Co-Captain), Tim Hunter, Mike Vernon, Rick Wamsley, Al MacInnis, Brad McCrimmon, Dana Murzyn, Ric Nattress, Joe Mullen, Gary Roberts, Colin Patterson, Hakan Loob, Theoren Fleury, Jiri Hrdina, Gary Suter, Mark Hunter, Joe Nieuwendyk, Brian MacLellan, Joel Otto, Jamie Macoun, Doug Gilmour, Rob Ramage; Norman Green, Harley Hotchkiss, Norman Kwong, Sonia Scurfield, B.J. Seaman, D.K. Seaman (Owners), Cliff Fletcher (President/General Manager), Al MacNeil (Assistant General Manager), Al Coates (Assistant to the President), Terry Crisp (Head Coach), Doug Risebrough, Tom Watt (Assistant Coaches), Glenn Hall (Goaltending Consultant), Jim Murray (Trainer), Al Murray (Assistant Trainer), Bob Stewart (Equipment Manager).
Scores: May 14, at Calgary — Calgary 3, Montreal 2; May 17, at Calgary— Montreal 4, Calgary 2; May 19, at Montreal — Montreal 4, Calgary 3; May 21, at Montreal — Calgary 4, Montreal 2; May 23, at Calgary — Calgary 3, Montreal 2; May 25, at Montreal — Calgary 4, Montreal 2.

1987-88 — Edmonton Oilers — Wayne Gretzky (Captain), Keith Acton, Glenn Anderson, Jeff Beukeboom, Geoff Courtnall, Grant Fuhr, Randy Gregg, Dave Hannan, Charlie Huddy, Mike Krushelnyski, Jari Kurri, Normand Lacombe, Kevin Lowe, Craig MacTavish, Kevin McClelland, Marty McSorley, Mark Messier, Craig Muni, Bill Ranford, Craig Simpson, Steve Smith, Esa Tikkanen; Peter Pocklington (Owner), Glen Sather (General Manager/Coach), John Muckler (Co-Coach), Ted Green (Assistant Coach), Bruce MacGregor (Assistant General Manager), Barry Fraser (Director of Player Personnel), Bill Tuele (Director of Public Relations), Dr. Gordon Cameron (Team Doctor), Peter Millar (Athletic Therapist), Juergen Merz (Massage Therapist), Barrie Stafford (Trainer), Lyle Kulchisky (Assistant Trainer).
Scores: May 18, at Edmonton — Edmonton 2, Boston 1; May 20, at Edmonton — Edmonton 4, Boston 2; May 22, at Boston — Edmonton 6, Boston 3; May 24, at Boston — Boston 3, Edmonton 3 (suspended due to power failure); May 26, at Edmonton — Edmonton 6, Boston 3.

1986-87 — Edmonton Oilers — Wayne Gretzky (Captain), Glenn Anderson, Jeff Beukeboom, Kelly Buchberger, Paul Coffey, Grant Fuhr, Randy Gregg, Charlie Huddy, Dave Hunter, Mike Krushelnyski, Jari Kurri, Moe Lemay, Kevin Lowe, Craig MacTavish, Kevin McClelland, Marty McSorley, Mark Messier, Andy Moog, Craig Muni, Kent Nilsson, Jaroslav Pouzar, Reijo Ruotsalainen, Steve Smith, Esa Tikkanen; Peter Pocklington (Owner), Glen Sather (General Manager/Coach), Bruce MacGregor (Assistant General Manager), John Muckler (Co-Coach), Ted Green, Ron Low (Assistant Coaches), Barry Fraser (Director of Player Personnel), Garnet Bailey, Ed Chadwick, Lorne Davis, Matti Vaisanen (Scouts), Peter Millar (Athletic Therapist), Juergen Merz (Massage Therapist), Dr. Gordon Cameron (Team Doctor), Barrie Stafford (Trainer), Lyle Kulchisky (Assistant Trainer).
Scores: May 17, at Edmonton — Edmonton 4, Philadelphia 2; May 20, at Edmonton — Edmonton 3, Philadelphia 2; May 22, at Philadelphia — Philadelphia 5, Edmonton 3; May 24, at Philadelphia — Edmonton 4, Philadelphia 1; May 26, at Edmonton — Philadelphia 4, Edmonton 3; May 28, at Philadelphia — Philadelphia 3, Edmonton 2; May 31, at Edmonton — Edmonton 3, Philadelphia 1.

1985-86 — Montreal Canadiens — Bob Gainey (Captain), Doug Soetaert, Patrick Roy, Rick Green, David Maley, Ryan Walter, Serge Boisvert, Mario Tremblay, Bobby Smith, Craig Ludwig, Tom Kurvers, Kjell Dahlin, Larry Robinson, Guy Carbonneau, Chris Chelios, Petr Svoboda, Mats Naslund, Lucien DeBlois, Steve Rooney, Gaston Gingras, Mike Lalor, Chris Nilan, John Kordic, Claude Lemieux, Mike McPhee, Brian Skrudland, Stephane Richer; Ronald Corey (President), Serge Savard (General Manager), Jean Perron (Coach), Jacques Laperrière (Assistant Coach), Jean Béliveau, Francois-Xavier Seigneur, Fred Steer (Vice Presidents), Jacques Lemaire, André Boudrias (Assistant General Managers), Claude Ruel (Player Development), Yves Belanger (Athletic Therapist), Gaetan Lefebvre (Assistant Athletic Therapist), Eddy Palchak (Trainer), Sylvain Toupin (Assistant Trainer).
Scores: May 16, at Calgary — Calgary 5, Montreal 2; May 18, at Calgary — Montreal 3, Calgary 2; May 20, at Montreal — Montreal 5, Calgary 3; May 22, at Montreal — Montreal 1, Calgary 0; May 24, at Calgary — Montreal 4, Calgary 3.

1984-85 — Edmonton Oilers — Wayne Gretzky (Captain), Glenn Anderson, Billy Carroll, Paul Coffey, Lee Fogolin Jr., Grant Fuhr, Randy Gregg, Charlie Huddy, Pat Hughes, Dave Hunter, Don Jackson, Mike Krushelnyski, Jari Kurri, Willy Lindstrom, Kevin Lowe, Dave Lumley, Kevin McClelland, Larry Melnyk, Mark Messier, Andy Moog, Mark Napier, Jaroslav Pouzar, Dave Semenko, Esa Tikkanen; Peter Pocklington (Owner), Glen Sather (General Manager/Coach), Bruce MacGregor (Assistant General Manager), John Muckler, Ted Green (Assistant Coaches), Barry Fraser (Director of Player Personnel/Chief Scout), Garnet Bailey, Ed Chadwick, Lorne Davis, Matti Vaisanen (Scouts), Peter Millar (Athletic Therapist), Dr. Gordon Cameron (Team Doctor), Barrie Stafford (Trainer), Lyle Kulchisky (Assistant Trainer).
Scores: May 21, at Philadelphia — Philadelphia 4, Edmonton 1; May 23, at Philadelphia — Edmonton 3, Philadelphia 1; May 25, at Edmonton — Edmonton 4, Philadelphia 3; May 28, at Edmonton — Edmonton 5, Philadelphia 3; May 30, at Edmonton — Edmonton 8, Philadelphia 3.

1983-84 — Edmonton Oilers — Wayne Gretzky (Captain), Glenn Anderson, Paul Coffey, Pat Conacher, Lee Fogolin Jr., Grant Fuhr, Randy Gregg, Charlie Huddy, Pat Hughes, Dave Hunter, Don Jackson, Jari Kurri, Willy Lindstrom, Ken Linseman, Kevin Lowe, Dave Lumley, Kevin McClelland, Mark Messier, Andy Moog, Jaroslav Pouzar, Dave Semenko; Peter Pocklington (Owner), Glen Sather (General Manager/Coach), Bruce MacGregor (Assistant General Manager), John Muckler, Ted Green (Assistant Coaches), Barry Fraser (Director of Player Personnel/Chief Scout), Pete Millar (Athletic Therapist), Barrie Stafford (Trainer), Lyle Kulchisky (Assistant Trainer).
Scores: May 10, at New York — Edmonton 1, NY Islanders 0; May 12, at New York — NY Islanders 6, Edmonton 1; May 15, at Edmonton — Edmonton 7, NY Islanders 2; May 17, at Edmonton — Edmonton 7, NY Islanders 2; May 19, at Edmonton — Edmonton 5, NY Islanders 2.

1982-83 — New York Islanders — Denis Potvin (Captain), Mike Bossy, Bob Bourne, Paul Boutilier, Billy Carroll, Greg Gilbert, Clark Gillies, Butch Goring, Mats Hallin, Tomas Jonsson, Anders Kallur, Gord Lane, Dave Langevin, Mike McEwen, Roland Melanson, Wayne Merrick, Ken Morrow, Bob Nystrom, Stefan Persson, Billy Smith, Brent Sutter, Duane Sutter, John Tonelli, Bryan Trottier; Bill Torrey (President/General Manager), John Pickett Jr. (Chairman), Gerry Ehman (Assistant General Manager/Director of Scouting), Al Arbour (Coach), Lorne Henning (Assistant Coach), Ron Waske (Trainer), Jim Pickard (Assistant Trainer).
Scores: May 10, at Edmonton — NY Islanders 2, Edmonton 0; May 12, at Edmonton — NY Islanders 6, Edmonton 3; May 14, at New York — NY Islanders 5, Edmonton 1; May 17, at New York — NY Islanders 4, Edmonton 2

1981-82 — New York Islanders — Denis Potvin (Captain), Mike Bossy, Bob Bourne, Billy Carroll, Greg Gilbert, Clark Gillies, Butch Goring, Tomas Jonsson, Anders Kallur, Gord Lane, Dave Langevin, Hector Marini, Mike McEwen, Roland Melanson, Wayne Merrick, Ken Morrow, Bob Nystrom, Stefan Persson, Billy Smith, Brent Sutter, Duane Sutter, John Tonelli, Bryan Trottier; Bill Torrey (President/General Manager), John Pickett Jr. (Chairman), Jim Devellano (Assistant General Manager/Director of Scouting), Al Arbour (Coach), Lorne Henning (Assistant Coach), Gerry Ehman (Head Scout), Ron Waske (Trainer), Jim Pickard (Assistant Trainer).
Scores: May 8, at New York — NY Islanders 6, Vancouver 5; May 11, at New York — NY Islanders 6, Vancouver 4; May 13, at Vancouver — NY Islanders 3, Vancouver 0; May 16, at Vancouver — NY Islanders 3, Vancouver 1

1980-81 — New York Islanders — Denis Potvin (Captain), Mike Bossy, Bob Bourne, Billy Carroll, Clark Gillies, Butch Goring, Garry Howatt, Anders Kallur, Gord Lane, Dave Langevin, Bob Lorimer, Hector Marini, Mike McEwen, Roland Melanson, Wayne Merrick, Ken Morrow, Bob Nystrom, Stefan Persson, Jean Potvin, Billy Smith, Duane Sutter, John Tonelli, Bryan Trottier; Bill Torrey (President/General Manager), John Pickett Jr. (Chairman), Al Arbour (Coach), Lorne Henning (Player/Assistant Coach), Jim Devellano (Chief Scout), Gerry Ehman, Mario Saraceno, Harry Boyd (Scouts), Ron Waske (Trainer), Jim Pickard (Assistant Trainer).
Scores: May 12, at New York — NY Islanders 6, Minnesota 3; May 14, at New York — NY Islanders 6, Minnesota 3; May 17, at Minnesota — NY Islanders 7, Minnesota 5; May 19, at Minnesota— Minnesota 4, NY Islanders 2; May 21, at New York — NY Islanders 5, Minnesota 1.

1979-80 — New York Islanders — Denis Potvin (Captain), Mike Bossy, Bob Bourne, Clark Gillies, Butch Goring, Lorne Henning, Garry Howatt, Anders Kallur, Gord Lane, Dave Langevin, Bob Lorimer, Alex McKendry, Wayne Merrick, Ken Morrow, Bob Nystrom, Stefan Persson, Jean Potvin, Glenn Resch, Billy Smith, Duane Sutter, Steve Tambellini, John Tonelli, Bryan Trottier; Bill Torrey (President/General Manager), John Pickett Jr. (Chairman), Al Arbour (Coach), Billy MacMillan (Assistant Coach), Jim Devellano (Chief Scout), Gerry Ehman, Mario Saraceno, Harry Boyd (Scouts), Ron Waske (Trainer), Jim Pickard (Assistant Trainer).
Scores: May 13, at Philadelphia — NY Islanders 4, Philadelphia 3; May 15, at Philadelphia — Philadelphia 8, NY Islanders 3; May 17, at New York — NY Islanders 6, Philadelphia 2; May 19, at New York — NY Islanders 5, Philadelphia 2; May 22, at Philadelphia — Philadelphia 6, NY Islanders 3; May 24, at New York — NY Islanders 5, Philadelphia 4.

1978-79 — Montreal Canadiens — Yvan Cournoyer (Captain), Guy Lafleur, Ken Dryden, Rick Chartraw, Brian Engblom, Bob Gainey, Mario Tremblay, Guy Lapointe, Doug Risebrough, Réjean Houle, Pat Hughes, Michel Larocque, Doug Jarvis, Yvon Lambert, Pierre Larouche, Gilles Lupien, Rod Langway, Jacques Lemaire, Pierre Mondou, Larry Robinson, Mark Napier, Serge Savard, Steve Shutt, Cam Connor, Richard Sévigny; Jacques Courtois (President), Sam Pollock (Director), Irving Grundman (Vice President/Managing Director), Jean Beliveau (Vice President - Corporate Affairs), Scotty Bowman (Coach), Claude Ruel (Director of Player Development), Al MacNeil (Director of Player Personnel), Morgan McCammon (Director), Ron Caron (Director of Recruitment), Eddy Palchak (Trainer), Pierre Meilleur (Assistant Trainer).
Scores: May 13, at Montreal — NY Rangers 4, Montreal 1; May 15, at Montreal — Montreal 6, NY Rangers 2; May 17, at New York — Montreal 4, NY Rangers 1; May 19, at New York — Montreal 4, NY Rangers 3; May 21, at Montreal — Montreal 4, NY Rangers 1.

1977-78 — Montreal Canadiens — Yvan Cournoyer (Captain), Guy Lafleur, Ken Dryden, Michel Larocque, Rick Chartraw, Réjean Houle, Pierre Larouche, Brian Engblom, Yvon Lambert, Jacques Lemaire, Bob Gainey, Guy Lapointe, Doug Jarvis, Gilles Lupien, Pierre Mondou, Larry Robinson, Bill Nyrop, Murray Wilson, Serge Savard, Steve Shutt, Mario Tremblay, Pierre Bouchard, Doug Risebrough; Jacques Courtois (President), Sam Pollock (Vice President/General Manager), Jean Beliveau (Vice President/Director of Corporate Relations), Scotty Bowman (Coach), Peter Bronfman, Edward Bronfman (Directors), Al MacNeil (Director of Player Development), Eddy Palchak (Trainer), Pierre Meilleur (Assistant Trainer), Claude Ruel (Director of Player Development), Floyd Curry, Ron Caron (Assistant General Managers).
Scores: May 13, at Montreal — Montreal 4, Boston 1; May 16, at Montreal — Montreal 3, Boston 2; May 18, at Boston — Boston 4, Montreal 0; May 21, at Boston — Boston 4, Montreal 3; May 23, at Montreal — Montreal 4, Boston 1; May 25, at Boston — Montreal 4, Boston 1.

1976-77 — Montreal Canadiens — Yvan Cournoyer (Captain), Larry Robinson, Guy Lafleur, Pierre Bouchard, Rejean Houle, Yvon Lambert, Bob Gainey, Jacques Lemaire, Guy Lapointe, Ken Dryden, Rick Chartraw, Bill Nyrop, Michel Larocque, Pierre Mondou, Serge Savard, Steve Shutt, Mario Tremblay, Murray Wilson, Doug Jarvis, Mike Polich, Jimmy Roberts, Pete Mahovlich, Doug Risebrough, Jacques Courtois (President), Sam Pollock (Vice President/General Manager), Jean Beliveau (Vice President/Director of Corporate Relations), Scotty Bowman (Coach), Peter Bronfman, Edward Bronfman (Directors), Claude Ruel (Director of Player Development), Floyd Curry, Ron Caron (Assistant General Managers), Pierre Meilleur (Assistant Trainer), Eddy Palchak (Trainer).
Scores: May 7, at Montreal — Montreal 7, Boston 3; May 10, at Montreal — Montreal 3, Boston 0; May 12, at Boston — Montreal 4, Boston 2; May 14, at Boston — Montreal 2, Boston 1.

1975-76 — Montreal Canadiens — Yvan Cournoyer (Captain), Bob Gainey, Larry Robinson, Pierre Bouchard, Rick Chartraw, Ken Dryden, Pete Mahovlich, Guy Lafleur, Yvon Lambert, Michel Larocque, Serge Savard, Doug Jarvis, Jacques Lemaire, Guy Lapointe, Jimmy Roberts, Doug Risebrough, Steve Shutt, Murray Wilson, Mario Tremblay, Bill Nyrop; Jacques Courtois (President), Jean Beliveau (Vice President), Peter Bronfman (Chairman), Edward Bronfman (Director), Sam Pollock (Vice President/General Manager), Scotty Bowman (Coach), Eddy Palchak (Trainer), Pierre Meilleur (Assistant Trainer), Claude Ruel (Director of Player Development).
Scores: May 9, at Montreal — Montreal 4, Philadelphia 3; May 11, at Montreal — Montreal 2, Philadelphia 1; May 13, at Philadelphia — Montreal 3, Philadelphia 2; May 16, at Philadelphia — Montreal 5, Philadelphia 3.

1974-75 — Philadelphia Flyers — Bobby Clarke (Captain), Bernie Parent, Bobby Taylor, Wayne Stephenson, Ed Van Impe, Don Saleski, Tom Bladon, Larry Goodenough, Bill Barber, Gary Dornhoefer, Dave Schultz, Joe Watson, Ross Lonsberry, André Dupont, Terry Crisp, Orest Kindrachuk, Bill Clement, Bob Kelly, Rick MacLeish, Jimmy Watson, Reggie Leach, Ted Harris; Ed Snider (Chairman), Joe Scott (President), Eugene Dixon Jr. (Vice Chairman), Fred Shero (Coach), Keith Allen (Vice President/General Manager), Lou Scheinfeld (Vice President), Mike Nykoluk (Assistant Coach), Marcel Pelletier (Player Personnel Director), Barry Ashbee (Assistant Coach), Frank Lewis (Trainer), Jim McKenzie (Assistant Trainer).
Scores: May 15, at Philadelphia — Philadelphia 4, Buffalo 1; May 18, at Philadelphia — Philadelphia 2, Buffalo 1; May 20, at Buffalo — Buffalo 5, Philadelphia 4; May 22, at Buffalo — Buffalo 4, Philadelphia 2; May 25, at Philadelphia — Philadelphia 5, Buffalo 1; May 27, at Buffalo — Philadelphia 2, Buffalo 0.

1973-74 — Philadelphia Flyers — Bobby Clarke (Captain), Bernie Parent, Bobby Taylor, Bill Clement, Ross Lonsberry, Bill Barber, Orest Kindrachuk, Ed Van Impe, Don Saleski, Gary Dornhoefer, Barry Ashbee, Jimmy Watson, Dave Schultz, André Dupont, Bruce Cowick, Rick MacLeish, Terry Crisp, Bill Flett, Simon Nolet, Joe Watson, Bob Kelly, Tom Bladon; Ed Snider (Chairman), Joe Scott (President), Eugene Dixon Jr. (Vice Chairman), Fred Shero (Coach), Keith Allen (Vice President/General Manager), Mike Nykoluk (Assistant Coach), Marcel Pelletier (Player Personnel Director), Frank Lewis (Trainer), Jim McKenzie (Assistant Trainer).
Scores: May 7, at Boston — Boston 3, Philadelphia 2; May 9, at Boston — Philadelphia 3, Boston 2; May 12, at Philadelphia — Philadelphia 4, Boston 1; May 14, at Philadelphia — Philadelphia 4, Boston 2; May 16, at Boston — Boston 5, Philadelphia 1; May 19, at Philadelphia — Philadelphia 1, Boston 0.

1972-73 — Montreal Canadiens — Henri Richard (Captain), Jacques Laperrière, Ken Dryden, Yvan Cournoyer, Jacques Lemaire, Marc Tardif, Serge Savard, Pete Mahovlich, Guy Lapointe, Réjean Houle, Claude Larose, Pierre Bouchard, Frank Mahovlich, Jimmy Roberts, Chuck Lefley, Guy Lafleur, Bob Murdoch, Michel Plasse, Murray Wilson, Larry Robinson, Steve Shutt; Jacques Courtois (President), Jean Beliveau (Vice President), Peter Bronfman (Chairman), Sam Pollock (Vice President/General Manager), Edward Bronfman (Executive Director), Scotty Bowman (Coach), Bob Williams (Trainer).
Scores: April 29, at Montreal — Montreal 8, Chicago 3; May 1, at Montreal — Montreal 4, Chicago 1; May 3, at Chicago — Chicago 7, Montreal 4; May 6, at Chicago — Montreal 4, Chicago 0; May 8, at Montreal — Chicago 8, Montreal 7; May 10, at Chicago — Montreal 6, Chicago 4.

1971-72 — Boston Bruins — Bobby Orr, Gerry Cheevers, Eddie Johnston, Dallas Smith, Derek Sanderson, Carol Vadnais, Phil Esposito, Fred Stanfield, Don Awrey, Ted Green, Ken Hodge, John Bucyk, Wayne Cashman, John McKenzie, Ed Westfall, Mike Walton, Garnet Bailey, Don Marcotte; Weston Adams (Chairman), Weston Adams Jr. (President), Shelby Davis (Vice President), Charles Mulcahy (Junior Vice President/General Counsel), Eddie Powers (Vice President/Treasurer), Milt Schmidt (General Manager), Tom Johnson (Coach), Dan Canney (Trainer), John Forristall (Assistant Trainer).
Scores: April 30, at Boston — Boston 6, NY Rangers 5; May 2, at Boston — Boston 2, NY Rangers 1; May 4, at New York — NY Rangers 5, Boston 2; May 7, at New York — Boston 3, NY Rangers 2; May 9, at Boston — NY Rangers 3, Boston 2; May 11, at New York — Boston 3, NY Rangers 0.

1970-71 — Montreal Canadiens — Jean Béliveau (Captain), Pierre Bouchard, Yvan Cournoyer, John Ferguson, Jacques Laperrière, Terry Harper, Réjean Houle, Guy Lapointe, Claude Larose, Marc Tardif, Chuck Lefley, Jacques Lemaire, Frank Mahovlich, Henri Richard, Phil Roberto, Pete Mahovlich, Bob Murdoch, Serge Savard (37GP – injured), Bobby Sheehan, Leon Rochefort, J.C. Tremblay, Ken Dryden, Rogie Vachon; David Molson (President), William Molson, Peter Molson (Vice Presidents), Sam Pollock (Vice President/General Manager), Ron Caron (Assistant General Manager), Al MacNeil (Coach), Yves Belanger (Trainer), Phil Langlois, Eddie Palchak (Assistant Trainers).
Scores: May 4, at Chicago — Chicago 2, Montreal 1; May 6, at Chicago — Chicago 5, Montreal 3; May 9, at Montreal — Montreal 4, Chicago 2; May 11, at Montreal — Montreal 5, Chicago 2; May 13, at Chicago — Chicago 2, Montreal 0; May 16, at Montreal — Montreal 4, Chicago 3; May 18, at Chicago — Montreal 3, Chicago 2.

1969-70 — Boston Bruins — Don Awrey, John Bucyk, Garnet Bailey, Wayne Carleton, Wayne Cashman, Gary Doak, Phil Esposito, Ted Green, Ken Hodge, Bobby Orr, Don Marcotte, John McKenzie, Derek Sanderson, Dallas Smith, Rick Smith, Bill Speer, Fred Stanfield, Ed Westfall, Gerry Cheevers, Eddie Johnston, John Adams, Jim Lorentz, Ron Murphy, Bill Lesuk, Ivan Boldirev, Danny Schock; Weston Adams Sr. (Chairman), Weston Adams Jr. (President), Charles Mulcahy, Eddie Powers, Shelby Davis (Vice Presidents), Harry Sinden (Coach), Milt Schmidt (General Manager), Tom Johnson (Assistant General Manager), Dan Canney (Trainer), John Forristall (Assistant Trainer).
Scores: May 3, at St. Louis — Boston 6, St. Louis 1; May 5, at St. Louis — Boston 6, St. Louis 2; May 7, at Boston — Boston 4, St. Louis 1; May 10, at Boston — Boston 4, St. Louis 3.

1968-69 — Montreal Canadiens — Jean Béliveau (Captain), Ralph Backstrom, Jacques Lemaire, Dick Duff, Christian Bordeleau, Mickey Redmond, Yvan Cournoyer, Henri Richard, Bobby Rousseau, John Ferguson, Serge Savard, Terry Harper, Gilles Tremblay, Ted Harris, J.C. Tremblay, Larry Hillman, Jacques Laperrière, Claude Provost, Tony Esposito, Rogie Vachon, Gump Worsley; David Molson (President), William Molson, Peter Molson (Vice Presidents), Sam Pollock (Vice President/General Manager), Claude Ruel (Coach), Larry Aubut (Trainer), Eddie Palchak (Assistant Trainer).
Scores: April 27, at Montreal — Montreal 3, St. Louis 1; April 29, at Montreal — Montreal 3, St. Louis 1; May 1, at St. Louis — Montreal 4, St. Louis 0; May 4, at St. Louis — Montreal 2, St. Louis 1.

1967-68 — Montreal Canadiens — Jean Béliveau (Captain), Ralph Backstrom, Yvan Cournoyer, Dick Duff, John Ferguson, Danny Grant, Terry Harper, Ted Harris, Serge Savard, Jacques Laperrière, Claude Larose, Jacques Lemaire, Claude Provost, Mickey Redmond, Henri Richard, Bobby Rousseau, Gilles Tremblay, J.C. Tremblay, Carol Vadnais, Rogie Vachon, Ernie Wakely, Gump Worsley; Hartland Molson (Chairman), David Molson (President), Sam Pollock (Vice President/General Manager), Toe Blake (Coach), Larry Aubut (Trainer), Eddie Palchak (Assistant Trainer).
Scores: May 5, at St. Louis — Montreal 3, St. Louis 2; May 7, at St. Louis — Montreal 1, St. Louis 0; May 9, at Montreal — Montreal 4, St. Louis 3; May 11, at Montreal — Montreal 3, St. Louis 2.

1966-67 — Toronto Maple Leafs — George Armstrong (Captain), Bob Baun, Johnny Bower, Brian Conacher, Ron Ellis, Aut Erickson, Larry Hillman, Tim Horton, Red Kelly, Larry Jeffrey, Dave Keon, Frank Mahovlich, Milan Marcetta, Jim Pappin, Marcel Pronovost, Bob Pulford, Terry Sawchuk, Eddie Shack, Allan Stanley, Pete Stemkowski, Mike Walton; Stafford Smythe (President), Harold Ballard (Executive Vice President), John Bassett (Chairman), Punch Imlach (General Manager/Coach), King Clancy (Assistant Coach/Assistant General Manager), Bob Davidson (Chief Scout), John Anderson (Business Manager), Bob Haggert (Trainer), Tom Nayler (Assistant Trainer), Karl Elieff (Physiotherapist), Richard Smythe (Mascot).
Scores: April 20, at Montreal — Toronto 2, Montreal 6; April 22, at Montreal — Toronto 3, Montreal 0; April 25, at Toronto — Toronto 3, Montreal 2; April 27, at Toronto — Toronto 2, Montreal 6; April 29, at Montreal — Toronto 4, Montreal 1; May 2, at Toronto — Toronto 3, Montreal 1.

1965-66 — Montreal Canadiens — Jean Béliveau (Captain), Ralph Backstrom, Dave Balon, Yvan Cournoyer, Bobby Rousseau, Dick Duff, John Ferguson, Terry Harper, Ted Harris, Charlie Hodge, Jacques Laperrière, Claude Larose, Noel Price, Claude Provost, Henri Richard, Jimmy Roberts, Leon Rochefort, Jean-Guy Talbot, Gilles Tremblay, J.C. Tremblay, Gump Worsley; Hartland Molson (Chairman), David Molson (President), Sam Pollock (General Manager), Toe Blake (Coach), Andy Galley (Trainer), Larry Aubut (Assistant Trainer).
Scores: April 24, at Montreal — Detroit 3, Montreal 2; April 26, at Montreal — Detroit 5, Montreal 2; April 28, at Detroit — Montreal 4, Detroit 2; May 1, at Detroit — Montreal 2, Detroit 1; May 3, at Montreal — Montreal 5, Detroit 1; May 5, at Detroit — Montreal 3, Detroit 2.

1964-65 — Montreal Canadiens — Jean Béliveau (Captain), Ralph Backstrom, Dave Balon, Red Berenson, Yvan Cournoyer, Dick Duff, John Ferguson, Jean Gauthier, Charlie Hodge, Terry Harper, Ted Harris, Jacques Laperrière, Claude Larose, Garry Peters, Noel Picard, Claude Provost, Henri Richard, Jimmy Roberts, Bobby Rousseau, Jean-Guy Talbot, Gilles Tremblay, J.C. Tremblay, Ernie Wakely, Bryan Watson, Gump Worsley; Hartland Molson (Chairman), David Molson (President), Maurice Richard (Assistant to the President), Sam Pollock (General Manager), Toe Blake (Coach), Andy Galley (Trainer), Larry Aubut (Assistant Trainer).
Scores: April 17, at Montreal — Montreal 3, Chicago 2; April 20, at Montreal — Montreal 2, Chicago 0; April 22, at Chicago — Montreal 1, Chicago 3; April 25, at Chicago — Montreal 1, Chicago 5; April 7, at Montreal — Montreal 6, Chicago 0; April 29, at Chicago — Montreal 1, Chicago 2; May 1, at Montreal — Montreal 4, Chicago 0.

1963-64 — Toronto Maple Leafs — George Armstrong (Captain), Andy Bathgate, Bob Baun, Johnny Bower, Carl Brewer, Gerry Ehman, Billy Harris, Larry Hillman, Dave Keon, Tim Horton, Red Kelly, Frank Mahovlich, Don McKenney, Jim Pappin, Bob Pulford, Eddie Shack, Don Simmons, Allan Stanley, Ron Stewart, Al Arbour, Ed Litzenberger; Stafford Smythe (President), Harold Ballard (Executive Vice President), John Bassett (Chairman), Punch Imlach (Coach/General Manager), King Clancy (Assistant Coach/Assistant General Manager), Bob Haggert (Trainer), Tom Nayler (Assistant Trainer), Hugh Hoult (Stick Boy).
Scores April 11, at Toronto — Toronto 3, Detroit 2; April 14, at Toronto — Toronto 3, Detroit 4; April 16, at Detroit — Toronto 3, Detroit 4; April 18, at Detroit — Toronto 4, Detroit 2; April 21, at Toronto — Toronto 1, Detroit 2; April 23, at Detroit — Toronto 4, Detroit 3; April 25, at Toronto — Toronto 4, Detroit 0.

1962-63 — Toronto Maple Leafs — George Armstrong (Captain), Bob Baun, Johnny Bower, Carl Brewer, Kent Douglas, Dick Duff, Billy Harris, Larry Hillman, Tim Horton, Red Kelly, Dave Keon, Ed Litzenberger, John MacMillan, Frank Mahovlich, Bob Nevin, Bob Pulford, Eddie Shack, Don Simmons, Allan Stanley, Ron Stewart; Stafford Smythe (President), Harold Ballard (Executive Vice President), John Bassett (Chairman), Punch Imlach (Coach/General Manager), King Clancy (Assistant Coach/Assistant General Manager), Bob Haggert (Trainer), Tom Nayler (Assistant Trainer), Hugh Hoult (Stick Boy).
Scores: April 9, at Toronto — Toronto 4, Detroit 2; April 11, at Toronto — Toronto 4, Detroit 2; April 14, at Detroit — Toronto 2, Detroit 3; April 16, at Detroit — Toronto 4, Detroit 2; April 18, at Toronto — Toronto 3, Detroit 1.

1961-62 — Toronto Maple Leafs — George Armstrong (Captain), Al Arbour, Bob Baun, Johnny Bower, Carl Brewer, Dick Duff, Billy Harris, Larry Hillman, Dave Keon, Tim Horton, Red Kelly, Ed Litzenberger, John MacMillan, Frank Mahovlich, Bob Nevin, Bert Olmstead, Bob Pulford, Eddie Shack, Allan Stanley, Don Simmons, Ron Stewart; Stafford Smythe (President), Harold Ballard (Executive Vice President), John Bassett (Vice President), Conn Smythe (Chairman), Punch Imlach (Coach/General Manager), King Clancy (Assistant Coach), Bob Davidson (Chief Scout), Bob Haggert (Trainer), Tom Nayler (Assistant Trainer), Hugh Hoult (Stick Boy).
Scores: April 10, at Toronto — Toronto 4, Chicago 1; April 12, at Toronto — Toronto 3, Chicago 2; April 15, at Chicago — Toronto 0, Chicago 3; April 17, at Chicago — Toronto 1, Chicago 4; April 19, at Toronto —Toronto 8, Chicago 4; April 22, at Chicago — Toronto 2, Chicago 1.

1960-61 — Chicago Black Hawks — Ed Litzenberger (Captain), Al Arbour, Earl Balfour, Murray Balfour, Glenn Hall, Jack Evans, Roy Edwards, Denis DeJordy, Bill Hay, Wayne Hicks, Reggie Fleming, Wayne Hillman, Bobby Hull, Chico Maki, Ab McDonald, Moose Vasko, Stan Mikita, Ron Murphy, Eric Nesterenko, Pierre Pilote, Tod Sloan, Dollard St. Laurent, Kenny Wharram; Arthur Wirtz (President), Arthur Wirtz Jr. (Vice President), James Norris (Chairman), Tommy Ivan (General Manager), Rudy Pilous (Coach), Nick Garen, Walter Humeniuk (Trainers).
Scores: April 6, at Chicago — Chicago 3, Detroit 2; April 8, at Detroit — Detroit 3, Chicago 1; April 10, at Chicago — Chicago 3, Detroit 1; April 12, at Detroit — Detroit 2, Chicago 1; April 14, at Chicago — Chicago 6, Detroit 3; April 16, at Detroit — Chicago 5, Detroit 1.

Red Wings stars Gordie Howe, Sid Abel and Ted Lindsay were known as the Production Line. The high-scoring trio helped Detroit win the Stanley Cup in 1950 and 1952. Howe and Lindsay won again in 1954 and 1955.

1959-60 — Montreal Canadiens — Maurice Richard (Captain), Ralph Backstrom, Marcel Bonin, Jean Béliveau, Bernie Geoffrion, Phil Goyette, Doug Harvey, Bill Hicke, Charlie Hodge, Tom Johnson, Albert Langlois, Don Marshall, Dickie Moore, Ab McDonald, Jacques Plante, Henri Richard, André Pronovost, Claude Provost, Bob Turner, Jean-Guy Talbot; Senator Hartland Molson (President), Frank Selke (Managing Director), Ken Reardon (Vice President), Sam Pollock (Personnel Director), Toe Blake (Coach), Hector Dubois, Larry Aubut (Trainers).
Scores: April 7, at Montreal — Montreal 4, Toronto 2; April 9, at Montreal — Montreal 2, Toronto 1; April 12, at Toronto — Montreal 5, Toronto 2; April 14, at Toronto — Montreal 4, Toronto 0.

1958-59 — Montreal Canadiens — Maurice Richard (Captain), Ralph Backstrom, Marcel Bonin, Jean Béliveau, Ian Cushenan, Bernie Geoffrion, Charlie Hodge, Phil Goyette, Doug Harvey, Bill Hicke, Tom Johnson, Albert Langlois, Don Marshall, Ab McDonald, Dickie Moore, Jacques Plante, Ken Mosdell, André Pronovost, Claude Provost, Henri Richard, Jean-Guy Talbot, Bob Turner; Senator Hartland Molson (President), Frank Selke (Managing Director), Ken Reardon (Vice President), Sam Pollock (Personnel Director), Toe Blake (Coach), Hector Dubois, Larry Aubut (Trainers).
Scores: April 9, at Montreal — Montreal 5, Toronto 3; April 11, at Montreal — Montreal 3, Toronto 1; April 14, at Toronto — Toronto 3, Montreal 2; April 16, at Toronto — Montreal 3, Toronto 2; April 18, at Montreal — Montreal 5, Toronto 3.

1957-58 — Montreal Canadiens — Maurice Richard (Captain), Jean Béliveau, Marcel Bonin, Floyd Curry, Connie Broden, Bernie Geoffrion, Phil Goyette, Doug Harvey, Charlie Hodge, Tom Johnson, Albert Langlois, Don Marshall, Ab McDonald, Gerry McNeil, Dickie Moore, Bert Olmstead, Jacques Plante, André Pronovost, Henri Richard, Claude Provost, Dollard St. Laurent, Jean-Guy Talbot, Bob Turner; Senator Hartland Molson (President), Frank Selke (Managing Director), Ken Reardon (Vice President), Toe Blake (Coach), Hector Dubois, Larry Aubut (Trainers).
Scores: April 8, at Montreal —Montreal 2, Boston 1; April 10, at Montreal — Boston 5, Montreal 2; April 13, at Boston — Montreal 3, Boston 0; April 15, at Boston — Boston 3, Montreal 1; April 17, at Montreal — Montreal 3, Boston 2; April 20, at Boston — Montreal 5, Boston 3.

1956-57 — Montreal Canadiens — Maurice Richard (Captain), Jean Béliveau, Connie Broden, Floyd Curry, Bernie Geoffrion, Phil Goyette, Doug Harvey, Tom Johnson, Don Marshall, Gerry McNeil, Dickie Moore, Bert Olmstead, Jacques Plante, André Pronovost, Claude Provost, Henri Richard, Dollard St. Laurent, Jean-Guy Talbot, Bob Turner; William Northey (President), Donat Raymond (Chairman), Ken Reardon (Vice President), Frank Selke (Managing Director), Toe Blake (Coach), Hector Dubois, Larry Aubut (Trainers).
Scores: April 6, at Montreal — Montreal 5, Boston 1; April 9, at Montreal — Montreal 1, Boston 0; April 11, at Boston — Montreal 4, Boston 2; April 14, at Boston — Boston 2, Montreal 0; April 16, at Montreal — Montreal 5, Boston 1.

1955-56 — Montreal Canadiens — Butch Bouchard (Captain), Bob Turner, Jean Béliveau, Bert Olmstead, Floyd Curry, Bernie Geoffrion, Jacques Plante, Doug Harvey, Claude Provost, Charlie Hodge, Henri Richard, Tom Johnson, Maurice Richard, Jackie LeClair, Dollard St. Laurent, Don Marshall, Jean-Guy Talbot, Dickie Moore, Ken Mosdell; Donat Raymond (President), Frank Selke (Managing Director), D'Alton Coleman, William Northey (Vice Presidents), Ken Reardon (Assistant Manager), Toe Blake (Coach), Hector Dubois, Gaston Bettez (Trainers).
Scores: March 31, at Montreal — Montreal 6, Detroit 4; April 3, at Montreal — Montreal 5, Detroit 1; April 5, at Detroit — Detroit 3, Montreal 1; April 8, at Detroit — Montreal 3, Detroit 0; April 10, at Montreal — Montreal 3, Detroit 1.

1954-55 — Detroit Red Wings — Dutch Reibel, Terry Sawchuk, Jim Hay, Vic Stasiuk, Johnny Wilson, Gordie Howe, Red Kelly, Tony Leswick, Ted Lindsay (Captain), Marty Pavelich, Marcel Pronovost, Marcel Bonin, Alex Delvecchio, Bill Dineen, Bob Goldham, Benny Woit, Larry Hillman, Glen Skov; Bruce Norris (President), Marguerite Norris (President), Jack Adams (Manager), Jimmy Skinner (Coach), John Mitchell (Chief Scout), Fred Huber (Publicity Director), Carl Mattson, Lefty Wilson (Trainers).
Scores: April 3, at Detroit — Detroit 4, Montreal 2; April 5, at Detroit — Detroit 7, Montreal; April 7, at Montreal — Montreal 4, Detroit 2; April 9, at Montreal — Montreal 5, Detroit 3; April 10, at Detroit — Detroit 5, Montreal 1; April 12, at Montreal — Montreal 6, Detroit 3; April 14, at Detroit — Detroit 3, Montreal 1.

1953-54 — Detroit Red Wings — Marty Pavelich, Jimmy Peters, Marcel Pronovost, Metro Prystai, Dutch Reibel, Terry Sawchuk, Bob Goldham, Gordie Howe, Earl Johnson, Red Kelly, Tony Leswick, Ted Lindsay (Captain), Keith Allen, Al Arbour, Alex Delvecchio, Bill Dineen, Gilles Dube, Dave Gatherum, Glen Skov, Johnny Wilson, Benny Woit; Bruce Norris (Owner), Marguerite Norris (President), Jack Adams (Manager), Tommy Ivan (Coach), John Mitchell (Chief Scout), Fred Huber (Publicity Director), Carl Mattson, Lefty Wilson (Trainers), Wally Crossman (Assistant Trainer).
Scores: April 4, at Detroit — Detroit 3, Montreal 1; April 6, at Detroit — Montreal 3, Detroit 1; April 8, at Montreal — Detroit 5, Montreal 2; April 10, at Montreal — Detroit 2, Montreal 0; April 11, at Detroit — Montreal 1, Detroit 0; April 13, at Montreal — Montreal 4, Detroit 1; April 16, at Detroit — Detroit 2, Montreal 1.

1952-53 — Montreal Canadiens — Floyd Curry, Bernie Geoffrion, Bert Olmstead, Paul Meger, Dick Gamble, Dickie Moore, Tom Johnson, Bud MacPherson, Billy Reay, Ken Mosdell, Paul Masnick, John McCormack, Butch Bouchard (Captain), Maurice Richard, Elmer Lach, Gerry McNeil, Doug Harvey, Dollard St. Laurent, Jacques Plante, Lorne Davis, Calum MacKay, Eddie Mazur, Donat Raymond (President), Dalton Coleman (Director), William Northey (Special Advisor), Frank Selke (Manager), Dick Irvin (Coach), Hector Dubois, Gaston Bettez (Trainers).
Scores: April 9, at Montreal — Montreal 4, Boston 2; April 11, at Montreal — Boston 4, Montreal 1; April 12, at Boston — Montreal 3, Boston 0; April 14, at Boston — Montreal 7, Boston 3; April 16, at Montreal — Montreal 1, Boston 0.

1951-52 — Detroit Red Wings — Metro Prystai, Leo Reise Jr., Terry Sawchuk, Enio Sclisizzi, Glen Skov, Vic Stasiuk, Gordie Howe, Red Kelly, Tony Leswick, Ted Lindsay, Marty Pavelich, Marcel Pronovost, Sid Abel (Captain), Alex Delvecchio, Fred Glover, Bob Goldham, Glenn Hall, Benny Woit, Johnny Wilson, Larry Zeidel; James Norris (President), Bruce Norris (Owner), Jack Adams (Manager), Tommy Ivan (Coach), Fred Huber (Publicity Director), Carson Cooper (Scout), Carl Mattson, Lefty Wilson (Trainers), Wally Crossman (Assistant Trainer).
Scores: April 10, at Montreal — Detroit 3, Montreal 1; April 12, at Montreal — Detroit 2, Montreal 1; April 13, at Detroit — Detroit 3, Montreal 0; April 15, at Detroit — Detroit 3, Montreal 0.

1950-51 — Toronto Maple Leafs — Bill Barilko, Max Bentley, Hugh Bolton, Turk Broda, Fern Flaman, Cal Gardner, Bob Hassard, Bill Juzda, Ted Kennedy (Captain), Joe Klukay, Danny Lewicki, Fleming MacKell, Howie Meeker, Gus Mortson, John McCormack, Al Rollins, Tod Sloan, Sid Smith, Jimmy Thomson, Ray Timgren, Harry Watson; Joe Primeau (Coach), Bill MacBrien (Chairman), Conn Smythe (President/Manager), Hap Day (Assistant Manager), George McCullagh, J.Y. Murdoch (Vice Presidents), J.P. Bickell, Ed Bickle (Directors), Tim Daly (Trainer), Archie Campbell, Tommy Naylor (Assistant Trainers), Dr. Norman Delarue, Dr. James Murray, Dr. Horace MacIntyre (Club Doctors), Ed Fitkin (Publicity Director), Squib Walker (Chief Scout).
Scores: April 11, at Toronto — Toronto 3, Montreal 2; April 14, at Toronto — Montreal 3, Toronto 2; April 17, at Montreal — Toronto 2, Montreal 1; April 19, at Montreal — Toronto 3, Montreal 2; April 21, at Toronto — Toronto 3, Montreal 2.

1949-50 — Detroit Red Wings — Sid Abel (Captain), Pete Babando, Steve Black, Joe Carveth, Gerry Couture, Al Dewsbury, Lee Fogolin, George Gee, Gordie Howe, Red Kelly, Ted Lindsay, Harry Lumley, Clare Martin, Jim McFadden, Max McNab, Marty Pavelich, Jimmy Peters, Marcel Pronovost, Leo Reise Jr., Jack Stewart, Johnny Wilson, Larry Wilson, Doug McKay; James Norris (President), James Norris Jr. (Vice President), Arthur Wirtz (Secretary Treasurer), Jack Adams (Manager), Tommy Ivan (Coach), Fred Huber Jr. (Publicity Director), Carson Cooper (Head Scout), Carl Mattson (Trainer), Walter Humeniuk (Assistant Trainer).
Scores: April 11, at Detroit — Detroit 4, NY Rangers 1; April 13, at Toronto* — NY Rangers 3, Detroit 1; April 15, at Toronto* — Detroit 4, NY Rangers 0; April 18, at Detroit — NY Rangers 4, Detroit 3; April 20, at Detroit — NY Rangers 2, Detroit 1; April 22, at Detroit — Detroit 5, NY Rangers 4; April 23, at Detroit — Detroit 4, NY Rangers 3.
*Ice was unavailable in Madison Square Garden and NY Rangers elected to play second and third games on Toronto ice.

1948-49 — Toronto Maple Leafs — Bill Barilko, Max Bentley, Garth Boesch, Turk Broda, Bob Dawes, Bill Ezinicki, Cal Gardner, Bill Juzda, Ted Kennedy (Captain), Joe Klukay, Vic Lynn, Howie Meeker, Don Metz, Fleming MacKell, Gus Mortson, Sid Smith, Harry Taylor, Ray Timgren, Jimmy Thomson, Harry Watson; Hap Day (Coach), Bill MacBrien (Chairman), Conn Smythe (President/Manager), George McCullagh, J.Y. Murdoch (Vice Presidents), J.P. Bickell, Ed Bickle (Directors), Tim Daly (Trainer), Archie Campbell (Assistant Trainer), Dr. Norman Delarue, Dr. James Murray, Dr. Horace MacIntyre (Club Doctors), Ed Fitkin (Publicity Director), Squib Walker (Chief Scout), Kerry Day (Mascot).
Scores: April 8, at Detroit — Toronto 3, Detroit 2; April 10, at Detroit — Toronto 3, Detroit 1; April 13, at Toronto — Toronto 3, Detroit 1; April 16, at Toronto — Toronto 3, Detroit 1.

1947-48 — Toronto Maple Leafs — Syl Apps (Captain), Bill Barilko, Max Bentley, Garth Boesch, Turk Broda, Les Costello, Bill Ezinicki, Ted Kennedy, Joe Klukay, Vic Lynn, Howie Meeker, Nick Metz, Don Metz, Gus Mortson, Phil Samis, Sid Smith, Wally Stanowski, Jimmy Thomson, Harry Watson; Hap Day (Coach), Conn Smythe (Manager), Tim Daly (Trainer).
Scores: April 7, at Toronto — Toronto 5, Detroit 3; April 10, at Toronto — Toronto 4, Detroit 2; April 11, at Detroit — Toronto 2, Detroit 0; April 14, at Detroit — Toronto 7, Detroit 2.

1946-47 — Toronto Maple Leafs — Turk Broda, Garth Boesch, Gus Mortson, Jimmy Thomson, Wally Stanowski, Bill Barilko, Harry Watson, Bud Poile, Ted Kennedy, Syl Apps (Captain), Don Metz, Nick Metz, Bill Ezinicki, Vic Lynn, Howie Meeker, Gaye Stewart, Joe Klukay, Gus Bodnar, Bob Goldham; Conn Smythe (Manager), Hap Day (Coach), Tim Daly (Trainer).
Scores: April 8, at Montreal — Montreal 6, Toronto 0; April 10, at Montreal — Toronto 4, Montreal 0; April 12, at Toronto — Toronto 4, Montreal 2; April 15, at Toronto — Toronto 2, Montreal 1; April 17, at Montreal — Montreal 3, Toronto 1; April 19, at Toronto — Toronto 2, Montreal 1.

1945-46 — Montreal Canadiens — Elmer Lach, Toe Blake (Captain), Maurice Richard, Bob Fillion, Dutch Hiller, Murph Chamberlain, Ken Mosdell, Buddy O'Connor, Glen Harmon, Jimmy Peters, Butch Bouchard, Billy Reay, Ken Reardon, Leo Lamoureux, Frank Eddolls, Gerry Plamondon, Joe Benoit, Bill Durnan; Tommy Gorman (Manager), Dick Irvin (Coach), Ernie Cook (Trainer).
Scores: March 30, at Montreal — Montreal 4, Boston 3; April 2, at Montreal — Montreal 3, Boston 2; April 4, at Boston — Montreal 4, Boston 2; April 7, at Boston — Boston 3, Montreal 2; April 9, at Montreal — Montreal 6, Boston 3.

1944-45 — Toronto Maple Leafs — Don Metz, Frank McCool, Wally Stanowski, Reg Hamilton, Moe Morris, John McCreedy, Tom O'Neill, Ted Kennedy, Babe Pratt, Gus Bodnar, Art Jackson, Jack McLean, Mel Hill, Nick Metz, Bob Davidson (Captain), Sweeney Schriner, Lorne Carr, Pete Backor, Ross Johnstone; Conn Smythe (Manager), Frank Selke (Business Manager), Hap Day (Coach), Tim Daly (Trainer).
Scores: April 6, at Detroit — Toronto 1, Detroit 0; April 8, at Detroit — Toronto 2, Detroit 0; April 12, at Toronto — Toronto 1, Detroit 0; April 14, at Toronto — Detroit 5, Toronto 3; April 19, at Detroit — Detroit 2, Toronto 0; April 21, at Toronto — Detroit 1, Toronto 0; April 22, at Detroit — Toronto 2, Detroit 1.

1943-44 — Montreal Canadiens — Toe Blake (Captain), Maurice Richard, Elmer Lach, Ray Getliffe, Murph Chamberlain, Phil Watson, Butch Bouchard, Glen Harmon, Buddy O'Connor, Gerry Heffernan, Mike McMahon, Leo Lamoureux, Fern Majeau, Bob Fillion, Bill Durnan; Tommy Gorman (Manager), Dick Irvin (Coach), Ernie Cook (Trainer).
Scores: April 4, at Montreal — Montreal 5, Chicago 1; April 6, at Chicago — Montreal 3, Chicago 1; April 9, at Chicago — Montreal 3, Chicago 2; April 13, at Montreal — Montreal 5, Chicago 4.

1942-43 — Detroit Red Wings — Jack Stewart, Jimmy Orlando, Sid Abel (captain), Alex Motter, Harry Watson, Joe Carveth, Mud Bruneteau, Eddie Wares, Johnny Mowers, Cully Simon, Don Grosso, Carl Liscombe, Connie Brown, Syd Howe, Les Douglas, Harold Jackson, Joe Fisher, Adam Brown; Jack Adams (Manager), Ebbie Goodfellow (Playing Coach), Honey Walker (Trainer).
Scores: April 1, at Detroit — Detroit 6, Boston 2; April 4, at Detroit — Detroit 4, Boston 3; April 7, at Boston — Detroit 4, Boston 0; April 8, at Boston — Detroit 2, Boston 0.

1941-42 — Toronto Maple Leafs — Wally Stanowski, Syl Apps (Captain), Bob Goldham, Gordie Drillon, Hank Goldup, Ernie Dickens, Sweeney Schriner, Bucko McDonald, Bob Davidson, Nick Metz, Bingo Kampman, Don Metz, Gaye Stewart, Turk Broda, John McCreedy, Lorne Carr, Pete Langelle, Billy Taylor, Reg Hamilton; Conn Smythe (Manager), Hap Day (Coach), Frank Selke (Business Manager), Tim Daly (Trainer).
Scores: April 4, at Toronto — Detroit 3, Toronto 2; April 7, at Toronto — Detroit 4, Toronto 2; April 9, at Detroit — Detroit 5, Toronto 2; April 12, at Detroit — Toronto 4, Detroit 3; April 14, at Toronto — Toronto 9, Detroit 3; April 16, at Detroit — Toronto 3, Detroit 0; April 18, at Toronto — Toronto 3, Detroit 1.

1940-41 — Boston Bruins — Bill Cowley, Des Smith, Dit Clapper (Captain), Frank Brimsek, Flash Hollett, Jack Crawford, Bobby Bauer, Pat McReavy, Herb Cain, Mel Hill, Milt Schmidt, Woody Dumart, Roy Conacher, Terry Reardon, Art Jackson, Eddie Wiseman, Jack Shewchuck; Art Ross (Manager), Cooney Weiland (Coach), Win Green (Trainer).
Scores: April 6, at Boston — Detroit 2, Boston 3; April 8, at Boston — Detroit 1, Boston 2; April 10, at Detroit — Boston 4, Detroit 2; April 12, at Detroit — Boston 3, Detroit 1.

1939-40 — New York Rangers — Dave Kerr, Art Coulter (Captain), Ott Heller, Alex Shibicky, Mac Colville, Neil Colville, Phil Watson, Lynn Patrick, Clint Smith, Muzz Patrick, Babe Pratt, Bryan Hextall, Kilby MacDonald, Dutch Hiller, Alf Pike, Stan Smith; Lester Patrick (Manager), Frank Boucher (Coach), Harry Westerby (Trainer).
Scores: April 2, at New York — NY Rangers 2, Toronto 1; April 3, at New York — NY Rangers 6, Toronto 2; April 6, at Toronto — NY Rangers 1, Toronto 2; April 9, at Toronto — NY Rangers 0, Toronto 3; April 11, at Toronto — NY Rangers 2, Toronto 1; April 13, at Toronto — NY Rangers 3, Toronto 2.

1938-39 — Boston Bruins — Bobby Bauer, Mel Hill, Flash Hollett, Roy Conacher, Gord Pettinger, Charlie Sands, Milt Schmidt, Woody Dumart, Jack Crawford, Ray Getliffe, Frank Brimsek, Eddie Shore, Dit Clapper, Bill Cowley, Jack Portland, Red Hamill, Harry Frost, Cooney Weiland (Captain); Art Ross (Manager/Coach), Win Green (Trainer).
Scores: April 6, at Boston — Toronto 1, Boston 2; April 9, at Boston — Toronto 3, Boston 2; April 11, at Toronto — Toronto 1, Boston 3; April 13, at Toronto — Toronto 0, Boston 2; April 16, at Boston — Toronto 1, Boston 3.

1937-38 — Chicago Black Hawks — Art Wiebe, Carl Voss, Harold Jackson, Mike Karakas, Mush March, Jack Shill, Earl Seibert, Cully Dahlstrom, Alex Levinsky, Johnny Gottselig (Captain), Lou Trudel, Pete Palangio, Bill MacKenzie, Doc Romnes, Paul Thompson, Roger Jenkins, Alfie Moore, Bert Connelly, Virgil Johnson, Paul Goodman; Bill Stewart (Manager/Coach), Eddie Froelich (Trainer).
Scores: April 5, at Toronto — Chicago 3, Toronto 1; April 7, at Toronto — Chicago 1, Toronto 5; April 10, at Chicago — Chicago 2, Toronto 1; April 12, at Chicago — Chicago 4, Toronto 1.

1936-37 — Detroit Red Wings — Normie Smith, Pete Kelly, Larry Aurie, Herbie Lewis, Hec Kilrea, Mud Bruneteau, Syd Howe, Wally Kilrea, Jimmy Franks, Bucko McDonald, Gord Pettinger, Ebbie Goodfellow, John Gallagher, Ralph Bowman, John Sorrell, Marty Barry, Earl Robertson, John Sherf, Howie Mackie, Rolly Roulston, Doug Young (Captain); Jack Adams (Manager/Coach), Honey Walker (Trainer).
Scores: April 6, at New York — Detroit 1, NY Rangers 5; April 8, at Detroit — Detroit 4, NY Rangers 2; April 11, at Detroit — Detroit 0, NY Rangers 1; April 13, at Detroit — Detroit 1, NY Rangers 0; April 15, at Detroit — Detroit 3, NY Rangers 0.

1935-36 — Detroit Red Wings — John Sorrell, Syd Howe, Marty Barry, Herbie Lewis, Mud Bruneteau, Wally Kilrea, Hec Kilrea, Gord Pettinger, Bucko McDonald, Ralph Bowman, Pete Kelly, Doug Young (Captain), Ebbie Goodfellow, Normie Smith, Larry Aurie; Jack Adams (Manager/Coach), Honey Walker (Trainer).
Scores: April 5, at Detroit — Detroit 3, Toronto 1; April 7, at Detroit — Detroit 9, Toronto 4; April 9, at Toronto — Detroit 3, Toronto 4; April 11, at Toronto — Detroit 3, Toronto 2.

1934-35 — Montreal Maroons — Lionel Conacher, Cy Wentworth, Alec Connell, Toe Blake, Stewart Evans, Earl Robinson, Bill Miller, Dave Trottier, Jimmy Ward, Baldy Northcott, Hooley Smith (Captain), Russ Blinco, Al Shields, Sammy McManus, Gus Marker, Bob Gracie, Herb Cain, Dutch Gainor; Tommy Gorman (Manager/Coach), Bill O'Brien (Trainer).
Scores: April 4, at Toronto — Mtl. Maroons 3, Toronto 2; April 6, at Toronto — Mtl. Maroons 3, Toronto 1; April 9, at Montreal — Mtl. Maroons 4, Toronto 1.

1933-34 — Chicago Black Hawks — Clarence Abel, Rosie Couture, Lou Trudel, Lionel Conacher, Paul Thompson, Leroy Goldsworthy, Art Coulter, Roger Jenkins, Don McFadyen, Tom Cook, Doc Romnes, Johnny Gottselig, Mush March, Johnny Sheppard, Charlie Gardiner (Captain), Bill Kendall, Jack Leswick; Tommy Gorman (Manager/Coach), Eddie Froelich (Trainer).
Scores: April 3, at Detroit — Chicago 2, Detroit 1; April 5, at Detroit — Chicago 4, Detroit 1; April 8, at Chicago — Detroit 5, Chicago 2; April 10, at Chicago — Chicago 1, Detroit 0.

1932-33 — New York Rangers — Ching Johnson, Butch Keeling, Frank Boucher, Art Somers, Babe Siebert, Bun Cook, Andy Aitkenhead, Ott Heller, Oscar Asmundson, Gord Pettinger, Doug Brennan, Cecil Dillon, Bill Cook (Captain), Murray Murdoch, Earl Seibert; Lester Patrick (Manager/Coach), Harry Westerby (Trainer).
Scores: April 4, at New York — NY Rangers 5, Toronto 1; April 8, at Toronto — NY Rangers 3, Toronto 1; April 11, at Toronto — Toronto 3, NY Rangers 2; April 13, at Toronto — NY Rangers 1, Toronto 0.

1931-32 — Toronto Maple Leafs — Charlie Conacher, Busher Jackson, King Clancy, Andy Blair, Red Horner, Lorne Chabot, Alex Levinsky, Joe Primeau, Harold Darragh, Baldy Cotton, Frank Finnigan, Hap Day (Captain), Ace Bailey, Bob Gracie, Fred Robertson, Earl Miller; Conn Smythe (Manager), Dick Irvin (Coach), Tim Daly (Trainer).
Scores: April 5, at New York — Toronto 6, NY Rangers 4; April 7, at Boston* — Toronto 6, NY Rangers 2; April 9, at Toronto — Toronto 6, NY Rangers 4.

1930-31 — Montreal Canadiens — George Hainsworth, Wildor Larochelle, Marty Burke, Sylvio Mantha (Captain), Howie Morenz, Johnny Gagnon, Aurel Joliat, Armand Mondou, Pit Lepine, Albert Leduc, Georges Mantha, Art Lesieur, Nick Wasnie, Gus Rivers, Jean Pusie; Léo Dandurand (Manager), Cecil Hart (Coach), Ed Dufour (Trainer).
Scores: April 3, at Chicago — Montreal 2, Chicago 1; April 5, at Chicago — Chicago 2, Montreal 1; April 9, at Montreal — Chicago 3, Montreal 2; April 11, at Montreal — Montreal 4, Chicago 2; April 14, at Montreal — Montreal 2, Chicago 0.

1929-30 — Montreal Canadiens — George Hainsworth, Marty Burke, Sylvio Mantha (Captain), Howie Morenz, Bert McCaffrey, Aurel Joliat, Albert Leduc, Pit Lepine, Wildor Larochelle, Nick Wasnie, Gerry Carson, Armand Mondou, Georges Mantha, Gus Rivers; Léo Dandurand (Manager), Cecil Hart (Coach), Ed Dufour (Trainer).
Scores: April 1, at Boston — Montreal 3, Boston 0; April 3, at Montreal — Montreal 4, Boston 3.

1928-29 — Boston Bruins — Tiny Thompson, Eddie Shore, Lionel Hitchman (Captain), Percy Galbraith, Mickey MacKay, Red Green, Dutch Gainor, Harry Oliver, Eddie Rodden, Dit Clapper, Cooney Weiland, Lloyd Klein, Cy Denneny, Bill Carson, George Owen, Myles Lane; Art Ross (Manager/Coach), Win Green (Trainer).
Scores: March 28, at Boston — Boston 2, NY Rangers 0; March 29, at New York — Boston 2, NY Rangers 1.

Almost no players were left from the Ottawa dynasty of 1903 to 1906 (known today as the Silver Seven) by the time Ottawa won the Stanley Cup again in 1909. That Senators team of 100 years ago featured future Hall of Famers Percy LeSueur, Cyclone Taylor, Marty Walsh, Billy Gilmour and captain Bruce Stuart.

1927-28 — New York Rangers — Lorne Chabot, Clarence Abel, Leo Bourgeault, Ching Johnson, Bill Cook (Captain), Bun Cook, Frank Boucher, Bill Boyd, Murray Murdoch, Paul Thompson, Alex Gray, Joe Miller, Patsy Callighen; Lester Patrick (Manager/Coach), Harry Westerby (Trainer).
Scores: April 5, at Montreal — Mtl. Maroons 2, NY Rangers 0; April 7, at Montreal — NY Rangers 2, Mtl. Maroons 1; April 10, at Montreal — Mtl. Maroons 2, NY Rangers 0; April 12, at Montreal — NY Rangers 1, Mtl. Maroons 0; April 14, at Montreal — NY Rangers 2, Mtl. Maroons 1.

1926-27 — Ottawa Senators — Alec Connell, King Clancy, Georges Boucher (Captain), Ed Gorman, Frank Finnigan, Alex Smith, Hec Kilrea, Hooley Smith, Cy Denneny, Frank Nighbor, Jack Adams, Milt Halliday; Dave Gill (Manager/Coach).
Scores: April 7, at Boston — Ottawa 0, Boston 0; April 9, at Boston — Ottawa 3, Boston 1; April 11, at Ottawa — Boston 1, Ottawa 1; April 13, at Ottawa — Ottawa 3, Boston 1.

1925-26 — Montreal Maroons — Clint Benedict, Reg Noble, Frank Carson, Dunc Munro (Captain), Nels Stewart, Punch Broadbent, Babe Siebert, Chuck Dinsmore, Merlyn Phillips, Hobie Kitchen, Sam Rothschild, Albert Holway, George Horne, Bernie Brophy; Eddie Gerard (Manager/Coach), Bill O'Brien (Trainer).
Scores: March 30, at Montreal — Mtl. Maroons 3, Victoria 0; April 1, at Montreal — Mtl. Maroons 3, Victoria 0; April 3, at Montreal — Victoria 3, Mtl. Maroons 2; April 6, at Montreal — Mtl. Maroons 2, Victoria 0.

The series in the spring of 1926 ended the annual playoffs between the champions of the East and the champions of the West. Since 1926-27 the annual playoffs in the National Hockey League have decided the Stanley Cup champions.

1924-25 — Victoria Cougars — Hap Holmes, Clem Loughlin (Captain), Gord Fraser, Frank Fredrickson, Jack Walker, Gizzy Hart, Harold Halderson, Frank Foyston, Wally Elmer, Harry Meeking, Jocko Anderson; Lester Patrick (Manager/Coach).
Scores: March 21, at Victoria — Victoria 5, Montreal 2; March 23, at Vancouver — Victoria 3, Montreal 1; March 27, at Victoria — Montreal 4, Victoria 2; March 30, at Victoria — Victoria 6, Montreal 1.

1923-24 — Montreal Canadiens — Georges Vezina, Sprague Cleghorn (Captain), Billy Coutu, Howie Morenz, Aurel Joliat, Billy Boucher, Odie Cleghorn, Sylvio Mantha, Bobby Boucher, Billy Bell, Billy Cameron, Joe Malone, Charles Fortier; Leo Dandurand (Manager/Coach).
Scores: March 22, at Montreal — Montreal 6, Cgy. Tigers 1; March 25, at Ottawa* — Montreal 3, Cgy. Tigers 0.

* Game transferred to Ottawa to benefit from artificial ice surface.

1922-23 — Ottawa Senators — Georges Boucher, Lionel Hitchman, Frank Nighbor, King Clancy, Harry Helman, Clint Benedict, Jack Darragh, Eddie Gerard (Captain), Cy Denneny, Punch Broadbent; Tommy Gorman (Manager), Pete Green (Coach), F. Dolan (Trainer).
Scores: March 29, at Vancouver — Ottawa 2, Edm. Eskimos 1; March 31, at Vancouver — Ottawa 1, Edm. Eskimos 0.

1921-22 — Toronto St. Patricks — Ted Stackhouse, Corb Denneny, Rod Smylie, Lloyd Andrews, John Ross Roach, Harry Cameron, Billy Stuart, Babe Dye, Ken Randall, Reg Noble (Captain), Eddie Gerard (borrowed for one game from Ottawa), Stan Jackson, Ivan Mitchell; Charlie Querrie (Manager), George O'Donoghue (Coach).
Scores: March 17, at Toronto — Van. Millionaires 4, Toronto 3; March 20, at Toronto — Toronto 2, Van. Millionaires 1; March 23, at Toronto — Van. Millionaires 3, Toronto 0; March 25, at Toronto — Toronto 6, Van. Millionaires 0; March 28, at Toronto — Toronto 5, Van. Millionaires 1.

1920-21 — Ottawa Senators — Jack MacKell, Jack Darragh, Morley Bruce, Georges Boucher, Eddie Gerard (Captain), Clint Benedict, Sprague Cleghorn, Frank Nighbor, Punch Broadbent, Cy Denneny, Leth Graham; Tommy Gorman (Manager), Pete Green (Coach), F. Dolan (Trainer).
Scores: March 21, at Vancouver — Van. Millionaires 2, Ottawa 1; March 24, at Vancouver — Ottawa 4, Van. Millionaires 3; March 28, at Vancouver — Ottawa 3, Van. Millionaires 2; March 31, at Vancouver — Van. Millionaires 3, Ottawa 2; April 4, at Vancouver — Ottawa 2, Van. Millionaires 1

1919-20 — Ottawa Senators — Jack MacKell, Jack Darragh, Morley Bruce, Horace Merrill, Georges Boucher, Eddie Gerard (Captain), Clint Benedict, Sprague Cleghorn, Frank Nighbor, Punch Broadbent, Cy Denneny, Tommy Gorman (Manager), Pete Green (Coach).
Scores: March 22, at Ottawa — Ottawa 3, Seattle 2; March 24, at Ottawa — Ottawa 3, Seattle 0; March 27, at Ottawa — Seattle 3, Ottawa 1; March 30, at Toronto* — Seattle 5, Ottawa 2; April 1, at Toronto* — Ottawa 6, Seattle 1.

* Games transferred to Toronto to benefit from artificial ice surface.

1918-19 — No decision, Series halted by Spanish influenza epidemic, illness of several players and death of Joe Hall of Montreal Canadiens from the flu. Five games had been played when the series was halted, each team having won two and tied one. Final scores are listed below.
Scores: March 19, at Seattle — Seattle 7, Montreal 0; March 22, at Seattle — Montreal 4, Seattle 2; March 24, at Seattle — Seattle 7, Montreal 2; March 26, at Seattle — Montreal 0, Seattle 0; March 30, at Seattle — Montreal 4, Seattle 3.

1917-18 — Toronto Arenas — Rusty Crawford, Harry Meeking, Ken Randall (Captain), Corb Denneny, Harry Cameron, Jack Adams, Alf Skinner, Harry Mummery, Hap Holmes, Reg Noble, Sammy Hebert, Jack Marks, Jack Coughlin; Charlie Querrie (Manager), Dick Carroll (Coach), Frank Carroll (Trainer).
Scores: March 20, at Toronto — Toronto 5, Van. Millionaires 3; March 23, at Toronto — Van. Millionaires 6, Toronto 4; March 26, at Toronto — Toronto 6, Van. Millionaires 3; March 28, at Toronto — Van. Millionaires 8, Toronto 1; March 30, at Toronto — Toronto 2, Van. Millionaires 1.

1916-17 — Seattle Metropolitans — Hap Holmes, Ed Carpenter, Cully Wilson, Jack Walker, Bernie Morris, Frank Foyston, Roy Rickey, Jim Riley, Bobby Rowe (Captain); Peter Muldoon (Manager).
Scores: March 17, at Seattle — Montreal 8, Seattle 4; March 20, at Seattle — Seattle 6, Montreal 1; March 23, at Seattle — Seattle 4, Montreal 1; March 25, at Seattle — Seattle 9, Montreal 1.

1915-16 — Montreal Canadiens — Georges Vezina, Bert Corbeau, Jack Laviolette, Newsy Lalonde, Louis Berlinquette, Goldie Prodgers, Howard McNamara (Captain), Didier Pitre, Skene Ronan, Amos Arbour, Skinner Poulin, Jack Fournier; George Kennedy (Manager).
Scores: March 20, at Montreal — Portland 2, Montreal 0; March 22, at Montreal — Montreal 2, Portland 1; March 25, at Montreal — Montreal 6, Portland 3; March 28, at Montreal — Portland 6, Montreal 5; March 30, at Montreal — Montreal 2, Portland 1.

1914-15 — Vancouver Millionaires — Ken Mallen, Frank Nighbor, Cyclone Taylor, Hugh Lehman, Lloyd Cook, Mickey MacKay, Barney Stanley, Jim Seaborn, Si Griffis (Captain), Johnny Matz; Frank Patrick (Playing Manager).
Scores: March 22, at Vancouver — Van. Millionaires 6, Ottawa 2; March 24, at Vancouver — Van. Millionaires 8, Ottawa 3; March 26, at Vancouver — Van. Millionaires 12, Ottawa 3.

1913-14 — Toronto Blueshirts — Con Corbeau, Roy McGiffen, Jack Walker, George McNamara, Cully Wilson, Frank Foyston, Harry Cameron, Hap Holmes, Scotty Davidson (Captain), Harriston; Jack Marshall (Playing Manager), Frank Carroll, Dick Carroll (Trainers).
Scores: March 14, at Toronto — Toronto 5, Victoria 2; March 17, at Toronto — Toronto 6, Victoria 5; March 19, at Toronto — Toronto 2, Victoria 1.

Prior to 1914, teams could challenge the Stanley Cup champions for the title, thus there was more than one Championship Series played in most of the seasons between 1894 and 1913.

1912-13 — Quebec Bulldogs — Joe Malone (Captain), Joe Hall, Paddy Moran, Harry Mummery, Tommy Smith, Jack Marks, Rusty Crawford, Billy Creighton, Jeff Malone, Rocket Power; M.J. Quinn (Manager), D. Beland (Trainer).
Scores: March 8, at Quebec — Que. Bulldogs 14, Sydney 3; March 10, at Quebec — Que. Bulldogs 6, Sydney 2.

Victoria challenged Quebec but the Bulldogs refused to put the Stanley Cup in competition so the two teams played an exhibition series with Victoria winning two games to one by scores of 7-5, 3-6, 6-1. It was the first meeting between the Eastern champions and the Western champions. The following year, and until the Western Hockey League disbanded after the 1926 playoffs, the Cup went to the winner of the series between East and West.

1911-12 — Quebec Bulldogs — Goldie Prodgers, Joe Hall, Walter Rooney, Paddy Moran, Jack Marks, Jack McDonald, Eddie Oatman, George Leonard, Joe Malone (Captain); Charley Nolan (Coach), M.J. Quinn (Manager), D. Beland (Trainer).
Scores: March 11, at Quebec — Que. Bulldogs 9, Moncton 3; March 13, at Quebec — Que. Bulldogs 8, Moncton 0.

1910-11 — Ottawa Senators — Hamby Shore, Percy LeSueur (Captain), Jack Darragh, Bruce Stuart, Marty Walsh, Bruce Ridpath, Fred Lake, Dubbie Kerr, Alex Currie, Horace Gaul.
Scores: March 13, at Ottawa — Ottawa 7, Galt 4; March 16, at Ottawa — Ottawa 13, Port Arthur 4.

1909-10 — (March) **— Montreal Wanderers —** Cecil Blachford, Moose Johnson, Ernie Russell, Riley Hern, Harry Hyland, Jack Marshall, Pud Glass (Captain), Jimmy Gardner; Dickie Boon (Manager).
Scores: March 12, at Montreal — Mtl. Wanderers 7, Berlin (Kitchener) 3.

By winning the 1910 NHA title, the Montreal Wanderers took possession of the Stanley Cup from Ottawa and accepted a challenge from Berlin, 1910 champions of the OPHL

1909-10 — (January) **— Ottawa Senators —** Dubbie Kerr, Fred Lake, Percy LeSueur, Ken Mallen, Bruce Ridpath, Gord Roberts, Hamby Shore, Bruce Stuart (Captain), Marty Walsh.

The Senators accepted two challenges as defending Cup champions. The first was against Galt in a 2-game, total-goals series, and the second was against Edmonton, also a 2-game, total-goals series.
Scores: January 5, at Ottawa — Ottawa 12, Galt 3; January 7, at Ottawa — Ottawa 3, Galt 1; January 18, at Ottawa — Ottawa 8, Edm. Eskimos 4; January 20, at Ottawa — Ottawa 13, Edm. Eskimos 7.

1908-09 — Ottawa Senators — Fred Lake, Percy LeSueur, Cyclone Taylor, Billy Gilmour, Dubbie Kerr, Edgar Dey, Marty Walsh, Bruce Stuart (Captain).

Ottawa, as champions of the Eastern Canada Hockey Association took over the Stanley Cup in 1909 and, although a challenge was accepted by the Cup trustees from Winnipeg Shamrocks, games could not be arranged because of the lateness of the season. No other challenges were made in 1909.

1907-08 — Montreal Wanderers — Riley Hern, Art Ross, Walter Smaill, Pud Glass, Bruce Stuart, Ernie Russell, Moose Johnson, Cecil Blachford (Captain), Tom Hooper, Larry Gilmour, Ernie Liffiton; Dickie Boon (Manager).
Scores: Wanderers accepted four challenges for the Cup: January 9, at Montreal — Mtl. Wanderers 9, Ott. Victorias 3; January 13, at Montreal — Mtl. Wanderers 13, Ott. Victorias 1; March 10, at Montreal — Mtl. Wanderers 11, Wpg. Maple Leafs 5; March 12, at Montreal — Mtl. Wanderers 9, Wpg. Maple Leafs 3; March 14, at Montreal — Mtl. Wanderers 6, Toronto (OPHL) 4. At start of following season, 1908-09, Wanderers were challenged by Edmonton. Results: December 28, at Montreal — Mtl. Wanderers 7, Edm. Eskimos 3; December 30, at Montreal — Edm. Eskimos 7, Mtl. Wanderers 6. Total goals: Mtl. Wanderers 13, Edm. Eskimos 10.

1906-07 — (March 25) **— Montreal Wanderers —** Billy Strachan, Riley Hern, Lester Patrick, Hod Stuart, Pud Glass, Ernie Russell, Cecil Blachford (Captain), Moose Johnson, Rod Kennedy, Jack Marshall; Dickie Boon (Manager).

1906-07 — (March 18) **— Kenora Thistles —** Eddie Giroux, Si Griffis, Tom Hooper, Fred Whitcroft, Alf Smith, Harry Westwick, Roxy Beaudro, Tommy Phillips (Captain), Russell Phillips.
Scores: March 16, at Winnipeg — Kenora 8, Brandon 6; March 18, at Winnipeg — Kenora 4, Brandon 1; March 23, at Winnipeg — Mtl. Wanderers 7, Kenora 2; March 25, at Winnipeg — Kenora 6, Mtl. Wanderers 5. Total goals: Mtl. Wanderers 12, Kenora 8.

1906-07 — (January) **— Kenora Thistles —** Eddie Giroux, Art Ross, Si Griffis, Tom Hooper, Billy McGimsie, Roxy Beaudro, Tommy Phillips (Captain), Joe Hall, Russell Phillips.
Scores: January 17, at Montreal — Kenora 4, Mtl. Wanderers 2; Jan. 21, at Montreal — Kenora 8, Mtl. Wanderers 6.

1906-07 — (December) **— Montreal Wanderers —** Riley Hern, Billy Strachan, Rod Kennedy, Lester Patrick, Pud Glass, Ernie Russell, Moose Johnson, Cecil Blachford (Captain), Dickie Boon (Manager).

1905-06 — (March) **— Montreal Wanderers —** Henri Menard, Billy Strachan, Rod Kennedy, Lester Patrick, Pud Glass, Ernie Russell, Moose Johnson, Cecil Blachford (Captain), Josh Arnold; Dickie Boon (Manager).
Scores: March 14, at Montreal — Mtl. Wanderers 9, Ottawa 1; March 17, at Ottawa — Ottawa 9, Mtl. Wanderers 3. Total goals: Mtl. Wanderers 12, Ottawa 10. Wanderers accepted a challenge from New Glasgow, N.S., prior to the start of the 1906-07 season. Results: December 27, at Montreal — Mtl. Wanderers 10, New Glasgow 3; December 29, at Montreal — Mtl. Wanderers 7, New Glasgow 2.

1905-06 — (February) **— Ottawa Silver Seven —** Harvey Pulford (Captain), Arthur Moore, Harry Westwick, Frank McGee, Alf Smith (Playing Coach), Billy Gilmour, Billy Hague, Percy LeSueur, Harry Smith, Tommy Smith, Dion, Ebbs.
Scores: February 27, at Ottawa — Ottawa 16, Queen's University 7; February 28, at Ottawa — Ottawa 12, Queen's University 7; March 6, at Ottawa — Ottawa 6, Smiths Falls 5; March 8, at Ottawa — Ottawa 8, Smiths Falls 2.

1904-05 — Ottawa Silver Seven — Dave Finnie, Harvey Pulford (Captain), Arthur Moore, Harry Westwick, Frank McGee, Alf Smith (Playing Coach), Billy Gilmour, Frank White, Horace Gaul, Hamby Shore, Bones Allen.
Scores: January 13, at Ottawa — Ottawa 9, Dawson City 2; January 16, at Ottawa — Ottawa 23, Dawson City 2; March 7, at Ottawa — Rat Portage 9, Ottawa 3; March 9, at Ottawa — Ottawa 4, Rat Portage 2; March 11, at Ottawa — Ottawa 5, Rat Portage 4.

1903-04 — Ottawa Silver Seven — Suddy Gilmour, Arthur Moore, Frank McGee, Bouse Hutton, Billy Gilmour, Jim McGee, Harry Westwick, Harvey Pulford (Captain), Scott, Alf Smith (Playing Coach).
Scores: December 30, at Ottawa — Ottawa 9, Wpg. Rowing Club 1; January 1, at Ottawa — Wpg. Rowing Club 6, Ottawa 2; January 4, at Ottawa — Ottawa 2, Wpg. Rowing Club 0. February 23, at Ottawa — Ottawa 6, Tor. Marlboros 3; February 25, at Ottawa — Ottawa 11, Tor. Marlboros 2; March 2, at Montreal — Ottawa 5, Mtl. Wanderers 5. Following the tie game, a new two-game series was ordered to be played in Ottawa but the Wanderers refused unless the tie game was replayed in Montreal. When no settlement could be reached, the series was abandoned and Ottawa retained the Cup and accepted a two-game challenge from Brandon. Results: (both games at Ottawa), March 9, Ottawa 6, Brandon 3; March 11, Ottawa 9, Brandon 3.

1902-03 — (March) — Ottawa Silver Seven — Suddy Gilmour, Percy Sims, Bouse Hutton, Dave Gilmour, Billy Gilmour, Harry Westwick, Frank McGee, F.H. Wood, A.A. Fraser, Charles Spittal, Harvey Pulford (Captain), Arthur Moore; Alf Smith (Coach).
Scores: March 7, at Montreal — Ottawa 1, Mtl. Victorias 1; March 10, at Ottawa — Ottawa 8, Mtl. Victorias 0. Total goals: Ottawa 9, Mtl. Victorias 1; March 12, at Ottawa — Ottawa 6, Rat Portage 2; March 14, at Ottawa — Ottawa 4, Rat Portage 2.

1902-03 — (February) — Montreal AAA — Tom Hodge, Dickie Boon, Billy Nicholson, Tommy Phillips, Art Hooper, Billy Bellingham, Charles Liffiton, Jack Marshall, Jimmy Gardner, Cecil Blachford, George Smith.
Scores: January 29, at Montreal — Mtl. AAA 8, Wpg. Victorias 1; January 31, at Montreal — Wpg. Victorias 2, Mtl. AAA 2; February 2, at Montreal — Wpg. Victorias 4, Mtl. AAA 2; February 4, at Montreal — Mtl. AAA 5, Wpg. Victorias 1.

1901-02 — (March) — Montreal AAA — Tom Hodge, Dickie Boon, Billy Nicholson, Art Hooper, Billy Bellingham, Charles Liffiton, Jack Marshall, Roland Elliot, Jimmy Gardner.
Scores: March 13, at Winnipeg — Wpg. Victorias 1, Mtl. AAA 0; March 15, at Winnipeg — Mtl. AAA 5, Wpg. Victorias 0; March 17, at Winnipeg — Mtl. AAA 2, Wpg. Victorias 1.

1901-02 — (January) — Winnipeg Victorias — Burke Wood, Tony Gingras, Charles Johnstone, Rod Flett, Magnus Flett, Dan Bain (Captain), Fred Scanlon, F. Cadham, Art Brown.
Scores: January 21, at Winnipeg — Wpg. Victorias 5, Tor Wellingtons 3; January 23, at Winnipeg — Wpg. Victorias 5, Tor. Wellingtons 3.

1900-01 — Winnipeg Victorias — Burke Wood, Jack Marshall, Tony Gingras, Charles Johnstone, Rod Flett, Magnus Flett, Dan Bain (Captain), Art Brown, George Carruthers.
Scores: January 29, at Montreal — Wpg. Victorias 4, Mtl. Shamrocks 3; January 31, at Montreal — Wpg. Victorias 2, Mtl. Shamrocks 1.

1899-1900 — Montreal Shamrocks — oe McKenna, Frank Tansey, Frank Wall, Art Farrell, Fred Scanlon, Harry Trihey (Captain), Jack Brannen.
Scores: February 12, at Montreal — Mtl. Shamrocks 4, Wpg. Victorias 3; February 14, at Montreal — Wpg. Victorias 3, Mtl. Shamrocks 2; February 16, at Montreal — Mtl. Shamrocks 5, Wpg. Victorias 4; March 5, at Montreal — Mtl. Shamrocks 10, Halifax 2; March 7, at Montreal — Mtl. Shamrocks 11, Halifax 0.

1898-99 — (March) — Montreal Shamrocks — Joe McKenna, Frank Tansey, Frank Wall, Harry Trihey (Captain), Art Farrell, Fred Scanlon, Jack Brannen, John Dobby, Charles Hoerner.
Scores: March 14, at Montreal — Mtl. Shamrocks 6, Queen's University 2.

1898-99 — (February) — Montreal Victorias — Gordon Lewis, Mike Grant (Captain), Graham Drinkwater, Cam Davidson, Bob McDougall, Ernie McLea, Frank Richardson, Jack Ewing, Russell Bowie, Douglas Acer, Fred McRobie.
Scores: February 15, at Montreal — Mtl. Victorias 2, Wpg. Victorias 1; February 18, at Montreal — Mtl. Victorias 3, Wpg. Victorias 2.

1897-98 — Montreal Victorias — Gordon Lewis, Hartland McDougall, Mike Grant, Graham Drinkwater, Cam Davidson, Bob McDougall, Ernie McLea, Frank Richardson (Captain), Jack Ewing.

1896-97 — Montreal Victorias — Gordon Lewis, Harold Henderson, Mike Grant (Captain), Cam Davidson, Graham Drinkwater, Bob McDougall, Ernie McLea, Shirley Davidson, Hartland McDougall, Jack Ewing, Percy Molson, David Gillilan, McLellan.
Scores: December 27, at Montreal — Mtl. Victorias 15, Ott. Capitals 2.

1895-96 — (December) — Montreal Victorias — Harold Henderson, Mike Grant (Captain), Bob McDougall, Graham Drinkwater, Shirley Davidson, Hartland McDougall, Ernie McLea, Cam Davidson, David Gillilan, Stanley Willett, Gordon Lewis, W. Wallace.
Scores: December 30, at Winnipeg — Mtl. Victorias 6, Wpg. Victorias 5.

1895-96 — (February) — Winnipeg Victorias — Whitey Merritt, Rod Flett, Fred Higginbotham, Jack Armitage (Captain), Tote Campbell, Dan Bain, Charles Johnstone, Attie Howard.
Scores: February 14, at Montreal — Wpg. Victorias 2, Mtl. Victorias 0.

1894-95 — Montreal Victorias — Robert Jones, Harold Henderson, Mike Grant (Captain), Shirley Davidson, Hartland McDougall, Bob McDougall, Norman Rankin, Graham Drinkwater, Roland Elliot, William Pullan, Arthur Fenwick, A. McDougall.

1893-94 — Montreal AAA — Herb Collins, Allan Cameron, George James, Billy Barlow, Clare Mussen, Archie Hodgson, Haviland Routh, Alex Irving, James Stewart, E. O'Brien, Toad Wand, Alex Kingan.
Scores: March 17, at Mtl. Victorias — Mtl. AAA 3, Mtl. Victorias 2; March 22, at Montreal — Mtl. AAA 3, Ott. Capitals 1.

1892-93 — Montreal AAA — Tom Paton, James Stewart, Allan Cameron, Haviland Routh, Archie Hodgson, Billy Barlow, Alex Irving, Alex Kingan, G.S. Low.

All-Time NHL Playoff Formats

1917-18 — The regular-season was split into two halves. The winners of both halves faced each other in a two-game, total-goals series for the NHL championship and the right to meet the PCHA champion in the best-of-five Stanley Cup Finals.

1918-19 — Same as 1917-18, except that the Stanley Cup Finals was extended to a best-of-seven series.

1919-20 — Same as 1917-1918, except that Ottawa won both halves of the split regular-season schedule to earn an automatic berth into the best-of-five Stanley Cup Finals against the PCHA champions.

1921-22 — The top two teams at the conclusion of the regular-season faced each other in a two-game, total-goals series for the NHL championship. The NHL champion then moved on to play the winner of the PCHA-WCHL playoff series in the best-of-five Stanley Cup Finals.

1922-23 — The top two teams at the conclusion of the regular-season faced each other in a two-game, total-goals series for the NHL championship. The NHL champion then moved on to play the PCHA champion in the best-of-three Stanley Cup Semi-Finals, and the winner of the Semi-Finals played the WCHL champion, which had been given a bye, in the best-of-three Stanley Cup Finals.

1923-24 — The top two teams at the conclusion of the regular-season faced each other in a two-game, total-goals series for the NHL championship. The NHL champion then moved on to play the loser of the PCHA-WCHL playoff (the winner of the PCHA-WCHL playoff earned a bye into the Stanley Cup Finals) in the best-of-three Stanley Cup Semi-Finals. The winner of this series met the PCHA-WCHL playoff winner in the best-of-three Stanley Cup Finals.

1924-25 — The first place team (Hamilton) at the conclusion of the regular-season was supposed to play the winner of a two-game, total-goals series between the second (Toronto) and third (Montreal) place clubs. However, Hamilton refused to abide by this new format, demanding greater compensation than offered by the League. Thus, Toronto and Montreal played their two-game, total-goals series, and the winner (Montreal) earned the NHL title and then played the WCHL champion (Victoria) in the best-of-five Stanley Cup Finals.

1925-26 — The format which was intended for 1924-25 went into effect. The winner of the two-game, total-goals series between the second and third place teams squared off against the first place team in the two-game, total-goals NHL championship series. The NHL champion then moved on to play the WHL champion in the best-of-five Stanley Cup Finals.

After the 1925-26 season, the NHL was the only major professional hockey league still in existence and consequently took over sole control of the Stanley Cup competition.

1926-27 — The 10-team league was divided into two divisions — Canadian and American — of five teams apiece. In each division, the winner of the two-game, total-goals series between the second and third place teams faced the first place team in a two-game, total-goals series for the division title. The two division title winners then met in the best-of-five Stanley Cup Finals.

1928-29 — Both first place teams in the two divisions played each other in a best-of-five series. Both second place teams in the two divisions played each other in a two-game, total-goals series as did the two third place teams. The winners of these latter two series then played each other in a best-of-three series for the right to meet the winner of the series between the two first place clubs. This Stanley Cup Final was a best-of-three.

Series A: First in Canadian Division vs. first in American (best-of-five)
Series B: Second in Canadian Division vs. second in American (two-game, total-goals)
Series C: Third in Canadian Division vs. third in American (two-game, total-goals)
Series D: Winner of Series B vs. winner of Series C (best-of-three)
Series E: Winner of Series A vs. winner of Series D (best-of-three) for Stanley Cup

1931-32 — Same as 1928-29, except that Series D was changed to a two-game, total-goals format and Series E was changed to best-of-five.

1936-37 — Same as 1931-32, except that Series B, C, and D were each best-of-three.

1938-39 — With the NHL reduced to seven teams, the two-division system was replaced by one seven-team league. Based on final regular-season standings, the following playoff format was adopted:

Series A: First vs. Second (best-of-seven)
Series B: Third vs. Fourth (best-of-three)
Series C: Fifth vs. Sixth (best-of-three)
Series D: Winner of Series B vs. winner of Series C (best-of-three)
Series E: Winner of Series A vs. winner of Series D (best-of-seven)

1942-43 — With the NHL reduced to six teams (the "original six"), only the top four finishers qualified for playoff action. The best-of-seven Semi-Finals pitted Team #1 vs. Team #3 and Team #2 vs. Team #4. The winners of each Semi-Final series met in the best-of-seven Stanley Cup Finals.

1967-68 — When it doubled in size from 6 to 12 teams, the NHL once again was divided into two divisions — East and West — of six teams apiece. The top four clubs in each division qualified for the playoffs (all series were best-of-seven):

Series A: Team #1 (East) vs. Team #3 (East)
Series B: Team #2 (East) vs. Team #4 (East)
Series C: Team #1 (West) vs. Team #3 (West)
Series D: Team #2 (West) vs. Team #4 (West)
Series E: Winner of Series A vs. winner of Series B
Series F: Winner of Series C vs. winner of Series D
Series G: Winner of Series E vs. Winner of Series F

1970-71 — Same as 1967-68 except that Series E matched the winners of Series A and D, and Series F matched the winners of Series B and C.

1971-72 — Same as 1970-71, except that Series A and C matched Team #1 vs. Team #4, and Series B and D matched Team #2 vs. Team #3.

1974-75 — With the League now expanded to 18 teams in four divisions, a completely new playoff format was introduced. First, the #2 and #3 teams in each of the four divisions were pooled together in the Preliminary round. These eight (#2 and #3) clubs were ranked #1 to #8 based on regular-season record:

Series A: Team #1 vs. Team #8 (best-of-three)
Series B: Team #2 vs. Team #7 (best-of-three)
Series C: Team #3 vs. Team #6 (best-of-three)
Series D: Team #4 vs. Team #5 (best-of-three)
The winners of this Preliminary round then pooled together with the four division winners, which had received byes into this Quarter-Final round. These eight teams were again ranked #1 to #8 based on regular-season record:
Series E: Team #1 vs. Team #8 (best-of-seven)
Series F: Team #2 vs. Team #7 (best-of-seven)
Series G: Team #3 vs. Team #6 (best-of-seven)
Series H: Team #4 vs. Team #5 (best-of-seven)
The four Quarter-Finals winners, which moved on to the Semi-Finals, were then ranked #1 to #4 based on regular season record:
Series I: Team #1 vs. Team #4 (best-of-seven)
Series J: Team #2 vs. Team #3 (best-of-seven)
Series K: Winner of Series I vs. winner of Series J (best-of-seven)

1977-78 — Same as 1974-75, except that the Preliminary round consisted of the #2 teams in the four divisions and the next four teams based on regular-season record (not their standings within their divisions).

1979-80 — With the addition of four WHA franchises, the League expanded its playoff structure to include 16 of its 21 teams. The four first place teams in the four divisions automatically earned playoff berths. Among the 17 other clubs, the top 12, according to regular-season record, also earned berths. All 16 teams were then pooled together and ranked #1 to #16 based on regular-season record:

Series A: Team #1 vs. Team #16 (best-of-five)
Series B: Team #2 vs. Team #15 (best-of-five)
Series C: Team #3 vs. Team #14 (best-of-five)
Series D: Team #4 vs. Team #13 (best-of-five)
Series E: Team #5 vs. Team #12 (best-of-five)
Series F: Team #6 vs. Team #11 (best-of-five)
Series G: Team #7 vs. Team #10 (best-of-five)
Series H: Team #8 vs. Team # 9 (best-of-five)
The eight Preliminary round winners, ranked #1 to #8 based on regular-season record, moved on to the Quarter-Finals:
Series I: Team #1 vs. Team #8 (best-of-seven)
Series J: Team #2 vs. Team #7 (best-of-seven)
Series K: Team #3 vs. Team #6 (best-of-seven)
Series L: Team #4 vs. Team #5 (best-of-seven)
The four Quarter-Finals winners, ranked #1 to #4 based on regular-season record, moved on to the semi-finals:
Series M: Team #1 vs. Team #4 (best-of-seven)
Series N: Team #2 vs. Team #3 (best-of-seven)
Series O: Winner of Series M vs. winner of Series N (best-of-seven)

1981-82 — The first four teams in each division earned playoff berths. In each division, the first-place team opposed the fourth-place team and the second-place team opposed the third-place team in a best-of-five Division Semi-Final series (DSF). In each division, the two winners of the DSF met in a best-of-seven Division Final series (DF). The two DF winners in each conference met in a best-of-seven Conference Final series (CF). In the Prince of Wales Conference, the Adams Division winner opposed the Patrick Division winner; in the Clarence Campbell Conference, the Smythe Division winner opposed the Norris Division winner. The two CF winners met in a best-of-seven Stanley Cup Final (F) series.

1986-87 — Division Semi-Final series changed from best-of-five to best-of-seven.

1993-94 — The NHL's playoff draw is conference-based rather than division-based. At the conclusion of the regular season, the top eight teams in each of the Eastern and Western Conferences qualify for the playoffs. The teams that finish in first place in each of the League's divisions are seeded first and second in each conference's playoff draw and are assured of home ice advantage in the first two playoff rounds. The remaining teams are seeded based on their regular-season point totals. In each conference, the team seeded #1 plays #8; #2 vs. #7; #3 vs. #6; and #4 vs. #5. All series are best-of-seven with home ice rotating on a 2-2-1-1-1 basis, with the exception of matchups between Central and Pacific Division teams. These matchups will be played on a 2-3-2 basis to reduce travel. In a 2-3-2 series, the team with the most points will have its choice to start the series at home or on the road. The Eastern Conference champion will face the Western Conference champion in the Stanley Cup Final.

1994-95 — Same as 1993-94, except that in first, second or third-round playoff series involving Central and Pacific Division teams, the team with the better record has the choice of using either a 2-3-2 or a 2-2-1-1-1 format. When a 2-3-2 format is selected, the higher-ranked team also has the choice of playing games 1, 2, 6 and 7 at home or playing games 3, 4 and 5 at home. The format for the Stanley Cup Final remains 2-2-1-1-1.

1998-99 — The NHL's clubs are re-aligned into two conferences each consisting of three divisions. The number of teams qualifying for the Stanley Cup Playoffs remains unchanged at 16.

First-round playoff berths will be awarded to the first-place team in each division as well as to the next five best teams based on regular-season point totals in each conference. The three division winners in each conference will be seeded first through third, in order of points, for the playoffs and the next five best teams, in order of points, will be seeded fourth through eighth. In each conference, the team seeded #1 will play #8; #2 vs. #7; #3 vs. #6; and #4 vs. #5 in the quarterfinal round. Home-ice in the Conference Quarter-Finals is granted to those teams seeded first through fourth in each conference.

In the Conference Semi-Finals and Conference Finals, teams will be re-seeded according to the same criteria as the Conference Quarter-Finals. Higher seeded teams will have home-ice advantage.

Home-ice advantage for the Stanley Cup Finals will be determined by points.

All series remain best-of-seven.

Captain Nicklas Lidstrom and his teammates celebrate Detroit's Stanley Cup victory in 2008. The win marked the 11th championship in Red Wings history in their 23rd appearance in the Stanley Cup Final.

Team Records

1918-2008

GAMES PLAYED

MOST GAMES PLAYED BY ALL TEAMS, ONE PLAYOFF YEAR:
92 — 1991. There were 51 DSF, 24 DF, 11 CF and 6 F games.
90 — 1994. There were 48 CQF, 23 CSF, 12 CF and 7 F games.
— 2002. There were 47 CQF, 25 CSF, 13 CF and 5 F games.

MOST GAMES PLAYED, ONE TEAM, ONE PLAYOFF YEAR:
26 — Philadelphia Flyers, 1987. Won DSF 4-2 vs. NY Rangers, DF 4-3 vs. NY Islanders, CF 4-2 vs. Montreal, and lost F 4-3 vs. Edmonton.
— Calgary Flames, 2004. Won DSF 4-3 vs. Vancouver, DF 4-2 vs. Detroit, CF 4-2 vs. San Jose, and lost F 4-3 vs. Tampa Bay.
25 — New Jersey Devils, 2001. Won CQF 4-2 vs. Carolina, CSF 4-3 vs. Toronto, CF 4-1 vs. Pittsburgh, and lost F 4-3 vs. Colorado.
— Carolina Hurricanes, 2006. Won CQF 4-2 vs. Montreal, CSF 4-1 vs. New Jersey, CF 4-3 vs. Buffalo, and F 4-3 vs. Edmonton

PLAYOFF APPEARANCES

MOST STANLEY CUP CHAMPIONSHIPS:
23 — Montreal Canadiens (1924-30-31-44-46-53-56-57-58-59-60-65-66-68-69-71-73-76-77-78-79-86-93)
13 — Toronto Maple Leafs (1918-22-32-42-45-47-48-49-51-62-63-64-67)
11 — Detroit Red Wings (1936-37-43-50-52-54-55-97-98-2002-08)

MOST CONSECUTIVE STANLEY CUP CHAMPIONSHIPS:
5 — Montreal Canadiens (1956-57-58-59-60)
4 — Montreal Canadiens (1976-77-78-79)
— NY Islanders (1980-81-82-83)

MOST FINAL SERIES APPEARANCES:
32 — Montreal Canadiens in 91-year history.
23 — Detroit Red Wings in 82-year history.
21 — Toronto Maple Leafs in 91-year history.

MOST CONSECUTIVE FINAL SERIES APPEARANCES:
10 — Montreal Canadiens, (1951-60, inclusive)
5 — Montreal Canadiens, (1965-69, inclusive)
— NY Islanders, (1980-84, inclusive)

MOST YEARS IN PLAYOFFS:
75 — Montreal Canadiens in 91-year history.
64 — Toronto Maple Leafs in 91-year history.
62 — Boston Bruins in 84-year history.

MOST CONSECUTIVE PLAYOFF APPEARANCES:
29 — Boston Bruins (1968-96, inclusive)
28 — Chicago Blackhawks (1970-97, inclusive)
25 — St. Louis Blues (1980-2004, inclusive)
24 — Montreal Canadiens (1971-94, inclusive)
21 — Montreal Canadiens (1949-69, inclusive)

TEAM WINS

MOST HOME WINS, ONE TEAM, ONE PLAYOFF YEAR:
12 — New Jersey Devils, 2003 in 13 home games.
11 — Edmonton Oilers, 1988 in 11 home games.
10 — Edmonton Oilers, 1985 in 10 home games.
— Montreal Canadiens, 1986 in 11 home games.
— Montreal Canadiens, 1993 in 11 home games.
— Carolina Hurricanes, 2006 in 14 home games.
— Anaheim Ducks, 2007 in 12 home games.

MOST HOME WINS, ALL TEAMS, ONE PLAYOFF YEAR:
57 — 1991. Of 92 games played, home teams won 57 (29 DSF, 17 DF, 8 CF and 3 in F).

MOST ROAD WINS, ONE TEAM, ONE PLAYOFF YEAR:
10 — New Jersey Devils, 1995. Won three at Boston in CQF; two at Pittsburgh in CSF; three at Philadelphia in CF; and two at Detroit in F.
— New Jersey Devils, 2000. Won two at Florida in CQF; two at Toronto in CSF; three at Philadelphia in CF; and three at Dallas in F.
— Calgary Flames, 2004. Won three at Vancouver in DSF; two at Detroit in DF; three at San Jose in CF; and two at Tampa Bay in F.
8 — NY Islanders, 1980. Won two at Los Angeles in PR; three at Boston in QF; two at Buffalo in SF; and one at Philadelphia in F.
— Philadelphia Flyers, 1987. Won two at NY Rangers in DSF; two at NY Islanders in DF; three at Montreal in CF; and one at Edmonton in F.
— Edmonton Oilers, 1990. Won one at Winnipeg in DSF; two at Los Angeles in DF; two at Chicago in CF and three at Boston in F.
— Pittsburgh Penguins, 1992. Won two at Washington in DSF; two at NY Rangers in DF; two at Boston in CF; and two at Chicago in F.
— Vancouver Canucks, 1994. Won three at Calgary in CQF; two at Dallas in CSF; one at Toronto in CF; and two at NY Rangers in F.
— Colorado Avalanche, 1996. Won two at Vancouver in CQF; two at Chicago in CSF; two at Detroit in CF; and two at Florida in F.
— Detroit Red Wings, 1998. Won two at Phoenix in CQF; three at St. Louis in CSF; one at Dallas in CF; and two at Washington in F.
— Colorado Avalanche, 1999. Won three at San Jose in CQF; three at Detroit in CSF; and two at Dallas in CF.
— New Jersey Devils, 2001. Won two at Carolina in CQF; two at Toronto in CSF; two at Pittsburgh in CF; and two at Colorado in F.
— Detroit Red Wings, 2002. Won three at Vancouver in CQF; one at St. Louis in CSF; two at Colorado in CF; and two at Carolina in F.

MOST ROAD WINS, ALL TEAMS, ONE PLAYOFF YEAR:
46 — 1987. Of 87 games played, road teams won 46 (22 DSF, 14 DF, 8 CF and 2 in F).

MOST OVERTIME WINS, ONE TEAM, ONE PLAYOFF YEAR:
10 — Montreal Canadiens, 1993. Won two vs. Quebec in DSF; three vs. Buffalo in DF; two vs. NY Islanders in CF; and three vs. Los Angeles in F.
7 — Carolina Hurricanes, 2002. Won two vs. New Jersey in CQF; one vs. Montreal in CSF; three vs. Toronto in CF; and one vs. Detroit in F.
— Anaheim Mighty Ducks, 2003. Won two vs. Detroit in CQF; two vs. Dallas in CSF; one vs. Minnestoa in CF; and two vs. New Jersey in F.

MOST OVERTIME WINS AT HOME, ONE TEAM, ONE PLAYOFF YEAR:
4 — St. Louis Blues, 1968. Won one vs. Philadelphia in QF; three vs. Minnesota in SF.
— Montreal Canadiens, 1993. Won one vs. Quebec in DSF; one vs. Buffalo in DF, one vs. NY Islanders in CF; one vs. Los Angeles in F.

MOST OVERTIME WINS ON THE ROAD, ONE TEAM, ONE PLAYOFF YEAR:
6 — **Montreal Canadiens, 1993.** Won one vs. Quebec in DSF; two vs. Buffalo in DF; one vs. NY Islanders in CF; two vs. Los Angeles in F.

TEAM LOSSES

MOST LOSSES, ONE TEAM, ONE PLAYOFF YEAR:
11 — **Philadelphia Flyers, 1987.** Lost two vs. NY Rangers in DSF; three vs. NY Islanders in DF; two vs. Montreal in CF; four vs. Edmonton in F.
— **Calgary Flames, 2004.** Lost three vs. Vancouver in CQF; two vs. Detroit in CSF; two vs. San Jose in CF; four vs. Tampa Bay in F

MOST HOME LOSSES, ONE TEAM, ONE PLAYOFF YEAR:
7 — **Calgary Flames, 2004.** Lost two vs. Vancouver in DSF; one vs. Detroit in DF; two vs. San Jose in CF; two vs. Tampa Bay in F.
6 — Philadelphia Flyers, 1987. Lost one vs. NY Rangers in DSF; two vs. NY Islanders in DF; two vs. Montreal in CF; one vs. Edmonton in F.
— Washington Capitals, 1998. Lost two vs. Boston in CQF; two vs. Buffalo in CF; two vs. Detroit in F.
— Colorado Avalanche, 1999. Lost two vs. San Jose in CQF; two vs. Detroit in CSF; two vs. Dallas in CF.
— New Jersey Devils, 2001. Lost one vs. Carolina in CQF; two vs. Toronto in CSF; one vs. Pittsburgh in CF; two vs Colorado in F.
— Minnesota Wild, 2003. Lost two vs. Colorado in CQF; two vs. Vancouver in CSF; two vs. Anaheim in CF.

MOST ROAD LOSSES, ONE TEAM, ONE PLAYOFF YEAR:
7 — **New Jersey Devils, 2003.** Lost one at Boston in CQF; one at Tampa Bay in CSF; two at Ottawa in CF; three at Anaheim in F.

MOST OVERTIME LOSSES, ONE TEAM, ONE PLAYOFF YEAR:
4 — **Montreal Canadiens, 1951.** Lost four vs. Toronto in F.
— **St. Louis Blues, 1968.** Lost one vs. Philadelphia in QF; one vs. Minnesota in SF; two vs. Montreal in F.
— **New York Rangers, 1979.** Lost one vs. Philadelphia in QF; two vs. NY Islanders in SF; one vs. Montreal in F.
— **Los Angeles Kings, 1991.** Lost one vs. Vancouver in DSF; three vs. Edmonton in DF.
— **Los Angeles Kings, 1993.** Lost one vs. Toronto in CF; three vs. Montreal in F.
— **New Jersey Devils, 1994.** Lost one vs. Buffalo in CQF; one vs. Boston in CSF; two vs. NY Rangers in CF.
— **Chicago Blackhawks, 1995.** Lost one vs. Toronto in CQF; three vs. Detroit in CF.
— **Philadelphia Flyers, 1996.** Lost two vs. Tampa Bay in CQF; two vs. Florida in CSF.
— **Dallas Stars, 1999.** Lost two vs. St. Louis in CSF; one vs. Colorado in CF; one vs. Buffalo in F.
— **Detroit Red Wings, 2002.** Lost one vs. Vancouver in CQF; two vs. Colorado in CF; one vs. Carolina in F.
— **New Jersey Devils, 2003.** Lost two vs. Ottawa in CF; two vs. Anaheim in F.

MOST OVERTIME LOSSES AT HOME, ONE TEAM, ONE PLAYOFF YEAR:
4 — **Detroit Red Wings, 2002.** Lost one vs. Vancouver in CQF; two vs. Colorado in CF; one vs. Carolina in F.

MOST OVERTIME LOSSES ON THE ROAD, ONE TEAM, ONE PLAYOFF YEAR:
3 — **Los Angeles Kings, 1991.** Lost one at Vancouver in DSF; two at Edmonton in DF.
— **Chicago Blackhawks, 1995.** Lost one at Toronto in CQF; two at Detroit in CF.
— **St. Louis Blues, 1996.** Lost two at Toronto in CQF; one at Detroit in CSF.
— **Dallas Stars, 1999.** Lost two at St. Louis in CSF; one at Colorado in CF.
— **New Jersey Devils, 2003.** Lost one at Ottawa in CF; two at Anaheim in F.

PLAYOFF WINNING STREAKS

LONGEST PLAYOFF WINNING STREAK:
14 — **Pittsburgh Penguins.** Streak started May 9, 1992 as Pittsburgh won the first of three straight games in DF vs. NY Rangers. Continued with four wins vs. Boston in 1992 CF and four wins vs. Chicago in 1992 F. Pittsburgh then won the first three games of 1993 DSF vs. New Jersey. New Jersey ended the streak April 25, 1993, at New Jersey with a 4-1 win vs. Pittsburgh in the fourth game of 1993 DSF.
12 — Edmonton Oilers. Streak started May 15, 1984 as Edmonton won the first of three straight games in F vs. NY Islanders. Continued with three wins vs. Los Angeles in 1985 DSF and four wins vs. Winnipeg in 1985 DF. Edmonton then won the first two games of 1985 CF vs. Chicago. Chicago ended the streak May 9, 1985, at Chicago with a 5-2 win vs. Edmonton in the third game of 1985 CF.

MOST CONSECUTIVE WINS, ONE TEAM, ONE PLAYOFF YEAR:
11 — **Chicago Blackhawks** in 1992. Chicago won last three games of DSF vs. St. Louis to win series 4-2, defeated Detroit 4-0 in DF and Edmonton 4-0 in CF.
— **Pittsburgh Penguins** in 1992. Pittsburgh won last three games of DF vs. NY Rangers to win series 4-2, defeated Boston 4-0 in CF and Chicago 4-0 in F.
— **Montreal Canadiens** in 1993. Montreal won last four games of DSF vs. Quebec to win series 4-2, defeated Buffalo 4-0 in DF and won first three games of CF vs. NY Islanders.

PLAYOFF LOSING STREAKS

LONGEST PLAYOFF LOSING STREAK:
16 — **Chicago Black Hawks.** Streak started April 20, 1975 at Chicago with a 6-2 loss in fourth game of QF vs. Buffalo, won by Buffalo 4-1. Continued with four consecutive losses vs. Montreal, in 1976 QF and two straight losses vs. NY Islanders in 1977 best-of-three PRE. Chicago then lost four games vs. Boston in 1978 QF and four games vs. NY Islanders in 1979 QF. Chicago ended the streak April 8, 1980, at Chicago with a 3-2 win vs. St. Louis in the opening game of 1980 PRE.
— **Los Angeles Kings.** Streak started June 3, 1993 at Montreal with a 3-2 loss in second game of F vs. Montreal, won by Montreal 4-1. Los Angeles failed to qualify for the playoffs for the next four years. Then Los Angeles lost four games vs. St. Louis in 1998 CQF; missed the 1999 playoffs and lost four games vs. Detroit in 2002 CQF. Los Angeles then lost the first two games of 2001 CQF vs. Detroit. Los Angeles ended the streak April 15, 2001, at Los Angeles with a 2-1 win vs. Detroit in the third game of 2001 CQF.

The Montreal Canadiens of 1924-25 wore globes on their sweaters to symbolize the "World Championship" they had won in 1924. The victory was the second Stanley Cup title in franchise history, but the team's first since the formation of the NHL in 1917.

MOST GOALS IN A SERIES, ONE TEAM

MOST GOALS, ONE TEAM, ONE PLAYOFF SERIES:
44 — Edmonton Oilers in 1985. Edmonton won best-of-seven CF 4-2, outscoring Chicago 44-25.
35 — Edmonton Oilers in 1983. Edmonton won best-of-seven DF 4-1, outscoring Calgary 35-13.
— Calgary Flames in 1995. Calgary lost best-of-seven CQF 4-3, outscoring San Jose 35-26.

MOST GOALS, ONE TEAM, TWO-GAME SERIES:
11 — Buffalo Sabres in 1977. Buffalo won best-of-three PRE 2-0, outscoring Minnesota 11-3.
— Toronto Maple Leafs in 1978. Toronto won best-of-three PRE 2-0, outscoring Los Angeles 11-3.

MOST GOALS, ONE TEAM, THREE-GAME SERIES:
23 — Chicago Blackhawks in 1985. Chicago won best-of-five DSF 3-0, outscoring Detroit 23-8.
20 — Minnesota North Stars in 1981. Minnesota won best-of-five PRE 3-0, outscoring Boston 20-13.
— NY Islanders in 1981. NY Islanders won best-of-five PRE 3-0, outscoring Toronto 20-4.

MOST GOALS, ONE TEAM, FOUR-GAME SERIES:
28 — Boston Bruins in 1972. Boston won best-of-seven SF 4-0, outscoring St. Louis 28-8.

MOST GOALS, ONE TEAM, FIVE-GAME SERIES:
35 — Edmonton Oilers in 1983. Edmonton won best-of-seven DF 4-1, outscoring Calgary 35-13.
32 — Edmonton Oilers in 1987. Edmonton won best-of-seven DSF 4-1, outscoring Los Angeles 32-20.
30 — Calgary Flames in 1988. Calgary won best-of-seven DSF 4-1, outscoring Los Angeles 30-18.

MOST GOALS, ONE TEAM, SIX-GAME SERIES:
44 — Edmonton Oilers in 1985. Edmonton won best-of-seven CF 4-2, outscoring Chicago 44-25.
33 — Montreal Canadiens in 1973. Montreal won best-of-seven F 4-2, outscoring Chicago 33-23.
— Chicago Blackhawks in 1985. Chicago won best-of-seven DF 4-2, outscoring Minnesota 33-29.
— Los Angeles Kings in 1993. Los Angeles won best-of-seven DSF 4-2, outscoring Calgary 33-28.

MOST GOALS, ONE TEAM, SEVEN-GAME SERIES:
35 — Calgary Flames in 1995. Calgary lost best-of-seven CQF 4-3, outscoring San Jose 35-26.
33 — Philadelphia Flyers in 1976. Philadelphia won best-of-seven QF 4-3, outscoring Toronto 33-23.
— Boston Bruins in 1983. Boston won best-of-seven DF 4-3, outscoring Buffalo 33-23.
— Edmonton Oilers in 1984. Edmonton won best-of-seven DF 4-3, outscoring Calgary 33-27.

Babe Dye led the NHL in goals scored three times and points twice, but neither he nor any of his St. Pats teammates managed a single goal in Toronto's 1921 two-game league final versus Ottawa.

FEWEST GOALS IN A SERIES, ONE TEAM

FEWEST GOALS, ONE TEAM, TWO-GAME SERIES:
0 — Toronto St. Patricks in 1921. Toronto lost two-game, total-goals NHL F 7-0 vs. Ottawa.
— New York Americans in 1929. NY Americans lost two-game, total-goals QF 1-0 vs. NY Rangers.
— New York Rangers in 1931. NY Rangers lost two-game, total-goals SF 3-0 vs. Chicago.
— Chicago Black Hawks in 1935. Chicago lost two-game, total-goals SF 1-0 vs. Mtl. Maroons.
— Montreal Maroons in 1937. Mtl. Maroons lost best-of-three SF 2-0, outscored by NY Rangers 5-0.
— New York Americans in 1939. NY Americans lost best-of-three QF 2-0, outscored by Toronto 5-0.

FEWEST GOALS, ONE TEAM, THREE-GAME SERIES:
1 — Montreal Maroons in 1936. Mtl. Maroons lost best-of-five SF 3-0, outscored by Detroit 6-1.

FEWEST GOALS, ONE TEAM, FOUR-GAME SERIES:
1 — Minnesota Wild in 2003. Minnesota lost best-of-seven CF 4-0, outscored by Anaheim 9-1.

FEWEST GOALS, ONE TEAM, FIVE-GAME SERIES:
2 — Philadelphia Flyers in 2002. Ottawa won best-of-seven CQF 4-1, while outscoring Philadelphia 11-2.

FEWEST GOALS, ONE TEAM, SIX-GAME SERIES:
5 — Boston Bruins in 1951. Toronto won best-of-seven SF 4-1 with 1 tie, outscoring Boston 17-5.

FEWEST GOALS, ONE TEAM, SEVEN-GAME SERIES:
9 — Toronto Maple Leafs, in 1945. Toronto won best-of- seven F 4-3; teams tied in scoring 9-9.
— Detroit Red Wings, in 1945. Toronto won best-of-seven F 4-3; teams tied in scoring 9-9.

MOST GOALS IN A SERIES, BOTH TEAMS

MOST GOALS, BOTH TEAMS, ONE PLAYOFF SERIES:
69 — Edmonton Oilers (44), Chicago Black Hawks (25) in 1985. Edmonton won best-of-seven CF 4-2.
62 — Chicago Black Hawks (33), Minnesota North Stars (29) in 1985. Chicago won best-of-seven DF 4-2.
61 — Los Angeles Kings (33), Calgary Flames (28) in 1993. Los Angeles won best-of-seven DSF 4-2.
— Calgary Flames (35), San Jose Sharks (26) in 1995. San Jose won best-of-seven CQF 4-3.

MOST GOALS, BOTH TEAMS, TWO-GAME SERIES:
17 — Toronto St. Patricks (10), Montreal Canadiens (7) in 1918. Toronto won two-game total-goals NHL F.
15 — Boston Bruins (10), Chicago Black Hawks (5) in 1927. Boston won two-game total-goals QF.
— Pittsburgh Penguins (9), St. Louis Blues (6) in 1975. Pittsburgh won best-of-three PRE 2-0.

MOST GOALS, BOTH TEAMS, THREE-GAME SERIES:
33 — Minnesota North Stars (20), Boston Bruins (13) in 1981. Minnesota won best-of-five PRE 3-0.
31 — Chicago Black Hawks (23), Detroit Red Wings (8) in 1985. Chicago won best-of-five DSF 3-0.
28 — Toronto Maple Leafs (18), New York Rangers (10) in 1932. Toronto won best-of-five F 3-0.

MOST GOALS, BOTH TEAMS, FOUR-GAME SERIES:
36 — Boston Bruins (28), St. Louis Blues (8) in 1972. Boston won best-of-seven SF 4-0.
— Minnesota North Stars (18), Toronto Maple Leafs (18) in 1983. Minnesota won best-of-five DSF 3-1.
— Edmonton Oilers (25), Chicago Black Hawks (11) in 1983. Edmonton won best-of-seven CF 4-0.
35 — New York Rangers (23), Los Angeles Kings (12) in 1981. NY Rangers won best-of-five PRE 3-1.

MOST GOALS, BOTH TEAMS, FIVE-GAME SERIES:
52 — Edmonton Oilers (32), Los Angeles Kings (20) in 1987. Edmonton won best-of-seven DSF 4-1.
50 — Los Angeles Kings (27), Edmonton Oilers (23) in 1982. Los Angeles won best-of-five DSF 3-2.
48 — Edmonton Oilers (35), Calgary Flames (13) in 1983. Edmonton won best-of-seven DF 4-1.
— Calgary Flames (30), Los Angeles Kings (18) in 1988. Calgary won best-of-seven DSF 4-1.

MOST GOALS, BOTH TEAMS, SIX-GAME SERIES:
69 — Edmonton Oilers (44), Chicago Black Hawks (25) in 1985. Edmonton won best-of-seven CF 4-2.
62 — Chicago Black Hawks (33), Minnesota North Stars (29) in 1985. Chicago won best-of-seven DF 4-2.
61 — Los Angeles Kings (33), Calgary Flames (28) in 1993. Los Angeles won best-of-seven DSF 4-2.

MOST GOALS, BOTH TEAMS, SEVEN-GAME SERIES:
61 — Calgary Flames (35), San Jose Sharks (26) in 1995. San Jose won best-of-seven CQF 4-3.
60 — Edmonton Oilers (33), Calgary Flames (27) in 1984. Edmonton won best-of-seven DF 4-3.

FEWEST GOALS IN A SERIES, BOTH TEAMS

FEWEST GOALS, BOTH TEAMS, TWO-GAME SERIES:
1 — New York Rangers (1), New York Americans (0) in 1929. NY Rangers won two-game total-goals QF.
— Montreal Maroons (1), Chicago Black Hawks (0) in 1935. Mtl. Maroons won two-game total-goals SF.

FEWEST GOALS, BOTH TEAMS, THREE-GAME SERIES:
7 — Boston Bruins (5), Montreal Canadiens (2) in 1929. Boston won best-of-five SF 3-0.
— Detroit Red Wings (6), Montreal Maroons (1) in 1936. Detroit won best-of-five SF 3-0.

FEWEST GOALS, BOTH TEAMS, FOUR-GAME SERIES:
9 — Toronto Maple Leafs (7), Boston Bruins (2) in 1935. Toronto won best-of-five SF 3-1.

FEWEST GOALS, BOTH TEAMS, FIVE-GAME SERIES:
11 — Montreal Maroons (6), New York Rangers (5) in 1928. NY Rangers won best-of-five F 3-2.

FEWEST GOALS, BOTH TEAMS, SIX-GAME SERIES:
16 — Carolina Hurricanes (10), Toronto Maple Leafs (6) in 2002. Carolina won best-of-seven CF 4-2.

FEWEST GOALS, BOTH TEAMS, SEVEN-GAME SERIES:
18 — Toronto Maple Leafs (9), Detroit Red Wings (9) in 1945. Toronto won best-of-seven F 4-3.

MOST GOALS IN A GAME OR PERIOD

MOST GOALS, ONE TEAM, ONE GAME:
13 — Edmonton Oilers April 9, 1987, vs. Los Angeles at Edmonton. Edmonton won 13-3.
12 — Los Angeles Kings, April 10, 1990, vs. Calgary at Los Angeles. Los Angeles won 12-4.
11 — Montreal Canadiens, March 30, 1944, vs. Toronto at Montreal. Montreal won 11-0.
— Edmonton Oilers, May 4, 1985, vs. Chicago at Edmonton. Edmonton won 11-2.

MOST GOALS, ONE TEAM, ONE PERIOD:
7 — Montreal Canadiens, March 30, 1944, vs. Toronto at Montreal, third period. Montreal won 11-0.

MOST GOALS, BOTH TEAMS, ONE GAME:
18 — Los Angeles Kings (10), Edmonton Oilers (8), April 7, 1982, at Edmonton. Los Angeles won best-of-five DSF 3-2.
17 — Pittsburgh Penguins (10), Philadelphia Flyers (7), April 25, 1989, at Pittsburgh. Pittsburgh won best-of-seven DF 4-3.
16 — Edmonton Oilers (13), Los Angeles Kings (3), April 9, 1987, at Edmonton. Edmonton won best-of-seven DSF 4-1.
— Los Angeles Kings (12), Calgary Flames (4), April 10, 1990, at Los Angeles. Los Angeles won best-of-seven DF 4-2.

MOST GOALS, BOTH TEAMS, ONE PERIOD:
9 — New York Rangers (6), Philadelphia Flyers (3), April 24, 1979, third period, at Philadelphia. NY Rangers won 8-3.
— Los Angeles Kings (5), Calgary Flames (4), April 10, 1990, second period, at Los Angeles. Los Angeles won 12-4.
8 — Chicago Black Hawks (5), Montreal Canadiens (3), May 8, 1973, second period, at Montreal. Chicago won 8-7.
— Chicago Black Hawks (5), Edmonton Oilers (3), May 12, 1985, first period, at Chicago. Chicago won 8-6.
— Edmonton Oilers (6), Winnipeg Jets (2), April 6, 1988, third period, at Edmonton. Edmonton won 7-4.
— Hartford Whalers (5), Montreal Canadiens (3), April 10, 1988, third period, at Montreal. Hartford won 7-5.
— Vancouver Canucks (5), New York Rangers (3), June 9, 1994, third period, at NY Rangers. Vancouver won 6-3.

TEAM POWER-PLAY GOALS

MOST POWER-PLAY GOALS BY ALL TEAMS, ONE PLAYOFF YEAR:
199 — 1988 in 83 games.

MOST POWER-PLAY GOALS, ONE TEAM, ONE PLAYOFF YEAR:
35 — Minnesota North Stars, 1991 in 23 games.
32 — Edmonton Oilers, 1988 in 18 games.
31 — New York Islanders, 1981 in 18 games.

MOST POWER-PLAY GOALS, ONE TEAM, ONE SERIES:
15 — New York Islanders in 1980 F vs. Philadelphia. NY Islanders won series 4-2.
— Minnesota North Stars in 1991 DSF vs. Chicago. Minnesota won series 4-2.
13 — New York Islanders in 1981 QF vs. Edmonton. NY Islanders won series 4-2.
— Calgary Flames in 1986 CF vs. St. Louis. Calgary won series 4-3.
12 — Toronto Maple Leafs in 1976 QF vs. Philadelphia. Philadelphia won series 4-3.

MOST POWER-PLAY GOALS, BOTH TEAMS, ONE SERIES:
21 — New York Islanders (15), Philadelphia Flyers (6) in 1980 best-of-seven F won by NY Islanders 4-2.
— New York Islanders (13), Edmonton Oilers (8) in 1981 best-of-seven QF won by NY Islanders 4-2.
— Philadelphia Flyers (11), Pittsburgh Penguins (10) in 1989 best-of-seven DF won by Philadelphia 4-3.
— Minnesota North Stars (15), Chicago Black Hawks (6) in 1991 best-of-seven DSF won by Minnesota 4-2.
20 — Toronto Maple Leafs (12), Philadelphia Flyers (8) in 1976 best-of-seven QF won by Philadelphia 4-3.

MOST POWER-PLAY GOALS, ONE TEAM, ONE GAME:
6 — Boston Bruins, April 2, 1969, at Boston vs. Toronto. Boston won 10-0.

MOST POWER-PLAY GOALS, BOTH TEAMS, ONE GAME:
8 — Minnesota North Stars (4), St. Louis Blues (4), April 24, 1991, at Minnesota. Minnesota won 8-4.
7 — Minnesota North Stars (4), Edmonton Oilers (3), April 28, 1984, at Minnesota. Edmonton won 8-5.
— Philadelphia Flyers (4), NY Rangers (3), April 13, 1985, at NY Rangers. Philadelphia won 6-5.
— Chicago Black Hawks (5), Edmonton Oilers (2), May 14, 1985, at Edmonton. Edmonton won 10-5.
— Edmonton Oilers (5), Los Angeles Kings (2), April 9, 1987, at Edmonton. Edmonton won 13-3.
— Vancouver Canucks (4), Calgary Flames (3), April 9, 1989, at Vancouver. Vancouver won 5-3.

MOST POWER-PLAY GOALS, ONE TEAM, ONE PERIOD:
4 — Toronto Maple Leafs, March 26, 1936, second period vs. Boston at Toronto. Toronto won 8-3.
— Minnesota North Stars, April 28, 1984, second period vs. Edmonton at Minnesota. Edmonton won 8-5.
— Boston Bruins, April 11, 1991, third period vs. Hartford at Boston. Boston won 6-1.
— Minnesota North Stars, April 24, 1991, second period vs. St. Louis at Minnesota. Minnesota won 8-4.
— St. Louis Blues, April 27, 1998, third period at Los Angeles. St. Louis won 4-3.

MOST POWER-PLAY GOALS, BOTH TEAMS, ONE PERIOD:
5 — Minnesota North Stars (4), Edmonton Oilers (1), April 28, 1984, at Minnesota. Edmonton won 8-5.
— Vancouver Canucks (3), Calgary Flames (2), April 9, 1989, at Vancouver. Vancouver won 5-3.
— Minnesota North Stars (4), St. Louis Blues (1), April 24, 1991, at Minnesota. Minnesota won 8-4.

TEAM SHORTHAND GOALS

MOST SHORTHAND GOALS BY ALL TEAMS, ONE PLAYOFF YEAR:
33 — 1988, in 83 games.

MOST SHORTHAND GOALS, ONE TEAM, ONE PLAYOFF YEAR:
10 — Edmonton Oilers, 1983, in 16 games.
9 — New York Islanders, 1981, in 19 games.
8 — Philadelphia Flyers, 1989, in 19 games.

MOST SHORTHAND GOALS, ONE TEAM, ONE SERIES:
6 — Calgary Flames in 1995 vs. San Jose in best-of-seven CQF won by San Jose 4-3.
— Vancouver Canucks in 1995 vs. St. Louis in best-of-seven CQF won by Vancouver 4-3.
5 — NY Rangers in 1979 vs. Philadelphia in best-of-seven QF won by NY Rangers 4-1.
— Edmonton Oilers in 1983 vs. Calgary in best-of-seven DF won by Edmonton 4-1.

MOST SHORTHAND GOALS, BOTH TEAMS, ONE SERIES:
7 — Boston Bruins (4), NY Rangers (3), in 1958 SF won by Boston 4-2.
— Edmonton Oilers (5), Calgary Flames (2), in 1983 DF won by Edmonton 4-1.
— Vancouver Canucks (6), St. Louis Blues (1), in 1995 CQF won by Vancouver 4-3.

MOST SHORTHAND GOALS, ONE TEAM, ONE GAME:
3 — Boston Bruins, April 11, 1981, at Minnesota North Stars. Minnesota won 6-3.
— New York Islanders, April 17, 1983, at NY Rangers. NY Rangers won 7-6.
— Toronto Maple Leafs, May 8, 1994, at San Jose Sharks. Toronto won 8-3.

MOST SHORTHAND GOALS, BOTH TEAMS, ONE GAME:

4 — Boston Bruins (3), Minnesota North Stars (1), April 11, 1981, at Minnesota. Minnesota won 6-3.
— New York Islanders (3), New York Rangers (1), April 17, 1983, at NY Rangers. NY Rangers won 7-6.
— Toronto Maple Leafs (3), San Jose Sharks (1), May 8, 1994, at San Jose. Toronto won 8-3.
3 — Toronto Maple Leafs (2), Detroit Red Wings (1), April 5, 1947, at Toronto. Toronto won 6-1.
— New York Rangers (2), Boston Bruins (1), April 1, 1958, at Boston. NY Rangers won 5-2.
— Minnesota North Stars (2), Philadelphia Flyers (1), May 4, 1980, at Minnesota. Philadelphia won 5-3.
— Winnipeg Jets (2), Edmonton Oilers (1), April 9, 1988, at Winnipeg. Winnipeg won 6-4.
— New York Islanders (2), New Jersey Devils (1), April 14, 1988, at New Jersey. New Jersey won 6-5.
— Montreal Canadiens (2), New Jersey Devils (1), April 17, 1997, at New Jersey. New Jersey won 5-2.
— Dallas Stars (2), San Jose Sharks (1), May 5, 2000, at San Jose. Dallas won 5-4.
— Detroit Red Wings (2), Calgary Flames (1), April 21, 2007, at Detroit. Detroit won 5-1.

MOST SHORTHAND GOALS, ONE TEAM, ONE PERIOD:

2 — Toronto Maple Leafs, April 5, 1947, first period vs. Detroit at Toronto. Toronto won 6-1.
— Toronto Maple Leafs, April 13, 1965, first period vs. Montreal at Toronto. Montreal won 4-3.
— Boston Bruins, April 20, 1969, first period vs. Montreal at Boston. Boston won 3-2.
— Boston Bruins, April 8, 1970, second period vs. NY Rangers at Boston. Boston won 8-2.
— Boston Bruins, April 30, 1972, first period vs. NY Rangers at Boston. Boston won 6-5.
— Chicago Black Hawks, May 3, 1973, first period vs. Montreal at Chicago. Chicago won 7-4.
— Montreal Canadiens, April 23, 1978, first period at Detroit. Montreal won 8-0.
— New York Islanders, April 8, 1980, second period vs. Los Angeles at NY Islanders. NY Islanders won 8-1.
— Los Angeles Kings, April 9, 1980, first period at NY Islanders. Los Angeles won 6-3.
— Boston Bruins, April 13, 1980, second period at Pittsburgh. Boston won 8-3.
— Minnesota North Stars, May 4, 1980, second period vs. Philadelphia at Minnesota. Philadelphia won 5-3.
— Boston Bruins, April 11, 1981, third period at Minnesota North Stars. Minnesota won 6-3.
— New York Islanders, May 12, 1981, first period vs. Minnesota North Stars at NY Islanders. NY Islanders won 6-3.
— Montreal Canadiens, April 7, 1982, third period vs. Quebec at Montreal. Montreal won 5-1.
— Edmonton Oilers, April 24, 1983, third period vs. Chicago at Edmonton. Edmonton won 8-4.
— Winnipeg Jets, April 14, 1985, second period at Calgary. Winnipeg won 5-3.
— Boston Bruins, April 6, 1988, first period vs. Buffalo at Boston. Boston won 7-3.
— New York Islanders, April 14, 1988, third period at New Jersey. New Jersey won 6-5.
— Detroit Red Wings, April 29, 1993, second period at Toronto. Detroit won 7-3.
— Toronto Maple Leafs, May 8, 1994, third period at San Jose. Toronto won 8-3.
— Calgary Flames, May 11, 1995, first period at San Jose. Calgary won 9-2.
— Vancouver Canucks, May 15, 1995, second period at St. Louis. Vancouver won 6-5.
— Montreal Canadiens, April 17, 1997, second period at New Jersey. New Jersey won 5-2.
— Philadelphia Flyers, April 26, 1997, first period vs. Pittsburgh at Philadelphia. Philadelphia won 6-3.
— Phoenix Coyotes, April 24, 1998, second period at Detroit. Phoenix won 7-4.
— Buffalo Sabres, April 27, 1998, second period vs. Philadelphia at Buffalo. Buffalo won 6-1.
— San Jose Sharks, April 30, 1999, third period at Colorado. San Jose won 7-3.
— Detroit Red Wings, April 27, 2002, second period at Vancouver. Detroit won 6-4.
— Detroit Red Wings, April 21, 2007, second period at Detroit. Detroit won 5-1.

MOST SHORTHAND GOALS, BOTH TEAMS, ONE PERIOD:

3 — Toronto Maple Leafs (2), Detroit Red Wings (1), April 5, 1947, first period at Toronto. Toronto won 6-1.
— Toronto Maple Leafs (2), San Jose Sharks (1), May 8, 1994, third period at San Jose. Toronto won 8-3.

FASTEST GOALS

FASTEST FIVE GOALS, BOTH TEAMS:

3:06 — Minnesota North Stars, Chicago Black Hawks, April 21, 1985, at Chicago. Keith Brown scored for Chicago at 1:12 of the second period; Ken Yaremchuk, Chicago, 1:27; Dino Ciccarelli, Minnesota, 2:48; Tony McKegney, Minnesota, 4:07; and Curt Fraser, Chicago, 4:18. Chicago won 6-2 and won best-of-seven DF 4-2.
3:20 — Minnesota North Stars, Philadelphia Flyers, April 29, 1980, at Philadelphia. Paul Shmyr scored for Minnesota at 13:20 of the first period; Steve Christoff, Minnesota, 13:59; Ken Linseman, Philadelphia, 14:54; Tom Gorence, Philadelphia, 15:36; and Ken Linseman, Philadelphia, 16:40. Minnesota won 6-5. Philadelphia won best-of-seven SF 4-1.
4:00 — Los Angeles Kings, Detroit Red Wings, April 15, 2000, at Detroit. Brendan Shanahan scored for Detroit at 0:55 of the first period; Martin Lapointe, Detroit, 1:33; Luc Robitaille, Los Angeles, 2:04; Kris Draper, Detroit, 3:32; and Ziggy Palffy, Los Angeles, 4:55. Detroit won 8-5 and won best-of-seven CQF 4-0.

FASTEST FIVE GOALS, ONE TEAM:

3:36 — Montreal Canadiens, March 30, 1944, at Montreal vs. Toronto. Toe Blake scored at 7:58 and 8:37 of the third period; Maurice Richard, 9:17; Ray Getliffe, 10:33; and Buddy O'Connor, 11:34. Canadiens won 11-0 and won best-of-seven SF 4-1.

FASTEST FOUR GOALS, BOTH TEAMS:

1:33 — Toronto Maple Leafs, Philadelphia Flyers, April 20, 1976, at Philadelphia. Don Saleski scored for Philadelphia at 10:04 of the second period; Bob Neely, Toronto, 10:42; Gary Dornhoefer, Philadelphia, 11:24; and Don Saleski, Philadelphia, 11:37. Philadelphia won 7-1 and won best-of-seven SF 4-3.
1:34 — Calgary Flames, Montreal Canadiens, May 20, 1986, at Montreal. Joel Otto scored for Calgary at 17:59 of the first period; Bobby Smith, Montreal, 18:25; Mats Naslund, Montreal, 19:17; and Bob Gainey, Montreal, 19:33. Montreal won 5-3 and won best-of-seven F 4-1.
1:38 — Boston Bruins, Philadelphia Flyers, April 26, 1977, at Philadelphia. Gregg Sheppard scored for Boston at 14:01 of the second period; Mike Milbury, Boston, 15:01; Gary Dornhoefer, Philadelphia, 15:16; and Jean Ratelle, Boston, 15:39. Boston won 5-4 and won best-of-seven SF 4-0.

FASTEST FOUR GOALS, ONE TEAM:

2:35 — Montreal Canadiens, March 30, 1944, at Montreal. Toe Blake scored at 7:58 and 8:37 of the third period; Maurice Richard, 9:17; and Ray Getliffe, 10:33. Montreal won 11-0 and won best-of-seven SF 4-1.

FASTEST THREE GOALS, BOTH TEAMS:

0:21 — Chicago Black Hawks, Edmonton Oilers, May 7, 1985, at Edmonton. Behn Wilson scored for Chicago at 19:22 of the third period; Jari Kurri, Edmonton, 19:36; and Glenn Anderson, Edmonton, 19:43. Edmonton won 7-3 and won best-of-seven CF 4-2.
0:27 — Phoenix Coyotes, Detroit Red Wings, April 24, 1998, at Detroit. Jeremy Roenick scored for Phoenix at 13:24 of the second period; Mathieu Dandenault, Detroit, 13:32; and Keith Tkachuk, Phoenix, 13:51. Phoenix won 7-4. Detroit won best-of-seven CQF 4-2.
0:30 — Pittsburgh Penguins, Chicago Blackhawks, June 1, 1992, at Chicago. Dirk Graham scored for Chicago at 6:21 of the first period; Kevin Stevens, Pittsburgh, 6:33; and Dirk Graham, Chicago, 6:51. Pittsburgh won 6-5 and won best-of-seven F 4-0.

FASTEST THREE GOALS, ONE TEAM:

0:23 — Toronto Maple Leafs, April 12, 1979, at Toronto vs. Atlanta Flames. Darryl Sittler scored at 4:04 and 4:16 of the first period; and Ron Ellis, 4:27. Toronto won 7-4 and won best-of-three PRE 2-0.
0:38 — New York Rangers, April 12, 1986, at NY Rangers vs. Philadelphia. Jim Weimer scored at 12:29 of the third period; Bob Brooke, 12:43; and Ron Greschner, 13:07. NY Rangers won 5-2 and won best-of-five DSF 3-2.
— Colorado Avalanche, April 18, 2001, at Vancouver. Peter Forsberg scored at 9:11 of the third period; Joe Sakic, 9:28; and Eric Messier, 9:49. Colorado won 5-1 and won best-of-seven CQF 4-0.

FASTEST TWO GOALS, BOTH TEAMS:

0:05 — Pittsburgh Penguins, Buffalo Sabres, April 14, 1979, at Buffalo. Gilbert Perreault scored for Buffalo at 12:59 of the first period; and Jim Hamilton, Pittsburgh, 13:04. Pittsburgh won 4-3 and won best-of-three PRE 2-1.
0:08 — St. Louis Blues, Minnesota North Stars, April 9, 1989, at Minnesota. Bernie Federko scored for St. Louis at 2:28 of the third period; and Perry Berezan, Minnesota, 2:36. Minnesota won 5-4. St. Louis won best-of-seven DSF 4-1.
— Phoenix Coyotes, Detroit Red Wings, April 24, 1998, at Detroit. Jeremy Roenick scored for Phoenix at 13:24 of the second period; and Mathieu Dandenault, Detroit, 13:32. Phoenix won 7-4. Detroit won best-of-seven CQF 4-2.

FASTEST TWO GOALS, ONE TEAM:

0:05 — Detroit Red Wings, April 11, 1965, at Detroit vs. Chicago. Norm Ullman scored at 17:35 and 17:40 of the second period. Detroit won 4-2. Chicago won best-of-seven SF 4-3.

With shorthanded goals in games three and four of San Jose's 2008 second-round series with Dallas, Patrick Marleau became the first player to score a shorthanded goal in back-to-back playoff games since Brett Hull in 2002.

After starting the playoffs on the bench, Chris Osgood took over in the fourth game of the opening round and starred all the way to the Stanley Cup. He led all goalies with a 1.55 average in the playoffs and tied Marc-Andre Fleury for the lead with 14 wins and three shutouts.

OVERTIME

SHORTEST OVERTIME:
0:09 — Montreal Canadiens, Calgary Flames, May 18, 1986, at Calgary. Montreal won 3-2 on Brian Skrudland's goal at 0:09 of the first overtime period. Montreal won best-of-seven F 4-1.
0:11 — New York Islanders, New York Rangers, April 11, 1975, at NY Rangers. NY Islanders won 4-3 on J.P. Parise's goal at 0:11 of the first overtime period. NY Islanders won best-of-three PRE 2-1.

LONGEST OVERTIME:
116:30 — Detroit Red Wings, Montreal Maroons, March 24, 1936, at Montreal. Mtl. Maroons won 1-0 on Mud Bruneteau's goal at 16:30 of the sixth overtime period. Detroit won best-of-five SF 3-0.

MOST OVERTIME GAMES, ONE PLAYOFF YEAR:
28 — 1993. Of 85 games played, 28 went into overtime.
26 — 2001. Of 86 games played, 26 went into overtime.
22 — 2003. Of 89 games played, 22 went into overtime.

FEWEST OVERTIME GAMES, ONE PLAYOFF YEAR:
0 — 1963. None of the 16 games went into overtime, the only year since 1926 that no overtime was required in any playoff series.

MOST OVERTIME GAMES, ONE SERIES:
5 — Toronto Maple Leafs, Montreal Canadiens in 1951. Toronto won best-of-seven F 4-1.
4 — Toronto Maple Leafs, Boston Bruins in 1933. Toronto won best-of-five SF 3-2.
— Boston Bruins, NY Rangers in 1939. Boston won best-of-seven SF 4-3.
— St. Louis Blues, Minnesota North Stars in 1968. St. Louis won best-of-seven SF 4-3.
— Dallas Stars, St. Louis Blues in 1999. Dallas won best-of-seven CSF 4-2.
— Dallas Stars, Edmonton Oilers in 2001. Dallas won best-of-seven CQF 4-2.
— Dallas Stars, San Jose Sharks in 2008. Dallas won best-of-seven CSF 4-2

TEAM HAT-TRICKS

MOST HAT-TRICKS, BY ALL TEAMS, ONE PLAYOFF YEAR:
12 — 1983 in 66 games.
— 1988 in 83 games.
11 — 1985 in 70 games.
— 1992 in 86 games.

MOST HAT-TRICKS, ONE TEAM, ONE PLAYOFF YEAR:
6 — Edmonton Oilers in 16 games, 1983.
— Edmonton Oilers in 18 games, 1985.

SHUTOUTS

MOST SHUTOUTS, ONE PLAYOFF YEAR, ALL TEAMS:
25 — 2002. Of 90 games played, Detroit had 6; Ottawa had 4; Carolina, Colorado, St. Louis and Toronto had 3 each; while Los Angeles, New Jersey and Philadelphia had 1 each.
23 — 2004. Of 89 games played, Tampa Bay and Calgary had 5 each; Toronto and San Jose had 3 each; while Boston, Colorado, Detroit, Montreal, Nashville, NY Islanders and Philadelphia had 1 each.
19 — 2001. Of 86 games played, Colorado and New Jersey had 4 each, Toronto had 3, Pittsburgh and Los Angeles had 2 each, while Buffalo, Washington, Detroit and San Jose had 1 each.

FEWEST SHUTOUTS, ONE PLAYOFF YEAR, ALL TEAMS:
0 — 1959. 18 games played.

MOST SHUTOUTS, BOTH TEAMS, ONE SERIES:
5 — Toronto Maple Leafs (3), Detroit Red Wings (2), in 1945. Toronto won best-of-seven F 4-3.
— Toronto Maple Leafs (3), Detroit Red Wings (2), in 1950. Detroit won best-of-seven SF 4-3.

TEAM PENALTIES

FEWEST PENALTIES, BOTH TEAMS, BEST-OF-SEVEN SERIES:
19 — Detroit Red Wings, Toronto Maple Leafs in 1945. Detroit received 10 minors, Toronto received 9 minors. Detroit won best-of-seven F 4-3.

FEWEST PENALTIES, ONE TEAM, BEST-OF-SEVEN SERIES:
9 — Toronto Maple Leafs in 1945 vs. Detroit. Toronto received 9 minors. Detroit won best-of-seven F 4-3.

MOST PENALTIES, BOTH TEAMS, ONE SERIES:
218 — New Jersey Devils, Washington Capitals in 1988. New Jersey received 97 minors, 11 majors, 9 misconducts and 1 match penalty. Washington received 80 minors, 11 majors, 8 misconducts and 1 match penalty. New Jersey won best-of-seven DF 4-3.

MOST PENALTY MINUTES, BOTH TEAMS, ONE SERIES:
654 — New Jersey Devils (349), Washington Capitals (305) in 1988. New Jersey won best-of-seven DF 4-3.

MOST PENALTIES, ONE TEAM, ONE SERIES:
118 — New Jersey Devils in 1988 vs. Washington. New Jersey received 97 minors, 11 majors, 9 misconducts and 1 match penalty. New Jersey won best-of-seven DF 4-3.

MOST PENALTY MINUTES, ONE TEAM, ONE SERIES:
349 — New Jersey Devils in 1988 vs. Washington. New Jersey won best-of-seven DF 4-3.

MOST PENALTIES, BOTH TEAMS, ONE GAME:
66 — Detroit Red Wings (33), St. Louis Blues (33), April 12, 1991, at St. Louis. St. Louis won 6-1.
63 — Minnesota North Stars (34), Chicago Blackhawks (29), April 6, 1990, at Chicago. Chicago won 5-3.
62 — New Jersey Devils (32), Washington Capitals (30), April 22, 1988, at New Jersey. New Jersey won 10-4.

MOST PENALTY MINUTES, BOTH TEAMS, ONE GAME:
298 — Detroit Red Wings (152), St. Louis Blues (146), April 12, 1991, at St. Louis. Detroit received 33 penalties; St. Louis received 33 penalties. St. Louis won 6-1.
267 — New York Rangers (142), Los Angeles Kings (125), April 9, 1981, at Los Angeles. NY Rangers received 31 penalties; Los Angeles received 28 penalties. Los Angeles won 5-4.

MOST PENALTIES, ONE TEAM, ONE GAME:
34 — Minnesota North Stars, April 6, 1990, at Chicago. Chicago won 5-3.
33 — Detroit Red Wings, April 12, 1991, at St. Louis. St. Louis won 6-1.
— St. Louis Blues, April 12, 1991, at St. Louis vs. Detroit. St. Louis won 6-1.

MOST PENALTY MINUTES, ONE TEAM, ONE GAME:
152 — Detroit Red Wings, April 12, 1991, at St. Louis. St. Louis won 6-1.
146 — St. Louis Blues, April 12, 1991, at St. Louis vs. Detroit. St. Louis won 6-1.
142 — New York Rangers, April 9, 1981, at Los Angeles. Los Angeles won 5-4.

MOST PENALTIES, BOTH TEAMS, ONE PERIOD:
43 — New York Rangers (24), Los Angeles Kings (19), April 9, 1981, first period at Los Angeles. Los Angeles won 5-4.

MOST PENALTY MINUTES, BOTH TEAMS, ONE PERIOD:
248 — New York Islanders (124), Boston Bruins (124), April 17, 1980, first period at Boston. NY Islanders won 5-4.

MOST PENALTIES, ONE TEAM, ONE PERIOD:
24 — New York Rangers, April 9, 1981, first period at Los Angeles. Los Angeles won 5-4.

MOST PENALTY MINUTES, ONE TEAM, ONE PERIOD:
125 — New York Rangers, April 9, 1981, first period at Los Angeles. Los Angeles won 5-4.

Individual Records

GAMES PLAYED

MOST YEARS IN PLAYOFFS:
23 — Chris Chelios, Montreal, Chicago, Detroit (1984-97 inclusive; 1999-2004 inclusive, 2006-2008 inclusive)
21 — Raymond Bourque, Boston, Colorado (1980-96 inclusive; 98-2001 inclusive)
20 — Gordie Howe, Detroit, Hartford
— Larry Robinson, Montreal, Los Angeles
— Larry Murphy, Los Angeles, Washington, Minnesota, Pittsburgh, Toronto, Detroit
— Scott Stevens, Washington, St. Louis, New Jersey
— Steve Yzerman, Detroit

MOST CONSECUTIVE YEARS IN PLAYOFFS:
20 — Larry Robinson, Montreal, Los Angeles (1973-92, inclusive).
19 — Brett Hull, Calgary, St. Louis, Dallas, Detroit (1986-2004, inclusive).
18 — Larry Murphy, Los Angeles, Washington, Minnesota, Pittsburgh, Toronto, Detroit (1984-2001, inclusive).
17 — Brad Park, NY Rangers, Boston, Detroit (1969-85, inclusive).
— Raymond Bourque, Boston (1980-96, inclusive).

MOST PLAYOFF GAMES:
260 — Chris Chelios, Montreal, Chicago, Detroit
247 — Patrick Roy, Montreal, Colorado
236 — Mark Messier, Edmonton, NY Rangers
233 — Claude Lemieux, Montreal, New Jersey, Colorado, Phoenix
— Scott Stevens, Washington, St. Louis, New Jersey

GOALS

MOST GOALS IN PLAYOFFS (CAREER):
122 — Wayne Gretzky, Edmonton, Los Angeles, St. Louis, NY Rangers
109 — Mark Messier, Edmonton, NY Rangers
106 — Jari Kurri, Edmonton, Los Angeles, NY Rangers, Anaheim
103 — Brett Hull, Calgary, St. Louis, Dallas, Detroit
93 — Glenn Anderson, Edmonton, Toronto, NY Rangers, St. Louis

MOST GOALS, ONE PLAYOFF YEAR:
19 — Reggie Leach, Philadelphia, 1976. 16 games.
— Jari Kurri, Edmonton, 1985. 18 games.
18 — Joe Sakic, Colorado, 1996. 22 games.
17 — Newsy Lalonde, Montreal, 1919. 10 games.
— Mike Bossy, NY Islanders, 1981. 18 games.
— Steve Payne, Minnesota, 1981. 19 games.
— Mike Bossy, NY Islanders, 1982. 19 games.
— Mike Bossy, NY Islanders, 1983. 19 games
— Wayne Gretzky, Edmonton, 1985. 18 games.
— Kevin Stevens, Pittsburgh, 1991. 24 games.

MOST GOALS IN ONE SERIES (OTHER THAN FINAL):
12 — Jari Kurri, Edmonton, in 1985 CF, 6 games vs. Chicago.
11 — Newsy Lalonde, Montreal, in 1919 NHL F, 5 games vs. Ottawa.
10 — Tim Kerr, Philadelphia, in 1989 DF, 7 games vs. Pittsburgh.
9 — Reggie Leach, Philadelphia, in 1976 SF, 5 games vs. Boston.
— Bill Barber, Philadelphia, in 1980 SF, 5 games vs. Minnesota.
— Mike Bossy, NY Islanders, in 1983 CF, 6 games vs. Boston.
— Mario Lemieux, Pittsburgh, in 1989 DF, 7 games vs. Philadelphia.
— Johan Franzen, Detroit, in 2008 CSF, 4 games vs. Colorado

MOST GOALS IN FINAL SERIES (NHL PLAYERS ONLY):
9 — Babe Dye, Toronto, in 1922, 5 games vs. Van. Millionaires.
8 — Alf Skinner, Toronto, in 1918, 5 games vs. Van. Millionaires.
7 — Jean Beliveau, Montreal, in 1956, 5 games vs. Detroit.
— Mike Bossy, NY Islanders, in 1982, 4 games vs. Vancouver.
— Wayne Gretzky, Edmonton, in 1985, 5 games vs. Philadelphia.

MOST GOALS, ONE GAME:
5 — Newsy Lalonde, Montreal, March 1, 1919, at Montreal. Final score: Montreal 6, Ottawa 3.
— Maurice Richard, Montreal, March 23, 1944, at Montreal. Final score: Montreal 5, Toronto 1.
— Darryl Sittler, Toronto, April 22, 1976, at Toronto. Final score: Toronto 8, Philadelphia 5.
— Reggie Leach, Philadelphia, May 6, 1976, at Philadelphia. Final score: Philadelphia 6, Boston 3.
— Mario Lemieux, Pittsburgh, April 25, 1989, at Pittsburgh. Final score: Pittsburgh 10, Philadelphia 7.

MOST GOALS, ONE PERIOD:
4 — Tim Kerr, Philadelphia, April 13, 1985, at NY Rangers, second period. Final score: Philadelphia 6, NY Rangers 5.
— Mario Lemieux, Pittsburgh, April 25, 1989, at Pittsburgh vs. Philadelphia, first period. Final score: Pittsburgh 10, Philadelphia 7.

ASSISTS

MOST ASSISTS IN PLAYOFFS (CAREER):
260 — Wayne Gretzky, Edmonton, Los Angeles, St. Louis, NY Rangers
186 — Mark Messier, Edmonton, NY Rangers
139 — Raymond Bourque, Boston, Colorado
137 — Paul Coffey, Edmonton, Pittsburgh, Los Angeles, Detroit, Philadelphia, Carolina
128 — Doug Gilmour, St. Louis, Calgary, Toronto, New Jersey, Buffalo, Montreal

MOST ASSISTS, ONE PLAYOFF YEAR:
31 — Wayne Gretzky, Edmonton, 1988. 19 games.
30 — Wayne Gretzky, Edmonton, 1985. 18 games.
29 — Wayne Gretzky, Edmonton, 1987. 21 games.
28 — Mario Lemieux, Pittsburgh, 1991. 23 games.
26 — Wayne Gretzky, Edmonton, 1983. 16 games.

MOST ASSISTS IN ONE SERIES (OTHER THAN FINAL):
14 — Rick Middleton, Boston, in 1983 DF, 7 games vs. Buffalo.
— Wayne Gretzky, Edmonton, in 1985 CF, 6 games vs. Chicago.
13 — Wayne Gretzky, Edmonton, in 1987 DSF, 5 games vs. Los Angeles.
— Doug Gilmour, Toronto, in 1994 CSF, 7 games vs. San Jose.
11 — Al MacInnis, Calgary, in 1984 DF, 7 games vs. Edmonton.
— Mark Messier, Edmonton, in 1989 DSF, 7 games vs. Los Angeles.
— Mike Ridley, Washington, in 1992 DSF, 7 games vs. Pittsburgh.
— Ron Francis, Pittsburgh, in 1995 CQF, 7 games vs. Washington.
10 — Fleming Mackell, Boston, in 1958 SF, 6 games vs. NY Rangers.
— Stan Mikita, Chicago, in 1962 SF, 6 games vs. Montreal.
— Bob Bourne, NY Islanders, in 1983 DF, 6 games vs. NY Rangers.
— Wayne Gretzky, Edmonton, in 1988 DSF, 5 games vs. Winnipeg.
— Mario Lemieux, Pittsburgh, in 1992 DSF, 6 games vs. Washington.

MOST ASSISTS IN FINAL SERIES:
10 — Wayne Gretzky, Edmonton, in 1988, 4 games plus suspended game vs. Boston.
9 — Jacques Lemaire, Montreal, in 1973, 6 games vs. Chicago.
— Wayne Gretzky, Edmonton, in 1987, 7 games vs. Philadelphia.
— Larry Murphy, Pittsburgh, in 1991, 6 games vs. Minnesota.

MOST ASSISTS, ONE GAME:
6 — Mikko Leinonen, NY Rangers, April 8, 1982, at NY Rangers. Final score: NY Rangers 7, Philadelphia 3.
— Wayne Gretzky, Edmonton, April 9, 1987, at Edmonton. Final score: Edmonton 13, Los Angeles 3.
5 — Toe Blake, Montreal, March 23, 1944, at Montreal. Final score: Montreal 5, Toronto 1.
— Maurice Richard, Montreal, March 27, 1956, at Montreal. Final score: Montreal 7, NY Rangers 0.
— Bert Olmstead, Montreal, March 30, 1957, at Montreal. Final score: Montreal 8, NY Rangers 3.
— Don McKenney, Boston, April 5, 1958, at Boston. Final score: Boston 8, NY Rangers 2.
— Stan Mikita, Chicago, April 4, 1973, at Chicago. Final score: Chicago 7, St. Louis 1.
— Wayne Gretzky, Edmonton, April 8, 1981, at Montreal. Final score: Edmonton 6, Montreal 3.
— Paul Coffey, Edmonton, May 14, 1985, at Edmonton. Final score: Edmonton 10, Chicago 5.
— Doug Gilmour, St. Louis, April 15, 1986, at Minnesota. Final score: St. Louis 6, Minnesota 3.
— Risto Siltanen, Quebec, April 14, 1987, at Hartford. Final score: Quebec 7, Hartford 5.
— Patrik Sundstrom, New Jersey, April 22, 1988, at New Jersey. Final score: New Jersey 10, Washington 4.
— Geoff Courtnall, St. Louis, April 23, 1998, at St. Louis. Final score: St. Louis 8, Los Angeles 3.

MOST ASSISTS, ONE PERIOD:
3 — Three assists by one player in one period of a playoff game has been recorded on 81 occasions. Brad Richards of the Dallas Stars is the most recent to equal this mark with 3 assists in the third period at San Jose, April 27, 2008. Final score: Dallas 5, San Jose 2.
— Wayne Gretzky has had 3 assists in one period 5 times; Raymond Bourque, 3 times; Toe Blake, Jean Beliveau, Doug Harvey and Bobby Orr, twice each. Joe Primeau of Toronto was the first player to be credited with 3 assists in one period of a playoff game; third period at Boston vs. NY Rangers, April 7, 1932. Final score: Toronto 6, NY Rangers 2.

POINTS

MOST POINTS IN PLAYOFFS (CAREER):
382 — Wayne Gretzky, Edmonton, Los Angeles, St. Louis, NY Rangers, 122G, 260A
295 — Mark Messier, Edmonton, NY Rangers, 109G, 186A
233 — Jari Kurri, Edmonton, Los Angeles, NY Rangers, Anaheim, 106G, 127A
214 — Glenn Anderson, Edmonton, Toronto, NY Rangers, St. Louis, 93G, 121A
196 — Paul Coffey, Edmonton, Pittsburgh, Los Angeles, Detroit, Philadelphia, Carolina, 59G, 137A

MOST POINTS, ONE PLAYOFF YEAR:
47 — Wayne Gretzky, Edmonton, in 1985. 17 goals, 30 assists in 18 games.
44 — Mario Lemieux, Pittsburgh, in 1991. 16 goals, 28 assists in 23 games.
43 — Wayne Gretzky, Edmonton, in 1988. 12 goals, 31 assists in 19 games.
40 — Wayne Gretzky, Los Angeles, in 1993. 15 goals, 25 assists in 24 games.
38 — Wayne Gretzky, Edmonton, in 1983. 12 goals, 26 assists in 16 games.

MOST POINTS IN ONE SERIES (OTHER THAN FINAL):
19 — Rick Middleton, Boston, in 1983 DF, 7 games vs. Buffalo. 5 goals, 14 assists.
18 — Wayne Gretzky, Edmonton, in 1985 CF, 6 games vs. Chicago. 4 goals, 14 assists.
17 — Mario Lemieux, Pittsburgh, in 1992 DSF, 6 games vs. Washington. 7 goals, 10 assists.
16 — Barry Pederson, Boston, in 1983 DF, 7 games vs. Buffalo. 7 goals, 9 assists.
— Doug Gilmour, Toronto, in 1994 CSF, 7 games vs. San Jose. 3 goals, 13 assists.
15 — Jari Kurri, Edmonton, in 1985 CF, 6 games vs. Chicago. 12 goals, 3 assists.
— Wayne Gretzky, Edmonton, in 1987 DSF, 5 games vs. Los Angeles. 2 goals, 13 assists.
— Tim Kerr, Philadelphia, in 1989 DF, 7 games vs. Pittsburgh. 10 goals, 5 assists.
— Mario Lemieux, Pittsburgh, in 1991 CF, 6 games vs. Boston. 6 goals, 9 assists.

MOST POINTS IN FINAL SERIES:
13 — Wayne Gretzky, Edmonton, in 1988, 4 games plus suspended game vs. Boston. 3 goals, 10 assists.
12 — Gordie Howe, Detroit, in 1955, 7 games vs. Montreal. 5 goals, 7 assists.
— Yvan Cournoyer, Montreal, in 1973, 6 games vs. Chicago. 6 goals, 6 assists.
— Jacques Lemaire, Montreal, in 1973, 6 games vs. Chicago. 3 goals, 9 assists.
— Mario Lemieux, Pittsburgh, in 1991, 5 games vs. Minnesota. 5 goals, 7 assists.

MOST POINTS, ONE GAME:
8 — Patrik Sundstrom, New Jersey, April 22, 1988, at New Jersey in 10-4 win over Washington. Sundstrom had 3 goals, 5 assists.
— Mario Lemieux, Pittsburgh, April 25, 1989, at Pittsburgh in 10-7 win over Philadelphia. Lemieux had 5 goals, 3 assists.
7 — Wayne Gretzky, Edmonton, April 17, 1983, at Calgary in 10-2 win. Gretzky had 4 goals, 3 assists.
— Wayne Gretzky, Edmonton, April 25,1985, at Winnipeg in 8-3 win. Gretzky had 3 goals, 4 assists.
— Wayne Gretzky, Edmonton, April 9, 1987, at Edmonton in 13-3 win over Los Angeles. Gretzky had 1 goal, 6 assists.
6 — Dickie Moore, Montreal, March 25, 1954, at Montreal in 8-1 win over Boston. Moore had 2 goals, 4 assists.
— Phil Esposito, Boston, April 2, 1969, at Boston in 10-0 win over Toronto. Esposito had 4 goals, 2 assists.
— Darryl Sittler, Toronto, April 22, 1976, at Toronto in 8-5 win over Philadelphia. Sittler had 5 goals, 1 assist.
— Guy Lafleur, Montreal, April 11, 1977, at Montreal in 7-2 win over St. Louis. Lafleur had 3 goals, 3 assists.
— Mikko Leinonen, NY Rangers, April 8, 1982, at NY Rangers in 7-3 win over Philadelphia. Leinonen had 6 assists.
— Paul Coffey, Edmonton, May 14, 1985, at Edmonton in 10-5 win over Chicago. Coffey had 1 goal, 5 assists.
— John Anderson, Hartford, April 12, 1986, at Hartford in 9-4 win over Quebec. Anderson had 2 goals, 4 assists.
— Mario Lemieux, Pittsburgh, April 23, 1992, at Pittsburgh in 6-4 win over Washington. Lemieux had 3 goals, 3 assists.
— Geoff Courtnall, St. Louis, April 23, 1998, at St. Louis in 8-3 win over Los Angeles. Courtnall had 1 goal, 5 assists.

MOST POINTS, ONE PERIOD:
4 — Maurice Richard, Montreal, March 29, 1945, at Montreal, third period, in 10-3 win vs. Toronto. 3 goals, 1 assist.
— Dickie Moore, Montreal, March 25, 1954, at Montreal, first period, in 8-1 win vs. Boston. 2 goals, 2 assists.
— Barry Pederson, Boston, April 8, 1982, at Boston, second period, in 7-3 win vs. Buffalo. 3 goals, 1 assist.
— Peter McNab, Boston, April 11, 1982, at Buffalo, second period, in 5-2 win vs. Buffalo. 1 goal, 3 assists.
— Tim Kerr, Philadelphia, April 13, 1985, at NY Rangers, second period, in 6-5 win vs. NY Rangers. 4 goals.
— Ken Linseman, Boston, April 14, 1985, at Boston, second period, in 7-6 win vs. Montreal. 2 goals, 2 assists.
— Wayne Gretzky, Edmonton, April 12, 1987, at Los Angeles, third period, in 6-3 win vs. Los Angeles. 1 goal, 3 assists.
— Glenn Anderson, Edmonton, April 6, 1988, at Edmonton, third period, in 7-4 win vs. Winnipeg. 3 goals, 1 assist.
— Mario Lemieux, Pittsburgh, April 25, 1989, at Pittsburgh, first period, in 10-7 win vs. Philadelphia. 4 goals.
— Dave Gagner, Minnesota North Stars, April 8, 1991, at Minnesota, first period, in 6-5 loss vs. Chicago. 2 goals, 2 assists.
— Mario Lemieux, Pittsburgh, April 23, 1992, at Pittsburgh, second period, in 6-4 win vs. Washington. 2 goals, 2 assists.
— Alexander Mogilny, New Jersey, April 28, 2001, at New Jersey, second period, in 6-5 win vs. Toronto. 1 goal, 3 assists.
— Brad Richards, Dallas, April 27, 2008, at San Jose, third period, in 5-2 win vs. San Jose. 1 goal, 3 assists.

POWER-PLAY GOALS

MOST POWER-PLAY GOALS IN PLAYOFFS (CAREER):
38 — Brett Hull, St. Louis, Dallas, Detroit
35 — Mike Bossy, NY Islanders
34 — Dino Ciccarelli, Minnesota, Washington, Detroit
— Wayne Gretzky, Edmonton, Los Angeles, St. Louis, NY Rangers
29 — Mario Lemieux, Pittsburgh

MOST POWER-PLAY GOALS, ONE PLAYOFF YEAR:
9 — Mike Bossy, NY Islanders, 1981. 18 games vs. Toronto, Edmonton, NY Rangers and Minnesota.
— Cam Neely, Boston, 1991. 19 games vs. Hartford, Montreal and Pittsburgh.
8 — Tim Kerr, Philadelphia, 1989. 19 games.
— John Druce, Washington, 1990. 15 games.
— Brian Propp, Minnesota, 1991. 23 games.
— Mario Lemieux, Pittsburgh, 1992. 15 games.

MOST POWER-PLAY GOALS, ONE PLAYOFF SERIES:
6 — Chris Kontos, Los Angeles, 1989 DSF vs. Edmonton, won by Los Angeles 4-3.
5 — Andy Bathgate, Detroit, 1966 SF vs. Chicago, won by Detroit 4-2.
— Denis Potvin, NY Islanders, 1981 QF vs. Edmonton, won by NY Islanders 4-2.
— Ken Houston, Calgary, 1981 QF vs. Philadelphia, won by Calgary 4-3.
— Rick Vaive, Chicago, 1988 DSF vs. St. Louis, won by St. Louis 4-1.
— Tim Kerr, Philadelphia, 1989 DF vs. Pittsburgh, won by Philadelphia 4-3.
— Mario Lemieux, Pittsburgh, 1989 DF vs. Philadelphia, won by Philadelphia 4-3.
— John Druce, Washington, 1990 DF vs. NY Rangers, won by Washington 4-1.
— Pat LaFontaine, Buffalo, 1992 DSF vs. Boston, won by Boston 4-3.
— Adam Graves, NY Rangers, 1996 CQF vs Montreal, won by NY Rangers 4-2.

MOST POWER-PLAY GOALS, ONE GAME:
3 — Syd Howe, Detroit, March 23, 1939, at Detroit vs. Montreal. Detroit won 7-3.
— Sid Smith, Toronto, April 10, 1949, at Detroit. Toronto won 3-1.
— Phil Esposito, Boston, April 2, 1969, at Boston vs. Toronto. Boston won 10-0.
— John Bucyk, Boston, April 21, 1974, at Boston vs. Chicago. Boston won 8-6.
— Denis Potvin, NY Islanders, April 17, 1981, at NY Islanders vs. Edmonton. NY Islanders won 6-3.
— Tim Kerr, Philadelphia, April 13, 1985, at NY Rangers. Philadelphia won 6-5.
— Jari Kurri, Edmonton, April 9, 1987, at Edmonton vs. Los Angeles. Edmonton won 13-3.
— Mark Johnson, New Jersey, April 22, 1988, at New Jersey vs. Washington. New Jersey won 10-4.
— Dino Ciccarelli, Detroit, April 29, 1993, at Toronto. Detroit won 7-3.
— Dino Ciccarelli, Detroit, May 11, 1995, at Dallas. Detroit won 5-1.
— Valeri Kamensky, Colorado, April 24, 1997, at Colorado vs. Chicago. Colorado won 7-0.

MOST POWER-PLAY GOALS, ONE PERIOD:
3 — Tim Kerr, Philadelphia, April 13, 1985, at NY Rangers, second period in 6-5 win.
2 — Two power-play goals have been scored by one player in one period on 55 occasions. Charlie Conacher of Toronto was the first to score two power-play goals in one period, setting the mark with two power-play goals in the second period at Toronto vs. Boston, March 26, 1936. Final score: Toronto 8, Boston 3. Brad Richards of the Tampa Bay Lightning is the most recent to equal this mark with two power-play goals in the second period at Calgary, June 5, 2004. Final score: Tampa Bay 3, Calgary 2.

SHORTHAND GOALS

MOST SHORTHAND GOALS IN PLAYOFFS (CAREER):
14 — Mark Messier, Edmonton, NY Rangers
11 — Wayne Gretzky, Edmonton, Los Angeles, St. Louis
10 — Jari Kurri, Edmonton, Los Angeles, NY Rangers
8 — Ed Westfall, Boston, NY Islanders
— Hakan Loob, Calgary

MOST SHORTHAND GOALS, ONE PLAYOFF YEAR:
3 — Derek Sanderson, Boston, 1969. 1 vs. Toronto in QF, won by Boston 4-0; 2 vs. Montreal in SF, won by Montreal, 4-2.
— Bill Barber, Philadelphia, 1980. All vs. Minnesota in SF, won by Philadelphia 4-1.
— Lorne Henning, NY Islanders, 1980. 1 vs. Boston in QF, won by NY Islanders 4-1; 1 vs. Buffalo in SF, won by NY Islanders 4-2, 1 vs. Philadelphia in F, won by NY Islanders 4-2.
— Wayne Gretzky, Edmonton, 1983. 2 vs. Winnipeg in DSF, won by Edmonton 3-0; 1 vs. Calgary in DF, won by Edmonton 4-1.
— Wayne Presley, Chicago, 1989. All vs. Detroit in DSF, won by Chicago 4-2.
— Todd Marchant, Edmonton, 1997. 1 vs. Dallas in CQF, won by Edmonton 4-3; 2 vs. Colorado in CSF, won by Colorado 4-1.

Chris Kontos was a little-known journeyman before exploding for nine goals in 11 playoff games with Los Angeles in 1989. His six power-play goals in the opening round helped the Kings knock off the defending champion Edmonton Oilers.

MOST SHORTHAND GOALS, ONE PLAYOFF SERIES:
3 — Bill Barber, Philadelphia, 1980 SF vs. Minnesota, won by Philadelphia 4-1.
— Wayne Presley, Chicago, 1989 DSF vs. Detroit, won by Chicago 4-2.
2 — Mac Colville, NY Rangers, 1940 SF vs. Boston, won by NY Rangers 4-2.
— Jerry Toppazzini, Boston, 1958 SF vs. NY Rangers, won by Boston 4-2.
— Dave Keon, Toronto, 1963 F vs. Detroit, won by Toronto 4-1.
— Bob Pulford, Toronto, 1964 F vs. Detroit, won by Toronto 4-3.
— Serge Savard, Montreal, 1968 F vs. St. Louis, won by Montreal 4-0.
— Derek Sanderson, Boston, 1969 SF vs. Montreal, won by Montreal 4-2.
— Bryan Trottier, NY Islanders, 1980 PR vs. Los Angeles, won by NY Islanders 3-1.
— Bobby Lalonde, Boston, 1981 PR vs. Minnesota, won by Minnesota 3-0.
— Butch Goring, NY Islanders, 1981 SF vs. NY Rangers, won by NY Islanders 4-0.
— Wayne Gretzky, Edmonton, 1983 DSF vs. Winnipeg, won by Edmonton 3-0.
— Mark Messier, Edmonton, 1983 DF vs. Calgary, won by Edmonton 4-1.
— Jari Kurri, Edmonton, 1983 CF vs. Chicago, won by Edmonton 4-0.
— Wayne Gretzky, Edmonton, 1985 DF vs. Winnipeg, won by Edmonton 4-0.
— Kevin Lowe, Edmonton, 1987 F vs. Philadelphia, won by Edmonton 4-3.
— Bob Gould, Washington, 1988 DSF vs. Philadelphia, won by Washington 4-3.
— Dave Poulin, Philadelphia, 1989 DF vs. Pittsburgh, won by Philadelphia 4-3.
— Russ Courtnall, Montreal, 1991 DF vs. Boston, won by Boston 4-3.
— Sergei Fedorov, Detroit, 1992 DSF vs. Minnesota, won by Detroit 4-3.
— Mark Messier, NY Rangers, 1992 DSF vs. New Jersey, won by NY Rangers 4-3.
— Tom Fitzgerald, NY Islanders, 1993 DF vs. Pittsburgh, won by NY Islanders 4-3.
— Mark Osborne, Toronto, 1994 CSF vs. San Jose, won by Toronto 4-3.
— Tony Amonte, Chicago, 1997 CQF vs. Colorado, won by Colorado 4-2.
— Brian Rolston, New Jersey, 1997 CQF vs. Montreal, won by New Jersey 4-1.
— Rod Brind'Amour, Philadelphia, 1997 CQF vs. Pittsburgh, won by Philadelphia 4-1.
— Todd Marchant, Edmonton, 1997 CSF vs. Colorado, won by Colorado 4-1.
— Jeremy Roenick, Phoenix, 1998 CQF vs. Detroit, won by Detroit 4-2.
— Vincent Damphousse, San Jose, 1999 CQF vs. Colorado, won by Colorado 4-2.
— Dixon Ward, Buffalo, 1999 CF vs. Toronto, won by Buffalo 4-1.
— Curtis Brown, Buffalo, 2001 CSF vs. Pittsburgh, won by Pittsburgh 4-3.
— John Madden, New Jersey, 2006 CQF vs. NY Rangers, won by New Jersey 4-0.

MOST SHORTHAND GOALS, ONE GAME:
2 — Dave Keon, Toronto, April 18, 1963, at Toronto, in 3-1 win vs. Detroit.
— Bryan Trottier, NY Islanders, April 8, 1980, at NY Islanders, in 8-1 win vs. Los Angeles.
— Bobby Lalonde, Boston, April 11, 1981, at Minnesota, in 6-3 loss vs. Minnesota.
— Wayne Gretzky, Edmonton, April 6, 1983, at Edmonton, in 6-3 win vs. Winnipeg.
— Jari Kurri, Edmonton, April 24, 1983, at Edmonton, in 8-3 win vs. Chicago.
— Wayne Gretzky, Edmonton, April 25, 1985, at Winnipeg, in 8-3 win by Edmonton.
— Mark Messier, NY Rangers, April 21, 1992, at NY Rangers, in 7-3 loss vs. New Jersey.
— Tom Fitzgerald, NY Islanders, May 8, 1993, at NY Islanders, in 6-5 win vs. Pittsburgh.
— Rod Brind'Amour, Philadelphia, April 26, 1997, at Philadelphia, in 6-3 win vs. Pittsburgh.
— Jeremy Roenick, Phoenix, April 24, 1998, at Detroit, in 7-4 win by Phoenix.
— Vincent Damphousse, San Jose, April 30, 1999, at Colorado, in 7-3 win by San Jose.
— John Madden, New Jersey, April 24, 2006, at New Jersey, in 4-1 win vs. NY Rangers.

MOST SHORTHAND GOALS, ONE PERIOD:
2 — Bryan Trottier, NY Islanders, April 8, 1980, second period, at NY Islanders, in 8-1 win vs. Los Angeles.
— Bobby Lalonde, Boston, April 11, 1981, third period, at Minnesota, in 6-3 loss vs. Minnesota.
— Jari Kurri, Edmonton, April 24, 1983, third period, at Edmonton, in 8-4 win vs. Chicago.
— Rod Brind'Amour, Philadelphia, April 26, 1997, first period, at Philadelphia, in 6-3 win vs. Pittsburgh.
— Jeremy Roenick, Phoenix, April 24, 1998, second period, at Detroit, in 7-4 win by Phoenix.
— Vincent Damphousse, San Jose, April 30, 1999, third period, at Colorado, in 7-3 win vs. Colorado.

GAME-WINNING GOALS

MOST GAME-WINNING GOALS IN PLAYOFFS, CAREER:
24 — Wayne Gretzky, Edmonton, Los Angeles, St. Louis, NY Rangers
— Brett Hull, St. Louis, Dallas, Detroit
19 — Claude Lemieux, Montreal, New Jersey, Colorado
18 — Maurice Richard, Montreal
— Joe Sakic, Colorado

MOST GAME-WINNING GOALS, ONE PLAYOFF YEAR:
7 — Brad Richards, Tampa Bay, 2004. 23 games.
6 — Joe Sakic, Colorado, 1996. 22 games.
— Joe Nieuwendyk, Dallas, 1999. 23 games.
5 — Mike Bossy, NY Islanders, 1983. 19 games.
— Jari Kurri, Edmonton, 1987. 21 games.
— Bobby Smith, Minnesota, 1991. 23 games.
— Mario Lemieux, Pittsburgh, 1992. 15 games.
— Fernando Pisani, Edmonton, 2006. 24 games.
— Johan Franzen, Detroit, 2008. 16 games.

MOST GAME-WINNING GOALS, ONE PLAYOFF SERIES:
4 — Mike Bossy, NY Islanders, 1983 CF vs. Boston, won by NY Islanders 4-2.

OVERTIME GOALS

MOST OVERTIME GOALS IN PLAYOFFS, CAREER:
7 — Joe Sakic, Colorado (2 in 1996; 1 in 1998; 1 in 2001; 2 in 2004; 1 in 2006)
6 — Maurice Richard, Montreal
5 — Glenn Anderson, Edmonton, Toronto, St. Louis
4 — Bob Nystrom, NY Islanders
— Dale Hunter, Quebec, Washington
— Wayne Gretzky, Edmonton, Los Angeles
— Stephane Richer, Montreal, New Jersey
— Joe Murphy, Edmonton, Chicago
— Esa Tikkanen, Edmonton, NY Rangers
— Jaromir Jagr, Pittsburgh
— Kirk Muller, Montreal, Dallas
— Jeremy Roenick, Chicago, Philadelphia
— Chris Drury, Colorado, Buffalo
— Jamie Langenbrunner, Dallas, New Jersey

MOST OVERTIME GOALS, ONE PLAYOFF YEAR:
3 — Mel Hill, Boston, 1939. All vs. NY Rangers in best-of-seven SF, won by Boston 4-3.
— Maurice Richard, Montreal, 1951. 2 vs. Detroit in best-of-seven SF, won by Montreal 4-2; 1 vs. Toronto best-of-seven F, won by Toronto 4-1.

MOST OVERTIME GOALS, ONE PLAYOFF SERIES:
3 — Mel Hill, Boston, 1939, SF vs. NY Rangers, won by Boston 4-3. Hill scored at 59:25 of overtime March 21 for a 2-1 win; at 8:24 of overtime, March 23 for a 3-2 win; and at 48:00 of overtime, April 2 for a 2-1 win.

SCORING BY A DEFENSEMAN

MOST GOALS BY A DEFENSEMAN, ONE PLAYOFF YEAR:
12 — Paul Coffey, Edmonton, 1985. 18 games.
11 — Brian Leetch, NY Rangers, 1994. 23 games.
9 — Bobby Orr, Boston, 1970. 14 games.
— Brad Park, Boston, 1978. 15 games.
8 — Denis Potvin, NY Islanders, 1981. 18 games.
— Raymond Bourque, Boston, 1983. 17 games.
— Denis Potvin, NY Islanders, 1983. 20 games.
— Paul Coffey, Edmonton, 1984. 19 games.

MOST GOALS BY A DEFENSEMAN, ONE GAME:
3 — Bobby Orr, Boston, April 11, 1971, at Montreal.
Final score: Boston 5, Montreal 2.
— Dick Redmond, Chicago, April 4, 1973, at Chicago.
Final score: Chicago 7, St. Louis 1.
— Denis Potvin, NY Islanders, April 17, 1981, at NY Islanders.
Final score: NY Islanders 6, Edmonton 3.
— Paul Reinhart, Calgary, April 14, 1983, at Edmonton.
Final score: Edmonton 6, Calgary 3.
— Doug Halward, Vancouver, April 7, 1984, at Vancouver.
Final score: Vancouver 7, Calgary 0.
— Paul Reinhart, Calgary, April 8, 1984, at Vancouver.
Final score: Calgary 5, Vancouver 1.
— Al Iafrate, Washington, April 26, 1993, at Washington.
Final score: Washington 6, NY Islanders 4.
— Eric Desjardins, Montreal, June 3, 1993, at Montreal.
Final score: Montreal 3, Los Angeles 2.
— Gary Suter, Chicago, April 24, 1994, at Chicago.
Final score: Chicago 4, Toronto 3.
— Brian Leetch, NY Rangers, May 22, 1995, at Philadelphia.
Final score: Philadelphia 4, NY Rangers 3.
— Andy Delmore, Philadelphia, May 7, 2000, at Philadelphia.
Final score: Philadelphia 6, Pittsburgh 3.

MOST ASSISTS BY A DEFENSEMAN, ONE PLAYOFF YEAR:
25 — Paul Coffey, Edmonton, 1985. 18 games.
24 — Al MacInnis, Calgary, 1989. 22 games.
23 — Brian Leetch, NY Rangers, 1994. 23 games.
19 — Bobby Orr, Boston, 1972. 15 games.
18 — Raymond Bourque, Boston, 1988. 23 games.
— Raymond Bourque, Boston, 1991. 19 games.
— Larry Murphy, Pittsburgh, 1991. 23 games.

MOST ASSISTS BY A DEFENSEMAN, ONE GAME:
5 — Paul Coffey, Edmonton, May 14, 1985, at Edmonton vs. Chicago. Edmonton won 10-5.
— Risto Siltanen, Quebec, April 14, 1987, at Hartford. Quebec won 7-5.

MOST POINTS BY A DEFENSEMAN, ONE PLAYOFF YEAR:
37 — Paul Coffey, Edmonton, 1985. 12 goals, 25 assists in 18 games.
34 — Brian Leetch, NY Rangers, 1994. 11 goals, 23 assists in 23 games.
31 — Al MacInnis, Calgary, 1989. 7 goals, 24 assists in 22 games.
25 — Denis Potvin, NY Islanders, 1981. 8 goals, 17 assists in 18 games.
— Raymond Bourque, Boston, 1991. 7 goals, 18 assists in 19 games.

MOST POINTS BY A DEFENSEMAN, ONE GAME:
6 — Paul Coffey, Edmonton, May 14, 1985, at Edmonton vs. Chicago. 1 goal, 5 assists. Edmonton won 10-5.
5 — Eddie Bush, Detroit, April 9, 1942, at Detroit vs. Toronto. 1 goal, 4 assists. Detroit won 5-2.
— Bob Dailey, Philadelphia, May 1, 1980, at Philadelphia vs. Minnesota. 1 goal, 4 assists. Philadelphia won 7-0.
— Denis Potvin, NY Islanders, April 17, 1981, at NY Islanders vs. Edmonton. 3 goals, 2 assists. NY Islanders won 6-3.
— Risto Siltanen, Quebec, April 14, 1987, at Hartford. 5 assists. Quebec won 7-5.

SCORING BY A ROOKIE

MOST GOALS BY A ROOKIE, ONE PLAYOFF YEAR:

14 — Dino Ciccarelli, Minnesota, 1981. 19 games.
11 — Jeremy Roenick, Chicago, 1990. 20 games.
10 — Claude Lemieux, Montreal, 1986. 20 games.
9 — Pat Flatley, NY Islanders, 1984. 21 games
8 — Steve Christoff, Minnesota, 1980. 14 games.
— Brad Palmer, Minnesota, 1981. 19 games.
— Mike Krushelnyski, Boston, 1983. 17 games.
— Bob Joyce, Boston, 1988. 23 games.

MOST POINTS BY A ROOKIE, ONE PLAYOFF YEAR:

21 — Dino Ciccarelli, Minnesota, 1981. 14 goals, 7 assists in 19 games.
20 — Don Maloney, NY Rangers, 1979. 7 goals, 13 assists in 18 games.

THREE-OR-MORE-GOAL GAMES

MOST THREE-OR-MORE-GOAL GAMES IN PLAYOFFS, CAREER:

10 — Wayne Gretzky, Edmonton, Los Angeles, NY Rangers. Eight three-goal games; two four-goal games.
7 — Maurice Richard, Montreal. Four three-goal games; two four-goal games; one five-goal game.
— Jari Kurri, Edmonton. Six three-goal games; one four-goal game.
6 — Dino Ciccarelli, Minnesota, Washington, Detroit. Five three-goal games; one four-goal game.
5 — Mike Bossy, NY Islanders. Four three-goal games; one four-goal game.

MOST THREE-OR-MORE-GOAL GAMES, ONE PLAYOFF YEAR:

4 — Jari Kurri, Edmonton, 1985. 1 four-goal game, 3 three-goal games.
3 — Mark Messier, Edmonton, 1983. 3 three-goal games.
— Mike Bossy, NY Islanders, 1983. 1 four-goal game, 2 three-goal games
2 — Newsy Lalonde, Montreal, 1919. 1 five-goal game, 1 four-goal game.
— Maurice Richard, Montreal, 1944. 1 five-goal game; 1 three-goal game.
— Doug Bentley, Chicago, 1944. 2 three-goal games.
— Norm Ullman, Detroit, 1964. 2 three-goal games.
— Phil Esposito, Boston, 1970. 2 three-goal games.
— Pit Martin, Chicago, 1973. 2 three-goal games.
— Rick MacLeish, Philadelphia, 1975. 2 three-goal games.
— Lanny McDonald, Toronto, 1977. 1 four-goal game; 1 three-goal game.
— Wayne Gretzky, Edmonton, 1981. 2 three-goal games.
— Wayne Gretzky, Edmonton, 1983. 2 four-goal games.
— Wayne Gretzky, Edmonton, 1985. 2 three-goal games.
— Petr Klima, Detroit, 1988. 2 three-goal games.
— Cam Neely, Boston, 1991. 2 three-goal games.
— Wayne Gretzky, NY Rangers, 1997. 2 three-goal games.
— Daniel Alfredsson, Ottawa, 1998. 2 three-goal games.
— Patrick Marleau, San Jose, 2004. 2 three-goal games.
— Johan Franzen, Detroit, 2008. 2 three-goal games.

MOST THREE-OR-MORE-GOAL GAMES, ONE PLAYOFF SERIES:

3 — Jari Kurri, Edmonton, 1985 CF vs. Chicago, won by Edmonton 4-2. Kurri scored 3 goals May 7 at Edmonton in 7-3 win, 3 goals May 14 at Edmonton in 10-5 win and 4 goals May 16 at Chicago in 8-2 win.
2 — Doug Bentley, Chicago, 1944 SF vs. Detroit, won by Chicago 4-1. Bentley scored 3 goals March 28 at Chicago in 7-1 win and 3 goals March 30 at Detroit in 5-2 win.
— Norm Ullman, Detroit, 1964 SF vs. Chicago, won by Detroit 4-3. Ullman scored 3 goals March 29 at Chicago in 5-4 win and 3 goals April 7 at Detroit in 7-2 win.
— Mark Messier, Edmonton, 1983 DF vs. Calgary, won by Edmonton 4-1. Messier scored 4 goals April 14 at Edmonton in 6-3 win and 3 goals April 17 at Calgary in 10-2 win.
— Mike Bossy, NY Islanders, 1983 CF vs. Boston, won by NY Islanders 4-2. Bossy scored 3 goals May 3 at NY Islanders in 8-3 win and 4 goals May 7 at New York in 8-4 win.
— Johan Franzen, Detroit, 2008 CSF vs. Colorado, won by Detroit 4-0. Franzen scored 3 goals Apr. 26 at Detroit in 5-1 win and 3 goals May 1 at Colorado in 8-2 win.

SCORING STREAKS

LONGEST CONSECUTIVE GOAL-SCORING STREAK, ONE PLAYOFF YEAR:

10 Games — Reggie Leach, Philadelphia, 1976. Streak started April 17 at Toronto and ended May 9 at Montreal. He scored one goal in each of eight games; two in one game; and five in another; a total of 15 goals.

LONGEST CONSECUTIVE POINT-SCORING STREAK, ONE PLAYOFF YEAR:

18 games — Bryan Trottier, NY Islanders, 1981. 11 goals, 18 assists, 29 points.
17 games — Wayne Gretzky, Edmonton, 1988. 12 goals, 29 assists, 41 points.
— Al MacInnis, Calgary, 1989. 7 goals, 19 assists, 26 points.

LONGEST CONSECUTIVE POINT-SCORING STREAK, MORE THAN ONE PLAYOFF YEAR:

27 games — Bryan Trottier, NY Islanders, 1980, 1981 and 1982. 7 games in 1980 (3 goals, 5 assists, 8 points), 18 games in 1981 (11 goals, 18 assists, 29 points), and two games in 1982 (2 goals, 3 assists, 5 points). Total points, 42.
19 games — Wayne Gretzky, Edmonton, Los Angeles, 1988 and 1989. 17 games in 1988 (12 goals, 29 assists, 41 points with Edmonton), 2 games in 1989 (1 goal, 2 assists, 3 points with Los Angeles). Total points, 44.
— Al MacInnis, Calgary, 1989 and 1990. 17 games in 1989 (7 goals, 19 assists, 26 points), and two games in 1990 (2 goals, 1 assist, 3 points). Total points, 29.

FASTEST GOALS

FASTEST GOAL FROM START OF GAME:

0:06 — Don Kozak, Los Angeles, April 17, 1977, at Los Angeles vs. Boston and goaltender Gerry Cheevers. Los Angeles won 7-4.
0:07 — Bob Gainey, Montreal, May 5, 1977, at NY Islanders vs. goaltender Chico Resch. Montreal won 2-1.
— Terry Murray, Philadelphia, April 12, 1981, at Quebec vs. goaltender Dan Bouchard. Quebec won 4-3 in overtime.

FASTEST GOAL FROM START OF PERIOD (OTHER THAN FIRST):

0:06 — Pelle Eklund, Philadelphia, April 25, 1989, at Pittsburgh vs. goaltender Tom Barrasso, second period. Pittsburgh won 10-7.
0:09 — Bill Collins, Minnesota, April 9, 1968, at Minnesota vs. Los Angeles and goaltender Wayne Rutledge, third period. Minnesota won 7-5.
— Dave Balon, Minnesota, April 25, 1968, at St. Louis vs. goaltender Glenn Hall, third period. Minnesota won 5-1.
— Murray Oliver, Minnesota, April 8, 1971, at St. Louis vs. goaltender Ernie Wakely, third period. St. Louis won 4-2.
— Clark Gillies, NY Islanders, April 15, 1977, at Buffalo vs. goaltender Don Edwards, third period. NY Islanders won 4-3.
— Eric Vail, Atlanta, April 11, 1978, at Atlanta vs. Detroit and goaltender Ron Low, third period. Detroit won 5-3.
— Stan Smyl, Vancouver, April 10, 1979, at Philadelphia vs. goaltender Wayne Stephenson, third period. Vancouver won 3-2.
— Wayne Gretzky, Edmonton, April 6, 1983, at Edmonton vs. Winnipeg and goaltender Brian Hayward, second period. Edmonton won 6-3.
— Mark Messier, Edmonton, April 16, 1984, at Calgary vs. goaltender Don Edwards, third period. Edmonton won 5-3.
— Brian Skrudland, Montreal, May 18, 1986, at Calgary vs. goaltender Mike Vernon, first overtime period. Montreal won 3-2.

FASTEST TWO GOALS:

0:05 — Norm Ullman, Detroit, April 11, 1965, at Detroit vs. Chicago and goaltender Glenn Hall. Ullman scored at 17:35 and 17:40 of second period. Detroit won 4-2.

FASTEST TWO GOALS FROM START OF A GAME:

1:08 — Dick Duff, Toronto, April 9, 1963, at Toronto vs. Detroit and goaltender Terry Sawchuk. Duff scored at 0:49 and 1:08. Toronto won 4-2.

FASTEST TWO GOALS FROM START OF A PERIOD:

0:35 — Pat LaFontaine, NY Islanders, May 19, 1984, at Edmonton vs. goaltender Andy Moog. LaFontaine scored at 0:13 and 0:35 of third period. Edmonton won 5-2.

PENALTIES

MOST PENALTY MINUTES IN PLAYOFFS, CAREER:

729 — Dale Hunter, Quebec, Washington, Colorado
541 — Chris Nilan, Montreal, NY Rangers, Boston
529 — Claude Lemieux, Montreal, New Jersey, Colorado, Phoenix
471 — Rick Tocchet, Philadelphia, Pittsburgh, Boston, Phoenix
466 — Willi Plett, Atlanta, Calgary, Minnesota, Boston

MOST PENALTIES, ONE GAME:

8 — Forbes Kennedy, Toronto, April 2, 1969, at Boston. Kennedy was assessed 4 minors, 2 majors, 1 10-minute misconduct, 1 game misconduct. Boston won 10-0.
— Kim Clackson, Pittsburgh, April 14, 1980, at Boston. Clackson was assessed 5 minors, 2 majors, 1 10-minute misconduct. Boston won 6-2.

MOST PENALTY MINUTES, ONE GAME:

42 — Dave Schultz, Philadelphia, April 22, 1976, at Toronto. Schultz was assessed 1 minor, 2 majors, 1 10-minute misconduct and 2 game-misconducts. Toronto won 8-5.

MOST PENALTIES, ONE PERIOD AND MOST PENALTY MINUTES, ONE PERIOD:

6 Penalties; 39 Minutes — Ed Hospodar, NY Rangers, April 9, 1981, at Los Angeles, first period. Hospodar was assessed 2 minors, 1 major, 1 10-minute misconduct, 2 game misconducts. Los Angeles won 5-4.

GOALTENDING

MOST PLAYOFF GAMES APPEARED IN BY A GOALTENDER, CAREER:

247 — Patrick Roy, Montreal, Colorado
169 — Martin Brodeur, New Jersey
161 — Ed Belfour, Chicago, Dallas, Toronto
150 — Grant Fuhr, Edmonton, Buffalo, St. Louis
138 — Mike Vernon, Calgary, Detroit, San Jose, Florida

MOST MINUTES PLAYED BY A GOALTENDER, CAREER:

15,209 — Patrick Roy, Montreal, Colorado
10,520 — Martin Brodeur, New Jersey
9,945 — Ed Belfour, Chicago, Dallas, Toronto
8,834 — Grant Fuhr, Edmonton, Buffalo, St. Louis
8,214 — Mike Vernon, Calgary, Detroit, San Jose, Florida

MOST MINUTES PLAYED BY A GOALTENDER, ONE PLAYOFF YEAR:

1,655 — Miikka Kiprusoff, Calgary, 2004. 26 games.
1,544 — Kirk McLean, Vancouver, 1994. 24 games.
— Ed Belfour, Dallas, 1999. 23 games.
1,540 — Ron Hextall, Philadelphia, 1987. 26 games.
1,505 — Martin Brodeur, New Jersey, 2001. 25 games.

MOST SHUTOUTS IN PLAYOFFS (CAREER):

23 — Patrick Roy, Montreal, Colorado
22 — Martin Brodeur, New Jersey
16 — Curtis Joseph, St. Louis, Edmonton, Toronto

MOST SHUTOUTS, ONE PLAYOFF YEAR:
7 — **Martin Brodeur, New Jersey,** 2003. 24 games.
6 — Dominik Hasek, Detroit, 2002. 23 games.
5 — Jean-Sebastien Giguere, Anaheim, 2003. 21 games.
— Nikolai Khabibulin, Tampa Bay, 2004. 23 games.
— Miikka Kiprusoff, Calgary, 2004. 26 games.

MOST SHUTOUTS, ONE PLAYOFF SERIES:
3 — **Clint Benedict, Mtl. Maroons,** 1926 F vs. Victoria. 4 games.
— **Dave Kerr, NY Rangers,** 1940 SF vs. Boston. 6 games.
— **Frank McCool, Toronto,** 1945 F vs. Detroit. 7 games.
— **Turk Broda, Toronto,** 1950 SF vs. Detroit. 7 games.
— **Felix Potvin, Toronto,** 1994 CQF vs. Chicago. 6 games.
— **Martin Brodeur, New Jersey,** 1995 CQF vs. Boston. 7 games.
— **Brent Johnson, St. Louis,** 2002 CQF vs. Chicago. 5 games.
— **Patrick Lalime, Ottawa,** 2002 CQF vs. Philadelphia. 5 games.
— **Jean-Sebastien Giguere, Anaheim,** 2003 CF vs. Minnesota. 4 games.
— **Martin Brodeur, New Jersey,** 2003 F vs. Anaheim. 7 games.
— **Ed Belfour, Toronto,** 2004 CQF vs. Ottawa. 7 games.
— **Nikolai Khabibulin, Tampa Bay,** 2004 CQF vs. NY Islanders. 5 games.

MOST WINS BY A GOALTENDER, (CAREER):
151 — Patrick Roy, Montreal, Colorado
95 — Martin Brodeur, New Jersey
92 — Grant Fuhr, Edmonton, Buffalo, St. Louis
88 — Billy Smith, NY Islanders
— Ed Belfour, Chicago, Dallas, Toronto

MOST WINS BY A GOALTENDER, ONE PLAYOFF YEAR:
16 — Sixteen wins by a goaltender in one playoff year has been recorded on 16 occasions. Nikolai Khabibulin of the Tampa Bay Lightning is the most recent to equal this mark, posting a record of 16 wins and 7 losses in 23 games in 2004. It was first accomplished by Grant Fuhr in 1988.

MOST CONSECUTIVE WINS BY A GOALTENDER, MORE THAN ONE PLAYOFF YEAR:
14 — **Tom Barrasso, Pittsburgh,** 1992, 1993; 3 wins vs. NY Rangers in 1992 DF, won by Pittsburgh 4-2; 4 wins vs. Boston in 1992 CF, won by Pittsburgh 4-0; 4 wins vs. Chicago in 1992 F, won by Pittsburgh 4-0; 3 wins vs. New Jersey in 1993 DSF, won by Pittsburgh 4-1.

MOST CONSECUTIVE WINS BY A GOALTENDER, ONE PLAYOFF YEAR:
11 — **Ed Belfour, Chicago,** 1992. 3 wins vs. St. Louis in DSF, won by Chicago 4-2; 4 wins vs. Detroit in DF, won by Chicago 4-0; and 4 wins vs. Edmonton in CF, won by Chicago 4-0.
— **Tom Barrasso, Pittsburgh,** 1992. 3 wins vs. NY Rangers in DF, won by Pittsburgh 4-2; 4 wins vs. Boston in CF, won by Pittsburgh 4-0; and 4 wins vs. Chicago in F, won by Pittsburgh 4-0.
— **Patrick Roy, Montreal,** 1993. 4 wins vs. Quebec in DSF, won by Montreal 4-2; 4 wins vs. Buffalo in DF, won by Montreal 4-0; and 3 wins vs. NY Islanders in CF, won by Montreal 4-1.

LONGEST SHUTOUT SEQUENCE:
270:08 — George Hainsworth, Montreal, 1930. Hainsworth's shutout streak began after Murray Murdoch scored a goal for the NY Rangers at 15:34 of the first period in the first game of a SF series on March 28, 1930. Hainsworth did not allow another goal in the final 113:18 of that game, won by Montreal 2-1 at 8:52 of the 4th overtime period. Hainsworth then shutout the NY Rangers in the next and final game of the series on March 30, 1930, won by Montreal 2-0. The streak continued with a 3-0 win over Boston in the opening game of the F series on April 1, 1930. His streak ended on April 3, 1930 when Boston's Eddie Shore scored at 16:50 of the second period in the second game of the F series.

MOST CONSECUTIVE SHUTOUTS:
3 — **Clint Benedict, Mtl. Maroons,** 1926. Benedict shut out Ottawa 1-0, Mar. 27; he then shut out Victoria twice, 3-0, Mar. 30; 3-0, Apr. 1. Mtl. Maroons won NHL F vs. Ottawa 2 goals to 1 and won the best-of-five F vs. Victoria 3-1.
— **John Ross Roach, NY Rangers,** 1929. Roach shut out NY Americans twice, 0-0, Mar. 19; 1-0, Mar. 21; he then shut out Toronto 1-0, Mar. 24. NY Rangers won QF vs. NY Americans 1 goal to 0 and won the best-of-three SF vs. Toronto 2-0.
— **Frank McCool, Toronto,** 1945. McCool shut out Detroit 1-0, April 6; 2-0, April 8; 1-0, April 12. Toronto won the best-of-seven F 4-3.
— **Brent Johnson, St. Louis,** 2002. Johnson shut out Chicago three times; 2-0, April 20; 4-0, April 21; 1-0, April 23. St. Louis won the best-of-seven CQF 4-1.
— **Patrick Lalime, Ottawa,** 2002. Lalime shut out Philadelphia three times; 3-0, April 20; 3-0, April 22; 3-0, April 24. Ottawa won the best-of-seven CQF 4-1.
— **Jean-Sebastien Giguere, Anaheim,** 2003. Giguere shut out Minnesota 1-0, May 10; 2-0, May 12; 4-0, May 14. Anaheim won the best-of-seven CF 4-0.

Early Playoff Records

1893-1918

Team Records

MOST GOALS, BOTH TEAMS, ONE GAME:
25 — **Ottawa Silver Seven, Dawson City** at Ottawa, Jan. 16, 1905. Ottawa 23, Dawson City 2. Ottawa won best-of-three series 2-0.

MOST GOALS, ONE TEAM, ONE GAME:
23 — **Ottawa Silver Seven** at Ottawa, Jan. 16, 1905. Ottawa defeated Dawson City 23-2.

MOST GOALS, BOTH TEAMS, BEST-OF-THREE SERIES:
42 — **Ottawa Silver Seven, Queen's University** at Ottawa, 1906. Ottawa defeated Queen's 16-7, Feb. 27, and 12-7, Feb. 28.

MOST GOALS, ONE TEAM, BEST-OF-THREE SERIES:
32 — **Ottawa Silver Seven** in 1905 at Ottawa. Defeated Dawson City 9-2, Jan. 13, and 23-2, Jan. 16.

MOST GOALS, BOTH TEAMS, BEST-OF-FIVE SERIES:
39 — **Toronto Arenas, Vancouver Millionaires** at Toronto, 1918. Toronto won 5-3, Mar. 20; 6-3, Mar. 26; 2-1, Mar. 30. Vancouver won 6-4, Mar. 23, and 8-1, Mar. 28. Toronto scored 18 goals; Vancouver 21.

MOST GOALS, ONE TEAM, BEST-OF-FIVE SERIES:
26 — **Vancouver Millionaires** in 1915 at Vancouver. Defeated Ottawa Senators 6-2, Mar. 22; 8-3, Mar. 24; and 12-3, Mar. 26.

Individual Records

MOST GOALS IN PLAYOFFS:
63 — **Frank McGee, Ottawa Silver Seven,** in 22 playoff games. Seven goals in four games, 1903; 21 goals in eight games, 1904; 18 goals in four games, 1905; 17 goals in six games, 1906.

MOST GOALS, ONE PLAYOFF SERIES:
15 — **Frank McGee, Ottawa Silver Seven,** in two games in 1905 at Ottawa. Scored one goal, Jan. 13, in 9-2 victory over Dawson City and 14 goals, Jan. 16, in 23-2 victory.

MOST GOALS, ONE PLAYOFF GAME:
14 — **Frank McGee, Ottawa Silver Seven,** at Ottawa, Jan. 16, 1905, in 23-2 victory over Dawson City.

FASTEST THREE GOALS:
40 Seconds — Marty Walsh, Ottawa Senators, at Ottawa, March 16, 1911, at 3:00, 3:10, and 3:40 of third period. Ottawa defeated Port Arthur 13-4.

Edmonton's Grant Fuhr was the first goalie to win 16 playoff games in one year, posting a record of 16-2 in 1988. Fuhr played in all 19 Oilers playoff games that year, including the May 24 game that was suspended due to a power failure in Boston.

All-Time Playoff Goal Leaders since 1918

(40 or more goals)

Player	Teams	Yrs.	GP	G
Wayne Gretzky	Edm., L.A., St.L., NYR	16	208	122
Mark Messier	Edm., NYR, Van.	17	236	109
Jari Kurri	Edm., L.A., NYR, Ana., Col.	15	200	106
Brett Hull	Cgy., St.L., Dal., Det., Phx.	19	202	103
Glenn Anderson	Edm., Tor., NYR, St.L.	15	225	93
Mike Bossy	NYI	10	129	85
*Joe Sakic	Que., Col.	13	172	84
Maurice Richard	Mtl.	15	133	82
Claude Lemieux	Mtl., N.J., Col., Phx., Dal.	17	233	80
Jean Beliveau	Mtl.	17	162	79
*Jaromir Jagr	Pit., Wsh., NYR	15	169	77
Mario Lemieux	Pit.	8	107	76
Dino Ciccarelli	Min., Wsh., Det., T.B., Fla.	14	141	73
Esa Tikkanen	Edm., NYR, St.L., N.J., Van., Fla., Wsh.	13	186	72
Bryan Trottier	NYI, Pit.	17	221	71
Steve Yzerman	Det.	20	196	70
Gordie Howe	Det., Hfd.	20	157	68
Joe Nieuwendyk	Cgy., Dal., N.J., Tor., Fla.	16	158	66
Denis Savard	Chi., Mtl., T.B.	16	169	66
Yvan Cournoyer	Mtl.	12	147	64
*Peter Forsberg	Que., Col., Phi., Nsh.	13	151	64
Brian Propp	Phi., Bos., Min., Hfd.	13	160	64
Bobby Smith	Min., Mtl.	13	184	64
Bobby Hull	Chi., Wpg., Hfd.	14	119	62
Phil Esposito	Chi., Bos., NYR	15	130	61
Jacques Lemaire	Mtl.	11	145	61
Joe Mullen	St.L., Cgy., Pit., Bos.	15	143	60
Doug Gilmour	St.L., Cgy., Tor., N.J., Chi., Buf., Mtl.	17	182	60
Stan Mikita	Chi.	18	155	59
*Brendan Shanahan	N.J., St.L., Hfd., Det., NYR	18	177	59
Paul Coffey	Edm., Pit., L.A., Det., Hfd., Phi., Chi., Car., Bos.	16	194	59
Guy Lafleur	Mtl., NYR, Que.	14	128	58
Bernie Geoffrion	Mtl., NYR	16	132	58
Luc Robitaille	L.A., Pit., NYR, Det.	15	159	58
*Mike Modano	Min., Dal.	15	174	58
Cam Neely	Van., Bos.	9	93	57
Steve Larmer	Chi., NYR	13	140	56
Denis Potvin	NYI	14	185	56
Rick MacLeish	Phi., Hfd., Pit., Det.	11	114	54
Steve Thomas	Tor., Chi., NYI, N.J., Ana., Det.	16	174	54
Bill Barber	Phi.	11	129	53
Stephane Richer	Mtl., N.J., T.B., St.L., Pit.	13	134	53
*Jeremy Roenick	Chi., Phx., Phi., L.A., S.J.	16	148	53
Rick Tocchet	Phi., Pit., L.A., Bos., Wsh., Phx.	13	145	52
Frank Mahovlich	Tor., Det., Mtl.	14	137	51
Brian Bellows	Min., Mtl., T.B., Ana., Wsh.	13	143	51
*Sergei Fedorov	Det., Ana., CBJ, Wsh.	14	169	51
Steve Shutt	Mtl., L.A.	12	99	50
*Rod Brind'Amour	St.L., Phi., Car.	11	141	50
Henri Richard	Mtl.	18	180	49
Reggie Leach	Bos., Cal., Phi., Det.	8	94	47
Ted Lindsay	Det., Chi.	16	133	47
*Mark Recchi	Pit., Phi., Mtl., Car., Atl.	12	140	47
Clark Gillies	NYI, Buf.	13	164	47
Kevin Stevens	Pit., Bos., L.A., NYR, Phi.	7	103	46
*Chris Drury	Col., Cgy., Buf., NYR	7	124	46
Dickie Moore	Mtl., Tor., St.L.	14	135	46
Ron Francis	Hfd., Pit., Car., Tor.	17	171	46
Rick Middleton	NYR, Bos.	12	114	45
Lanny McDonald	Tor., Col., Cgy.	13	117	44
Scott Young	Hfd., Pit., Que., Col., Ana., St.L., Dal.	14	141	44
*Daniel Alfredsson	Ott.	11	101	43
Ken Linseman	Phi., Edm., Bos., Tor.	11	113	43
Mike Gartner	Wsh., Min., NYR, Tor., Phx.	15	122	43
Dave Andreychuk	Buf., Tor., N.J., Bos., Col., T.B.	18	162	43
*Alex Kovalev	NYR, Pit., Mtl.	9	112	42
*Vyacheslav Kozlov	Det., Buf., Atl.	10	118	42
Bernie Nicholls	L.A., NYR, Edm., N.J., Chi., S.J.	13	118	42
Bobby Clarke	Phi.	13	136	42
John LeClair	Mtl., Phi., Pit.	14	154	42
Adam Oates	Det., St.L., Bos., Wsh., Phi., Ana., Edm.	15	163	42
Dale Hunter	Que., Wsh., Col.	18	186	42
*Nicklas Lidstrom	Det.	16	214	42
John Bucyk	Det., Bos.	14	124	41
Vincent Damphousse	Tor., Edm., Mtl., S.J.	14	140	41
Raymond Bourque	Bos., Col.	21	214	41
Tim Kerr	Phi., NYR, Hfd.	10	81	40
Peter McNab	Buf., Bos., Van., N.J.	10	107	40
Bob Bourne	NYI, L.A.	13	139	40
John Tonelli	NYI, Cgy., L.A., Chi., Que.	13	172	40

*Active

All-Time Playoff Assist Leaders since 1918

(65 or more assists)

Player	Teams	Yrs.	GP	A
Wayne Gretzky	Edm., L.A., St.L., NYR	16	208	260
Mark Messier	Edm., NYR, Van.	17	236	186
Raymond Bourque	Bos., Col.	21	214	139
Paul Coffey	Edm., Pit., L.A., Det., Hfd., Phi., Chi., Car., Bos.	16	194	137
Doug Gilmour	St.L., Cgy., Tor., N.J., Chi., Buf., Mtl.	17	182	128
Jari Kurri	Edm., L.A., NYR, Ana., Col.	15	200	127
Al MacInnis	Cgy., St.L.	19	177	121
Glenn Anderson	Edm., Tor., NYR, St.L.	15	225	121
*Sergei Fedorov	Det., Ana., CBJ, Wsh.	14	169	117
Larry Robinson	Mtl., L.A.	20	227	116
Steve Yzerman	Det.	20	196	115
Larry Murphy	L.A., Wsh., Min., Pit., Tor., Det.	20	215	115
Adam Oates	Det., St.L., Bos., Wsh., Phi., Ana., Edm.	15	163	114
Bryan Trottier	NYI, Pit.	17	221	113
*Chris Chelios	Mtl., Chi., Det.	23	260	113
Denis Savard	Chi., Mtl., T.B.	16	169	109
Denis Potvin	NYI	14	185	108
*Peter Forsberg	Que., Col., Phi., Nsh.	13	151	107
*Nicklas Lidstrom	Det.	16	214	107
*Jaromir Jagr	Pit., Wsh., NYR	15	169	104
*Joe Sakic	Que., Col.	13	172	104
Jean Beliveau	Mtl.	17	162	97
Ron Francis	Hfd., Pit., Car., Tor.	17	171	97
Mario Lemieux	Pit.	8	107	96
Bobby Smith	Min., Mtl.	13	184	96
*Sergei Zubov	NYR, Pit., Dal.	13	164	93
Gordie Howe	Det., Hfd.	20	157	92
Scott Stevens	Wsh., St.L., N.J.	20	233	92
Stan Mikita	Chi.	18	155	91
Brad Park	NYR, Bos., Det.	17	161	90
*Mike Modano	Min., Dal.	15	174	87
Brett Hull	Cgy., St.L., Dal., Det., Phx.	19	202	87
Craig Janney	Bos., St.L., S.J., Wpg., Phx., T.B., NYI	11	120	86
Brian Propp	Phi., Bos., Min., Hfd.	13	160	84
Henri Richard	Mtl.	18	180	80
Jacques Lemaire	Mtl.	11	145	78
Claude Lemieux	Mtl., N.J., Col., Phx., Dal.	17	233	78
Ken Linseman	Phi., Edm., Bos., Tor.	11	113	77
Bobby Clarke	Phi.	13	136	77
Guy Lafleur	Mtl., NYR, Que.	14	128	76
Phil Esposito	Chi., Bos., NYR	15	130	76
Dale Hunter	Que., Wsh., Col.	18	186	76
Mike Bossy	NYI	10	129	75
Steve Larmer	Chi., NYR	13	140	75
John Tonelli	NYI, Cgy., L.A., Chi., Que.	13	172	75
Peter Stastny	Que., N.J., St.L.	12	93	72
Bernie Nicholls	L.A., NYR, Edm., N.J., Chi., S.J.	13	118	72
*Chris Pronger	Hfd., St.L., Edm., Ana.	12	134	72
*Brendan Shanahan	N.J., St.L., Hfd., Det., NYR	18	177	72
*Patrik Elias	N.J.	11	126	71
Brian Bellows	Min., Mtl., T.B., Ana., Wsh.	13	143	71
Gilbert Perreault	Buf.	11	90	70
*Mark Recchi	Pit., Phi., Mtl., Car., Atl.	12	140	70
Geoff Courtnall	Bos., Edm., Wsh., St.L., Van.	15	156	70
Brian Leetch	NYR, Tor., Bos.	8	95	69
Dale Hawerchuk	Wpg., Buf., St.L., Phi.	15	97	69
Alex Delvecchio	Det.	14	121	69
Luc Robitaille	L.A., Pit., NYR, Det.	15	159	69
*Jeremy Roenick	Chi., Phx., Phi., L.A., S.J.	16	148	68
Bobby Hull	Chi., Wpg., Hfd.	14	119	67
*Sandis Ozolinsh	S.J., Col., Car., Fla., Ana., NYR	10	137	67
Frank Mahovlich	Tor., Det., Mtl.	14	137	67
Igor Larionov	Van., S.J., Det., Fla., N.J.	13	150	67
Bobby Orr	Bos., Chi.	8	74	66
Bernie Federko	St.L., Det.	11	91	66
Jean Ratelle	NYR, Bos.	15	123	66
Charlie Huddy	Edm., L.A., Buf., St.L.	14	183	66
*Scott Niedermayer	N.J., Ana.	14	189	66
Trevor Linden	Van., NYI, Mtl., Wsh.	12	124	65

All-Time Playoff Point Leaders since 1918

(110 or more points)

Player	Teams	Yrs.	GP	G	A	Pts.
Wayne Gretzky	Edm., L.A., St.L., NYR	16	208	122	260	382
Mark Messier	Edm., NYR, Van.	17	236	109	186	295
Jari Kurri	Edm., L.A., NYR, Ana., Col.	15	200	106	127	233
Glenn Anderson	Edm., Tor., NYR, St.L.	15	225	93	121	214
Paul Coffey	Edm., Pit., L.A., Det., Hfd., Phi., Chi., Car., Bos.	16	194	59	137	196
Brett Hull	Cgy., St.L., Dal., Det., Phx.	19	202	103	87	190
*Joe Sakic	Que., Col.	13	172	84	104	188
Doug Gilmour	St.L., Cgy., Tor., N.J., Chi., Buf., Mtl.	17	182	60	128	188
Steve Yzerman	Det.	20	196	70	115	185
Bryan Trottier	NYI, Pit.	17	221	71	113	184
*Jaromir Jagr	Pit., Wsh., NYR	15	169	77	104	181
Raymond Bourque	Bos., Col.	21	214	41	139	180
Jean Beliveau	Mtl.	17	162	79	97	176
Denis Savard	Chi., Mtl., T.B.	16	169	66	109	175
Mario Lemieux	Pit.	8	107	76	96	172
*Peter Forsberg	Que., Col., Phi., Nsh.	13	151	64	107	171
*Sergei Fedorov	Det., Ana., CBJ, Wsh.	14	169	51	117	168
Denis Potvin	NYI	14	185	56	108	164
Mike Bossy	NYI	10	129	85	75	160
Gordie Howe	Det., Hfd.	20	157	68	92	160
Al MacInnis	Cgy., St.L.	19	177	39	121	160
Bobby Smith	Min., Mtl.	13	184	64	96	160
Claude Lemieux	Mtl., N.J., Col., Phx., Dal.	17	233	80	78	158
Adam Oates	Det., St.L., Bos., Wsh., Phi., Ana., Edm.	15	163	42	114	156
Larry Murphy	L.A., Wsh., Min., Pit., Tor., Det.	20	215	37	115	152
Stan Mikita	Chi.	18	155	59	91	150
*Nicklas Lidstrom	Det.	16	214	42	107	149
Brian Propp	Phi., Bos., Min., Hfd.	13	160	64	84	148
*Mike Modano	Min., Dal.	15	174	58	87	145
Larry Robinson	Mtl., L.A.	20	227	28	116	144
*Chris Chelios	Mtl., Chi., Det.	23	260	31	113	144
Ron Francis	Hfd., Pit., Car., Tor.	17	171	46	97	143
Jacques Lemaire	Mtl.	11	145	61	78	139
Phil Esposito	Chi., Bos., NYR	15	130	61	76	137
Guy Lafleur	Mtl., NYR, Que.	14	128	58	76	134
Esa Tikkanen	Edm., NYR, St.L., N.J., Van., Fla., Wsh.	13	186	72	60	132
Steve Larmer	Chi., NYR	13	140	56	75	131
*Brendan Shanahan	N.J., St.L., Hfd., Det., NYR	18	177	59	72	131
Bobby Hull	Chi., Wpg., Hfd.	14	119	62	67	129
Henri Richard	Mtl.	18	180	49	80	129
Yvan Cournoyer	Mtl.	12	147	64	63	127
Luc Robitaille	L.A., Pit., NYR, Det.	15	159	58	69	127
Maurice Richard	Mtl.	15	133	82	44	126
Brad Park	NYR, Bos., Det.	17	161	35	90	125
Brian Bellows	Min., Mtl., T.B., Ana., Wsh.	13	143	51	71	122
*Jeremy Roenick	Chi., Phx., Phi., L.A., S.J.	16	148	53	68	121
Ken Linseman	Phi., Edm., Bos., Tor.	11	113	43	77	120
Bobby Clarke	Phi.	13	136	42	77	119
Bernie Geoffrion	Mtl., NYR	16	132	58	60	118
Frank Mahovlich	Tor., Det., Mtl.	14	137	51	67	118
Dino Ciccarelli	Min., Wsh., Det., T.B., Fla.	14	141	73	45	118
Dale Hunter	Que., Wsh., Col.	18	186	42	76	118
Scott Stevens	Wsh., St.L., N.J.	20	233	26	92	118
*Mark Recchi	Pit., Phi., Mtl., Car., Atl.	12	140	47	70	117
*Sergei Zubov	NYR, Pit., Dal.	13	164	24	93	117
Joe Nieuwendyk	Cgy., Dal., N.J., Tor., Fla.	16	158	66	50	116
John Tonelli	NYI, Cgy., L.A., Chi., Que.	13	172	40	75	115
Bernie Nicholls	L.A., NYR, Edm., N.J., Chi., S.J.	13	118	42	72	114
Rick Tocchet	Phi., Pit., L.A., Bos., Wsh., Phx.	13	145	52	60	112
Craig Janney	Bos., St.L., S.J., Wpg., Phx., T.B., NYI	11	120	24	86	110
*Patrik Elias	N.J.	11	126	39	71	110
Dickie Moore	Mtl., Tor., St.L.	14	135	46	64	110

Pittsburgh's Sidney Crosby was slowed by an ankle injury during the regular season, but he led all playoff performers with 21 assists in 20 games played, and tied Henrik Zetterberg for the lead with 27 points in 2008.

Leading Playoff Scorers, 1918–2008

Season	Player and Club	Games Played	Goals	Assists	Points
2007-08	Henrik Zetterberg, Detroit	22	13	14	27
	Sidney Crosby, Pittsburgh	20	6	21	27
2006-07	Daniel Alfredsson, Ottawa	20	14	8	22
	Dany Heatley, Ottawa	20	7	15	22
	Jason Spezza, Ottawa	20	7	15	22
2005-06	Eric Staal, Carolina	25	9	19	28
2004-05	*Season Cancelled*				
2003-04	Brad Richards, Tampa Bay	23	12	14	26
2002-03	Jamie Langenbrunner, New Jersey	24	11	7	18
	Scott Niedermayer, New Jersey	24	2	16	18
2001-02	Peter Forsberg, Colorado	20	9	18	27
2000-01	Joe Sakic, Colorado	21	13	13	26
99-2000	Brett Hull, Dallas	23	11	13	24
1998-99	Peter Forsberg, Colorado	19	8	16	24
1997-98	Steve Yzerman, Detroit	22	6	18	24
1996-97	Eric Lindros, Philadelphia	19	12	14	26
1995-96	Joe Sakic, Colorado	22	18	16	34
1994-95	Sergei Fedorov, Detroit	17	7	17	24
1993-94	Brian Leetch, NY Rangers	23	11	23	34
1992-93	Wayne Gretzky, Los Angeles	24	15	25	40
1991-92	Mario Lemieux, Pittsburgh	15	16	18	34
1990-91	Mario Lemieux, Pittsburgh	23	16	28	44
1989-90	Craig Simpson, Edmonton	22	16	15	31
	Mark Messier, Edmonton	22	9	22	31
1988-89	Al MacInnis, Calgary	22	7	24	31
1987-88	Wayne Gretzky, Edmonton	19	12	31	43
1986-87	Wayne Gretzky, Edmonton	21	5	29	34
1985-86	Doug Gilmour, St. Louis	19	9	12	21
	Bernie Federko, St. Louis	19	7	14	21
1984-85	Wayne Gretzky, Edmonton	18	17	30	47
1983-84	Wayne Gretzky, Edmonton	19	13	22	35
1982-83	Wayne Gretzky, Edmonton	16	12	26	38
1981-82	Bryan Trottier, NY Islanders	19	6	23	29
1980-81	Mike Bossy, NY Islanders	18	17	18	35
1979-80	Bryan Trottier, NY Islanders	21	12	17	29
1978-79	Jacques Lemaire, Montreal	16	11	12	23
	Guy Lafleur, Montreal	16	10	13	23
1977-78	Guy Lafleur, Montreal	15	10	11	21
	Larry Robinson, Montreal	15	4	17	21
1976-77	Guy Lafleur, Montreal	14	9	17	26
1975-76	Reggie Leach, Philadelphia	16	19	5	24
1974-75	Rick MacLeish, Philadelphia	17	11	9	20
1973-74	Rick MacLeish, Philadelphia	17	13	9	22
1972-73	Yvan Cournoyer, Montreal	17	15	10	25
1971-72	Phil Esposito, Boston	15	9	15	24
	Bobby Orr, Boston	15	5	19	24
1970-71	Frank Mahovlich, Montreal	20	14	13	27
1969-70	Phil Esposito, Boston	14	13	14	27
1968-69	Phil Esposito, Boston	10	8	10	18
1967-68	Bill Goldsworthy, Minnesota	14	8	7	15
1966-67	Jim Pappin, Toronto	12	7	8	15
1965-66	Norm Ullman, Detroit	12	6	9	15
1964-65	Bobby Hull, Chicago	14	10	7	17
1963-64	Gordie Howe, Detroit	14	9	10	19
1962-63	Gordie Howe, Detroit	11	7	9	16
	Norm Ullman, Detroit	11	4	12	16
1961-62	Stan Mikita, Chicago	12	6	15	21
1960-61	Gordie Howe, Detroit	11	4	11	15
	Pierre Pilote, Chicago	12	3	12	15
1959-60	Henri Richard, Montreal	8	3	9	12
	Bernie Geoffrion, Montreal	8	2	10	12
1958-59	Dickie Moore, Montreal	11	5	12	17
1957-58	Fleming MacKell, Boston	12	5	14	19
1956-57	Bernie Geoffrion, Montreal	11	11	7	18
1955-56	Jean Béliveau, Montreal	10	12	7	19
1954-55	Gordie Howe, Detroit	11	9	11	20
1953-54	Dickie Moore, Montreal	11	5	8	13
1952-53	Ed Sandford, Boston	11	8	3	11
1951-52	Ted Lindsay, Detroit	8	5	2	7
	Floyd Curry, Montreal	11	4	3	7
	Metro Prystai, Detroit	8	2	5	7
	Gordie Howe, Detroit	8	2	5	7
1950-51	Maurice Richard, Montreal	11	9	4	13
	Max Bentley, Toronto	11	2	11	13
1949-50	Pentti Lund, NY Rangers	12	6	5	11
1948-49	Gordie Howe, Detroit	11	8	3	11
1947-48	Ted Kennedy, Toronto	9	8	6	14
1946-47	Maurice Richard, Montreal	10	6	5	11
1945-46	Elmer Lach, Montreal	9	5	12	17
1944-45	Joe Carveth, Detroit	14	5	6	11
1943-44	Toe Blake, Montreal	9	7	11	18
1942-43	Carl Liscombe, Detroit	10	6	8	14
1941-42	Don Grosso, Detroit	12	8	6	14
	Syl Apps, Toronto	13	5	9	14
1940-41	Milt Schmidt, Boston	11	5	6	11
1939-40	Phil Watson, NY Rangers	12	3	6	9
	Neil Colville, NY Rangers	12	2	7	9
1938-39	Bill Cowley, Boston	12	3	11	14
1937-38	Johnny Gottselig, Chicago	10	5	3	8
	Gordie Drillon, Toronto	7	7	1	8
1936-37	Marty Barry, Detroit	10	4	7	11
1935-36	Frank Boll, Toronto	9	7	3	10
1934-35	Baldy Northcott, Mtl. Maroons	7	4	1	5
	Busher Jackson, Toronto	7	3	2	5
	Cy Wentworth, Mtl. Maroons	7	3	2	5
	Charlie Conacher, Toronto	7	1	4	5
1933-34	Larry Aurie, Detroit	9	3	7	10
1932-33	Cecil Dillon, NY Rangers	8	8	2	10
1931-32	Frank Boucher, NY Rangers	7	3	6	9
1930-31	Cooney Weiland, Boston	5	6	3	9
1929-30	Marty Barry, Boston	6	3	3	6
	Cooney Weiland, Boston	6	1	5	6
1928-29	Andy Blair, Toronto	4	3	0	3
	Butch Keeling, NY Rangers	6	3	0	3
	Ace Bailey, Toronto	4	1	2	3
1927-28	Frank Boucher, NY Rangers	9	7	3	10
1926-27	Harry Oliver, Boston	8	4	2	6
	Percy Galbraith, Boston	8	3	3	6
1925-26	Nels Stewart, Mtl. Maroons	8	6	3	9
1924-25	Howie Morenz, Montreal	6	7	1	8
1923-24	Howie Morenz, Montreal	6	7	3	10
1922-23	Punch Broadbent, Ottawa	8	6	1	7
1921-22	Babe Dye, Toronto	7	11	1	12
1920-21	Cy Denneny, Ottawa	7	4	2	6
1919-20	Frank Nighbor, Ottawa	5	6	1	7
	Jack Darragh, Ottawa	5	5	2	7
1918-19	Newsy Lalonde, Montreal	10	17	2	19
1917-18	Alf Skinner, Toronto	7	8	3	11

Three-or-more-Goal Games, Playoffs 1918 –2008

Player	Team	Date	City	Total Goals	Opposing Goaltender	Score
Wayne Gretzky (10)	Edm.	Apr. 11/81	Edm.	3	Richard Sevigny	Edm. 6 Mtl. 2
		Apr. 19/81	Edm.	3	Billy Smith	Edm. 5 NYI 2
		Apr. 6/83	Edm.	4	Brian Hayward	Edm. 6 Wpg. 3
		Apr. 17/83	Cgy.	4	Reggie Lemelin	Edm. 10 Cgy. 2
		Apr. 25/85	Wpg.	3	Brian Hayward (2)	
					Marc Behrend (1)	Edm. 8 Wpg. 3
		May 25/85	Edm.	3	Pelle Lindbergh	Edm. 4 Phi. 3
		Apr. 24/86	Cgy.	3	Mike Vernon	Edm. 7 Cgy. 4
	L.A.	May 29/93	Tor.	3	Felix Potvin	L.A. 5 Tor. 4
	NYR	Apr. 23/97	NYR	3	John Vanbiesbrouck	NYR 3 Fla. 2
		May 18/97	Phi.	3	Garth Snow	NYR 5 Phi. 4
Maurice Richard (7)	Mtl.	Mar. 23/44	Mtl.	5	Paul Bibeault	Mtl. 5 Tor. 1
		Apr. 6/44	Chi.	3	Mike Karakas	Mtl. 3 Chi. 1
		Mar. 29/45	Mtl.	4	Frank McCool	Mtl. 10 Tor. 3
		Apr. 14/53	Bos.	3	Gord Henry	Mtl. 7 Bos. 3
		Mar. 20/56	Mtl.	3	Gump Worsley	Mtl. 7 NYR 1
		Apr. 6/57	Mtl.	4	Don Simmons	Mtl. 5 Bos. 1
		Apr. 1/58	Det.	3	Terry Sawchuk	Mtl. 4 Det. 3
Jari Kurri (7)	Edm.	Apr. 4/84	Edm.	3	Doug Soetaert (1)	
					Mike Veisor (2)	Edm. 9 Wpg. 2
		Apr. 25/85	Wpg.	3	Brian Hayward (2)	
					Marc Behrend (1)	Edm. 8 Wpg. 3
		May 7/85	Edm.	3	Murray Bannerman	Edm. 7 Chi. 3
		May 14/85	Edm.	3	Murray Bannerman	Edm. 10 Chi. 5
		May 16/85	Chi.	4	Murray Bannerman	Edm. 8 Chi. 2
		Apr. 9/87	Edm.	4	Rollie Melanson (2)	
					Darren Eliot (2)	Edm. 13 L.A. 3
		May 18/90	Bos.	3	Andy Moog (2)	
					Reggie Lemelin (1)	Edm. 7 Bos. 2
Dino Ciccarelli (6)	Min.	May 5/81	Min.	3	Pat Riggin	Min. 7 Cgy. 4
		Apr. 10/82	Min.	3	Murray Bannerman	Min. 7 Chi. 1
	Wsh.	Apr. 5/90	N.J.	3	Sean Burke	Wsh. 5 N.J. 4
		Apr. 25/92	Pit.	4	Tom Barrasso (1)	
					Ken Wregget (3)	Wsh. 7 Pit. 2
	Det.	Apr. 29/93	Tor.	3	Felix Potvin (2)	
					Daren Puppa (1)	Det. 7 Tor. 3
		May 11/95	Dal.	3	Andy Moog (2)	
					Darcy Wakaluk (1)	Det. 5 Dal. 1
Mike Bossy (5)	NYI	Apr. 16/79	NYI	3	Tony Esposito	NYI 6 Chi. 2
		May 8/82	NYI	3	Richard Brodeur	NYI 6 Van. 5
		Apr. 10/83	Wsh.	3	Al Jensen	NYI 6 Wsh. 3
		May 3/83	NYI	3	Pete Peeters	NYI 8 Bos. 3
		May 7/83	NYI	4	Pete Peeters	NYI 8 Bos. 4
Phil Esposito (4)	Bos.	Apr. 2/69	Bos.	4	Bruce Gamble	Bos. 10 Tor. 0
		Apr. 8/70	Bos.	3	Ed Giacomin	Bos. 8 NYR 2
		Apr. 19/70	Chi.	3	Tony Esposito	Bos. 6 Chi. 3
		Apr. 8/75	Bos.	3	Tony Esposito (2)	
					Michel Dumas (1)	Bos. 8 Chi. 2
Mark Messier (4)	Edm.	Apr. 14/83	Edm.	4	Reggie Lemelin	Edm. 6 Cgy. 3
		Apr. 17/83	Cgy.	3	Reggie Lemelin (1)	Edm. 10 Cgy. 2
					Don Edwards (2)	
		Apr. 26/83	Edm.	3	Murray Bannerman	Edm. 8 Chi. 2
	NYR	May 25/94	N.J.	3	Martin Brodeur (2)	NYR 4 N.J. 2
					ENG (1)	
Steve Yzerman (4)	Det.	Apr. 6/89	Det.	3	Alain Chevrier	Chi. 5 Det. 4
		Apr. 4/91	St.L.	3	Vincent Riendeau (2)	Det. 6 St.L. 3
					Pat Jablonski (1)	
		May 8/96	St.L.	3	Jon Casey	St.L. 5 Det. 4
		Apr. 21/99	Det.	3	Guy Hebert (2)	Det. 5 Ana. 3
					Pat Jablonski (1)	
Bernie Geoffrion (3)	Mtl.	Mar. 27/52	Mtl.	3	Jim Henry	Mtl. 4 Bos. 0
		Apr. 7/55	Mtl.	3	Terry Sawchuk	Mtl. 4 Det. 2
		Mar. 30/57	Mtl.	3	Gump Worsley	Mtl. 8 NYR 3
Norm Ullman (3)	Det.	Mar. 29/64	Chi.	3	Glenn Hall	Det. 5 Chi. 4
		Apr. 7/64	Det.	3	Glenn Hall (2)	
					Denis DeJordy (1)	Det. 7 Chi. 2
		Apr. 11/65	Det.	3	Glenn Hall	Det. 4 Chi. 2
John Bucyk (3)	Bos.	May 3/70	St.L.	3	Jacques Plante (1)	
					Ernie Wakely (2)	Bos. 6 St.L. 1
		Apr. 20/72	Bos.	3	Jacques Caron (1)	
					Ernie Wakely (2)	Bos. 10 St.L. 2
		Apr. 21/74	Bos.	3	Tony Esposito	Bos. 8 Chi. 6
Rick MacLeish (3)	Phi.	Apr. 11/74	Phi.	3	Phil Myre	Phi. 5 Atl. 1
		Apr. 13/75	Phi.	3	Gord McRae	Phi. 6 Tor. 3
		May 13/75	Phi.	3	Glenn Resch	Phi. 4 NYI 1
Denis Savard (3)	Chi.	Apr. 19/82	Chi.	3	Mike Liut	Chi. 7 StL. 4
		Apr. 10/86	Chi.	4	Ken Wregget	Tor. 6 Chi. 4
		Apr. 9/88	St.L.	3	Greg Millen	Chi. 6 St.L. 3
Tim Kerr (3)	Phi.	Apr. 13/85	NYR	4	Glen Hanlon	Phi. 6 NYR 5
		Apr. 20/87	Phi.	3	Kelly Hrudey	Phi. 4 NYI 2
		Apr. 19/89	Pit.	3	Tom Barrasso	Phi. 4 Pit. 2
Cam Neely (3)	Bos.	Apr. 9/87	Mtl.	3	Patrick Roy	Mtl. 4 Bos. 3
		Apr. 5/91	Bos.	3	Peter Sidorkiewicz	Bos. 4 Hfd. 3
		Apr. 25/91	Bos.	3	Patrick Roy	Bos. 4 Mtl. 1
Petr Klima (3)	Det.	Apr. 7/88	Tor.	3	Allan Bester (2)	
					Ken Wregett (1)	Det. 6 Tor. 2
		Apr. 21/88	St.L.	3	Greg Millen	Det. 6 St.L. 0
	Edm.	May 4/91	Edm.	3	Jon Casey	Edm. 7 Min. 2
Esa Tikkanen (3)	Edm.	May 22/88	Edm.	3	Reggie Lemelin	Edm. 6 Bos. 3
		Apr. 16/91	Cgy.	3	Mike Vernon	Edm. 5 Cgy. 4
		Apr. 26/92	L.A.	3	Kelly Hrudey (2)	Edm. 5 L.A. 2
					Tom Askey (1)	
Mike Gartner (3)	NYR	Apr. 13/90	NYR	3	Mark Fitzpatrick (2)	
					Glenn Healy (1)	NYR 6 NYI 5
		Apr. 27/92	NYR	3	Chris Terreri	NYR 8 N.J. 5
	Tor.	Apr. 25/96	Tor.	3	Jon Casey	Tor. 5 St.L. 4
Mario Lemieux (3)	Pit.	Apr. 25/89	Pit.	5	Ron Hextall	Pit. 10 Phi. 7
		Apr. 23/92	Pit.	3	Don Beaupre	Pit. 6 Wsh. 4
		May 11/96	Pit.	3	Mike Richter	Pit. 7 NYR 3
Patrick Marleau (3)	S.J.	Apr. 10/04	S.J.	3	Chris Osgood	S.J. 3 St.L. 1
		Apr. 22/04	S.J.	3	David Aebischer	S.J. 5 Col. 2
		Apr. 27/06	S.J.	3	Chris Mason	Nsh. 4 S.J. 5
Newsy Lalonde (2)	Mtl.	Mar. 1/19	Mtl.	5	Clint Benedict	Mtl. 6 Ott. 3
		Mar. 22/19	Sea.	4	Hap Holmes	Mtl. 4 Sea. 2
Howie Morenz (2)	Mtl.	Mar. 22/24	Mtl.	3	Charles Reid	Mtl. 6 Cgy.T. 1
		Mar. 27/25	Mtl.	3	Hap Holmes	Mtl. 4 Vic. 2
Doug Bentley (2)	Chi.	Mar. 28/44	Chi.	3	Connie Dion	Chi. 7 Det. 1
		Mar. 30/44	Det.	3	Connie Dion	Chi. 5 Det. 2
Toe Blake (2)	Mtl.	Mar. 22/38	Mtl.	3	Mike Karakas	Mtl. 6 Chi. 4
		Mar. 26/46	Chi.	3	Mike Karakas	Mtl. 7 Chi. 2
Ted Kennedy (2)	Tor.	Apr. 14/45	Tor.	3	Harry Lumley	Det. 5 Tor. 3
		Mar. 27/48	Tor.	4	Frank Brimsek	Tor. 5 Bos. 3
F. St. Marseille (2)	St.L.	Apr. 28/70	St.L.	3	Al Smith	St.L. 5 Pit. 0
		Apr. 6/72	Min.	3	Cesare Maniago	Min. 6 St.L. 5
Bobby Hull (2)	Chi.	Apr. 7/63	Det.	3	Terry Sawchuk	Det. 7 Chi. 4
		Apr. 9/72	Pit.	3	Jim Rutherford	Chi. 6 Pit. 5
Pit Martin (2)	Chi.	Apr. 4/73	Chi.	3	Wayne Stephenson	Chi. 7 St.L. 1
		May 10/73	Chi.	3	Ken Dryden	Mtl. 6 Chi. 4
Yvan Cournoyer (2)	Mtl.	Apr. 5/73	Mtl.	3	Dave Dryden	Mtl. 7 Buf. 3
		Apr. 11/74	Mtl.	3	Ed Giacomin	Mtl. 4 NYR 1
Guy Lafleur (2)	Mtl.	May 1/75	Mtl.	3	Roger Crozier (1)	
					Gerry Desjardins (2)	Mtl. 7 Buf. 0
		Apr. 11/77	Mtl.	3	Ed Staniowski	Mtl. 7 St.L. 2
Lanny McDonald (2)	Tor.	Apr. 9/77	Pit.	3	Denis Herron	Tor. 5 Pit. 2
		Apr. 17/77	Tor.	4	Wayne Stephenson	Phi. 6 Tor. 5
Bill Barber (2)	Phi.	May 4/80	Min.	4	Gilles Meloche	Phi. 5 Min. 3
		Apr. 9/81	Phi.	3	Dan Bouchard	Phi. 8 Que. 5
Bryan Trottier (2)	NYI	Apr. 8/80	NYI	3	Doug Keans	NYI 8 L.A. 1
		Apr. 9/81	NYI	3	Michel Larocque	NYI 5 Tor. 1
Butch Goring (2)	L.A.	Apr. 9/77	L.A.	3	Phil Myre	L.A. 4 Atl. 2
	NYI	May 17/81	Min.	3	Gilles Meloche	NYI 7 Min. 5
Paul Reinhart (2)	Cgy.	Apr. 14/83	Edm.	3	Andy Moog	Edm. 6 Cgy. 3
		Apr. 8/84	Van	3	Richard Brodeur	Cgy. 5 Van. 1
Brian Propp (2)	Phi.	Apr. 22/81	Phi.	3	Pat Riggin	Phi. 9 Cgy. 4
		Apr. 21/85	Phi.	3	Billy Smith	Phi. 5 NYI 2
Peter Stastny (2)	Que.	Apr. 5/83	Bos.	3	Pete Peeters	Bos. 4 Que. 3
		Apr. 11/87	Que.	3	Mike Liut (2)	
					Steve Weeks (1)	Que. 5 Hfd. 1
Michel Goulet (2)	Que.	Apr. 23/85	Que.	3	Steve Penney	Que. 7 Mtl. 6
		Apr. 12/87	Que.	3	Mike Liut	Que. 4 Hfd. 1
Glenn Anderson (2)	Edm.	Apr. 26/83	Edm.	4	Murray Bannerman	Edm. 8 Chi. 2
		Apr. 6/88	Wpg.	3	Daniel Berthiaume	Edm. 7 Wpg. 4
Peter Zezel (2)	Phi.	Apr. 13/86	NYR	3	John Vanbiesbrouck	Phi. 7 NYR 1
	St.L.	Apr. 11/89	St.L.	3	Jon Casey (2)	
					Kari Takko (1)	St.L. 6 Min. 1
Geoff Courtnall (2)	Van.	Apr. 4/91	L.A.	3	Kelly Hrudey	Van. 6 L.A. 5
		Apr. 30/92	Van.	3	Rick Tabaracci	Van. 5 Win. 0
Joe Sakic (2)	Que.	May 6/95	Que.	3	Mike Richter	Que. 5 NYR 4
	Col.	Apr. 25/96	Col.	3	Corey Hirsch	Col. 5 Van. 4
Daniel Alfredsson (2)	Ott.	Apr. 28/98	Ott.	3	Martin Brodeur	Ott. 4 N.J. 3
		May 11/98	Ott.	3	Olaf Kolzig	Ott. 4 Wsh. 3
Johan Franzen (2)	Det.	Apr. 26/08	Det.	3	Jose Theodore (2)	
					Peter Budaj (1)	Det. 5 Col. 1
	Det.	May 1/08	Col.	3	Jose Theodore (1)	Det. 8 Col. 2
					Peter Budaj (2)	
Harry Meeking	Tor.	Mar. 11/18	Tor.	3	Georges Vezina	Tor. 7 Mtl. 3
Alf Skinner	Tor.	Mar. 23/18	Tor.	3	Hugh Lehman	Van.M. 6 Tor. 4
Joe Malone	Mtl.	Feb. 23/19	Mtl.	3	Clint Benedict	Mtl. 8 Ott. 4
Odie Cleghorn	Mtl.	Feb. 27/19	Ott.	3	Clint Benedict	Mtl. 5 Ott. 3
Jack Darragh	Ott.	Apr. 1/20	Tor.	3	Hap Holmes	Ott. 6 Sea. 1
George Boucher	Ott.	Mar. 10/21	Ott.	3	Jake Forbes	Ott. 5 Tor. 0
Babe Dye	Tor.	Mar. 28/22	Tor.	4	Hugh Lehman	Tor. 5 Van.M. 1
Percy Galbraith	Bos.	Mar. 31/27	Bos.	3	Hugh Lehman	Bos. 4 Chi. 4
Busher Jackson	Tor.	Apr. 5/32	NYR	3	John Ross Roach	Tor. 6 NYR 4
Frank Boucher	NYR	Apr. 9/32	Tor.	3	Lorne Chabot	Tor. 6 NYR 4
Charlie Conacher	Tor.	Mar. 26/36	Tor.	3	Tiny Thompson	Tor. 8 Bos. 3
Syd Howe	Det.	Mar. 23/39	Det.	3	Claude Bourque	Det. 7 Mtl. 3
Bryan Hextall	NYR	Apr. 3/40	NYR	3	Turk Broda	NYR 6 Tor. 2
Joe Benoit	Mtl.	Mar. 22/41	Mtl.	3	Sam LoPresti	Mtl. 4 Chi. 3
Syl Apps	Tor.	Mar. 25/41	Tor.	3	Frank Brimsek	Tor. 7 Bos. 2
Jack McGill	Bos.	Mar. 29/42	Bos.	3	Johnny Mowers	Det. 6 Bos. 4
Don Metz	Tor.	Apr. 14/42	Tor.	3	Johnny Mowers	Tor. 9 Det. 3
Mud Bruneteau	Det.	Apr. 1/43	Det.	3	Frank Brimsek	Det. 6 Bos. 2
Don Grosso	Det.	Apr. 7/43	Bos.	3	Frank Brimsek	Det. 4 Bos. 0
Carl Liscombe	Det.	Apr. 3/45	Bos.	4	Paul Bibeault	Det. 5 Bos. 3
Billy Reay	Mtl.	Apr. 1/47	Bos.	4	Frank Brimsek	Mtl. 5 Bos. 1
Gerry Plamondon	Mtl.	Mar. 24/49	Det.	3	Harry Lumley	Mtl. 4 Det. 3
Sid Smith	Tor.	Apr. 10/49	Det.	3	Harry Lumley	Tor. 3 Det. 1

Three-or-more-Goal Games, Playoffs *— continued*

Player	Team	Date	City	Total Goals	Opposing Goaltender	Score	
Pentti Lund	NYR	Apr. 2/50	NYR	3	Bill Durnan	NYR 4	Mtl. 1
Ted Lindsay	Det.	Apr. 5/55	Det.	4	Charlie Hodge (1)		
					Jacques Plante (3)	Det. 7	Mtl. 1
Gordie Howe	Det.	Apr. 10/55	Det.	3	Jacques Plante	Det. 5	Mtl. 1
Phil Goyette	Mtl.	Mar. 25/58	Mtl.	3	Terry Sawchuk	Mtl. 8	Det. 1
Jerry Toppazzini	Bos.	Apr. 5/58	Bos.	3	Gump Worsley	Bos. 8	NYR 2
Bob Pulford	Tor.	Apr. 19/62	Tor.	3	Glenn Hall	Tor. 8	Chi. 4
Dave Keon	Tor.	Apr. 9/64	Mtl.	3	Charlie Hodge (2)	Tor. 3	Mtl. 1
					ENG (1)		
Henri Richard	Mtl.	Apr. 20/67	Mtl.	3	Terry Sawchuk (2)		
					Johnny Bower (1)	Mtl. 6	Tor. 2
Rosaire Paiement	Phi.	Apr. 13/68	Phi.	3	Glenn Hall (1)		
					Seth Martin (2)	Phi. 6	St.L. 1
Jean Beliveau	Mtl.	Apr. 20/68	Mtl.	3	Denis DeJordy	Mtl. 4	Chi. 1
Red Berenson	St.L.	Apr. 15/69	St.L.	3	Gerry Desjardins	St.L. 4	L.A. 0
Ken Schinkel	Pit.	Apr. 11/70	Oak.	3	Gary Smith	Pit. 5	Oak. 2
Jim Pappin	Chi.	Apr. 11/71	Phi.	3	Bruce Gamble	Chi. 6	Phi. 2
Bobby Orr	Bos.	Apr. 11/71	Mtl.	3	Ken Dryden	Bos. 5	Mtl. 2
Jacques Lemaire	Mtl.	Apr. 20/71	Mtl.	3	Gump Worsley	Mtl. 7	Min. 2
Vic Hadfield	NYR	Apr. 22/71	NYR	3	Tony Esposito	NYR 4	Chi. 1
Fred Stanfield	Bos.	Apr. 18/72	Bos.	3	Jacques Caron	Bos. 6	St.L. 1
Ken Hodge	Bos.	Apr. 30/72	Bos.	3	Ed Giacomin	Bos. 6	NYR 5
Dick Redmond	Chi.	Apr. 4/73	Chi.	3	Wayne Stephenson	Chi. 7	St.L. 1
Steve Vickers	NYR	Apr. 10/73	Bos.	3	Ross Brooks (2)		
					Eddie Johnston (1)	NYR 6	Bos. 3
Tom Williams	L.A.	Apr. 14/74	L.A.	3	Mike Veisor	L.A. 5	Chi. 1
Marcel Dionne	L.A.	Apr. 15/76	L.A.	3	Gilles Gilbert	L.A. 6	Bos. 4
Don Saleski	Phi.	Apr. 20/76	Phi.	3	Wayne Thomas	Phi. 7	Tor. 1
Darryl Sittler	Tor.	Apr. 22/76	Tor.	5	Bernie Parent	Tor. 8	Phi. 5
Reggie Leach	Phi.	May 6/76	Phi.	5	Gilles Gilbert	Phi. 6	Bos. 3
Jim Lorentz	Buf.	Apr. 7/77	Min.	3	Pete LoPresti (2)		
					Gary Smith (1)	Buf. 7	Min. 1
Bobby Schmautz	Bos.	Apr. 11/77	Bos.	3	Rogie Vachon	Bos. 8	L.A. 3
Billy Harris	NYI	Apr. 23/77	Mtl.	3	Ken Dryden	Mtl. 4	NYI 3
George Ferguson	Tor.	Apr. 11/78	Tor.	3	Rogie Vachon	Tor. 7	L.A. 3
Jean Ratelle	Bos.	May 3/79	Bos.	3	Ken Dryden	Bos. 4	Mtl. 3
Stan Jonathan	Bos.	May 8/79	Bos.	3	Ken Dryden	Bos. 5	Mtl. 2
Ron Duguay	NYR	Apr. 20/80	NYR	3	Pete Peeters	NYR 4	Phi. 2
Steve Shutt	Mtl.	Apr. 22/80	Mtl.	3	Gilles Meloche	Mtl. 6	Min. 2
Gilbert Perreault	Buf.	May 6/80	NYI	3	Billy Smith (2)		
					ENG (1)	Buf. 7	NYI 4
Paul Holmgren	Phi.	May 15/80	Phi.	3	Billy Smith	Phi. 8	NYI 3
Steve Payne	Min.	Apr. 8/81	Bos.	3	Rogie Vachon	Min. 5	Bos. 4
Denis Potvin	NYI	Apr. 17/81	NYI	3	Andy Moog	NYI 6	Edm. 3
Barry Pederson	Bos.	Apr. 8/82	Bos.	3	Don Edwards	Bos. 7	Buf. 3
Duane Sutter	NYI	Apr. 15/83	NYI	3	Glen Hanlon	NYI 5	NYR 0
Doug Halward	Van.	Apr. 7/84	Van.	3	Reggie Lemelin (2)		
					Don Edwards (1)	Van. 7	Cgy. 0
Jorgen Pettersson	St.L.	Apr. 8/84	Det.	3	Eddie Mio	St.L. 3	Det. 2
Clark Gillies	NYI	May 12/84	NYI	3	Grant Fuhr	NYI 6	Edm. 1
Ken Linseman	Bos.	Apr. 14/85	Bos.	3	Steve Penney	Bos. 7	Mtl. 6
Dave Andreychuk	Buf.	Apr. 14/85	Buf.	3	Dan Bouchard	Buf. 7	Que. 4
Greg Paslawski	St.L.	Apr. 15/86	Min.	3	Don Beaupre	St.L. 6	Min. 3
Doug Risebrough	Cgy.	May 4/86	Cgy.	3	Rick Wamsley	Cgy. 8	St.L. 2
Mike McPhee	Mtl.	Apr. 11/87	Bos.	3	Doug Keans	Mtl. 5	Bos. 4
John Ogrodnick	Que.	Apr. 14/87	Hfd.	3	Mike Liut	Que. 7	Hfd. 5
Pelle Eklund	Phi.	May 10/87	Mtl.	3	Patrick Roy (1)		
					Brian Hayward (2)	Phi. 6	Mtl. 3
John Tucker	Buf.	Apr. 9/88	Bos.	4	Andy Moog	Buf. 6	Bos. 2
Tony Hrkac	St.L.	Apr. 10/88	St.L.	4	Darren Pang	St.L. 6	Chi. 5
Hakan Loob	Cgy.	Apr. 10/88	Cgy.	3	Glenn Healy	Cgy. 7	L.A. 3
Ed Olczyk	Tor.	Apr. 12/88	Tor.	3	Greg Stefan (2)		
					Glen Hanlon (1)	Tor. 6	Det. 5
Aaron Broten	N.J.	Apr. 20/88	N.J.	3	Pete Peeters	N.J. 5	Wsh. 2
Mark Johnson	N.J.	Apr. 22/88	Wsh.	4	Pete Peeters	N.J. 10	Wsh. 4
Patrik Sundstrom	N.J.	Apr. 22/88	Wsh.	3	Pete Peeters (2)		
					Clint Malarchuk (1)	N.J. 10	Wsh. 4
Bob Brooke	Min.	Apr. 5/89	St.L.	3	Greg Millen	St.L. 4	Min. 3
Chris Kontos	L.A.	Apr. 6/89	L.A.	3	Grant Fuhr	L.A. 5	Edm. 2
Wayne Presley	Chi.	Apr. 13/89	Chi.	3	Greg Stefan (1)		
					Glen Hanlon (2)	Chi. 7	Det. 1
Tony Granato	L.A.	Apr. 10/90	L.A.	3	Mike Vernon (1)		
					Rick Wamsley (2)	L.A. 12	Cgy. 4
Tomas Sandstrom	L.A.	Apr. 10/90	L.A.	3	Mike Vernon (1)		
					Rick Wamsley (2)	L.A. 12	Cgy. 4
Dave Taylor	L.A.	Apr. 10/90	L.A.	3	Mike Vernon (1)		
					Rick Wamsley (2)	L.A. 12	Cgy. 4
Bernie Nicholls	NYR	Apr. 19/90	NYR	3	Mike Liut	NYR 7	Wsh. 3
John Druce	Wsh.	Apr. 21/90	NYR	3	John Vanbiesbrouck	Wsh. 6	NYR 3
Adam Oates	St.L.	Apr. 12/91	St.L.	3	Tim Chevaldae	St.L. 6	Det. 1
Luc Robitaille	L.A.	Apr. 26/91	L.A.	3	Grant Fuhr	L.A. 5	Edm. 2
Ray Sheppard	Det.	Apr. 24/92	Min.	3	Jon Casey	Min. 5	Det. 2
Pavel Bure	Van.	Apr. 28/92	Wpg.	3	Rick Tabaracci	Van. 8	Wpg. 3
Joe Murphy	Edm.	May 6/92	Edm.	3	Kirk McLean	Edm. 5	Van. 2
Ron Francis	Pit.	May 9/92	Pit.	3	Mike Richter (2)		
					John V'brouck (1)	Pit. 5	NYR. 4
Kevin Stevens	Pit.	May 21/92	Bos.	4	Andy Moog	Pit. 5	Bos. 2
Dirk Graham	Chi.	Jun. 1/92	Chi.	3	Tom Barrasso	Pit. 6	Chi. 5
Brian Noonan	Chi.	Apr. 18/93	Chi.	3	Curtis Joseph	St.L. 4	Chi. 3
Dale Hunter	Wsh.	Apr. 20/93	Wsh.	3	Glenn Healy	NYI 5	Wsh. 4
Teemu Selanne	Wpg.	Apr. 23/93	Wpg.	3	Kirk McLean	Wpg. 5	Van. 4
Ray Ferraro	NYI	Apr. 26/93	Wsh.	4	Don Beaupre	Wsh. 6	NYI 4
Al Iafrate	Wsh.	Apr. 26/93	Wsh.	3	Glenn Healy (2)		
					Mark Fitzpatrick (1)	Wsh. 6	NYI 4
Paul DiPietro	Mtl.	Apr. 28/93	Mtl.	3	Ron Hextall	Mtl. 6	Que. 2
Wendel Clark	Tor.	May 27/93	L.A.	3	Kelly Hrudey	L.A. 5	Tor. 4
Eric Desjardins	Mtl.	Jun. 3/93	Mtl.	3	Kelly Hrudey	Mtl. 3	L.A. 2
Tony Amonte	Chi.	Apr. 23/94	Chi.	4	Felix Potvin	Chi. 5	Tor. 4
Gary Suter	Chi.	Apr. 24/94	Chi.	3	Felix Potvin	Chi. 4	Tor. 3
Ulf Dahlen	S.J.	May 6/94	S.J.	3	Felix Potvin	S.J. 5	Tor. 2
Mike Sullivan	Cgy.	May 11/95	S.J.	3	Arturs Irbe (2)		
					Wade Flaherty (1)	Cgy. 9	S.J. 2
Theoren Fleury	Cgy.	May 13/95	S.J.	4	Arturs Irbe (3)		
					ENG (1)	Cgy. 6	S.J. 4
Brendan Shanahan	St.L.	May 13/95	Van.	3	Kirk McLean	St.L. 5	Van. 2
John LeClair	Phi.	May 21/95	Phi.	3	Mike Richter	Phi. 5	NYR 4
Brian Leetch	NYR	May 22/95	Phi.	3	Ron Hextall	Phi. 4	NYR 3
Trevor Linden	Van.	Apr. 25/96	Col.	3	Patrick Roy	Col. 5	Van. 4
Jaromir Jagr	Pit.	May 11/96	Pit.	3	Mike Richter	Pit. 7	NYR 3
Peter Forsberg	Col.	Jun. 6/96	Col.	3	John Vanbiesbrouck	Col. 8	Fla. 1
Valeri Zelepukin	N.J.	Apr. 22/97	Mtl.	3	Jocelyn Thibault	N.J. 6	Mtl. 4
Valeri Kamensky	Col.	Apr. 24/97	Col.	3	Jeff Hackett (2)		
					Chris Terreri (1)	Col. 7	Chi. 0
Eric Lindros	Phi.	May 20/97	NYR	3	Mike Richter	Phi. 6	NYR 3
Matthew Barnaby	Buf.	May 10/98	Buf.	3	Andy Moog (2)	Buf. 6	Mtl. 3
					ENG (1)		
Martin Straka	Pit.	Apr. 25/99	Pit.	3	Martin Brodeur	Pit. 4	N.J. 2
Martin Lapointe	Det.	Apr. 15/00	Det.	3	Stephane Fiset (2)	Det. 8	L.A. 5
					Jamie Storr (1)		
Doug Weight	Edm.	Apr. 16/00	Edm.	3	Ed Belfour	Edm. 5	Dal. 2
Bill Guerin	Edm.	Apr. 18/00	Edm.	3	Ed Belfour	Dal. 4	Edm. 3
Scott Young	St.L.	Apr. 23/00	S.J.	3	Steve Shields	St.L. 6	S.J. 2
Andy Delmore	Phi.	May 7/00	Phi.	3	Ron Tugnutt (2)	Phi. 6	Pit. 3
					Peter Skudra (1)		
Brett Hull	Det.	Apr. 27/02	Van.	3	Peter Skudra	Det. 6	Van. 4
Keith Tkachuk	St.L.	May 7/02	St.L.	3	Dominik Hasek	St.L. 6	Det. 1
Darren McCarty	Det.	May 18/02	Det.	3	Patrick Roy	Det. 5	Col. 3
Alexander Mogilny	Tor.	Apr. 9/03	Phi.	3	Roman Cechmanek (2)	Tor. 5	Phi. 3
					ENG (1)		
Mike Sillinger	St.L.	Apr. 12/04	St.L.	3	Evgeni Nabokov (2)	St.L. 4	S.J. 1
					ENG (1)		
Keith Primeau	Phi.	May 2/04	Phi.	3	Ed Belfour (2)	Phi. 7	Tor. 2
					Trevor Kidd (1)		
J.P. Dumont	Buf.	Apr. 24/06	Buf.	3	Antero Niittymaki (1)	Phi. 2	Buf. 8
					Robert Esche (2)		
John Madden	N.J.	Apr. 24/06	N.J.	3	Kevin Weekes	NYR 1	N.J. 4
Jason Pominville	Buf.	Apr. 24/06	Buf.	3	Antero Niittymaki (2)	Phi. 2	Buf. 8
					Robert Esche (1)		
Joffrey Lupul	Ana.	May 9/06	Col.	4	Jose Theodore	Ana. 4	Col. 3
Michael Nylander	NYR	Apr. 17/07	NYR	3	Kari Lehtonen	NYR 7	Atl. 0
Andy McDonald	Ana.	Apr. 25/07	Ana.	3	Dany Sabourin (1)	Ana. 5	Van. 1
					Roberto Luongo (2)		
Pavel Datsyuk	Det.	May 12/08	Dal.	3	Marty Turco	Det. 5	Dal. 2

Johan Franzen's late-season scoring surge carried over into the playoffs, where he tied teammate Henrik Zetterberg for the lead with 13 goals despite missing six games due to injuries. Franzen had a pair of hat tricks in Detroit's second-round sweep of Colorado.

Overtime Games since 1918

Abbreviations: Teams/Cities: — **Ana.** - Anaheim; **Atl.** - Atlanta; **Bos.** - Boston; **Buf.** - Buffalo; **Cgy.** - Calgary; **Cgy. T.** - Calgary Tigers (Western Canada Hockey League); **Chi.** - Chicago; **Col.** - Colorado; **Dal.** - Dallas; **Det.** - Detroit; **Edm.** - Edmonton; **Edm. E.** - Edmonton Eskimos (WCHL); **Fla.** - Florida; **Hfd.** - Hartford; **L.A.** - Los Angeles; **Min.** - Minnesota; **Mtl.** - Montreal; **Mtl. M.** - Montreal Maroons; **N.J.** - New Jersey; **NYA** - NY Americans; **NYI** - New York Islanders; **NYR** - New York Rangers; **Oak.** - Oakland; **Ott.** - Ottawa; **Phi.** - Philadelphia; **Phx.** - Phoenix; **Pit.** - Pittsburgh; **Que.** - Quebec; **St.L.** - St. Louis; **Sea.** - Seattle Metropolitans (Pacific Coast Hockey Association); **S.J.** - San Jose; **T.B.** - Tampa Bay; **Tor.** - Toronto; **Van.** - Vancouver; **Van. M.** - Vancouver Millionaires (PCHA); **Vic.** - Victoria Cougars (WCHL); **Wpg.** - Winnipeg; **Wsh.** - Washington.

SERIES — **CF** - conference final; **CQF** - conference quarter-final; **CSF** - conference semi-final; **DF** - division final; **DSF** - division semi-final; **F** - final; **PRE** - preliminary round; **QF** - quarter-final; **SF** - semi-final.

Date	City	Series	Score		Scorer	Overtime	Series Winner
Mar. 26/19	Sea.	F	Mtl. 0	Sea. 0	no scorer	20:00	....
Mar. 30/19	Sea.	F	Mtl. 4	Sea. 3	Odie Cleghorn	15:57	....
Mar. 20/22	Tor.	F	Tor. 2	Van. M. 1	Babe Dye	4:50	Tor.
Mar. 29/23	Van.	F	Ott. 2	Edm. E. 1	Cy Denneny	2:08	Ott.
Mar. 31/27	Mtl.	QF	Mtl. 1	Mtl. M. 0	Howie Morenz	12:05	Mtl.
Apr. 7/27	Bos.	F	Ott. 0	Bos. 0	no scorer	20:00	Ott.
Apr. 11/27	Ott.	F	Bos. 1	Ott. 1	no scorer	20:00	Ott.
Apr. 3/28	Mtl.	QF	Mtl. M. 1	Mtl. 0	Russell Oatman	8:20	Mtl. M.
Apr. 7/28	Mtl.	F	NYR 2	Mtl. M. 1	Frank Boucher	7:05	NYR
Mar. 21/29	NYR	QF	NYR 1	NYA 0	Butch Keeling	29:50	NYR
Mar. 26/29	Tor.	SF	NYR 2	Tor. 1	Frank Boucher	2:03	NYR
Mar. 20/30	Mtl.	SF	Bos. 2	Mtl. M. 1	Harry Oliver	45:35	Bos.
Mar. 25/30	Bos.	SF	Mtl. M. 1	Bos. 0	Archie Wilcox	26:27	Bos.
Mar. 26/30	Mtl.	QF	Chi. 2	Mtl. 2	Howie Morenz (Mtl.)	51:43	Mtl.
Mar. 28/30	Mtl.	SF	Mtl. 2	NYR 1	Gus Rivers	68:52	Mtl.
Mar. 24/31	Bos.	SF	Bos. 5	Mtl. 4	Cooney Weiland	18:56	Mtl.
Mar. 26/31	Chi.	QF	Chi. 2	Tor. 1	Stew Adams	19:20	Chi.
Mar. 28/31	Mtl.	SF	Mtl. 4	Bos. 3	Georges Mantha	5:10	Mtl.
Apr. 1/31	Mtl.	SF	Mtl. 3	Bos. 2	Wildor Larochelle	19:00	Mtl.
Apr. 5/31	Chi.	F	Chi. 2	Mtl. 1	Johnny Gottselig	24:50	Mtl.
Apr. 9/31	Mtl.	F	Chi. 3	Mtl. 2	Cy Wentworth	53:50	Mtl.
Mar. 26/32	Mtl.	SF	NYR 4	Mtl. 3	Fred Cook	59:32	NYR
Apr. 2/32	Tor.	SF	Tor. 3	Mtl. M. 2	Bob Gracie	17:59	Tor.
Mar. 25/33	Bos.	SF	Bos. 2	Tor. 1	Marty Barry	14:14	Tor.
Mar. 28/33	Bos.	SF	Tor. 1	Bos. 0	Busher Jackson	15:03	Tor.
Mar. 30/33	Tor.	SF	Bos. 2	Tor. 1	Eddie Shore	4:23	Tor.
Apr. 3/33	Tor.	SF	Tor. 1	Bos. 0	Ken Doraty	104:46	Tor.
Apr. 13/33	Tor.	F	NYR 1	Tor. 0	Bill Cook	7:33	NYR
Mar. 22/34	Tor.	SF	Det. 2	Tor. 1	Herbie Lewis	1:33	Det.
Mar. 25/34	Chi.	QF	Chi. 1	Mtl. 1	Mush March (Chi)	11:05	Chi.
Apr. 3/34	Det.	F	Chi. 2	Det. 1	Paul Thompson	21:10	Chi.
Apr. 10/34	Chi.	F	Chi. 1	Det. 0	Mush March	30:05	Chi.
Mar. 23/35	Bos.	SF	Bos. 1	Tor. 0	Dit Clapper	33:26	Tor.
Mar. 26/35	Chi.	QF	Mtl. M. 1	Chi. 0	Baldy Northcott	4:02	Mtl. M.
Mar. 30/35	Tor.	SF	Tor. 2	Bos. 1	Pep Kelly	1:36	Tor.
Apr. 4/35	Tor.	F	Mtl. M. 3	Tor. 2	Dave Trottier	5:28	Mtl. M.
Mar. 24/36	Mtl.	SF	Det. 1	Mtl. M. 0	Mud Bruneteau	116:30	Det.
Apr. 9/36	Tor.	F	Tor. 4	Det. 3	Buzz Boll	0:31	Det.
Mar. 25/37	NYR	QF	NYR 2	Tor. 1	Babe Pratt	13:05	NYR
Apr. 1/37	Mtl.	SF	Det. 2	Mtl. 1	Hec Kilrea	51:49	Det.
Mar. 22/38	NYR	QF	NYA 2	NYR 1	John Sorrell	21:25	NYA
Mar. 24/38	Tor.	SF	Tor. 1	Bos. 0	George Parsons	21:31	Tor.
Mar. 26/38	Mtl.	QF	Chi. 3	Mtl. 2	Paul Thompson	11:49	Chi.
Mar. 27/38	NYR	QF	NYA 3	NYR 2	Lorne Carr	60:40	NYA
Mar. 29/38	Bos.	SF	Tor. 3	Bos. 2	Gordie Drillon	10:04	Tor.
Mar. 31/38	Chi.	SF	Chi. 1	NYA 0	Cully Dahlstrom	33:01	Chi.
Mar. 21/39	NYR	SF	Bos. 2	NYR 1	Mel Hill	59:25	Bos.
Mar. 23/39	Bos.	SF	Bos. 3	NYR 2	Mel Hill	8:24	Bos.
Mar. 26/39	Det.	QF	Det. 1	Mtl. 0	Marty Barry	7:47	Det.
Mar. 30/39	Bos.	SF	NYR 2	Bos. 1	Clint Smith	17:19	Bos.
Apr. 1/39	Tor.	SF	Tor. 5	Det. 4	Gordie Drillon	5:42	Tor.
Apr. 2/39	Bos.	SF	Bos. 2	NYR 1	Mel Hill	48:00	Bos.
Apr. 9/39	Bos.	F	Tor. 3	Bos. 2	Doc Romnes	10:38	Bos.
Mar. 19/40	Det.	QF	Det. 2	NYA 1	Syd Howe	0:25	Det.
Mar. 19/40	Tor.	QF	Tor. 3	Chi. 2	Syl Apps	6:35	Tor.
Apr. 2/40	NYR	F	NYR 2	Tor. 1	Alf Pike	15:30	NYR
Apr. 11/40	Tor.	F	NYR 2	Tor. 1	Muzz Patrick	31:43	NYR
Apr. 13/40	Tor.	F	NYR 3	Tor. 2	Bryan Hextall	2:07	NYR
Mar. 20/41	Det.	QF	Det. 2	NYR 1	Syd Howe	12:01	Det.
Mar. 22/41	Mtl.	QF	Mtl. 4	Chi. 3	Charlie Sands	34:04	Chi.
Mar. 29/41	Bos.	SF	Tor. 2	Bos. 1	Pete Langelle	17:31	Bos.
Mar. 30/41	Chi.	SF	Det. 2	Chi. 1	Gus Giesebrecht	9:15	Det.
Mar. 22/42	Chi.	QF	Bos. 2	Chi. 1	Des Smith	6:51	Bos.
Mar. 21/43	Bos.	SF	Bos. 5	Mtl. 4	Don Gallinger	12:30	Bos.
Mar. 23/43	Det.	SF	Tor. 3	Det. 2	Jack McLean	70:18	Det.
Mar. 25/43	Mtl.	SF	Bos. 3	Mtl. 2	Busher Jackson	3:20	Bos.
Mar. 30/43	Tor.	SF	Det. 3	Tor. 2	Adam Brown	9:21	Det.
Mar. 30/43	Bos.	SF	Bos. 5	Mtl. 4	Ab DeMarco	3:41	Bos.
Apr. 13/44	Mtl.	F	Mtl. 5	Chi. 4	Toe Blake	9:12	Mtl.
Mar. 27/45	Tor.	SF	Tor. 4	Mtl. 3	Gus Bodnar	12:36	Tor.
Mar. 29/45	Det.	SF	Det. 3	Bos. 2	Mud Bruneteau	17:12	Det.
Apr. 21/45	Tor.	F	Det. 1	Tor. 0	Eddie Bruneteau	14:16	Tor.
Mar. 28/46	Bos.	SF	Bos. 4	Det. 3	Don Gallinger	9:51	Bos.
Mar. 30/46	Mtl.	F	Mtl. 4	Bos. 3	Maurice Richard	9:08	Mtl.
Apr. 2/46	Mtl.	F	Mtl. 3	Bos. 2	Jimmy Peters	16:55	Mtl.
Apr. 7/46	Bos.	F	Bos. 3	Mtl. 2	Terry Reardon	15:13	Mtl.
Mar. 26/47	Tor.	SF	Tor. 3	Det. 2	Howie Meeker	3:05	Tor.
Mar. 27/47	Mtl.	SF	Mtl. 2	Bos. 1	Ken Mosdell	5:38	Mtl.
Apr. 3/47	Mtl.	SF	Mtl. 4	Bos. 3	John Quilty	36:40	Mtl.
Apr. 15/47	Tor.	F	Tor. 2	Mtl. 1	Syl Apps	16:36	Tor.
Mar. 24/48	Tor.	SF	Tor. 5	Bos. 4	Nick Metz	17:03	Tor.
Mar. 22/49	Det.	SF	Det. 2	Mtl. 1	Max McNab	44:52	Det.
Mar. 24/49	Det.	SF	Mtl. 4	Det. 3	Gerry Plamondon	2:59	Det.
Mar. 26/49	Tor.	SF	Bos. 5	Tor. 4	Woody Dumart	16:14	Tor.
Apr. 8/49	Det.	F	Tor. 3	Det. 2	Joe Klukay	17:31	Tor.
Apr. 4/50	Tor.	SF	Det. 2	Tor. 1	Leo Reise Jr.	20:38	Det.
Apr. 4/50	Mtl.	SF	Mtl. 3	NYR 2	Elmer Lach	15:19	NYR
Apr. 9/50	Det.	SF	Det. 1	Tor. 0	Leo Reise Jr.	8:39	Det.
Apr. 18/50	Det.	F	NYR 4	Det. 3	Don Raleigh	8:34	Det.
Apr. 20/50	Det.	F	NYR 2	Det. 1	Don Raleigh	1:38	Det.
Apr. 23/50	Det.	F	Det. 4	NYR 3	Pete Babando	28:31	Det.
Mar. 27/51	Det.	SF	Mtl. 3	Det. 2	Maurice Richard	61:09	Mtl.
Mar. 29/51	Det.	SF	Mtl. 1	Det. 0	Maurice Richard	42:20	Mtl.
Mar. 31/51	Tor.	SF	Bos. 1	Tor. 1	no scorer	20:00	Tor.
Apr. 11/51	Tor.	F	Tor. 3	Mtl. 2	Sid Smith	5:51	Tor.
Apr. 14/51	Tor.	F	Mtl. 3	Tor. 2	Maurice Richard	2:55	Tor.
Apr. 17/51	Mtl.	F	Tor. 2	Mtl. 1	Ted Kennedy	4:47	Tor.
Apr. 19/51	Mtl.	F	Tor. 3	Mtl. 2	Harry Watson	5:15	Tor.
Apr. 21/51	Tor.	F	Tor. 3	Mtl. 2	Bill Barilko	2:53	Tor.
Apr. 6/52	Bos.	SF	Mtl. 3	Bos. 2	Paul Masnick	27:49	Mtl.
Mar. 29/53	Bos.	SF	Bos. 2	Det. 1	Jack McIntyre	12:29	Bos.
Mar. 29/53	Chi.	SF	Chi. 2	Mtl. 1	Al Dewsbury	5:18	Mtl.
Apr. 16/53	Mtl.	F	Mtl. 1	Bos. 0	Elmer Lach	1:22	Mtl.
Apr. 1/54	Det.	SF	Det. 4	Tor. 3	Ted Lindsay	21:01	Det.
Apr. 11/54	Det.	F	Mtl. 1	Det. 0	Ken Mosdell	5:45	Det.
Apr. 16/54	Det.	F	Det. 2	Mtl. 1	Tony Leswick	4:29	Det.
Mar. 29/55	Bos.	SF	Mtl. 4	Bos. 3	Don Marshall	3:05	Mtl.
Mar. 24/56	Tor.	SF	Det. 5	Tor. 4	Ted Lindsay	4:22	Det.
Mar. 28/57	NYR	SF	NYR 4	Mtl. 3	Andy Hebenton	13:38	Mtl.
Apr. 4/57	Mtl.	SF	Mtl. 4	NYR 3	Maurice Richard	1:11	Mtl.
Mar. 27/58	NYR	SF	Bos. 4	NYR 3	Jerry Toppazzini	4:46	Bos.
Mar. 30/58	Det.	SF	Mtl. 2	Det. 1	André Pronovost	11:52	Mtl.
Apr. 17/58	Mtl.	F	Mtl. 3	Bos. 2	Maurice Richard	5:45	Mtl.
Mar. 28/59	Tor.	SF	Tor. 3	Bos. 2	Gerry Ehman	5:02	Tor.
Mar. 31/59	Tor.	SF	Tor. 3	Bos. 2	Frank Mahovlich	11:21	Tor.
Apr. 14/59	Tor.	F	Tor. 3	Mtl. 2	Dick Duff	10:06	Mtl.
Mar. 26/60	Mtl.	SF	Mtl. 4	Chi. 3	Doug Harvey	8:38	Mtl.
Mar. 27/60	Det.	SF	Tor. 5	Det. 4	Frank Mahovlich	43:00	Tor.
Mar. 29/60	Det.	SF	Det. 2	Tor. 1	Gerry Melnyk	1:54	Tor.
Mar. 22/61	Tor.	SF	Tor. 3	Det. 2	George Armstrong	24:51	Det.
Mar. 26/61	Chi.	SF	Chi. 2	Mtl. 1	Murray Balfour	52:12	Chi.
Apr. 5/62	Tor.	SF	Tor. 3	NYR 2	Red Kelly	24:23	Tor.
Apr. 2/64	Det.	SF	Chi. 3	Det. 2	Murray Balfour	8:21	Det.
Apr. 14/64	Tor.	F	Det. 4	Tor. 3	Larry Jeffrey	7:52	Tor.
Apr. 23/64	Det.	F	Tor. 4	Det. 3	Bob Baun	1:43	Tor.
Apr. 6/65	Tor.	SF	Tor. 3	Mtl. 2	Dave Keon	4:17	Mtl.
Apr. 13/65	Tor.	SF	Mtl. 4	Tor. 3	Claude Provost	16:33	Mtl.
May 5/66	Det.	F	Mtl. 3	Det. 2	Henri Richard	2:20	Mtl.
Apr. 13/67	NYR	SF	Mtl. 2	NYR 1	John Ferguson	6:28	Mtl.
Apr. 25/67	Tor.	F	Tor. 3	Mtl. 2	Bob Pulford	28:26	Tor.
Apr. 10/68	St.L.	QF	St.L. 3	Phi. 2	Larry Keenan	24:10	St.L.
Apr. 16/68	St.L.	QF	Phi. 2	St.L. 1	Don Blackburn	31:18	St.L.
Apr. 16/68	Min.	QF	Min. 4	L.A. 3	Milan Marcetta	9:11	Min.
Apr. 22/68	Min.	SF	Min. 3	St.L. 2	Parker MacDonald	3:41	St.L.
Apr. 27/68	St.L.	SF	St.L. 4	Min. 3	Gary Sabourin	1:32	St.L.
Apr. 28/68	Mtl.	SF	Mtl. 4	Chi. 3	Jacques Lemaire	2:14	Mtl.
Apr. 29/68	St.L.	SF	St.L. 3	Min. 2	Bill McCreary	17:27	St.L.
May 3/68	St.L.	SF	St.L. 2	Min. 1	Ron Schock	22:50	St.L.
May 5/68	St.L.	F	Mtl. 3	St.L. 2	Jacques Lemaire	1:41	Mtl.
May 9/68	Mtl.	F	Mtl. 4	St.L. 3	Bobby Rousseau	1:13	Mtl.
Apr. 2/69	Oak.	QF	L.A. 5	Oak. 4	Ted Irvine	0:19	L.A.
Apr. 10/69	Mtl.	SF	Mtl. 3	Bos. 2	Ralph Backstrom	0:42	Mtl.
Apr. 13/69	Mtl.	SF	Mtl. 4	Bos. 3	Mickey Redmond	4:55	Mtl.
Apr. 24/69	Bos.	SF	Mtl. 2	Bos. 1	Jean Béliveau	31:28	Mtl.
Apr. 12/70	Oak.	QF	Pit. 3	Oak. 2	Michel Briere	8:28	Pit.
May 10/70	Bos.	F	Bos. 4	St.L. 3	Bobby Orr	0:40	Bos.
Apr. 15/71	Tor.	QF	NYR 2	Tor. 1	Bob Nevin	9:07	NYR
Apr. 18/71	Chi.	SF	NYR 2	Chi. 1	Pete Stemkowski	1:37	Chi.
Apr. 27/71	Chi.	SF	Chi. 3	NYR 2	Bobby Hull	6:35	Chi.
Apr. 29/71	NYR	SF	NYR 3	Chi. 2	Pete Stemkowski	41:29	Chi.
May 4/71	Chi.	F	Chi. 2	Mtl. 1	Jim Pappin	21:11	Mtl.
Apr. 6/72	Bos.	QF	Tor. 4	Bos. 3	Jim Harrison	2:58	Bos.
Apr. 6/72	Min.	QF	Min. 6	St.L. 5	Bill Goldsworthy	1:36	St.L.
Apr. 9/72	Pit.	QF	Chi. 6	Pit. 5	Pit Martin	0:12	Chi.
Apr. 16/72	Min.	QF	St.L. 2	Min. 1	Kevin O'Shea	10:07	St.L.
Apr. 1/73	Mtl.	QF	Buf. 3	Mtl. 2	René Robert	9:18	Mtl.
Apr. 10/73	Phi.	QF	Phi. 3	Min. 2	Gary Dornhoefer	8:35	Phi.
Apr. 14/73	Mtl.	SF	Phi. 5	Mtl. 4	Rick MacLeish	2:56	Mtl.
Apr. 17/73	Mtl.	SF	Mtl. 4	Phi. 3	Larry Robinson	6:45	Mtl.
Apr. 14/74	Tor.	QF	Bos. 4	Tor. 3	Ken Hodge	1:27	Bos.
Apr. 14/74	Atl.	QF	Phi. 4	Atl. 3	Dave Schultz	5:40	Phi.
Apr. 16/74	Mtl.	QF	NYR 3	Mtl. 2	Ron Harris	4:07	NYR
Apr. 23/74	Chi.	SF	Chi. 4	Bos. 3	Jim Pappin	3:48	Bos.
Apr. 28/74	NYR	SF	NYR 2	Phi. 1	Rod Gilbert	4:20	Phi.
May 9/74	Bos.	F	Phi. 3	Bos. 2	Bobby Clarke	12:01	Phi.
Apr. 8/75	L.A.	PRE	L.A. 3	Tor. 2	Mike Murphy	8:53	Tor.
Apr. 10/75	Tor.	PRE	Tor. 3	L.A. 2	Blaine Stoughton	10:19	Tor.
Apr. 10/75	Chi.	PRE	Chi. 4	Bos. 3	Ivan Boldirev	7:33	Chi.
Apr. 11/75	NYR	PRE	NYI 4	NYR 3	J.P. Parise	0:11	NYI
Apr. 17/75	Chi.	QF	Chi. 5	Buf. 4	Stan Mikita	2:31	Buf.
Apr. 19/75	Tor.	QF	Phi. 4	Tor. 3	André Dupont	1:45	Phi.
Apr. 22/75	Mtl.	QF	Mtl. 5	Van. 4	Guy Lafleur	17:06	Mtl.
Apr. 27/75	Buf.	SF	Buf. 6	Mtl. 5	Danny Gare	4:42	Buf.
May 1/75	Phi.	SF	Phi. 5	NYI 4	Bobby Clarke	2:56	Phi.
May 6/75	Buf.	SF	Buf. 5	Mtl. 4	René Robert	5:56	Buf.
May 7/75	NYI	SF	NYI 4	Phi. 3	Jude Drouin	1:53	Phi.
May 20/75	Buf.	F	Buf. 5	Phi. 4	René Robert	18:29	Phi.
Apr. 8/76	Buf.	PRE	Buf. 3	St.L. 2	Danny Gare	11:43	Buf.

Overtime Games since 1918 — *continued*

Date	City	Series	Score		Scorer	Overtime	Series Winner
Apr. 9/76	Buf.	PRE	Buf. 2	St.L. 1	Don Luce	14:27	Buf.
Apr. 13/76	Bos.	QF	L.A. 3	Bos. 2	Butch Goring	0:27	Bos.
Apr. 13/76	Buf.	QF	Buf. 3	NYI 2	Danny Gare	14:04	NYI
Apr. 22/76	L.A.	QF	L.A. 4	Bos. 3	Butch Goring	18:28	Bos.
Apr. 29/76	Phi.	SF	Phi. 2	Bos. 1	Reggie Leach	13:38	Phi.
Apr. 15/77	Tor.	QF	Phi. 4	Tor. 3	Rick MacLeish	2:55	Phi.
Apr. 17/77	Tor.	QF	Phi. 6	Tor. 5	Reggie Leach	19:10	Phi.
Apr. 24/77	Phi.	SF	Bos. 4	Phi. 3	Rick Middleton	2:57	Bos.
Apr. 26/77	Phi.	SF	Bos. 5	Phi. 4	Terry O'Reilly	30:07	Bos.
May 3/77	Mtl.	SF	NYI 4	Mtl. 3	Billy Harris	3:58	Mtl.
May 14/77	Bos.	F	Mtl. 2	Bos. 1	Jacques Lemaire	4:32	Mtl.
Apr. 11/78	Phi.	PRE	Phi. 3	Col. 2	Mel Bridgman	0:23	Phi.
Apr. 13/78	NYR	PRE	NYR 4	Buf. 3	Don Murdoch	1:37	Buf.
Apr. 19/78	Bos.	QF	Bos. 4	Chi. 3	Terry O'Reilly	1:50	Bos.
Apr. 19/78	NYI	QF	NYI 3	Tor. 2	Mike Bossy	2:50	Tor.
Apr. 21/78	Chi.	QF	Bos. 4	Chi. 3	Peter McNab	10:17	Bos.
Apr. 25/78	NYI	QF	NYI 2	Tor. 1	Bob Nystrom	8:02	Tor.
Apr. 29/78	NYI	QF	Tor. 2	NYI 1	Lanny McDonald	4:13	Tor.
May 2/78	Bos.	SF	Bos. 3	Phi. 2	Rick Middleton	1:43	Bos.
May 16/78	Mtl.	F	Mtl. 3	Bos. 2	Guy Lafleur	13:09	Mtl.
May 21/78	Bos.	F	Bos. 4	Mtl. 3	Bobby Schmautz	6:22	Mtl.
Apr. 12/79	L.A.	PRE	NYR 2	L.A. 1	Phil Esposito	6:11	NYR
Apr. 14/79	Buf.	PRE	Pit. 4	Buf. 3	George Ferguson	0:47	Pit.
Apr. 16/79	Phi.	QF	Phi. 3	NYR 2	Ken Linseman	0:44	NYR
Apr. 18/79	NYI	QF	NYI 1	Chi. 0	Mike Bossy	2:31	NYI
Apr. 21/79	Tor.	QF	Mtl. 4	Tor. 3	Cam Connor	25:25	Mtl.
Apr. 22/79	Tor.	QF	Mtl. 5	Tor. 4	Larry Robinson	4:14	Mtl.
Apr. 28/79	NYI	SF	NYI 4	NYR 3	Denis Potvin	8:02	NYR
May 3/79	NYR	SF	NYI 3	NYR 2	Bob Nystrom	3:40	NYR
May 3/79	Bos.	SF	Bos. 4	Mtl. 3	Jean Ratelle	3:46	Mtl.
May 10/79	Mtl.	SF	Mtl. 5	Bos. 4	Yvon Lambert	9:33	Mtl.
May 19/79	NYR	F	Mtl. 4	NYR 3	Serge Savard	7:25	Mtl.
Apr. 8/80	NYR	PRE	NYR 2	Atl. 1	Steve Vickers	0:33	NYR
Apr. 8/80	Phi.	PRE	Phi. 4	Edm. 3	Bobby Clarke	8:06	Phi.
Apr. 8/80	Chi.	PRE	Chi. 3	St.L. 2	Doug Lecuyer	12:34	Chi.
Apr. 11/80	Hfd.	PRE	Mtl. 4	Hfd. 3	Yvon Lambert	0:29	Mtl.
Apr. 11/80	Tor.	PRE	Min. 4	Tor. 3	Al MacAdam	0:32	Min.
Apr. 11/80	L.A.	PRE	NYI 4	L.A. 3	Ken Morrow	6:55	NYI
Apr. 11/80	Edm.	PRE	Phi. 3	Edm. 2	Ken Linseman	23:56	Phi.
Apr. 16/80	Bos.	QF	NYI 2	Bos. 1	Clark Gillies	1:02	NYI
Apr. 17/80	Bos.	QF	NYI 5	Bos. 4	Bob Bourne	1:24	NYI
Apr. 21/80	NYI	QF	Bos. 4	NYI 3	Terry O'Reilly	17:13	NYI
May 1/80	Buf.	SF	NYI 2	Buf. 1	Bob Nystrom	21:20	NYI
May 13/80	Phi.	F	NYI 4	Phi. 3	Denis Potvin	4:07	NYI
May 24/80	NYI	F	NYI 5	Phi. 4	Bob Nystrom	7:11	NYI
Apr. 8/81	Buf.	PRE	Buf. 3	Van. 2	Alan Haworth	5:00	Buf.
Apr. 8/81	Bos.	PRE	Min. 5	Bos. 4	Steve Payne	3:34	Min.
Apr. 11/81	Chi.	PRE	Cgy. 5	Chi. 4	Willi Plett	35:17	Cgy.
Apr. 12/81	Que.	PRE	Que. 4	Phi. 3	Dale Hunter	0:37	Phi.
Apr. 14/81	St.L.	PRE	St.L. 4	Pit. 3	Mike Crombeen	25:16	St.L.
Apr. 16/81	Buf.	QF	Min. 4	Buf. 3	Steve Payne	0:22	Min.
Apr. 20/81	Min.	QF	Buf. 5	Min. 4	Craig Ramsay	16:32	Min.
Apr. 20/81	Edm.	QF	NYI 5	Edm. 4	Ken Morrow	5:41	NYI
Apr. 7/82	Min.	DSF	Chi. 3	Min. 2	Greg Fox	3:34	Chi.
Apr. 8/82	Edm.	DSF	Edm. 3	L.A. 2	Wayne Gretzky	6:20	L.A.
Apr. 8/82	Van.	DSF	Van. 2	Cgy. 1	Tiger Williams	14:20	Van.
Apr. 10/82	Pit.	DSF	Pit. 2	NYI 1	Rick Kehoe	4:14	NYI
Apr. 10/82	L.A.	DSF	L.A. 6	Edm. 5	Daryl Evans	2:35	L.A.
Apr. 13/82	Mtl.	DSF	Que. 3	Mtl. 2	Dale Hunter	0:22	Que.
Apr. 13/82	NYI	DSF	NYI 4	Pit. 3	John Tonelli	6:19	NYI
Apr. 16/82	Van.	DF	L.A. 3	Van. 2	Steve Bozek	4:33	Van.
Apr. 18/82	Que.	DF	Que. 3	Bos. 2	Wilf Paiement	11:44	Que.
Apr. 18/82	NYR	DF	NYI 4	NYR 3	Bryan Trottier	3:00	NYI
Apr. 18/82	L.A.	DF	Van. 4	L.A. 3	Colin Campbell	1:23	Van.
Apr. 21/82	St.L.	DF	St.L. 3	Chi. 2	Bernie Federko	3:28	Chi.
Apr. 23/82	Que.	DF	Bos. 6	Que. 5	Peter McNab	10:54	Que.
Apr. 27/82	Chi.	CF	Van. 2	Chi. 1	Jim Nill	28:58	Van.
May 1/82	Que.	CF	NYI 5	Que. 4	Wayne Merrick	16:52	NYI
May 8/82	NYI	F	NYI 6	Van. 5	Mike Bossy	19:58	NYI
Apr. 5/83	Bos.	DSF	Bos. 4	Que. 3	Barry Pederson	1:46	Bos.
Apr. 6/83	Cgy.	DSF	Cgy. 4	Van. 3	Eddy Beers	12:27	Cgy.
Apr. 7/83	Min.	DSF	Min. 5	Tor. 4	Bobby Smith	5:03	Min.
Apr. 10/83	Tor.	DSF	Min. 5	Tor. 4	Dino Ciccarelli	8:05	Min.
Apr. 10/83	Van.	DSF	Cgy. 4	Van. 3	Greg Meredith	1:06	Cgy.
Apr. 18/83	Min.	DF	Chi. 4	Min. 3	Rich Preston	10:34	Chi.
Apr. 24/83	Bos.	DF	Bos. 3	Buf. 2	Brad Park	1:52	Bos.
Apr. 5/84	Edm.	DSF	Edm. 5	Wpg. 4	Randy Gregg	0:21	Edm.
Apr. 7/84	Det.	DSF	St.L. 4	Det. 3	Mark Reeds	37:07	St.L.
Apr. 8/84	Det.	DSF	St.L. 3	Det. 2	Jorgen Pettersson	2:42	St.L.
Apr. 10/84	NYI	DSF	NYI 3	NYR 2	Ken Morrow	8:56	NYI
Apr. 13/84	Min.	DF	St.L. 4	Min. 3	Doug Gilmour	16:16	Min.
Apr. 13/84	Edm.	DF	Cgy. 6	Edm. 5	Carey Wilson	3:42	Edm.
Apr. 13/84	NYI	DF	NYI 5	Wsh. 4	Anders Kallur	7:35	NYI
Apr. 16/84	Mtl.	DF	Que. 4	Mtl. 3	Bo Berglund	3:00	Mtl.
Apr. 20/84	Cgy.	DF	Cgy. 5	Edm. 4	Lanny McDonald	1:04	Edm.
Apr. 22/84	Min.	DF	Min. 4	St.L. 3	Steve Payne	6:00	Min.
Apr. 10/85	Phi.	DSF	Phi. 5	NYR 4	Mark Howe	8:01	Phi.
Apr. 10/85	Wsh.	DSF	Wsh. 4	NYI 3	Alan Haworth	2:28	NYI
Apr. 10/85	Edm.	DSF	Edm. 3	L.A. 2	Lee Fogolin	3:01	Edm.
Apr. 10/85	Wpg.	DSF	Wpg. 5	Cgy. 4	Brian Mullen	7:56	Wpg.
Apr. 11/85	Wsh.	DSF	Wsh. 2	NYI 1	Mike Gartner	21:23	NYI
Apr. 13/85	L.A.	DSF	Edm. 4	L.A. 3	Glenn Anderson	0:46	Edm.
Apr. 18/85	Mtl.	DF	Que. 2	Mtl. 1	Mark Kumpel	12:23	Que.
Apr. 23/85	Que.	DF	Que. 7	Mtl. 6	Dale Hunter	18:36	Que.

Date	City	Series	Score		Scorer	Overtime	Series Winner
Apr. 25/85	Min.	DF	Chi. 7	Min. 6	Darryl Sutter	21:57	Chi.
Apr. 28/85	Chi.	DF	Min. 5	Chi. 4	Dennis Maruk	1:14	Chi.
Apr. 30/85	Min.	DF	Chi. 6	Min. 5	Darryl Sutter	15:41	Chi.
May 2/85	Mtl.	DF	Que. 3	Mtl. 2	Peter Stastny	2:22	Que.
May 5/85	Que.	CF	Que. 2	Phi. 1	Peter Stastny	6:20	Phi.
Apr. 9/86	Que.	DSF	Hfd. 3	Que. 2	Sylvain Turgeon	2:36	Hfd.
Apr. 12/86	Wpg.	DSF	Cgy. 4	Wpg. 3	Lanny McDonald	8:25	Cgy.
Apr. 17/86	Wsh.	DF	NYR 4	Wsh. 3	Brian MacLellan	1:16	NYR
Apr. 20/86	Edm.	DF	Edm. 6	Cgy. 5	Glenn Anderson	1:04	Cgy.
Apr. 23/86	Hfd.	DF	Hfd. 2	Mtl. 1	Kevin Dineen	1:07	Mtl.
Apr. 23/86	NYR	DF	NYR 6	Wsh. 5	Bob Brooke	2:40	NYR
Apr. 26/86	St L.	DF	St L. 4	Tor. 3	Mark Reeds	7:11	St L.
Apr. 29/86	Mtl.	DF	Mtl. 2	Hfd. 1	Claude Lemieux	5:55	Mtl.
May 5/86	NYR	CF	Mtl. 4	NYR 3	Claude Lemieux	9:41	Mtl.
May 12/86	St L.	CF	St L. 6	Cgy. 5	Doug Wickenheiser	7:30	Cgy.
May 18/86	Cgy.	F	Mtl. 3	Cgy. 2	Brian Skrudland	0:09	Mtl.
Apr. 8/87	Hfd.	DSF	Hfd. 3	Que. 2	Paul MacDermid	2:20	Que.
Apr. 9/87	Mtl.	DSF	Mtl. 4	Bos. 3	Mats Naslund	2:38	Mtl.
Apr. 9/87	St.L.	DSF	Tor. 3	St.L. 2	Rick Lanz	10:17	Tor.
Apr. 11/87	Wpg.	DSF	Cgy. 3	Wpg. 2	Mike Bullard	3:53	Wpg.
Apr. 11/87	Chi.	DSF	Det. 4	Chi. 3	Shawn Burr	4:51	Det.
Apr. 16/87	Que.	DSF	Que. 5	Hfd. 4	Peter Stastny	6:05	Que.
Apr. 18/87	Wsh.	DSF	NYI 3	Wsh. 2	Pat LaFontaine	68:47	NYI
Apr. 21/87	Edm.	DF	Edm. 3	Wpg. 2	Glenn Anderson	0:36	Edm.
Apr. 26/87	Que.	DF	Mtl. 3	Que. 2	Mats Naslund	5:30	Mtl.
Apr. 27/87	Tor.	DF	Tor. 3	Det. 2	Mike Allison	9:31	Det.
May 4/87	Phi.	CF	Phi. 4	Mtl. 3	Ilkka Sinislao	9:11	Phi.
May 20/87	Edm.	F	Edm. 3	Phi. 2	Jari Kurri	6:50	Edm.
Apr. 6/88	NYI	DSF	NYI 4	N.J. 3	Pat LaFontaine	6:11	N.J.
Apr. 10/88	Phi.	DSF	Phi. 5	Wsh. 4	Murray Craven	1:18	Wsh.
Apr. 10/88	N.J.	DSF	NYI 5	N.J. 4	Brent Sutter	15:07	N.J.
Apr. 10/88	Buf.	DSF	Buf. 6	Bos. 5	John Tucker	5:32	Bos.
Apr. 12/88	Det.	DSF	Tor. 6	Det. 5	Ed Olczyk	0:34	Det.
Apr. 16/88	Wsh.	DSF	Wsh. 5	Phi. 4	Dale Hunter	5:57	Wsh.
Apr. 21/88	Cgy.	DF	Edm. 5	Cgy. 4	Wayne Gretzky	7:54	Edm.
May 4/88	Bos.	CF	N.J. 3	Bos. 2	Doug Brown	17:46	Bos.
May 9/88	Det.	CF	Edm. 4	Det. 3	Jari Kurri	11:02	Edm.
Apr. 5/89	St.L.	DSF	St.L. 4	Min. 3	Brett Hull	11:55	St.L.
Apr. 5/89	Cgy.	DSF	Van. 4	Cgy. 3	Paul Reinhart	2:47	Cgy.
Apr. 6/89	St.L.	DSF	St.L. 4	Min. 3	Rick Meagher	5:30	St.L.
Apr. 6/89	Det.	DSF	Chi. 5	Det. 4	Duane Sutter	14:36	Chi.
Apr. 8/89	Hfd.	DSF	Mtl. 5	Hfd. 4	Stephane Richer	5:01	Mtl.
Apr. 8/89	Phi.	DSF	Wsh. 4	Phi. 3	Kelly Miller	0:51	Phi.
Apr. 9/89	Hfd.	DSF	Mtl. 4	Hfd. 3	Russ Courtnall	15:12	Mtl.
Apr. 15/89	Cgy.	DSF	Cgy. 4	Van. 3	Joel Otto	19:21	Cgy.
Apr. 18/89	Cgy.	DF	Cgy. 4	L.A. 3	Doug Gilmour	7:47	Cgy.
Apr. 19/89	Mtl.	DF	Mtl. 3	Bos. 2	Bobby Smith	12:24	Mtl.
Apr. 20/89	St.L.	DF	St.L. 5	Chi. 4	Tony Hrkac	33:49	Chi.
Apr. 21/89	Phi.	DF	Pit. 4	Phi. 3	Phil Bourque	12:08	Phi.
May 8/89	Chi.	CF	Cgy. 2	Chi. 1	Al MacInnis	15:05	Cgy.
May 9/89	Mtl.	CF	Phi. 2	Mtl. 1	Dave Poulin	5:02	Mtl.
May 19/89	Mtl.	F	Mtl. 4	Cgy. 3	Ryan Walter	38:08	Cgy.
Apr. 5/90	N.J.	DSF	Wsh. 5	N.J. 4	Dino Ciccarelli	5:34	Wsh.
Apr. 6/90	Edm.	DSF	Edm. 3	Wpg. 2	Mark Lamb	4:21	Edm.
Apr. 8/90	Tor.	DSF	St.L. 6	Tor. 5	Sergio Momesso	6:04	St.L.
Apr. 8/90	L.A.	DSF	L.A. 2	Cgy. 1	Tony Granato	8:37	L.A.
Apr. 9/90	Mtl.	DSF	Mtl. 2	Buf. 1	Brian Skrudland	12:35	Mtl.
Apr. 9/90	NYI	DSF	NYI 4	NYR 3	Brent Sutter	20:59	NYR
Apr. 10/90	Wpg.	DSF	Wpg. 4	Edm. 3	Dave Ellett	21:08	Edm.
Apr. 14/90	L.A.	DSF	L.A. 4	Cgy. 3	Mike Krushelnyski	23:14	L.A.
Apr. 15/90	Hfd.	DSF	Hfd. 3	Bos. 2	Kevin Dineen	12:30	Bos.
Apr. 21/90	Bos.	DF	Bos. 5	Mtl. 4	Garry Galley	3:42	Bos.
Apr. 24/90	L.A.	DF	Edm. 6	L.A. 5	Joe Murphy	4:42	Edm.
Apr. 25/90	Wsh.	DF	Wsh. 4	NYR 3	Rod Langway	0:34	Wsh.
Apr. 27/90	NYR	DF	Wsh. 2	NYR 1	John Druce	6:48	Wsh.
May 15/90	Bos.	F	Edm. 3	Bos. 2	Petr Klima	55:13	Edm.
Apr. 4/91	Chi.	DSF	Min. 4	Chi. 3	Brian Propp	4:14	Min.
Apr. 5/91	Pit.	DSF	Pit. 5	N.J. 4	Jaromir Jagr	8:52	Pit.
Apr. 6/91	L.A.	DSF	L.A. 3	Van. 2	Wayne Gretzky	11:08	L.A.
Apr. 8/91	Van.	DSF	Van. 2	L.A. 1	Cliff Ronning	3:12	L.A.
Apr. 11/91	NYR	DSF	Wsh. 5	NYR 4	Dino Ciccarelli	6:44	Wsh.
Apr. 11/91	Mtl.	DSF	Mtl. 4	Buf. 3	Russ Courtnall	5:56	Mtl.
Apr. 14/91	Edm.	DSF	Cgy. 2	Edm. 1	Theoren Fleury	4:40	Edm.
Apr. 16/91	Cgy.	DSF	Edm. 5	Cgy. 4	Esa Tikkanen	6:58	Edm.
Apr. 18/91	L.A.	DF	L.A. 4	Edm. 3	Luc Robitaille	2:13	Edm.
Apr. 19/91	Bos.	DF	Mtl. 4	Bos. 3	Stephane Richer	0:27	Bos.
Apr. 19/91	Pit.	DF	Pit. 7	Wsh. 6	Kevin Stevens	8:10	Pit.
Apr. 20/91	L.A.	DF	Edm. 4	L.A. 3	Petr Klima	24:48	Edm.
Apr. 22/91	Edm.	DF	Edm. 4	L.A. 3	Esa Tikkanen	20:48	Edm.
Apr. 27/91	Mtl.	DF	Mtl. 3	Bos. 2	Shayne Corson	17:47	Bos.
Apr. 28/91	Edm.	DF	Edm. 4	L.A. 3	Craig MacTavish	16:57	Edm.
May 3/91	Bos.	CF	Bos. 5	Pit. 4	Vladimir Ruzicka	8:14	Pit.
Apr. 21/92	Bos.	DSF	Bos. 3	Buf. 2	Adam Oates	11:14	Bos.
Apr. 22/92	Min.	DSF	Det. 5	Min. 4	Yves Racine	1:15	Det.
Apr. 22/92	St.L.	DSF	St.L. 5	Chi. 4	Brett Hull	23:33	Chi.
Apr. 25/92	Buf.	DSF	Bos. 5	Buf. 4	Ted Donato	2:08	Bos.
Apr. 28/92	Min.	DSF	Det. 1	Min. 0	Sergei Fedorov	16:13	Det.
Apr. 29/92	Hfd.	DSF	Hfd. 2	Mtl. 1	Yvon Corriveau	0:24	Mtl.
May 1/92	Mtl.	DSF	Mtl. 3	Hfd. 2	Russ Courtnall	25:26	Mtl.
May 3/92	Van.	DF	Edm. 4	Van. 3	Joe Murphy	8:36	Edm.
May 5/92	Mtl.	DF	Bos. 3	Mtl. 2	Peter Douris	3:12	Bos.
May 7/92	Pit.	DF	NYR 6	Pit. 5	Kris King	1:29	Pit.
May 9/92	Pit.	DF	Pit. 5	NYR 4	Ron Francis	2:47	Pit.
May 17/92	Pit.	CF	Pit. 4	Bos. 3	Jaromir Jagr	9:44	Pit.

Pittsburgh's Petr Sykora celebrates with Ryan Whitney after keeping the Penguins alive with a triple-overtime goal in game five of the 2008 Stanley Cup Final against Detroit.

Date	City	Series	Score		Scorer	Overtime	Series Winner
May 20/92	Edm.	CF	Chi. 4	Edm. 3	Jeremy Roenick	2:45	Chi.
Apr. 18/93	Bos.	DSF	Buf. 5	Bos. 4	Bob Sweeney	11:03	Buf.
Apr. 18/93	Que.	DSF	Que. 3	Mtl. 2	Scott Young	16:49	Mtl.
Apr. 20/93	Wsh.	DSF	NYI 5	Wsh. 4	Brian Mullen	34:50	NYI
Apr. 22/93	Mtl.	DSF	Mtl. 2	Que. 1	Vincent Damphousse	10:30	Mtl.
Apr. 22/93	Buf.	DSF	Buf. 4	Bos. 3	Yuri Khmylev	1:05	Buf.
Apr. 22/93	NYI	DSF	NYI 4	Wsh. 3	Ray Ferraro	4:46	NYI
Apr. 24/93	Buf.	DSF	Buf. 6	Bos. 5	Brad May	4:48	Buf.
Apr. 24/93	NYI	DSF	NYI 4	Wsh. 3	Ray Ferraro	25:40	NYI
Apr. 25/93	St.L.	DSF	St.L. 4	Chi. 3	Craig Janney	10:43	St.L.
Apr. 26/93	Que.	DSF	Mtl. 5	Que. 4	Kirk Muller	8:17	Mtl.
Apr. 27/93	Det.	DSF	Tor. 5	Det. 4	Mike Foligno	2:05	Tor.
Apr. 27/93	Van.	DSF	Wpg. 4	Van. 3	Teemu Selanne	6:18	Van.
Apr. 29/93	Wpg.	DSF	Van. 4	Wpg. 3	Greg Adams	4:30	Van.
May 1/93	Det.	DSF	Tor. 4	Det. 3	Nikolai Borschevsky	2:35	Tor.
May 3/93	Tor.	DF	Tor. 2	St.L. 1	Doug Gilmour	23:16	Tor.
May 4/93	Mtl.	DF	Mtl. 4	Buf. 3	Guy Carbonneau	2:50	Mtl.
May 5/93	Tor.	DF	St.L. 2	Tor. 1	Jeff Brown	23:03	Tor.
May 6/93	Buf.	DF	Mtl. 4	Buf. 3	Gilbert Dionne	8:28	Mtl.
May 8/93	Buf.	DF	Mtl. 4	Buf. 3	Kirk Muller	11:37	Mtl.
May 11/93	Van.	DF	L.A. 4	Van. 3	Gary Shuchuk	26:31	L.A.
May 14/93	Pit.	DF	NYI 4	Pit. 3	Dave Volek	5:16	NYI
May 18/93	Mtl.	CF	Mtl. 4	NYI 3	Stephan Lebeau	26:21	Mtl.
May 20/93	NYI	CF	Mtl. 2	NYI 1	Guy Carbonneau	12:34	Mtl.
May 25/93	Tor.	CF	Tor. 3	L.A. 2	Glenn Anderson	19:20	L.A.
May 27/93	L.A.	CF	L.A. 5	Tor. 4	Wayne Gretzky	1:41	L.A.
Jun. 3/93	Mtl.	F	Mtl. 3	L.A. 2	Eric Desjardins	0:51	Mtl.
Jun. 5/93	L.A.	F	Mtl. 4	L.A. 3	John LeClair	0:34	Mtl.
Jun. 7/93	L.A.	F	Mtl. 3	L.A. 2	John LeClair	14:37	Mtl.
Apr. 20/94	Tor.	CQF	Tor. 1	Chi. 0	Todd Gill	2:15	Tor.
Apr. 22/94	St.L.	CQF	Dal. 5	St.L. 4	Paul Cavallini	8:34	Dal.
Apr. 24/94	Chi.	CQF	Chi. 4	Tor. 3	Jeremy Roenick	1:23	Tor.
Apr. 25/94	Bos.	CQF	Mtl. 2	Bos. 1	Kirk Muller	17:18	Bos.
Apr. 26/94	Cgy.	CQF	Van. 2	Cgy. 1	Geoff Courtnall	7:15	Van.
Apr. 27/94	Buf.	CQF	Buf. 1	N.J. 0	Dave Hannan	65:43	N.J.
Apr. 28/94	Van.	CQF	Van. 3	Cgy. 2	Trevor Linden	16:43	Van.
Apr. 30/94	Cgy.	CQF	Van. 4	Cgy. 3	Pavel Bure	22:20	Van.
May 3/94	N.J.	CSF	Bos. 6	N.J. 5	Don Sweeney	9:08	N.J.
May 7/94	Bos.	CSF	N.J. 5	Bos. 4	Stephane Richer	14:19	N.J.
May 8/94	Van.	CSF	Van. 2	Dal. 1	Sergio Momesso	11:01	Van.
May 12/94	Tor.	CSF	Tor. 3	S.J. 2	Mike Gartner	8:53	Tor.
May 15/94	NYR	CF	N.J. 4	NYR 3	Stephane Richer	35:23	NYR
May 16/94	Tor.	CF	Tor. 3	Van. 2	Peter Zezel	16:55	Van.
May 19/94	N.J.	CF	NYR 3	N.J. 2	Stephane Matteau	26:13	NYR
May 24/94	Van.	CF	Van. 4	Tor. 3	Greg Adams	20:14	Van.
May 27/94	NYR	CF	NYR 2	N.J. 1	Stephane Matteau	24:24	NYR
May 31/94	NYR	F	Van. 3	NYR 2	Greg Adams	19:26	NYR
May 7/95	Phi.	CQF	Phi. 4	Buf. 3	Karl Dykhuis	10:06	Phi.
May 9/95	Cgy.	CQF	S.J. 5	Cgy. 4	Ulf Dahlen	12:21	S.J.
May 12/95	NYR	CQF	NYR 3	Que. 2	Steve Larmer	8:09	NYR
May 12/95	N.J.	CQF	N.J. 1	Bos. 0	Randy McKay	8:51	N.J.
May 14/95	Pit.	CQF	Pit. 6	Wsh. 5	Luc Robitaille	4:30	Pit.
May 15/95	St.L.	CQF	Van. 6	St.L. 5	Cliff Ronning	1:48	Van.
May 17/95	Tor.	CQF	Tor. 5	Chi. 4	Randy Wood	10:00	Chi.
May 19/95	Cgy.	CQF	S.J. 5	Cgy. 4	Ray Whitney	21:54	S.J.
May 21/95	Phi.	CSF	Phi. 5	NYR 4	Eric Desjardins	7:03	Phi.
May 21/95	Chi.	CSF	Chi. 2	Van. 1	Joe Murphy	9:04	Chi.
May 22/95	Phi.	CSF	Phi. 4	NYR 3	Kevin Haller	0:25	Phi.
May 25/95	Van.	CSF	Chi. 3	Van. 2	Chris Chelios	6:22	Chi.
May 26/95	N.J.	CSF	N.J. 2	Pit. 1	Neal Broten	18:36	N.J.
May 27/95	Van.	CSF	Chi. 4	Van. 3	Chris Chelios	5:35	Chi.
Jun. 1/95	Det.	CF	Det. 2	Chi. 1	Nicklas Lidstrom	1:01	Det.
Jun. 6/95	Chi.	CF	Det. 4	Chi. 3	Vladimir Konstantinov	29:25	Det.
Jun. 7/95	N.J.	CF	Phi. 3	N.J. 2	Eric Lindros	4:19	N.J.
Jun. 11/95	Det.	CF	Det. 2	Chi. 1	Vyacheslav Kozlov	22:25	Det.
Apr. 16/96	NYR	CQF	Mtl. 3	NYR 2	Vincent Damphousse	5:04	NYR
Apr. 18/96	Tor.	CQF	Tor. 5	St.L. 4	Mats Sundin	4:02	St.L.
Apr. 18/96	Phi.	CQF	T.B. 2	Phi. 1	Brian Bellows	9:05	Phi.
Apr. 21/96	St.L.	CQF	St.L. 3	Tor. 2	Glenn Anderson	1:24	St.L.
Apr. 21/96	T.B.	CQF	T.B. 5	Phi. 4	Alexander Selivanov	2:04	Phi.
Apr. 23/96	Cgy.	CQF	Chi. 2	Cgy. 1	Joe Murphy	50:02	Chi.
Apr. 24/96	Wsh.	CQF	Pit. 3	Wsh. 2	Petr Nedved	79:15	Pit.
Apr. 25/96	Col.	CQF	Col. 5	Van. 4	Joe Sakic	0:51	Col.
Apr. 25/96	Tor.	CQF	Tor. 5	St.L. 4	Mike Gartner	7:31	St.L.
May 2/96	Col.	CSF	Chi. 3	Col. 2	Jeremy Roenick	6:29	Col.
May 6/96	Chi.	CSF	Chi. 4	Col. 3	Sergei Krivokrasov	0:46	Col.
May 8/96	St.L.	CSF	St.L. 5	Det. 4	Igor Kravchuk	3:23	Det.
May 8/96	Chi.	CSF	Col. 3	Chi. 2	Joe Sakic	44:33	Col.
May 9/96	Fla.	CSF	Fla. 4	Phi. 3	Dave Lowry	4:06	Fla.
May 12/96	Phi.	CSF	Fla. 2	Phi. 1	Mike Hough	28:05	Fla.
May 13/96	Chi.	CSF	Col. 4	Chi. 3	Sandis Ozolinsh	25:18	Col.
May 16/96	Det.	CSF	Det. 1	St.L. 0	Steve Yzerman	21:15	Det.
May 19/96	Det.	CF	Col. 3	Det. 2	Mike Keane	17:31	Col.
Jun. 10/96	Fla.	F	Col. 1	Fla. 0	Uwe Krupp	44:31	Col.
Apr. 20/97	Chi.	CQF	Chi. 4	Col. 3	Sergei Krivokrasov	31:03	Col.
Apr. 20/97	Edm.	CQF	Edm. 4	Dal. 3	Kelly Buchberger	9:15	Edm.
Apr. 22/97	NYR	CQF	NYR 4	Fla. 3	Esa Tikkanen	16:29	NYR
Apr. 23/97	Ott.	CQF	Ott. 1	Buf. 0	Daniel Alfredsson	2:34	Buf.
Apr. 24/97	Mtl.	CQF	Mtl. 4	N.J. 3	Patrice Brisebois	47:37	N.J.
Apr. 25/97	Fla.	CQF	NYR 3	Fla. 2	Esa Tikkanen	12:02	NYR
Apr. 25/97	Dal.	CQF	Edm. 1	Dal. 0	Ryan Smyth	20:22	Edm.
Apr. 27/97	Phx.	CQF	Ana. 3	Phx. 2	Paul Kariya	7:29	Ana.
Apr. 29/97	Buf.	CQF	Buf. 3	Ott. 2	Derek Plante	5:24	Buf.
Apr. 29/97	Dal.	CQF	Edm. 4	Dal. 3	Todd Marchant	12:26	Edm.
May 2/97	Det.	CSF	Det. 2	Ana. 1	Martin Lapointe	0:59	Det.
May 4/97	Det.	CSF	Det. 3	Ana. 2	Vyacheslav Kozlov	41:31	Det.
May 8/97	Ana.	CSF	Det. 3	Ana. 2	Brendan Shanahan	37:03	Det.
May 9/97	Phi.	CSF	Buf. 5	Phi. 4	Ed Ronan	6:24	Phi.
May 9/97	Edm.	CSF	Col. 3	Edm. 2	Claude Lemieux	8:35	Col.
May 11/97	N.J.	CSF	NYR 2	N.J. 1	Adam Graves	14:08	NYR
Apr. 22/98	N.J.	CQF	Ott. 2	N.J. 1	Bruce Gardiner	5:58	Ott.
Apr. 23/98	Pit.	CQF	Mtl. 3	Pit. 2	Benoit Brunet	18:43	Mtl.
Apr. 24/98	Wsh.	CQF	Bos. 4	Wsh. 3	Darren Van Impe	20:54	Wsh.
Apr. 26/98	Ott.	CQF	Ott. 2	N.J. 1	Alexei Yashin	2:47	Ott.
Apr. 26/98	Bos.	CQF	Wsh. 3	Bos. 2	Joe Juneau	26:31	Wsh.
Apr. 26/98	Edm.	CQF	Col. 5	Edm. 4	Joe Sakic	15:25	Edm.
Apr. 28/98	S.J.	CQF	S.J. 1	Dal. 0	Andrei Zyuzin	6:31	Dal.
May 1/98	Phi.	CQF	Buf. 3	Phi. 2	Michal Grosek	5:40	Buf.
May 2/98	S.J.	CQF	Dal. 3	S.J. 2	Mike Keane	3:43	Dal.
May 3/98	Bos.	CQF	Wsh. 3	Bos. 2	Brian Bellows	15:24	Wsh.
May 3/98	Buf.	CSF	Buf. 3	Mtl. 2	Geoff Sanderson	2:37	Buf.
May 11/98	Edm.	CSF	Dal. 1	Edm. 0	Benoit Hogue	13:07	Dal.
May 12/98	Mtl.	CSF	Buf. 5	Mtl. 4	Michael Peca	21:24	Buf.
May 12/98	St.L.	CSF	Det. 3	St.L. 2	Brendan Shanahan	31:12	Det.
May 25/98	Wsh.	CF	Wsh. 3	Buf. 2	Todd Krygier	3:01	Wsh.
May 28/98	Buf.	CF	Wsh. 4	Buf. 3	Peter Bondra	9:37	Wsh.
Jun. 3/98	Dal.	CF	Dal. 3	Det. 2	Jamie Langenbrunner	0:46	Det.
Jun. 4/98	Buf.	CF	Wsh. 3	Buf. 2	Joe Juneau	6:24	Wsh.
Jun. 11/98	Det.	F	Det. 5	Wsh. 4	Kris Draper	15:24	Det.
Apr. 23/99	Ott.	CQF	Buf. 3	Ott. 2	Miroslav Satan	30:35	Buf.
Apr. 24/99	Car.	CQF	Car. 3	Bos. 2	Ray Sheppard	17:05	Bos.
Apr. 24/99	Phx.	CQF	Phx. 4	St.L. 3	Shane Doan	8:58	St.L.
Apr. 26/99	S.J.	CQF	Col. 2	S.J. 1	Milan Hejduk	7:53	Col.
Apr. 27/99	Edm.	CQF	Dal. 3	Edm. 2	Joe Nieuwendyk	57:34	Dal.
Apr. 30/99	Tor.	CQF	Tor. 2	Phi. 1	Yanic Perreault	11:51	Tor.
Apr. 30/99	Car.	CQF	Bos. 4	Car. 3	Anson Carter	34:45	Bos.
Apr. 30/99	Phx.	CQF	St.L. 2	Phx. 1	Scott Young	5:43	St.L.
May 2/99	Pit.	CQF	Pit. 3	N.J. 2	Jaromir Jagr	8:59	Pit.
May 3/99	S.J.	CQF	Col. 3	S.J. 2	Milan Hejduk	13:12	Col.
May 4/99	Phx.	CQF	St.L. 1	Phx. 0	Pierre Turgeon	17:59	St.L.
May 7/99	Col.	CSF	Det. 3	Col. 2	Kirk Maltby	4:18	Col.
May 8/99	Dal.	CSF	Dal. 5	St.L. 4	Joe Nieuwendyk	8:22	Dal.
May 10/99	St.L.	CSF	St.L. 3	Dal. 2	Pavol Demitra	2:43	Dal.
May 12/99	St.L.	CSF	St.L. 3	Dal. 2	Pierre Turgeon	5:52	Dal.
May 13/99	Pit.	CSF	Tor. 3	Pit. 2	Sergei Berezin	2:18	Tor.
May 17/99	Pit.	CSF	Tor. 4	Pit. 3	Garry Valk	1:57	Tor.

Overtime Games since 1918 *— continued*

Date	City	Series	Score		Scorer	Overtime	Series Winner
May 17/99	St.L.	CSF	Dal. 2	St.L. 1	Mike Modano	2:21	Dal.
May 28/99	Col.	CF	Col. 3	Dal. 2	Chris Drury	19:29	Dal.
Jun. 8/99	Dal.	F	Buf. 3	Dal. 2	Jason Woolley	15:30	Dal.
Jun. 19/99	Buf.	F	Dal. 2	Buf. 1	Brett Hull	54:51	Dal.
Apr. 15/00	Pit.	CQF	Pit. 2	Wsh. 1	Jaromir Jagr	5:49	Pit.
Apr. 18/00	Buf.	CQF	Buf. 3	Phi. 2	Stu Barnes	4:42	Phi.
Apr. 22/00	Tor.	CQF	Tor. 2	Ott. 1	Steve Thomas	14:47	Tor.
May 2/00	Pit.	CSF	Phi. 4	Pit. 3	Andy Delmore	11:01	Phi.
May 3/00	Det.	CSF	Col. 3	Det. 2	Chris Drury	10:21	Col.
May 4/00	Pit.	CSF	Phi. 2	Pit. 1	Keith Primeau	92:01	Phi.
May 23/00	Dal.	CF	Dal. 3	Col. 2	Joe Nieuwendyk	12:10	Dal.
Jun. 8/00	N.J.	F	Dal. 1	N.J. 0	Mike Modano	46:21	N.J.
Jun. 10/00	Dal.	F	N.J. 2	Dal. 1	Jason Arnott	28:20	N.J.
Apr. 11/01	Dal.	CQF	Dal. 2	Edm. 1	Jamie Langenbrunner	2:08	Dal.
Apr. 13/01	Ott.	CQF	Tor. 1	Ott. 0	Mats Sundin	10:49	Tor.
Apr. 14/01	Phi.	CQF	Buf. 4	Phi. 3	Jay McKee	18:02	Buf.
Apr. 15/01	Edm.	CQF	Dal. 3	Edm. 2	Benoit Hogue	19:48	Dal.
Apr. 16/01	Tor.	CQF	Tor. 3	Ott. 2	Cory Cross	2:16	Tor.
Apr. 16/01	Van.	CQF	Col. 4	Van. 3	Peter Forsberg	2:50	Col.
Apr. 17/01	Buf.	CQF	Buf. 4	Phi. 3	Curtis Brown	6:13	Buf.
Apr. 17/01	Edm.	CQF	Edm. 2	Dal. 1	Mike Comrie	17:19	Dal.
Apr. 18/01	Car.	CQF	Car. 3	N.J. 2	Rod Brind'Amour	:46	N.J.
Apr. 18/01	Pit.	CQF	Wsh. 4	Pit. 3	Jeff Halpern	4:01	Pit.
Apr. 18/01	L.A.	CQF	L.A. 4	Det. 3	Eric Belanger	2:36	L.A.
Apr. 19/01	Dal.	CQF	Dal. 4	Edm. 3	Kirk Muller	8:01	Dal.
Apr. 19/01	St.L.	CQF	St.L. 3	S.J. 2	Bryce Salvador	9:54	St.L.
Apr. 23/01	Pit.	CQF	Pit. 4	Wsh. 3	Martin Straka	13:04	Pit.
Apr. 23/01	L.A.	CQF	L.A. 3	Det. 2	Adam Deadmarsh	4:48	L.A.
Apr. 26/01	Col.	CSF	L.A. 4	Col. 3	Jaroslav Modry	14:23	Col.
Apr. 28/01	N.J.	CSF	N.J. 6	Tor. 5	Randy McKay	5:31	N.J.
May 1/01	Tor.	CSF	N.J. 3	Tor. 2	Brian Rafalski	7:00	N.J.
May 1/01	St.L.	CSF	St.L. 3	Dal. 2	Cory Stillman	29:26	St.L.
May 5/01	Buf.	CSF	Buf. 3	Pit. 2	Stu Barnes	8:34	Pit.
May 6/01	L.A.	CSF	L.A. 1	Col. 0	Glen Murray	22:41	Col.
May 8/01	Pit.	CSF	Pit. 3	Buf. 2	Martin Straka	11:29	Pit.
May 10/01	Buf.	CSF	Pit. 3	Buf. 2	Darius Kasparaitis	13:01	Pit.
May 16/01	St.L.	CF	St.L. 4	Col. 3	Scott Young	30:27	Col.
May 18/01	St.L.	CF	Col. 4	St.L. 3	Stephane Yelle	4:23	Col.
May 21/01	Col.	CF	Col. 2	St.L. 1	Joe Sakic	:24	Col.
Apr. 17/02	Phi.	CQF	Phi. 1	Ott. 0	Ruslan Fedotenko	7:47	Ott.
Apr. 17/02	Det.	CQF	Van. 4	Det. 3	Henrik Sedin	13:59	Det.
Apr. 19/02	Car.	CQF	Car. 2	N.J. 1	Bates Battaglia	15:26	Car.
Apr. 24/02	Car.	CQF	Car. 3	N.J. 2	Josef Vasicek	8:16	Car.
Apr. 25/02	Col.	CQF	L.A. 1	Col. 0	Craig Johnson	2:19	Col.
Apr. 26/02	Phi.	CQF	Ott. 2	Phi. 1	Martin Havlat	7:33	Ott.
May 4/02	Tor.	CSF	Tor. 3	Ott. 2	Gary Roberts	44:30	Tor.
May 7/02	Mtl.	CSF	Mtl. 2	Car. 1	Donald Audette	2:26	Car.
May 9/02	Mtl.	CSF	Car. 4	Mtl. 3	Niclas Wallin	3:14	Car.
May 13/02	S.J.	CSF	Col. 2	S.J. 1	Peter Forsberg	2:47	Col.
May 19/02	Car.	CF	Car. 2	Tor. 1	Niclas Wallin	13:42	Car.
May 20/02	Det.	CF	Col. 4	Det. 3	Chris Drury	2:17	Det.
May 21/02	Tor.	CF	Car. 2	Tor. 1	Jeff O'Neill	6:01	Car.
May 22/02	Col.	CF	Det. 2	Col. 1	Fredrik Olausson	12:44	Det.
May 27/02	Det.	CF	Col. 2	Det. 1	Peter Forsberg	6:24	Det.
May 28/02	Tor.	CF	Car. 2	Tor. 1	Martin Gelinas	8:05	Car.
Jun. 4/02	Det.	F	Car. 3	Det. 2	Ron Francis	:58	Det.
Jun. 8/02	Car.	F	Det. 3	Car. 2	Igor Larionov	54:47	Det.
Apr. 10/03	Det.	CQF	Ana. 2	Det. 1	Paul Kariya	43:18	Ana.
Apr. 14/03	NYI	CQF	Ott. 3	NYI 2	Todd White	22:25	Ott.
Apr. 14/03	Tor.	CQF	Tor. 4	Phi. 3	Tomas Kaberle	27:20	Phi.
Apr. 15/03	Wsh.	CQF	T.B. 4	Wsh. 3	Vincent Lecavalier	2:29	T.B.
Apr. 16/03	Tor.	CQF	Phi. 3	Tor. 2	Mark Recchi	53:54	Phi.
Apr. 16/03	Ana.	CQF	Ana. 3	Det. 2	Steve Rucchin	6:53	Ana.
Apr. 20/03	Wsh.	CQF	T.B. 2	Wsh. 1	Martin St. Louis	44:03	T.B.
Apr. 21/03	Tor.	CQF	Tor. 2	Phi. 1	Travis Green	30:51	Phi.
Apr. 21/03	Min.	CQF	Min. 3	Col. 2	Richard Park	4:22	Min.
Apr. 22/03	Col.	CQF	Min. 3	Col. 2	Andrew Brunette	3:25	Min.
Apr. 24/03	Dal.	CSF	Ana. 4	Dal. 3	Petr Sykora	80:48	Ana.
Apr. 25/03	Van.	CSF	Van. 4	Min. 3	Trent Klatt	3:42	Min.
Apr. 26/03	N.J.	CSF	N.J. 3	T.B. 2	Jamie Langenbrunner	2:09	N.J.
Apr. 26/03	Dal.	CSF	Ana. 3	Dal. 2	Mike Leclerc	1:44	Ana.
Apr. 29/03	Phi.	CSF	Ott. 3	Phi. 2	Wade Redden	6:43	Ott.
May 2/03	Min.	CSF	Van. 3	Min. 2	Brent Sopel	15:52	Min.
May 2/03	N.J.	CSF	N.J. 2	T.B. 1	Grant Marshall	51:12	N.J.
May 10/03	Min.	CF	Ana. 1	Min. 0	Petr Sykora	28:06	Ana.
May 10/03	Ott.	CF	Ott. 3	N.J. 2	Shaun Van Allen	3:08	N.J.
May 21/03	N.J.	CF	Ott. 2	N.J. 1	Chris Phillips	15:51	N.J.
May 31/03	Ana.	F	Ana. 3	N.J. 2	Ruslan Salei	6:59	N.J.
Jun. 2/03	Ana.	F	Ana. 1	N.J. 0	Steve Thomas	0:39	N.J.
Apr. 8/04	S.J.	CQF	S.J. 1	St.L. 0	Niko Dimitrakos	9:16	S.J.
Apr. 9/04	Bos.	CQF	Bos. 2	Mtl. 1	Patrice Bergeron	1:26	Mtl.
Apr. 12/04	Dal.	CQF	Dal. 4	Col. 3	Steve Ott	2:11	Col.
Apr. 13/04	Mtl.	CQF	Bos. 4	Mtl. 3	Glen Murray	29:27	Mtl.
Apr. 14/04	Dal.	CQF	Col. 3	Dal. 2	Marek Svatos	25:21	Col.
Apr. 16/04	T.B.	CQF	T.B. 3	NYI 2	Martin St. Louis	4:07	T.B.
Apr. 17/04	Cgy.	CQF	Van. 5	Cgy. 4	Brendan Morrison	42:28	Cgy.
Apr. 18/04	Ott.	CQF	Ott. 2	Tor. 1	Mike Fisher	21:47	Tor.
Apr. 19/04	Van.	CQF	Cgy. 3	Van. 2	Martin Gelinas	1:25	Cgy.
Apr. 22/04	Det.	CSF	Cgy. 2	Det. 1	Marcus Nilson	2:39	Cgy.
Apr. 27/04	Mtl.	CSF	T.B. 4	Mtl 3	Brad Richards	1:05	T.B.
Apr. 28/04	Col	CSF	Col. 1	S.J. 0	Joe Sakic	5:15	S.J.
May 1/04	S.J.	CSF	Col. 2	S.J. 1	Joe Sakic	1:54	S.J.
May 3/04	Cgy	CSF	Cgy. 1	Det. 0	Martin Gelinas	19:13	Cgy.
May 4/04	Phi.	CSF	Phi. 3	Tor. 2	Jeremy Roenick	7:39	Phi.
May 9/04	S.J.	CF	Cgy. 4	S.J. 3	Steve Montador	18:43	Cgy.
May 20/04	Phi.	CF	Phi. 5	T.B. 4	Simon Gagne	18:18	T.B.
Jun. 3/04	T.B.	F	Cgy. 3	T.B. 2	Oleg Saprykin	14:40	T.B.
Jun. 5/04	Cgy.	F	T.B. 3	Cgy. 2	Martin St. Louis	20:33	T.B.
Apr. 21/06	Det.	CQF	Det. 3	Edm. 2	Kirk Maltby	22:39	Edm.
Apr. 21/06	Cgy.	CQF	Cgy. 2	Ana. 1	Darren McCarty	9:45	Ana.
Apr. 22/06	Buf.	CQF	Buf. 3	Phi. 2	Daniel Briere	27:31	Buf.
Apr. 24/06	Car.	CQF	Mtl. 6	Car. 5	Michael Ryder	22:32	Car.
Apr. 24/06	Dal.	CQF	Col. 5	Dal. 4	Joe Sakic	4:36	Col.
Apr. 25/06	Edm.	CQF	Edm. 4	Det. 3	Jarret Stoll	28:44	Edm.
Apr. 26/06	Mtl.	CQF	Car. 2	Mtl. 1	Eric Staal	3:38	Car.
Apr. 26/06	Col.	CQF	Col. 4	Dal. 3	Alex Tanguay	1:09	Col.
Apr. 27/06	Ana.	CQF	Ana. 3	Cgy. 2	Sean O'Donnell	1:36	Ana.
Apr. 30/06	Dal.	CQF	Col. 3	Dal. 2	Andrew Brunette	13:55	Col.
May 2/06	Mtl.	CQF	Car. 2	Mtl. 1	Cory Stillman	1:19	Car.
May 5/06	Ott.	CSF	Buf. 7	Ott. 6	Chris Drury	0:18	Buf.
May 8/06	Car.	CSF	Car. 3	N.J. 2	Niclas Wallin	3:09	Car.
May 9/06	Col.	CSF	Ana. 4	Col. 3	Joffrey Lupul	16:30	Ana.
May 10/06	Buf.	CSF	Buf. 3	Ott. 2	J.P. Dumont	5:05	Buf.
May 10/06	Edm.	CSF	Edm. 3	S.J. 2	Shawn Horcoff	42:24	Edm.
May 13/06	Ott.	CSF	Buf. 3	Ott. 2	Jason Pominville	2:26	Buf.
May 28/06	Car.	CF	Car. 4	Buf. 3	Cory Stillman	8:46	Car.
May 30/06	Buf.	CF	Buf. 2	Car. 1	Daniel Briere	4:22	Car.
June 14/06	Car.	F	Edm. 4	Car. 3	Fernando Pisani	3:31	Car.
Apr. 11/07	Nsh.	CQF	S.J. 5	Nsh. 4	Patrick Rissmiller	28:14	S.J.
Apr. 11/07	Van.	CQF	Van. 5	Dal. 4	Henrik Sedin	78:06	Van.
Apr. 15/07	Dal.	CQF	Van. 2	Dal. 1	Taylor Pyatt	7:47	Van.
Apr. 18/07	T.B.	CQF	N.J. 4	T.B. 3	Scott Gomez	12:54	N.J.
Apr. 19/07	Van.	CQF	Dal. 1	Van. 0	Brenden Morrow	6:22	Van.
Apr. 22/07	Cgy.	CQF	Det. 2	Cgy. 1	Johan Franzen	24:23	Det.
Apr. 27/07	Ana.	CSF	Van. 2	Ana. 1	Jeff Cowan	27:49	Ana.
Apr. 28/07	N.J.	CSF	N.J. 3	Ott. 2	Jamie Langenbrunner	21:55	Ott.
Apr. 29/07	NYR	CSF	NYR 2	Buf. 1	Michal Rozsival	36:43	Buf.
May 1/07	Van.	CSF	Ana. 3	Van. 2	Travis Moen	2:07	Ana.
May 2/07	S.J.	CSF	Det. 3	S.J. 2	Mathieu Schneider	16:04	Det.
May 3/07	Ana.	CSF	Ana. 2	Van. 1	Scott Niedermayer	24:30	Ana.
May 4/07	Buf.	CSF	Buf. 2	NYR 1	Maxim Afinogenov	4:39	Buf.
May 12/07	Buf.	CF	Ott. 4	Buf. 3	Joe Corvo	24:58	Ott.
May 13/07	Det.	CF	Ana. 4	Det. 3	Scott Niedermayer	14:17	Ana.
May 19/07	Buf.	CF	Ott. 3	Buf. 2	Daniel Alfredsson	9:32	Ott.
May 20/07	Det.	CF	Ana. 2	Det. 1	Teemu Selanne	11:57	Ana.
Apr. 9/08	Min.	CQF	Col. 3	Min. 2	Joe Sakic	11:11	Col.
Apr. 11/08	Min.	CQF	Min. 3	Col. 2	Keith Carney	1:14	Col.
Apr. 12/08	Mtl.	CQF	Mtl. 3	Bos. 2	Alex Kovalev	2:30	Mtl.
Apr. 13/08	Mtl.	CQF	Bos. 2	Mtl.1	Marc Savard	9:25	Mtl.
Apr. 13/08	NYR	CQF	N.J. 4	NYR 3	John Madden	6:01	NYR
Apr. 14/08	Col.	CQF	Min. 3	Col. 2	Pierre-Marc Bouchard	11:58	Col.
Apr. 17/08	Phi.	CQF	Phi. 4	Wsh. 3	Mike Knuble	26:40	Phi.
Apr. 18/08	Det.	CQF	Det. 2	Nsh. 1	Johan Franzen	1:48	Det.
Apr. 22/08	Wsh.	CQF	Phi. 3	Wsh. 2	Joffrey Lupul	6:06	Phi.
Apr. 24/08	Mtl.	CSF	Mtl. 4	Phi. 3	Tom Kostopoulos	0:48	Phi.
Apr. 25/08	S.J.	CSF	Dal. 3	S.J. 2	Brenden Morrow	4:39	Dal.
Apr. 29/08	Dal.	CSF	Dal. 2	S.J. 1	Mattias Norstrom	4:37	Dal.
May 1/08	S.J.	CSF	S.J. 3	Dal. 2	Joe Pavelski	1:05	Dal.
May 4/08	Pit.	CSF	Pit. 3	NYR 2	Marian Hossa	7:10	Pit.
May 4/08	Dal.	CSF	Dal. 2	S.J. 1	Brenden Morrow	69:03	Dal.
June 2/08	Det.	F	Pit. 3	Det. 2	Petr Sykora	49:57	Det.

Ten Longest Overtime Games

Date	City	Series	Score		Scorer	Overtime	Series Winner
Mar. 24/36	Mtl.	SF	Det. 1	Mtl. M. 0	Mud Bruneteau	116:30	Det.
Apr. 3/33	Tor.	SF	Tor. 1	Bos. 0	Ken Doraty	104:46	Tor.
May 4/00	Pit.	CSF	Phi. 2	Pit. 1	Keith Primeau	92:01	Phi.
Apr. 24/03	Dal.	CSF	Ana. 4	Dal. 3	Petr Sykora	80:48	Ana.
Apr. 24/96	Wsh.	CQF	Pit. 3	Wsh. 2	Petr Nedved	79:15	Pit.
Apr. 11/07	Van.	CQF	Van. 5	Dal. 4	Henrik Sedin	78:06	Van.
Mar. 23/43	Det.	SF	Tor. 3	Det. 2	Jack McLean	70:18	Det.
May 4/08	**Dal.**	**CSF**	**Dal. 2**	**S.J. 1**	**Brenden Morrow**	**69:03**	**Dal.**
Mar. 28/30	Mtl.	SF	Mtl. 2	NYR 1	Gus Rivers	68:52	Mtl.
Apr. 18/87	Wsh.	DSF	NYI 3	Wsh. 2	Pat LaFontaine	68:47	NYI

Overtime Record of Current Teams

(Listed by number of OT games played)

	Overall				Home					Road				
Team	GP	W	L	T	GP	W	L	T	Last OT Game	GP	W	L	T	Last OT Game
Montreal	131	73	56	2	63	39	23	1	Apr. 24/08	68	34	33	1	Apr. 13/08
Toronto	106	54	51	1	68	36	31	1	May 4/04	38	18	20	0	Apr. 18/04
Boston	103	41	59	3	47	22	24	1	Apr. 13/08	56	19	35	2	Apr. 12/08
Detroit	84	37	47	0	50	18	32	0	Jun. 2/08	34	19	15	0	May 2/07
NY Rangers	67	32	36	0	29	13	16	0	Apr. 13/08	38	18	20	0	May 4/08
Dallas[1]	64	28	36	0	32	13	19	0	May 4/08	32	15	17	0	May 2/08
Chicago	62	30	30	2	30	16	13	1	Apr. 20/97	32	14	17	1	May 2/96
Philadelphia	62	30	32	0	27	14	13	0	Apr. 17/08	35	16	19	0	Apr. 24/08
Buffalo	56	31	25	0	32	20	12	0	May 19/07	24	11	13	0	Apr. 29/07
Colorado[2]	56	32	24	0	22	10	12	0	Apr. 14/08	34	22	12	0	Apr. 11/08
St. Louis	50	27	23	0	26	20	6	0	May 18/01	24	7	17	0	Apr. 8/04
Edmonton	42	24	18	0	23	13	10	0	May 10/06	19	11	8	0	Jun. 14/06
Vancouver	41	20	21	0	18	7	11	0	May 1/07	23	13	10	0	May 3/07
NY Islanders	40	29	11	0	18	14	4	0	Apr. 14/03	22	15	7	0	Apr. 16/04
Calgary[3]	40	17	23	0	19	6	13	0	Apr. 22/07	21	11	10	0	Apr. 27/06
New Jersey[4]	37	13	24	0	15	6	9	0	Apr. 28/07	22	7	15	0	Apr. 13/08
Los Angeles	35	17	18	0	19	11	8	0	May 6/01	16	6	10	0	Apr. 25/02
Washington	33	14	19	0	13	5	8	0	Apr. 22/08	20	9	11	0	Apr. 17/08
Carolina[5]	30	18	12	0	18	11	7	0	Jun. 14/06	12	7	5	0	May 30/06
Pittsburgh	30	17	13	0	19	11	8	0	May 4/08	11	6	5	0	Jun. 2/08
Ottawa	22	11	11	0	8	4	4	0	May 13/06	14	7	7	0	May 19/07
San Jose	20	6	14	0	11	3	8	0	May 2/08	9	3	6	0	May 4/08
Anaheim	19	14	5	0	7	5	2	0	May 3/07	12	9	3	0	May 20/07
Tampa Bay	12	7	5	0	4	2	2	0	Apr. 18/07	8	5	3	0	Jun. 5/04
Phoenix[6]	12	5	7	0	8	3	5	0	May 4/99	4	2	2	0	Apr. 27/93
Minnesota	8	4	4	0	5	2	3	0	Apr. 11/08	3	2	1	0	Apr. 14/08
Florida	5	2	3	0	3	1	2	0	Apr. 25/97	2	1	1	0	Apr. 22/97
Nashville	2	0	2	0	1	0	1	0	Apr. 11/07	1	0	1	0	Apr. 18/08

[1] Totals include those of Minnesota North Stars 1967-93.
[2] Totals include those of Quebec 1979-95.
[3] Totals include those of Atlanta Flames 1972-80.
[4] Totals include those of Kansas City and Colorado Rockies 1974-82.
[5] Totals include those of Hartford 1979-97.
[6] Totals include those of Winnipeg 1979-96.

Dallas captain Brenden Morrow was the only player to score two overtime goals in the 2008 playoffs. He got the winner in game one of a second-round series with Dallas, and then clinched the series in quadruple overtime in game six.

Penalty Shots in Stanley Cup Playoff Games

Date	Player, Team	Goaltender, Team	Scored	Final Score	Series
Mar. 25/37	Lionel Conacher, Mtl. Maroons	Tiny Thompson, Boston	No	Mtl. M. 0 at Bos. 4	QF
Apr. 15/37	Alex Shibicky, NY Rangers	Earl Robertson, Detroit	No	NYR 0 at Det. 3	F
Mar. 24/38	Mush March, Chicago	Wilf Cude, Montreal	No	Mtl. 0 at Chi. 4	QF
Mar. 29/38	Lorne Carr, NY Americans	Mike Karakas, Chicago	No	Chi. 1 at NYA 3	SF
Apr. 10/38	Art Wiebe, Chicago	Turk Broda, Toronto	No	Tor. 1 at Chi. 2	F
Mar. 24/42	Charlie Sands, Montreal	Johnny Mowers, Detroit	No	Det. 0 at Mtl. 5	QF
Apr. 13/44	Virgil Johnson, Chicago	Bill Durnan, Montreal	No	Chi. 4 at Mtl. 5*	F
Apr. 9/68	Wayne Connelly, Minnesota	Terry Sawchuk, Los Angeles	Yes	L.A. 5 at Min. 7	QF
Apr. 27/68	Jim Roberts, St. Louis	Cesare Maniago, Minnesota	No	St.L. 4 at Min. 3	SF
May 16/71	Frank Mahovlich, Montreal	Tony Esposito, Chicago	No	Chi. 3 at Mtl. 4	F
May 7/75	Bill Barber, Philadelphia	Glenn Resch, NY Islanders	No	Phi. 3 at NYI 4*	SF
Apr. 20/79	Mike Walton, Chicago	Glenn Resch, NY Islanders	No	NYI 4 at Chi. 0	QF
Apr. 9/81	Peter McNab, Boston	Don Beaupre, Minnesota	No	Min. 5 at Bos. 4*	PR
Apr. 17/81	Anders Hedberg, NY Rangers	Mike Liut, St. Louis	Yes	NYR 6 at St.L. 4	QF
Apr. 9/83	Denis Potvin, NY Islanders	Pat Riggin, Washington	No	NYI 6 at Wsh. 2	DSF
Apr. 28/84	Wayne Gretzky, Edmonton	Don Beaupre, Minnesota	Yes	Edm. 8 at Min. 5	CF
May 1/84	Mats Naslund, Montreal	Billy Smith, NY Islanders	No	Mtl. 1 at NYI 3	CF
Apr. 14/85	Bob Carpenter, Washington	Billy Smith, NY Islanders	No	Wsh. 4 at NYI. 6	DF
May 28/85	Ron Sutter, Philadelphia	Grant Fuhr, Edmonton	No	Phi. 3 at Edm. 5	F
May 30/85	Dave Poulin, Philadelphia	Grant Fuhr, Edmonton	No	Phi. 3 at Edm. 8	F
Apr. 9/88	John Tucker, Buffalo	Andy Moog, Boston	Yes	Bos. 2 at Buf. 6	DSF
Apr. 9/88	Petr Klima, Detroit	Allan Bester, Toronto	Yes	Det. 6 at Tor. 3	DSF
Apr. 8/89	Neal Broten, Minnesota	Greg Millen, St. Louis	Yes	St.L. 5 at Min. 3	DSF
Apr. 4/90	Al MacInnis, Calgary	Kelly Hrudey, Los Angeles	Yes	L.A. 5 at Cgy. 3	DSF
Apr. 5/90	Randy Wood, NY Islanders	Mike Richter, NY Rangers	No	NYI 1 at NYR 2	DSF
May 3/90	Kelly Miller, Washington	Andy Moog, Boston	No	Wsh. 3 at Bos. 5	CF
May 18/90	Petr Klima, Edmonton	Reggie Lemelin, Boston	No	Edm. 7 at Bos. 2	F
Apr. 6/91	Basil McRae, Minnesota	Ed Belfour, Chicago	Yes	Min. 2 at Chi. 5	DSF
Apr. 10/91	Steve Duchesne, Los Angeles	Kirk McLean, Vancouver	Yes	L.A. 6 at Van. 1	DSF
May 11/92	Jaromir Jagr, Pittsburgh	John Vanbiesbrouck, NYR	Yes	Pit. 3 at NYR 2	DF
May 13/92	Shawn McEachern, Pittsburgh	John Vanbiesbrouck, NYR	No	NYR 1 at Pit. 5	DF
June 7/94	Pavel Bure, Vancouver	Mike Richter, NYR	No	NYR 4 at Van. 2	F
May 9/95	Patrick Poulin, Chicago	Felix Potvin, Toronto	No	Tor. 3 at Chi. 0	CQF
May 10/95	Michal Pivonka, Washington	Tom Barrasso, Pittsburgh	No	Pit. 2 at Wsh. 6	CQF
Apr. 24/96	Joe Juneau, Washington	Ken Wregget, Pittsburgh	No	Pit. 3 at Wsh. 2**	CQF
May 11/97	Eric Lindros, Philadelphia	Steve Shields, Buffalo	Yes	Phi. 6 at Buf. 3	CSF
Apr. 23/98	Aleksey Morozov, Pittsburgh	Andy Moog, Montreal	No	Mtl. 3 at Pit. 2**	CQF
Apr. 22/99	Mats Sundin, Toronto	John Vanbiesbrouck, Phi.	No	Phi. 3 at Tor. 0	CQF
May 29/99	Mats Sundin, Toronto	Dominik Hasek, Buffalo	Yes	Tor. 2 at Buf. 5	CF
Apr. 16/00	Eric Desjardins, Philadelphia	Dominik Hasek, Buffalo	No	Phi. 2 at Buf. 0	CQF
Apr. 11/01	Mark Recchi, Philadelphia	Dominik Hasek, Buffalo	No	Buf. 2 at Phi. 1	CQF
May 2/01	Martin Straka, Pittsburgh	Dominik Hasek, Buffalo	No	Buf. 5 at Pit. 2	CSF
May 12/01	Joe Sakic, Colorado	Roman Turek, St. Louis	Yes	St.L. 1 at Col. 4	CF
Apr. 21/02	Todd Bertuzzi, Vancouver	Dominik Hasek, Detroit	No	Det. 3 at Van. 1	CQF
Apr. 24/02	Shawn Bates, NY Islanders	Curtis Joseph, Toronto	Yes	Tor. 3 at NYI 4	CQF
Apr. 26/02	Mike Johnson, Phoenix	Evgeni Nabokov, San Jose	Yes	Phx. 1 at S.J. 4	CQF
Apr. 15/03	Dainius Zubrus, Washington	Nikolai Khabibulin, Tampa Bay	No	T.B. 4 at Wsh. 3	CQF
Apr. 21/03	Robert Reichel, Toronto	Roman Cechmanek, Philadelphia	No	Phi. 1 at Tor. 2	CQF
Apr. 7/04	Steve Sullivan, Nashville	Manny Legace, Detroit	No	Nsh. 1 at Det. 3	CQF
Apr. 28/06	Derek Roy, Buffalo	Robert Esche, Philadelphia	No	Buf. 4 at Phi. 5	CQF
June 5/06	Chris Pronger, Edmonton***	Cam Ward, Carolina	Yes	Edm. 4 at Car. 5	F
Apr. 21/07	Daniel Cleary, Detroit	Miikka Kiprusoff, Calgary	Yes	Cgy. 1 at Det. 5	CQF
June 5/07	Antoine Vermette, Ottawa	J.S. Giguere, Anaheim	No	Ott. 2 at Ana. 6	F
Apr. 9/08	Ryan Smyth, Colorado	Niklas Backstrom, Minnesota	No	Col. 3 at Min. 2	CQF
Apr. 15/08	Mike Richards, Philadelphia	Cristobal Huet, Washington	Yes	Wsh. 3 at Phi. 6	CQF
Apr. 18/08	John Madden, New Jersey	Henrik Lundqvist, NY Rangers	No	NYR 5 at N.J. 3	CQF
Apr. 24/08	Andrei Kostitsyn, Montreal	Martin Biron, Philadelphia	No	Phi. 3 at Mtl. 4	CSF
Apr. 29/08	Niklas Hagman, Dallas	Evgeni Nabokov, San Jose	No	S.J. 1 at Dal. 2	CSF
May 1/08	Evgeni Malkin, Pittsburgh	Henrik Lundqvist, NY Rangers	No	Pit. 0 at NYR 3	CSF

* Game was decided in overtime, but shot taken during regulation time.
** Shot taken in overtime.
*** First penalty shot scored in Stanley Cup Final history

A record six penalty shots were taken during the 2008 playoffs, but Philadelphia's Mike Richards was the only player to score a goal, beating Washington's Cristobal Huet in game three of their opening-round series.

All-Time Playoff NHL Coaching Register

Playoffs, 1917-2008

Coach	Team	Games Coached	Wins	Losses	Ties	Years	Cup Wins	Career
Abel, Sid	Chicago	7	3	4		1		
	Detroit	69	29	40		8		
	Totals	**76**	**32**	**44**		**9**		**1952-76**
Adams, Jack	**Detroit**	**105**	**52**	**52**	**1**	**15**	**3**	**1927-47**
Allen, Keith	**Philadelphia**	**11**	**3**	**8**		**2**		**1967-69**
Arbour, Al	St. Louis	11	4	7		1		
	NY Islanders	198	119	79		15	4	
	Totals	**209**	**123**	**86**		**16**	**4**	**1970-08**
Babcock, Mike	Anaheim	21	15	6		1		
	Detroit	46	28	18		3	1	
	Totals	**67**	**43**	**24**		**4**	**1**	**2002-08**
Barber, Bill	**Philadelphia**	**11**	**3**	**8**		**2**		**2000-02**
Berenson, Red	**St. Louis**	**14**	**5**	**9**		**2**		**1979-82**
Bergeron, Michel	**Quebec**	**68**	**31**	**37**		**7**		**1980-90**
Berry, Bob	Los Angeles	10	2	8		3		
	Montreal	8	2	6		2		
	St. Louis	15	7	8		2		
	Totals	**33**	**11**	**22**		**7**		**1978-94**
Beverley, Nick	**Toronto**	**6**	**2**	**4**		**1**		**1995-96**
Blackburn, Don	**Hartford**	**3**	**0**	**3**		**1**		**1979-81**
Blair, Wren	**Minnesota**	**14**	**7**	**7**		**1**		**1967-70**
Blake, Toe	**Montreal**	**119**	**82**	**37**		**13**	**8**	**1955-68**
Boileau, Marc	**Pittsburgh**	**9**	**5**	**4**		**1**		**1973-76**
Boivin, Leo	**St. Louis**	**3**	**1**	**2**		**1**		**1975-78**
Boucher, Georges	**Mtl. Maroons**	**2**	**0**	**2**	**0**	**1**		**1930-50**
Boucher, Frank	**NY Rangers**	**27**	**13**	**14**		**4**	**1**	**1939-54**
Boudreau, Bruce	**Washington**	**7**	**3**	**4**		**1**		**2007-08**
Bowman, Scotty	St. Louis	52	26	26		4		
	Montreal	98	70	28		8	5	
	Buffalo	36	18	18		5		
	Pittsburgh	33	23	10		2	1	
	Detroit	134	86	48		9	3	
	Totals	**353**	**223**	**130**		**28**	**9**	**1967-02**
Bowness, Rick	**Boston**	**15**	**8**	**7**		**1**		**1988-05**
Brooks, Herb	NY Rangers	24	12	12		3		
	New Jersey	5	1	4		1		
	Pittsburgh	11	6	5		1		
	Totals	**40**	**19**	**21**		**5**		**1981-00**
Brophy, John	**Toronto**	**19**	**9**	**10**		**2**		**1986-89**
Burns, Pat	Montreal	56	30	26		4		
	Toronto	46	23	23		3		
	Boston	18	8	10		2		
	New Jersey	29	17	12		2	1	
	Totals	**149**	**78**	**71**		**11**	**1**	**1988-05**
Burns, Charlie	**Minnesota**	**6**	**2**	**4**		**1**		**1969-75**
Campbell, Colin	**NY Rangers**	**36**	**18**	**18**		**3**		**1994-98**
Carbonneau, Guy	**Montreal**	**12**	**5**	**7**		**1**		**2006-08**
Carlyle, Randy	**Anaheim**	**43**	**27**	**16**		**3**	**1**	**2005-08**
Carpenter, Doug	**Toronto**	**5**	**1**	**4**		**1**		**1984-91**
Carroll, Dick	**Toronto**	**2**	**1**	**1**	**0**	**1**	**1**	**1917-19**
Carroll, Frank	**Toronto**	**2**	**0**	**2**	**0**	**1**		**1920-21**
Cassidy, Bruce	**Washington**	**6**	**2**	**4**		**1**		**2002-04**
Cheevers, Gerry	**Boston**	**34**	**15**	**19**		**4**		**1980-85**
Cherry, Don	**Boston**	**55**	**31**	**24**		**5**		**1974-80**
Clancy, King	**Toronto**	**14**	**2**	**12**		**3**		**1937-56**
Clapper, Dit	**Boston**	**25**	**8**	**17**		**4**		**1945-49**
Cleghorn, Sprague	**Mtl. Maroons**	**4**	**1**	**1**	**2**	**1**		**1931-32**
Cleghorn, Odie	**Pittsburgh**	**4**	**1**	**2**	**1**	**2**		**1925-29**
Constantine, Kevin	San Jose	25	11	14		2		
	Pittsburgh	19	8	11		2		
	New Jersey	6	2	4		1		
	Totals	**50**	**21**	**29**		**5**		**1993-02**
Crawford, Marc	Quebec	6	2	4		1		
	Colorado	46	29	17		3	1	
	Vancouver	27	12	15		3		
	Totals	**79**	**43**	**36**		**7**	**1**	**1994-08**
Creighton, Fred	**Atlanta**	**9**	**2**	**7**		**4**		**1974-80**
Crisp, Terry	Calgary	37	22	15		3	1	
	Tampa Bay	6	2	4		1		
	Totals	**43**	**24**	**19**		**4**	**1**	**1987-98**
Crozier, Joe	**Buffalo**	**6**	**2**	**4**		**1**		**1971-81**
Cunniff, John	**New Jersey**	**6**	**2**	**4**		**1**		**1982-91**
Curry, Alex	**Ottawa**	**2**	**0**	**1**	**1**	**1**		**1925-26**
Dandurand, Leo	**Montreal**	**8**	**5**	**3**	**0**	**4**	**1**	**1921-35**
Day, Hap	**Toronto**	**80**	**49**	**31**		**9**	**5**	**1940-50**
Demers, Jacques	St. Louis	33	16	17		3		
	Detroit	38	20	18		3		
	Montreal	27	19	8		2	1	
	Totals	**98**	**55**	**43**		**8**	**1**	**1979-99**
Denneny, Cy	**Boston**	**5**	**5**	**0**	**0**	**1**	**1**	**1928-33**
Dudley, Rick	**Buffalo**	**12**	**4**	**8**		**2**		**1989-04**
Dugal, Jules	**Montreal**	**3**	**1**	**2**		**1**		**1938-39**
Duncan, Art	**Toronto**	**2**	**0**	**1**	**1**	**1**		**1926-32**
Dutton, Red	**NY Americans**	**16**	**6**	**10**	**0**	**4**		**1935-42**
Esposito, Phil	**NY Rangers**	**10**	**2**	**8**		**2**		**1986-89**
Evans, Jack	**Hartford**	**16**	**8**	**8**		**2**		**1975-88**
Ferguson, John	**Winnipeg**	**3**	**0**	**3**		**1**		**1975-86**

Coach	Team	Games Coached	Wins	Losses	Ties	Years	Cup Wins	Career
Francis, Emile	NY Rangers	75	34	41		9		
	St. Louis	14	5	9		2		
	Totals	**89**	**39**	**50**		**11**		**1965-83**
Francis, Bob	**Phoenix**	**10**	**2**	**8**		**2**		**1999-04**
Ftorek, Robbie	Los Angeles	16	5	11		2		
	New Jersey	7	3	4		1		
	Boston	6	2	4		1		
	Totals	**29**	**10**	**19**		**4**		**1987-03**
Gainey, Bob	Minnesota	30	17	13		2		
	Dallas	14	6	8		2		
	Montreal	6	2	4		1		
	Totals	**50**	**25**	**25**		**5**		**1990-06**
Geoffrion, Bernie	**Atlanta**	**4**	**0**	**4**		**1**		**1968-80**
Gerard, Eddie	**Mtl. Maroons**	**21**	**8**	**8**	**5**	**5**	**1**	**1917-35**
Gill, David	**Ottawa**	**8**	**3**	**2**	**3**	**2**	**1**	**1926-29**
Glover, Fred	**Oakland**	**11**	**3**	**8**		**2**		**1968-74**
Gordon, Jackie	**Minnesota**	**25**	**11**	**14**		**3**		**1970-75**
Goring, Butch	**Boston**	**3**	**0**	**3**		**1**		**1985-01**
Gorman, Tommy	NY Americans	2	0	1	1	1		
	Chicago	8	6	1	1	1	1	
	Mtl. Maroons	15	7	6	2	3	1	
	Totals	**25**	**13**	**8**	**4**	**5**	**2**	**1925-38**
Gottselig, Johnny	**Chicago**	**4**	**0**	**4**		**1**		**1944-48**
Granato, Tony	**Colorado**	**18**	**9**	**9**		**2**		**2002-04**
Green, Pete	**Ottawa**	**8**	**3**	**4**	**1**	**4**	**3**	**1919-25**
Green, Ted	**Edmonton**	**16**	**8**	**8**		**1**		**1991-94**
Guidolin, Bep	**Boston**	**21**	**11**	**10**		**2**		**1972-76**
Harris, Ted	**Minnesota**	**2**	**0**	**2**		**1**		**1975-78**
Hart, Cecil	**Montreal**	**37**	**16**	**17**	**4**	**8**	**2**	**1926-39**
Hartley, Bob	Colorado	80	49	31		4	1	
	Atlanta	4	0	4		1		
	Totals	**84**	**49**	**35**		**5**	**1**	**1998-08**
Hartsburg, Craig	Chicago	16	8	8		2		
	Anaheim	4	0	4		1		
	Totals	**20**	**8**	**12**		**3**		**1995-01**
Harvey, Doug	**NY Rangers**	**6**	**2**	**4**		**1**		**1961-62**
Hay, Don	**Phoenix**	**7**	**3**	**4**		**1**		**1996-01**
Henning, Lorne	**Minnesota**	**5**	**2**	**3**		**1**		**1985-01**
Hitchcock, Ken	Dallas	80	47	33		5	1	
	Philadelphia	37	19	18		3		
	Totals	**117**	**66**	**51**		**8**	**1**	**1995-08**
Hlinka, Ivan	**Pittsburgh**	**18**	**9**	**9**		**1**		**2000-02**
Holmgren, Paul	**Philadelphia**	**19**	**10**	**9**		**1**		**1988-96**
Imlach, Punch	**Toronto**	**92**	**44**	**48**		**11**	**4**	**1958-80**
Inglis, Bill	**Buffalo**	**3**	**1**	**2**		**1**		**1978-79**
Irvin, Dick	Chicago	9	5	3	1	1		
	Toronto	66	33	32	1	9	1	
	Montreal	115	62	53		14	3	
	Totals	**190**	**100**	**88**	**2**	**24**	**4**	**1928-56**
Ivan, Tommy	**Detroit**	**67**	**36**	**31**		**7**	**3**	**1947-58**
Johnson, Tom	**Boston**	**22**	**15**	**7**		**2**	**1**	**1970-73**
Johnson, Bob	Calgary	52	25	27		5		
	Pittsburgh	24	16	8		1	1	
	Totals	**76**	**41**	**35**		**6**	**1**	**1982-91**
Johnston, Eddie	Chicago	7	3	4		1		
	Pittsburgh	46	22	24		5		
	Totals	**53**	**25**	**28**		**6**		**1979-97**
Julien, Claude	Montreal	11	4	7		1		
	Boston	7	3	4		1		
	Totals	**18**	**7**	**11**		**2**		**2002-08**
Kasper, Steve	**Boston**	**5**	**1**	**4**		**1**		**1995-97**
Keenan, Mike	Philadelphia	57	32	25		4		
	Chicago	60	33	27		4		
	NY Rangers	23	16	7		1	1	
	St. Louis	20	10	10		2		
	Calgary	7	3	4		1		
	Totals	**167**	**94**	**73**		**12**	**1**	**1984-08**
Kelly, Pat	**Colorado**	**2**	**0**	**2**		**1**		**1977-79**
Kelly, Red	Los Angeles	18	7	11		2		
	Pittsburgh	14	6	8		2		
	Toronto	30	11	19		4		
	Totals	**62**	**24**	**38**		**8**		**1967-77**
King, Dave	**Calgary**	**20**	**8**	**12**		**3**		**1992-03**
Kromm, Bobby	**Detroit**	**7**	**3**	**4**		**1**		**1977-80**
Lalonde, Newsy	Montreal	11	5	4	2	4		
	Ottawa	2	0	1	1	1		
	Totals	**13**	**5**	**5**	**3**	**5**		**1917-35**
Lamoriello, Lou	**New Jersey**	**20**	**10**	**10**		**2**		**2005-07**
Laviolette, Peter	NY Islanders	12	4	8		2		
	Carolina	25	16	9		1	1	
	Totals	**37**	**20**	**17**		**3**	**1**	**2001-08**
Lemaire, Jacques	Montreal	27	15	12		2		
	New Jersey	56	34	22		4	1	
	Minnesota	29	11	18		3		
	Totals	**112**	**60**	**52**		**9**	**1**	**1983-08**
Lewis, Dave	**Minnesota**	**16**	**6**	**10**		**2**		**1998-07**
Ley, Rick	Hartford	13	5	8		2		
	Vancouver	11	4	7		1		
	Totals	**24**	**9**	**15**		**3**		**1989-96**
Long, Barry	**Winnipeg**	**11**	**3**	**8**		**2**		**1983-86**
Loughlin, Clem	**Chicago**	**4**	**1**	**2**	**1**	**2**		**1934-37**
Low, Ron	**Edmonton**	**28**	**10**	**18**		**3**		**1994-02**
Lowe, Kevin	**Edmonton**	**5**	**1**	**4**		**1**		**1999-00**
MacLean, Doug	**Florida**	**27**	**13**	**14**		**2**		**1995-04**

Coach	Team	Games Coached	Wins	Losses	Ties	Years	Cup Wins	Career
MacNeil, Al	Montreal	20	12	8		1	1	
	Atlanta	4	1	3		1		
	Calgary	19	9	10		2		
	Totals	43	22	21		4	1	1970-03
MacTavish, Craig	Edmonton	30	17	13		2		2000-08
Magnuson, Keith	Chicago	3	0	3		1		1980-82
Mahoney, Bill	Minnesota	16	7	9		1		1983-85
Maloney, Dan	Toronto	10	6	4		1		
	Winnipeg	15	5	10		2		
	Totals	25	11	14		3		1984-89
Maloney, Phil	Vancouver	7	1	6		2		1973-77
Martin, Jacques	St. Louis	16	7	9		2		
	Ottawa	69	31	38		8		
	Totals	85	38	47		10		1986-08
Maurice, Paul	Carolina	35	17	18		3		1995-08
McCammon, Bob	Philadelphia	10	1	9		3		
	Vancouver	7	3	4		1		
	Totals	17	4	13		4		1978-91
McLellan, John	Toronto	11	3	8		2		1969-73
McVie, Tom	New Jersey	14	6	8		2		1975-92
Melrose, Barry	Los Angeles	24	13	11		1		1992-95
Milbury, Mike	Boston	40	23	17		2		1989-99
Muckler, John	Edmonton	40	25	15		2	1	
	Buffalo	27	11	16		4		
	Totals	67	36	31		6	1	1968-00
Muldoon, Pete	Chicago	2	0	1	1	1		1926-27
Munro, Dunc	Mtl. Maroons	4	1	3	0	1		1929-31
Murdoch, Bob	Chicago	5	1	4		1		
	Winnipeg	7	3	4		1		
	Totals	12	4	8		2		1987-91
Murphy, Mike	Los Angeles	5	1	4		1		1986-98
Murray, Andy	Los Angeles	24	10	14		3		1999-08
Murray, Terry	Washington	39	18	21		4		
	Philadelphia	46	28	18		3		
	Florida	4	0	4		1		
	Totals	89	46	43		8		1989-01
Murray, Bryan	Washington	53	24	29		7		
	Detroit	25	10	15		3		
	Ottawa	34	18	16		3		
	Totals	112	52	60		13		1981-08
Neale, Harry	Vancouver	14	3	11		4		1978-86
Neilson, Roger	Toronto	19	8	11		2		
	Buffalo	8	4	4		1		
	Vancouver	21	12	9		2		
	NY Rangers	29	13	16		3		
	Philadelphia	29	14	15		3		
	Totals	106	51	55		11		1977-02
Nolan, Ted	Buffalo	12	5	7		1		
	NY Islanders	5	1	4		1		
	Totals	17	6	11		2		1995-08
Nykoluk, Mike	Toronto	7	1	6		2		1980-84
O'Connell, Mike	Boston	5	1	4		1		2002-03
O'Donoghue, George	Toronto	2	1	0	1	1	1	1921-23
Oliver, Murray	Minnesota	13	5	8		2		1981-83
O'Reilly, Terry	Boston *	37	17	19	1	3		1986-89
	* Playoff game May 24, 1988 suspended due to power failure. Score tied.							
Paddock, John	Winnipeg	13	5	8		2		1991-08
Page, Pierre	Minnesota	12	4	8		2		
	Quebec	6	2	4		1		
	Calgary	4	0	4		1		
	Totals	22	6	16		4		1988-98
Patrick, Lester	NY Rangers	65	32	26	7	12	2	1926-39
Patrick, Craig	NY Rangers	17	7	10		2		
	Pittsburgh	5	1	4		1		
	Totals	22	8	14		3		1980-97
Patrick, Lynn	NY Rangers	12	7	5		1		
	Boston *	28	9	18	1	4		
	Totals	40	16	23	1	5		1948-76
	* Playoff game March 31, 1951 suspended due to Toronto city curfew. Score tied.							
Patrick, Frank	Boston	6	2	4	0	2		1934-36
Perron, Jean	Montreal	48	30	18		3	1	1985-89
Perry, Don	Los Angeles	10	4	6		1		1981-84
Pilous, Rudy	Chicago	41	19	22		5	1	1957-63
Plager, Barclay	St. Louis	4	1	3		1		1977-83
Playfair, Jim	Calgary	6	2	4		1		2006-07
Pleau, Larry	Hartford	10	2	8		2		1980-89
Polano, Nick	Detroit	7	1	6		2		1982-85
Powers, Eddie	Toronto	2	0	2	0	1		1924-26
Primeau, Joe	Toronto *	15	8	6	1	2	1	1950-53
	* Playoff game March 31, 1951 suspended due to Toronto city curfew. Score tied.							
Pronovost, Marcel	Buffalo	8	3	5		1		1977-79
Pulford, Bob	Los Angeles	26	10	16		4		
	Chicago	45	17	28		6		
	Totals	71	27	44		10		1972-00
Quenneville, Joel	St. Louis	68	34	34		7		
	Colorado	19	8	11		2		
	Totals	87	42	45		9		1996-08
Quinn, Pat	Philadelphia	39	22	17		3		
	Los Angeles	3	0	3		1		
	Vancouver	61	31	30		5		
	Toronto	80	41	39		6		
	Totals	183	94	89		15		1978-06
Reay, Billy	Chicago	116	56	60		12		1957-77
Renney, Tom	NY Rangers	24	11	13		3		1996-08
Risebrough, Doug	Calgary	7	3	4		1		1990-92
Roberts, Jim	Hartford	7	3	4		1		1981-97
Robinson, Larry	Los Angeles	4	0	4		1		
	New Jersey	48	31	17		2	1	
	Totals	52	31	21		3	1	1995-06
Ross, Art	Boston	65	27	33	5	11	1	1917-45
Ruel, Claude	Montreal	27	18	9		3	1	1968-81
Ruff, Lindy	Buffalo	88	52	36		6		1997-08
Sather, Glen	Edmonton *	127	89	37	1	10	4	1979-04
	* Playoff game May 24, 1988 suspended due to power failure. Score tied.							
Sator, Ted	NY Rangers	16	8	8		1		
	Buffalo	11	3	8		2		
	Totals	27	11	16		3		1985-89
Schinkel, Ken	Pittsburgh	6	2	4		2		1972-77
Schmidt, Milt	Boston	34	15	19		4		1954-76
Schoenfeld, Jim	New Jersey	20	11	9		1		
	Washington	24	10	14		3		
	Phoenix	13	5	8		2		
	Totals	57	26	31		6		1985-99
Shero, Fred	Philadelphia	83	48	35		6	2	
	NY Rangers	27	15	12		2		
	Totals	110	63	47		8	2	1971-81
Simpson, Terry	NY Islanders	20	9	11		2		
	Winnipeg	6	2	4		1		
	Totals	26	11	15		3		1986-96
Sinden, Harry	Boston	43	24	19		5	1	1966-85
Skinner, Jimmy	Detroit	26	14	12		3	1	1954-58
Smith, Alf	Ottawa	5	1	4	0	1		1918-19
Smith, Floyd	Buffalo	32	16	16		3		1971-80
Smythe, Conn	Toronto	4	2	2	0	1		1927-31
Sonmor, Glen	Minnesota	43	25	18		3		1978-87
Stasiuk, Vic	Philadelphia	4	0	4		1		1969-73
Stevens, John	Philadelphia	17	9	8		1		2006-08
Stewart, Ron	Los Angeles	2	0	2		1		1975-78
Stewart, Bill	Chicago	10	7	3		1	1	1937-39
Sutter, Brent	New Jersey	5	1	4		1		2007-08
Sutter, Brian	St. Louis	41	20	21		4		
	Boston	22	7	15		3		
	Chicago	5	1	4		1		
	Totals	68	28	40		8		1988-05
Sutter, Darryl	Chicago	26	11	15		3		
	San Jose	42	18	24		5		
	Calgary	33	18	15		2		
	Totals	101	47	54		10		1992-06
Talbot, Jean-Guy	St. Louis	5	1	4		1		
	NY Rangers	3	1	2		1		
	Totals	8	2	6		2		1972-78
Tessier, Orval	Chicago	18	9	9		2		1982-85
Therrien, Michel	Montreal	12	6	6		1		
	Pittsburgh	25	15	10		2		
	Totals	37	21	16		3		2000-08
Thompson, Paul	Chicago	19	7	12		4		1938-45
Tippett, Dave	Dallas	47	21	26		5		2002-08
Tobin, Bill	Chicago	4	1	2	1	2		1929-32
Tortorella, John	Tampa Bay	45	24	21		4	1	1999-08
Tremblay, Mario	Montreal	11	3	8		2		1995-97
Trotz, Barry	Nashville	22	6	16		4		1998-08
Ubriaco, Gene	Pittsburgh	11	7	4		1		1988-90
Vigneault, Alain	Montreal	10	4	6		1		
	Vancouver	12	5	7		1		
	Totals	22	9	13		2		1997-08
Watson, Phil	NY Rangers	16	4	12		3		1955-63
Watt, Tom	Winnipeg	7	1	6		2		
	Vancouver	3	0	3		1		
	Totals	10	1	9		3		1981-92
Webster, Tom	Los Angeles	28	12	16		3		1986-92
Weiland, Cooney	Boston	17	10	7		2	1	1939-41
White, Bill	Chicago	2	0	2		1		1976-77
Wilson, Ron	Anaheim	11	4	7		1		
	Washington	32	15	17		3		
	San Jose	52	28	24		4		
	Totals	95	47	48		8		1993-08
Wilson, Johnny	Pittsburgh	12	4	8		2		1969-80
Young, Garry	St. Louis	2	0	2		1		1972-76

Key to Prospect, NHL Player and Goaltender Registers

Demographics: Position, shooting side (catching hand for goaltenders), height, weight, place and date of birth as well as draft information, if any, is located on this line.

Major and tier-II junior, NCAA, minor pro, European and NHL clubs form a permanent part of each player's data panel. If a player sees action with more than one club in any of the above categories, a separate line is included for each one.

Olympic Team statistics are also listed.

Player's NHL organization as of August 21, 2008. This includes players under contract, unsigned draft choices and other players on reserve lists. Free agents as of this date show a blank here.

The complete career data panels of players with NHL experience who announced their retirement before the start of the 2008-09 season are included in the Player Register and Golatender Register.

These newly-retired players also show a blank here.

Each NHL club's minor-pro affiliates are listed on page 14.

CLEARY, Daniel (KLIH-ree, DAN-yehl) **DET.**

Right wing. Shoots left. 6', 210 lbs. Born, Carbonear, Nfld., December 18, 1978. Chicago's 1st choice, 13th overall, in 1997 Entry Draft.

			Regular Season														Playoffs								
Season	Club	League	GP	G	A	Pts	PIM	PP	SH	GW	S	%	+/-	TF	F%	Min	GP	G	A	Pts	PIM	PP	SH	GW	Min
1993-94	Kingston	MTJHL	41	18	28	46	33	....	....	....	....	....	....	....	....	....	2	0	1	1	0	....	....	....	....
1994-95	Belleville Bulls	OHL	62	26	55	81	62	....	....	....	....	....	....	....	....	....	16	7	10	17	23	....	....	....	....
1995-96	Belleville Bulls	OHL	64	53	62	115	74	....	....	....	....	....	....	....	....	....	14	10	17	27	40	....	....	....	....
1996-97	Belleville Bulls	OHL	64	32	48	80	88	....	....	....	....	....	....	....	....	....	6	3	4	7	6	....	....	....	....
1997-98	**Chicago**	**NHL**	**6**	**0**	**0**	**0**	**0**	**0**	**0**	**0**	**4**	**0.0**	**–2**	....	....	....	....	....	....	....	....	....	....	....	....
	Belleville Bulls	OHL	30	16	31	47	14	....	....	....	....	....	....	....	....	....	10	6	*17	*23	0	....	....	....	....
	Indianapolis Ice	IHL	4	2	1	3	6	....	....	....	....	....	....	....	....	....	....	....	....	....	....	....	....	....	....
1998-99	**Chicago**	**NHL**	**35**	**4**	**5**	**9**	**24**	**0**	**0**	**0**	**49**	**8.2**	**–1**	**13**	**46.2**	**14:21**	....	....	....	....	....	....	....	....	....
	Portland Pirates	AHL	30	9	17	26	74	....	....	....	....	....	....	....	....	....	....	....	....	....	....	....	....	....	....
	Hamilton	AHL	9	0	1	1	7	....	....	....	....	....	....	....	....	....	3	0	0	0	0	....	....	....	....
99-2000	**Edmonton**	**NHL**	**17**	**3**	**2**	**5**	**8**	**0**	**0**	**1**	**18**	**16.7**	**–1**	**1**	**100.0**	**9:44**	**4**	[illegible]	**1**	**1**	**2**	**0**	**0**	**0**	**8:40**
	Hamilton	AHL	58	22	52	74	108	....	....	....	....	....	....	....	....	....	5	2	3	5	18	....	....	....	....
2000-01	**Edmonton**	**NHL**	**81**	**14**	**21**	**35**	**37**	**2**	**0**	**2**	**107**	**13.1**	**5**	**13**	**23.1**	**12:58**	**6**	**1**	**1**	**2**	**8**	**1**	**0**	**0**	**14:09**
2001-02	**Edmonton**	**NHL**	**65**	**10**	**19**	**29**	**51**	**2**	**1**	**1**	**75**	**13.3**	**–1**	**5**	**60.0**	**12:43**	....	....	....	....	....	....	....	....	....
2002-03	**Edmonton**	**NHL**	**57**	**4**	**13**	**17**	**31**	**0**	**0**	**1**	**89**	**4.5**	**5**	**5**	**40.0**	**11:58**	....	....	....	....	....	....	....	....	....
2003-04	**Phoenix**	**NHL**	**68**	**6**	**11**	**17**	**42**	**0**	**3**	**0**	**83**	**7.2**	**–8**	**51**	**39.2**	**13:12**	....	....	....	....	....	....	....	....	....
2004-05	Mora IK	Sweden	47	11	26	37	138	....	....	....	....	....	....	....	....	....	....	....	....	....	....	....	....	....	....
2005-06	**Detroit**	**NHL**	**77**	**3**	**12**	**15**	**40**	**0**	**0**	**1**	**106**	**2.8**	**5**	**286**	**45.8**	**10:30**	[illegible]	**0**	**1**	**1**	**6**	**0**	**0**	**0**	**10:44**
2006-07	**Detroit**	**NHL**	**71**	**20**	**20**	**40**	**24**	**6**	**2**	**5**	**135**	**14.8**	**6**	**411**	**51.1**	**15:28**	**18**	**4**	**8**	**12**	**30**	[illegible]	**2**	**0**	**16:28**
2007-08♦	**Detroit**	**NHL**	**63**	**20**	**22**	**42**	**33**	**5**	**0**	**3**	**177**	**11.3**	**21**	**110**	**50.9**	**17:23**	**22**	**2**	**1**	**3**	**4**	**0**	**1**	**0**	**17:50**
	NHL Totals		**540**	**84**	**125**	**209**	**290**	**15**	**6**	**14**	**843**	**10.0**		**895**	**48.3**	**13:21**	**56**	**7**	**12**	**19**	**50**	**2**	**3**	**0**	**15:35**

OHL All-Rookie Team (1995) • OHL First All-Star Team (1996, 1997) • AHL Second All-Star Team (2000)

Traded to **Edmonton** by **Chicago** with Chad Kilger, Ethan Moreau and Christian Laflamme for Boris Mironov, Dean McAmmond and Jonas Elofsson, March 20, 1999. Signed as a free agent by **Phoenix**, July 15, 2003. Signed as a free agent by **Mora** (Sweden), September 6, 2004. Signed as a free agent by **Detroit**, October 4, 2005.

Diamond (♦) indicates member of Stanley Cup-winning team.

"Did not play" Indicates that a player did not participate in a professional, junior or college league for an entire season.

Asterisks (*) indicates league leader in individual statistical categories.

All trades, free agent signings and other transactions involving NHL clubs are listed in chronological order. First draft selection for players who re-enter the NHL Entry Draft is noted here. Other special notes are also listed here. These are highlighted with a bullet (•).

Dates for trades or free agent signings often differ depending upon source. Signings can be reported based on when contracts are filed with NHL Central Registry or on the date a club announces that it has made a trade or come to terms with a free agent.

All-Star Team selections and awards are listed below player's year-by-year data.

NHL All-Star Game appearances are listed above trade notes.

Pronunciation of Player Names

United Press International phonetic style.

AY	long A as in mate
A	short A as in cat
AI	nasal A as on air
AH	short A as in father
AW	broad A as in talk
EE	long E as in meat
EH	short E as in get
UH	hollow E as in the
AY	French long E with acute accent as in Pathe
IH	middle E as in pretty
EW	EW dipthong as in few
IGH	long I as in time
EE	French long I as in machine
IH	short I as in pity
OH	long O as in note
AH	short O as in hot
AW	broad O as in fought
OI	OI dipthong as in noise
OO	long double OO as in fool
U	short double O as in foot
OW	OW dipthong as in how
EW	long U as in mule
OO	long U as in rule
U	middle U as in put
UH	short U as in shut or hurt
K	hard C as in cat
S	soft C as in cease
SH	soft CH as in machine
CH	hard CH or TCH as in catch
Z	hard S as in bells
S	soft S as in sun
G	hard G as in gang
J	soft G as in general
ZH	soft J as in French version of Joliet
KH	gutteral CH as in Scottish version of Loch

THIS 77TH EDITION OF THE *NHL Official Guide & Record Book* is the tenth to include additional statistical categories for forwards and defensemen in the National Hockey League. These categories are, from left to right in the sample panel above, power-play goals (PP), shorthand goals (SH), game-winning goals (GW), shots on goal (S), percentage of shots that score (%), plus-minus rating (+/–), total faceoffs taken (TF), faceoff winning percentage (F%), and average time-on-ice per game played (Min).

To integrate this data, the Player Register has been is split into two sections. The Prospect Register presents data on players who have yet to play in the NHL. The NHL Player Register, containing more information and a photo of each player, lists all active players who have appeared in an NHL regular-season or playoff game at any time.

Goaltenders, whether prospects or active NHLers, are included in one register. With the addition of the shootout to NHL regular-season play, the column formerly used to record tie games for goaltenders has been renamed "O/T." For NHL goaltenders beginning in 2005-06, it lists overtime losses and shootout losses; previous to 2005-06, it lists tie games.

Registers (with their starting page) are presented in the following order: Prospects (273), NHL Players (344), Goaltenders (579), Retired Players (604) and Retired Goaltenders (642).

League abbreviations, page 654. Late additions to the Registers, page 603.

Some information is unavailable at press time. Readers are encouraged to contribute. See page 5 for contact names and addresses.

2008-09 Prospect Register

Note: The 2008-09 Prospect Register lists forwards and defensemen only. Goaltenders are listed separately. The Prospect Register lists every player drafted in the 2008 Entry Draft, players on NHL Reserve Lists and other players who have not yet played in the NHL. Trades and roster changes are current as of August 21, 2008.

Abbreviations: GP – games played; **G** – goals; **A** – assists; **Pts** – points; **PIM** – penalties in minutes; * – league-leading total.

NHL Player Register begins on page 344.
Goaltender Register begins on page 579.
League Abbreviations are listed on page 654.

ADAM, Luke (A-duhm, LEWK) BUF.

Center. Shoots left. 6'2", 210 lbs. Born, St. John's, Nfld., June 18, 1990.
(Buffalo's 3rd choice, 44th overall, in 2008 Entry Draft).

			Regular Season					Playoffs				
Season	Club	League	GP	G	A	Pts	PIM	GP	G	A	Pts	PIM
2006-07	St. John's	QMJHL	63	6	9	15	51	4	0	2	2	4
2007-08	St. John's	QMJHL	70	36	30	66	72	6	3	5	8	8

AHNELOV, Jonas (AH-neh-lawv, YOH-nuhs) PHX.

Defense. Shoots left. 6'3", 205 lbs. Born, Huddinge, Sweden, December 11, 1987.
(Phoenix's 3rd choice, 88th overall, in 2006 Entry Draft).

			Regular Season					Playoffs				
Season	Club	League	GP	G	A	Pts	PIM	GP	G	A	Pts	PIM
2003-04	Huddinge IK U18	Swe-U18	6	0	3	3	8	....	....	....	....	....
	Huddinge IK Jr.	Swe-Jr.	9	0	1	1	6	....	....	....	....	....
2004-05	Huddinge IK U18	Swe-U18	2	0	0	0	2	....	....	....	....	....
	Huddinge IK Jr.	Swe-Jr.	29	3	3	6	94	3	0	0	0	2
2005-06	Frolunda Jr.	Swe-Jr.	29	4	11	15	84	7	2	4	6	22
	Frolunda	Sweden	15	0	0	0	2	....	....	....	....	....
2006-07	Frolunda Jr.	Swe-Jr.	9	4	5	9	22	8	2	3	5	8
	Frolunda	Sweden	46	1	3	4	20	....	....	....	....	....
2007-08	Boras HC	Sweden-2	1	0	0	0	0	....	....	....	....	....
	Frolunda	Sweden	51	3	4	7	30	6	0	0	0	0

AIELLO, Anthony (igh-EHL-oh, AN-thu-nee) MIN.

Defense. Shoots left. 6'1", 187 lbs. Born, Braintree, MA, May 19, 1986.
(Minnesota's 6th choice, 129th overall, in 2005 Entry Draft).

			Regular Season					Playoffs				
Season	Club	League	GP	G	A	Pts	PIM	GP	G	A	Pts	PIM
2003-04	Thayer Academy	High-MA	33	11	26	37	....	....	....	....	....	....
2004-05	Thayer Academy	High-MA	30	7	27	34	42	....	....	....	....	....
2005-06	Boston College	H-East	40	1	8	9	50	....	....	....	....	....
2006-07	Boston College	H-East	22	1	8	9	24	....	....	....	....	....
2007-08	Boston College	H-East	43	3	10	13	40	....	....	....	....	....

ALBERS, Paul (AL-buhrs, PAWL) MIN.

Defense. Shoots left. 6'1", 189 lbs. Born, Melville, Sask., October 15, 1985.

			Regular Season					Playoffs				
Season	Club	League	GP	G	A	Pts	PIM	GP	G	A	Pts	PIM
2001-02	Calgary Hitmen	WHL	54	1	5	6	32	7	0	0	0	6
2002-03	Calgary Hitmen	WHL	72	4	20	24	51	5	0	0	0	0
2003-04	Calgary Hitmen	WHL	8	0	1	1	6	....	....	....	....	....
	Regina Pats	WHL	54	5	18	23	30	4	0	0	0	2
2004-05	Regina Pats	WHL	23	0	4	4	6	....	....	....	....	....
	Vancouver Giants	WHL	48	4	19	23	42	6	2	3	5	0
2005-06	Vancouver Giants	WHL	70	17	45	62	33	18	3	*16	19	8
2006-07	Houston Aeros	AHL	5	0	0	0	2	....	....	....	....	....
	Texas Wildcatters	ECHL	68	12	31	43	32	9	1	5	6	8
2007-08	Houston Aeros	AHL	69	5	16	21	26	4	0	0	0	0

WHL West First All-Star Team (2006) • Memorial Cup Tournament All-Star Team (2006) • ECHL All-Rookie Team (2007)

Signed as a free agent by **Minnesota**, July 5, 2006.

ALBERT, John (AL-buhrt, JAWN) ATL.

Center. Shoots left. 5'10", 180 lbs. Born, Cleveland, OH, January 19, 1989.
(Atlanta's 3rd choice, 175th overall, in 2007 Entry Draft).

			Regular Season					Playoffs				
Season	Club	League	GP	G	A	Pts	PIM	GP	G	A	Pts	PIM
2004-05	Cleveland Barons	MWEHL	67	34	60	94	....	....	....	....	....	....
	Cleveland Barons	NAHL	3	0	0	0	0	....	....	....	....	....
2005-06	USNTDP	U-17	19	8	15	23	25	....	....	....	....	....
	USNTDP	NAHL	36	8	15	23	23	....	....	....	....	....
2006-07	USNTDP	U-18	41	8	16	24	10	....	....	....	....	....
	USNTDP	NAHL	15	4	9	13	4	....	....	....	....	....
2007-08	Ohio State	CCHA	41	4	17	21	10	....	....	....	....	....

ALCEN, Johan (AL-sehn, YOH-hahn) COL.

Right wing. Shoots left. 6'1", 189 lbs. Born, Sandviken, Sweden, March 11, 1988.
(Colorado's 9th choice, 195th overall, in 2007 Entry Draft).

			Regular Season					Playoffs				
Season	Club	League	GP	G	A	Pts	PIM	GP	G	A	Pts	PIM
2003-04	Sandvikens IK	Sweden-4	STATISTICS NOT AVAILABLE									
2004-05	Brynas IF Gavle Jr.	Swe-Jr.	30	9	12	21	16	....	....	....	....	....
2005-06	Brynas U18	Swe-U18	2	1	3	4	4	....	....	....	....	....
	Brynas IF Gavle Jr.	Swe-Jr.	39	16	19	35	48	2	0	2	2	0
	Brynas IF Gavle	Sweden	3	0	0	0	0	....	....	....	....	....
2006-07	Brynas IF Gavle Jr.	Swe-Jr.	26	17	29	46	46	4	1	1	2	0
	IFK Arboga IK	Sweden-2	2	0	0	0	2	....	....	....	....	....
	Brynas IF Gavle	Sweden	32	0	0	0	0	1	0	0	0	0
2007-08	Brynas IF Gavle Jr.	Swe-Jr.	7	12	9	21	6	....	....	....	....	....
	Brynas IF Gavle	Sweden	39	4	6	10	14	....	....	....	....	....
	Brynas IF Gavle	Sweden-Q	10	1	2	3	2	....	....	....	....	....

ALEN, Juha (AL-ehn, YOO-haw) VAN.

Defense. Shoots left. 6'4", 218 lbs. Born, Tampere, Finland, October 25, 1981.
(Anaheim's 4th choice, 90th overall, in 2003 Entry Draft).

			Regular Season					Playoffs				
Season	Club	League	GP	G	A	Pts	PIM	GP	G	A	Pts	PIM
1998-99	KooVee Jr.	Fin-Jr.	36	6	7	13	42	....	....	....	....	....
99-2000	KooVee Jr.	Fin-Jr.	22	2	4	6	28	....	....	....	....	....
2000-01	Ilves Tampere Jr.	Fin-Jr.	42	2	12	14	62	....	....	....	....	....
2001-02	Soo Indians	NAHL	54	10	10	20	46	2	0	1	1	0
2002-03	Northern Mich.	CCHA	40	4	19	23	64	....	....	....	....	....
2003-04	Cincinnati	AHL	59	2	3	5	64	9	0	0	0	14
2004-05	Ilves Tampere	Finland	7	0	0	0	16	2	0	0	0	0
2005-06	Ilves Tampere	Finland	52	5	5	10	104	4	0	0	0	6
2006-07	Ilves Tampere	Finland	27	4	4	8	42	....	....	....	....	....
	Blues Espoo	Finland	12	0	0	0	4	....	....	....	....	....
2007-08	Lukko Rauma	Finland	49	2	1	3	56	3	0	0	0	6

• Missed majority of 2004-05 season recovering from off-season foot injury. Traded to **Vancouver** by **Anaheim** with Keith Carney for Brett Skinner and NY Islanders' 2nd round choice (previously acquired, Anaheim selected Bryce Swan) in 2006 Entry Draft, March 9, 2006.

ALEXANDROV, Yuri (al-ehx-AN-drawv, YOO-ree) BOS.

Defense. Shoots left. 6', 185 lbs. Born, Cherepovets, USSR, June 24, 1988.
(Boston's 2nd choice, 37th overall, in 2006 Entry Draft).

			Regular Season					Playoffs				
Season	Club	League	GP	G	A	Pts	PIM	GP	G	A	Pts	PIM
2003-04	Cherepovets 2	Russia-3	32	0	2	2	10	4	0	0	0	0
2004-05	Cherepovets 2	Russia-3	STATISTICS NOT AVAILABLE									
2005-06	Cherepovets	Russia	37	1	0	1	18	2	0	0	0	2
2006-07	Cherepovets	Russia	45	1	1	2	38	5	0	0	0	8
2007-08	Cherepovets	Russia	45	5	4	9	32	8	0	0	0	8

ALIU, Akim (a-LEE-00, A-kihm) CHI.

Center. Shoots right. 6'2", 200 lbs. Born, Okene, Nigeria, April 24, 1989.
(Chicago's 3rd choice, 56th overall, in 2007 Entry Draft).

			Regular Season					Playoffs				
Season	Club	League	GP	G	A	Pts	PIM	GP	G	A	Pts	PIM
2004-05	Toronto Marlboros	GTHL	68	35	50	85	197	....	....	....	....	....
2005-06	Windsor Spitfires	OHL	18	3	4	7	25	....	....	....	....	....
	Sudbury Wolves	OHL	29	7	6	13	54	6	0	1	1	7
2006-07	Sudbury Wolves	OHL	53	20	22	42	104	21	1	5	6	50
2007-08	London Knights	OHL	60	28	33	61	133	5	2	1	3	15
	Rockford IceHogs	AHL	2	0	0	0	2	....	....	....	....	....

ALLARD, Jean-Simon (a-LAHR, ZHAWN-SEE-mohn) BUF.

Center. Shoots right. 6'2", 186 lbs. Born, St. Bruno, Que., May 24, 1989.
(Buffalo's 5th choice, 147th overall, in 2007 Entry Draft).

			Regular Season					Playoffs				
Season	Club	League	GP	G	A	Pts	PIM	GP	G	A	Pts	PIM
2004-05	Jonquiere Elites	QAAA	40	19	18	37	30	10	4	13	17	0
2005-06	St. John's	QMJHL	65	4	13	17	34	5	0	0	0	2
2006-07	St. John's	QMJHL	69	12	38	50	47	4	0	1	1	4
2007-08	St. John's	QMJHL	67	16	44	60	48	6	4	8	12	6

ALMOND, Cody (al-MUHND, KOH-dee) MIN.

Center. Shoots left. 6'2", 199 lbs. Born, Calgary, Alta., July 24, 1989.
(Minnesota's 3rd choice, 140th overall, in 2007 Entry Draft).

			Regular Season					Playoffs				
Season	Club	League	GP	G	A	Pts	PIM	GP	G	A	Pts	PIM
2004-05	Cgy. Stampeders	SAMHL	30	28	15	43	108	....	....	....	....	....
2005-06	Kelowna Rockets	WHL	23	2	1	3	7	8	0	0	0	0
2006-07	Kelowna Rockets	WHL	68	15	28	43	72	....	....	....	....	....
2007-08	Kelowna Rockets	WHL	69	22	34	56	114	7	1	2	3	2

ALZNER, Karl (ALZ-nuhr, KARL) WSH.

Defense. Shoots left. 6'2", 205 lbs. Born, Burnaby, B.C., September 24, 1988.
(Washington's 1st choice, 5th overall, in 2007 Entry Draft).

			Regular Season					Playoffs				
Season	Club	League	GP	G	A	Pts	PIM	GP	G	A	Pts	PIM
2002-03	Burnaby W.C.	Minor-BC	64	17	31	48	24	....	....	....	....	....
2003-04	Richmond	PIJHL	41	3	9	12	8	13	0	2	2	0
	Calgary Hitmen	WHL	1	0	0	0	0	....	....	....	....	....
2004-05	Calgary Hitmen	WHL	66	0	10	10	19	12	0	3	3	9
2005-06	Calgary Hitmen	WHL	70	4	20	24	28	13	1	3	4	4
2006-07	Calgary Hitmen	WHL	63	8	39	47	32	18	1	12	13	4
2007-08	Calgary Hitmen	WHL	60	7	29	36	15	16	6	2	8	4

WHL East Second All-Star Team (2007) • WHL East First All-Star Team (2008) • WHL Defenseman of the Year (2008) • WHL Player of the Year (2008) • Canadian Major Junior First All-Star Team (2008) • Canadian Major Junior Defenseman of the Year (2008)

ANDERSEN, Niclas (AN-duhr-suhn, NIHK-luhs) L.A.

Defense. Shoots left. 6'1", 207 lbs. Born, Grums, Sweden, April 28, 1988.
(Los Angeles' 6th choice, 114th overall, in 2006 Entry Draft).

			Regular Season					Playoffs				
Season	Club	League	GP	G	A	Pts	PIM	GP	G	A	Pts	PIM
2003-04	Grums IK	Sweden-3	30	4	5	9	45	....	....	....	....	....
2004-05	Leksands IF Jr.	Swe-Jr.	26	3	2	5	91	5	0	2	2	2
2005-06	Leksands IF U18	Swe-U18	3	0	3	3	8	2	0	0	0	10
	Leksands IF Jr.	Swe-Jr.	36	5	6	11	214	....	....	....	....	....
	Leksands IF	Sweden-Q	3	0	0	0	2	....	....	....	....	....
	Leksands IF	Sweden	8	0	0	0	8	....	....	....	....	....
2006-07	Leksands IF Jr.	Swe-Jr.	4	1	1	2	47	....	....	....	....	....
	Leksands IF	Sweden-2	35	0	5	5	38	....	....	....	....	....
2007-08	AIK IF Solna	Sweden-2	3	1	1	2	2	....	....	....	....	....
	Brynas IF Gavle Jr.	Swe-Jr.	5	0	1	1	35	....	....	....	....	....
	Brynas IF Gavle	Sweden	38	0	3	3	26	....	....	....	....	....
	Brynas IF Gavle	Sweden-Q	10	1	2	3	10	....	....	....	....	....

ANDERSON, Chad (AN-duhr-suhn, CHAD) MTL.

Defense. Shoots right. 6'4", 217 lbs. Born, Chisago City, MN, June 16, 1982.

			Regular Season					Playoffs				
Season	Club	League	GP	G	A	Pts	PIM	GP	G	A	Pts	PIM
2000-01	Tri-City Storm	USHL	50	0	1	1	34	7	0	1	1	2
2001-02	Tri-City Storm	USHL	60	3	10	13	53	....	....	....	....	....
2002-03	Tri-City Storm	USHL	60	8	20	28	119	3	0	0	0	10
2003-04	Alaska Anchorage	WCHA	38	2	6	8	24	....	....	....	....	....
2004-05	Alaska Anchorage	WCHA	36	4	11	15	46	....	....	....	....	....
2005-06	Alaska Anchorage	WCHA	30	3	3	6	49	....	....	....	....	....
2006-07	Alaska Anchorage	WCHA	34	7	13	20	96	....	....	....	....	....
	Las Vegas	ECHL	2	0	0	0	0	....	....	....	....	....
2007-08	Philadelphia	AHL	55	2	11	13	35	12	0	2	2	8

Signed as a free agent by **Montreal**, August 6, 2008.

ANDERSON, R.J. (AN-duhr-suhn, AHR-JAY) PHI.

Defense. Shoots right. 5'11", 190 lbs. Born, Maple Wood, MN, July 16, 1986.
(Philadelphia's 2nd choice, 101st overall, in 2004 Entry Draft).

			Regular Season					Playoffs				
Season	Club	League	GP	G	A	Pts	PIM	GP	G	A	Pts	PIM
2002-03	Centennial	High-MN	24	6	35	41	10	....	....	....	....	....
2003-04	Centennial	High-MN	30	29	56	85	34	....	....	....	....	....
	Team Northeast	UMEHL	24	9	16	25	....	....	....	....	....	....
2004-05	Centennial	High-MN	28	23	36	59	....	....	....	....	....	....
2005-06	U. of Minnesota	WCHA	37	0	4	4	32	....	....	....	....	....
2006-07	U. of Minnesota	WCHA	32	0	6	6	20	....	....	....	....	....
2007-08	U. of Minnesota	WCHA	45	5	7	12	28	....	....	....	....	....

ANDERSSON, Joakim (AN-duhr-suhn, YOH-ah-kihm) DET.

Center. Shoots left. 6'2", 198 lbs. Born, Munkedal, Sweden, February 5, 1989.
(Detroit's 2nd choice, 88th overall, in 2007 Entry Draft).

			Regular Season					Playoffs				
Season	Club	League	GP	G	A	Pts	PIM	GP	G	A	Pts	PIM
2004-05	Munkedals BK	Sweden-5	STATISTICS NOT AVAILABLE									
2005-06	Frolunda U18	Swe-U18	1	0	0	0	0	2	0	1	1	0
	Frolunda Jr.	Swe-Jr.	35	9	11	20	10	7	2	5	7	4
2006-07	Frolunda U18	Swe-U18	2	1	2	3	2	6	3	2	5	28
	Frolunda Jr.	Swe-Jr.	41	20	26	46	60	8	0	7	7	4
	Frolunda	Sweden	1	0	0	0	0	....	....	....	....	....
2007-08	Boras HC	Sweden-2	33	6	17	23	26	....	....	....	....	....
	Frolunda Jr.	Swe-Jr.	6	8	2	10	30	5	6	3	9	4
	Frolunda	Sweden	9	1	0	1	2	4	1	1	2	0

ANGELIDIS, Mike (AN-gehl-EE-dihs, MIGHK) CAR.

Left wing. Shoots left. 6'1", 210 lbs. Born, Woodbridge, Ont., June 27, 1985.

			Regular Season					Playoffs				
Season	Club	League	GP	G	A	Pts	PIM	GP	G	A	Pts	PIM
2002-03	Owen Sound	OHL	65	7	10	17	81	4	1	1	2	0
2003-04	Owen Sound	OHL	66	9	9	18	118	7	4	1	5	4
2004-05	Owen Sound	OHL	41	9	10	19	126	8	3	2	5	10
2005-06	Owen Sound	OHL	68	53	25	78	167	11	5	9	14	38
2006-07	Albany River Rats	AHL	27	4	5	9	44	4	0	0	0	10
	Florida Everblades	ECHL	24	10	8	18	54	....	....	....	....	....
2007-08	Albany River Rats	AHL	74	11	16	27	151	7	1	1	2	6

OHL First All-Star Team (2006) • Canadian Major Junior Humanitarian Player of the Year (2006)

Signed as a free agent by **Carolina**, July 27, 2006.

ANIKEYENKO, Vitali (ah-nih-KEH-ehn-koh, vih-TAL-ee) OTT.

Defense. Shoots right. 6'3", 198 lbs. Born, Kiev, USSR, January 2, 1987.
(Ottawa's 2nd choice, 70th overall, in 2005 Entry Draft).

			Regular Season					Playoffs				
Season	Club	League	GP	G	A	Pts	PIM	GP	G	A	Pts	PIM
2003-04	Yaroslavl 2	Russia-3	40	2	9	11	68	....	....	....	....	....
2004-05	Yaroslavl 2	Russia-3	58	3	11	14	62	....	....	....	....	....
2005-06	Yaroslavl 2	Russia-3	19	3	5	8	20	....	....	....	....	....
	Yaroslavl	Russia	26	0	1	1	28	1	0	0	0	0
2006-07	Yaroslavl 2	Russia-3	15	1	6	7	59	....	....	....	....	....
	Yaroslavl	Russia	25	1	3	4	16	3	0	0	0	12
2007-08	Novokuznetsk	Russia	10	1	1	2	10	....	....	....	....	....
	Yaroslavl	Russia	40	4	9	13	48	16	0	0	0	20

ANISIMOV, Artem (a-NEE-see-mawv, AHR-tehm) NYR

Center. Shoots left. 6'3", 187 lbs. Born, Yaroslavl, USSR, May 24, 1988.
(NY Rangers' 2nd choice, 54th overall, in 2006 Entry Draft).

			Regular Season					Playoffs				
Season	Club	League	GP	G	A	Pts	PIM	GP	G	A	Pts	PIM
2004-05	Yaroslavl 2	Russia-3	24	3	5	8	10	....	....	....	....	....
2005-06	Yaroslavl 2	Russia-3	32	15	12	27	28	....	....	....	....	....
	Yaroslavl	Russia	10	0	1	1	4	....	....	....	....	....
2006-07	Yaroslavl 2	Russia-3	2	2	0	2	0	....	....	....	....	....
	Yaroslavl	Russia	39	2	8	10	26	7	3	2	5	4
2007-08	Hartford Wolf Pack	AHL	74	16	27	43	30	5	1	0	1	2

ANSHAKOV, Sergei (an-sha-KAHV, SAIR-gay) PIT.

Left wing. Shoots left. 6'3", 179 lbs. Born, Moscow, USSR, January 13, 1984.
(Los Angeles' 2nd choice, 50th overall, in 2002 Entry Draft).

			Regular Season					Playoffs				
Season	Club	League	GP	G	A	Pts	PIM	GP	G	A	Pts	PIM
2000-01	Dyn'o Moscow 18	Exhib.	6	7	1	8	2	....	....	....	....	....
2001-02	HK CSKA 2	Russia-3	3	3	1	4	0	....	....	....	....	....
	HK CSKA Moscow	Russia-2	46	20	12	22	10	....	....	....	....	....
2002-03	CSKA Moscow	Russia	25	1	2	3	4	....	....	....	....	....
2003-04	CSKA Moscow	Russia	33	3	2	5	12	....	....	....	....	....
2004-05	CSKA Moscow	Russia	11	0	0	0	2	....	....	....	....	....
	Ufa	Russia	23	9	3	12	4	....	....	....	....	....
2005-06	Ufa	Russia	6	1	1	2	12	....	....	....	....	....
	Dynamo Moscow	Russia	1	0	0	0	0	....	....	....	....	....
	HK MVD-THK Tver	Russia-3	1	2	0	2	0	....	....	....	....	....
	MVD	Russia	12	1	3	4	2	2	0	1	1	0
2006-07	CSKA Moscow	Russia	29	2	3	5	12	....	....	....	....	....
	Sibir Novosibirsk 2	Russia-3	2	2	1	3	0	....	....	....	....	....
	Sibir Novosibirsk	Russia	17	2	4	6	4	3	1	0	1	2
2007-08	Khabarovsk 2	Russia-3	2	0	0	0	2	....	....	....	....	....
	Amur Khabarovsk	Russia	22	4	2	6	4	....	....	....	....	....

Traded to **Pittsburgh** by **Los Angeles** with Martin Strbak for Martin Straka, November 30, 2003.

ANTTILA, Marko (AN-tih-la, MAHR-koh) CHI.

Right wing. Shoots right. 6'7", 226 lbs. Born, Lempaala, Finland, May 27, 1985.
(Chicago's 17th choice, 260th overall, in 2004 Entry Draft).

			Regular Season					Playoffs				
Season	Club	League	GP	G	A	Pts	PIM	GP	G	A	Pts	PIM
2002-03	LeKi Lempaala U18	Fin-U18	11	17	8	25	41	....	....	....	....	....
2003-04	LeKi Lempaala Jr.	Fin-Jr.	12	11	11	22	26	....	....	....	....	....
	LeKi Lempaala	Finland-4	21	18	18	36	20	....	....	....	....	....
2004-05	Ilves Tampere Jr.	Fin-Jr.	27	14	6	20	44	9	5	7	12	14
	Ilves Tampere	Finland	28	2	1	3	10	3	0	0	0	0
2005-06	Ilves Tampere Jr.	Fin-Jr.	10	4	2	6	6	2	1	1	2	4
	Ilves Tampere	Finland	50	4	3	7	46	4	0	0	0	0
2006-07	Ilves Tampere	Finland	53	2	2	4	34	7	1	0	1	8
2007-08	Ilves Tampere	Finland	56	14	9	23	90	9	2	2	4	4

ARCHER, Andrew (AHR-chuhr, AN-droo)

Defense. Shoots right. 6'4", 213 lbs. Born, Calgary, Alta., May 15, 1983.
(Montreal's 7th choice, 203rd overall, in 2001 Entry Draft).

			Regular Season					Playoffs				
Season	Club	League	GP	G	A	Pts	PIM	GP	G	A	Pts	PIM
99-2000	Oshawa Generals	OHL	47	0	1	1	24	3	0	1	1	2
2000-01	Oshawa Generals	OHL	2	0	0	0	4	....	....	....	....	....
	Guelph Storm	OHL	50	0	2	2	59	4	0	0	0	4
2001-02	Guelph Storm	OHL	58	3	10	13	76	9	0	2	2	16
2002-03	Guelph Storm	OHL	65	2	16	18	138	11	2	2	4	18
2003-04	Hamilton Bulldogs	AHL	30	0	1	1	23	3	0	0	0	0
	Columbus	ECHL	6	0	1	1	19	....	....	....	....	....
2004-05	Hamilton Bulldogs	AHL	68	1	10	11	112	3	0	0	0	2
2005-06	Hamilton Bulldogs	AHL	42	0	3	3	62	....	....	....	....	....
2006-07	Hamilton Bulldogs	AHL	16	0	1	1	24	19	0	3	3	21
2007-08	Hamilton Bulldogs	AHL	64	1	10	11	49	....	....	....	....	....

• Missed majority of 2003-04 season recovering from hernia injury suffered in training camp, September 15, 2003. • Missed majority of 2006-07 season recovering from off-season knee surgery.

ARDELAN, Mark (AHR-deh-lan, MAHRK)

Defense. Shoots left. 5'11", 202 lbs. Born, Regina, Sask., March 16, 1983.

			Regular Season					Playoffs				
Season	Club	League	GP	G	A	Pts	PIM	GP	G	A	Pts	PIM
99-2000	Brandon	WHL	63	4	16	20	60	....	....	....	....	....
2000-01	Brandon	WHL	66	2	14	16	65	6	0	1	1	9
2001-02	Vancouver Giants	WHL	66	8	29	37	50	....	....	....	....	....
2002-03	Vancouver Giants	WHL	71	13	35	48	64	4	0	1	1	0
2003-04	Prince Albert	WHL	72	19	54	73	29	6	1	4	5	0
2004-05	Portland Pirates	AHL	1	0	1	1	2	....	....	....	....	....
	South Carolina	ECHL	72	15	32	47	24	4	0	0	0	2
2005-06	Manchester	AHL	62	9	21	30	36	7	2	0	2	0
2006-07	Iowa Stars	AHL	79	8	30	38	32	11	0	5	5	4
2007-08	Wilkes-Barre	AHL	60	7	20	27	33	23	6	7	13	2

Signed as a free agent by **Pittsburgh**, July 16, 2007.

ARMSTRONG, John (AHRM-stawng, JAWN) CGY.

Center. Shoots right. 6'2", 210 lbs. Born, Unionville, Ont., February 26, 1988.
(Calgary's 2nd choice, 87th overall, in 2006 Entry Draft).

			Regular Season					Playoffs				
Season	Club	League	GP	G	A	Pts	PIM	GP	G	A	Pts	PIM
2004-05	Plymouth Whalers	OHL	52	6	13	19	39	4	0	0	0	4
2005-06	Plymouth Whalers	OHL	65	14	23	37	75	13	4	7	11	18
2006-07	Plymouth Whalers	OHL	34	8	13	21	26	....	....	....	....	....
	Peterborough	OHL	27	11	13	24	34	....	....	....	....	....
2007-08	Peterborough	OHL	65	21	36	57	77	5	0	1	1	6

ARMSTRONG, Riley (AHRM-stawng, RIGH-lee) S.J.

Right wing. Shoots right. 5'11", 190 lbs. Born, Saskatoon, Sask., November 8, 1984.

			Regular Season					Playoffs				
Season	Club	League	GP	G	A	Pts	PIM	GP	G	A	Pts	PIM
2001-02	Yorkton Terriers	SMHL	42	43	34	77	....	....	....	....	....	....
2002-03	Kootenay Ice	WHL	65	6	10	16	69	10	0	1	1	14
2003-04	Everett Silvertips	WHL	69	18	26	44	119	21	5	4	9	46
2004-05	Cleveland Barons	AHL	70	8	11	19	117	....	....	....	....	....
2005-06	Cleveland Barons	AHL	64	4	5	9	67	....	....	....	....	....
2006-07	Worcester Sharks	AHL	73	19	17	36	108	6	0	1	1	12
2007-08	Worcester Sharks	AHL	64	15	19	34	91	....	....	....	....	....

Signed as a free agent by **San Jose**, September 15, 2004.

ARNIEL, Jamie (ahr-NEEL, JAY-mee) BOS.

Center. Shoots right. 5'11", 183 lbs. Born, Kingston, Ont., November 16, 1989.
(Boston's 4th choice, 97th overall, in 2008 Entry Draft).

			Regular Season					Playoffs				
Season	Club	League	GP	G	A	Pts	PIM	GP	G	A	Pts	PIM
2005-06	Guelph Storm	OHL	61	11	8	19	30	15	2	0	2	4
2006-07	Guelph Storm	OHL	68	31	31	62	51	4	2	2	4	0
2007-08	Guelph Storm	OHL	20	9	4	13	16	....	....	....	....	....
	Sarnia Sting	OHL	40	18	16	34	22	9	2	2	4	6

ASTON, Peter (AS-tuhn, PEE-tuhr) FLA.

Defense. Shoots right. 6'1", 205 lbs. Born, Toronto, Ont., February 24, 1986.
(Florida's 5th choice, 155th overall, in 2006 Entry Draft).

			Regular Season					Playoffs				
Season	Club	League	GP	G	A	Pts	PIM	GP	G	A	Pts	PIM
2002-03	Pickering Panthers	OPJHL	45	4	20	24	52	....	....	....	....	....
2003-04	Peterborough	OHL	36	2	3	5	17	....	....	....	....	....
2004-05	Peterborough	OHL	52	0	15	15	16	14	0	4	4	6
2005-06	Peterborough	OHL	16	4	15	19	10	....	....	....	....	....
	Windsor Spitfires	OHL	49	12	21	33	21	7	2	1	3	2
2006-07	Assat Pori	Finland	21	2	1	3	14	....	....	....	....	....
	Oshawa Generals	OHL	41	8	24	32	38	9	1	7	8	8
2007-08	Rochester	AHL	56	3	10	13	35	....	....	....	....	....
	Florida Everblades	ECHL	6	1	2	3	4	2	0	1	1	2

ATKINSON, Cam (AT-kihn-suhn, KAM-ih-RUHN) CBJ

Right wing. Shoots right. 5'9", 165 lbs. Born, Riverside, CT, June 5, 1989.
(Columbus' 8th choice, 157th overall, in 2008 Entry Draft).

			Regular Season					Playoffs				
Season	Club	League	GP	G	A	Pts	PIM	GP	G	A	Pts	PIM
2005-06	Avon Old Farms	High-CT	25	15	20	35	16	....	....	....	....	....
2006-07	Avon Old Farms	High-CT	27	28	24	52	12	....	....	....	....	....
2007-08	Avon Old Farms	High-CT	28	26	37	63	10	....	....	....	....	....

- Signed Letter of Intent to attend **Boston College** (Hockey East) in fall of 2008.

ATYUSHOV, Vitali (a-tew-SHAWF, vih-TAL-ee) OTT.

Defense. Shoots left. 6'1", 205 lbs. Born, Penza, USSR, July 4, 1979.
(Ottawa's 8th choice, 276th overall, in 2002 Entry Draft).

			Regular Season					Playoffs				
Season	Club	League	GP	G	A	Pts	PIM	GP	G	A	Pts	PIM
1997-98	Krylja Sovetov	Russia	4	0	0	0	2	....	....	....	....	....
1998-99	Dizelist Penza 2	Russia-4	2	1	1	2	2	....	....	....	....	....
	Dizelist Penza	Russia-2	22	0	0	0	22	....	....	....	....	....
	Krylja Sovetov	Russia	17	1	0	1	20	....	....	....	....	....
	Krylja Sovetov	Russia-Q	21	0	5	5	50	....	....	....	....	....
99-2000	Perm	Russia	38	4	0	4	50	3	0	0	0	12
2000-01	Perm	Russia	44	3	9	12	32	....	....	....	....	....
2001-02	Perm	Russia	51	4	8	12	66	....	....	....	....	....
2002-03	Ak Bars Kazan	Russia	33	0	9	9	12	2	0	0	0	0
2003-04	Magnitogorsk	Russia	56	5	9	14	26	14	2	3	5	6
2004-05	Magnitogorsk	Russia	58	6	18	24	42	5	2	0	2	0
2005-06	Magnitogorsk	Russia	51	7	12	19	64	11	2	0	2	4
2006-07	Magnitogorsk	Russia	54	7	20	27	46	15	3	9	12	10
2007-08	Magnitogorsk	Russia	56	10	33	43	32	10	1	4	5	2

AUBIN, Brent (OH-behn, BREHNT) TOR.

Right wing. Shoots left. 5'9", 181 lbs. Born, St-Sophie, Que., June 18, 1986.

			Regular Season					Playoffs				
Season	Club	League	GP	G	A	Pts	PIM	GP	G	A	Pts	PIM
2002-03	Rouyn-Noranda	QMJHL	65	14	20	34	98	4	1	0	1	6
2003-04	Rouyn-Noranda	QMJHL	70	29	36	65	116	11	4	3	7	22
2004-05	Rouyn-Noranda	QMJHL	70	41	43	84	78	10	5	4	9	14
2005-06	Rouyn-Noranda	QMJHL	40	31	33	64	58	....	....	....	....	....
	Quebec Remparts	QMJHL	32	26	27	53	34	23	12	15	27	24
2006-07	Quebec Remparts	QMJHL	68	51	54	105	124	5	3	5	8	8
	Toronto Marlies	AHL	8	0	2	2	4	....	....	....	....	....
2007-08	Toronto Marlies	AHL	75	10	12	22	76	17	5	0	5	6

Signed as a free agent by **Toronto**, September 15, 2006.

AUBIN, Mathieu (oh-BEHN, MAT-yew) MTL.

Center. Shoots right. 6'2", 202 lbs. Born, Sorel, Que., September 18, 1986.
(Montreal's 4th choice, 130th overall, in 2005 Entry Draft).

			Regular Season					Playoffs				
Season	Club	League	GP	G	A	Pts	PIM	GP	G	A	Pts	PIM
2001-02	Antoine-Girouard	QAAA	19	5	10	15	10	....	....	....	....	....
2002-03	Antoine-Girouard	QAAA	42	19	35	54	28	....	....	....	....	....
	Sherbrooke	QMJHL	1	0	0	0	0	....	....	....	....	....
2003-04	Lewiston	QMJHL	68	19	23	42	34	7	1	1	2	2
2004-05	Lewiston	QMJHL	49	19	26	45	24	8	3	6	9	6
2005-06	Lewiston	QMJHL	70	47	56	103	63	6	3	4	7	4
2006-07	Hamilton Bulldogs	AHL	17	2	3	5	4	....	....	....	....	....
	Cincinnati	ECHL	38	12	25	37	32	10	4	5	9	10
2007-08	Hamilton Bulldogs	AHL	20	2	4	6	8	....	....	....	....	....
	Cincinnati	ECHL	47	30	27	57	56	22	8	6	14	34

AUGER, Chris (AW-zhay, KRIHS) CHI.

Center. Shoots left. 5'10", 161 lbs. Born, Belleville, Ont., December 16, 1987.
(Chicago's 8th choice, 169th overall, in 2006 Entry Draft).

			Regular Season					Playoffs				
Season	Club	League	GP	G	A	Pts	PIM	GP	G	A	Pts	PIM
2004-05	Wellington Dukes	OPJHL	44	25	30	55	16	14	9	11	20	37
2005-06	Wellington Dukes	OPJHL	47	41	51	92	46	12	8	14	22	2
2006-07	U. Mass-Lowell	H-East	34	2	10	12	6	....	....	....	....	....
2007-08	U. Mass-Lowell	H-East	33	4	10	14	16	....	....	....	....	....

OPJHL East MVP (2006)

AULIE, Keith (AW-lee, KEETH) CGY.

Defense. Shoots left. 6'6", 220 lbs. Born, Regina, Sask., June 11, 1989.
(Calgary's 3rd choice, 116th overall, in 2007 Entry Draft).

			Regular Season					Playoffs				
Season	Club	League	GP	G	A	Pts	PIM	GP	G	A	Pts	PIM
2004-05	Notre Dame	SJHL	38	2	7	9	53	....	....	....	....	....
2005-06	Brandon	WHL	38	0	2	2	32	4	0	0	0	4
2006-07	Brandon	WHL	66	1	8	9	82	11	0	2	2	14
2007-08	Brandon	WHL	72	5	12	17	81	6	0	3	3	11

AXELSSON, Anton (AHX-ehl-suhn, AN-tawn) DET.

Left wing. Shoots left. 6', 183 lbs. Born, Ytterby, Sweden, January 16, 1986.
(Detroit's 5th choice, 192nd overall, in 2004 Entry Draft).

			Regular Season					Playoffs				
Season	Club	League	GP	G	A	Pts	PIM	GP	G	A	Pts	PIM
2003-04	V.Frolunda Jr.	Swe-Jr.	28	7	10	17	14	10	2	3	5	2
2004-05	Frolunda Jr.	Swe-Jr.	33	12	30	42	14	6	2	5	7	0
2005-06	Frolunda Jr.	Swe-Jr.	12	6	11	17	2	1	0	1	1	0
	Frolunda	Sweden	39	3	3	6	8	11	0	0	0	6
2006-07	Frolunda Jr.	Swe-Jr.	2	4	2	6	4	....	....	....	....	....
	Kungalvs IK	Sweden-3	1	1	3	4	0	....	....	....	....	....
	Frolunda	Sweden	52	5	7	12	14	....	....	....	....	....
2007-08	Timra IK	Sweden	54	10	10	20	10	11	2	2	4	4

AXELSSON, Dick (AHX-ehl-suhn, DIHK) DET.

Wing. Shoots left. 6'2", 198 lbs. Born, Stockholm, Sweden, April 25, 1987.
(Detroit's 3rd choice, 62nd overall, in 2006 Entry Draft).

			Regular Season					Playoffs				
Season	Club	League	GP	G	A	Pts	PIM	GP	G	A	Pts	PIM
2003-04	Huddinge IK U18	Swe-U18	13	3	1	4	38	....	....	....	....	....
2004-05	Huddinge IK U18	Swe-U18	1	0	0	0	0	....	....	....	....	....
	Huddinge IK Jr.	Swe-Jr.	31	12	4	16	34	3	1	0	1	0
2005-06	Huddinge IK Jr.	Swe-Jr.	28	19	15	34	157	....	....	....	....	....
2006-07	Huddinge IK	Sweden-2	33	16	15	31	145	....	....	....	....	....
2007-08	Djurgarden	Sweden	47	12	13	25	44	5	1	0	1	2

AXELSSON, Emil (AHX-ehl-suhn, eh-MIHL) NYI

Defense. Shoots left. 6'3", 198 lbs. Born, Orebro, Sweden, March 19, 1986.
(NY Islanders' 7th choice, 210th overall, in 2004 Entry Draft).

			Regular Season					Playoffs				
Season	Club	League	GP	G	A	Pts	PIM	GP	G	A	Pts	PIM
2002-03	HC Orebro 90 Jr.	Swe-Jr.	27	7	9	16	2	....	....	....	....	....
2003-04	HC Orebro 90	Sweden-2	49	4	0	4	116	....	....	....	....	....
2004-05	Linkopings HC Jr.	Swe-Jr.	21	0	1	1	32	....	....	....	....	....
2005-06	IFK Arboga IK	Sweden-2	39	1	2	3	30	....	....	....	....	....
2006-07	IFK Arboga IK	Sweden-2	38	1	5	6	85	....	....	....	....	....
	Linkopings HC	Sweden	2	0	0	0	0	....	....	....	....	....
	VIK Vasteras HK	Sweden-2	5	0	0	0	2	2	0	0	0	0
2007-08	VIK Vasteras HK	Sweden-2	54	0	5	5	151	5	0	0	0	4

AZEVEDO, Justin (a-zeh-VAY-doh, JUHS-tihn) L.A.

Center. Shoots right. 5'7", 183 lbs. Born, West Lorne, Ont., April 1, 1988.
(Los Angeles' 8th choice, 153rd overall, in 2008 Entry Draft).

			Regular Season					Playoffs				
Season	Club	League	GP	G	A	Pts	PIM	GP	G	A	Pts	PIM
2004-05	Kitchener Rangers	OHL	58	18	21	39	34	15	3	1	4	14
2005-06	Kitchener Rangers	OHL	60	29	40	69	80	5	0	3	3	12
2006-07	Kitchener Rangers	OHL	50	17	39	56	42	9	4	11	15	22
2007-08	Kitchener Rangers	OHL	67	43	*81	*124	69	20	10	*26	*36	33

OHL First All-Star Team (2008) • Memorial Cup All-Star Team (2008) • Ed Chynoweth Trophy (Memorial Cup Tournament - Leading Scorer) (2008) • Canadian Major Junior First All-Star Team (2008) • Canadian Major Junior Player of the Year (2008)

BABIN, Noah (BA-bihn, NOH-ah) CAR.

Defense. Shoots right. 6', 200 lbs. Born, Palm Beach Gardens, FL, March 11, 1984.

			Regular Season					Playoffs				
Season	Club	League	GP	G	A	Pts	PIM	GP	G	A	Pts	PIM
2002-03	Green Bay	USHL	57	3	11	14	54	....	....	....	....	....
2003-04	U. of Notre Dame	CCHA	31	0	1	1	20	....	....	....	....	....
2004-05	U. of Notre Dame	CCHA	38	5	6	11	34	....	....	....	....	....
2005-06	U. of Notre Dame	CCHA	35	3	12	15	20	....	....	....	....	....
2006-07	U. of Notre Dame	CCHA	42	2	20	22	32	....	....	....	....	....
	Albany River Rats	AHL	11	1	6	7	2	5	0	0	0	2
2007-08	Albany River Rats	AHL	46	0	4	4	20	....	....	....	....	....

Signed as a free agent by **Carolina**, March 26, 2007.

BACKLUND, Mikael (BAHK-luhnd, mih-KIGH-ehl) CGY.

Center. Shoots left. 6'2", 181 lbs. Born, Vasteras, Sweden, March 17, 1989.
(Calgary's 1st choice, 24th overall, in 2007 Entry Draft).

			Regular Season					Playoffs				
Season	Club	League	GP	G	A	Pts	PIM	GP	G	A	Pts	PIM
2004-05	Vasteras U18	Swe-U18	14	5	6	11	14	4	2	1	3	2
2005-06	Vasteras Jr.	Swe-Jr.	25	15	16	31	30	....	....	....	....	....
	VIK Vasteras HK	Sweden-2	12	2	2	4	14	....	....	....	....	....
2006-07	Vasteras U18	Swe-U18	2	2	1	3	2	1	0	0	0	10
	Vasteras Jr.	Swe-Jr.	7	5	4	9	8	5	1	0	1	4
	VIK Vasteras HK	Sweden-2	18	1	2	3	14	....	....	....	....	....
2007-08	Vasteras Jr.	Swe-Jr.	9	7	6	13	20	....	....	....	....	....
	VIK Vasteras HK	Sweden-2	46	11	4	15	28	5	4	3	7	0

BACKSTROM, Nils (BAK-struhm, NIHLZ) **DET.**

Defense. Shoots right. 6', 183 lbs. Born, Stockholm, Sweden, June 29, 1986.
(Detroit's 8th choice, 290th overall, in 2004 Entry Draft).

			Regular Season					Playoffs				
Season	Club	League	GP	G	A	Pts	PIM	GP	G	A	Pts	PIM
2003-04	Stocksund Jr.	Swe-Jr.	12	1	6	7	26	....	....	....	....	....
2004-05	Djurgarden Jr.	Swe-Jr.	31	0	5	5	75	....	....	....	....	....
2005-06	Djurgarden Jr.	Swe-Jr.	41	7	11	18	70	4	0	1	1	4
	Djurgarden	Sweden	1	0	0	0	0	....	....	....	....	....
2006-07	Alaska Anchorage	WCHA	33	1	9	10	44	....	....	....	....	....
2007-08	Alaska-Anchorage	WCHA	16	1	2	3	18	....	....	....	....	....

BAGNALL, Drew (BAG-nuhl, DROO) **L.A.**

Defense. Shoots left. 6'3", 220 lbs. Born, Oakbank, Man., October 26, 1983.
(Dallas' 9th choice, 195th overall, in 2003 Entry Draft).

			Regular Season					Playoffs				
Season	Club	League	GP	G	A	Pts	PIM	GP	G	A	Pts	PIM
2000-01	Battlefords	SJHL	58	7	20	27	205	....	....	....	....	....
2001-02	Battlefords	SJHL	60	16	23	39	247	....	....	....	....	....
2002-03	Battlefords	SJHL	55	17	46	63	248	4	0	1	1	4
2003-04	St. Lawrence	ECAC	40	5	13	18	61	....	....	....	....	....
2004-05	St. Lawrence	ECAC	37	7	12	19	68	....	....	....	....	....
2005-06	St. Lawrence	ECAC	24	1	9	10	32	....	....	....	....	....
2006-07	St. Lawrence	ECAC	39	6	19	25	74	....	....	....	....	....
2007-08	Manchester	AHL	54	1	11	12	115	4	0	0	0	4
	Reading Royals	ECHL	10	1	2	3	32	....	....	....	....	....

Traded to **Florida** by **Dallas** with Dallas' 2nd round compensatory choice (later traded to Phoenix - Phoenix selected Enver Lisin) in 2004 Entry Draft for Valeri Bure, March 8, 2004. Signed as a free agent by **Los Angeles**, August 23, 2007.

BAIER, Paul (BAI-uhr, PAWL)

Defense. Shoots right. 6'3", 212 lbs. Born, Summit, NJ, February 2, 1985.
(Los Angeles' 2nd choice, 95th overall, in 2004 Entry Draft).

			Regular Season					Playoffs				
Season	Club	League	GP	G	A	Pts	PIM	GP	G	A	Pts	PIM
2002-03	Deerfield Academy	High-MA	25	2	15	17	24	....	....	....	....	....
2003-04	Deerfield Academy	High-MA	23	6	4	10	22	....	....	....	....	....
2004-05	Brown U.	ECAC	32	2	8	10	24	....	....	....	....	....
2005-06	Brown U.	ECAC	30	0	6	6	18	....	....	....	....	....
2006-07	Brown U.	ECAC	32	1	4	5	55	....	....	....	....	....
2007-08	Brown U.	ECAC	31	2	5	7	38	....	....	....	....	....
	Rochester	AHL	9	1	3	4	5	....	....	....	....	....

BAILEY, Jason (BAY-lee, JAY-sohn) **ANA.**

Right wing. Shoots right. 6', 209 lbs. Born, Ottawa, Ont., June 4, 1987.
(Anaheim's 3rd choice, 63rd overall, in 2005 Entry Draft).

			Regular Season					Playoffs				
Season	Club	League	GP	G	A	Pts	PIM	GP	G	A	Pts	PIM
2003-04	Nepean Raiders	CJHL	45	14	14	28	119	18	2	7	9	35
2004-05	USNTDP	U-18	26	3	2	5	91	....	....	....	....	....
	USNTDP	NAHL	13	2	4	6	50	....	....	....	....	....
2005-06	U. of Michigan	CCHA	27	5	2	7	57	....	....	....	....	....
2006-07	U. of Michigan	CCHA	19	0	0	0	28	....	....	....	....	....
	Ottawa 67's	OHL	35	7	9	16	88	4	0	0	0	6
2007-08	Ottawa 67's	OHL	34	8	9	17	78	4	0	2	2	11

BAILEY, Joshua (BAY-lee, JAWSH-oo-aw) **NYI**

Center. Shoots left. 6'1", 188 lbs. Born, Oshawa, Ont., October 2, 1989.
(NY Islanders' 1st choice, 9th overall, in 2008 Entry Draft).

			Regular Season					Playoffs				
Season	Club	League	GP	G	A	Pts	PIM	GP	G	A	Pts	PIM
2004-05	Clarington	Minor-ON	69	53	59	112	38	....	....	....	....	....
2005-06	Owen Sound	OHL	55	7	19	26	8	11	0	0	0	0
2006-07	Owen Sound	OHL	27	11	15	26	8	....	....	....	....	....
	Windsor Spitfires	OHL	42	11	24	35	16	....	....	....	....	....
2007-08	Windsor Spitfires	OHL	67	29	67	96	32	5	1	5	6	2

BAINES, Ajay (BAYNZ, AY-JAY)

Center. Shoots left. 5'9", 183 lbs. Born, Kamloops, B.C., March 25, 1978.

			Regular Season					Playoffs				
Season	Club	League	GP	G	A	Pts	PIM	GP	G	A	Pts	PIM
1994-95	Kamloops	Minor-BC	52	45	79	124	139	....	....	....	....	....
1995-96	Kamloops Blazers	WHL	68	14	29	43	43	....	....	....	....	....
1996-97	Kamloops Blazers	WHL	70	32	43	75	106	5	4	1	5	6
1997-98	Kamloops Blazers	WHL	72	34	25	59	88	....	....	....	....	....
1998-99	Kamloops Blazers	WHL	72	33	32	65	145	15	7	6	13	20
99-2000	Greenville Grrrowl	ECHL	67	24	31	55	102	15	2	5	7	13
2000-01	Norfolk Admirals	AHL	73	18	18	36	92	9	0	1	1	2
2001-02	Norfolk Admirals	AHL	80	16	28	44	70	4	0	1	1	0
2002-03	Norfolk Admirals	AHL	74	8	14	22	108	9	2	1	3	18
2003-04	Norfolk Admirals	AHL	80	15	27	42	81	8	1	3	4	13
2004-05	Norfolk Admirals	AHL	70	7	16	23	60	6	3	2	5	16
2005-06	Norfolk Admirals	AHL	32	4	4	8	45	....	....	....	....	....
	Omaha	AHL	24	8	4	12	26	....	....	....	....	....
2006-07	Hamilton Bulldogs	AHL	77	13	13	26	72	22	6	4	10	8
2007-08	Hamilton Bulldogs	AHL	58	6	3	9	61	....	....	....	....	....

Signed as a free agent by **Chicago**, August 1, 2001. Signed as a free agent by **Hamilton** (AHL), August 4, 2006.

BALAN, Stanislav (BAY-luhn, STAN-ihs-lahv) **NSH.**

Center. Shoots left. 6'2", 161 lbs. Born, Hodonin, Czech., January 30, 1986.
(Nashville's 8th choice, 209th overall, in 2004 Entry Draft).

			Regular Season					Playoffs				
Season	Club	League	GP	G	A	Pts	PIM	GP	G	A	Pts	PIM
2001-02	HC Zlin Jr.	CzRep-Jr.	48	21	23	44	60	4	1	1	2	0
2002-03	HC Zlin Jr.	CzRep-Jr.	35	24	21	45	59	3	2	0	2	16
2003-04	HC Zlin Jr.	CzRep-Jr.	53	23	33	56	122	5	2	0	2	31
	HC Hame Zlin	CzRep	4	1	0	1	0	....	....	....	....	....
2004-05	SHK Hodonin	CzRep-3	5	3	2	5	20	....	....	....	....	....
	HC Zlin Jr.	CzRep-Jr.	37	10	13	23	131	2	0	0	0	2
2005-06	Portland	WHL	67	14	23	37	102	12	1	4	5	18
2006-07	HC Hame Zlin	CzRep	44	4	3	7	48	5	0	0	0	2
	Trebic	CzRep-2	7	3	2	5	12	....	....	....	....	....
2007-08	RI Okna Zlin	CzRep	57	4	6	10	54	....	....	....	....	....

BALDWIN, Gord (BAHLD-wihn, GOHRD) **CGY.**

Defense. Shoots left. 6'5", 205 lbs. Born, Winnipeg, Man., March 1, 1987.
(Calgary's 2nd choice, 69th overall, in 2005 Entry Draft).

			Regular Season					Playoffs				
Season	Club	League	GP	G	A	Pts	PIM	GP	G	A	Pts	PIM
2003-04	Wpg. Thrashers	MMHL	39	5	16	21	66	....	....	....	....	....
2004-05	Medicine Hat	WHL	66	3	8	11	73	....	....	....	....	....
2005-06	Medicine Hat	WHL	71	4	20	24	119	13	0	9	9	22
2006-07	Medicine Hat	WHL	53	7	19	26	70	23	2	6	8	32
2007-08	Quad City Flames	AHL	37	0	5	5	26	....	....	....	....	....
	Las Vegas	ECHL	12	0	1	1	9	....	....	....	....	....

BARANOV, Konstantin (buh-RA-nawf, KAWN-stan-tihn) **PHI.**

Right wing. Shoots left. 6'2", 185 lbs. Born, Omsk, USSR, January 11, 1982.
(Philadelphia's 3rd choice, 126th overall, in 2002 Entry Draft).

			Regular Season					Playoffs				
Season	Club	League	GP	G	A	Pts	PIM	GP	G	A	Pts	PIM
1998-99	Omsk 2	Russia-4	23	18	8	26	40	....	....	....	....	....
	Avangard Omsk	Russia	1	0	0	0	0	2	0	0	0	0
99-2000	Omsk 2	Russia-3	33	15	8	23	46	....	....	....	....	....
	Avangard Omsk	Russia	1	0	0	0	2	....	....	....	....	....
2000-01	Kristall Saratov	Russia-2	26	6	9	15	26	....	....	....	....	....
	Ufa	Russia	8	1	0	1	4	....	....	....	....	....
2001-02	Avangard Omsk	Russia	5	0	0	0	6	....	....	....	....	....
	Mechel	Russia	6	1	2	3	2	....	....	....	....	....
	Lada Togliatti	Russia	20	2	4	6	18	3	0	2	2	0
2002-03	Avangard Omsk	Russia	6	0	1	1	2	....	....	....	....	....
	Ufa	Russia	11	2	2	4	0	....	....	....	....	....
	CSKA Moscow	Russia	14	4	1	5	10	....	....	....	....	....
	Omsk 2	Russia-3	3	4	6	10	2	....	....	....	....	....
2003-04	Avangard Omsk	Russia	51	6	10	16	50	11	2	2	4	6
2004-05	Omsk 2	Russia-3	7	5	7	12	20	....	....	....	....	....
	Avangard Omsk	Russia	21	3	2	5	16	....	....	....	....	....
2005-06	Dynamo Moscow	Russia	19	0	5	5	10	....	....	....	....	....
	SKA St. Petersburg	Russia	12	1	2	3	18	3	0	0	0	2
2006-07	Amur Khabarovsk	Russia	7	0	1	1	16	....	....	....	....	....
	Novokuznetsk	Russia	21	2	2	4	28	3	3	1	4	0
2007-08	Avtomobilist	Russia-2	4	0	0	0	26	....	....	....	....	....
	Avtomobilist 2	Russia-3	6	3	2	5	10	....	....	....	....	....
	HK Dmitrov	Russia-2	33	5	14	19	56	2	1	0	1	0

BARBERIO, Mark (bahr-BAIR-ee-oh, MAHRK) **T.B.**

Defense. Shoots left. 6', 201 lbs. Born, Montreal, Que., March 23, 1990.
(Tampa Bay's 5th choice, 152nd overall, in 2008 Entry Draft).

			Regular Season					Playoffs				
Season	Club	League	GP	G	A	Pts	PIM	GP	G	A	Pts	PIM
2005-06	Lac St-Louis Lions	QAAA	43	2	12	14	80	10	1	7	8	26
2006-07	Cape Breton	QMJHL	41	2	8	10	42	....	....	....	....	....
	Moncton Wildcats	QMJHL	19	1	6	7	21	7	0	2	2	8
2007-08	Moncton Wildcats	QMJHL	70	11	35	46	75	....	....	....	....	....

BARNES, Joe (BAHRNZ, JOH) **NYR**

Center. Shoots left. 6'3", 225 lbs. Born, Winnipeg, Man., June 16, 1986.
(Carolina's 3rd choice, 64th overall, in 2005 Entry Draft).

			Regular Season					Playoffs				
Season	Club	League	GP	G	A	Pts	PIM	GP	G	A	Pts	PIM
2001-02	Winnipeg Sharks	MMHL	STATISTICS NOT AVAILABLE									
	Saskatoon Blades	WHL	1	0	0	0	0	....	....	....	....	....
2002-03	Saskatoon Blades	WHL	54	9	7	16	48	....	....	....	....	....
2003-04	Saskatoon Blades	WHL	58	5	17	22	90	....	....	....	....	....
2004-05	Saskatoon Blades	WHL	72	30	32	62	73	4	0	1	1	0
2005-06	Saskatoon Blades	WHL	55	25	27	52	55	7	2	4	6	8
2006-07	Albany River Rats	AHL	15	2	1	3	19	....	....	....	....	....
2007-08	Charlotte	ECHL	5	2	1	3	8	....	....	....	....	....

Traded to **NY Rangers** by **Carolina** with Andrew Hutchinson and Carolina's 3rd round choice (Evgeny Grachev) in 2008 Entry Draft for Matt Cullen, July 17, 2007. • Missed majority of 2007-08 season recovering from knee injury.

BARRIBALL, Jay (BEHR-ih-bahl, JAY) **ST.L.**

Left wing. Shoots left. 5'9", 155 lbs. Born, Prior Lake, MN, May 27, 1987.
(San Jose's 6th choice, 203rd overall, in 2006 Entry Draft).

			Regular Season					Playoffs				
Season	Club	League	GP	G	A	Pts	PIM	GP	G	A	Pts	PIM
2004-05	Holy Angels	High-MN	30	32	49	81	....	....	....	....	....	....
2005-06	Holy Angels	High-MN	20	28	38	66		....	....	....	....	....
	Sioux Falls	USHL	13	5	7	12	2	5	2	1	3	0
2006-07	U. of Minnesota	WCHA	44	20	23	43	16	....	....	....	....	....
2007-08	U. of Minnesota	WCHA	41	6	15	21	34	....	....	....	....	....

Traded to **St. Louis** by **San Jose** with Ville Nieminen and New Jersey's 1st round choice (previously acquired, St. Louis selected David Perron) in 2007 Entry Draft for Bill Guerin, February 27, 2007.

BARTKOWSKI, Matthew (bahrt-KOW-skee, MA-thew) **FLA.**

Defense. Shoots left. 6'1", 196 lbs. Born, Pittsburgh, PA, June 4, 1988.
(Florida's 5th choice, 190th overall, in 2008 Entry Draft).

			Regular Season					Playoffs				
Season	Club	League	GP	G	A	Pts	PIM	GP	G	A	Pts	PIM
2006-07	Lincoln Stars	USHL	57	3	6	9	95	3	0	0	0	2
2007-08	Lincoln Stars	USHL	60	4	37	41	135	8	1	4	5	10

• Signed Letter of Intent to attend **Ohio State University** (CCHA) in fall of 2008.

BARTULIS, Oskars (bahr-TEW-lihs, AWZ-kahrz) **PHI.**

Defense. Shoots left. 6'2", 195 lbs. Born, Ogre, Latvia, January 21, 1987.
(Philadelphia's 2nd choice, 91st overall, in 2005 Entry Draft).

			Regular Season					Playoffs				
Season	Club	League	GP	G	A	Pts	PIM	GP	G	A	Pts	PIM
2001-02	Prizma '83 Riga	EEHL-B	3	0	1	1	2	....	....	....	....	....
	Prizma '83 Riga	Latvia	6	0	1	1	2	....	....	....	....	....
2002-03	Prizma '83 Riga	EEHL-B	12	5	5	10	12	....	....	....	....	....
	Vilki Riga	Latvia	....	0	1	1	12	....	....	....	....	....
2003-04	CSKA Moscow 2	Russia-3	65	3	9	12	....	....	....	....	....	....
2004-05	Moncton Wildcats	QMJHL	62	5	19	24	55	12	1	1	2	16
2005-06	Moncton Wildcats	QMJHL	54	6	25	31	84	21	1	9	10	22
2006-07	Cape Breton	QMJHL	55	13	35	48	52	16	3	9	12	24
2007-08	Philadelphia	AHL	57	1	20	21	42	....	....	....	....	....

QMJHL All-Rookie Team (2005) • Canadian Major Junior All-Rookie Team (2005) • QMJHL Second All-Star Team (2007)

BASHKIROV, Ruslan (bash-KIHR-ahv, roos-LAHN) OTT.

Left wing. Shoots left. 5'11", 199 lbs. Born, Moscow, USSR, March 7, 1989.
(Ottawa's 2nd choice, 60th overall, in 2007 Entry Draft).

			Regular Season					Playoffs				
Season	Club	League	GP	G	A	Pts	PIM	GP	G	A	Pts	PIM
2005-06	Spartak Moscow 2	Russia-3	35	16	9	25	44	....	....	....	....	....
2006-07	Quebec Remparts	QMJHL	64	30	37	67	117	5	1	3	4	6
2007-08	Mytischi	Russia	4	0	0	0	0	....	....	....	....	....
	Kristall Elektrostal	Russia-2	12	4	0	4	22	....	....	....	....	....

Signed as a free agent by **Mytischi** (Russia), August 23, 2007.

BEACH, Kyle (BEECH, KIGH-uhl) CHI.

Center. Shoots right. 6'3", 203 lbs. Born, Vancouver, B.C., January 13, 1990.
(Chicago's 1st choice, 11th overall, in 2008 Entry Draft).

			Regular Season					Playoffs				
Season	Club	League	GP	G	A	Pts	PIM	GP	G	A	Pts	PIM
2005-06	Okanagan Rockets	Minor-BC	25	23	18	41	220	....	....	....	....	....
	Everett Silvertips	WHL	4	2	1	3	4	9	1	3	4	31
2006-07	Everett Silvertips	WHL	65	29	32	61	196	11	5	6	11	19
2007-08	Everett Silvertips	WHL	60	27	33	60	222	4	0	0	0	4

BEAGLE, Jay (BEE-guhl, JAY) WSH.

Right wing. Shoots right. 6'3", 207 lbs. Born, Calgary, Alta., October 16, 1985.

			Regular Season					Playoffs				
Season	Club	League	GP	G	A	Pts	PIM	GP	G	A	Pts	PIM
2003-04	Calgary Royals	AJHL	58	10	27	37	100	....	....	....	....	....
2004-05	Calgary Royals	AJHL	64	28	42	70	114	....	....	....	....	....
2005-06	Alaska Anchorage	WCHA	31	4	6	10	40	....	....	....	....	....
2006-07	Alaska Anchorage	WCHA	36	10	10	20	93	....	....	....	....	....
	Idaho Steelheads	ECHL	8	2	8	10	4	18	1	2	3	22
2007-08	Hershey Bears	AHL	64	19	18	37	41	5	0	1	1	2

Signed as a free agent by **Washington**, March 26, 2008.

BEARSON, Zach (BEER-suhn, ZAK) FLA.

Right wing. Shoots right. 6'1", 180 lbs. Born, Houston, TX, June 13, 1987.
(Florida's 8th choice, 224th overall, in 2005 Entry Draft).

			Regular Season					Playoffs				
Season	Club	League	GP	G	A	Pts	PIM	GP	G	A	Pts	PIM
2002-03	Team Illinois	MWEHL	....	21	29	50	....	....	....	....	....	....
2003-04	Waterloo	USHL	53	7	11	18	65	9	4	1	5	12
2004-05	Waterloo	USHL	51	18	18	36	56	5	0	1	1	2
2005-06	Waterloo	USHL	56	13	21	34	73	....	....	....	....	....
2006-07	U. of Wisconsin	WCHA	5	0	0	0	2	....	....	....	....	....
2007-08	U. of Wisconsin	WCHA	1	0	0	0	0	....	....	....	....	....

BEAULIEU, Josh (BOI-loh, JAWSH) PHI.

Right wing. Shoots left. 6'1", 180 lbs. Born, Windsor, Ont., January 10, 1987.
(Philadelphia's 4th choice, 152nd overall, in 2005 Entry Draft).

			Regular Season					Playoffs				
Season	Club	League	GP	G	A	Pts	PIM	GP	G	A	Pts	PIM
2003-04	London Knights	OHL	41	3	6	9	32	9	0	0	0	5
2004-05	London Knights	OHL	65	9	13	22	159	13	2	3	5	13
2005-06	London Knights	OHL	60	15	13	28	140	18	4	5	9	12
2006-07	London Knights	OHL	44	10	6	16	93	10	3	6	9	31
2007-08	Philadelphia	AHL	50	3	3	6	50	....	....	....	....	....

BEAVERSON, Luke (BEE-vuhr-suhn, LEWK) FLA.

Defense. Shoots left. 6'4", 208 lbs. Born, St. Paul, MN, December 11, 1984.
(Florida's 7th choice, 283rd overall, in 2004 Entry Draft).

			Regular Season					Playoffs				
Season	Club	League	GP	G	A	Pts	PIM	GP	G	A	Pts	PIM
2003-04	Green Bay	USHL	57	1	6	7	141	....	....	....	....	....
2004-05	Alaska Anchorage	WCHA	37	0	2	2	48	....	....	....	....	....
2005-06	Alaska Anchorage	WCHA	34	1	3	4	53	....	....	....	....	....
2006-07	Alaska Anchorage	WCHA	37	5	4	9	44	....	....	....	....	....
2007-08	Alaska-Anchorage	WCHA	30	1	2	3	24	....	....	....	....	....
	Rochester	AHL	6	0	0	0	13	....	....	....	....	....

BELESKEY, Matt (beh-LEH-skee, MAT) ANA.

Left wing. Shoots left. 6', 206 lbs. Born, Windsor, Ont., June 7, 1988.
(Anaheim's 4th choice, 112th overall, in 2006 Entry Draft).

			Regular Season					Playoffs				
Season	Club	League	GP	G	A	Pts	PIM	GP	G	A	Pts	PIM
2004-05	Belleville Bulls	OHL	68	10	13	23	118	5	0	0	0	18
2005-06	Belleville Bulls	OHL	61	20	20	40	119	6	1	2	3	10
2006-07	Belleville Bulls	OHL	66	27	41	68	124	15	4	10	14	18
2007-08	Belleville Bulls	OHL	62	41	49	90	106	21	12	21	33	23

BELLAMY, Rob (BEHL-ah-mee, RAWB) PHI.

Right wing. Shoots right. 6', 205 lbs. Born, Providence, RI, May 30, 1985.
(Philadelphia's 1st choice, 92nd overall, in 2004 Entry Draft).

			Regular Season					Playoffs				
Season	Club	League	GP	G	A	Pts	PIM	GP	G	A	Pts	PIM
2002-03	Berkshire Bears	High-MA	32	21	21	42	128	....	....	....	....	....
2003-04	N.E. Jr. Coyotes	EJHL	36	19	21	40	95	....	....	....	....	....
2004-05	U. of Maine	H-East	28	3	4	7	34	....	....	....	....	....
2005-06	U. of Maine	H-East	40	6	9	15	77	....	....	....	....	....
2006-07	U. of Maine	H-East	37	1	7	8	82	....	....	....	....	....
2007-08	U. of Maine	H-East	33	5	13	18	61	....	....	....	....	....
	Philadelphia	AHL	1	0	0	0	0	....	....	....	....	....

BELLEMORE, Brett (BEHL-mohr, BREHT) CAR.

Defense. Shoots right. 6'4", 205 lbs. Born, Windsor, Ont., June 25, 1988.
(Carolina's 5th choice, 162nd overall, in 2007 Entry Draft).

			Regular Season					Playoffs				
Season	Club	League	GP	G	A	Pts	PIM	GP	G	A	Pts	PIM
2005-06	Plymouth Whalers	OHL	46	0	0	0	16	10	0	0	0	0
2006-07	Plymouth Whalers	OHL	50	0	12	12	50	20	0	5	5	28
2007-08	Plymouth Whalers	OHL	56	6	18	24	70	4	0	2	2	8
	Albany River Rats	AHL	4	0	0	0	6	5	0	0	0	6

BELLER, Greg (BEHL-uhr, GREHG) NYR

Wing. Shoots right. 6'3", 210 lbs. Born, Vancouver, B.C., January 22, 1987.
(NY Rangers' 8th choice, 178th overall, in 2005 Entry Draft).

			Regular Season					Playoffs				
Season	Club	League	GP	G	A	Pts	PIM	GP	G	A	Pts	PIM
2004-05	Lake of the Woods	High-MN	21	23	25	48	38	....	....	....	....	....
	Borderland	SIJHL	6	2	5	7	0	2	0	1	1	2
2005-06	Green Bay	USHL	3	1	0	1	2	....	....	....	....	....
2006-07	Yale	ECAC	24	2	3	5	18	....	....	....	....	....
2007-08	Yale	ECAC	2	0	0	0	2	....	....	....	....	....

• Missed majority of 2005-06 season recovering from collarbone injury suffered during the pre-season and re-injured in game at Chicago (USHL), November 29, 2005.

BENDFELD, Jordan (BENHD-felhd, JOHR-dahn) EDM.

Defense. Shoots right. 6'2", 222 lbs. Born, Leduc, Alta., February 9, 1988.
(Edmonton's 5th choice, 193rd overall, in 2008 Entry Draft).

			Regular Season					Playoffs				
Season	Club	League	GP	G	A	Pts	PIM	GP	G	A	Pts	PIM
2003-04	Leduc Oil Kings	AMHL	36	0	9	9	22	....	....	....	....	....
2004-05	Leduc Oil Kings	AMHL	21	1	5	6	96	....	....	....	....	....
	Medicine Hat	WHL	16	0	0	0	4	2	0	0	0	2
2005-06	Medicine Hat	WHL	65	2	10	12	92	13	0	4	4	27
2006-07	Medicine Hat	WHL	72	9	21	30	136	23	0	5	5	*62
2007-08	Medicine Hat	WHL	72	6	19	25	160	5	0	2	2	2

• Re-entered NHL Entry Draft. Originally Phoenix's 6th choice, 152nd overall, in 2006 Entry Draft.

BENN, Jamie (BEHN, JAY-mee) DAL.

Left wing. Shoots left. 6'2", 185 lbs. Born, Victoria, B.C., July 18, 1989.
(Dallas' 5th choice, 129th overall, in 2007 Entry Draft).

			Regular Season					Playoffs				
Season	Club	League	GP	G	A	Pts	PIM	GP	G	A	Pts	PIM
2004-05	Peninsula Eagles	Minor-BC	STATISTICS NOT AVAILABLE									
	Peninsula Panthers	VIJHL	4	1	2	3	2	2	0	0	0	0
2005-06	Peninsula Panthers	VIJHL	38	31	24	55	92	7	5	7	10	20
2006-07	Victoria Grizzlies	BCHL	53	42	23	65	78	11	5	4	9	12
2007-08	Kelowna Rockets	WHL	51	33	32	65	68	7	3	8	11	4

BENTIVOGLIO, Sean (behn-tih-VOHG-lee-oh, SHAWN) NYI

Left wing. Shoots left. 5'10", 190 lbs. Born, Thorold, Ont., October 16, 1985.

			Regular Season					Playoffs				
Season	Club	League	GP	G	A	Pts	PIM	GP	G	A	Pts	PIM
2003-04	Niagara University	CHA	39	2	19	21	14	....	....	....	....	....
2004-05	Niagara University	CHA	36	9	18	27	20	....	....	....	....	....
2005-06	Niagara University	CHA	33	16	22	38	55	....	....	....	....	....
2006-07	Niagara University	CHA	37	16	30	46	53	....	....	....	....	....
	Providence Bruins	AHL	15	3	11	14	8	13	3	6	9	14
2007-08	Bridgeport	AHL	68	9	23	32	28	....	....	....	....	....

Signed as a free agent by **NY Islanders**, May 19, 2007.

BERGIN, Mike (BUHR-gihn, MIGHK) DAL.

Defense. Shoots left. 6'3", 197 lbs. Born, Kanata, Ont., June 30, 1988.
(Dallas' 5th choice, 209th overall, in 2008 Entry Draft).

			Regular Season					Playoffs				
Season	Club	League	GP	G	A	Pts	PIM	GP	G	A	Pts	PIM
2006-07	Smiths Falls Bears	CJHL	53	10	35	45	116	11	2	7	9	18
2007-08	Smiths Falls Bears	CJHL	45	14	27	41	60	15	2	5	7	19

• Signed Letter of Intent to attend **RPI** (ECAC) in fall of 2008.

BERGLUND, Kristofer (BUHR-gluhnd, KRIHS-toh-fuhr) ST.L.

Defense. Shoots left. 5'10", 180 lbs. Born, Umea, Sweden, August 12, 1988.
(St. Louis' 8th choice, 125th overall, in 2008 Entry Draft).

			Regular Season					Playoffs				
Season	Club	League	GP	G	A	Pts	PIM	GP	G	A	Pts	PIM
2003-04	Bjorkloven U18	Swe-U18	10	4	4	8	2	....	....	....	....	....
2004-05	Bjorkloven U18	Swe-U18	STATISTICS NOT AVAILABLE									
2005-06	Bjorkloven Jr.	Swe-Jr.	38	3	11	14	36	6	0	3	3	8
	IF Bjorkloven Umea	Sweden-2	1	0	0	0	0	....	....	....	....	....
2006-07	Bjorkloven Jr.	Swe-Jr.	30	4	22	26	38	....	....	....	....	....
	Tegs SK Umea	Sweden-3	2	0	1	1	2	....	....	....	....	....
	IF Bjorkloven Umea	Sweden-2	42	0	4	4	18	....	....	....	....	....
2007-08	Bjorkloven Jr.	Swe-Jr.	1	0	0	0	0	....	....	....	....	....
	IF Bjorkloven Umea	Sweden-2	42	4	21	25	14	2	0	1	1	0

BERGLUND, Patrik (BUHRG-luhnd, PAT-rihk) ST.L.

Center. Shoots left. 6'4", 187 lbs. Born, Vasteras, Sweden, June 2, 1988.
(St. Louis' 2nd choice, 25th overall, in 2006 Entry Draft).

			Regular Season					Playoffs				
Season	Club	League	GP	G	A	Pts	PIM	GP	G	A	Pts	PIM
2002-03	Vasteras U18	Swe-U18	1	0	1	1	0	....	....	....	....	....
2003-04	Vasteras U18	Swe-U18	10	4	1	5	18	....	....	....	....	....
2004-05	Vasteras U18	Swe-U18	5	2	1	3	4	3	0	1	1	6
	Vasteras Jr.	Swe-Jr.	25	5	5	10	14	....	....	....	....	....
2005-06	Vasteras Jr.	Swe-Jr.	27	17	12	29	38	....	....	....	....	....
	VIK Vasteras HK	Sweden-2	21	3	1	4	4	....	....	....	....	....
2006-07	VIK Vasteras HK	Sweden-2	35	21	27	48	30	1	0	0	0	2
	Vasteras Jr.	Swe-Jr.	....	....	....	....	....	5	4	5	9	6
2007-08	VIK Vasteras HK	Sweden-2	46	22	32	54	26	5	1	2	3	6

BERNIKOV, Ruslan (BAIR-nih-kahf, roos-LAHN) DAL.

Right wing. Shoots left. 6'3", 216 lbs. Born, Vidnoye, USSR, December 4, 1977.
(Dallas' 6th choice, 139th overall, in 2000 Entry Draft).

			Regular Season					Playoffs				
Season	Club	League	GP	G	A	Pts	PIM	GP	G	A	Pts	PIM
1996-97	Dyn'o Moscow 2	Russia-3	32	11	4	15	20	....	....	....	....	....
	Dynamo Moscow	Russia	2	0	0	0	0	....	....	....	....	....
1997-98	Yekaterinburg 2	Russia-3	2	1	1	2	0	....	....	....	....	....
	Yekaterinburg	Russia	43	7	7	14	55	....	....	....	....	....
1998-99	Dynamo Moscow	Russia	6	0	1	1	2	....	....	....	....	....
	Krylja Sovetov	Russia	20	3	1	4	24	....	....	....	....	....
	CSKA Moscow	Russia	1	0	0	0	0	....	....	....	....	....
	Cherepovets	Russia	5	0	0	0	0	1	0	0	0	0
99-2000	Dynamo Moscow	Russia	6	2	1	3	2	....	....	....	....	....
	Amur Khabarovsk	Russia	14	3	6	9	10	5	3	1	4	2
2000-01	Amur Khabarovsk	Russia	33	1	4	5	40	....	....	....	....	....
2001-02	Amur Khabarovsk	Russia	38	7	10	17	20	....	....	....	....	....
2002-03	Krylja Sovetov	Russia	50	15	10	25	40	....	....	....	....	....
2003-04	Lada Togliatti	Russia	49	8	10	18	51	6	0	0	0	4
2004-05	Lada Togliatti	Russia	16	3	1	4	14	....	....	....	....	....
	Cherepovets	Russia	33	9	6	15	8	....	....	....	....	....
2005-06	Mytischi	Russia	21	2	3	5	40	....	....	....	....	....
	Ak Bars Kazan	Russia	5	0	0	0	0	....	....	....	....	....
	Ufa	Russia	16	3	2	5	26	6	1	0	1	4
2006-07	Ufa	Russia	32	6	3	9	14	5	1	1	2	6
	Ufa 2	Russia-3	4	4	3	7	28	....	....	....	....	....
2007-08	Sibir Novosibirsk	Russia	20	3	4	7	16	....	....	....	....	....
	Nizhnekamsk	Russia	27	8	3	11	34	5	1	2	3	2

BERRY, Alex (BAIR-ee, AL-ehx) TOR.

Right wing. Shoots right. 6'2", 212 lbs. Born, Danvers, MA, March 6, 1986.
(Toronto's 3rd choice, 153rd overall, in 2005 Entry Draft).

			Regular Season					Playoffs				
Season	Club	League	GP	G	A	Pts	PIM	GP	G	A	Pts	PIM
2003-04	Cushing	High-MA	31	19	16	35	50	....	....	....	....	....
2004-05	Junior Bruins	EJHL	53	17	25	42	170	....	....	....	....	....
2005-06	Massachusetts	H-East	24	1	1	2	33	....	....	....	....	....
2006-07	Massachusetts	H-East	29	7	6	13	34	....	....	....	....	....
2007-08	Massachusetts	H-East	34	10	7	17	63	....	....	....	....	....

BERTRAM, Dan (BUHR-truhm, DAN) CHI.

Right wing. Shoots right. 5'11", 182 lbs. Born, Calgary, Alta., January 14, 1987.
(Chicago's 3rd choice, 54th overall, in 2005 Entry Draft).

			Regular Season					Playoffs				
Season	Club	League	GP	G	A	Pts	PIM	GP	G	A	Pts	PIM
2003-04	Camrose Kodiaks	AJHL	44	22	33	55	....	....	....	....	....	....
2004-05	Boston College	H-East	39	9	8	17	58	....	....	....	....	....
2005-06	Boston College	H-East	39	10	16	26	38	....	....	....	....	....
2006-07	Boston College	H-East	40	8	17	25	48	....	....	....	....	....
2007-08	Boston College	H-East	43	10	27	37	26	....	....	....	....	....

AJHL Rookie of the Year (2004)

BERUBE, Jean-Sebastien (beh-ROO-bay, ZHAWN-seh-BAS-tee-yeh) N.J.

Left wing. Shoots left. 6'3", 185 lbs. Born, Matane, Que., July 20, 1990.
(New Jersey's 9th choice, 205th overall, in 2008 Entry Draft).

			Regular Season					Playoffs				
Season	Club	League	GP	G	A	Pts	PIM	GP	G	A	Pts	PIM
2006-07	Rouyn-Noranda	QMJHL	40	3	7	10	22	16	0	0	0	4
2007-08	Rouyn-Noranda	QMJHL	64	12	12	24	118	17	1	3	4	16

BEZRUKOV, Dmitri (behz-ROO-kahv, dih-MEE-tree) T.B.

Left wing. Shoots left. 6'3", 187 lbs. Born, Kazan, USSR, November 9, 1977.
(Tampa Bay's 11th choice, 259th overall, in 2001 Entry Draft).

			Regular Season					Playoffs				
Season	Club	League	GP	G	A	Pts	PIM	GP	G	A	Pts	PIM
1997-98	Nizhnekamsk 2	Russia-3	8	0	1	1	6	....	....	....	....	....
	Nizhnekamsk	Russia	14	5	3	8	4	....	....	....	....	....
1998-99	Nizhnekamsk 2	Russia-4	1	3	0	3	0	....	....	....	....	....
	Nizhnekamsk	Russia	39	4	6	10	18	3	1	0	1	2
99-2000	Nizhnekamsk 2	Russia-3	4	0	0	0	6	....	....	....	....	....
	Leninogorsk	Russia-2	8	2	1	3	8	....	....	....	....	....
	Nizhnekamsk	Russia	28	5	6	11	45	3	0	1	1	2
2000-01	Nizhnekamsk	Russia	35	7	10	17	54	4	0	2	2	2
2001-02	Nizhnekamsk	Russia	38	5	6	11	45	....	....	....	....	....
2002-03	Spartak Moscow	Russia	51	10	12	22	24	....	....	....	....	....
2003-04	Nizhnekamsk	Russia	17	1	3	4	10	....	....	....	....	....
	Cherepovets	Russia	8	0	0	0	0	....	....	....	....	....
	Cherepovets 2	Russia-3	12	7	10	17	20	....	....	....	....	....
2004-05	Perm	Russia	27	1	3	4	18	....	....	....	....	....
	Nizhny Novgorod	Russia-2	18	7	5	12	16	6	0	1	1	4
2005-06	Nizhny Novgorod	Russia-2	25	4	4	8	32	....	....	....	....	....
	Almetjevsk 2	Russia-3	3	2	0	2	0	....	....	....	....	....
	Almetjevsk	Russia-2	18	3	4	7	18	8	0	0	0	8
2006-07	Almetjevsk	Russia-2	36	5	8	13	65	3	0	0	0	0
2007-08			DID NOT PLAY									

BICKEL, Stu (BIH-kuhl, STEW) ANA.

Defense. Shoots right. 6'4", 215 lbs. Born, Chanhassen, MN, October 2, 1986.

			Regular Season					Playoffs				
Season	Club	League	GP	G	A	Pts	PIM	GP	G	A	Pts	PIM
2004-05	Green Bay	USHL	13	0	0	0	20	....	....	....	....	....
2005-06	Green Bay	USHL	14	0	0	0	25	....	....	....	....	....
2006-07	Sioux Falls	USHL	57	2	11	13	*215	8	0	3	3	29
2007-08	U. of Minnesota	WCHA	45	1	6	7	*92	....	....	....	....	....

Signed as a free agent by **Anaheim**, July 2, 2008.

BIEGA, Alex (bee-AY-guh, AL-ehx) BUF.

Defense. Shoots right. 5'10", 191 lbs. Born, Montreal, Que., April 4, 1988.
(Buffalo's 5th choice, 147th overall, in 2006 Entry Draft).

			Regular Season					Playoffs				
Season	Club	League	GP	G	A	Pts	PIM	GP	G	A	Pts	PIM
2004-05	Salisbury School	High-CT	27	9	22	31	45	....	....	....	....	....
2005-06	Salisbury School	High-CT	28	10	17	27	51	....	....	....	....	....
2006-07	Harvard Crimson	ECAC	33	6	12	18	36	....	....	....	....	....
2007-08	Harvard Crimson	ECAC	34	3	19	22	28	....	....	....	....	....

ECAC All-Rookie Team (2007)

BILLINGSLEY, Tim (BIHL-ihngz-lee, TIHM) PHX.

Defense. Shoots right. 6'1", 177 lbs. Born, Ottawa, Ont., January 17, 1990.
(Phoenix's 8th choice, 189th overall, in 2008 Entry Draft).

			Regular Season					Playoffs				
Season	Club	League	GP	G	A	Pts	PIM	GP	G	A	Pts	PIM
2005-06	Cumberland	Minor-ON	31	6	12	18	16	....	....	....	....	....
2006-07	St. Michael's	OHL	49	2	6	8	24	....	....	....	....	....
2007-08	St. Michael's	OHL	68	5	22	27	95	2	0	0	0	2

BIRCH, Braden (BUHRCH, BRAY-duhn) CHI.

Defense. Shoots left. 6'3", 185 lbs. Born, Hamilton, Ont., September 25, 1989.
(Chicago's 6th choice, 179th overall, in 2008 Entry Draft).

			Regular Season					Playoffs				
Season	Club	League	GP	G	A	Pts	PIM	GP	G	A	Pts	PIM
2006-07	Stoney Creek	OJHL-B	43	10	11	21	86	....	....	....	....	....
2007-08	Nanaimo Clippers	BCHL	19	0	2	2	15	....	....	....	....	....
	Oakville Blades	OPJHL	13	1	4	5	6	19	0	2	2	4

• Signed Letter of Intent to attend **Cornell University** (ECAC) in fall of 2009.

BIRNER, Michal (BUHR-nuhr, MEE-khahl) ANA.

Left wing. Shoots left. 6', 183 lbs. Born, Litomerice, Czech., March 2, 1986.
(St. Louis' 4th choice, 116th overall, in 2004 Entry Draft).

			Regular Season					Playoffs				
Season	Club	League	GP	G	A	Pts	PIM	GP	G	A	Pts	PIM
2000-01	Slavia U17	CzR-U17	48	16	24	40	20	7	0	1	1	6
2001-02	Slavia U17	CzR-U17	46	24	34	58	28	21	1	0	1	0
2002-03	Slavia U17	CzR-U17	5	5	6	11	14	5	4	3	7	20
	HC Slavia Praha Jr.	CzRep-Jr.	31	4	8	12	10	3	1	0	1	2
2003-04	HC Slavia Praha Jr.	CzRep-Jr.	55	25	35	60	112	2	0	1	1	4
	HC Slavia Praha	CzRep	1	0	0	0	0	....	....	....	....	....
2004-05	Barrie Colts	OHL	28	4	10	14	12	....	....	....	....	....
	Saginaw Spirit	OHL	31	7	21	28	29	....	....	....	....	....
2005-06	Saginaw Spirit	OHL	60	31	54	85	91	4	1	3	4	8
2006-07	Peoria Rivermen	AHL	66	11	17	28	20	....	....	....	....	....
2007-08	Peoria Rivermen	AHL	18	2	5	7	4	....	....	....	....	....
	Portland Pirates	AHL	40	7	6	13	14	15	2	1	3	6

Traded to **Anaheim** by **St. Louis** with Doug Weight and St. Louis' 7th round choice (later traded to Los Angeles - later traded back to St. Louis - St. Louis selected Paul Karpowich) in 2008 Entry Draft for Andy McDonald, December 14, 2007.

BISSONNETTE, Paul (bih-sawn-EHT, PAWL) PIT.

Defense. Shoots left. 6'2", 211 lbs. Born, Welland, Ont., March 11, 1985.
(Pittsburgh's 5th choice, 121st overall, in 2003 Entry Draft).

			Regular Season					Playoffs				
Season	Club	League	GP	G	A	Pts	PIM	GP	G	A	Pts	PIM
2001-02	North Bay	OHL	57	3	3	6	21	5	0	0	0	2
2002-03	Saginaw Spirit	OHL	67	7	16	23	57	....	....	....	....	....
2003-04	Saginaw Spirit	OHL	67	5	14	19	96	....	....	....	....	....
2004-05	Saginaw Spirit	OHL	28	1	6	7	46	....	....	....	....	....
	Owen Sound	OHL	35	2	11	13	46	8	1	3	4	2
2005-06	Wilkes-Barre	AHL	55	1	5	6	60	11	0	1	1	4
	Wheeling Nailers	ECHL	14	3	7	10	4	....	....	....	....	....
2006-07	Wilkes-Barre	AHL	3	0	0	0	6	....	....	....	....	....
	Wheeling Nailers	ECHL	65	10	32	42	115	....	....	....	....	....
2007-08	Wilkes-Barre	AHL	46	3	5	8	145	7	0	0	0	11
	Wheeling Nailers	ECHL	22	3	14	17	43	....	....	....	....	....

BITZ, Byron (BIHTZ, BIGH-ruhn) BOS.

Right wing. Shoots right. 6'5", 215 lbs. Born, Saskatoon, Sask., July 21, 1984.
(Boston's 4th choice, 107th overall, in 2003 Entry Draft).

			Regular Season					Playoffs				
Season	Club	League	GP	G	A	Pts	PIM	GP	G	A	Pts	PIM
2000-01	Saskatoon	SMBHL	40	17	35	52	....	....	....	....	....	....
2001-02	Saskatoon	SMHL	41	25	48	73	69	11	12	10	22	9
2002-03	Nanaimo Clippers	BCHL	58	27	46	73	59	....	....	....	....	....
2003-04	Cornell Big Red	ECAC	31	5	16	21	36	....	....	....	....	....
2004-05	Cornell Big Red	ECAC	29	5	10	15	20	....	....	....	....	....
2005-06	Cornell Big Red	ECAC	35	10	18	28	52	....	....	....	....	....
2006-07	Cornell Big Red	ECAC	29	8	16	24	49	....	....	....	....	....
2007-08	Providence Bruins	AHL	61	13	14	27	70	10	1	1	2	6

BIZYAYEV, Vasily (bihz-AY-yehv, va-SEE-lee) BUF.

Right wing. Shoots left. 6'1", 185 lbs. Born, Moscow, USSR, June 6, 1982.
(Buffalo's 5th choice, 213th overall, in 2000 Entry Draft).

			Regular Season					Playoffs				
Season	Club	League	GP	G	A	Pts	PIM	GP	G	A	Pts	PIM
99-2000	CSKA Moscow 2	Russia-3	20	28	14	42	22	....	....	....	....	....
	HK Moscow	Russia-2	STATISTICS NOT AVAILABLE									
2000-01	Kitchener Rangers	OHL	53	10	14	24	10	....	....	....	....	....
2001-02	CSKA Moscow	Russia	3	0	1	1	0	....	....	....	....	....
	HK CSKA Moscow	Russia-2	4	2	0	2	0	....	....	....	....	....
2002-03	MGU Moscow	Russia-3	STATISTICS NOT AVAILABLE									
2003-04	HK Rybinsk	Russia-2	13	1	1	2	2	....	....	....	....	....
	Kedr Novouralsk	Russia-2	1	1	0	1	0	....	....	....	....	....
	Desna Bryansk	Russia-4	5	1	0	1	0	....	....	....	....	....
2004-05	Krylja Sovetov 2	Russia-3	22	8	15	23	18	....	....	....	....	....
	Krylja Sovetov	Russia-2	31	3	3	6	8	....	....	....	....	....
2005-06	Krylja Sovetov	Russia-2	17	0	2	2	4	....	....	....	....	....
	HK Brest	BelOpen	9	1	0	1	10	....	....	....	....	....
2006-07	Yuzhny Ural Orsk	Russia-2	38	7	7	14	20	3	2	0	2	4
2007-08	Yuzhny Ural Orsk	Russia-2	37	7	12	19	0	....	....	....	....	....

BLANCHARD, Nicolas (BLAN-shard, NIHK-oh-las) CAR.

Center/Right wing. Shoots left. 6'3", 200 lbs. Born, Granby, Que., May 31, 1987.
(Carolina's 8th choice, 192nd overall, in 2005 Entry Draft).

			Regular Season					Playoffs				
Season	Club	League	GP	G	A	Pts	PIM	GP	G	A	Pts	PIM
2003-04	Antoine-Girouard	QAAA	42	24	28	52	28	13	9	6	15	4
2004-05	Chicoutimi	QMJHL	69	13	26	39	31	17	2	2	4	10
2005-06	Chicoutimi	QMJHL	60	15	29	44	51	9	1	2	3	4
2006-07	Chicoutimi	QMJHL	62	22	35	57	41	4	0	2	2	8
	Albany River Rats	AHL	7	1	2	3	2	5	0	0	0	2
2007-08	Albany River Rats	AHL	64	11	12	23	70	7	0	2	2	2

BLIZNAK, Mario (BLIZH-nak, MAHR-ee-oh) **VAN.**

Center. Shoots left. 6', 200 lbs. Born, Trencin, Czech., March 6, 1987.
(Vancouver's 6th choice, 205th overall, in 2005 Entry Draft).

			Regular Season					Playoffs				
Season	Club	League	GP	G	A	Pts	PIM	GP	G	A	Pts	PIM
2003-04	Dubnica U18	Svk-U18	46	25	26	51	62	....	....	....	....	....
	Dubnica Jr.	Slovak-Jr.	2	1	0	1	2	....	....	....	....	....
2004-05	Dubnica U18	Svk-U18	14	5	8	13	45	....	....	....	....	....
	Dubnica Jr.	Slovak-Jr.	36	22	17	39	38	....	....	....	....	....
	Dubnica	Slovakia	19	0	0	0	14	....	....	....	....	....
2005-06	Vancouver Giants	WHL	69	9	12	21	29	18	4	1	5	14
2006-07	Vancouver Giants	WHL	47	8	14	22	20	22	6	6	12	14
2007-08	Vancouver Giants	WHL	67	19	32	51	36	10	3	5	8	2

BLOOD, Ben (BLUHD, BEHN) **OTT.**

Defense. Shoots left. 6'3", 212 lbs. Born, Plymouth, MN, March 15, 1989.
(Ottawa's 4th choice, 120th overall, in 2007 Entry Draft).

			Regular Season					Playoffs				
Season	Club	League	GP	G	A	Pts	PIM	GP	G	A	Pts	PIM
2005-06	Shat.-St. Mary's	High-MN	73	3	22	25	32	....	....	....	....	....
2006-07	Shat.-St. Mary's	High-MN	63	11	25	36	144	....	....	....	....	....
2007-08	Des Moines	USHL	11	0	7	7	17	....	....	....	....	....
	Indiana Ice	USHL	46	10	6	16	83	4	1	2	3	14

• Signed Letter of Intent to attend **University of North Dakota** (WCHA) in fall of 2008.

BLUM, Jonathon (BLUHM, JAWN-ah-thuhn) **NSH.**

Defense. Shoots right. 6'1", 177 lbs. Born, Long Beach, CA, January 30, 1989.
(Nashville's 1st choice, 23rd overall, in 2007 Entry Draft).

			Regular Season					Playoffs				
Season	Club	League	GP	G	A	Pts	PIM	GP	G	A	Pts	PIM
2004-05	California Wave	Minor-CA	55	15	50	65	65	....	....	....	....	....
2005-06	Vancouver Giants	WHL	61	7	17	24	25	18	1	7	8	16
2006-07	Vancouver Giants	WHL	72	8	43	51	48	22	3	6	9	8
2007-08	Vancouver Giants	WHL	64	18	45	63	44	10	3	4	7	10

WHL West Second All-Star Team (2008)

BODIE, Troy (BOH-dee, TROI) **ANA.**

Right wing. Shoots right. 6'4", 196 lbs. Born, Portage La Prairie, Man., January 25, 1985.
(Edmonton's 12th choice, 278th overall, in 2003 Entry Draft).

			Regular Season					Playoffs				
Season	Club	League	GP	G	A	Pts	PIM	GP	G	A	Pts	PIM
2001-02	Central Plains	MMMHL	40	22	21	43	10	....	....	....	....	....
2002-03	Kelowna Rockets	WHL	35	4	4	8	36	11	1	1	2	2
2003-04	Kelowna Rockets	WHL	71	8	12	20	112	17	7	3	10	6
2004-05	Kelowna Rockets	WHL	72	24	24	48	96	24	4	13	17	26
2005-06	Kelowna Rockets	WHL	72	28	25	53	117	12	5	4	9	8
2006-07	Hamilton Bulldogs	AHL	20	0	1	1	29	....	....	....	....	....
	Stockton Thunder	ECHL	46	21	17	38	80	6	0	2	2	6
2007-08	Springfield Falcons	AHL	62	9	6	15	108	....	....	....	....	....

Signed as a free agent by **Anaheim**, July 22, 2008.

BODNARCHUK, Andrew (BAWD-nahr-chuhk, AN-droo) **BOS.**

Defense. Shoots left. 5'11", 185 lbs. Born, Drumheller, Alta., July 11, 1988.
(Boston's 5th choice, 128th overall, in 2006 Entry Draft).

			Regular Season					Playoffs				
Season	Club	League	GP	G	A	Pts	PIM	GP	G	A	Pts	PIM
2003-04	Dartmouth	NSMHL	58	16	23	39	81	....	....	....	....	....
2004-05	St. Paul's School	High-NH	36	3	15	18	....	....	....	....	....	....
2005-06	Halifax	QMJHL	68	6	17	23	136	11	0	2	2	22
2006-07	Halifax	QMJHL	63	16	41	57	96	12	1	10	11	25
	Providence Bruins	AHL	....	....	....	....	....	1	0	0	0	0
2007-08	Halifax	QMJHL	65	10	33	43	89	14	0	9	9	16

QMJHL All-Rookie Team (2006)

BODROV, Denis (bawd-RAWV, DEH-nihs) **PHI.**

Defense. Shoots left. 6', 185 lbs. Born, Togliatti, USSR, August 22, 1986.
(Philadelphia's 4th choice, 55th overall, in 2006 Entry Draft).

			Regular Season					Playoffs				
Season	Club	League	GP	G	A	Pts	PIM	GP	G	A	Pts	PIM
2002-03	Lada Togliatti 2	Russia-3	9	0	0	0	2	....	....	....	....	....
2003-04	Lada Togliatti 2	Russia-3	45	3	4	7	58	....	....	....	....	....
2004-05	CSK VVS Samara	Russia-2	33	1	6	7	57	....	....	....	....	....
2005-06	Lada Togliatti	Russia	35	2	2	4	42	8	0	0	0	8
2006-07	Lada Togliatti	Russia	49	1	5	6	70	3	0	1	1	6
2007-08	Lada Togliatti 2	Russia-3	8	3	4	7	38	....	....	....	....	....
	Lada Togliatti	Russia	46	2	9	11	74	4	1	0	1	2

BOEDKER, Mikkel (BAWD-kuhr, MIH-kehl) **PHX.**

Right wing. Shoots left. 5'11", 195 lbs. Born, Brondby, Denmark, December 16, 1989.
(Phoenix's 1st choice, 8th overall, in 2008 Entry Draft).

			Regular Season					Playoffs				
Season	Club	League	GP	G	A	Pts	PIM	GP	G	A	Pts	PIM
2004-05	Rodovre IK	Denmark-2	1	0	1	1	0	....	....	....	....	....
2005-06	Frolunda U18	Swe-U18	5	2	0	2	0	2	0	1	1	0
	Frolunda Jr.	Swe-Jr.	37	9	8	17	22	2	1	2	3	0
2006-07	Frolunda U18	Swe-U18	3	3	2	5	2	6	5	4	9	2
	Frolunda Jr.	Swe-Jr.	39	19	30	49	14	8	6	5	11	6
	Frolunda	Sweden	2	0	0	0	0	....	....	....	....	....
2007-08	Kitchener Rangers	OHL	62	29	44	73	14	20	9	*26	35	2

BOGOSIAN, Zach (buh-GOH-zhuhn, ZAK) **ATL.**

Defense. Shoots right. 6'2", 200 lbs. Born, Massena, NY, July 15, 1990.
(Atlanta's 1st choice, 3rd overall, in 2008 Entry Draft).

			Regular Season					Playoffs				
Season	Club	League	GP	G	A	Pts	PIM	GP	G	A	Pts	PIM
2005-06	Cushing	High-MA	36	1	16	17	....	....	....	....	....	....
2006-07	Peterborough	OHL	67	7	26	33	63	....	....	....	....	....
2007-08	Peterborough	OHL	60	11	50	61	72	5	0	3	3	8

OHL First All-Star Team (2008)

BOLDUC, Alexandre (bohl-DUHK, ahl-ehx-AHN-druh) **VAN.**

Center. Shoots left. 6'1", 178 lbs. Born, Montreal, Que., June 26, 1985.
(St. Louis' 6th choice, 127th overall, in 2003 Entry Draft).

			Regular Season					Playoffs				
Season	Club	League	GP	G	A	Pts	PIM	GP	G	A	Pts	PIM
2000-01	Notre Dame	SMHL	61	17	35	52	....	....	....	....	....	....
2001-02	Rouyn-Noranda	QMJHL	64	6	14	20	69	4	1	1	2	4
2002-03	Rouyn-Noranda	QMJHL	66	14	29	43	131	4	0	2	2	2
2003-04	Rouyn-Noranda	QMJHL	65	23	35	58	115	11	3	4	7	18
2004-05	Rouyn-Noranda	QMJHL	33	7	10	17	46	....	....	....	....	....
	Shawinigan	QMJHL	29	7	11	18	14	3	0	0	0	0
2005-06	Manitoba Moose	AHL	29	3	7	10	35	....	....	....	....	....
	Bakersfield	ECHL	24	10	6	16	56	11	4	4	8	28
2006-07	Manitoba Moose	AHL	32	4	5	9	35	5	0	0	0	8
	Bakersfield	ECHL	16	7	17	24	42	6	2	4	6	9
2007-08	Manitoba Moose	AHL	70	18	19	37	93	6	1	0	1	6

Signed as a free agent by **Vancouver**, July 2, 2008.

BOLT, Bobby (BOHLT, BAW-bee) **ANA.**

Left wing. Shoots left. 6'4", 226 lbs. Born, Thunder Bay, Ont., April 29, 1987.
(Anaheim's 4th choice, 127th overall, in 2005 Entry Draft).

			Regular Season					Playoffs				
Season	Club	League	GP	G	A	Pts	PIM	GP	G	A	Pts	PIM
2003-04	Strathroy Rockets	OHA-B	39	5	14	19	41	....	....	....	....	....
	London Knights	OHL	8	1	0	1	2	....	....	....	....	....
2004-05	Kingston	OHL	67	11	14	25	92	....	....	....	....	....
2005-06	Kingston	OHL	68	5	10	15	89	6	0	0	0	4
2006-07	Kingston	OHL	62	22	28	50	70	5	0	6	6	4
	Portland Pirates	AHL	5	1	1	2	2	....	....	....	....	....
2007-08	Portland Pirates	AHL	4	0	0	0	0	....	....	....	....	....
	Augusta Lynx	ECHL	62	15	11	26	45	5	1	0	1	7

BONINO, Nick (boh-NEE-noh, NIHK) **S.J.**

Center. Shoots left. 6'1", 180 lbs. Born, Hartford, CT, April 20, 1988.
(San Jose's 6th choice, 173rd overall, in 2007 Entry Draft).

			Regular Season					Playoffs				
Season	Club	League	GP	G	A	Pts	PIM	GP	G	A	Pts	PIM
2003-04	Farmington	High-CT	24	44	23	67	10	....	....	....	....	....
2004-05	Farmington	High-CT	24	68	23	91	12	....	....	....	....	....
2005-06	Avon Old Farms	High-CT	25	26	30	56	10	....	....	....	....	....
2006-07	Avon Old Farms	High-CT	26	24	42	66	14	....	....	....	....	....
2007-08	Boston University	H-East	39	16	13	29	10	....	....	....	....	....

BONNEAU, Jimmy (BAW-noh, JIHM-mee) **BUF.**

Left wing. Shoots left. 6'3", 214 lbs. Born, Baie-Comeau, Que., March 22, 1985.
(Montreal's 10th choice, 241st overall, in 2003 Entry Draft).

			Regular Season					Playoffs				
Season	Club	League	GP	G	A	Pts	PIM	GP	G	A	Pts	PIM
2000-01	Jonquiere Elites	QAAA	1	0	0	0	0	....	....	....	....	....
2001-02	Jonquiere Elites	QAAA	40	5	10	15	55	3	1	1	2	2
2002-03	Montreal Rocket	QMJHL	65	1	5	6	261	7	0	0	0	12
2003-04	PEI Rocket	QMJHL	70	7	12	19	263	11	1	0	1	12
2004-05	PEI Rocket	QMJHL	70	11	11	22	234	....	....	....	....	....
2005-06	Long Beach	ECHL	65	1	5	6	137	....	....	....	....	....
2006-07	Hamilton Bulldogs	AHL	9	0	0	0	59	....	....	....	....	....
	Cincinnati	ECHL	46	2	5	7	89	10	0	0	0	23
2007-08	Hamilton Bulldogs	AHL	6	1	0	1	5	....	....	....	....	....
	Cincinnati	ECHL	18	0	4	4	61	3	0	0	0	0

Signed as a free agent by **Buffalo**, August 13, 2008.

BOOGAARD, Aaron (BOO-gard, AIR-ruhn) **PIT.**

Right wing. Shoots right. 6'3", 220 lbs. Born, Newmarket, Ont., August 11, 1986.
(Minnesota's 9th choice, 175th overall, in 2004 Entry Draft).

			Regular Season					Playoffs				
Season	Club	League	GP	G	A	Pts	PIM	GP	G	A	Pts	PIM
2002-03	Calgary Hitmen	WHL	39	3	0	3	52	5	0	0	0	0
2003-04	Calgary Hitmen	WHL	12	0	1	1	24	....	....	....	....	....
	Tri-City Americans	WHL	23	3	1	4	33	6	0	0	0	8
2004-05	Tri-City Americans	WHL	65	4	11	15	96	5	0	0	0	4
2005-06	Tri-City Americans	WHL	65	6	4	10	211	5	0	2	2	4
2006-07	Tri-City Americans	WHL	69	10	11	21	173	5	1	0	1	14
2007-08	Wilkes-Barre	AHL	2	0	0	0	5	....	....	....	....	....
	Wheeling Nailers	ECHL	58	6	9	15	105	....	....	....	....	....

Signed as a free agent by **Pittsburgh**, April 23, 2007.

BOROWIECKI, Mark (boh-roh-WIH-kee, MAHRK) **OTT.**

Defense. Shoots left. 6'1", 188 lbs. Born, Ottawa, Ont., July 12, 1989.
(Ottawa's 6th choice, 139th overall, in 2008 Entry Draft).

			Regular Season					Playoffs				
Season	Club	League	GP	G	A	Pts	PIM	GP	G	A	Pts	PIM
2006-07	Smiths Falls Bears	CJHL	53	3	25	28	85	6	0	0	0	10
2007-08	Smiths Falls Bears	CJHL	46	2	24	26	80	15	1	10	11	22

• Signed Letter of Intent to attend **Clarkson University** (ECAC) in fall of 2008.

BORTUZZO, Robert (bohr-TOOZ-oh, RAW-buhrt) **PIT.**

Defense. Shoots right. 6'3", 196 lbs. Born, Thunder Bay, Ont., March 18, 1989.
(Pittsburgh's 3rd choice, 78th overall, in 2007 Entry Draft).

			Regular Season					Playoffs				
Season	Club	League	GP	G	A	Pts	PIM	GP	G	A	Pts	PIM
2005-06	F-Wm. North Stars	SIJHL	40	4	18	22	....	....	....	....	....	....
2006-07	Kitchener Rangers	OHL	63	2	12	14	67	9	1	2	3	8
2007-08	Kitchener Rangers	OHL	52	3	15	18	61	18	0	8	8	14

BOUCHARD, Francois (BOO-shahrd, frahn-SWUH) **WSH.**

Right wing. Shoots left. 6'1", 193 lbs. Born, Sherbrooke, Que., April 26, 1988.
(Washington's 4th choice, 35th overall, in 2006 Entry Draft).

			Regular Season					Playoffs				
Season	Club	League	GP	G	A	Pts	PIM	GP	G	A	Pts	PIM
2004-05	Baie-Comeau	QMJHL	54	11	13	24	13	6	1	1	2	2
2005-06	Baie-Comeau	QMJHL	69	33	69	102	66	4	1	0	1	6
2006-07	Baie-Comeau	QMJHL	68	45	*80	*125	72	11	7	11	18	4
2007-08	Baie-Comeau	QMJHL	68	36	56	92	70	5	1	1	2	6
	Hershey Bears	AHL	4	1	0	1	2	1	0	0	0	2

QMJHL Second All-Star Team (2007)

BOUMA, Lance (BOW-ma, LANTZ) CGY.

Center. Shoots left. 6'1", 210 lbs. Born, Provost, Alta., March 25, 1990.
(Calgary's 3rd choice, 78th overall, in 2008 Entry Draft).

			Regular Season					Playoffs				
Season	Club	League	GP	G	A	Pts	PIM	GP	G	A	Pts	PIM
2005-06	Wainwright	RAMHL	37	21	29	50	....	....	....	....	....	....
	Vancouver Giants	WHL	5	1	3	4	0	....	....	....	....	....
2006-07	Vancouver Giants	WHL	49	3	5	8	31	22	3	3	6	12
2007-08	Vancouver Giants	WHL	71	12	23	35	93	10	0	1	1	8

BOURDON, Marc-Andre (boor-DAWN, MAHRK-AHN-dray) PHI.

Defense. Shoots left. 6', 206 lbs. Born, St-Hyacinthe, Que., September 17, 1989.
(Philadelphia's 2nd choice, 67th overall, in 2008 Entry Draft).

			Regular Season					Playoffs				
Season	Club	League	GP	G	A	Pts	PIM	GP	G	A	Pts	PIM
2006-07	Rouyn-Noranda	QMJHL	63	2	26	28	80	16	0	4	4	21
2007-08	Rouyn-Noranda	QMJHL	69	12	47	59	114	17	2	16	18	25

QMJHL First All-Star Team (2008) • Canadian Major Junior Second All-Star Team (2008)

BOURRET, Alex (BUHR-ray, AL-ehx) PHX.

Right wing. Shoots left. 5'11", 205 lbs. Born, Drummondville, Que., October 5, 1986.
(Atlanta's 1st choice, 16th overall, in 2005 Entry Draft).

			Regular Season					Playoffs				
Season	Club	League	GP	G	A	Pts	PIM	GP	G	A	Pts	PIM
2001-02	Magog	QAAA	40	26	34	60	105	....	....	....	....	....
2002-03	Sherbrooke	QMJHL	61	13	15	28	73	12	1	1	2	10
2003-04	Lewiston	QMJHL	65	22	41	63	94	7	4	5	9	20
2004-05	Lewiston	QMJHL	65	31	55	86	172	8	6	8	14	25
2005-06	Shawinigan	QMJHL	67	44	70	114	133	7	3	4	7	14
2006-07	Chicago Wolves	AHL	45	11	21	32	46	....	....	....	....	....
	Hartford Wolf Pack	AHL	23	5	13	18	12	7	3	8	11	2
2007-08	Hartford Wolf Pack	AHL	54	9	24	33	78	5	1	3	4	17

QMJHL Second All-Star Team (2005, 2006)

Traded to **NY Rangers** by **Atlanta** for Pascal Dupuis and NY Rangers' 3rd round choice (later traded to Pittsburgh - Pittsburgh selected Robert Bortuzzo) in 2007 Entry Draft, February 27, 2007. Traded to **Phoenix** by **NY Rangers** for Pittsburgh's 3rd round choice (previously acquired, NY Rangers selected Tomas Kundratek) in 2008 Entry Draft, June 21, 2008.

BOWMAN, Drayson (BOH-muhn, DRAY-suhn) CAR.

Center/Left wing. Shoots left. 6', 181 lbs. Born, Grand Rapids, MI, March 8, 1989.
(Carolina's 2nd choice, 72nd overall, in 2007 Entry Draft).

			Regular Season					Playoffs				
Season	Club	League	GP	G	A	Pts	PIM	GP	G	A	Pts	PIM
2004-05	Kimberly	KIJHL	47	29	30	59	108	....	....	....	....	....
	Spokane Chiefs	WHL	4	0	0	0	0	....	....	....	....	....
2005-06	Spokane Chiefs	WHL	72	17	17	34	51	....	....	....	....	....
2006-07	Spokane Chiefs	WHL	61	24	19	43	55	6	2	5	7	4
2007-08	Spokane Chiefs	WHL	66	42	40	82	62	21	11	9	20	8

WHL West Second All-Star Team (2008) • Memorial Cup All-Star Team (2008)

BOYCHUK, Zach (BOY-chuhk, ZAK) CAR.

Center. Shoots left. 5'10", 180 lbs. Born, Airdrie, Alta., October 4, 1989.
(Carolina's 1st choice, 14th overall, in 2008 Entry Draft).

			Regular Season					Playoffs				
Season	Club	League	GP	G	A	Pts	PIM	GP	G	A	Pts	PIM
2004-05	Strathmore	AMHL	36	13	14	27	18	16	10	5	15	....
2005-06	Lethbridge	WHL	64	18	33	51	30	6	0	5	5	2
2006-07	Lethbridge	WHL	69	31	60	91	52	....	....	....	....	....
2007-08	Lethbridge	WHL	61	33	39	72	80	18	*13	8	21	6

WHL East Second All-Star Team (2008)

BRADFORD, Brock (BRAD-fohrd, BRAWK) BOS.

Center. Shoots right. 5'9", 168 lbs. Born, Burnaby, B.C., January 7, 1987.
(Boston's 8th choice, 217th overall, in 2005 Entry Draft).

			Regular Season					Playoffs				
Season	Club	League	GP	G	A	Pts	PIM	GP	G	A	Pts	PIM
2002-03	Richmond	PIJHL	18	12	12	24	....	....	....	....	....	....
	Coquitlam Express	BCHL	36	11	23	34	14	....	....	....	....	....
2003-04	Coquitlam Express	BCHL	57	36	49	85	....	....	....	....	....	....
2004-05	Omaha Lancers	USHL	60	24	33	57	16	5	0	1	1	0
2005-06	Boston College	H-East	42	6	12	18	8	....	....	....	....	....
2006-07	Boston College	H-East	42	19	26	45	28	....	....	....	....	....
2007-08	Boston College	H-East	5	3	2	5	2	....	....	....	....	....

BRAUN, Constantin (BRAWN, kawn-stuhn-TIHN) L.A.

Left wing. Shoots left. 6'3", 198 lbs. Born, Lampertheim, West Germany, March 11, 1988.
(Los Angeles' 9th choice, 164th overall, in 2006 Entry Draft).

			Regular Season					Playoffs				
Season	Club	League	GP	G	A	Pts	PIM	GP	G	A	Pts	PIM
2003-04	Mannheim Jr.	Ger-Jr.	30	12	5	17	42	....	....	....	....	....
2004-05	Eisb. Jrs. Berlin	German-3	1	0	0	0	0	....	....	....	....	....
	Eisb. Jrs. Berl. Jr.	Ger-Jr.	29	14	20	34	125	6	5	4	9	16
2005-06	Eisbaren Berlin	Germany	6	0	0	0	0	....	....	....	....	....
	Eisb. Jrs. Berl. Jr.	Ger-Jr.	7	8	4	12	14	1	1	0	1	6
	Eisb. Jrs. Berlin	German-3	24	13	10	23	34	....	....	....	....	....
2006-07	Eisb. Jrs. Berlin	German-3	10	4	3	7	37	2	2	1	3	0
	Eisbaren Berlin	Germany	34	1	3	4	14	....	....	....	....	....
2007-08	Eisb. Jrs. Berlin	German-3	2	0	0	0	0	....	....	....	....	....
	Eisbaren Berlin	Germany	50	4	7	11	32	14	3	7	10	2

BRAUN, Justin (BRAWN, JUHS-tihn) S.J.

Defense. Shoots right. 6'1", 180 lbs. Born, St. Paul, MN, February 10, 1987.
(San Jose's 7th choice, 201st overall, in 2007 Entry Draft).

			Regular Season					Playoffs				
Season	Club	League	GP	G	A	Pts	PIM	GP	G	A	Pts	PIM
2004-05	White Bear Lake	High-MN	STATISTICS NOT AVAILABLE									
	Green Bay	USHL	10	0	0	0	2	....	....	....	....	....
2005-06	Green Bay	USHL	59	2	11	13	69	3	0	0	0	2
2006-07	Massachusetts	H-East	39	4	10	14	20	....	....	....	....	....
2007-08	Massachusetts	H-East	36	4	16	20	20	....	....	....	....	....

Hockey East All-Rookie Team (2007)

BRENNAN, Mike (BREH-nan, MIGHK) CHI.

Defense. Shoots right. 6', 190 lbs. Born, Smithtown, NY, January 24, 1986.

			Regular Season					Playoffs				
Season	Club	League	GP	G	A	Pts	PIM	GP	G	A	Pts	PIM
2002-03	USNTDP	U-17	18	2	4	6	8	....	....	....	....	....
	USNTDP	NAHL	44	1	2	3	89	....	....	....	....	....
2003-04	USNTDP	U-17	43	2	5	7	58	....	....	....	....	....
	USNTDP	NAHL	11	2	3	5	19	....	....	....	....	....
2004-05	Boston College	H-East	40	2	6	8	46	....	....	....	....	....
2005-06	Boston College	H-East	40	2	9	11	89	....	....	....	....	....
2006-07	Boston College	H-East	42	0	11	11	89	....	....	....	....	....
2007-08	Boston College	H-East	44	3	5	8	52	....	....	....	....	....

Signed as a free agent by **Chicago**, April 16, 2008.

BRENNAN, T.J. (BREH-nan, TEE-JAY) BUF.

Defense. Shoots left. 6', 204 lbs. Born, Willingboro, NJ, April 3, 1989.
(Buffalo's 1st choice, 31st overall, in 2007 Entry Draft).

			Regular Season					Playoffs				
Season	Club	League	GP	G	A	Pts	PIM	GP	G	A	Pts	PIM
2005-06	Phi. Little Flyers	AtJHL	42	9	23	32	....	....	....	....	....	....
2006-07	Saint John	QMJHL	68	16	25	41	79	4	1	1	2	4
2007-08	St. John's	QMJHL	65	16	25	41	92	6	2	4	6	12

BRITTAIN, Josh (BRIH-tehn, JAWSH) ANA.

Left wing. Shoots left. 6'4", 210 lbs. Born, Milton, Ont., January 3, 1990.
(Anaheim's 5th choice, 71st overall, in 2008 Entry Draft).

			Regular Season					Playoffs				
Season	Club	League	GP	G	A	Pts	PIM	GP	G	A	Pts	PIM
2005-06	Tor. Jr. Canadiens	GTHL	33	19	21	40	47	....	....	....	....	....
2006-07	Kingston	OHL	54	5	12	17	38	2	0	0	0	0
2007-08	Kingston	OHL	68	28	23	51	106	....	....	....	....	....

BRODA, Joel (BROH-da, JOHL) WSH.

Center. Shoots left. 6'1", 200 lbs. Born, Yorkton, Sask., November 24, 1989.
(Washington's 6th choice, 144th overall, in 2008 Entry Draft).

			Regular Season					Playoffs				
Season	Club	League	GP	G	A	Pts	PIM	GP	G	A	Pts	PIM
2004-05	Beardy's	SMHL	44	13	13	26	28	....	....	....	....	....
	Tri-City Americans	WHL	2	0	0	0	0	....	....	....	....	....
2005-06	Tri-City Americans	WHL	51	3	1	4	10	5	0	0	0	0
2006-07	Tri-City Americans	WHL	71	16	28	44	62	6	2	0	2	0
2007-08	Tri-City Americans	WHL	3	2	1	3	2	....	....	....	....	....
	Moose Jaw	WHL	70	28	22	50	72	6	1	1	2	0

BRODEUR, Mathieu (broh-DUHR, MA-tyew) PHX.

Defense. Shoots left. 6'5", 190 lbs. Born, Laval, Que., June 21, 1990.
(Phoenix's 5th choice, 76th overall, in 2008 Entry Draft).

			Regular Season					Playoffs				
Season	Club	League	GP	G	A	Pts	PIM	GP	G	A	Pts	PIM
2006-07	Laurentides	QAAA	44	5	7	12	58	15	2	4	6	18
2007-08	Cape Breton	QMJHL	69	1	6	7	27	11	0	0	0	6

BRODIE, T.J. (BROH-dee, TEE-JAY) CGY.

Defense. Shoots left. 6'1", 170 lbs. Born, Chatham, Ont., June 7, 1990.
(Calgary's 5th choice, 114th overall, in 2008 Entry Draft).

			Regular Season					Playoffs				
Season	Club	League	GP	G	A	Pts	PIM	GP	G	A	Pts	PIM
2006-07	Leamington Flyers	OJHL-B	43	8	38	46	104	5	1	2	3	12
	Saginaw Spirit	OHL	20	0	4	4	23	3	0	1	1	2
2007-08	Saginaw Spirit	OHL	68	4	26	30	73	4	0	3	3	2

BROPHEY, Evan (BROH-fee, EN-vuhn) CHI.

Center/Left wing. Shoots left. 6'1", 203 lbs. Born, Kitchener, Ont., December 3, 1986.
(Chicago's 4th choice, 68th overall, in 2005 Entry Draft).

			Regular Season					Playoffs				
Season	Club	League	GP	G	A	Pts	PIM	GP	G	A	Pts	PIM
2002-03	Barrie Colts	OHL	61	12	14	26	36	6	0	0	0	2
2003-04	Barrie Colts	OHL	67	14	11	25	63	12	4	3	7	4
2004-05	Barrie Colts	OHL	10	3	7	10	13	....	....	....	....	....
	Belleville Bulls	OHL	53	25	36	61	42	5	2	1	3	2
2005-06	Belleville Bulls	OHL	22	9	17	26	39	....	....	....	....	....
	Plymouth Whalers	OHL	40	10	25	35	42	13	4	7	11	18
2006-07	Plymouth Whalers	OHL	68	36	71	107	91	20	9	14	23	26
2007-08	Rockford IceHogs	AHL	74	4	15	19	64	1	0	0	0	0

BROSNIHAN, Pat (BRAWS-nih-han, PAT) PHX.

Right wing. Shoots right. 6'4", 214 lbs. Born, Worcester, MA, August 20, 1986.
(Phoenix's 5th choice, 212th overall, in 2005 Entry Draft).

			Regular Season					Playoffs				
Season	Club	League	GP	G	A	Pts	PIM	GP	G	A	Pts	PIM
2003-04	Worcester	High-MA	25	28	26	54	30	....	....	....	....	....
2004-05	Worcester	High-MA	26	20	44	64	48	....	....	....	....	....
2005-06	Yale	ECAC	19	0	1	1	31	....	....	....	....	....
2006-07	Yale	ECAC	27	3	2	5	37	....	....	....	....	....
2007-08	Yale	ECAC	19	3	1	4	14	....	....	....	....	....

BRUNNSTROM, Fabian (BRUHN-struhm, FAY-bee-yehn) DAL.

Left wing. Shoots left. 6'1", 202 lbs. Born, Jonstorp, Sweden, February 6, 1985.

			Regular Season					Playoffs				
Season	Club	League	GP	G	A	Pts	PIM	GP	G	A	Pts	PIM
2002-03	Jonstorps IF	Sweden-3	STATISTICS NOT AVAILABLE									
2003-04	Helsingborgs HC	Sweden-4	....	6	7	13	....	....	....	....	....	....
2004-05	Helsingborgs HC	Sweden-4	....	18	11	29	....	....	....	....	....	....
2005-06	Jonstorps IF	Sweden-3	38	21	23	44	8	....	....	....	....	....
	Rogle	Sweden-2	3	0	0	0	2	....	....	....	....	....
2006-07	Boras HC	Sweden-3	49	38	41	79	32	2	1	3	4	0
2007-08	Farjestad	Sweden	54	9	28	37	16	12	1	0	1	6

Signed as a free agent by **Dallas**, May 8, 2008.

BUCKLEY, Brendan (BUHK-lee, BREHN-duhn) S.J.

Defense. Shoots right. 6'1", 205 lbs. Born, Boston, MA, February 26, 1977.
(Anaheim's 3rd choice, 117th overall, in 1996 Entry Draft).

			Regular Season					Playoffs				
Season	Club	League	GP	G	A	Pts	PIM	GP	G	A	Pts	PIM
1994-95	Boston Jr. Bruins	Exhib.	48	22	43	65	164	....	....	....	....	....
1995-96	Boston College	H-East	34	0	4	4	72	....	....	....	....	....
1996-97	Boston College	H-East	38	2	6	8	90	....	....	....	....	....
1997-98	Boston College	H-East	41	1	12	13	69	....	....	....	....	....
1998-99	Boston College	H-East	43	1	13	14	75	....	....	....	....	....
99-2000	Cincinnati	AHL	4	0	0	0	6	....	....	....	....	....
	Quad City	UHL	61	1	10	11	73	9	1	0	1	10
2000-01	Wilkes-Barre	AHL	63	2	8	10	62	21	0	2	2	33
2001-02	Wilkes-Barre	AHL	80	1	19	20	116	....	....	....	....	....
2002-03	Wilkes-Barre	AHL	80	2	6	8	99	6	0	0	0	2
2003-04	Wilkes-Barre	AHL	45	2	4	6	61	....	....	....	....	....
	Syracuse Crunch	AHL	30	0	4	4	40	7	0	0	0	14
2004-05	Worcester IceCats	AHL	63	3	13	16	128	....	....	....	....	....
2005-06	Peoria Rivermen	AHL	73	2	9	11	104	4	0	0	0	4
2006-07	Manchester	AHL	63	2	7	9	107	16	0	3	3	13
2007-08	Iserlohn Roosters	Germany	43	0	4	4	119	6	1	0	1	31

Signed as a free agent by **Pittsburgh**, September 28, 2000. Traded to **Columbus** by **Pittsburgh** for Pauli Levokari, February 10, 2004. Signed as a free agent by **Worcester** (AHL), October 25, 2004. Signed as a free agent by **Los Angeles**, July 10, 2006. Signed as a free agent by **San Jose**, July 15, 2008.

BUMAGIN, Alexander (buh-MAH-gihn, al-EHX-AN-duhr) EDM.

Wing. Shoots left. 6', 180 lbs. Born, Togliatti, USSR, March 1, 1987.
(Edmonton's 5th choice, 170th overall, in 2006 Entry Draft).

			Regular Season					Playoffs				
Season	Club	League	GP	G	A	Pts	PIM	GP	G	A	Pts	PIM
2002-03	Lada Togliatti 2	Russia-3	9	4	1	5	2	....	....	....	....	....
2003-04	Lada Togliatti 2	Russia-3	22	4	9	13	12	4	0	1	1	4
2004-05	Lada Togliatti 2	Russia-3	STATISTICS NOT AVAILABLE									
	Lada Togliatti	Russia	7	2	0	2	2	....	....	....	....	....
	Lada Togliatti	Russia	7	2	0	2	2	....	....	....	....	....
2005-06	Lada Togliatti	Russia	40	9	12	21	28	8	0	3	3	4
2006-07	Lada Togliatti	Russia	41	2	3	5	18	3	0	0	0	0
2007-08	Mytischi	Russia	31	8	7	15	37	5	0	0	0	0

BURAVCHIKOV, Vyacheslav (burh-AV-chih-kawf, V'YATCH-ih-slav) BUF.

Defense. Shoots left. 6', 189 lbs. Born, Moscow, USSR, May 22, 1987.
(Buffalo's 7th choice, 191st overall, in 2005 Entry Draft).

			Regular Season					Playoffs				
Season	Club	League	GP	G	A	Pts	PIM	GP	G	A	Pts	PIM
2003-04	Krylja Sovetov 2	Russia-3	STATISTICS NOT AVAILABLE									
2004-05	Krylja Sovetov 2	Russia-3	15	5	6	11	22	....	....	....	....	....
	Krylja Sovetov	Russia-2	26	4	1	5	14	3	0	0	0	2
2005-06	Mytischi	Russia	43	1	2	3	24	9	1	0	1	4
2006-07	Ak Bars Kazan	Russia	35	0	3	3	20	....	....	....	....	....
2007-08	Ak Bars Kazan	Russia	46	1	0	1	12	10	1	0	1	4

BURKE, Greg (BUHRK, GREHG) WSH.

Left wing. Shoots left. 6', 200 lbs. Born, Portsmouth, NH, May 16, 1990.
(Washington's 7th choice, 174th overall, in 2008 Entry Draft).

			Regular Season					Playoffs				
Season	Club	League	GP	G	A	Pts	PIM	GP	G	A	Pts	PIM
2006-07	N.H. Jr. Monarchs	EJHL	34	6	12	18	22	....	....	....	....	....
2007-08	N.H. Jr. Monarchs	EJHL	40	21	25	46	46	6	5	4	9	6

• Signed Letter of Intent to attend **University of New Hampshire** (Hockey East) in fall of 2009.

BURKI, Codey (BUHR-kee, KOH-dee) COL.

Center. Shoots left. 6', 190 lbs. Born, Winnipeg, Man., November 17, 1987.
(Colorado's 3rd choice, 59th overall, in 2006 Entry Draft).

			Regular Season					Playoffs				
Season	Club	League	GP	G	A	Pts	PIM	GP	G	A	Pts	PIM
2004-05	Brandon	WHL	68	10	13	23	48	24	6	5	11	13
2005-06	Brandon	WHL	70	27	34	61	69	6	0	3	3	2
2006-07	Brandon	WHL	70	36	49	85	83	11	6	5	11	4
2007-08	Lake Erie Monsters	AHL	40	2	7	9	22	....	....	....	....	....
	Johnstown Chiefs	ECHL	12	3	4	7	14	4	0	0	0	4

BURLON, Brandon (BUHR-lohn, BRAN-duhn) N.J.

Defense. Shoots left. 6', 190 lbs. Born, Nobleton, Ont., March 5, 1990.
(New Jersey's 2nd choice, 52nd overall, in 2008 Entry Draft).

			Regular Season					Playoffs				
Season	Club	League	GP	G	A	Pts	PIM	GP	G	A	Pts	PIM
2005-06	Vaughan Kings	GTHL	55	19	29	48	38	....	....	....	....	....
2006-07	St. Michael's	OPJHL	45	4	19	23	46	4	0	1	1	4
2007-08	St. Michael's	OPJHL	32	7	17	24	41	10	2	4	6	8

• Signed Letter of Intent to attend **University of Michigan** (CCHA) in fall of 2008.

BUSTO, Michael (BUHS-toh, MIGH-kuhl) NYR

Defense. Shoots right. 6'2", 220 lbs. Born, Burnaby, B.C., June 20, 1986.

			Regular Season					Playoffs				
Season	Club	League	GP	G	A	Pts	PIM	GP	G	A	Pts	PIM
2001-02	Moose Jaw	WHL	3	0	0	0	2	....	....	....	....	....
2002-03	Moose Jaw	WHL	50	1	7	8	54	7	1	0	1	0
2003-04	Moose Jaw	WHL	42	4	13	17	51	....	....	....	....	....
	Swift Current	WHL	26	0	0	0	29	5	0	0	0	2
2004-05	Kootenay Ice	WHL	71	8	21	29	79	16	1	5	6	27
2005-06	Kootenay Ice	WHL	69	8	35	43	77	4	0	4	4	4
2006-07	Kootenay Ice	WHL	70	20	43	63	79	6	1	2	3	9
2007-08	Charlotte	ECHL	48	4	12	16	10	....	....	....	....	....

Signed as a free agent by **NY Rangers**, April 27, 2007.

BUT, Anton (BOOT, AN-tawn) T.B.

Left wing. Shoots left. 6'1", 189 lbs. Born, Kharkov, USSR, July 3, 1980.
(New Jersey's 7th choice, 119th overall, in 1998 Entry Draft).

			Regular Season					Playoffs				
Season	Club	League	GP	G	A	Pts	PIM	GP	G	A	Pts	PIM
1995-96	Yaroslavl 2	CIS-2	60	30	12	42	10	....	....	....	....	....
1996-97	Yaroslavl 2	Russia-3	70	30	20	50	20	....	....	....	....	....
1997-98	Yaroslavl 2	Russia-2	48	12	5	17	28	....	....	....	....	....
1998-99	Yaroslavl 2	Russia-3	22	12	8	20	59	....	....	....	....	....
	Torpedo Yaroslavl	Russia	5	0	0	0	0	....	....	....	....	....
99-2000	Yaroslavl 2	Russia-3	1	0	0	0	2	....	....	....	....	....
	Torpedo Yaroslavl	Russia	26	2	5	7	16	8	2	1	3	0
2000-01	Yaroslavl	Russia	42	14	6	20	14	11	1	3	4	8
2001-02	Yaroslavl	Russia	48	14	11	25	14	6	0	1	1	2
2002-03	Yaroslavl	Russia	44	16	13	29	16	9	1	2	3	6
2003-04	Yaroslavl	Russia	51	11	10	21	24	3	0	0	0	0
2004-05	Yaroslavl	Russia	60	12	22	34	58	8	3	3	6	0
2005-06	Yaroslavl	Russia	49	16	21	37	26	11	2	1	3	2
2006-07	SKA St. Petersburg	Russia	52	13	13	26	61	2	0	1	1	2
2007-08	SKA St. Petersburg	Russia	57	15	13	28	40	9	4	1	5	6

Rights traded to **Tampa Bay** by **New Jersey** with Josef Boumedienne and Sascha Goc for Andrei Zyuzin, November 9, 2001.

BUTCHER, Matt (BUH-chuhr, MAT) VAN.

Center. Shoots left. 6'1", 188 lbs. Born, Bellingham, WA, January 1, 1987.
(Vancouver's 4th choice, 138th overall, in 2005 Entry Draft).

			Regular Season					Playoffs				
Season	Club	League	GP	G	A	Pts	PIM	GP	G	A	Pts	PIM
2003-04	Chilliwack Chiefs	BCHL	48	7	18	25	73	11	3	1	4	14
2004-05	Chilliwack Chiefs	BCHL	58	27	28	55	94	....	....	....	....	....
2005-06	Chilliwack Chiefs	BCHL	57	38	63	101	109	10	12	11	23	12
2006-07	Northern Mich.	CCHA	40	0	4	4	28	....	....	....	....	....
2007-08	Northern Mich.	CCHA	44	8	15	23	45	....	....	....	....	....

BUTLER, Chris (BUHT-luhr, KRIHS) BUF.

Defense. Shoots left. 6'1", 199 lbs. Born, St. Louis, MO, October 27, 1986.
(Buffalo's 4th choice, 96th overall, in 2005 Entry Draft).

			Regular Season					Playoffs				
Season	Club	League	GP	G	A	Pts	PIM	GP	G	A	Pts	PIM
2003-04	Sioux City	USHL	55	3	6	9	37	7	0	1	1	6
2004-05	Sioux City	USHL	60	6	22	28	90	13	1	6	7	10
2005-06	U. of Denver	WCHA	35	7	15	22	28	....	....	....	....	....
2006-07	U. of Denver	WCHA	39	10	17	27	42	....	....	....	....	....
2007-08	U. of Denver	WCHA	41	3	14	17	38	....	....	....	....	....

USHL First All-Star Team (2005) • WCHA All-Rookie Team (2006) • WCHA Second All-Star Team (2008) • NCAA West Second All-American Team (2008)

BYRNE, Trevor (BUHR-ne, TREH-vuhr) DAL.

Defense. Shoots left. 6'3", 205 lbs. Born, Weymouth, MA, May 7, 1980.
(St. Louis' 4th choice, 143rd overall, in 1999 Entry Draft).

			Regular Season					Playoffs				
Season	Club	League	GP	G	A	Pts	PIM	GP	G	A	Pts	PIM
1997-98	Deerfield Academy	High-MA	25	5	14	19	16	....	....	....	....	....
1998-99	Deerfield Academy	High-MA	25	9	19	28	22	....	....	....	....	....
99-2000	Dartmouth	ECAC	30	3	9	12	40	....	....	....	....	....
2000-01	Dartmouth	ECAC	34	5	21	26	52	....	....	....	....	....
2001-02	Dartmouth	ECAC	32	5	16	21	38	....	....	....	....	....
2002-03	Dartmouth	ECAC	34	8	16	24	28	....	....	....	....	....
2003-04	Worcester IceCats	AHL	63	7	13	20	22	9	2	2	4	2
	Peoria Rivermen	ECHL	6	0	0	0	0	....	....	....	....	....
2004-05	Worcester IceCats	AHL	40	1	6	7	18	....	....	....	....	....
	Peoria Rivermen	ECHL	33	6	12	18	28	....	....	....	....	....
2005-06	Peoria Rivermen	AHL	51	3	18	21	47	3	0	1	1	0
	Wheeling Nailers	ECHL	2	0	3	3	0	....	....	....	....	....
2006-07	Hershey Bears	AHL	35	1	13	14	46	....	....	....	....	....
	Chicago Wolves	AHL	9	0	0	0	6	15	2	4	6	18
2007-08	Iowa Stars	AHL	73	3	13	16	79	....	....	....	....	....

ECAC Second All-Star Team (2001, 2002, 2003)

Signed as a free agent by **Washington**, July 25, 2006. Signed as a free agent by **Dallas**, July 6, 2007.

BYRON, Paul (BIGH-ruhn, PAWL) BUF.

Center. Shoots left. 5'8", 142 lbs. Born, Ottawa, Ont., April 27, 1989.
(Buffalo's 6th choice, 179th overall, in 2007 Entry Draft).

			Regular Season					Playoffs				
Season	Club	League	GP	G	A	Pts	PIM	GP	G	A	Pts	PIM
2005-06	Ottawa West	OJHL-B	33	20	23	43	33	7	3	8	11	4
2006-07	Gatineau	QMJHL	68	21	23	44	46	5	5	1	6	2
2007-08	Gatineau	QMJHL	52	37	31	68	25	19	*21	11	32	12

CABANA, Frederik (kah-BAH-nuh, FREHD-uhr-ihk) PHI.

Center. Shoots left. 6', 200 lbs. Born, Fleurimont, Que., May 16, 1986.
(Philadelphia's 7th choice, 171st overall, in 2004 Entry Draft).

			Regular Season					Playoffs				
Season	Club	League	GP	G	A	Pts	PIM	GP	G	A	Pts	PIM
2001-02	Magog	QAAA	37	20	16	36	124	7	1	4	5	12
2002-03	Halifax	QMJHL	62	4	10	14	65	24	7	1	8	50
2003-04	Halifax	QMJHL	70	17	21	38	78	....	....	....	....	....
2004-05	Halifax	QMJHL	59	10	24	34	47	11	6	6	12	11
2005-06	Halifax	QMJHL	68	17	24	41	85	11	1	3	4	17
2006-07	Philadelphia	AHL	61	4	15	19	78	....	....	....	....	....
2007-08	Philadelphia	AHL	48	9	7	16	75	3	0	0	0	5

CALLA, Brady (KAL-luh, BRAY-dee) FLA.

Right wing. Shoots right. 6', 190 lbs. Born, North Vancouver, B.C., March 14, 1988.
(Florida's 2nd choice, 73rd overall, in 2006 Entry Draft).

			Regular Season					Playoffs				
Season	Club	League	GP	G	A	Pts	PIM	GP	G	A	Pts	PIM
2004-05	Everett Silvertips	WHL	68	11	10	21	38	11	1	1	2	0
2005-06	Everett Silvertips	WHL	66	8	25	33	52	11	1	2	3	4
2006-07	Everett Silvertips	WHL	29	3	6	9	23	....	....	....	....	....
	Moose Jaw	WHL	39	12	20	32	19	....	....	....	....	....
2007-08	Moose Jaw	WHL	14	2	8	10	10	....	....	....	....	....
	Kamloops Blazers	WHL	52	10	20	30	52	4	0	2	2	4
	Rochester	AHL	6	2	2	4	2	....	....	....	....	....

CALLAHAN, Joe (kal-AH-han, JOH) NYI

Defense. Shoots right. 6'3", 221 lbs. Born, Brockton, MA, December 20, 1982.
(Phoenix's 4th choice, 70th overall, in 2002 Entry Draft).

			Regular Season					Playoffs				
Season	Club	League	GP	G	A	Pts	PIM	GP	G	A	Pts	PIM
2001-02	Yale	ECAC	31	3	8	11	20	....	....	....	....	....
2002-03	Yale	ECAC	32	2	11	13	38	....	....	....	....	....
2003-04 •	Yale	ECAC	31	6	14	20	38	....	....	....	....	....
	Springfield Falcons	AHL	13	0	4	4	12	....	....	....	....	....
2004-05	Utah Grizzlies	AHL	75	4	7	11	66	....	....	....	....	....
2005-06	San Antonio	AHL	80	1	5	6	88	....	....	....	....	....
2006-07	San Antonio	AHL	78	1	13	14	65	....	....	....	....	....
2007-08	Portland Pirates	AHL	65	1	23	24	59	18	1	11	12	25

Signed as a free agent by **Anaheim**, July 12, 2007. Signed as a free agent by **NY Islanders**, July 8, 2008.

CALVERT, Matthew (KAL-vuhrt, MA-thew) CBJ

Left wing. Shoots left. 5'9", 164 lbs. Born, Brandon, Man., December 24, 1989.
(Columbus' 5th choice, 127th overall, in 2008 Entry Draft).

			Regular Season					Playoffs				
Season	Club	League	GP	G	A	Pts	PIM	GP	G	A	Pts	PIM
2005-06	Brandon	MMHL	38	24	30	54	48	6	3	6	9	18
2006-07	Brandon	MMHL	30	28	55	83	46	16	5	13	18	16
	Winkler Flyers	MJHL	1	0	0	0	15	....	....	....	....	....
2007-08	Brandon	WHL	72	24	40	64	53	6	1	2	3	2

CAMERON, Bryan (KAM-ih-RUHN, BRIGH-uhn) L.A.

Center. Shoots right. 5'10", 180 lbs. Born, Brampton, Ont., February 25, 1989.
(Los Angeles' 4th choice, 82nd overall, in 2007 Entry Draft).

			Regular Season					Playoffs				
Season	Club	League	GP	G	A	Pts	PIM	GP	G	A	Pts	PIM
2004-05	Toronto Marlboros	GTHL	75	73	47	120	76	....	....	....	....	....
2005-06	Belleville Bulls	OHL	64	20	9	29	46	6	1	2	3	6
2006-07	Belleville Bulls	OHL	60	33	25	58	50	15	4	8	12	15
2007-08	Belleville Bulls	OHL	68	41	37	78	56	21	4	9	13	10

CAMERON, Randy (KAM-ih-RUHN, RAN-dee) DET.

Center. Shoots right. 5'11", 175 lbs. Born, Cornwall, P.E.I., January 28, 1989.
(Detroit's 3rd choice, 148th overall, in 2007 Entry Draft).

			Regular Season					Playoffs				
Season	Club	League	GP	G	A	Pts	PIM	GP	G	A	Pts	PIM
2005-06	Summerside	MJrHL	52	21	50	71	16	11	2	6	8	6
2006-07	Moncton Wildcats	QMJHL	70	17	22	39	44	7	1	1	2	0
2007-08	Moncton Wildcats	QMJHL	62	12	27	39	30	....	....	....	....	....

CAMPBELL, Andrew (KAM-buhl, AN-droo) L.A.

Defense. Shoots left. 6'4", 208 lbs. Born, Hamilton, Ont., February 4, 1988.
(Los Angeles' 5th choice, 74th overall, in 2008 Entry Draft).

			Regular Season					Playoffs				
Season	Club	League	GP	G	A	Pts	PIM	GP	G	A	Pts	PIM
2005-06	Sault Ste. Marie	OHL	31	1	3	4	23	3	0	0	0	4
2006-07	Sault Ste. Marie	OHL	63	4	14	18	75	13	0	1	1	6
2007-08	Sault Ste. Marie	OHL	68	13	22	35	64	14	2	3	5	13

CAMPBELL, Max (KAM-behl, MAX) NYR

Center. Shoots left. 6', 178 lbs. Born, Strathroy, Ont., December 21, 1988.
(NY Rangers' 3rd choice, 138th overall, in 2007 Entry Draft).

			Regular Season					Playoffs				
Season	Club	League	GP	G	A	Pts	PIM	GP	G	A	Pts	PIM
2005-06	Strathroy Rockets	OJHL-B	48	17	18	35	10	....	....	....	....	....
2006-07	Strathroy Rockets	OJHL-B	46	46	49	95	84	....	....	....	....	....
2007-08	Western Mich.	CCHA	38	6	16	22	10	....	....	....	....	....

CAPORUSSO, Louie (kap-oh-ROO-soh, LOO-ee) OTT.

Center/Left wing. Shoots left. 5'9", 190 lbs. Born, Toronto, Ont., June 21, 1989.
(Ottawa's 3rd choice, 90th overall, in 2007 Entry Draft).

			Regular Season					Playoffs				
Season	Club	League	GP	G	A	Pts	PIM	GP	G	A	Pts	PIM
2004-05	Tor. Red Wings	GTHL	53	38	28	66	28	....	....	....	....	....
2005-06	St. Michael's	OPJHL	48	29	44	73	44	25	8	10	18	16
2006-07	St. Michael's	OPJHL	37	23	27	50	45	20	14	19	33	14
2007-08	U. of Michigan	CCHA	33	12	9	21	18	....	....	....	....	....

CAPUTI, Luca (ka-POO-tee, LOO-ka) PIT.

Left wing. Shoots left. 6'2", 184 lbs. Born, Toronto, Ont., October 1, 1988.
(Pittsburgh's 5th choice, 111th overall, in 2007 Entry Draft).

			Regular Season					Playoffs				
Season	Club	League	GP	G	A	Pts	PIM	GP	G	A	Pts	PIM
2003-04	Tor. Jr. Canadiens	GTHL	53	52	55	107	127	....	....	....	....	....
2004-05	Mississauga	OHL	48	5	1	6	25	....	....	....	....	....
2005-06	Mississauga	OHL	32	3	0	3	43	....	....	....	....	....
2006-07	Mississauga	OHL	68	27	38	65	66	5	2	1	3	0
2007-08	Niagara Ice Dogs	OHL	66	51	60	111	107	10	8	9	17	14
	Wilkes-Barre	AHL	....	....	....	....	....	19	4	4	8	8

OHL Second All-Star Team (2008)

CAREY, Paul (KAIR-ee, PAWL) COL.

Center. Shoots left. 6', 175 lbs. Born, Boston, MA, September 24, 1988.
(Colorado's 7th choice, 135th overall, in 2007 Entry Draft).

			Regular Season					Playoffs				
Season	Club	League	GP	G	A	Pts	PIM	GP	G	A	Pts	PIM
2005-06	Salisbury School	High-CT	27	14	11	25	18	....	....	....	....	....
2006-07	Salisbury School	High-CT	24	16	11	27	16	....	....	....	....	....
2007-08	Indiana Ice	USHL	60	34	32	66	32	4	1	2	3	2

CARLE, David (KARL, DAY-vihd) T.B.

Defense. Shoots left. 5'11", 180 lbs. Born, Anchorage, AK, November 9, 1989.
(Tampa Bay's 8th choice, 203rd overall, in 2008 Entry Draft).

			Regular Season					Playoffs				
Season	Club	League	GP	G	A	Pts	PIM	GP	G	A	Pts	PIM
2006-07	Shat.-St. Mary's	High-MN	61	4	9	13	66	....	....	....	....	....
2007-08	Shat.-St. Mary's	High-MN	61	13	38	51	61	....	....	....	....	....

• Signed Letter of Intent to attend **University of Denver** (WCHA) in fall of 2008. • Forced to retire from hockey due to a heart condition detected by doctors at the NHL Entry Draft combine, May 30, 2008.

CARLE, Mathieu (KAHRL, MA-tyew) MTL.

Defense. Shoots right. 6', 211 lbs. Born, Gatineau, Que., September 30, 1987.
(Montreal's 3rd choice, 53rd overall, in 2006 Entry Draft).

			Regular Season					Playoffs				
Season	Club	League	GP	G	A	Pts	PIM	GP	G	A	Pts	PIM
2004-05	Acadie-Bathurst	QMJHL	69	4	29	33	53	....	....	....	....	....
2005-06	Acadie-Bathurst	QMJHL	67	18	51	69	122	17	1	14	15	29
2006-07	Acadie-Bathurst	QMJHL	38	12	39	51	52	....	....	....	....	....
	Rouyn-Noranda	QMJHL	25	4	15	19	27	16	6	10	16	16
2007-08	Hamilton Bulldogs	AHL	64	7	17	24	43	....	....	....	....	....

QMJHL All-Rookie Team (2004)

CARLSON, John (KAHRL-suhn, JAWN) WSH.

Defense. Shoots right. 6'2", 218 lbs. Born, Natick, MA, January 10, 1990.
(Washington's 2nd choice, 27th overall, in 2008 Entry Draft).

			Regular Season					Playoffs				
Season	Club	League	GP	G	A	Pts	PIM	GP	G	A	Pts	PIM
2005-06	N.J. Rockets	AtJHL	38	2	10	12	42	....	....	....	....	....
2006-07	N.J. Rockets	AtJHL	44	12	38	50	96	....	....	....	....	....
	Indiana Ice	USHL	2	0	0	0	6	....	....	....	....	....
2007-08	Indiana Ice	USHL	59	12	31	43	72	4	1	0	1	0

CARLSSON, Jonathan (KAHRL-suhn, JAWN-ah-thuhn) CHI.

Defense. Shoots right. 6'1", 198 lbs. Born, Uppsala, Sweden, August 5, 1988.
(Chicago's 4th choice, 162nd overall, in 2008 Entry Draft).

			Regular Season					Playoffs				
Season	Club	League	GP	G	A	Pts	PIM	GP	G	A	Pts	PIM
2004-05	Brynas IF Gavle Jr.	Swe-Jr.	19	1	0	1	6	....	....	....	....	....
2005-06	Brynas U18	Swe-U18	1	0	0	0	0	....	....	....	....	....
	Brynas IF Gavle Jr.	Swe-Jr.	37	2	9	11	24	2	0	1	1	0
2006-07	Brynas IF Gavle Jr.	Swe-Jr.	39	12	5	17	16	4	2	1	3	6
	Brynas IF Gavle	Sweden	6	1	0	1	2	....	....	....	....	....
2007-08	Brynas IF Gavle Jr.	Swe-Jr.	8	3	2	5	6	4	2	0	2	0
	IF Bjorkloven Umea	Sweden-2	16	2	3	5	6	....	....	....	....	....
	Brynas IF Gavle	Sweden	26	0	0	0	27	....	....	....	....	....
	Brynas IF Gavle	Sweden-Q	9	0	0	0	2	....	....	....	....	....

CARMAN, Michael (KAR-mahn, MIGH-kuhl) COL.

Center. Shoots left. 6', 180 lbs. Born, Augusta, GA, April 14, 1988.
(Colorado's 4th choice, 81st overall, in 2006 Entry Draft).

			Regular Season					Playoffs				
Season	Club	League	GP	G	A	Pts	PIM	GP	G	A	Pts	PIM
2003-04	Holy Angels	High-MN	29	19	40	59	....	....	....	....	....	....
2004-05	USNTDP	U-17	14	2	9	11	40	....	....	....	....	....
	USNTDP	NAHL	39	12	15	27	38	10	2	4	6	10
2005-06	USNTDP	U-18	43	15	23	38	78	....	....	....	....	....
	USNTDP	NAHL	17	6	10	16	24	....	....	....	....	....
2006-07	U. of Minnesota	WCHA	41	9	11	20	55	....	....	....	....	....
2007-08	U. of Minnesota	WCHA	23	4	7	11	28	....	....	....	....	....

CARPENTIER, Hugo (kar-PUHNT-yay, HEW-goh) CGY.

Center. Shoots left. 6'2", 205 lbs. Born, Hull, Que., March 17, 1988.
(Calgary's 4th choice, 118th overall, in 2006 Entry Draft).

			Regular Season					Playoffs				
Season	Club	League	GP	G	A	Pts	PIM	GP	G	A	Pts	PIM
2004-05	Rouyn-Noranda	QMJHL	49	6	9	15	32	5	0	1	1	6
2005-06	Rouyn-Noranda	QMJHL	70	31	39	70	64	5	1	2	3	4
2006-07	Rouyn-Noranda	QMJHL	69	17	37	54	86	16	0	6	6	24
2007-08	Rouyn-Noranda	QMJHL	69	27	38	65	114	17	14	8	22	20

CARSON, Brett (KAR-suhn, BREHT) CAR.

Defense. Shoots right. 6'5", 220 lbs. Born, Regina, Sask., November 29, 1985.
(Carolina's 4th choice, 109th overall, in 2004 Entry Draft).

			Regular Season					Playoffs				
Season	Club	League	GP	G	A	Pts	PIM	GP	G	A	Pts	PIM
99-2000	Pipestone Valley	SSMHL	8	0	0	0	0	....	....	....	....	....
2000-01	Pipestone Valley	SSMHL	31	5	17	22	20	....	....	....	....	....
2001-02	Yorkton Terriers	SMHL	41	16	37	53	32	....	....	....	....	....
	Moose Jaw	WHL	6	0	0	0	0	12	2	0	2	0
2002-03	Moose Jaw	WHL	28	1	4	5	28	....	....	....	....	....
	Calgary Hitmen	WHL	30	3	6	9	4	5	2	1	3	0
2003-04	Calgary Hitmen	WHL	71	5	27	32	49	7	0	0	0	6
2004-05	Calgary Hitmen	WHL	61	8	16	24	61	8	2	2	4	8
2005-06	Calgary Hitmen	WHL	72	11	29	40	62	13	1	6	7	20
2006-07	Florida Everblades	ECHL	3	1	1	2	0	....	....	....	....	....
	Albany River Rats	AHL	63	2	16	18	26	5	0	2	2	0
2007-08	Albany River Rats	AHL	77	2	22	24	32	7	1	3	4	11

WHL East First All-Star Team (2006)

CARUANA, Matt (CAHR-wah-na, MAT) ANA.

Forward. Shoots left. 6', 185 lbs. Born, Oshawa, Ont., June 7, 1985.

			Regular Season					Playoffs				
Season	Club	League	GP	G	A	Pts	PIM	GP	G	A	Pts	PIM
2004-05	Niagara University	CHA	36	8	8	16	32	....	....	....	....	....
2005-06	Niagara University	CHA	36	12	24	36	20	....	....	....	....	....
2006-07	Niagara University	CHA	37	14	24	38	26	....	....	....	....	....
2007-08	Niagara University	CHA	37	17	22	39	30	....	....	....	....	....
	Portland Pirates	AHL	5	0	1	1	2	13	0	0	0	2

CHA Second All-Star Team (2008)

Signed as a free agent by **Anaheim**, April 4, 2008.

CARUSO, Michael (kah-ROO-soh, MIGH-kuhl) FLA.

Defense. Shoots left. 6'2", 191 lbs. Born, Mississauga, Ont., July 5, 1988.
(Florida's 3rd choice, 103rd overall, in 2006 Entry Draft).

			Regular Season					Playoffs				
Season	Club	League	GP	G	A	Pts	PIM	GP	G	A	Pts	PIM
2004-05	Guelph Storm	OHL	56	0	3	3	31	4	0	0	0	2
2005-06	Guelph Storm	OHL	66	1	15	16	85	15	1	2	3	24
2006-07	Guelph Storm	OHL	64	4	16	20	119	4	0	0	0	8
2007-08	Guelph Storm	OHL	62	10	24	34	103	10	2	6	8	22

CAYER, Julien (KAY-uhr, JOO-lee-ehn) DET.

Center. Shoots left. 6'4", 186 lbs. Born, Longueuil, Que., July 6, 1989.
(Detroit's 4th choice, 151st overall, in 2008 Entry Draft).

			Regular Season					Playoffs				
Season	Club	League	GP	G	A	Pts	PIM	GP	G	A	Pts	PIM
2005-06	C.C. Lemoyne	QAAA	42	11	21	32	46	8	1	2	3	14
2006-07	St-Jerome	QJHL	45	6	23	29	84	10	1	3	4	2
2007-08	Northwood	High-NY	42	24	32	56	56	....	....	....	....	....

• Signed Letter of Intent to attend **Clarkson University** (ECAC) in fall of 2008.

CHAMPAGNE, Joel (sham-PAYN, JOHL) TOR.

Center. Shoots left. 6'4", 210 lbs. Born, Chateauguay, Que., January 24, 1990.
(Toronto's 5th choice, 129th overall, in 2008 Entry Draft).

			Regular Season					Playoffs				
Season	Club	League	GP	G	A	Pts	PIM	GP	G	A	Pts	PIM
2005-06	Chateauguay	QAAA	42	9	29	38	22	19	7	10	17	20
2006-07	Chicoutimi	QMJHL	62	6	16	22	51	4	0	0	0	6
2007-08	Chicoutimi	QMJHL	70	18	22	40	45	6	1	1	2	6

CHAPUT, Stefan (sha-PEW, STEH-fan) CAR.

Center. Shoots left. 6', 190 lbs. Born, Montreal, Que., March 11, 1988.
(Carolina's 4th choice, 153rd overall, in 2006 Entry Draft).

			Regular Season					Playoffs				
Season	Club	League	GP	G	A	Pts	PIM	GP	G	A	Pts	PIM
2003-04	West Island Lions	QAAA	29	7	12	19	32	7	1	3	4	4
2004-05	West Island Lions	QAAA	39	29	25	54	86	5	2	2	4	16
	Lewiston	QMJHL	8	2	3	5	2	8	1	0	1	2
2005-06	Lewiston	QMJHL	69	19	29	48	44	6	0	1	1	4
2006-07	Lewiston	QMJHL	57	17	29	46	43	17	6	5	11	20
2007-08	Lewiston	QMJHL	62	33	36	69	56	6	2	1	3	12
	Albany River Rats	AHL	1	0	0	0	0	....	....	....	....	....

CHARLEBOIS, Joe (SHAHR-luh-bwah, JOH) CHI.

Defense. Shoots right. 6'1", 210 lbs. Born, Potsdam, NY, February 18, 1986.
(Chicago's 10th choice, 188th overall, in 2005 Entry Draft).

			Regular Season					Playoffs				
Season	Club	League	GP	G	A	Pts	PIM	GP	G	A	Pts	PIM
2002-03	Cornwall Colts	CJHL	59	2	18	20	....	....	....	....	....	....
2003-04	USNTDP	U-18	35	0	2	2	10	....	....	....	....	....
	USNTDP	NAHL	12	1	0	1	6	7	0	1	1	4
2004-05	Sioux City	USHL	59	1	24	25	146	7	1	1	2	6
2005-06	New Hampshire	H-East	32	2	3	5	35	....	....	....	....	....
2006-07	New Hampshire	H-East	39	0	4	4	50	....	....	....	....	....
2007-08	New Hampshire	H-East	38	1	8	9	40	....	....	....	....	....

CHEREPANOV, Alexei (chair-ih-PAN-ahv, al-EHX-ay) NYR

Right wing. Shoots left. 6'1", 183 lbs. Born, Ozerki, USSR, January 15, 1989.
(NY Rangers' 1st choice, 17th overall, in 2007 Entry Draft).

			Regular Season					Playoffs				
Season	Club	League	GP	G	A	Pts	PIM	GP	G	A	Pts	PIM
2005-06	Omsk 2	Russia-3	5	2	0	2	2	....	....	....	....	....
2006-07	Avangard Omsk 2	Russia-3	3	1	0	1	0	....	....	....	....	....
	Avangard Omsk	Russia	46	18	11	29	45	10	3	5	8	0
2007-08	Avangard Omsk	Russia	46	15	12	27	12	4	2	1	3	0

CHORNEY, Taylor (CHOHR-nee, TAY-luhr) EDM.

Defense. Shoots left. 6', 196 lbs. Born, Thunder Bay, Ont., April 27, 1987.
(Edmonton's 2nd choice, 36th overall, in 2005 Entry Draft).

			Regular Season					Playoffs				
Season	Club	League	GP	G	A	Pts	PIM	GP	G	A	Pts	PIM
2003-04	Shat.-St. Mary's	High-MN	74	12	44	56	58	....	....	....	....	....
2004-05	Shat.-St. Mary's	High-MN	50	4	30	34	52	....	....	....	....	....
2005-06	North Dakota	WCHA	44	3	15	18	54	....	....	....	....	....
2006-07	North Dakota	WCHA	39	8	23	31	48	....	....	....	....	....
2007-08	North Dakota	WCHA	43	3	21	24	24	....	....	....	....	....

WCHA Second All-Star Team (2007) • NCAA West Second All-American Team (2007) • WCHA First All-Star Team (2008)

CHOUINARD, Joel (SHWEE-nahrd, JOHL) COL.

Defense. Shoots left. 6'1", 186 lbs. Born, Longueuil, Que., April 8, 1990.
(Colorado's 5th choice, 167th overall, in 2008 Entry Draft).

			Regular Season					Playoffs				
Season	Club	League	GP	G	A	Pts	PIM	GP	G	A	Pts	PIM
2005-06	Magog	QAAA	44	4	14	18	70	13	1	5	6	6
2006-07	Magog	QAAA	33	8	30	38	88	....	....	....	....	....
	Victoriaville Tigres	QMJHL	23	3	3	6	20	6	0	1	1	0
2007-08	Victoriaville Tigres	QMJHL	69	7	28	35	95	6	2	0	2	4

CHUCKO, Kris (CHUH-koh, KRIHS) CGY.

Left wing. Shoots right. 6'2", 200 lbs. Born, Burnaby, B.C., March 13, 1986.
(Calgary's 1st choice, 24th overall, in 2004 Entry Draft).

			Regular Season					Playoffs				
Season	Club	League	GP	G	A	Pts	PIM	GP	G	A	Pts	PIM
2002-03	Salmon Arm	BCHL	59	14	19	33	80	11	5	3	8	12
2003-04	Salmon Arm	BCHL	53	32	55	87	161	14	10	9	19	36
2004-05	U. of Minnesota	WCHA	44	10	11	21	61	....	....	....	....	....
2005-06	U. of Minnesota	WCHA	33	4	9	13	40	....	....	....	....	....
2006-07	Omaha	AHL	80	14	14	28	72	6	0	0	0	2
2007-08	Quad City Flames	AHL	80	15	15	30	38	....	....	....	....	....

CLACKSON, Matt (KLAK-suhn, MA-thyew) PHI.

Left wing. Shoots right. 6', 196 lbs. Born, Saskatoon, Sask., April 26, 1985.
(Philadelphia's 6th choice, 215th overall, in 2005 Entry Draft).

			Regular Season					Playoffs				
Season	Club	League	GP	G	A	Pts	PIM	GP	G	A	Pts	PIM
2002-03	Pittsburgh Hornets	MWEHL	64	22	22	44	169	....	....	....	....	....
2003-04	Chicago Steel	USHL	42	5	4	9	108	5	0	1	1	8
2004-05	Chicago Steel	USHL	56	10	15	25	270	....	....	....	....	....
2005-06	Western Mich.	CCHA	34	1	1	2	52	....	....	....	....	....
2006-07	Western Mich.	CCHA	36	0	8	8	80	....	....	....	....	....
2007-08	Western Mich.	CCHA	35	3	3	6	87	....	....	....	....	....
	Philadelphia	AHL	2	0	0	0	19	....	....	....	....	....

CLICHE, Marc-Andre (KLEESH, MAHRK-AWN-dray) L.A.

Center. Shoots right. 6'1", 190 lbs. Born, Rouyn-Noranda, Que., March 23, 1987.
(NY Rangers' 3rd choice, 56th overall, in 2005 Entry Draft).

			Regular Season					Playoffs				
Season	Club	League	GP	G	A	Pts	PIM	GP	G	A	Pts	PIM
2003-04	Lewiston	QMJHL	52	8	10	18	17	7	1	2	3	0
2004-05	Lewiston	QMJHL	19	4	4	8	8	....	....	....	....	....
2005-06	Lewiston	QMJHL	66	37	45	82	60	6	2	2	4	0
2006-07	Lewiston	QMJHL	52	24	30	54	42	16	6	16	22	10
2007-08	Manchester	AHL	52	11	10	21	25	4	0	1	1	2

Traded to **Los Angeles** by **NY Rangers** with Jason Ward, Jan Marek and NY Rangers' 3rd round choice (later traded to Buffalo - Buffalo selected Corey Fienhage) in 2008 Entry Draft for Sean Avery and John Seymour, February 5, 2007.

CLITSOME, Grant (KLIHT-suhm, GRANT) CBJ

Defense. Shoots left. 6', 208 lbs. Born, Gloucester, Ont., April 14, 1985.
(Columbus' 12th choice, 271st overall, in 2004 Entry Draft).

			Regular Season					Playoffs				
Season	Club	League	GP	G	A	Pts	PIM	GP	G	A	Pts	PIM
2003-04	Nepean Raiders	CJHL	55	13	26	39	67	17	1	10	11	6
2004-05	Clarkson Knights	ECAC	39	2	11	13	36	....	....	....	....	....
2005-06	Clarkson Knights	ECAC	34	2	17	19	20	....	....	....	....	....
2006-07	Clarkson Knights	ECAC	38	7	12	19	38	....	....	....	....	....
2007-08	Clarkson Knights	ECAC	39	5	17	22	28	....	....	....	....	....
	Syracuse Crunch	AHL	....	....	....	....	....	1	0	0	0	0

ECAC First All-Star Team (2008) • NCAA East Second All-American Team (2008)

CLUNE, Richard (KLOON, RIH-chuhrd) L.A.

Left wing. Shoots left. 6', 195 lbs. Born, Toronto, Ont., April 25, 1987.
(Dallas' 3rd choice, 71st overall, in 2005 Entry Draft).

			Regular Season					Playoffs				
Season	Club	League	GP	G	A	Pts	PIM	GP	G	A	Pts	PIM
2003-04	Sarnia Sting	OHL	58	3	13	16	72	5	0	1	1	0
2004-05	Sarnia Sting	OHL	68	21	13	34	103	....	....	....	....	....
2005-06	Sarnia Sting	OHL	61	20	32	52	126	....	....	....	....	....
2006-07	Barrie Colts	OHL	67	32	46	78	151	8	3	4	7	8
	Iowa Stars	AHL	1	0	0	0	2	....	....	....	....	....
2007-08	Iowa Stars	AHL	38	3	5	8	137	....	....	....	....	....
	Idaho Steelheads	ECHL	19	1	9	10	41	....	....	....	....	....

Traded to **Los Angeles** by **Dallas** for Lauri Tukonen, July 21, 2008.

COHEN, Colby (KOH-uhn, KOHL-bee) COL.

Defense. Shoots right. 6'2", 200 lbs. Born, Villanova, PA, April 25, 1989.
(Colorado's 2nd choice, 45th overall, in 2007 Entry Draft).

			Regular Season					Playoffs				
Season	Club	League	GP	G	A	Pts	PIM	GP	G	A	Pts	PIM
2004-05	Syracuse Stars	EmJHL	50	13	30	41	....	....	....	....	....	....
2005-06	USNTDP	U-17	18	2	3	5	22	....	....	....	....	....
	USNTDP	NAHL	37	5	9	14	33	10	1	1	2	0
2006-07	Lincoln Stars	USHL	53	13	47	60	110	4	0	0	0	2
	USNTDP	NAHL	4	1	3	4	0	....	....	....	....	....
2007-08	Boston University	H-East	39	3	13	16	34	....	....	....	....	....

COLBERT, Will (KOHL-buhrt, WIHL) S.J.

Defense. Shoots left. 6'3", 225 lbs. Born, Arnprior, Ont., February 6, 1985.
(San Jose's 7th choice, 183rd overall, in 2005 Entry Draft).

			Regular Season					Playoffs				
Season	Club	League	GP	G	A	Pts	PIM	GP	G	A	Pts	PIM
2001-02	Pembroke	CJHL	52	2	6	8	20	....	....	....	....	....
2002-03	Ottawa 67's	OHL	56	1	6	7	23	23	1	5	6	7
2003-04	Ottawa 67's	OHL	55	3	18	21	28	7	0	4	4	0
2004-05	Ottawa 67's	OHL	68	6	26	32	65	21	3	8	11	8
2005-06	St. FX University	AUAA	28	3	8	11	10	....	....	....	....	....
2006-07	St. FX University	AUAA	27	2	9	11	28	....	....	....	....	....
2007-08	St. FX University	AUAA	28	2	13	15	22	....	....	....	....	....

• Re-entered NHL Entry Draft. Originally Ottawa's 7th choice, 228th overall, in 2003 Entry Draft.
CIS All-Rookie Team (2006)

COLBORNE, Joe (KOHL-bohrn, JOH) BOS.

Center. Shoots left. 6'6", 196 lbs. Born, Calgary, Alta., January 30, 1990.
(Boston's 1st choice, 16th overall, in 2008 Entry Draft).

			Regular Season					Playoffs				
Season	Club	League	GP	G	A	Pts	PIM	GP	G	A	Pts	PIM
2005-06	Notre Dame	SMHL	48	13	14	27	26	....	....	....	....	....
2006-07	Camrose Kodiaks	AJHL	53	20	28	48	44	16	5	1	6	10
2007-08	Camrose Kodiaks	AJHL	55	33	*57	90	48	18	8	8	*16	26

• Signed Letter of Intent to attend **University of Denver** (WCHA) in fall of 2008.

COLE, Brad (KOHL, BRAD) CGY.

Defense. Shoots left. 6'4", 200 lbs. Born, Miniota, Man., October 21, 1986.

			Regular Season					Playoffs				
Season	Club	League	GP	G	A	Pts	PIM	GP	G	A	Pts	PIM
2003-04	Seattle	WHL	6	0	0	0	12	....	....	....	....	....
	Kootenay Ice	WHL	52	0	1	1	39	4	1	0	1	2
2004-05	Kootenay Ice	WHL	39	1	2	3	35	8	0	1	1	2
2005-06	Kootenay Ice	WHL	16	1	2	3	20	....	....	....	....	....
	Saskatoon Blades	WHL	56	3	12	15	64	9	1	0	1	23
2006-07	Saskatoon Blades	WHL	63	16	25	41	83	....	....	....	....	....
2007-08	Quad City Flames	AHL	25	1	4	5	13	....	....	....	....	....
	Las Vegas	ECHL	19	0	4	4	11	....	....	....	....	....

Signed as a free agent by **Calgary**, May 22, 2007.

COLE, Ian (KOHL, EE-an) ST.L.

Defense. Shoots left. 6'1", 211 lbs. Born, Ann Arbour, MI, February 21, 1989.
(St. Louis' 2nd choice, 18th overall, in 2007 Entry Draft).

			Regular Season					Playoffs				
Season	Club	League	GP	G	A	Pts	PIM	GP	G	A	Pts	PIM
2004-05	Det. Victory Honda	MWEHL	60	15	25	40	....	....	....	....	....	....
2005-06	USNTDP	U-17	18	2	1	3	14	....	....	....	....	....
	USNTDP	NAHL	40	2	8	10	75	12	0	3	3	14
2006-07	USNTDP	U-18	42	6	11	17	36	....	....	....	....	....
	USNTDP	NAHL	16	2	7	9	28	....	....	....	....	....
2007-08	U. of Notre Dame	CCHA	43	8	12	20	40	....	....	....	....	....

COLLINS, Chris (KAW-lihns, KRIHS)

Left wing. Shoots right. 5'10", 181 lbs. Born, Fairport, NY, June 8, 1984.

			Regular Season					Playoffs				
Season	Club	League	GP	G	A	Pts	PIM	GP	G	A	Pts	PIM
2001-02	Des Moines	USHL	60	26	39	65	112	3	1	2	3	10
2002-03	Boston College	H-East	39	11	12	23	53	....	....	....	....	....
2003-04	Boston College	H-East	41	9	10	19	42	....	....	....	....	....
2004-05	Boston College	H-East	40	9	8	17	58	....	....	....	....	....
2005-06	Boston College	H-East	40	*31	29	*60	26	....	....	....	....	....
2006-07	Providence Bruins	AHL	17	2	0	2	12	1	0	0	0	0
	Long Beach	ECHL	51	18	19	37	79	....	....	....	....	....
2007-08	Providence Bruins	AHL	72	22	19	41	75	10	1	3	4	10

Hockey East First All-Star Team (2006) • NCAA East First All-American Team (2006) • NCAA Championship All-Tournament Team (2006)

Signed as a free agent by **Boston**, July 11, 2006.

COLLINS, Dan (KAW-lihns, DAN) FLA.

Right wing. Shoots right. 6'1", 185 lbs. Born, Syracuse, NY, February 26, 1987.
(Florida's 3rd choice, 90th overall, in 2005 Entry Draft).

			Regular Season					Playoffs				
Season	Club	League	GP	G	A	Pts	PIM	GP	G	A	Pts	PIM
2002-03	Syracuse	OPJHL	35	14	12	26	58	....	....	....	....	....
2003-04	Plymouth Whalers	OHL	59	9	13	22	30	9	0	1	1	0
2004-05	Plymouth Whalers	OHL	68	25	21	46	60	4	0	0	0	6
2005-06	Plymouth Whalers	OHL	44	26	23	49	56	4	3	2	5	2
2006-07	Plymouth Whalers	OHL	66	26	42	68	87	20	9	11	20	30
2007-08	Rochester	AHL	35	5	6	11	21	....	....	....	....	....
	Florida Everblades	ECHL	28	4	14	18	34	....	....	....	....	....

COLLINS, Sean (KAW-lihns, SHAWN) WSH.

Defense. Shoots right. 6'1", 212 lbs. Born, Troy, MI, October 30, 1983.

			Regular Season					Playoffs				
Season	Club	League	GP	G	A	Pts	PIM	GP	G	A	Pts	PIM
2002-03	Sioux City	USHL	59	6	22	28	89	4	0	1	1	2
2003-04	Ohio State	CCHA	41	3	12	15	57	....	....	....	....	....
2004-05	Ohio State	CCHA	40	9	17	26	40	....	....	....	....	....
2005-06	Ohio State	CCHA	39	7	11	18	63	....	....	....	....	....
2006-07	Ohio State	CCHA	37	9	19	28	50	....	....	....	....	....
	Hershey Bears	AHL	3	0	0	0	2	....	....	....	....	....
2007-08	Hershey Bears	AHL	12	0	0	0	11	....	....	....	....	....
	South Carolina	ECHL	31	1	13	14	16	20	1	8	9	24

Signed as a free agent by **Washington**, March 19, 2007.

COLLINS, Sean (KAWL-ihns, SHAWN) CBJ

Center. Shoots left. 6'3", 184 lbs. Born, Saskatoon, Sask., December 29, 1988.
(Columbus' 9th choice, 187th overall, in 2008 Entry Draft).

			Regular Season					Playoffs				
Season	Club	League	GP	G	A	Pts	PIM	GP	G	A	Pts	PIM
2006-07	Waywayseecappo	MJHL	70	20	69	89	34	....	....	....	....	....
2007-08	Waywayseecappo	MJHL	60	51	64	115	34	7	9	4	13	10

• Signed Letter of Intent to attend **Cornell University** (ECAC) in fall of 2008.

COMRIE, Adam (KAWM-ree, A-duhm) FLA.

Defense. Shoots left. 6'4", 205 lbs. Born, Kanata, Ont., July 31, 1990.
(Florida's 3rd choice, 80th overall, in 2008 Entry Draft).

			Regular Season					Playoffs				
Season	Club	League	GP	G	A	Pts	PIM	GP	G	A	Pts	PIM
2006-07	Ohio	USHL	19	6	4	10	28	....	....	....	....	....
	Omaha Lancers	USHL	38	1	6	7	27	5	0	0	0	4
2007-08	Saginaw Spirit	OHL	58	10	18	28	90	4	0	0	0	4

CONBOY, Andrew (KAWN-boi, AN-droo) MTL.

Left wing. Shoots left. 6'4", 191 lbs. Born, Burnsville, MN, May 16, 1988.
(Montreal's 7th choice, 142nd overall, in 2007 Entry Draft).

			Regular Season					Playoffs				
Season	Club	League	GP	G	A	Pts	PIM	GP	G	A	Pts	PIM
2005-06	Wichita Falls	NAHL	51	7	8	15	158	5	0	2	2	2
2006-07	Omaha Lancers	USHL	56	25	25	50	105	....	....	....	....	....
2007-08	Omaha Lancers	USHL	58	17	21	38	188	14	*9	1	10	24

CONDON, Nate (KOHN-duhn, NAY-thun) COL.

Center. Shoots left. 6', 180 lbs. Born, Wausau, WI, May 29, 1990.
(Colorado's 7th choice, 200th overall, in 2008 Entry Draft).

			Regular Season					Playoffs				
Season	Club	League	GP	G	A	Pts	PIM	GP	G	A	Pts	PIM
2004-05	Wausau West	High-WI	22	1	4	5	4	....	....	....	....	....
2005-06	Wausau West	High-WI	22	21	22	43	6	....	....	....	....	....
	Team Wisconsin	UMHSEL	24	16	13	29	10	....	....	....	....	....
2006-07	Wausau West	High-WI	21	21	27	48	10	....	....	....	....	....
	Team Wisconsin	UMHSEL	23	14	9	23	6	....	....	....	....	....
2007-08	Wausau West	High-WI	23	33	26	59	10	....	....	....	....	....
	Team Wisconsin	UMHSEL	24	20	25	45	6	....	....	....	....	....

• Signed Letter of Intent to attend **University of Minnesota** (WCHA) in fall of 2009.

CONDRA, Erik (KAWN-druh, AIR-ihk) OTT.

Right wing. Shoots right. 6', 188 lbs. Born, Trenton, MI, August 6, 1986.
(Ottawa's 7th choice, 211th overall, in 2006 Entry Draft).

			Regular Season					Playoffs				
Season	Club	League	GP	G	A	Pts	PIM	GP	G	A	Pts	PIM
2004-05	Lincoln Stars	USHL	60	30	30	60	56	4	0	2	2	4
2005-06	U. of Notre Dame	CCHA	36	6	28	34	32	....	....	....	....	....
2006-07	U. of Notre Dame	CCHA	42	14	34	48	18	....	....	....	....	....
2007-08	U. of Notre Dame	CCHA	41	15	23	38	26	....	....	....	....	....

CCHA All-Rookie Team (2006)

COOPER, Joe (KOO-puhr, JOH) TOR.

Right wing. Shoots right. 6', 200 lbs. Born, Toronto, Ont., June 7, 1985.
(Ottawa's 9th choice, 219th overall, in 2004 Entry Draft).

			Regular Season					Playoffs				
Season	Club	League	GP	G	A	Pts	PIM	GP	G	A	Pts	PIM
2002-03	St. Mike's B's	OPJHL	44	15	30	45	121	....	....	....	....	....
2003-04	Miami U.	CCHA	34	1	0	1	66	....	....	....	....	....
2004-05	Miami U.	CCHA	36	1	7	8	43	....	....	....	....	....
2005-06	Miami U.	CCHA	39	3	7	10	64	....	....	....	....	....
2006-07	Miami U.	CCHA	36	3	1	4	58	....	....	....	....	....
2007-08	Columbia Inferno	ECHL	5	0	0	0	12	3	0	0	0	9

Signed as a free agent by **Toronto** (AHL), October 3, 2007.

CORMIER, Kevin (KOHR-mee-ay, KEH-vihn) PHX.

Left wing. Shoots left. 6'3", 249 lbs. Born, Moncton, N.B., January 27, 1986.
(Phoenix's 6th choice, 168th overall, in 2004 Entry Draft).

			Regular Season					Playoffs				
Season	Club	League	GP	G	A	Pts	PIM	GP	G	A	Pts	PIM
2003-04	Moncton	MJrHL	42	3	2	5	235	4	0	0	0	52
	Halifax	QMJHL	1	0	0	0	5	....	....	....	....	....
2004-05	Halifax	QMJHL	60	2	5	7	235	9	0	0	0	8
2005-06	Halifax	QMJHL	69	16	11	27	202	11	0	1	1	18
2006-07	Rimouski Oceanic	QMJHL	28	5	4	9	97	....	....	....	....	....
	Shawinigan	QMJHL	25	7	5	12	70	3	0	0	0	4
2007-08	Arizona Sundogs	CHL	23	3	2	5	104	....	....	....	....	....

CORMIER, Patrice (KOHR-mee-ay, pa-TREEZ) N.J.

Center. Shoots left. 6'2", 200 lbs. Born, Moncton, N. B., June 14, 1990.
(New Jersey's 3rd choice, 54th overall, in 2008 Entry Draft).

			Regular Season					Playoffs				
Season	Club	League	GP	G	A	Pts	PIM	GP	G	A	Pts	PIM
2006-07	Rimouski Oceanic	QMJHL	53	11	10	21	73	....	....	....	....	....
2007-08	Rimouski Oceanic	QMJHL	51	18	23	41	84	9	4	5	9	10

CORNET, Philippe (kohr-NAY, fihl-LEEP) EDM.

Left wing. Shoots left. 6', 173 lbs. Born, Val-Senneville, Que., March 28, 1990.
(Edmonton's 3rd choice, 133rd overall, in 2008 Entry Draft).

			Regular Season					Playoffs				
Season	Club	League	GP	G	A	Pts	PIM	GP	G	A	Pts	PIM
2006-07	Rimouski Oceanic	QMJHL	46	7	14	21	8	....	....	....	....	....
2007-08	Rimouski Oceanic	QMJHL	61	23	26	49	24	9	3	3	6	6

CORRENTE, Matthew (kohr-REHN-tay, MA-thew) N.J.

Defense. Shoots right. 6', 195 lbs. Born, Mississauga, Ont., March 17, 1988.
(New Jersey's 1st choice, 30th overall, in 2006 Entry Draft).

			Regular Season					Playoffs				
Season	Club	League	GP	G	A	Pts	PIM	GP	G	A	Pts	PIM
2004-05	Saginaw Spirit	OHL	62	6	9	15	89	....	....	....	....	....
2005-06	Saginaw Spirit	OHL	61	6	24	30	172	4	1	1	2	8
2006-07	Saginaw Spirit	OHL	29	2	13	15	67	....	....	....	....	....
	Mississauga	OHL	14	1	10	11	27	5	0	1	1	8
2007-08	Niagara Ice Dogs	OHL	21	2	13	15	64	10	0	5	5	33

COURTNALL, Justin (KOHRT-nawl, JUHS-tihn) T.B.

Left wing. Shoots left. 6'3", 185 lbs. Born, Victoria, B.C., May 21, 1989.
(Tampa Bay's 9th choice, 210th overall, in 2007 Entry Draft).

			Regular Season					Playoffs				
Season	Club	League	GP	G	A	Pts	PIM	GP	G	A	Pts	PIM
2005-06	Victoria Cougars	VIJHL	33	17	17	34	51	....	....	....	....	....
2006-07	Victoria Grizzlies	BCHL	5	0	0	0	14	....	....	....	....	....
	Burnaby Express	BCHL	48	5	9	14	55	12	0	2	2	19
2007-08	Victoria Grizzlies	BCHL	60	19	32	51	88	11	3	2	5	12

COUTURE, Derek (koh-TYOOR, DAIR-ihk)

Right wing. Shoots right. 6'2", 206 lbs. Born, Calgary, Alta., April 24, 1984.

			Regular Season					Playoffs				
Season	Club	League	GP	G	A	Pts	PIM	GP	G	A	Pts	PIM
2001-02	Saskatoon Blades	WHL	61	6	10	16	159	7	0	0	0	10
2002-03	Saskatoon Blades	WHL	70	17	20	37	160	6	1	2	3	13
2003-04	Saskatoon Blades	WHL	45	3	9	12	99	....	....	....	....	....
2004-05	Seattle	WHL	71	20	18	38	154	12	3	6	9	18
2005-06	Omaha	AHL	66	7	12	19	88	....	....	....	....	....
2006-07	Omaha	AHL	46	3	6	9	76	6	0	1	1	4
2007-08	Quad City Flames	AHL	76	10	8	18	129	....	....	....	....	....

Signed as a free agent by **Calgary**, August 5, 2005.

COUTURE, Logan (koh-TYOOR, LOH-guhn) S.J.

Center. Shoots left. 6', 195 lbs. Born, Guelph, Ont., March 28, 1989.
(San Jose's 1st choice, 9th overall, in 2007 Entry Draft).

			Regular Season					Playoffs				
Season	Club	League	GP	G	A	Pts	PIM	GP	G	A	Pts	PIM
2004-05	St. Thomas Stars	OJHL-B	48	24	22	46		....	....	....	....	....
2005-06	Ottawa 67's	OHL	65	25	39	64	52	6	3	4	7	0
2006-07	Ottawa 67's	OHL	54	26	52	78	24	5	1	7	8	4
2007-08	Ottawa 67's	OHL	51	21	37	58	37	4	2	1	3	0

CRABB, Joey (KRAB, JOH-ee) ATL.

Right wing. Shoots right. 6'1", 190 lbs. Born, Anchorage, AK, April 3, 1983.
(NY Rangers' 7th choice, 226th overall, in 2002 Entry Draft).

			Regular Season					Playoffs				
Season	Club	League	GP	G	A	Pts	PIM	GP	G	A	Pts	PIM
99-2000	USNTDP	NAHL	55	13	10	23	69	3	1	0	1	4
2000-01	USNTDP	U-18	39	10	10	20	22	....	....	....	....	....
	USNTDP	USHL	21	2	3	5	18	....	....	....	....	....
2001-02	Green Bay	USHL	61	15	27	42	94	7	4	8	12	21
2002-03	Colorado College	WCHA	35	4	4	8	40	....	....	....	....	....
2003-04	Colorado College	WCHA	39	15	12	27	20	....	....	....	....	....
2004-05	Colorado College	WCHA	43	16	16	32	44	....	....	....	....	....
2005-06	Colorado College	WCHA	42	18	25	43	45	....	....	....	....	....
2006-07	Chicago Wolves	AHL	63	7	15	22	25	6	0	0	0	0
2007-08	Chicago Wolves	AHL	72	9	26	35	78	24	1	4	5	20

Signed as a free agent by **Atlanta**, August 31, 2006.

CRACKNELL, Adam (krak-NEHL, A-duhm) **CGY.**

Right wing. Shoots right. 6'3", 214 lbs. Born, Prince Albert, Sask., July 15, 1985.
(Calgary's 10th choice, 279th overall, in 2004 Entry Draft).

			Regular Season					Playoffs				
Season	Club	League	GP	G	A	Pts	PIM	GP	G	A	Pts	PIM
2002-03	Kootenay Ice	WHL	67	7	4	11	37	11	0	0	0	2
2003-04	Kootenay Ice	WHL	72	26	35	61	63	4	1	1	2	2
2004-05	Kootenay Ice	WHL	72	19	29	48	65	16	8	8	16	6
2005-06	Kootenay Ice	WHL	72	42	51	93	85	6	1	4	5	6
	Omaha	AHL	6	1	2	3	2	....	....	....	....	....
2006-07	Las Vegas	ECHL	31	8	14	22	35	8	3	3	6	6
2007-08	Quad City Flames	AHL	4	1	0	1	0	....	....	....	....	....
	Las Vegas	ECHL	61	29	30	59	47	21	9	13	22	4

WHL West Second All-Star Team (2006)

CRAWFORD, Nick (KRAW-fuhrd, NIHK) **BUF.**

Defense. Shoots left. 6'1", 191 lbs. Born, Brampton, Ont., February 23, 1990.
(Buffalo's 8th choice, 164th overall, in 2008 Entry Draft).

			Regular Season					Playoffs				
Season	Club	League	GP	G	A	Pts	PIM	GP	G	A	Pts	PIM
2006-07	Saginaw Spirit	OHL	63	1	7	8	32	5	0	1	1	0
2007-08	Saginaw Spirit	OHL	68	4	16	20	58	4	1	1	2	2

CROSS, Tommy (KRAWS, TAW-mee) **BOS.**

Defense. Shoots left. 6'3", 198 lbs. Born, Hartford, CT, September 12, 1989.
(Boston's 2nd choice, 35th overall, in 2007 Entry Draft).

			Regular Season					Playoffs				
Season	Club	League	GP	G	A	Pts	PIM	GP	G	A	Pts	PIM
2004-05	Simsbury	High-CT	23	5	40	45	18	....	....	....	....	....
2005-06	Simsbury	High-CT	22	15	35	50	....	....	....	....	....	....
2006-07	Westminster	High-CT	25	8	12	20	20	....	....	....	....	....
	USNTDP	NAHL	2	0	2	2	0	....	....	....	....	....
	USNTDP	U-18	11	0	1	1	8	....	....	....	....	....
2007-08	Westminster	High-CT	25	9	12	21	....	....	....	....	....	....
	Ohio	USHL	9	0	4	4	8	....	....	....	....	....

• Signed Letter of Intent to attend **Boston College** (Hockey East) in fall of 2008.

CROWDER, Tim (KROW-duhr, TIHM) **PIT.**

Right wing. Shoots right. 6'2", 180 lbs. Born, Victoria, B.C., October 16, 1986.
(Pittsburgh's 5th choice, 126th overall, in 2005 Entry Draft).

			Regular Season					Playoffs				
Season	Club	League	GP	G	A	Pts	PIM	GP	G	A	Pts	PIM
2002-03	Powell River Kings	BCHL	52	6	6	12	....	....	....	....	....	....
2003-04	Powell River Kings	BCHL	57	21	34	55	44	7	3	3	6	8
2004-05	South Surrey	BCHL	56	23	27	50	30	....	....	....	....	....
2005-06	Michigan State	CCHA	44	17	13	30	29	....	....	....	....	....
2006-07	Michigan State	CCHA	41	14	11	25	18	....	....	....	....	....
2007-08	Michigan State	CCHA	42	15	23	38	36	....	....	....	....	....

CUMA, Tyler (KOO-ma, TIGH-luhr) **MIN.**

Defense. Shoots left. 6'2", 180 lbs. Born, Toronto, Ont., January 19, 1990.
(Minnesota's 1st choice, 23rd overall, in 2008 Entry Draft).

			Regular Season					Playoffs				
Season	Club	League	GP	G	A	Pts	PIM	GP	G	A	Pts	PIM
2005-06	Mississauga Reps	GTHL	40	15	20	35	52	....	....	....	....	....
2006-07	Ottawa 67's	OHL	63	3	16	19	55	5	0	2	2	6
2007-08	Ottawa 67's	OHL	59	4	28	32	69	4	1	1	2	2

CUNNING, Cam (KUH-nihng, KAM) **CGY.**

Left wing. Shoots left. 6'1", 213 lbs. Born, Powell River, B.C., June 4, 1985.
(Calgary's 8th choice, 240th overall, in 2003 Entry Draft).

			Regular Season					Playoffs				
Season	Club	League	GP	G	A	Pts	PIM	GP	G	A	Pts	PIM
2002-03	Kamloops Blazers	WHL	71	7	12	19	54	6	1	0	1	2
2003-04	Kamloops Blazers	WHL	65	14	13	27	62	5	1	1	2	10
2004-05	Kamloops Blazers	WHL	39	14	8	22	63	....	....	....	....	....
	Vancouver Giants	WHL	30	3	7	10	19	6	1	3	4	14
2005-06	Red Deer Rebels	WHL	40	19	13	32	52	....	....	....	....	....
	Omaha	AHL	30	2	4	6	24	....	....	....	....	....
2006-07	Omaha	AHL	60	12	5	17	45	6	0	2	2	2
2007-08	Quad City Flames	AHL	68	11	4	15	80	....	....	....	....	....

CUNTI, Luca (KOON-tee, LOO-ka) **T.B.**

Center. Shoots left. 6', 190 lbs. Born, Zurich, Switz., July 4, 1989.
(Tampa Bay's 2nd choice, 75th overall, in 2007 Entry Draft).

			Regular Season					Playoffs				
Season	Club	League	GP	G	A	Pts	PIM	GP	G	A	Pts	PIM
2004-05	GCK Zurich Jr.	Swiss-Jr.	32	12	10	22	18	....	....	....	....	....
2005-06	GCK Zurich Jr.	Swiss-Jr.	48	20	24	44	34	....	....	....	....	....
	GCK Lions Zurich	Swiss-2	7	0	0	0	2	....	....	....	....	....
2006-07	GCK Zurich Jr.	Swiss-Jr.	13	9	7	16	22	....	....	....	....	....
	Switzerland U20	Swiss-2	3	0	0	0	2	....	....	....	....	....
	HC Thurgau	Swiss-2	5	1	0	1	6	....	....	....	....	....
	GCK Lions Zurich	Swiss-2	5	1	1	2	0	....	....	....	....	....
	EHC Dubendorf	Swiss-3	STATISTICS NOT AVAILABLE									
2007-08	Chicago Steel	USHL	34	11	21	32	37	6	2	3	5	2

CURRY, Mike (KUH-ree, MIGHK) **L.A.**

Right wing. Shoots right. 6'4", 190 lbs. Born, Fort Benning, GA, September 20, 1984.
(Los Angeles' 6th choice, 205th overall, in 2004 Entry Draft).

			Regular Season					Playoffs				
Season	Club	League	GP	G	A	Pts	PIM	GP	G	A	Pts	PIM
2002-03	Sioux City	USHL	52	6	13	19	58	4	1	2	3	2
2003-04	Sioux City	USHL	60	20	20	40	119	7	2	5	7	16
2004-05	U. Minn-Duluth	WCHA	22	3	6	9	35	....	....	....	....	....
2005-06	U. Minn-Duluth	WCHA	36	2	3	5	68	....	....	....	....	....
2006-07	U. Minn-Duluth	WCHA	36	3	11	14	60	....	....	....	....	....
2007-08	U. Minn-Duluth	WCHA	21	3	4	7	34	....	....	....	....	....

CURRY, Sean (KUH-ree, SHAWN) **PHI.**

Defense. Shoots right. 6'4", 230 lbs. Born, Burnsville, MN, April 29, 1982.
(Carolina's 6th choice, 211th overall, in 2001 Entry Draft).

			Regular Season					Playoffs				
Season	Club	League	GP	G	A	Pts	PIM	GP	G	A	Pts	PIM
99-2000	Burnsville	High-MN	23	8	18	26	....	....	....	....	....	....
2000-01	Tri-City Americans	WHL	72	5	12	17	113	....	....	....	....	....
2001-02	Tri-City Americans	WHL	36	6	6	12	84	....	....	....	....	....
	Medicine Hat	WHL	24	4	13	17	43	....	....	....	....	....
2002-03	Lowell	AHL	35	0	2	2	62	....	....	....	....	....
	Florida Everblades	ECHL	32	1	6	7	77	1	0	0	0	0
2003-04	Lowell	AHL	74	1	8	9	66	....	....	....	....	....
2004-05	Lowell	AHL	61	2	7	9	103	7	0	1	1	4
2005-06	Providence Bruins	AHL	72	4	4	8	144	6	0	1	1	20
2006-07	Providence Bruins	AHL	64	5	8	13	122	13	2	9	11	28
2007-08	Providence Bruins	AHL	72	13	25	38	139	10	0	4	4	27

Signed as a free agent by **Boston**, August 8, 2007. Signed as a free agent by **Philadelphia**, July 1, 2008.

CZARNIK, Robert (CHAHR-nihk, RAW-buhrt) **L.A.**

Right wing. Shoots right. 6', 178 lbs. Born, Roseville, MI, January 25, 1990.
(Los Angeles' 4th choice, 63rd overall, in 2008 Entry Draft).

			Regular Season					Playoffs				
Season	Club	League	GP	G	A	Pts	PIM	GP	G	A	Pts	PIM
2005-06	Det. Honeybaked	MWEHL	....	53	78	131	....	....	....	....	....	....
2006-07	USNTDP	U-17	19	10	2	12	22	....	....	....	....	....
	USNTDP	NAHL	46	7	10	17	46	....	....	....	....	....
2007-08	USNTDP	U-18	43	15	18	33	30	....	....	....	....	....
	USNTDP	NAHL	14	4	2	6	12	....	....	....	....	....

• Signed Letter of Intent to attend **University of Michigan** (CCHA) in fall of 2008.

DADONOV, Evgeni (do-DON-nauv, ehv-GEH-nee) **FLA.**

Right wing. Shoots left. 5'10", 178 lbs. Born, Chelyabinsk, USSR, March 12, 1989.
(Florida's 3rd choice, 71st overall, in 2007 Entry Draft).

			Regular Season					Playoffs				
Season	Club	League	GP	G	A	Pts	PIM	GP	G	A	Pts	PIM
2005-06	Chelyabinsk 2	Russia-3	12	1	4	5	2	....	....	....	....	....
	Chelyabinsk	Russia-2	....	....	....	....	....	1	0	0	0	0
2006-07	Chelyabinsk 2	Russia-3	4	2	0	2	14	....	....	....	....	....
	Chelyabinsk	Russia	24	1	1	2	8	....	....	....	....	....
2007-08	Chelyabinsk 2	Russia-3	12	4	7	11	32	....	....	....	....	....
	Chelyabinsk	Russia	43	7	13	20	20	2	0	0	0	0

D'AGOSTINO, Nicholas (DA-goh-STEE-noh, NIHK-oh-las) **PIT.**

Defense. Shoots left. 6'1", 177 lbs. Born, Mississauga, Ont., June 24, 1990.
(Pittsburgh's 4th choice, 210th overall, in 2008 Entry Draft).

			Regular Season					Playoffs				
Season	Club	League	GP	G	A	Pts	PIM	GP	G	A	Pts	PIM
2006-07	Young Nats	GTHL	30	5	21	26	....	5	0	4	4	....
	Young Nats	Exhib.	8	1	5	6	....	....	....	....	....	....
2007-08	St. Michael's	OPJHL	46	5	18	23	22	10	0	3	3	8

• Signed Letter of Intent to attend **Cornell University** (ECAC) in fall of 2009.

DALPE, Zac (DAL-pee, ZAK) **CAR.**

Right wing. Shoots right. 6'1", 180 lbs. Born, Paris, Ont., November 1, 1989.
(Carolina's 2nd choice, 45th overall, in 2008 Entry Draft).

			Regular Season					Playoffs				
Season	Club	League	GP	G	A	Pts	PIM	GP	G	A	Pts	PIM
2006-07	Stratford Cullitons	OJHL-B	52	30	43	73	68	....	....	....	....	....
2007-08	Penticton Vees	BCHL	46	27	36	63	14	15	8	9	17	4

• Signed Letter of Intent to attend **Ohio State University** (CCHA) in fall of 2008.

DANIELS, Drew (DA-nyehlz, DROO) **S.J.**

Right wing. Shoots right. 6'1", 158 lbs. Born, Suffern, NY, June 7, 1989.
(San Jose's 7th choice, 194th overall, in 2008 Entry Draft).

			Regular Season					Playoffs				
Season	Club	League	GP	G	A	Pts	PIM	GP	G	A	Pts	PIM
2006-07	Kent Prep School	High-CT	....	12	22	34	....	....	....	....	....	....
2007-08	Kent Prep School	High-CT	25	12	35	47	14	....	....	....	....	....

• Signed Letter of Intent to attend **Northeastern University** (Hockey East) in fall of 2009.

DANIELS, Justin (DA-nyehlz, JUHS-tihn) **S.J.**

Center. Shoots right. 6'1", 156 lbs. Born, Suffern, NY, June 7, 1989.
(San Jose's 1st choice, 62nd overall, in 2008 Entry Draft).

			Regular Season					Playoffs				
Season	Club	League	GP	G	A	Pts	PIM	GP	G	A	Pts	PIM
2006-07	Kent Prep School	High-CT	....	14	32	46	....	....	....	....	....	....
2007-08	Kent Prep School	High-CT	25	17	37	54	10	....	....	....	....	....

• Signed Letter of Intent to attend **Northeastern University** (Hockey East) in fall of 2009.

DANIS-PEPIN, Simon (da-NEE-peh-PEH, see-MOHN) **CHI.**

Defense. Shoots right. 6'7", 217 lbs. Born, Gatineau, Que., April 11, 1988.
(Chicago's 3rd choice, 61st overall, in 2006 Entry Draft).

			Regular Season					Playoffs				
Season	Club	League	GP	G	A	Pts	PIM	GP	G	A	Pts	PIM
2003-04	Gatineau Intrepide	QAAA	33	2	14	16	20	2	0	0	0	0
2004-05	Gatineau Intrepide	QAAA	39	6	31	37	64	14	6	7	13	25
2005-06	N.H. Jr. Monarchs	EJHL	2	0	0	0	0	....	....	....	....	....
	U. of Maine	H-East	23	0	5	5	14	....	....	....	....	....
2006-07	U. of Maine	H-East	40	2	4	6	18	....	....	....	....	....
2007-08	U. of Maine	H-East	34	4	8	12	20	....	....	....	....	....

DASILVA, Dan (duh-SIHL-vah, DAN)

Right wing. Shoots right. 6'1", 195 lbs. Born, Saskatoon, Sask., April 30, 1985.

			Regular Season					Playoffs				
Season	Club	League	GP	G	A	Pts	PIM	GP	G	A	Pts	PIM
2002-03	Portland	WHL	64	9	13	22	81	7	0	4	4	16
2003-04	Portland	WHL	65	36	20	56	120	5	0	1	1	6
2004-05	Portland	WHL	71	31	42	73	127	5	1	1	2	6
2005-06	Lowell	AHL	25	3	2	5	27	....	....	....	....	....
	San Diego Gulls	ECHL	4	5	3	8	2	....	....	....	....	....
2006-07	Albany River Rats	AHL	43	11	8	19	33	....	....	....	....	....
	Arizona Sundogs	CHL	14	9	13	22	10	....	....	....	....	....
2007-08	Lake Erie Monsters	AHL	54	9	14	23	50	....	....	....	....	....

Signed as a free agent by **Colorado**, October 11, 2005.

DAUGAVINS, Kaspars (DAH-gah-vihnsh, KAS-purz) **OTT.**

Left wing. Shoots left. 5'11", 212 lbs. Born, Riga, Latvia, May 18, 1988.
(Ottawa's 3rd choice, 91st overall, in 2006 Entry Draft).

			Regular Season					Playoffs				
Season	Club	League	GP	G	A	Pts	PIM	GP	G	A	Pts	PIM
2003-04	HK Riga 2000	EEHL	2	0	1	1	0	....	....	....	....	....
	Prizma/Riga 86	Latvia	14	6	6	12	10	2	1	1	2	4
2004-05	CSKA Moscow 2	Russia-3	STATISTICS NOT AVAILABLE									
2005-06	HK Riga 2000	Latvia	....	4	6	10	16	....	....	....	....	....
	HK Riga 2000	BelOpen	45	4	11	15	16	....	....	....	....	....
2006-07	St. Michael's	OHL	61	18	42	60	64	....	....	....	....	....
	Binghamton	AHL	11	2	0	2	9	....	....	....	....	....
2007-08	St. Michael's	OHL	62	40	34	74	42	4	2	1	3	4
	Binghamton	AHL	3	0	1	1	0	....	....	....	....	....

OHL All-Rookie Team (2007)

D'AVERSA, Jonathan (dah-VEHR-sah, JAWN-ah-thuhn) **PIT.**

Defense. Shoots right. 6'2", 200 lbs. Born, Richmond Hill, Ont., March 2, 1986.

			Regular Season					Playoffs				
Season	Club	League	GP	G	A	Pts	PIM	GP	G	A	Pts	PIM
2002-03	Stouffville Spirit	OPJHL	49	4	21	25	18	....	....	....	....	....
2003-04	Sudbury Wolves	OHL	63	1	14	15	22	7	0	1	1	2
2004-05	Sudbury Wolves	OHL	67	5	24	29	42	12	4	6	10	8
2005-06	Sudbury Wolves	OHL	62	7	39	46	83	10	2	0	2	17
2006-07	Sudbury Wolves	OHL	67	13	47	60	53	21	3	15	18	16
2007-08	Wilkes-Barre	AHL	27	4	2	6	6	....	....	....	....	....
	Wheeling Nailers	ECHL	25	1	13	14	10	....	....	....	....	....

Signed as a free agent by **Pittsburgh**, May 24, 2007.

DAVIS, Nathan (DAY-vihs, NAY-thuhn) **CHI.**

Center/Left wing. Shoots left. 6'1", 193 lbs. Born, Cleveland, OH, May 23, 1986.
(Chicago's 6th choice, 113th overall, in 2005 Entry Draft).

			Regular Season					Playoffs				
Season	Club	League	GP	G	A	Pts	PIM	GP	G	A	Pts	PIM
2002-03	USNTDP	NAHL	20	2	3	5	23	....	....	....	....	....
2003-04	USNTDP	U-18	46	7	8	15	16	....	....	....	....	....
	USNTDP	NAHL	11	3	6	9	17	....	....	....	....	....
2004-05	Miami U.	CCHA	38	14	11	25	30	....	....	....	....	....
2005-06	Miami U.	CCHA	37	20	20	40	34	....	....	....	....	....
2006-07	Miami U.	CCHA	42	21	29	50	24	....	....	....	....	....
2007-08	Miami U.	CCHA	21	8	9	17	14	....	....	....	....	....

CCHA First All-Star Team (2006) • CCHA Second All-Star Team (2007) • NCAA West Second All-American Team (2007)

DAVIS, Patrick (DAY-vihs, PAT-rihk) **N.J.**

Center. Shoots right. 6'3", 210 lbs. Born, Sterling, MI, December 28, 1986.
(New Jersey's 4th choice, 99th overall, in 2005 Entry Draft).

			Regular Season					Playoffs				
Season	Club	League	GP	G	A	Pts	PIM	GP	G	A	Pts	PIM
2002-03	Detroit Belle Tire	MWEHL	STATISTICS NOT AVAILABLE									
	Sioux City	USHL	16	3	2	5	8	1	0	0	0	2
2003-04	Kitchener Rangers	OHL	27	8	10	18	21	....	....	....	....	....
2004-05	Kitchener Rangers	OHL	59	20	30	50	41	14	3	4	7	20
2005-06	Kitchener Rangers	OHL	22	13	4	17	30	....	....	....	....	....
	Windsor Spitfires	OHL	38	22	29	51	64	7	2	6	8	12
	Albany River Rats	AHL	3	0	0	0	2	....	....	....	....	....
2006-07	Lowell Devils	AHL	41	5	13	18	26	....	....	....	....	....
2007-08	Lowell Devils	AHL	60	7	12	19	58	....	....	....	....	....

DAY, Brian (DAY, BRIGH-uhn) **NYI**

Right wing. Shoots right. 6', 186 lbs. Born, Boston, MA, August 4, 1988.
(NY Islanders' 11th choice, 171st overall, in 2006 Entry Draft).

			Regular Season					Playoffs				
Season	Club	League	GP	G	A	Pts	PIM	GP	G	A	Pts	PIM
2003-04	Gov. Dummer	High-MA	25	8	15	23	....	....	....	....	....	....
2004-05	Gov. Dummer	High-MA	25	11	13	24	30	....	....	....	....	....
2005-06	Gov. Dummer	High-MA	28	9	13	22	34	....	....	....	....	....
2006-07	Gov. Academy	High-MA	27	20	18	38	....	....	....	....	....	....
2007-08	Colgate	ECAC	41	9	13	22	53	....	....	....	....	....

De COSTE, Kyle (duh KAWS-tuh, KIGH-uhl) **T.B.**

Right wing. Shoots right. 6'1", 178 lbs. Born, London, Ont., June 30, 1990.
(Tampa Bay's 4th choice, 147th overall, in 2008 Entry Draft).

			Regular Season					Playoffs				
Season	Club	League	GP	G	A	Pts	PIM	GP	G	A	Pts	PIM
2005-06	Elgin	Minor-ON	58	20	18	38	40	....	....	....	....	....
2006-07	Brampton	OHL	45	1	3	4	29	3	1	0	1	0
2007-08	Brampton	OHL	66	10	12	22	48	5	0	0	0	2

DEE, Robby (DEE, RAW-bee) **EDM.**

Center/Wing. Shoots left. 6'2", 185 lbs. Born, Minneapolis, MN, April 9, 1987.
(Edmonton's 4th choice, 86th overall, in 2005 Entry Draft).

			Regular Season					Playoffs				
Season	Club	League	GP	G	A	Pts	PIM	GP	G	A	Pts	PIM
2004-05	Breck Mustangs	High-MN	28	49	38	87	14	....	....	....	....	....
2005-06	Omaha Lancers	USHL	32	6	6	12	20	3	1	0	1	2
2006-07	Omaha Lancers	USHL	34	11	14	25	60	....	....	....	....	....
2007-08	U. of Maine	H-East	24	1	2	3	18	....	....	....	....	....

DEGON, Marvin (DEE-gawn, MAR-vihn)

Defense. Shoots right. 5'11", 190 lbs. Born, Worcester, MA, July 20, 1983.

			Regular Season					Playoffs				
Season	Club	League	GP	G	A	Pts	PIM	GP	G	A	Pts	PIM
2002-03	Massachusetts	H-East	36	2	14	16	14	....	....	....	....	....
2003-04	Massachusetts	H-East	36	5	15	20	18	....	....	....	....	....
2004-05	Massachusetts	H-East	38	10	8	18	44	....	....	....	....	....
2005-06	Massachusetts	H-East	36	10	19	29	33	....	....	....	....	....
	Hartford Wolf Pack	AHL	14	2	4	6	4	13	0	5	5	6
2006-07	Hartford Wolf Pack	AHL	71	8	26	34	40	7	0	1	1	0
2007-08	Hamilton Bulldogs	AHL	79	9	22	31	56	....	....	....	....	....

Signed as a free agent by **Montreal**, July 5, 2007.

DEGRAY, John (DIH-gray, JAWN) **ANA.**

Defense. Shoots left. 6'4", 213 lbs. Born, Richmond Hill, Ont., March 14, 1988.
(Anaheim's 3rd choice, 83rd overall, in 2006 Entry Draft).

			Regular Season					Playoffs				
Season	Club	League	GP	G	A	Pts	PIM	GP	G	A	Pts	PIM
2003-04	Richmond Hill	Minor-ON	76	5	35	40	107	....	....	....	....	....
2004-05	Brampton	OHL	52	2	8	10	51	6	0	0	0	2
2005-06	Brampton	OHL	68	0	10	10	103	11	0	0	0	8
2006-07	Brampton	OHL	65	4	13	17	75	4	1	0	1	10
2007-08	Brampton	OHL	67	4	13	17	140	5	0	0	0	12
	Portland Pirates	AHL	6	0	0	0	0	3	0	0	0	0

DEILERT, Alexander (DAY-luhrt, al-ehx-AN-duhr) **CGY.**

Defense. Shoots right. 5'11", 180 lbs. Born, Stockholm, Sweden, February 10, 1989.
(Calgary's 7th choice, 198th overall, in 2008 Entry Draft).

			Regular Season					Playoffs				
Season	Club	League	GP	G	A	Pts	PIM	GP	G	A	Pts	PIM
2004-05	Hammarby U18	Swe-U18	2	2	1	3	....	....	....	....	....	....
2005-06	Djurgarden U18	Swe-U18	24	6	8	14	41	4	0	0	0	4
2006-07	Djurgarden U18	Swe-U18	11	2	2	4	41	2	0	1	1	6
	Djurgarden Jr.	Swe-Jr.	28	1	4	5	10	7	0	0	0	0
2007-08	Djurgarden Jr.	Swe-Jr.	38	6	12	18	70	7	1	2	3	14

DEL ZOTTO, Michael (DEHL ZAW-toh, MIGH-kuhl) **NYR**

Defense. Shoots left. 6'1", 200 lbs. Born, Stouffville, Ont., June 24, 1990.
(NY Rangers' 1st choice, 20th overall, in 2008 Entry Draft).

			Regular Season					Playoffs				
Season	Club	League	GP	G	A	Pts	PIM	GP	G	A	Pts	PIM
2005-06	Markham Waxers	Minor-ON	73	30	90	120	90	....	....	....	....	....
2006-07	Oshawa Generals	OHL	64	10	47	57	78	9	3	9	12	14
2007-08	Oshawa Generals	OHL	64	16	47	63	82	15	2	6	8	38

DELAHEY, Matt (dehl-A-hay, MAT) **N.J.**

Defense. Shoots left. 6'3", 215 lbs. Born, Moose Jaw, Sask., September 25, 1989.
(New Jersey's 5th choice, 112th overall, in 2008 Entry Draft).

			Regular Season					Playoffs				
Season	Club	League	GP	G	A	Pts	PIM	GP	G	A	Pts	PIM
2004-05	Moose Jaw	SMHL	STATISTICS NOT AVAILABLE									
	Regina Pats	WHL	1	0	0	0	0	....	....	....	....	....
2005-06	Moose Jaw	SMHL	STATISTICS NOT AVAILABLE									
	Regina Pats	WHL	3	0	0	0	2	1	0	0	0	0
2006-07	Regina Pats	WHL	60	1	5	6	42	10	0	0	0	4
2007-08	Regina Pats	WHL	68	3	16	19	68	6	0	3	3	6

DELISLE, Steven (duh-LIGH-uhl, STEE-vehn) **CBJ**

Defense. Shoots right. 6'6", 209 lbs. Born, Levise, Que., July 30, 1990.
(Columbus' 3rd choice, 107th overall, in 2008 Entry Draft).

			Regular Season					Playoffs				
Season	Club	League	GP	G	A	Pts	PIM	GP	G	A	Pts	PIM
2006-07	Gatineau	QMJHL	56	1	11	12	47	5	0	0	0	0
2007-08	Gatineau	QMJHL	70	6	23	29	82	19	0	10	10	16

DELLA ROVERE, Stefan (DEHL-ah ROH-vair, STEH-fan) **WSH.**

Left wing. Shoots left. 5'11", 196 lbs. Born, Richmond Hill, Ont., February 25, 1990.
(Washington's 8th choice, 204th overall, in 2008 Entry Draft).

			Regular Season					Playoffs				
Season	Club	League	GP	G	A	Pts	PIM	GP	G	A	Pts	PIM
2005-06	Tor. Jr. Canadiens	GTHL	47	25	31	56	69	....	....	....	....	....
2006-07	Barrie Colts	OHL	48	7	7	14	37	6	0	0	0	0
2007-08	Barrie Colts	OHL	68	13	19	32	171	9	1	2	3	16

DELORY, James (deh-LOR-ee, JAYMZ) **FLA.**

Defense. Shoots right. 6'4", 220 lbs. Born, Scarborough, Ont., March 3, 1988.
(San Jose's 3rd choice, 98th overall, in 2006 Entry Draft).

			Regular Season					Playoffs				
Season	Club	League	GP	G	A	Pts	PIM	GP	G	A	Pts	PIM
2004-05	Oshawa Generals	OHL	61	1	4	5	82	....	....	....	....	....
2005-06	Oshawa Generals	OHL	67	6	26	32	136	....	....	....	....	....
2006-07	Oshawa Generals	OHL	61	4	21	25	167	9	0	4	4	16
2007-08	Oshawa Generals	OHL	54	2	20	22	154	15	1	8	9	26

Signed as a free agent by **Florida**, July 3, 2008.

DEMEN-WILLAUME, Richard (deh-MEHN-WIHL-awm, RIH-kahrd) **COL.**

Defense. Shoots left. 6'3", 210 lbs. Born, Asa, Sweden, January 28, 1986.
(Colorado's 4th choice, 154th overall, in 2004 Entry Draft).

			Regular Season					Playoffs				
Season	Club	League	GP	G	A	Pts	PIM	GP	G	A	Pts	PIM
2001-02	V.Frolunda U18	Swe-U18	13	2	2	4	14	3	1	0	1	2
	V.Frolunda Jr.	Swe-Jr.	1	0	0	0	0	....	....	....	....	....
2002-03	V.Frolunda Jr.	Swe-Jr.	22	0	6	6	14	5	0	1	1	6
	V.Frolunda U18	Swe-U18	1	0	0	0	2	7	1	2	3	4
2003-04	V.Frolunda Jr.	Swe-Jr.	35	6	7	13	22	....	....	....	....	....
2004-05	Frolunda	Sweden	9	0	0	0	0	1	0	0	0	0
	Frolunda Jr.	Swe-Jr.	32	3	12	15	63	6	1	1	2	22
2005-06	Frolunda Jr.	Swe-Jr.	10	4	8	12	8	6	3	5	8	31
	Frolunda	Sweden	42	2	1	3	26	....	....	....	....	....
2006-07	Arizona Sundogs	CHL	9	0	2	2	16	....	....	....	....	....
2007-08	Rogle	Sweden-2	52	10	10	20	50	....	....	....	....	....

DEMERS, Jason (duh-MAIRZ, JAY-suhn) **S.J.**

Defense. Shoots right. 6'1", 185 lbs. Born, Dorval, Que., June 9, 1988.
(San Jose's 6th choice, 186th overall, in 2008 Entry Draft).

			Regular Season					Playoffs				
Season	Club	League	GP	G	A	Pts	PIM	GP	G	A	Pts	PIM
2004-05	Moncton Wildcats	QMJHL	25	0	1	1	10	....	....	....	....	....
2005-06	Moncton Wildcats	QMJHL	21	1	3	4	15	....	....	....	....	....
	Victoriaville Tigres	QMJHL	33	2	13	15	58	5	0	2	2	10
2006-07	Victoriaville Tigres	QMJHL	69	5	19	24	98	6	0	0	0	2
2007-08	Victoriaville Tigres	QMJHL	67	9	55	64	91	6	1	5	6	6

DEMERS, Julien (duh-MAIRZ, JOO-lee-ehn) **S.J.**

Defense. Shoots left. 6', 218 lbs. Born, Ottawa, Ont., September 25, 1989.
(San Jose's 4th choice, 146th overall, in 2008 Entry Draft).

			Regular Season					Playoffs				
Season	Club	League	GP	G	A	Pts	PIM	GP	G	A	Pts	PIM
2006-07	Nepean Raiders	CJHL	35	7	24	31	38	....	....	....	....	....
	Ottawa 67's	OHL	31	2	4	6	29	5	0	0	0	6
2007-08	Ottawa 67's	OHL	65	5	28	33	94	4	0	2	2	0

DENISOV, Denis (den-NEES-ahf, deh-NEES) **BUF.**

Left wing. Shoots left. 6', 183 lbs. Born, Kalinin, USSR, December 31, 1981.
(Buffalo's 4th choice, 149th overall, in 2000 Entry Draft).

			Regular Season					Playoffs				
Season	Club	League	GP	G	A	Pts	PIM	GP	G	A	Pts	PIM
1997-98	HK CSKA Moscow	Russia	7	0	0	0	4	....	....	....	....	....
1998-99	HK CSKA Moscow	Russia-2	42	1	6	7	16	....	....	....	....	....
99-2000	HK Moscow	Russia-2	39	1	8	9	16	....	....	....	....	....
2000-01	HK Moscow	Russia-2	41	0	3	3	6	....	....	....	....	....
2001-02	Krylja Sovetov	Russia	47	3	4	7	37	....	....	....	....	....
	Krylja Sovetov 2	Russia-3	3	0	1	1	18	....	....	....	....	....
2002-03	Ufa	Russia	50	2	8	10	12	3	0	1	1	0
2003-04	Ak Bars Kazan	Russia	51	4	11	15	34	7	0	0	0	4
2004-05	Ak Bars Kazan	Russia	57	4	7	11	30	4	0	0	0	2
2005-06	Ak Bars Kazan	Russia	22	0	2	2	51	2	0	0	0	4
2006-07	Avangard Omsk	Russia	52	2	10	12	32	9	1	2	3	4
2007-08	Avangard Omsk	Russia	51	7	12	19	34	4	0	2	2	4

DENISOV, Vladimir (den-NEES-ahf) **NYR**

Defense. Shoots left. 5'11", 207 lbs. Born, Novopolotzk, USSR, June 29, 1984.

			Regular Season					Playoffs				
Season	Club	League	GP	G	A	Pts	PIM	GP	G	A	Pts	PIM
2003-04	Yunior Minsk	Belarus	1	0	0	0	2	....	....	....	....	....
	Novopolotsk	Belarus	41	3	8	11	107	2	0	0	0	8
2004-05	Dynamo Minsk	Belarus	1	0	0	0	0	....	....	....	....	....
	Keramin Minsk 2	Bel-2	9	3	2	5	20	....	....	....	....	....
	Keramin Minsk	Belarus	12	0	1	1	12	4	0	0	0	0
2005-06	Keramin Minsk 2	Belarus-2	1	0	1	1	0	....	....	....	....	....
	Keramin Minsk	Belarus	39	1	3	4	71	....	....	....	....	....
2006-07	Lada Togliatti	Russia	39	0	3	3	76	3	0	0	0	6
2007-08	Lake Erie Monsters	AHL	66	2	6	8	111	....	....	....	....	....
	Johnstown Chiefs	ECHL	5	0	2	2	26	....	....	....	....	....

Signed as a free agent by **NY Rangers**, July 10, 2008.

DENNY, Chad (DEHN-ee, CHAD) **ATL.**

Defense. Shoots left. 6'3", 220 lbs. Born, Sydney, N.S., March 27, 1987.
(Atlanta's 3rd choice, 49th overall, in 2005 Entry Draft).

			Regular Season					Playoffs				
Season	Club	League	GP	G	A	Pts	PIM	GP	G	A	Pts	PIM
2003-04	Lewiston	QMJHL	41	3	6	9	19	7	0	0	0	11
2004-05	Lewiston	QMJHL	53	8	18	26	98	8	2	2	4	14
2005-06	Lewiston	QMJHL	62	19	28	47	150	6	0	3	3	10
2006-07	Lewiston	QMJHL	59	17	48	65	89	17	10	9	19	32
2007-08	Chicago Wolves	AHL	11	2	4	6	19	....	....	....	....	....
	Gwinnett	ECHL	48	7	6	13	48	8	0	0	0	12

DERLYUK, Roman (duhr-LYUHK, ROH-muhn) **FLA.**

Defense. Shoots left. 6'3", 198 lbs. Born, Leningrad, USSR, October 27, 1986.
(Florida's 7th choice, 164th overall, in 2005 Entry Draft).

			Regular Season					Playoffs				
Season	Club	League	GP	G	A	Pts	PIM	GP	G	A	Pts	PIM
2003-04	Lokom. St. Pete.	Russia-3	STATISTICS NOT AVAILABLE									
2004-05	Spartak St. Pet.	Russia-2	51	0	3	3	74	....	....	....	....	....
2005-06	SKA St. Petersburg	Russia	32	0	3	3	63	2	1	0	1	0
	St. Petersburg 2	Russia-3	2	0	1	1	0	....	....	....	....	....
2006-07	SKA St. Petersburg	Russia	6	0	1	1	4	....	....	....	....	....
	St. Petersburg 2	Russia-3	6	1	4	5	6	....	....	....	....	....
	THK Tver	Russia-3	2	0	2	2	0	....	....	....	....	....
	MVD	Russia	19	0	3	3	14	1	0	0	0	0
2007-08	MVD 2	Russia-3	24	1	5	6	36	....	....	....	....	....
	MVD	Russia	26	3	3	6	26	3	0	0	0	2

DESCHAMPS, Nicolas (day-SHAWMP, NIHK-oh-las) **ANA.**

Center. Shoots left. 6', 173 lbs. Born, Lasalle, Que., January 6, 1990.
(Anaheim's 2nd choice, 35th overall, in 2008 Entry Draft).

			Regular Season					Playoffs				
Season	Club	League	GP	G	A	Pts	PIM	GP	G	A	Pts	PIM
2005-06	C.C. Lemoyne	QAAA	23	5	4	9	14	8	0	0	0	12
2006-07	C.C. Lemoyne	QAAA	35	20	28	48	60	10	4	7	11	22
2007-08	Chicoutimi	QMJHL	70	24	43	67	63	6	2	3	5	6

QMJHL All-Rookie Team (2008) • Canadian Major Junior All-Rookie Team (2008)

DESIMONE, Phil (dih-SEE-mohn, FIHL) **WSH.**

Center. Shoots left. 6', 195 lbs. Born, East Amherst, NY, March 19, 1987.
(Washington's 4th choice, 84th overall, in 2007 Entry Draft).

			Regular Season					Playoffs				
Season	Club	League	GP	G	A	Pts	PIM	GP	G	A	Pts	PIM
2004-05	Sioux City	USHL	44	2	7	9	28	6	0	1	1	4
2005-06	Sioux City	USHL	60	15	38	53	71	....	....	....	....	....
2006-07	Sioux City	USHL	60	26	47	73	60	7	6	6	12	2
2007-08	New Hampshire	H-East	38	3	10	13	28	....	....	....	....	....

DEVEAUX, Andre (de-VOH, AWN-dray) **TOR.**

Center. Shoots right. 6'3", 240 lbs. Born, Welland, Ont., February 23, 1984.
(Montreal's 4th choice, 182nd overall, in 2002 Entry Draft).

			Regular Season					Playoffs				
Season	Club	League	GP	G	A	Pts	PIM	GP	G	A	Pts	PIM
2000-01	Belleville Bulls	OHL	58	3	6	9	65	10	3	6	9	6
2001-02	Belleville Bulls	OHL	64	8	13	21	89	11	1	2	3	30
2002-03	Belleville Bulls	OHL	34	6	12	18	93	....	....	....	....	....
	Owen Sound	OHL	29	9	10	19	33	4	2	2	4	6
2003-04	Owen Sound	OHL	64	16	30	46	151	7	3	3	6	21
2004-05	Springfield Falcons	AHL	73	4	8	12	210	....	....	....	....	....
2005-06	Springfield Falcons	AHL	59	6	5	11	135	....	....	....	....	....
	Johnstown Chiefs	ECHL	11	4	7	11	36	5	1	1	2	2
2006-07	Springfield Falcons	AHL	8	1	2	3	8	....	....	....	....	....
	Johnstown Chiefs	ECHL	21	6	8	14	51	....	....	....	....	....
	Chicago Wolves	AHL	28	4	4	8	105	14	3	2	5	48
2007-08	Chicago Wolves	AHL	66	7	11	18	232	24	0	2	2	67

Signed as a free agent by **Tampa Bay**, September 15, 2004. Traded to **Atlanta** by **Tampa Bay** with Andy Delmore for and Stephen Baby and Kyle Wanvig, February 1, 2007. Signed as a free agent by **Toronto**, July 21, 2008.

DIBENEDETTO, Justin (dih-behn-ih-DEH-toh, JUHS-tihn) **NYI**

Center. Shoots left. 5'11", 194 lbs. Born, Etobicoke, Ont., August 25, 1988.
(NY Islanders' 13th choice, 175th overall, in 2008 Entry Draft).

			Regular Season					Playoffs				
Season	Club	League	GP	G	A	Pts	PIM	GP	G	A	Pts	PIM
2004-05	St. Michael's	OHL	64	3	6	9	37	9	0	0	0	0
2005-06	St. Michael's	OHL	61	17	13	30	58	4	1	0	1	11
2006-07	Sarnia Sting	OHL	58	28	35	63	46	4	2	1	3	4
2007-08	Sarnia Sting	OHL	58	39	54	93	61	9	3	7	10	12

DiCASMIRRO, Nate (dee-KAZ-MIHR-oh, NAYT)

Left wing. Shoots left. 5'11", 205 lbs. Born, Atikokan, Ont., September 27, 1978.

			Regular Season					Playoffs				
Season	Club	League	GP	G	A	Pts	PIM	GP	G	A	Pts	PIM
1996-97	North Iowa	USHL	51	18	22	40	86	12	0	6	6	22
1997-98	North Iowa	USHL	52	29	45	74	118	11	5	5	10	34
1998-99	St. Cloud State	WCHA	34	6	8	14	46	....	....	....	....	....
99-2000	St. Cloud State	WCHA	40	19	24	43	26	....	....	....	....	....
2000-01	St. Cloud State	WCHA	32	9	20	29	26	....	....	....	....	....
2001-02	St. Cloud State	WCHA	41	17	33	50	58	....	....	....	....	....
	Hamilton Bulldogs	AHL	1	0	0	0	0	10	0	5	5	6
2002-03	Hamilton Bulldogs	AHL	49	5	12	17	22	16	2	1	3	8
2003-04	Toronto	AHL	71	17	18	35	37	2	0	1	1	0
2004-05	Edmonton	AHL	77	7	18	25	48	....	....	....	....	....
2005-06	Grand Rapids	AHL	72	16	36	52	97	16	3	3	6	20
2006-07	Providence Bruins	AHL	68	10	18	28	59	13	4	0	4	10
2007-08	Providence Bruins	AHL	20	2	3	5	12	....	....	....	....	....
	San Antonio	AHL	23	6	2	8	16	....	....	....	....	....
	Syracuse Crunch	AHL	20	3	10	13	8	13	3	4	7	12

USHL First All-Star Team (1998) • USHL MVP (1998) • WCHA Second All-Star Team (2002)

Signed as a free agent by **Edmonton**, May 28, 2002. Signed as a free agent by **Boston**, July 17, 2006. Traded to **Phoenix** by **Boston** with Boston's 5th round choice in 2009 Entry Draft for Alex Auld, December 6, 2007. Traded to **Columbus** by **Phoenix** for Steven Goertzen, February 28, 2008.

DIDOMENICO, Christopher dee-DOH-mehn-ih-koh, KRIHS-tuh-fuhr **TOR.**

Center. Shoots right. 5'11", 165 lbs. Born, Toronto, Ont., February 20, 1989.
(Toronto's 5th choice, 164th overall, in 2007 Entry Draft).

			Regular Season					Playoffs				
Season	Club	League	GP	G	A	Pts	PIM	GP	G	A	Pts	PIM
2005-06	North York	GTHL	36	28	35	63		....	....	....	....	....
	North York	OPJHL	2	2	0	2	0	....	....	....	....	....
2006-07	Saint John	QMJHL	70	25	50	75	60	....	....	....	....	....
2007-08	Saint John	QMJHL	70	39	56	95	103	14	8	11	19	20

QMJHL All-Rookie Team (2007)

DIETRICH, Robert (DEET-rihkh, RAW-buhrt) **NSH.**

Defense. Shoots right. 5'10", 172 lbs. Born, Ordzhonikidze, USSR, July 25, 1986.
(Nashville's 8th choice, 174th overall, in 2007 Entry Draft).

			Regular Season					Playoffs				
Season	Club	League	GP	G	A	Pts	PIM	GP	G	A	Pts	PIM
2001-02	Kaufbeuren Jr.	Ger-Jr.	9	1	2	3	2	....	....	....	....	....
2002-03	Mannheim Jr.	Ger-Jr.	33	4	13	17	39	3	0	1	1	4
2003-04	EC Peiting	German-3	42	5	9	24	83	....	....	....	....	....
2004-05	ETC Crimmitschau	German-2	45	3	14	17	34	10	0	0	0	6
2005-06	Straubing Tigers	German-2	46	5	3	8	55	15	0	1	1	8
	Dusseldorf	Germany	4	0	0	0	2	....	....	....	....	....
2006-07	Dusseldorf	Germany	52	3	19	22	28	9	2	4	6	22
2007-08	Dusseldorf	Germany	9	1	1	2	12	13	1	2	3	4

DINGLE, Ryan (DIHN-guhl, RIGH-uhn) **ANA.**

Left wing. Shoots left. 5'10", 190 lbs. Born, Steamboat Springs, CO, April 4, 1984.

			Regular Season					Playoffs				
Season	Club	League	GP	G	A	Pts	PIM	GP	G	A	Pts	PIM
2001-02	Des Moines	USHL	61	7	10	17	63	3	1	0	1	2
2002-03	Tri-City Storm	USHL	32	17	17	34	31	3	0	0	0	6
	Des Moines	USHL	26	8	6	14	16	....	....	....	....	....
2003-04	Tri-City Storm	USHL	38	13	23	36	14	9	3	7	10	4
2004-05	U. of Denver	WCHA	41	6	12	18	32	....	....	....	....	....
2005-06	U. of Denver	WCHA	38	27	16	43	37	....	....	....	....	....
2006-07	U. of Denver	WCHA	40	22	15	37	38	....	....	....	....	....
	Portland Pirates	AHL	4	0	1	1	4	....	....	....	....	....
2007-08	Portland Pirates	AHL	19	1	5	6	10	2	0	1	1	0
	Augusta Lynx	ECHL	50	10	17	27	51	5	0	1	1	4

Signed as a free agent by **Anaheim**, March 26, 2007.

DIXON, Stephen (DIHX-uhn, STEE-vehn)

Center. Shoots left. 5'11", 188 lbs. Born, Halifax, N.S., September 7, 1985.
(Pittsburgh's 9th choice, 229th overall, in 2003 Entry Draft).

			Regular Season					Playoffs				
Season	Club	League	GP	G	A	Pts	PIM	GP	G	A	Pts	PIM
2001-02	Cape Breton	QMJHL	64	16	15	31	12	16	3	5	8	12
2002-03	Cape Breton	QMJHL	72	28	42	70	54	4	0	0	0	6
2003-04	Cape Breton	QMJHL	55	22	50	72	33	5	1	0	1	0
2004-05	Cape Breton	QMJHL	45	17	34	51	40	....	....	....	....	....
2005-06	Wilkes-Barre	AHL	80	12	17	29	45	11	0	1	1	4
2006-07	Wilkes-Barre	AHL	80	17	24	41	43	11	2	3	5	6
2007-08	Portland Pirates	AHL	80	17	28	45	43	18	6	4	10	10

Traded to **Anaheim** by **Pittsburgh** for Tim Brent, June 23, 2007.

DOBRYSHKIN, Yuri (doh-BRIHSH-kihn, YOO-ree) **ATL.**

Right wing. Shoots right. 6', 190 lbs. Born, Penza, USSR, July 19, 1979.
(Atlanta's 7th choice, 159th overall, in 1999 Entry Draft).

			Regular Season					Playoffs				
Season	Club	League	GP	G	A	Pts	PIM	GP	G	A	Pts	PIM
1996-97	Krylja Sovetov 2	Russia-3	35	13	5	18	42	....	....	....	....	....
	Krylja Sovetov	Russia	2	0	0	0	0	2	0	0	0	0
1997-98	Krylja Sovetov 2	Russia-3	26	12	5	17	68	....	....	....	....	....
	Krylja Sovetov	Russia	22	4	0	4	12	....	....	....	....	....
1998-99	Krylja Sovetov	Russia	50	11	5	16	86	....	....	....	....	....
99-2000	Ak Bars Kazan	Russia	27	6	9	15	24	17	2	0	2	10
2000-01	Ak Bars Kazan	Russia	40	10	5	15	32	4	2	0	2	2
2001-02	Ak Bars Kazan	Russia	38	9	8	17	22	11	0	2	2	6
2002-03	Cherepovets	Russia	49	19	7	26	82	12	5	2	7	12
2003-04	Cherepovets	Russia	53	11	7	18	75	....	....	....	....	....
2004-05	Magnitogorsk	Russia	54	14	6	20	42	2	0	0	0	0
2005-06	Magnitogorsk	Russia	15	3	1	4	22	8	0	0	0	0
	Magnitogorsk 2	Russia-3	2	3	1	4	2	....	....	....	....	....
2006-07	CSKA Moscow	Russia	50	5	10	15	65	12	3	0	3	12
2007-08	Nizhny Novgorod	Russia	48	15	6	21	60	....	....	....	....	....

DODGE, Nick (DAWGE, NIHK) **CAR.**

Right wing. Shoots right. 5'10", 175 lbs. Born, Oakville, Ont., May 1, 1986.
(Carolina's 5th choice, 183rd overall, in 2006 Entry Draft).

			Regular Season					Playoffs				
Season	Club	League	GP	G	A	Pts	PIM	GP	G	A	Pts	PIM
2004-05	Clarkson Knights	ECAC	37	6	12	18	42	....	....	....	....	....
2005-06	Clarkson Knights	ECAC	38	16	25	41	72	....	....	....	....	....
2006-07	Clarkson Knights	ECAC	36	18	21	39	32	....	....	....	....	....
2007-08	Clarkson Knights	ECAC	39	12	14	26	26	....	....	....	....	....

ECAC First All-Star Team (2007) • NCAA East Second All-American Team (2007)

DONALLY, Ryan (DAWN-ah-lee, RIGH-uhn) **ANA.**

Left wing. Shoots left. 6'5", 224 lbs. Born, Tecumseh, Ont., February 4, 1985.
(Calgary's 3rd choice, 97th overall, in 2003 Entry Draft).

			Regular Season					Playoffs				
Season	Club	League	GP	G	A	Pts	PIM	GP	G	A	Pts	PIM
2001-02	Windsor Spitfires	OHL	53	6	7	13	77	16	0	2	2	6
2002-03	Windsor Spitfires	OHL	65	11	15	26	108	7	0	1	1	8
2003-04	Windsor Spitfires	OHL	44	8	14	22	93	....	....	....	....	....
2004-05	Windsor Spitfires	OHL	29	2	3	5	87	....	....	....	....	....
	Kitchener Rangers	OHL	21	1	2	3	45	13	0	0	0	12
2005-06	Kitchener Rangers	OHL	8	0	0	0	29	....	....	....	....	....
	Sudbury Wolves	OHL	39	5	5	10	76	10	0	1	1	27
2006-07	Omaha	AHL	18	3	2	5	38	....	....	....	....	....
	Las Vegas	ECHL	33	3	5	8	79	3	0	0	0	4
2007-08	Quad City Flames	AHL	10	0	0	0	21	....	....	....	....	....
	Las Vegas	ECHL	53	15	22	37	176	4	2	2	4	6

Signed as a free agent by **Anaheim**, July 22, 2008.

DONIKA, Mikhail (DAW-nih-ka, mih-kigh-EHL) **DAL.**

Defense. Shoots left. 6', 185 lbs. Born, Yaroslavl, USSR, May 15, 1979.
(Dallas' 11th choice, 272nd overall, in 1999 Entry Draft).

			Regular Season					Playoffs				
Season	Club	League	GP	G	A	Pts	PIM	GP	G	A	Pts	PIM
1996-97	Yaroslavl 2	Russia-3	15	3	5	8	6	....	....	....	....	....
	Torpedo Yaroslavl	Russia	22	1	0	1	6	2	0	0	0	0
1997-98	Yaroslavl 2	Russia-2	19	1	2	3	32	....	....	....	....	....
	Torpedo Yaroslavl	Russia	30	0	2	2	14	....	....	....	....	....
1998-99	Yaroslavl 2	Russia-3	6	2	1	3	4	....	....	....	....	....
	Torpedo Yaroslavl	Russia	37	0	1	1	10	....	....	....	....	....
99-2000	Torpedo Yaroslavl	Russia	35	0	1	1	22	10	0	0	0	4
2000-01	Dynamo Moscow	Russia	43	1	3	4	12	....	....	....	....	....
2001-02	Amur Khabarovsk	Russia	51	1	3	4	66	....	....	....	....	....
2002-03	Spartak Moscow	Russia	51	4	7	11	16	....	....	....	....	....
2003-04	Spartak Moscow	Russia-2	55	4	14	18	14	12	2	1	3	2
2004-05	Spartak Moscow	Russia	49	0	2	2	34	....	....	....	....	....
2005-06	Perm	Russia	26	0	0	0	18	....	....	....	....	....
	Sibir Novosibirsk	Russia	14	1	3	4	8	3	0	1	1	0
2006-07	Nizhny Novgorod	Russia-2	47	8	16	24	38	14	3	0	3	14
2007-08	Nizhny Novgorod	Russia	31	0	5	5	28	....	....	....	....	....
	Lada Togliatti	Russia	2	0	0	0	0	....	....	....	....	....
	Yunost Minsk	Belarus	10	1	1	2	2	....	....	....	....	....
	Yunior Minsk	Belarus-2	....	....	....	....	....	1	0	0	0	0

DONOVAN, Matt (DAWN-uh-vuhn, MAT) **NYI**

Defense. Shoots left. 5'11", 185 lbs. Born, Edmond, OK, May 9, 1990.
(NY Islanders' 8th choice, 96th overall, in 2008 Entry Draft).

			Regular Season					Playoffs				
Season	Club	League	GP	G	A	Pts	PIM	GP	G	A	Pts	PIM
2006-07	Dallas Stars AAA	NTHL	....	22	46	68	54	....	....	....	....	....
2007-08	Cedar Rapids	USHL	59	12	18	30	41	3	0	1	1	4

• Signed Letter of Intent to attend **University of Denver** (WCHA) in fall of 2009.

DORSETT, Derek (DORH-seht, DAIR-ihk) **CBJ**

Right wing. Shoots right. 5'11", 187 lbs. Born, Kindersley, Sask., December 20, 1986.
(Columbus' 9th choice, 189th overall, in 2006 Entry Draft).

			Regular Season					Playoffs				
Season	Club	League	GP	G	A	Pts	PIM	GP	G	A	Pts	PIM
2004-05	Medicine Hat	WHL	51	5	11	16	108	13	5	1	6	35
2005-06	Medicine Hat	WHL	68	25	23	48	*279	13	8	4	12	53
2006-07	Medicine Hat	WHL	61	19	45	64	206	17	8	8	16	56
2007-08	Syracuse Crunch	AHL	64	10	8	18	289	12	0	1	1	56

DOUGHTY, Drew (DOW-tee, DROO) **L.A.**

Defense. Shoots right. 6'1", 219 lbs. Born, London, Ont., December 8, 1989.
(Los Angeles' 1st choice, 2nd overall, in 2008 Entry Draft).

			Regular Season					Playoffs				
Season	Club	League	GP	G	A	Pts	PIM	GP	G	A	Pts	PIM
2004-05	Lon. Jr. Knights	Minor-ON	55	19	30	49	31	....	....	....	....	....
2005-06	Guelph Storm	OHL	65	5	28	33	40	14	0	13	13	18
2006-07	Guelph Storm	OHL	67	21	53	74	76	4	2	3	5	8
2007-08	Guelph Storm	OHL	58	13	37	50	68	10	3	6	9	14

OHL First All-Star Team (2008) • Canadian Major Junior First All-Star Team (2008)

DOVGAN, Viktor (DAWV-guhn, VIHK-tohr) **WSH.**

Defense. Shoots left. 6'1", 205 lbs. Born, Moscow, USSR, February 27, 1987.
(Washington's 7th choice, 209th overall, in 2005 Entry Draft).

			Regular Season					Playoffs				
Season	Club	League	GP	G	A	Pts	PIM	GP	G	A	Pts	PIM
2003-04	CSKA Moscow 2	Russia-3	STATISTICS NOT AVAILABLE									
2004-05	CSKA Moscow 2	Russia-3	STATISTICS NOT AVAILABLE									
2005-06	CSKA Moscow 2	Russia-3	STATISTICS NOT AVAILABLE									
	CSK VVS Samara	Russia-2	8	1	2	3	20	3	0	1	1	4
2006-07	Hershey Bears	AHL	1	0	0	0	2	....	....	....	....	....
	South Carolina	ECHL	56	5	6	11	95	....	....	....	....	....
2007-08	CSKA Moscow	Russia	16	0	0	0	10	....	....	....	....	....

DOYLE, Chris (DOYL, KRIHS) **NYR**

Center. Shoots left. 6', 194 lbs. Born, Charlottetown, PEI, March 22, 1990.
(NY Rangers' 6th choice, 141st overall, in 2008 Entry Draft).

			Regular Season					Playoffs				
Season	Club	League	GP	G	A	Pts	PIM	GP	G	A	Pts	PIM
2006-07	PEI Rocket	QMJHL	50	18	18	36	50	7	1	3	4	4
2007-08	PEI Rocket	QMJHL	63	27	36	63	81	4	1	5	6	6

DRAVECKY, Vladimir (dra-VEH-kee, vla-DIH-meer) **L.A.**

Right wing. Shoots left. 5'11", 195 lbs. Born, Kosice, Czech., June 3, 1985.

			Regular Season					Playoffs				
Season	Club	League	GP	G	A	Pts	PIM	GP	G	A	Pts	PIM
2002-03	Trebisov	Slovak-2	2	0	1	1	0	....	....	....	....	....
2003-04	Presov Jr.	Slovak-Jr.	1	0	1	1	0	....	....	....	....	....
	Presov	Slovak-2	4	1	1	2	4	7	7	2	9	4
	HC Kosice	Slovakia	43	1	3	4	4	....	....	....	....	....
2004-05	HC Kosice Jr.	Slovak-Jr.	10	4	10	14	8	5	1	3	4	2
	HC Kosice	Slovakia	51	5	6	11	8	10	0	1	1	0
2005-06	HC Kosice	Slovakia	54	8	18	26	18	8	1	0	1	8
	HKm Humenne	Slovak-2	2	1	3	4	0	....	....	....	....	....
2006-07	HC Kosice	Slovakia	52	9	14	23	16	11	5	3	8	2
	HKm Humenne	Slovak-2	1	2	1	3	2	....	....	....	....	....
2007-08	Manchester	AHL	31	3	9	12	19	....	....	....	....	....
	Reading Royals	ECHL	26	4	20	24	20	6	0	1	1	4

Signed as a free agent by **Los Angeles**, May 31, 2007.

DRAZENOVIC, Nicholas (DRAY-zehn-oh-vihk, NIHK-oh-las) **ST.L.**

Center. Shoots left. 6', 172 lbs. Born, Prince George, B.C., January 14, 1987.
(St. Louis' 6th choice, 171st overall, in 2005 Entry Draft).

			Regular Season					Playoffs				
Season	Club	League	GP	G	A	Pts	PIM	GP	G	A	Pts	PIM
2003-04	Prince George	WHL	65	7	30	37	38	....	....	....	....	....
2004-05	Prince George	WHL	72	18	38	56	24	....	....	....	....	....
2005-06	Prince George	WHL	71	30	33	63	51	5	0	0	0	4
2006-07	Prince George	WHL	58	18	32	50	63	15	9	10	19	6
2007-08	Peoria Rivermen	AHL	69	16	26	42	38	....	....	....	....	....

DREWISKE, Davis (droo-WIHS-kee, DAY-vihs) **L.A.**

Defense. Shoots left. 6'1", 215 lbs. Born, Hudson, WI, November 22, 1984.

			Regular Season					Playoffs				
Season	Club	League	GP	G	A	Pts	PIM	GP	G	A	Pts	PIM
2003-04	Des Moines	USHL	60	4	19	23	63	3	0	0	0	4
2004-05	U. of Wisconsin	WCHA	34	1	5	6	20	....	....	....	....	....
2005-06	U. of Wisconsin	WCHA	35	2	2	4	22	....	....	....	....	....
2006-07	U. of Wisconsin	WCHA	41	4	6	10	46	....	....	....	....	....
2007-08	U. of Wisconsin	WCHA	40	5	16	21	46	....	....	....	....	....
	Manchester	AHL	5	0	0	0	6	4	0	1	1	6

Signed as a free agent by **Los Angeles**, April 1, 2008.

DROZDETSKY, Alexander (drawz-DEHT-skee, al-EHX-AN-duhr) **PHI.**

Right wing. Shoots left. 6', 180 lbs. Born, Moscow, USSR, November 10, 1981.
(Philadelphia's 2nd choice, 94th overall, in 2000 Entry Draft).

			Regular Season					Playoffs				
Season	Club	League	GP	G	A	Pts	PIM	GP	G	A	Pts	PIM
1997-98	St. Petersburg 2	Russia-3	19	0	1	1	0	....	....	....	....	....
1998-99	St. Petersburg 2	Russia-4	24	5	3	8	12	....	....	....	....	....
99-2000	St. Petersburg 2	Russia-3	4	4	1	5	2	....	....	....	....	....
	SKA St. Petersburg	Russia	32	2	0	2	10	4	0	0	0	0
2000-01	SKA St. Petersburg	Russia	42	6	7	13	74	....	....	....	....	....
2001-02	CSKA Moscow	Russia	49	11	6	17	26	....	....	....	....	....
2002-03	CSKA Moscow	Russia	46	14	13	27	30	....	....	....	....	....
2003-04	Ak Bars Kazan	Russia	57	16	15	31	62	1	0	0	0	2
2004-05	Ak Bars Kazan	Russia	32	3	4	7	28	....	....	....	....	....
	Ak Bars Kazan 2	Russia-3	....	10	8	18	....	....	....	....	....	....
	Nizhnekamsk	Russia	7	5	1	6	4	....	....	....	....	....
2005-06	Avangard Omsk	Russia	30	6	6	12	26	....	....	....	....	....
	SKA St. Petersburg	Russia	16	4	10	14	6	3	0	0	0	0
2006-07	SKA St. Petersburg	Russia	45	11	15	26	66	3	0	2	2	0
2007-08	St. Petersburg 2	Russia-3	12	9	9	18	6	....	....	....	....	....
	Spartak Moscow	Russia	32	11	6	17	40	5	4	3	7	2

DUCO, Mike (DOO-koh, MIGHK) **FLA.**

Left wing. Shoots left. 5'10", 200 lbs. Born, Toronto, Ont., July 8, 1987.

			Regular Season					Playoffs				
Season	Club	League	GP	G	A	Pts	PIM	GP	G	A	Pts	PIM
2003-04	Kitchener Rangers	OHL	5	1	2	3	4	4	0	1	1	4
2004-05	Kitchener Rangers	OHL	62	24	26	50	78	15	0	0	0	11
2005-06	Kitchener Rangers	OHL	59	22	22	44	113	5	2	1	3	10
2006-07	Kitchener Rangers	OHL	54	20	20	40	121	9	1	1	2	12
2007-08	Kitchener Rangers	OHL	62	32	22	54	173	20	*16	6	22	37

Signed as a free agent by **Florida**, October 8, 2007.

DUFFY, Matt (DUHF-ee, MAT) **FLA.**

Defense. Shoots right. 6'2", 180 lbs. Born, Portland, ME, March 21, 1986.
(Florida's 5th choice, 104th overall, in 2005 Entry Draft).

			Regular Season					Playoffs				
Season	Club	League	GP	G	A	Pts	PIM	GP	G	A	Pts	PIM
2003-04	N.H. Jr. Monarchs	EJHL	33	9	13	22	....	....	....	....	....	....
2004-05	N.H. Jr. Monarchs	EJHL	54	19	26	45	147	....	....	....	....	....
2005-06	U. of Maine	H-East	28	3	5	8	43	....	....	....	....	....
2006-07	U. of Maine	H-East	39	5	5	10	41	....	....	....	....	....
2007-08	U. of Maine	H-East	30	6	2	8	16	....	....	....	....	....

DUPONT, Brodie (DOO-pawnt, BROH-dee) **NYR**

Center. Shoots left. 6'2", 210 lbs. Born, Russell, Man., February 17, 1987.
(NY Rangers' 4th choice, 66th overall, in 2005 Entry Draft).

			Regular Season					Playoffs				
Season	Club	League	GP	G	A	Pts	PIM	GP	G	A	Pts	PIM
2003-04	Swan Valley	MJHL	51	25	16	41	88	12	5	1	6	36
	Calgary Hitmen	WHL	2	0	1	1	0	....	....	....	....	....
2004-05	Calgary Hitmen	WHL	70	14	11	25	111	12	2	8	10	21
2005-06	Calgary Hitmen	WHL	72	30	23	53	123	13	4	5	9	24
2006-07	Calgary Hitmen	WHL	70	37	33	70	90	18	9	7	16	33
2007-08	Hartford Wolf Pack	AHL	66	9	13	22	75	1	0	0	0	0

DUPUIS, Philippe (doo-PWEE, fihl-EEP) **COL.**

Center. Shoots right. 6', 196 lbs. Born, Laval, Que., April 24, 1985.
(Columbus' 5th choice, 104th overall, in 2003 Entry Draft).

			Regular Season					Playoffs				
Season	Club	League	GP	G	A	Pts	PIM	GP	G	A	Pts	PIM
2000-01	Laval-Laurentides	QAAA	46	16	27	43	74	8	1	5	6	30
2001-02	Hull Olympiques	QMJHL	67	7	14	21	59	12	6	5	11	14
2002-03	Hull Olympiques	QMJHL	68	22	34	56	89	20	2	4	6	22
2003-04	Gatineau	QMJHL	60	18	37	55	77	15	6	10	16	14
2004-05	Rouyn-Noranda	QMJHL	62	34	50	84	60	10	5	3	8	8
2005-06	Moncton Wildcats	QMJHL	56	32	76	108	52	19	14	18	32	14
2006-07	Syracuse Crunch	AHL	51	11	11	22	18	....	....	....	....	....
	Dayton Bombers	ECHL	8	3	2	5	8	19	6	9	15	28
2007-08	Syracuse Crunch	AHL	29	7	4	11	2	....	....	....	....	....
	Lake Erie Monsters	AHL	17	5	3	8	12	....	....	....	....	....

Traded to **Colorado** by **Columbus** with Darcy Campbell for Mark Rycroft, January 22, 2008.

DURNO, Chris (DUHR-noh, KRIHS) **COL.**

Center. Shoots left. 6'4", 205 lbs. Born, Scarborough, Ont., October 31, 1980.

			Regular Season					Playoffs				
Season	Club	League	GP	G	A	Pts	PIM	GP	G	A	Pts	PIM
99-2000	Michigan Tech	WCHA	24	1	1	2	30	....	....	....	....	....
2000-01	Michigan Tech	WCHA	35	9	6	15	46	....	....	....	....	....
2001-02	Michigan Tech	WCHA	36	7	8	15	48	....	....	....	....	....
2002-03	Michigan Tech	WCHA	35	5	11	16	60	....	....	....	....	....
2003-04	Gwinnett	ECHL	68	20	26	46	46	13	7	5	12	10
2004-05	Gwinnett	ECHL	66	20	36	56	101	8	5	2	7	8
2005-06	Gwinnett	ECHL	13	12	10	22	19	....	....	....	....	....
	Milwaukee	AHL	57	20	20	40	52	21	2	2	4	18
2006-07	Norfolk Admirals	AHL	22	4	1	5	61	....	....	....	....	....
	Portland Pirates	AHL	12	1	1	2	2	....	....	....	....	....
	Milwaukee	AHL	29	13	3	16	24	4	1	2	3	10
2007-08	San Antonio	AHL	80	23	26	49	109	7	0	2	2	26

Signed as a free agent by **Chicago**, September 25, 2006. Traded to **Anaheim** by **Chicago** with Sebastiien Caron and Matt Keith for Pierre Parenteau and Bruno St. Jacques, December 28, 2006. Traded to **Nashville** by **Anaheim** for Shane Endicott, January 26, 2007. Signed as a free agent by **Colorado**, July 3, 2008.

DWYER, Patrick (DWIGH-uhr, PAT-rihk) **CAR.**

Right wing. Shoots right. 5'11", 175 lbs. Born, Spokane, WA, June 22, 1983.
(Atlanta's 3rd choice, 116th overall, in 2002 Entry Draft).

			Regular Season					Playoffs				
Season	Club	League	GP	G	A	Pts	PIM	GP	G	A	Pts	PIM
2000-01	Great Falls	NWJHL	40	33	57	90	106	12	10	12	22	....
2001-02	Western Mich.	CCHA	38	17	17	34	26	....	....	....	....	....
2002-03	Western Mich.	CCHA	33	9	10	19	20	....	....	....	....	....
2003-04	Western Mich.	CCHA	35	13	13	26	22	....	....	....	....	....
2004-05	Western Mich.	CCHA	36	6	16	22	56	....	....	....	....	....
2005-06	Chicago Wolves	AHL	73	16	29	45	49	....	....	....	....	....
2006-07	Albany River Rats	AHL	79	16	25	41	39	5	0	1	1	5
2007-08	Albany River Rats	AHL	59	13	12	25	29	7	0	2	2	0

CCHA All-Rookie Team (2002) • CCHA Rookie of the Year (2002)

Signed as a free agent by **Carolina**, July 7, 2006.

EBERLE, Jordan (EH-buhr-lee, JOHR-dahn) **EDM.**

Center. Shoots right. 5'10", 174 lbs. Born, Regina, Sask., May 15, 1990.
(Edmonton's 1st choice, 22nd overall, in 2008 Entry Draft).

			Regular Season					Playoffs				
Season	Club	League	GP	G	A	Pts	PIM	GP	G	A	Pts	PIM
2005-06	Calgary Buffaloes	AMHL	31	14	20	34	6	11	7	1	8	8
2006-07	Regina Pats	WHL	66	28	27	55	32	6	2	5	7	2
2007-08	Regina Pats	WHL	70	42	33	75	20	5	2	4	6	7

WHL East First All-Star Team (2008)

ECKFORD, Tyler (EHK-fuhrd, TIGH-luhr) **N.J.**

Defense. Shoots left. 6'3", 220 lbs. Born, Vancouver, B.C., September 8, 1985.
(New Jersey's 5th choice, 217th overall, in 2004 Entry Draft).

			Regular Season					Playoffs				
Season	Club	League	GP	G	A	Pts	PIM	GP	G	A	Pts	PIM
2003-04	South Surrey	BCHL	58	7	30	37	101	13	2	8	10	34
2004-05	South Surrey	BCHL	60	22	43	65	93	25	4	15	19	46
2005-06	Alaska	CCHA	38	3	15	18	43	....	....	....	....	....
2006-07	Alaska	CCHA	39	5	17	22	54	....	....	....	....	....
2007-08	Alaska	CCHA	35	8	23	31	55	....	....	....	....	....

CCHA All-Rookie Team (2006) • CCHA First All-Star Team (2008) • NCAA West First All-American Team (2008)

EGENER, Mike (EHG-eh-nuhr, MIGHK) **BOS.**

Defense. Shoots left. 6'4", 216 lbs. Born, Lahr, West Germany, September 26, 1984.
(Tampa Bay's 1st choice, 34th overall, in 2003 Entry Draft).

			Regular Season					Playoffs				
Season	Club	League	GP	G	A	Pts	PIM	GP	G	A	Pts	PIM
99-2000	Calgary Bruins	CMHA	27	4	9	13	88	....	....	....	....	....
2000-01	Calgary Hitmen	WHL	52	1	0	1	91	6	0	0	0	5
2001-02	Calgary Hitmen	WHL	68	2	7	9	175	6	0	0	0	23
2002-03	Calgary Hitmen	WHL	40	2	8	10	210	3	1	0	1	8
2003-04	Calgary Hitmen	WHL	64	1	16	17	228	7	1	1	2	47
2004-05	Springfield Falcons	AHL	45	3	2	5	183	....	....	....	....	....
2005-06	Springfield Falcons	AHL	38	2	1	3	142	....	....	....	....	....
	Johnstown Chiefs	ECHL	18	2	2	4	66	....	....	....	....	....
2006-07	Springfield Falcons	AHL	75	0	3	3	152	....	....	....	....	....
2007-08	Norfolk Admirals	AHL	17	1	2	3	28	....	....	....	....	....
	Mississippi	ECHL	9	1	0	1	13	....	....	....	....	....

Signed as a free agent by **Boston**, July 15, 2008.

ELLER, Lars (EHL-uhr, LARZ) **ST.L.**

Center. Shoots left. 6', 198 lbs. Born, Herlev, Denmark, May 8, 1989.
(St. Louis' 1st choice, 13th overall, in 2007 Entry Draft).

			Regular Season					Playoffs				
Season	Club	League	GP	G	A	Pts	PIM	GP	G	A	Pts	PIM
2004-05	Rodovre IK Jr.	Den-Jr.	28	21	26	47	20	....	....	....	....	....
	Rodovre	Denmark	1	3	1	4	0	....	....	....	....	....
2005-06	Frolunda U18	Swe-U18	8	2	4	6	10	2	0	0	0	0
	Frolunda Jr.	Swe-Jr.	36	7	7	14	6	2	0	0	0	0
2006-07	Frolunda U18	Swe-U18	3	1	4	5	6	6	3	2	5	8
	Frolunda Jr.	Swe-Jr.	39	18	37	55	58	8	4	1	5	24
2007-08	Boras HC	Sweden-2	19	2	6	8	8	....	....	....	....	....
	Frolunda Jr.	Swe-Jr.	9	4	4	8	10	7	5	6	11	14
	Frolunda	Sweden	14	0	2	2	4	7	0	1	1	2

ELLERBY, Keaton (EHL-uhr-bee, KEE-tuhn) **FLA.**

Defense. Shoots left. 6'4", 186 lbs. Born, Strathmore, Alta., November 5, 1988.
(Florida's 1st choice, 10th overall, in 2007 Entry Draft).

			Regular Season					Playoffs				
Season	Club	League	GP	G	A	Pts	PIM	GP	G	A	Pts	PIM
2003-04	Okotoks Oilers	AMHA	30	7	32	39	69	....	....	....	....	....
2004-05	Kamloops Blazers	WHL	60	0	1	1	77	6	0	0	0	16
2005-06	Kamloops Blazers	WHL	68	2	6	8	121	....	....	....	....	....
2006-07	Kamloops Blazers	WHL	69	2	23	25	120	4	1	2	3	12
2007-08	Kamloops Blazers	WHL	16	0	3	3	29	....	....	....	....	....
	Moose Jaw	WHL	53	2	21	23	81	5	0	2	2	15

ELLINGTON, Taylor (EHL-ihng-tuhn, TAY-luhr) **VAN.**

Defense. Shoots left. 6', 205 lbs. Born, Victoria, B.C., October 31, 1988.
(Vancouver's 2nd choice, 33rd overall, in 2007 Entry Draft).

			Regular Season					Playoffs				
Season	Club	League	GP	G	A	Pts	PIM	GP	G	A	Pts	PIM
2004-05	Everett Silvertips	WHL	47	0	0	0	48	8	0	1	1	4
2005-06	Everett Silvertips	WHL	63	0	7	7	62	15	1	2	3	16
2006-07	Everett Silvertips	WHL	60	5	8	13	65	6	1	0	1	2
2007-08	Everett Silvertips	WHL	48	3	11	14	66	4	0	0	0	0

ELO, Eero (EH-loh, EE-roh) **MIN.**

Left wing. Shoots right. 6'3", 189 lbs. Born, Rauma, Finland, April 26, 1990.
(Minnesota's 4th choice, 145th overall, in 2008 Entry Draft).

			Regular Season					Playoffs				
Season	Club	League	GP	G	A	Pts	PIM	GP	G	A	Pts	PIM
2005-06	Lukko Rauma U18	Fin-U18	30	10	10	20	18	....	....	....	....	....
2006-07	Lukko Rauma U18	Fin-U18	18	8	12	20	36	....	....	....	....	....
	Lukko Rauma Jr.	Fin-Jr.	22	1	2	3	8	....	....	....	....	....
2007-08	Lukko Rauma U18	Fin-U18	5	2	3	5	2	2	2	1	3	0
	Lukko Rauma Jr.	Fin-Jr.	42	12	15	27	34	....	....	....	....	....

EMMERSON, Riley (EHM-uhr-sohn, RIGH-lee) **MIN.**

Right wing. Shoots left. 6'8", 230 lbs. Born, Burnaby, B.C., February 7, 1986.
(Minnesota's 7th choice, 199th overall, in 2005 Entry Draft).

			Regular Season					Playoffs				
Season	Club	League	GP	G	A	Pts	PIM	GP	G	A	Pts	PIM
2003-04	Chilliwack Chiefs	BCHL	52	0	6	6	137	6	0	0	0	0
2004-05	Tri-City Americans	WHL	35	0	0	0	61	....	....	....	....	....
2005-06	Tri-City Americans	WHL	66	1	1	2	109	2	0	0	0	0
2006-07	Texas Wildcatters	ECHL	42	2	1	3	99	....	....	....	....	....
2007-08	Texas Wildcatters	ECHL	51	2	2	4	142	4	0	0	0	16

EMMERTON, Cory (EHM-uhr-tuhn, KOH-ree) **DET.**

Center. Shoots left. 6', 177 lbs. Born, St. Thomas, Ont., June 1, 1988.
(Detroit's 1st choice, 41st overall, in 2006 Entry Draft).

			Regular Season					Playoffs				
Season	Club	League	GP	G	A	Pts	PIM	GP	G	A	Pts	PIM
2003-04	Elgin	Minor-ON	32	33	24	57	26	....	....	....	....	....
2004-05	Kingston	OHL	58	17	21	38	8	....	....	....	....	....
2005-06	Kingston	OHL	66	26	64	90	32	6	2	0	2	6
2006-07	Kingston	OHL	40	29	37	66	22	5	5	2	7	2
	Grand Rapids	AHL	....	....	....	....	....	2	0	0	0	0
2007-08	Kingston	OHL	24	13	18	31	6	....	....	....	....	....
	Brampton	OHL	30	12	18	30	10	5	0	2	2	2
	Grand Rapids	AHL	7	0	1	1	0	....	....	....	....	....

ENGASSER, Will (EHN-gahs-uhr, WIHL-yuhm) **PHX.**

Left wing. Shoots left. 6'2", 237 lbs. Born, Edina, MN, September 25, 1985.
(Phoenix's 9th choice, 261st overall, in 2004 Entry Draft).

			Regular Season					Playoffs				
Season	Club	League	GP	G	A	Pts	PIM	GP	G	A	Pts	PIM
2000-01	Blake Bears	High-MN	5	1	2	3	....	....	....	....	....	....
2001-02	Blake Bears	High-MN	26	7	24	31	....	....	....	....	....	....
2002-03	Blake Bears	High-MN	28	17	26	43	52	....	....	....	....	....
2003-04	Blake Bears	High-MN	28	22	30	52	20	....	....	....	....	....
	Team Southwest	UMEHL	24	9	5	14	....	....	....	....	....	....
2004-05	Yale	ECAC	21	2	0	2	10	....	....	....	....	....
2005-06	Yale	ECAC	18	2	2	4	6	....	....	....	....	....
2006-07	Yale	ECAC	25	7	1	8	22	....	....	....	....	....
2007-08	Yale	ECAC	25	4	11	15	30	....	....	....	....	....

ENGELHARDT, Brett (ehn-GEHL-hahrt, BREHT)

Right wing. Shoots right. 6'2", 210 lbs. Born, Sheboygan, WI, August 12, 1980.

			Regular Season					Playoffs				
Season	Club	League	GP	G	A	Pts	PIM	GP	G	A	Pts	PIM
1997-98	USNTDP	USHL	11	0	0	0	18	....	....	....	....	....
	USNTDP	NAHL	35	3	5	8	30	....	....	....	....	....
1998-99	Green Bay	USHL	54	12	18	30	76	6	2	0	2	8
99-2000	Green Bay	USHL	58	24	27	51	167	14	7	8	15	28
2000-01	Michigan Tech	WCHA	35	6	10	16	73	....	....	....	....	....
2001-02	Michigan Tech	WCHA	38	16	16	32	40	....	....	....	....	....
2002-03	Michigan Tech	WCHA	38	17	15	32	67	....	....	....	....	....
2003-04	Michigan Tech	WCHA	38	12	13	25	68	....	....	....	....	....
	Philadelphia	AHL	2	0	1	1	0	....	....	....	....	....
2004-05	Gwinnett	ECHL	21	14	9	23	18	....	....	....	....	....
	St. John's	AHL	44	7	5	12	32	4	1	0	1	2
2005-06	Toronto Marlies	AHL	71	12	32	44	89	5	1	1	2	6
2006-07	Toronto Marlies	AHL	79	25	23	48	129	....	....	....	....	....
2007-08	Grand Rapids	AHL	42	8	8	16	33	....	....	....	....	....
	Hamilton Bulldogs	AHL	25	5	5	10	29	....	....	....	....	....

Signed as a free agent by **Detroit**, July 18, 2007. Traded to **Montreal** by **Detroit** for Francis Lemieux, February 8, 2008.

ENGELLAND, Deryk (ehn-GUHL-uhnd, DEH-rihk) PIT.

Defense. Shoots right. 6'2", 202 lbs. Born, Edmonton, Alta., April 5, 1982.
(New Jersey's 11th choice, 194th overall, in 2000 Entry Draft).

			Regular Season					Playoffs				
Season	Club	League	GP	G	A	Pts	PIM	GP	G	A	Pts	PIM
1998-99	Moose Jaw	WHL	2	0	0	0	0	....	....	....	....	....
99-2000	Moose Jaw	WHL	55	0	5	5	62	4	0	0	0	0
2000-01	Moose Jaw	WHL	65	4	11	15	157	4	0	0	0	10
2001-02	Moose Jaw	WHL	56	7	10	17	102	12	0	2	2	27
2002-03	Moose Jaw	WHL	65	3	8	11	199	13	1	1	2	20
2003-04	Lowell	AHL	26	0	0	0	34	....	....	....	....	....
	Las Vegas	ECHL	35	2	11	13	63	2	0	0	0	0
2004-05	Las Vegas	ECHL	72	5	16	21	138	....	....	....	....	....
2005-06	South Carolina	ECHL	35	3	13	16	20	....	....	....	....	....
	Hershey Bears	AHL	37	0	4	4	77	1	0	0	0	0
2006-07	Hershey Bears	AHL	44	4	6	10	95	14	0	0	0	14
	Reading Royals	ECHL	6	0	3	3	8	....	....	....	....	....
2007-08	Wilkes-Barre	AHL	80	2	15	17	141	23	1	3	4	14

Signed as a free agent by **Calgary**, July, 2003. Signed as a free agent by **Pittsburgh**, July 16, 2007.

ENLUND, Jonas (EHN-luhnd, YOH-nuhs) ATL.

Center. Shoots left. 6', 185 lbs. Born, Helsinki, Finland, November 3, 1987.
(Atlanta's 5th choice, 165th overall, in 2006 Entry Draft).

			Regular Season					Playoffs				
Season	Club	League	GP	G	A	Pts	PIM	GP	G	A	Pts	PIM
2002-03	HIFK Helsinki U18	Fin-U18	24	11	3	14	0	2	1	0	1	0
2003-04	HIFK Helsinki U18	Fin-U18	30	15	16	31	30	7	3	5	8	2
	HIFK Helsinki Jr.	Fin-Jr.	3	0	0	0	0	....	....	....	....	....
2004-05	HIFK Helsinki U18	Fin-U18	....	....	....	....	....	7	4	3	7	8
	HIFK Helsinki Jr.	Fin-Jr.	38	15	15	30	18	2	1	1	2	0
2005-06	Suomi U20	Finland-2	4	1	1	2	0	....	....	....	....	....
	HIFK Helsinki Jr.	Fin-Jr.	37	24	18	42	14	....	....	....	....	....
2006-07	Tappara Jr.	Fin-Jr.	10	2	7	9	12	4	3	0	3	2
	Suomi U20	Finland-2	5	0	1	1	0	....	....	....	....	....
	Tappara Tampere	Finland	46	2	1	3	8	5	0	0	0	0
2007-08	Tappara Tampere	Finland	56	19	22	41	10	11	3	3	6	4

ENNIS, Tyler (EH-nihs, TIGH-luhr) BUF.

Center. Shoots left. 5'9", 160 lbs. Born, Edmonton, Alta., October 6, 1989.
(Buffalo's 2nd choice, 26th overall, in 2008 Entry Draft).

			Regular Season					Playoffs				
Season	Club	League	GP	G	A	Pts	PIM	GP	G	A	Pts	PIM
2004-05	K of C Pats	AMHL	36	15	17	32	10	....	....	....	....	....
2005-06	Medicine Hat	WHL	43	3	7	10	10	7	0	0	0	0
2006-07	Medicine Hat	WHL	71	26	24	50	30	22	8	4	12	6
2007-08	Medicine Hat	WHL	70	43	48	91	42	5	0	4	4	6

WHL East First All-Star Team (2008)

ERSTAD, Travis (UHR-stad, TRA-vihs) ST.L.

Center/Right wing. Shoots right. 6'4", 182 lbs. Born, Madison, WI, November 9, 1988.
(St. Louis' 8th choice, 100th overall, in 2007 Entry Draft).

			Regular Season					Playoffs				
Season	Club	League	GP	G	A	Pts	PIM	GP	G	A	Pts	PIM
2005-06	Stevens Point High	High-WI	STATISTICS NOT AVAILABLE									
2006-07	Stevens Point High	High-WI	24	31	33	64	....	....	....	....	....	....
	Lincoln Stars	USHL	8	0	0	0	4	3	1	0	1	0
2007-08	Lincoln Stars	USHL	52	9	10	19	104	8	1	2	3	8

• Signed Letter of Intent to attend **University of Wisconsin** (WCHA) in fall of 2008.

ESPOSITO, Angelo (EHS-poh-ZEE-toh, AN-jul-loh) ATL.

Center. Shoots left. 6'1", 180 lbs. Born, Montreal, Que., February 20, 1989.
(Pittsburgh's 1st choice, 20th overall, in 2007 Entry Draft).

			Regular Season					Playoffs				
Season	Club	League	GP	G	A	Pts	PIM	GP	G	A	Pts	PIM
2004-05	Shat.-St. Mary's	High-MN	68	31	35	66	47	....	....	....	....	....
2005-06	Quebec Remparts	QMJHL	57	39	59	98	45	23	6	5	11	4
2006-07	Quebec Remparts	QMJHL	60	27	52	79	63	5	4	3	7	2
2007-08	Quebec Remparts	QMJHL	56	30	39	69	69	11	4	6	10	6
	Chicago Wolves	AHL	1	0	0	0	0	....	....	....	....	....

QMJHL All-Rookie Team (2006) • QMJHL Offensive Rookie of the Year (2006)

Traded to **Atlanta** by **Pittsburgh** with Colby Armstrong, Erik Christensen and Pittsburgh's 1st round choice (Daultan Leveille) in 2008 Entry Draft for Marian Hossa and Pascal Dupuis, February 26, 2008.

EVSEEV, Vladislav (yehv-SAY-ehv, VLA-dih-slav) BOS.

Left wing. Shoots left. 6'2", 196 lbs. Born, Moscow, USSR, September 10, 1984.
(Boston's 2nd choice, 56th overall, in 2002 Entry Draft).

			Regular Season					Playoffs				
Season	Club	League	GP	G	A	Pts	PIM	GP	G	A	Pts	PIM
99-2000	Dyn'o Moscow 2	Russia-3	5	2	3	5	6	....	....	....	....	....
2000-01	Dyn'o Moscow 2	Russia-3	6	5	2	7	2	....	....	....	....	....
2001-02	CSKA Moscow 2	Russia-3	8	2	1	3	2	....	....	....	....	....
	HK CSKA Moscow	Russia-2	15	2	5	7	10	....	....	....	....	....
2002-03	Dynamo Moscow	Russia	22	1	1	2	2	1	0	0	0	0
2003-04	Vityaz Podolsk	Russia-2	8	1	2	3	2	7	0	0	0	2
2004-05	Dynamo Moscow	Russia	12	1	1	2	2	....	....	....	....	....
	Ufa	Russia	5	0	0	0	2	....	....	....	....	....
2005-06	Cherepovets	Russia	30	3	0	3	18	....	....	....	....	....
2006-07	Dynamo Moscow	Russia	30	1	3	4	32	2	0	0	0	0
2007-08	Dynamo Moscow	Russia	3	0	0	0	12	....	....	....	....	....
	Vityaz Chekhov	Russia	30	5	5	10	10	....	....	....	....	....

EZHOV, Denis (YEHZH-awf, DEH-nihs) BUF.

Defense. Shoots left. 5'11", 200 lbs. Born, Togliatti, USSR, February 28, 1985.
(Buffalo's 5th choice, 114th overall, in 2003 Entry Draft).

			Regular Season					Playoffs				
Season	Club	League	GP	G	A	Pts	PIM	GP	G	A	Pts	PIM
99-2000	Lada Togliatti 2	Russia-3	4	0	0	0	4	....	....	....	....	....
2000-01	Lada Togliatti 2	Russia-3	STATISTICS NOT AVAILABLE									
2001-02	Lada Togliatti 2	Russia-3	4	2	4	6	6	....	....	....	....	....
	Lada Togliatti	Russia	15	0	0	0	6	....	....	....	....	....
2002-03	Lada Togliatti 2	Russia-3	15	2	7	9	4	....	....	....	....	....
	CSK VVS Samara	Russia-2	9	0	1	1	8	....	....	....	....	....
2003-04	Novokuznetsk	Russia	19	0	1	1	2	3	0	0	0	0
	CSKA Moscow 2	Russia-3	4	1	2	3	2	....	....	....	....	....
2004-05	Novokuznetsk	Russia	28	0	0	0	16	4	0	0	0	2
2005-06	Mytischi	Russia	24	1	0	1	10	....	....	....	....	....
	Kristall Elektrostal	Russia-3	STATISTICS NOT AVAILABLE									
2006-07	Chelyabinsk	Russia	54	2	6	8	73	....	....	....	....	....
2007-08	Chelyabinsk	Russia	57	4	9	13	64	3	0	0	0	10

FADDEN, Mitch (FA-dehn, MIHTCH) T.B.

Center. Shoots left. 6', 174 lbs. Born, Victoria, B.C., April 3, 1988.
(Tampa Bay's 4th choice, 107th overall, in 2007 Entry Draft).

			Regular Season					Playoffs				
Season	Club	League	GP	G	A	Pts	PIM	GP	G	A	Pts	PIM
2003-04	Victoria Cougars	VIJHL	47	36	31	67	63	11	11	4	15	24
	Seattle	WHL	2	0	0	0	0	....	....	....	....	....
2004-05	Seattle	WHL	64	9	12	21	30	12	2	0	2	4
2005-06	Seattle	WHL	38	9	11	20	19	....	....	....	....	....
	Lethbridge	WHL	30	11	17	28	22	6	2	5	7	14
2006-07	Lethbridge	WHL	71	36	48	84	54	....	....	....	....	....
2007-08	Lethbridge	WHL	72	34	55	89	72	19	5	15	20	19

WHL East Second All-Star Team (2008)

FAHEY, Brian (FAY-hee, BRIGH-uhn) NYR

Defense. Shoots right. 6'1", 215 lbs. Born, Des Plaines, IL, March 2, 1981.
(Colorado's 7th choice, 119th overall, in 2000 Entry Draft).

			Regular Season					Playoffs				
Season	Club	League	GP	G	A	Pts	PIM	GP	G	A	Pts	PIM
1997-98	USNTDP	U-18	17	1	10	11	12	....	....	....	....	....
	USNTDP	USHL	5	1	1	2	8	....	....	....	....	....
	USNTDP	NAHL	39	5	10	15	35	7	0	0	0	2
1998-99	USNTDP	U-18	6	1	0	1	4	....	....	....	....	....
	USNTDP	USHL	52	9	9	18	34	....	....	....	....	....
99-2000	U. of Wisconsin	WCHA	41	6	11	17	42	....	....	....	....	....
2000-01	U. of Wisconsin	WCHA	38	1	5	6	16	....	....	....	....	....
2001-02	U. of Wisconsin	WCHA	38	2	8	10	55	....	....	....	....	....
2002-03	U. of Wisconsin	WCHA	39	5	4	9	34	....	....	....	....	....
2003-04	Worcester IceCats	AHL	2	0	0	0	2	....	....	....	....	....
	Atlantic City	ECHL	55	11	26	37	49	2	0	0	0	2
	Hershey Bears	AHL	12	0	1	1	6	....	....	....	....	....
2004-05	Worcester IceCats	AHL	20	0	4	4	12	....	....	....	....	....
	Atlantic City	ECHL	46	10	16	26	47	3	0	2	2	0
2005-06	Idaho Steelheads	ECHL	3	1	1	2	4	....	....	....	....	....
	Iowa Stars	AHL	64	6	11	17	74	7	0	1	1	8
2006-07	Chicago Wolves	AHL	75	11	18	29	81	15	3	2	5	20
2007-08	Chicago Wolves	AHL	76	14	23	37	123	24	2	8	10	24

WCHA All-Rookie Team (2000) • ECHL All-Rookie Team (2004)

Signed as a free agent by **Chicago** (AHL), August 31, 2006. Signed as a free agent by **NY Rangers**, July 17, 2008.

FAIRCHILD, Cade (FAIR-chighld, KAYD) ST.L.

Defense. Shoots left. 5'10", 186 lbs. Born, Duluth, MN, January 15, 1989.
(St. Louis' 7th choice, 96th overall, in 2007 Entry Draft).

			Regular Season					Playoffs				
Season	Club	League	GP	G	A	Pts	PIM	GP	G	A	Pts	PIM
2004-05	Duluth East	High-MN	29	10	32	42	....	....	....	....	....	....
2005-06	USNTDP	U-17	18	2	7	9	4	....	....	....	....	....
	USNTDP	NAHL	36	8	9	17	10	2	0	0	0	0
2006-07	USNTDP	U-18	36	3	16	19	34	....	....	....	....	....
	USNTDP	NAHL	13	1	6	7	16	....	....	....	....	....
2007-08	U. of Minnesota	WCHA	40	2	13	15	22	....	....	....	....	....

WCHA All-Rookie Team (2008)

FALK, Justin (FAWLK, JUHS-tihn) MIN.

Defense. Shoots left. 6'5", 215 lbs. Born, Snowflake, Man., October 11, 1988.
(Minnesota's 2nd choice, 110th overall, in 2007 Entry Draft).

			Regular Season					Playoffs				
Season	Club	League	GP	G	A	Pts	PIM	GP	G	A	Pts	PIM
2004-05	Swan Valley	MJHL	56	0	8	8	46	....	....	....	....	....
	Calgary Hitmen	WHL	4	0	0	0	2	5	0	0	0	0
2005-06	Calgary Hitmen	WHL	5	0	2	2	0	....	....	....	....	....
	Spokane Chiefs	WHL	48	0	8	8	35	....	....	....	....	....
2006-07	Spokane Chiefs	WHL	62	3	12	15	88	6	0	0	0	8
2007-08	Spokane Chiefs	WHL	72	4	22	26	98	21	1	4	5	12

Memorial Cup All-Star Team (2008)

FAST, T.J. (FAST, TEE-JAY) **ST.L.**

Defense. Shoots left. 6'1", 190 lbs. Born, Calgary, Alta., September 2, 1987.
(Los Angeles' 3rd choice, 60th overall, in 2005 Entry Draft).

			Regular Season					Playoffs				
Season	Club	League	GP	G	A	Pts	PIM	GP	G	A	Pts	PIM
2003-04	Cgy. North Stars	AMHL	31	7	7	14	42	....	....	....	....	....
2004-05	Camrose Kodiaks	AJHL	58	8	28	36	40	....	....	....	....	....
2005-06	U. of Denver	WCHA	39	1	6	7	26	....	....	....	....	....
2006-07	U. of Denver	WCHA	19	0	4	4	14	....	....	....	....	....
	Tri-City Americans	WHL	26	3	19	22	30	6	0	1	1	14
2007-08	Tri-City Americans	WHL	71	17	37	54	92	16	1	8	9	16

AJHL All-Rookie Team (2005) • WHL West First All-Star Team (2008)

Traded to **St. Louis** by **Los Angeles** for St. Louis' 5th round choice in 2009 Entry Draft, June 4, 2008.

FAYNE, Mark (FAYN, MAHRK) **N.J.**

Defense. Shoots right. 6'3", 195 lbs. Born, Nashua, NH, May 15, 1987.
(New Jersey's 5th choice, 155th overall, in 2005 Entry Draft).

			Regular Season					Playoffs				
Season	Club	League	GP	G	A	Pts	PIM	GP	G	A	Pts	PIM
2003-04	Nobles	High-MA	20	3	5	8	14	....	....	....	....	....
2004-05	Nobles	High-MA	24	1	17	18	16	....	....	....	....	....
2005-06	Nobles	High-MA	29	10	24	34	....	....	....	....	....	....
2006-07	Providence College	H-East	36	5	7	12	43	....	....	....	....	....
2007-08	Providence College	H-East	36	2	4	6	18	....	....	....	....	....

FEDOROV, Yevgeny (FEH-duh-rahf, yehv-GEH-nee) **DAL.**

Center. Shoots left. 5'10", 187 lbs. Born, Sverdlovsk, USSR, November 11, 1980.
(Los Angeles' 6th choice, 201st overall, in 2000 Entry Draft).

			Regular Season					Playoffs				
Season	Club	League	GP	G	A	Pts	PIM	GP	G	A	Pts	PIM
1997-98	Krylja Sovetov 2	Russia-3	20	1	6	7	48	....	....	....	....	....
	Krylja Sovetov	Russia	32	1	0	1	12	....	....	....	....	....
1998-99	Krylja Sovetov	Russia	52	5	3	8	61	....	....	....	....	....
99-2000	Perm	Russia	37	5	5	10	20	3	0	1	1	4
2000-01	Perm	Russia	43	9	9	18	18	....	....	....	....	....
2001-02	Ak Bars Kazan	Russia	45	10	12	22	12	11	0	0	0	2
2002-03	Ak Bars Kazan	Russia	46	4	11	15	26	5	1	0	1	2
2003-04	Ak Bars Kazan	Russia	47	7	4	11	14	4	0	0	0	0
2004-05	Ak Bars Kazan	Russia	47	4	10	14	10	....	....	....	....	....
2005-06	Dynamo Moscow	Russia	35	7	9	16	16	....	....	....	....	....
2006-07	Dynamo Moscow	Russia	48	15	9	24	42	3	0	0	0	0
2007-08	Magnitogorsk	Russia	49	9	10	19	64	13	1	1	2	2

Traded to **Dallas** by **Los Angeles** for Dallas' 6th round choice (later traded to Chicago - Chicago selected Braden Birch) in 2008 Entry Draft, December 10, 2007.

FENTON, P.J. (FEHN-tuhn, PEE-JAY) **S.J.**

Left wing. Shoots left. 5'11", 180 lbs. Born, Springfield, MA, August 26, 1985.
(San Jose's 6th choice, 162nd overall, in 2005 Entry Draft).

			Regular Season					Playoffs				
Season	Club	League	GP	G	A	Pts	PIM	GP	G	A	Pts	PIM
2002-03	N.E. Jr. Coyotes	EJHL	35	8	17	25	....	....	....	....	....	....
2003-04	N.E. Jr. Coyotes	EJHL	37	16	17	33	61	....	....	....	....	....
2004-05	Massachusetts	H-East	36	12	12	24	24	....	....	....	....	....
2005-06	Massachusetts	H-East	35	5	12	17	61	....	....	....	....	....
2006-07	Massachusetts	H-East	39	10	15	25	16	....	....	....	....	....
2007-08	Massachusetts	H-East	36	9	19	28	24	....	....	....	....	....
	Worcester Sharks	AHL	4	0	0	0	4	....	....	....	....	....

Hockey East All-Rookie Team (2005)

FERNHOLM, Daniel (FUHRN-hohlm, DAN-yehl) **PIT.**

Defense. Shoots left. 6'4", 218 lbs. Born, Stockholm, Sweden, December 20, 1983.
(Pittsburgh's 4th choice, 101st overall, in 2002 Entry Draft).

			Regular Season					Playoffs				
Season	Club	League	GP	G	A	Pts	PIM	GP	G	A	Pts	PIM
99-2000	Mora IK Jr.	Swe-Jr.	33	3	3	6	8	1	0	0	0	0
2000-01	Mora IK Jr.	Swe-Jr.	3	0	1	1	2	....	....	....	....	....
	Mora IK	Sweden-2	2	0	0	0	0	....	....	....	....	....
2001-02	Djurgarden Jr.	Swe-Jr.	8	6	13	19	12	3	0	0	0	0
2002-03	Huddinge IK	Sweden-2	39	6	10	16	20	2	1	0	1	0
	Huddinge IK Jr.	Swe-Jr.	1	0	0	0	2	....	....	....	....	....
2003-04	Djurgarden	Sweden	37	4	7	11	28	4	0	0	0	4
	Hammarby	Sweden-2	15	1	3	4	6	....	....	....	....	....
2004-05	Djurgarden Jr.	Swe-Jr.	2	0	0	0	4	....	....	....	....	....
	HC Forst Bolzano	Italy	7	0	2	2	2	....	....	....	....	....
	Djurgarden	Sweden	31	3	2	5	22	11	0	0	0	14
2005-06	Wilkes-Barre	AHL	27	1	6	7	10	....	....	....	....	....
	Wheeling Nailers	ECHL	29	2	4	6	20	9	1	3	4	6
2006-07	Wheeling Nailers	ECHL	13	0	3	3	14	....	....	....	....	....
	Djurgarden	Sweden	32	4	12	16	16	....	....	....	....	....
2007-08	Linkopings HC	Sweden	54	8	21	29	28	16	3	7	10	20

FERRIERO, Benn (fuh-RAIR-oh, BEHN) **PHX.**

Center. Shoots right. 5'10", 191 lbs. Born, Boston, MA, April 29, 1987.
(Phoenix's 8th choice, 196th overall, in 2006 Entry Draft).

			Regular Season					Playoffs				
Season	Club	League	GP	G	A	Pts	PIM	GP	G	A	Pts	PIM
2001-02	Gov. Dummer	High-MA	STATISTICS NOT AVAILABLE									
2002-03	Gov. Dummer	High-MA	....	8	10	18	....	....	....	....	....	....
2003-04	Gov. Dummer	High-MA	28	19	24	43	....	....	....	....	....	....
2004-05	Gov. Dummer	High-MA	28	15	27	42	....	....	....	....	....	....
2005-06	Boston College	H-East	42	16	9	25	36	....	....	....	....	....
2006-07	Boston College	H-East	42	23	23	46	43	....	....	....	....	....
2007-08	Boston College	H-East	44	17	25	42	71	....	....	....	....	....

Hockey East All-Rookie Team (2006)

FESTERLING, Brett (FEHS-tuhr-lihng, BREHT) **ANA.**

Defense. Shoots left. 6'1", 210 lbs. Born, Quesnel, B.C., March 3, 1986.

			Regular Season					Playoffs				
Season	Club	League	GP	G	A	Pts	PIM	GP	G	A	Pts	PIM
2001-02	Quesnel Thunder	Minor-BC	40	18	26	44	44	....	....	....	....	....
	Quesnel	BCHL	7	0	0	0	0	....	....	....	....	....
	Tri-City Americans	WHL	3	0	0	0	0	....	....	....	....	....
2002-03	Tri-City Americans	WHL	55	3	8	11	26	....	....	....	....	....
2003-04	Tri-City Americans	WHL	54	1	9	10	34	11	1	1	2	2
2004-05	Tri-City Americans	WHL	33	3	11	14	20	....	....	....	....	....
	Vancouver Giants	WHL	32	2	4	6	10	5	0	0	0	6
2005-06	Vancouver Giants	WHL	67	1	6	7	35	18	0	1	1	10
2006-07	Vancouver Giants	WHL	70	5	16	21	80	22	1	6	7	24
2007-08	Portland Pirates	AHL	74	3	11	14	64	15	1	3	4	6

Signed as a free agent by **Anaheim**, September 14, 2005.

FIEDLER, Jonas (FIHD-luhr, YOH-nuhs) **CAR.**

Right wing. Shoots right. 6'2", 173 lbs. Born, Jihlava, Czech., May 29, 1984.
(Carolina's 7th choice, 235th overall, in 2004 Entry Draft).

			Regular Season					Playoffs				
Season	Club	League	GP	G	A	Pts	PIM	GP	G	A	Pts	PIM
99-2000	Jihlava Jr.	CzRep-Jr.	48	11	11	22	48	....	....	....	....	....
2000-01	Jihlava Jr.	CzRep-Jr.	44	29	33	62	167	....	....	....	....	....
2001-02	Plymouth Whalers	OHL	68	8	12	20	27	6	0	1	1	4
2002-03	Plymouth Whalers	OHL	63	7	21	28	59	18	5	9	14	10
2003-04	Plymouth Whalers	OHL	63	18	28	46	83	9	1	6	7	16
2004-05	Plymouth Whalers	OHL	61	19	18	37	71	4	1	0	1	2
	Florida Everblades	ECHL	2	0	0	0	0	....	....	....	....	....
2005-06	HC Dukla Jihlava	CzRep-2	46	8	9	17	122	6	0	2	2	22
2006-07	HC Dukla Jihlava	CzRep-2	51	6	25	31	149	4	0	0	0	30
2007-08	HC Dukla Jihlava	CzRep-2	11	1	1	2	20	....	....	....	....	....
	BK Mlada Boleslav	CzRep-2	5	0	1	1	29	17	2	5	7	26

• Re-entered NHL Entry Draft. Originally San Jose's 3rd choice, 86th overall, in 2002 Entry Draft.

FIENHAGE, Corey (fihn-AW-gee, KOH-ree) **BUF.**

Defense. Shoots right. 6'2", 190 lbs. Born, Topeka, KS, May 4, 1990.
(Buffalo's 4th choice, 81st overall, in 2008 Entry Draft).

			Regular Season					Playoffs				
Season	Club	League	GP	G	A	Pts	PIM	GP	G	A	Pts	PIM
2005-06	Eastview High	High-MN	25	1	6	7	32	....	....	....	....	....
2006-07	Eastview High	High-MN	20	4	11	15	....	....	....	....	....	....
	Team Southeast	UMWEHL	11	4	4	8		....	....	....	....	....
2007-08	Eastview High	High-MN	26	6	10	16	87	....	....	....	....	....
	Team Southeast	UMWEHL	12	2	4	6	....	....	....	....	....	....
	Indiana Ice	USHL	12	1	2	3	12	2	0	0	0	0

• Signed Letter of Intent to attend **University of North Dakota** (WCHA).

FIGREN, Robin (FIH-grehn, RAW-bihn) **NYI**

Wing. Shoots right. 5'11", 176 lbs. Born, Stockholm, Sweden, March 7, 1988.
(NY Islanders' 3rd choice, 70th overall, in 2006 Entry Draft).

			Regular Season					Playoffs				
Season	Club	League	GP	G	A	Pts	PIM	GP	G	A	Pts	PIM
2003-04	Hammarby U18	Swe-U18	11	5	5	10	22	....	....	....	....	....
2004-05	Frolunda U18	Swe-U18	12	13	8	21	94	7	4	4	8	10
	Frolunda Jr.	Swe-Jr.	4	1	2	3	0	....	....	....	....	....
2005-06	Frolunda Jr.	Swe-Jr.	38	10	18	28	72	7	4	2	6	6
	Frolunda	Sweden	2	0	0	0	0	....	....	....	....	....
	Frolunda U18	Swe-U18	1	1	0	1	2	2	2	0	2	0
2006-07	Calgary Hitmen	WHL	62	10	17	27	54	18	4	4	8	18
2007-08	Edmonton	WHL	35	18	13	31	46	....	....	....	....	....

FILATOV, Nikita (fihl-A-tawv, nih-KEE-ta) **CBJ**

Left wing. Shoots right. 6', 172 lbs. Born, Moscow, USSR, May 25, 1990.
(Columbus' 1st choice, 6th overall, in 2008 Entry Draft).

			Regular Season					Playoffs				
Season	Club	League	GP	G	A	Pts	PIM	GP	G	A	Pts	PIM
2005-06	CSKA Moscow 2	Russia-3	STATISTICS NOT AVAILABLE									
2006-07	CSKA Moscow 2	Russia-3	STATISTICS NOT AVAILABLE									
2007-08	CSKA Moscow 2	Russia-3	23	24	23	47	62	11	14	9	23	28
	CSKA Moscow	Russia	5	0	0	0	0	....	....	....	....	....

FILLIER, Matt (FIHL-ee-uhr, MAT) **L.A.**

Center. Shoots left. 6'1", 184 lbs. Born, New Glasgow, N.S., October 5, 1988.
(Los Angeles' 10th choice, 188th overall, in 2007 Entry Draft).

			Regular Season					Playoffs				
Season	Club	League	GP	G	A	Pts	PIM	GP	G	A	Pts	PIM
2003-04	Pictou	NSMHL	27	3	8	11	10	....	....	....	....	....
2004-05	Pictou	NSMHL	31	19	37	56	36	8	2	8	10	6
2005-06	St. John's	QMJHL	59	7	12	19	75	5	0	0	0	4
2006-07	St. John's	QMJHL	63	18	18	36	118	4	0	1	1	2
2007-08	St. John's	QMJHL	65	11	14	25	154	5	0	1	1	9

FINLEY, Joe (FIHN-lee, JOH) **WSH.**

Defense. Shoots left. 6'7", 229 lbs. Born, Edina, MN, June 29, 1987.
(Washington's 2nd choice, 27th overall, in 2005 Entry Draft).

			Regular Season					Playoffs				
Season	Club	League	GP	G	A	Pts	PIM	GP	G	A	Pts	PIM
2004-05	Sioux Falls	USHL	55	3	10	13	181	....	....	....	....	....
2005-06	North Dakota	WCHA	43	0	3	3	96	....	....	....	....	....
2006-07	North Dakota	WCHA	41	1	6	7	72	....	....	....	....	....
2007-08	North Dakota	WCHA	43	4	11	15	79	....	....	....	....	....

FISCHER, David (FIH-shuhr, DAY-vihd) **MTL.**

Defense. Shoots right. 6'4", 198 lbs. Born, Minneapolis, MN, February 19, 1988.
(Montreal's 1st choice, 20th overall, in 2006 Entry Draft).

			Regular Season					Playoffs				
Season	Club	League	GP	G	A	Pts	PIM	GP	G	A	Pts	PIM
2003-04	Apple Valley	High-MN	27	2	9	11	10	....	....	....	....	....
2004-05	Apple Valley	High-MN	28	8	20	28	36	....	....	....	....	....
2005-06	Apple Valley	High-MN	28	8	31	39	22	....	....	....	....	....
2006-07	U. of Minnesota	WCHA	42	0	5	5	14	....	....	....	....	....
2007-08	U. of Minnesota	WCHA	45	2	12	14	18	....	....	....	....	....

FLAAKE, Jerome (FLAH-keh, juh-ROHM) **TOR.**

Left wing. Shoots left. 6'2", 187 lbs. Born, Guben, East Germany, March 2, 1990.
(Toronto's 6th choice, 130th overall, in 2008 Entry Draft).

			Regular Season					Playoffs				
Season	Club	League	GP	G	A	Pts	PIM	GP	G	A	Pts	PIM
2005-06	Riessersee Jr.	Ger-Jr.	36	20	18	38	36	3	0	2	2	0
2006-07	Heil./Mann. Jr.	Ger-Jr.	36	32	31	63	36	6	4	3	7	8
2007-08	Kolner Haie	Germany	30	0	1	1	4	....	....	....	....	....
	Koln Jr.	Ger-Jr.	32	33	41	74	68	4	2	4	6	41

FLETCHER, Justin (FLEHTCH-uhr, JUHS-tihn) **T.B.**

Defense. Shoots left. 5'11", 180 lbs. Born, Maryville, IL, March 30, 1983.

			Regular Season					Playoffs				
Season	Club	League	GP	G	A	Pts	PIM	GP	G	A	Pts	PIM
2000-01	Sioux City	USHL	38	0	5	5	28	3	0	0	0	0
2001-02	Sioux City	USHL	56	3	10	13	48	12	2	1	3	6
2002-03	Sioux City	USHL	60	12	31	43	28	4	0	3	3	6
2003-04	St. Cloud State	WCHA	29	6	7	13	22	....	....	....	....	....
2004-05	St. Cloud State	WCHA	36	8	14	22	86	....	....	....	....	....
2005-06	St. Cloud State	WCHA	40	6	21	27	55	....	....	....	....	....
2006-07	St. Cloud State	WCHA	38	6	18	24	37	....	....	....	....	....
	Springfield Falcons	AHL	10	3	1	4	4	....	....	....	....	....
2007-08	Norfolk Admirals	AHL	39	1	4	5	37	....	....	....	....	....
	Rockford IceHogs	AHL	20	4	7	11	43	11	0	1	1	6

Signed as a free agent by **Tampa Bay**, April 30, 2007.

FLOOD, Mark (FLUD, MAHRK) **CAR.**

Defense. Shoots right. 6'1", 190 lbs. Born, Charlottetown, PEI, September 29, 1984.
(Montreal's 8th choice, 188th overall, in 2003 Entry Draft).

			Regular Season					Playoffs				
Season	Club	League	GP	G	A	Pts	PIM	GP	G	A	Pts	PIM
2000-01	Charlotwn AAA	PEIHA	STATISTICS NOT AVAILABLE									
	Charlotwn Abbies	MJrHL	11	0	2	2	2	....	....	....	....	....
2001-02	Peterborough	OHL	57	1	4	5	21	6	0	0	0	2
2002-03	Peterborough	OHL	68	5	24	29	18	7	1	2	3	0
2003-04	Peterborough	OHL	68	15	29	44	30	....	....	....	....	....
2004-05	Peterborough	OHL	60	4	38	42	14	14	2	7	9	0
2005-06	Syracuse Crunch	AHL	9	1	1	2	2	....	....	....	....	....
	Dayton Bombers	ECHL	50	11	14	25	20	....	....	....	....	....
2006-07	Syracuse Crunch	AHL	8	1	1	2	2	....	....	....	....	....
	Albany River Rats	AHL	36	3	7	10	20	....	....	....	....	....
2007-08	Albany River Rats	AHL	53	10	12	22	18	....	....	....	....	....

Signed as a free agent by **Columbus**, August 22, 2005. Traded to **Carolina** by **Columbus** for Derrick Walser, November 29, 2006.

FLYNN, Ryan (FLIHN, RIGH-uhn) **NSH.**

Right wing. Shoots right. 6'2", 212 lbs. Born, St. Paul, MN, March 22, 1988.
(Nashville's 4th choice, 176th overall, in 2006 Entry Draft).

			Regular Season					Playoffs				
Season	Club	League	GP	G	A	Pts	PIM	GP	G	A	Pts	PIM
2003-04	Centennial	High-MN	30	29	39	68	....	....	....	....	....	....
2004-05	USNTDP	U-17	14	4	5	9	12	....	....	....	....	....
	USNTDP	NAHL	41	11	8	19	31	9	2	4	6	7
2005-06	USNTDP	U-18	42	10	12	22	57	....	....	....	....	....
	USNTDP	NAHL	17	6	5	11	20	....	....	....	....	....
2006-07	U. of Minnesota	WCHA	43	5	8	13	58	....	....	....	....	....
2007-08	U. of Minnesota	WCHA	38	4	11	15	51	....	....	....	....	....

FORD, Matthew (FOHRD, MA-thew) **CHI.**

Right wing. Shoots right. 6'1", 206 lbs. Born, West Hills, CA, October 9, 1984.
(Chicago's 16th choice, 256th overall, in 2004 Entry Draft).

			Regular Season					Playoffs				
Season	Club	League	GP	G	A	Pts	PIM	GP	G	A	Pts	PIM
2003-04	Sioux Falls	USHL	60	*37	31	68	60	....	....	....	....	....
2004-05	U. of Wisconsin	WCHA	21	5	5	10	18	....	....	....	....	....
2005-06	U. of Wisconsin	WCHA	31	5	2	7	14	....	....	....	....	....
2006-07	U. of Wisconsin	WCHA	39	7	6	13	38	....	....	....	....	....
2007-08	U. of Wisconsin	WCHA	33	4	5	9	30	....	....	....	....	....

FORNEY, Michael (FOHR-NEE, MIGH-kuhl) **ATL.**

Right wing. Shoots right. 6'2", 185 lbs. Born, Thief River Falls, MN, May 14, 1988.
(Atlanta's 3rd choice, 80th overall, in 2006 Entry Draft).

			Regular Season					Playoffs				
Season	Club	League	GP	G	A	Pts	PIM	GP	G	A	Pts	PIM
2002-03	Thief River Falls	High-MN	28	4	10	14	....	....	....	....	....	....
2003-04	Thief River Falls	High-MN	24	14	22	36	....	....	....	....	....	....
2004-05	Thief River Falls	High-MN	28	34	33	67	....	....	....	....	....	....
2005-06	Thief River Falls	High-MN	21	23	37	60	28	....	....	....	....	....
	Des Moines	USHL	3	0	0	0	0	....	....	....	....	....
2006-07	North Dakota	WCHA	16	0	2	2	10	....	....	....	....	....
2007-08	North Dakota	WCHA	3	0	0	0	2	....	....	....	....	....

FORTIER, Olivier (FOHR-t'yay, OH-lihv-ee-ay) **MTL.**

Center. Shoots left. 5'11", 179 lbs. Born, Quebec City, Que., May 2, 1989.
(Montreal's 4th choice, 65th overall, in 2007 Entry Draft).

			Regular Season					Playoffs				
Season	Club	League	GP	G	A	Pts	PIM	GP	G	A	Pts	PIM
2004-05	St-Francois	QAAA	31	7	17	24	8	4	2	1	3	4
2005-06	Drummondville	QMJHL	13	2	2	4	14	....	....	....	....	....
	Rimouski Oceanic	QMJHL	27	4	8	12	16	....	....	....	....	....
2006-07	Rimouski Oceanic	QMJHL	69	28	36	64	28	....	....	....	....	....
2007-08	Rimouski Oceanic	QMJHL	67	23	23	46	37	3	1	0	1	4

FORTUNUS, Maxime (fohr-TOON-uhs, MAX-eem) **DAL.**

Defense. Shoots right. 6'1", 190 lbs. Born, La Prairie, Que., July 28, 1983.

			Regular Season					Playoffs				
Season	Club	League	GP	G	A	Pts	PIM	GP	G	A	Pts	PIM
99-2000	Baie-Comeau	QMJHL	68	6	15	21	36	6	0	0	0	2
2000-01	Baie-Comeau	QMJHL	71	10	31	41	106	11	2	4	6	6
2001-02	Baie-Comeau	QMJHL	72	11	30	41	76	5	0	1	1	2
2002-03	Baie-Comeau	QMJHL	69	12	32	44	44	12	2	4	6	6
2003-04	Baie-Comeau	QMJHL	5	1	0	1	15	....	....	....	....	....
	Houston Aeros	AHL	12	0	2	2	2	1	0	0	0	0
	Louisiana	ECHL	64	3	15	18	27	4	1	1	2	0
2004-05	Houston Aeros	AHL	13	0	0	0	4	....	....	....	....	....
	Louisiana	ECHL	59	8	16	24	26	....	....	....	....	....
2005-06	Manitoba Moose	AHL	76	3	10	13	36	13	0	0	0	10
2006-07	Manitoba Moose	AHL	72	2	18	20	64	13	1	4	5	10
2007-08	Manitoba Moose	AHL	65	8	13	21	28	6	0	1	1	4

Signed as a free agent by **Dallas**, July 3, 2008.

FOSS, Jeffrey (FAWS, JEHF-ree) **NSH.**

Defense. Shoots right. 6'2", 208 lbs. Born, Fargo, ND, December 12, 1988.
(Nashville's 5th choice, 166th overall, in 2008 Entry Draft).

			Regular Season					Playoffs				
Season	Club	League	GP	G	A	Pts	PIM	GP	G	A	Pts	PIM
2004-05	Moorhead Spuds	High-MN	22	1	4	5	6	....	....	....	....	....
2005-06	Moorhead Spuds	High-MN	26	4	17	21	16	....	....	....	....	....
	Team Great Plains	UMWEHL	11	4	9	13	....	....	....	....	....	....
2006-07	Moorhead Spuds	High-MN	26	15	31	46	28	....	....	....	....	....
	Team Great Plains	UMWEHL	12	3	13	16	....	....	....	....	....	....
	Sioux Falls	USHL	11	0	1	1	10	4	0	1	1	2
2007-08	RPI Engineers	ECAC	38	1	3	4	28	....	....	....	....	....

FOX, T.J. (FAWX, TEE-JAY) **S.J.**

Left wing. Shoots left. 6'1", 200 lbs. Born, Oswego, NY, June 11, 1984.

			Regular Season					Playoffs				
Season	Club	League	GP	G	A	Pts	PIM	GP	G	A	Pts	PIM
2002-03	Green Bay	USHL	32	3	3	6	24	....	....	....	....	....
2003-04	Chicago Steel	USHL	56	11	16	27	62	5	1	0	1	4
2004-05	Chicago Steel	USHL	60	21	29	50	90	7	2	3	5	8
2005-06	Union College	ECAC	30	8	12	20	34	....	....	....	....	....
2006-07	Union College	ECAC	36	13	24	37	54	....	....	....	....	....
2007-08	Worcester Sharks	AHL	71	12	12	24	33	....	....	....	....	....

Signed as a free agent by **San Jose**, March 8, 2007.

FRANK, Chris (FRANK, KRIHS) **PHX.**

Defense. Shoots left. 6'1", 231 lbs. Born, Lynnwood, WA, January 8, 1986.
(Phoenix's 7th choice, 188th overall, in 2006 Entry Draft).

			Regular Season					Playoffs				
Season	Club	League	GP	G	A	Pts	PIM	GP	G	A	Pts	PIM
2003-04	Cowichan Valley	BCHL	55	3	16	19	277	6	1	0	1	26
2004-05	Cowichan Valley	BCHL	55	6	30	36	207	....	....	....	....	....
2005-06	Western Mich.	CCHA	38	2	2	4	127	....	....	....	....	....
2006-07	Western Mich.	CCHA	36	2	10	12	*109	....	....	....	....	....
2007-08	Western Mich.	CCHA	37	2	4	6	91	....	....	....	....	....

FRANSON, Cody (FRAN-suhn, KOH-dee) **NSH.**

Defense. Shoots right. 6'5", 227 lbs. Born, Salmon Arm, B.C., August 8, 1987.
(Nashville's 3rd choice, 79th overall, in 2005 Entry Draft).

			Regular Season					Playoffs				
Season	Club	League	GP	G	A	Pts	PIM	GP	G	A	Pts	PIM
2002-03	Sicamous	Minor-BC	65	44	82	126	42	....	....	....	....	....
	Vancouver Giants	WHL	3	0	0	0	0	....	....	....	....	....
2003-04	Beaver Valley	KIJHL	48	10	22	32	70	....	....	....	....	....
	Trail Smoke Eaters	BCHL	2	0	1	1	0	....	....	....	....	....
	Vancouver Giants	WHL	2	0	0	0	0	....	....	....	....	....
2004-05	Vancouver Giants	WHL	64	2	11	13	44	4	0	1	1	0
2005-06	Vancouver Giants	WHL	71	15	40	55	61	18	5	15	20	12
2006-07	Vancouver Giants	WHL	59	17	34	51	88	19	3	4	7	10
2007-08	Milwaukee	AHL	76	11	25	36	40	6	0	2	2	2

WHL West Second All-Star Team (2006) • WHL West First All-Star Team (2007) • Memorial Cup Tournament All-Star Team (2007)

FRANSSON, Johan (FRAN-suhn, YOH-han) **L.A.**

Defense. Shoots left. 6'1", 183 lbs. Born, Kalix, Sweden, February 18, 1985.
(Dallas' 2nd choice, 34th overall, in 2004 Entry Draft).

			Regular Season					Playoffs				
Season	Club	League	GP	G	A	Pts	PIM	GP	G	A	Pts	PIM
2000-01	Kalix HF	Sweden-3	19	0	6	6	8	....	....	....	....	....
2001-02	Lulea HF U18	Swe-U18	5	2	0	2	0	....	....	....	....	....
	Lulea HF Jr.	Swe-Jr.	29	4	4	8	28	5	0	1	1	8
2002-03	Lulea HF Jr.	Swe-Jr.	24	2	4	6	67	....	....	....	....	....
	Lulea HF U18	Swe-U18	2	0	0	0	2	....	....	....	....	....
	Lulea HF	Sweden	3	0	0	0	0	....	....	....	....	....
2003-04	Lulea HF Jr.	Swe-Jr.	5	0	2	2	10	....	....	....	....	....
	Lulea HF	Sweden	44	3	3	6	28	2	0	0	0	4
2004-05	Lulea HF Jr.	Swe-Jr.	1	1	1	2	0	7	1	2	3	4
	Lulea HF	Sweden	43	1	6	7	30	3	0	0	0	0
2005-06	Lulea HF	Sweden	50	3	5	8	74	6	1	1	2	6
2006-07	Frolunda	Sweden	35	0	6	6	18	....	....	....	....	....
	Assat Pori	Finland	6	0	1	1	2	....	....	....	....	....
	Linkopings HC	Sweden	8	0	0	0	4	15	0	0	0	2
2007-08	Linkopings HC	Sweden	48	5	9	14	24	16	0	5	5	16

Rights traded to **Los Angeles** by **Dallas** with Jaroslav Modry, Dallas' 2nd (Oscar Moller) and 3rd (Bryan Cameron) round choices in 2007 Entry Draft and Dallas' 1st round choice (later traded to Phoenix - Phoenix selected Viktor Tikhonov) in 2008 Entry Draft for Mattias Norstrom, Konstantin Pushkarev and Los Angeles' 3rd (Sergei Korostin) and 4th (later traded to Columbus - Columbus selected Maxim Mayorov) round choices in 2007 Entry Draft, February 27, 2007.

FRASER, Jamie (FRAY-zuhr, JAY-mee) NYI

Defense. Shoots left. 6'1", 200 lbs. Born, Sarnia, Ont., November 17, 1985.

			Regular Season					Playoffs				
Season	**Club**	**League**	**GP**	**G**	**A**	**Pts**	**PIM**	**GP**	**G**	**A**	**Pts**	**PIM**
2002-03	Brampton	OHL	57	3	11	14	13	10	0	2	2	2
2003-04	Brampton	OHL	61	4	13	17	36	12	3	1	4	6
2004-05	Sarnia Sting	OHL	66	10	21	31	22	....	....	....	....	....
2005-06	Sarnia Sting	OHL	65	16	26	42	68	....	....	....	....	....
	South Carolina	ECHL	3	1	0	1	2	6	1	1	2	2
2006-07	Syracuse Crunch	AHL	2	0	0	0	0	....	....	....	....	....
	South Carolina	ECHL	27	5	23	28	6	....	....	....	....	....
	Bridgeport	AHL	43	3	11	14	16	....	....	....	....	....
2007-08	Bridgeport	AHL	70	11	13	24	20	....	....	....	....	....

Signed as a free agent by **NY Islanders**, February 22, 2007.

FRATTIN, Matt (FRA-tihn, MAT) TOR.

Right wing. Shoots right. 5'11", 187 lbs. Born, Edmonton, Alta., January 3, 1988.
(Toronto's 2nd choice, 99th overall, in 2007 Entry Draft).

			Regular Season					Playoffs				
Season	**Club**	**League**	**GP**	**G**	**A**	**Pts**	**PIM**	**GP**	**G**	**A**	**Pts**	**PIM**
2004-05	Gregg Distributors	AMHL	34	12	13	25	14	....	....	....	....	....
2005-06	Gregg Distributors	AMHL	34	20	17	37	48	6	5	1	6	4
	Ft. Saskatchewan	AJHL	3	2	0	2	0	....	....	....	....	....
2006-07	Ft. Saskatchewan	AJHL	58	49	34	83	75	15	5	6	11	10
2007-08	North Dakota	WCHA	43	4	11	15	18	....	....	....	....	....

FREDHEIM, Kris (FREHD-highm, KRIHS) VAN.

Defense. Shoots right. 6'2", 174 lbs. Born, Campbell River, B.C., February 23, 1987.
(Vancouver's 5th choice, 185th overall, in 2005 Entry Draft).

			Regular Season					Playoffs				
Season	**Club**	**League**	**GP**	**G**	**A**	**Pts**	**PIM**	**GP**	**G**	**A**	**Pts**	**PIM**
2003-04	Notre Dame	SMHL	41	9	21	30	38	....	....	....	....	....
2004-05	Notre Dame	SJHL	50	2	15	17	28	....	....	....	....	....
2005-06	Notre Dame	SJHL	52	12	23	35	75	11	2	9	11	15
2006-07	Colorado College	WCHA	23	1	3	4	16	....	....	....	....	....
2007-08	Colorado College	WCHA	34	1	4	5	24	....	....	....	....	....

FRETTER, Colton (FREH-tuhr, KOHL-tuhn) BUF.

Right wing. Shoots right. 5'10", 187 lbs. Born, Harrow, Ont., March 12, 1982.
(Atlanta's 8th choice, 230th overall, in 2002 Entry Draft).

			Regular Season					Playoffs				
Season	**Club**	**League**	**GP**	**G**	**A**	**Pts**	**PIM**	**GP**	**G**	**A**	**Pts**	**PIM**
99-2000	Chatham Maroons	OHA-B	40	12	22	34	34	....	....	....	....	....
2000-01	Chatham Maroons	OHA-B	54	33	39	72	....	15	7	6	13	....
2001-02	Chatham Maroons	OHA-B	52	51	53	104	62	15	5	3	8	2
2002-03	Michigan State	CCHA	35	7	15	22	36	....	....	....	....	....
2003-04	Michigan State	CCHA	39	6	11	17	22	....	....	....	....	....
2004-05	Michigan State	CCHA	40	20	24	44	28	....	....	....	....	....
2005-06	Michigan State	CCHA	45	10	19	29	28	....	....	....	....	....
2006-07	Gwinnett	ECHL	51	36	32	68	46	4	3	0	3	4
2007-08	Chicago Wolves	AHL	8	1	3	4	2	....	....	....	....	....
	Gwinnett	ECHL	2	2	0	2	4	....	....	....	....	....
	Bridgeport	AHL	18	9	2	11	14	....	....	....	....	....

ECHL All-Rookie Team (2007) • ECHL Rookie of the Year (2007)

Signed as a free agent by **Buffalo**, August 4, 2008.

FRITSCHE, Tom (FRIHCH, TAWM) COL.

Left wing. Shoots left. 5'11", 183 lbs. Born, Parma, OH, September 30, 1986.
(Colorado's 3rd choice, 47th overall, in 2005 Entry Draft).

			Regular Season					Playoffs				
Season	**Club**	**League**	**GP**	**G**	**A**	**Pts**	**PIM**	**GP**	**G**	**A**	**Pts**	**PIM**
2002-03	USNTDP	U-17	19	7	11	18	16	....	....	....	....	....
	USNTDP	NAHL	44	14	9	23	43	....	....	....	....	....
2003-04	USNTDP	U-18	46	19	23	42	46	....	....	....	....	....
	USNTDP	NAHL	11	5	4	9	0	....	....	....	....	....
2004-05	Ohio State	CCHA	42	11	*34	45	38	....	....	....	....	....
2005-06	Ohio State	CCHA	37	11	19	30	16	....	....	....	....	....
2006-07	Ohio State	CCHA	19	5	8	13	8	....	....	....	....	....
2007-08	Ohio State	CCHA	39	5	14	19	28	....	....	....	....	....
	Lake Erie Monsters	AHL	15	2	3	5	2	....	....	....	....	....

CCHA All-Rookie Team (2005) • CCHA Second All-Star Team (2005)

FRITZ, Mitch (FRIHTZ, MIHTCH) NYI

Left wing. Shoots left. 6'8", 258 lbs. Born, Osoyoos, B.C., November 24, 1980.

			Regular Season					Playoffs				
Season	**Club**	**League**	**GP**	**G**	**A**	**Pts**	**PIM**	**GP**	**G**	**A**	**Pts**	**PIM**
1998-99	Kelowna Rockets	WHL	52	9	0	9	156	2	0	0	0	0
99-2000	Kelowna Rockets	WHL	58	4	2	6	204	5	0	0	0	0
2000-01	Lowell	AHL	5	0	0	0	20	....	....	....	....	....
	Tallahassee	ECHL	42	5	3	8	79	....	....	....	....	....
2001-02	Hamilton Bulldogs	AHL	13	0	0	0	37	....	....	....	....	....
	Saint John Flames	AHL	11	0	0	0	34	....	....	....	....	....
	Columbus	ECHL	45	3	7	10	284	....	....	....	....	....
2002-03	Milwaukee	AHL	13	1	2	3	33	....	....	....	....	....
	Columbus	ECHL	33	2	4	6	144	....	....	....	....	....
2003-04	Worcester IceCats	AHL	4	0	0	0	10	4	0	0	0	4
	Columbus	ECHL	64	3	9	12	149	....	....	....	....	....
2004-05	Springfield Falcons	AHL	45	3	1	4	179	....	....	....	....	....
2005-06	Springfield Falcons	AHL	69	6	5	11	212	....	....	....	....	....
2006-07	Springfield Falcons	AHL	63	0	1	1	144	....	....	....	....	....
2007-08	Hartford Wolf Pack	AHL	11	1	4	5	34	2	0	0	0	4

Yanick Dupre Memorial Award (Outstanding Humanitarian Contribution - AHL) (2006)

Signed as a free agent by **Tampa Bay**, August 5, 2005. Rights traded to **NY Rangers** by **Tampa Bay** for the rights to Bryce Lampman, July 4, 2007. • Missed majority of 2007-08 season recovering from shoulder surgery. Signed as a free agent by **NY Islanders**, July 3, 2008.

FROGREN, Jonas (FREW-grehn, YOH-nuhs) TOR.

Defense. Shoots left. 6'2", 194 lbs. Born, Falun, Sweden, August 28, 1980.
(Calgary's 8th choice, 206th overall, in 1998 Entry Draft).

			Regular Season					Playoffs				
Season	**Club**	**League**	**GP**	**G**	**A**	**Pts**	**PIM**	**GP**	**G**	**A**	**Pts**	**PIM**
1996-97	Farjestad Jr.	Swe-Jr.	20	2	7	9	4	....	....	....	....	....
1997-98	Farjestad Jr.	Swe-Jr.	28	5	6	11	12	2	1	0	1	0
1998-99	Farjestad Jr.	Swe-Jr.	28	10	8	18	16	6	0	2	2	10
	Farjestad	Sweden	22	0	0	0	2	....	....	....	....	....
	Farjestad	EuroHL	5	0	0	0	0	2	0	0	0	0
99-2000	Bofors	Sweden-2	43	2	7	9	40	....	....	....	....	....
2000-01	Farjestad	Sweden	49	3	0	3	10	16	0	0	0	4
	Farjestad Jr.	Swe-Jr.	1	0	0	0	0	....	....	....	....	....
2001-02	Farjestad	Sweden	50	3	6	9	18	10	0	0	0	4
2002-03	Farjestad	Sweden	50	1	7	8	48	14	0	0	0	16
2003-04	Farjestad	Sweden	47	5	5	10	38	17	2	0	2	6
2004-05	Farjestad	Sweden	34	1	0	1	26	15	0	2	2	2
2005-06	Farjestad	Sweden	46	3	3	6	84	17	1	1	2	6
2006-07	Farjestad	Sweden	53	4	4	8	40	7	1	0	1	0
2007-08	Farjestad	Sweden	47	0	1	1	38	12	0	1	1	12

Signed as a free agent by **Toronto**, July 9, 2008.

FROLIK, Michael (FROH-lihk, MIGH-kuhl) FLA.

Center. Shoots left. 6'1", 185 lbs. Born, Kladno, Czech., February 17, 1988.
(Florida's 1st choice, 10th overall, in 2006 Entry Draft).

			Regular Season					Playoffs				
Season	**Club**	**League**	**GP**	**G**	**A**	**Pts**	**PIM**	**GP**	**G**	**A**	**Pts**	**PIM**
2002-03	HC Kladno U17	CzR-U17	46	37	21	58	36	9	9	1	10	18
	HC Kladno Jr.	CzRep-Jr.	....	....	....	....	....	1	0	0	0	2
2003-04	HC Kladno U17	CzR-U17	1	0	1	1	2	....	....	....	....	....
	HC Kladno Jr.	CzRep-Jr.	53	21	23	44	22	7	3	1	4	6
2004-05	HC Kladno U17	CzR-U17	....	....	....	....	....	1	1	0	1	0
	HC Kladno Jr.	CzRep-Jr.	15	9	11	20	18	5	1	0	1	0
	HC Rabat Kladno	CzRep	27	3	1	4	6	1	0	0	0	0
2005-06	HC Kladno Jr.	CzRep-Jr.	3	1	2	3	0	6	3	9	12	6
	HC Rabat Kladno	CzRep	48	2	7	9	32	....	....	....	....	....
2006-07	Rimouski Oceanic	QMJHL	52	31	42	73	40	....	....	....	....	....
2007-08	Rimouski Oceanic	QMJHL	45	24	41	65	22	9	2	4	6	12

QMJHL All-Rookie Team (2007)

FROSHAUG , Mats (FRAWZ-howg, MATS) VAN.

Center. Shoots left. 6'1", 198 lbs. Born, Oslo, Norway, July 31, 1988.
(Vancouver's 4th choice, 161st overall, in 2008 Entry Draft).

			Regular Season					Playoffs				
Season	**Club**	**League**	**GP**	**G**	**A**	**Pts**	**PIM**	**GP**	**G**	**A**	**Pts**	**PIM**
2004-05	Sunne IK U18	Swe-U18	18	8	8	16	35	....	....	....	....	....
	Sunne IK Jr.	Swe-Jr.	16	0	3	3	4	....	....	....	....	....
2005-06	Sunne IK U18	Swe-U18	16	8	11	19	10	....	....	....	....	....
	Sunne IK Jr.	Swe-Jr.	17	14	10	24	6	....	....	....	....	....
	Sunne IK	Sweden-3	14	1	1	2	0	....	....	....	....	....
2006-07	Linkopings HC Jr.	Swe-Jr.	37	10	11	21	20	5	0	1	1	6
2007-08	Linkopings HC Jr.	Swe-Jr.	35	18	18	36	41	5	3	4	7	2
	Nykoping	Sweden-2	2	0	1	1	2	....	....	....	....	....
	Linkopings HC	Sweden	2	0	0	0	0	....	....	....	....	....

FULTON, Jordan (FUL-tuhn, JOHR-dahn) CGY.

Center. Shoots left. 6'1", 191 lbs. Born, St. Louis Park, MN, September 12, 1987.
(Calgary's 6th choice, 179th overall, in 2006 Entry Draft).

			Regular Season					Playoffs				
Season	**Club**	**League**	**GP**	**G**	**A**	**Pts**	**PIM**	**GP**	**G**	**A**	**Pts**	**PIM**
2002-03	Breck Mustangs	High-MN	26	24	7	31	12	....	....	....	....	....
2003-04	Breck Mustangs	High-MN	31	30	36	66	24	....	....	....	....	....
2004-05	Breck Mustangs	High-MN	28	29	41	70	68	....	....	....	....	....
2005-06	Breck Mustangs	High-MN	28	45	36	81	76	....	....	....	....	....
2006-07	U. Minn-Duluth	WCHA	38	3	7	10	22	....	....	....	....	....
2007-08	U. Minn-Duluth	WCHA	36	5	9	14	40	....	....	....	....	....

GAGNON, Aaron (GAN-YAWN, AIR-ruhn) DAL.

Center. Shoots right. 5'10", 185 lbs. Born, Quesnel, B.C., April 24, 1986.
(Phoenix's 8th choice, 240th overall, in 2004 Entry Draft).

			Regular Season					Playoffs				
Season	**Club**	**League**	**GP**	**G**	**A**	**Pts**	**PIM**	**GP**	**G**	**A**	**Pts**	**PIM**
2001-02	North Okanoghan	Minor-BC	41	59	59	118	60	....	....	....	....	....
	Seattle	WHL	2	0	0	0	0	....	....	....	....	....
2002-03	Seattle	WHL	60	5	13	18	14	15	3	2	5	4
2003-04	Seattle	WHL	63	21	15	36	29	....	....	....	....	....
2004-05	Seattle	WHL	72	31	34	65	29	12	4	5	9	16
2005-06	Seattle	WHL	62	24	21	45	40	7	5	3	8	6
2006-07	Seattle	WHL	59	42	38	80	58	11	6	2	8	10
2007-08	Iowa Stars	AHL	25	0	1	1	8	....	....	....	....	....
	Idaho Steelheads	ECHL	22	7	14	21	4	4	1	1	2	2

WHL West First All-Star Team (2005, 2007)

Signed as a free agent by **Dallas**, February 2, 2007.

GALIARDI, T.J. (gal-ee-AR-dee, TEE-JAY) COL.

Wing. Shoots left. 6'2", 172 lbs. Born, Calgary, Alta., April 22, 1988.
(Colorado's 4th choice, 55th overall, in 2007 Entry Draft).

			Regular Season					Playoffs				
Season	**Club**	**League**	**GP**	**G**	**A**	**Pts**	**PIM**	**GP**	**G**	**A**	**Pts**	**PIM**
2004-05	Cgy. North Stars	AMHL	36	14	16	30	32	....	....	....	....	....
2005-06	Calgary Royals	AJHL	56	19	37	56	60	....	....	....	....	....
2006-07	Dartmouth	ECAC	33	14	17	31	30	....	....	....	....	....
2007-08	Calgary Hitmen	WHL	72	18	52	70	77	16	5	*19	*24	20

ECAC All-Rookie Team (2007)

GARDINER, Jake (GAHR-dih-nuhr, JAYK) ANA.

Defense. Shoots left. 6'1", 173 lbs. Born, Deephaven, MN, July 4, 1990.
(Anaheim's 1st choice, 17th overall, in 2008 Entry Draft).

			Regular Season					Playoffs				
Season	**Club**	**League**	**GP**	**G**	**A**	**Pts**	**PIM**	**GP**	**G**	**A**	**Pts**	**PIM**
2005-06	Minnetonka High	High-MN	21	2	14	16	6	....	....	....	....	....
2006-07	Minnetonka High	High-MN	19	10	22	32	20	....	....	....	....	....
	Team Southwest	UMWEHL	11	4	3	7	....	....	....	....	....	....
2007-08	Minnetonka High	High-MN	24	20	28	48	14	....	....	....	....	....
	Team Southwest	UMWEHL	11	8	7	15	....	....	....	....	....	....

• Signed Letter of Intent to attend **University of Wisconsin** (WCHA) in fall of 2008.

GAULTON, Mitch (GAWL-tuhn, MIHTCH) NYR

Defense. Shoots left. 6', 207 lbs. Born, St. Catherines, Ont., April 25, 1990.
(NY Rangers' 7th choice, 171st overall, in 2008 Entry Draft).

			Regular Season					Playoffs				
Season	Club	League	GP	G	A	Pts	PIM	GP	G	A	Pts	PIM
2005-06	Tor. Red Wings	GTHL	55	22	26	48	71	....	....	....	....	....
2006-07	Erie Otters	OHL	54	5	11	16	53	....	....	....	....	....
2007-08	Erie Otters	OHL	20	2	5	7	19	....	....	....	....	....

GAUNCE, Cameron (GAWNS, KAM-ih-RUHN) COL.

Defense. Shoots left. 6'1", 203 lbs. Born, Sudbury, Ont., March 19, 1990.
(Colorado's 1st choice, 50th overall, in 2008 Entry Draft).

			Regular Season					Playoffs				
Season	Club	League	GP	G	A	Pts	PIM	GP	G	A	Pts	PIM
2005-06	Markham Waxers	Minor-ON	72	11	60	71	122	....	....	....	....	....
2006-07	Markham Waxers	OPJHL	45	2	12	14	68	11	0	3	3	26
2007-08	St. Michael's	OHL	63	10	30	40	99	4	0	1	1	6

GAWRYLETZ, Travis (GAW-reh-lehtz, TRA-vihs) PHI.

Defense. Shoots right. 6'2", 190 lbs. Born, Trail, B.C., November 2, 1985.
(Philadelphia's 9th choice, 253rd overall, in 2004 Entry Draft).

			Regular Season					Playoffs				
Season	Club	League	GP	G	A	Pts	PIM	GP	G	A	Pts	PIM
2002-03	Trail Smoke Eaters	BCHL	56	4	28	32	42	14	6	6	12	10
2003-04	Trail Smoke Eaters	BCHL	51	9	21	30	51	10	1	3	4	6
2004-05	U. Minn-Duluth	WCHA	35	4	1	5	26	....	....	....	....	....
2005-06	U. Minn-Duluth	WCHA	32	0	7	7	12	....	....	....	....	....
2006-07	U. Minn-Duluth	WCHA	37	0	5	5	57	....	....	....	....	....
2007-08	U. Minn-Duluth	WCHA	36	1	5	6	30	....	....	....	....	....

BCHL All-Rookie Team (2003) • BCHL Interior Division First All-Star Team (2004)

GAZDIC, Luke (GAZ-dihk, LEWK) DAL.

Left wing. Shoots left. 6'3", 210 lbs. Born, Toronto, Ont., July 25, 1989.
(Dallas' 8th choice, 172nd overall, in 2007 Entry Draft).

			Regular Season					Playoffs				
Season	Club	League	GP	G	A	Pts	PIM	GP	G	A	Pts	PIM
2005-06	Wexford Raiders	OPJHL	47	17	16	33	105	....	....	....	....	....
	North York	GTHL	38	13	16	29	24	....	....	....	....	....
2006-07	Erie Otters	OHL	58	5	8	13	136	....	....	....	....	....
2007-08	Erie Otters	OHL	67	17	12	29	144	....	....	....	....	....

GELECH, Randall (GEH-lehkh, RAN-duhl)

Center. Shoots right. 6'3", 220 lbs. Born, Wynard, Sask., February 2, 1984.
(Phoenix's 5th choice, 208th overall, in 2003 Entry Draft).

			Regular Season					Playoffs				
Season	Club	League	GP	G	A	Pts	PIM	GP	G	A	Pts	PIM
2000-01	Kelowna Rockets	WHL	51	1	9	10	19	6	0	0	0	4
2001-02	Kelowna Rockets	WHL	48	6	2	8	33	15	2	1	3	15
2002-03	Kelowna Rockets	WHL	67	25	20	45	93	19	8	4	12	17
2003-04	Kelowna Rockets	WHL	71	30	19	49	117	17	10	4	14	22
2004-05	Utah Grizzlies	AHL	76	15	12	27	72	....	....	....	....	....
2005-06	San Antonio	AHL	75	9	12	21	39	....	....	....	....	....
2006-07	San Antonio	AHL	79	17	17	34	64	....	....	....	....	....
2007-08	Grand Rapids	AHL	70	7	8	15	37	....	....	....	....	....

Memorial Cup Tournament All-Star Team (2004)

Signed as a free agent by **Detroit**, July 16, 2007.

GENDUR, Dan (JEHN-duhr, DAN) VAN.

Right wing. Shoots right. 5'11", 195 lbs. Born, Vancouver, B.C., May 21, 1987.
(Vancouver's 6th choice, 206th overall, in 2007 Entry Draft).

			Regular Season					Playoffs				
Season	Club	League	GP	G	A	Pts	PIM	GP	G	A	Pts	PIM
2003-04	Victoria Cougars	VIJHL	31	26	30	56	70	....	....	....	....	....
	Cowichan Valley	BCHL	17	3	8	11	22	1	0	0	0	0
2004-05	Prince George	WHL	60	2	6	8	75	....	....	....	....	....
2005-06	Prince George	WHL	19	2	1	3	24	....	....	....	....	....
2006-07	Prince George	WHL	13	2	5	7	18	....	....	....	....	....
	Everett Silvertips	WHL	48	20	22	42	44	12	4	4	8	8
2007-08	Everett Silvertips	WHL	60	29	55	84	68	4	1	2	3	8

WHL West Second All-Star Team (2008)

GENEROUS, Matt (GEHN-uhr-uhs, MAT) BUF.

Defense. Shoots right. 6'3", 204 lbs. Born, Methuen, MA, May 4, 1985.
(Buffalo's 8th choice, 208th overall, in 2005 Entry Draft).

			Regular Season					Playoffs				
Season	Club	League	GP	G	A	Pts	PIM	GP	G	A	Pts	PIM
2003-04	N.E. Jr. Falcons	EJHL	43	6	9	15	134	....	....	....	....	....
2004-05	N.E. Jr. Falcons	EJHL	49	8	16	24	105	....	....	....	....	....
2005-06	St. Lawrence	ECAC	34	4	11	15	34	....	....	....	....	....
2006-07	St. Lawrence	ECAC	37	3	6	9	34	....	....	....	....	....
2007-08	St. Lawrence	ECAC	33	3	12	15	31	....	....	....	....	....

ECAC All-Rookie Team (2006)

GENOWAY, Colby (JEHN-oh-way, KOHL-bee) VAN.

Right wing. Shoots right. 6'1", 201 lbs. Born, Morden, Man., December 12, 1983.

			Regular Season					Playoffs				
Season	Club	League	GP	G	A	Pts	PIM	GP	G	A	Pts	PIM
2002-03	North Dakota	WCHA	31	1	2	3	24	....	....	....	....	....
2003-04	North Dakota	WCHA	40	11	23	34	22	....	....	....	....	....
2004-05	North Dakota	WCHA	42	13	31	44	38	....	....	....	....	....
	Hartford Wolf Pack	AHL	4	0	0	0	0	....	....	....	....	....
2005-06	Hartford Wolf Pack	AHL	77	26	35	61	78	13	4	8	12	10
2006-07	Portland Pirates	AHL	41	8	21	29	36	....	....	....	....	....
	Manitoba Moose	AHL	32	1	11	12	12	13	1	1	2	6
2007-08	Manitoba Moose	AHL	67	15	34	49	37	6	0	4	4	6

Signed as a free agent by **Anaheim**, July 11, 2006. Traded to **Vancouver** by **Anaheim** for Joe Rullier, January 24, 2007.

GEOFFRION, Blake (JEHF-REE-ohn, BLAYK) NSH.

Left wing. Shoots left. 6'1", 191 lbs. Born, Plantation, FL, February 3, 1988.
(Nashville's 1st choice, 56th overall, in 2006 Entry Draft).

			Regular Season					Playoffs				
Season	Club	League	GP	G	A	Pts	PIM	GP	G	A	Pts	PIM
2003-04	Culver Academy	High-IN	45	....	....	65	....	....	....	....	....	....
2004-05	USNTDP	U-17	11	2	3	5	24	....	....	....	....	....
	USNTDP	NAHL	37	7	15	22	62	10	2	5	7	23
2005-06	USNTDP	U-18	41	12	14	26	38	....	....	....	....	....
	USNTDP	NAHL	13	6	9	15	30	....	....	....	....	....
2006-07	U. of Wisconsin	WCHA	36	2	4	6	62	....	....	....	....	....
2007-08	U. of Wisconsin	WCHA	36	10	20	30	52	....	....	....	....	....

GERBE, Nathan (GUHR-bee, NAY-thuhn) BUF.

Center. Shoots left. 5'5", 172 lbs. Born, Oxford, MI, July 24, 1987.
(Buffalo's 5th choice, 142nd overall, in 2005 Entry Draft).

			Regular Season					Playoffs				
Season	Club	League	GP	G	A	Pts	PIM	GP	G	A	Pts	PIM
2002-03	River City Lancers	USHL	25	3	3	6	49	7	1	1	2	2
2003-04	USNTDP	U-17	32	14	12	26	66	....	....	....	....	....
	USNTDP	NAHL	26	11	7	18	87	....	....	....	....	....
2004-05	USNTDP	U-18	26	6	11	17	48	....	....	....	....	....
	USNTDP	NAHL	12	7	5	12	25	....	....	....	....	....
2005-06	Boston College	H-East	39	11	7	18	75	....	....	....	....	....
2006-07	Boston College	H-East	41	*25	22	47	76	....	....	....	....	....
2007-08	Boston College	H-East	43	*35	33	*68	65	....	....	....	....	....

Hockey East Second Alll-Star Team (2007) • NCAA Championship All-Tournament Team (2007, 2008) • Hockey East First All-Star Team (2008) • NCAA East First All-American Team (2008) • NCAA Championship Tournament MVP (2008)

GERGEN, Michael (GUHR-gehn, MIGH-kuhl) PIT.

Left wing. Shoots left. 5'11", 185 lbs. Born, Hastings, MN, February 17, 1987.
(Pittsburgh's 2nd choice, 61st overall, in 2005 Entry Draft).

			Regular Season					Playoffs				
Season	Club	League	GP	G	A	Pts	PIM	GP	G	A	Pts	PIM
2003-04	Shat.-St. Mary's	High-MN	71	29	26	55	52	....	....	....	....	....
2004-05	Shat.-St. Mary's	High-MN	69	64	53	117	110	....	....	....	....	....
2005-06	U. Minn-Duluth	WCHA	39	14	8	22	63	....	....	....	....	....
2006-07	U. Minn-Duluth	WCHA	39	5	11	16	34	....	....	....	....	....
2007-08	U. Minn-Duluth	WCHA	33	6	7	13	49	....	....	....	....	....

GIFFORD, Brian (GIH-fuhrd, BRIGH-uhn) PIT.

Center. Shoots left. 6'1", 173 lbs. Born, Fargo, ND, November 12, 1985.
(Pittsburgh's 5th choice, 85th overall, in 2004 Entry Draft).

			Regular Season					Playoffs				
Season	Club	League	GP	G	A	Pts	PIM	GP	G	A	Pts	PIM
2002-03	Moorhead Spuds	High-MN	30	18	20	38	32	....	....	....	....	....
2003-04	Moorhead Spuds	High-MN	26	19	37	56	26	....	....	....	....	....
2004-05	Indiana Ice	USHL	55	13	10	23	80	3	1	0	1	0
2005-06	Indiana Ice	USHL	56	12	14	26	55	5	0	2	2	0
2006-07	U. of Denver	WCHA	40	3	10	13	49	....	....	....	....	....
2007-08	U. of Denver	WCHA	36	2	5	7	16	....	....	....	....	....

GILIATI, Stefano TOR.

Left wing. Shoots left. 5'11", 200 lbs. Born, Montreal, Que., October 7, 1987.

			Regular Season					Playoffs				
Season	Club	League	GP	G	A	Pts	PIM	GP	G	A	Pts	PIM
2004-05	Shawinigan	QMJHL	54	9	5	14	23	3	0	0	0	2
2005-06	Lewiston	QMJHL	70	21	28	49	72	6	2	0	2	6
2006-07	Lewiston	QMJHL	68	24	33	57	73	17	4	11	15	22
2007-08	Lewiston	QMJHL	65	40	47	87	103	....	....	....	....	....
	Toronto Marlies	AHL	1	0	0	0	0	....	....	....	....	....

QMJHL First All-Star Team (2008)

Signed as a free agent by **Toronto**, April 3, 2008.

GILLIES, Colton (GIHL-eez, KOHL-tuhn) MIN.

Center. Shoots left. 6'4", 194 lbs. Born, White Rock, B.C., February 12, 1989.
(Minnesota's 1st choice, 16th overall, in 2007 Entry Draft).

			Regular Season					Playoffs				
Season	Club	League	GP	G	A	Pts	PIM	GP	G	A	Pts	PIM
2004-05	North Delta Flyers	PIJHL	44	9	17	26	....	6	2	1	3	....
	South Surrey	BCHL	3	1	0	1	0	....	....	....	....	....
	Saskatoon Blades	WHL	9	1	1	2	8	2	0	0	0	0
2005-06	Saskatoon Blades	WHL	63	6	6	12	57	8	0	0	0	4
2006-07	Saskatoon Blades	WHL	65	13	17	30	148	....	....	....	....	....
2007-08	Saskatoon Blades	WHL	58	24	23	47	97	....	....	....	....	....
	Houston Aeros	AHL	11	1	7	8	4	5	0	0	0	2

GIMAYEV, Sergei (gih-MIGH-ehv, SAIR-gay) OTT.

Defense. Shoots left. 6'1", 183 lbs. Born, Moscow, USSR, February 16, 1984.
(Ottawa's 6th choice, 166th overall, in 2003 Entry Draft).

			Regular Season					Playoffs				
Season	Club	League	GP	G	A	Pts	PIM	GP	G	A	Pts	PIM
2001-02	CSKA Moscow 2	Russia-3	36	0	10	10	50	....	....	....	....	....
2002-03	Cherepovets	Russia	11	0	0	0	4	....	....	....	....	....
2003-04	Cherepovets	Russia	50	1	3	4	32	....	....	....	....	....
2004-05	Cherepovets	Russia	5	0	1	1	2	....	....	....	....	....
	Sibir Novosibirsk	Russia	31	1	6	7	34	....	....	....	....	....
2005-06	Dynamo Moscow	Russia	46	1	3	4	36	2	0	0	0	0
2006-07	Dynamo Moscow	Russia	23	0	2	2	28	2	0	0	0	6
2007-08	Cherepovets	Russia	39	1	0	1	30	8	1	1	2	4

GIONTA, Stephen (jee-OHN-tuh, STEE-vehn) N.J.

Right wing. Shoots right. 5'7", 180 lbs. Born, Rochester, NY, October 9, 1983.

			Regular Season					Playoffs				
Season	Club	League	GP	G	A	Pts	PIM	GP	G	A	Pts	PIM
2002-03	Boston College	H-East	33	5	10	15	36	....	....	....	....	....
2003-04	Boston College	H-East	41	9	15	24	36	....	....	....	....	....
2004-05	Boston College	H-East	38	8	11	19	44	....	....	....	....	....
2005-06	Boston College	H-East	37	11	21	32	66	....	....	....	....	....
	Albany River Rats	AHL	3	5	1	6	2	....	....	....	....	....
2006-07	Lowell Devils	AHL	67	7	8	15	15	....	....	....	....	....
2007-08	Lowell Devils	AHL	63	16	13	29	33	....	....	....	....	....

Signed to an ATO (tryout) contract by **Albany** (AHL), April 12, 2006. Signed as a free agent by **New Jersey**, September 26, 2006.

GLADSKIKH, Evgeny (glad-SKEEKH, ehv-GEH-nee) VAN.

Right wing. Shoots left. 6', 198 lbs. Born, Magnitogorsk, USSR, April 24, 1982.
(Vancouver's 3rd choice, 114th overall, in 2001 Entry Draft).

			Regular Season					Playoffs				
Season	Club	League	GP	G	A	Pts	PIM	GP	G	A	Pts	PIM
1998-99	Magnitogorsk 2	Russia-4	16	3	3	6	6	....	....	....	....	....
99-2000	Magnitogorsk 2	Russia-3	39	17	2	19	24	....	....	....	....	....
	Magnitogorsk	Russia	1	0	0	0	0	....	....	....	....	....
2000-01	Magnitogorsk 2	Russia-3	11	10	7	17	6	....	....	....	....	....
	Magnitogorsk	Russia	31	3	5	8	10	12	0	2	2	2
2001-02	Magnitogorsk	Russia	32	5	6	11	6	4	0	0	0	4
2002-03	Magnitogorsk	Russia	42	4	7	11	18	3	0	0	0	2
2003-04	Magnitogorsk	Russia	47	13	13	26	22	14	3	1	4	10
2004-05	Magnitogorsk 2	Russia-3	2	0	2	2	0	....	....	....	....	....
	Magnitogorsk	Russia	42	11	12	23	24	4	1	0	1	4
2005-06	Magnitogorsk	Russia	43	12	8	20	20	7	1	1	2	2
2006-07	Magnitogorsk	Russia	47	5	9	14	16	15	2	4	6	6
2007-08	Magnitogorsk	Russia	52	12	12	24	12	12	2	2	4	2

GLASS, Andrew (GLAS, AN-droo) WSH.

Left wing. Shoots left. 6', 175 lbs. Born, Wrentham, MA, July 14, 1989.
(Washington's 10th choice, 199th overall, in 2007 Entry Draft).

			Regular Season					Playoffs				
Season	Club	League	GP	G	A	Pts	PIM	GP	G	A	Pts	PIM
2003-04	Junior Bruins	Minor-MA	61	15	23	38	2	....	....	....	....	....
2004-05	Little Bruins	Minor-MA	33	5	13	18	15	....	....	....	....	....
	Nobles	High-MA	29	7	15	22	6	....	....	....	....	....
2005-06	Little Bruins	Minor-MA	19	9	11	20	17	....	....	....	....	....
	Nobles	High-MA	29	15	24	39	8	....	....	....	....	....
2006-07	Little Bruins	Minor-MA	12	7	8	15	4	....	....	....	....	....
	Nobles	High-MA	18	7	10	17	6	....	....	....	....	....
2007-08	Nobles	High-MA	29	27	23	50	....	....	....	....	....	....

• Signed Letter of Intent to attend **Boston University** (Hockey East) in fall of 2008.

GLASSER, Matthew (GLAS-uhr, MA-thew) EDM.

Left wing. Shoots left. 5'10", 175 lbs. Born, Saskatoon, Sask., January 11, 1987.
(Edmonton's 8th choice, 220th overall, in 2005 Entry Draft).

			Regular Season					Playoffs				
Season	Club	League	GP	G	A	Pts	PIM	GP	G	A	Pts	PIM
2003-04	Fort McMurray	AJHL	55	13	12	25	24	....	....	....	....	....
2004-05	Fort McMurray	AJHL	62	25	24	49	14	....	....	....	....	....
2005-06	Fort McMurray	AJHL	58	15	20	35	36	17	5	2	7	38
2006-07	U. of Denver	WCHA	12	0	0	0	2	....	....	....	....	....
2007-08	U. of Denver	WCHA	40	6	2	8	20	....	....	....	....	....

GLAZACHEV, Konstantin (GLAH-zuh-chehv, KAWN-stan-tihn) NSH.

Left wing. Shoots right. 6', 186 lbs. Born, Arkhangelsk, USSR, February 18, 1985.
(Nashville's 2nd choice, 35th overall, in 2003 Entry Draft).

			Regular Season					Playoffs				
Season	Club	League	GP	G	A	Pts	PIM	GP	G	A	Pts	PIM
2001-02	Yaroslavl 2	Russia-3	7	5	6	11	6	....	....	....	....	....
2002-03	Yaroslavl 2	Russia-3	STATISTICS NOT AVAILABLE									
	Yaroslavl	Russia	13	3	4	7	4	4	0	0	0	0
2003-04	Yaroslavl 2	Russia-3	9	6	5	11	8	....	....	....	....	....
	Yaroslavl	Russia	35	4	3	7	4	2	0	0	0	0
2004-05	Sibir Novosibirsk	Russia	24	4	9	13	6	....	....	....	....	....
	Yaroslavl	Russia	9	0	3	3	2	....	....	....	....	....
	Yaroslavl 2	Russia-3	20	17	9	26	14	....	....	....	....	....
2005-06	Yaroslavl	Russia	29	7	4	11	8	9	0	2	2	0
2006-07	Yaroslavl	Russia	14	4	1	5	10	....	....	....	....	....
	Yaroslavl 2	Russia-3	4	2	5	7	0	....	....	....	....	....
	Amur Khabarovsk	Russia	22	4	7	11	14	....	....	....	....	....
2007-08	Novokuznetsk	Russia	50	7	9	16	10	....	....	....	....	....

GLEASON, Joe (GLEE-suhn, JOH) CHI.

Defense. Shoots right. 5'9", 178 lbs. Born, Edina, MN, March 30, 1990.
(Chicago's 7th choice, 192nd overall, in 2008 Entry Draft).

			Regular Season					Playoffs				
Season	Club	League	GP	G	A	Pts	PIM	GP	G	A	Pts	PIM
2006-07	Edina Hornets	High-MN	21	10	23	33	....	....	....	....	....	....
	Team Southwest	UMWEHL	11	4	6	10	....	....	....	....	....	....
2007-08	Edina Hornets	High-MN	23	9	33	42	....	....	....	....	....	....
	Team Southwest	UMWEHL	12	6	14	20	....	....	....	....	....	....

• Signed Letter of Intent to attend **University of North Dakota** (WCHA) in fall of 2009.

GLUKHOV, Alexei (GLUH-khawv, al-EHX-ay) T.B.

Right wing. Shoots left. 6'3", 176 lbs. Born, Voskresensk, USSR, April 5, 1984.
(Tampa Bay's 12th choice, 286th overall, in 2002 Entry Draft).

			Regular Season					Playoffs				
Season	Club	League	GP	G	A	Pts	PIM	GP	G	A	Pts	PIM
99-2000	Voskresensk 2	Russia-3	10	2	2	4	2	....	....	....	....	....
2000-01	Voskresensk	Russia-2	9	0	1	1	6	....	....	....	....	....
2001-02	Voskresensk 2	Russia-3	34	8	22	30	54	....	....	....	....	....
	Voskresensk	Russia-2	4	0	0	0	0	....	....	....	....	....
2002-03	Voskresensk	Russia-2	38	4	4	8	30	....	....	....	....	....
2003-04	Voskresensk	Russia	28	0	0	0	12	....	....	....	....	....
2004-05	Voskresensk	Russia	9	0	0	0	6	....	....	....	....	....
	Springfield Falcons	AHL	3	0	1	1	6	....	....	....	....	....
2005-06	Mytischi	Russia	45	2	14	16	70	9	2	1	3	10
2006-07	Cherepovets	Russia	52	2	14	16	97	5	0	0	0	4
2007-08	Cherepovets	Russia	57	7	13	20	86	8	2	0	2	12

Signed to PTO (tryout) contract by **Springfield** (AHL), April 14, 2005.

GODFREY, Josh (GAWD-free, JAWSH) WSH.

Defense. Shoots right. 6', 202 lbs. Born, Collingwood, Ont., January 15, 1988.
(Washington's 2nd choice, 34th overall, in 2007 Entry Draft).

			Regular Season					Playoffs				
Season	Club	League	GP	G	A	Pts	PIM	GP	G	A	Pts	PIM
2004-05	Guelph Storm	OHL	18	0	4	4	9	1	0	0	0	0
2005-06	Guelph Storm	OHL	33	2	8	10	38	....	....	....	....	....
	Sault Ste. Marie	OHL	30	6	5	11	26	1	0	1	1	0
2006-07	Sault Ste. Marie	OHL	68	24	33	57	80	13	9	5	14	18
2007-08	Sault Ste. Marie	OHL	60	17	34	51	61	14	5	1	6	20
	Hershey Bears	AHL	....	....	....	....	....	1	0	0	0	0

GOGGIN, Mark (GAW-gihn, MAHRK) BOS.

Center. Shoots left. 5'11", 186 lbs. Born, Chicago, IL, July 29, 1990.
(Boston's 6th choice, 197th overall, in 2008 Entry Draft).

			Regular Season					Playoffs				
Season	Club	League	GP	G	A	Pts	PIM	GP	G	A	Pts	PIM
2006-07	Choate-Rosemary	High-CT	....	15	20	35	....	....	....	....	....	....
2007-08	Choate-Rosemary	High-CT	21	15	21	36	10	....	....	....	....	....
	USNTDP	U-17	3	1	1	2	0	....	....	....	....	....
	USNTDP	NAHL	5	1	1	2	2	....	....	....	....	....

• Signed Letter of Intent to attend **Dartmouth College** (ECAC) in fall of 2009.

GOGULLA, Philip (GOH-goo-lah, FIHL-ihp) BUF.

Right wing. Shoots left. 6'2", 180 lbs. Born, Dusseldorf, West Germany, July 31, 1987.
(Buffalo's 2nd choice, 48th overall, in 2005 Entry Draft).

			Regular Season					Playoffs				
Season	Club	League	GP	G	A	Pts	PIM	GP	G	A	Pts	PIM
2002-03	Krefelder EV Jr.	Ger-Jr.	32	11	23	34	42	2	0	0	0	2
2003-04	Krefelder EV Jr.	Ger-Jr.	35	35	44	79	22	2	0	2	2	27
2004-05	Essen	German-2	3	0	0	0	0	....	....	....	....	....
	Koln Jr.	Ger-Jr.	7	4	5	9	18	....	....	....	....	....
	Kolner Haie	Germany	47	1	1	2	14	7	0	0	0	2
2005-06	Kolner Haie	Germany	48	7	15	22	49	9	3	2	5	40
2006-07	Kolner Haie	Germany	44	8	13	21	26	7	0	0	0	8
2007-08	Kolner Haie	Germany	51	11	33	44	30	14	3	9	12	6

GOLOUBEF, Cody (GAW-luh-behf, KOH-dee) CBJ

Defense. Shoots right. 6', 195 lbs. Born, Mississauga, Ont., November 30, 1989.
(Columbus' 2nd choice, 37th overall, in 2008 Entry Draft).

			Regular Season					Playoffs				
Season	Club	League	GP	G	A	Pts	PIM	GP	G	A	Pts	PIM
2003-04	Toronto Marlboros	GTHL	89	10	27	37	44	....	....	....	....	....
2004-05	Toronto Marlboros	GTHL	69	14	47	61	56	....	....	....	....	....
2005-06	Milton Icehawks	OPJHL	42	9	29	38	38	7	1	3	4	10
2006-07	Oakville Blades	OPJHL	9	5	5	10	46	10	2	10	12	18
2007-08	U. of Wisconsin	WCHA	40	4	6	10	36	....	....	....	....	....

• Missed majority of 2006-07 season due to injury.

GONCHAROV, Maxim (gohn-CHAR-ahv, mahx-EEM) PHX.

Defense. Shoots right. 6', 176 lbs. Born, Moscow, USSR, June 15, 1989.
(Phoenix's 6th choice, 123rd overall, in 2007 Entry Draft).

			Regular Season					Playoffs				
Season	Club	League	GP	G	A	Pts	PIM	GP	G	A	Pts	PIM
2005-06	CSKA Moscow 2	Russia-3	STATISTICS NOT AVAILABLE									
2006-07	CSKA Moscow 2	Russia-3	STATISTICS NOT AVAILABLE									
	CSKA Moscow	Russia	18	0	0	0	10	5	0	0	0	2
2007-08	CSKA Moscow	Russia	47	3	2	5	38	6	0	2	2	0
	CSKA Moscow 2	Russia-3	4	0	2	2	35	3	0	0	0	8

GORDON, Andrew (GOHR-duhn, AN-droo) WSH.

Right wing. Shoots right. 6', 198 lbs. Born, Halifax, N.S., December 13, 1985.
(Washington's 11th choice, 197th overall, in 2004 Entry Draft).

			Regular Season					Playoffs				
Season	Club	League	GP	G	A	Pts	PIM	GP	G	A	Pts	PIM
2002-03	Notre Dame	SJHL	58	20	27	47	12	....	....	....	....	....
2003-04	Notre Dame	SJHL	55	20	44	64	12	....	....	....	....	....
2004-05	St. Cloud State	WCHA	38	9	8	17	6	....	....	....	....	....
2005-06	St. Cloud State	WCHA	42	20	20	40	22	....	....	....	....	....
2006-07	St. Cloud State	WCHA	40	22	23	45	16	....	....	....	....	....
2007-08	Hershey Bears	AHL	58	16	35	51	39	5	3	2	5	2
	South Carolina	ECHL	11	8	6	14	6	9	5	3	8	8

WCHA First All-Star Team (2007)

GOULET, Alain (goo-LAY, AL-eh) BOS.

Defense. Shoots right. 6'3", 195 lbs. Born, Kapuskasing, Ont., September 22, 1988.
(Boston's 4th choice, 159th overall, in 2007 Entry Draft).

			Regular Season					Playoffs				
Season	Club	League	GP	G	A	Pts	PIM	GP	G	A	Pts	PIM
2005-06	Ottawa Jr. Sens	CJHL	41	6	14	20	22	....	....	....	....	....
2006-07	Aurora Tigers	OPJHL	43	10	32	42	34	25	5	16	21	32
2007-08	Nebraska-Omaha	CCHA	37	6	8	14	14	....	....	....	....	....

GOULET, Stephane (goo-LAY, STEH-fan) EDM.

Right wing. Shoots left. 6'3", 185 lbs. Born, Levis, Que., January 7, 1986.
(Edmonton's 8th choice, 208th overall, in 2004 Entry Draft).

			Regular Season					Playoffs				
Season	Club	League	GP	G	A	Pts	PIM	GP	G	A	Pts	PIM
2002-03	Levis	QAAA	42	39	29	68	70	....	....	....	....	....
2003-04	Quebec Remparts	QMJHL	54	6	8	14	14	5	0	0	0	2
2004-05	Moncton Wildcats	QMJHL	69	22	25	47	37	12	3	7	10	12
2005-06	Moncton Wildcats	QMJHL	67	51	42	93	80	13	7	8	15	16
2006-07	Grand Rapids	AHL	2	0	0	0	2	....	....	....	....	....
	Stockton Thunder	ECHL	69	17	23	40	58	5	0	1	1	2
2007-08	Springfield Falcons	AHL	36	9	5	14	22	....	....	....	....	....
	Stockton Thunder	ECHL	12	4	10	14	10	6	5	4	9	0

GRABNER, Michael (GRAB-nuhr, MIGH-kuhl) VAN.

Right wing. Shoots left. 6', 187 lbs. Born, Villach, Austria, October 5, 1987.
(Vancouver's 1st choice, 14th overall, in 2006 Entry Draft).

			Regular Season					Playoffs				
Season	Club	League	GP	G	A	Pts	PIM	GP	G	A	Pts	PIM
2002-03	EC Villacher SV Jr.	Austria-Jr.	13	6	4	10	4	....	....	....	....	....
2003-04	EC Villacher SV Jr.	Austria-Jr.	23	32	5	37	58	....	....	....	....	....
	EC Villacher SV	Austria	18	2	1	3	0	....	....	....	....	....
2004-05	Spokane Chiefs	WHL	58	13	11	24	18	....	....	....	....	....
2005-06	Spokane Chiefs	WHL	67	36	14	50	28	....	....	....	....	....
2006-07	Spokane Chiefs	WHL	55	39	16	55	34	6	0	1	1	2
	Manitoba Moose	AHL	2	1	1	2	0	6	0	0	0	0
2007-08	Manitoba Moose	AHL	74	22	22	44	8	6	3	0	3	2

GRACHEV, Yevgeny (gra-CHAWF, yehv-GEH-nee) **NYR**

Center. Shoots left. 6'4", 217 lbs. Born, Khabarovsk, USSR, February 21, 1990.
(NY Rangers' 3rd choice, 75th overall, in 2008 Entry Draft).

			Regular Season					Playoffs				
Season	Club	League	GP	G	A	Pts	PIM	GP	G	A	Pts	PIM
2005-06	Yaroslavl 2	Russia-3	1	0	0	0	2	....	....	....	....	....
2006-07	Yaroslavl 2	Russia-3	28	7	6	13	6	....	....	....	....	....
2007-08	Yaroslavl 2	Russia-3	STATISTICS NOT AVAILABLE									
	Yaroslavl	Russia	1	0	0	0	0	....	....	....	....	....

GRACIK, Juraj (GRAH-chihk, YUHR-ay) **ATL.**

Right wing. Shoots right. 6'3", 190 lbs. Born, Topolcany, Czech., August 14, 1986.
(Atlanta's 5th choice, 142nd overall, in 2004 Entry Draft).

			Regular Season					Playoffs				
Season	Club	League	GP	G	A	Pts	PIM	GP	G	A	Pts	PIM
2002-03	Topolcany Jr.	Slovak-Jr.	24	10	7	17	28	....	....	....	....	....
2003-04	Topolcany Jr.	Slovak-Jr.	28	22	12	34	78	....	....	....	....	....
	Topolcany	Slovak-2	28	16	8	24	8	4	1	0	1	0
2004-05	Tri-City Americans	WHL	33	4	2	6	18	....	....	....	....	....
2005-06	Tri-City Americans	WHL	53	22	23	45	36	....	....	....	....	....
2006-07	Bratislava	Slovakia	37	5	1	6	6	3	0	0	0	0
	HC Topolcany	Slovak-2	7	8	1	9	18	....	....	....	....	....
	Ruzinov	Slovak-2	13	7	5	12	16	3	1	1	2	0
2007-08	Bratislava	Slovakia	40	3	4	7	10	11	0	0	0	0
	Ruzinov	Slovak-2	10	5	3	8	10	4	1	2	3	4

Signed as a free agent by **Bratislava** (Slovakia), October 14, 2006.

GRANT, Alex (GRANT, AL-ehx) **PIT.**

Defense. Shoots right. 6'2", 185 lbs. Born, Antigonish, N.S., January 20, 1989.
(Pittsburgh's 6th choice, 118th overall, in 2007 Entry Draft).

			Regular Season					Playoffs				
Season	Club	League	GP	G	A	Pts	PIM	GP	G	A	Pts	PIM
2004-05	Antigonish	MJrHL	50	7	9	16	36	3	1	1	2	2
2005-06	Saint John	QMJHL	47	4	9	13	58	....	....	....	....	....
2006-07	Saint John	QMJHL	68	12	20	32	108	....	....	....	....	....
2007-08	Saint John	QMJHL	70	15	33	48	96	14	3	11	14	12

GRANT, Derek (GRANT, DAIR-ihk) **OTT.**

Center. Shoots left. 6'2", 176 lbs. Born, Abbotsford, B.C., April 20, 1990.
(Ottawa's 5th choice, 119th overall, in 2008 Entry Draft).

			Regular Season					Playoffs				
Season	Club	League	GP	G	A	Pts	PIM	GP	G	A	Pts	PIM
2006-07	Abbotsford Pilots	PIJHL	47	31	20	51	42	11	6	5	11	20
2007-08	Langley Chiefs	BCHL	57	24	39	63	44	12	5	5	10	15

• Signed Letter of Intent to attend **Michigan State University** (CCHA) in fall of 2009.

GRANTHAM, Ryley (GRAN-thum, RIGH-lee) **CGY.**

Center. Shoots left. 6'3", 207 lbs. Born, Hanna, Alta., January 7, 1988.
(Calgary's 6th choice, 168th overall, in 2008 Entry Draft).

			Regular Season					Playoffs				
Season	Club	League	GP	G	A	Pts	PIM	GP	G	A	Pts	PIM
2005-06	Brooks Bandits	AJHL	43	6	3	9	98	13	2	0	2	16
2006-07	Brooks Bandits	AJHL	....	3	11	14	....	....	....	....	....	....
	Moose Jaw	WHL	33	1	1	2	50	....	....	....	....	....
2007-08	Moose Jaw	WHL	66	10	9	19	163	6	0	0	0	8

GRATCHEV, Maxim (GRAT-chehv, mahx-EEM) **NYI**

Left wing. Shoots left. 5'11", 196 lbs. Born, Novosibirsk, USSR, September 26, 1988.
(NY Islanders' 3rd choice, 106th overall, in 2007 Entry Draft).

			Regular Season					Playoffs				
Season	Club	League	GP	G	A	Pts	PIM	GP	G	A	Pts	PIM
2003-04	Thayer Academy	High-MA	....	7	9	16	....	....	....	....	....	....
2004-05	Quebec Remparts	QMJHL	54	7	11	18	36	....	....	....	....	....
2005-06	Quebec Remparts	QMJHL	22	5	5	10	40	....	....	....	....	....
	Rimouski Oceanic	QMJHL	33	6	11	17	57	....	....	....	....	....
2006-07	Rimouski Oceanic	QMJHL	70	35	42	77	88	....	....	....	....	....
2007-08	Rimouski Oceanic	QMJHL	39	9	20	29	48	9	2	0	2	12

GREENING, Colin (GREEN-ihng, KAW-lihn) **OTT.**

Center/Left wing. Shoots left. 6'2", 211 lbs. Born, St. John's, Nfld., March 9, 1986.
(Ottawa's 8th choice, 204th overall, in 2005 Entry Draft).

			Regular Season					Playoffs				
Season	Club	League	GP	G	A	Pts	PIM	GP	G	A	Pts	PIM
2002-03	St. John's	NFAHA	60	24	34	58	48	....	....	....	....	....
2003-04	Upper Canada	High-ON	53	30	43	73	40	....	....	....	....	....
2004-05	Upper Canada	High-ON	35	24	22	46	24	....	....	....	....	....
2005-06	Nanaimo Clippers	BCHL	56	27	35	62	46	5	3	0	3	2
2006-07	Cornell Big Red	ECAC	31	11	8	19	26	....	....	....	....	....
2007-08	Cornell Big Red	ECAC	36	14	19	33	41	....	....	....	....	....

ECAC Second All-Star Team (2008)

GREENOP, Richard (GREEN-awp, RIH-chuhrd) **CHI.**

Center. Shoots right. 6'3", 210 lbs. Born, Oshawa, Ont., February 24, 1989.
(Chicago's 7th choice, 156th overall, in 2007 Entry Draft).

			Regular Season					Playoffs				
Season	Club	League	GP	G	A	Pts	PIM	GP	G	A	Pts	PIM
2005-06	Oshawa	OPJHL	47	10	4	14	97	....	....	....	....	....
2006-07	Windsor Spitfires	OHL	48	3	9	12	149	....	....	....	....	....
2007-08	Windsor Spitfires	OHL	60	2	3	5	194	5	0	0	0	2

GREER, Matt (GREER, MAT) **CBJ**

Left wing. Shoots right. 6'2", 190 lbs. Born, St. Paul, MN, November 21, 1985.
(Columbus' 11th choice, 233rd overall, in 2004 Entry Draft).

			Regular Season					Playoffs				
Season	Club	League	GP	G	A	Pts	PIM	GP	G	A	Pts	PIM
2003-04	White Bear Lake	High-MN	27	25	19	44	....	....	....	....	....	....
2004-05	Des Moines	USHL	60	14	18	32	16	....	....	....	....	....
2005-06	U. Minn-Duluth	WCHA	40	2	3	5	12	....	....	....	....	....
2006-07	U. Minn-Duluth	WCHA	32	4	4	8	24	....	....	....	....	....
2007-08	U. Minn-Duluth	WCHA	36	2	5	7	12	....	....	....	....	....

GREGOIRE, Jason (GREHG-wahr, JAY-suhn) **NYI**

Left wing. Shoots left. 5'11", 175 lbs. Born, Winnipeg, Man., February 24, 1989.
(NY Islanders' 2nd choice, 76th overall, in 2007 Entry Draft).

			Regular Season					Playoffs				
Season	Club	League	GP	G	A	Pts	PIM	GP	G	A	Pts	PIM
2005-06	Winnipeg South	MJHL	57	22	28	50	46	14	12	11	23	....
2006-07	Lincoln Stars	USHL	32	16	20	36	10	4	4	0	4	2
2007-08	Lincoln Stars	USHL	54	*37	32	69	41	8	3	9	*12	6

• Signed Letter of Intent to attend **University of North Dakota** (WCHA) in fall of 2008.

GRIGORENKO, Igor (grih-goh-REHN-koh, EE-gohr) **DET.**

Right wing. Shoots right. 5'11", 183 lbs. Born, Togliatti, USSR, April 9, 1983.
(Detroit's 1st choice, 62nd overall, in 2001 Entry Draft).

			Regular Season					Playoffs				
Season	Club	League	GP	G	A	Pts	PIM	GP	G	A	Pts	PIM
1998-99	Lada Togliatti 2	Russia-4	19	3	3	6	2	....	....	....	....	....
99-2000	Lada Togliatti 2	Russia-3	38	17	18	35	36	....	....	....	....	....
2000-01	Lada Togliatti 2	Russia-3	6	5	4	9	....	....	....	....	....	....
	CSK VVS Samara	Russia-2	39	10	10	20	....	....	....	....	....	....
	Lada Togliatti	Russia	....	....	....	....	....	5	1	0	1	4
2001-02	Lada Togliatti	Russia	41	8	9	17	58	4	1	0	1	2
2002-03	Lada Togliatti	Russia	47	19	11	30	82	10	1	*6	7	10
2003-04	Lada Togliatti 2	Russia-3	6	2	2	4	0	2	0	1	1	0
	Lada Togliatti	Russia	....	....	....	....	....	3	0	0	0	0
2004-05	Lada Togliatti	Russia	11	0	1	1	6	....	....	....	....	....
	Ufa	Russia	30	11	7	18	22	....	....	....	....	....
2005-06	Cherepovets	Russia	50	13	20	33	26	4	1	1	2	8
2006-07	Lada Togliatti	Russia	49	14	13	27	71	2	2	1	3	2
2007-08	Grand Rapids	AHL	5	0	0	0	4	....	....	....	....	....
	Ufa	Russia	27	4	6	10	24	5	0	1	1	0

• Missed majority of 2003-04 season recovering from injuries suffered in automobile accident, May 16, 2003.

GROT, Denis (GROHT, DEH-nihs) **VAN.**

Defense. Shoots left. 6'1", 185 lbs. Born, Minsk, USSR, January 6, 1984.
(Vancouver's 2nd choice, 55th overall, in 2002 Entry Draft).

			Regular Season					Playoffs				
Season	Club	League	GP	G	A	Pts	PIM	GP	G	A	Pts	PIM
2000-01	Yaroslavl 2	Russia-3	34	5	1	6	10	....	....	....	....	....
	Russia	Nat-Tm	5	0	2	2	8	....	....	....	....	....
2001-02	Yaroslavl 2	Russia-3	14	1	0	1	10	....	....	....	....	....
	Elektrostal 2	Russia-3	3	0	1	1	2	....	....	....	....	....
	Elektrostal	Russia-2	33	1	1	2	42	....	....	....	....	....
2002-03	HK Lipetsk	Russia-2	27	4	4	8	28	....	....	....	....	....
2003-04	Yaroslavl	Russia	31	0	2	2	4	3	0	0	0	2
2004-05	Yaroslavl 2	Russia-3	20	2	3	5	22	....	....	....	....	....
	Yaroslavl	Russia	1	0	0	0	2	....	....	....	....	....
	Sibir Novosibirsk	Russia	23	0	4	4	32	....	....	....	....	....
	Amur Khabarovsk	Russia-2	9	1	5	6	2	12	0	0	0	31
2005-06	Spartak Moscow	Russia	48	1	4	5	28	3	0	0	0	0
2006-07	Nizhnekamsk	Russia	38	2	7	9	59	1	0	0	0	2
2007-08	Nizhnekamsk	Russia	48	0	3	3	32	5	0	0	0	4

GROULX, Samuel (GROOL, SAM-ew-l) **S.J.**

Defense. Shoots left. 6'2", 165 lbs. Born, Gatineau, Que., June 28, 1990.
(San Jose's 2nd choice, 92nd overall, in 2008 Entry Draft).

			Regular Season					Playoffs				
Season	Club	League	GP	G	A	Pts	PIM	GP	G	A	Pts	PIM
2005-06	Gatineau Intrepide	QAAA	44	1	13	14	24	3	0	0	0	4
2006-07	Gatineau Intrepide	QAAA	36	2	9	11	62	3	0	1	1	8
	Quebec Remparts	QMJHL	9	1	1	2	2	1	0	0	0	0
2007-08	Quebec Remparts	QMJHL	70	5	20	25	100	11	0	3	3	14

QMJHL All-Rookie Team (2008)

GRYBA, Eric (GREE-buh, AIR-ihk) **OTT.**

Defense. Shoots right. 6'3", 214 lbs. Born, Saskatoon, Sask., April 14, 1988.
(Ottawa's 2nd choice, 68th overall, in 2006 Entry Draft).

			Regular Season					Playoffs				
Season	Club	League	GP	G	A	Pts	PIM	GP	G	A	Pts	PIM
2003-04	Sask. Contacts	SMHL	39	1	10	11	89	10	4	8	12	20
2004-05	Sask. Contacts	SMHL	32	11	29	40	83	11	5	7	12	22
2005-06	Green Bay	USHL	56	3	12	15	*205	3	1	1	2	27
2006-07	Boston University	H-East	38	1	3	4	76	....	....	....	....	....
2007-08	Boston University	H-East	32	1	1	2	54	....	....	....	....	....

GUGGISBERG, Peter (GUH-gihs-buhrg, PEE-tuhr) **WSH.**

Right wing. Shoots right. 5'11", 183 lbs. Born, Davos, Switzerland, January 20, 1985.
(Washington's 10th choice, 166th overall, in 2004 Entry Draft).

			Regular Season					Playoffs				
Season	Club	League	GP	G	A	Pts	PIM	GP	G	A	Pts	PIM
2000-01	Langnau Jr.	Swiss-Jr.	12	3	3	6	0	2	1	0	1	2
2001-02	Langnau Jr.	Swiss-Jr.	15	12	4	16	2	4	2	3	5	4
	Langnau	Swiss	....	....	....	....	....	6	0	1	1	0
2002-03	Langnau Jr.	Swiss-Jr.	10	7	10	17	0	5	2	1	3	32
	Langnau	Swiss	34	6	7	13	0	....	....	....	....	....
2003-04	HC Davos	Swiss	39	11	9	20	2	6	0	0	0	4
2004-05	HC Davos	Swiss	36	12	7	19	8	15	3	5	8	4
2005-06	HC Davos	Swiss	43	7	9	16	10	15	3	2	5	2
2006-07	HC Davos	Swiss	43	6	6	12	6	19	6	5	11	4
2007-08	HC Davos	Swiss	48	11	9	20	4	13	5	4	9	2

GUNNARSSON, Carl (GUHN-nuhr-suhn, KARL) **TOR.**

Defense. Shoots left. 6'2", 189 lbs. Born, Orebro, Sweden, November 9, 1986.
(Toronto's 6th choice, 194th overall, in 2007 Entry Draft).

			Regular Season					Playoffs				
Season	Club	League	GP	G	A	Pts	PIM	GP	G	A	Pts	PIM
2003-04	HC Orebro 90	Sweden-2	43	0	4	4	16	....	....	....	....	....
2004-05	Linkopings HC U18	Swe-U18	1	0	1	1	2	....	....	....	....	....
	Linkopings HC Jr.	Swe-Jr.	22	2	5	7	24	....	....	....	....	....
2005-06	Linkopings HC Jr.	Swe-Jr.	30	7	6	13	26	4	1	0	1	4
	IFK Arboga IK	Sweden-2	12	1	5	6	8	....	....	....	....	....
	Linkopings HC	Sweden	14	0	0	0	0	....	....	....	....	....
2006-07	Linkopings HC Jr.	Swe-Jr.	6	0	5	5	6	....	....	....	....	....
	VIK Vasteras HK	Sweden-2	15	2	3	5	14	....	....	....	....	....
	Linkopings HC	Sweden	30	2	2	4	8	15	0	4	4	4
2007-08	Linkopings HC	Sweden	53	2	7	9	26	16	0	4	4	10

GUSTAFSSON, Anton (goos-TAHF-suhn, AN-tawn) WSH.

Center. Shoots left. 6'2", 194 lbs. Born, Karlskoga, Sweden, February 25, 1990.
(Washington's 1st choice, 21st overall, in 2008 Entry Draft).

			Regular Season					Playoffs				
Season	**Club**	**League**	**GP**	**G**	**A**	**Pts**	**PIM**	**GP**	**G**	**A**	**Pts**	**PIM**
2005-06	Karlskoga HC	Sweden-4	....	3	0	3	0	....	....	....	....	....
2006-07	Frolunda U18	Swe-U18	8	3	4	7	8	6	3	1	4	2
	Frolunda Jr.	Swe-Jr.	26	5	3	8	24	8	0	0	0	8
2007-08	Frolunda U18	Swe-U18	1	0	1	1	2	....	....	....	....	....
	Frolunda Jr.	Swe-Jr.	33	15	17	32	55	2	1	0	1	2
	Frolunda	Sweden	1	0	0	0	0	....	....	....	....	....

GUTHRIE, Shea (GUHTH-ree, SHAY) NYI

Wing. Shoots right. 6', 200 lbs. Born, Almonte, Ont., July 30, 1987.
(NY Islanders' 3rd choice, 76th overall, in 2005 Entry Draft).

			Regular Season					Playoffs				
Season	**Club**	**League**	**GP**	**G**	**A**	**Pts**	**PIM**	**GP**	**G**	**A**	**Pts**	**PIM**
2004-05	St. George's	High-RI	25	31	26	57	20	....	....	....	....	....
2005-06	Clarkson Knights	ECAC	33	9	17	26	60	....	....	....	....	....
2006-07	Clarkson Knights	ECAC	36	8	23	31	30	....	....	....	....	....
2007-08	Clarkson Knights	ECAC	38	9	13	22	20	....	....	....	....	....

ECAC All-Rookie Team (2006)

HAGELIN, Carl (HAG-eh-lihn, KARL) NYR

Left wing. Shoots left. 5'11", 176 lbs. Born, Sodertalje, Sweden, August 23, 1988.
(NY Rangers' 4th choice, 168th overall, in 2007 Entry Draft).

			Regular Season					Playoffs				
Season	**Club**	**League**	**GP**	**G**	**A**	**Pts**	**PIM**	**GP**	**G**	**A**	**Pts**	**PIM**
2004-05	Sodertalje SK U18	Swe-U18	14	10	7	17	16	2	0	2	2	0
2005-06	Sodertalje SK U18	Swe-U18	7	4	8	12	2	....	....	....	....	....
	Sodertalje SK Jr.	Swe-Jr.	41	20	20	40	42	4	1	2	3	22
2006-07	Sodertalje SK Jr.	Swe-Jr.	40	24	31	55	42	3	1	5	6	20
2007-08	U. of Michigan	CCHA	41	11	11	22	28	....	....	....	....	....

HALISCHUK, Matt (huh-LIHS-chuhk, MAT) N.J.

Right wing. Shoots right. 5'11", 175 lbs. Born, Toronto, Ont., June 1, 1988.
(New Jersey's 4th choice, 117th overall, in 2007 Entry Draft).

			Regular Season					Playoffs				
Season	**Club**	**League**	**GP**	**G**	**A**	**Pts**	**PIM**	**GP**	**G**	**A**	**Pts**	**PIM**
2003-04	Tor. Jr. Canadiens	GTHL	53	37	48	85	27	....	....	....	....	....
2004-05	St. Michael's	OHL	30	3	3	6	4	....	....	....	....	....
	St. Mike's B's	OPJHL	17	5	11	16	8	32	10	15	25	4
2005-06	St. Michael's	OHL	61	13	18	31	16	4	1	1	2	0
2006-07	Kitchener Rangers	OHL	67	33	33	66	20	9	4	1	5	10
2007-08	Kitchener Rangers	OHL	40	13	46	59	16	20	*16	16	32	0

OHL First All-Star Team (2008) • George Parsons Trophy (Memorial Cup Tournament - Most Sportsmanlike Player) (2008)

HAMBLY, Tim (HAM-blee, TIHM) CHI.

Defense. Shoots left. 6', 185 lbs. Born, White Bear Lake, MN, June 23, 1983.

			Regular Season					Playoffs				
Season	**Club**	**League**	**GP**	**G**	**A**	**Pts**	**PIM**	**GP**	**G**	**A**	**Pts**	**PIM**
2000-01	Waterloo	USHL	17	1	8	9	4	....	....	....	....	....
2001-02	U. Minn-Duluth	WCHA	39	1	10	11	26	....	....	....	....	....
2002-03	U. Minn-Duluth	WCHA	29	2	3	5	18	....	....	....	....	....
2003-04	U. Minn-Duluth	WCHA	39	5	19	24	52	....	....	....	....	....
2004-05	U. Minn-Duluth	WCHA	34	5	15	20	36	....	....	....	....	....
	Las Vegas	ECHL	8	0	2	2	4	....	....	....	....	....
2005-06	Iowa Stars	AHL	2	0	0	0	4	....	....	....	....	....
	Omaha	AHL	45	1	16	17	33	....	....	....	....	....
	Las Vegas	ECHL	31	9	12	21	23	9	3	2	5	4
2006-07	Omaha	AHL	67	3	15	18	28	5	1	0	1	0
2007-08	Quad City Flames	AHL	72	4	26	30	40	....	....	....	....	....

Signed as a free agent by **Chicago**, June 24, 2008.

HAMILL, Zach (HA-mihl, ZAK) BOS.

Center. Shoots right. 5'11", 175 lbs. Born, Vancouver, B.C., September 23, 1988.
(Boston's 1st choice, 8th overall, in 2007 Entry Draft).

			Regular Season					Playoffs				
Season	**Club**	**League**	**GP**	**G**	**A**	**Pts**	**PIM**	**GP**	**G**	**A**	**Pts**	**PIM**
2002-03	Port Coquitlam	Minor-BC	61	120	83	203	....	....	....	....	....	....
2003-04	Port Coquitlam	PIJHL	39	30	31	51	50	....	....	....	....	....
	Everett Silvertips	WHL	4	0	2	2	0	20	3	2	5	2
2004-05	Everett Silvertips	WHL	57	8	25	33	29	11	2	3	5	8
2005-06	Everett Silvertips	WHL	53	21	38	59	28	15	3	11	14	4
2006-07	Everett Silvertips	WHL	69	32	*61	*93	90	12	2	8	10	16
2007-08	Everett Silvertips	WHL	67	26	49	75	88	4	0	3	3	2
	Providence Bruins	AHL	7	0	5	5	6	9	1	3	4	0

WHL West First All-Star Team (2007)

HAMILTON, Mike (HAM-ihl-tuhn, MIGHK)

Left wing. Shoots left. 6'1", 190 lbs. Born, Vancouver, B.C., May 2, 1983.
(Atlanta's 6th choice, 175th overall, in 2003 Entry Draft).

			Regular Season					Playoffs				
Season	**Club**	**League**	**GP**	**G**	**A**	**Pts**	**PIM**	**GP**	**G**	**A**	**Pts**	**PIM**
99-2000	Peninsula Panthers	VIJHL	44	33	42	75	94	....	....	....	....	....
2000-01	Peninsula Panthers	VIJHL	19	15	20	35	106	....	....	....	....	....
	Victoria Salsa	BCHL	31	2	5	7	18	....	....	....	....	....
2001-02	Victoria Salsa	BCHL	13	5	2	7	14	....	....	....	....	....
	Merritt	BCHL	45	23	36	59	64	....	....	....	....	....
2002-03	Merritt	BCHL	56	42	51	95	133	....	....	....	....	....
2003-04	U. of Maine	H-East	29	7	6	13	40	....	....	....	....	....
2004-05	U. of Maine	H-East	38	3	15	18	49	....	....	....	....	....
2005-06	U. of Maine	H-East	30	1	10	11	56	....	....	....	....	....
2006-07	U. of Maine	H-East	40	9	13	22	63	....	....	....	....	....
2007-08	Gwinnett	ECHL	72	23	27	50	121	8	2	6	8	16
	Chicago Wolves	AHL	....	....	....	....	....	6	1	0	1	2

Signed as a free agent by **Chicago** (AHL), September 24, 2007.

HAMILTON, Ryan (HAM-ihl-tuhn, RIGH-uhn) MIN.

Left wing. Shoots left. 6'2", 215 lbs. Born, Oshawa, Ont., April 15, 1985.

			Regular Season					Playoffs				
Season	**Club**	**League**	**GP**	**G**	**A**	**Pts**	**PIM**	**GP**	**G**	**A**	**Pts**	**PIM**
2002-03	Couchiching	OPJHL	11	5	8	13	2	....	....	....	....	....
	Peterborough Bees	OPJHL	27	3	10	13	43	....	....	....	....	....
	Trenton Sting	OPJHL	17	3	8	11	24	....	....	....	....	....
	Barrie Colts	OHL	24	3	2	5	10	6	1	0	1	0
2003-04	Kingston	OPJHL	14	1	5	6	23	....	....	....	....	....
	Barrie Colts	OHL	46	17	10	27	21	7	0	1	1	8
2004-05	Barrie Colts	OHL	37	13	11	24	6	6	2	0	2	2
2005-06	Barrie Colts	OHL	63	46	26	72	58	14	8	9	17	11
	Houston Aeros	AHL	....	....	....	....	....	1	0	0	0	0
2006-07	Houston Aeros	AHL	62	7	9	16	36	....	....	....	....	....
2007-08	Houston Aeros	AHL	72	20	19	39	38	2	1	0	1	0

Signed as a free agent by **Minnesota**, July 5, 2006.

HAMONIC, Travis (HA-mohn-ihk, TRA-vihs) NYI

Defense. Shoots right. 6', 192 lbs. Born, Winnipeg, Man., August 16, 1990.
(NY Islanders' 4th choice, 53rd overall, in 2008 Entry Draft).

			Regular Season					Playoffs				
Season	**Club**	**League**	**GP**	**G**	**A**	**Pts**	**PIM**	**GP**	**G**	**A**	**Pts**	**PIM**
2006-07	Winnipeg Saints	MJHL	....	2	13	15	....	....	....	....	....	....
	Moose Jaw	WHL	22	0	3	3	30	....	....	....	....	....
2007-08	Moose Jaw	WHL	61	5	17	22	101	6	0	1	1	6

HANSEN, Jake (HAHN-suhn, JAYK) CBJ

Wing. Shoots right. 6'1", 170 lbs. Born, St.Paul, MN, August 21, 1989.
(Columbus' 4th choice, 68th overall, in 2007 Entry Draft).

			Regular Season					Playoffs				
Season	**Club**	**League**	**GP**	**G**	**A**	**Pts**	**PIM**	**GP**	**G**	**A**	**Pts**	**PIM**
2005-06	White Bear Lake	High-MN		STATISTICS NOT AVAILABLE								
2006-07	White Bear Lake	High-MN	25	28	43	71	....	....	....	....	....	....
	Sioux Falls	USHL	15	4	4	8	14	7	0	2	2	6
2007-08	Sioux Falls	USHL	60	31	27	58	57	3	1	0	1	0

• Signed Letter of Intent to attend **University of Minnesota** (WCHA) in fall of 2008.

HARJU, Johan (HAHR-yoo, YOH-hahn) T.B.

Left wing. Shoots left. 6'3", 205 lbs. Born, Overtornea, Sweden, May 15, 1986.
(Tampa Bay's 6th choice, 167th overall, in 2007 Entry Draft).

			Regular Season					Playoffs				
Season	**Club**	**League**	**GP**	**G**	**A**	**Pts**	**PIM**	**GP**	**G**	**A**	**Pts**	**PIM**
2002-03	Lulea HF U18	Swe-U18	11	7	2	9	14	....	....	....	....	....
	Lulea HF Jr.	Swe-Jr.	7	2	0	2	0	....	....	....	....	....
2003-04	Lulea HF U18	Swe-U18	3	1	3	4	0	7	4	3	7	8
	Lulea HF Jr.	Swe-Jr.	35	14	12	26	8	....	....	....	....	....
2004-05	Lulea HF Jr.	Swe-Jr.	33	18	13	31	14	7	2	2	4	2
	Pitea HC	Sweden-2	1	0	0	0	0	....	....	....	....	....
	Lulea HF	Sweden	4	0	0	0	0	....	....	....	....	....
2005-06	Lulea HF Jr.	Swe-Jr.	17	14	9	23	4	4	3	1	4	8
	Lulea HF	Sweden	39	3	1	4	8	4	0	0	0	20
2006-07	Lulea HF	Sweden	55	12	10	22	30	4	2	0	2	4
2007-08	Lulea HF	Sweden	51	20	8	28	55	....	....	....	....	....

HARRINGTON, Chris (HAYR-ihng-tuhn, KRIHS)

Right wing. Shoots right. 6', 185 lbs. Born, St. Cloud, MN, May 7, 1982.

			Regular Season					Playoffs				
Season	**Club**	**League**	**GP**	**G**	**A**	**Pts**	**PIM**	**GP**	**G**	**A**	**Pts**	**PIM**
2000-01	Omaha Lancers	USHL	50	7	11	18	66	10	2	6	8	12
2001-02	Omaha Lancers	USHL	57	9	33	42	68	13	3	3	6	32
2002-03	U. of Minnesota	WCHA	45	4	14	18	60	....	....	....	....	....
2003-04	U. of Minnesota	WCHA	41	5	24	29	42	....	....	....	....	....
2004-05	U. of Minnesota	WCHA	43	2	24	26	98	....	....	....	....	....
2005-06	U. of Minnesota	WCHA	40	3	33	36	64	....	....	....	....	....
2006-07	Toronto Marlies	AHL	68	10	18	28	58	....	....	....	....	....
2007-08	Toronto Marlies	AHL	73	9	11	20	35	17	3	2	5	9

WCHA All-Rookie Team (2003)

Signed as a free agent by **Toronto**. April 19, 2006.

HARTIKAINEN, Teemu (har-tih-KIGH-nehn, TEE-moo) EDM.

Center. Shoots left. 6'1", 198 lbs. Born, Kuopio, Finland, May 3, 1990.
(Edmonton's 4th choice, 163rd overall, in 2008 Entry Draft).

			Regular Season					Playoffs				
Season	**Club**	**League**	**GP**	**G**	**A**	**Pts**	**PIM**	**GP**	**G**	**A**	**Pts**	**PIM**
2006-07	KalPa Kuopio U18	Fin-U18	19	24	13	37	51	....	....	....	....	....
	KalPa Kuopio Jr.	Fin-Jr.	11	2	1	3	0	3	0	0	0	4
2007-08	KalPa Kuopio U18	Fin-U18	7	9	6	15	6	....	....	....	....	....
	KalPa Kuopio Jr.	Fin-Jr.	37	10	7	17	24	11	1	4	5	6
	KalPa Kuopio	Finland	1	0	0	0	0	....	....	....	....	....

HAYES, Jimmy (HAYZ, JIH-mee) TOR.

Right wing. Shoots right. 6'5", 210 lbs. Born, Boston, MA, November 21, 1989.
(Toronto's 2nd choice, 60th overall, in 2008 Entry Draft).

			Regular Season					Playoffs				
Season	**Club**	**League**	**GP**	**G**	**A**	**Pts**	**PIM**	**GP**	**G**	**A**	**Pts**	**PIM**
2006-07	USNTDP	U-17	42	17	14	31	37	....	....	....	....	....
	USNTDP	NAHL	14	6	8	14	4	....	....	....	....	....
2007-08	USNTDP	U-18	18	2	5	7	6	....	....	....	....	....
	USNTDP	NAHL	19	2	8	10	6	....	....	....	....	....
	Lincoln Stars	USHL	21	4	11	15	18	8	4	5	9	8

• Signed Letter of Intent to attend **Boston College** (Hockey East) in fall of 2008.

HEDMAN, Anton (HEHD-man, AN-tawn) BOS.

Center. Shoots left. 6'2", 207 lbs. Born, Stockholm, Sweden, May 15, 1986.
(Boston's 7th choice, 255th overall, in 2004 Entry Draft).

			Regular Season					Playoffs				
Season	**Club**	**League**	**GP**	**G**	**A**	**Pts**	**PIM**	**GP**	**G**	**A**	**Pts**	**PIM**
2003-04	Stocksund Jr.	Swe-Jr.	14	5	5	10	14	....	....	....	....	....
2004-05	Djurgarden Jr.	Swe-Jr.	32	14	9	23	119	....	....	....	....	....
2005-06	Sudbury Wolves	OHL	60	18	16	34	126	8	1	3	4	19
2006-07	Owen Sound	OHL	39	12	12	24	73	....	....	....	....	....
	Guelph Storm	OHL	28	5	7	12	38	4	0	1	1	8
2007-08	Almtuna	Sweden-2	9	0	2	2	47	....	....	....	....	....
	Hammarby	Sweden-2	11	1	2	3	12	....	....	....	....	....
	VIK Vasteras HK	Sweden-2	9	0	1	1	39	....	....	....	....	....

HEDMAN, Oscar (HEHD-man, AWZ-kuhr) **WSH.**

Defense. Shoots left. 6', 209 lbs. Born, Ornskoldsvik, Sweden, April 21, 1986.
(Washington's 8th choice, 132nd overall, in 2004 Entry Draft).

			Regular Season					Playoffs				
Season	Club	League	GP	G	A	Pts	PIM	GP	G	A	Pts	PIM
2002-03	MODO U18	Swe-U18	14	4	5	9	8	6	2	1	3	32
	Malmo Jr.	Swe-Jr.	5	0	1	1	2	....	....	....	....	....
2003-04	Malmo Jr.	Swe-Jr.	25	7	11	18	28	8	3	3	6	6
	MODO U18	Swe-U18	3	3	1	4	2	2	0	3	3	0
	MODO	Sweden	24	1	2	3	6	6	0	0	0	0
2004-05	MODO Jr.	Swe-Jr.	7	2	2	4	12	5	0	1	1	4
	MODO	Sweden	43	1	3	4	18	4	0	0	0	0
2005-06	MODO Jr.	Swe-Jr.	7	3	2	5	10	....	....	....	....	....
	MODO	Sweden	44	3	2	5	30	5	0	1	1	0
2006-07	MODO	Sweden	55	2	7	9	42	20	1	4	5	14
2007-08	MODO	Sweden	53	4	9	13	30	5	1	1	2	0

HEGARTY, Ryan (HEH-gahr-tee, RIGH-uhn) **ANA.**

Defense. Shoots left. 6', 196 lbs. Born, Stoneham, MA, May 16, 1990.
(Anaheim's 8th choice, 113th overall, in 2008 Entry Draft).

			Regular Season					Playoffs				
Season	Club	League	GP	G	A	Pts	PIM	GP	G	A	Pts	PIM
2006-07	USNTDP	U-17	15	1	2	3	10	....	....	....	....	....
	USNTDP	NAHL	43	2	2	4	54	6	0	0	0	4
2007-08	USNTDP	U-18	41	5	8	13	38	....	....	....	....	....
	USNTDP	NAHL	14	2	8	10	18	....	....	....	....	....

• Signed Letter of Intent to attend **University of Maine** (Hockey East) in fall of 2008.

HELLGREN, Jens (HEHL-grehn, YEHNZ) **COL.**

Defense. Shoots left. 6'3", 192 lbs. Born, Bjorbo, Sweden, March 6, 1989.
(Colorado's 8th choice, 155th overall, in 2007 Entry Draft).

			Regular Season					Playoffs				
Season	Club	League	GP	G	A	Pts	PIM	GP	G	A	Pts	PIM
2004-05	Leksands IF U18	Swe-U18	STATISTICS NOT AVAILABLE									
2005-06	Frolunda U18	Swe-U18	12	1	0	1	2	2	0	0	0	2
	Frolunda Jr.	Swe-Jr.	22	0	0	0	4	6	0	0	0	0
2006-07	Frolunda U18	Swe-U18	3	0	2	2	0	4	2	2	4	6
	Frolunda Jr.	Swe-Jr.	40	4	6	10	26	7	0	0	0	2
2007-08	Frolunda Jr.	Swe-Jr.	40	4	10	14	20	8	0	1	1	2

HELLSTROM, Alexander (HEHL-struhm, al-EHX-AN-duhr) **ST.L.**

Defense. Shoots left. 6'2", 207 lbs. Born, Falun, Sweden, April 17, 1987.
(St. Louis' 9th choice, 184th overall, in 2006 Entry Draft).

			Regular Season					Playoffs				
Season	Club	League	GP	G	A	Pts	PIM	GP	G	A	Pts	PIM
2003-04	Bjorkloven U18	Swe-U18	7	0	2	2	8	....	....	....	....	....
2004-05	Bjorkloven U18	Swe-U18	STATISTICS NOT AVAILABLE									
	Bjorkloven Jr.	Swe-Jr.	3	0	2	2	2	....	....	....	....	....
	IF Bjorkloven Umea	Sweden-2	15	0	1	1	8	....	....	....	....	....
2005-06	Bjorkloven Jr.	Swe-Jr.	11	1	3	4	20	6	0	3	3	4
	IF Bjorkloven Umea	Sweden-2	31	1	0	1	45	....	....	....	....	....
2006-07	Bjorkloven Jr.	Swe-Jr.	8	2	2	4	26	....	....	....	....	....
	IF Bjorkloven Umea	Sweden-2	55	0	7	7	153	6	0	0	0	6
2007-08	Peoria Rivermen	AHL	35	3	2	5	38	....	....	....	....	....

HELMINEN, Dwight (HEHL-mih-nehn, DWIGHT) **CAR.**

Center. Shoots left. 5'10", 191 lbs. Born, Hancock, MI, June 22, 1983.
(Edmonton's 12th choice, 244th overall, in 2002 Entry Draft).

			Regular Season					Playoffs				
Season	Club	League	GP	G	A	Pts	PIM	GP	G	A	Pts	PIM
1998-99	Det. Compuware	MNHL	32	9	7	16	....	....	....	....	....	....
99-2000	USNTDP	USHL	30	5	7	12	10	....	....	....	....	....
	USNTDP	NAHL	30	7	10	17	8	....	....	....	....	....
2000-01	USNTDP	U-18	42	9	36	45	20	....	....	....	....	....
	USNTDP	USHL	24	12	7	19	8	....	....	....	....	....
	USNTDP	NAHL	1	0	1	1	2	....	....	....	....	....
2001-02	U. of Michigan	CCHA	39	10	8	18	10	....	....	....	....	....
2002-03	U. of Michigan	CCHA	39	17	16	33	34	....	....	....	....	....
2003-04	U. of Michigan	CCHA	41	17	11	28	4	....	....	....	....	....
2004-05	Hartford Wolf Pack	AHL	41	2	7	9	10	....	....	....	....	....
	Charlotte	ECHL	28	5	16	21	10	15	7	3	10	2
2005-06	Hartford Wolf Pack	AHL	77	32	24	56	40	13	3	5	8	10
2006-07	Hartford Wolf Pack	AHL	80	15	24	39	32	7	1	1	2	2
2007-08	JYP Jyvaskyla	Finland	52	20	25	45	10	6	3	3	6	0

Traded to **NY Rangers** by **Edmonton** with Steve Valiquette and Edmonton's 2nd round compensatory choice (Dane Byers) in 2004 Entry Draft for Petr Nedved and Jussi Markkanen, March 3, 2004. Signed as a free agent by **Jyvaskyla** (Finland), July 7, 2007. Signed as a free agent by **Carolina**, July 3, 2008.

HENDRICKS, Matt (HEHN-drihks, MAT) **COL.**

Center. Shoots left. 6', 215 lbs. Born, Blaine, MN, June 17, 1981.
(Nashville's 5th choice, 131st overall, in 2000 Entry Draft).

			Regular Season					Playoffs				
Season	Club	League	GP	G	A	Pts	PIM	GP	G	A	Pts	PIM
1998-99	Blaine Bengals	High-MN	22	23	34	57	42	....	....	....	....	....
99-2000	Blaine Bengals	High-MN	21	23	30	53	28	....	....	....	....	....
2000-01	St. Cloud State	WCHA	37	3	9	12	23	....	....	....	....	....
2001-02	St. Cloud State	WCHA	42	19	20	39	74	....	....	....	....	....
2002-03	St. Cloud State	WCHA	37	18	18	36	64	....	....	....	....	....
2003-04	St. Cloud State	WCHA	36	13	11	24	32	....	....	....	....	....
	Milwaukee	AHL	1	0	0	0	2	....	....	....	....	....
2004-05	Lowell	AHL	15	1	2	3	10	....	....	....	....	....
	Florida Everblades	ECHL	54	24	26	50	94	4	0	0	0	4
2005-06	Rochester	AHL	56	13	14	27	84	....	....	....	....	....
2006-07	Hershey Bears	AHL	65	18	26	44	105	19	8	4	12	18
2007-08	Providence Bruins	AHL	67	22	30	52	121	10	0	3	3	6

Signed as a free agent by **Boston**, July 9, 2007. Traded to **Colorado** by **Boston** for Johnny Boychuk, June 24, 2008.

HENDRIKX, Trevor (HEHN-drihx, TREH-vuhr) **CBJ**

Defense. Shoots right. 6'1", 208 lbs. Born, Russell, Ont., March 29, 1985.
(Columbus' 8th choice, 201st overall, in 2005 Entry Draft).

			Regular Season					Playoffs				
Season	Club	League	GP	G	A	Pts	PIM	GP	G	A	Pts	PIM
2000-01	Gloucester	OPJHL	26	2	3	5	25	....	....	....	....	....
2001-02	Peterborough	OHL	46	1	3	4	37	5	0	0	0	4
2002-03	Peterborough	OHL	56	1	8	9	128	7	0	0	0	4
2003-04	Peterborough	OHL	63	8	24	32	208	....	....	....	....	....
2004-05	Peterborough	OHL	68	15	33	48	100	14	5	7	12	14
2005-06	Peterborough	OHL	60	9	47	56	123	19	5	10	15	40
2006-07	Dayton Bombers	ECHL	41	5	6	11	88	15	2	2	4	6
2007-08	Elmira Jackals	ECHL	72	8	23	31	170	6	0	0	0	8

• Re-entered NHL Entry Draft. Originally Columbus' 10th choice, 283rd overall, in 2003 Entry Draft.

HENRICH, Adam (HEHN-rihch, A-duhm) **PIT.**

Left wing. Shoots left. 6'4", 231 lbs. Born, Thornhill, Ont., January 19, 1984.
(Tampa Bay's 1st choice, 60th overall, in 2002 Entry Draft).

			Regular Season					Playoffs				
Season	Club	League	GP	G	A	Pts	PIM	GP	G	A	Pts	PIM
99-2000	Don Mills Flyers	GTHL	54	30	52	82	86	....	....	....	....	....
2000-01	Brampton	OHL	48	5	4	9	27	9	0	0	0	6
2001-02	Brampton	OHL	66	33	30	63	92	....	....	....	....	....
2002-03	Brampton	OHL	63	31	33	64	84	11	4	1	5	25
2003-04	Brampton	OHL	65	29	29	58	146	12	5	1	6	24
2004-05	Springfield Falcons	AHL	63	10	16	26	97	....	....	....	....	....
	Johnstown Chiefs	ECHL	6	2	1	3	15	....	....	....	....	....
2005-06	Springfield Falcons	AHL	12	0	3	3	14	....	....	....	....	....
	Johnstown Chiefs	ECHL	51	18	23	41	78	5	2	4	6	8
2006-07	Springfield Falcons	AHL	27	3	6	9	31	....	....	....	....	....
	Johnstown Chiefs	ECHL	32	15	19	34	119	2	0	0	0	2
2007-08	Norfolk Admirals	AHL	43	14	17	31	88	....	....	....	....	....
	Wheeling Nailers	ECHL	12	10	10	20	34	....	....	....	....	....

Signed as a free agent by **Pittsburgh**, July 8, 2008.

HENRIQUE, Adam (HEHN-reek, A-duhm) **N.J.**

Center. Shoots left. 5'11", 185 lbs. Born, Brantford, Ont., February 6, 1990.
(New Jersey's 4th choice, 82nd overall, in 2008 Entry Draft).

			Regular Season					Playoffs				
Season	Club	League	GP	G	A	Pts	PIM	GP	G	A	Pts	PIM
2006-07	Windsor Spitfires	OHL	62	23	21	44	20	....	....	....	....	....
2007-08	Windsor Spitfires	OHL	66	20	24	44	28	5	2	3	5	4

HERSLEY, Patrik (HUHRS-lee, PAT-rihk) **PHI.**

Defense. Shoots right. 6'3", 205 lbs. Born, Malmo, Sweden, June 23, 1986.
(Los Angeles' 5th choice, 139th overall, in 2005 Entry Draft).

			Regular Season					Playoffs				
Season	Club	League	GP	G	A	Pts	PIM	GP	G	A	Pts	PIM
2002-03	Malmo U18	Swe-U18	9	3	4	7	53	4	1	2	3	4
	Malmo Jr.	Swe-Jr.	16	0	2	2	4	1	0	0	0	0
2003-04	Malmo U18	Swe-U18	2	2	0	2	4	....	....	....	....	....
	Malmo Jr.	Swe-Jr.	17	1	4	5	16	8	0	2	2	2
2004-05	Malmo Jr.	Swe-Jr.	31	8	14	22	104	3	2	1	3	6
	Malmo	Sweden	8	0	1	1	0	....	....	....	....	....
	Malmo	Sweden-Q	6	0	0	0	2	....	....	....	....	....
2005-06	Malmo Jr.	Swe-Jr.	13	10	9	19	38	....	....	....	....	....
	Malmo	Sweden-2	41	6	8	14	38	....	....	....	....	....
2006-07	Malmo Jr.	Swe-Jr.	2	1	3	4	14	....	....	....	....	....
	Malmo	Sweden	28	1	1	2	10	....	....	....	....	....
	IK Pantern Malmo	Sweden-3	2	1	1	2	8	....	....	....	....	....
2007-08	Manchester	AHL	42	1	8	9	27	....	....	....	....	....
	Reading Royals	ECHL	20	3	15	18	18	13	3	6	9	10

Traded to **Philadelphia** by **Los Angeles** with Ned Lukacevic for Denis Gauthier and Philadelphia's 2nd round choice in 2010 Entry Draft, July 1, 2008.

HESHKA, Shaun (HEHSH-kah, SHAWN) **VAN.**

Defense. Shoots right. 6'1", 198 lbs. Born, Melville, Sask., July 30, 1985.

			Regular Season					Playoffs				
Season	Club	League	GP	G	A	Pts	PIM	GP	G	A	Pts	PIM
2002-03	Melville	SJHL	53	6	14	20	53	....	....	....	....	....
2003-04	Everett Silvertips	WHL	66	3	7	10	25	21	0	2	2	8
2004-05	Everett Silvertips	WHL	72	12	26	38	21	11	2	0	2	6
2005-06	Everett Silvertips	WHL	66	10	49	59	91	14	3	10	13	10
2006-07	Manitoba Moose	AHL	57	2	4	6	14	7	0	0	0	8
	Victoria	ECHL	3	0	1	1	4	....	....	....	....	....
2007-08	Manitoba Moose	AHL	77	9	21	30	59	6	0	1	1	4

WHL West First All-Star Team (2006)

Signed as a free agent by **Vancouver**, July 24, 2006.

HEXTALL, Brett (HEHX-tahl, BREHT) **PHX.**

Center. Shoots right. 5'10", 176 lbs. Born, Philadelphia, PA, April 2, 1988.
(Phoenix's 7th choice, 159th overall, in 2008 Entry Draft).

			Regular Season					Playoffs				
Season	Club	League	GP	G	A	Pts	PIM	GP	G	A	Pts	PIM
2006-07	Penticton Vees	BCHL	59	18	27	45	156	11	2	2	4	8
2007-08	Penticton Vees	BCHL	54	24	48	72	52	15	*12	3	15	12

• Signed Letter of Intent to attend **University of North Dakota** (WCHA) in fall of 2008.

HICKEY, Chris (HIH-kee, KRIHS) **MIN.**

Center. Shoots right. 6'1", 196 lbs. Born, St. Paul, MN, September 2, 1988.
(Minnesota's 7th choice, 192nd overall, in 2006 Entry Draft).

			Regular Season					Playoffs				
Season	Club	League	GP	G	A	Pts	PIM	GP	G	A	Pts	PIM
2003-04	Cretin-Derham	High-MN	27	19	13	32	32	....	....	....	....	....
2004-05	Cretin-Derham	High-MN	28	25	21	46	48	....	....	....	....	....
2005-06	Cretin-Derham	High-MN	31	37	28	65	36	....	....	....	....	....
2006-07	Cretin-Derham	High-MN	17	21	15	36	....	....	....	....	....	....
	Tri-City Storm	USHL	1	0	0	0	0	....	....	....	....	....
2007-08	Tri-City Storm	USHL	55	15	16	31	34	....	....	....	....	....

HICKEY, Thomas (HIH-kee, TAW-muhs) L.A.

Defense. Shoots left. 5'11", 182 lbs. Born, Calgary, Alta., February 8, 1989.
(Los Angeles' 1st choice, 4th overall, in 2007 Entry Draft).

			Regular Season					Playoffs				
Season	Club	League	GP	G	A	Pts	PIM	GP	G	A	Pts	PIM
2003-04	Cgy. Royals	CBHL	32	13	25	38	51	....	....	....	....	....
2004-05	Calgary Royals	AMHL	33	9	13	22	36	....	....	....	....	....
	Seattle	WHL	5	2	1	3	6	....	....	....	....	....
2005-06	Seattle	WHL	69	1	27	28	53	7	1	3	4	10
2006-07	Seattle	WHL	68	9	41	50	70	11	3	4	7	4
2007-08	Seattle	WHL	63	11	34	45	49	9	1	9	10	4

WHL West Second All-Star Team (2007) • WHL West First All-Star Team (2008)

HILLIER, Ryan (HIHL-lee-uhr, RIGH-uhn) NYR

Left wing. Shoots left. 6'1", 195 lbs. Born, Halifax, N.S., January 25, 1988.
(NY Rangers' 3rd choice, 84th overall, in 2006 Entry Draft).

			Regular Season					Playoffs				
Season	Club	League	GP	G	A	Pts	PIM	GP	G	A	Pts	PIM
2003-04	Dartmouth	NSMHL	55	31	36	67	97	....	....	....	....	....
2004-05	Halifax	QMJHL	21	1	1	2	13	7	0	2	2	2
2005-06	Halifax	QMJHL	68	19	38	57	76	11	2	2	4	12
2006-07	Halifax	QMJHL	70	32	27	59	79	12	3	6	9	20
2007-08	Halifax	QMJHL	70	34	38	72	55	14	8	7	15	22

HJALMARSSON, Simon (H'YAHL-muhr-suhn, SEE-muhn) ST.L.

Right wing. Shoots left. 5'11", 161 lbs. Born, Varnamo, Sweden, February 1, 1989.
(St. Louis' 4th choice, 39th overall, in 2007 Entry Draft).

			Regular Season					Playoffs				
Season	Club	League	GP	G	A	Pts	PIM	GP	G	A	Pts	PIM
2004-05	Gislaveds SK Jr.	Swe-Jr.	STATISTICS NOT AVAILABLE									
2005-06	Frolunda U18	Swe-U18	6	2	3	5	4	2	0	0	0	2
	Frolunda Jr.	Swe-Jr.	31	8	10	18	8	7	2	3	5	2
2006-07	Frolunda U18	Swe-U18	3	4	3	7	33	6	3	8	11	2
	Gislaveds SK	Sweden-3	2	0	1	1	0	....	....	....	....	....
	Frolunda Jr.	Swe-Jr.	41	31	23	54	91	8	1	1	2	6
2007-08	Boras HC	Sweden-2	10	2	4	6	4	....	....	....	....	....
	Frolunda	Sweden	1	0	0	0	2	....	....	....	....	....
	Frolunda Jr.	Swe-Jr.	37	16	30	46	104	8	3	9	12	8

HOBBS, Danny (HAWBZ, DA-nee) NYR

Center/Right wing. Shoots left. 5'11", 178 lbs. Born, Shawville, Ont., June 21, 1989.
(NY Rangers' 6th choice, 198th overall, in 2007 Entry Draft).

			Regular Season					Playoffs				
Season	Club	League	GP	G	A	Pts	PIM	GP	G	A	Pts	PIM
2005-06	Stanstead	QJHL	46	58	32	90	15	....	....	....	....	....
2006-07	Ohio	USHL	60	10	11	21	36	4	0	2	2	2
2007-08	Ohio	USHL	54	15	16	31	22	....	....	....	....	....

• Signed Letter of Intent to attend **University of Massachusetts** (Hockey East) in fall of 2008.

HOBSON, Adam (HAWB-sohn, A-duhm) CHI.

Center. Shoots left. 6', 210 lbs. Born, Lund, Sweden, January 9, 1987.
(Chicago's 12th choice, 203rd overall, in 2005 Entry Draft).

			Regular Season					Playoffs				
Season	Club	League	GP	G	A	Pts	PIM	GP	G	A	Pts	PIM
2002-03	Abbotsford Pilots	PIJHL	38	20	28	48	....	....	....	....	....	....
	Spokane Chiefs	WHL	1	0	0	0	2	....	....	....	....	....
2003-04	Spokane Chiefs	WHL	63	4	5	9	35	4	0	0	0	0
2004-05	Spokane Chiefs	WHL	72	10	27	37	47	....	....	....	....	....
2005-06	Spokane Chiefs	WHL	72	23	27	50	124	....	....	....	....	....
2006-07	Spokane Chiefs	WHL	43	14	18	32	59	6	3	0	3	6
2007-08	Rockford IceHogs	AHL	25	1	4	5	36	....	....	....	....	....
	Pensacola	ECHL	24	10	5	15	30	....	....	....	....	....

HODGSON, Cody (HAWJ-suhn, KOH-dee) VAN.

Center. Shoots right. 6', 185 lbs. Born, Toronto, Ont., February 18, 1990.
(Vancouver's 1st choice, 10th overall, in 2008 Entry Draft).

			Regular Season					Playoffs				
Season	Club	League	GP	G	A	Pts	PIM	GP	G	A	Pts	PIM
2005-06	Markham Waxers	Minor-ON	30	27	24	51	22	15	13	14	27	8
2006-07	Brampton	OHL	63	23	23	46	24	4	1	3	4	0
2007-08	Brampton	OHL	68	40	45	85	36	5	5	0	5	2

HOEFFEL, Mike (HOH-fuhl, MIGHK) N.J.

Left wing. Shoots left. 6'2", 185 lbs. Born, North Oaks, MN, April 9, 1989.
(New Jersey's 1st choice, 57th overall, in 2007 Entry Draft).

			Regular Season					Playoffs				
Season	Club	League	GP	G	A	Pts	PIM	GP	G	A	Pts	PIM
2004-05	Hill-Murray	High-MN	26	24	19	43	10	....	....	....	....	....
2005-06	Hill-Murray	High-MN	30	27	46	73	20	....	....	....	....	....
2006-07	USNTDP	U-18	33	10	2	12	18	....	....	....	....	....
	USNTDP	NAHL	11	6	5	11	10	....	....	....	....	....
2007-08	U. of Minnesota	WCHA	45	9	10	19	22	....	....	....	....	....

HOFFMAN, Mike (HAWF-muhn, MIGHK) ATL.

Right wing. Shoots right. 6'5", 250 lbs. Born, Weymouth, MA, September 20, 1980.

			Regular Season					Playoffs				
Season	Club	League	GP	G	A	Pts	PIM	GP	G	A	Pts	PIM
2002-03	Connecticut	MAAC	28	2	8	10	24	....	....	....	....	....
2003-04	Connecticut	MAAC	3	0	0	0	2	....	....	....	....	....
	Worcester IceCats	AHL	15	0	0	0	20	....	....	....	....	....
	Peoria Rivermen	ECHL	25	2	7	9	16	8	0	1	1	6
2004-05	Cleveland Barons	AHL	58	1	7	8	170	....	....	....	....	....
2005-06	Toronto Marlies	AHL	54	2	5	7	103	1	0	0	0	0
2006-07	Manchester	AHL	35	6	7	13	96	....	....	....	....	....
	Portland Pirates	AHL	21	4	5	9	43	....	....	....	....	....
2007-08	Portland Pirates	AHL	38	5	3	8	81	11	1	1	2	11

Signed as a free agent by **Cleveland** (AHL), September 22, 2004. Signed as a free agent by **Toronto**, August 12, 2005. Signed to a PTO (tryout) contract by **Manchester** (AHL), October 25, 2006. Signed as a free agent by **Anaheim**, February 23, 2007. Signed as a free agent by **Atlanta**, July 9, 2008.

HOLDEN, Nick CBJ

Defense. Shoots left. 6'4", 200 lbs. Born, St. Albert, Alta., May 15, 1987.

			Regular Season					Playoffs				
Season	Club	League	GP	G	A	Pts	PIM	GP	G	A	Pts	PIM
2004-05	Camrose Kodiaks	AJHL	4	0	0	0	0	....	....	....	....	....
2005-06	Sherwood Park	AJHL	57	7	23	30	46	....	....	....	....	....
2006-07	Chilliwack Bruins	WHL	67	8	23	31	62	5	1	1	2	6
2007-08	Chilliwack Bruins	WHL	70	22	38	60	54	4	1	3	4	0
	Syracuse Crunch	AHL	1	0	0	0	2	....	....	....	....	....

Signed as a free agent by **Columbus**, March 28, 2008.

HOLLOWAY, Bud (HAHL-OH-way, BUHD) L.A.

Center. Shoots right. 6'1", 192 lbs. Born, Wapella, Sask., March 1, 1988.
(Los Angeles' 5th choice, 86th overall, in 2006 Entry Draft).

			Regular Season					Playoffs				
Season	Club	League	GP	G	A	Pts	PIM	GP	G	A	Pts	PIM
2003-04	Yorkton Harvest	SMHL	43	15	21	36	22	....	....	....	....	....
	Seattle	WHL	2	0	0	0	0	....	....	....	....	....
2004-05	Seattle	WHL	67	4	11	15	27	12	0	1	1	0
2005-06	Seattle	WHL	72	21	13	34	18	7	3	2	5	4
2006-07	Seattle	WHL	71	27	38	65	50	11	3	3	6	8
2007-08	Seattle	WHL	70	43	40	83	55	12	5	5	10	4

HOLMQVIST, Andreas (HOHLM-kvihst, awn-DRAY-uhs) T.B.

Defense. Shoots right. 6'4", 195 lbs. Born, Stockholm, Sweden, July 23, 1981.
(Tampa Bay's 3rd choice, 61st overall, in 2001 Entry Draft).

			Regular Season					Playoffs				
Season	Club	League	GP	G	A	Pts	PIM	GP	G	A	Pts	PIM
99-2000	Hammarby Jr.	Swe-Jr.	33	8	12	20	16	6	1	2	3	4
2000-01	Hammarby Jr.	Swe-Jr.	47	6	15	21	40	....	....	....	....	....
2001-02	Hammarby	Sweden-2	42	11	13	24	97	....	....	....	....	....
2002-03	Linkopings HC	Sweden	43	4	9	13	28	....	....	....	....	....
	Linkopings HC	Sweden-Q	10	0	0	0	4	....	....	....	....	....
2003-04	Hamilton Bulldogs	AHL	4	0	0	0	0	....	....	....	....	....
	Pensacola	ECHL	63	4	33	37	16	5	0	4	4	0
2004-05	Springfield Falcons	AHL	42	3	9	12	22	....	....	....	....	....
2005-06	Linkopings HC	Sweden	46	6	16	22	64	13	1	3	4	24
2006-07	Linkopings HC	Sweden	49	7	21	28	54	12	4	5	9	35
2007-08	Frolunda	Sweden	49	3	23	26	40	4	0	0	0	2

HOLOS, Jonas (hoh-LAWS, YOH-nuhs) COL.

Defense. Shoots right. 5'11", 196 lbs. Born, Sarpsborg, Norway, August 27, 1987.
(Colorado's 6th choice, 170th overall, in 2008 Entry Draft).

			Regular Season					Playoffs				
Season	Club	League	GP	G	A	Pts	PIM	GP	G	A	Pts	PIM
2002-03	Sarpsborg Jr.	Norway-Jr.	20	1	1	2	0	....	....	....	....	....
2003-04	Sarpsborg Jr.	Norway-Jr.	35	10	7	17	24	1	0	1	1	2
	Sarpsborg	Norway	1	0	0	0	0	....	....	....	....	....
2004-05	Sarpsborg Jr.	Norway-Jr.	1	1	1	2	0	1	0	0	0	0
	Sarpsborg	Norway	41	3	2	5	18	4	0	0	0	2
2005-06	Sarpsborg	Norway	26	3	4	7	14	6	0	0	0	0
2006-07	Sarpsborg 2	Norway-2	1	2	0	2	0	....	....	....	....	....
	Sarpsborg	Norway	40	11	19	30	32	13	2	2	4	18
2007-08	Sarpsborg	Norway	40	2	20	22	67	6	1	0	1	2

HOLTET, Marius (HOHL-teht, MAIR-ee-uhs)

Center. Shoots right. 6'1", 188 lbs. Born, Hamar, Norway, August 31, 1984.
(Dallas' 4th choice, 42nd overall, in 2002 Entry Draft).

			Regular Season					Playoffs				
Season	Club	League	GP	G	A	Pts	PIM	GP	G	A	Pts	PIM
2000-01	Farjestad U18	Swe-U18	5	3	1	4	16	....	....	....	....	....
	Farjestad Jr.	Swe-Jr.	18	2	2	4	18	....	....	....	....	....
2001-02	Farjestad Jr.	Swe-Jr.	37	12	7	19	70	....	....	....	....	....
2002-03	Skare BK Karlstad	Sweden-3	STATISTICS NOT AVAILABLE									
	Bofors	Sweden-2	14	1	1	2	8	2	0	0	0	2
2003-04	Bofors	Sweden-2	43	11	3	14	90	5	2	0	2	4
2004-05	Louisiana	ECHL	4	0	0	0	0	....	....	....	....	....
	Houston Aeros	AHL	54	7	5	12	48	1	0	0	0	0
2005-06	Iowa Stars	AHL	68	9	13	22	61	7	2	0	2	2
2006-07	Iowa Stars	AHL	66	16	15	31	48	11	2	0	2	6
2007-08	Iowa Stars	AHL	67	10	9	19	37	....	....	....	....	....

HOLZAPFEL, Riley (HOHL-za-fehl, RIGH-lee) ATL.

Center. Shoots left. 6', 185 lbs. Born, Regina, Sask., August 18, 1988.
(Atlanta's 2nd choice, 43rd overall, in 2006 Entry Draft).

			Regular Season					Playoffs				
Season	Club	League	GP	G	A	Pts	PIM	GP	G	A	Pts	PIM
2004-05	Moose Jaw	WHL	63	15	13	28	32	5	1	2	3	8
2005-06	Moose Jaw	WHL	64	19	38	57	46	22	7	9	16	20
2006-07	Moose Jaw	WHL	72	39	43	82	94	....	....	....	....	....
2007-08	Moose Jaw	WHL	49	18	23	41	43	6	3	5	8	12
	Chicago Wolves	AHL	1	0	0	0	0	....	....	....	....	....

WHL East First All-Star Team (2007)

HOLZER, Korbinian (HOHL-zuhr, kohr-BEEHN-yuhn) TOR.

Defense. Shoots right. 6'3", 190 lbs. Born, Munich, West Germany, February 16, 1988.
(Toronto's 4th choice, 111th overall, in 2006 Entry Draft).

			Regular Season					Playoffs				
Season	Club	League	GP	G	A	Pts	PIM	GP	G	A	Pts	PIM
2004-05	EC Bad Tolz Jr.	Ger-Jr.	34	7	11	18	66	5	0	2	2	2
2005-06	EC Bad Tolz Jr.	Ger-Jr.	2	1	1	2	6	....	....	....	....	....
	Tolzer Lowen	German-2	46	3	3	6	94	....	....	....	....	....
2006-07	Regensburg	German-2	42	2	6	8	68	4	0	0	0	2
2007-08	Dusseldorf	Germany	35	2	5	7	66	13	0	2	2	20

HORNQVIST, Patric (HOHRN-kwihst, PAT-rihk) NSH.

Right wing. Shoots left. 5'11", 194 lbs. Born, Sollentuna, Sweden, January 1, 1987.
(Nashville's 7th choice, 230th overall, in 2005 Entry Draft).

			Regular Season					Playoffs				
Season	Club	League	GP	G	A	Pts	PIM	GP	G	A	Pts	PIM
2003-04	Vasby Jr.	Swe-Jr.	10	7	10	17	30	....	....	....	....	....
	Vasby	Sweden-3	32	8	5	13	26	....	....	....	....	....
2004-05	Vasby	Sweden-3	28	12	12	24	36	....	....	....	....	....
	Djurgarden Jr.	Swe-Jr.	5	3	0	3	2	....	....	....	....	....
2005-06	Djurgarden Jr.	Swe-Jr.	4	2	1	3	2	4	1	2	3	2
	Djurgarden	Sweden	47	5	2	7	36	....	....	....	....	....
2006-07	Djurgarden	Sweden	49	23	11	34	38	....	....	....	....	....
	Djurgarden Jr.	Swe-Jr.	....	....	....	....	....	7	2	5	7	14
2007-08	Djurgarden	Sweden	53	18	12	30	58	5	0	1	1	6

HRABAL, Josef (huh-RA-buhl, YOH-sehf) EDM.

Defense. Shoots left. 6'1", 176 lbs. Born, Prerov, Czech., August 17, 1985.
(Edmonton's 11th choice, 248th overall, in 2003 Entry Draft).

			Regular Season					Playoffs				
Season	Club	League	GP	G	A	Pts	PIM	GP	G	A	Pts	PIM
2001-02	HC Vsetin U17	CzR-U17	38	4	2	6	18	....	....	....	....	....
2002-03	HC Vsetin Jr.	CzRep-Jr.	30	6	7	13	12	9	2	4	6	10
	HC Vsetin	CzRep	6	0	0	0	4	....	....	....	....	....
2003-04	HC Vsetin	CzRep	13	0	0	0	2	....	....	....	....	....
	HC Vsetin Jr.	CzRep-Jr.	46	12	8	20	54	7	1	0	1	2
2004-05	HC Vsetin	CzRep	23	0	2	2	8	....	....	....	....	....
	HC Kometa Brno	CzRep-2	1	0	0	0	0	....	....	....	....	....
	HC Olomouc	CzRep-2	7	0	0	0	6	....	....	....	....	....
	HC Vsetin Jr.	CzRep-Jr.	19	6	8	14	42	8	3	4	7	16
2005-06	HC Vsetin	CzRep	34	3	9	12	34	....	....	....	....	....
	HC Vsetin Jr.	CzRep-Jr.	1	1	0	1	2	....	....	....	....	....
	HC Vsetin	CzRep-Q	....	....	....	....	....	6	0	2	2	2
2006-07	HC Vsetin	CzRep	21	3	7	10	30	....	....	....	....	....
	Cherepovets	Russia	20	3	4	7	24	5	0	1	1	2
2007-08	Cherepovets	Russia	56	3	11	14	73	8	0	1	1	12

HROMAS, Karel (huh-ROM-mahs, KAH-rehl) CHI.

Left wing. Shoots left. 6'2", 208 lbs. Born, Beroun, Czech., January 27, 1986.
(Chicago's 8th choice, 123rd overall, in 2004 Entry Draft).

			Regular Season					Playoffs				
Season	Club	League	GP	G	A	Pts	PIM	GP	G	A	Pts	PIM
2000-01	Sparta U17	CzR-U17	34	4	18	22	6	....	....	....	....	....
2001-02	Sparta U17	CzR-U17	39	19	15	34	55	6	3	2	5	6
2002-03	Sparta U17	CzR-U17	1	3	1	4	0	....	....	....	....	....
	Sparta Jr.	CzRep-Jr.	32	6	7	13	14	3	0	1	1	4
2003-04	Sparta Jr.	CzRep-Jr.	21	10	10	20	16	....	....	....	....	....
	HC Sparta Praha	CzRep	13	0	0	0	0	2	0	0	0	0
2004-05	Everett Silvertips	WHL	65	18	11	29	22	11	2	2	4	4
2005-06	Everett Silvertips	WHL	52	11	11	22	14	14	2	0	2	10
2006-07	HC Sparta Praha	CzRep	48	1	0	1	20	11	1	0	1	0
2007-08	HC Sparta Praha	CzRep	52	0	1	1	42	4	0	0	0	0

HUGHES, Bobby (HEWZ, BAW-bee) CAR.

Center. Shoots left. 5'10", 180 lbs. Born, Richmond Hill, Ont., November 11, 1987.
(Carolina's 3rd choice, 123rd overall, in 2006 Entry Draft).

			Regular Season					Playoffs				
Season	Club	League	GP	G	A	Pts	PIM	GP	G	A	Pts	PIM
2003-04	Kingston	OHL	62	11	16	27	20	5	0	1	1	2
2004-05	Kingston	OHL	66	17	38	55	36	....	....	....	....	....
2005-06	Kingston	OHL	56	35	40	75	47	6	1	1	2	4
2006-07	Kingston	OHL	59	40	56	96	76	5	0	3	3	0
	Albany River Rats	AHL	....	....	....	....	....	1	0	0	0	0
2007-08	Albany River Rats	AHL	26	6	10	16	4	....	....	....	....	....

HUNTER, Dylan (HUHN-tuhr, DIH-luhn) BUF.

Left wing. Shoots left. 6', 193 lbs. Born, Quebec City, Que., May 21, 1985.
(Buffalo's 8th choice, 273rd overall, in 2004 Entry Draft).

			Regular Season					Playoffs				
Season	Club	League	GP	G	A	Pts	PIM	GP	G	A	Pts	PIM
2001-02	London Knights	OHL	54	6	21	27	38	6	1	1	2	10
2002-03	London Knights	OHL	68	11	31	42	41	14	3	3	6	8
2003-04	London Knights	OHL	64	26	53	79	47	15	4	10	14	10
2004-05	London Knights	OHL	67	31	73	104	64	18	10	11	21	16
2005-06	London Knights	OHL	62	32	85	117	50	19	13	23	36	16
2006-07	Rochester	AHL	67	8	20	28	42	6	1	2	3	2
2007-08	Rochester	AHL	70	20	27	47	69	....	....	....	....	....

OHL First All-Star Team (2005) • OHL Second All-Star Team (2006)

HUNTER, Eric (HUHN-tuhr, AIR-ihk) NYR

Center. Shoots left. 6'2", 195 lbs. Born, Winnipeg, Man., August 11, 1986.
(NY Rangers' 6th choice, 174th overall, in 2006 Entry Draft).

			Regular Season					Playoffs				
Season	Club	League	GP	G	A	Pts	PIM	GP	G	A	Pts	PIM
2002-03	Prince George	WHL	66	16	18	34	70	5	1	0	1	6
2003-04	Prince George	WHL	70	19	23	42	122	....	....	....	....	....
2004-05	Prince George	WHL	47	12	18	30	57	....	....	....	....	....
2005-06	Prince George	WHL	71	40	32	72	125	5	3	1	4	10
2006-07	Prince George	WHL	69	24	31	55	109	6	2	2	4	6
2007-08	U. of Alberta	CIS	24	11	15	26	16	....	....	....	....	....

• Re-entered NHL Entry Draft. Originally Chicago's 15th choice, 229th overall, in 2004 Entry Draft.

IGNATUSHKIN, Igor (ihg-nah-TOOSH-kihn, EE-gohr) WSH.

Center. Shoots left. 5'11", 161 lbs. Born, Elektrostal, USSR, April 7, 1984.
(Washington's 12th choice, 242nd overall, in 2002 Entry Draft).

			Regular Season					Playoffs				
Season	Club	League	GP	G	A	Pts	PIM	GP	G	A	Pts	PIM
99-2000	Elektrostal 2	Russia-3	5	0	0	0	0	....	....	....	....	....
2000-01	Team Center 84	Exhib.	5	1	1	2	0	....	....	....	....	....
	Elektrostal 2	Russia-3	STATISTICS NOT AVAILABLE									
2001-02	Elektrostal 2	Russia-3	6	2	3	5	6	....	....	....	....	....
	Elektrostal	Russia-2	46	1	4	5	20	....	....	....	....	....
2002-03	Elektrostal	Russia-2	36	9	10	19	8	....	....	....	....	....
2003-04	Kristall Elektrostal	Russia-2	49	6	2	8	22	....	....	....	....	....
2004-05	Kristall Elektrostal	Russia-2	45	9	3	12	28	....	....	....	....	....
	Leninogorsk	Russia-2	6	1	1	2	6	4	1	0	1	4
2005-06	Mytischi	Russia	7	0	0	0	2	....	....	....	....	....
	Kristall Elektrostal	Russia-3	STATISTICS NOT AVAILABLE									
2006-07	Kristall Elektrostal	Russia-2	49	14	23	37	48	....	....	....	....	....
2007-08	Khabarovsk 2	Russia-3	2	0	0	0	0	....	....	....	....	....
	Amur Khabarovsk	Russia	49	4	4	8	12	4	0	0	0	2

ILVONEN, Harri (ihl-VOH-nehn, HAIR-ree) MIN.

Defense. Shoots left. 6'2", 187 lbs. Born, Helsinki, Finland, November 3, 1988.
(Minnesota's 4th choice, 170th overall, in 2007 Entry Draft).

			Regular Season					Playoffs				
Season	Club	League	GP	G	A	Pts	PIM	GP	G	A	Pts	PIM
2004-05	Tappara U18	Fin-U18	27	2	10	12	14	2	0	0	0	2
2005-06	Tappara U18	Fin-U18	10	3	5	8	10	3	0	2	2	4
	Tappara Jr.	Fin-Jr.	24	2	1	3	24	....	....	....	....	....
2006-07	Tappara Jr.	Fin-Jr.	39	9	21	30	38	10	0	2	2	22
	Suomi U20	Finland-2	10	0	2	2	12	....	....	....	....	....
	Tappara Tampere	Finland	7	0	0	0	2	....	....	....	....	....
2007-08	Suomi U20	Finland-2	4	0	2	2	2	....	....	....	....	....
	Tappara Jr.	Fin-Jr.	14	2	10	12	22	....	....	....	....	....
	Tappara Tampere	Finland	2	0	0	0	0	....	....	....	....	....
	LeKi Lempaala	Finland-2	7	0	1	1	4	....	....	....	....	....
	HPK Hameenlinna	Finland	9	2	2	4	2	....	....	....	....	....

IRMEN, Danny (UHR-mehn, DA-nee) MIN.

Center. Shoots right. 6', 190 lbs. Born, Fargo, ND, September 6, 1984.
(Minnesota's 3rd choice, 78th overall, in 2003 Entry Draft).

			Regular Season					Playoffs				
Season	Club	League	GP	G	A	Pts	PIM	GP	G	A	Pts	PIM
2001-02	Lincoln Stars	USHL	61	17	36	53	....	....	....	....	....	....
2002-03	Lincoln Stars	USHL	45	21	34	55	78	10	8	6	14	17
2003-04	U. of Minnesota	WCHA	44	14	8	22	40	....	....	....	....	....
2004-05	U. of Minnesota	WCHA	44	24	19	43	66	....	....	....	....	....
2005-06	U. of Minnesota	WCHA	30	16	22	38	40	....	....	....	....	....
	Houston Aeros	AHL	4	0	2	2	0	7	0	0	0	4
2006-07	Houston Aeros	AHL	80	17	20	37	45	....	....	....	....	....
2007-08	Houston Aeros	AHL	77	10	13	23	51	5	0	1	1	0

USHL Second All-Star Team (2003) • USHL Playoff MVP (2003)

ISAKOV, Evgeni (ih-SA-kawf, ehv-GEH-nee) PIT.

Right wing. Shoots left. 6'1", 196 lbs. Born, Krasnoyarsk, USSR, October 13, 1984.
(Pittsburgh's 6th choice, 161st overall, in 2003 Entry Draft).

			Regular Season					Playoffs				
Season	Club	League	GP	G	A	Pts	PIM	GP	G	A	Pts	PIM
99-2000	Rubin Tyumen 2	Russia-3	7	0	2	2	16	....	....	....	....	....
2000-01	Rubin Tyumen 2	Russia-3	....	....	....	....	....	....	....	....	....	....
	Gazovik Tyumen	Russia-3	11	1	1	2	12	....	....	....	....	....
2001-02	Gazovik Tyumen	Russia-2	19	2	2	4	2	....	....	....	....	....
	Elektrostal	Russia-2	29	3	2	5	24	....	....	....	....	....
	Elektrostal 2	Russia-3	11	3	3	6	43	....	....	....	....	....
2002-03	Cherepovets	Russia	36	0	3	3	12	1	0	0	0	0
2003-04	Cherepovets	Russia	38	3	2	5	18	....	....	....	....	....
	Cherepovets 2	Russia-3	14	4	8	12	48	....	....	....	....	....
2004-05	Kristall Saratov	Russia-2	1	0	0	0	0	....	....	....	....	....
	Tyumen 2	Russia-3	2	1	3	4	14	....	....	....	....	....
	Gazovik Tyumen	Russia-2	4	0	2	2	2	3	0	0	0	2
2005-06	Gazovik Tyumen	Russia-2	46	9	12	21	90	3	0	0	0	6
2006-07	Gazovik Tyumen	Russia-2	51	6	11	17	48	....	....	....	....	....
	Tyumen 2	Russia-3	2	1	2	3	0	....	....	....	....	....
2007-08	Gazovik Tyumen	Russia-2	43	10	11	21	119	....	....	....	....	....

ISTOMIN, Denis (ihs-TOH-mihn, DEH-nihs) CHI.

Right wing. Shoots left. 6', 189 lbs. Born, Chelyabinsk, USSR, January 12, 1987.
(Chicago's 7th choice, 117th overall, in 2005 Entry Draft).

			Regular Season					Playoffs				
Season	Club	League	GP	G	A	Pts	PIM	GP	G	A	Pts	PIM
2003-04	Magnitogorsk 2	Russia-3	3	2	1	3	2	....	....	....	....	....
2004-05	Chelyabinsk 2	Russia-3	1	0	0	0	0	....	....	....	....	....
	Chelyabinsk	Russia-2	42	11	5	16	24	8	1	1	2	4
2005-06	Vityaz Chekhov	Russia	46	4	4	8	6	....	....	....	....	....
	Nizhny Novgorod	Russia-2	4	0	3	3	2	3	2	1	3	0
2006-07	Magnitogorsk	Russia	6	0	1	1	6	....	....	....	....	....
	Vityaz Chekhov	Russia	15	0	3	3	6	....	....	....	....	....
2007-08	Kapitan Stupino	Russia-2	20	2	11	13	4	....	....	....	....	....

JACKSON, Scott (JAK-suhn, SKAWT) T.B.

Defense. Shoots left. 6'4", 213 lbs. Born, Salmon Arm, B.C., February 5, 1987.
(St. Louis' 2nd choice, 37th overall, in 2005 Entry Draft).

			Regular Season					Playoffs				
Season	Club	League	GP	G	A	Pts	PIM	GP	G	A	Pts	PIM
2002-03	Sicamous Eagles	KIJHL	45	2	20	22	20	....	....	....	....	....
	Seattle	WHL	2	0	0	0	2	....	....	....	....	....
2003-04	Seattle	WHL	66	4	9	13	17	....	....	....	....	....
2004-05	Seattle	WHL	72	6	16	22	46	12	1	2	3	4
2005-06	Seattle	WHL	57	3	23	26	48	7	1	4	5	12
2006-07	Seattle	WHL	71	4	31	35	52	11	0	5	5	9
2007-08	Seattle	WHL	58	6	17	23	44	12	2	2	4	8

Signed as a free agent by **Tampa Bay**, July 3, 2008.

JAMTIN, Andreas (yahm-TEEN, ahn-DRAY-uhs) NYR

Right wing. Shoots left. 6', 192 lbs. Born, Stockholm, Sweden, May 4, 1983.
(Detroit's 4th choice, 157th overall, in 2001 Entry Draft).

			Regular Season					Playoffs				
Season	Club	League	GP	G	A	Pts	PIM	GP	G	A	Pts	PIM
1998-99	AIK Solna Jr.	Swe-Jr.	44	33	29	62	105	....	....	....	....	....
99-2000	Farjestad Jr.	Swe-Jr.	28	6	6	12	36	....	....	....	....	....
2000-01	Farjestad U18	Swe-U18	1	1	0	1	2	....	....	....	....	....
	Farjestad Jr.	Swe-Jr.	13	5	8	13	83	....	....	....	....	....
	Farjestad	Sweden	1	0	0	0	0	....	....	....	....	....
2001-02	AIK Solna	Sweden	42	2	3	5	55	....	....	....	....	....
	AIK Solna Jr.	Swe-Jr.	12	12	15	27	61	1	2	2	4	2
	AIK Solna	Sweden-Q	10	1	2	3	4	....	....	....	....	....
2002-03	AIK Solna	Sweden-2	28	14	15	29	62	....	....	....	....	....
2003-04	HV 71 Jonkoping	Sweden	39	5	13	18	105	16	3	3	6	*68
2004-05	HV 71 Jonkoping	Sweden	42	6	12	18	155	....	....	....	....	....
2005-06	TPS Turku	Finland	37	8	7	15	81	....	....	....	....	....
	HV 71 Jonkoping	Sweden	8	1	1	2	28	12	3	2	5	28
2006-07	HV 71 Jonkoping	Sweden	49	14	11	25	150	11	2	1	3	36
2007-08	HV 71 Jonkoping	Sweden	51	17	13	30	167	17	1	5	6	36

Signed as a free agent by **NY Rangers**, July 1, 2008.

JEFFREY, Dustin (JEHF-ree, DUHS-tihn) PIT.

Center. Shoots left. 6'1", 205 lbs. Born, Sarnia, Ont., February 27, 1988.
(Pittsburgh's 8th choice, 171st overall, in 2007 Entry Draft).

			Regular Season					Playoffs				
Season	Club	League	GP	G	A	Pts	PIM	GP	G	A	Pts	PIM
2003-04	Lambton Sting	Minor-ON	40	44	23	67	22	....	....	....	....	....
2004-05	Mississauga	OHL	53	10	15	25	20	....	....	....	....	....
2005-06	Mississauga	OHL	30	6	9	15	26	....	....	....	....	....
	Sault Ste. Marie	OHL	39	12	11	23	10	4	1	2	3	2
2006-07	Sault Ste. Marie	OHL	68	34	58	92	40	13	6	12	18	11
2007-08	Sault Ste. Marie	OHL	56	38	59	97	30	14	3	8	11	12
	Wilkes-Barre	AHL	....	....	....	....	....	15	2	1	3	4

JENKS, A.J. (JEHKS, AY-JAY) FLA.

Left wing. Shoots left. 6'2", 206 lbs. Born, Detroit, MI, June 27, 1990.
(Florida's 4th choice, 100th overall, in 2008 Entry Draft).

			Regular Season					Playoffs				
Season	Club	League	GP	G	A	Pts	PIM	GP	G	A	Pts	PIM
2004-05	Det. Compuware	MWEHL	28	7	12	19	54	....	....	....	....	....
2005-06	Det. Honeybaked	MWEHL	21	7	10	17	23	....	....	....	....	....
2006-07	Plymouth Whalers	OHL	68	9	14	23	50	20	0	1	1	8
2007-08	Plymouth Whalers	OHL	68	26	29	55	94	4	1	0	1	4

JENSEN, Christian (JEHN-suhn, KRIHS-tyehn) S.J.

Defense. Shoots right. 6'3", 190 lbs. Born, Brooklyn, NY, January 6, 1986.
(San Jose's 10th choice, 289th overall, in 2004 Entry Draft).

			Regular Season					Playoffs				
Season	Club	League	GP	G	A	Pts	PIM	GP	G	A	Pts	PIM
2003-04	New Jersey Jrs.	AtJHL	48	6	23	29	62	....	....	....	....	....
2004-05	Jersey Hitmen	EJHL	48	1	9	10	22	....	....	....	....	....
2005-06	Chicago Steel	USHL	24	0	4	4	8	....	....	....	....	....
	Waterloo	USHL	18	1	4	5	14	....	....	....	....	....
2006-07	RPI Engineers	ECAC	24	1	3	4	28	....	....	....	....	....
2007-08	RPI Engineers	ECAC	31	2	5	7	41	....	....	....	....	....

JESSIMAN, Hugh (JEHS-ih-muhn, HEW) NYR

Right wing. Shoots right. 6'6", 230 lbs. Born, New York, NY, March 28, 1984.
(NY Rangers' 1st choice, 12th overall, in 2003 Entry Draft).

			Regular Season					Playoffs				
Season	Club	League	GP	G	A	Pts	PIM	GP	G	A	Pts	PIM
2001-02	Brunswick Bruins	High-CT	18	25	27	52	40	....	....	....	....	....
2002-03	Dartmouth	ECAC	34	23	24	47	48	....	....	....	....	....
2003-04	Dartmouth	ECAC	34	16	17	33	71	....	....	....	....	....
2004-05	Dartmouth	ECAC	12	1	1	2	18	....	....	....	....	....
2005-06	Hartford Wolf Pack	AHL	46	7	11	18	66	2	0	0	0	0
	Charlotte	ECHL	25	13	10	23	56	....	....	....	....	....
2006-07	Hartford Wolf Pack	AHL	49	7	6	13	79	7	1	0	1	9
	Charlotte	ECHL	20	12	10	22	52	....	....	....	....	....
2007-08	Hartford Wolf Pack	AHL	71	18	24	42	154	5	0	1	1	21

ECAC All-Rookie Team (2003) • ECAC Rookie of the Year (2003) • ECAC Second All-Star Team (2004)

JOENSUU, Jesse (YOH-ehn-soo, YEH-see) NYI

Wing. Shoots left. 6'4", 207 lbs. Born, Pori, Finland, October 5, 1987.
(NY Islanders' 2nd choice, 60th overall, in 2006 Entry Draft).

			Regular Season					Playoffs				
Season	Club	League	GP	G	A	Pts	PIM	GP	G	A	Pts	PIM
2002-03	Assat Pori U18	Fin-U18	26	8	10	18	53	3	1	2	3	0
	Assat Pori Jr.	Fin-Jr.	3	0	1	1	2	....	....	....	....	....
2003-04	Assat Pori U18	Fin-U18	6	7	2	9	8	....	....	....	....	....
	Assat Pori Jr.	Fin-Jr.	28	7	9	16	18	3	0	1	1	2
	Assat Pori	Finland	6	0	0	0	0	....	....	....	....	....
2004-05	Assat Pori Jr.	Fin-Jr.	17	7	13	20	20	2	1	1	2	2
	Assat Pori	Finland	39	1	1	2	4	....	....	....	....	....
	Assat Pori	Finland	39	1	1	2	4	....	....	....	....	....
2005-06	Assat Pori	Finland	51	4	8	12	57	14	0	2	2	12
	Suomi U20	Finland-2	2	1	0	1	12	....	....	....	....	....
2006-07	Assat Pori Jr.	Fin-Jr.	5	2	1	3	6	....	....	....	....	....
	Suomi U20	Finland-2	2	0	2	2	6	....	....	....	....	....
	Assat Pori	Finland	52	9	17	26	74	....	....	....	....	....
2007-08	Assat Pori	Finland	56	17	18	35	89	....	....	....	....	....
	Bridgeport	AHL	1	0	0	0	0	....	....	....	....	....

JOHANSSON, Fredrik (yoh-HAHN-suhn, FREHD-rihk)

Center. Shoots left. 6', 187 lbs. Born, Goteburg, Sweden, February 27, 1984.
(Edmonton's 14th choice, 274th overall, in 2002 Entry Draft).

			Regular Season					Playoffs				
Season	Club	League	GP	G	A	Pts	PIM	GP	G	A	Pts	PIM
2000-01	V.Frolunda Jr.	Swe-Jr.	22	3	4	7	8	3	0	1	1	4
	V.Frolunda U18	Swe-U18	6	5	1	6	4	....	....	....	....	....
2001-02	V.Frolunda Jr.	Swe-Jr.	42	13	23	36	39	....	....	....	....	....
	V.Frolunda U18	Swe-U18	1	0	1	1	0	....	....	....	....	....
2002-03	V.Frolunda Jr.	Swe-Jr.	30	13	34	47	24	3	0	2	2	2
	V.Frolunda	Sweden	9	0	0	0	2	5	0	0	0	0
2003-04	V.Frolunda Jr.	Swe-Jr.	7	1	2	3	4	4	2	4	6	0
	Halmstad	Sweden-2	1	0	0	0	0	....	....	....	....	....
	V.Frolunda	Sweden	48	1	3	4	6	10	0	0	0	0
2004-05	Vasteras	Sweden-2	46	15	15	30	32	5	0	3	3	8
2005-06	VIK Vasteras HK	Sweden-2	41	7	15	22	26	....	....	....	....	....
2006-07	Frolunda	Sweden	53	1	4	5	20	....	....	....	....	....
	Frolunda Jr.	Swe-Jr.	1	1	1	2	2	....	....	....	....	....
2007-08	Springfield Falcons	AHL	25	4	1	5	8	....	....	....	....	....
	Stockton Thunder	ECHL	37	5	13	18	16	....	....	....	....	....

JOHNSON, Nick (JAWN-suhn, NIHK) PIT.

Right wing. Shoots right. 6'1", 183 lbs. Born, Calgary, Alta., December 24, 1985.
(Pittsburgh's 4th choice, 67th overall, in 2004 Entry Draft).

			Regular Season					Playoffs				
Season	Club	League	GP	G	A	Pts	PIM	GP	G	A	Pts	PIM
2002-03	St. Albert Saints	AJHL	60	21	30	51	10	....	....	....	....	....
2003-04	St. Albert Saints	AJHL	51	35	36	71	33	4	0	2	2	0
2004-05	Dartmouth	ECAC	35	18	17	35	16	....	....	....	....	....
2005-06	Dartmouth	ECAC	33	15	10	25	24	....	....	....	....	....
2006-07	Dartmouth	ECAC	33	14	16	30	46	....	....	....	....	....
2007-08	Dartmouth	ECAC	32	10	25	35	20	....	....	....	....	....
	Wilkes-Barre	AHL	4	0	1	1	0	10	0	1	1	2

ECAC All-Rookie Team 2005) • ECAC First All-Star Team (2008)

JOHNSON, Patrick (JAWN-suhn, PAT-rihk) MTL.

Center. Shoots left. 5'9", 155 lbs. Born, Madison, WI, April 21, 1989.
(Montreal's 5th choice, 206th overall, in 2008 Entry Draft).

			Regular Season					Playoffs				
Season	Club	League	GP	G	A	Pts	PIM	GP	G	A	Pts	PIM
2006-07	Lincoln Stars	USHL	49	11	16	27	50	4	1	0	1	14
2007-08	U. of Wisconsin	WCHA	40	8	13	21	36	....	....	....	....	....

JOHNSTON, Stephen (JAWN-stuhn, STEE-vehn) DET.

Left wing. Shoots left. 6'1", 175 lbs. Born, Guelph, Ont., February 24, 1990.
(Detroit's 5th choice, 181st overall, in 2008 Entry Draft).

			Regular Season					Playoffs				
Season	Club	League	GP	G	A	Pts	PIM	GP	G	A	Pts	PIM
2005-06	Guelph AAA	Minor-ON	57	26	30	56	32	....	....	....	....	....
2006-07	Guelph AAA	Minor-ON	STATISTICS NOT AVAILABLE									
	John F. Ross	High-ON	48	37	39	76	....	....	....	....	....	....
2007-08	Belleville Bulls	OHL	56	2	7	9	12	21	5	2	7	6

JOKINEN, Justin (YOH-kihn-ihn, JUHS-tihn) BUF.

Right wing. Shoots right. 6'2", 165 lbs. Born, Cloquet, MN, November 25, 1989.
(Buffalo's 5th choice, 101st overall, in 2008 Entry Draft).

			Regular Season					Playoffs				
Season	Club	League	GP	G	A	Pts	PIM	GP	G	A	Pts	PIM
2005-06	Cloquet	High-MN	....	7	11	18	....	....	....	....	....	....
2006-07	Cloquet	High-MN	....	26	25	51	18	....	....	....	....	....
	Team North	UMWEHL	11	6	5	11	....	....	....	....	....	....
2007-08	Cloquet	High-MN	30	22	21	43	....	....	....	....	....	....
	Team North	UMWEHL	12	5	13	18	....	....	....	....	....	....

• Signed Letter of Intent to attend **Minnesota State University** (WCHA) in fall of 2008.

JONES, Matt (JOHNZ, MAT) S.J.

Right wing. Shoots right. 6'4", 205 lbs. Born, Kentwood, MI, January 13, 1986.

			Regular Season					Playoffs				
Season	Club	League	GP	G	A	Pts	PIM	GP	G	A	Pts	PIM
2005-06	Sioux City	USHL	51	11	8	19	71	....	....	....	....	....
2006-07	Merrimack College	H-East	32	4	2	6	70	....	....	....	....	....
2007-08	Merrimack College	H-East	34	15	7	22	60	....	....	....	....	....
	Worcester Sharks	AHL	7	2	1	3	8	....	....	....	....	....

Signed as a free agent by **San Jose**, March 28, 2008.

JONES, Ryan (JOHNZ, RIGH-uhn) NSH.

Right wing. Shoots left. 6'1", 207 lbs. Born, Chatham, Ont., June 14, 1984.
(Minnesota's 5th choice, 111th overall, in 2004 Entry Draft).

			Regular Season					Playoffs				
Season	Club	League	GP	G	A	Pts	PIM	GP	G	A	Pts	PIM
2002-03	Chatham Maroons	OHA-B	38	12	11	23	42	....	....	....	....	....
2003-04	Chatham Maroons	OHA-B	46	39	30	69	64	17	17	9	26	25
2004-05	Miami U.	CCHA	38	8	7	15	79	....	....	....	....	....
2005-06	Miami U.	CCHA	39	22	13	35	72	....	....	....	....	....
2006-07	Miami U.	CCHA	42	29	19	48	88	....	....	....	....	....
2007-08	Miami U.	CCHA	42	31	18	49	83	....	....	....	....	....
	Houston Aeros	AHL	4	0	0	0	2	4	1	1	2	2

CCHA Second All-Star Team (2006, 2007) • CCHA First All-Star Team (2008) • NCAA West First All-American Team (2008)

Traded to **Nashville** by **Minnesota** with Minnesota's 2nd round choice in 2009 Entry Draft for Marek Zidlicky, July 1, 2008

JONSSON, Per (YAWN-suhn, PAIR) CGY.

Forward. Shoots left. 6', 172 lbs. Born, Karlstad, Sweden, April 20, 1988.
(Calgary's 8th choice, 209th overall, in 2006 Entry Draft).

			Regular Season					Playoffs				
Season	Club	League	GP	G	A	Pts	PIM	GP	G	A	Pts	PIM
2004-05	Farjestad U18	Swe-U18	12	2	2	4	10	2	0	0	0	2
2005-06	Farjestad U18	Swe-U18	14	3	1	4	38	8	1	1	2	22
2006-07	Farjestad	Sweden	11	0	1	1	0	....	....	....	....	....
	Skare BK Karlstad	Sweden-3	25	3	4	7	42	....	....	....	....	....
2007-08	Skare BK	Sweden-3	38	3	15	18	102	....	....	....	....	....
	Farjestad	Sweden	16	0	1	1	0	....	....	....	....	....

JORDAN, Michal (JOHR-duhn, MEE-khuhl) CAR.

Defense. Shoots left. 6'1", 184 lbs. Born, Zlin, Czech., July 17, 1990.
(Carolina's 3rd choice, 105th overall, in 2008 Entry Draft).

			Regular Season					Playoffs				
Season	Club	League	GP	G	A	Pts	PIM	GP	G	A	Pts	PIM
2005-06	HC Zlin U17	CzR-U17	43	7	15	22	12	5	0	1	1	2
2006-07	HC Zlin U17	CzR-U17	1	0	0	0	4	....	....	....	....	....
	HC Zlin Jr.	CzRep-Jr.	40	7	11	18	20	12	1	5	6	12
2007-08	Windsor Spitfires	OHL	22	1	5	6	12	....	....	....	....	....
	Plymouth Whalers	OHL	39	5	17	22	32	4	0	3	3	6

JOSI, Roman (YAW-see, ROH-man) NSH.

Defense. Shoots left. 6'1", 185 lbs. Born, Bern, Switzerland, June 1, 1990.
(Nashville's 3rd choice, 38th overall, in 2008 Entry Draft).

			Regular Season					Playoffs				
Season	Club	League	GP	G	A	Pts	PIM	GP	G	A	Pts	PIM
2005-06	SC Bern Future Jr.	Swiss-Jr.	5	0	0	0	0	....	....	....	....	....
2006-07	SC Bern Future Jr.	Swiss-Jr.	33	14	16	30	28	14	1	3	4	2
	Switzerland U20	Swiss-2	5	1	1	2	2	....	....	....	....	....
	SC Bern	Swiss	3	0	1	1	0	....	....	....	....	....
2007-08	Switzerland U20	Swiss-2	2	0	1	1	0	....	....	....	....	....
	HC Neuchatel	Swiss-2	3	2	0	2	4	....	....	....	....	....
	SC Bern	Swiss	35	2	6	8	10	6	0	0	0	0

JOSLIN, Derek (JAWS-lihn, DAIR-ihk) S.J.

Defense. Shoots left. 6'1", 210 lbs. Born, Richmond Hill, Ont., March 17, 1987.
(San Jose's 5th choice, 149th overall, in 2005 Entry Draft).

			Regular Season					Playoffs				
Season	Club	League	GP	G	A	Pts	PIM	GP	G	A	Pts	PIM
2002-03	Vaughan	GTHL	60	9	18	27	72	....	....	....	....	....
2003-04	Aurora Tigers	OPJHL	36	4	12	16	....	....	....	....	....	....
	Ottawa 67's	OHL	7	0	0	0	4	....	....	....	....	....
2004-05	Ottawa 67's	OHL	68	6	24	30	44	21	0	3	3	24
2005-06	Ottawa 67's	OHL	68	11	37	48	40	6	1	5	6	10
	Cleveland Barons	AHL	2	0	0	0	0	....	....	....	....	....
2006-07	Ottawa 67's	OHL	68	11	38	49	66	5	1	4	5	4
	Worcester Sharks	AHL	3	0	0	0	0	4	0	0	0	2
2007-08	Worcester Sharks	AHL	80	10	24	34	44	....	....	....	....	....

JOUDREY, Andrew (JOO-dree, AN-droo) **WSH.**

Center. Shoots left. 5'11", 191 lbs. Born, Halifax, N.S., July 15, 1984.
(Washington's 5th choice, 249th overall, in 2003 Entry Draft).

			Regular Season					Playoffs				
Season	Club	League	GP	G	A	Pts	PIM	GP	G	A	Pts	PIM
2000-01	Dartmouth	NSMHL	82	51	70	121	....	....	....	....	....	....
2001-02	Notre Dame	SJHL	57	24	38	62	14	....	....	....	....	....
2002-03	Notre Dame	SJHL	53	27	51	78	16	....	....	....	....	....
2003-04	U. of Wisconsin	WCHA	42	7	15	22	2	....	....	....	....	....
2004-05	U. of Wisconsin	WCHA	41	7	17	24	18	....	....	....	....	....
2005-06	U. of Wisconsin	WCHA	37	8	10	18	14	....	....	....	....	....
2006-07	U. of Wisconsin	WCHA	40	9	20	29	18	....	....	....	....	....
	Hershey Bears	AHL	5	2	1	3	0	10	0	2	2	0
2007-08	Hershey Bears	AHL	61	11	14	25	22	5	0	1	1	0

JUNLAND, Jonas (YUHN-land, YOH-nuhs) **ST.L.**

Defense. Shoots left. 6'2", 198 lbs. Born, Linkoping, Sweden, November 15, 1987.
(St. Louis' 4th choice, 64th overall, in 2006 Entry Draft).

			Regular Season					Playoffs				
Season	Club	League	GP	G	A	Pts	PIM	GP	G	A	Pts	PIM
2002-03	Linkopings HC U18	Swe-U18	7	0	0	0	6	....	....	....	....	....
2003-04	Linkopings HC U18	Swe-U18	4	0	0	0	4	....	....	....	....	....
	Linkopings HC Jr.	Swe-Jr.	19	1	0	1	12	....	....	....	....	....
2004-05	Linkopings HC U18	Swe-U18	11	6	5	11	35	....	....	....	....	....
	Linkopings HC Jr.	Swe-Jr.	32	3	5	8	96	....	....	....	....	....
2005-06	Linkopings HC Jr.	Swe-Jr.	32	17	23	40	44	....	....	....	....	....
	Linkopings HC U18	Swe-U18	1	5	0	5	2	....	....	....	....	....
	Linkopings HC	Sweden	4	0	0	0	0	....	....	....	....	....
2006-07	Linkopings HC Jr.	Swe-Jr.	9	6	7	13	26	....	....	....	....	....
	IK Oskarshamn	Sweden-2	4	0	3	3	4	....	....	....	....	....
	Linkopings HC	Sweden	41	1	4	5	22	15	0	5	5	20
2007-08	Linkopings HC	Sweden	52	3	17	20	42	16	4	3	7	18

KABLUKOV, Ilja (ka-BLOO-hahv, IHL-yah) **VAN.**

Center. Shoots left. 6'2", 183 lbs. Born, Moscow, USSR, January 18, 1988.
(Vancouver's 4th choice, 146th overall, in 2007 Entry Draft).

			Regular Season					Playoffs				
Season	Club	League	GP	G	A	Pts	PIM	GP	G	A	Pts	PIM
2005-06	CSKA Moscow 2	Russia-3	STATISTICS NOT AVAILABLE									
2006-07	CSKA Moscow 2	Russia-3	STATISTICS NOT AVAILABLE									
	CSKA Moscow	Russia	24	0	0	0	2	2	0	0	0	2
2007-08	CSKA Moscow	Russia	50	4	9	13	18	6	1	3	4	2
	CSKA Moscow 2	Russia-3	....	....	....	....	....	2	1	3	4	2

KAIP, Rylan (KAYP, RIH-luhn) **ATL.**

Center. Shoots left. 6'1", 185 lbs. Born, Wilcox, Sask., March 19, 1984.
(Atlanta's 9th choice, 269th overall, in 2003 Entry Draft).

			Regular Season					Playoffs				
Season	Club	League	GP	G	A	Pts	PIM	GP	G	A	Pts	PIM
2000-01	Notre Dame	SJHL	5	0	0	0	0	1	0	0	0	0
2001-02	Notre Dame	SJHL	61	14	18	32	77	....	....	....	....	....
2002-03	Notre Dame	SJHL	57	20	36	56	164	6	1	6	7	21
2003-04	Notre Dame	SJHL	54	30	36	66	133	4	1	1	2	6
2004-05	North Dakota	WCHA	22	0	4	4	20	....	....	....	....	....
2005-06	North Dakota	WCHA	42	3	5	8	76	....	....	....	....	....
2006-07	North Dakota	WCHA	38	5	7	12	55	....	....	....	....	....
2007-08	North Dakota	WCHA	42	8	7	15	81	....	....	....	....	....

KALINSKI, Jonathon (kuh-LIHN-skee, JAWN-ah-thuhn) **PHI.**

Left wing. Shoots left. 6'1", 180 lbs. Born, Bonnyville , Alta., May 25, 1987.
(Philadelphia's 5th choice, 152nd overall, in 2007 Entry Draft).

			Regular Season					Playoffs				
Season	Club	League	GP	G	A	Pts	PIM	GP	G	A	Pts	PIM
2003-04	Bonnyville Pontiacs	AJHL	52	13	13	26	68	5	0	0	0	8
2004-05	Bonnyville Pontiacs	AJHL	58	16	25	41	195	4	2	0	2	6
2005-06	Minnesota State	WCHA	30	4	7	11	73	....	....	....	....	....
2006-07	Minnesota State	WCHA	37	17	10	27	74	....	....	....	....	....
2007-08	Minnesota State	WCHA	39	8	10	18	56	....	....	....	....	....
	Philadelphia	AHL	5	0	3	3	4	10	1	2	3	14

KAMPFER, Steven (KAMP-fuhr, STEE-vehn) **ANA.**

Defense. Shoots right. 5'11", 204 lbs. Born, Ann Arbour, MI, September 24, 1988.
(Anaheim's 5th choice, 93rd overall, in 2007 Entry Draft).

			Regular Season					Playoffs				
Season	Club	League	GP	G	A	Pts	PIM	GP	G	A	Pts	PIM
2004-05	Sioux City	USHL	47	6	13	19	91	13	2	5	7	12
2005-06	Sioux City	USHL	56	6	10	16	99	....	....	....	....	....
2006-07	U. of Michigan	CCHA	35	1	3	4	24	....	....	....	....	....
2007-08	U. of Michigan	CCHA	42	2	15	17	36	....	....	....	....	....

KANA, Tomas (KA-nah, TAW-mahsh) **ST.L.**

Center. Shoots right. 6', 202 lbs. Born, Opava, Czech., November 29, 1987.
(St. Louis' 3rd choice, 31st overall, in 2006 Entry Draft).

			Regular Season					Playoffs				
Season	Club	League	GP	G	A	Pts	PIM	GP	G	A	Pts	PIM
2002-03	HC Vitkovice U17	CzR-U17	44	20	14	34	72	2	2	0	2	4
	HC Vitkovice Jr.	CzRep-Jr.	3	2	0	2	4	....	....	....	....	....
2003-04	HC Vitkovice U17	CzR-U17	8	2	9	11	33	7	4	5	9	18
	HC Vitkovice Jr.	CzRep-Jr.	50	12	7	19	78	....	....	....	....	....
2004-05	HC Vitkovice Jr.	CzRep-Jr.	46	12	22	34	155	2	0	0	0	2
	HC Vitkovice Steel	CzRep	1	0	0	0	0	....	....	....	....	....
2005-06	HC Vitkovice Steel	CzRep	42	5	9	14	50	6	0	1	1	2
	HC Vitkovice Jr.	CzRep-Jr.	5	4	3	7	16	....	....	....	....	....
2006-07	HC Vitkovice Steel	CzRep	44	9	7	16	54	....	....	....	....	....
	BK Mlada Boleslav	CzRep-2	6	2	1	3	16	6	1	0	1	16
2007-08	Alaska Aces	ECHL	12	2	0	2	4	....	....	....	....	....
	HC Sareza Ostrava	CzRep-2	8	3	0	3	6	....	....	....	....	....
	HC Vitkovice Steel	CzRep	8	1	1	2	6	....	....	....	....	....
	Usti n. L.	CzRep	17	4	4	8	18	....	....	....	....	....
	Usti n. L.	CzRep-Q	....	....	....	....	....	3	0	0	0	2

KARIYA, Martin (kah-REE-ah, MAR-tihn)

Right wing. Shoots right. 5'9", 175 lbs. Born, Vancouver, B.C., October 5, 1981.

			Regular Season					Playoffs				
Season	Club	League	GP	G	A	Pts	PIM	GP	G	A	Pts	PIM
1998-99	Victoria Salsa	BCJHL	59	25	80	105	14	....	....	....	....	....
99-2000	U. of Maine	H-East	35	8	17	25	6	....	....	....	....	....
2000-01	U. of Maine	H-East	39	12	14	36	10	....	....	....	....	....
2001-02	U. of Maine	H-East	43	16	28	44	14	....	....	....	....	....
2002-03	U. of Maine	H-East	39	14	36	50	6	....	....	....	....	....
	Portland Pirates	AHL	....	....	....	....	....	3	0	0	0	0
2003-04	Bridgeport	AHL	70	8	17	25	16	7	0	1	1	2
2004-05	HC Nikko Icebucks	AsianHL	15	6	12	18	20	....	....	....	....	....
2005-06	Stjernen Hockey	Norway	39	15	37	52	49	11	3	10	13	8
2006-07	Blues Espoo	Finland	51	18	43	61	58	....	....	....	....	....
2007-08	Peoria Rivermen	AHL	71	16	37	53	29	....	....	....	....	....

Hockey East First All-Star Team (2003)

Signed to a PTO (tryout) contract by **Portland** (AHL), April 9, 2003. Signed as a free agent by **Bridgeport** (AHL), July 7, 2003. Signed as a free agent by **St. Louis**, June 1, 2007.

KARLSSON, Erik (KAHRL-suhn, AIR-ihk) **OTT.**

Defense. Shoots right. 5'11", 165 lbs. Born, Landsbro, Sweden, May 31, 1990.
(Ottawa's 1st choice, 15th overall, in 2008 Entry Draft).

			Regular Season					Playoffs				
Season	Club	League	GP	G	A	Pts	PIM	GP	G	A	Pts	PIM
2006-07	Sodertalje SK U18	Swe-U18	2	0	1	1	33	....	....	....	....	....
	Sodertalje SK Jr.	Swe-Jr.	10	2	8	10	8	....	....	....	....	....
2007-08	Frolunda U18	Swe-U18	3	1	2	3	2	2	0	1	1	10
	Frolunda Jr.	Swe-Jr.	38	13	24	37	68	5	1	0	1	4
	Frolunda	Sweden	7	1	0	1	0	6	0	0	0	0

KARLSSON, Mattias (KARL-suhn, mat-TEE-uhs) **OTT.**

Defense. Shoots left. 6'2", 230 lbs. Born, Stora, Sweden, April 15, 1985.
(Ottawa's 4th choice, 135th overall, in 2003 Entry Draft).

			Regular Season					Playoffs				
Season	Club	League	GP	G	A	Pts	PIM	GP	G	A	Pts	PIM
2001-02	Brynas U18	Swe-U18	5	2	1	3	6	....	....	....	....	....
	Brynas IF Gavle Jr.	Swe-Jr.	13	0	1	1	12	....	....	....	....	....
2002-03	Brynas IF Gavle Jr.	Swe-Jr.	27	11	6	17	93	2	0	0	0	4
	Brynas IF Gavle	Sweden	3	0	0	0	0	....	....	....	....	....
	Brynas IF Gavle	Sweden-Q	3	0	0	0	0	....	....	....	....	....
2003-04	Brynas IF Gavle Jr.	Swe-Jr.	20	5	8	13	67	5	0	4	4	10
	Brynas IF Gavle	Sweden	39	0	0	0	6	....	....	....	....	....
2004-05	Brynas IF Gavle Jr.	Swe-Jr.	13	3	5	8	40	....	....	....	....	....
	Almtuna	Sweden-2	22	0	2	2	18	....	....	....	....	....
	Brynas IF Gavle	Sweden	9	0	0	0	2	....	....	....	....	....
	Brynas IF Gavle	Sweden-Q	1	0	0	0	0	....	....	....	....	....
2005-06	Almtuna Jr.	Swe-Jr.	2	0	1	1	4	....	....	....	....	....
	Almtuna	Sweden-2	32	3	4	7	40	....	....	....	....	....
2006-07	Bofors	Sweden-2	44	11	21	32	34	....	....	....	....	....
2007-08	Binghamton	AHL	2	0	0	0	0	....	....	....	....	....
	Farjestad	Sweden	13	2	2	4	4	12	1	3	4	20

KARSUMS, Martins (KAHR-suhmz, MAHR-tihnsh) **BOS.**

Right wing. Shoots right. 5'10", 198 lbs. Born, Riga, Latvia, February 26, 1986.
(Boston's 2nd choice, 64th overall, in 2004 Entry Draft).

			Regular Season					Playoffs				
Season	Club	League	GP	G	A	Pts	PIM	GP	G	A	Pts	PIM
2000-01	Prizma '83 Riga Jr.	Latvia-Jr.	2	0	0	0	0	....	....	....	....	....
	Lido Nafta Jr.	Latvia-Jr.	18	8	6	14	....	....	....	....	....	....
2001-02	Prizma '83 Riga	EEHL-B	16	7	8	15	4	....	....	....	....	....
	Prizma '83 Riga	Latvia	6	4	1	5	4	....	....	....	....	....
2002-03	HK Riga 2000	EEHL	2	0	0	0	0	....	....	....	....	....
	Vilki Riga	Latvia	STATISTICS NOT AVAILABLE									
2003-04	Moncton Wildcats	QMJHL	60	30	23	53	76	20	8	9	17	14
2004-05	Moncton Wildcats	QMJHL	30	14	12	26	31	2	0	0	0	0
2005-06	Moncton Wildcats	QMJHL	49	34	31	65	89	21	15	11	26	22
2006-07	Providence Bruins	AHL	54	13	22	35	41	12	3	1	4	2
2007-08	Providence Bruins	AHL	79	20	43	63	57	10	7	3	10	6

QMJHL All-Rookie Team (2004)

KASSIAN, Matt (KAS-ee-uhn, MAT) **MIN.**

Left wing. Shoots left. 6'5", 245 lbs. Born, Edmonton, Alta., October 28, 1986.
(Minnesota's 2nd choice, 57th overall, in 2005 Entry Draft).

			Regular Season					Playoffs				
Season	Club	League	GP	G	A	Pts	PIM	GP	G	A	Pts	PIM
2002-03	Sherwood Park	AJHL	33	5	7	12	38	....	....	....	....	....
2003-04	Vancouver Giants	WHL	37	1	0	1	42	3	0	0	0	4
2004-05	Vancouver Giants	WHL	41	0	3	3	89	....	....	....	....	....
	Kamloops Blazers	WHL	28	3	0	3	83	6	1	2	3	14
2005-06	Kamloops Blazers	WHL	67	5	6	11	147	....	....	....	....	....
2006-07	Kamloops Blazers	WHL	72	8	10	18	162	4	0	1	1	0
2007-08	Houston Aeros	AHL	19	0	0	0	48	....	....	....	....	....
	Texas Wildcatters	ECHL	47	6	4	10	90	....	....	....	....	....

KATIC, Mark (KA-tihk, MAHRK) **NYI**

Defense. Shoots left. 5'10", 180 lbs. Born, Timmins, Ont., May 9, 1989.
(NY Islanders' 1st choice, 62nd overall, in 2007 Entry Draft).

			Regular Season					Playoffs				
Season	Club	League	GP	G	A	Pts	PIM	GP	G	A	Pts	PIM
2003-04	Timmins Majors	GNMHL	40	12	20	32	35	....	....	....	....	....
2004-05	Timmins Majors	GNMHL	35	11	21	32	74	....	....	....	....	....
2005-06	Sarnia Sting	OHL	51	5	29	34	33	....	....	....	....	....
2006-07	Sarnia Sting	OHL	68	5	35	40	31	4	1	3	4	8
2007-08	Sarnia Sting	OHL	45	5	26	31	28	6	0	3	3	8

KAZIONOV, Denis (ka-zee-OH-nahv, DEH-nihs) **T.B.**

Left wing. Shoots left. 6'3", 187 lbs. Born, Perm, USSR, December 8, 1987.
(Tampa Bay's 4th choice, 198th overall, in 2006 Entry Draft).

			Regular Season					Playoffs				
Season	Club	League	GP	G	A	Pts	PIM	GP	G	A	Pts	PIM
2003-04	CSKA Moscow 2	Russia-3	2	0	1	1	2	....	....	....	....	....
2004-05	Dyn'o Moscow 2	Russia-3	STATISTICS NOT AVAILABLE									
2005-06	HK MVD-THK Tver	Russia-3	31	6	13	19	34	....	....	....	....	....
	MVD	Russia	26	0	0	0	12	3	0	0	0	0
2006-07	THK Tver	Russia-3	13	23	15	38	42	....	....	....	....	....
	MVD	Russia	24	2	0	2	8	2	0	0	0	2
2007-08	Novokuznetsk	Russia	8	0	0	0	8	....	....	....	....	....
	Avangard Omsk 2	Russia-3	13	10	6	16	16	....	....	....	....	....
	Avangard Omsk	Russia	18	0	0	0	4	3	0	0	0	6

KAZIONOV, Dmitri (ka-zee-OH-nahv, dih-MEE-tree) **T.B.**

Center. Shoots left. 6'3", 185 lbs. Born, Moscow, USSR, May 13, 1984.
(Tampa Bay's 2nd choice, 100th overall, in 2002 Entry Draft).

			Regular Season					Playoffs				
Season	**Club**	**League**	**GP**	**G**	**A**	**Pts**	**PIM**	**GP**	**G**	**A**	**Pts**	**PIM**
99-2000	Dyn'o Moscow 2	Russia-3	2	1	0	1	0	....	....	....	....	....
2000-01	THK Tver	Russia-2	33	1	1	2	6	....	....	....	....	....
2001-02	HK CSKA Moscow	Russia-2	2	0	1	1	0	....	....	....	....	....
	HK CSKA 2	Russia-3	10	1	0	1	4	....	....	....	....	....
	Lada Togliatti	Russia	3	0	0	0	0	....	....	....	....	....
	Lada Togliatti 2	Russia-3	16	10	9	19	0	....	....	....	....	....
2002-03	Lada Togliatti	Russia	5	0	1	1	4	....	....	....	....	....
	Lada Togliatti 2	Russia-3	34	14	13	27	26	....	....	....	....	....
2003-04	Lada Togliatti 2	Russia-3	5	3	2	5	0	4	0	0	0	0
	Lada Togliatti	Russia	47	5	5	10	34	5	0	0	0	4
2004-05	Lada Togliatti	Russia	46	3	7	10	32	2	0	0	0	0
2005-06	Lada Togliatti	Russia	13	0	3	3	18	....	....	....	....	....
	Dynamo Moscow	Russia	27	2	2	4	24	4	1	0	1	6
2006-07	Ak Bars Kazan	Russia	48	10	11	21	34	13	2	3	5	4
2007-08	Ak Bars Kazan	Russia	56	7	13	20	46	10	0	3	3	16

KELL, Trevor (KEHL, TREH-vuhr)

Right wing. Shoots right. 6', 185 lbs. Born, Thunder Bay, Ont., June 23, 1986.
(Chicago's 9th choice, 131st overall, in 2004 Entry Draft).

			Regular Season					Playoffs				
Season	**Club**	**League**	**GP**	**G**	**A**	**Pts**	**PIM**	**GP**	**G**	**A**	**Pts**	**PIM**
2002-03	Wellington Dukes	OPJHL	42	13	17	30	24	....	....	....	....	....
2003-04	London Knights	OHL	62	9	14	23	48	15	7	8	15	14
2004-05	London Knights	OHL	63	16	17	33	57	12	1	4	5	14
2005-06	London Knights	OHL	66	10	28	38	65	19	1	4	5	22
2006-07	Sarnia Sting	OHL	66	37	36	73	76	4	4	1	5	8
2007-08	Lowell Devils	AHL	9	2	5	7	6	....	....	....	....	....
	Trenton Devils	ECHL	61	16	20	36	77	....	....	....	....	....

KELLER, Justin (KEHL-uhr, JUHS-tihn) **T.B.**

Left wing. Shoots left. 5'11", 185 lbs. Born, Nelson, B.C., March 4, 1986.
(Tampa Bay's 8th choice, 245th overall, in 2004 Entry Draft).

			Regular Season					Playoffs				
Season	**Club**	**League**	**GP**	**G**	**A**	**Pts**	**PIM**	**GP**	**G**	**A**	**Pts**	**PIM**
2001-02	Spokane Chiefs	WHL	25	7	6	13	10	....	....	....	....	....
	Saskatoon Blades	WHL	36	7	6	13	6	2	0	0	0	2
2002-03	Saskatoon Blades	WHL	2	0	0	0	0	....	....	....	....	....
	Regina Pats	WHL	16	3	3	6	6	....	....	....	....	....
2003-04	Kelowna Rockets	WHL	72	25	21	46	44	17	4	5	9	18
2004-05	Kelowna Rockets	WHL	72	31	22	53	103	23	12	10	22	44
2005-06	Kelowna Rockets	WHL	72	*51	37	88	82	12	3	6	9	14
2006-07	Springfield Falcons	AHL	60	13	11	24	26	....	....	....	....	....
2007-08	Norfolk Admirals	AHL	70	15	22	37	45	....	....	....	....	....

WHL West First All-Star Team (2006)

KEMP, T.J. (KEHMP, TEE-JAY) **PIT.**

Defense. Shoots left. 5'11", 197 lbs. Born, Pickering, Ont., July 3, 1981.

			Regular Season					Playoffs				
Season	**Club**	**League**	**GP**	**G**	**A**	**Pts**	**PIM**	**GP**	**G**	**A**	**Pts**	**PIM**
2001-02	Mercyhurst	MAAC	31	6	13	19	18	....	....	....	....	....
2002-03	Mercyhurst	MAAC	37	11	16	27	39	....	....	....	....	....
2003-04	Mercyhurst	AH	34	5	21	26	42	....	....	....	....	....
2004-05	Mercyhurst	AH	31	10	18	28	78	....	....	....	....	....
	Missouri	UHL	6	1	2	3	4	....	....	....	....	....
2005-06	Peoria Rivermen	AHL	3	0	0	0	2	....	....	....	....	....
	Iowa Stars	AHL	3	0	0	0	0	....	....	....	....	....
	Milwaukee	AHL	2	0	0	0	2	....	....	....	....	....
	Bridgeport	AHL	6	0	0	0	0	....	....	....	....	....
	Reading Royals	ECHL	60	13	27	40	54	4	1	1	2	2
2006-07	Manchester	AHL	65	5	33	38	56	14	2	5	7	12
2007-08	Springfield Falcons	AHL	73	8	38	46	44	....	....	....	....	....

Signed as a free agent by **Edmonton**, July 17, 2007. Signed as a free agent by **Pittsburgh**, July 8, 2008.

KEMPE, Mario (KEHM-peh, MAHR-ee-oh) **PHI.**

Center. Shoots left. 6', 185 lbs. Born, Kramfors, Sweden, September 19, 1988.
(Philadelphia's 4th choice, 122nd overall, in 2007 Entry Draft).

			Regular Season					Playoffs				
Season	**Club**	**League**	**GP**	**G**	**A**	**Pts**	**PIM**	**GP**	**G**	**A**	**Pts**	**PIM**
2003-04	Hoga Kusten	Sweden-4	STATISTICS NOT AVAILABLE									
2004-05	MODO U18	Swe-U18	14	5	7	12	40	4	1	1	2	4
2005-06	MODO U18	Swe-U18	6	4	2	6	29	2	0	2	2	0
	MODO Jr.	Swe-Jr.	36	20	12	32	16	2	0	0	0	10
2006-07	St. John's	QMJHL	62	23	19	42	51	4	0	0	0	2
2007-08	St. John's	QMJHL	48	25	24	49	36	6	4	3	7	8

KENNEDY, Tim (KEH-nuh-dee, TIHM) **BUF.**

Left wing. Shoots left. 5'9", 176 lbs. Born, Buffalo, NY, April 30, 1986.
(Washington's 6th choice, 181st overall, in 2005 Entry Draft).

			Regular Season					Playoffs				
Season	**Club**	**League**	**GP**	**G**	**A**	**Pts**	**PIM**	**GP**	**G**	**A**	**Pts**	**PIM**
2003-04	Sioux City	USHL	56	9	10	19	42	7	2	2	4	6
2004-05	Sioux City	USHL	54	30	31	61	112	13	*6	*11	*17	18
2005-06	Michigan State	CCHA	29	4	15	19	31	....	....	....	....	....
2006-07	Michigan State	CCHA	42	18	25	43	49	....	....	....	....	....
2007-08	Michigan State	CCHA	42	20	23	43	50	....	....	....	....	....

USHL Second All-Star Team (2005) • NCAA Championship All-Tournament Team (2007) • CCHA Second All-Star Team (2008)

Traded to **Buffalo** by **Washington** for Buffalo's 6th round choice (Mathieu Perreault) in 2006 Entry Draft, July 30, 2005.

KESSEL, Blake (KEH-suhl, BLAYK) **NYI**

Defense. Shoots right. 6'1", 210 lbs. Born, Madison, WI, April 13, 1989.
(NY Islanders' 4th choice, 166th overall, in 2007 Entry Draft).

			Regular Season					Playoffs				
Season	**Club**	**League**	**GP**	**G**	**A**	**Pts**	**PIM**	**GP**	**G**	**A**	**Pts**	**PIM**
2005-06	Madison Capitols	MAHL	62	33	47	80	....	....	....	....	....	....
2006-07	Waterloo	USHL	59	11	27	38	38	9	1	5	6	8
2007-08	Waterloo	USHL	59	19	38	57	26	11	1	*10	11	12

• Signed Letter of Intent to attend **University of New Hampshire** (Hockey East) in fall of 2008.

KHOMITSKI, Vadim (khoh-MIHT-skee, va-DEEM) **DAL.**

Defense. Shoots left. 6'1", 185 lbs. Born, Voskresensk, USSR, July 21, 1982.
(Dallas' 5th choice, 123rd overall, in 2000 Entry Draft).

			Regular Season					Playoffs				
Season	**Club**	**League**	**GP**	**G**	**A**	**Pts**	**PIM**	**GP**	**G**	**A**	**Pts**	**PIM**
1998-99	Voskresensk	Russia	9	0	0	0	10	....	....	....	....	....
99-2000	Voskresensk	Russia-2	17	0	0	0	31	....	....	....	....	....
	HK Moscow	Russia-2	11	0	1	1	10	....	....	....	....	....
2000-01	HK Moscow	Russia-2	44	2	7	9	89	....	....	....	....	....
2001-02	HK CSKA Moscow	Russia-2	68	2	18	20	63	....	....	....	....	....
2002-03	CSKA Moscow	Russia	51	3	2	5	58	....	....	....	....	....
2003-04	CSKA Moscow	Russia	54	3	3	6	46	....	....	....	....	....
2004-05	CSKA Moscow	Russia	60	1	5	6	105	....	....	....	....	....
2005-06	CSKA Moscow	Russia	51	5	6	11	110	7	0	0	0	6
2006-07	Iowa Stars	AHL	9	1	6	7	24	....	....	....	....	....
	Mytischi	Russia	29	6	5	11	50	9	1	1	2	22
2007-08	Iowa Stars	AHL	7	1	0	1	10	....	....	....	....	....
	Mytischi	Russia	27	1	3	4	34	5	1	2	3	8

KHOMUTOV, Ivan (khoh-moo-TAWF, ee-VAHN) **N.J.**

Center. Shoots left. 6'3", 210 lbs. Born, Saratov, USSR, March 11, 1985.
(New Jersey's 3rd choice, 93rd overall, in 2003 Entry Draft).

			Regular Season					Playoffs				
Season	**Club**	**League**	**GP**	**G**	**A**	**Pts**	**PIM**	**GP**	**G**	**A**	**Pts**	**PIM**
2001-02	HK CSKA 2	Russia-3	30	11	8	19	14	....	....	....	....	....
2002-03	Elektrostal	Russia-2	20	1	1	2	8	....	....	....	....	....
2003-04	London Knights	OHL	40	9	12	21	25	15	3	1	4	7
2004-05	Albany River Rats	AHL	66	6	11	17	30	....	....	....	....	....
2005-06	Albany River Rats	AHL	60	9	20	29	44	....	....	....	....	....
2006-07	Lowell Devils	AHL	3	1	1	2	2	....	....	....	....	....
	Trenton Titans	ECHL	5	0	1	1	2	....	....	....	....	....
2007-08	Lowell Devils	AHL	72	13	19	32	53	....	....	....	....	....

KIDD, Josh (KIHD, JAWSH) **L.A.**

Defense. Shoots right. 6'5", 220 lbs. Born, Sundridge, Ont., November 16, 1988.
(Los Angeles' 9th choice, 184th overall, in 2007 Entry Draft).

			Regular Season					Playoffs				
Season	**Club**	**League**	**GP**	**G**	**A**	**Pts**	**PIM**	**GP**	**G**	**A**	**Pts**	**PIM**
2003-04	Richmond Hill	Minor-ON	75	7	14	21	126	....	....	....	....	....
2004-05	Erie Otters	OHL	57	0	0	0	11	4	0	0	0	0
2005-06	Erie Otters	OHL	68	4	6	10	53	....	....	....	....	....
2006-07	Erie Otters	OHL	64	9	18	27	96	....	....	....	....	....
2007-08	Erie Otters	OHL	43	5	8	13	69	....	....	....	....	....
	Manchester	AHL	9	1	3	4	0	....	....	....	....	....

KILLORN, Alexander (KIHL-ohrn, al-ehx-AN-duhr) **T.B.**

Center. Shoots left. 6', 161 lbs. Born, Halifax, N.S., September 14, 1989.
(Tampa Bay's 3rd choice, 77th overall, in 2007 Entry Draft).

			Regular Season					Playoffs				
Season	**Club**	**League**	**GP**	**G**	**A**	**Pts**	**PIM**	**GP**	**G**	**A**	**Pts**	**PIM**
2005-06	Lac St-Louis Lions	QAAA	43	18	34	52	94	10	9	6	15	8
2006-07	Deerfield Academy	High-MA	25	18	14	32	....	....	....	....	....	....
2007-08	Deerfield Academy	High-MA	24	28	27	55	....	....	....	....	....	....

• Signed Letter of Intent to attend **Harvard University** (ECAC) in fall of 2008.

KINCH, Matt (KIHNCH, MATT) **S.J.**

Defense. Shoots left. 5'11", 185 lbs. Born, Red Deer, Alta., February 17, 1980.
(Buffalo's 8th choice, 146th overall, in 1999 Entry Draft).

			Regular Season					Playoffs				
Season	**Club**	**League**	**GP**	**G**	**A**	**Pts**	**PIM**	**GP**	**G**	**A**	**Pts**	**PIM**
1995-96	Red Deer	AMHL	35	6	17	23	31	....	....	....	....	....
	Calgary Hitmen	WHL	1	0	1	1	2	....	....	....	....	....
1996-97	Calgary Hitmen	WHL	64	10	22	32	31	....	....	....	....	....
1997-98	Calgary Hitmen	WHL	55	7	24	31	13	18	3	2	5	4
1998-99	Calgary Hitmen	WHL	68	14	69	83	16	21	8	15	23	59
99-2000	Calgary Hitmen	WHL	62	14	61	75	24	13	2	12	14	8
2000-01	Calgary Hitmen	WHL	70	18	66	84	52	12	3	6	9	6
2001-02	Hartford Wolf Pack	AHL	40	1	7	8	4	....	....	....	....	....
	Charlotte	ECHL	26	3	12	15	13	5	3	2	5	0
2002-03	Hartford Wolf Pack	AHL	66	7	22	29	28	2	0	0	0	0
2003-04	Hartford Wolf Pack	AHL	67	1	19	20	38	1	0	0	0	0
2004-05	Salzburg	Austria	37	1	12	13	18	....	....	....	....	....
2005-06	Langnau	Swiss	25	1	4	5	14	....	....	....	....	....
	ERC Ingolstadt	Germany	16	1	2	3	16	7	0	0	0	4
2006-07	Straubing Tigers	Germany	51	4	20	24	36	....	....	....	....	....
2007-08	Binghamton	AHL	73	9	16	25	73	....	....	....	....	....

WHL East First All-Star Team (1999, 2001) • Memorial Cup Tournament All-Star Team (1999) • Canadian Major Junior Sportsman of the Year (1999) • WHL East Second All-Star Team (2000) • Canadian Major Junior First All-Star Team (2001)

Signed as a free agent by **NY Rangers**, June 26, 2001. Signed as a free agent by **Salzburg** (Austria), August 11, 2004. Signed as a free agent by **Ottawa**, July 17, 2007. Signed as a free agent by **San Jose**, July 17, 2008.

KINDL, Jakub (KEEHN-duhl, YA-kuhb) **DET.**

Defense. Shoots left. 6'3", 199 lbs. Born, Sumperk, Czech., February 10, 1987.
(Detroit's 1st choice, 19th overall, in 2005 Entry Draft).

			Regular Season					Playoffs				
Season	**Club**	**League**	**GP**	**G**	**A**	**Pts**	**PIM**	**GP**	**G**	**A**	**Pts**	**PIM**
2002-03	HC Pardubice U17	CzR-U17	3	0	3	3	10	....	....	....	....	....
	HC Pardubice Jr.	CzRep-Jr.	27	0	3	3	46	....	....	....	....	....
	Pardubice	CzRep	1	0	0	0	0	....	....	....	....	....
2003-04	HC Pardubice U17	CzR-U17	2	0	1	1	6	....	....	....	....	....
	HC Pardubice Jr.	CzRep-Jr.	48	4	14	18	108	....	....	....	....	....
	Hr. Kralove	CzRep-2	1	0	0	0	0	1	0	0	0	0
2004-05	Kitchener Rangers	OHL	62	3	11	14	92	12	0	0	0	22
2005-06	Kitchener Rangers	OHL	60	12	46	58	112	5	1	0	1	10
	Grand Rapids	AHL	3	0	1	1	2	....	....	....	....	....
2006-07	Kitchener Rangers	OHL	54	11	44	55	142	9	2	9	11	8
	Grand Rapids	AHL	....	....	....	....	....	7	0	2	2	0
2007-08	Grand Rapids	AHL	75	3	14	17	82	....	....	....	....	....

OHL Second All-Star Team (2007)

KING, Dwight (KIHNG, DWIGHT) L.A.

Center/Left wing. Shoots left. 6'3", 221 lbs. Born, Meadowlake, Sask., July 5, 1989.
(Los Angeles' 6th choice, 109th overall, in 2007 Entry Draft).

			Regular Season					Playoffs				
Season	Club	League	GP	G	A	Pts	PIM	GP	G	A	Pts	PIM
2004-05	Beardy's	SMHL	44	26	30	56	16	3	0	1	1	4
	Lethbridge	WHL	7	0	0	0	2	4	0	0	0	2
2005-06	Lethbridge	WHL	68	8	8	16	22	6	0	0	0	6
2006-07	Lethbridge	WHL	62	12	32	44	39	....	....	....	....	....
2007-08	Lethbridge	WHL	72	34	35	69	56	19	8	6	14	12

KISHEL, Scott (KIH-shuhl, SKAWT) MTL.

Defense. Shoots left. 5'11", 172 lbs. Born, Virginia, MN, April 21, 1989.
(Montreal's 9th choice, 192nd overall, in 2007 Entry Draft).

			Regular Season					Playoffs				
Season	Club	League	GP	G	A	Pts	PIM	GP	G	A	Pts	PIM
2004-05	Virginia Blue Devils	High-MN	....	4	9	13	....	....	....	....	....	....
2005-06	Virginia Blue Devils	High-MN	....	5	25	30	....	....	....	....	....	....
2006-07	Virginia Blue Devils	High-MN	24	14	34	48	....	....	....	....	....	....
2007-08	Sioux Falls	USHL	57	3	11	14	34	3	0	0	0	0

• Signed Letter of Intent to attend **University of Minnesota-Duluth** (WCHA) in fall of 2008.

KLIMOV, Valeri (KLEE-mawf, VAL-uhr-ee) N.J.

Defense. Shoots left. 6'3", 200 lbs. Born, Moscow, USSR, July 17, 1986.
(New Jersey's 7th choice, 282nd overall, in 2004 Entry Draft).

			Regular Season					Playoffs				
Season	Club	League	GP	G	A	Pts	PIM	GP	G	A	Pts	PIM
2001-02	Spartak Moscow 2	Russia-3	24	1	1	2	6	....	....	....	....	....
2002-03	Spartak Moscow 2	Russia-3	5	2	1	3	8	....	....	....	....	....
2003-04	Spartak Moscow 2	Russia-3	4	1	0	1	0	....	....	....	....	....
2004-05	Spartak Moscow	Russia	6	0	0	0	2	....	....	....	....	....
2005-06	Spartak Moscow 2	Russia-3	17	1	4	5	20	....	....	....	....	....
	Spartak Moscow	Russia	23	1	0	1	4	2	0	0	0	2
2006-07	Khimik	Russia-2	3	0	1	1	2	....	....	....	....	....
2007-08			DID NOT PLAY									

KLOTZ, Garrett (KLAWTZ, GAIR-reht) PHI.

Left wing. Shoots left. 6'6", 225 lbs. Born, Regina, Sask., November 27, 1988.
(Philadelphia's 3rd choice, 66th overall, in 2007 Entry Draft).

			Regular Season					Playoffs				
Season	Club	League	GP	G	A	Pts	PIM	GP	G	A	Pts	PIM
2004-05	Reg. Midget Hawks	SMMHL	STATISTICS NOT AVAILABLE									
	Reg. Pat Canadians	SMHL	5	0	1	1	0	....	....	....	....	....
2005-06	Red Deer Rebels	WHL	35	2	0	2	26	....	....	....	....	....
2006-07	Saskatoon Blades	WHL	63	2	2	4	107	....	....	....	....	....
2007-08	Saskatoon Blades	WHL	52	1	3	4	96	....	....	....	....	....

KNACKSTEDT, Jordan (NAK-stehd, JOHR-dahn) BOS.

Right wing. Shoots right. 6'3", 191 lbs. Born, Saskatoon, Sask., September 28, 1988.
(Boston's 6th choice, 189th overall, in 2007 Entry Draft).

			Regular Season					Playoffs				
Season	Club	League	GP	G	A	Pts	PIM	GP	G	A	Pts	PIM
2003-04	Beardy's	SMHL	44	22	19	41	20	4	2	1	3	0
2004-05	Red Deer Rebels	WHL	52	1	2	3	34	7	0	0	0	2
2005-06	Red Deer Rebels	WHL	72	12	28	40	36	....	....	....	....	....
2006-07	Red Deer Rebels	WHL	33	10	7	17	54	....	....	....	....	....
	Moose Jaw	WHL	39	13	26	39	44	....	....	....	....	....
2007-08	Moose Jaw	WHL	72	31	54	85	116	6	1	1	2	8
	Providence Bruins	AHL	5	2	0	2	2	4	1	0	1	0

KNYAZEV, Igor (kuh-NYA-zhev, EE-gohr) PHX.

Defense. Shoots left. 6', 208 lbs. Born, Elektrostal, USSR, January 27, 1983.
(Carolina's 1st choice, 15th overall, in 2001 Entry Draft).

			Regular Season					Playoffs				
Season	Club	League	GP	G	A	Pts	PIM	GP	G	A	Pts	PIM
99-2000	Spartak Moscow 2	Russia-3	13	2	4	6	74	....	....	....	....	....
	Spartak Moscow	Russia-2	26	1	1	2	6	....	....	....	....	....
2000-01	Spartak Moscow	Russia-2	53	6	5	11	101	....	....	....	....	....
2001-02	Spartak Moscow	Russia	3	0	0	0	8	....	....	....	....	....
	Spartak Moscow 2	Russia-3	2	0	1	1	0	....	....	....	....	....
	Ak Bars Kazan	Russia	14	0	1	1	4	3	0	0	0	0
2002-03	Lowell	AHL	68	2	5	7	68	....	....	....	....	....
2003-04	Springfield Falcons	AHL	72	1	6	7	61	....	....	....	....	....
2004-05	Voskresensk	Russia	29	0	2	2	57	....	....	....	....	....
2005-06	Mytischi	Russia	21	3	1	4	36	....	....	....	....	....
2006-07	Dynamo Moscow	Russia	14	0	2	2	22	....	....	....	....	....
	Vityaz Chekhov	Russia	12	0	0	0	82	3	0	0	0	2
2007-08	MVD	Russia	8	0	2	2	6	3	0	2	2	2

Traded to **Phoenix** by **Carolina** with David Tanabe for Danny Markov and Edmonton's 3rd round choice (previously acquired, later traded to NY Rangers - NY Rangers selected Billy Ryan) in 2004 Entry Draft, June 21, 2003. Signed as a free agent by **Voskresensk** (Russia), September, 2004.

KOHN, Dustin (KOHN, DUHS-tihn) NYI

Defense. Shoots left. 6'2", 182 lbs. Born, Edmonton, Alta., February 2, 1987.
(NY Islanders' 2nd choice, 46th overall, in 2005 Entry Draft).

			Regular Season					Playoffs				
Season	Club	League	GP	G	A	Pts	PIM	GP	G	A	Pts	PIM
2003-04	Calgary Hitmen	WHL	52	3	6	9	13	7	0	1	1	2
2004-05	Calgary Hitmen	WHL	71	8	35	43	61	12	0	4	4	6
2005-06	Calgary Hitmen	WHL	38	2	12	14	20	....	....	....	....	....
	Brandon	WHL	31	2	13	15	30	6	0	4	4	10
	Bridgeport	AHL	2	0	0	0	0	....	....	....	....	....
2006-07	Brandon	WHL	61	5	45	50	77	11	1	8	9	18
2007-08	Bridgeport	AHL	62	3	9	12	28	....	....	....	....	....

KOLARIK, Chad (koh-LAHR-ihk, CHAD) PHX.

Center. Shoots right. 5'10", 175 lbs. Born, Abington, PA, January 26, 1986.
(Phoenix's 7th choice, 199th overall, in 2004 Entry Draft).

			Regular Season					Playoffs				
Season	Club	League	GP	G	A	Pts	PIM	GP	G	A	Pts	PIM
2002-03	USNTDP	U-17	21	14	10	24	4	....	....	....	....	....
	USNTDP	NAHL	44	16	22	38	43	....	....	....	....	....
2003-04	USNTDP	U-18	45	18	20	38	16	....	....	....	....	....
	USNTDP	NAHL	10	3	4	7	4	....	....	....	....	....
2004-05	U. of Michigan	CCHA	42	18	17	35	53	....	....	....	....	....
2005-06	U. of Michigan	CCHA	41	12	26	38	30	....	....	....	....	....
2006-07	U. of Michigan	CCHA	41	18	27	45	24	....	....	....	....	....
2007-08	U. of Michigan	CCHA	39	30	26	56	24	....	....	....	....	....
	San Antonio	AHL	....	....	....	....	....	7	4	2	6	0

CCHA First All-Star Team (2008) • NCAA West Second All-American Team (2008)

KOLOSOV, Sergei (KOH-leh-sawf, SAIR-gay) DET.

Defense. Shoots left. 6'4", 187 lbs. Born, Novopolotsk, USSR, May 22, 1986.
(Detroit's 3rd choice, 151st overall, in 2004 Entry Draft).

			Regular Season					Playoffs				
Season	Club	League	GP	G	A	Pts	PIM	GP	G	A	Pts	PIM
2003-04	Dynamo Minsk	Belarus	STATISTICS NOT AVAILABLE									
2004-05	Dynamo Minsk	BelOpen	37	2	6	8	24	....	....	....	....	....
	Yunost-Minsk	BelOpen	1	0	0	0	2	9	0	0	0	4
2005-06	Cedar Rapids	USHL	50	2	8	10	66	8	0	0	0	10
2006-07	Cedar Rapids	USHL	51	1	10	11	79	5	0	0	0	4
2007-08	Dynamo Minsk	Belarus	55	5	9	14	83					

KOLTSOV, Ivan (kohlt-SAHV, ee-VAHN) EDM.

Defense. Shoots left. 6'2", 182 lbs. Born, Cherepovets, USSR, March 7, 1984.
(Edmonton's 6th choice, 106th overall, in 2002 Entry Draft).

			Regular Season					Playoffs				
Season	Club	League	GP	G	A	Pts	PIM	GP	G	A	Pts	PIM
2001-02	Cherepovets 2	Russia-3	27	2	2	4	24	....	....	....	....	....
2002-03	Leninogorsk	Russia-2	1	0	1	1	2	....	....	....	....	....
	Cherepovets 2	Russia-3	34	4	7	11	26	....	....	....	....	....
2003-04	Cherepovets 2	Russia-3	14	2	2	4	20	....	....	....	....	....
2004-05	HK Lipetsk	Russia-2	10	2	0	2	2	....	....	....	....	....
	HK Belgorod	Russia-2	30	1	2	3	32	....	....	....	....	....
2005-06	Dizel Penza	Russia-2	40	0	4	4	22	8	0	0	0	4
2006-07	Mechel	Russia-2	17	0	1	1	12	....	....	....	....	....
2007-08			DID NOT PLAY									

KOLTSOV, Kirill (kohlt-SAHV, kih-RIHL) VAN.

Defense. Shoots left. 5'11", 183 lbs. Born, Chelyabinsk, USSR, February 1, 1983.
(Vancouver's 1st choice, 49th overall, in 2002 Entry Draft).

			Regular Season					Playoffs				
Season	Club	League	GP	G	A	Pts	PIM	GP	G	A	Pts	PIM
1998-99	Streetsville Derbys	OPJHL	20	5	7	12	4	....	....	....	....	....
99-2000	Omsk 2	Russia-3	27	0	7	7	30	....	....	....	....	....
	Avangard Omsk	Russia	2	0	0	0	0	....	....	....	....	....
2000-01	Avangard Omsk	Russia	39	0	1	1	20	16	1	3	4	12
2001-02	Avangard Omsk	Russia	41	1	5	6	34	11	1	0	1	8
2002-03	Avangard Omsk	Russia	45	4	8	12	54	12	1	3	4	8
2003-04	Manitoba Moose	AHL	74	7	25	32	62	....	....	....	....	....
2004-05	Manitoba Moose	AHL	28	3	14	17	42	....	....	....	....	....
	Avangard Omsk	Russia	22	2	2	4	46	10	0	1	1	18
2005-06	Avangard Omsk	Russia	43	9	8	17	98	13	4	5	9	10
2006-07	Avangard Omsk	Russia	51	9	31	40	46	9	3	3	6	12
2007-08	Ufa	Russia	50	5	18	23	42	11	0	6	6	6

KORNEEV, Konstantin (kor-NEE-ehv, KAWN-stan-tihn) MTL.

Defense. Shoots right. 5'11", 181 lbs. Born, Moscow, USSR, June 5, 1984.
(Montreal's 6th choice, 275th overall, in 2002 Entry Draft).

			Regular Season					Playoffs				
Season	Club	League	GP	G	A	Pts	PIM	GP	G	A	Pts	PIM
99-2000	Krylja Sovetov 2	Russia-3	1	0	0	0	0	....	....	....	....	....
2000-01	Russia Jr.	Exhib.	12	0	4	4	10	....	....	....	....	....
2001-02	Krylja Sovetov 2	Russia-3	26	9	19	28	44	....	....	....	....	....
	Krylja Sovetov	Russia	4	0	2	2	0	2	0	0	0	2
2002-03	Krylja Sovetov	Russia	49	2	8	10	28	....	....	....	....	....
2003-04	Ak Bars Kazan	Russia	55	1	4	5	8	8	0	1	1	2
2004-05	Ak Bars Kazan 2	Russia-3	....	6	16	22	....	....	....	....	....	....
	Ak Bars Kazan	Russia	35	0	4	4	10	1	0	0	0	0
2005-06	Ak Bars Kazan	Russia	30	1	3	4	14	4	0	0	0	0
2006-07	CSKA Moscow	Russia	54	8	14	22	40	12	2	4	6	6
2007-08	CSKA Moscow	Russia	57	6	18	24	52	6	0	1	1	0

KOROSTIN, Sergei (koh-ROH-stihn, SAIR-gay) DAL.

Right wing. Shoots left. 5'11", 180 lbs. Born, Prokopjevsk, USSR, July 5, 1989.
(Dallas' 2nd choice, 64th overall, in 2007 Entry Draft).

			Regular Season					Playoffs				
Season	Club	League	GP	G	A	Pts	PIM	GP	G	A	Pts	PIM
2005-06	Dyn'o Moscow 2	Russia-3	STATISTICS NOT AVAILABLE									
	Dynamo Moscow	Russia	1	0	0	0	0	....	....	....	....	....
2006-07	Dyn'o Moscow 2	Russia-3	STATISTICS NOT AVAILABLE									
	Dynamo Moscow	Russia	7	0	0	0	8	....	....	....	....	....
2007-08	Dynamo Moscow	Russia	2	0	0	0	2	....	....	....	....	....
	Prokopjevsk	Russia-3	2	2	2	4	0	....	....	....	....	....
	Texas Tornado	NAHL	19	8	10	18	12	3	2	0	2	2

KOSMACHEV, Dmitry (kaws-ma-CHEHV, dih-MEE-tree) CBJ

Defense. Shoots right. 6'3", 209 lbs. Born, Nizhny Novgorod, USSR, June 7, 1985.
(Columbus' 3rd choice, 71st overall, in 2003 Entry Draft).

			Regular Season					Playoffs				
Season	Club	League	GP	G	A	Pts	PIM	GP	G	A	Pts	PIM
2001-02	HK CSKA 2	Russia-3	6	1	0	1	2	....	....	....	....	....
	HK CSKA Moscow	Russia-2	49	0	1	1	12	....	....	....	....	....
2002-03	CSKA Moscow	Russia	27	0	0	0	2	....	....	....	....	....
2003-04	CSKA Moscow	Russia	34	0	2	2	12	....	....	....	....	....
2004-05	Nizhny Novgorod	Russia-2	34	3	4	7	22	15	0	1	1	0
2005-06	Mytischi	Russia	38	2	2	4	14	9	0	0	0	4
	Kristall Elektrostal	Russia-3	STATISTICS NOT AVAILABLE									
2006-07	Mytischi	Russia	32	0	0	0	18	9	0	0	0	2
2007-08	Mytischi	Russia	56	0	6	6	34	4	0	0	0	2

KOSTKA, Mike (KOHST-kuh, MIGHK) BUF.

Defense. Shoots right. 6'2", 210 lbs. Born, Ajax, Ont., November 28, 1985.

			Regular Season					Playoffs				
Season	Club	League	GP	G	A	Pts	PIM	GP	G	A	Pts	PIM
2001-02	Ajax Axemen	OPJHL	19	1	4	5	8	....	....	....	....	....
2002-03	Ajax Axemen	OPJHL	39	4	11	15	32	....	....	....	....	....
2003-04	Aurora Tigers	OPJHL	42	9	27	36	4	....	....	....	....	....
2004-05	Massachusetts	H-East	32	1	5	6	14	....	....	....	....	....
2005-06	Massachusetts	H-East	36	2	6	8	20	....	....	....	....	....
2006-07	Massachusetts	H-East	39	3	15	18	20	....	....	....	....	....
2007-08	Massachusetts	H-East	36	9	12	21	20	....	....	....	....	....
	Rochester	AHL	1	0	0	0	2	....	....	....	....	....

Signed as a free agent by **Buffalo**, March 25, 2008.

KOZEK, Andrew (KOH-zehk, AN-droo) ATL.

Left wing. Shoots left. 5'11", 190 lbs. Born, Revelstoke, B.C., May 26, 1986.
(Atlanta's 4th choice, 53rd overall, in 2005 Entry Draft).

			Regular Season					Playoffs				
Season	Club	League	GP	G	A	Pts	PIM	GP	G	A	Pts	PIM
2003-04	South Surrey	BCHL	58	19	22	41	67	....	....	....	....	....
2004-05	South Surrey	BCHL	60	48	49	97	81	....	....	....	....	....
2005-06	North Dakota	WCHA	46	7	6	13	22	....	....	....	....	....
2006-07	North Dakota	WCHA	41	5	6	11	12	....	....	....	....	....
2007-08	North Dakota	WCHA	42	18	3	21	18	....	....	....	....	....

KRIKUNOV, Ilia (krih-koo-NAWF, IHL-yah) VAN.

Left wing. Shoots left. 5'11", 169 lbs. Born, Elektrostal, USSR, February 27, 1984.
(Vancouver's 8th choice, 223rd overall, in 2002 Entry Draft).

			Regular Season					Playoffs				
Season	Club	League	GP	G	A	Pts	PIM	GP	G	A	Pts	PIM
2000-01	Elektrostal 2	Russia-3	4	0	0	0	2	....	....	....	....	....
2001-02	Elektrostal 2	Russia-3	5	3	6	9	4	....	....	....	....	....
	Elektrostal	Russia-2	48	12	10	22	28	....	....	....	....	....
2002-03	Elektrostal	Russia-2	48	19	9	28	34	....	....	....	....	....
2003-04	Voskresensk	Russia	50	10	9	19	14	....	....	....	....	....
2004-05	Voskresensk	Russia	58	9	14	23	20	....	....	....	....	....
2005-06	Mytischi	Russia	46	10	5	15	57	8	1	1	2	2
	Kristall Elektrostal	Russia-3		STATISTICS NOT AVAILABLE								
2006-07	Mytischi	Russia	48	9	6	15	56	9	2	1	3	12
2007-08	Mytischi	Russia	34	7	12	19	18	5	1	1	2	4

KRISTO, Danny (KRIHS-toh, DAN-ee) MTL.

Right wing. Shoots right. 5'11", 176 lbs. Born, Edina, MN, June 18, 1990.
(Montreal's 1st choice, 56th overall, in 2008 Entry Draft).

			Regular Season					Playoffs				
Season	Club	League	GP	G	A	Pts	PIM	GP	G	A	Pts	PIM
2006-07	USNTDP	U-17	14	4	5	9	0	....	....	....	....	....
	USNTDP	NAHL	39	8	10	18	34	6	0	1	1	2
2007-08	USNTDP	U-18	43	18	14	32	18	....	....	....	....	....
	USNTDP	NAHL	14	4	4	8	6	....	....	....	....	....

• Signed Letter of Intent to attend **University of North Dakota** (WCHA) in fall of 2009.

KRUEGER, Justin (KROO-guhr, JUHS-tihn) CAR.

Defense. Shoots right. 6'2", 205 lbs. Born, Dusseldorf, West Germany, October 6, 1986.
(Carolina's 6th choice, 213th overall, in 2006 Entry Draft).

			Regular Season					Playoffs				
Season	Club	League	GP	G	A	Pts	PIM	GP	G	A	Pts	PIM
2002-03	HC Davos Jr.	Swiss-Jr.	12	0	0	0	4	2	0	0	0	0
2003-04	HC Davos Jr.	Swiss-Jr.	33	2	0	2	14	....	....	....	....	....
2004-05	HC Davos Jr.	Swiss-Jr.	38	5	12	17	76	4	1	2	3	2
2005-06	Penticton Vees	BCHL	55	7	15	22	25	....	....	....	....	....
2006-07	Cornell Big Red	ECAC	31	1	5	6	24	....	....	....	....	....
2007-08	Cornell Big Red	ECAC	35	4	5	9	33	....	....	....	....	....

KRYSANOV, Anton (KREE-sa-nahf, AN-tawn) PHX.

Center. Shoots left. 6'3", 198 lbs. Born, Togliatti, USSR, March 25, 1987.
(Phoenix's 4th choice, 148th overall, in 2005 Entry Draft).

			Regular Season					Playoffs				
Season	Club	League	GP	G	A	Pts	PIM	GP	G	A	Pts	PIM
2002-03	Lada Togliatti 2	Russia-3	9	1	3	4	2	....	....	....	....	....
2003-04	Lada Togliatti 2	Russia-3	18	2	3	5	2	....	....	....	....	....
2004-05	Lada Togliatti 2	Russia-3	34	13	13	26	32	....	....	....	....	....
	Lada Togliatti	Russia	15	1	0	1	2	....	....	....	....	....
2005-06	Lada Togliatti	Russia	46	3	3	6	24	8	0	0	0	2
2006-07	Lada Togliatti	Russia	48	1	15	16	14	3	0	0	0	4
2007-08	Lada Togliatti 2	Russia-3	2	2	1	3	2	....	....	....	....	....
	Lada Togliatti	Russia	54	9	11	20	22	4	0	1	1	0

KRYUKOV, Artem (KREE-oo-kahf, AHR-tehm) BUF.

Center. Shoots left. 6'3", 180 lbs. Born, Novosibirsk, USSR, March 5, 1982.
(Buffalo's 1st choice, 15th overall, in 2000 Entry Draft).

			Regular Season					Playoffs				
Season	Club	League	GP	G	A	Pts	PIM	GP	G	A	Pts	PIM
1997-98	Torpedo Yaroslavl	Russia	7	0	0	0	2	....	....	....	....	....
1998-99	Yaroslavl 2	Russia-3	20	2	2	4	6	....	....	....	....	....
99-2000	Yaroslavl 2	Russia-3	14	1	1	2	12	....	....	....	....	....
	Torpedo Yaroslavl	Russia	3	0	0	0	4	....	....	....	....	....
2000-01	Yaroslavl 2	Russia-3	6	0	0	0	2	11	0	0	0	8
	SKA St. Petersburg	Russia	14	0	2	2	14	....	....	....	....	....
2001-02	Yaroslavl	Russia	15	1	3	4	10	6	1	0	1	8
2002-03	Sibir Novosibirsk	Russia	9	0	0	0	27	....	....	....	....	....
2003-04	Yaroslavl 2	Russia-3	30	5	4	9	26	....	....	....	....	....
	Yaroslavl	Russia	4	0	2	2	0	....	....	....	....	....
2004-05	Yaroslavl	Russia	60	8	9	17	44	7	1	0	1	4
2005-06	Yaroslavl	Russia	33	1	2	3	42	1	0	0	0	0
	Yaroslavl 2	Russia-3	6	3	3	6	18	....	....	....	....	....
2006-07	Vityaz Chekhov	Russia	12	0	0	0	20	....	....	....	....	....
	Yaroslavl 2	Russia-3	13	4	10	14	10	....	....	....	....	....
	Yaroslavl	Russia	19	1	3	4	20	....	....	....	....	....
2007-08	SKA St. Petersburg	Russia	51	7	8	15	54	9	0	2	2	8

KUBALIK, Tomas (koo-BAHL-ihk, TAW-mahsh) CBJ

Right wing. Shoots right. 6'2", 189 lbs. Born, Plzen, Czech., May 1, 1990.
(Columbus' 6th choice, 135th overall, in 2008 Entry Draft).

			Regular Season					Playoffs				
Season	Club	League	GP	G	A	Pts	PIM	GP	G	A	Pts	PIM
2003-04	HC Plzen U17	CzR-U17	4	0	0	0	0	....	....	....	....	....
2004-05	HC Plzen U17	CzR-U17	37	4	1	5	18	....	....	....	....	....
2005-06	HC Plzen U17	CzR-U17	35	26	21	47	91	6	1	5	6	16
	HC Plzen Jr.	CzRep-Jr.	5	1	2	3	6	....	....	....	....	....
2006-07	HC Plzen U17	CzR-U17	2	4	1	5	6	8	5	5	10	30
	HC Plzen Jr.	CzRep-Jr.	34	23	15	38	76	3	1	2	3	24
	Plzen	CzRep	23	1	0	1	18	....	....	....	....	....
2007-08	HC Plzen Jr.	CzRep-Jr.	22	8	13	21	50	5	1	3	4	22
	Beroun	CzRep-2	7	0	0	0	2	....	....	....	....	....
	Plzen	CzRep	20	2	1	3	8	1	0	0	0	0

KUDELKA, Tomas (koo-DEHL-kah, TAW-mahsh) OTT.

Defense. Shoots left. 6'2", 198 lbs. Born, Gottwaldov, Czech., March 10, 1987.
(Ottawa's 6th choice, 136th overall, in 2005 Entry Draft).

			Regular Season					Playoffs				
Season	Club	League	GP	G	A	Pts	PIM	GP	G	A	Pts	PIM
2002-03	HC Zlin U17	CzR-U17	45	1	16	17	28	3	1	0	1	12
2003-04	HC Zlin U17	CzR-U17	1	0	0	0	2	3	0	0	0	0
	HC Zlin Jr.	CzRep-Jr.	51	1	12	13	95	7	0	0	0	0
	HC Hame Zlin	CzRep	3	0	0	0	0	....	....	....	....	....
2004-05	HC Zlin Jr.	CzRep-Jr.	38	9	8	17	38	....	....	....	....	....
	HC Hame Zlin	CzRep	4	0	0	0	6	....	....	....	....	....
2005-06	Lethbridge	WHL	64	6	25	31	77	6	1	1	2	12
	Binghamton	AHL	5	0	0	0	4	....	....	....	....	....
2006-07	Lethbridge	WHL	59	14	27	41	74	....	....	....	....	....
	Binghamton	AHL	11	1	2	3	8	....	....	....	....	....
2007-08	Binghamton	AHL	35	1	1	2	17	....	....	....	....	....
	Elmira Jackals	ECHL	23	5	14	19	26	1	0	0	0	0

KUGRYSHEV, Dmitry (koo-GRIH-shev, dih-MEE-tree) WSH.

Right wing. Shoots right. 5'11", 185 lbs. Born, Balakovo, USSR, January 18, 1990.
(Washington's 4th choice, 58th overall, in 2008 Entry Draft).

			Regular Season					Playoffs				
Season	Club	League	GP	G	A	Pts	PIM	GP	G	A	Pts	PIM
2005-06	CSKA Moscow 2	Russia-3		STATISTICS NOT AVAILABLE								
2006-07	CSKA Moscow 2	Russia-3		STATISTICS NOT AVAILABLE								
2007-08	CSKA Moscow 2	Russia-3	29	25	25	50	60	7	5	6	11	6

KUKUSHKIN, Sergei (koo-KOOSH-kihn, SAIR-gay) DAL.

Center. Shoots left. 6'2", 187 lbs. Born, Minsk, USSR, July 24, 1985.
(Dallas' 8th choice, 218th overall, in 2004 Entry Draft).

			Regular Season					Playoffs				
Season	Club	League	GP	G	A	Pts	PIM	GP	G	A	Pts	PIM
2003-04	Yunost Minsk	Belarus		STATISTICS NOT AVAILABLE								
2004-05	N.E. Jr. Falcons	EJHL	21	9	13	22	30	....	....	....	....	....
	Indiana Ice	USHL	19	1	2	3	50	....	....	....	....	....
2005-06	Kapitan Stupino	Russia-2	45	21	11	32	67	8	4	3	7	10
2006-07	Dynamo Moscow	Russia	5	1	1	2	8	....	....	....	....	....
	Lada Togliatti	Russia	25	4	1	5	12	1	0	0	0	2
2007-08	Metallurg Zhlobin	Belarus	39	16	13	29	50	....	....	....	....	....

KULDA , Arturs (KOOL-da, AHR-tuhrs) ATL.

Defense. Shoots left. 6'2", 200 lbs. Born, Riga, Latvia, July 25, 1988.
(Atlanta's 7th choice, 200th overall, in 2006 Entry Draft).

			Regular Season					Playoffs				
Season	Club	League	GP	G	A	Pts	PIM	GP	G	A	Pts	PIM
2003-04	Prizma/Riga 86	Latvia	11	0	0	0	8	2	0	0	0	0
2004-05	CSKA Moscow 2	Russia-3		STATISTICS NOT AVAILABLE								
2005-06	CSKA Moscow 2	Russia-3	44	5	12	17	....	....	....	....	....	....
2006-07	Peterborough	OHL	58	2	9	11	83	....	....	....	....	....
2007-08	Peterborough	OHL	55	7	27	34	87	5	1	3	4	6
	Chicago Wolves	AHL	5	0	1	1	10	22	1	5	6	32

KULEMIN, Nikolai (koo-LAY-mihn, NIH-koh-ligh) TOR.

Wing. Shoots left. 6'1", 183 lbs. Born, Magnitogorsk, USSR, July 14, 1986.
(Toronto's 2nd choice, 44th overall, in 2006 Entry Draft).

			Regular Season					Playoffs				
Season	Club	League	GP	G	A	Pts	PIM	GP	G	A	Pts	PIM
2003-04	Magnitogorsk 2	Russia-3	43	8	18	26	91	....	....	....	....	....
2004-05	Magnitogorsk 2	Russia-3	43	9	13	22	44	....	....	....	....	....
2005-06	Magnitogorsk 2	Russia-3	4	3	1	4	6	....	....	....	....	....
	Magnitogorsk	Russia	31	5	7	12	8	11	2	4	6	6
2006-07	Magnitogorsk	Russia	54	27	12	39	42	15	10	1	11	10
2007-08	Magnitogorsk	Russia	57	21	12	33	63	11	2	2	4	29

KULYASH, Denis (kuh-L'YASH, DEH-nihs) NSH.

Defense. Shoots left. 6'3", 199 lbs. Born, Omsk, USSR, May 31, 1983.
(Nashville's 9th choice, 243rd overall, in 2004 Entry Draft).

			Regular Season					Playoffs				
Season	Club	League	GP	G	A	Pts	PIM	GP	G	A	Pts	PIM
2003-04	CSK VVS Samara 2	Russia-3		STATISTICS NOT AVAILABLE								
	CSKA Moscow	Russia	10	1	0	1	8	....	....	....	....	....
2004-05	CSKA Moscow	Russia	59	8	10	18	58	....	....	....	....	....
2005-06	Dynamo Moscow	Russia	44	12	5	17	117	4	0	2	2	6
2006-07	Dynamo Moscow	Russia	48	3	9	12	58	2	0	0	0	2
2007-08	CSKA Moscow	Russia	53	9	13	22	79	6	1	1	2	34

KUNDRATEK, Tomas (kuhn-DRAT-ehk, TAW-mahsh) NYR

Defense. Shoots right. 6'1", 190 lbs. Born, Prerov, Czech., December 26, 1989.
(NY Rangers' 4th choice, 90th overall, in 2008 Entry Draft).

			Regular Season					Playoffs				
Season	Club	League	GP	G	A	Pts	PIM	GP	G	A	Pts	PIM
2003-04	HC Prerov U17	CzR-U17	6	0	0	0	0	....	....	....	....	....
2004-05	HC Prerov U17	CzR-U17	38	2	7	9	26	4	0	1	1	4
2005-06	HC Trinec U17	CzR-U17	39	5	13	18	96	2	0	1	1	10
	HC Trinec Jr.	CzRep-Jr.	12	1	1	2	16	7	1	1	2	4
2006-07	HC Trinec Jr.	CzRep-Jr.	33	4	13	17	93	3	1	1	2	10
	HC Ocelari Trinec	CzRep	22	0	1	1	4	4	0	0	0	6
2007-08	HC Trinec Jr.	CzRep-Jr.	14	3	6	9	28	....	....	....	....	....
	Prostejov	CzRep-2	15	1	0	1	10	....	....	....	....	....
	HC Havirov	CzRep-2	2	0	0	0	2	....	....	....	....	....
	HC Ocelari Trinec	CzRep	14	0	1	1	10	7	0	2	2	8

KUNES, Tim (KOONZ, TIHM) **CAR.**

Defense. Shoots left. 6'1", 170 lbs. Born, Red Bank, NJ, February 12, 1987.
(Carolina's 6th choice, 145th overall, in 2005 Entry Draft).

			Regular Season					Playoffs				
Season	**Club**	**League**	**GP**	**G**	**A**	**Pts**	**PIM**	**GP**	**G**	**A**	**Pts**	**PIM**
2003-04	N.E. Jr. Falcons	EJHL	45	4	19	23	20	....	....	....	....	....
2004-05	N.E. Jr. Falcons	EJHL	50	12	28	40	51	....	....	....	....	....
2005-06	Boston College	H-East	28	1	3	4	31	....	....	....	....	....
2006-07	Boston College	H-East	27	1	4	5	6	....	....	....	....	....
2007-08	Boston College	H-East	43	1	7	8	6	....	....	....	....	....

KVETON, David (KVEH-tuhn, DAY-vihd) **NYR**

Right wing. Shoots left. 6', 190 lbs. Born, Novy Jicin, Czech., January 3, 1988.
(NY Rangers' 4th choice, 104th overall, in 2006 Entry Draft).

			Regular Season					Playoffs				
Season	**Club**	**League**	**GP**	**G**	**A**	**Pts**	**PIM**	**GP**	**G**	**A**	**Pts**	**PIM**
2003-04	HC Vsetin U17	CzR-U17	14	9	11	20	35	....	....	....	....	....
	HC Vsetin Jr.	CzRep-Jr.	41	12	11	23	14	5	2	3	5	2
	TJ Novy Jicin	CzRep-3	1	0	1	1	0	....	....	....	....	....
	HC Vsetin	CzRep	1	0	0	0	0	....	....	....	....	....
2004-05	HC Vsetin U17	CzR-U17	1	1	0	1	0	....	....	....	....	....
	HC Vsetin Jr.	CzRep-Jr.	36	21	27	48	66	8	6	5	11	4
	TJ Novy Jicin	CzRep-3	7	0	1	1	6	....	....	....	....	....
	HC Vsetin	CzRep	6	1	0	1	0	....	....	....	....	....
2005-06	HC Vsetin Jr.	CzRep-Jr.	1	1	1	2	0	1	0	1	1	0
	HC Sareza Ostrava	CzRep-2	7	2	1	3	2	....	....	....	....	....
	HC Vsetin	CzRep	45	6	4	10	18	....	....	....	....	....
	TJ Novy Jicin	CzRep-3	....	....	....	....	....	5	5	0	5	18
	HC Vsetin	CzRep-Q	....	....	....	....	....	3	1	1	2	2
2006-07	Gatineau	QMJHL	31	5	27	32	17	5	0	0	0	4
	HC Vsetin	CzRep	19	2	0	2	8	....	....	....	....	....
2007-08	HC Ocelari Trinec	CzRep	28	10	5	15	10	....	....	....	....	....

KYTNAR, Milan (KIHT-nahr, MEE-lan) **EDM.**

Center. Shoots left. 6', 180 lbs. Born, Topolcany, Czech., May 19, 1989.
(Edmonton's 5th choice, 127th overall, in 2007 Entry Draft).

			Regular Season					Playoffs				
Season	**Club**	**League**	**GP**	**G**	**A**	**Pts**	**PIM**	**GP**	**G**	**A**	**Pts**	**PIM**
2003-04	Topolcany U18	Svk-U18	42	17	22	39	90	....	....	....	....	....
2004-05	Topolcany U18	Svk-U18	53	36	65	101	105	....	....	....	....	....
	Topolcany Jr.	Slovak-Jr.	10	2	2	4	8	....	....	....	....	....
2005-06	HK Trnava U18	Svk-U18	30	18	23	41	106	....	....	....	....	....
	HK Trnava Jr.	Slovak-Jr.	12	1	2	3	20	....	....	....	....	....
	Topolcany U18	Svk-U18	8	4	4	8	4	....	....	....	....	....
	Topolcany Jr.	Slovak-Jr.	6	6	4	10	8	....	....	....	....	....
2006-07	HC Topolcany U18	Svk-U18	53	37	54	91	84	....	....	....	....	....
	HC Topolcany	Slovak-2	22	4	7	11	53	5	1	1	2	4
2007-08	Kelowna Rockets	WHL	62	9	13	22	66	7	0	0	0	4

LAAKSO, Teemu (LAK-soh, TEE-moo) **NSH.**

Defense. Shoots right. 6'1", 211 lbs. Born, Tuusula, Finland, August 27, 1987.
(Nashville's 2nd choice, 78th overall, in 2005 Entry Draft).

			Regular Season					Playoffs				
Season	**Club**	**League**	**GP**	**G**	**A**	**Pts**	**PIM**	**GP**	**G**	**A**	**Pts**	**PIM**
2002-03	KJT Jarvenpaa U18	Fin-U18	18	2	5	7	24	....	....	....	....	....
2003-04	HIFK Helsinki Jr.	Fin-Jr.	41	3	6	9	20	3	0	1	1	0
2004-05	HIFK Helsinki U18	Fin-U18	....	....	....	....	....	1	0	0	0	0
	HIFK Helsinki Jr.	Fin-Jr.	20	5	4	9	18	....	....	....	....	....
	HIFK Helsinki	Finland	15	0	2	2	2	....	....	....	....	....
2005-06	HIFK Helsinki Jr.	Fin-Jr.	6	1	2	3	32	....	....	....	....	....
	Suomi U20	Finland-2	6	2	0	2	10	....	....	....	....	....
	HIFK Helsinki	Finland	47	2	1	3	20	8	1	0	1	0
2006-07	Suomi U20	Finland-2	2	0	1	1	4	....	....	....	....	....
	HIFK Helsinki	Finland	50	3	6	9	70	5	0	1	1	0
2007-08	HIFK Helsinki	Finland	53	3	7	10	40	7	0	0	0	2

LABRIE, Pierre-Cedric (la-BREE, pee-AIR-SHE-drihk) **VAN.**

Left wing. Shoots right. 6'2", 218 lbs. Born, Baie Comeau, Que., December 6, 1986.

			Regular Season					Playoffs				
Season	**Club**	**League**	**GP**	**G**	**A**	**Pts**	**PIM**	**GP**	**G**	**A**	**Pts**	**PIM**
2003-04	Coaticook	QJHL	46	13	12	25	96	....	....	....	....	....
	Quebec Remparts	QMJHL	1	0	0	0	0	....	....	....	....	....
2004-05	Coaticook	QJHL	15	3	4	7	59	....	....	....	....	....
2005-06	Restigouche Tigers	MJrHL	54	43	43	86	153	....	....	....	....	....
	Baie-Comeau	QMJHL	....	....	....	....	....	4	2	2	4	6
2006-07	Baie-Comeau	QMJHL	68	35	28	63	113	11	8	6	14	35
2007-08	Manitoba Moose	AHL	67	7	11	18	108	3	0	0	0	2

Signed as a free agent by **Vancouver**, July 3, 2007.

LACROIX, Maxime (luh-KWAH, max-EEM)

Left wing. Shoots left. 6', 195 lbs. Born, Quebec City, Que., June 5, 1987.
(Washington's 8th choice, 127th overall, in 2006 Entry Draft).

			Regular Season					Playoffs				
Season	**Club**	**League**	**GP**	**G**	**A**	**Pts**	**PIM**	**GP**	**G**	**A**	**Pts**	**PIM**
2003-04	St-Francois	QAAA	42	21	21	42	47	8	3	1	4	8
2004-05	Quebec Remparts	QMJHL	49	6	8	14	34	13	0	0	0	8
2005-06	Quebec Remparts	QMJHL	70	25	22	47	79	23	7	5	12	21
2006-07	Quebec Remparts	QMJHL	68	22	31	53	85	5	2	1	3	2
2007-08	Quebec Remparts	QMJHL	67	30	32	62	89	8	1	5	6	16
	Hershey Bears	AHL	....	....	....	....	....	2	1	0	1	0

LACROIX, Simon (luh-KWAH, see-MOHN) **NYI**

Defense. Shoots right. 6'2", 172 lbs. Born, Ottawa, Ont., May 29, 1989.
(NY Islanders' 5th choice, 196th overall, in 2007 Entry Draft).

			Regular Season					Playoffs				
Season	**Club**	**League**	**GP**	**G**	**A**	**Pts**	**PIM**	**GP**	**G**	**A**	**Pts**	**PIM**
2005-06	Cumberland	CJHL	65	6	13	19	90	....	....	....	....	....
2006-07	Shawinigan	QMJHL	60	11	27	38	66	4	0	2	2	6
2007-08	Shawinigan	QMJHL	52	5	29	34	41	5	1	3	4	6

QMJHL All-Rookie Team (2007)

LAGACE, Jacob (LEH-gah-see, JAY-kawb) **BUF.**

Left wing. Shoots left. 5'11", 190 lbs. Born, Beloeil, Que., January 9, 1990.
(Buffalo's 7th choice, 134th overall, in 2008 Entry Draft).

			Regular Season					Playoffs				
Season	**Club**	**League**	**GP**	**G**	**A**	**Pts**	**PIM**	**GP**	**G**	**A**	**Pts**	**PIM**
2005-06	C.A.-Girouord	QAAA	38	10	11	21	....	8	0	2	2	4
2006-07	C.A.-Girouord	QAAA	44	24	29	53	46	4	1	4	5	2
2007-08	Chicoutimi	QMJHL	67	23	39	62	40	6	3	2	5	7

QMJHL All-Rookie Team (2008)

LAGERSTROM, Tony (LA-guhr-struhm, TOH-nee) **CHI.**

Center. Shoots left. 6'1", 189 lbs. Born, Stockholm, Sweden, July 19, 1988.
(Chicago's 4th choice, 76th overall, in 2006 Entry Draft).

			Regular Season					Playoffs				
Season	**Club**	**League**	**GP**	**G**	**A**	**Pts**	**PIM**	**GP**	**G**	**A**	**Pts**	**PIM**
2003-04	Huddinge IK U18	Swe-U18	12	5	1	6	6	....	....	....	....	....
2004-05	Sodertalje SK U18	Swe-U18	2	3	2	5	4	1	0	0	0	0
	Sodertalje SK Jr.	Swe-Jr.	28	13	11	24	16	3	2	1	3	2
2005-06	Sodertalje SK U18	Swe-U18	7	9	5	14	2	1	0	0	0	0
	Sodertalje SK Jr.	Swe-Jr.	37	14	19	33	69	4	1	2	3	14
	Sodertalje SK	Sweden	1	0	0	0	0	....	....	....	....	....
2006-07	Sodertalje SK Jr.	Swe-Jr.	23	7	11	18	16	3	0	3	3	6
	Sodertalje SK	Sweden-2	36	0	1	1	2	....	....	....	....	....
2007-08	Sodertalje SK Jr.	Swe-Jr.	3	1	2	3	0	....	....	....	....	....
	Huddinge IK	Sweden-2	37	9	5	14	30	....	....	....	....	....

LAHTI, Janne (LAH-tee, yah-NAY)

Left wing. Shoots left. 6', 200 lbs. Born, Riihimaki, Finland, July 20, 1982.

			Regular Season					Playoffs				
Season	**Club**	**League**	**GP**	**G**	**A**	**Pts**	**PIM**	**GP**	**G**	**A**	**Pts**	**PIM**
1998-99	HPK U18	Fin-U18	36	10	6	16	18	....	....	....	....	....
99-2000	HPK U18	Fin-U18	12	5	7	12	2	....	....	....	....	....
	HPK Jr.	Fin-Jr.	18	6	5	11	8	....	....	....	....	....
2000-01	HPK Jr.	Fin-Jr.	35	9	11	20	16	....	....	....	....	....
2001-02	HPK Hameenlinna	Finland	36	1	0	1	2	4	0	0	0	0
	HPK Jr.	Fin-Jr.	22	22	11	33	18	4	1	3	4	2
2002-03	HPK Hameenlinna	Finland	17	1	0	1	2	1	0	0	0	0
	HPK Jr.	Fin-Jr.	22	23	19	42	35	....	....	....	....	....
2003-04	HPK Hameenlinna	Finland	43	14	6	20	26	8	1	0	1	0
2004-05	HPK Hameenlinna	Finland	52	6	9	15	22	8	2	2	4	4
	Haukat Jarvenpaa	Finland-2	4	2	2	4	2	....	....	....	....	....
2005-06	HPK Hameenlinna	Finland	51	9	13	22	30	13	5	4	9	6
2006-07	HPK Hameenlinna	Finland	56	20	14	34	87	9	8	1	9	4
2007-08	Hamilton Bulldogs	AHL	65	9	9	18	47	....	....	....	....	....

Signed as a free agent by **Montreal**, May 31, 2007.

LAJUNEN, Jani (LA-joo-nehn, YAH-nee) **NSH.**

Center. Shoots left. 6'1", 174 lbs. Born, Helsinki, Finland, June 16, 1990.
(Nashville's 6th choice, 201st overall, in 2008 Entry Draft).

			Regular Season					Playoffs				
Season	**Club**	**League**	**GP**	**G**	**A**	**Pts**	**PIM**	**GP**	**G**	**A**	**Pts**	**PIM**
2005-06	K-Vantaa U18	Fin-U18	2	0	0	0	0	....	....	....	....	....
2006-07	Blues Espoo U18	Fin-U18	28	5	12	17	20	6	1	1	2	4
2007-08	Blues Espoo U18	Fin-U18	1	1	0	1	2	4	2	2	4	0
	Blues Espoo Jr.	Fin-Jr.	25	4	10	14	14	3	0	0	0	0
	Blues Espoo	Finland	1	0	0	0	0					

LALIBERTE, David (la-LIH-buhr-tee, DAY-vihd) **PHI.**

Right wing. Shoots right. 6'1", 194 lbs. Born, St-Jean-Sur-Richelieu, Que., March 17, 1986.
(Philadelphia's 3rd choice, 124th overall, in 2004 Entry Draft).

			Regular Season					Playoffs				
Season	**Club**	**League**	**GP**	**G**	**A**	**Pts**	**PIM**	**GP**	**G**	**A**	**Pts**	**PIM**
2001-02	Antoine-Girouard	QAAA	41	21	21	42	14	15	8	9	17	6
2002-03	Montreal Rocket	QMJHL	66	15	14	29	10	6	3	0	3	2
2003-04	PEI Rocket	QMJHL	70	21	22	43	51	11	1	3	4	6
2004-05	PEI Rocket	QMJHL	41	23	13	36	36	....	....	....	....	....
2005-06	PEI Rocket	QMJHL	34	12	11	23	41	6	3	1	4	6
2006-07	PEI Rocket	QMJHL	68	50	48	98	86	7	5	4	9	4
2007-08	Philadelphia	AHL	27	3	6	9	13	....	....	....	....	....
	Wheeling Nailers	ECHL	27	10	14	24	16	....	....	....	....	....

LALONDE, Shawn (la-LAWND, SHAWN) **CHI.**

Defense. Shoots right. 6'1", 175 lbs. Born, Ottawa, Ont., March 10, 1990.
(Chicago's 2nd choice, 68th overall, in 2008 Entry Draft).

			Regular Season					Playoffs				
Season	**Club**	**League**	**GP**	**G**	**A**	**Pts**	**PIM**	**GP**	**G**	**A**	**Pts**	**PIM**
2005-06	Cumberland	Minor-ON	60	18	36	54	98	....	....	....	....	....
2006-07	Belleville Bulls	OHL	58	6	20	26	71	13	1	1	2	6
2007-08	Belleville Bulls	OHL	66	9	22	31	67	21	2	7	9	25

LAMMERS, John (LA-muhrs, JAWN) **DAL.**

Left wing. Shoots left. 5'11", 184 lbs. Born, Bowmanville, Ont., January 29, 1986.
(Dallas' 5th choice, 86th overall, in 2004 Entry Draft).

			Regular Season					Playoffs				
Season	**Club**	**League**	**GP**	**G**	**A**	**Pts**	**PIM**	**GP**	**G**	**A**	**Pts**	**PIM**
2001-02	Langley Bantams	Minor-BC	64	51	69	120	30	....	....	....	....	....
	Lethbridge	WHL	5	0	0	0	0	....	....	....	....	....
2002-03	Lethbridge	WHL	53	17	15	32	11	....	....	....	....	....
2003-04	Lethbridge	WHL	62	21	24	45	31	....	....	....	....	....
2004-05	Lethbridge	WHL	66	17	30	47	43	5	0	0	0	2
2005-06	Everett Silvertips	WHL	70	38	37	75	25	15	5	6	11	12
2006-07	Iowa Stars	AHL	52	6	8	14	14	....	....	....	....	....
	Idaho Steelheads	ECHL	9	2	2	4	4	22	7	12	19	2
2007-08	Iowa Stars	AHL	1	0	0	0	0	....	....	....	....	....
	Idaho Steelheads	ECHL	36	27	16	43	22	4	0	3	3	2
	Assat Pori	Finland	23	0	4	4	24	....	....	....	....	....

LANDRY, Jon (LAN-dree, JAWN) CBJ

Defense. Shoots right. 6', 193 lbs. Born, Lexington, MA, May 29, 1984.

			Regular Season					Playoffs				
Season	Club	League	GP	G	A	Pts	PIM	GP	G	A	Pts	PIM
2003-04	Holy Cross	AH	33	3	12	15	28	....	....	....	....	....
2004-05	Holy Cross	AH	35	3	12	15	52	....	....	....	....	....
2005-06	Holy Cross	AH	38	9	20	29	54	....	....	....	....	....
2006-07	Holy Cross	AH	27	9	18	27	54	....	....	....	....	....
	Augusta Lynx	ECHL	2	1	0	1	2	....	....	....	....	....
2007-08	Arizona Sundogs	CHL	60	9	33	42	70	17	3	6	9	14

AH First All-Star Team (2006, 2007)

Signed as a free agent by **Columbus**, March 19, 2007.

LANNON, Ryan (LA-nuhn, RIGH-uhn) PHX.

Defense. Shoots left. 6'1", 198 lbs. Born, Worcester, MA, December 14, 1982.
(Pittsburgh's 10th choice, 239th overall, in 2002 Entry Draft).

			Regular Season					Playoffs				
Season	Club	League	GP	G	A	Pts	PIM	GP	G	A	Pts	PIM
1998-99	USNTDP	NAHL	56	3	4	7	36	....	....	....	....	....
99-2000	Cushing	High-MA	STATISTICS NOT AVAILABLE									
2000-01	Cushing	High-MA	STATISTICS NOT AVAILABLE									
2001-02	Harvard Crimson	ECAC	34	0	2	2	38	....	....	....	....	....
2002-03	Harvard Crimson	ECAC	34	3	11	14	39	....	....	....	....	....
2003-04	Harvard Crimson	ECAC	35	0	9	9	36	....	....	....	....	....
2004-05	Harvard Crimson	ECAC	33	1	12	13	34	....	....	....	....	....
2005-06	Wilkes-Barre	AHL	74	2	8	10	65	11	0	0	0	8
2006-07	Wilkes-Barre	AHL	68	0	19	19	71	11	0	2	2	14
2007-08	Wilkes-Barre	AHL	75	3	10	13	29	23	1	6	7	2

Signed as a free agent by **Phoenix**, July 15, 2008.

LAPOINT, Derrick (luh-POYNT, DAIR-ihk) FLA.

Defense. Shoots left. 6'3", 175 lbs. Born, Eau Claire, MA, May 13, 1988.
(Florida's 4th choice, 116th overall, in 2006 Entry Draft).

			Regular Season					Playoffs				
Season	Club	League	GP	G	A	Pts	PIM	GP	G	A	Pts	PIM
2004-05	Eau Claire North	High-WI	23	9	28	37	14	....	....	....	....	....
2005-06	Eau Claire North	High-WI	23	6	26	32	34	....	....	....	....	....
2006-07	Green Bay	USHL	59	13	36	49	48	4	0	2	2	2
2007-08	North Dakota	WCHA	31	2	5	7	34	....	....	....	....	....

LARSEN, Philip (LAHR-suhn, FIHL-ihp) DAL.

Defense. Shoots right. 5'11", 185 lbs. Born, Esbjerg, Denmark, December 7, 1989.
(Dallas' 3rd choice, 149th overall, in 2008 Entry Draft).

			Regular Season					Playoffs				
Season	Club	League	GP	G	A	Pts	PIM	GP	G	A	Pts	PIM
2004-05	Esbjerg IK Jr.	Denmark-Jr.	10	1	0	1	2	....	....	....	....	....
2005-06	Rogle Jr.	Swe-Jr.	32	1	4	5	24	....	....	....	....	....
	Rogle	Sweden-2	13	0	0	0	0	....	....	....	....	....
2006-07	Frolunda U18	Swe-U18	3	1	2	3	2	4	2	1	3	8
	Frolunda Jr.	Swe-Jr.	37	3	15	18	50	8	0	1	1	6
	Frolunda	Sweden	5	0	0	0	0	....	....	....	....	....
2007-08	Frolunda Jr.	Swe-Jr.	8	1	4	5	12	7	0	4	4	6
	Boras HC	Sweden-2	24	5	5	10	32	....	....	....	....	....
	Frolunda	Sweden	16	0	0	0	2	....	....	....	....	....

LARSON, Nick (LAHR-suhn, NIHK-oh-las) CGY.

Left wing. Shoots left. 6'1", 193 lbs. Born, St.Paul, MN, November 14, 1989.
(Calgary's 4th choice, 108th overall, in 2008 Entry Draft).

			Regular Season					Playoffs				
Season	Club	League	GP	G	A	Pts	PIM	GP	G	A	Pts	PIM
2006-07	St. Thomas	High-MN	25	20	30	50	....	....	....	....	....	....
	Team Southeast	UMWEHL	11	5	6	11	....	....	....	....	....	....
2007-08	Waterloo	USHL	57	19	19	38	66	9	3	2	5	31

• Signed Letter of Intent to attend **University of Notre Dame** (CCHA) in fall of 2009.

LASU, Nicklas (LA-soo, NIHK-luhs) ATL.

Left wing. Shoots left. 5'11", 180 lbs. Born, Molndal, Sweden, September 16, 1989.
(Atlanta's 5th choice, 124th overall, in 2008 Entry Draft).

			Regular Season					Playoffs				
Season	Club	League	GP	G	A	Pts	PIM	GP	G	A	Pts	PIM
2005-06	Frolunda U18	Swe-U18	14	3	3	6	2	2	1	0	1	2
2006-07	Frolunda U18	Swe-U18	5	5	5	10	12	7	2	6	8	6
	Frolunda Jr.	Swe-Jr.	39	11	14	25	30	7	0	0	0	4
2007-08	Frolunda Jr.	Swe-Jr.	41	19	34	53	42	8	5	5	10	4
	Frolunda	Sweden	2	0	0	0	0	....	....	....	....	....

LATENDRESSE, Olivier (lah-TEHN-drehs, oh-LIHV-ee-ay) MTL.

Center. Shoots left. 5'10", 195 lbs. Born, LaSalle, Que., February 12, 1986.

			Regular Season					Playoffs				
Season	Club	League	GP	G	A	Pts	PIM	GP	G	A	Pts	PIM
2002-03	Val-d'Or Foreurs	QMJHL	55	11	14	25	22	8	0	2	2	0
2003-04	Val-d'Or Foreurs	QMJHL	53	19	46	65	44	7	1	5	6	14
2004-05	Val-d'Or Foreurs	QMJHL	68	27	47	74	34	....	....	....	....	....
2005-06	Val-d'Or Foreurs	QMJHL	70	41	84	125	83	4	5	2	7	2
2006-07	San Antonio	AHL	17	1	3	4	14	....	....	....	....	....
	Phoenix	ECHL	47	12	15	27	22	....	....	....	....	....
2007-08	San Antonio	AHL	7	1	2	3	25	....	....	....	....	....
	Arizona Sundogs	CHL	37	22	30	52	30	....	....	....	....	....
	Cincinnati	ECHL	24	7	28	35	29	22	7	12	19	30

Signed as a free agent by **Phoenix**, September 15, 2004. Traded to **Montreal** by **Phoenix** for Cory Urquhart, April 7, 2008.

LAVIN, Joseph (LA-vihn, JOH-sehf) CHI.

Defense. Shoots left. 6'1", 195 lbs. Born, Worcester, MA, July 17, 1989.
(Chicago's 6th choice, 126th overall, in 2007 Entry Draft).

			Regular Season					Playoffs				
Season	Club	League	GP	G	A	Pts	PIM	GP	G	A	Pts	PIM
2004-05	Boston Jr. Bruins	EmJHL	64	11	44	55	....	....	....	....	....	....
2005-06	USNTDP	U-17	19	2	1	3	30	....	....	....	....	....
	USNTDP	NAHL	37	8	10	18	16	12	3	2	5	4
2006-07	USNTDP	U-18	23	1	0	1	18	....	....	....	....	....
	USNTDP	NAHL	18	1	8	9	22	6	0	2	2	4
2007-08	Providence College	H-East	36	0	8	8	26	....	....	....	....	....

LAVRENTIEV, Anton (lahv-REHN-tee-yehv, AN-tawn) NSH.

Defense. Shoots right. 6'4", 196 lbs. Born, Kazan, USSR, August 25, 1983.
(Nashville's 7th choice, 178th overall, in 2001 Entry Draft).

			Regular Season					Playoffs				
Season	Club	League	GP	G	A	Pts	PIM	GP	G	A	Pts	PIM
2000-01	Ak Bars Kazan 2	Russia-3	STATISTICS NOT AVAILABLE									
2001-02	Sudbury Wolves	OHL	10	0	0	0	17	....	....	....	....	....
	Ak Bars Kazan 2	Russia-3	STATISTICS NOT AVAILABLE									
2002-03	Yuzhny Ural Orsk	Russia-2	13	0	1	1	14	....	....	....	....	....
2003-04	HK Rybinsk	Russia-2	31	2	1	3	49	....	....	....	....	....
2004-05	Novopolotsk	BelOpen	23	2	3	5	26	1	0	0	0	2
2005-06	Naber. Chelny	Russia-3	70	8	6	14	214	....	....	....	....	....
2006-07	Naber. Chelny	Russia-3	67	10	21	31	270	....	....	....	....	....
2007-08	Naber. Chelny	Russia-3	63	9	10	19	127	....	....	....	....	....

LAWRENCE, Chris (LOH-rehnts, KRIHS) T.B.

Center. Shoots right. 6'4", 199 lbs. Born, Toronto, Ont., February 5, 1987.
(Tampa Bay's 3rd choice, 89th overall, in 2005 Entry Draft).

			Regular Season					Playoffs				
Season	Club	League	GP	G	A	Pts	PIM	GP	G	A	Pts	PIM
2003-04	Sault Ste. Marie	OHL	62	7	6	13	34	....	....	....	....	....
2004-05	Sault Ste. Marie	OHL	68	11	40	51	57	7	3	3	6	4
2005-06	Sault Ste. Marie	OHL	29	3	14	17	31	....	....	....	....	....
	Mississauga	OHL	38	20	16	36	60	....	....	....	....	....
2006-07	Mississauga	OHL	64	47	41	88	113	5	3	1	4	14
2007-08	Norfolk Admirals	AHL	53	5	11	16	32	....	....	....	....	....

LAWSON, Kyle (LAW-suhn, KIGHL) CAR.

Defense. Shoots right. 5'11", 192 lbs. Born, Southfield, MI, January 11, 1987.
(Carolina's 9th choice, 198th overall, in 2005 Entry Draft).

			Regular Season					Playoffs				
Season	Club	League	GP	G	A	Pts	PIM	GP	G	A	Pts	PIM
2003-04	Det. Honeybaked	MWEHL	61	17	41	58	68	....	....	....	....	....
	Texarkana Bandits	NAHL	....	....	....	....	....	3	0	1	1	0
2004-05	USNTDP	U-18	23	2	12	14	6	....	....	....	....	....
	USNTDP	NAHL	8	1	3	4	0	....	....	....	....	....
2005-06	Tri-City Storm	USHL	49	9	13	22	40	1	0	0	0	0
2006-07	U. of Notre Dame	CCHA	38	4	15	19	14	....	....	....	....	....
2007-08	U. of Notre Dame	CCHA	45	5	21	26	36	....	....	....	....	....

CCHA All-Rookie Team (2007) • NCAA Championship All-Tournament Team (2008)

LEAVITT, Alex (LEH-viht, ALEHX)

Center. Shoots right. 5'10", 175 lbs. Born, Edmonton, Alta., January 31, 1984.

			Regular Season					Playoffs				
Season	Club	League	GP	G	A	Pts	PIM	GP	G	A	Pts	PIM
2001-02	U. of Wisconsin	WCHA	39	11	13	24	42	....	....	....	....	....
2002-03	U. of Wisconsin	WCHA	28	2	13	15	24	....	....	....	....	....
2003-04	Swift Current	WHL	71	27	41	68	67	5	2	2	4	8
2004-05	Swift Current	WHL	15	3	11	14	27	....	....	....	....	....
	Everett Silvertips	WHL	49	13	35	48	43	11	6	5	11	6
2005-06	Alaska Aces	ECHL	72	26	*65	*91	58	16	1	12	13	28
2006-07	Houston Aeros	AHL	23	2	9	11	14	....	....	....	....	....
	Texas Wildcatters	ECHL	30	10	14	24	30	....	....	....	....	....
	San Antonio	AHL	16	10	10	20	22	....	....	....	....	....
2007-08	San Antonio	AHL	4	1	2	3	6	....	....	....	....	....
	Arizona Sundogs	CHL	58	40	*88	*128	111	17	10	*20	*30	28

CHL First All-Star Team (2008)

Signed as a free agent by **Phoenix**, March 15, 2007.

LEBLANC, Peter (luh-BLAHNK, PEE-tuhr) CHI.

Center. Shoots left. 5'10", 196 lbs. Born, Hamilton, Ont., February 3, 1988.
(Chicago's 9th choice, 186th overall, in 2006 Entry Draft).

			Regular Season					Playoffs				
Season	Club	League	GP	G	A	Pts	PIM	GP	G	A	Pts	PIM
2004-05	Hamilton	OPJHL	49	14	22	36	....	....	....	....	....	....
2005-06	Hamilton	OPJHL	22	10	12	22	25	....	....	....	....	....
2006-07	New Hampshire	H-East	39	1	4	5	4	....	....	....	....	....
2007-08	New Hampshire	H-East	37	5	10	15	37	....	....	....	....	....

OPJHL Rookie of the Year (2005)

• Missed majority of 2005-06 season due to mononucleosis.

LEDIN, Per (lay-DEEN, PAIR) COL.

Left wing. Shoots left. 6', 194 lbs. Born, Lulea, Sweden, September 14, 1978.

			Regular Season					Playoffs				
Season	Club	League	GP	G	A	Pts	PIM	GP	G	A	Pts	PIM
1996-97	Bjorkloven Jr.	Swe-Jr.	27	19	11	30	....	....	....	....	....	....
	IF Bjorkloven Umea	Sweden-2	6	0	0	0	2	....	....	....	....	....
1997-98	Bjorkloven Jr.	Swe-Jr.	11	8	4	12	44	....	....	....	....	....
	IF Bjorkloven Umea	Sweden-2	44	14	15	29	30	....	....	....	....	....
1998-99	IF Bjorkloven Umea	Sweden	46	6	4	10	32	....	....	....	....	....
	IF Bjorkloven Umea	Sweden-Q	9	1	0	1	29	....	....	....	....	....
99-2000	IF Bjorkloven Umea	Sweden-2	47	14	7	21	69	....	....	....	....	....
2000-01	Baton Rouge	ECHL	27	4	8	12	37	....	....	....	....	....
	Lulea HF	Sweden	18	1	0	1	14	12	0	0	0	6
2001-02	Lulea HF Jr.	Swe-Jr.	4	5	2	7	4	....	....	....	....	....
	Lulea HF	Sweden	50	0	5	5	47	6	0	0	0	8
2002-03	Lulea HF Jr.	Swe-Jr.	1	2	0	2	0	....	....	....	....	....
	Lulea HF	Sweden	50	8	7	15	72	4	0	0	0	6
2003-04	Lulea HF	Sweden	50	6	9	15	112	5	1	1	2	8
2004-05	Lulea HF	Sweden	46	16	20	36	94	4	0	1	1	37
2005-06	Farjestad	Sweden	46	8	15	23	123	18	3	7	10	55
2006-07	Farjestad	Sweden	55	9	15	24	148	....	....	....	....	....
2007-08	HV 71 Jonkoping	Sweden	52	16	17	33	137	17	2	5	7	63

Signed as a free agent by **Colorado**, July 1, 2008.

LEE, Carter (LEE, KAHR-tuhr) S.J.

Right wing. Shoots right. 6'1", 190 lbs. Born, Toms River, NJ, July 2, 1984.
(San Jose's 11th choice, 276th overall, in 2003 Entry Draft).

			Regular Season					Playoffs				
Season	Club	League	GP	G	A	Pts	PIM	GP	G	A	Pts	PIM
2001-02	Christian Bros.	High-NJ	34	10	9	19	45	....	....	....	....	....
2002-03	Canterbury	High-CT	35	38	22	60	40	....	....	....	....	....
2003-04	Canterbury	High-CT	30	19	26	45	40	....	....	....	....	....
2004-05	Northeastern	H-East	11	2	1	3	4	....	....	....	....	....
2005-06	Northeastern	H-East	9	0	1	1	21	....	....	....	....	....
2006-07	Lake Superior	CCHA	DID NOT PLAY – TRANSFERRED COLLEGES									
2007-08	Lake Superior	CCHA	17	1	1	2	8	....	....	....	....	....

LEE, Chris (LEE, KRIHS) NYI

Defense. Shoots left. 6', 185 lbs. Born, MacTier, Ont., October 3, 1980.

			Regular Season					Playoffs				
Season	Club	League	GP	G	A	Pts	PIM	GP	G	A	Pts	PIM
2004-05	Florida Everblades	ECHL	68	5	22	27	16	15	2	9	11	6
2005-06	Florida Everblades	ECHL	52	10	27	37	56	8	2	1	3	4
2006-07	Albany River Rats	AHL	3	0	1	1	4	....	....	....	....	....
	Bridgeport	AHL	1	0	0	0	0	....	....	....	....	....
	Omaha	AHL	32	4	13	17	16	6	3	0	3	6
	Florida Everblades	ECHL	37	6	19	25	22	9	3	1	4	0
2007-08	Iowa Stars	AHL	68	7	21	28	42	....	....	....	....	....

Signed as a free agent by **NY Islanders**, July 3, 2008.

LEE, John (LEE, JAWN) FLA.

Defense. Shoots right. 6'2", 173 lbs. Born, Fargo, ND, January 16, 1989.
(Florida's 5th choice, 131st overall, in 2007 Entry Draft).

			Regular Season					Playoffs				
Season	Club	League	GP	G	A	Pts	PIM	GP	G	A	Pts	PIM
2004-05	Moorhead Spuds	High-MN	3	0	1	1	0	....	....	....	....	....
2005-06	Moorhead Spuds	High-MN	26	6	21	27	50	....	....	....	....	....
2006-07	Moorhead Spuds	High-MN	26	6	33	39	62	....	....	....	....	....
	Waterloo	USHL	27	2	7	9	56	9	0	3	3	4
2007-08	Waterloo	USHL	59	1	11	12	106	11	0	4	4	24

• Signed Letter of Intent to attend **University of Denver** (WCHA) in fall of 2008.

LEFFLER, Brett (LEHF-luhr, BREHT) WSH.

Right wing. Shoots right. 6'2", 190 lbs. Born, Wynyard, Sask., May 19, 1989.
(Washington's 6th choice, 125th overall, in 2007 Entry Draft).

			Regular Season					Playoffs				
Season	Club	League	GP	G	A	Pts	PIM	GP	G	A	Pts	PIM
2004-05	Tisdale Trojans	SMHL	43	20	27	80	....	5	1	0	1	8
	Regina Pats	WHL	7	0	1	1	2	....	....	....	....	....
2005-06	Regina Pats	WHL	42	2	7	9	54	....	....	....	....	....
2006-07	Regina Pats	WHL	69	13	13	26	114	10	2	0	2	14
2007-08	Regina Pats	WHL	56	9	5	14	77	3	0	0	0	4

LEGEIN, Stefan (LEE-gihn, STEH-fan) CBJ

Right wing. Shoots right. 5'11", 180 lbs. Born, Oakville, Ont., November 24, 1988.
(Columbus' 2nd choice, 37th overall, in 2007 Entry Draft).

			Regular Season					Playoffs				
Season	Club	League	GP	G	A	Pts	PIM	GP	G	A	Pts	PIM
2003-04	Tor. Red Wings	GTHL	33	19	14	33	63	....	....	....	....	....
2004-05	Milton Icehawks	OPJHL	26	7	12	19	18	....	....	....	....	....
	Mississauga	OHL	49	3	5	8	37	5	0	1	1	0
2005-06	Mississauga	OHL	59	7	9	16	101	....	....	....	....	....
2006-07	Mississauga	OHL	64	43	32	75	115	5	3	2	5	0
2007-08	Niagara Ice Dogs	OHL	30	24	13	37	80	10	7	11	18	28
	Syracuse Crunch	AHL	....	....	....	....	....	2	0	0	0	0

OHL Second All-Star Team (2008)

LEHMAN, Scott (LAY-man, SKAWT) ATL.

Defense. Shoots left. 6'2", 200 lbs. Born, Fort McMurray, Alta., January 6, 1986.
(Atlanta's 3rd choice, 76th overall, in 2004 Entry Draft).

			Regular Season					Playoffs				
Season	Club	League	GP	G	A	Pts	PIM	GP	G	A	Pts	PIM
2002-03	St. Michael's	OHL	53	3	10	13	50	19	1	3	4	34
2003-04	St. Michael's	OHL	66	5	27	32	189	18	2	2	4	38
2004-05	St. Michael's	OHL	57	2	19	21	189	10	2	2	4	31
2005-06	St. Michael's	OHL	68	5	50	55	175	4	0	2	2	15
2006-07	Chicago Wolves	AHL	3	0	0	0	14	....	....	....	....	....
	Gwinnett	ECHL	72	2	12	14	86	4	0	0	0	11
2007-08	Chicago Wolves	AHL	40	2	5	7	109	....	....	....	....	....
	Gwinnett	ECHL	6	0	2	2	18	....	....	....	....	....

LEHTERA, Jori (LEH-tuhr-a, YOHR-ee) ST.L.

Center. Shoots left. 6'2", 191 lbs. Born, Helsinki, Finland, December 23, 1987.
(St. Louis' 4th choice, 65th overall, in 2008 Entry Draft).

			Regular Season					Playoffs				
Season	Club	League	GP	G	A	Pts	PIM	GP	G	A	Pts	PIM
2003-04	Jokerit U18	Fin-U18	19	0	6	6	2	5	3	1	4	0
2004-05	Jokerit U18	Fin-U18	30	13	37	50	24	7	6	5	11	2
2005-06	Suomi U20	Finland-2	2	0	0	0	0	....	....	....	....	....
	Jokerit Helsinki Jr.	Fin-Jr.	39	14	33	47	16	4	1	4	5	0
2006-07	Suomi U20	Finland-2	10	4	7	11	10	....	....	....	....	....
	Jokerit Helsinki Jr.	Fin-Jr.	24	18	48	66	20	5	1	7	8	2
	Jokerit Helsinki	Finland	28	6	6	12	14	....	....	....	....	....
2007-08	Tappara Tampere	Finland	54	13	29	42	32	11	4	2	6	8

LEHTIVUORI, Joonas (leh-tee-VWOO-aw-ree, YOH-nuhs) PHI.

Defense. Shoots left. 5'11", 170 lbs. Born, Tampere, Finland, July 19, 1988.
(Philadelphia's 6th choice, 101st overall, in 2006 Entry Draft).

			Regular Season					Playoffs				
Season	Club	League	GP	G	A	Pts	PIM	GP	G	A	Pts	PIM
2004-05	Ilves Tampere U18	Fin-U18	25	5	11	16	12	5	1	1	2	8
2005-06	Ilves Tampere U18	Fin-U18	2	0	1	1	0	6	1	4	5	4
	Ilves Tampere Jr.	Fin-Jr.	39	9	16	25	22	3	0	0	0	4
	Ilves Tampere	Finland	1	0	0	0	0	....	....	....	....	....
2006-07	Ilves Tampere Jr.	Fin-Jr.	15	3	8	11	51	5	0	1	1	2
	Suomi U20	Finland-2	2	0	0	0	0	....	....	....	....	....
	Ilves Tampere	Finland	40	0	0	0	18	4	0	0	0	0
2007-08	Suomi U20	Finland-2	2	0	1	1	2	....	....	....	....	....
	Ilves Tampere	Finland	48	8	13	21	10	9	1	1	2	2

LEHTONEN, Mikko (LEH-tuh-nehn, MEE-koh) BOS.

Right wing. Shoots right. 6'5", 203 lbs. Born, Espoo, Finland, April 1, 1987.
(Boston's 3rd choice, 83rd overall, in 2005 Entry Draft).

			Regular Season					Playoffs				
Season	Club	League	GP	G	A	Pts	PIM	GP	G	A	Pts	PIM
2002-03	Blues Espoo U18	Fin-U18	11	1	3	4	2	1	0	0	0	0
2003-04	Blues Espoo U18	Fin-U18	20	8	7	15	22	....	....	....	....	....
	Blues Espoo Jr.	Fin-Jr.	19	3	0	3	0	5	0	0	0	0
2004-05	Blues Espoo U18	Fin-U18	2	0	2	2	0	....	....	....	....	....
	Blues Espoo Jr.	Fin-Jr.	37	6	9	15	38	6	3	1	4	0
	Blues Espoo	Finland	1	0	0	0	0	....	....	....	....	....
2005-06	Blues Espoo Jr.	Fin-Jr.	15	3	4	7	12	10	5	2	7	6
	Suomi U20	Finland-2	3	1	0	1	2	....	....	....	....	....
	Blues Espoo	Finland	25	4	0	4	0	....	....	....	....	....
2006-07	Suomi U20	Finland-2	3	0	3	3	0	....	....	....	....	....
	Blues Espoo	Finland	39	6	9	15	24	9	1	1	2	4
2007-08	Blues Espoo	Finland	42	8	12	20	12	17	1	8	9	4

LEINO, Ville (LAY-noh, VIHL-ee) DET.

Left wing. Shoots left. 6', 183 lbs. Born, Savonlinna, Finland, October 6, 1983.

			Regular Season					Playoffs				
Season	Club	League	GP	G	A	Pts	PIM	GP	G	A	Pts	PIM
2002-03	Ilves Tampere Jr.	Fin-Jr.	26	14	21	35	24	....	....	....	....	....
	Ilves Tampere	Finland	23	1	1	2	0	....	....	....	....	....
2003-04	Ilves Tampere Jr.	Fin-Jr.	5	4	6	10	6	....	....	....	....	....
	Ilves Tampere	Finland	54	9	15	24	26	7	1	1	2	4
2004-05	Ilves Tampere	Finland	56	8	11	19	32	7	1	0	1	2
2005-06	HPK Hameenlinna	Finland	56	12	31	43	65	13	3	*9	12	4
2006-07	HPK Hameenlinna	Finland	50	11	29	40	73	8	1	9	10	31
2007-08	Jokerit Helsinki	Finland	55	28	*49	77	18	14	8	11	19	8

Signed as a free agent by **Detroit**, May 10, 2008.

LEMIEUX, Francis (leh-M'YOO, FRAN-sihs) DET.

Center. Shoots right. 5'11", 187 lbs. Born, Sherbrooke, Que., February 22, 1984.

			Regular Season					Playoffs				
Season	Club	League	GP	G	A	Pts	PIM	GP	G	A	Pts	PIM
2001-02	Chicoutimi	QMJHL	66	17	22	39	44	3	0	0	0	0
2002-03	Chicoutimi	QMJHL	66	28	35	63	36	4	0	0	0	2
2003-04	Chicoutimi	QMJHL	70	22	44	66	49	18	6	4	10	10
2004-05	Chicoutimi	QMJHL	70	32	50	82	52	13	4	5	9	6
2005-06	Hamilton Bulldogs	AHL	67	18	23	41	76	....	....	....	....	....
2006-07	Hamilton Bulldogs	AHL	44	6	11	17	34	11	0	2	2	6
2007-08	Hamilton Bulldogs	AHL	33	0	6	6	27	....	....	....	....	....
	Grand Rapids	AHL	26	6	5	11	28	....	....	....	....	....

Signed as a free agent by **Montreal**, December 8, 2005. Traded to **Detroit** by **Montreal** for Brett Engelhardt, February 8, 2008.

LEMTYUGOV, Nikolai (LEHM-tyuh-gawf, NIH-koh-ligh) ST.L.

Right wing. Shoots left. 6', 183 lbs. Born, Miass, USSR, January 15, 1986.
(St. Louis' 7th choice, 219th overall, in 2005 Entry Draft).

			Regular Season					Playoffs				
Season	Club	League	GP	G	A	Pts	PIM	GP	G	A	Pts	PIM
2003-04	CSKA Moscow 2	Russia-3	STATISTICS NOT AVAILABLE									
2004-05	CSKA Moscow 2	Russia-3	STATISTICS NOT AVAILABLE									
	CSKA Moscow	Russia	11	1	1	2	16	....	....	....	....	....
2005-06	CSKA Moscow	Russia	37	9	11	20	45	7	1	1	2	8
2006-07	Cherepovets	Russia	52	11	8	19	50	5	0	1	1	8
2007-08	Peoria Rivermen	AHL	69	22	15	37	71	....	....	....	....	....

LERG, Bryan (LEHRG, BRIGH-uhn EDM.

Center. Shoots left. 5'10", 175 lbs. Born, Livonia, MI, January 20, 1986.

			Regular Season					Playoffs				
Season	Club	League	GP	G	A	Pts	PIM	GP	G	A	Pts	PIM
2002-03	USNTDP	U-17	19	11	6	17	5	....	....	....	....	....
	USNTDP	NAHL	46	10	12	22	32	....	....	....	....	....
2003-04	USNTDP	U-18	46	22	25	47	....	....	....	....	....	....
	USNTDP	NAHL	11	5	7	12	10	....	....	....	....	....
2004-05	Michigan State	CCHA	41	10	5	15	14	....	....	....	....	....
2005-06	Michigan State	CCHA	45	15	23	38	26	....	....	....	....	....
2006-07	Michigan State	CCHA	41	23	13	36	21	....	....	....	....	....
2007-08	Michigan State	CCHA	42	20	19	39	18	....	....	....	....	....
	Springfield Falcons	AHL	4	0	2	2	2	....	....	....	....	....

Signed as a free agent by **Edmonton**, April 2, 2008.

LETESTU, Mark (luh-TEHS- too, MAHRK) PIT.

Center. Shoots right. 5'11", 195 lbs. Born, Elk Point, Alta., February 4, 1985.

			Regular Season					Playoffs				
Season	Club	League	GP	G	A	Pts	PIM	GP	G	A	Pts	PIM
2003-04	Bonnyville Pontiacs	AJHL	58	22	27	49	24	....	....	....	....	....
2004-05	Bonnyville Pontiacs	AJHL	63	39	47	86	32	....	....	....	....	....
2005-06	Bonnyville Pontiacs	AJHL	58	50	55	105	59	....	....	....	....	....
2006-07	Western Mich.	CCHA	37	24	22	46	14	....	....	....	....	....
	Wilkes-Barre	AHL	3	0	0	0	0	2	0	0	0	2
2007-08	Wilkes-Barre	AHL	52	6	12	18	28	13	0	3	3	0
	Wheeling Nailers	ECHL	6	1	2	3	4	....	....	....	....	....

Signed as a free agent by **Pittsburgh**, March 22, 2007.

LETOURNEAU-LEBLOND, Pierre-Luc (leh-TOOR-noh-leh-BLAWN) N.J.

Right wing. Shoots left. 6'2", 220 lbs. Born, Levis, Que., June 4, 1985.
(New Jersey's 4th choice, 216th overall, in 2004 Entry Draft).

			Regular Season					Playoffs				
Season	Club	League	GP	G	A	Pts	PIM	GP	G	A	Pts	PIM
2003-04	Baie-Comeau	QMJHL	62	2	3	5	198	4	0	0	0	6
2004-05	Baie-Comeau	QMJHL	67	1	6	7	229	6	0	1	1	10
2005-06	Albany River Rats	AHL	27	1	1	2	130	....	....	....	....	....
	Adirondack	UHL	31	3	6	9	165	6	0	1	1	29
2006-07	Trenton Titans	ECHL	52	4	9	13	183	4	0	0	0	15
2007-08	Lowell Devils	AHL	36	3	3	6	98	....	....	....	....	....
	Trenton Devils	ECHL	6	0	1	1	46	....	....	....	....	....

LEVEILLE, Daultan (leh-VAY-yay, DAWL-tuhn) **ATL.**

Center. Shoots left. 5'11", 165 lbs. Born, St. Catharines, Ont., August 10, 1990.
(Atlanta's 2nd choice, 29th overall, in 2008 Entry Draft).

			Regular Season					Playoffs				
Season	Club	League	GP	G	A	Pts	PIM	GP	G	A	Pts	PIM
2005-06	St. Catharines	Minor-ON	46	25	31	56	32	....	....	....	....	....
2006-07	St. Catharines	OJHL-B	48	19	26	45	30	....	....	....	....	....
2007-08	St. Catharines	OJHL-B	45	29	27	56	38	16	*14	16	30	14

• Signed Letter of Intent to attend **Michigan State University** (CCHA) in fall of 2008.

LEWIS, Grant (LOO-ihs, GRANT) **ATL.**

Defense. Shoots right. 6'3", 200 lbs. Born, Pittsburgh, PA, January 20, 1985.
(Atlanta's 2nd choice, 40th overall, in 2004 Entry Draft).

			Regular Season					Playoffs				
Season	Club	League	GP	G	A	Pts	PIM	GP	G	A	Pts	PIM
2002-03	Pittsburgh Forge	NAHL	50	2	7	9	59	....	....	....	....	....
2003-04	Dartmouth	ECAC	34	3	22	25	57	....	....	....	....	....
2004-05	Dartmouth	ECAC	33	5	17	22	32	....	....	....	....	....
2005-06	Dartmouth	ECAC	29	4	11	15	53	....	....	....	....	....
2006-07	Dartmouth	ECAC	24	1	14	15	30	....	....	....	....	....
2007-08	Chicago Wolves	AHL	43	2	14	16	44	2	0	0	0	2

ECAC All-Rookie Team (2004) • ECAC First All-Star Team (2004) • ECAC Second All-Star Team (2006)

LEWIS, Trevor (LOO-ihs, TREH-vuhr) **L.A.**

Center. Shoots right. 6'1", 200 lbs. Born, Salt Lake City, UT, January 8, 1987.
(Los Angeles' 2nd choice, 17th overall, in 2006 Entry Draft).

			Regular Season					Playoffs				
Season	Club	League	GP	G	A	Pts	PIM	GP	G	A	Pts	PIM
2004-05	Des Moines	USHL	52	10	12	22	70	....	....	....	....	....
2005-06	Des Moines	USHL	56	35	40	75	69	11	3	*13	*16	16
2006-07	Owen Sound	OHL	62	29	44	73	51	4	1	2	3	0
	Manchester	AHL	8	4	2	6	2	2	0	0	0	0
2007-08	Manchester	AHL	76	12	16	28	43	4	0	0	0	2

LINDGREN, Perttu (LIHND-gruhn, PUHR-too) **DAL.**

Center. Shoots left. 6', 185 lbs. Born, Tampere, Finland, August 26, 1987.
(Dallas' 4th choice, 75th overall, in 2005 Entry Draft).

			Regular Season					Playoffs				
Season	Club	League	GP	G	A	Pts	PIM	GP	G	A	Pts	PIM
2003-04	Ilves Tampere U18	Fin-U18	24	11	17	28	26	....	....	....	....	....
	Ilves Tampere Jr.	Fin-Jr.	2	0	0	0	0	....	....	....	....	....
2004-05	Ilves Tampere Jr.	Fin-Jr.	38	12	29	41	2	10	7	10	17	4
	Ilves Tampere	Finland	2	0	0	0	0	....	....	....	....	....
2005-06	Ilves Tampere Jr.	Fin-Jr.	2	1	0	1	0	....	....	....	....	....
	Suomi U20	Finland-2	3	0	3	3	0	....	....	....	....	....
	Ilves Tampere	Finland	51	13	24	37	16	4	0	0	0	0
2006-07	Suomi U20	Finland-2	2	1	1	2	2	....	....	....	....	....
	Ilves Tampere	Finland	43	4	22	26	38	7	4	2	6	2
2007-08	Iowa Stars	AHL	69	10	24	34	6	....	....	....	....	....

LINGLET, Charles (LIHNG-leht, CHAHR-uhlz) **ST.L.**

Left wing. Shoots left. 6'2", 205 lbs. Born, Montreal, Que., June 22, 1982.

			Regular Season					Playoffs				
Season	Club	League	GP	G	A	Pts	PIM	GP	G	A	Pts	PIM
99-2000	Baie-Comeau	QMJHL	64	14	20	34	13	6	3	3	6	4
2000-01	Baie-Comeau	QMJHL	70	21	34	55	61	11	2	2	4	10
2001-02	Baie-Comeau	QMJHL	72	52	71	123	34	5	1	3	4	2
2002-03	Baie-Comeau	QMJHL	47	21	27	48	35	12	3	8	11	18
2003-04	Utah Grizzlies	AHL	7	0	0	0	2	....	....	....	....	....
	Alaska Aces	ECHL	62	20	35	55	61	7	2	5	7	4
2004-05	Alaska Aces	ECHL	72	28	34	62	44	15	6	10	16	14
2005-06	Peoria Rivermen	AHL	38	14	7	21	10	....	....	....	....	....
	Las Vegas	ECHL	16	5	9	14	15	12	5	4	9	20
2006-07	Peoria Rivermen	AHL	73	31	29	60	30	....	....	....	....	....
2007-08	Peoria Rivermen	AHL	80	24	42	66	65	....	....	....	....	....

QMJHL First All-Star Team (2002)

Signed as a free agent by **St. Louis**, Jauary 1, 2007.

LIVINGSTON, James (LIH-vihng-stuhn, JAYMZ) **ST.L.**

Right wing. Shoots right. 6'1", 200 lbs. Born, Halifax, N. S., March 8, 1990.
(St. Louis' 5th choice, 70th overall, in 2008 Entry Draft).

			Regular Season					Playoffs				
Season	Club	League	GP	G	A	Pts	PIM	GP	G	A	Pts	PIM
2005-06	York Simcoe	Minor-ON	51	25	32	57	....	....	....	....	....	....
2006-07	Sault Ste. Marie	OHL	60	2	5	7	95	13	1	0	1	15
2007-08	Sault Ste. Marie	OHL	68	21	23	44	135	14	2	3	5	14

LOGINOV, Denis (LOG-gih-nawv, DEH-nihs) **ATL.**

Center. Shoots left. 6'1", 210 lbs. Born, Kazan, USSR, May 5, 1985.
(Atlanta's 7th choice, 203rd overall, in 2003 Entry Draft).

			Regular Season					Playoffs				
Season	Club	League	GP	G	A	Pts	PIM	GP	G	A	Pts	PIM
99-2000	Ak Bars Kazan 2	Russia-3	4	0	0	0	0	....	....	....	....	....
2000-01	Ak Bars Kazan 2	Russia-3	STATISTICS NOT AVAILABLE									
2001-02	Ak Bars Kazan 2	Russia-3	38	6	10	16	40	....	....	....	....	....
	Team Volga	Exhib.	3	0	3	3	27	....	....	....	....	....
2002-03	Ak Bars Kazan 2	Russia-3	52	17	24	41	98	....	....	....	....	....
	Perm	Russia	1	0	0	0	0	....	....	....	....	....
2003-04	Ak Bars Kazan	Russia	16	2	1	3	0	7	1	0	1	6
2004-05	Ak Bars Kazan	Russia	2	0	0	0	0	....	....	....	....	....
2005-06	Almetjevsk	Russia-2	7	1	0	1	8	....	....	....	....	....
	Ak Bars Kazan	Russia	16	1	1	2	10	....	....	....	....	....
2006-07	Ak Bars Kazan 2	Russia-3	STATISTICS NOT AVAILABLE									
2007-08	Nizhnekamsk	Russia	6	0	0	0	6	....	....	....	....	....
	Volzhsk	Russia-2	10	2	3	5	14	....	....	....	....	....
	Orenburg	Russia-2	12	3	3	6	30	....	....	....	....	....

LOKTIONOV, Andrei (lawk-too-OH-nawf, ahn-DRAY) **L.A.**

Center. Shoots left. 5'11", 187 lbs. Born, Voskresensk, USSR, May 30, 1990.
(Los Angeles' 7th choice, 123rd overall, in 2008 Entry Draft).

			Regular Season					Playoffs				
Season	Club	League	GP	G	A	Pts	PIM	GP	G	A	Pts	PIM
2005-06	Spartak Moscow 2	Russia-3	4	1	1	2	2	....	....	....	....	....
2006-07	Yaroslavl 2	Russia-3	31	7	21	28	26	....	....	....	....	....
2007-08	Yaroslavl 2	Russia-3	STATISTICS NOT AVAILABLE									
	Yaroslavl	Russia	5	0	1	1	0	1	0	0	0	0

LONG, Colin (LAWNG, KAW-lihn) **PHX.**

Center. Shoots right. 5'11", 186 lbs. Born, Santa Ana, CA, June 19, 1989.
(Phoenix's 6th choice, 99th overall, in 2008 Entry Draft).

			Regular Season					Playoffs				
Season	Club	League	GP	G	A	Pts	PIM	GP	G	A	Pts	PIM
2005-06	Kelowna Rockets	WHL	20	1	3	4	6	3	0	0	0	0
2006-07	Kelowna Rockets	WHL	69	11	17	28	38	....	....	....	....	....
2007-08	Kelowna Rockets	WHL	72	31	69	100	41	7	2	10	12	6

WHL West First All-Star Team (2008)

LORENZ, Sean (lohr-EHNZ, SHAWN) **MIN.**

Defense. Shoots right. 6'1", 191 lbs. Born, Littleton, CO, March 10, 1990.
(Minnesota's 3rd choice, 115th overall, in 2008 Entry Draft).

			Regular Season					Playoffs				
Season	Club	League	GP	G	A	Pts	PIM	GP	G	A	Pts	PIM
2006-07	USNTDP	U-17	6	6	9	15	28	....	....	....	....	....
	USNTDP	NAHL	45	1	7	8	26	6	0	0	0	2
2007-08	USNTDP	U-18	50	0	8	8	28	....	....	....	....	....
	USNTDP	NAHL	14	2	1	3	4	....	....	....	....	....

• Signed Letter of Intent to attend **University of Notre Dame** (CCHA) in fall of 2008.

LOVE, Mitch (LUHV, MIHTCH)

Defense. Shoots left. 6', 200 lbs. Born, Quesnel, B.C., June 15, 1984.

			Regular Season					Playoffs				
Season	Club	League	GP	G	A	Pts	PIM	GP	G	A	Pts	PIM
2000-01	Moose Jaw	WHL	51	5	4	9	97	4	0	0	0	2
2001-02	Moose Jaw	WHL	16	0	1	1	40	....	....	....	....	....
	Swift Current	WHL	52	5	11	16	132	12	0	0	0	37
2002-03	Swift Current	WHL	70	2	15	17	*327	4	1	0	1	16
2003-04	Everett Silvertips	WHL	70	12	15	27	163	21	2	6	8	47
2004-05	Everett Silvertips	WHL	59	9	20	29	142	4	0	2	2	6
2005-06	Lowell	AHL	27	0	4	4	68	....	....	....	....	....
2006-07	Albany River Rats	AHL	69	1	5	6	184	....	....	....	....	....
2007-08	Lake Erie Monsters	AHL	59	2	5	7	213	....	....	....	....	....
	Johnstown Chiefs	ECHL	4	0	0	0	16	....	....	....	....	....

Signed as a free agent by **Colorado**, October 25, 2005.

LoVECCHIO, Jeff (LOH-veh-kee-oh, JEHF) **BOS.**

Left wing. Shoots left. 6'2", 194 lbs. Born, Arlington Heights, IL, August 26, 1985.

			Regular Season					Playoffs				
Season	Club	League	GP	G	A	Pts	PIM	GP	G	A	Pts	PIM
2003-04	River City Lancers	USHL	58	16	13	29	29	3	0	1	1	2
2004-05	Omaha Lancers	USHL	57	17	27	44	82	5	1	0	1	0
2005-06	Western Mich.	CCHA	40	7	11	18	46	....	....	....	....	....
2006-07	Western Mich.	CCHA	37	19	16	35	24	....	....	....	....	....
2007-08	Western Mich.	CCHA	36	9	12	21	28	....	....	....	....	....
	Providence Bruins	AHL	14	3	2	5	6	6	0	1	1	2

Signed as a free agent by **Boston**, March 18, 2008.

LOVEJOY, Ben (LUHV-joi, BEHN) **PIT.**

Defense. Shoots right. 6'2", 214 lbs. Born, Concord, NH, February 20, 1984.

			Regular Season					Playoffs				
Season	Club	League	GP	G	A	Pts	PIM	GP	G	A	Pts	PIM
2002-03	Boston College	H-East	22	0	6	6	6	....	....	....	....	....
2003-04	Dartmouth	ECAC	DID NOT PLAY – TRANSFERRED COLLEGES									
2004-05	Dartmouth	ECAC	32	2	11	13	28	....	....	....	....	....
2005-06	Dartmouth	ECAC	32	2	16	18	24	....	....	....	....	....
2006-07	Dartmouth	ECAC	32	7	16	23	28	....	....	....	....	....
	Norfolk Admirals	AHL	5	0	0	0	6	....	....	....	....	....
2007-08	Wilkes-Barre	AHL	72	2	18	20	63	23	2	8	10	18

Signed as a free agent by **Wilkes-Barre/Scranton** (AHL), June 14, 2007. Signed as a free agent by **Pittsburgh**, July 7, 2008.

LUCENIUS, Niclas (loo-SEHN-ee-uhs, NIHK-luhs) **ATL.**

Center. Shoots left. 6', 190 lbs. Born, Turku, Finland, May 3, 1989.
(Atlanta's 2nd choice, 115th overall, in 2007 Entry Draft).

			Regular Season					Playoffs				
Season	Club	League	GP	G	A	Pts	PIM	GP	G	A	Pts	PIM
2005-06	Tappara U18	Fin-U18	11	6	5	11	10	3	2	0	2	25
	Tappara Jr.	Fin-Jr.	23	5	4	9	18	....	....	....	....	....
2006-07	Tappara U18	Fin-U18	7	5	3	8	32	....	....	....	....	....
	Tappara Jr.	Fin-Jr.	33	14	14	28	44	10	2	3	5	14
	Tappara Tampere	Finland	5	0	0	0	0	....	....	....	....	....
2007-08	Suomi U20	Finland-2	5	1	2	3	12	....	....	....	....	....
	Tappara Jr.	Fin-Jr.	15	6	13	19	28	....	....	....	....	....
	Tappara Tampere	Finland	28	0	2	2	10	....	....	....	....	....
	LeKi Lempaala	Finland-2	6	2	1	3	4	3	0	2	2	4

LUCHINKIN, Sergei (loo-CHIHN-kihn, SAIR-gay) **CBJ**

Center. Shoots left. 5'11", 172 lbs. Born, Dmitrov, USSR, October 16, 1976.
(Dallas' 9th choice, 202nd overall, in 1995 Entry Draft).

			Regular Season					Playoffs				
Season	Club	League	GP	G	A	Pts	PIM	GP	G	A	Pts	PIM
1994-95	Dynamo Moscow	CIS	6	1	0	1	4	....	....	....	....	....
1995-96	Dynamo Moscow	CIS	21	6	2	8	14	10	0	1	1	6
1996-97	Dynamo Moscow	Russia	18	1	5	6	4	....	....	....	....	....
	Dynamo Moscow	EuroHL	4	0	1	1	4	....	....	....	....	....
1997-98	Dynamo Moscow	EuroHL	1	0	0	0	0	....	....	....	....	....
	Dynamo Moscow	Russia	6	0	1	1	0	....	....	....	....	....
	Spartak Moscow	Russia	10	0	1	1	4	....	....	....	....	....
1998-99	Spartak Moscow	Russia	33	4	5	9	18	....	....	....	....	....
99-2000	Spartak Moscow 2	Russia-3	1	2	0	2	2	....	....	....	....	....
	Spartak Moscow	Russia-2	58	19	17	36	54	....	....	....	....	....
2000-01	Spartak Moscow	Russia-2	42	19	16	35	44	....	....	....	....	....
2001-02	HK CSKA Moscow	Russia-2	60	14	20	34	32	....	....	....	....	....
	Spartak Moscow	Russia	57	23	18	41	46	....	....	....	....	....
2002-03	CSKA Moscow	Russia	16	7	4	11	6	....	....	....	....	....
2003-04	CSKA Moscow	Russia	40	1	2	3	14	....	....	....	....	....
2004-05	HK MVD Tver	Russia-2	42	6	19	25	28	....	....	....	....	....
2005-06	MVD	Russia	27	3	1	4	22	....	....	....	....	....
	HK MVD-THK Tver	Russia-3	1	0	0	0	0	....	....	....	....	....
	Nizhnekamsk	Russia	17	4	5	9	10	5	0	2	2	10
2006-07	Nizhnekamsk	Russia	4	0	0	0	0	....	....	....	....	....
	Lada Togliatti	Russia	8	1	1	2	8	....	....	....	....	....
2007-08	Khimik	Russia-2	51	25	13	38	48	14	2	6	8	4

Claimed by **Columbus** from **Dallas** in Expansion Draft, June 23, 2000.

LUCIA, Tony (loo-CHEE-ah, TOH-nee) S.J.

Left wing. Shoots left. 6', 180 lbs. Born, Wayzata, MN, August 23, 1987.
(San Jose's 8th choice, 193rd overall, in 2005 Entry Draft).

			Regular Season					Playoffs				
Season	Club	League	GP	G	A	Pts	PIM	GP	G	A	Pts	PIM
2003-04	Wayzata	High-MN	31	13	22	35	....	....	....	....	....	....
2004-05	Wayzata	High-MN	24	27	36	63	32	....	....	....	....	....
	Omaha Lancers	USHL	11	1	0	1	0	....	....	....	....	....
2005-06	Omaha Lancers	USHL	56	12	23	35	25	5	0	0	0	2
2006-07	U. of Minnesota	WCHA	43	7	12	19	28	....	....	....	....	....
2007-08	U. of Minnesota	WCHA	44	7	11	18	41	....	....	....	....	....

LUDWIG, Trevor (LUHD-wihg, TREH-vuhr) DAL.

Defense. Shoots left. 6'1", 200 lbs. Born, Rhinelander, WI, May 24, 1985.
(Dallas' 7th choice, 183rd overall, in 2004 Entry Draft).

			Regular Season					Playoffs				
Season	Club	League	GP	G	A	Pts	PIM	GP	G	A	Pts	PIM
2002-03	Texas Tornado	NAHL	55	4	5	9	39	....	....	....	....	....
2003-04	Texas Tornado	NAHL	54	5	25	30	50	....	....	....	....	....
2004-05	Providence College	H-East	33	1	6	7	36	....	....	....	....	....
2005-06	Providence College	H-East	27	0	2	2	6	....	....	....	....	....
2006-07	Providence College	H-East	26	0	2	2	37	....	....	....	....	....
2007-08	Providence College	H-East	29	1	3	4	28	....	....	....	....	....
	Iowa Stars	AHL	7	0	3	3	12	....	....	....	....	....

NAHL All-Rookie Team (2003) • NAHL First All-Star Team (2004)

LUKACEVIC, Ned (loo-kuh-SAY-vihk, NEHD) PHI.

Left wing. Shoots left. 6', 185 lbs. Born, Podgorica, Serbia, February 11, 1986.
(Los Angeles' 3rd choice, 110th overall, in 2004 Entry Draft).

			Regular Season					Playoffs				
Season	Club	League	GP	G	A	Pts	PIM	GP	G	A	Pts	PIM
2000-01	Port Coquitlam	Minor-BC	60	42	48	90	....	....	....	....	....	....
2001-02	Port Coquitlam	Minor-BC	70	40	55	95	60	....	....	....	....	....
	Spokane Chiefs	WHL	1	1	0	1	0	....	....	....	....	....
2002-03	Spokane Chiefs	WHL	31	0	4	4	29	4	0	1	1	0
2003-04	Spokane Chiefs	WHL	72	19	14	33	65	4	1	1	2	2
2004-05	Spokane Chiefs	WHL	71	18	28	46	52	....	....	....	....	....
2005-06	Swift Current	WHL	63	25	28	53	71	4	1	0	1	5
	Manchester	AHL	....	....	....	....	....	7	1	0	1	4
2006-07	Manchester	AHL	12	1	0	1	9	....	....	....	....	....
	Reading Royals	ECHL	53	7	17	24	38	....	....	....	....	....
2007-08	Reading Royals	ECHL	61	17	19	36	52	8	0	2	2	2

Traded to **Philadelphia** by **Los Angeles** with Patrik Hersley for Denis Gauthier and Philadelphia's 2nd round choice in 2010 Entry Draft, July 1, 2008.

LUNDBOHM, Bryan (LUHND-bawm, BRIGH-uhn) MIN.

Center. Shoots right. 5'10", 185 lbs. Born, Roseau, MN, August 24, 1977.

			Regular Season					Playoffs				
Season	Club	League	GP	G	A	Pts	PIM	GP	G	A	Pts	PIM
1996-97	Lincoln Stars	USHL	52	12	33	45	33	14	8	4	12	20
1997-98	Lincoln Stars	USHL	55	26	38	64	10	9	2	7	9	0
1998-99	North Dakota	WCHA	32	2	9	11	4	....	....	....	....	....
99-2000	North Dakota	WCHA	44	22	22	44	14	....	....	....	....	....
2000-01	North Dakota	WCHA	46	*32	37	69	38	....	....	....	....	....
2001-02	Milwaukee	AHL	79	11	23	34	63	....	....	....	....	....
2002-03	Milwaukee	AHL	80	9	17	26	63	6	1	5	6	0
2003-04	HC Sierre	Swiss-2	10	6	8	14	8	....	....	....	....	....
	Milwaukee	AHL	28	6	8	14	8	....	....	....	....	....
2004-05	Fort Worth	CHL	26	10	20	30	28	....	....	....	....	....
	Grand Rapids	AHL	3	0	0	0	0	....	....	....	....	....
	Milwaukee	AHL	47	7	12	19	36	4	0	0	0	0
2005-06	Houston Aeros	AHL	78	9	21	30	46	8	3	5	8	4
2006-07	Houston Aeros	AHL	77	9	21	30	34	....	....	....	....	....
2007-08	KalPa Kuopio	Finland	5	0	1	1	0	....	....	....	....	....
	Vojens	Denmark	33	12	15	27	12	13	4	4	8	6

USHL First All-Star Team (1998) • WCHA First All-Star Team (2001) • NCAA West Second All-American Team (2001) • NCAA Championship All-Tournament Team (2001)

Signed as a free agent by **Nashville**, May 1, 2001. Signed as a free agent by **Sierre** (Swiss-2), September 5, 2003. Signed as a free agent by **Milwaukee** (AHL), November 25, 2003. • Missed majority of 2003-04 season recovering from groin injury suffered in game vs. Philadelphia (AHL), January 31, 2004. Signed as a free agent by **Fort Worth** (CHL), October 19, 2004. Signed as a free agent by **Grand Rapids** (AHL), November 17, 2004. Signed as a free agent by **Milwaukee** (AHL), December 28, 2004. Signed as a free agent by **Minnesota**, July 15, 2008.

LYAMIN, Kirill (L'YAH-mihn, kih-RIHL) OTT.

Defense. Shoots left. 6'3", 198 lbs. Born, Moscow, USSR, January 13, 1986.
(Ottawa's 2nd choice, 58th overall, in 2004 Entry Draft).

			Regular Season					Playoffs				
Season	Club	League	GP	G	A	Pts	PIM	GP	G	A	Pts	PIM
2001-02	Moscow 18	Exhib.	5	0	3	3	4	....	....	....	....	....
2002-03	CSKA Moscow 2	Russia-3	5	0	0	0	10	....	....	....	....	....
	Moscow 18	Exhib.	5	0	0	0	6	....	....	....	....	....
2003-04	CSKA Moscow 2	Russia-3	STATISTICS NOT AVAILABLE									
	CSKA Moscow	Russia	28	0	3	3	12	....	....	....	....	....
2004-05	CSKA Moscow 2	Russia-3	STATISTICS NOT AVAILABLE									
2005-06	CSKA Moscow	Russia	25	0	1	1	28	2	0	0	0	0
2006-07	CSKA Moscow	Russia	47	1	7	8	48	12	1	0	1	8
2007-08	Mytischi	Russia	40	1	6	7	77	3	0	0	0	0

LYUBUSHIN, Mikhail (l'yoo-BOOSH-ihn, mih-kigh-EHL) L.A.

Defense. Shoots left. 6'1", 183 lbs. Born, Moscow, USSR, July 24, 1983.
(Los Angeles' 9th choice, 215th overall, in 2002 Entry Draft).

			Regular Season					Playoffs				
Season	Club	League	GP	G	A	Pts	PIM	GP	G	A	Pts	PIM
99-2000	Vityaz Podolsk 2	Russia-3	24	2	2	4	69	....	....	....	....	....
2000-01	Krylja Sovetov	Russia-2	2	0	1	1	0	1	0	0	0	0
2001-02	Krylja Sovetov 2	Russia-3	20	3	6	9	24	....	....	....	....	....
	THK Tver	Russia-2	22	1	0	1	18	....	....	....	....	....
	Krylja Sovetov	Russia	13	0	1	1	14	3	0	0	0	0
2002-03	Krylja Sovetov	Russia	49	0	6	6	26	....	....	....	....	....
2003-04	Dynamo Moscow	Russia	38	1	2	3	18	2	0	0	0	2
2004-05	Voskresensk	Russia	21	1	2	3	16	....	....	....	....	....
	Vityaz Chekhov	Russia-2	8	0	2	2	6	14	1	0	1	8
2005-06	Cherepovets	Russia	23	1	4	5	10	....	....	....	....	....
	Avangard Omsk	Russia	26	0	1	1	20	8	0	0	0	4
2006-07	Avangard Omsk	Russia	21	0	1	1	16	3	0	0	0	2
	Avangard Omsk 2	Russia-3	2	0	1	1	4	....	....	....	....	....
2007-08	Avangard Omsk	Russia	42	1	3	4	28	4	0	0	0	2

MacDONALD, Andrew (MAK-DAWN-uhld, AN-droo) NYI

Defense. Shoots left. 6'1", 188 lbs. Born, Judique, N.S., September 7, 1986.
(NY Islanders' 10th choice, 160th overall, in 2006 Entry Draft).

			Regular Season					Playoffs				
Season	Club	League	GP	G	A	Pts	PIM	GP	G	A	Pts	PIM
2003-04	Truro Bearcats	MJrHL	50	8	20	28	43	10	0	0	0	....
2004-05	Truro Bearcats	MJrHL	56	11	22	33	60	17	6	7	13	....
2005-06	Moncton Wildcats	QMJHL	68	6	40	46	62	21	2	11	13	10
2006-07	Moncton Wildcats	QMJHL	65	14	44	58	81	7	1	5	6	4
	Bridgeport	AHL	3	0	0	0	0	....	....	....	....	....
2007-08	Bridgeport	AHL	21	2	3	5	10	....	....	....	....	....
	Utah Grizzlies	ECHL	37	1	11	12	39	15	3	9	12	12

QMJHL First All-Star Team (2007)

MacDONALD, Franklin (MAK-DAWN-uhld, FRAN-klihn) FLA.

Defense. Shoots left. 6', 198 lbs. Born, Sydney, N.S., April 8, 1985.

			Regular Season					Playoffs				
Season	Club	League	GP	G	A	Pts	PIM	GP	G	A	Pts	PIM
2002-03	Truro Bearcats	MJrHL	48	2	10	12	65	....	....	....	....	....
2003-04	Halifax	QMJHL	63	4	8	12	52	....	....	....	....	....
2004-05	Halifax	QMJHL	65	5	11	16	93	13	0	5	5	24
2005-06	Halifax	QMJHL	58	12	33	45	129	11	4	2	6	22
2006-07	Rochester	AHL	11	0	2	2	12	....	....	....	....	....
	Florida Everblades	ECHL	56	4	20	24	58	16	1	5	6	20
2007-08	Rochester	AHL	51	1	13	14	49	....	....	....	....	....
	Florida Everblades	ECHL	11	2	6	8	20	3	0	1	1	0

Signed as a free agent by **Florida**, September 14, 2006.

MACENAUER, Maxime (MAK-ehn-owr, mahx-EEM) ANA.

Center. Shoots left. 6', 195 lbs. Born, Laval, Que., January 4, 1989.
(Anaheim's 3rd choice, 63rd overall, in 2007 Entry Draft).

			Regular Season					Playoffs				
Season	Club	League	GP	G	A	Pts	PIM	GP	G	A	Pts	PIM
2004-05	Ecole Montpetit	QAAA	37	17	22	39	56	3	0	0	0	0
2005-06	Rimouski Oceanic	QMJHL	41	8	14	22	30	....	....	....	....	....
2006-07	Rouyn-Noranda	QMJHL	14	1	3	4	10	....	....	....	....	....
2007-08	Rouyn-Noranda	QMJHL	67	23	37	60	53	17	6	10	16	8

MACHACEK, Spencer (muh-HA-chehk, SPEHN-suhr) ATL.

Right wing. Shoots right. 6'1", 195 lbs. Born, Lethbridge, Alta., October 14, 1988.
(Atlanta's 1st choice, 67th overall, in 2007 Entry Draft).

			Regular Season					Playoffs				
Season	Club	League	GP	G	A	Pts	PIM	GP	G	A	Pts	PIM
2004-05	Brooks Bandits	AJHL	59	16	20	36	41	10	2	2	4	8
2005-06	Vancouver Giants	WHL	70	23	22	45	53	18	6	8	14	8
2006-07	Vancouver Giants	WHL	63	21	24	45	32	22	9	11	20	14
2007-08	Vancouver Giants	WHL	70	33	45	78	69	10	5	2	7	6

MACIAS, Ray (mah-CHEE-ahs, RAY) COL.

Defense. Shoots right. 6'2", 195 lbs. Born, Long Beach, CA, September 18, 1986.
(Colorado's 6th choice, 124th overall, in 2005 Entry Draft).

			Regular Season					Playoffs				
Season	Club	League	GP	G	A	Pts	PIM	GP	G	A	Pts	PIM
2002-03	L.A. Jr. Kings	Minor-CA	49	37	26	63	100	....	....	....	....	....
	Kamloops Blazers	WHL	4	0	0	0	0	2	0	0	0	0
2003-04	Kamloops Blazers	WHL	69	12	17	29	14	5	2	0	2	0
2004-05	Kamloops Blazers	WHL	69	12	35	47	18	2	0	0	0	0
2005-06	Kamloops Blazers	WHL	68	12	26	38	34	....	....	....	....	....
2006-07	Kamloops Blazers	WHL	70	30	40	70	58	....	....	....	....	....
2007-08	Lake Erie Monsters	AHL	42	4	9	13	18	....	....	....	....	....
	Johnstown Chiefs	ECHL	5	0	5	5	0	6	1	3	4	2

WHL West First All-Star Team (2007)

MacINTYRE, Steve (MAK-ihn-tighr, STEEV) FLA.

Left wing. Shoots left. 6'6", 265 lbs. Born, Brock, Sask., August 8, 1980.

			Regular Season					Playoffs				
Season	Club	League	GP	G	A	Pts	PIM	GP	G	A	Pts	PIM
2002-03	St. Jean Mission	QSPHL	10	1	1	2	68	....	....	....	....	....
	Muskegon Fury	UHL	54	2	1	3	279	5	0	0	0	24
2003-04	Hartford Wolf Pack	AHL	3	0	0	0	0	....	....	....	....	....
	Charlotte	ECHL	61	1	4	5	217	....	....	....	....	....
	Jacksonville	WHA2	6	0	2	2	18	5	0	1	1	17
2004-05	Hartford Wolf Pack	AHL	27	1	1	2	207	....	....	....	....	....
	Charlotte	ECHL	46	1	4	5	214	11	0	4	4	17
2005-06	Charlotte	ECHL	61	3	2	5	238	1	0	0	0	4
2006-07	Quad City	UHL	46	2	1	3	168	5	0	0	0	6
2007-08	Providence Bruins	AHL	62	2	3	5	213	5	0	0	0	9

Signed as a free agent by **NY Rangers**, August 15, 2005. Signed as a free agent by **Quad City** (UHL), August 24, 2006. Signed as a free agent by **Florida**, July 3, 2008.

MacKENZIE, Aaron (muh-KEHN-zee, AIR-ruhn) COL.

Defense. Shoots left. 6', 193 lbs. Born, Terrace Bay, Ont., March 7, 1981.

			Regular Season					Playoffs				
Season	Club	League	GP	G	A	Pts	PIM	GP	G	A	Pts	PIM
1998-99	Thunder Bay Flyers	USHL	49	8	12	20	123	3	0	1	1	0
99-2000	U. of Denver	WCHA	40	1	9	10	56	....	....	....	....	....
2000-01	U. of Denver	WCHA	37	2	6	8	45	....	....	....	....	....
2001-02	U. of Denver	WCHA	39	5	18	23	30	....	....	....	....	....
2002-03	U. of Denver	WCHA	41	11	21	32	33	....	....	....	....	....
2003-04	Worcester IceCats	AHL	66	5	9	14	108	10	0	2	2	10
2004-05	Worcester IceCats	AHL	75	2	13	15	106	....	....	....	....	....
2005-06	Peoria Rivermen	AHL	51	2	7	9	35	4	0	0	0	6
2006-07	Peoria Rivermen	AHL	67	1	6	7	46	....	....	....	....	....
2007-08	Peoria Rivermen	AHL	55	0	5	5	20	....	....	....	....	....

WCHA First All-Star Team (2003)

Signed as a free agent by **Worcester** (AHL), October 6, 2003. Signed as a free agent by **St. Louis**, June 29, 2004. Signed as a free agent by **Peoria** (AHL), August 24, 2007. Signed as a free agent by **Colorado**, July 14, 2008.

MACKENZIE, Drew (muh-KEHN-zee , DROO) BUF.

Defense. Shoots left. 6'2", 200 lbs. Born, Stamford, CT, December 17, 1988.
(Buffalo's 8th choice, 209th overall, in 2007 Entry Draft).

			Regular Season					Playoffs				
Season	Club	League	GP	G	A	Pts	PIM	GP	G	A	Pts	PIM
2004-05	Taft Rhinos	High-CT	....	0	1	1	....	....	....	....	....	....
2005-06	Taft Rhinos	High-CT	....	0	11	11	....	....	....	....	....	....
2006-07	Taft Rhinos	High-CT	24	3	10	13	10	....	....	....	....	....
2007-08	Waterloo	USHL	57	4	14	18	103	11	0	6	6	4

• Signed Letter of Intent to attend **University of Vermont** (Hockey East) in fall of 2008.

MACLEAN, Brett (muh-KLAIN, BREHT) PHX.

Left wing. Shoots right. 6'2", 197 lbs. Born, Port Elgin, Ont., December 24, 1988.
(Phoenix's 3rd choice, 32nd overall, in 2007 Entry Draft).

			Regular Season					Playoffs				
Season	Club	League	GP	G	A	Pts	PIM	GP	G	A	Pts	PIM
2003-04	Grey-Bruce	Minor-ON	66	71	47	118	117	....	....	....	....	....
	Listowel Cyclones	OJHL-B	9	4	6	10	10	2	3	2	5	12
2004-05	Erie Otters	OHL	68	7	16	23	31	6	1	1	2	6
2005-06	Erie Otters	OHL	13	3	5	8	6	....	....	....	....	....
	Oshawa Generals	OHL	35	13	25	38	29	....	....	....	....	....
2006-07	Oshawa Generals	OHL	68	47	53	100	43	7	6	9	15	9
2007-08	Oshawa Generals	OHL	61	*61	58	119	42	15	5	11	16	12

OHL Second All-Star Team (2007) • OHL First All-Star Team (2008) • Canadian Major Junior Second All-Star Team (2008)

MacMILLAN, Logan (muhk-MIHL-uhn , LOH-guhn) ANA.

Center. Shoots left. 6'1", 182 lbs. Born, Charlottetown, PEI, July 5, 1989.
(Anaheim's 1st choice, 19th overall, in 2007 Entry Draft).

			Regular Season					Playoffs				
Season	Club	League	GP	G	A	Pts	PIM	GP	G	A	Pts	PIM
2004-05	Notre Dame	SJHL	41	9	19	28	27	....	....	....	....	....
2005-06	Halifax	QMJHL	62	9	9	18	31	11	1	0	1	0
2006-07	Halifax	QMJHL	68	20	35	55	82	12	9	11	20	6
2007-08	Halifax	QMJHL	46	15	26	41	77	15	3	10	13	20

MacWILLIAM, Andrew (MAK-WIHL-yuhm, AN-droo) TOR.

Defense. Shoots left. 6'2", 214 lbs. Born, Calgary, Alta., March 25, 1990.
(Toronto's 8th choice, 188th overall, in 2008 Entry Draft).

			Regular Season					Playoffs				
Season	Club	League	GP	G	A	Pts	PIM	GP	G	A	Pts	PIM
2006-07	Calgary Royals	AMHL	35	5	13	18	125	....	....	....	....	....
	Camrose Kodiaks	AJHL	2	0	0	0	0	1	0	0	0	0
2007-08	Camrose Kodiaks	AJHL	54	0	13	13	130	18	0	5	5	49

• Signed Letter of Intent to attend **University of North Dakota** (WCHA) in fall of 2008..

MADSEN, Morten (MAD-sehn, MOHR-tuhn) MIN.

Right wing. Shoots left. 6'2", 205 lbs. Born, Rodovre, Denmark, January 16, 1987.
(Minnesota's 5th choice, 122nd overall, in 2005 Entry Draft).

			Regular Season					Playoffs				
Season	Club	League	GP	G	A	Pts	PIM	GP	G	A	Pts	PIM
2003-04	V.Frolunda U18	Swe-U18	11	13	8	21	0	7	3	1	4	4
	V.Frolunda Jr.	Swe-Jr.	16	3	2	5	0	1	0	0	0	0
2004-05	Frolunda U18	Swe-U18	2	1	2	3	0	6	7	7	14	6
	Frolunda Jr.	Swe-Jr.	32	7	14	21	14	6	3	2	5	0
2005-06	Frolunda Jr.	Swe-Jr.	36	10	32	42	60	7	5	3	8	4
	Frolunda	Sweden	5	0	0	0	2	....	....	....	....	....
2006-07	Victoriaville Tigres	QMJHL	62	32	68	100	86	6	3	6	9	4
2007-08	Houston Aeros	AHL	50	3	17	20	18	3	1	0	1	0

MAGNAN-GRENIER, Olivier (MAHG-nah-GREH-n'yay) N.J.

Defense. Shoots left. 6'2", 200 lbs. Born, Sherbrooke, Que., May 1, 1986.
(New Jersey's 6th choice, 148th overall, in 2006 Entry Draft).

			Regular Season					Playoffs				
Season	Club	League	GP	G	A	Pts	PIM	GP	G	A	Pts	PIM
2004-05	Rouyn-Noranda	QMJHL	70	5	15	20	82	10	0	2	2	14
2005-06	Rouyn-Noranda	QMJHL	69	14	27	41	97	5	0	1	1	6
2006-07	Lowell Devils	AHL	24	1	1	2	13	....	....	....	....	....
	Trenton Titans	ECHL	45	1	9	10	63	1	0	0	0	0
2007-08	Lowell Devils	AHL	75	1	15	16	69	....	....	....	....	....

MAKAROV, Igor (mak-AH-rawv, EE-gohr) CHI.

Right wing. Shoots right. 6'1", 183 lbs. Born, Moscow, USSR, September 19, 1987.
(Chicago's 2nd choice, 33rd overall, in 2006 Entry Draft).

			Regular Season					Playoffs				
Season	Club	League	GP	G	A	Pts	PIM	GP	G	A	Pts	PIM
2003-04	Krylja Sovetov 2	Russia-3	1	0	0	0	0	....	....	....	....	....
2004-05	Krylja Sovetov 2	Russia-3	38	13	15	28	44	....	....	....	....	....
	Krylja Sovetov	Russia-2	6	2	2	4	4	1	0	0	0	0
2005-06	Krylja Sovetov	Russia-2	35	9	7	16	20	17	3	4	7	20
2006-07	SKA St. Petersburg	Russia	49	7	2	9	47	3	1	0	1	2
2007-08	St. Petersburg 2	Russia-3	3	1	3	4	2	2	1	2	3	2
	SKA St. Petersburg	Russia	50	4	11	15	26	9	2	1	3	35

MAKI, Ryan (MA-kee, RIGH-uhn) NSH.

Right wing. Shoots right. 6'2", 207 lbs. Born, Medford, NJ, April 23, 1985.
(Nashville's 5th choice, 176th overall, in 2005 Entry Draft).

			Regular Season					Playoffs				
Season	Club	League	GP	G	A	Pts	PIM	GP	G	A	Pts	PIM
2001-02	USNTDP	U-17	17	3	11	14	6	....	....	....	....	....
	USNTDP	NAHL	31	4	11	15	24	....	....	....	....	....
2002-03	USNTDP	U-18	42	5	6	11	18	....	....	....	....	....
	USNTDP	NAHL	10	1	0	1	8	....	....	....	....	....
2003-04	Harvard Crimson	ECAC	34	4	4	8	18	....	....	....	....	....
2004-05	Harvard Crimson	ECAC	30	10	9	19	20	....	....	....	....	....
2005-06	Harvard Crimson	ECAC	33	10	12	22	32	....	....	....	....	....
2006-07	Harvard Crimson	ECAC	32	12	11	23	36	....	....	....	....	....
	Milwaukee	AHL	2	0	1	1	0	2	0	0	0	0
2007-08	Milwaukee	AHL	54	2	3	5	23	3	0	0	0	2
	Cincinnati	ECHL	5	1	0	1	4	6	1	0	1	4

MALENKYKH, Vladimir (MAH-lihn-keh, vla-DIH-meer) PIT.

Defense. Shoots left. 6'1", 187 lbs. Born, Togliatti, USSR, October 1, 1980.
(Pittsburgh's 7th choice, 157th overall, in 1999 Entry Draft).

			Regular Season					Playoffs				
Season	Club	League	GP	G	A	Pts	PIM	GP	G	A	Pts	PIM
1997-98	Lada Togliatti 2	Russia-3	39	6	4	10	112	....	....	....	....	....
1998-99	Lada Togliatti 2	Russia-4	38	6	3	9	68	....	....	....	....	....
	Lada Togliatti	Russia	9	0	0	0	2	....	....	....	....	....
99-2000	Lada Togliatti 2	Russia-3	34	7	9	16	98	....	....	....	....	....
	CSK VVS Samara	Russia	7	0	1	1	14	....	....	....	....	....
	Lada Togliatti	Russia	1	0	0	0	0	....	....	....	....	....
	CSK VVS Samara 2	Russia-3	1	0	1	1	2	....	....	....	....	....
2000-01	Lada Togliatti	Russia	25	1	1	2	14	5	0	0	0	26
2001-02	Lada Togliatti	Russia	47	5	4	9	88	4	0	0	0	2
2002-03	Lada Togliatti	Russia	30	3	1	4	36	10	0	0	0	6
2003-04	Lada Togliatti	Russia	44	2	4	6	42	3	0	0	0	0
2004-05	Lada Togliatti	Russia	37	1	4	5	20	....	....	....	....	....
2005-06	Magnitogorsk	Russia	36	0	2	2	8	11	0	1	1	16
	Magnitogorsk 2	Russia-3	5	1	1	2	2	....	....	....	....	....
2006-07	Magnitogorsk	Russia	54	2	9	11	92	15	1	2	3	28
2007-08	Magnitogorsk 2	Russia-3	1	1	0	1	0	....	....	....	....	....
	Magnitogorsk	Russia	19	0	2	2	18	12	0	0	0	8

MALONE, Brad (MA-lohn, BRAD) COL.

Center/Left wing. Shoots left. 6'2", 207 lbs. Born, Miramichi, N.B., May 20, 1989.
(Colorado's 5th choice, 105th overall, in 2007 Entry Draft).

			Regular Season					Playoffs				
Season	Club	League	GP	G	A	Pts	PIM	GP	G	A	Pts	PIM
2005-06	Cushing	High-MA	STATISTICS NOT AVAILABLE									
2006-07	Sioux Falls	USHL	57	14	19	33	134	8	3	1	4	24
2007-08	North Dakota	WCHA	34	1	2	3	44	....	....	....	....	....

MARCHAND, Brad (mahr-SHAHND, BRAD) BOS.

Center. Shoots left. 5'9", 187 lbs. Born, Halifax, N.S., May 11, 1988.
(Boston's 4th choice, 71st overall, in 2006 Entry Draft).

			Regular Season					Playoffs				
Season	Club	League	GP	G	A	Pts	PIM	GP	G	A	Pts	PIM
2003-04	Dartmouth	NSMHL	60	47	47	94	104	....	....	....	....	....
2004-05	Moncton Wildcats	QMJHL	61	9	20	29	52	11	1	0	1	7
2005-06	Moncton Wildcats	QMJHL	68	29	37	66	83	20	5	14	19	34
2006-07	Val-d'Or Foreurs	QMJHL	57	33	47	80	108	20	*16	*24	*40	36
2007-08	Val-d'Or Foreurs	QMJHL	33	21	23	44	36	....	....	....	....	....
	Halifax	QMJHL	26	10	19	29	40	14	3	16	19	18

MARCINKO, Tomas (mahr-TSIHN-koh, TAW-mahsh) NYI

Center. Shoots right. 6'4", 187 lbs. Born, Poprad, Czech., April 11, 1988.
(NY Islanders' 6th choice, 115th overall, in 2006 Entry Draft).

			Regular Season					Playoffs				
Season	Club	League	GP	G	A	Pts	PIM	GP	G	A	Pts	PIM
2003-04	HC Kosice U18	Svk-U18	42	19	23	42	60	2	0	0	0	4
	HC Kosice Jr.	Slovak-Jr.	7	0	2	2	4	3	0	1	1	0
2004-05	HC Kosice	Slovakia	6	0	0	0	0	....	....	....	....	....
	HC Kosice Jr.	Slovak-Jr.	38	11	18	29	28	8	1	2	3	6
	HC Kosice	Slovakia	6	0	0	0	0	....	....	....	....	....
2005-06	HC Kosice Jr.	Slovak-Jr.	35	26	21	47	50	3	1	0	1	4
	HKm Humenne	Slovak-2	9	3	5	8	10	....	....	....	....	....
	HC Kosice	Slovakia	18	2	0	2	2	5	0	0	0	0
2006-07	Barrie Colts	OHL	56	19	21	40	56	8	0	1	1	8
2007-08	Barrie Colts	OHL	48	19	26	45	54	9	4	3	7	14

MAREK, Jan (MAIR-ehk, YAHN) L.A.

Center. Shoots right. 5'10", 185 lbs. Born, Jindrichuv Hradec, Czech., December 31, 1979.
(NY Rangers' 10th choice, 243rd overall, in 2003 Entry Draft).

			Regular Season					Playoffs				
Season	Club	League	GP	G	A	Pts	PIM	GP	G	A	Pts	PIM
1998-99	Trinec	CzRep	32	2	2	4	2	6	0	0	0	0
99-2000	HC Trinec Jr.	CzRep-Jr.	6	5	5	10	10	1	0	0	0	0
	HC Slezan Opava	CzRep-2	3	0	1	1	4	....	....	....	....	....
	Jind. Hradec	CzRep-2	4	0	3	3	10	....	....	....	....	....
	HC Ocelari Trinec	CzRep	32	1	5	6	4	2	0	0	0	0
2000-01	HC Ocelari Trinec	CzRep	38	7	4	11	2	....	....	....	....	....
2001-02	HC Ocelari Trinec	CzRep	52	13	27	40	44	6	1	3	4	6
2002-03	HC Ocelari Trinec	CzRep	51	*32	30	62	42	12	6	4	10	22
2003-04	HC Sparta Praha	CzRep	50	21	30	51	62	11	4	9	13	26
2004-05	HC Sparta Praha	CzRep	38	7	21	28	26	5	2	2	4	2
2005-06	HC Sparta Praha	CzRep	48	22	32	*54	66	17	4	4	8	24
2006-07	Magnitogorsk	Russia	47	17	30	47	70	15	7	10	17	10
2007-08	Magnitogorsk	Russia	49	16	32	48	40	11	4	3	7	2

Traded to **Los Angeles** by **NY Rangers** with Jason Ward, Marc-Andre Cliche and NY Rangers' 3rd round choice (later traded to Buffalo - Buffalo selected Corey Fienhage) in 2008 Entry Draft for Sean Avery and John Seymour, February 5, 2007.

MAROON, Patrick (ma-ROON, PAT-rihk) PHI.

Left wing. Shoots left. 6'4", 225 lbs. Born, St Louis, MO, April 23, 1988.
(Philadelphia's 6th choice, 161st overall, in 2007 Entry Draft).

			Regular Season					Playoffs				
Season	Club	League	GP	G	A	Pts	PIM	GP	G	A	Pts	PIM
2005-06	Texarkana Bandits	NAHL	57	23	37	60	61	8	3	1	4	22
2006-07	St. Louis Bandits	NAHL	57	40	55	*95	152	12	*10	*13	*23	12
2007-08	London Knights	OHL	64	35	55	90	57	5	0	1	1	10
	Philadelphia	AHL	1	0	0	0	0					

MARQUARDT, Matt (MAR-kwart, MAT) BOS.

Left wing. Shoots left. 6'3", 216 lbs. Born, North Bay, Ont., July 19, 1987.
(Columbus' 10th choice, 194th overall, in 2006 Entry Draft).

			Regular Season					Playoffs				
Season	Club	League	GP	G	A	Pts	PIM	GP	G	A	Pts	PIM
2003-04	Huntsville Wildcats	OPJHL	STATISTICS NOT AVAILABLE									
	Brockville Braves	CJHL	11	1	2	3	17	....	....	....	....	....
2004-05	Brockville Braves	CJHL	55	19	22	41	78	7	2	1	3	8
2005-06	Moncton Wildcats	QMJHL	68	16	9	25	69	20	5	3	8	12
2006-07	Moncton Wildcats	QMJHL	67	41	29	70	68	7	1	3	4	14
2007-08	Moncton Wildcats	QMJHL	35	20	13	33	38	....	....	....	....	....
	Baie-Comeau	QMJHL	33	23	13	36	33	5	1	1	2	6

CJHL Rookie of the Year (2005)

Traded to **Boston** by **Columbus** for Jonathon Sigalet, May 27, 2008.

MARSH, Tyson (MAHRSH, TIGH-suhn)

Defense. Shoots left. 6'1", 190 lbs. Born, Quesnel, B.C, June 20, 1984.

			Regular Season					Playoffs				
Season	Club	League	GP	G	A	Pts	PIM	GP	G	A	Pts	PIM
2000-01	Quesnel	BCHL	52	4	2	6	25	....	....	....	....	....
2001-02	Vancouver Giants	WHL	69	2	14	16	85	....	....	....	....	....
2002-03	Vancouver Giants	WHL	68	3	15	18	143	3	0	1	1	4
2003-04	Vancouver Giants	WHL	67	3	18	21	102	11	0	3	3	4
2004-05	St. John's	AHL	21	0	1	1	30	....	....	....	....	....
	Pensacola	ECHL	23	1	2	3	29	4	0	0	0	2
2005-06	Toronto Marlies	AHL	12	0	0	0	23	....	....	....	....	....
2006-07	Toronto Marlies	AHL	1	0	1	1	5	....	....	....	....	....
	Columbia Inferno	ECHL	48	2	19	21	97	....	....	....	....	....
2007-08	Rockford IceHogs	AHL	11	2	2	4	19	12	0	2	2	4
	Columbia Inferno	ECHL	61	3	14	17	126	....	....	....	....	....

Signed as a free agent by **Toronto**, September 18, 2002. • Missed majority of 2005-06 season recovering from abdominal injury.

MARSHALL, Kevin (MAR-shuhl, KEH-vihn) PHI.

Defense. Shoots left. 6'1", 200 lbs. Born, Boucherville, Que., March 10, 1989.
(Philadelphia's 2nd choice, 41st overall, in 2007 Entry Draft).

			Regular Season					Playoffs				
Season	Club	League	GP	G	A	Pts	PIM	GP	G	A	Pts	PIM
2004-05	C.C. Lemoyne	QAAA	39	2	9	11	88	5	0	1	1	16
2005-06	Lewiston	QMJHL	60	1	10	11	112	6	0	1	1	14
2006-07	Lewiston	QMJHL	70	5	27	32	141	17	0	7	7	38
2007-08	Lewiston	QMJHL	66	11	24	35	143	6	1	1	2	12

QMJHL Second All-Star Team (2008)

MARSHALL, Matt (MAR-shuhl, MAT) T.B.

Center/Right wing. Shoots right. 6'1", 175 lbs. Born, Boston, MA, August 30, 1988.
(Tampa Bay's 5th choice, 150th overall, in 2007 Entry Draft).

			Regular Season					Playoffs				
Season	Club	League	GP	G	A	Pts	PIM	GP	G	A	Pts	PIM
2005-06	Hingham	High-MA	STATISTICS NOT AVAILABLE									
2006-07	Nobles	High-MA	27	14	10	24	6	....	....	....	....	....
2007-08	Nobles	High-MA	29	25	26	51	....	....	....	....	....	....

• Signed Letter of Intent to attend **University of Vermont** (Hockey East) in fall of 2008.

MARTIN, Jesse (MAHR-tihn, JEH-see) ATL.

Center. Shoots right. 5'11", 170 lbs. Born, Edmonton, Alta., September 7, 1988.
(Atlanta's 6th choice, 195th overall, in 2006 Entry Draft).

			Regular Season					Playoffs				
Season	Club	League	GP	G	A	Pts	PIM	GP	G	A	Pts	PIM
2003-04	K of C Pats	AMHL	34	10	11	21	6	....	....	....	....	....
2004-05	K of C Pats	AMHL	30	17	28	45	70	8	4	8	12	....
2005-06	Spruce Grove	AJHL	40	15	29	44	122	....	....	....	....	....
2006-07	Tri-City Storm	USHL	59	19	37	56	31	9	2	4	6	4
2007-08	U. of Denver	WCHA	41	7	8	15	26	....	....	....	....	....

MARTIN, Matt (MAHR-tihn, MA-thew) NYI

Left wing. Shoots left. 6'2", 192 lbs. Born, Windsor, Ont., May 8, 1989.
(NY Islanders' 11th choice, 148th overall, in 2008 Entry Draft).

			Regular Season					Playoffs				
Season	Club	League	GP	G	A	Pts	PIM	GP	G	A	Pts	PIM
2005-06	Blenheim Blast	OHA-C	40	11	12	23	102	....	....	....	....	....
2006-07	Sarnia Blast	OJHL-B	9	2	5	7	16	....	....	....	....	....
	Sarnia Sting	OHL	39	3	3	6	52	4	0	0	0	0
2007-08	Sarnia Sting	OHL	66	25	13	38	155	9	3	3	6	16

MARTINEZ, Alec (mar-TEE-nehz, AL-ehk) L.A.

Defense. Shoots left. 6', 188 lbs. Born, Rochester Hills, MI, July 26, 1987.
(Los Angeles' 5th choice, 95th overall, in 2007 Entry Draft).

			Regular Season					Playoffs				
Season	Club	League	GP	G	A	Pts	PIM	GP	G	A	Pts	PIM
2004-05	Cedar Rapids	USHL	58	10	11	21	30	11	1	2	3	8
2005-06	Miami U.	CCHA	39	3	8	11	31	....	....	....	....	....
2006-07	Miami U.	CCHA	42	9	15	24	40	....	....	....	....	....
2007-08	Miami U.	CCHA	42	9	23	32	42	....	....	....	....	....

CCHA First All-Star Team (2008) • NCAA West Second All-American Team (2008)

MARVIN, Aaron (MAHR-vihn, AIR-ruhn) CGY.

Forward. Shoots left. 6'3", 185 lbs. Born, Warrod, MN, May 27, 1988.
(Calgary's 3rd choice, 89th overall, in 2006 Entry Draft).

			Regular Season					Playoffs				
Season	Club	League	GP	G	A	Pts	PIM	GP	G	A	Pts	PIM
2004-05	Warroad Warriors	High-MN	31	23	25	48	18	....	....	....	....	....
2005-06	Warroad Warriors	High-MN	23	9	21	30	40	....	....	....	....	....
2006-07	Tri-City Storm	USHL	13	1	3	4	8	9	1	0	1	8
2007-08	St. Cloud State	WCHA	40	3	10	13	33	....	....	....	....	....

MASON, Tyrell (MAY-sohn, TIGH-rehl) NYI

Defense. Shoots left. 6'1", 167 lbs. Born, Grand Prairie, Alta., March 12, 1986.
(NY Islanders' 5th choice, 180th overall, in 2005 Entry Draft).

			Regular Season					Playoffs				
Season	Club	League	GP	G	A	Pts	PIM	GP	G	A	Pts	PIM
2003-04	Salmon Arm	BCHL	59	7	29	36	36	....	....	....	....	....
2004-05	Salmon Arm	BCHL	51	6	36	42	78	....	....	....	....	....
2005-06	Clarkson Knights	ECAC	38	1	5	6	38	....	....	....	....	....
2006-07	Clarkson Knights	ECAC	39	1	11	12	62	....	....	....	....	....
2007-08	Clarkson Knights	ECAC	37	1	9	10	60	....	....	....	....	....

MATSON, Taylor (MAT-suhn, TAY-luhr) VAN.

Center. Shoots right. 5'10", 165 lbs. Born, Mound, MN, September 16, 1988.
(Vancouver's 5th choice, 176th overall, in 2007 Entry Draft).

			Regular Season					Playoffs				
Season	Club	League	GP	G	A	Pts	PIM	GP	G	A	Pts	PIM
2005-06	Holy Angels	High-MN	27	30	40	70	28	....	....	....	....	....
2006-07	Holy Angels	High-MN	11	16	15	31	16	....	....	....	....	....
	Des Moines	USHL	10	1	2	3	6	6	0	1	1	10
2007-08	Des Moines	USHL	55	13	24	37	38	....	....	....	....	....

MATSUMOTO, Jonathan (mat-suh-MOH-toh, JAWN-ah-thuhn) PHI.

Center. Shoots left. 6', 184 lbs. Born, Ottawa, Ont., October 13, 1986.
(Philadelphia's 5th choice, 79th overall, in 2006 Entry Draft).

			Regular Season					Playoffs				
Season	Club	League	GP	G	A	Pts	PIM	GP	G	A	Pts	PIM
2002-03	Cumberland	CJHL	8	2	3	5	2	10	4	7	11	2
2003-04	Cumberland	CJHL	51	31	32	63	26	7	5	5	10	6
2004-05	Bowling Green	CCHA	36	18	14	32	22	....	....	....	....	....
2005-06	Bowling Green	CCHA	36	20	28	48	43	....	....	....	....	....
2006-07	Bowling Green	CCHA	38	11	22	33	70	....	....	....	....	....
	Philadelphia	AHL	16	2	2	4	10	....	....	....	....	....
2007-08	Philadelphia	AHL	77	20	24	44	52	12	2	2	4	10

MAXWELL, Ben (MAX-wehl, BEHN) MTL.

Center. Shoots left. 6'1", 185 lbs. Born, North Vancouver, B.C., March 30, 1988.
(Montreal's 2nd choice, 49th overall, in 2006 Entry Draft).

			Regular Season					Playoffs				
Season	Club	League	GP	G	A	Pts	PIM	GP	G	A	Pts	PIM
2003-04	North Delta Ice	PIJHL	40	17	28	45	46	5	3	6	9	0
	South Surrey	BCHL	2	0	0	0	0	....	....	....	....	....
	Kootenay Ice	WHL	3	0	1	1	2	1	0	0	0	0
2004-05	Kootenay Ice	WHL	68	8	10	18	37	16	0	1	1	6
2005-06	Kootenay Ice	WHL	69	28	32	60	52	6	3	5	8	0
2006-07	Kootenay Ice	WHL	39	19	34	53	42	7	1	4	5	21
2007-08	Kootenay Ice	WHL	31	9	18	27	26	10	6	3	9	14

MAYOROV, Maxim (may-YOHR-ahv, mahx-EEM) CBJ

Left wing. Shoots left. 6'2", 187 lbs. Born, Andizhan, USSR, March 26, 1989.
(Columbus' 5th choice, 94th overall, in 2007 Entry Draft).

			Regular Season					Playoffs				
Season	Club	League	GP	G	A	Pts	PIM	GP	G	A	Pts	PIM
2005-06	Ak Bars Kazan 2	Russia-3	STATISTICS NOT AVAILABLE									
2006-07	Leninogorsk	Russia-2	28	6	4	10	6	....	....	....	....	....
	Almetjevsk	Russia-2	6	1	1	2	0	4	0	0	0	2
2007-08	Ak Bars Kazan	Russia	11	1	0	1	16	....	....	....	....	....

McARDLE, Kenndal (muh-KAHR-duhl, KEHN-dahl) FLA.

Left wing. Shoots left. 5'11", 190 lbs. Born, Toronto, Ont., January 4, 1987.
(Florida's 1st choice, 20th overall, in 2005 Entry Draft).

			Regular Season					Playoffs				
Season	Club	League	GP	G	A	Pts	PIM	GP	G	A	Pts	PIM
2002-03	Burnaby W.C.	Minor-BC	30	1	9	10	131	....	....	....	....	....
	Moose Jaw	WHL	2	0	0	0	0	....	....	....	....	....
2003-04	Moose Jaw	WHL	54	8	8	16	57	10	3	2	5	6
2004-05	Moose Jaw	WHL	70	37	37	74	122	5	1	0	1	16
2005-06	Moose Jaw	WHL	72	28	43	71	135	22	6	10	16	43
2006-07	Moose Jaw	WHL	26	10	10	20	75	....	....	....	....	....
	Vancouver Giants	WHL	37	9	13	22	54	22	*11	9	20	49
2007-08	Rochester	AHL	36	5	5	10	31	....	....	....	....	....
	Florida Everblades	ECHL	6	3	1	4	26	3	0	0	0	2

McBAIN, Jamie (muhk-BAYN, JAY-mee) CAR.

Defense. Shoots right. 6'2", 200 lbs. Born, Edina, MN, February 25, 1988.
(Carolina's 1st choice, 63rd overall, in 2006 Entry Draft).

			Regular Season					Playoffs				
Season	Club	League	GP	G	A	Pts	PIM	GP	G	A	Pts	PIM
2003-04	Shat.-St. Mary's	High-MN	73	6	27	33	....	....	....	....	....	....
2004-05	USNTDP	U-17	14	1	6	7	16	....	....	....	....	....
	USNTDP	NAHL	38	2	7	9	22	10	0	3	3	4
2005-06	USNTDP	U-18	41	9	16	25	35	....	....	....	....	....
	USNTDP	NAHL	14	0	5	5	6	....	....	....	....	....
2006-07	U. of Wisconsin	WCHA	36	3	15	18	36	....	....	....	....	....
2007-08	U. of Wisconsin	WCHA	35	5	19	24	18	....	....	....	....	....

WCHA All-Rookie Team (2007)

McCARTHY, John (muh-KAHR-thee, JAWN) S.J.

Left wing. Shoots left. 6'1", 205 lbs. Born, Boston, MA, August 9, 1986.
(San Jose's 5th choice, 202nd overall, in 2006 Entry Draft).

			Regular Season					Playoffs				
Season	Club	League	GP	G	A	Pts	PIM	GP	G	A	Pts	PIM
2004-05	Des Moines	USHL	60	8	10	18	32	....	....	....	....	....
2005-06	Boston University	H-East	33	2	2	4	12	....	....	....	....	....
2006-07	Boston University	H-East	39	2	3	5	18	....	....	....	....	....
2007-08	Boston University	H-East	38	4	3	7	24	....	....	....	....	....

McCOLLEM, Matthew (muh-KAHL-uhm, MA-thew) ST.L.

Left wing. Shoots left. 6', 185 lbs. Born, Somerville, MA, May 6, 1988.
(St. Louis' 8th choice, 154th overall, in 2006 Entry Draft).

			Regular Season					Playoffs				
Season	Club	League	GP	G	A	Pts	PIM	GP	G	A	Pts	PIM
2004-05	Belmont Hill	High-MA	....	2	7	9	....	....	....	....	....	....
2005-06	Belmont Hill	High-MA	....	15	11	26	....	....	....	....	....	....
2006-07	Belmont Hill	High-MA	28	16	19	35	64	....	....	....	....	....
2007-08	Harvard Crimson	ECAC	31	5	9	14	28	....	....	....	....	....

McCRAE, Justin (muh-KRAY, JUHS-tihn) CAR.

Center. Shoots right. 6'1", 185 lbs. Born, Calgary, Alta., October 30, 1988.
(Carolina's 3rd choice, 102nd overall, in 2007 Entry Draft).

			Regular Season					Playoffs				
Season	Club	League	GP	G	A	Pts	PIM	GP	G	A	Pts	PIM
2003-04	Strathmore	AMHL	36	9	14	23	36	....	....	....	....	....
	Saskatoon Blades	WHL	6	0	0	0	2	....	....	....	....	....
2004-05	Saskatoon Blades	WHL	68	8	11	19	44	4	0	0	0	2
2005-06	Saskatoon Blades	WHL	71	17	24	41	58	9	1	2	3	10
2006-07	Saskatoon Blades	WHL	61	16	33	49	98	....	....	....	....	....
2007-08	Saskatoon Blades	WHL	35	11	13	24	22	....	....	....	....	....
	Spokane Chiefs	WHL	30	8	9	17	25	21	0	7	7	14

McCULLOCH, Scott (muh-KUHL-uh, SKAWT) CHI.

Left wing. Shoots left. 6', 212 lbs. Born, Edmonton, Alta., March 10, 1986.
(Chicago's 11th choice, 165th overall, in 2004 Entry Draft).

			Regular Season					Playoffs				
Season	Club	League	GP	G	A	Pts	PIM	GP	G	A	Pts	PIM
2003-04	Grand Prairie	AJHL	44	23	26	49	85	16	12	8	20	18
2004-05	Colorado College	WCHA	11	4	3	7	6	....	....	....	....	....
2005-06	Colorado College	WCHA	42	5	7	12	67	....	....	....	....	....
2006-07	Colorado College	WCHA	39	18	6	24	44	....	....	....	....	....
2007-08	Colorado College	WCHA	37	13	8	21	52	....	....	....	....	....

McCUTCHEON, Mark (muh-KUH-chuhn, MAHRK)

Center. Shoots right. 6', 190 lbs. Born, Ithaca, NY, May 21, 1984.
(Colorado's 3rd choice, 146th overall, in 2003 Entry Draft).

			Regular Season					Playoffs				
Season	Club	League	GP	G	A	Pts	PIM	GP	G	A	Pts	PIM
2001-02	N.E. Jr. Coyotes	EJHL	36	24	26	50	84	....	....	....	....	....
2002-03	N.E. Jr. Coyotes	EJHL	35	27	22	49	76	10	8	5	13	24
2003-04	Cornell Big Red	ECAC	32	0	4	4	12	....	....	....	....	....
2004-05	Cornell Big Red	ECAC	22	0	5	5	12	....	....	....	....	....
2005-06	Cornell Big Red	ECAC	34	9	6	15	34	....	....	....	....	....
2006-07	Cornell Big Red	ECAC	29	10	10	20	32	....	....	....	....	....
2007-08	Lake Erie Monsters	AHL	63	2	7	9	73	....	....	....	....	....

McDONAGH, Ryan (muhk-DUHN-uh, RIGH-uhn) MTL.

Defense. Shoots left. 6'1", 211 lbs. Born, St.Paul, MN, June 13, 1989.
(Montreal's 1st choice, 12th overall, in 2007 Entry Draft).

			Regular Season					Playoffs				
Season	Club	League	GP	G	A	Pts	PIM	GP	G	A	Pts	PIM
2004-05	Cretin-Derham	High-MN	28	12	18	30	....	....	....	....	....	....
2005-06	Cretin-Derham	High-MN	25	12	33	45	....	....	....	....	....	....
2006-07	Cretin-Derham	High-MN	26	14	26	40	....	....	....	....	....	....
2007-08	U. of Wisconsin	WCHA	40	5	7	12	42	....	....	....	....	....

WCHA All-Rookie Team (2008)

McDONALD, Colin (muhk-DAWN-uhld, KAW-lihn) EDM.

Right wing. Shoots right. 6'3", 205 lbs. Born, New Haven, CT, September 30, 1984.
(Edmonton's 2nd choice, 51st overall, in 2003 Entry Draft).

			Regular Season					Playoffs				
Season	Club	League	GP	G	A	Pts	PIM	GP	G	A	Pts	PIM
2001-02	N.E. Jr. Coyotes	EJHL	39	16	20	36	50	....	....	....	....	....
2002-03	N.E. Jr. Coyotes	EJHL	44	28	40	*68	59	....	....	....	....	....
2003-04	Providence College	H-East	37	10	6	16	47	....	....	....	....	....
2004-05	Providence College	H-East	26	11	5	16	14	....	....	....	....	....
2005-06	Providence College	H-East	36	9	19	28	29	....	....	....	....	....
2006-07	Providence College	H-East	36	13	4	17	30	....	....	....	....	....
2007-08	Springfield Falcons	AHL	73	12	11	23	46	....	....	....	....	....

Hockey East All-Rookie Team (2004)

McGINN, Jamie (muh-GIHN, JAY-mee) S.J.

Left wing. Shoots left. 6', 185 lbs. Born, Fergus, Ont., August 5, 1988.
(San Jose's 2nd choice, 36th overall, in 2006 Entry Draft).

			Regular Season					Playoffs				
Season	Club	League	GP	G	A	Pts	PIM	GP	G	A	Pts	PIM
2003-04	Tor. Jr. Canadiens	GTHL	31	....	....	48	....	18	14	18	32	....
2004-05	Ottawa 67's	OHL	59	10	12	22	35	18	4	7	11	0
2005-06	Ottawa 67's	OHL	65	26	31	57	113	6	2	2	4	4
2006-07	Ottawa 67's	OHL	68	46	43	89	49	5	5	1	6	2
	Worcester Sharks	AHL	4	1	1	2	4	6	0	0	0	8
2007-08	Ottawa 67's	OHL	51	29	29	58	54	4	2	2	4	4
	Worcester Sharks	AHL	8	0	2	2	0	....	....	....	....	....

McGRATH, Evan (muh-GRATH, EH-vuhn) DET.

Center. Shoots left. 6', 190 lbs. Born, Oakville, Ont., January 14, 1986.
(Detroit's 2nd choice, 128th overall, in 2004 Entry Draft).

			Regular Season					Playoffs				
Season	Club	League	GP	G	A	Pts	PIM	GP	G	A	Pts	PIM
2001-02	Oakville Blades	OPJHL	49	43	44	87	24	....	....	....	....	....
2002-03	Kitchener Rangers	OHL	64	16	31	47	40	21	6	2	8	6
2003-04	Kitchener Rangers	OHL	68	15	36	51	28	5	2	1	3	2
2004-05	Kitchener Rangers	OHL	67	28	59	87	51	15	7	6	13	6
2005-06	Kitchener Rangers	OHL	67	37	77	114	63	5	1	3	4	4
2006-07	Grand Rapids	AHL	59	6	8	14	41	7	0	0	0	0
	Toledo Storm	ECHL	9	6	9	15	12	....	....	....	....	....
2007-08	Grand Rapids	AHL	78	18	17	35	26	....	....	....	....	....

OHL All-Rookie Team (2003)

McGUIRK, Brian (muh-GUHRK, BRIGH-uhn)

Left wing. Shoots left. 6', 191 lbs. Born, Danvers, MA, July 11, 1985.
(Columbus' 10th choice, 231st overall, in 2004 Entry Draft).

			Regular Season					Playoffs				
Season	Club	League	GP	G	A	Pts	PIM	GP	G	A	Pts	PIM
2003-04	Gov. Dummer	High-MA	25	16	16	32	....	....	....	....	....	....
2004-05	Boston University	H-East	33	0	1	1	18	....	....	....	....	....
2005-06	Boston University	H-East	39	5	4	9	18	....	....	....	....	....
2006-07	Boston University	H-East	36	1	4	5	24	....	....	....	....	....
2007-08	Boston University	H-East	37	4	9	13	53	....	....	....	....	....
	Syracuse Crunch	AHL	6	2	1	3	11	....	....	....	....	....

McINTYRE, David (MAK-ihn-tigh-uhr, DAY-vihd) DAL.

Center. Shoots left. 5'11", 171 lbs. Born, Oakville, Ont., February 4, 1987.
(Dallas' 4th choice, 138th overall, in 2006 Entry Draft).

			Regular Season					Playoffs				
Season	Club	League	GP	G	A	Pts	PIM	GP	G	A	Pts	PIM
2004-05	Newmarket	OPJHL	46	17	14	31	33	16	8	7	15	20
2005-06	Newmarket	OPJHL	46	42	50	92	143	11	4	8	12	42
2006-07	Colgate	ECAC	40	9	8	17	75	....	....	....	....	....
2007-08	Colgate	ECAC	39	15	17	32	38	....	....	....	....	....

McKENZIE, Ian (muh-KEHN-zee, EE-an) NSH.

Right wing. Shoots right. 6'4", 205 lbs. Born, Weyburn, Sask., May 23, 1987.

			Regular Season					Playoffs				
Season	Club	League	GP	G	A	Pts	PIM	GP	G	A	Pts	PIM
2003-04	Saskatoon Blazers	SMHL	STATISTICS NOT AVAILABLE									
	Moose Jaw	WHL	8	0	0	0	0	....	....	....	....	....
2004-05	Moose Jaw	WHL	44	3	4	7	18	5	0	0	0	11
2005-06	Moose Jaw	WHL	42	4	3	7	68	22	5	3	8	8
2006-07	Moose Jaw	WHL	6	1	0	1	10	....	....	....	....	....
	Seattle	WHL	60	12	9	21	77	11	2	1	3	17
2007-08	Seattle	WHL	68	19	21	40	103	12	8	6	14	12

Signed as a free agent by **Nashville**, May 6, 2008.

McKENZIE, Jim (muh-KEHN-zee, JIHM) OTT.

Right wing. Shoots right. 6'2", 204 lbs. Born, St. Paul, MN, June 10, 1984.
(Ottawa's 7th choice, 141st overall, in 2004 Entry Draft).

			Regular Season					Playoffs				
Season	Club	League	GP	G	A	Pts	PIM	GP	G	A	Pts	PIM
2000-01	Hill-Murray	High-MN	27	9	13	22	....	....	....	....	....	....
2001-02	USNTDP	U-18	13	7	8	15	10	....	....	....	....	....
	USNTDP	USHL	2	0	1	1	9	....	....	....	....	....
	USNTDP	NAHL	4	0	2	2	4	....	....	....	....	....
	Green Bay	USHL	17	1	2	3	34	....	....	....	....	....
2002-03	Sioux Falls	USHL	45	6	18	24	108	....	....	....	....	....
2003-04	Sioux Falls	USHL	59	26	38	64	168	....	....	....	....	....
2004-05	Michigan State	CCHA	34	11	7	18	44	....	....	....	....	....
2005-06	Michigan State	CCHA	43	11	17	28	85	....	....	....	....	....
2006-07	Michigan State	CCHA	35	12	18	30	56	....	....	....	....	....
2007-08	Binghamton	AHL	18	2	1	3	15	....	....	....	....	....
	Elmira Jackals	ECHL	43	9	10	19	43	6	1	0	1	6

McKNIGHT, Matt (muhk-NIGHT, MAT) DAL.

Forward. Shoots right. 6'2", 190 lbs. Born, Red Deer, Alta., June 14, 1984.
(Dallas' 10th choice, 280th overall, in 2004 Entry Draft).

			Regular Season					Playoffs				
Season	Club	League	GP	G	A	Pts	PIM	GP	G	A	Pts	PIM
2003-04	Camrose Kodiaks	AJHL	42	20	36	56	31	....	....	....	....	....
2004-05	U. Minn-Duluth	WCHA	30	6	13	19	16	....	....	....	....	....
2005-06	U. Minn-Duluth	WCHA	40	9	16	25	24	....	....	....	....	....
2006-07	U. Minn-Duluth	WCHA	29	4	5	9	16	....	....	....	....	....
2007-08	U. Minn-Duluth	WCHA	33	6	10	16	24	....	....	....	....	....

McLAREN, Frazer (muh-KLAIR-uhn, FRAY-zuhr) S.J.

Left wing. Shoots left. 6'5", 230 lbs. Born, Winnipeg, Man., October 29, 1987.
(San Jose's 8th choice, 203rd overall, in 2007 Entry Draft).

			Regular Season					Playoffs				
Season	Club	League	GP	G	A	Pts	PIM	GP	G	A	Pts	PIM
2002-03	Kelvin	High-MB	56	27	24	51	136	....	....	....	....	....
2003-04	Portland	WHL	50	0	3	3	44	1	0	0	0	0
2004-05	Portland	WHL	71	6	5	11	124	7	0	0	0	10
2005-06	Portland	WHL	70	12	6	18	194	12	0	2	2	27
2006-07	Portland	WHL	61	19	12	31	186	....	....	....	....	....
2007-08	Portland	WHL	18	4	3	7	45	....	....	....	....	....
	Moose Jaw	WHL	48	15	18	33	119	6	1	1	2	8
	Worcester Sharks	AHL	4	0	1	1	17	....	....	....	....	....

McLEAN, Kurtis (muh-KLAYN, KUHR-this) NYI

Center. Shoots right. 5'11", 175 lbs. Born, Kirkland Lake, Ont., November 2, 1980.

			Regular Season					Playoffs				
Season	Club	League	GP	G	A	Pts	PIM	GP	G	A	Pts	PIM
2005-06	Wilkes-Barre	AHL	32	4	11	15	8	....	....	....	....	....
	Wheeling Nailers	ECHL	41	31	25	56	32	5	4	4	8	4
2006-07	Wilkes-Barre	AHL	55	16	16	32	24	10	4	3	7	4
	Wheeling Nailers	ECHL	16	11	12	23	21	....	....	....	....	....
2007-08	Wilkes-Barre	AHL	76	22	32	54	58	23	4	15	19	8

Signed as a free agent by **Wilkes-Barre-Scranton** (AHL), September 29, 2005. Signed as a free agent by **Pittsburgh**, September 7, 2006. Signed as a free agent by **NY Islanders**, July 3, 2008.

McMILLAN, Brandon (muhk-MIHL-uhn, BRAN-duhn) ANA.

Center. Shoots left. 5'11", 188 lbs. Born, Richmond, B.C., March 22, 1990.
(Anaheim's 7th choice, 85th overall, in 2008 Entry Draft).

			Regular Season					Playoffs				
Season	Club	League	GP	G	A	Pts	PIM	GP	G	A	Pts	PIM
2006-07	Kelowna Rockets	WHL	55	2	10	12	27	....	....	....	....	....
2007-08	Kelowna Rockets	WHL	71	15	26	41	56	7	0	0	0	6

McMILLAN, Carson (muhk-MIHL-lihn, KAHR-suhn) MIN.

Right wing. Shoots right. 6'1", 194 lbs. Born, Brandon, Man., September 10, 1988.
(Minnesota's 5th choice, 200th overall, in 2007 Entry Draft).

			Regular Season					Playoffs				
Season	Club	League	GP	G	A	Pts	PIM	GP	G	A	Pts	PIM
2003-04	Crocus Plains	High-MB	STATISTICS NOT AVAILABLE									
	Brandon	MMHL	4	0	0	0	0	....	....	....	....	....
2004-05	Brandon	MMHL	40	17	19	36	34	5	3	4	7	8
	Winkler Flyers	MJHL	4	1	1	2	2	....	....	....	....	....
2005-06	Calgary Hitmen	WHL	59	3	2	5	42	13	0	0	0	2
2006-07	Calgary Hitmen	WHL	72	7	15	22	76	18	2	0	2	17
2007-08	Calgary Hitmen	WHL	72	16	26	42	87	16	1	0	1	22

McNEILL, Patrick (muhk-NEEL, PAT-rihk) WSH.

Defense. Shoots left. 6', 198 lbs. Born, Strathroy, Ont., March 17, 1987.
(Washington's 4th choice, 118th overall, in 2005 Entry Draft).

			Regular Season					Playoffs				
Season	Club	League	GP	G	A	Pts	PIM	GP	G	A	Pts	PIM
2002-03	Strathroy Rockets	OHA-B	45	6	13	19	53	....	....	....	....	....
2003-04	Saginaw Spirit	OHL	57	3	11	14	28	....	....	....	....	....
2004-05	Saginaw Spirit	OHL	66	7	26	33	31	....	....	....	....	....
2005-06	Saginaw Spirit	OHL	68	21	56	77	64	4	1	3	4	6
2006-07	Saginaw Spirit	OHL	58	22	36	58	49	6	3	2	5	6
2007-08	Hershey Bears	AHL	48	1	13	14	16	2	0	0	0	0
	South Carolina	ECHL	19	5	11	16	16	5	0	2	2	4

OHL Second All-Star Team (2006)

McPHERSON, Corbin (muhk-FUHR-suhn, KOHR-bihn) N.J.

Defense. Shoots right. 6'4", 210 lbs. Born, Folsom, CA, September 7, 1988.
(New Jersey's 3rd choice, 87th overall, in 2007 Entry Draft).

			Regular Season					Playoffs				
Season	Club	League	GP	G	A	Pts	PIM	GP	G	A	Pts	PIM
2005-06	San Jose Jr. Sharks	Minor-CA	59	5	16	21	45	....	....	....	....	....
2006-07	Cowichan Valley	BCHL	44	4	10	14	63	18	1	3	4	14
2007-08	Cowichan Valley	BCHL	55	3	14	17	84	....	....	....	....	....

McQUAID, Adam (muhk-WAYD, A-duhm) BOS.

Defense. Shoots right. 6'5", 209 lbs. Born, Charlottetown, PEI, October 12, 1986.
(Columbus' 2nd choice, 55th overall, in 2005 Entry Draft).

			Regular Season					Playoffs				
Season	Club	League	GP	G	A	Pts	PIM	GP	G	A	Pts	PIM
2003-04	Sudbury Wolves	OHL	47	3	6	9	25	7	0	1	1	2
2004-05	Sudbury Wolves	OHL	66	3	16	19	98	8	0	2	2	10
2005-06	Sudbury Wolves	OHL	68	3	14	17	107	10	0	1	1	16
2006-07	Sudbury Wolves	OHL	65	9	22	31	110	21	1	5	6	24
2007-08	Providence Bruins	AHL	68	1	8	9	73	10	0	0	0	9

Traded to **Boston** by **Columbus** for Boston's 5th round choice (later traded to Dallas - Dallas selected Jamie Benn) in 2007 Entry Draft, May 16, 2007.

McRAE, Philip (muh-KRAY, FIHL-ihp) ST.L.

Center. Shoots left. 6'2", 189 lbs. Born, Minneapolis, MN, March 15, 1990.
(St. Louis' 2nd choice, 33rd overall, in 2008 Entry Draft).

			Regular Season					Playoffs				
Season	Club	League	GP	G	A	Pts	PIM	GP	G	A	Pts	PIM
2005-06	USNTDP	U-17	15	1	1	2	0	....	....	....	....	....
	USNTDP	NAHL	33	8	8	16	9	10	1	2	3	2
2006-07	London Knights	OHL	63	2	8	10	27	16	0	0	0	6
2007-08	London Knights	OHL	66	18	28	46	61	4	0	0	0	7

MECKLER, David (MEHK-luhr, DAY-vihd) L.A.

Center. Shoots right. 6', 204 lbs. Born, Highland Park, IL, July 9, 1987.
(Los Angeles' 7th choice, 134th overall, in 2006 Entry Draft).

			Regular Season					Playoffs				
Season	Club	League	GP	G	A	Pts	PIM	GP	G	A	Pts	PIM
2004-05	Waterloo	USHL	60	30	15	45	32	5	3	2	5	2
2005-06	Yale	ECAC	31	7	3	10	28	....	....	....	....	....
2006-07	London Knights	OHL	67	38	35	73	53	16	*15	7	22	20
2007-08	Manchester	AHL	76	23	13	36	24	4	1	1	2	2

MEDVEC, Kyle (MEHD-vek, KIGHL) MIN.

Defense. Shoots left. 6'6", 205 lbs. Born, Westminster, CO, June 16, 1988.
(Minnesota's 4th choice, 102nd overall, in 2006 Entry Draft).

			Regular Season					Playoffs				
Season	Club	League	GP	G	A	Pts	PIM	GP	G	A	Pts	PIM
2003-04	Apple Valley	High-MN	27	1	12	13	30	....	....	....	....	....
2004-05	Apple Valley	High-MN	23	4	16	20	18	....	....	....	....	....
2005-06	Apple Valley	High-MN	28	13	22	35	44	....	....	....	....	....
	Sioux City	USHL	3	0	0	0	0	....	....	....	....	....
2006-07	Sioux City	USHL	57	4	14	18	83	7	0	0	0	4
2007-08	U. of Vermont	H-East	30	1	4	5	18	....	....	....	....	....

MEGALINSKY, Dmitri (meh-gahl-IHN-skee, dih-MEE-tree) OTT.

Defense. Shoots left. 6'2", 212 lbs. Born, Perm, USSR, April 15, 1985.
(Ottawa's 7th choice, 186th overall, in 2005 Entry Draft).

			Regular Season					Playoffs				
Season	Club	League	GP	G	A	Pts	PIM	GP	G	A	Pts	PIM
2003-04	HK Voronezh	Russia-2	42	4	8	12	159	....	....	....	....	....
	Yaroslavl	Russia	1	0	0	0	0	....	....	....	....	....
	Yaroslavl 2	Russia-3	11	0	4	4	16	....	....	....	....	....
2004-05	Yaroslavl	Russia	1	0	0	0	2	....	....	....	....	....
	Yaroslavl 2	Russia-3	30	6	12	18	82	....	....	....	....	....
2005-06	Yaroslavl 2	Russia-3	12	4	10	14	6	....	....	....	....	....
	Yaroslavl	Russia	20	0	1	1	8	8	0	0	0	6
2006-07	Khimik	Russia-2	33	4	7	11	34	7	0	1	1	16
2007-08	Vityaz Chekhov	Russia	25	2	7	9	20	....	....	....	....	....

MELYAKOV, Igor (mehl-yuh-KAHF, EE-gohr) L.A.

Left wing. Shoots left. 5'10", 190 lbs. Born, Lipetsk, USSR, December 23, 1976.
(Los Angeles' 6th choice, 137th overall, in 1995 Entry Draft).

			Regular Season					Playoffs				
Season	Club	League	GP	G	A	Pts	PIM	GP	G	A	Pts	PIM
1993-94	Torpedo Yaroslavl	CIS	39	4	3	7	10	4	0	0	0	0
1994-95	Torpedo Yaroslavl	CIS	50	6	8	14	34	4	0	1	1	0
1995-96	Torpedo Yaroslavl	CIS	39	5	1	6	6	3	0	0	0	2
1996-97	Torpedo Yaroslavl	Russia	8	0	0	0	0	....	....	....	....	....
	Nizhny Novgorod	Russia	12	2	3	5	10	....	....	....	....	....
1997-98	Nizhny Novgorod	Russia	13	3	3	6	6	....	....	....	....	....
1998-99	Nizhny Novgorod	Russia-2	36	13	17	30	14	....	....	....	....	....
99-2000	Nizhny Novgorod	Russia	34	1	8	9	10	5	1	0	1	4
2000-01	Nizhny Novgorod	Russia	24	2	3	5	10	....	....	....	....	....
2001-02	HK Lipetsk	Russia-2	68	16	37	53	94	....	....	....	....	....
2002-03	Voskresensk	Russia-2	48	9	22	31	16	....	....	....	....	....
2003-04	Nizhny Novgorod	Russia	45	5	10	15	18	....	....	....	....	....
	Nizh. Novgorod 2	Russia-3	4	1	6	7	4	....	....	....	....	....
2004-05	Nizhny Novgorod	Russia-2	52	14	30	44	32	11	2	4	6	18
2005-06	Magnitogorsk	Russia	25	7	8	15	10	3	0	0	0	2
2006-07	Novokuznetsk	Russia	22	0	1	1	8	....	....	....	....	....
	Nizhny Novgorod	Russia-2	16	2	6	8	10	12	2	5	7	6
2007-08	Nizhny Novgorod	Russia	8	1	0	1	6	....	....	....	....	....
	Zauralje Kurgan	Russia-2	24	2	11	13	38	....	....	....	....	....

MERCIER, Justin (MUHR-see-uhr, JUHS-tihn) COL.

Forward. Shoots left. 5'11", 190 lbs. Born, Erie, PA, June 25, 1987.
(Colorado's 8th choice, 168th overall, in 2005 Entry Draft).

			Regular Season					Playoffs				
Season	Club	League	GP	G	A	Pts	PIM	GP	G	A	Pts	PIM
2003-04	St. Louis	USHL	60	12	9	21	....	....	....	....	....	....
2004-05	USNTDP	U-18	26	1	7	8	31	....	....	....	....	....
	USNTDP	NAHL	16	4	3	7	33	....	....	....	....	....
2005-06	Miami U.	CCHA	35	3	7	10	32	....	....	....	....	....
2006-07	Miami U.	CCHA	40	10	15	25	59	....	....	....	....	....
2007-08	Miami U.	CCHA	42	25	15	40	42	....	....	....	....	....

MESSIER, Charles-Antoine (MEH-see-ay, SHARL-AN-twuhn) VAN.

Center. Shoots left. 5'10", 183 lbs. Born, Boucherville, Que., November 4, 1988.
(Vancouver's 3rd choice, 145th overall, in 2007 Entry Draft).

			Regular Season					Playoffs				
Season	Club	League	GP	G	A	Pts	PIM	GP	G	A	Pts	PIM
2005-06	Baie-Comeau	QMJHL	57	4	11	15	33	4	2	0	2	2
2006-07	Baie-Comeau	QMJHL	69	27	21	48	67	11	0	3	3	14
2007-08	Acadie-Bathurst	QMJHL	34	9	11	20	69	....	....	....	....	....
	Chicoutimi	QMJHL	32	5	16	21	79	4	1	2	3	10

MESTERY, Eric (MEHS-tuhr-ee, AIR-ihk) WSH.

Defense. Shoots left. 6'5", 196 lbs. Born, Winnipeg, Man., May 28, 1990.
(Washington's 3rd choice, 57th overall, in 2008 Entry Draft).

			Regular Season					Playoffs				
Season	Club	League	GP	G	A	Pts	PIM	GP	G	A	Pts	PIM
2005-06	Wpg. Thrashers	MMHL	39	5	18	23	28	....	....	....	....	....
2006-07	Tri-City Americans	WHL	43	1	6	7	20	....	....	....	....	....
2007-08	Tri-City Americans	WHL	71	2	14	16	65	16	2	1	3	10

MEYERS, Josh (MIGH-uhrs, JAWSH) L.A.

Defense. Shoots right. 6'2", 180 lbs. Born, Alexandria, MN, December 7, 1985.
(Los Angeles' 7th choice, 206th overall, in 2005 Entry Draft).

			Regular Season					Playoffs				
Season	Club	League	GP	G	A	Pts	PIM	GP	G	A	Pts	PIM
2003-04	Minnesota Blizzard	NAHL	27	2	12	14	....	....	....	....	....	....
2004-05	Sioux City	USHL	57	8	24	32	92	13	1	9	10	18
2005-06	U. Minn-Duluth	WCHA	27	3	7	10	20	....	....	....	....	....
2006-07	U. Minn-Duluth	WCHA	37	11	13	24	30	....	....	....	....	....
2007-08	U. Minn-Duluth	WCHA	36	6	8	14	72	....	....	....	....	....

MIHALIK, Vladimir (mih-HAHL-ihk, vla-DIH-meer) T.B.

Defense. Shoots left. 6'7", 222 lbs. Born, Presov, Czech., January 29, 1987.
(Tampa Bay's 1st choice, 30th overall, in 2005 Entry Draft).

			Regular Season					Playoffs				
Season	Club	League	GP	G	A	Pts	PIM	GP	G	A	Pts	PIM
2003-04	Presov	Svk-U18	6	4	4	8	4	....	....	....	....	....
	Presov Jr.	Slovak-Jr.	23	6	10	16	44	....	....	....	....	....
2004-05	PHK Presov Jr.	Slovak-Jr.	23	6	10	16	44	....	....	....	....	....
	PHK Presov	Slovak-2	32	3	1	4	24	6	0	1	1	2
2005-06	Red Deer Rebels	WHL	62	3	9	12	86	....	....	....	....	....
2006-07	Prince George	WHL	53	7	19	26	91	15	1	2	3	17
2007-08	Norfolk Admirals	AHL	68	1	15	16	68	....	....	....	....	....

MIKHAILISHIN, Alexander (mih-khigh-LIHSH-ihn, al-EHX-AN-duh) N.J.

Defense. Shoots left. 6'4", 210 lbs. Born, Moscow, USSR, February 24, 1986.
(New Jersey's 2nd choice, 155th overall, in 2004 Entry Draft).

			Regular Season					Playoffs				
Season	Club	League	GP	G	A	Pts	PIM	GP	G	A	Pts	PIM
2001-02	Spartak Moscow 2	Russia-3	15	0	0	0	2	....	....	....	....	....
2002-03	Spartak Moscow 2	Russia-3	7	1	1	2	4	....	....	....	....	....
2003-04	Spartak Moscow 2	Russia-3	STATISTICS NOT AVAILABLE									
2004-05	Spartak Moscow	Russia	6	0	1	1	4	....	....	....	....	....
2005-06	Spartak Moscow 2	Russia-3	23	2	0	2	72	....	....	....	....	....
2006-07	Yuzhny Ural Orsk	Russia-2	22	0	0	0	128	....	....	....	....	....
	Krylja Sovetov 2	Russia-3	12	1	1	2	22	....	....	....	....	....
2007-08			DID NOT PLAY									

MIKKELSON, Brendan (MIGHK-ehl-sohn, BREHN-duhn) ANA.

Defense. Shoots left. 6'3", 202 lbs. Born, Regina, Sask., June 22, 1987.
(Anaheim's 2nd choice, 31st overall, in 2005 Entry Draft).

			Regular Season					Playoffs				
Season	Club	League	GP	G	A	Pts	PIM	GP	G	A	Pts	PIM
2003-04	Portland	WHL	65	3	12	15	43	5	1	0	1	0
2004-05	Portland	WHL	70	5	10	15	60	7	1	2	3	0
2005-06	Portland	WHL	3	1	1	2	4	....	....	....	....	....
	Vancouver Giants	WHL	19	1	8	9	37	....	....	....	....	....
2006-07	Vancouver Giants	WHL	69	6	23	29	60	21	3	7	10	10
2007-08	Portland Pirates	AHL	66	6	10	16	50	14	2	6	8	2

Memorial Cup Tournament All-Star Team (2007)

• Missed majority of 2005-06 season recovering from shoulder and knee injuries.

MIKUS, Juraj (MEE-kuhsh, YUHR-ay) TOR.

Defense. Shoots left. 6'4", 185 lbs. Born, Trencin, Czech., November 30, 1988.
(Toronto's 4th choice, 134th overall, in 2007 Entry Draft).

			Regular Season					Playoffs				
Season	Club	League	GP	G	A	Pts	PIM	GP	G	A	Pts	PIM
2004-05	Piestany U18	Svk-U18	2	1	2	3	2	....	....	....	....	....
	Dukla Trencin U18	Svk-U18	39	2	7	9	20	5	0	0	0	0
2005-06	Piestany Jr.	Slovak-Jr.	6	0	4	4	2	....	....	....	....	....
	Dukla Trencin Jr.	Slovak-Jr.	17	1	4	5	2	....	....	....	....	....
	Dukla Trencin U18	Svk-U18	40	3	18	21	36	7	1	5	6	12
2006-07	Dukla Trencin Jr.	Slovak-Jr.	42	9	15	24	72	7	2	1	3	10
	P. Bystrica	Slovak-2	7	0	3	3	2	1	0	0	0	0
	Dukla Trencin	Slovakia	22	0	0	0	2	7	0	0	0	0
2007-08	HK VSR SR 20	Slovakia	21	1	4	5	30	....	....	....	....	....
	Dukla Trencin	Slovakia	14	0	3	3	4	14	0	1	1	2

MILLER, Tyler (MIHL-luhr, TIGH-luhr) N.J.

Defense. Shoots left. 6'4", 210 lbs. Born, Placentia, CA, September 15, 1986.
(New Jersey's 5th choice, 107th overall, in 2006 Entry Draft).

			Regular Season					Playoffs				
Season	Club	League	GP	G	A	Pts	PIM	GP	G	A	Pts	PIM
2004-05	South Surrey	BCHL	53	3	9	12	85	....	....	....	....	....
2005-06	Penticton Vees	BCHL	60	16	32	48	73	....	....	....	....	....
2006-07	Northern Mich.	CCHA	37	2	12	14	12	....	....	....	....	....
2007-08	Northern Mich.	CCHA	42	2	7	9	53	....	....	....	....	....

MIRNOV, Igor (mihr-NAWF, EE-gohr) OTT.

Left wing. Shoots left. 6', 187 lbs. Born, Chita, USSR, September 19, 1984.
(Ottawa's 2nd choice, 67th overall, in 2003 Entry Draft).

			Regular Season					Playoffs				
Season	Club	League	GP	G	A	Pts	PIM	GP	G	A	Pts	PIM
2001-02	Dyn'o Moscow 2	Russia-3	30	33	17	50	34	....	....	....	....	....
	Dynamo Moscow	Russia	6	0	0	0	0	....	....	....	....	....
2002-03	Dynamo Moscow	Russia	50	3	7	10	49	5	0	0	0	2
2003-04	Dynamo Moscow	Russia	53	11	10	21	26	3	0	0	0	2
2004-05	Dynamo Moscow	Russia	55	13	13	26	50	9	2	4	6	0
2005-06	Dynamo Moscow	Russia	32	8	10	18	36	4	0	2	2	4
2006-07	Dynamo Moscow	Russia	49	21	25	46	54	3	2	1	3	4
2007-08	Dynamo Moscow	Russia	24	3	3	6	16	....	....	....	....	....
	Magnitogorsk	Russia	23	9	6	15	20	13	3	1	4	4

MISHARIN, Georgy (mih-SHAHR-ihn, g'YOHR-gee) **MIN.**

Defense. Shoots left. 6', 198 lbs. Born, Yekaterinburg, USSR, May 11, 1985.
(Minnesota's 6th choice, 207th overall, in 2003 Entry Draft).

			Regular Season					Playoffs				
Season	Club	League	GP	G	A	Pts	PIM	GP	G	A	Pts	PIM
2001-02	Yekaterinburg 2	Russia-3	STATISTICS NOT AVAILABLE									
	Magnitogorsk 2	Russia-3	STATISTICS NOT AVAILABLE									
2002-03	Yekaterinburg	Russia-2	28	1	3	4	16	....	....	....	....	....
2003-04	Saginaw Spirit	OHL	65	5	22	27	42	....	....	....	....	....
2004-05	Nizhnekamsk	Russia	47	1	3	4	38	3	0	0	0	4
2005-06	CSKA Moscow	Russia	50	4	9	13	46	7	0	0	0	31
2006-07	Dynamo Moscow	Russia	48	3	7	10	70	3	0	1	1	12
2007-08	CSKA Moscow	Russia	50	6	5	11	42	6	0	3	3	6

Signed as a free agent by **Dynamo Moscow** (Russia), August 31, 2006.

MITCHELL, Dale (MIH-chuhl, DAYL) **TOR.**

Right wing. Shoots right. 5'9", 205 lbs. Born, Etobicoke, Ont., April 9, 1989.
(Toronto's 1st choice, 74th overall, in 2007 Entry Draft).

			Regular Season					Playoffs				
Season	Club	League	GP	G	A	Pts	PIM	GP	G	A	Pts	PIM
2005-06	Oshawa Generals	OHL	65	20	23	43	63	....	....	....	....	....
2006-07	Oshawa Generals	OHL	67	43	37	80	81	9	1	4	5	12
2007-08	Oshawa Generals	OHL	63	24	36	60	79	15	10	6	16	23
	Toronto Marlies	AHL	....	....	....	....	....	2	0	1	1	2

MITCHELL, John (MIH-chuhl, JAWN) **TOR.**

Center. Shoots left. 6'2", 205 lbs. Born, Waterloo, Ont., January 22, 1985.
(Toronto's 4th choice, 158th overall, in 2003 Entry Draft).

			Regular Season					Playoffs				
Season	Club	League	GP	G	A	Pts	PIM	GP	G	A	Pts	PIM
2000-01	Waterloo Siskens	OPJHL	47	15	29	44	33	....	....	....	....	....
2001-02	Plymouth Whalers	OHL	62	9	9	18	23	6	1	0	1	4
2002-03	Plymouth Whalers	OHL	68	18	37	55	31	18	2	10	12	8
2003-04	Plymouth Whalers	OHL	65	28	54	82	45	9	6	6	12	6
2004-05	Plymouth Whalers	OHL	63	25	50	75	59	4	1	1	2	0
	St. John's	AHL	2	0	0	0	0	....	....	....	....	....
2005-06	Toronto Marlies	AHL	51	5	12	17	22	2	0	0	0	0
2006-07	Toronto Marlies	AHL	73	16	20	36	46	....	....	....	....	....
2007-08	Toronto Marlies	AHL	79	20	31	51	56	19	8	4	12	12

MITERA, Mark (MIH-tair-a, MAHRK) **ANA.**

Defense. Shoots left. 6'3", 211 lbs. Born, Royal Oak, MI, October 22, 1987.
(Anaheim's 1st choice, 19th overall, in 2006 Entry Draft).

			Regular Season					Playoffs				
Season	Club	League	GP	G	A	Pts	PIM	GP	G	A	Pts	PIM
2003-04	USNTDP	U-17	16	2	6	8	22	....	....	....	....	....
	USNTDP	NAHL	43	2	13	15	69	7	0	2	2	10
2004-05	USNTDP	U-18	45	5	10	15	91	....	....	....	....	....
	USNTDP	NAHL	16	2	6	8	32	....	....	....	....	....
2005-06	U. of Michigan	CCHA	39	0	10	10	59	....	....	....	....	....
2006-07	U. of Michigan	CCHA	41	1	17	18	52	....	....	....	....	....
2007-08	U. of Michigan	CCHA	43	2	21	23	60	....	....	....	....	....

CCHA Second All-Star Team (2008)

MOLLE, Ryan (MOHL, RIGH-uhn) **N.J.**

Defense. Shoots right. 6'3", 195 lbs. Born, Winnipeg, Man., January 29, 1989.
(New Jersey's 6th choice, 207th overall, in 2007 Entry Draft).

			Regular Season					Playoffs				
Season	Club	League	GP	G	A	Pts	PIM	GP	G	A	Pts	PIM
2004-05	Cgy. Stampeders	CBHL	STATISTICS NOT AVAILABLE									
	Vancouver Giants	WHL	1	0	0	0	0	....	....	....	....	....
2005-06	Calgary Flames	AMHL	35	3	16	19	60	....	....	....	....	....
	Vancouver Giants	WHL	2	0	0	0	0	....	....	....	....	....
2006-07	Swift Current	WHL	61	1	4	5	52	6	1	0	1	8
2007-08	Swift Current	WHL	62	2	8	10	57	12	0	2	2	14

MOLLER, Oscar (MOH-luhr, OAWZ-kuhr) **L.A.**

Center. Shoots right. 5'11", 182 lbs. Born, Stockholm, Sweden, January 22, 1989.
(Los Angeles' 2nd choice, 52nd overall, in 2007 Entry Draft).

			Regular Season					Playoffs				
Season	Club	League	GP	G	A	Pts	PIM	GP	G	A	Pts	PIM
2003-04	Spanga U18	Swe-U18	32	28	12	40	68	....	....	....	....	....
2004-05	Spanga U18	Swe-U18	24	28	16	44	52	....	....	....	....	....
	Spanga Jr.	Swe-Jr.	4	6	1	7	6	....	....	....	....	....
	Spanga	Sweden-4	6	6	4	10	0	....	....	....	....	....
2005-06	Djurgarden U18	Swe-U18	8	8	5	13	6	2	1	0	1	0
	Djurgarden Jr.	Swe-Jr.	25	8	5	13	41	4	2	0	2	0
2006-07	Chilliwack Bruins	WHL	68	32	37	69	50	5	0	3	3	6
2007-08	Chilliwack Bruins	WHL	63	39	43	82	42	4	2	1	3	4
	Manchester	AHL	....	....	....	....	....	2	0	1	1	0

WHL West First All-Star Team (2008)

MONDOU, Benoit (mawn-DOO, BEHN-wah) **N.J.**

Center. Shoots right. 5'10", 180 lbs. Born, Sorel, Que., May 3, 1985.
(Boston's 9th choice, 247th overall, in 2003 Entry Draft).

			Regular Season					Playoffs				
Season	Club	League	GP	G	A	Pts	PIM	GP	G	A	Pts	PIM
2001-02	Baie-Comeau	QMJHL	64	25	45	70	36	5	1	5	6	4
2002-03	Baie-Comeau	QMJHL	25	5	16	21	12	....	....	....	....	....
	Shawinigan	QMJHL	35	6	35	41	21	9	3	8	11	8
2003-04	Shawinigan	QMJHL	68	34	61	95	32	10	4	9	13	2
2004-05	Shawinigan	QMJHL	57	16	43	59	44	4	2	3	5	9
2005-06	Shawinigan	QMJHL	59	46	52	98	57	8	5	4	9	6
2006-07	Trenton Titans	ECHL	62	25	31	56	36	5	2	1	3	6
2007-08	Lowell Devils	AHL	51	11	18	29	14	....	....	....	....	....
	Trenton Devils	ECHL	3	4	1	5	2	....	....	....	....	....

QMJHL All-Rookie Team (2002) • Canadian Major Junior Sportsman of the Year (2004)
Signed as a free agent by **New Jersey**, June 24, 2006.

MONTGOMERY, Kevin (mawnt-GUHM-uhr-ee, KEH-vihn) **COL.**

Defense. Shoots left. 6'1", 185 lbs. Born, Rochester, NY, April 4, 1988.
(Colorado's 5th choice, 110th overall, in 2006 Entry Draft).

			Regular Season					Playoffs				
Season	Club	League	GP	G	A	Pts	PIM	GP	G	A	Pts	PIM
2003-04	Syracuse Jr. Stars	EmJHL	62	7	28	35	....	....	....	....	....	....
2004-05	USNTDP	U-17	8	1	4	5	4	....	....	....	....	....
	USNTDP	NAHL	38	4	12	16	46	9	1	3	4	6
2005-06	USNTDP	U-18	42	2	10	12	61	....	....	....	....	....
	USNTDP	NAHL	17	4	6	10	15	....	....	....	....	....
2006-07	Ohio State	CCHA	17	1	4	5	18	....	....	....	....	....
	London Knights	OHL	31	1	16	17	50	9	0	0	0	6
2007-08	London Knights	OHL	63	9	34	43	95	5	0	1	1	4
	Lake Erie Monsters	AHL	5	0	0	0	2	....	....	....	....	....

MOON, Nathan (MOON, NAY-thun) **PIT.**

Center. Shoots right. 5'11", 179 lbs. Born, Belleville, Ont., January 4, 1990.
(Pittsburgh's 1st choice, 120th overall, in 2008 Entry Draft).

			Regular Season					Playoffs				
Season	Club	League	GP	G	A	Pts	PIM	GP	G	A	Pts	PIM
2006-07	Kingston	OHL	56	13	27	40	39	5	2	0	2	0
2007-08	Kingston	OHL	68	35	42	77	79	....	....	....	....	....

MOORE, Mike (MOOR, MIGHK) **S.J.**

Defense. Shoots left. 6'1", 200 lbs. Born, Calgary, Alta., December 12, 1984.

			Regular Season					Playoffs				
Season	Club	League	GP	G	A	Pts	PIM	GP	G	A	Pts	PIM
2003-04	South Surrey	BCHL	52	6	21	27	148	10	0	2	2	6
2004-05	Princeton	ECAC	25	3	7	10	22	....	....	....	....	....
2005-06	Princeton	ECAC	30	0	4	4	42	....	....	....	....	....
2006-07	Princeton	ECAC	32	4	10	14	50	....	....	....	....	....
2007-08	Princeton	ECAC	34	7	17	24	40	....	....	....	....	....
	Worcester Sharks	AHL	3	0	0	0	16	....	....	....	....	....

ECAC First All-Star Team (2008) • NCAA East First All-American Team (2008)
Signed as a free agent by **San Jose**, April 8, 2008.

MORIN, Travis (moh-REHN, TRA-vihs) **WSH.**

Center. Shoots left. 6'2", 195 lbs. Born, Minneapolis, MN, January 9, 1984.
(Washington's 13th choice, 263rd overall, in 2004 Entry Draft).

			Regular Season					Playoffs				
Season	Club	League	GP	G	A	Pts	PIM	GP	G	A	Pts	PIM
2001-02	Chicago Steel	USHL	20	5	8	13	....	4	0	0	0	2
2002-03	Chicago Steel	USHL	60	21	26	47	46	....	....	....	....	....
2003-04	Minnesota State	WCHA	38	9	12	21	14	....	....	....	....	....
2004-05	Minnesota State	WCHA	36	12	19	31	20	....	....	....	....	....
2005-06	Minnesota State	WCHA	39	20	22	42	16	....	....	....	....	....
2006-07	Minnesota State	WCHA	38	17	22	39	34	....	....	....	....	....
	South Carolina	ECHL	8	2	1	3	0	....	....	....	....	....
2007-08	Hershey Bears	AHL	4	0	0	0	0	....	....	....	....	....
	South Carolina	ECHL	68	34	50	84	30	20	*10	7	17	18

WCHA Second All-Star Team (2007)

MORNEAU, Samuel (mohr-NOH, SAM-ew-l) **CAR.**

Left wing. Shoots left. 5'11", 190 lbs. Born, Cowansville, Que., February 10, 1990.
(Carolina's 5th choice, 195th overall, in 2008 Entry Draft).

			Regular Season					Playoffs				
Season	Club	League	GP	G	A	Pts	PIM	GP	G	A	Pts	PIM
2006-07	Acadie-Bathurst	QMJHL	51	6	10	16	34	10	1	0	1	0
2007-08	Baie-Comeau	QMJHL	68	23	19	42	54	5	0	1	1	8

MORRIS, Mike (MOHR-his, MIGHK) **S.J.**

Right wing. Shoots right. 6'1", 185 lbs. Born, Dorchester, MA, July 14, 1983.
(San Jose's 1st choice, 27th overall, in 2002 Entry Draft).

			Regular Season					Playoffs				
Season	Club	League	GP	G	A	Pts	PIM	GP	G	A	Pts	PIM
2000-01	St. Sebastian's	High-MA	28	20	28	48	18	....	....	....	....	....
2001-02	St. Sebastian's	High-MA	31	29	29	58	26	....	....	....	....	....
2002-03	Northeastern	H-East	26	9	12	21	16	....	....	....	....	....
2003-04	Northeastern	H-East	34	10	20	30	14	....	....	....	....	....
2004-05	Northeastern	H-East	34	19	20	39	22	....	....	....	....	....
2005-06	Northeastern	H-East	DID NOT PLAY – INJURED									
2006-07	Northeastern	H-East	20	7	11	18	22	....	....	....	....	....
2007-08	Worcester Sharks	AHL	9	1	1	2	2	....	....	....	....	....

Hockey East Second All-Star Team (2005)

• Missed entire 2005-06 season with post-concussion syndrome. • Missed majority of 2007-08 season recovering from a sports hernia injury.

MORRISON, Brett (MOHR-ih-suhn , BREHT) **ANA.**

Center. Shoots left. 5'11", 192 lbs. Born, Sydney, N.S., July 25, 1987.
(Anaheim's 8th choice, 151st overall, in 2007 Entry Draft).

			Regular Season					Playoffs				
Season	Club	League	GP	G	A	Pts	PIM	GP	G	A	Pts	PIM
2003-04	Cape Breton	NSMHL	36	43	41	84	22	....	....	....	....	....
2004-05	Gatineau	QMJHL	51	7	15	22	6	8	0	0	0	0
2005-06	Gatineau	QMJHL	64	33	39	72	53	16	2	5	7	4
2006-07	Gatineau	QMJHL	36	23	31	54	50	....	....	....	....	....
	PEI Rocket	QMJHL	28	12	24	36	26	7	8	8	16	10
2007-08	PEI Rocket	QMJHL	40	26	31	57	48	....	....	....	....	....
	Rouyn-Noranda	QMJHL	25	13	21	34	12	17	6	20	26	14

MOTIN, Johan (MOH-tihn, YOH-han) **EDM.**

Defense. Shoots right. 6'1", 202 lbs. Born, Karlskoga, Sweden, October 10, 1989.
(Edmonton's 2nd choice, 103rd overall, in 2008 Entry Draft).

			Regular Season					Playoffs				
Season	Club	League	GP	G	A	Pts	PIM	GP	G	A	Pts	PIM
2005-06	Farjestad U18	Swe-U18	14	0	7	7	6	8	0	2	2	8
2006-07	Farjestad U18	Swe-U18	1	0	0	0	0	1	1	1	2	0
	Skare BK Karlstad	Sweden-3	18	0	4	4	30	....	....	....	....	....
	Farjestad	Sweden	22	0	4	4	8	9	0	0	0	2
2007-08	Farjestad	Sweden	28	0	2	2	10	....	....	....	....	....
	Bofors	Sweden-2	15	2	3	5	18	....	....	....	....	....
	Skare BK	Sweden-3	3	0	2	2	2	....	....	....	....	....

MOZYAKIN, Sergei (mohz-YA-kihn, SAIR-gay) **CBJ**

Left wing. Shoots right. 5'10", 165 lbs. Born, Yaroslavl, USSR, March 30, 1981.
(Columbus' 13th choice, 263rd overall, in 2002 Entry Draft).

			Regular Season					Playoffs				
Season	Club	League	GP	G	A	Pts	PIM	GP	G	A	Pts	PIM
1998-99	Val-d'Or Foreurs	QMJHL	4	0	1	1	2	....	....	....	....	....
99-2000	HK Moscow 2	Russia-3	6	9	3	12	6	....	....	....	....	....
	HK Moscow	Russia-2	44	23	25	48	10	....	....	....	....	....
2000-01	HK Moscow	Russia-2	37	22	28	50	18	....	....	....	....	....
	CSKA Moscow	Russia	9	0	2	2	0	....	....	....	....	....
2001-02	HK CSKA Moscow	Russia-2	54	34	30	64	10	12	9	12	21	4
2002-03	CSKA Moscow	Russia	33	12	15	27	18	....	....	....	....	....
2003-04	CSKA Moscow	Russia	45	21	19	40	6	....	....	....	....	....
2004-05	CSKA Moscow	Russia	49	11	12	23	22	....	....	....	....	....
2005-06	CSKA Moscow	Russia	51	20	*31	*51	28	7	1	2	3	4
2006-07	Mytischi	Russia	54	27	33	60	10	9	5	3	8	4
2007-08	Mytischi	Russia	57	*37	29	*66	22	5	3	1	4	0

MURATOV, Yevgeny (muhr-A-tahf, yehv-GEH-nee) **EDM.**

Left wing. Shoots right. 5'10", 178 lbs. Born, Nizhny Tagil, USSR, January 28, 1981.
(Edmonton's 10th choice, 274th overall, in 2000 Entry Draft).

			Regular Season					Playoffs				
Season	Club	League	GP	G	A	Pts	PIM	GP	G	A	Pts	PIM
1997-98	Nizhnekamsk 2	Russia-3	39	7	7	14	2	....	....	....	....	....
1998-99	Nizhnekamsk 2	Russia-4	37	26	9	35	32	....	....	....	....	....
	Nizhnekamsk	Russia	4	0	0	0	0	3	1	0	1	2
99-2000	Nizhnekamsk	Russia	29	9	7	16	2	....	....	....	....	....
	Ak Bars Kazan	Russia	8	2	2	4	2	9	0	0	0	2
2000-01	Nizhnekamsk	Russia	42	9	8	17	14	4	0	0	0	0
2001-02	Nizhnekamsk	Russia	45	5	13	18	4	....	....	....	....	....
2002-03	Nizhnekamsk	Russia	51	10	11	21	41	....	....	....	....	....
2003-04	Nizhnekamsk	Russia	20	1	6	7	8	....	....	....	....	....
2004-05	Novokuznetsk	Russia	58	15	13	28	12	4	1	2	3	0
2005-06	SKA St. Petersburg	Russia	49	13	10	23	16	3	0	1	1	0
2006-07	SKA St. Petersburg	Russia	42	5	9	14	14	1	0	0	0	0
	St. Petersburg 2	Russia-3	5	5	5	10	2	....	....	....	....	....
2007-08	Nizhnekamsk	Russia	22	2	5	7	8	....	....	....	....	....
	Sibir Novosibirsk	Russia	30	3	2	5	6	....	....	....	....	....

Signed as a free agent by **Nizhnekamsk** (Russia), August 5, 2007.

MURPHY, Colin (MUHR-fee, KOHL-ihn) **BUF.**

Left wing. Shoots left. 6', 195 lbs. Born, Fort McMurray, Alta., April 11, 1980.

			Regular Season					Playoffs				
Season	Club	League	GP	G	A	Pts	PIM	GP	G	A	Pts	PIM
2001-02	Michigan Tech	WCHA	38	8	19	27	40	....	....	....	....	....
2002-03	Michigan Tech	WCHA	37	20	20	40	42	....	....	....	....	....
2003-04	Michigan Tech	WCHA	33	15	17	32	28	....	....	....	....	....
2004-05	Michigan Tech	WCHA	37	11	*42	53	40	....	....	....	....	....
	St. John's	AHL	12	1	7	8	34	5	1	3	4	17
2005-06	Toronto Marlies	AHL	53	16	17	33	44	4	0	0	0	0
2006-07	Toronto Marlies	AHL	73	20	36	56	126	....	....	....	....	....
2007-08	Toronto Marlies	AHL	68	11	27	38	152	11	2	3	5	34

WCHA First All-Star Team (2005) • NCAA West Second All-American Team (2005)

Signed as a free agent by **Toronto**, March 18, 2005. Signed as a free agent by **Buffalo**, August 4, 2008.

MURPHY, Ryan (MUHR-fee, RIGH-uhn) **N.J.**

Left wing. Shoots left. 6'1", 205 lbs. Born, Van Nuys, CA, March 21, 1979.
(Carolina's 4th choice, 113th overall, in 1999 Entry Draft).

			Regular Season					Playoffs				
Season	Club	League	GP	G	A	Pts	PIM	GP	G	A	Pts	PIM
1995-96	Thornhill Islanders	MTJHL	32	13	16	29	49	1	0	0	0	0
1996-97	Thornhill Islanders	MTJHL	41	22	32	54	36	12	7	8	15	....
1997-98	Bowling Green	CCHA	36	3	9	12	27	....	....	....	....	....
1998-99	Bowling Green	CCHA	34	10	23	33	38	....	....	....	....	....
99-2000	Bowling Green	CCHA	36	9	10	19	63	....	....	....	....	....
2000-01	Bowling Green	CCHA	38	23	15	38	22	....	....	....	....	....
2001-02	Florida Everblades	ECHL	66	13	18	31	38	6	1	2	3	4
2002-03	Lowell	AHL	12	1	2	3	4	....	....	....	....	....
	Florida Everblades	ECHL	58	28	17	45	47	1	0	0	0	0
2003-04	Albany River Rats	AHL	71	10	9	19	28	....	....	....	....	....
2004-05	Albany River Rats	AHL	75	13	23	36	44	....	....	....	....	....
2005-06	Albany River Rats	AHL	17	4	2	6	12	....	....	....	....	....
2006-07	Lowell Devils	AHL	69	17	21	38	22	....	....	....	....	....
2007-08	Lowell Devils	AHL	59	9	21	30	14	....	....	....	....	....

Signed as a free agent by **New Jersey**, July 20, 2003.

MURSAK , Jan (MUHR-sak, YAHN) **DET.**

Left wing. Shoots right. 5'11", 167 lbs. Born, Maribor, Yugoslavia, January 20, 1988.
(Detroit's 5th choice, 182nd overall, in 2006 Entry Draft).

			Regular Season					Playoffs				
Season	Club	League	GP	G	A	Pts	PIM	GP	G	A	Pts	PIM
2002-03	HK Maribor U18	Sloven-U18	13	27	18	45	14	....	....	....	....	....
2003-04	HK Maribor U18	Sloven-U18	22	27	17	44	14	....	....	....	....	....
	HK Maribor Jr.	Sloven-Jr.	19	8	8	16	37	....	....	....	....	....
	HK Maribor	Slovenia	14	3	3	6	16	....	....	....	....	....
2004-05	HK Maribor Jr.	Sloven-Jr.	19	17	16	33	39	....	....	....	....	....
	HK Maribor	Slovenia	24	16	29	45	10	....	....	....	....	....
2005-06	C. Budejovice Jr.	CzRep-Jr.	43	15	15	30	32	5	0	2	2	2
2006-07	Saginaw Spirit	OHL	62	27	53	80	50	6	1	2	3	10
	Grand Rapids	AHL	....	....	....	....	....	7	0	2	2	2
2007-08	Saginaw Spirit	OHL	26	6	20	26	15	....	....	....	....	....
	Belleville Bulls	OHL	31	11	27	38	8	21	9	15	24	10

MUZZIN, Jake (MUH-zihn, JAYK) **PIT.**

Defense. Shoots left. 6'2", 206 lbs. Born, Woodstock, Ont., February 21, 1989.
(Pittsburgh's 7th choice, 141st overall, in 2007 Entry Draft).

			Regular Season					Playoffs				
Season	Club	League	GP	G	A	Pts	PIM	GP	G	A	Pts	PIM
2004-05	Brantford 99ers	Minor-ON	57	20	23	43	78	....	....	....	....	....
2005-06	Sault Ste. Marie	OHL	DID NOT PLAY – INJURED									
2006-07	Soo Thunderbirds	NOJHL	4	0	3	3	2	....	....	....	....	....
	Sault Ste. Marie	OHL	37	1	3	4	10	13	0	4	4	6
2007-08	Sault Ste. Marie	OHL	67	6	12	18	53	10	1	3	4	4

• Missed entire 2005-06 season recovering from off-season back surgery.

MYERS, Tyler (MIGH-uhrz, TIGH-luhr) **BUF.**

Defense. Shoots right. 6'7", 210 lbs. Born, Houston, TX, February 1, 1990.
(Buffalo's 1st choice, 12th overall, in 2008 Entry Draft).

			Regular Season					Playoffs				
Season	Club	League	GP	G	A	Pts	PIM	GP	G	A	Pts	PIM
2005-06	Notre Dame	SMHL	34	4	6	10	78	....	....	....	....	....
	Kelowna Rockets	WHL	9	0	1	1	2	8	1	0	1	2
2006-07	Kelowna Rockets	WHL	59	2	13	15	78	....	....	....	....	....
2007-08	Kelowna Rockets	WHL	65	6	13	19	97	7	1	2	3	12

NAGY, Kory (NAH-gee, KOHR-ee) **N.J.**

Center. Shoots left. 5'11", 195 lbs. Born, London, Ont., October 12, 1989.
(New Jersey's 6th choice, 142nd overall, in 2008 Entry Draft).

			Regular Season					Playoffs				
Season	Club	League	GP	G	A	Pts	PIM	GP	G	A	Pts	PIM
2005-06	Lindsay Muskies	OPJHL	47	11	12	23	14	4	0	0	0	0
	Oshawa Generals	OHL	16	0	1	1	8	....	....	....	....	....
2006-07	Oshawa Generals	OHL	64	0	5	5	18	9	0	0	0	4
2007-08	Oshawa Generals	OHL	57	5	12	17	47	15	6	3	9	4

NASH, Riley (NASH, RIGH-lee) **EDM.**

Center. Shoots right. 6'1", 175 lbs. Born, Consort, Alta., May 9, 1989.
(Edmonton's 3rd choice, 21st overall, in 2007 Entry Draft).

			Regular Season					Playoffs				
Season	Club	League	GP	G	A	Pts	PIM	GP	G	A	Pts	PIM
2005-06	Thompson Blazers	Minor-BC	31	29	31	60	100	....	....	....	....	....
	Salmon Arm	BCHL	1	0	0	0	0	5	1	2	3	0
2006-07	Salmon Arm	BCHL	55	38	46	84	87	11	4	7	11	31
2007-08	Cornell Big Red	ECAC	36	12	20	32	28	....	....	....	....	....

ECAC All-Rookie Team (2008) • ECAC Rookie of the Year (2008)

NASLUND, Fredrik (NAZ-luhnd, FREHD-rihk) **DAL.**

Left wing. Shoots right. 6'4", 211 lbs. Born, Stockholm, Sweden, February 11, 1986.
(Dallas' 6th choice, 104th overall, in 2004 Entry Draft).

			Regular Season					Playoffs				
Season	Club	League	GP	G	A	Pts	PIM	GP	G	A	Pts	PIM
2002-03	Vasteras Jr.	Swe-Jr.	34	12	9	21	8	....	....	....	....	....
2003-04	Vasteras Jr.	Swe-Jr.	17	13	15	28	6	3	0	1	1	4
	Vasteras	Sweden-2	32	2	4	6	0	....	....	....	....	....
2004-05	Vasteras	Sweden-2	3	0	0	0	0	....	....	....	....	....
	Vasteras Jr.	Swe-Jr.	21	7	7	14	2	....	....	....	....	....
2005-06	Peterborough	OHL	66	9	21	30	30	19	6	5	11	6
2006-07	Nykoping	Sweden-2	45	13	13	26	38	5	2	2	4	4
2007-08	Nybro Vikings IF	Sweden-2	33	7	12	19	14	....	....	....	....	....

NAUROV, Alexander (naw-OO-rawf, al-EHX-AN-duhr) **DAL.**

Right wing. Shoots left. 5'11", 191 lbs. Born, Saratov, USSR, March 4, 1985.
(Dallas' 5th choice, 134th overall, in 2003 Entry Draft).

			Regular Season					Playoffs				
Season	Club	League	GP	G	A	Pts	PIM	GP	G	A	Pts	PIM
2001-02	Yaroslavl 2	Russia-3	12	0	0	0	16	....	....	....	....	....
2002-03	Yaroslavl 2	Russia-3	STATISTICS NOT AVAILABLE									
2003-04	Yaroslavl 2	Russia-3	24	9	5	14	73	....	....	....	....	....
2004-05	Yaroslavl	Russia	11	2	2	4	2	....	....	....	....	....
	Yaroslavl 2	Russia-3	35	19	16	35	61	....	....	....	....	....
2005-06	Kristall Saratov	Russia-2	52	11	13	24	42	....	....	....	....	....
2006-07	Idaho Steelheads	ECHL	16	1	6	7	8	8	0	0	0	2
	Assat Pori	Finland	11	0	2	2	8	....	....	....	....	....
	TuTo Turku	Finland-2	4	0	0	0	10	....	....	....	....	....
2007-08	Idaho Steelheads	ECHL	40	1	6	7	18	....	....	....	....	....
	Bakersfield	ECHL	13	1	9	10	8	6	2	3	5	10

NEAL, James (NEEL, JAYMS) **DAL.**

Left wing. Shoots left. 6'2", 185 lbs. Born, Oshawa, Ont., September 3, 1987.
(Dallas' 2nd choice, 33rd overall, in 2005 Entry Draft).

			Regular Season					Playoffs				
Season	Club	League	GP	G	A	Pts	PIM	GP	G	A	Pts	PIM
2003-04	Bowmanville	OPJHL	43	28	27	55	....	....	....	....	....	....
	Plymouth Whalers	OHL	9	2	4	6	0	....	....	....	....	....
2004-05	Plymouth Whalers	OHL	67	18	26	44	32	4	1	1	2	6
2005-06	Plymouth Whalers	OHL	66	21	37	58	109	13	9	7	16	33
2006-07	Plymouth Whalers	OHL	45	27	38	65	94	20	13	12	25	54
2007-08	Iowa Stars	AHL	62	18	19	37	63	....	....	....	....	....

OHL First All-Star Team (2007)

NEAL, Michael (NEEL, MIGH-kuhl) **DAL.**

Left wing. Shoots left. 6'2", 188 lbs. Born, Whitby, Ont., April 3, 1989.
(Dallas' 7th choice, 149th overall, in 2007 Entry Draft).

			Regular Season					Playoffs				
Season	Club	League	GP	G	A	Pts	PIM	GP	G	A	Pts	PIM
2004-05	Whitby Wildcats	Minor-ON	52	20	29	49	67	....	....	....	....	....
2005-06	Belleville Bulls	OHL	46	1	3	4	6	....	....	....	....	....
2006-07	Belleville Bulls	OHL	52	4	4	8	25	15	0	1	1	6
2007-08	Belleville Bulls	OHL	....	....	....	....	....	7	0	0	0	2

• Missed entire 2007-08 regular season recovering from knee injury.

NEGRIN, John (NEH-grihn, JAWN) **CGY.**

Defense. Shoots left. 6'3", 194 lbs. Born, West Vancouver, B.C., March 25, 1989.
(Calgary's 2nd choice, 70th overall, in 2007 Entry Draft).

			Regular Season					Playoffs				
Season	Club	League	GP	G	A	Pts	PIM	GP	G	A	Pts	PIM
2004-05	North Delta Flyers	PIJHL	45	3	12	15	53	....	....	....	....	....
	Kootenay Ice	WHL	2	0	0	0	0	....	....	....	....	....
2005-06	Kootenay Ice	WHL	55	3	7	10	48	6	0	0	0	6
2006-07	Kootenay Ice	WHL	44	1	15	16	57	7	0	2	2	8
2007-08	Kootenay Ice	WHL	71	1	41	42	68	10	1	1	2	8

NELSON, Levi (NELH-sohn, LEE-vigh) BOS.

Center. Shoots left. 6', 184 lbs. Born, Calgary, Alta., April 28, 1988.
(Boston's 6th choice, 158th overall, in 2006 Entry Draft).

			Regular Season					Playoffs				
Season	Club	League	GP	G	A	Pts	PIM	GP	G	A	Pts	PIM
2004-05	Cgy. North Stars	AMHL	35	15	13	28	70	....	....	....	....	....
	Swift Current	WHL	2	1	0	1	0	....	....	....	....	....
2005-06	Swift Current	WHL	63	21	17	38	63	4	0	0	0	4
2006-07	Swift Current	WHL	66	18	34	52	125	6	4	3	7	4
	Providence Bruins	AHL	1	0	0	0	2	4	1	0	1	2
2007-08	Swift Current	WHL	67	25	36	61	152	12	7	8	15	16

NEMISZ, Greg (NEH-mihtz, GREHG) CGY.

Center. Shoots right. 6'3", 200 lbs. Born, Courtice, Ont., June 5, 1990.
(Calgary's 1st choice, 25th overall, in 2008 Entry Draft).

			Regular Season					Playoffs				
Season	Club	League	GP	G	A	Pts	PIM	GP	G	A	Pts	PIM
2005-06	Clarington	Minor-ON	32	29	24	53	24	....	....	....	....	....
2006-07	Windsor Spitfires	OHL	62	11	23	34	23	....	....	....	....	....
2007-08	Windsor Spitfires	OHL	68	34	33	67	52	5	2	1	3	8

NEPRYAYEV, Ivan (neh-pree-YIGH-ehv, IGH-vuhn) WSH.

Center. Shoots left. 6'1", 180 lbs. Born, Yaroslavl, USSR, February 4, 1982.
(Washington's 5th choice, 163rd overall, in 2000 Entry Draft).

			Regular Season					Playoffs				
Season	Club	League	GP	G	A	Pts	PIM	GP	G	A	Pts	PIM
1997-98	Torpedo Yaroslavl	Russia	6	0	0	0	0	....	....	....	....	....
1998-99	Yaroslavl 2	Russia-3	15	1	0	1	0	....	....	....	....	....
99-2000	Yaroslavl 2	Russia-3	40	8	14	22	....	....	....	....	....	....
2000-01	Yaroslavl	Russia	10	0	0	0	2	....	....	....	....	....
2001-02	Yaroslavl 2	Russia-3	2	1	0	1	18	....	....	....	....	....
	Yaroslavl	Russia	36	3	8	11	28	....	....	....	....	....
2002-03	Yaroslavl	Russia	26	3	6	9	12	6	1	0	1	0
2003-04	Yaroslavl 2	Russia-3	13	5	10	15	12	....	....	....	....	....
2004-05	Yaroslavl	Russia	56	10	10	20	73	9	1	0	1	16
2005-06	Yaroslavl	Russia	43	7	16	23	70	11	0	0	0	8
	Russia	Olympics	2	0	0	0	2	....	....	....	....	....
2006-07	Yaroslavl	Russia	52	17	9	26	66	7	0	4	4	2
2007-08	Yaroslavl	Russia	56	9	17	26	84	15	3	6	9	41

NESBITT, Derek (NEHZ-biht, DAIR-ihk) PHX.

Right wing. Shoots left. 6', 185 lbs. Born, Egmondville, Ont., April 16, 1982.

			Regular Season					Playoffs				
Season	Club	League	GP	G	A	Pts	PIM	GP	G	A	Pts	PIM
2001-02	Ferris State	CCHA	36	9	11	20	16	....	....	....	....	....
2002-03	Ferris State	CCHA	42	20	33	53	26	....	....	....	....	....
2003-04	Ferris State	CCHA	38	11	17	28	36	....	....	....	....	....
2004-05	Ferris State	CCHA	38	19	21	40	44	....	....	....	....	....
	Bossier-Shreve.	CHL	7	0	5	5	0	....	....	....	....	....
2005-06	Gwinnett	ECHL	71	26	43	69	6	17	6	7	13	8
2006-07	Idaho Steelheads	ECHL	66	30	51	81	32	22	6	12	18	8
2007-08	Rockford IceHogs	AHL	46	17	18	35	6	12	3	3	6	12
	Gwinnett	ECHL	26	11	28	39	4	....	....	....	....	....

Signed as a free agent by **Phoenix**, July 2, 2008.

NESS, Aaron (NEHS, AIR-uhn) NYI

Defense. Shoots left. 5'10", 157 lbs. Born, Bemidji, MN, May 18, 1990.
(NY Islanders' 3rd choice, 40th overall, in 2008 Entry Draft).

			Regular Season					Playoffs				
Season	Club	League	GP	G	A	Pts	PIM	GP	G	A	Pts	PIM
2005-06	Roseau Rams	High-MN	30	3	18	21	8	....	....	....	....	....
2006-07	Roseau Rams	High-MN	31	13	38	51	12	....	....	....	....	....
	Team Great Plains	UMWEHL	11	0	8	8	....	....	....	....	....	....
2007-08	Roseau Rams	High-MN	31	28	44	72	16	....	....	....	....	....
	Great Plains	UMWEHL	11	2	11	13	....	....	....	....	....	....

• Signed Letter of Intent to attend **University of Minnesota** (WCHA) in fall of 2008.

NICASTRO, Max (nih-KAS-troh, MAX) DET.

Defense. Shoots right. 6'2", 189 lbs. Born, Thousand Oaks, CA, March 2, 1990.
(Detroit's 2nd choice, 91st overall, in 2008 Entry Draft).

			Regular Season					Playoffs				
Season	Club	League	GP	G	A	Pts	PIM	GP	G	A	Pts	PIM
2006-07	L.A. Jr. Kings	Minor-CA	48	17	19	36	44	....	....	....	....	....
2007-08	Chicago Steel	USHL	58	6	14	20	78	7	1	2	3	12

• Signed Letter of Intent to attend **Boston University** (Hockey East) in fall of 2009.

NIEMI, Jyri (nee-YEH-mee, YEW-ree) NYI

Defense. Shoots left. 6'2", 192 lbs. Born, Hameenkyro, Finland, June 15, 1990.
(NY Islanders' 6th choice, 72nd overall, in 2008 Entry Draft).

			Regular Season					Playoffs				
Season	Club	League	GP	G	A	Pts	PIM	GP	G	A	Pts	PIM
2006-07	HPK U18	Fin-U18	1	0	1	1	4	....	....	....	....	....
	HPK Jr.	Fin-Jr.	40	7	5	12	82	....	....	....	....	....
2007-08	Saskatoon Blades	WHL	49	14	20	34	57	....	....	....	....	....

NIGRO, Anthony (NIGH-groh, AN-thuh-nee) ST.L.

Center. Shoots left. 6', 189 lbs. Born, Vaughan, Ont., January 11, 1990.
(St. Louis' 9th choice, 155th overall, in 2008 Entry Draft).

			Regular Season					Playoffs				
Season	Club	League	GP	G	A	Pts	PIM	GP	G	A	Pts	PIM
2006-07	Guelph Storm	OHL	56	4	13	17	26	4	0	0	0	2
2007-08	Guelph Storm	OHL	67	24	24	48	65	10	2	3	5	7

NIKITIN, Nikita (nih-KEE-tihn, nih-KEE-tuh) ST.L.

Defense. Shoots left. 6'3", 178 lbs. Born, Omsk, USSR, June 16, 1986.
(St. Louis' 5th choice, 136th overall, in 2004 Entry Draft).

			Regular Season					Playoffs				
Season	Club	League	GP	G	A	Pts	PIM	GP	G	A	Pts	PIM
2002-03	Omsk 2	Russia-3	34	3	7	10	4	....	....	....	....	....
2003-04	Omsk 2	Russia-3	34	3	8	11	22	....	....	....	....	....
2004-05	Omsk 2	Russia-3	31	3	8	11	20	....	....	....	....	....
	Avangard Omsk	Russia	12	0	0	0	2	3	0	0	0	0
2005-06	Avangard Omsk	Russia	43	1	2	3	22	13	1	2	3	6
	Omsk 2	Russia-3	1	0	0	0	0	....	....	....	....	....
2006-07	Avangard Omsk	Russia	54	1	15	16	99	9	0	4	4	35
2007-08	Avangard Omsk	Russia	57	3	11	14	48	4	0	1	1	2

NIKULIN, Ilja (nih-KOO-lihn, IHL-yah) ATL.

Defense. Shoots left. 6'3", 210 lbs. Born, Moscow, USSR, March 12, 1982.
(Atlanta's 2nd choice, 31st overall, in 2000 Entry Draft).

			Regular Season					Playoffs				
Season	Club	League	GP	G	A	Pts	PIM	GP	G	A	Pts	PIM
1998-99	Dyn'o Moscow 2	Russia-3	23	0	2	2	18	....	....	....	....	....
99-2000	Dyn'o Moscow 2	Russia-3	4	2	1	3	10	....	....	....	....	....
	THK Tver	Russia-2	39	3	6	9	84	....	....	....	....	....
2000-01	Dynamo Moscow	Russia	44	0	4	4	61	....	....	....	....	....
2001-02	Dyn'o Moscow 2	Russia-3	2	0	1	1	2	....	....	....	....	....
	Dynamo Moscow	Russia	47	2	1	3	44	3	0	0	0	0
2002-03	Dynamo Moscow	Russia	40	1	4	5	46	5	0	1	1	4
2003-04	Dynamo Moscow	Russia	54	1	5	6	56	3	0	0	0	2
2004-05	Dynamo Moscow	Russia	50	1	9	10	65	10	0	3	3	8
2005-06	Ak Bars Kazan	Russia	49	9	9	18	48	13	4	0	4	36
2006-07	Ak Bars Kazan	Russia	51	11	14	25	99	16	4	5	9	18
2007-08	Ak Bars Kazan	Russia	57	3	15	18	95	10	1	3	4	14

NILL, Trevor (NIHL, TREH-vuhr) ST.L.

Center. Shoots right. 6'1", 180 lbs. Born, Detroit, MI, April 11, 1989.
(St. Louis' 10th choice, 190th overall, in 2007 Entry Draft).

			Regular Season					Playoffs				
Season	Club	League	GP	G	A	Pts	PIM	GP	G	A	Pts	PIM
2004-05	Det. Compuware	MWEHL	25	10	8	18	8	4	2	1	3	0
2005-06	Det. Compuware	MWEHL	21	4	9	13	20	4	1	0	1	2
2006-07	Det. Compuware	MWEHL	24	6	10	16	23	6	2	4	6	2
2007-08	Penticton Vees	BCHL	53	5	6	11	16	11	0	2	2	0

• Signed Letter of Intent to attend **Michigan State University** (CCHA) in fall of 2008.

NISKALA, Janne (NIHS-kah-lah, YAH-nee) T.B.

Defense. Shoots left. 5'11", 199 lbs. Born, Vasteras, Sweden, September 22, 1981.
(Nashville's 5th choice, 147th overall, in 2004 Entry Draft).

			Regular Season					Playoffs				
Season	Club	League	GP	G	A	Pts	PIM	GP	G	A	Pts	PIM
1997-98	Lukko Rauma U18	Fin-U18	34	7	16	23	40	....	....	....	....	....
1998-99	Lukko Rauma U18	Fin-U18	14	7	4	11	42	....	....	....	....	....
	Lukko Rauma Jr.	Fin-Jr.	2	0	0	0	12	....	....	....	....	....
99-2000	Lukko Rauma Jr.	Fin-Jr.	40	14	15	29	50	8	0	2	2	8
2000-01	Lukko Rauma Jr.	Fin-Jr.	13	4	8	12	40	....	....	....	....	....
	Lukko Rauma	Finland	18	0	0	0	0	....	....	....	....	....
	Jaa-Kotkat	Finland-2	13	4	1	5	43	....	....	....	....	....
	Manchester Storm	Britain	16	0	1	1	14	....	....	....	....	....
2001-02	Lukko Rauma Jr.	Fin-Jr.	3	1	1	2	2	....	....	....	....	....
	Lukko Rauma	Finland	55	7	13	20	81	....	....	....	....	....
2002-03	Lukko Rauma	Finland	46	4	5	9	40	....	....	....	....	....
2003-04	Lukko Rauma	Finland	55	21	15	36	73	4	0	0	0	16
2004-05	Lukko Rauma	Finland	44	9	12	21	63	9	5	2	7	4
2005-06	EV Zug	Swiss	43	12	17	29	50	7	0	2	2	10
2006-07	Farjestad	Sweden	53	19	30	49	62	9	3	3	6	14
2007-08	Milwaukee	AHL	80	19	25	44	81	6	0	1	1	8

Traded to **Philadelphia** by **Nashvile** for Triston Grant and a 7th round choice in 2009 Entry Draft, June 24, 2008. Traded to **Tampa Bay** by **Philadelphia** for Tampa Bay's 6th round choice in 2009 Entry Draft, June 30, 2008.

NODL, Andreas (NOHD'L, awn-DRAY-uhs) PHI.

Right wing. Shoots left. 6'1", 190 lbs. Born, Vienna, Austria, February 28, 1987.
(Philadelphia's 2nd choice, 39th overall, in 2006 Entry Draft).

			Regular Season					Playoffs				
Season	Club	League	GP	G	A	Pts	PIM	GP	G	A	Pts	PIM
2001-02	Wien Jr.	Austria-Jr.	1	0	0	0	0	....	....	....	....	....
2002-03	Wien Jr.	Austria-Jr.	STATISTICS NOT AVAILABLE									
2003-04	Vienna Capitals	Austria	25	15	22	37	26	....	....	....	....	....
	Wien Jr.	Austria-Jr.	15	11	10	21	47	....	....	....	....	....
2004-05	Sioux Falls	USHL	44	7	9	16	24	....	....	....	....	....
	Sioux Falls	USHL	44	7	9	16	24	....	....	....	....	....
2005-06	Sioux Falls	USHL	58	29	30	59	16	14	6	9	15	6
2006-07	St. Cloud State	WCHA	40	18	28	46	32	....	....	....	....	....
2007-08	St. Cloud State	WCHA	40	18	26	44	22	....	....	....	....	....
	Philadelphia	AHL	3	1	0	1	0	10	1	0	1	2

USHL First All-Star Team (2006) • WCHA All-Rookie Team (2007) • WCHA Rookie of the Year (2007) • WCHA Second All-Star Team (2008)

NOLET, Martin (noh-LAY, MAHR-tihn) L.A.

Defense. Shoots right. 6'3", 209 lbs. Born, Quebec, Que., October 2, 1986.
(Los Angeles' 8th choice, 144th overall, in 2006 Entry Draft).

			Regular Season					Playoffs				
Season	Club	League	GP	G	A	Pts	PIM	GP	G	A	Pts	PIM
2002-03	St-Francois	QAAA	31	3	3	6	62	....	....	....	....	....
2003-04	St-Francois	QAAA	31	5	11	16	91	8	2	2	4	24
2004-05	Champlain College	QJHL	43	4	23	27	97	14	2	3	5	14
2005-06	Champlain College	QJHL	19	5	7	12	26	10	1	1	2	24
2006-07	Massachusetts	H-East	32	1	3	4	35	....	....	....	....	....
2007-08	Massachusetts	H-East	31	2	4	6	53	....	....	....	....	....

• Missed majority of 2005-06 season recovering from off-season shoulder surgery.

NOREAU, Maxim (NOHR-oh, max-EEM) MIN.

Defense. Shoots right. 5'11", 190 lbs. Born, Montreal, Que., May 14, 1987.

			Regular Season					Playoffs				
Season	Club	League	GP	G	A	Pts	PIM	GP	G	A	Pts	PIM
2004-05	Victoriaville Tigres	QMJHL	65	5	8	13	47	7	0	0	0	8
2005-06	Victoriaville Tigres	QMJHL	69	22	43	65	116	5	2	4	6	7
2006-07	Victoriaville Tigres	QMJHL	69	17	53	70	106	6	2	1	3	8
2007-08	Houston Aeros	AHL	50	8	8	16	48	5	0	0	0	4
	Texas Wildcatters	ECHL	2	0	3	3	0	....	....	....	....	....

Signed as a free agent by **Minnesota**, May 22, 2008.

NORTON, Pierce (NOHR-tuhn, PIHRS) TOR.

Right wing. Shoots right. 6'2", 200 lbs. Born, Boston, MA, June 7, 1985.
(Toronto's 6th choice, 285th overall, in 2004 Entry Draft).

			Regular Season					Playoffs				
Season	Club	League	GP	G	A	Pts	PIM	GP	G	A	Pts	PIM
2002-03	Thayer Academy	High-MA	29	16	18	34	....	....	....	....	....	....
2003-04	Thayer Academy	High-MA	34	21	34	55	84	....	....	....	....	....
2004-05	Thayer Academy	High-MA	29	*30	20	50	....	....	....	....	....	....
2005-06	Providence College	H-East	35	1	2	3	22	....	....	....	....	....
2006-07	Providence College	H-East	31	6	5	11	46	....	....	....	....	....
2007-08	Providence College	H-East	36	14	10	24	65	....	....	....	....	....

NYQUIST, Gustav (NEW-kwihst, GUHS-tav) **DET.**

Right wing. Shoots left. 5'10", 169 lbs. Born, Halmstad, Sweden, September 1, 1989.
(Detroit's 3rd choice, 121st overall, in 2008 Entry Draft).

			Regular Season					Playoffs				
Season	Club	League	GP	G	A	Pts	PIM	GP	G	A	Pts	PIM
2005-06	Malmo U18	Swe-U18	14	9	3	12	10	6	1	3	4	0
2006-07	Malmo Jr.	Swe-Jr.	42	21	23	44	57	4	2	2	4	6
2007-08	Malmo Jr.	Swe-Jr.	24	11	20	31	20	7	5	5	10	6

• Signed Letter of Intent to attend **University of Maine** (Hockey East) in fall of 2008.

O'BRIEN, James (oh-BRIGH-uhn, JAYMZ) **OTT.**

Center. Shoots right. 6'3", 198 lbs. Born, Maplewood, MN, January 29, 1989.
(Ottawa's 1st choice, 29th overall, in 2007 Entry Draft).

			Regular Season					Playoffs				
Season	Club	League	GP	G	A	Pts	PIM	GP	G	A	Pts	PIM
2003-04	Det. Caesars	MWEHL	68	19	24	43	72	....	....	....	....	....
2004-05	USNTDP	U-17	13	6	6	12	10	....	....	....	....	....
	USNTDP	NAHL	40	10	12	22	41	1	0	0	0	0
2005-06	USNTDP	U-18	38	11	14	25	62	....	....	....	....	....
	USNTDP	NAHL	13	6	10	16	14	....	....	....	....	....
2006-07	U. of Minnesota	WCHA	43	7	8	15	51	....	....	....	....	....
2007-08	Seattle	WHL	70	21	34	55	66	12	2	6	8	14

O'DELL, Eric (OH-DEHL, AIR-ihk) **ANA.**

Center. Shoots right. 6', 174 lbs. Born, Ottawa, Ont., June 21, 1990.
(Anaheim's 3rd choice, 39th overall, in 2008 Entry Draft).

			Regular Season					Playoffs				
Season	Club	League	GP	G	A	Pts	PIM	GP	G	A	Pts	PIM
2006-07	Ottawa West	OJHL-B	40	28	20	48	45	....	....	....	....	....
	Ottawa Jr. Sens	CJHL	2	1	0	1	0	....	....	....	....	....
2007-08	Cumberland	CJHL	34	23	33	56	12	....	....	....	....	....
	Sudbury Wolves	OHL	26	14	18	32	19	....	....	....	....	....

OGORODNIKOV, Sergei (oh-goh-RAWD-nee-kawf, SAIR-gay) **NYI**

Center. Shoots left. 6', 178 lbs. Born, Irkutsk, USSR, January 21, 1986.
(NY Islanders' 3rd choice, 82nd overall, in 2004 Entry Draft).

			Regular Season					Playoffs				
Season	Club	League	GP	G	A	Pts	PIM	GP	G	A	Pts	PIM
2002-03	Dyn'o Moscow 2	Russia-3	STATISTICS NOT AVAILABLE									
2003-04	Dyn'o Moscow 2	Russia-3	STATISTICS NOT AVAILABLE									
	THK Tver	Russia-2	21	8	3	11	14	....	....	....	....	....
2004-05	CSKA Moscow	Russia	18	2	4	6	2	....	....	....	....	....
2005-06	CSKA Moscow	Russia	3	0	0	0	2	....	....	....	....	....
	Ufa	Russia	14	0	3	3	8	6	0	0	0	4
	CSKA Moscow 2	Russia-3	STATISTICS NOT AVAILABLE									
2006-07	Bridgeport	AHL	27	3	3	6	10	....	....	....	....	....
	Pensacola	ECHL	42	18	22	40	30	....	....	....	....	....
2007-08	CSKA Moscow	Russia	4	0	0	0	0	....	....	....	....	....
	Novokuznetsk	Russia	25	1	1	2	14	....	....	....	....	....

OLSON, Drew (OHL-suhn, DROO) **CBJ**

Defense. Shoots left. 5'11", 215 lbs. Born, Brainerd, MN, April 4, 1990.
(Columbus' 4th choice, 118th overall, in 2008 Entry Draft).

			Regular Season					Playoffs				
Season	Club	League	GP	G	A	Pts	PIM	GP	G	A	Pts	PIM
2006-07	Brainerd	High-MN	STATISTICS NOT AVAILABLE									
	Team North	UMWEHL	11	2	4	6	....	....	....	....	....	....
2007-08	Brainerd	High-MN	27	20	16	36	....	....	....	....	....	....
	Team North	UMWEHL	11	3	4	7	....	....	....	....	....	....

• Signed Letter of Intent to attend **University of Minnesota-Duluth** (WCHA) in fall of 2009.

OLVECKY, Peter (ohl-VEHT-skee, PEE-tuhr) **MIN.**

Center. Shoots left. 6'2", 214 lbs. Born, Trencin, Czech., October 11, 1985.
(Minnesota's 3rd choice, 78th overall, in 2004 Entry Draft).

			Regular Season					Playoffs				
Season	Club	League	GP	G	A	Pts	PIM	GP	G	A	Pts	PIM
2003-04	Dukla Trencin Jr.	Slovak-Jr.	40	16	20	36	74	2	0	0	0	12
	Dukla Trencin	Slovakia	16	0	0	0	18	....	....	....	....	....
	Dukla Trencin U18	Svk-U18	2	0	0	0	0	....	....	....	....	....
2004-05	SHK 37 Piestany	Slovak-2	1	0	0	0	10	....	....	....	....	....
	Dukla Trencin Jr.	Slovak-Jr.	8	1	3	4	10	2	1	4	5	4
	Dukla Trencin	Slovakia	45	10	9	19	49	12	1	0	1	6
2005-06	Houston Aeros	AHL	67	14	18	32	56	7	1	3	4	4
2006-07	Houston Aeros	AHL	69	12	15	27	46	....	....	....	....	....
2007-08	Houston Aeros	AHL	61	17	16	33	38	5	1	1	2	4

OLVER, Mark (AWL-vuhr, MAHRK) **COL.**

Center. Shoots left. 5'10", 155 lbs. Born, Burnaby, B.C., January 1, 1988.
(Colorado's 4th choice, 140th overall, in 2008 Entry Draft).

			Regular Season					Playoffs				
Season	Club	League	GP	G	A	Pts	PIM	GP	G	A	Pts	PIM
2005-06	Omaha Lancers	USHL	59	5	20	25	72	2	0	0	0	0
2006-07	Omaha Lancers	USHL	57	29	35	64	84	5	3	3	6	18
2007-08	Northern Mich.	CCHA	39	21	17	38	59	....	....	....	....	....

OMARK, Linus (OH-mahrk, LIH-nuhs) **EDM.**

Left wing. Shoots left. 5'9", 170 lbs. Born, Overtornea, Sweden, February 5, 1987.
(Edmonton's 4th choice, 97th overall, in 2007 Entry Draft).

			Regular Season					Playoffs				
Season	Club	League	GP	G	A	Pts	PIM	GP	G	A	Pts	PIM
2003-04	Lulea HF U18	Swe-U18	14	14	8	22	18	7	3	4	7	0
	Lulea HF Jr.	Swe-Jr.	1	0	0	0	0	....	....	....	....	....
2004-05	Lulea HF U18	Swe-U18	1	2	0	2	0	....	....	....	....	....
	Lulea HF Jr.	Swe-Jr.	32	8	9	17	44	7	4	2	6	2
2005-06	Lulea HF Jr.	Swe-Jr.	32	22	21	43	56	5	1	2	3	28
	Lulea HF	Sweden	19	0	1	1	10	3	0	0	0	0
2006-07	Lulea HF	Sweden	50	8	9	17	32	4	1	0	1	2
2007-08	Lulea HF	Sweden	55	11	21	32	46	....	....	....	....	....

O'MARRA, Ryan (oh-MAHR-ah, RIGH-uhn) **EDM.**

Center. Shoots right. 6'2", 207 lbs. Born, Tokyo, Japan, June 9, 1987.
(NY Islanders' 1st choice, 15th overall, in 2005 Entry Draft).

			Regular Season					Playoffs				
Season	Club	League	GP	G	A	Pts	PIM	GP	G	A	Pts	PIM
2002-03	Miss. Senators	GTHL	76	51	60	111	83	....	....	....	....	....
	Georgetown	OPJHL	3	0	2	2	0	....	....	....	....	....
	Streetsville Derbys	OPJHL	6	0	1	1	2	....	....	....	....	....
2003-04	Erie Otters	OHL	63	16	16	32	33	9	5	5	10	6
2004-05	Erie Otters	OHL	64	25	38	63	60	6	4	1	5	0
2005-06	Erie Otters	OHL	61	27	50	77	134	....	....	....	....	....
	Bridgeport	AHL	8	4	1	5	4	3	0	1	1	2
2006-07	Erie Otters	OHL	13	8	6	14	26	....	....	....	....	....
	Saginaw Spirit	OHL	33	18	19	37	48	3	2	1	3	4
2007-08	Springfield Falcons	AHL	31	2	7	9	31	....	....	....	....	....
	Stockton Thunder	ECHL	24	11	9	20	45	6	2	7	9	10

Traded to **Edmonton** by **NY Islanders** with Robert Nilsson and NY Islanders' 1st round choice (Alex Plante) in 2007 Entry Draft for Ryan Smyth, February 27, 2007.

O'NEILL, Wes (oh-NEEL, WEHS) **COL.**

Defense. Shoots left. 6'4", 200 lbs. Born, Windsor, Ont., March 3, 1986.
(NY Islanders' 4th choice, 115th overall, in 2004 Entry Draft).

			Regular Season					Playoffs				
Season	Club	League	GP	G	A	Pts	PIM	GP	G	A	Pts	PIM
2000-01	Chatham Maroons	OHA-B	51	6	9	15	50	....	....	....	....	....
2001-02	Chatham Maroons	OHA-B	51	9	36	45	....	....	....	....	....	....
2002-03	Green Bay	USHL	50	2	15	17	79	....	....	....	....	....
2003-04	U. of Notre Dame	CCHA	39	2	10	12	28	....	....	....	....	....
2004-05	U. of Notre Dame	CCHA	38	6	14	20	52	....	....	....	....	....
2005-06	U. of Notre Dame	CCHA	35	6	19	25	40	....	....	....	....	....
2006-07	U. of Notre Dame	CCHA	42	3	18	21	40	....	....	....	....	....
2007-08	Lake Erie Monsters	AHL	51	2	4	6	50	....	....	....	....	....
	Johnstown Chiefs	ECHL	6	0	1	1	2	6	0	0	0	8

Signed as a free agent by **Colorado**, August 20, 2007.

O'NEILL, Will (oh-NEEL, WIHL) **ATL.**

Defense. Shoots left. 6', 195 lbs. Born, Boston, MA, April 28, 1988.
(Atlanta's 8th choice, 210th overall, in 2006 Entry Draft).

			Regular Season					Playoffs				
Season	Club	League	GP	G	A	Pts	PIM	GP	G	A	Pts	PIM
2004-05	Tabor	High-MA	....	1	16	17	....	....	....	....	....	....
2005-06	Tabor	High-MA	28	5	25	30	38	....	....	....	....	....
2006-07	Omaha Lancers	USHL	57	4	9	13	73	5	0	0	0	8
2007-08	Omaha Lancers	USHL	58	5	19	24	95	14	1	6	7	38

O'REILLY, Cal (oh-RIGH-lee, KAL) **NSH.**

Center. Shoots left. 6', 187 lbs. Born, Toronto, Ont., September 30, 1986.
(Nashville's 4th choice, 150th overall, in 2005 Entry Draft).

			Regular Season					Playoffs				
Season	Club	League	GP	G	A	Pts	PIM	GP	G	A	Pts	PIM
2002-03	St. Mary's Lincolns	OJHL-B	46	11	19	30	2	....	....	....	....	....
2003-04	Windsor Spitfires	OHL	61	3	18	21	2	3	0	1	1	0
2004-05	Windsor Spitfires	OHL	68	24	50	74	16	11	4	5	9	4
2005-06	Windsor Spitfires	OHL	68	18	81	99	8	7	3	8	11	0
	Milwaukee	AHL	2	0	0	0	0	10	0	1	1	0
2006-07	Milwaukee	AHL	78	18	47	65	20	4	1	2	3	0
2007-08	Milwaukee	AHL	80	16	63	79	22	6	1	2	3	0

ORESKOVIC, Phil (oh-rehs-KOH-vihch, FIHL) **TOR.**

Defense. Shoots right. 6'3", 217 lbs. Born, North York, Ont., January 26, 1987.
(Toronto's 2nd choice, 82nd overall, in 2005 Entry Draft).

			Regular Season					Playoffs				
Season	Club	League	GP	G	A	Pts	PIM	GP	G	A	Pts	PIM
2003-04	Brampton	OHL	66	0	7	7	64	12	0	2	2	16
2004-05	Brampton	OHL	61	1	6	7	147	6	0	0	0	4
2005-06	Brampton	OHL	65	3	9	12	202	11	0	0	0	34
2006-07	Brampton	OHL	36	2	12	14	113	....	....	....	....	....
	Owen Sound	OHL	26	1	7	8	66	4	0	0	0	2
	Toronto Marlies	AHL	3	0	1	1	2	....	....	....	....	....
2007-08	Toronto Marlies	AHL	54	1	9	10	68	7	0	1	1	11
	Columbia Inferno	ECHL	13	0	4	4	19	....	....	....	....	....

ORLOV, Maxim (ohr-LAHF, max-EEM) **WSH.**

Center. Shoots left. 6', 176 lbs. Born, Moscow, USSR, March 31, 1981.
(Washington's 9th choice, 219th overall, in 1999 Entry Draft).

			Regular Season					Playoffs				
Season	Club	League	GP	G	A	Pts	PIM	GP	G	A	Pts	PIM
1998-99	CSKA Moscow	Russia	2	0	0	0	2	1	0	0	0	0
99-2000	CSKA Moscow	Russia	25	0	0	0	2	2	0	0	0	2
2000-01	CSKA Moscow	Russia	41	5	4	9	14	....	....	....	....	....
2001-02	CSKA Moscow 2	Russia-3	7	7	4	11	4	....	....	....	....	....
	CSKA Moscow	Russia	35	3	5	8	14	....	....	....	....	....
2002-03	MGU Moscow	Russia-3	2	0	0	0	0	....	....	....	....	....
	Leninogorsk	Russia-2	25	3	8	11	24	....	....	....	....	....
2003-04	Leninogorsk	Russia-2	35	5	9	14	39	2	0	0	0	0
2004-05	Kristall Saratov	Russia-2	47	13	23	36	46	4	0	0	0	2
2005-06	Ufa 2	Russia-3	20	8	8	16	10	....	....	....	....	....
	Ufa	Russia	5	0	0	0	0	....	....	....	....	....
2006-07	Toros Neftekamsk	Russia-2	55	5	22	27	46	....	....	....	....	....
2007-08	Toros Neftekamsk	Russia-2	50	7	12	19	20	3	1	2	3	0

ORPIK, Andrew (OHR-pihk, AN-droo) **BUF.**

Defense. Shoots right. 6'3", 214 lbs. Born, East Amherst, NY, March 12, 1986.
(Buffalo's 9th choice, 227th overall, in 2005 Entry Draft).

			Regular Season					Playoffs				
Season	Club	League	GP	G	A	Pts	PIM	GP	G	A	Pts	PIM
2003-04	Thayer Academy	High-MA	32	9	8	17	18	....	....	....	....	....
2004-05	Thayer Academy	High-MA	31	8	12	20	24	....	....	....	....	....
2005-06	Boston College	H-East	40	3	5	8	32	....	....	....	....	....
2006-07	Boston College	H-East	38	3	6	9	22	....	....	....	....	....
2007-08	Boston College	H-East	41	7	6	13	57	....	....	....	....	....

OSALA, Oskar (OH-sa-la, AWZ-kuhr) WSH.

Left wing. Shoots left. 6'4", 225 lbs. Born, Vaasa, Finland, December 26, 1987.
(Washington's 6th choice, 97th overall, in 2006 Entry Draft).

			Regular Season					Playoffs				
Season	Club	League	GP	G	A	Pts	PIM	GP	G	A	Pts	PIM
2003-04	Sport Vaasa U18	Fin-U18	25	19	18	37	32	....	....	....	....	....
	Sport Vaasa Jr.	Fin-Jr.	2	0	0	0	4	....	....	....	....	....
	Sport Vaasa	Finland-2	5	0	0	0	0	....	....	....	....	....
2004-05	Sport Vaasa U18	Fin-U18	4	4	2	6	16	....	....	....	....	....
	Sport Vaasa Jr.	Fin-Jr.	19	13	14	27	28	2	0	0	0	2
	Sport Vaasa	Finland-2	21	1	4	5	6	7	0	0	0	6
2005-06	Mississauga	OHL	68	17	26	43	86	....	....	....	....	....
2006-07	Mississauga	OHL	54	22	22	44	81	5	2	2	4	0
	Suomi U20	Finland-2	2	1	0	1	0	....	....	....	....	....
2007-08	Blues Espoo	Finland	53	18	17	35	62	17	7	3	10	8

Signed as a free agent by **Espoo** (Finland), July 23, 2007.

OSHIE, T.J. (OH-shee, TEE-JAY) ST.L.

Center. Shoots right. 5'10", 170 lbs. Born, Mt. Vernon, WA, December 23, 1986.
(St. Louis' 1st choice, 24th overall, in 2005 Entry Draft).

			Regular Season					Playoffs				
Season	Club	League	GP	G	A	Pts	PIM	GP	G	A	Pts	PIM
2004-05	Warroad Warriors	High-MN	31	37	62	99	22	....	....	....	....	....
	Sioux Falls	USHL	11	3	2	5	6	....	....	....	....	....
2005-06	North Dakota	WCHA	44	24	21	45	33	....	....	....	....	....
2006-07	North Dakota	WCHA	43	17	*35	52	30	....	....	....	....	....
2007-08	North Dakota	WCHA	42	18	27	45	57	....	....	....	....	....

WCHA All-Rookie Team (2006) • WCHA First All-Star Team (2008) • NCAA West First All-American Team (2008)

OSLUND, Nick (OZ-luhnd, NIHK) DET.

Right wing. Shoots right. 6'3", 195 lbs. Born, Burnsville, MN, November 15, 1987.
(Detroit's 6th choice, 191st overall, in 2006 Entry Draft).

			Regular Season					Playoffs				
Season	Club	League	GP	G	A	Pts	PIM	GP	G	A	Pts	PIM
2004-05	Burnsville	High-MN	27	29	18	47	28	....	....	....	....	....
2005-06	Burnsville	High-MN	26	22	30	52	30	....	....	....	....	....
2006-07	Tri-City Storm	USHL	56	7	14	21	24	9	0	1	1	0
2007-08	St. Cloud State	WCHA	38	4	1	5	27	....	....	....	....	....

OSTRCIL, Radim (AWS-tuhr-chihl, RA-dihm) BOS.

Defense. Shoots left. 5'11", 200 lbs. Born, Vsetin, Czech., January 15, 1989.
(Boston's 5th choice, 169th overall, in 2007 Entry Draft).

			Regular Season					Playoffs				
Season	Club	League	GP	G	A	Pts	PIM	GP	G	A	Pts	PIM
2002-03	HC Vsetin U17	CzR-U17	33	1	2	3	8	11	1	1	2	2
2003-04	HC Vsetin U17	CzR-U17	43	0	12	12	44	2	0	0	0	0
2004-05	HC Vsetin U17	CzR-U17	31	8	15	23	85	3	1	3	4	4
	HC Vsetin Jr.	CzRep-Jr.	19	0	3	3	14	3	0	0	0	2
2005-06	HC Vsetin U17	CzR-U17	1	1	1	2	0	3	2	2	4	0
	HC Vsetin Jr.	CzRep-Jr.	41	6	8	14	50	5	1	1	2	6
	Hr. Kralove	CzRep-2	1	0	0	0	0	1	0	0	0	0
	HC Vsetin	CzRep	3	0	0	0	6	....	....	....	....	....
2006-07	HC Vsetin Jr.	CzRep-Jr.	25	8	13	21	69	8	4	4	8	6
	HC Vsetin	CzRep	37	1	1	2	20	....	....	....	....	....
2007-08	Ottawa 67's	OHL	59	0	13	13	69	4	0	0	0	2

OULAHEN, Ryan (OO-la-hehn, RIGH-uhn) DET.

Center. Shoots left. 6', 180 lbs. Born, Newmarket, Ont., March 26, 1985.
(Detroit's 3rd choice, 164th overall, in 2003 Entry Draft).

			Regular Season					Playoffs				
Season	Club	League	GP	G	A	Pts	PIM	GP	G	A	Pts	PIM
2000-01	Wexford Raiders	Minor-ON	66	38	58	96	18	....	....	....	....	....
2001-02	Newmarket	OPJHL	48	18	17	35	4	....	....	....	....	....
2002-03	Brampton	OHL	61	21	22	43	6	11	2	1	3	2
2003-04	Brampton	OHL	57	17	18	35	26	12	3	7	10	6
2004-05	Brampton	OHL	64	27	31	58	22	5	1	4	5	4
2005-06	Grand Rapids	AHL	75	9	10	19	20	16	0	0	0	2
2006-07	Grand Rapids	AHL	79	11	16	27	42	7	0	2	2	4
2007-08	Grand Rapids	AHL	75	14	16	30	47	....	....	....	....	....

OYSTRICK, Nathan (OI-strihk, NAY-thuhn) ATL.

Defense. Shoots left. 6', 215 lbs. Born, Regina, Sask., December 17, 1982.
(Atlanta's 7th choice, 198th overall, in 2002 Entry Draft).

			Regular Season					Playoffs				
Season	Club	League	GP	G	A	Pts	PIM	GP	G	A	Pts	PIM
99-2000	Reg. Pat Cdns.	SMHL	43	6	22	28	214	....	....	....	....	....
2000-01	South Surrey	BCHL	STATISTICS NOT AVAILABLE									
2001-02	South Surrey	BCHL	50	15	42	57	142	....	....	....	....	....
2002-03	Northern Mich.	CCHA	34	2	10	12	26	....	....	....	....	....
2003-04	Northern Mich.	CCHA	39	8	20	28	98	....	....	....	....	....
2004-05	Northern Mich.	CCHA	40	7	13	20	87	....	....	....	....	....
2005-06	Northern Mich.	CCHA	38	9	20	29	58	....	....	....	....	....
	Chicago Wolves	AHL	2	0	1	1	4	....	....	....	....	....
2006-07	Chicago Wolves	AHL	80	15	32	47	105	15	0	6	6	16
2007-08	Chicago Wolves	AHL	80	15	28	43	112	24	3	8	11	35

CCHA Second All-Star Team (2004) • CCHA First All-Star Team (2005, 2006) • NCAA West Second All-American Team (2006) • AHL All-Rookie Team (2007) • AHL Second All-Star Team (2007)

PACIORETTY, Max (pahk-OHR-eht-tee, MAX) MTL.

Left wing. Shoots left. 6'2", 199 lbs. Born, New Canaan, CT, November 20, 1988.
(Montreal's 2nd choice, 22nd overall, in 2007 Entry Draft).

			Regular Season					Playoffs				
Season	Club	League	GP	G	A	Pts	PIM	GP	G	A	Pts	PIM
2004-05	Taft Rhinos	High-CT	23	5	14	19	....					
2005-06	Taft Rhinos	High-CT	26	7	26	33	....					
2006-07	Sioux City	USHL	60	21	42	63	119	7	4	6	10	10
2007-08	U. of Michigan	CCHA	37	15	24	39	59	....	....	....	....	....

CCHA All-Rookie Team (2008) • CCHA Rookie of the Year (2008)

PACKARD, Dennis (PA-kuhrd, DEH-nihs)

Left wing. Shoots left. 6'4", 235 lbs. Born, St. Catherines, Ont., February 9, 1982.
(Tampa Bay's 8th choice, 219th overall, in 2001 Entry Draft).

			Regular Season					Playoffs				
Season	Club	League	GP	G	A	Pts	PIM	GP	G	A	Pts	PIM
99-2000	USNTDP	U-18	6	0	1	1	2	....	....	....	....	....
	USNTDP	USHL	55	11	14	25	85	....	....	....	....	....
2000-01	Harvard Crimson	ECAC	33	4	4	8	28	....	....	....	....	....
2001-02	Harvard Crimson	ECAC	32	9	10	19	34	....	....	....	....	....
2002-03	Harvard Crimson	ECAC	30	8	8	16	32	....	....	....	....	....
2003-04	Harvard Crimson	ECAC	36	11	11	22	16	....	....	....	....	....
2004-05	Springfield Falcons	AHL	47	2	8	10	25	....	....	....	....	....
	Johnstown Chiefs	ECHL	15	3	4	7	6	....	....	....	....	....
2005-06	Springfield Falcons	AHL	46	3	6	9	34	....	....	....	....	....
	Johnstown Chiefs	ECHL	16	2	9	11	12	5	0	1	1	4
2006-07	Providence Bruins	AHL	68	6	12	18	55	13	1	1	2	2
2007-08	Worcester Sharks	AHL	76	11	19	30	31	....	....	....	....	....

Signed as a free agent by **Boston**, July 17, 2006.

PADDOCK, Cam (PA-dawk, KAM) ST.L.

Center. Shoots right. 6'1", 191 lbs. Born, Vancouver, B.C., March 22, 1983.
(Pittsburgh's 6th choice, 137th overall, in 2002 Entry Draft).

			Regular Season					Playoffs				
Season	Club	League	GP	G	A	Pts	PIM	GP	G	A	Pts	PIM
99-2000	Kelowna Rockets	WHL	46	5	5	10	42	5	0	0	0	0
2000-01	Kelowna Rockets	WHL	72	14	10	24	110	6	0	0	0	4
2001-02	Kelowna Rockets	WHL	72	38	35	73	122	15	8	6	14	35
2002-03	Kelowna Rockets	WHL	71	33	26	59	107	19	11	8	19	18
2003-04	Kelowna Rockets	WHL	62	17	22	39	86	16	3	4	7	22
	Wilkes-Barre	AHL	1	0	0	0	2	....	....	....	....	....
2004-05	Wilkes-Barre	AHL	16	0	0	0	13	....	....	....	....	....
	Wheeling Nailers	ECHL	53	11	18	29	70	....	....	....	....	....
2005-06	Wilkes-Barre	AHL	4	0	0	0	2	....	....	....	....	....
	Wheeling Nailers	ECHL	61	14	24	38	90	9	0	0	0	12
2006-07	San Antonio	AHL	22	0	2	2	13	....	....	....	....	....
	Phoenix	ECHL	46	11	20	31	117	3	2	0	2	9
2007-08	San Antonio	AHL	78	12	13	25	107	7	0	2	2	18

Signed as a free agent by **San Antonio** (AHL), December 26, 2006. Signed as a free agent by **St. Louis**, July 15, 2008.

PAINCHAUD, Chad (PAYN-show, CHAD) ATL.

Left wing. Shoots left. 6'1", 185 lbs. Born, Mississauga, Ont., May 27, 1986.
(Atlanta's 4th choice, 106th overall, in 2004 Entry Draft).

			Regular Season					Playoffs				
Season	Club	League	GP	G	A	Pts	PIM	GP	G	A	Pts	PIM
2002-03	Mississauga Reps	GTHL	52	47	47	94	....	....	....	....	....	....
2003-04	Mississauga	OHL	68	17	25	42	25	24	4	6	10	23
2004-05	Mississauga	OHL	8	3	3	6	11	....	....	....	....	....
	Sarnia Sting	OHL	49	18	16	34	22	....	....	....	....	....
2005-06	Sarnia Sting	OHL	49	31	34	65	65	....	....	....	....	....
2006-07	Gwinnett	ECHL	72	22	32	54	71	4	0	5	5	4
2007-08	Chicago Wolves	AHL	22	1	2	3	13	....	....	....	....	....
	Gwinnett	ECHL	10	8	6	14	17	4	0	1	1	0

PALIN, Brett (PAY-lihn, BREHT) CGY.

Defense. Shoots right. 6'2", 200 lbs. Born, Nanaimo, B.C., June 23, 1984.

			Regular Season					Playoffs				
Season	Club	League	GP	G	A	Pts	PIM	GP	G	A	Pts	PIM
2000-01	Kelowna Rockets	WHL	39	0	0	0	25	....	....	....	....	....
2001-02	Kelowna Rockets	WHL	70	0	1	1	88	15	0	0	0	4
2002-03	Kelowna Rockets	WHL	71	1	17	18	118	19	0	4	4	12
2003-04	Kelowna Rockets	WHL	72	1	16	17	106	17	0	5	5	24
2004-05	Kelowna Rockets	WHL	72	4	21	25	71	24	4	6	10	52
2005-06	Omaha	AHL	64	0	5	5	46	....	....	....	....	....
2006-07	Omaha	AHL	78	1	9	10	71	6	1	0	1	0
2007-08	Quad City Flames	AHL	67	0	10	10	68	....	....	....	....	....

Signed as a free agent by **Calgary**, August 5, 2005.

PALMIERI, Nick (pawl-mee-AIR-ee, NIHK) N.J.

Right wing. Shoots right. 6'3", 215 lbs. Born, Utica, NY, July 12, 1989.
(New Jersey's 2nd choice, 79th overall, in 2007 Entry Draft).

			Regular Season					Playoffs				
Season	Club	League	GP	G	A	Pts	PIM	GP	G	A	Pts	PIM
2004-05	Northwood	High-NY	STATISTICS NOT AVAILABLE									
2005-06	Erie Otters	OHL	68	13	10	23	79	....	....	....	....	....
2006-07	Erie Otters	OHL	56	24	21	45	99	....	....	....	....	....
2007-08	Erie Otters	OHL	50	28	18	46	122	....	....	....	....	....
	Lowell Devils	AHL	9	1	0	1	4	....	....	....	....	....

PALUSHAJ, Aaron (puh-LOO-shigh, AIR-ruhn) ST.L.

Right wing. Shoots right. 5'11", 187 lbs. Born, Livonia, MI, September 7, 1989.
(St. Louis' 5th choice, 44th overall, in 2007 Entry Draft).

			Regular Season					Playoffs				
Season	Club	League	GP	G	A	Pts	PIM	GP	G	A	Pts	PIM
2005-06	Des Moines	USHL	58	10	23	33	53	11	2	4	6	15
2006-07	Des Moines	USHL	56	22	45	67	62	8	6	5	11	6
2007-08	U. of Michigan	CCHA	43	10	*34	44	22	....	....	....	....	....

PAQUET, Philippe (pa-KEHT, fihl-EEP) MTL.

Defense. Shoots right. 6'3", 210 lbs. Born, Quebec City, Que., March 12, 1987.
(Montreal's 7th choice, 229th overall, in 2005 Entry Draft).

			Regular Season					Playoffs				
Season	Club	League	GP	G	A	Pts	PIM	GP	G	A	Pts	PIM
2003-04	St-Francois	QAAA	39	6	14	20	136	7	0	3	3	10
2004-05	Salisbury School	High-CT	26	1	4	5	10	....	....	....	....	....
2005-06	Clarkson Knights	ECAC	37	2	5	7	91	....	....	....	....	....
2006-07	Clarkson Knights	ECAC	37	3	4	7	*116	....	....	....	....	....
2007-08	Clarkson Knights	ECAC	27	1	3	4	63	....	....	....	....	....

PAQUETTE, Danick (pa-KETT, DA-nihk) ATL.

Right wing. Shoots right. 6', 210 lbs. Born, Montreal, Que., July 17, 1990.
(Atlanta's 3rd choice, 64th overall, in 2008 Entry Draft).

			Regular Season					Playoffs				
Season	Club	League	GP	G	A	Pts	PIM	GP	G	A	Pts	PIM
2005-06	Ecole Montpetit	QAAA	36	17	16	33	191	3	0	1	1	6
2006-07	Lewiston	QMJHL	63	4	14	18	112	14	0	0	0	18
2007-08	Lewiston	QMJHL	63	29	13	42	213	5	1	2	3	30

PARDY, Adam (PAHR-dee, A-duhm) **CGY.**

Defense. Shoots left. 6'4", 220 lbs. Born, Bonavista, Nfld., March 29, 1984.
(Calgary's 6th choice, 173rd overall, in 2004 Entry Draft).

			Regular Season					Playoffs				
Season	**Club**	**League**	**GP**	**G**	**A**	**Pts**	**PIM**	**GP**	**G**	**A**	**Pts**	**PIM**
2002-03	Yarmouth	MJrHL	1	0	0	0	2	....	....	....	....	....
	Antigonish	MJrHL	31	5	16	21	42	....	....	....	....	....
	Cape Breton	QMJHL	7	0	1	1	2	2	0	0	0	0
2003-04	Cape Breton	QMJHL	68	4	12	16	137	5	0	1	1	8
2004-05	Cape Breton	QMJHL	65	12	27	39	163	5	2	2	4	8
2005-06	Omaha	AHL	24	0	0	0	18	....	....	....	....	....
	Las Vegas	ECHL	41	1	11	12	55	10	2	1	3	12
2006-07	Omaha	AHL	70	2	6	8	60	6	1	1	2	0
2007-08	Quad City Flames	AHL	65	5	13	18	67	....	....	....	....	....

PARSE, Scott (PARS, SKAWT) **L.A.**

Center. Shoots right. 6'1", 188 lbs. Born, Portage, MI, September 5, 1984.
(Los Angeles' 5th choice, 174th overall, in 2004 Entry Draft).

			Regular Season					Playoffs				
Season	**Club**	**League**	**GP**	**G**	**A**	**Pts**	**PIM**	**GP**	**G**	**A**	**Pts**	**PIM**
2002-03	Tri-City Storm	USHL	48	21	23	44	32	3	2	1	3	8
2003-04	Nebraska-Omaha	CCHA	39	16	19	35	52	....	....	....	....	....
2004-05	Nebraska-Omaha	CCHA	39	19	30	49	32	....	....	....	....	....
2005-06	Nebraska-Omaha	CCHA	41	20	*41	*61	40	....	....	....	....	....
2006-07	Nebraska-Omaha	CCHA	40	24	28	52	36	....	....	....	....	....
	Grand Rapids	AHL	10	2	5	7	6	7	1	0	1	8
2007-08	Manchester	AHL	14	0	3	3	4	....	....	....	....	....
	Reading Royals	ECHL	18	5	11	16	14	....	....	....	....	....

USHL All-Rookie Team (2003) • CCHA First All-Star Team (2005, 2007) • CCHA Player of the Year (2006) • NCAA West First All-American Team (2006) • NCAA West Second All-American Team (2007)

PARSHIN, Denis (PAHR-shihn, DEH-nihs) **COL.**

Right wing. Shoots left. 5'10", 165 lbs. Born, Rybinsk, USSR, February 1, 1986.
(Colorado's 3rd choice, 72nd overall, in 2004 Entry Draft).

			Regular Season					Playoffs				
Season	**Club**	**League**	**GP**	**G**	**A**	**Pts**	**PIM**	**GP**	**G**	**A**	**Pts**	**PIM**
2002-03	CSKA Moscow 2	Russia-3	4	1	0	1	2	....	....	....	....	....
2003-04	CSKA Moscow	Russia	27	2	4	6	4	....	....	....	....	....
	CSKA Moscow 2	Russia-3	STATISTICS NOT AVAILABLE									
2004-05	CSKA Moscow	Russia	42	3	4	7	18	....	....	....	....	....
2005-06	CSKA Moscow 2	Russia-3	STATISTICS NOT AVAILABLE									
	CSKA Moscow	Russia	37	2	8	10	22	6	0	2	2	2
2006-07	CSKA Moscow	Russia	54	18	14	32	24	12	2	2	4	8
2007-08	CSKA Moscow	Russia	56	12	23	35	46	6	1	0	1	0

PATERYN, Greg (PA-tuhr-ihn, GREHG) **MTL.**

Defense. Shoots right. 6'2", 223 lbs. Born, Sterling Heights, MI, June 20, 1990.
(Toronto's 4th choice, 128th overall, in 2008 Entry Draft).

			Regular Season					Playoffs				
Season	**Club**	**League**	**GP**	**G**	**A**	**Pts**	**PIM**	**GP**	**G**	**A**	**Pts**	**PIM**
2004-05	Brother Rice	High-MI	29	2	8	10	42	....	....	....	....	....
2005-06	Brother Rice	High-MI	24	0	8	8	34	....	....	....	....	....
2006-07	Brother Rice	High-MI	27	9	19	28	44	....	....	....	....	....
2007-08	Ohio	USHL	60	3	24	27	145	....	....	....	....	....

• Signed Letter of Intent to attend **University of Michigan** (CCHA) in fall of 2008. Traded to **Montreal** by **Toronto** with Toronto's 2nd round choice in 2009 Entry Draft for Mikhail Grabovski, July 3, 2008.

PAUKOVICH, Geoff (paw-KOH-vihch, JEHF) **EDM.**

Left wing. Shoots left. 6'4", 208 lbs. Born, Englewood, CO, April 24, 1986.
(Edmonton's 4th choice, 57th overall, in 2004 Entry Draft).

			Regular Season					Playoffs				
Season	**Club**	**League**	**GP**	**G**	**A**	**Pts**	**PIM**	**GP**	**G**	**A**	**Pts**	**PIM**
2002-03	Tri-City Storm	USHL	31	1	3	4	29	....	....	....	....	....
2003-04	USNTDP	U-18	44	6	9	15	46	....	....	....	....	....
	USNTDP	NAHL	11	4	2	6	31	....	....	....	....	....
2004-05	U. of Denver	WCHA	41	12	10	22	120	....	....	....	....	....
2005-06	U. of Denver	WCHA	37	4	6	10	72	....	....	....	....	....
2006-07	U. of Denver	WCHA	39	8	9	17	65	....	....	....	....	....
2007-08	Stockton Thunder	ECHL	70	13	13	26	94	6	1	0	1	4

PELECH, Matt (PEH-lihk, MAT) **CGY.**

Defense. Shoots right. 6'5", 227 lbs. Born, Toronto, Ont., September 4, 1987.
(Calgary's 1st choice, 26th overall, in 2005 Entry Draft).

			Regular Season					Playoffs				
Season	**Club**	**League**	**GP**	**G**	**A**	**Pts**	**PIM**	**GP**	**G**	**A**	**Pts**	**PIM**
2002-03	Vaughan	GTHL	44	3	13	16	113	....	....	....	....	....
2003-04	Sarnia Sting	OHL	62	4	6	10	39	5	0	1	1	12
2004-05	Sarnia Sting	OHL	31	1	5	6	74	....	....	....	....	....
2005-06	Sarnia Sting	OHL	18	0	2	2	59	....	....	....	....	....
	London Knights	OHL	34	1	7	8	80	19	0	0	0	48
2006-07	Belleville Bulls	OHL	58	5	30	35	171	12	0	3	3	22
2007-08	Quad City Flames	AHL	77	3	6	9	141	....	....	....	....	....

PELTIER, Derek (PEHL-tyay, DAIR-ihk) **COL.**

Defense. Shoots left. 5'11", 190 lbs. Born, Plymouth, MN, March 14, 1985.
(Colorado's 5th choice, 184th overall, in 2004 Entry Draft).

			Regular Season					Playoffs				
Season	**Club**	**League**	**GP**	**G**	**A**	**Pts**	**PIM**	**GP**	**G**	**A**	**Pts**	**PIM**
2003-04	Cedar Rapids	USHL	55	7	26	33	34	4	0	0	0	4
2004-05	U. of Minnesota	WCHA	43	6	13	19	22	....	....	....	....	....
2005-06	U. of Minnesota	WCHA	41	1	17	18	30	....	....	....	....	....
2006-07	U. of Minnesota	WCHA	44	4	11	15	28	....	....	....	....	....
2007-08	U. of Minnesota	WCHA	45	4	17	21	38	....	....	....	....	....
	Lake Erie Monsters	AHL	6	0	1	1	4	....	....	....	....	....

PELUSO, Anthony (puh-LOO-soh, AN-toh-nee) **ST.L.**

Defense. Shoots right. 6'3", 222 lbs. Born, North York, Ont., April 18, 1989.
(St. Louis' 9th choice, 160th overall, in 2007 Entry Draft).

			Regular Season					Playoffs				
Season	**Club**	**League**	**GP**	**G**	**A**	**Pts**	**PIM**	**GP**	**G**	**A**	**Pts**	**PIM**
2004-05	Richmond Hill	Minor-ON	30	22	20	42	80	....	....	....	....	....
2005-06	Erie Otters	OHL	68	5	3	8	66	....	....	....	....	....
2006-07	Erie Otters	OHL	52	7	3	10	176	....	....	....	....	....
2007-08	Erie Otters	OHL	21	3	3	6	41	....	....	....	....	....
	Sault Ste. Marie	OHL	42	4	11	15	83	14	2	1	3	12

PELUSO, Chris (puh-LOO-soh, KRIHS) **PIT.**

Defense. Shoots left. 5'11", 180 lbs. Born, Wadena, MN, August 21, 1986.
(Pittsburgh's 9th choice, 194th overall, in 2004 Entry Draft).

			Regular Season					Playoffs				
Season	**Club**	**League**	**GP**	**G**	**A**	**Pts**	**PIM**	**GP**	**G**	**A**	**Pts**	**PIM**
2003-04	Brainerd	High-MN	25	10	33	43	....	....	....	....	....	....
2004-05	Sioux Falls	USHL	53	1	7	8	54	....	....	....	....	....
2005-06	Sioux Falls	USHL	57	5	19	24	49	14	0	4	4	8
2006-07	Bemidji State	CHA	26	0	6	6	24	....	....	....	....	....
2007-08	Bemidji State	CHA	36	1	9	10	26	....	....	....	....	....

PENNER, Jeff (PEH-nuhr, JEHF) **BOS.**

Defense. Shoots left. 5'10", 191 lbs. Born, Steinbach, Man., April 13, 1987.

			Regular Season					Playoffs				
Season	**Club**	**League**	**GP**	**G**	**A**	**Pts**	**PIM**	**GP**	**G**	**A**	**Pts**	**PIM**
2005-06	Dauphin Kings	MJHL	44	8	27	35	46	....	....	....	....	....
2006-07	Dauphin Kings	MJHL	45	9	44	53	....	....	....	....	....	....
2007-08	Alaska	CCHA	35	5	7	12	49	....	....	....	....	....
	Providence Bruins	AHL	2	0	0	0	0	....	....	....	....	....

MJHL Rookie All-Star Team (2006) • MJHL First All-Star Team (2007)

Signed as a free agent by **Boston**, March 29, 2008.

PERKOVICH, Nathan (puhr-KOH-vihch, NAY-thuhn) **N.J.**

Right wing. Shoots right. 6'5", 195 lbs. Born, Canton, MI, October 15, 1985.
(New Jersey's 6th choice, 250th overall, in 2004 Entry Draft).

			Regular Season					Playoffs				
Season	**Club**	**League**	**GP**	**G**	**A**	**Pts**	**PIM**	**GP**	**G**	**A**	**Pts**	**PIM**
2003-04	Cedar Rapids	USHL	35	1	7	8	23	4	1	0	1	0
2004-05	Chicago Steel	USHL	37	6	2	8	55	7	2	2	4	4
2005-06	Chicago Steel	USHL	56	28	24	52	121	....	....	....	....	....
2006-07	Lake Superior	CCHA	42	15	7	22	59	....	....	....	....	....
2007-08	Lake Superior	CCHA	36	17	8	25	52	....	....	....	....	....

PERREAULT, Mathieu (pair-OH, MA-tyew) **WSH.**

Center. Shoots left. 5'10", 165 lbs. Born, Drummondville, Que., January 5, 1988.
(Washington's 10th choice, 177th overall, in 2006 Entry Draft).

			Regular Season					Playoffs				
Season	**Club**	**League**	**GP**	**G**	**A**	**Pts**	**PIM**	**GP**	**G**	**A**	**Pts**	**PIM**
2004-05	Magog	QAAA	41	25	47	72	68	9	5	10	15	12
2005-06	Acadie-Bathurst	QMJHL	62	18	34	52	42	17	10	11	21	8
2006-07	Acadie-Bathurst	QMJHL	67	41	78	119	66	12	6	8	14	8
2007-08	Acadie-Bathurst	QMJHL	65	34	*80	*114	61	12	3	19	22	6
	Hershey Bears	AHL	....	....	....	....	....	3	0	0	0	0

QMJHL First All-Star Team (2007) • QMJHL Player of the Year (2007) • QMJHL Second All-Star Team (2008) • Canadian Major Junior Second All-Star Team (2008)

PERRY, Todd (PAIHR-ee, TAWD) **TOR.**

Defense. Shoots left. 6'3", 215 lbs. Born, Ingleside, Ont., December 13, 1986.

			Regular Season					Playoffs				
Season	**Club**	**League**	**GP**	**G**	**A**	**Pts**	**PIM**	**GP**	**G**	**A**	**Pts**	**PIM**
2002-03	Brockville Braves	CJHL	55	3	28	31	....	....	....	....	....	....
2003-04	Brockville Braves	CJHL	38	7	16	23	....	....	....	....	....	....
2004-05	Boston College	H-East	4	0	0	0	0	....	....	....	....	....
	Barrie Colts	OHL	29	0	8	8	46	6	0	0	0	13
2005-06	Barrie Colts	OHL	67	4	20	24	165	14	2	3	5	29
2006-07	London Knights	OHL	67	1	18	19	129	16	2	4	6	36
2007-08	Toronto Marlies	AHL	8	0	1	1	8	....	....	....	....	....
	Columbia Inferno	ECHL	55	6	22	28	73	13	0	0	0	14

Signed by **Barrie** (OHL) after leaving **Boston College** (H-East), January 2, 2005. Signed as a free agent by **Toronto** (AHL), October 3, 2007.

PERSSON, Dennis (PAIR-suhn, DEH-nihs) **BUF.**

Defense. Shoots left. 6'1", 187 lbs. Born, Nykoping, Sweden, June 2, 1988.
(Buffalo's 1st choice, 24th overall, in 2006 Entry Draft).

			Regular Season					Playoffs				
Season	**Club**	**League**	**GP**	**G**	**A**	**Pts**	**PIM**	**GP**	**G**	**A**	**Pts**	**PIM**
2004-05	Vasteras U18	Swe-U18	3	0	1	1	2	4	0	1	1	0
	Vasteras Jr.	Swe-Jr.	27	3	3	6	24	....	....	....	....	....
2005-06	Vasteras Jr.	Swe-Jr.	28	11	15	26	22	....	....	....	....	....
	VIK Vasteras HK	Sweden-2	19	0	2	2	6	....	....	....	....	....
2006-07	Djurgarden	Sweden	9	0	0	0	2	....	....	....	....	....
	Almtuna	Sweden-2	3	0	0	0	2	....	....	....	....	....
	Nykoping	Sweden-2	29	4	4	8	38	....	....	....	....	....
	Djurgarden Jr.	Swe-Jr.	11	1	3	4	8	5	2	3	5	2
2007-08	Djurgarden Jr.	Swe-Jr.	4	0	0	0	10	....	....	....	....	....
	Djurgarden	Sweden	21	0	1	1	6	....	....	....	....	....
	Nykoping	Sweden-2	21	1	3	4	14	....	....	....	....	....

PERVYSHIN, Andrei (pair-VIHSH-ihn, AWN-dray) **ST.L.**

Defense. Shoots left. 5'8", 156 lbs. Born, Arkhangelsk, USSR, February 2, 1985.
(St. Louis' 11th choice, 253rd overall, in 2003 Entry Draft).

			Regular Season					Playoffs				
Season	**Club**	**League**	**GP**	**G**	**A**	**Pts**	**PIM**	**GP**	**G**	**A**	**Pts**	**PIM**
2003-04	Spartak Moscow	Russia-2	59	3	6	9	14	13	0	1	1	4
2004-05	Ak Bars Kazan 2	Russia-3	....	0	1	1	....	....	....	....	....	....
	Ak Bars Kazan	Russia	52	0	3	3	10	2	0	0	0	0
2005-06	Ak Bars Kazan	Russia	48	3	7	10	22	13	0	3	3	14
2006-07	Ak Bars Kazan	Russia	45	5	8	13	71	12	2	3	5	8
2007-08	Ak Bars Kazan	Russia	55	7	8	15	40	10	1	1	2	2

PESONEN, Janne (PEHS-oh-nihn, YAH-nee) **PIT.**

Left wing. Shoots left. 5'11", 180 lbs. Born, Suomussalmi, Finland, May 11, 1982.
(Anaheim's 8th choice, 269th overall, in 2004 Entry Draft).

			Regular Season					Playoffs				
Season	**Club**	**League**	**GP**	**G**	**A**	**Pts**	**PIM**	**GP**	**G**	**A**	**Pts**	**PIM**
1998-99	Hokki Kajaani	Finland-3	2	0	0	0	0	....	....	....	....	....
99-2000	Karpat Oulu U18	Fin-U18	33	6	12	18	30	3	0	1	1	0
2000-01	Karpat Oulu Jr.	Fin-Jr.	41	9	22	31	18	6	1	1	2	0
2001-02	Karpat Oulu Jr.	Fin-Jr.	42	12	19	31	18	3	2	0	2	2
	Karpat Oulu	Finland	9	2	0	2	0	1	0	0	0	0
2002-03	Hokki Kajaani	Finland-2	40	15	21	36	62	3	2	0	2	4
2003-04	Karpat Oulu	Finland	56	17	13	30	28	15	1	1	2	4
2004-05	Karpat Oulu	Finland	55	11	18	29	42	12	2	0	2	0
2005-06	Karpat Oulu	Finland	53	8	14	22	34	11	4	0	4	8
2006-07	Karpat Oulu	Finland	56	22	33	55	38	9	4	3	7	10
2007-08	Karpat Oulu	Finland	56	*34	44	*78	58	14	7	9	16	10

Signed as a free agent by **Pittsburgh**, July 7, 2008.

PESTUNOV, Dmitri (pehs-too-NAWF, dih-MEE-tree) **PHX.**

Center. Shoots left. 5'9", 196 lbs. Born, Ust-Kamenogorsk, USSR, January 22, 1985.
(Phoenix's 2nd choice, 80th overall, in 2003 Entry Draft).

			Regular Season					Playoffs				
Season	Club	League	GP	G	A	Pts	PIM	GP	G	A	Pts	PIM
2002-03	Magnitogorsk	Russia	32	4	0	4	0	....	....	....	....	....
2003-04	Magnitogorsk	Russia	51	6	7	13	40	14	0	3	3	25
	Magnitogorsk 2	Russia-3	6	3	15	18	2	3	0	2	2	4
2004-05	Magnitogorsk	Russia	37	4	4	8	46	....	....	....	....	....
	Spartak Moscow	Russia	12	1	1	2	14	....	....	....	....	....
2005-06	Magnitogorsk	Russia	48	6	13	19	58	4	0	1	1	0
2006-07	Magnitogorsk	Russia	53	5	18	23	26	11	0	0	0	8
2007-08	Spartak Moscow	Russia	51	8	17	25	56	5	0	0	0	16

Signed as a free agent by **Spartak Moscow** (Russia), February 16, 2005.

PETERS, Warren (PEE-tuhrz, WAHR-ihn) **CGY.**

Center. Shoots left. 6', 200 lbs. Born, Saskatoon, Sask., July 10, 1982.

			Regular Season					Playoffs				
Season	Club	League	GP	G	A	Pts	PIM	GP	G	A	Pts	PIM
1998-99	Saskatoon Blades	WHL	53	8	6	14	111	....	....	....	....	....
99-2000	Saskatoon Blades	WHL	70	11	17	28	97	10	1	2	3	13
2000-01	Saskatoon Blades	WHL	63	27	14	41	111	....	....	....	....	....
2001-02	Saskatoon Blades	WHL	72	34	26	60	115	7	1	4	5	13
2002-03	Saskatoon Blades	WHL	71	31	44	75	108	6	1	6	7	6
	Portland Pirates	AHL	1	0	0	0	0	....	....	....	....	....
2003-04	Utah Grizzlies	AHL	55	4	4	8	63	....	....	....	....	....
	Idaho Steelheads	ECHL	21	6	7	13	33	....	....	....	....	....
2004-05	Idaho Steelheads	ECHL	69	23	23	46	131	4	0	1	1	12
2005-06	Omaha	AHL	77	15	10	25	133	....	....	....	....	....
2006-07	Omaha	AHL	79	17	16	33	95	6	2	1	3	4
2007-08	Quad City Flames	AHL	75	11	13	24	74	....	....	....	....	....

Signed as a free agent by **Calgary**, August 5, 2005.

PETERSSON, Andre (PEH-tuhr-suhn, AHN-dray) **OTT.**

Right wing. Shoots right. 5'9", 168 lbs. Born, Olofstrom, Sweden, September 11, 1990.
(Ottawa's 4th choice, 109th overall, in 2008 Entry Draft).

			Regular Season					Playoffs				
Season	Club	League	GP	G	A	Pts	PIM	GP	G	A	Pts	PIM
2005-06	Tingsryds AIF U18	Swe-U18	9	5	3	8	0	....	....	....	....	....
2006-07	HV 71 U18	Swe-U18	10	14	10	24	6	2	1	2	3	0
	HV 71 Jr.	Swe-Jr.	6	1	1	2	8	....	....	....	....	....
2007-08	HV 71 U18	Swe-U18	4	4	5	9	4	....	....	....	....	....
	HV 71 Jr.	Swe-Jr.	36	16	22	38	34	3	0	0	0	2

PETRECKI, Nicholas (peh-TREH-kee, NIHK-oh-las) **S.J.**

Defense. Shoots left. 6'3", 215 lbs. Born, Schenectady, NY, July 11, 1989.
(San Jose's 2nd choice, 28th overall, in 2007 Entry Draft).

			Regular Season					Playoffs				
Season	Club	League	GP	G	A	Pts	PIM	GP	G	A	Pts	PIM
2004-05	Capital District	EmJHL	53	5	18	23	159	....	....	....	....	....
2005-06	Omaha Lancers	USHL	53	0	3	3	110	5	0	0	0	0
2006-07	Omaha Lancers	USHL	54	11	14	25	177	5	0	0	0	10
2007-08	Boston College	H-East	42	5	7	12	*102	....	....	....	....	....

PETRELL, Lennart (peh-TREHL, LEH-nahrt) **CBJ**

Center. Shoots left. 6'3", 198 lbs. Born, Helsinki, Finland, April 13, 1984.
(Columbus' 8th choice, 190th overall, in 2004 Entry Draft).

			Regular Season					Playoffs				
Season	Club	League	GP	G	A	Pts	PIM	GP	G	A	Pts	PIM
2000-01	K-Kissat Jr.	Fin-Jr.	4	3	2	5	0	....	....	....	....	....
	K-Kissat	Finland-4	1	0	0	0	0	....	....	....	....	....
2001-02	HIFK Helsinki U18	Fin-U18	18	10	8	18	12	8	2	0	2	2
	HIFK Helsinki Jr.	Fin-Jr.	5	0	0	0	0	....	....	....	....	....
2002-03	HIFK Helsinki Jr.	Fin-Jr.	28	2	2	4	35	7	3	1	4	29
2003-04	Suomi U20	Finland-2	7	1	0	1	0	....	....	....	....	....
	HIFK Helsinki Jr.	Fin-Jr.	33	11	17	28	28	10	6	7	13	2
	HIFK Helsinki	Finland	8	0	0	0	2	1	0	0	0	0
2004-05	HIFK Helsinki Jr.	Fin-Jr.	12	5	5	10	10	2	0	1	1	0
	HIFK Helsinki	Finland	35	3	2	5	35	4	0	1	1	2
2005-06	HIFK Helsinki	Finland	51	12	8	20	88	10	1	2	3	20
2006-07	HIFK Helsinki	Finland	53	19	11	30	74	5	0	0	0	2
2007-08	HIFK Helsinki	Finland	48	10	17	27	34	7	1	1	2	2

PETROCHININ, Evgeny (peht-roh-CHIH-nihn, ehv-GEH-nee) **CBJ**

Defense. Shoots left. 6'2", 190 lbs. Born, Murmansk, USSR, February 7, 1976.
(Dallas' 5th choice, 150th overall, in 1994 Entry Draft).

			Regular Season					Playoffs				
Season	Club	League	GP	G	A	Pts	PIM	GP	G	A	Pts	PIM
1993-94	Spartak Moscow	CIS	2	0	0	0	0	....	....	....	....	....
1994-95	Spartak Moscow	CIS	45	0	2	2	14	....	....	....	....	....
1995-96	Spartak Moscow	CIS	50	5	17	22	18	5	3	0	3	0
1996-97	Spartak Moscow	Russia	32	5	6	11	52	....	....	....	....	....
1997-98	Spartak Moscow	Russia	46	12	6	18	100	....	....	....	....	....
1998-99	Spartak Moscow	Russia	21	4	6	10	14	....	....	....	....	....
	Ak Bars Kazan	Russia	6	0	2	2	2	9	1	1	2	24
99-2000	Magnitogorsk	Russia	33	7	10	17	38	14	2	1	3	26
2000-01	Cherepovets	Russia	40	8	7	15	38	9	2	0	2	40
2001-02	Cherepovets	Russia	35	35	2	8	10	1	0	0	0	0
2002-03	Cherepovets	Russia	29	3	6	9	14	10	1	0	1	0
2003-04	Cherepovets	Russia	43	4	9	13	85	....	....	....	....	....
	Cherepovets 2	Russia-3	1	0	2	2	0	....	....	....	....	....
2004-05	Magnitogorsk	Russia	48	3	4	7	14	3	0	0	0	2
2005-06	Magnitogorsk 2	Russia-3	1	0	0	0	0	....	....	....	....	....
	Vityaz Chekhov	Russia	18	0	3	3	6	....	....	....	....	....
2006-07	HK Dmitrov	Russia-2	9	3	1	4	32	....	....	....	....	....
	Nizhny Novgorod	Russia-2	1	0	0	0	0	....	....	....	....	....
2007-08	HK Dmitrov	Russia-2	42	9	16	25	96	7	0	4	4	6

Rights traded to **Columbus** by **Dallas** for Kirk Muller, September 28, 2001.

PETROV, Kirill (peh-TRAWF, kih-RIHL) **NYI**

Right wing. Shoots left. 6'3", 198 lbs. Born, Kazan, USSR, April 13, 1990.
(NY Islanders' 7th choice, 73rd overall, in 2008 Entry Draft).

			Regular Season					Playoffs				
Season	Club	League	GP	G	A	Pts	PIM	GP	G	A	Pts	PIM
2005-06	Ak Bars Kazan 2	Russia-3		STATISTICS NOT AVAILABLE								
2006-07	Ak Bars Kazan 2	Russia-3		STATISTICS NOT AVAILABLE								
	Ak Bars Kazan	Russia	9	1	1	2	8	3	0	0	0	2
2007-08	Ak Bars Kazan	Russia	47	4	6	10	54	8	1	1	2	0

PETRUZALEK, Jakub (peh-troo-ZAL-ehk, YA-kuhb) **CAR.**

Center/Right wing. Shoots right. 5'10", 176 lbs. Born, Most, Czech., April 24, 1985.
(NY Rangers' 13th choice, 266th overall, in 2004 Entry Draft).

			Regular Season					Playoffs				
Season	Club	League	GP	G	A	Pts	PIM	GP	G	A	Pts	PIM
2002-03	Litvinov Jr.	CzRep-Jr.	21	17	13	30	10	....	....	....	....	....
	Litvinov	CzRep	5	0	0	0	0	....	....	....	....	....
2003-04	Litvinov Jr.	CzRep-Jr.	53	38	51	89	110	2	0	0	0	2
	Litvinov	CzRep	7	0	0	0	2	....	....	....	....	....
	SK HC Banik Most	CzRep-3	1	0	0	0	0	....	....	....	....	....
2004-05	Ottawa 67's	OHL	59	23	40	63	64	21	8	10	18	30
2005-06	Litvinov Jr.	CzRep-Jr.	3	4	2	6	4	....	....	....	....	....
	Litvinov	CzRep	19	1	1	2	6	....	....	....	....	....
	Barrie Colts	OHL	24	11	20	31	28	14	8	11	19	14
2006-07	Hartford Wolf Pack	AHL	6	0	2	2	0	....	....	....	....	....
	Charlotte	ECHL	7	1	9	10	4	....	....	....	....	....
	Albany River Rats	AHL	54	10	18	28	16	5	2	2	4	10
2007-08	Albany River Rats	AHL	78	14	31	45	52	7	2	1	3	8

Traded to **Carolina** by **NY Rangers** with future considerations for Brad Isbister, November 21, 2006.

PETRY, Jeff (PEH-tree, JEHF) **EDM.**

Defense. Shoots right. 6'3", 180 lbs. Born, Ann Arbor, MI, December 9, 1987.
(Edmonton's 1st choice, 45th overall, in 2006 Entry Draft).

			Regular Season					Playoffs				
Season	Club	League	GP	G	A	Pts	PIM	GP	G	A	Pts	PIM
2004-05	St. Mary's Prep	High-MI	23	2	8	10	....	6	2	5	7	....
2005-06	Det. Caesers	MWEHL	33	7	21	28	24	....	....	....	....	....
	Des Moines	USHL	48	1	14	15	68	11	2	5	7	8
2006-07	Des Moines	USHL	55	18	27	45	71	8	0	6	6	10
2007-08	Michigan State	CCHA	42	3	21	24	28	....	....	....	....	....

CCHA All-Rookie Team (2008)

PIERRO-ZABOTEL, Casey (PEE-air-oh-ZA-boh-tuhl, KAY-see) **PIT.**

Center. Shoots left. 6'1", 205 lbs. Born, Ashcroft, B.C., November 8, 1988.
(Pittsburgh's 4th choice, 80th overall, in 2007 Entry Draft).

			Regular Season					Playoffs				
Season	Club	League	GP	G	A	Pts	PIM	GP	G	A	Pts	PIM
2004-05	Merritt	BCHL	58	6	6	12	19	5	0	0	0	0
2005-06	Merritt	BCHL	60	20	35	55	29	9	9	4	13	10
2006-07	Merritt	BCHL	55	51	65	116	42	7	8	3	11	13
2007-08	Vancouver Giants	WHL	49	19	29	48	8	10	2	4	6	4

PIETRANGELO, Alex (puh-TRAN-geh-loh, AL-ehx) **ST.L.**

Defense. Shoots right. 6'3", 206 lbs. Born, King City, Ont., January 18, 1990.
(St. Louis' 1st choice, 4th overall, in 2008 Entry Draft).

			Regular Season					Playoffs				
Season	Club	League	GP	G	A	Pts	PIM	GP	G	A	Pts	PIM
2005-06	Tor. Jr. Canadiens	GTHL	44	13	31	44	33	....	....	....	....	....
2006-07	Mississauga	OHL	59	7	45	52	45	4	0	0	0	8
2007-08	Niagara Ice Dogs	OHL	60	13	40	53	94	6	5	4	9	4

PINIZZOTTO, Steve (pih-nih-ZAW-toh, STEEV) **WSH.**

Center. Shoots right. 6'1", 196 lbs. Born, Mississauga, Ont., April 26, 1984.

			Regular Season					Playoffs				
Season	Club	League	GP	G	A	Pts	PIM	GP	G	A	Pts	PIM
2001-02	Oakville Blades	OPJHL	34	10	16	26	40	....	....	....	....	....
2002-03	Oakville Blades	OPJHL	44	16	24	40	152	2	0	0	0	2
2003-04	Oakville Blades	OPJHL	39	17	34	51	177	....	....	....	....	....
2004-05	Oakville Blades	OPJHL	48	33	62	95	86	....	....	....	....	....
2005-06	RIT Tigers	NCAA	20	7	6	13	32	....	....	....	....	....
2006-07	RIT Tigers	AH	34	13	31	44	76	....	....	....	....	....
	Hershey Bears	AHL	5	0	0	0	4	....	....	....	....	....
2007-08	Hershey Bears	AHL	23	0	4	4	12	5	0	0	0	13
	South Carolina	ECHL	40	15	17	32	58	10	1	2	3	34

Signed as a free agent by **Washington**, March 16, 2007.

PISELLINI, Gino (pih-sehl-EE-nee, JEE-noh) **PHI.**

Right wing. Shoots right. 6', 210 lbs. Born, Melrose Park, IL, August 5, 1986.
(Philadelphia's 5th choice, 149th overall, in 2004 Entry Draft).

			Regular Season					Playoffs				
Season	Club	League	GP	G	A	Pts	PIM	GP	G	A	Pts	PIM
2003-04	Plymouth Whalers	OHL	68	15	15	30	214	9	0	3	3	23
2004-05	Plymouth Whalers	OHL	59	4	6	10	137	4	0	1	1	9
2005-06	Plymouth Whalers	OHL	63	15	16	31	194	13	0	3	3	28
2006-07	Philadelphia	AHL	32	1	1	2	53	....	....	....	....	....
	Trenton Titans	ECHL	23	1	3	4	65	5	0	1	1	11
2007-08	Wheeling Nailers	ECHL	34	0	5	5	123	....	....	....	....	....

PITTON, Jason (PIH-tuhn, JAY-suhn) **NYI**

Left wing. Shoots left. 6'3", 216 lbs. Born, Mississauga, Ont., May 23, 1986.
(NY Islanders' 9th choice, 244th overall, in 2004 Entry Draft).

			Regular Season					Playoffs				
Season	Club	League	GP	G	A	Pts	PIM	GP	G	A	Pts	PIM
2002-03	Brampton Capitals	OPJHL	47	23	18	41	46	....	....	....	....	....
	Sault Ste. Marie	OHL	1	0	0	0	0	....	....	....	....	....
2003-04	Sault Ste. Marie	OHL	67	9	11	20	37	....	....	....	....	....
2004-05	Sault Ste. Marie	OHL	68	23	19	42	35	7	2	2	4	4
2005-06	Sault Ste. Marie	OHL	37	18	9	27	29	....	....	....	....	....
	Guelph Storm	OHL	31	10	5	15	21	15	5	3	8	18
2006-07	Bridgeport	AHL	76	9	10	19	65	....	....	....	....	....
2007-08	Bridgeport	AHL	21	1	4	5	16	....	....	....	....	....
	Utah Grizzlies	ECHL	23	5	8	13	29	....	....	....	....	....

PLANTE, Alex (PLAWNT, AL-ehx) **EDM.**

Defense. Shoots right. 6'4", 225 lbs. Born, Brandon, Man., May 9, 1989.
(Edmonton's 2nd choice, 15th overall, in 2007 Entry Draft).

			Regular Season					Playoffs				
Season	Club	League	GP	G	A	Pts	PIM	GP	G	A	Pts	PIM
2004-05	Brandon	MMHL	37	5	21	26	120	....	....	....	....	....
	Calgary Hitmen	WHL	8	0	0	0	6	11	0	0	0	17
2005-06	Calgary Hitmen	WHL	54	1	3	4	72	13	0	0	0	6
2006-07	Calgary Hitmen	WHL	58	8	30	38	81	13	5	6	11	14
2007-08	Calgary Hitmen	WHL	36	1	1	2	28	15	0	4	4	10

PLATONOV, Denis (PLAH-tah-nahv, DEH-nihs) **NSH.**

Right wing. Shoots left. 6'3", 205 lbs. Born, Saratov, USSR, November 6, 1981.
(Nashville's 4th choice, 75th overall, in 2001 Entry Draft).

			Regular Season					Playoffs				
Season	Club	League	GP	G	A	Pts	PIM	GP	G	A	Pts	PIM
1997-98	Kristall Saratov 2	Russia-3	20	4	2	6	34	....	....	....	....	....
1998-99	Kristall Saratov	Russia-2	14	1	0	1	61	....	....	....	....	....
99-2000	Kristall Saratov 2	Russia-3	5	0	0	0	37	....	....	....	....	....
	Kristall Saratov	Russia-2	32	9	4	13	60	....	....	....	....	....
2000-01	Kristall Saratov	Russia-2	51	14	6	20	75	....	....	....	....	....
2001-02	Kristall Saratov	Russia-2	50	18	14	32	96	....	....	....	....	....
2002-03	Ak Bars Kazan	Russia	47	8	9	17	49	5	0	0	0	2
2003-04	Milwaukee	AHL	3	0	0	0	0	....	....	....	....	....
	Ak Bars Kazan	Russia	28	5	3	8	18	8	1	0	1	2
	Ak Bars Kazan 2	Russia-3	STATISTICS NOT AVAILABLE									
2004-05	Ak Bars Kazan	Russia	38	3	7	10	10	....	....	....	....	....
	Nizhnekamsk	Russia	11	3	1	4	34	3	0	1	1	2
2005-06	Magnitogorsk	Russia	49	11	8	19	60	8	4	0	4	6
2006-07	Magnitogorsk	Russia	53	17	8	25	87	14	5	3	8	14
2007-08	Magnitogorsk	Russia	57	16	11	27	76	13	3	4	7	16

Assigned to **Kazan** (Russia) by **Nashville**, October 29, 2003.

PLEKHANOV, Andrey (pleh-HAN-awf, AWN-dray) **CBJ**

Defense. Shoots right. 6'2", 206 lbs. Born, Nizhnekamsk, USSR, July 12, 1986.
(Columbus' 5th choice, 96th overall, in 2004 Entry Draft).

			Regular Season					Playoffs				
Season	Club	League	GP	G	A	Pts	PIM	GP	G	A	Pts	PIM
2003-04	Nizhnekamsk 2	Russia-3	STATISTICS NOT AVAILABLE									
2004-05	Sarnia Sting	OHL	2	0	0	0	0	....	....	....	....	....
	Nizhnekamsk	Russia	2	0	0	0	2	....	....	....	....	....
	Leninogorsk	Russia-2	1	0	0	0	4	....	....	....	....	....
	Perm 2	Russia-3	2	0	0	0	4	....	....	....	....	....
2005-06	Nizhnekamsk	Russia	45	1	1	2	22	5	0	0	0	0
2006-07	Nizhnekamsk	Russia	16	1	2	3	28	....	....	....	....	....
2007-08	Elmira Jackals	ECHL	7	0	1	1	2	....	....	....	....	....
	Syracuse Crunch	AHL	40	9	16	25	10	8	1	2	3	2

POHL, Petr (PAWL, PEE-tuhr) **CBJ**

Right wing. Shoots right. 5'11", 188 lbs. Born, Prostejov, Czech., August 28, 1986.
(Columbus' 6th choice, 133rd overall, in 2004 Entry Draft).

			Regular Season					Playoffs				
Season	Club	League	GP	G	A	Pts	PIM	GP	G	A	Pts	PIM
2001-02	HC Vitkovice U17	CzR-U17	38	34	19	53	65	2	1	0	1	4
	HC Vitkovice Jr.	CzRep-Jr.	10	0	2	2	2	....	....	....	....	....
2002-03	HC Vitkovice Jr.	CzRep-Jr.	36	13	22	35	30	2	1	0	1	6
2003-04	Gatineau	QMJHL	70	23	27	50	16	8	0	2	2	2
2004-05	Gatineau	QMJHL	62	27	32	59	16	10	6	4	10	4
2005-06	Acadie-Bathurst	QMJHL	62	27	43	70	44	17	6	10	16	12
2006-07	Syracuse Crunch	AHL	1	0	0	0	0	....	....	....	....	....
	Dayton Bombers	ECHL	65	8	16	24	18	18	3	3	6	10
2007-08	Syracuse Crunch	AHL	2	0	0	0	5	....	....	....	....	....
	Dayton Bombers	ECHL	7	1	8	9	0	2	0	1	1	4
	Youngstown	CHL	56	24	41	65	28					

POKULOK, Sasha (poh-KUH-lawk, SA-shuh) **WSH.**

Defense. Shoots left. 6'6", 220 lbs. Born, Montreal, Que., May 25, 1986.
(Washington's 1st choice, 14th overall, in 2005 Entry Draft).

			Regular Season					Playoffs				
Season	Club	League	GP	G	A	Pts	PIM	GP	G	A	Pts	PIM
2003-04	Notre Dame	SJHL	39	7	16	23	34	....	....	....	....	....
2004-05	Cornell Big Red	ECAC	26	3	7	10	33	....	....	....	....	....
2005-06	Cornell Big Red	ECAC	27	4	9	13	49	....	....	....	....	....
2006-07	Hershey Bears	AHL	1	0	0	0	0	....	....	....	....	....
	South Carolina	ECHL	16	3	6	9	22	....	....	....	....	....
2007-08	Hershey Bears	AHL	44	1	6	7	43	....	....	....	....	....
	South Carolina	ECHL	5	0	6	6	6	18	0	6	6	18

ECAC All-Rookie Team (2005)

POPOV, Andrei (PAH-pawv, AWN-dray) **PHI.**

Right wing. Shoots left. 6', 187 lbs. Born, Chelyabinsk, USSR, July 15, 1988.
(Philadelphia's 10th choice, 205th overall, in 2006 Entry Draft).

			Regular Season					Playoffs				
Season	Club	League	GP	G	A	Pts	PIM	GP	G	A	Pts	PIM
2003-04	Chelyabinsk 2	Russia-3	6	3	0	3	4	....	....	....	....	....
2004-05	Chelyabinsk 2	Russia-3	17	7	1	8	4	....	....	....	....	....
2005-06	Chelyabinsk 2	Russia-3	2	1	4	5	0	....	....	....	....	....
	Chelyabinsk	Russia-2	37	8	8	16	26	5	2	0	2	2
2006-07	Chelyabinsk 2	Russia-3	2	1	1	2	0	....	....	....	....	....
	Chelyabinsk	Russia	44	2	10	12	36	....	....	....	....	....
2007-08	Chelyabinsk 2	Russia-3	6	4	3	7	4	....	....	....	....	....
	Chelyabinsk	Russia	33	5	2	7	12	2	0	0	0	4

PORTER, Chris (POHR-tuhr, KRIHS) **ST.L.**

Center. Shoots left. 6'1", 203 lbs. Born, Toronto, Ont., May 29, 1984.
(Chicago's 10th choice, 282nd overall, in 2003 Entry Draft).

			Regular Season					Playoffs				
Season	Club	League	GP	G	A	Pts	PIM	GP	G	A	Pts	PIM
2001-02	Shat.-St. Mary's	High-MN	75	10	25	35	32	....	....	....	....	....
2002-03	Lincoln Stars	USHL	59	13	22	35	74	10	4	3	7	10
2003-04	North Dakota	WCHA	41	10	15	25	46	....	....	....	....	....
2004-05	North Dakota	WCHA	45	12	3	15	36	....	....	....	....	....
2005-06	North Dakota	WCHA	46	7	16	23	40	....	....	....	....	....
2006-07	North Dakota	WCHA	43	13	17	30	38	....	....	....	....	....
2007-08	Peoria Rivermen	AHL	80	12	25	37	72	....	....	....	....	....

Signed as a free agent by **St. Louis**, August 21, 2007.

PORTER, Kevin (POHR-tuhr, KEH-vihn) **PHX.**

Left wing. Shoots left. 5'11", 194 lbs. Born, Detroit, MI, March 12, 1986.
(Phoenix's 5th choice, 119th overall, in 2004 Entry Draft).

			Regular Season					Playoffs				
Season	Club	League	GP	G	A	Pts	PIM	GP	G	A	Pts	PIM
2002-03	USNTDP	U-17	19	9	11	20	8	....	....	....	....	....
	USNTDP	U-18	13	1	2	3	2	....	....	....	....	....
	USNTDP	NAHL	40	19	9	28	17	....	....	....	....	....
2003-04	USNTDP	U-18	44	5	21	26	26	....	....	....	....	....
	USNTDP	NAHL	11	3	8	11	4	....	....	....	....	....
2004-05	U. of Michigan	CCHA	39	11	13	24	51	....	....	....	....	....
2005-06	U. of Michigan	CCHA	39	17	21	38	30	....	....	....	....	....
2006-07	U. of Michigan	CCHA	41	24	34	58	16	....	....	....	....	....
2007-08	U. of Michigan	CCHA	43	*33	30	*63	18	....	....	....	....	....
	San Antonio	AHL	....	....	....	....	....	7	0	4	4	0

CCHA Second All-Star Team (2007) • CCHA First All-Star Team (2008) • CCHA Player of the Year (2008) • NCAA West First All-American Team (2008)

POSPISIL, Tomas (PAWS-pih-shihl, TAW-mahsh) **ATL.**

Right wing. Shoots right. 6', 185 lbs. Born, Sumperk, Czech., August 25, 1987.
(Atlanta's 6th choice, 135th overall, in 2005 Entry Draft).

			Regular Season					Playoffs				
Season	Club	League	GP	G	A	Pts	PIM	GP	G	A	Pts	PIM
2002-03	HC Trinec U17	CzR-U17	41	24	28	52	44	2	0	1	1	2
	HC Trinec Jr.	CzRep-Jr.	2	0	0	0	0	2	0	0	0	0
2003-04	HC Trinec U17	CzR-U17	3	3	3	6	14	5	5	2	7	26
	HC Trinec Jr.	CzRep-Jr.	45	14	11	25	40	2	1	1	2	0
2004-05	HC Ocelari Trinec	CzRep	14	0	0	0	0	....	....	....	....	....
	HC Trinec Jr.	CzRep-Jr.	38	19	18	37	44	5	4	1	5	27
2005-06	Sarnia Sting	OHL	60	25	30	55	61	....	....	....	....	....
2006-07	Sarnia Sting	OHL	55	29	38	67	38	4	1	5	6	4
2007-08	Chicago Wolves	AHL	11	0	2	2	2	....	....	....	....	....
	Gwinnett	ECHL	54	18	23	41	18	8	2	3	5	6

POSTMA, Paul (POHST-muh, PAWL) **ATL.**

Defense. Shoots right. 6'2", 180 lbs. Born, Red Deer, Alta., February 22, 1989.
(Atlanta's 4th choice, 205th overall, in 2007 Entry Draft).

			Regular Season					Playoffs				
Season	Club	League	GP	G	A	Pts	PIM	GP	G	A	Pts	PIM
2004-05	Red Deer	AMHL	36	6	5	11	24	....	....	....	....	....
	Swift Current	WHL	4	0	0	0	0	....	....	....	....	....
2005-06	Swift Current	WHL	58	2	9	11	6	4	0	0	0	0
2006-07	Swift Current	WHL	70	5	19	24	42	6	0	1	1	0
2007-08	Swift Current	WHL	2	0	0	0	2	....	....	....	....	....
	Calgary Hitmen	WHL	66	14	28	42	30	16	6	4	10	4

POTTER, Corey (PAW-tuhr, KOHR-ee) **NYR**

Defense. Shoots right. 6'3", 200 lbs. Born, Lansing, MI, January 5, 1984.
(NY Rangers' 4th choice, 122nd overall, in 2003 Entry Draft).

			Regular Season					Playoffs				
Season	Club	League	GP	G	A	Pts	PIM	GP	G	A	Pts	PIM
99-2000	Det. Honeybaked	MWEHL	58	10	38	48	....	....	....	....	....	....
2000-01	USNTDP	U-17	13	0	0	0	6	....	....	....	....	....
	USNTDP	NAHL	53	4	4	8	20	....	....	....	....	....
2001-02	USNTDP	U-18	38	4	6	10	49	....	....	....	....	....
	USNTDP	USHL	13	2	2	4	12	....	....	....	....	....
	USNTDP	NAHL	10	0	3	3	4	....	....	....	....	....
2002-03	Michigan State	CCHA	35	4	4	8	30	....	....	....	....	....
2003-04	Michigan State	CCHA	38	0	8	8	63	....	....	....	....	....
2004-05	Michigan State	CCHA	32	0	6	6	73	....	....	....	....	....
2005-06	Michigan State	CCHA	45	4	18	22	117	....	....	....	....	....
2006-07	Hartford Wolf Pack	AHL	30	2	8	10	21	7	1	4	5	12
	Charlotte	ECHL	43	6	13	19	56	....	....	....	....	....
2007-08	Hartford Wolf Pack	AHL	80	5	27	32	102	5	0	1	1	14

POTULNY, Grant (poh-TUHL-nee, GRANT)

Center. Shoots left. 6'3", 205 lbs. Born, Grand Forks, ND, March 4, 1980.
(Ottawa's 7th choice, 157th overall, in 2000 Entry Draft).

			Regular Season					Playoffs				
Season	Club	League	GP	G	A	Pts	PIM	GP	G	A	Pts	PIM
1998-99	Lincoln Stars	USHL	46	7	11	18	76	10	2	1	3	7
99-2000	Lincoln Stars	USHL	56	25	30	55	85	10	3	4	7	4
2000-01	U. of Minnesota	WCHA	42	22	11	33	38	....	....	....	....	....
2001-02	U. of Minnesota	WCHA	43	15	19	34	38	....	....	....	....	....
2002-03	U. of Minnesota	WCHA	23	15	8	23	12	....	....	....	....	....
2003-04	U. of Minnesota	WCHA	38	16	10	26	28	....	....	....	....	....
	Binghamton	AHL	3	0	1	1	0	2	0	0	0	0
2004-05	Binghamton	AHL	50	4	6	10	104	6	0	0	0	2
2005-06	Binghamton	AHL	78	23	23	46	122	....	....	....	....	....
2006-07	Binghamton	AHL	47	10	10	20	85	....	....	....	....	....
2007-08	Hershey Bears	AHL	50	19	12	31	71	....	....	....	....	....
	Springfield Falcons	AHL	25	9	6	15	33	....	....	....	....	....

NCAA Championship All-Tournament Team (2002) • NCAA Championship Tournament MVP (2002)

Signed as a free agent by **Hershey** (AHL), August 16, 2007.

POWE, Darroll (POW, DAIR-ohl) **PHI.**

Left wing. Shoots left. 5'11", 212 lbs. Born, Saskatoon, Sask., June 22, 1985.

			Regular Season					Playoffs				
Season	Club	League	GP	G	A	Pts	PIM	GP	G	A	Pts	PIM
2003-04	Princeton	ECAC	29	4	5	9	28	....	....	....	....	....
2004-05	Princeton	ECAC	30	5	2	7	41	....	....	....	....	....
2005-06	Princeton	ECAC	27	6	10	16	48	....	....	....	....	....
2006-07	Princeton	ECAC	34	13	15	28	63	....	....	....	....	....
	Philadelphia	AHL	11	2	2	4	20	....	....	....	....	....
2007-08	Philadelphia	AHL	76	9	14	23	133	10	1	0	1	6

Signed as a free agent by **Philadelphia**, April 17, 2008.

PRUDDEN, Josh (PROO-dehn, JAWSH)

Left wing. Shoots left. 5'11", 190 lbs. Born, Andover, MA, January 10, 1980.

			Regular Season					Playoffs				
Season	Club	League	GP	G	A	Pts	PIM	GP	G	A	Pts	PIM
99-2000	New Hampshire	H-East	16	2	3	5	12	....	....	....	....	....
2000-01	New Hampshire	H-East	37	8	8	16	28	....	....	....	....	....
2001-02	New Hampshire	H-East	36	14	16	30	32	....	....	....	....	....
2002-03	New Hampshire	H-East	42	9	13	22	52	....	....	....	....	....
2003-04	Atlantic City	ECHL	60	18	34	52	54	4	0	0	0	2
2004-05	Cleveland Barons	AHL	73	14	8	22	54	....	....	....	....	....
2005-06	Cleveland Barons	AHL	76	9	12	21	46	....	....	....	....	....
2006-07	Worcester Sharks	AHL	56	9	22	31	34	6	0	1	1	9
	Fresno Falcons	ECHL	18	7	10	17	26	....	....	....	....	....
2007-08	Worcester Sharks	AHL	32	5	4	9	14	....	....	....	....	....
	Fresno Falcons	ECHL	18	7	14	21	25	6	1	2	3	4
	Manitoba Moose	AHL	7	1	0	1	0	....	....	....	....	....

Signed as a free agent by **San Jose**, August 15, 2005.

PRYOR, Nick (PRIGH-uhr, NIHK) **ANA.**

Defense. Shoots left. 5'11", 184 lbs. Born, St. Paul, MN, September 9, 1990.
(Anaheim's 10th choice, 208th overall, in 2008 Entry Draft).

			Regular Season					Playoffs				
Season	Club	League	GP	G	A	Pts	PIM	GP	G	A	Pts	PIM
2006-07	USNTDP	U-17	7	2	3	5	2	....	....	....	....	....
	USNTDP	NAHL	37	1	3	4	10	4	1	0	1	0
2007-08	USNTDP	U-18	41	3	9	12	6	....	....	....	....	....
	USNTDP	NAHL	12	0	2	2	6	....	....	....	....	....

• Signed Letter of Intent to attend **University of Wisconsin** (WCHA) in fall of 2009.

PUUSTINEN, Juuso (POOS-tih-nehn, YUH-soh) **CGY.**

Right wing. Shoots right. 6'2", 188 lbs. Born, Kuopio, Finland, April 5, 1988.
(Calgary's 5th choice, 149th overall, in 2006 Entry Draft).

			Regular Season					Playoffs				
Season	Club	League	GP	G	A	Pts	PIM	GP	G	A	Pts	PIM
2004-05	KalPa Kuopio U18	Fin-U18	26	14	15	29	81	6	1	2	3	4
	KalPa Kuopio Jr.	Fin-Jr.	1	0	0	0	0	....	....	....	....	....
2005-06	KalPa Kuopio U18	Fin-U18	7	8	7	15	18	1	0	0	0	2
	KalPa Kuopio Jr.	Fin-Jr.	29	9	5	14	46	5	0	0	0	0
2006-07	Kamloops Blazers	WHL	64	32	39	71	52	4	0	3	3	4
	Suomi U20	Finland-2	2	0	1	1	2	....	....	....	....	....
2007-08	Kamloops Blazers	WHL	60	27	26	53	26	4	1	1	2	2

PYATT, Tom (PIGH-at, TAWM) **NYR**

Center. Shoots left. 6', 185 lbs. Born, Thunder Bay, Ont., February 14, 1987.
(NY Rangers' 6th choice, 107th overall, in 2005 Entry Draft).

			Regular Season					Playoffs				
Season	Club	League	GP	G	A	Pts	PIM	GP	G	A	Pts	PIM
2003-04	Saginaw Spirit	OHL	67	9	9	18	21	....	....	....	....	....
2004-05	Saginaw Spirit	OHL	57	18	30	48	14	....	....	....	....	....
2005-06	Saginaw Spirit	OHL	58	24	29	53	29	4	1	2	3	4
2006-07	Saginaw Spirit	OHL	58	43	38	81	18	6	3	5	8	0
	Hartford Wolf Pack	AHL	1	0	0	0	0	....	....	....	....	....
2007-08	Hartford Wolf Pack	AHL	41	4	7	11	6	3	0	0	0	0
	Charlotte	ECHL	16	6	9	15	8	3	0	0	0	0

PYETT, Logan (PIGH-eht, LOH-guhn) **DET.**

Defense. Shoots right. 5'10", 199 lbs. Born, Regina, Sask., May 26, 1988.
(Detroit's 7th choice, 212th overall, in 2006 Entry Draft).

			Regular Season					Playoffs				
Season	Club	League	GP	G	A	Pts	PIM	GP	G	A	Pts	PIM
2002-03	Balgonie	SSMHL	35	27	46	73	40	....	....	....	....	....
2003-04	Regina Pat Cdns.	SMHL	44	18	27	45	34	....	....	....	....	....
	Regina Pats	WHL	2	0	1	1	0	3	0	0	0	0
2004-05	Regina Pats	WHL	67	5	19	24	67	....	....	....	....	....
2005-06	Regina Pats	WHL	71	10	35	45	89	6	1	6	7	12
2006-07	Regina Pats	WHL	71	14	48	62	84	10	3	6	9	4
2007-08	Regina Pats	WHL	62	20	34	54	54	6	1	3	4	0

WHL East First All-Star Team (2008) • Canadian Major Junior Second All-Star Team (2008)

QUAILER, Steve (KWAY-luhr, STEEV) **MTL.**

Right wing. Shoots left. 6'4", 180 lbs. Born, Arvada, CO, August 5, 1989.
(Montreal's 2nd choice, 86th overall, in 2008 Entry Draft).

			Regular Season					Playoffs				
Season	Club	League	GP	G	A	Pts	PIM	GP	G	A	Pts	PIM
2006-07	Rocky Mountain	Minor-CO	53	14	23	37	25	....	....	....	....	....
2007-08	Sioux City	USHL	60	19	30	49	55	4	1	2	3	4

• Signed Letter of Intent to attend **Northeastern University** (Hockey East) in fall of 2008.

QUICK, Kevin (KWIHK, KEH-vihn) **T.B.**

Defense. Shoots left. 6', 175 lbs. Born, Buffalo, NY, March 29, 1988.
(Tampa Bay's 2nd choice, 78th overall, in 2006 Entry Draft).

			Regular Season					Playoffs				
Season	Club	League	GP	G	A	Pts	PIM	GP	G	A	Pts	PIM
2004-05	Salisbury School	High-CT	27	3	9	12	3	....	....	....	....	....
2005-06	Salisbury School	High-CT	28	3	20	23	6	....	....	....	....	....
2006-07	Salisbury School	High-CT	25	1	10	11	10	....	....	....	....	....
2007-08	U. of Michigan	CCHA	21	2	2	4	12	....	....	....	....	....
	Norfolk Admirals	AHL	18	0	4	4	6	....	....	....	....	....

QUIST, William (KVIHST, WILL-yuhm) **EDM.**

Left wing. Shoots left. 6'3", 185 lbs. Born, Nybro, Sweden, July 31, 1989.
(Edmonton's 6th choice, 157th overall, in 2007 Entry Draft).

			Regular Season					Playoffs				
Season	Club	League	GP	G	A	Pts	PIM	GP	G	A	Pts	PIM
2005-06	Tingsryds AIF U18	Swe-U18	12	6	3	9	12	....	....	....	....	....
	Tingsryds AIF Jr.	Swe-Jr.	10	0	4	4	14	....	....	....	....	....
2006-07	Tingsryds AIF U18	Swe-U18	16	8	10	18	18	....	....	....	....	....
	Tingsryds AIF Jr.	Swe-Jr.	22	10	15	25	86	....	....	....	....	....
	Tingsryds AIF	Sweden-3	7	0	0	0	0	1	0	0	0	0
2007-08	Linkopings HC U18	Swe-U18	2	1	0	1	2	....	....	....	....	....
	Linkopings HC Jr.	Swe-Jr.	9	3	2	5	31	....	....	....	....	....
	Tingsryds AIF U18	Swe-U18	4	1	2	3	6	....	....	....	....	....
	Tingsryds AIF Jr.	Swe-Jr.	6	4	7	11	4	....	....	....	....	....
	Tingsryds AIF	Sweden-3	17	6	7	13	6	....	....	....	....	....

RABBIT, Wacey (RA-biht, WAY-see) **BOS.**

Center. Shoots left. 5'10", 171 lbs. Born, Lethbridge, Alta., November 16, 1986.
(Boston's 6th choice, 154th overall, in 2005 Entry Draft).

			Regular Season					Playoffs				
Season	Club	League	GP	G	A	Pts	PIM	GP	G	A	Pts	PIM
2001-02	Cgy. North Stars	AMHL	35	24	28	52	....	....	....	....	....	....
	Saskatoon Blades	WHL	3	0	1	1	0	....	....	....	....	....
2002-03	Saskatoon Blades	WHL	62	21	24	45	33	5	1	3	4	6
2003-04	Saskatoon Blades	WHL	60	9	8	17	51	....	....	....	....	....
2004-05	Saskatoon Blades	WHL	70	22	45	67	70	4	1	2	3	0
2005-06	Saskatoon Blades	WHL	64	28	28	56	45	10	5	3	8	4
2006-07	Vancouver Giants	WHL	30	11	25	36	34	22	*11	9	20	16
	Providence Bruins	AHL	22	1	2	3	25	....	....	....	....	....
2007-08	Providence Bruins	AHL	66	9	17	26	51	4	2	0	2	2

RADUNS, Nate (RAH-duhnz, NAYT) **PHI.**

Right wing. Shoots right. 6'3", 205 lbs. Born, Sauk Rapids, MN, May 17, 1984.

			Regular Season					Playoffs				
Season	Club	League	GP	G	A	Pts	PIM	GP	G	A	Pts	PIM
2001-02	USNTDP	USHL	13	3	3	6	14	....	....	....	....	....
	USNTDP	NAHL	10	0	4	4	7	....	....	....	....	....
2002-03	River City Lancers	USHL	48	5	17	22	50	11	1	3	4	8
2003-04	St. Cloud State	WCHA	34	4	7	11	40	....	....	....	....	....
2004-05	St. Cloud State	WCHA	28	4	8	12	32	....	....	....	....	....
2005-06	St. Cloud State	WCHA	41	5	10	15	50	....	....	....	....	....
2006-07	St. Cloud State	WCHA	40	6	6	12	53	....	....	....	....	....
2007-08	Worcester Sharks	AHL	56	12	15	27	42	....	....	....	....	....

Signed as a free agent by **Philadelphia**, July 1, 2008.

RAHIMI, Daniel (RA-hih-mee, DAN-yehl) **VAN.**

Defense. Shoots left. 6'3", 221 lbs. Born, Umea, Sweden, April 28, 1987.
(Vancouver's 2nd choice, 82nd overall, in 2006 Entry Draft).

			Regular Season					Playoffs				
Season	Club	League	GP	G	A	Pts	PIM	GP	G	A	Pts	PIM
2003-04	Bjorkloven U18	Swe-U18	10	0	3	3	14	....	....	....	....	....
2004-05	Bjorkloven U18	Swe-U18	STATISTICS NOT AVAILABLE									
	Bjorkloven Jr.	Swe-Jr.	3	1	0	1	8	....	....	....	....	....
2005-06	Bjorkloven Jr.	Swe-Jr.	40	3	10	13	78	6	3	2	5	37
	IF Bjorkloven Umea	Sweden-2	6	0	0	0	4	....	....	....	....	....
2006-07	Manitoba Moose	AHL	1	0	0	0	0	4	0	0	0	2
	Bjorkloven Jr.	Swe-Jr.	8	0	2	2	18	....	....	....	....	....
	IF Bjorkloven Umea	Sweden-2	43	0	3	3	112	6	0	0	0	6
2007-08	Manitoba Moose	AHL	41	3	2	5	37	....	....	....	....	....
	Victoria	ECHL	19	0	5	5	14	....	....	....	....	....

RAI, Prab (RIGH, PRAB) **VAN.**

Center. Shoots left. 5'11", 191 lbs. Born, Surrey, B.C., November 22, 1989.
(Vancouver's 3rd choice, 131st overall, in 2008 Entry Draft).

			Regular Season					Playoffs				
Season	Club	League	GP	G	A	Pts	PIM	GP	G	A	Pts	PIM
2006-07	Prince George	WHL	24	2	3	5	12	....	....	....	....	....
	Seattle	WHL	38	5	14	19	18	8	1	4	5	0
2007-08	Seattle	WHL	72	20	45	65	21	11	2	4	6	4

RAKHSHANI, Rhett (rahk-SHAH-nee, REHT) **NYI**

Right wing. Shoots right. 5'10", 170 lbs. Born, Orange, CA, March 6, 1988.
(NY Islanders' 4th choice, 100th overall, in 2006 Entry Draft).

			Regular Season					Playoffs				
Season	Club	League	GP	G	A	Pts	PIM	GP	G	A	Pts	PIM
2003-04	California Wave	Minor-CA	56	54	67	121	....	....	....	....	....	....
2004-05	USNTDP	U-17	14	6	5	11	32	....	....	....	....	....
	USNTDP	NAHL	40	12	15	27	21	9	1	4	5	2
2005-06	USNTDP	U-18	43	11	12	23	30	....	....	....	....	....
	USNTDP	NAHL	16	13	13	26	35	....	....	....	....	....
2006-07	U. of Denver	WCHA	40	10	26	36	38	....	....	....	....	....
2007-08	U. of Denver	WCHA	37	14	14	28	52	....	....	....	....	....

RATCHUK, Michael (RAT-chuhk, MIGH-kuhl) **PHI.**

Defense. Shoots left. 5'10", 180 lbs. Born, Buffalo, NY, February 20, 1988.
(Philadelphia's 3rd choice, 42nd overall, in 2006 Entry Draft).

			Regular Season					Playoffs				
Season	Club	League	GP	G	A	Pts	PIM	GP	G	A	Pts	PIM
2004-05	USNTDP	U-17	15	1	4	5	16	....	....	....	....	....
	USNTDP	NAHL	33	3	6	9	14	10	1	1	2	2
2005-06	USNTDP	U-18	39	8	14	22	52	....	....	....	....	....
	USNTDP	NAHL	16	4	4	8	4	....	....	....	....	....
2006-07	Michigan State	CCHA	40	4	8	12	28	....	....	....	....	....
2007-08	Michigan State	CCHA	42	6	19	25	48	....	....	....	....	....
	Philadelphia	AHL	3	1	2	3	2	5	0	1	1	0

RAU, Chad (ROW, CHAD) **TOR.**

Center. Shoots right. 5'11", 185 lbs. Born, Eden Prairie, MN, January 18, 1987.
(Toronto's 6th choice, 228th overall, in 2005 Entry Draft).

			Regular Season					Playoffs				
Season	Club	League	GP	G	A	Pts	PIM	GP	G	A	Pts	PIM
2004-05	Des Moines	USHL	57	31	40	71	32	....	....	....	....	....
2005-06	Colorado College	WCHA	42	13	17	30	8	....	....	....	....	....
2006-07	Colorado College	WCHA	39	14	17	31	4	....	....	....	....	....
2007-08	Colorado College	WCHA	40	*28	14	42	8	....	....	....	....	....

USHL All-Rookie Team (2005) • USHL First All-Star Team (2005) • USHL Rookie of the Year (2005) • WCHA First All-Star Team (2008) • NCAA West Second All-American Team (2008)

REANEY, Les (RAY-nee, LEHS) **EDM.**

Center. Shoots left. 6'2", 221 lbs. Born, Ceylon, Sask., July 8, 1984.

			Regular Season					Playoffs				
Season	Club	League	GP	G	A	Pts	PIM	GP	G	A	Pts	PIM
2005-06	Niagara University	CHA	35	13	27	40	63	....	....	....	....	....
2006-07	Niagara University	CHA	37	16	28	44	80	....	....	....	....	....
2007-08	Niagara University	CHA	25	5	10	15	48	....	....	....	....	....
	Stockton Thunder	ECHL	5	0	1	1	0	....	....	....	....	....

Signed as a free agent by **Edmonton**, February 15, 2008.

REAVES, Ryan (REEVZ, RIGH-uhn) **ST.L.**

Right wing. Shoots right. 6'1", 193 lbs. Born, Winnipeg, Man., January 20, 1987.
(St. Louis' 4th choice, 156th overall, in 2005 Entry Draft).

			Regular Season					Playoffs				
Season	Club	League	GP	G	A	Pts	PIM	GP	G	A	Pts	PIM
2004-05	Brandon	WHL	64	7	9	16	79	23	2	4	6	43
2005-06	Brandon	WHL	68	14	14	28	91	6	0	1	1	8
2006-07	Brandon	WHL	69	15	20	35	76	11	1	4	5	19
2007-08	Peoria Rivermen	AHL	31	4	3	7	46	....	....	....	....	....
	Alaska Aces	ECHL	9	2	0	2	42	2	0	0	0	22

RECHLICZ, Joel (WRECK-lidge, JOHL) **NYI**

Right wing. Shoots right. 6'4", 220 lbs. Born, Brookfield, WI, June 14, 1987.

			Regular Season					Playoffs				
Season	Club	League	GP	G	A	Pts	PIM	GP	G	A	Pts	PIM
2004-05	Santa Fe	NAHL	3	0	1	1	29	....	....	....	....	....
2005-06	Des Moines	USHL	2	0	0	0	4	....	....	....	....	....
	Indiana Ice	USHL	2	0	0	0	16	....	....	....	....	....
	Gatineau	QMJHL	3	0	0	0	17	....	....	....	....	....
2006-07	Chicoutimi	QMJHL	55	0	1	1	159	1	0	0	0	2
	Chicago Hounds	UHL	2	0	0	0	9	....	....	....	....	....
2007-08	Albany River Rats	AHL	25	0	1	1	106	....	....	....	....	....
	Kalamazoo Wings	IHL	25	1	0	1	100	....	....	....	....	....

Signed as a free agent by **NY Islanders**, May 6, 2008.

REDMOND, Zach (REHD-muhnd, ZAK) **ATL.**

Defense. Shoots right. 6'2", 200 lbs. Born, Houston, TX, July 26, 1988.
(Atlanta's 7th choice, 184th overall, in 2008 Entry Draft).

			Regular Season					Playoffs				
Season	Club	League	GP	G	A	Pts	PIM	GP	G	A	Pts	PIM
2005-06	Sioux Falls	USHL	48	4	7	11	57	11	1	2	3	4
2006-07	Sioux Falls	USHL	60	8	31	39	37	8	3	7	10	8
2007-08	Ferris State	CCHA	37	6	13	19	33	....	....	....	....	....

REED, Harrison (REED, HAIR-rih-suhn) **CAR.**

Center/Right wing. Shoots right. 6'1", 185 lbs. Born, Newmarket, Ont., January 18, 1988.
(Carolina's 2nd choice, 93rd overall, in 2006 Entry Draft).

			Regular Season					Playoffs				
Season	Club	League	GP	G	A	Pts	PIM	GP	G	A	Pts	PIM
2004-05	Petrolia Jets	OJHL-B	43	11	18	29	43	....	....	....	....	....
	London Knights	OHL	6	0	0	0	0	4	0	1	1	0
2005-06	Sarnia Sting	OHL	68	26	24	50	50	....	....	....	....	....
2006-07	Sarnia Sting	OHL	67	29	52	81	30	4	0	4	4	8
2007-08	Sarnia Sting	OHL	28	6	12	18	20	....	....	....	....	....
	Guelph Storm	OHL	41	8	21	29	20	10	3	2	5	12

REESE, Dylan (REES, DIH-luhn)

Defense. Shoots right. 6', 205 lbs. Born, Pittsburgh, PA, August 29, 1984.
(NY Rangers' 9th choice, 209th overall, in 2003 Entry Draft).

			Regular Season					Playoffs				
Season	Club	League	GP	G	A	Pts	PIM	GP	G	A	Pts	PIM
2000-01	Pittsburgh Hornets	MWEHL	66	14	42	66		....	....	....	....	....
2001-02	Pittsburgh Forge	NAHL	48	7	16	23	70	7	0	2	2	4
2002-03	Pittsburgh Forge	NAHL	56	11	30	41	98	5	2	3	5	6
2003-04	Harvard Crimson	ECAC	21	1	4	5	18	....	....	....	....	....
2004-05	Harvard Crimson	ECAC	34	7	12	19	44	....	....	....	....	....
2005-06	Harvard Crimson	ECAC	33	4	15	19	36	....	....	....	....	....
2006-07	Harvard Crimson	ECAC	33	9	9	18	26	....	....	....	....	....
	Hartford Wolf Pack	AHL	10	0	4	4	12	2	0	0	0	2
2007-08	San Antonio	AHL	59	1	6	7	49	3	1	1	2	4

ECAC Second All-Star Team (2006, 2007)

Signed as a free agent by **San Antonio** (AHL), September 5, 2007.

REGIN, Peter (REE-gihn, PEE-tuhr) **OTT.**

Center. Shoots left. 6'2", 193 lbs. Born, Herning, Denmark, April 16, 1986.
(Ottawa's 4th choice, 87th overall, in 2004 Entry Draft).

			Regular Season					Playoffs				
Season	Club	League	GP	G	A	Pts	PIM	GP	G	A	Pts	PIM
2002-03	Herning IK	Denmark	24	0	1	1	4	10	1	3	4	4
2003-04	Herning IK	Denmark	33	9	11	20	14	....	....	....	....	....
2004-05	Herning Blue Fox	Denmark	36	19	27	46	43	16	5	8	13	2
2005-06	Timra IK	Sweden	44	4	7	11	14	....	....	....	....	....
2006-07	Timra IK	Sweden	51	9	7	16	16	7	2	2	4	2
2007-08	Timra IK	Sweden	55	12	19	31	36	11	2	7	9	2

REGNER, Brent (RAY-nuhr, BREHNT) **CBJ**

Defense. Shoots right. 5'11", 175 lbs. Born, Westlock, Alta., May 17, 1989.
(Columbus' 7th choice, 137th overall, in 2008 Entry Draft).

			Regular Season					Playoffs				
Season	Club	League	GP	G	A	Pts	PIM	GP	G	A	Pts	PIM
2004-05	Ft. Saskatchewan	AMHL	36	2	13	15	24	....	....	....	....	....
2005-06	Ft. Saskatchewan	AMHL	36	9	25	34	30	14	1	7	8	2
	Vancouver Giants	WHL	1	0	0	0	0	....	....	....	....	....
2006-07	Vancouver Giants	WHL	64	1	5	6	19	22	0	6	6	10
2007-08	Vancouver Giants	WHL	72	8	39	47	45	10	0	10	10	10

RENAUD, Mickey (RAY-noh, MIH-kee)

Center. Shoots left. 6'2", 217 lbs. Born, Tecumseh, Ont., October 5, 1988.
(Calgary's 4th choice, 143rd overall, in 2007 Entry Draft).

			Regular Season					Playoffs				
Season	Club	League	GP	G	A	Pts	PIM	GP	G	A	Pts	PIM
2004-05	Tecumseh Chiefs	OJHL-B	39	9	14	23	8	....	....	....	....	....
2005-06	Windsor Spitfires	OHL	68	8	18	26	70	7	0	3	3	12
2006-07	Windsor Spitfires	OHL	68	22	32	54	76	....	....	....	....	....
2007-08	Windsor Spitfires	OHL	56	21	20	41	73	....	....	....	....	....

• Died on February 18, 2008. His doctor issued the following statement : "...suddenly collapsed at his Tecumseh home and was transported to Windsor Regional Hospital with absent vital signs. All attempts were made at resuscitation and were unsuccessful at the emergency room."

REPIK, Michal (REH-pihk, MEE-khahl) **FLA.**

Right wing. Shoots right. 5'10", 180 lbs. Born, Vlasim, Czech., December 31, 1988.
(Florida's 2nd choice, 40th overall, in 2007 Entry Draft).

			Regular Season					Playoffs				
Season	Club	League	GP	G	A	Pts	PIM	GP	G	A	Pts	PIM
2002-03	Sparta U17	CzR-U17	18	7	10	17	6	2	0	0	0	0
2003-04	Sparta U17	CzR-U17	33	25	17	42	42	3	0	0	0	0
	Sparta Jr.	CzRep-Jr.	23	12	5	17	10	....	....	....	....	....
2004-05	Sparta U17	CzR-U17	2	2	3	5	6	....	....	....	....	....
	Sparta Jr.	CzRep-Jr.	45	26	31	57	24	8	2	4	6	10
2005-06	Vancouver Giants	WHL	69	24	28	52	55	14	3	3	6	19
2006-07	Vancouver Giants	WHL	56	24	31	55	56	22	10	*16	*26	24
2007-08	Vancouver Giants	WHL	51	27	34	61	62	10	5	6	11	18

Memorial Cup Tournament All-Star Team (2007) • Ed Chynoweth Trophy (Memorial Cup Tournament - Leading Scorer) (2007)

REUL, Denis (ROIL, DEH-nihs) **BOS.**

Defense. Shoots right. 6'4", 215 lbs. Born, Marktredwitz, West Germany, June 29, 1989.
(Boston's 3rd choice, 130th overall, in 2007 Entry Draft).

			Regular Season					Playoffs				
Season	Club	League	GP	G	A	Pts	PIM	GP	G	A	Pts	PIM
2004-05	Mannheimer ERC	German-5	1	0	0	0	0	....	....	....	....	....
	Mannheim Jr.	Ger-Jr.	34	0	3	3	18	7	1	0	1	12
2005-06	Mannheim Jr.	Ger-Jr.	36	6	13	19	40	5	0	1	1	4
2006-07	Heilbronner Falken	German-3	16	0	1	1	16	....	....	....	....	....
	Heil./Mann. Jr.	Ger-Jr.	34	9	17	26	82	6	0	1	1	16
2007-08	Lewiston	QMJHL	67	3	11	14	99	6	0	0	0	4

Signed as a free agent by **Lewiston** (QMJHL), Asugust 14, 2007.

RIDDLE, Troy (RIH-duhl, TROI)

Center. Shoots right. 5'10", 175 lbs. Born, Minneapolis, MN, August 24, 1981.
(St. Louis' 5th choice, 129th overall, in 2000 Entry Draft).

			Regular Season					Playoffs				
Season	Club	League	GP	G	A	Pts	PIM	GP	G	A	Pts	PIM
1997-98	St. Margaret's	High-MN	29	33	35	68	....					
1998-99	St. Margaret's	High-MN	29	54	45	99	....	....	....	....	....	....
99-2000	Des Moines	USHL	53	36	30	66	95	8	2	2	4	31
2000-01	U. of Minnesota	WCHA	38	16	14	30	49	....	....	....	....	....
2001-02	U. of Minnesota	WCHA	44	16	31	47	46	....	....	....	....	....
2002-03	U. of Minnesota	WCHA	45	26	26	52	50	....	....	....	....	....
2003-04	U. of Minnesota	WCHA	44	24	25	49	52	....	....	....	....	....
2004-05	Worcester IceCats	AHL	42	9	6	15	35	....	....	....	....	....
	Peoria Rivermen	ECHL	14	4	8	12	16	....	....	....	....	....
2005-06	Peoria Rivermen	AHL	55	11	11	22	47	....	....	....	....	....
	Alaska Aces	ECHL	7	2	2	4	6	21	4	3	7	28
2006-07	Philadelphia	AHL	3	0	0	0	0	....	....	....	....	....
	Trenton Titans	ECHL	68	28	37	65	60	5	3	2	5	10
2007-08	Houston Aeros	AHL	32	4	5	9	19	....	....	....	....	....
	Texas Wildcatters	ECHL	22	6	12	18	26	8	1	0	1	8

USHL Second All-Star Team (2000) • USHL Rookie of the Year (2000)

Signed as a free agent by **Houston** (AHL), August 15, 2007.

RINALDO, Zac (rih-NAL-doh, ZAK) **PHI.**

Center. Shoots left. 5'11", 169 lbs. Born, Mississauga, Ont., June 15, 1990.
(Philadelphia's 4th choice, 178th overall, in 2008 Entry Draft).

			Regular Season					Playoffs				
Season	Club	League	GP	G	A	Pts	PIM	GP	G	A	Pts	PIM
2006-07	Hamilton	OPJHL	44	16	16	32	193	16	4	4	8	48
	St. Michael's	OHL	6	0	0	0	2	....	....	....	....	....
2007-08	St. Michael's	OHL	63	7	7	14	191	4	0	0	0	9

ROBAK, Colby (ROH-bak, KOHL-bee) **FLA.**

Defense. Shoots left. 6'3", 194 lbs. Born, Dauphin, Man., April 24, 1990.
(Florida's 2nd choice, 46th overall, in 2008 Entry Draft).

			Regular Season					Playoffs				
Season	Club	League	GP	G	A	Pts	PIM	GP	G	A	Pts	PIM
2005-06	Parkland Rangers	MMHL	40	14	20	34	14	....	....	....	....	....
2006-07	Brandon	WHL	39	2	3	5	12	1	0	0	0	0
2007-08	Brandon	WHL	71	6	24	30	25	6	0	2	2	8

ROBINS, Bobby (RAW-bihns, BAW-bee)

Right wing. Shoots right. 6'1", 220 lbs. Born, Peshtigo, WI, October 17, 1981.

			Regular Season					Playoffs				
Season	Club	League	GP	G	A	Pts	PIM	GP	G	A	Pts	PIM
2001-02	Tri-City Storm	USHL	60	16	14	30	176	....	....	....	....	....
2002-03	U. Mass-Lowell	H-East	26	5	3	8	24	....	....	....	....	....
2003-04	U. Mass-Lowell	H-East	32	5	7	12	49	....	....	....	....	....
2004-05	U. Mass-Lowell	H-East	34	9	9	18	86	....	....	....	....	....
2005-06	U. Mass-Lowell	H-East	35	13	18	31	*94	....	....	....	....	....
	Binghamton	AHL	16	4	3	7	19	....	....	....	....	....
2006-07	Binghamton	AHL	80	7	8	15	110	....	....	....	....	....
2007-08	Rochester	AHL	5	0	0	0	13	....	....	....	....	....
	Elmira Jackals	ECHL	68	18	17	35	151	6	2	3	5	8
	Albany River Rats	AHL	1	0	0	0	0	....	....	....	....	....
	Syracuse Crunch	AHL	1	0	0	0	2	....	....	....	....	....

Signed as a free agent by **Ottawa**, July 13, 2006.

RODNEY, Bryan (ROHD-nee, BRIGH-uhn) **CAR.**

Defense. Shoots right. 6', 204 lbs. Born, London, Ont., April 22, 1984.

			Regular Season					Playoffs				
Season	Club	League	GP	G	A	Pts	PIM	GP	G	A	Pts	PIM
2000-01	Ottawa 67's	OHL	65	0	15	15	26	20	1	4	5	20
2001-02	Ottawa 67's	OHL	30	3	8	11	14	....	....	....	....	....
	Kingston	OHL	18	2	8	10	8	1	0	0	0	0
2002-03	Kingston	OHL	67	8	52	60	60	....	....	....	....	....
2003-04	Kingston	OHL	67	11	65	76	68	5	1	4	5	8
2004-05	London Knights	OHL	64	23	39	62	48	12	5	10	15	20
2005-06	Hartford Wolf Pack	AHL	8	1	2	3	0	....	....	....	....	....
	Charlotte	ECHL	59	4	21	25	47	3	0	1	1	0
2006-07	Charlotte	ECHL	31	2	19	21	14	....	....	....	....	....
	Columbia Inferno	ECHL	14	2	9	11	12	....	....	....	....	....
2007-08	Albany River Rats	AHL	42	4	11	15	22	7	3	3	6	2
	Columbia Inferno	ECHL	17	2	9	11	10	....	....	....	....	....
	Elmira Jackals	ECHL	6	5	5	10	2	....	....	....	....	....

Signed as a free agent by **Charlotte** (ECHL), October 21, 2005. Signed as a free agent by **Albany** (AHL), December 16, 2007. Signed as a free agent by **Carolina**, May 12, 2008.

ROE, Garrett (ROH, GAIR-eht) L.A.

Left wing. Shoots left. 5'8", 162 lbs. Born, Vienna, VA, February 22, 1988.
(Los Angeles' 9th choice, 183rd overall, in 2008 Entry Draft).

			Regular Season					Playoffs				
Season	Club	League	GP	G	A	Pts	PIM	GP	G	A	Pts	PIM
2004-05	Indiana Ice	USHL	49	6	15	21	62	3	0	3	3	4
2005-06	Indiana Ice	USHL	49	21	32	53	93	2	3	0	3	0
2006-07	Indiana Ice	USHL	57	24	39	63	143	6	3	10	13	8
2007-08	St. Cloud State	WCHA	39	18	27	45	55	....	....	....	....	....

ROGERS, Andy (RAW-juhrs, AN-dee) T.B.

Defense. Shoots left. 6'5", 206 lbs. Born, Calgary, Alta., August 25, 1986.
(Tampa Bay's 1st choice, 30th overall, in 2004 Entry Draft).

			Regular Season					Playoffs				
Season	Club	League	GP	G	A	Pts	PIM	GP	G	A	Pts	PIM
2000-01	Calgary AA Gold	CMHA	32	2	7	9	32	....	....	....	....	....
2001-02	Calgary AAA Gold	CBHL	30	1	13	14	80	....	....	....	....	....
2002-03	Calgary Hitmen	WHL	25	0	3	3	17	....	....	....	....	....
2003-04	Calgary Hitmen	WHL	64	1	3	4	89	7	0	0	0	11
2004-05	Calgary Hitmen	WHL	18	1	4	5	36	....	....	....	....	....
	Prince George	WHL	30	1	5	6	49	....	....	....	....	....
2005-06	Prince George	WHL	21	0	3	3	51	....	....	....	....	....
2006-07	Springfield Falcons	AHL	48	0	7	7	39	....	....	....	....	....
2007-08	Norfolk Admirals	AHL	30	0	1	1	35	....	....	....	....	....
	Mississippi	ECHL	4	1	0	1	10	....	....	....	....	....

ROGERS, Brandon (RAW-juhrs, BRAN-duhn) MIN.

Defense. Shoots right. 6'1", 195 lbs. Born, Rochester, NH, February 27, 1982.
(Anaheim's 6th choice, 118th overall, in 2001 Entry Draft).

			Regular Season					Playoffs				
Season	Club	League	GP	G	A	Pts	PIM	GP	G	A	Pts	PIM
1998-99	Hotchkiss	High-CT	22	8	13	21	....	....	....	....	....	....
99-2000	Hotchkiss	High-CT	25	9	12	21	35	....	....	....	....	....
2000-01	Hotchkiss	High-CT	22	10	13	23	45	....	....	....	....	....
2001-02	U. of Michigan	CCHA	32	2	1	3	30	....	....	....	....	....
2002-03	U. of Michigan	CCHA	43	4	21	25	65	....	....	....	....	....
2003-04	U. of Michigan	CCHA	43	7	16	23	46	....	....	....	....	....
2004-05	U. of Michigan	CCHA	42	5	22	27	70	....	....	....	....	....
2005-06	Omaha	AHL	42	0	8	8	24	....	....	....	....	....
	Norfolk Admirals	AHL	27	3	7	10	28	2	0	0	0	4
2006-07	Norfolk Admirals	AHL	64	0	9	9	92	6	0	0	0	14
2007-08	Houston Aeros	AHL	63	4	24	28	77	5	0	1	1	2

CCHA Second All-Star Team (2004)

Signed as a free agent by **Minnesota**, July 15, 2008.

ROGERS, Doug (RAW-juhrs, DUHG) NYI

Center. Shoots right. 6', 175 lbs. Born, Watertown, MA, January 20, 1988.
(NY Islanders' 7th choice, 119th overall, in 2006 Entry Draft).

			Regular Season					Playoffs				
Season	Club	League	GP	G	A	Pts	PIM	GP	G	A	Pts	PIM
2003-04	St. Sebastian's	High-MA	28	24	24	48	....	....	....	....	....	....
2004-05	St. Sebastian's	High-MA	28	17	26	43	....	....	....	....	....	....
2005-06	St. Sebastian's	High-MA	28	24	38	62	20	....	....	....	....	....
2006-07	Harvard Crimson	ECAC	33	7	17	24	18	....	....	....	....	....
2007-08	Harvard Crimson	ECAC	34	13	19	32	30	....	....	....	....	....

ROGERS, Kyle (RAW-juhrs, KIGHL) TOR.

Right wing. Shoots right. 6'3", 215 lbs. Born, Philadelphia, PA, December 20, 1984.

			Regular Season					Playoffs				
Season	Club	League	GP	G	A	Pts	PIM	GP	G	A	Pts	PIM
2005-06	Niagara University	CHA	28	2	2	4	12	....	....	....	....	....
2006-07	Niagara University	CHA	35	6	7	13	37	....	....	....	....	....
2007-08	Niagara University	CHA	34	10	13	23	40	....	....	....	....	....
	Toronto Marlies	AHL	2	0	0	0	0	10	0	0	0	7

Signed as a free agent by **Toronto**, March 31, 2008.

ROHLFS, David (ROHLFS, DAY-vihd) EDM.

Right wing. Shoots right. 6'3", 225 lbs. Born, Ann Arbor, MI, June 4, 1984.
(Edmonton's 7th choice, 154th overall, in 2003 Entry Draft).

			Regular Season					Playoffs				
Season	Club	League	GP	G	A	Pts	PIM	GP	G	A	Pts	PIM
2000-01	Det. Compuware	MWEHL	70	35	21	56	....	....	....	....	....	....
	Det. Compuware	NAHL	4	0	1	1	0	....	....	....	....	....
2001-02	Det. Compuware	NAHL	60	13	10	23	36	....	....	....	....	....
2002-03	Det. Compuware	NAHL	53	30	14	44	36	5	2	1	3	8
2003-04	U. of Michigan	CCHA	43	7	6	13	26	....	....	....	....	....
2004-05	U. of Michigan	CCHA	34	5	5	10	14	....	....	....	....	....
2005-06	U. of Michigan	CCHA	40	2	10	12	43	....	....	....	....	....
2006-07	U. of Michigan	CCHA	41	17	17	34	30	....	....	....	....	....
2007-08	Springfield Falcons	AHL	2	0	0	0	2	....	....	....	....	....
	Stockton Thunder	ECHL	65	16	16	32	41	2	0	0	0	0

ROMAN, Ondrej (ROH-mahn, AWN-dray) DAL.

Center. Shoots left. 6', 168 lbs. Born, Ostrava, Czech., April 8, 1989.
(Dallas' 6th choice, 136th overall, in 2007 Entry Draft).

			Regular Season					Playoffs				
Season	Club	League	GP	G	A	Pts	PIM	GP	G	A	Pts	PIM
2002-03	HC Ostrava U17	CzR-U17	6	1	1	2	0	....	....	....	....	....
2003-04	HC Ostrava U17	CzR-U17	55	38	27	65	61	....	....	....	....	....
2004-05	HC Ostrava U17	CzR-U17	8	8	16	24	22	....	....	....	....	....
	HC Ostrava Jr.	CzRep-Jr.	7	2	2	4	6	....	....	....	....	....
	HC Vitkovice U17	CzR-U17	2	0	3	3	2	....	....	....	....	....
	HC Vitkovice Jr.	CzRep-Jr.	30	8	3	11	12	....	....	....	....	....
2005-06	HC Vitkovice U17	CzR-U17	....	....	....	....	....	4	1	8	9	0
	HC Vitkovice Jr.	CzRep-Jr.	46	17	27	44	42	5	0	3	3	4
	HC Vitkovice Steel	CzRep	1	0	0	0	0	....	....	....	....	....
2006-07	Spokane Chiefs	WHL	70	4	44	48	42	6	1	4	5	0
2007-08	Spokane Chiefs	WHL	72	15	46	61	28	21	9	11	20	6

ROMANO, Tony (roh-MAHN-oh, TOH-nee) N.J.

Center. Shoots right. 5'11", 175 lbs. Born, Smithtown, NY, January 5, 1988.
(New Jersey's 7th choice, 178th overall, in 2006 Entry Draft).

			Regular Season					Playoffs				
Season	Club	League	GP	G	A	Pts	PIM	GP	G	A	Pts	PIM
2004-05	New York Bobcats	AtJHL	....	47	54	101	....	....	....	....	....	....
2005-06	New York Bobcats	AtJHL	40	*50	52	*102	38	....	....	....	....	....
2006-07	Cornell Big Red	ECAC	29	9	10	19	18	....	....	....	....	....
2007-08	London Knights	OHL	66	12	10	22	40	4	1	0	1	0

ROME, Ashton (ROHM, ASH-tuhn) S.J.

Right wing. Shoots right. 6'1", 205 lbs. Born, Nesbitt, Man., December 31, 1985.
(San Jose's 4th choice, 143rd overall, in 2006 Entry Draft).

			Regular Season					Playoffs				
Season	Club	League	GP	G	A	Pts	PIM	GP	G	A	Pts	PIM
2002-03	Moose Jaw	WHL	61	5	10	15	103	13	1	1	2	6
2003-04	Moose Jaw	WHL	72	15	22	37	139	10	6	2	8	18
2004-05	Moose Jaw	WHL	41	10	17	27	84	....	....	....	....	....
	Red Deer Rebels	WHL	31	9	10	19	39	7	3	1	4	14
2005-06	Red Deer Rebels	WHL	14	11	6	17	27	....	....	....	....	....
	Kamloops Blazers	WHL	51	19	28	47	103	....	....	....	....	....
2006-07	Worcester Sharks	AHL	65	8	3	11	63	6	1	0	1	2
2007-08	Worcester Sharks	AHL	60	7	8	15	49	....	....	....	....	....

• Re-entered NHL Entry Draft. Originally Boston's 3rd choice, 108th overall, in 2004 Entry Draft.

ROSEHILL, Jay (ROHZ-hihl, JAY) T.B.

Defense. Shoots left. 6'3", 195 lbs. Born, Olds, Alta., July 16, 1985.
(Tampa Bay's 6th choice, 227th overall, in 2003 Entry Draft).

			Regular Season					Playoffs				
Season	Club	League	GP	G	A	Pts	PIM	GP	G	A	Pts	PIM
2002-03	Olds Grizzlys	AJHL	59	1	4	5	219	....	....	....	....	....
2003-04	Olds Grizzlys	AJHL	42	4	12	16	172	14	2	2	4	....
2004-05	U. Minn-Duluth	WCHA	34	0	5	5	103	....	....	....	....	....
2005-06	Springfield Falcons	AHL	45	1	2	3	68	....	....	....	....	....
	Johnstown Chiefs	ECHL	5	0	0	0	13	5	0	0	0	4
2006-07	Springfield Falcons	AHL	64	0	6	6	85	....	....	....	....	....
	Johnstown Chiefs	ECHL	1	0	0	0	2	....	....	....	....	....
2007-08	Norfolk Admirals	AHL	66	3	4	7	194	....	....	....	....	....
	Mississippi	ECHL	2	0	0	0	6	....	....	....	....	....

ROSS, Jared (RAWS, JAIR-uhd) PHI.

Center. Shoots left. 5'9", 165 lbs. Born, Huntsville, AL, September 18, 1982.

			Regular Season					Playoffs				
Season	Club	League	GP	G	A	Pts	PIM	GP	G	A	Pts	PIM
2001-02	AL-Huntsville	CHA	37	11	17	28	8	....	....	....	....	....
2002-03	AL-Huntsville	CHA	35	20	20	40	30	....	....	....	....	....
2003-04	AL-Huntsville	CHA	31	19	31	50	46	....	....	....	....	....
2004-05	AL-Huntsville	CHA	30	22	18	40	53	....	....	....	....	....
	Motor City	UHL	12	3	5	8	2	....	....	....	....	....
2005-06	Chicago Wolves	AHL	62	10	27	37	37	....	....	....	....	....
	Gwinnett	ECHL	1	0	0	0	0	....	....	....	....	....
2006-07	Chicago Wolves	AHL	41	7	8	15	14	....	....	....	....	....
	Philadelphia	AHL	21	4	10	14	6	....	....	....	....	....
2007-08	Philadelphia	AHL	67	23	39	62	56	12	5	4	9	4

Traded to **Philadelphia** (AHL) by **Chicago** (AHL) for the loan of Niko Dimitrakos, March 1, 2007. Signed as a free agent by **Philadelphia**, April 8, 2008.

ROSS, Nick (RAWS, NIHK) PHX.

Defense. Shoots left. 6'1", 188 lbs. Born, Edmonton, Alta., February 10, 1989.
(Phoenix's 2nd choice, 30th overall, in 2007 Entry Draft).

			Regular Season					Playoffs				
Season	Club	League	GP	G	A	Pts	PIM	GP	G	A	Pts	PIM
2004-05	Lethbridge	AMHL	33	8	20	28	123	....	....	....	....	....
	Regina Pats	WHL	10	0	1	1	2	....	....	....	....	....
2005-06	Regina Pats	WHL	62	7	16	23	38	6	0	1	1	2
2006-07	Regina Pats	WHL	70	7	24	31	87	10	1	5	6	14
2007-08	Regina Pats	WHL	41	3	25	28	60	....	....	....	....	....
	Kamloops Blazers	WHL	31	5	14	19	55	4	0	2	2	10
	San Antonio	AHL	4	1	0	1	0	....	....	....	....	....

RUDENKO, Konstantin (roo-DEHN-koh, KAWN-stan-tihn) PHI.

Left wing. Shoots right. 5'11", 180 lbs. Born, Ust-Kamenogorsk, USSR, July 23, 1981.
(Philadelphia's 3rd choice, 160th overall, in 1999 Entry Draft).

			Regular Season					Playoffs				
Season	Club	League	GP	G	A	Pts	PIM	GP	G	A	Pts	PIM
1997-98	Omsk 2	Russia-3	22	7	8	15	4	....	....	....	....	....
1998-99	Cherepovets	Russia	28	15	9	24	67	....	....	....	....	....
	Cherepovets 2	Russia-3	3	0	1	1	4	....	....	....	....	....
99-2000	St. Petersburg 2	Russia-3	7	2	4	6	2	....	....	....	....	....
	SKA St. Petersburg	Russia	19	1	1	2	10	1	0	0	0	0
2000-01	Yaroslavl	Russia	18	2	3	5	28	9	2	1	3	8
2001-02	Yaroslavl 2	Russia-3	2	1	1	2	2	....	....	....	....	....
	Yaroslavl	Russia	8	0	2	2	12	1	0	0	0	0
2002-03	Yaroslavl	Russia	20	3	4	7	20	2	0	0	0	0
2003-04	Yaroslavl	Russia	43	10	12	22	18	3	0	0	0	0
	Yaroslavl 2	Russia-3	4	4	2	6	4	....	....	....	....	....
2004-05	Yaroslavl 2	Russia-3	20	13	14	27	42	....	....	....	....	....
	Yaroslavl	Russia	21	1	0	1	8	2	0	0	0	0
2005-06	Yaroslavl	Russia	49	11	17	28	55	11	1	2	3	0
2006-07	Yaroslavl	Russia	35	11	8	19	30	7	2	2	4	6
2007-08	Yaroslavl	Russia	46	6	16	22	28	7	0	1	1	8

RUEGSEGGER, Tyler (ROOG-suh-guhr, TIGH-luhr) TOR.

Center. Shoots right. 5'11", 170 lbs. Born, Denver, CO, January 19, 1988.
(Toronto's 6th choice, 166th overall, in 2006 Entry Draft).

			Regular Season					Playoffs				
Season	Club	League	GP	G	A	Pts	PIM	GP	G	A	Pts	PIM
2004-05	Shat.-St. Mary's	High-MN	69	26	54	80	30	....	....	....	....	....
2005-06	Shat.-St. Mary's	High-MN	60	38	51	89	70	....	....	....	....	....
2006-07	U. of Denver	WCHA	40	15	19	34	25	....	....	....	....	....
2007-08	U. of Denver	WCHA	31	10	12	22	39	....	....	....	....	....

RUFENACH, Bryan (RUHF-ehn-ak, BRIGH-uhn) DET.

Defense. Shoots left. 5'11", 184 lbs. Born, Cameron, Ont., April 15, 1989.
(Detroit's 5th choice, 208th overall, in 2007 Entry Draft).

			Regular Season					Playoffs				
Season	Club	League	GP	G	A	Pts	PIM	GP	G	A	Pts	PIM
2005-06	Lindsay Muskies	OPJHL	48	11	15	26	50	4	1	1	2	6
2006-07	Lindsay Muskies	OPJHL	31	11	21	32	28	5	1	2	3	8
2007-08	Clarkson Knights	ECAC	35	3	3	6	12	....	....	....	....	....

RUGGERI, Rosario (ROO-zhee-AIR-ee, roh-ZAHR-ee-oh) N.J.

Defense. Shoots right. 6'1", 215 lbs. Born, Montreal, Que., June 8, 1984.
(Philadelphia's 2nd choice, 105th overall, in 2002 Entry Draft).

			Regular Season					Playoffs				
Season	**Club**	**League**	**GP**	**G**	**A**	**Pts**	**PIM**	**GP**	**G**	**A**	**Pts**	**PIM**
99-2000	Lac St-Louis Lions	QAAA	40	0	7	7	70	....	....	....	....	....
2000-01	Lac St-Louis Lions	QAAA	24	6	11	17	117	5	1	3	4	4
	Montreal Rocket	QMJHL	9	0	0	0	8	....	....	....	....	....
2001-02	Chicoutimi	QMJHL	60	2	15	17	131	4	1	1	2	10
2002-03	Chicoutimi	QMJHL	70	10	37	47	64	3	0	0	0	21
2003-04	Chicoutimi	QMJHL	65	12	36	48	98	18	2	2	4	28
2004-05	Philadelphia	AHL	5	0	0	0	0	....	....	....	....	....
	Trenton Titans	ECHL	49	2	12	14	77	20	0	2	2	26
2005-06	Philadelphia	AHL	2	0	0	0	2	....	....	....	....	....
	Trenton Titans	ECHL	32	2	8	10	28	....	....	....	....	....
2006-07	Philadelphia	AHL	15	0	2	2	0	....	....	....	....	....
	Trenton Titans	ECHL	49	4	25	29	46	5	0	0	0	6
2007-08	Lowell Devils	AHL	60	4	14	18	26	....	....	....	....	....

Signed as a free agent by **New Jersey**, August, 2008.

RULLIER, Joe (ROO-yay, JOH)

Defense. Shoots right. 6'3", 230 lbs. Born, Montreal, Que., January 28, 1980.
(Los Angeles' 5th choice, 133rd overall, in 1998 Entry Draft).

			Regular Season					Playoffs				
Season	**Club**	**League**	**GP**	**G**	**A**	**Pts**	**PIM**	**GP**	**G**	**A**	**Pts**	**PIM**
1996-97	Montreal-Bourassa	QAAA	24	5	10	15	....	....	....	....	....	....
	Rimouski Oceanic	QMJHL	23	0	3	3	87	4	0	0	0	11
1997-98	Rimouski Oceanic	QMJHL	55	1	10	11	176	16	1	4	5	34
1998-99	Rimouski Oceanic	QMJHL	54	7	32	39	202	11	2	3	5	26
99-2000	Rimouski Oceanic	QMJHL	49	3	32	35	161	14	1	8	9	34
2000-01	Lowell	AHL	63	1	1	2	162	4	0	1	1	2
2001-02	Manchester	AHL	62	2	2	4	133	3	0	0	0	5
2002-03	Manchester	AHL	62	3	6	9	166	3	0	0	0	2
2003-04	Manchester	AHL	73	3	12	15	186	6	0	0	0	4
2004-05	Manchester	AHL	71	3	13	16	322	6	0	2	2	27
2005-06	Hartford Wolf Pack	AHL	51	6	22	28	123	....	....	....	....	....
	Manchester	AHL	16	2	1	3	37	7	0	3	3	14
2006-07	Manitoba Moose	AHL	24	2	6	8	62	....	....	....	....	....
	Portland Pirates	AHL	6	0	1	1	14	....	....	....	....	....
	Springfield Falcons	AHL	10	0	5	5	18	....	....	....	....	....
2007-08	Bridgeport	AHL	20	1	6	7	58	....	....	....	....	....
	Kloten Flyers	Swiss	12	0	1	1	40	1	0	0	0	0

Signed as a free agent by **NY Rangers**, August 10, 2005. Signed as a free agent by **Vancouver**, July 24, 2006. Traded to **Anaheim** by **Vancouver** for Colby Genoway, January 24, 2007. Traded to **Tampa Bay** by **Anaheim** for Doug O'Brien, February 27, 2007.

RUSSELL, Ryan (RUH-sehl, RIGH-uhn) MTL.

Center. Shoots left. 5'10", 176 lbs. Born, Caroline, Alta., May 2, 1987.
(NY Rangers' 9th choice, 211th overall, in 2005 Entry Draft).

			Regular Season					Playoffs				
Season	**Club**	**League**	**GP**	**G**	**A**	**Pts**	**PIM**	**GP**	**G**	**A**	**Pts**	**PIM**
2003-04	Kootenay Ice	WHL	67	3	9	12	27	4	0	0	0	0
2004-05	Kootenay Ice	WHL	66	32	21	53	18	16	6	7	13	12
2005-06	Kootenay Ice	WHL	72	33	42	75	30	6	3	5	8	2
2006-07	Kootenay Ice	WHL	58	30	46	76	40	7	3	6	9	2
2007-08	Hamilton Bulldogs	AHL	25	2	1	3	4	....	....	....	....	....
	Cincinnati	ECHL	12	6	4	10	4	15	3	4	7	0

Traded to **Montreal** by **NY Rangers** for Montreal's 7th round choice (David Skokan) in 2007 Entry Draft, May 31, 2007.

RUST, Matt (RUHST, MAT) FLA.

Center. Shoots left. 5'10", 192 lbs. Born, Bloomfield Hills, MI, March 23, 1989.
(Florida's 4th choice, 101st overall, in 2007 Entry Draft).

			Regular Season					Playoffs				
Season	**Club**	**League**	**GP**	**G**	**A**	**Pts**	**PIM**	**GP**	**G**	**A**	**Pts**	**PIM**
2004-05	Det. Honeybaked	MWEHL	50	16	24	40	....	....	....	....	....	....
2005-06	USNTDP	U-17	20	5	5	10	22	....	....	....	....	....
	USNTDP	NAHL	36	9	8	17	36	12	2	0	2	0
2006-07	USNTDP	U-18	36	3	16	19	34	....	....	....	....	....
	USNTDP	NAHL	15	9	6	15	31	....	....	....	....	....
2007-08	U. of Michigan	CCHA	38	12	11	23	69	....	....	....	....	....

RUTH, Theo (ROOTH, THEE-oh) CBJ

Defense. Shoots right. 6'1", 199 lbs. Born, Naperville, IL, February 14, 1989.
(Washington's 3rd choice, 46th overall, in 2007 Entry Draft).

			Regular Season					Playoffs				
Season	**Club**	**League**	**GP**	**G**	**A**	**Pts**	**PIM**	**GP**	**G**	**A**	**Pts**	**PIM**
2004-05	Chicago Mission	MAHL	46	8	8	16	....	....	....	....	....	....
2005-06	USNTDP	U-17	18	2	3	5	22	....	....	....	....	....
	USNTDP	NAHL	36	1	2	3	33	12	0	2	2	8
2006-07	USNTDP	U-18	39	2	6	8	52	....	....	....	....	....
	USNTDP	NAHL	9	3	6	9	14	....	....	....	....	....
2007-08	U. of Notre Dame	CCHA	42	2	3	5	36	....	....	....	....	....

Traded to **Columbus** by **Washington** for Sergei Fedorov, February 26, 2008.

RUZICKA, Vladimir (roo-ZHEECH-kuh, vla-DIH-meer) PHX.

Center. Shoots left. 6'1", 196 lbs. Born, Most, Czech., February 17, 1989.
(Phoenix's 5th choice, 103rd overall, in 2007 Entry Draft).

			Regular Season					Playoffs				
Season	**Club**	**League**	**GP**	**G**	**A**	**Pts**	**PIM**	**GP**	**G**	**A**	**Pts**	**PIM**
2002-03	Slavia U17	CzR-U17	20	1	5	6	2	1	0	0	0	0
2003-04	Slavia U17	CzR-U17	51	18	35	53	24	7	5	8	13	4
2004-05	Slavia U17	CzR-U17	38	22	39	61	38	6	4	4	8	10
2005-06	Slavia U17	CzR-U17	3	3	6	9	22	6	5	7	12	14
	HC Slavia Praha Jr.	CzRep-Jr.	37	15	26	41	42	1	0	1	1	0
	HC Slavia Praha	CzRep	13	1	1	2	4	....	....	....	....	....
2006-07	HC Slavia Praha Jr.	CzRep-Jr.	37	24	34	58	54	4	1	2	3	4
	HC Slavia Praha	CzRep	3	0	0	0	0	....	....	....	....	....
2007-08	HC Slavia Praha Jr.	CzRep-Jr.	1	0	0	0	4	1	0	0	0	2
	HC Slavia Praha	CzRep	42	7	8	15	18	19	1	0	1	4

RYAN, Ben (RIGH-uhn, BEHN) NSH.

Center. Shoots right. 5'11", 190 lbs. Born, Detroit, MI, October 16, 1988.
(Nashville's 5th choice, 114th overall, in 2007 Entry Draft).

			Regular Season					Playoffs				
Season	**Club**	**League**	**GP**	**G**	**A**	**Pts**	**PIM**	**GP**	**G**	**A**	**Pts**	**PIM**
2005-06	Des Moines	USHL	60	14	23	37	38	11	4	1	5	4
2006-07	Des Moines	USHL	59	22	42	64	66	8	3	5	8	8
2007-08	U. of Notre Dame	CCHA	47	10	16	26	22	....	....	....	....	....

RYDER, Dan (RIGH-duhr, DAN) CGY.

Center. Shoots right. 5'11", 193 lbs. Born, Bonavista, Nfld., January 12, 1987.
(Calgary's 3rd choice, 74th overall, in 2005 Entry Draft).

			Regular Season					Playoffs				
Season	**Club**	**League**	**GP**	**G**	**A**	**Pts**	**PIM**	**GP**	**G**	**A**	**Pts**	**PIM**
2003-04	Peterborough	OHL	63	20	32	52	16	....	....	....	....	....
2004-05	Peterborough	OHL	68	29	53	82	55	....	....	....	....	....
2005-06	Peterborough	OHL	65	38	44	82	57	19	*15	16	31	22
2006-07	Peterborough	OHL	29	24	35	59	21	....	....	....	....	....
	Plymouth Whalers	OHL	28	16	17	33	4	20	8	9	17	10
2007-08	Quad City Flames	AHL	6	1	4	5	2	....	....	....	....	....

RYNO, Johan (RYUH-noh, YOH-han) DET.

Right wing. Shoots left. 6'4", 198 lbs. Born, Orebro, Sweden, June 5, 1986.
(Detroit's 6th choice, 137th overall, in 2005 Entry Draft).

			Regular Season					Playoffs				
Season	**Club**	**League**	**GP**	**G**	**A**	**Pts**	**PIM**	**GP**	**G**	**A**	**Pts**	**PIM**
2003-04	IFK Hallsberg	Sweden-3	28	9	18	27	30	....	....	....	....	....
2004-05	IFK Kumla Jr.	Swe-Jr.	29	20	18	38	14	....	....	....	....	....
	IFK Arboga IK	Sweden-2	2	0	0	0	0	....	....	....	....	....
2005-06	IK Oskarshamn	Sweden-2	34	13	10	23	64	....	....	....	....	....
2006-07	Frolunda Jr.	Swe-Jr.	2	1	0	1	2	....	....	....	....	....
	Frolunda	Sweden	14	0	0	0	14	....	....	....	....	....
	AIK IF Solna	Sweden-2	14	2	7	9	14	....	....	....	....	....
	Timra IK	Sweden	25	5	6	11	8	5	0	1	1	0
2007-08	Grand Rapids	AHL	12	3	4	7	8	....	....	....	....	....
	Djurgarden	Sweden	30	2	7	9	18	5	0	0	0	0

SACCHETTI, Nico (SA-sheh-tee, NEE-koh) DAL.

Center. Shoots right. 5'11", 189 lbs. Born, Virginia, MN, August 21, 1989.
(Dallas' 1st choice, 50th overall, in 2007 Entry Draft).

			Regular Season					Playoffs				
Season	**Club**	**League**	**GP**	**G**	**A**	**Pts**	**PIM**	**GP**	**G**	**A**	**Pts**	**PIM**
2004-05	Virginia Blue Devils	High-MN	29	25	29	54	....	....	....	....	....	....
2005-06	Virginia Blue Devils	High-MN	27	29	45	74	....	....	....	....	....	....
2006-07	Virginia Blue Devils	High-MN	25	38	52	90	22	....	....	....	....	....
2007-08	Omaha Lancers	USHL	56	10	14	24	51	14	1	2	3	10

SACKRISON, Andy (sak-RIH-suhn, AN-dee) ST.L.

Center. Shoots left. 6'1", 178 lbs. Born, St. Louis Park, MN, November 12, 1987.
(St. Louis' 7th choice, 124th overall, in 2006 Entry Draft).

			Regular Season					Playoffs				
Season	**Club**	**League**	**GP**	**G**	**A**	**Pts**	**PIM**	**GP**	**G**	**A**	**Pts**	**PIM**
2004-05	St. Louis Park	High-MN	26	18	15	33	....	....	....	....	....	....
2005-06	St. Louis Park	High-MN	25	42	27	69	....	....	....	....	....	....
2006-07	Tri-City Storm	USHL	59	12	15	27	19	9	2	0	2	6
2007-08	Minnesota State	WCHA	36	6	14	20	4	....	....	....	....	....

SALCIDO, Brian (sal-SEE-doh, BRIGH-uhn) ANA.

Defense. Shoots left. 6'2", 202 lbs. Born, Los Angeles, CA, April 14, 1985.
(Anaheim's 5th choice, 141st overall, in 2005 Entry Draft).

			Regular Season					Playoffs				
Season	**Club**	**League**	**GP**	**G**	**A**	**Pts**	**PIM**	**GP**	**G**	**A**	**Pts**	**PIM**
2002-03	Shat.-St. Mary's	High-MN	53	8	35	43	....	....	....	....	....	....
2003-04	Colorado College	WCHA	12	1	0	1	48	....	....	....	....	....
2004-05	Colorado College	WCHA	38	7	23	30	52	....	....	....	....	....
2005-06	Colorado College	WCHA	42	8	32	40	69	....	....	....	....	....
2006-07	Portland Pirates	AHL	76	7	20	27	80	....	....	....	....	....
2007-08	Portland Pirates	AHL	71	11	42	53	58	18	0	6	6	18

WCHA Second All-Star Team (2006) • AHL Second All-Star Team (2008)

SALMELA, Anssi (sahl-MEHL-ah, AN-see) N.J.

Defense. Shoots left. 5'11", 190 lbs. Born, Tampere, Finland, August 13, 1984.

			Regular Season					Playoffs				
Season	**Club**	**League**	**GP**	**G**	**A**	**Pts**	**PIM**	**GP**	**G**	**A**	**Pts**	**PIM**
2000-01	Tappara U18	Fin-U18	32	7	3	10	24	2	0	1	1	4
2001-02	Tappara U18	Fin-U18	11	6	4	10	12	....	....	....	....	....
	Tappara Jr.	Fin-Jr.	26	3	4	7	22	2	2	1	3	0
2002-03	Tappara Jr.	Fin-Jr.	23	5	9	14	22	....	....	....	....	....
2003-04	Suomi U20	Finland-2	5	2	2	4	0	....	....	....	....	....
	Tappara Jr.	Fin-Jr.	27	10	9	19	22	12	5	3	8	4
	Tappara Tampere	Finland	10	0	0	0	2	3	0	0	0	2
2004-05	Tappara Jr.	Fin-Jr.	10	2	4	6	6	1	0	0	0	0
	Tappara Tampere	Finland	48	1	5	6	49	8	0	0	0	0
2005-06	Tappara Tampere	Finland	8	0	1	1	0	....	....	....	....	....
	Pelicans Lahti	Finland	40	8	7	15	59	....	....	....	....	....
2006-07	Pelicans Lahti	Finland	56	11	12	23	58	6	1	1	2	4
2007-08	Tappara Tampere	Finland	56	16	16	32	40	11	0	6	6	14

Signed as a free agent by **New Jersey**, May 30, 2008.

SALMONSSON, Johannes (sal-MUHN-suhn, yoh-HA-nuhs) PIT.

Left wing. Shoots left. 6'2", 183 lbs. Born, Uppsala, Sweden, February 7, 1986.
(Pittsburgh's 2nd choice, 31st overall, in 2004 Entry Draft).

			Regular Season					Playoffs				
Season	**Club**	**League**	**GP**	**G**	**A**	**Pts**	**PIM**	**GP**	**G**	**A**	**Pts**	**PIM**
2002-03	Almtuna	Sweden-2	26	10	14	24	4	....	....	....	....	....
2003-04	Djurgarden Jr.	Swe-Jr.	6	4	9	13	6	....	....	....	....	....
	Djurgarden	Sweden	25	0	3	3	4	....	....	....	....	....
	Almtuna	Sweden-2	2	0	0	0	0	....	....	....	....	....
2004-05	Almtuna	Sweden-2	8	0	2	2	6	....	....	....	....	....
	Djurgarden Jr.	Swe-Jr.	4	2	0	2	4	....	....	....	....	....
	Djurgarden	Sweden	30	2	2	4	6	9	0	0	0	0
2005-06	Spokane Chiefs	WHL	54	12	15	27	30	....	....	....	....	....
2006-07	Brynas IF Gavle Jr.	Swe-Jr.	2	0	7	7	0	....	....	....	....	....
	Brynas IF Gavle	Sweden	45	8	3	11	28	....	....	....	....	....
2007-08	Brynas IF Gavle Jr.	Swe-Jr.	2	0	2	2	2	....	....	....	....	....
	Brynas IF Gavle	Sweden	9	0	1	1	2	....	....	....	....	....
	Rogle	Sweden-2	34	15	9	24	36	....	....	....	....	....

Signed as a free agent by **Brynas** (Sweden), September 18, 2006.

SALONEN, Pasi (SAH-loh-nehn, PA-see) **WSH.**

Left wing. Shoots left. 5'11", 187 lbs. Born, Helsinki, Finland, December 18, 1985.
(Washington's 9th choice, 138th overall, in 2004 Entry Draft).

			Regular Season					Playoffs				
Season	Club	League	GP	G	A	Pts	PIM	GP	G	A	Pts	PIM
2000-01	HIFK Helsinki U18	Fin-U18	28	6	8	14	4	....	....	....	....	....
2001-02	HIFK Helsinki U18	Fin-U18	16	10	14	24	39	8	6	4	10	4
	HIFK Helsinki Jr.	Fin-Jr.	19	5	6	11	2	....	....	....	....	....
2002-03	HIFK Helsinki Jr.	Fin-Jr.	32	16	11	27	10	10	8	3	11	2
2003-04	Suomi U20	Finland-2	3	0	0	0	0	....	....	....	....	....
	HIFK Helsinki Jr.	Fin-Jr.	30	12	10	22	60	9	4	4	8	8
	HIFK Helsinki	Finland	3	0	0	0	0	....	....	....	....	....
2004-05			DID NOT PLAY – INJURED									
2005-06	HIFK Helsinki Jr.	Fin-Jr.	10	4	2	6	4	....	....	....	....	....
	HIFK Helsinki	Finland	49	5	9	14	6	8	0	0	0	0
2006-07	HIFK Helsinki	Finland	51	5	7	12	55	2	0	0	0	0
2007-08	HPK Hameenlinna	Finland	53	11	17	28	39	....	....	....	....	....

SAMSON, Jerome (SAM-sohn, jeh-ROHM) **CAR.**

Right wing. Shoots right. 5'11", 175 lbs. Born, Greenfield Park, Que., September 4, 1987.

			Regular Season					Playoffs				
Season	Club	League	GP	G	A	Pts	PIM	GP	G	A	Pts	PIM
2004-05	Moncton Wildcats	QMJHL	63	6	11	17	22	12	1	4	5	8
2005-06	Moncton Wildcats	QMJHL	62	20	32	52	46	21	6	12	18	15
2006-07	Moncton Wildcats	QMJHL	38	19	33	52	20	....	....	....	....	....
	Val-d'Or Foreurs	QMJHL	33	25	22	47	16	20	14	12	26	10
2007-08	Albany River Rats	AHL	65	21	18	39	38	7	1	1	2	2

Signed as a free agent by **Carolina**, July 2, 2007.

SAMUELSSON, Jesper (SA-mewl-suhn, YEHS-puhr) **DET.**

Center. Shoots left. 5'11", 178 lbs. Born, Stockholm, Sweden, June 13, 1988.
(Detroit's 6th choice, 211th overall, in 2008 Entry Draft).

			Regular Season					Playoffs				
Season	Club	League	GP	G	A	Pts	PIM	GP	G	A	Pts	PIM
2004-05	Hasten	Sweden-3	1	0	0	0	0	....	....	....	....	....
2005-06	Hasten	Sweden-3	36	8	11	19	67	....	....	....	....	....
2006-07	Hasten	Sweden-3	36	15	29	44	38	....	....	....	....	....
2007-08	HC Vita Hasten	Sweden-3	40	20	42	62	73	....	....	....	....	....

SANDIN, Emil (san-DEEN, eh-MIHL) **OTT.**

Left wing. Shoots left. 5'10", 178 lbs. Born, Uppsala, Sweden, February 28, 1988.
(Ottawa's 7th choice, 199th overall, in 2008 Entry Draft).

			Regular Season					Playoffs				
Season	Club	League	GP	G	A	Pts	PIM	GP	G	A	Pts	PIM
2004-05	Brynas IF Gavle Jr.	Swe-Jr.	2	0	0	0	0	....	....	....	....	....
2005-06	Brynas U18	Swe-U18	4	2	3	5	14	....	....	....	....	....
	Brynas IF Gavle Jr.	Swe-Jr.	31	9	9	18	8	2	2	0	2	0
2006-07	Brynas IF Gavle Jr.	Swe-Jr.	39	10	20	30	40	4	1	0	1	4
2007-08	Brynas IF Gavle Jr.	Swe-Jr.	28	10	25	35	50	7	1	4	5	8
	Brynas IF Gavle	Sweden	19	0	4	4	0	....	....	....	....	....
	Brynas IF Gavle	Sweden-Q	2	0	0	0	0	....	....	....	....	....

SANGUINETTI, Bobby (san-GIH-neh-tee, BAW-bee) **NYR**

Defense. Shoots right. 6'3", 190 lbs. Born, Trenton, NJ, February 29, 1988.
(NY Rangers' 1st choice, 21st overall, in 2006 Entry Draft).

			Regular Season					Playoffs				
Season	Club	League	GP	G	A	Pts	PIM	GP	G	A	Pts	PIM
2003-04	Lawrenceville	High-NJ	26	4	17	21	....	....	....	....	....	....
2004-05	Owen Sound	OHL	67	4	20	24	12	5	0	2	2	0
2005-06	Owen Sound	OHL	68	14	51	65	44	11	5	10	15	4
2006-07	Owen Sound	OHL	67	23	30	53	48	4	3	3	6	2
	Hartford Wolf Pack	AHL	5	0	3	3	2	7	0	1	1	2
2007-08	Brampton	OHL	61	29	41	70	38	5	1	3	4	10
	Hartford Wolf Pack	AHL	6	0	1	1	2	5	0	0	0	2

OHL Second All-Star Team (2008)

SANNITZ, Raffaele (ZAH-nihts, ra-FIGH-ehl-lay) **CBJ**

Center. Shoots left. 6'1", 212 lbs. Born, Mendrisio, Switz., May 18, 1983.
(Columbus' 9th choice, 204th overall, in 2001 Entry Draft).

			Regular Season					Playoffs				
Season	Club	League	GP	G	A	Pts	PIM	GP	G	A	Pts	PIM
1997-98	HC Lugano Jr.	Swiss-Jr.	33	7	12	19	54	....	....	....	....	....
1998-99	HC Lugano Jr.	Swiss-Jr.	38	5	12	17	62	....	....	....	....	....
	HC Lugano	Swiss	8	0	1	1	0	....	....	....	....	....
99-2000	HC Lugano Jr.	Swiss-Jr.	33	13	16	29	47	....	....	....	....	....
	HC Lugano	Swiss	1	0	0	0	2	....	....	....	....	....
2000-01	HC Sierre	Swiss-2	2	0	0	0	0	....	....	....	....	....
	HC Lugano Jr.	Swiss-Jr.	35	22	30	52	152	2	0	0	0	0
	HC Lugano	Swiss	13	1	0	1	0	2	0	0	0	0
2001-02	HC Lugano Jr.	Swiss-Jr.	14	14	13	27	18	3	3	2	5	4
	HC Lugano	Swiss	38	3	4	7	37	12	1	1	2	2
2002-03	HC Lugano	Swiss	14	1	1	2	37	....	....	....	....	....
2003-04	HC Lugano	Swiss	48	7	9	16	20	16	2	1	3	8
	EHC Chur	Swiss-2	2	2	1	3	2	....	....	....	....	....
2004-05	Syracuse Crunch	AHL	53	6	3	9	38	....	....	....	....	....
	Dayton Bombers	ECHL	2	0	3	3	0	....	....	....	....	....
2005-06	HC Lugano	Swiss	33	5	9	14	85	17	4	8	12	16
2006-07	HC Lugano	Swiss	38	6	20	26	50	6	3	3	6	41
2007-08	HC Lugano	Swiss	50	7	10	17	36	5	3	1	4	31

• Missed majority of 2002-03 season recovering from shoulder injury suffered in game vs. Kloten (Swiss), October 12, 2002.

SANTORELLI, Mark (san-toh-REHL-ee, MAHRK) **NSH.**

Center. Shoots right. 6'1", 191 lbs. Born, Burnaby, B.C., August 6, 1988.
(Nashville's 6th choice, 119th overall, in 2007 Entry Draft).

			Regular Season					Playoffs				
Season	Club	League	GP	G	A	Pts	PIM	GP	G	A	Pts	PIM
2003-04	Abbotsford Pilots	PIJHL	40	12	19	31	33	....	....	....	....	....
	Chilliwack Chiefs	BCHL	1	0	1	1	0	....	....	....	....	....
2004-05	Salmon Arm	BCHL	59	9	16	25	10	11	2	3	5	6
2005-06	Salmon Arm	BCHL	20	2	10	12	11	....	....	....	....	....
	Burnaby Express	BCHL	39	15	28	43	16	20	2	14	16	14
2006-07	Chilliwack Bruins	WHL	72	29	53	82	46	5	2	3	5	2
2007-08	Chilliwack Bruins	WHL	72	27	*74	*101	40	4	1	3	5	4
	Milwaukee	AHL	1	0	0	0	0	2	0	0	0	0

WHL West Second All-Star Team (2008)

SANTORELLI, Mike (san-toh-REHL-ee, MIGHK) **NSH.**

Center. Shoots right. 6', 196 lbs. Born, Vancouver, B.C., December 14, 1985.
(Nashville's 6th choice, 178th overall, in 2004 Entry Draft).

			Regular Season					Playoffs				
Season	Club	League	GP	G	A	Pts	PIM	GP	G	A	Pts	PIM
2003-04	Vernon Vipers	BCHL	60	43	53	96	26	5	0	2	2	0
2004-05	Northern Mich.	CCHA	40	16	14	30	22	....	....	....	....	....
2005-06	Northern Mich.	CCHA	40	15	18	33	24	....	....	....	....	....
2006-07	Northern Mich.	CCHA	41	*30	17	47	28	....	....	....	....	....
2007-08	Milwaukee	AHL	80	21	21	42	60	6	0	0	0	2

CCHA All-Rookie Team (2005) • CCHA First All-Star Team (2007) • NCAA West Second All-American Team (2007)

SAPONARI, Vinny (sa-pawn-AIR-ee, VIH-nee) **ATL.**

Right wing. Shoots right. 6', 180 lbs. Born, Powder Springs, GA, February 15, 1990.
(Atlanta's 4th choice, 94th overall, in 2008 Entry Draft).

			Regular Season					Playoffs				
Season	Club	League	GP	G	A	Pts	PIM	GP	G	A	Pts	PIM
2006-07	USNTDP	U-17	4	11	6	17	....	....	....	....	....	....
	USNTDP	U-18	21	4	3	7	6	....	....	....	....	....
	USNTDP	NAHL	35	9	10	19	43	....	....	....	....	....
2007-08	USNTDP	U-18	42	12	16	28	42	....	....	....	....	....
	USNTDP	NAHL	15	1	7	8	0	....	....	....	....	....

• Signed Letter of Intent to attend **Boston University** (Hockey East) in fall of 2008.

SAUER, Michael (SAW-uhr, MIGH-kuhl) **NYR**

Defense. Shoots right. 6'3", 215 lbs. Born, St. Cloud, MN, August 7, 1987.
(NY Rangers' 2nd choice, 40th overall, in 2005 Entry Draft).

			Regular Season					Playoffs				
Season	Club	League	GP	G	A	Pts	PIM	GP	G	A	Pts	PIM
2003-04	St. Cloud Tech	High-MN	18	12	16	28	34	....	....	....	....	....
2004-05	Portland	WHL	32	2	11	13	10	....	....	....	....	....
2005-06	Portland	WHL	59	8	23	31	68	12	4	2	6	8
2006-07	Portland	WHL	33	4	8	12	46	....	....	....	....	....
	Medicine Hat	WHL	32	1	10	11	29	23	1	5	6	34
2007-08	Hartford Wolf Pack	AHL	71	4	7	11	80	2	0	0	0	0

• Missed majority of 2004-05 season due to hip injury and resulting surgery.

SAUVE, Maxime (soh-VAY, max-EEM) **BOS.**

Center. Shoots left. 6', 182 lbs. Born, Tours, France, January 30, 1990.
(Boston's 2nd choice, 47th overall, in 2008 Entry Draft).

			Regular Season					Playoffs				
Season	Club	League	GP	G	A	Pts	PIM	GP	G	A	Pts	PIM
2005-06	Laval-Laurentides	QAAA	41	16	30	46	54	5	1	3	4	2
2006-07	Quebec Remparts	QMJHL	60	10	6	16	24	2	0	0	0	2
2007-08	Quebec Remparts	QMJHL	38	12	20	32	22	....	....	....	....	....
	Val-d'Or Foreurs	QMJHL	32	14	19	33	8	4	2	3	5	2

SAUVE, Yann (soh-VAY, YAHN) **VAN.**

Defense. Shoots left. 6'3", 209 lbs. Born, Montreal, Que., February 18, 1990.
(Vancouver's 2nd choice, 41st overall, in 2008 Entry Draft).

			Regular Season					Playoffs				
Season	Club	League	GP	G	A	Pts	PIM	GP	G	A	Pts	PIM
2005-06	Chateauguay	QAAA	42	14	15	29	63	19	2	12	14	44
2006-07	Saint John	QMJHL	60	2	13	15	75	....	....	....	....	....
2007-08	Saint John	QMJHL	69	6	15	21	92	14	1	2	3	23

SAWADA, Raymond (suh-WAW-duh, RAY-muhnd) **DAL.**

Right wing. Shoots right. 6'2", 195 lbs. Born, Richmond, B.C., February 19, 1985.
(Dallas' 3rd choice, 52nd overall, in 2004 Entry Draft).

			Regular Season					Playoffs				
Season	Club	League	GP	G	A	Pts	PIM	GP	G	A	Pts	PIM
2002-03	Richmond	PIJHL	36	7	17	24	155	....	....	....	....	....
2003-04	Nanaimo Clippers	BCHL	54	20	32	52	93	25	6	16	22	22
2004-05	Cornell Big Red	ECAC	35	4	5	9	48	....	....	....	....	....
2005-06	Cornell Big Red	ECAC	35	7	13	20	20	....	....	....	....	....
2006-07	Cornell Big Red	ECAC	31	10	11	21	29	....	....	....	....	....
2007-08	Cornell Big Red	ECAC	36	10	16	26	34	....	....	....	....	....
	Iowa Stars	AHL	10	2	7	9	14	....	....	....	....	....

SAWYER, Jean-Claude (SOI-uhr, ZHAWN-KLOHD) **CHI.**

Defense. Shoots left. 6'3", 194 lbs. Born, Saint John, N.B., August 12, 1986.
(Minnesota's 8th choice, 161st overall, in 2004 Entry Draft).

			Regular Season					Playoffs				
Season	Club	League	GP	G	A	Pts	PIM	GP	G	A	Pts	PIM
2002-03	Cape Breton	QMJHL	31	3	2	5	44	3	0	0	0	2
2003-04	Cape Breton	QMJHL	56	5	13	18	48	2	0	0	0	2
2004-05	Cape Breton	QMJHL	58	10	22	32	53	5	2	2	4	4
2005-06	Cape Breton	QMJHL	69	12	41	53	108	9	4	0	4	15
2006-07	Cape Breton	QMJHL	68	15	62	77	87	16	3	16	19	6
2007-08	Rockford IceHogs	AHL	4	0	0	0	4	....	....	....	....	....
	Pensacola	ECHL	65	7	25	32	50	....	....	....	....	....

QMJHL Second All-Star Team (2007)

Signed as a free agent by **Chicago**, July 2, 2007.

SBISA, Luca (S'BEE-za, LOO-ka) **PHI.**

Defense. Shoots left. 6'2", 190 lbs. Born, Ozieri, Italy, January 30, 1990.
(Philadelphia's 1st choice, 19th overall, in 2008 Entry Draft).

			Regular Season					Playoffs				
Season	Club	League	GP	G	A	Pts	PIM	GP	G	A	Pts	PIM
2005-06	EV Zug Jr.	Swiss-Jr.	18	0	3	3	18	....	....	....	....	....
2006-07	EV Zug Jr.	Swiss-Jr.	STATISTICS NOT AVAILABLE									
	EHC Seewen	Swiss-3	6	1	2	3	4	....	....	....	....	....
	EV Zug	Swiss	7	0	0	0	0	1	0	0	0	0
2007-08	Lethbridge	WHL	62	6	27	33	63	19	3	12	15	17

SCALZO, Mario (SKAL-zoh, MAHR-ee-oh)

Defense. Shoots left. 5'9", 187 lbs. Born, St-Hubert, Que., November 11, 1984.

			Regular Season					Playoffs				
Season	Club	League	GP	G	A	Pts	PIM	GP	G	A	Pts	PIM
2001-02	Antoine-Girouard	QAAA	40	8	27	35	50	....	....	....	....	....
	Victoriaville Tigres	QMJHL	1	0	1	1	0	1	0	0	0	0
2002-03	Victoriaville Tigres	QMJHL	72	10	34	44	134	4	0	3	3	6
2003-04	Victoriaville Tigres	QMJHL	68	16	52	68	113	....	....	....	....	....
2004-05	Victoriaville Tigres	QMJHL	39	11	19	30	73	....	....	....	....	....
	Rimouski Oceanic	QMJHL	23	13	31	44	31	13	7	14	21	10
2005-06	Iowa Stars	AHL	74	4	29	33	42	7	0	2	2	8
2006-07	Iowa Stars	AHL	73	4	21	25	89	9	0	3	3	10
2007-08	Iowa Stars	AHL	15	1	8	9	10	....	....	....	....	....
	Norfolk Admirals	AHL	48	4	16	20	27	....	....	....	....	....

QMJHL All-Rookie Team (2003) • QMJHL Second All-Star Team (2004) • QMJHL First All-Star Team (2005) • Memorial Cup All-Star Team (2005)

Signed as a free agent by **Dallas**, August 5, 2005. Traded to **Tampa Bay** by **Dallas** for Bryce Lampman, November 19, 2007.

SCANDELLA, Marco (skan-DEHL-a, MAHR-koh) MIN.

Defense. Shoots left. 6'2", 190 lbs. Born, Montreal, Que., February 23, 1990.
(Minnesota's 2nd choice, 55th overall, in 2008 Entry Draft).

			Regular Season					Playoffs				
Season	Club	League	GP	G	A	Pts	PIM	GP	G	A	Pts	PIM
2005-06	Ecole Montpetit	QAAA	42	3	4	7	40	3	0	0	0	2
2006-07	Mtl. Predators	QAAA	42	7	13	20	66	3	0	1	1	10
2007-08	Val-d'Or Foreurs	QMJHL	65	4	10	14	35	4	0	1	1	4

SCEVIOUR, Colton (SEE-vee-yuhr, KOHL-tuhn) DAL.

Center/Right wing. Shoots right. 6', 201 lbs. Born, Red Deer, Alta., April 20, 1989.
(Dallas' 3rd choice, 112th overall, in 2007 Entry Draft).

			Regular Season					Playoffs				
Season	Club	League	GP	G	A	Pts	PIM	GP	G	A	Pts	PIM
2004-05	Red Deer	AMHL	36	15	22	37	32	....	....	....	....	....
	Portland	WHL	6	1	0	1	6	4	0	0	0	0
2005-06	Portland	WHL	58	3	6	9	25	12	0	1	1	4
2006-07	Portland	WHL	49	12	26	38	38	....	....	....	....	....
2007-08	Portland	WHL	17	2	8	10	9	....	....	....	....	....
	Lethbridge	WHL	52	31	23	54	36	19	3	10	13	15

SCHAEFFER, Kevin (SHAY-fuhr, KEH-vihn)

Defense. Shoots right. 6', 203 lbs. Born, Huntington, NY, October 16, 1984.
(Nashville's 7th choice, 193rd overall, in 2004 Entry Draft).

			Regular Season					Playoffs				
Season	Club	League	GP	G	A	Pts	PIM	GP	G	A	Pts	PIM
2002-03	NY Apple Core	EJHL	65	20	38	58	60	....	....	....	....	....
2003-04	Boston University	H-East	38	5	12	17	20	....	....	....	....	....
2004-05	Boston University	H-East	41	2	12	14	26	....	....	....	....	....
2005-06	Boston University	H-East	40	4	9	13	18	....	....	....	....	....
2006-07	Boston University	H-East	33	6	4	10	22	....	....	....	....	....
2007-08	Providence Bruins	AHL	31	1	1	2	6	....	....	....	....	....
	Reading Royals	ECHL	19	2	5	7	21	11	1	3	4	8

Hockey East All-Rookie Team (2004)

SCHENN, Luke (SHEHN, LEWK) TOR.

Defense. Shoots right. 6'2", 216 lbs. Born, Saskatoon, Sask., November 2, 1989.
(Toronto's 1st choice, 5th overall, in 2008 Entry Draft).

			Regular Season					Playoffs				
Season	Club	League	GP	G	A	Pts	PIM	GP	G	A	Pts	PIM
2004-05	Sask. Contacts	SMHL	41	5	22	27	69	....	....	....	....	....
2005-06	Kelowna Rockets	WHL	60	3	8	11	86	12	0	0	0	14
2006-07	Kelowna Rockets	WHL	72	2	27	29	139	....	....	....	....	....
2007-08	Kelowna Rockets	WHL	57	7	21	28	100	7	2	2	4	6

WHL West Second All-Star Team (2008)

SCHEVJEV, Maxim (shehv-YAWF-yehv, MAX-ihm) BUF.

Center. Shoots left. 6', 178 lbs. Born, Noginsk, USSR, July 5, 1984.
(Buffalo's 7th choice, 178th overall, in 2002 Entry Draft).

			Regular Season					Playoffs				
Season	Club	League	GP	G	A	Pts	PIM	GP	G	A	Pts	PIM
99-2000	Elektrostal 2	Russia-3	11	0	1	1	2	....	....	....	....	....
2000-01	Elektrostal	Russia-2	7	0	0	0	6	....	....	....	....	....
2001-02	Elektrostal 2	Russia-3	6	1	2	3	2	....	....	....	....	....
	Elektrostal	Russia-2	49	6	9	15	34	....	....	....	....	....
2002-03	Amur Khabarovsk	Russia	21	0	0	0	10	....	....	....	....	....
	Khabarovsk 2	Russia-3	5	2	1	3	4	....	....	....	....	....
2003-04	Kristall Elektrostal	Russia-2	26	4	5	9	20	....	....	....	....	....
	Voskresensk	Russia	18	1	0	1	2	....	....	....	....	....
2004-05	Kristall Elektrostal	Russia-2	48	4	7	11	109	....	....	....	....	....
2005-06	Yuzhny Ural Orsk	Russia-2	38	3	10	13	38	....	....	....	....	....
	Yuzhny Ural Orsk 2	Russia-3	3	1	3	4	0	....	....	....	....	....
	Kristall Elektrostal	Russia-3	STATISTICS NOT AVAILABLE									
2006-07	Kristall Elektrostal	Russia-2	47	4	7	11	52	....	....	....	....	....
2007-08	Kristall Elektrostal	Russia-2	58	6	11	17	68	....	....	....	....	....

SCHIESTEL, Drew (SHIGHS-tuhl, DROO) BUF.

Defense. Shoots right. 6'1", 189 lbs. Born, Hamilton, Ont., March 9, 1989.
(Buffalo's 2nd choice, 59th overall, in 2007 Entry Draft).

			Regular Season					Playoffs				
Season	Club	League	GP	G	A	Pts	PIM	GP	G	A	Pts	PIM
2004-05	Hamilton Reps	Minor-ON	68	21	27	46	....	....	....	....	....	....
2005-06	Mississauga	OHL	40	1	4	5	42	....	....	....	....	....
2006-07	Mississauga	OHL	66	6	15	21	40	5	0	6	6	2
2007-08	Niagara Ice Dogs	OHL	68	8	29	37	40	10	1	6	7	10

SCHLEMKO, David (SHLEHM-koh, DAY-vihd) PHX.

Defense. Shoots left. 6'1", 195 lbs. Born, Edmonton, Alta., May 7, 1987.

			Regular Season					Playoffs				
Season	Club	League	GP	G	A	Pts	PIM	GP	G	A	Pts	PIM
2004-05	Medicine Hat	WHL	65	5	24	29	23	13	0	3	3	10
2005-06	Medicine Hat	WHL	69	9	35	44	44	13	2	5	7	15
2006-07	Medicine Hat	WHL	64	8	50	58	78	23	3	13	16	12
2007-08	San Antonio	AHL	1	0	0	0	4	....	....	....	....	....
	Arizona Sundogs	CHL	58	10	29	39	24	14	3	5	8	6

Signed as a free agent by **Phoenix**, July 19, 2007.

SCHNEIDER, Andy (SHNIGH-duhr, AN-dee) TOR.

Defense. Shoots left. 6'1", 215 lbs. Born, Grand Forks, ND, July 31, 1981.
(Pittsburgh's 7th choice, 156th overall, in 2001 Entry Draft).

			Regular Season					Playoffs				
Season	Club	League	GP	G	A	Pts	PIM	GP	G	A	Pts	PIM
1998-99	Lincoln Stars	USHL	9	0	4	4	8	4	0	0	0	2
99-2000	Lincoln Stars	USHL	46	7	10	17	102	10	6	4	10	27
2000-01	Lincoln Stars	USHL	54	12	24	36	134	....	....	....	....	....
2001-02	North Dakota	WCHA	35	3	11	14	65	....	....	....	....	....
2002-03	North Dakota	WCHA	43	11	30	41	52	....	....	....	....	....
2003-04	North Dakota	WCHA	39	2	10	12	54	....	....	....	....	....
2004-05	North Dakota	WCHA	42	2	8	10	58	....	....	....	....	....
2005-06	Wilkes-Barre	AHL	50	3	13	16	54	....	....	....	....	....
	Wheeling Nailers	ECHL	4	0	1	1	2	....	....	....	....	....
2006-07	Dusseldorf	Germany	48	6	20	26	73	9	3	7	10	18
2007-08	Portland Pirates	AHL	57	3	8	11	81	11	2	3	5	6

Signed as a free agent by **Toronto**, July 27, 2008.

SCHNEIDER, David (SHNIGH-duhr, DAY-vihd)

Defense. Shoots left. 5'9", 190 lbs. Born, Melrose Park, IL, August 24, 1979.

			Regular Season					Playoffs				
Season	Club	League	GP	G	A	Pts	PIM	GP	G	A	Pts	PIM
1998-99	Princeton	ECAC	21	1	0	1	24	....	....	....	....	....
99-2000	Princeton	ECAC	30	5	11	16	22	....	....	....	....	....
2000-01	Princeton	ECAC	23	8	7	15	22	....	....	....	....	....
2001-02	Princeton	ECAC	24	4	14	18	20	....	....	....	....	....
	Trenton Titans	ECHL	2	0	1	1	5	....	....	....	....	....
2002-03	Trenton Titans	ECHL	26	5	11	16	22	....	....	....	....	....
2003-04	TPS Turku	Finland	54	8	11	19	72	13	2	3	5	20
2004-05	TPS Turku	Finland	26	2	3	5	49	6	0	1	1	25
2005-06	HPK Hameenlinna	Finland	51	8	18	26	98	13	1	3	4	16
2006-07	HPK Hameenlinna	Finland	53	8	17	25	72	9	3	2	5	16
2007-08	Norfolk Admirals	AHL	71	2	25	27	70	....	....	....	....	....

Signed as a free agent by **Tampa Bay**, July 3, 2007.

SCHULTZ, Ian (SHUHLTZ, EE-an) ST.L.

Right wing. Shoots right. 6'1", 179 lbs. Born, Calgary, Alta., February 4, 1990.
(St. Louis' 6th choice, 87th overall, in 2008 Entry Draft).

			Regular Season					Playoffs				
Season	Club	League	GP	G	A	Pts	PIM	GP	G	A	Pts	PIM
2006-07	Calgary Buffaloes	AMHL	32	13	25	38	92	7	2	7	9	26
	Calgary Hitmen	WHL	1	1	0	1	0	....	....	....	....	....
2007-08	Calgary Hitmen	WHL	67	15	15	30	128	16	2	7	9	19

SCHULTZ, Justin (SHUHLTZ, JUHS-tihn) ANA.

Defense. Shoots right. 6'1", 163 lbs. Born, Kelowna, B.C., July 6, 1990.
(Anaheim's 4th choice, 43rd overall, in 2008 Entry Draft).

			Regular Season					Playoffs				
Season	Club	League	GP	G	A	Pts	PIM	GP	G	A	Pts	PIM
2006-07	Westside Warriors	Minor-BC	....	29	29	58	29	....	....	....	....	....
2007-08	Westside Warriors	BCHL	57	9	31	40	28	11	3	5	8	4

• Signed Letter of Intent to attend **University of Wisconsin** (WCHA) in fall of 2009.

SCHUTZ, Felix (SCHUTZ, FEEL-ihx) BUF.

Center. Shoots left. 5'11", 190 lbs. Born, Erding, West Germany, November 3, 1987.
(Buffalo's 4th choice, 117th overall, in 2006 Entry Draft).

			Regular Season					Playoffs				
Season	Club	League	GP	G	A	Pts	PIM	GP	G	A	Pts	PIM
2003-04	Mannheim Jr.	Ger-Jr.	30	22	22	44	12	....	....	....	....	....
2004-05	EV Landshut Jr.	Ger-Jr.	9	6	8	14	33	2	2	3	5	0
	Landshut Cann.	German-2	24	1	2	3	8	5	0	0	0	2
2005-06	Saint John	QMJHL	65	21	31	52	61	....	....	....	....	....
2006-07	Saint John	QMJHL	18	4	7	11	16	....	....	....	....	....
	Val-d'Or Foreurs	QMJHL	27	15	18	33	28	20	5	10	15	22
2007-08	ERC Ingolstadt	Germany	46	12	13	25	76	3	0	1	1	2

QMJHL All-Rookie Team (2006)

SCOTT, Greg (SKAWT, GREHG) TOR.

Right wing. Shoots right. 6', 178 lbs. Born, Victoria, B.C., June 3, 1988.

			Regular Season					Playoffs				
Season	Club	League	GP	G	A	Pts	PIM	GP	G	A	Pts	PIM
2004-05	Peninsula Panthers	VIJHL	48	34	40	74	65	....	....	....	....	....
	Victoria Salsa	BCHL	7	1	1	2	0	....	....	....	....	....
2005-06	Seattle	WHL	69	8	14	22	37	7	1	3	4	4
2006-07	Seattle	WHL	72	18	14	32	62	11	0	2	2	2
2007-08	Seattle	WHL	72	38	37	75	56	12	5	4	9	9

Signed as a free agent by **Toronto**, July 3, 2008.

SCOTT, John (SKAWT, JAWN) MIN.

Defense. Shoots left. 6'8", 255 lbs. Born, St. Catharines, Ont., September 26, 1982.

			Regular Season					Playoffs				
Season	Club	League	GP	G	A	Pts	PIM	GP	G	A	Pts	PIM
2002-03	Michigan Tech	WCHA	31	1	3	4	64	....	....	....	....	....
2003-04	Michigan Tech	WCHA	35	1	3	4	100	....	....	....	....	....
2004-05	Michigan Tech	WCHA	36	2	3	5	101	....	....	....	....	....
2005-06	Michigan Tech	WCHA	24	3	2	5	87	....	....	....	....	....
2006-07	Houston Aeros	AHL	65	1	5	6	107	....	....	....	....	....
2007-08	Houston Aeros	AHL	64	3	0	3	184	5	0	0	0	13

Signed as a free agent by **Houston** (AHL), September 26, 2006. Signed as a free agent by **Minnesota**, December 31, 2006.

SEABROOK, Keith (SEE-bruk, KEETH) WSH.

Defense. Shoots right. 6', 197 lbs. Born, Delta, B.C., August 2, 1988.
(Washington's 5th choice, 52nd overall, in 2006 Entry Draft).

			Regular Season					Playoffs				
Season	Club	League	GP	G	A	Pts	PIM	GP	G	A	Pts	PIM
2004-05	Coquitlam Express	BCHL	58	8	20	28	70	....	....	....	....	....
2005-06	Burnaby Express	BCHL	57	10	24	34	81	....	....	....	....	....
2006-07	U. of Denver	WCHA	37	2	11	13	24	....	....	....	....	....
2007-08	Calgary Hitmen	WHL	59	4	13	17	47	14	0	5	5	13

• Left **University of Denver** (WCHA) and signed with **Calgary** (WHL), July 30, 2007.

SEDOV, Pavel (se-DAHF, PAH-vehl) **T.B.**

Right wing. Shoots left. 6'3", 200 lbs. Born, Voskresensk, USSR, January 12, 1982.
(Tampa Bay's 5th choice, 161st overall, in 2000 Entry Draft).

			Regular Season					Playoffs				
Season	Club	League	GP	G	A	Pts	PIM	GP	G	A	Pts	PIM
99-2000	Voskresensk	Russia-2	10	0	0	0	2	....	....	....	....	....
	Voskresensk 2	Russia-3	21	5	5	-10	26	....	....	....	....	....
2000-01	Voskresensk	Russia-2	38	2	1	3	10	....	....	....	....	....
2001-02	Voskresensk 2	Russia-3	12	4	1	5	0	....	....	....	....	....
	Voskresensk	Russia-2	18	3	1	4	0	....	....	....	....	....
2002-03	Voskresensk 2	Russia-3	7	2	4	6	4	....	....	....	....	....
	Voskresensk	Russia-2	25	1	5	6	6	....	....	....	....	....
2003-04	THK Tver	Russia-2	26	2	6	8	6	....	....	....	....	....
	Voskresensk	Russia	10	1	0	1	2	....	....	....	....	....
	Voskresensk 2	Russia-3	STATISTICS NOT AVAILABLE									
2004-05	HK Tver	Russia-3	STATISTICS NOT AVAILABLE									
	HK Dmitrov	Russia-3	STATISTICS NOT AVAILABLE									
	HK Ryazan	Russia-4	STATISTICS NOT AVAILABLE									
2005-06			DID NOT PLAY									
2006-07	HK Ryazan	Russia-3	70	24	29	53	16	....	....	....	....	....
2007-08	HK Ryazan	Russia-2	50	6	10	16	14	....	....	....	....	....

SEGAL, Brandon (SEE-guhl, BRAN-duhn) **T.B.**

Right wing. Shoots right. 6'3", 213 lbs. Born, Richmond, B.C., July 12, 1983.
(Nashville's 2nd choice, 102nd overall, in 2002 Entry Draft).

			Regular Season					Playoffs				
Season	Club	League	GP	G	A	Pts	PIM	GP	G	A	Pts	PIM
99-2000	Calgary Hitmen	WHL	44	2	6	8	76	13	1	1	2	13
	Delta Ice Hawks	PIJHL	....	....	....	....	....	3	0	1	1	2
2000-01	Calgary Hitmen	WHL	72	16	11	27	103	12	1	1	2	17
2001-02	Calgary Hitmen	WHL	71	43	40	83	122	7	1	4	5	16
2002-03	Calgary Hitmen	WHL	71	31	27	58	104	5	2	2	4	4
2003-04	Calgary Hitmen	WHL	28	18	12	30	29	....	....	....	....	....
	Milwaukee	AHL	44	11	10	21	54	13	2	1	3	21
2004-05	Milwaukee	AHL	59	7	8	15	45	3	1	0	1	11
	Rockford IceHogs	UHL	10	5	4	9	27	11	11	5	16	10
2005-06	Milwaukee	AHL	79	18	15	33	126	21	1	2	3	16
2006-07	Milwaukee	AHL	77	20	9	29	84	4	1	0	1	2
2007-08	Portland Pirates	AHL	54	5	9	14	46	....	....	....	....	....
	Norfolk Admirals	AHL	22	7	6	13	25	....	....	....	....	....

Traded to **Anaheim** by **Nashville** for future considerations, June 25, 2007. Traded to **Tampa Bay** by **Anaheim** with Anaheim's 7th round choice (David Carle) in 2008 Entry Draft for Jay Leach, February 26, 2008.

SEITSONEN, Aki (SIGHT-soh-nehn, AH-kee) **CGY.**

Center. Shoots right. 6'3", 203 lbs. Born, Riihimaki, Finland, February 5, 1986.
(Calgary's 4th choice, 118th overall, in 2004 Entry Draft).

			Regular Season					Playoffs				
Season	Club	League	GP	G	A	Pts	PIM	GP	G	A	Pts	PIM
2002-03	HPK U18	Fin-U18	28	15	18	33	6	2	1	1	2	0
	HPK Jr.	Fin-Jr.	1	1	0	1	0	....	....	....	....	....
2003-04	Prince Albert	WHL	71	16	24	40	18	5	0	0	0	0
2004-05	Prince Albert	WHL	67	24	28	52	14	17	5	9	14	10
2005-06	Prince Albert	WHL	66	20	15	35	22	....	....	....	....	....
	Omaha	AHL	7	0	0	0	2	....	....	....	....	....
2006-07	Omaha	AHL	13	1	3	4	0	....	....	....	....	....
	Las Vegas	ECHL	59	14	18	32	16	5	0	2	2	2
2007-08	Las Vegas	ECHL	70	18	18	36	14	21	7	3	10	4

SEMIN, Dmitri (SEH-min, dih-MEE-tree) **ST.L.**

Center. Shoots left. 5'10", 185 lbs. Born, Moscow, USSR, August 14, 1983.
(St. Louis' 4th choice, 159th overall, in 2001 Entry Draft).

			Regular Season					Playoffs				
Season	Club	League	GP	G	A	Pts	PIM	GP	G	A	Pts	PIM
99-2000	Spartak Moscow 2	Russia-3	27	9	10	19	10	....	....	....	....	....
	Spartak Moscow	Russia-2	1	0	0	0	0	....	....	....	....	....
2000-01	Spartak Moscow	Russia	21	6	3	9	4	11	2	3	5	4
2001-02	Spartak Moscow 2	Russia-3	4	5	0	5	4	....	....	....	....	....
	Spartak Moscow	Russia	44	2	6	8	14	....	....	....	....	....
2002-03	Spartak Moscow	Russia	51	9	13	22	30	....	....	....	....	....
2003-04	Spartak Moscow	Russia-2	60	15	23	38	34	13	2	2	4	2
2004-05	Spartak Moscow	Russia	53	7	7	14	34	....	....	....	....	....
2005-06	Spartak Moscow	Russia	51	12	14	26	38	3	0	1	1	0
2006-07	Yaroslavl	Russia	41	13	13	26	30	7	3	2	5	2
2007-08	Yaroslavl	Russia	54	9	14	23	46	16	1	2	3	10

SEPPANEN, Timo (SEH-pah-nehn, TEE-moh) **PIT.**

Defense. Shoots left. 6'1", 209 lbs. Born, Helsinki, Finland, July 22, 1987.
(Pittsburgh's 5th choice, 185th overall, in 2006 Entry Draft).

			Regular Season					Playoffs				
Season	Club	League	GP	G	A	Pts	PIM	GP	G	A	Pts	PIM
2002-03	HIFK Helsinki U18	Fin-U18	24	2	5	7	12	2	2	0	2	0
2003-04	HIFK Helsinki U18	Fin-U18	7	2	5	7	32	4	0	2	2	6
	HIFK Helsinki Jr.	Fin-Jr.	29	0	4	4	6	7	0	0	0	2
2004-05	HIFK Helsinki U18	Fin-U18	....	....	....	....	....	7	2	3	5	26
	HIFK Helsinki Jr.	Fin-Jr.	39	3	4	7	32	3	0	0	0	4
2005-06	Suomi U20	Finland-2	6	2	2	4	10	....	....	....	....	....
	HIFK Helsinki Jr.	Fin-Jr.	30	7	11	18	65	....	....	....	....	....
	HIFK Helsinki	Finland	21	0	0	0	2	5	0	1	1	0
2006-07	HIFK Helsinki Jr.	Fin-Jr.	12	2	2	4	10	....	....	....	....	....
	Suomi U20	Finland-2	6	1	0	1	6	....	....	....	....	....
	HIFK Helsinki	Finland	12	0	0	0	10	....	....	....	....	....
	HPK Jr.	Fin-Jr.	9	1	4	5	8	3	1	2	3	0
	HPK Hameenlinna	Finland	16	2	1	3	10	....	....	....	....	....
2007-08	HIFK Helsinki Jr.	Fin-Jr.	1	1	0	1	2	....	....	....	....	....
	HIFK Helsinki	Finland	3	0	0	0	0	....	....	....	....	....
	KalPa Kuopio	Finland	49	6	6	12	30	....	....	....	....	....

SERSEN, Michal (suhr-SEHN, MEE-khahl) **PIT.**

Defense. Shoots left. 6'2", 200 lbs. Born, Celnica, Czech., December 28, 1985.
(Pittsburgh's 7th choice, 130th overall, in 2004 Entry Draft).

			Regular Season					Playoffs				
Season	Club	League	GP	G	A	Pts	PIM	GP	G	A	Pts	PIM
2002-03	Bratislava Jr.	Slovak-Jr.	33	5	4	9	51	....	....	....	....	....
	Bratislava	Slovakia	17	0	0	0	0	....	....	....	....	....
2003-04	Rimouski Oceanic	QMJHL	45	7	18	25	30	9	1	5	6	6
2004-05	Rimouski Oceanic	QMJHL	67	9	33	42	74	13	0	8	8	18
2005-06	Quebec Remparts	QMJHL	63	22	57	79	76	23	3	18	21	36
2006-07	Bratislava	Slovakia	42	1	4	5	28	14	0	1	1	2
2007-08	Bratislava	Slovakia	54	9	9	18	58	18	1	2	3	6

QMJHL Second All-Star Team (2006) • Memorial Cup Tournament All-Star Team (2006)

Signed as a free agent by **Bratislava** (Slovakia), October 14, 2006.

SERTICH, Marty (SUHR-tihch, MAHR-tee) **COL.**

Center. Shoots left. 5'9", 165 lbs. Born, Roseville, MN, October 13, 1982.

			Regular Season					Playoffs				
Season	Club	League	GP	G	A	Pts	PIM	GP	G	A	Pts	PIM
2001-02	Sioux Falls	USHL	61	19	33	52	30	3	1	0	1	0
2002-03	Colorado College	WCHA	42	9	20	29	26	....	....	....	....	....
2003-04	Colorado College	WCHA	39	11	28	39	12	....	....	....	....	....
2004-05	Colorado College	WCHA	42	27	37	*64	26	....	....	....	....	....
2005-06	Colorado College	WCHA	42	14	36	50	55	....	....	....	....	....
2006-07	Iowa Stars	AHL	44	13	20	33	24	2	0	1	1	0
2007-08	Iowa Stars	AHL	79	27	25	52	42	....	....	....	....	....

WCHA Second All-Star Team (2006)

Signed as a free agent by **Dallas**, July 10, 2006. Traded to **Colorado** by **Dallas** for future considerations, June 10, 2008.

SESTITO, Tim (sehs-TEE-toh, TIHM) **EDM.**

Center. Shoots left. 6', 195 lbs. Born, Rome, NY, August 28, 1984.

			Regular Season					Playoffs				
Season	Club	League	GP	G	A	Pts	PIM	GP	G	A	Pts	PIM
2001-02	Plymouth Whalers	OHL	51	10	11	21	40	6	0	0	0	0
2002-03	Plymouth Whalers	OHL	61	11	7	18	49	18	2	3	5	4
2003-04	Plymouth Whalers	OHL	57	10	20	30	68	9	4	1	5	14
2004-05	Plymouth Whalers	OHL	67	14	18	32	93	4	0	0	0	14
	Bridgeport	AHL	9	2	1	3	12	....	....	....	....	....
2005-06	Greenville Grrrowl	ECHL	72	21	23	44	127	6	2	2	4	24
2006-07	Wilkes-Barre	AHL	4	0	0	0	6	....	....	....	....	....
	Stockton Thunder	ECHL	66	13	13	26	132	6	2	1	3	6
2007-08	Springfield Falcons	AHL	77	7	10	17	175	....	....	....	....	....

Signed as a free agent by **Edmonton**, August 28, 2006.

SEVERYN, C.J. (SEH-vuhr-ihn, SEE-JAY) **CGY.**

Left wing. Shoots left. 6', 185 lbs. Born, Beaver, PA, June 2, 1989.
(Calgary's 5th choice, 186th overall, in 2007 Entry Draft).

			Regular Season					Playoffs				
Season	Club	League	GP	G	A	Pts	PIM	GP	G	A	Pts	PIM
2004-05	Pittsburgh Hornets	MWEHL	65	27	44	71	....	....	....	....	....	....
2005-06	USNTDP	U-17	19	2	3	5	40	....	....	....	....	....
	USNTDP	NAHL	32	2	13	15	77	12	1	0	1	12
2006-07	USNTDP	U-18	42	8	8	16	32	....	....	....	....	....
	USNTDP	NAHL	15	0	3	3	22	....	....	....	....	....
2007-08	Ohio State	CCHA	32	0	2	2	20	....	....	....	....	....

SHADILOV, Igor (sha-DEE-lahf, EE-gohr) **WSH.**

Defense. Shoots left. 6'2", 189 lbs. Born, Moscow, USSR, June 7, 1980.
(Washington's 10th choice, 249th overall, in 1999 Entry Draft).

			Regular Season					Playoffs				
Season	Club	League	GP	G	A	Pts	PIM	GP	G	A	Pts	PIM
1996-97	Dyn'o Moscow 2	Russia-3	30	3	7	10	30	....	....	....	....	....
1997-98	Dynamo Moscow	Russia	38	1	0	1	6	....	....	....	....	....
1998-99	Dyn'o Moscow 2	Russia-3	28	2	9	11	15	....	....	....	....	....
	Dynamo Moscow	Russia	2	0	0	0	0	....	....	....	....	....
	Krylja Sovetov	Russia	9	0	0	0	0	....	....	....	....	....
99-2000	THK Tver	Russia-2	14	0	3	3	6	....	....	....	....	....
	Dynamo Moscow	Russia	26	0	2	2	8	16	0	0	0	2
2000-01	Dynamo Moscow	Russia	34	1	5	6	12	....	....	....	....	....
2001-02	Cherepovets	Russia	33	7	3	10	10	4	0	0	0	2
2002-03	Cherepovets	Russia	32	3	3	6	28	12	1	3	4	4
2003-04	Dynamo Moscow	Russia	56	4	8	12	16	3	0	1	1	2
2004-05	Dynamo Moscow	Russia	34	0	5	5	12	....	....	....	....	....
2005-06	Ak Bars Kazan	Russia	49	3	9	12	20	13	1	1	2	6
2006-07	Ak Bars Kazan	Russia	49	5	10	15	32	16	1	1	2	41
2007-08	Ufa	Russia	45	5	11	16	18	16	0	2	2	8

SHAFIGULIN, Grigory (sha-fih-GOO-lihn, grih-GOH-ree) **NSH.**

Center. Shoots left. 6'2", 185 lbs. Born, Chelyabinsk, USSR, January 13, 1985.
(Nashville's 8th choice, 98th overall, in 2003 Entry Draft).

			Regular Season					Playoffs				
Season	Club	League	GP	G	A	Pts	PIM	GP	G	A	Pts	PIM
2000-01	Chelyabinsk 2	Russia-3	6	3	2	5	8	....	....	....	....	....
2001-02	Yaroslavl 2	Russia-3	19	2	2	4	12	....	....	....	....	....
2002-03	Yaroslavl 2	Russia-3	33	18	12	30	46	7	0	4	4	31
	Yaroslavl	Russia	11	0	1	1	4	8	0	0	0	4
2003-04	Yaroslavl	Russia	29	3	0	3	4	2	0	0	0	0
	Yaroslavl 2	Russia-3	11	3	8	11	22	....	....	....	....	....
2004-05	Yaroslavl 2	Russia-3	1	0	2	2	0	....	....	....	....	....
	Yaroslavl	Russia	46	5	6	11	49	9	0	0	0	10
2005-06	Yaroslavl	Russia	32	3	6	9	20	3	0	0	0	6
	Yaroslavl 2	Russia-3	7	1	3	4	18	....	....	....	....	....
2006-07	Yaroslavl	Russia	54	5	16	21	46	7	3	0	3	14
2007-08	Ak Bars Kazan	Russia	39	5	5	10	112	8	1	0	1	4

SHARROW, Jim (SHA-row, JIHM) **VAN.**

Defense. Shoots right. 6'2", 198 lbs. Born, Framingham, MA, January 31, 1985.
(Atlanta's 2nd choice, 110th overall, in 2003 Entry Draft).

			Regular Season					Playoffs				
Season	Club	League	GP	G	A	Pts	PIM	GP	G	A	Pts	PIM
2001-02	USNTDP	U-17	17	2	11	13	2	....	....	....	....	....
	USNTDP	NAHL	44	3	5	8	28	....	....	....	....	....
2002-03	Halifax	QMJHL	70	2	14	16	54	25	2	4	6	24
2003-04	Halifax	QMJHL	52	12	26	38	67	....	....	....	....	....
2004-05	Halifax	QMJHL	69	16	31	47	76	13	5	6	11	6
2005-06	Chicago Wolves	AHL	47	2	17	19	17	....	....	....	....	....
	Gwinnett	ECHL	23	3	7	10	12	....	....	....	....	....
2006-07	Chicago Wolves	AHL	42	4	14	18	38	....	....	....	....	....
2007-08	Manitoba Moose	AHL	44	5	17	22	26	2	0	1	1	0

QMJHL All-Rookie Team (2003)

Traded to **Vancouver** by **Atlanta** for Jesse Schultz, June 23, 2007.

SHATTENKIRK, Kevin (SHAH-tehn-kuhrk, KEH-vihn) **COL.**

Defense. Shoots right. 5'11", 193 lbs. Born, Greenwich, CT, January 29, 1989.
(Colorado's 1st choice, 14th overall, in 2007 Entry Draft).

			Regular Season					Playoffs				
Season	Club	League	GP	G	A	Pts	PIM	GP	G	A	Pts	PIM
2004-05	Brunswick Bruins	High-CT	22	10	18	28	....	....	....	....	....	....
2005-06	USNTDP	U-17	13	4	4	8	4	....	....	....	....	....
	USNTDP	NAHL	28	6	9	15	17	12	3	7	10	10
2006-07	USNTDP	U-18	43	8	19	27	36	....	....	....	....	....
	USNTDP	NAHL	14	5	8	13	26	....	....	....	....	....
2007-08	Boston University	H-East	40	4	17	21	38	....	....	....	....	....

Hockey East All-Rookie Team (2008)

SHEFER, Andrei (SHEH-fuhr, AWN-dray) **L.A.**

Left wing. Shoots left. 6'1", 194 lbs. Born, Yekaterinburg, USSR, July 26, 1981.
(Los Angeles' 1st choice, 43rd overall, in 1999 Entry Draft).

			Regular Season					Playoffs				
Season	Club	League	GP	G	A	Pts	PIM	GP	G	A	Pts	PIM
1997-98	Yekaterinburg 2	Russia-3	16	3	3	6	18	....	....	....	....	....
1998-99	Cherepovets 3	Russia-4	6	2	2	4	18	....	....	....	....	....
	Cherepovets 2	Russia-3	21	6	5	11	20	....	....	....	....	....
	Cherepovets	Russia	8	1	0	1	4	....	....	....	....	....
99-2000	Halifax	QMJHL	72	34	42	76	30	10	0	5	5	4
2000-01	SKA St. Petersburg	Russia	11	6	1	7	4	....	....	....	....	....
	Cherepovets	Russia	20	1	1	2	10	6	1	0	1	0
2001-02	Cherepovets 2	Russia-3	3	1	2	3	2	....	....	....	....	....
	Cherepovets	Russia	8	0	0	0	6	....	....	....	....	....
	SKA St. Petersburg	Russia	28	4	4	8	10	....	....	....	....	....
2002-03	Cherepovets	Russia	37	2	4	6	10	10	0	0	0	0
	Cherepovets 2	Russia-3	3	1	2	3	2	....	....	....	....	....
2003-04	Cherepovets	Russia	55	4	6	10	46	....	....	....	....	....
2004-05	Cherepovets	Russia	46	1	11	12	18	....	....	....	....	....
2005-06	Cherepovets	Russia	45	2	1	3	32	4	0	1	1	0
2006-07	CSKA Moscow	Russia	45	7	7	14	48	2	0	0	0	2
2007-08	CSKA Moscow	Russia	53	3	14	17	34	6	1	1	2	0

SHELAST, Tyler (SHEE-last, TIGH-luhr) **DAL.**

Wing. Shoots right. 6'1", 202 lbs. Born, Edmonton, Alta., December 26, 1984.

			Regular Season					Playoffs				
Season	Club	League	GP	G	A	Pts	PIM	GP	G	A	Pts	PIM
2003-04	Powell River Kings	BCHL	58	25	42	67	131	7	1	3	4	6
2004-05	Michigan Tech	WCHA	37	11	8	19	42	....	....	....	....	....
2005-06	Michigan Tech	WCHA	37	9	9	18	44	....	....	....	....	....
2006-07	Michigan Tech	WCHA	38	15	9	24	18	....	....	....	....	....
2007-08	Michigan Tech	WCHA	39	16	10	26	26	....	....	....	....	....
	Iowa Stars	AHL	11	1	1	2	0	....	....	....	....	....

Signed as a free agent by **Dallas**, March 19, 2008.

SHIROKOV, Sergei (sheer-OH-kawv, SAIR-gay) **VAN.**

Wing. Shoots right. 5'10", 176 lbs. Born, Moscow, USSR, March 10, 1986.
(Vancouver's 3rd choice, 163rd overall, in 2006 Entry Draft).

			Regular Season					Playoffs				
Season	Club	League	GP	G	A	Pts	PIM	GP	G	A	Pts	PIM
2001-02	HK CSKA 2	Russia-3	18	2	3	5	0	....	....	....	....	....
2002-03	CSKA Moscow 2	Russia-3	2	0	0	0	0	....	....	....	....	....
2003-04	CSKA Moscow 2	Russia-3	66	39	41	80	66	....	....	....	....	....
2004-05	CSKA Moscow	Russia	8	0	0	0	0	....	....	....	....	....
	CSKA Moscow 2	Russia-3	25	16	13	29	47	....	....	....	....	....
	CSKA Moscow	Russia	8	0	0	0	0	....	....	....	....	....
2005-06	CSKA Moscow	Russia	39	7	7	14	26	4	0	0	0	0
2006-07	CSKA Moscow	Russia	52	16	19	35	36	12	4	6	10	4
2007-08	CSKA Moscow	Russia	57	12	21	33	28	6	0	3	3	4

SIDDALL, Matt (sih-DUHL, MAT) **ATL.**

Right wing. Shoots right. 6'1", 210 lbs. Born, North Vancouver, B.C., September 26, 1984.
(Atlanta's 9th choice, 270th overall, in 2004 Entry Draft).

			Regular Season					Playoffs				
Season	Club	League	GP	G	A	Pts	PIM	GP	G	A	Pts	PIM
2003-04	Powell River Kings	BCHL	45	25	36	61	216	7	4	2	6	10
2004-05	Northern Mich.	CCHA	33	4	4	8	62	....	....	....	....	....
2005-06	Northern Mich.	CCHA	36	6	6	12	72	....	....	....	....	....
2006-07	Northern Mich.	CCHA	37	4	16	20	107	....	....	....	....	....
2007-08	Northern Mich.	CCHA	41	18	18	36	*116	....	....	....	....	....

SIDORENKO, Kirill (sih-dohr-EHN-koh, kih-RIHL) **DAL.**

Center. Shoots left. 6'3", 187 lbs. Born, Omsk, USSR, March 30, 1983.
(Dallas' 9th choice, 180th overall, in 2002 Entry Draft).

			Regular Season					Playoffs				
Season	Club	League	GP	G	A	Pts	PIM	GP	G	A	Pts	PIM
1998-99	Omsk 2	Russia-4	2	0	0	0	2	....	....	....	....	....
99-2000	Omsk 2	Russia-3	26	2	11	13	14	....	....	....	....	....
2000-01	Omsk 2	Russia-3	30	8	7	15	44	....	....	....	....	....
2001-02	Mostovik Kurgan	Russia-2	50	11	6	17	64	....	....	....	....	....
2002-03	Sibir Novosibirsk	Russia	30	1	1	2	2	....	....	....	....	....
2003-04	Energiya Kemerovo	Russia-2	14	1	1	2	6	....	....	....	....	....
	Zauralje Kurgan	Russia-2	32	3	3	6	6	4	0	0	0	27
2004-05	Omsk 2	Russia-3	18	7	4	11	12	....	....	....	....	....
	CSK VVS Samara	Russia-2	16	2	2	4	0	....	....	....	....	....
2005-06	CSK VVS Samara	Russia-2	47	8	11	19	62	....	....	....	....	....
	Krylja Sovetov	Russia-2	6	3	3	6	8	17	1	3	4	4
2006-07	Krylja Sovetov 2	Russia-3	4	2	1	3	6	....	....	....	....	....
	Krylja Sovetov	Russia	35	5	4	9	22	....	....	....	....	....
2007-08	Titan Klin	Russia-2	53	6	12	18	43	....	....	....	....	....

SIFERS, Jaime (SIH-fuhrs, JAY-mee) **TOR.**

Defense. Shoots right. 5'11", 210 lbs. Born, Stratford, CT, January 18, 1983.

			Regular Season					Playoffs				
Season	Club	League	GP	G	A	Pts	PIM	GP	G	A	Pts	PIM
2002-03	U. of Vermont	ECAC	34	4	14	18	66	....	....	....	....	....
2003-04	U. of Vermont	ECAC	35	4	14	18	93	....	....	....	....	....
2004-05	U. of Vermont	ECAC	36	4	12	16	57	....	....	....	....	....
2005-06	U. of Vermont	H-East	38	3	15	18	60	....	....	....	....	....
	Toronto Marlies	AHL	2	0	0	0	2	....	....	....	....	....
2006-07	Toronto Marlies	AHL	80	7	18	25	75	....	....	....	....	....
2007-08	Toronto Marlies	AHL	80	3	10	13	57	19	2	3	5	6

ECAC Second All-Star Team (2005)

Signed as a free agent by **Toronto**, July 20, 2006.

SIMEK, Juraj (SEE-mehk, YUHR-ay) **VAN.**

Wing. Shoots left. 6'1", 192 lbs. Born, Presov, Czech., September 29, 1987.
(Vancouver's 4th choice, 167th overall, in 2006 Entry Draft).

			Regular Season					Playoffs				
Season	Club	League	GP	G	A	Pts	PIM	GP	G	A	Pts	PIM
2002-03	SC Bern Jr.	Swiss-Jr.	2	1	0	1	0	2	0	0	0	0
2003-04	Kloten Flyers Jr.	Swiss-Jr.	36	8	6	14	28	....	....	....	....	....
2004-05	Kloten Flyers Jr.	Swiss-Jr.	39	17	13	30	62	9	2	3	5	10
	Kloten Flyers	Swiss	18	0	0	0	0	....	....	....	....	....
	Kloten Flyers	Swiss	18	0	0	0	0	....	....	....	....	....
2005-06	Kloten Flyers Jr.	Swiss-Jr.	45	24	44	68	202	....	....	....	....	....
	Kloten Flyers	Swiss	8	0	1	1	4	....	....	....	....	....
	EHC Biel-Bienne	Swiss-2	3	0	0	0	2	....	....	....	....	....
2006-07	Brandon	WHL	58	28	29	57	41	9	1	5	6	6
2007-08	Manitoba Moose	AHL	66	7	10	17	30	1	1	0	1	0

SIMMONDS, Wayne (SIH-muhnz, WAYN) **L.A.**

Right wing. Shoots right. 6'2", 174 lbs. Born, Scarborough, Ont., August 26, 1988.
(Los Angeles' 3rd choice, 61st overall, in 2007 Entry Draft).

			Regular Season					Playoffs				
Season	Club	League	GP	G	A	Pts	PIM	GP	G	A	Pts	PIM
2004-05	Tor. Jr. Canadiens	GTHL	67	32	40	72	97	....	....	....	....	....
2005-06	Brockville Braves	CJHL	49	24	19	43	127	7	4	2	6	12
2006-07	Owen Sound	OHL	66	23	26	49	112	4	1	1	2	4
2007-08	Owen Sound	OHL	29	17	22	39	43	....	....	....	....	....
	Sault Ste. Marie	OHL	31	16	20	36	68	14	5	9	14	22

SIMS, Shane (SIHMZ, SHAYN) **NYI**

Defense. Shoots right. 6', 192 lbs. Born, East Amherst, NY, April 30, 1988.
(NY Islanders' 8th choice, 126th overall, in 2006 Entry Draft).

			Regular Season					Playoffs				
Season	Club	League	GP	G	A	Pts	PIM	GP	G	A	Pts	PIM
2004-05	Buffalo Lightning	OPJHL	48	14	26	40	47	....	....	....	....	....
2005-06	Des Moines	USHL	59	10	12	22	80	11	2	0	2	12
2006-07	Des Moines	USHL	59	10	19	29	137	8	1	3	4	8
2007-08	Ohio State	CCHA	39	1	10	11	45	....	....	....	....	....

USHL All-Rookie Team (2006)

SINDEL, Jakub (SHIHN-dehl, YA-kuhb) **CHI.**

Center. Shoots right. 6', 172 lbs. Born, Jihlava, Czech., January 24, 1986.
(Chicago's 5th choice, 54th overall, in 2004 Entry Draft).

			Regular Season					Playoffs				
Season	Club	League	GP	G	A	Pts	PIM	GP	G	A	Pts	PIM
99-2000	Slavia U17	CzR-U17	32	10	6	16	6	....	....	....	....	....
2000-01	Slavia U17	CzR-U17	26	12	15	27	2	6	1	0	1	0
2001-02	Slavia U17	CzR-U17	34	32	14	46	34	2	0	1	1	2
	HC Slavia Praha Jr.	CzRep-Jr.	14	7	4	11	10	....	....	....	....	....
2002-03	HC Slavia Praha Jr.	CzRep-Jr.	35	12	11	23	39	2	0	1	1	0
2003-04	HC Sparta Praha	CzRep	34	5	1	6	14	13	1	1	2	2
	Sparta Jr.	CzRep-Jr.	13	8	14	22	4	....	....	....	....	....
	HC Dukla Jihlava	CzRep-2	1	0	0	0	0	....	....	....	....	....
2004-05	Sparta Jr.	CzRep-Jr.	9	5	16	21	16	....	....	....	....	....
	HC Sparta Praha	CzRep	10	0	2	2	0	....	....	....	....	....
	Trebic	CzRep-2	5	0	0	0	0	....	....	....	....	....
	Brandon	WHL	35	16	13	29	12	24	7	4	11	22
2005-06	HC Sparta Praha	CzRep	12	1	1	2	6	....	....	....	....	....
	Plzen	CzRep	31	11	8	19	18	....	....	....	....	....
2006-07	Plzen	CzRep	50	16	10	26	30	....	....	....	....	....
	BK Mlada Boleslav	CzRep-2	4	1	0	1	4	8	5	5	10	20
2007-08	Plzen	CzRep	45	19	4	23	16	4	0	2	2	4
	BK Mlada Boleslav	CzRep-2	....	....	....	....	....	11	5	2	7	8

SIPOTZ, Brian (SIHP-awtz, BRIGH-uhn)

Defense. Shoots right. 6'7", 235 lbs. Born, South Bend, IN, September 16, 1981.
(Atlanta's 3rd choice, 100th overall, in 2001 Entry Draft).

			Regular Season					Playoffs				
Season	Club	League	GP	G	A	Pts	PIM	GP	G	A	Pts	PIM
99-2000	Culver Academy	High-IN	45	14	22	36	56	....	....	....	....	....
2000-01	Miami U.	CCHA	32	0	1	1	48	....	....	....	....	....
2001-02	Miami U.	CCHA	25	0	1	1	28	....	....	....	....	....
2002-03	Miami U.	CCHA	26	0	0	0	24	....	....	....	....	....
2003-04	Miami U.	CCHA	36	0	3	3	39	....	....	....	....	....
2004-05	Chicago Wolves	AHL	75	2	6	8	31	18	1	2	3	6
	Gwinnett	ECHL	2	0	0	0	0	....	....	....	....	....
2005-06	Chicago Wolves	AHL	57	2	12	14	41	....	....	....	....	....
2006-07	Chicago Wolves	AHL	73	2	10	12	36	8	0	0	0	2
2007-08	Chicago Wolves	AHL	54	1	4	5	22	21	0	4	4	14

SKACHKOV, Evgeny (skatch-KAWF, yehv-GEH-nee) ST.L.

Left wing. Shoots right. 6', 187 lbs. Born, Penza, USSR, July 14, 1984.
(St. Louis' 10th choice, 221st overall, in 2003 Entry Draft).

			Regular Season					Playoffs				
Season	Club	League	GP	G	A	Pts	PIM	GP	G	A	Pts	PIM
2000-01	Dizelist Penza	Russia-2	9	0	0	0	0	....	....	....	....	....
2001-02	Kapitan Stupino	Russia-3		STATISTICS NOT AVAILABLE								
2002-03	Stupino	Russia-3		STATISTICS NOT AVAILABLE								
	Kapitan Stupino	EEHL	34	4	4	8	2	....	....	....	....	....
2003-04	CSKA Moscow 2	Russia-3		DID NOT PLAY – INJURED								
	CSKA Moscow	Russia	1	0	0	0	2	....	....	....	....	....
2004-05	Spartak Moscow	Russia	9	0	2	2	0	....	....	....	....	....
2005-06	Spartak Moscow 2	Russia-3	55	25	31	56	98	....	....	....	....	....
	Spartak Moscow	Russia	2	0	0	0	6	....	....	....	....	....
2006-07	Chelyabinsk	Russia	52	13	9	22	52	....	....	....	....	....
2007-08	Chelyabinsk	Russia	53	14	13	27	58	3	1	0	1	6

SKINNER, Brett (SKIH-nuhr, BREHT) NYI

Defense. Shoots left. 6'1", 195 lbs. Born, Brandon, Man., June 28, 1983.
(Vancouver's 3rd choice, 68th overall, in 2002 Entry Draft).

			Regular Season					Playoffs				
Season	Club	League	GP	G	A	Pts	PIM	GP	G	A	Pts	PIM
1998-99	Brandon Kings	MMBHL	29	3	18	21	20	....	....	....	....	....
99-2000	Brandon Kings	MMMHL	40	8	27	35	48	....	....	....	....	....
2000-01	Trail Smoke Eaters	BCHL	59	11	24	35	43	....	....	....	....	....
2001-02	Des Moines	USHL	44	9	38	47	25	3	0	1	1	0
2002-03	U. of Denver	WCHA	37	4	13	17	27	....	....	....	....	....
2003-04	U. of Denver	WCHA	44	7	23	30	32	....	....	....	....	....
2004-05	U. of Denver	WCHA	43	4	36	40	30	....	....	....	....	....
2005-06	Manitoba Moose	AHL	65	4	21	25	33	13	0	4	4	19
2006-07	Portland Pirates	AHL	41	6	12	18	24	....	....	....	....	....
	Augusta Lynx	ECHL	5	1	3	4	8	....	....	....	....	....
	Omaha	AHL	21	0	6	6	2	5	0	3	3	2
2007-08	Providence Bruins	AHL	68	7	40	47	47	10	0	1	1	0

USHL First All-Star Team (2002) • USHL Defenseman of the Year (2002) • WCHA First All-Star Team (2005) • NCAA West Second All-American Team (2005) • NCAA Championship All-Tournament Team (2005)

Traded to **Anaheim** by **Vancouver** with NY Islanders' 2nd round choice (previously acquired, Anaheim selected Bryce Swan) in 2006 Entry Draft for Keith Carney and Juha Alen, March 9, 2006. Traded to **Boston** by **Anaheim** with Nathan Saunders for Mark Mowers, September 24, 2007. Signed as a free agent by **NY Islanders**, July 3, 2008.

SKOKAN, David (SKOH-kahn, DAY-vihd) NYR

Center. Shoots left. 6', 191 lbs. Born, Poprad, Czech., December 6, 1988.
(NY Rangers' 5th choice, 193rd overall, in 2007 Entry Draft).

			Regular Season					Playoffs				
Season	Club	League	GP	G	A	Pts	PIM	GP	G	A	Pts	PIM
2003-04	Poprad U18	Svk-U18	38	17	28	45	110	6	1	5	6	37
	HK SKP Poprad Jr.	Slovak-Jr.	7	2	0	2	7	....	....	....	....	....
2004-05	Poprad U18	Svk-U18	4	4	6	10	37	....	....	....	....	....
	HK SKP Poprad Jr.	Slovak-Jr.	24	5	19	24	52	....	....	....	....	....
	HK SKP Poprad	Slovakia	8	0	0	0	6	2	0	0	0	25
2005-06	Rimouski Oceanic	QMJHL	53	6	15	21	143	....	....	....	....	....
2006-07	Rimouski Oceanic	QMJHL	52	14	21	35	62	....	....	....	....	....
2007-08	Rimouski Oceanic	QMJHL	53	19	21	40	92	8	0	5	5	10

SLOAN, Tyler (SLOHN, TIGH-luhr) WSH.

Defense. Shoots left. 6'4", 190 lbs. Born, Calgary, Alta., March 15, 1981.

			Regular Season					Playoffs				
Season	Club	League	GP	G	A	Pts	PIM	GP	G	A	Pts	PIM
1997-98	Calgary Buffaloes	AMHL	36	2	11	13	24	10	0	4	4	2
1998-99	Calgary Royals	AJHL		STATISTICS NOT AVAILABLE								
99-2000	Calgary Royals	AJHL	45	5	26	31	80	....	....	....	....	....
2000-01	Kamloops Blazers	WHL	70	5	28	33	146	4	0	0	0	4
2001-02	Kamloops Blazers	WHL	70	3	29	32	89	4	0	0	0	15
	Syracuse Crunch	AHL	2	0	0	0	5	....	....	....	....	....
2002-03	Syracuse Crunch	AHL	39	2	1	3	46	....	....	....	....	....
	Dayton Bombers	ECHL	14	1	2	3	22	....	....	....	....	....
2003-04	Syracuse Crunch	AHL	69	2	4	6	50	7	0	0	0	8
2004-05	Syracuse Crunch	AHL	14	0	2	2	18	....	....	....	....	....
	Dayton Bombers	ECHL	43	6	11	17	84	....	....	....	....	....
2005-06	Las Vegas	ECHL	48	4	16	20	71	13	0	4	4	27
	Manitoba Moose	AHL	4	0	0	0	0	....	....	....	....	....
	Hershey Bears	AHL	....	....	....	....	....	2	0	1	1	2
2006-07	Hershey Bears	AHL	68	2	9	11	104	17	0	7	7	30
2007-08	Hershey Bears	AHL	56	1	7	8	90	5	0	0	0	8

Signed as a free agent by **Columbus**, September 24, 2000. Signed as a free agent by **Hershey** (AHL), August 15, 2007. Signed as a free agent by **Washington**, July 2, 2008.

SMITH, Austin (SMIHTH, AUZ-tihn) DAL.

Right wing. Shoots right. 5'11", 160 lbs. Born, Dallas, TX, November 7, 1988.
(Dallas' 4th choice, 128th overall, in 2007 Entry Draft).

			Regular Season					Playoffs				
Season	Club	League	GP	G	A	Pts	PIM	GP	G	A	Pts	PIM
2003-04	Dallas Jesuit Prep	High-TX		STATISTICS NOT AVAILABLE								
2004-05	Dallas Jesuit Prep	High-TX		STATISTICS NOT AVAILABLE								
	Alliance Bulldogs	NTHL	53	29	46	75	24	....	....	....	....	....
2005-06	The Gunnery	High-CT	31	23	20	43	22	....	....	....	....	....
2006-07	The Gunnery	High-CT	30	25	38	63	36	....	....	....	....	....
2007-08	Penticton Vees	BCHL	60	32	35	67	42	15	11	11	22	12

• Signed Letter of Intent to attend **Colgate University** (ECAC) in fall of 2008.

SMITH, Ben (SMIHTH, BEHN) CHI.

Right wing. Shoots right. 5'11", 195 lbs. Born, Winston-Salem, NC, July 11, 1988.
(Chicago's 5th choice, 169th overall, in 2008 Entry Draft).

			Regular Season					Playoffs				
Season	Club	League	GP	G	A	Pts	PIM	GP	G	A	Pts	PIM
2006-07	Boston College	H-East	42	10	8	18	10	....	....	....	....	....
2007-08	Boston College	H-East	44	25	25	50	12	....	....	....	....	....

SMITH, Brendan (SMIHTH, BREHN-duhn) DET.

Defense. Shoots left. 6'1", 170 lbs. Born, Toronto, Ont., February 8, 1989.
(Detroit's 1st choice, 27th overall, in 2007 Entry Draft).

			Regular Season					Playoffs				
Season	Club	League	GP	G	A	Pts	PIM	GP	G	A	Pts	PIM
2004-05	Toronto Marlboros	GTHL	66	22	63	85	120	....	....	....	....	....
2005-06	St. Michael's	OPJHL	39	5	21	26	55	17	1	5	6	44
2006-07	St. Michael's	OPJHL	39	12	24	36	90	16	6	14	20	30
2007-08	U. of Wisconsin	WCHA	22	2	10	12	26	....	....	....	....	....

SMITH, Derek (SMIHTH, dair-IHK) OTT.

Defense. Shoots left. 6'1", 197 lbs. Born, Belleville, Ont., October 13, 1984.

			Regular Season					Playoffs				
Season	Club	League	GP	G	A	Pts	PIM	GP	G	A	Pts	PIM
2002-03	Wellington Dukes	OPJHL	21	6	10	16	26	....	....	....	....	....
2003-04	Wellington Dukes	OPJHL	44	8	26	34	34	....	....	....	....	....
2004-05	Lake Superior	CCHA	38	1	4	5	28	....	....	....	....	....
2005-06	Lake Superior	CCHA	36	2	8	10	18	....	....	....	....	....
2006-07	Lake Superior	CCHA	43	10	20	30	10	....	....	....	....	....
2007-08	Binghamton	AHL	52	2	11	13	18	....	....	....	....	....
	Elmira Jackals	ECHL	1	0	1	1	0	....	....	....	....	....

Signed as a free agent by **Ottawa**, April 12, 2007.

SMITH, Trevor (SMIHTH, TREH-vuhr) NYI

Left wing. Shoots left. 6'1", 195 lbs. Born, North Vancouver, B.C., February 8, 1985.

			Regular Season					Playoffs				
Season	Club	League	GP	G	A	Pts	PIM	GP	G	A	Pts	PIM
2003-04	Quesnel	BCHL	44	28	19	47	50	....	....	....	....	....
2004-05	Omaha Lancers	USHL	60	29	39	68	78	5	3	1	4	2
2005-06	New Hampshire	H-East	39	10	10	20	34	....	....	....	....	....
2006-07	New Hampshire	H-East	39	21	22	43	39	....	....	....	....	....
	Bridgeport	AHL	8	1	2	3	2	....	....	....	....	....
2007-08	Bridgeport	AHL	53	20	17	37	16	....	....	....	....	....
	Utah Grizzlies	ECHL	22	11	14	25	28	....	....	....	....	....

NCAA East Second All-American Team (2007)

Signed as a free agent by **NY Islanders**, April 2, 2007.

SMITH, Zack (SMIHTH, ZAK) OTT.

Center. Shoots left. 6'2", 196 lbs. Born, Medicine Hat, Alta., April 5, 1988.
(Ottawa's 3rd choice, 79th overall, in 2008 Entry Draft).

			Regular Season					Playoffs				
Season	Club	League	GP	G	A	Pts	PIM	GP	G	A	Pts	PIM
2004-05	Swift Current	SMHL	43	15	27	42	83	....	....	....	....	....
	Swift Current	WHL	14	1	1	2	0	....	....	....	....	....
2005-06	Swift Current	WHL	64	2	5	7	78	3	0	0	0	9
2006-07	Swift Current	WHL	71	16	15	31	130	6	0	2	2	11
2007-08	Swift Current	WHL	72	22	47	69	136	12	5	5	10	29
	Manitoba Moose	AHL	....	....	....	....	....	6	0	1	1	0

SMOLENAK, Radek (SMOH-lehn-ahk, RA-dehk) T.B.

Left wing. Shoots left. 6'3", 180 lbs. Born, Prague, Czech., December 3, 1986.
(Tampa Bay's 2nd choice, 73rd overall, in 2005 Entry Draft).

			Regular Season					Playoffs				
Season	Club	League	GP	G	A	Pts	PIM	GP	G	A	Pts	PIM
2001-02	HC Kladno U17	CzR-U17	47	29	20	49	38	....	....	....	....	....
2002-03	HC Kladno U17	CzR-U17	41	39	27	66	50	9	7	3	10	18
	HC Kladno Jr.	CzRep-Jr.	4	2	0	2	6	....	....	....	....	....
2003-04	HC Kladno Jr.	CzRep-Jr.	54	27	25	52	51	7	3	4	7	0
2004-05	Kingston	OHL	67	32	28	60	58	....	....	....	....	....
2005-06	Kingston	OHL	65	42	42	84	109	6	1	3	4	20
2006-07	Springfield Falcons	AHL	20	0	1	1	8	....	....	....	....	....
	Johnstown Chiefs	ECHL	43	15	20	35	35	1	0	0	0	0
2007-08	Norfolk Admirals	AHL	56	15	11	26	108	....	....	....	....	....
	Mississippi	ECHL	19	7	8	15	14	....	....	....	....	....

SMOLYANINOV, Vitali (smoh-LEE-ya-NEE-nohv, vih-TAL-ee) T.B.

Left wing. Shoots left. 6'3", 205 lbs. Born, Nizhnekamsk, USSR, August 5, 1983.
(Tampa Bay's 12th choice, 261st overall, in 2001 Entry Draft).

			Regular Season					Playoffs				
Season	Club	League	GP	G	A	Pts	PIM	GP	G	A	Pts	PIM
1998-99	Nizhnekamsk 2	Russia-4	12	1	0	1	0	....	....	....	....	....
99-2000	Nizhnekamsk 2	Russia-3	54	7	7	14	28	....	....	....	....	....
2000-01	Nizhnekamsk 2	Russia-3		STATISTICS NOT AVAILABLE								
2001-02	Nizhnekamsk	Russia	1	0	0	0	0	....	....	....	....	....
2002-03	HK Voronezh	Russia-2	14	1	1	2	12	....	....	....	....	....
2003-04	Karaganda	Kazakh.	9	2	3	5	0	....	....	....	....	....
	Karaganda	Russia-2	19	0	1	1	32	....	....	....	....	....
2004-05	Karaganda	Kazakh.	7	5	3	8	2	....	....	....	....	....
	Karaganda	Russia-2	20	1	5	6	10	....	....	....	....	....
2005-06	Irtysh Pavlodar	Kazakh.	14	8	6	14	12	....	....	....	....	....
	Irtysh Pavlodar	Russia-3		STATISTICS NOT AVAILABLE								
2006-07	Barys Astana	Russia-3	42	8	19	27	36	....	....	....	....	....
	Barys Astana	Kazakh.	22	10	6	16	52	....	....	....	....	....
2007-08	Barys Astana	Russia-2	51	18	21	39	54	7	1	1	2	2

SNEEP, Carl (SNEEP, KAHRL) PIT.

Defense. Shoots right. 6'4", 210 lbs. Born, St. Louis Park, MN, November 5, 1987.
(Pittsburgh's 2nd choice, 32nd overall, in 2006 Entry Draft).

			Regular Season					Playoffs				
Season	Club	League	GP	G	A	Pts	PIM	GP	G	A	Pts	PIM
2004-05	Brainerd	High-MN	26	20	21	41	25	....	....	....	....	....
2005-06	Brainerd	High-MN	26	14	23	37	34	....	....	....	....	....
	Lincoln Stars	USHL	13	1	3	4	9	9	0	1	1	6
2006-07	Boston College	H-East	38	1	9	10	8	....	....	....	....	....
2007-08	Boston College	H-East	44	3	12	15	15	....	....	....	....	....

SNELLMAN , Niko (SNEHL-mahn, NEE-KOH) NSH.

Left wing. Shoots left. 6'3", 208 lbs. Born, Tampere, Finland, March 12, 1988.
(Nashville's 2nd choice, 105th overall, in 2006 Entry Draft).

			Regular Season					Playoffs				
Season	Club	League	GP	G	A	Pts	PIM	GP	G	A	Pts	PIM
2004-05	Ilves Tampere U18	Fin-U18	22	5	1	6	44	5	0	0	0	2
2005-06	Ilves Tampere U18	Fin-U18	6	3	8	11	28	6	2	5	7	64
	Ilves Tampere Jr.	Fin-Jr.	23	4	4	8	74	3	0	0	0	4
2006-07	Regina Pats	WHL	32	5	5	10	65	....	....	....	....	....
2007-08	Ilves Tampere Jr.	Fin-Jr.	31	5	11	16	137	1	0	0	0	0
	Ilves Tampere	Finland	....	....	....	....	....	1	0	1	1	0

SNETSINGER, Brad (SNEHT-sihng-uhr, BRAD) N.J.

Left wing. Shoots left. 6'1", 185 lbs. Born, Ajax, Ont., April 8, 1987.

			Regular Season					Playoffs				
Season	Club	League	GP	G	A	Pts	PIM	GP	G	A	Pts	PIM
2003-04	Milton IceHawks	OPJHL	40	10	9	19	30	....	....	....	....	....
	Mississauga	OHL	8	2	1	3	2	1	0	0	0	0
2004-05	Mississauga	OHL	54	8	5	13	30	5	0	0	0	0
2005-06	Windsor Spitfires	OHL	60	29	15	44	29	7	2	3	5	8
2006-07	Windsor Spitfires	OHL	63	29	33	62	86	....	....	....	....	....
2007-08	Windsor Spitfires	OHL	68	37	52	89	45	2	0	0	0	5

Signed as a free agent by **New Jersey**, December 20, 2007.

SODERBERG, Carl (SOH-dehr-buhrg, KAHRL) BOS.

Center. Shoots left. 6'3", 198 lbs. Born, Malmo, Sweden, October 12, 1985.
(St. Louis' 2nd choice, 49th overall, in 2004 Entry Draft).

			Regular Season					Playoffs				
Season	Club	League	GP	G	A	Pts	PIM	GP	G	A	Pts	PIM
2000-01	Skane	Exhib.	8	1	2	3	2	....	....	....	....	....
	Malmo U18	Swe-U18	3	1	1	2	0	....	....	....	....	....
2001-02	Malmo U18	Swe-U18	13	9	20	29	18	....	....	....	....	....
	Malmo Jr.	Swe-Jr.	4	0	2	2	2	7	0	2	2	4
2002-03	Malmo U18	Swe-U18	4	6	3	9	25	....	....	....	....	....
	Malmo Jr.	Swe-Jr.	28	17	18	35	22	6	2	4	6	8
2003-04	Malmo	Sweden	24	1	1	2	8	....	....	....	....	....
	Malmo U18	Swe-U18	27	23	25	48	30	6	1	2	3	10
	Malmo	Sweden-Q	8	1	1	2	4	....	....	....	....	....
2004-05	Morrums GoIS IK	Sweden-2	14	5	6	11	8	....	....	....	....	....
	Malmo Jr.	Swe-Jr.	12	13	6	19	43	3	2	1	3	12
	Malmo	Sweden	38	0	5	5	8	....	....	....	....	....
	Malmo	Sweden-Q	7	0	0	0	0	....	....	....	....	....
2005-06	Malmo	Sweden-2	49	20	27	47	47	....	....	....	....	....
2006-07	Malmo	Sweden	31	12	18	30	14	....	....	....	....	....
2007-08	Malmo	Sweden-2	42	22	36	58	18	....	....	....	....	....

Traded to **Boston** by **St. Louis** for Hannu Toivonen, July 23, 2007.

SOIN, Sergei (SOY-ihn, SAIR-gay) NSH.

Center/Left wing. Shoots left. 6', 185 lbs. Born, Moscow, USSR, March 31, 1982.
(Colorado's 3rd choice, 50th overall, in 2000 Entry Draft).

			Regular Season					Playoffs				
Season	Club	League	GP	G	A	Pts	PIM	GP	G	A	Pts	PIM
1997-98	Krylja Sovetov 2	Russia-3	2	0	0	0	0	....	....	....	....	....
1998-99	Krylja Sovetov	Russia	34	1	4	5	12	....	....	....	....	....
99-2000	Krylja Sovetov 2	Russia-3	8	2	3	5	12	....	....	....	....	....
	Krylja Sovetov	Russia-2	32	8	8	16	28	14	0	2	2	6
2000-01	Krylja Sovetov 2	Russia-3	8	2	3	5	12	....	....	....	....	....
	Krylja Sovetov	Russia-2	19	6	3	9	8	11	2	2	4	2
2001-02	Krylja Sovetov 2	Russia-3	5	2	6	8	20	....	....	....	....	....
	Krylja Sovetov	Russia	41	5	7	12	8	....	....	....	....	....
2002-03	Krylja Sovetov	Russia	49	8	6	14	40	....	....	....	....	....
2003-04	CSKA Moscow	Russia	49	1	6	7	32	....	....	....	....	....
2004-05	CSKA Moscow	Russia	19	3	3	6	10	....	....	....	....	....
2005-06	Cherepovets	Russia	48	5	12	17	36	4	1	1	2	0
2006-07	Cherepovets	Russia	52	12	12	24	78	5	2	1	3	0
2007-08	Cherepovets	Russia	52	9	11	20	22	7	1	1	2	4

Traded to **Nashville** by **Colorado** for Tomas Slovak, June 21, 2003.

SOINTU, Matias (SOYN-too, mat-TEE-uhs) T.B.

Right wing. Shoots left. 5'10", 154 lbs. Born, Tampere, Finland, February 10, 1990.
(Tampa Bay's 7th choice, 182nd overall, in 2008 Entry Draft).

			Regular Season					Playoffs				
Season	Club	League	GP	G	A	Pts	PIM	GP	G	A	Pts	PIM
2006-07	Ilves Tampere U18	Fin-U18	34	22	23	45	32	3	0	0	0	0
2007-08	Ilves Tampere U18	Fin-U18	10	8	6	14	6	....	....	....	....	....
	Ilves Tampere Jr.	Fin-Jr.	41	21	19	40	38	5	3	1	4	4

SOLAREV, Ilja (SOH-luh-rehv, IHL-yuh) T.B.

Left wing. Shoots left. 6'3", 176 lbs. Born, Perm, USSR, August 2, 1982.
(Tampa Bay's 13th choice, 281st overall, in 2001 Entry Draft).

			Regular Season					Playoffs				
Season	Club	League	GP	G	A	Pts	PIM	GP	G	A	Pts	PIM
1997-98	Perm 2	Russia-3	4	1	0	1	0	....	....	....	....	....
1998-99	Perm 2	Russia-4	20	2	6	8	10	....	....	....	....	....
99-2000	Perm 2	Russia-3	35	3	2	5	24	....	....	....	....	....
2000-01	Perm 2	Russia-3	STATISTICS NOT AVAILABLE									
	Perm	Russia	5	0	1	1	0	....	....	....	....	....
2001-02	Leninogorsk	Russia-2	31	3	5	8	20	....	....	....	....	....
	HK Tambov	Russia-3	2	0	0	0	0	....	....	....	....	....
2002-03	Perm 2	Russia-3	STATISTICS NOT AVAILABLE									
	HK Brest	Belarus	STATISTICS NOT AVAILABLE									
2003-04	Motor Barnaul	Russia-2	34	6	6	12	20	1	0	0	0	0
2004-05	Energiya Kemerovo	Russia-2	36	3	2	5	28	....	....	....	....	....
2005-06	HK Lipetsk	Russia-2	49	4	6	10	30	3	0	0	0	0
2006-07	Satpayev	Russia-2	44	17	16	33	24	....	....	....	....	....
	Satpayev	Kazakh.	21	7	2	9	12	....	....	....	....	....
2007-08	Satpayev	Russia-2	29	10	10	20	24	....	....	....	....	....
	Barys Astana	Russia-2	22	4	9	13	26	7	2	1	3	6

SONNE, Brett (SOHNE, BREHT) ST.L.

Center/Left wing. Shoots left. 5'11", 200 lbs. Born, Chilliwack, B.C., March 16, 1989.
(St. Louis' 6th choice, 85th overall, in 2007 Entry Draft).

			Regular Season					Playoffs				
Season	Club	League	GP	G	A	Pts	PIM	GP	G	A	Pts	PIM
2004-05	Port Coquitlam	PIJHL	47	21	34	55	125	....	....	....	....	....
	Calgary Hitmen	WHL	6	0	0	0	2	....	....	....	....	....
2005-06	Calgary Hitmen	WHL	64	12	9	21	38	13	1	2	3	8
2006-07	Calgary Hitmen	WHL	71	21	9	30	65	18	5	1	6	22
2007-08	Calgary Hitmen	WHL	29	8	12	20	12	16	3	1	4	14

SOPANEN, Vili (SOH-puh-nehn, VIHL-ee) N.J.

Right wing. Shoots right. 6'4", 210 lbs. Born, Valkeala, Finland, October 21, 1987.
(New Jersey's 5th choice, 177th overall, in 2007 Entry Draft).

			Regular Season					Playoffs				
Season	Club	League	GP	G	A	Pts	PIM	GP	G	A	Pts	PIM
2003-04	K-Reipas U18	Fin-U18	20	1	2	3	14	....	....	....	....	....
2004-05	K-Reipas U18	Fin-U18	25	11	15	26	4	3	0	2	2	22
2005-06	Pelicans Lahti Jr.	Fin-Jr.	38	15	17	32	22	....	....	....	....	....
	Pelicans Lahti	Finland	3	0	0	0	0	....	....	....	....	....
2006-07	Pelicans Lahti Jr.	Fin-Jr.	33	18	21	39	40	15	5	13	18	18
	Suomi U20	Finland-2	6	1	1	2	4	....	....	....	....	....
	Pelicans Lahti	Finland	7	1	0	1	0	....	....	....	....	....
2007-08	Pelicans Lahti Jr.	Fin-Jr.	2	1	1	2	0	....	....	....	....	....
	Pelicans Lahti	Finland	54	15	15	30	8	6	0	4	4	2

SORYAL, Justin (SOHR-yahl, JUHS-tihn) NYR

Left wing. Shoots left. 6'2", 210 lbs. Born, Newmarket, Ont., June 29, 2007.

			Regular Season					Playoffs				
Season	Club	League	GP	G	A	Pts	PIM	GP	G	A	Pts	PIM
2003-04	Aurora Tigers	OPJHL	3	0	0	0	2	....	....	....	....	....
2004-05	Peterborough	OHL	29	0	1	1	54	14	0	1	1	21
2005-06	Peterborough	OHL	53	3	3	6	136	17	0	1	1	16
2006-07	Peterborough	OHL	60	26	27	53	125	....	....	....	....	....
2007-08	Peterborough	OHL	59	17	22	39	140	5	2	0	2	8

Signed as a free agent by **NY Rangers**, March 12, 2008.

SOUTHORN, Jordon (SUH-thohrn, JOHR-dahn) BUF.

Defense. Shoots left. 6'2", 185 lbs. Born, Montreal, Que., May 15, 1990.
(Buffalo's 6th choice, 104th overall, in 2008 Entry Draft).

			Regular Season					Playoffs				
Season	Club	League	GP	G	A	Pts	PIM	GP	G	A	Pts	PIM
2005-06	Lac St-Louis Tigres	Minor-QC	26	7	15	22	90	....	....	....	....	....
2006-07	PEI Rocket	QMJHL	58	5	5	10	76	7	0	0	0	2
2007-08	PEI Rocket	QMJHL	69	12	19	31	70	4	0	1	1	4

SPALING, Nick (SPAHL-ihng, NIHK) NSH.

Center. Shoots left. 6'1", 185 lbs. Born, Palmerston, Ont., September 19, 1988.
(Nashville's 3rd choice, 58th overall, in 2007 Entry Draft).

			Regular Season					Playoffs				
Season	Club	League	GP	G	A	Pts	PIM	GP	G	A	Pts	PIM
2004-05	Listowel Cyclones	OJHL-B	61	25	27	52	58	....	....	....	....	....
2005-06	Kitchener Rangers	OHL	62	10	15	25	22	5	0	3	3	0
2006-07	Kitchener Rangers	OHL	61	23	36	59	41	9	2	3	5	4
2007-08	Kitchener Rangers	OHL	56	38	34	72	18	20	14	16	30	9

SPANG, Dan (SPANG, DAN) CGY.

Defense. Shoots left. 6', 205 lbs. Born, Winchester, MA, August 18, 1983.
(San Jose's 2nd choice, 52nd overall, in 2002 Entry Draft).

			Regular Season					Playoffs				
Season	Club	League	GP	G	A	Pts	PIM	GP	G	A	Pts	PIM
2000-01	Winchester High	High-MA	24	8	37	45	14	....	....	....	....	....
2001-02	Winchester High	High-MA	6	9	8	17	14	....	....	....	....	....
2002-03	Boston University	H-East	27	3	6	9	14	....	....	....	....	....
2003-04	Boston University	H-East	38	5	9	14	12	....	....	....	....	....
2004-05	Boston University	H-East	41	3	13	16	22	....	....	....	....	....
2005-06	Boston University	H-East	40	9	22	31	14	....	....	....	....	....
	Cleveland Barons	AHL	8	0	0	0	8	....	....	....	....	....
2006-07	Worcester Sharks	AHL	48	4	21	25	18	....	....	....	....	....
2007-08	Worcester Sharks	AHL	77	8	23	31	41	....	....	....	....	....

Hockey East First All-Star Team (2006) • NCAA East First All-American Team (2006)

• Missed majority of 2001-02 season recovering from head injuries suffered in automobile accident, October, 2001. Signed as a free agent by **Quad City** (AHL), July 22, 2008.

SPINA, David (SPEE-nuh, DAY-vihd) PHX.

Left wing. Shoots left. 5'10", 185 lbs. Born, Mesa, AZ, June 5, 1983.

			Regular Season					Playoffs				
Season	Club	League	GP	G	A	Pts	PIM	GP	G	A	Pts	PIM
99-2000	Texas Tornado	NAHL	54	15	26	41	31	....	....	....	....	....
2000-01	USNTDP	USHL	23	3	7	10	28	....	....	....	....	....
2001-02	Boston College	H-East	36	13	13	26	39	....	....	....	....	....
2002-03	Boston College	H-East	37	17	20	37	34	....	....	....	....	....
2003-04	Boston College	H-East	25	6	6	12	20	....	....	....	....	....
2004-05	Boston College	H-East	40	13	15	28	42	....	....	....	....	....
	Utah Grizzlies	AHL	9	0	0	0	2	....	....	....	....	....
2005-06	Springfield Falcons	AHL	54	11	13	24	36	....	....	....	....	....
	South Carolina	ECHL	11	7	0	7	6	....	....	....	....	....
2006-07	Springfield Falcons	AHL	73	15	20	35	80	....	....	....	....	....
	Johnstown Chiefs	ECHL	6	4	2	6	4	....	....	....	....	....
2007-08	San Antonio	AHL	76	21	29	50	35	7	3	0	3	2

Signed as a free agent by **Phoenix**, July 2, 2008.

SPRUNGER, Julien (SRUHN-guhr, JEW-lee-ehn) MIN.

Right wing. Shoots right. 6'4", 197 lbs. Born, Fribourg, Switz., January 4, 1986.
(Minnesota's 7th choice, 117th overall, in 2004 Entry Draft).

			Regular Season					Playoffs				
Season	Club	League	GP	G	A	Pts	PIM	GP	G	A	Pts	PIM
2002-03	Fribourg Jr.	Swiss-Jr.	24	21	19	40	32	....	....	....	....	....
	Fribourg	Swiss	2	0	0	0	0	....	....	....	....	....
	HC Dudingen	Swiss-3	9	7	1	8	....	2	1	1	2	....
2003-04	Fribourg	Swiss	42	2	3	5	14	4	0	0	0	4
2004-05	Fribourg Jr.	Swiss-Jr.	4	3	4	7	4	....	....	....	....	....
	Chaux-de-Fonds	Swiss-2	1	0	0	0	0	....	....	....	....	....
	Fribourg	Swiss	41	9	7	16	35	11	2	1	3	14
2005-06	Fribourg Jr.	Swiss-Jr.	2	2	1	3	6	....	....	....	....	....
	Fribourg	Swiss	38	19	14	33	36	10	5	2	7	25
	Fribourg	Swiss-Q	....	....	....	....	....	5	2	1	3	4
2006-07	Fribourg	Swiss	34	10	10	20	46	....	....	....	....	....
2007-08	Fribourg	Swiss	49	27	20	47	34	5	2	1	3	20

SPURGEON, Jared (SPUHR-juhn, JAIR-uhd) NYI

Defense. Shoots right. 5'8", 175 lbs. Born, Edmonton, Alta., November 29, 1989.
(NY Islanders' 12th choice, 156th overall, in 2008 Entry Draft).

			Regular Season					Playoffs				
Season	Club	League	GP	G	A	Pts	PIM	GP	G	A	Pts	PIM
2004-05	K of C Pats	AMHL	26	9	21	30	16	....	....	....	....	....
2005-06	Spokane Chiefs	WHL	46	3	9	12	28	....	....	....	....	....
2006-07	Spokane Chiefs	WHL	38	4	15	19	16	....	....	....	....	....
2007-08	Spokane Chiefs	WHL	69	12	31	43	19	21	0	5	5	16

SPURGEON, Tyler (SPUHR-juhn, TIGH-luhr) **EDM.**

Center. Shoots left. 5'11", 188 lbs. Born, Edmonton, Alta., April 10, 1986.
(Edmonton's 9th choice, 242nd overall, in 2004 Entry Draft).

Season	Club	League	Regular Season GP	G	A	Pts	PIM	Playoffs GP	G	A	Pts	PIM
2001-02	Edmonton MLAC	AMHL	35	39	36	75	12	....	....	....	....	....
	Kelowna Rockets	WHL	2	0	1	1	0	....	....	....	....	....
2002-03	Kelowna Rockets	WHL	50	7	6	13	21	19	2	5	7	6
2003-04	Kelowna Rockets	WHL	49	8	16	24	24	17	4	5	9	9
2004-05	Kelowna Rockets	WHL	72	21	41	62	32	24	11	6	17	12
2005-06	Kelowna Rockets	WHL	39	7	17	24	22	12	0	3	3	14
2006-07	Wilkes-Barre	AHL	34	5	10	15	10	6	1	0	1	4
	Stockton Thunder	ECHL	39	12	17	29	26	....	....	....	....	....
2007-08	Springfield Falcons	AHL	12	1	7	8	2	....	....	....	....	....

STAAL, Jared (STAWL, JAIR-uhd) **PHX.**

Right wing. Shoots right. 6'3", 198 lbs. Born, Thunder Bay, Ont., August 21, 1990.
(Phoenix's 3rd choice, 49th overall, in 2008 Entry Draft).

Season	Club	League	Regular Season GP	G	A	Pts	PIM	Playoffs GP	G	A	Pts	PIM
2005-06	Thunder Bay Kings	Minor-ON	64	24	25	49	72	....	....	....	....	....
2006-07	Sudbury Wolves	OHL	63	2	1	3	18	21	1	0	1	2
2007-08	Sudbury Wolves	OHL	60	21	28	49	44	....	....	....	....	....

STAHLBERG, Viktor (STAHL-buhrg, VIHK-tohr) **TOR.**

Left wing. Shoots left. 6'3", 196 lbs. Born, Stockholm, Sweden, January 17, 1986.
(Toronto's 5th choice, 161st overall, in 2006 Entry Draft).

Season	Club	League	Regular Season GP	G	A	Pts	PIM	Playoffs GP	G	A	Pts	PIM
2003-04	Molndal U18	Swe-U18	13	14	13	27	....	....	....	....	....	....
	Molndal Jr.	Swe-Jr.	18	25	10	35	....	....	....	....	....	....
	IF Molndal Hockey	Sweden-4	....	11	9	20	....	....	....	....	....	....
2004-05	Molndal Jr.	Swe-Jr.	11	16	7	23	....	....	....	....	....	....
	IF Molndal Hockey	Sweden-3	29	6	9	15	54	....	....	....	....	....
2005-06	Frolunda Jr.	Swe-Jr.	41	27	26	53	89	7	6	5	11	6
2006-07	U. of Vermont	H-East	39	7	8	15	53	....	....	....	....	....
2007-08	U. of Vermont	H-East	39	10	13	23	34	....	....	....	....	....

STAMKOS, Steven (STAM-kohs, STEE-vehn) **T.B.**

Center. Shoots right. 6', 176 lbs. Born, Markham, Ont., February 7, 1990.
(Tampa Bay's 1st choice, 1st overall, in 2008 Entry Draft).

Season	Club	League	Regular Season GP	G	A	Pts	PIM	Playoffs GP	G	A	Pts	PIM
2005-06	Markham Waxers	Minor-ON	66	105	92	197	87	....	....	....	....	....
2006-07	Sarnia Sting	OHL	63	42	50	92	56	4	3	3	6	0
2007-08	Sarnia Sting	OHL	61	58	47	105	88	9	11	0	11	20

OHL Second All-Star Team (2008) • Canadian Major Junior First All-Star Team (2008)

STAMLER, Bretton (STAM-lehr, BREH-tuhn)

Defense. Shoots right. 6'1", 201 lbs. Born, Calgary, Alta., March 10, 1987.
(Detroit's 9th choice, 214th overall, in 2005 Entry Draft).

Season	Club	League	Regular Season GP	G	A	Pts	PIM	Playoffs GP	G	A	Pts	PIM
2002-03	Sherwood Park	AMHL	34	3	8	11	22	....	....	....	....	....
2003-04	Seattle	WHL	61	0	9	9	27	....	....	....	....	....
2004-05	Seattle	WHL	72	4	9	13	106	1	0	0	0	0
2005-06	Seattle	WHL	56	5	10	15	102	7	0	4	4	8
2006-07	Seattle	WHL	72	8	24	32	135	11	0	1	1	14
2007-08	Edmonton	WHL	43	1	16	17	82	....	....	....	....	....
	Swift Current	WHL	28	3	6	9	56	12	0	4	4	4

STAPLETON, Tim (STAY-puhl-TOHN, TIHM) **TOR.**

Center. Shoots right. 5'9", 160 lbs. Born, La Grange, IL, July 9, 1982.

Season	Club	League	Regular Season GP	G	A	Pts	PIM	Playoffs GP	G	A	Pts	PIM
2000-01	Green Bay	USHL	52	7	15	22	8	4	1	2	3	4
2001-02	Green Bay	USHL	61	24	36	60	10	7	4	7	11	0
2002-03	U. Minn-Duluth	WCHA	42	14	28	42	6	....	....	....	....	....
2003-04	U. Minn-Duluth	WCHA	43	16	25	41	18	....	....	....	....	....
2004-05	U. Minn-Duluth	WCHA	38	19	20	39	6	....	....	....	....	....
2005-06	U. Minn-Duluth	WCHA	39	14	16	30	4	....	....	....	....	....
	Portland Pirates	AHL	9	0	5	5	4	4	0	0	0	2
2006-07	Jokerit Helsinki	Finland	56	19	29	48	24	10	6	4	10	8
2007-08	Jokerit Helsinki	Finland	55	29	33	62	36	14	*9	8	17	8

Signed as a free agent by **Toronto**, June 6, 2008.

STARKOV, Kirill (stahr-KAWF, kih-RIHL) **CBJ**

Center. Shoots left. 6', 199 lbs. Born, Sverdlovsk, USSR, March 31, 1987.
(Columbus' 7th choice, 189th overall, in 2005 Entry Draft).

Season	Club	League	Regular Season GP	G	A	Pts	PIM	Playoffs GP	G	A	Pts	PIM
2002-03	Esbjerg Oilers	Denmark	28	2	4	6	6	14	0	0	0	0
2003-04	V.Frolunda U18	Swe-U18	9	6	6	12	2	7	2	3	5	2
	V.Frolunda Jr.	Swe-Jr.	25	3	10	13	4	5	2	0	2	0
2004-05	Frolunda U18	Swe-U18	1	0	0	0	4	3	2	1	3	0
	Frolunda Jr.	Swe-Jr.	34	18	12	30	6	6	2	2	4	2
2005-06	Frolunda Jr.	Swe-Jr.	19	8	16	24	16	6	3	4	7	2
	Frolunda	Sweden	34	1	2	3	4	....	....	....	....	....
2006-07	Red Deer Rebels	WHL	72	34	37	71	41	7	2	4	6	4
2007-08	Syracuse Crunch	AHL	20	4	4	8	4	....	....	....	....	....
	Elmira Jackals	ECHL	8	0	0	0	0	....	....	....	....	....
	Youngstown	CHL	25	10	12	22	0	....	....	....	....	....

STASYUK, Denis (stah-S'YUHK, DEH-nihs) **FLA.**

Center. Shoots left. 6'1", 165 lbs. Born, Novokuznetsk, USSR, September 2, 1985.
(Florida's 9th choice, 171st overall, in 2003 Entry Draft).

Season	Club	League	Regular Season GP	G	A	Pts	PIM	Playoffs GP	G	A	Pts	PIM
2002-03	Novokuznetsk 2	Russia-3		STATISTICS NOT AVAILABLE								
	Novokuznetsk	Russia	11	1	0	1	0	....	....	....	....	....
2003-04	Novokuznetsk	Russia	5	0	0	0	0	....	....	....	....	....
	Novokuznetsk 2	Russia-3		STATISTICS NOT AVAILABLE								
2004-05	Amur Khabarovsk	Russia-2	44	11	10	21	12	10	1	2	3	6
2005-06	Novokuznetsk	Russia	41	7	2	9	18	3	0	0	0	0
2006-07	Novokuznetsk	Russia	26	0	1	1	16	3	0	0	0	0
2007-08	Novokuznetsk	Russia	33	4	2	6	14	....	....	....	....	....

STAUBITZ, Brad (STAW-bihtz, BRAD) **S.J.**

Right wing. Shoots right. 6'1", 215 lbs. Born, Bright's Grove, Ont., July 28, 1984.

Season	Club	League	Regular Season GP	G	A	Pts	PIM	Playoffs GP	G	A	Pts	PIM
2001-02	Sault Ste. Marie	OHL	45	0	3	3	46	3	0	0	0	2
2002-03	Sault Ste. Marie	OHL	55	2	6	8	116	4	0	0	0	7
2003-04	Sault Ste. Marie	OHL	66	6	18	24	140	....	....	....	....	....
2004-05	Sault Ste. Marie	OHL	40	2	11	13	101	....	....	....	....	....
	Ottawa 67's	OHL	30	5	8	13	80	21	4	16	20	70
2005-06	Cleveland Barons	AHL	71	0	6	6	245	....	....	....	....	....
2006-07	Worcester Sharks	AHL	51	1	4	5	137	5	0	0	0	13
2007-08	Worcester Sharks	AHL	73	6	14	20	195	....	....	....	....	....

Signed as a free agent by **San Jose**, September 19, 2005.

STEFANOVICH, Mikhail (steh-fan-AWV-ihch, mih-kigh-EHL) **TOR.**

Right wing. Shoots right. 6'2", 202 lbs. Born, Minsk, USSR, November 27, 1989.
(Toronto's 3rd choice, 98th overall, in 2008 Entry Draft).

Season	Club	League	Regular Season GP	G	A	Pts	PIM	Playoffs GP	G	A	Pts	PIM
2004-05	Dynamo Minsk 2	Belarus-2	19	3	7	10	8	....	....	....	....	....
	HK Gomel 2	Belarus-2	14	3	0	3	6	....	....	....	....	....
2005-06	HK Gomel 2	Belarus-2	37	18	12	30	64	....	....	....	....	....
2006-07	HK Gomel 2	Belarus-2	3	3	1	4	4	....	....	....	....	....
	HK Gomel	Belarus	41	16	9	25	43	5	1	0	1	2
2007-08	Quebec Remparts	QMJHL	62	32	34	66	32	11	4	4	8	10
	HK Gomel	Belarus	1	0	0	0	0	....	....	....	....	....

STEFISHEN, Taylor (STEH-fih-shehn, TAY-luhr) **NSH.**

Left wing. Shoots right. 5'11", 170 lbs. Born, North Vancouver, B.C., August 15, 1990.
(Nashville's 4th choice, 136th overall, in 2008 Entry Draft).

Season	Club	League	Regular Season GP	G	A	Pts	PIM	Playoffs GP	G	A	Pts	PIM
2006-07	Langley Chiefs	BCHL	59	25	31	56	73	7	5	1	6	8
2007-08	Langley Chiefs	BCHL	57	33	48	81	71	12	6	10	16	19

• Signed Letter of Intent to attend **Ohio State University** (CCHA) in fall of 2008.

STEJSKAL, Joe (STAY-kuhl, JOH) **MTL.**

Defense. Shoots right. 6'3", 196 lbs. Born, Grand Rapids, MN, April 30, 1988.
(Montreal's 6th choice, 133rd overall, in 2007 Entry Draft).

Season	Club	League	Regular Season GP	G	A	Pts	PIM	Playoffs GP	G	A	Pts	PIM
2003-04	Grand Rapids	High-MN	....	1	7	8	....	....	....	....	....	....
2004-05	Grand Rapids	High-MN	....	2	8	10	....	....	....	....	....	....
2005-06	Grand Rapids	High-MN	....	7	18	25	....	....	....	....	....	....
2006-07	Grand Rapids	High-MN	24	11	17	28	42	....	....	....	....	....
2007-08	Dartmouth	ECAC	32	1	4	5	46	....	....	....	....	....

STEPAN, Derek (STEH-pan, DAIR-ihk) **NYR**

Center. Shoots right. 6', 175 lbs. Born, Hastings, MN, June 18, 1990.
(NY Rangers' 2nd choice, 51st overall, in 2008 Entry Draft).

Season	Club	League	Regular Season GP	G	A	Pts	PIM	Playoffs GP	G	A	Pts	PIM
2006-07	Shat.-St. Mary's	High-MN	63	38	32	70	22	....	....	....	....	....
2007-08	Shat.-St. Mary's	High-MN	60	44	67	111	22	....	....	....	....	....

• Signed Letter of Intent to attend **University of Wisconsin** (WCHA) in fall of 2008.

STEPHENSON, Logan (STEE-vehn-suhn, LOH-guhn) **PHX.**

Defense. Shoots left. 6'3", 197 lbs. Born, Saskatoon, Sask., February 19, 1986.
(Phoenix's 2nd choice, 35th overall, in 2004 Entry Draft).

Season	Club	League	Regular Season GP	G	A	Pts	PIM	Playoffs GP	G	A	Pts	PIM
2001-02	Notre Dame	SMHL	37	4	2	6	74	....	....	....	....	....
	Tri-City Americans	WHL	....	....	....	....	....	3	0	0	0	0
2002-03	Tri-City Americans	WHL	50	0	6	6	121	....	....	....	....	....
2003-04	Tri-City Americans	WHL	69	3	8	11	112	11	1	1	2	10
2004-05	Tri-City Americans	WHL	59	6	9	15	86	5	0	0	0	2
2005-06	Tri-City Americans	WHL	71	10	43	53	162	5	1	0	1	18
2006-07	San Antonio	AHL	73	3	5	8	90	....	....	....	....	....
2007-08	San Antonio	AHL	74	1	7	8	94	7	0	1	1	6

WHL West Second All-Star Team (2006)

STEWART, Chris (STEW-ahrt, KRIHS) **COL.**

Right wing. Shoots right. 6'2", 228 lbs. Born, Toronto, Ont., October 30, 1987.
(Colorado's 1st choice, 18th overall, in 2006 Entry Draft).

Season	Club	League	Regular Season GP	G	A	Pts	PIM	Playoffs GP	G	A	Pts	PIM
2004-05	Kingston	OHL	64	18	12	30	45	....	....	....	....	....
2005-06	Kingston	OHL	62	37	50	87	118	6	2	0	2	13
2006-07	Kingston	OHL	61	36	46	82	108	5	4	2	6	6
	Albany River Rats	AHL	5	1	2	3	2	1	0	0	0	0
2007-08	Lake Erie Monsters	AHL	77	25	19	44	93	....	....	....	....	....

STOA, Ryan (STOH-ah, RIGH-uhn) **COL.**

Center. Shoots left. 6'3", 200 lbs. Born, Bloomington, MN, April 13, 1987.
(Colorado's 1st choice, 34th overall, in 2005 Entry Draft).

Season	Club	League	Regular Season GP	G	A	Pts	PIM	Playoffs GP	G	A	Pts	PIM
2003-04	USNTDP	U-17	18	9	8	17		....	....	....	....	....
	USNTDP	NAHL	42	10	12	22	26	7	7	1	8	2
2004-05	USNTDP	U-18	23	4	11	15	16	....	....	....	....	....
	USNTDP	NAHL	15	10	13	23	20	....	....	....	....	....
2005-06	U. of Minnesota	WCHA	41	10	15	25	43	....	....	....	....	....
2006-07	U. of Minnesota	WCHA	41	12	12	24	44	....	....	....	....	....
2007-08	U. of Minnesota	WCHA	2	1	1	2	2	....	....	....	....	....

• Missed remainder of 2007-08 season recovering from knee injury suffered in game vs. University of Michigan, October 13, 2007.

STOESZ, Myles (STOHZ, MIGH-uhlz) ATL.

Right wing. Shoots right. 6'2", 215 lbs. Born, Steinbach, Man., February 15, 1987.
(Atlanta's 8th choice, 207th overall, in 2005 Entry Draft).

			Regular Season					Playoffs				
Season	Club	League	GP	G	A	Pts	PIM	GP	G	A	Pts	PIM
2003-04	Spokane Chiefs	WHL	43	1	1	2	133	0	0	0	0	0
2004-05	Spokane Chiefs	WHL	67	1	8	9	238	....	....	....	....	....
2005-06	Spokane Chiefs	WHL	56	0	2	2	260	....	....	....	....	....
2006-07	Chilliwack Bruins	WHL	40	3	2	5	135	....	....	....	....	....
	Regina Pats	WHL	29	4	2	6	89	9	0	0	0	21
2007-08	Gwinnett	ECHL	64	4	2	6	*291	1	0	0	0	0

STOKES, Ryan (STOHKS, RIGH-uhn) BOS.

Defense. Shoots left. 6'4", 220 lbs. Born, Sarnia, Ont., June 23, 1983.

			Regular Season					Playoffs				
Season	Club	League	GP	G	A	Pts	PIM	GP	G	A	Pts	PIM
2001-02	Barrie Colts	OHL	53	0	5	5	31	20	0	0	0	16
2002-03	Mississauga	OHL	59	2	7	9	139	5	0	1	1	22
2003-04	Mississauga	OHL	66	4	20	24	179	24	2	9	11	74
2004-05	Houston Aeros	AHL	7	0	0	0	7	....	....	....	....	....
	Pensacola	ECHL	59	1	15	16	119	....	....	....	....	....
2005-06	Houston Aeros	AHL	75	2	3	5	164	6	0	1	1	10
2006-07	Houston Aeros	AHL	72	2	8	10	158	....	....	....	....	....
2007-08	Rockford IceHogs	AHL	55	4	6	10	93	12	0	0	0	14

Signed as a free agent by **Minnesota**, May 25, 2004. Signed as a free agent by **Boston**, July 22, 2008.

STOLYAROV, Gennady (stohl-yah-RAWF, gehn-AH-dee) DET.

Right wing. Shoots left. 6'4", 187 lbs. Born, Moscow, USSR, August 20, 1986.
(Detroit's 7th choice, 257th overall, in 2004 Entry Draft).

			Regular Season					Playoffs				
Season	Club	League	GP	G	A	Pts	PIM	GP	G	A	Pts	PIM
2003-04	Dyn'o Moscow 2	Russia-3	STATISTICS NOT AVAILABLE									
	THK Tver	Russia-2	24	3	1	4	4	....	....	....	....	....
2004-05	Vityaz Chekhov	Russia-2	25	0	1	1	2	....	....	....	....	....
2005-06	Kapitan Stupino	Russia-2	17	3	5	8	20	5	1	2	3	36
	Dynamo Moscow	Russia	12	0	0	0	4	3	0	1	1	0
2006-07	Dynamo Moscow	Russia	37	6	3	9	39	2	0	0	0	0
2007-08	Dynamo Moscow	Russia	37	3	3	6	22	8	1	0	1	2

STONE, Michael (STOHN, MIGH-kuhl) PHX.

Defense. Shoots right. 6'3", 200 lbs. Born, Winnipeg, Man., June 7, 1990.
(Phoenix's 4th choice, 69th overall, in 2008 Entry Draft).

			Regular Season					Playoffs				
Season	Club	League	GP	G	A	Pts	PIM	GP	G	A	Pts	PIM
2005-06	Wpg. Thrashers	MMHL	40	14	18	32	14	....	....	....	....	....
2006-07	Calgary Hitmen	WHL	55	2	18	20	32	17	0	3	3	14
2007-08	Calgary Hitmen	WHL	71	10	25	35	28	14	3	4	7	10

STONER, Clayton (STOH-nuhr, KLAY-tuhn) MIN.

Defense. Shoots left. 6'4", 212 lbs. Born, Port McNeill, B.C., February 19, 1985.
(Minnesota's 4th choice, 79th overall, in 2004 Entry Draft).

			Regular Season					Playoffs				
Season	Club	League	GP	G	A	Pts	PIM	GP	G	A	Pts	PIM
2000-01	Campbell River	VIJHL	47	4	16	20	57	....	....	....	....	....
2001-02	Campbell River	VIJHL	42	12	35	47	199	....	....	....	....	....
2002-03	Tri-City Americans	WHL	58	4	12	16	85	....	....	....	....	....
2003-04	Tri-City Americans	WHL	71	7	24	31	109	11	1	1	2	8
2004-05	Tri-City Americans	WHL	60	12	34	46	81	4	0	3	3	2
2005-06	Houston Aeros	AHL	73	6	18	24	92	3	1	1	2	7
2006-07	Houston Aeros	AHL	65	1	6	7	104	....	....	....	....	....
2007-08	Houston Aeros	AHL	56	3	12	15	78	....	....	....	....	....

WHL West Second All-Star Team (2005)

STRACHAN, Tyson (STRAWN, TIGH-suhn)

Defense. Shoots right. 6'3", 205 lbs. Born, Melfort, Sask., October 30, 1984.
(Carolina's 6th choice, 137th overall, in 2003 Entry Draft).

			Regular Season					Playoffs				
Season	Club	League	GP	G	A	Pts	PIM	GP	G	A	Pts	PIM
2001-02	Tisdale Trojans	SMHL	42	5	18	23	70	....	....	....	....	....
	Melville	SJHL	2	0	0	0	0	....	....	....	....	....
2002-03	Vernon Vipers	BCHL	56	6	22	28	99	....	....	....	....	....
2003-04	Ohio State	CCHA	30	2	5	7	8	....	....	....	....	....
2004-05	Ohio State	CCHA	31	1	4	5	32	....	....	....	....	....
2005-06	Ohio State	CCHA	23	3	2	5	37	....	....	....	....	....
2006-07	Ohio State	CCHA	35	7	11	18	55	....	....	....	....	....
	Albany River Rats	AHL	1	0	0	0	0	....	....	....	....	....
2007-08	Peoria Rivermen	AHL	34	1	2	3	61	....	....	....	....	....
	Las Vegas	ECHL	25	2	7	9	68	16	0	4	4	12

STRAIT, Brian (STRAYT, BRIGH-uhn) PIT.

Defense. Shoots left. 6'1", 200 lbs. Born, Boston, MA, January 4, 1988.
(Pittsburgh's 3rd choice, 65th overall, in 2006 Entry Draft).

			Regular Season					Playoffs				
Season	Club	League	GP	G	A	Pts	PIM	GP	G	A	Pts	PIM
2003-04	NMH School	High-MA	30	5	15	20	....	....	....	....	....	....
2004-05	USNTDP	U-17	18	1	5	6	8	....	....	....	....	....
	USNTDP	NAHL	42	4	8	12	42	10	0	2	2	2
2005-06	USNTDP	U-18	40	2	7	9	31	....	....	....	....	....
	USNTDP	NAHL	15	0	5	5	41	....	....	....	....	....
2006-07	Boston University	H-East	36	3	3	6	47	....	....	....	....	....
2007-08	Boston University	H-East	37	0	10	10	20	....	....	....	....	....

SUBBAN, P.K. (soo-BAHN, PEE-KAY) MTL.

Defense. Shoots right. 5'11", 206 lbs. Born, Toronto, Ont., May 13, 1989.
(Montreal's 3rd choice, 43rd overall, in 2007 Entry Draft).

			Regular Season					Playoffs				
Season	Club	League	GP	G	A	Pts	PIM	GP	G	A	Pts	PIM
2004-05	Markham	GTHL	67	15	28	43	179	....	....	....	....	....
2005-06	Belleville Bulls	OHL	52	5	7	12	70	3	0	0	0	2
2006-07	Belleville Bulls	OHL	68	15	41	56	89	15	5	8	13	26
2007-08	Belleville Bulls	OHL	58	8	38	46	100	21	8	15	23	28

SUBBOTIN, Dmitri (soo-BOH-tihn, dih-MEE-tree) CBJ

Left wing. Shoots left. 6'1", 183 lbs. Born, Tomsk, USSR, October 20, 1977.
(NY Rangers' 3rd choice, 76th overall, in 1996 Entry Draft).

			Regular Season					Playoffs				
Season	Club	League	GP	G	A	Pts	PIM	GP	G	A	Pts	PIM
1993-94	Yekaterinburg	CIS	12	0	3	3	4	....	....	....	....	....
1994-95	Yekaterinburg	CIS	52	9	6	15	75	2	0	0	0	2
1995-96	CSKA Moscow	CIS	41	6	5	11	62	3	0	0	0	0
1996-97	CSKA Moscow	Russia-2	8	1	0	1	8	....	....	....	....	....
	HK CSKA Moscow	Russia	17	5	3	8	22	2	0	0	0	2
1997-98	HK CSKA Moscow	Russia	16	1	1	2	47	....	....	....	....	....
1998-99	Dynamo Moscow	Russia	1	0	1	1	0	....	....	....	....	....
	Lada Togliatti	Russia	31	8	3	11	47	7	0	0	0	4
99-2000	Lada Togliatti	Russia	27	10	4	14	26	7	1	1	2	4
	Lada Togliatti 2	Russia-3	2	0	1	1	0	....	....	....	....	....
2000-01	Dynamo Moscow	Russia	39	11	15	26	48	....	....	....	....	....
2001-02	Magnitogorsk	Russia	38	8	3	11	18	9	0	2	2	10
2002-03	Cherepovets	Russia	10	0	1	1	31	....	....	....	....	....
	CSKA Moscow	Russia	20	3	9	12	6	....	....	....	....	....
2003-04	CSKA Moscow	Russia	20	0	3	3	14	....	....	....	....	....
	Avangard Omsk	Russia	26	6	6	12	36	11	2	3	5	6
2004-05	Avangard Omsk	Russia	55	5	6	11	66	7	0	0	0	10
2005-06	Ufa	Russia	5	0	1	1	8	....	....	....	....	....
	MVD	Russia	27	6	8	14	52	4	1	3	4	4
2006-07	MVD	Russia	51	16	20	36	96	2	0	1	1	6
2007-08	Vityaz Chekhov	Russia	44	12	13	25	22	....	....	....	....	....

Claimed by **Columbus** from **NY Rangers** in Expansion Draft, June 23, 2000.

SUCHARSKI, Nick (soo-CHAR-skee, NIHK) CBJ

Left wing. Shoots left. 6'1", 165 lbs. Born, Toronto, Ont., November 15, 1987.
(Columbus' 6th choice, 136th overall, in 2006 Entry Draft).

			Regular Season					Playoffs				
Season	Club	League	GP	G	A	Pts	PIM	GP	G	A	Pts	PIM
2003-04	Wexford Raiders	OPJHL	43	15	29	44	48	....	....	....	....	....
2004-05	Wexford Raiders	OPJHL	46	26	27	53	78	13	6	10	16	20
2005-06	Michigan State	CCHA	36	2	5	7	18	....	....	....	....	....
2006-07	Michigan State	CCHA	41	9	15	24	32	....	....	....	....	....
2007-08	Michigan State	CCHA	41	9	17	26	32	....	....	....	....	....

SULLIVAN, Sean (SUHL-ih-vuhn, SHAWN) PHX.

Defense. Shoots left. 6', 188 lbs. Born, Boston, MA, March 29, 1984.
(Phoenix's 7th choice, 272nd overall, in 2003 Entry Draft).

			Regular Season					Playoffs				
Season	Club	League	GP	G	A	Pts	PIM	GP	G	A	Pts	PIM
2001-02	St. Sebastian's	High-MA	31	3	11	14	4	....	....	....	....	....
2002-03	St. Sebastian's	High-MA	41	9	30	39	59	....	....	....	....	....
2003-04	Boston University	H-East	36	2	5	7	14	....	....	....	....	....
2004-05	Boston University	H-East	41	1	3	4	10	....	....	....	....	....
2005-06	Boston University	H-East	40	3	14	17	32	....	....	....	....	....
2006-07	Boston University	H-East	38	3	12	15	12	....	....	....	....	....
	San Antonio	AHL	7	0	0	0	0	....	....	....	....	....
2007-08	San Antonio	AHL	34	0	8	8	13	1	0	0	0	4
	Arizona Sundogs	CHL	22	9	16	25	19	....	....	....	....	....

NCAA East Second All-American Team (2007)

SULZER, Alexander (ZUHLT-suhr, al-EHX-AN-duhr) NSH.

Defense. Shoots left. 6'1", 207 lbs. Born, Kaufbeuren, West Germany, May 30, 1984.
(Nashville's 7th choice, 92nd overall, in 2003 Entry Draft).

			Regular Season					Playoffs				
Season	Club	League	GP	G	A	Pts	PIM	GP	G	A	Pts	PIM
2000-01	ESV Kaufbeuren	German-3	38	3	6	9	20	....	....	....	....	....
	Kaufbeuren Jr.	Ger-Jr.	1	0	2	2	2	....	....	....	....	....
2001-02	ESV Kaufbeuren	German-3	19	1	9	10	14	....	....	....	....	....
	Kaufbeuren Jr.	Ger-Jr.	1	0	0	0	4	....	....	....	....	....
2002-03	ESV Kaufbeuren	German-2	26	5	3	8	38	1	0	1	1	4
	Hamburg Freezers	Germany	18	0	1	1	18	5	0	0	0	12
2003-04	Dusseldorf	Germany	46	4	1	5	56	4	0	0	0	8
2004-05	Dusseldorf	Germany	42	5	6	11	68	....	....	....	....	....
	EV Duisburg	German-2	....	....	....	....	....	7	0	3	3	6
2005-06	Dusseldorf	Germany	48	3	15	18	82	13	3	6	9	22
	Germany	Olympics	5	0	1	1	2	....	....	....	....	....
2006-07	Dusseldorf	Germany	44	4	11	15	82	9	2	1	3	20
2007-08	Milwaukee	AHL	61	7	25	32	47	....	....	....	....	....

SUMMERS, Chris (SUHM-mehrs, KRIHS) PHX.

Defense. Shoots left. 6'2", 180 lbs. Born, Ann Arbor, MI, February 5, 1988.
(Phoenix's 2nd choice, 29th overall, in 2006 Entry Draft).

			Regular Season					Playoffs				
Season	Club	League	GP	G	A	Pts	PIM	GP	G	A	Pts	PIM
2004-05	USNTDP	U-17	13	2	2	4	10	....	....	....	....	....
	USNTDP	NAHL	31	2	5	7	20	7	1	0	1	0
2005-06	USNTDP	U-18	42	4	9	13	67	....	....	....	....	....
	USNTDP	NAHL	17	2	2	4	20	....	....	....	....	....
2006-07	U. of Michigan	CCHA	41	6	8	14	58	....	....	....	....	....
2007-08	U. of Michigan	CCHA	41	2	11	13	65	....	....	....	....	....

SUTTER, Brandon (SUH-tuhr, BRAN-duhn) CAR.

Center/Right wing. Shoots right. 6'3", 183 lbs. Born, Huntington, NY, February 14, 1989.
(Carolina's 1st choice, 11th overall, in 2007 Entry Draft).

			Regular Season					Playoffs				
Season	Club	League	GP	G	A	Pts	PIM	GP	G	A	Pts	PIM
2003-04	Red Deer Chiefs	AMBHL	35	25	34	59	28	11	5	4	9	....
2004-05	Red Deer	AMHL	34	4	16	20	28	....	....	....	....	....
	Red Deer Rebels	WHL	7	0	2	2	8	7	1	4	5	2
2005-06	Red Deer Rebels	WHL	68	22	24	46	36	....	....	....	....	....
2006-07	Red Deer Rebels	WHL	71	20	37	57	54	7	0	3	3	14
2007-08	Red Deer Rebels	WHL	59	26	23	49	38	....	....	....	....	....
	Albany River Rats	AHL	7	1	1	2	2	7	0	2	2	4

SUTTER, Brett (SUH-tuhr, BREHT) CGY.

Center/Left wing. Shoots left. 6', 195 lbs. Born, Viking, Alta., June 2, 1987.
(Calgary's 7th choice, 179th overall, in 2005 Entry Draft).

			Regular Season					Playoffs				
Season	Club	League	GP	G	A	Pts	PIM	GP	G	A	Pts	PIM
2003-04	Kootenay Ice	WHL	44	5	7	12	26	4	0	0	0	4
2004-05	Kootenay Ice	WHL	70	8	11	19	70	16	1	2	3	16
2005-06	Kootenay Ice	WHL	16	8	7	15	21	....	....	....	....	....
	Red Deer Rebels	WHL	57	9	26	35	80	....	....	....	....	....
2006-07	Red Deer Rebels	WHL	67	28	29	57	77	7	3	4	7	11
2007-08	Quad City Flames	AHL	75	4	6	10	63	....	....	....	....	....

SWEATT, Bill (SWEHT, BIHL) CHI.

Left wing. Shoots left. 6', 180 lbs. Born, Elburn, IL, September 21, 1988.
(Chicago's 2nd choice, 38th overall, in 2007 Entry Draft).

			Regular Season					Playoffs				
Season	Club	League	GP	G	A	Pts	PIM	GP	G	A	Pts	PIM
2003-04	Team Illinois	MWEHL	74	33	37	70	....	....	....	....	....	....
2004-05	USNTDP	U-17	11	5	10	15	54	....	....	....	....	....
	USNTDP	NAHL	41	7	9	16	12	10	4	3	7	6
2005-06	USNTDP	U-18	42	19	11	30	24	....	....	....	....	....
	USNTDP	NAHL	17	10	15	25	4	....	....	....	....	....
2006-07	Colorado College	WCHA	30	9	17	26	18	....	....	....	....	....
2007-08	Colorado College	WCHA	37	10	17	27	38	....	....	....	....	....

SWITZER, Craig (SWIHT-zuhr, KRAYG)

Defense. Shoots left. 6'1", 195 lbs. Born, Calgary, Alta., October 16, 1984.
(Nashville's 11th choice, 275th overall, in 2004 Entry Draft).

			Regular Season					Playoffs				
Season	Club	League	GP	G	A	Pts	PIM	GP	G	A	Pts	PIM
2003-04	Salmon Arm	BCHL	57	14	40	54	117	14	0	12	12	16
2004-05	New Hampshire	H-East	41	1	13	14	22	....	....	....	....	....
2005-06	New Hampshire	H-East	40	2	14	16	54	....	....	....	....	....
2006-07	New Hampshire	H-East	39	3	14	17	50	....	....	....	....	....
2007-08	New Hampshire	H-East	38	6	14	20	53	....	....	....	....	....

Hockey East Second All-Star Team (2008)

SYVRET, Corey (SIHV-reht, KOHR-ee) FLA.

Defense. Shoots left. 6'2", 193 lbs. Born, Millgrove, Ont., February 12, 1989.
(Florida's 6th choice, 181st overall, in 2007 Entry Draft).

			Regular Season					Playoffs				
Season	Club	League	GP	G	A	Pts	PIM	GP	G	A	Pts	PIM
2004-05	Cambridge	OJHL-B	46	2	3	5	56	....	....	....	....	....
2005-06	London Knights	OHL	59	0	5	5	35	11	0	1	1	6
2006-07	London Knights	OHL	34	0	2	2	29	....	....	....	....	....
	Guelph Storm	OHL	27	5	9	14	32	4	0	0	0	2
2007-08	Guelph Storm	OHL	50	7	11	18	60	10	2	2	4	4

SZCZECHURA, Paul (sha-HUR-uh, PAWL) T.B.

Right wing. Shoots right. 5'11", 175 lbs. Born, Brantford, Ont., November 30, 1985.

			Regular Season					Playoffs				
Season	Club	League	GP	G	A	Pts	PIM	GP	G	A	Pts	PIM
2003-04	Western Mich.	CCHA	39	9	11	20	12	....	....	....	....	....
2004-05	Western Mich.	CCHA	37	6	23	29	22	....	....	....	....	....
2005-06	Western Mich.	CCHA	40	10	26	36	47	....	....	....	....	....
2006-07	Western Mich.	CCHA	37	19	26	45	26	....	....	....	....	....
	Iowa Stars	AHL	14	3	4	7	19	10	3	1	4	8
2007-08	Iowa Stars	AHL	29	2	3	5	15	....	....	....	....	....
	Norfolk Admirals	AHL	24	14	12	26	16	....	....	....	....	....

Signed as a free agent by **Tampa Bay**, April 24, 2008.

TALBOT, Julian (TAL-buht, JOO-lee-uhn) ST.L.

Center. Shoots left. 5'11", 181 lbs. Born, Wahnapitae, Ont., March 24, 1985.

			Regular Season					Playoffs				
Season	Club	League	GP	G	A	Pts	PIM	GP	G	A	Pts	PIM
2002-03	Ottawa 67's	OHL	62	10	18	28	13	23	1	7	8	2
2003-04	Ottawa 67's	OHL	68	18	31	49	56	7	1	4	5	6
2004-05	Ottawa 67's	OHL	68	25	41	66	50	21	8	12	20	31
2005-06	Ottawa 67's	OHL	65	30	47	77	70	3	1	2	3	8
2006-07	Providence Bruins	AHL	7	1	2	3	0	....	....	....	....	....
	Alaska Aces	ECHL	66	20	33	53	54	15	9	11	20	8
2007-08	Peoria Rivermen	AHL	78	24	26	50	53	....	....	....	....	....

Signed as a free agent by **St. Louis**, March 19, 2008.

TANGRADI, Eric (tan-GRAY-dee, AIR-ihk) ANA.

Center. Shoots left. 6'3", 214 lbs. Born, Philadelphia, PA, February 10, 1989.
(Anaheim's 2nd choice, 42nd overall, in 2007 Entry Draft).

			Regular Season					Playoffs				
Season	Club	League	GP	G	A	Pts	PIM	GP	G	A	Pts	PIM
2005-06	Wyoming Prep	High-PA	38	21	23	44	120	....	....	....	....	....
2006-07	Belleville Bulls	OHL	65	5	15	20	32	15	8	9	17	14
2007-08	Belleville Bulls	OHL	56	24	36	60	41	21	7	11	18	20

TANGUAY, Maxime (TAN-guay, mahx-EEM) CHI.

Center. Shoots left. 5'11", 175 lbs. Born, Ste-Justine, Que., November 16, 1988.
(Chicago's 4th choice, 69th overall, in 2007 Entry Draft).

			Regular Season					Playoffs				
Season	Club	League	GP	G	A	Pts	PIM	GP	G	A	Pts	PIM
2004-05	Levis	QAAA	36	19	29	48	50	....	....	....	....	....
	Chicoutimi	QMJHL	23	1	1	2	6	11	2	3	5	2
2005-06	Chicoutimi	QMJHL	36	2	9	11	28	....	....	....	....	....
	Rimouski Oceanic	QMJHL	29	3	13	16	22	....	....	....	....	....
2006-07	Rimouski Oceanic	QMJHL	54	24	36	60	32	....	....	....	....	....
2007-08	Rimouski Oceanic	QMJHL	26	7	9	16	15	....	....	....	....	....
	Victoriaville Tigres	QMJHL	27	9	12	21	32	3	0	0	0	2

TARKIR, Zach (TAHR-kihr, ZAK)

Defense. Shoots right. 6'1", 195 lbs. Born, Fresno, CA, June 28, 1984.
(New Jersey's 4th choice, 167th overall, in 2003 Entry Draft).

			Regular Season					Playoffs				
Season	Club	League	GP	G	A	Pts	PIM	GP	G	A	Pts	PIM
2001-02	Great Falls	AWHL	24	3	5	8	....	8	0	3	3	....
2002-03	Chilliwack Chiefs	BCHL	53	5	28	33	86	....	....	....	....	....
2003-04	Northern Mich.	CCHA	36	2	3	5	40	....	....	....	....	....
2004-05	Northern Mich.	CCHA	35	2	8	10	51	....	....	....	....	....
2005-06	Northern Mich.	CCHA	39	3	11	14	57	....	....	....	....	....
2006-07	Northern Mich.	CCHA	41	7	13	20	46	....	....	....	....	....
	Lowell Devils	AHL	2	0	0	0	0	....	....	....	....	....
2007-08	Lowell Devils	AHL	11	0	5	5	2	....	....	....	....	....
	Trenton Devils	ECHL	49	1	14	15	32	....	....	....	....	....

TASSONE, Matthew (tah-SOH-nee, MA-thew) DAL.

Center. Shoots left. 6', 200 lbs. Born, Edmonton, Alta., September 28, 1989.
(Dallas' 4th choice, 176th overall, in 2008 Entry Draft).

			Regular Season					Playoffs				
Season	Club	League	GP	G	A	Pts	PIM	GP	G	A	Pts	PIM
2005-06	Ft. Saskatchewan	AMHL	25	14	19	33	91	12	4	8	12	24
	Swift Current	WHL	4	0	1	1	0	....	....	....	....	....
2006-07	Swift Current	WHL	38	6	2	8	60	....	....	....	....	....
2007-08	Swift Current	WHL	60	19	17	36	111	12	3	5	8	12

TAYLOR, Justin (TAY-luhr, JUHS-tihn) WSH.

Center. Shoots left. 5'11", 184 lbs. Born, London, Ont., February 8, 1989.
(Washington's 8th choice, 180th overall, in 2007 Entry Draft).

			Regular Season					Playoffs				
Season	Club	League	GP	G	A	Pts	PIM	GP	G	A	Pts	PIM
2005-06	Wellington Dukes	OPJHL	48	18	13	31	12	12	0	3	3	8
2006-07	Wellington Dukes	OPJHL	37	20	32	52	36	....	....	....	....	....
	London Knights	OHL	31	6	12	18	18	16	4	6	10	17
2007-08	London Knights	OHL	68	26	29	55	79	5	0	0	0	5

TAYLOR, Max (TAY-luhr, MAX) TOR.

Center. Shoots left. 5'10", 185 lbs. Born, Ottawa, Ont., December 20, 1983.

			Regular Season					Playoffs				
Season	Club	League	GP	G	A	Pts	PIM	GP	G	A	Pts	PIM
2003-04	St. Lawrence	ECAC	35	1	6	7	10	....	....	....	....	....
2004-05	St. Lawrence	ECAC	37	11	15	26	18	....	....	....	....	....
2005-06	St. Lawrence	ECAC	34	4	11	15	24	....	....	....	....	....
2006-07	St. Lawrence	ECAC	39	13	18	31	32	....	....	....	....	....
2007-08	Texas Wildcatters	ECHL	59	25	20	45	51	6	5	6	11	10
	Toronto Marlies	AHL	13	2	3	5	28	....	....	....	....	....

Signed as a free agent by **Toronto** (AHL), March 11, 2008.

TEDENBY, Mattias (TEH-dehn-bew, muh-TIGH-uhs) N.J.

Left wing. Shoots left. 5'10", 175 lbs. Born, Vetlanda, Sweden, February 21, 1990.
(New Jersey's 1st choice, 24th overall, in 2008 Entry Draft).

			Regular Season					Playoffs				
Season	Club	League	GP	G	A	Pts	PIM	GP	G	A	Pts	PIM
2005-06	HV 71 U18	Swe-U18	13	8	7	15	24	5	1	0	1	10
2006-07	HV 71 U18	Swe-U18	2	4	0	4	2	5	7	2	9	14
	HV 71 Jr.	Swe-Jr.	27	10	10	20	43	4	3	1	4	2
2007-08	HV 71 U18	Swe-U18	1	1	0	1	0	....	....	....	....	....
	HV 71 Jr.	Swe-Jr.	25	14	16	30	14	2	0	0	0	0
	HV 71 Jonkoping	Sweden	23	3	3	6	6	5	0	0	0	0

TENKANEN, Valtteri (TEHN-kah-nehn, vahl-TEH-ree) L.A.

Center. Shoots left. 5'11", 183 lbs. Born, Jamsa, Finland, March 27, 1985.
(Los Angeles' 10th choice, 264th overall, in 2004 Entry Draft).

			Regular Season					Playoffs				
Season	Club	League	GP	G	A	Pts	PIM	GP	G	A	Pts	PIM
2001-02	JYP Jyvaskyla U18	Fin-U18	25	14	12	26	2	7	1	0	1	0
	JYP Jyvaskyla Jr.	Fin-Jr.	3	0	1	1	0	....	....	....	....	....
2002-03	JYP Jyvaskyla U18	Fin-U18	1	2	1	3	0	....	....	....	....	....
	JYP Jyvaskyla Jr.	Fin-Jr.	30	8	7	15	14	4	1	1	2	0
2003-04	Suomi U20	Finland-2	2	0	1	1	0	....	....	....	....	....
	JYP Jyvaskyla Jr.	Fin-Jr.	10	3	2	5	2	9	2	3	5	0
	JYP Jyvaskyla	Finland	25	1	3	4	2	2	0	0	0	0
2004-05	JYP Jyvaskyla Jr.	Fin-Jr.	12	1	5	6	14	6	2	1	3	25
	JYP Jyvaskyla	Finland	10	0	1	1	0	....	....	....	....	....
2005-06	JYP Jyvaskyla	Finland	35	0	6	6	4	3	0	1	1	0
2006-07	JYP Jyvaskyla	Finland	34	4	9	13	4	....	....	....	....	....
2007-08	JYP Jyvaskyla	Finland	13	0	0	0	2	....	....	....	....	....
	SaiPa	Finland	25	3	6	9	29	....	....	....	....	....
	SaPKo Savonlinna	Finland-2	2	1	3	4	0	....	....	....	....	....

TERESCHENKO, Alexei (teh-reh-SHEHN-koh, al-EHX-ay) DAL.

Center. Shoots left. 5'11", 176 lbs. Born, Mozhaisk, USSR, December 16, 1980.
(Dallas' 4th choice, 91st overall, in 2000 Entry Draft).

			Regular Season					Playoffs				
Season	Club	League	GP	G	A	Pts	PIM	GP	G	A	Pts	PIM
1996-97	Dyn'o Moscow 2	Russia-3	9	0	0	0	2	....	....	....	....	....
1997-98	Dynamo Moscow	Russia	26	6	7	13	30	....	....	....	....	....
1998-99	Dyn'o Moscow 2	Russia-3	28	4	17	21	20	....	....	....	....	....
	THK Tver	Russia-2	12	3	4	7	4	....	....	....	....	....
	Dynamo Moscow	Russia	1	0	1	1	0	2	0	0	0	0
99-2000	Dynamo Moscow	Russia	27	1	1	2	10	17	1	1	2	8
2000-01	Dynamo Moscow	Russia	39	3	2	5	18	....	....	....	....	....
2001-02	Yaroslavl 2	Russia-3	1	0	0	0	0	....	....	....	....	....
	Dynamo Moscow	Russia	40	3	6	9	20	3	0	0	0	0
2002-03	Dynamo Moscow	Russia	40	7	9	16	14	5	1	0	1	2
2003-04	Dynamo Moscow	Russia	47	8	12	20	26	3	0	0	0	4
2004-05	Dynamo Moscow	Russia	31	3	6	9	8	10	0	1	1	2
2005-06	Ak Bars Kazan	Russia	36	3	12	15	12	10	0	4	4	12
2006-07	Ak Bars Kazan	Russia	53	8	22	30	38	16	3	6	9	6
2007-08	Ufa	Russia	51	16	24	40	22	16	5	4	9	6

TERNAVSKY, Artem (tuhr-NAV-skee, AHR-tehm) WSH.

Defense. Shoots left. 6'2", 208 lbs. Born, Magnitogorsk, USSR, June 2, 1983.
(Washington's 4th choice, 160th overall, in 2001 Entry Draft).

			Regular Season					Playoffs				
Season	Club	League	GP	G	A	Pts	PIM	GP	G	A	Pts	PIM
99-2000	CSKA Moscow 2	Russia-3	2	0	1	1	0	....	....	....	....	....
	HK Moscow 2	Russia-3	25	0	4	4	42	....	....	....	....	....
2000-01	Sherbrooke	QMJHL	65	3	15	18	143	....	....	....	....	....
2001-02	Mostovik Kurgan	Russia-2	25	0	0	0	46	....	....	....	....	....
2002-03	Sibir Novosibirsk	Russia	42	1	1	2	20	....	....	....	....	....
2003-04	Ufa	Russia	12	0	0	0	4	....	....	....	....	....
	Magnitogorsk 2	Russia-3	7	1	0	1	0	....	....	....	....	....
2004-05	Nizhny Novgorod	Russia-2	16	0	1	1	18	....	....	....	....	....
	Motor Barnaul	Russia-2	8	0	1	1	14	....	....	....	....	....
2005-06	Karaganda	Kazakh.	17	1	1	2	12	....	....	....	....	....
	Karaganda	Russia-2	39	3	2	5	26	6	0	1	1	2
2006-07	Gazovik Tyumen	Russia-2	56	3	12	15	78	3	1	0	1	4
	Ust-Kamenogorsk	Kazakh.	14	3	2	5	12	....	....	....	....	....
2007-08	Novokuznetsk	Russia	56	6	7	13	46	....	....	....	....	....

TERRY, Chris (TAIR-ee, KRIHS) CAR.

Left wing. Shoots left. 5'10", 195 lbs. Born, Brampton, Ont., April 7, 1989.
(Carolina's 4th choice, 132nd overall, in 2007 Entry Draft).

			Regular Season					Playoffs				
Season	Club	League	GP	G	A	Pts	PIM	GP	G	A	Pts	PIM
2003-04	Markham	GTHL	66	39	50	89	....	....	....	....	....	....
2004-05	Markham	GTHL	60	42	53	95	113	9	0	9	9	14
2005-06	Plymouth Whalers	OHL	64	9	19	28	72	11	3	2	5	4
2006-07	Plymouth Whalers	OHL	68	22	44	66	98	20	8	10	18	21
2007-08	Plymouth Whalers	OHL	68	44	57	101	107	4	4	3	7	6
	Albany River Rats	AHL	1	0	0	0	0	....	....	....	....	....

TESSIER, Kelsey (TEHS-ee-ay, KEHL-see) COL.

Center. Shoots right. 5'9", 168 lbs. Born, Moncton, N. B., January 16, 1990.
(Colorado's 3rd choice, 110th overall, in 2008 Entry Draft).

			Regular Season					Playoffs				
Season	Club	League	GP	G	A	Pts	PIM	GP	G	A	Pts	PIM
2005-06	Colorado Outlaws	Minor-CO		STATISTICS NOT AVAILABLE								
2006-07	Quebec Remparts	QMJHL	63	23	27	50	40	5	1	5	6	0
2007-08	Quebec Remparts	QMJHL	68	36	45	81	73	11	8	7	15	10

TEUBERT, Colten (TEW-buhrt, KOHL-tuhn) L.A.

Defense. Shoots right. 6'4", 185 lbs. Born, Whiterock, B.C., March 8, 1990.
(Los Angeles' 2nd choice, 13th overall, in 2008 Entry Draft).

			Regular Season					Playoffs				
Season	Club	League	GP	G	A	Pts	PIM	GP	G	A	Pts	PIM
2005-06	South West Hawks	Minor-BC	29	8	12	20	122	....	....	....	....	....
	Regina Pats	WHL	14	0	2	2	16	6	0	1	1	4
2006-07	Regina Pats	WHL	63	3	8	11	91	10	0	1	1	13
2007-08	Regina Pats	WHL	66	7	16	23	135	6	1	4	5	6

THANG, Ryan (THAYNG, RIGH-uhn) NSH.

Left wing. Shoots right. 5'11", 190 lbs. Born, Chicago, IL, May 11, 1987.
(Nashville's 4th choice, 81st overall, in 2007 Entry Draft).

			Regular Season					Playoffs				
Season	Club	League	GP	G	A	Pts	PIM	GP	G	A	Pts	PIM
2004-05	Sioux Falls	USHL	58	9	22	31	45	....	....	....	....	....
2005-06	Sioux Falls	USHL	32	8	14	22	52	....	....	....	....	....
	Omaha Lancers	USHL	25	15	15	30	26	5	2	1	3	2
2006-07	U. of Notre Dame	CCHA	42	20	21	41	22	....	....	....	....	....
2007-08	U. of Notre Dame	CCHA	47	18	14	32	48	....	....	....	....	....

CCHA All-Rookie Team (2007)

THURESSON, Andreas (THUR-reh-suhn, an-DRAY-uhs) NSH.

Center. Shoots right. 6'1", 208 lbs. Born, Kristianstad, Sweden, November 18, 1987.
(Nashville's 7th choice, 144th overall, in 2007 Entry Draft).

			Regular Season					Playoffs				
Season	Club	League	GP	G	A	Pts	PIM	GP	G	A	Pts	PIM
2003-04	Malmo U18	Swe-U18	3	0	0	0	4	....	....	....	....	....
	Tyringe SoSS	Sweden-3	12	0	1	1	0	....	....	....	....	....
	Malmo Jr.	Swe-Jr.	19	2	2	4	16	8	0	0	0	6
2004-05	Malmo U18	Swe-U18	3	1	1	2	4	....	....	....	....	....
	Malmo Jr.	Swe-Jr.	30	4	4	8	28	3	2	1	3	2
2005-06	Malmo U18	Swe-U18	2	1	0	1	4	....	....	....	....	....
	Malmo Jr.	Swe-Jr.	38	15	18	33	71	....	....	....	....	....
	Malmo	Sweden-2	20	0	2	2	10	....	....	....	....	....
2006-07	Malmo	Sweden	48	10	5	15	26	....	....	....	....	....
	Malmo	Sweden-Q	10	2	2	4	2	....	....	....	....	....
2007-08	Milwaukee	AHL	77	11	7	18	37	6	0	0	0	4

TIKHONOV, Viktor (TIHK-uh-nawf, VIHK-tohr) PHX.

Center. Shoots right. 6'2", 187 lbs. Born, Riga, Latvia, May 12, 1988.
(Phoenix's 2nd choice, 28th overall, in 2008 Entry Draft).

			Regular Season					Playoffs				
Season	Club	League	GP	G	A	Pts	PIM	GP	G	A	Pts	PIM
2004-05	CSKA Moscow 2	Russia-3		STATISTICS NOT AVAILABLE								
2005-06	CSKA Moscow 2	Russia-3		STATISTICS NOT AVAILABLE								
	HK Dmitrov	Russia-2	36	6	8	14	10	....	....	....	....	....
2006-07	Cherepovets 2	Russia-3		STATISTICS NOT AVAILABLE								
	Cherepovets	Russia	4	0	0	0	0	....	....	....	....	....
2007-08	Cherepovets	Russia	43	7	5	12	43	8	0	1	1	4

TIMKIN, Alexei (TIHM-kihn, al-EHX-ay) DAL.

Right wing. Shoots left. 6'2", 194 lbs. Born, Kirov, USSR, April 21, 1979.
(Dallas' 6th choice, 160th overall, in 1997 Entry Draft).

			Regular Season					Playoffs				
Season	Club	League	GP	G	A	Pts	PIM	GP	G	A	Pts	PIM
1996-97	Yaroslavl 2	Russia-3	47	16	6	22	54	....	....	....	....	....
	Torpedo Yaroslavl	Russia	3	0	1	1	0	....	....	....	....	....
1997-98	Torpedo Yaroslavl	Russia	16	4	5	9	14	....	....	....	....	....
1998-99	Kirovo-Chepetsk	Russia-3	30	4	3	7	36	....	....	....	....	....
	St. Petersburg 2	Russia-4	1	0	0	0	2	....	....	....	....	....
99-2000	Kirovo-Chepetsk	Russia-3	49	29	13	42	26	....	....	....	....	....
2000-01	Kirovo-Chepetsk	Russia-3		STATISTICS NOT AVAILABLE								
2001-02	Kapitan Stupino	Russia-3	2	0	0	0	0	....	....	....	....	....
	Kirovo-Chepetsk	Russia-2	46	9	8	17	18	....	....	....	....	....
2002-03	Kirovo-Chepetsk	Russia-2	22	2	1	3	10	....	....	....	....	....
	HC Vitebsk	EEHL	12	4	2	6	2	....	....	....	....	....
2003-04	Kirovo-Chepetsk	Russia-2	3	0	1	1	4	....	....	....	....	....
	Karaganda	Russia-2	11	0	1	1	6	....	....	....	....	....
2004-05	Kirovo-Chepetsk	Russia-2	50	12	9	21	28	....	....	....	....	....
2005-06	Kirovo-Chepetsk	Russia-2	37	6	6	12	22	3	0	1	1	4
	HK Dmitrov	Russia-2	2	0	0	0	2	....	....	....	....	....
2006-07	Kirovo-Chepetsk	Russia-2	47	7	11	18	44	....	....	....	....	....
2007-08	Volzhsk	Russia-2	50	14	11	25	53	....	....	....	....	....

TKACHENKO, Ivan (t'kuh-CHEHN-koh, ee-VAHN) CBJ

Left wing. Shoots left. 5'10", 183 lbs. Born, Yaroslavl, USSR, November 9, 1979.
(Columbus' 5th choice, 98th overall, in 2002 Entry Draft).

			Regular Season					Playoffs				
Season	Club	League	GP	G	A	Pts	PIM	GP	G	A	Pts	PIM
1997-98	Yaroslavl 2	Russia-2		STATISTICS NOT AVAILABLE								
	Torpedo Yaroslavl	Russia	....	....	....	....	....	1	0	0	0	0
1998-99	Yaroslavl 2	Russia-3	28	15	13	28	26	....	....	....	....	....
99-2000	Yaroslavl 2	Russia-3	1	1	0	1	0	....	....	....	....	....
	Motor Zavolzhje	Russia-2	43	15	14	29	22	....	....	....	....	....
	Nizhnekamsk 2	Russia-3	8	6	3	9	24	....	....	....	....	....
	Nizhnekamsk	Russia	5	1	0	1	0	4	0	1	1	0
2000-01	Nizhnekamsk	Russia	28	2	2	4	14	4	0	1	1	0
2001-02	Yaroslavl 2	Russia-3	1	0	1	1	2	....	....	....	....	....
	Yaroslavl	Russia	44	13	20	33	57	9	5	2	7	4
2002-03	Yaroslavl	Russia	44	11	6	17	57	10	2	3	5	6
2003-04	Yaroslavl	Russia	56	7	11	18	22	3	0	0	0	0
2004-05	Yaroslavl	Russia	59	15	15	30	30	9	2	3	5	8
2005-06	Yaroslavl	Russia	45	10	21	31	30	11	1	2	3	16
	Yaroslavl 2	Russia-3	1	0	1	1	2	....	....	....	....	....
2006-07	Yaroslavl	Russia	52	9	24	33	30	7	1	2	3	6
2007-08	Yaroslavl	Russia	56	14	15	29	34	16	1	3	4	6

TOEWS, David (TAYVZ, DAY-vihd) NYI

Center. Shoots right. 5'10", 175 lbs. Born, Winnipeg, Man., June 7, 1990.
(NY Islanders' 5th choice, 66th overall, in 2008 Entry Draft).

			Regular Season					Playoffs				
Season	Club	League	GP	G	A	Pts	PIM	GP	G	A	Pts	PIM
2005-06	Colorado Outlaws	Minor-CO		STATISTICS NOT AVAILABLE								
2006-07	Shat.-St. Mary's	High-MN	61	34	47	81	52	....	....	....	....	....
2007-08	Shat.-St. Mary's	High-MN	51	44	56	100	20	....	....	....	....	....

• Signed Letter of Intent to attend **University of North Dakota** (WCHA) in fall of 2008.

TOPOL, Sergei (TOH-puhl, SAIR-gay) VAN.

Center. Shoots left. 6'2", 183 lbs. Born, Omsk, USSR, February 15, 1985.
(Vancouver's 8th choice, 252nd overall, in 2003 Entry Draft).

			Regular Season					Playoffs				
Season	Club	League	GP	G	A	Pts	PIM	GP	G	A	Pts	PIM
2002-03	Omsk 2	Russia-3	45	16	5	21	18	....	....	....	....	....
2003-04	Avangard Omsk	Russia	9	0	0	0	2	....	....	....	....	....
	Omsk 2	Russia-3	39	25	14	39	10	....	....	....	....	....
2004-05	Mechel	Russia-2	19	1	0	1	6	....	....	....	....	....
	Mechel 2	Russia-3	5	2	1	3	8	....	....	....	....	....
	Omsk 2	Russia-3	18	6	4	10	4	....	....	....	....	....
	Avangard Omsk	Russia	2	1	0	1	0	....	....	....	....	....
2005-06	Omsk 2	Russia-3	33	24	15	39	26	....	....	....	....	....
	Avangard Omsk	Russia	17	1	0	1	12	....	....	....	....	....
2006-07	Avangard Omsk 2	Russia-3	26	18	14	32	30	....	....	....	....	....
	Avangard Omsk	Russia	27	0	1	1	12	1	0	0	0	2
2007-08	Avtomobilist	Russia-2	16	0	7	7	10	....	....	....	....	....
	Avtomobilist 2	Russia-3	6	6	4	10	14	....	....	....	....	....
	Nizhny Tagil	Russia-2	6	1	0	1	0	....	....	....	....	....

TORP, Nichlas (TOHRP, NIHK-luhs) MTL.

Defense. Shoots left. 5'10", 197 lbs. Born, Jonkoping, Sweden, April 10, 1989.
(Montreal's 8th choice, 163rd overall, in 2007 Entry Draft).

			Regular Season					Playoffs				
Season	Club	League	GP	G	A	Pts	PIM	GP	G	A	Pts	PIM
2004-05	HV 71 U18	Swe-U18	11	5	2	7	20	....	....	....	....	....
2005-06	HV 71 U18	Swe-U18	8	3	1	4	45	5	1	1	2	12
	HV 71 Jr.	Swe-Jr.	7	0	0	0	34	....	....	....	....	....
2006-07	HV 71 U18	Swe-U18	1	0	0	0	2	3	1	0	1	43
	HV 71 Jr.	Swe-Jr.	17	3	1	4	42	4	0	2	2	10
2007-08	HV 71 Jonkoping	Sweden		DID NOT PLAY – INJURED								

TORQUATO, Zack (tohr-KAH-toh, ZAK) DET.

Center. Shoots right. 6', 195 lbs. Born, Sault Ste Marie, Ont., June 8, 1989.
(Detroit's 4th choice, 178th overall, in 2007 Entry Draft).

			Regular Season					Playoffs				
Season	Club	League	GP	G	A	Pts	PIM	GP	G	A	Pts	PIM
2004-05	Stratford Cullitons	OJHL-B	47	34	41	75	52	....	....	....	....	....
2005-06	Saginaw Spirit	OHL	65	19	18	37	56	4	1	0	1	6
2006-07	Saginaw Spirit	OHL	22	10	13	23	24	....	....	....	....	....
	Erie Otters	OHL	43	20	26	46	69	....	....	....	....	....
2007-08	Erie Otters	OHL	66	25	42	67	112	....	....	....	....	....
	Grand Rapids	AHL	11	1	0	1	8	....	....	....	....	....

TREMBLAY, Jonathan (TRAHM-blay, JAWN-ah-thuhn) CGY.

Right wing. Shoots right. 6'3", 240 lbs. Born, Fauquier, Ont., March 3, 1984.
(San Jose's 6th choice, 201st overall, in 2003 Entry Draft).

			Regular Season					Playoffs				
Season	Club	League	GP	G	A	Pts	PIM	GP	G	A	Pts	PIM
2001-02	Timmins Majors	GNML		STATISTICS NOT AVAILABLE								
	Acadie-Bathurst	QMJHL	2	0	0	0	5	1	0	0	0	0
2002-03	Acadie-Bathurst	QMJHL	62	0	1	1	232	9	0	0	0	45
2003-04	Acadie-Bathurst	QMJHL	60	3	0	3	*316	....	....	....	....	....
2004-05	Cleveland Barons	AHL	1	0	0	0	0	....	....	....	....	....
	Johnstown Chiefs	ECHL	46	2	3	5	136	....	....	....	....	....
2005-06	Toledo Storm	ECHL	1	0	0	0	0	....	....	....	....	....
	Kalamazoo Wings	UHL	8	0	0	0	20	....	....	....	....	....
	Quad City	UHL	37	0	2	2	62	....	....	....	....	....
2006-07	Worcester Sharks	AHL	3	0	0	0	5	....	....	....	....	....
	Fresno Falcons	ECHL	63	0	2	2	133	....	....	....	....	....
2007-08	Worcester Sharks	AHL	17	0	1	1	37	....	....	....	....	....

Signed as a free agent by **Quad City** (AHL), July 22, 2008.

TREMBLAY, Nick (TRAWM-blay, NIHK-oh-las) BOS.

Center. Shoots left. 5'11", 179 lbs. Born, Ottawa, Ont., April 5, 1988.
(Boston's 5th choice, 173rd overall, in 2008 Entry Draft).

			Regular Season					Playoffs				
Season	Club	League	GP	G	A	Pts	PIM	GP	G	A	Pts	PIM
2005-06	Champlain College	QJHL	48	13	22	35	36	9	1	1	2	8
2006-07	Champlain College	QJHL	53	26	26	52	58	7	1	2	3	2
2007-08	Smiths Falls Bears	CJHL	57	*51	59	110	12	9	5	8	13	10

• Signed Letter of Intent to attend **Clarkson University** (ECAC) in fall of 2008.

TREVELYAN, T.J. (truh-VEHL-yuhn, TEE-JAY)

Left wing. Shoots left. 5'10", 187 lbs. Born, Mississauga, Ont., March 6, 1984.

			Regular Season					Playoffs				
Season	Club	League	GP	G	A	Pts	PIM	GP	G	A	Pts	PIM
2002-03	St. Lawrence	ECAC	34	10	12	22	38	....	....	....	....	....
2003-04	St. Lawrence	ECAC	38	*23	16	39	62	....	....	....	....	....
2004-05	St. Lawrence	ECAC	38	*25	20	45	61	....	....	....	....	....
2005-06	St. Lawrence	ECAC	40	20	28	*48	43	....	....	....	....	....
2006-07	Providence Bruins	AHL	60	28	24	52	41	13	3	6	9	12
	Long Beach	ECHL	15	9	8	17	16	....	....	....	....	....
2007-08	Providence Bruins	AHL	72	18	20	38	23	10	5	3	8	6

ECAC First All-Star Team (2005, 2006) • ECAC Player of the Year (2006) • NCAA East First All-American Team (2006)

Signed as a free agent by **Boston**, August 17, 2006.

TRIVINO, Corey (trih-VEE-noh, KOH-ree) **NYI**

Center. Shoots left. 6'1", 170 lbs. Born, Etobicoke, Ont., January 12, 1990.
(NY Islanders' 2nd choice, 36th overall, in 2008 Entry Draft).

			Regular Season					Playoffs				
Season	Club	League	GP	G	A	Pts	PIM	GP	G	A	Pts	PIM
2005-06	Toronto Marlboros	GTHL	30	17	22	39	4	....	....	....	....	....
2006-07	Stouffville Spirit	OPJHL	49	24	34	58	24	9	1	6	7	16
2007-08	Stouffville Spirit	OPJHL	39	19	50	69	22	15	5	17	22	10

• Signed Letter of Intent to attend **Boston University** (Hockey East) in fall of 2008.

TROPP, Corey (TROHP, KOHR-ee) **BUF.**

Right wing. Shoots right. 5'11", 183 lbs. Born, Grosse Pointe, MI, July 25, 1989.
(Buffalo's 3rd choice, 89th overall, in 2007 Entry Draft).

			Regular Season					Playoffs				
Season	Club	League	GP	G	A	Pts	PIM	GP	G	A	Pts	PIM
2005-06	Sioux Falls	USHL	46	7	8	15	21	14	2	3	5	8
2006-07	Sioux Falls	USHL	54	26	36	62	76	8	4	9	*13	0
2007-08	Michigan State	CCHA	42	6	11	17	16	....	....	....	....	....

TROTTER, Brock (TRAW-tuhr, BRAWK) **MTL.**

Center. Shoots right. 5'10", 170 lbs. Born, Brandon, Man., September 18, 1987.

			Regular Season					Playoffs				
Season	Club	League	GP	G	A	Pts	PIM	GP	G	A	Pts	PIM
2003-04	Dauphin Kings	MJHL	63	32	33	65	108	....	....	....	....	....
2004-05	Lincoln Stars	USHL	60	20	38	58	84	4	2	3	5	0
2005-06	U. of Denver	WCHA	5	3	2	5	2	....	....	....	....	....
2006-07	U. of Denver	WCHA	40	16	24	40	22	....	....	....	....	....
2007-08	U. of Denver	WCHA	24	13	18	31	18	....	....	....	....	....
	Hamilton Bulldogs	AHL	21	3	6	9	4	....	....	....	....	....

• Missed majority of 2005-06 season recovering from achilles tendon injury suffered in game vs. North Dakota (WCHA), October 29, 2005. Signed as a free agent by **Montreal**, February 7, 2008.

TRUKHNO, Vyacheslav (trookh-NOH, V'YTACH-ih-slav) **EDM.**

Left wing. Shoots left. 6'1", 197 lbs. Born, Khimki, USSR, February 22, 1987.
(Edmonton's 6th choice, 120th overall, in 2005 Entry Draft).

			Regular Season					Playoffs				
Season	Club	League	GP	G	A	Pts	PIM	GP	G	A	Pts	PIM
2002-03	Rungstead IK	Denmark-2	1	2	3	5	0	....	....	....	....	....
	Rungstead	Denmark	27	7	4	11	8	12	0	1	1	8
2003-04	Rungstead	Denmark	35	12	11	23	18	7	0	0	0	8
2004-05	PEI Rocket	QMJHL	64	25	34	59	57	....	....	....	....	....
2005-06	PEI Rocket	QMJHL	60	28	68	96	81	3	2	2	4	0
2006-07	Gatineau	QMJHL	60	25	77	102	67	5	0	6	6	19
2007-08	Springfield Falcons	AHL	64	14	21	35	44	....	....	....	....	....

QMJHL All-Rookie Team (2005) • Canadian Major Junior All-Rookie Team (2005) • QMJHL First All-Star Team (2007)

TRUNEV, Maxim (troo-NAWF, max-EEM) **MTL.**

Right wing. Shoots right. 5'11", 174 lbs. Born, Kirovo-Chepetsk, USSR, September 7, 1990.
(Montreal's 4th choice, 138th overall, in 2008 Entry Draft).

			Regular Season					Playoffs				
Season	Club	League	GP	G	A	Pts	PIM	GP	G	A	Pts	PIM
2005-06	Cherepovets 2	Russia-3	STATISTICS NOT AVAILABLE									
2006-07	Cherepovets 2	Russia-3	STATISTICS NOT AVAILABLE									
2007-08	Cherepovets 2	Russia-3	STATISTICS NOT AVAILABLE									
	Cherepovets	Russia	1	0	0	0	0	....	....	....	....	....

TUOMAINEN, Miikka (too-oh-MAY-nehn, MEE-kah) **ATL.**

Left wing. Shoots left. 6'3", 250 lbs. Born, Turku, Finland, May 22, 1986.
(Atlanta's 7th choice, 204th overall, in 2004 Entry Draft).

			Regular Season					Playoffs				
Season	Club	League	GP	G	A	Pts	PIM	GP	G	A	Pts	PIM
2001-02	TuTo Turku U18	Fin-U18	14	8	5	13	14	....	....	....	....	....
	TuTo Turku Jr.	Fin-Jr.	1	1	0	1	0	....	....	....	....	....
2002-03	TuTo Turku U18	Fin-U18	24	3	4	7	52	4	0	0	0	0
	TuTo Turku Jr.	Fin-Jr.	2	0	0	0	4	....	....	....	....	....
	TuTo Turku	Finland-2	6	0	0	0	0	....	....	....	....	....
2003-04	TuTo Turku Jr.	Fin-Jr.	20	10	7	17	6	....	....	....	....	....
	TuTo Turku U18	Fin-U18	20	10	7	17	6	....	....	....	....	....
	TuTo Turku	Finland-2	30	4	3	7	2	....	....	....	....	....
2004-05	TuTo Turku Jr.	Fin-Jr.	5	1	4	5	0	....	....	....	....	....
	TuTo Turku	Finland-2	42	4	4	8	22	7	1	0	1	2
2005-06	Lukko Rauma Jr.	Fin-Jr.	16	5	3	8	4	9	5	3	8	8
	Suomi U20	Finland-2	2	0	0	0	2	....	....	....	....	....
	Lukko Rauma	Finland	33	2	2	4	12	....	....	....	....	....
2006-07	Lukko Rauma Jr.	Fin-Jr.	5	0	1	1	0	....	....	....	....	....
	Lukko Rauma	Finland	54	6	8	14	77	3	1	0	1	0
2007-08	Lukko Rauma	Finland	50	1	2	3	55	3	0	0	0	0

TUREK, Ryan (TOOR-ehk, RIGH-uhn) **ST.L.**

Center. Shoots right. 5'11", 170 lbs. Born, Southfield, MI, September 22, 1987.
(St. Louis' 5th choice, 94th overall, in 2006 Entry Draft).

			Regular Season					Playoffs				
Season	Club	League	GP	G	A	Pts	PIM	GP	G	A	Pts	PIM
2004-05	Omaha Lancers	USHL	45	3	8	11	52	4	1	0	1	2
2005-06	Omaha Lancers	USHL	52	17	11	28	71	5	1	1	2	2
2006-07	Michigan State	CCHA	31	0	2	2	18	....	....	....	....	....
2007-08	Michigan State	CCHA	35	0	5	5	16	....	....	....	....	....

TURNBULL, Joshua (TUHRN-buhl, JAWSH-oo-uh) **L.A.**

Center. Shoots right. 5'10", 172 lbs. Born, Hayward, WI, July 12, 1988.
(Los Angeles' 8th choice, 137th overall, in 2007 Entry Draft).

			Regular Season					Playoffs				
Season	Club	League	GP	G	A	Pts	PIM	GP	G	A	Pts	PIM
2005-06	Duluth East	High-MN	STATISTICS NOT AVAILABLE									
2006-07	Waterloo	USHL	60	25	29	54	66	9	3	1	4	12
2007-08	U. of Wisconsin	WCHA	37	4	7	11	44	....	....	....	....	....

TURNER, Brennan (TUHR-nuhr, BREH-nuhn) **CHI.**

Defense. Shoots left. 6'3", 221 lbs. Born, Winnipeg, Man., December 5, 1986.
(Chicago's 8th choice, 134th overall, in 2005 Entry Draft).

			Regular Season					Playoffs				
Season	Club	League	GP	G	A	Pts	PIM	GP	G	A	Pts	PIM
2003-04	Notre Dame	SJHL	35	2	8	10	110	....	....	....	....	....
2004-05	Notre Dame	SJHL	41	5	12	17	207	8	0	1	1	25
2005-06	Yale	ECAC	16	0	2	2	53	....	....	....	....	....
2006-07	Yale	ECAC	27	0	0	0	71	....	....	....	....	....
2007-08	Yale	ECAC	15	0	1	1	22	....	....	....	....	....
	Rockford IceHogs	AHL	4	0	0	0	14	....	....	....	....	....

TYRELL, Dana (TIH-rehl, DAY-nuh) **T.B.**

Center/Right wing. Shoots left. 5'10", 185 lbs. Born, Airdrie, Alta., April 23, 1989.
(Tampa Bay's 1st choice, 47th overall, in 2007 Entry Draft).

			Regular Season					Playoffs				
Season	Club	League	GP	G	A	Pts	PIM	GP	G	A	Pts	PIM
2003-04	Airdrie Xtreme	AMBHL	35	21	47	68	28	7	6	4	10	....
2004-05	Strathmore	AMBHL	34	16	23	39	32	16	8	9	*17	....
	Prince George	WHL	1	0	0	0	2	....	....	....	....	....
2005-06	Prince George	WHL	69	7	11	18	44	5	0	0	0	2
2006-07	Prince George	WHL	72	30	26	56	51	15	1	6	7	4
2007-08	Prince George	WHL	68	25	40	65	47	....	....	....	....	....
	Norfolk Admirals	AHL	11	1	5	6	6	....	....	....	....	....

ULLSTROM, David (UHL-struhm, DAY-vihd) **NYI**

Center. Shoots left. 6'3", 198 lbs. Born, Jonkoping, Sweden, April 22, 1989.
(NY Islanders' 9th choice, 102nd overall, in 2008 Entry Draft).

			Regular Season					Playoffs				
Season	Club	League	GP	G	A	Pts	PIM	GP	G	A	Pts	PIM
2005-06	HV 71 U18	Swe-U18	13	5	8	13	14	5	4	1	5	14
	HV 71 Jr.	Swe-Jr.	1	0	0	0	0	....	....	....	....	....
2006-07	HV 71 U18	Swe-U18	1	0	0	0	2	5	2	6	8	10
	HV 71 Jr.	Swe-Jr.	39	16	14	30	30	4	0	2	2	0
2007-08	HV 71 Jr.	Swe-Jr.	40	27	27	54	86	3	2	2	4	0
	HV 71 Jonkoping	Sweden	7	0	0	0	0	....	....	....	....	....

UTKIN, Dmitri (OOT-kihn, dih-MEE-tree) **BOS.**

Left wing. Shoots left. 6', 170 lbs. Born, Yaroslavl, USSR, June 10, 1984.
(Boston's 5th choice, 228th overall, in 2002 Entry Draft).

			Regular Season					Playoffs				
Season	Club	League	GP	G	A	Pts	PIM	GP	G	A	Pts	PIM
2000-01	Yaroslavl 2	Russia-3	49	12	1	13	10	....	....	....	....	....
2001-02	Yaroslavl 2	Russia-3	32	15	7	22	33	....	....	....	....	....
2002-03	Yaroslavl	Russia	4	0	1	1	0	....	....	....	....	....
2003-04	Spartak Moscow	Russia-2	57	10	10	20	8	13	3	3	6	2
2004-05	Keramin Minsk	BelOpen	8	2	0	2	31	....	....	....	....	....
	HK Brest	BelOpen	20	4	12	16	4	....	....	....	....	....
	HK Riga 2000	BelOpen	....	....	....	....	....	3	0	0	0	0
	HK Riga 2000	Latvia	....	....	....	....	....	6	3	2	5	0
2005-06	Spartak Moscow	Russia	33	3	1	4	4	2	0	0	0	0
	Spartak Moscow 2	Russia-3	10	5	2	7	8	....	....	....	....	....
2006-07	Chelyabinsk	Russia	50	6	8	14	20	....	....	....	....	....
2007-08	Chelyabinsk 2	Russia-3	16	4	3	7	2	....	....	....	....	....
	Chelyabinsk	Russia	5	1	0	1	2	....	....	....	....	....
	Avtomobilist	Russia-2	11	2	0	2	0	6	1	0	1	0

VAGNER, Martin (VAHG-nuhr, MAHR-tihn) **CAR.**

Defense. Shoots left. 6'1", 214 lbs. Born, Jaromer, Czech., March 16, 1984.
(Carolina's 8th choice, 268th overall, in 2004 Entry Draft).

			Regular Season					Playoffs				
Season	Club	League	GP	G	A	Pts	PIM	GP	G	A	Pts	PIM
99-2000	Sparta Jr.	CzRep-Jr.	46	2	8	10	34	....	....	....	....	....
2000-01	HC Pardubice Jr.	CzRep-Jr.	53	2	12	14	46	....	....	....	....	....
2001-02	Hull Olympiques	QMJHL	64	6	28	34	81	8	0	1	1	10
2002-03	Hull Olympiques	QMJHL	53	1	12	13	98	20	1	4	5	38
2003-04	Gatineau	QMJHL	38	6	12	18	85	13	0	3	3	16
2004-05	Acadie-Bathurst	QMJHL	48	3	10	13	84	....	....	....	....	....
2005-06	Pardubice	CzRep	36	0	0	0	14	....	....	....	....	....
	Hr. Kralove	CzRep-2	12	0	1	1	12	....	....	....	....	....
2006-07	C. Budejovice	CzRep	40	0	0	0	20	3	0	0	0	0
2007-08	Usti n. L.	CzRep	45	3	3	6	40	....	....	....	....	....

• Re-entered NHL Entry Draft. Originally Dallas' 1st choice, 26th overall, in 2002 Entry Draft.

QMJHL All-Rookie Team (2002)

VAIVE, Justin (VIGHV, JUHS-tihn) **ANA.**

Left wing. Shoots left. 6'5", 210 lbs. Born, Buffalo, NY, July 8, 1989.
(Anaheim's 4th choice, 92nd overall, in 2007 Entry Draft).

			Regular Season					Playoffs				
Season	Club	League	GP	G	A	Pts	PIM	GP	G	A	Pts	PIM
2004-05	Toronto Marlboros	GTHL	72	38	64	102		....	....	....	....	....
2005-06	USNTDP	U-17	13	3	5	8	18	....	....	....	....	....
	USNTDP	NAHL	24	4	8	12	34	5	1	1	2	6
2006-07	USNTDP	U-18	43	7	8	15	49	....	....	....	....	....
	USNTDP	NAHL	15	4	1	5	22	....	....	....	....	....
2007-08	Miami U.	CCHA	41	3	7	10	65	....	....	....	....	....

VALENTENKO, Pavel (val-ehn-TEHN-koh, PAH-vehl) **MTL.**

Defense. Shoots left. 6'2", 218 lbs. Born, Nizhnekamsk, USSR, October 20, 1987.
(Montreal's 5th choice, 139th overall, in 2006 Entry Draft).

			Regular Season					Playoffs				
Season	Club	League	GP	G	A	Pts	PIM	GP	G	A	Pts	PIM
2002-03	Lada Togliatti 2	Russia-3	6	0	0	0	4	....	....	....	....	....
2003-04	Nizhnekamsk 2	Russia-3	26	0	1	1	28	....	....	....	....	....
2004-05	Nizhnekamsk 2	Russia-3	STATISTICS NOT AVAILABLE									
2005-06	Nizhnekamsk 2	Russia-3	STATISTICS NOT AVAILABLE									
	Nizhnekamsk	Russia	2	0	0	0	2	....	....	....	....	....
2006-07	Nizhnekamsk	Russia	50	0	2	2	62	4	0	0	0	2
2007-08	Hamilton Bulldogs	AHL	57	1	15	16	58	....	....	....	....	....

VALETTE, Craig (va-LEHT, KRAIG)

Center. Shoots left. 6', 200 lbs. Born, Shellbrook, Sask., October 7, 1982.

			Regular Season					Playoffs				
Season	Club	League	GP	G	A	Pts	PIM	GP	G	A	Pts	PIM
1998-99	Sask. Contacts	SMHL	36	19	22	41	....	....	....	....	....	....
99-2000	Saskatoon Blades	WHL	47	2	1	3	25	3	0	0	0	0
2000-01	Saskatoon Blades	WHL	24	2	0	2	19	....	....	....	....	....
	Portland	WHL	39	8	6	14	39	16	0	2	2	27
2001-02	Portland	WHL	67	8	14	22	160	7	2	1	3	6
2002-03	Portland	WHL	71	30	26	56	192	7	5	4	9	18
2003-04	Cleveland Barons	AHL	56	6	10	16	77	5	0	0	0	2
2004-05	Cleveland Barons	AHL	79	6	6	12	94	....	....	....	....	....
2005-06	Cleveland Barons	AHL	69	5	6	11	95	....	....	....	....	....
2006-07	Worcester Sharks	AHL	55	15	11	26	77	1	0	0	0	0
2007-08	Worcester Sharks	AHL	69	4	10	14	97	....	....	....	....	....

Signed as a free agent by **San Jose**, April 4, 2003.

VAN DER GULIK, David (VAN DUHR-GOO-lihk, DAY-vihd) CGY.

Right wing. Shoots left. 5'11", 183 lbs. Born, Abbotsford, B.C., April 20, 1983.
(Calgary's 10th choice, 206th overall, in 2002 Entry Draft).

			Regular Season					Playoffs				
Season	Club	League	GP	G	A	Pts	PIM	GP	G	A	Pts	PIM
99-2000	Chilliwack Chiefs	BCHL	41	35	46	81	....	....	....	....	....	....
2000-01	Chilliwack Chiefs	BCHL	60	42	38	80	....	....	....	....	....	....
2001-02	Chilliwack Chiefs	BCHL	56	38	62	100	90	13	8	11	19	....
2002-03	Boston University	H-East	40	10	10	20	56	....	....	....	....	....
2003-04	Boston University	H-East	35	13	7	20	74	....	....	....	....	....
2004-05	Boston University	H-East	41	18	13	31	48	....	....	....	....	....
2005-06	Boston University	H-East	25	11	11	22	26	....	....	....	....	....
2006-07	Omaha	AHL	80	16	27	43	69	6	0	2	2	4
2007-08	Quad City Flames	AHL	80	19	23	42	62	....	....	....	....	....

Hockey East All-Rookie Team (2003)

VANDE VELDE, Chris (VAN-deh VEHLD, KRIHS) EDM.

Center. Shoots left. 6'2", 204 lbs. Born, Moorhead, MN, March 15, 1987.
(Edmonton's 5th choice, 97th overall, in 2005 Entry Draft).

			Regular Season					Playoffs				
Season	Club	League	GP	G	A	Pts	PIM	GP	G	A	Pts	PIM
2003-04	Moorhead Spuds	High-MN	29	19	24	43	....	....	....	....	....	....
2004-05	Moorhead Spuds	High-MN	30	35	32	67	28	....	....	....	....	....
	Lincoln Stars	USHL	7	1	4	5	0	4	0	2	2	0
2005-06	Lincoln Stars	USHL	56	16	20	36	70	9	1	3	4	10
2006-07	North Dakota	WCHA	38	3	6	9	37	....	....	....	....	....
2007-08	North Dakota	WCHA	43	15	17	32	38	....	....	....	....	....

vanRIEMSDYK, James (VAN REEMZ-dighk, JAYMZ) PHI.

Left wing. Shoots left. 6'3", 205 lbs. Born, Middletown, NJ, May 4, 1989.
(Philadelphia's 1st choice, 2nd overall, in 2007 Entry Draft).

			Regular Season					Playoffs				
Season	Club	League	GP	G	A	Pts	PIM	GP	G	A	Pts	PIM
2004-05	Christian Bros.	High-NJ	30	36	24	60	....	....	....	....	....	....
2005-06	USNTDP	U-17	11	7	5	12	18	....	....	....	....	....
	USNTDP	U-18	14	1	3	4	6	....	....	....	....	....
	USNTDP	NAHL	37	18	11	29	36	7	1	0	1	8
2006-07	USNTDP	U-18	39	25	28	53	48	....	....	....	....	....
	USNTDP	NAHL	12	13	12	25	37	....	....	....	....	....
2007-08	New Hampshire	H-East	31	11	23	34	36	....	....	....	....	....

Hockey East All-Rookie Team (2008)

VAS, Janos (VAHSH, YAH-nohsh)

Left wing. Shoots left. 6'1", 205 lbs. Born, Dunaujvaros, Hungary, January 29, 1984.
(Dallas' 2nd choice, 32nd overall, in 2002 Entry Draft).

			Regular Season					Playoffs				
Season	Club	League	GP	G	A	Pts	PIM	GP	G	A	Pts	PIM
99-2000	Dunaferr SE	Hungary	2	2	0	0	0	....	....	....	....	....
2000-01	Malmo Jr.	Swe-Jr.	23	4	4	8	12	....	....	....	....	....
	Malmo U18	Swe-U18	3	2	0	2	4	....	....	....	....	....
2001-02	Malmo Jr.	Swe-Jr.	36	15	19	34	52	7	8	2	10	4
2002-03	Malmo Jr.	Swe-Jr.	17	5	12	17	14	....	....	....	....	....
	IK Pantern Malmo	Sweden-3	STATISTICS NOT AVAILABLE									
	IF Troja-Ljungby	Sweden-2	17	2	2	4	20	....	....	....	....	....
	Malmo	Sweden	14	1	0	1	2	....	....	....	....	....
2003-04	Malmo U18	Swe-U18	15	5	3	8	14	8	5	2	7	33
	Malmo	Sweden	6	0	0	0	0	....	....	....	....	....
	IK Pantern Malmo	Sweden-3	3	0	2	2	....	....	....	....	....	....
	Malmo	Sweden-Q	1	0	0	0	0	....	....	....	....	....
2004-05	Halmstad	Sweden-2	39	9	8	17	10	2	0	1	1	2
2005-06	Iowa Stars	AHL	35	2	9	11	18	7	1	1	2	2
	Idaho Steelheads	ECHL	10	4	5	9	15	....	....	....	....	....
2006-07	Iowa Stars	AHL	72	13	13	26	42	10	1	1	2	2
2007-08	Iowa Stars	AHL	80	17	24	41	51	....	....	....	....	....

VASYUNOV, Alexander (vahs-YUH-nawv, al-EHX-AN-duhr) N.J.

Left wing. Shoots right. 6', 190 lbs. Born, Yaroslavl, USSR, April 22, 1988.
(New Jersey's 2nd choice, 58th overall, in 2006 Entry Draft).

			Regular Season					Playoffs				
Season	Club	League	GP	G	A	Pts	PIM	GP	G	A	Pts	PIM
2004-05	Yaroslavl 2	Russia-3	28	10	2	12	6	....	....	....	....	....
2005-06	Yaroslavl 2	Russia-3	29	29	6	35	14	....	....	....	....	....
	Yaroslavl	Russia	2	0	0	0	2	....	....	....	....	....
2006-07	Yaroslavl	Russia	17	0	0	0	4	....	....	....	....	....
	Yaroslavl 2	Russia-3	30	16	9	25	52	....	....	....	....	....
2007-08	Yaroslavl	Russia	22	4	0	4	4	16	2	0	2	2

VEILLEUX, Keven (VAY-oo, KEH-vihn) PIT.

Center. Shoots right. 6'5", 202 lbs. Born, Saint-Renee, Que., June 27, 1989.
(Pittsburgh's 2nd choice, 51st overall, in 2007 Entry Draft).

			Regular Season					Playoffs				
Season	Club	League	GP	G	A	Pts	PIM	GP	G	A	Pts	PIM
2004-05	Levis	QAAA	11	1	0	1	0	2	0	1	1	0
2005-06	Levis	QAAA	26	12	23	35	53	....	....	....	....	....
	Victoriaville Tigres	QMJHL	33	2	13	15	4	5	0	1	1	2
2006-07	Victoriaville Tigres	QMJHL	70	20	35	55	53	6	1	5	6	4
2007-08	Victoriaville Tigres	QMJHL	42	10	32	42	54	....	....	....	....	....
	Rimouski Oceanic	QMJHL	19	7	15	22	22	9	3	4	7	2

VERNACE, Michael (vuhr-NAYS, MIGH-kuhl) COL.

Defense. Shoots left. 6'2", 200 lbs. Born, Toronto, Ont., May 26, 1986.
(San Jose's 6th choice, 201st overall, in 2004 Entry Draft).

			Regular Season					Playoffs				
Season	Club	League	GP	G	A	Pts	PIM	GP	G	A	Pts	PIM
2003-04	Bramalea Blues	OPJHL	33	3	12	15	16	....	....	....	....	....
	Brampton	OHL	2	1	1	2	0	11	2	3	5	8
2004-05	Brampton	OHL	68	12	38	50	42	6	2	2	4	0
2005-06	Brampton	OHL	68	10	62	72	54	11	1	5	6	6
2006-07	Albany River Rats	AHL	30	1	11	12	35	....	....	....	....	....
	Arizona Sundogs	CHL	24	3	11	14	20	....	....	....	....	....
2007-08	Lake Erie Monsters	AHL	79	3	26	29	59	....	....	....	....	....

OHL All-Rookie Team (2005)

Rights traded to **Colorado** by **San Jose** for Colorado's 6th round choice (Patrick Zackrisson) in 2007 Entry Draft, June 1, 2006.

VESCE, Ryan (veks-KEE, RIGH-uhn) S.J.

Center. Shoots right. 5'8", 165 lbs. Born, Lloyd Harbor, NY, April 7, 1982.

			Regular Season					Playoffs				
Season	Club	League	GP	G	A	Pts	PIM	GP	G	A	Pts	PIM
2000-01	Cornell Big Red	ECAC	33	7	20	27	10	....	....	....	....	....
2001-02	Cornell Big Red	ECAC	35	10	20	30	10	....	....	....	....	....
2002-03	Cornell Big Red	ECAC	36	19	26	45	16	....	....	....	....	....
2003-04	Cornell Big Red	ECAC	27	10	16	26	14	....	....	....	....	....
2004-05	Rogle	Sweden-2	43	20	25	45	51	....	....	....	....	....
2005-06	Springfield Falcons	AHL	80	18	49	67	50	....	....	....	....	....
2006-07	Binghamton	AHL	80	16	35	51	51	....	....	....	....	....
2007-08	HIFK Helsinki	Finland	56	26	18	44	42	7	1	2	3	2

Signed as a free agent by **Ottawa**, July 17, 2006. Signed as a free agent by **HIFK Helsinki** (Finland), July 17, 2007. Signed as a free agent by **San Jose**, August 13, 2008.

VIGILANTE, John (vih-jih-LAN-tee, JAWN) CBJ

Left wing. Shoots left. 6', 190 lbs. Born, Dearborn, MI, May 24, 1985.

			Regular Season					Playoffs				
Season	Club	League	GP	G	A	Pts	PIM	GP	G	A	Pts	PIM
2002-03	Plymouth Whalers	OHL	65	15	24	39	31	18	6	3	9	8
2003-04	Plymouth Whalers	OHL	66	30	38	68	25	9	1	7	8	8
2004-05	Plymouth Whalers	OHL	68	24	38	62	17	4	0	0	0	0
2005-06	Plymouth Whalers	OHL	55	24	53	77	34	13	4	12	16	0
2006-07	Milwaukee	AHL	62	8	19	27	10	2	0	0	0	2
2007-08	Milwaukee	AHL	73	15	31	46	12	6	0	1	1	0

Signed as a free agent by **Nashville**. December 7, 2005. Signed as a free agent by **Columbus**. July 8, 2008.

VISHNEVSKIY, Ivan (vihsh-NEHV-skee, ee-VAHN) DAL.

Defense. Shoots left. 5'11", 176 lbs. Born, Barnaul, USSR, February 18, 1988.
(Dallas' 1st choice, 27th overall, in 2006 Entry Draft).

			Regular Season					Playoffs				
Season	Club	League	GP	G	A	Pts	PIM	GP	G	A	Pts	PIM
2003-04	Lada Togliatti 2	Russia-3	16	0	0	0	10	....	....	....	....	....
2004-05	Lada Togliatti 2	Russia-3	STATISTICS NOT AVAILABLE									
2005-06	Rouyn-Noranda	QMJHL	54	13	35	48	57	5	2	1	3	2
2006-07	Rouyn-Noranda	QMJHL	60	14	37	51	90	16	5	8	13	8
2007-08	Rouyn-Noranda	QMJHL	45	17	28	45	50	17	0	6	6	16

QMJHL All-Rookie Team (2006) • QMJHL Second All-Star Team (2008)

VISHNYAKOV, Albert (vihsh-nyeh-KAWF, al-BAIRT) T.B.

Left wing. Shoots left. 6', 185 lbs. Born, Almyetevsk, USSR, December 30, 1983.
(Tampa Bay's 9th choice, 273rd overall, in 2003 Entry Draft).

			Regular Season					Playoffs				
Season	Club	League	GP	G	A	Pts	PIM	GP	G	A	Pts	PIM
99-2000	Almetjevsk 2	Russia-3	41	11	5	16	68	....	....	....	....	....
2000-01	Almetjevsk	Russia-2	29	0	0	0	2	....	....	....	....	....
2001-02	Ak Bars Kazan	Russia	9	0	1	1	2	....	....	....	....	....
	Nizhny Novgorod	Russia	6	1	0	1	0	....	....	....	....	....
	Nizh. Novgorod 2	Russia-3	4	2	2	4	10	....	....	....	....	....
2002-03	Ak Bars Kazan	Russia	47	7	6	13	47	5	1	0	1	0
2003-04	Nizhnekamsk	Russia	10	2	3	5	10	....	....	....	....	....
	Ak Bars Kazan 2	Russia-3	STATISTICS NOT AVAILABLE									
	Ak Bars Kazan	Russia	10	1	1	2	8	....	....	....	....	....
2004-05	Dynamo Moscow	Russia	28	1	2	3	10	....	....	....	....	....
2005-06	Dynamo Moscow	Russia	48	9	3	12	78	3	0	0	0	0
2006-07	Dynamo Moscow	Russia	33	9	6	15	36	1	0	0	0	0
2007-08	Spartak Moscow	Russia	8	2	0	2	14	....	....	....	....	....
	Novokuznetsk	Russia	19	1	7	8	12	....	....	....	....	....

VITALE, Joe (vih-TA-lee, JOH) PIT.

Center. Shoots right. 6', 205 lbs. Born, St. Louis, MO, August 20, 1985.
(Pittsburgh's 7th choice, 195th overall, in 2005 Entry Draft).

			Regular Season					Playoffs				
Season	Club	League	GP	G	A	Pts	PIM	GP	G	A	Pts	PIM
2003-04	St. Louis Jr. Blues	CSJHL	43	21	29	50	42	....	....	....	....	....
2004-05	Sioux Falls	USHL	53	11	20	31	62	....	....	....	....	....
2005-06	Northeastern	H-East	31	8	8	16	71	....	....	....	....	....
2006-07	Northeastern	H-East	35	7	9	16	54	....	....	....	....	....
2007-08	Northeastern	H-East	37	12	23	35	75	....	....	....	....	....

Hockey East Second All-Star Team (2008)

VOGELHUBER, Trent (VOH-guhl-hew-buhr, TREHNT) CBJ

Right wing. Shoots right. 6'2", 185 lbs. Born, Cleveland, OH, July 13, 1988.
(Columbus' 7th choice, 211th overall, in 2007 Entry Draft).

			Regular Season					Playoffs				
Season	Club	League	GP	G	A	Pts	PIM	GP	G	A	Pts	PIM
2004-05	Ohio AAA	Ind.	67	32	30	62	77	....	....	....	....	....
2005-06	Ohio AAA	GLHL	44	27	52	79	28	....	....	....	....	....
2006-07	St. Louis Bandits	NAHL	31	10	16	26	24	....	....	....	....	....
2007-08	Des Moines	USHL	2	0	1	1	0	....	....	....	....	....

• Signed Letter of Intent to attend **Miami University** (CCHA) in fall of 2008.

VOLOSHENKO, Roman (voh-loh-SHEHN-koh, ROH-muhn) **MIN.**

Left wing. Shoots right. 6'1", 207 lbs. Born, Brest, USSR, May 12, 1986.
(Minnesota's 2nd choice, 42nd overall, in 2004 Entry Draft).

			Regular Season					Playoffs				
Season	Club	League	GP	G	A	Pts	PIM	GP	G	A	Pts	PIM
2001-02	Krylja Sovetov 2	Russia-3	8	2	3	5	0	....	....	....	....	....
2002-03	Krylja Sovetov 2	Russia-3	6	3	1	4	2	....	....	....	....	....
	Krylja Sovetov	Russia	5	0	1	1	2	....	....	....	....	....
2003-04	Krylja Sovetov	Russia-2	46	7	8	15	40	4	1	1	2	4
2004-05	Krylja Sovetov 2	Russia-3	1	0	0	0	2	....	....	....	....	....
	Krylja Sovetov	Russia-2	38	16	13	29	22	3	0	1	1	2
2005-06	Houston Aeros	AHL	69	33	27	60	36	7	0	1	1	0
2006-07	Houston Aeros	AHL	76	11	19	30	22	....	....	....	....	....
2007-08	Dynamo Moscow	Russia	18	1	1	2	6	3	0	0	0	2

VOMELA, Lukas (voh-MEH-luh, LOO-kahsh) **DAL.**

Defense. Shoots left. 6'3", 189 lbs. Born, Ceske Budejovice, Czech., September 25, 1985.
(Dallas' 9th choice, 248th overall, in 2004 Entry Draft).

			Regular Season					Playoffs				
Season	Club	League	GP	G	A	Pts	PIM	GP	G	A	Pts	PIM
2000-01	C. Budejovice U17	CzR-U17	39	1	1	2	8	....	....	....	....	....
2001-02	C. Budejovice U17	CzR-U17	47	9	9	18	87	....	....	....	....	....
	C. Budejovice Jr.	CzRep-Jr.	1	0	0	0	0	....	....	....	....	....
2002-03	C. Budejovice Jr.	CzRep-Jr.	36	2	2	4	24	....	....	....	....	....
	C. Budejovice	CzRep	1	0	0	0	4	....	....	....	....	....
2003-04	C. Budejovice Jr.	CzRep-Jr.	21	1	7	8	45	....	....	....	....	....
	C. Budejovice	CzRep	15	0	1	1	8	....	....	....	....	....
2004-05	C. Budejovice	CzRep-2	2	0	0	0	0	....	....	....	....	....
	Jind. Hradec	CzRep-3	5	0	3	3	0	....	....	....	....	....
	C. Budejovice Jr.	CzRep-Jr.	30	3	10	13	68	2	0	1	1	4
2005-06	C. Budejovice	CzRep	1	0	0	0	0	....	....	....	....	....
	Jind. Hradec	CzRep-2	49	1	4	5	42	....	....	....	....	....
2006-07	HC Slavia Praha	CzRep	5	0	0	0	2	....	....	....	....	....
	HC Sparta Praha	CzRep	1	0	0	0	0	....	....	....	....	....
	Trebic	CzRep-2	36	2	5	7	91	2	0	0	0	2
2007-08	Prostejov	CzRep-2	28	1	2	3	42	....	....	....	....	....
	HC Vrchlabi	CzRep-2	6	0	2	2	4	9	0	2	2	6

VORACEK, Jakub (voh-RA-chehk, YA-kuhb) **CBJ**

Right wing. Shoots left. 6'1", 205 lbs. Born, Kladno, Czech., August 15, 1989.
(Columbus' 1st choice, 7th overall, in 2007 Entry Draft).

			Regular Season					Playoffs				
Season	Club	League	GP	G	A	Pts	PIM	GP	G	A	Pts	PIM
2002-03	HC Kladno U17	CzR-U17	2	1	1	2	2	2	1	1	2	0
2003-04	HC Kladno U17	CzR-U17	52	30	24	54	26	2	0	0	0	2
2004-05	HC Kladno U17	CzR-U17	30	23	39	62	44	7	5	4	9	14
	HC Kladno Jr.	CzRep-Jr.	16	5	7	12	6	1	1	0	1	2
2005-06	HC Kladno U17	CzR-U17	....	....	....	....	....	2	1	3	4	31
	HC Kladno Jr.	CzRep-Jr.	46	21	38	59	54	6	7	4	11	2
	HC Rabat Kladno	CzRep	1	0	0	0	0	....	....	....	....	....
2006-07	Halifax	QMJHL	59	23	63	86	26	12	7	17	24	6
2007-08	Halifax	QMJHL	53	33	68	101	42	15	5	13	18	14

QMJHL All-Rookie Team (2007) • QMJHL Rookie of the Year (2007) • QMJHL Second All-Star Team (2008)

VOROBIEV, Dmitri (voh-roh-BEE-ehf, dih-MEE-tree) **TOR.**

Defense. Shoots left. 6'2", 211 lbs. Born, Togliatti, USSR, October 18, 1985.
(Toronto's 3rd choice, 157th overall, in 2004 Entry Draft).

			Regular Season					Playoffs				
Season	Club	League	GP	G	A	Pts	PIM	GP	G	A	Pts	PIM
2002-03	Lada Togliatti 2	Russia-3	31	3	5	8	12	....	....	....	....	....
2003-04	Lada Togliatti 2	Russia-3	10	1	1	2	4	....	....	....	....	....
	Lada Togliatti	Russia	23	1	0	1	12	4	0	0	0	4
2004-05	Lada Togliatti	Russia	53	2	6	8	30	10	0	0	0	8
2005-06	Lada Togliatti	Russia	42	1	7	8	73	8	0	0	0	8
2006-07	Lada Togliatti	Russia	54	10	7	17	48	3	0	0	0	6
2007-08	Lada Togliatti	Russia	55	16	12	28	74	4	3	0	3	2

VOROSHNIN, Pavel (vo-rohsh-NIHN, PAH-vehl) **BUF.**

Defense. Shoots left. 6'3", 175 lbs. Born, Chelyabinsk, USSR, March 23, 1984.
(Buffalo's 7th choice, 172nd overall, in 2003 Entry Draft).

			Regular Season					Playoffs				
Season	Club	League	GP	G	A	Pts	PIM	GP	G	A	Pts	PIM
2001-02	Chelyabinsk	Russia-2	32	0	2	2	10	....	....	....	....	....
2002-03	Mississauga	OHL	68	9	27	36	81	1	0	0	0	2
2003-04	Mississauga	OHL	18	0	4	4	6	....	....	....	....	....
	Owen Sound	OHL	40	3	18	21	36	7	0	2	2	4
2004-05	Metallurg Serov	Russia-2	34	0	1	1	12	....	....	....	....	....
2005-06	Lada Togliatti	Russia	33	0	1	1	18	8	0	1	1	0
2006-07	Lada Togliatti	Russia	3	0	0	0	2	....	....	....	....	....
	Mytischi	Russia	9	0	1	1	0	....	....	....	....	....
2007-08	Mytischi	Russia	18	0	0	0	12	....	....	....	....	....

VOYNOV, Viatcheslav (VOY-nawf, v'ya-cheh-SLAV) **L.A.**

Defense. Shoots right. 6', 190 lbs. Born, Chelyabinsk, USSR, January 15, 1990.
(Los Angeles' 3rd choice, 32nd overall, in 2008 Entry Draft).

			Regular Season					Playoffs				
Season	Club	League	GP	G	A	Pts	PIM	GP	G	A	Pts	PIM
2005-06	Chelyabinsk 2	Russia-3	2	0	0	0	0	....	....	....	....	....
2006-07	Chelyabinsk	Russia	31	0	0	0	12	....	....	....	....	....
2007-08	Chelyabinsk 2	Russia-3	2	1	0	1	0	....	....	....	....	....
	Chelyabinsk	Russia	36	1	3	4	20	2	0	0	0	0

VRANA, Petr (vuh-RA-nuh, PEE-tuhr) **N.J.**

Center. Shoots left. 5'10", 190 lbs. Born, Sternberk, Czech., March 29, 1985.
(New Jersey's 2nd choice, 42nd overall, in 2003 Entry Draft).

			Regular Season					Playoffs				
Season	Club	League	GP	G	A	Pts	PIM	GP	G	A	Pts	PIM
2001-02	HC Havirov Jr.	CzRep-Jr.	38	11	12	23	....	....	....	....	....	....
	HC Femax Havirov	CzRep	6	0	0	0	4	....	....	....	....	....
2002-03	Halifax	QMJHL	72	37	46	83	32	24	5	15	20	12
2003-04	Halifax	QMJHL	48	13	25	38	56	....	....	....	....	....
2004-05	Halifax	QMJHL	60	16	35	51	77	12	10	4	14	12
2005-06	Albany River Rats	AHL	74	12	23	35	91	....	....	....	....	....
2006-07	Lowell Devils	AHL	61	13	19	32	44	....	....	....	....	....
2007-08	Lowell Devils	AHL	80	20	41	61	64	....	....	....	....	....

QMJHL All-Rookie Team (2003) • QMJHL Rookie of the Year (2003)

WAHL, Mitch (WAWL, MIHTCH) **CGY.**

Center. Shoots right. 6', 174 lbs. Born, Long Beach, CA, January 22, 1990.
(Calgary's 2nd choice, 48th overall, in 2008 Entry Draft).

			Regular Season					Playoffs				
Season	Club	League	GP	G	A	Pts	PIM	GP	G	A	Pts	PIM
2005-06	L.A. Jr. Kings	Minor-CA	64	40	50	90	95	....	....	....	....	....
	Spokane Chiefs	WHL	2	0	0	0	0	....	....	....	....	....
2006-07	Spokane Chiefs	WHL	69	16	32	48	50	4	0	1	1	5
2007-08	Spokane Chiefs	WHL	67	20	53	73	63	21	6	8	14	20

Memorial Cup All-Star Team (2008)

WALKER, Julian (WAH-kuhr, JEW-lee-ehn) **MIN.**

Wing. Shoots right. 6'2", 209 lbs. Born, Bern, Switz., September 10, 1986.
(Minnesota's 6th choice, 162nd overall, in 2006 Entry Draft).

			Regular Season					Playoffs				
Season	Club	League	GP	G	A	Pts	PIM	GP	G	A	Pts	PIM
2001-02	SC Bern Jr.	Swiss-Jr.	....	....	....	....	....	1	0	0	0	0
2002-03	SC Bern Jr.	Swiss-Jr.	34	2	5	7	14	3	0	0	0	4
2003-04	SC Bern Jr.	Swiss-Jr.	35	15	15	30	91	7	2	3	5	8
2004-05	SC Bern Jr.	Swiss-Jr.	42	25	32	57	84	9	1	11	12	10
	SC Langenthal	Swiss-2	3	0	0	0	0	....	....	....	....	....
2005-06	EHC Basel Jr.	Swiss-Jr.	6	3	2	5	6	....	....	....	....	....
	EHC Olten	Swiss-2	2	0	0	0	2	....	....	....	....	....
	EHC Basel	Swiss	36	2	0	2	41	5	1	0	1	6
2006-07	EHC Basel	Swiss	40	4	4	8	16	13	0	1	1	6
	EHC Olten	Swiss-2	8	8	4	12	0	....	....	....	....	....
2007-08	EHC Basel	Swiss	50	0	6	6	22	8	2	0	2	10
	EHC Basel	Swiss-Q	....	....	....	....	....	4	2	1	3	2

WALLACE, Tim (WAHL-las, TIHM) **PIT.**

Right wing. Shoots right. 6'1", 207 lbs. Born, Anchorage, AK, August 6, 1984.

			Regular Season					Playoffs				
Season	Club	League	GP	G	A	Pts	PIM	GP	G	A	Pts	PIM
2002-03	U. of Notre Dame	CCHA	40	6	5	11	28	....	....	....	....	....
2003-04	U. of Notre Dame	CCHA	39	3	8	11	10	....	....	....	....	....
2004-05	U. of Notre Dame	CCHA	38	5	9	14	20	....	....	....	....	....
2005-06	U. of Notre Dame	CCHA	36	11	12	23	28	....	....	....	....	....
2006-07	Wilkes-Barre	AHL	32	5	9	14	39	11	1	1	2	2
	Wheeling Nailers	ECHL	19	6	11	17	23	....	....	....	....	....
2007-08	Wilkes-Barre	AHL	74	12	14	26	82	23	2	6	8	21

Signed as a free agent by **Pittsburgh**, May 29, 2007.

WANDELL, Tom (VAHN-dehl, TAWM) **DAL.**

Center. Shoots left. 6'1", 183 lbs. Born, Sodertalje, Sweden, January 29, 1987.
(Dallas' 5th choice, 146th overall, in 2005 Entry Draft).

			Regular Season					Playoffs				
Season	Club	League	GP	G	A	Pts	PIM	GP	G	A	Pts	PIM
2002-03	Sodertalje SK U18	Swe-U18	13	8	7	15	6	....	....	....	....	....
2003-04	Sodertalje SK U18	Swe-U18	6	5	7	12	6	2	0	0	0	0
	Sodertalje SK Jr.	Swe-Jr.	33	7	15	22	14	2	0	0	0	0
2004-05	Sodertalje SK Jr.	Swe-Jr.	5	1	2	3	4	....	....	....	....	....
2005-06	Sodertalje SK Jr.	Swe-Jr.	41	19	20	39	45	4	1	0	1	2
	Sodertalje SK	Sweden	6	0	0	0	0	....	....	....	....	....
	Sodertalje SK	Sweden-Q	1	1	0	1	0	....	....	....	....	....
2006-07	Assat Pori Jr.	Fin-Jr.	4	1	1	2	0	....	....	....	....	....
	Assat Pori	Finland	50	6	6	12	20	....	....	....	....	....
2007-08	Iowa Stars	AHL	53	10	9	19	16	....	....	....	....	....
	Idaho Steelheads	ECHL	3	3	0	3	2	....	....	....	....	....

WARD, Michael (WOHRD, MIGH-kuhl) **T.B.**

Defense. Shoots left. 6'2", 180 lbs. Born, Shippagan, N.B., August 13, 1989.
(Tampa Bay's 8th choice, 197th overall, in 2007 Entry Draft).

			Regular Season					Playoffs				
Season	Club	League	GP	G	A	Pts	PIM	GP	G	A	Pts	PIM
2005-06	Miramichi	NBPEI	34	6	17	23	24	....	....	....	....	....
2006-07	Lewiston	QMJHL	58	0	7	7	39	11	0	1	1	16
2007-08	Lewiston	QMJHL	70	4	16	20	91	5	0	3	3	13

WARG, Stefan (WAHRG, STEH-fan) **ANA.**

Defense. Shoots right. 6'2", 187 lbs. Born, Stockholm, Sweden, February 6, 1990.
(Anaheim's 9th choice, 143rd overall, in 2008 Entry Draft).

			Regular Season					Playoffs				
Season	Club	League	GP	G	A	Pts	PIM	GP	G	A	Pts	PIM
2006-07	Vasteras U18	Swe-U18	14	0	6	6	14	5	0	0	0	6
2007-08	Vasteras U18	Swe-U18	1	0	0	0	12	....	....	....	....	....
	Vasteras Jr.	Swe-Jr.	33	2	6	8	61	3	0	0	0	14
	VIK Vasteras HK	Sweden-2	3	0	0	0	0	....	....	....	....	....

WARN, Max (VAHRN, MAX) **DAL.**

Left wing. Shoots left. 6'2", 194 lbs. Born, Helsinki, Finland, June 10, 1988.
(Dallas' 5th choice, 150th overall, in 2006 Entry Draft).

			Regular Season					Playoffs				
Season	Club	League	GP	G	A	Pts	PIM	GP	G	A	Pts	PIM
2004-05	HIFK Helsinki U18	Fin-U18	22	6	9	15	30	7	1	3	4	4
	HIFK Helsinki Jr.	Fin-Jr.	4	0	0	0	0	2	0	0	0	0
2005-06	HIFK Helsinki U18	Fin-U18	7	5	4	9	6	7	4	2	6	6
	HIFK Helsinki Jr.	Fin-Jr.	24	3	10	13	39	....	....	....	....	....
2006-07	HIFK Helsinki Jr.	Fin-Jr.	13	5	6	11	10	10	4	6	10	6
	HIFK Helsinki	Finland	1	0	0	0	0	....	....	....	....	....
2007-08	Suomi U20	Finland-2	4	0	0	0	4	....	....	....	....	....
	HPK Hameenlinna	Finland	4	0	0	0	0	....	....	....	....	....
	Kiekko-Vantaa	Finland-2	1	2	0	2	0	....	....	....	....	....
	HIFK Helsinki Jr.	Fin-Jr.	14	3	3	6	12	....	....	....	....	....
	HIFK Helsinki	Finland	23	0	0	0	4	5	0	0	0	0

WARSOFSKY, David (wawr-SAWF-skee, DAY-vihd) **ST.L.**

Defense. Shoots left. 5'8", 160 lbs. Born, Marshfield, MA, May 30, 1990.
(St. Louis' 7th choice, 95th overall, in 2008 Entry Draft).

			Regular Season					Playoffs				
Season	Club	League	GP	G	A	Pts	PIM	GP	G	A	Pts	PIM
2005-06	Cushing	High-MA	....	8	26	34	....	....	....	....	....	....
2006-07	Cushing	High-MA	29	15	34	49	55	....	....	....	....	....
2007-08	USNTDP	U-18	41	5	29	34	26	....	....	....	....	....
	USNTDP	NAHL	15	4	2	6	8	....	....	....	....	....

• Signed Letter of Intent to attend **Boston University** (Hockey East) in fall of 2008.

WATHIER, Francis (waw-TEE-ay, FRAN-sihs) DAL.

Left wing. Shoots left. 6'3", 198 lbs. Born, St Isidore, Ont., December 7, 1984.
(Dallas' 8th choice, 185th overall, in 2003 Entry Draft).

			Regular Season					Playoffs				
Season	Club	League	GP	G	A	Pts	PIM	GP	G	A	Pts	PIM
2001-02	Hull Olympiques	QMJHL	63	1	3	4	68	12	1	2	3	30
2002-03	Hull Olympiques	QMJHL	72	9	18	27	143	20	1	6	7	20
2003-04	Gatineau	QMJHL	51	9	16	25	127	15	0	2	2	23
2004-05	Gatineau	QMJHL	67	15	20	35	96	10	0	2	2	8
2005-06	Iowa Stars	AHL	11	0	1	1	26	....	....	....	....	....
2006-07	Iowa Stars	AHL	57	14	3	17	78	12	0	4	4	25
	Idaho Steelheads	ECHL	17	4	9	13	31	7	1	1	2	4
2007-08	Iowa Stars	AHL	19	2	3	5	17	....	....	....	....	....

• Missed majority of 2005-06 season recovering from two shoulder injuries.

WATKINS, Matt (WAHT-kihns, MAT) DAL.

Right wing. Shoots left. 5'10", 180 lbs. Born, Aylesbury, Sask., November 22, 1986.
(Dallas' 6th choice, 160th overall, in 2005 Entry Draft).

			Regular Season					Playoffs				
Season	Club	League	GP	G	A	Pts	PIM	GP	G	A	Pts	PIM
2003-04	Tisdale Trojans	SMHL	44	34	37	71	52	....	....	....	....	....
2004-05	Vernon Vipers	BCHL	60	36	38	74	53	....	....	....	....	....
2005-06	North Dakota	WCHA	46	5	4	9	45	....	....	....	....	....
2006-07	North Dakota	WCHA	38	6	11	17	31	....	....	....	....	....
2007-08	North Dakota	WCHA	43	8	10	18	34	....	....	....	....	....

WATSON, Ryan (WAWT-suhn , RIGH-uhn) FLA.

Left wing. Shoots left. 6'1", 175 lbs. Born, Cambridge, Ont., March 1, 1988.
(Florida's 7th choice, 191st overall, in 2007 Entry Draft).

			Regular Season					Playoffs				
Season	Club	League	GP	G	A	Pts	PIM	GP	G	A	Pts	PIM
2005-06	Cambridge	OJHL-B	46	7	19	26	58	16	5	5	10	14
2006-07	Cambridge	OJHL-B	37	27	29	56	55	9	2	7	9	18
2007-08	Western Mich.	CCHA	34	4	4	8	16	....	....	....	....	....

WATT, J.D. (WAHT , JAY-DEE) CGY.

Right wing. Shoots right. 6'2", 205 lbs. Born, Calgary, Alta., May 25, 1987.
(Calgary's 4th choice, 111th overall, in 2005 Entry Draft).

			Regular Season					Playoffs				
Season	Club	League	GP	G	A	Pts	PIM	GP	G	A	Pts	PIM
2003-04	Drumheller	AJHL	59	20	17	37	245	....	....	....	....	....
	Vancouver Giants	WHL	3	1	0	1	0	10	0	3	3	14
2004-05	Vancouver Giants	WHL	66	6	7	13	213	....	....	....	....	....
2005-06	Vancouver Giants	WHL	58	8	29	37	199	18	4	3	7	42
2006-07	Vancouver Giants	WHL	70	34	19	53	182	21	2	3	5	72
2007-08	Red Deer Rebels	WHL	29	7	8	15	87	....	....	....	....	....
	Regina Pats	WHL	29	6	16	22	82	6	2	6	8	19

WAUGH, Geoff (WAW, JEHF) OTT.

Defense. Shoots right. 6'4", 215 lbs. Born, Winnipeg, Man., August 25, 1983.
(Dallas' 6th choice, 78th overall, in 2002 Entry Draft).

			Regular Season					Playoffs				
Season	Club	League	GP	G	A	Pts	PIM	GP	G	A	Pts	PIM
2000-01	Kindersley Klippers	SJHL	57	2	5	7	74	....	....	....	....	....
2001-02	Kindersley Klippers	SJHL	59	4	21	25	125	18	0	8	8	59
2002-03	Northern Mich.	CCHA	39	0	7	7	41	....	....	....	....	....
2003-04	Northern Mich.	CCHA	41	2	13	15	72	....	....	....	....	....
2004-05	Northern Mich.	CCHA	39	2	8	10	89	....	....	....	....	....
2005-06	Northern Mich.	CCHA	39	0	7	7	74	....	....	....	....	....
2006-07	Springfield Falcons	AHL	10	0	0	0	25	....	....	....	....	....
	Johnstown Chiefs	ECHL	56	1	12	13	91	2	1	0	1	4
2007-08	Binghamton	AHL	71	3	3	6	139	....	....	....	....	....

Signed as a free agent by **Ottawa**, August 11, 2008.

WEBER, Will (WEH-buhr, WIHL) CBJ

Defense. Shoots left. 6'4", 205 lbs. Born, Gaylord, MI, October 28, 1988.
(Columbus' 3rd choice, 53rd overall, in 2007 Entry Draft).

			Regular Season					Playoffs				
Season	Club	League	GP	G	A	Pts	PIM	GP	G	A	Pts	PIM
2003-04	Gaylord	High-MI	Statistics Not Available									
2004-05	Gaylord	High-MI	Statistics Not Available									
2005-06	Gaylord	High-MI	Statistics Not Available									
2006-07	Gaylord	High-MI	25	18	20	38	104	....	....	....	....	....
2007-08	Chicago Steel	USHL	46	8	10	18	137	....	....	....	....	....

• Signed Letter of Intent to attend **Miami University** (CCHA) in fall of 2008.

WEBER, Yannick (WEH-buhr, YAH-nihk) MTL.

Defense. Shoots right. 5'10", 199 lbs. Born, Morges, Switz., September 23, 1988.
(Montreal's 5th choice, 73rd overall, in 2007 Entry Draft).

			Regular Season					Playoffs				
Season	Club	League	GP	G	A	Pts	PIM	GP	G	A	Pts	PIM
2003-04	SC Bern Jr.	Swiss-Jr.	32	2	3	5	39	8	2	0	2	8
2004-05	SC Bern Jr.	Swiss-Jr.	37	5	4	9	62	5	0	0	0	22
2005-06	SC Bern Future Jr.	Swiss-Jr.	17	1	6	7	46	....	....	....	....	....
	SC Langenthal	Swiss-2	28	3	0	3	8	....	....	....	....	....
2006-07	SC Bern Future Jr.	Swiss-Jr.	1	0	0	0	2	....	....	....	....	....
	Kitchener Rangers	OHL	51	13	28	41	42	9	3	6	9	8
2007-08	Kitchener Rangers	OHL	59	20	35	55	79	17	4	13	17	24

OHL Second All-Star Team (2008)

WEISE, Dale (WIHGS, DAYL) NYR

Right wing. Shoots right. 6'2", 209 lbs. Born, Winnipeg, Man., August 5, 1988.
(NY Rangers' 5th choice, 111th overall, in 2008 Entry Draft).

			Regular Season					Playoffs				
Season	Club	League	GP	G	A	Pts	PIM	GP	G	A	Pts	PIM
2005-06	Swift Current	WHL	53	4	14	18	57	4	0	0	0	2
2006-07	Swift Current	WHL	67	18	25	43	94	6	0	1	1	8
2007-08	Swift Current	WHL	53	29	22	51	84	12	7	6	13	20

WELLER, Shawn (WEHL-uhr, SHAWN) OTT.

Left wing. Shoots left. 6'1", 206 lbs. Born, Glens Falls, NY, July 8, 1986.
(Ottawa's 3rd choice, 77th overall, in 2004 Entry Draft).

			Regular Season					Playoffs				
Season	Club	League	GP	G	A	Pts	PIM	GP	G	A	Pts	PIM
2001-02	South Glen Falls	High-NY	25	32	21	53	....	....	....	....	....	....
2002-03	Capital District	EJHL	Statistics Not Available									
2003-04	Capital District	EJHL	37	18	25	43	110	3	3	3	6	6
	Capital District	Exhib.	30	16	19	35	78	....	....	....	....	....
2004-05	Clarkson Knights	ECAC	33	3	11	14	72	....	....	....	....	....
2005-06	Clarkson Knights	ECAC	37	14	10	24	*103	....	....	....	....	....
2006-07	Clarkson Knights	ECAC	39	19	21	40	62	....	....	....	....	....
	Binghamton	AHL	5	0	0	0	4	....	....	....	....	....
2007-08	Binghamton	AHL	59	8	8	16	40	....	....	....	....	....
	Elmira Jackals	ECHL	10	4	5	9	11	....	....	....	....	....

WERNER, Steve (WUHR-nuhr, STEEV)

Right wing. Shoots right. 6'1", 200 lbs. Born, Washington, DC, August 8, 1984.
(Washington's 2nd choice, 83rd overall, in 2003 Entry Draft).

			Regular Season					Playoffs				
Season	Club	League	GP	G	A	Pts	PIM	GP	G	A	Pts	PIM
99-2000	Wsh. Jr. Capitals	MetroHL	42	32	45	77	....	....	....	....	....	....
2000-01	USNTDP	U-17	13	5	2	7	2	....	....	....	....	....
	USNTDP	NAHL	56	7	21	28	24	....	....	....	....	....
2001-02	USNTDP	U-18	34	10	16	26	10	....	....	....	....	....
	USNTDP	USHL	10	2	3	5	9	....	....	....	....	....
	USNTDP	NAHL	10	4	1	5	23	....	....	....	....	....
2002-03	Massachusetts	H-East	37	16	22	38	4	....	....	....	....	....
2003-04	Massachusetts	H-East	33	7	17	24	18	....	....	....	....	....
2004-05	Massachusetts	H-East	38	14	13	27	12	....	....	....	....	....
2005-06	Massachusetts	H-East	35	13	14	27	26	....	....	....	....	....
	Hershey Bears	AHL	4	0	3	3	2	....	....	....	....	....
2006-07	Hershey Bears	AHL	26	3	3	6	26	....	....	....	....	....
	South Carolina	ECHL	26	10	7	17	14	....	....	....	....	....
2007-08	Hershey Bears	AHL	8	1	4	5	2	....	....	....	....	....
	Springfield Falcons	AHL	30	9	4	13	23	....	....	....	....	....

Hockey East All-Rookie Team (2003)

WESSBECKER, John (WEHS-beh-kuhr, JAWN) T.B.

Defense. Shoots right. 6'1", 180 lbs. Born, Edina, MN, September 15, 1986.
(Tampa Bay's 9th choice, 225th overall, in 2005 Entry Draft).

			Regular Season					Playoffs				
Season	Club	League	GP	G	A	Pts	PIM	GP	G	A	Pts	PIM
2004-05	Blake Bears	High-MN	16	6	16	22	38	....	....	....	....	....
2005-06	Massachusetts	H-East	36	0	3	3	30	....	....	....	....	....
2006-07	Massachusetts	H-East	38	1	0	1	14	....	....	....	....	....
2007-08	Massachusetts	H-East	14	0	3	3	2	....	....	....	....	....

WESTGARTH, Brett (WEHST-garth, BREHT) S.J.

Defense. Shoots right. 6'2", 215 lbs. Born, Amherstburg, Ont., February 4, 1982.

			Regular Season					Playoffs				
Season	Club	League	GP	G	A	Pts	PIM	GP	G	A	Pts	PIM
2002-03	Princeton	ECAC	27	1	0	1	30	....	....	....	....	....
2003-04	Princeton	ECAC	23	0	1	1	18	....	....	....	....	....
2004-05			Did Not Play									
2005-06	Princeton	ECAC	31	3	8	11	30	....	....	....	....	....
2006-07	Princeton	ECAC	33	0	11	11	32	....	....	....	....	....
	Syracuse Crunch	AHL	5	0	1	1	6	....	....	....	....	....
2007-08	Iowa Stars	AHL	37	2	3	5	89	....	....	....	....	....
	Flint Generals	IHL	27	2	10	12	39	....	....	....	....	....

Signed as a free agent by **San Jose**, July 17, 2008.

WESTGARTH, Kevin (WEHST-garth, KEH-vihn) L.A.

Right wing. Shoots right. 6'5", 247 lbs. Born, Amherstburg, Ont., February 7, 1984.

			Regular Season					Playoffs				
Season	Club	League	GP	G	A	Pts	PIM	GP	G	A	Pts	PIM
2003-04	Princeton	ECAC	25	3	3	6	48	....	....	....	....	....
2004-05	Princeton	ECAC	29	4	3	7	36	....	....	....	....	....
2005-06	Princeton	ECAC	29	10	13	23	36	....	....	....	....	....
2006-07	Princeton	ECAC	33	8	16	24	40	....	....	....	....	....
	Manchester	AHL	14	1	2	3	44	....	....	....	....	....
2007-08	Manchester	AHL	69	6	6	12	191	4	0	0	0	6

Signed as a free agent by **Los Angeles**, March 16, 2007.

WHARTON, Kyle (WAWR-tuhn, KIGHL) CBJ

Defense. Shoots left. 6'3", 196 lbs. Born, Ottawa, Ont., March 3, 1986.
(Columbus' 3rd choice, 59th overall, in 2004 Entry Draft).

			Regular Season					Playoffs				
Season	Club	League	GP	G	A	Pts	PIM	GP	G	A	Pts	PIM
2001-02	Ottawa Valley	Minor-ON	34	18	24	42	....	....	....	....	....	....
2002-03	Ottawa 67's	OHL	39	3	5	8	16	....	....	....	....	....
2003-04	Ottawa 67's	OHL	43	4	10	14	50	7	2	3	5	4
2004-05	Ottawa 67's	OHL	29	1	12	13	23	....	....	....	....	....
	Sault Ste. Marie	OHL	28	4	12	16	22	7	1	5	6	4
2005-06	Sault Ste. Marie	OHL	34	6	16	22	62	....	....	....	....	....
	Guelph Storm	OHL	24	2	14	16	34	15	4	8	12	20
2006-07	Syracuse Crunch	AHL	2	0	0	0	4	....	....	....	....	....
	Eisbaren Berlin	Germany	30	2	6	8	36	3	0	0	0	14
2007-08	Syracuse Crunch	AHL	13	2	1	3	29	....	....	....	....	....
	Elmira Jackals	ECHL	32	4	7	11	46	....	....	....	....	....

Assigned to **Berlin** (Germany) by **Columbus**, October 25, 2006.

WHEELER, Blake (WEE-luhr, BLAYK) BOS.

Right wing. Shoots right. 6'5", 208 lbs. Born, Robbinsdale, MN, August 31, 1986.
(Phoenix's 1st choice, 5th overall, in 2004 Entry Draft).

			Regular Season					Playoffs				
Season	Club	League	GP	G	A	Pts	PIM	GP	G	A	Pts	PIM
2002-03	Breck Mustangs	High-MN	26	15	27	42	....	....	....	....	....	....
2003-04	Team Northwest	UMEHL	24	5	6	11	....	....	....	....	....	....
	Breck Mustangs	High-MN	27	39	50	89	34	3	6	5	11	0
2004-05	Green Bay	USHL	58	19	28	47	43	....	....	....	....	....
2005-06	U. of Minnesota	WCHA	39	9	14	23	41	....	....	....	....	....
2006-07	U. of Minnesota	WCHA	44	18	20	38	42	....	....	....	....	....
2007-08	U. of Minnesota	WCHA	44	15	20	35	72	....	....	....	....	....

USHL All-Rookie Team (2005)

Signed as a free agent by **Boston**, July 1, 2008.

WHITE, Patrick (WIGHT, PAT-rihk) VAN.

Center. Shoots right. 6'1", 186 lbs. Born, Grand Rapids, MN, January 20, 1989.
(Vancouver's 1st choice, 25th overall, in 2007 Entry Draft).

			Regular Season					Playoffs				
Season	Club	League	GP	G	A	Pts	PIM	GP	G	A	Pts	PIM
2003-04	Grand Rapids	High-MN	....	3	6	9	....	....	....	....	....	....
2004-05	Grand Rapids	High-MN	....	17	15	32	....	....	....	....	....	....
2005-06	Grand Rapids	High-MN	....	24	28	52	....	....	....	....	....	....
2006-07	Grand Rapids	High-MN	....	19	35	54	....	....	....	....	....	....
	Tri-City Storm	USHL	12	8	1	9	4	....	....	....	....	....
2007-08	U. of Minnesota	WCHA	45	6	4	10	20	....	....	....	....	....

WHITE, Ryan (WIGHT, RIGH-uhn) MTL.

Center. Shoots right. 6', 202 lbs. Born, Brandon, Man., March 17, 1988.
(Montreal's 4th choice, 66th overall, in 2006 Entry Draft).

			Regular Season					Playoffs				
Season	Club	League	GP	G	A	Pts	PIM	GP	G	A	Pts	PIM
2003-04	Brandon	MMHL	39	21	41	62	90	11	7	7	14	22
2004-05	Calgary Hitmen	WHL	63	9	14	23	95	12	2	1	3	26
2005-06	Calgary Hitmen	WHL	72	20	33	53	121	13	3	4	7	18
2006-07	Calgary Hitmen	WHL	72	34	55	89	97	18	6	8	14	36
2007-08	Calgary Hitmen	WHL	68	28	44	72	98	16	6	11	17	8

WHL East First All-Star Team (2007) • WHL East Second All-Star Team (2008)

WHITMORE, Derek (WHIHT-mohr, DAIR-ihk) BUF.

Forward. Shoots left. 5'11", 185 lbs. Born, Rochester, NY, December 17, 1984.

			Regular Season					Playoffs				
Season	Club	League	GP	G	A	Pts	PIM	GP	G	A	Pts	PIM
2002-03	Waterloo	USHL	58	15	13	28	51	6	1	0	1	0
2003-04	Waterloo	USHL	10	2	0	2	6	....	....	....	....	....
	Lincoln Stars	USHL	45	19	23	42	22	....	....	....	....	....
2004-05	Bowling Green	CCHA	33	11	6	17	14	....	....	....	....	....
2005-06	Bowling Green	CCHA	34	13	6	19	17	....	....	....	....	....
2006-07	Bowling Green	CCHA	38	19	10	29	20	....	....	....	....	....
2007-08	Bowling Green	CCHA	38	27	10	37	33	....	....	....	....	....
	Rochester	AHL	8	1	0	1	2	....	....	....	....	....

CCHA Second All-Star Team (2008)

Signed as a free agent by **Buffalo**, March 26, 2008.

WICK, Roman (WIHK, ROH-muhn) OTT.

Right wing. Shoots left. 6'2", 192 lbs. Born, Kloten, Switz., December 30, 1985.
(Ottawa's 8th choice, 156th overall, in 2004 Entry Draft).

			Regular Season					Playoffs				
Season	Club	League	GP	G	A	Pts	PIM	GP	G	A	Pts	PIM
2000-01	Kloten Flyers Jr.	Swiss-Jr.	26	4	1	5	6	5	1	0	1	2
2001-02	Kloten Flyers Jr.	Swiss-Jr.	34	19	27	46	32	8	1	2	3	4
2002-03	Kloten Flyers Jr.	Swiss-Jr.	28	29	22	51	68	2	0	1	1	0
	Kloten Flyers	Swiss	9	1	0	1	4	1	0	0	0	0
2003-04	Kloten Flyers	Swiss	20	1	1	2	6	....	....	....	....	....
	Kloten Flyers	Swiss-Q	7	3	1	4	0	....	....	....	....	....
	GCK Lions Zurich	Swiss-2	6	4	0	4	6	....	....	....	....	....
2004-05	Red Deer Rebels	WHL	66	32	38	70	25	7	1	2	3	6
2005-06	Red Deer Rebels	WHL	23	7	10	17	8	....	....	....	....	....
	Lethbridge	WHL	38	14	17	31	20	6	4	3	7	6
2006-07	Kloten Flyers	Swiss	44	12	11	23	20	11	1	1	2	2
2007-08	Kloten Flyers	Swiss	50	12	15	27	46	4	1	2	3	2

WIERCIOCH, Patrick (WEER-kawsh, PAT-rihk) OTT.

Defense. Shoots left. 6'4", 185 lbs. Born, Burnaby, B.C., September 12, 1990.
(Ottawa's 2nd choice, 42nd overall, in 2008 Entry Draft).

			Regular Season					Playoffs				
Season	Club	League	GP	G	A	Pts	PIM	GP	G	A	Pts	PIM
2006-07	Burnaby Express	BCHL	42	9	16	25	46	14	3	4	7	10
2007-08	Omaha Lancers	USHL	40	3	18	21	24	14	2	9	11	22

• Signed Letter of Intent to attend **University of Wisconsin** (WCHA) in fall of 2008.

WILD, Cody (WIGHLD, KOH-dee) EDM.

Defense. Shoots left. 6'1", 185 lbs. Born, Limestone, ME, June 5, 1987.
(Edmonton's 4th choice, 140th overall, in 2006 Entry Draft).

			Regular Season					Playoffs				
Season	Club	League	GP	G	A	Pts	PIM	GP	G	A	Pts	PIM
2003-04	Junior Bruins	EJHL	53	5	24	29	12	....	....	....	....	....
2004-05	Junior Bruins	EJHL	64	16	36	52	44	....	....	....	....	....
2005-06	Providence College	H-East	36	6	15	21	24	....	....	....	....	....
2006-07	Providence College	H-East	32	6	8	14	28	....	....	....	....	....
2007-08	Providence College	H-East	32	4	18	22	28	....	....	....	....	....
	Springfield Falcons	AHL	13	1	2	3	8	....	....	....	....	....

Hockey East All-Rookie Team (2006)

WILFORD, Marty (WIHL-fohrd, MAHR-tee)

Defense. Shoots left. 6'1", 212 lbs. Born, Cobourg, Ont., April 17, 1977.
(Chicago's 7th choice, 149th overall, in 1995 Entry Draft).

			Regular Season					Playoffs				
Season	Club	League	GP	G	A	Pts	PIM	GP	G	A	Pts	PIM
1993-94	Peterborough	OPJHL	40	3	19	22	*107	....	....	....	....	....
1994-95	Oshawa Generals	OHL	63	1	6	7	95	7	1	1	2	4
1995-96	Oshawa Generals	OHL	65	3	24	27	107	5	0	1	1	4
1996-97	Oshawa Generals	OHL	62	19	43	62	126	16	2	18	20	28
1997-98	Indianapolis Ice	IHL	26	0	4	4	16	....	....	....	....	....
	Columbus Chill	ECHL	46	8	27	35	123	....	....	....	....	....
1998-99	Indianapolis Ice	IHL	80	3	13	16	116	7	0	1	1	16
99-2000	Cleveland	IHL	7	0	3	3	24	....	....	....	....	....
	Houston Aeros	IHL	45	0	9	9	30	11	2	2	4	18
2000-01	Norfolk Admirals	AHL	80	7	41	48	102	9	1	5	6	8
2001-02	St. John's	AHL	60	4	21	25	70	....	....	....	....	....
	Milwaukee	AHL	8	1	3	4	12	....	....	....	....	....
	Hartford Wolf Pack	AHL	9	0	2	2	2	10	3	3	6	4
2002-03	Norfolk Admirals	AHL	80	13	35	48	87	9	0	3	3	16
2003-04	Norfolk Admirals	AHL	80	5	35	40	67	8	0	3	3	18
2004-05	Norfolk Admirals	AHL	78	7	30	37	80	6	0	4	4	15
2005-06	Manchester	AHL	79	5	36	41	81	7	0	3	3	19
2006-07	Iowa Stars	AHL	65	5	25	30	72	12	0	2	2	18
2007-08	Hamburg Freezers	Germany	56	8	34	42	70	8	0	3	3	20

OHL Second All-Star Team (1997)

Traded to **Toronto** by **Chicago** for Shawn Thornton, September 30, 2001. Traded to **Nashville** by **Toronto** with D.J. Smith for Marc Moro, March 1, 2002. Signed as a free agent by **Chicago**, July 8, 2003. Signed as a free agent by **Los Angeles**, August 10, 2005. Signed as a free agent by **Iowa** (AHL), July 25, 2006. Signed as a free agent by **Hamburg** (Germany), July 8, 2007.

WILLIAMS, Nigel (WIHL-yuhms, NIGH-juhl) COL.

Defense. Shoots left. 6'4", 226 lbs. Born, Aurora, IL, April 18, 1988.
(Colorado's 2nd choice, 51st overall, in 2006 Entry Draft).

			Regular Season					Playoffs				
Season	Club	League	GP	G	A	Pts	PIM	GP	G	A	Pts	PIM
2004-05	Team Illinois	MWEHL	60	14	18	32	....	....	....	....	....	....
	USNTDP	U-17	3	2	1	3	4	....	....	....	....	....
2005-06	USNTDP	U-18	40	3	6	9	40	....	....	....	....	....
	USNTDP	NAHL	19	3	4	7	23	....	....	....	....	....
2006-07	U. of Wisconsin	WCHA	1	0	0	0	2	....	....	....	....	....
	Saginaw Spirit	OHL	46	17	19	36	92	6	2	1	3	10
2007-08	Saginaw Spirit	OHL	29	5	19	24	60	....	....	....	....	....
	Belleville Bulls	OHL	38	10	12	22	40	21	7	11	18	20

WILSON, Colin (WIHL-suhn, KAW-lihn) NSH.

Center. Shoots left. 6'1", 213 lbs. Born, Greenwich, CT, October 20, 1989.
(Nashville's 1st choice, 7th overall, in 2008 Entry Draft).

			Regular Season					Playoffs				
Season	Club	League	GP	G	A	Pts	PIM	GP	G	A	Pts	PIM
2005-06	USNTDP	U-17	15	9	7	16	2	....	....	....	....	....
	USNTDP	U-18	16	2	4	6	8	....	....	....	....	....
	USNTDP	NAHL	34	10	11	21	10	2	0	0	0	2
2006-07	USNTDP	U-18	41	19	31	50	32	....	....	....	....	....
	USNTDP	NAHL	15	11	13	24	21	....	....	....	....	....
2007-08	Boston University	H-East	37	12	23	35	22	....	....	....	....	....

WILSON, Kelsey (WIHL-suhn, KEHL-see) NSH.

Left wing. Shoots left. 6'1", 218 lbs. Born, Sault Ste. Marie, Ont., January 22, 1986.

			Regular Season					Playoffs				
Season	Club	League	GP	G	A	Pts	PIM	GP	G	A	Pts	PIM
2003-04	Sarnia Sting	OHL	62	5	11	16	106	5	0	0	0	4
2004-05	Sarnia Sting	OHL	37	0	3	3	118	....	....	....	....	....
	Guelph Storm	OHL	23	7	4	11	78	4	0	0	0	9
2005-06	Guelph Storm	OHL	67	38	31	69	196	15	12	6	18	33
2006-07	Milwaukee	AHL	74	9	10	19	215	4	0	0	0	6
2007-08	Milwaukee	AHL	66	8	11	19	179	6	1	0	1	22

Signed as a free agent by **Nashville**, October 6, 2006.

WILSON, Kyle (WIHL-suhn, KIGHL) WSH.

Center. Shoots right. 6', 200 lbs. Born, Oakville, Ont., December 15, 1984.
(Minnesota's 12th choice, 272nd overall, in 2004 Entry Draft).

			Regular Season					Playoffs				
Season	Club	League	GP	G	A	Pts	PIM	GP	G	A	Pts	PIM
2000-01	Strathroy Rockets	OHA-B	33	12	17	29	15	5	2	2	4	2
2001-02	Strathroy Rockets	OHA-B	53	42	25	67	16	....	....	....	....	....
2002-03	Colgate	ECAC	33	4	2	6	15	....	....	....	....	....
2003-04	Colgate	ECAC	37	14	17	31	23	....	....	....	....	....
2004-05	Colgate	ECAC	30	5	18	23	12	....	....	....	....	....
2005-06	Colgate	ECAC	39	*23	18	41	22	....	....	....	....	....
2006-07	San Antonio	AHL	7	1	0	1	2	....	....	....	....	....
	South Carolina	ECHL	5	3	2	5	4	....	....	....	....	....
	Hershey Bears	AHL	54	24	30	54	26	19	7	9	16	8
2007-08	Hershey Bears	AHL	80	30	31	61	26	5	0	3	3	2

ECAC Second All-Star Team (2006)

Signed as a free agent by **San Antonio** (AHL), October 6, 2006. Signed as a free agent by **Washington**, July 5, 2007.

WILSON, Ryan (WIHL-suhn, RIGH-uhn) CGY.

Defense. Shoots left. 6'1", 207 lbs. Born, Windsor, Ont., February 3, 1987.

			Regular Season					Playoffs				
Season	Club	League	GP	G	A	Pts	PIM	GP	G	A	Pts	PIM
2003-04	St. Michael's	OHL	58	3	22	25	88	18	3	7	10	16
2004-05	St. Michael's	OHL	68	13	24	37	149	10	4	5	9	12
2005-06	St. Michael's	OHL	64	12	49	61	145	4	1	3	4	12
2006-07	Sarnia Sting	OHL	68	17	58	75	136	4	1	3	4	14
2007-08	Sarnia Sting	OHL	58	7	64	71	84	9	0	7	7	19

Signed as a free agent by **Calgary**, July 1, 2008.

WINGELS, Tommy (WIHN-guhls, TAW-mee) S.J.

Center. Shoots right. 6', 184 lbs. Born, Evanston, IL, April 12, 1988.
(San Jose's 5th choice, 177th overall, in 2008 Entry Draft).

			Regular Season					Playoffs				
Season	Club	League	GP	G	A	Pts	PIM	GP	G	A	Pts	PIM
2006-07	Cedar Rapids	USHL	47	10	18	28	52	6	3	0	3	6
2007-08	Miami U.	CCHA	42	15	14	29	22	....	....	....	....	....

WINKLER, Scott (WIHNK-luhr, SKAWT) DAL.

Center. Shoots right. 6'2", 194 lbs. Born, Asker, Norway, February 22, 1990.
(Dallas' 2nd choice, 89th overall, in 2008 Entry Draft).

			Regular Season					Playoffs				
Season	Club	League	GP	G	A	Pts	PIM	GP	G	A	Pts	PIM
2005-06	Frisk Asker IF/NTG	Norway-Jr.	3	1	0	1	0	....	....	....	....	....
2006-07	Frisk Asker IF/NTG	Norway-Jr.	26	34	30	64	20	8	5	3	8	2
	Asker 2	Norway-2	25	6	6	12	2	....	....	....	....	....
2007-08	Russell Stover	Minor-MO	70	40	52	92	36	....	....	....	....	....

• Signed Letter of Intent to attend **Colorado College** (WCHA) in fall of 2009.

WINNETT, Ben (wih-NEHT, BEHN) TOR.

Left wing. Shoots right. 5'11", 173 lbs. Born, New Westminster, B.C., April 3, 1989.
(Toronto's 3rd choice, 104th overall, in 2007 Entry Draft).

			Regular Season					Playoffs				
Season	Club	League	GP	G	A	Pts	PIM	GP	G	A	Pts	PIM
2005-06	Salmon Arm	BCHL	60	18	31	49	31	1	1	1	2	6
2006-07	Salmon Arm	BCHL	39	27	30	57	58	11	3	7	10	12
2007-08	U. of Michigan	CCHA	41	6	5	11	12	....	....	....	....	....

WISHART, Ty (wih-SHAHRT, TIGH) T.B.

Defense. Shoots left. 6'4", 205 lbs. Born, Belleville, Ont., May 19, 1988.
(San Jose's 1st choice, 16th overall, in 2006 Entry Draft).

			Regular Season					Playoffs				
Season	Club	League	GP	G	A	Pts	PIM	GP	G	A	Pts	PIM
2003-04	Comox Valley	Minor-BC	47	26	27	53	48	....	....	....	....	....
2004-05	Prince George	WHL	58	1	7	8	41	....	....	....	....	....
2005-06	Prince George	WHL	70	5	32	37	68	5	0	0	0	4
2006-07	Prince George	WHL	62	11	38	49	59	15	3	8	11	6
2007-08	Prince George	WHL	40	12	28	40	34	....	....	....	....	....
	Moose Jaw	WHL	32	4	23	27	18	6	1	3	4	2
	Worcester Sharks	AHL	5	0	0	0	0	....	....	....	....	....

WHL West Second All-Star Team (2007) • WHL East Second All-Star Team (2008)

Traded to **Tampa Bay** by **San Jose** with Matt Carle, San Jose's 1st round choice in 2009 Entry Draft and San Jose's 4th round choice in 2010 Entry Draft for Dan Boyle and Brad Lukowich, July 4, 2008.

WITKOWSKI, Luke (wiht-KOW-skee, LEWK) T.B.

Defense. Shoots right. 6'2", 200 lbs. Born, Holland, MI, April 14, 1990.
(Tampa Bay's 6th choice, 160th overall, in 2008 Entry Draft).

			Regular Season					Playoffs				
Season	Club	League	GP	G	A	Pts	PIM	GP	G	A	Pts	PIM
2006-07	Team nXi Majors	Minor-MI	59	18	22	40	172	....	....	....	....	....
2007-08	Ohio	USHL	58	3	10	13	139	....	....	....	....	....

• Signed Letter of Intent to attend **Western Michigan University** (CCHA) in fall of 2009.

WOHLBERG, David (WOHL-buhrg, DAY-vihd) N.J.

Center. Shoots left. 6'1", 192 lbs. Born, South Lyon, MI, July 18, 1990.
(New Jersey's 7th choice, 172nd overall, in 2008 Entry Draft).

			Regular Season					Playoffs				
Season	Club	League	GP	G	A	Pts	PIM	GP	G	A	Pts	PIM
2006-07	USNTDP	U-17	12	2	6	8	42	....	....	....	....	....
	USNTDP	NAHL	45	10	10	20	99	6	3	0	3	6
2007-08	USNTDP	U-18	37	9	7	16	48	....	....	....	....	....
	USNTDP	NAHL	22	10	5	15	27	....	....	....	....	....

• Signed Letter of Intent to attend **University of Michigan** (CCHA) in fall of 2008.

WRIGHT, James (RIGHT, JAYMZ) T.B.

Center. Shoots left. 6'3", 175 lbs. Born, Saskatoon, Sask., March 24, 1990.
(Tampa Bay's 2nd choice, 117th overall, in 2008 Entry Draft).

			Regular Season					Playoffs				
Season	Club	League	GP	G	A	Pts	PIM	GP	G	A	Pts	PIM
2005-06	Sask. Contacts	SMHL	41	13	19	32	43	....	....	....	....	....
	Vancouver Giants	WHL	2	0	0	0	2	....	....	....	....	....
2006-07	Vancouver Giants	WHL	48	5	7	12	31	14	3	1	4	0
2007-08	Vancouver Giants	WHL	60	13	23	36	21	6	1	0	1	2

WUDRICK, Geordie (WUD-rihk, JOHR-dee) L.A.

Left wing. Shoots left. 6'3", 204 lbs. Born, New Westminster, B.C., April 9, 1990.
(Los Angeles' 6th choice, 88th overall, in 2008 Entry Draft).

			Regular Season					Playoffs				
Season	Club	League	GP	G	A	Pts	PIM	GP	G	A	Pts	PIM
2005-06	Notre Dame	SMHL	42	14	16	30	30	....	....	....	....	....
	Swift Current	WHL	14	0	1	1	4	4	0	0	0	2
2006-07	Swift Current	WHL	67	13	11	24	60	6	1	1	2	4
2007-08	Swift Current	WHL	66	20	24	44	72	12	5	2	7	12

WYMAN, James (WIGH-muhn, JAYMZ) MTL.

Right wing. Shoots right. 6'2", 205 lbs. Born, Edina, MN, February 27, 1986.
(Montreal's 3rd choice, 100th overall, in 2004 Entry Draft).

			Regular Season					Playoffs				
Season	Club	League	GP	G	A	Pts	PIM	GP	G	A	Pts	PIM
2001-02	Blake Bears	High-MN	26	7	5	12	....	....	....	....	....	....
2002-03	Blake Bears	High-MN	28	17	23	40	12	....	....	....	....	....
2003-04	Blake Bears	High-MN	27	31	24	55	4	....	....	....	....	....
	Team Southwest	UMEHL	24	8	8	16	....	....	....	....	....	....
2004-05	Dartmouth	ECAC	33	5	6	11	4	....	....	....	....	....
2005-06	Dartmouth	ECAC	28	8	12	20	6	....	....	....	....	....
2006-07	Dartmouth	ECAC	33	13	11	24	20	....	....	....	....	....
2007-08	Dartmouth	ECAC	29	15	15	30	18	....	....	....	....	....

YACHMENEV, Denis (YATCH-muh-nehv, DEH-nihs) FLA.

Left wing. Shoots left. 6'1", 185 lbs. Born, Chelyabinsk, USSR, June 4, 1984.
(Florida's 9th choice, 200th overall, in 2002 Entry Draft).

			Regular Season					Playoffs				
Season	Club	League	GP	G	A	Pts	PIM	GP	G	A	Pts	PIM
2000-01	Chelyabinsk 2	Russia-3	36	40	27	67	....	....	....	....	....	....
2001-02	North Bay	OHL	65	17	12	29	32	5	2	0	2	0
2002-03	Saginaw Spirit	OHL	68	17	28	45	69	....	....	....	....	....
2003-04	Omsk 2	Russia-3	13	12	4	16	10	....	....	....	....	....
	Amur Khabarovsk	Russia	25	0	1	1	4	....	....	....	....	....
2004-05	Amur Khabarovsk	Russia-2	42	7	14	21	28	13	3	1	4	8
2005-06	Amur Khabarovsk	Russia-2	46	9	14	23	43	11	2	3	5	6
2006-07	Sibir Novosibirsk	Russia	16	0	0	0	8	1	0	0	0	0
	Sibir Novosibirsk 2	Russia-3	6	0	3	3	8	....	....	....	....	....
2007-08	Chelyabinsk	Russia	40	2	7	9	22	2	0	0	0	0

YEMELIN, Alexei (yeh-MUH-lehn, al-EHX-ay) MTL.

Defense. Shoots left. 6', 187 lbs. Born, Togliatti, USSR, April 25, 1986.
(Montreal's 2nd choice, 84th overall, in 2004 Entry Draft).

			Regular Season					Playoffs				
Season	Club	League	GP	G	A	Pts	PIM	GP	G	A	Pts	PIM
2002-03	Lada Togliatti 2	Russia-3	31	1	1	2	20	....	....	....	....	....
2003-04	Lada Togliatti 2	Russia-3	2	0	0	0	10	....	....	....	....	....
	CSK VVS Samara	Russia-2	52	2	4	6	180	1	0	0	0	18
2004-05	Lada Togliatti	Russia	12	0	1	1	24	2	0	0	0	2
2005-06	Lada Togliatti	Russia	44	6	6	12	131	6	0	1	1	*47
2006-07	Lada Togliatti	Russia	43	2	5	7	74	3	0	0	0	4
2007-08	Ak Bars Kazan	Russia	56	0	5	5	123	10	0	1	1	10

YIP, Brandon (YIHP, BRAN-duhn) COL.

Right wing. Shoots right. 6'1", 180 lbs. Born, Vancouver, B.C., April 25, 1985.
(Colorado's 7th choice, 239th overall, in 2004 Entry Draft).

			Regular Season					Playoffs				
Season	Club	League	GP	G	A	Pts	PIM	GP	G	A	Pts	PIM
2003-04	Coquitlam Express	BCHL	56	31	38	69	87	4	1	2	3	14
2004-05	Coquitlam Express	BCHL	43	20	42	62	92	7	6	1	7	12
2005-06	Boston University	H-East	39	9	22	31	59	....	....	....	....	....
2006-07	Boston University	H-East	18	5	6	11	29	....	....	....	....	....
2007-08	Boston University	H-East	37	11	12	23	28	....	....	....	....	....

Hockey East All-Rookie Team (2006) • Hockey East Rookie of the Year (2006)

YOUNG, Harry (YUHNG, HAIR-ee) N.J.

Defense. Shoots left. 6'4", 205 lbs. Born, Windsor, Ont., November 12, 1989.
(New Jersey's 8th choice, 202nd overall, in 2008 Entry Draft).

			Regular Season					Playoffs				
Season	Club	League	GP	G	A	Pts	PIM	GP	G	A	Pts	PIM
2005-06	Guelph Storm	OHL	44	0	4	4	20	....	....	....	....	....
2006-07	Guelph Storm	OHL	7	0	2	2	11	....	....	....	....	....
	Windsor Spitfires	OHL	47	0	3	3	72	....	....	....	....	....
2007-08	Windsor Spitfires	OHL	68	2	12	14	155	5	0	1	1	8

YUNKOV, Mikhail (yuhn-KAWF, mih-kigh-EHL) WSH.

Center. Shoots left. 6', 180 lbs. Born, Voskresensk, USSR, February 16, 1986.
(Washington's 5th choice, 62nd overall, in 2004 Entry Draft).

			Regular Season					Playoffs				
Season	Club	League	GP	G	A	Pts	PIM	GP	G	A	Pts	PIM
2001-02	Krylja Sovetov 2	Russia-3	4	0	1	1	0	....	....	....	....	....
2002-03	Krylja Sovetov 2	Russia-3	3	0	1	1	0	....	....	....	....	....
	Krylja Sovetov	Russia	7	1	0	1	2	....	....	....	....	....
2003-04	Krylja Sovetov	Russia-2	38	5	10	15	12	4	0	1	1	0
	Krylja Sovetov 2	Russia-3	STATISTICS NOT AVAILABLE									
2004-05	Krylja Sovetov 2	Russia-3	1	0	0	0	0	....	....	....	....	....
	Krylja Sovetov	Russia-2	38	9	14	23	22	3	0	1	1	4
2005-06	Ak Bars Kazan	Russia	33	3	4	7	35	11	0	1	1	6
2006-07	Ak Bars Kazan	Russia	47	3	6	9	12	16	1	2	3	8
2007-08	Spartak Moscow	Russia	57	4	6	10	20	5	1	0	1	6

ZABORSKY, Tomas (za-BOHR-skee, TAW-mahsh) NYR

Wing. Shoots left. 6'1", 188 lbs. Born, Banska Bystrica, Czech., November 14, 1987.
(NY Rangers' 5th choice, 137th overall, in 2006 Entry Draft).

			Regular Season					Playoffs				
Season	Club	League	GP	G	A	Pts	PIM	GP	G	A	Pts	PIM
2003-04	Dukla Trencin U18	Svk-U18	46	20	12	32	8	7	4	2	6	4
2004-05	Dukla Trencin U18	Svk-U18	46	44	25	69	53	7	4	4	8	39
	Dukla Trencin Jr.	Slovak-Jr.	7	1	2	3	0	1	0	1	1	0
2005-06	Dukla Trencin Jr.	Slovak-Jr.	42	39	22	61	18	7	10	5	15	2
	Dukla Trencin	Slovakia	4	0	0	0	2	....	....	....	....	....
	P. Bystrica	Slovak-2	5	0	1	1	2	....	....	....	....	....
2006-07	Saginaw Spirit	OHL	59	19	24	43	18	6	1	2	3	4
2007-08	Saginaw Spirit	OHL	68	31	39	70	42	4	2	1	3	2
	Hartford Wolf Pack	AHL	2	0	1	1	0	....	....	....	....	....

ZACKRISSON, Patrik (ZAK-rihs-suhn, PAT-rihk) S.J.

Right wing. Shoots right. 5'11", 190 lbs. Born, Ekero, Sweden, March 27, 1987.
(San Jose's 5th choice, 165th overall, in 2007 Entry Draft).

			Regular Season					Playoffs				
Season	Club	League	GP	G	A	Pts	PIM	GP	G	A	Pts	PIM
2002-03	Ska IK	Sweden-3	17	3	6	9	4	....	....	....	....	....
2003-04	V.Frolunda U18	Swe-U18	14	5	9	14	4	7	2	3	5	0
	V.Frolunda Jr.	Swe-Jr.	2	0	1	1	0	....	....	....	....	....
2004-05	Frolunda U18	Swe-U18	2	2	1	3	29	6	3	3	6	4
	Frolunda Jr.	Swe-Jr.	32	16	9	25	22	6	1	2	3	0
2005-06	Frolunda Jr.	Swe-Jr.	39	26	19	45	34	7	4	5	9	4
	Frolunda	Sweden	10	0	1	1	0	....	....	....	....	....
2006-07	Rogle	Sweden-2	38	17	23	40	32	....	....	....	....	....
2007-08	Linkopings HC	Sweden	55	4	9	13	35	16	3	1	4	12

ZAGRAPAN, Marek (ZAG-rah-pahn, MAIR-ehk) BUF.

Center. Shoots left. 6'1", 195 lbs. Born, Presov, Czech., December 6, 1986.
(Buffalo's 1st choice, 13th overall, in 2005 Entry Draft).

			Regular Season					Playoffs				
Season	Club	League	GP	G	A	Pts	PIM	GP	G	A	Pts	PIM
2001-02	HC Zlin U17	CzR-U17	48	23	14	37	24	6	1	0	1	2
2002-03	HC Zlin U17	CzR-U17	15	18	16	34	14	3	1	0	1	6
	HC Zlin Jr.	CzRep-Jr.	25	9	13	22	10	....	....	....	....	....
	HC Hame Zlin	CzRep	13	1	1	2	10	....	....	....	....	....
2003-04	HC Zlin Jr.	CzRep-Jr.	42	23	12	35	40	7	1	3	4	4
	HC Hame Zlin	CzRep	5	0	0	0	0	....	....	....	....	....
	HC Kometa Brno	CzRep-2	5	0	1	1	0	....	....	....	....	....
2004-05	Chicoutimi	QMJHL	59	32	50	82	50	17	11	6	17	28
2005-06	Chicoutimi	QMJHL	59	35	52	87	63	8	4	6	10	4
2006-07	Rochester	AHL	71	17	21	38	39	6	1	0	1	2
2007-08	Rochester	AHL	76	18	22	40	66	....	....	....	....	....

ZAHN, Teigan (ZAWN, TEE-guhn) CHI.

Defense. Shoots left. 6'1", 217 lbs. Born, Regina, Sask., January 4, 1990.
(Chicago's 3rd choice, 132nd overall, in 2008 Entry Draft).

			Regular Season					Playoffs				
Season	Club	League	GP	G	A	Pts	PIM	GP	G	A	Pts	PIM
2005-06	Moose Jaw	SMHL	STATISTICS NOT AVAILABLE									
	Saskatoon Blades	WHL	1	0	0	0	2	....	....	....	....	....
2006-07	Saskatoon Blades	WHL	39	0	3	3	68	....	....	....	....	....
2007-08	Saskatoon Blades	WHL	69	4	15	19	104	....	....	....	....	....

ZALEWSKI, Steven (zuh-LOO-skee, STEE-vehn) S.J.

Center. Shoots left. 6', 190 lbs. Born, Utica, NY, August 20, 1986.
(San Jose's 5th choice, 153rd overall, in 2004 Entry Draft).

			Regular Season					Playoffs				
Season	Club	League	GP	G	A	Pts	PIM	GP	G	A	Pts	PIM
2003-04	Northwood	High-NY	40	32	34	66	22	....	....	....	....	....
2004-05	Clarkson Knights	ECAC	39	12	7	19	60	....	....	....	....	....
2005-06	Clarkson Knights	ECAC	35	9	13	22	50	....	....	....	....	....
2006-07	Clarkson Knights	ECAC	39	16	18	34	44	....	....	....	....	....
2007-08	Clarkson Knights	ECAC	38	21	12	33	34	....	....	....	....	....
	Worcester Sharks	AHL	7	2	4	6	0	....	....	....	....	....

ECAC First All-Star Team (2008)

ZAPLETAL, Jan (ZAH-pleht-tuhl, YAHN) T.B.

Defense. Shoots right. 6'3", 190 lbs. Born, Brno, Czech., August 21, 1986.
(Tampa Bay's 6th choice, 188th overall, in 2004 Entry Draft).

			Regular Season					Playoffs				
Season	**Club**	**League**	**GP**	**G**	**A**	**Pts**	**PIM**	**GP**	**G**	**A**	**Pts**	**PIM**
2001-02	HC Ytong Brno Jr.	CzRep-Jr.	27	3	0	3	8	....	....	....	....	....
2002-03	HC Vsetin Jr.	CzRep-Jr.	27	4	3	7	8	10	0	0	0	2
2003-04	HC Vsetin Jr.	CzRep-Jr.	51	2	4	6	26	4	0	0	0	0
2004-05	Regina Pats	WHL	55	3	2	5	20	....	....	....	....	....
2005-06	HC Vsetin Jr.	CzRep-Jr.	9	0	3	3	2	....	....	....	....	....
	HC Vsetin	CzRep	16	0	0	0	10	....	....	....	....	....
	Jind. Hradec	CzRep-2	20	0	0	0	16	....	....	....	....	....
2006-07	VSK Technika Brno	CzRep-3	22	1	5	6	32	....	....	....	....	....
2007-08	HC Olomouc	CzRep-2	10	0	0	0	10	....	....	....	....	....
	HC TJ Sternberk	CzRep-3	11	2	3	5	12	....	....	....	....	....
	SHK Hodonin	CzRep-3	16	2	2	4	22	3	0	1	1	2

ZARB, Chris (ZAHRB, KRIHS) PHI.

Defense. Shoots right. 6'4", 210 lbs. Born, San Diego, CA, January 11, 1985.
(Philadelphia's 4th choice, 144th overall, in 2004 Entry Draft).

			Regular Season					Playoffs				
Season	**Club**	**League**	**GP**	**G**	**A**	**Pts**	**PIM**	**GP**	**G**	**A**	**Pts**	**PIM**
2002-03	Det. Caesars	MWEHL	60	15	35	50	60	....	....	....	....	....
2003-04	Tri-City Storm	USHL	43	4	20	24	78	11	0	4	4	17
2004-05	Tri-City Storm	USHL	48	9	14	23	147	....	....	....	....	....
2005-06	Ferris State	CCHA	29	0	10	10	35	....	....	....	....	....
2006-07	Ferris State	CCHA	29	1	13	14	75	....	....	....	....	....
2007-08	Ferris State	CCHA	21	1	4	5	20	....	....	....	....	....

ZELISKA, Lukas (zeh-LIHS-kah, LOO-kahsh) NYR

Center. Shoots right. 5'11", 175 lbs. Born, Martin, Czech., January 8, 1988.
(NY Rangers' 7th choice, 204th overall, in 2006 Entry Draft).

			Regular Season					Playoffs				
Season	**Club**	**League**	**GP**	**G**	**A**	**Pts**	**PIM**	**GP**	**G**	**A**	**Pts**	**PIM**
2003-04	HC Trinec U17	CzR-U17	48	39	41	80	166	5	2	2	4	4
	HC Trinec Jr.	CzRep-Jr.	7	1	1	2	2	....	....	....	....	....
2004-05	HC Trinec U17	CzR-U17	11	7	11	18	40	....	....	....	....	....
	HC Trinec Jr.	CzRep-Jr.	13	1	2	3	6	....	....	....	....	....
2005-06	HC Trinec Jr.	CzRep-Jr.	29	8	3	11	81	7	4	1	5	22
	HC Ocelari Trinec	CzRep	1	0	0	0	0	....	....	....	....	....
2006-07	Prince Albert	WHL	61	4	25	29	77	5	1	4	5	4
2007-08	Prostejov	CzRep-2	2	0	0	0	0	....	....	....	....	....
	HC Trinec Jr.	CzRep-Jr.	38	23	29	52	236	7	2	4	6	10

ZHARKOV, Vladimir (zhar-KAWV, vla-DIH-meer) N.J.

Right wing. Shoots left. 6', 185 lbs. Born, Elektrostal, USSR, January 10, 1988.
(New Jersey's 4th choice, 77th overall, in 2006 Entry Draft).

			Regular Season					Playoffs				
Season	**Club**	**League**	**GP**	**G**	**A**	**Pts**	**PIM**	**GP**	**G**	**A**	**Pts**	**PIM**
2004-05	CSKA Moscow 2	Russia-3	STATISTICS NOT AVAILABLE									
2005-06	CSKA Moscow	Russia	4	0	1	1	4	1	0	0	0	0
	CSKA Moscow 2	Russia-3	48	17	22	39	86	....	....	....	....	....
2006-07	CSKA Moscow	Russia	47	4	1	5	18	12	0	1	1	2
2007-08	CSKA Moscow	Russia	30	5	2	7	6	....	....	....	....	....
	CSKA Moscow 2	Russia-3	4	3	4	7	4	12	8	7	15	8

ZIMAKOV, Sergei (zih-MAH-kahv, SAIR-gay) WSH.

Defense. Shoots left. 6'1", 194 lbs. Born, Moscow, USSR, January 15, 1978.
(Washington's 4th choice, 58th overall, in 1996 Entry Draft).

			Regular Season					Playoffs				
Season	**Club**	**League**	**GP**	**G**	**A**	**Pts**	**PIM**	**GP**	**G**	**A**	**Pts**	**PIM**
1994-95	Omaha Lancers	USHL	48	14	46	60	22	....	....	....	....	....
1995-96	Krylja Sovetov	CIS	49	2	7	9	36	....	....	....	....	....
1996-97	Krylja Sovetov	Russia	39	4	3	7	57	2	0	0	0	0
1997-98	Krylja Sovetov	Russia	42	4	1	5	48	....	....	....	....	....
1998-99	Ak Bars Kazan	Russia	28	1	0	1	6	8	0	1	1	6
99-2000	Perm	Russia	31	1	2	3	34	3	0	1	1	0
2000-01	CSKA Moscow 2	Russia-3	3	2	2	4	2	....	....	....	....	....
	CSKA Moscow	Russia	26	1	5	6	28	....	....	....	....	....
2001-02	CSKA Moscow	Russia	42	3	10	13	74	....	....	....	....	....
2002-03	Ufa	Russia	11	0	0	0	8	....	....	....	....	....
	Ufa 2	Russia-3	STATISTICS NOT AVAILABLE									
2003-04	Spartak Moscow	Russia-2	60	11	17	28	38	12	0	1	1	10
2004-05	Spartak Moscow	Russia	23	2	2	4	20	....	....	....	....	....
2005-06	Spartak Moscow	Russia	46	3	11	14	55	3	0	0	0	4
2006-07	Vityaz Chekhov	Russia	36	3	2	5	38	3	0	0	0	0
2007-08	Spartak Moscow	Russia	11	1	1	2	10	....	....	....	....	....
	Krylja Sovetov	Russia-2	17	7	5	12	34	....	....	....	....	....

ZIMMERMAN, Sean (ZIH-mehr-man, SHAWN) N.J.

Defense. Shoots right. 6'2", 210 lbs. Born, Denver, CO, May 24, 1987.
(New Jersey's 6th choice, 170th overall, in 2005 Entry Draft).

			Regular Season					Playoffs				
Season	**Club**	**League**	**GP**	**G**	**A**	**Pts**	**PIM**	**GP**	**G**	**A**	**Pts**	**PIM**
2002-03	Spokane Braves	KIJHL	45	3	5	8	70	....	....	....	....	....
2003-04	Spokane Chiefs	WHL	67	4	4	8	16	4	0	0	0	0
2004-05	Spokane Chiefs	WHL	71	2	14	16	36	....	....	....	....	....
2005-06	Spokane Chiefs	WHL	72	2	19	21	44	....	....	....	....	....
	Albany River Rats	AHL	6	0	0	0	4	....	....	....	....	....
2006-07	Spokane Chiefs	WHL	60	2	12	14	69	6	0	2	2	2
	Lowell Devils	AHL	1	0	0	0	2	....	....	....	....	....
2007-08	Lowell Devils	AHL	66	0	6	6	47	....	....	....	....	....
	Trenton Devils	ECHL	8	0	1	1	10	....	....	....	....	....

ZUBAREV, Andrei (ZOO-bah-rehv, AWN-dray) ATL.

Defense. Shoots left. 6'1", 200 lbs. Born, Ufa, USSR, March 3, 1987.
(Atlanta's 7th choice, 187th overall, in 2005 Entry Draft).

			Regular Season					Playoffs				
Season	**Club**	**League**	**GP**	**G**	**A**	**Pts**	**PIM**	**GP**	**G**	**A**	**Pts**	**PIM**
2003-04	Ufa 2	Russia-3	STATISTICS NOT AVAILABLE									
	Ufa	Russia	6	0	1	1	4	....	....	....	....	....
2004-05	Ufa 2	Russia-3	28	2	4	6	32	....	....	....	....	....
	Ufa	Russia	5	0	0	0	4	....	....	....	....	....
2005-06	Ak Bars Kazan	Russia	40	2	11	13	40	....	....	....	....	....
2006-07	Ak Bars Kazan	Russia	20	0	0	0	32	....	....	....	....	....
2007-08	Ak Bars Kazan	Russia	39	4	3	7	86	2	0	0	0	0

2008-09 NHL Player Register

Note: The 2008-09 NHL Player Register lists forwards and defensemen only. Goaltenders are listed separately. The NHL Player Register lists every active skater who played in the NHL in 2007-08 plus additional players with NHL experience. Trades and roster changes are current as of August 21, 2008.

Abbreviations: GP – games played; **G** – goals; **A** – assists; **Pts** – points; **PIM** – penalties in minutes; **PP** – power-play goals; **SH** – shorthanded goals; **GW** – game-winning goals; **S** – shots; **%** – shooting percentage; **+/–** – plus/minus; **TF** – total faceoffs taken; **F%** – faceoff winning percentage; **Min** – average time on ice per game; ***** – league-leading total
♦ – member of Stanley Cup-winning team.

Prospect Register begins on page 273.
Goaltender Register begins on page 579.
League abbreviations are listed on page 654.

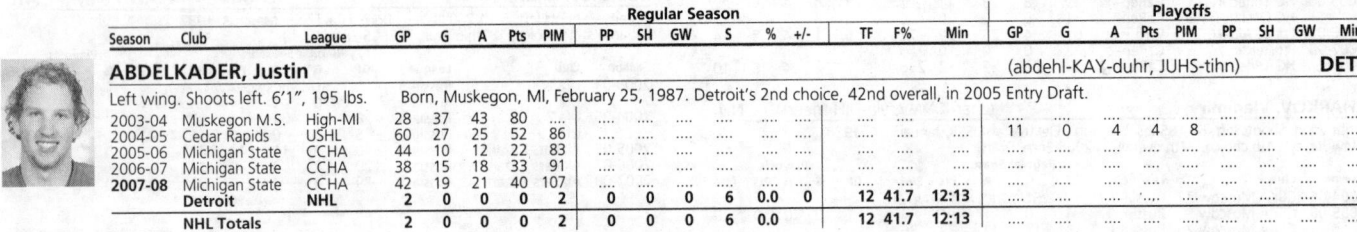

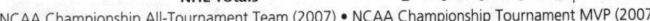

ABDELKADER, Justin

(abdehl-KAY-duhr, JUHS-tihn) **DET.**

Left wing. Shoots left. 6'1", 195 lbs. Born, Muskegon, MI, February 25, 1987. Detroit's 2nd choice, 42nd overall, in 2005 Entry Draft.

			Regular Season														Playoffs								
Season	Club	League	GP	G	A	Pts	PIM	PP	SH	GW	S	%	+/-	TF	F%	Min	GP	G	A	Pts	PIM	PP	SH	GW	Min
2003-04	Muskegon M.S.	High-MI	28	37	43	80	....	....	....	....	....	....	....	....	....	....	....	....	....	....	....	....	....	....	....
2004-05	Cedar Rapids	USHL	60	27	25	52	86	....	....	....	....	....	....	....	....	....	11	0	4	4	8	....	....	....	....
2005-06	Michigan State	CCHA	44	10	12	22	83	....	....	....	....	....	....	....	....	....	....	....	....	....	....	....	....	....	....
2006-07	Michigan State	CCHA	38	15	18	33	91	....	....	....	....	....	....	....	....	....	....	....	....	....	....	....	....	....	....
2007-08	Michigan State	CCHA	42	19	21	40	107	....	....	....	....	....	....	....	....	....	....	....	....	....	....	....	....	....	....
	Detroit	**NHL**	**2**	**0**	**0**	**0**	**2**	**0**	**0**	**0**	**6**	**0.0**	**0**	**12**	**41.7**	**12:13**	....	....	....	....	....	....	....	....	....
	NHL Totals		**2**	**0**	**0**	**0**	**2**	**0**	**0**	**0**	**6**	**0.0**		**12**	**41.7**	**12:13**	....	....	....	....	....	....	....	....	....

NCAA Championship All-Tournament Team (2007) • NCAA Championship Tournament MVP (2007)

ABID, Ramzi

(a-BIHD, RAM-zee)

Left wing. Shoots left. 6'2", 210 lbs. Born, Montreal, Que., March 24, 1980. Phoenix's 3rd choice, 85th overall, in 2000 Entry Draft.

			Regular Season														Playoffs								
Season	Club	League	GP	G	A	Pts	PIM	PP	SH	GW	S	%	+/-	TF	F%	Min	GP	G	A	Pts	PIM	PP	SH	GW	Min
1995-96	Richelieu Riverains	QAAA	42	10	14	24	18	....	....	....	....	....	....	....	....	....	4	1	2	3	2	....	....	....	....
1996-97	Chicoutimi	QMJHL	65	13	24	37	141	....	....	....	....	....	....	....	....	....	21	2	12	14	28	....	....	....	....
1997-98	Chicoutimi	QMJHL	68	50	*85	*135	266	....	....	....	....	....	....	....	....	....	6	3	4	7	10	....	....	....	....
1998-99	Chicoutimi	QMJHL	21	11	15	26	97	....	....	....	....	....	....	....	....	....	....	....	....	....	....	....	....	....	....
	Acadie-Bathurst	QMJHL	24	14	22	36	102	....	....	....	....	....	....	....	....	....	23	14	20	34	*84	....	....	....	....
99-2000	Acadie-Bathurst	QMJHL	13	10	11	21	61	....	....	....	....	....	....	....	....	....	....	....	....	....	....	....	....	....	....
	Halifax	QMJHL	59	57	80	137	148	....	....	....	....	....	....	....	....	....	10	10	13	23	18	....	....	....	....
2000-01	Springfield	AHL	17	6	4	10	38	....	....	....	....	....	....	....	....	....	....	....	....	....	....	....	....	....	....
2001-02	Springfield	AHL	66	18	25	43	214	....	....	....	....	....	....	....	....	....	....	....	....	....	....	....	....	....	....
2002-03	**Phoenix**	**NHL**	**30**	**10**	**8**	**18**	**30**	**4**	**0**	**3**	**52**	**19.2**	**1**	**1**	**100.0**	**12:30**	....	....	....	....	....	....	....	....	....
	Springfield	AHL	27	15	10	25	50	....	....	....	....	....	....	....	....	....	....	....	....	....	....	....	....	....	....
	Pittsburgh	**NHL**	**3**	**0**	**0**	**0**	**2**	**0**	**0**	**0**	**7**	**0.0**	**–5**	**1**	**0.0**	**17:33**	....	....	....	....	....	....	....	....	....
2003-04	**Pittsburgh**	**NHL**	**16**	**3**	**2**	**5**	**27**	**2**	**0**	**1**	**35**	**8.6**	**–5**	**2**	**0.0**	**12:56**	....	....	....	....	....	....	....	....	....
2004-05	Wilkes-Barre	AHL	78	26	29	55	119	....	....	....	....	....	....	....	....	....	7	0	2	2	18	....	....	....	....
2005-06	**Atlanta**	**NHL**	**6**	**0**	**2**	**2**	**6**	**0**	**0**	**0**	**6**	**0.0**	**1**	**0**	**0.0**	**8:10**	....	....	....	....	....	....	....	....	....
	Chicago Wolves	AHL	75	34	42	76	165	....	....	....	....	....	....	....	....	....	....	....	....	....	....	....	....	....	....
2006-07	**Nashville**	**NHL**	**13**	**1**	**4**	**5**	**13**	**0**	**0**	**0**	**12**	**8.3**	**–3**	**1**	**0.0**	**10:51**	**2**	**0**	**0**	**0**	**0**	**0**	**0**	**0**	**5:18**
	Milwaukee	AHL	57	19	30	49	70	....	....	....	....	....	....	....	....	....	2	0	1	1	6	....	....	....	....
2007-08	SC Bern	Swiss	41	20	11	31	56	....	....	....	....	....	....	....	....	....	5	3	2	5	14	....	....	....	....
	NHL Totals		**68**	**14**	**16**	**30**	**78**	**6**	**0**	**4**	**112**	**12.5**		**5**	**20.0**	**12:08**	**2**	**0**	**0**	**0**	**0**	**0**	**0**	**0**	**5:18**

• Re-entered NHL Entry Draft. Originally Colorado's 5th choice, 28th overall, in 1998 Entry Draft.

QMJHL First All-Star Team (1998, 2000) • Jean Beliveau Trophy (QMJHL - Leading Scorer) (1998) • Michel Briere Trophy (QMJHL - MVP) (1998) • Canadian Major Junior First All-Star Team (2000) • Ed Chynoweth Trophy (Memorial Cup Tournament - Leading Scorer) (2000)

• Missed majority of 2000-01 season recovering from a wrist injury suffered in game vs. Louisville (AHL), October 27, 2000. Traded to **Pittsburgh** by **Phoenix** with Dan Focht and Guillaume Lefebvre for Jan Hrdina and Francois Leroux, March 11, 2003. • Missed majority of 2003-04 season recovering from knee injury suffered in game vs. Edmonton, December 6, 2003. Signed as a free agent by **Atlanta**, August 8, 2005. Signed as a free agent by **Nashville**, July 21, 2006. Signed as a free agent by **Bern** (Swiss), July 10, 2007.

ADAMS, Craig

(A-duhms, KRAYG) **CHI.**

Right wing. Shoots right. 6', 200 lbs. Born, Seria, Brunei, April 26, 1977. Hartford's 9th choice, 223rd overall, in 1996 Entry Draft.

			Regular Season														Playoffs								
Season	Club	League	GP	G	A	Pts	PIM	PP	SH	GW	S	%	+/-	TF	F%	Min	GP	G	A	Pts	PIM	PP	SH	GW	Min
1995-96	Harvard Crimson	ECAC	34	8	9	17	56	....	....	....	....	....	....	....	....	....	....	....	....	....	....	....	....	....	....
1996-97	Harvard Crimson	ECAC	32	6	4	10	36	....	....	....	....	....	....	....	....	....	....	....	....	....	....	....	....	....	....
1997-98	Harvard Crimson	ECAC	12	6	6	12	12	....	....	....	....	....	....	....	....	....	....	....	....	....	....	....	....	....	....
1998-99	Harvard Crimson	ECAC	31	9	14	23	53	....	....	....	....	....	....	....	....	....	....	....	....	....	....	....	....	....	....
99-2000	Cincinnati	IHL	73	12	12	24	124	....	....	....	....	....	....	....	....	....	8	0	1	1	14	....	....	....	....
2000-01	**Carolina**	**NHL**	**44**	**1**	**0**	**1**	**20**	**0**	**0**	**0**	**15**	**6.7**	**–7**	**4**	**25.0**	**4:30**	**3**	**0**	**0**	**0**	**0**	**0**	**0**	**0**	**3:45**
	Cincinnati	IHL	4	0	1	1	9	....	....	....	....	....	....	....	....	....	1	0	0	0	2	....	....	....	....
2001-02	**Carolina**	**NHL**	**33**	**0**	**1**	**1**	**38**	**0**	**0**	**0**	**17**	**0.0**	**2**	**9**	**33.3**	**5:54**	**1**	**0**	**0**	**0**	**0**	**0**	**0**	**0**	**7:41**
	Lowell	AHL	22	5	4	9	51	....	....	....	....	....	....	....	....	....	....	....	....	....	....	....	....	....	....
2002-03	**Carolina**	**NHL**	**81**	**6**	**12**	**18**	**71**	**1**	**0**	**1**	**107**	**5.6**	**–11**	**20**	**35.0**	**12:12**	....	....	....	....	....	....	....	....	....
2003-04	**Carolina**	**NHL**	**80**	**7**	**10**	**17**	**69**	**0**	**1**	**0**	**110**	**6.4**	**–5**	**20**	**45.0**	**13:41**	....	....	....	....	....	....	....	....	....
2004-05	Milano Vipers	Italy	30	15	14	29	57	....	....	....	....	....	....	....	....	....	15	4	7	11	26	....	....	....	....
2005-06 ♦	**Carolina**	**NHL**	**67**	**10**	**11**	**21**	**51**	**1**	**1**	**2**	**68**	**14.7**	**1**	**13**	**53.9**	**12:18**	**25**	**0**	**0**	**0**	**10**	**0**	**0**	**0**	**8:16**
	Lowell	AHL	13	4	3	7	20	....	....	....	....	....	....	....	....	....	....	....	....	....	....	....	....	....	....
2006-07	**Carolina**	**NHL**	**82**	**7**	**7**	**14**	**54**	**0**	**1**	**1**	**71**	**9.9**	**–9**	**36**	**30.6**	**10:04**	....	....	....	....	....	....	....	....	....
2007-08	**Carolina**	**NHL**	**40**	**2**	**3**	**5**	**34**	**0**	**0**	**0**	**31**	**6.5**	**–8**	**11**	**27.3**	**9:48**	....	....	....	....	....	....	....	....	....
	Chicago	**NHL**	**35**	**2**	**4**	**6**	**24**	**0**	**1**	**1**	**32**	**6.3**	**–8**	**30**	**53.3**	**11:56**	....	....	....	....	....	....	....	....	....
	NHL Totals		**462**	**35**	**48**	**83**	**361**	**2**	**4**	**5**	**451**	**7.8**		**143**	**39.9**	**10:41**	**29**	**0**	**0**	**0**	**10**	**0**	**0**	**0**	**7:46**

Rights transferred to **Carolina** after **Hartford** franchise relocated, June 25, 1997. • Missed majority of 1997-98 season recovering from shoulder injury suffered in game vs. University of Wisconsin (WCHA), December 27, 1997. Signed as a free agent by **Milano**, (Italy), July 28, 2004. Signed as a free agent by **Anaheim**, August 25, 2005. Traded to **Carolina** by **Anaheim** for Bruno St. Jacques, October 3, 2005. Traded to **Chicago** by **Carolina** for future considerations, January 17, 2008.

			Regular Season														Playoffs								
Season	Club	League	GP	G	A	Pts	PIM	PP	SH	GW	S	%	+/-	TF	F%	Min	GP	G	A	Pts	PIM	PP	SH	GW	Min

ADAMS, Kevyn

(A-duhms, KEH-vihn)

Center. Shoots right. 6'1", 200 lbs. Born, Washington, DC, October 8, 1974. Boston's 1st choice, 25th overall, in 1993 Entry Draft.

Season	Club	League	GP	G	A	Pts	PIM	PP	SH	GW	S	%	+/-	TF	F%	Min	GP	G	A	Pts	PIM	PP	SH	GW	Min
1990-91	Niagara Scenics	NAHL	55	17	20	37	24	....	....	....	....	....	....	....	....	....	....	....	....	....	....	....	....	....	....
1991-92	Niagara Scenics	NAHL	40	25	33	58	51	....	....	....	....	....	....	....	....	....	....	....	....	....	....	....	....	....	....
1992-93	Miami U.	CCHA	40	17	15	32	18	....	....	....	....	....	....	....	....	....	....	....	....	....	....	....	....	....	....
1993-94	Miami U.	CCHA	36	15	28	43	24	....	....	....	....	....	....	....	....	....	....	....	....	....	....	....	....	....	....
1994-95	Miami U.	CCHA	38	20	29	49	30	....	....	....	....	....	....	....	....	....	....	....	....	....	....	....	....	....	....
1995-96	Miami U.	CCHA	36	17	30	47	30	....	....	....	....	....	....	....	....	....	....	....	....	....	....	....	....	....	....
1996-97	Grand Rapids	IHL	82	22	25	47	47	....	....	....	....	....	....	....	....	....	5	1	1	2	4	....	....	....	....
1997-98	**Toronto**	**NHL**	**5**	**0**	**0**	**0**	**7**	**0**	**0**	**0**	**3**	**0.0**	**0**	....	....	....	....	....	....	....	....	....	....	....	....
	St. John's	AHL	59	17	20	37	99	....	....	....	....	....	....	....	....	....	4	0	0	0	4	....	....	....	....
1998-99	**Toronto**	**NHL**	**1**	**0**	**0**	**0**	**0**	**0**	**0**	**0**	**1**	**0.0**	**0**	**9**	**44.4**	**7:56**	**7**	**0**	**2**	**2**	**14**	**0**	**0**	**0**	**11:18**
	St. John's	AHL	80	15	35	50	85	....	....	....	....	....	....	....	....	....	5	2	0	2	4	....	....	....	....
99-2000	**Toronto**	**NHL**	**52**	**5**	**8**	**13**	**39**	**0**	**0**	**0**	**70**	**7.1**	**-7**	**604**	**56.5**	**12:23**	**12**	**1**	**0**	**1**	**7**	**0**	**1**	**0**	**11:06**
	St. John's	AHL	23	6	11	17	24	....	....	....	....	....	....	....	....	....	....	....	....	....	....	....	....	....	....
2000-01	**Columbus**	**NHL**	**66**	**8**	**12**	**20**	**52**	**0**	**0**	**1**	**84**	**9.5**	**-4**	**1152**	**57.4**	**15:18**	....	....	....	....	....	....	....	....	....
	Florida	**NHL**	**12**	**3**	**6**	**9**	**2**	**0**	**0**	**2**	**21**	**14.3**	**7**	**198**	**47.5**	**17:25**	....	....	....	....	....	....	....	....	....
2001-02	**Florida**	**NHL**	**44**	**4**	**8**	**12**	**28**	**0**	**0**	**1**	**71**	**5.6**	**-3**	**572**	**57.9**	**13:21**	....	....	....	....	....	....	....	....	....
	Carolina	**NHL**	**33**	**2**	**3**	**5**	**15**	**0**	**0**	**1**	**37**	**5.4**	**-2**	**187**	**58.8**	**9:05**	**23**	**1**	**0**	**1**	**4**	**0**	**0**	**0**	**7:29**
2002-03	**Carolina**	**NHL**	**77**	**9**	**9**	**18**	**57**	**0**	**0**	**0**	**169**	**5.3**	**-8**	**1018**	**53.1**	**14:39**	....	....	....	....	....	....	....	....	....
2003-04	**Carolina**	**NHL**	**73**	**10**	**12**	**22**	**43**	**0**	**5**	**1**	**141**	**7.1**	**6**	**722**	**51.9**	**13:17**	....	....	....	....	....	....	....	....	....
2004-05	Dusseldorf	Germany	9	1	2	3	4	....	....	....	....	....	....	....	....	....	....	....	....	....	....	....	....	....	....
2005-06 ♦	**Carolina**	**NHL**	**82**	**15**	**8**	**23**	**36**	**0**	**2**	**2**	**160**	**9.4**	**0**	**633**	**49.1**	**12:53**	**25**	**0**	**0**	**0**	**14**	**0**	**0**	**0**	**11:44**
2006-07	**Carolina**	**NHL**	**35**	**2**	**2**	**4**	**17**	**0**	**1**	**0**	**36**	**5.6**	**-10**	**206**	**45.2**	**8:39**	....	....	....	....	....	....	....	....	....
	Phoenix	**NHL**	**33**	**1**	**7**	**8**	**8**	**0**	**0**	**0**	**51**	**2.0**	**-10**	**106**	**45.3**	**13:20**	....	....	....	....	....	....	....	....	....
2007-08	**Chicago**	**NHL**	**27**	**0**	**2**	**2**	**13**	**0**	**0**	**0**	**32**	**0.0**	**-7**	**207**	**49.8**	**10:56**	....	....	....	....	....	....	....	....	....
	NHL Totals		**540**	**59**	**77**	**136**	**317**	**0**	**8**	**8**	**876**	**6.7**		**5614**	**53.6**	**13:00**	**67**	**2**	**2**	**4**	**39**	**0**	**1**	**0**	**10:07**

CCHA Second All-Star Team (1995)

Signed as a free agent by **Toronto**, August 7, 1997. Claimed by **Columbus** from **Toronto** in Expansion Draft, June 23, 2000. Traded to **Florida** by **Columbus** with Columbus's 4th round choice (Mike Woodford) in 2001 Entry Draft for Ray Whitney and future considerations, March 13, 2001. Traded to **Carolina** by **Florida** with Bret Hedican and Tomas Malec for Sandis Ozolinsh and Byron Ritchie, January 16, 2002. Signed as a free agent by **Dusseldorf** (Germany), February 13, 2005. Traded to **Phoenix** by **Carolina** for Dennis Seidenberg, January 8, 2007. Traded to **Chicago** by **Phoenix** for Radim Vrbata, August 11, 2007. • Missed majority of 2007-08 season recovering from knee injury suffered in game vs. Columbus, November 7, 2007.

AFANASENKOV, Dmitry

(a-fahn-A-sehn-kahv, dih-MEE-tree)

Left wing. Shoots right. 6'2", 209 lbs. Born, Arkhangelsk, USSR, May 12, 1980. Tampa Bay's 3rd choice, 72nd overall, in 1998 Entry Draft.

Season	Club	League	GP	G	A	Pts	PIM	PP	SH	GW	S	%	+/-	TF	F%	Min	GP	G	A	Pts	PIM	PP	SH	GW	Min
1995-96	Yaroslavl 2	CIS-2	25	10	5	15	10	....	....	....	....	....	....	....	....	....	....	....	....	....	....	....	....	....	....
1996-97	Yaroslavl 2	Russia-3	45	20	15	35	14	....	....	....	....	....	....	....	....	....	....	....	....	....	....	....	....	....	....
1997-98	Yaroslavl 2	Russia-2	48	14	7	21	20	....	....	....	....	....	....	....	....	....	....	....	....	....	....	....	....	....	....
1998-99	Moncton Wildcats	QMJHL	15	5	5	10	12	....	....	....	....	....	....	....	....	....	....	....	....	....	....	....	....	....	....
	Sherbrooke	QMJHL	51	23	30	53	22	....	....	....	....	....	....	....	....	....	13	10	6	16	6	....	....	....	....
99-2000	Sherbrooke	QMJHL	60	56	43	99	70	....	....	....	....	....	....	....	....	....	5	3	2	5	4	....	....	....	....
2000-01	**Tampa Bay**	**NHL**	**9**	**1**	**1**	**2**	**4**	**0**	**0**	**0**	**8**	**12.5**	**1**	**7**	**28.6**	**11:24**	....	....	....	....	....	....	....	....	....
	Detroit Vipers	IHL	65	15	22	37	26	....	....	....	....	....	....	....	....	....	....	....	....	....	....	....	....	....	....
2001-02	**Tampa Bay**	**NHL**	**5**	**0**	**0**	**0**	**0**	**0**	**0**	**0**	**1**	**0.0**	**-1**	**0**	**0.0**	**4:54**	....	....	....	....	....	....	....	....	....
	Springfield	AHL	28	4	5	9	4	....	....	....	....	....	....	....	....	....	....	....	....	....	....	....	....	....	....
	Grand Rapids	AHL	18	1	2	3	2	....	....	....	....	....	....	....	....	....	....	....	....	....	....	....	....	....	....
2002-03	Springfield	AHL	41	4	9	13	25	....	....	....	....	....	....	....	....	....	....	....	....	....	....	....	....	....	....
	Kloten Flyers	Swiss	....	....	....	....	....	....	....	....	....	....	....	....	....	....	5	1	1	2	0	....	....	....	....
2003-04 ♦	**Tampa Bay**	**NHL**	**71**	**6**	**10**	**16**	**12**	**0**	**0**	**1**	**98**	**6.1**	**-4**	**2**	**0.0**	**12:21**	**23**	**1**	**2**	**3**	**6**	**0**	**0**	**0**	**13:06**
2004-05	Lada Togliatti	Russia	30	2	9	11	12	....	....	....	....	....	....	....	....	....	9	0	0	0	4	....	....	....	....
2005-06	**Tampa Bay**	**NHL**	**68**	**9**	**6**	**15**	**16**	**1**	**0**	**0**	**78**	**11.5**	**-7**	**17**	**29.4**	**9:44**	**5**	**0**	**1**	**1**	**2**	**0**	**0**	**0**	**15:46**
2006-07	**Tampa Bay**	**NHL**	**33**	**3**	**3**	**6**	**8**	**0**	**0**	**0**	**31**	**9.7**	**-6**	**12**	**33.3**	**9:02**	....	....	....	....	....	....	....	....	....
	Philadelphia	**NHL**	**41**	**8**	**7**	**15**	**12**	**0**	**0**	**0**	**65**	**12.3**	**-19**	**7**	**14.3**	**11:44**	....	....	....	....	....	....	....	....	....
2007-08	Dynamo Moscow	Russia	45	13	5	18	56	....	....	....	....	....	....	....	....	....	9	1	3	4	2	....	....	....	....
	NHL Totals		**227**	**27**	**27**	**54**	**52**	**1**	**0**	**1**	**281**	**9.6**		**45**	**26.7**	**10:46**	**28**	**1**	**3**	**4**	**8**	**0**	**0**	**0**	**13:34**

• Assigned to **Kloten** (Swiss) by **Tampa Bay**, February 19, 2003. Signed as a free agent by **Togliatti** (Russia), September 28, 2004. Claimed on waivers by **Philadelphia** from **Tampa Bay**, December 30, 2006. Signed as a free agent by **Dynamo Moscow** (Russia), August 1, 2007.

AFINOGENOV, Maxim

(ah-fihn-ah-GEHN-ahf, max-EEM) **BUF.**

Right wing. Shoots left. 6', 192 lbs. Born, Moscow, USSR, September 4, 1979. Buffalo's 3rd choice, 69th overall, in 1997 Entry Draft.

Season	Club	League	GP	G	A	Pts	PIM	PP	SH	GW	S	%	+/-	TF	F%	Min	GP	G	A	Pts	PIM	PP	SH	GW	Min
1996-97	Dynamo Moscow	Russia	29	6	5	11	10	....	....	....	....	....	....	....	....	....	4	0	2	2	0	....	....	....	....
	Dynamo Moscow	EuroHL	3	0	0	0	0	....	....	....	....	....	....	....	....	....	3	1	0	1	4	....	....	....	....
1997-98	Dynamo Moscow	Russia	35	10	5	15	53	....	....	....	....	....	....	....	....	....	....	....	....	....	....	....	....	....	....
	Dynamo Moscow	EuroHL	6	3	1	4	27	....	....	....	....	....	....	....	....	....	....	....	....	....	....	....	....	....	....
1998-99	Dynamo Moscow	Russia	38	8	13	21	24	....	....	....	....	....	....	....	....	....	16	*10	6	*16	14	....	....	....	....
	Dynamo Moscow	EuroHL	5	3	5	8	29	....	....	....	....	....	....	....	....	....	4	2	1	3	27	....	....	....	....
99-2000	**Buffalo**	**NHL**	**65**	**16**	**18**	**34**	**41**	**2**	**0**	**2**	**128**	**12.5**	**-4**	**0**	**0.0**	**13:09**	**5**	**0**	**1**	**1**	**2**	**0**	**0**	**0**	**12:53**
	Rochester	AHL	15	6	12	18	8	....	....	....	....	....	....	....	....	....	8	3	1	4	4	....	....	....	....
2000-01	**Buffalo**	**NHL**	**78**	**14**	**22**	**36**	**40**	**3**	**0**	**5**	**190**	**7.4**	**1**	**2**	**0.0**	**14:32**	**11**	**2**	**3**	**5**	**4**	**0**	**0**	**0**	**10:56**
2001-02	**Buffalo**	**NHL**	**81**	**21**	**19**	**40**	**69**	**3**	**1**	**0**	**234**	**9.0**	**-9**	**1**	**100.0**	**15:22**	....	....	....	....	....	....	....	....	....
	Russia	Olympics	6	2	2	4	4	....	....	....	....	....	....	....	....	....	....	....	....	....	....	....	....	....	....
2002-03	**Buffalo**	**NHL**	**35**	**5**	**6**	**11**	**21**	**2**	**0**	**2**	**77**	**6.5**	**-12**	**4**	**50.0**	**13:24**	....	....	....	....	....	....	....	....	....
2003-04	**Buffalo**	**NHL**	**73**	**17**	**14**	**31**	**57**	**3**	**0**	**4**	**148**	**11.5**	**-4**	**9**	**22.2**	**13:46**	....	....	....	....	....	....	....	....	....
2004-05	Dynamo Moscow	Russia	36	13	14	27	91	....	....	....	....	....	....	....	....	....	10	4	4	8	8	....	....	....	....
2005-06	**Buffalo**	**NHL**	**77**	**22**	**51**	**73**	**84**	**11**	**0**	**3**	**241**	**9.1**	**6**	**17**	**17.7**	**16:20**	**18**	**3**	**5**	**8**	**10**	**0**	**0**	**0**	**16:53**
	Russia	Olympics	8	0	1	1	10	....	....	....	....	....	....	....	....	....	....	....	....	....	....	....	....	....	....
2006-07	**Buffalo**	**NHL**	**56**	**23**	**38**	**61**	**66**	**7**	**0**	**3**	**151**	**15.2**	**19**	**3**	**66.7**	**17:03**	**15**	**5**	**4**	**9**	**6**	**3**	**0**	**2**	**15:24**
2007-08	**Buffalo**	**NHL**	**56**	**10**	**18**	**28**	**42**	**1**	**0**	**1**	**114**	**8.8**	**-16**	**5**	**20.0**	**16:03**	....	....	....	....	....	....	....	....	....
	NHL Totals		**521**	**128**	**186**	**314**	**420**	**32**	**1**	**20**	**1283**	**10.0**		**41**	**26.8**	**15:00**	**49**	**10**	**13**	**23**	**22**	**3**	**0**	**2**	**14:41**

• Missed majority of 2002-03 season recovering from head injury suffered prior to training camp, August, 2002. Signed as a free agent by **Dynamo Moscow** (Russia), June 19, 2004.

ALBERTS, Andrew

(AL-buhrts, AN-droo) **BOS.**

Defense. Shoots left. 6'5", 218 lbs. Born, Minneapolis, MN, June 30, 1981. Boston's 5th choice, 179th overall, in 2001 Entry Draft.

Season	Club	League	GP	G	A	Pts	PIM	PP	SH	GW	S	%	+/-	TF	F%	Min	GP	G	A	Pts	PIM	PP	SH	GW	Min
1998-99	Benide	High-MN	26	10	25	35		....	....	....	....	....	....	....	....	....	....	....	....	....	....	....	....	....	....
99-2000	Waterloo	USHL	49	2	2	4	55	....	....	....	....	....	....	....	....	....	....	....	....	....	....	....	....	....	....
2000-01	Waterloo	USHL	54	4	10	14	128	....	....	....	....	....	....	....	....	....	4	0	0	0	12	....	....	....	....
2001-02	Boston College	H-East	38	2	10	12	52	....	....	....	....	....	....	....	....	....	....	....	....	....	....	....	....	....	....
2002-03	Boston College	H-East	39	6	16	22	60	....	....	....	....	....	....	....	....	....	....	....	....	....	....	....	....	....	....
2003-04	Boston College	H-East	42	4	12	16	64	....	....	....	....	....	....	....	....	....	....	....	....	....	....	....	....	....	....
2004-05	Boston College	H-East	30	4	12	16	67	....	....	....	....	....	....	....	....	....	....	....	....	....	....	....	....	....	....
	Providence Bruins	AHL	8	0	0	0	16	....	....	....	....	....	....	....	....	....	16	1	4	5	40	....	....	....	....
2005-06	**Boston**	**NHL**	**73**	**1**	**6**	**7**	**68**	**0**	**1**	**0**	**30**	**3.3**	**3**	**2**	**50.0**	**12:50**	....	....	....	....	....	....	....	....	....
	Providence Bruins	AHL	6	0	1	1	7	....	....	....	....	....	....	....	....	....	....	....	....	....	....	....	....	....	....
2006-07	**Boston**	**NHL**	**76**	**0**	**10**	**10**	**124**	**0**	**0**	**0**	**41**	**0.0**	**-15**	**1**	**0.0**	**19:40**	....	....	....	....	....	....	....	....	....
2007-08	**Boston**	**NHL**	**35**	**0**	**2**	**2**	**39**	**0**	**0**	**0**	**25**	**0.0**	**4**	**2**	**50.0**	**20:37**	**2**	**0**	**0**	**0**	**0**	**0**	**0**	**0**	**11:07**
	NHL Totals		**184**	**1**	**18**	**19**	**231**	**0**	**1**	**0**	**96**	**1.0**		**5**	**40.0**	**17:08**	**2**	**0**	**0**	**0**	**0**	**0**	**0**	**0**	**11:07**

Hockey East Second All-Star Team (2004) • NCAA East First All-American Team (2004, 2005) • Hockey East First All-Star Team (2005)

• Missed majority of 2007-08 season recovering from post-concussion symptoms.

			Regular Season														Playoffs								
Season	Club	League	GP	G	A	Pts	PIM	PP	SH	GW	S	%	+/-	TF	F%	Min	GP	G	A	Pts	PIM	PP	SH	GW	Min

ALEXEEV, Nikita

(uh-LEHX-ee-ehv, nih-KEE-tuh)

Right wing. Shoots left. 6'5", 227 lbs. Born, Murmansk, USSR, December 27, 1981. Tampa Bay's 1st choice, 8th overall, in 2000 Entry Draft.

Season	Club	League	GP	G	A	Pts	PIM	PP	SH	GW	S	%	+/-	TF	F%	Min	GP	G	A	Pts	PIM	PP	SH	GW	Min
1996-97	Krylja Sovetov 2	Russia-3	45	4	6	10	8	....	....	....	....	....	....	....	....	....	....	....	....	....	....	....	....	....	....
1997-98	Krylja Sovetov 2	Russia-3	61	11	4	15	36	....	....	....	....	....	....	....	....	....	....	....	....	....	....	....	....	....	....
1998-99	Erie Otters	OHL	61	17	18	35	14	....	....	....	....	....	....	....	....	....	5	1	1	2	4	....	....	....	....
99-2000	Erie Otters	OHL	64	24	29	53	42	....	....	....	....	....	....	....	....	....	13	4	3	7	6	....	....	....	....
2000-01	Erie Otters	OHL	64	31	41	72	45	....	....	....	....	....	....	....	....	....	12	7	7	14	12	....	....	....	....
2001-02	**Tampa Bay**	**NHL**	**44**	**4**	**4**	**8**	**8**	**1**	**0**	**1**	**47**	**8.5**	**–9**	**0**	**0.0**	**11:26**	....	....	....	....	....	....	....	....	....
	Springfield	AHL	35	5	9	14	16	....	....	....	....	....	....	....	....	....	....	....	....	....	....	....	....	....	....
2002-03	**Tampa Bay**	**NHL**	**37**	**4**	**2**	**6**	**8**	**1**	**0**	**1**	**52**	**7.7**	**–6**	**3**	**33.3**	**11:31**	**11**	**1**	**0**	**1**	**0**	**0**	**0**	**0**	**10:12**
	Springfield	AHL	36	7	5	12	8	....	....	....	....	....	....	....	....	....	....	....	....	....	....	....	....	....	....
2003-04	Hershey Bears	AHL	14	0	1	1	8	....	....	....	....	....	....	....	....	....	....	....	....	....	....	....	....	....	....
2004-05	Springfield	AHL	72	13	9	22	16	....	....	....	....	....	....	....	....	....	....	....	....	....	....	....	....	....	....
2005-06	Avangard Omsk	Russia	40	6	3	9	14	....	....	....	....	....	....	....	....	....	5	0	0	0	2	....	....	....	....
2006-07	**Tampa Bay**	**NHL**	**63**	**10**	**11**	**21**	**12**	**2**	**0**	**2**	**102**	**9.8**	**10**	**12**	**16.7**	**14:19**	....	....	....	....	....	....	....	....	....
	Chicago	**NHL**	**15**	**2**	**0**	**2**	**0**	**0**	**0**	**0**	**15**	**13.3**	**–3**	**1**	**100.0**	**11:33**	....	....	....	....	....	....	....	....	....
2007-08	Ak Bars Kazan	Russia	37	3	2	5	26	....	....	....	....	....	....	....	....	....	5	0	3	3	0	....	....	....	....
	NHL Totals		**159**	**20**	**17**	**37**	**28**	**4**	**0**	**4**	**216**	**9.3**		**16**	**25.0**	**12:36**	**11**	**1**	**0**	**1**	**0**	**0**	**0**	**0**	**10:12**

• Missed majority of 2003-04 season recovering from shoulder injury suffered in game vs. Philadelphia (AHL) on November 2, 2003. Traded to **Chicago** by **Tampa Bay** for Karl Stewart and Florida's 6th round choice (previously acquired, Tampa Bay selected Luke Witkowski) in 2008 Entry Draft, February 27, 2007. Signed as a free agent by **Kazan** (Russia), August 23, 2007.

ALFREDSSON, Daniel

(AHL-frehd-suhn, DAN-yehl) **OTT.**

Right wing. Shoots right. 5'11", 205 lbs. Born, Gothenburg, Sweden, December 11, 1972. Ottawa's 5th choice, 133rd overall, in 1994 Entry Draft.

Season	Club	League	GP	G	A	Pts	PIM	PP	SH	GW	S	%	+/-	TF	F%	Min	GP	G	A	Pts	PIM	PP	SH	GW	Min
1990-91	Molndal Hockey	Sweden-2	3	0	0	0	2	....	....	....	....	....	....	....	....	....	8	4	4	8	4	....	....	....	....
1991-92	Molndal	Sweden-2	32	12	8	20	43	....	....	....	....	....	....	....	....	....	....	....	....	....	....	....	....	....	....
1992-93	V.Frolunda	Sweden	20	1	5	6	8	....	....	....	....	....	....	....	....	....	....	....	....	....	....	....	....	....	....
1993-94	V.Frolunda	Sweden	39	20	10	30	18	....	....	....	....	....	....	....	....	....	4	1	1	2	....	....	....	....	....
1994-95	V.Frolunda	Sweden	22	7	11	18	22	....	....	....	....	....	....	....	....	....	....	....	....	....	....	....	....	....	....
1995-96	**Ottawa**	**NHL**	**82**	**26**	**35**	**61**	**28**	**8**	**2**	**3**	**212**	**12.3**	**–18**	....	....	....	....	....	....	....	....	....	....	....	....
1996-97	**Ottawa**	**NHL**	**76**	**24**	**47**	**71**	**30**	**11**	**1**	**1**	**247**	**9.7**	**5**	....	....	....	**7**	**5**	**2**	**7**	**6**	**3**	**0**	**2**	....
1997-98	**Ottawa**	**NHL**	**55**	**17**	**28**	**45**	**18**	**7**	**0**	**7**	**149**	**11.4**	**7**	....	....	....	**11**	**7**	**2**	**9**	**20**	**2**	**1**	**1**	....
	Sweden	Olympics	4	2	3	5	2	....	....	....	....	....	....	....	....	....	....	....	....	....	....	....	....	....	....
1998-99	**Ottawa**	**NHL**	**58**	**11**	**22**	**33**	**14**	**3**	**0**	**5**	**163**	**6.7**	**8**	**7**	**57.1**	**17:22**	**4**	**1**	**2**	**3**	**4**	**1**	**0**	**0**	**22:23**
99-2000	**Ottawa**	**NHL**	**57**	**21**	**38**	**59**	**28**	**4**	**2**	**0**	**164**	**12.8**	**11**	**3**	**66.7**	**18:45**	**6**	**1**	**3**	**4**	**2**	**1**	**0**	**0**	**20:22**
2000-01	**Ottawa**	**NHL**	**68**	**24**	**46**	**70**	**30**	**10**	**0**	**3**	**206**	**11.7**	**11**	**8**	**50.0**	**18:47**	**4**	**1**	**0**	**1**	**2**	**0**	**0**	**0**	**21:20**
2001-02	**Ottawa**	**NHL**	**78**	**37**	**34**	**71**	**45**	**9**	**1**	**4**	**243**	**15.2**	**3**	**30**	**30.0**	**20:19**	**12**	**7**	**6**	**13**	**4**	**3**	**0**	**3**	**21:43**
	Sweden	Olympics	4	1	4	5	2	....	....	....	....	....	....	....	....	....	....	....	....	....	....	....	....	....	....
2002-03	**Ottawa**	**NHL**	**78**	**27**	**51**	**78**	**42**	**9**	**0**	**6**	**240**	**11.3**	**15**	**40**	**40.0**	**19:32**	**18**	**4**	**4**	**8**	**12**	**4**	**0**	**1**	**18:00**
2003-04	**Ottawa**	**NHL**	**77**	**32**	**48**	**80**	**24**	**9**	**0**	**5**	**230**	**13.9**	**12**	**33**	**24.2**	**19:24**	**7**	**1**	**2**	**3**	**2**	**0**	**0**	**0**	**20:03**
2004-05	Frolunda	Sweden	15	8	9	17	10	....	....	....	....	....	....	....	....	....	14	*12	6	*18	8	....	....	....	....
2005-06	**Ottawa**	**NHL**	**77**	**43**	**60**	**103**	**50**	**16**	**5**	**8**	**249**	**17.3**	**29**	**44**	**20.5**	**21:41**	**10**	**2**	**8**	**10**	**4**	**1**	**0**	**0**	**21:10**
	Sweden	Olympics	8	5	5	10	4	....	....	....	....	....	....	....	....	....	....	....	....	....	....	....	....	....	....
2006-07	**Ottawa**	**NHL**	**77**	**29**	**58**	**87**	**42**	**7**	**2**	**7**	**240**	**12.1**	**42**	**43**	**34.9**	**21:35**	**20**	***14**	**8**	***22**	**10**	**6**	**1**	**4**	**23:20**
2007-08	**Ottawa**	**NHL**	**70**	**40**	**49**	**89**	**34**	**9**	**7**	**5**	**217**	**18.4**	**15**	**39**	**53.9**	**22:17**	**2**	**0**	**0**	**0**	**0**	**0**	**0**	**0**	**19:20**
	NHL Totals		**853**	**331**	**516**	**847**	**385**	**102**	**20**	**54**	**2560**	**12.9**		**247**	**35.6**	**20:04**	**101**	**43**	**37**	**80**	**66**	**21**	**2**	**11**	**20:57**

NHL All-Rookie Team (1996) • Calder Memorial Trophy (1996) • NHL Second All-Star Team (2006)

Played in NHL All-Star Game (1996, 1997, 1998, 2004, 2008)

Signed as a free agent by **Frolunda** (Sweden), November 10, 2004.

ALLEN, Bobby

(AHL-lehn, BAW-bee)

Defense. Shoots left. 6', 201 lbs. Born, Weymouth, MA, November 14, 1978. Boston's 2nd choice, 52nd overall, in 1998 Entry Draft.

Season	Club	League	GP	G	A	Pts	PIM	PP	SH	GW	S	%	+/-	TF	F%	Min	GP	G	A	Pts	PIM	PP	SH	GW	Min
1996-97	Cushing	High-MA	36	11	33	44	28	....	....	....	....	....	....	....	....	....	....	....	....	....	....	....	....	....	....
1997-98	Boston College	H-East	40	7	21	28	49	....	....	....	....	....	....	....	....	....	....	....	....	....	....	....	....	....	....
1998-99	Boston College	H-East	43	9	23	32	34	....	....	....	....	....	....	....	....	....	....	....	....	....	....	....	....	....	....
99-2000	Boston College	H-East	42	4	23	27	40	....	....	....	....	....	....	....	....	....	....	....	....	....	....	....	....	....	....
2000-01	Boston College	H-East	42	5	18	23	28	....	....	....	....	....	....	....	....	....	....	....	....	....	....	....	....	....	....
2001-02	Providence Bruins	AHL	49	5	10	15	18	....	....	....	....	....	....	....	....	....	....	....	....	....	....	....	....	....	....
	Hamilton	AHL	10	1	6	7	0	....	....	....	....	....	....	....	....	....	14	0	3	3	6	....	....	....	....
2002-03	**Edmonton**	**NHL**	**1**	**0**	**0**	**0**	**0**	**0**	**0**	**0**	**0**	**0.0**	**0**	**0**	**0.0**	**2:53**	....	....	....	....	....	....	....	....	....
	Hamilton	AHL	56	1	12	13	24	....	....	....	....	....	....	....	....	....	23	0	5	5	10	....	....	....	....
2003-04	Toronto	AHL	56	5	10	15	18	....	....	....	....	....	....	....	....	....	3	0	2	2	4	....	....	....	....
2004-05	Albany River Rats	AHL	66	5	11	16	20	....	....	....	....	....	....	....	....	....	....	....	....	....	....	....	....	....	....
2005-06	Albany River Rats	AHL	68	4	14	18	28	....	....	....	....	....	....	....	....	....	....	....	....	....	....	....	....	....	....
2006-07	**Boston**	**NHL**	**31**	**0**	**3**	**3**	**10**	**0**	**0**	**0**	**14**	**0.0**	**–1**	**0**	**0.0**	**13:02**	....	....	....	....	....	....	....	....	....
	Providence Bruins	AHL	31	5	13	18	14	....	....	....	....	....	....	....	....	....	....	....	....	....	....	....	....	....	....
2007-08	**Boston**	**NHL**	**19**	**0**	**0**	**0**	**2**	**0**	**0**	**0**	**10**	**0.0**	**–2**	**0**	**0.0**	**9:53**	....	....	....	....	....	....	....	....	....
	NHL Totals		**51**	**0**	**3**	**3**	**12**	**0**	**0**	**0**	**24**	**0.0**		**0**	**0.0**	**11:40**	....	....	....	....	....	....	....	....	....

Hockey East Second All-Star Team (2000) • Hockey East First All-Star Team (2001) • NCAA East First All-American Team (2001)

Traded to **Edmonton** by **Boston** for Sean Brown, March 19, 2002. Signed as a free agent by **New Jersey**, July 22, 2004. Signed as a free agent by **Boston**, July 17, 2006. • Missed majority of 2007-08 season with arm injury, recurring back spasms and as a healthy reserve.

ALLEN, Bryan

(AHL-lehn, BRIGH-uhn) **FLA.**

Defense. Shoots left. 6'4", 220 lbs. Born, Kingston, Ont., August 21, 1980. Vancouver's 1st choice, 4th overall, in 1998 Entry Draft.

Season	Club	League	GP	G	A	Pts	PIM	PP	SH	GW	S	%	+/-	TF	F%	Min	GP	G	A	Pts	PIM	PP	SH	GW	Min
1995-96	Ernestown Jets	OHA-C	36	1	16	17	71	....	....	....	....	....	....	....	....	....	....	....	....	....	....	....	....	....	....
1996-97	Oshawa Generals	OHL	60	2	4	6	76	....	....	....	....	....	....	....	....	....	18	1	3	4	26	....	....	....	....
1997-98	Oshawa Generals	OHL	48	6	13	19	126	....	....	....	....	....	....	....	....	....	5	0	5	5	18	....	....	....	....
1998-99	Oshawa Generals	OHL	37	7	15	22	77	....	....	....	....	....	....	....	....	....	15	0	3	3	26	....	....	....	....
99-2000	Oshawa Generals	OHL	3	0	2	2	12	....	....	....	....	....	....	....	....	....	3	0	0	0	13	....	....	....	....
	Syracuse Crunch	AHL	9	1	1	2	11	....	....	....	....	....	....	....	....	....	2	0	0	0	2	....	....	....	....
2000-01	**Vancouver**	**NHL**	**6**	**0**	**0**	**0**	**0**	**0**	**0**	**0**	**2**	**0.0**	**0**	**0**	**0.0**	**9:20**	**2**	**0**	**0**	**0**	**2**	**0**	**0**	**0**	**13:47**
	Kansas City	IHL	75	5	20	25	99	....	....	....	....	....	....	....	....	....	....	....	....	....	....	....	....	....	....
2001-02	**Vancouver**	**NHL**	**11**	**0**	**0**	**0**	**6**	**0**	**0**	**0**	**4**	**0.0**	**1**	**0**	**0.0**	**10:47**	....	....	....	....	....	....	....	....	....
	Manitoba Moose	AHL	68	7	18	25	121	....	....	....	....	....	....	....	....	....	5	0	1	1	8	....	....	....	....
2002-03	**Vancouver**	**NHL**	**48**	**5**	**3**	**8**	**73**	**0**	**0**	**1**	**43**	**11.6**	**8**	**0**	**0.0**	**12:56**	**1**	**0**	**0**	**0**	**2**	**0**	**0**	**0**	**10:35**
	Manitoba Moose	AHL	7	0	1	1	4	....	....	....	....	....	....	....	....	....	....	....	....	....	....	....	....	....	....
2003-04	**Vancouver**	**NHL**	**74**	**2**	**5**	**7**	**94**	**0**	**0**	**0**	**70**	**2.9**	**–10**	**0**	**0.0**	**16:51**	**4**	**0**	**0**	**0**	**2**	**0**	**0**	**0**	**14:37**
2004-05	Voskresensk	Russia	19	0	3	3	34	....	....	....	....	....	....	....	....	....	....	....	....	....	....	....	....	....	....
2005-06	**Vancouver**	**NHL**	**77**	**7**	**10**	**17**	**115**	**1**	**0**	**0**	**88**	**8.0**	**4**	**0**	**0.0**	**20:27**	....	....	....	....	....	....	....	....	....
2006-07	**Florida**	**NHL**	**82**	**4**	**21**	**25**	**112**	**0**	**0**	**0**	**99**	**4.0**	**7**	**1**	**0.0**	**21:36**	....	....	....	....	....	....	....	....	....
2007-08	**Florida**	**NHL**	**73**	**2**	**14**	**16**	**67**	**0**	**0**	**0**	**67**	**3.0**	**5**	**0**	**0.0**	**21:17**	....	....	....	....	....	....	....	....	....
	NHL Totals		**371**	**20**	**53**	**73**	**467**	**1**	**0**	**1**	**373**	**5.4**		**1**	**0.0**	**18:43**	**7**	**0**	**0**	**0**	**6**	**0**	**0**	**0**	**13:48**

OHL First All-Star Team (1999)

• Missed majority of 1999-2000 season recovering from knee injury suffered in training camp, September 21, 1999. Signed as a free agent by **Voskresensk** (Russia), December 20, 2004. Traded to **Florida** by **Vancouver** with Todd Bertuzzi and Alex Auld for Roberto Luongo, Lukas Krajicek and Florida's 6th round choice (Sergei Shirokov) in 2006 Entry Draft, June 23, 2006.

ANDERSSON, Jonas

(AN-duhr-suhn, YOH-nuhs) **NSH.**

Right wing. Shoots left. 6'2", 202 lbs. Born, Stockholm, Sweden, February 24, 1981. Nashville's 2nd choice, 33rd overall, in 1999 Entry Draft.

Season	Club	League	GP	G	A	Pts	PIM	PP	SH	GW	S	%	+/-	TF	F%	Min	GP	G	A	Pts	PIM	PP	SH	GW	Min
1997-98	AIK Solna Jr.	Swe-Jr.	33	14	16	30	32	....	....	....	....	....	....	....	....	....	....	....	....	....	....	....	....	....	....
1998-99	AIK Solna Jr.	Swe-Jr.	16	3	7	10	18	....	....	....	....	....	....	....	....	....	....	....	....	....	....	....	....	....	....
	London Knights	Britain	12	2	3	5	0	....	....	....	....	....	....	....	....	....	....	....	....	....	....	....	....	....	....
99-2000	North Bay	OHL	67	31	36	67	27	....	....	....	....	....	....	....	....	....	6	2	2	4	2	....	....	....	....
	Milwaukee	IHL	2	1	0	1	0	....	....	....	....	....	....	....	....	....	2	0	0	0	2	....	....	....	....
2000-01	Milwaukee	IHL	52	6	7	13	44	....	....	....	....	....	....	....	....	....	5	0	0	0	2	....	....	....	....

Season	Club	League	GP	G	A	Pts	PIM	PP	SH	GW	S	%	+/-	TF	F%	Min	GP	G	A	Pts	PIM	PP	SH	GW	Min
			Regular Season														Playoffs								
2001-02	Nashville	NHL	5	0	0	0	2	0	0	0	4	0.0	–2	0	0.0	9:06									
	Milwaukee	AHL	71	13	17	30	19																		
2002-03	Milwaukee	AHL	49	7	4	11	12										5	0	1	1	4				
2003-04			DID NOT PLAY – INJURED																						
2004-05	Sodertalje SK	Sweden	34	0	4	4	8																		
	Brynas IF Gavle	Sweden	7	2	0	2	2																		
2005-06	Ilves Tampere	Finland	48	8	10	18	26										4	2	0	2	0				
2006-07	HPK Hameenlinna	Finland	23	6	7	13	20										9	0	1	1	8				
2007-08	HPK Hameenlinna	Finland	42	11	13	24	42																		
	Karpat Oulu	Finland	13	1	7	8	4										10	3	7	10	4				
	NHL Totals		5	0	0	0	2	0	0	0	4	0.0		0	0.0	9:06									

• Missed entire 2003-04 season recovering from wrist injury suffered in training camp, September 30, 2003. Signed as a free agent by **Sodertalje** (Sweden), April 28, 2004. Signed as a free agent by **Gavle** (Sweden), January 22, 2005.

ANTROPOV, Nik

(an-TROH-pahv, NIHK) **TOR.**

Center. Shoots left. 6'6", 230 lbs. Born, Ust-Kamenogorsk, USSR, February 18, 1980. Toronto's 1st choice, 10th overall, in 1998 Entry Draft.

Season	Club	League	GP	G	A	Pts	PIM	PP	SH	GW	S	%	+/-	TF	F%	Min	GP	G	A	Pts	PIM	PP	SH	GW	Min
1996-97	Ust-Kamenogorsk	Russia-2	8	2	1	3	6																		
1997-98	Ust-Kamenogorsk	Russia-2	42	15	24	39	62																		
1998-99	Dynamo Moscow	Russia	30	5	9	14	30										11	0	1	1	4				
99-2000	Toronto	NHL	66	12	18	30	41	0	0	2	89	13.5	14	501	46.3	12:48	3	0	0	0	4	0	0	0	10:14
	St. John's	AHL	2	0	0	0	4																		
2000-01	Toronto	NHL	52	6	11	17	30	0	0	1	71	8.5	5	431	44.3	10:02	9	2	1	3	12	1	0	1	11:04
2001-02	Toronto	NHL	11	1	1	2	4	0	0	0	12	8.3	–1	31	38.7	8:57									
	St. John's	AHL	34	11	24	35	47																		
2002-03	Toronto	NHL	72	16	29	45	124	2	1	6	102	15.7	11	621	40.1	15:00	3	0	0	0	0	0	0	0	19:17
2003-04	Toronto	NHL	62	13	18	31	62	1	1	2	89	14.6	7	309	40.8	15:18	13	0	2	2	18	0	0	0	15:56
2004-05	Ak Bars Kazan	Russia	10	2	3	5	6																		
	Yaroslavl	Russia	26	4	15	19	44										9	3	4	7	18				
2005-06	Toronto	NHL	57	12	19	31	56	2	1	0	113	10.6	13	172	34.3	15:34									
	Kazakhstan	Olympics	5	1	0	1	4																		
2006-07	Toronto	NHL	54	18	15	33	44	4	0	4	125	14.4	8	34	35.3	16:36									
2007-08	Toronto	NHL	72	26	30	56	92	12	0	5	165	15.8	10	271	42.1	20:07									
	NHL Totals		446	104	141	245	453	21	3	20	766	13.6		2370	42.0	15:05	28	2	3	5	34	1	0	1	14:07

Signed as a free agent by **Kazan** (Russia), October 27, 2004. Signed as a free agent by **Yaroslavl** (Russia), December 20, 2004.

ARKHIPOV, Denis

(AHR-kih-pahv, DEH-nihs)

Center. Shoots left. 6'3", 214 lbs. Born, Kazan, USSR, May 19, 1979. Nashville's 2nd choice, 60th overall, in 1998 Entry Draft.

Season	Club	League	GP	G	A	Pts	PIM	PP	SH	GW	S	%	+/-	TF	F%	Min	GP	G	A	Pts	PIM	PP	SH	GW	Min
1994-95	Itil Kazan 2	CIS-2	40	20	12	32	10																		
1995-96	Ak Bars Kazan	CIS	15	10	8	18	10																		
1996-97	Ak Bars Kazan 2	Russia-3	50	17	23	40	20																		
	Ak Bars Kazan	Russia	1	1	0	1	0																		
1997-98	Ak Bars Kazan	Russia	29	2	2	4	2																		
1998-99	Ak Bars Kazan	Russia	34	12	1	13	22										9	2	3	5	6				
	Ak Bars Kazan	EuroHL	4	0	0	0	0										1	0	0	0	0				
99-2000	Ak Bars Kazan	Russia	32	7	9	16	14										18	5	5	10	6				
2000-01	Nashville	NHL	40	6	7	13	4	0	0	0	42	14.3	0	299	43.8	9:56									
	Milwaukee	IHL	40	9	8	17	11																		
2001-02	Nashville	NHL	82	20	22	42	16	7	0	6	118	16.9	–18	1108	44.8	15:43									
2002-03	Nashville	NHL	79	11	24	35	32	3	0	1	148	7.4	–18	1069	46.7	15:09									
2003-04	Nashville	NHL	72	9	12	21	22	3	0	3	91	9.9	–2	926	44.7	13:58									
2004-05	Ak Bars Kazan	Russia	45	9	8	17	28										4	0	0	0	0				
2005-06	Mytischi	Russia	50	8	8	16	28										9	2	1	3	0				
2006-07	Chicago	NHL	79	10	17	27	54	2	1	1	112	8.9	–13	981	49.2	15:43									
2007-08	Ak Bars Kazan	Russia	56	10	17	27	22										9	1	3	4	6				
	NHL Totals		352	56	82	138	128	15	1	11	511	11.0		4383	46.2	14:34									

Signed as a free agent by **Kazan** (Russia), July 27, 2004. Signed as a free agent by **Chicago**, July 6, 2006. Signed as a free agent by **Kazan** (Russia), June 4, 2007.

ARMSTRONG, Colby

(AHRM-stawng, KOHL-bee) **ATL.**

Right wing. Shoots right. 6'2", 190 lbs. Born, Lloydminster, Sask., November 23, 1982. Pittsburgh's 1st choice, 21st overall, in 2001 Entry Draft.

Season	Club	League	GP	G	A	Pts	PIM	PP	SH	GW	S	%	+/-	TF	F%	Min	GP	G	A	Pts	PIM	PP	SH	GW	Min
1998-99	Sask. Contacts	SMHL	33	21	19	40	103																		
	Red Deer Rebels	WHL	1	0	1	1	0																		
99-2000	Red Deer Rebels	WHL	68	13	25	38	122										2	0	1	1	11				
2000-01	Red Deer Rebels	WHL	72	36	42	78	156										21	6	6	12	29				
2001-02	Red Deer Rebels	WHL	64	27	41	68	115										23	6	10	16	32				
2002-03	Wilkes-Barre	AHL	73	7	11	18	76										3	0	0	0	4				
2003-04	Wilkes-Barre	AHL	67	10	17	27	71										24	3	1	4	45				
2004-05	Wilkes-Barre	AHL	80	18	37	55	89										10	4	2	6	14				
2005-06	Pittsburgh	NHL	47	16	24	40	58	7	2	3	86	18.6	15	44	27.3	19:04									
	Wilkes-Barre	AHL	31	11	18	29	44																		
2006-07	Pittsburgh	NHL	80	12	22	34	67	1	1	3	145	8.3	2	13	15.4	16:50	5	0	1	1	11	0	0	0	15:18
2007-08	Pittsburgh	NHL	54	9	15	24	50	0	0	2	84	10.7	6	12	25.0	15:24									
	Atlanta	NHL	18	4	7	11	6	1	0	1	29	13.8	–2	3	0.0	18:02									
	NHL Totals		199	41	68	109	181	9	3	9	344	11.9		72	23.6	17:05	5	0	1	1	11	0	0	0	15:18

Traded to **Atlanta** by **Pittsburgh** with Erik Christensen, Angelo Esposito and Pittsburgh's 1st round choice (Daultan Leveille) in 2008 Entry Draft for Marian Hossa and Pascal Dupuis, February 26, 2008.

ARMSTRONG, Derek

(AHRM-stawng, DAIR-ihk) **L.A.**

Center. Shoots right. 6', 197 lbs. Born, Ottawa, Ont., April 23, 1973. NY Islanders' 5th choice, 128th overall, in 1992 Entry Draft.

Season	Club	League	GP	G	A	Pts	PIM	PP	SH	GW	S	%	+/-	TF	F%	Min	GP	G	A	Pts	PIM	PP	SH	GW	Min
1989-90	Hawkesbury	CJHL	48	8	10	18	30																		
1990-91	Hawkesbury	CJHL	54	27	45	72	49																		
	Sudbury Wolves	OHL	2	0	2	2	0																		
1991-92	Sudbury Wolves	OHL	66	31	54	85	22										9	2	2	4	2				
1992-93	Sudbury Wolves	OHL	66	44	62	106	56										14	9	10	19	26				
1993-94	NY Islanders	NHL	1	0	0	0	0	0	0	0	2	0.0	0												
	Salt Lake	IHL	76	23	35	58	61																		
1994-95	Denver Grizzlies	IHL	59	13	18	31	65										6	0	2	2	0				
1995-96	NY Islanders	NHL	19	1	3	4	14	0	0	0	23	4.3	–6												
	Worcester IceCats	AHL	51	11	15	26	33										4	2	1	3	0				
1996-97	NY Islanders	NHL	50	6	7	13	33	0	0	2	36	16.7	–8												
	Utah Grizzlies	IHL	17	4	8	12	10										6	0	4	4	4				
1997-98	Ottawa	NHL	9	2	0	2	9	0	0	1	8	25.0	1												
	Detroit Vipers	IHL	10	0	1	1	2																		
	Hartford	AHL	54	16	30	46	40										15	2	6	8	22				
1998-99	NY Rangers	NHL	3	0	0	0	0	0	0	0	1	0.0	0	0	0.0	2:50									
	Hartford	AHL	59	29	51	80	73										7	5	4	9	10				
99-2000	NY Rangers	NHL	1	0	0	0	0	0	0	0	1	0.0	0	3	33.3	3:10									
	Hartford	AHL	77	28	54	82	101										23	7	16	23	24				
2000-01	NY Rangers	NHL	3	0	0	0	0	0	0	0	6	0.0	0	30	50.0	11:22									
	Hartford	AHL	75	32	*69	*101	73										5	0	6	6	6				
2001-02	SC Bern	Swiss	44	17	36	53	62										6	3	5	8	8				
2002-03	Los Angeles	NHL	66	12	26	38	30	2	0	1	106	11.3	5	708	50.0	15:40									
	Manchester	AHL	2	3	0	3	4																		
2003-04	Los Angeles	NHL	57	14	21	35	33	5	0	1	101	13.9	4	912	52.0	17:00									
2004-05	Geneve	Swiss	9	6	7	13	18																		
	Rapperswil	Swiss	3	1	3	4	4																		
2005-06	Los Angeles	NHL	62	13	28	41	46	7	0	1	100	13.0	–2	546	50.7	15:31									

			Regular Season														Playoffs								
Season	Club	League	GP	G	A	Pts	PIM	PP	SH	GW	S	%	+/-	TF	F%	Min	GP	G	A	Pts	PIM	PP	SH	GW	Min
2006-07	Los Angeles	NHL	67	11	33	44	62	3	0	0	109	10.1	13	842	47.9	15:04	....	....	....	....	....	....	....	....	....
2007-08	Los Angeles	NHL	77	8	27	35	63	1	0	2	118	6.8	4	750	50.7	13:17	....	....	....	....	....	....	....	....	....
	NHL Totals		415	67	145	212	290	18	0	8	611	11.0		3791	50.2	15:01	....	....	....	....	....	....	....	....	....

AHL Second All-Star Team (2000) • Jack A. Butterfield Trophy (Playoff MVP – AHL) (2000) • AHL First All-Star Team (2001) • John P. Sollenberger Trophy (Leading Scorer – AHL) (2001) • Les Cunningham Award (MVP – AHL) (2001)

Signed as a free agent by **Ottawa**, July 28, 1997. Loaned to **Hartford** (AHL) by **Ottawa**, October 28, 1997. Signed as a free agent by **NY Rangers**, August 10, 1998. Signed as a free agent by **Bern** (Swiss) with NY Rangers retaining NHL rights, July 18, 2001. Traded to **Los Angeles** by **NY Rangers** for Los Angeles' 6th round choice (Chris Holt) in 2003 Entry Draft, July 16, 2002. Signed as a free agent by **Geneve** (Swiss), October 12, 2004. Signed as a free agent by **Rapperswil** (Swiss), February 13, 2005.

ARNASON, Tyler

(AHR-na-suhn, TIGH-luhr) **COL.**

Center. Shoots left. 5'11", 204 lbs. Born, Oklahoma City, OK, March 16, 1979. Chicago's 6th choice, 183rd overall, in 1998 Entry Draft.

1996-97	Winnipeg South	MJHL	50	35	50	85	15	....	....	....	....	....	....	....	....	....	6	3	3	6	18	....	....	....	....
1997-98	Fargo-Moorhead	USHL	52	37	45	82	16	....	....	....	....	....	....	....	....	....	4	1	1	2	2	....	....	....	....
1998-99	St. Cloud State	WCHA	38	14	17	31	16	....	....	....	....	....	....	....	....	....	....	....	....	....	....	....	....	....	....
99-2000	St. Cloud State	WCHA	39	19	30	49	18	....	....	....	....	....	....	....	....	....	....	....	....	....	....	....	....	....	....
2000-01	St. Cloud State	WCHA	41	28	28	56	14	....	....	....	....	....	....	....	....	....	....	....	....	....	....	....	....	....	....
2001-02	**Chicago**	**NHL**	21	3	1	4	4	0	0	0	19	15.8	–3	112	41.1	9:28	3	0	0	0	0	0	0	0	7:43
	Norfolk Admirals	AHL	60	26	30	56	42	....	....	....	....	....	....	....	....	....	....	....	....	....	....	....	....	....	....
2002-03	**Chicago**	**NHL**	82	19	20	39	20	3	0	6	178	10.7	7	626	40.3	14:30	....	....	....	....	....	....	....	....	....
2003-04	**Chicago**	**NHL**	82	22	33	55	16	6	0	2	222	9.9	–13	904	43.1	16:34	....	....	....	....	....	....	....	....	....
2004-05	Brynas IF Gavle	Sweden	4	0	0	0	0	....	....	....	....	....	....	....	....	....	....	....	....	....	....	....	....	....	....
2005-06	**Chicago**	**NHL**	60	13	28	41	40	5	0	1	161	8.1	5	492	44.7	14:58	....	....	....	....	....	....	....	....	....
	Ottawa	**NHL**	19	0	4	4	4	0	0	0	42	0.0	–4	172	51.7	12:19	....	....	....	....	....	....	....	....	....
2006-07	**Colorado**	**NHL**	82	16	33	49	26	1	0	3	211	7.6	–8	422	43.8	14:20	....	....	....	....	....	....	....	....	....
2007-08	**Colorado**	**NHL**	70	10	21	31	16	3	0	1	179	5.6	–1	792	47.4	15:16	10	2	3	5	2	1	0	0	14:12
	NHL Totals		416	83	140	223	126	18	0	13	1012	8.2		3520	44.2	14:43	13	2	3	5	2	1	0	0	12:42

USHL First All-Star Team (1998) • WCHA All-Rookie Team (1999) • WCHA Second All-Star Team (2000) • AHL All-Rookie Team (2002) • Dudley "Red" Garrett Memorial Award (Rookie of the Year – AHL) (2002) • NHL All-Rookie Team (2003)

Signed as a free agent by **Gavle** (Sweden), October 29, 2004. Traded to **Ottawa** by **Chicago** for Brandon Bochenski and Ottawa's 2nd round choice (Simon Danis-Pepin) in 2006 Entry Draft, March 9, 2006. Signed as a free agent by **Colorado**, July 1, 2006.

ARNOTT, Jason

(AHR-nawt, JAY-suhn) **NSH.**

Center. Shoots right. 6'4", 220 lbs. Born, Collingwood, Ont., October 11, 1974. Edmonton's 1st choice, 7th overall, in 1993 Entry Draft.

1989-90	Stayner Siskins	OHA-C	34	21	31	52	12	....	....	....	....	....	....	....	....	....	....	....	....	....	....	....	....	....	....
1990-91	Lindsay Bears	OHA-B	42	17	44	61	10	....	....	....	....	....	....	....	....	....	8	9	8	17	6	....	....	....	....
1991-92	Oshawa Generals	OHL	57	9	15	24	12	....	....	....	....	....	....	....	....	....	....	....	....	....	....	....	....	....	....
1992-93	Oshawa Generals	OHL	56	41	57	98	74	....	....	....	....	....	....	....	....	....	13	9	9	18	20	....	....	....	....
1993-94	**Edmonton**	**NHL**	78	33	35	68	104	10	0	4	194	17.0	1	....	....	....	....	....	....	....	....	....	....	....	....
1994-95	**Edmonton**	**NHL**	42	15	22	37	128	7	0	1	156	9.6	–14	....	....	....	....	....	....	....	....	....	....	....	....
1995-96	**Edmonton**	**NHL**	64	28	31	59	87	8	0	5	244	11.5	–6	....	....	....	....	....	....	....	....	....	....	....	....
1996-97	**Edmonton**	**NHL**	67	19	38	57	92	10	1	2	248	7.7	–21	....	....	....	12	3	6	9	18	1	0	0	....
1997-98	**Edmonton**	**NHL**	35	5	13	18	78	1	0	0	100	5.0	–16	....	....	....	....	....	....	....	....	....	....	....	....
	New Jersey	**NHL**	35	5	10	15	21	3	0	2	99	5.1	–8	....	....	....	5	0	2	2	0	0	0	0	....
1998-99	**New Jersey**	**NHL**	74	27	27	54	79	8	0	3	200	13.5	10	872	49.3	15:24	7	2	2	4	4	1	0	0	16:48
99-2000♦	**New Jersey**	**NHL**	76	22	34	56	51	7	0	4	244	9.0	22	1172	46.9	17:05	23	8	12	20	18	3	0	1	16:29
2000-01	**New Jersey**	**NHL**	54	21	34	55	75	8	0	3	138	15.2	23	760	49.6	16:12	23	8	7	15	16	5	0	0	15:49
2001-02	**New Jersey**	**NHL**	63	22	19	41	59	8	0	1	169	13.0	3	934	47.8	17:13	....	....	....	....	....	....	....	....	....
	Dallas	**NHL**	10	3	1	4	6	2	0	2	28	10.7	–1	77	52.0	18:13	....	....	....	....	....	....	....	....	....
2002-03	**Dallas**	**NHL**	72	23	24	47	51	7	0	6	169	13.6	9	1130	53.3	16:12	11	3	2	5	6	1	0	0	15:35
2003-04	**Dallas**	**NHL**	73	21	36	57	66	5	0	5	143	14.7	23	1203	53.0	17:00	5	1	1	2	2	1	0	0	17:23
2004-05			DID NOT PLAY																						
2005-06	**Dallas**	**NHL**	81	32	44	76	102	11	1	5	167	19.2	13	1306	51.2	17:12	5	0	3	3	4	0	0	0	20:04
2006-07	**Nashville**	**NHL**	68	27	27	54	48	12	0	6	190	14.2	15	1145	50.6	17:59	5	2	1	3	2	1	0	0	19:17
2007-08	**Nashville**	**NHL**	79	28	44	72	54	13	0	3	248	11.3	19	1260	48.7	18:59	4	1	0	1	4	0	0	1	18:29
	NHL Totals		971	331	439	770	1101	120	2	52	2737	12.1		9859	50.1	17:05	100	28	36	64	74	13	0	2	16:44

NHL All-Rookie Team (1994)

Played in NHL All-Star Game (1997, 2008)

Traded to **New Jersey** by **Edmonton** with Bryan Muir for Valeri Zelepukin and Bill Guerin, January 4, 1998. Traded to **Dallas** by **New Jersey** with Randy McKay and New Jersey's 1st round choice (later traded to Columbus – later traded to Buffalo – Buffalo selected Dan Paille) in 2002 Entry Draft for Joe Nieuwendyk and Jamie Langenbrunner, March 19, 2002. Signed as a free agent by **Nashville**, July 2, 2006.

ARTYUKHIN, Evgeny

(ahr-TYEW-khin, ehv-GEH-nee) **T.B.**

Right wing. Shoots left. 6'5", 254 lbs. Born, Moscow, USSR, April 4, 1983. Tampa Bay's 4th choice, 94th overall, in 2001 Entry Draft.

99-2000	Vityaz Podolsk 2	Russia-3	26	9	8	17	46	....	....	....	....	....	....	....	....	....	....	....	....	....	....	....	....	....	....
	Vityaz Podolsk	Russia-2	3	0	0	0	2	....	....	....	....	....	....	....	....	....	....	....	....	....	....	....	....	....	....
2000-01	Vityaz Podolsk	Russia	24	0	1	1	14	....	....	....	....	....	....	....	....	....	....	....	....	....	....	....	....	....	....
2001-02	Vityaz Podolsk 2	Russia-3	4	3	1	4	6	....	....	....	....	....	....	....	....	....	....	....	....	....	....	....	....	....	....
	Vityaz Podolsk	Russia-2	49	15	7	22	94	....	....	....	....	....	....	....	....	....	12	0	1	1	18	....	....	....	....
2002-03	Moncton Wildcats	QMJHL	53	13	27	40	204	....	....	....	....	....	....	....	....	....	6	1	2	3	29	....	....	....	....
2003-04	Hershey Bears	AHL	36	3	3	6	111	....	....	....	....	....	....	....	....	....	....	....	....	....	....	....	....	....	....
	Pensacola	ECHL	6	1	0	1	14	....	....	....	....	....	....	....	....	....	....	....	....	....	....	....	....	....	....
2004-05	Springfield	AHL	62	9	19	28	142	....	....	....	....	....	....	....	....	....	....	....	....	....	....	....	....	....	....
2005-06	**Tampa Bay**	**NHL**	72	4	13	17	90	1	0	0	79	5.1	–4	0	0.0	8:43	5	1	0	1	6	0	0	0	8:14
2006-07	Yaroslavl	Russia	44	5	8	13	183	....	....	....	....	....	....	....	....	....	1	0	0	0	0	....	....	....	....
2007-08	Avangard Omsk	Russia	19	3	2	5	40	....	....	....	....	....	....	....	....	....	....	....	....	....	....	....	....	....	....
	CSKA Moscow	Russia	23	3	5	8	99	....	....	....	....	....	....	....	....	....	6	4	0	4	6	....	....	....	....
	NHL Totals		72	4	13	17	90	1	0	0	79	5.1		0	0.0	8:43	5	1	0	1	6	0	0	0	8:14

Signed as a free agent by **Yaroslavl** (Russia), August 5, 2006.

ASHAM, Arron

(ASH-uhm, AIR-ruhn) **PHI.**

Right wing. Shoots right. 5'11", 205 lbs. Born, Portage La Prairie, Man., April 13, 1978. Montreal's 3rd choice, 71st overall, in 1996 Entry Draft.

1993-94	Portage	MAHA	21	18	19	37	82	....	....	....	....	....	....	....	....	....	....	....	....	....	....	....	....	....	....
1994-95	Red Deer Rebels	WHL	62	11	16	27	126	....	....	....	....	....	....	....	....	....	....	....	....	....	....	....	....	....	....
1995-96	Red Deer Rebels	WHL	70	32	45	77	174	....	....	....	....	....	....	....	....	....	10	6	3	9	20	....	....	....	....
1996-97	Red Deer Rebels	WHL	67	45	51	96	149	....	....	....	....	....	....	....	....	....	16	12	14	26	36	....	....	....	....
1997-98	Red Deer Rebels	WHL	67	43	49	92	153	....	....	....	....	....	....	....	....	....	5	0	2	2	8	....	....	....	....
	Fredericton	AHL	2	1	1	2	0	....	....	....	....	....	....	....	....	....	2	0	1	1	0	....	....	....	....
1998-99	**Montreal**	**NHL**	7	0	0	0	0	0	0	0	5	0.0	–4	0	0.0	7:27	....	....	....	....	....	....	....	....	....
	Fredericton	AHL	60	16	18	34	118	....	....	....	....	....	....	....	....	....	13	8	6	14	11	....	....	....	....
99-2000	**Montreal**	**NHL**	33	4	2	6	24	0	1	1	29	13.8	–7	1	0.0	10:14	....	....	....	....	....	....	....	....	....
	Quebec Citadelles	AHL	13	4	5	9	32	....	....	....	....	....	....	....	....	....	2	0	0	0	2	....	....	....	....
2000-01	**Montreal**	**NHL**	46	2	3	5	59	0	0	0	32	6.3	–9	3	100.0	8:28	....	....	....	....	....	....	....	....	....
	Quebec Citadelles	AHL	15	7	9	16	51	....	....	....	....	....	....	....	....	....	7	1	2	3	2	....	....	....	....
2001-02	**Montreal**	**NHL**	35	5	4	9	55	0	0	0	30	16.7	7	4	25.0	8:13	3	0	1	1	0	0	0	0	5:39
	Quebec Citadelles	AHL	24	9	14	23	35	....	....	....	....	....	....	....	....	....	....	....	....	....	....	....	....	....	....
2002-03	**NY Islanders**	**NHL**	78	15	19	34	57	4	0	1	114	13.2	1	17	41.2	12:13	5	0	0	0	16	0	0	0	15:09
2003-04	**NY Islanders**	**NHL**	79	12	12	24	92	1	0	0	108	11.1	–12	23	34.8	13:13	5	0	1	1	4	0	0	0	8:44
2004-05	EHC Visp	Swiss-2	5	2	4	6	6	....	....	....	....	....	....	....	....	....	4	1	1	2	8	....	....	....	....
2005-06	**NY Islanders**	**NHL**	63	9	15	24	103	2	1	0	99	9.1	–5	63	41.3	13:33	....	....	....	....	....	....	....	....	....
2006-07	**NY Islanders**	**NHL**	80	11	12	23	63	0	0	2	85	12.9	3	10	60.0	9:20	5	1	0	1	0	0	0	0	10:08
2007-08	**New Jersey**	**NHL**	77	6	4	10	84	0	0	2	68	8.8	–6	3	0.0	8:33	5	0	1	1	2	0	0	0	5:04
	NHL Totals		498	64	71	135	537	7	2	6	570	11.2		124	41.1	10:41	23	1	3	4	22	0	0	0	9:14

Traded to **NY Islanders** by **Montreal** with Montreal's 5th round choice (Marcus Paulsson) in 2002 Entry Draft for Mariusz Czerkawski, June 22, 2002. Signed as a free agent by **Visp** (Swiss-2), January 19, 2005. Signed as a free agent by **New Jersey**, August 7, 2007. Signed as a free agent by **Philadelphia**, July 7, 2008.

AUCOIN, Adrian
(oh-KOIN, AY-dree-uhn) **CGY.**

Defense. Shoots right. 6'2", 212 lbs. Born, Ottawa, Ont., July 3, 1973. Vancouver's 7th choice, 117th overall, in 1992 Entry Draft.

			Regular Season														Playoffs								
Season	Club	League	GP	G	A	Pts	PIM	PP	SH	GW	S	%	+/-	TF	F%	Min	GP	G	A	Pts	PIM	PP	SH	GW	Min
1989-90	Nepean Raiders	CJHL	54	2	14	16	95	....	....	....	....	....	....	....	....	....	4	0	1	1	....	....	....	....	....
1990-91	Nepean Raiders	CJHL	56	17	33	50	125	....	....	....	....	....	....	....	....	....	....	....	....	....	....	....	....	....	....
1991-92	Boston University	H-East	32	2	10	12	60	....	....	....	....	....	....	....	....	....	....	....	....	....	....	....	....	....	....
1992-93	Canada	Nat-Tm	42	8	10	18	71	....	....	....	....	....	....	....	....	....	....	....	....	....	....	....	....	....	....
1993-94	Canada	Nat-Tm	59	5	12	17	80	....	....	....	....	....	....	....	....	....	....	....	....	....	....	....	....	....	....
	Canada	Olympics	4	0	0	0	2	....	....	....	....	....	....	....	....	....	....	....	....	....	....	....	....	....	....
	Hamilton	AHL	13	1	2	3	19	....	....	....	....	....	....	....	....	....	4	0	2	2	6	....	....	....	....
1994-95	Syracuse Crunch	AHL	71	13	18	31	52	....	....	....	....	....	....	....	....	....	....	....	....	....	....	....	....	....	....
	Vancouver	NHL	1	1	0	1	0	0	0	0	2	50.0	1	....	....	....	4	1	0	1	0	1	0	0	....
1995-96	Vancouver	NHL	49	4	14	18	34	2	0	0	85	4.7	8	....	....	....	6	0	0	0	2	0	0	0	....
	Syracuse Crunch	AHL	29	5	13	18	47	....	....	....	....	....	....	....	....	....	....	....	....	....	....	....	....	....	....
1996-97	Vancouver	NHL	70	5	16	21	63	1	0	0	116	4.3	0	....	....	....	....	....	....	....	....	....	....	....	....
1997-98	Vancouver	NHL	35	3	3	6	21	1	0	1	44	6.8	–4	....	....	....	....	....	....	....	....	....	....	....	....
1998-99	Vancouver	NHL	82	23	11	34	77	18	2	3	174	13.2	–14	1	100.0	23:52	....	....	....	....	....	....	....	....	....
99-2000	Vancouver	NHL	57	10	14	24	30	4	0	1	126	7.9	7	0	0.0	23:06	....	....	....	....	....	....	....	....	....
2000-01	Vancouver	NHL	47	3	13	16	20	1	0	0	99	3.0	13	0	0.0	18:21	....	....	....	....	....	....	....	....	....
	Tampa Bay	NHL	26	1	11	12	25	1	0	0	60	1.7	–8	0	0.0	23:34	....	....	....	....	....	....	....	....	....
2001-02	NY Islanders	NHL	81	12	22	34	62	7	0	1	232	5.2	23	0	0.0	28:54	7	2	5	7	4	2	0	0	32:19
2002-03	NY Islanders	NHL	73	8	27	35	70	5	0	1	175	4.6	–5	0	0.0	29:01	5	1	2	3	4	0	0	0	31:43
2003-04	NY Islanders	NHL	81	13	31	44	54	4	0	2	213	6.1	29	0	0.0	26:38	5	0	0	0	6	0	0	0	28:21
2004-05	MODO	Sweden	14	2	4	6	32	....	....	....	....	....	....	....	....	....	6	1	0	1	16	....	....	....	....
2005-06	Chicago	NHL	33	1	5	6	38	1	0	0	59	1.7	–13	0	0.0	22:58	....	....	....	....	....	....	....	....	....
2006-07	Chicago	NHL	59	4	12	16	50	2	0	3	96	4.2	–22	0	0.0	20:50	....	....	....	....	....	....	....	....	....
2007-08	Calgary	NHL	76	10	25	35	37	5	0	1	121	8.3	13	0	0.0	20:58	7	0	3	3	4	0	0	0	18:13
	NHL Totals		**770**	**98**	**204**	**302**	**581**	**52**	**2**	**13**	**1602**	**6.1**		**1**	**100.0**	**24:18**	**34**	**4**	**10**	**14**	**20**	**3**	**0**	**0**	**27:15**

Played in NHL All-Star Game (2004)

• Missed majority of 1997-98 season recovering from ankle (October 4, 1997 vs. Anaheim) and groin (November 1, 1997 vs. Pittsburgh) injuries. Traded to **Tampa Bay** by **Vancouver** with Vancouver's 2nd round choice (Alexander Polushin) in 2001 Entry Draft for Dan Cloutier, February 7, 2001. Traded to **NY Islanders** by **Tampa Bay** with Alexander Kharitonov for Mathieu Biron and NY Islanders' 2nd round choice (later traded to Washington – later traded to Vancouver – Vancouver selected Denis Grot) in 2002 Entry Draft, June 22, 2001. Signed as a free agent by **MODO** (Sweden), December 21, 2004. Signed as a free agent by **Chicago**, August 2, 2005. Traded to **Calgary** by **Chicago** with Chicago's 7th round choice (C.J. Severyn) in 2007 Entry Draft for Andrei Zyuzin and Steve Marr, June 22, 2007.

AUCOIN, Keith
(oh-KOIN, KEETH) **WSH.**

Center. Shoots right. 5'9", 187 lbs. Born, Waltham, MA, November 6, 1978.

Season	Club	League	GP	G	A	Pts	PIM	PP	SH	GW	S	%	+/-	TF	F%	Min	GP	G	A	Pts	PIM	PP	SH	GW	Min
1997-98	Norwich U.	ECAC-3	26	19	14	33	....	....	....	....	....	....	....	....	....	....	....	....	....	....	....	....	....	....	....
1998-99	Norwich U.	ECAC-3	31	33	39	72	....	....	....	....	....	....	....	....	....	....	....	....	....	....	....	....	....	....	....
99-2000	Norwich U.	ECAC-3	31	36	41	77	14	....	....	....	....	....	....	....	....	....	....	....	....	....	....	....	....	....	....
2000-01	Norwich U.	ECAC-3	28	26	30	56	26	....	....	....	....	....	....	....	....	....	....	....	....	....	....	....	....	....	....
2001-02	Lowell	AHL	30	6	10	16	8	....	....	....	....	....	....	....	....	....	....	....	....	....	....	....	....	....	....
	Florida Everblades	ECHL	1	0	2	2	0	....	....	....	....	....	....	....	....	....	....	....	....	....	....	....	....	....	....
	BC Icemen	UHL	44	23	35	58	42	....	....	....	....	....	....	....	....	....	10	3	5	8	4	....	....	....	....
2002-03	Providence Bruins	AHL	78	25	49	74	71	....	....	....	....	....	....	....	....	....	4	0	1	1	6	....	....	....	....
2003-04	Cincinnati	AHL	80	18	30	48	64	....	....	....	....	....	....	....	....	....	9	0	3	3	4	....	....	....	....
2004-05	Memphis	CHL	5	4	5	9	10	....	....	....	....	....	....	....	....	....	....	....	....	....	....	....	....	....	....
	Providence Bruins	AHL	72	21	45	66	49	....	....	....	....	....	....	....	....	....	17	4	*14	18	18	....	....	....	....
2005-06	Carolina	NHL	7	0	1	1	4	0	0	0	3	0.0	–4	4	100.0	5:19	....	....	....	....	....	....	....	....	....
	Lowell	AHL	72	29	56	85	68	....	....	....	....	....	....	....	....	....	....	....	....	....	....	....	....	....	....
2006-07	Carolina	NHL	8	0	1	1	0	0	0	0	6	0.0	1	29	65.5	6:17	....	....	....	....	....	....	....	....	....
	Albany River Rats	AHL	65	27	72	99	108	....	....	....	....	....	....	....	....	....	5	1	3	4	7	....	....	....	....
2007-08	Carolina	NHL	38	5	8	13	10	0	0	0	65	7.7	3	327	37.9	13:28	....	....	....	....	....	....	....	....	....
	Albany River Rats	AHL	38	8	37	45	38	....	....	....	....	....	....	....	....	....	....	....	....	....	....	....	....	....	....
	NHL Totals		**53**	**5**	**10**	**15**	**14**	**0**	**0**	**0**	**74**	**6.8**		**360**	**40.8**	**11:18**	....	....	....	....	....	....	....	....	....

ECAC-3 First All-Star Team (2000, 2001) • ECAC-3 Player of the Year (2000, 2001) • AHL Second All-Star Team (2006, 2007)

Signed as a free agent by **Lowell** (AHL), June 19, 2001. Signed as a free agent by **Providence** (AHL), August 2, 2002. Signed as a free agent by **Anaheim**, August 29, 2003. Signed to a PTO (tryout) contract by **Providence** (AHL), November 4, 2004, Signed as a free agent by **Providence** (AHL), December 9, 2004. Signed as a free agent by **Carolina**, August 4, 2005. Signed as a free agent by **Washington**, July 3, 2008.

AVERY, Sean
(AY-vuhr-ee, SHAWN) **DAL.**

Center. Shoots left. 5'10", 195 lbs. Born, Pickering, Ont., April 10, 1980.

Season	Club	League	GP	G	A	Pts	PIM	PP	SH	GW	S	%	+/-	TF	F%	Min	GP	G	A	Pts	PIM	PP	SH	GW	Min
1995-96	Markham	Minor-ON	70	34	81	115	180	....	....	....	....	....	....	....	....	....	....	....	....	....	....	....	....	....	....
	Markham Waxers	MTJHL	1	0	0	0	4	....	....	....	....	....	....	....	....	....	....	....	....	....	....	....	....	....	....
1996-97	Owen Sound	OHL	58	10	21	31	86	....	....	....	....	....	....	....	....	....	4	1	0	1	4	....	....	....	....
1997-98	Owen Sound	OHL	47	13	41	54	105	....	....	....	....	....	....	....	....	....	....	....	....	....	....	....	....	....	....
1998-99	Owen Sound	OHL	28	22	23	45	70	....	....	....	....	....	....	....	....	....	....	....	....	....	....	....	....	....	....
	Kingston	OHL	33	14	25	39	88	....	....	....	....	....	....	....	....	....	5	1	3	4	13	....	....	....	....
99-2000	Kingston	OHL	55	28	56	84	215	....	....	....	....	....	....	....	....	....	5	2	2	4	26	....	....	....	....
2000-01	Cincinnati	AHL	58	8	15	23	304	....	....	....	....	....	....	....	....	....	4	1	0	1	19	....	....	....	....
2001-02	Detroit	NHL	36	2	2	4	68	0	0	1	30	6.7	1	299	51.8	7:51	....	....	....	....	....	....	....	....	....
	Cincinnati	AHL	36	14	7	21	106	....	....	....	....	....	....	....	....	....	....	....	....	....	....	....	....	....	....
2002-03	Detroit	NHL	39	5	6	11	120	0	0	2	40	12.5	7	224	58.0	7:03	....	....	....	....	....	....	....	....	....
	Grand Rapids	AHL	15	6	6	12	82	....	....	....	....	....	....	....	....	....	....	....	....	....	....	....	....	....	....
	Los Angeles	NHL	12	1	3	4	33	0	0	0	19	5.3	0	49	46.9	13:50	....	....	....	....	....	....	....	....	....
	Manchester	AHL	....	....	....	....	....	....	....	....	....	....	....	....	....	....	3	2	1	3	8	....	....	....	....
2003-04	Los Angeles	NHL	76	9	19	28	*261	0	0	2	125	7.2	2	124	54.8	11:41	....	....	....	....	....	....	....	....	....
2004-05	Pelicans Lahti	Finland	2	3	0	3	26	....	....	....	....	....	....	....	....	....	....	....	....	....	....	....	....	....	....
	Motor City	UHL	16	15	11	26	149	....	....	....	....	....	....	....	....	....	....	....	....	....	....	....	....	....	....
2005-06	Los Angeles	NHL	75	15	24	39	*257	1	3	1	189	7.9	–5	226	44.3	13:37	....	....	....	....	....	....	....	....	....
2006-07	Los Angeles	NHL	55	10	18	28	116	1	1	2	160	6.3	–10	180	47.2	16:52	....	....	....	....	....	....	....	....	....
	NY Rangers	NHL	29	8	12	20	58	1	0	0	89	9.0	11	110	52.7	17:49	10	1	4	5	27	0	0	0	19:27
2007-08	NY Rangers	NHL	57	15	18	33	154	2	0	4	125	12.0	6	28	39.3	15:50	8	4	3	7	6	1	0	1	14:14
	NHL Totals		**379**	**65**	**102**	**167**	**1067**	**5**	**4**	**12**	**777**	**8.4**		**1240**	**50.8**	**13:08**	**18**	**5**	**7**	**12**	**33**	**1**	**0**	**1**	**17:08**

Signed as a free agent by **Detroit**, September 21, 1999. Traded to **Los Angeles** by **Detroit** with Maxim Kuznetsov, Detroit's 1st round choice (Jeff Tambellini) in 2003 Entry Draft and Detroit's 2nd round choice (later traded to Boston – Boston selected Martins Karsums) in 2004 Entry Draft for Mathieu Schneider, March 11, 2003. Signed as a free agent by **Lahti** (Finland), November 24, 2004. Signed as a free agent by **Motor City** (UHL), February 11, 2005. Traded to **NY Rangers** by **Los Angeles** with John Seymour for Jason Ward, Jan Marek, Marc-Andre Cliche and NY Rangers' 3rd round choice (later traded to Buffalo - Buffalo selected Corey Fienhage) in 2008 Entry Draft, February 5, 2007. Signed as a free agent by **Dallas**, July 2, 2008.

AXELSSON, P.J.
(AHX-ehl-suhn, PEE-JAY) **BOS.**

Left wing. Shoots left. 6'1", 188 lbs. Born, Kungalv, Sweden, February 26, 1975. Boston's 7th choice, 177th overall, in 1995 Entry Draft.

Season	Club	League	GP	G	A	Pts	PIM	PP	SH	GW	S	%	+/-	TF	F%	Min	GP	G	A	Pts	PIM	PP	SH	GW	Min
1992-93	V.Frolunda Jr.	Swe-Jr.	16	9	5	14	12	....	....	....	....	....	....	....	....	....	....	....	....	....	....	....	....	....	....
	V.Frolunda	Sweden	1	0	0	0	0	....	....	....	....	....	....	....	....	....	....	....	....	....	....	....	....	....	....
1993-94	V.Frolunda	Sweden	11	0	0	0	4	....	....	....	....	....	....	....	....	....	4	0	0	0	0	....	....	....	....
1994-95	V.Frolunda Jr.	Swe-Jr.	19	16	9	25	22	....	....	....	....	....	....	....	....	....	....	....	....	....	....	....	....	....	....
	V.Frolunda	Sweden	11	2	1	3	6	....	....	....	....	....	....	....	....	....	5	0	0	0	0	....	....	....	....
1995-96	V.Frolunda	Sweden	36	15	5	20	10	....	....	....	....	....	....	....	....	....	13	3	0	3	10	....	....	....	....
1996-97	V.Frolunda	Sweden	50	19	15	34	34	....	....	....	....	....	....	....	....	....	3	0	2	2	0	....	....	....	....
	V.Frolunda	EuroHL	3	1	1	2	0	....	....	....	....	....	....	....	....	....	3	0	0	0	2	....	....	....	....
1997-98	Boston	NHL	82	8	19	27	38	2	0	1	144	5.6	–14	....	....	....	6	1	0	1	0	0	0	0	....
1998-99	Boston	NHL	77	7	10	17	18	0	0	2	146	4.8	–14	8	75.0	16:38	12	1	1	2	4	0	0	0	15:11
99-2000	Boston	NHL	81	10	16	26	24	0	0	4	186	5.4	1	22	27.3	16:43	....	....	....	....	....	....	....	....	....
2000-01	Boston	NHL	81	8	15	23	27	0	0	2	146	5.5	–12	41	36.6	12:30	....	....	....	....	....	....	....	....	....
2001-02	Boston	NHL	78	7	17	24	16	0	2	0	127	5.5	6	17	35.3	14:42	6	2	1	3	6	0	1	1	16:48
	Sweden	Olympics	4	0	0	0	2	....	....	....	....	....	....	....	....	....	....	....	....	....	....	....	....	....	....
2002-03	Boston	NHL	66	17	19	36	24	2	2	1	122	13.9	8	17	23.5	16:37	5	0	0	0	6	0	0	0	13:23
2003-04	Boston	NHL	68	6	14	20	42	0	0	1	107	5.6	2	13	15.4	16:19	7	0	0	0	4	0	0	0	14:43
2004-05	Frolunda	Sweden	45	8	9	17	95	....	....	....	....	....	....	....	....	....	14	1	*10	11	18	....	....	....	....

			Regular Season														Playoffs								
Season	Club	League	GP	G	A	Pts	PIM	PP	SH	GW	S	%	+/-	TF	F%	Min	GP	G	A	Pts	PIM	PP	SH	GW	Min
2005-06	**Boston**	**NHL**	**59**	**10**	**18**	**28**	**4**	**1**	**2**	**1**	**113**	**8.8**	**–3**	**27**	**40.7**	**17:36**	....	....	....	....	....	....	....	....	....
	Sweden	Olympics	8	3	3	6	0	....	....	....	....	....	....	....	....	....	....	....	....	....	....	....	....	....	....
2006-07	**Boston**	**NHL**	**55**	**11**	**16**	**27**	**52**	**3**	**2**	**0**	**81**	**13.6**	**–10**	**38**	**34.2**	**19:34**	....	....	....	....	....	....	....	....	....
2007-08	**Boston**	**NHL**	**75**	**13**	**16**	**29**	**15**	**0**	**2**	**2**	**100**	**13.0**	**11**	**45**	**37.8**	**17:36**	**7**	**0**	**0**	**0**	**2**	**0**	**0**	**0**	**16:57**
	NHL Totals		**722**	**97**	**160**	**257**	**260**	**8**	**10**	**14**	**1272**	**7.6**		**228**	**35.1**	**16:18**	**43**	**4**	**2**	**6**	**22**	**0**	**1**	**1**	**15:27**

Signed as a free agent by **Frolunda** (Sweden), September 15, 2004.

BABCHUK, Anton

(bab-CHUHK, AN-tawn) **CAR.**

Defense. Shoots right. 6'5", 212 lbs. Born, Kiev, USSR, May 6, 1984. Chicago's 1st choice, 21st overall, in 2002 Entry Draft.

99-2000	Elektrostal 2	Russia-3	6	0	0	0	8	....	....	....	....	....	....	....	....	....	....	....	....	....	....	....	....	....	....
	Elektrostal 2	Russia-3	18	0	1	1	18	....	....	....	....	....	....	....	....	....	....	....	....	....	....	....	....	....	....
2000-01	Elektrostal	Russia-2	7	0	0	0	12	....	....	....	....	....	....	....	....	....	....	....	....	....	....	....	....	....	....
	Russia 17	Nat-Tm	15	1	3	4	12	....	....	....	....	....	....	....	....	....	....	....	....	....	....	....	....	....	....
2001-02	Elektrostal	Russia-2	40	7	8	15	90	....	....	....	....	....	....	....	....	....	....	....	....	....	....	....	....	....	....
	Elektrostal 2	Russia-3	3	0	0	0	8	....	....	....	....	....	....	....	....	....	....	....	....	....	....	....	....	....	....
2002-03	Ak Bars Kazan	Russia	10	0	0	0	4	....	....	....	....	....	....	....	....	....	....	....	....	....	....	....	....	....	....
	St. Petersburg	Russia	20	3	0	3	10	....	....	....	....	....	....	....	....	....	....	....	....	....	....	....	....	....	....
	Spartak St. Pet.	Russia-2	1	1	0	1	0	....	....	....	....	....	....	....	....	....	....	....	....	....	....	....	....	....	....
2003-04	**Chicago**	**NHL**	**5**	**0**	**2**	**2**	**2**	**0**	**0**	**0**	**11**	**0.0**	**–1**	**0**	**0.0**	**12:43**	....	....	....	....	....	....	....	....	....
	Norfolk Admirals	AHL	73	8	14	22	89	....	....	....	....	....	....	....	....	....	8	0	2	2	6	....	....	....	....
2004-05	Norfolk Admirals	AHL	66	8	16	24	88	....	....	....	....	....	....	....	....	....	2	0	0	0	2	....	....	....	....
2005-06	**Chicago**	**NHL**	**17**	**2**	**3**	**5**	**16**	**1**	**0**	**0**	**24**	**8.3**	**–5**	**0**	**0.0**	**16:38**	....	....	....	....	....	....	....	....	....
	Norfolk Admirals	AHL	24	5	7	12	22	....	....	....	....	....	....	....	....	....	....	....	....	....	....	....	....	....	....
	♦ **Carolina**	**NHL**	**22**	**3**	**2**	**5**	**6**	**2**	**0**	**0**	**32**	**9.4**	**–2**	**0**	**0.0**	**13:22**	....	....	....	....	....	....	....	....	....
	Lowell	AHL	5	1	3	4	0	....	....	....	....	....	....	....	....	....	....	....	....	....	....	....	....	....	....
2006-07	**Carolina**	**NHL**	**52**	**2**	**12**	**14**	**30**	**0**	**0**	**2**	**63**	**3.2**	**–6**	**0**	**0.0**	**17:26**	....	....	....	....	....	....	....	....	....
	Albany River Rats	AHL	9	1	6	7	2	....	....	....	....	....	....	....	....	....	....	....	....	....	....	....	....	....	....
2007-08	Avangard Omsk	Russia	57	9	17	26	30	....	....	....	....	....	....	....	....	....	4	1	1	2	6	....	....	....	....
	NHL Totals		**96**	**7**	**19**	**26**	**54**	**3**	**0**	**2**	**130**	**5.4**		**0**	**0.0**	**16:07**									

Traded to **Carolina** by **Chicago** for Danny Richmond and Columbus' 4th round choice (previously acquired, later traded to Toronto - Toronto selected James Reimer) in 2006 Entry Draft, January 20, 2006.

BACKES, David

(BA-kuhs, DAY-vihd) **ST.L.**

Center. Shoots right. 6'3", 216 lbs. Born, Blaine, MN, May 1, 1984. St. Louis' 2nd choice, 62nd overall, in 2003 Entry Draft.

99-2000	Spring Lake Park	High-MN	24	17	20	37	....	....	....	....	....	....	....	....	....	....	....	....	....	....	....	....	....	....	....
2000-01	Spring Lake Park	High-MN	24	29	46	75	....	....	....	....	....	....	....	....	....	....	....	....	....	....	....	....	....	....	....
2001-02	Chicago Steel	USHL	25	31	36	67	....	....	....	....	....	....	....	....	....	....	2	1	1	2	....	....	....	....	....
	Lincoln Stars	USHL	30	11	10	21	54	....	....	....	....	....	....	....	....	....	3	0	0	0	2	....	....	....	....
2002-03	Lincoln Stars	USHL	57	28	41	69	126	....	....	....	....	....	....	....	....	....	7	4	1	5	17	....	....	....	....
2003-04	Minnesota State	WCHA	39	16	21	37	66	....	....	....	....	....	....	....	....	....	....	....	....	....	....	....	....	....	....
2004-05	Minnesota State	WCHA	38	17	23	40	55	....	....	....	....	....	....	....	....	....	....	....	....	....	....	....	....	....	....
2005-06	Minnesota State	WCHA	38	13	29	42	91	....	....	....	....	....	....	....	....	....	....	....	....	....	....	....	....	....	....
	Peoria Rivermen	AHL	12	5	5	10	10	....	....	....	....	....	....	....	....	....	3	1	1	2	8	....	....	....	....
2006-07	**St. Louis**	**NHL**	**49**	**10**	**13**	**23**	**37**	**2**	**0**	**2**	**89**	**11.2**	**6**	**26**	**46.2**	**13:25**	....	....	....	....	....	....	....	....	....
	Peoria Rivermen	AHL	31	10	3	13	47	....	....	....	....	....	....	....	....	....	....	....	....	....	....	....	....	....	....
2007-08	**St. Louis**	**NHL**	**72**	**13**	**18**	**31**	**99**	**3**	**0**	**2**	**129**	**10.1**	**–11**	**67**	**44.8**	**14:41**	....	....	....	....	....	....	....	....	....
	NHL Totals		**121**	**23**	**31**	**54**	**136**	**5**	**0**	**4**	**218**	**10.6**		**93**	**45.2**	**14:10**	....	....	....	....	....	....	....	....	....

USHL First All-Star Team (2003) • WCHA All-Rookie Team (2004) • WCHA Second All-Star Team (2006) • NCAA West Second All-American Team (2006)

BACKMAN, Christian

(BAK-man, KRIH-stan) **CBJ**

Defense. Shoots Left. 6'4", 210 lbs. Born, Alingsas, Alingsas, April 28, 1980. St. Louis' 1st choice, 24th overall, in 1998 Entry Draft.

1996-97	V.Frolunda Jr.	Swe-Jr.	26	2	5	7	16	....	....	....	....	....	....	....	....	....	....	....	....	....	....	....	....	....	....
1997-98	V.Frolunda U18	Swe-U18	4	4	1	5	2	....	....	....	....	....	....	....	....	....	5	2	2	4	2	....	....	....	....
	V.Frolunda Jr.	Swe-Jr.	28	5	14	19	12	....	....	....	....	....	....	....	....	....	2	0	1	1	4	....	....	....	....
1998-99	V.Frolunda Jr.	Swe-Jr.	4	0	2	2	4	....	....	....	....	....	....	....	....	....	....	....	....	....	....	....	....	....	....
	V.Frolunda	Sweden	49	0	4	4	4	....	....	....	....	....	....	....	....	....	4	0	0	0	0	....	....	....	....
99-2000	V.Frolunda Jr.	Swe-Jr.	5	1	1	2	0	....	....	....	....	....	....	....	....	....	3	1	1	2	0	....	....	....	....
	Gislaveds SK	Sweden-2	21	5	2	7	8	....	....	....	....	....	....	....	....	....	....	....	....	....	....	....	....	....	....
	V.Frolunda	Sweden	27	1	0	1	14	....	....	....	....	....	....	....	....	....	5	0	0	0	0	....	....	....	....
2000-01	V.Frolunda	Sweden	50	1	10	11	32	....	....	....	....	....	....	....	....	....	3	0	2	2	2	....	....	....	....
2001-02	V.Frolunda	Sweden	44	7	4	11	38	....	....	....	....	....	....	....	....	....	10	0	0	0	8	....	....	....	....
2002-03	**St. Louis**	**NHL**	**4**	**0**	**0**	**0**	**0**	**0**	**0**	**0**	**4**	**0.0**	**–3**	**0**	**0.0**	**12:22**	....	....	....	....	....	....	....	....	....
	Worcester IceCats	AHL	72	8	19	27	66	....	....	....	....	....	....	....	....	....	3	0	1	1	5	....	....	....	....
2003-04	**St. Louis**	**NHL**	**66**	**5**	**13**	**18**	**16**	**1**	**0**	**0**	**92**	**5.4**	**3**	**0**	**0.0**	**19:20**	**5**	**0**	**2**	**2**	**4**	**0**	**0**	**0**	**23:06**
	Worcester IceCats	AHL	4	1	2	3	2	....	....	....	....	....	....	....	....	....	....	....	....	....	....	....	....	....	....
2004-05	Frolunda	Sweden	50	4	15	19	40	....	....	....	....	....	....	....	....	....	14	2	7	9	10	....	....	....	....
2005-06	**St. Louis**	**NHL**	**52**	**6**	**12**	**18**	**48**	**3**	**0**	**1**	**70**	**8.6**	**–15**	**0**	**0.0**	**24:49**	....	....	....	....	....	....	....	....	....
	Sweden	Olympics	8	1	2	3	6	....	....	....	....	....	....	....	....	....	....	....	....	....	....	....	....	....	....
2006-07	**St. Louis**	**NHL**	**61**	**7**	**11**	**18**	**36**	**1**	**0**	**0**	**80**	**8.8**	**13**	**0**	**0.0**	**22:10**	....	....	....	....	....	....	....	....	....
2007-08	**St. Louis**	**NHL**	**45**	**1**	**9**	**10**	**30**	**0**	**0**	**0**	**30**	**3.3**	**–4**	**0**	**0.0**	**19:22**	....	....	....	....	....	....	....	....	....
	NY Rangers	**NHL**	**18**	**2**	**6**	**8**	**20**	**1**	**0**	**0**	**21**	**9.5**	**2**	**0**	**0.0**	**18:49**	**8**	**0**	**0**	**0**	**12**	**0**	**0**	**0**	**18:16**
	NHL Totals		**246**	**21**	**51**	**72**	**150**	**6**	**0**	**1**	**297**	**7.1**		**0**	**0.0**	**21:03**	**13**	**0**	**2**	**2**	**16**	**0**	**0**	**0**	**20:07**

Signed as a free agent by **Frolunda** (Sweden), September 15, 2004. Traded to **NY Rangers** by **St. Louis** for NY Rangers' 4th round choice (later traded back to NY Rangers - NY Rangers selected Dale Weise) in 2008 Entry Draft, February 26, 2008. Traded to **Columbus** by **NY Rangers** with Fedor Tyutin for Nikolai Zherdev and Dan Fritsche, July 2, 2008.

BACKSTROM, Nicklas

(BAK-struhm, NIHK-luhs) **WSH.**

Center. Shoots left. 6', 183 lbs. Born, Gavle, Sweden, November 23, 1987. Washington's 1st choice, 4th overall, in 2006 Entry Draft.

2001-02	Brynas U18	Swe-U18	2	0	0	0	0	....	....	....	....	....	....	....	....	....	....	....	....	....	....	....	....	....	....
2002-03	Brynas U18	Swe-U18	STATISTICS NOT AVAILABLE																						
2003-04	Brynas U18	Swe-U18	6	9	5	14	4	....	....	....	....	....	....	....	....	....	3	0	3	3	0	....	....	....	....
	Brynas IF Gavle Jr.	Swe-Jr.	21	2	6	8	2	....	....	....	....	....	....	....	....	....	5	0	0	0	4	....	....	....	....
2004-05	Brynas IF Gavle Jr.	Swe-Jr.	29	17	17	34	24	....	....	....	....	....	....	....	....	....	....	....	....	....	....	....	....	....	....
	Brynas IF Gavle	Sweden	19	0	0	0	2	....	....	....	....	....	....	....	....	....	....	....	....	....	....	....	....	....	....
2005-06	Brynas IF Gavle	Sweden	46	10	16	26	30	....	....	....	....	....	....	....	....	....	4	1	0	1	2	....	....	....	....
	Brynas IF Gavle Jr.	Swe-Jr.	....	....	....	....	....	....	....	....	....	....	....	....	....	....	1	0	0	0	2	....	....	....	....
2006-07	Brynas IF Gavle	Sweden	45	12	28	40	46	....	....	....	....	....	....	....	....	....	7	3	3	6	6	....	....	....	....
2007-08	**Washington**	**NHL**	**82**	**14**	**55**	**69**	**24**	**3**	**0**	**4**	**153**	**9.2**	**13**	**874**	**46.3**	**19:00**	**7**	**4**	**2**	**6**	**2**	**3**	**0**	**0**	**20:26**
	NHL Totals		**82**	**14**	**55**	**69**	**24**	**3**	**0**	**4**	**153**	**9.2**		**874**	**46.3**	**19:00**	**7**	**4**	**2**	**6**	**2**	**3**	**0**	**0**	**20:26**

NHL All-Rookie Team (2008)

BALEJ, Jozef

(BAH-lay, YOH-zehf)

Right wing. Shoots right. 6'1", 195 lbs. Born, Myjava, Czech., February 22, 1982. Montreal's 3rd choice, 78th overall, in 2000 Entry Draft.

1996-97	Dukla Trencin Jr.	Slovak-Jr.	51	31	25	56	36	....	....	....	....	....	....	....	....	....	....	....	....	....	....	....	....	....	....
1997-98	Dukla Trencin Jr.	Slovak-Jr.	52	57	40	97	60	....	....	....	....	....	....	....	....	....	....	....	....	....	....	....	....	....	....
1998-99	Thunder Bay	USHL	38	8	7	15	9	....	....	....	....	....	....	....	....	....	....	....	....	....	....	....	....	....	....
	Rochester	USHL	17	0	1	1	2	....	....	....	....	....	....	....	....	....	....	....	....	....	....	....	....	....	....
99-2000	Portland	WHL	65	22	23	45	33	....	....	....	....	....	....	....	....	....	....	....	....	....	....	....	....	....	....
2000-01	Portland	WHL	46	32	21	53	18	....	....	....	....	....	....	....	....	....	16	9	6	15	6	....	....	....	....
2001-02	Portland	WHL	65	51	41	92	52	....	....	....	....	....	....	....	....	....	7	0	2	2	6	....	....	....	....
2002-03	Hamilton	AHL	56	5	15	20	29	....	....	....	....	....	....	....	....	....	....	....	....	....	....	....	....	....	....
2003-04	**Montreal**	**NHL**	**4**	**0**	**0**	**0**	**0**	**0**	**0**	**0**	**4**	**0.0**	**–1**	**2**	**50.0**	**12:38**	....	....	....	....	....	....	....	....	....
	Hamilton	AHL	55	25	33	58	32	....	....	....	....	....	....	....	....	....	....	....	....	....	....	....	....	....	....
	NY Rangers	**NHL**	**13**	**1**	**4**	**5**	**4**	**0**	**0**	**0**	**25**	**4.0**	**0**	**1**	**0.0**	**13:06**	....	....	....	....	....	....	....	....	....
	Hartford	AHL	5	1	3	4	21	....	....	....	....	....	....	....	....	....	16	9	7	16	10	....	....	....	....
2004-05	Hartford	AHL	69	20	22	42	46	....	....	....	....	....	....	....	....	....	6	0	0	0	4	....	....	....	....

			Regular Season														Playoffs								
Season	Club	League	GP	G	A	Pts	PIM	PP	SH	GW	S	%	+/-	TF	F%	Min	GP	G	A	Pts	PIM	PP	SH	GW	Min
2005-06	**Vancouver**	**NHL**	**1**	**0**	**1**	**1**	**0**	**0**	**0**	**0**	**3**	**0.0**	**1**	**0**	**0.0**	**7:56**	....	....	....	....	....	....	....	....	....
	Manitoba Moose	AHL	39	14	15	29	20	....	....	....	....	....	....	....	....	....	4	1	0	1	4	....	....	....	....
2006-07	Fribourg	Swiss	37	13	17	30	44	....	....	....	....	....	....	....	....	....	4	4	1	5	2	....	....	....	....
2007-08	Manitoba Moose	AHL	16	4	9	13	10	....	....	....	....	....	....	....	....	....	....	....	....	....	....	....	....	....	....
	NHL Totals		**18**	**1**	**5**	**6**	**4**	**0**	**0**	**0**	**32**	**3.1**		**3**	**33.3**	**12:43**	....	....	....	....	....	....	....	....	....

WHL West First All-Star Team (2002)

Traded to **NY Rangers** by **Montreal** with Montreal's 2nd round choice (Bruce Graham) in 2004 Entry Draft for Alex Kovalev, March 2, 2004. Traded to **Vancouver** by **NY Rangers** with future consdierations for Fedor Fedorov, October 7, 2005. Signed as a free agent by **Fribourg** (Austria), July 24, 2006.

BALLARD, Keith

(BAL-uhrd, KEETH) **FLA.**

Defense. Shoots left. 5'11", 208 lbs. Born, Baudette, MN, November 26, 1982. Buffalo's 1st choice, 11th overall, in 2002 Entry Draft.

Season	Club	League	GP	G	A	Pts	PIM	PP	SH	GW	S	%	+/-	TF	F%	Min	GP	G	A	Pts	PIM	PP	SH	GW	Min
99-2000	USNTDP	U-18	6	1	1	2	4	....	....	....	....	....	....	....	....	....	....	....	....	....	....	....	....	....	....
	USNTDP	USHL	58	12	21	33	119	....	....	....	....	....	....	....	....	....	....	....	....	....	....	....	....	....	....
2000-01	Omaha Lancers	USHL	56	22	29	51	168	....	....	....	....	....	....	....	....	....	10	1	6	7	8	....	....	....	....
2001-02	U. of Minnesota	WCHA	41	10	13	23	42	....	....	....	....	....	....	....	....	....	....	....	....	....	....	....	....	....	....
2002-03	U. of Minnesota	WCHA	41	12	29	41	78	....	....	....	....	....	....	....	....	....	....	....	....	....	....	....	....	....	....
2003-04	U. of Minnesota	WCHA	37	11	25	36	83	....	....	....	....	....	....	....	....	....	....	....	....	....	....	....	....	....	....
2004-05	Utah Grizzlies	AHL	60	2	18	20	88	....	....	....	....	....	....	....	....	....	....	....	....	....	....	....	....	....	....
2005-06	**Phoenix**	**NHL**	**82**	**8**	**31**	**39**	**99**	**1**	**3**	**1**	**102**	**7.8**	**–18**	**0**	**0.0**	**19:59**	....	....	....	....	....	....	....	....	....
2006-07	**Phoenix**	**NHL**	**69**	**5**	**22**	**27**	**59**	**2**	**0**	**0**	**79**	**6.3**	**–7**	**0**	**0.0**	**22:00**	....	....	....	....	....	....	....	....	....
2007-08	**Phoenix**	**NHL**	**82**	**6**	**15**	**21**	**85**	**2**	**1**	**1**	**105**	**5.7**	**7**	**0**	**0.0**	**21:16**	....	....	....	....	....	....	....	....	....
	NHL Totals		**233**	**19**	**68**	**87**	**243**	**5**	**4**	**2**	**286**	**6.6**		**0**	**0.0**	**21:02**	....	....	....	....	....	....	....	....	....

USHL First All-Star Team (2001) • WCHA All-Rookie Team (2002) • WCHA First All-Star Team (2003, 2004) • NCAA West First All-American Team (2004)

Traded to **Colorado** by **Buffalo** for Steve Reinprecht, July 3, 2003. Traded to **Phoenix** by **Colorado** with Derek Morris for Ossi Vaananen, Chris Gratton and Phoenix's 2nd round choice (Paul Stastny) in 2005 Entry Draft, March 9, 2004. Traded to **Florida** by **Phoenix** with Nick Boynton and Ottawa's 2nd round choice (previously acquired, later traded back to Phoenix - Phoenix selected Jared Staal) in 2008 Entry Draft for Olli Jokinen, June 20, 2008.

BARANKA, Ivan

(ba-RAN-kuh, IGH-vuhn) **NYR**

Defense. Shoots left. 6'3", 205 lbs. Born, Ilava, Czech., May 19, 1985. NY Rangers' 2nd choice, 50th overall, in 2003 Entry Draft.

Season	Club	League	GP	G	A	Pts	PIM	PP	SH	GW	S	%	+/-	TF	F%	Min	GP	G	A	Pts	PIM	PP	SH	GW	Min
2002-03	Dubnica Jr.	Slovak-Jr.	27	1	7	8	44	....	....	....	....	....	....	....	....	....	....	....	....	....	....	....	....	....	....
	Dubnica	Slovak-2	2	0	0	0	0	....	....	....	....	....	....	....	....	....	....	....	....	....	....	....	....	....	....
2003-04	Everett Silvertips	WHL	58	3	12	15	69	....	....	....	....	....	....	....	....	....	20	3	5	8	26	....	....	....	....
2004-05	Everett Silvertips	WHL	64	7	16	23	64	....	....	....	....	....	....	....	....	....	11	3	1	4	6	....	....	....	....
	Hartford	AHL	....	....	....	....	....	....	....	....	....	....	....	....	....	....	1	0	0	0	0	....	....	....	....
2005-06	Hartford	AHL	59	5	16	21	87	....	....	....	....	....	....	....	....	....	....	....	....	....	....	....	....	....	....
2006-07	Hartford	AHL	54	3	20	23	50	....	....	....	....	....	....	....	....	....	....	....	....	....	....	....	....	....	....
2007-08	**NY Rangers**	**NHL**	**1**	**0**	**1**	**1**	**0**	**0**	**0**	**0**	**1**	**0.0**	**1**	**0**	**0.0**	**12:44**	....	....	....	....	....	....	....	....	....
	Hartford	AHL	61	5	21	26	53	....	....	....	....	....	....	....	....	....	5	0	2	2	2	....	....	....	....
	NHL Totals		**1**	**0**	**1**	**1**	**0**	**0**	**0**	**0**	**1**	**0.0**		**0**	**0.0**	**12:44**	....	....	....	....	....	....	....	....	....

BARCH, Krys

(BAHRCH, KRIHS) **DAL.**

Right wing. Shoots left. 6'2", 220 lbs. Born, Hamilton, Ont., March 26, 1980. Washington's 3rd choice, 106th overall, in 1998 Entry Draft.

Season	Club	League	GP	G	A	Pts	PIM	PP	SH	GW	S	%	+/-	TF	F%	Min	GP	G	A	Pts	PIM	PP	SH	GW	Min
1995-96	Georgetown	OPJHL	41	6	8	14	10	....	....	....	....	....	....	....	....	....	....	....	....	....	....	....	....	....	....
1996-97	Georgetown	OPJHL	51	18	26	44	58	....	....	....	....	....	....	....	....	....	....	....	....	....	....	....	....	....	....
1997-98	London Knights	OHL	65	9	27	36	62	....	....	....	....	....	....	....	....	....	16	4	3	7	16	....	....	....	....
1998-99	London Knights	OHL	66	18	20	38	66	....	....	....	....	....	....	....	....	....	25	9	17	26	15	....	....	....	....
99-2000	London Knights	OHL	56	23	26	49	78	....	....	....	....	....	....	....	....	....	....	....	....	....	....	....	....	....	....
	Portland Pirates	AHL	....	....	....	....	....	....	....	....	....	....	....	....	....	....	4	0	2	2	2	....	....	....	....
2000-01	Portland Pirates	AHL	76	10	15	25	91	....	....	....	....	....	....	....	....	....	2	0	0	0	0	....	....	....	....
2001-02	Portland Pirates	AHL	29	3	8	11	28	....	....	....	....	....	....	....	....	....	....	....	....	....	....	....	....	....	....
	Richmond	ECHL	25	6	4	10	43	....	....	....	....	....	....	....	....	....	....	....	....	....	....	....	....	....	....
2002-03	Portland Pirates	AHL	36	1	7	8	49	....	....	....	....	....	....	....	....	....	....	....	....	....	....	....	....	....	....
2003-04			DID NOT PLAY																						
2004-05	Norfolk Admirals	AHL	9	1	0	1	37	....	....	....	....	....	....	....	....	....	....	....	....	....	....	....	....	....	....
	Greenville	ECHL	55	11	19	30	154	....	....	....	....	....	....	....	....	....	3	0	0	0	36	....	....	....	....
2005-06	Iowa Stars	AHL	43	7	6	13	129	....	....	....	....	....	....	....	....	....	7	0	1	1	37	....	....	....	....
	Greenville	ECHL	14	10	4	14	75	....	....	....	....	....	....	....	....	....	....	....	....	....	....	....	....	....	....
2006-07	**Dallas**	**NHL**	**26**	**3**	**2**	**5**	**107**	**0**	**0**	**2**	**12**	**25.0**	**2**	**1**	**0.0**	**5:38**	....	....	....	....	....	....	....	....	....
	Iowa Stars	AHL	31	3	5	8	110	....	....	....	....	....	....	....	....	....	....	....	....	....	....	....	....	....	....
2007-08	**Dallas**	**NHL**	**48**	**1**	**2**	**3**	**105**	**0**	**0**	**0**	**23**	**4.3**	**–3**	**2**	**0.0**	**6:30**	**3**	**0**	**0**	**0**	**2**	**0**	**0**	**0**	**2:21**
	NHL Totals		**74**	**4**	**4**	**8**	**212**	**0**	**0**	**2**	**35**	**11.4**		**3**	**0.0**	**6:12**	**3**	**0**	**0**	**0**	**2**	**0**	**0**	**0**	**2:21**

Signed as a free agent by **Dallas**, July 18, 2006.

BARKER, Cam

(BAR-kuhr, KAM) **CHI.**

Defense. Shoots left. 6'3", 222 lbs. Born, Winnipeg, Man., April 4, 1986. Chicago's 1st choice, 3rd overall, in 2004 Entry Draft.

Season	Club	League	GP	G	A	Pts	PIM	PP	SH	GW	S	%	+/-	TF	F%	Min	GP	G	A	Pts	PIM	PP	SH	GW	Min
2001-02	Cornwall Colts	CJHL	72	6	23	29	132	....	....	....	....	....	....	....	....	....	....	....	....	....	....	....	....	....	....
	Medicine Hat	WHL	3	0	1	1	0	....	....	....	....	....	....	....	....	....	....	....	....	....	....	....	....	....	....
2002-03	Medicine Hat	WHL	64	10	37	47	79	....	....	....	....	....	....	....	....	....	11	3	4	7	17	....	....	....	....
2003-04	Medicine Hat	WHL	69	21	44	65	105	....	....	....	....	....	....	....	....	....	20	3	9	12	18	....	....	....	....
2004-05	Medicine Hat	WHL	52	15	33	48	99	....	....	....	....	....	....	....	....	....	12	3	3	6	16	....	....	....	....
2005-06	**Chicago**	**NHL**	**1**	**0**	**0**	**0**	**0**	**0**	**0**	**0**	**1**	**0.0**	**0**	**0**	**0.0**	**11:02**	....	....	....	....	....	....	....	....	....
	Medicine Hat	WHL	26	5	13	18	63	....	....	....	....	....	....	....	....	....	13	4	8	12	*59	....	....	....	....
2006-07	**Chicago**	**NHL**	**35**	**1**	**7**	**8**	**44**	**1**	**0**	**0**	**38**	**2.6**	**–12**	**0**	**0.0**	**19:19**	....	....	....	....	....	....	....	....	....
	Norfolk Admirals	AHL	34	5	10	15	53	....	....	....	....	....	....	....	....	....	6	1	3	4	13	....	....	....	....
2007-08	**Chicago**	**NHL**	**45**	**6**	**12**	**18**	**52**	**2**	**0**	**0**	**42**	**14.3**	**–3**	**0**	**0.0**	**17:12**	....	....	....	....	....	....	....	....	....
	Rockford IceHogs	AHL	29	8	11	19	67	....	....	....	....	....	....	....	....	....	....	....	....	....	....	....	....	....	....
	NHL Totals		**81**	**7**	**19**	**26**	**96**	**3**	**0**	**0**	**81**	**8.6**		**0**	**0.0**	**18:02**	....	....	....	....	....	....	....	....	....

BARNES, Stu

(BAHRNZ, STEW) **DAL.**

Center. Shoots right. 5'11", 182 lbs. Born, Spruce Grove, Alta., December 25, 1970. Winnipeg's 1st choice, 4th overall, in 1989 Entry Draft.

Season	Club	League	GP	G	A	Pts	PIM	PP	SH	GW	S	%	+/-	TF	F%	Min	GP	G	A	Pts	PIM	PP	SH	GW	Min
1986-87	St. Albert Saints	AJHL	53	41	34	*75	103	....	....	....	....	....	....	....	....	....	19	7	15	22	....	....	....	....	....
1987-88	New Westminster	WHL	71	37	64	101	88	....	....	....	....	....	....	....	....	....	5	2	3	5	6	....	....	....	....
1988-89	Tri-City	WHL	70	59	82	141	117	....	....	....	....	....	....	....	....	....	7	6	5	11	10	....	....	....	....
1989-90	Tri-City	WHL	63	52	92	144	165	....	....	....	....	....	....	....	....	....	7	1	5	6	26	....	....	....	....
1990-91	Canada	Nat-Tm	53	22	27	49	68	....	....	....	....	....	....	....	....	....	....	....	....	....	....	....	....	....	....
1991-92	**Winnipeg**	**NHL**	**46**	**8**	**9**	**17**	**26**	**4**	**0**	**0**	**75**	**10.7**	**–2**	....	....	....	....	....	....	....	....	....	....	....	....
	Moncton Hawks	AHL	30	13	19	32	10	....	....	....	....	....	....	....	....	....	11	3	9	12	6	....	....	....	....
1992-93	**Winnipeg**	**NHL**	**38**	**12**	**10**	**22**	**10**	**3**	**0**	**3**	**73**	**16.4**	**–3**	....	....	....	**6**	**1**	**3**	**4**	**2**	**0**	**0**	**0**	....
	Moncton Hawks	AHL	42	23	31	54	58	....	....	....	....	....	....	....	....	....	....	....	....	....	....	....	....	....	....
1993-94	**Winnipeg**	**NHL**	**18**	**5**	**4**	**9**	**8**	**2**	**0**	**0**	**24**	**20.8**	**–1**	....	....	....	....	....	....	....	....	....	....	....	....
	Florida	**NHL**	**59**	**18**	**20**	**38**	**30**	**6**	**1**	**3**	**148**	**12.2**	**5**	....	....	....	....	....	....	....	....	....	....	....	....
1994-95	**Florida**	**NHL**	**41**	**10**	**19**	**29**	**8**	**1**	**0**	**2**	**93**	**10.8**	**7**	....	....	....	....	....	....	....	....	....	....	....	....
1995-96	**Florida**	**NHL**	**72**	**19**	**25**	**44**	**46**	**8**	**0**	**5**	**158**	**12.0**	**–12**	....	....	....	**22**	**6**	**10**	**16**	**4**	**2**	**0**	**2**	....
1996-97	**Florida**	**NHL**	**19**	**2**	**8**	**10**	**10**	**1**	**0**	**0**	**44**	**4.5**	**–3**	....	....	....	....	....	....	....	....	....	....	....	....
	Pittsburgh	**NHL**	**62**	**17**	**22**	**39**	**16**	**4**	**0**	**3**	**132**	**12.9**	**–20**	....	....	....	**5**	**0**	**1**	**1**	**0**	**0**	**0**	**0**	....
1997-98	**Pittsburgh**	**NHL**	**78**	**30**	**35**	**65**	**30**	**15**	**1**	**5**	**196**	**15.3**	**15**	....	....	....	**6**	**3**	**3**	**6**	**2**	**0**	**0**	**1**	....
1998-99	**Pittsburgh**	**NHL**	**64**	**20**	**12**	**32**	**20**	**13**	**0**	**3**	**155**	**12.9**	**–12**	**720**	**51.9**	**17:52**	....	....	....	....	....	....	....	....	....
	Buffalo	**NHL**	**17**	**0**	**4**	**4**	**10**	**0**	**0**	**0**	**25**	**0.0**	**1**	**236**	**51.3**	**18:20**	**21**	**7**	**3**	**10**	**6**	**4**	**0**	**1**	**14:40**
99-2000	**Buffalo**	**NHL**	**82**	**20**	**25**	**45**	**16**	**8**	**2**	**2**	**137**	**14.6**	**–3**	**778**	**48.5**	**17:23**	**5**	**3**	**0**	**3**	**2**	**2**	**0**	**1**	**17:02**
2000-01	**Buffalo**	**NHL**	**75**	**19**	**24**	**43**	**26**	**3**	**2**	**5**	**160**	**11.9**	**–2**	**1470**	**48.3**	**19:06**	**13**	**4**	**4**	**8**	**2**	**2**	**0**	**2**	**18:30**
2001-02	**Buffalo**	**NHL**	**68**	**17**	**31**	**48**	**26**	**5**	**0**	**4**	**127**	**13.4**	**6**	**984**	**47.2**	**18:35**	....	....	....	....	....	....	....	....	....
2002-03	**Buffalo**	**NHL**	**68**	**11**	**21**	**32**	**20**	**2**	**1**	**2**	**124**	**8.9**	**–13**	**923**	**49.0**	**18:29**	....	....	....	....	....	....	....	....	....
	Dallas	**NHL**	**13**	**2**	**5**	**7**	**8**	**2**	**0**	**1**	**25**	**8.0**	**2**	**76**	**44.7**	**17:23**	**12**	**2**	**3**	**5**	**0**	**0**	**0**	**2**	**19:06**
2003-04	**Dallas**	**NHL**	**77**	**11**	**18**	**29**	**18**	**0**	**1**	**4**	**135**	**8.1**	**7**	**879**	**52.9**	**18:05**	**5**	**0**	**0**	**0**	**0**	**0**	**0**	**0**	**14:59**

			Regular Season														Playoffs								
Season	Club	League	GP	G	A	Pts	PIM	PP	SH	GW	S	%	+/-	TF	F%	Min	GP	G	A	Pts	PIM	PP	SH	GW	Min
2004-05			DID NOT PLAY																						
2005-06	**Dallas**	**NHL**	**78**	**15**	**21**	**36**	**44**	**0**	**1**	**2**	**123**	**12.2**	**9**	**649**	**50.1**	**16:29**	**5**	**1**	**1**	**2**	**0**	**0**	**1**	**0**	**17:33**
2006-07	**Dallas**	**NHL**	**82**	**13**	**12**	**25**	**40**	**1**	**0**	**2**	**118**	**11.0**	**–2**	**734**	**48.6**	**16:06**	**7**	**1**	**3**	**4**	**4**	**1**	**0**	**0**	**18:45**
2007-08	**Dallas**	**NHL**	**79**	**12**	**11**	**23**	**26**	**0**	**2**	**4**	**71**	**16.9**	**–3**	**627**	**54.7**	**13:38**	**9**	**2**	**1**	**3**	**2**	**0**	**0**	**2**	**15:33**
	NHL Totals		**1136**	**261**	**336**	**597**	**438**	**78**	**11**	**50**	**2143**	**12.2**		**8076**	**49.8**	**17:16**	**116**	**30**	**32**	**62**	**24**	**11**	**1**	**11**	**16:51**

WHL West Second All-Star Team (1988, 1989) • WHL Rookie of the Year (1988) • WHL Player of the Year (1989)

Traded to **Florida** by **Winnipeg** with St. Louis' 6th round choice (previously acquired, later traded to Edmonton – later traded back to Winnipeg – Winnipeg selected Chris Kibermanis) in 1994 Entry Draft for Randy Gilhen, November 25, 1993. Traded to **Pittsburgh** by **Florida** with Jason Woolley for Chris Wells, November 19, 1996. Traded to **Buffalo** by **Pittsburgh** for Matthew Barnaby, March 11, 1999. Traded to **Dallas** by **Buffalo** for Michael Ryan and Dallas's 2nd round choice (Branislav Fabry) in 2003 Entry Draft, March 10, 2003.

BARNEY, Scott

(BAHR-nee, SKAWT)

Center. Shoots right. 6'4", 210 lbs. Born, Oshawa, Ont., March 27, 1979. Los Angeles' 3rd choice, 29th overall, in 1997 Entry Draft.

1994-95	North York	MTJHL	41	16	19	35	88	....	....	....	....	....	....	....	....	....	....	....	....	....	....	....	....	....	....
1995-96	Peterborough	OHL	60	22	24	46	52	....	....	....	....	....	....	....	....	....	24	6	8	14	38	....	....	....	....
1996-97	Peterborough	OHL	64	21	33	54	110	....	....	....	....	....	....	....	....	....	9	0	3	3	16	....	....	....	....
1997-98	Peterborough	OHL	62	44	32	76	60	....	....	....	....	....	....	....	....	....	4	1	0	1	6	....	....	....	....
1998-99	Peterborough	OHL	44	41	26	67	80	....	....	....	....	....	....	....	....	....	5	4	1	5	4	....	....	....	....
	Springfield	AHL	5	0	0	0	2	....	....	....	....	....	....	....	....	....	1	0	0	0	2	....	....	....	....
99-2000			DID NOT PLAY – INJURED																						
2000-01			DID NOT PLAY – INJURED																						
2001-02			DID NOT PLAY – INJURED																						
2002-03	**Los Angeles**	**NHL**	**5**	**0**	**0**	**0**	**0**	**0**	**0**	**0**	**5**	**0.0**	**–1**	**0**	**0.0**	**9:04**	....	....	....	....	....	....	....	....	....
	Manchester	AHL	57	13	5	18	74	....	....	....	....	....	....	....	....	....	....	....	....	....	....	....	....	....	....
2003-04	**Los Angeles**	**NHL**	**19**	**5**	**6**	**11**	**4**	**2**	**0**	**0**	**31**	**16.1**	**3**	**7**	**14.3**	**11:12**	....	....	....	....	....	....	....	....	....
	Manchester	AHL	44	20	14	34	28	....	....	....	....	....	....	....	....	....	6	2	3	5	8	....	....	....	....
2004-05			DID NOT PLAY																						
2005-06	**Atlanta**	**NHL**	**3**	**0**	**0**	**0**	**0**	**0**	**0**	**0**	**4**	**0.0**	**–1**	**0**	**0.0**	**6:45**	....	....	....	....	....	....	....	....	....
	Chicago Wolves	AHL	53	32	19	51	56	....	....	....	....	....	....	....	....	....	....	....	....	....	....	....	....	....	....
2006-07	Grand Rapids	AHL	40	4	8	12	26	....	....	....	....	....	....	....	....	....	....	....	....	....	....	....	....	....	....
	Hershey Bears	AHL	11	6	4	10	6	....	....	....	....	....	....	....	....	....	19	*10	9	19	14	....	....	....	....
2007-08	Hershey Bears	AHL	66	21	20	41	60	....	....	....	....	....	....	....	....	....	....	....	....	....	....	....	....	....	....
	NHL Totals		**27**	**5**	**6**	**11**	**4**	**2**	**0**	**0**	**40**	**12.5**		**7**	**14.3**	**10:19**	....	....	....	....	....	....	....	....	....

• Missed entire 1999-2000, 2000-01 and 2001-02 seasons recovering from back injury suffered in training camp, September 28, 1999. Signed as a free agent by **Atlanta**, August 8, 2005.

BASS, Cody

(BAS, KOH-dee) **OTT.**

Center. Shoots right. 6', 212 lbs. Born, Owen Sound, Ont., January 7, 1987. Ottawa's 3rd choice, 95th overall, in 2005 Entry Draft.

2003-04	Mississauga	OHL	61	3	7	10	30	....	....	....	....	....	....	....	....	....	24	2	3	5	21	....	....	....	....
2004-05	Mississauga	OHL	66	11	17	28	103	....	....	....	....	....	....	....	....	....	5	1	1	2	8	....	....	....	....
2005-06	Mississauga	OHL	67	16	25	41	152	....	....	....	....	....	....	....	....	....	....	....	....	....	....	....	....	....	....
	Binghamton	AHL	9	1	0	1	2	....	....	....	....	....	....	....	....	....	....	....	....	....	....	....	....	....	....
2006-07	Mississauga	OHL	23	5	11	16	37	....	....	....	....	....	....	....	....	....	....	....	....	....	....	....	....	....	....
	Saginaw Spirit	OHL	30	5	24	29	49	....	....	....	....	....	....	....	....	....	6	1	2	3	10	....	....	....	....
	Binghamton	AHL	5	0	2	2	9	....	....	....	....	....	....	....	....	....	....	....	....	....	....	....	....	....	....
2007-08	**Ottawa**	**NHL**	**21**	**2**	**2**	**4**	**19**	**0**	**1**	**1**	**12**	**16.7**	**–1**	**73**	**43.8**	**5:19**	**4**	**1**	**0**	**1**	**6**	**0**	**0**	**0**	**8:21**
	Binghamton	AHL	24	3	5	8	44	....	....	....	....	....	....	....	....	....	....	....	....	....	....	....	....	....	....
	NHL Totals		**21**	**2**	**2**	**4**	**19**	**0**	**1**	**1**	**12**	**16.7**		**73**	**43.8**	**5:19**	**4**	**1**	**0**	**1**	**6**	**0**	**0**	**0**	**8:21**

BATES, Shawn

(BAYTS, SHAWN)

Center. Shoots right. 6', 210 lbs. Born, Melrose, MA, April 3, 1975. Boston's 4th choice, 103rd overall, in 1993 Entry Draft.

1990-91	Medford	High-MA	22	18	43	61	6	....	....	....	....	....	....	....	....	....	....	....	....	....	....	....	....	....	....
1991-92	Medford	High-MA	22	38	41	79	10	....	....	....	....	....	....	....	....	....	....	....	....	....	....	....	....	....	....
1992-93	Medford	High-MA	25	49	46	95	20	....	....	....	....	....	....	....	....	....	....	....	....	....	....	....	....	....	....
1993-94	Boston University	H-East	41	10	19	29	24	....	....	....	....	....	....	....	....	....	....	....	....	....	....	....	....	....	....
1994-95	Boston University	H-East	38	18	12	30	48	....	....	....	....	....	....	....	....	....	....	....	....	....	....	....	....	....	....
1995-96	Boston University	H-East	40	28	22	50	54	....	....	....	....	....	....	....	....	....	....	....	....	....	....	....	....	....	....
1996-97	Boston University	H-East	41	17	18	35	64	....	....	....	....	....	....	....	....	....	....	....	....	....	....	....	....	....	....
1997-98	**Boston**	**NHL**	**13**	**2**	**0**	**2**	**2**	**0**	**0**	**0**	**12**	**16.7**	**–3**	....	....	....	....	....	....	....	....	....	....	....	....
	Providence Bruins	AHL	50	15	19	34	22	....	....	....	....	....	....	....	....	....	....	....	....	....	....	....	....	....	....
1998-99	**Boston**	**NHL**	**33**	**5**	**4**	**9**	**2**	**0**	**0**	**0**	**30**	**16.7**	**3**	**178**	**51.1**	**8:35**	**12**	**0**	**0**	**0**	**4**	**0**	**0**	**0**	**5:12**
	Providence Bruins	AHL	37	25	21	46	39	....	....	....	....	....	....	....	....	....	....	....	....	....	....	....	....	....	....
99-2000	**Boston**	**NHL**	**44**	**5**	**7**	**12**	**14**	**0**	**0**	**1**	**65**	**7.7**	**–17**	**460**	**47.0**	**10:52**	....	....	....	....	....	....	....	....	....
2000-01	**Boston**	**NHL**	**45**	**2**	**3**	**5**	**26**	**0**	**0**	**0**	**59**	**3.4**	**–12**	**413**	**50.6**	**9:19**	....	....	....	....	....	....	....	....	....
	Providence Bruins	AHL	11	5	8	13	12	....	....	....	....	....	....	....	....	....	8	2	6	8	8	....	....	....	....
2001-02	**NY Islanders**	**NHL**	**71**	**17**	**35**	**52**	**30**	**1**	**4**	**4**	**150**	**11.3**	**18**	**306**	**49.4**	**18:45**	**7**	**2**	**4**	**6**	**11**	**1**	**0**	**1**	**20:27**
2002-03	**NY Islanders**	**NHL**	**74**	**13**	**29**	**42**	**52**	**1**	**6**	**1**	**126**	**10.3**	**–9**	**398**	**57.0**	**18:26**	**5**	**1**	**0**	**1**	**0**	**1**	**0**	**0**	**18:36**
2003-04	**NY Islanders**	**NHL**	**69**	**9**	**23**	**32**	**46**	**0**	**1**	**1**	**115**	**7.8**	**–8**	**603**	**55.9**	**18:26**	**5**	**0**	**0**	**0**	**4**	**0**	**0**	**0**	**17:14**
2004-05			DID NOT PLAY																						
2005-06	**NY Islanders**	**NHL**	**66**	**15**	**19**	**34**	**60**	**1**	**1**	**4**	**95**	**15.8**	**–11**	**1063**	**51.3**	**17:12**	....	....	....	....	....	....	....	....	....
2006-07	**NY Islanders**	**NHL**	**48**	**4**	**6**	**10**	**34**	**0**	**1**	**0**	**50**	**8.0**	**13**	**455**	**53.2**	**12:32**	....	....	....	....	....	....	....	....	....
2007-08	**NY Islanders**	**NHL**	**2**	**0**	**0**	**0**	**0**	**0**	**0**	**0**	**0**	**0.0**	**–2**	**4**	**25.0**	**7:00**	....	....	....	....	....	....	....	....	....
	Bridgeport	AHL	3	2	0	2	6	....	....	....	....	....	....	....	....	....	....	....	....	....	....	....	....	....	....
	NHL Totals		**465**	**72**	**126**	**198**	**266**	**3**	**13**	**11**	**702**	**10.3**		**3880**	**52.0**	**15:16**	**29**	**3**	**4**	**7**	**19**	**2**	**0**	**1**	**13:16**

NCAA Championship All-Tournament Team (1995)

Signed as a free agent by **NY Islanders**, July 8, 2001.

BATTAGLIA, Bates

(buh-TAG-lee-ah, BAYTS) **TOR.**

Left wing. Shoots left. 6'2", 205 lbs. Born, Chicago, IL, December 13, 1975. Anaheim's 6th choice, 132nd overall, in 1994 Entry Draft.

1992-93	Team Illinois	MEHL	60	42	42	84	68	....	....	....	....	....	....	....	....	....	....	....	....	....	....	....	....	....	....
1993-94	Caledon	MTJHL	44	15	33	48	104	....	....	....	....	....	....	....	....	....	....	....	....	....	....	....	....	....	....
1994-95	Lake Superior	CCHA	38	6	14	20	34	....	....	....	....	....	....	....	....	....	....	....	....	....	....	....	....	....	....
1995-96	Lake Superior	CCHA	40	13	22	35	48	....	....	....	....	....	....	....	....	....	....	....	....	....	....	....	....	....	....
1996-97	Lake Superior	CCHA	38	12	27	39	80	....	....	....	....	....	....	....	....	....	....	....	....	....	....	....	....	....	....
1997-98	**Carolina**	**NHL**	**33**	**2**	**4**	**6**	**10**	**0**	**0**	**1**	**21**	**9.5**	**–1**	....	....	....	....	....	....	....	....	....	....	....	....
	New Haven	AHL	48	15	21	36	48	....	....	....	....	....	....	....	....	....	1	0	0	0	0	....	....	....	....
1998-99	**Carolina**	**NHL**	**60**	**7**	**11**	**18**	**97**	**0**	**0**	**0**	**52**	**13.5**	**7**	**144**	**39.6**	**9:53**	**6**	**0**	**3**	**3**	**8**	**0**	**0**	**0**	**15:22**
99-2000	**Carolina**	**NHL**	**77**	**16**	**18**	**34**	**39**	**3**	**0**	**3**	**86**	**18.6**	**20**	**23**	**26.1**	**15:12**	....	....	....	....	....	....	....	....	....
2000-01	**Carolina**	**NHL**	**80**	**12**	**15**	**27**	**76**	**2**	**0**	**3**	**133**	**9.0**	**–14**	**5**	**60.0**	**14:28**	**6**	**0**	**2**	**2**	**2**	**0**	**0**	**0**	**11:25**
2001-02	**Carolina**	**NHL**	**82**	**21**	**25**	**46**	**44**	**5**	**1**	**2**	**167**	**12.6**	**–6**	**12**	**33.3**	**19:05**	**23**	**5**	**9**	**14**	**14**	**1**	**0**	**1**	**20:42**
2002-03	**Carolina**	**NHL**	**70**	**5**	**14**	**19**	**90**	**0**	**1**	**1**	**96**	**5.2**	**–17**	**16**	**25.0**	**18:39**	....	....	....	....	....	....	....	....	....
	Colorado	**NHL**	**13**	**1**	**5**	**6**	**10**	**1**	**0**	**1**	**27**	**3.7**	**–2**	**3**	**0.0**	**15:19**	**7**	**0**	**2**	**2**	**4**	**0**	**0**	**0**	**14:39**
2003-04	**Colorado**	**NHL**	**4**	**0**	**1**	**1**	**4**	**0**	**0**	**0**	**1**	**0.0**	**–1**	**1**	**100.0**	**11:04**	....	....	....	....	....	....	....	....	....
	Washington	**NHL**	**66**	**4**	**6**	**10**	**38**	**0**	**0**	**1**	**69**	**5.8**	**–23**	**116**	**32.8**	**13:37**	....	....	....	....	....	....	....	....	....
2004-05	Mississippi	ECHL	25	6	11	17	24	....	....	....	....	....	....	....	....	....	4	0	0	0	10	....	....	....	....
2005-06	Toronto Marlies	AHL	79	20	47	67	86	....	....	....	....	....	....	....	....	....	5	1	1	2	6	....	....	....	....
2006-07	**Toronto**	**NHL**	**82**	**12**	**19**	**31**	**45**	**0**	**0**	**0**	**94**	**12.8**	**9**	**4**	**0.0**	**12:27**	....	....	....	....	....	....	....	....	....
2007-08	**Toronto**	**NHL**	**13**	**0**	**0**	**0**	**7**	**0**	**0**	**0**	**6**	**0.0**	**–6**	**1**	**0.0**	**4:46**	....	....	....	....	....	....	....	....	....
	Toronto Marlies	AHL	56	12	14	26	42	....	....	....	....	....	....	....	....	....	19	6	2	8	28	....	....	....	....
	NHL Totals		**580**	**80**	**118**	**198**	**460**	**11**	**2**	**12**	**752**	**10.6**		**325**	**34.8**	**14:39**	**42**	**5**	**16**	**21**	**28**	**1**	**0**	**1**	**17:36**

Traded to **Hartford** by **Anaheim** with Anaheim's 4th round choice (Josef Vasicek) in 1998 Entry Draft for Mark Janssens, March 18, 1997. Rights transferred to **Carolina** after **Hartford** franchise relocated, June 25, 1997. Traded to **Colorado** by **Carolina** for Radim Vrbata, March 11, 2003. Traded to **Washington** by **Colorado** with Jonas Johansson for Steve Konowalchuk and Washington's 3rd round choice (later traded to Carolina – Carolina selected Casey Borer) in 2004 Entry Draft, October 22, 2003. Signed as a free agent by **Mississippi** (ECHL), February 21, 2005. Signed to a PTO (tryout) contract by **Toronto** (AHL), October 2, 2005. Signed as a free agent by **Toronto**, July 8, 2006.

BAUMGARTNER, Nolan

(BAWM-gahrt-nuhr, NOH-luhn) **VAN.**

Defense. Shoots right. 6'2", 205 lbs. Born, Calgary, Alta., March 23, 1976. Washington's 1st choice, 10th overall, in 1994 Entry Draft.

			Regular Season														Playoffs								
Season	Club	League	GP	G	A	Pts	PIM	PP	SH	GW	S	%	+/-	TF	F%	Min	GP	G	A	Pts	PIM	PP	SH	GW	Min
1991-92	Cgy. AAA Flames	AMHL	39	11	29	40	40																		
1992-93	Kamloops Blazers	WHL	43	0	5	5	30										11	1	1	2	0				
1993-94	Kamloops Blazers	WHL	69	13	42	55	109										19	3	14	17	33				
1994-95	Kamloops Blazers	WHL	62	8	36	44	71										21	4	13	17	16				
1995-96	Kamloops Blazers	WHL	28	13	15	28	45										16	1	9	10	26				
	Washington	NHL	1	0	0	0	0	0	0	0	0	0.0	–1				1	0	0	0	10	0	0	0	
1996-97	Portland Pirates	AHL	8	2	2	4	4																		
1997-98	Washington	NHL	4	0	1	1	0	0	0	0	4	0.0	0												
	Portland Pirates	AHL	70	2	24	26	70										10	1	4	5	10				
1998-99	Washington	NHL	5	0	0	0	0	0	0	0	1	0.0	–3	0	0.0	8:41									
	Portland Pirates	AHL	38	5	14	19	62																		
99-2000	Washington	NHL	8	0	1	1	2	0	0	0	6	0.0	1	0	0.0	10:31									
	Portland Pirates	AHL	71	5	18	23	56										4	1	2	3	10				
2000-01	Chicago	NHL	8	0	0	0	6	0	0	0	7	0.0	–4	2	50.0	12:40									
	Norfolk Admirals	AHL	63	5	28	33	75										9	2	3	5	11				
2001-02	Norfolk Admirals	AHL	76	10	24	34	72										4	0	1	1	2				
2002-03	Vancouver	NHL	8	1	2	3	4	1	0	0	7	14.3	4	0	0.0	11:36	2	0	0	0	0	0	0	0	11:07
	Manitoba Moose	AHL	59	8	31	39	82										1	0	0	0	4				
2003-04	Pittsburgh	NHL	5	0	0	0	2	0	0	0	6	0.0	–7	0	0.0	19:20									
	Vancouver	NHL	9	0	3	3	2	0	0	0	9	0.0	3	0	0.0	11:52									
	Manitoba Moose	AHL	55	6	21	27	101																		
2004-05	Manitoba Moose	AHL	78	9	30	39	51										14	0	4	4	10				
2005-06	Vancouver	NHL	70	5	29	34	30	4	1	1	73	6.8	11	1	0.0	16:29									
2006-07	Philadelphia	NHL	6	0	1	1	21	0	0	0	4	0.0	0	0	0.0	15:00									
	Philadelphia	AHL	51	6	20	26	46																		
	Dallas	NHL	7	0	2	2	0	0	0	0	4	0.0	0	0	0.0	12:14									
2007-08	Iowa Stars	AHL	56	5	13	18	47																		
	Manitoba Moose	AHL	18	0	6	6	10										3	0	1	1	4				
	NHL Totals		131	6	39	45	67	5	1	1	121	5.0		3	33.3	14:43	3	0	0	0	10	0	0	0	11:06

Memorial Cup Tournement All-Star Team (1994, 1995) • WHL West First All-Star Team (1995, 1996) • Canadian Major Junior First All-Star Team (1995) • Canadian Major Junior Defenseman of the Year (1995)

Traded to **Chicago** by **Washington** for Remi Royer, July 20, 2000. Signed as a free agent by **Vancouver**, July 11, 2002. Claimed by **Pittsburgh** from **Vancouver** in Waiver Draft, October 3, 2003. Claimed on waivers by **Vancouver** from **Pittsburgh**, November 1, 2003. Signed as a free agent by **Philadelphia**, July 1, 2006. Claimed on waivers by **Dallas** from **Philadelphia**, February 24, 2007. Signed as a free agent by **Vancouver**, July 2, 2008.

BAYDA, Ryan

(BAY-duh, RIGH-uhn) **CAR.**

Left wing. Shoots left. 5'11", 185 lbs. Born, Saskatoon, Sask., December 9, 1980. Carolina's 2nd choice, 80th overall, in 2000 Entry Draft.

			Regular Season														Playoffs								
Season	Club	League	GP	G	A	Pts	PIM	PP	SH	GW	S	%	+/-	TF	F%	Min	GP	G	A	Pts	PIM	PP	SH	GW	Min
1995-96	Saskatoon Flyers	SMHL	60	85	74	159	85																		
1996-97	Sask. Contacts	SMHL	44	22	23	45	18																		
1997-98	Sask. Contacts	SMHL	41	29	49	78	103																		
1998-99	Vernon Vipers	BCHL	45	24	58	82	15																		
99-2000	North Dakota	WCHA	44	17	23	40	30																		
2000-01	North Dakota	WCHA	46	25	34	59	48																		
2001-02	North Dakota	WCHA	37	19	28	47	52																		
	Lowell	AHL	3	1	1	2	0										5	3	0	3	0				
2002-03	Carolina	NHL	25	4	10	14	16	0	0	1	49	8.2	–5	2	100.0	17:15									
	Lowell	AHL	53	11	32	43	32																		
2003-04	Carolina	NHL	44	3	3	6	22	0	0	1	65	4.6	–14	4	0.0	10:57									
	Lowell	AHL	34	7	15	22	28																		
2004-05	Lowell	AHL	80	13	27	40	91										9	3	3	6	4				
2005-06	Manitoba Moose	AHL	59	13	25	38	52										13	1	6	7	27				
2006-07	Carolina	NHL	9	1	1	2	2	0	0	0	10	10.0	–1	0	0.0	8:41									
	Albany River Rats	AHL	55	29	25	54	66										5	3	2	5	4				
2007-08	Carolina	NHL	31	3	3	6	28	0	0	0	58	5.2	–2	2	0.0	12:36									
	Albany River Rats	AHL	21	7	10	17	6																		
	NHL Totals		109	11	17	28	68	0	0	2	182	6.0		8	25.0	12:40									

BCHL Rookie of the Year (1999) • WCHA All-Rookie Team (2000) • WCHA Second All-Star Team (2001, 2002)

BEAUCHEMIN, Francois

(boh-sheh-MEH, frahn-SWUH) **ANA.**

Defense. Shoots left. 6', 213 lbs. Born, Sorel, Que., June 4, 1980. Montreal's 3rd choice, 75th overall, in 1998 Entry Draft.

			Regular Season														Playoffs								
Season	Club	League	GP	G	A	Pts	PIM	PP	SH	GW	S	%	+/-	TF	F%	Min	GP	G	A	Pts	PIM	PP	SH	GW	Min
1995-96	Richelieu Riverains	QAAA	40	9	23	32	59																		
1996-97	Laval Titan	QMJHL	66	7	21	28	132										3	0	0	0	2				
1997-98	Laval Titan	QMJHL	70	12	35	47	132										16	1	3	4	23				
1998-99	Acadie-Bathurst	QMJHL	31	4	17	21	53										23	2	16	18	55				
99-2000	Acadie-Bathurst	QMJHL	38	11	36	47	64																		
	Moncton Wildcats	QMJHL	33	8	31	39	35										16	2	11	13	14				
2000-01	Quebec Citadelles	AHL	56	3	6	9	44																		
2001-02	Quebec Citadelles	AHL	56	8	11	19	88										3	0	1	1	0				
	Mississippi	ECHL	7	1	3	4	2																		
2002-03	Montreal	NHL	1	0	0	0	0	0	0	0	1	0.0	–1	0	0.0	17:11									
	Hamilton	AHL	75	7	21	28	92										23	1	9	10	16				
2003-04	Hamilton	AHL	77	9	27	36	57										10	2	4	6	18				
2004-05	Syracuse Crunch	AHL	72	3	27	30	55																		
2005-06	Columbus	NHL	11	0	2	2	11	0	0	0	16	0.0	–6	0	0.0	17:16									
	Anaheim	NHL	61	8	26	34	41	4	0	3	121	6.6	8	1	0.0	24:14	16	3	6	9	11	3	0	0	27:26
2006-07♦	Anaheim	NHL	71	7	21	28	49	2	0	0	128	5.5	7	1	0.0	25:28	20	4	4	8	16	4	0	0	30:33
2007-08	Anaheim	NHL	82	2	19	21	59	0	0	2	144	1.4	–9	1	0.0	25:32	6	0	0	0	26	0	0	0	21:02
	NHL Totals		226	17	68	85	160	6	0	5	410	4.1		3	0.0	24:43	42	7	10	17	53	7	0	0	28:00

QMJHL All-Rookie Team (1997) • QMJHL Second All-Star Team (2000)

Claimed on waivers by **Columbus** from **Montreal**, September 15, 2004. Traded to **Anaheim** by **Columbus** with Tyler Wright for Sergei Fedorov and Anaheim's 5th round choice (Maxime Frechette) in 2006 Entry Draft, November 15, 2005.

BEECH, Kris

(BEECH, KRIHS) **PIT.**

Center. Shoots left. 6'3", 211 lbs. Born, Salmon Arm, B.C., February 5, 1981. Washington's 1st choice, 7th overall, in 1999 Entry Draft.

			Regular Season														Playoffs								
Season	Club	League	GP	G	A	Pts	PIM	PP	SH	GW	S	%	+/-	TF	F%	Min	GP	G	A	Pts	PIM	PP	SH	GW	Min
1996-97	Sicamous Eagles	KIJHL	49	34	36	70	80																		
	Calgary Hitmen	WHL	8	1	1	2	0																		
1997-98	Calgary Hitmen	WHL	58	10	25	35	24										12	4	5	9	32				
1998-99	Calgary Hitmen	WHL	68	26	41	67	103										6	1	4	5	8				
99-2000	Calgary Hitmen	WHL	66	32	54	86	99										5	3	5	8	16				
2000-01	Washington	NHL	4	0	0	0	2	0	0	0	0	0.0	–2	25	36.0	7:29									
	Calgary Hitmen	WHL	40	22	44	66	103										10	2	8	10	26				
2001-02	Pittsburgh	NHL	79	10	15	25	45	2	0	0	126	7.9	–25	604	45.2	13:33									
2002-03	Pittsburgh	NHL	12	0	1	1	6	0	0	0	6	0.0	–3	96	42.7	10:34									
	Wilkes-Barre	AHL	50	19	24	43	76										5	1	1	2	0				
2003-04	Pittsburgh	NHL	4	0	1	1	6	0	0	0	6	0.0	0	45	40.0	12:32									
	Wilkes-Barre	AHL	53	20	25	45	97										22	9	6	15	22				
2004-05	Wilkes-Barre	AHL	68	14	48	62	146										11	4	6	10	14				
2005-06	Nashville	NHL	5	1	2	3	0	0	0	0	6	16.7	1	81	54.3	14:40									
	Milwaukee	AHL	48	18	32	50	48																		
	Washington	NHL	5	0	0	0	4	0	0	0	6	0.0	0	36	50.0	9:24									
	Hershey Bears	AHL	10	8	6	14	6										21	14	14	28	30				
2006-07	Washington	NHL	64	8	18	26	46	3	0	0	77	10.4	–11	744	48.4	12:28									

			Regular Season														Playoffs								
Season	Club	League	GP	G	A	Pts	PIM	PP	SH	GW	S	%	+/-	TF	F%	Min	GP	G	A	Pts	PIM	PP	SH	GW	Min
2007-08	Columbus	NHL	16	5	4	9	2	2	0	0	24	20.8	3	205	53.2	13:00	....	....	....	....	....	....	....	....	....
	Syracuse Crunch	AHL	16	5	10	15	22	....	....	....	....	....	....	....	....	....	....	....	....	....	....	....	....	....	....
	Vancouver	NHL	4	1	1	2	0	0	0	0	6	16.7	1	37	48.7	9:37	....	....	....	....	....	....	....	....	....
	Pittsburgh	NHL	5	0	0	0	2	0	0	0	6	0.0	–1	34	50.0	8:14	....	....	....	....	....	....	....	....	....
	NHL Totals		198	25	42	67	113	7	0	0	263	9.5		1907	47.6	12:33	....	....	....	....	....	....	....	....	....

Traded to **Pittsburgh** by **Washington** with Michal Sivek, Ross Lupaschuk and future considerations for Jaromir Jagr and Frantisek Kucera, July 11, 2001. Traded to **Nashville** by **Pittsburgh** for Nashville's 4th round choice (later traded to Florida - Florida selected Derrick Lapoint) in 2006 Entry Draft, September 9, 2005. Traded to **Washington** by **Nashville** with Nashville's 1st round choice (Simeon Varlamov) in 2006 Entry Draft for Brendan Witt, March 9, 2006. Signed as a free agent by **Columbus**, August 7, 2007. Claimed on waivers by **Vancouver** from **Columbus**, January 10, 2008. Claimed on waivers by **Washington** from **Vancouver**, January 23, 2008. Claimed on waivers by **Pittsburgh** from **Washington**, January 26, 2008.

BEGIN, Steve
(bay-ZHIN, STEEV) **MTL.**

Center. Shoots left. 6', 187 lbs. Born, Trois-Rivieres, Que., June 14, 1978. Calgary's 3rd choice, 40th overall, in 1996 Entry Draft.

Season	Club	League	GP	G	A	Pts	PIM	PP	SH	GW	S	%	+/-	TF	F%	Min	GP	G	A	Pts	PIM	PP	SH	GW	Min
1993-94	Cap-d-Madelaine	QAAA	8	0	1	1	6	....	....	....	....	....	....	....	....	....	2	0	0	0	0	....	....	....	....
1994-95	Cap-d-Madelaine	QAAA	35	9	15	24	48	....	....	....	....	....	....	....	....	....	3	0	0	0	2	....	....	....	....
1995-96	Val-d'Or Foreurs	QMJHL	64	13	23	36	218	....	....	....	....	....	....	....	....	....	13	1	3	4	33	....	....	....	....
1996-97	Val-d'Or Foreurs	QMJHL	58	13	33	46	229	....	....	....	....	....	....	....	....	....	10	0	3	3	8	....	....	....	....
	Saint John Flames	AHL	....	....	....	....	....	....	....	....	....	....	....	....	....	....	4	0	2	2	6	....	....	....	....
1997-98	Calgary	NHL	5	0	0	0	23	0	0	0	2	0.0	0	....	....	....	....	....	....	....	....	....	....	....	....
	Val-d'Or Foreurs	QMJHL	35	18	17	35	73	....	....	....	....	....	....	....	....	....	15	2	12	14	34	....	....	....	....
1998-99	Saint John Flames	AHL	73	11	9	20	156	....	....	....	....	....	....	....	....	....	7	2	0	2	18	....	....	....	....
99-2000	Calgary	NHL	13	1	1	2	18	0	0	0	3	33.3	–3	19	47.4	7:13	....	....	....	....	....	....	....	....	....
	Saint John Flames	AHL	47	13	12	25	99	....	....	....	....	....	....	....	....	....	....	....	....	....	....	....	....	....	....
2000-01	Calgary	NHL	4	0	0	0	21	0	0	0	3	0.0	0	0	0.0	6:04	....	....	....	....	....	....	....	....	....
	Saint John Flames	AHL	58	14	14	28	109	....	....	....	....	....	....	....	....	....	19	10	7	17	18	....	....	....	....
2001-02	Calgary	NHL	51	7	5	12	79	1	0	0	65	10.8	–3	129	53.5	9:25	....	....	....	....	....	....	....	....	....
2002-03	Calgary	NHL	50	3	1	4	51	0	0	1	59	5.1	–7	50	60.0	9:13	....	....	....	....	....	....	....	....	....
2003-04	Montreal	NHL	52	10	5	15	41	0	1	1	91	11.0	6	436	48.6	12:32	9	0	1	1	10	0	0	0	12:26
2004-05	Hamilton	AHL	21	10	3	13	20	....	....	....	....	....	....	....	....	....	4	0	2	2	8	....	....	....	....
2005-06	Montreal	NHL	76	11	12	23	113	1	2	2	134	8.2	9	573	50.1	14:19	2	0	0	0	2	0	0	0	13:42
2006-07	Montreal	NHL	52	5	5	10	46	0	0	0	64	7.8	–6	159	49.7	11:55	....	....	....	....	....	....	....	....	....
2007-08	Montreal	NHL	44	3	5	8	48	0	0	0	67	4.5	0	69	34.8	11:38	12	0	3	3	8	0	0	0	12:45
	NHL Totals		347	40	34	74	440	2	3	4	488	8.2		1435	49.5	11:29	23	0	4	4	20	0	0	0	12:43

Jack A. Butterfield Trophy (Playoff MVP – AHL) (2001)

Traded to **Buffalo** by **Calgary** with Chris Drury for Steve Reinprecht and Rhett Warrener, July 3, 2003. Claimed by **Montreal** from **Buffalo** in Waiver Draft, October 3, 2003.

BELAK, Wade
(BEE-lak, WAYD) **FLA.**

Defense. Shoots right. 6'5", 221 lbs. Born, Saskatoon, Sask., July 3, 1976. Quebec's 1st choice, 12th overall, in 1994 Entry Draft.

Season	Club	League	GP	G	A	Pts	PIM	PP	SH	GW	S	%	+/-	TF	F%	Min	GP	G	A	Pts	PIM	PP	SH	GW	Min
1991-92	North Battleford	SMBHL	57	6	20	26	186	....	....	....	....	....	....	....	....	....	....	....	....	....	....	....	....	....	....
1992-93	North Battleford	SJHL	50	5	15	20	146	....	....	....	....	....	....	....	....	....	....	....	....	....	....	....	....	....	....
	Saskatoon Blades	WHL	7	0	0	0	23	....	....	....	....	....	....	....	....	....	7	0	0	0	0	....	....	....	....
1993-94	Saskatoon Blades	WHL	69	4	13	17	226	....	....	....	....	....	....	....	....	....	16	2	2	4	43	....	....	....	....
1994-95	Saskatoon Blades	WHL	72	4	14	18	290	....	....	....	....	....	....	....	....	....	9	0	0	0	36	....	....	....	....
	Cornwall Aces	AHL	....	....	....	....	....	....	....	....	....	....	....	....	....	....	11	1	2	3	40	....	....	....	....
1995-96	Saskatoon Blades	WHL	63	3	15	18	207	....	....	....	....	....	....	....	....	....	4	0	0	0	9	....	....	....	....
	Cornwall Aces	AHL	5	0	0	0	18	....	....	....	....	....	....	....	....	....	2	0	0	0	2	....	....	....	....
1996-97	Colorado	NHL	5	0	0	0	11	0	0	0	1	0.0	–1	....	....	....	....	....	....	....	....	....	....	....	....
	Hershey Bears	AHL	65	1	7	8	320	....	....	....	....	....	....	....	....	....	16	0	1	1	61	....	....	....	....
1997-98	Colorado	NHL	8	1	1	2	27	0	0	1	2	50.0	–3	....	....	....	....	....	....	....	....	....	....	....	....
	Hershey Bears	AHL	11	0	0	0	30	....	....	....	....	....	....	....	....	....	....	....	....	....	....	....	....	....	....
1998-99	Colorado	NHL	22	0	0	0	71	0	0	0	5	0.0	–2	0	0.0	6:48	....	....	....	....	....	....	....	....	....
	Hershey Bears	AHL	17	0	1	1	49	....	....	....	....	....	....	....	....	....	....	....	....	....	....	....	....	....	....
	Calgary	NHL	9	0	1	1	23	0	0	0	2	0.0	3	0	0.0	10:46	....	....	....	....	....	....	....	....	....
	Saint John Flames	AHL	12	0	2	2	43	....	....	....	....	....	....	....	....	....	6	0	1	1	23	....	....	....	....
99-2000	Calgary	NHL	40	0	2	2	122	0	0	0	11	0.0	–4	1	0.0	7:33	....	....	....	....	....	....	....	....	....
2000-01	Calgary	NHL	23	0	0	0	79	0	0	0	8	0.0	–2	0	0.0	6:54	....	....	....	....	....	....	....	....	....
	Toronto	NHL	16	1	1	2	31	0	0	0	8	12.5	–4	0	0.0	13:38	....	....	....	....	....	....	....	....	....
2001-02	Toronto	NHL	63	1	3	4	142	0	0	0	47	2.1	2	0	0.0	9:14	16	1	0	1	18	0	0	0	7:28
2002-03	Toronto	NHL	55	3	6	9	196	0	0	0	33	9.1	–2	0	0.0	10:50	2	0	0	0	4	0	0	0	8:22
2003-04	Toronto	NHL	34	1	1	2	109	0	0	0	15	6.7	0	0	0.0	7:00	4	0	0	0	14	0	0	0	9:59
2004-05	Coventry Blaze	Britain	20	3	5	8	109	....	....	....	....	....	....	....	....	....	8	1	1	2	16	....	....	....	....
2005-06	Toronto	NHL	55	0	3	3	109	0	0	0	16	0.0	–13	0	0.0	9:59	....	....	....	....	....	....	....	....	....
2006-07	Toronto	NHL	65	0	3	3	110	0	0	0	16	0.0	–8	0	0.0	5:02	....	....	....	....	....	....	....	....	....
2007-08	Toronto	NHL	30	1	0	1	66	0	0	0	13	7.7	–2	1	0.0	4:02	....	....	....	....	....	....	....	....	....
	Florida	NHL	17	0	0	0	12	0	0	0	4	0.0	0	0	0.0	4:09	....	....	....	....	....	....	....	....	....
	NHL Totals		442	8	21	29	1108	0	0	1	181	4.4		2	0.0	7:57	22	1	0	1	36	0	0	0	8:00

Rights transferred to **Colorado** after **Quebec** franchise relocated, June 21, 1995. Traded to **Calgary** by **Colorado** with Rene Corbet, Robyn Regehr and Colorado's 2nd round compensatory choice (Jarret Stoll) in 2000 Entry Draft for Theoren Fleury and Chris Dingman, February 28, 1999. • Missed majority of 1999-2000 and 2000-01 seasons recovering from shoulder injury suffered in game vs. Colorado, February 10, 2000. Claimed on waivers by **Toronto** from **Calgary**, February 16, 2001. • Missed majority of 2003-04 season recovering from abdomen (November 20, 2003 vs. Edmonton) and knee (January 6, 2004 vs. Nashville) injuries. Signed as a free agent by **Coventry** (Britain), November 8, 2004. Traded to **Florida** by **Toronto** for Florida's 5th round choice (Jerome Flaake) in 2008 Entry Draft, February 26, 2008.

BELANGER, Eric
(buh-LAWN-zhay, AIR-ihk) **MIN.**

Center. Shoots left. 6', 185 lbs. Born, Sherbrooke, Que., December 16, 1977. Los Angeles' 5th choice, 96th overall, in 1996 Entry Draft.

Season	Club	League	GP	G	A	Pts	PIM	PP	SH	GW	S	%	+/-	TF	F%	Min	GP	G	A	Pts	PIM	PP	SH	GW	Min
1993-94	Magog	QAAA	32	19	24	43	24	....	....	....	....	....	....	....	....	....	13	5	6	11	36	....	....	....	....
1994-95	Beauport	QMJHL	71	12	28	40	24	....	....	....	....	....	....	....	....	....	18	5	9	14	25	....	....	....	....
1995-96	Beauport	QMJHL	59	35	48	83	18	....	....	....	....	....	....	....	....	....	20	13	14	27	6	....	....	....	....
1996-97	Beauport	QMJHL	31	13	37	50	30	....	....	....	....	....	....	....	....	....	....	....	....	....	....	....	....	....	....
	Rimouski Oceanic	QMJHL	31	26	41	67	36	....	....	....	....	....	....	....	....	....	4	2	3	5	10	....	....	....	....
1997-98	Fredericton	AHL	56	17	34	51	28	....	....	....	....	....	....	....	....	....	4	2	1	3	2	....	....	....	....
1998-99	Springfield	AHL	33	8	18	26	10	....	....	....	....	....	....	....	....	....	3	0	1	1	2	....	....	....	....
	Long Beach	IHL	1	0	0	0	0	....	....	....	....	....	....	....	....	....	....	....	....	....	....	....	....	....	....
99-2000	Lowell	AHL	65	15	25	40	20	....	....	....	....	....	....	....	....	....	7	3	3	6	2	....	....	....	....
2000-01	Los Angeles	NHL	62	9	12	21	16	1	2	1	80	11.3	14	849	56.4	13:25	13	1	4	5	2	0	0	1	13:47
	Lowell	AHL	13	8	10	18	4	....	....	....	....	....	....	....	....	....	....	....	....	....	....	....	....	....	....
2001-02	Los Angeles	NHL	53	8	16	24	21	2	1	1	67	11.9	2	882	57.7	14:33	7	0	0	0	4	0	0	0	12:57
2002-03	Los Angeles	NHL	62	16	19	35	26	0	3	1	114	14.0	–5	1143	51.8	17:42	....	....	....	....	....	....	....	....	....
2003-04	Los Angeles	NHL	81	13	20	33	44	0	1	2	132	9.8	–16	1418	53.7	17:01	....	....	....	....	....	....	....	....	....
2004-05	HC Forst Bolzano	Italy	12	13	10	23	20	....	....	....	....	....	....	....	....	....	9	3	7	10	33	....	....	....	....
2005-06	Los Angeles	NHL	65	17	20	37	62	5	0	1	119	14.3	–5	1179	49.0	17:33	....	....	....	....	....	....	....	....	....
2006-07	Carolina	NHL	56	8	12	20	14	3	0	1	100	8.0	–2	689	53.4	14:51	....	....	....	....	....	....	....	....	....
	Atlanta	NHL	24	9	6	15	12	1	0	0	49	18.4	0	517	52.6	19:29	4	1	0	1	12	1	0	0	16:47
2007-08	Minnesota	NHL	75	13	24	37	30	7	1	3	115	11.3	–6	1195	49.1	17:13	6	0	0	0	4	0	0	0	18:34
	NHL Totals		478	93	129	222	225	19	8	10	776	12.0		7872	52.7	16:20	30	2	4	6	22	1	0	1	14:57

Signed as a free agent by **Bolzano** (Italy), December 22, 2004. Traded to **Carolina** by **Los Angeles** with Tim Gleason for Oleg Tverdovsky and Jack Johnson, September 29, 2006. Traded to **Nashville** by **Carolina** for Josef Vasicek, February 9, 2007. Traded to **Atlanta** by **Nashville** for Vitaly Vishnevski, February 10, 2007. Signed as a free agent by **Minnesota**, July 3, 2007.

BELL, Brendan
(BEHL, BREHN-duhn) **OTT.**

Defense. Shoots left. 6'1", 205 lbs. Born, Ottawa, Ont., March 31, 1983. Toronto's 3rd choice, 65th overall, in 2001 Entry Draft.

Season	Club	League	GP	G	A	Pts	PIM	PP	SH	GW	S	%	+/-	TF	F%	Min	GP	G	A	Pts	PIM	PP	SH	GW	Min
1998-99	Ott. Jr. Senators	CJHL	54	7	20	27	46	....	....	....	....	....	....	....	....	....	....	....	....	....	....	....	....	....	....
99-2000	Ottawa 67's	OHL	48	1	32	33	34	....	....	....	....	....	....	....	....	....	5	0	1	1	4	....	....	....	....
2000-01	Ottawa 67's	OHL	68	7	32	39	59	....	....	....	....	....	....	....	....	....	20	1	11	12	22	....	....	....	....
2001-02	Ottawa 67's	OHL	67	10	36	46	56	....	....	....	....	....	....	....	....	....	13	2	5	7	25	....	....	....	....
2002-03	Ottawa 67's	OHL	55	14	39	53	46	....	....	....	....	....	....	....	....	....	23	8	19	27	25	....	....	....	....
2003-04	St. John's	AHL	74	7	18	25	72	....	....	....	....	....	....	....	....	....	....	....	....	....	....	....	....	....	....
2004-05	St. John's	AHL	75	6	25	31	57	....	....	....	....	....	....	....	....	....	5	0	1	1	2	....	....	....	....
2005-06	Toronto	NHL	1	0	0	0	0	0	0	0	2	0.0	0	0	0.0	14:00	....	....	....	....	....	....	....	....	....
	Toronto Marlies	AHL	70	6	37	43	99	....	....	....	....	....	....	....	....	....	5	0	4	4	10	....	....	....	....

			Regular Season														Playoffs								
Season	Club	League	GP	G	A	Pts	PIM	PP	SH	GW	S	%	+/-	TF	F%	Min	GP	G	A	Pts	PIM	PP	SH	GW	Min
2006-07	Toronto	NHL	31	1	4	5	19	1	0	0	29	3.4	–3	1	0.0	12:08	....	....	....	....	....	....	....	....	....
	Phoenix	NHL	14	0	2	2	8	0	0	0	18	0.0	–8	0	0.0	17:07	....	....	....	....	....	....	....	....	....
2007-08	Phoenix	NHL	2	0	0	0	0	0	0	0	0	0.0	–2	0	0.0	14:49	....	....	....	....	....	....	....	....	....
	San Antonio	AHL	69	7	24	31	80	....	....	....	....	....	....	....	....	....	7	2	5	7	10	....	....	....	....
	NHL Totals		48	1	6	7	27	1	0	0	49	2.0		1	0.0	13:44	....	....	....	....	....	....	....	....	....

OHL First All-Star Team (2003) • Canadian Major Junior First All-Star Team (2003) • Canadian Major Junior Defenseman of the Year (2003)

Traded to **Phoenix** by **Toronto** with Toronto's 2nd round choice (later traded to Nashville - Nashville selected Roman Josi) in 2008 Entry Draft for Yanic Perreault and Phoenix's 5th round choice (Joel Champagne) in 2008 Entry Draft, February 27, 2007. Signed as a free agent by **Ottawa**, July 11, 2008.

BELL, Mark

(BEHL, MAHRK) **TOR.**

Center. Shoots left. 6'4", 220 lbs. Born, St. Pauls, Ont., August 5, 1980. Chicago's 1st choice, 8th overall, in 1998 Entry Draft.

1995-96	Stratford Cullitons	OHA-B	47	8	15	23	32	....	....	....	....	....	....	....	....	....	....	....	....	....	....	....	....	....	....
1996-97	Ottawa 67's	OHL	65	8	12	20	40	....	....	....	....	....	....	....	....	....	24	4	7	11	13	....	....	....	....
1997-98	Ottawa 67's	OHL	55	34	26	60	87	....	....	....	....	....	....	....	....	....	13	6	5	11	14	....	....	....	....
1998-99	Ottawa 67's	OHL	44	29	26	55	69	....	....	....	....	....	....	....	....	....	9	6	5	11	8	....	....	....	....
99-2000	Ottawa 67's	OHL	48	34	38	72	95	....	....	....	....	....	....	....	....	....	2	0	1	1	0	....	....	....	....
2000-01	Chicago	NHL	13	0	1	1	4	0	0	0	14	0.0	0	141	48.9	12:00	....	....	....	....	....	....	....	....	....
	Norfolk Admirals	AHL	61	15	27	42	126	....	....	....	....	....	....	....	....	....	9	4	3	7	10	....	....	....	....
2001-02	Chicago	NHL	80	12	16	28	124	1	0	1	120	10.0	–6	47	42.6	12:39	5	0	0	0	8	0	0	0	9:18
2002-03	Chicago	NHL	82	14	15	29	113	0	2	0	127	11.0	0	377	52.5	14:04	....	....	....	....	....	....	....	....	....
2003-04	Chicago	NHL	82	21	24	45	106	2	0	1	202	10.4	–14	387	48.3	17:37	....	....	....	....	....	....	....	....	....
2004-05	Trondheim IK	Norway	25	10	17	27	87	....	....	....	....	....	....	....	....	....	11	6	6	12	44	....	....	....	....
2005-06	Chicago	NHL	82	25	23	48	107	11	1	1	227	11.0	–14	1034	48.5	17:37	....	....	....	....	....	....	....	....	....
2006-07	San Jose	NHL	71	11	10	21	83	3	0	2	116	9.5	–9	108	48.2	12:57	4	0	0	0	2	0	0	0	10:16
2007-08	Toronto	NHL	35	4	6	10	60	0	0	0	42	9.5	–2	179	41.3	9:45	....	....	....	....	....	....	....	....	....
	NHL Totals		445	87	95	182	597	17	3	5	848	10.3		2273	48.4	14:33	9	0	0	0	10	0	0	0	9:44

Signed as a free agent by **Trondheim** (Norway), November 6, 2004. Traded to **San Jose** by **Chicago** for Tom Preissing and Josh Hennessy, July 10, 2006. Traded to **Toronto** by **San Jose** with Vesa Toskala for Toronto's 1st (later traded to St. Louis - St. Louis selected Lars Eller) and 2nd (later traded to St. Louis - St. Louis selected Aaron Palushaj) round choices in 2007 Entry Draft and Toronto's 4th round choice in 2009 Entry Draft, June 22, 2007.

BELLE, Shawn

(BEHL, SHAWN) **MTL.**

Defense. Shoots left. 6'2", 232 lbs. Born, Edmonton, Alta., January 3, 1985. St. Louis' 1st choice, 30th overall, in 2003 Entry Draft.

99-2000	K of C Squires	AMBHL	34	7	20	27	36	....	....	....	....	....	....	....	....	....	....	....	....	....	....	....	....	....	....
2000-01	K of C Squires	AMBHL	39	18	30	48	69	....	....	....	....	....	....	....	....	....	....	....	....	....	....	....	....	....	....
	Regina Pats	WHL	4	0	3	3	0	....	....	....	....	....	....	....	....	....	....	....	....	....	....	....	....	....	....
	Tri-City	WHL	2	0	1	1	0	....	....	....	....	....	....	....	....	....	....	....	....	....	....	....	....	....	....
2001-02	Tri-City	WHL	64	1	17	18	51	....	....	....	....	....	....	....	....	....	5	2	1	3	2	....	....	....	....
2002-03	Tri-City	WHL	66	7	14	21	79	....	....	....	....	....	....	....	....	....	....	....	....	....	....	....	....	....	....
2003-04	Tri-City	WHL	55	9	20	29	68	....	....	....	....	....	....	....	....	....	11	3	5	8	15	....	....	....	....
2004-05	Tri-City	WHL	62	13	32	45	76	....	....	....	....	....	....	....	....	....	5	1	1	2	6	....	....	....	....
2005-06	Iowa Stars	AHL	45	1	2	3	63	....	....	....	....	....	....	....	....	....	....	....	....	....	....	....	....	....	....
	Houston Aeros	AHL	16	1	1	2	18	....	....	....	....	....	....	....	....	....	8	1	0	1	4	....	....	....	....
2006-07	Minnesota	NHL	9	0	1	1	0	0	0	0	3	0.0	4	0	0.0	9:56	....	....	....	....	....	....	....	....	....
	Houston Aeros	AHL	57	4	14	18	73	....	....	....	....	....	....	....	....	....	....	....	....	....	....	....	....	....	....
2007-08	Houston Aeros	AHL	63	1	2	3	74	....	....	....	....	....	....	....	....	....	3	0	0	0	2	....	....	....	....
	NHL Totals		9	0	1	1	0	0	0	0	3	0.0		0	0.0	9:56	....	....	....	....	....	....	....	....	....

Rights traded to **Dallas** by **St. Louis** for Jason Bacashihua, June 25, 2004. Traded to **Minnesota** by **Dallas** with Martin Skoula for Willie Mitchell and Minnesota's 2nd round choice (Nico Saccheti) in 2007 Entry Draft, March 9, 2006. Traded to **Montreal** by **Minnesota** for Cory Locke, July 11, 2008.

BERARD, Bryan

(buh-RAHRD, BRIGH-uhn)

Defense. Shoots left. 6'2", 220 lbs. Born, Woonsocket, RI, March 5, 1977. Ottawa's 1st choice, 1st overall, in 1995 Entry Draft.

1991-92	Mount St. Charles	High-RI	15	3	15	18	4	....	....	....	....	....	....	....	....	....	....	....	....	....	....	....	....	....	....
1992-93	Mount St. Charles	High-RI	15	8	12	20	18	....	....	....	....	....	....	....	....	....	....	....	....	....	....	....	....	....	....
1993-94	Mount St. Charles	High-RI	15	11	26	37	4.5	....	....	....	....	....	....	....	....	....	4	3	3	6	6	....	....	....	....
1994-95	Detroit	OHL	58	20	55	75	97	....	....	....	....	....	....	....	....	....	21	4	20	24	38	....	....	....	....
1995-96	Detroit	OHL	56	31	58	89	116	....	....	....	....	....	....	....	....	....	17	7	18	25	41	....	....	....	....
1996-97	NY Islanders	NHL	82	8	40	48	86	3	0	1	172	4.7	1	....	....	....	....	....	....	....	....	....	....	....	....
1997-98	NY Islanders	NHL	75	14	32	46	59	8	1	2	192	7.3	–32	....	....	....	....	....	....	....	....	....	....	....	....
	United States	Olympics	2	0	0	0	0	....	....	....	....	....	....	....	....	....	....	....	....	....	....	....	....	....	....
1998-99	NY Islanders	NHL	31	4	11	15	26	2	0	3	72	5.6	–6	0	0.0	24:45	....	....	....	....	....	....	....	....	....
	Toronto	NHL	38	5	14	19	22	2	0	2	63	7.9	7	0	0.0	22:38	17	1	8	9	8	1	0	0	21:11
99-2000	Toronto	NHL	64	3	27	30	42	1	0	0	98	3.1	11	0	0.0	19:34	....	....	....	....	....	....	....	....	....
2000-01	Toronto	NHL	DID NOT PLAY – INJURED																						
2001-02	NY Rangers	NHL	82	2	21	23	60	0	0	0	132	1.5	–1	0	0.0	19:38	....	....	....	....	....	....	....	....	....
2002-03	Boston	NHL	80	10	28	38	64	4	0	1	205	4.9	–4	0	0.0	21:21	3	1	0	1	2	0	0	0	21:50
2003-04	Chicago	NHL	58	13	34	47	53	6	0	0	203	6.4	–24	0	0.0	21:46	....	....	....	....	....	....	....	....	....
2004-05			DID NOT PLAY																						
2005-06	Columbus	NHL	44	12	20	32	32	11	0	2	126	9.5	–29	0	0.0	22:40	....	....	....	....	....	....	....	....	....
2006-07	Columbus	NHL	11	0	3	3	8	0	0	0	22	0.0	–4	0	0.0	18:58	....	....	....	....	....	....	....	....	....
2007-08	NY Islanders	NHL	54	5	17	22	48	4	0	2	87	5.7	–17	0	0.0	17:38	....	....	....	....	....	....	....	....	....
	NHL Totals		619	76	247	323	500	41	1	13	1372	5.5		0	0.0	20:49	20	2	8	10	10	1	0	0	21:17

OHL All-Rookie Team (1995) • OHL First All-Star Team (1995, 1996) • OHL Rookie of the Year (1995) • Canadian Major Junior First All-Star Team (1995, 1996) • Canadian Major Junior Rookie of the Year (1995) • Canadian Major Junior Defenseman of the Year (1996) • NHL All-Rookie Team (1997) • Calder Memorial Trophy (1997) • Bill Masterton Memorial Trophy (2004)

Traded to **NY Islanders** by **Ottawa** with Don Beaupre and Martin Straka for Damian Rhodes and Wade Redden, January 23, 1996. Traded to **Toronto** by **NY Islanders** with NY Islanders' 6th round choice (Jan Sochor) in 1999 Entry Draft for Felix Potvin and Toronto's 6th round choice (later traded to Tampa Bay – Tampa Bay selected Fedor Fedorov) in 1999 Entry Draft, January 9, 1999. • Missed remainder of 1999-2000 season and entire 2000-01 season recovering from eye injury suffered in game vs. Ottawa, March 11, 2000. Signed as a free agent by **NY Rangers**, October 5, 2001. Signed as a free agent by **Boston**, August 13, 2002. Signed as a free agent by **Chicago**, October 31, 2003. Signed as a free agent by **Columbus**, August 3, 2005. • Missed majority of 2006-07 season due to recurring back injury. Signed as a free agent by **NY Islanders**, October 9, 2007.

BERGENHEIM, Sean

(BUHR-gehn-highm, SHAWN) **NYI**

Left wing. Shoots left. 5'11", 205 lbs. Born, Helsinki, Finland, February 8, 1984. NY Islanders' 1st choice, 22nd overall, in 2002 Entry Draft.

99-2000	Jokerit U18	Fin-U18	30	22	11	33	34	....	....	....	....	....	....	....	....	....	3	1	0	1	0	....	....	....	....
	Jokerit U18	Fin-U18	17	10	8	18	14	....	....	....	....	....	....	....	....	....	3	1	0	1	2	....	....	....	....
2000-01	Jokerit U18	Fin-U18	1	1	0	1	4	....	....	....	....	....	....	....	....	....	6	9	5	14	8	....	....	....	....
	Jokerit Helsinki Jr.	Fin-Jr.	18	6	4	10	26	....	....	....	....	....	....	....	....	....	2	0	0	0	4	....	....	....	....
2001-02	Jokerit U18	Fin-U18	....	....	....	....	....	....	....	....	....	....	....	....	....	....	5	6	2	8	18	....	....	....	....
	Jokerit Helsinki Jr.	Fin-Jr.	23	11	19	30	36	....	....	....	....	....	....	....	....	....	1	0	0	0	2	....	....	....	....
	Kiekko-Vantaa	Finland-2	4	0	0	0	52	....	....	....	....	....	....	....	....	....	....	....	....	....	....	....	....	....	....
	Jokerit Helsinki	Finland	28	2	2	4	4	....	....	....	....	....	....	....	....	....	....	....	....	....	....	....	....	....	....
2002-03	Jokerit Helsinki Jr.	Fin-Jr.	2	3	0	3	2	....	....	....	....	....	....	....	....	....	....	....	....	....	....	....	....	....	....
	Jokerit Helsinki	Finland	38	3	3	6	4	....	....	....	....	....	....	....	....	....	2	0	0	0	0	....	....	....	....
2003-04	NY Islanders	NHL	18	1	1	2	4	0	1	0	12	8.3	–4	2	50.0	8:55	....	....	....	....	....	....	....	....	....
	Jokerit Helsinki	Finland	20	2	2	4	18	....	....	....	....	....	....	....	....	....	3	1	1	2	0	....	....	....	....
	Bridgeport	AHL	....	....	....	....	....	....	....	....	....	....	....	....	....	....	7	2	3	5	10	....	....	....	....
2004-05	Bridgeport	AHL	61	15	14	29	69	....	....	....	....	....	....	....	....	....	....	....	....	....	....	....	....	....	....
2005-06	NY Islanders	NHL	28	4	5	9	20	0	0	1	63	6.3	–11	14	28.6	13:17	....	....	....	....	....	....	....	....	....
	Bridgeport	AHL	55	25	22	47	112	....	....	....	....	....	....	....	....	....	7	0	2	2	24	....	....	....	....
2006-07	Yaroslavl	Russia	9	1	4	5	26	....	....	....	....	....	....	....	....	....	....	....	....	....	....	....	....	....	....
	Frolunda	Sweden	36	16	17	33	80	....	....	....	....	....	....	....	....	....	....	....	....	....	....	....	....	....	....
2007-08	NY Islanders	NHL	78	10	12	22	62	1	0	1	155	6.5	–3	15	60.0	11:15	....	....	....	....	....	....	....	....	....
	NHL Totals		124	15	18	33	86	1	1	2	230	6.5		31	45.2	11:22	....	....	....	....	....	....	....	....	....

Signed as a free agent by **Yaroslavl** (Russia), August 5, 2006. Signed as a free agent by **Frolunda** (Sweden), November 3, 2006.

BERGERON, Marc-Andre
(BAIR-zhur-uhn, MAHRK-AWN-dray) **MIN.**

Defense. Shoots left. 5'10", 197 lbs. Born, St-Louis-de-France, Que., October 13, 1980.

			Regular Season														Playoffs								
Season	Club	League	GP	G	A	Pts	PIM	PP	SH	GW	S	%	+/-	TF	F%	Min	GP	G	A	Pts	PIM	PP	SH	GW	Min
1996-97	Cap-d-Madeleine	QAAA	4	0	1	1	0	....	....	....	....	....	....	....	....	....	2	0	0	0	0	....	....	....	....
1997-98	Baie-Comeau	QMJHL	40	6	14	20	48	....	....	....	....	....	....	....	....	....	....	....	....	....	....	....	....	....	....
1998-99	Baie-Comeau	QMJHL	46	8	14	22	57	....	....	....	....	....	....	....	....	....	....	....	....	....	....	....	....	....	....
	Shawinigan	QMJHL	24	6	7	13	66	....	....	....	....	....	....	....	....	....	5	2	2	4	24	....	....	....	....
99-2000	Shawinigan	QMJHL	70	24	50	74	173	....	....	....	....	....	....	....	....	....	13	4	7	11	45	....	....	....	....
2000-01	Shawinigan	QMJHL	69	42	59	101	185	....	....	....	....	....	....	....	....	....	10	4	11	15	24	....	....	....	....
2001-02	Hamilton	AHL	50	2	13	15	61	....	....	....	....	....	....	....	....	....	9	1	4	5	8	....	....	....	....
2002-03	**Edmonton**	**NHL**	**5**	**1**	**1**	**2**	**9**	**0**	**0**	**0**	**5**	**20.0**	**2**	**0**	**0.0**	**16:30**	**1**	**0**	**1**	**1**	**0**	**0**	**0**	**0**	**19:20**
	Hamilton	AHL	66	8	31	39	73	....	....	....	....	....	....	....	....	....	20	0	7	7	25	....	....	....	....
2003-04	**Edmonton**	**NHL**	**54**	**9**	**17**	**26**	**26**	**3**	**0**	**0**	**105**	**8.6**	**13**	**0**	**0.0**	**17:39**	....	....	....	....	....	....	....	....	....
	Toronto	AHL	17	4	3	7	23	....	....	....	....	....	....	....	....	....	....	....	....	....	....	....	....	....	....
2004-05	Brynas IF Gavle	Sweden	10	3	2	5	72	....	....	....	....	....	....	....	....	....	....	....	....	....	....	....	....	....	....
	Brynas IF Gavle	Sweden-Q	9	1	2	3	8	....	....	....	....	....	....	....	....	....	....	....	....	....	....	....	....	....	....
2005-06	**Edmonton**	**NHL**	**75**	**15**	**20**	**35**	**38**	**8**	**0**	**1**	**144**	**10.4**	**3**	**0**	**0.0**	**21:14**	**18**	**2**	**1**	**3**	**14**	**2**	**0**	**0**	**14:56**
2006-07	**Edmonton**	**NHL**	**55**	**8**	**17**	**25**	**28**	**6**	**0**	**3**	**111**	**7.2**	**–9**	**0**	**0.0**	**17:27**	....	....	....	....	....	....	....	....	....
	NY Islanders	**NHL**	**23**	**6**	**15**	**21**	**10**	**4**	**0**	**1**	**55**	**10.9**	**5**	**0**	**0.0**	**23:07**	**5**	**1**	**1**	**2**	**6**	**1**	**0**	**1**	**27:21**
2007-08	**NY Islanders**	**NHL**	**46**	**9**	**9**	**18**	**16**	**8**	**0**	**1**	**96**	**9.4**	**–14**	**0**	**0.0**	**18:17**	....	....	....	....	....	....	....	....	....
	Anaheim	**NHL**	**9**	**0**	**1**	**1**	**4**	**0**	**0**	**0**	**12**	**0.0**	**–2**	**0**	**0.0**	**12:50**	....	....	....	....	....	....	....	....	....
	NHL Totals		**267**	**48**	**80**	**128**	**131**	**29**	**0**	**6**	**528**	**9.1**		**0**	**0.0**	**19:01**	**24**	**3**	**3**	**6**	**20**	**3**	**0**	**1**	**17:42**

QMJHL First All-Star Team (2001) • Canadian Major Junior First All-Star Team (2001) • Canadian Major Junior Defenseman of the Year (2001) • AHL Second All-Star Team (2003)

Signed as a free agent by **Edmonton**, July 20, 2001. Signed as a free agent by **Gavle** (Sweden), January 23, 2005. Traded to **NY Islanders** by **Edmonton** with Edmonton's 3rd round choice (later traded back to Edmonton - later traded to Anaheim - later traded back to NY Islanders - NY Islanders selected Kirill Petrov) in 2008 Entry Draft for Denis Grebeshkov, February 18, 2007. Traded to **Anaheim** by **NY Islanders** for Edmonton's 3rd round choice (previously acquired, NY Islanders selected Kirill Petrov) in 2008 Entry Draft, February 26, 2008. Traded to **Minnesota** by **Anaheim** for Minnesota's 3rd round choice (Brandon McMillan) in 2008 Entry Draft, June 10, 2008.

BERGERON, Patrice
(BAIR-zhuhr-uhn, pa-TREEZ) **BOS.**

Center. Shoots right. 6'2", 194 lbs. Born, Ancienne-Lorette, Que., July 24, 1985. Boston's 2nd choice, 45th overall, in 2003 Entry Draft.

			Regular Season														Playoffs								
Season	Club	League	GP	G	A	Pts	PIM	PP	SH	GW	S	%	+/-	TF	F%	Min	GP	G	A	Pts	PIM	PP	SH	GW	Min
2000-01	Ste-Foy	QAAA	5	1	2	3	0	....	....	....	....	....	....	....	....	....	....	....	....	....	....	....	....	....	....
2001-02	St-Francois	QAAA	38	25	37	62	18	....	....	....	....	....	....	....	....	....	8	6	4	10	10	....	....	....	....
	Acadie-Bathurst	QMJHL	4	0	1	1	0	....	....	....	....	....	....	....	....	....	....	....	....	....	....	....	....	....	....
2002-03	Acadie-Bathurst	QMJHL	70	23	50	73	62	....	....	....	....	....	....	....	....	....	11	6	9	15	6	....	....	....	....
2003-04	**Boston**	**NHL**	**71**	**16**	**23**	**39**	**22**	**7**	**0**	**2**	**133**	**12.0**	**5**	**699**	**49.4**	**16:21**	**7**	**1**	**3**	**4**	**0**	**0**	**0**	**1**	**17:13**
2004-05	Providence Bruins	AHL	68	21	40	61	59	....	....	....	....	....	....	....	....	....	16	5	7	12	4	....	....	....	....
2005-06	**Boston**	**NHL**	**81**	**31**	**42**	**73**	**22**	**12**	**1**	**6**	**310**	**10.0**	**3**	**1447**	**54.7**	**20:36**	....	....	....	....	....	....	....	....	....
2006-07	**Boston**	**NHL**	**77**	**22**	**48**	**70**	**26**	**14**	**0**	**6**	**224**	**9.8**	**–28**	**1560**	**51.2**	**20:49**	....	....	....	....	....	....	....	....	....
2007-08	**Boston**	**NHL**	**10**	**3**	**4**	**7**	**2**	**2**	**0**	**0**	**24**	**12.5**	**2**	**175**	**50.3**	**18:10**	....	....	....	....	....	....	....	....	....
	NHL Totals		**239**	**72**	**117**	**189**	**72**	**35**	**1**	**14**	**691**	**10.4**		**3881**	**52.1**	**19:18**	**7**	**1**	**3**	**4**	**0**	**0**	**0**	**1**	**17:13**

QAAA Second All-Star Team (2002)

• Missed majority of 2007-08 season recovering from concussion suffered in game vs. Philadelphia, October 27, 2007.

BERGFORS, Nicklas
(BUHRG-fohrs, NIHK-luhs) **N.J.**

Right wing. Shoots right. 5'11", 190 lbs. Born, Sodertalje, Sweden, March 7, 1987. New Jersey's 1st choice, 23rd overall, in 2005 Entry Draft.

			Regular Season														Playoffs								
Season	Club	League	GP	G	A	Pts	PIM	PP	SH	GW	S	%	+/-	TF	F%	Min	GP	G	A	Pts	PIM	PP	SH	GW	Min
2002-03	Sodertalje SK U18	Swe-U18	4	4	4	8	0	....	....	....	....	....	....	....	....	....	....	....	....	....	....	....	....	....	....
	Sodertalje SK Jr.	Swe-Jr.	13	1	5	6	4	....	....	....	....	....	....	....	....	....	....	....	....	....	....	....	....	....	....
2003-04	Sodertalje SK U18	Swe-U18	5	14	4	18	4	....	....	....	....	....	....	....	....	....	2	0	1	1	6	....	....	....	....
	Sodertalje SK Jr.	Swe-Jr.	31	13	17	30	22	....	....	....	....	....	....	....	....	....	2	1	1	2	0	....	....	....	....
2004-05	Sodertalje SK Jr.	Swe-Jr.	21	18	16	34	25	....	....	....	....	....	....	....	....	....	3	0	3	3	4	....	....	....	....
	Sodertalje SK	Sweden	25	1	0	1	2	....	....	....	....	....	....	....	....	....	2	0	0	0	0	....	....	....	....
2005-06	Albany River Rats	AHL	65	17	23	40	10	....	....	....	....	....	....	....	....	....	....	....	....	....	....	....	....	....	....
2006-07	Lowell Devils	AHL	60	13	19	32	8	....	....	....	....	....	....	....	....	....	....	....	....	....	....	....	....	....	....
2007-08	**New Jersey**	**NHL**	**1**	**0**	**0**	**0**	**0**	**0**	**0**	**0**	**3**	**0.0**	**–1**	**1**	**0.0**	**11:17**	....	....	....	....	....	....	....	....	....
	Lowell Devils	AHL	66	12	15	27	22	....	....	....	....	....	....	....	....	....	....	....	....	....	....	....	....	....	....
	NHL Totals		**1**	**0**	**0**	**0**	**0**	**0**	**0**	**0**	**3**	**0.0**		**1**	**0.0**	**11:17**	....	....	....	....	....	....	....	....	....

BERNIER, Steve
(BAIRN-yay, STEEV) **VAN.**

Right wing. Shoots right. 6'2", 225 lbs. Born, Quebec City, Que., March 31, 1985. San Jose's 2nd choice, 16th overall, in 2003 Entry Draft.

			Regular Season														Playoffs								
Season	Club	League	GP	G	A	Pts	PIM	PP	SH	GW	S	%	+/-	TF	F%	Min	GP	G	A	Pts	PIM	PP	SH	GW	Min
1998-99	Quebec AA Aces	QAHA	28	33	23	56	24	....	....	....	....	....	....	....	....	....	....	....	....	....	....	....	....	....	....
99-2000	Quebec AA Aces	QAHA	26	12	23	35	42	....	....	....	....	....	....	....	....	....	....	....	....	....	....	....	....	....	....
2000-01	Ste-Foy	QAAA	39	17	35	52	48	....	....	....	....	....	....	....	....	....	16	9	17	26	8	....	....	....	....
2001-02	Moncton Wildcats	QMJHL	66	31	28	59	51	....	....	....	....	....	....	....	....	....	....	....	....	....	....	....	....	....	....
2002-03	Moncton Wildcats	QMJHL	71	49	52	101	90	....	....	....	....	....	....	....	....	....	2	1	0	1	2	....	....	....	....
2003-04	Moncton Wildcats	QMJHL	66	36	46	82	80	....	....	....	....	....	....	....	....	....	20	7	10	17	17	....	....	....	....
2004-05	Moncton Wildcats	QMJHL	68	35	36	71	114	....	....	....	....	....	....	....	....	....	12	6	13	19	22	....	....	....	....
2005-06	**San Jose**	**NHL**	**39**	**14**	**13**	**27**	**35**	**2**	**1**	**1**	**75**	**18.7**	**4**	**8**	**62.5**	**14:08**	**11**	**1**	**5**	**6**	**8**	**1**	**0**	**1**	**15:17**
	Cleveland Barons	AHL	49	20	23	43	33	....	....	....	....	....	....	....	....	....	....	....	....	....	....	....	....	....	....
2006-07	**San Jose**	**NHL**	**62**	**15**	**16**	**31**	**29**	**6**	**0**	**4**	**104**	**14.4**	**5**	**18**	**27.8**	**13:35**	**11**	**0**	**1**	**1**	**2**	**0**	**0**	**0**	**10:39**
	Worcester Sharks	AHL	10	3	4	7	12	....	....	....	....	....	....	....	....	....	....	....	....	....	....	....	....	....	....
2007-08	**San Jose**	**NHL**	**59**	**13**	**10**	**23**	**62**	**4**	**0**	**0**	**96**	**13.5**	**–2**	**10**	**50.0**	**13:07**	....	....	....	....	....	....	....	....	....
	Buffalo	**NHL**	**17**	**3**	**6**	**9**	**2**	**0**	**0**	**0**	**35**	**8.6**	**1**	**5**	**20.0**	**14:06**	....	....	....	....	....	....	....	....	....
	NHL Totals		**177**	**45**	**45**	**90**	**128**	**12**	**1**	**5**	**310**	**14.5**		**41**	**39.0**	**13:36**	**22**	**1**	**6**	**7**	**10**	**1**	**0**	**1**	**12:58**

QMJHL All-Rookie Team (2002) • QMJHL Second All-Star Team (2003, 2004)

Traded to **Buffalo** by **San Jose** with San Jose's 1st round choice (Tyler Ennis) in 2008 Entry Draft for Brian Campbell and Buffalo's 7th round choice (Drew Daniels) in 2008 Entry Draft, February 26, 2008. Traded to **Vancouver** by **Buffalo** for Los Angeles' 3rd round choice (previously acquired) in 2009 Entry Draft and Vancouver's 2nd round choice in 2010 Entry Draft, July 4, 2008.

BERRY, Rick
(BAIR-ee, RIHK)

Defense. Shoots left. 6'2", 210 lbs. Born, Birtle, Man., November 4, 1978. Colorado's 3rd choice, 55th overall, in 1997 Entry Draft.

			Regular Season														Playoffs								
Season	Club	League	GP	G	A	Pts	PIM	PP	SH	GW	S	%	+/-	TF	F%	Min	GP	G	A	Pts	PIM	PP	SH	GW	Min
1994-95	Yellowhead	MMMHL	33	12	19	31	90	....	....	....	....	....	....	....	....	....	....	....	....	....	....	....	....	....	....
1995-96	Seattle	WHL	59	4	9	13	103	....	....	....	....	....	....	....	....	....	1	0	0	0	0	....	....	....	....
1996-97	Seattle	WHL	72	12	21	33	125	....	....	....	....	....	....	....	....	....	15	3	7	10	23	....	....	....	....
1997-98	Seattle	WHL	37	5	12	17	100	....	....	....	....	....	....	....	....	....	....	....	....	....	....	....	....	....	....
	Spokane Chiefs	WHL	22	4	9	13	31	....	....	....	....	....	....	....	....	....	17	1	4	5	26	....	....	....	....
1998-99	Hershey Bears	AHL	62	2	6	8	153	....	....	....	....	....	....	....	....	....	....	....	....	....	....	....	....	....	....
99-2000	Hershey Bears	AHL	64	9	16	25	148	....	....	....	....	....	....	....	....	....	13	2	3	5	24	....	....	....	....
2000-01	**Colorado**	**NHL**	**19**	**0**	**4**	**4**	**38**	**0**	**0**	**0**	**10**	**0.0**	**5**	**0**	**0.0**	**12:08**	....	....	....	....	....	....	....	....	....
	Hershey Bears	AHL	48	6	17	23	87	....	....	....	....	....	....	....	....	....	12	2	2	4	18	....	....	....	....
2001-02	**Colorado**	**NHL**	**57**	**0**	**0**	**0**	**60**	**0**	**0**	**0**	**29**	**0.0**	**1**	**0**	**0.0**	**9:29**	....	....	....	....	....	....	....	....	....
	Pittsburgh	**NHL**	**13**	**0**	**2**	**2**	**21**	**0**	**0**	**0**	**20**	**0.0**	**–4**	**0**	**0.0**	**19:39**	....	....	....	....	....	....	....	....	....
2002-03	**Washington**	**NHL**	**43**	**2**	**1**	**3**	**87**	**0**	**0**	**1**	**40**	**5.0**	**–3**	**0**	**0.0**	**12:58**	....	....	....	....	....	....	....	....	....
2003-04	**Washington**	**NHL**	**65**	**0**	**6**	**6**	**108**	**0**	**0**	**0**	**43**	**0.0**	**–5**	**2**	**50.0**	**12:11**	....	....	....	....	....	....	....	....	....
	Portland Pirates	AHL	10	2	1	3	12	....	....	....	....	....	....	....	....	....	....	....	....	....	....	....	....	....	....
2004-05	Utah Grizzlies	AHL	45	2	6	8	83	....	....	....	....	....	....	....	....	....	....	....	....	....	....	....	....	....	....
2005-06	San Antonio	AHL	5	0	0	0	4	....	....	....	....	....	....	....	....	....	....	....	....	....	....	....	....	....	....
	Milwaukee	AHL	64	1	11	12	121	....	....	....	....	....	....	....	....	....	7	0	0	0	15	....	....	....	....
2006-07	Bridgeport	AHL	76	3	15	18	155	....	....	....	....	....	....	....	....	....	....	....	....	....	....	....	....	....	....
2007-08	Springfield	AHL	54	2	8	10	77	....	....	....	....	....	....	....	....	....	....	....	....	....	....	....	....	....	....
	NHL Totals		**197**	**2**	**13**	**15**	**314**	**0**	**0**	**1**	**142**	**1.4**		**2**	**50.0**	**12:04**	....	....	....	....	....	....	....	....	....

Traded to **Pittsburgh** by **Colorado** with Ville Nieminen for Darius Kasparaitis, March 19, 2002. Claimed by **Washington** from **Pittsburgh** in Waiver Draft, October 4, 2002. Signed as a free agent by **Phoenix**, September 2, 2004. Traded to **Nashville** by **Phoenix** for future considerations, October 24, 2005. Signed as a free agent by **NY Islanders**, July 20, 2006. Signed as a free agent by **Springfield** (AHL), July 26, 2007.

Season	Club	League	Regular Season GP	G	A	Pts	PIM	PP	SH	GW	S	%	+/-	TF	F%	Min	Playoffs GP	G	A	Pts	PIM	PP	SH	GW	Min

BERTI, Adam

(BUHR-tee, A-duhm) **CHI.**

Left wing. Shoots left. 6'3", 198 lbs. Born, Scarborough, Ont., July 1, 1986. Chicago's 6th choice, 68th overall, in 2004 Entry Draft.

2002-03	Oshawa Generals	OHL	15	3	3	6	12	....	....	....	....	....	....	....	....	....	....	....	....	....	....	....	....	....	....
2003-04	Oshawa Generals	OHL	66	17	29	46	44	....	....	....	....	....	....	....	....	....	7	0	2	2	4	....	....	....	....
2004-05	Oshawa Generals	OHL	66	23	28	51	53	....	....	....	....	....	....	....	....	....	....	....	....	....	....	....	....	....	....
2005-06	Oshawa Generals	OHL	23	16	18	34	28	....	....	....	....	....	....	....	....	....	....	....	....	....	....	....	....	....	....
	Erie Otters	OHL	39	17	12	29	24	....	....	....	....	....	....	....	....	....	....	....	....	....	....	....	....	....	....
2006-07	Norfolk Admirals	AHL	48	6	6	12	50	....	....	....	....	....	....	....	....	....	....	....	....	....	....	....	....	....	....
2007-08	**Chicago**	**NHL**	**2**	**0**	**0**	**0**	**0**	**0**	**0**	**0**	**1**	**0.0**	**0**	**0**	**0.0**	**10:07**	....	....	....	....	....	....	....	....	....
	Rockford IceHogs	AHL	42	2	5	7	68	....	....	....	....	....	....	....	....	....	5	1	0	1	2	....	....	....	....
	Pensacola	ECHL	4	2	3	5	0	....	....	....	....	....	....	....	....	....	....	....	....	....	....	....	....	....	....
	NHL Totals		**2**	**0**	**0**	**0**	**0**	**0**	**0**	**0**	**1**	**0.0**		**0**	**0.0**	**10:07**	....	....	....	....	....	....	....	....	....

BERTUZZI, Todd

(buhr-TOO-zee, TAWD) **CGY.**

Right wing. Shoots left. 6'3", 231 lbs. Born, Sudbury, Ont., February 2, 1975. NY Islanders' 1st choice, 23rd overall, in 1993 Entry Draft.

1990-91	Sudbury Legion	NOHA	48	25	46	71	247	....	....	....	....	....	....	....	....	....	....	....	....	....	....	....	....	....	....
	Sudbury Cubs	NOJHA	3	3	2	5	10	....	....	....	....	....	....	....	....	....	....	....	....	....	....	....	....	....	....
1991-92	Guelph Storm	OHL	47	7	14	21	145	....	....	....	....	....	....	....	....	....	....	....	....	....	....	....	....	....	....
1992-93	Guelph Storm	OHL	59	27	32	59	164	....	....	....	....	....	....	....	....	....	5	2	2	4	6	....	....	....	....
1993-94	Guelph Storm	OHL	61	28	54	82	165	....	....	....	....	....	....	....	....	....	9	2	6	8	30	....	....	....	....
1994-95	Guelph Storm	OHL	62	54	65	119	58	....	....	....	....	....	....	....	....	....	14	*15	18	33	41	....	....	....	....
1995-96	**NY Islanders**	**NHL**	**76**	**18**	**21**	**39**	**83**	**4**	**0**	**2**	**127**	**14.2**	**–14**	....	....	....	....	....	....	....	....	....	....	....	....
1996-97	**NY Islanders**	**NHL**	**64**	**10**	**13**	**23**	**68**	**3**	**0**	**1**	**79**	**12.7**	**–3**	....	....	....	....	....	....	....	....	....	....	....	....
	Utah Grizzlies	IHL	13	5	5	10	16	....	....	....	....	....	....	....	....	....	....	....	....	....	....	....	....	....	....
1997-98	**NY Islanders**	**NHL**	**52**	**7**	**11**	**18**	**58**	**1**	**0**	**1**	**63**	**11.1**	**–19**	....	....	....	....	....	....	....	....	....	....	....	....
	Vancouver	**NHL**	**22**	**6**	**9**	**15**	**63**	**1**	**1**	**1**	**39**	**15.4**	**2**	....	....	....	....	....	....	....	....	....	....	....	....
1998-99	**Vancouver**	**NHL**	**32**	**8**	**8**	**16**	**44**	**1**	**0**	**3**	**72**	**11.1**	**–6**	**191**	**43.5**	**18:28**	....	....	....	....	....	....	....	....	....
99-2000	**Vancouver**	**NHL**	**80**	**25**	**25**	**50**	**126**	**4**	**0**	**2**	**173**	**14.5**	**–2**	**476**	**46.6**	**15:24**	....	....	....	....	....	....	....	....	....
2000-01	**Vancouver**	**NHL**	**79**	**25**	**30**	**55**	**93**	**14**	**0**	**3**	**203**	**12.3**	**–18**	**84**	**45.2**	**17:13**	**4**	**2**	**2**	**4**	**8**	**0**	**0**	**0**	**19:01**
2001-02	**Vancouver**	**NHL**	**72**	**36**	**49**	**85**	**110**	**14**	**0**	**3**	**203**	**17.7**	**21**	**151**	**49.0**	**19:40**	**6**	**2**	**2**	**4**	**14**	**1**	**0**	**0**	**21:50**
2002-03	**Vancouver**	**NHL**	**82**	**46**	**51**	**97**	**144**	**25**	**0**	**7**	**243**	**18.9**	**2**	**208**	**47.1**	**20:34**	**14**	**2**	**4**	**6**	***60**	**0**	**0**	**0**	**21:05**
2003-04	**Vancouver**	**NHL**	**69**	**17**	**43**	**60**	**122**	**8**	**0**	**2**	**156**	**10.9**	**21**	**111**	**45.1**	**21:00**	....	....	....	....	....	....	....	....	....
2004-05	DID NOT PLAY – SUSPENDED													....	....	....	....	....	....	....	....	....	....	....	....
2005-06	**Vancouver**	**NHL**	**82**	**25**	**46**	**71**	**120**	**12**	**0**	**3**	**200**	**12.5**	**–17**	**363**	**43.8**	**19:08**	....	....	....	....	....	....	....	....	....
	Canada	Olympics	6	0	3	3	6	....	....	....	....	....	....	....	....	....	....	....	....	....	....	....	....	....	....
2006-07	**Florida**	**NHL**	**7**	**1**	**6**	**7**	**13**	**1**	**0**	**0**	**8**	**12.5**	**–4**	**0**	**0.0**	**16:32**	....	....	....	....	....	....	....	....	....
	Detroit	**NHL**	**8**	**2**	**2**	**4**	**6**	**0**	**0**	**0**	**15**	**13.3**	**3**	**2**	**50.0**	**15:32**	**16**	**3**	**4**	**7**	**15**	**1**	**0**	**0**	**14:25**
2007-08	**Anaheim**	**NHL**	**68**	**14**	**26**	**40**	**97**	**4**	**0**	**2**	**121**	**11.6**	**8**	**110**	**45.5**	**16:27**	**6**	**0**	**2**	**2**	**14**	**0**	**0**	**0**	**14:15**
	NHL Totals		**793**	**240**	**340**	**580**	**1147**	**92**	**1**	**30**	**1702**	**14.1**		**1696**	**45.7**	**18:25**	**46**	**9**	**14**	**23**	**111**	**2**	**0**	**0**	**17:47**

OHL Second All-Star Team (1995) • NHL First All-Star Team (2003)

Played in NHL All-Star Game (2003, 2004)

Traded to **Vancouver** by **NY Islanders** with Bryan McCabe and NY Islanders' 3rd round choice (Jarkko Ruutu) in 1998 Entry Draft for Trevor Linden, February 6, 1998. • Missed majority of 1998-99 season recovering from leg injury suffered in game vs. Washington, November 1, 1998. • Suspended indefinitely by NHL for deliberate injury to Steve Moore in game vs. Colorado, March 8, 2004. • Reinstated by NHL on August 8, 2005. Traded to **Florida** by **Vancouver** with Bryan Allen and Alex Auld for Roberto Luongo, Lukas Krajicek and Florida's 6th round choice (Sergei Shirokov) in 2006 Entry Draft, June 23, 2006. Traded to **Detroit** by **Florida** for Shawn Matthias and Detroit's 2nd round choice (later traded to Nashville - Nashville selected Nick Spaling) in 2007 Entry Draft, February 27, 2007. • Missed majority of 2006-07 season recovering from recurring back injury. Signed as a free agent by **Anaheim**, July 2, 2007. Signed as a free agent by **Calgary**, July 7, 2008.

BETTS, Blair

(BEHTS, BLAIR) **NYR**

Center. Shoots left. 6'3", 210 lbs. Born, Edmonton, Alta., February 16, 1980. Calgary's 2nd choice, 33rd overall, in 1998 Entry Draft.

1995-96	Sherwood Park	AMHL	34	22	19	41	69	....	....	....	....	....	....	....	....	....	....	....	....	....	....	....	....	....	....
1996-97	Prince George	WHL	58	12	18	30	19	....	....	....	....	....	....	....	....	....	15	2	2	4	6	....	....	....	....
1997-98	Prince George	WHL	71	35	41	76	38	....	....	....	....	....	....	....	....	....	11	4	6	10	8	....	....	....	....
1998-99	Prince George	WHL	42	20	22	42	39	....	....	....	....	....	....	....	....	....	7	3	2	5	8	....	....	....	....
99-2000	Prince George	WHL	44	24	35	59	38	....	....	....	....	....	....	....	....	....	13	11	11	22	6	....	....	....	....
2000-01	Saint John Flames	AHL	75	13	15	28	28	....	....	....	....	....	....	....	....	....	19	2	3	5	4	....	....	....	....
2001-02	**Calgary**	**NHL**	**6**	**1**	**0**	**1**	**2**	**0**	**0**	**1**	**4**	**25.0**	**–1**	**39**	**48.7**	**7:05**	....	....	....	....	....	....	....	....	....
	Saint John Flames	AHL	67	20	29	49	10	....	....	....	....	....	....	....	....	....	....	....	....	....	....	....	....	....	....
2002-03	**Calgary**	**NHL**	**9**	**1**	**3**	**4**	**0**	**0**	**0**	**0**	**16**	**6.3**	**3**	**71**	**53.5**	**11:33**	....	....	....	....	....	....	....	....	....
	Saint John Flames	AHL	19	6	7	13	6	....	....	....	....	....	....	....	....	....	....	....	....	....	....	....	....	....	....
2003-04	**Calgary**	**NHL**	**20**	**1**	**2**	**3**	**10**	**1**	**0**	**1**	**21**	**4.8**	**–1**	**248**	**54.0**	**12:46**	....	....	....	....	....	....	....	....	....
2004-05	Hartford	AHL	16	5	4	9	4	....	....	....	....	....	....	....	....	....	....	....	....	....	....	....	....	....	....
2005-06	**NY Rangers**	**NHL**	**66**	**8**	**2**	**10**	**24**	**0**	**1**	**0**	**94**	**8.5**	**–10**	**817**	**53.4**	**12:55**	**4**	**1**	**1**	**2**	**2**	**0**	**0**	**0**	**16:12**
2006-07	**NY Rangers**	**NHL**	**82**	**9**	**4**	**13**	**24**	**1**	**1**	**0**	**120**	**7.5**	**–4**	**1186**	**52.3**	**14:02**	**10**	**0**	**0**	**0**	**4**	**0**	**0**	**0**	**11:15**
2007-08	**NY Rangers**	**NHL**	**75**	**2**	**5**	**7**	**20**	**0**	**0**	**0**	**85**	**2.4**	**–4**	**771**	**50.3**	**11:52**	**8**	**0**	**0**	**0**	**2**	**0**	**0**	**0**	**7:16**
	NHL Totals		**258**	**22**	**16**	**38**	**80**	**2**	**2**	**2**	**340**	**6.5**		**3132**	**52.2**	**12:46**	**22**	**1**	**1**	**2**	**8**	**0**	**0**	**0**	**10:42**

• Missed majority of 2002-03 season recovering from shoulder injury suffered in training camp, September 27, 2002. • Missed majority of 2003-04 season recovering from shoulder injuries suffered in games vs. Chicago (November 22, 2003) and Colorado (December 31, 2003). Traded to **NY Rangers** by **Calgary** with Jamie McLennan and Greg Moore for Chris Simon and NY Rangers' 7th round choice (Matt Schneider) in 2004 Entry Draft, March 6, 2004.

BICKELL, Bryan

(bih-KEHL, BRIGH-uhn) **CHI.**

Left wing. Shoots left. 6'4", 223 lbs. Born, Bowmanville, Ont., March 9, 1986. Chicago's 3rd choice, 41st overall, in 2004 Entry Draft.

2000-01	Tor. Red Wings	GTHL	68	24	26	50	20	....	....	....	....	....	....	....	....	....	5	3	1	4	4	....	....	....	....
2001-02	Tor. Red Wings	GTHL	65	31	41	72	76	....	....	....	....	....	....	....	....	....	2	2	2	4	0	....	....	....	....
2002-03	Ottawa 67's	OHL	50	7	10	17	4	....	....	....	....	....	....	....	....	....	20	5	3	8	12	....	....	....	....
2003-04	Ottawa 67's	OHL	59	20	16	36	76	....	....	....	....	....	....	....	....	....	7	3	0	3	11	....	....	....	....
2004-05	Ottawa 67's	OHL	66	22	32	54	95	....	....	....	....	....	....	....	....	....	21	5	12	17	32	....	....	....	....
2005-06	Ottawa 67's	OHL	41	28	22	50	41	....	....	....	....	....	....	....	....	....	....	....	....	....	....	....	....	....	....
	Windsor Spitfires	OHL	26	17	16	33	19	....	....	....	....	....	....	....	....	....	7	5	5	10	10	....	....	....	....
2006-07	**Chicago**	**NHL**	**3**	**2**	**0**	**2**	**0**	**0**	**0**	**0**	**10**	**20.0**	**1**	**0**	**0.0**	**11:49**	....	....	....	....	....	....	....	....	....
	Norfolk Admirals	AHL	48	10	15	25	66	....	....	....	....	....	....	....	....	....	2	0	0	0	0	....	....	....	....
2007-08	**Chicago**	**NHL**	**4**	**0**	**0**	**0**	**2**	**0**	**0**	**0**	**3**	**0.0**	**–1**	**0**	**0.0**	**9:08**	....	....	....	....	....	....	....	....	....
	Rockford IceHogs	AHL	73	19	20	39	52	....	....	....	....	....	....	....	....	....	12	2	3	5	11	....	....	....	....
	NHL Totals		**7**	**2**	**0**	**2**	**2**	**0**	**0**	**0**	**13**	**15.4**		**0**	**0.0**	**10:17**	....	....	....	....	....	....	....	....	....

BIEKSA, Kevin

(BEEKS-ah, KEH-vihn) **VAN.**

Defense. Shoots right. 6'1", 205 lbs. Born, Grimsby, Ont., June 16, 1981. Vancouver's 4th choice, 151st overall, in 2001 Entry Draft.

1997-98	Burlington	OPJHL	27	0	3	3	10	....	....	....	....	....	....	....	....	....	....	....	....	....	....	....	....	....	....
1998-99	Burlington	OPJHL	49	8	29	37	83	....	....	....	....	....	....	....	....	....	....	....	....	....	....	....	....	....	....
99-2000	Burlington	OPJHL	49	6	27	33	139	....	....	....	....	....	....	....	....	....	....	....	....	....	....	....	....	....	....
2000-01	Bowling Green	CCHA	35	4	9	13	90	....	....	....	....	....	....	....	....	....	....	....	....	....	....	....	....	....	....
2001-02	Bowling Green	CCHA	40	5	10	15	68	....	....	....	....	....	....	....	....	....	....	....	....	....	....	....	....	....	....
2002-03	Bowling Green	CCHA	34	8	17	25	92	....	....	....	....	....	....	....	....	....	....	....	....	....	....	....	....	....	....
2003-04	Bowling Green	CCHA	38	7	15	22	66	....	....	....	....	....	....	....	....	....	....	....	....	....	....	....	....	....	....
	Manitoba Moose	AHL	4	0	2	2	2	....	....	....	....	....	....	....	....	....	....	....	....	....	....	....	....	....	....
2004-05	Manitoba Moose	AHL	80	12	27	39	192	....	....	....	....	....	....	....	....	....	14	1	1	2	52	....	....	....	....
2005-06	**Vancouver**	**NHL**	**39**	**0**	**6**	**6**	**77**	**0**	**0**	**0**	**38**	**0.0**	**–1**	**0**	**0.0**	**16:06**	....	....	....	....	....	....	....	....	....
	Manitoba Moose	AHL	23	3	17	20	71	....	....	....	....	....	....	....	....	....	13	0	10	10	38	....	....	....	....
2006-07	**Vancouver**	**NHL**	**81**	**12**	**30**	**42**	**134**	**6**	**0**	**2**	**203**	**5.9**	**1**	**0**	**0.0**	**24:16**	**9**	**0**	**0**	**0**	**20**	**0**	**0**	**0**	**28:01**
2007-08	**Vancouver**	**NHL**	**34**	**2**	**10**	**12**	**90**	**1**	**0**	**1**	**64**	**3.1**	**–11**	**0**	**0.0**	**23:24**	....	....	....	....	....	....	....	....	....
	Manitoba Moose	AHL	1	0	1	1	2	....	....	....	....	....	....	....	....	....	....	....	....	....	....	....	....	....	....
	NHL Totals		**154**	**14**	**46**	**60**	**301**	**7**	**0**	**3**	**305**	**4.6**		**0**	**0.0**	**22:01**	**9**	**0**	**0**	**0**	**20**	**0**	**0**	**0**	**28:01**

AHL All-Rookie Team (2005)

BIRON, Mathieu

(BEE-rawn, MA-tyew)

Defense. Shoots right. 6'6", 230 lbs. Born, Lac-St-Charles, Que., April 29, 1980. Los Angeles' 1st choice, 21st overall, in 1998 Entry Draft.

			Regular Season														Playoffs								
Season	Club	League	GP	G	A	Pts	PIM	PP	SH	GW	S	%	+/-	TF	F%	Min	GP	G	A	Pts	PIM	PP	SH	GW	Min
1996-97	Ste-Foy	QAAA	40	4	22	26	49	....	....	....	....	....	....	....	....	....	10	3	4	7	....	....	....	....	....
1997-98	Shawinigan	QMJHL	59	8	28	36	60	....	....	....	....	....	....	....	....	....	6	0	1	1	10	....	....	....	....
1998-99	Shawinigan	QMJHL	69	13	32	45	116	....	....	....	....	....	....	....	....	....	6	0	2	2	6	....	....	....	....
99-2000	**NY Islanders**	**NHL**	**60**	**4**	**4**	**8**	**38**	**2**	**0**	**2**	**70**	**5.7**	**–13**	**2**	**0.0**	**15:02**	....	....	....	....	....	....	....	....	....
2000-01	**NY Islanders**	**NHL**	**14**	**0**	**1**	**1**	**12**	**0**	**0**	**0**	**10**	**0.0**	**2**	**0**	**0.0**	**12:21**	....	....	....	....	....	....	....	....	....
	Lowell	AHL	22	1	3	4	17	....	....	....	....	....	....	....	....	....	....	....	....	....	....	....	....	....	....
	Springfield	AHL	34	0	6	6	18	....	....	....	....	....	....	....	....	....	....	....	....	....	....	....	....	....	....
2001-02	**Tampa Bay**	**NHL**	**36**	**0**	**0**	**0**	**12**	**0**	**0**	**0**	**35**	**0.0**	**–16**	**0**	**0.0**	**14:47**	....	....	....	....	....	....	....	....	....
	Springfield	AHL	35	4	9	13	16	....	....	....	....	....	....	....	....	....	....	....	....	....	....	....	....	....	....
2002-03	**Florida**	**NHL**	**34**	**1**	**8**	**9**	**14**	**0**	**1**	**0**	**52**	**1.9**	**–18**	**0**	**0.0**	**21:08**	....	....	....	....	....	....	....	....	....
	San Antonio	AHL	43	3	8	11	58	....	....	....	....	....	....	....	....	....	....	....	....	....	....	....	....	....	....
2003-04	**Florida**	**NHL**	**57**	**3**	**10**	**13**	**51**	**0**	**0**	**1**	**75**	**4.0**	**–13**	**0**	**0.0**	**18:13**	....	....	....	....	....	....	....	....	....
2004-05			DID NOT PLAY																						
2005-06	**Washington**	**NHL**	**52**	**4**	**9**	**13**	**50**	**3**	**0**	**0**	**61**	**6.6**	**–11**	**0**	**0.0**	**12:14**	....	....	....	....	....	....	....	....	....
2006-07	Worcester Sharks	AHL	24	3	15	18	42	....	....	....	....	....	....	....	....	....	....	....	....	....	....	....	....	....	....
	Hamilton	AHL	53	7	14	21	52	....	....	....	....	....	....	....	....	....	22	2	6	8	33	....	....	....	....
2007-08	Hamilton	AHL	35	6	6	12	38	....	....	....	....	....	....	....	....	....	....	....	....	....	....	....	....	....	....
	NHL Totals		**253**	**12**	**32**	**44**	**177**	**5**	**1**	**3**	**303**	**4.0**		**2**	**0.0**	**15:49**	....	....	....	....	....	....	....	....	....

Traded to **NY Islanders** by **Los Angeles** with Olli Jokinen, Josh Green and Los Angeles' 1st round choice (Taylor Pyatt) in 1999 Entry Draft for Ziggy Palffy, Brian Smolinski, Marcel Cousineau and New Jersey's 4th round choice (previously acquired, Los Angeles selected Daniel Johansson) in 1999 Entry Draft, June 20, 1999. Traded to **Tampa Bay** by **NY Islanders** with NY Islanders' 2nd round choice (later traded to Washington – later traded to Vancouver – Vancouver selected Denis Grot) in 2002 Entry Draft for Adrian Aucoin and Alexander Kharitonov, June 22, 2001. Claimed by **Columbus** from **Tampa Bay** in Waiver Draft, October 4, 2002. Traded to **Florida** by **Columbus** for Petr Tenkrat, October 4, 2002. Signed as a free agent by **Washington**, August 10, 2005. Signed as a free agent by **San Jose**, August 9, 2006. Traded to **Montreal** by **San Jose** for Patrick Traverse, December 15, 2006.

BISAILLON, Sebastien

(BIH-sigh-awn, suh-BAS-tee-yeh) **EDM.**

Defense. Shoots right. 6', 205 lbs. Born, Mont-Laurier, Que., December 8, 1986.

Season	Club	League	GP	G	A	Pts	PIM	PP	SH	GW	S	%	+/-	TF	F%	Min	GP	G	A	Pts	PIM	PP	SH	GW	Min
2002-03	Val-d'Or Foreurs	QMJHL	1	0	0	0	0	....	....	....	....	....	....	....	....	....	....	....	....	....	....	....	....	....	....
2003-04	Val-d'Or Foreurs	QMJHL	67	4	14	18	39	....	....	....	....	....	....	....	....	....	7	2	0	2	2	....	....	....	....
2004-05	Val-d'Or Foreurs	QMJHL	69	15	33	48	39	....	....	....	....	....	....	....	....	....	....	....	....	....	....	....	....	....	....
2005-06	Val-d'Or Foreurs	QMJHL	63	35	36	71	56	....	....	....	....	....	....	....	....	....	5	0	4	4	2	....	....	....	....
2006-07	**Edmonton**	**NHL**	**2**	**0**	**0**	**0**	**0**	**0**	**0**	**0**	**3**	**0.0**	**–1**	**0**	**0.0**	**14:12**	....	....	....	....	....	....	....	....	....
	Val-d'Or Foreurs	QMJHL	63	12	40	52	30	....	....	....	....	....	....	....	....	....	20	2	10	12	12	....	....	....	....
2007-08	Springfield	AHL	21	3	7	10	10	....	....	....	....	....	....	....	....	....	....	....	....	....	....	....	....	....	....
	Stockton Thunder	ECHL	7	4	2	6	2	....	....	....	....	....	....	....	....	....	6	0	1	1	2	....	....	....	....
	NHL Totals		**2**	**0**	**0**	**0**	**0**	**0**	**0**	**0**	**3**	**0.0**		**0**	**0.0**	**14:12**	....	....	....	....	....	....	....	....	....

Signed as a free agent by **Edmonton**, September 27, 2006.

BLAKE, Jason

(BLAYK, JAY-suhn) **TOR.**

Center. Shoots left. 5'10", 180 lbs. Born, Moorhead, MN, September 2, 1973.

Season	Club	League	GP	G	A	Pts	PIM	PP	SH	GW	S	%	+/-	TF	F%	Min	GP	G	A	Pts	PIM	PP	SH	GW	Min
1991-92	Moorhead Spuds	High-MN	25	30	30	60	....	....	....	....	....	....	....	....	....	....	....	....	....	....	....	....	....	....	....
1992-93	Waterloo	USHL	45	24	27	51	107	....	....	....	....	....	....	....	....	....	....	....	....	....	....	....	....	....	....
1993-94	Waterloo	USHL	47	50	50	100	76	....	....	....	....	....	....	....	....	....	....	....	....	....	....	....	....	....	....
1994-95	Ferris State	CCHA	36	16	16	32	46	....	....	....	....	....	....	....	....	....	....	....	....	....	....	....	....	....	....
1995-96	North Dakota	WCHA	DID NOT PLAY – TRANSFERRED COLLEGES																						
1996-97	North Dakota	WCHA	43	19	32	51	44	....	....	....	....	....	....	....	....	....	....	....	....	....	....	....	....	....	....
1997-98	North Dakota	WCHA	38	24	27	51	62	....	....	....	....	....	....	....	....	....	....	....	....	....	....	....	....	....	....
1998-99	North Dakota	WCHA	38	*28	*41	*69	49	....	....	....	....	....	....	....	....	....	....	....	....	....	....	....	....	....	....
	Los Angeles	**NHL**	**1**	**1**	**0**	**1**	**0**	**0**	**0**	**0**	**5**	**20.0**	**1**	**14**	**35.7**	**17:13**	....	....	....	....	....	....	....	....	....
	Orlando	IHL	5	3	5	8	6	....	....	....	....	....	....	....	....	....	13	3	4	7	20	....	....	....	....
99-2000	**Los Angeles**	**NHL**	**64**	**5**	**18**	**23**	**26**	**0**	**0**	**1**	**131**	**3.8**	**4**	**269**	**43.9**	**11:17**	**3**	**0**	**0**	**0**	**0**	**0**	**0**	**0**	**9:35**
	Long Beach	IHL	7	3	6	9	2	....	....	....	....	....	....	....	....	....	....	....	....	....	....	....	....	....	....
2000-01	**Los Angeles**	**NHL**	**17**	**1**	**3**	**4**	**10**	**0**	**0**	**0**	**27**	**3.7**	**–8**	**13**	**61.5**	**10:03**	....	....	....	....	....	....	....	....	....
	Lowell	AHL	2	0	1	1	2	....	....	....	....	....	....	....	....	....	....	....	....	....	....	....	....	....	....
	NY Islanders	**NHL**	**30**	**4**	**8**	**12**	**24**	**1**	**1**	**0**	**73**	**5.5**	**–12**	**118**	**44.1**	**15:43**	....	....	....	....	....	....	....	....	....
2001-02	**NY Islanders**	**NHL**	**82**	**8**	**10**	**18**	**36**	**0**	**0**	**1**	**136**	**5.9**	**–11**	**23**	**43.5**	**12:54**	**7**	**0**	**1**	**1**	**13**	**0**	**0**	**0**	**12:13**
2002-03	**NY Islanders**	**NHL**	**81**	**25**	**30**	**55**	**58**	**3**	**1**	**4**	**253**	**9.9**	**16**	**22**	**18.2**	**17:38**	**5**	**0**	**1**	**1**	**2**	**0**	**0**	**0**	**19:39**
2003-04	**NY Islanders**	**NHL**	**75**	**22**	**25**	**47**	**56**	**1**	**4**	**3**	**243**	**9.1**	**11**	**70**	**41.4**	**18:49**	**4**	**2**	**0**	**2**	**2**	**0**	**0**	**0**	**18:09**
2004-05	HC Lugano	Swiss	7	2	2	4	4	....	....	....	....	....	....	....	....	....	....	....	....	....	....	....	....	....	....
2005-06	**NY Islanders**	**NHL**	**76**	**28**	**29**	**57**	**60**	**12**	**2**	**2**	**304**	**9.2**	**0**	**152**	**42.8**	**18:47**	....	....	....	....	....	....	....	....	....
	United States	Olympics	6	0	0	0	2	....	....	....	....	....	....	....	....	....	....	....	....	....	....	....	....	....	....
2006-07	**NY Islanders**	**NHL**	**82**	**40**	**29**	**69**	**34**	**14**	**0**	**7**	**305**	**13.1**	**1**	**117**	**57.3**	**18:09**	**5**	**1**	**2**	**3**	**2**	**0**	**0**	**0**	**17:04**
2007-08	**Toronto**	**NHL**	**82**	**15**	**37**	**52**	**28**	**2**	**0**	**0**	**332**	**4.5**	**–4**	**28**	**50.0**	**17:49**	....	....	....	....	....	....	....	....	....
	NHL Totals		**590**	**149**	**189**	**338**	**332**	**33**	**8**	**18**	**1809**	**8.2**		**826**	**45.0**	**16:22**	**24**	**3**	**4**	**7**	**19**	**0**	**0**	**0**	**15:26**

WCHA First All-Star Team (1997, 1998, 1999) • NCAA West Second All-American Team (1998) • WCHA Player of the Year (1999) • NCAA West First All-American Team (1999) • Bill Masterton Memorial Trophy (2008)

Played in NHL All-Star Game (2007)

Signed as a free agent by **Los Angeles**, April 20, 1999. Traded to **NY Islanders** by **Los Angeles** for NY Islanders' 5th round choice (Joel Andresen) in 2002 Entry Draft, January 3, 2001. Signed as a free agent by **Lugano** (Swiss), December 1, 2004. Signed as a free agent by **Toronto**, July 1, 2007.

BLAKE, Rob

(BLAYK, RAWB) **S.J.**

Defense. Shoots right. 6'4", 225 lbs. Born, Simcoe, Ont., December 10, 1969. Los Angeles' 4th choice, 70th overall, in 1988 Entry Draft.

Season	Club	League	GP	G	A	Pts	PIM	PP	SH	GW	S	%	+/-	TF	F%	Min	GP	G	A	Pts	PIM	PP	SH	GW	Min
1985-86	Brantford Classics	OHA-B	39	3	13	16	43	....	....	....	....	....	....	....	....	....	....	....	....	....	....	....	....	....	....
1986-87	Stratford Cullitons	OHA-B	31	11	20	31	115	....	....	....	....	....	....	....	....	....	....	....	....	....	....	....	....	....	....
1987-88	Bowling Green	CCHA	43	5	8	13	88	....	....	....	....	....	....	....	....	....	....	....	....	....	....	....	....	....	....
1988-89	Bowling Green	CCHA	46	11	21	32	140	....	....	....	....	....	....	....	....	....	....	....	....	....	....	....	....	....	....
1989-90	Bowling Green	CCHA	42	23	36	59	140	....	....	....	....	....	....	....	....	....	....	....	....	....	....	....	....	....	....
	Los Angeles	**NHL**	**4**	**0**	**0**	**0**	**4**	**0**	**0**	**0**	**3**	**0.0**	**0**	....	....	....	**8**	**1**	**3**	**4**	**4**	**1**	**0**	**0**	....
1990-91	**Los Angeles**	**NHL**	**75**	**12**	**34**	**46**	**125**	**9**	**0**	**2**	**150**	**8.0**	**3**	....	....	....	**12**	**1**	**4**	**5**	**26**	**1**	**0**	**0**	....
1991-92	**Los Angeles**	**NHL**	**57**	**7**	**13**	**20**	**102**	**5**	**0**	**0**	**131**	**5.3**	**–5**	....	....	....	**6**	**2**	**1**	**3**	**12**	**0**	**0**	**0**	....
1992-93	**Los Angeles**	**NHL**	**76**	**16**	**43**	**59**	**152**	**10**	**0**	**4**	**243**	**6.6**	**18**	....	....	....	**23**	**4**	**6**	**10**	**46**	**1**	**1**	**0**	....
1993-94	**Los Angeles**	**NHL**	**84**	**20**	**48**	**68**	**137**	**7**	**0**	**6**	**304**	**6.6**	**–7**	....	....	....	....	....	....	....	....	....	....	....	....
1994-95	**Los Angeles**	**NHL**	**24**	**4**	**7**	**11**	**38**	**4**	**0**	**1**	**76**	**5.3**	**–16**	....	....	....	....	....	....	....	....	....	....	....	....
1995-96	**Los Angeles**	**NHL**	**6**	**1**	**2**	**3**	**8**	**0**	**0**	**0**	**13**	**7.7**	**0**	....	....	....	....	....	....	....	....	....	....	....	....
1996-97	**Los Angeles**	**NHL**	**62**	**8**	**23**	**31**	**82**	**4**	**0**	**1**	**169**	**4.7**	**–28**	....	....	....	....	....	....	....	....	....	....	....	....
1997-98	**Los Angeles**	**NHL**	**81**	**23**	**27**	**50**	**94**	**11**	**0**	**4**	**261**	**8.8**	**–3**	....	....	....	**4**	**0**	**0**	**0**	**6**	**0**	**0**	**0**	....
	Canada	Olympics	6	1	1	2	2	....	....	....	....	....	....	....	....	....	....	....	....	....	....	....	....	....	....
1998-99	**Los Angeles**	**NHL**	**62**	**12**	**23**	**35**	**128**	**5**	**1**	**2**	**216**	**5.6**	**–7**	**0**	**0.0**	**24:52**	....	....	....	....	....	....	....	....	....
99-2000	**Los Angeles**	**NHL**	**77**	**18**	**39**	**57**	**112**	**12**	**0**	**5**	**327**	**5.5**	**10**	**0**	**0.0**	**28:30**	**4**	**0**	**2**	**2**	**4**	**0**	**0**	**0**	**30:10**
2000-01	**Los Angeles**	**NHL**	**54**	**17**	**32**	**49**	**69**	**9**	**0**	**1**	**223**	**7.6**	**–8**	**0**	**0.0**	**28:11**	....	....	....	....	....	....	....	....	....
	♦ Colorado	**NHL**	**13**	**2**	**8**	**10**	**8**	**1**	**0**	**1**	**44**	**4.5**	**11**	**0**	**0.0**	**26:03**	**23**	**6**	**13**	**19**	**16**	**3**	**0**	**0**	**29:26**
2001-02	**Colorado**	**NHL**	**75**	**16**	**40**	**56**	**58**	**10**	**0**	**2**	**229**	**7.0**	**16**	**0**	**0.0**	**27:35**	**20**	**6**	**6**	**12**	**16**	**1**	**0**	**0**	**26:38**
	Canada	Olympics	6	1	2	3	2	....	....	....	....	....	....	....	....	....	....	....	....	....	....	....	....	....	....
2002-03	**Colorado**	**NHL**	**79**	**17**	**28**	**45**	**57**	**8**	**2**	**3**	**269**	**6.3**	**20**	**0**	**0.0**	**26:21**	**7**	**1**	**2**	**3**	**8**	**0**	**0**	**0**	**27:28**
2003-04	**Colorado**	**NHL**	**74**	**13**	**33**	**46**	**61**	**8**	**0**	**3**	**242**	**5.4**	**6**	**1**	**0.0**	**24:23**	**9**	**0**	**5**	**5**	**6**	**0**	**0**	**0**	**20:17**
2004-05			DID NOT PLAY																						
2005-06	**Colorado**	**NHL**	**81**	**14**	**37**	**51**	**94**	**7**	**1**	**1**	**264**	**5.3**	**2**	**2**	**0.0**	**24:22**	**9**	**3**	**1**	**4**	**8**	**2**	**0**	**1**	**28:19**
	Canada	Olympics	6	0	1	1	2	....	....	....	....	....	....	....	....	....	....	....	....	....	....	....	....	....	....

			Regular Season														Playoffs								
Season	Club	League	GP	G	A	Pts	PIM	PP	SH	GW	S	%	+/-	TF	F%	Min	GP	G	A	Pts	PIM	PP	SH	GW	Min
2006-07	**Los Angeles**	**NHL**	**72**	**14**	**20**	**34**	**82**	**11**	**0**	**1**	**208**	**6.7**	**–26**	**3**	**33.3**	**24:24**	....	....	....	....	....	....	....	....	....
2007-08	**Los Angeles**	**NHL**	**71**	**9**	**22**	**31**	**98**	**5**	**0**	**2**	**144**	**6.3**	**–19**	**8**	**50.0**	**22:44**	....	....	....	....	....	....	....	....	....
	NHL Totals		**1127**	**223**	**479**	**702**	**1509**	**126**	**4**	**39**	**3516**	**6.3**		**14**	**35.7**	**25:41**	**125**	**24**	**43**	**67**	**152**	**9**	**1**	**1**	**27:13**

CCHA Second All-Star Team (1989) • CCHA First All-Star Team (1990) • NCAA West First All-American Team (1990) • NHL All-Rookie Team (1991) • NHL First All-Star Team (1998) • James Norris Memorial Trophy (1998) • NHL Second All-Star Team (2000, 2001, 2002)

Played in NHL All-Star Game (1994, 1999, 2000, 2001, 2002, 2003, 2004)

• Missed majority of 1995-96 season recovering from knee injury suffered in game vs. Washington, October 20, 1995. Traded to **Colorado** by **Los Angeles** with Steve Reinprecht for Adam Deadmarsh, Aaron Miller, a player to be named later (Jared Aulin, March 22, 2001) and Colorado's 1st round choices in 2001 (Dave Steckel) and 2003 (Brian Boyle) Entry Drafts, February 21, 2001. Signed as a free agent by **Los Angeles**, July 1, 2006. Signed as a free agent by **San Jose**, July 3, 2008.

BLUNDEN, Michael

(BLUHN-dehn, MIGH-kuhl) **CHI.**

Right wing. Shoots right. 6'3", 207 lbs. Born, Toronto, Ont., December 15, 1986. Chicago's 2nd choice, 43rd overall, in 2005 Entry Draft.

2002-03	Erie Otters	OHL	63	10	7	17	55	....	....	....	....	....	....	....	....	....	....	....	....	....	....	....	....	....	....
2003-04	Erie Otters	OHL	52	22	17	39	53	....	....	....	....	....	....	....	....	....	3	0	0	0	0	....	....	....	....
2004-05	Erie Otters	OHL	61	22	19	41	75	....	....	....	....	....	....	....	....	....	2	0	0	0	2	....	....	....	....
2005-06	Erie Otters	OHL	60	46	38	84	63	....	....	....	....	....	....	....	....	....	....	....	....	....	....	....	....	....	....
	Norfolk Admirals	AHL	11	1	5	6	2	....	....	....	....	....	....	....	....	....	1	0	0	0	0	....	....	....	....
2006-07	**Chicago**	**NHL**	**9**	**0**	**0**	**0**	**10**	**0**	**0**	**0**	**10**	**0.0**	**–5**	**1**	**0.0**	**11:23**	....	....	....	....	....	....	....	....	....
	Norfolk Admirals	AHL	17	4	5	9	15	....	....	....	....	....	....	....	....	....	....	....	....	....	....	....	....	....	....
2007-08	**Chicago**	**NHL**	**1**	**0**	**0**	**0**	**0**	**0**	**0**	**0**	**1**	**0.0**	**–1**	**0**	**0.0**	**7:51**	....	....	....	....	....	....	....	....	....
	Rockford IceHogs	AHL	74	16	21	37	83	....	....	....	....	....	....	....	....	....	12	1	3	4	35	....	....	....	....
	NHL Totals		**10**	**0**	**0**	**0**	**10**	**0**	**0**	**0**	**11**	**0.0**		**1**	**0.0**	**11:02**	....	....	....	....	....	....	....	....	....

• Missed majority of 2006-07 season recovering from shoulder injury sufffered in game vs. Hershey (AHL), December 10, 2006.

BOCHENSKI, Brandon

(boh-CHEHN-skee, BRAN-duhn) **T.B.**

Right wing. Shoots right. 6'1", 187 lbs. Born, Blaine, MN, April 4, 1982. Ottawa's 9th choice, 223rd overall, in 2001 Entry Draft.

99-2000	Blaine Bengals	High-MN	28	32	30	62	....	....	....	....	....	....	....	....	....	....	....	....	....	....	....	....	....	....	....
2000-01	Lincoln Stars	USHL	55	*47	33	80	22	....	....	....	....	....	....	....	....	....	11	5	7	12	4	....	....	....	....
2001-02	North Dakota	WCHA	36	17	15	32	36	....	....	....	....	....	....	....	....	....	....	....	....	....	....	....	....	....	....
2002-03	North Dakota	WCHA	43	35	27	62	42	....	....	....	....	....	....	....	....	....	....	....	....	....	....	....	....	....	....
2003-04	North Dakota	WCHA	41	27	33	60	40	....	....	....	....	....	....	....	....	....	....	....	....	....	....	....	....	....	....
2004-05	Binghamton	AHL	75	34	36	70	16	....	....	....	....	....	....	....	....	....	6	1	0	1	2	....	....	....	....
2005-06	**Ottawa**	**NHL**	**20**	**6**	**7**	**13**	**14**	**2**	**0**	**0**	**39**	**15.4**	**7**	**4**	**50.0**	**12:17**	....	....	....	....	....	....	....	....	....
	Binghamton	AHL	33	22	24	46	36	....	....	....	....	....	....	....	....	....	....	....	....	....	....	....	....	....	....
	Chicago	**NHL**	**20**	**2**	**2**	**4**	**8**	**0**	**0**	**0**	**23**	**8.7**	**–9**	**8**	**37.5**	**8:53**	....	....	....	....	....	....	....	....	....
	Norfolk Admirals	AHL	....	....	....	....	....	....	....	....	....	....	....	....	....	....	3	1	1	2	0	....	....	....	....
2006-07	**Chicago**	**NHL**	**10**	**2**	**0**	**2**	**2**	**0**	**0**	**0**	**20**	**10.0**	**–2**	**1**	**0.0**	**9:59**	....	....	....	....	....	....	....	....	....
	Norfolk Admirals	AHL	35	33	33	66	31	....	....	....	....	....	....	....	....	....	....	....	....	....	....	....	....	....	....
	Boston	**NHL**	**31**	**11**	**11**	**22**	**14**	**3**	**0**	**2**	**72**	**15.3**	**3**	**4**	**25.0**	**14:59**	....	....	....	....	....	....	....	....	....
2007-08	**Boston**	**NHL**	**20**	**0**	**6**	**6**	**6**	**0**	**0**	**0**	**30**	**0.0**	**2**	**6**	**33.3**	**12:48**	....	....	....	....	....	....	....	....	....
	Providence Bruins	AHL	2	1	0	1	0	....	....	....	....	....	....	....	....	....	....	....	....	....	....	....	....	....	....
	Anaheim	**NHL**	**12**	**2**	**2**	**4**	**6**	**1**	**0**	**0**	**17**	**11.8**	**2**	**1**	**0.0**	**12:28**	....	....	....	....	....	....	....	....	....
	Nashville	**NHL**	**8**	**1**	**2**	**3**	**0**	**0**	**0**	**0**	**9**	**11.1**	**2**	**0**	**0.0**	**9:01**	**3**	**0**	**0**	**0**	**0**	**0**	**0**	**0**	**6:36**
	NHL Totals		**121**	**24**	**30**	**54**	**50**	**6**	**0**	**2**	**210**	**11.4**		**24**	**33.3**	**12:07**	**3**	**0**	**0**	**0**	**0**	**0**	**0**	**0**	**6:36**

USHL First All-Star Team (2001) • USHL Rookie of the Year (2001) • WCHA All-Rookie Team (2002) • WCHA Rookie of the Year (2002) • WCHA Second All-Star Team (2003) • WCHA First All-Star Team (2004) • NCAA West First All-American Team (2004) • AHL All-Rookie Team (2005)

Traded to **Chicago** by **Ottawa** with Ottawa's 2nd round choice (Simon Danis-Pepin) in 2006 Entry Draft for Tyler Arnason, March 9, 2006. Traded to **Boston** by **Chicago** for Kris Versteeg and future considerations, February 3, 2007. Traded to **Anaheim** by **Boston** for Shane Hnidy and Anaheim's 6th round choice (Nicholas Tremblay) in 2008 Entry Draft, January 2, 2008. Traded to **Nashville** by **Anaheim** for future considerations, February 26, 2008. Signed as a free agent by **Tampa Bay**, July 8, 2008.

BOGUNIECKI, Eric

(BOH-guhn-ih-kee, AIR-ihk) **ANA.**

Center. Shoots right. 5'8", 192 lbs. Born, New Haven, CT, May 6, 1975. St. Louis' 6th choice, 193rd overall, in 1993 Entry Draft.

1992-93	Westminster	High-CT	24	30	24	54	55	....	....	....	....	....	....	....	....	....	....	....	....	....	....	....	....	....	....
1993-94	New Hampshire	H-East	40	17	16	33	66	....	....	....	....	....	....	....	....	....	....	....	....	....	....	....	....	....	....
1994-95	New Hampshire	H-East	34	12	16	28	62	....	....	....	....	....	....	....	....	....	....	....	....	....	....	....	....	....	....
1995-96	New Hampshire	H-East	32	23	28	51	46	....	....	....	....	....	....	....	....	....	....	....	....	....	....	....	....	....	....
1996-97	New Hampshire	H-East	36	26	31	57	58	....	....	....	....	....	....	....	....	....	....	....	....	....	....	....	....	....	....
1997-98	Dayton Bombers	ECHL	26	19	18	37	36	....	....	....	....	....	....	....	....	....	....	....	....	....	....	....	....	....	....
	Fort Wayne	IHL	35	4	8	12	29	....	....	....	....	....	....	....	....	....	4	1	2	3	10	....	....	....	....
1998-99	Fort Wayne	IHL	72	32	34	66	100	....	....	....	....	....	....	....	....	....	2	0	1	1	2	....	....	....	....
99-2000	**Florida**	**NHL**	**4**	**0**	**0**	**0**	**2**	**0**	**0**	**0**	**5**	**0.0**	**–1**	**25**	**36.0**	**8:35**	....	....	....	....	....	....	....	....	....
	Louisville Panthers	AHL	57	33	42	75	148	....	....	....	....	....	....	....	....	....	4	3	2	5	20	....	....	....	....
2000-01	Louisville Panthers	AHL	28	13	12	25	56	....	....	....	....	....	....	....	....	....	....	....	....	....	....	....	....	....	....
	St. Louis	**NHL**	**1**	**0**	**0**	**0**	**0**	**0**	**0**	**0**	**1**	**0.0**	**–1**	**0**	**0.0**	**13:44**	....	....	....	....	....	....	....	....	....
	Worcester IceCats	AHL	45	17	28	45	100	....	....	....	....	....	....	....	....	....	9	3	2	5	10	....	....	....	....
2001-02	**St. Louis**	**NHL**	**8**	**0**	**1**	**1**	**4**	**0**	**0**	**0**	**10**	**0.0**	**–2**	**21**	**38.1**	**11:42**	**1**	**0**	**1**	**1**	**0**	**0**	**0**	**0**	**8:01**
	Worcester IceCats	AHL	63	*38	46	84	181	....	....	....	....	....	....	....	....	....	3	2	0	2	4	....	....	....	....
2002-03	**St. Louis**	**NHL**	**80**	**22**	**27**	**49**	**38**	**3**	**1**	**5**	**117**	**18.8**	**22**	**5**	**40.0**	**14:00**	**7**	**1**	**2**	**3**	**2**	**1**	**0**	**0**	**13:09**
2003-04	**St. Louis**	**NHL**	**27**	**6**	**4**	**10**	**20**	**2**	**0**	**2**	**40**	**15.0**	**–1**	**1**	**0.0**	**14:42**	**1**	**0**	**0**	**0**	**0**	**0**	**0**	**0**	**12:52**
	Worcester IceCats	AHL	3	0	1	1	0	....	....	....	....	....	....	....	....	....	....	....	....	....	....	....	....	....	....
2004-05	Worcester IceCats	AHL	30	14	11	25	46	....	....	....	....	....	....	....	....	....	....	....	....	....	....	....	....	....	....
	SC Langenthal	Swiss-2	10	5	3	8	47	....	....	....	....	....	....	....	....	....	....	....	....	....	....	....	....	....	....
2005-06	**St. Louis**	**NHL**	**9**	**1**	**4**	**5**	**4**	**1**	**0**	**0**	**12**	**8.3**	**–1**	**1**	**100.0**	**12:15**	....	....	....	....	....	....	....	....	....
	Peoria Rivermen	AHL	2	0	0	0	4	....	....	....	....	....	....	....	....	....	....	....	....	....	....	....	....	....	....
	Pittsburgh	**NHL**	**38**	**5**	**6**	**11**	**29**	**1**	**0**	**0**	**36**	**13.9**	**–2**	**74**	**48.7**	**10:50**	....	....	....	....	....	....	....	....	....
2006-07	Syracuse Crunch	AHL	6	0	0	0	8	....	....	....	....	....	....	....	....	....	....	....	....	....	....	....	....	....	....
	NY Islanders	**NHL**	**11**	**0**	**0**	**0**	**8**	**0**	**0**	**0**	**2**	**0.0**	**0**	**0**	**0.0**	**4:54**	....	....	....	....	....	....	....	....	....
	Bridgeport	AHL	48	22	32	54	48	....	....	....	....	....	....	....	....	....	....	....	....	....	....	....	....	....	....
2007-08	ERC Ingolstadt	Germany	16	4	14	18	24	....	....	....	....	....	....	....	....	....	3	1	3	4	2	....	....	....	....
	NHL Totals		**178**	**34**	**42**	**76**	**105**	**7**	**1**	**7**	**223**	**15.2**		**127**	**44.1**	**12:33**	**9**	**1**	**3**	**4**	**2**	**1**	**0**	**0**	**12:33**

Hockey East Second All-Star Team (1997) • AHL First All-Star Team (2002) • Les Cunningham Award (MVP – AHL) (2002)

Signed as a free agent by **Florida**, July 7, 1999. Traded to **St. Louis** by **Florida** for Andrei Podkonicky, December 17, 2000. • Missed majority of 2003-04 season recovering from shoulder (September 23, 2003 in training camp) and head (February 28, 2004 vs. Vancouver) injuries. Signed as a free agent by **Langenthal** (Swiss-2), October 4, 2004. Traded to **Pittsburgh** by **St. Louis** for Steve Poapst, December 9, 2005. Signed as a free agent by **Columbus**, August 22, 2006. Traded to **NY Islanders** by **Columbus** for Ryan Caldwell, October 25, 2006. Signed as a free agent by **Ingolstadt** (Germany), June 29, 2007. Signed as a free agent by **Anaheim**, July 22, 2008.

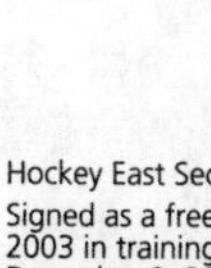

BOIS, Danny

(BOIZ, DA-nee) **OTT.**

Right wing. Shoots right. 6'1", 202 lbs. Born, Thunder Bay, Ont., June 1, 1983. Colorado's 2nd choice, 97th overall, in 2001 Entry Draft.

1998-99	T. Bay Kings	TBMHL	15	7	12	19	28	....	....	....	....	....	....	....	....	....	....	....	....	....	....	....	....	....	....
99-2000	Wellington Dukes	OPJHL	37	15	20	35	115	....	....	....	....	....	....	....	....	....	....	....	....	....	....	....	....	....	....
2000-01	London Knights	OHL	66	21	16	37	218	....	....	....	....	....	....	....	....	....	5	2	1	3	19	....	....	....	....
2001-02	London Knights	OHL	62	16	14	30	256	....	....	....	....	....	....	....	....	....	12	2	2	4	47	....	....	....	....
2002-03	London Knights	OHL	56	19	13	32	207	....	....	....	....	....	....	....	....	....	13	4	6	10	38	....	....	....	....
2003-04	London Knights	OHL	52	14	25	39	242	....	....	....	....	....	....	....	....	....	7	4	4	8	29	....	....	....	....
2004-05	Binghamton	AHL	72	2	4	6	287	....	....	....	....	....	....	....	....	....	6	0	1	1	2	....	....	....	....
2005-06	Binghamton	AHL	79	18	17	35	224	....	....	....	....	....	....	....	....	....	....	....	....	....	....	....	....	....	....
2006-07	**Ottawa**	**NHL**	**1**	**0**	**0**	**0**	**7**	**0**	**0**	**0**	**1**	**0.0**	**0**	**2**	**50.0**	**3:53**	....	....	....	....	....	....	....	....	....
	Binghamton	AHL	65	14	13	27	153	....	....	....	....	....	....	....	....	....	....	....	....	....	....	....	....	....	....
2007-08	Binghamton	AHL	54	8	13	21	153	....	....	....	....	....	....	....	....	....	....	....	....	....	....	....	....	....	....
	NHL Totals		**1**	**0**	**0**	**0**	**7**	**0**	**0**	**0**	**1**	**0.0**		**2**	**50.0**	**3:53**	....	....	....	....	....	....	....	....	....

Signed as a free agent by **Ottawa**, April 30, 2004.

BOLL, Jared

(BAWL, JAIR-ehd) **CBJ**

Right wing. Shoots right. 6'2", 206 lbs. Born, Crystal Lake, IL, May 13, 1986. Columbus' 4th choice, 101st overall, in 2005 Entry Draft.

			Regular Season														Playoffs								
Season	Club	League	GP	G	A	Pts	PIM	PP	SH	GW	S	%	+/-	TF	F%	Min	GP	G	A	Pts	PIM	PP	SH	GW	Min
2003-04	Lincoln Stars	USHL	57	6	8	14	*176	....	....	....	....	....	....	....	....	....	....	....	....	....	....	....	....	....	....
2004-05	Lincoln Stars	USHL	59	23	24	47	*294	....	....	....	....	....	....	....	....	....	4	1	3	4	25	....	....	....	....
2005-06	Plymouth Whalers	OHL	65	19	22	41	205	....	....	....	....	....	....	....	....	....	13	2	4	6	21	....	....	....	....
2006-07	Plymouth Whalers	OHL	66	28	27	55	198	....	....	....	....	....	....	....	....	....	20	6	4	10	*66	....	....	....	....
2007-08	**Columbus**	**NHL**	**75**	**5**	**5**	**10**	**226**	**0**	**0**	**3**	**63**	**7.9**	**–4**	**6**	**33.3**	**8:01**	....	....	....	....	....	....	....	....	....
	NHL Totals		**75**	**5**	**5**	**10**	**226**	**0**	**0**	**3**	**63**	**7.9**		**6**	**33.3**	**8:01**	....	....	....	....	....	....	....	....	....

BOLLAND, Dave

(BOHL-uhnd, DAYV) **CHI.**

Center. Shoots right. 6', 176 lbs. Born, Toronto, Ont., June 5, 1986. Chicago's 2nd choice, 32nd overall, in 2004 Entry Draft.

			Regular Season														Playoffs								
Season	Club	League	GP	G	A	Pts	PIM	PP	SH	GW	S	%	+/-	TF	F%	Min	GP	G	A	Pts	PIM	PP	SH	GW	Min
2000-01	Tor. Red Wings	GTHL	95	79	67	146	....	....	....	....	....	....	....	....	....	....	....	....	....	....	....	....	....	....	....
2001-02	Tor. Red Wings	GTHL	36	35	35	70	40	....	....	....	....	....	....	....	....	....	....	....	....	....	....	....	....	....	....
2002-03	London Knights	OHL	64	7	10	17	21	....	....	....	....	....	....	....	....	....	14	2	1	3	2	....	....	....	....
2003-04	London Knights	OHL	65	37	30	67	58	....	....	....	....	....	....	....	....	....	15	3	10	13	18	....	....	....	....
2004-05	London Knights	OHL	66	34	51	85	97	....	....	....	....	....	....	....	....	....	18	11	14	25	30	....	....	....	....
2005-06	London Knights	OHL	59	*57	73	130	104	....	....	....	....	....	....	....	....	....	15	*15	9	24	41	....	....	....	....
2006-07	**Chicago**	**NHL**	**1**	**0**	**0**	**0**	**0**	**0**	**0**	**0**	**1**	**0.0**	**–1**	**11**	**36.4**	**11:17**	....	....	....	....	....	....	....	....	....
	Norfolk Admirals	AHL	65	17	32	49	53	....	....	....	....	....	....	....	....	....	6	0	4	4	17	....	....	....	....
2007-08	**Chicago**	**NHL**	**39**	**4**	**13**	**17**	**28**	**0**	**0**	**0**	**49**	**8.2**	**6**	**385**	**46.5**	**13:43**	....	....	....	....	....	....	....	....	....
	Rockford IceHogs	AHL	16	6	4	10	22	....	....	....	....	....	....	....	....	....	7	0	0	0	8	....	....	....	....
	NHL Totals		**40**	**4**	**13**	**17**	**28**	**0**	**0**	**0**	**50**	**8.0**		**396**	**46.2**	**13:39**	....	....	....	....	....	....	....	....	....

OHL First All-Star Team (2006)

BONK, Radek

(BOHNK, RA-dehk) **NSH.**

Center. Shoots left. 6'3", 213 lbs. Born, Krnov, Czech., January 9, 1976. Ottawa's 1st choice, 3rd overall, in 1994 Entry Draft.

			Regular Season														Playoffs								
Season	Club	League	GP	G	A	Pts	PIM	PP	SH	GW	S	%	+/-	TF	F%	Min	GP	G	A	Pts	PIM	PP	SH	GW	Min
1990-91	Opava Jr.	Czech-Jr.	35	47	42	89	25	....	....	....	....	....	....	....	....	....	....	....	....	....	....	....	....	....	....
1991-92	AC ZPS Zlin Jr.	Czech-Jr.	45	47	36	83	30	....	....	....	....	....	....	....	....	....	....	....	....	....	....	....	....	....	....
1992-93	AC ZPS Zlin	Czech	30	5	5	10	10	....	....	....	....	....	....	....	....	....	....	....	....	....	....	....	....	....	....
1993-94	Las Vegas	IHL	76	42	45	87	208	....	....	....	....	....	....	....	....	....	5	1	2	3	10	....	....	....	....
1994-95	Las Vegas	IHL	33	7	13	20	62	....	....	....	....	....	....	....	....	....	....	....	....	....	....	....	....	....	....
	Ottawa	**NHL**	**42**	**3**	**8**	**11**	**28**	**1**	**0**	**0**	**40**	**7.5**	**–5**	....	....	....	....	....	....	....	....	....	....	....	....
	P.E.I. Senators	AHL	....	....	....	....	....	....	....	....	....	....	....	....	....	....	1	0	0	0	0	....	....	....	....
1995-96	**Ottawa**	**NHL**	**76**	**16**	**19**	**35**	**36**	**5**	**0**	**1**	**161**	**9.9**	**–5**	....	....	....	....	....	....	....	....	....	....	....	....
1996-97	**Ottawa**	**NHL**	**53**	**5**	**13**	**18**	**14**	**0**	**1**	**0**	**82**	**6.1**	**–4**	....	....	....	**7**	**0**	**1**	**1**	**4**	**0**	**0**	**0**	....
1997-98	**Ottawa**	**NHL**	**65**	**7**	**9**	**16**	**16**	**1**	**0**	**0**	**93**	**7.5**	**–13**	....	....	....	**5**	**0**	**0**	**0**	**2**	**0**	**0**	**0**	....
1998-99	**Ottawa**	**NHL**	**81**	**16**	**16**	**32**	**48**	**0**	**1**	**6**	**110**	**14.5**	**15**	**1184**	**50.1**	**13:44**	**4**	**0**	**0**	**0**	**6**	**0**	**0**	**0**	**16:16**
99-2000	Pardubice	CzRep	3	1	0	1	4	....	....	....	....	....	....	....	....	....	....	....	....	....	....	....	....	....	....
	Ottawa	**NHL**	**80**	**23**	**37**	**60**	**53**	**10**	**0**	**5**	**167**	**13.8**	**–2**	**1654**	**52.0**	**18:14**	**6**	**0**	**0**	**0**	**8**	**0**	**0**	**0**	**15:37**
2000-01	**Ottawa**	**NHL**	**74**	**23**	**36**	**59**	**52**	**5**	**2**	**3**	**139**	**16.5**	**27**	**1506**	**51.2**	**18:16**	**2**	**0**	**0**	**0**	**2**	**0**	**0**	**0**	**14:32**
2001-02	**Ottawa**	**NHL**	**82**	**25**	**45**	**70**	**52**	**6**	**2**	**5**	**170**	**14.7**	**3**	**1530**	**51.0**	**17:57**	**12**	**3**	**7**	**10**	**6**	**2**	**0**	**1**	**18:53**
2002-03	**Ottawa**	**NHL**	**70**	**22**	**32**	**54**	**36**	**11**	**0**	**4**	**146**	**15.1**	**6**	**1218**	**46.2**	**17:32**	**18**	**6**	**5**	**11**	**10**	**2**	**0**	**0**	**17:43**
2003-04	**Ottawa**	**NHL**	**66**	**12**	**32**	**44**	**66**	**6**	**0**	**1**	**98**	**12.2**	**2**	**1184**	**44.9**	**17:38**	**7**	**0**	**2**	**2**	**0**	**0**	**0**	**0**	**18:29**
2004-05	HC Ocelari Trinec	CzRep	27	6	10	16	44	....	....	....	....	....	....	....	....	....	....	....	....	....	....	....	....	....	....
	HC Hame Zlin	CzRep	6	3	2	5	4	....	....	....	....	....	....	....	....	....	6	0	2	2	8	....	....	....	....
2005-06	**Montreal**	**NHL**	**61**	**6**	**15**	**21**	**52**	**0**	**2**	**1**	**76**	**7.9**	**–3**	**963**	**47.4**	**15:10**	**6**	**2**	**0**	**2**	**2**	**0**	**0**	**1**	**15:36**
2006-07	**Montreal**	**NHL**	**74**	**13**	**10**	**23**	**54**	**1**	**2**	**1**	**111**	**11.7**	**0**	**1198**	**49.8**	**15:52**	....	....	....	....	....	....	....	....	....
2007-08	**Nashville**	**NHL**	**79**	**14**	**15**	**29**	**40**	**6**	**0**	**1**	**138**	**10.1**	**–31**	**879**	**52.0**	**15:56**	**6**	**1**	**0**	**1**	**2**	**0**	**0**	**0**	**17:56**
	NHL Totals		**903**	**185**	**287**	**472**	**547**	**52**	**10**	**28**	**1531**	**12.1**		**11316**	**49.6**	**16:42**	**73**	**12**	**15**	**27**	**42**	**4**	**0**	**2**	**17:26**

Garry F. Longman Memorial Trophy (Rookie of the Year – IHL) (1994)

Played in NHL All-Star Game (2000, 2001)

Traded to **Los Angeles** by **Ottawa** for Los Angeles' 3rd round choice (Shawn Weller) in 2004 Entry Draft, June 26, 2004. Traded to **Montreal** by **Los Angeles** with Cristobal Huet for Mathieu Garon and San Jose's 3rd round choice (previously acquired, Los Angeles selected Paul Baier) in 2004 Entry Draft, June 26, 2004. Signed as a free agent by **Trinec** (CzRep), September 17, 2004. Signed as a free agent by **Zlin** (CzRep), January 31, 2005. Signed as a free agent by **Nashville**, July 2, 2007.

BOOGAARD, Derek

(BOO-gard, DAIR-ihk) **MIN.**

Left wing. Shoots right. 6'7", 258 lbs. Born, Saskatoon, Sask., June 23, 1982. Minnesota's 6th choice, 202nd overall, in 2001 Entry Draft.

			Regular Season														Playoffs								
Season	Club	League	GP	G	A	Pts	PIM	PP	SH	GW	S	%	+/-	TF	F%	Min	GP	G	A	Pts	PIM	PP	SH	GW	Min
1998-99	Regina Caps	SJHL	35	2	3	5	166	....	....	....	....	....	....	....	....	....	....	....	....	....	....	....	....	....	....
99-2000	Regina Pats	WHL	5	0	0	0	17	....	....	....	....	....	....	....	....	....	....	....	....	....	....	....	....	....	....
	Prince George	WHL	33	0	0	0	149	....	....	....	....	....	....	....	....	....	....	....	....	....	....	....	....	....	....
2000-01	Prince George	WHL	61	1	8	9	245	....	....	....	....	....	....	....	....	....	6	1	0	1	31	....	....	....	....
2001-02	Prince George	WHL	2	0	0	0	16	....	....	....	....	....	....	....	....	....	....	....	....	....	....	....	....	....	....
	Medicine Hat	WHL	46	1	8	9	178	....	....	....	....	....	....	....	....	....	....	....	....	....	....	....	....	....	....
2002-03	Medicine Hat	WHL	27	1	2	3	65	....	....	....	....	....	....	....	....	....	....	....	....	....	....	....	....	....	....
	Louisiana	ECHL	33	1	2	3	240	....	....	....	....	....	....	....	....	....	2	0	0	0	0	....	....	....	....
2003-04	Houston Aeros	AHL	53	0	4	4	207	....	....	....	....	....	....	....	....	....	2	0	1	1	16	....	....	....	....
2004-05	Houston Aeros	AHL	56	1	4	5	259	....	....	....	....	....	....	....	....	....	5	0	0	0	38	....	....	....	....
2005-06	**Minnesota**	**NHL**	**65**	**2**	**4**	**6**	**158**	**0**	**0**	**1**	**15**	**13.3**	**2**	**0**	**0.0**	**5:23**	....	....	....	....	....	....	....	....	....
2006-07	**Minnesota**	**NHL**	**48**	**0**	**1**	**1**	**120**	**0**	**0**	**0**	**11**	**0.0**	**0**	**0**	**0.0**	**4:38**	**4**	**0**	**1**	**1**	**20**	**0**	**0**	**0**	**5:59**
2007-08	**Minnesota**	**NHL**	**34**	**0**	**0**	**0**	**74**	**0**	**0**	**0**	**6**	**0.0**	**–5**	**0**	**0.0**	**3:56**	**6**	**0**	**0**	**0**	**24**	**0**	**0**	**0**	**4:48**
	NHL Totals		**147**	**2**	**5**	**7**	**352**	**0**	**0**	**1**	**32**	**6.3**		**0**	**0.0**	**4:48**	**10**	**0**	**1**	**1**	**44**	**0**	**0**	**0**	**5:16**

BOOTH, David

(BOOTH, DAY-vihd) **FLA.**

Left wing. Shoots left. 6', 212 lbs. Born, Detroit, MI, November 24, 1984. Florida's 3rd choice, 53rd overall, in 2004 Entry Draft.

			Regular Season														Playoffs								
Season	Club	League	GP	G	A	Pts	PIM	PP	SH	GW	S	%	+/-	TF	F%	Min	GP	G	A	Pts	PIM	PP	SH	GW	Min
2000-01	Det. Compuware	NAHL	42	17	13	30	44	....	....	....	....	....	....	....	....	....	2	1	0	1	2	....	....	....	....
2001-02	USNTDP	U-18	40	12	6	18	17	....	....	....	....	....	....	....	....	....	....	....	....	....	....	....	....	....	....
	USNTDP	USHL	12	4	3	7	6	....	....	....	....	....	....	....	....	....	....	....	....	....	....	....	....	....	....
	USNTDP	NAHL	6	1	3	4	18	....	....	....	....	....	....	....	....	....	....	....	....	....	....	....	....	....	....
2002-03	Michigan State	CCHA	39	17	19	36	53	....	....	....	....	....	....	....	....	....	....	....	....	....	....	....	....	....	....
2003-04	Michigan State	CCHA	30	8	10	18	30	....	....	....	....	....	....	....	....	....	....	....	....	....	....	....	....	....	....
2004-05	Michigan State	CCHA	29	7	9	16	30	....	....	....	....	....	....	....	....	....	....	....	....	....	....	....	....	....	....
2005-06	Michigan State	CCHA	37	13	22	35	50	....	....	....	....	....	....	....	....	....	....	....	....	....	....	....	....	....	....
2006-07	**Florida**	**NHL**	**48**	**3**	**7**	**10**	**12**	**0**	**0**	**1**	**86**	**3.5**	**0**	**11**	**36.4**	**9:34**	....	....	....	....	....	....	....	....	....
	Rochester	AHL	25	7	7	14	26	....	....	....	....	....	....	....	....	....	6	0	2	2	4	....	....	....	....
2007-08	**Florida**	**NHL**	**73**	**22**	**18**	**40**	**26**	**1**	**0**	**6**	**228**	**9.6**	**13**	**38**	**34.2**	**16:10**	....	....	....	....	....	....	....	....	....
	NHL Totals		**121**	**25**	**25**	**50**	**38**	**1**	**0**	**7**	**314**	**8.0**		**49**	**34.7**	**13:33**	....	....	....	....	....	....	....	....	....

CCHA All-Rookie Team (2003)

BOOTLAND, Darryl

(BOOT-land, DAIR-uhl)

Right wing. Shoots right. 6'1", 197 lbs. Born, Toronto, Ont., November 2, 1981. Colorado's 12th choice, 252nd overall, in 2000 Entry Draft.

			Regular Season														Playoffs								
Season	Club	League	GP	G	A	Pts	PIM	PP	SH	GW	S	%	+/-	TF	F%	Min	GP	G	A	Pts	PIM	PP	SH	GW	Min
1997-98	Orangeville	OHA-B	44	22	26	48	177	....	....	....	....	....	....	....	....	....	....	....	....	....	....	....	....	....	....
1998-99	Barrie Colts	OHL	38	18	11	29	89	....	....	....	....	....	....	....	....	....	....	....	....	....	....	....	....	....	....
	St. Michael's	OHL	28	12	6	18	80	....	....	....	....	....	....	....	....	....	....	....	....	....	....	....	....	....	....
99-2000	St. Michael's	OHL	65	24	30	54	166	....	....	....	....	....	....	....	....	....	....	....	....	....	....	....	....	....	....
2000-01	St. Michael's	OHL	56	32	33	65	136	....	....	....	....	....	....	....	....	....	11	3	1	4	20	....	....	....	....
2001-02	St. Michael's	OHL	61	41	56	97	137	....	....	....	....	....	....	....	....	....	15	8	10	18	50	....	....	....	....
2002-03	Toledo Storm	ECHL	54	17	19	36	322	....	....	....	....	....	....	....	....	....	....	....	....	....	....	....	....	....	....
	Grand Rapids	AHL	16	1	4	5	41	....	....	....	....	....	....	....	....	....	15	3	2	5	46	....	....	....	....
2003-04	**Detroit**	**NHL**	**22**	**1**	**1**	**2**	**74**	**0**	**0**	**1**	**13**	**7.7**	**–3**	**1**	**100.0**	**6:07**	....	....	....	....	....	....	....	....	....
	Grand Rapids	AHL	54	12	2	14	175	....	....	....	....	....	....	....	....	....	4	0	1	1	2	....	....	....	....
2004-05	Grand Rapids	AHL	78	14	20	34	336	....	....	....	....	....	....	....	....	....	....	....	....	....	....	....	....	....	....
2005-06	Grand Rapids	AHL	77	27	29	56	392	....	....	....	....	....	....	....	....	....	16	5	7	12	50	....	....	....	....

			Regular Season														Playoffs								
Season	Club	League	GP	G	A	Pts	PIM	PP	SH	GW	S	%	+/-	TF	F%	Min	GP	G	A	Pts	PIM	PP	SH	GW	Min
2006-07	**Detroit**	**NHL**	**6**	**0**	**0**	**0**	**9**	**0**	**0**	**0**	**4**	**0.0**	**0**	**2**	**100.0**	**4:08**	....	....	....	....	....	....	....	....	....
	Grand Rapids	AHL	68	18	13	31	222	....	....	....	....	....	....	....	....	....	6	1	0	1	32	....	....	....	....
2007-08	**NY Islanders**	**NHL**	**4**	**0**	**1**	**1**	**2**	**0**	**0**	**0**	**3**	**0.0**	**0**	**0**	**0.0**	**4:42**	....	....	....	....	....	....	....	....	....
	Bridgeport	AHL	28	2	8	10	93	....	....	....	....	....	....	....	....	....	....	....	....	....	....	....	....	....	....
	Portland Pirates	AHL	35	2	5	7	132	....	....	....	....	....	....	....	....	....	16	1	1	2	21	....	....	....	....
	NHL Totals		**32**	**1**	**2**	**3**	**85**	**0**	**0**	**1**	**20**	**5.0**		**3**	**100.0**	**5:34**	....	....	....	....	....	....	....	....	....

Signed as a free agent by **Detroit**, July 25, 2002. Signed as a free agent by **NY Islanders**, July 9, 2007. Traded to **Anaheim** by **NY Islanders** for Matt Keith, January 9, 2008.

BORER, Casey

(BOHR-uhr, KAY-see) **CAR.**

Defense. Shoots left. 6'2", 205 lbs. Born, Minneapolis, MN, July 28, 1985. Carolina's 3rd choice, 69th overall, in 2004 Entry Draft.

Season	Club	League	GP	G	A	Pts	PIM	PP	SH	GW	S	%	+/-	TF	F%	Min	GP	G	A	Pts	PIM	PP	SH	GW	Min
2002-03	USNTDP	U-18	46	2	2	4	36	....	....	....	....	....	....	....	....	....	....	....	....	....	....	....	....	....	....
	USNTDP	NAHL	10	1	2	3	10	....	....	....	....	....	....	....	....	....	....	....	....	....	....	....	....	....	....
2003-04	St. Cloud State	WCHA	31	0	8	8	18	....	....	....	....	....	....	....	....	....	....	....	....	....	....	....	....	....	....
2004-05	St. Cloud State	WCHA	35	0	11	11	40	....	....	....	....	....	....	....	....	....	....	....	....	....	....	....	....	....	....
2005-06	St. Cloud State	WCHA	42	3	8	11	24	....	....	....	....	....	....	....	....	....	....	....	....	....	....	....	....	....	....
2006-07	St. Cloud State	WCHA	40	2	9	11	30	....	....	....	....	....	....	....	....	....	....	....	....	....	....	....	....	....	....
	Albany River Rats	AHL	1	0	0	0	0	....	....	....	....	....	....	....	....	....	....	....	....	....	....	....	....	....	....
2007-08	**Carolina**	**NHL**	**11**	**1**	**2**	**3**	**4**	**0**	**0**	**0**	**5**	**20.0**	**–3**	**0**	**0.0**	**15:17**	....	....	....	....	....	....	....	....	....
	Albany River Rats	AHL	61	6	13	19	58	....	....	....	....	....	....	....	....	....	....	....	....	....	....	....	....	....	....
	NHL Totals		**11**	**1**	**2**	**3**	**4**	**0**	**0**	**0**	**5**	**20.0**		**0**	**0.0**	**15:17**	....	....	....	....	....	....	....	....	....

BOUCHARD, Joel

(BOO-shahrd, JOHL)

Defense. Shoots left. 6'1", 209 lbs. Born, Montreal, Que., January 23, 1974. Calgary's 7th choice, 129th overall, in 1992 Entry Draft.

Season	Club	League	GP	G	A	Pts	PIM	PP	SH	GW	S	%	+/-	TF	F%	Min	GP	G	A	Pts	PIM	PP	SH	GW	Min
1989-90	Mtl-Bourassa	QAAA	41	7	17	24	10	....	....	....	....	....	....	....	....	....	1	1	0	1	0	....	....	....	....
1990-91	Longueuil	QMJHL	53	3	19	22	34	....	....	....	....	....	....	....	....	....	8	1	0	1	11	....	....	....	....
1991-92	Verdun	QMJHL	70	9	20	29	55	....	....	....	....	....	....	....	....	....	19	1	7	8	20	....	....	....	....
1992-93	Verdun	QMJHL	60	10	49	59	126	....	....	....	....	....	....	....	....	....	4	0	2	2	4	....	....	....	....
1993-94	Verdun	QMJHL	60	15	55	70	62	....	....	....	....	....	....	....	....	....	4	1	0	1	6	....	....	....	....
	Saint John Flames	AHL	1	0	0	0	0	....	....	....	....	....	....	....	....	....	2	0	0	0	0	....	....	....	....
1994-95	Saint John Flames	AHL	77	6	25	31	63	....	....	....	....	....	....	....	....	....	5	1	0	1	4	....	....	....	....
	Calgary	**NHL**	**2**	**0**	**0**	**0**	**0**	**0**	**0**	**0**	**0**	**0.0**	**0**	....	....	....	....	....	....	....	....	....	....	....	....
1995-96	**Calgary**	**NHL**	**4**	**0**	**0**	**0**	**4**	**0**	**0**	**0**	**0**	**0.0**	**0**	....	....	....	....	....	....	....	....	....	....	....	....
	Saint John Flames	AHL	74	8	25	33	104	....	....	....	....	....	....	....	....	....	16	1	4	5	10	....	....	....	....
1996-97	**Calgary**	**NHL**	**76**	**4**	**5**	**9**	**49**	**0**	**1**	**0**	**61**	**6.6**	**–23**	....	....	....	....	....	....	....	....	....	....	....	....
1997-98	**Calgary**	**NHL**	**44**	**5**	**7**	**12**	**57**	**0**	**1**	**1**	**51**	**9.8**	**0**	....	....	....	....	....	....	....	....	....	....	....	....
	Saint John Flames	AHL	3	2	1	3	6	....	....	....	....	....	....	....	....	....	....	....	....	....	....	....	....	....	....
1998-99	**Nashville**	**NHL**	**64**	**4**	**11**	**15**	**60**	**0**	**0**	**0**	**78**	**5.1**	**–10**	**0**	**0.0**	**22:34**	....	....	....	....	....	....	....	....	....
99-2000	**Nashville**	**NHL**	**52**	**1**	**4**	**5**	**23**	**0**	**0**	**0**	**60**	**1.7**	**–11**	**0**	**0.0**	**18:41**	....	....	....	....	....	....	....	....	....
	Dallas	**NHL**	**2**	**0**	**0**	**0**	**2**	**0**	**0**	**0**	**1**	**0.0**	**1**	**0**	**0.0**	**9:45**	....	....	....	....	....	....	....	....	....
2000-01	**Phoenix**	**NHL**	**32**	**1**	**2**	**3**	**22**	**0**	**0**	**0**	**26**	**3.8**	**–8**	**0**	**0.0**	**14:28**	....	....	....	....	....	....	....	....	....
	Grand Rapids	IHL	19	3	9	12	8	....	....	....	....	....	....	....	....	....	....	....	....	....	....	....	....	....	....
2001-02	**New Jersey**	**NHL**	**1**	**0**	**1**	**1**	**0**	**0**	**0**	**0**	**0**	**0.0**	**1**	**0**	**0.0**	**19:26**	....	....	....	....	....	....	....	....	....
	Albany River Rats	AHL	70	9	22	31	28	....	....	....	....	....	....	....	....	....	....	....	....	....	....	....	....	....	....
2002-03	**NY Rangers**	**NHL**	**27**	**5**	**7**	**12**	**14**	**1**	**0**	**2**	**41**	**12.2**	**6**	**0**	**0.0**	**20:07**	....	....	....	....	....	....	....	....	....
	Hartford	AHL	22	6	14	20	22	....	....	....	....	....	....	....	....	....	....	....	....	....	....	....	....	....	....
	Pittsburgh	**NHL**	**7**	**0**	**1**	**1**	**0**	**0**	**0**	**0**	**6**	**0.0**	**–6**	**0**	**0.0**	**21:49**	....	....	....	....	....	....	....	....	....
2003-04	**NY Rangers**	**NHL**	**28**	**1**	**7**	**8**	**10**	**0**	**0**	**0**	**34**	**2.9**	**2**	**0**	**0.0**	**16:42**	....	....	....	....	....	....	....	....	....
2004-05	Hartford	AHL	7	1	2	3	6	....	....	....	....	....	....	....	....	....	6	0	2	2	20	....	....	....	....
2005-06	**NY Islanders**	**NHL**	**25**	**1**	**8**	**9**	**23**	**0**	**0**	**0**	**45**	**2.2**	**5**	**0**	**0.0**	**21:56**	....	....	....	....	....	....	....	....	....
	Bridgeport	AHL	15	4	9	13	10	....	....	....	....	....	....	....	....	....	....	....	....	....	....	....	....	....	....
2006-07	Bridgeport	AHL	4	0	3	3	0	....	....	....	....	....	....	....	....	....	....	....	....	....	....	....	....	....	....
2007-08	Hamilton	AHL	20	1	6	7	18	....	....	....	....	....	....	....	....	....	....	....	....	....	....	....	....	....	....
	NHL Totals		**364**	**22**	**53**	**75**	**264**	**1**	**2**	**3**	**403**	**5.5**		**0**	**0.0**	**19:27**	....	....	....	....	....	....	....	....	....

QMJHL First All-Star Team (1994)

Claimed by **Nashville** from **Calgary** in Expansion Draft, June 26, 1998. Claimed on waivers by **Dallas** from **Nashville**, March 14, 2000. Signed as a free agent by **Phoenix**, August 31, 2000. Signed as a free agent by **New Jersey**, October 25, 2001. Signed as a free agent by **NY Rangers**, August 5, 2002. Traded to **Pittsburgh** by **NY Rangers** with Richard Lintner, Rico Fata and Mikael Samuelsson for Mike Wilson, Alex Kovalev, Janne Laukkanen and Dan LaCouture, February 10, 2003. Signed as a free agent by **Buffalo**, July 14, 2003. Claimed by **NY Rangers** from **Buffalo** in Waiver Draft, October 3, 2003. • Spent majority of 2003-04 season as a healthy reserve. Signed as a free agent by **Hartford** (AHL), March 17, 2005. Signed as a free agent by **NY Islanders**, August 18, 2005. • Missed majority of 2006-07 season recovering from recurring hamstring injury.

BOUCHARD, Pierre-Marc

(BOO-shahrd, PEE-air- MAHRK) **MIN.**

Center. Shoots left. 5'10", 171 lbs. Born, Sherbrooke, Que., April 27, 1984. Minnesota's 1st choice, 8th overall, in 2002 Entry Draft.

Season	Club	League	GP	G	A	Pts	PIM	PP	SH	GW	S	%	+/-	TF	F%	Min	GP	G	A	Pts	PIM	PP	SH	GW	Min
1998-99	Mtl.-Bourassa	QAHA	28	23	41	64	....	....	....	....	....	....	....	....	....	....	....	....	....	....	....	....	....	....	....
99-2000	Charles-Lemoyne	QAAA	42	28	*45	*74	20	....	....	....	....	....	....	....	....	....	9	4	8	12	6	....	....	....	....
2000-01	Chicoutimi	QMJHL	67	38	57	95	20	....	....	....	....	....	....	....	....	....	6	5	8	13	0	....	....	....	....
2001-02	Chicoutimi	QMJHL	69	46	*94	*140	54	....	....	....	....	....	....	....	....	....	4	2	3	5	4	....	....	....	....
2002-03	**Minnesota**	**NHL**	**50**	**7**	**13**	**20**	**18**	**5**	**0**	**1**	**53**	**13.2**	**1**	**474**	**40.7**	**13:16**	**5**	**0**	**1**	**1**	**2**	**0**	**0**	**0**	**13:15**
2003-04	**Minnesota**	**NHL**	**61**	**4**	**18**	**22**	**22**	**2**	**0**	**0**	**60**	**6.7**	**–7**	**60**	**50.0**	**14:00**	....	....	....	....	....	....	....	....	....
2004-05	Houston Aeros	AHL	67	12	42	54	46	....	....	....	....	....	....	....	....	....	5	0	1	1	0	....	....	....	....
2005-06	**Minnesota**	**NHL**	**80**	**17**	**42**	**59**	**28**	**7**	**0**	**3**	**118**	**14.4**	**3**	**15**	**46.7**	**15:15**	....	....	....	....	....	....	....	....	....
2006-07	**Minnesota**	**NHL**	**82**	**20**	**37**	**57**	**14**	**5**	**0**	**3**	**173**	**11.6**	**13**	**18**	**33.3**	**15:59**	**5**	**1**	**1**	**2**	**0**	**0**	**0**	**0**	**14:48**
2007-08	**Minnesota**	**NHL**	**81**	**13**	**50**	**63**	**34**	**6**	**0**	**4**	**129**	**10.1**	**11**	**10**	**40.0**	**16:51**	**6**	**2**	**2**	**4**	**2**	**1**	**0**	**1**	**17:47**
	NHL Totals		**354**	**61**	**160**	**221**	**116**	**25**	**0**	**11**	**533**	**11.4**		**577**	**41.6**	**15:18**	**16**	**3**	**4**	**7**	**4**	**1**	**0**	**1**	**15:26**

QMJHL Rookie of the Year (2001) • QMJHL First All-Star Team (2002) • Canadian Major Junior First All-Star Team (2002) • Canadian Major Junior Player of the Year (2002)

BOUCHER, Philippe

(boo-SHAY, fihl-EEP) **DAL.**

Defense. Shoots right. 6'3", 218 lbs. Born, Ste-Apollinaire, Que., March 24, 1973. Buffalo's 1st choice, 13th overall, in 1991 Entry Draft.

Season	Club	League	GP	G	A	Pts	PIM	PP	SH	GW	S	%	+/-	TF	F%	Min	GP	G	A	Pts	PIM	PP	SH	GW	Min
1988-89	Ste-Foy	QAAA	5	0	0	0	2	....	....	....	....	....	....	....	....	....	....	....	....	....	....	....	....	....	....
1989-90	Ste-Foy	QAAA	42	26	60	86	76	....	....	....	....	....	....	....	....	....	12	6	*19	25	16	....	....	....	....
1990-91	Granby Bisons	QMJHL	69	21	46	67	92	....	....	....	....	....	....	....	....	....	....	....	....	....	....	....	....	....	....
1991-92	Granby Bisons	QMJHL	49	22	37	59	47	....	....	....	....	....	....	....	....	....	....	....	....	....	....	....	....	....	....
	Laval Titan	QMJHL	16	7	11	18	36	....	....	....	....	....	....	....	....	....	10	5	6	11	8	....	....	....	....
1992-93	Laval Titan	QMJHL	16	12	15	27	37	....	....	....	....	....	....	....	....	....	13	6	15	21	12	....	....	....	....
	Buffalo	**NHL**	**18**	**0**	**4**	**4**	**14**	**0**	**0**	**0**	**28**	**0.0**	**1**	....	....	....	....	....	....	....	....	....	....	....	....
	Rochester	AHL	5	4	3	7	8	....	....	....	....	....	....	....	....	....	3	0	1	1	2	....	....	....	....
1993-94	**Buffalo**	**NHL**	**38**	**6**	**8**	**14**	**29**	**4**	**0**	**1**	**67**	**9.0**	**–1**	....	....	....	**7**	**1**	**1**	**2**	**2**	**1**	**0**	**0**	....
	Rochester	AHL	31	10	22	32	51	....	....	....	....	....	....	....	....	....	....	....	....	....	....	....	....	....	....
1994-95	Rochester	AHL	43	14	27	41	26	....	....	....	....	....	....	....	....	....	....	....	....	....	....	....	....	....	....
	Buffalo	**NHL**	**9**	**1**	**4**	**5**	**0**	**0**	**0**	**0**	**15**	**6.7**	**6**	....	....	....	....	....	....	....	....	....	....	....	....
	Los Angeles	**NHL**	**6**	**1**	**0**	**1**	**4**	**0**	**0**	**0**	**15**	**6.7**	**–3**	....	....	....	....	....	....	....	....	....	....	....	....
1995-96	**Los Angeles**	**NHL**	**53**	**7**	**16**	**23**	**31**	**5**	**0**	**1**	**145**	**4.8**	**–26**	....	....	....	....	....	....	....	....	....	....	....	....
	Phoenix	IHL	10	4	3	7	4	....	....	....	....	....	....	....	....	....	....	....	....	....	....	....	....	....	....
1996-97	**Los Angeles**	**NHL**	**60**	**7**	**18**	**25**	**25**	**2**	**0**	**1**	**159**	**4.4**	**0**	....	....	....	....	....	....	....	....	....	....	....	....
1997-98	**Los Angeles**	**NHL**	**45**	**6**	**10**	**16**	**49**	**1**	**0**	**0**	**80**	**7.5**	**6**	....	....	....	....	....	....	....	....	....	....	....	....
	Long Beach	IHL	2	0	1	1	4	....	....	....	....	....	....	....	....	....	....	....	....	....	....	....	....	....	....
1998-99	**Los Angeles**	**NHL**	**45**	**2**	**6**	**8**	**32**	**1**	**0**	**0**	**87**	**2.3**	**–12**	**0**	**0.0**	**17:51**	....	....	....	....	....	....	....	....	....
99-2000	**Los Angeles**	**NHL**	**1**	**0**	**0**	**0**	**0**	**0**	**0**	**0**	**3**	**0.0**	**0**	**0**	**0.0**	**17:04**	....	....	....	....	....	....	....	....	....
	Long Beach	IHL	14	4	11	15	8	....	....	....	....	....	....	....	....	....	6	0	9	9	8	....	....	....	....
2000-01	**Los Angeles**	**NHL**	**22**	**2**	**4**	**6**	**20**	**2**	**0**	**0**	**40**	**5.0**	**4**	**0**	**0.0**	**18:25**	**13**	**0**	**1**	**1**	**2**	**0**	**0**	**0**	**15:48**
	Manitoba Moose	IHL	45	10	22	32	39	....	....	....	....	....	....	....	....	....	....	....	....	....	....	....	....	....	....
2001-02	**Los Angeles**	**NHL**	**80**	**7**	**23**	**30**	**94**	**4**	**0**	**2**	**198**	**3.5**	**0**	**0**	**0.0**	**21:36**	**5**	**0**	**1**	**1**	**2**	**0**	**0**	**0**	**19:31**
2002-03	**Dallas**	**NHL**	**80**	**7**	**20**	**27**	**94**	**1**	**1**	**3**	**137**	**5.1**	**28**	**1**	**0.0**	**20:29**	**11**	**1**	**2**	**3**	**11**	**0**	**0**	**0**	**21:28**
2003-04	**Dallas**	**NHL**	**70**	**8**	**16**	**24**	**64**	**2**	**0**	**2**	**134**	**6.0**	**15**	**0**	**0.0**	**22:24**	**5**	**1**	**0**	**1**	**6**	**0**	**0**	**0**	**23:57**
2004-05			DID NOT PLAY																						
2005-06	**Dallas**	**NHL**	**66**	**16**	**27**	**43**	**77**	**8**	**0**	**3**	**174**	**9.2**	**28**	**1**	**100.0**	**23:25**	**5**	**0**	**1**	**1**	**2**	**0**	**0**	**0**	**21:35**

			Regular Season														Playoffs								
Season	Club	League	GP	G	A	Pts	PIM	PP	SH	GW	S	%	+/-	TF	F%	Min	GP	G	A	Pts	PIM	PP	SH	GW	Min
2006-07	Dallas	NHL	76	19	32	51	104	12	0	4	222	8.6	2	1	0.0	22:54	7	0	1	1	6	0	0	0	27:22
2007-08	Dallas	NHL	38	2	12	14	26	0	1	0	72	2.8	3	0	0.0	21:31	3	0	0	0	4	0	0	0	20:04
	NHL Totals		707	91	200	291	663	42	2	17	1576	5.8		3	33.3	21:28	56	3	7	10	35	1	0	0	20:47

QMJHL Second All-Star Team (1991, 1992) • QMJHL Defensive Rookie of the Year (1991) • Canadian Major Junior Rookie of the Year (1991)

Played in NHL All-Star Game (2007)

Traded to **Los Angeles** by **Buffalo** with Denis Tsygurov and Grant Fuhr for Alexei Zhitnik, Robb Stauber, Charlie Huddy and Los Angeles' 5th round choice (Marian Menhart) in 1995 Entry Draft, February 14, 1995. • Missed majority of 1999-2000 season recovering from foot injury suffered in training camp, September, 1999. Signed as a free agent by **Dallas**, July 2, 2002. • Missed majority of 2007-08 season recovering from shoulder surgery, December 5, 2007.

BOUCK, Tyler

(BOWK, TIGH-luhr) **BUF.**

Center. Shoots left. 6', 196 lbs. Born, Camrose, Alta., January 13, 1980. Dallas' 2nd choice, 57th overall, in 1998 Entry Draft.

Season	Club	League	GP	G	A	Pts	PIM	PP	SH	GW	S	%	+/-	TF	F%	Min	GP	G	A	Pts	PIM	PP	SH	GW	Min
1995-96	Sherwood Park	AMHL	22	10	21	31	58	....	....	....	....	....	....	....	....	....	....	....	....	....	....	....	....	....	....
1996-97	Prince George	WHL	12	0	2	2	11	....	....	....	....	....	....	....	....	....	....	....	....	....	....	....	....	....	....
1997-98	Prince George	WHL	65	11	26	37	90	....	....	....	....	....	....	....	....	....	11	1	0	1	21	....	....	....	....
1998-99	Prince George	WHL	56	22	25	47	178	....	....	....	....	....	....	....	....	....	2	0	2	2	10	....	....	....	....
99-2000	Prince George	WHL	57	30	33	63	183	....	....	....	....	....	....	....	....	....	13	6	13	19	36	....	....	....	....
2000-01	**Dallas**	**NHL**	48	2	5	7	29	0	0	1	41	4.9	−3	1	0.0	8:59	1	0	0	0	0	0	0	0	9:02
	Utah Grizzlies	IHL	24	2	6	8	39	....	....	....	....	....	....	....	....	....	....	....	....	....	....	....	....	....	....
2001-02	**Phoenix**	**NHL**	7	0	0	0	4	0	0	0	3	0.0	−1	0	0.0	6:54	....	....	....	....	....	....	....	....	....
	Springfield	AHL	21	1	2	3	33	....	....	....	....	....	....	....	....	....	....	....	....	....	....	....	....	....	....
	Manitoba Moose	AHL	20	4	4	8	25	....	....	....	....	....	....	....	....	....	....	....	....	....	....	....	....	....	....
2002-03	Manitoba Moose	AHL	76	10	28	38	103	....	....	....	....	....	....	....	....	....	14	2	2	4	10	....	....	....	....
2003-04	**Vancouver**	**NHL**	18	1	2	3	23	0	1	0	12	8.3	−4	0	0.0	9:18	1	0	0	0	0	0	0	0	5:15
	Manitoba Moose	AHL	49	11	14	25	100	....	....	....	....	....	....	....	....	....	....	....	....	....	....	....	....	....	....
2004-05	TPS Turku	Finland	40	3	7	10	100	....	....	....	....	....	....	....	....	....	6	1	0	1	12	....	....	....	....
2005-06	**Vancouver**	**NHL**	12	1	1	2	21	0	0	0	6	16.7	0	0	0.0	6:22	....	....	....	....	....	....	....	....	....
	Manitoba Moose	AHL	8	0	1	1	8	....	....	....	....	....	....	....	....	....	....	....	....	....	....	....	....	....	....
2006-07	**Vancouver**	**NHL**	6	0	0	0	16	0	0	0	7	0.0	−1	0	0.0	7:55	....	....	....	....	....	....	....	....	....
	Manitoba Moose	AHL	24	1	3	4	36	....	....	....	....	....	....	....	....	....	....	....	....	....	....	....	....	....	....
2007-08	Portland Pirates	AHL	79	11	18	29	86	....	....	....	....	....	....	....	....	....	13	0	2	2	8	....	....	....	....
	NHL Totals		91	4	8	12	93	0	1	1	69	5.8		1	0.0	8:28	2	0	0	0	0	0	0	0	7:09

WHL West First All-Star Team (2000)

Traded to **Phoenix** by **Dallas** for Jyrki Lumme, June 23, 2001. Traded to **Vancouver** by **Phoenix** with Todd Warriner, Trevor Letowski and Phoenix's 3rd round choice (later traded back to Phoenix – Phoenix selected Dimitri Pestunov) in 2003 Entry Draft for Drake Berehowsky and Denis Pederson, December 28, 2001. Signed as a free agent by **Turku** (Finland), October 22, 2004. • Missed majority of 2005-06 season recovering from groin injury suffered in training camp (October 4, 2005) and as a healthy reserve. • Missed majority of 2006-07 season recovering from shoulder injury suffered in game vs. Hamilton (AHL), December 27, 2006. Signed as a free agent by **Buffalo**, August 8, 2008.

BOUILLON, Francis

(BOO-liawn, FRAN-sihs) **MTL.**

Defense. Shoots left. 5'8", 196 lbs. Born, New York, NY, October 17, 1975.

Season	Club	League	GP	G	A	Pts	PIM	PP	SH	GW	S	%	+/-	TF	F%	Min	GP	G	A	Pts	PIM	PP	SH	GW	Min
1991-92	Mtl-Bourassa	QAAA	42	2	5	7	28	....	....	....	....	....	....	....	....	....	9	1	0	1	6	....	....	....	....
1992-93	Laval Titan	QMJHL	46	0	7	7	45	....	....	....	....	....	....	....	....	....	....	....	....	....	....	....	....	....	....
1993-94	Laval Titan	QMJHL	68	3	15	18	129	....	....	....	....	....	....	....	....	....	19	2	9	11	48	....	....	....	....
1994-95	Laval Titan	QMJHL	72	8	25	33	115	....	....	....	....	....	....	....	....	....	20	3	11	14	21	....	....	....	....
1995-96	Granby	QMJHL	68	11	35	46	156	....	....	....	....	....	....	....	....	....	21	2	12	14	30	....	....	....	....
1996-97	Wheeling Nailers	ECHL	69	10	32	42	77	....	....	....	....	....	....	....	....	....	3	0	2	2	10	....	....	....	....
1997-98	Quebec Rafales	IHL	71	8	27	35	76	....	....	....	....	....	....	....	....	....	....	....	....	....	....	....	....	....	....
1998-99	Fredericton	AHL	79	19	36	55	174	....	....	....	....	....	....	....	....	....	5	2	1	3	0	....	....	....	....
99-2000	**Montreal**	**NHL**	74	3	13	16	38	2	0	1	76	3.9	−7	1	0.0	15:52	....	....	....	....	....	....	....	....	....
2000-01	**Montreal**	**NHL**	29	0	6	6	26	0	0	0	24	0.0	3	0	0.0	13:24	....	....	....	....	....	....	....	....	....
	Quebec Citadelles	AHL	4	0	0	0	0	....	....	....	....	....	....	....	....	....	....	....	....	....	....	....	....	....	....
2001-02	**Montreal**	**NHL**	28	0	5	5	33	0	0	0	24	0.0	−5	0	0.0	18:47	....	....	....	....	....	....	....	....	....
	Quebec Citadelles	AHL	38	8	14	22	30	....	....	....	....	....	....	....	....	....	....	....	....	....	....	....	....	....	....
2002-03	**Nashville**	**NHL**	4	0	0	0	2	0	0	0	0	0.0	−1	0	0.0	12:52	....	....	....	....	....	....	....	....	....
	Montreal	**NHL**	20	3	1	4	2	0	1	0	30	10.0	−1	0	0.0	20:24	....	....	....	....	....	....	....	....	....
	Hamilton	AHL	29	1	12	13	31	....	....	....	....	....	....	....	....	....	....	....	....	....	....	....	....	....	....
2003-04	**Montreal**	**NHL**	73	2	16	18	70	0	0	0	86	2.3	1	0	0.0	19:39	11	0	0	0	7	0	0	0	18:00
2004-05	Leksands IF	Sweden-2	31	10	21	31	46	....	....	....	....	....	....	....	....	....	....	....	....	....	....	....	....	....	....
2005-06	**Montreal**	**NHL**	67	3	19	22	34	3	0	1	75	4.0	−6	0	0.0	20:47	6	1	2	3	10	1	0	0	22:24
2006-07	**Montreal**	**NHL**	62	3	11	14	52	1	0	1	56	5.4	−10	0	0.0	18:19									
2007-08	**Montreal**	**NHL**	74	2	6	8	61	0	0	0	60	3.3	9	0	0.0	17:22	7	1	2	3	4	0	0	0	15:55
	NHL Totals		431	16	77	93	318	6	1	3	431	3.7		1	0.0	18:05	24	2	4	6	21	1	0	0	18:29

Signed as a free agent by **Montreal**, August 18, 1998. • Missed majority of 2000-01 season recovering from ankle injury suffered in game vs. Calgary, December 31, 2000. Claimed by **Nashville** from **Montreal** in Waiver Draft, October 4, 2002. Claimed on waivers by **Montreal** from **Nashville**, October 25, 2002. Signed as a free agent by **Leksands** (Sweden-2), November 15, 2004.

BOULERICE, Jesse

(BOO-luhr-ighs, JEH-see)

Right wing. Shoots right. 6'2", 215 lbs. Born, Plattsburgh, NY, August 10, 1978. Philadelphia's 4th choice, 133rd overall, in 1996 Entry Draft.

Season	Club	League	GP	G	A	Pts	PIM	PP	SH	GW	S	%	+/-	TF	F%	Min	GP	G	A	Pts	PIM	PP	SH	GW	Min
1994-95	Hawkesbury	CJHL	46	1	8	9	160	....	....	....	....	....	....	....	....	....	....	....	....	....	....	....	....	....	....
1995-96	Detroit	OHL	64	2	5	7	150	....	....	....	....	....	....	....	....	....	16	0	0	0	12	....	....	....	....
1996-97	Detroit	OHL	33	10	14	24	209	....	....	....	....	....	....	....	....	....	....	....	....	....	....	....	....	....	....
1997-98	Plymouth Whalers	OHL	53	20	23	43	170	....	....	....	....	....	....	....	....	....	13	2	4	6	35	....	....	....	....
1998-99	Philadelphia	AHL	24	1	2	3	82	....	....	....	....	....	....	....	....	....	....	....	....	....	....	....	....	....	....
	New Orleans	ECHL	12	0	1	1	38	....	....	....	....	....	....	....	....	....	....	....	....	....	....	....	....	....	....
99-2000	Philadelphia	AHL	40	3	4	7	85	....	....	....	....	....	....	....	....	....	4	0	2	2	4	....	....	....	....
	Trenton Titans	ECHL	25	8	8	16	90	....	....	....	....	....	....	....	....	....	....	....	....	....	....	....	....	....	....
2000-01	Philadelphia	AHL	60	3	4	7	256	....	....	....	....	....	....	....	....	....	10	1	1	2	28	....	....	....	....
2001-02	**Philadelphia**	**NHL**	3	0	0	0	5	0	0	0	1	0.0	−1	0	0.0	4:18	....	....	....	....	....	....	....	....	....
	Philadelphia	AHL	41	2	5	7	204	....	....	....	....	....	....	....	....	....	....	....	....	....	....	....	....	....	....
	Lowell	AHL	15	2	4	6	80	....	....	....	....	....	....	....	....	....	5	0	2	2	6	....	....	....	....
2002-03	**Carolina**	**NHL**	48	2	1	3	108	0	0	0	12	16.7	−2	0	0.0	3:54	....	....	....	....	....	....	....	....	....
2003-04	**Carolina**	**NHL**	76	6	1	7	127	0	0	0	46	13.0	−5	0	0.0	6:32	....	....	....	....	....	....	....	....	....
2004-05			DID NOT PLAY																						
2005-06	**Carolina**	**NHL**	26	0	0	0	51	0	0	0	3	0.0	−3	0	0.0	2:30	....	....	....	....	....	....	....	....	....
	St. Louis	**NHL**	12	0	0	0	13	0	0	0	2	0.0	−4	0	0.0	2:39	....	....	....	....	....	....	....	....	....
2006-07	Albany River Rats	AHL	16	4	3	7	36	....	....	....	....	....	....	....	....	....	....	....	....	....	....	....	....	....	....
2007-08	**Philadelphia**	**NHL**	5	0	0	0	29	0	0	0	1	0.0	−2	0	0.0	3:52	....	....	....	....	....	....	....	....	....
	Philadelphia	AHL	36	2	4	6	101	....	....	....	....	....	....	....	....	....	7	0	0	0	2	....	....	....	....
	NHL Totals		170	8	2	10	333	0	0	0	65	12.3		0	0.0	4:47	....	....	....	....	....	....	....	....	....

Traded to **Carolina** by **Philadelphia** for Greg Koehler, February 13, 2002. Traded to **St. Louis** by **Carolina** with Mike Zigomanis, the rights to Magnus Kahnberg, Carolina's 1st round choice (later traded to New Jersey - New Jersey selected Matthew Corrente) in 2006 Entry Draft, Toronto's 4th round choice (previously acquired, St. Louis selected Reto Berra) in 2006 Entry Draft and Chicago's 4th round choice (previously acquired, St. Louis selected Cade Fairchild) in 2007 Entry Draft for Doug Weight and Erkki Rajamaki, January 30, 2006. Signed as a free agent by **Carolina**, August 2, 2006. Signed as a free agent by **Philadelphia**, October 3, 2007.

BOULTON, Eric

(BOHL-tuhn, AIR-ihk) **ATL.**

Left wing. Shoots left. 6'1", 225 lbs. Born, Halifax, N.S., August 17, 1976. NY Rangers' 12th choice, 234th overall, in 1994 Entry Draft.

Season	Club	League	GP	G	A	Pts	PIM	PP	SH	GW	S	%	+/-	TF	F%	Min	GP	G	A	Pts	PIM	PP	SH	GW	Min
1992-93	Cole Harbour	MJrHL	44	12	15	27	212	....	....	....	....	....	....	....	....	....	....	....	....	....	....	....	....	....	....
1993-94	Oshawa Generals	OHL	45	4	3	7	149	....	....	....	....	....	....	....	....	....	5	0	0	0	16	....	....	....	....
1994-95	Oshawa Generals	OHL	27	7	5	12	125	....	....	....	....	....	....	....	....	....	....	....	....	....	....	....	....	....	....
	Sarnia Sting	OHL	24	3	7	10	134	....	....	....	....	....	....	....	....	....	4	0	1	1	10	....	....	....	....
1995-96	Sarnia Sting	OHL	66	14	29	43	243	....	....	....	....	....	....	....	....	....	9	0	3	3	29	....	....	....	....
1996-97	Binghamton	AHL	23	2	3	5	67	....	....	....	....	....	....	....	....	....	3	0	0	0	4	....	....	....	....
	Charlotte	ECHL	44	14	11	25	325	....	....	....	....	....	....	....	....	....	3	0	1	1	6	....	....	....	....
1997-98	Charlotte	ECHL	53	11	16	27	202	....	....	....	....	....	....	....	....	....	4	1	0	1	0	....	....	....	....
	Fort Wayne	IHL	8	0	2	2	42	....	....	....	....	....	....	....	....	....	....	....	....	....	....	....	....	....	....
1998-99	Kentucky	AHL	34	3	3	6	154	....	....	....	....	....	....	....	....	....	10	0	1	1	36	....	....	....	....
	Florida Everblades	ECHL	26	9	13	22	143	....	....	....	....	....	....	....	....	....	....	....	....	....	....	....	....	....	....
	Houston Aeros	IHL	7	1	0	1	41	....	....	....	....	....	....	....	....	....	....	....	....	....	....	....	....	....	....

			Regular Season														Playoffs								
Season	Club	League	GP	G	A	Pts	PIM	PP	SH	GW	S	%	+/-	TF	F%	Min	GP	G	A	Pts	PIM	PP	SH	GW	Min
99-2000	Rochester	AHL	76	2	2	4	276	....	....	....	....	....	....	....	....	....	18	2	1	3	53	....	....	....	....
2000-01	**Buffalo**	**NHL**	**35**	**1**	**2**	**3**	**94**	**0**	**0**	**0**	**20**	**5.0**	**–1**	**2**	**0.0**	**5:42**	....	....	....	....	....	....	....	....	....
2001-02	**Buffalo**	**NHL**	**35**	**2**	**3**	**5**	**129**	**0**	**0**	**1**	**21**	**9.5**	**–1**	**0**	**0.0**	**6:08**	....	....	....	....	....	....	....	....	....
2002-03	**Buffalo**	**NHL**	**58**	**1**	**5**	**6**	**178**	**0**	**0**	**0**	**33**	**3.0**	**1**	**6**	**33.3**	**6:35**	....	....	....	....	....	....	....	....	....
2003-04	**Buffalo**	**NHL**	**44**	**1**	**2**	**3**	**110**	**0**	**0**	**0**	**20**	**5.0**	**–2**	**1**	**0.0**	**4:52**	....	....	....	....	....	....	....	....	....
2004-05	Columbia Inferno	ECHL	48	23	16	39	124	....	....	....	....	....	....	....	....	....	4	2	3	5	8	....	....	....	....
2005-06	**Atlanta**	**NHL**	**51**	**4**	**5**	**9**	**87**	**0**	**0**	**0**	**28**	**14.3**	**–4**	**2**	**50.0**	**4:54**	....	....	....	....	....	....	....	....	....
2006-07	**Atlanta**	**NHL**	**45**	**3**	**4**	**7**	**49**	**0**	**0**	**0**	**42**	**7.1**	**2**	**2**	**50.0**	**6:16**	**4**	**0**	**0**	**0**	**24**	**0**	**0**	**0**	**5:04**
2007-08	**Atlanta**	**NHL**	**74**	**4**	**5**	**9**	**127**	**0**	**0**	**0**	**64**	**6.3**	**–10**	**4**	**25.0**	**7:27**	....	....	....	....	....	....	....	....	....
	NHL Totals		**342**	**16**	**26**	**42**	**774**	**0**	**0**	**1**	**228**	**7.0**		**17**	**29.4**	**6:07**	**4**	**0**	**0**	**0**	**24**	**0**	**0**	**0**	**5:04**

Signed as a free agent by **Buffalo**, September 14, 1999. Signed as a free agent by **Columbia** (ECHL), November 24, 2004. Signed as a free agent by **Atlanta**, August 8, 2005.

BOUMEDIENNE, Josef

(BOO-mih-dyehn, JOH-sehf) **TOR.**

Defense. Shoots left. 6'1", 200 lbs. Born, Stockholm, Sweden, January 12, 1978. New Jersey's 7th choice, 91st overall, in 1996 Entry Draft.

Season	Club	League	GP	G	A	Pts	PIM	PP	SH	GW	S	%	+/-	TF	F%	Min	GP	G	A	Pts	PIM	PP	SH	GW	Min
1994-95	Huddinge IK Jr.	Swe-Jr.	10	0	2	2	57	....	....	....	....	....	....	....	....	....	....	....	....	....	....	....	....	....	....
1995-96	Huddinge IK Jr.	Swe-Jr.	25	2	4	6	66	....	....	....	....	....	....	....	....	....	....	....	....	....	....	....	....	....	....
	Huddinge IK	Sweden-2	7	0	0	0	14	....	....	....	....	....	....	....	....	....	....	....	....	....	....	....	....	....	....
1996-97	Sodertalje SK	Sweden	32	1	1	2	32	....	....	....	....	....	....	....	....	....	....	....	....	....	....	....	....	....	....
1997-98	Sodertalje SK	Sweden	26	3	3	6	28	....	....	....	....	....	....	....	....	....	....	....	....	....	....	....	....	....	....
1998-99	Tappara Tampere	Finland	51	6	8	14	119	....	....	....	....	....	....	....	....	....	....	....	....	....	....	....	....	....	....
99-2000	Tappara Tampere	Finland	50	8	24	32	160	....	....	....	....	....	....	....	....	....	4	1	2	3	10	....	....	....	....
2000-01	Albany River Rats	AHL	79	8	28	36	117	....	....	....	....	....	....	....	....	....	....	....	....	....	....	....	....	....	....
2001-02	**New Jersey**	**NHL**	**1**	**1**	**0**	**1**	**2**	**0**	**0**	**0**	**1**	**100.0**	**–1**	**0**	**0.0**	**20:23**	....	....	....	....	....	....	....	....	....
	Albany River Rats	AHL	9	0	3	3	10	....	....	....	....	....	....	....	....	....	....	....	....	....	....	....	....	....	....
	Tampa Bay	**NHL**	**3**	**0**	**0**	**0**	**4**	**0**	**0**	**0**	**0**	**0.0**	**–1**	**0**	**0.0**	**10:58**	....	....	....	....	....	....	....	....	....
	Springfield	AHL	53	7	25	32	57	....	....	....	....	....	....	....	....	....	....	....	....	....	....	....	....	....	....
2002-03	Binghamton	AHL	26	2	15	17	62	....	....	....	....	....	....	....	....	....	....	....	....	....	....	....	....	....	....
	Washington	**NHL**	**6**	**1**	**0**	**1**	**0**	**0**	**0**	**1**	**7**	**14.3**	**–1**	**0**	**0.0**	**19:33**	....	....	....	....	....	....	....	....	....
	Portland Pirates	AHL	44	8	22	30	77	....	....	....	....	....	....	....	....	....	....	....	....	....	....	....	....	....	....
2003-04	**Washington**	**NHL**	**37**	**2**	**12**	**14**	**30**	**2**	**0**	**0**	**44**	**4.5**	**–10**	**0**	**0.0**	**23:02**	....	....	....	....	....	....	....	....	....
	Portland Pirates	AHL	13	1	8	9	10	....	....	....	....	....	....	....	....	....	....	....	....	....	....	....	....	....	....
2004-05	Brynas IF Gavle	Sweden	13	6	0	6	43	....	....	....	....	....	....	....	....	....	....	....	....	....	....	....	....	....	....
	Karpat Oulu	Finland	32	5	10	15	58	....	....	....	....	....	....	....	....	....	12	1	5	6	12	....	....	....	....
2005-06	ZSC Lions Zurich	Swiss	17	1	10	11	22	....	....	....	....	....	....	....	....	....	....	....	....	....	....	....	....	....	....
	Sodertalje SK	Sweden	26	1	19	20	62	....	....	....	....	....	....	....	....	....	....	....	....	....	....	....	....	....	....
	Sodertalje SK	Sweden-Q	10	2	7	9	18	....	....	....	....	....	....	....	....	....	....	....	....	....	....	....	....	....	....
2006-07	Karpat Oulu	Finland	18	2	2	4	36	....	....	....	....	....	....	....	....	....	10	1	3	4	16	....	....	....	....
2007-08	Hershey Bears	AHL	52	7	35	42	81	....	....	....	....	....	....	....	....	....	1	0	0	0	2	....	....	....	....
	NHL Totals		**47**	**4**	**12**	**16**	**36**	**2**	**0**	**1**	**52**	**7.7**		**0**	**0.0**	**21:46**	....	....	....	....	....	....	....	....	....

Traded to **Tampa Bay** by **New Jersey** with Sascha Goc and the rights to Anton But for Andrei Zyuzin, November 9, 2001. Traded to **Ottawa** by **Tampa Bay** for Ottawa's 7th round choice (Fredrik Norrena) in 2002 Entry Draft, June 23, 2002. Traded to **Washington** by **Ottawa** for Dean Melanson, December 16, 2002. Signed as a free agent by **Brynas** (Sweden), September 25, 2004. Signed as a free agent by **Karpat** (Finland), November 10, 2004. Signed as a free agent by **ZSC** (Swiss), September 7, 2005. Signed as a free agent by **Toronto**, August, 2008.

BOURDON, Luc

(BOOR-duhn, LEWK)

Defense. Shoots left. 6'3", 211 lbs. Born, Shippagan, N.B., February 16, 1987. Vancouver's 1st choice, 10th overall, in 2005 Entry Draft.

Season	Club	League	GP	G	A	Pts	PIM	PP	SH	GW	S	%	+/-	TF	F%	Min	GP	G	A	Pts	PIM	PP	SH	GW	Min
2002-03	Miramichi	NBMHL	20	2	12	14	106	....	....	....	....	....	....	....	....	....	....	....	....	....	....	....	....	....	....
2003-04	Val-d'Or Foreurs	QMJHL	64	2	6	8	58	....	....	....	....	....	....	....	....	....	7	1	0	1	4	....	....	....	....
2004-05	Val-d'Or Foreurs	QMJHL	70	13	19	32	117	....	....	....	....	....	....	....	....	....	....	....	....	....	....	....	....	....	....
2005-06	Val-d'Or Foreurs	QMJHL	20	2	18	20	54	....	....	....	....	....	....	....	....	....	....	....	....	....	....	....	....	....	....
	Moncton Wildcats	QMJHL	10	1	7	8	8	....	....	....	....	....	....	....	....	....	16	0	3	3	22	....	....	....	....
2006-07	**Vancouver**	**NHL**	**9**	**0**	**0**	**0**	**4**	**0**	**0**	**0**	**3**	**0.0**	**–1**	**0**	**0.0**	**8:50**	....	....	....	....	....	....	....	....	....
	Moncton Wildcats	QMJHL	13	3	11	14	28	....	....	....	....	....	....	....	....	....	....	....	....	....	....	....	....	....	....
	Cape Breton	QMJHL	23	1	5	6	45	....	....	....	....	....	....	....	....	....	16	2	11	13	28	....	....	....	....
	Manitoba Moose	AHL	....	....	....	....	....	....	....	....	....	....	....	....	....	....	5	0	0	0	2	....	....	....	....
2007-08	**Vancouver**	**NHL**	**27**	**2**	**0**	**2**	**20**	**1**	**0**	**0**	**26**	**7.7**	**7**	**0**	**0.0**	**12:52**	....	....	....	....	....	....	....	....	....
	Manitoba Moose	AHL	41	6	8	14	68	....	....	....	....	....	....	....	....	....	6	0	0	0	8	....	....	....	....
	NHL Totals		**36**	**2**	**0**	**2**	**24**	**1**	**0**	**0**	**29**	**6.9**		**0**	**0.0**	**11:52**	....	....	....	....	....	....	....	....	....

• Died as a result of motorcycle accident, May 29, 2008.

BOURQUE, Chris

(BOHRK, KRIHS) **WSH.**

Center. Shoots left. 5'9", 173 lbs. Born, Boston, MA, January 29, 1986. Washington's 4th choice, 33rd overall, in 2004 Entry Draft.

Season	Club	League	GP	G	A	Pts	PIM	PP	SH	GW	S	%	+/-	TF	F%	Min	GP	G	A	Pts	PIM	PP	SH	GW	Min
2002-03	Cushing	High-MA	28	31	26	57	49	....	....	....	....	....	....	....	....	....	....	....	....	....	....	....	....	....	....
2003-04	Cushing	High-MA	31	37	53	90	96	....	....	....	....	....	....	....	....	....	....	....	....	....	....	....	....	....	....
2004-05	Boston University	H-East	35	10	13	23	50	....	....	....	....	....	....	....	....	....	....	....	....	....	....	....	....	....	....
	Portland Pirates	AHL	6	1	1	2	2	....	....	....	....	....	....	....	....	....	....	....	....	....	....	....	....	....	....
2005-06	Hershey Bears	AHL	52	8	28	36	40	....	....	....	....	....	....	....	....	....	1	0	0	0	0	....	....	....	....
2006-07	Hershey Bears	AHL	76	25	33	58	49	....	....	....	....	....	....	....	....	....	19	2	6	8	18	....	....	....	....
2007-08	**Washington**	**NHL**	**4**	**0**	**0**	**0**	**2**	**0**	**0**	**0**	**4**	**0.0**	**0**	**1**	**0.0**	**8:42**	....	....	....	....	....	....	....	....	....
	Hershey Bears	AHL	73	28	35	63	56	....	....	....	....	....	....	....	....	....	5	1	3	4	8	....	....	....	....
	NHL Totals		**4**	**0**	**0**	**0**	**2**	**0**	**0**	**0**	**4**	**0.0**		**1**	**0.0**	**8:42**	....	....	....	....	....	....	....	....	....

Hockey East All-Rookie Team (2005)

BOURQUE, Rene

(BOHRK, reh-NAY) **CGY.**

Left wing. Shoots left. 6'2", 213 lbs. Born, Lac La Biche, Alta., December 10, 1981.

Season	Club	League	GP	G	A	Pts	PIM	PP	SH	GW	S	%	+/-	TF	F%	Min	GP	G	A	Pts	PIM	PP	SH	GW	Min
2000-01	U. of Wisconsin	WCHA	32	10	5	15	18	....	....	....	....	....	....	....	....	....	....	....	....	....	....	....	....	....	....
2001-02	U. of Wisconsin	WCHA	38	12	7	19	26	....	....	....	....	....	....	....	....	....	....	....	....	....	....	....	....	....	....
2002-03	U. of Wisconsin	WCHA	40	19	8	27	54	....	....	....	....	....	....	....	....	....	....	....	....	....	....	....	....	....	....
2003-04	U. of Wisconsin	WCHA	42	16	20	36	74	....	....	....	....	....	....	....	....	....	....	....	....	....	....	....	....	....	....
2004-05	Norfolk Admirals	AHL	78	33	27	60	105	....	....	....	....	....	....	....	....	....	6	1	0	1	8	....	....	....	....
2005-06	**Chicago**	**NHL**	**77**	**16**	**18**	**34**	**56**	**4**	**0**	**2**	**180**	**8.9**	**3**	**11**	**36.4**	**15:20**	....	....	....	....	....	....	....	....	....
2006-07	**Chicago**	**NHL**	**44**	**7**	**10**	**17**	**38**	**2**	**1**	**1**	**82**	**8.5**	**–4**	**9**	**22.2**	**16:01**	....	....	....	....	....	....	....	....	....
	Norfolk Admirals	AHL	1	0	0	0	0	....	....	....	....	....	....	....	....	....	....	....	....	....	....	....	....	....	....
2007-08	**Chicago**	**NHL**	**62**	**10**	**14**	**24**	**42**	**0**	**5**	**2**	**103**	**9.7**	**6**	**8**	**25.0**	**15:16**	....	....	....	....	....	....	....	....	....
	NHL Totals		**183**	**33**	**42**	**75**	**136**	**6**	**6**	**5**	**365**	**9.0**		**28**	**28.6**	**15:29**	....	....	....	....	....	....	....	....	....

AHL All-Rookie Team (2005) • Dudley "Red" Garrett Memorial Trophy (Top Rookie - AHL) (2005)

Signed as a free agent by **Chicago**, July 29, 2004. Traded to **Calgary** by **Chicago** for future considerations, July 1, 2008.

BOUWMEESTER, Jay

(BOW-mee-stuhr, JAY) **FLA.**

Defense. Shoots left. 6'4", 212 lbs. Born, Edmonton, Alta., September 27, 1983. Florida's 1st choice, 3rd overall, in 2002 Entry Draft.

Season	Club	League	GP	G	A	Pts	PIM	PP	SH	GW	S	%	+/-	TF	F%	Min	GP	G	A	Pts	PIM	PP	SH	GW	Min
1998-99	Edmonton SSAC	AMHL	32	14	29	43	36	....	....	....	....	....	....	....	....	....	....	....	....	....	....	....	....	....	....
	Medicine Hat	WHL	8	2	1	3	2	....	....	....	....	....	....	....	....	....	....	....	....	....	....	....	....	....	....
99-2000	Medicine Hat	WHL	64	13	21	34	26	....	....	....	....	....	....	....	....	....	....	....	....	....	....	....	....	....	....
2000-01	Medicine Hat	WHL	61	14	39	53	44	....	....	....	....	....	....	....	....	....	....	....	....	....	....	....	....	....	....
2001-02	Medicine Hat	WHL	61	11	50	61	42	....	....	....	....	....	....	....	....	....	....	....	....	....	....	....	....	....	....
2002-03	**Florida**	**NHL**	**82**	**4**	**12**	**16**	**14**	**2**	**0**	**0**	**110**	**3.6**	**–29**	**0**	**0.0**	**20:09**	....	....	....	....	....	....	....	....	....
2003-04	**Florida**	**NHL**	**61**	**2**	**18**	**20**	**30**	**0**	**0**	**0**	**85**	**2.4**	**–15**	**0**	**0.0**	**23:02**	....	....	....	....	....	....	....	....	....
	San Antonio	AHL	2	0	1	1	2	....	....	....	....	....	....	....	....	....	....	....	....	....	....	....	....	....	....
2004-05	San Antonio	AHL	64	4	13	17	50	....	....	....	....	....	....	....	....	....	....	....	....	....	....	....	....	....	....
	Chicago Wolves	AHL	18	6	3	9	12	....	....	....	....	....	....	....	....	....	18	0	0	0	14	....	....	....	....
2005-06	**Florida**	**NHL**	**82**	**5**	**41**	**46**	**79**	**0**	**0**	**0**	**189**	**2.6**	**1**	**1**	**0.0**	**25:29**	....	....	....	....	....	....	....	....	....
	Canada	Olympics	6	0	0	0	0	....	....	....	....	....	....	....	....	....	....	....	....	....	....	....	....	....	....

			Regular Season														Playoffs								
Season	Club	League	GP	G	A	Pts	PIM	PP	SH	GW	S	%	+/-	TF	F%	Min	GP	G	A	Pts	PIM	PP	SH	GW	Min
2006-07	Florida	NHL	82	12	30	42	66	3	0	3	174	6.9	23	0	0.0	26:09	....	....	....	....	....	....	....	....	....
2007-08	Florida	NHL	82	15	22	37	72	4	0	0	182	8.2	–5	0	0.0	27:28	....	....	....	....	....	....	....	....	....
	NHL Totals		389	38	123	161	261	9	0	3	740	5.1		1	0.0	24:32	....	....	....	....	....	....	....	....	....

WHL East First All-Star Team (2002) • NHL All-Rookie Team (2003)
Played in NHL All-Star Game (2007)
Loaned to **Chicago** (AHL) by **Florida** (San Antonio-AHL) for cash, March 8, 2005.

BOYCE, Darryl (BOIS, DAIR-uhl) TOR.

Center. Shoots left. 6', 200 lbs. Born, Summerside, PEI, July 7, 1984.

Season	Club	League	GP	G	A	Pts	PIM	PP	SH	GW	S	%	+/-	TF	F%	Min	GP	G	A	Pts	PIM	PP	SH	GW	Min
2001-02	St. Michael's	OHL	67	10	11	21	71	....	....	....	....	....	....	....	....	....	15	2	5	7	46	....	....	....	....
2002-03	St. Michael's	OHL	64	16	21	37	119	....	....	....	....	....	....	....	....	....	19	1	3	4	28	....	....	....	....
2003-04	St. Michael's	OHL	64	13	24	37	110	....	....	....	....	....	....	....	....	....	18	1	3	4	23	....	....	....	....
2004-05	St. Michael's	OHL	67	15	35	50	152	....	....	....	....	....	....	....	....	....	10	2	5	7	28	....	....	....	....
2005-06	New Brunswick	AUAA	28	15	17	32	50	....	....	....	....	....	....	....	....	....	....	....	....	....	....	....	....	....	....
2006-07	New Brunswick	AUAA	25	14	19	33	63	....	....	....	....	....	....	....	....	....	....	....	....	....	....	....	....	....	....
2007-08	Toronto Marlies	AHL	41	8	16	24	71	....	....	....	....	....	....	....	....	....	....	....	....	....	....	....	....	....	....
	Toronto	**NHL**	**1**	**0**	**0**	**0**	**0**	**0**	**0**	**0**	**0**	**0.0**	**0**	**2**	**100.0**	**3:20**	....	....	....	....	....	....	....	....	....
	NHL Totals		**1**	**0**	**0**	**0**	**0**	**0**	**0**	**0**	**0**	**0.0**		**2**	**100.0**	**3:20**	....	....	....	....	....	....	....	....	....

Signed as a free agent by **Toronto** (AHL), April, 2007. Signed as a free agent by **Toronto**, January 1, 2008.

BOYCHUK, Johnny (BOI-chuhk, JAW-nee) BOS.

Defense. Shoots right. 6'2", 225 lbs. Born, Edmonton, Alta., January 19, 1984. Colorado's 2nd choice, 61st overall, in 2002 Entry Draft.

Season	Club	League	GP	G	A	Pts	PIM	PP	SH	GW	S	%	+/-	TF	F%	Min	GP	G	A	Pts	PIM	PP	SH	GW	Min
1998-99	Edm. Cycle	AMBHL	36	8	20	28	59	....	....	....	....	....	....	....	....	....	....	....	....	....	....	....	....	....	....
99-2000	Edm. Cycle	AMHL	35	6	17	23	59	....	....	....	....	....	....	....	....	....	....	....	....	....	....	....	....	....	....
2000-01	Calgary Hitmen	WHL	66	4	8	12	61	....	....	....	....	....	....	....	....	....	12	1	1	2	17	....	....	....	....
2001-02	Calgary Hitmen	WHL	70	8	32	40	85	....	....	....	....	....	....	....	....	....	7	1	1	2	6	....	....	....	....
2002-03	Calgary Hitmen	WHL	40	8	18	26	58	....	....	....	....	....	....	....	....	....	....	....	....	....	....	....	....	....	....
	Moose Jaw	WHL	27	5	17	22	32	....	....	....	....	....	....	....	....	....	13	2	6	8	29	....	....	....	....
2003-04	Moose Jaw	WHL	62	13	20	33	71	....	....	....	....	....	....	....	....	....	10	1	9	10	9	....	....	....	....
2004-05	Hershey Bears	AHL	80	3	12	15	69	....	....	....	....	....	....	....	....	....	....	....	....	....	....	....	....	....	....
2005-06	Lowell	AHL	74	6	26	32	73	....	....	....	....	....	....	....	....	....	....	....	....	....	....	....	....	....	....
2006-07	Albany River Rats	AHL	80	10	18	28	125	....	....	....	....	....	....	....	....	....	5	1	1	2	4	....	....	....	....
2007-08	**Colorado**	**NHL**	**4**	**0**	**0**	**0**	**0**	**0**	**0**	**0**	**3**	**0.0**	**1**	**1**	**0.0**	**8:57**	....	....	....	....	....	....	....	....	....
	Lake Erie	AHL	60	8	18	26	63	....	....	....	....	....	....	....	....	....	....	....	....	....	....	....	....	....	....
	NHL Totals		**4**	**0**	**0**	**0**	**0**	**0**	**0**	**0**	**3**	**0.0**		**1**	**0.0**	**8:57**	....	....	....	....	....	....	....	....	....

Traded to **Boston** by **Colorado** for Matt Hendricks, June 24, 2008.

BOYD, Dustin (BOID, DUHS-tihn) CGY.

Center. Shoots left. 6', 193 lbs. Born, Winnipeg, Man., July 16, 1986. Calgary's 3rd choice, 98th overall, in 2004 Entry Draft.

Season	Club	League	GP	G	A	Pts	PIM	PP	SH	GW	S	%	+/-	TF	F%	Min	GP	G	A	Pts	PIM	PP	SH	GW	Min
2001-02	Wpg. Warriors	MMMHL	40	50	57	107	16	....	....	....	....	....	....	....	....	....	....	....	....	....	....	....	....	....	....
2002-03	Moose Jaw	WHL	63	11	17	28	15	....	....	....	....	....	....	....	....	....	13	0	3	3	2	....	....	....	....
2003-04	Moose Jaw	WHL	72	18	20	38	40	....	....	....	....	....	....	....	....	....	10	2	2	4	8	....	....	....	....
2004-05	Moose Jaw	WHL	66	26	35	61	57	....	....	....	....	....	....	....	....	....	5	1	2	3	2	....	....	....	....
2005-06	Moose Jaw	WHL	64	48	42	90	34	....	....	....	....	....	....	....	....	....	22	7	11	18	10	....	....	....	....
2006-07	**Calgary**	**NHL**	**13**	**2**	**2**	**4**	**4**	**0**	**0**	**1**	**8**	**25.0**	**5**	**16**	**50.0**	**10:09**	....	....	....	....	....	....	....	....	....
	Omaha	AHL	66	27	33	60	34	....	....	....	....	....	....	....	....	....	6	1	1	2	0	....	....	....	....
2007-08	**Calgary**	**NHL**	**48**	**7**	**5**	**12**	**6**	**0**	**0**	**1**	**46**	**15.2**	**–11**	**129**	**50.4**	**9:49**	....	....	....	....	....	....	....	....	....
	Quad City Flames	AHL	18	2	7	9	4	....	....	....	....	....	....	....	....	....	....	....	....	....	....	....	....	....	....
	NHL Totals		**61**	**9**	**7**	**16**	**10**	**0**	**0**	**2**	**54**	**16.7**		**145**	**50.3**	**9:53**	....	....	....	....	....	....	....	....	....

WHL East First All-Star Team (2006)

BOYES, Brad (BOIZ, BRAD) ST.L.

Center. Shoots right. 6', 195 lbs. Born, Mississauga, Ont., April 17, 1982. Toronto's 1st choice, 24th overall, in 2000 Entry Draft.

Season	Club	League	GP	G	A	Pts	PIM	PP	SH	GW	S	%	+/-	TF	F%	Min	GP	G	A	Pts	PIM	PP	SH	GW	Min
1997-98	Mississauga Reps	MTHL	44	27	50	77	....	....	....	....	....	....	....	....	....	....	....	....	....	....	....	....	....	....	....
1998-99	Erie Otters	OHL	59	24	36	60	30	....	....	....	....	....	....	....	....	....	5	1	2	3	10	....	....	....	....
99-2000	Erie Otters	OHL	68	36	46	82	38	....	....	....	....	....	....	....	....	....	13	6	8	14	10	....	....	....	....
2000-01	Erie Otters	OHL	59	45	45	90	42	....	....	....	....	....	....	....	....	....	15	10	13	23	8	....	....	....	....
2001-02	Erie Otters	OHL	47	36	41	77	42	....	....	....	....	....	....	....	....	....	21	22	*19	41	27	....	....	....	....
2002-03	St. John's	AHL	65	23	28	51	45	....	....	....	....	....	....	....	....	....	....	....	....	....	....	....	....	....	....
	Cleveland Barons	AHL	15	7	6	13	21	....	....	....	....	....	....	....	....	....	....	....	....	....	....	....	....	....	....
2003-04	**San Jose**	**NHL**	**1**	**0**	**0**	**0**	**2**	**0**	**0**	**0**	**0**	**0.0**	**–2**	**0**	**0.0**	**13:03**	....	....	....	....	....	....	....	....	....
	Cleveland Barons	AHL	61	25	35	60	38	....	....	....	....	....	....	....	....	....	....	....	....	....	....	....	....	....	....
	Providence Bruins	AHL	17	6	6	12	13	....	....	....	....	....	....	....	....	....	2	1	0	1	0	....	....	....	....
2004-05	Providence Bruins	AHL	80	33	42	75	58	....	....	....	....	....	....	....	....	....	16	8	7	15	23	....	....	....	....
2005-06	**Boston**	**NHL**	**82**	**26**	**43**	**69**	**30**	**8**	**0**	**3**	**203**	**12.8**	**11**	**265**	**53.6**	**15:46**	....	....	....	....	....	....	....	....	....
2006-07	**Boston**	**NHL**	**62**	**13**	**21**	**34**	**25**	**1**	**1**	**1**	**139**	**9.4**	**–17**	**220**	**44.1**	**16:04**	....	....	....	....	....	....	....	....	....
	St. Louis	**NHL**	**19**	**4**	**8**	**12**	**4**	**0**	**0**	**1**	**43**	**9.3**	**0**	**93**	**58.1**	**17:25**	....	....	....	....	....	....	....	....	....
2007-08	**St. Louis**	**NHL**	**82**	**43**	**22**	**65**	**20**	**11**	**0**	**9**	**207**	**20.8**	**1**	**236**	**44.5**	**17:57**	....	....	....	....	....	....	....	....	....
	NHL Totals		**246**	**86**	**94**	**180**	**81**	**20**	**1**	**14**	**592**	**14.5**		**814**	**48.9**	**16:41**	....	....	....	....	....	....	....	....	....

Canadian Major Junior Scholastic Player of the Year (2000) • OHL Second All-Star Team (2001) • OHL First All-Star Team (2002) • Canadian Major Junior Sportsman of the Year (2002) • AHL All-Rookie Team (2003) • AHL Second All-Star Team (2004) • NHL All-Rookie Team (2006)

Traded to **San Jose** by **Toronto** with Alyn McCauley and Toronto's 1st round choice (later traded to Boston – Boston selected Mark Stuart) in 2003 Entry Draft for Owen Nolan, March 5, 2003. Traded to **Boston** by **San Jose** for Jeff Jillson, March 9, 2004. Traded to **St. Louis** by **Boston** for Dennis Wideman, February 27, 2007.

BOYLE, Brian (BOIL, BRIGH-uhn) L.A.

Center. Shoots left. 6'7", 244 lbs. Born, Hingham, MA, December 18, 1984. Los Angeles' 2nd choice, 26th overall, in 2003 Entry Draft.

Season	Club	League	GP	G	A	Pts	PIM	PP	SH	GW	S	%	+/-	TF	F%	Min	GP	G	A	Pts	PIM	PP	SH	GW	Min
2000-01	St. Sebastian's	High-MA	25	20	19	39	....	....	....	....	....	....	....	....	....	....	....	....	....	....	....	....	....	....	....
2001-02	St. Sebastian's	High-MA	28	21	26	47	22	....	....	....	....	....	....	....	....	....	....	....	....	....	....	....	....	....	....
2002-03	St. Sebastian's	High-MA	31	32	31	62	46	....	....	....	....	....	....	....	....	....	....	....	....	....	....	....	....	....	....
2003-04	Boston College	H-East	35	5	3	8	36	....	....	....	....	....	....	....	....	....	....	....	....	....	....	....	....	....	....
2004-05	Boston College	H-East	40	19	8	27	64	....	....	....	....	....	....	....	....	....	....	....	....	....	....	....	....	....	....
2005-06	Boston College	H-East	42	22	*30	52	90	....	....	....	....	....	....	....	....	....	....	....	....	....	....	....	....	....	....
2006-07	Boston College	H-East	42	19	*34	*53	*104	....	....	....	....	....	....	....	....	....	....	....	....	....	....	....	....	....	....
	Manchester	AHL	2	0	0	0	2	....	....	....	....	....	....	....	....	....	16	3	5	8	13	....	....	....	....
2007-08	**Los Angeles**	**NHL**	**8**	**4**	**1**	**5**	**4**	**0**	**0**	**0**	**19**	**21.1**	**4**	**80**	**46.3**	**13:38**	....	....	....	....	....	....	....	....	....
	Manchester	AHL	70	31	31	62	87	....	....	....	....	....	....	....	....	....	....	....	....	....	....	....	....	....	....
	NHL Totals		**8**	**4**	**1**	**5**	**4**	**0**	**0**	**0**	**19**	**21.1**		**80**	**46.3**	**13:38**	....	....	....	....	....	....	....	....	....

Hockey East First All-Star Team (2006, 2007) • NCAA East Second All-American Team (2006) • NCAA East First All-American Team (2007) • NCAA Championship All-Tournament Team (2007)

BOYLE, Dan (BOIL, DAN) S.J.

Defense. Shoots right. 5'11", 190 lbs. Born, Ottawa, Ont., July 12, 1976.

Season	Club	League	GP	G	A	Pts	PIM	PP	SH	GW	S	%	+/-	TF	F%	Min	GP	G	A	Pts	PIM	PP	SH	GW	Min
1992-93	Gloucester	CJHL	55	22	51	73	60	....	....	....	....	....	....	....	....	....	....	....	....	....	....	....	....	....	....
1993-94	Gloucester	CJHL	53	27	54	81	155	....	....	....	....	....	....	....	....	....	....	....	....	....	....	....	....	....	....
1994-95	Miami U.	CCHA	35	8	18	26	24	....	....	....	....	....	....	....	....	....	....	....	....	....	....	....	....	....	....
1995-96	Miami U.	CCHA	36	7	20	27	70	....	....	....	....	....	....	....	....	....	....	....	....	....	....	....	....	....	....
1996-97	Miami U.	CCHA	40	11	43	54	52	....	....	....	....	....	....	....	....	....	....	....	....	....	....	....	....	....	....
1997-98	Miami U.	CCHA	37	14	26	40	58	....	....	....	....	....	....	....	....	....	....	....	....	....	....	....	....	....	....
1998-99	**Florida**	**NHL**	**22**	**3**	**5**	**8**	**6**	**1**	**0**	**1**	**31**	**9.7**	**0**	**1**	**100.0**	**18:50**	....	....	....	....	....	....	....	....	....
	Kentucky	AHL	53	8	34	42	87	....	....	....	....	....	....	....	....	....	12	3	5	8	16	....	....	....	....
99-2000	**Florida**	**NHL**	**13**	**0**	**3**	**3**	**4**	**0**	**0**	**0**	**9**	**0.0**	**–2**	**0**	**0.0**	**16:57**	....	....	....	....	....	....	....	....	....
	Louisville Panthers	AHL	58	14	38	52	75	....	....	....	....	....	....	....	....	....	4	0	2	2	8	....	....	....	....

			Regular Season														Playoffs								
Season	Club	League	GP	G	A	Pts	PIM	PP	SH	GW	S	%	+/-	TF	F%	Min	GP	G	A	Pts	PIM	PP	SH	GW	Min
2000-01	**Florida**	**NHL**	69	4	18	22	28	1	0	0	83	4.8	−14	0	0.0	16:56	....	....	....	....	....	....	....	....	....
	Louisville Panthers	AHL	6	0	5	5	12	....	....	....	....	....	....	....	....	....	....	....	....	....	....	....	....	....	....
2001-02	**Florida**	**NHL**	25	3	3	6	12	1	0	0	31	9.7	−1	2	50.0	15:40	....	....	....	....	....	....	....	....	....
	Tampa Bay	**NHL**	41	5	15	20	27	2	0	1	68	7.4	−15	0	0.0	22:28	....	....	....	....	....	....	....	....	....
2002-03	**Tampa Bay**	**NHL**	77	13	40	53	44	8	0	1	136	9.6	9	2	0.0	24:31	11	0	7	7	6	0	0	0	27:45
2003-04♦	**Tampa Bay**	**NHL**	78	9	30	39	60	3	0	2	137	6.6	23	0	0.0	22:46	23	2	8	10	16	1	0	0	21:27
2004-05	Djurgarden	Sweden	32	9	9	18	47	....	....	....	....	....	....	....	....	....	12	2	3	5	26	....	....	....	....
2005-06	**Tampa Bay**	**NHL**	79	15	38	53	38	6	0	4	153	9.8	−8	1	0.0	23:26	5	1	3	4	6	0	0	0	25:54
	Canada	Olympics	DID NOT PLAY																						
2006-07	**Tampa Bay**	**NHL**	82	20	43	63	62	10	1	4	203	9.9	−5	1	0.0	27:03	6	0	1	1	2	0	0	0	28:03
2007-08	**Tampa Bay**	**NHL**	37	4	21	25	57	2	0	1	74	5.4	−29	0	0.0	27:24	....	....	....	....	....	....	....	....	....
	NHL Totals		**523**	**76**	**216**	**292**	**338**	**34**	**1**	**14**	**925**	**8.2**		**7**	**28.6**	**22:41**	**45**	**3**	**19**	**22**	**30**	**1**	**0**	**0**	**24:22**

CCHA First All-Star Team (1997, 1998) • NCAA West First All-American Team (1997, 1998) • AHL All-Rookie Team (1999 • AHL Second All-Star Team (1999, 2000) • NHL Second All-Star Team (2007)

Signed as a free agent by **Florida**, March 30, 1998. Traded to **Tampa Bay** by **Florida** for Tampa Bay's 5th round choice (Martin Tuma) in 2003 Entry Draft, January 7, 2002. Signed as a free agent by **Djurgarden** (Sweden), November 14, 2004. • Missed majority of 2007-08 season recovering from off-ice wrist injury, September 22, 2007 and follow-up surgery, November 6, 2007. Traded to **San Jose** by **Tampa Bay** with Brad Lukowich for Matt Carle, Ty Wishart, San Jose's 1st round choice in 2009 Entry Draft and San Jose's 4th round choice in 2010 Entry Draft, July 4, 2008.

BOYNTON, Nick

(BOIN-tuhn, NIHK) **FLA.**

Defense. Shoots right. 6'2", 210 lbs. Born, Nobleton, Ont., January 14, 1979. Boston's 1st choice, 21st overall, in 1999 Entry Draft.

Season	Club	League	GP	G	A	Pts	PIM	PP	SH	GW	S	%	+/-	TF	F%	Min	GP	G	A	Pts	PIM	PP	SH	GW	Min
1993-94	Caledon	MTJHL	4	0	1	1	0	....	....	....	....	....	....	....	....	....	....	....	....	....	....	....	....	....	....
1994-95	Caledon	MTJHL	44	10	35	45	139	....	....	....	....	....	....	....	....	....	....	....	....	....	....	....	....	....	....
1995-96	Ottawa 67's	OHL	64	10	14	24	90	....	....	....	....	....	....	....	....	....	4	0	3	3	10	....	....	....	....
1996-97	Ottawa 67's	OHL	63	13	51	64	143	....	....	....	....	....	....	....	....	....	24	4	*24	28	38	....	....	....	....
1997-98	Ottawa 67's	OHL	40	7	31	38	94	....	....	....	....	....	....	....	....	....	13	0	4	4	24	....	....	....	....
1998-99	Ottawa 67's	OHL	51	11	48	59	83	....	....	....	....	....	....	....	....	....	9	1	9	10	18	....	....	....	....
99-2000	**Boston**	**NHL**	5	0	0	0	0	0	0	0	6	0.0	−5	0	0.0	21:21	....	....	....	....	....	....	....	....	....
	Providence Bruins	AHL	53	5	14	19	66	....	....	....	....	....	....	....	....	....	12	1	0	1	6	....	....	....	....
2000-01	**Boston**	**NHL**	1	0	0	0	0	0	0	0	1	0.0	−1	0	0.0	14:27	•....	....	....	....	....	....	....	....	....
	Providence Bruins	AHL	78	6	27	33	105	....	....	....	....	....	....	....	....	....	17	0	2	2	35	....	....	....	....
2001-02	**Boston**	**NHL**	80	4	14	18	107	0	0	1	136	2.9	18	0	0.0	18:30	6	1	2	3	8	0	0	0	21:30
2002-03	**Boston**	**NHL**	78	7	17	24	99	0	1	2	160	4.4	8	1	0.0	22:41	5	0	1	1	4	0	0	0	23:22
2003-04	**Boston**	**NHL**	81	6	24	30	98	1	1	1	178	3.4	17	0	0.0	22:32	7	0	2	2	2	0	0	0	24:44
2004-05	Nottingham	Britain	9	1	3	4	4	....	....	....	....	....	....	....	....	....	6	1	2	3	22	....	....	....	....
2005-06	**Boston**	**NHL**	54	5	7	12	93	1	1	0	89	5.6	−7	1	100.0	20:39	....	....	....	....	....	....	....	....	....
2006-07	**Phoenix**	**NHL**	59	2	9	11	138	1	0	0	53	3.8	−13	1	0.0	16:48	....	....	....	....	....	....	....	....	....
2007-08	**Phoenix**	**NHL**	79	3	9	12	125	0	1	0	94	3.2	−9	0	0.0	17:01	....	....	....	....	....	....	....	....	....
	NHL Totals		**437**	**27**	**80**	**107**	**660**	**3**	**4**	**4**	**717**	**3.8**		**3**	**33.3**	**19:47**	**18**	**1**	**5**	**6**	**14**	**0**	**0**	**0**	**23:16**

• Re-entered NHL Entry Draft. Originally Washington's 1st choice, 9th overall, in 1997 Entry Draft.

OHL All-Rookie Team (1996) • Memorial Cup Tournament All-Star Team (1999) • Stafford Smythe Memorial Trophy (Memorial Cup Tournament - MVP) (1999) • NHL All-Rookie Team (2002)

Played in NHL All-Star Game (2004)

Signed as a free agent by **Nottingham** (Britain), January 26, 2005. Traded to **Phoenix** by **Boston** with Boston's 4th round choice (later traded to Toronto - Toronto selected Matt Frattin) in 2007 Entry Draft for Paul Mara and Phoenix's 3rd round choice (later traded to Anaheim - Anaheim selected Maxime Macenauer) in 2007 Entry Draft, June 26, 2006. Traded to **Florida** by **Phoenix** with Keith Ballard and Ottawa's 2nd round choice (previously acquired, later traded back to Phoenix - Phoenix selected Jared Staal) in 2008 Entry Draft for Olli Jokinen, June 20, 2008.

BRADLEY, Matt

(BRAD-lee, MAT) **WSH.**

Right wing. Shoots right. 6'3", 210 lbs. Born, Stittsville, Ont., June 13, 1978. San Jose's 4th choice, 102nd overall, in 1996 Entry Draft.

Season	Club	League	GP	G	A	Pts	PIM	PP	SH	GW	S	%	+/-	TF	F%	Min	GP	G	A	Pts	PIM	PP	SH	GW	Min
1994-95	Cumberland	CJHL	49	13	20	33	18	....	....	....	....	....	....	....	....	....	....	....	....	....	....	....	....	....	....
1995-96	Kingston	OHL	55	10	14	24	17	....	....	....	....	....	....	....	....	....	6	0	1	1	6	....	....	....	....
1996-97	Kingston	OHL	65	24	24	48	41	....	....	....	....	....	....	....	....	....	5	0	4	4	2	....	....	....	....
	Kentucky	AHL	1	0	1	1	0	....	....	....	....	....	....	....	....	....	....	....	....	....	....	....	....	....	....
1997-98	Kingston	OHL	55	33	50	83	24	....	....	....	....	....	....	....	....	....	8	3	4	7	7	....	....	....	....
1998-99	Kentucky	AHL	79	23	20	43	57	....	....	....	....	....	....	....	....	....	10	1	4	5	4	....	....	....	....
99-2000	Kentucky	AHL	80	22	19	41	81	....	....	....	....	....	....	....	....	....	9	6	3	9	9	....	....	....	....
2000-01	**San Jose**	**NHL**	21	1	1	2	19	0	0	0	16	6.3	0	0	0.0	6:58	....	....	....	....	....	....	....	....	....
	Kentucky	AHL	22	5	8	13	16	....	....	....	....	....	....	....	....	....	1	1	0	1	5	....	....	....	....
2001-02	**San Jose**	**NHL**	54	9	13	22	43	0	0	2	63	14.3	22	2	0.0	8:27	10	0	0	0	0	0	0	0	5:16
2002-03	**San Jose**	**NHL**	46	2	3	5	37	0	0	0	21	9.5	−1	1	0.0	7:54	....	....	....	....	....	....	....	....	....
2003-04	**Pittsburgh**	**NHL**	82	7	9	16	65	0	0	1	85	8.2	−27	29	41.4	12:48	....	....	....	....	....	....	....	....	....
2004-05	Bulldogs Dornbirn	Austria-2	6	5	2	7	18	....	....	....	....	....	....	....	....	....	....	....	....	....	....	....	....	....	....
2005-06	**Washington**	**NHL**	74	7	12	19	72	0	0	1	87	8.0	−8	25	52.0	12:36	....	....	....	....	....	....	....	....	....
2006-07	**Washington**	**NHL**	57	4	9	13	47	0	0	0	77	5.2	−5	20	45.0	11:55	....	....	....	....	....	....	....	....	....
2007-08	**Washington**	**NHL**	77	7	11	18	74	1	1	2	111	6.3	1	32	43.8	10:00	7	0	2	2	2	0	0	0	11:40
	NHL Totals		**411**	**37**	**58**	**95**	**357**	**1**	**1**	**6**	**460**	**8.0**		**109**	**44.0**	**10:42**	**17**	**0**	**2**	**2**	**2**	**0**	**0**	**0**	**7:54**

Traded to **Pittsburgh** by **San Jose** for Wayne Primeau, March 11, 2003. Signed as a free agent by **Dornbirn** (Austria-2), November 14, 2004. Signed as a free agent by **Washington**, August 18, 2005.

BRASHEAR, Donald

(bra-SHEER, DAWN-uohld) **WSH.**

Left wing. Shoots left. 6'3", 239 lbs. Born, Bedford, IN, January 7, 1972.

Season	Club	League	GP	G	A	Pts	PIM	PP	SH	GW	S	%	+/-	TF	F%	Min	GP	G	A	Pts	PIM	PP	SH	GW	Min
1988-89	Ste-Foy	QAAA	10	1	2	3	10	....	....	....	....	....	....	....	....	....	....	....	....	....	....	....	....	....	....
1989-90	Longueuil	QMJHL	64	12	14	26	169	....	....	....	....	....	....	....	....	....	7	0	0	0	11	....	....	....	....
1990-91	Longueuil	QMJHL	68	12	26	38	195	....	....	....	....	....	....	....	....	....	8	0	3	3	33	....	....	....	....
1991-92	Verdun	QMJHL	65	18	24	42	283	....	....	....	....	....	....	....	....	....	18	4	2	6	98	....	....	....	....
1992-93	Fredericton	AHL	76	11	3	14	261	....	....	....	....	....	....	....	....	....	5	0	0	0	8	....	....	....	....
1993-94	**Montreal**	**NHL**	14	2	2	4	34	0	0	0	15	13.3	0	....	....	....	2	0	0	0	0	0	0	0	
	Fredericton	AHL	62	38	28	66	250	....	....	....	....	....	....	....	....	....	....	....	....	....	....	....	....	....	....
1994-95	Fredericton	AHL	29	10	9	19	182	....	....	....	....	....	....	....	....	....	17	7	5	12	77	....	....	....	....
	Montreal	**NHL**	20	1	1	2	63	0	0	1	10	10.0	−5	....	....	....	....	....	....	....	....	....	....	....	....
1995-96	**Montreal**	**NHL**	67	0	4	4	223	0	0	0	25	0.0	−10	....	....	....	6	0	0	0	2	0	0	0	
1996-97	**Montreal**	**NHL**	10	0	0	0	38	0	0	0	6	0.0	−2	....	....	....	....	....	....	....	....	....	....	....	....
	Vancouver	**NHL**	59	8	5	13	207	0	0	2	55	14.5	−6	....	....	....	....	....	....	....	....	....	....	....	....
1997-98	**Vancouver**	**NHL**	77	9	9	18	*372	0	0	1	64	14.1	−9	....	....	....	....	....	....	....	....	....	....	....	....
1998-99	**Vancouver**	**NHL**	82	8	10	18	209	2	0	1	112	7.1	−25	6	16.7	13:25	....	....	....	....	....	....	....	....	....
99-2000	**Vancouver**	**NHL**	60	11	2	13	136	1	0	3	83	13.3	−9	11	36.4	13:07	....	....	....	....	....	....	....	....	....
2000-01	**Vancouver**	**NHL**	79	9	19	28	145	0	0	1	127	7.1	0	6	16.7	13:27	4	0	0	0	0	0	0	0	14:47
2001-02	**Vancouver**	**NHL**	31	5	8	13	90	1	0	0	45	11.1	−8	4	25.0	13:58	....	....	....	....	....	....	....	....	....
	Philadelphia	**NHL**	50	4	15	19	109	0	0	2	62	6.5	0	1	0.0	13:00	5	0	0	0	19	0	0	0	9:55
2002-03	**Philadelphia**	**NHL**	80	8	17	25	161	0	0	1	99	8.1	5	27	33.3	13:23	13	1	2	3	21	0	0	0	11:09
2003-04	**Philadelphia**	**NHL**	64	6	7	13	212	0	0	0	72	8.3	−1	18	38.9	11:02	18	1	3	4	61	1	0	0	8:56
2004-05	Quebec RadioX	QNAHL	47	18	32	50	260	....	....	....	....	....	....	....	....	....	8	4	6	10	42	....	....	....	....
2005-06	**Philadelphia**	**NHL**	76	4	5	9	166	0	0	0	73	5.5	−2	7	28.6	8:36	1	0	0	0	0	0	0	0	4:20
2006-07	**Washington**	**NHL**	77	4	9	13	156	0	0	0	47	8.5	1	8	25.0	7:58	....	....	....	....	....	....	....	....	....
2007-08	**Washington**	**NHL**	80	5	3	8	119	0	0	0	59	8.5	−7	1	0.0	7:52	7	1	1	2	0	0	0	0	7:30
	NHL Totals		**926**	**84**	**116**	**200**	**2440**	**4**	**0**	**12**	**954**	**8.8**		**89**	**30.3**	**11:21**	**56**	**3**	**6**	**9**	**103**	**1**	**0**	**0**	**9:49**

Signed as a free agent by **Montreal**, July 28, 1992. Traded to **Vancouver** by **Montreal** for Jassen Cullimore, November 13, 1996. Traded to **Philadelphia** by **Vancouver** with Vancouver's 6th round choice (later traded to Columbus – Columbus selected Jaroslav Balastik) in 2002 Entry Draft for Jan Hlavac and Tampa Bay's 3rd round choice (previously acquired, Vancouver selected Brett Skinner) in 2002 Entry Draft, December 17, 2001. Signed as a free agent by **Quebec** (QNAHL), September 21, 2004. Signed as a free agent by **Washington**, July 14, 2006.

BRASSARD, Derick

(bra-SAHRD, DAIR-ihk) **CBJ**

Center. Shoots left. 6', 188 lbs. Born, Hull, Que., September 22, 1987. Columbus' 1st choice, 6th overall, in 2006 Entry Draft.

Season	Club	League	GP	G	A	Pts	PIM	PP	SH	GW	S	%	+/-	TF	F%	Min	GP	G	A	Pts	PIM	PP	SH	GW	Min
2004-05	Drummondville	QMJHL	69	25	51	76	25	....	....	....	....	....	....	....	....	....	6	1	5	6	6	....	....	....	....
2005-06	Drummondville	QMJHL	58	44	72	116	92	....	....	....	....	....	....	....	....	....	7	5	4	9	10	....	....	....	....
2006-07	Drummondville	QMJHL	14	6	19	25	24	....	....	....	....	....	....	....	....	....	12	9	15	24	12	....	....	....	....

			Regular Season														Playoffs								
Season	Club	League	GP	G	A	Pts	PIM	PP	SH	GW	S	%	+/-	TF	F%	Min	GP	G	A	Pts	PIM	PP	SH	GW	Min
2007-08	Columbus	NHL	17	1	1	2	6	0	0	0	13	7.7	–4	80	42.5	9:03	....	....	....	....	....	....	....	....	....
	Syracuse Crunch	AHL	42	15	36	51	51	....	....	....	....	....	....	....	....	....	13	4	9	13	10	....	....	....	....
	NHL Totals		17	1	1	2	6	0	0	0	13	7.7		80	42.5	9:03	....	....	....	....	....	....	....	....	....

QMJHL First All-Star Team (2006)

• Missed majority of 2006-07 season recovering from shoulder injury.

BRENNAN, Kip

(BREH-nan, KIHP)

Left wing. Shoots left. 6'4", 230 lbs. Born, Kingston, Ont., August 27, 1980. Los Angeles' 4th choice, 103rd overall, in 1998 Entry Draft.

Season	Club	League	GP	G	A	Pts	PIM	PP	SH	GW	S	%	+/-	TF	F%	Min	GP	G	A	Pts	PIM	PP	SH	GW	Min
1995-96	St. Mike's B's	OPJHL	40	0	11	11	155	....	....	....	....	....	....	....	....	....	7	0	1	1	20	....	....	....	....
1996-97	Windsor Spitfires	OHL	42	0	10	10	156	....	....	....	....	....	....	....	....	....	5	0	1	1	16	....	....	....	....
1997-98	Windsor Spitfires	OHL	24	0	7	7	103	....	....	....	....	....	....	....	....	....	....	....	....	....	....	....	....	....	....
	Sudbury Wolves	OHL	24	0	3	3	85	....	....	....	....	....	....	....	....	....	....	....	....	....	....	....	....	....	....
1998-99	Sudbury Wolves	OHL	38	9	12	21	160	....	....	....	....	....	....	....	....	....	....	....	....	....	....	....	....	....	....
99-2000	Sudbury Wolves	OHL	55	16	16	32	228	....	....	....	....	....	....	....	....	....	12	3	3	6	67	....	....	....	....
2000-01	Lowell	AHL	23	2	3	5	117	....	....	....	....	....	....	....	....	....	....	....	....	....	....	....	....	....	....
	Sudbury Wolves	OHL	27	7	14	21	94	....	....	....	....	....	....	....	....	....	12	5	6	11	*92	....	....	....	....
2001-02	Los Angeles	NHL	4	0	0	0	22	0	0	0	0	0.0	1	0	0.0	4:40	....	....	....	....	....	....	....	....	....
	Manchester	AHL	44	4	1	5	269	....	....	....	....	....	....	....	....	....	4	0	1	1	26	....	....	....	....
2002-03	Los Angeles	NHL	19	0	0	0	57	0	0	0	6	0.0	0	2	0.0	4:52	....	....	....	....	....	....	....	....	....
	Manchester	AHL	35	3	2	5	195	....	....	....	....	....	....	....	....	....	3	0	0	0	0	....	....	....	....
2003-04	Los Angeles	NHL	18	1	0	1	79	0	0	0	6	16.7	–1	0	0.0	5:01	....	....	....	....	....	....	....	....	....
	Manchester	AHL	2	0	0	0	6	....	....	....	....	....	....	....	....	....	....	....	....	....	....	....	....	....	....
	Atlanta	NHL	5	0	0	0	17	0	0	0	2	0.0	0	0	0.0	3:37	....	....	....	....	....	....	....	....	....
2004-05	Chicago Wolves	AHL	48	7	6	13	267	....	....	....	....	....	....	....	....	....	18	1	1	2	*105	....	....	....	....
2005-06	Anaheim	NHL	12	0	1	1	35	0	0	0	5	0.0	–2	1	0.0	4:16	....	....	....	....	....	....	....	....	....
	Portland Pirates	AHL	9	2	1	3	22	....	....	....	....	....	....	....	....	....	....	....	....	....	....	....	....	....	....
2006-07	Hershey Bears	AHL	26	4	2	6	67	....	....	....	....	....	....	....	....	....	6	0	1	1	30	....	....	....	....
	Toronto Marlies	AHL	1	0	0	0	6	....	....	....	....	....	....	....	....	....	....	....	....	....	....	....	....	....	....
	Long Beach	ECHL	11	2	3	5	74	....	....	....	....	....	....	....	....	....	....	....	....	....	....	....	....	....	....
2007-08	NY Islanders	NHL	3	0	0	0	12	0	0	0	0	0.0	0	0	0.0	4:21	....	....	....	....	....	....	....	....	....
	Bridgeport	AHL	49	2	1	3	247	....	....	....	....	....	....	....	....	....	....	....	....	....	....	....	....	....	....
	NHL Totals		61	1	1	2	222	0	0	0	19	5.3		3	0.0	4:39	....	....	....	....	....	....	....	....	....

Traded to **Atlanta** by **Los Angeles** for Jeff Cowan, March 9, 2004. • Spent the majority of the 2003-04 season as a healthy reserve. Signed as a free agent by **Chicago** (AHL), September 27, 2004. Traded to **Anaheim** by **Atlanta** for Mark Popovic, August 23, 2005. Signed as a free agent by **NY Islanders**, July 3, 2007.

BRENT, Tim

(BREHNT, TIHM) **CHI.**

Center. Shoots right. 6', 188 lbs. Born, Cambridge, Ont., March 10, 1984. Anaheim's 3rd choice, 75th overall, in 2004 Entry Draft.

Season	Club	League	GP	G	A	Pts	PIM	PP	SH	GW	S	%	+/-	TF	F%	Min	GP	G	A	Pts	PIM	PP	SH	GW	Min
99-2000	Cambridge	OHA-B	40	19	16	35	42	....	....	....	....	....	....	....	....	....	....	....	....	....	....	....	....	....	....
2000-01	St. Michael's	OHL	64	9	19	28	31	....	....	....	....	....	....	....	....	....	18	2	8	10	6	....	....	....	....
2001-02	St. Michael's	OHL	61	19	40	59	52	....	....	....	....	....	....	....	....	....	14	7	12	19	20	....	....	....	....
2002-03	St. Michael's	OHL	60	24	42	66	74	....	....	....	....	....	....	....	....	....	19	7	17	24	14	....	....	....	....
2003-04	St. Michael's	OHL	53	26	41	67	105	....	....	....	....	....	....	....	....	....	18	4	13	17	24	....	....	....	....
2004-05	Cincinnati	AHL	46	5	13	18	42	....	....	....	....	....	....	....	....	....	12	0	1	1	6	....	....	....	....
2005-06	Portland Pirates	AHL	37	15	9	24	32	....	....	....	....	....	....	....	....	....	15	4	4	8	16	....	....	....	....
2006-07	Anaheim	NHL	15	1	0	1	6	0	0	0	14	7.1	–5	86	48.8	6:55	....	....	....	....	....	....	....	....	....
	Portland Pirates	AHL	48	16	14	30	40	....	....	....	....	....	....	....	....	....	....	....	....	....	....	....	....	....	....
2007-08	Pittsburgh	NHL	1	0	0	0	0	0	0	0	0	0.0	–1	5	60.0	4:34	....	....	....	....	....	....	....	....	....
	Wilkes-Barre	AHL	74	18	43	61	79	....	....	....	....	....	....	....	....	....	23	*12	15	27	10	....	....	....	....
	NHL Totals		16	1	0	1	6	0	0	0	14	7.1		91	49.5	6:46	....	....	....	....	....	....	....	....	....

• Re-entered NHL Entry Draft. Originally Anaheim's 2nd choice, 37th overall, in 2002 Entry Draft.

Traded to **Pittsburgh** by **Anaheim** for Stephen Dixon, June 23, 2007. Traded to **Chicago** by **Pittsburgh** for Danny Richmond, July 17, 2008.

BREWER, Eric

(BREW-uhr, AIR-ihk) **ST.L.**

Defense. Shoots left. 6'3", 222 lbs. Born, Vernon, B.C., April 17, 1979. NY Islanders' 2nd choice, 5th overall, in 1997 Entry Draft.

Season	Club	League	GP	G	A	Pts	PIM	PP	SH	GW	S	%	+/-	TF	F%	Min	GP	G	A	Pts	PIM	PP	SH	GW	Min
1994-95	Kamloops	Minor-BC	40	19	19	38	62	....	....	....	....	....	....	....	....	....	....	....	....	....	....	....	....	....	....
1995-96	Prince George	WHL	63	4	10	14	25	....	....	....	....	....	....	....	....	....	....	....	....	....	....	....	....	....	....
1996-97	Prince George	WHL	71	5	24	29	81	....	....	....	....	....	....	....	....	....	15	2	4	6	16	....	....	....	....
1997-98	Prince George	WHL	34	5	28	33	45	....	....	....	....	....	....	....	....	....	11	4	2	6	19	....	....	....	....
1998-99	NY Islanders	NHL	63	5	6	11	32	2	0	0	63	7.9	–14	0	0.0	15:28	....	....	....	....	....	....	....	....	....
99-2000	NY Islanders	NHL	26	0	2	2	20	0	0	0	30	0.0	–11	0	0.0	18:33	....	....	....	....	....	....	....	....	....
	Lowell	AHL	25	2	2	4	26	....	....	....	....	....	....	....	....	....	7	0	0	0	0	....	....	....	....
2000-01	Edmonton	NHL	77	7	14	21	53	2	0	2	91	7.7	15	0	0.0	18:31	6	1	5	6	2	1	0	0	28:12
2001-02	Edmonton	NHL	81	7	18	25	45	6	0	2	165	4.2	–5	0	0.0	23:56	....	....	....	....	....	....	....	....	....
	Canada	Olympics	6	2	0	2	0	....	....	....	....	....	....	....	....	....	....	....	....	....	....	....	....	....	....
2002-03	Edmonton	NHL	80	8	21	29	45	1	0	1	147	5.4	–11	1	100.0	24:56	6	1	3	4	6	0	0	0	25:31
2003-04	Edmonton	NHL	77	7	18	25	67	3	0	1	135	5.2	–6	0	0.0	24:40	....	....	....	....	....	....	....	....	....
2004-05			DID NOT PLAY																						
2005-06	St. Louis	NHL	32	6	3	9	45	1	0	1	64	9.4	–17	0	0.0	23:28	....	....	....	....	....	....	....	....	....
2006-07	St. Louis	NHL	82	6	23	29	69	2	0	1	111	5.4	–10	0	0.0	24:32	....	....	....	....	....	....	....	....	....
2007-08	St. Louis	NHL	77	1	21	22	91	0	0	0	101	1.0	–18	0	0.0	24:38	....	....	....	....	....	....	....	....	....
	NHL Totals		595	47	126	173	467	17	0	8	907	5.2		1	100.0	22:28	12	2	8	10	8	1	0	0	26:51

WHL West Second All-Star Team (1998)

Played in NHL All-Star Game (2003)

Traded to **Edmonton** by **NY Islanders** with Josh Green and NY Islanders' 2nd round choice (Brad Winchester) in 2000 Entry Draft for Roman Hamrlik, June 24, 2000. Traded to **St. Louis** by **Edmonton** with Doug Lynch and Jeff Woywitka for Chris Pronger, August 2, 2005. • Missed majority of 2005-06 season recovering from shoulder injuries suffered in games at Columbus (November 16, 2005) and Atlanta (January 13, 2006).

BRIERE, Daniel

(bree-AIR, DAN-yehl) **PHI.**

Center. Shoots right. 5'10", 179 lbs. Born, Gatineau, Que., October 6, 1977. Phoenix's 2nd choice, 24th overall, in 1996 Entry Draft.

Season	Club	League	GP	G	A	Pts	PIM	PP	SH	GW	S	%	+/-	TF	F%	Min	GP	G	A	Pts	PIM	PP	SH	GW	Min
1992-93	Abitibi Regents	QAAA	42	24	30	54	28	....	....	....	....	....	....	....	....	....	3	0	3	3	8	....	....	....	....
1993-94	Gatineau	QAAA	44	56	47	103	56	....	....	....	....	....	....	....	....	....	....	....	....	....	....	....	....	....	....
1994-95	Drummondville	QMJHL	72	51	72	123	54	....	....	....	....	....	....	....	....	....	4	2	3	5	2	....	....	....	....
1995-96	Drummondville	QMJHL	67	*67	*96	*163	84	....	....	....	....	....	....	....	....	....	6	6	12	18	8	....	....	....	....
1996-97	Drummondville	QMJHL	59	52	78	130	94	....	....	....	....	....	....	....	....	....	8	7	7	14	14	....	....	....	....
1997-98	Phoenix	NHL	5	1	0	1	2	0	0	0	4	25.0	1	....	....	....	....	....	....	....	....	....	....	....	....
	Springfield	AHL	68	36	56	92	42	....	....	....	....	....	....	....	....	....	4	1	2	3	4	....	....	....	....
1998-99	Phoenix	NHL	64	8	14	22	30	2	0	2	90	8.9	–3	484	47.5	11:13	....	....	....	....	....	....	....	....	....
	Las Vegas	IHL	1	1	1	2	0	....	....	....	....	....	....	....	....	....	....	....	....	....	....	....	....	....	....
	Springfield	AHL	13	2	6	8	20	....	....	....	....	....	....	....	....	....	3	0	1	1	2	....	....	....	....
99-2000	Phoenix	NHL	13	1	1	2	0	0	0	0	9	11.1	0	65	49.2	7:41	1	0	0	0	0	0	0	0	6:16
	Springfield	AHL	58	29	42	71	56	....	....	....	....	....	....	....	....	....	....	....	....	....	....	....	....	....	....
2000-01	Phoenix	NHL	30	11	4	15	12	9	0	1	43	25.6	–2	210	50.0	10:50	....	....	....	....	....	....	....	....	....
	Springfield	AHL	30	21	25	46	30	....	....	....	....	....	....	....	....	....	....	....	....	....	....	....	....	....	....
2001-02	Phoenix	NHL	78	32	28	60	52	12	0	5	149	21.5	6	951	51.8	15:44	5	2	1	3	2	1	0	1	16:25
2002-03	Phoenix	NHL	68	17	29	46	50	4	0	3	142	12.0	–21	1108	52.5	17:02	....	....	....	....	....	....	....	....	....
	Buffalo	NHL	14	7	5	12	12	5	0	1	39	17.9	1	206	50.0	17:49	....	....	....	....	....	....	....	....	....
2003-04	Buffalo	NHL	82	28	37	65	70	11	0	3	194	14.4	–7	1066	47.1	18:20	....	....	....	....	....	....	....	....	....
2004-05	SC Bern	Swiss	36	16	29	45	26	....	....	....	....	....	....	....	....	....	11	1	6	7	2	....	....	....	....
2005-06	Buffalo	NHL	48	25	33	58	48	11	0	4	147	17.0	3	517	50.7	19:04	18	8	11	19	12	3	0	2	18:48

			Regular Season														Playoffs								
Season	Club	League	GP	G	A	Pts	PIM	PP	SH	GW	S	%	+/-	TF	F%	Min	GP	G	A	Pts	PIM	PP	SH	GW	Min
2006-07	**Buffalo**	NHL	81	32	63	95	89	9	0	6	234	13.7	17	1089	49.6	19:19	16	3	12	15	16	2	0	1	20:53
2007-08	**Philadelphia**	NHL	79	31	41	72	68	14	0	3	182	17.0	–22	1250	50.5	18:52	17	9	7	16	20	6	0	3	18:26
	NHL Totals		562	193	255	448	433	77	0	28	1233	15.7		6946	50.1	16:37	57	22	31	53	50	12	0	7	18:51

QMJHL All-Rookie Team (1995) • QMJHL Offensive Rookie of the Year (1995) • QMJHL Second All-Star Team (1996, 1997) • AHL All-Rookie Team (1998) • AHL First All-Star Team (1998) • Dudley "Red" Garrett Memorial Award (Rookie of the Year – AHL) (1998)

Played in NHL All-Star Game (2007)

Traded to **Buffalo** by **Phoenix** with Phoenix's 3rd round choice (Andrej Sekera) in 2004 Entry Draft for Chris Gratton and Buffalo's 4th round choice (later traded to Edmonton – Edmonton selected Liam Reddox) in 2004 Entry Draft, March 10, 2003. Signed as a free agent by **Bern** (Swiss), September 28, 2004. Signed as a free agent by **Philadelphia**, July 1, 2007.

BRIND'AMOUR, Rod

(BRIHND-uh-MOHR, RAWD) **CAR.**

Center. Shoots left. 6'1", 205 lbs. Born, Ottawa, Ont., August 9, 1970. St. Louis' 1st choice, 9th overall, in 1988 Entry Draft.

1986-87	Notre Dame	SMHL	33	38	50	88	66	....	....	....	....	....	....	....	....	....	....	....	....	....	....	....	....	....	....
1987-88	Notre Dame	SJHL	56	46	61	107	136	....	....	....	....	....	....	....	....	....	....	....	....	....	....	....	....	....	....
1988-89	Michigan State	CCHA	42	27	32	59	63	....	....	....	....	....	....	....	....	....	....	....	....	....	....	....	....	....	....
	St. Louis	NHL	....	....	....	....	....	....	....	....	....	....	....	....	....	....	5	2	0	2	4	0	0	0	....
1989-90	**St. Louis**	NHL	79	26	35	61	46	10	0	1	160	16.3	23	....	....	....	12	5	8	13	6	1	0	0	....
1990-91	**St. Louis**	NHL	78	17	32	49	93	4	0	3	169	10.1	2	....	....	....	13	2	5	7	10	1	0	0	....
1991-92	**Philadelphia**	NHL	80	33	44	77	100	8	4	5	202	16.3	–3	....	....	....	....	....	....	....	....	....	....	....	....
1992-93	**Philadelphia**	NHL	81	37	49	86	89	13	4	4	206	18.0	–8	....	....	....	....	....	....	....	....	....	....	....	....
1993-94	**Philadelphia**	NHL	84	35	62	97	85	14	1	4	230	15.2	–9	....	....	....	....	....	....	....	....	....	....	....	....
1994-95	**Philadelphia**	NHL	48	12	27	39	33	4	1	2	86	14.0	–4	....	....	....	15	6	9	15	8	2	1	1	....
1995-96	**Philadelphia**	NHL	82	26	61	87	110	4	4	5	213	12.2	20	....	....	....	12	2	5	7	6	1	0	0	....
1996-97	**Philadelphia**	NHL	82	27	32	59	41	8	2	3	205	13.2	2	....	....	....	19	*13	8	21	10	4	2	1	....
1997-98	**Philadelphia**	NHL	82	36	38	74	54	10	2	8	205	17.6	–2	....	....	....	5	2	2	4	7	0	0	0	....
	Canada	Olympics	6	1	2	3	0	....	....	....	....	....	....	....	....	....	....	....	....	....	....	....	....	....	....
1998-99	**Philadelphia**	NHL	82	24	50	74	47	10	0	3	191	12.6	3	1773	56.5	21:29	6	1	3	4	0	0	0	0	25:08
99-2000	**Philadelphia**	NHL	12	5	3	8	4	4	0	0	26	19.2	–1	291	60.5	20:50	....	....	....	....	....	....	....	....	....
	Carolina	NHL	33	4	10	14	22	0	1	1	61	6.6	–12	704	55.5	20:35	....	....	....	....	....	....	....	....	....
2000-01	**Carolina**	NHL	79	20	36	56	47	5	1	5	163	12.3	–7	1907	60.4	22:07	6	1	3	4	6	0	0	1	23:27
2001-02	**Carolina**	NHL	81	23	32	55	40	5	2	5	162	14.2	3	2058	59.2	22:07	23	4	8	12	16	2	1	1	24:52
2002-03	**Carolina**	NHL	48	14	23	37	37	7	1	0	110	12.7	–9	1242	56.5	23:46	....	....	....	....	....	....	....	....	....
2003-04	**Carolina**	NHL	78	12	26	38	28	1	0	1	141	8.5	0	1817	61.1	21:23	....	....	....	....	....	....	....	....	....
2004-05	Kloten Flyers	Swiss	2	2	1	3	0	....	....	....	....	....	....	....	....	....	5	2	4	6	6	....	....	....	....
2005-06 ♦	**Carolina**	NHL	78	31	39	70	68	19	2	5	198	15.7	8	2145	59.1	24:18	25	12	6	18	16	6	0	4	23:52
2006-07	**Carolina**	NHL	78	26	56	82	46	9	2	5	181	14.4	7	2047	59.3	23:19	....	....	....	....	....	....	....	....	....
2007-08	**Carolina**	NHL	59	19	32	51	38	6	0	4	151	12.6	0	1460	58.3	22:27	....	....	....	....	....	....	....	....	....
	NHL Totals		1324	427	687	1114	1028	141	27	64	3060	14.0		15444	58.8	22:25	141	50	57	107	89	17	4	8	24:20

CCHA Rookie of the Year (1989) • NHL All-Rookie Team (1990) • Frank J. Selke Trophy (2006, 2007)

Played in NHL All-Star Game (1992)

Traded to **Philadelphia** by **St. Louis** with Dan Quinn for Ron Sutter and Murray Baron, September 22, 1991. Traded to **Carolina** by **Philadelphia** with Jean-Marc Pelletier and Philadelphia's 2nd round choice (later traded to Colorado – Colorado selected Agris Saviels) in 2000 Entry Draft for Keith Primeau and Carolina's 5th round choice (later traded to NY Islanders – NY Islanders selected Kristofer Ottosson) in 2000 Entry Draft, January 23, 2000. Signed as a free agent by **Kloten** (Swiss), February 16, 2005.

BRINE, David

(BRIGHN, DAY-vihd) **FLA.**

Center. Shoots left. 6'1", 201 lbs. Born, Truro, N.S., January 6, 1985.

2002-03	Truro Bearcats	MJrHL	52	21	32	53	29	....	....	....	....	....	....	....	....	....	....	....	....	....	....	....	....	....	....
2003-04	Halifax	QMJHL	70	22	25	47	20	....	....	....	....	....	....	....	....	....	....	....	....	....	....	....	....	....	....
2004-05	Halifax	QMJHL	67	14	37	51	36	....	....	....	....	....	....	....	....	....	13	6	7	13	8	....	....	....	....
2005-06	Halifax	QMJHL	70	34	66	100	80	....	....	....	....	....	....	....	....	....	11	1	5	6	23	....	....	....	....
	Manitoba Moose	AHL	....	....	....	....	....	....	....	....	....	....	....	....	....	....	9	0	1	1	2	....	....	....	....
2006-07	Rochester	AHL	22	4	4	8	4	....	....	....	....	....	....	....	....	....	....	....	....	....	....	....	....	....	....
	Florida Everblades	ECHL	52	9	21	30	22	....	....	....	....	....	....	....	....	....	15	6	4	10	22	....	....	....	....
2007-08	**Florida**	NHL	9	0	1	1	4	0	0	0	3	0.0	–1	44	38.6	6:02	....	....	....	....	....	....	....	....	....
	Rochester	AHL	66	9	11	20	26	....	....	....	....	....	....	....	....	....	....	....	....	....	....	....	....	....	....
	NHL Totals		9	0	1	1	4	0	0	0	3	0.0		44	38.6	6:02	....	....	....	....	....	....	....	....	....

Signed as a free agent by **Florida**, September 14, 2006.

BRISEBOIS, Patrice

(BREES-bwah, pa-TREEZ)

Defense. Shoots right. 6'2", 196 lbs. Born, Montreal, Que., January 27, 1971. Montreal's 2nd choice, 30th overall, in 1989 Entry Draft.

1986-87	Mtl-Bourassa	QAAA	39	15	19	34	66	....	....	....	....	....	....	....	....	....	....	....	....	....	....	....	....	....	....
1987-88	Laval Titan	QMJHL	48	10	34	44	95	....	....	....	....	....	....	....	....	....	6	0	2	2	2	....	....	....	....
1988-89	Laval Titan	QMJHL	50	20	45	65	95	....	....	....	....	....	....	....	....	....	17	8	14	22	45	....	....	....	....
1989-90	Laval Titan	QMJHL	56	18	70	88	108	....	....	....	....	....	....	....	....	....	13	7	9	16	26	....	....	....	....
1990-91	Drummondville	QMJHL	54	17	44	61	72	....	....	....	....	....	....	....	....	....	14	6	18	24	49	....	....	....	....
	Montreal	NHL	10	0	2	2	4	0	0	0	11	0.0	1	....	....	....	....	....	....	....	....	....	....	....	....
1991-92	**Montreal**	NHL	26	2	8	10	20	0	0	1	37	5.4	9	....	....	....	11	2	4	6	6	1	0	1	....
	Fredericton	AHL	53	12	27	39	51	....	....	....	....	....	....	....	....	....	....	....	....	....	....	....	....	....	....
1992-93 ♦	**Montreal**	NHL	70	10	21	31	79	4	0	2	123	8.1	6	....	....	....	20	0	4	4	18	0	0	0	....
1993-94	**Montreal**	NHL	53	2	21	23	63	1	0	0	71	2.8	5	....	....	....	7	0	4	4	6	0	0	0	....
1994-95	**Montreal**	NHL	35	4	8	12	26	0	0	2	67	6.0	–2	....	....	....	....	....	....	....	....	....	....	....	....
1995-96	**Montreal**	NHL	69	9	27	36	65	3	0	1	127	7.1	10	....	....	....	6	1	2	3	6	0	0	0	....
1996-97	**Montreal**	NHL	49	2	13	15	24	0	0	1	72	2.8	–7	....	....	....	3	1	1	2	24	0	0	1	....
1997-98	**Montreal**	NHL	79	10	27	37	67	5	0	1	125	8.0	16	....	....	....	10	1	0	1	0	0	0	0	....
1998-99	**Montreal**	NHL	54	3	9	12	28	1	0	1	90	3.3	–8	0	0.0	22:26	....	....	....	....	....	....	....	....	....
99-2000	**Montreal**	NHL	54	10	25	35	18	5	0	2	88	11.4	–1	0	0.0	23:14	....	....	....	....	....	....	....	....	....
2000-01	**Montreal**	NHL	77	15	21	36	28	11	0	4	178	8.4	–31	1	100.0	24:43	....	....	....	....	....	....	....	....	....
2001-02	**Montreal**	NHL	71	4	29	33	25	2	1	1	95	4.2	9	0	0.0	23:53	10	1	1	2	2	0	0	0	22:05
2002-03	**Montreal**	NHL	73	4	25	29	32	1	0	1	105	3.8	–14	0	0.0	23:23	....	....	....	....	....	....	....	....	....
2003-04	**Montreal**	NHL	71	4	27	31	22	2	0	0	96	4.2	17	0	0.0	21:20	11	2	1	3	4	1	0	0	22:30
2004-05	Kloten Flyers	Swiss	10	3	1	4	2	....	....	....	....	....	....	....	....	....	....	....	....	....	....	....	....	....	....
2005-06	**Colorado**	NHL	80	10	28	38	55	4	0	2	107	9.3	1	2	0.0	22:19	9	0	1	1	4	0	0	0	22:19
2006-07	**Colorado**	NHL	33	1	10	11	22	1	0	0	36	2.8	–5	0	0.0	19:23	....	....	....	....	....	....	....	....	....
2007-08	**Montreal**	NHL	43	3	8	11	26	2	0	0	42	7.1	–2	0	0.0	16:50	10	1	5	6	6	1	0	1	16:33
	NHL Totals		947	93	309	402	604	42	1	19	1470	6.3		3	33.3	22:22	97	9	23	32	76	3	0	3	20:52

QMJHL Second All-Star Team (1990) • QMJHL First All-Star Team (1991) • Canadian Major Junior Defenseman of the Year (1991) • Memorial Cup Tournament All-Star Team (1991)

Signed as a free agent by **Kloten** (Swiss), October 13, 2004. Signed as a free agent by **Colorado**, August 3, 2005. • Missed remainder of 2006-07 season recovering from back injury suffered in game vs. Dallas, December 27, 2006. Signed as a free agent by **Montreal**, August 3, 2007.

BRODZIAK, Kyle

(brohd-ZEE-ak, KIGHL) **EDM.**

Center. Shoots right. 6'2", 209 lbs. Born, St. Paul, Alta., May 25, 1984. Edmonton's 9th choice, 214th overall, in 2003 Entry Draft.

99-2000	Ft. Saskatchewan	AMBHL	36	23	33	56	57	....	....	....	....	....	....	....	....	....	....	....	....	....	....	....	....	....	....
	Moose Jaw	WHL	2	0	0	0	0	....	....	....	....	....	....	....	....	....	....	....	....	....	....	....	....	....	....
2000-01	Moose Jaw	WHL	57	2	8	10	49	....	....	....	....	....	....	....	....	....	3	0	0	0	0	....	....	....	....
2001-02	Moose Jaw	WHL	72	8	12	20	56	....	....	....	....	....	....	....	....	....	12	0	3	3	11	....	....	....	....
2002-03	Moose Jaw	WHL	72	32	30	62	84	....	....	....	....	....	....	....	....	....	13	5	3	8	16	....	....	....	....
2003-04	Moose Jaw	WHL	70	39	54	93	58	....	....	....	....	....	....	....	....	....	10	5	4	9	10	....	....	....	....
2004-05	Edmonton	AHL	56	6	26	32	49	....	....	....	....	....	....	....	....	....	....	....	....	....	....	....	....	....	....
2005-06	**Edmonton**	NHL	10	0	0	0	4	0	0	0	7	0.0	–4	75	52.0	11:02	....	....	....	....	....	....	....	....	....
	Iowa Stars	AHL	55	12	19	31	41	....	....	....	....	....	....	....	....	....	7	1	3	4	2	....	....	....	....
2006-07	**Edmonton**	NHL	6	1	0	1	2	0	0	0	11	9.1	0	48	52.1	17:08	....	....	....	....	....	....	....	....	....
	Wilkes-Barre	AHL	62	24	32	56	44	....	....	....	....	....	....	....	....	....	11	1	5	6	14	....	....	....	....
2007-08	**Edmonton**	NHL	80	14	17	31	33	0	1	3	125	11.2	–6	297	51.5	12:55	....	....	....	....	....	....	....	....	....
	NHL Totals		96	15	17	32	39	0	1	3	143	10.5		420	51.7	12:59	....	....	....	....	....	....	....	....	....

WHL East First All-Star Team (2004)

BROOKBANK, Sheldon

(BRUK-bank, SHEHL-duhn) **N.J.**

Defense. Shoots right. 6'2", 215 lbs. Born, Lanigan, Sask., October 3, 1980.

Season	Club	League	GP	G	A	Pts	PIM	PP	SH	GW	S	%	+/-	TF	F%	Min	Playoffs GP	G	A	Pts	PIM	PP	SH	GW	Min
2000-01	Humboldt	SJHL	59	14	35	49	281	....	....	....	....	....	....	....	....	....	....	....	....	....	....	....	....	....	....
2001-02	Grand Rapids	AHL	6	0	1	1	24	....	....	....	....	....	....	....	....	....	....	....	....	....	....	....	....	....	....
	Mississippi	ECHL	62	8	21	29	137	....	....	....	....	....	....	....	....	....	10	1	4	5	27	....	....	....	....
2002-03	Grand Rapids	AHL	69	2	11	13	136	....	....	....	....	....	....	....	....	....	15	1	3	4	28	....	....	....	....
2003-04	Cincinnati	AHL	74	2	9	11	216	....	....	....	....	....	....	....	....	....	9	0	2	2	20	....	....	....	....
2004-05	Cincinnati	AHL	60	1	11	12	181	....	....	....	....	....	....	....	....	....	11	0	0	0	40	....	....	....	....
2005-06	Milwaukee	AHL	73	9	26	35	232	....	....	....	....	....	....	....	....	....	21	1	8	9	49	....	....	....	....
2006-07	**Nashville**	**NHL**	**3**	**0**	**1**	**1**	**12**	**0**	**0**	**0**	**3**	**0.0**	**0**	**0**	**0.0**	**8:16**	....	....	....	....	....	....	....	....	....
	Milwaukee	AHL	78	15	38	53	176	....	....	....	....	....	....	....	....	....	4	0	0	0	6	....	....	....	....
2007-08	**New Jersey**	**NHL**	**44**	**0**	**8**	**8**	**63**	**0**	**0**	**0**	**43**	**0.0**	**0**	**0**	**0.0**	**15:08**	....	....	....	....	....	....	....	....	....
	Lowell Devils	AHL	1	0	0	0	5	....	....	....	....	....	....	....	....	....	....	....	....	....	....	....	....	....	....
	NHL Totals		**47**	**0**	**9**	**9**	**75**	**0**	**0**	**0**	**46**	**0.0**		**0**	**0.0**	**14:42**	....	....	....	....	....	....	....	....	....

AHL First All-Star Team (2007) • Eddie Shore Award (Outstanding Defenseman - AHL) (2007)

Signed as a free agent by **Anaheim**, July 21, 2003. Signed as a free agent by **Nashville**, August 4, 2005. Signed as a free agent by **Columbus**, July 1, 2007. Claimed on waivers by **New Jersey** from **Columbus**, October 2, 2007.

BROOKBANK, Wade

(BRUK-bank, WAYD) **CAR.**

Left wing. Shoots left. 6'4", 225 lbs. Born, Lanigan, Sask., September 29, 1977.

Season	Club	League	GP	G	A	Pts	PIM	PP	SH	GW	S	%	+/-	TF	F%	Min	Playoffs GP	G	A	Pts	PIM	PP	SH	GW	Min
1997-98	Melville	SJHL	58	8	21	29	330	....	....	....	....	....	....	....	....	....	....	....	....	....	....	....	....	....	....
	Anchorage Aces	WCHL	7	0	0	0	46	....	....	....	....	....	....	....	....	....	4	0	0	0	20	....	....	....	....
1998-99	Anchorage Aces	WCHL	56	0	4	4	337	....	....	....	....	....	....	....	....	....	....	....	....	....	....	....	....	....	....
99-2000	Oklahoma City	CHL	68	3	9	12	354	....	....	....	....	....	....	....	....	....	7	1	1	2	29	....	....	....	....
2000-01	Orlando	IHL	29	0	1	1	122	....	....	....	....	....	....	....	....	....	4	0	0	0	6	....	....	....	....
	Oklahoma City	CHL	46	1	13	14	267	....	....	....	....	....	....	....	....	....	5	0	0	0	24	....	....	....	....
2001-02	Grand Rapids	AHL	73	1	6	7	337	....	....	....	....	....	....	....	....	....	3	0	1	1	14	....	....	....	....
2002-03	Binghamton	AHL	8	0	0	0	28	....	....	....	....	....	....	....	....	....	....	....	....	....	....	....	....	....	....
2003-04	**Nashville**	**NHL**	**9**	**0**	**0**	**0**	**38**	**0**	**0**	**0**	**1**	**0.0**	**–4**	**0**	**0.0**	**3:28**	....	....	....	....	....	....	....	....	....
	Milwaukee	AHL	6	0	0	0	6	....	....	....	....	....	....	....	....	....	....	....	....	....	....	....	....	....	....
	Binghamton	AHL	4	0	0	0	31	....	....	....	....	....	....	....	....	....	....	....	....	....	....	....	....	....	....
	Vancouver	**NHL**	**20**	**2**	**0**	**2**	**95**	**0**	**0**	**1**	**6**	**33.3**	**3**	**0**	**0.0**	**3:50**	....	....	....	....	....	....	....	....	....
	Manitoba Moose	AHL	4	0	0	0	12	....	....	....	....	....	....	....	....	....	....	....	....	....	....	....	....	....	....
2004-05	Manitoba Moose	AHL	68	0	10	10	285	....	....	....	....	....	....	....	....	....	9	0	0	0	10	....	....	....	....
2005-06	**Vancouver**	**NHL**	**32**	**1**	**2**	**3**	**81**	**0**	**0**	**0**	**10**	**10.0**	**3**	**0**	**0.0**	**4:56**	....	....	....	....	....	....	....	....	....
2006-07	**Boston**	**NHL**	**7**	**1**	**0**	**1**	**15**	**0**	**0**	**0**	**1**	**100.0**	**–1**	**1**	**0.0**	**4:25**	....	....	....	....	....	....	....	....	....
	Providence Bruins	AHL	4	0	0	0	15	....	....	....	....	....	....	....	....	....	....	....	....	....	....	....	....	....	....
	Wilkes-Barre	AHL	39	1	0	1	116	....	....	....	....	....	....	....	....	....	5	0	0	0	6	....	....	....	....
2007-08	**Carolina**	**NHL**	**32**	**1**	**1**	**2**	**76**	**0**	**0**	**0**	**12**	**8.3**	**4**	**4**	**25.0**	**3:48**	....	....	....	....	....	....	....	....	....
	Albany River Rats	AHL	25	0	2	2	28	....	....	....	....	....	....	....	....	....	....	....	....	....	....	....	....	....	....
	NHL Totals		**100**	**5**	**3**	**8**	**305**	**0**	**0**	**1**	**30**	**16.7**		**5**	**20.0**	**4:11**	....	....	....	....	....	....	....	....	....

Signed as a free agent by **Orlando** (IHL), September 1, 2000. Signed as a free agent by **Ottawa**, July 27, 2001. • Missed majority of 2002-03 season recovering from knee injury suffered in game vs. Wilkes-Barre (AHL), November 2, 2002. Claimed by **Nashville** from **Ottawa** in Waiver Draft, October 3, 2003. Traded to **Vancouver** by **Nashville** for future considerations, December 17, 2003. Claimed on waivers by **Ottawa** from **Vancouver**, December 19, 2003. Traded to **Florida** by **Ottawa** for future considerations, December 29, 2003. Claimed on waivers by **Vancouver** from **Florida**, January 3, 2004. • Missed majority of 2005-06 season recovering from two head injuries suffered during the season and as a healthy reserve. Signed as a free agent by **Boston**, July 21, 2006. Traded to **Pittsburgh** by **Boston** for future considerations, December 19, 2006. Signed as a free agent by **Carolina**, July 1, 2007.

BROOKS, Alex

(BROOKS, AL-ehx)

Defense. Shoots right. 6'1", 195 lbs. Born, Madison, WI, August 21, 1976.

Season	Club	League	GP	G	A	Pts	PIM	PP	SH	GW	S	%	+/-	TF	F%	Min	Playoffs GP	G	A	Pts	PIM	PP	SH	GW	Min
1993-94	Madison Capitols	USHL	13	3	11	14	....	....	....	....	....	....	....	....	....	....	....	....	....	....	....	....	....	....	....
1994-95	Madison West	High-WI	24	13	28	41	....	....	....	....	....	....	....	....	....	....	....	....	....	....	....	....	....	....	....
1995-96	Green Bay	USHL	46	3	22	25	....	....	....	....	....	....	....	....	....	....	....	....	....	....	....	....	....	....	....
1996-97	U. of Wisconsin	WCHA	DID NOT PLAY – INJURED																						
1997-98	U. of Wisconsin	WCHA	40	1	4	5	72	....	....	....	....	....	....	....	....	....	....	....	....	....	....	....	....	....	....
1998-99	U. of Wisconsin	WCHA	37	0	3	3	73	....	....	....	....	....	....	....	....	....	....	....	....	....	....	....	....	....	....
99-2000	U. of Wisconsin	WCHA	41	4	10	14	78	....	....	....	....	....	....	....	....	....	....	....	....	....	....	....	....	....	....
2000-01	U. of Wisconsin	WCHA	41	3	16	19	76	....	....	....	....	....	....	....	....	....	....	....	....	....	....	....	....	....	....
2001-02	Jokerit Helsinki	Finland	53	1	3	4	109	....	....	....	....	....	....	....	....	....	12	0	0	0	11	....	....	....	....
2002-03	Albany River Rats	AHL	66	0	7	7	56	....	....	....	....	....	....	....	....	....	....	....	....	....	....	....	....	....	....
2003-04	Albany River Rats	AHL	77	2	6	8	100	....	....	....	....	....	....	....	....	....	....	....	....	....	....	....	....	....	....
2004-05	Albany River Rats	AHL	63	0	6	6	83	....	....	....	....	....	....	....	....	....	....	....	....	....	....	....	....	....	....
2005-06	Albany River Rats	AHL	58	1	4	5	81	....	....	....	....	....	....	....	....	....	....	....	....	....	....	....	....	....	....
2006-07	**New Jersey**	**NHL**	**19**	**0**	**1**	**1**	**4**	**0**	**0**	**0**	**4**	**0.0**	**–1**	**0**	**0.0**	**8:39**	....	....	....	....	....	....	....	....	....
	Lowell Devils	AHL	21	0	2	2	6	....	....	....	....	....	....	....	....	....	....	....	....	....	....	....	....	....	....
2007-08	Peoria Rivermen	AHL	70	0	8	8	90	....	....	....	....	....	....	....	....	....	....	....	....	....	....	....	....	....	....
	NHL Totals		**19**	**0**	**1**	**1**	**4**	**0**	**0**	**0**	**4**	**0.0**		**0**	**0.0**	**8:39**	....	....	....	....	....	....	....	....	....

• Missed entire 1996-97 season recovering from back injury suffered during off-season training, August, 1996. Signed as a free agent by **New Jersey**, July 12, 2002. Signed as a free agent by **St. Louis**, August 9, 2007.

BROUWER, Troy

(BROW-uhr, TROI) **CHI.**

Right wing. Shoots right. 6'3", 220 lbs. Born, Vancouver, B.C., August 17, 1985. Chicago's 13th choice, 214th overall, in 2004 Entry Draft.

Season	Club	League	GP	G	A	Pts	PIM	PP	SH	GW	S	%	+/-	TF	F%	Min	Playoffs GP	G	A	Pts	PIM	PP	SH	GW	Min
2001-02	Moose Jaw	WHL	13	0	0	0	7	....	....	....	....	....	....	....	....	....	....	....	....	....	....	....	....	....	....
2002-03	Moose Jaw	WHL	59	9	12	21	54	....	....	....	....	....	....	....	....	....	13	1	2	3	14	....	....	....	....
2003-04	Moose Jaw	WHL	72	23	26	49	111	....	....	....	....	....	....	....	....	....	10	3	0	3	12	....	....	....	....
2004-05	Moose Jaw	WHL	71	22	25	47	132	....	....	....	....	....	....	....	....	....	5	1	2	3	8	....	....	....	....
2005-06	Moose Jaw	WHL	72	49	53	*102	122	....	....	....	....	....	....	....	....	....	17	10	4	14	34	....	....	....	....
2006-07	**Chicago**	**NHL**	**10**	**0**	**0**	**0**	**7**	**0**	**0**	**0**	**7**	**0.0**	**–7**	**0**	**0.0**	**9:55**	....	....	....	....	....	....	....	....	....
	Norfolk Admirals	AHL	66	41	38	79	70	....	....	....	....	....	....	....	....	....	6	1	0	1	4	....	....	....	....
2007-08	**Chicago**	**NHL**	**2**	**0**	**1**	**1**	**0**	**0**	**0**	**0**	**0**	**0.0**	**1**	**0**	**0.0**	**11:56**	....	....	....	....	....	....	....	....	....
	Rockford IceHogs	AHL	75	35	19	54	154	....	....	....	....	....	....	....	....	....	12	5	4	9	16	....	....	....	....
	NHL Totals		**12**	**0**	**1**	**1**	**7**	**0**	**0**	**0**	**7**	**0.0**		**0**	**0.0**	**10:15**	....	....	....	....	....	....	....	....	....

WHL East First All-Star Team (2006) • AHL All-Rookie Team (2007) • AHL Second All-Star Team (2007)

BROWN, Curtis

(BROWN, KUHR-tihs)

Center/Left wing. Shoots left. 6', 200 lbs. Born, Unity, Sask., February 12, 1976. Buffalo's 2nd choice, 43rd overall, in 1994 Entry Draft.

Season	Club	League	GP	G	A	Pts	PIM	PP	SH	GW	S	%	+/-	TF	F%	Min	Playoffs GP	G	A	Pts	PIM	PP	SH	GW	Min
1990-91	Unity Bantams	SBHL	60	93	104	197	55	....	....	....	....	....	....	....	....	....	....	....	....	....	....	....	....	....	....
1991-92	Moose Jaw	SMHL	36	35	30	65	44	....	....	....	....	....	....	....	....	....	....	....	....	....	....	....	....	....	....
1992-93	Moose Jaw	WHL	71	13	16	29	30	....	....	....	....	....	....	....	....	....	....	....	....	....	....	....	....	....	....
1993-94	Moose Jaw	WHL	72	27	38	65	82	....	....	....	....	....	....	....	....	....	....	....	....	....	....	....	....	....	....
1994-95	Moose Jaw	WHL	70	51	53	104	63	....	....	....	....	....	....	....	....	....	10	8	7	15	20	....	....	....	....
	Buffalo	**NHL**	**1**	**1**	**1**	**2**	**2**	**0**	**0**	**0**	**4**	**25.0**	**2**	....	....	....	....	....	....	....	....	....	....	....	....
1995-96	Moose Jaw	WHL	25	20	18	38	30	....	....	....	....	....	....	....	....	....	....	....	....	....	....	....	....	....	....
	Prince Albert	WHL	19	12	21	33	8	....	....	....	....	....	....	....	....	....	18	10	15	25	18	....	....	....	....
	Buffalo	**NHL**	**4**	**0**	**0**	**0**	**0**	**0**	**0**	**0**	**1**	**0.0**	**0**	....	....	....	....	....	....	....	....	....	....	....	....
	Rochester	AHL	....	....	....	....	....	....	....	....	....	....	....	....	....	....	12	0	1	1	2	....	....	....	....
1996-97	**Buffalo**	**NHL**	**28**	**4**	**3**	**7**	**18**	**0**	**0**	**1**	**31**	**12.9**	**4**	....	....	....	....	....	....	....	....	....	....	....	....
	Rochester	AHL	51	22	21	43	30	....	....	....	....	....	....	....	....	....	10	4	6	10	4	....	....	....	....
1997-98	**Buffalo**	**NHL**	**63**	**12**	**12**	**24**	**34**	**1**	**1**	**2**	**91**	**13.2**	**11**	....	....	....	**13**	**1**	**2**	**3**	**10**	**1**	**0**	**0**	....
1998-99	**Buffalo**	**NHL**	**78**	**16**	**31**	**47**	**56**	**5**	**1**	**3**	**128**	**12.5**	**23**	**1198**	**45.0**	**17:30**	**21**	**7**	**6**	**13**	**10**	**3**	**0**	**3**	**18:51**
99-2000	**Buffalo**	**NHL**	**74**	**22**	**29**	**51**	**42**	**5**	**0**	**4**	**149**	**14.8**	**19**	**1318**	**48.6**	**18:11**	**5**	**1**	**3**	**4**	**6**	**1**	**0**	**0**	**17:11**
2000-01	**Buffalo**	**NHL**	**70**	**10**	**22**	**32**	**34**	**2**	**1**	**0**	**105**	**9.5**	**15**	**1159**	**50.4**	**16:34**	**13**	**5**	**0**	**5**	**8**	**0**	**2**	**1**	**18:14**
2001-02	**Buffalo**	**NHL**	**82**	**20**	**17**	**37**	**32**	**4**	**1**	**5**	**171**	**11.7**	**–4**	**1608**	**49.0**	**17:48**	....	....	....	....	....	....	....	....	....
2002-03	**Buffalo**	**NHL**	**74**	**15**	**16**	**31**	**40**	**3**	**4**	**4**	**144**	**10.4**	**4**	**1387**	**49.5**	**16:53**	....	....	....	....	....	....	....	....	....
2003-04	**Buffalo**	**NHL**	**68**	**9**	**12**	**21**	**30**	**2**	**1**	**2**	**117**	**7.7**	**2**	**1182**	**51.5**	**16:36**	....	....	....	....	....	....	....	....	....
	San Jose	**NHL**	**12**	**2**	**2**	**4**	**6**	**0**	**0**	**0**	**21**	**9.5**	**1**	**105**	**47.6**	**16:26**	**17**	**0**	**2**	**2**	**18**	**0**	**0**	**0**	**14:37**

			Regular Season														Playoffs								
Season	Club	League	GP	G	A	Pts	PIM	PP	SH	GW	S	%	+/-	TF	F%	Min	GP	G	A	Pts	PIM	PP	SH	GW	Min
2004-05	San Diego Gulls	ECHL	47	9	29	38	24	....	....	....	....	....	....	....	....	....	....	....	....	....	....	....	....	....	....
2005-06	Chicago	NHL	71	5	10	15	38	0	1	0	84	6.0	–9	881	50.6	13:39	....	....	....	....	....	....	....	....	....
2006-07	San Jose	NHL	78	8	12	20	56	0	2	3	84	9.5	–2	881	51.4	13:10	11	0	2	2	2	0	0	0	12:10
2007-08	San Jose	NHL	33	5	4	9	10	0	0	0	38	13.2	4	179	59.2	10:49	7	0	0	0	4	0	0	0	9:11
	NHL Totals		736	129	171	300	398	22	12	24	1168	11.0		9898	49.5	16:02	87	14	15	29	58	5	2	4	15:45

WHL East First All-Star Team (1995) • WHL East Second All-Star Team (1996)

Traded to **San Jose** by **Buffalo** with Andy Delmore for Jeff Jillson and San Jose's compensatory 7th round choice (Andrew Orpik) in 2005 Entry Draft, March 9, 2004. Signed as a free agent by **Chicago**, July 2, 2004. Signed as a free agent by **San Diego** (ECHL), November 16, 2004. Signed as a free agent by **San Jose**, July 3, 2006.

BROWN, Dustin

(BROWN, DUHS-tihn) **L.A.**

Left wing. Shoots right. 6', 205 lbs. Born, Ithaca, NY, November 4, 1984. Los Angeles' 1st choice, 13th overall, in 2003 Entry Draft.

Season	Club	League	GP	G	A	Pts	PIM	PP	SH	GW	S	%	+/-	TF	F%	Min	GP	G	A	Pts	PIM	PP	SH	GW	Min
1998-99	Ithaca	High-NY	18	4	13	17	....	....	....	....	....	....	....	....	....	....	....	....	....	....	....	....	....	....	....
99-2000	Ithaca	High-NY	24	33	21	53	....	....	....	....	....	....	....	....	....	....	....	....	....	....	....	....	....	....	....
2000-01	Guelph Storm	OHL	53	23	22	45	45	....	....	....	....	....	....	....	....	....	4	0	0	0	10	....	....	....	....
2001-02	Guelph Storm	OHL	63	41	32	73	56	....	....	....	....	....	....	....	....	....	9	8	5	13	14	....	....	....	....
2002-03	Guelph Storm	OHL	58	34	42	76	89	....	....	....	....	....	....	....	....	....	11	7	8	15	6	....	....	....	....
2003-04	Los Angeles	NHL	31	1	4	5	16	0	0	0	40	2.5	0	1	0.0	10:29	....	....	....	....	....	....	....	....	....
2004-05	Manchester	AHL	79	29	45	74	96	....	....	....	....	....	....	....	....	....	6	5	2	7	10	....	....	....	....
2005-06	Los Angeles	NHL	79	14	14	28	80	6	0	2	159	8.8	–10	15	66.7	13:59	....	....	....	....	....	....	....	....	....
2006-07	Los Angeles	NHL	81	17	29	46	54	13	0	1	195	8.7	–21	77	49.4	18:43	....	....	....	....	....	....	....	....	....
2007-08	Los Angeles	NHL	78	33	27	60	55	12	2	4	219	15.1	–13	40	50.0	20:18	....	....	....	....	....	....	....	....	....
	NHL Totals		269	65	74	139	205	31	2	7	613	10.6		133	51.1	16:50	....	....	....	....	....	....	....	....	....

OHL All-Rookie Team (2001) • Canadian Major Junior Scholastic Player of the Year (2003)

• Missed majority of 2003-04 season recovering from ankle injury suffered in game vs. Chicago, November 29, 2003.

BROWN, Mike

(BROWN, MIGHK) **VAN.**

Right wing. Shoots right. 6', 210 lbs. Born, Northbrook, IL, June 24, 1985. Vancouver's 4th choice, 159th overall, in 2004 Entry Draft.

Season	Club	League	GP	G	A	Pts	PIM	PP	SH	GW	S	%	+/-	TF	F%	Min	GP	G	A	Pts	PIM	PP	SH	GW	Min
2000-01	Chicago Chill	USAHA	66	27	23	50	....	....	....	....	....	....	....	....	....	....	....	....	....	....	....	....	....	....	....
2001-02	USNTDP	U-17	17	6	4	10	13	....	....	....	....	....	....	....	....	....	....	....	....	....	....	....	....	....	....
	USNTDP	NAHL	46	5	11	16	56	....	....	....	....	....	....	....	....	....	....	....	....	....	....	....	....	....	....
2002-03	USNTDP	U-18	34	5	3	8	16	....	....	....	....	....	....	....	....	....	....	....	....	....	....	....	....	....	....
	USNTDP	NAHL	9	0	3	3	29	....	....	....	....	....	....	....	....	....	....	....	....	....	....	....	....	....	....
2003-04	U. of Michigan	CCHA	42	8	5	13	51	....	....	....	....	....	....	....	....	....	....	....	....	....	....	....	....	....	....
2004-05	U. of Michigan	CCHA	35	3	5	8	95	....	....	....	....	....	....	....	....	....	....	....	....	....	....	....	....	....	....
2005-06	Manitoba Moose	AHL	73	7	8	15	139	....	....	....	....	....	....	....	....	....	13	1	2	3	17	....	....	....	....
2006-07	Manitoba Moose	AHL	62	3	0	3	194	....	....	....	....	....	....	....	....	....	13	0	2	2	16	....	....	....	....
2007-08	Vancouver	NHL	19	1	0	1	55	0	0	0	9	11.1	–2	0	0.0	6:19	....	....	....	....	....	....	....	....	....
	Manitoba Moose	AHL	54	10	3	13	201	....	....	....	....	....	....	....	....	....	6	2	0	2	11	....	....	....	....
	NHL Totals		19	1	0	1	55	0	0	0	9	11.1		0	0.0	6:19	....	....	....	....	....	....	....	....	....

BRULE, Gilbert

(broo-LAY, zhihl-BAIR) **EDM.**

Center. Shoots right. 5'10", 180 lbs. Born, Edmonton, Alta., January 1, 1987. Columbus' 1st choice, 6th overall, in 2005 Entry Draft.

Season	Club	League	GP	G	A	Pts	PIM	PP	SH	GW	S	%	+/-	TF	F%	Min	GP	G	A	Pts	PIM	PP	SH	GW	Min
2002-03	Quesnel	BCHL	48	32	25	57	71	....	....	....	....	....	....	....	....	....	....	....	....	....	....	....	....	....	....
	Vancouver Giants	WHL	1	0	0	0	0	....	....	....	....	....	....	....	....	....	4	1	0	1	0	....	....	....	....
2003-04	Vancouver Giants	WHL	67	25	35	60	100	....	....	....	....	....	....	....	....	....	11	4	5	9	10	....	....	....	....
2004-05	Vancouver Giants	WHL	70	39	48	87	169	....	....	....	....	....	....	....	....	....	6	1	3	4	8	....	....	....	....
2005-06	Columbus	NHL	7	2	2	4	0	0	0	0	11	18.2	–2	60	43.3	13:11	....	....	....	....	....	....	....	....	....
	Vancouver Giants	WHL	27	23	15	38	40	....	....	....	....	....	....	....	....	....	18	*16	14	*30	44	....	....	....	....
2006-07	Columbus	NHL	78	9	10	19	28	3	0	0	98	9.2	–21	268	45.9	10:39	....	....	....	....	....	....	....	....	....
2007-08	Columbus	NHL	61	1	8	9	24	0	0	1	74	1.4	–4	78	51.3	9:54	....	....	....	....	....	....	....	....	....
	Syracuse Crunch	AHL	16	5	5	10	44	....	....	....	....	....	....	....	....	....	13	2	3	5	16	....	....	....	....
	NHL Totals		146	12	20	32	52	3	0	1	183	6.6		406	46.6	10:27	....	....	....	....	....	....	....	....	....

WHL West First All-Star Team (2005) • Canadian Major Junior Scholastic Player of the Year (2005) • WHL West Second All-Star Team (2006) • Memorial Cup Tournament All-Star Team (2006) • Ed Chynoweth Trophy (Memorial Cup Tournament - Leading Scorer) (2006)

• Missed majority of 2005-06 season recovering from sternum (October 7, 2005 vs. Calgary) and leg (November 30, 2005 at Minnesota) injuries. Traded to **Edmonton** by **Columbus** for Raffi Torres, July 1, 2008.

BRUNETTE, Andrew

(broo-NEHT, AN-droo) **MIN.**

Left wing. Shoots left. 6'1", 212 lbs. Born, Sudbury, Ont., August 24, 1973. Washington's 6th choice, 174th overall, in 1993 Entry Draft.

Season	Club	League	GP	G	A	Pts	PIM	PP	SH	GW	S	%	+/-	TF	F%	Min	GP	G	A	Pts	PIM	PP	SH	GW	Min
1989-90	Rayside-Balfour	NOHA	32	38	*65	*103	....	....	....	....	....	....	....	....	....	....	....	....	....	....	....	....	....	....	....
	Rayside-Balfour	NOJHA	4	1	1	2	0	....	....	....	....	....	....	....	....	....	....	....	....	....	....	....	....	....	....
1990-91	Owen Sound	OHL	63	15	20	35	15	....	....	....	....	....	....	....	....	....	....	....	....	....	....	....	....	....	....
1991-92	Owen Sound	OHL	66	51	47	98	42	....	....	....	....	....	....	....	....	....	5	5	0	5	8	....	....	....	....
1992-93	Owen Sound	OHL	66	*62	*100	*162	91	....	....	....	....	....	....	....	....	....	8	8	6	14	16	....	....	....	....
1993-94	Portland Pirates	AHL	23	9	11	20	10	....	....	....	....	....	....	....	....	....	2	0	1	1	0	....	....	....	....
	Providence Bruins	AHL	3	0	0	0	0	....	....	....	....	....	....	....	....	....	....	....	....	....	....	....	....	....	....
	Hampton Roads	ECHL	20	12	18	30	32	....	....	....	....	....	....	....	....	....	7	7	6	13	18	....	....	....	....
1994-95	Portland Pirates	AHL	79	30	50	80	53	....	....	....	....	....	....	....	....	....	7	3	3	6	10	....	....	....	....
1995-96	Washington	NHL	11	3	3	6	0	0	0	1	16	18.8	5	....	....	....	6	1	3	4	0	0	0	0	....
	Portland Pirates	AHL	69	28	66	94	125	....	....	....	....	....	....	....	....	....	20	11	18	29	15	....	....	....	....
1996-97	Washington	NHL	23	4	7	11	12	2	0	0	23	17.4	–3	....	....	....	....	....	....	....	....	....	....	....	....
	Portland Pirates	AHL	50	22	51	73	48	....	....	....	....	....	....	....	....	....	5	1	2	3	0	....	....	....	....
1997-98	Washington	NHL	28	11	12	23	12	4	0	2	42	26.2	2	....	....	....	....	....	....	....	....	....	....	....	....
	Portland Pirates	AHL	43	21	46	67	64	....	....	....	....	....	....	....	....	....	10	1	11	12	12	....	....	....	....
1998-99	Nashville	NHL	77	11	20	31	26	7	0	1	65	16.9	–10	8	50.0	13:13	....	....	....	....	....	....	....	....	....
99-2000	Atlanta	NHL	81	23	27	50	30	9	0	2	107	21.5	–32	8	25.0	15:42	....	....	....	....	....	....	....	....	....
2000-01	Atlanta	NHL	77	15	44	59	26	6	0	4	104	14.4	–5	11	54.6	16:58	....	....	....	....	....	....	....	....	....
2001-02	Minnesota	NHL	81	21	48	69	18	10	0	2	106	19.8	–4	111	58.6	16:02	....	....	....	....	....	....	....	....	....
2002-03	Minnesota	NHL	82	18	28	46	30	9	0	2	97	18.6	–10	59	44.1	14:29	18	7	6	13	4	4	0	1	15:00
2003-04	Minnesota	NHL	82	15	34	49	12	7	0	3	90	16.7	3	49	46.9	15:32	....	....	....	....	....	....	....	....	....
2004-05			DID NOT PLAY																						
2005-06	Colorado	NHL	82	24	39	63	48	11	0	2	129	18.6	9	18	33.3	15:01	9	3	6	9	8	1	0	1	17:47
2006-07	Colorado	NHL	82	27	56	83	36	9	0	2	173	15.6	–8	8	62.5	17:31	....	....	....	....	....	....	....	....	....
2007-08	Colorado	NHL	82	19	40	59	14	7	0	2	125	15.2	5	8	37.5	15:33	10	5	3	8	2	3	0	0	17:02
	NHL Totals		788	191	358	549	264	81	0	23	1077	17.7		280	50.0	15:34	43	16	18	34	14	8	0	2	16:13

OHL First All-Star Team (1993) • Canadian Major Junior Second All-Star Team (1993) • AHL Second All-Star Team (1995)

Claimed by **Nashville** from **Washington** in Expansion Draft, June 26, 1998. Traded to **Atlanta** by **Nashville** for Atlanta's 5th round choice (Matt Hendricks) in 2000 Entry Draft, June 21, 1999. Signed as a free agent by **Minnesota**, July 17, 2001. Signed as a free agent by **Colorado**, August 6, 2005. Signed as a free agent by **Minnesota**, July 1, 2008.

BRYLIN, Sergei

(BRIH-lin, SAIR-gay)

Left wing. Shoots left. 5'10", 190 lbs. Born, Moscow, USSR, January 13, 1974. New Jersey's 2nd choice, 42nd overall, in 1992 Entry Draft.

Season	Club	League	GP	G	A	Pts	PIM	PP	SH	GW	S	%	+/-	TF	F%	Min	GP	G	A	Pts	PIM	PP	SH	GW	Min
1991-92	CSKA Moscow	CIS	44	1	6	7	4	....	....	....	....	....	....	....	....	....	....	....	....	....	....	....	....	....	....
	CSKA Moscow 2	CIS-3	1	0	0	0	0	....	....	....	....	....	....	....	....	....	....	....	....	....	....	....	....	....	....
1992-93	CSKA Moscow	CIS	42	5	4	9	36	....	....	....	....	....	....	....	....	....	....	....	....	....	....	....	....	....	....
1993-94	CSKA Moscow	CIS	39	4	6	10	36	....	....	....	....	....	....	....	....	....	....	....	....	....	....	....	....	....	....
	Russian Penguins	IHL	13	4	5	9	18	....	....	....	....	....	....	....	....	....	....	....	....	....	....	....	....	....	....
1994-95	Albany River Rats	AHL	63	19	35	54	78	....	....	....	....	....	....	....	....	....	....	....	....	....	....	....	....	....	....
	♦ New Jersey	NHL	26	6	8	14	8	0	0	0	41	14.6	12	....	....	....	12	1	2	3	4	0	0	0	....
1995-96	New Jersey	NHL	50	4	5	9	26	0	0	1	51	7.8	–2	....	....	....	....	....	....	....	....	....	....	....	....
1996-97	New Jersey	NHL	29	2	2	4	20	0	0	0	34	5.9	–13	....	....	....	....	....	....	....	....	....	....	....	....
	Albany River Rats	AHL	43	17	24	41	38	....	....	....	....	....	....	....	....	....	16	4	8	12	12	....	....	....	....
1997-98	New Jersey	NHL	18	2	3	5	0	0	0	0	20	10.0	4	....	....	....	....	....	....	....	....	....	....	....	....
	Albany River Rats	AHL	44	21	22	43	60	....	....	....	....	....	....	....	....	....	....	....	....	....	....	....	....	....	....
1998-99	New Jersey	NHL	47	5	10	15	28	3	0	1	51	9.8	8	184	50.5	12:55	5	3	1	4	4	1	0	1	18:21

			Regular Season														Playoffs								
Season	Club	League	GP	G	A	Pts	PIM	PP	SH	GW	S	%	+/-	TF	F%	Min	GP	G	A	Pts	PIM	PP	SH	GW	Min
99-2000♦	New Jersey	NHL	64	9	11	20	20	1	0	1	84	10.7	0	72	41.7	13:23	17	3	5	8	0	0	0	0	13:02
2000-01	New Jersey	NHL	75	23	29	52	24	3	1	0	130	17.7	25	43	44.2	15:31	20	3	4	7	6	1	0	1	13:07
2001-02	New Jersey	NHL	76	16	28	44	10	5	0	3	133	12.0	21	17	47.1	17:11	6	0	2	2	2	0	0	0	19:05
2002-03♦	New Jersey	NHL	52	11	8	19	16	3	1	1	86	12.8	-2	90	32.2	16:11	19	1	3	4	8	0	0	1	17:03
2003-04	New Jersey	NHL	82	14	19	33	20	7	0	1	98	14.3	10	695	46.6	16:25	5	0	0	0	0	0	0	0	15:02
2004-05	Voskresensk	Russia	35	8	19	27	40	....	....	....	....	....	....	....	....	....	....	....	....	....	....	....	....	....	....
2005-06	New Jersey	NHL	82	15	22	37	46	4	0	3	126	11.9	-4	807	48.7	15:44	9	2	0	2	2	0	0	0	16:34
2006-07	New Jersey	NHL	82	16	24	40	35	8	0	2	97	16.5	-5	277	45.5	17:45	11	1	2	3	6	1	0	0	18:12
2007-08	New Jersey	NHL	82	6	10	16	20	0	0	1	65	9.2	-5	192	45.8	13:33	5	1	0	1	0	0	0	0	11:39
	NHL Totals		765	129	179	308	273	34	2	14	1016	12.7		2377	46.7	15:32	109	15	19	34	32	3	0	3	15:26

Signed as a free agent by **Voskresensk** (Russia), November 4, 2004.

BULIS, Jan

(BOO-lihs, YAHN)

Center. Shoots left. 6'1", 208 lbs. Born, Pardubice, Czech., March 18, 1978. Washington's 3rd choice, 43rd overall, in 1996 Entry Draft.

Season	Club	League	GP	G	A	Pts	PIM	PP	SH	GW	S	%	+/-	TF	F%	Min	GP	G	A	Pts	PIM	PP	SH	GW	Min
1993-94	HC Pardubice Jr.	CzRep-Jr.	25	16	11	27	....	....	....	....	....	....	....	....	....	....	....	....	....	....	....	....	....	....	....
1994-95	Kelowna Spartans	BCJHL	51	23	25	48	36	....	....	....	....	....	....	....	....	....	17	7	9	16	0	....	....	....	....
1995-96	Barrie Colts	OHL	59	29	30	59	22	....	....	....	....	....	....	....	....	....	7	2	3	5	2	....	....	....	....
1996-97	Barrie Colts	OHL	64	42	61	103	42	....	....	....	....	....	....	....	....	....	9	3	7	10	10	....	....	....	....
1997-98	Kingston	OHL	2	0	1	1	0	....	....	....	....	....	....	....	....	....	12	8	10	18	12	....	....	....	....
	Washington	NHL	48	5	11	16	18	0	0	0	37	13.5	-5	....	....	....	....	....	....	....	....	....	....	....	....
	Portland Pirates	AHL	3	1	4	5	12	....	....	....	....	....	....	....	....	....	....	....	....	....	....	....	....	....	....
1998-99	Washington	NHL	38	7	16	23	6	3	0	3	57	12.3	3	599	48.9	14:27	....	....	....	....	....	....	....	....	....
	Cincinnati	IHL	10	2	2	4	14	....	....	....	....	....	....	....	....	....	....	....	....	....	....	....	....	....	....
99-2000	Washington	NHL	56	9	22	31	30	0	0	1	92	9.8	7	609	45.5	13:55	....	....	....	....	....	....	....	....	....
2000-01	Washington	NHL	39	5	13	18	26	1	0	0	41	12.2	0	224	46.9	11:53	....	....	....	....	....	....	....	....	....
	Portland Pirates	AHL	4	0	2	2	0	....	....	....	....	....	....	....	....	....	....	....	....	....	....	....	....	....	....
	Montreal	NHL	12	0	5	5	0	0	0	0	20	0.0	-1	230	48.3	18:25	....	....	....	....	....	....	....	....	....
2001-02	Montreal	NHL	53	9	10	19	8	1	0	3	87	10.3	-2	156	43.0	13:34	6	0	0	0	6	0	0	0	12:25
2002-03	Montreal	NHL	82	16	24	40	30	0	0	2	160	10.0	9	153	42.5	15:42	....	....	....	....	....	....	....	....	....
2003-04	Montreal	NHL	72	13	17	30	30	1	1	4	147	8.8	-8	103	46.6	17:07	11	1	1	2	4	0	0	0	17:23
2004-05	Pardubice	CzRep	45	24	25	49	113	....	....	....	....	....	....	....	....	....	16	7	4	11	43	....	....	....	....
2005-06	Montreal	NHL	73	20	20	40	50	6	1	3	131	15.3	2	129	44.2	15:37	6	1	1	2	2	0	0	0	16:42
	Czech Republic	Olympics	8	0	0	0	10	....	....	....	....	....	....	....	....	....	....	....	....	....	....	....	....	....	....
2006-07	Vancouver	NHL	79	12	11	23	70	1	1	2	122	9.8	-8	132	38.6	14:23	12	1	1	2	2	0	0	0	19:46
2007-08	Mytischi	Russia	57	18	29	47	106	....	....	....	....	....	....	....	....	....	5	0	0	0	4	....	....	....	....
	NHL Totals		552	96	149	245	268	13	3	18	894	10.7		2335	46.0	14:56	35	3	3	6	14	0	0	0	17:14

Traded to **Montreal** by **Washington** with Richard Zednik and Washington's 1st round choice (Alexander Perezhogin) in 2001 Entry Draft for Trevor Linden, Dainius Zubrus and New Jersey's 2nd round choice (previously acquired, later traded to Tampa Bay – Tampa Bay selected Andreas Holmqvist) in 2001 Entry Draft, March 13, 2001. Signed as a free agent by **Pardubice** (CzRep), September 17, 2004. Signed as a free agent by **Vancouver**, July 25, 2006. Signed as a free agent by **Khimik Mytischi** (Russia), August 31, 2007.

BURISH, Adam

(BUHR-ish, A-duhm) **CHI.**

Right wing. Shoots right. 6'1", 189 lbs. Born, Madison, WI, January 6, 1983. Chicago's 9th choice, 282nd overall, in 2002 Entry Draft.

Season	Club	League	GP	G	A	Pts	PIM	PP	SH	GW	S	%	+/-	TF	F%	Min	GP	G	A	Pts	PIM	PP	SH	GW	Min
2000-01	Edgewood	High-WI	22	25	30	55	22	....	....	....	....	....	....	....	....	....	....	....	....	....	....	....	....	....	....
2001-02	Green Bay	USHL	61	24	33	57	122	....	....	....	....	....	....	....	....	....	1	0	0	0	0	....	....	....	....
2002-03	U. of Wisconsin	WCHA	19	0	6	6	32	....	....	....	....	....	....	....	....	....	....	....	....	....	....	....	....	....	....
2003-04	U. of Wisconsin	WCHA	43	6	13	19	63	....	....	....	....	....	....	....	....	....	....	....	....	....	....	....	....	....	....
2004-05	U. of Wisconsin	WCHA	41	13	7	20	41	....	....	....	....	....	....	....	....	....	....	....	....	....	....	....	....	....	....
2005-06	U. of Wisconsin	WCHA	42	9	24	33	67	....	....	....	....	....	....	....	....	....	....	....	....	....	....	....	....	....	....
2006-07	Chicago	NHL	9	0	0	0	2	0	0	0	12	0.0	-4	6	50.0	11:08	....	....	....	....	....	....	....	....	....
	Norfolk Admirals	AHL	64	11	10	21	146	....	....	....	....	....	....	....	....	....	6	1	1	2	4	....	....	....	....
2007-08	Chicago	NHL	81	4	4	8	214	0	1	1	69	5.8	-13	264	42.1	11:45	....	....	....	....	....	....	....	....	....
	NHL Totals		90	4	4	8	216	0	1	1	81	4.9		270	42.2	11:41	....	....	....	....	....	....	....	....	....

NCAA Championship All-Tournament Team (2006)

BURNS, Brent

(BUHRNZ, BREHNT) **MIN.**

Defense. Shoots right. 6'5", 219 lbs. Born, Ajax, Ont., March 9, 1985. Minnesota's 1st choice, 20th overall, in 2003 Entry Draft.

Season	Club	League	GP	G	A	Pts	PIM	PP	SH	GW	S	%	+/-	TF	F%	Min	GP	G	A	Pts	PIM	PP	SH	GW	Min
2000-01	North York	MTHL	46	4	7	11	16	....	....	....	....	....	....	....	....	....	....	....	....	....	....	....	....	....	....
2001-02	Couchiching	OPJHL	68	15	25	40	14	....	....	....	....	....	....	....	....	....	....	....	....	....	....	....	....	....	....
2002-03	Brampton	OHL	68	15	25	40	14	....	....	....	....	....	....	....	....	....	11	5	6	11	6	....	....	....	....
2003-04	Minnesota	NHL	36	1	5	6	12	0	0	0	34	2.9	-10	7	28.6	13:29	....	....	....	....	....	....	....	....	....
	Houston Aeros	AHL	1	0	1	1	2	....	....	....	....	....	....	....	....	....	....	....	....	....	....	....	....	....	....
2004-05	Houston Aeros	AHL	73	11	16	27	57	....	....	....	....	....	....	....	....	....	5	0	0	0	4	....	....	....	....
2005-06	Minnesota	NHL	72	4	12	16	32	1	0	1	73	5.5	-7	11	54.6	14:07	....	....	....	....	....	....	....	....	....
2006-07	Minnesota	NHL	77	7	18	25	26	3	0	3	108	6.5	16	4	25.0	15:48	5	0	1	1	14	0	0	0	18:59
2007-08	Minnesota	NHL	82	15	28	43	80	8	0	4	158	9.5	12	1	100.0	23:06	6	0	2	2	6	0	0	0	27:35
	NHL Totals		267	27	63	90	150	12	0	8	373	7.2		23	43.5	17:16	11	0	3	3	20	0	0	0	23:40

• Spent majority of 2003-04 season on assignment to Team Canada and as a healthy reserve.

BURROWS, Alexandre

(BUHR-ohz, al-ehx-AHN-druh) **VAN.**

Left wing. Shoots left. 6'1", 190 lbs. Born, Pincourt, Que., April 11, 1981.

Season	Club	League	GP	G	A	Pts	PIM	PP	SH	GW	S	%	+/-	TF	F%	Min	GP	G	A	Pts	PIM	PP	SH	GW	Min
2000-01	Shawinigan	QMJHL	63	16	14	30	105	....	....	....	....	....	....	....	....	....	10	2	1	3	8	....	....	....	....
2001-02	Shawinigan	QMJHL	64	35	35	70	184	....	....	....	....	....	....	....	....	....	10	9	10	19	20	....	....	....	....
2002-03	Greenville	ECHL	53	9	17	26	201	....	....	....	....	....	....	....	....	....	....	....	....	....	....	....	....	....	....
	Baton Rouge	ECHL	13	4	2	6	64	....	....	....	....	....	....	....	....	....	....	....	....	....	....	....	....	....	....
2003-04	Manitoba Moose	AHL	2	0	0	0	0	....	....	....	....	....	....	....	....	....	....	....	....	....	....	....	....	....	....
	Columbia Inferno	ECHL	64	29	44	73	194	....	....	....	....	....	....	....	....	....	4	2	0	2	28	....	....	....	....
2004-05	Manitoba Moose	AHL	72	9	17	26	107	....	....	....	....	....	....	....	....	....	14	0	3	3	37	....	....	....	....
	Columbia Inferno	ECHL	4	5	1	6	4	....	....	....	....	....	....	....	....	....	....	....	....	....	....	....	....	....	....
2005-06	Vancouver	NHL	43	7	5	12	61	0	1	1	49	14.3	5	19	47.4	10:24	....	....	....	....	....	....	....	....	....
	Manitoba Moose	AHL	33	12	18	30	57	....	....	....	....	....	....	....	....	....	13	6	7	13	27	....	....	....	....
2006-07	Vancouver	NHL	81	3	6	9	93	0	0	1	70	4.3	-7	16	43.8	11:26	11	1	0	1	14	0	0	0	10:34
2007-08	Vancouver	NHL	82	12	19	31	179	1	3	3	126	9.5	11	37	35.1	15:06	....	....	....	....	....	....	....	....	....
	NHL Totals		206	22	30	52	333	1	4	5	245	9.0		72	40.3	12:41	11	1	0	1	14	0	0	0	10:34

Signed as a free agent by **Manitoba** (AHL), October 21, 2003. Signed as a free agent by **Vancouver**, November 8, 2005.

BYERS, Dane

(BIGH-uhrs, DAYN) **NYR**

Left wing. Shoots left. 6'3", 195 lbs. Born, Nipawin, Sask., February 21, 1986. NY Rangers' 4th choice, 48th overall, in 2004 Entry Draft.

Season	Club	League	GP	G	A	Pts	PIM	PP	SH	GW	S	%	+/-	TF	F%	Min	GP	G	A	Pts	PIM	PP	SH	GW	Min
2002-03	Prince Albert	WHL	49	8	6	14	46	....	....	....	....	....	....	....	....	....	....	....	....	....	....	....	....	....	....
2003-04	Prince Albert	WHL	51	9	8	17	134	....	....	....	....	....	....	....	....	....	6	1	2	3	17	....	....	....	....
2004-05	Prince Albert	WHL	65	11	9	20	181	....	....	....	....	....	....	....	....	....	17	4	6	10	18	....	....	....	....
2005-06	Prince Albert	WHL	71	21	27	48	157	....	....	....	....	....	....	....	....	....	....	....	....	....	....	....	....	....	....
	Hartford	AHL	5	0	2	2	6	....	....	....	....	....	....	....	....	....	....	....	....	....	....	....	....	....	....
2006-07	Hartford	AHL	78	17	30	47	213	....	....	....	....	....	....	....	....	....	7	2	0	2	16	....	....	....	....
2007-08	NY Rangers	NHL	1	0	0	0	0	0	0	0	0	0.0	-1	0	0.0	5:05	....	....	....	....	....	....	....	....	....
	Hartford	AHL	73	23	23	46	184	....	....	....	....	....	....	....	....	....	5	2	1	3	2	....	....	....	....
	NHL Totals		1	0	0	0	0	0	0	0	0	0.0		0	0.0	5:05	....	....	....	....	....	....	....	....	....

BYFUGLIEN, Dustin

(bigh-FEWG-lehn, DUHS-tihn) **CHI.**

Right wing. Shoots right. 6'3", 246 lbs. Born, Minneapolis, MN, March 27, 1985. Chicago's 8th choice, 245th overall, in 2003 Entry Draft.

			Regular Season														Playoffs								
Season	Club	League	GP	G	A	Pts	PIM	PP	SH	GW	S	%	+/-	TF	F%	Min	GP	G	A	Pts	PIM	PP	SH	GW	Min
2001-02	Chicago Mission	MAHL	52	32	30	62	40	....	....	....	....	....	....	....	....	....	....	....	....	....	....	....	....	....	....
	Brandon	WHL	3	0	0	0	0	....	....	....	....	....	....	....	....	....	....	....	....	....	....	....	....	....	....
2002-03	Brandon	WHL	8	1	1	2	4	....	....	....	....	....	....	....	....	....	....	....	....	....	....	....	....	....	....
	Prince George	WHL	48	9	28	37	74	....	....	....	....	....	....	....	....	....	5	1	3	4	12	....	....	....	....
2003-04	Prince George	WHL	66	16	29	45	137	....	....	....	....	....	....	....	....	....	....	....	....	....	....	....	....	....	....
2004-05	Prince George	WHL	64	22	36	58	184	....	....	....	....	....	....	....	....	....	....	....	....	....	....	....	....	....	....
2005-06	**Chicago**	**NHL**	**25**	**3**	**2**	**5**	**24**	**0**	**0**	**1**	**45**	**6.7**	**–6**	**0**	**0.0**	**17:19**	....	....	....	....	....	....	....	....	....
	Norfolk Admirals	AHL	53	8	15	23	75	....	....	....	....	....	....	....	....	....	4	1	2	3	4	....	....	....	....
2006-07	**Chicago**	**NHL**	**9**	**1**	**2**	**3**	**10**	**0**	**0**	**0**	**18**	**5.6**	**–2**	**0**	**0.0**	**17:18**	....	....	....	....	....	....	....	....	....
	Norfolk Admirals	AHL	63	16	28	44	146	....	....	....	....	....	....	....	....	....	6	0	2	2	18	....	....	....	....
2007-08	**Chicago**	**NHL**	**67**	**19**	**17**	**36**	**59**	**7**	**0**	**4**	**163**	**11.7**	**–7**	**1**	**0.0**	**17:02**	....	....	....	....	....	....	....	....	....
	Rockford IceHogs	AHL	8	2	5	7	25	....	....	....	....	....	....	....	....	....	....	....	....	....	....	....	....	....	....
	NHL Totals		**101**	**23**	**21**	**44**	**93**	**7**	**0**	**5**	**226**	**10.2**		**1**	**0.0**	**17:08**	....	....	....	....	....	....	....	....	....

AHL Second All-Star Team (2007)

CAJANEK, Petr

(chuh-YA-nihk, PEE-tuhr)

Right wing. Shoots left. 5'11", 193 lbs. Born, Gottwaldov/Zlin, Czech., August 18, 1975. St. Louis' 6th choice, 253rd overall, in 2001 Entry Draft.

Season	Club	League	GP	G	A	Pts	PIM	PP	SH	GW	S	%	+/-	TF	F%	Min	GP	G	A	Pts	PIM	PP	SH	GW	Min
1993-94	AC ZPS Zlin	CzRep	34	5	4	9		....	....	....	....	....	....	....	....	....	3	0	0	0	....	....	....	....	....
1994-95	AC ZPS Zlin	CzRep	35	7	9	16	8	....	....	....	....	....	....	....	....	....	12	2	6	8	4	....	....	....	....
1995-96	AC ZPS Zlin	CzRep	36	8	11	19	32	....	....	....	....	....	....	....	....	....	8	2	6	8	8	....	....	....	....
1996-97	AC ZPS Zlin	CzRep	50	9	30	39	46	....	....	....	....	....	....	....	....	....	....	....	....	....	....	....	....	....	....
1997-98	Zlin	CzRep	46	19	27	46	117	....	....	....	....	....	....	....	....	....	....	....	....	....	....	....	....	....	....
1998-99	Zlin	CzRep	49	15	33	48	123	....	....	....	....	....	....	....	....	....	11	5	7	12	12	....	....	....	....
99-2000	Zlin	CzRep	50	23	34	57	66	....	....	....	....	....	....	....	....	....	4	1	0	1	0	....	....	....	....
2000-01	Zlin	CzRep	52	18	31	49	105	....	....	....	....	....	....	....	....	....	6	0	4	4	22	....	....	....	....
2001-02	Zlin	CzRep	49	20	44	64	64	....	....	....	....	....	....	....	....	....	11	5	7	12	10	....	....	....	....
	Czech Republic	Olympics	4	0	0	0	0	....	....	....	....	....	....	....	....	....	....	....	....	....	....	....	....	....	....
2002-03	**St. Louis**	**NHL**	**51**	**9**	**29**	**38**	**20**	**2**	**2**	**1**	**90**	**10.0**	**16**	**793**	**48.4**	**15:56**	**2**	**0**	**0**	**0**	**2**	**0**	**0**	**0**	**11:07**
2003-04	**St. Louis**	**NHL**	**70**	**12**	**14**	**26**	**16**	**3**	**0**	**4**	**126**	**9.5**	**12**	**1000**	**47.6**	**17:48**	**5**	**0**	**2**	**2**	**2**	**0**	**0**	**0**	**19:27**
2004-05	HC Hame Zlin	CzRep	49	10	15	25	91	....	....	....	....	....	....	....	....	....	17	5	4	9	24	....	....	....	....
2005-06	**St. Louis**	**NHL**	**71**	**10**	**31**	**41**	**54**	**3**	**0**	**0**	**150**	**6.7**	**–22**	**888**	**49.7**	**18:53**	....	....	....	....	....	....	....	....	....
	Czech Republic	Olympics	7	1	0	1	4	....	....	....	....	....	....	....	....	....	....	....	....	....	....	....	....	....	....
2006-07	**St. Louis**	**NHL**	**77**	**15**	**33**	**48**	**54**	**1**	**0**	**1**	**167**	**9.0**	**9**	**539**	**50.3**	**16:15**	....	....	....	....	....	....	....	....	....
2007-08	Peoria Rivermen	AHL	4	1	0	1	0	....	....	....	....	....	....	....	....	....	....	....	....	....	....	....	....	....	....
	Ak Bars Kazan	Russia	33	13	20	33	56	....	....	....	....	....	....	....	....	....	10	5	6	11	4	....	....	....	....
	NHL Totals		**269**	**46**	**107**	**153**	**144**	**9**	**2**	**6**	**533**	**8.6**		**3220**	**48.8**	**17:17**	**7**	**0**	**2**	**2**	**4**	**0**	**0**	**0**	**17:04**

Signed as a free agent by **Zlin** (CzRep), September 5, 2004. • Re-assigned to **Kazan** (Russia) by **St. Louis**, October 25, 2007.

CALDER, Kyle

(KAWL-dehr, KIGHL) **L.A.**

Left wing. Shoots left. 5'11", 180 lbs. Born, Mannville, Alta., January 5, 1979. Chicago's 7th choice, 130th overall, in 1997 Entry Draft.

Season	Club	League	GP	G	A	Pts	PIM	PP	SH	GW	S	%	+/-	TF	F%	Min	GP	G	A	Pts	PIM	PP	SH	GW	Min
1994-95	Leduc Oil Barons	AMHL	27	25	32	57	22	....	....	....	....	....	....	....	....	....	....	....	....	....	....	....	....	....	....
1995-96	Regina Pats	WHL	27	1	7	8	10	....	....	....	....	....	....	....	....	....	11	0	0	0	0	....	....	....	....
1996-97	Regina Pats	WHL	62	25	34	59	17	....	....	....	....	....	....	....	....	....	5	3	0	3	6	....	....	....	....
1997-98	Regina Pats	WHL	62	27	50	77	58	....	....	....	....	....	....	....	....	....	2	0	1	1	0	....	....	....	....
1998-99	Regina Pats	WHL	34	23	28	51	29	....	....	....	....	....	....	....	....	....	....	....	....	....	....	....	....	....	....
	Kamloops Blazers	WHL	27	19	18	37	30	....	....	....	....	....	....	....	....	....	15	6	10	16	6	....	....	....	....
99-2000	**Chicago**	**NHL**	**8**	**1**	**1**	**2**	**2**	**0**	**0**	**0**	**5**	**20.0**	**–3**	**2**	**0.0**	**9:59**	....	....	....	....	....	....	....	....	....
	Cleveland	IHL	74	14	22	36	43	....	....	....	....	....	....	....	....	....	9	2	2	4	14	....	....	....	....
2000-01	**Chicago**	**NHL**	**43**	**5**	**10**	**15**	**14**	**0**	**0**	**1**	**63**	**7.9**	**–4**	**2**	**0.0**	**12:43**	....	....	....	....	....	....	....	....	....
	Norfolk Admirals	AHL	37	12	15	27	21	....	....	....	....	....	....	....	....	....	9	2	6	8	2	....	....	....	....
2001-02	**Chicago**	**NHL**	**81**	**17**	**36**	**53**	**47**	**6**	**0**	**3**	**133**	**12.8**	**8**	**0**	**0.0**	**16:33**	**5**	**2**	**0**	**2**	**2**	**1**	**0**	**0**	**16:45**
2002-03	**Chicago**	**NHL**	**82**	**15**	**27**	**42**	**40**	**7**	**0**	**2**	**164**	**9.1**	**–6**	**4**	**25.0**	**16:43**	....	....	....	....	....	....	....	....	....
2003-04	**Chicago**	**NHL**	**66**	**21**	**18**	**39**	**29**	**10**	**0**	**1**	**144**	**14.6**	**–18**	**13**	**30.8**	**17:08**	....	....	....	....	....	....	....	....	....
2004-05	Sodertalje SK	Sweden	12	5	1	6	6	....	....	....	....	....	....	....	....	....	10	5	1	6	2	....	....	....	....
2005-06	**Chicago**	**NHL**	**79**	**26**	**33**	**59**	**52**	**6**	**2**	**6**	**183**	**14.2**	**–4**	**13**	**46.2**	**18:23**	....	....	....	....	....	....	....	....	....
2006-07	**Philadelphia**	**NHL**	**59**	**9**	**12**	**21**	**36**	**2**	**2**	**0**	**88**	**10.2**	**–31**	**10**	**30.0**	**15:02**	....	....	....	....	....	....	....	....	....
	Detroit	**NHL**	**19**	**5**	**9**	**14**	**22**	**1**	**0**	**2**	**42**	**11.9**	**6**	**2**	**50.0**	**17:05**	**13**	**0**	**1**	**1**	**8**	**0**	**0**	**0**	**8:59**
2007-08	**Los Angeles**	**NHL**	**65**	**7**	**13**	**20**	**18**	**3**	**0**	**0**	**70**	**10.0**	**–11**	**18**	**38.9**	**13:00**	....	....	....	....	....	....	....	....	....
	NHL Totals		**502**	**106**	**159**	**265**	**260**	**35**	**4**	**15**	**892**	**11.9**		**64**	**34.4**	**15:54**	**18**	**2**	**1**	**3**	**10**	**1**	**0**	**0**	**11:09**

Signed as a free agent by **Sodertalje** (Sweden), January 20, 2005. Traded to **Philadelphia** by **Chicago** for Michael Handzus, August 4, 2006. Traded to **Chicago** by **Philadelphia** for Lasse Kukkonen and Chicago's 3rd round choice (Garrett Klotz) in 2007 Entry Draft, February 26, 2007. Traded to **Detroit** by **Chicago** for Jason Williams, February 26, 2007. Signed as a free agent by **Los Angeles**, July 2, 2007.

CALDWELL, Ryan

(KAWLD-wehl, RIGH-uhn)

Defense. Shoots left. 6'2", 174 lbs. Born, Deloraine, Man., June 15, 1981. NY Islanders' 7th choice, 202nd overall, in 2000 Entry Draft.

Season	Club	League	GP	G	A	Pts	PIM	PP	SH	GW	S	%	+/-	TF	F%	Min	GP	G	A	Pts	PIM	PP	SH	GW	Min
1998-99	Shat.-St. Mary's	High-MN	29	24	55	79	22	....	....	....	....	....	....	....	....	....	....	....	....	....	....	....	....	....	....
99-2000	Thunder Bay	USHL	46	3	20	23	152	....	....	....	....	....	....	....	....	....	....	....	....	....	....	....	....	....	....
2000-01	U. of Denver	WCHA	36	3	20	23	76	....	....	....	....	....	....	....	....	....	....	....	....	....	....	....	....	....	....
2001-02	U. of Denver	WCHA	40	3	16	19	76	....	....	....	....	....	....	....	....	....	....	....	....	....	....	....	....	....	....
2002-03	U. of Denver	WCHA	38	5	14	19	58	....	....	....	....	....	....	....	....	....	....	....	....	....	....	....	....	....	....
2003-04	U. of Denver	WCHA	42	15	12	27	96	....	....	....	....	....	....	....	....	....	....	....	....	....	....	....	....	....	....
2004-05	Bridgeport	AHL	73	2	19	21	65	....	....	....	....	....	....	....	....	....	....	....	....	....	....	....	....	....	....
2005-06	**NY Islanders**	**NHL**	**2**	**0**	**0**	**0**	**2**	**0**	**0**	**0**	**2**	**0.0**	**–2**	**0**	**0.0**	**16:33**	....	....	....	....	....	....	....	....	....
	Bridgeport	AHL	61	2	13	15	38	....	....	....	....	....	....	....	....	....	7	1	1	2	2	....	....	....	....
2006-07	Syracuse Crunch	AHL	61	7	23	30	94	....	....	....	....	....	....	....	....	....	....	....	....	....	....	....	....	....	....
2007-08	**Phoenix**	**NHL**	**2**	**0**	**0**	**0**	**2**	**0**	**0**	**0**	**1**	**0.0**	**0**	**0**	**0.0**	**6:08**	....	....	....	....	....	....	....	....	....
	San Antonio	AHL	71	3	18	21	94	....	....	....	....	....	....	....	....	....	7	0	0	0	4	....	....	....	....
	NHL Totals		**4**	**0**	**0**	**0**	**4**	**0**	**0**	**0**	**3**	**0.0**		**0**	**0.0**	**11:20**	....	....	....	....	....	....	....	....	....

WCHA All-Rookie Team (2001) • WCHA Second All-Star Team (2004) • NCAA West First All-American Team (2004) • NCAA Championship All-Tournament Team (2004)

Traded to **Columbus** by **NY Islanders** for Eric Boguniecki, October 25, 2006. Signed as a free agent by **Phoenix**, July 23, 2007.

CALLAHAN, Ryan

(kal-AH-han, RIGH-uhn) **NYR**

Right wing. Shoots right. 5'11", 190 lbs. Born, Rochester, NY, March 21, 1985. NY Rangers' 9th choice, 127th overall, in 2004 Entry Draft.

Season	Club	League	GP	G	A	Pts	PIM	PP	SH	GW	S	%	+/-	TF	F%	Min	GP	G	A	Pts	PIM	PP	SH	GW	Min
2002-03	Guelph Storm	OHL	59	14	17	31	47	....	....	....	....	....	....	....	....	....	11	0	3	3	2	....	....	....	....
2003-04	Guelph Storm	OHL	68	36	32	68	86	....	....	....	....	....	....	....	....	....	22	*13	8	21	20	....	....	....	....
2004-05	Guelph Storm	OHL	60	28	26	54	108	....	....	....	....	....	....	....	....	....	4	1	1	2	6	....	....	....	....
2005-06	Guelph Storm	OHL	62	52	32	84	126	....	....	....	....	....	....	....	....	....	13	7	17	24	20	....	....	....	....
2006-07	**NY Rangers**	**NHL**	**14**	**4**	**2**	**6**	**9**	**0**	**0**	**1**	**40**	**10.0**	**5**	**3**	**66.7**	**10:31**	**10**	**2**	**1**	**3**	**6**	**1**	**0**	**0**	**12:19**
	Hartford	AHL	60	35	20	55	74	....	....	....	....	....	....	....	....	....	....	....	....	....	....	....	....	....	....
2007-08	**NY Rangers**	**NHL**	**52**	**8**	**5**	**13**	**31**	**0**	**1**	**1**	**92**	**8.7**	**7**	**5**	**20.0**	**12:22**	**10**	**2**	**2**	**4**	**10**	**0**	**1**	**1**	**15:55**
	Hartford	AHL	11	7	8	15	27	....	....	....	....	....	....	....	....	....	....	....	....	....	....	....	....	....	....
	NHL Totals		**66**	**12**	**7**	**19**	**40**	**0**	**1**	**2**	**132**	**9.1**		**8**	**37.5**	**11:59**	**20**	**4**	**3**	**7**	**16**	**1**	**1**	**1**	**14:07**

OHL Second All-Star Team (2006) • AHL All-Rookie Team (2007)

CAMMALLERI, Michael
(kam-UH-LAIR-ee, MIGH-kuhl) **CGY.**

Center. Shoots left. 5'9", 185 lbs. Born, Richmond Hill, Ont., June 8, 1982. Los Angeles' 3rd choice, 49th overall, in 2001 Entry Draft.

			Regular Season														Playoffs								
Season	Club	League	GP	G	A	Pts	PIM	PP	SH	GW	S	%	+/-	TF	F%	Min	GP	G	A	Pts	PIM	PP	SH	GW	Min
1997-98	Bramalea Blues	OPJHL	46	36	52	88	30	....	....	....	....	....	....	....	....	....	....	....	....	....	....	....	....	....	....
1998-99	Bramalea Blues	OPJHL	41	31	72	103	51	....	....	....	....	....	....	....	....	....	....	....	....	....	....	....	....	....	....
99-2000	U. of Michigan	CCHA	39	13	13	26	32	....	....	....	....	....	....	....	....	....	....	....	....	....	....	....	....	....	....
2000-01	U. of Michigan	CCHA	42	*29	32	61	24	....	....	....	....	....	....	....	....	....	....	....	....	....	....	....	....	....	....
2001-02	U. of Michigan	CCHA	29	23	21	44	28	....	....	....	....	....	....	....	....	....	....	....	....	....	....	....	....	....	....
2002-03	**Los Angeles**	**NHL**	**28**	**5**	**3**	**8**	**22**	**2**	**0**	**2**	**40**	**12.5**	**-4**	**253**	**51.4**	**14:05**	....	....	....	....	....	....	....	....	....
	Manchester	AHL	13	5	15	20	12	....	....	....	....	....	....	....	....	....	....	....	....	....	....	....	....	....	....
2003-04	**Los Angeles**	**NHL**	**31**	**9**	**6**	**15**	**20**	**2**	**0**	**2**	**53**	**17.0**	**1**	**280**	**53.6**	**13:18**	....	....	....	....	....	....	....	....	....
	Manchester	AHL	41	20	19	39	28	....	....	....	....	....	....	....	....	....	1	0	1	1	0	....	....	....	....
2004-05	Manchester	AHL	79	*46	63	109	60	....	....	....	....	....	....	....	....	....	6	1	5	6	0	....	....	....	....
2005-06	**Los Angeles**	**NHL**	**80**	**26**	**29**	**55**	**50**	**15**	**0**	**4**	**206**	**12.6**	**-14**	**578**	**53.5**	**16:45**	....	....	....	....	....	....	....	....	....
2006-07	**Los Angeles**	**NHL**	**81**	**34**	**46**	**80**	**48**	**16**	**0**	**5**	**299**	**11.4**	**5**	**301**	**54.2**	**18:03**	....	....	....	....	....	....	....	....	....
2007-08	**Los Angeles**	**NHL**	**63**	**19**	**28**	**47**	**30**	**10**	**0**	**1**	**210**	**9.0**	**-16**	**380**	**54.2**	**18:35**	....	....	....	....	....	....	....	....	....
	NHL Totals		**283**	**93**	**112**	**205**	**170**	**45**	**0**	**14**	**808**	**11.5**		**1792**	**53.5**	**16:53**	....	....	....	....	....	....	....	....	....

CCHA First All-Star Team (2001) • NCAA West Second All-American Team (2001) • CCHA Second All-Star Team (2002) • NCAA West First All-American Team (2002) • AHL Second All-Star Team (2005) • Willie Marshall Award (Top Goal-scorer - AHL) (2005)

• Missed majority of 2002-03 season recovering from head injury suffered in game vs. San Jose, January 28, 2003. Traded to **Calgary** by **Los Angeles** with Calgary's 2nd round choice (previously acquired, Calgary selected Mitch Wahl) in 2008 Entry Draft for Calgary's 1st round choice (later traded to Anaheim - Anaheim selected Jake Gardiner) in 2008 Entry Draft and Calgary's 2nd round choice in 2009 Entry Draft, June 20, 2008.

CAMPBELL, Brian
(KAM-behl, BRIGH-uhn) **CHI.**

Defense. Shoots left. 6', 191 lbs. Born, Strathroy, Ont., May 23, 1979. Buffalo's 7th choice, 156th overall, in 1997 Entry Draft.

Season	Club	League	GP	G	A	Pts	PIM	PP	SH	GW	S	%	+/-	TF	F%	Min	GP	G	A	Pts	PIM	PP	SH	GW	Min
1994-95	Petrolia Oil Barons	OHA-B	49	11	27	38	43	....	....	....	....	....	....	....	....	....	....	....	....	....	....	....	....	....	....
1995-96	Ottawa 67's	OHL	66	5	22	27	23	....	....	....	....	....	....	....	....	....	4	0	1	1	2	....	....	....	....
1996-97	Ottawa 67's	OHL	66	7	36	43	12	....	....	....	....	....	....	....	....	....	24	2	11	13	8	....	....	....	....
1997-98	Ottawa 67's	OHL	66	14	39	53	31	....	....	....	....	....	....	....	....	....	13	1	14	15	0	....	....	....	....
1998-99	Ottawa 67's	OHL	62	12	75	87	27	....	....	....	....	....	....	....	....	....	9	2	10	12	6	....	....	....	....
	Rochester	AHL	....	....	....	....	....	....	....	....	....	....	....	....	....	....	2	0	0	0	0	....	....	....	....
99-2000	**Buffalo**	**NHL**	**12**	**1**	**4**	**5**	**4**	**0**	**0**	**0**	**10**	**10.0**	**-2**	**0**	**0.0**	**15:48**	....	....	....	....	....	....	....	....	....
	Rochester	AHL	67	2	24	26	22	....	....	....	....	....	....	....	....	....	21	0	3	3	0	....	....	....	....
2000-01	**Buffalo**	**NHL**	**8**	**0**	**0**	**0**	**2**	**0**	**0**	**0**	**7**	**0.0**	**-2**	**0**	**0.0**	**15:40**	....	....	....	....	....	....	....	....	....
	Rochester	AHL	65	7	25	32	24	....	....	....	....	....	....	....	....	....	4	0	1	1	0	....	....	....	....
2001-02	**Buffalo**	**NHL**	**29**	**3**	**3**	**6**	**12**	**0**	**0**	**0**	**30**	**10.0**	**0**	**1**	**0.0**	**15:18**	....	....	....	....	....	....	....	....	....
	Rochester	AHL	45	2	35	37	13	....	....	....	....	....	....	....	....	....	....	....	....	....	....	....	....	....	....
2002-03	**Buffalo**	**NHL**	**65**	**2**	**17**	**19**	**20**	**0**	**0**	**1**	**90**	**2.2**	**-8**	**1**	**0.0**	**18:40**	....	....	....	....	....	....	....	....	....
2003-04	**Buffalo**	**NHL**	**53**	**3**	**8**	**11**	**12**	**0**	**0**	**0**	**45**	**6.7**	**-8**	**0**	**0.0**	**16:02**	....	....	....	....	....	....	....	....	....
2004-05	Jokerit Helsinki	Finland	44	12	13	25	12	....	....	....	....	....	....	....	....	....	12	3	4	7	6	....	....	....	....
2005-06	**Buffalo**	**NHL**	**79**	**12**	**32**	**44**	**16**	**5**	**0**	**5**	**105**	**11.4**	**-14**	**0**	**0.0**	**17:43**	**18**	**0**	**6**	**6**	**12**	**0**	**0**	**0**	**20:29**
2006-07	**Buffalo**	**NHL**	**82**	**6**	**42**	**48**	**35**	**1**	**0**	**1**	**92**	**6.5**	**28**	**0**	**0.0**	**21:53**	**16**	**3**	**4**	**7**	**14**	**2**	**0**	**0**	**21:39**
2007-08	**Buffalo**	**NHL**	**63**	**5**	**38**	**43**	**12**	**3**	**0**	**0**	**102**	**4.9**	**-1**	**0**	**0.0**	**25:06**	....	....	....	....	....	....	....	....	....
	San Jose	**NHL**	**20**	**3**	**16**	**19**	**8**	**2**	**0**	**0**	**40**	**7.5**	**9**	**0**	**0.0**	**25:07**	**13**	**1**	**6**	**7**	**4**	**0**	**0**	**0**	**29:19**
	NHL Totals		**411**	**35**	**160**	**195**	**121**	**11**	**0**	**7**	**521**	**6.7**		**2**	**0.0**	**19:42**	**47**	**4**	**16**	**20**	**30**	**2**	**0**	**0**	**23:19**

OHL First All-Star Team (1999) • OHL MVP (1999) • Canadian Major Junior First All-Star Team (1999) • Canadian Major Junior Player of the Year (1999) • George Parsons Trophy (Memorial Cup Tournament - Most Sportsmanlike Player) (1999) • NHL Second All-Star Team (2008)

Played in NHL All-Star Game (2007, 2008)

Signed as a free agent by **Jokerit Helsinki** (Finland), October 19, 2004. Traded to **San Jose** by **Buffalo** with Buffalo's 7th round choice (Drew Daniels) in 2008 Entry Draft for Steve Bernier and San Jose's 1st round choice (Tyler Ennis) in 2008 Entry Draft, February 26, 2008. Signed as a free agent by **Chicago**, July 1, 2008.

CAMPBELL, Darcy
(KAM-behl, DAHR-see) **COL.**

Defense. Shoots left. 6'1", 180 lbs. Born, Airdrie, Alta., May 12, 1984.

Season	Club	League	GP	G	A	Pts	PIM	PP	SH	GW	S	%	+/-	TF	F%	Min	GP	G	A	Pts	PIM	PP	SH	GW	Min
2002-03	Canmore Eagles	AJHL	62	10	37	47	112	....	....	....	....	....	....	....	....	....	9	2	2	4	6	....	....	....	....
2003-04	Canmore Eagles	AJHL	24	6	15	21	25	....	....	....	....	....	....	....	....	....	14	2	7	9	2	....	....	....	....
	Olds Grizzlys	AJHL	36	9	19	28	40	....	....	....	....	....	....	....	....	....	....	....	....	....	....	....	....	....	....
2004-05	Alaska	CCHA	37	2	10	12	56	....	....	....	....	....	....	....	....	....	....	....	....	....	....	....	....	....	....
2005-06	Alaska	CCHA	38	5	9	14	67	....	....	....	....	....	....	....	....	....	....	....	....	....	....	....	....	....	....
2006-07	Alaska	CCHA	39	4	20	24	54	....	....	....	....	....	....	....	....	....	....	....	....	....	....	....	....	....	....
	Columbus	**NHL**	**1**	**0**	**0**	**0**	**0**	**0**	**0**	**0**	**0**	**0.0**	**0**	**0**	**0.0**	**5:41**	....	....	....	....	....	....	....	....	....
2007-08	Syracuse Crunch	AHL	28	1	5	6	26	....	....	....	....	....	....	....	....	....	....	....	....	....	....	....	....	....	....
	Lake Erie	AHL	8	1	0	1	2	....	....	....	....	....	....	....	....	....	....	....	....	....	....	....	....	....	....
	NHL Totals		**1**	**0**	**0**	**0**	**0**	**0**	**0**	**0**	**0**	**0.0**		**0**	**0.0**	**5:41**	....	....	....	....	....	....	....	....	....

AJHL South All-Rookie Team (2003) • AJHL South First All-Star Team (2004)

Signed as a free agent by **Columbus**, March 24, 2007. Traded to **Colorado** by **Columbus** with Phillipe Dupuis for Mark Rycroft, January 22, 2008.

CAMPBELL, Gregory
(KAM-behl, GREH-goh-ree) **FLA.**

Left wing. Shoots left. 6', 194 lbs. Born, London, Ont., December 17, 1983. Florida's 4th choice, 67th overall, in 2002 Entry Draft.

Season	Club	League	GP	G	A	Pts	PIM	PP	SH	GW	S	%	+/-	TF	F%	Min	GP	G	A	Pts	PIM	PP	SH	GW	Min
1998-99	Aylmer Aces	OHA-B	49	5	9	14	44	....	....	....	....	....	....	....	....	....	....	....	....	....	....	....	....	....	....
99-2000	St. Thomas Stars	OHA-B	51	12	8	20	51	....	....	....	....	....	....	....	....	....	....	....	....	....	....	....	....	....	....
2000-01	Plymouth Whalers	OHL	65	2	12	14	40	....	....	....	....	....	....	....	....	....	10	0	0	0	7	....	....	....	....
2001-02	Plymouth Whalers	OHL	65	17	36	53	105	....	....	....	....	....	....	....	....	....	6	0	2	2	13	....	....	....	....
2002-03	Kitchener Rangers	OHL	55	23	33	56	116	....	....	....	....	....	....	....	....	....	21	15	4	19	34	....	....	....	....
2003-04	**Florida**	**NHL**	**2**	**0**	**0**	**0**	**5**	**0**	**0**	**0**	**0**	**0.0**	**-1**	**1**	**0.0**	**9:09**	....	....	....	....	....	....	....	....	....
	San Antonio	AHL	76	13	16	29	73	....	....	....	....	....	....	....	....	....	....	....	....	....	....	....	....	....	....
2004-05	San Antonio	AHL	70	12	16	28	113	....	....	....	....	....	....	....	....	....	....	....	....	....	....	....	....	....	....
2005-06	**Florida**	**NHL**	**64**	**3**	**6**	**9**	**40**	**0**	**0**	**0**	**59**	**5.1**	**-11**	**38**	**34.2**	**8:38**	....	....	....	....	....	....	....	....	....
	Rochester	AHL	11	3	3	6	30	....	....	....	....	....	....	....	....	....	....	....	....	....	....	....	....	....	....
2006-07	**Florida**	**NHL**	**79**	**6**	**3**	**9**	**66**	**0**	**1**	**0**	**103**	**5.8**	**-10**	**588**	**45.2**	**10:34**	....	....	....	....	....	....	....	....	....
2007-08	**Florida**	**NHL**	**81**	**5**	**13**	**18**	**72**	**0**	**2**	**1**	**113**	**4.4**	**-12**	**460**	**51.1**	**12:27**	....	....	....	....	....	....	....	....	....
	NHL Totals		**226**	**14**	**22**	**36**	**183**	**0**	**3**	**1**	**275**	**5.1**		**1087**	**47.3**	**10:41**	....	....	....	....	....	....	....	....	....

Memorial Cup Tournament All-Star Team (2003) • George Parsons Trophy (Memorial Cup Tournament - Most Sportsmanlike Player) (2003) • Ed Chynoweth Trophy (Memorial Cup Tournament - Leading Scorer) (2003)

CAMPOLI, Chris
(kam-POH-lee, KRIHS) **NYI**

Defense. Shoots left. 5'11", 190 lbs. Born, North York, Ont., July 9, 1984. NY Islanders' 8th choice, 227th overall, in 2004 Entry Draft.

Season	Club	League	GP	G	A	Pts	PIM	PP	SH	GW	S	%	+/-	TF	F%	Min	GP	G	A	Pts	PIM	PP	SH	GW	Min
2001-02	Erie Otters	OHL	68	2	24	26	117	....	....	....	....	....	....	....	....	....	20	0	5	5	18	....	....	....	....
2002-03	Erie Otters	OHL	60	8	40	48	82	....	....	....	....	....	....	....	....	....	....	....	....	....	....	....	....	....	....
2003-04	Erie Otters	OHL	67	20	46	66	66	....	....	....	....	....	....	....	....	....	8	0	6	6	16	....	....	....	....
2004-05	Bridgeport	AHL	79	15	34	49	78	....	....	....	....	....	....	....	....	....	....	....	....	....	....	....	....	....	....
2005-06	**NY Islanders**	**NHL**	**80**	**9**	**25**	**34**	**46**	**2**	**0**	**2**	**123**	**7.3**	**-16**	**0**	**0.0**	**18:32**	....	....	....	....	....	....	....	....	....
2006-07	**NY Islanders**	**NHL**	**51**	**1**	**13**	**14**	**23**	**0**	**0**	**0**	**41**	**2.4**	**-3**	**0**	**0.0**	**14:50**	**5**	**1**	**1**	**2**	**2**	**0**	**0**	**0**	**13:30**
	Bridgeport	AHL	15	3	3	6	8	....	....	....	....	....	....	....	....	....	....	....	....	....	....	....	....	....	....
2007-08	**NY Islanders**	**NHL**	**46**	**4**	**14**	**18**	**16**	**2**	**1**	**0**	**68**	**5.9**	**-1**	**0**	**0.0**	**19:09**	....	....	....	....	....	....	....	....	....
	NHL Totals		**177**	**14**	**52**	**66**	**85**	**4**	**1**	**2**	**232**	**6.0**		**0**	**0.0**	**17:38**	**5**	**1**	**1**	**2**	**2**	**0**	**0**	**0**	**13:30**

OHL Humanitarian Player of the Year (2004) • Canadian Major Junior Humanitarian Player of the Year (2004) • AHL All-Rookie Team (2005)

CARCILLO, Daniel

(KAR-sihl-oh, DAN-yuhl) **PHX.**

Left wing. Shoots left. 5'11", 203 lbs. Born, King City, Ont., January 28, 1985. Pittsburgh's 4th choice, 73rd overall, in 2003 Entry Draft.

			Regular Season														Playoffs								
Season	Club	League	GP	G	A	Pts	PIM	PP	SH	GW	S	%	+/-	TF	F%	Min	GP	G	A	Pts	PIM	PP	SH	GW	Min
2001-02	Milton Merchants	OHA-B	47	15	16	31	162	....	....	....	....	....	....	....	....	....	....	....	....	....	....	....	....	....	....
2002-03	Sarnia Sting	OHL	68	29	37	66	157	....	....	....	....	....	....	....	....	....	6	0	4	4	14	....	....	....	....
2003-04	Sarnia Sting	OHL	61	30	29	59	148	....	....	....	....	....	....	....	....	....	4	1	2	3	12	....	....	....	....
2004-05	Sarnia Sting	OHL	12	2	7	9	40	....	....	....	....	....	....	....	....	....	....	....	....	....	....	....	....	....	....
	Mississauga	OHL	20	8	10	18	75	....	....	....	....	....	....	....	....	....	5	3	1	4	18	....	....	....	....
2005-06	Wilkes-Barre	AHL	51	11	13	24	311	....	....	....	....	....	....	....	....	....	11	1	0	1	47	....	....	....	....
	Wheeling Nailers	ECHL	6	3	2	5	32	....	....	....	....	....	....	....	....	....	....	....	....	....	....	....	....	....	....
2006-07	Wilkes-Barre	AHL	52	21	9	30	183	....	....	....	....	....	....	....	....	....	....	....	....	....	....	....	....	....	....
	Phoenix	**NHL**	**18**	**4**	**3**	**7**	**74**	**3**	**0**	**0**	**32**	**12.5**	**–7**	**0**	**0.0**	**14:56**	....	....	....	....	....	....	....	....	....
2007-08	**Phoenix**	**NHL**	**57**	**13**	**11**	**24**	***324**	**3**	**0**	**1**	**106**	**12.3**	**1**	**5**	**80.0**	**12:43**	....	....	....	....	....	....	....	....	....
	San Antonio	AHL	5	2	1	3	16	....	....	....	....	....	....	....	....	....	....	....	....	....	....	....	....	....	....
	NHL Totals		**75**	**17**	**14**	**31**	**398**	**6**	**0**	**1**	**138**	**12.3**		**5**	**80.0**	**13:15**	....	....	....	....	....	....	....	....	....

Traded to **Phoenix** by **Pittsburgh** with Pittsburgh's 3rd round choice (later traded to NY Rangers - NY Rangers selected Tomas Kundratek) in 2008 Entry Draft for Georges Laraque, February 27, 2007.

CARD, Mike

(KARD, MIGHK) **BUF.**

Defense. Shoots right. 6', 189 lbs. Born, Kitchener, Ont., February 18, 1986. Buffalo's 7th choice, 241st overall, in 2004 Entry Draft.

			Regular Season														Playoffs								
Season	Club	League	GP	G	A	Pts	PIM	PP	SH	GW	S	%	+/-	TF	F%	Min	GP	G	A	Pts	PIM	PP	SH	GW	Min
2002-03	Kelowna Rockets	WHL	61	7	22	29	41	....	....	....	....	....	....	....	....	....	19	2	6	8	12	....	....	....	....
2003-04	Kelowna Rockets	WHL	72	6	12	18	47	....	....	....	....	....	....	....	....	....	17	2	4	6	20	....	....	....	....
2004-05	Kelowna Rockets	WHL	72	10	35	45	85	....	....	....	....	....	....	....	....	....	24	2	5	7	38	....	....	....	....
2005-06	Kelowna Rockets	WHL	64	12	43	55	103	....	....	....	....	....	....	....	....	....	12	0	3	3	8	....	....	....	....
2006-07	**Buffalo**	**NHL**	**4**	**0**	**0**	**0**	**0**	**0**	**0**	**0**	**0**	**0.0**	**0**	**0**	**0.0**	**4:34**	....	....	....	....	....	....	....	....	....
	Rochester	AHL	50	1	8	9	38	....	....	....	....	....	....	....	....	....	6	0	0	0	8	....	....	....	....
	Florida Everblades	ECHL	6	1	3	4	2	....	....	....	....	....	....	....	....	....	9	1	4	5	14	....	....	....	....
2007-08	Rochester	AHL	23	1	4	5	32	....	....	....	....	....	....	....	....	....	....	....	....	....	....	....	....	....	....
	NHL Totals		**4**	**0**	**0**	**0**	**0**	**0**	**0**	**0**	**0**	**0.0**		**0**	**0.0**	**4:34**	....	....	....	....	....	....	....	....	....

CARKNER, Matt

(KARK-nehr, MAT) **OTT.**

Defense. Shoots right. 6'4", 231 lbs. Born, Winchester, Ont., November 3, 1980. Montreal's 2nd choice, 58th overall, in 1999 Entry Draft.

			Regular Season														Playoffs								
Season	Club	League	GP	G	A	Pts	PIM	PP	SH	GW	S	%	+/-	TF	F%	Min	GP	G	A	Pts	PIM	PP	SH	GW	Min
1996-97	Winchester	OHA-B	29	1	18	19	....	....	....	....	....	....	....	....	....	....	....	....	....	....	....	....	....	....	....
1997-98	Peterborough	OHL	57	0	6	6	121	....	....	....	....	....	....	....	....	....	4	0	0	0	2	....	....	....	....
1998-99	Peterborough	OHL	60	2	16	18	173	....	....	....	....	....	....	....	....	....	5	0	0	0	20	....	....	....	....
99-2000	Peterborough	OHL	62	3	13	16	177	....	....	....	....	....	....	....	....	....	5	0	1	1	6	....	....	....	....
2000-01	Peterborough	OHL	53	8	8	16	128	....	....	....	....	....	....	....	....	....	7	0	3	3	25	....	....	....	....
2001-02	Cleveland Barons	AHL	74	0	3	3	335	....	....	....	....	....	....	....	....	....	....	....	....	....	....	....	....	....	....
2002-03	Cleveland Barons	AHL	39	1	4	5	104	....	....	....	....	....	....	....	....	....	....	....	....	....	....	....	....	....	....
2003-04	Cleveland Barons	AHL	60	2	11	13	115	....	....	....	....	....	....	....	....	....	9	0	3	3	39	....	....	....	....
2004-05	Cleveland Barons	AHL	73	0	10	10	192	....	....	....	....	....	....	....	....	....	....	....	....	....	....	....	....	....	....
2005-06	**San Jose**	**NHL**	**1**	**0**	**1**	**1**	**2**	**0**	**0**	**0**	**0**	**0.0**	**0**	**0**	**0.0**	**6:01**	....	....	....	....	....	....	....	....	....
	Cleveland Barons	AHL	69	10	21	31	202	....	....	....	....	....	....	....	....	....	....	....	....	....	....	....	....	....	....
2006-07	Wilkes-Barre	AHL	75	6	24	30	167	....	....	....	....	....	....	....	....	....	8	1	0	1	19	....	....	....	....
2007-08	Binghamton	AHL	67	10	15	25	218	....	....	....	....	....	....	....	....	....	....	....	....	....	....	....	....	....	....
	NHL Totals		**1**	**0**	**1**	**1**	**2**	**0**	**0**	**0**	**0**	**0.0**		**0**	**0.0**	**6:01**	....	....	....	....	....	....	....	....	....

Yanick Dupre Memorial Award (Outstanding Humanitarian Contribution - AHL) (2007)

Signed as a free agent by **San Jose**, June 6, 2001. • Missed majority of 2002-03 season recovering from knee injury suffered in game vs. Utah (AHL), January 4, 2003. Signed as a free agent by **Pittsburgh**, July 23, 2006. Signed as a free agent by **Ottawa**, July 3, 2007.

CARLE, Matt

(KAHRL, MAT) **T.B.**

Defense. Shoots left. 6', 205 lbs. Born, Anchorage, AK, September 25, 1984. San Jose's 4th choice, 47th overall, in 2003 Entry Draft.

			Regular Season														Playoffs								
Season	Club	League	GP	G	A	Pts	PIM	PP	SH	GW	S	%	+/-	TF	F%	Min	GP	G	A	Pts	PIM	PP	SH	GW	Min
99-2000	Alaska All-Stars	AASHA	42	14	28	42	....	....	....	....	....	....	....	....	....	....	....	....	....	....	....	....	....	....	....
2000-01	USNTDP	U-17	13	0	1	1	....	....	....	....	....	....	....	....	....	....	....	....	....	....	....	....	....	....	....
	USNTDP	NAHL	55	1	4	5	33	....	....	....	....	....	....	....	....	....	....	....	....	....	....	....	....	....	....
2001-02	USNTDP	U-18	45	3	13	16	30	....	....	....	....	....	....	....	....	....	....	....	....	....	....	....	....	....	....
	USNTDP	NAHL	7	1	2	3	0	....	....	....	....	....	....	....	....	....	....	....	....	....	....	....	....	....	....
	USNTDP	USHL	12	0	0	0	21	....	....	....	....	....	....	....	....	....	....	....	....	....	....	....	....	....	....
2002-03	River City Lancers	USHL	59	12	30	42	98	....	....	....	....	....	....	....	....	....	11	2	2	4	20	....	....	....	....
2003-04	U. of Denver	WCHA	30	5	20	25	33	....	....	....	....	....	....	....	....	....	....	....	....	....	....	....	....	....	....
2004-05	U. of Denver	WCHA	43	13	31	44	68	....	....	....	....	....	....	....	....	....	....	....	....	....	....	....	....	....	....
2005-06	U. of Denver	WCHA	39	11	*42	53	58	....	....	....	....	....	....	....	....	....	....	....	....	....	....	....	....	....	....
	San Jose	**NHL**	**12**	**3**	**3**	**6**	**14**	**2**	**0**	**1**	**11**	**27.3**	**–2**	**0**	**0.0**	**16:07**	**11**	**0**	**3**	**3**	**4**	**0**	**0**	**0**	**15:17**
2006-07	**San Jose**	**NHL**	**77**	**11**	**31**	**42**	**30**	**8**	**0**	**1**	**111**	**9.9**	**9**	**1**	**0.0**	**18:08**	**11**	**2**	**3**	**5**	**0**	**1**	**0**	**1**	**14:51**
	Worcester Sharks	AHL	3	0	2	2	0	....	....	....	....	....	....	....	....	....	....	....	....	....	....	....	....	....	....
2007-08	**San Jose**	**NHL**	**62**	**2**	**13**	**15**	**26**	**2**	**0**	**1**	**63**	**3.2**	**–8**	**1**	**100.0**	**16:33**	**11**	**0**	**1**	**1**	**4**	**0**	**0**	**0**	**13:56**
	NHL Totals		**151**	**16**	**47**	**63**	**70**	**12**	**0**	**3**	**185**	**8.6**		**2**	**50.0**	**17:20**	**33**	**2**	**7**	**9**	**8**	**1**	**0**	**1**	**14:42**

USHL First All-Star Team (2003) • USHL Defenseman of the Year (2003) • WCHA All-Rookie Team (2004) • WCHA First All-Star Team (2005, 2006) • NCAA West First All-American Team (2005, 2006) • NCAA Championship All-Tournament Team (2005) • WCHA Player of the Year (2006) • Hobey Baker Memorial Award (Top U.S. Collegiate Player) (2006) • NHL All-Rookie Team (2007)

Traded to **Tampa Bay** by **San Jose** with Ty Wishart, San Jose's 1st round choice in 2009 Entry Draft and San Jose's 4th round choice in 2010 Entry Draft for Dan Boyle and Brad Lukowich, July 4, 2008.

CARNEY, Keith

(KAHRN-nee, KEETH)

Defense. Shoots left. 6'1", 207 lbs. Born, Providence, RI, February 3, 1970. Buffalo's 3rd choice, 76th overall, in 1988 Entry Draft.

			Regular Season														Playoffs								
Season	Club	League	GP	G	A	Pts	PIM	PP	SH	GW	S	%	+/-	TF	F%	Min	GP	G	A	Pts	PIM	PP	SH	GW	Min
1987-88	Mount St. Charles	High-RI	23	12	43	55	....	....	....	....	....	....	....	....	....	....	....	....	....	....	....	....	....	....	....
1988-89	U. of Maine	H-East	40	4	22	26	24	....	....	....	....	....	....	....	....	....	....	....	....	....	....	....	....	....	....
1989-90	U. of Maine	H-East	41	3	41	44	43	....	....	....	....	....	....	....	....	....	....	....	....	....	....	....	....	....	....
1990-91	U. of Maine	H-East	40	7	49	56	38	....	....	....	....	....	....	....	....	....	....	....	....	....	....	....	....	....	....
1991-92	United States	Nat-Tm	49	2	17	19	16	....	....	....	....	....	....	....	....	....	....	....	....	....	....	....	....	....	....
	Buffalo	**NHL**	**14**	**1**	**2**	**3**	**18**	**1**	**0**	**0**	**17**	**5.9**	**–3**	....	....	....	**7**	**0**	**3**	**3**	**0**	**0**	**0**	**0**	....
	Rochester	AHL	24	1	10	11	2	....	....	....	....	....	....	....	....	....	2	0	2	2	0	....	....	....	....
1992-93	**Buffalo**	**NHL**	**30**	**2**	**4**	**6**	**55**	**0**	**0**	**1**	**26**	**7.7**	**3**	....	....	....	**8**	**0**	**3**	**3**	**6**	**0**	**0**	**0**	....
	Rochester	AHL	41	5	21	26	32	....	....	....	....	....	....	....	....	....	....	....	....	....	....	....	....	....	....
1993-94	**Buffalo**	**NHL**	**7**	**1**	**3**	**4**	**4**	**0**	**0**	**0**	**6**	**16.7**	**–1**	....	....	....	....	....	....	....	....	....	....	....	....
	Chicago	**NHL**	**30**	**3**	**5**	**8**	**35**	**0**	**0**	**0**	**31**	**9.7**	**15**	....	....	....	**6**	**0**	**1**	**1**	**4**	**0**	**0**	**0**	....
	Indianapolis Ice	IHL	28	0	14	14	20	....	....	....	....	....	....	....	....	....	....	....	....	....	....	....	....	....	....
1994-95	**Chicago**	**NHL**	**18**	**1**	**0**	**1**	**11**	**0**	**0**	**1**	**14**	**7.1**	**–1**	....	....	....	**4**	**0**	**1**	**1**	**0**	**0**	**0**	**0**	....
1995-96	**Chicago**	**NHL**	**82**	**5**	**14**	**19**	**94**	**1**	**0**	**1**	**69**	**7.2**	**31**	....	....	....	**10**	**0**	**3**	**3**	**4**	**0**	**0**	**0**	....
1996-97	**Chicago**	**NHL**	**81**	**3**	**15**	**18**	**62**	**0**	**0**	**1**	**77**	**3.9**	**26**	....	....	....	**6**	**1**	**1**	**2**	**2**	**0**	**0**	**0**	....
1997-98	**Chicago**	**NHL**	**60**	**2**	**13**	**15**	**73**	**0**	**1**	**0**	**53**	**3.8**	**–7**	....	....	....	....	....	....	....	....	....	....	....	....
	United States	Olympics	4	0	0	0	2	....	....	....	....	....	....	....	....	....	....	....	....	....	....	....	....	....	....
	Phoenix	**NHL**	**20**	**1**	**6**	**7**	**18**	**1**	**0**	**0**	**18**	**5.6**	**5**	....	....	....	**6**	**0**	**0**	**0**	**4**	**0**	**0**	**0**	....
1998-99	**Phoenix**	**NHL**	**82**	**2**	**14**	**16**	**62**	**0**	**2**	**0**	**62**	**3.2**	**15**	**0**	**0.0**	**22:46**	**7**	**1**	**2**	**3**	**10**	**0**	**0**	**0**	**23:59**
99-2000	**Phoenix**	**NHL**	**82**	**4**	**20**	**24**	**87**	**0**	**0**	**1**	**73**	**5.5**	**11**	**0**	**0.0**	**21:12**	**5**	**0**	**0**	**0**	**17**	**0**	**0**	**0**	**22:38**
2000-01	**Phoenix**	**NHL**	**82**	**2**	**14**	**16**	**86**	**0**	**0**	**0**	**65**	**3.1**	**15**	**0**	**0.0**	**20:53**	....	....	....	....	....	....	....	....	....
2001-02	**Anaheim**	**NHL**	**60**	**5**	**9**	**14**	**30**	**0**	**0**	**1**	**66**	**7.6**	**14**	**0**	**0.0**	**20:47**	....	....	....	....	....	....	....	....	....
2002-03	**Anaheim**	**NHL**	**81**	**4**	**18**	**22**	**65**	**0**	**0**	**1**	**87**	**4.6**	**8**	**0**	**0.0**	**22:34**	**21**	**0**	**4**	**4**	**16**	**0**	**0**	**0**	**26:40**
2003-04	**Anaheim**	**NHL**	**69**	**2**	**5**	**7**	**42**	**1**	**0**	**0**	**58**	**3.4**	**–5**	**0**	**0.0**	**21:43**	....	....	....	....	....	....	....	....	....
2004-05			DID NOT PLAY																						
2005-06	**Anaheim**	**NHL**	**61**	**2**	**16**	**18**	**48**	**1**	**0**	**1**	**71**	**2.8**	**13**	**1**	**0.0**	**19:19**	....	....	....	....	....	....	....	....	....
	Vancouver	**NHL**	**18**	**0**	**2**	**2**	**14**	**0**	**0**	**0**	**14**	**0.0**	**–5**	**0**	**0.0**	**24:30**	....	....	....	....	....	....	....	....	....

			Regular Season														Playoffs								
Season	Club	League	GP	G	A	Pts	PIM	PP	SH	GW	S	%	+/-	TF	F%	Min	GP	G	A	Pts	PIM	PP	SH	GW	Min
2006-07	**Minnesota**	**NHL**	80	4	13	17	58	0	0	1	31	12.9	22	2	100.0	15:31	5	0	0	0	4	0	0	0	13:57
2007-08	**Minnesota**	**NHL**	61	1	10	11	42	0	0	0	27	3.7	8	0	0.0	13:22	6	1	1	2	0	0	0	1	15:13
	NHL Totals		1018	45	183	228	904	5	3	9	865	5.2		3	66.7	20:04	91	3	19	22	67	0	0	1	22:46

Hockey East Second All-Star Team (1990) • NCAA East Second All-American Team (1990) • Hockey East First All-Star Team (1991) • NCAA East First All-American Team (1991)

Traded to **Chicago** by **Buffalo** with Buffalo's 6th round choice (Marc Magliarditi) in 1995 Entry Draft for Craig Muni and Chicago's 5th round choice (Daniel Bienvenue) in 1995 Entry Draft, October 26, 1993. Traded to **Phoenix** by **Chicago** with Jim Cummins for Chad Kilger and Jayson More, March 4, 1998. Traded to **Anaheim** by **Phoenix** for Calgary's 2nd round choice (previously acquired, later traded back to Calgary – Calgary selected Andrei Taratukhin) in 2001 Entry Draft, June 19, 2001. Traded to **Vancouver** by **Anaheim** with Juha Alen for Brett Skinner and NY Islanders' 2nd round choice (previously acquired, Anaheim selected Bryce Swan) in 2006 Entry Draft, March 9, 2006. Signed as a free agent by **Minnesota**, July 1, 2006.

CARTER, Jeff

(KAHR-tuhr, JEHF) **PHI.**

Center. Shoots right. 6'3", 200 lbs. Born, London, Ont., January 1, 1985. Philadelphia's 1st choice, 11th overall, in 2003 Entry Draft.

			Regular Season														Playoffs								
Season	Club	League	GP	G	A	Pts	PIM	PP	SH	GW	S	%	+/-	TF	F%	Min	GP	G	A	Pts	PIM	PP	SH	GW	Min
2000-01	Strathroy Rockets	OHA-B	49	27	20	47	10	....	....	....	....	....	....	....	....	....	....	....	....	....	....	....	....	....	....
2001-02	Sault Ste. Marie	OHL	63	18	17	35	12	....	....	....	....	....	....	....	....	....	4	0	0	0	2	....	....	....	....
2002-03	Sault Ste. Marie	OHL	61	35	36	71	55	....	....	....	....	....	....	....	....	....	4	0	2	2	2	....	....	....	....
2003-04	Sault Ste. Marie	OHL	57	36	30	66	26	....	....	....	....	....	....	....	....	....	....	....	....	....	....	....	....	....	....
	Philadelphia	AHL	....	....	....	....	....	....	....	....	....	....	....	....	....	....	12	4	1	5	0	....	....	....	....
2004-05	Sault Ste. Marie	OHL	55	34	40	74	40	....	....	....	....	....	....	....	....	....	7	5	5	10	6	....	....	....	....
	Philadelphia	AHL	3	0	1	1	4	....	....	....	....	....	....	....	....	....	21	12	11	23	12	....	....	....	....
2005-06	**Philadelphia**	**NHL**	81	23	19	42	40	6	2	7	189	12.2	10	683	48.2	12:04	6	0	0	0	10	0	0	0	13:04
2006-07	**Philadelphia**	**NHL**	62	14	23	37	48	3	2	1	215	6.5	–17	1062	45.4	19:00	....	....	....	....	....	....	....	....	....
2007-08	**Philadelphia**	**NHL**	82	29	24	53	55	7	2	5	260	11.2	6	1378	47.7	18:51	17	6	5	11	12	3	0	1	20:08
	NHL Totals		225	66	66	132	143	16	6	13	664	9.9		3123	47.0	16:27	23	6	5	11	22	3	0	1	18:17

OHL Second All-Star Team (2004) • OHL First All-Star Team (2005) • Canadian Major Junior Sportsman of the Year (2005) • Canadian Major Junior First All-Star Team (2005)

CARTER, Ryan

(KAHR-tuhr, RIGH-uhn) **ANA.**

Center. Shoots left. 6'2", 203 lbs. Born, White Bear Lake, MN, August 3, 1983.

			Regular Season														Playoffs								
Season	Club	League	GP	G	A	Pts	PIM	PP	SH	GW	S	%	+/-	TF	F%	Min	GP	G	A	Pts	PIM	PP	SH	GW	Min
2002-03	Green Bay	USHL	55	19	17	36	94	....	....	....	....	....	....	....	....	....	....	....	....	....	....	....	....	....	....
2003-04	Green Bay	USHL	59	22	23	45	131	....	....	....	....	....	....	....	....	....	....	....	....	....	....	....	....	....	....
2004-05	Minnesota State	WCHA	37	15	8	23	44	....	....	....	....	....	....	....	....	....	....	....	....	....	....	....	....	....	....
2005-06	Minnesota State	WCHA	39	19	16	35	71	....	....	....	....	....	....	....	....	....	....	....	....	....	....	....	....	....	....
2006-07	Portland Pirates	AHL	76	16	20	36	85	....	....	....	....	....	....	....	....	....	....	....	....	....	....	....	....	....	....
	♦ Anaheim	**NHL**	....	....	....	....	....	....	....	....	....	....	....	....	....	....	4	0	0	0	0	0	0	0	3:12
2007-08	**Anaheim**	**NHL**	34	4	4	8	36	0	0	1	56	7.1	–2	299	61.5	10:29	6	0	0	0	6	0	0	0	11:03
	Portland Pirates	AHL	13	3	2	5	38	....	....	....	....	....	....	....	....	....	....	....	....	....	....	....	....	....	....
	NHL Totals		34	4	4	8	36	0	0	1	56	7.1		299	61.5	10:29	10	0	0	0	6	0	0	0	7:54

Signed as a free agent by **Anaheim**, July 12, 2006.

CAVANAGH, Tom

(KAV-a-naw, TAWM) **S.J.**

Left wing. Shoots left. 6', 200 lbs. Born, Warwick, RI, March 24, 1982. San Jose's 6th choice, 182nd overall, in 2001 Entry Draft.

			Regular Season														Playoffs								
Season	Club	League	GP	G	A	Pts	PIM	PP	SH	GW	S	%	+/-	TF	F%	Min	GP	G	A	Pts	PIM	PP	SH	GW	Min
1997-98	Toll Gate Titans	High-RI	15	5	17	22	6	....	....	....	....	....	....	....	....	....	4	2	8	10	4	....	....	....	....
1998-99	Toll Gate Titans	High-RI	15	9	20	29	26	....	....	....	....	....	....	....	....	....	5	5	4	9	6	....	....	....	....
99-2000	Toll Gate Titans	High-RI	18	25	29	*54	28	....	....	....	....	....	....	....	....	....	5	0	12	12	9	....	....	....	....
2000-01	Exeter	High-NH	31	*42	40	82	34	....	....	....	....	....	....	....	....	....	....	....	....	....	....	....	....	....	....
2001-02	Harvard Crimson	ECAC	34	8	17	25	4	....	....	....	....	....	....	....	....	....	....	....	....	....	....	....	....	....	....
2002-03	Harvard Crimson	ECAC	34	14	13	27	31	....	....	....	....	....	....	....	....	....	....	....	....	....	....	....	....	....	....
2003-04	Harvard Crimson	ECAC	36	16	20	36	26	....	....	....	....	....	....	....	....	....	....	....	....	....	....	....	....	....	....
2004-05	Harvard Crimson	ECAC	34	10	19	29	22	....	....	....	....	....	....	....	....	....	....	....	....	....	....	....	....	....	....
2005-06	Cleveland Barons	AHL	62	10	11	21	36	....	....	....	....	....	....	....	....	....	....	....	....	....	....	....	....	....	....
2006-07	Worcester Sharks	AHL	74	12	32	44	56	....	....	....	....	....	....	....	....	....	6	1	0	1	6	....	....	....	....
2007-08	**San Jose**	**NHL**	1	0	1	1	0	0	0	0	0	0.0	1	3	33.3	13:54	....	....	....	....	....	....	....	....	....
	Worcester Sharks	AHL	77	19	36	55	55	....	....	....	....	....	....	....	....	....	....	....	....	....	....	....	....	....	....
	NHL Totals		1	0	1	1	0	0	0	0	0	0.0		3	33.3	13:54	....	....	....	....	....	....	....	....	....

ECAC Second All-Star Team (2005)

CHARA, Zdeno

(CHAH-rah, z'DEHN-oh) **BOS.**

Defense. Shoots left. 6'9", 255 lbs. Born, Trencin, Czech., March 18, 1977. NY Islanders' 3rd choice, 56th overall, in 1996 Entry Draft.

			Regular Season														Playoffs								
Season	Club	League	GP	G	A	Pts	PIM	PP	SH	GW	S	%	+/-	TF	F%	Min	GP	G	A	Pts	PIM	PP	SH	GW	Min
1994-95	Dukla Trencin U18	Svk-U18	30	22	22	44	113	....	....	....	....	....	....	....	....	....	....	....	....	....	....	....	....	....	....
	Dukla Trencin Jr.	Slovak-Jr.	2	0	0	0	0	....	....	....	....	....	....	....	....	....	....	....	....	....	....	....	....	....	....
1995-96	Dukla Trencin Jr.	Slovak-Jr.	22	1	13	14	80	....	....	....	....	....	....	....	....	....	....	....	....	....	....	....	....	....	....
	HK VTJ Piestany	Slovak-2	10	1	3	4	10	....	....	....	....	....	....	....	....	....	....	....	....	....	....	....	....	....	....
	Sparta Jr.	CzRep-Jr.	15	1	2	3	42	....	....	....	....	....	....	....	....	....	....	....	....	....	....	....	....	....	....
	HC Sparta Praha	CzRep	1	0	0	0	0	....	....	....	....	....	....	....	....	....	....	....	....	....	....	....	....	....	....
1996-97	Prince George	WHL	49	3	19	22	120	....	....	....	....	....	....	....	....	....	15	1	7	8	45	....	....	....	....
1997-98	**NY Islanders**	**NHL**	25	0	1	1	50	0	0	0	10	0.0	1	....	....	....	....	....	....	....	....	....	....	....	....
	Kentucky	AHL	48	4	9	13	125	....	....	....	....	....	....	....	....	....	1	0	0	0	4	....	....	....	....
1998-99	**NY Islanders**	**NHL**	59	2	6	8	83	0	1	0	56	3.6	–8	0	0.0	18:54	....	....	....	....	....	....	....	....	....
	Lowell	AHL	23	2	2	4	47	....	....	....	....	....	....	....	....	....	....	....	....	....	....	....	....	....	....
99-2000	**NY Islanders**	**NHL**	65	2	9	11	57	0	0	1	47	4.3	–27	0	0.0	22:52	....	....	....	....	....	....	....	....	....
2000-01	**NY Islanders**	**NHL**	82	2	7	9	157	0	1	0	83	2.4	–27	0	0.0	22:20	....	....	....	....	....	....	....	....	....
2001-02	Dukla Trencin	Slovakia	8	2	2	4	32	....	....	....	....	....	....	....	....	....	....	....	....	....	....	....	....	....	....
	Ottawa	**NHL**	75	10	13	23	156	4	1	2	105	9.5	30	0	0.0	22:16	10	0	1	1	12	0	0	0	26:07
2002-03	**Ottawa**	**NHL**	74	9	30	39	116	3	0	2	168	5.4	29	0	0.0	24:57	18	1	6	7	14	0	0	0	25:07
2003-04	**Ottawa**	**NHL**	79	16	25	41	147	7	0	3	185	8.6	33	0	0.0	24:38	7	1	1	2	8	0	0	0	24:38
2004-05	Farjestad	Sweden	33	10	15	25	132	....	....	....	....	....	....	....	....	....	13	3	5	8	82	....	....	....	....
2005-06	**Ottawa**	**NHL**	71	16	27	43	135	10	1	3	212	7.5	17	24	41.7	27:11	10	1	3	4	23	1	0	0	27:32
	Slovakia	Olympics	6	1	1	2	2	....	....	....	....	....	....	....	....	....	....	....	....	....	....	....	....	....	....
2006-07	**Boston**	**NHL**	80	11	32	43	100	9	0	3	204	5.4	–21	1	0.0	27:58	....	....	....	....	....	....	....	....	....
2007-08	**Boston**	**NHL**	77	17	34	51	114	9	1	0	207	8.2	14	0	0.0	26:50	7	1	1	2	12	1	0	0	25:52
	NHL Totals		687	85	184	269	1115	42	5	14	1277	6.7		25	40.0	24:22	52	4	12	16	69	2	0	0	25:48

AHL All-Rookie Team (1998) • NHL First All-Star Team (2004) • NHL Second All-Star Team (2006, 2008)

Played in NHL All-Star Game (2003, 2007, 2008)

Traded to **Ottawa** by **NY Islanders** with Bill Muckalt and NY Islanders' 1st round choice (Jason Spezza) in 2001 Entry Draft for Alexei Yashin, June 23, 2001. Signed as a free agent by **Farjestad** (Sweden), September 24, 2004. Signed as a free agent by **Boston**, July 1, 2006.

CHEECHOO, Jonathan

(CHEE-choo, JAWN-ah-thuhn) **S.J.**

Right wing. Shoots right. 6'1", 205 lbs. Born, Moose Factory, Ont., July 15, 1980. San Jose's 2nd choice, 29th overall, in 1998 Entry Draft.

			Regular Season														Playoffs								
Season	Club	League	GP	G	A	Pts	PIM	PP	SH	GW	S	%	+/-	TF	F%	Min	GP	G	A	Pts	PIM	PP	SH	GW	Min
1996-97	Kitchener	OHA-B	43	35	41	76	33	....	....	....	....	....	....	....	....	....	....	....	....	....	....	....	....	....	....
1997-98	Belleville Bulls	OHL	64	31	45	76	62	....	....	....	....	....	....	....	....	....	10	4	2	6	10	....	....	....	....
1998-99	Belleville Bulls	OHL	63	35	47	82	74	....	....	....	....	....	....	....	....	....	21	15	15	30	27	....	....	....	....
99-2000	Belleville Bulls	OHL	66	45	46	91	102	....	....	....	....	....	....	....	....	....	16	5	12	17	16	....	....	....	....
2000-01	Kentucky	AHL	75	32	34	66	63	....	....	....	....	....	....	....	....	....	3	0	0	0	0	....	....	....	....
2001-02	Cleveland Barons	AHL	53	21	25	46	54	....	....	....	....	....	....	....	....	....	....	....	....	....	....	....	....	....	....
2002-03	**San Jose**	**NHL**	66	9	7	16	39	0	0	3	94	9.6	–5	8	37.5	10:43	....	....	....	....	....	....	....	....	....
	Cleveland Barons	AHL	9	3	4	7	16	....	....	....	....	....	....	....	....	....	....	....	....	....	....	....	....	....	....
2003-04	**San Jose**	**NHL**	81	28	19	47	33	8	0	9	175	16.0	5	7	14.3	16:12	17	4	6	10	10	1	0	0	17:37
2004-05	HV 71 Jonkoping	Sweden	20	5	0	5	10	....	....	....	....	....	....	....	....	....	....	....	....	....	....	....	....	....	....
2005-06	**San Jose**	**NHL**	82	*56	37	93	58	24	2	11	317	17.7	23	20	20.0	19:57	11	4	5	9	8	1	0	1	24:00

			Regular Season														Playoffs								
Season	Club	League	GP	G	A	Pts	PIM	PP	SH	GW	S	%	+/-	TF	F%	Min	GP	G	A	Pts	PIM	PP	SH	GW	Min
2006-07	San Jose	NHL	76	37	32	69	69	15	0	5	250	14.8	11	32	31.3	17:34	11	3	3	6	6	1	0	1	16:25
2007-08	San Jose	NHL	69	23	14	37	46	10	0	4	220	10.5	11	20	20.0	16:36	13	4	4	8	4	0	0	1	18:21
	NHL Totals		374	153	109	262	245	57	2	32	1056	14.5		87	25.3	16:24	52	15	18	33	28	3	0	3	18:54

OHL All-Rookie Team (1998) • AHL All-Rookie Team (2001) • Maurice "Rocket" Richard Trophy (2006)

Played in NHL All-Star Game (2007)

Signed as a free agent by **Jonkoping** (Sweden), December 21, 2004.

CHELIOS, Chris (CHELL-EE-ohs, KRIHS) DET.

Defense. Shoots right. 6', 191 lbs. Born, Chicago, IL, January 25, 1962. Montreal's 5th choice, 40th overall, in 1981 Entry Draft.

Season	Club	League	GP	G	A	Pts	PIM	PP	SH	GW	S	%	+/-	TF	F%	Min	GP	G	A	Pts	PIM	PP	SH	GW	Min
1979-80	Moose Jaw	SJHL	53	12	31	43	118	....	....	....	....	....	....	....	....	....	....	....	....	....	....	....	....	....	....
1980-81	Moose Jaw	SJHL	54	23	64	87	175	....	....	....	....	....	....	....	....	....	....	....	....	....	....	....	....	....	....
1981-82	U. of Wisconsin	WCHA	43	6	43	49	50	....	....	....	....	....	....	....	....	....	....	....	....	....	....	....	....	....	....
1982-83	U. of Wisconsin	WCHA	26	9	17	26	50	....	....	....	....	....	....	....	....	....	....	....	....	....	....	....	....	....	....
1983-84	United States	Nat-Tm	60	14	35	49	58	....	....	....	....	....	....	....	....	....	....	....	....	....	....	....	....	....	....
	United States	Olympics	6	0	4	4	8	....	....	....	....	....	....	....	....	....	....	....	....	....	....	....	....	....	....
	Montreal	**NHL**	**12**	**0**	**2**	**2**	**12**	**0**	**0**	**0**	**23**	**0.0**	**–5**	....	....	....	**15**	**1**	**9**	**10**	**17**	**1**	**0**	**0**	....
1984-85	**Montreal**	**NHL**	**74**	**9**	**55**	**64**	**87**	**2**	**1**	**0**	**199**	**4.5**	**11**	....	....	....	**9**	**2**	**8**	**10**	**17**	**2**	**0**	**0**	....
1985-86 ♦	**Montreal**	**NHL**	**41**	**8**	**26**	**34**	**67**	**2**	**0**	**0**	**101**	**7.9**	**4**	....	....	....	**20**	**2**	**9**	**11**	**49**	**1**	**0**	**0**	....
1986-87	**Montreal**	**NHL**	**71**	**11**	**33**	**44**	**124**	**6**	**0**	**2**	**141**	**7.8**	**–5**	....	....	....	**17**	**4**	**9**	**13**	**38**	**2**	**1**	**0**	....
1987-88	**Montreal**	**NHL**	**71**	**20**	**41**	**61**	**172**	**10**	**1**	**5**	**199**	**10.1**	**14**	....	....	....	**11**	**3**	**1**	**4**	**29**	**1**	**0**	**0**	....
1988-89	**Montreal**	**NHL**	**80**	**15**	**58**	**73**	**185**	**8**	**0**	**6**	**206**	**7.3**	**35**	....	....	....	**21**	**4**	**15**	**19**	**28**	**1**	**0**	**2**	....
1989-90	**Montreal**	**NHL**	**53**	**9**	**22**	**31**	**136**	**1**	**2**	**1**	**123**	**7.3**	**20**	....	....	....	**5**	**0**	**1**	**1**	**8**	**0**	**0**	**0**	....
1990-91	**Chicago**	**NHL**	**77**	**12**	**52**	**64**	**192**	**5**	**2**	**2**	**187**	**6.4**	**23**	....	....	....	**6**	**1**	**7**	**8**	**46**	**1**	**0**	**0**	....
1991-92	**Chicago**	**NHL**	**80**	**9**	**47**	**56**	**245**	**2**	**2**	**2**	**239**	**3.8**	**24**	....	....	....	**18**	**6**	**15**	**21**	**37**	**3**	**0**	**1**	....
1992-93	**Chicago**	**NHL**	**84**	**15**	**58**	**73**	**282**	**8**	**0**	**2**	**290**	**5.2**	**14**	....	....	....	**4**	**0**	**2**	**2**	**14**	**0**	**0**	**0**	....
1993-94	**Chicago**	**NHL**	**76**	**16**	**44**	**60**	**212**	**7**	**1**	**2**	**219**	**7.3**	**12**	....	....	....	**6**	**1**	**1**	**2**	**8**	**1**	**0**	**0**	....
1994-95	EHC Biel-Bienne	Swiss	3	0	3	3	4	....	....	....	....	....	....	....	....	....	....	....	....	....	....	....	....	....	....
	Chicago	**NHL**	**48**	**5**	**33**	**38**	**72**	**3**	**1**	**0**	**166**	**3.0**	**17**	....	....	....	**16**	**4**	**7**	**11**	**12**	**0**	**1**	**3**	....
1995-96	**Chicago**	**NHL**	**81**	**14**	**58**	**72**	**140**	**7**	**0**	**3**	**219**	**6.4**	**25**	....	....	....	**9**	**0**	**3**	**3**	**8**	**0**	**0**	**0**	....
1996-97	**Chicago**	**NHL**	**72**	**10**	**38**	**48**	**112**	**2**	**0**	**2**	**194**	**5.2**	**16**	....	....	....	**6**	**0**	**1**	**1**	**8**	**0**	**0**	**0**	....
1997-98	**Chicago**	**NHL**	**81**	**3**	**39**	**42**	**151**	**1**	**0**	**0**	**205**	**1.5**	**–7**	....	....	....	....	....	....	....	....	....	....	....	....
	United States	Olympics	4	2	0	2	2	....	....	....	....	....	....	....	....	....	....	....	....	....	....	....	....	....	....
1998-99	**Chicago**	**NHL**	**65**	**8**	**26**	**34**	**89**	**2**	**1**	**0**	**172**	**4.7**	**–4**	**4**	**25.0**	**27:19**	....	....	....	....	....	....	....	....	....
	Detroit	**NHL**	**10**	**1**	**1**	**2**	**4**	**1**	**0**	**1**	**15**	**6.7**	**5**	**0**	**0.0**	**22:21**	**10**	**0**	**4**	**4**	**14**	**0**	**0**	**0**	**27:15**
99-2000	**Detroit**	**NHL**	**81**	**3**	**31**	**34**	**103**	**0**	**0**	**0**	**135**	**2.2**	**48**	**0**	**0.0**	**25:16**	**9**	**0**	**1**	**1**	**8**	**0**	**0**	**0**	**24:06**
2000-01	**Detroit**	**NHL**	**24**	**0**	**3**	**3**	**45**	**0**	**0**	**0**	**26**	**0.0**	**4**	**0**	**0.0**	**22:51**	**5**	**1**	**0**	**1**	**2**	**0**	**0**	**0**	**19:41**
2001-02 ♦	**Detroit**	**NHL**	**79**	**6**	**33**	**39**	**126**	**1**	**0**	**1**	**128**	**4.7**	**40**	**0**	**0.0**	**25:18**	**23**	**1**	**13**	**14**	**44**	**1**	**0**	**0**	**26:22**
	United States	Olympics	6	1	0	1	4	....	....	....	....	....	....	....	....	....	....	....	....	....	....	....	....	....	....
2002-03	**Detroit**	**NHL**	**66**	**2**	**17**	**19**	**78**	**0**	**1**	**1**	**92**	**2.2**	**4**	**0**	**0.0**	**24:15**	**4**	**0**	**0**	**0**	**2**	**0**	**0**	**0**	**25:43**
2003-04	**Detroit**	**NHL**	**69**	**2**	**19**	**21**	**61**	**0**	**0**	**0**	**113**	**1.8**	**12**	**0**	**0.0**	**21:21**	**8**	**0**	**1**	**1**	**4**	**0**	**0**	**0**	**21:13**
2004-05	Motor City	UHL	23	5	19	24	25	....	....	....	....	....	....	....	....	....	....	....	....	....	....	....	....	....	....
2005-06	**Detroit**	**NHL**	**81**	**4**	**7**	**11**	**108**	**1**	**1**	**0**	**83**	**4.8**	**22**	**4**	**25.0**	**18:29**	**6**	**0**	**0**	**0**	**6**	**0**	**0**	**0**	**19:25**
	United States	Olympics	6	0	1	1	2	....	....	....	....	....	....	....	....	....	....	....	....	....	....	....	....	....	....
2006-07	**Detroit**	**NHL**	**71**	**0**	**11**	**11**	**34**	**0**	**0**	**0**	**72**	**0.0**	**11**	**1**	**0.0**	**18:08**	**18**	**1**	**6**	**7**	**12**	**0**	**1**	**0**	**20:07**
2007-08 ♦	**Detroit**	**NHL**	**69**	**3**	**9**	**12**	**36**	**0**	**0**	**1**	**60**	**5.0**	**11**	**0**	**0.0**	**16:58**	**14**	**0**	**0**	**0**	**10**	**0**	**0**	**0**	**12:54**
	NHL Totals		**1616**	**185**	**763**	**948**	**2873**	**69**	**13**	**31**	**3607**	**5.1**		**9**	**22.2**	**22:09**	**260**	**31**	**113**	**144**	**421**	**14**	**3**	**6**	**21:55**

WCHA Second All-Star Team (1983) • NCAA Championship All-Tournament Team (1983) • NHL All-Rookie Team (1985) • NHL First All-Star Team (1989, 1993, 1995, 1996, 2002) • James Norris Memorial Trophy (1989, 1993, 1996) • NHL Second All-Star Team (1991, 1997) • Bud Light Plus/Minus Award (2002)

Played in NHL All-Star Game (1985, 1990, 1991, 1992, 1993, 1994, 1996, 1997, 1998, 2000, 2002)

Traded to **Chicago** by **Montreal** with Montreal's 2nd round choice (Michael Pomichter) in 1991 Entry Draft for Denis Savard, June 29, 1990. Traded to **Detroit** by **Chicago** for Anders Eriksson and Detroit's 1st round choices in 1999 (Steve McCarthy) and 2001 (Adam Munro) Entry Drafts, March 23, 1999. • Missed majority of 2000-01 season recovering from knee injury suffered in game vs. Dallas, November 17, 2000. Signed as a free agent by **Motor City** (UHL), February 1, 2005.

CHIMERA, Jason (chihm-AIR-a, JAY-suhn) CBJ

Left wing. Shoots left. 6'2", 216 lbs. Born, Edmonton, Alta., May 2, 1979. Edmonton's 5th choice, 121st overall, in 1997 Entry Draft.

Season	Club	League	GP	G	A	Pts	PIM	PP	SH	GW	S	%	+/-	TF	F%	Min	GP	G	A	Pts	PIM	PP	SH	GW	Min
1994-95	Edmonton Pats	AMHL	33	27	31	58	42	....	....	....	....	....	....	....	....	....	....	....	....	....	....	....	....	....	....
1995-96	Edmonton Pats	AMHL	34	23	24	47	44	....	....	....	....	....	....	....	....	....	....	....	....	....	....	....	....	....	....
1996-97	Medicine Hat	WHL	71	16	23	39	64	....	....	....	....	....	....	....	....	....	4	0	1	1	4	....	....	....	....
1997-98	Medicine Hat	WHL	72	34	32	66	93	....	....	....	....	....	....	....	....	....	....	....	....	....	....	....	....	....	....
	Hamilton	AHL	4	0	0	0	8	....	....	....	....	....	....	....	....	....	....	....	....	....	....	....	....	....	....
1998-99	Medicine Hat	WHL	37	18	22	40	84	....	....	....	....	....	....	....	....	....	....	....	....	....	....	....	....	....	....
	Brandon	WHL	21	14	12	26	32	....	....	....	....	....	....	....	....	....	5	4	1	5	8	....	....	....	....
99-2000	Hamilton	AHL	78	15	13	28	77	....	....	....	....	....	....	....	....	....	10	0	2	2	12	....	....	....	....
2000-01	**Edmonton**	**NHL**	**1**	**0**	**0**	**0**	**0**	**0**	**0**	**0**	**0**	**0.0**	**0**	**0**	**0.0**	**6:58**	....	....	....	....	....	....	....	....	....
	Hamilton	AHL	78	29	25	54	93	....	....	....	....	....	....	....	....	....	....	....	....	....	....	....	....	....	....
2001-02	**Edmonton**	**NHL**	**3**	**1**	**0**	**1**	**0**	**0**	**0**	**0**	**3**	**33.3**	**–3**	**0**	**0.0**	**12:44**	....	....	....	....	....	....	....	....	....
	Hamilton	AHL	77	26	51	77	158	....	....	....	....	....	....	....	....	....	15	4	6	10	10	....	....	....	....
2002-03	**Edmonton**	**NHL**	**66**	**14**	**9**	**23**	**36**	**0**	**1**	**4**	**90**	**15.6**	**–2**	**11**	**54.6**	**10:46**	**2**	**0**	**2**	**2**	**0**	**0**	**0**	**0**	**10:55**
2003-04	**Edmonton**	**NHL**	**60**	**4**	**8**	**12**	**57**	**0**	**0**	**1**	**79**	**5.1**	**–1**	**22**	**31.8**	**10:07**	....	....	....	....	....	....	....	....	....
2004-05	AS Varese Hockey	Italy	15	7	3	10	34	....	....	....	....	....	....	....	....	....	5	2	1	3	31	....	....	....	....
2005-06	**Columbus**	**NHL**	**80**	**17**	**13**	**30**	**95**	**1**	**1**	**5**	**127**	**13.4**	**–10**	**16**	**50.0**	**12:41**	....	....	....	....	....	....	....	....	....
2006-07	**Columbus**	**NHL**	**82**	**15**	**21**	**36**	**91**	**2**	**2**	**2**	**151**	**9.9**	**2**	**38**	**36.8**	**15:22**	....	....	....	....	....	....	....	....	....
2007-08	**Columbus**	**NHL**	**81**	**14**	**17**	**31**	**98**	**1**	**1**	**3**	**198**	**7.1**	**–5**	**35**	**45.7**	**17:30**	....	....	....	....	....	....	....	....	....
	NHL Totals		**373**	**65**	**68**	**133**	**377**	**4**	**5**	**15**	**648**	**10.0**		**122**	**41.8**	**13:33**	**2**	**0**	**2**	**2**	**0**	**0**	**0**	**0**	**10:55**

AHL First All-Star Team (2002)

Traded to **Phoenix** by **Edmonton** with Edmonton's 3rd round choice (later traded to Carolina – later traded to NY Rangers – NY Rangers selected Billy Ryan) in 2004 Entry Draft for New Jersey's 2nd round choice (previously acquired, Edmonton selected Geoff Paukovich) in 2004 Entry Draft and Buffalo's 4th round choice (previously acquired, Edmonton selected Liam Reddox) in 2004 Entry Draft, June 26, 2004. Signed as a free agent by **Varese** (Italy), December 15, 2004. Traded to **Columbus** by **Phoenix** with Cale Hulse and Mike Rupp for Geoff Sanderson and Tim Jackman, October 8, 2005.

CHIPCHURA, Kyle (chip-CHUHR-a, KIGHL) MTL.

Center. Shoots left. 6'2", 204 lbs. Born, Westlock, Alta., February 19, 1986. Montreal's 1st choice, 18th overall, in 2004 Entry Draft.

Season	Club	League	GP	G	A	Pts	PIM	PP	SH	GW	S	%	+/-	TF	F%	Min	GP	G	A	Pts	PIM	PP	SH	GW	Min
2000-01	Spruce Grove	AMBHL	36	26	34	60	48	....	....	....	....	....	....	....	....	....	....	....	....	....	....	....	....	....	....
2001-02	Ft. Saskatchewan	AMHL	33	15	36	51	78	....	....	....	....	....	....	....	....	....	17	16	20	36	....	....	....	....	....
2002-03	Prince Albert	WHL	63	9	21	30	89	....	....	....	....	....	....	....	....	....	....	....	....	....	....	....	....	....	....
2003-04	Prince Albert	WHL	64	15	33	48	118	....	....	....	....	....	....	....	....	....	6	2	4	6	12	....	....	....	....
2004-05	Prince Albert	WHL	28	14	18	32	32	....	....	....	....	....	....	....	....	....	14	4	7	11	25	....	....	....	....
2005-06	Prince Albert	WHL	59	21	34	55	81	....	....	....	....	....	....	....	....	....	....	....	....	....	....	....	....	....	....
	Hamilton	AHL	8	1	2	3	6	....	....	....	....	....	....	....	....	....	....	....	....	....	....	....	....	....	....
2006-07	Hamilton	AHL	80	12	27	39	56	....	....	....	....	....	....	....	....	....	22	6	7	13	20	....	....	....	....
2007-08	**Montreal**	**NHL**	**36**	**4**	**7**	**11**	**10**	**0**	**0**	**0**	**36**	**11.1**	**–1**	**317**	**43.9**	**11:22**	....	....	....	....	....	....	....	....	....
	Hamilton	AHL	39	10	11	21	27	....	....	....	....	....	....	....	....	....	....	....	....	....	....	....	....	....	....
	NHL Totals		**36**	**4**	**7**	**11**	**10**	**0**	**0**	**0**	**36**	**11.1**		**317**	**43.8**	**11:22**	....	....	....	....	....	....	....	....	....

WHL East Second All-Star Team (2006)

CHOUINARD, Marc (shwee-NAHR, MAHRK)

Center. Shoots right. 6'5", 218 lbs. Born, Charlesbourg, Que., May 6, 1977. Winnipeg's 2nd choice, 32nd overall, in 1995 Entry Draft.

Season	Club	League	GP	G	A	Pts	PIM	PP	SH	GW	S	%	+/-	TF	F%	Min	GP	G	A	Pts	PIM	PP	SH	GW	Min
1992-93	Beaubourg Selects	QAHA	28	26	45	71	42	....	....	....	....	....	....	....	....	....	....	....	....	....	....	....	....	....	....
	Ste-Foy	QAAA	3	1	1	2	2	....	....	....	....	....	....	....	....	....	....	....	....	....	....	....	....	....	....
1993-94	Beauport	QMJHL	62	11	19	30	23	....	....	....	....	....	....	....	....	....	13	2	5	7	2	....	....	....	....
1994-95	Beauport	QMJHL	68	24	40	64	32	....	....	....	....	....	....	....	....	....	18	1	6	7	4	....	....	....	....
1995-96	Beauport	QMJHL	30	14	21	35	19	....	....	....	....	....	....	....	....	....	....	....	....	....	....	....	....	....	....
	Halifax	QMJHL	24	6	12	18	17	....	....	....	....	....	....	....	....	....	6	2	1	3	2	....	....	....	....
1996-97	Halifax	QMJHL	63	24	49	73	74	....	....	....	....	....	....	....	....	....	18	9	16	25	12	....	....	....	....
1997-98	Cincinnati	AHL	8	1	2	3	4	....	....	....	....	....	....	....	....	....	....	....	....	....	....	....	....	....	....
1998-99	Cincinnati	AHL	69	7	8	15	20	....	....	....	....	....	....	....	....	....	3	0	0	0	4	....	....	....	....

Season	Club	League	Regular Season GP	G	A	Pts	PIM	PP	SH	GW	S	%	+/-	TF	F%	Min	Playoffs GP	G	A	Pts	PIM	PP	SH	GW	Min
99-2000	Cincinnati	AHL	70	17	16	33	29																		
2000-01	**Anaheim**	**NHL**	**44**	**3**	**4**	**7**	**12**	**0**	**0**	**1**	**26**	**11.5**	**–5**	**414**	**60.9**	**7:50**									
	Cincinnati	AHL	32	10	9	19	4																		
2001-02	**Anaheim**	**NHL**	**45**	**4**	**5**	**9**	**10**	**0**	**0**	**0**	**40**	**10.0**	**2**	**581**	**54.9**	**10:36**									
2002-03	**Anaheim**	**NHL**	**70**	**3**	**4**	**7**	**40**	**0**	**1**	**0**	**52**	**5.8**	**–9**	**662**	**54.5**	**9:25**	**15**	**1**	**0**	**1**	**0**	**0**	**0**	**0**	**7:16**
2003-04	**Minnesota**	**NHL**	**45**	**11**	**10**	**21**	**17**	**3**	**1**	**2**	**70**	**15.7**	**4**	**809**	**53.7**	**15:58**									
2004-05	Frisk-Asker IF	Norway	16	9	8	17	26										3	5	2	7	29				
2005-06	**Minnesota**	**NHL**	**74**	**14**	**16**	**30**	**34**	**6**	**2**	**3**	**112**	**12.5**	**1**	**1089**	**52.7**	**16:29**									
2006-07	**Vancouver**	**NHL**	**42**	**2**	**2**	**4**	**10**	**1**	**0**	**0**	**15**	**13.3**	**–2**	**392**	**48.7**	**9:26**									
	Manitoba Moose	AHL	13	3	1	4	5										4	0	0	0	4				
2007-08	Fribourg	Swiss	44	13	11	24	52										9	2	6	8	10				
	NHL Totals		**320**	**37**	**41**	**78**	**123**	**10**	**4**	**6**	**315**	**11.7**		**3947**	**54.0**	**11:55**	**15**	**1**	**0**	**1**	**0**	**0**	**0**	**0**	**7:16**

Traded to **Anaheim** by **Winnipeg** with Teemu Selanne and Winnipeg's 4th round choice (later traded to Toronto – later traded to Montreal – Montreal selected Kim Staal) in 1996 Entry Draft for Chad Kilger, Oleg Tverdovsky and Anaheim's 3rd round choice (Per-Anton Lundstrom) in 1996 Entry Draft, February 7, 1996. Signed as a free agent by **Minnesota**, July 28, 2003. Signed as a free agent by **Frisk-Asker** (Norway), January 1, 2005. Signed as a free agent by **Vancouver**, July 20, 2006.

CHRISTENSEN, Erik

(KRIHS-tehn-suhn, AIR-ihk) **ATL.**

Center. Shoots left. 6'1", 210 lbs. Born, Edmonton, Alta., December 17, 1983. Pittsburgh's 3rd choice, 69th overall, in 2002 Entry Draft.

Season	Club	League	GP	G	A	Pts	PIM	PP	SH	GW	S	%	+/-	TF	F%	Min	GP	G	A	Pts	PIM	PP	SH	GW	Min
1998-99	Leduc Oil Kings	AMBHL	36	34	42	76	70																		
99-2000	Kamloops Blazers	WHL	66	9	5	14	41										4	0	0	0	2				
2000-01	Kamloops Blazers	WHL	72	21	23	44	36										4	1	1	2	0				
2001-02	Kamloops Blazers	WHL	70	22	36	58	68										4	0	0	0	4				
2002-03	Kamloops Blazers	WHL	67	*54	54	*108	60										6	1	7	8	14				
2003-04	Kamloops Blazers	WHL	29	10	14	24	40																		
	Brandon	WHL	34	17	21	38	20										11	8	4	12	8				
2004-05	Wilkes-Barre	AHL	77	14	13	27	33										11	1	6	7	4				
2005-06	**Pittsburgh**	**NHL**	**33**	**6**	**7**	**13**	**34**	**2**	**0**	**0**	**85**	**7.1**	**–3**	**381**	**53.0**	**14:17**									
	Wilkes-Barre	AHL	48	24	22	46	50										11	2	2	4	2				
2006-07	**Pittsburgh**	**NHL**	**61**	**18**	**15**	**33**	**26**	**6**	**0**	**1**	**133**	**13.5**	**–3**	**240**	**56.3**	**11:38**	**4**	**0**	**0**	**0**	**6**	**0**	**0**	**0**	**8:15**
	Wilkes-Barre	AHL	16	12	12	24	8																		
2007-08	**Pittsburgh**	**NHL**	**49**	**9**	**11**	**20**	**28**	**2**	**0**	**0**	**109**	**8.3**	**–3**	**314**	**58.6**	**12:37**									
	Atlanta	**NHL**	**10**	**2**	**2**	**4**	**2**	**0**	**0**	**0**	**23**	**8.7**	**–7**	**160**	**58.1**	**16:57**									
	NHL Totals		**153**	**35**	**35**	**70**	**90**	**10**	**0**	**1**	**350**	**10.0**		**1095**	**56.1**	**12:52**	**4**	**0**	**0**	**0**	**6**	**0**	**0**	**0**	**8:15**

WHL West First All-Star Team (2003)

Traded to **Atlanta** by **Pittsburgh** with Colby Armstrong, Angelo Esposito and Pittsburgh's 1st round choice (Daultan Leveille) in 2008 Entry Draft for Marian Hossa and Pascal Dupuis, February 26, 2008.

CLARK, Brett

(KLAHRK, BREHT) **COL.**

Defense. Shoots left. 6', 195 lbs. Born, Wapella, Sask., December 23, 1976. Montreal's 7th choice, 154th overall, in 1996 Entry Draft.

Season	Club	League	GP	G	A	Pts	PIM	PP	SH	GW	S	%	+/-	TF	F%	Min	GP	G	A	Pts	PIM	PP	SH	GW	Min
1994-95	Melville	SJHL	62	19	32	51	77																		
1995-96	U. of Maine	H-East	39	7	31	38	22																		
1996-97	Canada	Nat-Tm	57	6	21	27	52																		
1997-98	**Montreal**	**NHL**	**41**	**1**	**0**	**1**	**20**	**0**	**0**	**0**	**26**	**3.8**	**–3**												
	Fredericton	AHL	20	0	6	6	6										4	0	1	1	17				
1998-99	**Montreal**	**NHL**	**61**	**2**	**2**	**4**	**16**	**0**	**0**	**0**	**36**	**5.6**	**–3**	**0**	**0.0**	**13:11**									
	Fredericton	AHL	3	1	0	1	0																		
99-2000	**Atlanta**	**NHL**	**14**	**0**	**1**	**1**	**4**	**0**	**0**	**0**	**13**	**0.0**	**–12**	**0**	**0.0**	**16:51**									
	Orlando	IHL	63	9	17	26	31										6	0	1	1	0				
2000-01	**Atlanta**	**NHL**	**28**	**1**	**2**	**3**	**14**	**0**	**0**	**0**	**35**	**2.9**	**–12**	**0**	**0.0**	**18:02**									
	Orlando	IHL	43	2	9	11	32										15	1	6	7	2				
2001-02	**Atlanta**	**NHL**	**2**	**0**	**0**	**0**	**0**	**0**	**0**	**0**	**0**	**0.0**	**–3**	**1**	**100.0**	**15:32**									
	Chicago Wolves	AHL	42	3	17	20	18																		
	Hershey Bears	AHL	32	7	9	16	12										8	0	2	2	6				
2002-03	Hershey Bears	AHL	80	8	27	35	26										5	0	4	4	4				
2003-04	**Colorado**	**NHL**	**12**	**1**	**1**	**2**	**6**	**0**	**0**	**0**	**14**	**7.1**	**3**	**0**	**0.0**	**10:26**									
	Hershey Bears	AHL	64	11	21	32	37																		
2004-05	Hershey Bears	AHL	67	7	37	44	54																		
2005-06	**Colorado**	**NHL**	**80**	**9**	**27**	**36**	**56**	**4**	**0**	**1**	**148**	**6.1**	**3**	**1**	**0.0**	**19:39**	**9**	**2**	**2**	**4**	**2**	**0**	**1**	**0**	**24:17**
2006-07	**Colorado**	**NHL**	**82**	**10**	**29**	**39**	**50**	**4**	**0**	**1**	**140**	**7.1**	**5**	**1**	**100.0**	**23:41**									
2007-08	**Colorado**	**NHL**	**57**	**5**	**16**	**21**	**33**	**1**	**0**	**0**	**87**	**5.7**	**5**	**0**	**0.0**	**23:09**									
	NHL Totals		**377**	**29**	**78**	**107**	**199**	**9**	**0**	**2**	**499**	**5.8**		**3**	**66.7**	**19:27**	**9**	**2**	**2**	**4**	**2**	**0**	**1**	**0**	**24:17**

Claimed by **Atlanta** from **Montreal** in Expansion Draft, June 25, 1999. Traded to **Colorado** by **Atlanta** for Frederic Cassivi, January 24, 2002.

CLARK, Chris

(KLAHRK, KRIHS) **WSH.**

Right wing. Shoots right. 6', 202 lbs. Born, South Windsor, CT, March 8, 1976. Calgary's 3rd choice, 77th overall, in 1994 Entry Draft.

Season	Club	League	GP	G	A	Pts	PIM	PP	SH	GW	S	%	+/-	TF	F%	Min	GP	G	A	Pts	PIM	PP	SH	GW	Min
1990-91	South Windsor	High-CT	23	16	15	31	24																		
1991-92	Spring. Olympics	NEJHL	49	21	29	50	56																		
1992-93	Spring. Olympics	NEJHL	43	17	60	77	120																		
1993-94	Spring. Olympics	NEJHL	35	31	26	57	185																		
1994-95	Clarkson Knights	ECAC	32	12	11	23	92																		
1995-96	Clarkson Knights	ECAC	38	10	8	18	108																		
1996-97	Clarkson Knights	ECAC	37	23	25	48	*86																		
1997-98	Clarkson Knights	ECAC	35	18	21	39	*106																		
1998-99	Saint John Flames	AHL	73	13	27	40	123										7	2	4	6	15				
99-2000	**Calgary**	**NHL**	**22**	**0**	**1**	**1**	**14**	**0**	**0**	**0**	**17**	**0.0**	**–3**	**0**	**0.0**	**9:02**									
	Saint John Flames	AHL	48	16	17	33	134																		
2000-01	**Calgary**	**NHL**	**29**	**5**	**1**	**6**	**38**	**1**	**0**	**0**	**43**	**11.6**	**0**	**3**	**33.3**	**11:56**									
	Saint John Flames	AHL	48	18	17	35	131										18	4	10	14	49				
2001-02	**Calgary**	**NHL**	**64**	**10**	**7**	**17**	**79**	**2**	**1**	**4**	**109**	**9.2**	**–12**	**21**	**33.3**	**13:57**									
2002-03	**Calgary**	**NHL**	**81**	**10**	**12**	**22**	**126**	**2**	**0**	**2**	**156**	**6.4**	**–11**	**40**	**32.5**	**14:24**									
2003-04	**Calgary**	**NHL**	**82**	**10**	**15**	**25**	**106**	**4**	**0**	**2**	**137**	**7.3**	**–3**	**97**	**36.1**	**14:05**	**26**	**3**	**3**	**6**	**30**	**1**	**0**	**0**	**14:34**
2004-05	SC Bern	Swiss	3	0	0	0	6																		
	Storhamar	Norway	15	10	4	14	86										7	4	4	8	14				
2005-06	**Washington**	**NHL**	**78**	**20**	**19**	**39**	**110**	**1**	**3**	**0**	**144**	**13.9**	**9**	**209**	**49.3**	**15:24**									
2006-07	**Washington**	**NHL**	**74**	**30**	**24**	**54**	**66**	**9**	**4**	**2**	**164**	**18.3**	**–10**	**118**	**50.9**	**18:25**									
2007-08	**Washington**	**NHL**	**18**	**5**	**4**	**9**	**43**	**1**	**0**	**1**	**29**	**17.2**	**0**	**13**	**46.2**	**16:54**									
	NHL Totals		**448**	**90**	**83**	**173**	**582**	**20**	**8**	**11**	**799**	**11.3**		**501**	**44.9**	**14:48**	**26**	**3**	**3**	**6**	**30**	**1**	**0**	**0**	**14:34**

ECAC Second All-Star Team (1998)

Signed as a free agent by **Bern** (Swiss), October 3, 2004. Signed as a free agent by **Storhamar** (Norway), December 29, 2004. Traded to **Washington** by **Calgary** with Calgary's 7th round choice (Andrew Glass) in 2007 Entry Draft for Washington's 7th round choice (Devin Didiomete) in 2006 Entry Draft and Washington's 6th round choice (later traded to Colorado - Colorado selected Jens Hellgren) in 2007 Entry Draft, August 4, 2005.

CLARKE, Noah

(KLAHRK, NOH-uh)

Left wing. Shoots left. 5'9", 190 lbs. Born, La Verne, CA, June 11, 1979. Los Angeles' 10th choice, 250th overall, in 1999 Entry Draft.

Season	Club	League	GP	G	A	Pts	PIM	PP	SH	GW	S	%	+/-	TF	F%	Min	GP	G	A	Pts	PIM	PP	SH	GW	Min
1996-97	Shat.-St. Mary's	High-MN	30	33	44	77																			
1997-98	Des Moines	USHL	54	19	30	49	29										12	2	9	11	23				
1998-99	Des Moines	USHL	52	31	32	63	47										13	8	2	10	16				
99-2000	Colorado College	WCHA	39	17	20	37	30																		
2000-01	Colorado College	WCHA	41	12	20	32	22																		
2001-02	Colorado College	WCHA	42	13	24	37	32																		
2002-03	Colorado College	WCHA	42	21	*49	70	15																		
	Manchester	AHL	3	1	1	2	0																		
2003-04	**Los Angeles**	**NHL**	**2**	**0**	**1**	**1**	**0**	**0**	**0**	**0**	**3**	**0.0**	**1**	**0**	**0.0**	**9:39**									
	Manchester	AHL	71	25	26	51	24										6	3	1	4	4				
2004-05	Manchester	AHL	61	21	24	45	24										6	1	0	1	4				
2005-06	**Los Angeles**	**NHL**	**5**	**0**	**0**	**0**	**0**	**0**	**0**	**0**	**3**	**0.0**	**0**	**3**	**33.3**	**7:23**									
	Manchester	AHL	69	14	30	44	33										7	4	4	8	2				

			Regular Season														Playoffs								
Season	Club	League	GP	G	A	Pts	PIM	PP	SH	GW	S	%	+/-	TF	F%	Min	GP	G	A	Pts	PIM	PP	SH	GW	Min
2006-07	**Los Angeles**	**NHL**	**13**	**2**	**0**	**2**	**4**	**0**	**1**	**0**	**11**	**18.2**	**-6**	**43**	**39.5**	**8:36**	....	....	....	....	....	....	....	....	....
	Manchester	AHL	63	24	33	57	27	....	....	....	....	....	....	....	....	....	16	1	3	4	4	....	....	....	....
2007-08	**New Jersey**	**NHL**	**1**	**1**	**0**	**1**	**0**	**0**	**0**	**0**	**3**	**33.3**	**0**	**0**	**0.0**	**10:39**	....	....	....	....	....	....	....	....	....
	Lowell Devils	AHL	47	14	17	31	25	....	....	....	....	....	....	....	....	....	....	....	....	....	....	....	....	....	....
	NHL Totals		**21**	**3**	**1**	**4**	**4**	**0**	**1**	**0**	**20**	**15.0**		**46**	**39.1**	**8:30**	....	....	....	....	....	....	....	....	....

USHL All-Rookie Team (1998) • USHL First All-Star Team (1999) • Curt Hammer Award (Most Gentlemanly Player - USHL) (1999) • WCHA All-Rookie Team (2000) • WCHA Second All-Star Team (2003) • NCAA West First All-American Team (2003) • AHL All-Rookie Team (2004)

Signed as a free agent by **New Jersey**, July 24, 2007.

CLARKSON, David

(KLAHRK-suhn, DAYV-ihd) **N.J.**

Right wing. Shoots right. 6'1", 200 lbs. Born, Toronto, Ont., March 31, 1984.

Season	Club	League	GP	G	A	Pts	PIM	PP	SH	GW	S	%	+/-	TF	F%	Min	GP	G	A	Pts	PIM	PP	SH	GW	Min
2001-02	Belleville Bulls	OHL	22	2	7	9	34	....	....	....	....	....	....	....	....	....	8	1	1	2	6	....	....	....	....
2002-03	Belleville Bulls	OHL	3	0	0	0	11	....	....	....	....	....	....	....	....	....	....	....	....	....	....	....	....	....	....
	Kitchener Rangers	OHL	54	17	11	28	122	....	....	....	....	....	....	....	....	....	21	4	3	7	23	....	....	....	....
2003-04	Kitchener Rangers	OHL	55	22	17	39	173	....	....	....	....	....	....	....	....	....	....	....	....	....	....	....	....	....	....
2004-05	Kitchener Rangers	OHL	51	33	21	54	145	....	....	....	....	....	....	....	....	....	15	6	2	8	40	....	....	....	....
2005-06	Albany River Rats	AHL	56	13	21	34	233	....	....	....	....	....	....	....	....	....	....	....	....	....	....	....	....	....	....
2006-07	**New Jersey**	**NHL**	**7**	**3**	**1**	**4**	**6**	**2**	**0**	**1**	**18**	**16.7**	**-1**	**1**	**0.0**	**17:02**	**3**	**0**	**0**	**0**	**2**	**0**	**0**	**0**	**6:42**
	Lowell Devils	AHL	67	20	18	38	150	....	....	....	....	....	....	....	....	....	....	....	....	....	....	....	....	....	....
2007-08	**New Jersey**	**NHL**	**81**	**9**	**13**	**22**	**183**	**0**	**0**	**1**	**151**	**6.0**	**1**	**15**	**40.0**	**12:02**	**5**	**0**	**0**	**0**	**4**	**0**	**0**	**0**	**12:20**
	NHL Totals		**88**	**12**	**14**	**26**	**189**	**2**	**0**	**2**	**169**	**7.1**		**16**	**37.5**	**12:26**	**8**	**0**	**0**	**0**	**6**	**0**	**0**	**0**	**10:13**

Signed as a free agent by **New Jersey**, August 12, 2005.

CLASSEN, Greg

(KLAW-sehn, GREHG)

Center. Shoots left. 6'1", 200 lbs. Born, Aylsham, Sask., August 24, 1977.

Season	Club	League	GP	G	A	Pts	PIM	PP	SH	GW	S	%	+/-	TF	F%	Min	GP	G	A	Pts	PIM	PP	SH	GW	Min
1997-98	Nipawin Hawks	SJHL	59	32	50	82	50	....	....	....	....	....	....	....	....	....	14	8	13	21	6	....	....	....	....
1998-99	Merrimack	H-East	36	14	11	25	28	....	....	....	....	....	....	....	....	....	....	....	....	....	....	....	....	....	....
99-2000	Merrimack	H-East	36	14	16	30	16	....	....	....	....	....	....	....	....	....	....	....	....	....	....	....	....	....	....
	Milwaukee	IHL	11	1	0	1	2	....	....	....	....	....	....	....	....	....	2	0	0	0	2	....	....	....	....
2000-01	**Nashville**	**NHL**	**27**	**2**	**4**	**6**	**14**	**1**	**0**	**0**	**18**	**11.1**	**-4**	**195**	**42.1**	**10:16**	....	....	....	....	....	....	....	....	....
	Milwaukee	IHL	23	5	10	15	31	....	....	....	....	....	....	....	....	....	5	0	0	0	0	....	....	....	....
2001-02	**Nashville**	**NHL**	**55**	**5**	**6**	**11**	**30**	**0**	**1**	**0**	**32**	**15.6**	**1**	**389**	**43.2**	**10:09**	....	....	....	....	....	....	....	....	....
	Milwaukee	AHL	8	2	4	6	12	....	....	....	....	....	....	....	....	....	....	....	....	....	....	....	....	....	....
2002-03	**Nashville**	**NHL**	**8**	**0**	**0**	**0**	**4**	**0**	**0**	**0**	**2**	**0.0**	**-3**	**65**	**52.3**	**10:02**	....	....	....	....	....	....	....	....	....
	Milwaukee	AHL	72	20	28	48	61	....	....	....	....	....	....	....	....	....	6	1	1	2	4	....	....	....	....
2003-04	Milwaukee	AHL	68	18	29	47	95	....	....	....	....	....	....	....	....	....	20	4	3	7	12	....	....	....	....
2004-05	Assat Pori	Finland	42	8	10	18	74	....	....	....	....	....	....	....	....	....	2	0	0	0	0	....	....	....	....
2005-06	Milwaukee	AHL	76	24	26	50	67	....	....	....	....	....	....	....	....	....	21	1	15	16	18	....	....	....	....
2006-07	Hamburg Freezers	Germany	50	9	26	35	70	....	....	....	....	....	....	....	....	....	7	1	0	1	14	....	....	....	....
2007-08	Manitoba Moose	AHL	77	11	15	26	67	....	....	....	....	....	....	....	....	....	6	1	1	2	6	....	....	....	....
	NHL Totals		**90**	**7**	**10**	**17**	**48**	**1**	**1**	**0**	**52**	**13.5**		**649**	**43.8**	**10:10**	....	....	....	....	....	....	....	....	....

Hockey East All-Rookie Team (1999)

Signed as a free agent by **Nashville**, March 27, 2000. Signed as a free agent by **Pori** (Finland), July 25, 2004. Signed as a free agent by **Hamburg** (Germany), August 2, 2006. Signed as a free agent by **Vancouver**, July 3, 2007.

CLEARY, Daniel

(KLIH-ree, DAN-yehl) **DET.**

Right wing. Shoots left. 6', 210 lbs. Born, Carbonear, Nfld., December 18, 1978. Chicago's 1st choice, 13th overall, in 1997 Entry Draft.

Season	Club	League	GP	G	A	Pts	PIM	PP	SH	GW	S	%	+/-	TF	F%	Min	GP	G	A	Pts	PIM	PP	SH	GW	Min
1993-94	Kingston	MTJHL	41	18	28	46	33	....	....	....	....	....	....	....	....	....	2	0	1	1	0	....	....	....	....
1994-95	Belleville Bulls	OHL	62	26	55	81	62	....	....	....	....	....	....	....	....	....	16	7	10	17	23	....	....	....	....
1995-96	Belleville Bulls	OHL	64	53	62	115	74	....	....	....	....	....	....	....	....	....	14	10	17	27	40	....	....	....	....
1996-97	Belleville Bulls	OHL	64	32	48	80	88	....	....	....	....	....	....	....	....	....	6	3	4	7	6	....	....	....	....
1997-98	**Chicago**	**NHL**	**6**	**0**	**0**	**0**	**0**	**0**	**0**	**0**	**4**	**0.0**	**-2**	....	....	....	....	....	....	....	....	....	....	....	....
	Belleville Bulls	OHL	30	16	31	47	14	....	....	....	....	....	....	....	....	....	10	6	*17	*23	10	....	....	....	....
	Indianapolis Ice	IHL	4	2	1	3	6	....	....	....	....	....	....	....	....	....	....	....	....	....	....	....	....	....	....
1998-99	**Chicago**	**NHL**	**35**	**4**	**5**	**9**	**24**	**0**	**0**	**0**	**49**	**8.2**	**-1**	**13**	**46.2**	**14:21**	....	....	....	....	....	....	....	....	....
	Portland Pirates	AHL	30	9	17	26	74	....	....	....	....	....	....	....	....	....	....	....	....	....	....	....	....	....	....
	Hamilton	AHL	9	0	1	1	7	....	....	....	....	....	....	....	....	....	3	0	0	0	0	....	....	....	....
99-2000	**Edmonton**	**NHL**	**17**	**3**	**2**	**5**	**8**	**0**	**0**	**1**	**18**	**16.7**	**-1**	**1**	**100.0**	**9:44**	**4**	**0**	**1**	**1**	**2**	**0**	**0**	**0**	**8:40**
	Hamilton	AHL	58	22	52	74	108	....	....	....	....	....	....	....	....	....	5	2	3	5	18	....	....	....	....
2000-01	**Edmonton**	**NHL**	**81**	**14**	**21**	**35**	**37**	**2**	**0**	**2**	**107**	**13.1**	**5**	**13**	**23.1**	**12:58**	**6**	**1**	**1**	**2**	**8**	**1**	**0**	**0**	**14:09**
2001-02	**Edmonton**	**NHL**	**65**	**10**	**19**	**29**	**51**	**2**	**1**	**1**	**75**	**13.3**	**-1**	**5**	**60.0**	**12:43**	....	....	....	....	....	....	....	....	....
2002-03	**Edmonton**	**NHL**	**57**	**4**	**13**	**17**	**31**	**0**	**0**	**1**	**89**	**4.5**	**5**	**5**	**40.0**	**11:58**	....	....	....	....	....	....	....	....	....
2003-04	**Phoenix**	**NHL**	**68**	**6**	**11**	**17**	**42**	**0**	**3**	**0**	**83**	**7.2**	**-8**	**51**	**39.2**	**13:12**	....	....	....	....	....	....	....	....	....
2004-05	Mora IK	Sweden	47	11	26	37	138	....	....	....	....	....	....	....	....	....	....	....	....	....	....	....	....	....	....
2005-06	**Detroit**	**NHL**	**77**	**3**	**12**	**15**	**40**	**0**	**0**	**1**	**106**	**2.8**	**5**	**286**	**45.8**	**10:30**	**6**	**0**	**1**	**1**	**6**	**0**	**0**	**0**	**10:44**
2006-07	**Detroit**	**NHL**	**71**	**20**	**20**	**40**	**24**	**6**	**2**	**5**	**135**	**14.8**	**6**	**411**	**51.1**	**15:28**	**18**	**4**	**8**	**12**	**30**	**1**	**2**	**0**	**16:28**
2007-08♦	**Detroit**	**NHL**	**63**	**20**	**22**	**42**	**33**	**5**	**0**	**3**	**177**	**11.3**	**21**	**110**	**50.9**	**17:23**	**22**	**2**	**1**	**3**	**4**	**0**	**1**	**0**	**17:50**
	NHL Totals		**540**	**84**	**125**	**209**	**290**	**15**	**6**	**14**	**843**	**10.0**		**895**	**48.3**	**13:21**	**56**	**7**	**12**	**19**	**50**	**2**	**3**	**0**	**15:35**

OHL All-Rookie Team (1995) • OHL First All-Star Team (1996, 1997) • AHL Second All-Star Team (2000)

Traded to **Edmonton** by **Chicago** with Chad Kilger, Ethan Moreau and Christian Laflamme for Boris Mironov, Dean McAmmond and Jonas Elofsson, March 20, 1999. Signed as a free agent by **Phoenix**, July 15, 2003. Signed as a free agent by **Mora** (Sweden), September 6, 2004. Signed as a free agent by **Detroit**, October 4, 2005.

CLOWE, Ryane

(KLOH, RIGH-uhn) **S.J.**

Right wing. Shoots right. 6'2", 225 lbs. Born, St. John's, Nfld., September 30, 1982. San Jose's 5th choice, 175th overall, in 2001 Entry Draft.

Season	Club	League	GP	G	A	Pts	PIM	PP	SH	GW	S	%	+/-	TF	F%	Min	GP	G	A	Pts	PIM	PP	SH	GW	Min
2000-01	Rimouski Oceanic	QMJHL	32	15	10	25	43	....	....	....	....	....	....	....	....	....	11	8	1	9	12	....	....	....	....
2001-02	Rimouski Oceanic	QMJHL	53	28	45	73	120	....	....	....	....	....	....	....	....	....	7	1	6	7	2	....	....	....	....
2002-03	Rimouski Oceanic	QMJHL	17	8	19	27	44	....	....	....	....	....	....	....	....	....	....	....	....	....	....	....	....	....	....
	Montreal Rocket	QMJHL	43	18	30	48	60	....	....	....	....	....	....	....	....	....	7	3	7	10	6	....	....	....	....
2003-04	Cleveland Barons	AHL	72	11	29	40	97	....	....	....	....	....	....	....	....	....	8	3	1	4	9	....	....	....	....
2004-05	Cleveland Barons	AHL	74	27	35	62	101	....	....	....	....	....	....	....	....	....	....	....	....	....	....	....	....	....	....
2005-06	**San Jose**	**NHL**	**18**	**0**	**2**	**2**	**9**	**0**	**0**	**0**	**14**	**0.0**	**-2**	**2**	**0.0**	**9:40**	**1**	**0**	**0**	**0**	**0**	**0**	**0**	**0**	**5:06**
	Cleveland Barons	AHL	35	13	21	34	35	....	....	....	....	....	....	....	....	....	....	....	....	....	....	....	....	....	....
2006-07	**San Jose**	**NHL**	**58**	**16**	**18**	**34**	**78**	**4**	**0**	**3**	**93**	**17.2**	**4**	**5**	**60.0**	**13:11**	**11**	**4**	**2**	**6**	**17**	**0**	**0**	**1**	**15:19**
2007-08	**San Jose**	**NHL**	**15**	**3**	**5**	**8**	**22**	**2**	**0**	**0**	**22**	**13.6**	**-1**	**14**	**35.7**	**14:17**	**13**	**5**	**4**	**9**	**12**	**2**	**0**	**0**	**19:00**
	NHL Totals		**91**	**19**	**25**	**44**	**109**	**6**	**0**	**3**	**129**	**14.7**		**21**	**38.1**	**12:40**	**25**	**9**	**6**	**15**	**29**	**2**	**0**	**1**	**16:49**

• Missed majority of 2007-08 season recovering from knee injury suffered in game at Columbus, October 27, 2007.

CLUTTERBUCK, Cal

(KLUH-tuhr-buhck, KAL) **MIN.**

Right wing. Shoots right. 5'11", 205 lbs. Born, Welland, Ont., November 18, 1987. Minnesota's 3rd choice, 72nd overall, in 2006 Entry Draft.

Season	Club	League	GP	G	A	Pts	PIM	PP	SH	GW	S	%	+/-	TF	F%	Min	GP	G	A	Pts	PIM	PP	SH	GW	Min
2004-05	St. Michael's	OHL	38	10	6	16	55	....	....	....	....	....	....	....	....	....	....	....	....	....	....	....	....	....	....
	Oshawa Generals	OHL	27	9	9	18	42	....	....	....	....	....	....	....	....	....	....	....	....	....	....	....	....	....	....
2005-06	Oshawa Generals	OHL	66	35	33	68	139	....	....	....	....	....	....	....	....	....	....	....	....	....	....	....	....	....	....
2006-07	Oshawa Generals	OHL	65	35	54	89	153	....	....	....	....	....	....	....	....	....	9	8	5	13	21	....	....	....	....
2007-08	**Minnesota**	**NHL**	**2**	**0**	**0**	**0**	**0**	**0**	**0**	**0**	**0**	**0.0**	**0**	**1**	**100.0**	**7:05**	....	....	....	....	....	....	....	....	....
	Houston Aeros	AHL	73	11	13	24	97	....	....	....	....	....	....	....	....	....	5	0	0	0	14	....	....	....	....
	NHL Totals		**2**	**0**	**0**	**0**	**0**	**0**	**0**	**0**	**0**	**0.0**		**1**	**100.0**	**7:05**	....	....	....	....	....	....	....	....	....

CLYMER, Ben
(KLIH-mehr, BEHN)

Right wing. Shoots right. 6'1", 200 lbs. Born, Bloomington, MN, April 11, 1978. Boston's 3rd choice, 27th overall, in 1997 Entry Draft.

			Regular Season														Playoffs								
Season	Club	League	GP	G	A	Pts	PIM	PP	SH	GW	S	%	+/-	TF	F%	Min	GP	G	A	Pts	PIM	PP	SH	GW	Min
1993-94	Jefferson Jaguars	High-MN	23	3	7	10	20	....	....	....	....	....	....	....	....	....	....	....	....	....	....	....	....	....	....
1994-95	Jefferson Jaguars	High-MN	28	11	22	33	36	....	....	....	....	....	....	....	....	....	....	....	....	....	....	....	....	....	....
1995-96	Jefferson Jaguars	High-MN	18	12	34	46	34	....	....	....	....	....	....	....	....	....	5	0	6	6	6	....	....	....	....
1996-97	U. of Minnesota	WCHA	29	7	13	20	64	....	....	....	....	....	....	....	....	....	....	....	....	....	....	....	....	....	....
1997-98	U. of Minnesota	WCHA	1	0	0	0	2	....	....	....	....	....	....	....	....	....	....	....	....	....	....	....	....	....	....
1998-99	Seattle	WHL	70	12	44	56	93	....	....	....	....	....	....	....	....	....	11	1	5	6	12	....	....	....	....
99-2000	**Tampa Bay**	**NHL**	**60**	**2**	**6**	**8**	**87**	**2**	**0**	**0**	**98**	**2.0**	**-26**	**3**	**66.7**	**19:37**	....	....	....	....	....	....	....	....	....
	Detroit Vipers	IHL	19	1	9	10	30	....	....	....	....	....	....	....	....	....	....	....	....	....	....	....	....	....	....
2000-01	**Tampa Bay**	**NHL**	**23**	**5**	**1**	**6**	**21**	**3**	**0**	**0**	**25**	**20.0**	**-7**	**8**	**25.0**	**13:03**	....	....	....	....	....	....	....	....	....
	Detroit Vipers	IHL	53	5	8	13	88	....	....	....	....	....	....	....	....	....	....	....	....	....	....	....	....	....	....
2001-02	**Tampa Bay**	**NHL**	**81**	**14**	**20**	**34**	**36**	**4**	**0**	**2**	**151**	**9.3**	**-10**	**14**	**28.6**	**17:26**	....	....	....	....	....	....	....	....	....
2002-03	**Tampa Bay**	**NHL**	**65**	**6**	**12**	**18**	**57**	**1**	**0**	**1**	**103**	**5.8**	**-2**	**15**	**0.0**	**13:39**	**11**	**0**	**2**	**2**	**6**	**0**	**0**	**0**	**13:30**
2003-04♦	**Tampa Bay**	**NHL**	**66**	**2**	**8**	**10**	**50**	**0**	**0**	**0**	**96**	**2.1**	**5**	**25**	**28.0**	**9:48**	**5**	**0**	**0**	**0**	**0**	**0**	**0**	**0**	**7:46**
2004-05	EHC Biel-Bienne	Swiss-2	19	11	12	23	30	....	....	....	....	....	....	....	....	....	11	6	11	17	24	....	....	....	....
2005-06	**Washington**	**NHL**	**77**	**16**	**17**	**33**	**72**	**3**	**0**	**3**	**149**	**10.7**	**-7**	**11**	**45.5**	**14:10**	....	....	....	....	....	....	....	....	....
2006-07	**Washington**	**NHL**	**66**	**7**	**13**	**20**	**44**	**0**	**0**	**0**	**78**	**9.0**	**-17**	**7**	**14.3**	**13:57**	....	....	....	....	....	....	....	....	....
2007-08	Hershey Bears	AHL	50	11	16	27	83	....	....	....	....	....	....	....	....	....	....	....	....	....	....	....	....	....	....
	NHL Totals		**438**	**52**	**77**	**129**	**367**	**13**	**0**	**6**	**700**	**7.4**		**83**	**25.3**	**14:41**	**16**	**0**	**2**	**2**	**6**	**0**	**0**	**0**	**11:42**

• Missed majority of 1997-98 season recovering from shoulder injury suffered in game vs. University of Michigan (CCHA), October 10, 1997. Signed as a free agent by **Tampa Bay**, October 2, 1999. Signed as a free agent by **Biel-Bienne** (Swiss-2), December 2, 2004. Signed as a free agent by **Washington**, August 8, 2005.

COBURN, Braydon
(KOH-buhrn, BRAY-duhn) **PHI.**

Defense. Shoots left. 6'5", 220 lbs. Born, Calgary, Alta., February 27, 1985. Atlanta's 1st choice, 8th overall, in 2003 Entry Draft.

			Regular Season														Playoffs								
Season	Club	League	GP	G	A	Pts	PIM	PP	SH	GW	S	%	+/-	TF	F%	Min	GP	G	A	Pts	PIM	PP	SH	GW	Min
2000-01	Notre Dame	SMHL	32	3	19	22	70	....	....	....	....	....	....	....	....	....	....	....	....	....	....	....	....	....	....
	Portland	WHL	2	0	1	1	0	....	....	....	....	....	....	....	....	....	14	0	4	4	2	....	....	....	....
2001-02	Portland	WHL	68	4	33	37	100	....	....	....	....	....	....	....	....	....	7	1	1	2	9	....	....	....	....
2002-03	Portland	WHL	53	3	16	19	147	....	....	....	....	....	....	....	....	....	7	0	1	1	8	....	....	....	....
2003-04	Portland	WHL	55	10	20	30	92	....	....	....	....	....	....	....	....	....	5	0	1	1	10	....	....	....	....
2004-05	Portland	WHL	60	12	32	44	144	....	....	....	....	....	....	....	....	....	7	1	5	6	6	....	....	....	....
	Chicago Wolves	AHL	3	0	1	1	5	....	....	....	....	....	....	....	....	....	18	0	1	1	36	....	....	....	....
2005-06	**Atlanta**	**NHL**	**9**	**0**	**1**	**1**	**4**	**0**	**0**	**0**	**4**	**0.0**	**-2**	**0**	**0.0**	**7:43**	....	....	....	....	....	....	....	....	....
	Chicago Wolves	AHL	73	6	20	26	134	....	....	....	....	....	....	....	....	....	....	....	....	....	....	....	....	....	....
2006-07	**Atlanta**	**NHL**	**29**	**0**	**4**	**4**	**30**	**0**	**0**	**0**	**21**	**0.0**	**1**	**0**	**0.0**	**11:41**	....	....	....	....	....	....	....	....	....
	Chicago Wolves	AHL	15	1	10	11	36	....	....	....	....	....	....	....	....	....	....	....	....	....	....	....	....	....	....
	Philadelphia	**NHL**	**20**	**3**	**4**	**7**	**16**	**1**	**0**	**0**	**33**	**9.1**	**-2**	**0**	**0.0**	**20:58**	....	....	....	....	....	....	....	....	....
2007-08	**Philadelphia**	**NHL**	**78**	**9**	**27**	**36**	**74**	**5**	**0**	**2**	**113**	**8.0**	**17**	**0**	**0.0**	**21:14**	**14**	**0**	**6**	**6**	**14**	**0**	**0**	**0**	**22:25**
	NHL Totals		**136**	**12**	**36**	**48**	**124**	**6**	**0**	**2**	**171**	**7.0**		**0**	**0.0**	**18:16**	**14**	**0**	**6**	**6**	**14**	**0**	**0**	**0**	**22:25**

WHL Rookie of the Year (2002) • WHL West First All-Star Team (2004, 2005)

Traded to **Philadelphia** by **Atlanta** for Alexei Zhitnik, February 24, 2007.

COGLIANO, Andrew
(kawg-lee-A-noh, AN-droo) **EDM.**

Center. Shoots left. 5'10", 184 lbs. Born, Toronto, Ont., June 14, 1987. Edmonton's 1st choice, 25th overall, in 2005 Entry Draft.

			Regular Season														Playoffs								
Season	Club	League	GP	G	A	Pts	PIM	PP	SH	GW	S	%	+/-	TF	F%	Min	GP	G	A	Pts	PIM	PP	SH	GW	Min
2002-03	Vaughan	GTHL	58	39	54	93	122	....	....	....	....	....	....	....	....	....	....	....	....	....	....	....	....	....	....
2003-04	St. Mike's B's	OPJHL	36	26	47	73	14	....	....	....	....	....	....	....	....	....	24	11	20	31	12	....	....	....	....
2004-05	St. Mike's B's	OPJHL	49	36	*66	*102	33	....	....	....	....	....	....	....	....	....	25	*22	*24	*46	20	....	....	....	....
2005-06	U. of Michigan	CCHA	39	12	16	28	38	....	....	....	....	....	....	....	....	....	....	....	....	....	....	....	....	....	....
2006-07	U. of Michigan	CCHA	38	24	26	50	12	....	....	....	....	....	....	....	....	....	....	....	....	....	....	....	....	....	....
2007-08	**Edmonton**	**NHL**	**82**	**18**	**27**	**45**	**20**	**1**	**2**	**5**	**98**	**18.4**	**1**	**542**	**39.5**	**13:40**	....	....	....	....	....	....	....	....	....
	NHL Totals		**82**	**18**	**27**	**45**	**20**	**1**	**2**	**5**	**98**	**18.4**		**542**	**39.5**	**13:40**	....	....	....	....	....	....	....	....	....

CCHA All-Rookie Team (2006)

COLAIACOVO, Carlo
(koh-lee-A-KOH-voh, KAHR-loh) **TOR.**

Defense. Shoots left. 6'1", 200 lbs. Born, Toronto, Ont., January 27, 1983. Toronto's 1st choice, 17th overall, in 2001 Entry Draft.

			Regular Season														Playoffs								
Season	Club	League	GP	G	A	Pts	PIM	PP	SH	GW	S	%	+/-	TF	F%	Min	GP	G	A	Pts	PIM	PP	SH	GW	Min
1998-99	Mississauga Reps	GTHL	44	10	12	23	28	....	....	....	....	....	....	....	....	....	....	....	....	....	....	....	....	....	....
99-2000	Erie Otters	OHL	52	4	18	22	12	....	....	....	....	....	....	....	....	....	13	2	4	6	9	....	....	....	....
2000-01	Erie Otters	OHL	62	12	27	39	59	....	....	....	....	....	....	....	....	....	14	4	7	11	16	....	....	....	....
2001-02	Erie Otters	OHL	60	13	27	40	49	....	....	....	....	....	....	....	....	....	21	7	10	17	20	....	....	....	....
2002-03	**Toronto**	**NHL**	**2**	**0**	**1**	**1**	**0**	**0**	**0**	**0**	**1**	**0.0**	**0**	**0**	**0.0**	**13:43**	....	....	....	....	....	....	....	....	....
	Erie Otters	OHL	35	14	21	35	12	....	....	....	....	....	....	....	....	....	....	....	....	....	....	....	....	....	....
2003-04	**Toronto**	**NHL**	**2**	**0**	**1**	**1**	**2**	**0**	**0**	**0**	**0**	**0.0**	**1**	**0**	**0.0**	**13:56**	....	....	....	....	....	....	....	....	....
	St. John's	AHL	62	6	25	31	50	....	....	....	....	....	....	....	....	....	....	....	....	....	....	....	....	....	....
2004-05	St. John's	AHL	49	4	20	24	59	....	....	....	....	....	....	....	....	....	5	0	1	1	2	....	....	....	....
2005-06	**Toronto**	**NHL**	**21**	**2**	**5**	**7**	**17**	**1**	**0**	**0**	**21**	**9.5**	**0**	**1**	**0.0**	**15:26**	....	....	....	....	....	....	....	....	....
	Toronto Marlies	AHL	14	5	6	11	14	....	....	....	....	....	....	....	....	....	....	....	....	....	....	....	....	....	....
2006-07	**Toronto**	**NHL**	**48**	**8**	**9**	**17**	**22**	**0**	**0**	**1**	**60**	**13.3**	**5**	**0**	**0.0**	**17:57**	....	....	....	....	....	....	....	....	....
	Toronto Marlies	AHL	5	1	5	6	4	....	....	....	....	....	....	....	....	....	....	....	....	....	....	....	....	....	....
2007-08	**Toronto**	**NHL**	**28**	**2**	**4**	**6**	**10**	**0**	**0**	**1**	**30**	**6.7**	**-4**	**0**	**0.0**	**17:26**	....	....	....	....	....	....	....	....	....
	Toronto Marlies	AHL	2	0	0	0	0	....	....	....	....	....	....	....	....	....	....	....	....	....	....	....	....	....	....
	NHL Totals		**101**	**12**	**20**	**32**	**51**	**1**	**0**	**2**	**112**	**10.7**		**1**	**0.0**	**17:07**	....	....	....	....	....	....	....	....	....

OHL Second All-Star Team (2002, 2003)

• Missed remainder of 2005-06 season recovering from head injury suffered in game at Ottawa, January 23, 2006. • Missed majority of 2007-08 season recovering from recurring knee injury.

COLE, Erik
(KOHL, AIR-ihk) **EDM.**

Left wing. Shoots left. 6'2", 205 lbs. Born, Oswego, NY, November 6, 1978. Carolina's 3rd choice, 71st overall, in 1998 Entry Draft.

			Regular Season														Playoffs								
Season	Club	League	GP	G	A	Pts	PIM	PP	SH	GW	S	%	+/-	TF	F%	Min	GP	G	A	Pts	PIM	PP	SH	GW	Min
1995-96	Oswego	High-NY	40	49	41	90	....	....	....	....	....	....	....	....	....	....	....	....	....	....	....	....	....	....	....
1996-97	Des Moines	USHL	48	30	34	64	140	....	....	....	....	....	....	....	....	....	5	2	0	2	6	....	....	....	....
1997-98	Clarkson Knights	ECAC	34	11	20	31	55	....	....	....	....	....	....	....	....	....	....	....	....	....	....	....	....	....	....
1998-99	Clarkson Knights	ECAC	36	*22	20	42	50	....	....	....	....	....	....	....	....	....	....	....	....	....	....	....	....	....	....
99-2000	Clarkson Knights	ECAC	33	19	11	30	46	....	....	....	....	....	....	....	....	....	....	....	....	....	....	....	....	....	....
	Cincinnati	IHL	9	4	3	7	2	....	....	....	....	....	....	....	....	....	7	1	1	2	2	....	....	....	....
2000-01	Cincinnati	IHL	69	23	20	43	28	....	....	....	....	....	....	....	....	....	5	1	0	1	2	....	....	....	....
2001-02	**Carolina**	**NHL**	**81**	**16**	**24**	**40**	**35**	**3**	**0**	**2**	**159**	**10.1**	**-10**	**17**	**47.1**	**16:04**	**23**	**6**	**3**	**9**	**30**	**1**	**0**	**1**	**18:27**
2002-03	**Carolina**	**NHL**	**53**	**14**	**13**	**27**	**72**	**6**	**2**	**3**	**125**	**11.2**	**1**	**56**	**39.3**	**17:08**	....	....	....	....	....	....	....	....	....
2003-04	**Carolina**	**NHL**	**80**	**18**	**24**	**42**	**93**	**2**	**2**	**3**	**172**	**10.5**	**-4**	**15**	**46.7**	**18:06**	....	....	....	....	....	....	....	....	....
2004-05	Eisbaren Berlin	Germany	39	6	21	27	76	....	....	....	....	....	....	....	....	....	8	5	1	6	37	....	....	....	....
2005-06♦	**Carolina**	**NHL**	**60**	**30**	**29**	**59**	**54**	**3**	**3**	**8**	**164**	**18.3**	**19**	**19**	**36.8**	**19:18**	**2**	**0**	**0**	**0**	**0**	**0**	**0**	**0**	**15:29**
	United States	Olympics	6	1	2	3	0	....	....	....	....	....	....	....	....	....	....	....	....	....	....	....	....	....	....
2006-07	**Carolina**	**NHL**	**71**	**29**	**32**	**61**	**76**	**9**	**0**	**4**	**166**	**17.5**	**2**	**27**	**40.7**	**18:01**	....	....	....	....	....	....	....	....	....
2007-08	**Carolina**	**NHL**	**73**	**22**	**29**	**51**	**76**	**10**	**0**	**4**	**216**	**10.2**	**5**	**38**	**23.7**	**19:22**	....	....	....	....	....	....	....	....	....
	NHL Totals		**418**	**129**	**151**	**280**	**406**	**33**	**7**	**24**	**1002**	**12.9**		**172**	**37.2**	**17:58**	**25**	**6**	**3**	**9**	**30**	**1**	**0**	**1**	**18:13**

ECAC Rookie of the Year (1998) (co-winner - Willie Mitchell) • ECAC First All-Star Team (1999) • NCAA East Second All-American Team (1999) • ECAC Second All-Star Team (2000)

Signed as a free agent by **Berlin** (Germany), October 24, 2004. Traded to **Edmonton** by **Carolina** for Joni Pitkanen, July 1, 2008.

COLLITON, Jeremy

(KAW-lih-tuhn, JAIR-eh-mee) **NYI**

Center. Shoots right. 6'2", 195 lbs. Born, Blackie, Alta., January 13, 1985. NY Islanders' 4th choice, 58th overall, in 2003 Entry Draft.

Season	Club	League	GP	G	A	Pts	PIM	PP	SH	GW	S	%	+/-	TF	F%	Min	Playoffs GP	G	A	Pts	PIM	PP	SH	GW	Min
99-2000	Airdrie Express	AMHL	33	16	25	41	28	....	....	....	....	....	....	....	....	....	....	....	....	....	....	....	....	....	....
2000-01	Crowsnest Pass	AJHL	63	18	30	48	98	....	....	....	....	....	....	....	....	....	....	....	....	....	....	....	....	....	....
2001-02	Prince Albert	WHL	68	11	21	32	53	....	....	....	....	....	....	....	....	....	....	....	....	....	....	....	....	....	....
2002-03	Prince Albert	WHL	58	20	28	48	76	....	....	....	....	....	....	....	....	....	....	....	....	....	....	....	....	....	....
2003-04	Prince Albert	WHL	62	24	26	50	73	....	....	....	....	....	....	....	....	....	6	5	5	10	8	....	....	....	....
2004-05	Prince Albert	WHL	41	16	30	46	25	....	....	....	....	....	....	....	....	....	17	3	4	7	21	....	....	....	....
2005-06	**NY Islanders**	**NHL**	**19**	**1**	**1**	**2**	**6**	**0**	**0**	**0**	**9**	**11.1**	**2**	**76**	**40.8**	**6:18**	....	....	....	....	....	....	....	....	....
	Bridgeport	AHL	66	20	32	52	44	....	....	....	....	....	....	....	....	....	6	0	1	1	2	....	....	....	....
2006-07	**NY Islanders**	**NHL**	**1**	**0**	**0**	**0**	**0**	**0**	**0**	**0**	**0**	**0.0**	**–1**	**0**	**0.0**	**4:40**	....	....	....	....	....	....	....	....	....
	Bridgeport	AHL	45	10	12	22	32	....	....	....	....	....	....	....	....	....	....	....	....	....	....	....	....	....	....
2007-08	**NY Islanders**	**NHL**	**16**	**0**	**0**	**0**	**8**	**0**	**0**	**0**	**16**	**0.0**	**–4**	**104**	**51.9**	**8:46**	....	....	....	....	....	....	....	....	....
	Bridgeport	AHL	65	9	11	20	44	....	....	....	....	....	....	....	....	....	....	....	....	....	....	....	....	....	....
	NHL Totals		**36**	**1**	**1**	**2**	**14**	**0**	**0**	**0**	**25**	**4.0**		**180**	**47.2**	**7:21**	....	....	....	....	....	....	....	....	....

COMEAU, Blake

(KOH-moh, BLAYK) **NYI**

Right wing. Shoots right. 6'1", 207 lbs. Born, Meadow Lake, Sask., February 18, 1986. NY Islanders' 2nd choice, 47th overall, in 2004 Entry Draft.

Season	Club	League	GP	G	A	Pts	PIM	PP	SH	GW	S	%	+/-	TF	F%	Min	Playoffs GP	G	A	Pts	PIM	PP	SH	GW	Min
2001-02	Sask. Contacts	SMHL	42	27	33	60	72	....	....	....	....	....	....	....	....	....	....	....	....	....	....	....	....	....	....
	Kelowna Rockets	WHL	3	0	0	0	4	....	....	....	....	....	....	....	....	....	....	....	....	....	....	....	....	....	....
2002-03	Kelowna Rockets	WHL	54	5	18	23	77	....	....	....	....	....	....	....	....	....	19	2	1	3	20	....	....	....	....
2003-04	Kelowna Rockets	WHL	71	10	23	33	123	....	....	....	....	....	....	....	....	....	17	4	2	6	23	....	....	....	....
2004-05	Kelowna Rockets	WHL	65	24	23	47	108	....	....	....	....	....	....	....	....	....	24	6	12	18	34	....	....	....	....
2005-06	Kelowna Rockets	WHL	60	21	53	74	85	....	....	....	....	....	....	....	....	....	12	4	9	13	22	....	....	....	....
	Bridgeport	AHL	....	....	....	....	....	....	....	....	....	....	....	....	....	....	7	0	3	3	0	....	....	....	....
2006-07	**NY Islanders**	**NHL**	**3**	**0**	**0**	**0**	**0**	**0**	**0**	**0**	**1**	**0.0**	**0**	**0**	**0.0**	**9:25**	....	....	....	....	....	....	....	....	....
	Bridgeport	AHL	61	12	31	43	46	....	....	....	....	....	....	....	....	....	....	....	....	....	....	....	....	....	....
2007-08	**NY Islanders**	**NHL**	**51**	**8**	**7**	**15**	**22**	**1**	**0**	**1**	**67**	**11.9**	**1**	**27**	**29.6**	**11:40**	....	....	....	....	....	....	....	....	....
	Bridgeport	AHL	31	4	15	19	30	....	....	....	....	....	....	....	....	....	....	....	....	....	....	....	....	....	....
	NHL Totals		**54**	**8**	**7**	**15**	**22**	**1**	**0**	**1**	**68**	**11.8**		**27**	**29.6**	**11:33**	....	....	....	....	....	....	....	....	....

WHL West First All-Star Team (2006)

COMMODORE, Mike

(KAWM-uh-dohr, MIGHK) **CBJ**

Defense. Shoots right. 6'5", 228 lbs. Born, Fort Saskatchewan, Alta., November 7, 1979. New Jersey's 2nd choice, 42nd overall, in 1999 Entry Draft.

Season	Club	League	GP	G	A	Pts	PIM	PP	SH	GW	S	%	+/-	TF	F%	Min	Playoffs GP	G	A	Pts	PIM	PP	SH	GW	Min
1996-97	Ft. Saskatchewan	AJHL	51	3	8	11	244	....	....	....	....	....	....	....	....	....	....	....	....	....	....	....	....	....	....
1997-98	North Dakota	WCHA	29	0	5	5	74	....	....	....	....	....	....	....	....	....	....	....	....	....	....	....	....	....	....
1998-99	North Dakota	WCHA	39	5	8	13	154	....	....	....	....	....	....	....	....	....	....	....	....	....	....	....	....	....	....
99-2000	North Dakota	WCHA	38	5	7	12	*154	....	....	....	....	....	....	....	....	....	....	....	....	....	....	....	....	....	....
2000-01	**New Jersey**	**NHL**	**20**	**1**	**4**	**5**	**14**	**0**	**0**	**0**	**11**	**9.1**	**5**	**0**	**0.0**	**12:46**	....	....	....	....	....	....	....	....	....
	Albany River Rats	AHL	41	2	5	7	59	....	....	....	....	....	....	....	....	....	....	....	....	....	....	....	....	....	....
2001-02	**New Jersey**	**NHL**	**37**	**0**	**1**	**1**	**30**	**0**	**0**	**0**	**22**	**0.0**	**–12**	**0**	**0.0**	**12:37**	....	....	....	....	....	....	....	....	....
	Albany River Rats	AHL	14	0	3	3	31	....	....	....	....	....	....	....	....	....	....	....	....	....	....	....	....	....	....
2002-03	Cincinnati	AHL	61	2	9	11	210	....	....	....	....	....	....	....	....	....	....	....	....	....	....	....	....	....	....
	Calgary	**NHL**	**6**	**0**	**1**	**1**	**19**	**0**	**0**	**0**	**5**	**0.0**	**2**	**0**	**0.0**	**11:35**	....	....	....	....	....	....	....	....	....
	Saint John Flames	AHL	7	0	3	3	18	....	....	....	....	....	....	....	....	....	....	....	....	....	....	....	....	....	....
2003-04	**Calgary**	**NHL**	**12**	**0**	**0**	**0**	**25**	**0**	**0**	**0**	**10**	**0.0**	**–4**	**0**	**0.0**	**15:17**	**20**	**0**	**2**	**2**	**19**	**0**	**0**	**0**	**11:34**
	Lowell	AHL	37	5	11	16	75	....	....	....	....	....	....	....	....	....	....	....	....	....	....	....	....	....	....
2004-05	Lowell	AHL	73	6	29	35	175	....	....	....	....	....	....	....	....	....	11	1	2	3	18	....	....	....	....
2005-06♦	**Carolina**	**NHL**	**72**	**3**	**10**	**13**	**138**	**0**	**0**	**2**	**72**	**4.2**	**12**	**1**	**0.0**	**15:30**	**25**	**2**	**2**	**4**	**33**	**0**	**1**	**0**	**19:27**
2006-07	**Carolina**	**NHL**	**82**	**7**	**22**	**29**	**113**	**0**	**2**	**1**	**136**	**5.1**	**0**	**0**	**0.0**	**19:54**	....	....	....	....	....	....	....	....	....
2007-08	**Carolina**	**NHL**	**41**	**3**	**9**	**12**	**74**	**0**	**0**	**0**	**67**	**4.5**	**2**	**0**	**0.0**	**19:16**	....	....	....	....	....	....	....	....	....
	Ottawa	**NHL**	**26**	**0**	**2**	**2**	**26**	**0**	**0**	**0**	**30**	**0.0**	**–9**	**0**	**0.0**	**16:33**	**4**	**0**	**2**	**2**	**0**	**0**	**0**	**0**	**20:14**
	NHL Totals		**296**	**14**	**49**	**63**	**439**	**0**	**2**	**3**	**353**	**4.0**		**1**	**0.0**	**16:42**	**49**	**2**	**6**	**8**	**52**	**0**	**1**	**0**	**16:18**

NCAA Championship All-Tournament Team (2000)

Traded to **Anaheim** by **New Jersey** with Petr Sykora, Jean-Francois Damphousse and Igor Pohanka for Jeff Friesen, Oleg Tverdovsky and Maxim Balmochnykh, July 6, 2002. Traded to **Calgary** by **Anaheim** with Jean-Francois Damphousse for Rob Niedermayer, March 11, 2003. Traded to **Carolina** by **Calgary** for Atlanta's 3rd round choice (previously acquired, Calgary selected Gord Baldwin) in 2005 Entry Draft, July 29, 2005. Traded to **Ottawa** by **Carolina** with Cory Stillman for Joe Corvo and Patrick Eaves, February 11, 2008. Signed as a free agent by **Columbus**, July 1, 2008.

COMRIE, Mike

(KAWM-ree, MIGHK) **NYI**

Center. Shoots left. 5'10", 185 lbs. Born, Edmonton, Alta., September 11, 1980. Edmonton's 5th choice, 91st overall, in 1999 Entry Draft.

Season	Club	League	GP	G	A	Pts	PIM	PP	SH	GW	S	%	+/-	TF	F%	Min	Playoffs GP	G	A	Pts	PIM	PP	SH	GW	Min
1995-96	Edmonton SSAC	AMHL	33	51	52	103	....	....	....	....	....	....	....	....	....	....	....	....	....	....	....	....	....	....	....
1996-97	St. Albert Saints	AJHL	63	37	41	78	44	....	....	....	....	....	....	....	....	....	....	....	....	....	....	....	....	....	....
1997-98	St. Albert Saints	AJHL	58	*60	*78	*138	134	....	....	....	....	....	....	....	....	....	19	*24	*24	*48	51	....	....	....	....
1998-99	U. of Michigan	CCHA	42	19	25	44	38	....	....	....	....	....	....	....	....	....	....	....	....	....	....	....	....	....	....
99-2000	U. of Michigan	CCHA	40	24	35	59	95	....	....	....	....	....	....	....	....	....	....	....	....	....	....	....	....	....	....
2000-01	Kootenay Ice	WHL	37	39	40	79	79	....	....	....	....	....	....	....	....	....	....	....	....	....	....	....	....	....	....
	Edmonton	**NHL**	**41**	**8**	**14**	**22**	**14**	**3**	**0**	**1**	**62**	**12.9**	**6**	**372**	**43.3**	**11:23**	**6**	**1**	**2**	**3**	**0**	**1**	**0**	**1**	**15:00**
2001-02	**Edmonton**	**NHL**	**82**	**33**	**27**	**60**	**45**	**8**	**0**	**5**	**170**	**19.4**	**16**	**1198**	**47.3**	**17:32**	....	....	....	....	....	....	....	....	....
2002-03	**Edmonton**	**NHL**	**69**	**20**	**31**	**51**	**90**	**8**	**0**	**6**	**170**	**11.8**	**–18**	**1069**	**47.1**	**17:51**	**6**	**1**	**0**	**1**	**10**	**0**	**0**	**0**	**13:07**
2003-04	**Philadelphia**	**NHL**	**21**	**4**	**5**	**9**	**12**	**0**	**0**	**1**	**36**	**11.1**	**2**	**165**	**50.9**	**12:51**	....	....	....	....	....	....	....	....	....
	Phoenix	**NHL**	**28**	**8**	**7**	**15**	**16**	**1**	**1**	**1**	**65**	**12.3**	**–8**	**304**	**50.3**	**17:50**	....	....	....	....	....	....	....	....	....
2004-05	Farjestad	Sweden	10	1	6	7	10	....	....	....	....	....	....	....	....	....	....	....	....	....	....	....	....	....	....
2005-06	**Phoenix**	**NHL**	**80**	**30**	**30**	**60**	**55**	**10**	**0**	**4**	**190**	**15.8**	**2**	**781**	**52.8**	**16:01**	....	....	....	....	....	....	....	....	....
2006-07	**Phoenix**	**NHL**	**24**	**7**	**13**	**20**	**20**	**4**	**0**	**1**	**38**	**18.4**	**1**	**210**	**48.6**	**16:36**	....	....	....	....	....	....	....	....	....
	Ottawa	**NHL**	**41**	**13**	**12**	**25**	**24**	**3**	**0**	**2**	**87**	**14.9**	**–1**	**244**	**50.0**	**14:27**	**20**	**2**	**4**	**6**	**17**	**0**	**0**	**0**	**12:41**
2007-08	**NY Islanders**	**NHL**	**76**	**21**	**28**	**49**	**87**	**4**	**0**	**3**	**194**	**10.8**	**–21**	**1227**	**46.0**	**19:11**	....	....	....	....	....	....	....	....	....
	NHL Totals		**462**	**144**	**167**	**311**	**363**	**41**	**1**	**24**	**1012**	**14.2**		**5570**	**47.9**	**16:32**	**32**	**4**	**6**	**10**	**27**	**1**	**0**	**1**	**13:12**

CCHA All-Rookie Team (1999) • CCHA First All-Star Team (1999) • CCHA Rookie of the Year (1999) • CCHA First All-Star Team (2000) • NCAA West Second All-American Team (2000)

• Left **University of Michigan** (CCHA) and signed as a free agent by **Kootenay** (WHL), August 23, 2000. • Left **Kootenay** (WHL) and signed with **Edmonton**, December 30, 2000. Traded to **Philadelphia** by **Edmonton** for Jeff Woywitka, Philadelphia's 1st round choice (Rob Schremp) in 2004 Entry Draft and Philadelphia's 3rd round choice (Danny Syvret) in 2005 Entry Draft, December 16, 2003. Traded to **Phoenix** by **Philadelphia** for Sean Burke, Branko Radivojevic and Ben Eager, February 9, 2004. Signed as a free agent by **Farjestad** (Sweden), October 30, 2004. Traded to **Ottawa** by **Phoenix** for Alexei Kaigorodov, January 3, 2007. Signed as a free agent by **NY Islanders**, July 5, 2007.

CONBOY, Tim

(KAWN-boi, TIHM) **CAR.**

Defense. Shoots right. 6'2", 210 lbs. Born, Farmington, MN, March 22, 1982. San Jose's 6th choice, 217th overall, in 2002 Entry Draft.

Season	Club	League	GP	G	A	Pts	PIM	PP	SH	GW	S	%	+/-	TF	F%	Min	Playoffs GP	G	A	Pts	PIM	PP	SH	GW	Min
99-2000	Brainerd	High-MN	22	20	26	46		....	....	....	....	....	....	....	....	....	....	....	....	....	....	....	....	....	....
2000-01	Rochester	USHL	51	5	9	14	256	....	....	....	....	....	....	....	....	....	....	....	....	....	....	....	....	....	....
2001-02	Rochester	USHL	14	1	6	7	65	....	....	....	....	....	....	....	....	....	....	....	....	....	....	....	....	....	....
	Topeka	USHL	29	4	15	19	128	....	....	....	....	....	....	....	....	....	....	....	....	....	....	....	....	....	....
2002-03	St. Cloud State	WCHA	31	3	12	15	48	....	....	....	....	....	....	....	....	....	....	....	....	....	....	....	....	....	....
2003-04	St. Cloud State	WCHA	32	5	5	10	68	....	....	....	....	....	....	....	....	....	....	....	....	....	....	....	....	....	....
	Cleveland Barons	AHL	....	....	....	....	....	....	....	....	....	....	....	....	....	....	3	0	3	3	4	....	....	....	....
2004-05	Cleveland Barons	AHL	61	4	11	15	134	....	....	....	....	....	....	....	....	....	....	....	....	....	....	....	....	....	....
2005-06	Cleveland Barons	AHL	78	6	14	20	124	....	....	....	....	....	....	....	....	....	....	....	....	....	....	....	....	....	....
2006-07	Albany River Rats	AHL	75	3	7	10	163	....	....	....	....	....	....	....	....	....	5	0	1	1	6	....	....	....	....
2007-08	**Carolina**	**NHL**	**19**	**0**	**5**	**5**	**60**	**0**	**0**	**0**	**16**	**0.0**	**1**	**0**	**0.0**	**6:58**	....	....	....	....	....	....	....	....	....
	Albany River Rats	AHL	52	2	2	4	191	....	....	....	....	....	....	....	....	....	1	0	0	0	21	....	....	....	....
	NHL Totals		**19**	**0**	**5**	**5**	**60**	**0**	**0**	**0**	**16**	**0.0**		**0**	**0.0**	**6:58**	....	....	....	....	....	....	....	....	....

Signed as a free agent by **Carolina**, July 21, 2006.

CONNER, Chris
(KAWN-uhr, KRIHS) **DAL.**

Wing. Shoots left. 5'8", 180 lbs. Born, Westland, MI, December 23, 1983.

Season	Club	League	GP	G	A	Pts	PIM	PP	SH	GW	S	%	+/-	TF	F%	Min	GP	G	A	Pts	PIM	PP	SH	GW	Min
			Regular Season														Playoffs								
2002-03	Michigan Tech	WCHA	38	13	24	37	8																		
2003-04	Michigan Tech	WCHA	38	25	14	39	12																		
2004-05	Michigan Tech	WCHA	37	14	10	24	6																		
2005-06	Michigan Tech	WCHA	38	17	12	29	18																		
	Iowa Stars	AHL	15	2	3	5	0										7	1	1	2	2				
2006-07	**Dallas**	**NHL**	11	1	2	3	4	0	0	0	18	5.6	–3	1	100.0	11:15									
	Iowa Stars	AHL	48	19	18	37	24										12	2	5	7	2				
2007-08	**Dallas**	**NHL**	22	3	2	5	6	0	0	0	27	11.1	0	1	100.0	12:00	1	0	0	0	0	0	0	0	4:17
	Iowa Stars	AHL	55	13	26	39	17																		
	NHL Totals		33	4	4	8	10	0	0	0	45	8.9		2	100.0	11:45	1	0	0	0	0	0	0	0	4:17

WCHA Second All-Star Team (2004)

Signed as a free agent by **Dallas**, July 13, 2006.

CONNOLLY, Tim
(KAW-nuhl-lee, TIHM) **BUF.**

Center. Shoots right. 6'1", 193 lbs. Born, Syracuse, NY, May 7, 1981. NY Islanders' 1st choice, 5th overall, in 1999 Entry Draft.

Season	Club	League	GP	G	A	Pts	PIM	PP	SH	GW	S	%	+/-	TF	F%	Min	GP	G	A	Pts	PIM	PP	SH	GW	Min
1996-97	Syracuse	MTJHL	50	42	62	104	34																		
1997-98	Erie Otters	OHL	59	30	32	62	32										7	1	6	7	6				
1998-99	Erie Otters	OHL	46	34	34	68	50																		
99-2000	**NY Islanders**	**NHL**	81	14	20	34	44	2	1	1	114	12.3	–25	786	36.3	16:18									
2000-01	**NY Islanders**	**NHL**	82	10	31	41	42	5	0	0	171	5.8	–14	989	41.7	20:02									
2001-02	**Buffalo**	**NHL**	82	10	35	45	34	3	0	3	126	7.9	4	1074	39.6	16:58									
2002-03	**Buffalo**	**NHL**	80	12	13	25	32	6	0	2	159	7.5	–28	845	42.8	16:00									
2003-04	**Buffalo**	**NHL**	DID NOT PLAY – INJURED																						
2004-05	Langnau	Swiss	16	7	3	10	14																		
2005-06	**Buffalo**	**NHL**	63	16	39	55	28	7	0	3	99	16.2	5	844	42.5	18:00	8	5	6	11	0	1	1	1	17:29
2006-07	**Buffalo**	**NHL**	2	1	0	1	2	0	0	0	2	50.0	1	13	53.9	13:07	16	0	9	9	4	0	0	0	16:56
2007-08	**Buffalo**	**NHL**	48	7	33	40	8	3	1	3	111	6.3	4	463	48.0	18:41									
	NHL Totals		438	70	171	241	190	26	2	12	782	9.0		5014	41.3	17:33	24	5	15	20	4	1	1	1	17:07

Traded to **Buffalo** by **NY Islanders** with Taylor Pyatt for Michael Peca, June 24, 2001. • Missed entire 2003-04 season recovering from head injury suffered in pre-season game vs. Chicago, October 2, 2003. Signed as a free agent by **Langnau** (Swiss), October 10, 2004. • Missed majority of 2006-07 season recovering from concussion suffered in game vs. Ottawa, May 8, 2006.

CONROY, Craig
(KAWN-roi, KRAYG) **CGY.**

Center. Shoots right. 6'2", 193 lbs. Born, Potsdam, NY, September 4, 1971. Montreal's 7th choice, 123rd overall, in 1990 Entry Draft.

Season	Club	League	GP	G	A	Pts	PIM	PP	SH	GW	S	%	+/-	TF	F%	Min	GP	G	A	Pts	PIM	PP	SH	GW	Min
1989-90	Northwood	High-NY	31	33	43	76																			
1990-91	Clarkson Knights	ECAC	40	8	21	29	24																		
1991-92	Clarkson Knights	ECAC	31	19	17	36	36																		
1992-93	Clarkson Knights	ECAC	35	10	23	33	26																		
1993-94	Clarkson Knights	ECAC	34	26	*40	*66	46																		
1994-95	Fredericton	AHL	55	26	18	44	29										11	7	3	10	6				
	Montreal	**NHL**	6	1	0	1	0	0	0	0	4	25.0	–1												
1995-96	**Montreal**	**NHL**	7	0	0	0	2	0	0	0	1	0.0	–4												
	Fredericton	AHL	67	31	38	69	65										10	5	7	12	6				
1996-97	Fredericton	AHL	9	10	6	16	10																		
	St. Louis	**NHL**	61	6	11	17	43	0	0	1	74	8.1	0				6	0	0	0	8	0	0	0	
	Worcester IceCats	AHL	5	5	6	11	2																		
1997-98	**St. Louis**	**NHL**	81	14	29	43	46	0	3	1	118	11.9	20				10	1	2	3	8	0	0	1	
1998-99	**St. Louis**	**NHL**	69	14	25	39	38	0	1	1	134	10.4	14	1190	54.6	16:39	13	2	1	3	6	0	0	0	15:09
99-2000	**St. Louis**	**NHL**	79	12	15	27	36	1	2	3	98	12.2	5	1339	53.6	14:48	7	0	2	2	2	0	0	0	13:13
2000-01	**St. Louis**	**NHL**	69	11	14	25	46	0	3	2	101	10.9	2	729	55.1	14:01									
	Calgary	**NHL**	14	3	4	7	14	0	1	0	32	9.4	0	264	52.7	18:08									
2001-02	**Calgary**	**NHL**	81	27	48	75	32	7	2	4	146	18.5	24	1654	54.3	20:56									
2002-03	**Calgary**	**NHL**	79	22	37	59	36	5	0	2	143	15.4	–4	1579	57.0	19:47									
2003-04	**Calgary**	**NHL**	63	8	39	47	44	2	0	0	112	7.1	13	1402	53.9	19:13	26	6	11	17	12	2	0	1	20:23
2004-05			DID NOT PLAY																						
2005-06	**Los Angeles**	**NHL**	78	22	44	66	78	5	3	3	154	14.3	13	1429	51.2	19:13									
	United States	Olympics	6	1	4	5	2																		
2006-07	**Los Angeles**	**NHL**	52	5	11	16	38	4	0	2	73	6.8	–13	802	51.5	15:29									
	Calgary	**NHL**	28	8	13	21	18	0	1	0	39	20.5	10	443	50.3	16:00	6	1	1	2	8	0	0	0	15:33
2007-08	**Calgary**	**NHL**	79	12	22	34	71	1	0	4	116	10.3	6	1411	51.5	17:09	7	0	2	2	8	0	0	0	16:43
	NHL Totals		846	165	312	477	542	25	16	23	1345	12.3		12242	53.5	17:32	75	10	19	29	52	2	0	2	17:27

ECAC First All-Star Team (1994) • NCAA East First All-American Team (1994) • NCAA Final Four All-Tournament Team (1994)

Traded to **St. Louis** by **Montreal** with Pierre Turgeon and Rory Fitzpatrick for Murray Baron, Shayne Corson and St. Louis' 5th round choice (Gennady Razin) in 1997 Entry Draft, October 29, 1996. Traded to **Calgary** by **St. Louis** with St. Louis' 7th round choice (David Moss) in 2001 Entry Draft for Cory Stillman, March 13, 2001. Signed as a free agent by **Los Angeles**, July 6, 2004. Traded to **Calgary** by **Los Angeles** for Jamie Lundmark, Calgary's 4th round choice (Dwight King) in 2007 Entry Draft and Calgary's 2nd round choice (later traded back to Calgary - Calgary selected Mitch Wahl) in 2008 Entry Draft, January 29, 2007.

COOKE, Matt
(KUK, MAT) **PIT.**

Center. Shoots left. 5'11", 205 lbs. Born, Belleville, Ont., September 7, 1978. Vancouver's 8th choice, 144th overall, in 1997 Entry Draft.

Season	Club	League	GP	G	A	Pts	PIM	PP	SH	GW	S	%	+/-	TF	F%	Min	GP	G	A	Pts	PIM	PP	SH	GW	Min
1994-95	Wellington Dukes	MTJHL	46	9	23	32	62																		
1995-96	Windsor Spitfires	OHL	61	8	11	19	102										7	1	3	4	6				
1996-97	Windsor Spitfires	OHL	65	45	50	95	146										5	5	5	10	10				
1997-98	Windsor Spitfires	OHL	23	14	19	33	50																		
	Kingston	OHL	25	8	13	21	49										12	8	8	16	20				
1998-99	**Vancouver**	**NHL**	30	0	2	2	27	0	0	0	22	0.0	–12	189	40.2	8:07									
	Syracuse Crunch	AHL	37	15	18	33	119																		
99-2000	**Vancouver**	**NHL**	51	5	7	12	39	0	1	1	58	8.6	3	71	39.4	11:48									
	Syracuse Crunch	AHL	18	5	8	13	27																		
2000-01	**Vancouver**	**NHL**	81	14	13	27	94	0	2	0	121	11.6	5	321	43.0	14:35	4	0	0	0	4	0	0	0	12:04
2001-02	**Vancouver**	**NHL**	82	13	20	33	111	1	0	2	103	12.6	4	28	32.1	14:03	6	3	2	5	0	1	0	0	15:09
2002-03	**Vancouver**	**NHL**	82	15	27	42	82	1	4	0	118	12.7	21	31	35.5	13:24	14	2	1	3	12	0	0	0	14:07
2003-04	**Vancouver**	**NHL**	53	11	12	23	73	1	1	4	79	13.9	5	34	52.9	14:06	7	3	1	4	12	0	0	1	18:23
2004-05			DID NOT PLAY																						
2005-06	**Vancouver**	**NHL**	45	8	10	18	71	0	0	2	67	11.9	–8	25	24.0	13:57									
2006-07	**Vancouver**	**NHL**	81	10	20	30	64	1	0	3	133	7.5	0	19	47.4	15:37	1	0	0	0	2	0	0	0	9:51
2007-08	**Vancouver**	**NHL**	61	7	9	16	64	0	0	1	68	10.3	–4	26	42.3	13:24									
	Washington	**NHL**	17	3	4	7	27	0	1	0	18	16.7	5	2	50.0	12:19	7	0	0	0	4	0	0	0	13:55
	NHL Totals		583	86	124	210	652	4	9	13	787	10.9		746	41.2	13:37	39	8	4	12	34	1	0	1	14:41

Traded to **Washington** by **Vancouver** for Matt Pettinger, February 26, 2008. Signed as a free agent by **Pittsburgh**, July 6, 2008.

CORAZZINI, Carl
(koh-ra-ZEE-nee, KAHRL) **EDM.**

Center. Shoots right. 5'10", 182 lbs. Born, Framingham, MA, April 21, 1979.

Season	Club	League	GP	G	A	Pts	PIM	PP	SH	GW	S	%	+/-	TF	F%	Min	GP	G	A	Pts	PIM	PP	SH	GW	Min
1996-97	St. Sebastian's	High-MA	25	29	31	60																			
1997-98	Boston University	H-East	36	9	6	15	4																		
1998-99	Boston University	H-East	37	15	9	24	12																		
99-2000	Boston University	H-East	42	22	20	42	44																		
2000-01	Boston University	H-East	35	16	20	36	48																		
2001-02	Providence Bruins	AHL	61	7	8	15	10																		
2002-03	Providence Bruins	AHL	33	7	6	13	4										4	0	0	0	0				
	Atlantic City	ECHL	27	13	8	21	14																		
2003-04	**Boston**	**NHL**	12	2	0	2	0	0	1	0	16	12.5	2	6	33.3	10:41									
	Providence Bruins	AHL	62	16	9	25	6										2	1	0	1	2				
2004-05	Providence Bruins	AHL	8	0	0	0	0																		
	Hershey Bears	AHL	52	10	13	23	6																		

			Regular Season														Playoffs								
Season	Club	League	GP	G	A	Pts	PIM	PP	SH	GW	S	%	+/-	TF	F%	Min	GP	G	A	Pts	PIM	PP	SH	GW	Min
2005-06	Norfolk Admirals	AHL	75	26	29	55	16	....	....	....	....	....	....	....	....	....	4	2	2	4	0	....	....	....	....
2006-07	**Chicago**	**NHL**	**7**	**0**	**1**	**1**	**2**	**0**	**0**	**0**	**5**	**0.0**	**0**	**1**	**0.0**	**10:47**	....	....	....	....	....	....	....	....	....
	Norfolk Admirals	AHL	68	28	29	57	18	....	....	....	....	....	....	....	....	....	6	4	1	5	2	....	....	....	....
2007-08	Grand Rapids	AHL	80	24	36	60	14	....	....	....	....	....	....	....	....	....	....	....	....	....	....	....	....	....	....
	NHL Totals		**19**	**2**	**1**	**3**	**2**	**0**	**1**	**0**	**21**	**9.5**		**7**	**28.6**	**10:44**	....	....	....	....	....	....	....	....	....

Hockey East All-Rookie Team (1998) • Hockey East First All-Star Team (2001) • NCAA East Second All-American Team (2001)

Signed as a free agent by **Boston**, August 8, 2001. Signed as a free agent by **Providence** (AHL), October 1, 2004. Traded to **Hershey** (AHL) by **Providence** (AHL) for Darrel Scoville, November 15, 2004. Signed as a free agent by **Norfolk** (AHL), October 18, 2005. Signed as a free agent by **Chicago**, July 17, 2006. Signed as a free agent by **Detroit**, July 16, 2007. Signed as a free agent by **Edmonton**, July 17, 2008.

CORSO, Daniel

(KOHR-soh, DAN-yehl)

Center. Shoots left. 5'10", 187 lbs. Born, Montreal, Que., April 3, 1978. St. Louis' 6th choice, 169th overall, in 1996 Entry Draft.

1993-94	Magog	QAAA	36	17	22	39	....	....	....	....	....	....	....	....	....	....	12	10	12	22	....	....	....	....	....
1994-95	Victoriaville Tigres	QMJHL	65	27	26	53	6	....	....	....	....	....	....	....	....	....	4	2	5	7	2	....	....	....	....
1995-96	Victoriaville Tigres	QMJHL	65	49	65	114	77	....	....	....	....	....	....	....	....	....	12	6	7	13	4	....	....	....	....
1996-97	Victoriaville Tigres	QMJHL	54	51	68	119	50	....	....	....	....	....	....	....	....	....	....	....	....	....	....	....	....	....	....
1997-98	Victoriaville Tigres	QMJHL	35	24	51	75	20	....	....	....	....	....	....	....	....	....	3	1	1	2	2	....	....	....	....
1998-99	Worcester IceCats	AHL	63	14	14	28	26	....	....	....	....	....	....	....	....	....	....	....	....	....	....	....	....	....	....
99-2000	Worcester IceCats	AHL	71	21	34	55	19	....	....	....	....	....	....	....	....	....	9	2	3	5	10	....	....	....	....
2000-01	**St. Louis**	**NHL**	**28**	**10**	**3**	**13**	**14**	**5**	**0**	**4**	**42**	**23.8**	**0**	**296**	**56.1**	**13:56**	**12**	**0**	**1**	**1**	**0**	**0**	**0**	**0**	**8:52**
	Worcester IceCats	AHL	52	19	37	56	47	....	....	....	....	....	....	....	....	....	....	....	....	....	....	....	....	....	....
2001-02	**St. Louis**	**NHL**	**41**	**4**	**7**	**11**	**6**	**1**	**0**	**2**	**25**	**16.0**	**3**	**423**	**54.9**	**11:13**	**2**	**0**	**0**	**0**	**0**	**0**	**0**	**0**	**8:51**
2002-03	**St. Louis**	**NHL**	**1**	**0**	**0**	**0**	**0**	**0**	**0**	**0**	**0**	**0.0**	**–1**	**8**	**50.0**	**7:44**	....	....	....	....	....	....	....	....	....
	Worcester IceCats	AHL	1	0	0	0	0	....	....	....	....	....	....	....	....	....	....	....	....	....	....	....	....	....	....
2003-04	Binghamton	AHL	32	7	11	18	16	....	....	....	....	....	....	....	....	....	....	....	....	....	....	....	....	....	....
	Atlanta	**NHL**	**7**	**0**	**1**	**1**	**0**	**0**	**0**	**0**	**2**	**0.0**	**–2**	**105**	**47.6**	**12:59**	....	....	....	....	....	....	....	....	....
	Chicago Wolves	AHL	29	8	18	26	15	....	....	....	....	....	....	....	....	....	10	1	5	6	0	....	....	....	....
2004-05	Kassel Huskies	Germany	45	8	30	38	32	....	....	....	....	....	....	....	....	....	7	1	5	6	20	....	....	....	....
2005-06	Frankfurt Lions	Germany	29	11	17	28	57	....	....	....	....	....	....	....	....	....	....	....	....	....	....	....	....	....	....
2006-07	Philadelphia	AHL	6	2	4	6	4	....	....	....	....	....	....	....	....	....	....	....	....	....	....	....	....	....	....
	Springfield	AHL	58	13	33	46	35	....	....	....	....	....	....	....	....	....	....	....	....	....	....	....	....	....	....
2007-08	Nizhny Novgorod	Russia	22	2	5	7	18	....	....	....	....	....	....	....	....	....	....	....	....	....	....	....	....	....	....
	Hamilton	AHL	35	7	18	25	12	....	....	....	....	....	....	....	....	....	....	....	....	....	....	....	....	....	....
	NHL Totals		**77**	**14**	**11**	**25**	**20**	**6**	**0**	**6**	**69**	**20.3**		**832**	**54.3**	**12:19**	**14**	**0**	**1**	**1**	**0**	**0**	**0**	**0**	**8:52**

QMJHL All-Rookie Team (1995) • QMJHL First All-Star Team (1997) • QMJHL MVP (1997)

• Missed majority of 2002-03 season recovering from shoulder injury suffered in game vs. Anaheim, October 10, 2003. Signed as a free agent by **Ottawa**, September 2, 2003. Traded to **Atlanta** by **Ottawa** for Brad Tapper, January 6, 2004. Signed as a free agent by **Kassel** (Germany), August 7, 2004. Signed as a free agent by **Frankfurt** (Germany), June 9, 2005. Signed as a free agent by **Philadelphia**, July 13, 2006. Traded to **Tampa Bay** by **Philadelphia** for Darren Reid, November 9, 2006. Signed as a free agent by **Nizhny Novgorod** (Russia), September 3, 2007.

CORVO, Joe

(KOHR-voh, JOH) **CAR.**

Defense. Shoots right. 6', 204 lbs. Born, Oak Park, IL, June 20, 1977. Los Angeles' 4th choice, 83rd overall, in 1997 Entry Draft.

1995-96	Western Mich.	CCHA	41	5	25	30	38	....	....	....	....	....	....	....	....	....	....	....	....	....	....	....	....	....	....
1996-97	Western Mich.	CCHA	32	12	21	33	85	....	....	....	....	....	....	....	....	....	....	....	....	....	....	....	....	....	....
1997-98	Western Mich.	CCHA	32	5	12	17	93	....	....	....	....	....	....	....	....	....	....	....	....	....	....	....	....	....	....
1998-99	Springfield	AHL	50	5	15	20	32	....	....	....	....	....	....	....	....	....	....	....	....	....	....	....	....	....	....
	Hampton Roads	ECHL	5	0	0	0	15	....	....	....	....	....	....	....	....	....	4	0	1	1	0	....	....	....	....
99-2000			DID NOT PLAY																						
2000-01	Lowell	AHL	77	10	23	33	31	....	....	....	....	....	....	....	....	....	4	3	1	4	0	....	....	....	....
2001-02	Manchester	AHL	80	13	37	50	30	....	....	....	....	....	....	....	....	....	5	0	5	5	0	....	....	....	....
2002-03	**Los Angeles**	**NHL**	**50**	**5**	**7**	**12**	**14**	**2**	**0**	**0**	**84**	**6.0**	**2**	**0**	**0.0**	**18:37**	....	....	....	....	....	....	....	....	....
	Manchester	AHL	26	8	18	26	8	....	....	....	....	....	....	....	....	....	3	0	0	0	0	....	....	....	....
2003-04	**Los Angeles**	**NHL**	**72**	**8**	**17**	**25**	**36**	**0**	**0**	**3**	**150**	**5.3**	**7**	**1**	**0.0**	**21:09**	....	....	....	....	....	....	....	....	....
2004-05	Chicago Wolves	AHL	23	7	7	14	14	....	....	....	....	....	....	....	....	....	18	4	5	9	12	....	....	....	....
2005-06	**Los Angeles**	**NHL**	**81**	**14**	**26**	**40**	**38**	**7**	**0**	**3**	**190**	**7.4**	**16**	**0**	**0.0**	**19:59**	....	....	....	....	....	....	....	....	....
2006-07	**Ottawa**	**NHL**	**76**	**8**	**29**	**37**	**42**	**3**	**0**	**2**	**160**	**5.0**	**8**	**0**	**0.0**	**18:04**	**20**	**2**	**7**	**9**	**6**	**1**	**0**	**1**	**17:18**
2007-08	**Ottawa**	**NHL**	**51**	**6**	**21**	**27**	**18**	**1**	**0**	**1**	**111**	**5.4**	**13**	**0**	**0.0**	**17:41**	....	....	....	....	....	....	....	....	....
	Carolina	**NHL**	**23**	**7**	**14**	**21**	**8**	**5**	**0**	**2**	**56**	**12.5**	**4**	**0**	**0.0**	**20:46**	....	....	....	....	....	....	....	....	....
	NHL Totals		**353**	**48**	**114**	**162**	**156**	**18**	**0**	**11**	**751**	**6.4**		**1**	**0.0**	**19:20**	**20**	**2**	**7**	**9**	**6**	**1**	**0**	**1**	**17:18**

CCHA All-Rookie Team (1996) • CCHA Second All-Star Team (1997)

• Missed entire 1999-2000 season after failing to come to contract terms with **Los Angeles.** Signed as a free agent by **Chicago** (AHL), February 24, 2005. Signed as a free agent by **Ottawa**, July 1, 2006. Traded to **Carolina** by **Ottawa** with Patrick Eaves for Cory Stillman and Mike Commodore, February 11, 2008

COTE, Jean-Philippe

(KOH-tay, ZHAWN-fihl-EEP)

Defense. Shoots left. 6'3", 213 lbs. Born, Charlesbourg, Que., April 22, 1982. Toronto's 10th choice, 265th overall, in 2000 Entry Draft.

1998-99	Ste-Foy	QAAA	38	10	24	34	34	....	....	....	....	....	....	....	....	....	17	1	8	9	17	....	....	....	....
	Quebec Remparts	QMJHL	8	0	0	0	2	....	....	....	....	....	....	....	....	....	....	....	....	....	....	....	....	....	....
99-2000	Quebec Remparts	QMJHL	34	0	10	10	15	....	....	....	....	....	....	....	....	....	....	....	....	....	....	....	....	....	....
	Cape Breton	QMJHL	28	0	4	4	21	....	....	....	....	....	....	....	....	....	4	0	1	1	4	....	....	....	....
2000-01	Cape Breton	QMJHL	71	6	29	35	90	....	....	....	....	....	....	....	....	....	12	0	0	0	18	....	....	....	....
2001-02	Cape Breton	QMJHL	61	4	20	24	72	....	....	....	....	....	....	....	....	....	16	1	6	7	38	....	....	....	....
2002-03	Cape Breton	QMJHL	16	1	3	4	12	....	....	....	....	....	....	....	....	....	....	....	....	....	....	....	....	....	....
	Acadie-Bathurst	QMJHL	48	8	18	26	87	....	....	....	....	....	....	....	....	....	11	2	3	5	20	....	....	....	....
2003-04	Hamilton	AHL	75	2	7	9	79	....	....	....	....	....	....	....	....	....	10	0	4	4	24	....	....	....	....
2004-05	Hamilton	AHL	51	1	8	9	58	....	....	....	....	....	....	....	....	....	4	0	1	1	0	....	....	....	....
2005-06	**Montreal**	**NHL**	**8**	**0**	**0**	**0**	**4**	**0**	**0**	**0**	**2**	**0.0**	**2**	**0**	**0.0**	**11:02**	....	....	....	....	....	....	....	....	....
	Hamilton	AHL	61	3	8	11	113	....	....	....	....	....	....	....	....	....	....	....	....	....	....	....	....	....	....
2006-07	Hamilton	AHL	68	3	9	12	115	....	....	....	....	....	....	....	....	....	6	0	0	0	2	....	....	....	....
2007-08	Hamilton	AHL	79	1	12	13	112	....	....	....	....	....	....	....	....	....	....	....	....	....	....	....	....	....	....
	NHL Totals		**8**	**0**	**0**	**0**	**4**	**0**	**0**	**0**	**2**	**0.0**		**0**	**0.0**	**11:02**	....	....	....	....	....	....	....	....	....

Signed as a free agent by **Montreal**, August 19, 2004.

COTE, Riley

(KOH-tay, RIGH-lee) **PHI.**

Right wing. Shoots left. 6'1", 210 lbs. Born, Winnipeg, Man., March 16, 1982.

1998-99	Prince Albert	WHL	37	3	2	5	63	....	....	....	....	....	....	....	....	....	9	0	0	0	9	....	....	....	....
99-2000	Prince Albert	WHL	67	6	7	13	71	....	....	....	....	....	....	....	....	....	3	1	0	1	2	....	....	....	....
2000-01	Prince Albert	WHL	64	17	35	52	114	....	....	....	....	....	....	....	....	....	....	....	....	....	....	....	....	....	....
2001-02	Prince Albert	WHL	67	28	23	51	134	....	....	....	....	....	....	....	....	....	....	....	....	....	....	....	....	....	....
2002-03	St. John's	AHL	6	0	0	0	5	....	....	....	....	....	....	....	....	....	....	....	....	....	....	....	....	....	....
	Memphis	CHL	51	8	6	14	241	....	....	....	....	....	....	....	....	....	14	1	0	1	54	....	....	....	....
2003-04	Syracuse Crunch	AHL	9	0	0	0	19	....	....	....	....	....	....	....	....	....	....	....	....	....	....	....	....	....	....
	Dayton Bombers	ECHL	57	6	11	17	258	....	....	....	....	....	....	....	....	....	....	....	....	....	....	....	....	....	....
2004-05	Philadelphia	AHL	61	4	7	11	280	....	....	....	....	....	....	....	....	....	13	0	0	0	6	....	....	....	....
2005-06	Philadelphia	AHL	70	3	1	4	259	....	....	....	....	....	....	....	....	....	....	....	....	....	....	....	....	....	....
2006-07	**Philadelphia**	**NHL**	**8**	**0**	**0**	**0**	**11**	**0**	**0**	**0**	**3**	**0.0**	**0**	**0**	**0.0**	**4:30**	....	....	....	....	....	....	....	....	....
	Philadelphia	AHL	37	1	4	5	125	....	....	....	....	....	....	....	....	....	....	....	....	....	....	....	....	....	....
2007-08	**Philadelphia**	**NHL**	**70**	**1**	**3**	**4**	**202**	**0**	**0**	**0**	**17**	**5.9**	**2**	**2**	**50.0**	**4:17**	**3**	**0**	**0**	**0**	**0**	**0**	**0**	**0**	**4:08**
	NHL Totals		**78**	**1**	**3**	**4**	**213**	**0**	**0**	**0**	**20**	**5.0**		**2**	**50.0**	**4:18**	**3**	**0**	**0**	**0**	**0**	**0**	**0**	**0**	**4:08**

Signed as a free agent by **Philadelphia**, August 23, 2005.

COULOMBE, Patrick (KOO-lawmb, PAT-rihk) VAN.

Defense. Shoots left. 5'11", 185 lbs. Born, St-Fabien, Quebec, April 23, 1985.

			Regular Season														Playoffs								
Season	Club	League	GP	G	A	Pts	PIM	PP	SH	GW	S	%	+/-	TF	F%	Min	GP	G	A	Pts	PIM	PP	SH	GW	Min
2001-02	Rimouski Oceanic	QMJHL	34	0	8	8	30	....	....	....	....	....	....	....	....	....	7	0	3	3	2	....	....	....	....
2002-03	Rimouski Oceanic	QMJHL	72	6	25	31	48	....	....	....	....	....	....	....	....	....	....	....	....	....	....	....	....	....	....
2003-04	Rimouski Oceanic	QMJHL	59	7	38	45	32	....	....	....	....	....	....	....	....	....	9	0	5	5	0	....	....	....	....
2004-05	Rimouski Oceanic	QMJHL	70	8	60	68	46	....	....	....	....	....	....	....	....	....	13	2	17	19	6	....	....	....	....
2005-06	Rimouski Oceanic	QMJHL	29	5	23	28	18	....	....	....	....	....	....	....	....	....	....	....	....	....	....	....	....	....	....
	Chicoutimi	QMJHL	33	18	31	49	22	....	....	....	....	....	....	....	....	....	9	2	10	12	6	....	....	....	....
2006-07	**Vancouver**	**NHL**	**7**	**0**	**1**	**1**	**4**	**0**	**0**	**0**	**11**	**0.0**	**-6**	**0**	**0.0**	**13:38**	....	....	....	....	....	....	....	....	....
	Manitoba Moose	AHL	44	3	6	9	22	....	....	....	....	....	....	....	....	....	1	0	0	0	0	....	....	....	....
	Victoria	ECHL	6	0	3	3	2	....	....	....	....	....	....	....	....	....	6	0	2	2	0	....	....	....	....
2007-08	Manitoba Moose	AHL	2	0	0	0	0	....	....	....	....	....	....	....	....	....	....	....	....	....	....	....	....	....	....
	Victoria	ECHL	58	8	22	30	40	....	....	....	....	....	....	....	....	....	11	0	5	5	4	....	....	....	....
	NHL Totals		**7**	**0**	**1**	**1**	**4**	**0**	**0**	**0**	**11**	**0.0**		**0**	**0.0**	**13:38**	....	....	....	....	....	....	....	....	....

Signed as a free agent by **Vancouver**, November 3, 2006.

COWAN, Jeff (KOW-an, JEHF) VAN.

Left wing. Shoots left. 6'2", 205 lbs. Born, Scarborough, Ont., September 27, 1976.

			Regular Season														Playoffs								
Season	Club	League	GP	G	A	Pts	PIM	PP	SH	GW	S	%	+/-	TF	F%	Min	GP	G	A	Pts	PIM	PP	SH	GW	Min
1992-93	Guelph Platers	OHA-B	45	8	8	16	22	....	....	....	....	....	....	....	....	....	....	....	....	....	....	....	....	....	....
1993-94	Guelph Platers	OHA-B	43	30	26	56	96	....	....	....	....	....	....	....	....	....	....	....	....	....	....	....	....	....	....
	Guelph Storm	OHL	17	1	0	1	5	....	....	....	....	....	....	....	....	....	....	....	....	....	....	....	....	....	....
1994-95	Guelph Storm	OHL	51	10	7	17	14	....	....	....	....	....	....	....	....	....	14	1	1	2	0	....	....	....	....
1995-96	Barrie Colts	OHL	66	38	14	52	29	....	....	....	....	....	....	....	....	....	5	1	2	3	6	....	....	....	....
1996-97	Saint John Flames	AHL	22	5	5	10	8	....	....	....	....	....	....	....	....	....	....	....	....	....	....	....	....	....	....
	Roanoke Express	ECHL	47	21	13	34	42	....	....	....	....	....	....	....	....	....	....	....	....	....	....	....	....	....	....
1997-98	Saint John Flames	AHL	69	15	13	28	23	....	....	....	....	....	....	....	....	....	13	4	1	5	14	....	....	....	....
1998-99	Saint John Flames	AHL	71	7	12	19	117	....	....	....	....	....	....	....	....	....	4	0	1	1	10	....	....	....	....
99-2000	**Calgary**	**NHL**	**13**	**4**	**1**	**5**	**16**	**0**	**0**	**0**	**26**	**15.4**	**2**	**0**	**0.0**	**10:22**	....	....	....	....	....	....	....	....	....
	Saint John Flames	AHL	47	15	10	25	77	....	....	....	....	....	....	....	....	....	....	....	....	....	....	....	....	....	....
2000-01	**Calgary**	**NHL**	**51**	**9**	**4**	**13**	**74**	**2**	**0**	**1**	**48**	**18.8**	**-8**	**5**	**20.0**	**9:06**	....	....	....	....	....	....	....	....	....
2001-02	**Calgary**	**NHL**	**19**	**1**	**0**	**1**	**40**	**0**	**0**	**1**	**13**	**7.7**	**-3**	**2**	**50.0**	**7:44**	....	....	....	....	....	....	....	....	....
	Atlanta	**NHL**	**38**	**4**	**1**	**5**	**50**	**0**	**0**	**1**	**51**	**7.8**	**-11**	**5**	**20.0**	**12:27**	....	....	....	....	....	....	....	....	....
2002-03	**Atlanta**	**NHL**	**66**	**3**	**5**	**8**	**115**	**0**	**0**	**0**	**52**	**5.8**	**-15**	**10**	**30.0**	**8:24**	....	....	....	....	....	....	....	....	....
2003-04	**Atlanta**	**NHL**	**58**	**9**	**15**	**24**	**68**	**1**	**0**	**1**	**74**	**12.2**	**2**	**9**	**22.2**	**10:04**	....	....	....	....	....	....	....	....	....
	Los Angeles	**NHL**	**13**	**2**	**1**	**3**	**24**	**1**	**0**	**0**	**15**	**13.3**	**-1**	**2**	**50.0**	**11:43**	....	....	....	....	....	....	....	....	....
2004-05			DID NOT PLAY																						
2005-06	**Los Angeles**	**NHL**	**46**	**8**	**1**	**9**	**73**	**0**	**0**	**0**	**53**	**15.1**	**-8**	**4**	**25.0**	**8:26**	....	....	....	....	....	....	....	....	....
2006-07	**Los Angeles**	**NHL**	**21**	**0**	**2**	**2**	**32**	**0**	**0**	**0**	**28**	**0.0**	**-1**	**1**	**0.0**	**7:37**	....	....	....	....	....	....	....	....	....
	Vancouver	**NHL**	**42**	**7**	**3**	**10**	**93**	**0**	**1**	**0**	**46**	**15.2**	**4**	**0**	**0.0**	**8:15**	**10**	**2**	**0**	**2**	**22**	**0**	**0**	**1**	**11:38**
2007-08	**Vancouver**	**NHL**	**46**	**0**	**1**	**1**	**110**	**0**	**0**	**0**	**35**	**0.0**	**-5**	**1**	**0.0**	**8:45**	....	....	....	....	....	....	....	....	....
	NHL Totals		**413**	**47**	**34**	**81**	**695**	**4**	**1**	**4**	**441**	**10.7**		**39**	**25.6**	**9:13**	**10**	**2**	**0**	**2**	**22**	**0**	**0**	**1**	**11:38**

Signed as a free agent by **Calgary**, October 2, 1995. Traded to **Atlanta** by **Calgary** with the rights to Kurtis Foster for Petr Buzek and Atlanta's 6th round choice (Adam Pardy) in 2004 Entry Draft, December 18, 2001. Traded to **Los Angeles** by **Atlanta** for Kip Brennan, March 9, 2004. Claimed on waivers by **Vancouver** from **Los Angeles**, December 30, 2006.

CRAIG, Ryan (KRAIG, RIGH-uhn) T.B.

Center. Shoots left. 6'2", 212 lbs. Born, Abbotsford, B.C., January 6, 1982. Tampa Bay's 10th choice, 255th overall, in 2002 Entry Draft.

			Regular Season														Playoffs								
Season	Club	League	GP	G	A	Pts	PIM	PP	SH	GW	S	%	+/-	TF	F%	Min	GP	G	A	Pts	PIM	PP	SH	GW	Min
1997-98	Abbotsford	Minor-BC	80	118	120	238	110	....	....	....	....	....	....	....	....	....	....	....	....	....	....	....	....	....	....
	Brandon	WHL	1	0	0	0	0	....	....	....	....	....	....	....	....	....	....	....	....	....	....	....	....	....	....
1998-99	Brandon	WHL	54	11	12	23	46	....	....	....	....	....	....	....	....	....	5	0	0	0	4	....	....	....	....
99-2000	Brandon	WHL	65	17	19	36	40	....	....	....	....	....	....	....	....	....	....	....	....	....	....	....	....	....	....
2000-01	Brandon	WHL	70	38	33	71	49	....	....	....	....	....	....	....	....	....	6	3	0	3	7	....	....	....	....
2001-02	Brandon	WHL	52	29	35	64	52	....	....	....	....	....	....	....	....	....	19	11	10	21	13	....	....	....	....
2002-03	Brandon	WHL	60	42	32	74	69	....	....	....	....	....	....	....	....	....	17	5	8	13	29	....	....	....	....
2003-04	Hershey Bears	AHL	61	4	8	12	24	....	....	....	....	....	....	....	....	....	....	....	....	....	....	....	....	....	....
	Pensacola	ECHL	5	3	5	8	0	....	....	....	....	....	....	....	....	....	2	0	1	1	0	....	....	....	....
2004-05	Springfield	AHL	80	27	14	41	50	....	....	....	....	....	....	....	....	....	....	....	....	....	....	....	....	....	....
2005-06	**Tampa Bay**	**NHL**	**48**	**15**	**13**	**28**	**6**	**6**	**0**	**0**	**81**	**18.5**	**-4**	**95**	**46.3**	**15:21**	**5**	**0**	**0**	**0**	**10**	**0**	**0**	**0**	**12:59**
	Springfield	AHL	28	12	10	22	14	....	....	....	....	....	....	....	....	....	....	....	....	....	....	....	....	....	....
2006-07	**Tampa Bay**	**NHL**	**72**	**14**	**13**	**27**	**55**	**4**	**0**	**2**	**130**	**10.8**	**-11**	**110**	**40.0**	**15:20**	**6**	**0**	**0**	**0**	**12**	**0**	**0**	**0**	**7:02**
2007-08	**Tampa Bay**	**NHL**	**7**	**1**	**1**	**2**	**0**	**1**	**0**	**0**	**8**	**12.5**	**-1**	**1**	**100.0**	**13:04**	....	....	....	....	....	....	....	....	....
	Norfolk Admirals	AHL	2	1	2	3	2	....	....	....	....	....	....	....	....	....	....	....	....	....	....	....	....	....	....
	NHL Totals		**127**	**30**	**27**	**57**	**61**	**11**	**0**	**2**	**219**	**13.7**		**206**	**43.2**	**15:13**	**11**	**0**	**0**	**0**	**22**	**0**	**0**	**0**	**9:44**

WHL East First All-Star Team (2003) • Canadian Major Junior Humanitarian Player of the Year (2003)
• Missed majority of 2007-08 season recovering from back and knee injuries.

CROMBEEN, B.J. (KRAWM-been, BEE-JAY) DAL.

Right wing. Shoots right. 6'2", 212 lbs. Born, Denver, CO, July 10, 1985. Dallas' 3rd choice, 54th overall, in 2003 Entry Draft.

			Regular Season														Playoffs								
Season	Club	League	GP	G	A	Pts	PIM	PP	SH	GW	S	%	+/-	TF	F%	Min	GP	G	A	Pts	PIM	PP	SH	GW	Min
2000-01	Newmarket	OPJHL	35	14	14	28	63	....	....	....	....	....	....	....	....	....	....	....	....	....	....	....	....	....	....
2001-02	Barrie Colts	OHL	60	12	13	25	118	....	....	....	....	....	....	....	....	....	20	1	1	2	31	....	....	....	....
2002-03	Barrie Colts	OHL	63	22	24	46	133	....	....	....	....	....	....	....	....	....	6	1	0	1	8	....	....	....	....
2003-04	Barrie Colts	OHL	62	21	29	50	154	....	....	....	....	....	....	....	....	....	12	5	7	12	35	....	....	....	....
2004-05	Barrie Colts	OHL	63	31	18	49	111	....	....	....	....	....	....	....	....	....	6	2	4	6	35	....	....	....	....
2005-06	Iowa Stars	AHL	52	5	7	12	97	....	....	....	....	....	....	....	....	....	5	1	0	1	9	....	....	....	....
	Idaho Steelheads	ECHL	8	5	3	8	5	....	....	....	....	....	....	....	....	....	....	....	....	....	....	....	....	....	....
2006-07	Assat Pori	Finland	55	13	9	22	152	....	....	....	....	....	....	....	....	....	....	....	....	....	....	....	....	....	....
	Idaho Steelheads	ECHL	13	7	4	11	43	....	....	....	....	....	....	....	....	....	22	5	5	10	45	....	....	....	....
2007-08	**Dallas**	**NHL**	**8**	**0**	**2**	**2**	**39**	**0**	**0**	**0**	**9**	**0.0**	**1**	**1**	**0.0**	**6:38**	**5**	**0**	**0**	**0**	**0**	**0**	**0**	**0**	**4:16**
	Iowa Stars	AHL	65	14	14	28	158	....	....	....	....	....	....	....	....	....	....	....	....	....	....	....	....	....	....
	NHL Totals		**8**	**0**	**2**	**2**	**39**	**0**	**0**	**0**	**9**	**0.0**		**1**	**0.0**	**6:38**	**5**	**0**	**0**	**0**	**0**	**0**	**0**	**0**	**4:16**

Signed as a free agent by **Assat Pori** (Finland), August 2, 2006.

CROSBY, Sidney (KRAWZ-bee, SIHD-nee) PIT.

Center. Shoots left. 5'11", 200 lbs. Born, Cole Harbour, N.S., August 7, 1987. Pittsburgh's 1st choice, 1st overall, in 2005 Entry Draft.

			Regular Season														Playoffs								
Season	Club	League	GP	G	A	Pts	PIM	PP	SH	GW	S	%	+/-	TF	F%	Min	GP	G	A	Pts	PIM	PP	SH	GW	Min
2001-02	Dartmouth	NSMHL	74	95	98	193	114	....	....	....	....	....	....	....	....	....	....	....	....	....	....	....	....	....	....
2002-03	Shat.-St. Mary's	High-MN	57	72	90	162	....	....	....	....	....	....	....	....	....	....	....	....	....	....	....	....	....	....	....
2003-04	Rimouski Oceanic	QMJHL	59	54	*81	*135	74	....	....	....	....	....	....	....	....	....	9	7	9	16	10	....	....	....	....
2004-05	Rimouski Oceanic	QMJHL	62	*66	*102	*168	84	....	....	....	....	....	....	....	....	....	13	*14	*17	*31	16	....	....	....	....
2005-06	**Pittsburgh**	**NHL**	**81**	**39**	**63**	**102**	**110**	**16**	**0**	**5**	**278**	**14.0**	**-1**	**1174**	**45.5**	**20:08**	....	....	....	....	....	....	....	....	....
2006-07	**Pittsburgh**	**NHL**	**79**	**36**	**84**	***120**	**60**	**13**	**0**	**4**	**250**	**14.4**	**10**	**1686**	**49.8**	**20:46**	**5**	**3**	**2**	**5**	**4**	**1**	**0**	**1**	**21:40**
2007-08	**Pittsburgh**	**NHL**	**53**	**24**	**48**	**72**	**39**	**6**	**0**	**4**	**173**	**13.9**	**18**	**1103**	**51.4**	**20:51**	**20**	**6**	***21**	***27**	**12**	**2**	**0**	**1**	**20:42**
	NHL Totals		**213**	**99**	**195**	**294**	**209**	**35**	**0**	**13**	**701**	**14.1**		**3963**	**49.0**	**20:32**	**25**	**9**	**23**	**32**	**16**	**3**	**0**	**2**	**20:53**

QMJHL All-Rookie Team (2004) • QMJHL First All-Star Team (2004, 2005) • QMJHL Player of the Year (2004, 2005) • Canadian Major Junior First All-Star Team (2004, 2005) • Canadian Major Junior Rookie of the Year (2004) • Canadian Major Junior Player of the Year (2004, 2005) • Memorial Cup All-Star Team (2005) • Ed Chynoweth Trophy (Memorial Cup Tournament - Leading Scorer) (2005) • NHL All-Rookie Team (2006) • NHL First All-Star Team (2007) • Art Ross Trophy (2007) • Lester B. Pearson Award (2007) • Hart Memorial Trophy (2007)

Played in NHL All-Star Game (2007)

Regular Season / Playoffs

Season	Club	League	GP	G	A	Pts	PIM	PP	SH	GW	S	%	+/-	TF	F%	Min	GP	G	A	Pts	PIM	PP	SH	GW	Min

CULLEN, Mark (KUH-lehn, MAHRK) **VAN.**

Center. Shoots left. 5'11", 190 lbs. Born, Moorhead, MN, October 28, 1978.

1996-97	Fargo High	High-ND	30	20	45	65	....	....	....	....	....	....	....	....	....	....	....	....	....	....	....	....	....	....	....
1997-98	Fargo-Moorhead	USHL	30	17	37	54	16	....	....	....	....	....	....	....	....	....	4	3	0	3	25	....	....	....	....
1998-99	Colorado College	WCHA	42	8	25	33	22	....	....	....	....	....	....	....	....	....	....	....	....	....	....	....	....	....	....
99-2000	Colorado College	WCHA	37	11	20	31	22	....	....	....	....	....	....	....	....	....	....	....	....	....	....	....	....	....	....
2000-01	Colorado College	WCHA	31	20	33	53	26	....	....	....	....	....	....	....	....	....	....	....	....	....	....	....	....	....	....
2001-02	Colorado College	WCHA	43	14	36	50	14	....	....	....	....	....	....	....	....	....	....	....	....	....	....	....	....	....	....
2002-03	Houston Aeros	AHL	72	22	25	47	20	....	....	....	....	....	....	....	....	....	15	3	7	10	4	....	....	....	....
2003-04	Houston Aeros	AHL	53	10	28	38	28	....	....	....	....	....	....	....	....	....	2	0	0	0	0	....	....	....	....
2004-05	Houston Aeros	AHL	64	10	24	34	26	....	....	....	....	....	....	....	....	....	5	1	1	2	0	....	....	....	....
2005-06	**Chicago**	**NHL**	**29**	**7**	**9**	**16**	**2**	**0**	**0**	**0**	**45**	**15.6**	**7**	**281**	**48.8**	**13:15**	....	....	....	....	....	....	....	....	....
	Norfolk Admirals	AHL	54	29	39	68	48	....	....	....	....	....	....	....	....	....	4	2	2	4	0	....	....	....	....
2006-07	**Philadelphia**	**NHL**	**3**	**0**	**0**	**0**	**0**	**0**	**0**	**0**	**4**	**0.0**	**–3**	**14**	**50.0**	**6:15**	....	....	....	....	....	....	....	....	....
	Philadelphia	AHL	56	16	36	52	34	....	....	....	....	....	....	....	....	....	....	....	....	....	....	....	....	....	....
2007-08	Grand Rapids	AHL	59	16	31	47	61	....	....	....	....	....	....	....	....	....	....	....	....	....	....	....	....	....	....
	NHL Totals		**32**	**7**	**9**	**16**	**2**	**0**	**0**	**0**	**49**	**14.3**		**295**	**48.8**	**12:36**	....	....	....	....	....	....	....	....	....

USHL All-Rookie Team (1998) • USHL Rookie of the Year (1998) • WCHA First All-Star Team (2001, 2002) • NCAA West Second All-American Team (2001) • Fred Hunt Memorial Trophy (Sportsmanship - AHL) (2006)

Signed as a free agent by **Minnesota**, April 8, 2002. Signed as a free agent by **Chicago**, August 4, 2005. Signed as a free agent by **Philadelphia**, July 5, 2006. Signed as a free agent by **Detroit**, July 16, 2007. Signed as a free agent by **Vancouver**, July 4, 2008.

CULLEN, Matt (KUH-lehn, MAT) **CAR.**

Center. Shoots left. 6'1", 200 lbs. Born, Virginia, MN, November 2, 1976. Anaheim's 2nd choice, 35th overall, in 1996 Entry Draft.

1994-95	Moorhead Spuds	High-MN	28	47	42	89	78	....	....	....	....	....	....	....	....	....	....	....	....	....	....	....	....	....	....
1995-96	St. Cloud State	WCHA	39	12	29	41	28	....	....	....	....	....	....	....	....	....	....	....	....	....	....	....	....	....	....
1996-97	St. Cloud State	WCHA	36	15	30	45	70	....	....	....	....	....	....	....	....	....	....	....	....	....	....	....	....	....	....
	Baltimore Bandits	AHL	6	3	3	6	7	....	....	....	....	....	....	....	....	....	3	0	2	2	0	....	....	....	....
1997-98	**Anaheim**	**NHL**	**61**	**6**	**21**	**27**	**23**	**2**	**0**	**0**	**75**	**8.0**	**–4**	....	....	....	....	....	....	....	....	....	....	....	....
	Cincinnati	AHL	18	15	12	27	2	....	....	....	....	....	....	....	....	....	....	....	....	....	....	....	....	....	....
1998-99	**Anaheim**	**NHL**	**75**	**11**	**14**	**25**	**47**	**5**	**1**	**1**	**112**	**9.8**	**–12**	**1047**	**47.7**	**15:31**	**4**	**0**	**0**	**0**	**0**	**0**	**0**	**0**	**15:30**
	Cincinnati	AHL	3	1	2	3	8	....	....	....	....	....	....	....	....	....	....	....	....	....	....	....	....	....	....
99-2000	**Anaheim**	**NHL**	**80**	**13**	**26**	**39**	**24**	**1**	**0**	**1**	**137**	**9.5**	**5**	**1247**	**44.6**	**16:54**	....	....	....	....	....	....	....	....	....
2000-01	**Anaheim**	**NHL**	**82**	**10**	**30**	**40**	**38**	**4**	**0**	**1**	**159**	**6.3**	**–23**	**1478**	**48.0**	**18:15**	....	....	....	....	....	....	....	....	....
2001-02	**Anaheim**	**NHL**	**79**	**18**	**30**	**48**	**24**	**3**	**1**	**4**	**164**	**11.0**	**–1**	**1283**	**51.4**	**17:01**	....	....	....	....	....	....	....	....	....
2002-03	**Anaheim**	**NHL**	**50**	**7**	**14**	**21**	**12**	**1**	**0**	**1**	**77**	**9.1**	**–4**	**271**	**50.6**	**14:18**	....	....	....	....	....	....	....	....	....
	Florida	**NHL**	**30**	**6**	**6**	**12**	**22**	**2**	**1**	**1**	**54**	**11.1**	**–4**	**423**	**47.3**	**14:43**	....	....	....	....	....	....	....	....	....
2003-04	**Florida**	**NHL**	**56**	**6**	**13**	**19**	**24**	**1**	**0**	**2**	**75**	**8.0**	**–2**	**735**	**50.6**	**14:12**	....	....	....	....	....	....	....	....	....
2004-05	SG Cortina	Italy	36	*27	33	60	64	....	....	....	....	....	....	....	....	....	18	8	14	22	32	....	....	....	....
2005-06♦	**Carolina**	**NHL**	**78**	**25**	**24**	**49**	**40**	**8**	**0**	**5**	**214**	**11.7**	**4**	**583**	**52.1**	**16:26**	**25**	**4**	**14**	**18**	**12**	**2**	**0**	**1**	**15:37**
2006-07	**NY Rangers**	**NHL**	**80**	**16**	**25**	**41**	**52**	**2**	**3**	**2**	**217**	**7.4**	**0**	**1134**	**54.6**	**17:10**	**10**	**1**	**3**	**4**	**6**	**0**	**0**	**1**	**16:55**
2007-08	**Carolina**	**NHL**	**59**	**13**	**36**	**49**	**32**	**8**	**0**	**1**	**137**	**9.5**	**2**	**649**	**56.1**	**16:52**	....	....	....	....	....	....	....	....	....
	NHL Totals		**730**	**131**	**239**	**370**	**338**	**37**	**6**	**19**	**1421**	**9.2**		**8850**	**50.0**	**16:23**	**39**	**5**	**17**	**22**	**18**	**2**	**0**	**2**	**15:57**

WCHA Second All-Star Team (1997)

Traded to **Florida** by **Anaheim** with Pavel Trnka and Anaheim's 4th round choice (James Pemberton) in 2003 Entry Draft for Sandis Ozolinsh and Lance Ward, January 30, 2003. Signed as a free agent by **Carolina**, August 5, 2004. Signed as a free agent by **Cortina** (Italy), September 18, 2004. Signed as a free agent by **NY Rangers**, July 1, 2006. Traded to **Carolina** by **NY Rangers** for Andrew Hutchinson, Joe Barnes and Carolina's 3rd round choice (Evgeny Grachev) in 2008 Entry Draft, July 17, 2007.

CULLIMORE, Jassen (KUHL-ih-mohr, JAY-suhn)

Defense. Shoots left. 6'5", 235 lbs. Born, Simcoe, Ont., December 4, 1972. Vancouver's 2nd choice, 29th overall, in 1991 Entry Draft.

1986-87	Caledonia	OHA-C	18	2	0	2	9	....	....	....	....	....	....	....	....	....	....	....	....	....	....	....	....	....	....
1987-88	Simcoe Rams	OHA-C	35	11	14	25	92	....	....	....	....	....	....	....	....	....	....	....	....	....	....	....	....	....	....
1988-89	Peterborough	OHA-B	29	11	17	28	88	....	....	....	....	....	....	....	....	....	....	....	....	....	....	....	....	....	....
	Peterborough	OHL	20	2	1	3	6	....	....	....	....	....	....	....	....	....	....	....	....	....	....	....	....	....	....
1989-90	Peterborough	OHL	59	2	6	8	61	....	....	....	....	....	....	....	....	....	11	0	2	2	8	....	....	....	....
1990-91	Peterborough	OHL	62	8	16	24	74	....	....	....	....	....	....	....	....	....	4	1	0	1	7	....	....	....	....
1991-92	Peterborough	OHL	54	9	37	46	65	....	....	....	....	....	....	....	....	....	10	3	6	9	8	....	....	....	....
1992-93	Hamilton	AHL	56	5	7	12	60	....	....	....	....	....	....	....	....	....	....	....	....	....	....	....	....	....	....
1993-94	Hamilton	AHL	71	8	20	28	86	....	....	....	....	....	....	....	....	....	3	0	1	1	2	....	....	....	....
1994-95	Syracuse Crunch	AHL	33	2	7	9	66	....	....	....	....	....	....	....	....	....	....	....	....	....	....	....	....	....	....
	Vancouver	**NHL**	**34**	**1**	**2**	**3**	**39**	**0**	**0**	**0**	**30**	**3.3**	**–2**	....	....	....	**11**	**0**	**0**	**0**	**12**	**0**	**0**	**0**	....
1995-96	**Vancouver**	**NHL**	**27**	**1**	**1**	**2**	**21**	**0**	**0**	**1**	**12**	**8.3**	**4**	....	....	....	....	....	....	....	....	....	....	....	....
1996-97	**Vancouver**	**NHL**	**3**	**0**	**0**	**0**	**2**	**0**	**0**	**0**	**2**	**0.0**	**–2**	....	....	....	....	....	....	....	....	....	....	....	....
	Montreal	**NHL**	**49**	**2**	**6**	**8**	**42**	**0**	**1**	**1**	**52**	**3.8**	**4**	....	....	....	**2**	**0**	**0**	**0**	**2**	**0**	**0**	**0**	....
1997-98	**Montreal**	**NHL**	**3**	**0**	**0**	**0**	**4**	**0**	**0**	**0**	**1**	**0.0**	**0**	....	....	....	....	....	....	....	....	....	....	....	....
	Fredericton	AHL	5	1	0	1	8	....	....	....	....	....	....	....	....	....	....	....	....	....	....	....	....	....	....
	Tampa Bay	**NHL**	**25**	**1**	**2**	**3**	**22**	**1**	**0**	**0**	**17**	**5.9**	**–4**	....	....	....	....	....	....	....	....	....	....	....	....
1998-99	**Tampa Bay**	**NHL**	**78**	**5**	**12**	**17**	**81**	**1**	**1**	**1**	**73**	**6.8**	**–22**	**0**	**0.0**	**20:14**	....	....	....	....	....	....	....	....	....
99-2000	Providence Bruins	AHL	16	5	10	15	31	....	....	....	....	....	....	....	....	....	....	....	....	....	....	....	....	....	....
	Tampa Bay	**NHL**	**46**	**1**	**1**	**2**	**66**	**0**	**0**	**0**	**23**	**4.3**	**–12**	**2**	**0.0**	**15:38**	....	....	....	....	....	....	....	....	....
2000-01	**Tampa Bay**	**NHL**	**74**	**1**	**6**	**7**	**80**	**0**	**0**	**0**	**56**	**1.8**	**–6**	**0**	**0.0**	**19:43**	....	....	....	....	....	....	....	....	....
2001-02	**Tampa Bay**	**NHL**	**78**	**4**	**9**	**13**	**58**	**0**	**0**	**1**	**84**	**4.8**	**–1**	**0**	**0.0**	**20:07**	....	....	....	....	....	....	....	....	....
2002-03	**Tampa Bay**	**NHL**	**28**	**1**	**3**	**4**	**31**	**0**	**0**	**0**	**23**	**4.3**	**3**	**0**	**0.0**	**18:25**	**11**	**1**	**1**	**2**	**4**	**0**	**0**	**0**	**22:11**
2003-04♦	**Tampa Bay**	**NHL**	**79**	**2**	**5**	**7**	**58**	**0**	**0**	**1**	**78**	**2.6**	**8**	**0**	**0.0**	**19:02**	**11**	**0**	**2**	**2**	**6**	**0**	**0**	**0**	**15:15**
2004-05			DID NOT PLAY																						
2005-06	**Chicago**	**NHL**	**54**	**1**	**6**	**7**	**53**	**1**	**0**	**1**	**23**	**4.3**	**–24**	**0**	**0.0**	**16:58**	....	....	....	....	....	....	....	....	....
2006-07	**Chicago**	**NHL**	**65**	**1**	**6**	**7**	**64**	**0**	**0**	**0**	**17**	**5.9**	**–6**	**0**	**0.0**	**16:17**	....	....	....	....	....	....	....	....	....
2007-08	**Florida**	**NHL**	**65**	**3**	**10**	**13**	**38**	**0**	**0**	**1**	**55**	**5.5**	**21**	**1**	**100.0**	**18:04**	....	....	....	....	....	....	....	....	....
	Rochester	AHL	3	0	1	1	4	....	....	....	....	....	....	....	....	....	....	....	....	....	....	....	....	....	....
	NHL Totals		**708**	**24**	**69**	**93**	**659**	**3**	**2**	**7**	**546**	**4.4**		**3**	**33.3**	**18:30**	**35**	**1**	**3**	**4**	**24**	**0**	**0**	**0**	**18:43**

OHL Second All-Star Team (1992)

Traded to **Montreal** by **Vancouver** for Donald Brashear, November 13, 1996. Claimed on waivers by **Tampa Bay** from **Montreal**, January 22, 1998. Loaned to **Providence** (AHL) by **Tampa Bay**, October 1, 1999. • Missed majority of 2002-03 season recovering from elbow injury suffered in game vs. Vancouver, November 29, 2002. Signed as a free agent by **Chicago**, July 22, 2004. Traded to **Montreal** by **Chicago** with Tony Salmelainen for Sergei Samsonov, June 16, 2007. Signed as a free agent by **Florida**, October 26, 2007.

CUMISKEY, Kyle (kuh-MIHS-kee, KIGHL) **COL.**

Defense. Shoots left. 5'10", 185 lbs. Born, Abbotsford, B.C., December 2, 1986. Colorado's 9th choice, 222nd overall, in 2005 Entry Draft.

2002-03	Penticton	BCHL	59	10	11	21	36	....	....	....	....	....	....	....	....	....	....	....	....	....	....	....	....	....	....
2003-04	Kelowna Rockets	WHL	54	2	7	9	20	....	....	....	....	....	....	....	....	....	17	0	0	0	0	....	....	....	....
2004-05	Kelowna Rockets	WHL	72	4	36	40	47	....	....	....	....	....	....	....	....	....	24	0	13	13	12	....	....	....	....
2005-06	Kelowna Rockets	WHL	51	6	24	30	52	....	....	....	....	....	....	....	....	....	12	0	6	6	8	....	....	....	....
2006-07	**Colorado**	**NHL**	**9**	**1**	**1**	**2**	**2**	**0**	**0**	**0**	**8**	**12.5**	**0**	**0**	**0.0**	**13:28**	....	....	....	....	....	....	....	....	....
	Albany River Rats	AHL	63	7	26	33	32	....	....	....	....	....	....	....	....	....	5	0	2	2	6	....	....	....	....
2007-08	**Colorado**	**NHL**	**38**	**0**	**5**	**5**	**16**	**0**	**0**	**0**	**19**	**0.0**	**–3**	**0**	**0.0**	**12:08**	....	....	....	....	....	....	....	....	....
	Lake Erie	AHL	5	1	1	2	4	....	....	....	....	....	....	....	....	....	....	....	....	....	....	....	....	....	....
	NHL Totals		**47**	**1**	**6**	**7**	**18**	**0**	**0**	**0**	**27**	**3.7**		**0**	**0.0**	**12:23**	....	....	....	....	....	....	....	....	....

D'AGOSTINI, Matt (DAG-uh-stee-noh, MAT) MTL.

Right wing. Shoots right. 6', 201 lbs. Born, Sault Ste. Marie, Ont., October 23, 1986. Montreal's 5th choice, 190th overall, in 2005 Entry Draft.

Season	Club	League	GP	G	A	Pts	PIM	PP	SH	GW	S	%	+/-	TF	F%	Min	Playoffs GP	G	A	Pts	PIM	PP	SH	GW	Min
2003-04	Soo North Stars	GNML	36	36	23	59	41																		
2004-05	Guelph Storm	OHL	59	24	22	46	29										4	0	2	2	8				
2005-06	Guelph Storm	OHL	66	25	54	79	81										15	8	20	28	16				
2006-07	Hamilton	AHL	63	21	28	49	33										22	4	9	13	18				
2007-08	**Montreal**	**NHL**	**1**	**0**	**0**	**0**	**2**	**0**	**0**	**0**	**0**	**0.0**	**0**	**0**	**0.0**	**8:49**									
	Hamilton	AHL	76	23	30	53	38																		
	NHL Totals		**1**	**0**	**0**	**0**	**2**	**0**	**0**	**0**	**0**	**0.0**		**0**	**0.0**	**8:49**									

DALEY, Trevor (DAY-lee, TREH-vuhr) DAL.

Defense. Shoots left. 5'11", 207 lbs. Born, Toronto, Ont., October 9, 1983. Dallas' 5th choice, 43rd overall, in 2002 Entry Draft.

Season	Club	League	GP	G	A	Pts	PIM	PP	SH	GW	S	%	+/-	TF	F%	Min	Playoffs GP	G	A	Pts	PIM	PP	SH	GW	Min
1998-99	Vaughan Vipers	OPJHL	44	10	36	46	79																		
99-2000	Sault Ste. Marie	OHL	54	16	30	46	77										15	3	7	10	12				
2000-01	Sault Ste. Marie	OHL	58	14	27	41	105																		
2001-02	Sault Ste. Marie	OHL	47	9	39	48	38										6	2	2	4	4				
2002-03	Sault Ste. Marie	OHL	57	20	33	53	128										1	0	0	0	2				
2003-04	**Dallas**	**NHL**	**27**	**1**	**5**	**6**	**14**	**1**	**0**	**0**	**34**	**2.9**	**-6**	**0**	**0.0**	**16:02**	**1**	**0**	**0**	**0**	**0**	**0**	**0**	**0**	**10:21**
	Utah Grizzlies	AHL	40	8	6	14	76																		
2004-05	Hamilton	AHL	78	7	27	34	109										4	0	1	1	2				
2005-06	**Dallas**	**NHL**	**81**	**3**	**11**	**14**	**87**	**0**	**0**	**1**	**91**	**3.3**	**-2**	**0**	**0.0**	**18:40**	**3**	**0**	**0**	**0**	**0**	**0**	**0**	**0**	**11:30**
2006-07	**Dallas**	**NHL**	**74**	**4**	**8**	**12**	**63**	**0**	**0**	**1**	**68**	**5.9**	**2**	**0**	**0.0**	**19:23**	**7**	**1**	**0**	**1**	**4**	**0**	**0**	**0**	**22:26**
2007-08	**Dallas**	**NHL**	**82**	**5**	**19**	**24**	**85**	**0**	**0**	**1**	**87**	**5.7**	**-1**	**1**	**100.0**	**19:48**	**18**	**1**	**0**	**1**	**20**	**0**	**0**	**0**	**18:52**
	NHL Totals		**264**	**13**	**43**	**56**	**249**	**1**	**0**	**3**	**280**	**4.6**		**1**	**100.0**	**18:57**	**29**	**2**	**0**	**2**	**24**	**0**	**0**	**0**	**18:40**

DALLMAN, Kevin (DAL-mahn, KEH-vihn)

Defense. Shoots right. 5'11", 195 lbs. Born, Niagara Falls, Ont., February 26, 1981.

Season	Club	League	GP	G	A	Pts	PIM	PP	SH	GW	S	%	+/-	TF	F%	Min	Playoffs GP	G	A	Pts	PIM	PP	SH	GW	Min
1996-97	Niagara Falls	OHA-B	3	0	1	1	2																		
1997-98	Niagara Falls	OHA-B	47	13	25	38	42																		
1998-99	Guelph Storm	OHL	68	8	30	38	52										11	1	4	5	2				
99-2000	Guelph Storm	OHL	67	13	46	59	38										6	0	2	2	11				
2000-01	Guelph Storm	OHL	66	25	52	77	88										1	0	0	0	0				
2001-02	Guelph Storm	OHL	67	23	63	86	68										9	8	8	16	22				
2002-03	Providence Bruins	AHL	72	2	19	21	53																		
2003-04	Providence Bruins	AHL	65	6	23	29	44										2	0	0	0	0				
2004-05	Providence Bruins	AHL	71	8	26	34	48										17	4	6	10	20				
2005-06	**Boston**	**NHL**	**21**	**0**	**1**	**1**	**8**	**0**	**0**	**0**	**42**	**0.0**	**1**	**0**	**0.0**	**19:24**									
	St. Louis	**NHL**	**46**	**4**	**9**	**13**	**21**	**3**	**0**	**0**	**89**	**4.5**	**-15**	**11**	**18.2**	**18:49**									
2006-07	**Los Angeles**	**NHL**	**53**	**1**	**9**	**10**	**12**	**0**	**0**	**0**	**76**	**1.3**	**-13**	**20**	**20.0**	**12:48**									
	Manchester	AHL	3	4	0	4	4																		
2007-08	**Los Angeles**	**NHL**	**34**	**3**	**4**	**7**	**4**	**0**	**0**	**1**	**41**	**7.3**	**4**	**2**	**0.0**	**12:53**									
	Manchester	AHL	5	1	4	5	2																		
	NHL Totals		**154**	**8**	**23**	**31**	**45**	**3**	**0**	**1**	**248**	**3.2**		**33**	**18.2**	**15:31**									

Memorial Cup Tournament All-Star Team (2002)

Signed as a free agent by **Boston**, July 18, 2002. Claimed on waivers by **St. Louis** from **Boston**, December 3, 2005. Signed as a free agent by **Los Angeles**, July 10, 2006.

DANDENAULT, Mathieu (DAHN-deh-noh, MA-tyew) MTL.

Defense. Shoots right. 6', 204 lbs. Born, Sherbrooke, Que., February 3, 1976. Detroit's 2nd choice, 49th overall, in 1994 Entry Draft.

Season	Club	League	GP	G	A	Pts	PIM	PP	SH	GW	S	%	+/-	TF	F%	Min	Playoffs GP	G	A	Pts	PIM	PP	SH	GW	Min
1990-91	Gloucester	Minor-ON	44	52	50	102	30																		
1991-92	Vanier Voyageurs	OHA-B	33	27	31	58	20																		
	Gloucester	CJHL	6	3	4	7	0																		
1992-93	Gloucester	CJHL	55	11	26	37	64																		
1993-94	Sherbrooke	QMJHL	67	17	36	53	67										12	4	10	14	12				
1994-95	Sherbrooke	QMJHL	67	37	70	107	76										7	1	7	8	10				
1995-96	**Detroit**	**NHL**	**34**	**5**	**7**	**12**	**6**	**1**	**0**	**0**	**32**	**15.6**	**6**												
	Adirondack	AHL	4	0	0	0	0																		
1996-97♦	**Detroit**	**NHL**	**65**	**3**	**9**	**12**	**28**	**0**	**0**	**0**	**81**	**3.7**	**-10**												
1997-98♦	**Detroit**	**NHL**	**68**	**5**	**12**	**17**	**43**	**0**	**0**	**0**	**75**	**6.7**	**5**				**3**	**1**	**0**	**1**	**0**	**1**	**0**	**0**	
1998-99	**Detroit**	**NHL**	**75**	**4**	**10**	**14**	**59**	**0**	**0**	**0**	**94**	**4.3**	**17**	**3**	**0.0**	**15:10**	**10**	**0**	**1**	**1**	**0**	**0**	**0**	**0**	**11:51**
99-2000	**Detroit**	**NHL**	**81**	**6**	**12**	**18**	**20**	**0**	**0**	**0**	**98**	**6.1**	**-12**	**1**	**100.0**	**12:10**	**6**	**0**	**0**	**0**	**2**	**0**	**0**	**0**	**8:31**
2000-01	**Detroit**	**NHL**	**73**	**10**	**15**	**25**	**38**	**2**	**0**	**2**	**95**	**10.5**	**11**	**0**	**0.0**	**16:06**	**6**	**0**	**1**	**1**	**0**	**0**	**0**	**0**	**14:11**
2001-02♦	**Detroit**	**NHL**	**81**	**8**	**12**	**20**	**44**	**2**	**0**	**3**	**97**	**8.2**	**-5**	**1**	**0.0**	**16:43**	**23**	**1**	**2**	**3**	**8**	**0**	**1**	**0**	**13:29**
2002-03	**Detroit**	**NHL**	**74**	**4**	**15**	**19**	**64**	**1**	**0**	**0**	**74**	**5.4**	**25**	**0**	**0.0**	**19:08**	**4**	**0**	**0**	**0**	**2**	**0**	**0**	**0**	**25:51**
2003-04	**Detroit**	**NHL**	**65**	**3**	**9**	**12**	**40**	**0**	**1**	**0**	**68**	**4.4**	**9**	**1**	**0.0**	**13:47**	**12**	**1**	**1**	**2**	**6**	**0**	**0**	**1**	**13:33**
2004-05	Asiago	Italy	10	0	2	2	2										9	1	6	7	4				
2005-06	**Montreal**	**NHL**	**82**	**5**	**15**	**20**	**83**	**0**	**0**	**1**	**101**	**5.0**	**8**	**0**	**0.0**	**18:38**	**6**	**0**	**3**	**3**	**4**	**0**	**0**	**0**	**19:48**
2006-07	**Montreal**	**NHL**	**68**	**2**	**6**	**8**	**40**	**0**	**0**	**0**	**54**	**3.7**	**-8**	**3**	**0.0**	**16:07**									
2007-08	**Montreal**	**NHL**	**61**	**9**	**5**	**14**	**34**	**0**	**1**	**0**	**69**	**13.0**	**-11**	**1**	**0.0**	**11:08**	**9**	**0**	**0**	**0**	**2**	**0**	**0**	**0**	**8:45**
	NHL Totals		**827**	**64**	**127**	**191**	**499**	**6**	**2**	**6**	**938**	**6.8**		**10**	**10.0**	**15:33**	**79**	**3**	**8**	**11**	**24**	**1**	**1**	**1**	**13:32**

Signed as a free agent by **Asiago** (Italy), December 27, 2004. Signed as a free agent by **Montreal**, August 3, 2005.

DARCHE, Mathieu (DAHRSH, MA-thew) BUF.

Left wing. Shoots left. 6'1", 220 lbs. Born, St. Laurent, Que., November 26, 1976.

Season	Club	League	GP	G	A	Pts	PIM	PP	SH	GW	S	%	+/-	TF	F%	Min	Playoffs GP	G	A	Pts	PIM	PP	SH	GW	Min
1995-96	Choate-Rosemary	High-CT	STATISTICS NOT AVAILABLE																						
1996-97	McGill Redmen	OUAA	23	1	2	3	27																		
1997-98	McGill Redmen	OUAA	40	28	17	45	69																		
1998-99	McGill Redmen	OUAA	32	16	24	40	60																		
99-2000	McGill Redmen	OUAA	33	31	41	*72	38										5	2	8	10	16				
2000-01	**Columbus**	**NHL**	**9**	**0**	**0**	**0**	**0**	**0**	**0**	**0**	**9**	**0.0**	**-4**	**1**	**0.0**	**10:07**									
	Syracuse Crunch	AHL	66	16	24	40	21										5	0	1	1	4				
2001-02	**Columbus**	**NHL**	**14**	**1**	**1**	**2**	**6**	**0**	**0**	**0**	**15**	**6.7**	**-5**	**3**	**33.3**	**9:49**									
	Syracuse Crunch	AHL	63	22	23	45	26										10	2	5	7	2				
2002-03	**Columbus**	**NHL**	**1**	**0**	**0**	**0**	**0**	**0**	**0**	**0**	**0**	**0.0**	**-1**	**0**	**0.0**	**6:57**									
	Syracuse Crunch	AHL	76	32	32	64	38																		
2003-04	**Nashville**	**NHL**	**2**	**0**	**0**	**0**	**0**	**0**	**0**	**0**	**1**	**0.0**	**-1**	**0**	**0.0**	**6:39**									
	Milwaukee	AHL	76	28	31	59	41										22	6	8	14	8				
2004-05	Hershey Bears	AHL	79	29	25	54	49																		
2005-06	Fuchse Duisburg	Germany	52	12	13	25	88										5	1	3	4	4				
2006-07	**San Jose**	**NHL**	**2**	**0**	**0**	**0**	**0**	**0**	**0**	**0**	**3**	**0.0**	**0**	**0**	**0.0**	**9:13**									
	Worcester Sharks	AHL	76	35	45	80	72										5	2	2	4	2				
2007-08	**Tampa Bay**	**NHL**	**73**	**7**	**15**	**22**	**20**	**1**	**1**	**0**	**120**	**5.8**	**-14**	**89**	**48.3**	**14:26**									
	Norfolk Admirals	AHL	4	3	7	10	2																		
	NHL Totals		**101**	**8**	**16**	**24**	**26**	**1**	**1**	**0**	**148**	**5.4**		**93**	**47.3**	**13:04**									

OUAA East Second All-Star Team (1998) • OUAA East First All-Star Team (1999) • OUAA First All-Star Team (2000) • CIAU All-Canadian Team (2000)

Signed as a free agent by **Columbus**, May 16, 2000. Signed as a free agent by **Nashville**, September 10, 2003. Signed as a free agent by **Colorado**, July 26, 2004. Signed as a free agent by **San Jose**, July 10, 2006. Signed as a free agent by **Tampa Bay**, July 2, 2007. Signed as a free agent by **Buffalo**, July 24, 2008.

DATSYUK, Pavel

(daht-SOOK, PAH-vehl) **DET.**

Center. Shoots left. 5'11", 197 lbs. Born, Sverdlovsk, USSR, July 20, 1978. Detroit's 8th choice, 171st overall, in 1998 Entry Draft.

			Regular Season														Playoffs								
Season	Club	League	GP	G	A	Pts	PIM	PP	SH	GW	S	%	+/-	TF	F%	Min	GP	G	A	Pts	PIM	PP	SH	GW	Min
1996-97	Yekaterinburg 2	Russia-3	18	2	2	4	4	....	....	....	....	....	....	....	....	....	....	....	....	....	....	....	....	....	....
	Yekaterinburg	Russia	36	12	10	22	12	....	....	....	....	....	....	....	....	....	....	....	....	....	....	....	....	....	....
1997-98	Yekaterinburg	Russia	24	3	5	8	4	....	....	....	....	....	....	....	....	....	....	....	....	....	....	....	....	....	....
	Yekaterinburg 2	Russia-3	22	7	8	15	4	....	....	....	....	....	....	....	....	....	....	....	....	....	....	....	....	....	....
1998-99	Yekaterinburg 2	Russia-4	10	14	14	28	4	....	....	....	....	....	....	....	....	....	....	....	....	....	....	....	....	....	....
	Yekaterinburg	Russia-2	35	21	23	44	14	....	....	....	....	....	....	....	....	....	9	3	7	10	10	....	....	....	....
99-2000	Yekaterinburg	Russia	15	1	3	4	4	....	....	....	....	....	....	....	....	....	....	....	....	....	....	....	....	....	....
2000-01	Ak Bars Kazan	Russia	42	9	18	27	10	....	....	....	....	....	....	....	....	....	4	0	1	1	2	....	....	....	....
2001-02 ♦	**Detroit**	**NHL**	**70**	**11**	**24**	**35**	**4**	**2**	**0**	**1**	**79**	**13.9**	**4**	**794**	**47.7**	**13:39**	**21**	**3**	**3**	**6**	**2**	**1**	**0**	**1**	**10:40**
	Russia	Olympics	6	1	2	3	0	....	....	....	....	....	....	....	....	....	....	....	....	....	....	....	....	....	....
2002-03	**Detroit**	**NHL**	**64**	**12**	**39**	**51**	**16**	**1**	**0**	**1**	**82**	**14.6**	**20**	**778**	**48.2**	**15:28**	**4**	**0**	**0**	**0**	**0**	**0**	**0**	**0**	**18:48**
2003-04	**Detroit**	**NHL**	**75**	**30**	**38**	**68**	**35**	**8**	**1**	**4**	**136**	**22.1**	**−2**	**1314**	**54.0**	**18:16**	**12**	**0**	**6**	**6**	**2**	**0**	**0**	**0**	**17:23**
2004-05	Dynamo Moscow	Russia	47	15	17	32	16	....	....	....	....	....	....	....	....	....	10	*6	3	9	4	....	....	....	....
2005-06	**Detroit**	**NHL**	**75**	**28**	**59**	**87**	**22**	**11**	**0**	**4**	**145**	**19.3**	**26**	**1059**	**53.1**	**17:53**	**5**	**0**	**3**	**3**	**0**	**0**	**0**	**0**	**20:05**
	Russia	Olympics	8	1	7	8	10	....	....	....	....	....	....	....	....	....	....	....	....	....	....	....	....	....	....
2006-07	**Detroit**	**NHL**	**79**	**27**	**60**	**87**	**20**	**5**	**2**	**5**	**207**	**13.0**	**36**	**845**	**56.2**	**19:57**	**18**	**8**	**8**	**16**	**8**	**4**	**0**	**2**	**22:03**
2007-08 ♦	**Detroit**	**NHL**	**82**	**31**	**66**	**97**	**20**	**10**	**1**	**6**	**264**	**11.7**	**41**	**833**	**54.4**	**21:23**	**22**	**10**	**13**	**23**	**6**	**4**	**0**	**1**	**21:40**
	NHL Totals		**445**	**139**	**286**	**425**	**117**	**37**	**4**	**21**	**913**	**15.2**		**5623**	**52.5**	**17:57**	**82**	**21**	**33**	**54**	**18**	**9**	**0**	**4**	**18:05**

Lady Byng Memorial Trophy (2006, 2007, 2008) • Frank J. Selke Trophy (2008)

Played in NHL All-Star Game (2004, 2008)

• Spent majority of 1999-2000 season on **Kazan** (Russia) reserve squad. Signed as a free agent by **Dynamo Moscow** (Russia), June 19, 2004.

DAVISON, Rob

(DAY-vihs-ohn, RAWB) **VAN.**

Defense. Shoots left. 6'3", 220 lbs. Born, St. Catharines, Ont., May 1, 1980. San Jose's 4th choice, 98th overall, in 1998 Entry Draft.

1996-97	St. Mike's B's	OPJHL	45	2	6	8	93	....	....	....	....	....	....	....	....	....	6	0	0	0	9	....	....	....	....
1997-98	North Bay	OHL	59	0	11	11	200	....	....	....	....	....	....	....	....	....	....	....	....	....	....	....	....	....	....
1998-99	North Bay	OHL	59	2	17	19	150	....	....	....	....	....	....	....	....	....	4	0	1	1	12	....	....	....	....
99-2000	North Bay	OHL	67	4	6	10	194	....	....	....	....	....	....	....	....	....	6	0	1	1	8	....	....	....	....
2000-01	Kentucky	AHL	72	0	4	4	230	....	....	....	....	....	....	....	....	....	3	0	0	0	0	....	....	....	....
2001-02	Cleveland Barons	AHL	70	1	3	4	206	....	....	....	....	....	....	....	....	....	....	....	....	....	....	....	....	....	....
2002-03	**San Jose**	**NHL**	**15**	**1**	**2**	**3**	**22**	**0**	**0**	**0**	**15**	**6.7**	**4**	**0**	**0.0**	**17:53**	....	....	....	....	....	....	....	....	....
	Cleveland Barons	AHL	42	1	3	4	82	....	....	....	....	....	....	....	....	....	....	....	....	....	....	....	....	....	....
2003-04	**San Jose**	**NHL**	**55**	**0**	**3**	**3**	**92**	**0**	**0**	**0**	**33**	**0.0**	**−3**	**0**	**0.0**	**14:22**	**5**	**0**	**2**	**2**	**4**	**0**	**0**	**0**	**9:01**
2004-05	Cardiff Devils	Britain	24	2	3	5	114	....	....	....	....	....	....	....	....	....	8	0	1	1	12	....	....	....	....
2005-06	**San Jose**	**NHL**	**69**	**1**	**5**	**6**	**76**	**0**	**0**	**0**	**36**	**2.8**	**6**	**0**	**0.0**	**13:50**	**1**	**0**	**0**	**0**	**0**	**0**	**0**	**0**	**8:00**
2006-07	**San Jose**	**NHL**	**22**	**0**	**2**	**2**	**27**	**0**	**0**	**0**	**14**	**0.0**	**−2**	**0**	**0.0**	**9:19**	....	....	....	....	....	....	....	....	....
2007-08	**San Jose**	**NHL**	**15**	**0**	**0**	**0**	**21**	**0**	**0**	**0**	**10**	**0.0**	**−3**	**0**	**0.0**	**7:47**	....	....	....	....	....	....	....	....	....
	NY Islanders	**NHL**	**19**	**1**	**1**	**2**	**32**	**0**	**1**	**0**	**22**	**4.5**	**−3**	**0**	**0.0**	**18:40**	....	....	....	....	....	....	....	....	....
	NHL Totals		**195**	**3**	**13**	**16**	**270**	**0**	**1**	**0**	**130**	**2.3**		**0**	**0.0**	**13:48**	**6**	**0**	**2**	**2**	**4**	**0**	**0**	**0**	**8:51**

Signed as a free agent by **Cardiff** (Britain), October 5, 2004. Traded to **NY Islanders** by **San Jose** for NY Islanders' 7th round choice (Jason Demers) in 2008 Entry Draft, February 26, 2008. Signed as a free agent by **Vancouver**, July 10, 2008.

DAWES, Nigel

(DAWZ, NIGH-juhl) **NYR**

Left wing. Shoots left. 5'9", 190 lbs. Born, Winnipeg, Man., February 9, 1985. NY Rangers' 5th choice, 149th overall, in 2003 Entry Draft.

2000-01	Wpg. Warriors	MMMHL	36	55	41	96	74	....	....	....	....	....	....	....	....	....	....	....	....	....	....	....	....	....	....
2001-02	Kootenay Ice	WHL	54	15	19	34	14	....	....	....	....	....	....	....	....	....	22	9	6	15	8	....	....	....	....
2002-03	Kootenay Ice	WHL	72	47	45	92	54	....	....	....	....	....	....	....	....	....	11	4	8	12	6	....	....	....	....
2003-04	Kootenay Ice	WHL	56	47	23	70	31	....	....	....	....	....	....	....	....	....	4	1	2	3	10	....	....	....	....
	Hartford	AHL	4	0	0	0	0	....	....	....	....	....	....	....	....	....	....	....	....	....	....	....	....	....	....
2004-05	Kootenay Ice	WHL	63	50	26	76	30	....	....	....	....	....	....	....	....	....	12	5	10	15	5	....	....	....	....
2005-06	Hartford	AHL	77	35	31	66	21	....	....	....	....	....	....	....	....	....	13	6	6	12	9	....	....	....	....
2006-07	**NY Rangers**	**NHL**	**8**	**1**	**0**	**1**	**0**	**0**	**0**	**0**	**7**	**14.3**	**−4**	**1**	**0.0**	**6:44**	**1**	**0**	**0**	**0**	**0**	**0**	**0**	**0**	**9:02**
	Hartford	AHL	65	27	33	60	29	....	....	....	....	....	....	....	....	....	7	5	6	11	9	....	....	....	....
2007-08	**NY Rangers**	**NHL**	**61**	**14**	**15**	**29**	**10**	**3**	**0**	**4**	**121**	**11.6**	**11**	**2**	**50.0**	**12:59**	**10**	**2**	**2**	**4**	**0**	**0**	**0**	**0**	**12:31**
	Hartford	AHL	20	14	20	34	2	....	....	....	....	....	....	....	....	....	....	....	....	....	....	....	....	....	....
	NHL Totals		**69**	**15**	**15**	**30**	**10**	**3**	**0**	**4**	**128**	**11.7**		**3**	**33.3**	**12:16**	**11**	**2**	**2**	**4**	**0**	**0**	**0**	**0**	**12:12**

WHL West Second All-Star Team (2003) • WHL West First All-Star Team (2004, 2005)

DEMITRA, Pavol

(deh-MEET-rah, PAH-vohl) **VAN.**

Left wing. Shoots left. 6', 200 lbs. Born, Dubnica, Czech., November 29, 1974. Ottawa's 9th choice, 227th overall, in 1993 Entry Draft.

1991-92	Dubnica	Czech-2	28	13	10	23	12	....	....	....	....	....	....	....	....	....	....	....	....	....	....	....	....	....	....
1992-93	Dubnica	Czech-2	4	3	0	3	....	....	....	....	....	....	....	....	....	....	....	....	....	....	....	....	....	....	....
	Dukla Trencin	Czech	46	11	17	28	0	....	....	....	....	....	....	....	....	....	....	....	....	....	....	....	....	....	....
1993-94	**Ottawa**	**NHL**	**12**	**1**	**1**	**2**	**4**	**1**	**0**	**0**	**10**	**10.0**	**−7**	....	....	....	....	....	....	....	....	....	....	....	....
	P.E.I. Senators	AHL	41	18	23	41	8	....	....	....	....	....	....	....	....	....	....	....	....	....	....	....	....	....	....
1994-95	P.E.I. Senators	AHL	61	26	48	74	23	....	....	....	....	....	....	....	....	....	5	0	7	7	0	....	....	....	....
	Ottawa	**NHL**	**16**	**4**	**3**	**7**	**0**	**1**	**0**	**0**	**21**	**19.0**	**−4**	....	....	....	....	....	....	....	....	....	....	....	....
1995-96	**Ottawa**	**NHL**	**31**	**7**	**10**	**17**	**6**	**2**	**0**	**1**	**66**	**10.6**	**−3**	....	....	....	....	....	....	....	....	....	....	....	....
	P.E.I. Senators	AHL	48	28	53	81	44	....	....	....	....	....	....	....	....	....	....	....	....	....	....	....	....	....	....
1996-97	Dukla Trencin	Slovakia	1	1	1	2	....	....	....	....	....	....	....	....	....	....	....	....	....	....	....	....	....	....	....
	Las Vegas	IHL	22	8	13	21	10	....	....	....	....	....	....	....	....	....	....	....	....	....	....	....	....	....	....
	St. Louis	**NHL**	**8**	**3**	**0**	**3**	**2**	**2**	**0**	**1**	**15**	**20.0**	**0**	....	....	....	**6**	**1**	**3**	**4**	**6**	**0**	**0**	**0**	....
	Grand Rapids	IHL	42	20	30	50	24	....	....	....	....	....	....	....	....	....	....	....	....	....	....	....	....	....	....
1997-98	**St. Louis**	**NHL**	**61**	**22**	**30**	**52**	**22**	**4**	**4**	**6**	**147**	**15.0**	**11**	....	....	....	**10**	**3**	**3**	**6**	**2**	**0**	**0**	**0**	....
1998-99	**St. Louis**	**NHL**	**82**	**37**	**52**	**89**	**16**	**14**	**0**	**10**	**259**	**14.3**	**13**	**250**	**44.0**	**20:10**	**13**	**5**	**4**	**9**	**4**	**3**	**0**	**1**	**19:10**
99-2000	**St. Louis**	**NHL**	**71**	**28**	**47**	**75**	**8**	**8**	**0**	**4**	**241**	**11.6**	**34**	**41**	**39.0**	**19:13**	....	....	....	....	....	....	....	....	....
2000-01	**St. Louis**	**NHL**	**44**	**20**	**25**	**45**	**16**	**5**	**0**	**5**	**124**	**16.1**	**27**	**8**	**37.5**	**18:03**	**15**	**2**	**4**	**6**	**2**	**0**	**0**	**1**	**18:13**
2001-02	**St. Louis**	**NHL**	**82**	**35**	**43**	**78**	**46**	**11**	**0**	**10**	**212**	**16.5**	**13**	**1224**	**48.1**	**19:11**	**10**	**4**	**7**	**11**	**6**	**2**	**1**	**1**	**19:45**
	Slovakia	Olympics	2	1	2	3	2	....	....	....	....	....	....	....	....	....	....	....	....	....	....	....	....	....	....
2002-03	**St. Louis**	**NHL**	**78**	**36**	**57**	**93**	**32**	**11**	**0**	**4**	**205**	**17.6**	**0**	**1253**	**46.1**	**19:47**	**7**	**2**	**4**	**6**	**2**	**1**	**0**	**0**	**18:20**
2003-04	**St. Louis**	**NHL**	**68**	**23**	**35**	**58**	**18**	**8**	**0**	**5**	**179**	**12.8**	**1**	**770**	**47.3**	**20:30**	**5**	**1**	**0**	**1**	**4**	**0**	**0**	**0**	**18:07**
2004-05	Dukla Trencin	Slovakia	54	*28	*54	*82	39	....	....	....	....	....	....	....	....	....	12	4	13	17	14	....	....	....	....
2005-06	**Los Angeles**	**NHL**	**58**	**25**	**37**	**62**	**42**	**7**	**5**	**7**	**184**	**13.6**	**21**	**114**	**49.1**	**21:04**	....	....	....	....	....	....	....	....	....
	Slovakia	Olympics	6	2	5	7	2	....	....	....	....	....	....	....	....	....	....	....	....	....	....	....	....	....	....
2006-07	**Minnesota**	**NHL**	**71**	**25**	**39**	**64**	**28**	**9**	**1**	**4**	**175**	**14.3**	**0**	**513**	**47.8**	**20:39**	**5**	**1**	**3**	**4**	**0**	**0**	**0**	**0**	**19:47**
2007-08	**Minnesota**	**NHL**	**68**	**15**	**39**	**54**	**24**	**2**	**0**	**1**	**126**	**11.9**	**9**	**890**	**45.3**	**19:42**	**6**	**1**	**2**	**3**	**2**	**1**	**0**	**0**	**21:09**
	NHL Totals		**750**	**281**	**418**	**699**	**264**	**85**	**10**	**58**	**1964**	**14.3**		**5063**	**46.7**	**19:51**	**77**	**20**	**30**	**50**	**28**	**7**	**1**	**3**	**19:05**

Lady Byng Memorial Trophy (2000)

Played in NHL All-Star Game (1999, 2000, 2002)

Traded to **St. Louis** by **Ottawa** for Christer Olsson, November 27, 1996. Signed as a free agent by **Trencin** (Slovakia), September 17, 2004. Signed as a free agent by **Los Angeles**, August 2, 2005. Traded to **Minnesota** by **Los Angeles** for Patrick O'Sullivan and Edmonton's 1st round choice (previously acquired, Los Angeles selected Trevor Lewis) in 2006 Entry Draft, June 24, 2006. Signed as a free agent by **Vancouver**, July 10, 2008.

DEVEREAUX, Boyd

(DEH-vuhr-oh, BOID) **TOR.**

Center. Shoots left. 6'2", 195 lbs. Born, Seaforth, Ont., April 16, 1978. Edmonton's 1st choice, 6th overall, in 1996 Entry Draft.

1992-93	Seaforth Sailors	OHA-D	34	7	20	27	13	....	....	....	....	....	....	....	....	....	....	....	....	....	....	....	....	....	....
1993-94	Stratford Cullitons	OHA-B	46	12	27	39	8	....	....	....	....	....	....	....	....	....	....	....	....	....	....	....	....	....	....
1994-95	Stratford Cullitons	OHA-B	45	31	74	105	21	....	....	....	....	....	....	....	....	....	....	....	....	....	....	....	....	....	....
1995-96	Kitchener Rangers	OHL	66	20	38	58	35	....	....	....	....	....	....	....	....	....	12	3	7	10	4	....	....	....	....
1996-97	Kitchener Rangers	OHL	54	28	41	69	37	....	....	....	....	....	....	....	....	....	13	4	11	15	8	....	....	....	....
	Hamilton	AHL	....	....	....	....	....	....	....	....	....	....	....	....	....	....	1	0	1	1	0	....	....	....	....

			Regular Season														Playoffs								
Season	Club	League	GP	G	A	Pts	PIM	PP	SH	GW	S	%	+/-	TF	F%	Min	GP	G	A	Pts	PIM	PP	SH	GW	Min
1997-98	Edmonton	NHL	38	1	4	5	6	0	0	0	27	3.7	–5												
	Hamilton	AHL	14	5	6	11	6										9	1	1	2	8				
1998-99	Edmonton	NHL	61	6	8	14	23	0	1	4	39	15.4	2	409	42.8	10:09	1	0	0	0	0	0	0	0	32:46
	Hamilton	AHL	7	4	6	10	2										8	0	3	3	4				
99-2000	Edmonton	NHL	76	8	19	27	20	0	1	2	108	7.4	7	241	34.9	12:36									
2000-01	Detroit	NHL	55	5	6	11	14	0	0	0	66	7.6	1	124	37.1	10:08	2	0	0	0	0	0	0	0	10:39
2001-02 ♦	Detroit	NHL	79	9	16	25	24	0	0	2	116	7.8	9	12	33.3	11:30	21	2	4	6	4	0	0	0	10:58
2002-03	Detroit	NHL	61	3	9	12	16	0	0	1	72	4.2	4	7	42.9	9:26									
2003-04	Detroit	NHL	61	6	9	15	20	0	0	2	62	9.7	–1	14	50.0	9:58	3	1	0	1	0	0	0	0	6:36
2004-05			DID NOT PLAY																						
2005-06	Phoenix	NHL	78	8	14	22	44	1	0	1	76	10.5	–13	281	36.7	12:47									
2006-07	Toronto	NHL	33	8	11	19	12	0	0	0	57	14.0	4	42	26.2	15:17									
	Toronto Marlies	AHL	30	6	8	14	14																		
2007-08	Toronto	NHL	62	7	11	18	24	0	1	1	81	8.6	–6	6	33.3	13:58									
	NHL Totals		604	61	107	168	203	1	3	13	704	8.7		1136	38.3	11:39	27	3	4	7	4	0	0	0	11:16

Canadian Major Junior Scholastic Player of the Year (1996)

Signed as a free agent by **Detroit**, August 23, 2000. Signed as a free agent by **Phoenix**, July 5, 2004. Signed as a free agent by **Toronto**, October 7, 2006.

de VRIES, Greg

(deh-VREES, GREHG) **NSH.**

Defense. Shoots left. 6'2", 215 lbs. Born, Sundridge, Ont., January 4, 1973.

1988-89	Cortina Astros	Minor-ON	35	28	40	68																			
1989-90	Aurora Eagles	OHA-B	42	1	16	17	32																		
1990-91	Stratford Cullitons	OHA-B	40	8	32	40	120										3	2	1	3	20				
1991-92	Thorold	OHA-B	3	0	0	0	0																		
	Bowling Green	CCHA	24	0	3	3	20																		
1992-93	Niagara Falls	OHL	62	3	23	26	86										4	0	1	1	6				
1993-94	Niagara Falls	OHL	64	5	40	45	135																		
	Cape Breton	AHL	9	0	0	0	11										1	0	0	0	0				
1994-95	Cape Breton	AHL	77	5	19	24	68																		
1995-96	Edmonton	NHL	13	1	1	2	12	0	0	0	8	12.5	–2												
	Cape Breton	AHL	58	9	30	39	174																		
1996-97	Edmonton	NHL	37	0	4	4	52	0	0	0	31	0.0	–2				12	0	1	1	8	0	0	0	
	Hamilton	AHL	34	4	14	18	26																		
1997-98	Edmonton	NHL	65	7	4	11	80	1	0	0	53	13.2	–17				7	0	0	0	21	0	0	0	
1998-99	Nashville	NHL	6	0	0	0	4	0	0	0	1	1.0	–4	0	0.0	18:11									
	Colorado	NHL	67	1	3	4	60	0	0	0	56	56.0	–3	1	100.0	16:23	19	0	2	2	22	0	0	0	12:09
99-2000	Colorado	NHL	69	2	7	9	73	0	0	0	40	5.0	–7	0	0.0	14:59	5	0	0	0	4	0	0	0	8:09
2000-01 ♦	Colorado	NHL	79	5	12	17	51	0	0	0	76	6.6	23	0	0.0	17:06	23	0	1	1	20	0	0	0	14:17
2001-02	Colorado	NHL	82	8	12	20	57	1	1	3	148	5.4	18	1	0.0	23:03	21	4	9	13	2	0	0	1	24:12
2002-03	Colorado	NHL	82	6	26	32	70	0	0	2	112	5.4	15	1	100.0	22:15	7	2	0	2	0	0	0	0	22:11
2003-04	NY Rangers	NHL	53	3	12	15	37	0	0	0	58	5.2	12	0	0.0	19:01									
	Ottawa	NHL	13	0	1	1	6	0	0	0	12	0.0	0	0	0.0	17:51	7	0	1	1	8	0	0	0	17:51
2004-05			DID NOT PLAY																						
2005-06	Atlanta	NHL	82	7	28	35	76	3	0	2	111	6.3	1	1	100.0	22:01									
2006-07	Atlanta	NHL	82	3	21	24	66	0	0	0	102	2.9	–3	0	0.0	22:14	4	1	0	1	4	0	0	0	19:17
2007-08	Nashville	NHL	77	4	11	15	71	0	0	1	66	6.1	7	0	0.0	18:52	6	1	0	1	2	0	0	1	19:41
	NHL Totals		807	47	142	189	715	5	1	8	874	5.4		4	75.0	19:42	111	8	14	22	91	0	0	2	17:13

Signed as a free agent by **Edmonton**, March 20, 1994. Traded to **Nashville** by **Edmonton** with Eric Fichaud and Drake Berehowsky for Mikhail Shtalenkov and Jim Dowd, October 1, 1998. Traded to **Colorado** by **Nashville** for Colorado's 3rd round choice (later traded back to Colorado - Colorado selected Branko Radivojevic) in 1999 Entry Draft, October 24, 1998. Signed as a free agent by **NY Rangers**, July 14, 2003. Traded to **Ottawa** by **NY Rangers** for Karel Rachunek and Alexandre Giroux, March 9, 2004. Traded to **Atlanta** by **Ottawa** with Marian Hossa for Dany Heatley, August 23, 2005. Signed as a free agent by **Nashville**, July 2, 2007.

DIMITRAKOS, Niko

(DIH-mih-tra-kohs, NEE-KOH)

Right wing. Shoots right. 5'11", 205 lbs. Born, Somerville, MA, May 21, 1979. San Jose's 4th choice, 155th overall, in 1999 Entry Draft.

1994-95	Matignon	High-MA	23	10	12	22																			
1995-96	Matignon	High-MA	25	12	28	40																			
1996-97	Matignon	High-MA	25	23	32	55																			
1997-98	Avon Old Farms	High-CT	26	27	28	55																			
1998-99	U. of Maine	H-East	35	8	19	27	33																		
99-2000	U. of Maine	H-East	32	11	16	27	16																		
2000-01	U. of Maine	H-East	29	11	14	25	43																		
2001-02	U. of Maine	H-East	43	20	31	51	44																		
2002-03	San Jose	NHL	21	6	7	13	8	3	0	0	34	17.6	–7	2	50.0	14:15									
	Cleveland Barons	AHL	55	15	29	44	30																		
2003-04	San Jose	NHL	68	9	15	24	49	2	0	4	116	7.8	6	4	50.0	13:20	15	1	8	9	8	0	0	1	14:31
	Cleveland Barons	AHL	7	4	4	8	4																		
2004-05	Langnau	Swiss	3	0	1	1	2										6	3	3	6	16				
2005-06	San Jose	NHL	45	4	12	16	26	0	0	0	66	6.1	0	8	25.0	11:54									
	Philadelphia	NHL	19	5	4	9	6	1	0	1	27	18.5	4	2	50.0	10:52	5	0	0	0	2	0	0	0	10:07
2006-07	Philadelphia	NHL	5	0	0	0	6	0	0	0	4	0.0	–4	0	0.0	8:32									
	Philadelphia	AHL	45	15	13	28	34																		
	Chicago Wolves	AHL	17	4	10	14	20										15	3	7	10	8				
2007-08	Binghamton	AHL	64	20	20	40	67																		
	NHL Totals		158	24	38	62	95	6	0	5	247	9.7		16	37.5	12:36	20	1	8	9	10	0	0	1	13:25

NCAA Championship All-Tournament Team (1999) • Hockey East Second All-Star Team (2002)

Signed as a free agent by **Langnau** (Swiss), February 2, 2005. Traded to **Philadelphia** by **San Jose** for Philadelphia's 3rd round choice (later traded to Columbus - Columbus selected Tommy Sestito) in 2006 Entry Draft, March 9, 2006. Loaned to **Chicago** (AHL) by **Philadelphia** (AHL) for Jared Ross, March 1, 2007. Signed as a free agent by **Ottawa**, July 13, 2007.

DiPENTA, Joe

(DIH-pehn-tah, JOH)

Defense. Shoots left. 6'2", 199 lbs. Born, Barrie, Ont., February 25, 1979. Florida's 2nd choice, 61st overall, in 1998 Entry Draft.

1996-97	Smiths Falls Bears	CJHL	54	13	22	35	92																		
1997-98	Boston University	H-East	38	2	16	18	50																		
1998-99	Boston University	H-East	36	2	15	17	72																		
99-2000	Halifax	QMJHL	63	13	43	56	83										10	3	4	7	26				
2000-01	Philadelphia	AHL	71	3	5	8	65										10	1	2	3	15				
2001-02	Philadelphia	AHL	61	2	4	6	71																		
	Chicago Wolves	AHL	15	0	2	2	15										25	1	3	4	22				
2002-03	Atlanta	NHL	3	1	1	2	0	0	0	0	2	50.0	3	0	0.0	15:47									
	Chicago Wolves	AHL	76	2	17	19	107										9	0	1	1	7				
2003-04	Chicago Wolves	AHL	73	0	6	6	105										10	1	0	1	13				
2004-05	Manitoba Moose	AHL	73	2	10	12	48										14	0	5	5	2				
2005-06	Anaheim	NHL	72	2	6	8	46	0	0	0	27	7.4	8	0	0.0	13:31	16	0	0	0	13	0	0	0	11:34
2006-07 ♦	Anaheim	NHL	76	2	6	8	48	0	0	1	33	6.1	1	1	0.0	12:09	16	0	0	0	4	0	0	0	8:12
2007-08	Anaheim	NHL	23	1	4	5	16	0	0	0	5	20.0	3	0	0.0	10:39									
	NHL Totals		174	6	17	23	110	0	0	1	67	9.0		1	0.0	12:35	32	0	0	0	17	0	0	0	9:53

• Left **Boston University** (Hockey East) and signed with **Halifax** (QMJHL), May 2, 1999. Signed as a free agent by **Philadelphia**, July 12, 2000. Traded to **Atlanta** by **Philadelphia** for Jarrod Skalde, March 5, 2002. Signed as a free agent by **Vancouver**, August 19, 2004. Signed as a free agent by **Anaheim**, August 11, 2005. • Spent majority of 2007-08 season as a healthy reserve. Signed as a free agent by **Frolunda** (Sweden), July 15, 2008.

			Regular Season														Playoffs								
Season	Club	League	GP	G	A	Pts	PIM	PP	SH	GW	S	%	+/-	TF	F%	Min	GP	G	A	Pts	PIM	PP	SH	GW	Min

DiSALVATORE, Jon

(dih-sal-vuh-TOH-ray, JAWN) **N.J.**

Right wing. Shoots right. 6'1", 200 lbs. Born, Bangor, ME, March 30, 1981. San Jose's 2nd choice, 104th overall, in 2000 Entry Draft.

Season	Club	League	GP	G	A	Pts	PIM	PP	SH	GW	S	%	+/-	TF	F%	Min	GP	G	A	Pts	PIM	PP	SH	GW	Min
1997-98	N.E. Jr. Coyotes	EJHL	38	24	41	65	....	....	....	....	....	....	....	....	....	....	....	....	....	....	....	....	....	....	....
1998-99	N.E. Jr. Coyotes	EJHL	48	44	76	*120	38	....	....	....	....	....	....	....	....	....	....	....	....	....	....	....	....	....	....
99-2000	Providence	H-East	38	15	12	27	12	....	....	....	....	....	....	....	....	....	....	....	....	....	....	....	....	....	....
2000-01	Providence	H-East	36	9	16	25	29	....	....	....	....	....	....	....	....	....	....	....	....	....	....	....	....	....	....
2001-02	Providence	H-East	38	16	26	42	6	....	....	....	....	....	....	....	....	....	....	....	....	....	....	....	....	....	....
2002-03	Providence	H-East	36	19	29	48	12	....	....	....	....	....	....	....	....	....	....	....	....	....	....	....	....	....	....
2003-04	Cleveland Barons	AHL	74	22	24	46	30	....	....	....	....	....	....	....	....	....	8	1	1	2	2	....	....	....	....
2004-05	Worcester IceCats	AHL	79	22	23	45	42	....	....	....	....	....	....	....	....	....	....	....	....	....	....	....	....	....	....
2005-06	**St. Louis**	**NHL**	**5**	**0**	**0**	**0**	**2**	**0**	**0**	**0**	**3**	**0.0**	**–1**	**0**	**0.0**	**8:27**	....	....	....	....	....	....	....	....	....
	Peoria Rivermen	AHL	72	22	45	67	42	....	....	....	....	....	....	....	....	....	4	0	0	0	0	....	....	....	....
2006-07	Peoria Rivermen	AHL	76	21	39	60	50	....	....	....	....	....	....	....	....	....	....	....	....	....	....	....	....	....	....
2007-08	San Antonio	AHL	66	22	24	46	46	....	....	....	....	....	....	....	....	....	7	2	1	3	9	....	....	....	....
	NHL Totals		**5**	**0**	**0**	**0**	**2**	**0**	**0**	**0**	**3**	**0.0**		**0**	**0.0**	**8:27**	....	....	....	....	....	....	....	....	....

Signed as a free agent by **St. Louis**, June 30, 2004. Signed as a free agent by **Phoenix**, July 9, 2007. Signed as a free agent by **New Jersey**, July 17, 2008.

DOAN, Shane

(DOHN, SHAYN) **PHX.**

Right wing. Shoots right. 6'2", 216 lbs. Born, Halkirk, Alta., October 10, 1976. Winnipeg's 1st choice, 7th overall, in 1995 Entry Draft.

Season	Club	League	GP	G	A	Pts	PIM	PP	SH	GW	S	%	+/-	TF	F%	Min	GP	G	A	Pts	PIM	PP	SH	GW	Min
1991-92	Killam Selects	AAHA	56	80	84	164	74	....	....	....	....	....	....	....	....	....	....	....	....	....	....	....	....	....	....
1992-93	Kamloops Blazers	WHL	51	7	12	19	65	....	....	....	....	....	....	....	....	....	13	0	1	1	8	....	....	....	....
1993-94	Kamloops Blazers	WHL	52	24	24	48	88	....	....	....	....	....	....	....	....	....	....	....	....	....	....	....	....	....	....
1994-95	Kamloops Blazers	WHL	71	37	57	94	106	....	....	....	....	....	....	....	....	....	21	6	10	16	16	....	....	....	....
1995-96	**Winnipeg**	**NHL**	**74**	**7**	**10**	**17**	**101**	**1**	**0**	**3**	**106**	**6.6**	**–9**	....	....	....	**6**	**0**	**0**	**0**	**6**	**0**	**0**	**0**	....
1996-97	**Phoenix**	**NHL**	**63**	**4**	**8**	**12**	**49**	**0**	**0**	**0**	**100**	**4.0**	**–3**	....	....	....	**4**	**0**	**0**	**0**	**2**	**0**	**0**	**0**	....
1997-98	**Phoenix**	**NHL**	**33**	**5**	**6**	**11**	**35**	**0**	**0**	**3**	**42**	**11.9**	**–3**	....	....	....	**6**	**1**	**0**	**1**	**6**	**0**	**0**	**0**	....
	Springfield	AHL	39	21	21	42	64	....	....	....	....	....	....	....	....	....	....	....	....	....	....	....	....	....	....
1998-99	**Phoenix**	**NHL**	**79**	**6**	**16**	**22**	**54**	**0**	**0**	**0**	**156**	**3.8**	**–5**	**6**	**16.7**	**12:42**	**7**	**2**	**2**	**4**	**6**	**0**	**0**	**2**	**17:58**
99-2000	**Phoenix**	**NHL**	**81**	**26**	**25**	**51**	**66**	**1**	**1**	**4**	**221**	**11.8**	**6**	**25**	**36.0**	**16:51**	**4**	**1**	**2**	**3**	**8**	**1**	**0**	**0**	**18:11**
2000-01	**Phoenix**	**NHL**	**76**	**26**	**37**	**63**	**89**	**6**	**1**	**6**	**220**	**11.8**	**0**	**15**	**40.0**	**19:32**	....	....	....	....	....	....	....	....	....
2001-02	**Phoenix**	**NHL**	**81**	**20**	**29**	**49**	**61**	**6**	**0**	**2**	**205**	**9.8**	**11**	**52**	**44.2**	**18:10**	**5**	**2**	**2**	**4**	**6**	**0**	**0**	**0**	**17:21**
2002-03	**Phoenix**	**NHL**	**82**	**21**	**37**	**58**	**86**	**7**	**0**	**2**	**225**	**9.3**	**3**	**623**	**39.8**	**18:47**	....	....	....	....	....	....	....	....	....
2003-04	**Phoenix**	**NHL**	**79**	**27**	**41**	**68**	**47**	**9**	**2**	**1**	**254**	**10.6**	**–11**	**55**	**40.0**	**21:46**	....	....	....	....	....	....	....	....	....
2004-05			DID NOT PLAY																						
2005-06	**Phoenix**	**NHL**	**82**	**30**	**36**	**66**	**123**	**17**	**0**	**7**	**254**	**11.8**	**–9**	**126**	**43.7**	**19:08**	....	....	....	....	....	....	....	....	....
	Canada	Olympics	6	2	1	3	2	....	....	....	....	....	....	....	....	....	....	....	....	....	....	....	....	....	....
2006-07	**Phoenix**	**NHL**	**73**	**27**	**28**	**55**	**73**	**11**	**0**	**7**	**209**	**12.9**	**–14**	**174**	**39.1**	**20:27**	....	....	....	....	....	....	....	....	....
2007-08	**Phoenix**	**NHL**	**80**	**28**	**50**	**78**	**59**	**9**	**2**	**5**	**243**	**11.5**	**4**	**187**	**41.2**	**20:46**	....	....	....	....	....	....	....	....	....
	NHL Totals		**883**	**227**	**323**	**550**	**843**	**67**	**6**	**40**	**2235**	**10.2**		**1263**	**40.3**	**18:40**	**32**	**6**	**6**	**12**	**34**	**1**	**0**	**2**	**17:50**

Memorial Cup Tournament All-Star Team (1995) • Stafford Smythe Memorial Trophy (Memorial Cup Tournament - MVP) (1995)
Played in NHL All-Star Game (2004)
Transferred to **Phoenix** after **Winnipeg** franchise relocated, July 1, 1996.

DOELL, Kevin

(DOH-ehl, KEH-vihn)

Center. Shoots left. 5'11", 190 lbs. Born, Saskatoon, Sask., July 15, 1979.

Season	Club	League	GP	G	A	Pts	PIM	PP	SH	GW	S	%	+/-	TF	F%	Min	GP	G	A	Pts	PIM	PP	SH	GW	Min
99-2000	U. of Denver	WCHA	40	8	15	23	18	....	....	....	....	....	....	....	....	....	....	....	....	....	....	....	....	....	....
2000-01	U. of Denver	WCHA	36	9	10	19	26	....	....	....	....	....	....	....	....	....	....	....	....	....	....	....	....	....	....
2001-02	U. of Denver	WCHA	41	20	23	43	28	....	....	....	....	....	....	....	....	....	....	....	....	....	....	....	....	....	....
2002-03	U. of Denver	WCHA	41	25	26	51	34	....	....	....	....	....	....	....	....	....	....	....	....	....	....	....	....	....	....
2003-04	Chicago Wolves	AHL	8	1	1	2	6	....	....	....	....	....	....	....	....	....	1	0	0	0	0	....	....	....	....
	Gwinnett	ECHL	63	33	41	74	88	....	....	....	....	....	....	....	....	....	13	1	6	7	12	....	....	....	....
2004-05	Chicago Wolves	AHL	45	4	8	12	69	....	....	....	....	....	....	....	....	....	....	....	....	....	....	....	....	....	....
	Gwinnett	ECHL	11	6	9	15	14	....	....	....	....	....	....	....	....	....	8	2	1	3	14	....	....	....	....
2005-06	Chicago Wolves	AHL	78	17	34	51	72	....	....	....	....	....	....	....	....	....	....	....	....	....	....	....	....	....	....
2006-07	Chicago Wolves	AHL	80	14	19	33	107	....	....	....	....	....	....	....	....	....	15	2	4	6	14	....	....	....	....
2007-08	**Atlanta**	**NHL**	**8**	**0**	**1**	**1**	**4**	**0**	**0**	**0**	**6**	**0.0**	**–2**	**53**	**47.2**	**9:40**	....	....	....	....	....	....	....	....	....
	Chicago Wolves	AHL	68	16	17	33	75	....	....	....	....	....	....	....	....	....	24	4	5	9	41	....	....	....	....
	NHL Totals		**8**	**0**	**1**	**1**	**4**	**0**	**0**	**0**	**6**	**0.0**		**53**	**47.2**	**9:40**	....	....	....	....	....	....	....	....	....

ECHL All-Rookie Team (2004) • ECHL Rookie of the Year (2004)
Signed as a free agent by **Atlanta**, June 30, 2004. Signed as a free agent by **Leksands** (Sweden), July 31, 2008.

DONOVAN, Shean

(DAW-nuh-vuhn, SHAWN) **OTT.**

Right wing. Shoots right. 6'2", 215 lbs. Born, Timmins, Ont., January 22, 1975. San Jose's 2nd choice, 28th overall, in 1993 Entry Draft.

Season	Club	League	GP	G	A	Pts	PIM	PP	SH	GW	S	%	+/-	TF	F%	Min	GP	G	A	Pts	PIM	PP	SH	GW	Min
1990-91	Kanata Valley	CJHL	44	8	5	13	8	....	....	....	....	....	....	....	....	....	....	....	....	....	....	....	....	....	....
1991-92	Ottawa 67's	OHL	58	11	8	19	14	....	....	....	....	....	....	....	....	....	11	1	0	1	5	....	....	....	....
1992-93	Ottawa 67's	OHL	66	29	23	52	33	....	....	....	....	....	....	....	....	....	....	....	....	....	....	....	....	....	....
1993-94	Ottawa 67's	OHL	62	35	49	84	63	....	....	....	....	....	....	....	....	....	17	10	11	21	14	....	....	....	....
1994-95	Ottawa 67's	OHL	29	22	19	41	41	....	....	....	....	....	....	....	....	....	....	....	....	....	....	....	....	....	....
	San Jose	**NHL**	**14**	**0**	**0**	**0**	**6**	**0**	**0**	**0**	**13**	**0.0**	**–6**	....	....	....	**7**	**0**	**1**	**1**	**6**	**0**	**0**	**0**	....
	Kansas City	IHL	5	0	2	2	7	....	....	....	....	....	....	....	....	....	14	5	3	8	23	....	....	....	....
1995-96	**San Jose**	**NHL**	**74**	**13**	**8**	**21**	**39**	**0**	**1**	**2**	**73**	**17.8**	**–17**	....	....	....	....	....	....	....	....	....	....	....	....
	Kansas City	IHL	4	0	0	0	8	....	....	....	....	....	....	....	....	....	5	0	0	0	8	....	....	....	....
1996-97	**San Jose**	**NHL**	**73**	**9**	**6**	**15**	**42**	**0**	**1**	**0**	**115**	**7.8**	**–18**	....	....	....	....	....	....	....	....	....	....	....	....
	Kentucky	AHL	3	1	3	4	18	....	....	....	....	....	....	....	....	....	....	....	....	....	....	....	....	....	....
1997-98	**San Jose**	**NHL**	**20**	**3**	**3**	**6**	**22**	**0**	**0**	**0**	**24**	**12.5**	**3**	....	....	....	....	....	....	....	....	....	....	....	....
	Colorado	**NHL**	**47**	**5**	**7**	**12**	**48**	**0**	**0**	**0**	**57**	**8.8**	**3**	....	....	....	....	....	....	....	....	....	....	....	....
1998-99	**Colorado**	**NHL**	**68**	**7**	**12**	**19**	**37**	**1**	**0**	**1**	**81**	**8.6**	**4**	**9**	**22.2**	**8:46**	**5**	**0**	**0**	**0**	**2**	**0**	**0**	**0**	**4:55**
99-2000	**Colorado**	**NHL**	**18**	**1**	**0**	**1**	**8**	**0**	**0**	**0**	**13**	**7.7**	**–4**	**1**	**0.0**	**5:20**	....	....	....	....	....	....	....	....	....
	Atlanta	**NHL**	**33**	**4**	**7**	**11**	**18**	**1**	**0**	**1**	**53**	**7.5**	**–13**	**22**	**31.8**	**14:19**	....	....	....	....	....	....	....	....	....
2000-01	**Atlanta**	**NHL**	**63**	**12**	**11**	**23**	**47**	**1**	**3**	**1**	**93**	**12.9**	**–14**	**218**	**45.9**	**14:03**	....	....	....	....	....	....	....	....	....
2001-02	**Atlanta**	**NHL**	**48**	**6**	**6**	**12**	**40**	**1**	**0**	**2**	**64**	**9.4**	**–16**	**12**	**50.0**	**13:30**	....	....	....	....	....	....	....	....	....
	Pittsburgh	**NHL**	**13**	**2**	**1**	**3**	**4**	**0**	**0**	**0**	**18**	**11.1**	**–5**	**4**	**0.0**	**14:34**	....	....	....	....	....	....	....	....	....
2002-03	**Pittsburgh**	**NHL**	**52**	**4**	**5**	**9**	**30**	**0**	**1**	**0**	**66**	**6.1**	**–6**	**37**	**24.3**	**13:01**	....	....	....	....	....	....	....	....	....
	Calgary	**NHL**	**13**	**1**	**2**	**3**	**7**	**0**	**0**	**1**	**22**	**4.5**	**–2**	**3**	**66.7**	**15:39**	....	....	....	....	....	....	....	....	....
2003-04	**Calgary**	**NHL**	**82**	**18**	**24**	**42**	**72**	**3**	**3**	**8**	**138**	**13.0**	**14**	**53**	**39.6**	**14:55**	**24**	**5**	**5**	**10**	**23**	**0**	**0**	**2**	**15:27**
2004-05	Geneve	Swiss	12	5	3	8	30	....	....	....	....	....	....	....	....	....	....	....	....	....	....	....	....	....	....
2005-06	**Calgary**	**NHL**	**80**	**9**	**11**	**20**	**82**	**0**	**1**	**0**	**132**	**6.8**	**9**	**26**	**30.8**	**11:47**	**7**	**0**	**0**	**0**	**6**	**0**	**0**	**0**	**11:24**
2006-07	**Boston**	**NHL**	**76**	**6**	**11**	**17**	**56**	**0**	**0**	**0**	**108**	**5.6**	**–13**	**41**	**43.9**	**14:09**	....	....	....	....	....	....	....	....	....
2007-08	**Ottawa**	**NHL**	**82**	**5**	**7**	**12**	**73**	**0**	**0**	**3**	**91**	**5.5**	**–3**	**29**	**37.9**	**9:35**	**4**	**1**	**0**	**1**	**2**	**0**	**0**	**0**	**14:00**
	NHL Totals		**856**	**105**	**121**	**226**	**631**	**7**	**10**	**19**	**1161**	**9.0**		**455**	**40.4**	**12:25**	**47**	**6**	**6**	**12**	**39**	**0**	**0**	**2**	**13:16**

Traded to **Colorado** by **San Jose** with San Jose's 1st round choice (Alex Tanguay) in 1998 Entry Draft for Mike Ricci and Colorado's 2nd round choice (later traded to Buffalo – Buffalo selected Jaroslav Kristek) in 1998 Entry Draft, November 21, 1997. Traded to **Atlanta** by **Colorado** for Rick Tabaracci, December 8, 1999. Claimed on waivers by **Pittsburgh** from **Atlanta**, March 15, 2002. Traded to **Calgary** by **Pittsburgh** for Micki Dupont and Mathias Johansson, March 11, 2003. Signed as a free agent by **Geneve** (Swiss), November 13, 2004. Signed as a free agent by **Boston**, July 2, 2006. Traded to **Ottawa** by **Boston** for Peter Schaefer, July 17, 2007.

DOWD, Jim

(DOWD, JIHM)

Center. Shoots right. 6', 180 lbs. Born, Brick, NJ, December 25, 1968. New Jersey's 7th choice, 149th overall, in 1987 Entry Draft.

Season	Club	League	GP	G	A	Pts	PIM	PP	SH	GW	S	%	+/-	TF	F%	Min	GP	G	A	Pts	PIM	PP	SH	GW	Min
1983-84	Brick Township	High-NJ	20	19	30	49	....	....	....	....	....	....	....	....	....	....	....	....	....	....	....	....	....	....	....
1984-85	Brick Township	High-NJ	24	58	55	113	....	....	....	....	....	....	....	....	....	....	....	....	....	....	....	....	....	....	....
1985-86	Brick Township	High-NJ	24	47	51	98	....	....	....	....	....	....	....	....	....	....	....	....	....	....	....	....	....	....	....
1986-87	Brick Township	High-NJ	24	22	33	55	....	....	....	....	....	....	....	....	....	....	....	....	....	....	....	....	....	....	....
1987-88	Lake Superior	CCHA	45	18	27	45	16	....	....	....	....	....	....	....	....	....	....	....	....	....	....	....	....	....	....
1988-89	Lake Superior	CCHA	46	24	35	59	40	....	....	....	....	....	....	....	....	....	....	....	....	....	....	....	....	....	....
1989-90	Lake Superior	CCHA	46	25	*67	92	30	....	....	....	....	....	....	....	....	....	....	....	....	....	....	....	....	....	....

			Regular Season														Playoffs								
Season	Club	League	GP	G	A	Pts	PIM	PP	SH	GW	S	%	+/-	TF	F%	Min	GP	G	A	Pts	PIM	PP	SH	GW	Min
1990-91	Lake Superior	CCHA	44	24	*54	*78	53																		
1991-92	**New Jersey**	**NHL**	**1**	**0**	**0**	**0**	**0**	**0**	**0**	**0**	**0**	**0.0**	**0**												
	Utica Devils	AHL	78	17	42	59	47										4	2	2	4	4				
1992-93	**New Jersey**	**NHL**	**1**	**0**	**0**	**0**	**0**	**0**	**0**	**0**	**1**	**0.0**	**–1**												
	Utica Devils	AHL	78	27	45	72	62										5	1	7	8	10				
1993-94	**New Jersey**	**NHL**	**15**	**5**	**10**	**15**	**0**	**2**	**0**	**0**	**26**	**19.2**	**8**				**19**	**2**	**6**	**8**	**8**	**0**	**0**	**0**	
	Albany River Rats	AHL	58	26	37	63	76																		
1994-95♦	**New Jersey**	**NHL**	**10**	**1**	**4**	**5**	**0**	**1**	**0**	**0**	**14**	**7.1**	**–5**				**11**	**2**	**1**	**3**	**8**	**0**	**0**	**1**	
1995-96	**New Jersey**	**NHL**	**28**	**4**	**9**	**13**	**17**	**0**	**0**	**0**	**41**	**9.8**	**–1**												
	Vancouver	**NHL**	**38**	**1**	**6**	**7**	**6**	**0**	**0**	**0**	**35**	**2.9**	**–8**				**1**	**0**	**0**	**0**	**0**	**0**	**0**	**0**	
1996-97	**NY Islanders**	**NHL**	**3**	**0**	**0**	**0**	**0**	**0**	**0**	**0**	**0**	**0.0**	**–1**												
	Utah Grizzlies	IHL	48	10	21	31	27																		
	Saint John Flames	AHL	24	5	11	16	18										5	1	2	3	0				
1997-98	**Calgary**	**NHL**	**48**	**6**	**8**	**14**	**12**	**0**	**1**	**0**	**58**	**10.3**	**10**												
	Saint John Flames	AHL	35	8	30	38	20										19	3	13	16	10				
1998-99	**Edmonton**	**NHL**	**1**	**0**	**0**	**0**	**0**	**0**	**0**	**0**	**1**	**0.0**	**0**	**7**	**14.3**	**9:47**									
	Hamilton	AHL	51	15	29	44	82										11	3	6	9	8				
99-2000	**Edmonton**	**NHL**	**69**	**5**	**18**	**23**	**45**	**2**	**0**	**1**	**103**	**4.9**	**10**	**720**	**54.0**	**13:08**	**5**	**2**	**1**	**3**	**4**	**0**	**0**	**0**	**15:22**
2000-01	**Minnesota**	**NHL**	**68**	**7**	**22**	**29**	**80**	**0**	**0**	**0**	**92**	**7.6**	**–6**	**1154**	**50.7**	**17:50**									
2001-02	**Minnesota**	**NHL**	**82**	**13**	**30**	**43**	**54**	**5**	**0**	**1**	**111**	**11.7**	**–14**	**1243**	**52.9**	**15:34**									
2002-03	**Minnesota**	**NHL**	**78**	**8**	**17**	**25**	**31**	**3**	**1**	**2**	**78**	**10.3**	**–1**	**930**	**47.9**	**13:03**	**15**	**0**	**2**	**2**	**0**	**0**	**0**	**0**	**12:58**
2003-04	**Minnesota**	**NHL**	**55**	**4**	**20**	**24**	**38**	**2**	**0**	**2**	**41**	**9.8**	**6**	**712**	**48.5**	**14:07**									
	Montreal	**NHL**	**14**	**3**	**2**	**5**	**6**	**0**	**1**	**0**	**13**	**23.1**	**6**	**167**	**47.3**	**13:30**	**11**	**0**	**2**	**2**	**2**	**0**	**0**	**0**	**15:34**
2004-05	Hamburg Freezers	Germany	20	4	9	13	12																		
2005-06	**Chicago**	**NHL**	**60**	**3**	**12**	**15**	**38**	**0**	**0**	**0**	**55**	**5.5**	**–5**	**664**	**51.7**	**12:43**									
	Colorado	**NHL**	**18**	**2**	**1**	**3**	**2**	**0**	**1**	**0**	**12**	**16.7**	**–6**	**180**	**51.7**	**12:04**	**9**	**2**	**3**	**5**	**20**	**0**	**1**	**0**	**14:11**
2006-07	**New Jersey**	**NHL**	**66**	**4**	**4**	**8**	**20**	**0**	**1**	**1**	**44**	**9.1**	**–5**	**274**	**51.8**	**8:17**	**11**	**0**	**0**	**0**	**4**	**0**	**0**	**0**	**4:33**
2007-08	**Philadelphia**	**NHL**	**73**	**5**	**5**	**10**	**41**	**0**	**1**	**0**	**41**	**12.2**	**0**	**446**	**53.8**	**8:26**	**17**	**1**	**2**	**3**	**4**	**0**	**0**	**0**	**8:55**
	NHL Totals		**728**	**71**	**168**	**239**	**390**	**15**	**6**	**7**	**766**	**9.3**		**6497**	**51.1**	**12:54**	**99**	**9**	**17**	**26**	**50**	**0**	**1**	**1**	**11:21**

CCHA Second All-Star Team (1990) • NCAA West Second All-American Team (1990) • CCHA First All-Star Team (1991) • CCHA Player of the Year (1991) • NCAA West First All-American Team (1991)

• Missed majority of 1994-95 season recovering from shoulder injury suffered in game vs. Quebec, February 2, 1995. Traded to **Hartford** by **New Jersey** with New Jersey's 2nd round choice (later traded to Calgary – Calgary selected Dmitri Kokorev) in 1997 Entry Draft for Jocelyn Lemieux and Hartford's 2nd round choice (later traded to Dallas – Dallas selected John Erskine) in 1998 Entry Draft, December 19, 1995. Traded to **Vancouver** by **Hartford** with Frantisek Kucera and Hartford's 2nd round choice (Ryan Bonni) in 1997 Entry Draft for Jeff Brown and Vancouver's 3rd round choice (later traded to Calgary – Calgary selected Paul Manning) in 1998 Entry Draft, December 19, 1995. Claimed by **NY Islanders** from **Vancouver** in Waiver Draft, September 30, 1996. Signed as a free agent by **Calgary**, August, 1997. Traded to **Nashville** by **Calgary** for future considerations, June 26, 1998. Traded to **Edmonton** by **Nashville** with Mikhail Shtalenkov for Eric Fichaud, Drake Berehowsky and Greg de Vries, October 1, 1998. Claimed by **Minnesota** from **Edmonton** in Expansion Draft, June 23, 2000. Traded to **Montreal** by **Minnesota** for Montreal's 4th round choice (Julien Sprunger) in 2004 Entry Draft, March 4, 2004. Signed as a free agent by **Hamburg** (Germany), October 1, 2004. Signed as a free agent by **Chicago**, August 5, 2005. Traded to **Colorado** by **Chicago** for Colorado's 4th round choice (later traded to Toronto - Toronto selected James Reimer) in 2006 Entry Draft, March 9, 2006. Signed as a free agent by **New Jersey**, November 2, 2006. Signed as a free agent by **Philadelphia**, October 3, 2007.

DOWELL, Jake

(DOW-uhl, JAYK) **CHI.**

Center. Shoots left. 6', 202 lbs. Born, Eau Claire, WI, March 4, 1985. Chicago's 10th choice, 140th overall, in 2004 Entry Draft.

			Regular Season														Playoffs								
Season	Club	League	GP	G	A	Pts	PIM	PP	SH	GW	S	%	+/-	TF	F%	Min	GP	G	A	Pts	PIM	PP	SH	GW	Min
2000-01	Eau Claire Mem.	High-WI	24	25	30	55																			
2001-02	USNTDP	U-17	11	5	1	6	14																		
	USNTDP	NAHL	44	5	12	17	51																		
2002-03	USNTDP	U-18	54	8	17	25	54																		
	USNTDP	NAHL	9	2	2	4	13																		
2003-04	U. of Wisconsin	WCHA	37	6	13	19	48																		
2004-05	U. of Wisconsin	WCHA	38	12	14	26	74																		
2005-06	U. of Wisconsin	WCHA	43	5	15	20	42																		
2006-07	U. of Wisconsin	WCHA	41	19	6	25	54																		
	Norfolk Admirals	AHL	9	2	3	5	8										6	0	3	3	4				
2007-08	**Chicago**	**NHL**	**19**	**2**	**1**	**3**	**10**	**0**	**1**	**0**	**19**	**10.5**	**1**	**170**	**46.5**	**11:56**									
	Rockford IceHogs	AHL	49	7	10	17	64										12	1	1	2	6				
	NHL Totals		**19**	**2**	**1**	**3**	**10**	**0**	**1**	**0**	**19**	**10.5**		**170**	**46.5**	**11:56**									

DOWNEY, Aaron

(DOW-nee, AIR-ruhn) **DET.**

Right wing. Shoots right. 6'1", 215 lbs. Born, Shelburne, Ont., August 27, 1974.

			Regular Season														Playoffs								
Season	Club	League	GP	G	A	Pts	PIM	PP	SH	GW	S	%	+/-	TF	F%	Min	GP	G	A	Pts	PIM	PP	SH	GW	Min
1990-91	Grand Valley	OHA-C	27	6	8	14	57																		
1991-92	Collingwood	OHA-B	40	9	8	17	111																		
1992-93	Guelph Storm	OHL	53	3	3	6	88										5	1	0	1	0				
1993-94	Cole Harbour	NSMHL	35	8	20	28	210																		
1994-95	Cole Harbour	NSMHL	40	10	31	41	320																		
1995-96	Hampton Roads	ECHL	65	12	11	23	354																		
1996-97	Manitoba Moose	IHL	2	0	0	0	17																		
	Portland Pirates	AHL	3	0	0	0	19																		
	Hampton Roads	ECHL	64	8	8	16	338										9	0	3	3	26				
1997-98	Providence Bruins	AHL	78	5	10	15	*407																		
1998-99	Providence Bruins	AHL	75	10	12	22	*401										19	1	1	2	46				
99-2000	**Boston**	**NHL**	**1**	**0**	**0**	**0**	**0**	**0**	**0**	**0**	**0**	**0.0**	**0**	**0**	**0.0**	**8:31**									
	Providence Bruins	AHL	47	6	4	10	221										14	1	0	1	24				
2000-01	**Chicago**	**NHL**	**3**	**0**	**0**	**0**	**6**	**0**	**0**	**0**	**2**	**0.0**	**–1**	**0**	**0.0**	**5:30**									
	Norfolk Admirals	AHL	67	6	15	21	234										9	0	0	0	4				
2001-02	**Chicago**	**NHL**	**36**	**1**	**0**	**1**	**76**	**0**	**0**	**1**	**10**	**10.0**	**–2**	**0**	**0.0**	**5:06**	**4**	**0**	**0**	**0**	**8**	**0**	**0**	**0**	**6:29**
	Norfolk Admirals	AHL	12	0	2	2	21																		
2002-03	**Dallas**	**NHL**	**43**	**1**	**1**	**2**	**69**	**0**	**0**	**0**	**14**	**7.1**	**1**	**0**	**0.0**	**4:47**									
2003-04	**Dallas**	**NHL**	**37**	**1**	**1**	**2**	**77**	**0**	**0**	**1**	**11**	**9.1**	**2**	**0**	**0.0**	**4:30**									
2004-05			DID NOT PLAY																						
2005-06	**St. Louis**	**NHL**	**17**	**2**	**0**	**2**	**45**	**0**	**0**	**0**	**11**	**18.2**	**0**	**0**	**0.0**	**3:56**									
	Montreal	**NHL**	**25**	**1**	**4**	**5**	**50**	**0**	**0**	**0**	**10**	**10.0**	**2**	**1**	**0.0**	**6:43**	**1**	**0**	**0**	**0**	**0**	**0**	**0**	**0**	**6:17**
2006-07	**Montreal**	**NHL**	**21**	**1**	**0**	**1**	**48**	**0**	**0**	**1**	**10**	**10.0**	**–6**	**0**	**0.0**	**4:59**									
	Providence Bruins	AHL	15	0	0	0	30										1	0	0	0	12				
2007-08♦	**Detroit**	**NHL**	**56**	**0**	**3**	**3**	**116**	**0**	**0**	**0**	**15**	**0.0**	**0**	**0**	**0.0**	**4:35**									
	NHL Totals		**239**	**7**	**9**	**16**	**487**	**0**	**0**	**3**	**83**	**8.4**		**1**	**0.0**	**4:56**	**5**	**0**	**0**	**0**	**8**	**0**	**0**	**0**	**6:27**

Signed as a free agent by **Boston**, January 20, 1998. Signed as a free agent by **Chicago**, August 13, 2000. Signed as a free agent by **Dallas**, July 3, 2002. • Spent majority of 2003-04 season as a healthy reserve. Signed as a free agent by **St. Louis**, August 1, 2005. Claimed on waivers by **Montreal** from **St. Louis**, January 23, 2006. Signed as a free agent by **Detroit**, October 3, 2007.

DOWNIE, Steve

(DOW-nee, STEEV) **PHI.**

Right wing. Shoots right. 5'11", 200 lbs. Born, Newmarket, Ont., April 3, 1987. Philadelphia's 1st choice, 29th overall, in 2005 Entry Draft.

			Regular Season														Playoffs								
Season	Club	League	GP	G	A	Pts	PIM	PP	SH	GW	S	%	+/-	TF	F%	Min	GP	G	A	Pts	PIM	PP	SH	GW	Min
2002-03	Aurora Tigers	OPJHL	34	12	13	25	55																		
2003-04	Windsor Spitfires	OHL	49	7	9	16	90										4	0	1	1	27				
2004-05	Windsor Spitfires	OHL	61	21	52	73	179										11	4	5	9	49				
2005-06	Windsor Spitfires	OHL	1	3	0	3	4																		
	Peterborough	OHL	34	16	34	50	109										19	6	15	21	38				
2006-07	Peterborough	OHL	28	23	36	59	92																		
	Kitchener Rangers	OHL	17	12	21	33	32										9	8	14	22	15				
	Philadelphia	AHL	1	0	0	0	0																		
2007-08	**Philadelphia**	**NHL**	**32**	**6**	**6**	**12**	**73**	**0**	**1**	**1**	**25**	**24.0**	**2**	**15**	**33.3**	**9:51**	**6**	**0**	**1**	**1**	**10**	**0**	**0**	**0**	**6:04**
	Philadelphia	AHL	21	5	12	17	114																		
	NHL Totals		**32**	**6**	**6**	**12**	**73**	**0**	**1**	**1**	**25**	**24.0**		**15**	**33.3**	**9:51**	**6**	**0**	**1**	**1**	**10**	**0**	**0**	**0**	**6:04**

DRAKE, Dallas

(DRAYK, DAL-uhs)

Right wing. Shoots left. 6'1", 186 lbs. Born, Trail, B.C., February 4, 1969. Detroit's 6th choice, 116th overall, in 1989 Entry Draft.

			Regular Season														Playoffs								
Season	Club	League	GP	G	A	Pts	PIM	PP	SH	GW	S	%	+/-	TF	F%	Min	GP	G	A	Pts	PIM	PP	SH	GW	Min
1984-85	Rossland	KIJHL	30	13	37	50	....	....	....	....	....	....	....	....	....	....	....	....	....	....	....	....	....	....	....
1985-86	Rossland	KIJHL	41	53	73	126	....	....	....	....	....	....	....	....	....	....	....	....	....	....	....	....	....	....	....
1986-87	Rossland	KIJHL	40	55	80	135	....	....	....	....	....	....	....	....	....	....	....	....	....	....	....	....	....	....	....
1987-88	Vernon Lakers	BCJHL	47	39	85	124	50	....	....	....	....	....	....	....	....	....	11	9	17	26	30	....	....	....	....
1988-89	Northern Mich.	WCHA	38	17	22	39	22	....	....	....	....	....	....	....	....	....	7	1	2	3	4	....	....	....	....
1989-90	Northern Mich.	WCHA	36	13	24	37	42	....	....	....	....	....	....	....	....	....	....	....	....	....	....	....	....	....	....
1990-91	Northern Mich.	WCHA	44	22	36	58	89	....	....	....	....	....	....	....	....	....	....	....	....	....	....	....	....	....	....
1991-92	Northern Mich.	WCHA	38	*39	41	*80	46	....	....	....	....	....	....	....	....	....	....	....	....	....	....	....	....	....	....
1992-93	**Detroit**	**NHL**	**72**	**18**	**26**	**44**	**93**	**3**	**2**	**5**	**89**	**20.2**	**15**	....	....	....	**7**	**3**	**3**	**6**	**6**	**1**	**0**	**0**	....
1993-94	**Detroit**	**NHL**	**47**	**10**	**22**	**32**	**37**	**0**	**1**	**2**	**78**	**12.8**	**5**	....	....	....	....	....	....	....	....	....	....	....	....
	Adirondack	AHL	1	2	0	2	0	....	....	....	....	....	....	....	....	....	....	....	....	....	....	....	....	....	....
	Winnipeg	**NHL**	**15**	**3**	**5**	**8**	**12**	**1**	**1**	**1**	**34**	**8.8**	**–6**	....	....	....	....	....	....	....	....	....	....	....	....
1994-95	**Winnipeg**	**NHL**	**43**	**8**	**18**	**26**	**30**	**0**	**0**	**1**	**66**	**12.1**	**–6**	....	....	....	....	....	....	....	....	....	....	....	....
1995-96	**Winnipeg**	**NHL**	**69**	**19**	**20**	**39**	**36**	**4**	**4**	**2**	**121**	**15.7**	**–7**	....	....	....	**3**	**0**	**0**	**0**	**0**	**0**	**0**	**0**	....
1996-97	**Phoenix**	**NHL**	**63**	**17**	**19**	**36**	**52**	**5**	**1**	**1**	**113**	**15.0**	**–11**	....	....	....	**7**	**0**	**1**	**1**	**2**	**0**	**0**	**0**	....
1997-98	**Phoenix**	**NHL**	**60**	**11**	**29**	**40**	**71**	**3**	**0**	**2**	**112**	**9.8**	**17**	....	....	....	**4**	**0**	**1**	**1**	**2**	**0**	**0**	**0**	....
1998-99	**Phoenix**	**NHL**	**53**	**9**	**22**	**31**	**65**	**0**	**0**	**3**	**105**	**8.6**	**17**	**5**	**60.0**	**15:38**	**7**	**4**	**3**	**7**	**4**	**2**	**0**	**1**	**19:51**
99-2000	**Phoenix**	**NHL**	**79**	**15**	**30**	**45**	**62**	**0**	**2**	**5**	**127**	**11.8**	**11**	**4**	**25.0**	**15:48**	**5**	**0**	**1**	**1**	**4**	**0**	**0**	**0**	**15:30**
2000-01	**St. Louis**	**NHL**	**82**	**12**	**29**	**41**	**71**	**2**	**0**	**3**	**142**	**8.5**	**18**	**11**	**45.5**	**14:44**	**15**	**4**	**2**	**6**	**16**	**0**	**1**	**1**	**14:08**
2001-02	**St. Louis**	**NHL**	**80**	**11**	**15**	**26**	**87**	**1**	**3**	**2**	**116**	**9.5**	**8**	**92**	**32.6**	**13:26**	**8**	**0**	**0**	**0**	**8**	**0**	**0**	**0**	**11:59**
2002-03	**St. Louis**	**NHL**	**80**	**20**	**10**	**30**	**66**	**4**	**1**	**2**	**113**	**17.7**	**–7**	**56**	**39.3**	**14:48**	**7**	**1**	**4**	**5**	**23**	**0**	**0**	**1**	**13:04**
2003-04	**St. Louis**	**NHL**	**79**	**13**	**22**	**35**	**65**	**3**	**2**	**1**	**121**	**10.7**	**10**	**92**	**45.7**	**16:57**	**5**	**1**	**1**	**2**	**2**	**0**	**0**	**1**	**16:45**
2004-05			DID NOT PLAY																						
2005-06	**St. Louis**	**NHL**	**62**	**2**	**24**	**26**	**59**	**1**	**0**	**1**	**88**	**2.3**	**–13**	**122**	**45.9**	**16:55**	....	....	....	....	....	....	....	....	....
2006-07	**St. Louis**	**NHL**	**60**	**6**	**6**	**12**	**38**	**0**	**2**	**2**	**74**	**8.1**	**–14**	**202**	**53.0**	**12:53**	....	....	....	....	....	....	....	....	....
2007-08♦	**Detroit**	**NHL**	**65**	**3**	**3**	**6**	**41**	**0**	**1**	**0**	**46**	**6.5**	**–12**	**70**	**41.4**	**10:42**	**22**	**1**	**3**	**4**	**12**	**0**	**0**	**0**	**11:22**
	NHL Totals		**1009**	**177**	**300**	**477**	**885**	**27**	**20**	**33**	**1545**	**11.5**		**654**	**45.1**	**14:41**	**90**	**14**	**19**	**33**	**79**	**3**	**1**	**4**	**13:46**

WCHA First All-Star Team (1992) • NCAA West First All-American Team (1992)

Traded to **Winnipeg** by **Detroit** with Tim Cheveldae for Bob Essensa and Sergei Bautin, March 8, 1994. Transferred to **Phoenix** after **Winnipeg** franchise relocated, July 1, 1996. Claimed by **Minnesota** from **Phoenix** in Expansion Draft, June 23, 2000. Signed as a free agent by **St. Louis**, July 1, 2000. Signed as a free agent by **Detroit**, July 9, 2007. • Officially announced his retirement, July 15, 2008.

DRAPER, Kris

(DRAY-puhr, KRIHS) **DET.**

Center. Shoots left. 5'10", 188 lbs. Born, Toronto, Ont., May 24, 1971. Winnipeg's 4th choice, 62nd overall, in 1989 Entry Draft.

Season	Club	League	GP	G	A	Pts	PIM	PP	SH	GW	S	%	+/-	TF	F%	Min	GP	G	A	Pts	PIM	PP	SH	GW	Min
1987-88	Don Mills Flyers	MTHL	40	35	32	67	46	....	....	....	....	....	....	....	....	....	....	....	....	....	....	....	....	....	....
1988-89	Canada	Nat-Tm	60	11	15	26	16	....	....	....	....	....	....	....	....	....	....	....	....	....	....	....	....	....	....
1989-90	Canada	Nat-Tm	61	12	22	34	44	....	....	....	....	....	....	....	....	....	....	....	....	....	....	....	....	....	....
1990-91	Ottawa 67's	OHL	39	19	42	61	35	....	....	....	....	....	....	....	....	....	17	8	11	19	20	....	....	....	....
	Winnipeg	**NHL**	**3**	**1**	**0**	**1**	**5**	**0**	**0**	**0**	**1**	**100.0**	**0**	....	....	....	....	....	....	....	....	....	....	....	....
	Moncton Hawks	AHL	7	2	1	3	2	....	....	....	....	....	....	....	....	....	....	....	....	....	....	....	....	....	....
1991-92	**Winnipeg**	**NHL**	**10**	**2**	**0**	**2**	**2**	**0**	**0**	**0**	**19**	**10.5**	**0**	....	....	....	**2**	**0**	**0**	**0**	**0**	**0**	**0**	**0**	....
	Moncton Hawks	AHL	61	11	18	29	113	....	....	....	....	....	....	....	....	....	4	0	1	1	6	....	....	....	....
1992-93	**Winnipeg**	**NHL**	**7**	**0**	**0**	**0**	**2**	**0**	**0**	**0**	**5**	**0.0**	**–6**	....	....	....	....	....	....	....	....	....	....	....	....
	Moncton Hawks	AHL	67	12	23	35	40	....	....	....	....	....	....	....	....	....	5	2	2	4	18	....	....	....	....
1993-94	**Detroit**	**NHL**	**39**	**5**	**8**	**13**	**31**	**0**	**1**	**0**	**55**	**9.1**	**11**	....	....	....	**7**	**2**	**2**	**4**	**4**	**0**	**1**	**0**	....
	Adirondack	AHL	46	20	23	43	49	....	....	....	....	....	....	....	....	....	....	....	....	....	....	....	....	....	....
1994-95	**Detroit**	**NHL**	**36**	**2**	**6**	**8**	**22**	**0**	**0**	**0**	**44**	**4.5**	**1**	....	....	....	**18**	**4**	**1**	**5**	**12**	**0**	**1**	**1**	....
1995-96	**Detroit**	**NHL**	**52**	**7**	**9**	**16**	**32**	**0**	**1**	**0**	**51**	**13.7**	**2**	....	....	....	**18**	**4**	**2**	**6**	**18**	**0**	**1**	**0**	....
1996-97♦	**Detroit**	**NHL**	**76**	**8**	**5**	**13**	**73**	**1**	**0**	**1**	**85**	**9.4**	**–11**	....	....	....	**20**	**2**	**4**	**6**	**12**	**0**	**1**	**0**	....
1997-98♦	**Detroit**	**NHL**	**64**	**13**	**10**	**23**	**45**	**1**	**0**	**4**	**96**	**13.5**	**5**	....	....	....	**19**	**1**	**3**	**4**	**12**	**0**	**0**	**1**	....
1998-99	**Detroit**	**NHL**	**80**	**4**	**14**	**18**	**79**	**0**	**1**	**1**	**78**	**5.1**	**2**	**887**	**54.6**	**12:43**	**10**	**0**	**1**	**1**	**6**	**0**	**0**	**0**	**11:35**
99-2000	**Detroit**	**NHL**	**51**	**5**	**7**	**12**	**28**	**0**	**0**	**3**	**76**	**6.6**	**3**	**380**	**57.6**	**13:33**	**9**	**2**	**0**	**2**	**6**	**0**	**0**	**0**	**12:26**
2000-01	**Detroit**	**NHL**	**75**	**8**	**17**	**25**	**38**	**0**	**1**	**1**	**123**	**6.5**	**17**	**997**	**56.5**	**13:26**	**6**	**0**	**1**	**1**	**2**	**0**	**0**	**0**	**16:08**
2001-02♦	**Detroit**	**NHL**	**82**	**15**	**15**	**30**	**56**	**0**	**2**	**3**	**137**	**10.9**	**26**	**756**	**53.2**	**15:35**	**23**	**2**	**3**	**5**	**20**	**0**	**0**	**0**	**17:00**
2002-03	**Detroit**	**NHL**	**82**	**14**	**21**	**35**	**82**	**0**	**1**	**2**	**142**	**9.9**	**6**	**1059**	**56.9**	**16:12**	**4**	**0**	**0**	**0**	**4**	**0**	**0**	**0**	**17:29**
2003-04	**Detroit**	**NHL**	**67**	**24**	**16**	**40**	**31**	**2**	**5**	**1**	**149**	**16.1**	**22**	**1058**	**56.9**	**17:44**	**12**	**1**	**3**	**4**	**6**	**0**	**0**	**0**	**18:29**
2004-05			DID NOT PLAY																						
2005-06	**Detroit**	**NHL**	**80**	**10**	**22**	**32**	**58**	**0**	**1**	**1**	**153**	**6.5**	**3**	**1287**	**57.7**	**17:46**	**6**	**0**	**0**	**0**	**6**	**0**	**0**	**0**	**19:58**
	Canada	Olympics	6	0	0	0	0	....	....	....	....	....	....	....	....	....	....	....	....	....	....	....	....	....	....
2006-07	**Detroit**	**NHL**	**81**	**14**	**15**	**29**	**58**	**0**	**5**	**1**	**157**	**8.9**	**7**	**1242**	**57.3**	**16:45**	**18**	**2**	**0**	**2**	**24**	**0**	**0**	**0**	**16:36**
2007-08♦	**Detroit**	**NHL**	**65**	**9**	**8**	**17**	**68**	**0**	**2**	**2**	**97**	**9.3**	**–2**	**944**	**58.6**	**15:38**	**22**	**3**	**1**	**4**	**10**	**0**	**0**	**1**	**15:27**
	NHL Totals		**950**	**141**	**173**	**314**	**710**	**4**	**20**	**20**	**1468**	**9.6**		**8610**	**56.7**	**15:33**	**194**	**23**	**21**	**44**	**142**	**0**	**4**	**3**	**16:03**

Frank J. Selke Trophy (2004)

Traded to **Detroit** by **Winnipeg** for future considerations, June 30, 1993.

DRURY, Chris

(DROO-ree, KRIHS) **NYR**

Center. Shoots right. 5'10", 190 lbs. Born, Trumbull, CT, August 20, 1976. Quebec's 5th choice, 72nd overall, in 1994 Entry Draft.

Season	Club	League	GP	G	A	Pts	PIM	PP	SH	GW	S	%	+/-	TF	F%	Min	GP	G	A	Pts	PIM	PP	SH	GW	Min
1991-92	Fairfield Prep	High-CT	25	22	27	49	....	....	....	....	....	....	....	....	....	....	....	....	....	....	....	....	....	....	....
1992-93	Fairfield Prep	High-CT	24	25	32	57	15	....	....	....	....	....	....	....	....	....	....	....	....	....	....	....	....	....	....
1993-94	Fairfield Prep	High-CT	24	37	18	55	....	....	....	....	....	....	....	....	....	....	....	....	....	....	....	....	....	....	....
1994-95	Boston University	H-East	39	12	15	27	38	....	....	....	....	....	....	....	....	....	....	....	....	....	....	....	....	....	....
1995-96	Boston University	H-East	37	35	33	*68	46	....	....	....	....	....	....	....	....	....	....	....	....	....	....	....	....	....	....
1996-97	Boston University	H-East	41	*38	24	62	64	....	....	....	....	....	....	....	....	....	....	....	....	....	....	....	....	....	....
1997-98	Boston University	H-East	38	28	29	57	88	....	....	....	....	....	....	....	....	....	....	....	....	....	....	....	....	....	....
1998-99	**Colorado**	**NHL**	**79**	**20**	**24**	**44**	**62**	**6**	**0**	**3**	**138**	**14.5**	**9**	**418**	**46.9**	**13:15**	**19**	**6**	**2**	**8**	**4**	**0**	**0**	**4**	**11:28**
99-2000	**Colorado**	**NHL**	**82**	**20**	**47**	**67**	**42**	**7**	**0**	**2**	**213**	**9.4**	**8**	**1321**	**53.1**	**18:33**	**17**	**4**	**10**	**14**	**4**	**1**	**0**	**2**	**18:30**
2000-01♦	**Colorado**	**NHL**	**71**	**24**	**41**	**65**	**47**	**11**	**0**	**5**	**204**	**11.8**	**6**	**552**	**55.1**	**18:03**	**23**	**11**	**5**	**16**	**4**	**2**	**0**	**2**	**19:06**
2001-02	**Colorado**	**NHL**	**82**	**21**	**25**	**46**	**38**	**5**	**0**	**6**	**236**	**8.9**	**1**	**1139**	**53.2**	**17:57**	**21**	**5**	**7**	**12**	**10**	**1**	**0**	**3**	**17:01**
	United States	Olympics	6	0	0	0	0	....	....	....	....	....	....	....	....	....	....	....	....	....	....	....	....	....	....
2002-03	**Calgary**	**NHL**	**80**	**23**	**30**	**53**	**33**	**5**	**1**	**5**	**224**	**10.3**	**–9**	**942**	**53.8**	**18:33**	....	....	....	....	....	....	....	....	....
2003-04	**Buffalo**	**NHL**	**76**	**18**	**35**	**53**	**68**	**5**	**1**	**2**	**152**	**11.8**	**8**	**1491**	**54.9**	**18:04**	....	....	....	....	....	....	....	....	....
2004-05			DID NOT PLAY																						
2005-06	**Buffalo**	**NHL**	**81**	**30**	**37**	**67**	**32**	**16**	**2**	**5**	**172**	**17.4**	**–11**	**1641**	**55.5**	**18:06**	**18**	**9**	**9**	**18**	**10**	**5**	**1**	**1**	**19:20**
	United States	Olympics	6	0	3	3	2	....	....	....	....	....	....	....	....	....	....	....	....	....	....	....	....	....	....
2006-07	**Buffalo**	**NHL**	**77**	**37**	**32**	**69**	**30**	**17**	**3**	**9**	**199**	**18.6**	**1**	**1613**	**58.8**	**18:47**	**16**	**8**	**5**	**13**	**2**	**3**	**0**	**3**	**20:45**
2007-08	**NY Rangers**	**NHL**	**82**	**25**	**33**	**58**	**45**	**12**	**0**	**7**	**220**	**11.4**	**–3**	**1359**	**54.9**	**19:48**	**10**	**3**	**3**	**6**	**8**	**0**	**0**	**1**	**18:27**
	NHL Totals		**710**	**218**	**304**	**522**	**397**	**84**	**7**	**44**	**1758**	**12.4**		**10476**	**54.8**	**17:54**	**124**	**46**	**41**	**87**	**42**	**12**	**1**	**16**	**17:41**

Hockey East Second All-Star Team (1996, 1997) • NCAA East Second All-American Team (1996) • Hockey East Player of the Year (1997, 1998) • NCAA East First All-American Team (1997, 1998) • NCAA Championship All-Tournament Team (1997) • Hockey East First All-Star Team (1998) • Hobey Baker Memorial Award (Top U.S. Collegiate Player) (1998) • NHL All-Rookie Team (1999) • Calder Memorial Trophy (1999)

Rights transferred to **Colorado** after **Quebec** franchise relocated, June 21, 1995. Traded to **Calgary** by **Colorado** with Stephane Yelle for Derek Morris, Jeff Shantz and Dean McAmmond, October 1, 2002. Traded to **Buffalo** by **Calgary** with Steve Begin for Steve Reinprecht and Rhett Warrener, July 3, 2003. Signed as a free agent by **NY Rangers**, July 1, 2007.

DUBINSKY, Brandon

(DOO-bihn-skee, BRAN-duhn) **NYR**

Center. Shoots left. 6'1", 210 lbs. Born, Anchorage, AK, April 29, 1986. NY Rangers' 6th choice, 60th overall, in 2004 Entry Draft.

Season	Club	League	GP	G	A	Pts	PIM	PP	SH	GW	S	%	+/-	TF	F%	Min	GP	G	A	Pts	PIM	PP	SH	GW	Min
2001-02	Alaska All-Stars	AASHA	37	14	24	38	....	....	....	....	....	....	....	....	....	....	....	....	....	....	....	....	....	....	....
2002-03	Portland	WHL	44	8	18	26	35	....	....	....	....	....	....	....	....	....	7	2	2	4	10	....	....	....	....
2003-04	Portland	WHL	71	30	48	78	137	....	....	....	....	....	....	....	....	....	5	0	2	2	6	....	....	....	....
2004-05	Portland	WHL	68	23	36	59	160	....	....	....	....	....	....	....	....	....	7	4	5	9	8	....	....	....	....
2005-06	Portland	WHL	51	21	46	67	98	....	....	....	....	....	....	....	....	....	12	5	10	15	24	....	....	....	....
	Hartford	AHL	....	....	....	....	....	....	....	....	....	....	....	....	....	....	11	5	5	10	14	....	....	....	....

			Regular Season														Playoffs								
Season	Club	League	GP	G	A	Pts	PIM	PP	SH	GW	S	%	+/-	TF	F%	Min	GP	G	A	Pts	PIM	PP	SH	GW	Min
2006-07	**NY Rangers**	**NHL**	**6**	**0**	**0**	**0**	**2**	**0**	**0**	**0**	**9**	**0.0**	**0**	**26**	**46.2**	**8:10**	....	....	....	....	....	....	....	....	....
	Hartford	AHL	71	21	22	43	115	....	....	....	....	....	....	....	....	....	7	1	3	4	12	....	....	....	....
2007-08	**NY Rangers**	**NHL**	**82**	**14**	**26**	**40**	**79**	**1**	**0**	**0**	**157**	**8.9**	**8**	**995**	**51.5**	**14:30**	**10**	**4**	**4**	**8**	**12**	**2**	**0**	**0**	**18:59**
	NHL Totals		**88**	**14**	**26**	**40**	**81**	**1**	**0**	**0**	**166**	**8.4**		**1021**	**51.3**	**14:04**	**10**	**4**	**4**	**8**	**12**	**2**	**0**	**0**	**18:59**

WHL West Second All-Star Team (2004, 2006)

DUMONT, J.P.

(DOO-mawnt, JAY-pee) **NSH.**

Right wing. Shoots left. 6'1", 205 lbs. Born, Montreal, Que., April 1, 1978. NY Islanders' 1st choice, 3rd overall, in 1996 Entry Draft.

Season	Club	League	GP	G	A	Pts	PIM	PP	SH	GW	S	%	+/-	TF	F%	Min	GP	G	A	Pts	PIM	PP	SH	GW	Min
1993-94	Mtl-Bourassa	QAAA	44	27	20	47	44	....	....	....	....	....	....	....	....	....	4	2	3	5	4	....	....	....	....
1994-95	Mtl-Bourassa	QAAA	10	2	7	9	12	....	....	....	....	....	....	....	....	....	....	....	....	....	....	....	....	....	....
	Val-d'Or Foreurs	QMJHL	48	5	14	19	24	....	....	....	....	....	....	....	....	....	....	....	....	....	....	....	....	....	....
1995-96	Val-d'Or Foreurs	QMJHL	66	48	57	105	109	....	....	....	....	....	....	....	....	....	13	12	8	20	22	....	....	....	....
1996-97	Val-d'Or Foreurs	QMJHL	62	44	64	108	86	....	....	....	....	....	....	....	....	....	13	9	7	16	12	....	....	....	....
1997-98	Val-d'Or Foreurs	QMJHL	55	57	42	99	63	....	....	....	....	....	....	....	....	....	19	31	15	46	18	....	....	....	....
1998-99	**Chicago**	**NHL**	**25**	**9**	**6**	**15**	**10**	**0**	**0**	**2**	**42**	**21.4**	**7**	**10**	**50.0**	**14:14**	....	....	....	....	....	....	....	....	....
	Portland Pirates	AHL	50	32	14	46	39	....	....	....	....	....	....	....	....	....	....	....	....	....	....	....	....	....	....
	Chicago Wolves	IHL	....	....	....	....	....	....	....	....	....	....	....	....	....	....	10	4	1	5	6	....	....	....	....
99-2000	**Chicago**	**NHL**	**47**	**10**	**8**	**18**	**18**	**0**	**0**	**1**	**86**	**11.6**	**-6**	**12**	**33.3**	**12:54**	....	....	....	....	....	....	....	....	....
	Cleveland	IHL	7	5	2	7	8	....	....	....	....	....	....	....	....	....	....	....	....	....	....	....	....	....	....
	Rochester	AHL	13	7	10	17	18	....	....	....	....	....	....	....	....	....	21	14	7	21	32	....	....	....	....
2000-01	**Buffalo**	**NHL**	**79**	**23**	**28**	**51**	**54**	**9**	**0**	**5**	**156**	**14.7**	**1**	**3**	**33.3**	**15:01**	**13**	**4**	**3**	**7**	**8**	**0**	**0**	**0**	**14:32**
2001-02	**Buffalo**	**NHL**	**76**	**23**	**21**	**44**	**42**	**7**	**0**	**3**	**154**	**14.9**	**-10**	**4**	**50.0**	**15:14**	....	....	....	....	....	....	....	....	....
2002-03	**Buffalo**	**NHL**	**76**	**14**	**21**	**35**	**44**	**2**	**0**	**2**	**135**	**10.4**	**-14**	**15**	**20.0**	**15:04**	....	....	....	....	....	....	....	....	....
2003-04	**Buffalo**	**NHL**	**77**	**22**	**31**	**53**	**40**	**10**	**0**	**1**	**156**	**14.1**	**-9**	**32**	**43.8**	**17:00**	....	....	....	....	....	....	....	....	....
2004-05	SC Bern	Swiss	3	2	2	4	6	....	....	....	....	....	....	....	....	....	10	4	1	5	16	....	....	....	....
2005-06	**Buffalo**	**NHL**	**54**	**20**	**20**	**40**	**38**	**9**	**0**	**4**	**116**	**17.2**	**-1**	**9**	**11.1**	**16:00**	**18**	**7**	**7**	**14**	**14**	**3**	**0**	**1**	**16:39**
2006-07	**Nashville**	**NHL**	**82**	**21**	**45**	**66**	**28**	**5**	**0**	**3**	**143**	**14.7**	**14**	**6**	**16.7**	**16:12**	**5**	**4**	**2**	**6**	**0**	**1**	**1**	**1**	**21:03**
2007-08	**Nashville**	**NHL**	**80**	**29**	**43**	**72**	**34**	**7**	**0**	**8**	**192**	**15.1**	**5**	**13**	**23.1**	**18:30**	**6**	**0**	**2**	**2**	**4**	**0**	**0**	**0**	**17:23**
	NHL Totals		**596**	**171**	**223**	**394**	**308**	**49**	**0**	**29**	**1180**	**14.5**		**104**	**32.7**	**15:50**	**42**	**15**	**14**	**29**	**26**	**4**	**1**	**2**	**16:37**

QMJHL Second All-Star Team (1997) • AHL All-Rookie Team (1999)

Rights traded to **Chicago** by **NY Islanders** with NY Islanders' 5th round choice (later traded to Philadelphia – Philadelphia selected Francis Belanger) in 1998 Entry Draft for Dmitri Nabokov, May 30, 1998. Traded to **Buffalo** by **Chicago** with Doug Gilmour for Michal Grosek, March 10, 2000. Signed as a free agent by **Bern** (Swiss), February 9, 2005. Signed as a free agent by **Nashville**, August 29, 2006.

DuPONT, Micki

(DOO-pawnt, MIH-kee)

Defense. Shoots right. 5'10", 186 lbs. Born, Calgary, Alta., April 15, 1980. Calgary's 9th choice, 270th overall, in 2000 Entry Draft.

Season	Club	League	GP	G	A	Pts	PIM	PP	SH	GW	S	%	+/-	TF	F%	Min	GP	G	A	Pts	PIM	PP	SH	GW	Min
1995-96	Calgary Blazers	AMHL	35	10	35	45	68	....	....	....	....	....	....	....	....	....	....	....	....	....	....	....	....	....	....
1996-97	Kamloops Blazers	WHL	59	8	27	35	39	....	....	....	....	....	....	....	....	....	5	0	4	4	8	....	....	....	....
1997-98	Kamloops Blazers	WHL	71	13	41	54	91	....	....	....	....	....	....	....	....	....	7	0	1	1	10	....	....	....	....
1998-99	Kamloops Blazers	WHL	59	8	27	35	110	....	....	....	....	....	....	....	....	....	15	2	8	10	22	....	....	....	....
99-2000	Kamloops Blazers	WHL	70	26	62	88	156	....	....	....	....	....	....	....	....	....	4	0	2	2	17	....	....	....	....
	Long Beach	IHL	1	0	0	0	0	....	....	....	....	....	....	....	....	....	....	....	....	....	....	....	....	....	....
	San Diego Gulls	WCHL	....	....	....	....	....	....	....	....	....	....	....	....	....	....	7	2	2	4	0	....	....	....	....
2000-01	Saint John Flames	AHL	67	8	21	29	28	....	....	....	....	....	....	....	....	....	19	1	9	10	14	....	....	....	....
2001-02	**Calgary**	**NHL**	**2**	**0**	**0**	**0**	**2**	**0**	**0**	**0**	**2**	**0.0**	**0**	**0**	**0.0**	**14:44**	....	....	....	....	....	....	....	....	....
	Saint John Flames	AHL	77	7	33	40	77	....	....	....	....	....	....	....	....	....	....	....	....	....	....	....	....	....	....
2002-03	**Calgary**	**NHL**	**16**	**1**	**2**	**3**	**4**	**0**	**0**	**0**	**27**	**3.7**	**-5**	**0**	**0.0**	**16:45**	....	....	....	....	....	....	....	....	....
	Saint John Flames	AHL	44	12	21	33	73	....	....	....	....	....	....	....	....	....	....	....	....	....	....	....	....	....	....
	Wilkes-Barre	AHL	14	1	4	5	16	....	....	....	....	....	....	....	....	....	6	3	0	3	21	....	....	....	....
2003-04	Eisbaren Berlin	Germany	45	10	22	32	76	....	....	....	....	....	....	....	....	....	10	3	6	9	35	....	....	....	....
2004-05	Eisbaren Berlin	Germany	51	11	22	33	93	....	....	....	....	....	....	....	....	....	11	2	5	7	41	....	....	....	....
2005-06	Eisbaren Berlin	Germany	52	11	21	32	78	....	....	....	....	....	....	....	....	....	11	4	10	*14	10	....	....	....	....
2006-07	**Pittsburgh**	**NHL**	**3**	**0**	**1**	**1**	**4**	**0**	**0**	**0**	**6**	**0.0**	**-3**	**0**	**0.0**	**13:48**	....	....	....	....	....	....	....	....	....
	Wilkes-Barre	AHL	78	18	33	51	101	....	....	....	....	....	....	....	....	....	11	5	9	14	16	....	....	....	....
2007-08	**St. Louis**	**NHL**	**2**	**0**	**0**	**0**	**2**	**0**	**0**	**0**	**3**	**0.0**	**1**	**0**	**0.0**	**12:34**	....	....	....	....	....	....	....	....	....
	Peoria Rivermen	AHL	76	10	36	46	77	....	....	....	....	....	....	....	....	....	....	....	....	....	....	....	....	....	....
	NHL Totals		**23**	**1**	**3**	**4**	**12**	**0**	**0**	**0**	**38**	**2.6**		**0**	**0.0**	**15:49**	....	....	....	....	....	....	....	....	....

AHL All-Rookie Team (2001) • AHL First All-Star Team (2007)

Traded to **Pittsburgh** by **Calgary** with Mathias Johansson for Shean Donovan, March 11, 2003. Signed as a free agent by **Berlin** (Germany), August 6, 2003. Signed as a free agent by **St. Louis**, July 3, 2007.

DUPUIS, Pascal

(doo-PWEE, pas-KAL) **PIT.**

Left wing. Shoots left. 6'1", 205 lbs. Born, Laval, Que., April 7, 1979.

Season	Club	League	GP	G	A	Pts	PIM	PP	SH	GW	S	%	+/-	TF	F%	Min	GP	G	A	Pts	PIM	PP	SH	GW	Min
1995-96	Laval-Laurentides	QAAA	41	10	15	25		....	....	....	....	....	....	....	....	....	14	11	11	22		....	....	....	....
1996-97	Rouyn-Noranda	QMJHL	44	9	15	24	20	....	....	....	....	....	....	....	....	....	....	....	....	....	....	....	....	....	....
1997-98	Rouyn-Noranda	QMJHL	39	9	17	26	36	....	....	....	....	....	....	....	....	....	....	....	....	....	....	....	....	....	....
	Shawinigan	QMJHL	28	7	13	20	10	....	....	....	....	....	....	....	....	....	6	2	0	2	4	....	....	....	....
1998-99	Shawinigan	QMJHL	57	30	42	72	118	....	....	....	....	....	....	....	....	....	6	1	8	9	18	....	....	....	....
99-2000	Shawinigan	QMJHL	61	50	55	105	99	....	....	....	....	....	....	....	....	....	13	*15	7	22	4	....	....	....	....
2000-01	**Minnesota**	**NHL**	**4**	**1**	**0**	**1**	**4**	**1**	**0**	**0**	**8**	**12.5**	**0**	**0**	**0.0**	**15:36**	....	....	....	....	....	....	....	....	....
	Cleveland	IHL	70	19	24	43	37	....	....	....	....	....	....	....	....	....	4	0	0	0	0	....	....	....	....
2001-02	**Minnesota**	**NHL**	**76**	**15**	**12**	**27**	**16**	**3**	**2**	**0**	**154**	**9.7**	**-10**	**40**	**32.5**	**15:08**	....	....	....	....	....	....	....	....	....
2002-03	**Minnesota**	**NHL**	**80**	**20**	**28**	**48**	**44**	**6**	**0**	**4**	**183**	**10.9**	**17**	**186**	**40.9**	**17:30**	**16**	**4**	**4**	**8**	**8**	**2**	**0**	**1**	**16:58**
2003-04	**Minnesota**	**NHL**	**59**	**11**	**15**	**26**	**20**	**2**	**0**	**1**	**127**	**8.7**	**5**	**129**	**45.7**	**15:48**	....	....	....	....	....	....	....	....	....
2004-05	HC Ajoie	Swiss-2	8	5	5	10	26	....	....	....	....	....	....	....	....	....	6	6	8	14	8	....	....	....	....
2005-06	**Minnesota**	**NHL**	**67**	**10**	**16**	**26**	**40**	**4**	**0**	**2**	**151**	**6.6**	**-10**	**93**	**29.0**	**16:30**	....	....	....	....	....	....	....	....	....
2006-07	**Minnesota**	**NHL**	**48**	**10**	**3**	**13**	**38**	**2**	**2**	**0**	**106**	**9.4**	**-7**	**110**	**27.3**	**15:07**	....	....	....	....	....	....	....	....	....
	NY Rangers	**NHL**	**6**	**1**	**0**	**1**	**0**	**0**	**0**	**0**	**10**	**10.0**	**-4**	**2**	**50.0**	**15:30**	....	....	....	....	....	....	....	....	....
	Atlanta	**NHL**	**17**	**3**	**2**	**5**	**4**	**0**	**0**	**1**	**40**	**7.5**	**-6**	**19**	**52.6**	**16:44**	**4**	**1**	**2**	**3**	**4**	**0**	**0**	**0**	**20:28**
2007-08	**Atlanta**	**NHL**	**62**	**10**	**5**	**15**	**24**	**0**	**3**	**1**	**111**	**9.0**	**-4**	**13**	**38.5**	**14:46**	....	....	....	....	....	....	....	....	....
	Pittsburgh	**NHL**	**16**	**2**	**10**	**12**	**8**	**0**	**0**	**0**	**32**	**6.3**	**4**	**3**	**0.0**	**16:50**	**20**	**2**	**5**	**7**	**18**	**0**	**0**	**0**	**16:14**
	NHL Totals		**435**	**83**	**91**	**174**	**198**	**18**	**7**	**9**	**922**	**9.0**		**595**	**37.1**	**15:57**	**40**	**7**	**11**	**18**	**30**	**2**	**0**	**1**	**16:57**

Signed as a free agent by **Minnesota**, August 18, 2000. Signed as a free agent by **Ajoie** (Swiss-2), January 14, 2005. Traded to **NY Rangers** by **Minnesota** for Adam Hall, February 9, 2007. Traded to **Atlanta** by **NY Rangers** with NY Rangers' 3rd round choice (later traded to Pittsburgh - Pittsburgh selected Robert Bortuzzo) in 2007 Entry Draft for Alex Bourret, February 27, 2007. Traded to **Pittsburgh** by **Atlanta** with Marian Hossa for Colby Armstrong, Erik Christensen, Angelo Esposito and Pittsburgh's 1st round choice (Daulton Leveille) in 2008 Entry Draft, February 26, 2008.

DVORAK, Radek

(duh-VOHR-ak, RA-dehk) **FLA.**

Right wing. Shoots right. 6'2", 200 lbs. Born, Tabor, Czech., March 9, 1977. Florida's 1st choice, 10th overall, in 1995 Entry Draft.

Season	Club	League	GP	G	A	Pts	PIM	PP	SH	GW	S	%	+/-	TF	F%	Min	GP	G	A	Pts	PIM	PP	SH	GW	Min
1992-93	C. Budejovice Jr.	Czech-Jr.	35	44	46	90	....	....	....	....	....	....	....	....	....	....	....	....	....	....	....	....	....	....	....
1993-94	C. Budejovice Jr.	CzRep-Jr.	20	17	18	35	....	....	....	....	....	....	....	....	....	....	....	....	....	....	....	....	....	....	....
	C. Budejovice	CzRep	8	0	0	0	0	....	....	....	....	....	....	....	....	....	....	....	....	....	....	....	....	....	....
1994-95	C. Budejovice	CzRep	10	3	5	8	2	....	....	....	....	....	....	....	....	....	9	5	1	6	....	....	....	....	....
1995-96	**Florida**	**NHL**	**77**	**13**	**14**	**27**	**20**	**0**	**0**	**4**	**126**	**10.3**	**5**	....	....	....	**16**	**1**	**3**	**4**	**0**	**0**	**0**	**0**	....
1996-97	**Florida**	**NHL**	**78**	**18**	**21**	**39**	**30**	**2**	**0**	**1**	**139**	**12.9**	**-2**	....	....	....	**3**	**0**	**0**	**0**	**0**	**0**	**0**	**0**	....
1997-98	**Florida**	**NHL**	**64**	**12**	**24**	**36**	**33**	**2**	**3**	**0**	**112**	**10.7**	**-1**	....	....	....	....	....	....	....	....	....	....	....	....
1998-99	**Florida**	**NHL**	**82**	**19**	**24**	**43**	**29**	**0**	**4**	**0**	**182**	**10.4**	**7**	**98**	**46.9**	**16:13**	....	....	....	....	....	....	....	....	....
99-2000	**Florida**	**NHL**	**35**	**7**	**10**	**17**	**6**	**0**	**0**	**1**	**67**	**10.4**	**5**	**16**	**37.5**	**15:25**	....	....	....	....	....	....	....	....	....
	NY Rangers	**NHL**	**46**	**11**	**22**	**33**	**10**	**2**	**1**	**0**	**90**	**12.2**	**0**	**34**	**35.3**	**18:24**	....	....	....	....	....	....	....	....	....
2000-01	**NY Rangers**	**NHL**	**82**	**31**	**36**	**67**	**20**	**5**	**2**	**3**	**230**	**13.5**	**9**	**20**	**30.0**	**19:04**	....	....	....	....	....	....	....	....	....
2001-02	**NY Rangers**	**NHL**	**65**	**17**	**20**	**37**	**14**	**3**	**3**	**1**	**210**	**8.1**	**-20**	**5**	**0.0**	**19:44**	....	....	....	....	....	....	....	....	....
	Czech Republic	Olympics	4	0	0	0	0	....	....	....	....	....	....	....	....	....	....	....	....	....	....	....	....	....	....
2002-03	**NY Rangers**	**NHL**	**63**	**6**	**21**	**27**	**16**	**2**	**0**	**0**	**134**	**4.5**	**-3**	**9**	**44.4**	**15:42**	....	....	....	....	....	....	....	....	....
	Edmonton	**NHL**	**12**	**4**	**4**	**8**	**14**	**1**	**0**	**0**	**32**	**12.5**	**-3**	**1**	**0.0**	**16:07**	**4**	**1**	**0**	**1**	**0**	**0**	**0**	**1**	**15:05**
2003-04	**Edmonton**	**NHL**	**78**	**15**	**35**	**50**	**26**	**6**	**0**	**0**	**188**	**8.0**	**18**	**24**	**29.2**	**16:56**	....	....	....	....	....	....	....	....	....
2004-05	C. Budejovice	CzRep-2	32	23	35	58	18	....	....	....	....	....	....	....	....	....	16	5	13	18	20	....	....	....	....
2005-06	**Edmonton**	**NHL**	**64**	**8**	**20**	**28**	**26**	**2**	**0**	**2**	**131**	**6.1**	**-2**	**14**	**28.6**	**16:34**	**16**	**0**	**2**	**2**	**4**	**0**	**0**	**0**	**13:29**

			Regular Season														Playoffs								
Season	Club	League	GP	G	A	Pts	PIM	PP	SH	GW	S	%	+/-	TF	F%	Min	GP	G	A	Pts	PIM	PP	SH	GW	Min
2006-07	**St. Louis**	**NHL**	**82**	**10**	**27**	**37**	**48**	**1**	**1**	**1**	**139**	**7.2**	**–6**	**26**	**38.5**	**15:38**									
2007-08	**Florida**	**NHL**	**67**	**8**	**9**	**17**	**16**	**0**	**1**	**1**	**146**	**5.5**	**–1**	**12**	**16.7**	**15:07**									
	NHL Totals		**895**	**179**	**287**	**466**	**308**	**26**	**15**	**14**	**1926**	**9.3**		**259**	**37.5**	**16:54**	**39**	**2**	**5**	**7**	**4**	**0**	**0**	**1**	**13:48**

Traded to **San Jose** by **Florida** for Mike Vernon and San Jose's 3rd round choice (Sean O'Connor) in 2000 Entry Draft, December 30, 1999. Traded to **NY Rangers** by **San Jose** for Todd Harvey and NY Rangers' 4th round choice (Dimitri Patzold) in 2001 Entry Draft, December 30, 1999. Traded to **Edmonton** by **NY Rangers** with Cory Cross for Anson Carter and Ales Pisa, March 11, 2003. Signed as a free agent by **Ceske Budejovice** (CzRep-2), September 15, 2004. Signed as a free agent by **St. Louis**, September 14, 2006. Signed as a free agent by **Florida**, July 1, 2007.

EAGER, Ben
(EE-guhr, BEHN) **CHI.**

Left wing. Shoots left. 6'3", 225 lbs. Born, Ottawa, Ont., January 22, 1984. Phoenix's 2nd choice, 23rd overall, in 2002 Entry Draft.

Season	Club	League	GP	G	A	Pts	PIM	PP	SH	GW	S	%	+/-	TF	F%	Min	GP	G	A	Pts	PIM	PP	SH	GW	Min
99-2000	Ott. Jr. Senators	CJHL	50	8	11	19	119																		
2000-01	Oshawa Generals	OHL	61	4	6	10	120																		
2001-02	Oshawa Generals	OHL	63	14	23	37	255										5	0	1	1	13				
2002-03	Oshawa Generals	OHL	58	16	24	40	216										8	0	4	4	8				
2003-04	Oshawa Generals	OHL	61	25	27	52	204										7	2	3	5	31				
	Philadelphia	AHL	5	0	0	0	0										3	0	1	1	8				
2004-05	Philadelphia	AHL	66	7	10	17	232										16	1	1	2	71				
2005-06	**Philadelphia**	**NHL**	**25**	**3**	**5**	**8**	**18**	**0**	**0**	**0**	**21**	**14.3**	**0**	**0**	**0.0**	**7:24**	**2**	**0**	**0**	**0**	**26**	**0**	**0**	**0**	**7:06**
	Philadelphia	AHL	49	6	12	18	256																		
2006-07	**Philadelphia**	**NHL**	**63**	**6**	**5**	**11**	***233**	**0**	**0**	**0**	**48**	**12.5**	**–13**	**1**	**100.0**	**8:14**									
	Philadelphia	AHL	3	0	0	0	21																		
2007-08	**Philadelphia**	**NHL**	**23**	**0**	**0**	**0**	**62**	**0**	**0**	**0**	**11**	**0.0**	**–8**	**5**	**20.0**	**5:29**									
	Chicago	**NHL**	**9**	**0**	**2**	**2**	**27**	**0**	**0**	**0**	**5**	**0.0**	**–1**	**0**	**0.0**	**6:37**									
	NHL Totals		**120**	**9**	**12**	**21**	**340**	**0**	**0**	**0**	**85**	**10.6**		**6**	**33.3**	**7:25**	**2**	**0**	**0**	**0**	**26**	**0**	**0**	**0**	**7:06**

Traded to **Philadelphia** by **Phoenix** with Sean Burke and Branko Radivojevic for Mike Comrie, February 9, 2004. Traded to **Chicago** by **Philadelphia** for Jim Vandermeer, December 18, 2007.

EARL, Robbie
(UHRL, RAW-bee) **TOR.**

Left wing. Shoots left. 6', 195 lbs. Born, Chicago, IL, June 6, 1985. Toronto's 4th choice, 187th overall, in 2004 Entry Draft.

Season	Club	League	GP	G	A	Pts	PIM	PP	SH	GW	S	%	+/-	TF	F%	Min	GP	G	A	Pts	PIM	PP	SH	GW	Min
2000-01	L.A. Jr. Kings	Minor-CA	29	48	22	70																			
2001-02	USNTDP	U-17	15	8	9	17																			
	USNTDP	NAHL	43	14	7	21	43																		
2002-03	USNTDP	U-18	43	16	8	24	58																		
	USNTDP	NAHL	10	4	5	9	18																		
2003-04	U. of Wisconsin	WCHA	42	14	13	27	46																		
2004-05	U. of Wisconsin	WCHA	41	20	24	44	62																		
2005-06	U. of Wisconsin	WCHA	42	24	26	50	56																		
	Toronto Marlies	AHL	1	0	0	0	0										3	0	0	0	0				
2006-07	Toronto Marlies	AHL	67	12	18	30	50																		
2007-08	**Toronto**	**NHL**	**9**	**0**	**1**	**1**	**0**	**0**	**0**	**0**	**9**	**0.0**	**–2**	**2**	**100.0**	**9:14**									
	Toronto Marlies	AHL	66	14	33	47	56																		
	NHL Totals		**9**	**0**	**1**	**1**	**0**	**0**	**0**	**0**	**9**	**0.0**		**2**	**100.0**	**9:14**									

WCHA All-Rookie Team (2004) • WCHA Second All-Star Team (2005) • NCAA Championship All-Tournament Team (2006) • NCAA Championship Tournament MVP (2006)

EATON, Mark
(EE-tohn, MAHRK) **PIT.**

Defense. Shoots left. 6'2", 204 lbs. Born, Wilmington, DE, May 6, 1977.

Season	Club	League	GP	G	A	Pts	PIM	PP	SH	GW	S	%	+/-	TF	F%	Min	GP	G	A	Pts	PIM	PP	SH	GW	Min
1995-96	Waterloo	USHL	50	4	21	25																			
1996-97	Waterloo	USHL	50	6	32	38	62																		
1997-98	U. of Notre Dame	CCHA	41	12	17	29	32																		
1998-99	Philadelphia	AHL	74	9	27	36	38										16	4	8	12	0				
99-2000	**Philadelphia**	**NHL**	**27**	**1**	**1**	**2**	**8**	**0**	**0**	**1**	**25**	**4.0**	**1**	**0**	**0.0**	**18:17**	**7**	**0**	**0**	**0**	**0**	**0**	**0**	**0**	**13:36**
	Philadelphia	AHL	47	9	17	26	6																		
2000-01	**Nashville**	**NHL**	**34**	**3**	**8**	**11**	**14**	**1**	**0**	**1**	**32**	**9.4**	**7**	**0**	**0.0**	**17:13**									
	Milwaukee	IHL	34	3	12	15	27																		
2001-02	**Nashville**	**NHL**	**58**	**3**	**5**	**8**	**24**	**0**	**0**	**0**	**52**	**5.8**	**–12**	**0**	**0.0**	**17:12**									
2002-03	**Nashville**	**NHL**	**50**	**2**	**7**	**9**	**22**	**0**	**0**	**0**	**52**	**3.8**	**1**	**0**	**0.0**	**15:45**									
	Milwaukee	AHL	3	1	0	1	2																		
2003-04	**Nashville**	**NHL**	**75**	**4**	**9**	**13**	**26**	**0**	**0**	**1**	**82**	**4.9**	**16**	**0**	**0.0**	**20:56**	**6**	**0**	**0**	**0**	**2**	**0**	**0**	**0**	**19:51**
2004-05	Grand Rapids	AHL	29	3	3	6	21																		
2005-06	**Nashville**	**NHL**	**69**	**3**	**1**	**4**	**44**	**0**	**0**	**0**	**28**	**10.7**	**–2**	**0**	**0.0**	**19:43**	**5**	**0**	**0**	**0**	**8**	**0**	**0**	**0**	**17:49**
2006-07	**Pittsburgh**	**NHL**	**35**	**0**	**3**	**3**	**16**	**0**	**0**	**0**	**22**	**0.0**	**–6**	**0**	**0.0**	**19:12**	**5**	**0**	**0**	**0**	**0**	**0**	**0**	**0**	**18:31**
2007-08	**Pittsburgh**	**NHL**	**36**	**0**	**3**	**3**	**4**	**0**	**0**	**0**	**28**	**0.0**	**6**	**0**	**0.0**	**19:40**									
	NHL Totals		**384**	**16**	**37**	**53**	**158**	**1**	**0**	**3**	**321**	**5.0**		**0**	**0.0**	**18:41**	**23**	**0**	**0**	**0**	**10**	**0**	**0**	**0**	**17:13**

USHL Second All-Star Team (1997) • Curt Hammer Award (Most Gentlemanly Player – USHL) (1997) • CCHA Rookie of the Year (1998)

Signed as a free agent by **Philadelphia**, August 4, 1998. Traded to **Nashville** by **Philadelphia** for Detroit's 3rd round choice (previously acquired, Philadelphia selected Patrick Sharp) in 2001 Entry Draft, September 29, 2000. Signed as a free agent by **Grand Rapids** (AHL), February 16, 2005. Signed as a free agent by **Pittsburgh**, July 3, 2006.

EAVES, Patrick
(EEVZ, PAT-rihk) **CAR.**

Right wing. Shoots right. 5'11", 190 lbs. Born, Calgary, Alta., May 1, 1984. Ottawa's 1st choice, 29th overall, in 2003 Entry Draft.

Season	Club	League	GP	G	A	Pts	PIM	PP	SH	GW	S	%	+/-	TF	F%	Min	GP	G	A	Pts	PIM	PP	SH	GW	Min
99-2000	Shat.-St. Mary's	High-MN	50	23	24	47																			
2000-01	USNTDP	U-17	13	7	8	15	3																		
	USNTDP	NAHL	34	12	11	23	75																		
2001-02	USNTDP	U-18	32	19	21	40	87																		
	USNTDP	USHL	9	1	4	5	18																		
	USNTDP	NAHL	8	5	3	8	37																		
2002-03	Boston College	H-East	14	10	8	18	61																		
2003-04	Boston College	H-East	34	18	23	41	66																		
2004-05	Boston College	H-East	36	19	29	48	36																		
2005-06	**Ottawa**	**NHL**	**58**	**20**	**9**	**29**	**22**	**5**	**1**	**4**	**100**	**20.0**	**7**	**14**	**21.4**	**12:29**	**10**	**1**	**0**	**1**	**10**	**0**	**0**	**0**	**11:40**
	Binghamton	AHL	18	5	8	13	10																		
2006-07	**Ottawa**	**NHL**	**73**	**14**	**18**	**32**	**36**	**3**	**1**	**1**	**130**	**10.8**	**1**	**9**	**11.1**	**12:13**	**7**	**0**	**2**	**2**	**2**	**0**	**0**	**0**	**7:23**
2007-08	**Ottawa**	**NHL**	**26**	**4**	**6**	**10**	**6**	**1**	**0**	**1**	**59**	**6.8**	**0**	**1**	**100.0**	**12:44**									
	Carolina	**NHL**	**11**	**1**	**4**	**5**	**4**	**1**	**0**	**0**	**22**	**4.5**	**–2**	**2**	**0.0**	**12:51**									
	NHL Totals		**168**	**39**	**37**	**76**	**68**	**10**	**2**	**6**	**311**	**12.5**		**26**	**19.2**	**12:26**	**17**	**1**	**2**	**3**	**12**	**0**	**0**	**0**	**9:54**

Hockey East Second All-Star Team (2004) • NCAA East Second All-American Team (2004) • Hockey East First All-Star Team (2005) • NCAA East First All-American Team (2005)

• Missed majority of 2002-03 season recovering from neck injury suffered in game vs. Maine (Hockey East), December 7, 2002. Traded to **Carolina** by **Ottawa** with Joe Corvo for Cory Stillman and Mike Commodore, February 11, 2008. • Missed majority of 2007-08 season recovering from shoulder injury suffered in game at Buffalo, November 21, 2007.

EBBETT, Andrew
(EH-beht, AN-droo) **ANA.**

Center. Shoots left. 5'10", 174 lbs. Born, Vernon, B.C., January 2, 1983.

Season	Club	League	GP	G	A	Pts	PIM	PP	SH	GW	S	%	+/-	TF	F%	Min	GP	G	A	Pts	PIM	PP	SH	GW	Min
2002-03	U. of Michigan	CCHA	43	9	18	27	22																		
2003-04	U. of Michigan	CCHA	43	9	28	37	56																		
2004-05	U. of Michigan	CCHA	40	6	31	37	28																		
2005-06	U. of Michigan	CCHA	41	14	28	42	25																		
2006-07	Binghamton	AHL	71	26	39	65	44																		
2007-08	**Anaheim**	**NHL**	**3**	**0**	**0**	**0**	**2**	**0**	**0**	**0**	**3**	**0.0**	**3**	**29**	**58.6**	**13:18**									
	Portland Pirates	AHL	74	18	54	72	66										18	6	11	17	4				
	NHL Totals		**3**	**0**	**0**	**0**	**2**	**0**	**0**	**0**	**3**	**0.0**		**29**	**58.6**	**13:18**									

Signed as a free agent by **Anaheim**, May 16, 2007.

EDLER, Alexander
(EHD-luhr, al-EHX-AN-duhr) **VAN.**

Defense. Shoots left. 6'3", 220 lbs. Born, Ostersund, Sweden, April 21, 1986. Vancouver's 2nd choice, 91st overall, in 2004 Entry Draft.

			Regular Season														Playoffs								
Season	Club	League	GP	G	A	Pts	PIM	PP	SH	GW	S	%	+/-	TF	F%	Min	GP	G	A	Pts	PIM	PP	SH	GW	Min
2001-02	Jamtland	Exhib.	8	0	1	1	2																		
2002-03	Jamtland	Exhib.	8	2	1	3	0																		
2003-04	Jamtland Jr.	Swe-Jr.	6	0	3	3	6																		
	Jamtland	Sweden-3	24	3	6	9	20																		
2004-05	MODO Jr.	Swe-Jr.	33	8	15	23	40										5	1	0	1	6				
2005-06	Kelowna Rockets	WHL	62	13	40	53	44										12	3	5	8	12				
2006-07	**Vancouver**	**NHL**	**22**	**1**	**2**	**3**	**6**	**0**	**0**	**0**	**10**	**10.0**	**3**	**0**	**0.0**	**11:27**	**3**	**0**	**0**	**0**	**2**	**0**	**0**	**0**	**11:51**
	Manitoba Moose	AHL	49	5	21	26	28										8	0	0	0	2				
2007-08	**Vancouver**	**NHL**	**75**	**8**	**12**	**20**	**42**	**4**	**0**	**0**	**124**	**6.5**	**6**	**1**	**100.0**	**21:20**									
	Manitoba Moose	AHL	2	0	1	1	0																		
	NHL Totals		**97**	**9**	**14**	**23**	**48**	**4**	**0**	**0**	**134**	**6.7**		**1**	**100.0**	**19:06**	**3**	**0**	**0**	**0**	**2**	**0**	**0**	**0**	**11:51**

EHRHOFF, Christian
(AIR-hawf, KRIHS-tyehn) **S.J.**

Defense. Shoots left. 6'2", 205 lbs. Born, Moers, West Germany, July 6, 1982. San Jose's 2nd choice, 106th overall, in 2001 Entry Draft.

Season	Club	League	GP	G	A	Pts	PIM	PP	SH	GW	S	%	+/-	TF	F%	Min	GP	G	A	Pts	PIM	PP	SH	GW	Min
1998-99	Krefelder EV Jr.	Ger-Jr.	22	10	14	24	46																		
99-2000	EV Duisburg	German-3	41	3	12	15	50																		
	Krefeld Pinguine	Germany	9	1	0	1	6										3	0	0	0	0				
2000-01	EV Duisburg	German-3	6	1	2	3	12																		
	Krefeld Pinguine	Germany	58	3	11	14	73																		
2001-02	Krefeld Pinguine	Germany	46	7	17	24	81										3	0	0	0	2				
	Germany	Olympics	7	0	0	0	8																		
2002-03	Krefeld Pinguine	Germany	48	10	17	27	54										14	3	6	9	24				
2003-04	**San Jose**	**NHL**	**41**	**1**	**11**	**12**	**14**	**0**	**0**	**1**	**58**	**1.7**	**4**	**0**	**0.0**	**15:23**									
	Cleveland Barons	AHL	27	4	10	14	43										9	2	6	8	11				
2004-05	Cleveland Barons	AHL	79	12	23	35	103																		
2005-06	**San Jose**	**NHL**	**64**	**5**	**18**	**23**	**32**	**2**	**0**	**2**	**124**	**4.0**	**10**	**0**	**0.0**	**17:48**	**11**	**2**	**6**	**8**	**18**	**1**	**0**	**1**	**19:47**
	Germany	Olympics	5	1	1	2	4																		
2006-07	**San Jose**	**NHL**	**82**	**10**	**23**	**33**	**63**	**6**	**0**	**2**	**164**	**6.1**	**8**	**1**	**0.0**	**18:34**	**11**	**0**	**2**	**2**	**6**	**0**	**0**	**0**	**17:47**
2007-08	**San Jose**	**NHL**	**77**	**1**	**21**	**22**	**72**	**1**	**0**	**1**	**97**	**1.0**	**9**	**0**	**0.0**	**21:44**	**10**	**0**	**5**	**5**	**14**	**0**	**0**	**0**	**23:04**
	NHL Totals		**264**	**17**	**73**	**90**	**181**	**9**	**0**	**6**	**443**	**3.8**		**1**	**0.0**	**18:49**	**32**	**2**	**13**	**15**	**38**	**1**	**0**	**1**	**20:07**

EKMAN, Nils
(EHK-mahn, NIHLZ)

Left wing. Shoots left. 6', 185 lbs. Born, Stockholm, Sweden, March 11, 1976. Calgary's 6th choice, 107th overall, in 1994 Entry Draft.

Season	Club	League	GP	G	A	Pts	PIM	PP	SH	GW	S	%	+/-	TF	F%	Min	GP	G	A	Pts	PIM	PP	SH	GW	Min
1993-94	Hammarby Jr.	Swe-Jr.	11	4	5	9	14																		
	Hammarby	Sweden-2	18	7	2	9	4																		
1994-95	Hammarby Jr.	Swe-Jr.	2	2	1	3	0																		
	Hammarby	Sweden-2	32	10	8	18	18																		
1995-96	Hammarby	Sweden-2	26	9	7	16	53										1	0	0	0	0				
1996-97	Kiekko-Espoo	Finland	50	24	19	43	60										4	2	0	2	4				
1997-98	Kiekko-Espoo	Finland	43	14	14	28	86										7	2	2	4	27				
	Saint John Flames	AHL															1	0	0	0	2				
1998-99	Blues Espoo	Finland	52	20	14	34	96										3	1	1	2	6				
99-2000	Detroit Vipers	IHL	10	7	2	9	8																		
	Tampa Bay	**NHL**	**28**	**2**	**2**	**4**	**36**	**1**	**0**	**0**	**42**	**4.8**	**–8**	**3**	**0.0**	**11:12**									
	Long Beach	IHL	27	11	12	23	26										5	3	3	6	4				
2000-01	**Tampa Bay**	**NHL**	**43**	**9**	**11**	**20**	**40**	**2**	**1**	**1**	**72**	**12.5**	**–15**	**16**	**37.5**	**15:45**									
	Detroit Vipers	IHL	33	22	14	36	63																		
2001-02	Djurgarden	Sweden	38	16	15	31	57										4	1	0	1	32				
2002-03	Hartford	AHL	57	30	36	66	73										2	0	2	2	4				
2003-04	**San Jose**	**NHL**	**82**	**22**	**33**	**55**	**34**	**1**	**4**	**5**	**147**	**15.0**	**30**	**23**	**21.7**	**14:54**	**16**	**0**	**3**	**3**	**8**	**0**	**0**	**0**	**13:02**
2004-05	Djurgarden	Sweden	44	18	27	45	106										12	4	5	9	20				
2005-06	**San Jose**	**NHL**	**77**	**21**	**36**	**57**	**54**	**5**	**0**	**2**	**176**	**11.9**	**20**	**39**	**46.2**	**15:12**	**11**	**2**	**2**	**4**	**8**	**1**	**0**	**0**	**15:14**
2006-07	**Pittsburgh**	**NHL**	**34**	**6**	**9**	**15**	**24**	**2**	**0**	**0**	**69**	**8.7**	**–14**	**6**	**0.0**	**13:49**	**1**	**0**	**0**	**0**	**0**	**0**	**0**	**0**	**10:03**
2007-08	Mytischi	Russia	57	21	23	44	87										4	0	1	1	0				
	NHL Totals		**264**	**60**	**91**	**151**	**188**	**11**	**5**	**8**	**506**	**11.9**		**87**	**33.3**	**14:36**	**28**	**2**	**5**	**7**	**16**	**1**	**0**	**0**	**13:48**

Garry F. Longman Memorial Trophy (Rookie of the Year – IHL) (2000)

Traded to **Tampa Bay** by **Calgary** with Calgary's 4th round choice (later traded to NY Islanders – NY Islanders selected Vladimir Gorbunov) in 2000 Entry Draft for Andreas Johansson, November 20, 1999. Traded to **NY Rangers** by **Tampa Bay** with Kyle Freadrich for Tim Taylor, June 30, 2001. Traded to **San Jose** by **NY Rangers** for Chad Wiseman, August 12, 2003. Signed as a free agent by **Djurgarden** (Sweden), September 16, 2004. Traded to **Pittsburgh** by **San Jose** with Patrick Ehelechner for Carolina's 2nd round choice (previously acquired, later traded to Philadelphia - Philadelphia selected Kevin Marshall) in 2007 Entry Draft, July 20, 2006. • Missed majority of 2006-07 season recovering from elbow injury suffered in game vs. Toronto, December 29, 2006. Signed as a free agent by **Khimik Mytischi** (Russia), August 12, 2007.

ELIAS, Patrik
(ehl-EE-ahsh, PAT-rihk) **N.J.**

Left wing. Shoots left. 6'1", 195 lbs. Born, Trebic, Czech., April 13, 1976. New Jersey's 2nd choice, 51st overall, in 1994 Entry Draft.

Season	Club	League	GP	G	A	Pts	PIM	PP	SH	GW	S	%	+/-	TF	F%	Min	GP	G	A	Pts	PIM	PP	SH	GW	Min
1992-93	Poldi Kladno	Czech	2	0	0	0																			
1993-94	HC Kladno	CzRep	15	1	2	3											11	2	2	4					
1994-95	HC Kladno	CzRep	28	4	3	7	37										7	1	2	3	12				
1995-96	**New Jersey**	**NHL**	**1**	**0**	**0**	**0**	**0**	**0**	**0**	**0**	**2**	**0.0**	**–1**												
	Albany River Rats	AHL	74	27	36	63	83										4	1	1	2	2				
1996-97	**New Jersey**	**NHL**	**17**	**2**	**3**	**5**	**2**	**0**	**0**	**0**	**23**	**8.7**	**–4**				**8**	**2**	**3**	**5**	**4**	**1**	**0**	**0**	
	Albany River Rats	AHL	57	24	43	67	76										6	1	2	3	8				
1997-98	**New Jersey**	**NHL**	**74**	**18**	**19**	**37**	**28**	**5**	**0**	**6**	**147**	**12.2**	**18**				**4**	**0**	**1**	**1**	**0**	**0**	**0**	**0**	
	Albany River Rats	AHL	3	3	0	3	2																		
1998-99	**New Jersey**	**NHL**	**74**	**17**	**33**	**50**	**34**	**3**	**0**	**2**	**157**	**10.8**	**19**	**99**	**38.4**	**15:50**	**7**	**0**	**5**	**5**	**6**	**0**	**0**	**0**	**18:07**
99-2000	Trebic	CzRep-2	2	2	1	3	2																		
	Pardubice	CzRep	5	1	4	5	31																		
	♦ **New Jersey**	**NHL**	**72**	**35**	**37**	**72**	**58**	**9**	**0**	**9**	**183**	**19.1**	**16**	**134**	**45.5**	**17:28**	**23**	**7**	***13**	**20**	**9**	**2**	**1**	**1**	**17:44**
2000-01	**New Jersey**	**NHL**	**82**	**40**	**56**	**96**	**51**	**8**	**3**	**6**	**220**	**18.2**	**45**	**155**	**41.3**	**18:44**	**25**	**9**	**14**	**23**	**10**	**3**	**1**	**2**	**18:14**
2001-02	**New Jersey**	**NHL**	**75**	**29**	**32**	**61**	**36**	**8**	**1**	**8**	**199**	**14.6**	**4**	**128**	**45.3**	**18:57**	**6**	**2**	**4**	**6**	**6**	**2**	**0**	**0**	**20:33**
	Czech Republic	Olympics	4	1	1	2	0																		
2002-03 ♦	**New Jersey**	**NHL**	**81**	**28**	**29**	**57**	**22**	**6**	**0**	**4**	**255**	**11.0**	**17**	**427**	**43.8**	**18:05**	**24**	**5**	**8**	**13**	**26**	**2**	**0**	**2**	**17:14**
2003-04	**New Jersey**	**NHL**	**82**	**38**	**43**	**81**	**44**	**9**	**3**	**9**	**300**	**12.7**	**26**	**49**	**36.7**	**18:46**	**5**	**3**	**2**	**5**	**2**	**1**	**0**	**1**	**18:59**
2004-05	Znojmo	CzRep	28	8	20	28	65																		
	Magnitogorsk	Russia	17	5	9	14	28																		
2005-06	**New Jersey**	**NHL**	**38**	**16**	**29**	**45**	**20**	**6**	**0**	**3**	**142**	**11.3**	**11**	**10**	**20.0**	**18:34**	**9**	**6**	**10**	**16**	**4**	**4**	**0**	**0**	**18:43**
	Czech Republic	Olympics	1	0	0	0	2																		
2006-07	**New Jersey**	**NHL**	**75**	**21**	**48**	**69**	**38**	**8**	**0**	**5**	**267**	**7.9**	**1**	**18**	**38.9**	**18:37**	**10**	**1**	**9**	**10**	**4**	**1**	**0**	**0**	**19:13**
2007-08	**New Jersey**	**NHL**	**74**	**20**	**35**	**55**	**38**	**7**	**0**	**8**	**263**	**7.6**	**10**	**776**	**45.6**	**18:28**	**5**	**4**	**2**	**6**	**4**	**3**	**0**	**0**	**20:30**
	NHL Totals		**745**	**264**	**364**	**628**	**371**	**69**	**7**	**60**	**2158**	**12.2**		**1796**	**43.9**	**18:10**	**126**	**39**	**71**	**110**	**75**	**19**	**2**	**6**	**18:18**

NHL All-Rookie Team (1998) • NHL First All-Star Team (2001) • Bud Light Plus/Minus Award (2001) (tied with Joe Sakic)

Played in NHL All-Star Game (2000, 2002)

Signed as a free agent by **Znojmo** (CzRep), September 6, 2004. Signed as a free agent by **Magnitogorsk** (Russia), December 9, 2004. • Missed majority of 2005-06 season recovering from hepatitis-A.

ELLIS, Matt
(EHL-ihs, MAT) **L.A.**

Left wing. Shoots left. 6', 207 lbs. Born, Welland, Ont., August 31, 1981.

Season	Club	League	GP	G	A	Pts	PIM	PP	SH	GW	S	%	+/-	TF	F%	Min	GP	G	A	Pts	PIM	PP	SH	GW	Min
1998-99	St. Michael's	OHL	47	10	8	18	6																		
99-2000	St. Michael's	OHL	59	15	20	35	20																		
2000-01	St. Michael's	OHL	68	21	24	45	19										18	4	8	12	6				
2001-02	St. Michael's	OHL	66	38	51	89	20										15	8	6	14	6				
2002-03	Toledo Storm	ECHL	71	27	32	59	34										7	3	5	8	0				
2003-04	Grand Rapids	AHL	64	5	10	15	23										4	0	0	0	2				
2004-05	Grand Rapids	AHL	79	18	23	41	59																		
2005-06	Grand Rapids	AHL	74	20	28	48	61										16	4	1	5	20				

			Regular Season														Playoffs								
Season	Club	League	GP	G	A	Pts	PIM	PP	SH	GW	S	%	+/-	TF	F%	Min	GP	G	A	Pts	PIM	PP	SH	GW	Min
2006-07	Detroit	NHL	16	0	0	0	6	0	0	0	22	0.0	–1	48	47.9	5:35	....	....	....	....	....	....	....	....	....
	Grand Rapids	AHL	65	26	23	49	44	....	....	....	....	....	....	....	....	....	7	4	3	7	4	....	....	....	....
2007-08	Detroit	NHL	35	2	4	6	12	0	0	1	28	7.1	1	87	49.4	5:23	....	....	....	....	....	....	....	....	....
	Los Angeles	NHL	19	1	1	2	14	0	1	0	38	2.6	2	27	37.0	12:41	....	....	....	....	....	....	....	....	....
	NHL Totals		70	3	5	8	32	0	1	1	88	3.4		162	46.9	7:25	....	....	....	....	....	....	....	....	....

Signed as a free agent by **Detroit**, May 10, 2002. Claimed on waivers by **Los Angeles** from **Detroit**, February 21, 2008

ELLISON, Matt

(EHL-ih-suhn, MAT) **NSH.**

Right wing. Shoots right. 6', 192 lbs. Born, Duncan, B.C., December 8, 1983. Chicago's 4th choice, 128th overall, in 2002 Entry Draft.

1997-98	Cowichan Valley	Minor-BC	24	27	31	58	10	....	....	....	....	....	....	....	....	....	....	....	....	....	....	....	....	....	....
1998-99	Kerry Park	VIJHL	38	40	47	87	110	....	....	....	....	....	....	....	....	....	....	....	....	....	....	....	....	....	....
99-2000	Cowichan Valley	BCHL	60	11	23	34	95	....	....	....	....	....	....	....	....	....	....	....	....	....	....	....	....	....	....
2000-01	Cowichan Valley	BCHL	60	22	44	66	102	....	....	....	....	....	....	....	....	....	....	....	....	....	....	....	....	....	....
2001-02	Cowichan Valley	BCHL	60	42	*75	*117	76	....	....	....	....	....	....	....	....	....	10	5	6	11	8	....	....	....	....
2002-03	Red Deer Rebels	WHL	72	40	56	96	80	....	....	....	....	....	....	....	....	....	22	7	13	20	28	....	....	....	....
2003-04	Chicago	NHL	10	0	1	1	0	0	0	0	4	0.0	–3	46	39.1	12:40	....	....	....	....	....	....	....	....	....
	Norfolk Admirals	AHL	71	14	21	35	115	....	....	....	....	....	....	....	....	....	7	0	1	1	4	....	....	....	....
2004-05	Norfolk Admirals	AHL	71	14	37	51	44	....	....	....	....	....	....	....	....	....	5	0	1	1	2	....	....	....	....
2005-06	Chicago	NHL	26	3	9	12	17	1	0	0	47	6.4	–4	76	43.4	14:45	....	....	....	....	....	....	....	....	....
	Philadelphia	NHL	5	0	1	1	2	0	0	0	2	0.0	2	10	50.0	6:28	....	....	....	....	....	....	....	....	....
	Philadelphia	AHL	48	12	13	25	35	....	....	....	....	....	....	....	....	....	....	....	....	....	....	....	....	....	....
2006-07	Philadelphia	NHL	2	0	0	0	0	0	0	0	1	0.0	0	8	37.5	5:58	....	....	....	....	....	....	....	....	....
	Philadelphia	AHL	62	12	27	39	43	....	....	....	....	....	....	....	....	....	....	....	....	....	....	....	....	....	....
2007-08	Milwaukee	AHL	75	26	32	58	55	....	....	....	....	....	....	....	....	....	5	0	0	0	2	....	....	....	....
	NHL Totals		43	3	11	14	19	1	0	0	54	5.6		140	42.1	12:53	....	....	....	....	....	....	....	....	....

WHL East Second All-Star Team (2003) • WHL Rookie of the Year (2003) • Canadian Major Junior Rookie of the Year (2003)

Traded to **Philadelphia** by **Chicago** with Chicago's 3rd round choice (later traded to Montreal - Montreal selected Ryan White) in 2006 Entry Draft for Patrick Sharp and Eric Meloche, December 5, 2005. Traded to **Nashville** by **Philadelphia** for future considerations, June 4, 2007.

EMINGER, Steve

(EH-mihn-juhr, STEEV) **PHI.**

Defense. Shoots right. 6'2", 212 lbs. Born, Woodbridge, Ont., October 31, 1983. Washington's 1st choice, 12th overall, in 2002 Entry Draft.

1998-99	Bramalea Blues	OPJHL	47	6	9	15	81	....	....	....	....	....	....	....	....	....	....	....	....	....	....	....	....	....	....
99-2000	Kitchener Rangers	OHL	50	2	14	16	74	....	....	....	....	....	....	....	....	....	5	0	0	0	0	....	....	....	....
2000-01	Kitchener Rangers	OHL	54	6	26	32	66	....	....	....	....	....	....	....	....	....	....	....	....	....	....	....	....	....	....
2001-02	Kitchener Rangers	OHL	64	19	39	58	93	....	....	....	....	....	....	....	....	....	4	0	2	2	10	....	....	....	....
2002-03	Washington	NHL	17	0	2	2	24	0	0	0	6	0.0	–3	0	0.0	10:08	....	....	....	....	....	....	....	....	....
	Kitchener Rangers	OHL	23	2	27	29	40	....	....	....	....	....	....	....	....	....	21	3	8	11	44	....	....	....	....
2003-04	Washington	NHL	41	0	4	4	45	0	0	0	12	0.0	–11	0	0.0	17:32	....	....	....	....	....	....	....	....	....
	Portland Pirates	AHL	41	0	4	4	40	....	....	....	....	....	....	....	....	....	7	0	1	1	2	....	....	....	....
2004-05	Portland Pirates	AHL	62	3	17	20	40	....	....	....	....	....	....	....	....	....	....	....	....	....	....	....	....	....	....
2005-06	Washington	NHL	66	5	13	18	81	1	0	0	50	10.0	–12	1	100.0	21:21	....	....	....	....	....	....	....	....	....
2006-07	Washington	NHL	68	1	16	17	63	0	0	0	27	3.7	–14	1	100.0	18:56	....	....	....	....	....	....	....	....	....
2007-08	Washington	NHL	20	0	2	2	8	0	0	0	14	0.0	–4	0	0.0	11:08	5	1	0	1	2	0	0	0	16:06
	NHL Totals		212	6	37	43	221	1	0	0	109	5.5		2	100.0	17:58	5	1	0	1	2	0	0	0	16:06

OHL Second All-Star Team (2002, 2003) • Memorial Cup Tournament All-Star Team (2003)

Traded to **Philadelphia** by **Washington** with Washington's 3rd round choice (Jacob Deserres) in 2008 Entry Draft for Philadelphia's 1st round choice (John Carlson) in 2008 Entry Draft, June 20, 2008.

ENSTROM, Tobias

(EHN-struhm, toh-BYE-uhs) **ATL.**

Defense. Shoots left. 5'10", 175 lbs. Born, Nordingra, Sweden, November 5, 1984. Atlanta's 8th choice, 239th overall, in 2003 Entry Draft.

99-2000	MoDo U18	Swe-U18	3	0	0	0	0	....	....	....	....	....	....	....	....	....	....	....	....	....	....	....	....	....	....
2000-01	MoDo U18	Swe-U18	16	7	6	13	18	....	....	....	....	....	....	....	....	....	....	....	....	....	....	....	....	....	....
	MoDo Jr.	Swe-Jr.	1	0	0	0	0	....	....	....	....	....	....	....	....	....	....	....	....	....	....	....	....	....	....
2001-02	MODO Jr.	Swe-Jr.	21	1	7	8	10	....	....	....	....	....	....	....	....	....	2	1	1	2	2	....	....	....	....
2002-03	MODO Jr.	Swe-Jr.	7	4	6	10	31	....	....	....	....	....	....	....	....	....	....	....	....	....	....	....	....	....	....
	MODO	Sweden	42	1	5	6	16	....	....	....	....	....	....	....	....	....	6	0	1	1	4	....	....	....	....
2003-04	MODO	Sweden	33	1	4	5	6	....	....	....	....	....	....	....	....	....	6	1	1	2	2	....	....	....	....
2004-05	MODO	Sweden	49	4	10	14	24	....	....	....	....	....	....	....	....	....	2	0	0	0	0	....	....	....	....
2005-06	MODO	Sweden	47	4	7	11	48	....	....	....	....	....	....	....	....	....	4	0	1	1	25	....	....	....	....
2006-07	MODO	Sweden	55	7	21	28	52	....	....	....	....	....	....	....	....	....	20	1	11	12	37	....	....	....	....
2007-08	Atlanta	NHL	82	5	33	38	42	4	0	0	105	4.8	–5	0	0.0	24:28	....	....	....	....	....	....	....	....	....
	NHL Totals		82	5	33	38	42	4	0	0	105	4.8		0	0.0	24:28	....	....	....	....	....	....	....	....	....

NHL All-Rookie Team (2008)

ERAT, Martin

(EE-rat, MAHR-tihn) **NSH.**

Right wing. Shoots left. 6', 195 lbs. Born, Trebic, Czech., August 29, 1981. Nashville's 12th choice, 191st overall, in 1999 Entry Draft.

1997-98	HC ZPS Zlin Jr.	CzRep-Jr.	46	35	30	65	....	....	....	....	....	....	....	....	....	....	....	....	....	....	....	....	....	....	....
1998-99	HC ZPS Zlin Jr.	CzRep-Jr.	35	21	23	44	....	....	....	....	....	....	....	....	....	....	....	....	....	....	....	....	....	....	....
	Zlin	CzRep	5	0	0	0	2	....	....	....	....	....	....	....	....	....	....	....	....	....	....	....	....	....	....
99-2000	Saskatoon Blades	WHL	66	27	26	53	82	....	....	....	....	....	....	....	....	....	11	4	8	12	16	....	....	....	....
2000-01	Saskatoon Blades	WHL	31	19	35	54	48	....	....	....	....	....	....	....	....	....	....	....	....	....	....	....	....	....	....
	Red Deer Rebels	WHL	17	4	24	28	24	....	....	....	....	....	....	....	....	....	22	*15	*21	*36	32	....	....	....	....
2001-02	Nashville	NHL	80	9	24	33	32	2	0	2	84	10.7	–11	3	66.7	13:10	....	....	....	....	....	....	....	....	....
2002-03	Nashville	NHL	27	1	7	8	14	1	0	0	39	2.6	–9	1	0.0	12:47	....	....	....	....	....	....	....	....	....
	Milwaukee	AHL	45	10	22	32	41	....	....	....	....	....	....	....	....	....	6	5	4	9	4	....	....	....	....
2003-04	Nashville	NHL	76	16	33	49	38	4	0	2	137	11.7	10	31	29.0	15:00	6	0	1	1	6	0	0	0	14:09
2004-05	HC Hame Zlin	CzRep	48	20	23	43	129	....	....	....	....	....	....	....	....	....	16	*7	5	12	12	....	....	....	....
2005-06	Nashville	NHL	80	20	29	49	76	5	0	1	143	14.0	0	25	16.0	14:45	5	1	1	2	6	1	0	0	19:31
	Czech Republic	Olympics	8	1	1	2	4	....	....	....	....	....	....	....	....	....	....	....	....	....	....	....	....	....	....
2006-07	Nashville	NHL	68	16	41	57	50	5	1	3	132	12.1	13	43	44.2	18:59	3	0	1	1	0	0	0	0	14:13
2007-08	Nashville	NHL	76	23	34	57	40	4	0	6	163	14.1	–3	41	36.6	18:39	6	1	3	4	8	0	0	0	20:56
	NHL Totals		407	85	168	253	250	21	1	14	698	12.2		144	34.0	15:47	20	2	6	8	20	1	0	0	17:32

Signed as a free agent by **Zlin** (CzRep), September 5, 2004.

ERICSSON, Jonathan

(AIR-ihk-suhn, JAWN-ah-thuhn) **DET.**

Defense. Shoots left. 6'4", 206 lbs. Born, Karlskrona, Sweden, March 2, 1984. Detroit's 10th choice, 291st overall, in 2002 Entry Draft.

2001-02	Hasten Jr.	Swe-Jr.	STATISTICS NOT AVAILABLE					....	....	....	....	....	....	....	....	....	....	....	....	....	....	....	....	....	....
2002-03	Vita Hasten	Sweden-3	40	2	4	6	36	....	....	....	....	....	....	....	....	....	....	....	....	....	....	....	....	....	....
2003-04	Sodertalje SK	Sweden	42	1	0	1	12	....	....	....	....	....	....	....	....	....	....	....	....	....	....	....	....	....	....
2004-05	Sodertalje SK	Sweden	15	0	0	0	4	....	....	....	....	....	....	....	....	....	1	0	0	0	0	....	....	....	....
2005-06	Sodertalje SK Jr.	Swe-Jr.	1	0	0	0	2	....	....	....	....	....	....	....	....	....	....	....	....	....	....	....	....	....	....
	Almtuna	Sweden-2	19	2	3	5	44	....	....	....	....	....	....	....	....	....	....	....	....	....	....	....	....	....	....
	Sodertalje SK	Sweden	24	0	0	0	20	....	....	....	....	....	....	....	....	....	....	....	....	....	....	....	....	....	....
	Sodertalje SK	Sweden-Q	7	0	1	1	4	....	....	....	....	....	....	....	....	....	....	....	....	....	....	....	....	....	....
2006-07	Grand Rapids	AHL	67	5	24	29	102	....	....	....	....	....	....	....	....	....	7	0	0	0	8	....	....	....	....
2007-08	Detroit	NHL	8	1	0	1	4	1	0	0	19	5.3	–3	0	0.0	15:58	....	....	....	....	....	....	....	....	....
	Grand Rapids	AHL	69	10	24	34	83	....	....	....	....	....	....	....	....	....	....	....	....	....	....	....	....	....	....
	NHL Totals		8	1	0	1	4	1	0	0	19	5.3		0	0.0	15:58	....	....	....	....	....	....	....	....	....

ERIKSSON, Anders

(AIR-ihk-suhn, AND-uhrs) **CGY.**

Defense. Shoots left. 6'3", 224 lbs. Born, Bollnas, Sweden, January 9, 1975. Detroit's 1st choice, 22nd overall, in 1993 Entry Draft.

Season	Club	League	GP	G	A	Pts	PIM	PP	SH	GW	S	%	+/-	TF	F%	Min	GP	G	A	Pts	PIM	PP	SH	GW	Min
			Regular Season														Playoffs								
1992-93	MoDo Jr.	Swe-Jr.	10	5	3	8	14	....	....	....	....	....	....	....	....	....	....	....	....	....	....	....	....	....	....
	MoDo	Sweden	20	0	2	2	2	....	....	....	....	....	....	....	....	....	1	0	0	0	0	....	....	....	....
1993-94	MoDo	Sweden	38	2	8	10	42	....	....	....	....	....	....	....	....	....	11	0	0	0	8	....	....	....	....
	MoDo Jr.	Swe-Jr.	3	1	2	3	34	....	....	....	....	....	....	....	....	....	....	....	....	....	....	....	....	....	....
1994-95	MoDo	Sweden	39	3	6	9	54	....	....	....	....	....	....	....	....	....	....	....	....	....	....	....	....	....	....
1995-96	Detroit	NHL	1	0	0	0	2	0	0	0	0	0.0	1	....	....	....	3	0	0	0	0	0	0	0	....
	Adirondack	AHL	75	6	36	42	64	....	....	....	....	....	....	....	....	....	3	0	0	0	0	....	....	....	....
1996-97	Detroit	NHL	23	0	6	6	10	0	0	0	27	0.0	5	....	....	....	....	....	....	....	....	....	....	....	....
	Adirondack	AHL	44	3	25	28	36	....	....	....	....	....	....	....	....	....	4	0	1	1	4	....	....	....	....
1997-98♦	Detroit	NHL	66	7	14	21	32	1	0	2	91	7.7	21	....	....	....	18	0	5	5	16	0	0	0	....
1998-99	Detroit	NHL	61	2	10	12	34	0	0	1	67	3.0	5	0	0.0	15:54	....	....	....	....	....	....	....	....	....
	Chicago	NHL	11	0	8	8	0	0	0	0	12	0.0	6	0	0.0	22:51	....	....	....	....	....	....	....	....	....
99-2000	Chicago	NHL	73	3	25	28	20	0	0	1	86	3.5	4	1	100.0	21:03	....	....	....	....	....	....	....	....	....
2000-01	Chicago	NHL	13	2	3	5	2	1	0	0	19	10.5	-4	0	0.0	21:20	....	....	....	....	....	....	....	....	....
	Florida	NHL	60	0	21	21	28	0	0	0	80	0.0	2	1	0.0	21:02	....	....	....	....	....	....	....	....	....
2001-02	Toronto	NHL	34	0	2	2	12	0	0	0	31	0.0	-1	0	0.0	15:55	10	0	0	0	0	0	0	0	17:24
	St. John's	AHL	25	4	6	10	14	....	....	....	....	....	....	....	....	....	11	0	5	5	6	....	....	....	....
2002-03	Toronto	NHL	4	0	0	0	0	0	0	0	7	0.0	1	0	0.0	19:02	....	....	....	....	....	....	....	....	....
	St. John's	AHL	72	5	34	39	133	....	....	....	....	....	....	....	....	....	....	....	....	....	....	....	....	....	....
2003-04	Columbus	NHL	66	7	20	27	18	2	0	1	84	8.3	-6	0	0.0	20:42	....	....	....	....	....	....	....	....	....
	Syracuse Crunch	AHL	9	1	3	4	12	....	....	....	....	....	....	....	....	....	....	....	....	....	....	....	....	....	....
2004-05	HV 71 Jonkoping	Sweden	32	1	9	10	54	....	....	....	....	....	....	....	....	....	....	....	....	....	....	....	....	....	....
2005-06	Magnitogorsk	Russia	17	2	7	9	10	....	....	....	....	....	....	....	....	....	11	3	2	5	16	....	....	....	....
	Springfield	AHL	12	1	8	9	10	....	....	....	....	....	....	....	....	....	....	....	....	....	....	....	....	....	....
2006-07	Columbus	NHL	79	0	23	23	46	0	0	0	78	0.0	12	1	100.0	20:12	....	....	....	....	....	....	....	....	....
2007-08	Calgary	NHL	61	1	17	18	36	1	0	0	50	2.0	-5	0	0.0	20:47	3	0	1	1	2	0	0	0	18:16
	NHL Totals		552	22	149	171	240	5	0	5	632	3.5		3	66.7	19:48	34	0	6	6	18	0	0	0	17:36

Traded to **Chicago** by **Detroit** with Detroit's 1st round choices in 1999 (Steve McCarthy) and 2001 (Adam Munro) Entry Drafts for Chris Chelios, March 23, 1999. Traded to **Florida** by **Chicago** for Jaroslav Spacek, November 6, 2000. Signed as a free agent by **Toronto**, July 9, 2001. Signed as a free agent by **Columbus**, October 10, 2003. Signed as a free agent by **Calgary**, September 16, 2004. Signed as a free agent by **Jonkoping** (Sweden), October 29, 2004. Signed as a fee agent by **Columbus**, July 1, 2006. Signed as a free agent by **Calgary**, July 5, 2007.

ERIKSSON, Loui

(AIR-ihk-suhn, LOO-ee) **DAL.**

Left wing. Shoots left. 6'1", 183 lbs. Born, Gothenburg, Sweden, July 17, 1985. Dallas' 1st choice, 33rd overall, in 2003 Entry Draft.

Season	Club	League	GP	G	A	Pts	PIM	PP	SH	GW	S	%	+/-	TF	F%	Min	GP	G	A	Pts	PIM	PP	SH	GW	Min
2000-01	V.Frolunda U18	Swe-U18	9	5	3	8	4	....	....	....	....	....	....	....	....	....	....	....	....	....	....	....	....	....	....
	V.Frolunda Jr.	Swe-Jr.	1	0	0	0	0	....	....	....	....	....	....	....	....	....	....	....	....	....	....	....	....	....	....
2001-02	V.Frolunda U18	Swe-U18	1	1	0	1	0	....	....	....	....	....	....	....	....	....	....	....	....	....	....	....	....	....	....
	V.Frolunda Jr.	Swe-Jr.	35	7	15	22	2	....	....	....	....	....	....	....	....	....	8	2	3	5	2	....	....	....	....
2002-03	V.Frolunda Jr.	Swe-Jr.	30	16	15	31	10	....	....	....	....	....	....	....	....	....	8	4	6	10	4	....	....	....	....
2003-04	V.Frolunda	Sweden	46	8	5	13	4	....	....	....	....	....	....	....	....	....	10	1	5	6	0	....	....	....	....
2004-05	Frolunda	Sweden	39	5	9	14	4	....	....	....	....	....	....	....	....	....	12	0	0	0	0	....	....	....	....
2005-06	Iowa Stars	AHL	78	31	29	60	27	....	....	....	....	....	....	....	....	....	7	2	5	7	0	....	....	....	....
2006-07	Dallas	NHL	59	6	13	19	18	2	0	0	78	7.7	-3	9	44.4	13:11	4	0	1	1	0	0	0	0	15:47
	Iowa Stars	AHL	15	5	3	8	13	....	....	....	....	....	....	....	....	....	9	2	5	7	0	....	....	....	....
2007-08	Dallas	NHL	69	14	17	31	28	4	0	0	120	11.7	5	13	15.4	14:02	18	4	4	8	8	1	0	0	18:12
	Iowa Stars	AHL	2	1	2	3	2	....	....	....	....	....	....	....	....	....	....	....	....	....	....	....	....	....	....
	NHL Totals		128	20	30	50	46	6	0	0	198	10.1		22	27.3	13:38	22	4	5	9	8	1	0	0	17:46

ERSKINE, John

(AIR-skign, JAWN) **WSH.**

Defense. Shoots left. 6'4", 218 lbs. Born, Kingston, Ont., June 26, 1980. Dallas' 1st choice, 39th overall, in 1998 Entry Draft.

Season	Club	League	GP	G	A	Pts	PIM	PP	SH	GW	S	%	+/-	TF	F%	Min	GP	G	A	Pts	PIM	PP	SH	GW	Min
1996-97	Quinte Hawks	MTJHL	48	4	16	20	241	....	....	....	....	....	....	....	....	....	....	....	....	....	....	....	....	....	....
1997-98	London Knights	OHL	55	0	9	9	205	....	....	....	....	....	....	....	....	....	16	0	5	5	25	....	....	....	....
1998-99	London Knights	OHL	57	8	12	20	208	....	....	....	....	....	....	....	....	....	25	5	10	15	38	....	....	....	....
99-2000	London Knights	OHL	58	12	31	43	177	....	....	....	....	....	....	....	....	....	....	....	....	....	....	....	....	....	....
2000-01	Utah Grizzlies	IHL	77	1	8	9	284	....	....	....	....	....	....	....	....	....	....	....	....	....	....	....	....	....	....
2001-02	Dallas	NHL	33	0	1	1	62	0	0	0	16	0.0	-8	0	0.0	10:44	....	....	....	....	....	....	....	....	....
	Utah Grizzlies	AHL	39	2	6	8	118	....	....	....	....	....	....	....	....	....	3	0	0	0	10	....	....	....	....
2002-03	Dallas	NHL	16	2	0	2	29	0	0	0	12	16.7	1	0	0.0	10:45	....	....	....	....	....	....	....	....	....
	Utah Grizzlies	AHL	52	2	8	10	274	....	....	....	....	....	....	....	....	....	1	0	1	1	15	....	....	....	....
2003-04	Dallas	NHL	32	0	1	1	84	0	0	0	23	0.0	-9	0	0.0	12:36	....	....	....	....	....	....	....	....	....
	Utah Grizzlies	AHL	5	0	0	0	18	....	....	....	....	....	....	....	....	....	....	....	....	....	....	....	....	....	....
2004-05	Houston Aeros	AHL	61	3	7	10	238	....	....	....	....	....	....	....	....	....	5	0	1	1	20	....	....	....	....
2005-06	Dallas	NHL	26	0	0	0	62	0	0	0	9	0.0	-3	0	0.0	11:00	....	....	....	....	....	....	....	....	....
	NY Islanders	NHL	34	1	0	1	99	0	0	0	23	4.3	-12	0	0.0	14:37	....	....	....	....	....	....	....	....	....
2006-07	Washington	NHL	29	1	6	7	69	0	0	0	14	7.1	-13	0	0.0	18:03	....	....	....	....	....	....	....	....	....
	Hershey Bears	AHL	4	0	2	2	9	....	....	....	....	....	....	....	....	....	....	....	....	....	....	....	....	....	....
2007-08	Washington	NHL	51	2	7	9	96	0	0	1	48	4.2	1	0	0.0	15:43	7	0	2	2	6	0	0	0	17:07
	NHL Totals		221	6	15	21	501	0	0	1	145	4.1		0	0.0	13:45	7	0	2	2	6	0	0	0	17:07

OHL First All-Star Team (2000)

• Missed majority of 2003-04 season recovering from ankle (December 27, 2003 vs. Columbus) and hernia (January 24, 2004 vs. St. Louis) injuries. Traded to **NY Islanders** by **Dallas** with Dallas' 2nd round choice (Jesse Joensuu) in 2006 Entry Draft for Janne Niinimaa and NY Islanders' 5th round choice (Ondrej Roman) in 2007 Entry Draft, January 10, 2005. Signed as a free agent by **Washington**, September 14, 2006. • Missed majority of 2006-07 season recovering from foot (December 16, 2006 vs. Philadelphia) and thumb (March 9, 2007 vs. Carolina) injuries.

EVANS, Brennan

(EH-vans, BREH-nuhn) **ANA.**

Defense. Shoots left. 6'3", 220 lbs. Born, North Battleford, Sask., January 16, 1982.

Season	Club	League	GP	G	A	Pts	PIM	PP	SH	GW	S	%	+/-	TF	F%	Min	GP	G	A	Pts	PIM	PP	SH	GW	Min
1998-99	Camrose Kodiaks	AJHL	47	1	6	7	98	....	....	....	....	....	....	....	....	....	5	0	2	2	0	....	....	....	....
	Seattle	WHL	....	....	....	....	....	....	....	....	....	....	....	....	....	....	1	0	0	0	0	....	....	....	....
99-2000	Seattle	WHL	52	1	2	3	40	....	....	....	....	....	....	....	....	....	1	0	0	0	0	....	....	....	....
2000-01	Seattle	WHL	11	1	0	1	25	....	....	....	....	....	....	....	....	....	....	....	....	....	....	....	....	....	....
	Kootenay Ice	WHL	55	2	7	9	105	....	....	....	....	....	....	....	....	....	11	0	0	0	25	....	....	....	....
2001-02	Kootenay Ice	WHL	72	2	3	5	121	....	....	....	....	....	....	....	....	....	22	0	6	6	38	....	....	....	....
2002-03	Kootenay Ice	WHL	67	6	17	23	182	....	....	....	....	....	....	....	....	....	11	1	1	2	24	....	....	....	....
2003-04	Lowell	AHL	64	1	9	10	65	....	....	....	....	....	....	....	....	....	....	....	....	....	....	....	....	....	....
	Calgary	NHL	....	....	....	....	....	....	....	....	....	....	....	....	....	....	2	0	0	0	0	0	0	0	2:52
2004-05	Lowell	AHL	51	0	7	7	79	....	....	....	....	....	....	....	....	....	5	0	0	0	2	....	....	....	....
2005-06	Binghamton	AHL	70	3	6	9	198	....	....	....	....	....	....	....	....	....	....	....	....	....	....	....	....	....	....
2006-07	Worcester Sharks	AHL	75	2	14	16	170	....	....	....	....	....	....	....	....	....	5	0	1	1	21	....	....	....	....
2007-08	Worcester Sharks	AHL	80	1	13	14	211	....	....	....	....	....	....	....	....	....	....	....	....	....	....	....	....	....	....
	NHL Totals		....	....	....	....	....	....	....	....	....	....		....	....	....	2	0	0	0	0	0	0	0	2:52

Signed as a free agent by **Calgary**, September 30, 2003. Signed as a free agent by **San Jose**, July 18, 2007. Signed as a free agent by **Anaheim**, July 11, 2008.

EXELBY, Garnet

(EHX-uhl-bee, GAHR-neht) **ATL.**

Defense. Shoots left. 6'1", 210 lbs. Born, Ste. Anne, Man., August 16, 1981. Atlanta's 9th choice, 217th overall, in 1999 Entry Draft.

Season	Club	League	GP	G	A	Pts	PIM	PP	SH	GW	S	%	+/-	TF	F%	Min	GP	G	A	Pts	PIM	PP	SH	GW	Min
1997-98	Winnipeg South	MJHL	46	5	11	16	110	....	....	....	....	....	....	....	....	....	....	....	....	....	....	....	....	....	....
1998-99	Saskatoon Blades	WHL	61	5	3	8	91	....	....	....	....	....	....	....	....	....	....	....	....	....	....	....	....	....	....
99-2000	Saskatoon Blades	WHL	63	1	8	9	79	....	....	....	....	....	....	....	....	....	11	0	2	2	21	....	....	....	....
2000-01	Saskatoon Blades	WHL	43	5	10	15	110	....	....	....	....	....	....	....	....	....	....	....	....	....	....	....	....	....	....
	Regina Pats	WHL	22	2	8	10	51	....	....	....	....	....	....	....	....	....	6	0	2	2	2	....	....	....	....
2001-02	Chicago Wolves	AHL	75	3	4	7	257	....	....	....	....	....	....	....	....	....	25	0	4	4	49	....	....	....	....
2002-03	Atlanta	NHL	15	0	2	2	41	0	0	0	9	0.0	0	0	0.0	18:04	....	....	....	....	....	....	....	....	....
	Chicago Wolves	AHL	53	3	6	9	140	....	....	....	....	....	....	....	....	....	9	0	1	1	27	....	....	....	....
2003-04	Atlanta	NHL	71	1	9	10	134	0	0	0	42	2.4	-10	0	0.0	19:32	....	....	....	....	....	....	....	....	....
2004-05			DID NOT PLAY																						
2005-06	Atlanta	NHL	75	1	9	10	75	0	0	0	44	2.3	11	0	0.0	15:41	....	....	....	....	....	....	....	....	....

			Regular Season														Playoffs								
Season	Club	League	GP	G	A	Pts	PIM	PP	SH	GW	S	%	+/-	TF	F%	Min	GP	G	A	Pts	PIM	PP	SH	GW	Min
2006-07	Atlanta	NHL	58	2	8	10	56	0	1	0	57	3.5	2	0	0.0	18:00	4	0	0	0	6	0	0	0	15:38
2007-08	Atlanta	NHL	79	2	5	7	85	0	0	0	37	5.4	-21	0	0.0	18:53	....	....	....	....	....	....	....	....	....
	NHL Totals		298	6	33	39	391	0	1	0	189	3.2		0	0.0	18:01	4	0	0	0	6	0	0	0	15:38

FAHEY, Jim

(FA-hee, JIHM)

Defense. Shoots right. 6', 205 lbs. Born, Boston, MA, May 11, 1979. San Jose's 9th choice, 212th overall, in 1998 Entry Draft.

Season	Club	League	GP	G	A	Pts	PIM	PP	SH	GW	S	%	+/-	TF	F%	Min	GP	G	A	Pts	PIM	PP	SH	GW	Min
1997-98	Catholic Memorial	High-MA	24	12	32	44	28	....	....	....	....	....	....	....	....	....	....	....	....	....	....	....	....	....	....
1998-99	Northeastern	H-East	32	5	13	18	34	....	....	....	....	....	....	....	....	....	....	....	....	....	....	....	....	....	....
99-2000	Northeastern	H-East	36	3	17	20	62	....	....	....	....	....	....	....	....	....	....	....	....	....	....	....	....	....	....
2000-01	Northeastern	H-East	36	4	23	27	48	....	....	....	....	....	....	....	....	....	....	....	....	....	....	....	....	....	....
2001-02	Northeastern	H-East	39	14	32	46	50	....	....	....	....	....	....	....	....	....	....	....	....	....	....	....	....	....	....
2002-03	San Jose	NHL	43	1	19	20	33	0	0	0	66	1.5	-3	1	100.0	18:20	....	....	....	....	....	....	....	....	....
	Cleveland Barons	AHL	25	3	14	17	42	....	....	....	....	....	....	....	....	....	....	....	....	....	....	....	....	....	....
2003-04	San Jose	NHL	15	0	2	2	18	0	0	0	19	0.0	-2	0	0.0	16:54	2	0	0	0	0	0	0	0	4:41
	Cleveland Barons	AHL	32	1	18	19	64	....	....	....	....	....	....	....	....	....	....	....	....	....	....	....	....	....	....
2004-05	Cleveland Barons	AHL	69	4	22	26	146	....	....	....	....	....	....	....	....	....	....	....	....	....	....	....	....	....	....
2005-06	San Jose	NHL	21	0	2	2	14	0	0	0	22	0.0	-11	0	0.0	12:39	....	....	....	....	....	....	....	....	....
2006-07	New Jersey	NHL	13	0	1	1	2	0	0	0	7	0.0	0	0	0.0	10:47	....	....	....	....	....	....	....	....	....
	Lowell Devils	AHL	28	0	9	9	37	....	....	....	....	....	....	....	....	....	....	....	....	....	....	....	....	....	....
2007-08	Rockford IceHogs	AHL	65	0	12	12	109	....	....	....	....	....	....	....	....	....	12	1	3	4	18	....	....	....	....
	NHL Totals		92	1	24	25	67	0	0	0	114	0.9		1	100.0	15:44	2	0	0	0	0	0	0	0	4:41

Hockey East Second All-Star Team (2001) • Hockey East First All-Star Team (2002)

• Spent majority of the 2005-06 season as a healthy reserve. Traded to **New Jersey** by **San Jose** with Alexander Korolyuk for Vladimir Malakhov and New Jersey's 1st round choice (later traded to St. Louis - St. Louis selected David Perron) in 2007 Entry Draft, October 1, 2006. Signed as a free agent by **Chicago**, July 27, 2007.

FATA, Drew

(FA-tuh, DROO) **PHX.**

Defense. Shoots left. 6'1", 220 lbs. Born, Sault Ste. Marie, Ont., July 28, 1983. Pittsburgh's 3rd choice, 86th overall, in 2001 Entry Draft.

Season	Club	League	GP	G	A	Pts	PIM	PP	SH	GW	S	%	+/-	TF	F%	Min	GP	G	A	Pts	PIM	PP	SH	GW	Min
1998-99	S.S. Marie AA	NOHA	46	4	16	20	55	....	....	....	....	....	....	....	....	....	....	....	....	....	....	....	....	....	....
99-2000	St. Mike's B's	OPJHL	49	9	18	27	144	....	....	....	....	....	....	....	....	....	....	....	....	....	....	....	....	....	....
2000-01	St. Michael's	OHL	58	5	15	20	134	....	....	....	....	....	....	....	....	....	18	1	3	4	26	....	....	....	....
2001-02	St. Michael's	OHL	67	7	21	28	175	....	....	....	....	....	....	....	....	....	15	1	9	10	38	....	....	....	....
2002-03	St. Michael's	OHL	35	6	13	19	66	....	....	....	....	....	....	....	....	....	....	....	....	....	....	....	....	....	....
	Kingston	OHL	34	2	17	19	64	....	....	....	....	....	....	....	....	....	....	....	....	....	....	....	....	....	....
2003-04	Wilkes-Barre	AHL	23	1	2	3	26	....	....	....	....	....	....	....	....	....	....	....	....	....	....	....	....	....	....
	Wheeling Nailers	ECHL	28	6	10	16	61	....	....	....	....	....	....	....	....	....	4	0	0	0	8	....	....	....	....
2004-05	Wilkes-Barre	AHL	32	1	1	2	88	....	....	....	....	....	....	....	....	....	5	0	1	1	37	....	....	....	....
	Wheeling Nailers	ECHL	22	0	1	1	55	....	....	....	....	....	....	....	....	....	....	....	....	....	....	....	....	....	....
2005-06	Wilkes-Barre	AHL	28	1	12	13	98	....	....	....	....	....	....	....	....	....	11	0	0	0	16	....	....	....	....
	Wheeling Nailers	ECHL	34	10	8	18	145	....	....	....	....	....	....	....	....	....	....	....	....	....	....	....	....	....	....
2006-07	Bridgeport	AHL	64	3	7	10	185	....	....	....	....	....	....	....	....	....	....	....	....	....	....	....	....	....	....
	NY Islanders	NHL	3	1	0	1	5	0	0	0	1	100.0	-2	0	0.0	10:17	1	0	0	0	0	0	0	0	6:04
2007-08	NY Islanders	NHL	5	0	1	1	4	0	0	0	4	0.0	-1	0	0.0	17:30	....	....	....	....	....	....	....	....	....
	Bridgeport	AHL	71	3	11	14	197	....	....	....	....	....	....	....	....	....	....	....	....	....	....	....	....	....	....
	NHL Totals		8	1	1	2	9	0	0	0	5	20.0		0	0.0	14:48	1	0	0	0	0	0	0	0	6:04

Signed as a free agent by **NY Islanders**, December 21, 2006. Signed as a free agent by **Phoenix**, July 2, 2008.

FATA, Rico

(FA-tuh, REE-koh)

Right wing. Shoots left. 6', 205 lbs. Born, Sault Ste. Marie, Ont., February 12, 1980. Calgary's 1st choice, 6th overall, in 1998 Entry Draft.

Season	Club	League	GP	G	A	Pts	PIM	PP	SH	GW	S	%	+/-	TF	F%	Min	GP	G	A	Pts	PIM	PP	SH	GW	Min
1994-95	Soo Legion	NOHA	51	52	51	103	....	....	....	....	....	....	....	....	....	....	....	....	....	....	....	....	....	....	....
1995-96	Sault Ste. Marie	OHL	62	11	15	26	52	....	....	....	....	....	....	....	....	....	4	0	0	0	0	....	....	....	....
1996-97	London Knights	OHL	59	19	34	53	76	....	....	....	....	....	....	....	....	....	....	....	....	....	....	....	....	....	....
1997-98	London Knights	OHL	64	43	33	76	110	....	....	....	....	....	....	....	....	....	16	9	5	14	*49	....	....	....	....
1998-99	Calgary	NHL	20	0	1	1	4	0	0	0	13	0.0	0	2	50.0	7:36	....	....	....	....	....	....	....	....	....
	London Knights	OHL	23	15	18	33	41	....	....	....	....	....	....	....	....	....	25	10	12	22	42	....	....	....	....
99-2000	Calgary	NHL	2	0	0	0	0	0	0	0	0	0.0	-1	0	0.0	10:06	....	....	....	....	....	....	....	....	....
	Saint John Flames	AHL	76	29	29	58	65	....	....	....	....	....	....	....	....	....	3	0	0	0	4	....	....	....	....
2000-01	Calgary	NHL	5	0	0	0	6	0	0	0	6	0.0	-3	0	0.0	9:25	....	....	....	....	....	....	....	....	....
	Saint John Flames	AHL	70	23	29	52	129	....	....	....	....	....	....	....	....	....	19	2	3	5	22	....	....	....	....
2001-02	NY Rangers	NHL	10	0	0	0	0	0	0	0	8	0.0	-2	55	47.3	8:31	....	....	....	....	....	....	....	....	....
	Hartford	AHL	61	35	36	71	36	....	....	....	....	....	....	....	....	....	10	2	5	7	4	....	....	....	....
2002-03	NY Rangers	NHL	36	2	4	6	6	0	0	0	30	6.7	-1	30	50.0	7:16	....	....	....	....	....	....	....	....	....
	Hartford	AHL	9	8	6	14	6	....	....	....	....	....	....	....	....	....	....	....	....	....	....	....	....	....	....
	Pittsburgh	NHL	27	5	8	13	10	0	0	0	49	10.2	-6	87	49.4	17:46	....	....	....	....	....	....	....	....	....
2003-04	Pittsburgh	NHL	73	16	18	34	54	6	2	1	163	9.8	-46	1205	47.1	17:58	....	....	....	....	....	....	....	....	....
2004-05	Asiago	Italy	35	18	20	38	36	....	....	....	....	....	....	....	....	....	9	7	5	12	10	....	....	....	....
2005-06	Pittsburgh	NHL	20	0	0	0	10	0	0	0	18	0.0	-5	204	41.7	13:06	....	....	....	....	....	....	....	....	....
	Wilkes-Barre	AHL	25	8	10	18	39	....	....	....	....	....	....	....	....	....	....	....	....	....	....	....	....	....	....
	Atlanta	NHL	6	0	1	1	4	0	0	0	1	0.0	-2	20	55.0	7:18	....	....	....	....	....	....	....	....	....
	Washington	NHL	21	3	3	6	8	1	0	0	31	9.7	3	3	33.3	8:11	....	....	....	....	....	....	....	....	....
2006-07	Washington	NHL	10	1	1	2	2	0	0	0	15	6.7	3	7	57.1	10:26	....	....	....	....	....	....	....	....	....
	Adler Mannheim	Germany	29	8	10	18	12	....	....	....	....	....	....	....	....	....	11	2	4	6	8	....	....	....	....
2007-08	Adler Mannheim	Germany	53	7	14	21	67	....	....	....	....	....	....	....	....	....	5	0	2	2	2	....	....	....	....
	NHL Totals		230	27	36	63	104	7	2	1	334	8.1		1613	46.7	12:47									

AHL All-Rookie Team (2000) • AHL Second All-Star Team (2002)

Claimed on waivers by **NY Rangers** from **Calgary**, October 3, 2001. Traded to **Pittsburgh** by **NY Rangers** with Joel Bouchard, Richard Lintner and Mikael Samuelsson for Mike Wilson, Alex Kovalev, Janne Laukkanen and Dan LaCouture, February 10, 2003. Signed as a free agent by **Asiago** (Italy), August 15, 2004. Claimed on waivers by **Atlanta** from **Pittsburgh**, January 31, 2006. Claimed on waivers by **Washington** from **Atlanta**, March 9, 2006. Signed as a free agent by **Mannheim**, November 8, 2006.

FEDOROV, Fedor

(FEH-duh-rahf, feh-DUHR) **N.J.**

Center. Shoots left. 6'4", 230 lbs. Born, Appatity, USSR, June 11, 1981. Vancouver's 2nd choice, 66th overall, in 2001 Entry Draft.

Season	Club	League	GP	G	A	Pts	PIM	PP	SH	GW	S	%	+/-	TF	F%	Min	GP	G	A	Pts	PIM	PP	SH	GW	Min
1997-98	Det. Caesars	MNHL	13	3	7	10	18	....	....	....	....	....	....	....	....	....	....	....	....	....	....	....	....	....	....
1998-99	Port Huron	UHL	42	2	5	7	20	....	....	....	....	....	....	....	....	....	....	....	....	....	....	....	....	....	....
99-2000	Windsor Spitfires	OHL	60	7	10	17	115	....	....	....	....	....	....	....	....	....	12	1	0	1	4	....	....	....	....
2000-01	Sudbury Wolves	OHL	67	33	45	78	88	....	....	....	....	....	....	....	....	....	12	4	6	10	36	....	....	....	....
2001-02	Manitoba Moose	AHL	8	2	1	3	6	....	....	....	....	....	....	....	....	....	....	....	....	....	....	....	....	....	....
	Columbia Inferno	ECHL	2	0	2	2	0	....	....	....	....	....	....	....	....	....	....	....	....	....	....	....	....	....	....
2002-03	Vancouver	NHL	7	0	1	1	4	0	0	0	2	0.0	0	26	46.2	9:10	....	....	....	....	....	....	....	....	....
	Manitoba Moose	AHL	50	10	13	23	61	....	....	....	....	....	....	....	....	....	3	1	2	3	0	....	....	....	....
2003-04	Vancouver	NHL	8	0	1	1	4	0	0	0	10	0.0	0	4	50.0	10:59	....	....	....	....	....	....	....	....	....
	Manitoba Moose	AHL	58	23	16	39	52	....	....	....	....	....	....	....	....	....	....	....	....	....	....	....	....	....	....
2004-05	Spartak Moscow	Russia	19	4	7	11	52	....	....	....	....	....	....	....	....	....	....	....	....	....	....	....	....	....	....
	Magnitogorsk	Russia	10	3	0	3	22	....	....	....	....	....	....	....	....	....	5	2	0	2	30	....	....	....	....
2005-06	NY Rangers	NHL	3	0	0	0	6	0	0	0	2	0.0	0	1	0.0	9:49	....	....	....	....	....	....	....	....	....
	Hartford	AHL	38	2	15	17	80	....	....	....	....	....	....	....	....	....	....	....	....	....	....	....	....	....	....
	Syracuse Crunch	AHL	12	2	3	5	22	....	....	....	....	....	....	....	....	....	3	0	0	0	2	....	....	....	....

			Regular Season														Playoffs								
Season	Club	League	GP	G	A	Pts	PIM	PP	SH	GW	S	%	+/-	TF	F%	Min	GP	G	A	Pts	PIM	PP	SH	GW	Min
2006-07	Yaroslavl	Russia	20	4	3	7	32																		
	Malmo	Sweden	8	2	4	6	51																		
	Malmo	Sweden-Q	10	4	10	14	55																		
2007-08	Dynamo Moscow	Russia	49	12	14	26	119										9	0	3	3	24				
	NHL Totals		**18**	**0**	**2**	**2**	**14**	**0**	**0**	**0**	**14**	**0.0**		**31**	**45.2**	**10:05**									

• Re-entered NHL Entry Draft. Originally Tampa Bay's 7th choice, 182nd overall, in 1999 Entry Draft.

Signed as an underage free agent by **Detroit** (IHL), August 5, 1998. Released by **Detroit** (IHL), September 30, 1998. Signed as an underage free agent by **Port Huron** (UHL), October 1, 1998. • Missed majority of 2001-02 season recovering from eye injury suffered in game vs. Macon (ECHL), November 17, 2001. Signed as a free agent by **Spartak Moscow** (Russia), November 15, 2004. Signed as a free agent by **Magnitogorsk** (Russia), February 16, 2005. Traded to **NY Rangers** by **Vancouver** for Jozef Balej and future considerations, October 7, 2005. Loaned to **Syracuse** (AHL) by **NY Rangers** (Hartford-AHL) for cash, March 11, 2006. Signed as a free agent by **Yaroslavl** (Russia), July 25, 2006. Signed as a free agent by **Malmo** (Sweden), January 30, 2007. Signed as a free agent by **New Jersey**, July 21, 2008.

FEDOROV, Sergei (FEH-duh-rahf, SAIR-gay) WSH.

Center. Shoots left. 6'2", 207 lbs. Born, Pskov, USSR, December 13, 1969. Detroit's 4th choice, 74th overall, in 1989 Entry Draft.

Season	Club	League	GP	G	A	Pts	PIM	PP	SH	GW	S	%	+/-	TF	F%	Min	GP	G	A	Pts	PIM	PP	SH	GW	Min
1985-86	Dynamo Minsk	USSR-2	15	6	1	7	10																		
1986-87	CSKA Moscow	USSR	29	6	6	12	12																		
1987-88	CSKA Moscow	USSR	48	7	9	16	20																		
1988-89	CSKA Moscow	USSR	44	9	8	17	35																		
1989-90	CSKA Moscow	USSR	48	19	10	29	22																		
	CSKA Moscow	Super-S	5	2	2	4	11																		
1990-91	**Detroit**	**NHL**	**77**	**31**	**48**	**79**	**66**	**11**	**3**	**5**	**259**	**12.0**	**11**				**7**	**1**	**5**	**6**	**4**	**0**	**0**	**1**	
1991-92	**Detroit**	**NHL**	**80**	**32**	**54**	**86**	**72**	**7**	**2**	**5**	**249**	**12.9**	**26**				**11**	**5**	**5**	**10**	**8**	**1**	**2**	**1**	
1992-93	**Detroit**	**NHL**	**73**	**34**	**53**	**87**	**72**	**13**	**4**	**3**	**217**	**15.7**	**33**				**7**	**3**	**6**	**9**	**23**	**1**	**1**	**0**	
1993-94	**Detroit**	**NHL**	**82**	**56**	**64**	**120**	**34**	**13**	**4**	**10**	**337**	**16.6**	**48**				**7**	**1**	**7**	**8**	**6**	**0**	**0**	**0**	
1994-95	**Detroit**	**NHL**	**42**	**20**	**30**	**50**	**24**	**7**	**3**	**5**	**147**	**13.6**	**6**				**17**	**7**	***17**	***24**	**6**	**3**	**0**	**0**	
1995-96	**Detroit**	**NHL**	**78**	**39**	**68**	**107**	**48**	**11**	**3**	**11**	**306**	**12.7**	**49**				**19**	**2**	***18**	**20**	**10**	**0**	**0**	**2**	
1996-97 ♦	**Detroit**	**NHL**	**74**	**30**	**33**	**63**	**30**	**9**	**2**	**4**	**273**	**11.0**	**29**				**20**	**8**	**12**	**20**	**12**	**3**	**0**	**4**	
1997-98	Russia	Olympics	6	1	5	6	8																		
	♦ Detroit	**NHL**	**21**	**6**	**11**	**17**	**25**	**2**	**0**	**2**	**68**	**8.8**	**10**				**22**	***10**	**10**	**20**	**12**	**2**	**1**	**1**	
1998-99	**Detroit**	**NHL**	**77**	**26**	**37**	**63**	**66**	**6**	**2**	**3**	**224**	**11.6**	**9**	**1414**	**51.7**	**19:21**	**10**	**1**	**8**	**9**	**8**	**0**	**0**	**0**	**19:54**
99-2000	**Detroit**	**NHL**	**68**	**27**	**35**	**62**	**22**	**4**	**4**	**7**	**263**	**10.3**	**8**	**1274**	**53.8**	**20:05**	**9**	**4**	**4**	**8**	**4**	**2**	**0**	**1**	**20:48**
2000-01	**Detroit**	**NHL**	**75**	**32**	**37**	**69**	**40**	**14**	**2**	**7**	**268**	**11.9**	**12**	**1601**	**55.8**	**21:05**	**6**	**2**	**5**	**7**	**0**	**1**	**0**	**1**	**22:19**
2001-02 ♦	**Detroit**	**NHL**	**81**	**31**	**37**	**68**	**36**	**10**	**0**	**6**	**256**	**12.1**	**20**	**1160**	**51.7**	**19:33**	**23**	**5**	**14**	**19**	**20**	**2**	**1**	**0**	**22:20**
	Russia	Olympics	6	2	2	4	4																		
2002-03	**Detroit**	**NHL**	**80**	**36**	**47**	**83**	**52**	**10**	**2**	**11**	**281**	**12.8**	**15**	**1580**	**53.4**	**21:11**	**4**	**1**	**2**	**3**	**0**	**0**	**0**	**0**	**22:07**
2003-04	**Anaheim**	**NHL**	**80**	**31**	**34**	**65**	**42**	**9**	**2**	**6**	**268**	**11.6**	**–5**	**1558**	**56.6**	**21:05**									
2004-05			DID NOT PLAY																						
2005-06	**Anaheim**	**NHL**	**5**	**0**	**1**	**1**	**2**	**0**	**0**	**0**	**18**	**0.0**	**–1**	**80**	**55.0**	**20:17**									
	Columbus	**NHL**	**62**	**12**	**31**	**43**	**64**	**3**	**1**	**2**	**142**	**8.5**	**–1**	**1169**	**51.8**	**21:06**									
2006-07	**Columbus**	**NHL**	**73**	**18**	**24**	**42**	**56**	**7**	**2**	**2**	**163**	**11.0**	**–7**	**680**	**52.4**	**19:56**									
2007-08	**Columbus**	**NHL**	**50**	**9**	**19**	**28**	**30**	**5**	**0**	**1**	**94**	**9.6**	**–3**	**685**	**54.5**	**17:28**									
	Washington	**NHL**	**18**	**2**	**11**	**13**	**8**	**1**	**0**	**1**	**34**	**5.9**	**–2**	**326**	**58.0**	**18:16**	**7**	**1**	**4**	**5**	**8**	**0**	**0**	**0**	**21:38**
	NHL Totals		**1196**	**472**	**674**	**1146**	**789**	**142**	**36**	**91**	**3867**	**12.2**		**11527**	**53.8**	**20:08**	**169**	**51**	**117**	**168**	**121**	**15**	**5**	**11**	**21:35**

NHL All-Rookie Team (1991) • NHL First All-Star Team (1994) • Frank J. Selke Trophy (1994, 1996) • Lester B. Pearson Award (1994) • Hart Memorial Trophy (1994)

Played in NHL All-Star Game (1992, 1994, 1996, 2001, 2002, 2003)

• Missed majority of 1997-98 season after failing to come to contract terms with **Detroit**. Signed as a free agent by **Anaheim**, July 19, 2003. Traded to **Columbus** by **Anaheim** with Anaheim's 5th round choice (Maxime Frechette) in 2006 Entry Draft for Tyler Wright and Francois Beauchemin, November 15, 2005. Traded to **Washington** by **Columbus** for Ted Ruth, February 26, 2008.

FEDORUK, Todd (FEH-duh-ruhk, TAWD) PHX.

Left wing. Shoots left. 6'2", 240 lbs. Born, Redwater, Alta., February 13, 1979. Philadelphia's 6th choice, 164th overall, in 1997 Entry Draft.

Season	Club	League	GP	G	A	Pts	PIM	PP	SH	GW	S	%	+/-	TF	F%	Min	GP	G	A	Pts	PIM	PP	SH	GW	Min
1994-95	Ft. Saskatchewan	AMHL	STATISTICS NOT AVAILABLE																						
1995-96	Kelowna Rockets	WHL	44	1	1	2	83										4	0	0	0	6				
1996-97	Kelowna Rockets	WHL	31	1	5	6	87										6	0	0	0	13				
1997-98	Kelowna Rockets	WHL	31	3	5	8	120																		
	Regina Pats	WHL	21	4	3	7	80										9	1	2	3	23				
1998-99	Regina Pats	WHL	39	12	12	24	107																		
	Prince Albert	WHL	28	6	4	10	75										13	1	6	7	49				
99-2000	Trenton Titans	ECHL	18	2	5	7	118																		
	Philadelphia	AHL	19	1	2	3	40										5	0	1	1	2				
2000-01	**Philadelphia**	**NHL**	**53**	**5**	**5**	**10**	**109**	**0**	**0**	**0**	**28**	**17.9**	**0**	**0**	**0.0**	**7:02**	**2**	**0**	**0**	**0**	**20**	**0**	**0**	**0**	**5:57**
	Philadelphia	AHL	14	0	1	1	49																		
2001-02	**Philadelphia**	**NHL**	**55**	**3**	**4**	**7**	**141**	**0**	**0**	**0**	**21**	**14.3**	**–2**	**5**	**0.0**	**6:21**	**3**	**0**	**0**	**0**	**0**	**0**	**0**	**0**	**2:46**
	Philadelphia	AHL	7	0	1	1	54																		
2002-03	**Philadelphia**	**NHL**	**63**	**1**	**5**	**6**	**105**	**0**	**0**	**0**	**33**	**3.0**	**1**	**1**	**0.0**	**6:30**	**1**	**0**	**0**	**0**	**0**	**0**	**0**	**0**	**4:52**
2003-04	**Philadelphia**	**NHL**	**49**	**1**	**4**	**5**	**136**	**0**	**0**	**1**	**33**	**3.0**	**–4**	**0**	**0.0**	**6:47**	**1**	**0**	**0**	**0**	**2**	**0**	**0**	**0**	**6:42**
	Philadelphia	AHL	2	0	2	2	2																		
2004-05	Philadelphia	AHL	42	4	12	16	142										16	2	2	4	33				
2005-06	**Anaheim**	**NHL**	**76**	**4**	**19**	**23**	**174**	**0**	**0**	**1**	**69**	**5.8**	**6**	**8**	**37.5**	**8:24**	**12**	**0**	**0**	**0**	**16**	**0**	**0**	**0**	**8:19**
2006-07	**Anaheim**	**NHL**	**10**	**0**	**3**	**3**	**36**	**0**	**0**	**0**	**2**	**0.0**	**2**	**1**	**0.0**	**7:30**									
	Philadelphia	**NHL**	**48**	**3**	**8**	**11**	**84**	**0**	**0**	**0**	**28**	**10.7**	**–11**	**2**	**0.0**	**9:03**									
2007-08	**Dallas**	**NHL**	**11**	**0**	**2**	**2**	**33**	**0**	**0**	**0**	**6**	**0.0**	**2**	**0**	**0.0**	**6:50**									
	Minnesota	**NHL**	**58**	**6**	**5**	**11**	**106**	**2**	**0**	**0**	**51**	**11.8**	**0**	**4**	**0.0**	**10:59**	**6**	**1**	**1**	**2**	**16**	**1**	**0**	**0**	**13:38**
	NHL Totals		**423**	**23**	**55**	**78**	**924**	**2**	**0**	**2**	**271**	**8.5**		**21**	**14.3**	**7:51**	**25**	**1**	**1**	**2**	**54**	**1**	**0**	**0**	**8:32**

Traded to **Anaheim** by **Philadelphia** for Anaheim's 2nd round choice (later traded to Phoenix - Phoenix selected Pier-Olivier Pelletier) in 2005 Entry Draft, July 29, 2005. Traded to **Philadelphia** by **Anaheim** for Philadelphia's 4th round choice (Justin Vaive) in 2007 Entry Draft, November 13, 2006. Signed as a free agent by **Dallas**, July 9, 2007. Claimed on waivers by **Minnesota** from **Dallas**, November 22, 2007. Signed as a free agent by **Phoenix**, July 1, 2008.

FEDOTENKO, Ruslan (feh-doh-TEHN-koh, roos-LAHN) PIT.

Left wing. Shoots left. 6'2", 195 lbs. Born, Kiev, USSR, January 18, 1979.

Season	Club	League	GP	G	A	Pts	PIM	PP	SH	GW	S	%	+/-	TF	F%	Min	GP	G	A	Pts	PIM	PP	SH	GW	Min
1995-96	Kiev 2	EEHL	33	9	11	20	12																		
	Sokol Kiev	CIS	2	0	0	0	0																		
1996-97	TPS Turku U18	Fin-U18	3	3	2	5	2																		
	TPS Turku Jr.	Fin-Jr.	11	1	1	2	2																		
	Kiekko-67 Turku	Finland-2	22	4	3	7	16																		
	Kiekko Turku	Finland-3															3	1	0	1	2				
1997-98	Melfort Mustangs	SJHL	68	35	31	66	55																		
1998-99	Sioux City	USHL	55	43	34	77	139										5	5	1	6	9				
99-2000	Trenton Titans	ECHL	8	5	3	8	9																		
	Philadelphia	AHL	67	16	34	50	42										2	0	0	0	0				
2000-01	**Philadelphia**	**NHL**	**74**	**16**	**20**	**36**	**72**	**3**	**0**	**4**	**119**	**13.4**	**8**	**7**	**71.4**	**14:38**	**6**	**0**	**1**	**1**	**4**	**0**	**0**	**0**	**11:18**
	Philadelphia	AHL	8	1	0	1	8																		
2001-02	**Philadelphia**	**NHL**	**78**	**17**	**9**	**26**	**43**	**0**	**1**	**3**	**121**	**14.0**	**15**	**41**	**43.9**	**13:56**	**5**	**1**	**0**	**1**	**2**	**0**	**0**	**1**	**14:11**
	Ukraine	Olympics	1	1	0	1	4																		
2002-03	**Tampa Bay**	**NHL**	**76**	**19**	**13**	**32**	**44**	**6**	**0**	**6**	**114**	**16.7**	**–7**	**90**	**48.9**	**16:01**	**11**	**0**	**1**	**1**	**2**	**0**	**0**	**0**	**13:58**
2003-04 ♦	**Tampa Bay**	**NHL**	**77**	**17**	**22**	**39**	**30**	**0**	**0**	**3**	**116**	**14.7**	**14**	**58**	**55.2**	**14:39**	**22**	**12**	**2**	**14**	**14**	**5**	**0**	**3**	**16:40**
2004-05			DID NOT PLAY																						
2005-06	**Tampa Bay**	**NHL**	**80**	**26**	**15**	**41**	**44**	**4**	**0**	**6**	**164**	**15.9**	**–4**	**28**	**42.9**	**15:21**	**5**	**0**	**0**	**0**	**20**	**0**	**0**	**0**	**14:38**
2006-07	**Tampa Bay**	**NHL**	**80**	**12**	**20**	**32**	**52**	**2**	**0**	**1**	**154**	**7.8**	**–3**	**8**	**25.0**	**16:15**	**4**	**0**	**0**	**0**	**4**	**0**	**0**	**0**	**17:27**
2007-08	**NY Islanders**	**NHL**	**67**	**16**	**17**	**33**	**40**	**8**	**0**	**2**	**121**	**13.2**	**–9**	**28**	**39.3**	**16:42**									
	NHL Totals		**532**	**123**	**116**	**239**	**325**	**23**	**1**	**25**	**909**	**13.5**		**260**	**47.7**	**15:20**	**53**	**13**	**4**	**17**	**46**	**5**	**0**	**4**	**15:08**

Signed as a free agent by **Philadelphia**, August 3, 1999. Traded to **Tampa Bay** by **Philadelphia** with Tampa Bay's 2nd round choice (previously acquired, later traded to Dallas – Dallas selected Tobias Stephan) in 2002 Entry Draft and Phoenix's 2nd round choice (previously acquired, later traded to San Jose – San Jose selected Dan Spang) in 2002 Entry Draft for Tampa Bay's 1st round choice (Joni Pitkanen) in 2002 Entry Draft, June 21, 2002. Signed as a free agent by **NY Islanders**, July 4, 2007. Signed as a free agent by **Pittsburgh**, July 3, 2008.

			Regular Season													Playoffs								
Season	Club	League	GP	G	A	Pts	PIM	PP	SH	GW	S	%	+/-	TF	F%	Min	GP	G	A	Pts	PIM	PP	SH	GW	Min

FEHR, Eric

(FAIR, AIR-ihk) **WSH.**

Right wing. Shoots right. 6'4", 212 lbs. Born, Winkler, Man., September 7, 1985. Washington's 1st choice, 18th overall, in 2003 Entry Draft.

Season	Club	League	GP	G	A	Pts	PIM	PP	SH	GW	S	%	+/-	TF	F%	Min	GP	G	A	Pts	PIM	PP	SH	GW	Min
2000-01	Pembina Valley	MMMHL	36	45	13	58	30	....	....	....	....	....	....	....	....	....	....	....	....	....	....	....	....	....	....
	Brandon	WHL	4	0	0	0	0	....	....	....	....	....	....	....	....	....	....	....	....	....	....	....	....	....	....
2001-02	Brandon	WHL	63	11	16	27	29	....	....	....	....	....	....	....	....	....	12	1	1	2	0	....	....	....	....
2002-03	Brandon	WHL	70	26	29	55	76	....	....	....	....	....	....	....	....	....	17	4	8	12	26	....	....	....	....
2003-04	Brandon	WHL	71	50	34	84	129	....	....	....	....	....	....	....	....	....	7	5	0	5	16	....	....	....	....
2004-05	Brandon	WHL	71	*59	52	*111	91	....	....	....	....	....	....	....	....	....	24	16	16	*32	47	....	....	....	....
2005-06	**Washington**	**NHL**	**11**	**0**	**0**	**0**	**2**	**0**	**0**	**0**	**10**	**0.0**	**0**	**4**	**25.0**	**5:45**	....	....	....	....	....	....	....	....	....
	Hershey Bears	AHL	70	25	28	53	70	....	....	....	....	....	....	....	....	....	19	8	3	11	8	....	....	....	....
2006-07	**Washington**	**NHL**	**14**	**2**	**1**	**3**	**8**	**0**	**0**	**1**	**25**	**8.0**	**3**	**6**	**16.7**	**10:43**	....	....	....	....	....	....	....	....	....
	Hershey Bears	AHL	40	22	19	41	63	....	....	....	....	....	....	....	....	....	....	....	....	....	....	....	....	....	....
2007-08	**Washington**	**NHL**	**23**	**1**	**5**	**6**	**6**	**0**	**0**	**0**	**40**	**2.5**	**4**	**2**	**0.0**	**10:31**	**5**	**1**	**0**	**1**	**0**	**0**	**0**	**0**	**9:41**
	Hershey Bears	AHL	11	3	4	7	4	....	....	....	....	....	....	....	....	....	2	1	3	4	2	....	....	....	....
	NHL Totals		**48**	**3**	**6**	**9**	**16**	**0**	**0**	**1**	**75**	**4.0**		**12**	**16.7**	**9:29**	**5**	**1**	**0**	**1**	**0**	**0**	**0**	**0**	**9:41**

WHL East First All-Star Team (2005) • WHL Player of the Year (2005)

FERENCE, Andrew

(FAIR-ehns, AN-droo) **BOS.**

Defense. Shoots left. 5'11", 189 lbs. Born, Edmonton, Alta., March 17, 1979. Pittsburgh's 8th choice, 208th overall, in 1997 Entry Draft.

Season	Club	League	GP	G	A	Pts	PIM	PP	SH	GW	S	%	+/-	TF	F%	Min	GP	G	A	Pts	PIM	PP	SH	GW	Min
1994-95	Sherwood Park	AMHL	31	4	14	18	74	....	....	....	....	....	....	....	....	....	....	....	....	....	....	....	....	....	....
	Portland	WHL	2	0	0	0	4	....	....	....	....	....	....	....	....	....	....	....	....	....	....	....	....	....	....
1995-96	Portland	WHL	72	9	31	40	159	....	....	....	....	....	....	....	....	....	7	1	3	4	12	....	....	....	....
1996-97	Portland	WHL	72	12	32	44	163	....	....	....	....	....	....	....	....	....	6	1	2	3	12	....	....	....	....
1997-98	Portland	WHL	72	11	57	68	142	....	....	....	....	....	....	....	....	....	16	2	18	20	28	....	....	....	....
1998-99	Portland	WHL	40	11	21	32	104	....	....	....	....	....	....	....	....	....	4	1	4	5	10	....	....	....	....
	Kansas City	IHL	5	1	2	3	4	....	....	....	....	....	....	....	....	....	3	0	0	0	9	....	....	....	....
99-2000	**Pittsburgh**	**NHL**	**30**	**2**	**4**	**6**	**20**	**0**	**0**	**1**	**26**	**7.7**	**3**	**0**	**0.0**	**16:19**	....	....	....	....	....	....	....	....	....
	Wilkes-Barre	AHL	44	8	20	28	58	....	....	....	....	....	....	....	....	....	....	....	....	....	....	....	....	....	....
2000-01	**Pittsburgh**	**NHL**	**36**	**4**	**11**	**15**	**28**	**1**	**0**	**1**	**47**	**8.5**	**6**	**0**	**0.0**	**18:51**	**18**	**3**	**7**	**10**	**16**	**1**	**0**	**1**	**22:02**
	Wilkes-Barre	AHL	43	6	18	24	95	....	....	....	....	....	....	....	....	....	3	1	0	1	12	....	....	....	....
2001-02	**Pittsburgh**	**NHL**	**75**	**4**	**7**	**11**	**73**	**1**	**0**	**0**	**82**	**4.9**	**–12**	**2**	**0.0**	**18:34**	....	....	....	....	....	....	....	....	....
2002-03	**Pittsburgh**	**NHL**	**22**	**1**	**3**	**4**	**36**	**1**	**0**	**0**	**22**	**4.5**	**–16**	**1**	**100.0**	**19:33**	....	....	....	....	....	....	....	....	....
	Wilkes-Barre	AHL	1	0	0	0	2	....	....	....	....	....	....	....	....	....	....	....	....	....	....	....	....	....	....
	Calgary	**NHL**	**16**	**0**	**4**	**4**	**6**	**0**	**0**	**0**	**17**	**0.0**	**1**	**0**	**0.0**	**17:38**	....	....	....	....	....	....	....	....	....
2003-04	**Calgary**	**NHL**	**72**	**4**	**12**	**16**	**53**	**1**	**0**	**0**	**86**	**4.7**	**5**	**0**	**0.0**	**18:40**	**26**	**0**	**3**	**3**	**25**	**0**	**0**	**0**	**24:13**
2004-05	C. Budejovice	CzRep-2	19	5	6	11	45	....	....	....	....	....	....	....	....	....	12	2	7	9	10	....	....	....	....
2005-06	**Calgary**	**NHL**	**82**	**4**	**27**	**31**	**85**	**2**	**0**	**0**	**111**	**3.6**	**–12**	**1**	**0.0**	**20:08**	**7**	**0**	**4**	**4**	**12**	**0**	**0**	**0**	**23:09**
2006-07	**Calgary**	**NHL**	**54**	**2**	**10**	**12**	**66**	**1**	**0**	**0**	**51**	**3.9**	**7**	**3**	**33.3**	**18:29**	....	....	....	....	....	....	....	....	....
	Boston	**NHL**	**26**	**1**	**2**	**3**	**31**	**0**	**0**	**0**	**29**	**3.4**	**–2**	**0**	**0.0**	**22:22**	....	....	....	....	....	....	....	....	....
2007-08	**Boston**	**NHL**	**59**	**1**	**14**	**15**	**50**	**0**	**0**	**0**	**71**	**1.4**	**–14**	**1**	**100.0**	**22:15**	**7**	**0**	**4**	**4**	**6**	**0**	**0**	**0**	**21:39**
	NHL Totals		**472**	**23**	**94**	**117**	**448**	**7**	**0**	**2**	**542**	**4.2**		**8**	**37.5**	**19:24**	**58**	**3**	**18**	**21**	**59**	**1**	**0**	**1**	**23:06**

WHL West First All-Star Team (1998) • WHL West Second All-Star Team (1999)

• Missed majority of 2002-03 season recovering from groin (November 18, 2002 vs. Montreal) and ankle (March 20, 2003 vs. Los Angeles) injuries. Traded to **Calgary** by **Pittsburgh** for Calgary's 3rd round choice (Brian Gifford) in 2004 Entry Draft, February 9, 2003. Signed as a free agent by **Ceske Budejovice** (CzRep-2), December 1, 2004. Traded to **Boston** by **Calgary** with Chuck Kobasew for Brad Stuart, Wayne Primeau and Washington's 4th round choice (previously acquired, Calgary selected T.J. Brodie) in 2008 Entry Draft, February 10, 2007.

FERENCE, Brad

(FAIR-ehns, BRAD)

Defense. Shoots right. 6'3", 218 lbs. Born, Calgary, Alta., April 2, 1979. Vancouver's 1st choice, 10th overall, in 1997 Entry Draft.

Season	Club	League	GP	G	A	Pts	PIM	PP	SH	GW	S	%	+/-	TF	F%	Min	GP	G	A	Pts	PIM	PP	SH	GW	Min
1994-95	Calgary Royals	ABHL	60	19	47	66	220	....	....	....	....	....	....	....	....	....	....	....	....	....	....	....	....	....	....
1995-96	Calgary Royals	ABHL	22	7	21	28	140	....	....	....	....	....	....	....	....	....	....	....	....	....	....	....	....	....	....
	Spokane Chiefs	WHL	5	0	2	2	18	....	....	....	....	....	....	....	....	....	....	....	....	....	....	....	....	....	....
1996-97	Spokane Chiefs	WHL	67	6	20	26	324	....	....	....	....	....	....	....	....	....	9	0	4	4	21	....	....	....	....
1997-98	Spokane Chiefs	WHL	54	9	30	39	213	....	....	....	....	....	....	....	....	....	18	0	7	7	59	....	....	....	....
1998-99	Spokane Chiefs	WHL	31	3	22	25	125	....	....	....	....	....	....	....	....	....	....	....	....	....	....	....	....	....	....
	Tri-City	WHL	20	6	15	21	116	....	....	....	....	....	....	....	....	....	12	1	9	10	63	....	....	....	....
99-2000	**Florida**	**NHL**	**13**	**0**	**2**	**2**	**46**	**0**	**0**	**0**	**10**	**0.0**	**2**	**0**	**0.0**	**13:40**	....	....	....	....	....	....	....	....	....
	Louisville Panthers	AHL	58	2	7	9	231	....	....	....	....	....	....	....	....	....	2	0	0	0	2	....	....	....	....
2000-01	**Florida**	**NHL**	**14**	**0**	**1**	**1**	**14**	**0**	**0**	**0**	**5**	**0.0**	**–10**	**0**	**0.0**	**13:03**	....	....	....	....	....	....	....	....	....
	Louisville Panthers	AHL	52	3	21	24	200	....	....	....	....	....	....	....	....	....	....	....	....	....	....	....	....	....	....
2001-02	**Florida**	**NHL**	**80**	**2**	**15**	**17**	**254**	**0**	**0**	**0**	**65**	**3.1**	**–13**	**1**	**0.0**	**19:44**	....	....	....	....	....	....	....	....	....
2002-03	**Florida**	**NHL**	**60**	**2**	**6**	**8**	**118**	**0**	**0**	**0**	**41**	**4.9**	**2**	**0**	**0.0**	**15:58**	....	....	....	....	....	....	....	....	....
	Phoenix	**NHL**	**15**	**0**	**1**	**1**	**28**	**0**	**0**	**0**	**8**	**0.0**	**–5**	**0**	**0.0**	**16:33**	....	....	....	....	....	....	....	....	....
2003-04	**Phoenix**	**NHL**	**63**	**0**	**5**	**5**	**103**	**0**	**0**	**0**	**39**	**0.0**	**–19**	**0**	**0.0**	**14:03**	....	....	....	....	....	....	....	....	....
2004-05	Morzine-Avoriaz	France	17	2	10	12	138	....	....	....	....	....	....	....	....	....	4	1	4	5	10	....	....	....	....
2005-06	San Antonio	AHL	19	2	9	11	39	....	....	....	....	....	....	....	....	....	....	....	....	....	....	....	....	....	....
	Albany River Rats	AHL	43	3	8	11	96	....	....	....	....	....	....	....	....	....	....	....	....	....	....	....	....	....	....
2006-07	**Calgary**	**NHL**	**5**	**0**	**0**	**0**	**2**	**0**	**0**	**0**	**1**	**0.0**	**–1**	**0**	**0.0**	**11:46**	....	....	....	....	....	....	....	....	....
	Omaha	AHL	73	3	23	26	210	....	....	....	....	....	....	....	....	....	6	0	0	0	6	....	....	....	....
2007-08	Grand Rapids	AHL	32	1	1	2	78	....	....	....	....	....	....	....	....	....	....	....	....	....	....	....	....	....	....
	NHL Totals		**250**	**4**	**30**	**34**	**565**	**0**	**0**	**0**	**169**	**2.4**		**1**	**0.0**	**16:21**	....	....	....	....	....	....	....	....	....

Memorial Cup Tournament All-Star Team (1998)

Traded to **Florida** by **Vancouver** with Pavel Bure, Bret Hedican and Vancouver's 3rd round choice (Robert Fried) in 2000 Entry Draft for Ed Jovanovski, Dave Gagner, Mike Brown, Kevin Weekes and Florida's 1st round choice (Nathan Smith) in 2000 Entry Draft, January 17, 1999. Traded to **Phoenix** by **Florida** for Darcy Hordichuk and Phoenix's 2nd round choice (later traded to Tampa Bay – Tampa Bay selected Matt Smaby) in 2003 Entry Draft, March 8, 2003. Signed as a free agent by **Morzine-Avoriaz** (France), October 28, 2004. Traded to **New Jersey** by **Phoenix** for Pascal Rheaume, Ray Schultz and Steven Spencer, November 25, 2005. Signed as a free agent by **Calgary**, July 27, 2006. Signed as a free agent by **Detroit**, July 3, 2007.

FERLAND, Jonathan

(fair-LAWN, JAWN-ah-thuhn)

Right wing. Shoots right. 6'2", 212 lbs. Born, Ste-Marie-de-Beauce, Que., February 9, 1983. Montreal's 5th choice, 212th overall, in 2002 Entry Draft.

Season	Club	League	GP	G	A	Pts	PIM	PP	SH	GW	S	%	+/-	TF	F%	Min	GP	G	A	Pts	PIM	PP	SH	GW	Min
1998-99	Laval-Laurentides	QAAA	42	18	17	35	50	....	....	....	....	....	....	....	....	....	....	....	....	....	....	....	....	....	....
99-2000	Moncton Wildcats	QMJHL	52	3	6	9	21	....	....	....	....	....	....	....	....	....	11	0	1	1	0	....	....	....	....
2000-01	Acadie-Bathurst	QMJHL	70	17	11	28	135	....	....	....	....	....	....	....	....	....	13	0	4	4	47	....	....	....	....
2001-02	Acadie-Bathurst	QMJHL	55	28	46	74	104	....	....	....	....	....	....	....	....	....	16	5	12	17	16	....	....	....	....
2002-03	Acadie-Bathurst	QMJHL	68	45	44	89	94	....	....	....	....	....	....	....	....	....	11	4	5	9	16	....	....	....	....
2003-04	Hamilton	AHL	70	5	10	15	43	....	....	....	....	....	....	....	....	....	10	0	0	0	6	....	....	....	....
2004-05	Hamilton	AHL	62	6	8	14	24	....	....	....	....	....	....	....	....	....	4	0	0	0	4	....	....	....	....
2005-06	**Montreal**	**NHL**	**7**	**1**	**0**	**1**	**2**	**0**	**0**	**0**	**9**	**11.1**	**–2**	**2**	**0.0**	**6:37**	....	....	....	....	....	....	....	....	....
	Hamilton	AHL	39	7	8	15	65	....	....	....	....	....	....	....	....	....	....	....	....	....	....	....	....	....	....
2006-07	Hamilton	AHL	78	23	14	37	87	....	....	....	....	....	....	....	....	....	22	3	6	9	19	....	....	....	....
2007-08	Hamilton	AHL	80	16	24	40	97	....	....	....	....	....	....	....	....	....	....	....	....	....	....	....	....	....	....
	NHL Totals		**7**	**1**	**0**	**1**	**2**	**0**	**0**	**0**	**9**	**11.1**		**2**	**0.0**	**6:37**	....	....	....	....	....	....	....	....	....

FIDDLER, Vernon

(FIHD-luhr, VUHR-nuhn) **NSH.**

Center. Shoots left. 5'11", 204 lbs. Born, Edmonton, Alta., May 9, 1980.

Season	Club	League	GP	G	A	Pts	PIM	PP	SH	GW	S	%	+/-	TF	F%	Min	GP	G	A	Pts	PIM	PP	SH	GW	Min
1997-98	Kelowna Rockets	WHL	65	10	11	21	31	....	....	....	....	....	....	....	....	....	7	0	1	1	4	....	....	....	....
1998-99	Kelowna Rockets	WHL	68	22	21	43	82	....	....	....	....	....	....	....	....	....	6	2	0	2	8	....	....	....	....
99-2000	Kelowna Rockets	WHL	64	20	28	48	60	....	....	....	....	....	....	....	....	....	5	1	3	4	4	....	....	....	....
2000-01	Kelowna Rockets	WHL	3	0	2	2	0	....	....	....	....	....	....	....	....	....	....	....	....	....	....	....	....	....	....
	Medicine Hat	WHL	67	33	38	71	100	....	....	....	....	....	....	....	....	....	....	....	....	....	....	....	....	....	....
	Arkansas	ECHL	3	0	1	1	2	....	....	....	....	....	....	....	....	....	5	3	0	3	5	....	....	....	....
2001-02	Norfolk Admirals	AHL	38	8	5	13	28	....	....	....	....	....	....	....	....	....	4	1	3	4	2	....	....	....	....
	Roanoke Express	ECHL	44	27	28	55	71	....	....	....	....	....	....	....	....	....	....	....	....	....	....	....	....	....	....
2002-03	**Nashville**	**NHL**	**19**	**4**	**2**	**6**	**14**	**0**	**0**	**1**	**20**	**20.0**	**2**	**171**	**53.8**	**9:40**	....	....	....	....	....	....	....	....	....
	Milwaukee	AHL	54	8	16	24	70	....	....	....	....	....	....	....	....	....	6	1	2	3	14	....	....	....	....
2003-04	**Nashville**	**NHL**	**17**	**0**	**0**	**0**	**23**	**0**	**0**	**0**	**8**	**0.0**	**–6**	**123**	**49.6**	**8:06**	....	....	....	....	....	....	....	....	....
	Milwaukee	AHL	47	9	15	24	72	....	....	....	....	....	....	....	....	....	22	5	3	8	36	....	....	....	....

			Regular Season														Playoffs								
Season	Club	League	GP	G	A	Pts	PIM	PP	SH	GW	S	%	+/-	TF	F%	Min	GP	G	A	Pts	PIM	PP	SH	GW	Min
2004-05	Milwaukee	AHL	73	20	22	42	70	....	....	....	....	....	....	....	....	....	7	0	0	0	18	....	....	....	....
2005-06	**Nashville**	**NHL**	**40**	**8**	**4**	**12**	**42**	**3**	**0**	**2**	**46**	**17.4**	**–2**	**464**	**52.6**	**13:49**	**2**	**0**	**1**	**1**	**0**	**0**	**0**	**0**	**8:48**
	Milwaukee	AHL	11	1	6	7	20	....	....	....	....	....	....	....	....	....	....	....	....	....	....	....	....	....	....
2006-07	**Nashville**	**NHL**	**72**	**11**	**15**	**26**	**40**	**0**	**1**	**1**	**90**	**12.2**	**11**	**680**	**51.6**	**13:38**	**5**	**1**	**1**	**2**	**4**	**0**	**0**	**0**	**12:21**
2007-08	**Nashville**	**NHL**	**79**	**11**	**21**	**32**	**47**	**2**	**1**	**1**	**97**	**11.3**	**–4**	**384**	**50.3**	**13:56**	**6**	**0**	**0**	**0**	**0**	**0**	**0**	**0**	**16:48**
	NHL Totals		**227**	**34**	**42**	**76**	**166**	**5**	**2**	**5**	**261**	**13.0**		**1822**	**51.6**	**13:02**	**13**	**1**	**2**	**3**	**4**	**0**	**0**	**0**	**13:51**

ECHL All-Rookie Team (2002)

Signed as a free agent by **Arkansas** (ECHL), March 31, 2001. Traded to **Roanoke** (ECHL) by **Arkansas** (ECHL) for Calvin Elfring, August 11, 2001. Signed as a free agent by **Nashville**, May 6, 2002.

FILEWICH, Jonathan (FIGHL-uh-which, JAWN-ah-thuhn) PIT.

Right wing. Shoots right. 6'2", 208 lbs. Born, Kelowna, B.C., October 2, 1984. Pittsburgh's 3rd choice, 70th overall, in 2003 Entry Draft.

Season	Club	League	GP	G	A	Pts	PIM	PP	SH	GW	S	%	+/-	TF	F%	Min	GP	G	A	Pts	PIM	PP	SH	GW	Min
1998-99	Sherwood Park	AMBHL	36	29	43	72	90	....	....	....	....	....	....	....	....	....	....	....	....	....	....	....	....	....	....
99-2000	Sherwood Park	AMHL	33	28	20	48	59	....	....	....	....	....	....	....	....	....	....	....	....	....	....	....	....	....	....
	Prince George	WHL	3	0	0	0	0	....	....	....	....	....	....	....	....	....	....	....	....	....	....	....	....	....	....
2000-01	Prince George	WHL	61	9	16	25	32	....	....	....	....	....	....	....	....	....	....	....	....	....	....	....	....	....	....
2001-02	Prince George	WHL	66	13	19	32	23	....	....	....	....	....	....	....	....	....	7	2	0	2	2	....	....	....	....
2002-03	Prince George	WHL	51	27	27	54	45	....	....	....	....	....	....	....	....	....	5	1	1	2	2	....	....	....	....
2003-04	Prince George	WHL	72	30	25	55	52	....	....	....	....	....	....	....	....	....	....	....	....	....	....	....	....	....	....
2004-05	Lethbridge	WHL	68	42	38	80	26	....	....	....	....	....	....	....	....	....	5	1	1	2	2	....	....	....	....
2005-06	Wilkes-Barre	AHL	73	22	14	36	40	....	....	....	....	....	....	....	....	....	11	6	4	10	6	....	....	....	....
2006-07	Wilkes-Barre	AHL	80	30	26	56	38	....	....	....	....	....	....	....	....	....	11	4	2	6	8	....	....	....	....
2007-08	**Pittsburgh**	**NHL**	**5**	**0**	**0**	**0**	**0**	**0**	**0**	**0**	**3**	**0.0**	**–2**	**0**	**0.0**	**8:42**	....	....	....	....	....	....	....	....	....
	Wilkes-Barre	AHL	71	10	21	31	44	....	....	....	....	....	....	....	....	....	14	1	2	3	2	....	....	....	....
	NHL Totals		**5**	**0**	**0**	**0**	**0**	**0**	**0**	**0**	**3**	**0.0**		**0**	**0.0**	**8:42**	....	....	....	....	....	....	....	....	....

FILPPULA, Valtteri (FIHL-poo-luh, VAL-tuhr-ee) DET.

Center. Shoots left. 6', 193 lbs. Born, Vantaa, Finland, March 20, 1984. Detroit's 3rd choice, 95th overall, in 2002 Entry Draft.

Season	Club	League	GP	G	A	Pts	PIM	PP	SH	GW	S	%	+/-	TF	F%	Min	GP	G	A	Pts	PIM	PP	SH	GW	Min
2000-01	Jokerit U18	Fin-U18	31	18	29	47	4	....	....	....	....	....	....	....	....	....	6	4	4	8	0	....	....	....	....
	Jokerit Helsinki Jr.	Fin-Jr.	1	0	1	1	0	....	....	....	....	....	....	....	....	....	....	....	....	....	....	....	....	....	....
2001-02	Jokerit U18	Fin-U18	1	0	1	1	0	....	....	....	....	....	....	....	....	....	8	4	9	13	2	....	....	....	....
	Jokerit Helsinki Jr.	Fin-Jr.	40	8	15	23	14	....	....	....	....	....	....	....	....	....	1	0	0	0	0	....	....	....	....
2002-03	Jokerit Helsinki Jr.	Fin-Jr.	35	16	37	53	14	....	....	....	....	....	....	....	....	....	11	4	10	14	4	....	....	....	....
2003-04	Suomi U20	Finland-2	1	0	0	0	2	....	....	....	....	....	....	....	....	....	....	....	....	....	....	....	....	....	....
	Jokerit Helsinki	Finland	49	5	13	18	6	....	....	....	....	....	....	....	....	....	....	....	....	....	....	....	....	....	....
2004-05	Jokerit Helsinki	Finland	55	10	20	30	20	....	....	....	....	....	....	....	....	....	12	5	6	11	2	....	....	....	....
2005-06	**Detroit**	**NHL**	**4**	**0**	**1**	**1**	**2**	**0**	**0**	**0**	**1**	**0.0**	**1**	**21**	**47.6**	**7:19**	....	....	....	....	....	....	....	....	....
	Grand Rapids	AHL	74	20	51	71	30	....	....	....	....	....	....	....	....	....	16	7	9	16	4	....	....	....	....
2006-07	**Detroit**	**NHL**	**73**	**10**	**7**	**17**	**20**	**0**	**0**	**1**	**76**	**13.2**	**8**	**267**	**55.8**	**11:16**	**18**	**3**	**2**	**5**	**2**	**0**	**0**	**0**	**12:12**
	Grand Rapids	AHL	3	2	2	4	2	....	....	....	....	....	....	....	....	....	....	....	....	....	....	....	....	....	....
2007-08♦	**Detroit**	**NHL**	**78**	**19**	**17**	**36**	**28**	**3**	**0**	**3**	**122**	**15.6**	**16**	**621**	**50.6**	**16:58**	**22**	**5**	**6**	**11**	**2**	**0**	**0**	**0**	**16:40**
	NHL Totals		**155**	**29**	**25**	**54**	**50**	**3**	**0**	**4**	**199**	**14.6**		**909**	**52.0**	**14:02**	**40**	**8**	**8**	**16**	**4**	**0**	**0**	**0**	**14:39**

FINGER, Jeff (FIHN-guhr, JEHF) TOR.

Defense. Shoots right. 6'1", 205 lbs. Born, Hancock, MI, December 18, 1979. Colorado's 11th choice, 240th overall, in 1999 Entry Draft.

Season	Club	League	GP	G	A	Pts	PIM	PP	SH	GW	S	%	+/-	TF	F%	Min	GP	G	A	Pts	PIM	PP	SH	GW	Min
1997-98	Green Bay	USHL	51	5	9	14	208	....	....	....	....	....	....	....	....	....	4	0	0	0	18	....	....	....	....
1998-99	Green Bay	USHL	54	11	28	39	199	....	....	....	....	....	....	....	....	....	6	0	3	3	14	....	....	....	....
99-2000	Green Bay	USHL	55	13	35	48	15	....	....	....	....	....	....	....	....	....	14	3	11	14	40	....	....	....	....
2000-01	St. Cloud State	WCHA	41	4	5	9	84	....	....	....	....	....	....	....	....	....	....	....	....	....	....	....	....	....	....
2001-02	St. Cloud State	WCHA	42	6	20	26	105	....	....	....	....	....	....	....	....	....	....	....	....	....	....	....	....	....	....
2002-03	St. Cloud State	WCHA	24	5	8	13	46	....	....	....	....	....	....	....	....	....	....	....	....	....	....	....	....	....	....
2003-04	Reading Royals	ECHL	10	2	5	7	24	....	....	....	....	....	....	....	....	....	....	....	....	....	....	....	....	....	....
	Hershey Bears	AHL	63	2	9	11	88	....	....	....	....	....	....	....	....	....	....	....	....	....	....	....	....	....	....
2004-05	Hershey Bears	AHL	75	4	12	16	125	....	....	....	....	....	....	....	....	....	....	....	....	....	....	....	....	....	....
2005-06	Lowell	AHL	70	3	20	23	116	....	....	....	....	....	....	....	....	....	....	....	....	....	....	....	....	....	....
2006-07	**Colorado**	**NHL**	**22**	**1**	**4**	**5**	**11**	**0**	**0**	**0**	**16**	**6.3**	**10**	**0**	**0.0**	**13:48**	....	....	....	....	....	....	....	....	....
	Albany River Rats	AHL	44	3	10	13	65	....	....	....	....	....	....	....	....	....	5	1	1	2	4	....	....	....	....
2007-08	**Colorado**	**NHL**	**72**	**8**	**11**	**19**	**40**	**1**	**1**	**1**	**93**	**8.6**	**12**	**1**	**100.0**	**19:57**	**5**	**0**	**2**	**2**	**4**	**0**	**0**	**0**	**22:05**
	NHL Totals		**94**	**9**	**15**	**24**	**51**	**1**	**1**	**1**	**109**	**8.3**		**1**	**100.0**	**18:31**	**5**	**0**	**2**	**2**	**4**	**0**	**0**	**0**	**22:05**

Signed as a free agent by **Toronto**, July 1, 2008.

FISHER, Mike (FIH-shuhr, MIGHK) OTT.

Center. Shoots right. 6'1", 209 lbs. Born, Peterborough, Ont., June 5, 1980. Ottawa's 2nd choice, 44th overall, in 1998 Entry Draft.

Season	Club	League	GP	G	A	Pts	PIM	PP	SH	GW	S	%	+/-	TF	F%	Min	GP	G	A	Pts	PIM	PP	SH	GW	Min
1996-97	Peterborough	OPJHL	51	26	30	56	35	....	....	....	....	....	....	....	....	....	....	....	....	....	....	....	....	....	....
1997-98	Sudbury Wolves	OHL	66	24	25	49	65	....	....	....	....	....	....	....	....	....	9	2	2	4	13	....	....	....	....
1998-99	Sudbury Wolves	OHL	68	41	65	106	55	....	....	....	....	....	....	....	....	....	4	2	1	3	4	....	....	....	....
99-2000	**Ottawa**	**NHL**	**32**	**4**	**5**	**9**	**15**	**0**	**0**	**1**	**49**	**8.2**	**–6**	**356**	**47.8**	**12:57**	....	....	....	....	....	....	....	....	....
2000-01	**Ottawa**	**NHL**	**60**	**7**	**12**	**19**	**46**	**0**	**0**	**3**	**83**	**8.4**	**–1**	**709**	**50.2**	**11:38**	**4**	**0**	**1**	**1**	**4**	**0**	**0**	**0**	**13:41**
2001-02	**Ottawa**	**NHL**	**58**	**15**	**9**	**24**	**55**	**0**	**3**	**4**	**123**	**12.2**	**8**	**848**	**48.7**	**14:05**	**10**	**2**	**1**	**3**	**0**	**0**	**0**	**0**	**16:17**
2002-03	**Ottawa**	**NHL**	**74**	**18**	**20**	**38**	**54**	**5**	**1**	**3**	**142**	**12.7**	**13**	**1077**	**48.1**	**15:59**	**18**	**2**	**2**	**4**	**16**	**0**	**1**	**1**	**16:58**
2003-04	**Ottawa**	**NHL**	**24**	**4**	**6**	**10**	**39**	**1**	**0**	**0**	**47**	**8.5**	**–3**	**357**	**42.0**	**17:26**	**7**	**1**	**0**	**1**	**4**	**0**	**0**	**1**	**16:11**
2004-05	EV Zug	Swiss	21	9	18	27	34	....	....	....	....	....	....	....	....	....	9	2	3	5	10	....	....	....	....
2005-06	**Ottawa**	**NHL**	**68**	**22**	**22**	**44**	**64**	**2**	**4**	**3**	**150**	**14.7**	**23**	**883**	**50.3**	**17:09**	**10**	**2**	**2**	**4**	**12**	**0**	**1**	**0**	**18:50**
2006-07	**Ottawa**	**NHL**	**68**	**22**	**26**	**48**	**41**	**7**	**2**	**3**	**193**	**11.4**	**15**	**1191**	**52.1**	**18:25**	**20**	**5**	**5**	**10**	**24**	**2**	**1**	**1**	**17:43**
2007-08	**Ottawa**	**NHL**	**79**	**23**	**24**	**47**	**82**	**6**	**2**	**4**	**215**	**10.7**	**–10**	**1230**	**50.2**	**19:46**	....	....	....	....	....	....	....	....	....
	NHL Totals		**463**	**115**	**124**	**239**	**396**	**21**	**12**	**21**	**1002**	**11.5**		**6651**	**49.5**	**16:13**	**69**	**12**	**11**	**23**	**60**	**2**	**3**	**3**	**17:05**

• Missed majority of 1999-2000 season recovering from knee injury suffered in game vs. Boston, December 30, 1999. • Missed majority of 2003-04 season recovering from elbow injury suffered in practice, October 4, 2003. Signed as a free agent by **Zug** (Swiss), November 1, 2004.

FISTRIC, Mark (FIHST-rihc, MAHRK) DAL.

Defense. Shoots left. 6'2", 232 lbs. Born, Edmonton, Alta., June 1, 1986. Dallas' 1st choice, 28th overall, in 2004 Entry Draft.

Season	Club	League	GP	G	A	Pts	PIM	PP	SH	GW	S	%	+/-	TF	F%	Min	GP	G	A	Pts	PIM	PP	SH	GW	Min
2000-01	Edmonton MLAC	AMBHL	34	13	13	26	144	....	....	....	....	....	....	....	....	....	....	....	....	....	....	....	....	....	....
2001-02	Edmonton MLAC	AMHL	30	8	10	18	85	....	....	....	....	....	....	....	....	....	....	....	....	....	....	....	....	....	....
	Vancouver Giants	WHL	4	0	2	2	0	....	....	....	....	....	....	....	....	....	....	....	....	....	....	....	....	....	....
2002-03	Vancouver Giants	WHL	63	2	7	9	81	....	....	....	....	....	....	....	....	....	4	0	0	0	8	....	....	....	....
2003-04	Vancouver Giants	WHL	72	1	11	12	192	....	....	....	....	....	....	....	....	....	11	0	2	2	10	....	....	....	....
2004-05	Vancouver Giants	WHL	15	1	5	6	32	....	....	....	....	....	....	....	....	....	6	1	1	2	16	....	....	....	....
2005-06	Vancouver Giants	WHL	60	7	22	29	148	....	....	....	....	....	....	....	....	....	18	1	9	10	30	....	....	....	....
2006-07	Iowa Stars	AHL	80	2	22	24	83	....	....	....	....	....	....	....	....	....	12	0	0	0	16	....	....	....	....
2007-08	**Dallas**	**NHL**	**37**	**0**	**2**	**2**	**24**	**0**	**0**	**0**	**17**	**0.0**	**3**	**0**	**0.0**	**12:44**	**9**	**0**	**0**	**0**	**6**	**0**	**0**	**0**	**14:51**
	Iowa Stars	AHL	30	1	4	5	48	....	....	....	....	....	....	....	....	....	....	....	....	....	....	....	....	....	....
	NHL Totals		**37**	**0**	**2**	**2**	**24**	**0**	**0**	**0**	**17**	**0.0**		**0**	**0.0**	**12:44**	**9**	**0**	**0**	**0**	**6**	**0**	**0**	**0**	**14:51**

FITZGERALD, Zach (fihtz-JAIR-uhld, ZAK) VAN.

Defense. Shoots left. 6'2", 214 lbs. Born, Two Harbors, MN, June 16, 1985. St. Louis' 4th choice, 88th overall, in 2003 Entry Draft.

Season	Club	League	GP	G	A	Pts	PIM	PP	SH	GW	S	%	+/-	TF	F%	Min	GP	G	A	Pts	PIM	PP	SH	GW	Min
2000-01	Duluth East	High-MN	26	1	7	8	44	....	....	....	....	....	....	....	....	....	....	....	....	....	....	....	....	....	....
2001-02	Seattle	WHL	61	3	7	10	214	....	....	....	....	....	....	....	....	....	10	0	2	2	19	....	....	....	....
2002-03	Seattle	WHL	64	8	14	22	232	....	....	....	....	....	....	....	....	....	15	0	4	4	33	....	....	....	....
2003-04	Seattle	WHL	58	4	15	19	163	....	....	....	....	....	....	....	....	....	....	....	....	....	....	....	....	....	....
2004-05	Seattle	WHL	65	7	18	25	*244	....	....	....	....	....	....	....	....	....	9	0	3	3	24	....	....	....	....
2005-06	Peoria Rivermen	AHL	13	1	1	2	47	....	....	....	....	....	....	....	....	....	....	....	....	....	....	....	....	....	....
	Alaska Aces	ECHL	12	1	1	2	108	....	....	....	....	....	....	....	....	....	....	....	....	....	....	....	....	....	....
2006-07	Peoria Rivermen	AHL	29	0	2	2	86	....	....	....	....	....	....	....	....	....	....	....	....	....	....	....	....	....	....
	Alaska Aces	ECHL	10	0	1	1	48	....	....	....	....	....	....	....	....	....	14	2	3	5	*82	....	....	....	....

			Regular Season														Playoffs								
Season	Club	League	GP	G	A	Pts	PIM	PP	SH	GW	S	%	+/-	TF	F%	Min	GP	G	A	Pts	PIM	PP	SH	GW	Min
2007-08	**Vancouver**	**NHL**	**1**	**0**	**0**	**0**	**0**	**0**	**0**	**0**	**1**	**0.0**	**0**	**0**	**0.0**	**13:20**	....	....	....	....	....	....	....	....	....
	Manitoba Moose	AHL	48	5	3	8	158	....	....	....	....	....	....	....	....	....	3	0	0	0	14	....	....	....	....
	NHL Totals		**1**	**0**	**0**	**0**	**0**	**0**	**0**	**0**	**1**	**0.0**		**0**	**0.0**	**13:20**	....	....	....	....	....	....	....	....	....

Traded to **Vancouver** by **St. Louis** for Francois-Pierre Guenette, August 1, 2007.

FITZPATRICK, Rory

(FIHTZ-pa-trihk, ROHR-ee) **FLA.**

Defense. Shoots right. 6'2", 208 lbs. Born, Rochester, NY, January 11, 1975. Montreal's 2nd choice, 47th overall, in 1993 Entry Draft.

Season	Club	League	GP	G	A	Pts	PIM	PP	SH	GW	S	%	+/-	TF	F%	Min	GP	G	A	Pts	PIM	PP	SH	GW	Min
1990-91	Rochester	EmJHL	40	0	5	5	....	....	....	....	....	....	....	....	....	....	....	....	....	....	....	....	....	....	....
1991-92	Rochester	EmJHL	28	8	28	36	141	....	....	....	....	....	....	....	....	....	....	....	....	....	....	....	....	....	....
1992-93	Sudbury Wolves	OHL	58	4	20	24	68	....	....	....	....	....	....	....	....	....	14	0	0	0	17	....	....	....	....
1993-94	Sudbury Wolves	OHL	65	12	34	46	112	....	....	....	....	....	....	....	....	....	10	2	5	7	10	....	....	....	....
1994-95	Sudbury Wolves	OHL	56	12	36	48	72	....	....	....	....	....	....	....	....	....	18	3	15	18	21	....	....	....	....
	Fredericton	AHL	....	....	....	....	....	....	....	....	....	....	....	....	....	....	10	1	2	3	5	....	....	....	....
1995-96	**Montreal**	**NHL**	**42**	**0**	**2**	**2**	**18**	**0**	**0**	**0**	**31**	**0.0**	**-7**	....	....	....	**6**	**1**	**1**	**2**	**0**	**0**	**0**	**0**	....
	Fredericton	AHL	18	4	6	10	36	....	....	....	....	....	....	....	....	....	....	....	....	....	....	....	....	....	....
1996-97	**Montreal**	**NHL**	**6**	**0**	**1**	**1**	**6**	**0**	**0**	**0**	**5**	**0.0**	**-2**	....	....	....	....	....	....	....	....	....	....	....	....
	St. Louis	**NHL**	**2**	**0**	**0**	**0**	**2**	**0**	**0**	**0**	**1**	**0.0**	**-2**	....	....	....	....	....	....	....	....	....	....	....	....
	Worcester IceCats	AHL	49	4	13	17	78	....	....	....	....	....	....	....	....	....	5	1	2	3	0	....	....	....	....
1997-98	Worcester IceCats	AHL	62	8	22	30	111	....	....	....	....	....	....	....	....	....	11	0	3	3	26	....	....	....	....
1998-99	**St. Louis**	**NHL**	**1**	**0**	**0**	**0**	**2**	**0**	**0**	**0**	**0**	**0.0**	**-3**	**0**	**0.0**	**4:49**	....	....	....	....	....	....	....	....	....
	Worcester IceCats	AHL	53	5	16	21	82	....	....	....	....	....	....	....	....	....	4	0	1	1	17	....	....	....	....
99-2000	Worcester IceCats	AHL	28	0	5	5	48	....	....	....	....	....	....	....	....	....	....	....	....	....	....	....	....	....	....
	Milwaukee	IHL	27	2	1	3	27	....	....	....	....	....	....	....	....	....	3	0	2	2	2	....	....	....	....
2000-01	**Nashville**	**NHL**	**2**	**0**	**0**	**0**	**2**	**0**	**0**	**0**	**0**	**0.0**	**-2**	**0**	**0.0**	**9:47**	....	....	....	....	....	....	....	....	....
	Milwaukee	IHL	22	0	2	2	32	....	....	....	....	....	....	....	....	....	....	....	....	....	....	....	....	....	....
	Hamilton	AHL	34	3	17	20	29	....	....	....	....	....	....	....	....	....	....	....	....	....	....	....	....	....	....
2001-02	**Buffalo**	**NHL**	**5**	**0**	**0**	**0**	**4**	**0**	**0**	**0**	**2**	**0.0**	**-2**	**0**	**0.0**	**11:54**	....	....	....	....	....	....	....	....	....
	Rochester	AHL	60	4	8	12	83	....	....	....	....	....	....	....	....	....	2	0	1	1	0	....	....	....	....
2002-03	**Buffalo**	**NHL**	**36**	**1**	**3**	**4**	**16**	**0**	**0**	**0**	**29**	**3.4**	**-7**	**0**	**0.0**	**17:02**	....	....	....	....	....	....	....	....	....
	Rochester	AHL	41	5	11	16	65	....	....	....	....	....	....	....	....	....	....	....	....	....	....	....	....	....	....
2003-04	**Buffalo**	**NHL**	**60**	**4**	**7**	**11**	**44**	**2**	**0**	**2**	**78**	**5.1**	**-5**	**1**	**100.0**	**19:02**	....	....	....	....	....	....	....	....	....
2004-05	Rochester	AHL	20	1	1	2	18	....	....	....	....	....	....	....	....	....	9	0	1	1	12	....	....	....	....
2005-06	**Buffalo**	**NHL**	**56**	**4**	**5**	**9**	**50**	**2**	**0**	**1**	**45**	**8.9**	**-18**	**1**	**0.0**	**16:22**	**11**	**0**	**4**	**4**	**16**	**0**	**0**	**0**	**17:12**
2006-07	**Vancouver**	**NHL**	**58**	**1**	**6**	**7**	**46**	**0**	**0**	**1**	**41**	**2.4**	**12**	**1**	**100.0**	**14:06**	**3**	**0**	**0**	**0**	**6**	**0**	**0**	**0**	**21:08**
2007-08	**Philadelphia**	**NHL**	**19**	**0**	**1**	**1**	**11**	**0**	**0**	**0**	**10**	**0.0**	**-12**	**0**	**0.0**	**12:44**	....	....	....	....	....	....	....	....	....
	Philadelphia	AHL	19	1	4	5	24	....	....	....	....	....	....	....	....	....	12	0	2	2	11	....	....	....	....
	NHL Totals		**287**	**10**	**25**	**35**	**201**	**4**	**0**	**4**	**242**	**4.1**		**3**	**66.7**	**16:06**	**20**	**1**	**5**	**6**	**22**	**0**	**0**	**0**	**18:02**

OHL All-Rookie Team (1993)

Traded to **St. Louis** by **Montreal** with Pierre Turgeon and Craig Conroy for Murray Baron, Shayne Corson and St. Louis' 5th round choice (Gennady Razin) in 1997 Entry Draft, October 29, 1996. Claimed by **Boston** from **St. Louis** in Waiver Draft, October 5, 1998. Claimed on waivers by **St. Louis** from **Boston**, October 7, 1998. Traded to **Nashville** by **St. Louis** for Dan Keczmer, February 9, 2000. Traded to **Edmonton** by **Nashville** for future considerations, January 12, 2001. Signed as a free agent by **Buffalo**, August 14, 2001. Signed as a free agent by **Rochester** (AHL), March 2, 2005. Signed as a free agent by **Vancouver**, August 18, 2006. Signed as a free agent by **Philadelphia**, October 9, 2007. Signed as a free agent by **Florida**, July 3, 2008.

FLEISCHMANN, Tomas

(FLIGHSH-muhn, TAW-mahsh) **WSH.**

Left wing. Shoots left. 6'1", 192 lbs. Born, Koprivnice, Czech., May 16, 1984. Detroit's 2nd choice, 63rd overall, in 2002 Entry Draft.

Season	Club	League	GP	G	A	Pts	PIM	PP	SH	GW	S	%	+/-	TF	F%	Min	GP	G	A	Pts	PIM	PP	SH	GW	Min
99-2000	HC Vitkovice Jr.	CzRep-Jr.	46	9	13	22	6	....	....	....	....	....	....	....	....	....	....	....	....	....	....	....	....	....	....
2000-01	HC Vitkovice U17	CzR-U17	30	28	34	62	8	....	....	....	....	....	....	....	....	....	....	....	....	....	....	....	....	....	....
	HC Vitkovice Jr.	CzRep-Jr.	21	4	9	13	8	....	....	....	....	....	....	....	....	....	....	....	....	....	....	....	....	....	....
2001-02	HC Vitkovice Jr.	CzRep-Jr.	46	26	35	51	16	....	....	....	....	....	....	....	....	....	....	....	....	....	....	....	....	....	....
	TJ Novy Jicin	CzRep-3	8	3	2	5	8	....	....	....	....	....	....	....	....	....	7	3	4	7	35	....	....	....	....
2002-03	Moose Jaw	WHL	65	21	50	71	36	....	....	....	....	....	....	....	....	....	12	4	11	15	6	....	....	....	....
2003-04	Moose Jaw	WHL	60	33	42	75	32	....	....	....	....	....	....	....	....	....	10	3	4	7	10	....	....	....	....
2004-05	Portland Pirates	AHL	53	7	12	19	14	....	....	....	....	....	....	....	....	....	....	....	....	....	....	....	....	....	....
2005-06	**Washington**	**NHL**	**14**	**0**	**2**	**2**	**0**	**0**	**0**	**0**	**11**	**0.0**	**-7**	**5**	**40.0**	**6:45**	....	....	....	....	....	....	....	....	....
	Hershey Bears	AHL	57	30	33	63	32	....	....	....	....	....	....	....	....	....	20	11	*21	32	15	....	....	....	....
2006-07	**Washington**	**NHL**	**29**	**4**	**4**	**8**	**8**	**1**	**0**	**1**	**52**	**7.7**	**-6**	**14**	**35.7**	**11:38**	....	....	....	....	....	....	....	....	....
	Hershey Bears	AHL	45	22	29	51	22	....	....	....	....	....	....	....	....	....	19	5	16	21	10	....	....	....	....
2007-08	**Washington**	**NHL**	**75**	**10**	**20**	**30**	**18**	**1**	**0**	**1**	**107**	**9.3**	**-7**	**30**	**50.0**	**12:37**	**2**	**0**	**0**	**0**	**0**	**0**	**0**	**0**	**9:49**
	NHL Totals		**118**	**14**	**26**	**40**	**26**	**2**	**0**	**2**	**170**	**8.2**		**49**	**44.9**	**11:41**	**2**	**0**	**0**	**0**	**0**	**0**	**0**	**0**	**9:49**

WHL East Second All-Star Team (2004)

Traded to **Washington** by **Detroit** with Detroit's 1st round choice (Mike Green) in 2004 Entry Draft and Detroit's 4th round choice (Luke Lynes) in 2006 Entry Draft for Robert Lang, February 27, 2004.

FLINN, Ryan

(FLIHN, RIGH-yan) **MTL.**

Left wing. Shoots left. 6'5", 248 lbs. Born, Halifax, N.S., April 20, 1980. New Jersey's 8th choice, 143rd overall, in 1998 Entry Draft.

Season	Club	League	GP	G	A	Pts	PIM	PP	SH	GW	S	%	+/-	TF	F%	Min	GP	G	A	Pts	PIM	PP	SH	GW	Min
1996-97	Laval Titan	QMJHL	23	3	2	5	56	....	....	....	....	....	....	....	....	....	2	0	0	0	0	....	....	....	....
1997-98	Laval Titan	QMJHL	59	4	12	16	217	....	....	....	....	....	....	....	....	....	15	1	0	1	63	....	....	....	....
1998-99	Acadie-Bathurst	QMJHL	44	3	4	7	195	....	....	....	....	....	....	....	....	....	23	2	0	2	37	....	....	....	....
99-2000	Halifax	QMJHL	67	14	19	33	365	....	....	....	....	....	....	....	....	....	....	....	....	....	....	....	....	....	....
2000-01	Cape Breton	QMJHL	57	16	17	33	280	....	....	....	....	....	....	....	....	....	9	1	1	2	43	....	....	....	....
2001-02	Reading Royals	ECHL	20	1	3	4	130	....	....	....	....	....	....	....	....	....	....	....	....	....	....	....	....	....	....
	Los Angeles	**NHL**	**10**	**0**	**0**	**0**	**51**	**0**	**0**	**0**	**2**	**0.0**	**0**	**0**	**0.0**	**3:29**	....	....	....	....	....	....	....	....	....
	Manchester	AHL	37	0	1	1	113	....	....	....	....	....	....	....	....	....	1	0	0	0	0	....	....	....	....
2002-03	**Los Angeles**	**NHL**	**19**	**1**	**0**	**1**	**28**	**0**	**0**	**0**	**13**	**7.7**	**0**	**0**	**0.0**	**5:28**	....	....	....	....	....	....	....	....	....
	Manchester	AHL	27	2	2	4	95	....	....	....	....	....	....	....	....	....	....	....	....	....	....	....	....	....	....
2003-04	Manchester	AHL	59	3	5	8	164	....	....	....	....	....	....	....	....	....	6	0	0	0	4	....	....	....	....
2004-05	Manchester	AHL	14	1	1	2	112	....	....	....	....	....	....	....	....	....	....	....	....	....	....	....	....	....	....
2005-06	**Los Angeles**	**NHL**	**2**	**0**	**0**	**0**	**5**	**0**	**0**	**0**	**0**	**0.0**	**0**	**0**	**0.0**	**0:25**	....	....	....	....	....	....	....	....	....
	Manchester	AHL	6	0	1	1	38	....	....	....	....	....	....	....	....	....	....	....	....	....	....	....	....	....	....
2006-07	San Antonio	AHL	61	2	4	6	166	....	....	....	....	....	....	....	....	....	....	....	....	....	....	....	....	....	....
2007-08	Springfield	AHL	24	0	1	1	82	....	....	....	....	....	....	....	....	....	....	....	....	....	....	....	....	....	....
	Hershey Bears	AHL	17	3	0	3	53	....	....	....	....	....	....	....	....	....	2	0	0	0	2	....	....	....	....
	NHL Totals		**31**	**1**	**0**	**1**	**84**	**0**	**0**	**0**	**15**	**6.7**		**0**	**0.0**	**4:30**	....	....	....	....	....	....	....	....	....

Signed as a free agent by **Los Angeles**, January 8, 2002. • Missed majority of 2004-05 season recovering from foot and leg injuries. • Missed majority of 2005-06 season recovering from head injury suffered in game vs. Chicago, November 26, 2005. Signed as a free agent by **Edmonton**, July 17, 2007. Signed as a free agent by **Montreal**, July 7, 2008.

FOLIGNO, Nick

(foh-LIHG-noh, NIHK) **OTT.**

Left wing. Shoots left. 6', 210 lbs. Born, Buffalo, NY, October 31, 1987. Ottawa's 1st choice, 28th overall, in 2006 Entry Draft.

Season	Club	League	GP	G	A	Pts	PIM	PP	SH	GW	S	%	+/-	TF	F%	Min	GP	G	A	Pts	PIM	PP	SH	GW	Min
2003-04	USNTDP	U-17	18	7	9	16	28	....	....	....	....	....	....	....	....	....	....	....	....	....	....	....	....	....	....
	USNTDP	NAHL	43	8	12	20	44	....	....	....	....	....	....	....	....	....	7	2	1	3	8	....	....	....	....
2004-05	USNTDP	U-18	4	2	1	3	0	....	....	....	....	....	....	....	....	....	....	....	....	....	....	....	....	....	....
	Sudbury Wolves	OHL	65	10	28	38	111	....	....	....	....	....	....	....	....	....	12	5	5	10	16	....	....	....	....
2005-06	Sudbury Wolves	OHL	65	24	46	70	146	....	....	....	....	....	....	....	....	....	10	1	3	4	28	....	....	....	....
2006-07	Sudbury Wolves	OHL	66	31	57	88	135	....	....	....	....	....	....	....	....	....	21	12	17	29	36	....	....	....	....
2007-08	**Ottawa**	**NHL**	**45**	**6**	**3**	**9**	**20**	**0**	**0**	**0**	**44**	**13.6**	**0**	**49**	**44.9**	**9:10**	**4**	**1**	**0**	**1**	**2**	**0**	**0**	**0**	**12:50**
	Binghamton	AHL	28	6	13	19	16	....	....	....	....	....	....	....	....	....	....	....	....	....	....	....	....	....	....
	NHL Totals		**45**	**6**	**3**	**9**	**20**	**0**	**0**	**0**	**44**	**13.6**		**49**	**44.9**	**9:10**	**4**	**1**	**0**	**1**	**2**	**0**	**0**	**0**	**12:50**

FOOTE, Adam

(FUT, A-duhm) **COL.**

Defense. Shoots right. 6'2", 226 lbs. Born, Toronto, Ont., July 10, 1971. Quebec's 2nd choice, 22nd overall, in 1989 Entry Draft.

			Regular Season														Playoffs								
Season	Club	League	GP	G	A	Pts	PIM	PP	SH	GW	S	%	+/-	TF	F%	Min	GP	G	A	Pts	PIM	PP	SH	GW	Min
1987-88	Whitby Midgets	Minor-ON	65	25	43	68	108	....	....	....	....	....	....	....	....	....	....	....	....	....	....	....	....	....	....
1988-89	Sault Ste. Marie	OHL	66	7	32	39	120	....	....	....	....	....	....	....	....	....	....	....	....	....	....	....	....	....	....
1989-90	Sault Ste. Marie	OHL	61	12	43	55	199	....	....	....	....	....	....	....	....	....	....	....	....	....	....	....	....	....	....
1990-91	Sault Ste. Marie	OHL	59	18	51	69	93	....	....	....	....	....	....	....	....	....	14	5	12	17	28	....	....	....	....
1991-92	**Quebec**	**NHL**	**46**	**2**	**5**	**7**	**44**	**0**	**0**	**0**	**55**	**3.6**	**–4**	....	....	....	....	....	....	....	....	....	....	....	....
	Halifax Citadels	AHL	6	0	1	1	2	....	....	....	....	....	....	....	....	....	....	....	....	....	....	....	....	....	....
1992-93	**Quebec**	**NHL**	**81**	**4**	**12**	**16**	**168**	**0**	**1**	**0**	**54**	**7.4**	**6**	....	....	....	**6**	**0**	**1**	**1**	**2**	**0**	**0**	**0**	....
1993-94	**Quebec**	**NHL**	**45**	**2**	**6**	**8**	**67**	**0**	**0**	**0**	**42**	**4.8**	**3**	....	....	....	....	....	....	....	....	....	....	....	....
1994-95	**Quebec**	**NHL**	**35**	**0**	**7**	**7**	**52**	**0**	**0**	**0**	**24**	**0.0**	**17**	....	....	....	**6**	**0**	**1**	**1**	**14**	**0**	**0**	**0**	....
1995-96 ♦	**Colorado**	**NHL**	**73**	**5**	**11**	**16**	**88**	**1**	**0**	**1**	**49**	**10.2**	**27**	....	....	....	**22**	**1**	**3**	**4**	**36**	**0**	**0**	**0**	....
1996-97	**Colorado**	**NHL**	**78**	**2**	**19**	**21**	**135**	**0**	**0**	**0**	**60**	**3.3**	**16**	....	....	....	**17**	**0**	**4**	**4**	**62**	**0**	**0**	**0**	....
1997-98	**Colorado**	**NHL**	**77**	**3**	**14**	**17**	**124**	**0**	**0**	**1**	**64**	**4.7**	**–3**	....	....	....	**7**	**0**	**0**	**0**	**23**	**0**	**0**	**0**	....
	Canada	Olympics	6	0	1	1	4	....	....	....	....	....	....	....	....	....	....	....	....	....	....	....	....	....	....
1998-99	**Colorado**	**NHL**	**64**	**5**	**16**	**21**	**92**	**3**	**0**	**0**	**83**	**6.0**	**20**	**0**	**0.0**	**24:50**	**19**	**2**	**3**	**5**	**24**	**1**	**0**	**0**	**28:34**
99-2000	**Colorado**	**NHL**	**59**	**5**	**13**	**18**	**98**	**1**	**0**	**2**	**63**	**7.9**	**5**	**0**	**0.0**	**25:51**	**16**	**0**	**7**	**7**	**28**	**0**	**0**	**0**	**26:05**
2000-01 ♦	**Colorado**	**NHL**	**35**	**3**	**12**	**15**	**42**	**1**	**1**	**1**	**59**	**5.1**	**6**	**0**	**0.0**	**25:22**	**23**	**3**	**4**	**7**	***47**	**1**	**0**	**1**	**28:22**
2001-02	**Colorado**	**NHL**	**55**	**5**	**22**	**27**	**55**	**1**	**1**	**0**	**85**	**5.9**	**7**	**0**	**0.0**	**25:59**	**21**	**1**	**6**	**7**	**28**	**0**	**0**	**0**	**27:46**
	Canada	Olympics	6	1	0	1	2	....	....	....	....	....	....	....	....	....	....	....	....	....	....	....	....	....	....
2002-03	**Colorado**	**NHL**	**78**	**11**	**20**	**31**	**88**	**3**	**0**	**2**	**106**	**10.4**	**30**	**0**	**0.0**	**25:43**	**6**	**0**	**1**	**1**	**8**	**0**	**0**	**0**	**24:12**
2003-04	**Colorado**	**NHL**	**73**	**8**	**22**	**30**	**87**	**5**	**0**	**1**	**105**	**7.6**	**13**	**0**	**0.0**	**24:03**	**11**	**0**	**4**	**4**	**10**	**0**	**0**	**0**	**25:06**
2004-05			Did not play																						
2005-06	**Columbus**	**NHL**	**65**	**6**	**16**	**22**	**89**	**2**	**2**	**1**	**67**	**9.0**	**–16**	**0**	**0.0**	**24:34**	....	....	....	....	....	....	....	....	....
	Canada	Olympics	6	0	1	1	6	....	....	....	....	....	....	....	....	....	....	....	....	....	....	....	....	....	....
2006-07	**Columbus**	**NHL**	**59**	**3**	**9**	**12**	**71**	**2**	**0**	**0**	**78**	**3.8**	**–17**	**0**	**0.0**	**24:44**	....	....	....	....	....	....	....	....	....
2007-08	**Columbus**	**NHL**	**63**	**1**	**14**	**15**	**95**	**0**	**1**	**0**	**57**	**1.8**	**3**	**0**	**0.0**	**24:02**	....	....	....	....	....	....	....	....	....
	Colorado	**NHL**	**12**	**0**	**1**	**1**	**12**	**0**	**0**	**0**	**9**	**0.0**	**–1**	**0**	**0.0**	**20:01**	**10**	**0**	**0**	**0**	**6**	**0**	**0**	**0**	**21:14**
	NHL Totals		**998**	**65**	**219**	**284**	**1407**	**19**	**6**	**9**	**1060**	**6.1**		**0**	**0.0**	**24:52**	**164**	**7**	**34**	**41**	**288**	**2**	**0**	**1**	**26:41**

OHL First All-Star Team (1991)

Transferred to **Colorado** after **Quebec** franchise relocated, June 21, 1995. • Missed majority of 2000-01 season recovering from shoulder injury suffered in game vs. Carolina, January 6, 2001. Signed as a free agent by **Columbus**, August 2, 2005. Traded to **Colorado** by **Columbus** for Colorado's 1st round choice (later traded to Philadelphia - Philadelphia selected Luca Sbisa) in 2008 Entry Draft and future considerations, February 26, 2008.

FORSBERG, Peter

(FOHRS-buhrg, PEE-tuhr)

Center. Shoots left. 6', 205 lbs. Born, Ornskoldsvik, Sweden, July 20, 1973. Philadelphia's 1st choice, 6th overall, in 1991 Entry Draft.

			Regular Season														Playoffs								
Season	Club	League	GP	G	A	Pts	PIM	PP	SH	GW	S	%	+/-	TF	F%	Min	GP	G	A	Pts	PIM	PP	SH	GW	Min
1989-90	MoDo Jr.	Swe-Jr.	30	15	12	27	42	....	....	....	....	....	....	....	....	....	....	....	....	....	....	....	....	....	....
	MoDo	Sweden	1	0	1	1	4	....	....	....	....	....	....	....	....	....	....	....	....	....	....	....	....	....	....
1990-91	MoDo Jr.	Swe-Jr.	39	38	64	102	56	....	....	....	....	....	....	....	....	....	....	....	....	....	....	....	....	....	....
	MoDo	Sweden	23	7	10	17	22	....	....	....	....	....	....	....	....	....	....	....	....	....	....	....	....	....	....
1991-92	MoDo	Sweden	39	9	18	27	78	....	....	....	....	....	....	....	....	....	....	....	....	....	....	....	....	....	....
1992-93	MoDo Jr.	Swe-Jr.	2	0	3	3	4	....	....	....	....	....	....	....	....	....	....	....	....	....	....	....	....	....	....
	MoDo	Sweden	39	23	24	47	92	....	....	....	....	....	....	....	....	....	3	4	1	5	0	....	....	....	....
1993-94	MoDo	Sweden	39	18	26	44	82	....	....	....	....	....	....	....	....	....	11	9	7	16	14	....	....	....	....
	Sweden	Olympics	8	2	6	8	6	....	....	....	....	....	....	....	....	....	....	....	....	....	....	....	....	....	....
1994-95	MoDo	Sweden	11	5	9	14	20	....	....	....	....	....	....	....	....	....	....	....	....	....	....	....	....	....	....
	Quebec	**NHL**	**47**	**15**	**35**	**50**	**16**	**3**	**0**	**3**	**86**	**17.4**	**17**	....	....	....	**6**	**2**	**4**	**6**	**4**	**1**	**0**	**0**	....
1995-96 ♦	**Colorado**	**NHL**	**82**	**30**	**86**	**116**	**47**	**7**	**3**	**3**	**217**	**13.8**	**26**	....	....	....	**22**	**10**	**11**	**21**	**18**	**3**	**0**	**1**	....
1996-97	**Colorado**	**NHL**	**65**	**28**	**58**	**86**	**73**	**5**	**4**	**4**	**188**	**14.9**	**31**	....	....	....	**14**	**5**	**12**	**17**	**10**	**3**	**0**	**0**	....
1997-98	**Colorado**	**NHL**	**72**	**25**	**66**	**91**	**94**	**7**	**3**	**7**	**202**	**12.4**	**6**	....	....	....	**7**	**6**	**5**	**11**	**12**	**2**	**0**	**0**	....
	Sweden	Olympics	4	1	4	5	6	....	....	....	....	....	....	....	....	....	....	....	....	....	....	....	....	....	....
1998-99	**Colorado**	**NHL**	**78**	**30**	**67**	**97**	**108**	**9**	**2**	**7**	**217**	**13.8**	**27**	**895**	**54.4**	**23:29**	**19**	**8**	**16**	***24**	**31**	**1**	**1**	**0**	**21:39**
99-2000	**Colorado**	**NHL**	**49**	**14**	**37**	**51**	**52**	**3**	**0**	**2**	**105**	**13.3**	**9**	**519**	**46.6**	**20:55**	**16**	**7**	**8**	**15**	**12**	**2**	**1**	**4**	**20:59**
2000-01 ♦	**Colorado**	**NHL**	**73**	**27**	**62**	**89**	**54**	**12**	**2**	**5**	**178**	**15.2**	**23**	**755**	**46.6**	**20:48**	**11**	**4**	**10**	**14**	**6**	**1**	**0**	**2**	**21:55**
2001-02	**Colorado**	**NHL**	....	....	....	....	....	....	....	....	....	....	....	....	....	....	**20**	**9**	***18**	***27**	**20**	**0**	**0**	**4**	**18:10**
2002-03	**Colorado**	**NHL**	**75**	**29**	***77**	***106**	**70**	**8**	**0**	**2**	**166**	**17.5**	**52**	**709**	**47.0**	**19:20**	**7**	**2**	**6**	**8**	**6**	**1**	**0**	**0**	**20:01**
2003-04	**Colorado**	**NHL**	**39**	**18**	**37**	**55**	**30**	**3**	**1**	**5**	**85**	**21.2**	**16**	**549**	**42.3**	**19:12**	**11**	**4**	**7**	**11**	**12**	**1**	**0**	**1**	**19:02**
2004-05	MODO	Sweden	33	13	26	39	88	....	....	....	....	....	....	....	....	....	1	0	0	0	2	....	....	....	....
2005-06	**Philadelphia**	**NHL**	**60**	**19**	**56**	**75**	**46**	**8**	**1**	**2**	**132**	**14.4**	**21**	**941**	**50.6**	**18:47**	**6**	**4**	**4**	**8**	**6**	**1**	**0**	**2**	**18:55**
	Sweden	Olympics	6	0	6	6	0	....	....	....	....	....	....	....	....	....	....	....	....	....	....	....	....	....	....
2006-07	**Philadelphia**	**NHL**	**40**	**11**	**29**	**40**	**72**	**5**	**0**	**2**	**63**	**17.5**	**2**	**690**	**50.9**	**17:44**	....	....	....	....	....	....	....	....	....
	Nashville	**NHL**	**17**	**2**	**13**	**15**	**16**	**1**	**0**	**1**	**36**	**5.6**	**5**	**267**	**47.6**	**19:36**	**5**	**2**	**2**	**4**	**12**	**0**	**0**	**0**	**20:57**
2007-08	**Colorado**	**NHL**	**9**	**1**	**13**	**14**	**8**	**0**	**0**	**0**	**15**	**6.7**	**7**	**4**	**100.0**	**19:15**	**7**	**1**	**4**	**5**	**14**	**0**	**0**	**0**	**18:17**
	NHL Totals		**706**	**249**	**636**	**885**	**686**	**71**	**16**	**43**	**1690**	**14.7**		**5329**	**48.9**	**20:16**	**151**	**64**	**107**	**171**	**163**	**16**	**2**	**14**	**20:04**

NHL All-Rookie Team (1995) • Calder Memorial Trophy (1995) • NHL First All-Star Team (1998, 1999, 2003) • Bud Light Plus/Minus Award (2003) (tied with Milan Hejduk) • Art Ross Trophy (2003) • Hart Memorial Trophy (2003).

Played in NHL All-Star Game (1996, 1998, 1999, 2001, 2003)

Traded to **Quebec** by **Philadelphia** with Steve Duchesne, Kerry Huffman, Mike Ricci, Ron Hextall, Philadelphia's 1st round choice (Jocelyn Thibault) in 1993 Entry Draft, $15,000,000 and future considerations (Chris Simon and Philadelphia's 1st round choice (later traded to Toronto – later traded to Washington – Washington selected Nolan Baumgartner) in 1994 Entry Draft, July 21, 1992) for Eric Lindros, June 30, 1992. Transferred to **Colorado** after **Quebec** franchise relocated, June 21, 1995. • Missed entire 2001-02 regular season recovering from spleen (May 9, 2001 vs. Los Angeles) and ankle (January 10, 2002 in practive) injuries. • Missed majority of 2003-04 season recovering from groin (October 28, 2003 vs. Calgary) and hip (February 16, 2004 vs. Vancouver) injuries. Signed as a free agent by **MODO** (Sweden), September 18, 2004. Signed as a free agent by **Philadelphia**, August 3, 2005. Traded to **Nashville** by **Philadelphia** for Scottie Upshall, Ryan Parent and Nashville's 1st (later traded back to Nashville - Nashville selected Jonathon Blum) and 3rd (later traded to Washington - Washington selected Phil Desimone) round choices in 2007 Entry Draft, February 15, 2007. Signed as a free agent by **Colorado**, February 25, 2008.

FOSTER, Alex

(FAW-stuhr, AL-ehx) **TOR.**

Center. Shoots left. 6'1", 195 lbs. Born, Canton, MI, August 26, 1984.

			Regular Season														Playoffs								
Season	Club	League	GP	G	A	Pts	PIM	PP	SH	GW	S	%	+/-	TF	F%	Min	GP	G	A	Pts	PIM	PP	SH	GW	Min
2002-03	Sioux Falls	USHL	57	6	15	21	72	....	....	....	....	....	....	....	....	....	3	0	1	1	8	....	....	....	....
2003-04	Sioux Falls	USHL	5	0	1	1	0	....	....	....	....	....	....	....	....	....	....	....	....	....	....	....	....	....	....
	Danville Wings	USHL	55	23	30	53	91	....	....	....	....	....	....	....	....	....	6	1	2	3	6	....	....	....	....
2004-05	Bowling Green	CCHA	34	8	23	31	31	....	....	....	....	....	....	....	....	....	....	....	....	....	....	....	....	....	....
2005-06	Bowling Green	CCHA	38	11	40	51	40	....	....	....	....	....	....	....	....	....	....	....	....	....	....	....	....	....	....
2006-07	Toronto Marlies	AHL	57	8	9	17	31	....	....	....	....	....	....	....	....	....	....	....	....	....	....	....	....	....	....
	Columbia Inferno	ECHL	9	1	10	11	6	....	....	....	....	....	....	....	....	....	....	....	....	....	....	....	....	....	....
2007-08	**Toronto**	**NHL**	**3**	**0**	**0**	**0**	**0**	**0**	**0**	**0**	**1**	**0.0**	**0**	**1**	**0.0**	**3:32**	....	....	....	....	....	....	....	....	....
	Toronto Marlies	AHL	67	18	28	46	30	....	....	....	....	....	....	....	....	....	19	2	6	8	12	....	....	....	....
	NHL Totals		**3**	**0**	**0**	**0**	**0**	**0**	**0**	**0**	**1**	**0.0**		**1**	**0.0**	**3:32**	....	....	....	....	....	....	....	....	....

CCHA Second All-Star Team (2006)

Signed as a free agent by **Toronto**, March 8, 2006.

FOSTER, Kurtis

(FAW-stuhr, KUHR-this) **MIN.**

Defense. Shoots right. 6'5", 220 lbs. Born, Carp, Ont., November 24, 1981. Calgary's 2nd choice, 40th overall, in 2000 Entry Draft.

			Regular Season														Playoffs								
Season	Club	League	GP	G	A	Pts	PIM	PP	SH	GW	S	%	+/-	TF	F%	Min	GP	G	A	Pts	PIM	PP	SH	GW	Min
1996-97	Ottawa Valley	ODMHA	36	7	18	25	88	....	....	....	....	....	....	....	....	....	....	....	....	....	....	....	....	....	....
1997-98	Peterborough	OHL	39	1	1	2	45	....	....	....	....	....	....	....	....	....	4	0	0	0	2	....	....	....	....
1998-99	Peterborough	OHL	54	2	13	15	59	....	....	....	....	....	....	....	....	....	5	0	0	0	6	....	....	....	....
99-2000	Peterborough	OHL	68	6	18	24	116	....	....	....	....	....	....	....	....	....	5	1	2	3	4	....	....	....	....
2000-01	Peterborough	OHL	62	17	24	41	78	....	....	....	....	....	....	....	....	....	7	1	1	2	10	....	....	....	....
2001-02	Peterborough	OHL	33	10	4	14	58	....	....	....	....	....	....	....	....	....	....	....	....	....	....	....	....	....	....
	Chicago Wolves	AHL	39	6	9	15	59	....	....	....	....	....	....	....	....	....	14	1	1	2	21	....	....	....	....
2002-03	**Atlanta**	**NHL**	**2**	**0**	**0**	**0**	**0**	**0**	**0**	**0**	**1**	**0.0**	**–2**	**0**	**0.0**	**11:06**	....	....	....	....	....	....	....	....	....
	Chicago Wolves	AHL	75	15	27	42	159	....	....	....	....	....	....	....	....	....	9	1	3	4	14	....	....	....	....
2003-04	**Atlanta**	**NHL**	**3**	**0**	**1**	**1**	**0**	**0**	**0**	**0**	**1**	**0.0**	**0**	**0**	**0.0**	**6:58**	....	....	....	....	....	....	....	....	....
	Chicago Wolves	AHL	67	11	19	30	95	....	....	....	....	....	....	....	....	....	10	0	3	3	12	....	....	....	....
2004-05	Cincinnati	AHL	78	17	25	42	71	....	....	....	....	....	....	....	....	....	9	2	3	5	28	....	....	....	....
2005-06	**Minnesota**	**NHL**	**58**	**10**	**18**	**28**	**60**	**6**	**0**	**2**	**124**	**8.1**	**–3**	**0**	**0.0**	**19:13**	....	....	....	....	....	....	....	....	....
	Houston Aeros	AHL	19	4	11	15	32	....	....	....	....	....	....	....	....	....	....	....	....	....	....	....	....	....	....

Season	Club	League	Regular Season GP	G	A	Pts	PIM	PP	SH	GW	S	%	+/-	TF	F%	Min	Playoffs GP	G	A	Pts	PIM	PP	SH	GW	Min
2006-07	Minnesota	NHL	57	3	20	23	52	0	0	0	135	2.2	-3	1	100.0	17:59	3	0	2	2	0	0	0	0	18:38
2007-08	Minnesota	NHL	56	7	12	19	37	3	0	2	118	5.9	0	3	66.7	16:24	....	....	....	....	....	....	....	....	....
	NHL Totals		176	20	51	71	149	9	0	4	379	5.3		4	75.0	17:37	3	0	2	2	0	0	0	0	18:38

Yanick Dupre Memorial Award (Outstanding Humanitarian Contribution - AHL) (2004)

Rights traded to **Atlanta** by **Calgary** with Jeff Cowan for Petr Buzek and Atlanta's 6th round choice (Adam Pardy) in 2004 Entry Draft, December 18, 2001. Traded to **Anaheim** by **Atlanta** for Niclas Havelid, June 26, 2004. Signed as a free agent by **Minnesota**, August 4, 2005.

FOY, Matt

(FOI, MAT) **ST.L.**

Right wing. Shoots right. 6'2", 228 lbs. Born, Oakville, Ont., May 18, 1983. Minnesota's 6th choice, 175th overall, in 2002 Entry Draft.

Season	Club	League	GP	G	A	Pts	PIM	PP	SH	GW	S	%	+/-	TF	F%	Min	GP	G	A	Pts	PIM	PP	SH	GW	Min
2000-01	Wexford Raiders	OPJHL	47	43	49	92	30																		
2001-02	Merrimack	H-East	31	7	17	24	48																		
2002-03	Ottawa 67's	OHL	68	61	71	132	112										21	11	20	31	47				
2003-04	Houston Aeros	AHL	51	11	13	24	74										1	0	0	0	0				
2004-05	Houston Aeros	AHL	69	12	13	25	78										5	1	2	3	6				
2005-06	**Minnesota**	**NHL**	**19**	**2**	**3**	**5**	**16**	**1**	**0**	**0**	**21**	**9.5**	**-4**	**1**	**0.0**	**10:59**									
	Houston Aeros	AHL	51	15	25	40	122										8	5	3	8	29				
2006-07	**Minnesota**	**NHL**	**9**	**0**	**0**	**0**	**4**	**0**	**0**	**0**	**6**	**0.0**	**-1**	**0**	**0.0**	**7:11**									
	Houston Aeros	AHL	62	27	23	50	121																		
2007-08	**Minnesota**	**NHL**	**28**	**4**	**4**	**8**	**28**	**0**	**0**	**1**	**38**	**10.5**	**-1**	**7**	**28.6**	**7:50**	**1**	**0**	**0**	**0**	**0**	**0**	**0**	**0**	**6:49**
	NHL Totals		**56**	**6**	**7**	**13**	**48**	**1**	**0**	**1**	**65**	**9.2**		**8**	**25.0**	**8:48**	**1**	**0**	**0**	**0**	**0**	**0**	**0**	**0**	**6:49**

OHL First All-Star Team (2003)

• Officially announced intention to withdraw from **Merrimack College** (Hockey East) for academic reasons, May 30, 2002. • Spent majority of 2007-08 season as a healthy reserve. Signed as a free agent by **St. Louis**, July 14, 2008..

FRANZEN, Johan

(FRAN-zehn, YOH-han) **DET.**

Left wing. Shoots left. 6'3", 220 lbs. Born, Landsbro, Sweden, December 23, 1979. Detroit's 1st choice, 97th overall, in 2004 Entry Draft.

Season	Club	League	GP	G	A	Pts	PIM	PP	SH	GW	S	%	+/-	TF	F%	Min	GP	G	A	Pts	PIM	PP	SH	GW	Min
2001-02	Linkopings HC	Sweden	36	2	6	8	64																		
2002-03	Linkopings HC	Sweden	37	2	4	6	14																		
2003-04	Linkopings HC	Sweden	49	12	18	30	26										5	0	1	1	8				
2004-05	Linkopings HC	Sweden	43	7	7	14	45										6	2	0	2	16				
2005-06	**Detroit**	**NHL**	**80**	**12**	**4**	**16**	**36**	**0**	**2**	**2**	**119**	**10.1**	**4**	**171**	**41.5**	**12:27**	**6**	**1**	**2**	**3**	**4**	**0**	**0**	**0**	**12:00**
2006-07	**Detroit**	**NHL**	**69**	**10**	**20**	**30**	**37**	**0**	**1**	**2**	**151**	**6.6**	**20**	**45**	**40.0**	**15:35**	**18**	**3**	**4**	**7**	**10**	**0**	**0**	**2**	**16:47**
2007-08♦	**Detroit**	**NHL**	**72**	**27**	**11**	**38**	**51**	**14**	**0**	**8**	**199**	**13.6**	**12**	**390**	**48.5**	**17:44**	**16**	***13**	**5**	**18**	**14**	**6**	**2**	**5**	**18:49**
	NHL Totals		**221**	**49**	**35**	**84**	**124**	**14**	**3**	**12**	**469**	**10.4**		**606**	**45.9**	**15:09**	**40**	**17**	**11**	**28**	**28**	**6**	**2**	**7**	**16:53**

FRASER, Colin

(FRAY-zuhr, KAW-lihn) **CHI.**

Center. Shoots left. 6'1", 190 lbs. Born, Surrey, B.C., January 28, 1985. Philadelphia's 3rd choice, 69th overall, in 2003 Entry Draft.

Season	Club	League	GP	G	A	Pts	PIM	PP	SH	GW	S	%	+/-	TF	F%	Min	GP	G	A	Pts	PIM	PP	SH	GW	Min
2000-01	Port Coquitlam	PIJHL	38	16	24	40	90										8	2	2	4	21				
2001-02	Red Deer Rebels	WHL	67	11	31	42	126										23	2	1	3	39				
2002-03	Red Deer Rebels	WHL	69	15	37	52	192										22	7	6	13	40				
2003-04	Red Deer Rebels	WHL	70	24	29	53	174										19	5	9	14	24				
2004-05	Red Deer Rebels	WHL	63	24	43	67	148										7	2	5	7	8				
	Norfolk Admirals	AHL	3	0	0	0	20										6	1	0	1	2				
2005-06	Norfolk Admirals	AHL	75	12	13	25	145										4	0	0	0	7				
2006-07	**Chicago**	**NHL**	**1**	**0**	**0**	**0**	**2**	**0**	**0**	**0**	**0**	**0.0**	**-1**	**2**	**0.0**	**3:18**									
	Norfolk Admirals	AHL	67	12	24	36	158										6	1	0	1	21				
2007-08	**Chicago**	**NHL**	**5**	**0**	**0**	**0**	**7**	**0**	**0**	**0**	**4**	**0.0**	**-2**	**38**	**36.8**	**10:19**									
	Rockford IceHogs	AHL	75	17	24	41	165										12	1	2	3	28				
	NHL Totals		**6**	**0**	**0**	**0**	**9**	**0**	**0**	**0**	**4**	**0.0**		**40**	**35.0**	**9:09**									

Canadian Major Junior Humanitarian Player of the Year (2005)

Traded to **Chicago** by **Philadelphia** with Jim Vandermeer and Los Angeles' 2nd round choice (previously acquired, Chicago selected Bryan Bickell) in 2004 Entry Draft for Alex Zhamnov and Washington's 4th round choice (previously acquired, Philadelphia selected R.J. Anderson) in 2004 Entry Draft, February 19, 2004.

FRASER, Mark

(FRAY-zuhr, MAHRK) **N.J.**

Defense. Shoots left. 6'3", 220 lbs. Born, Ottawa, Ont., September 29, 1986. New Jersey's 3rd choice, 84th overall, in 2005 Entry Draft.

Season	Club	League	GP	G	A	Pts	PIM	PP	SH	GW	S	%	+/-	TF	F%	Min	GP	G	A	Pts	PIM	PP	SH	GW	Min
2004-05	Gloucester	CJHL	STATISTICS NOT AVAILABLE																						
	Kitchener Rangers	OHL	58	0	8	8	96										15	0	3	3	26				
2005-06	Kitchener Rangers	OHL	59	0	5	5	129										5	0	1	1	4				
	Albany River Rats	AHL	4	0	0	0	2																		
2006-07	**New Jersey**	**NHL**	**7**	**0**	**0**	**0**	**7**	**0**	**0**	**0**	**1**	**0.0**	**-1**	**0**	**0.0**	**3:34**									
	Lowell Devils	AHL	71	1	8	9	73																		
2007-08	Lowell Devils	AHL	79	1	17	18	96																		
	NHL Totals		**7**	**0**	**0**	**0**	**7**	**0**	**0**	**0**	**1**	**0.0**		**0**	**0.0**	**3:34**									

FRIESEN, Jeff

(FREE-zuhn, JEHF)

Left wing. Shoots left. 6'1", 205 lbs. Born, Meadow Lake, Sask., August 5, 1976. San Jose's 1st choice, 11th overall, in 1994 Entry Draft.

Season	Club	League	GP	G	A	Pts	PIM	PP	SH	GW	S	%	+/-	TF	F%	Min	GP	G	A	Pts	PIM	PP	SH	GW	Min
1991-92	Sask. Contacts	SMHL	35	37	51	88	75																		
	Regina Pats	WHL	4	3	1	4	2																		
1992-93	Regina Pats	WHL	70	45	38	83	23										13	7	10	17	8				
1993-94	Regina Pats	WHL	66	51	67	118	48										4	3	2	5	2				
1994-95	Regina Pats	WHL	25	21	23	44	22																		
	San Jose	**NHL**	**48**	**15**	**10**	**25**	**14**	**5**	**1**	**2**	**86**	**17.4**	**-8**				**11**	**1**	**5**	**6**	**4**	**0**	**0**	**0**	
1995-96	**San Jose**	**NHL**	**79**	**15**	**31**	**46**	**42**	**2**	**0**	**0**	**123**	**12.2**	**-19**												
1996-97	**San Jose**	**NHL**	**82**	**28**	**34**	**62**	**75**	**6**	**2**	**5**	**200**	**14.0**	**-8**												
1997-98	**San Jose**	**NHL**	**79**	**31**	**32**	**63**	**40**	**7**	**6**	**7**	**186**	**16.7**	**8**				**6**	**0**	**1**	**1**	**2**	**0**	**0**	**0**	
1998-99	**San Jose**	**NHL**	**78**	**22**	**35**	**57**	**42**	**10**	**1**	**3**	**215**	**10.2**	**3**	**24**	**33.3**	**19:25**	**6**	**2**	**2**	**4**	**14**	**1**	**0**	**0**	**22:22**
99-2000	**San Jose**	**NHL**	**82**	**26**	**35**	**61**	**47**	**11**	**3**	**7**	**191**	**13.6**	**-2**	**3**	**66.7**	**19:48**	**11**	**2**	**2**	**4**	**10**	**0**	**0**	**0**	**17:21**
2000-01	**San Jose**	**NHL**	**64**	**12**	**24**	**36**	**56**	**2**	**0**	**1**	**120**	**10.0**	**7**	**7**	**28.6**	**18:51**									
	Anaheim	**NHL**	**15**	**2**	**10**	**12**	**10**	**2**	**0**	**0**	**29**	**6.9**	**-2**	**43**	**55.8**	**21:28**									
2001-02	**Anaheim**	**NHL**	**81**	**17**	**26**	**43**	**44**	**1**	**1**	**0**	**161**	**10.6**	**-1**	**45**	**48.9**	**17:59**									
2002-03♦	**New Jersey**	**NHL**	**81**	**23**	**28**	**51**	**26**	**3**	**0**	**4**	**179**	**12.8**	**23**	**11**	**45.5**	**15:33**	**24**	**10**	**4**	**14**	**6**	**1**	**0**	**4**	**16:02**
2003-04	**New Jersey**	**NHL**	**81**	**17**	**20**	**37**	**26**	**5**	**0**	**4**	**177**	**9.6**	**8**	**31**	**45.2**	**15:08**	**5**	**0**	**0**	**0**	**4**	**0**	**0**	**0**	**12:55**
2004-05			DID NOT PLAY																						
2005-06	**Washington**	**NHL**	**33**	**3**	**4**	**7**	**24**	**0**	**0**	**0**	**64**	**4.7**	**-11**	**13**	**46.2**	**14:45**									
	Anaheim	**NHL**	**18**	**1**	**3**	**4**	**8**	**0**	**0**	**1**	**11**	**9.1**	**-4**	**0**	**0.0**	**10:53**	**16**	**3**	**1**	**4**	**6**	**0**	**0**	**0**	**11:14**
2006-07	**Calgary**	**NHL**	**72**	**6**	**6**	**12**	**34**	**0**	**1**	**0**	**55**	**10.9**	**-2**	**21**	**38.1**	**12:11**	**5**	**0**	**0**	**0**	**2**	**0**	**0**	**0**	**10:50**
2007-08	Lake Erie	AHL	5	1	4	5	0																		
	NHL Totals		**893**	**218**	**298**	**516**	**488**	**54**	**15**	**34**	**1797**	**12.1**		**198**	**46.0**	**16:48**	**84**	**18**	**15**	**33**	**48**	**2**	**0**	**4**	**15:03**

WHL Rookie of the Year (1993) • Canadian Major Junior Rookie of the Year (1993) • NHL All-Rookie Team (1995)

Traded to **Anaheim** by **San Jose** with Steve Shields and San Jose's 2nd round choice (later traded to Dallas – Dallas selected Vojtech Polak) in 2003 Entry Draft for Teemu Selanne, March 5, 2001. Traded to **New Jersey** by **Anaheim** with Oleg Tverdovsky and Maxim Balmochnykh for Petr Sykora, Mike Commodore, Jean-Francois Damphousse and Igor Pohanka, July 6, 2002. Traded to **Washington** by **New Jersey** for Washington's 3rd round choice (Kirill Tulupov) in 2006 Entry Draft, September 26, 2005. Traded to **Anaheim** by **Washington** for Anaheim's 2nd round choice (Keith Seabrook) in 2006 Entry Draft, March 9, 2006. Signed as a free agent by **Calgary**, July 5, 2006. Signed as a free agent by **Lake Erie** (AHL), January 14, 2008.

FRITSCHE, Dan

(FRIH-tchee, DAN) **NYR**

Center. Shoots right. 6'1", 206 lbs. Born, Parma, OH, July 13, 1985. Columbus' 2nd choice, 46th overall, in 2003 Entry Draft.

Season	Club	League	GP	G	A	Pts	PIM	PP	SH	GW	S	%	+/-	TF	F%	Min	GP	G	A	Pts	PIM	PP	SH	GW	Min
2000-01	Cleveland Barons	NAHL	49	23	29	52	47										1	1	1	2	0				
2001-02	Sarnia Sting	OHL	17	5	13	18	20																		
2002-03	Sarnia Sting	OHL	61	32	39	71	79										5	2	2	4	4				
2003-04	Sarnia Sting	OHL	27	16	13	29	26										5	1	5	6	0				
	Columbus	**NHL**	**19**	**1**	**0**	**1**	**12**	**0**	**0**	**0**	**19**	**5.3**	**-5**	**139**	**38.1**	**8:24**									
	Syracuse Crunch	AHL	4	2	0	2	0										4	0	1	1	4				

			Regular Season														Playoffs								
Season	Club	League	GP	G	A	Pts	PIM	PP	SH	GW	S	%	+/-	TF	F%	Min	GP	G	A	Pts	PIM	PP	SH	GW	Min
2004-05	Sarnia Sting	OHL	2	1	1	2	0	....	....	....	....	....	....	....	....	....	....	....	....	....	....	....	....	....	....
	London Knights	OHL	28	17	18	35	18	....	....	....	....	....	....	....	....	....	17	9	13	22	12	....	....	....	....
2005-06	**Columbus**	**NHL**	**59**	**6**	**7**	**13**	**22**	**0**	**0**	**0**	**93**	**6.5**	**-14**	**270**	**48.9**	**10:17**	....	....	....	....	....	....	....	....	....
	Syracuse Crunch	AHL	19	5	4	9	12	....	....	....	....	....	....	....	....	....	6	2	2	4	8	....	....	....	....
2006-07	**Columbus**	**NHL**	**59**	**12**	**15**	**27**	**35**	**5**	**1**	**4**	**81**	**14.8**	**3**	**296**	**49.3**	**14:02**	....	....	....	....	....	....	....	....	....
2007-08	**Columbus**	**NHL**	**69**	**10**	**12**	**22**	**22**	**1**	**1**	**4**	**109**	**9.2**	**2**	**121**	**48.8**	**12:21**	....	....	....	....	....	....	....	....	....
	NHL Totals		**206**	**29**	**34**	**63**	**91**	**6**	**2**	**8**	**302**	**9.6**		**826**	**47.2**	**11:53**	....	....	....	....	....	....	....	....	....

Memorial Cup Tournament All-Star Team (2005)

• Missed majority of 2001-02 season recovering from shoulder surgery, December 12, 2001. Traded to **NY Rangers** by **Columbus** with Nikolai Zherdev for Fedor Tyutin and Christian Backman, July 2, 2008.

FROLOV, Alexander

(froh-LAHF, al-EHX-AN-duhr) **L.A.**

Left wing. Shoots right. 6'2", 216 lbs. Born, Moscow, USSR, June 19, 1982. Los Angeles' 1st choice, 20th overall, in 2000 Entry Draft.

Season	Club	League	GP	G	A	Pts	PIM	PP	SH	GW	S	%	+/-	TF	F%	Min	GP	G	A	Pts	PIM	PP	SH	GW	Min
1998-99	Spartak Moscow	Russia	1	0	0	0	0	....	....	....	....	....	....	....	....	....	....	....	....	....	....	....	....	....	....
99-2000	Yaroslavl 2	Russia-3	36	27	13	40	30	....	....	....	....	....	....	....	....	....	....	....	....	....	....	....	....	....	....
2000-01	Krylja Sovetov	Russia-2	44	20	19	39	8	....	....	....	....	....	....	....	....	....	....	....	....	....	....	....	....	....	....
2001-02	Krylja Sovetov	Russia	43	18	12	30	16	....	....	....	....	....	....	....	....	....	3	1	0	1	0	....	....	....	....
	Krylja Sovetov 2	Russia-3	2	0	0	0	4	....	....	....	....	....	....	....	....	....	....	....	....	....	....	....	....	....	....
2002-03	**Los Angeles**	**NHL**	**79**	**14**	**17**	**31**	**34**	**1**	**0**	**3**	**141**	**9.9**	**12**	**9**	**22.2**	**14:23**	....	....	....	....	....	....	....	....	....
2003-04	**Los Angeles**	**NHL**	**77**	**24**	**24**	**48**	**24**	**5**	**2**	**3**	**168**	**14.3**	**8**	**34**	**32.4**	**17:13**	....	....	....	....	....	....	....	....	....
	Nizhny Novgorod	Russia	1	0	0	0	0	....	....	....	....	....	....	....	....	....	....	....	....	....	....	....	....	....	....
2004-05	CSKA Moscow	Russia	42	20	17	37	10	....	....	....	....	....	....	....	....	....	....	....	....	....	....	....	....	....	....
	Dynamo Moscow	Russia	6	2	1	3	2	....	....	....	....	....	....	....	....	....	6	2	1	3	0	....	....	....	....
2005-06	**Los Angeles**	**NHL**	**69**	**21**	**33**	**54**	**40**	**4**	**3**	**4**	**174**	**12.1**	**17**	**4**	**50.0**	**19:18**	....	....	....	....	....	....	....	....	....
	Russia	Olympics	3	0	1	1	0	....	....	....	....	....	....	....	....	....	....	....	....	....	....	....	....	....	....
2006-07	**Los Angeles**	**NHL**	**82**	**35**	**36**	**71**	**34**	**10**	**1**	**6**	**195**	**17.9**	**-8**	**19**	**36.8**	**19:56**	....	....	....	....	....	....	....	....	....
2007-08	**Los Angeles**	**NHL**	**71**	**23**	**44**	**67**	**22**	**5**	**0**	**7**	**160**	**14.4**	**1**	**11**	**18.2**	**18:48**	....	....	....	....	....	....	....	....	....
	NHL Totals		**378**	**117**	**154**	**271**	**154**	**25**	**6**	**23**	**838**	**14.0**		**77**	**31.2**	**17:54**	....	....	....	....	....	....	....	....	....

Signed as a free agent by **CSKA Moscow** (Russia), July 14, 2004. Signed as a free agent by **Dynamo Moscow** (Russia), February 17, 2005.

FUNK, Michael

(FUHNK, MIGH-kuhl) **BUF.**

Defense. Shoots left. 6'4", 213 lbs. Born, Abbotsford, B.C., August 15, 1986. Buffalo's 2nd choice, 43rd overall, in 2004 Entry Draft.

Season	Club	League	GP	G	A	Pts	PIM	PP	SH	GW	S	%	+/-	TF	F%	Min	GP	G	A	Pts	PIM	PP	SH	GW	Min
2001-02	Abbotsford	Minor-BC	72	9	24	33	84	....	....	....	....	....	....	....	....	....	....	....	....	....	....	....	....	....	....
2002-03	Portland	WHL	68	1	15	16	54	....	....	....	....	....	....	....	....	....	7	0	1	1	15	....	....	....	....
2003-04	Portland	WHL	71	3	25	28	86	....	....	....	....	....	....	....	....	....	5	0	1	1	6	....	....	....	....
2004-05	Portland	WHL	71	8	22	30	84	....	....	....	....	....	....	....	....	....	7	1	1	2	4	....	....	....	....
2005-06	Portland	WHL	70	11	36	47	88	....	....	....	....	....	....	....	....	....	5	0	0	0	8	....	....	....	....
2006-07	**Buffalo**	**NHL**	**5**	**0**	**2**	**2**	**0**	**0**	**0**	**0**	**1**	**0.0**	**2**	**0**	**0.0**	**3:26**	....	....	....	....	....	....	....	....	....
	Rochester	AHL	61	2	5	7	57	....	....	....	....	....	....	....	....	....	6	0	1	1	4	....	....	....	....
2007-08	**Buffalo**	**NHL**	**4**	**0**	**0**	**0**	**0**	**0**	**0**	**0**	**1**	**0.0**	**-3**	**0**	**0.0**	**11:37**	....	....	....	....	....	....	....	....	....
	Rochester	AHL	58	0	10	10	104	....	....	....	....	....	....	....	....	....	....	....	....	....	....	....	....	....	....
	NHL Totals		**9**	**0**	**2**	**2**	**0**	**0**	**0**	**0**	**2**	**0.0**		**0**	**0.0**	**7:04**	....	....	....	....	....	....	....	....	....

GABORIK, Marian

(GAB-rihk, MAIR-ee-uhn) **MIN.**

Right wing. Shoots left. 6'1", 199 lbs. Born, Trencin, Czech., February 14, 1982. Minnesota's 1st choice, 3rd overall, in 2000 Entry Draft.

Season	Club	League	GP	G	A	Pts	PIM	PP	SH	GW	S	%	+/-	TF	F%	Min	GP	G	A	Pts	PIM	PP	SH	GW	Min
1997-98	Dukla Trencin Jr.	Slovak-Jr.	36	37	22	59	28	....	....	....	....	....	....	....	....	....	....	....	....	....	....	....	....	....	....
	Dukla Trencin	Slovakia	1	1	0	1	0	....	....	....	....	....	....	....	....	....	....	....	....	....	....	....	....	....	....
1998-99	Dukla Trencin	Slovakia	33	11	9	20	6	....	....	....	....	....	....	....	....	....	3	1	0	1	2	....	....	....	....
99-2000	Dukla Trencin	Slovakia	50	25	21	46	34	....	....	....	....	....	....	....	....	....	5	1	2	3	2	....	....	....	....
2000-01	**Minnesota**	**NHL**	**71**	**18**	**18**	**36**	**32**	**6**	**0**	**3**	**179**	**10.1**	**-6**	**3**	**33.3**	**15:26**	....	....	....	....	....	....	....	....	....
2001-02	**Minnesota**	**NHL**	**78**	**30**	**37**	**67**	**34**	**10**	**0**	**4**	**221**	**13.6**	**0**	**4**	**25.0**	**16:47**	....	....	....	....	....	....	....	....	....
2002-03	**Minnesota**	**NHL**	**81**	**30**	**35**	**65**	**46**	**5**	**1**	**8**	**280**	**10.7**	**12**	**16**	**25.0**	**17:24**	**18**	**9**	**8**	**17**	**6**	**4**	**0**	**0**	**18:12**
2003-04	Dukla Trencin	Slovakia	9	10	3	13	10	....	....	....	....	....	....	....	....	....	....	....	....	....	....	....	....	....	....
	Minnesota	**NHL**	**65**	**18**	**22**	**40**	**20**	**3**	**0**	**4**	**220**	**8.2**	**10**	**11**	**45.5**	**18:17**	....	....	....	....	....	....	....	....	....
2004-05	Dukla Trencin	Slovakia	29	25	27	52	46	....	....	....	....	....	....	....	....	....	12	8	9	17	26	....	....	....	....
	Farjestad	Sweden	12	6	4	10	45	....	....	....	....	....	....	....	....	....	....	....	....	....	....	....	....	....	....
2005-06	**Minnesota**	**NHL**	**65**	**38**	**28**	**66**	**64**	**10**	**2**	**7**	**252**	**15.1**	**6**	**11**	**27.3**	**18:26**	....	....	....	....	....	....	....	....	....
	Slovakia	Olympics	6	3	4	7	4	....	....	....	....	....	....	....	....	....	....	....	....	....	....	....	....	....	....
2006-07	**Minnesota**	**NHL**	**48**	**30**	**27**	**57**	**40**	**12**	**1**	**7**	**196**	**15.3**	**12**	**4**	**0.0**	**19:38**	**5**	**3**	**1**	**4**	**8**	**1**	**1**	**1**	**19:32**
2007-08	**Minnesota**	**NHL**	**77**	**42**	**41**	**83**	**63**	**11**	**1**	**8**	**278**	**15.1**	**17**	**21**	**28.6**	**19:36**	**6**	**0**	**1**	**1**	**4**	**0**	**0**	**0**	**21:51**
	NHL Totals		**485**	**206**	**208**	**414**	**299**	**57**	**5**	**41**	**1626**	**12.7**		**70**	**28.6**	**17:50**	**29**	**12**	**10**	**22**	**18**	**5**	**1**	**1**	**19:11**

Played in NHL All-Star Game (2003, 2008)

Signed as a free agent by **Trencin** (Slovakia), July 5, 2004. Signed as a free agent by **Farjestad** (Sweden), December 21, 2004.

GAGNE, Simon

(gah-N'YAY, see-MOHN) **PHI.**

Left wing. Shoots left. 6', 195 lbs. Born, Ste-Foy, Que., February 29, 1980. Philadelphia's 1st choice, 22nd overall, in 1998 Entry Draft.

Season	Club	League	GP	G	A	Pts	PIM	PP	SH	GW	S	%	+/-	TF	F%	Min	GP	G	A	Pts	PIM	PP	SH	GW	Min
1995-96	Ste-Foy	QAAA	27	13	9	22	18	....	....	....	....	....	....	....	....	....	15	7	8	15	8	....	....	....	....
1996-97	Beauport	QMJHL	51	9	22	31	49	....	....	....	....	....	....	....	....	....	....	....	....	....	....	....	....	....	....
1997-98	Quebec Remparts	QMJHL	53	30	39	69	26	....	....	....	....	....	....	....	....	....	12	11	5	16	23	....	....	....	....
1998-99	Quebec Remparts	QMJHL	61	50	*70	*120	42	....	....	....	....	....	....	....	....	....	13	9	8	17	4	....	....	....	....
99-2000	**Philadelphia**	**NHL**	**80**	**20**	**28**	**48**	**22**	**8**	**1**	**4**	**159**	**12.6**	**11**	**443**	**42.2**	**14:59**	**17**	**5**	**5**	**10**	**2**	**2**	**0**	**1**	**16:46**
2000-01	**Philadelphia**	**NHL**	**69**	**27**	**32**	**59**	**18**	**6**	**0**	**7**	**191**	**14.1**	**24**	**21**	**28.6**	**18:05**	**6**	**3**	**0**	**3**	**0**	**2**	**0**	**0**	**19:09**
2001-02	**Philadelphia**	**NHL**	**79**	**33**	**33**	**66**	**32**	**4**	**1**	**7**	**199**	**16.6**	**31**	**6**	**83.3**	**18:09**	**5**	**0**	**0**	**0**	**2**	**0**	**0**	**0**	**19:16**
	Canada	Olympics	6	1	3	4	0	....	....	....	....	....	....	....	....	....	....	....	....	....	....	....	....	....	....
2002-03	**Philadelphia**	**NHL**	**46**	**9**	**18**	**27**	**16**	**1**	**1**	**3**	**115**	**7.8**	**20**	**70**	**42.9**	**17:24**	**13**	**4**	**1**	**5**	**6**	**0**	**1**	**1**	**18:13**
2003-04	**Philadelphia**	**NHL**	**80**	**24**	**21**	**45**	**29**	**6**	**0**	**6**	**211**	**11.4**	**12**	**104**	**39.4**	**16:27**	**18**	**5**	**4**	**9**	**12**	**0**	**0**	**1**	**16:48**
2004-05			DID NOT PLAY																						
2005-06	**Philadelphia**	**NHL**	**72**	**47**	**32**	**79**	**38**	**12**	**2**	**7**	**334**	**14.1**	**31**	**18**	**38.9**	**20:46**	**6**	**3**	**1**	**4**	**2**	**1**	**0**	**0**	**21:45**
	Canada	Olympics	6	1	2	3	6	....	....	....	....	....	....	....	....	....	....	....	....	....	....	....	....	....	....
2006-07	**Philadelphia**	**NHL**	**76**	**41**	**27**	**68**	**30**	**13**	**2**	**4**	**291**	**14.1**	**2**	**49**	**42.9**	**21:02**	....	....	....	....	....	....	....	....	....
2007-08	**Philadelphia**	**NHL**	**25**	**7**	**11**	**18**	**4**	**5**	**0**	**2**	**76**	**9.2**	**-8**	**2**	**50.0**	**18:09**	....	....	....	....	....	....	....	....	....
	NHL Totals		**527**	**208**	**202**	**410**	**189**	**55**	**7**	**40**	**1576**	**13.2**		**713**	**41.8**	**18:07**	**65**	**20**	**11**	**31**	**24**	**5**	**1**	**3**	**17:56**

QMJHL Second All-Star Team (1999) • NHL All-Rookie Team (2000)

Played in NHL ALL-Star Game (2001, 2007)

• Missed majority of 2007-08 season recovering from head injury suffered in game at Pittsburgh, February 10, 2008.

GAGNER, Sam

(GAH-n'yay, SAM) **EDM.**

Center/Wing. Shoots right. 5'11", 191 lbs. Born, London, Ont., August 10, 1989. Edmonton's 1st choice, 6th overall, in 2007 Entry Draft.

Season	Club	League	GP	G	A	Pts	PIM	PP	SH	GW	S	%	+/-	TF	F%	Min	GP	G	A	Pts	PIM	PP	SH	GW	Min
2001-02	Tor. Marlboros	GTHL	68	56	61	117	42	....	....	....	....	....	....	....	....	....	....	....	....	....	....	....	....	....	....
2002-03	Tor. Marlboros	GTHL	72	68	86	154	35	....	....	....	....	....	....	....	....	....	....	....	....	....	....	....	....	....	....
2003-04	Tor. Marlboros	GTHL	85	64	108	171	36	....	....	....	....	....	....	....	....	....	....	....	....	....	....	....	....	....	....
2004-05	Tor. Marlboros	GTHL	70	62	118	180	56	....	....	....	....	....	....	....	....	....	....	....	....	....	....	....	....	....	....
2005-06	Sioux City	USHL	56	11	35	46	60	....	....	....	....	....	....	....	....	....	....	....	....	....	....	....	....	....	....
2006-07	London Knights	OHL	53	35	83	118	36	....	....	....	....	....	....	....	....	....	16	7	*22	29	22	....	....	....	....
2007-08	**Edmonton**	**NHL**	**79**	**13**	**36**	**49**	**23**	**4**	**0**	**1**	**135**	**9.6**	**-21**	**299**	**41.8**	**15:41**	....	....	....	....	....	....	....	....	....
	NHL Totals		**79**	**13**	**36**	**49**	**23**	**4**	**0**	**1**	**135**	**9.6**		**299**	**41.8**	**15:41**	....	....	....	....	....	....	....	....	....

USHL All-Rookie Team (2006) • OHL All-Rookie Team (2007)

			Regular Season														Playoffs								
Season	Club	League	GP	G	A	Pts	PIM	PP	SH	GW	S	%	+/-	TF	F%	Min	GP	G	A	Pts	PIM	PP	SH	GW	Min

GAMACHE, Simon

(ga-MOHSH, see-MOHN)

Center. Shoots left. 5'10", 186 lbs. Born, Thetford Mines, Que., January 3, 1981. Atlanta's 14th choice, 290th overall, in 2000 Entry Draft.

1997-98	Levis-Lauzon	QAAA	42	28	26	54	....	....	....	....	....	....	....	....	....	....	4	1	1	2	....	....	....	....	....
1998-99	Val-d'Or Foreurs	QMJHL	70	19	43	62	54	....	....	....	....	....	....	....	....	....	6	1	2	3	4	....	....	....	....
99-2000	Val-d'Or Foreurs	QMJHL	72	64	79	143	74	....	....	....	....	....	....	....	....	....	....	....	....	....	....	....	....	....	....
2000-01	Val-d'Or Foreurs	QMJHL	72	*74	*110	*184	70	....	....	....	....	....	....	....	....	....	21	*22	*35	*57	18	....	....	....	....
2001-02	Chicago Wolves	AHL	26	2	4	6	11	....	....	....	....	....	....	....	....	....	....	....	....	....	....	....	....	....	....
	Greenville	ECHL	31	19	19	38	35	....	....	....	....	....	....	....	....	....	17	*15	9	*24	22	....	....	....	....
2002-03	**Atlanta**	**NHL**	**2**	**0**	**0**	**0**	**2**	**0**	**0**	**0**	**3**	**0.0**	**–1**	**0**	**0.0**	**12:37**	....	....	....	....	....	....	....	....	....
	Chicago Wolves	AHL	76	35	42	77	37	....	....	....	....	....	....	....	....	....	9	7	2	9	4	....	....	....	....
2003-04	**Atlanta**	**NHL**	**2**	**0**	**1**	**1**	**0**	**0**	**0**	**0**	**1**	**0.0**	**0**	**0**	**0.0**	**6:39**	....	....	....	....	....	....	....	....	....
	Chicago Wolves	AHL	16	5	6	11	4	....	....	....	....	....	....	....	....	....	....	....	....	....	....	....	....	....	....
	Nashville	**NHL**	**7**	**1**	**0**	**1**	**0**	**1**	**0**	**0**	**4**	**25.0**	**–3**	**18**	**55.6**	**7:35**	....	....	....	....	....	....	....	....	....
	Milwaukee	AHL	52	18	27	45	26	....	....	....	....	....	....	....	....	....	22	6	*18	24	14	....	....	....	....
2004-05	Milwaukee	AHL	80	29	57	86	93	....	....	....	....	....	....	....	....	....	7	6	4	10	18	....	....	....	....
2005-06	**Nashville**	**NHL**	**11**	**0**	**0**	**0**	**0**	**0**	**0**	**0**	**4**	**0.0**	**–6**	**2**	**50.0**	**8:16**	....	....	....	....	....	....	....	....	....
	Milwaukee	AHL	39	18	19	37	46	....	....	....	....	....	....	....	....	....	21	12	16	28	22	....	....	....	....
	St. Louis	**NHL**	**15**	**3**	**4**	**7**	**10**	**0**	**0**	**0**	**32**	**9.4**	**1**	**4**	**50.0**	**13:53**	....	....	....	....	....	....	....	....	....
2006-07	SC Bern	Swiss	44	20	*46	*66	40	....	....	....	....	....	....	....	....	....	16	7	9	*16	10	....	....	....	....
2007-08	**Toronto**	**NHL**	**11**	**2**	**2**	**4**	**6**	**1**	**0**	**0**	**11**	**18.2**	**–1**	**0**	**0.0**	**9:36**	....	....	....	....	....	....	....	....	....
	Toronto Marlies	AHL	17	4	3	7	10	....	....	....	....	....	....	....	....	....	....	....	....	....	....	....	....	....	....
	SC Bern	Swiss	13	3	14	17	4	....	....	....	....	....	....	....	....	....	4	0	1	1	2	....	....	....	....
	NHL Totals		**48**	**6**	**7**	**13**	**18**	**2**	**0**	**0**	**55**	**10.9**		**24**	**54.2**	**10:20**	....	....	....	....	....	....	....	....	....

Canadian Major Junior Second All-Star Team (2000) • QMJHL First All-Star Team (2001) • Michel Briere Trophy (MVP – QMJHL) (2001) • Canadian Major Junior First All-Star Team (2001) • Canadian Major Junior Player of the Year (2001) • Memorial Cup Tournament All-Star Team (2001) • Ed Chynoweth Trophy (Memorial Cup Tournament - Leading Scorer) (2001) • ECHL All-Rookie Team (2002) • ECHL Playoff MVP (2002) (co-winner - Tyrone Garner) • AHL First All-Star Team (2005)

Traded to **Nashville** by **Atlanta** with Kirill Safronov for Ben Simon and Tomas Kloucek, December 2, 2003. Claimed on waivers by **St. Louis** from **Nashville**, November 29, 2005. Signed as a free agent by **Toronto**, June 25, 2007.

GAUSTAD, Paul

(GAW-stad, PAWL) **BUF.**

Center. Shoots left. 6'5", 214 lbs. Born, Fargo, ND, February 3, 1982. Buffalo's 6th choice, 220th overall, in 2000 Entry Draft.

1998-99	Portland Hawks	USAHA	45	47	53	100	81	....	....	....	....	....	....	....	....	....	....	....	....	....	....	....	....	....	....
99-2000	Portland	WHL	56	6	8	14	110	....	....	....	....	....	....	....	....	....	....	....	....	....	....	....	....	....	....
2000-01	Portland	WHL	70	11	30	41	168	....	....	....	....	....	....	....	....	....	16	10	6	16	59	....	....	....	....
2001-02	Portland	WHL	72	36	44	80	202	....	....	....	....	....	....	....	....	....	6	3	1	4	16	....	....	....	....
2002-03	**Buffalo**	**NHL**	**1**	**0**	**0**	**0**	**0**	**0**	**0**	**0**	**0**	**0.0**	**0**	**7**	**42.9**	**5:48**	....	....	....	....	....	....	....	....	....
	Rochester	AHL	80	14	39	53	137	....	....	....	....	....	....	....	....	....	3	0	0	0	4	....	....	....	....
2003-04	Rochester	AHL	78	9	22	31	169	....	....	....	....	....	....	....	....	....	16	3	10	13	30	....	....	....	....
2004-05	Rochester	AHL	76	18	25	43	192	....	....	....	....	....	....	....	....	....	9	6	5	11	16	....	....	....	....
2005-06	**Buffalo**	**NHL**	**78**	**9**	**15**	**24**	**65**	**0**	**0**	**0**	**113**	**8.0**	**4**	**829**	**52.2**	**12:08**	**18**	**0**	**4**	**4**	**14**	**0**	**0**	**0**	**12:21**
2006-07	**Buffalo**	**NHL**	**54**	**9**	**13**	**22**	**74**	**3**	**0**	**0**	**75**	**12.0**	**11**	**386**	**52.9**	**13:19**	**7**	**0**	**1**	**1**	**2**	**0**	**0**	**0**	**11:00**
2007-08	**Buffalo**	**NHL**	**82**	**10**	**26**	**36**	**85**	**5**	**0**	**2**	**136**	**7.4**	**–4**	**1165**	**54.9**	**17:10**	....	....	....	....	....	....	....	....	....
	NHL Totals		**215**	**28**	**54**	**82**	**224**	**8**	**0**	**2**	**324**	**8.6**		**2387**	**53.6**	**14:19**	**25**	**0**	**5**	**5**	**16**	**0**	**0**	**0**	**11:58**

GAUTHIER, Denis

(GOH-tyay, DEH-nihs) **L.A.**

Defense. Shoots left. 6'3", 224 lbs. Born, Montreal, Que., October 1, 1976. Calgary's 1st choice, 20th overall, in 1995 Entry Draft.

1991-92	Richelieu AA	QAHA	STATISTICS NOT AVAILABLE																						
1992-93	Drummondville	QMJHL	61	1	7	8	136	....	....	....	....	....	....	....	....	....	10	0	5	5	40	....	....	....	....
1993-94	Drummondville	QMJHL	60	0	7	7	176	....	....	....	....	....	....	....	....	....	9	2	0	2	41	....	....	....	....
1994-95	Drummondville	QMJHL	64	9	31	40	190	....	....	....	....	....	....	....	....	....	4	0	5	5	12	....	....	....	....
1995-96	Drummondville	QMJHL	53	25	49	74	140	....	....	....	....	....	....	....	....	....	6	4	4	8	32	....	....	....	....
	Saint John Flames	AHL	5	2	0	2	8	....	....	....	....	....	....	....	....	....	16	1	6	7	20	....	....	....	....
1996-97	Saint John Flames	AHL	73	3	28	31	74	....	....	....	....	....	....	....	....	....	5	0	0	0	6	....	....	....	....
1997-98	**Calgary**	**NHL**	**10**	**0**	**0**	**0**	**16**	**0**	**0**	**0**	**3**	**0.0**	**–5**	....	....	....	....	....	....	....	....	....	....	....	....
	Saint John Flames	AHL	68	4	20	24	154	....	....	....	....	....	....	....	....	....	21	0	4	4	83	....	....	....	....
1998-99	**Calgary**	**NHL**	**55**	**3**	**4**	**7**	**68**	**0**	**0**	**0**	**40**	**7.5**	**3**	**0**	**0.0**	**12:41**	....	....	....	....	....	....	....	....	....
	Saint John Flames	AHL	16	0	3	3	31	....	....	....	....	....	....	....	....	....	....	....	....	....	....	....	....	....	....
99-2000	**Calgary**	**NHL**	**39**	**1**	**1**	**2**	**50**	**0**	**0**	**0**	**29**	**3.4**	**–4**	**0**	**0.0**	**19:21**	....	....	....	....	....	....	....	....	....
2000-01	**Calgary**	**NHL**	**62**	**2**	**6**	**8**	**78**	**0**	**0**	**0**	**33**	**6.1**	**3**	**0**	**0.0**	**16:37**	....	....	....	....	....	....	....	....	....
2001-02	**Calgary**	**NHL**	**66**	**5**	**8**	**13**	**91**	**0**	**1**	**2**	**76**	**6.6**	**9**	**0**	**0.0**	**19:19**	....	....	....	....	....	....	....	....	....
2002-03	**Calgary**	**NHL**	**72**	**1**	**11**	**12**	**99**	**0**	**0**	**1**	**50**	**2.0**	**5**	**0**	**0.0**	**19:52**	....	....	....	....	....	....	....	....	....
2003-04	**Calgary**	**NHL**	**80**	**1**	**15**	**16**	**113**	**0**	**0**	**0**	**90**	**1.1**	**4**	**0**	**0.0**	**18:43**	**6**	**0**	**1**	**1**	**4**	**0**	**0**	**0**	**18:33**
2004-05			DID NOT PLAY																						
2005-06	**Phoenix**	**NHL**	**45**	**2**	**9**	**11**	**61**	**0**	**0**	**0**	**43**	**4.7**	**–4**	**0**	**0.0**	**16:58**	....	....	....	....	....	....	....	....	....
	Philadelphia	**NHL**	**17**	**0**	**0**	**0**	**37**	**0**	**0**	**0**	**13**	**0.0**	**6**	**0**	**0.0**	**15:21**	**6**	**0**	**1**	**1**	**19**	**0**	**0**	**0**	**18:21**
2006-07	**Philadelphia**	**NHL**	**43**	**0**	**4**	**4**	**45**	**0**	**0**	**0**	**23**	**0.0**	**–11**	**0**	**0.0**	**16:39**	....	....	....	....	....	....	....	....	....
2007-08	Philadelphia	AHL	78	3	15	18	80	....	....	....	....	....	....	....	....	....	11	0	1	1	17	....	....	....	....
	NHL Totals		**489**	**15**	**58**	**73**	**658**	**0**	**1**	**3**	**400**	**3.8**		**0**	**0.0**	**17:35**	**12**	**0**	**2**	**2**	**23**	**0**	**0**	**0**	**18:27**

QMJHL First All-Star Team (1996) • Canadian Major Junior First All-Star Team (1996)

• Missed majority of 1999-2000 season recovering from hip injury suffered in game vs. St. Louis, February 1, 2000. Traded to **Phoenix** by **Calgary** with Oleg Saprykin for Daymond Langkow, August 26, 2004. Traded to **Philadelphia** by **Phoenix** for Josh Gratton, Florida's 2nd round choice (previously acquired, later traded to Detroit - Detroit selected Cory Emerton) in 2006 Entry Draft and Tampa Bay's 2nd round choice (previously acquired, later traded to Detroit - Detroit selected Shawn Matthias) in 2006 Entry Draft, March 9, 2006. Traded to **Los Angeles** by **Philadelphia** with Philadelphia's 2nd round choice in 2010 Entry Draft for Patrik Hersley and Ned Lukacevic, July 1, 2008.

GAUTHIER, Gabe

(GOH-tyay, GAYB) **L.A.**

Left wing. Shoots left. 5'9", 205 lbs. Born, Torrance, CA, January 20, 1984.

2002-03	U. of Denver	WCHA	41	8	8	16	30	....	....	....	....	....	....	....	....	....	....	....	....	....	....	....	....	....	....
2003-04	U. of Denver	WCHA	42	18	25	43	32	....	....	....	....	....	....	....	....	....	....	....	....	....	....	....	....	....	....
2004-05	U. of Denver	WCHA	41	23	29	52	44	....	....	....	....	....	....	....	....	....	....	....	....	....	....	....	....	....	....
2005-06	U. of Denver	WCHA	38	15	24	39	35	....	....	....	....	....	....	....	....	....	....	....	....	....	....	....	....	....	....
2006-07	**Los Angeles**	**NHL**	**5**	**0**	**0**	**0**	**2**	**0**	**0**	**0**	**6**	**0.0**	**–1**	**23**	**47.8**	**9:57**	....	....	....	....	....	....	....	....	....
	Manchester	AHL	69	14	28	42	54	....	....	....	....	....	....	....	....	....	16	1	4	5	14	....	....	....	....
2007-08	**Los Angeles**	**NHL**	**3**	**0**	**0**	**0**	**0**	**0**	**0**	**0**	**2**	**0.0**	**0**	**17**	**47.1**	**7:08**	....	....	....	....	....	....	....	....	....
	Manchester	AHL	61	23	37	60	43	....	....	....	....	....	....	....	....	....	3	0	0	0	4	....	....	....	....
	NHL Totals		**8**	**0**	**0**	**0**	**2**	**0**	**0**	**0**	**8**	**0.0**		**40**	**47.5**	**8:53**	....	....	....	....	....	....	....	....	....

NCAA Championship All-Tournament Team (2005)

Signed as a free agent by **Los Angeles**, July 7, 2006.

GELINAS, Martin

(ZHEHL-in-nuh, MAHR-tihn)

Left wing. Shoots left. 5'11", 202 lbs. Born, Shawinigan, Que., June 5, 1970. Los Angeles' 1st choice, 7th overall, in 1988 Entry Draft.

1985-86	Noranda Aces	NOHA	5	1	1	2	0	....	....	....	....	....	....	....	....	....	....	....	....	....	....	....	....	....	....
1986-87	Montreal L'est	QAAA	41	36	42	78	36	....	....	....	....	....	....	....	....	....	7	7	5	12	2	....	....	....	....
1987-88	Hull Olympiques	QMJHL	65	63	68	131	74	....	....	....	....	....	....	....	....	....	17	15	18	33	32	....	....	....	....
1988-89	Hull Olympiques	QMJHL	41	38	39	77	31	....	....	....	....	....	....	....	....	....	9	5	4	9	14	....	....	....	....
	Edmonton	**NHL**	**6**	**1**	**2**	**3**	**0**	**0**	**0**	**0**	**14**	**7.1**	**–1**	....	....	....	....	....	....	....	....	....	....	....	....
1989-90 ♦	**Edmonton**	**NHL**	**46**	**17**	**8**	**25**	**30**	**5**	**0**	**2**	**71**	**23.9**	**0**	....	....	....	**20**	**2**	**3**	**5**	**6**	**0**	**0**	**0**	....
1990-91	**Edmonton**	**NHL**	**73**	**20**	**20**	**40**	**34**	**4**	**0**	**2**	**124**	**16.1**	**–7**	....	....	....	**18**	**3**	**6**	**9**	**25**	**0**	**0**	**1**	....
1991-92	**Edmonton**	**NHL**	**68**	**11**	**18**	**29**	**62**	**1**	**0**	**0**	**94**	**11.7**	**14**	....	....	....	**15**	**1**	**3**	**4**	**10**	**0**	**0**	**0**	....
1992-93	**Edmonton**	**NHL**	**65**	**11**	**12**	**23**	**30**	**0**	**0**	**1**	**93**	**11.8**	**3**	....	....	....	....	....	....	....	....	....	....	....	....
1993-94	**Quebec**	**NHL**	**31**	**6**	**6**	**12**	**8**	**0**	**0**	**0**	**53**	**11.3**	**–2**	....	....	....	....	....	....	....	....	....	....	....	....
	Vancouver	**NHL**	**33**	**8**	**8**	**16**	**26**	**3**	**0**	**1**	**54**	**14.8**	**–6**	....	....	....	**24**	**5**	**4**	**9**	**14**	**2**	**0**	**1**	....
1994-95	**Vancouver**	**NHL**	**46**	**13**	**10**	**23**	**36**	**1**	**0**	**4**	**75**	**17.3**	**8**	....	....	....	**3**	**0**	**1**	**1**	**0**	**0**	**0**	**0**	....
1995-96	**Vancouver**	**NHL**	**81**	**30**	**26**	**56**	**59**	**3**	**4**	**5**	**181**	**16.6**	**8**	....	....	....	**6**	**1**	**1**	**2**	**12**	**1**	**0**	**0**	....
1996-97	**Vancouver**	**NHL**	**74**	**35**	**33**	**68**	**42**	**6**	**1**	**3**	**177**	**19.8**	**6**	....	....	....	....	....	....	....	....	....	....	....	....

			Regular Season														Playoffs								
Season	Club	League	GP	G	A	Pts	PIM	PP	SH	GW	S	%	+/-	TF	F%	Min	GP	G	A	Pts	PIM	PP	SH	GW	Min
1997-98	**Vancouver**	**NHL**	**24**	**4**	**4**	**8**	**10**	**1**	**1**	**1**	**49**	**8.2**	**–6**	....	....	....	....	....	....	....	....	....	....	....	....
	Carolina	**NHL**	**40**	**12**	**14**	**26**	**30**	**2**	**1**	**4**	**98**	**12.2**	**1**	....	....	....	....	....	....	....	....	....	....	....	....
1998-99	**Carolina**	**NHL**	**76**	**13**	**15**	**28**	**67**	**0**	**0**	**2**	**111**	**11.7**	**3**	**6**	**50.0**	**13:13**	**6**	**0**	**3**	**3**	**2**	**0**	**0**	**0**	**19:33**
99-2000	**Carolina**	**NHL**	**81**	**14**	**16**	**30**	**40**	**3**	**0**	**0**	**139**	**10.1**	**–10**	**5**	**40.0**	**13:39**	....	....	....	....	....	....	....	....	....
2000-01	**Carolina**	**NHL**	**79**	**23**	**29**	**52**	**59**	**6**	**1**	**4**	**170**	**13.5**	**–4**	**6**	**0.0**	**17:54**	**6**	**0**	**1**	**1**	**6**	**0**	**0**	**0**	**17:51**
2001-02	**Carolina**	**NHL**	**72**	**13**	**16**	**29**	**30**	**3**	**0**	**1**	**121**	**10.7**	**–1**	**13**	**23.1**	**16:05**	**23**	**3**	**4**	**7**	**10**	**0**	**0**	**1**	**14:16**
2002-03	**Calgary**	**NHL**	**81**	**21**	**31**	**52**	**51**	**6**	**0**	**3**	**152**	**13.8**	**–3**	**96**	**51.0**	**16:33**	....	....	....	....	....	....	....	....	....
2003-04	**Calgary**	**NHL**	**76**	**17**	**18**	**35**	**70**	**5**	**0**	**3**	**139**	**12.2**	**10**	**27**	**48.2**	**14:50**	**26**	**8**	**7**	**15**	**35**	**2**	**0**	**3**	**15:58**
2004-05	Morges	Swiss-2	41	37	21	58	81	....	....	....	....	....	....	....	....	....	4	2	2	4	24	....	....	....	....
	HC Lugano	Swiss	1	0	0	0	0	....	....	....	....	....	....	....	....	....	5	0	1	1	2	....	....	....	....
2005-06	**Florida**	**NHL**	**82**	**17**	**24**	**41**	**80**	**4**	**0**	**3**	**186**	**9.1**	**27**	**24**	**41.7**	**15:59**	....	....	....	....	....	....	....	....	....
2006-07	**Florida**	**NHL**	**82**	**14**	**30**	**44**	**36**	**7**	**0**	**1**	**171**	**8.2**	**7**	**27**	**40.7**	**13:26**	....	....	....	....	....	....	....	....	....
2007-08	**Nashville**	**NHL**	**57**	**9**	**11**	**20**	**20**	**0**	**1**	**1**	**110**	**8.2**	**5**	**22**	**50.0**	**14:07**	....	....	....	....	....	....	....	....	....
	NHL Totals		**1273**	**309**	**351**	**660**	**820**	**60**	**9**	**41**	**2382**	**13.0**		**226**	**45.1**	**15:07**	**147**	**23**	**33**	**56**	**120**	**5**	**0**	**6**	**15:51**

QMJHL First All-Star Team (1988) • QMJHL Offensive Rookie of the Year (1988) • Canadian Major Junior Rookie of the Year (1988) • George Parsons Trophy (Memorial Cup Tournament - Most Sportsmanlike Player) (1988)

Traded to **Edmonton** by **Los Angeles** with Jimmy Carson and Los Angeles' 1st round choices in 1989 (later traded to New Jersey – New Jersey selected Jason Miller), 1991 (Martin Rucinsky) and 1993 (Nick Stajduhar) Entry Drafts and cash for Wayne Gretzky, Mike Krushelnyski and Marty McSorley, August 9, 1988. Traded to **Quebec** by **Edmonton** with Edmonton's 6th round choice (Nicholas Checco) in 1993 Entry Draft for Scott Pearson, June 20, 1993. Claimed on waivers by **Vancouver** from **Quebec**, January 15, 1994. Traded to **Carolina** by **Vancouver** with Kirk McLean for Sean Burke, Geoff Sanderson and Enrico Ciccone, January 3, 1998. Signed as a free agent by **Calgary**, July 2, 2002. Signed as a free agent by **Morges** (Swiss-2), September 23, 2004. Signed as a free agent by **Lugano** (Swiss), February 17, 2005. Signed as a free agent by **Florida**, August 2, 2005. Signed as a free agent by **Nashville**, July 26, 2007.

GERMYN, Carsen

(JUHR-mihn, KAHR-sehn) **CGY.**

Right wing. Shoots right. 5'10", 185 lbs. Born, Campbell River, B.C., February 22, 1982.

1998-99	Kelowna Rockets	WHL	59	6	10	16	61	....	....	....	....	....	....	....	....	....	5	0	0	0	2	....	....	....	....
99-2000	Kelowna Rockets	WHL	71	16	29	45	111	....	....	....	....	....	....	....	....	....	5	3	3	6	4	....	....	....	....
2000-01	Kelowna Rockets	WHL	71	35	52	87	102	....	....	....	....	....	....	....	....	....	6	2	6	8	10	....	....	....	....
2001-02	Kelowna Rockets	WHL	23	10	18	28	43	....	....	....	....	....	....	....	....	....	....	....	....	....	....	....	....	....	....
	Red Deer Rebels	WHL	37	23	25	48	83	....	....	....	....	....	....	....	....	....	23	4	12	16	24	....	....	....	....
2002-03	Red Deer Rebels	WHL	63	26	33	59	108	....	....	....	....	....	....	....	....	....	23	4	9	13	25	....	....	....	....
2003-04	Norfolk Admirals	AHL	77	11	16	27	104	....	....	....	....	....	....	....	....	....	6	1	0	1	2	....	....	....	....
2004-05	Lowell	AHL	60	9	11	20	115	....	....	....	....	....	....	....	....	....	10	0	0	0	25	....	....	....	....
2005-06	**Calgary**	**NHL**	**2**	**0**	**0**	**0**	**0**	**0**	**0**	**0**	**2**	**0.0**	**–1**	**0**	**0.0**	**5:00**	....	....	....	....	....	....	....	....	....
	Omaha	AHL	77	24	31	55	127	....	....	....	....	....	....	....	....	....	....	....	....	....	....	....	....	....	....
2006-07	**Calgary**	**NHL**	**2**	**0**	**0**	**0**	**0**	**0**	**0**	**0**	**3**	**0.0**	**0**	**2**	**50.0**	**8:26**	....	....	....	....	....	....	....	....	....
	Omaha	AHL	77	28	32	60	124	....	....	....	....	....	....	....	....	....	6	1	1	2	2	....	....	....	....
2007-08	Quad City Flames	AHL	77	19	29	48	133	....	....	....	....	....	....	....	....	....	....	....	....	....	....	....	....	....	....
	NHL Totals		**4**	**0**	**0**	**0**	**0**	**0**	**0**	**0**	**5**	**0.0**		**2**	**50.0**	**6:43**	....	....	....	....	....	....	....	....	....

Signed as a free agent by **Calgary**, July 6, 2004.

GERVAIS, Bruno

(ZHUR-vay, BROO-noh) **NYI**

Defense. Shoots right. 6', 188 lbs. Born, Longueuil, Que., October 3, 1984. NY Islanders' 6th choice, 182nd overall, in 2003 Entry Draft.

99-2000	Antoine-Girouard	QAAA	6	0	0	0	0	....	....	....	....	....	....	....	....	....	4	0	0	0	0	....	....	....	....
2000-01	Antoine-Girouard	QAAA	40	8	27	35	46	....	....	....	....	....	....	....	....	....	7	4	2	6	8	....	....	....	....
2001-02	Acadie-Bathurst	QMJHL	65	4	12	16	42	....	....	....	....	....	....	....	....	....	16	3	1	4	8	....	....	....	....
2002-03	Acadie-Bathurst	QMJHL	72	22	28	50	73	....	....	....	....	....	....	....	....	....	11	3	5	8	14	....	....	....	....
2003-04	Acadie-Bathurst	QMJHL	23	4	6	10	28	....	....	....	....	....	....	....	....	....	....	....	....	....	....	....	....	....	....
2004-05	Bridgeport	AHL	76	8	22	30	58	....	....	....	....	....	....	....	....	....	....	....	....	....	....	....	....	....	....
2005-06	**NY Islanders**	**NHL**	**27**	**3**	**4**	**7**	**8**	**1**	**0**	**0**	**21**	**14.3**	**–1**	**0**	**0.0**	**16:47**	....	....	....	....	....	....	....	....	....
	Bridgeport	AHL	55	17	25	42	70	....	....	....	....	....	....	....	....	....	7	1	2	3	0	....	....	....	....
2006-07	**NY Islanders**	**NHL**	**51**	**0**	**6**	**6**	**28**	**0**	**0**	**0**	**47**	**0.0**	**–10**	**0**	**0.0**	**15:23**	**5**	**1**	**1**	**2**	**2**	**0**	**0**	**0**	**15:36**
	Bridgeport	AHL	3	0	0	0	6	....	....	....	....	....	....	....	....	....	....	....	....	....	....	....	....	....	....
2007-08	**NY Islanders**	**NHL**	**60**	**0**	**13**	**13**	**34**	**0**	**0**	**0**	**59**	**0.0**	**–5**	**0**	**0.0**	**20:00**	....	....	....	....	....	....	....	....	....
	NHL Totals		**138**	**3**	**23**	**26**	**70**	**1**	**0**	**0**	**127**	**2.4**		**0**	**0.0**	**17:40**	**5**	**1**	**1**	**2**	**2**	**0**	**0**	**0**	**15:36**

QMJHL Second All-Star Team (2003)

• Missed majority of 2003-04 season recovering from knee injury suffered during Team Canada Jr. training camp, December 12, 2003.

GETZLAF, Ryan

(GEHTZ-laf, RIGH-uhn) **ANA.**

Center. Shoots right. 6'4", 221 lbs. Born, Regina, Sask., May 10, 1985. Anaheim's 1st choice, 19th overall, in 2003 Entry Draft.

2000-01	Regina Rangers	SBHL	41	33	41	74	189	....	....	....	....	....	....	....	....	....	....	....	....	....	....	....	....	....	....
	Reg. Pat Cdns.	SMHL	8	4	3	7	8	....	....	....	....	....	....	....	....	....	....	....	....	....	....	....	....	....	....
2001-02	Calgary Hitmen	WHL	63	9	9	18	34	....	....	....	....	....	....	....	....	....	7	2	1	3	4	....	....	....	....
2002-03	Calgary Hitmen	WHL	70	29	39	68	121	....	....	....	....	....	....	....	....	....	5	1	1	2	6	....	....	....	....
2003-04	Calgary Hitmen	WHL	49	28	47	75	97	....	....	....	....	....	....	....	....	....	7	5	1	6	12	....	....	....	....
2004-05	Calgary Hitmen	WHL	51	29	25	54	102	....	....	....	....	....	....	....	....	....	12	4	13	17	18	....	....	....	....
	Cincinnati	AHL	....	....	....	....	....	....	....	....	....	....	....	....	....	....	10	1	4	5	4	....	....	....	....
2005-06	**Anaheim**	**NHL**	**57**	**14**	**25**	**39**	**22**	**10**	**0**	**1**	**116**	**12.1**	**6**	**534**	**44.0**	**12:35**	**16**	**3**	**4**	**7**	**13**	**2**	**0**	**1**	**15:49**
	Portland Pirates	AHL	17	8	25	33	36	....	....	....	....	....	....	....	....	....	1	0	0	0	4	....	....	....	....
2006-07 ♦	**Anaheim**	**NHL**	**82**	**25**	**33**	**58**	**66**	**11**	**1**	**6**	**203**	**12.3**	**17**	**888**	**49.4**	**15:04**	**21**	**7**	**10**	**17**	**32**	**3**	**1**	**3**	**21:43**
2007-08	**Anaheim**	**NHL**	**77**	**24**	**58**	**82**	**94**	**4**	**1**	**2**	**185**	**13.0**	**32**	**1152**	**47.3**	**19:39**	**6**	**2**	**3**	**5**	**6**	**1**	**0**	**0**	**20:29**
	NHL Totals		**216**	**63**	**116**	**179**	**182**	**25**	**2**	**9**	**504**	**12.5**		**2574**	**47.4**	**16:02**	**43**	**12**	**17**	**29**	**51**	**6**	**1**	**4**	**19:21**

WHL East First All-Star Team (2004) • WHL East Second All-Star Team (2005)

Played in NHL All-Star Game (2008)

GILBERT, Tom

(GIHL-buhrt, TAWM) **EDM.**

Defense. Shoots right. 6'3", 206 lbs. Born, Minneapolis, MN, January 10, 1983. Colorado's 5th choice, 129th overall, in 2002 Entry Draft.

99-2000	Bloomington-Jeff.	High-MN	18	7	18	25	....	....	....	....	....	....	....	....	....	....	....	....	....	....	....	....	....	....	....
2000-01	Bloomington-Jeff.	High-MN	23	20	18	38	....	....	....	....	....	....	....	....	....	....	....	....	....	....	....	....	....	....	....
	Chicago Steel	USHL	1	0	0	0	0	....	....	....	....	....	....	....	....	....	....	....	....	....	....	....	....	....	....
2001-02	Chicago Steel	USHL	57	13	15	28	62	....	....	....	....	....	....	....	....	....	4	0	0	0	4	....	....	....	....
2002-03	U. of Wisconsin	WCHA	39	7	13	20	36	....	....	....	....	....	....	....	....	....	....	....	....	....	....	....	....	....	....
2003-04	U. of Wisconsin	WCHA	39	6	15	21	36	....	....	....	....	....	....	....	....	....	....	....	....	....	....	....	....	....	....
2004-05	U. of Wisconsin	WCHA	41	8	9	17	48	....	....	....	....	....	....	....	....	....	....	....	....	....	....	....	....	....	....
2005-06	U. of Wisconsin	WCHA	43	12	19	31	32	....	....	....	....	....	....	....	....	....	....	....	....	....	....	....	....	....	....
2006-07	**Edmonton**	**NHL**	**12**	**1**	**5**	**6**	**0**	**0**	**0**	**0**	**13**	**7.7**	**–1**	**0**	**0.0**	**20:05**	....	....	....	....	....	....	....	....	....
	Wilkes-Barre	AHL	48	4	26	30	32	....	....	....	....	....	....	....	....	....	10	1	7	8	10	....	....	....	....
2007-08	**Edmonton**	**NHL**	**82**	**13**	**20**	**33**	**20**	**3**	**0**	**1**	**98**	**13.3**	**–6**	**0**	**0.0**	**22:12**	....	....	....	....	....	....	....	....	....
	NHL Totals		**94**	**14**	**25**	**39**	**20**	**3**	**0**	**1**	**111**	**12.6**		**0**	**0.0**	**21:56**	....	....	....	....	....	....	....	....	....

WCHA First All-Star Team (2006) • NCAA West Second All-American Team (2006) • NCAA Championship All-Tournament Team (2006) • NHL All-Rookie Team (2008)

Traded to **Edmonton** by **Colorado** for Tommy Salo and Edmonton's 6th round choice (Justin Mercier) in 2005 Entry Draft, March 8, 2004.

GILL, Hal

(GIHL, HAL) **PIT.**

Defense. Shoots left. 6'7", 250 lbs. Born, Concord, MA, April 6, 1975. Boston's 8th choice, 207th overall, in 1993 Entry Draft.

1992-93	Nashoba	High-MA	20	25	25	50	....	....	....	....	....	....	....	....	....	....	....	....	....	....	....	....	....	....	....
1993-94	Providence	H-East	31	1	2	3	26	....	....	....	....	....	....	....	....	....	....	....	....	....	....	....	....	....	....
1994-95	Providence	H-East	26	1	3	4	22	....	....	....	....	....	....	....	....	....	....	....	....	....	....	....	....	....	....
1995-96	Providence	H-East	39	5	12	17	54	....	....	....	....	....	....	....	....	....	....	....	....	....	....	....	....	....	....
1996-97	Providence	H-East	35	5	16	21	52	....	....	....	....	....	....	....	....	....	....	....	....	....	....	....	....	....	....
1997-98	**Boston**	**NHL**	**68**	**2**	**4**	**6**	**47**	**0**	**0**	**0**	**56**	**3.6**	**4**	....	....	....	**6**	**0**	**0**	**0**	**4**	**0**	**0**	**0**	....
	Providence Bruins	AHL	4	1	0	1	23	....	....	....	....	....	....	....	....	....	....	....	....	....	....	....	....	....	....
1998-99	**Boston**	**NHL**	**80**	**3**	**7**	**10**	**63**	**0**	**0**	**2**	**102**	**2.9**	**–10**	**1**	**100.0**	**20:54**	**12**	**0**	**0**	**0**	**14**	**0**	**0**	**0**	**20:41**
99-2000	**Boston**	**NHL**	**81**	**3**	**9**	**12**	**51**	**0**	**0**	**0**	**120**	**2.5**	**0**	**0**	**0.0**	**17:15**	....	....	....	....	....	....	....	....	....
2000-01	**Boston**	**NHL**	**80**	**1**	**10**	**11**	**71**	**0**	**0**	**0**	**79**	**1.3**	**–2**	**0**	**0.0**	**18:21**	....	....	....	....	....	....	....	....	....

			Regular Season														Playoffs								
Season	Club	League	GP	G	A	Pts	PIM	PP	SH	GW	S	%	+/-	TF	F%	Min	GP	G	A	Pts	PIM	PP	SH	GW	Min
2001-02	**Boston**	**NHL**	**79**	**4**	**18**	**22**	**77**	**0**	**0**	**0**	**137**	**2.9**	**16**	**0**	**0.0**	**24:13**	**6**	**0**	**1**	**1**	**2**	**0**	**0**	**0**	**23:04**
2002-03	**Boston**	**NHL**	**76**	**4**	**13**	**17**	**56**	**0**	**0**	**0**	**114**	**3.5**	**21**	**0**	**0.0**	**20:42**	**5**	**0**	**0**	**0**	**4**	**0**	**0**	**0**	**20:19**
2003-04	**Boston**	**NHL**	**82**	**2**	**7**	**9**	**99**	**0**	**0**	**0**	**104**	**1.9**	**16**	**0**	**0.0**	**18:24**	**7**	**0**	**1**	**1**	**4**	**0**	**0**	**0**	**19:03**
2004-05	Lukko Rauma	Finland	31	2	8	10	110	....	....	....	....	....	....	....	....	....	8	0	0	0	*57	....	....	....	....
2005-06	**Boston**	**NHL**	**80**	**1**	**9**	**10**	**124**	**0**	**0**	**0**	**68**	**1.5**	**–4**	**0**	**0.0**	**18:37**	....	....	....	....	....	....	....	....	....
2006-07	**Toronto**	**NHL**	**82**	**6**	**14**	**20**	**91**	**0**	**0**	**1**	**79**	**7.6**	**11**	**1**	**0.0**	**18:53**	....	....	....	....	....	....	....	....	....
2007-08	**Toronto**	**NHL**	**63**	**2**	**18**	**20**	**52**	**0**	**0**	**0**	**69**	**2.9**	**0**	**0**	**0.0**	**20:42**	....	....	....	....	....	....	....	....	....
	Pittsburgh	**NHL**	**18**	**1**	**3**	**4**	**16**	**0**	**0**	**0**	**17**	**5.9**	**6**	**0**	**0.0**	**17:31**	**20**	**0**	**1**	**1**	**12**	**0**	**0**	**0**	**19:17**
	NHL Totals		**789**	**29**	**112**	**141**	**747**	**0**	**0**	**3**	**945**	**3.1**		**2**	**50.0**	**19:41**	**56**	**0**	**3**	**3**	**40**	**0**	**0**	**0**	**20:09**

Signed as a free agent by **Rauma** (Finland), November 25, 2004. Signed as a free agent by **Toronto**, July 1, 2006. Traded to **Pittsburgh** by **Toronto** for Pittsburgh's 2nd round choice (Jimmy Hayes) in 2008 Entry Draft and Pittsburgh's 5th round choice (later traded to NY Rangers) in 2009 Entry Draft, February 26, 2008.

GILLIES, Trevor

(GIHL-eez, TREH-vuhr) **CAR.**

Left wing. Shoots left. 6'3", 215 lbs. Born, Cambridge, Ont., January 30, 1979.

1996-97	North Bay	OHL	26	0	3	3	72	....	....	....	....	....	....	....	....	....	....	....	....	....	....	....	....	....	....
1997-98	North Bay	OHL	2	0	0	0	4	....	....	....	....	....	....	....	....	....	....	....	....	....	....	....	....	....	....
	Sarnia Sting	OHL	17	0	1	1	33	....	....	....	....	....	....	....	....	....	....	....	....	....	....	....	....	....	....
	Oshawa Generals	OHL	45	1	2	3	184	....	....	....	....	....	....	....	....	....	7	0	1	1	12	....	....	....	....
1998-99	Oshawa Generals	OHL	66	6	9	15	270	....	....	....	....	....	....	....	....	....	11	0	2	2	28	....	....	....	....
99-2000	Lowell	AHL	8	0	0	0	38	....	....	....	....	....	....	....	....	....	....	....	....	....	....	....	....	....	....
	Mississippi	ECHL	53	0	6	6	202	....	....	....	....	....	....	....	....	....	....	....	....	....	....	....	....	....	....
2000-01	Greensboro	ECHL	63	1	6	7	303	....	....	....	....	....	....	....	....	....	....	....	....	....	....	....	....	....	....
	Worcester IceCats	AHL	....	....	....	....	....	....	....	....	....	....	....	....	....	....	6	0	0	0	24	....	....	....	....
2001-02	Providence Bruins	AHL	5	0	0	0	21	....	....	....	....	....	....	....	....	....	....	....	....	....	....	....	....	....	....
	Augusta Lynx	ECHL	46	0	1	1	*269	....	....	....	....	....	....	....	....	....	....	....	....	....	....	....	....	....	....
	Richmond	ECHL	18	0	1	1	*51	....	....	....	....	....	....	....	....	....	....	....	....	....	....	....	....	....	....
2002-03	Lowell	AHL	25	0	1	1	132	....	....	....	....	....	....	....	....	....	....	....	....	....	....	....	....	....	....
	Richmond	ECHL	6	0	0	0	20	....	....	....	....	....	....	....	....	....	....	....	....	....	....	....	....	....	....
	Peoria Rivermen	ECHL	24	0	1	1	180	....	....	....	....	....	....	....	....	....	....	....	....	....	....	....	....	....	....
2003-04	Springfield	AHL	61	2	1	3	277	....	....	....	....	....	....	....	....	....	....	....	....	....	....	....	....	....	....
2004-05	Hartford	AHL	49	0	2	2	277	....	....	....	....	....	....	....	....	....	....	....	....	....	....	....	....	....	....
2005-06	**Anaheim**	**NHL**	**1**	**0**	**0**	**0**	**21**	**0**	**0**	**0**	**1**	**0.0**	**0**	**0**	**0.0**	**2:40**	....	....	....	....	....	....	....	....	....
	Portland Pirates	AHL	50	2	3	5	169	....	....	....	....	....	....	....	....	....	4	0	0	0	0	....	....	....	....
2006-07	Portland Pirates	AHL	51	1	6	7	151	....	....	....	....	....	....	....	....	....	....	....	....	....	....	....	....	....	....
	Augusta Lynx	ECHL	7	0	2	2	23	....	....	....	....	....	....	....	....	....	....	....	....	....	....	....	....	....	....
2007-08	Albany River Rats	AHL	51	1	1	2	112	....	....	....	....	....	....	....	....	....	7	0	0	0	19	....	....	....	....
	NHL Totals		**1**	**0**	**0**	**0**	**21**	**0**	**0**	**0**	**1**	**0.0**		**0**	**0.0**	**2:40**	....	....	....	....	....	....	....	....	....

Signed as a free agent by **NY Rangers**, July 20, 2004. Traded to **Anaheim** by **NY Rangers** with NY Rangers' 4th round choice (later traded back to NY Rangers - later traded to Washington - Washington selected Brett Bruneteau) in 2007 Entry Draft for Steve Rucchin, August 23, 2005. Signed as a free agent by **Carolina**, July 2, 2007.

GIONTA, Brian

(jee-OHN-tuh, BRIGH-uhn) **N.J.**

Right wing. Shoots right. 5'7", 175 lbs. Born, Rochester, NY, January 18, 1979. New Jersey's 4th choice, 82nd overall, in 1998 Entry Draft.

1994-95	Rochester	EmJHL	28	*52	37	*89	....	....	....	....	....	....	....	....	....	....	....	....	....	....	....	....	....	....	....
1995-96	Niagara Scenic	MTJHL	51	47	44	91	59	....	....	....	....	....	....	....	....	....	....	....	....	....	....	....	....	....	....
1996-97	Niagara Scenic	MTJHL	50	57	70	127	101	....	....	....	....	....	....	....	....	....	6	6	11	17	21	....	....	....	....
1997-98	Boston College	H-East	40	30	32	62	44	....	....	....	....	....	....	....	....	....	....	....	....	....	....	....	....	....	....
1998-99	Boston College	H-East	39	27	33	60	46	....	....	....	....	....	....	....	....	....	....	....	....	....	....	....	....	....	....
99-2000	Boston College	H-East	42	*33	23	56	66	....	....	....	....	....	....	....	....	....	....	....	....	....	....	....	....	....	....
2000-01	Boston College	H-East	43	*33	21	*54	47	....	....	....	....	....	....	....	....	....	....	....	....	....	....	....	....	....	....
2001-02	**New Jersey**	**NHL**	**33**	**4**	**7**	**11**	**8**	**0**	**0**	**0**	**58**	**6.9**	**10**	**36**	**44.4**	**13:25**	**6**	**2**	**2**	**4**	**0**	**0**	**1**	**2**	**17:08**
	Albany River Rats	AHL	37	9	16	25	18	....	....	....	....	....	....	....	....	....	....	....	....	....	....	....	....	....	....
2002-03 ♦	**New Jersey**	**NHL**	**58**	**12**	**13**	**25**	**23**	**2**	**0**	**3**	**129**	**9.3**	**5**	**14**	**57.1**	**14:48**	**24**	**1**	**8**	**9**	**6**	**0**	**0**	**0**	**14:31**
2003-04	**New Jersey**	**NHL**	**75**	**21**	**8**	**29**	**36**	**0**	**0**	**8**	**174**	**12.1**	**19**	**60**	**58.3**	**14:44**	**5**	**2**	**3**	**5**	**0**	**1**	**0**	**0**	**15:41**
2004-05	Albany River Rats	AHL	15	5	7	12	10	....	....	....	....	....	....	....	....	....	....	....	....	....	....	....	....	....	....
2005-06	**New Jersey**	**NHL**	**82**	**48**	**41**	**89**	**46**	**24**	**1**	**10**	**291**	**16.5**	**18**	**73**	**38.4**	**19:49**	**9**	**3**	**4**	**7**	**2**	**1**	**1**	**2**	**20:06**
	United States	Olympics	6	4	0	4	2	....	....	....	....	....	....	....	....	....	....	....	....	....	....	....	....	....	....
2006-07	**New Jersey**	**NHL**	**62**	**25**	**20**	**45**	**36**	**11**	**0**	**4**	**194**	**12.9**	**–3**	**31**	**38.7**	**18:49**	**11**	**8**	**1**	**9**	**4**	**3**	**0**	**1**	**19:15**
2007-08	**New Jersey**	**NHL**	**82**	**22**	**31**	**53**	**46**	**8**	**1**	**4**	**257**	**8.6**	**1**	**55**	**54.6**	**18:16**	**5**	**1**	**0**	**1**	**2**	**0**	**0**	**0**	**17:52**
	NHL Totals		**392**	**132**	**120**	**252**	**195**	**45**	**2**	**29**	**1103**	**12.0**		**269**	**48.0**	**17:05**	**60**	**17**	**18**	**35**	**14**	**5**	**2**	**5**	**16:52**

Hockey East Rookie of the Year (1998) • Hockey East Second All-Star Team (1998) • NCAA East Second All-American Team (1998) • Hockey East First All-Star Team (1999, 2000, 2001) • NCAA East First All-American Team (1999, 2000, 2001) • Hockey East Player of the Year (2001)

GIORDANO, Mark

(jee-ohr-DAN-oh, MAHRK) **CGY.**

Defense. Shoots left. 6', 203 lbs. Born, Toronto, Ont., October 3, 1983.

2002-03	Owen Sound	OHL	68	18	30	48	109	....	....	....	....	....	....	....	....	....	4	1	3	4	2	....	....	....	....
2003-04	Owen Sound	OHL	65	14	35	49	72	....	....	....	....	....	....	....	....	....	7	1	3	4	5	....	....	....	....
2004-05	Lowell	AHL	66	6	10	16	85	....	....	....	....	....	....	....	....	....	11	0	1	1	41	....	....	....	....
2005-06	**Calgary**	**NHL**	**7**	**0**	**1**	**1**	**8**	**0**	**0**	**0**	**5**	**0.0**	**2**	**0**	**0.0**	**12:05**	....	....	....	....	....	....	....	....	....
	Omaha	AHL	73	16	42	58	141	....	....	....	....	....	....	....	....	....	....	....	....	....	....	....	....	....	....
2006-07	**Calgary**	**NHL**	**48**	**7**	**8**	**15**	**36**	**3**	**0**	**2**	**49**	**14.3**	**7**	**0**	**0.0**	**13:27**	**4**	**1**	**0**	**1**	**0**	**1**	**0**	**0**	**12:16**
	Omaha	AHL	5	0	2	2	8	....	....	....	....	....	....	....	....	....	3	0	1	1	2	....	....	....	....
2007-08	Dynamo Moscow	Russia	50	4	8	12	89	....	....	....	....	....	....	....	....	....	9	1	5	6	35	....	....	....	....
	NHL Totals		**55**	**7**	**9**	**16**	**44**	**3**	**0**	**2**	**54**	**13.0**		**0**	**0.0**	**13:16**	**4**	**1**	**0**	**1**	**0**	**1**	**0**	**0**	**12:16**

Signed as a free agent by **Calgary**, July 6, 2004. Signed as a free agent by **Dynamo Moscow** (Russia) August 28, 2007. Signed as a free agent by **Calgary**, July 1, 2008.

GIRARDI, Dan

(jih-RAHR-dee, DAN) **NYR**

Defense. Shoots right. 6'2", 210 lbs. Born, Welland, Ont., April 29, 1984.

2000-01	Barrie Colts	OHL	6	0	0	0	0	....	....	....	....	....	....	....	....	....	....	....	....	....	....	....	....	....	....
2001-02	Barrie Colts	OHL	21	0	1	1	0	....	....	....	....	....	....	....	....	....	20	0	0	0	0	....	....	....	....
2002-03	Barrie Colts	OHL	31	3	13	16	24	....	....	....	....	....	....	....	....	....	....	....	....	....	....	....	....	....	....
	Guelph Storm	OHL	36	1	13	14	20	....	....	....	....	....	....	....	....	....	11	0	9	9	14	....	....	....	....
2003-04	Guelph Storm	OHL	68	8	39	47	55	....	....	....	....	....	....	....	....	....	22	2	17	19	10	....	....	....	....
2004-05	Guelph Storm	OHL	38	5	20	25	24	....	....	....	....	....	....	....	....	....	....	....	....	....	....	....	....	....	....
	London Knights	OHL	31	4	10	14	14	....	....	....	....	....	....	....	....	....	18	0	6	6	10	....	....	....	....
2005-06	Hartford	AHL	66	8	31	39	44	....	....	....	....	....	....	....	....	....	13	4	5	9	8	....	....	....	....
	Charlotte	ECHL	7	1	4	5	6	....	....	....	....	....	....	....	....	....	....	....	....	....	....	....	....	....	....
2006-07	**NY Rangers**	**NHL**	**34**	**0**	**6**	**6**	**8**	**0**	**0**	**0**	**33**	**0.0**	**7**	**0**	**0.0**	**15:50**	**10**	**0**	**0**	**0**	**4**	**0**	**0**	**0**	**19:52**
	Hartford	AHL	45	2	22	24	16	....	....	....	....	....	....	....	....	....	....	....	....	....	....	....	....	....	....
2007-08	**NY Rangers**	**NHL**	**82**	**10**	**18**	**28**	**14**	**5**	**0**	**1**	**147**	**6.8**	**0**	**1**	**0.0**	**21:12**	**10**	**0**	**3**	**3**	**6**	**0**	**0**	**0**	**20:42**
	NHL Totals		**116**	**10**	**24**	**34**	**22**	**5**	**0**	**1**	**180**	**5.6**		**1**	**0.0**	**19:37**	**20**	**0**	**3**	**3**	**10**	**0**	**0**	**0**	**20:17**

AHL All-Rookie Team (2006)

Signed as a free agent by **NY Rangers**, July 1, 2006.

GIROUX, Alexandre

(ZHIH-roo, al-ehx-AHN-druh) **WSH.**

Center/Left wing. Shoots left. 6'3", 190 lbs. Born, Quebec City, Que., June 16, 1981. Ottawa's 9th choice, 213th overall, in 1999 Entry Draft.

1997-98	Ste-Foy	QAAA	42	28	30	58	96	....	....	....	....	....	....	....	....	....	....	....	....	....	....	....	....	....	....
1998-99	Hull Olympiques	QMJHL	67	15	22	37	124	....	....	....	....	....	....	....	....	....	22	2	2	4	8	....	....	....	....
99-2000	Hull Olympiques	QMJHL	72	52	47	99	117	....	....	....	....	....	....	....	....	....	15	12	6	18	30	....	....	....	....
2000-01	Hull Olympiques	QMJHL	38	31	32	63	62	....	....	....	....	....	....	....	....	....	....	....	....	....	....	....	....	....	....
	Rouyn-Noranda	QMJHL	25	13	14	27	56	....	....	....	....	....	....	....	....	....	9	2	6	8	22	....	....	....	....
2001-02	Grand Rapids	AHL	70	11	16	27	74	....	....	....	....	....	....	....	....	....	....	....	....	....	....	....	....	....	....
2002-03	Binghamton	AHL	67	19	16	35	101	....	....	....	....	....	....	....	....	....	10	1	0	1	10	....	....	....	....
2003-04	Binghamton	AHL	59	19	23	42	79	....	....	....	....	....	....	....	....	....	....	....	....	....	....	....	....	....	....
	Hartford	AHL	16	6	3	9	13	....	....	....	....	....	....	....	....	....	16	3	4	7	28	....	....	....	....

			Regular Season														Playoffs								
Season	Club	League	GP	G	A	Pts	PIM	PP	SH	GW	S	%	+/-	TF	F%	Min	GP	G	A	Pts	PIM	PP	SH	GW	Min
2004-05	Hartford	AHL	78	32	22	54	128	....	....	....	....	....	....	....	....	....	6	3	3	6	23	....	....	....	....
2005-06	**NY Rangers**	**NHL**	**1**	**0**	**0**	**0**	**0**	0	0	0	0	0.0	–1	0	0.0	2:50	....	....	....	....	....	....	....	....	....
	Hartford	AHL	73	36	31	67	102	....	....	....	....	....	....	....	....	....	13	7	9	16	17	....	....	....	....
2006-07	**Washington**	**NHL**	**9**	**2**	**2**	**4**	**2**	0	0	0	11	18.2	–4	2	50.0	10:11	....	....	....	....	....	....	....	....	....
	Hershey Bears	AHL	67	42	28	70	82	....	....	....	....	....	....	....	....	....	19	4	7	11	27	....	....	....	....
2007-08	Chicago Wolves	AHL	44	19	22	41	47	....	....	....	....	....	....	....	....	....	....	....	....	....	....	....	....	....	....
	Hershey Bears	AHL	24	14	13	27	30	....	....	....	....	....	....	....	....	....	5	3	1	4	2	....	....	....	....
	NHL Totals		**10**	**2**	**2**	**4**	**2**	0	0	0	11	18.2		2	50.0	9:27	....	....	....	....	....	....	....	....	....

Traded to **NY Rangers** by **Ottawa** with Karel Rachunek for Greg De Vries, March 9, 2004. Signed as a free agent by **Washington**, July 14, 2006. Signed as a free agent by **Atlanta**, July 13, 2007. Traded to **Washington** by **Atlanta** for Joe Motzko, February 26, 2008.

GIROUX, Claude

(zhih-ROO, KLOHD) **PHI.**

Right wing. Shoots right. 5'11", 180 lbs. Born, Hearst, Ont., January 12, 1988. Philadelphia's 1st choice, 22nd overall, in 2006 Entry Draft.

Season	Club	League	GP	G	A	Pts	PIM	PP	SH	GW	S	%	+/-	TF	F%	Min	GP	G	A	Pts	PIM	PP	SH	GW	Min
2004-05	Cumberland	CJHL	48	13	27	40	30	....	....	....	....	....	....	....	....	....	....	....	....	....	....	....	....	....	....
2005-06	Gatineau	QMJHL	69	39	64	103	64	....	....	....	....	....	....	....	....	....	17	5	15	20	24	....	....	....	....
2006-07	Gatineau	QMJHL	63	48	64	112	49	....	....	....	....	....	....	....	....	....	5	2	5	7	2	....	....	....	....
	Philadelphia	AHL	5	1	1	2	6	....	....	....	....	....	....	....	....	....	....	....	....	....	....	....	....	....	....
2007-08	**Philadelphia**	**NHL**	**2**	**0**	**0**	**0**	**0**	0	0	0	2	0.0	–2	0	0.0	9:35	....	....	....	....	....	....	....	....	....
	Gatineau	QMJHL	55	38	68	106	37	....	....	....	....	....	....	....	....	....	19	17	*34	*51	6	....	....	....	....
	NHL Totals		**2**	**0**	**0**	**0**	**0**	0	0	0	2	0.0		0	0.0	9:35	....	....	....	....	....	....	....	....	....

QMJHL All-Rookie Team (2006) • QMJHL First All-Star Team (2008) • Canadian Major Junior First All-Star Team (2008)

GIULIANO, Jeff

(JOO-lee-A-noh, JEHF)

Left wing. Shoots left. 5'9", 205 lbs. Born, Nashua, NH, June 20, 1979.

Season	Club	League	GP	G	A	Pts	PIM	PP	SH	GW	S	%	+/-	TF	F%	Min	GP	G	A	Pts	PIM	PP	SH	GW	Min
1998-99	Boston College	H-East	43	5	15	20	10	....	....	....	....	....	....	....	....	....	....	....	....	....	....	....	....	....	....
99-2000	Boston College	H-East	42	10	13	23	16	....	....	....	....	....	....	....	....	....	....	....	....	....	....	....	....	....	....
2000-01	Boston College	H-East	43	14	22	36	28	....	....	....	....	....	....	....	....	....	....	....	....	....	....	....	....	....	....
2001-02	Boston College	H-East	38	11	24	35	14	....	....	....	....	....	....	....	....	....	....	....	....	....	....	....	....	....	....
2002-03	Manchester	AHL	47	4	11	15	8	....	....	....	....	....	....	....	....	....	3	1	0	1	0	....	....	....	....
	Reading Royals	ECHL	38	7	23	30	6	....	....	....	....	....	....	....	....	....	....	....	....	....	....	....	....	....	....
2003-04	Manchester	AHL	80	6	14	20	16	....	....	....	....	....	....	....	....	....	1	0	0	0	0	....	....	....	....
2004-05	Manchester	AHL	69	8	16	24	21	....	....	....	....	....	....	....	....	....	2	0	0	0	0	....	....	....	....
2005-06	**Los Angeles**	**NHL**	**48**	**3**	**4**	**7**	**26**	0	0	2	32	9.4	0	252	46.0	9:45	....	....	....	....	....	....	....	....	....
	Manchester	AHL	19	5	6	11	17	....	....	....	....	....	....	....	....	....	7	3	1	4	2	....	....	....	....
2006-07	Manchester	AHL	35	4	10	14	27	....	....	....	....	....	....	....	....	....	16	3	3	6	12	....	....	....	....
2007-08	**Los Angeles**	**NHL**	**53**	**0**	**6**	**6**	**14**	0	0	0	30	0.0	–9	239	45.2	11:49	....	....	....	....	....	....	....	....	....
	Manchester	AHL	23	3	1	4	14	....	....	....	....	....	....	....	....	....	....	....	....	....	....	....	....	....	....
	NHL Totals		**101**	**3**	**10**	**13**	**40**	0	0	2	62	4.8		491	45.6	10:50	....	....	....	....	....	....	....	....	....

Signed as a free agent by **Los Angeles**, August 12, 2005. • Missed majority of 2006-07 season recovering from recurring abdominal injury.

GLASS, Tanner

(GLAS, TA-nuhr) **FLA.**

Forward. Shoots left. 6', 196 lbs. Born, Regina, Sask., November 29, 1983. Florida's 13th choice, 265th overall, in 2003 Entry Draft.

Season	Club	League	GP	G	A	Pts	PIM	PP	SH	GW	S	%	+/-	TF	F%	Min	GP	G	A	Pts	PIM	PP	SH	GW	Min
2000-01	Yorkton Mallers	SMHL	39	31	29	60	120	....	....	....	....	....	....	....	....	....	4	3	1	4	10	....	....	....	....
2001-02	Penticton	BCHL	57	11	28	39	171	....	....	....	....	....	....	....	....	....	....	....	....	....	....	....	....	....	....
2002-03	Penticton	BCHL	32	15	25	40	108	....	....	....	....	....	....	....	....	....	....	....	....	....	....	....	....	....	....
	Nanaimo Clippers	BCHL	18	8	14	22	46	....	....	....	....	....	....	....	....	....	....	....	....	....	....	....	....	....	....
2003-04	Dartmouth	ECAC	26	4	7	11	18	....	....	....	....	....	....	....	....	....	....	....	....	....	....	....	....	....	....
2004-05	Dartmouth	ECAC	33	7	8	15	32	....	....	....	....	....	....	....	....	....	....	....	....	....	....	....	....	....	....
2005-06	Dartmouth	ECAC	33	12	16	28	56	....	....	....	....	....	....	....	....	....	....	....	....	....	....	....	....	....	....
2006-07	Dartmouth	ECAC	32	8	20	28	92	....	....	....	....	....	....	....	....	....	....	....	....	....	....	....	....	....	....
	Rochester	AHL	4	0	1	1	5	....	....	....	....	....	....	....	....	....	....	....	....	....	....	....	....	....	....
2007-08	**Florida**	**NHL**	**41**	**1**	**1**	**2**	**39**	0	0	0	11	9.1	–5	2	0.0	4:25	....	....	....	....	....	....	....	....	....
	Rochester	AHL	43	6	5	11	84	....	....	....	....	....	....	....	....	....	....	....	....	....	....	....	....	....	....
	NHL Totals		**41**	**1**	**1**	**2**	**39**	0	0	0	11	9.1		2	0.0	4:25	....	....	....	....	....	....	....	....	....

GLEASON, Tim

(GLEE-suhn, TIHM) **CAR.**

Defense. Shoots left. 6', 217 lbs. Born, Clawson, MI, January 29, 1983. Ottawa's 2nd choice, 23rd overall, in 2001 Entry Draft.

Season	Club	League	GP	G	A	Pts	PIM	PP	SH	GW	S	%	+/-	TF	F%	Min	GP	G	A	Pts	PIM	PP	SH	GW	Min
1998-99	Leamington Flyers	OHA-B	52	5	26	31	76	....	....	....	....	....	....	....	....	....	....	....	....	....	....	....	....	....	....
99-2000	Windsor Spitfires	OHL	55	5	13	18	101	....	....	....	....	....	....	....	....	....	12	2	4	6	14	....	....	....	....
2000-01	Windsor Spitfires	OHL	47	8	28	36	124	....	....	....	....	....	....	....	....	....	9	1	2	3	23	....	....	....	....
2001-02	Windsor Spitfires	OHL	67	17	42	59	109	....	....	....	....	....	....	....	....	....	16	7	13	20	40	....	....	....	....
2002-03	Windsor Spitfires	OHL	45	7	31	38	75	....	....	....	....	....	....	....	....	....	7	5	2	7	17	....	....	....	....
2003-04	**Los Angeles**	**NHL**	**47**	**0**	**7**	**7**	**21**	0	0	0	45	0.0	1	0	0.0	14:59	....	....	....	....	....	....	....	....	....
	Manchester	AHL	22	0	8	8	19	....	....	....	....	....	....	....	....	....	6	0	1	1	4	....	....	....	....
2004-05	Manchester	AHL	67	10	14	24	112	....	....	....	....	....	....	....	....	....	5	0	0	0	4	....	....	....	....
2005-06	**Los Angeles**	**NHL**	**78**	**2**	**19**	**21**	**77**	0	0	0	72	2.8	0	0	0.0	17:41	....	....	....	....	....	....	....	....	....
2006-07	**Carolina**	**NHL**	**57**	**2**	**4**	**6**	**57**	1	0	0	72	2.8	–10	0	0.0	18:53	....	....	....	....	....	....	....	....	....
2007-08	**Carolina**	**NHL**	**80**	**3**	**16**	**19**	**84**	0	0	0	98	3.1	5	0	0.0	18:38	....	....	....	....	....	....	....	....	....
	NHL Totals		**262**	**7**	**46**	**53**	**239**	1	0	0	287	2.4		0	0.0	17:45	....	....	....	....	....	....	....	....	....

Rights traded to **Los Angeles** by **Ottawa** for Bryan Smolinski, March 11, 2003. Traded to **Carolina** by **Los Angeles** with Eric Belanger for Oleg Tverdovsky and Jack Johnson, September 29, 2006.

GLENCROSS, Curtis

(GLEHN-kraws, KUHR-tihs) **CGY.**

Center. Shoots left. 6'1", 195 lbs. Born, Kindersley, Sask., December 28, 1982.

Season	Club	League	GP	G	A	Pts	PIM	PP	SH	GW	S	%	+/-	TF	F%	Min	GP	G	A	Pts	PIM	PP	SH	GW	Min
2001-02	Brooks Bandits	AJHL	....	42	26	68	....	....	....	....	....	....	....	....	....	....	....	....	....	....	....	....	....	....	....
2002-03	Alaska Anchorage	WCHA	35	11	12	23	79	....	....	....	....	....	....	....	....	....	....	....	....	....	....	....	....	....	....
2003-04	Alaska Anchorage	WCHA	37	21	13	34	79	....	....	....	....	....	....	....	....	....	....	....	....	....	....	....	....	....	....
	Cincinnati	AHL	7	2	1	3	6	....	....	....	....	....	....	....	....	....	9	1	6	7	10	....	....	....	....
2004-05	Cincinnati	AHL	51	6	3	9	63	....	....	....	....	....	....	....	....	....	12	2	0	2	10	....	....	....	....
2005-06	Portland Pirates	AHL	41	15	10	25	85	....	....	....	....	....	....	....	....	....	19	4	6	10	37	....	....	....	....
2006-07	**Anaheim**	**NHL**	**2**	**1**	**0**	**1**	**2**	0	0	0	5	20.0	–1	0	0.0	10:43	....	....	....	....	....	....	....	....	....
	Portland Pirates	AHL	31	6	10	16	74	....	....	....	....	....	....	....	....	....	....	....	....	....	....	....	....	....	....
	Columbus	**NHL**	**7**	**0**	**0**	**0**	**0**	0	0	0	3	0.0	–4	2	0.0	8:43	....	....	....	....	....	....	....	....	....
	Syracuse Crunch	AHL	29	19	16	35	53	....	....	....	....	....	....	....	....	....	....	....	....	....	....	....	....	....	....
2007-08	**Columbus**	**NHL**	**36**	**6**	**6**	**12**	**25**	1	0	1	63	9.5	3	14	57.1	12:07	....	....	....	....	....	....	....	....	....
	Edmonton	**NHL**	**26**	**9**	**4**	**13**	**28**	0	0	0	41	22.0	5	11	45.5	10:19	....	....	....	....	....	....	....	....	....
	NHL Totals		**71**	**16**	**10**	**26**	**55**	1	0	1	112	14.3		27	48.1	11:05	....	....	....	....	....	....	....	....	....

Signed as a free agent by **Anaheim**, March 25, 2004. Traded to **Columbus** by **Anaheim** with Zenon Konopka and Anaheim's 7th round choice (Trent Vogelhuber) in 2007 Entry Draft for Mark Hartigan, Joe Motzko and Columbus' 4th round choice (Sebastian Stefaniszin) in 2007 Entry Draft, January 26, 2007. Traded to **Edmonton** by **Columbus** for Dick Tarnstrom, February 1, 2008. Signed as a free agent by **Calgary**, July 2, 2008.

GLOBKE, Rob

(GLAWB-kee, RAWB) **FLA.**

Center. Shoots right. 6'2", 208 lbs. Born, Farmington, MI, October 24, 1982. Florida's 3rd choice, 40th overall, in 2002 Entry Draft.

Season	Club	League	GP	G	A	Pts	PIM	PP	SH	GW	S	%	+/-	TF	F%	Min	GP	G	A	Pts	PIM	PP	SH	GW	Min
1998-99	Det. Compuware	NAHL	55	8	14	22	111	....	....	....	....	....	....	....	....	....	7	1	2	3	2	....	....	....	....
99-2000	USNTDP	U-18	6	4	2	6	6	....	....	....	....	....	....	....	....	....	....	....	....	....	....	....	....	....	....
	USNTDP	USHL	54	15	21	36	68	....	....	....	....	....	....	....	....	....	....	....	....	....	....	....	....	....	....
2000-01	U. of Notre Dame	CCHA	33	17	9	26	74	....	....	....	....	....	....	....	....	....	....	....	....	....	....	....	....	....	....
2001-02	U. of Notre Dame	CCHA	33	11	11	22	79	....	....	....	....	....	....	....	....	....	....	....	....	....	....	....	....	....	....
2002-03	U. of Notre Dame	CCHA	40	21	15	36	44	....	....	....	....	....	....	....	....	....	....	....	....	....	....	....	....	....	....
2003-04	U. of Notre Dame	CCHA	39	19	21	40	42	....	....	....	....	....	....	....	....	....	....	....	....	....	....	....	....	....	....
2004-05	San Antonio	AHL	63	6	6	12	21	....	....	....	....	....	....	....	....	....	....	....	....	....	....	....	....	....	....
	Texas Wildcatters	ECHL	10	8	4	12	13	....	....	....	....	....	....	....	....	....	....	....	....	....	....	....	....	....	....
2005-06	**Florida**	**NHL**	**18**	**1**	**0**	**1**	**6**	0	0	0	18	5.6	0	1	0.0	7:17	....	....	....	....	....	....	....	....	....
	Rochester	AHL	52	6	9	15	54	....	....	....	....	....	....	....	....	....	....	....	....	....	....	....	....	....	....

			Regular Season														Playoffs								
Season	Club	League	GP	G	A	Pts	PIM	PP	SH	GW	S	%	+/-	TF	F%	Min	GP	G	A	Pts	PIM	PP	SH	GW	Min
2006-07	**Florida**	**NHL**	19	0	1	1	0	0	0	0	15	0.0	–3	0	0.0	6:04	....	....	....	....	....	....	....	....	....
	Rochester	AHL	48	7	11	18	37	....	....	....	....	....	....	....	....	....	4	0	0	0	0	....	....	....	....
2007-08	**Florida**	**NHL**	9	0	0	0	2	0	0	0	4	0.0	–3	1	0.0	7:44	....	....	....	....	....	....	....	....	....
	Rochester	AHL	64	9	12	21	42	....	....	....	....	....	....	....	....	....	....	....	....	....	....	....	....	....	....
	NHL Totals		46	1	1	2	8	0	0	0	37	2.7		2	0.0	6:52	....	....	....	....	....	....	....	....	....

CCHA Second All-Star Team (2004)

GLUMAC, Mike

(GLOO-kmak, MIGHK) **MTL.**

Right wing. Shoots right. 6'2", 200 lbs. Born, Niagara Falls, Ont., April 5, 1980.

Season	Club	League	GP	G	A	Pts	PIM	PP	SH	GW	S	%	+/-	TF	F%	Min	GP	G	A	Pts	PIM	PP	SH	GW	Min
1996-97	St. Mike's B's	OPJHL	50	13	25	38	33	....	....	....	....	....	....	....	....	....	6	1	0	1	2	....	....	....	....
1997-98	Newmarket	OPJHL	36	16	16	32	57	....	....	....	....	....	....	....	....	....	....	....	....	....	....	....	....	....	....
1998-99	Miami U.	CCHA	35	2	0	2	44	....	....	....	....	....	....	....	....	....	....	....	....	....	....	....	....	....	....
99-2000	Miami U.	CCHA	36	8	5	13	52	....	....	....	....	....	....	....	....	....	....	....	....	....	....	....	....	....	....
2000-01	Miami U.	CCHA	37	9	10	19	46	....	....	....	....	....	....	....	....	....	....	....	....	....	....	....	....	....	....
2001-02	Miami U.	CCHA	36	15	8	23	28	....	....	....	....	....	....	....	....	....	....	....	....	....	....	....	....	....	....
2002-03	Pee Dee Pride	ECHL	69	37	32	69	49	....	....	....	....	....	....	....	....	....	....	....	....	....	....	....	....	....	....
	Cleveland Barons	AHL	2	0	0	0	0	....	....	....	....	....	....	....	....	....	....	....	....	....	....	....	....	....	....
2003-04	Worcester IceCats	AHL	80	28	24	52	74	....	....	....	....	....	....	....	....	....	10	3	3	6	11	....	....	....	....
2004-05	Worcester IceCats	AHL	45	12	17	29	27	....	....	....	....	....	....	....	....	....	....	....	....	....	....	....	....	....	....
2005-06	**St. Louis**	**NHL**	33	7	5	12	33	5	0	0	55	12.7	–8	5	40.0	12:25	....	....	....	....	....	....	....	....	....
	Peoria Rivermen	AHL	49	25	32	57	64	....	....	....	....	....	....	....	....	....	4	1	1	2	5	....	....	....	....
2006-07	**St. Louis**	**NHL**	3	0	1	1	0	0	0	0	4	0.0	1	0	0.0	8:24	....	....	....	....	....	....	....	....	....
	Peoria Rivermen	AHL	72	27	30	57	115	....	....	....	....	....	....	....	....	....	....	....	....	....	....	....	....	....	....
2007-08	**St. Louis**	**NHL**	4	0	0	0	5	0	0	0	3	0.0	–1	3	33.3	10:08	....	....	....	....	....	....	....	....	....
	Peoria Rivermen	AHL	75	21	28	49	99	....	....	....	....	....	....	....	....	....	....	....	....	....	....	....	....	....	....
	NHL Totals		40	7	6	13	38	5	0	0	62	11.3		8	37.5	11:53	....	....	....	....	....	....	....	....	....

ECHL All-Rookie Team (2003)

Signed as a free agent by **Pee Dee** (ECHL), August 28, 2002. Signed as a free agent by **Worcester** (AHL), October 6, 2003. Signed as a free agent by **St. Louis**, June 29, 2004. Signed as a free agent by **Montreal**, July 16, 2008.

GOC, Marcel

(GAWCH, MAHR-sehl) **S.J.**

Center. Shoots left. 6', 205 lbs. Born, Calw, West Germany, August 24, 1983. San Jose's 1st choice, 20th overall, in 2001 Entry Draft.

Season	Club	League	GP	G	A	Pts	PIM	PP	SH	GW	S	%	+/-	TF	F%	Min	GP	G	A	Pts	PIM	PP	SH	GW	Min
1998-99	Schwenningen Jr.	Ger-Jr.	12	23	10	33	12	....	....	....	....	....	....	....	....	....	....	....	....	....	....	....	....	....	....
99-2000	Schwenningen	Germany	51	0	3	3	4	....	....	....	....	....	....	....	....	....	11	1	1	2	2	....	....	....	....
2000-01	Schwenningen	Germany	58	13	28	41	12	....	....	....	....	....	....	....	....	....	....	....	....	....	....	....	....	....	....
2001-02	Schwenningen	Germany	45	8	9	17	24	....	....	....	....	....	....	....	....	....	....	....	....	....	....	....	....	....	....
	Adler Mannheim	Germany	8	0	2	2	0	....	....	....	....	....	....	....	....	....	....	....	....	....	....	....	....	....	....
2002-03	Adler Mannheim	Germany	36	6	14	20	16	....	....	....	....	....	....	....	....	....	8	1	2	3	0	....	....	....	....
2003-04	Cleveland Barons	AHL	78	16	21	37	24	....	....	....	....	....	....	....	....	....	....	....	....	....	....	....	....	....	....
	San Jose	**NHL**	....	....	....	....	....	....	....	....	....	....	....	....	....	....	5	1	1	2	0	0	0	1	7:08
2004-05	Cleveland Barons	AHL	76	16	34	50	28	....	....	....	....	....	....	....	....	....	....	....	....	....	....	....	....	....	....
2005-06	**San Jose**	**NHL**	81	8	14	22	22	2	0	2	96	8.3	–7	808	47.9	11:42	11	0	3	3	0	0	0	0	12:38
	Germany	Olympics	5	1	0	1	0	....	....	....	....	....	....	....	....	....	....	....	....	....	....	....	....	....	....
2006-07	**San Jose**	**NHL**	78	5	8	13	24	0	1	0	96	5.2	–2	659	55.2	12:01	11	2	1	3	4	0	0	0	14:49
2007-08	**San Jose**	**NHL**	51	5	3	8	12	0	0	0	87	5.7	–15	208	51.4	10:41	4	0	0	0	2	0	0	0	8:03
	NHL Totals		210	18	25	43	58	2	1	2	279	6.5		1675	51.2	11:34	31	3	5	8	6	0	0	1	11:56

GODARD, Eric

(GAW-duhrd, AIR-ihk) **PIT.**

Right wing. Shoots right. 6'4", 214 lbs. Born, Vernon, B.C., March 7, 1980.

Season	Club	League	GP	G	A	Pts	PIM	PP	SH	GW	S	%	+/-	TF	F%	Min	GP	G	A	Pts	PIM	PP	SH	GW	Min
1997-98	Lethbridge	WHL	7	0	0	0	26	....	....	....	....	....	....	....	....	....	2	0	0	0	0	....	....	....	....
1998-99	Lethbridge	WHL	66	2	5	7	213	....	....	....	....	....	....	....	....	....	4	0	0	0	14	....	....	....	....
99-2000	Lethbridge	WHL	60	3	5	8	*310	....	....	....	....	....	....	....	....	....	....	....	....	....	....	....	....	....	....
	Louisville Panthers	AHL	4	0	1	1	16	....	....	....	....	....	....	....	....	....	....	....	....	....	....	....	....	....	....
2000-01	Louisville Panthers	AHL	45	0	0	0	132	....	....	....	....	....	....	....	....	....	....	....	....	....	....	....	....	....	....
2001-02	Bridgeport	AHL	67	1	4	5	198	....	....	....	....	....	....	....	....	....	20	0	4	4	30	....	....	....	....
2002-03	**NY Islanders**	**NHL**	19	0	0	0	48	0	0	0	6	0.0	–3	0	0.0	4:32	2	0	1	1	4	0	0	0	1:09
	Bridgeport	AHL	46	2	2	4	199	....	....	....	....	....	....	....	....	....	6	0	0	0	16	....	....	....	....
2003-04	**NY Islanders**	**NHL**	31	0	1	1	97	0	0	0	5	0.0	–2	1	0.0	3:46	....	....	....	....	....	....	....	....	....
	Bridgeport	AHL	7	0	0	0	13	....	....	....	....	....	....	....	....	....	....	....	....	....	....	....	....	....	....
2004-05	Bridgeport	AHL	75	7	11	18	295	....	....	....	....	....	....	....	....	....	....	....	....	....	....	....	....	....	....
2005-06	**NY Islanders**	**NHL**	57	2	2	4	115	0	0	0	17	11.8	–2	1	0.0	3:34	....	....	....	....	....	....	....	....	....
2006-07	**Calgary**	**NHL**	19	0	1	1	50	0	0	0	3	0.0	0	0	0.0	3:47	....	....	....	....	....	....	....	....	....
	Omaha	AHL	36	5	4	9	94	....	....	....	....	....	....	....	....	....	....	....	....	....	....	....	....	....	....
2007-08	**Calgary**	**NHL**	74	1	1	2	171	0	0	1	14	7.1	–8	1	0.0	4:43	5	0	0	0	2	0	0	0	3:31
	NHL Totals		200	3	5	8	481	0	0	1	45	6.7		3	0.0	4:08	7	0	1	1	6	0	0	0	2:50

Signed as a free agent by **Florida**, September 24, 1999. Traded to **NY Islanders** by **Florida** for Florida's 3rd round choice (previously acquired, Florida selected Gregory Campbell) in 2002 Entry Draft, June 22, 2002. • Spent majority of 2003-04 season as a healthy reserve. Signed as a free agent by **Calgary**, August 14, 2006. Signed as a free agent by **Pittsburgh**, July 1, 2008.

GOERTZEN, Steven

(GUHRT-sehn, STEE-vehn) **PHX.**

Right wing. Shoots right. 6'2", 216 lbs. Born, Stony Plain, Alta., May 26, 1984. Columbus' 11th choice, 225th overall, in 2002 Entry Draft.

Season	Club	League	GP	G	A	Pts	PIM	PP	SH	GW	S	%	+/-	TF	F%	Min	GP	G	A	Pts	PIM	PP	SH	GW	Min
99-2000	Spruce Grove	AMBHL	36	16	17	33	30	....	....	....	....	....	....	....	....	....	....	....	....	....	....	....	....	....	....
2000-01	St. Albert Raiders	AMHL	34	11	19	30	70	....	....	....	....	....	....	....	....	....	....	....	....	....	....	....	....	....	....
	St. Albert Saints	AJHL	1	0	0	0	0	....	....	....	....	....	....	....	....	....	....	....	....	....	....	....	....	....	....
2001-02	Seattle	WHL	66	6	9	15	45	....	....	....	....	....	....	....	....	....	11	2	0	2	4	....	....	....	....
2002-03	Seattle	WHL	71	12	19	31	95	....	....	....	....	....	....	....	....	....	14	4	3	7	9	....	....	....	....
2003-04	Seattle	WHL	69	15	18	33	115	....	....	....	....	....	....	....	....	....	....	....	....	....	....	....	....	....	....
	Syracuse Crunch	AHL	8	0	3	3	4	....	....	....	....	....	....	....	....	....	1	0	0	0	0	....	....	....	....
2004-05	Syracuse Crunch	AHL	57	2	7	9	100	....	....	....	....	....	....	....	....	....	....	....	....	....	....	....	....	....	....
2005-06	**Columbus**	**NHL**	39	0	0	0	44	0	0	0	23	0.0	–17	11	54.6	8:32	....	....	....	....	....	....	....	....	....
	Syracuse Crunch	AHL	40	7	8	15	55	....	....	....	....	....	....	....	....	....	6	0	1	1	34	....	....	....	....
2006-07	**Columbus**	**NHL**	7	0	0	0	10	0	0	0	1	0.0	0	0	0.0	5:21	....	....	....	....	....	....	....	....	....
	Syracuse Crunch	AHL	60	9	7	16	120	....	....	....	....	....	....	....	....	....	....	....	....	....	....	....	....	....	....
2007-08	Syracuse Crunch	AHL	59	8	5	13	72	....	....	....	....	....	....	....	....	....	....	....	....	....	....	....	....	....	....
	San Antonio	AHL	22	1	3	4	34	....	....	....	....	....	....	....	....	....	7	1	0	1	5	....	....	....	....
	NHL Totals		46	0	0	0	54	0	0	0	24	0.0		11	54.5	8:03	....	....	....	....	....	....	....	....	....

Traded to **Phoenix** by **Columbus** for Nat DiCasmirro, February 28, 2008.

GOLIGOSKI, Alex

(goh-lih-GAW-skee, AL-ehx) **PIT.**

Defense. Shoots right. 5'11", 180 lbs. Born, Grand Rapids, MN, July 30, 1985. Pittsburgh's 3rd choice, 61st overall, in 2004 Entry Draft.

Season	Club	League	GP	G	A	Pts	PIM	PP	SH	GW	S	%	+/-	TF	F%	Min	GP	G	A	Pts	PIM	PP	SH	GW	Min
2002-03	Grand Rapids	High-MN	28	14	20	34	22	....	....	....	....	....	....	....	....	....	....	....	....	....	....	....	....	....	....
2003-04	Grand Rapids	High-MN	26	25	31	56	16	....	....	....	....	....	....	....	....	....	....	....	....	....	....	....	....	....	....
	Sioux Falls	USHL	10	0	2	2	6	....	....	....	....	....	....	....	....	....	....	....	....	....	....	....	....	....	....
2004-05	U. of Minnesota	WCHA	33	5	15	20	44	....	....	....	....	....	....	....	....	....	....	....	....	....	....	....	....	....	....
2005-06	U. of Minnesota	WCHA	41	11	28	39	63	....	....	....	....	....	....	....	....	....	....	....	....	....	....	....	....	....	....
2006-07	U. of Minnesota	WCHA	44	9	30	39	51	....	....	....	....	....	....	....	....	....	....	....	....	....	....	....	....	....	....
2007-08	**Pittsburgh**	**NHL**	3	0	2	2	2	0	0	0	2	0.0	2	0	0.0	13:56	....	....	....	....	....	....	....	....	....
	Wilkes-Barre	AHL	70	10	28	38	53	....	....	....	....	....	....	....	....	....	23	4	24	28	18	....	....	....	....
	NHL Totals		3	0	2	2	2	0	0	0	2	0.0		0	0.0	13:56	....	....	....	....	....	....	....	....	....

WCHA All-Rookie Team (2005) • WCHA Second All-Star Team (2006) • WCHA First All-Star Team (2007) • NCAA West First All-American Team (2007)

GOMEZ, Scott

(GOH-mehz, SKAWT) **NYR**

Center. Shoots left. 5'11", 200 lbs. Born, Anchorage, AK, December 23, 1979. New Jersey's 2nd choice, 27th overall, in 1998 Entry Draft.

			Regular Season														Playoffs								
Season	Club	League	GP	G	A	Pts	PIM	PP	SH	GW	S	%	+/-	TF	F%	Min	GP	G	A	Pts	PIM	PP	SH	GW	Min
1994-95	East High	High-AK	28	30	48	78	....	....	....	....	....	....	....	....	....	....	....	....	....	....	....	....	....	....	....
1995-96	East High	High-AK	27	*56	49	*101	....	....	....	....	....	....	....	....	....	....	....	....	....	....	....	....	....	....	....
	Anchorage	AAHL	40	*70	*67	*137	44	....	....	....	....	....	....	....	....	....	....	....	....	....	....	....	....	....	....
1996-97	South Surrey	BCHL	56	48	76	124	94	....	....	....	....	....	....	....	....	....	21	18	23	41	57	....	....	....	....
1997-98	Tri-City	WHL	45	12	37	49	57	....	....	....	....	....	....	....	....	....	....	....	....	....	....	....	....	....	....
1998-99	Tri-City	WHL	58	30	*78	108	55	....	....	....	....	....	....	....	....	....	10	6	13	19	31	....	....	....	....
99-2000 ♦	**New Jersey**	**NHL**	**82**	**19**	**51**	**70**	**78**	**7**	**0**	**1**	**204**	**9.3**	**14**	**341**	**44.6**	**16:21**	**23**	**4**	**6**	**10**	**4**	**1**	**0**	**2**	**14:08**
2000-01	**New Jersey**	**NHL**	**76**	**14**	**49**	**63**	**46**	**2**	**0**	**4**	**155**	**9.0**	**–1**	**1010**	**44.6**	**15:46**	**25**	**5**	**9**	**14**	**24**	**0**	**0**	**0**	**16:06**
2001-02	**New Jersey**	**NHL**	**76**	**10**	**38**	**48**	**36**	**1**	**0**	**1**	**156**	**6.4**	**–4**	**628**	**48.7**	**16:46**	....	....	....	....	....	....	....	....	....
2002-03 ♦	**New Jersey**	**NHL**	**80**	**13**	**42**	**55**	**48**	**2**	**0**	**4**	**205**	**6.3**	**17**	**864**	**47.5**	**16:01**	**24**	**3**	**9**	**12**	**2**	**0**	**0**	**0**	**13:45**
2003-04	**New Jersey**	**NHL**	**80**	**14**	***56**	**70**	**70**	**3**	**0**	**1**	**189**	**7.4**	**18**	**1129**	**46.2**	**16:00**	**5**	**0**	**6**	**6**	**0**	**0**	**0**	**0**	**17:14**
2004-05	Alaska Aces	ECHL	61	13	*73	*86	69	....	....	....	....	....	....	....	....	....	4	1	3	4	4	....	....	....	....
2005-06	**New Jersey**	**NHL**	**82**	**33**	**51**	**84**	**42**	**9**	**0**	**5**	**244**	**13.5**	**8**	**1434**	**52.6**	**18:47**	**9**	**5**	**4**	**9**	**6**	**4**	**0**	**1**	**18:14**
	United States	Olympics	6	1	4	5	10	....	....	....	....	....	....	....	....	....	....	....	....	....	....	....	....	....	....
2006-07	**New Jersey**	**NHL**	**72**	**13**	**47**	**60**	**42**	**4**	**0**	**1**	**248**	**5.2**	**7**	**1204**	**52.2**	**18:56**	**11**	**4**	**10**	**14**	**14**	**0**	**0**	**1**	**20:01**
2007-08	**NY Rangers**	**NHL**	**81**	**16**	**54**	**70**	**36**	**7**	**0**	**3**	**242**	**6.6**	**3**	**1165**	**52.5**	**19:54**	**10**	**4**	**7**	**11**	**8**	**1**	**0**	**0**	**20:53**
	NHL Totals		**629**	**132**	**388**	**520**	**398**	**35**	**0**	**20**	**1643**	**8.0**		**7775**	**49.3**	**17:19**	**107**	**25**	**51**	**76**	**58**	**6**	**0**	**4**	**16:14**

WHL West First All-Star Team (1999) • NHL All-Rookie Team (2000) • Calder Memorial Trophy (2000) • ECHL First All-Star Team (2005) • ECHL MVP (2005)

Played in NHL All-Star Game (2000, 2008)

Signed as a free agent by **Alaska** (ECHL), October 25, 2004. Signed as a free agent by **NY Rangers**, July 1, 2007.

GONCHAR, Sergei

(gohn-CHAR, SAIR-gay) **PIT.**

Defense. Shoots left. 6'2", 211 lbs. Born, Chelyabinsk, USSR, April 13, 1974. Washington's 1st choice, 14th overall, in 1992 Entry Draft.

			Regular Season														Playoffs								
Season	Club	League	GP	G	A	Pts	PIM	PP	SH	GW	S	%	+/-	TF	F%	Min	GP	G	A	Pts	PIM	PP	SH	GW	Min
1990-91	Mechel	USSR-2	2	0	0	0	0	....	....	....	....	....	....	....	....	....	....	....	....	....	....	....	....	....	....
	Chelyabinsk	USSR-Q	11	0	0	0	4	....	....	....	....	....	....	....	....	....	....	....	....	....	....	....	....	....	....
1991-92	Chelyabinsk	CIS	31	1	0	1	6	....	....	....	....	....	....	....	....	....	....	....	....	....	....	....	....	....	....
1992-93	Dynamo Moscow	CIS	31	1	3	4	70	....	....	....	....	....	....	....	....	....	10	0	0	0	12	....	....	....	....
1993-94	Dynamo Moscow	CIS	44	4	5	9	36	....	....	....	....	....	....	....	....	....	....	....	....	....	....	....	....	....	....
	Portland Pirates	AHL	....	....	....	....	....	....	....	....	....	....	....	....	....	....	2	0	0	0	0	....	....	....	....
1994-95	Portland Pirates	AHL	61	10	32	42	67	....	....	....	....	....	....	....	....	....	....	....	....	....	....	....	....	....	....
	Washington	**NHL**	**31**	**2**	**5**	**7**	**22**	**0**	**0**	**0**	**38**	**5.3**	**4**	....	....	....	**7**	**2**	**2**	**4**	**2**	**0**	**0**	**1**	....
1995-96	**Washington**	**NHL**	**78**	**15**	**26**	**41**	**60**	**4**	**0**	**4**	**139**	**10.8**	**25**	....	....	....	**6**	**2**	**4**	**6**	**4**	**1**	**0**	**0**	....
1996-97	**Washington**	**NHL**	**57**	**13**	**17**	**30**	**36**	**3**	**0**	**3**	**129**	**10.1**	**–11**	....	....	....	....	....	....	....	....	....	....	....	....
1997-98	Lada Togliatti	Russia	7	3	2	5	4	....	....	....	....	....	....	....	....	....	....	....	....	....	....	....	....	....	....
	Washington	**NHL**	**72**	**5**	**16**	**21**	**66**	**2**	**0**	**0**	**134**	**3.7**	**2**	....	....	....	**21**	**7**	**4**	**11**	**30**	**3**	**1**	**2**	....
	Russia	Olympics	6	0	2	2	0	....	....	....	....	....	....	....	....	....	....	....	....	....	....	....	....	....	....
1998-99	**Washington**	**NHL**	**53**	**21**	**10**	**31**	**57**	**13**	**1**	**3**	**180**	**11.7**	**1**	**0**	**0.0**	**23:55**	....	....	....	....	....	....	....	....	....
99-2000	**Washington**	**NHL**	**73**	**18**	**36**	**54**	**52**	**5**	**0**	**3**	**181**	**9.9**	**26**	**0**	**0.0**	**21:46**	**5**	**1**	**0**	**1**	**6**	**0**	**0**	**0**	**19:58**
2000-01	**Washington**	**NHL**	**76**	**19**	**38**	**57**	**70**	**8**	**0**	**2**	**241**	**7.9**	**12**	**1**	**100.0**	**22:26**	**6**	**1**	**3**	**4**	**2**	**1**	**0**	**0**	**19:45**
2001-02	**Washington**	**NHL**	**76**	**26**	**33**	**59**	**58**	**7**	**0**	**2**	**216**	**12.0**	**–1**	**1**	**100.0**	**23:51**	....	....	....	....	....	....	....	....	....
	Russia	Olympics	6	0	0	0	2	....	....	....	....	....	....	....	....	....	....	....	....	....	....	....	....	....	....
2002-03	**Washington**	**NHL**	**82**	**18**	**49**	**67**	**52**	**7**	**0**	**2**	**224**	**8.0**	**13**	**0**	**0.0**	**26:35**	**6**	**0**	**5**	**5**	**4**	**0**	**0**	**0**	**29:00**
2003-04	**Washington**	**NHL**	**56**	**7**	**42**	**49**	**44**	**4**	**0**	**0**	**127**	**5.5**	**–20**	**0**	**0.0**	**27:57**	....	....	....	....	....	....	....	....	....
	Boston	**NHL**	**15**	**4**	**5**	**9**	**12**	**2**	**0**	**0**	**34**	**11.8**	**6**	**0**	**0.0**	**25:32**	**7**	**1**	**4**	**5**	**4**	**1**	**0**	**1**	**27:51**
2004-05	Magnitogorsk	Russia	40	2	17	19	54	....	....	....	....	....	....	....	....	....	4	1	1	2	6	....	....	....	....
2005-06	**Pittsburgh**	**NHL**	**75**	**12**	**46**	**58**	**100**	**8**	**0**	**2**	**192**	**6.3**	**–13**	**0**	**0.0**	**24:40**	....	....	....	....	....	....	....	....	....
	Russia	Olympics	8	0	2	2	8	....	....	....	....	....	....	....	....	....	....	....	....	....	....	....	....	....	....
2006-07	**Pittsburgh**	**NHL**	**82**	**13**	**54**	**67**	**72**	**10**	**1**	**3**	**191**	**6.8**	**–5**	**0**	**0.0**	**26:34**	**5**	**1**	**3**	**4**	**2**	**1**	**0**	**0**	**26:53**
2007-08	**Pittsburgh**	**NHL**	**78**	**12**	**53**	**65**	**66**	**8**	**0**	**2**	**173**	**6.9**	**13**	**0**	**0.0**	**25:55**	**20**	**1**	**13**	**14**	**8**	**1**	**0**	**0**	**25:13**
	NHL Totals		**904**	**185**	**430**	**615**	**767**	**81**	**2**	**26**	**2199**	**8.4**		**2**	**100.0**	**24:51**	**83**	**16**	**38**	**54**	**62**	**8**	**1**	**4**	**25:01**

NHL Second All-Star Team (2002, 2003)

Played in NHL All-Star Game (2001, 2002, 2003, 2008)

Traded to **Boston** by **Washington** for Shaonne Morrisonn and Boston's 1st (Jeff Schultz) and 2nd (Michail Yunkov) round choices in 2004 Entry Draft, March 3, 2004. Signed as a free agent by **Magnitogorsk** (Russia), September 21, 2004. Signed as a free agent by **Pittsburgh**, August 3, 2005.

GORDON, Boyd

(GOHR-duhn, BOID) **WSH.**

Center. Shoots right. 6'2", 201 lbs. Born, Unity, Sask., October 19, 1983. Washington's 3rd choice, 17th overall, in 2002 Entry Draft.

			Regular Season														Playoffs								
Season	Club	League	GP	G	A	Pts	PIM	PP	SH	GW	S	%	+/-	TF	F%	Min	GP	G	A	Pts	PIM	PP	SH	GW	Min
1997-98	Regina Flyers	SMHA	60	70	102	172	53	....	....	....	....	....	....	....	....	....	....	....	....	....	....	....	....	....	....
1998-99	Regina Rangers	SMBHL	60	70	102	172	53	....	....	....	....	....	....	....	....	....	....	....	....	....	....	....	....	....	....
99-2000	Red Deer Rebels	WHL	66	10	26	36	24	....	....	....	....	....	....	....	....	....	4	0	1	1	16	....	....	....	....
2000-01	Red Deer Rebels	WHL	72	12	27	39	39	....	....	....	....	....	....	....	....	....	22	3	6	9	2	....	....	....	....
2001-02	Red Deer Rebels	WHL	66	22	29	51	19	....	....	....	....	....	....	....	....	....	23	10	12	22	8	....	....	....	....
2002-03	Red Deer Rebels	WHL	56	33	48	81	28	....	....	....	....	....	....	....	....	....	23	8	12	20	14	....	....	....	....
2003-04	**Washington**	**NHL**	**41**	**1**	**5**	**6**	**8**	**0**	**0**	**0**	**42**	**2.4**	**–9**	**328**	**43.0**	**13:11**	....	....	....	....	....	....	....	....	....
	Portland Pirates	AHL	43	5	17	22	16	....	....	....	....	....	....	....	....	....	7	2	1	3	0	....	....	....	....
2004-05	Portland Pirates	AHL	80	17	22	39	35	....	....	....	....	....	....	....	....	....	....	....	....	....	....	....	....	....	....
2005-06	**Washington**	**NHL**	**25**	**0**	**1**	**1**	**4**	**0**	**0**	**0**	**12**	**0.0**	**–4**	**216**	**46.3**	**11:40**	....	....	....	....	....	....	....	....	....
	Hershey Bears	AHL	58	16	22	38	23	....	....	....	....	....	....	....	....	....	21	3	5	8	10	....	....	....	....
2006-07	**Washington**	**NHL**	**71**	**7**	**22**	**29**	**14**	**0**	**2**	**0**	**104**	**6.7**	**10**	**1214**	**52.1**	**15:53**	....	....	....	....	....	....	....	....	....
2007-08	**Washington**	**NHL**	**67**	**7**	**9**	**16**	**12**	**0**	**1**	**0**	**100**	**7.0**	**5**	**904**	**55.8**	**15:44**	**7**	**0**	**0**	**0**	**0**	**0**	**0**	**0**	**13:23**
	NHL Totals		**204**	**15**	**37**	**52**	**38**	**0**	**3**	**0**	**258**	**5.8**		**2662**	**51.7**	**14:46**	**7**	**0**	**0**	**0**	**0**	**0**	**0**	**0**	**13:23**

WHL East First All-Star Team (2003)

GOREN, Lee

(GOH-rehn, LEE)

Right wing. Shoots right. 6'3", 205 lbs. Born, Winnipeg, Man., December 26, 1977. Boston's 5th choice, 63rd overall, in 1997 Entry Draft.

			Regular Season														Playoffs								
Season	Club	League	GP	G	A	Pts	PIM	PP	SH	GW	S	%	+/-	TF	F%	Min	GP	G	A	Pts	PIM	PP	SH	GW	Min
1994-95	Wpg. Warriors	MMMHL	31	19	31	50	50	....	....	....	....	....	....	....	....	....	....	....	....	....	....	....	....	....	....
1995-96	Minot Top Guns	SJHL	56	25	35	61	....	....	....	....	....	....	....	....	....	....	12	5	20	25	....	....	....	....	....
	Saskatoon Blades	WHL	2	0	0	0	2	....	....	....	....	....	....	....	....	....	....	....	....	....	....	....	....	....	....
1996-97	North Dakota	WCHA	DID NOT PLAY																						
1997-98	North Dakota	WCHA	29	3	13	16	26	....	....	....	....	....	....	....	....	....	....	....	....	....	....	....	....	....	....
1998-99	North Dakota	WCHA	38	26	19	45	20	....	....	....	....	....	....	....	....	....	....	....	....	....	....	....	....	....	....
99-2000	North Dakota	WCHA	44	*34	29	63	42	....	....	....	....	....	....	....	....	....	....	....	....	....	....	....	....	....	....
2000-01	**Boston**	**NHL**	**21**	**2**	**0**	**2**	**7**	**1**	**0**	**0**	**9**	**22.2**	**–3**	**21**	**38.1**	**4:24**	....	....	....	....	....	....	....	....	....
	Providence Bruins	AHL	54	15	18	33	72	....	....	....	....	....	....	....	....	....	17	5	2	7	11	....	....	....	....
2001-02	Providence Bruins	AHL	71	11	26	37	121	....	....	....	....	....	....	....	....	....	2	0	0	0	0	....	....	....	....
2002-03	**Boston**	**NHL**	**14**	**2**	**1**	**3**	**7**	**2**	**0**	**0**	**15**	**13.3**	**–2**	**0**	**0.0**	**8:15**	**5**	**0**	**0**	**0**	**5**	**0**	**0**	**0**	**6:29**
	Providence Bruins	AHL	65	32	37	69	106	....	....	....	....	....	....	....	....	....	3	0	1	1	0	....	....	....	....
2003-04	**Florida**	**NHL**	**2**	**0**	**1**	**1**	**0**	**0**	**0**	**0**	**1**	**0.0**	**–4**	**1**	**100.0**	**13:20**	....	....	....	....	....	....	....	....	....
	San Antonio	AHL	65	27	22	49	72	....	....	....	....	....	....	....	....	....	....	....	....	....	....	....	....	....	....
2004-05	Manitoba Moose	AHL	79	32	30	62	117	....	....	....	....	....	....	....	....	....	14	*10	3	13	23	....	....	....	....
2005-06	**Vancouver**	**NHL**	**28**	**1**	**2**	**3**	**30**	**0**	**0**	**1**	**37**	**2.7**	**–6**	**9**	**22.2**	**7:25**	....	....	....	....	....	....	....	....	....
	Manitoba Moose	AHL	42	22	19	41	84	....	....	....	....	....	....	....	....	....	13	3	7	10	27	....	....	....	....
2006-07	**Vancouver**	**NHL**	**2**	**0**	**0**	**0**	**0**	**0**	**0**	**0**	**2**	**0.0**	**–1**	**0**	**0.0**	**11:21**	....	....	....	....	....	....	....	....	....
	Manitoba Moose	AHL	72	26	42	68	86	....	....	....	....	....	....	....	....	....	13	4	5	9	16	....	....	....	....
2007-08	Skelleftea AIK HK	Sweden	47	16	20	36	73	....	....	....	....	....	....	....	....	....	5	1	0	1	14	....	....	....	....
	NHL Totals		**67**	**5**	**4**	**9**	**44**	**3**	**0**	**1**	**64**	**7.8**		**31**	**35.5**	**6:56**	**5**	**0**	**0**	**0**	**5**	**0**	**0**	**0**	**6:29**

WCHA Second All-Star Team (2000) • NCAA West Second All-American Team (2000) • NCAA Championship All-Tournament Team (2000) • NCAA Championship Tournament MVP (2000)

• Ruled ineligible to play during 1996-97 season by NCAA due to appearance with **Saskatoon** (WHL) in 1995-96 season. Signed as a free agent by **Florida**, July 24, 2003. Signed as a free agent by **Vancouver**, July 7, 2004. Signed as a free agent by **Skelleftea** (Sweden), June 8, 2007.

GORGES, Josh

(GOHR-juhz, JAWSH) **MTL.**

Defense. Shoots left. 6'1", 195 lbs. Born, Kelowna, B.C., August 14, 1984.

Season	Club	League	GP	G	A	Pts	PIM	PP	SH	GW	S	%	+/-	TF	F%	Min	GP	G	A	Pts	PIM	PP	SH	GW	Min
			Regular Season														Playoffs								
2000-01	Kelowna Rockets	WHL	57	4	6	10	24	....	....	....	....	....	....	....	....	....	6	1	1	2	4	....	....	....	....
2001-02	Kelowna Rockets	WHL	72	7	34	41	74	....	....	....	....	....	....	....	....	....	15	1	7	8	8	....	....	....	....
2002-03	Kelowna Rockets	WHL	54	11	48	59	76	....	....	....	....	....	....	....	....	....	19	3	17	20	16	....	....	....	....
2003-04	Kelowna Rockets	WHL	62	11	31	42	38	....	....	....	....	....	....	....	....	....	17	2	13	15	6	....	....	....	....
2004-05	Cleveland Barons	AHL	74	4	8	12	37	....	....	....	....	....	....	....	....	....	....	....	....	....	....	....	....	....	....
2005-06	**San Jose**	**NHL**	**49**	**0**	**6**	**6**	**31**	**0**	**0**	**0**	**25**	**0.0**	**5**	**0**	**0.0**	**17:38**	**11**	**0**	**1**	**1**	**4**	**0**	**0**	**0**	**18:56**
	Cleveland Barons	AHL	18	2	3	5	12	....	....	....	....	....	....	....	....	....	....	....	....	....	....	....	....	....	....
2006-07	**San Jose**	**NHL**	**47**	**1**	**3**	**4**	**26**	**0**	**0**	**0**	**37**	**2.7**	**–3**	**0**	**0.0**	**17:48**	....	....	....	....	....	....	....	....	....
	Worcester Sharks	AHL	7	0	1	1	2	....	....	....	....	....	....	....	....	....	....	....	....	....	....	....	....	....	....
	Montreal	**NHL**	**7**	**0**	**0**	**0**	**0**	**0**	**0**	**0**	**3**	**0.0**	**–1**	**0**	**0.0**	**12:28**	....	....	....	....	....	....	....	....	....
2007-08	**Montreal**	**NHL**	**62**	**0**	**9**	**9**	**32**	**0**	**0**	**0**	**41**	**0.0**	**0**	**0**	**0.0**	**16:20**	**12**	**0**	**3**	**3**	**0**	**0**	**0**	**0**	**18:20**
	NHL Totals		**165**	**1**	**18**	**19**	**89**	**0**	**0**	**0**	**106**	**0.9**		**0**	**0.0**	**16:58**	**23**	**0**	**4**	**4**	**4**	**0**	**0**	**0**	**18:37**

WHL West Second All-Star Team (2003) • WHL West First All-Star Team (2004) • George Parsons Trophy (Memorial Cup Tournament - Most Sportsmanlike Player) (2004)

Signed as a free agent by **San Jose**, September 20, 2002. Traded to **Montreal** by **San Jose** with San Jose's 1st round choice (Max Pacioretty) in 2007 Entry Draft for Craig Rivet and Montreal's 5th round choice (Julien Demers) in 2008 Entry Draft, February 25, 2007.

GOVE, David

(GOHV, DAY-vihd) **PIT.**

Center/Right wing. Shoots left. 5'9", 190 lbs. Born, Centerville, MA, May 4, 1978.

Season	Club	League	GP	G	A	Pts	PIM	PP	SH	GW	S	%	+/-	TF	F%	Min	GP	G	A	Pts	PIM	PP	SH	GW	Min
1997-98	Western Mich.	CCHA	36	8	7	15	8	....	....	....	....	....	....	....	....	....	....	....	....	....	....	....	....	....	....
1998-99	Western Mich.	CCHA	33	9	14	23	12	....	....	....	....	....	....	....	....	....	....	....	....	....	....	....	....	....	....
99-2000	Western Mich.	CCHA	36	18	28	46	22	....	....	....	....	....	....	....	....	....	....	....	....	....	....	....	....	....	....
2000-01	Western Mich.	CCHA	39	22	37	59	16	....	....	....	....	....	....	....	....	....	....	....	....	....	....	....	....	....	....
	Orlando	IHL	9	1	1	2	2	....	....	....	....	....	....	....	....	....	1	0	0	0	0	....	....	....	....
2001-02	Grand Rapids	AHL	17	2	4	6	8	....	....	....	....	....	....	....	....	....	....	....	....	....	....	....	....	....	....
	Johnstown Chiefs	ECHL	54	17	32	49	32	....	....	....	....	....	....	....	....	....	8	1	3	4	4	....	....	....	....
2002-03	San Antonio	AHL	72	15	20	35	30	....	....	....	....	....	....	....	....	....	3	0	1	1	0	....	....	....	....
	Laredo Bucks	CHL	8	4	12	16	15	....	....	....	....	....	....	....	....	....	....	....	....	....	....	....	....	....	....
2003-04	Utah Grizzlies	AHL	75	14	22	36	28	....	....	....	....	....	....	....	....	....	....	....	....	....	....	....	....	....	....
2004-05	Providence Bruins	AHL	70	13	18	31	30	....	....	....	....	....	....	....	....	....	17	3	3	6	14	....	....	....	....
2005-06	**Carolina**	**NHL**	**1**	**0**	**1**	**1**	**0**	**0**	**0**	**0**	**0**	**0.0**	**2**	**0**	**0.0**	**7:12**	....	....	....	....	....	....	....	....	....
	Lowell	AHL	65	20	26	46	50	....	....	....	....	....	....	....	....	....	....	....	....	....	....	....	....	....	....
2006-07	**Carolina**	**NHL**	**1**	**0**	**0**	**0**	**0**	**0**	**0**	**0**	**0**	**0.0**	**0**	**0**	**0.0**	**3:16**	....	....	....	....	....	....	....	....	....
	Albany River Rats	AHL	49	8	13	21	27	....	....	....	....	....	....	....	....	....	4	0	2	2	4	....	....	....	....
2007-08	Albany River Rats	AHL	45	8	15	23	31	....	....	....	....	....	....	....	....	....	....	....	....	....	....	....	....	....	....
	Wilkes-Barre	AHL	36	15	7	22	10	....	....	....	....	....	....	....	....	....	23	5	7	12	10	....	....	....	....
	NHL Totals		**2**	**0**	**1**	**1**	**0**	**0**	**0**	**0**	**0**	**0.0**		**0**	**0.0**	**5:14**	....	....	....	....	....	....	....	....	....

Signed as a free agent by **Carolina**, August 4, 2005. Traded to **Pittsburgh** by **Carolina** for Joe Jensen, January 31, 2008.

GRABOVSKI, Mikhail

(gra-BAWV-skee, mih-kigh-EHL) **TOR.**

Center. Shoots left. 5'11", 179 lbs. Born, Potsdam, East Germany, January 31, 1984. Montreal's 4th choice, 150th overall, in 2004 Entry Draft.

Season	Club	League	GP	G	A	Pts	PIM	PP	SH	GW	S	%	+/-	TF	F%	Min	GP	G	A	Pts	PIM	PP	SH	GW	Min
2001-02	HC Minsk	Belarus	26	10	7	17	16	....	....	....	....	....	....	....	....	....	....	....	....	....	....	....	....	....	....
2002-03	HC Minsk	Belarus	STATISTICS NOT AVAILABLE																						
2003-04	Nizhnekamsk	Russia	45	6	11	17	26	....	....	....	....	....	....	....	....	....	5	0	0	0	4	....	....	....	....
2004-05	Nizhnekamsk	Russia	60	16	20	36	32	....	....	....	....	....	....	....	....	....	3	2	0	2	2	....	....	....	....
	Yunost-Minsk	BelOpen	....	....	....	....	....	....	....	....	....	....	....	....	....	....	5	2	4	6	6	....	....	....	....
2005-06	Dynamo Moscow	Russia	48	10	17	27	28	....	....	....	....	....	....	....	....	....	4	0	0	0	4	....	....	....	....
	Yunost-Minsk	BelOpen	8	6	8	14	10	....	....	....	....	....	....	....	....	....	....	....	....	....	....	....	....	....	....
2006-07	**Montreal**	**NHL**	**3**	**0**	**0**	**0**	**0**	**0**	**0**	**0**	**5**	**0.0**	**–2**	**31**	**41.9**	**13:18**	....	....	....	....	....	....	....	....	....
	Hamilton	AHL	66	17	37	54	34	....	....	....	....	....	....	....	....	....	20	4	7	11	21	....	....	....	....
2007-08	**Montreal**	**NHL**	**24**	**3**	**6**	**9**	**8**	**0**	**0**	**1**	**23**	**13.0**	**–4**	**154**	**33.1**	**11:14**	....	....	....	....	....	....	....	....	....
	Hamilton	AHL	12	8	12	20	6	....	....	....	....	....	....	....	....	....	....	....	....	....	....	....	....	....	....
	NHL Totals		**27**	**3**	**6**	**9**	**8**	**0**	**0**	**1**	**28**	**10.7**		**185**	**34.6**	**11:27**	....	....	....	....	....	....	....	....	....

Traded to **Toronto** by **Montreal** for Greg Pateryn and Toronto's 2nd round choice in 2009 Entry Draft, July 3, 2008.

GRAGNANI, Marc-Andre

(GRUH-na-nee, MAHRK-AWN-dray) **BUF.**

Defense. Shoots left. 6'1", 192 lbs. Born, Montreal, Que., March 11, 1987. Buffalo's 3rd choice, 87th overall, in 2005 Entry Draft.

Season	Club	League	GP	G	A	Pts	PIM	PP	SH	GW	S	%	+/-	TF	F%	Min	GP	G	A	Pts	PIM	PP	SH	GW	Min
2002-03	West Island Lions	QAAA	34	3	15	18	22	....	....	....	....	....	....	....	....	....	....	....	....	....	....	....	....	....	....
2003-04	PEI Rocket	QMJHL	61	2	13	15	42	....	....	....	....	....	....	....	....	....	11	0	0	0	4	....	....	....	....
2004-05	PEI Rocket	QMJHL	68	10	29	39	48	....	....	....	....	....	....	....	....	....	....	....	....	....	....	....	....	....	....
2005-06	PEI Rocket	QMJHL	62	16	55	71	75	....	....	....	....	....	....	....	....	....	6	1	4	5	14	....	....	....	....
2006-07	PEI Rocket	QMJHL	65	22	46	68	58	....	....	....	....	....	....	....	....	....	7	5	8	13	4	....	....	....	....
2007-08	**Buffalo**	**NHL**	**2**	**0**	**0**	**0**	**4**	**0**	**0**	**0**	**1**	**0.0**	**–2**	**0**	**0.0**	**6:18**	....	....	....	....	....	....	....	....	....
	Rochester	AHL	78	14	38	52	38	....	....	....	....	....	....	....	....	....	....	....	....	....	....	....	....	....	....
	NHL Totals		**2**	**0**	**0**	**0**	**4**	**0**	**0**	**0**	**1**	**0.0**		**0**	**0.0**	**6:18**	....	....	....	....	....	....	....	....	....

GRAND-PIERRE, Jean-Luc

(GRAHN pee-AIR, ZHAWN-LOOK)

Defense. Shoots right. 6'3", 225 lbs. Born, Montreal, Que., February 2, 1977. St. Louis' 6th choice, 179th overall, in 1995 Entry Draft.

Season	Club	League	GP	G	A	Pts	PIM	PP	SH	GW	S	%	+/-	TF	F%	Min	GP	G	A	Pts	PIM	PP	SH	GW	Min
1992-93	Lac St-Louis Lions	QAAA	1	0	0	0	2	....	....	....	....	....	....	....	....	....	....	....	....	....	....	....	....	....	....
1993-94	Beauport	QMJHL	46	1	4	5	27	....	....	....	....	....	....	....	....	....	1	0	0	0	0	....	....	....	....
1994-95	Val-d'Or Foreurs	QMJHL	59	10	13	23	126	....	....	....	....	....	....	....	....	....	....	....	....	....	....	....	....	....	....
1995-96	Val-d'Or Foreurs	QMJHL	67	13	21	34	209	....	....	....	....	....	....	....	....	....	13	1	4	5	47	....	....	....	....
1996-97	Val-d'Or Foreurs	QMJHL	58	9	24	33	186	....	....	....	....	....	....	....	....	....	13	5	8	13	46	....	....	....	....
1997-98	Rochester	AHL	75	4	6	10	211	....	....	....	....	....	....	....	....	....	4	0	0	0	2	....	....	....	....
1998-99	**Buffalo**	**NHL**	**16**	**0**	**1**	**1**	**17**	**0**	**0**	**0**	**11**	**0.0**	**0**	**0**	**0.0**	**13:36**	....	....	....	....	....	....	....	....	....
	Rochester	AHL	55	5	4	9	90	....	....	....	....	....	....	....	....	....	....	....	....	....	....	....	....	....	....
99-2000	**Buffalo**	**NHL**	**11**	**0**	**0**	**0**	**15**	**0**	**0**	**0**	**11**	**0.0**	**–1**	**0**	**0.0**	**15:11**	**4**	**0**	**0**	**0**	**4**	**0**	**0**	**0**	**17:34**
	Rochester	AHL	62	5	8	13	124	....	....	....	....	....	....	....	....	....	17	0	1	1	40	....	....	....	....
2000-01	**Columbus**	**NHL**	**64**	**1**	**4**	**5**	**73**	**0**	**0**	**0**	**33**	**3.0**	**–6**	**0**	**0.0**	**12:51**	....	....	....	....	....	....	....	....	....
2001-02	**Columbus**	**NHL**	**81**	**2**	**6**	**8**	**90**	**0**	**0**	**0**	**62**	**3.2**	**–28**	**3**	**0.0**	**15:20**	....	....	....	....	....	....	....	....	....
2002-03	**Columbus**	**NHL**	**41**	**1**	**0**	**1**	**64**	**0**	**0**	**0**	**32**	**3.1**	**–6**	**0**	**0.0**	**13:38**	....	....	....	....	....	....	....	....	....
	Syracuse Crunch	AHL	2	1	0	1	6	....	....	....	....	....	....	....	....	....	....	....	....	....	....	....	....	....	....
2003-04	**Columbus**	**NHL**	**16**	**0**	**0**	**0**	**12**	**0**	**0**	**0**	**15**	**0.0**	**–3**	**2**	**100.0**	**7:25**	....	....	....	....	....	....	....	....	....
	Atlanta	**NHL**	**27**	**2**	**2**	**4**	**26**	**0**	**1**	**0**	**19**	**10.5**	**–7**	**1**	**0.0**	**15:25**	....	....	....	....	....	....	....	....	....
	Washington	**NHL**	**13**	**1**	**0**	**1**	**14**	**0**	**0**	**0**	**19**	**5.3**	**–2**	**2**	**0.0**	**11:34**	....	....	....	....	....	....	....	....	....
2004-05	IF Troja-Ljungby	Sweden-2	21	2	3	5	69	....	....	....	....	....	....	....	....	....	....	....	....	....	....	....	....	....	....
2005-06	Fuchse Duisburg	Germany	45	10	9	19	176	....	....	....	....	....	....	....	....	....	5	2	2	4	8	....	....	....	....
2006-07	Dusseldorf	Germany	44	9	14	23	63	....	....	....	....	....	....	....	....	....	9	1	1	2	10	....	....	....	....
2007-08	Lowell Devils	AHL	63	3	5	8	82	....	....	....	....	....	....	....	....	....	....	....	....	....	....	....	....	....	....
	NHL Totals		**269**	**7**	**13**	**20**	**311**	**0**	**1**	**0**	**202**	**3.5**		**8**	**25.0**	**13:44**	**4**	**0**	**0**	**0**	**4**	**0**	**0**	**0**	**17:34**

Traded to **Buffalo** by **St. Louis** with Ottawa's 2nd round choice (previously acquired, Buffalo selected Cory Sarich) in 1996 Entry Draft and St. Louis' 3rd round choice (Maxim Afinogenov) in 1997 Entry Draft for Yuri Khmylev and Buffalo's 8th round choice (Andrei Podkonicky) in 1996 Entry Draft, March 20, 1996. Traded to **Columbus** by **Buffalo** with Matt Davidson, San Jose's 5th round choice (previously acquired, Columbus selected Tyler Kolarik) in 2000 Entry Draft and Buffalo's 5th round choice (later traded to Calgary – later traded to Detroit – Detroit selected Andreas Jamtin) in 2001 Entry Draft to complete Expansion Draft agreement which had Columbus select Geoff Sanderson and Dwayne Roloson from Buffalo, June 23, 2000. Traded to **Atlanta** by **Columbus** for future considerations, December 31, 2003. Claimed on waivers by **Washington** from **Atlanta**, March 9, 2004. Signed as a free agent by **Troja-Ljungby** (Sweden-2), December 10, 2004. Signed as a free agent by **Duisburg** (Germany), September 2, 2005. Signed as a free agent by **Dusseldorf** (Germany), July 28, 2006. Signed as a free agent by **New Jersey**, July 24, 2007.

GRANT, Triston
(GRANT, TRIHS-tuhn) **NSH.**

Left wing. Shoots left. 6'1", 215 lbs. Born, Neepawa, Man., February 2, 1984. Philadelphia's 10th choice, 286th overall, in 2004 Entry Draft.

			Regular Season														Playoffs								
Season	Club	League	GP	G	A	Pts	PIM	PP	SH	GW	S	%	+/-	TF	F%	Min	GP	G	A	Pts	PIM	PP	SH	GW	Min
2000-01	Neepawa Natives	MJHL	Statistics Not Available																						
	Lethbridge	WHL	23	2	0	2	75										5	0	0	0	11				
2001-02	Lethbridge	WHL	36	8	1	9	110																		
	Vancouver Giants	WHL	21	2	4	6	53																		
2002-03	Vancouver Giants	WHL	72	10	10	20	200										4	0	0	0	10				
2003-04	Vancouver Giants	WHL	69	10	8	18	267										11	1	1	2	33				
2004-05	Vancouver Giants	WHL	70	20	12	32	193										6	1	0	1	8				
2005-06	Philadelphia	AHL	64	2	3	5	190																		
2006-07	Philadelphia	NHL	8	0	1	1	10	0	0	0	3	0.0	-1	0	0.0	4:32									
	Philadelphia	AHL	61	5	6	11	199																		
2007-08	Philadelphia	AHL	72	10	11	21	181										12	0	2	2	34				
	NHL Totals		8	0	1	1	10	0	0	0	3	0.0		0	0.0	4:32									

Traded to **Nashville** by **Philadelphia** with Philadelphia's 7th round choice in 2009 Entry Draft for Janne Niskala, June 24, 2008.

GRATTON, Chris
(GRAHT-uhn, KRIHS) **T.B.**

Center. Shoots left. 6'4", 226 lbs. Born, Brantford, Ont., July 5, 1975. Tampa Bay's 1st choice, 3rd overall, in 1993 Entry Draft.

1989-90	Brantford Classics	OHA-B	1	0	2	2	2																		
1990-91	Brantford Classics	OHA-B	31	30	30	60	28																		
1991-92	Kingston	OHL	62	27	39	66	37																		
1992-93	Kingston	OHL	58	55	54	109	125										16	11	18	29	42				
1993-94	Tampa Bay	NHL	84	13	29	42	123	5	1	2	161	8.1	-25												
1994-95	Tampa Bay	NHL	46	7	20	27	89	2	0	0	91	7.7	-2												
1995-96	Tampa Bay	NHL	82	17	21	38	105	7	0	3	183	9.3	-13				6	0	2	2	27	0	0	0	
1996-97	Tampa Bay	NHL	82	30	32	62	201	9	0	4	230	13.0	-28												
1997-98	Philadelphia	NHL	82	22	40	62	159	5	0	2	182	12.1	11				5	2	0	2	10	0	0	0	
1998-99	Philadelphia	NHL	26	1	7	8	41	0	0	0	54	1.9	-8	38	42.1	14:25									
	Tampa Bay	NHL	52	7	19	26	102	1	0	1	127	5.5	-20	1032	53.9	18:20									
99-2000	Tampa Bay	NHL	58	14	27	41	121	4	0	1	168	8.3	-24	1341	55.9	20:03									
	Buffalo	NHL	14	1	7	8	15	0	0	0	34	2.9	1	256	54.3	16:40	5	0	1	1	4	0	0	0	14:56
2000-01	Buffalo	NHL	82	19	21	40	102	5	0	5	156	12.2	0	1161	57.3	14:37	13	6	4	10	14	2	0	1	12:33
2001-02	Buffalo	NHL	82	15	24	39	75	1	0	5	139	10.8	0	1297	53.8	14:57									
2002-03	Buffalo	NHL	66	15	29	44	86	4	0	2	187	8.0	-5	1099	58.9	16:26									
	Phoenix	NHL	14	0	1	1	21	0	0	0	28	0.0	-11	231	57.1	17:12									
2003-04	Phoenix	NHL	68	11	18	29	93	3	0	1	122	9.0	-19	1090	55.3	14:40									
	Colorado	NHL	13	2	1	3	18	0	0	0	28	7.1	1	252	57.5	16:55	11	0	0	0	27	0	0	0	12:14
2004-05			Did Not Play																						
2005-06	Florida	NHL	76	17	22	39	104	4	1	2	135	12.6	6	960	51.3	15:43									
2006-07	Florida	NHL	81	13	22	35	94	1	0	1	131	9.9	1	517	56.7	12:06									
2007-08	Tampa Bay	NHL	60	10	11	21	77	1	0	1	92	10.9	-7	618	54.5	12:42									
	NHL Totals		1068	214	351	565	1626	52	2	30	2248	9.5		9892	55.3	15:22	40	8	7	15	82	2	0	1	12:50

OHL All-Rookie Team (1992) • OHL Rookie of the Year (1992)

Signed as a free agent by **Philadelphia**, August 14, 1997. Traded to **Tampa Bay** by **Philadelphia** with Mike Sillinger for Mikael Renberg and Daymond Langkow, December 12, 1998. Traded to **Buffalo** by **Tampa Bay** with Tampa Bay's 2nd round choice (Derek Roy) in 2001 Entry Draft for Cory Sarich, Wayne Primeau, Brian Holzinger and Buffalo's 3rd round choice (Alexander Kharitonov) in 2000 Entry Draft, March 9, 2000. Traded to **Phoenix** by **Buffalo** with Buffalo's 4th round choice (later traded to Edmonton – Edmonton selected Liam Reddox) in 2004 Entry Draft for Daniel Briere and Phoenix's 3rd round choice (Andrej Sekera) in 2004 Entry Draft, March 10, 2003. Traded to **Colorado** by **Phoenix** with Ossi Vaananen and Phoenix's 2nd round choice (Paul Stastny) in 2005 Entry Draft for Derek Morris and Keith Ballard, March 9, 2004. Signed as a free agent by **Florida**, August 12, 2005. Traded to **Tampa Bay** by **Florida** for Tampa Bay's 2nd round choice (Jacob Markstrom) in 2008 Entry Draft, June 13, 2007.

GRATTON, Josh
(GRAHT-uhn, JAWSH) **NSH.**

Left wing. Shoots left. 6'2", 214 lbs. Born, Brantford, Ont., September 9, 1982.

2000-01	Sudbury Wolves	OHL	44	5	13	18	110										9	1	1	2	25				
2001-02	Sudbury Wolves	OHL	14	5	4	9	47																		
	Kingston	OHL	46	14	14	28	140										1	1	0	1	7				
2002-03	Windsor Spitfires	OHL	62	26	30	56	192										6	2	1	3	8				
2003-04	Cincinnati	AHL	21	2	2	4	69										8	0	0	0	35				
	San Diego Gulls	ECHL	30	4	6	10	239																		
2004-05	Philadelphia	AHL	57	9	5	14	246										21	3	3	6	78				
	Trenton Titans	ECHL	1	0	0	0	0																		
2005-06	Philadelphia	NHL	3	0	0	0	14	0	0	0	3	0.0	0	0	0.0	5:00									
	Philadelphia	AHL	53	9	10	19	265																		
	Phoenix	NHL	11	1	0	1	30	0	0	0	14	7.1	-3	0	0.0	8:00									
2006-07	Phoenix	NHL	52	1	1	2	188	0	0	0	29	3.4	-9	1	0.0	5:54									
	San Antonio	AHL	3	1	1	2	8																		
2007-08	Phoenix	NHL	1	0	0	0	5	0	0	0	0	0.0	1	0	0.0	9:40									
	San Antonio	AHL	38	5	9	14	124																		
	Hartford	AHL	20	6	6	12	72										4	0	1	1	11				
	NHL Totals		67	2	1	3	237	0	0	0	46	4.3		1	0.0	6:16									

Signed as a free agent by **Philadelphia**, July 27, 2004. Traded to **Phoenix** by **Philadelphia** with Florida's 2nd round choice (previously acquired, later traded to Detroit - Detroit selected Cory Emerton) in 2006 Entry Draft and Tampa Bay's 2nd round choice (previously acquired, later traded to Detroit - Detroit selected Shawn Matthias) in 2006 Entry Draft for Denis Gauthier, March 9, 2006. Traded to **NY Rangers** by **Phoenix** with Fredrik Sjostrom, David LeNeveu and future considerations for Al Montoya and Marcel Hossa, February 26, 2008. Signed as a free agent by **Nashville**, July 9, 2008.

GREBESHKOV, Denis
(greh-behsh-KAHV, DEH-nihs) **EDM.**

Defense. Shoots left. 6', 209 lbs. Born, Yaroslavl, USSR, October 11, 1983. Los Angeles' 1st choice, 18th overall, in 2002 Entry Draft.

99-2000	Yaroslavl 2	Russia-3	42	2	1	3	12										6	0	0	0	2				
2000-01	Yaroslavl 2	Russia-3	34	7	2	9	20																		
2001-02	Yaroslavl 2	Russia-3	7	1	1	2	2																		
	Yaroslavl	Russia	27	1	2	3	10																		
2002-03	Yaroslavl	Russia	48	0	7	7	26										10	0	1	1	2				
2003-04	Los Angeles	NHL	4	0	1	1	0	0	0	0	5	0.0	-4	0	0.0	18:29									
	Manchester	AHL	43	2	7	9	34										6	0	1	1	6				
2004-05	Manchester	AHL	75	5	44	49	87										6	0	4	4	2				
2005-06	Los Angeles	NHL	8	0	2	2	12	0	0	0	10	0.0	-4	0	0.0	15:16									
	Manchester	AHL	48	2	25	27	59																		
	NY Islanders	NHL	21	0	3	3	8	0	0	0	14	0.0	-8	0	0.0	17:11									
	Bridgeport	AHL															7	1	1	2	8				
2006-07	Yaroslavl	Russia	47	8	9	17	79										7	0	2	2	6				
2007-08	Edmonton	NHL	71	3	15	18	22	1	0	0	34	8.8	2	0	0.0	16:53									
	NHL Totals		104	3	21	24	42	1	0	0	63	4.8		0	0.0	16:53									

Traded to **NY Islanders** by **Los Angeles** with Jeff Tambellini for Mark Parrish and Brent Sopel, March 8, 2006. Signed as a free agent by **Yaroslavl** (Russia), July 10, 2006. Traded to **Edmonton** by **NY Islanders** for Marc-Andre Bergeron and Edmonton's 3rd round choice (later traded back to Edmonton - later traded to Anaheim - later traded back to NY Islanders - NY Islanders selected Kirill Petrov) in 2008 Entry Draft, February 18, 2007.

GREEN, Josh
(GREEN, JAWSH) **ANA.**

Left wing. Shoots left. 6'3", 215 lbs. Born, Camrose, Alta., November 16, 1977. Los Angeles' 1st choice, 30th overall, in 1996 Entry Draft.

1992-93	Camrose Kodiaks	ABHL	60	55	45	100	80																		
1993-94	Medicine Hat	WHL	63	22	22	44	43										3	0	0	0	4				
1994-95	Medicine Hat	WHL	68	32	23	55	64										5	5	1	6	2				
1995-96	Medicine Hat	WHL	46	18	25	43	55										5	2	2	4	4				
1996-97	Medicine Hat	WHL	51	25	32	57	61																		
	Swift Current	WHL	23	10	15	25	33										10	9	7	16	19				
1997-98	Swift Current	WHL	5	9	1	10	9																		
	Portland	WHL	26	26	18	44	27																		
	Fredericton	AHL	43	16	15	31	14										4	1	3	4	6				

			Regular Season														Playoffs								
Season	Club	League	GP	G	A	Pts	PIM	PP	SH	GW	S	%	+/-	TF	F%	Min	GP	G	A	Pts	PIM	PP	SH	GW	Min
1998-99	**Los Angeles**	**NHL**	**27**	**1**	**3**	**4**	**8**	1	0	0	35	2.9	-5	2	50.0	11:44	....	....	....	....	....	....	....	....	....
	Springfield	AHL	41	15	15	30	29	....	....	....	....	....	....	....	....	....	....	....	....	....	....	....	....	....	....
99-2000	**NY Islanders**	**NHL**	**49**	**12**	**14**	**26**	**41**	2	0	3	109	11.0	-7	12	50.0	13:36	....	....	....	....	....	....	....	....	....
	Lowell	AHL	17	6	2	8	19	....	....	....	....	....	....	....	....	....	....	....	....	....	....	....	....	....	....
2000-01	Hamilton	AHL	2	2	0	2	2	....	....	....	....	....	....	....	....	....	....	....	....	....	....	....	....	....	....
	Edmonton	**NHL**	....	....	....	....	....	....	....	....	....	....	....	....	....	....	3	0	0	0	0	0	0	0	7:55
2001-02	**Edmonton**	**NHL**	**61**	**10**	**5**	**15**	**52**	1	0	1	78	12.8	9	18	38.9	10:05	....	....	....	....	....	....	....	....	....
2002-03	**Edmonton**	**NHL**	**20**	**0**	**2**	**2**	**12**	0	0	0	20	0.0	-3	5	0.0	10:22	....	....	....	....	....	....	....	....	....
	NY Rangers	**NHL**	**4**	**0**	**0**	**0**	**2**	0	0	0	3	0.0	-1	0	0.0	9:07	....	....	....	....	....	....	....	....	....
	Washington	**NHL**	**21**	**1**	**2**	**3**	**7**	0	0	0	20	5.0	1	3	0.0	8:07	....	....	....	....	....	....	....	....	....
2003-04	**Calgary**	**NHL**	**36**	**2**	**4**	**6**	**24**	0	0	0	47	4.3	-3	39	30.8	11:18	....	....	....	....	....	....	....	....	....
	Lowell	AHL	22	6	9	15	46	....	....	....	....	....	....	....	....	....	....	....	....	....	....	....	....	....	....
	NY Rangers	**NHL**	**14**	**3**	**2**	**5**	**8**	0	0	1	29	10.3	0	9	55.6	14:16	....	....	....	....	....	....	....	....	....
2004-05	Manitoba Moose	AHL	67	21	19	40	72	....	....	....	....	....	....	....	....	....	14	9	5	14	26	....	....	....	....
2005-06	**Vancouver**	**NHL**	**33**	**4**	**2**	**6**	**14**	0	0	0	35	11.4	2	146	40.4	8:35	....	....	....	....	....	....	....	....	....
	Manitoba Moose	AHL	35	7	24	31	33	....	....	....	....	....	....	....	....	....	10	5	5	10	23	....	....	....	....
2006-07	**Vancouver**	**NHL**	**57**	**2**	**5**	**7**	**25**	0	0	2	74	2.7	0	266	40.6	11:25	9	0	1	1	12	0	0	0	10:13
2007-08	Salzburg	Austria	43	20	22	42	100	....	....	....	....	....	....	....	....	....	....	....	....	....	....	....	....	....	....
	NHL Totals		**322**	**35**	**39**	**74**	**193**	**4**	**0**	**7**	**450**	**7.8**		**500**	**39.6**	**11:02**	**12**	**0**	**1**	**1**	**12**	**0**	**0**	**0**	**9:38**

Traded to **NY Islanders** by **Los Angeles** with Olli Jokinen, Mathieu Biron and Los Angeles' 1st round choice (Taylor Pyatt) in 1999 Entry Draft for Ziggy Palffy, Brian Smolinski, Marcel Cousineau and New Jersey's 4th round choice (previously acquired, Los Angeles selected Daniel Johansson) in 1999 Entry Draft, June 20, 1999. Traded to **Edmonton** by **NY Islanders** with Eric Brewer and NY Islanders' 2nd round choice (Brad Winchester) in 2000 Entry Draft for Roman Hamrlik, June 24, 2000. • Missed majority of 2000-01 season recovering from shoulder injury suffered in game vs. Detroit, October 10, 2000. Traded to **NY Rangers** by **Edmonton** for future considerations, December 12, 2002. Claimed on waivers by **Washington** from **NY Rangers**, January 15, 2003. Signed as a free agent by **Calgary**, July 17, 2003. Claimed on waivers by **NY Rangers** from **Calgary**, March 6, 2004. Signed to a PTO (tryout) contract by **Manitoba** (AHL), September 27, 2004. Signed as a free agent by **Vancouver**, August 23, 2005. Signed as a free agent by **Salzburg** (Austria), July 30, 2007. Signed as a free agent by **Anaheim**, July 22, 2008.

GREEN, Mike

(GREEN, MIGHK) **WSH.**

Defense. Shoots right. 6'2", 201 lbs. Born, Calgary, Alta., October 12, 1985. Washington's 3rd choice, 29th overall, in 2004 Entry Draft.

2000-01	Cgy. North Stars	AMHL	36	4	23	27	34	....	....	....	....	....	....	....	....	....	....	....	....	....	....	....	....	....	....
	Saskatoon Blades	WHL	7	0	2	2	0	....	....	....	....	....	....	....	....	....	....	....	....	....	....	....	....	....	....
2001-02	Saskatoon Blades	WHL	62	3	20	23	57	....	....	....	....	....	....	....	....	....	7	0	1	1	2	....	....	....	....
2002-03	Saskatoon Blades	WHL	72	6	36	42	70	....	....	....	....	....	....	....	....	....	6	0	2	2	6	....	....	....	....
2003-04	Saskatoon Blades	WHL	59	14	25	39	92	....	....	....	....	....	....	....	....	....	....	....	....	....	....	....	....	....	....
2004-05	Saskatoon Blades	WHL	67	14	52	66	105	....	....	....	....	....	....	....	....	....	4	0	0	0	6	....	....	....	....
2005-06	**Washington**	**NHL**	**22**	**1**	**2**	**3**	**18**	0	0	0	13	7.7	-8	0	0.0	14:54	....	....	....	....	....	....	....	....	....
	Hershey Bears	AHL	56	9	34	43	79	....	....	....	....	....	....	....	....	....	21	3	15	18	30	....	....	....	....
2006-07	**Washington**	**NHL**	**70**	**2**	**10**	**12**	**36**	0	0	0	68	2.9	-10	0	0.0	15:29	....	....	....	....	....	....	....	....	....
2007-08	**Washington**	**NHL**	**82**	**18**	**38**	**56**	**62**	8	0	4	234	7.7	6	1	0.0	23:38	7	3	4	7	15	2	0	0	26:59
	NHL Totals		**174**	**21**	**50**	**71**	**116**	**8**	**0**	**4**	**315**	**6.7**		**1**	**0.0**	**19:15**	**7**	**3**	**4**	**7**	**15**	**2**	**0**	**0**	**26:59**

WHL East First All-Star Team (2005) • AHL All-Rookie Team (2006)

GREENE, Andy

(GREEN, AN-dee) **N.J.**

Defense. Shoots left. 5'11", 195 lbs. Born, Trenton, MI, October 30, 1982.

2002-03	Miami U.	CCHA	41	4	19	23	64	....	....	....	....	....	....	....	....	....	....	....	....	....	....	....	....	....	....
2003-04	Miami U.	CCHA	41	7	19	26	78	....	....	....	....	....	....	....	....	....	....	....	....	....	....	....	....	....	....
2004-05	Miami U.	CCHA	38	7	27	34	66	....	....	....	....	....	....	....	....	....	....	....	....	....	....	....	....	....	....
2005-06	Miami U.	CCHA	39	9	22	31	48	....	....	....	....	....	....	....	....	....	....	....	....	....	....	....	....	....	....
2006-07	**New Jersey**	**NHL**	**23**	**1**	**5**	**6**	**6**	1	0	0	23	4.3	-1	0	0.0	14:15	**11**	**2**	**1**	**3**	**2**	**0**	**0**	**1**	**17:04**
	Lowell Devils	AHL	52	5	16	21	28	....	....	....	....	....	....	....	....	....	....	....	....	....	....	....	....	....	....
2007-08	**New Jersey**	**NHL**	**59**	**2**	**8**	**10**	**22**	2	0	0	50	4.0	0	0	0.0	19:30	**2**	**0**	**0**	**0**	**0**	**0**	**0**	**0**	**15:11**
	NHL Totals		**82**	**3**	**13**	**16**	**28**	**3**	**0**	**0**	**73**	**4.1**		**0**	**0.0**	**18:02**	**13**	**2**	**1**	**3**	**2**	**0**	**0**	**1**	**16:46**

CCHA All-Rookie Team (2003) • CCHA First All-Star Team (2004, 2005, 2006) • NCAA West First All-American Team (2006)

Signed as a free agent by **New Jersey**, April 4, 2006.

GREENE, Matt

(GREEN, MAT) **L.A.**

Defense. Shoots right. 6'3", 233 lbs. Born, Grand Ledge, MI, May 13, 1983. Edmonton's 4th choice, 44th overall, in 2002 Entry Draft.

2000-01	USNTDP	U-18	34	0	9	9	8	....	....	....	....	....	....	....	....	....	....	....	....	....	....	....	....	....	....
	USNTDP	USHL	20	0	1	1	51	....	....	....	....	....	....	....	....	....	....	....	....	....	....	....	....	....	....
2001-02	Green Bay	USHL	55	4	20	24	150	....	....	....	....	....	....	....	....	....	7	0	1	1	31	....	....	....	....
2002-03	North Dakota	WCHA	39	0	4	4	*135	....	....	....	....	....	....	....	....	....	....	....	....	....	....	....	....	....	....
2003-04	North Dakota	WCHA	40	1	16	17	86	....	....	....	....	....	....	....	....	....	....	....	....	....	....	....	....	....	....
2004-05	North Dakota	WCHA	43	2	8	10	*126	....	....	....	....	....	....	....	....	....	....	....	....	....	....	....	....	....	....
2005-06	**Edmonton**	**NHL**	**27**	**0**	**2**	**2**	**43**	0	0	0	10	0.0	-6	0	0.0	11:13	**18**	**0**	**1**	**1**	**34**	**0**	**0**	**0**	**10:03**
	Iowa Stars	AHL	26	2	5	7	47	....	....	....	....	....	....	....	....	....	....	....	....	....	....	....	....	....	....
2006-07	**Edmonton**	**NHL**	**78**	**1**	**9**	**10**	**109**	0	0	0	52	1.9	-22	0	0.0	17:36	....	....	....	....	....	....	....	....	....
2007-08	**Edmonton**	**NHL**	**46**	**0**	**1**	**1**	**53**	0	0	0	28	0.0	-3	0	0.0	16:42	....	....	....	....	....	....	....	....	....
	NHL Totals		**151**	**1**	**12**	**13**	**205**	**0**	**0**	**0**	**90**	**1.1**		**0**	**0.0**	**16:11**	**18**	**0**	**1**	**1**	**34**	**0**	**0**	**0**	**10:03**

USHL Second All-Star Team (2002)

Traded to **Los Angeles** by **Edmonton** with Jarret Stoll for Lubomir Visnovsky, June 29, 2008.

GREENTREE, Kyle

(GREEN-TREE, KIGHL) **CGY.**

Left wing. Shoots left. 6'3", 212 lbs. Born, Victoria, B.C., November 15, 1983.

99-2000	Victoria Salsa	BCHL	28	7	6	13	11	....	....	....	....	....	....	....	....	....	....	....	....	....	....	....	....	....	....
2000-01	Victoria Salsa	BCHL	59	27	38	65	50	....	....	....	....	....	....	....	....	....	....	....	....	....	....	....	....	....	....
2001-02	Victoria Salsa	BCHL	57	42	43	85	125	....	....	....	....	....	....	....	....	....	....	....	....	....	....	....	....	....	....
2002-03	Victoria Salsa	BCHL	52	46	53	99	110	....	....	....	....	....	....	....	....	....	....	....	....	....	....	....	....	....	....
2003-04	Victoria Salsa	BCHL	59	62	53	115	170	....	....	....	....	....	....	....	....	....	5	4	5	9	29	....	....	....	....
2004-05	Alaska	CCHA	37	12	20	32	31	....	....	....	....	....	....	....	....	....	....	....	....	....	....	....	....	....	....
2005-06	Alaska	CCHA	39	8	19	27	58	....	....	....	....	....	....	....	....	....	....	....	....	....	....	....	....	....	....
2006-07	Alaska	CCHA	39	21	21	42	78	....	....	....	....	....	....	....	....	....	....	....	....	....	....	....	....	....	....
	Philadelphia	AHL	8	2	0	2	2	....	....	....	....	....	....	....	....	....	....	....	....	....	....	....	....	....	....
2007-08	**Philadelphia**	**NHL**	**2**	**0**	**0**	**0**	**0**	0	0	0	3	0.0	-1	0	0.0	9:12	....	....	....	....	....	....	....	....	....
	Philadelphia	AHL	72	24	24	48	83	....	....	....	....	....	....	....	....	....	12	1	3	4	11	....	....	....	....
	NHL Totals		**2**	**0**	**0**	**0**	**0**	**0**	**0**	**0**	**3**	**0.0**		**0**	**0.0**	**9:12**	....	....	....	....	....	....	....	....	....

Signed as a free agent by **Philadelphia**, March 14, 2007. Traded to **Calgary** by **Philadelphia** for Tim Ramholt, June 30, 2008.

GRENIER, Martin

(GREH-n'yay, MAHR-tihn)

Defense. Shoots left. 6'5", 245 lbs. Born, Laval, Que., November 2, 1980. Colorado's 2nd choice, 45th overall, in 1999 Entry Draft.

1996-97	Laval-Laurentides	QAAA	34	3	16	19	117	....	....	....	....	....	....	....	....	....	13	0	4	4	....	....	....	....	....
1997-98	Quebec Remparts	QMJHL	61	4	11	15	202	....	....	....	....	....	....	....	....	....	14	0	2	2	36	....	....	....	....
1998-99	Quebec Remparts	QMJHL	60	7	18	25	*479	....	....	....	....	....	....	....	....	....	13	0	4	4	29	....	....	....	....
99-2000	Quebec Remparts	QMJHL	67	11	35	46	302	....	....	....	....	....	....	....	....	....	7	1	4	5	27	....	....	....	....
2000-01	Quebec Remparts	QMJHL	26	5	16	21	82	....	....	....	....	....	....	....	....	....	....	....	....	....	....	....	....	....	....
	Victoriaville Tigres	QMJHL	28	9	19	28	108	....	....	....	....	....	....	....	....	....	13	2	8	10	51	....	....	....	....
2001-02	**Phoenix**	**NHL**	**5**	**0**	**0**	**0**	**5**	0	0	0	1	0.0	0	1	100.0	5:56	....	....	....	....	....	....	....	....	....
	Springfield	AHL	69	2	6	8	241	....	....	....	....	....	....	....	....	....	....	....	....	....	....	....	....	....	....
2002-03	**Phoenix**	**NHL**	**3**	**0**	**0**	**0**	**0**	0	0	0	0	0.0	-1	0	0.0	6:11	....	....	....	....	....	....	....	....	....
	Springfield	AHL	73	2	10	12	232	....	....	....	....	....	....	....	....	....	6	0	1	1	12	....	....	....	....
2003-04	**Vancouver**	**NHL**	**7**	**1**	**0**	**1**	**9**	0	0	0	6	16.7	3	0	0.0	6:50	....	....	....	....	....	....	....	....	....
	Manitoba Moose	AHL	38	5	4	9	145	....	....	....	....	....	....	....	....	....	....	....	....	....	....	....	....	....	....
	Hartford	AHL	12	0	2	2	105	....	....	....	....	....	....	....	....	....	9	0	1	1	32	....	....	....	....
2004-05	Hartford	AHL	23	2	5	7	136	....	....	....	....	....	....	....	....	....	5	0	0	0	32	....	....	....	....
	Charlotte	ECHL	4	0	2	2	10	....	....	....	....	....	....	....	....	....	....	....	....	....	....	....	....	....	....
2005-06	Hartford	AHL	76	4	8	12	278	....	....	....	....	....	....	....	....	....	11	0	0	0	33	....	....	....	....

Season	Club	League	Regular Season GP	G	A	Pts	PIM	PP	SH	GW	S	%	+/-	TF	F%	Min	Playoffs GP	G	A	Pts	PIM	PP	SH	GW	Min
2006-07	Philadelphia	NHL	3	0	0	0	0	0	0	0	0	0.0	–3	0	0.0	4:40	....	....	....	....	....	....	....	....	....
	Philadelphia	AHL	57	2	1	3	156	....	....	....	....	....	....	....	....	....	....	....	....	....	....	....	....	....	....
2007-08	Philadelphia	AHL	34	1	2	3	78	....	....	....	....	....	....	....	....	....	3	0	0	0	0	....	....	....	....
	NHL Totals		18	1	0	1	14	0	0	0	7	14.3			1100.0	6:07	....	....	....	....	....	....	....	....	....

Traded to **Boston** by **Colorado** with Brian Rolston, Samuel Pahlsson and New Jersey's 1st round choice (previously acquired, Boston selected Martin Samuelsson) in 2000 Entry Draft for Raymond Bourque and Dave Andreychuk, March 6, 2000. Signed as a free agent by **Phoenix**, June 27, 2001. Traded to **Vancouver** by **Phoenix** for Bryan Helmer, July 25, 2003. Traded to **NY Rangers** by **Vancouver** with R.J. Umberger for Martin Rucinsky, March 9, 2004. Signed as a free agent by **Philadelphia**, July 13, 2006.

GRIER, Mike

(GREER, MIGHK) **S.J.**

Right wing. Shoots right. 6'1", 225 lbs. Born, Detroit, MI, January 5, 1975. St. Louis' 7th choice, 219th overall, in 1993 Entry Draft.

Season	Club	League	GP	G	A	Pts	PIM	PP	SH	GW	S	%	+/-	TF	F%	Min	GP	G	A	Pts	PIM	PP	SH	GW	Min
1992-93	St. Sebastian's	High-MA	22	16	27	43	32	....	....	....	....	....	....	....	....	....	....	....	....	....	....	....	....	....	....
1993-94	Boston University	H-East	39	9	9	18	56	....	....	....	....	....	....	....	....	....	....	....	....	....	....	....	....	....	....
1994-95	Boston University	H-East	37	*29	26	55	85	....	....	....	....	....	....	....	....	....	....	....	....	....	....	....	....	....	....
1995-96	Boston University	H-East	38	21	25	46	82	....	....	....	....	....	....	....	....	....	....	....	....	....	....	....	....	....	....
1996-97	Edmonton	NHL	79	15	17	32	45	4	0	2	89	16.9	7	....	....	....	12	3	1	4	4	1	0	1	....
1997-98	Edmonton	NHL	66	9	6	15	73	1	0	1	90	10.0	–3	....	....	....	12	2	2	4	13	0	0	1	....
1998-99	Edmonton	NHL	82	20	24	44	54	3	2	1	143	14.0	5	34	20.6	15:57	4	1	1	2	6	0	0	0	23:26
99-2000	Edmonton	NHL	65	9	22	31	68	0	3	2	115	7.8	9	32	46.8	15:45	....	....	....	....	....	....	....	....	....
2000-01	Edmonton	NHL	74	20	16	36	20	2	3	2	124	16.1	11	36	38.9	16:44	6	0	0	0	8	0	0	0	21:23
2001-02	Edmonton	NHL	82	8	17	25	32	0	2	3	112	7.1	1	38	47.4	15:01	....	....	....	....	....	....	....	....	....
2002-03	Washington	NHL	82	15	17	32	36	2	2	2	133	11.3	–14	98	43.9	17:48	6	1	1	2	2	0	0	0	17:59
2003-04	Washington	NHL	68	8	12	20	32	1	1	0	115	7.0	–19	54	44.4	17:25	....	....	....	....	....	....	....	....	....
	Buffalo	NHL	14	1	8	9	4	0	0	0	18	5.6	10	11	63.6	17:29	....	....	....	....	....	....	....	....	....
2004-05			DID NOT PLAY																						
2005-06	Buffalo	NHL	81	7	16	23	28	0	0	4	109	6.4	–7	9	22.2	14:22	18	3	5	8	2	0	1	0	16:17
2006-07	San Jose	NHL	81	16	17	33	43	2	3	1	125	12.8	–5	46	41.3	16:26	11	2	2	4	27	0	0	0	17:16
2007-08	San Jose	NHL	78	9	13	22	24	1	3	4	132	6.8	–8	86	25.6	16:13	13	0	1	1	2	0	0	0	15:20
	NHL Totals		852	137	185	322	459	16	19	22	1305	10.5		444	38.5	16:12	82	12	13	25	64	1	1	2	17:27

Hockey East First All-Star Team (1995) • NCAA East First All-American Team (1995)

Rights traded to **Edmonton** by **St. Louis** with Curtis Joseph for St. Louis' 1st round choices in 1996 (previously acquired, St. Louis selected Marty Reasoner) and 1997 (previously acquired, later traded to Los Angeles – Los Angeles selected Matt Zultek) Entry Drafts, August 4, 1995. Traded to **Washington** by **Edmonton** for Washington's 2nd round choice (later traded to NY Islanders – NY Islanders selected Evgeni Tunik) in 2003 Entry Draft and Vancouver's 3rd round choice (previously acquired, Edmonton selected Zachery Stortini) in 2003 Entry Draft, October 7, 2002. Traded to **Buffalo** by **Washington** for Jakub Klepis, March 9, 2004. Signed as a free agent by **San Jose**, July 3, 2006.

GROSSMAN, Nicklas

(GROHS-man, NIHK-luhs) **DAL.**

Defense. Shoots left. 6'3", 206 lbs. Born, Stockholm, Sweden, January 22, 1985. Dallas' 4th choice, 56th overall, in 2004 Entry Draft.

Season	Club	League	GP	G	A	Pts	PIM	PP	SH	GW	S	%	+/-	TF	F%	Min	GP	G	A	Pts	PIM	PP	SH	GW	Min
2002-03	Sodertalje SK Jr.	Swe-Jr.	34	1	1	2	32	....	....	....	....	....	....	....	....	....	....	....	....	....	....	....	....	....	....
2003-04	Sodertalje SK Jr.	Swe-Jr.	33	1	2	3	32	....	....	....	....	....	....	....	....	....	2	0	0	0	0	....	....	....	....
	Sodertalje SK	Sweden	1	0	0	0	0	....	....	....	....	....	....	....	....	....	....	....	....	....	....	....	....	....	....
2004-05	Sodertalje SK Jr.	Swe-Jr.	12	3	6	9	8	....	....	....	....	....	....	....	....	....	1	0	0	0	0	....	....	....	....
	Sodertalje SK	Sweden	31	0	2	2	14	....	....	....	....	....	....	....	....	....	9	0	0	0	0	....	....	....	....
2005-06	Iowa Stars	AHL	61	2	3	5	49	....	....	....	....	....	....	....	....	....	7	0	1	1	4	....	....	....	....
2006-07	Dallas	NHL	8	0	0	0	4	0	0	0	8	0.0	–1	0	0.0	12:49	....	....	....	....	....	....	....	....	....
	Iowa Stars	AHL	67	2	8	10	40	....	....	....	....	....	....	....	....	....	8	0	0	0	10	....	....	....	....
2007-08	Dallas	NHL	62	0	7	7	22	0	0	0	34	0.0	10	0	0.0	15:33	18	1	1	2	6	0	0	0	18:37
	Iowa Stars	AHL	10	0	0	0	10	....	....	....	....	....	....	....	....	....	....	....	....	....	....	....	....	....	....
	NHL Totals		70	0	7	7	26	0	0	0	42	0.0		0	0.0	15:15	18	1	1	2	6	0	0	0	18:37

GUENIN, Nate

(GEH-nihn, NAYT) **PHI.**

Defense. Shoots right. 6'2", 210 lbs. Born, Sewickley, PA, December 10, 1982. NY Rangers' 3rd choice, 127th overall, in 2002 Entry Draft.

Season	Club	League	GP	G	A	Pts	PIM	PP	SH	GW	S	%	+/-	TF	F%	Min	GP	G	A	Pts	PIM	PP	SH	GW	Min
99-2000	Pittsburgh	AAHA	40	3	10	13	122	....	....	....	....	....	....	....	....	....	....	....	....	....	....	....	....	....	....
2000-01	Green Bay	USHL	54	2	11	13	70	....	....	....	....	....	....	....	....	....	4	1	1	2	6	....	....	....	....
2001-02	Green Bay	USHL	56	4	11	15	150	....	....	....	....	....	....	....	....	....	7	3	3	6	10	....	....	....	....
2002-03	Ohio State	CCHA	42	2	9	11	85	....	....	....	....	....	....	....	....	....	....	....	....	....	....	....	....	....	....
2003-04	Ohio State	CCHA	29	2	15	17	92	....	....	....	....	....	....	....	....	....	....	....	....	....	....	....	....	....	....
2004-05	Ohio State	CCHA	41	2	12	14	136	....	....	....	....	....	....	....	....	....	....	....	....	....	....	....	....	....	....
2005-06	Ohio State	CCHA	39	0	11	11	87	....	....	....	....	....	....	....	....	....	....	....	....	....	....	....	....	....	....
2006-07	Philadelphia	NHL	9	0	2	2	4	0	0	0	0	0.0	0	0	0.0	8:40	....	....	....	....	....	....	....	....	....
	Philadelphia	AHL	68	3	9	12	92	....	....	....	....	....	....	....	....	....	....	....	....	....	....	....	....	....	....
2007-08	Philadelphia	NHL	2	0	0	0	2	0	0	0	0	0.0	2	0	0.0	9:57	....	....	....	....	....	....	....	....	....
	Philadelphia	AHL	77	4	13	17	146	....	....	....	....	....	....	....	....	....	12	0	1	1	18	....	....	....	....
	NHL Totals		11	0	2	2	6	0	0	0	0	0.0		0	0.0	8:54	....	....	....	....	....	....	....	....	....

USHL All-Rookie Team (2001) • CCHA Second All-Star Team (2005)

Signed as a free agent by **Philadelphia**, August 16, 2006.

GUERIN, Bill

(GAIR-ihn, BIHL) **NYI**

Right wing. Shoots right. 6'2", 220 lbs. Born, Worcester, MA, November 9, 1970. New Jersey's 1st choice, 5th overall, in 1989 Entry Draft.

Season	Club	League	GP	G	A	Pts	PIM	PP	SH	GW	S	%	+/-	TF	F%	Min	GP	G	A	Pts	PIM	PP	SH	GW	Min
1985-86	Spring. Olympics	NEJHL	48	26	19	45	71	....	....	....	....	....	....	....	....	....	....	....	....	....	....	....	....	....	....
1986-87	Spring. Olympics	NEJHL	32	34	20	54	40	....	....	....	....	....	....	....	....	....	....	....	....	....	....	....	....	....	....
1987-88	Spring. Olympics	NEJHL	38	31	44	75	146	....	....	....	....	....	....	....	....	....	....	....	....	....	....	....	....	....	....
1988-89	Spring. Olympics	NEJHL	31	32	35	67	90	....	....	....	....	....	....	....	....	....	....	....	....	....	....	....	....	....	....
1989-90	Boston College	H-East	39	14	11	25	54	....	....	....	....	....	....	....	....	....	....	....	....	....	....	....	....	....	....
1990-91	Boston College	H-East	38	26	19	45	102	....	....	....	....	....	....	....	....	....	....	....	....	....	....	....	....	....	....
1991-92	United States	Nat-Tm	46	12	15	27	67	....	....	....	....	....	....	....	....	....	....	....	....	....	....	....	....	....	....
	New Jersey	NHL	5	0	1	1	9	0	0	0	8	0.0	1	....	....	....	6	3	0	3	4	0	0	0	....
	Utica Devils	AHL	22	13	10	23	6	....	....	....	....	....	....	....	....	....	4	1	3	4	14	....	....	....	....
1992-93	New Jersey	NHL	65	14	20	34	63	0	0	2	123	11.4	14	....	....	....	5	1	1	2	4	0	0	0	....
	Utica Devils	AHL	18	10	7	17	47	....	....	....	....	....	....	....	....	....	....	....	....	....	....	....	....	....	....
1993-94	New Jersey	NHL	81	25	19	44	101	2	0	3	195	12.8	14	....	....	....	17	2	1	3	35	0	0	1	....
1994-95 ♦	New Jersey	NHL	48	12	13	25	72	4	0	3	96	12.5	6	....	....	....	20	3	8	11	30	1	0	0	....
1995-96	New Jersey	NHL	80	23	30	53	116	8	0	6	216	10.6	7	....	....	....	....	....	....	....	....	....	....	....	....
1996-97	New Jersey	NHL	82	29	18	47	95	7	0	9	177	16.4	–2	....	....	....	8	2	1	3	18	1	0	1	....
1997-98	New Jersey	NHL	19	5	5	10	13	1	0	2	48	10.4	0	....	....	....	....	....	....	....	....	....	....	....	....
	Edmonton	NHL	40	13	16	29	80	8	0	2	130	10.0	1	....	....	....	12	7	1	8	17	4	0	0	....
	United States	Olympics	4	0	3	3	2	....	....	....	....	....	....	....	....	....	....	....	....	....	....	....	....	....	....
1998-99	Edmonton	NHL	80	30	34	64	133	13	0	2	261	11.5	7	74	40.5	19:42	3	0	2	2	2	0	0	0	26:14
99-2000	Edmonton	NHL	70	24	22	46	123	11	0	2	188	12.8	4	13	46.2	18:01	5	3	2	5	9	1	0	0	17:55
2000-01	Edmonton	NHL	21	12	10	22	18	4	0	1	64	18.8	11	0	0.0	19:49	....	....	....	....	....	....	....	....	....
	Boston	NHL	64	28	35	63	122	7	1	4	225	12.4	–4	36	41.7	22:43	....	....	....	....	....	....	....	....	....
2001-02	Boston	NHL	78	41	25	66	91	10	1	7	355	11.5	–1	17	52.9	20:45	6	4	2	6	6	3	0	0	21:17
	United States	Olympics	6	4	0	4	4	....	....	....	....	....	....	....	....	....	....	....	....	....	....	....	....	....	....
2002-03	Dallas	NHL	64	25	25	50	113	11	0	2	229	10.9	5	20	25.0	18:33	4	0	0	0	4	0	0	0	8:34
2003-04	Dallas	NHL	82	34	35	69	109	9	0	10	263	12.9	14	16	18.8	18:42	5	0	1	1	4	0	0	0	20:09
2004-05			DID NOT PLAY																						
2005-06	Dallas	NHL	70	13	27	40	115	3	0	2	210	6.2	0	16	50.0	16:25	5	3	1	4	0	1	0	0	16:14
	United States	Olympics	6	1	0	1	0	....	....	....	....	....	....	....	....	....	....	....	....	....	....	....	....	....	....

Season	Club	League	GP	G	A	Pts	PIM	PP	SH	GW	S	%	+/-	TF	F%	Min	GP	G	A	Pts	PIM	PP	SH	GW	Min
			Regular Season														Playoffs								
2006-07	St. Louis	NHL	61	28	19	47	52	7	0	6	189	14.8	8	10	50.0	17:26	....	....	....	....	....	....	....	....	....
	San Jose	NHL	16	8	1	9	14	2	0	1	36	22.2	2	2	50.0	15:22	9	0	2	2	12	0	0	0	17:06
2007-08	NY Islanders	NHL	81	23	21	44	65	7	0	5	227	10.1	–15	18	66.7	17:23	....	....	....	....	....	....	....	....	....
	NHL Totals		1107	387	376	763	1504	114	2	69	3240	11.9		222	42.3	18:48	105	28	22	50	145	11	0	2	18:00

NHL Second All-Star Team (2002)

Played in NHL All-Star Game (2001, 2003, 2004, 2007)

Traded to **Edmonton** by **New Jersey** with Valeri Zelepukin for Jason Arnott and Bryan Muir, January 4, 1998. Traded to **Boston** by **Edmonton** for Anson Carter, Boston's 1st (Ales Hemsky) and 2nd (Doug Lynch) round choices in 2001 Entry Draft and future considerations, November 15, 2000. Signed as a free agent by **Dallas**, July 3, 2002. Signed as a free agent by **St. Louis**, July 3, 2006. Traded to **San Jose** by **St. Louis** for Ville Nieminen, Jay Barriball and New Jersey's 1st round choice (previously acquired, St. Louis selected David Perron) in 2007 Entry Draft, February 27, 2007. Signed as a free agent by **NY Islanders**, July 5, 2007.

GUITE, Ben

(GEE-tay, BEHN) **COL.**

Right wing. Shoots right. 6'1", 211 lbs. Born, Montreal, Que., July 17, 1978. Montreal's 8th choice, 172nd overall, in 1997 Entry Draft.

Season	Club	League	GP	G	A	Pts	PIM	PP	SH	GW	S	%	+/-	TF	F%	Min	GP	G	A	Pts	PIM	PP	SH	GW	Min
1994-95	Lac St-Louis Lions	QAAA	40	9	12	21	....	....	....	....	....	....	....	....	....	....	4	0	0	0	0	....	....	....	....
1995-96	Capital District	Exhib.	STATISTICS NOT AVAILABLE																						
1996-97	U. of Maine	H-East	34	7	7	14	21	....	....	....	....	....	....	....	....	....	....	....	....	....	....	....	....	....	....
1997-98	U. of Maine	H-East	32	6	12	18	20	....	....	....	....	....	....	....	....	....	....	....	....	....	....	....	....	....	....
1998-99	U. of Maine	H-East	40	12	16	28	30	....	....	....	....	....	....	....	....	....	....	....	....	....	....	....	....	....	....
99-2000	U. of Maine	H-East	40	22	14	36	36	....	....	....	....	....	....	....	....	....	....	....	....	....	....	....	....	....	....
2000-01	Tallahassee	ECHL	68	11	18	29	34	....	....	....	....	....	....	....	....	....	....	....	....	....	....	....	....	....	....
2001-02	Bridgeport	AHL	68	12	18	30	39	....	....	....	....	....	....	....	....	....	....	....	....	....	....	....	....	....	....
	Cincinnati	AHL	10	2	5	7	4	....	....	....	....	....	....	....	....	....	3	0	0	0	2	....	....	....	....
2002-03	Cincinnati	AHL	80	13	16	29	44	....	....	....	....	....	....	....	....	....	....	....	....	....	....	....	....	....	....
2003-04	Bridgeport	AHL	79	6	18	24	73	....	....	....	....	....	....	....	....	....	7	0	0	0	6	....	....	....	....
2004-05	Providence Bruins	AHL	77	9	15	24	69	....	....	....	....	....	....	....	....	....	17	3	4	7	34	....	....	....	....
2005-06	Boston	NHL	1	0	0	0	0	0	0	0	2	0.0	0	11	18.2	8:53	....	....	....	....	....	....	....	....	....
	Providence Bruins	AHL	73	22	30	52	87	....	....	....	....	....	....	....	....	....	6	1	3	4	14	....	....	....	....
2006-07	Colorado	NHL	39	3	8	11	16	0	1	1	63	4.8	–4	388	49.5	12:17	....	....	....	....	....	....	....	....	....
	Albany River Rats	AHL	36	10	19	29	22	....	....	....	....	....	....	....	....	....	....	....	....	....	....	....	....	....	....
2007-08	Colorado	NHL	79	11	11	22	47	0	0	2	103	10.7	1	805	48.0	13:05	10	1	0	1	14	0	1	0	12:02
	NHL Totals		119	14	19	33	63	0	1	3	168	8.3		1204	48.2	12:47	10	1	0	1	14	0	1	0	12:02

Signed as a free agent by **NY Islanders**, August, 2001. Traded to **Anaheim** by **NY Islanders** with the rights to Bjorn Mellin for Dave Roche, March 19, 2002. Signed as a free agent by **NY Rangers**, September 16, 2003. Signed as a free agent by **Bridgeport** (AHL), October 10, 2003. Signed to a PTO (tryout) contract by **Providence** (AHL), September 28, 2004. Signed as a free agent by **Boston**, August 15, 2005. Signed as a free agent by **Colorado**, July 12, 2006.

HAGMAN, Niklas

(HAG-muhn, NIHK-luhs) **TOR.**

Left wing. Shoots left. 6', 205 lbs. Born, Espoo, Finland, December 5, 1979. Florida's 3rd choice, 70th overall, in 1999 Entry Draft.

Season	Club	League	GP	G	A	Pts	PIM	PP	SH	GW	S	%	+/-	TF	F%	Min	GP	G	A	Pts	PIM	PP	SH	GW	Min
1995-96	HIFK Helsinki U18	Fin-U18	26	12	21	33	32	....	....	....	....	....	....	....	....	....	4	3	0	3	2	....	....	....	....
	HIFK Helsinki Jr.	Fin-Jr.	12	3	1	4	0	....	....	....	....	....	....	....	....	....	....	....	....	....	....	....	....	....	....
1996-97	HIFK Helsinki Jr.	Fin-Jr.	30	13	12	25	30	....	....	....	....	....	....	....	....	....	....	....	....	....	....	....	....	....	....
	HIFK Helsinki U18	Fin-U18	21	19	12	31	46	....	....	....	....	....	....	....	....	....	4	1	1	2	0	....	....	....	....
1997-98	HIFK Helsinki U18	Fin-U18	1	0	1	1	0	....	....	....	....	....	....	....	....	....	....	....	....	....	....	....	....	....	....
	HIFK Helsinki Jr.	Fin-Jr.	26	9	5	14	16	....	....	....	....	....	....	....	....	....	....	....	....	....	....	....	....	....	....
	HIFK Helsinki	Finland	8	1	0	1	0	....	....	....	....	....	....	....	....	....	....	....	....	....	....	....	....	....	....
1998-99	HIFK Helsinki	Finland	17	1	1	2	14	....	....	....	....	....	....	....	....	....	....	....	....	....	....	....	....	....	....
	HIFK Helsinki Jr.	Fin-Jr.	15	4	10	14	43	....	....	....	....	....	....	....	....	....	....	....	....	....	....	....	....	....	....
	HIFK Helsinki	EuroHL	1	0	1	1	0	....	....	....	....	....	....	....	....	....	....	....	....	....	....	....	....	....	....
	Blues Espoo	Finland	14	1	1	2	2	....	....	....	....	....	....	....	....	....	4	1	0	1	0	....	....	....	....
99-2000	Karpat Oulu Jr.	Fin-Jr.	4	7	3	10	0	....	....	....	....	....	....	....	....	....	....	....	....	....	....	....	....	....	....
	Karpat Oulu	Finland-2	41	17	18	35	12	....	....	....	....	....	....	....	....	....	7	4	2	6	0	....	....	....	....
2000-01	Karpat Oulu	Finland	56	28	18	46	32	....	....	....	....	....	....	....	....	....	8	3	1	4	0	....	....	....	....
2001-02	Florida	NHL	78	10	18	28	8	0	1	2	134	7.5	–6	32	28.1	13:50	....	....	....	....	....	....	....	....	....
	Finland	Olympics	4	1	2	3	0	....	....	....	....	....	....	....	....	....	....	....	....	....	....	....	....	....	....
2002-03	Florida	NHL	80	8	15	23	20	2	0	0	132	6.1	–8	17	11.8	13:31	....	....	....	....	....	....	....	....	....
2003-04	Florida	NHL	75	10	13	23	22	0	1	2	122	8.2	–5	19	21.1	14:47	....	....	....	....	....	....	....	....	....
2004-05	HC Davos	Swiss	44	17	22	39	20	....	....	....	....	....	....	....	....	....	15	10	7	17	6	....	....	....	....
2005-06	Florida	NHL	30	2	4	6	2	0	0	0	52	3.8	–8	10	10.0	14:00	....	....	....	....	....	....	....	....	....
	Dallas	NHL	54	6	9	15	16	0	1	0	74	8.1	–2	6	66.7	11:17	5	2	1	3	4	0	0	1	10:50
	Finland	Olympics	8	0	1	1	2	....	....	....	....	....	....	....	....	....	....	....	....	....	....	....	....	....	....
2006-07	Dallas	NHL	82	17	12	29	34	2	1	2	152	11.2	3	15	20.0	14:26	7	0	1	1	10	0	0	0	16:26
2007-08	Dallas	NHL	82	27	14	41	51	4	4	8	178	15.2	4	19	10.5	15:36	18	2	1	3	14	0	0	0	13:25
	NHL Totals		481	80	85	165	153	8	8	14	844	9.5		118	21.2	14:03	30	4	3	7	28	0	0	1	13:41

Signed as a free agent by **Davos** (Swiss), July 23, 2004. Traded to **Dallas** by **Florida** for Dallas' 7th round choice (Sergei Gayduchenko) in 2007 Entry Draft, December 12, 2005. Signed as a free agent by **Toronto**, July 1, 2008.

HAINSEY, Ron

(HAYN-zee, RAWN) **ATL.**

Defense. Shoots left. 6'3", 210 lbs. Born, Bolton, CT, March 24, 1981. Montreal's 1st choice, 13th overall, in 2000 Entry Draft.

Season	Club	League	GP	G	A	Pts	PIM	PP	SH	GW	S	%	+/-	TF	F%	Min	GP	G	A	Pts	PIM	PP	SH	GW	Min
1997-98	USNTDP	U-17	18	2	7	9	28	....	....	....	....	....	....	....	....	....	....	....	....	....	....	....	....	....	....
	USNTDP	USHL	3	0	0	0	0	....	....	....	....	....	....	....	....	....	....	....	....	....	....	....	....	....	....
	USNTDP	NAHL	40	4	7	11	16	....	....	....	....	....	....	....	....	....	5	0	1	1	0	....	....	....	....
1998-99	USNTDP	USHL	48	5	12	17	45	....	....	....	....	....	....	....	....	....	....	....	....	....	....	....	....	....	....
99-2000	U. Mass-Lowell	H-East	30	3	8	11	20	....	....	....	....	....	....	....	....	....	....	....	....	....	....	....	....	....	....
2000-01	U. Mass-Lowell	H-East	33	10	26	36	51	....	....	....	....	....	....	....	....	....	....	....	....	....	....	....	....	....	....
	Quebec Citadelles	AHL	4	1	0	1	0	....	....	....	....	....	....	....	....	....	1	0	0	0	0	....	....	....	....
2001-02	Quebec Citadelles	AHL	63	7	24	31	26	....	....	....	....	....	....	....	....	....	3	0	0	0	0	....	....	....	....
2002-03	Montreal	NHL	21	0	0	0	2	0	0	0	12	0.0	–1	0	0.0	12:25	....	....	....	....	....	....	....	....	....
	Hamilton	AHL	33	2	11	13	26	....	....	....	....	....	....	....	....	....	23	1	10	11	20	....	....	....	....
2003-04	Montreal	NHL	11	1	1	2	4	0	0	0	11	9.1	3	0	0.0	13:15	....	....	....	....	....	....	....	....	....
	Hamilton	AHL	54	7	24	31	35	....	....	....	....	....	....	....	....	....	10	0	5	5	6	....	....	....	....
2004-05	Hamilton	AHL	68	9	14	23	45	....	....	....	....	....	....	....	....	....	4	1	1	2	0	....	....	....	....
2005-06	Hamilton	AHL	22	3	14	17	19	....	....	....	....	....	....	....	....	....	....	....	....	....	....	....	....	....	....
	Columbus	NHL	55	2	15	17	43	1	0	0	81	2.5	13	1	0.0	17:47	....	....	....	....	....	....	....	....	....
2006-07	Columbus	NHL	80	9	25	34	69	7	0	0	136	6.6	–19	2	50.0	22:53	....	....	....	....	....	....	....	....	....
2007-08	Columbus	NHL	78	8	24	32	25	8	0	0	161	5.0	–7	0	0.0	22:34	....	....	....	....	....	....	....	....	....
	NHL Totals		245	20	65	85	143	16	0	0	401	5.0		3	33.3	20:19	....	....	....	....	....	....	....	....	....

Hockey East First All-Star Team (2001) • NCAA East Second All-American Team (2001) • AHL All-Rookie Team (2002)

Claimed on waivers by **Columbus** from **Montreal**, November 29, 2005. Signed as a free agent by **Atlanta**, July 2, 2008.

HALE, David

(HAYL, DAY-vihd) **PHX.**

Defense. Shoots left. 6'2", 213 lbs. Born, Colorado Springs, CO, June 18, 1981. New Jersey's 1st choice, 22nd overall, in 2000 Entry Draft.

Season	Club	League	GP	G	A	Pts	PIM	PP	SH	GW	S	%	+/-	TF	F%	Min	GP	G	A	Pts	PIM	PP	SH	GW	Min
1997-98	Colorado North	High-CO	25	11	33	44	154	....	....	....	....	....	....	....	....	....	....	....	....	....	....	....	....	....	....
1998-99	Sioux City	USHL	56	3	15	18	127	....	....	....	....	....	....	....	....	....	5	0	0	0	18	....	....	....	....
99-2000	Sioux City	USHL	54	6	18	24	187	....	....	....	....	....	....	....	....	....	5	0	2	2	6	....	....	....	....
2000-01	North Dakota	WCHA	44	4	5	9	79	....	....	....	....	....	....	....	....	....	....	....	....	....	....	....	....	....	....
2001-02	North Dakota	WCHA	34	4	5	9	63	....	....	....	....	....	....	....	....	....	....	....	....	....	....	....	....	....	....
2002-03	North Dakota	WCHA	26	2	6	8	49	....	....	....	....	....	....	....	....	....	....	....	....	....	....	....	....	....	....
2003-04	New Jersey	NHL	65	0	4	4	72	0	0	0	45	0.0	12	0	0.0	15:01	1	0	0	0	0	0	0	0	8:59
2004-05	Albany River Rats	AHL	30	2	3	5	39	....	....	....	....	....	....	....	....	....	....	....	....	....	....	....	....	....	....
2005-06	New Jersey	NHL	38	0	4	4	21	0	0	0	19	0.0	5	0	0.0	12:03	8	0	2	2	12	0	0	0	12:06
	Albany River Rats	AHL	30	2	5	7	64	....	....	....	....	....	....	....	....	....	....	....	....	....	....	....	....	....	....

			Regular Season														Playoffs								
Season	Club	League	GP	G	A	Pts	PIM	PP	SH	GW	S	%	+/-	TF	F%	Min	GP	G	A	Pts	PIM	PP	SH	GW	Min
2006-07	**New Jersey**	**NHL**	**43**	**0**	**1**	**1**	**26**	**0**	**0**	**0**	**21**	**0.0**	**2**	**0**	**0.0**	**9:41**	....	....	....	....	....	....	....	....	....
	Lowell Devils	AHL	2	0	1	1	0	....	....	....	....	....	....	....	....	....	....	....	....	....	....	....	....	....	....
	Calgary	**NHL**	**11**	**0**	**0**	**0**	**10**	**0**	**0**	**0**	**12**	**0.0**	**–2**	**0**	**0.0**	**15:47**	**2**	**0**	**0**	**0**	**6**	**0**	**0**	**0**	**12:42**
2007-08	**Calgary**	**NHL**	**58**	**0**	**2**	**2**	**46**	**0**	**0**	**0**	**35**	**0.0**	**0**	**0**	**0.0**	**13:53**	**6**	**0**	**0**	**0**	**2**	**0**	**0**	**0**	**12:48**
	NHL Totals		**215**	**0**	**11**	**11**	**175**	**0**	**0**	**0**	**132**	**0.0**		**0**	**0.0**	**13:10**	**17**	**0**	**2**	**2**	**20**	**0**	**0**	**0**	**12:14**

USHL First All-Star Team (2000)

Traded to **Calgary** by **New Jersey** with New Jersey's 5th round choice (later traded to Buffalo - Buffalo selected Jean-Simon Allard) in 2007 Entry Draft for Calgary's 3rd round choice (Nick Palmieri) in 2007 Entry Draft, February 27, 2007. Signed as a free agent by **Phoenix**, July 3, 2008.

HALL, Adam

(HAWL, A-duhm) **T.B.**

Right wing. Shoots right. 6'3", 206 lbs. Born, Kalamazoo, MI, August 14, 1980. Nashville's 3rd choice, 52nd overall, in 1999 Entry Draft.

Season	Club	League	GP	G	A	Pts	PIM	PP	SH	GW	S	%	+/-	TF	F%	Min	GP	G	A	Pts	PIM	PP	SH	GW	Min
1996-97	Bramalea Blues	OPJHL	43	9	14	23	92	....	....	....	....	....	....	....	....	....	....	....	....	....	....	....	....	....	....
1997-98	USNTDP	U-18	29	18	9	27	19	....	....	....	....	....	....	....	....	....	....	....	....	....	....	....	....	....	....
	USNTDP	USHL	21	9	11	20	20	....	....	....	....	....	....	....	....	....	....	....	....	....	....	....	....	....	....
	USNTDP	NAHL	15	12	1	13	20	....	....	....	....	....	....	....	....	....	6	3	2	5	4	....	....	....	....
1998-99	Michigan State	CCHA	36	16	7	23	74	....	....	....	....	....	....	....	....	....	....	....	....	....	....	....	....	....	....
99-2000	Michigan State	CCHA	40	*26	13	39	38	....	....	....	....	....	....	....	....	....	....	....	....	....	....	....	....	....	....
2000-01	Michigan State	CCHA	42	18	12	30	42	....	....	....	....	....	....	....	....	....	....	....	....	....	....	....	....	....	....
2001-02	Michigan State	CCHA	41	19	15	34	36	....	....	....	....	....	....	....	....	....	....	....	....	....	....	....	....	....	....
	Nashville	**NHL**	**1**	**0**	**1**	**1**	**0**	**0**	**0**	**0**	**2**	**0.0**	**0**	**0**	**0.0**	**14:04**	....	....	....	....	....	....	....	....	....
	Milwaukee	AHL	6	2	2	4	4	....	....	....	....	....	....	....	....	....	....	....	....	....	....	....	....	....	....
2002-03	**Nashville**	**NHL**	**79**	**16**	**12**	**28**	**31**	**8**	**0**	**2**	**146**	**11.0**	**–8**	**17**	**52.9**	**14:09**	....	....	....	....	....	....	....	....	....
	Milwaukee	AHL	1	0	0	0	2	....	....	....	....	....	....	....	....	....	....	....	....	....	....	....	....	....	....
2003-04	**Nashville**	**NHL**	**79**	**13**	**14**	**27**	**37**	**6**	**0**	**1**	**151**	**8.6**	**–8**	**348**	**56.3**	**16:14**	**6**	**2**	**1**	**3**	**2**	**0**	**0**	**1**	**18:29**
2004-05	KalPa Kuopio	Finland-2	36	23	17	40	28	....	....	....	....	....	....	....	....	....	9	2	3	5	4	....	....	....	....
2005-06	**Nashville**	**NHL**	**75**	**14**	**15**	**29**	**40**	**10**	**0**	**5**	**122**	**11.5**	**0**	**470**	**48.9**	**16:47**	**5**	**1**	**0**	**1**	**0**	**1**	**0**	**1**	**12:10**
2006-07	**NY Rangers**	**NHL**	**49**	**4**	**8**	**12**	**18**	**3**	**0**	**0**	**61**	**6.6**	**–13**	**59**	**45.8**	**12:27**	....	....	....	....	....	....	....	....	....
	Minnesota	**NHL**	**23**	**2**	**3**	**5**	**8**	**0**	**0**	**0**	**42**	**4.8**	**2**	**11**	**72.7**	**12:13**	**3**	**0**	**0**	**0**	**7**	**0**	**0**	**0**	**10:06**
2007-08	**Pittsburgh**	**NHL**	**46**	**2**	**4**	**6**	**24**	**0**	**0**	**0**	**39**	**5.1**	**–2**	**290**	**50.3**	**11:52**	**17**	**3**	**1**	**4**	**8**	**0**	**0**	**1**	**10:59**
	NHL Totals		**352**	**51**	**57**	**108**	**158**	**27**	**0**	**8**	**563**	**9.1**		**1195**	**51.5**	**14:31**	**31**	**6**	**2**	**8**	**17**	**1**	**0**	**3**	**12:32**

CCHA Second All-Star Team (2000)

Signed as a free agent by **Kuopio** (Finland-2), October 11, 2004. Traded to **NY Rangers** by **Nashville** for Dominic Moore, July 19, 2006. Traded to **Minnesota** by **NY Rangers** for Pascal Dupuis, February 9, 2007. Signed as a free agent by **Pittsburgh**, October 1, 2007. Signed as a free agent by **Tampa Bay**, July 1, 2008.

HALPERN, Jeff

(HAL-pehrn, JEHF) **T.B.**

Center. Shoots right. 6', 203 lbs. Born, Potomac, MD, May 3, 1976.

Season	Club	League	GP	G	A	Pts	PIM	PP	SH	GW	S	%	+/-	TF	F%	Min	GP	G	A	Pts	PIM	PP	SH	GW	Min
1994-95	Stratford Cullitons	OHA-B	44	29	54	83	43	....	....	....	....	....	....	....	....	....	....	....	....	....	....	....	....	....	....
1995-96	Princeton	ECAC	29	3	11	14	30	....	....	....	....	....	....	....	....	....	....	....	....	....	....	....	....	....	....
1996-97	Princeton	ECAC	33	7	24	31	35	....	....	....	....	....	....	....	....	....	....	....	....	....	....	....	....	....	....
1997-98	Princeton	ECAC	36	*28	25	*53	46	....	....	....	....	....	....	....	....	....	....	....	....	....	....	....	....	....	....
1998-99	Princeton	ECAC	33	*22	22	44	32	....	....	....	....	....	....	....	....	....	....	....	....	....	....	....	....	....	....
	Portland Pirates	AHL	6	2	1	3	4	....	....	....	....	....	....	....	....	....	....	....	....	....	....	....	....	....	....
99-2000	**Washington**	**NHL**	**79**	**18**	**11**	**29**	**39**	**4**	**4**	**1**	**108**	**16.7**	**21**	**812**	**51.1**	**13:14**	**5**	**2**	**1**	**3**	**0**	**1**	**0**	**1**	**15:16**
2000-01	**Washington**	**NHL**	**80**	**21**	**21**	**42**	**60**	**2**	**1**	**5**	**110**	**19.1**	**13**	**1293**	**52.4**	**16:08**	**6**	**2**	**3**	**5**	**17**	**1**	**0**	**1**	**20:02**
2001-02	**Washington**	**NHL**	**48**	**5**	**14**	**19**	**29**	**0**	**0**	**4**	**74**	**6.8**	**–9**	**661**	**56.0**	**15:19**	....	....	....	....	....	....	....	....	....
2002-03	**Washington**	**NHL**	**82**	**13**	**21**	**34**	**88**	**1**	**2**	**2**	**126**	**10.3**	**6**	**1492**	**54.1**	**17:25**	**6**	**0**	**1**	**1**	**2**	**0**	**0**	**0**	**19:59**
2003-04	**Washington**	**NHL**	**79**	**19**	**27**	**46**	**56**	**7**	**0**	**2**	**114**	**16.7**	**–21**	**1509**	**54.3**	**19:03**	....	....	....	....	....	....	....	....	....
2004-05	HC Ajoie	Swiss-2	15	5	12	17	52	....	....	....	....	....	....	....	....	....	....	....	....	....	....	....	....	....	....
	Kloten Flyers	Swiss	9	7	4	11	6	....	....	....	....	....	....	....	....	....	....	....	....	....	....	....	....	....	....
2005-06	**Washington**	**NHL**	**70**	**11**	**33**	**44**	**79**	**6**	**0**	**1**	**151**	**7.3**	**–8**	**1454**	**55.2**	**20:00**	....	....	....	....	....	....	....	....	....
2006-07	**Dallas**	**NHL**	**76**	**8**	**17**	**25**	**78**	**1**	**0**	**4**	**106**	**7.5**	**–7**	**1135**	**51.8**	**16:48**	**7**	**2**	**1**	**3**	**4**	**0**	**0**	**1**	**18:57**
2007-08	**Dallas**	**NHL**	**64**	**10**	**14**	**24**	**40**	**1**	**1**	**0**	**86**	**11.6**	**–2**	**548**	**54.0**	**16:21**	....	....	....	....	....	....	....	....	....
	Tampa Bay	**NHL**	**19**	**10**	**8**	**18**	**14**	**3**	**0**	**2**	**46**	**21.7**	**2**	**185**	**46.0**	**18:12**	....	....	....	....	....	....	....	....	....
	NHL Totals		**597**	**115**	**166**	**281**	**483**	**25**	**8**	**21**	**921**	**12.5**		**9089**	**53.5**	**16:53**	**24**	**6**	**6**	**12**	**23**	**2**	**0**	**3**	**18:43**

ECAC Second All-Star Team (1998, 1999)

Signed as a free agent by **Washington**, March 29, 1999. Signed as a free agent by **Ajoie** (Swiss-2), October 8, 2004. Signed as a free agent by **Kloten** (Swiss), December 30, 2004. Signed as a free agent by **Dallas**, July 5, 2006. Traded to **Tampa Bay** by **Dallas** with Mike Smith, Jussi Jokinen and Dallas' 4th round choice in 2009 Entry Draft for Brad Richards and Johan Holmqvist, February 26, 2008.

HAMEL, Denis

(ha-MEHL, deh-NEE)

Left wing. Shoots left. 6'1", 201 lbs. Born, Lachute, Que., May 10, 1977. St. Louis' 5th choice, 153rd overall, in 1995 Entry Draft.

Season	Club	League	GP	G	A	Pts	PIM	PP	SH	GW	S	%	+/-	TF	F%	Min	GP	G	A	Pts	PIM	PP	SH	GW	Min
1992-93	Lachute Regents	QAAA	32	18	24	42	....	....	....	....	....	....	....	....	....	....	....	....	....	....	....	....	....	....	....
1993-94	Lac St-Louis Lions	QAAA	28	10	11	21	50	....	....	....	....	....	....	....	....	....	....	....	....	....	....	....	....	....	....
	Abitibi Foresters	QAAA	15	5	7	12	29	....	....	....	....	....	....	....	....	....	5	0	3	3	16	....	....	....	....
1994-95	Chicoutimi	QMJHL	66	15	12	27	155	....	....	....	....	....	....	....	....	....	12	2	0	2	27	....	....	....	....
1995-96	Chicoutimi	QMJHL	65	40	49	89	199	....	....	....	....	....	....	....	....	....	17	10	14	24	64	....	....	....	....
1996-97	Chicoutimi	QMJHL	70	50	50	100	357	....	....	....	....	....	....	....	....	....	20	15	10	25	58	....	....	....	....
1997-98	Rochester	AHL	74	10	15	25	98	....	....	....	....	....	....	....	....	....	4	1	2	3	0	....	....	....	....
1998-99	Rochester	AHL	74	16	17	33	121	....	....	....	....	....	....	....	....	....	20	3	4	7	10	....	....	....	....
99-2000	**Buffalo**	**NHL**	**3**	**1**	**0**	**1**	**0**	**0**	**0**	**0**	**3**	**33.3**	**–1**	**0**	**0.0**	**9:45**	....	....	....	....	....	....	....	....	....
	Rochester	AHL	76	34	24	58	122	....	....	....	....	....	....	....	....	....	21	6	7	13	49	....	....	....	....
2000-01	**Buffalo**	**NHL**	**41**	**8**	**3**	**11**	**22**	**1**	**1**	**3**	**55**	**14.5**	**–2**	**171**	**33.9**	**10:58**	....	....	....	....	....	....	....	....	....
2001-02	**Buffalo**	**NHL**	**61**	**2**	**6**	**8**	**28**	**0**	**0**	**0**	**80**	**2.5**	**–1**	**94**	**39.4**	**11:00**	....	....	....	....	....	....	....	....	....
2002-03	**Buffalo**	**NHL**	**25**	**2**	**0**	**2**	**17**	**0**	**0**	**1**	**41**	**4.9**	**–4**	**4**	**25.0**	**12:40**	....	....	....	....	....	....	....	....	....
	Rochester	AHL	48	27	20	47	64	....	....	....	....	....	....	....	....	....	3	3	2	5	4	....	....	....	....
2003-04	**Ottawa**	**NHL**	**5**	**0**	**0**	**0**	**0**	**0**	**0**	**0**	**6**	**0.0**	**–3**	**1**	**100.0**	**6:16**	....	....	....	....	....	....	....	....	....
	Binghamton	AHL	78	29	38	67	116	....	....	....	....	....	....	....	....	....	2	0	0	0	2	....	....	....	....
2004-05	Binghamton	AHL	80	39	39	78	75	....	....	....	....	....	....	....	....	....	5	1	0	1	4	....	....	....	....
2005-06	**Ottawa**	**NHL**	**4**	**1**	**0**	**1**	**0**	**0**	**0**	**0**	**9**	**11.1**	**1**	**1**	**0.0**	**9:10**	....	....	....	....	....	....	....	....	....
	Binghamton	AHL	77	*56	35	91	65	....	....	....	....	....	....	....	....	....	....	....	....	....	....	....	....	....	....
2006-07	**Ottawa**	**NHL**	**43**	**4**	**3**	**7**	**10**	**0**	**0**	**0**	**36**	**11.1**	**4**	**9**	**33.3**	**5:38**	....	....	....	....	....	....	....	....	....
	Atlanta	**NHL**	**3**	**1**	**0**	**1**	**0**	**0**	**0**	**0**	**3**	**33.3**	**0**	**2**	**0.0**	**10:25**	....	....	....	....	....	....	....	....	....
	Philadelphia	**NHL**	**7**	**0**	**0**	**0**	**0**	**0**	**0**	**0**	**3**	**0.0**	**–4**	**0**	**0.0**	**6:58**	....	....	....	....	....	....	....	....	....
2007-08	Binghamton	AHL	67	32	23	55	60	....	....	....	....	....	....	....	....	....	....	....	....	....	....	....	....	....	....
	NHL Totals		**192**	**19**	**12**	**31**	**77**	**1**	**1**	**4**	**236**	**8.1**		**282**	**35.5**	**9:40**	....	....	....	....	....	....	....	....	....

QMJHL All-Rookie Team (1995) • AHL First All-Star Team (2004) • Willie Marshall Award (Top Goal-scorer - AHL) (2006) (tied with Don MacLean) • Yanick Dupre Memorial Award (Outstanding Humanitarian Contribution - AHL) (2008)

Traded to **Buffalo** by **St. Louis** for Charlie Huddy and Buffalo's 7th round choice (Daniel Corso) in 1996 Entry Draft, March 19, 1996. • Missed majority of 2000-01 season recovering from knee injury suffered in game vs. NY Islanders, January 27, 2001. Signed as a free agent by **Ottawa**, July 5, 2003. Claimed by **Washington** from **Ottawa** in Waiver Draft, October 3, 2003. Traded to **Ottawa** by **Washington** for future considerations, October 5, 2003. Claimed on waivers by **Atlanta** from **Ottawa**, February 10, 2007. Claimed on waivers by **Philadelphia** from **Atlanta**, February 27, 2007. Signed as a free agent by **Ottawa** , July 6, 2007.

HAMHUIS, Dan

(HAM-HOOS, DAN) **NSH.**

Defense. Shoots left. 6'1", 200 lbs. Born, Smithers, B.C., December 13, 1982. Nashville's 1st choice, 12th overall, in 2001 Entry Draft.

Season	Club	League	GP	G	A	Pts	PIM	PP	SH	GW	S	%	+/-	TF	F%	Min	GP	G	A	Pts	PIM	PP	SH	GW	Min
1997-98	Smithers A's	Minor-BC	59	59	72	131	59	....	....	....	....	....	....	....	....	....	....	....	....	....	....	....	....	....	....
1998-99	Prince George	WHL	56	1	3	4	45	....	....	....	....	....	....	....	....	....	7	1	2	3	8	....	....	....	....
99-2000	Prince George	WHL	70	10	23	33	140	....	....	....	....	....	....	....	....	....	13	2	3	5	35	....	....	....	....
2000-01	Prince George	WHL	62	13	47	60	125	....	....	....	....	....	....	....	....	....	6	2	3	5	15	....	....	....	....
2001-02	Prince George	WHL	59	10	50	60	135	....	....	....	....	....	....	....	....	....	7	0	5	5	16	....	....	....	....
2002-03	Milwaukee	AHL	68	6	21	27	81	....	....	....	....	....	....	....	....	....	6	0	3	3	2	....	....	....	....
2003-04	**Nashville**	**NHL**	**80**	**7**	**19**	**26**	**57**	**2**	**0**	**4**	**115**	**6.1**	**–12**	**0**	**0.0**	**22:08**	**6**	**0**	**2**	**2**	**6**	**0**	**0**	**0**	**20:29**
2004-05	Milwaukee	AHL	76	13	38	51	85	....	....	....	....	....	....	....	....	....	7	0	2	2	10	....	....	....	....
2005-06	**Nashville**	**NHL**	**82**	**7**	**31**	**38**	**70**	**4**	**1**	**1**	**135**	**5.2**	**11**	**0**	**0.0**	**22:34**	**5**	**0**	**2**	**2**	**2**	**0**	**0**	**0**	**19:41**

			Regular Season														Playoffs								
Season	Club	League	GP	G	A	Pts	PIM	PP	SH	GW	S	%	+/-	TF	F%	Min	GP	G	A	Pts	PIM	PP	SH	GW	Min
2006-07	Nashville	NHL	81	6	14	20	66	0	0	1	84	7.1	8	1	0.0	21:20	5	0	1	1	2	0	0	0	21:36
2007-08	Nashville	NHL	80	4	23	27	66	1	0	1	127	3.1	–4	0	0.0	22:44	6	1	1	2	6	1	0	0	22:47
	NHL Totals		323	24	87	111	259	7	1	7	461	5.2		1	0.0	22:11	22	1	6	7	16	1	0	0	21:11

WHL West First All-Star Team (2001, 2002) • WHL Player of the Year (2002) • Canadian Major Junior First All-Star Team (2002) • Canadian Major Junior Defenseman of the Year (2002) • AHL Second All-Star Team (2005)

HAMILTON, Jeff

(HAM-ihl-tuhn, JEHF)

Center. Shoots right. 5'10", 185 lbs. Born, Englewood, OH, September 4, 1977.

Season	Club	League	GP	G	A	Pts	PIM	PP	SH	GW	S	%	+/-	TF	F%	Min	GP	G	A	Pts	PIM	PP	SH	GW	Min
1995-96	Avon Old Farms	High-CT	24	29	23	52	....	....	....	....	....	....	....	....	....	....	....	....	....	....	....	....	....	....	....
1996-97	Yale	ECAC	31	10	13	23	26	....	....	....	....	....	....	....	....	....	....	....	....	....	....	....	....	....	....
1997-98	Yale	ECAC	33	27	20	47	28	....	....	....	....	....	....	....	....	....	....	....	....	....	....	....	....	....	....
1998-99	Yale	ECAC	30	20	28	48	51	....	....	....	....	....	....	....	....	....	....	....	....	....	....	....	....	....	....
99-2000	Yale	ECAC	2	0	1	1	0	....	....	....	....	....	....	....	....	....	....	....	....	....	....	....	....	....	....
2000-01	Yale	ECAC	31	23	32	55	39	....	....	....	....	....	....	....	....	....	....	....	....	....	....	....	....	....	....
2001-02	Karpat Oulu	Finland	39	18	15	33	16	....	....	....	....	....	....	....	....	....	3	0	0	0	0	....	....	....	....
2002-03	Bridgeport	AHL	67	22	16	38	35	....	....	....	....	....	....	....	....	....	9	3	3	6	0	....	....	....	....
2003-04	NY Islanders	NHL	1	0	0	0	0	0	0	0	1	0.0	0	0	0.0	10:00	....	....	....	....	....	....	....	....	....
	Bridgeport	AHL	67	*43	25	68	26	....	....	....	....	....	....	....	....	....	7	4	0	4	4	....	....	....	....
2004-05	Hartford	AHL	60	23	30	53	32	....	....	....	....	....	....	....	....	....	6	4	3	7	0	....	....	....	....
2005-06	Ak Bars Kazan	Russia	8	0	1	1	16	....	....	....	....	....	....	....	....	....	....	....	....	....	....	....	....	....	....
	NY Islanders	NHL	13	2	6	8	8	1	0	0	29	6.9	0	6	16.7	10:33	....	....	....	....	....	....	....	....	....
	Bridgeport	AHL	39	24	26	50	28	....	....	....	....	....	....	....	....	....	....	....	....	....	....	....	....	....	....
2006-07	Chicago	NHL	70	18	21	39	22	3	0	4	138	13.0	–4	55	36.4	12:56	....	....	....	....	....	....	....	....	....
2007-08	Carolina	NHL	58	9	15	24	10	7	0	1	116	7.8	–8	79	48.1	10:48	....	....	....	....	....	....	....	....	....
	Albany River Rats	AHL	9	3	6	9	6	....	....	....	....	....	....	....	....	....	....	....	....	....	....	....	....	....	....
	NHL Totals		142	29	42	71	40	11	0	5	284	10.2		140	42.1	11:49	....	....	....	....	....	....	....	....	....

ECAC All-Rookie Team (1997) • ECAC First All-Star Team (1998, 1999, 2001) • NCAA East Second All-American Team (1998, 1999) • NCAA East First All-American Team (2001) • AHL First All-Star Team (2004) • Willie Marshall Award (Top Goal-scorer - AHL) (2004)

• Missed majority of 1999-2000 season recovering from abdominal injury originally suffered in game vs. University of Michigan (CCHA), October 30, 1999. Signed as a free agent by **Oulu** (Finland), October 4, 2001. Signed as a free agent by **NY Islanders**, August 6, 2002. Signed as a free agent by **Hartford** (AHL), October 10, 2004. Signed as a free agent by **Kazan** (Russia), September 5, 2005. Signed as a free agent by **Chicago**, September 29, 2006. Signed as a free agent by **Carolina**, July 1, 2007.

HAMRLIK, Roman

(HAHM-reh-lik, ROH-muhn) **MTL.**

Defense. Shoots left. 6'2", 215 lbs. Born, Gottwaldov/Zlin, Czech., April 12, 1974. Tampa Bay's 1st choice, 1st overall, in 1992 Entry Draft.

Season	Club	League	GP	G	A	Pts	PIM	PP	SH	GW	S	%	+/-	TF	F%	Min	GP	G	A	Pts	PIM	PP	SH	GW	Min
1990-91	AC ZPS Zlin	Czech	14	2	2	4	18	....	....	....	....	....	....	....	....	....	....	....	....	....	....	....	....	....	....
1991-92	AC ZPS Zlin	Czech	34	5	5	10	50	....	....	....	....	....	....	....	....	....	....	....	....	....	....	....	....	....	....
1992-93	Tampa Bay	NHL	67	6	15	21	71	1	0	1	113	5.3	–21	....	....	....	....	....	....	....	....	....	....	....	....
	Atlanta Knights	IHL	2	1	1	2	2	....	....	....	....	....	....	....	....	....	....	....	....	....	....	....	....	....	....
1993-94	Tampa Bay	NHL	64	3	18	21	135	0	0	0	158	1.9	–14	....	....	....	....	....	....	....	....	....	....	....	....
1994-95	AC ZPS Zlin	CzRep	2	1	0	1	10	....	....	....	....	....	....	....	....	....	....	....	....	....	....	....	....	....	....
	Tampa Bay	NHL	48	12	11	23	86	7	1	2	134	9.0	–18	....	....	....	....	....	....	....	....	....	....	....	....
1995-96	Tampa Bay	NHL	82	16	49	65	103	12	0	2	281	5.7	–24	....	....	....	5	0	1	1	4	0	0	0	....
1996-97	Tampa Bay	NHL	79	12	28	40	57	6	0	0	238	5.0	–29	....	....	....	....	....	....	....	....	....	....	....	....
1997-98	Tampa Bay	NHL	37	3	12	15	22	1	0	0	86	3.5	–18	....	....	....	....	....	....	....	....	....	....	....	....
	Edmonton	NHL	41	6	20	26	48	4	1	3	112	5.4	3	....	....	....	12	0	6	6	12	0	0	0	....
	Czech Republic	Olympics	6	1	0	1	2	....	....	....	....	....	....	....	....	....	....	....	....	....	....	....	....	....	....
1998-99	Edmonton	NHL	75	8	24	32	70	3	0	0	172	4.7	9	0	0.0	23:49	3	0	0	0	2	0	0	0	16:23
99-2000	Zlin	CzRep	6	0	3	3	4	....	....	....	....	....	....	....	....	....	....	....	....	....	....	....	....	....	....
	Edmonton	NHL	80	8	37	45	68	5	0	0	180	4.4	1	0	0.0	25:18	5	0	1	1	4	0	0	0	24:44
2000-01	NY Islanders	NHL	76	16	30	46	92	5	1	4	232	6.9	–20	1	100.0	25:12	....	....	....	....	....	....	....	....	....
2001-02	NY Islanders	NHL	70	11	26	37	78	4	1	1	169	6.5	7	1	0.0	25:32	7	1	6	7	6	0	0	0	29:09
	Czech Republic	Olympics	4	0	1	1	2	....	....	....	....	....	....	....	....	....	....	....	....	....	....	....	....	....	....
2002-03	NY Islanders	NHL	73	9	32	41	87	3	0	2	151	6.0	21	0	0.0	26:34	5	0	2	2	2	0	0	0	29:24
2003-04	NY Islanders	NHL	81	7	22	29	68	2	0	2	182	3.8	2	0	0.0	24:35	5	0	1	1	2	0	0	0	25:30
2004-05	HC Hame Zlin	CzRep	45	2	14	16	70	....	....	....	....	....	....	....	....	....	17	1	3	4	24	....	....	....	....
2005-06	Calgary	NHL	51	7	19	26	56	1	1	0	89	7.9	8	0	0.0	21:51	7	0	2	2	2	0	0	0	19:44
2006-07	Calgary	NHL	75	7	31	38	88	1	0	1	125	5.6	22	0	0.0	24:52	6	0	1	1	8	0	0	0	26:53
2007-08	Montreal	NHL	77	5	21	26	38	3	0	3	129	3.9	7	0	0.0	23:08	12	1	2	3	8	0	0	0	22:55
	NHL Totals		1076	136	395	531	1167	58	5	21	2551	5.3		2	50.0	24:38	67	2	22	24	50	0	0	0	24:31

Played in NHL All-Star Game (1996, 1999, 2003)

Traded to **Edmonton** by **Tampa Bay** with Paul Comrie for Bryan Marchment, Steve Kelly and Jason Bonsignore, December 30, 1997. Traded to **NY Islanders** by **Edmonton** for Eric Brewer, Josh Green and NY Islanders' 2nd round choice (Brad Winchester) in 2000 Entry Draft, June 24, 2000. Signed as a free agent by **Zlin** (CzRep), August 4, 2004. Signed as a free agent by **Calgary**, August 14, 2005 Signed as a free agent by **Montreal**, July 2, 2007.

HANDZUS, Michal

(HAHND-zuhs, MIGH-kuhl) **L.A.**

Center. Shoots left. 6'5", 217 lbs. Born, Banska Bystrica, Czech., March 11, 1977. St. Louis' 3rd choice, 101st overall, in 1995 Entry Draft.

Season	Club	League	GP	G	A	Pts	PIM	PP	SH	GW	S	%	+/-	TF	F%	Min	GP	G	A	Pts	PIM	PP	SH	GW	Min
1993-94	B. Bystrica Jr.	Slovak-Jr.	40	23	36	59	....	....	....	....	....	....	....	....	....	....	....	....	....	....	....	....	....	....	....
1994-95	B. Bystrica	Slovak-2	22	15	14	29	10	....	....	....	....	....	....	....	....	....	....	....	....	....	....	....	....	....	....
1995-96	B. Bystrica	Slovakia	19	3	1	4	8	....	....	....	....	....	....	....	....	....	....	....	....	....	....	....	....	....	....
1996-97	HC SKP PS Poprad	Slovakia	44	15	18	33	....	....	....	....	....	....	....	....	....	....	....	....	....	....	....	....	....	....	....
1997-98	Worcester IceCats	AHL	69	27	36	63	54	....	....	....	....	....	....	....	....	....	11	2	6	8	10	....	....	....	....
1998-99	St. Louis	NHL	66	4	12	16	30	0	0	0	78	5.1	–9	794	49.9	14:48	11	0	2	2	8	0	0	0	16:52
99-2000	St. Louis	NHL	81	25	28	53	44	3	4	5	166	15.1	19	1243	51.5	17:43	7	0	3	3	6	0	0	0	16:35
2000-01	St. Louis	NHL	36	10	14	24	12	3	2	2	58	17.2	11	581	50.6	18:00	....	....	....	....	....	....	....	....	....
	Phoenix	NHL	10	4	4	8	21	0	1	0	14	28.6	5	111	60.4	15:26	....	....	....	....	....	....	....	....	....
2001-02	Phoenix	NHL	79	15	30	45	34	3	1	1	94	16.0	–8	1227	48.7	16:09	5	0	0	0	2	0	0	0	15:01
	Slovakia	Olympics	2	1	0	1	6	....	....	....	....	....	....	....	....	....	....	....	....	....	....	....	....	....	....
2002-03	Philadelphia	NHL	82	23	21	44	46	1	1	9	133	17.3	13	1350	52.3	17:33	13	2	6	8	6	0	0	1	18:23
2003-04	Philadelphia	NHL	82	20	38	58	82	7	1	2	135	14.8	18	1457	49.9	18:43	18	5	5	10	10	0	0	0	18:33
2004-05	HKm Zvolen	Slovakia	33	14	24	38	34	....	....	....	....	....	....	....	....	....	17	5	10	15	6	....	....	....	....
2005-06	Philadelphia	NHL	73	11	33	44	38	2	1	1	113	9.7	–2	1143	53.2	18:28	6	0	2	2	2	0	0	0	15:56
2006-07	Chicago	NHL	8	3	5	8	6	1	0	0	9	33.3	4	173	51.5	20:59	....	....	....	....	....	....	....	....	....
2007-08	Los Angeles	NHL	82	7	14	21	45	0	3	0	89	7.9	–21	1167	45.6	15:14	....	....	....	....	....	....	....	....	....
	NHL Totals		599	122	199	321	358	20	14	20	889	13.7		9246	50.4	17:05	60	7	18	25	34	0	0	1	17:25

Traded to **Phoenix** by **St. Louis** with Ladislav Nagy, the rights to Jeff Taffe and St. Louis' 1st round choice (Ben Eager) in 2002 Entry Draft for Keith Tkachuk, March 13, 2001. Traded to **Philadelphia** by **Phoenix** with Robert Esche for Brian Boucher and Nashville's 3rd round choice (previously acquired, Phoenix selected Joe Callahan) in 2002 Entry Draft, June 12, 2002. Signed as a free agent by **Zvolen** (Slovakia), October 27, 2004. Traded to **Chicago** by **Philadelphia** for Kyle Calder, August 4, 2006. • Missed remainder of 2006-07 season recovering from knee injury suffered in game vs. St. Louis, October 21, 2006. Signed as a free agent by **Los Angeles**, July 2, 2007.

HANNAN, Scott

(HAN-nan, SKAWT) **COL.**

Defense. Shoots left. 6'1", 225 lbs. Born, Richmond, B.C., January 23, 1979. San Jose's 2nd choice, 23rd overall, in 1997 Entry Draft.

Season	Club	League	GP	G	A	Pts	PIM	PP	SH	GW	S	%	+/-	TF	F%	Min	GP	G	A	Pts	PIM	PP	SH	GW	Min
1994-95	Surrey Wolves	Minor-BC	70	54	54	108	200	....	....	....	....	....	....	....	....	....	....	....	....	....	....	....	....	....	....
	Tacoma Rockets	WHL	2	0	0	0	0	....	....	....	....	....	....	....	....	....	....	....	....	....	....	....	....	....	....
1995-96	Kelowna Rockets	WHL	69	4	5	9	76	....	....	....	....	....	....	....	....	....	6	0	1	1	4	....	....	....	....
1996-97	Kelowna Rockets	WHL	70	17	26	43	101	....	....	....	....	....	....	....	....	....	6	0	0	0	8	....	....	....	....
1997-98	Kelowna Rockets	WHL	47	10	30	40	70	....	....	....	....	....	....	....	....	....	7	2	7	9	14	....	....	....	....
1998-99	San Jose	NHL	5	0	2	2	6	0	0	0	4	0.0	0	0	0.0	7:15	....	....	....	....	....	....	....	....	....
	Kelowna Rockets	WHL	47	15	30	45	92	....	....	....	....	....	....	....	....	....	6	1	2	3	14	....	....	....	....
	Kentucky	AHL	2	0	0	0	2	....	....	....	....	....	....	....	....	....	12	0	2	2	10	....	....	....	....
99-2000	San Jose	NHL	30	1	2	3	10	0	0	0	28	3.6	7	1	0.0	17:09	1	0	1	1	0	0	0	0	18:14
	Kentucky	AHL	41	5	12	17	40	....	....	....	....	....	....	....	....	....	....	....	....	....	....	....	....	....	....
2000-01	San Jose	NHL	75	3	14	17	51	0	0	1	96	3.1	10	0	0.0	19:02	6	0	1	1	6	0	0	0	25:10
2001-02	San Jose	NHL	75	2	12	14	57	0	0	1	68	2.9	10	1	100.0	20:19	12	0	2	2	12	0	0	0	20:46
2002-03	San Jose	NHL	81	3	19	22	61	1	0	0	103	2.9	0	3	33.3	24:16	....	....	....	....	....	....	....	....	....
2003-04	San Jose	NHL	82	6	15	21	48	0	0	0	114	5.3	10	0	0.0	23:41	17	1	5	6	22	1	0	1	26:38

			Regular Season														Playoffs								
Season	Club	League	GP	G	A	Pts	PIM	PP	SH	GW	S	%	+/-	TF	F%	Min	GP	G	A	Pts	PIM	PP	SH	GW	Min
2004-05			DID NOT PLAY																						
2005-06	**San Jose**	**NHL**	**81**	**6**	**18**	**24**	**58**	**2**	**0**	**1**	**104**	**5.8**	**7**	**0**	**0.0**	**24:34**	**11**	**0**	**1**	**1**	**6**	**0**	**0**	**0**	**25:16**
2006-07	**San Jose**	**NHL**	**79**	**4**	**20**	**24**	**38**	**0**	**1**	**1**	**79**	**5.1**	**1**	**0**	**0.0**	**22:49**	**11**	**0**	**2**	**2**	**33**	**0**	**0**	**0**	**21:42**
2007-08	**Colorado**	**NHL**	**82**	**2**	**19**	**21**	**55**	**0**	**0**	**0**	**79**	**2.5**	**–5**	**1**	**100.0**	**22:41**	**9**	**0**	**1**	**1**	**4**	**0**	**0**	**0**	**19:15**
	NHL Totals		**590**	**27**	**121**	**148**	**384**	**3**	**1**	**4**	**675**	**4.0**		**6**	**50.0**	**22:08**	**67**	**1**	**13**	**14**	**83**	**1**	**0**	**1**	**23:18**

WHL West First All-Star Team (1999)
Signed as a free agent by **Colorado**, July 1, 2007.

HANSEN, Jannik

(HAHN-suhn, YAH-nihk) **VAN.**

Left wing. Shoots right. 6'1", 194 lbs. Born, Herlev, Denmark, March 15, 1986. Vancouver's 7th choice, 287th overall, in 2004 Entry Draft.

Season	Club	League	GP	G	A	Pts	PIM	PP	SH	GW	S	%	+/-	TF	F%	Min	GP	G	A	Pts	PIM	PP	SH	GW	Min
2002-03	Rodovre	Denmark	15	0	0	0	0																		
	Malmo U18	Swe-U18	12	8	7	15	2										3	2	0	2	0				
2003-04	Rodovre	Denmark	35	12	7	19	48																		
2004-05	Rodovre	Denmark	32	17	17	34	40										5	3	1	4	24				
2005-06	Portland	WHL	64	24	40	64	67										12	7	6	13	16				
2006-07	Manitoba Moose	AHL	72	12	22	34	38										6	0	0	0	2				
	Vancouver	**NHL**															**10**	**0**	**1**	**1**	**4**	**0**	**0**	**0**	**12:41**
2007-08	**Vancouver**	**NHL**	**5**	**0**	**0**	**0**	**2**	**0**	**0**	**0**	**3**	**0.0**	**0**	**1**	**100.0**	**11:34**									
	Manitoba Moose	AHL	50	21	22	43	22										6	2	2	4	0				
	NHL Totals		**5**	**0**	**0**	**0**	**2**	**0**	**0**	**0**	**3**	**0.0**		**1**	**100.0**	**11:34**	**10**	**0**	**1**	**1**	**4**	**0**	**0**	**0**	**12:41**

HANZAL, Martin

(HAHN-zuhl, MAHR-tihn) **PHX.**

Center. Shoots left. 6'5", 208 lbs. Born, Pisek, Czech., February 20, 1987. Phoenix's 1st choice, 17th overall, in 2005 Entry Draft.

Season	Club	League	GP	G	A	Pts	PIM	PP	SH	GW	S	%	+/-	TF	F%	Min	GP	G	A	Pts	PIM	PP	SH	GW	Min
2002-03	C. Budejovice U17	CzR-U17	47	24	30	54	28										7	1	3	4	25				
2003-04	C. Budejovice U17	CzR-U17	2	0	2	2	2										2	1	0	1	4				
	C. Budejovice Jr.	CzRep-Jr.	53	15	7	22	32																		
2004-05	C. Budejovice Jr.	CzRep-Jr.	37	22	22	44	80										2	1	2	3	2				
	C. Budejovice	CzRep-2	15	1	2	3	2										6	0	0	0	6				
2005-06	C. Budejovice Jr.	CzRep-Jr.	7	3	5	8	20																		
	C. Budejovice	CzRep	19	0	1	1	10																		
	BK Mlada Boleslav	CzRep-2	5	2	0	2	0																		
	Omaha Lancers	USHL	19	4	15	19	30										5	1	0	1	4				
2006-07	Red Deer Rebels	WHL	60	26	59	85	94										6	2	7	9	19				
2007-08	**Phoenix**	**NHL**	**72**	**8**	**27**	**35**	**28**	**1**	**1**	**3**	**111**	**7.2**	**–7**	**1019**	**46.1**	**16:45**									
	NHL Totals		**72**	**8**	**27**	**35**	**28**	**1**	**1**	**3**	**111**	**7.2**		**1019**	**46.1**	**16:45**									

WHL East Second All-Star Team (2007)

HARRISON, Jay

(HAIR-ih-suhn, JAY)

Defense. Shoots left. 6'4", 211 lbs. Born, Oshawa, Ont., November 3, 1982. Toronto's 4th choice, 82nd overall, in 2001 Entry Draft.

Season	Club	League	GP	G	A	Pts	PIM	PP	SH	GW	S	%	+/-	TF	F%	Min	GP	G	A	Pts	PIM	PP	SH	GW	Min
1997-98	Oshawa	OHA-B	42	1	11	12	143																		
1998-99	Brampton	OHL	63	1	14	15	108																		
99-2000	Brampton	OHL	68	2	18	20	139										6	0	2	2	15				
2000-01	Brampton	OHL	53	4	15	19	112										9	1	1	2	17				
2001-02	Brampton	OHL	61	12	31	43	116																		
	St. John's	AHL	7	0	1	1	2										10	0	0	0	4				
	Memphis	CHL															1	0	0	0	2				
2002-03	St. John's	AHL	72	2	8	10	72																		
2003-04	St. John's	AHL	70	4	5	9	141																		
2004-05	St. John's	AHL	60	0	4	4	108										4	0	1	1	14				
2005-06	**Toronto**	**NHL**	**8**	**0**	**1**	**1**	**2**	**0**	**0**	**0**	**7**	**0.0**	**5**	**0**	**0.0**	**18:50**									
	Toronto Marlies	AHL	57	9	20	29	100										5	1	3	4	8				
2006-07	**Toronto**	**NHL**	**5**	**0**	**0**	**0**	**6**	**0**	**0**	**0**	**3**	**0.0**	**–5**	**0**	**0.0**	**8:22**									
	Toronto Marlies	AHL	41	4	14	18	68																		
2007-08	Toronto Marlies	AHL	69	13	14	27	73										18	2	10	12	35				
	NHL Totals		**13**	**0**	**1**	**1**	**8**	**0**	**0**	**0**	**10**	**0.0**		**0**	**0.0**	**14:48**									

OHL All-Rookie Team (1999)

HARROLD, Peter

(HAIR-ohld, PEE-tuhr) **L.A.**

Defense. Shoots right. 5'11", 195 lbs. Born, Kirtland Hills, OH, June 8, 1983.

Season	Club	League	GP	G	A	Pts	PIM	PP	SH	GW	S	%	+/-	TF	F%	Min	GP	G	A	Pts	PIM	PP	SH	GW	Min
2003-04	Boston College	H-East	40	2	12	14	12																		
2004-05	Boston College	H-East	35	4	10	14	22																		
2005-06	Boston College	H-East	42	7	23	30	32																		
2006-07	**Los Angeles**	**NHL**	**12**	**0**	**2**	**2**	**8**	**0**	**0**	**0**	**11**	**0.0**	**0**	**1**	**0.0**	**15:12**									
	Manchester	AHL	62	7	27	34	43										16	3	8	11	18				
2007-08	**Los Angeles**	**NHL**	**25**	**2**	**3**	**5**	**2**	**0**	**0**	**0**	**16**	**12.5**	**3**	**2**	**50.0**	**16:23**									
	Manchester	AHL	49	7	36	43	25										4	0	1	1	4				
	NHL Totals		**37**	**2**	**5**	**7**	**10**	**0**	**0**	**0**	**27**	**7.4**		**3**	**33.3**	**16:00**									

Hockey East First All-Star Team (2006) • NCAA East First All-American Team (2006)
Signed as a free agent by **Los Angeles**, April 12, 2006.

HARTIGAN, Mark

(HAHR-tih-guhn, MAHRK)

Center. Shoots left. 6', 200 lbs. Born, Fort St. John, B.C., October 15, 1977.

Season	Club	League	GP	G	A	Pts	PIM	PP	SH	GW	S	%	+/-	TF	F%	Min	GP	G	A	Pts	PIM	PP	SH	GW	Min
1996-97	Weyburn	SJHL	52	44	32	76																			
1997-98	Weyburn	SJHL	62	*59	46	*105	81										23	17	21	38	10				
1998-99	St. Cloud State	WCHA	DID NOT PLAY – FRESHMAN																						
99-2000	St. Cloud State	WCHA	37	22	20	42	24																		
2000-01	St. Cloud State	WCHA	40	27	21	48	20																		
2001-02	St. Cloud State	WCHA	42	*37	38	75	42																		
	Atlanta	**NHL**	**2**	**0**	**0**	**0**	**2**	**0**	**0**	**0**	**3**	**0.0**	**–2**	**18**	**38.9**	**13:16**									
2002-03	**Atlanta**	**NHL**	**23**	**5**	**2**	**7**	**6**	**1**	**0**	**0**	**25**	**20.0**	**–8**	**220**	**47.3**	**10:52**									
	Chicago Wolves	AHL	55	15	31	46	43										9	1	2	3	10				
2003-04	**Columbus**	**NHL**	**9**	**1**	**3**	**4**	**6**	**1**	**0**	**0**	**15**	**6.7**	**–2**	**138**	**40.6**	**16:19**									
	Syracuse Crunch	AHL	69	23	23	46	86										7	1	4	5	8				
2004-05	Syracuse Crunch	AHL	69	31	28	59	105																		
2005-06	**Columbus**	**NHL**	**33**	**9**	**3**	**12**	**22**	**3**	**0**	**1**	**54**	**16.7**	**–1**	**194**	**44.9**	**11:39**									
	Syracuse Crunch	AHL	49	34	41	75	48										6	1	2	3	33				
2006-07	**Columbus**	**NHL**	**6**	**1**	**2**	**3**	**2**	**1**	**0**	**0**	**11**	**9.1**	**2**	**83**	**45.8**	**13:51**									
	Syracuse Crunch	AHL	34	19	13	32	51																		
	♦ **Anaheim**	**NHL**	**6**	**0**	**0**	**0**	**4**	**0**	**0**	**0**	**4**	**0.0**	**–1**	**23**	**26.1**	**7:41**	**1**	**0**	**0**	**0**	**0**	**0**	**0**	**0**	**3:34**
	Portland Pirates	AHL	25	9	16	25	20																		
2007-08	**Detroit**	**NHL**	**23**	**3**	**1**	**4**	**16**	**0**	**0**	**0**	**19**	**15.8**	**–2**	**114**	**52.6**	**7:09**	**4**	**0**	**1**	**1**	**4**	**0**	**0**	**0**	**5:21**
	Grand Rapids	AHL	48	23	19	42	76																		
	NHL Totals		**102**	**19**	**11**	**30**	**58**	**6**	**0**	**1**	**131**	**14.5**		**790**	**45.3**	**10:48**	**5**	**0**	**1**	**1**	**4**	**0**	**0**	**0**	**5:00**

WCHA First All-Star Team (2002) • WCHA Player of the Year (2002)
Signed as a free agent by **Atlanta**, March 27, 2002. Signed as a free agent by **Columbus**, July 15, 2003. Traded to **Anaheim** by **Columbus** with Joe Motzko and Columbus'4th round choice (Sebastian Stefaniszin) in 2007 Entry Draft for Zenon Konopka, Curtis Glencross and Anaheim's 7th round choice (Trent Vogelhuber) in 2007 Entry Draft, January 26, 2007. Signed as a free agent by **Detroit**, July 16, 2007.

			Regular Season														Playoffs								
Season	Club	League	GP	G	A	Pts	PIM	PP	SH	GW	S	%	+/-	TF	F%	Min	GP	G	A	Pts	PIM	PP	SH	GW	Min

HARTNELL, Scott

(HAHRT-nuhl, SKAWT) **PHI.**

Left wing. Shoots left. 6'2", 210 lbs. Born, Regina, Sask., April 18, 1982. Nashville's 1st choice, 6th overall, in 2000 Entry Draft.

1997-98	Lloydminster	AJHL	56	9	25	34	82	....	....	....	....	....	....	....	....	....	4	2	1	3	8	....	....	....	....
	Prince Albert	WHL	1	0	1	1	2	....	....	....	....	....	....	....	....	....	....	....	....	....	....	....	....	....	....
1998-99	Prince Albert	WHL	65	10	34	44	104	....	....	....	....	....	....	....	....	....	14	0	5	5	22	....	....	....	....
99-2000	Prince Albert	WHL	62	27	55	82	124	....	....	....	....	....	....	....	....	....	6	3	2	5	6	....	....	....	....
2000-01	**Nashville**	**NHL**	**75**	**2**	**14**	**16**	**48**	**0**	**0**	**0**	**92**	**2.2**	**–8**	**3**	**33.3**	**10:54**	....	....	....	....	....	....	....	....	....
2001-02	**Nashville**	**NHL**	**75**	**14**	**27**	**41**	**111**	**3**	**0**	**4**	**162**	**8.6**	**5**	**12**	**25.0**	**16:58**	....	....	....	....	....	....	....	....	....
2002-03	**Nashville**	**NHL**	**82**	**12**	**22**	**34**	**101**	**2**	**0**	**2**	**221**	**5.4**	**–3**	**23**	**30.4**	**15:17**	....	....	....	....	....	....	....	....	....
2003-04	**Nashville**	**NHL**	**59**	**18**	**15**	**33**	**87**	**5**	**0**	**3**	**154**	**11.7**	**–5**	**48**	**37.5**	**16:16**	**6**	**1**	**2**	**3**	**2**	**0**	**0**	**0**	**15:37**
2004-05	Valerengen IF Oslo	Norway	28	17	12	29	103	....	....	....	....	....	....	....	....	....	11	12	7	19	24	....	....	....	....
2005-06	**Nashville**	**NHL**	**81**	**25**	**23**	**48**	**101**	**10**	**2**	**8**	**211**	**11.8**	**8**	**58**	**37.9**	**16:05**	**5**	**1**	**0**	**1**	**4**	**0**	**0**	**0**	**12:12**
2006-07	**Nashville**	**NHL**	**64**	**22**	**17**	**39**	**96**	**10**	**0**	**2**	**150**	**14.7**	**19**	**134**	**47.0**	**15:43**	**5**	**1**	**1**	**2**	**28**	**1**	**0**	**0**	**14:23**
2007-08	**Philadelphia**	**NHL**	**80**	**24**	**19**	**43**	**159**	**10**	**1**	**6**	**176**	**13.6**	**2**	**32**	**40.6**	**16:11**	**17**	**3**	**4**	**7**	**20**	**0**	**0**	**0**	**15:28**
	NHL Totals		**516**	**117**	**137**	**254**	**703**	**40**	**3**	**25**	**1166**	**10.0**		**310**	**41.0**	**15:20**	**33**	**6**	**7**	**13**	**54**	**1**	**0**	**0**	**14:50**

Signed as a free agent by **Oslo** (Norway), October 21, 2004. Traded to **Philadelphia** by **Nashville** with Kimmo Timmonen for Nashville's 1st round choice (previously acquired, Nashville selected Jonathon Blum) in 2007 Entry Draft, June 18, 2007.

HATCHER, Derian

(HAT-chuhr, DAIR-ee-an) **PHI.**

Defense. Shoots left. 6'5", 235 lbs. Born, Sterling Hts., MI, June 4, 1972. Minnesota's 1st choice, 8th overall, in 1990 Entry Draft.

1987-88	Detroit GPD	MNHL	25	5	13	18	52	....	....	....	....	....	....	....	....	....	....	....	....	....	....	....	....	....	....
1988-89	Detroit GPD	MNHL	51	19	35	54	100	....	....	....	....	....	....	....	....	....	....	....	....	....	....	....	....	....	....
1989-90	North Bay	OHL	64	14	38	52	81	....	....	....	....	....	....	....	....	....	5	2	3	5	8	....	....	....	....
1990-91	North Bay	OHL	64	13	49	62	163	....	....	....	....	....	....	....	....	....	10	2	10	12	28	....	....	....	....
1991-92	**Minnesota**	**NHL**	**43**	**8**	**4**	**12**	**88**	**0**	**0**	**2**	**51**	**15.7**	**7**	....	....	....	**5**	**0**	**2**	**2**	**8**	**0**	**0**	**0**	....
1992-93	**Minnesota**	**NHL**	**67**	**4**	**15**	**19**	**178**	**0**	**0**	**1**	**73**	**5.5**	**–27**	....	....	....	....	....	....	....	....	....	....	....	....
	Kalamazoo Wings	IHL	2	1	2	3	21	....	....	....	....	....	....	....	....	....	....	....	....	....	....	....	....	....	....
1993-94	**Dallas**	**NHL**	**83**	**12**	**19**	**31**	**211**	**2**	**1**	**2**	**132**	**9.1**	**19**	....	....	....	**9**	**0**	**2**	**2**	**14**	**0**	**0**	**0**	....
1994-95	**Dallas**	**NHL**	**43**	**5**	**11**	**16**	**105**	**2**	**0**	**2**	**74**	**6.8**	**3**	....	....	....	....	....	....	....	....	....	....	....	....
1995-96	**Dallas**	**NHL**	**79**	**8**	**23**	**31**	**129**	**2**	**0**	**1**	**125**	**6.4**	**–12**	....	....	....	....	....	....	....	....	....	....	....	....
1996-97	**Dallas**	**NHL**	**63**	**3**	**19**	**22**	**97**	**0**	**0**	**0**	**96**	**3.1**	**8**	....	....	....	**7**	**0**	**2**	**2**	**20**	**0**	**0**	**0**	....
1997-98	**Dallas**	**NHL**	**70**	**6**	**25**	**31**	**132**	**3**	**0**	**2**	**74**	**8.1**	**9**	....	....	....	**17**	**3**	**3**	**6**	**39**	**2**	**0**	**0**	....
	United States	Olympics	4	0	0	0	0	....	....	....	....	....	....	....	....	....	....	....	....	....	....	....	....	....	....
1998-99 ♦	**Dallas**	**NHL**	**80**	**9**	**21**	**30**	**102**	**3**	**0**	**2**	**125**	**7.2**	**21**	**0**	**0.0**	**24:44**	**18**	**1**	**6**	**7**	**24**	**0**	**0**	**0**	**29:06**
99-2000	**Dallas**	**NHL**	**57**	**2**	**22**	**24**	**68**	**0**	**0**	**0**	**90**	**2.2**	**6**	**0**	**0.0**	**27:33**	**23**	**1**	**3**	**4**	**29**	**0**	**0**	**0**	**27:40**
2000-01	**Dallas**	**NHL**	**80**	**2**	**21**	**23**	**77**	**1**	**0**	**2**	**97**	**2.1**	**5**	**0**	**0.0**	**25:53**	**10**	**0**	**1**	**1**	**16**	**0**	**0**	**0**	**28:53**
2001-02	**Dallas**	**NHL**	**80**	**4**	**21**	**25**	**87**	**1**	**0**	**0**	**111**	**3.6**	**12**	**0**	**0.0**	**26:40**	....	....	....	....	....	....	....	....	....
2002-03	**Dallas**	**NHL**	**82**	**8**	**22**	**30**	**106**	**1**	**1**	**2**	**159**	**5.0**	**37**	**0**	**0.0**	**25:51**	**11**	**1**	**2**	**3**	**33**	**0**	**0**	**0**	**30:02**
2003-04	**Detroit**	**NHL**	**15**	**0**	**4**	**4**	**8**	**0**	**0**	**0**	**18**	**0.0**	**4**	**0**	**0.0**	**19:38**	**12**	**0**	**1**	**1**	**15**	**0**	**0**	**0**	**22:54**
2004-05	Motor City	UHL	24	5	12	17	27	....	....	....	....	....	....	....	....	....	....	....	....	....	....	....	....	....	....
2005-06	**Philadelphia**	**NHL**	**77**	**4**	**13**	**17**	**93**	**1**	**1**	**0**	**98**	**4.1**	**2**	**0**	**0.0**	**23:30**	**6**	**0**	**2**	**2**	**10**	**0**	**0**	**0**	**21:36**
	United States	Olympics	6	0	0	0	12	....	....	....	....	....	....	....	....	....	....	....	....	....	....	....	....	....	....
2006-07	**Philadelphia**	**NHL**	**82**	**3**	**6**	**9**	**67**	**3**	**0**	**1**	**81**	**3.7**	**–24**	**0**	**0.0**	**23:40**	....	....	....	....	....	....	....	....	....
2007-08	**Philadelphia**	**NHL**	**44**	**2**	**5**	**7**	**33**	**0**	**0**	**1**	**27**	**7.4**	**4**	**0**	**0.0**	**21:06**	**15**	**1**	**2**	**3**	**40**	**0**	**0**	**0**	**21:14**
	NHL Totals		**1045**	**80**	**251**	**331**	**1581**	**19**	**3**	**18**	**1431**	**5.6**		**0**	**0.0**	**24:52**	**133**	**7**	**26**	**33**	**248**	**2**	**0**	**0**	**26:20**

NHL Second All-Star Team (2003)

Played in NHL All-Star Game (1997)

Transferred to **Dallas** after **Minnesota** franchise relocated, June 9, 1993. Signed as a free agent by **Detroit**, July 3, 2003. • Missed majority of 2003-04 season recovering from knee injury suffered in game vs. Vancouver, October 16, 2003. Signed as a free agent by **Motor City** (UHL), February 1, 2005. Signed as a free agent by **Philadelphia**, August 2, 2005.

HAVELID, Niclas

(HAHV-lihd, NIHK-luhs) **ATL.**

Defense. Shoots left. 6', 200 lbs. Born, Stockholm, Sweden, April 12, 1973. Anaheim's 2nd choice, 83rd overall, in 1999 Entry Draft.

1988-89	Enkopings SK	Sweden-3	7	0	1	1	0	....	....	....	....	....	....	....	....	....	....	....	....	....	....	....	....	....	....
1989-90	Enkopings SK	Sweden-3	24	1	2	3	28	....	....	....	....	....	....	....	....	....	....	....	....	....	....	....	....	....	....
1990-91	Arlanda	Sweden-2	30	2	3	5	22	....	....	....	....	....	....	....	....	....	....	....	....	....	....	....	....	....	....
1991-92	AIK Solna	Sweden	10	0	0	0	2	....	....	....	....	....	....	....	....	....	....	....	....	....	....	....	....	....	....
1992-93	AIK Solna	Sweden	30	1	2	3	22	....	....	....	....	....	....	....	....	....	3	0	0	0	2	....	....	....	....
1993-94	AIK Solna	Sweden-2	22	3	9	12	14	....	....	....	....	....	....	....	....	....	....	....	....	....	....	....	....	....	....
1994-95	AIK Solna	Sweden	40	3	7	10	38	....	....	....	....	....	....	....	....	....	....	....	....	....	....	....	....	....	....
1995-96	AIK Solna	Sweden	40	5	6	11	30	....	....	....	....	....	....	....	....	....	....	....	....	....	....	....	....	....	....
1996-97	AIK Solna	Sweden	49	3	6	9	42	....	....	....	....	....	....	....	....	....	7	1	2	3	8	....	....	....	....
1997-98	AIK Solna	Sweden	43	8	4	12	42	....	....	....	....	....	....	....	....	....	10	1	3	4	39	....	....	....	....
1998-99	Malmo	Sweden	50	10	12	22	42	....	....	....	....	....	....	....	....	....	8	0	4	4	10	....	....	....	....
99-2000	**Anaheim**	**NHL**	**50**	**2**	**7**	**9**	**20**	**0**	**0**	**2**	**70**	**2.9**	**0**	**1**	**0.0**	**19:10**	....	....	....	....	....	....	....	....	....
	Cincinnati	AHL	2	0	0	0	0	....	....	....	....	....	....	....	....	....	....	....	....	....	....	....	....	....	....
2000-01	**Anaheim**	**NHL**	**47**	**4**	**10**	**14**	**34**	**2**	**0**	**1**	**69**	**5.8**	**–6**	**4**	**0.0**	**21:51**	....	....	....	....	....	....	....	....	....
2001-02	**Anaheim**	**NHL**	**52**	**1**	**2**	**3**	**40**	**0**	**0**	**0**	**45**	**2.2**	**–13**	**1**	**0.0**	**17:01**	....	....	....	....	....	....	....	....	....
2002-03	**Anaheim**	**NHL**	**82**	**11**	**22**	**33**	**30**	**4**	**0**	**5**	**169**	**6.5**	**5**	**3**	**0.0**	**22:30**	**21**	**0**	**4**	**4**	**2**	**0**	**0**	**0**	**25:41**
2003-04	**Anaheim**	**NHL**	**79**	**6**	**20**	**26**	**28**	**5**	**0**	**3**	**122**	**4.9**	**–28**	**0**	**0.0**	**22:39**	....	....	....	....	....	....	....	....	....
2004-05	Sodertalje SK	Sweden	46	2	2	4	60	....	....	....	....	....	....	....	....	....	10	1	1	2	18	....	....	....	....
2005-06	**Atlanta**	**NHL**	**82**	**4**	**28**	**32**	**48**	**2**	**0**	**0**	**84**	**4.8**	**9**	**0**	**0.0**	**24:25**	....	....	....	....	....	....	....	....	....
	Sweden	Olympics	7	0	0	0	4	....	....	....	....	....	....	....	....	....	....	....	....	....	....	....	....	....	....
2006-07	**Atlanta**	**NHL**	**77**	**3**	**18**	**21**	**52**	**1**	**0**	**1**	**82**	**3.7**	**–2**	**1**	**0.0**	**25:16**	**4**	**0**	**2**	**2**	**0**	**0**	**0**	**0**	**24:14**
2007-08	**Atlanta**	**NHL**	**81**	**1**	**13**	**14**	**42**	**0**	**0**	**0**	**54**	**1.9**	**2**	**0**	**0.0**	**20:30**	....	....	....	....	....	....	....	....	....
	NHL Totals		**550**	**32**	**120**	**152**	**294**	**14**	**0**	**12**	**695**	**4.6**		**10**	**0.0**	**22:01**	**25**	**0**	**6**	**6**	**2**	**0**	**0**	**0**	**25:27**

Traded to **Atlanta** by **Anaheim** for Kurtis Foster, June 26, 2004. Signed as a free agent by **Sodertalje** (Sweden), August 9, 2004.

HAVLAT, Martin

(HAHV-lat, MAHR-tihn) **CHI.**

Right wing. Shoots left. 6'1", 204 lbs. Born, Mlada Boleslav, Czech., April 19, 1981. Ottawa's 1st choice, 26th overall, in 1999 Entry Draft.

1997-98	Ytong Brno Jr.	CzRep-Jr.	32	38	29	67	....	....	....	....	....	....	....	....	....	....	....	....	....	....	....	....	....	....	....
1998-99	HC Trinec Jr.	CzRep-Jr.	31	28	23	51	....	....	....	....	....	....	....	....	....	....	....	....	....	....	....	....	....	....	....
	Trinec	CzRep	24	2	3	5	4	....	....	....	....	....	....	....	....	....	8	0	0	0	....	....	....	....	....
99-2000	HC Ocelari Trinec	CzRep	46	13	29	42	42	....	....	....	....	....	....	....	....	....	4	0	2	2	8	....	....	....	....
2000-01	**Ottawa**	**NHL**	**73**	**19**	**23**	**42**	**20**	**7**	**0**	**5**	**133**	**14.3**	**8**	**40**	**30.0**	**13:47**	**4**	**0**	**0**	**0**	**2**	**0**	**0**	**0**	**14:04**
2001-02	**Ottawa**	**NHL**	**72**	**22**	**28**	**50**	**66**	**9**	**0**	**6**	**145**	**15.2**	**–7**	**15**	**40.0**	**14:46**	**12**	**2**	**5**	**7**	**14**	**2**	**0**	**2**	**16:19**
	Czech Republic	Olympics	4	3	1	4	27	....	....	....	....	....	....	....	....	....	....	....	....	....	....	....	....	....	....
2002-03	**Ottawa**	**NHL**	**67**	**24**	**35**	**59**	**30**	**9**	**0**	**4**	**179**	**13.4**	**20**	**7**	**14.3**	**16:27**	**18**	**5**	**6**	**11**	**14**	**1**	**0**	**2**	**16:27**
2003-04	HC Sparta Praha	CzRep	5	1	3	4	8	....	....	....	....	....	....	....	....	....	....	....	....	....	....	....	....	....	....
	Ottawa	**NHL**	**68**	**31**	**37**	**68**	**46**	**13**	**0**	**7**	**175**	**17.7**	**12**	**11**	**36.4**	**16:44**	**7**	**0**	**3**	**3**	**2**	**0**	**0**	**0**	**16:10**
2004-05	Znojmo	CzRep	12	10	4	14	16	....	....	....	....	....	....	....	....	....	....	....	....	....	....	....	....	....	....
	Dynamo Moscow	Russia	10	2	0	2	14	....	....	....	....	....	....	....	....	....	....	....	....	....	....	....	....	....	....
	HC Sparta Praha	CzRep	9	5	4	9	37	....	....	....	....	....	....	....	....	....	5	0	0	0	20	....	....	....	....
2005-06	**Ottawa**	**NHL**	**18**	**9**	**7**	**16**	**4**	**2**	**1**	**1**	**57**	**15.8**	**6**	**25**	**36.0**	**18:11**	**10**	**7**	**6**	**13**	**4**	**3**	**0**	**1**	**17:13**
2006-07	**Chicago**	**NHL**	**56**	**25**	**32**	**57**	**28**	**5**	**0**	**1**	**176**	**14.2**	**15**	**12**	**33.3**	**21:24**	....	....	....	....	....	....	....	....	....
2007-08	**Chicago**	**NHL**	**35**	**10**	**17**	**27**	**22**	**3**	**0**	**2**	**87**	**11.5**	**4**	**3**	**0.0**	**18:35**	....	....	....	....	....	....	....	....	....
	NHL Totals		**389**	**140**	**179**	**319**	**216**	**48**	**1**	**26**	**952**	**14.7**		**113**	**31.9**	**16:40**	**51**	**14**	**20**	**34**	**36**	**6**	**0**	**5**	**16:21**

NHL All-Rookie Team (2001)

Played in NHL All-Star Game (2007)

Signed as a free agent by **Znojmo** (CzRep), September 24, 2004. Signed as a free agent by **Dynamo Moscow** (Russia), November 10, 2004. Signed as a free agent by **Sparta Praha** (CzRep), January 31, 2005. • Missed majority of 2005-06 season recovering from shoulder injury suffered in game vs. Montreal, November 29, 2005. Traded to **Chicago** by **Ottawa** with Bryan Smolinski for Tom Preissing, Josh Hennessy, Michal Barinka and Chicago's 2nd round choice (Patrick Wiercioch) in 2008 Entry Draft, July 10, 2006. • Missed majority of 2007-08 season recovering from shoulder (October 4, 2007 at Minnesota) and groin (December 22, 2007 at Ottawa) injuries.

HAYDAR, Darren

(HAY-duhr, DAIR-ehn) **DET.**

Right wing. Shoots right. 5'9", 170 lbs. Born, Toronto, Ont., October 22, 1979. Nashville's 14th choice, 248th overall, in 1999 Entry Draft.

			Regular Season														Playoffs								
Season	Club	League	GP	G	A	Pts	PIM	PP	SH	GW	S	%	+/-	TF	F%	Min	GP	G	A	Pts	PIM	PP	SH	GW	Min
1995-96	Milton Merchants	OPJHL	6	1	2	3	4																		
1996-97	Milton Merchants	OPJHL	51	32	68	100	68																		
1997-98	Milton Merchants	OPJHL	51	*71	*69	*140	65																		
1998-99	New Hampshire	H-East	41	31	30	61	34																		
99-2000	New Hampshire	H-East	38	22	19	41	42																		
2000-01	New Hampshire	H-East	39	18	23	41	38																		
2001-02	New Hampshire	H-East	40	31	*45	*76	28																		
2002-03	**Nashville**	**NHL**	2	0	0	0	0	0	0	0	1	0.0	–1	0	0.0	8:54									
	Milwaukee	AHL	75	29	46	75	36										6	1	4	5	2				
2003-04	Milwaukee	AHL	79	22	37	59	35										22	*11	15	*26	10				
2004-05	Milwaukee	AHL	59	24	26	50	42										7	3	4	7	14				
2005-06	Milwaukee	AHL	80	35	57	92	50										21	*18	17	*35	18				
2006-07	**Atlanta**	**NHL**	4	0	0	0	0	0	0	0	4	0.0	0	3	66.7	8:01									
	Chicago Wolves	AHL	73	41	*81	*122	55										15	*10	*14	*24	14				
2007-08	**Atlanta**	**NHL**	16	1	7	8	2	0	0	0	14	7.1	4	2	0.0	11:46									
	Chicago Wolves	AHL	51	19	39	58	52										24	*12	15	27	8				
	NHL Totals		22	1	7	8	2	0	0	0	19	5.3		5	40.0	10:49									

Hockey East Second All-Star Team (1999, 2000) • Hockey East Rookie of the Year (1999) • Hockey East First All-Star Team (2002) • Hockey East Player of the Year (2002) • AHL All-Rookie Team (2003) • Dudley "Red" Garrett Memorial Award (Rookie of the Year – AHL) (2003) • AHL First All-Star Team (2007) • John P. Sollenberger Trophy (Top Scorer - AHL) (2007) • Les Cunningham Award (MVP - AHL) (2007)

Signed as a free agent by **Atlanta**, July 4, 2006. Signed as a free agent by **Detroit**, July 23, 2008.

HEALEY, Eric

(HEE-lee, AIR-ihk)

Left wing. Shoots left. 5'11", 201 lbs. Born, Hull, MA, January 20, 1975.

Season	Club	League	GP	G	A	Pts	PIM	PP	SH	GW	S	%	+/-	TF	F%	Min	GP	G	A	Pts	PIM	PP	SH	GW	Min
1993-94	New England	NEJHL	37	61	76	137																			
1994-95	RPI Engineers	ECAC	37	13	11	24	35																		
1995-96	RPI Engineers	ECAC	35	18	22	40	57																		
1996-97	RPI Engineers	ECAC	36	30	26	56	63																		
1997-98	RPI Engineers	ECAC	35	21	27	48	42																		
1998-99	Saint John Flames	AHL	64	14	24	38	77																		
	Orlando	IHL	13	5	4	9	13										8	1	0	1	12				
99-2000	Springfield	AHL	32	14	15	29	51										1	0	0	0	2				
2000-01	Springfield	AHL	66	16	17	33	53																		
2001-02	Jackson Bandits	ECHL	2	1	1	2	0																		
	Manchester	AHL	65	24	34	58	45										5	2	2	4	8				
2002-03	Manchester	AHL	75	*42	31	73	47										3	1	0	1	2				
2003-04	Chicago Wolves	AHL	71	31	20	51	52										10	3	6	9	10				
2004-05	Adler Mannheim	Germany	50	16	13	29	54										13	2	4	6	12				
2005-06	**Boston**	**NHL**	2	0	0	0	2	0	0	0	1	0.0	0	0	0.0	8:28									
	Providence Bruins	AHL	66	29	42	71	49										5	2	3	5	0				
2006-07	Springfield	AHL	80	27	48	75	51																		
2007-08	Lake Erie	AHL	74	22	36	58	48																		
	NHL Totals		2	0	0	0	2	0	0	0	1	0.0		0	0.0	8:28									

ECAC Second All-Star Team (1997) • NCAA East Second All-American Team (1997, 1998) • ECAC First All-Star Team (1998) • Fred T. Hunt Memorial Award (Sportsmanship – AHL) (2003) (co-winner - Chris Ferraro)

Signed as a free agent by **Calgary**, September 22, 1998. Signed as a free agent by **Phoenix**, July 26, 1999. Signed to a PTO (tryout) contract by **Manchester** (AHL), September 30, 2001. Signed as a free agent by **Atlanta**, August 12, 2003. Signed as a free agent by **Mannheim** (Germany), July 9, 2004. Signed as a free agent by **Boston**, August 15, 2005. Signed as a free agent by **Tampa Bay**, July 15, 2006. Signed as a free agent by **Colorado**, July 13, 2007.

HEATLEY, Dany

(HEET-lee, DA-nee) **OTT.**

Left wing. Shoots left. 6'3", 220 lbs. Born, Freiburg, West Germany, January 21, 1981. Atlanta's 1st choice, 2nd overall, in 2000 Entry Draft.

Season	Club	League	GP	G	A	Pts	PIM	PP	SH	GW	S	%	+/-	TF	F%	Min	GP	G	A	Pts	PIM	PP	SH	GW	Min
1996-97	Calgary Blazers	AMHL	25	30	42	72	26																		
1997-98	Calgary Buffaloes	AMHL	36	39	42	*81	34										10	10	12	*22	30				
1998-99	Calgary Canucks	AJHL	60	*70	56	*126	91										13	*22	13	*35	6				
99-2000	U. of Wisconsin	WCHA	38	28	28	56	32																		
2000-01	U. of Wisconsin	WCHA	39	24	33	57	74																		
2001-02	**Atlanta**	**NHL**	82	26	41	67	56	7	0	4	202	12.9	–19	116	32.8	19:53									
2002-03	**Atlanta**	**NHL**	77	41	48	89	58	19	1	6	252	16.3	–8	49	36.7	21:57									
2003-04	**Atlanta**	**NHL**	31	13	12	25	18	5	0	3	83	15.7	–8	41	24.4	19:53									
2004-05	SC Bern	Swiss	16	14	10	24	58																		
	Ak Bars Kazan	Russia	11	3	1	4	22										4	2	1	3	4				
2005-06	**Ottawa**	**NHL**	82	50	53	103	86	23	2	7	300	16.7	29	166	53.6	21:09	10	3	9	12	11	3	0	1	18:56
	Canada	Olympics	6	2	1	3	8																		
2006-07	**Ottawa**	**NHL**	82	50	55	105	74	17	3	10	310	16.1	31	60	38.3	21:02	20	7	*15	*22	14	2	0	2	21:18
2007-08	**Ottawa**	**NHL**	71	41	41	82	76	13	0	8	224	18.3	33	26	57.7	21:44	4	0	1	1	6	0	0	0	21:41
	NHL Totals		425	221	250	471	368	84	6	38	1371	16.1		458	42.1	21:02	34	10	25	35	31	5	0	3	20:39

WCHA First All-Star Team (2000) • WCHA Rookie of the Year (2000) • NCAA West Second All-American Team (2000) • WCHA Second All-Star Team (2001) • NCAA West First All-American Team (2001) • NHL All-Rookie Team (2002) • Calder Memorial Trophy (2002) • NHL Second All-Star Team (2006) • NHL First All-Star Team (2007)

Played in NHL All-Star Game (2003, 2007)

• Missed majority of 2003-04 season recovering from injuries suffered in automobile accident, September 29, 2003. Signed as a free agent by **Bern** (Swiss), October 13, 2004. Signed as a free agent by **Kazan** (Russia), February 9, 2005. Traded to **Ottawa** by **Atlanta** for Marian Hossa and Greg de Vries, August 23, 2005.

HECHT, Jochen

(HEHKHT, YOH-khehn) **BUF.**

Left wing. Shoots left. 6'1", 196 lbs. Born, Mannheim, West Germany, June 21, 1977. St. Louis' 1st choice, 49th overall, in 1995 Entry Draft.

Season	Club	League	GP	G	A	Pts	PIM	PP	SH	GW	S	%	+/-	TF	F%	Min	GP	G	A	Pts	PIM	PP	SH	GW	Min
1993-94	Mannheim Jr.	Ger-Jr.	28	27	13	40	103																		
1994-95	Adler Mannheim	Germany	43	11	12	23	68										10	5	4	9	12				
1995-96	Adler Mannheim	Germany	44	12	16	28	68										8	3	2	5	6				
1996-97	Adler Mannheim	Germany	46	21	21	42	36										9	3	3	6	4				
1997-98	Adler Mannheim	Germany	44	7	19	26	42										10	1	1	2	14				
	Adler Mannheim	EuroHL	5	0	4	4	8																		
	Germany	Olympics	4	1	0	1	6																		
1998-99	**St. Louis**	**NHL**	3	0	0	0	0	0	0	0	4	0.0	–2	19	21.1	13:16	5	2	0	2	0	0	0	0	16:40
	Worcester IceCats	AHL	74	21	35	56	48										4	1	1	2	2				
99-2000	**St. Louis**	**NHL**	63	13	21	34	28	5	0	1	140	9.3	20	75	49.3	15:25	7	4	6	10	2	1	0	1	17:02
2000-01	**St. Louis**	**NHL**	72	19	25	44	48	8	3	1	208	9.1	11	160	43.8	17:56	15	2	4	6	4	0	0	0	17:19
2001-02	**Edmonton**	**NHL**	82	16	24	40	60	5	0	3	211	7.6	4	26	53.9	15:00									
	Germany	Olympics	4	1	1	2	2																		
2002-03	**Buffalo**	**NHL**	49	10	16	26	30	2	0	2	145	6.9	4	33	30.3	17:55									
2003-04	**Buffalo**	**NHL**	64	15	37	52	49	2	1	0	174	8.6	17	141	43.3	19:00									
2004-05	Adler Mannheim	Germany	48	16	34	50	151										14	10	10	*20	14				
2005-06	**Buffalo**	**NHL**	64	18	24	42	34	4	2	4	179	10.1	10	156	39.7	18:07	15	2	6	8	8	0	0	1	17:29
2006-07	**Buffalo**	**NHL**	76	19	37	56	39	3	0	1	197	9.6	19	145	39.3	18:51	16	4	1	5	10	0	0	1	17:41
2007-08	**Buffalo**	**NHL**	75	22	27	49	38	3	1	2	229	9.6	1	905	42.0	19:19									
	NHL Totals		548	132	211	343	326	32	7	14	1487	8.9		1660	41.9	17:38	58	14	17	31	24	1	0	3	17:22

Traded to **Edmonton** by **St. Louis** with Marty Reasoner and Jan Horacek for Doug Weight and Michel Riesen, July 1, 2001. Traded to **Buffalo** by **Edmonton** for Atlanta's 2nd round choice (previously acquired, Edmonton selected Jeff Deslauriers) in 2002 Entry Draft and Nashville's 2nd round choice (previously acquired, Edmonton selected Jarret Stoll) in 2002 Entry Draft, June 22, 2002. Signed as a free agent by **Mannheim** (Germany), August 2, 2004.

HEDICAN, Bret

(HEH-dih-kan, BREHT)

Defense. Shoots left. 6'2", 210 lbs. Born, St. Paul, MN, August 10, 1970. St. Louis' 10th choice, 198th overall, in 1988 Entry Draft.

			Regular Season														Playoffs								
Season	Club	League	GP	G	A	Pts	PIM	PP	SH	GW	S	%	+/-	TF	F%	Min	GP	G	A	Pts	PIM	PP	SH	GW	Min
1987-88	North St. Paul	High-MN	23	15	19	34	16	....	....	....	....	....	....	....	....	....	....	....	....	....	....	....	....	....	....
1988-89	St. Cloud State	NCAA-3	28	5	3	8	28	....	....	....	....	....	....	....	....	....	....	....	....	....	....	....	....	....	....
1989-90	St. Cloud State	NCAA-3	36	4	17	21	37	....	....	....	....	....	....	....	....	....	....	....	....	....	....	....	....	....	....
1990-91	St. Cloud State	WCHA	41	21	26	47	26	....	....	....	....	....	....	....	....	....	....	....	....	....	....	....	....	....	....
1991-92	United States	Nat-Tm	54	1	8	9	59	....	....	....	....	....	....	....	....	....	....	....	....	....	....	....	....	....	....
	United States	Olympics	8	0	0	0	4	....	....	....	....	....	....	....	....	....	....	....	....	....	....	....	....	....	....
	St. Louis	**NHL**	**4**	**1**	**0**	**1**	**0**	**0**	**0**	**0**	**1**	**100.0**	**1**	....	....	....	**5**	**0**	**0**	**0**	**0**	**0**	**0**	**0**	....
1992-93	**St. Louis**	**NHL**	**42**	**0**	**8**	**8**	**30**	**0**	**0**	**0**	**40**	**0.0**	**–2**	....	....	....	**10**	**0**	**0**	**0**	**14**	**0**	**0**	**0**	....
	Peoria Rivermen	IHL	19	0	8	8	10	....	....	....	....	....	....	....	....	....	....	....	....	....	....	....	....	....	....
1993-94	**St. Louis**	**NHL**	**61**	**0**	**11**	**11**	**64**	**0**	**0**	**0**	**78**	**0.0**	**–8**	....	....	....	....	....	....	....	....	....	....	....	....
	Vancouver	**NHL**	**8**	**0**	**1**	**1**	**0**	**0**	**0**	**0**	**10**	**0.0**	**1**	....	....	....	**24**	**1**	**6**	**7**	**16**	**0**	**0**	**0**	....
1994-95	**Vancouver**	**NHL**	**45**	**2**	**11**	**13**	**34**	**0**	**0**	**0**	**56**	**3.6**	**–3**	....	....	....	**11**	**0**	**2**	**2**	**6**	**0**	**0**	**0**	....
1995-96	**Vancouver**	**NHL**	**77**	**6**	**23**	**29**	**83**	**1**	**0**	**0**	**113**	**5.3**	**8**	....	....	....	**6**	**0**	**1**	**1**	**10**	**0**	**0**	**0**	....
1996-97	**Vancouver**	**NHL**	**67**	**4**	**15**	**19**	**51**	**2**	**0**	**1**	**93**	**4.3**	**–3**	....	....	....	....	....	....	....	....	....	....	....	....
1997-98	**Vancouver**	**NHL**	**71**	**3**	**24**	**27**	**79**	**1**	**0**	**0**	**84**	**3.6**	**3**	....	....	....	....	....	....	....	....	....	....	....	....
1998-99	**Vancouver**	**NHL**	**42**	**2**	**11**	**13**	**34**	**0**	**2**	**0**	**52**	**3.8**	**7**	**0**	**0.0**	**18:40**	....	....	....	....	....	....	....	....	....
	Florida	**NHL**	**25**	**3**	**7**	**10**	**17**	**0**	**0**	**1**	**38**	**7.9**	**–2**	**0**	**0.0**	**22:24**	....	....	....	....	....	....	....	....	....
99-2000	**Florida**	**NHL**	**76**	**6**	**19**	**25**	**68**	**2**	**0**	**1**	**58**	**10.3**	**4**	**0**	**0.0**	**19:36**	**4**	**0**	**0**	**0**	**0**	**0**	**0**	**0**	**20:42**
2000-01	**Florida**	**NHL**	**70**	**5**	**15**	**20**	**72**	**4**	**0**	**1**	**104**	**4.8**	**–7**	**0**	**0.0**	**21:49**	....	....	....	....	....	....	....	....	....
2001-02	**Florida**	**NHL**	**31**	**3**	**7**	**10**	**12**	**0**	**0**	**0**	**46**	**6.5**	**–4**	**0**	**0.0**	**24:27**	....	....	....	....	....	....	....	....	....
	Carolina	**NHL**	**26**	**2**	**4**	**6**	**10**	**0**	**0**	**1**	**39**	**5.1**	**3**	**0**	**0.0**	**22:56**	**23**	**1**	**4**	**5**	**20**	**0**	**0**	**0**	**23:52**
2002-03	**Carolina**	**NHL**	**72**	**3**	**14**	**17**	**75**	**1**	**0**	**1**	**113**	**2.7**	**–24**	**0**	**0.0**	**23:02**	....	....	....	....	....	....	....	....	....
2003-04	**Carolina**	**NHL**	**81**	**7**	**17**	**24**	**64**	**2**	**0**	**3**	**112**	**6.3**	**–10**	**0**	**0.0**	**22:35**	....	....	....	....	....	....	....	....	....
2004-05			DID NOT PLAY																						
2005-06 ♦	**Carolina**	**NHL**	**74**	**5**	**22**	**27**	**58**	**2**	**1**	**1**	**73**	**6.8**	**11**	**0**	**0.0**	**20:19**	**25**	**2**	**9**	**11**	**42**	**0**	**0**	**0**	**22:40**
	United States	Olympics	6	0	1	1	6	....	....	....	....	....	....	....	....	....	....	....	....	....	....	....	....	....	....
2006-07	**Carolina**	**NHL**	**50**	**0**	**10**	**10**	**36**	**0**	**0**	**0**	**44**	**0.0**	**–8**	**0**	**0.0**	**19:58**	....	....	....	....	....	....	....	....	....
2007-08	**Carolina**	**NHL**	**66**	**2**	**15**	**17**	**70**	**0**	**0**	**0**	**80**	**2.5**	**17**	**0**	**0.0**	**19:18**	....	....	....	....	....	....	....	....	....
	NHL Totals		**988**	**54**	**234**	**288**	**857**	**15**	**3**	**10**	**1234**	**4.4**		**0**	**0.0**	**21:10**	**108**	**4**	**22**	**26**	**108**	**0**	**0**	**0**	**23:03**

WCHA First All-Star Team (1991)

Traded to **Vancouver** by **St. Louis** with Jeff Brown and Nathan LaFayette for Craig Janney, March 21, 1994. Traded to **Florida** by **Vancouver** with Pavel Bure, Brad Ference and Vancouver's 3rd round choice (Robert Fried) in 2000 Entry Draft for Ed Jovanovski, Dave Gagner, Mike Brown, Kevin Weekes and Florida's 1st round choice (Nathan Smith) in 2000 Entry Draft, January 17, 1999. Traded to **Carolina** by **Florida** with Kevyn Adams and Tomas Malec for Sandis Ozolinsh and Byron Ritchie, January 16, 2002.

HEJDA, Jan

(HAY-dah, YAHN) **CBJ**

Defense. Shoots left. 6'3", 229 lbs. Born, Prague, Czech., June 18, 1978. Buffalo's 4th choice, 106th overall, in 2003 Entry Draft.

Season	Club	League	GP	G	A	Pts	PIM	PP	SH	GW	S	%	+/-	TF	F%	Min	GP	G	A	Pts	PIM	PP	SH	GW	Min
1997-98	HC Slavia Praha	CzRep	44	2	5	7	51	....	....	....	....	....	....	....	....	....	5	0	0	0	6	....	....	....	....
1998-99	HC Slavia Praha	CzRep	34	1	2	3	38	....	....	....	....	....	....	....	....	....	....	....	....	....	....	....	....	....	....
99-2000	HC Slavia Praha	CzRep	26	1	2	3	14	....	....	....	....	....	....	....	....	....	....	....	....	....	....	....	....	....	....
	HC Femax Havirov	CzRep	7	0	2	2	6	....	....	....	....	....	....	....	....	....	....	....	....	....	....	....	....	....	....
	Liberec	CzRep-2	1	0	0	0	4	....	....	....	....	....	....	....	....	....	....	....	....	....	....	....	....	....	....
2000-01	HC Slavia Praha	CzRep	38	2	6	8	70	....	....	....	....	....	....	....	....	....	11	3	0	3	12	....	....	....	....
	SK Kadan	CzRep-2	8	1	0	1	6	....	....	....	....	....	....	....	....	....	....	....	....	....	....	....	....	....	....
2001-02	HC Slavia Praha	CzRep	42	9	8	17	52	....	....	....	....	....	....	....	....	....	9	1	1	2	14	....	....	....	....
2002-03	HC Slavia Praha	CzRep	52	6	11	17	44	....	....	....	....	....	....	....	....	....	17	5	8	13	12	....	....	....	....
2003-04	CSKA Moscow	Russia	60	1	5	6	26	....	....	....	....	....	....	....	....	....	....	....	....	....	....	....	....	....	....
2004-05	CSKA Moscow	Russia	60	2	11	13	59	....	....	....	....	....	....	....	....	....	....	....	....	....	....	....	....	....	....
2005-06	Mytischi	Russia	50	3	12	15	56	....	....	....	....	....	....	....	....	....	9	2	3	5	24	....	....	....	....
2006-07	**Edmonton**	**NHL**	**39**	**1**	**8**	**9**	**20**	**0**	**0**	**1**	**33**	**3.0**	**–6**	**0**	**0.0**	**20:23**	....	....	....	....	....	....	....	....	....
	Hamilton	AHL	5	0	3	3	21	....	....	....	....	....	....	....	....	....	....	....	....	....	....	....	....	....	....
2007-08	**Columbus**	**NHL**	**81**	**0**	**13**	**13**	**61**	**0**	**0**	**0**	**71**	**0.0**	**20**	**0**	**0.0**	**21:08**	....	....	....	....	....	....	....	....	....
	NHL Totals		**120**	**1**	**21**	**22**	**81**	**0**	**0**	**1**	**104**	**1.0**		**0**	**0.0**	**20:53**	....	....	....	....	....	....	....	....	....

Rights traded to **Edmonton** by **Buffalo** for Edmonton's 7th round choice (Nick Eno) in 2007 Entry Draft, July 10, 2006. Signed as a free agent by **Columbus**, July 5, 2007.

HEJDUK, Milan

(HAY-dook, MEE-lan) **COL.**

Right wing. Shoots right. 6', 190 lbs. Born, Usti nad Labem, Czech., February 14, 1976. Quebec's 6th choice, 87th overall, in 1994 Entry Draft.

Season	Club	League	GP	G	A	Pts	PIM	PP	SH	GW	S	%	+/-	TF	F%	Min	GP	G	A	Pts	PIM	PP	SH	GW	Min
1993-94	HC Pardubice	CzRep	22	6	3	9	....	....	....	....	....	....	....	....	....	....	10	5	1	6	....	....	....	....	....
1994-95	HC Pardubice	CzRep	43	11	13	24	6	....	....	....	....	....	....	....	....	....	6	3	1	4	0	....	....	....	....
1995-96	Pardubice	CzRep	37	13	7	20	....	....	....	....	....	....	....	....	....	....	....	....	....	....	....	....	....	....	....
1996-97	Pardubice	CzRep	51	27	11	38	10	....	....	....	....	....	....	....	....	....	10	6	0	6	27	....	....	....	....
1997-98	Pardubice	CzRep	48	26	19	45	20	....	....	....	....	....	....	....	....	....	3	0	0	0	2	....	....	....	....
	Czech Republic	Olympics	4	0	0	0	2	....	....	....	....	....	....	....	....	....	....	....	....	....	....	....	....	....	....
1998-99	**Colorado**	**NHL**	**82**	**14**	**34**	**48**	**26**	**4**	**0**	**5**	**178**	**7.9**	**8**	**2**	**50.0**	**15:45**	**16**	**6**	**6**	**12**	**4**	**1**	**0**	**3**	**15:53**
99-2000	**Colorado**	**NHL**	**82**	**36**	**36**	**72**	**16**	**13**	**0**	**9**	**228**	**15.8**	**14**	**3**	**100.0**	**19:58**	**17**	**5**	**4**	**9**	**6**	**3**	**0**	**1**	**19:56**
2000-01 ♦	**Colorado**	**NHL**	**80**	**41**	**38**	**79**	**36**	**12**	**1**	**9**	**213**	**19.2**	**32**	**3**	**33.3**	**19:52**	**23**	**7**	***16**	**23**	**6**	**4**	**0**	**1**	**21:33**
2001-02	**Colorado**	**NHL**	**62**	**21**	**23**	**44**	**24**	**7**	**1**	**5**	**139**	**15.1**	**0**	**5**	**40.0**	**20:11**	**16**	**3**	**3**	**6**	**4**	**1**	**0**	**0**	**18:24**
	Czech Republic	Olympics	4	1	0	1	0	....	....	....	....	....	....	....	....	....	....	....	....	....	....	....	....	....	....
2002-03	**Colorado**	**NHL**	**82**	***50**	**48**	**98**	**32**	**18**	**0**	**4**	**244**	**20.5**	**52**	**43**	**44.2**	**19:50**	**7**	**2**	**2**	**4**	**2**	**1**	**0**	**0**	**20:42**
2003-04	**Colorado**	**NHL**	**82**	**35**	**40**	**75**	**20**	**16**	**0**	**6**	**237**	**14.8**	**19**	**69**	**47.8**	**18:46**	**11**	**5**	**2**	**7**	**0**	**2**	**0**	**0**	**18:40**
2004-05	Pardubice	CzRep	48	25	26	51	14	....	....	....	....	....	....	....	....	....	16	6	2	8	6	....	....	....	....
2005-06	**Colorado**	**NHL**	**74**	**24**	**34**	**58**	**24**	**14**	**1**	**2**	**221**	**10.9**	**13**	**23**	**17.4**	**18:33**	**9**	**2**	**6**	**8**	**2**	**0**	**0**	**0**	**20:56**
	Czech Republic	Olympics	8	2	1	3	2	....	....	....	....	....	....	....	....	....	....	....	....	....	....	....	....	....	....
2006-07	**Colorado**	**NHL**	**80**	**35**	**35**	**70**	**44**	**12**	**1**	**6**	**257**	**13.6**	**10**	**109**	**45.0**	**17:53**	....	....	....	....	....	....	....	....	....
2007-08	**Colorado**	**NHL**	**77**	**29**	**25**	**54**	**36**	**8**	**1**	**4**	**205**	**14.1**	**8**	**136**	**39.7**	**19:21**	**10**	**3**	**3**	**6**	**4**	**2**	**0**	**0**	**19:05**
	NHL Totals		**701**	**285**	**313**	**598**	**258**	**104**	**5**	**50**	**1922**	**14.8**		**393**	**42.2**	**18:52**	**109**	**33**	**42**	**75**	**28**	**14**	**0**	**5**	**19:23**

NHL All-Rookie Team (1999) • NHL Second All-Star Team (2003) • Bud Light Plus/Minus Award (2003) (tied with Peter Forsberg) • Maurice "Rocket" Richard Trophy (2003)

Played in NHL All-Star Game (2000, 2001)

Rights transferred to **Colorado** after **Quebec** franchise relocated, June 21, 1995. Signed as a free agent by **Pardubice** (CzRep), September 18, 2004.

HELM, Darren

(HEHLM, DAIR-ehn) **DET.**

Center/Left wing. Shoots left. 5'11", 172 lbs. Born, Winnipeg, Man., January 21, 1987. Detroit's 5th choice, 132nd overall, in 2005 Entry Draft.

Season	Club	League	GP	G	A	Pts	PIM	PP	SH	GW	S	%	+/-	TF	F%	Min	GP	G	A	Pts	PIM	PP	SH	GW	Min
2003-04	Selkirk Fishermen	MJBHL	34	39	32	71	34	....	....	....	....	....	....	....	....	....	....	....	....	....	....	....	....	....	....
2004-05	Medicine Hat	WHL	72	10	14	24	27	....	....	....	....	....	....	....	....	....	13	2	6	8	10	....	....	....	....
2005-06	Medicine Hat	WHL	70	41	38	79	37	....	....	....	....	....	....	....	....	....	13	5	4	9	2	....	....	....	....
2006-07	Medicine Hat	WHL	59	25	39	64	53	....	....	....	....	....	....	....	....	....	23	10	12	22	14	....	....	....	....
2007-08 ♦	**Detroit**	**NHL**	**7**	**0**	**0**	**0**	**2**	**0**	**0**	**0**	**7**	**0.0**	**–2**	**23**	**21.7**	**7:00**	**18**	**2**	**2**	**4**	**2**	**0**	**0**	**0**	**7:30**
	Grand Rapids	AHL	67	16	15	31	30	....	....	....	....	....	....	....	....	....	....	....	....	....	....	....	....	....	....
	NHL Totals		**7**	**0**	**0**	**0**	**2**	**0**	**0**	**0**	**7**	**0.0**		**23**	**21.7**	**7:00**	**18**	**2**	**2**	**4**	**2**	**0**	**0**	**0**	**7:30**

WHL East First All-Star Team (2006) • WHL East Second All-Star Team (2007) • Memorial Cup Tournament All-Star Team (2007)

HELMER, Bryan

(HEHL-muhr, BRIGH-uhn)

Defense. Shoots right. 6'1", 208 lbs. Born, Sault Ste. Marie, Ont., July 15, 1972.

Season	Club	League	GP	G	A	Pts	PIM	PP	SH	GW	S	%	+/-	TF	F%	Min	GP	G	A	Pts	PIM	PP	SH	GW	Min
1989-90	Wellington Dukes	OHA-B	44	4	20	24	204	....	....	....	....	....	....	....	....	....	....	....	....	....	....	....	....	....	....
	Belleville Bulls	OHL	6	0	1	1	0	....	....	....	....	....	....	....	....	....	....	....	....	....	....	....	....	....	....
1990-91	Wellington Dukes	OHA-B	50	11	14	25	109	....	....	....	....	....	....	....	....	....	....	....	....	....	....	....	....	....	....
1991-92	Wellington Dukes	MTJHL	42	17	31	48	66	....	....	....	....	....	....	....	....	....	3	2	1	3	0	....	....	....	....
1992-93	Wellington Dukes	MTJHL	48	21	54	75	84	....	....	....	....	....	....	....	....	....	9	4	8	12	22	....	....	....	....
1993-94	Albany River Rats	AHL	65	4	19	23	79	....	....	....	....	....	....	....	....	....	5	0	0	0	9	....	....	....	....
1994-95	Albany River Rats	AHL	77	7	36	43	101	....	....	....	....	....	....	....	....	....	7	1	0	1	0	....	....	....	....
1995-96	Albany River Rats	AHL	80	14	30	44	107	....	....	....	....	....	....	....	....	....	4	2	0	2	6	....	....	....	....
1996-97	Albany River Rats	AHL	77	12	27	39	113	....	....	....	....	....	....	....	....	....	16	1	7	8	10	....	....	....	....
1997-98	Albany River Rats	AHL	80	14	49	63	101	....	....	....	....	....	....	....	....	....	13	4	9	13	18	....	....	....	....

			Regular Season														Playoffs								
Season	Club	League	GP	G	A	Pts	PIM	PP	SH	GW	S	%	+/-	TF	F%	Min	GP	G	A	Pts	PIM	PP	SH	GW	Min
1998-99	**Phoenix**	**NHL**	**11**	**0**	**0**	**0**	**23**	**0**	**0**	**0**	**11**	**0.0**	**2**	**0**	**0.0**	**7:43**	....	....	....	....	....	....	....	....	....
	Las Vegas	IHL	8	1	3	4	28	....	....	....	....	....	....	....	....	....	....	....	....	....	....	....	....	....	....
	St. Louis	**NHL**	**29**	**0**	**4**	**4**	**19**	**0**	**0**	**0**	**38**	**0.0**	**3**	**1**	**100.0**	**19:08**	....	....	....	....	....	....	....	....	....
	Worcester IceCats	AHL	16	7	8	15	18	....	....	....	....	....	....	....	....	....	4	0	0	0	12	....	....	....	....
99-2000	**St. Louis**	**NHL**	**15**	**1**	**1**	**2**	**10**	**1**	**0**	**1**	**19**	**5.3**	**-3**	**0**	**0.0**	**16:15**	....	....	....	....	....	....	....	....	....
	Worcester IceCats	AHL	54	10	25	35	124	....	....	....	....	....	....	....	....	....	9	1	4	5	10	....	....	....	....
2000-01	**Vancouver**	**NHL**	**20**	**2**	**4**	**6**	**18**	**0**	**0**	**0**	**28**	**7.1**	**0**	**0**	**0.0**	**16:51**	....	....	....	....	....	....	....	....	....
	Kansas City	IHL	42	4	15	19	76	....	....	....	....	....	....	....	....	....	....	....	....	....	....	....	....	....	....
2001-02	**Vancouver**	**NHL**	**40**	**5**	**5**	**10**	**53**	**2**	**0**	**1**	**43**	**11.6**	**10**	**0**	**0.0**	**12:04**	**6**	**0**	**0**	**0**	**0**	**0**	**0**	**0**	**9:09**
	Manitoba Moose	AHL	34	6	18	24	69	....	....	....	....	....	....	....	....	....	....	....	....	....	....	....	....	....	....
2002-03	**Vancouver**	**NHL**	**2**	**0**	**0**	**0**	**0**	**0**	**0**	**0**	**2**	**0.0**	**1**	**0**	**0.0**	**13:24**	....	....	....	....	....	....	....	....	....
	Manitoba Moose	AHL	60	7	24	31	82	....	....	....	....	....	....	....	....	....	14	0	4	4	20	....	....	....	....
2003-04	**Phoenix**	**NHL**	**17**	**0**	**1**	**1**	**10**	**0**	**0**	**0**	**10**	**0.0**	**-5**	**0**	**0.0**	**12:46**	....	....	....	....	....	....	....	....	....
	Springfield	AHL	9	1	6	7	6	....	....	....	....	....	....	....	....	....	....	....	....	....	....	....	....	....	....
2004-05	Grand Rapids	AHL	80	7	18	25	64	....	....	....	....	....	....	....	....	....	....	....	....	....	....	....	....	....	....
2005-06	Grand Rapids	AHL	80	12	44	56	138	....	....	....	....	....	....	....	....	....	16	1	8	9	24	....	....	....	....
2006-07	San Antonio	AHL	70	6	23	29	81	....	....	....	....	....	....	....	....	....	....	....	....	....	....	....	....	....	....
2007-08	San Antonio	AHL	66	5	15	20	53	....	....	....	....	....	....	....	....	....	7	0	0	0	6	....	....	....	....
	NHL Totals		**134**	**8**	**15**	**23**	**133**	**3**	**0**	**2**	**151**	**5.3**		**1**	**100.0**	**14:32**	**6**	**0**	**0**	**0**	**0**	**0**	**0**	**0**	**9:09**

AHL First All-Star Team (1998) • AHL Second All-Star Team (2006)

Signed as a free agent by **New Jersey**, July 10, 1994. Signed as a free agent by **Phoenix**, July 17, 1998. Claimed on waivers by **St. Louis** from **Phoenix**, December 19, 1998. Signed as a free agent by **Vancouver**, August 21, 2000. Traded to **Phoenix** by **Vancouver** for Martin Grenier, July 25, 2003. • Missed majority of 2003-04 season recovering from shoulder injury suffered in training camp, September 29, 2003. Signed as a free agent by **Detroit**, July 21, 2004. Signed as a free agent by **Phoenix**, July 19, 2006.

HEMSKY, Ales

(HEHM-skee, ahl-EHSH) **EDM.**

Right wing. Shoots right. 6', 192 lbs. Born, Pardubice, Czech., August 13, 1983. Edmonton's 1st choice, 13th overall, in 2001 Entry Draft.

Season	Club	League	GP	G	A	Pts	PIM	PP	SH	GW	S	%	+/-	TF	F%	Min	GP	G	A	Pts	PIM	PP	SH	GW	Min
99-2000	HC Pardubice Jr.	CzRep-Jr.	45	20	36	56	54	....	....	....	....	....	....	....	....	....	7	4	14	18	36	....	....	....	....
	Pardubice	CzRep	4	0	1	1	0	....	....	....	....	....	....	....	....	....	....	....	....	....	....	....	....	....	....
2000-01	Hull Olympiques	QMJHL	68	36	64	100	67	....	....	....	....	....	....	....	....	....	5	2	3	5	2	....	....	....	....
2001-02	Hull Olympiques	QMJHL	53	27	70	97	86	....	....	....	....	....	....	....	....	....	10	6	10	16	6	....	....	....	....
2002-03	**Edmonton**	**NHL**	**59**	**6**	**24**	**30**	**14**	**0**	**0**	**1**	**50**	**12.0**	**5**	**3**	**33.3**	**12:04**	**6**	**0**	**0**	**0**	**0**	**0**	**0**	**0**	**12:46**
2003-04	**Edmonton**	**NHL**	**71**	**12**	**22**	**34**	**14**	**4**	**0**	**3**	**87**	**13.8**	**-7**	**3**	**33.3**	**14:26**	....	....	....	....	....	....	....	....	....
2004-05	Pardubice	CzRep	47	13	18	31	28	....	....	....	....	....	....	....	....	....	16	4	*10	*14	26	....	....	....	....
2005-06	**Edmonton**	**NHL**	**81**	**19**	**58**	**77**	**64**	**7**	**1**	**4**	**178**	**10.7**	**-5**	**7**	**42.9**	**16:59**	**24**	**6**	**11**	**17**	**14**	**4**	**0**	**2**	**16:06**
	Czech Republic	Olympics	8	1	2	3	2	....	....	....	....	....	....	....	....	....	....	....	....	....	....	....	....	....	....
2006-07	**Edmonton**	**NHL**	**64**	**13**	**40**	**53**	**40**	**5**	**0**	**1**	**122**	**10.7**	**-7**	**10**	**30.0**	**16:59**	....	....	....	....	....	....	....	....	....
2007-08	**Edmonton**	**NHL**	**74**	**20**	**51**	**71**	**34**	**8**	**0**	**2**	**184**	**10.9**	**-9**	**5**	**20.0**	**18:35**	....	....	....	....	....	....	....	....	....
	NHL Totals		**349**	**70**	**195**	**265**	**166**	**24**	**1**	**11**	**621**	**11.3**		**28**	**32.1**	**15:58**	**30**	**6**	**11**	**17**	**14**	**4**	**0**	**2**	**15:26**

QMJHL Second All-Star Team (2002)

Signed as a free agent by **Pardubice** (CzRep), September 18, 2004.

HENDRY, Jordan

(HEHN-dree, JOHR-dahn) **CHI.**

Defense. Shoots left. 6', 196 lbs. Born, Nokomis, Sask., February 23, 1984.

Season	Club	League	GP	G	A	Pts	PIM	PP	SH	GW	S	%	+/-	TF	F%	Min	GP	G	A	Pts	PIM	PP	SH	GW	Min
2002-03	Alaska	CCHA	35	3	5	8	10	....	....	....	....	....	....	....	....	....	....	....	....	....	....	....	....	....	....
2003-04	Alaska	CCHA	36	4	9	13	38	....	....	....	....	....	....	....	....	....	....	....	....	....	....	....	....	....	....
2004-05	Alaska	CCHA	3	0	1	1	21	....	....	....	....	....	....	....	....	....	....	....	....	....	....	....	....	....	....
2005-06	Alaska	CCHA	38	4	10	14	74	....	....	....	....	....	....	....	....	....	....	....	....	....	....	....	....	....	....
	Norfolk Admirals	AHL	13	1	4	5	13	....	....	....	....	....	....	....	....	....	3	0	0	0	2	....	....	....	....
2006-07	Norfolk Admirals	AHL	80	4	12	16	84	....	....	....	....	....	....	....	....	....	6	0	2	2	6	....	....	....	....
2007-08	**Chicago**	**NHL**	**40**	**1**	**3**	**4**	**22**	**0**	**0**	**0**	**32**	**3.1**	**0**	**0**	**0.0**	**17:13**	....	....	....	....	....	....	....	....	....
	Rockford IceHogs	AHL	45	3	4	7	58	....	....	....	....	....	....	....	....	....	1	0	0	0	2	....	....	....	....
	NHL Totals		**40**	**1**	**3**	**4**	**22**	**0**	**0**	**0**	**32**	**3.1**		**0**	**0.0**	**17:13**	....	....	....	....	....	....	....	....	....

Signed as a free agent by **Chicago**, July 17, 2006.

HENNESSY, Josh

(HEHN-eh-see, JAWSH) **OTT.**

Center. Shoots left. 6', 192 lbs. Born, Brockton, MA, February 7, 1985. San Jose's 3rd choice, 43rd overall, in 2003 Entry Draft.

Season	Club	League	GP	G	A	Pts	PIM	PP	SH	GW	S	%	+/-	TF	F%	Min	GP	G	A	Pts	PIM	PP	SH	GW	Min
2000-01	Milton Academy	High-MA	28	20	30	50	20	....	....	....	....	....	....	....	....	....	....	....	....	....	....	....	....	....	....
2001-02	Quebec Remparts	QMJHL	70	20	20	40	24	....	....	....	....	....	....	....	....	....	9	3	9	12	8	....	....	....	....
2002-03	Quebec Remparts	QMJHL	72	33	51	84	44	....	....	....	....	....	....	....	....	....	11	6	9	15	10	....	....	....	....
2003-04	Quebec Remparts	QMJHL	59	40	42	82	55	....	....	....	....	....	....	....	....	....	....	....	....	....	....	....	....	....	....
2004-05	Quebec Remparts	QMJHL	68	35	50	85	39	....	....	....	....	....	....	....	....	....	12	2	9	11	6	....	....	....	....
2005-06	Cleveland Barons	AHL	80	24	39	63	60	....	....	....	....	....	....	....	....	....	....	....	....	....	....	....	....	....	....
2006-07	**Ottawa**	**NHL**	**10**	**1**	**0**	**1**	**4**	**0**	**0**	**0**	**6**	**16.7**	**0**	**43**	**37.2**	**5:39**	....	....	....	....	....	....	....	....	....
	Binghamton	AHL	76	27	30	57	54	....	....	....	....	....	....	....	....	....	....	....	....	....	....	....	....	....	....
2007-08	**Ottawa**	**NHL**	**5**	**0**	**0**	**0**	**0**	**0**	**0**	**0**	**2**	**0.0**	**-1**	**12**	**41.7**	**3:46**	....	....	....	....	....	....	....	....	....
	Binghamton	AHL	76	22	29	51	49	....	....	....	....	....	....	....	....	....	....	....	....	....	....	....	....	....	....
	NHL Totals		**15**	**1**	**0**	**1**	**4**	**0**	**0**	**0**	**8**	**12.5**		**55**	**38.2**	**5:01**	....	....	....	....	....	....	....	....	....

Traded to **Chicago** by **San Jose** with Tom Preissing for Mark Bell, July 9, 2006. Traded to **Ottawa** by **Chicago** with Tom Preissing, Michal Barinka and Chicago's 2nd round choice (Patrick Wiercioch) in 2008 Entry Draft for Martin Havlat and Bryan Smolinski, July 10, 2006.

HENRY, Alex

(HEHN-ree, AL-ehx) **MTL.**

Defense. Shoots left. 6'5", 220 lbs. Born, Elliot Lake, Ont., October 18, 1979. Edmonton's 2nd choice, 67th overall, in 1998 Entry Draft.

Season	Club	League	GP	G	A	Pts	PIM	PP	SH	GW	S	%	+/-	TF	F%	Min	GP	G	A	Pts	PIM	PP	SH	GW	Min
1995-96	Timmins Majors	NOHA	30	4	11	15	6	....	....	....	....	....	....	....	....	....	....	....	....	....	....	....	....	....	....
	Timmins	NOJHA	2	0	0	0	0	....	....	....	....	....	....	....	....	....	....	....	....	....	....	....	....	....	....
1996-97	London Knights	OHL	61	1	10	11	65	....	....	....	....	....	....	....	....	....	....	....	....	....	....	....	....	....	....
1997-98	London Knights	OHL	62	5	9	14	97	....	....	....	....	....	....	....	....	....	16	0	3	3	14	....	....	....	....
1998-99	London Knights	OHL	68	5	23	28	105	....	....	....	....	....	....	....	....	....	25	3	10	13	22	....	....	....	....
99-2000	Hamilton	AHL	60	1	0	1	69	....	....	....	....	....	....	....	....	....	....	....	....	....	....	....	....	....	....
2000-01	Hamilton	AHL	56	2	3	5	87	....	....	....	....	....	....	....	....	....	....	....	....	....	....	....	....	....	....
2001-02	Hamilton	AHL	69	4	8	12	143	....	....	....	....	....	....	....	....	....	15	1	2	3	16	....	....	....	....
2002-03	**Edmonton**	**NHL**	**3**	**0**	**0**	**0**	**0**	**0**	**0**	**0**	**0**	**0.0**	**-1**	**0**	**0.0**	**7:02**	....	....	....	....	....	....	....	....	....
	Washington	**NHL**	**38**	**0**	**0**	**0**	**80**	**0**	**0**	**0**	**8**	**0.0**	**-4**	**1**	**0.0**	**3:39**	....	....	....	....	....	....	....	....	....
	Portland Pirates	AHL	3	0	1	1	0	....	....	....	....	....	....	....	....	....	....	....	....	....	....	....	....	....	....
2003-04	**Minnesota**	**NHL**	**71**	**2**	**4**	**6**	**106**	**0**	**0**	**0**	**37**	**5.4**	**4**	**2**	**0.0**	**14:53**	....	....	....	....	....	....	....	....	....
2004-05	ESV Kaufbeuren	German-2	26	6	6	12	32	....	....	....	....	....	....	....	....	....	....	....	....	....	....	....	....	....	....
2005-06	**Minnesota**	**NHL**	**63**	**0**	**5**	**5**	**73**	**0**	**0**	**0**	**41**	**0.0**	**-4**	**2**	**50.0**	**11:26**	....	....	....	....	....	....	....	....	....
2006-07	Milwaukee	AHL	64	1	6	7	66	....	....	....	....	....	....	....	....	....	2	0	0	0	7	....	....	....	....
2007-08	Milwaukee	AHL	80	3	13	16	142	....	....	....	....	....	....	....	....	....	6	0	1	1	10	....	....	....	....
	NHL Totals		**175**	**2**	**9**	**11**	**259**	**0**	**0**	**0**	**86**	**2.3**		**5**	**20.0**	**11:04**	....	....	....	....	....	....	....	....	....

Claimed on waivers by **Washington** from **Edmonton**, October 24, 2002. Claimed on waivers by **Minnesota** from **Washington**, October 9, 2003. Signed as a free agent by **Kaufbeuren** (German-2), January 15, 2005. Signed as a free agent by **Nashville**, August 22, 2006. Signed as a free agent by **Montreal**, July 3, 2008.

HENSICK, T.J.

(HEHN-sihk, TEE-JAY) **COL.**

Center. Shoots right. 5'10", 185 lbs. Born, Lansing, MI, December 10, 1985. Colorado's 5th choice, 88th overall, in 2005 Entry Draft.

Season	Club	League	GP	G	A	Pts	PIM	PP	SH	GW	S	%	+/-	TF	F%	Min	GP	G	A	Pts	PIM	PP	SH	GW	Min
2001-02	USNTDP	U-17	17	10	5	15	....	....	....	....	....	....	....	....	....	....	....	....	....	....	....	....	....	....	....
	USNTDP	NAHL	46	15	25	40	10	....	....	....	....	....	....	....	....	....	....	....	....	....	....	....	....	....	....
2002-03	USNTDP	U-18	48	24	24	48	11	....	....	....	....	....	....	....	....	....	....	....	....	....	....	....	....	....	....
	USNTDP	NAHL	10	6	7	13	0	....	....	....	....	....	....	....	....	....	....	....	....	....	....	....	....	....	....
2003-04	U. of Michigan	CCHA	43	12	*34	46	38	....	....	....	....	....	....	....	....	....	....	....	....	....	....	....	....	....	....
2004-05	U. of Michigan	CCHA	39	23	32	55	24	....	....	....	....	....	....	....	....	....	....	....	....	....	....	....	....	....	....
2005-06	U. of Michigan	CCHA	41	17	35	52	44	....	....	....	....	....	....	....	....	....	....	....	....	....	....	....	....	....	....
2006-07	U. of Michigan	CCHA	41	23	*46	*69	38	....	....	....	....	....	....	....	....	....	....	....	....	....	....	....	....	....	....

			Regular Season														Playoffs								
Season	Club	League	GP	G	A	Pts	PIM	PP	SH	GW	S	%	+/-	TF	F%	Min	GP	G	A	Pts	PIM	PP	SH	GW	Min
2007-08	**Colorado**	**NHL**	**31**	**6**	**5**	**11**	**2**	**4**	**0**	**1**	**52**	**11.5**	**–4**	**256**	**42.2**	**11:59**	**2**	**0**	**1**	**1**	**0**	**0**	**0**	**0**	**15:29**
	Lake Erie	AHL	50	12	33	45	18	....	....	....	....	....	....	....	....	....	....	....	....	....	....	....	....	....	....
	NHL Totals		**31**	**6**	**5**	**11**	**2**	**4**	**0**	**1**	**52**	**11.5**		**256**	**42.2**	**11:59**	**2**	**0**	**1**	**1**	**0**	**0**	**0**	**0**	**15:29**

CCHA All-Rookie Team (2004) • CCHA First All-Star Team (2004, 2005, 2007) • CCHA Rookie of the Year (2004) • NCAA West First All-American Team (2005, 2007) • CCHA Second All-Star Team (2006)

HEWARD, Jamie

(HEW-uhrd, JAY-mee)

Defense. Shoots right. 6'2", 215 lbs. Born, Regina, Sask., March 30, 1971. Pittsburgh's 1st choice, 16th overall, in 1989 Entry Draft.

1987-88	Regina Pats	WHL	68	10	17	27	17	....	....	....	....	....	....	....	....	....	4	1	1	2	2	....	....	....	....
1988-89	Regina Pats	WHL	52	31	28	59	29	....	....	....	....	....	....	....	....	....	....	....	....	....	....	....	....	....	....
1989-90	Regina Pats	WHL	72	14	44	58	42	....	....	....	....	....	....	....	....	....	11	2	2	4	10	....	....	....	....
1990-91	Regina Pats	WHL	71	23	61	84	41	....	....	....	....	....	....	....	....	....	8	2	9	11	6	....	....	....	....
1991-92	Muskegon	IHL	54	6	21	27	37	....	....	....	....	....	....	....	....	....	14	1	4	5	4	....	....	....	....
1992-93	Cleveland	IHL	58	9	18	27	64	....	....	....	....	....	....	....	....	....	....	....	....	....	....	....	....	....	....
1993-94	Cleveland	IHL	73	8	16	24	72	....	....	....	....	....	....	....	....	....	....	....	....	....	....	....	....	....	....
1994-95	Canada	Nat-Tm	51	11	35	46	32	....	....	....	....	....	....	....	....	....	....	....	....	....	....	....	....	....	....
1995-96	**Toronto**	**NHL**	**5**	**0**	**0**	**0**	**0**	**0**	**0**	**0**	**8**	**0.0**	**–1**	....	....	....	....	....	....	....	....	....	....	....	....
	St. John's	AHL	73	22	34	56	33	....	....	....	....	....	....	....	....	....	3	1	1	2	6	....	....	....	....
1996-97	**Toronto**	**NHL**	**20**	**1**	**4**	**5**	**6**	**0**	**0**	**0**	**23**	**4.3**	**–6**	....	....	....	....	....	....	....	....	....	....	....	....
	St. John's	AHL	27	8	19	27	26	....	....	....	....	....	....	....	....	....	9	1	3	4	6	....	....	....	....
1997-98	Philadelphia	AHL	72	17	48	65	54	....	....	....	....	....	....	....	....	....	20	3	16	19	10	....	....	....	....
1998-99	**Nashville**	**NHL**	**63**	**6**	**12**	**18**	**44**	**4**	**0**	**1**	**124**	**4.8**	**–24**	**0**	**0.0**	**16:12**	....	....	....	....	....	....	....	....	....
99-2000	**NY Islanders**	**NHL**	**54**	**6**	**11**	**17**	**26**	**2**	**0**	**1**	**92**	**6.5**	**–9**	**0**	**0.0**	**19:58**	....	....	....	....	....	....	....	....	....
2000-01	**Columbus**	**NHL**	**69**	**11**	**16**	**27**	**33**	**9**	**0**	**1**	**108**	**10.2**	**3**	**0**	**0.0**	**14:21**	....	....	....	....	....	....	....	....	....
2001-02	**Columbus**	**NHL**	**28**	**1**	**2**	**3**	**7**	**0**	**0**	**0**	**38**	**2.6**	**–9**	**1**	**100.0**	**14:04**	....	....	....	....	....	....	....	....	....
	Syracuse Crunch	AHL	14	3	10	13	6	....	....	....	....	....	....	....	....	....	10	0	4	4	6	....	....	....	....
2002-03	Geneve	Swiss	40	8	23	31	60	....	....	....	....	....	....	....	....	....	6	1	1	2	22	....	....	....	....
2003-04	ZSC Lions Zurich	Swiss	25	5	9	14	57	....	....	....	....	....	....	....	....	....	6	0	1	1	24	....	....	....	....
2004-05	Langnau	Swiss	44	3	14	17	91	....	....	....	....	....	....	....	....	....	5	0	0	0	40	....	....	....	....
2005-06	**Washington**	**NHL**	**71**	**7**	**21**	**28**	**54**	**4**	**0**	**2**	**140**	**5.0**	**–5**	**1**	**0.0**	**21:52**	....	....	....	....	....	....	....	....	....
2006-07	**Washington**	**NHL**	**52**	**4**	**12**	**16**	**27**	**2**	**0**	**1**	**50**	**8.0**	**4**	**0**	**0.0**	**16:22**	....	....	....	....	....	....	....	....	....
	Los Angeles	**NHL**	**19**	**2**	**6**	**8**	**20**	**1**	**0**	**0**	**25**	**8.0**	**–2**	**0**	**0.0**	**19:44**	....	....	....	....	....	....	....	....	....
2007-08	St. Petersburg	Russia	53	2	15	17	98	....	....	....	....	....	....	....	....	....	9	2	0	2	10	....	....	....	....
	NHL Totals		**381**	**38**	**84**	**122**	**217**	**22**	**0**	**6**	**608**	**6.3**		**2**	**50.0**	**17:35**	....	....	....	....	....	....	....	....	....

WHL East First All-Star Team (1991) • AHL First All-Star Team (1996, 1998) • Eddie Shore Award (Outstanding Defenseman – AHL) (1998)

Signed as a free agent by **Toronto**, May 4, 1995. Signed as a free agent by **Philadelphia**, July 31, 1997. Signed as a free agent by **Nashville**, August 10, 1998. Signed as a free agent by **NY Islanders**, July 27, 1999. Claimed on waivers by **Columbus** from **NY Islanders**, May 26, 2000. Signed as a free agent by **Geneve** (Swiss), April 17, 2000. Signed as a free agent by **Washington**, August 12, 2005. Traded to **Los Angeles** by **Washington** for future considerations, February 27, 2007. Signed as a free agent by **St. Petersburg** (Russia), August 13, 2007.

HIGGINS, Christopher

(HIH-gihns, KRIHS-toh-fuhr) **MTL.**

Center. Shoots left. 6', 199 lbs. Born, Smithtown, NY, June 2, 1983. Montreal's 1st choice, 14th overall, in 2002 Entry Draft.

99-2000	Avon Old Farms	High-CT	27	19	20	39	10	....	....	....	....	....	....	....	....	....	....	....	....	....	....	....	....	....	....
2000-01	Avon Old Farms	High-CT	24	22	14	36	29	....	....	....	....	....	....	....	....	....	....	....	....	....	....	....	....	....	....
2001-02	Yale	ECAC	27	14	17	31	32	....	....	....	....	....	....	....	....	....	....	....	....	....	....	....	....	....	....
2002-03	Yale	ECAC	28	20	21	41	41	....	....	....	....	....	....	....	....	....	....	....	....	....	....	....	....	....	....
2003-04	**Montreal**	**NHL**	**2**	**0**	**0**	**0**	**0**	**0**	**0**	**0**	**0**	**0.0**	**0**	**9**	**22.2**	**6:18**	....	....	....	....	....	....	....	....	....
	Hamilton	AHL	67	21	27	48	18	....	....	....	....	....	....	....	....	....	10	3	2	5	0	....	....	....	....
2004-05	Hamilton	AHL	76	28	23	51	33	....	....	....	....	....	....	....	....	....	4	3	3	6	4	....	....	....	....
2005-06	**Montreal**	**NHL**	**80**	**23**	**15**	**38**	**26**	**7**	**3**	**3**	**148**	**15.5**	**–1**	**45**	**51.1**	**14:25**	**6**	**1**	**3**	**4**	**0**	**0**	**0**	**0**	**17:04**
2006-07	**Montreal**	**NHL**	**61**	**22**	**16**	**38**	**26**	**8**	**3**	**3**	**159**	**13.8**	**–11**	**53**	**34.0**	**17:54**	....	....	....	....	....	....	....	....	....
2007-08	**Montreal**	**NHL**	**82**	**27**	**25**	**52**	**22**	**12**	**0**	**5**	**241**	**11.2**	**0**	**62**	**35.5**	**17:57**	**12**	**3**	**2**	**5**	**2**	**0**	**0**	**0**	**18:27**
	NHL Totals		**225**	**72**	**56**	**128**	**74**	**27**	**6**	**11**	**548**	**13.1**		**169**	**38.5**	**16:35**	**18**	**4**	**5**	**9**	**2**	**0**	**0**	**0**	**17:59**

ECAC All-Rookie Team (2002) • ECAC Second All-Star Team (2002) • ECAC Rookie of the Year (2002) • ECAC First All-Star Team (2003) • ECAC Player of the Year (2003) (co-winner - David LeNeveu) • NCAA East First All-American Team (2003)

HILBERT, Andy

(HIHL-buhrt, AN-dee) **NYI**

Center/Left wing. Shoots left. 5'11", 194 lbs. Born, Lansing, MI, February 6, 1981. Boston's 3rd choice, 37th overall, in 2000 Entry Draft.

1997-98	USNTDP	U-17	29	14	10	24	34	....	....	....	....	....	....	....	....	....	....	....	....	....	....	....	....	....	....
	USNTDP	NAHL	39	19	16	35	102	....	....	....	....	....	....	....	....	....	7	1	4	5	12	....	....	....	....
1998-99	USNTDP	U-18	6	6	1	7	4	....	....	....	....	....	....	....	....	....	....	....	....	....	....	....	....	....	....
	USNTDP	USHL	46	23	35	58	140	....	....	....	....	....	....	....	....	....	....	....	....	....	....	....	....	....	....
99-2000	U. of Michigan	CCHA	35	17	15	32	39	....	....	....	....	....	....	....	....	....	....	....	....	....	....	....	....	....	....
2000-01	U. of Michigan	CCHA	42	26	38	64	72	....	....	....	....	....	....	....	....	....	....	....	....	....	....	....	....	....	....
2001-02	**Boston**	**NHL**	**6**	**1**	**0**	**1**	**2**	**0**	**0**	**0**	**11**	**9.1**	**–2**	**4**	**50.0**	**11:34**	....	....	....	....	....	....	....	....	....
	Providence Bruins	AHL	72	26	27	53	74	....	....	....	....	....	....	....	....	....	2	0	0	0	2	....	....	....	....
2002-03	**Boston**	**NHL**	**14**	**0**	**3**	**3**	**7**	**0**	**0**	**0**	**22**	**0.0**	**–1**	**34**	**44.1**	**11:30**	....	....	....	....	....	....	....	....	....
	Providence Bruins	AHL	64	35	35	70	119	....	....	....	....	....	....	....	....	....	4	0	1	1	4	....	....	....	....
2003-04	**Boston**	**NHL**	**18**	**2**	**0**	**2**	**9**	**0**	**0**	**0**	**27**	**7.4**	**1**	**11**	**54.6**	**8:57**	**5**	**1**	**0**	**1**	**0**	**0**	**0**	**0**	**5:32**
	Providence Bruins	AHL	19	3	5	8	20	....	....	....	....	....	....	....	....	....	....	....	....	....	....	....	....	....	....
2004-05	Providence Bruins	AHL	79	37	42	79	83	....	....	....	....	....	....	....	....	....	17	7	*14	*21	27	....	....	....	....
2005-06	**Chicago**	**NHL**	**28**	**5**	**4**	**9**	**22**	**0**	**0**	**1**	**50**	**10.0**	**–4**	**21**	**38.1**	**10:05**	....	....	....	....	....	....	....	....	....
	Norfolk Admirals	AHL	5	3	4	7	2	....	....	....	....	....	....	....	....	....	....	....	....	....	....	....	....	....	....
	Pittsburgh	**NHL**	**19**	**7**	**11**	**18**	**16**	**3**	**0**	**1**	**51**	**13.7**	**8**	**146**	**38.4**	**17:27**	....	....	....	....	....	....	....	....	....
2006-07	**NY Islanders**	**NHL**	**81**	**8**	**20**	**28**	**34**	**0**	**0**	**1**	**164**	**4.9**	**10**	**128**	**52.3**	**11:30**	**5**	**0**	**0**	**0**	**2**	**0**	**0**	**0**	**8:08**
2007-08	**NY Islanders**	**NHL**	**70**	**8**	**8**	**16**	**18**	**0**	**0**	**0**	**127**	**6.3**	**2**	**220**	**45.0**	**13:29**	....	....	....	....	....	....	....	....	....
	NHL Totals		**236**	**31**	**46**	**77**	**108**	**3**	**0**	**3**	**452**	**6.9**		**564**	**44.9**	**12:12**	**10**	**1**	**0**	**1**	**2**	**0**	**0**	**0**	**6:50**

CCHA First All-Star Team (2001) • NCAA West First All-American Team (2001) • AHL All-Rookie Team (2002) • AHL Second All-Star Team (2005)

• Missed majority of 2003-04 season recovering from groin injury suffered in pre-season game vs. Detroit, September 15, 2003. Traded to **Chicago** by **Boston** for Chicago's 5th round choice (later traded to NY Islanders - NY Islanders selected Shane Sims) in 2006 Entry Draft, November 6, 2005. Claimed on waivers by **Pittsburgh** from **Chicago**, March 9, 2006. Signed as a free agent by **NY Islanders**, July 4, 2006.

HILL, Sean

(HIHL, SHAWN)

Defense. Shoots right. 6', 204 lbs. Born, Duluth, MN, February 14, 1970. Montreal's 9th choice, 167th overall, in 1988 Entry Draft.

1986-87	Lakefield Chiefs	OHA-C	3	1	1	2	14	....	....	....	....	....	....	....	....	....	....	....	....	....	....	....	....	....	....
1987-88	Duluth East	High-MN	24	10	17	27	....	....	....	....	....	....	....	....	....	....	....	....	....	....	....	....	....	....	....
1988-89	U. of Wisconsin	WCHA	45	2	23	25	69	....	....	....	....	....	....	....	....	....	....	....	....	....	....	....	....	....	....
1989-90	U. of Wisconsin	WCHA	42	14	39	53	78	....	....	....	....	....	....	....	....	....	....	....	....	....	....	....	....	....	....
1990-91	U. of Wisconsin	WCHA	37	19	32	51	122	....	....	....	....	....	....	....	....	....	....	....	....	....	....	....	....	....	....
	Montreal	**NHL**	....	....	....	....	....	....	....	....	....	....	....	....	....	....	**1**	**0**	**0**	**0**	**0**	**0**	**0**	**0**	....
	Fredericton	AHL	....	....	....	....	....	....	....	....	....	....	....	....	....	....	3	0	2	2	2	....	....	....	....
1991-92	Fredericton	AHL	42	7	20	27	65	....	....	....	....	....	....	....	....	....	7	1	3	4	6	....	....	....	....
	United States	Nat-Tm	12	4	3	7	16	....	....	....	....	....	....	....	....	....	....	....	....	....	....	....	....	....	....
	United States	Olympics	8	2	0	2	6	....	....	....	....	....	....	....	....	....	....	....	....	....	....	....	....	....	....
	Montreal	**NHL**	....	....	....	....	....	....	....	....	....	....	....	....	....	....	**4**	**1**	**0**	**1**	**2**	**0**	**0**	**0**	....
1992-93 ♦	**Montreal**	**NHL**	**31**	**2**	**6**	**8**	**54**	**1**	**0**	**1**	**37**	**5.4**	**–5**	....	....	....	**3**	**0**	**0**	**0**	**4**	**0**	**0**	**0**	....
	Fredericton	AHL	6	1	3	4	10	....	....	....	....	....	....	....	....	....	....	....	....	....	....	....	....	....	....
1993-94	**Anaheim**	**NHL**	**68**	**7**	**20**	**27**	**78**	**2**	**1**	**1**	**165**	**4.2**	**–12**	....	....	....	....	....	....	....	....	....	....	....	....
1994-95	**Ottawa**	**NHL**	**45**	**1**	**14**	**15**	**30**	**0**	**0**	**0**	**107**	**0.9**	**–11**	....	....	....	....	....	....	....	....	....	....	....	....
1995-96	**Ottawa**	**NHL**	**80**	**7**	**14**	**21**	**94**	**2**	**0**	**2**	**157**	**4.5**	**–26**	....	....	....	....	....	....	....	....	....	....	....	....
1996-97	**Ottawa**	**NHL**	**5**	**0**	**0**	**0**	**4**	**0**	**0**	**0**	**9**	**0.0**	**1**	....	....	....	....	....	....	....	....	....	....	....	....
1997-98	**Ottawa**	**NHL**	**13**	**1**	**1**	**2**	**6**	**0**	**0**	**0**	**16**	**6.3**	**–3**	....	....	....	....	....	....	....	....	....	....	....	....
	Carolina	**NHL**	**42**	**0**	**5**	**5**	**48**	**0**	**0**	**0**	**37**	**0.0**	**–2**	....	....	....	....	....	....	....	....	....	....	....	....
1998-99	**Carolina**	**NHL**	**54**	**0**	**10**	**10**	**48**	**0**	**0**	**0**	**44**	**0.0**	**9**	**0**	**0.0**	**19:02**	....	....	....	....	....	....	....	....	....
99-2000	**Carolina**	**NHL**	**62**	**13**	**31**	**44**	**59**	**8**	**0**	**2**	**150**	**8.7**	**3**	**1**	**0.0**	**24:31**	....	....	....	....	....	....	....	....	....
2000-01	**St. Louis**	**NHL**	**48**	**1**	**10**	**11**	**51**	**0**	**0**	**0**	**47**	**2.1**	**5**	**1**	**0.0**	**17:23**	**15**	**0**	**1**	**1**	**12**	**0**	**0**	**0**	**13:46**
2001-02	**St. Louis**	**NHL**	**23**	**0**	**3**	**3**	**28**	**0**	**0**	**0**	**29**	**0.0**	**1**	**0**	**0.0**	**15:56**	....	....	....	....	....	....	....	....	....
	Carolina	**NHL**	**49**	**7**	**23**	**30**	**61**	**4**	**0**	**2**	**116**	**6.0**	**–1**	**1**	**0.0**	**23:58**	**23**	**4**	**4**	**8**	**20**	**4**	**0**	**1**	**25:55**

			Regular Season														Playoffs								
Season	Club	League	GP	G	A	Pts	PIM	PP	SH	GW	S	%	+/-	TF	F%	Min	GP	G	A	Pts	PIM	PP	SH	GW	Min
2002-03	**Carolina**	**NHL**	**82**	**5**	**24**	**29**	**141**	**1**	**0**	**0**	**188**	**2.7**	**4**	**1**	**0.0**	**24:21**	....	....	....	....	....	....	....	....	....
2003-04	**Carolina**	**NHL**	**80**	**13**	**26**	**39**	**84**	**6**	**0**	**1**	**228**	**5.7**	**–2**	**2**	**50.0**	**25:24**	....	....	....	....	....	....	....	....	....
2004-05			DID NOT PLAY																						
2005-06	**Florida**	**NHL**	**78**	**2**	**18**	**20**	**80**	**1**	**0**	**0**	**110**	**1.8**	**3**	**0**	**0.0**	**20:09**	....	....	....	....	....	....	....	....	....
2006-07	**NY Islanders**	**NHL**	**81**	**1**	**24**	**25**	**110**	**0**	**0**	**0**	**88**	**1.1**	**6**	**0**	**0.0**	**22:33**	**4**	**0**	**0**	**0**	**0**	**0**	**0**	**0**	**18:38**
2007-08	**Minnesota**	**NHL**	**35**	**2**	**7**	**9**	**32**	**1**	**0**	**1**	**18**	**11.1**	**–16**	**0**	**0.0**	**15:12**	**5**	**0**	**0**	**0**	**4**	**0**	**0**	**0**	**10:53**
	NHL Totals		**876**	**62**	**236**	**298**	**1008**	**26**	**1**	**10**	**1546**	**4.0**		**6**	**16.7**	**21:46**	**55**	**5**	**5**	**10**	**42**	**4**	**0**	**1**	**19:49**

WCHA Second All-Star Team (1990, 1991) • NCAA West Second All-American Team (1991)

Claimed by **Anaheim** from **Montreal** in Expansion Draft, June 24, 1993. Traded to **Ottawa** by **Anaheim** with Anaheim's 9th round choice (Frederic Cassivi) in 1994 Entry Draft for Ottawa's 3rd round choice (later traded to Tampa Bay – Tampa Bay selected Vadim Epanchintsev) in 1994 Entry Draft, June 29, 1994. • Missed remainder of 1996-97 season recovering from knee injury suffered in game vs. New Jersey, October 18, 1996. Traded to **Carolina** by **Ottawa** for Chris Murray, November 18, 1997. Signed as a free agent by **St. Louis**, July 1, 2000. Traded to **Carolina** by **St. Louis** for Steve Halko and Carolina's 4th round choice (later traded to Atlanta – Atlanta selected Lane Manson) in 2002 Entry Draft, December 5, 2001. Signed as a free agent by **Florida**, July 15, 2004. Signed as a free agent by **NY Islanders**, August 15, 2006. Signed as a free agent by **Minnesota**, July 6, 2007. • Suspended 20 games for violating NHL's performance-enhancing substances program, April 19, 2007. Signed as a free agent by **Biel** (Swiss), August 7, 2008.

HILLEN, Jack

(HIHL-uhn, JAK) **NYI**

Defense. Shoots left. 5'10", 190 lbs. Born, Portland, OR, January 24, 1986.

Season	Club	League	GP	G	A	Pts	PIM	PP	SH	GW	S	%	+/-	TF	F%	Min	GP	G	A	Pts	PIM	PP	SH	GW	Min
2003-04	Tri-City Storm	USHL	31	12	32	44	18	....	....	....	....	....	....	....	....	....	....	....	....	....	....	....	....	....	....
2004-05	Colorado College	WCHA	30	2	9	11	20	....	....	....	....	....	....	....	....	....	....	....	....	....	....	....	....	....	....
2005-06	Colorado College	WCHA	42	4	9	13	48	....	....	....	....	....	....	....	....	....	....	....	....	....	....	....	....	....	....
2006-07	Colorado College	WCHA	38	7	8	15	38	....	....	....	....	....	....	....	....	....	....	....	....	....	....	....	....	....	....
2007-08	Colorado College	WCHA	41	6	*31	37	60	....	....	....	....	....	....	....	....	....	....	....	....	....	....	....	....	....	....
	NY Islanders	**NHL**	**2**	**0**	**1**	**1**	**4**	**0**	**0**	**0**	**3**	**0.0**	**1**	**0**	**0.0**	**15:32**	....	....	....	....	....	....	....	....	....
	NHL Totals		**2**	**0**	**1**	**1**	**4**	**0**	**0**	**0**	**3**	**0.0**		**0**	**0.0**	**15:32**	....	....	....	....	....	....	....	....	....

WCHA First All-Star Team (2008) • NCAA West First All-American Team (2008)

Signed as a free agent by **NY Islanders**, April 1, 2008.

HINOTE, Dan

(HIGH-noht, DAN) **ST.L.**

Right wing. Shoots right. 6', 187 lbs. Born, Leesburg, FL, January 30, 1977. Colorado's 9th choice, 167th overall, in 1996 Entry Draft.

Season	Club	League	GP	G	A	Pts	PIM	PP	SH	GW	S	%	+/-	TF	F%	Min	GP	G	A	Pts	PIM	PP	SH	GW	Min
1993-94	Elk River Elks	High-MN	STATISTICS NOT AVAILABLE																						
1994-95	Army	NCAA	33	20	24	44	20	....	....	....	....	....	....	....	....	....	....	....	....	....	....	....	....	....	....
1995-96	Army	NCAA	34	21	24	45	22	....	....	....	....	....	....	....	....	....	....	....	....	....	....	....	....	....	....
1996-97	Oshawa Generals	OHL	60	15	13	28	58	....	....	....	....	....	....	....	....	....	18	4	5	9	8	....	....	....	....
1997-98	Oshawa Generals	OHL	35	12	15	27	39	....	....	....	....	....	....	....	....	....	5	2	2	4	7	....	....	....	....
	Hershey Bears	AHL	24	1	4	5	25	....	....	....	....	....	....	....	....	....	....	....	....	....	....	....	....	....	....
1998-99	Hershey Bears	AHL	65	4	16	20	95	....	....	....	....	....	....	....	....	....	5	3	1	4	6	....	....	....	....
99-2000	**Colorado**	**NHL**	**27**	**1**	**3**	**4**	**10**	**0**	**0**	**0**	**14**	**7.1**	**0**	**132**	**51.5**	**7:51**	....	....	....	....	....	....	....	....	....
	Hershey Bears	AHL	55	28	31	59	96	....	....	....	....	....	....	....	....	....	14	4	5	9	19	....	....	....	....
2000-01 ♦	**Colorado**	**NHL**	**76**	**5**	**10**	**15**	**51**	**1**	**0**	**1**	**69**	**7.2**	**1**	**506**	**49.8**	**10:21**	**23**	**2**	**4**	**6**	**21**	**0**	**0**	**0**	**8:22**
2001-02	**Colorado**	**NHL**	**58**	**6**	**6**	**12**	**39**	**0**	**1**	**3**	**75**	**8.0**	**8**	**267**	**51.3**	**12:27**	**19**	**1**	**2**	**3**	**9**	**0**	**0**	**0**	**10:46**
2002-03	**Colorado**	**NHL**	**60**	**6**	**4**	**10**	**49**	**0**	**0**	**3**	**65**	**9.2**	**4**	**218**	**46.8**	**10:36**	**7**	**1**	**2**	**3**	**2**	**0**	**0**	**0**	**14:19**
2003-04	**Colorado**	**NHL**	**59**	**4**	**7**	**11**	**57**	**0**	**2**	**0**	**53**	**7.5**	**–6**	**151**	**48.3**	**12:42**	**11**	**1**	**0**	**1**	**0**	**0**	**1**	**0**	**13:04**
2004-05	MODO	Sweden	18	2	1	3	106	....	....	....	....	....	....	....	....	....	5	0	0	0	56	....	....	....	....
2005-06	**Colorado**	**NHL**	**73**	**5**	**8**	**13**	**48**	**0**	**1**	**2**	**70**	**7.1**	**–5**	**335**	**42.1**	**10:41**	**9**	**1**	**1**	**2**	**31**	**0**	**0**	**0**	**13:27**
2006-07	**St. Louis**	**NHL**	**41**	**5**	**5**	**10**	**23**	**0**	**0**	**1**	**37**	**13.5**	**–8**	**173**	**49.1**	**13:04**	....	....	....	....	....	....	....	....	....
2007-08	**St. Louis**	**NHL**	**58**	**5**	**5**	**10**	**42**	**0**	**0**	**0**	**42**	**11.9**	**–3**	**33**	**42.4**	**10:31**	....	....	....	....	....	....	....	....	....
	NHL Totals		**452**	**37**	**48**	**85**	**319**	**1**	**4**	**10**	**425**	**8.7**		**1815**	**48.0**	**11:08**	**69**	**6**	**9**	**15**	**63**	**0**	**1**	**0**	**11:02**

Signed as a free agent by **MODO** (Sweden), December 22, 2004. Signed as a free agent by **St. Louis**, July 3, 2006.

HJALMARSSON, Niklas

(H'YAHL-muhr-suhn, NIHK-luhs) **CHI.**

Defense. Shoots left. 6'3", 196 lbs. Born, Eksjo, Sweden, June 6, 1987. Chicago's 5th choice, 108th overall, in 2005 Entry Draft.

Season	Club	League	GP	G	A	Pts	PIM	PP	SH	GW	S	%	+/-	TF	F%	Min	GP	G	A	Pts	PIM	PP	SH	GW	Min
2003-04	HV 71 Jr.	Swe-Jr.	15	1	3	4	14	....	....	....	....	....	....	....	....	....	2	0	0	0	8	....	....	....	....
2004-05	HV 71 U18	Swe-U18	3	0	2	2	4	....	....	....	....	....	....	....	....	....	....	....	....	....	....	....	....	....	....
	HV 71 Jr.	Swe-Jr.	31	4	11	15	87	....	....	....	....	....	....	....	....	....	....	....	....	....	....	....	....	....	....
	HV 71 Jonkoping	Sweden	14	0	0	0	0	....	....	....	....	....	....	....	....	....	....	....	....	....	....	....	....	....	....
2005-06	HV 71 Jr.	Swe-Jr.	7	3	2	5	12	....	....	....	....	....	....	....	....	....	....	....	....	....	....	....	....	....	....
	HV 71 Jonkoping	Sweden	4	1	2	3	0	....	....	....	....	....	....	....	....	....	12	0	1	1	4	....	....	....	....
2006-07	HV 71 Jonkoping	Sweden	37	2	0	2	24	....	....	....	....	....	....	....	....	....	14	1	1	2	0	....	....	....	....
	HV 71 Jr.	Swe-Jr.	7	0	2	2	14	....	....	....	....	....	....	....	....	....	....	....	....	....	....	....	....	....	....
	IK Oskarshamn	Sweden-2	8	1	2	3	6	....	....	....	....	....	....	....	....	....	....	....	....	....	....	....	....	....	....
2007-08	**Chicago**	**NHL**	**13**	**0**	**1**	**1**	**13**	**0**	**0**	**0**	**5**	**0.0**	**–2**	**0**	**0.0**	**13:37**	....	....	....	....	....	....	....	....	....
	Rockford IceHogs	AHL	47	4	9	13	31	....	....	....	....	....	....	....	....	....	12	0	4	4	8	....	....	....	....
	NHL Totals		**13**	**0**	**1**	**1**	**13**	**0**	**0**	**0**	**5**	**0.0**		**0**	**0.0**	**13:37**	....	....	....	....	....	....	....	....	....

HLAVAC, Jan

(huh-LAH-vahch, YAHN)

Left wing. Shoots left. 6', 201 lbs. Born, Prague, Czech., September 20, 1976. NY Islanders' 2nd choice, 28th overall, in 1995 Entry Draft.

Season	Club	League	GP	G	A	Pts	PIM	PP	SH	GW	S	%	+/-	TF	F%	Min	GP	G	A	Pts	PIM	PP	SH	GW	Min
1993-94	Sparta Jr.	CzRep-Jr.	27	12	15	27	....	....	....	....	....	....	....	....	....	....	....	....	....	....	....	....	....	....	....
	HC Sparta Praha	CzRep	9	1	1	2	....	....	....	....	....	....	....	....	....	....	....	....	....	....	....	....	....	....	....
1994-95	HC Sparta Praha	CzRep	38	7	6	13	18	....	....	....	....	....	....	....	....	....	5	0	2	2	0	....	....	....	....
1995-96	HC Sparta Praha	CzRep	34	8	5	13	....	....	....	....	....	....	....	....	....	....	12	1	2	3	....	....	....	....	....
1996-97	HC Sparta Praha	CzRep	38	8	13	21	24	....	....	....	....	....	....	....	....	....	10	5	2	7	2	....	....	....	....
	HC Sparta Praha	EuroHL	3	4	0	4	6	....	....	....	....	....	....	....	....	....	....	....	....	....	....	....	....	....	....
1997-98	HC Sparta Praha	CzRep	48	17	30	47	40	....	....	....	....	....	....	....	....	....	5	1	0	1	2	....	....	....	....
	HC Sparta Praha	EuroHL	5	0	3	3	4	....	....	....	....	....	....	....	....	....	....	....	....	....	....	....	....	....	....
1998-99	HC Sparta Praha	CzRep	49	*33	20	53	52	....	....	....	....	....	....	....	....	....	6	1	3	4	....	....	....	....	....
	HC Sparta Praha	EuroHL	5	4	2	6	0	....	....	....	....	....	....	....	....	....	1	1	1	2	0	....	....	....	....
99-2000	**NY Rangers**	**NHL**	**67**	**19**	**23**	**42**	**16**	**6**	**0**	**2**	**134**	**14.2**	**3**	**6**	**33.3**	**15:09**	....	....	....	....	....	....	....	....	....
	Hartford	AHL	3	1	0	1	0	....	....	....	....	....	....	....	....	....	....	....	....	....	....	....	....	....	....
2000-01	**NY Rangers**	**NHL**	**79**	**28**	**36**	**64**	**20**	**5**	**0**	**6**	**195**	**14.4**	**3**	**0**	**0.0**	**16:38**	....	....	....	....	....	....	....	....	....
2001-02	**Philadelphia**	**NHL**	**31**	**7**	**3**	**10**	**8**	**0**	**0**	**1**	**62**	**11.3**	**5**	**0**	**0.0**	**12:36**	....	....	....	....	....	....	....	....	....
	Vancouver	**NHL**	**46**	**9**	**12**	**21**	**10**	**1**	**0**	**2**	**70**	**12.9**	**4**	**2**	**100.0**	**14:46**	**5**	**0**	**1**	**1**	**0**	**0**	**0**	**0**	**9:38**
2002-03	**Vancouver**	**NHL**	**9**	**1**	**1**	**2**	**6**	**0**	**0**	**0**	**7**	**14.3**	**–1**	**0**	**0.0**	**10:51**	....	....	....	....	....	....	....	....	....
	Carolina	**NHL**	**52**	**9**	**15**	**24**	**22**	**6**	**0**	**1**	**116**	**7.8**	**–9**	**21**	**38.1**	**17:10**	....	....	....	....	....	....	....	....	....
2003-04	**NY Rangers**	**NHL**	**72**	**5**	**21**	**26**	**16**	**2**	**0**	**0**	**125**	**4.0**	**–8**	**7**	**42.9**	**13:52**	....	....	....	....	....	....	....	....	....
2004-05	HC Sparta Praha	CzRep	48	10	28	38	34	....	....	....	....	....	....	....	....	....	5	2	0	2	6	....	....	....	....
2005-06	Geneve	Swiss	42	12	22	34	28	....	....	....	....	....	....	....	....	....	4	1	0	1	2	....	....	....	....
2006-07	HC Sparta Praha	CzRep	41	20	11	31	85	....	....	....	....	....	....	....	....	....	16	8	2	10	16	....	....	....	....
2007-08	**Tampa Bay**	**NHL**	**62**	**9**	**13**	**22**	**32**	**0**	**0**	**0**	**123**	**7.3**	**–10**	**2**	**50.0**	**14:46**	....	....	....	....	....	....	....	....	....
	Nashville	**NHL**	**18**	**3**	**10**	**13**	**8**	**0**	**0**	**2**	**29**	**10.3**	**9**	**6**	**0.0**	**16:29**	**6**	**0**	**2**	**2**	**2**	**0**	**0**	**0**	**18:12**
	NHL Totals		**436**	**90**	**134**	**224**	**138**	**20**	**0**	**14**	**861**	**10.5**		**44**	**36.4**	**15:08**	**11**	**0**	**3**	**3**	**2**	**0**	**0**	**0**	**14:19**

Traded to **Calgary** by **NY Islanders** for Jorgen Jonsson, July 14, 1998. Rights traded to **NY Rangers** by **Calgary** with Calgary's 1st (Jamie Lundmark) and 3rd (later traded back to Calgary – Calgary selected Craig Andersson) round choices in 1999 Entry Draft for Marc Savard and NY Rangers' 1st round choice (Oleg Saprykin) in 1999 Entry Draft, June 26, 1999. Traded to **Philadelphia** by **NY Rangers** with Kim Johnsson, Pavel Brendl and NY Rangers' 3rd round choice (Stefan Ruzicka) in 2003 Entry Draft for Eric Lindros, August 20, 2001. Traded to **Vancouver** by **Philadelphia** with Tampa Bay's 3rd round choice (previously acquired, Vancouver selected Brett Skinner) in 2002 Entry Draft for Donald Brashear and Vancouver's 6th round choice (later traded to Columbus – Columbus selected Jaroslav Balastik) in 2002 Entry Draft, December 17, 2001. Traded to **Carolina** by **Vancouver** with Harold Druken for Darren Langdon and Marek Malik, November 1, 2002. Signed as a free agent by **NY Rangers**, August 28, 2003. Signed as a free agent by **Sparta Praha** (CzRep), August 9, 2004. Signed as a free agent by **Geneve** (Swiss), September, 2005. Signed as a free agent by **Sparta Praha** (CzRep), May 24, 2006. Signed as a free agent by **Tampa Bay**, June 14, 2007. Traded to **Nashville** by **Tampa Bay** for Nashville's 7th round choice (later traded to Philadelphia - Philadelphia selected Joacim Eriksson) in 2008 Entry Draft, February 26, 2008.

HLINKA, Jaroslav

(huh-LIHN-kuh, YAHR-oh-slav)

Center. Shoots left. 5'10", 185 lbs. Born, Prague, Czech., November 10, 1976.

			Regular Season														Playoffs								
Season	Club	League	GP	G	A	Pts	PIM	PP	SH	GW	S	%	+/-	TF	F%	Min	GP	G	A	Pts	PIM	PP	SH	GW	Min
1994-95	HC Sparta Praha	CzRep	4	0	2	2	0	....	....	....	....	....	....	....	....	....	5	1	1	2	0	....	....	....	....
1995-96	Usti n. L.	CzRep-2	3	1	1	2	2	....	....	....	....	....	....	....	....	....	....	....	....	....	....	....	....	....	....
	H+S Beroun	CzRep-2	6	2	1	3	0	....	....	....	....	....	....	....	....	....	....	....	....	....	....	....	....	....	....
	HC Sparta Praha	CzRep	18	3	1	4	6	....	....	....	....	....	....	....	....	....	12	1	4	5	0	....	....	....	....
1996-97	HC Sparta Praha	CzRep	48	8	18	26	12	....	....	....	....	....	....	....	....	....	6	0	0	0	0	....	....	....	....
	Karlovy Vary	CzRep-2	3	1	0	1	0	....	....	....	....	....	....	....	....	....	....	....	....	....	....	....	....	....	....
1997-98	HC Sparta Praha	CzRep	51	18	19	37	24	....	....	....	....	....	....	....	....	....	11	2	6	8	8	....	....	....	....
1998-99	HC Sparta Praha	CzRep	41	9	24	33	22	....	....	....	....	....	....	....	....	....	6	1	2	3	0	....	....	....	....
99-2000	HC Sparta Praha	CzRep	49	20	37	57	51	....	....	....	....	....	....	....	....	....	8	2	3	5	10	....	....	....	....
2000-01	HC Sparta Praha	CzRep	45	12	17	29	28	....	....	....	....	....	....	....	....	....	13	2	9	11	12	....	....	....	....
2001-02	HC Sparta Praha	CzRep	52	16	45	61	54	....	....	....	....	....	....	....	....	....	13	9	6	15	4	....	....	....	....
2002-03	Kloten Flyers	Swiss	41	18	30	48	16	....	....	....	....	....	....	....	....	....	....	....	....	....	....	....	....	....	....
2003-04	Kloten Flyers	Swiss	43	18	23	41	33	....	....	....	....	....	....	....	....	....	8	3	8	11	6	....	....	....	....
2004-05	Ak Bars Kazan	Russia	36	4	16	20	10	....	....	....	....	....	....	....	....	....	1	0	0	0	0	....	....	....	....
2005-06	Kloten Flyers	Swiss	37	12	23	35	18	....	....	....	....	....	....	....	....	....	....	....	....	....	....	....	....	....	....
	HC Sparta Praha	CzRep	9	3	8	11	14	....	....	....	....	....	....	....	....	....	17	10	6	16	10	....	....	....	....
2006-07	HC Sparta Praha	CzRep	46	19	38	57	46	....	....	....	....	....	....	....	....	....	16	4	12	16	38	....	....	....	....
2007-08	**Colorado**	**NHL**	**63**	**8**	**20**	**28**	**16**	**0**	**0**	**1**	**90**	**8.9**	**6**	**383**	**43.6**	**13:56**	**1**	**0**	**0**	**0**	**0**	**0**	**0**	**0**	**15:15**
	NHL Totals		**63**	**8**	**20**	**28**	**16**	**0**	**0**	**1**	**90**	**8.9**		**383**	**43.6**	**13:56**	**1**	**0**	**0**	**0**	**0**	**0**	**0**	**0**	**15:15**

Signed as a free agent by **Colorado**, June 1, 2007.

HNIDY, Shane

(NIGH-dee, SHAYN) **BOS.**

Defense. Shoots right. 6'2", 204 lbs. Born, Brandon, Man., November 8, 1975. Buffalo's 7th choice, 173rd overall, in 1994 Entry Draft.

1990-91	Yellowhead	MMMHL	36	9	11	20	92	....	....	....	....	....	....	....	....	....	....	....	....	....	....	....	....	....	....
1991-92	Swift Current	WHL	56	1	3	4	11	....	....	....	....	....	....	....	....	....	4	0	0	0	0	....	....	....	....
1992-93	Swift Current	WHL	45	5	12	17	62	....	....	....	....	....	....	....	....	....	....	....	....	....	....	....	....	....	....
	Prince Albert	WHL	27	2	10	12	43	....	....	....	....	....	....	....	....	....	....	....	....	....	....	....	....	....	....
1993-94	Prince Albert	WHL	69	7	26	33	113	....	....	....	....	....	....	....	....	....	....	....	....	....	....	....	....	....	....
1994-95	Prince Albert	WHL	72	5	29	34	169	....	....	....	....	....	....	....	....	....	15	4	7	11	29	....	....	....	....
1995-96	Prince Albert	WHL	58	11	42	53	100	....	....	....	....	....	....	....	....	....	18	4	11	15	34	....	....	....	....
1996-97	Baton Rouge	ECHL	21	3	10	13	50	....	....	....	....	....	....	....	....	....	....	....	....	....	....	....	....	....	....
	Saint John Flames	AHL	44	2	12	14	112	....	....	....	....	....	....	....	....	....	....	....	....	....	....	....	....	....	....
1997-98	Grand Rapids	IHL	77	6	12	18	210	....	....	....	....	....	....	....	....	....	3	0	2	2	23	....	....	....	....
1998-99	Adirondack	AHL	68	9	20	29	121	....	....	....	....	....	....	....	....	....	3	0	1	1	0	....	....	....	....
99-2000	Cincinnati	AHL	68	9	19	28	153	....	....	....	....	....	....	....	....	....	....	....	....	....	....	....	....	....	....
2000-01	**Ottawa**	**NHL**	**52**	**3**	**2**	**5**	**84**	**0**	**0**	**1**	**47**	**6.4**	**8**	**0**	**0.0**	**13:05**	**1**	**0**	**0**	**0**	**0**	**0**	**0**	**0**	**13:23**
	Grand Rapids	IHL	2	0	0	0	2	....	....	....	....	....	....	....	....	....	....	....	....	....	....	....	....	....	....
2001-02	**Ottawa**	**NHL**	**33**	**1**	**1**	**2**	**57**	**0**	**0**	**0**	**34**	**2.9**	**–10**	**0**	**0.0**	**16:56**	**12**	**1**	**1**	**2**	**12**	**0**	**0**	**0**	**16:00**
2002-03	**Ottawa**	**NHL**	**67**	**0**	**8**	**8**	**130**	**0**	**0**	**0**	**58**	**0.0**	**–1**	**1**	**0.0**	**13:55**	**1**	**0**	**0**	**0**	**0**	**0**	**0**	**0**	**9:38**
2003-04	**Ottawa**	**NHL**	**37**	**0**	**5**	**5**	**72**	**0**	**0**	**0**	**16**	**0.0**	**2**	**0**	**0.0**	**11:19**	....	....	....	....	....	....	....	....	....
	Nashville	**NHL**	**9**	**0**	**2**	**2**	**10**	**0**	**0**	**0**	**12**	**0.0**	**3**	**0**	**0.0**	**18:11**	**5**	**0**	**0**	**0**	**6**	**0**	**0**	**0**	**12:31**
2004-05	Florida Everblades	ECHL	19	1	4	5	56	....	....	....	....	....	....	....	....	....	17	0	4	4	6	....	....	....	....
2005-06	**Atlanta**	**NHL**	**66**	**0**	**3**	**3**	**33**	**0**	**0**	**0**	**50**	**0.0**	**1**	**0**	**0.0**	**10:14**	....	....	....	....	....	....	....	....	....
2006-07	**Atlanta**	**NHL**	**72**	**5**	**7**	**12**	**63**	**0**	**1**	**1**	**86**	**5.8**	**15**	**0**	**0.0**	**15:38**	**4**	**1**	**0**	**1**	**0**	**0**	**0**	**0**	**15:48**
2007-08	**Anaheim**	**NHL**	**33**	**1**	**2**	**3**	**30**	**0**	**0**	**0**	**21**	**4.8**	**2**	**0**	**0.0**	**13:08**	....	....	....	....	....	....	....	....	....
	Boston	**NHL**	**43**	**1**	**4**	**5**	**41**	**0**	**1**	**0**	**28**	**3.6**	**–4**	**0**	**0.0**	**14:42**	**7**	**1**	**1**	**2**	**9**	**0**	**0**	**0**	**17:11**
	NHL Totals		**412**	**11**	**34**	**45**	**520**	**0**	**2**	**2**	**352**	**3.1**		**1**	**0.0**	**13:39**	**30**	**3**	**2**	**5**	**27**	**0**	**0**	**0**	**15:22**

Signed as a free agent by **Detroit**, August 6, 1998. Traded to **Ottawa** by **Detroit** for Ottawa's 8th round choice (Todd Jackson) in 2000 Entry Draft, June 25, 2000. • Missed majority of 2001-02 season recovering from ankle injury suffered in game vs. Boston, December 26, 2001. Traded to **Nashville** by **Ottawa** for Colorado's 3rd round choice (previously acquired, Ottawa selected Peter Regin) in 2004 Entry Draft, March 9, 2004. Signed as a free agent by **Florida** (ECHL), December 6, 2004. Traded to **Atlanta** by **Nashville** for Atlanta's 4th round choice (Niko Snellman) in 2006 Entry Draft, July 30, 2005. Signed as a free agent by **Anaheim**, July 5, 2007. Traded to **Boston** by **Anaheim** with Anaheim's 6th round choice (Nicholas Tremblay) in 2008 Entry Draft for Brandon Bochenski, January 2, 2008.

HOGGAN, Jeff

(HOH-guhn, JEHF) **PHX.**

Left wing. Shoots left. 6'1", 188 lbs. Born, Hope, B.C., February 1, 1978.

1998-99	Powell River Kings	BCHL	STATISTICS NOT AVAILABLE																						
99-2000	Nebraska-Omaha	CCHA	34	16	9	25	82	....	....	....	....	....	....	....	....	....	....	....	....	....	....	....	....	....	....
2000-01	Nebraska-Omaha	CCHA	42	12	17	29	78	....	....	....	....	....	....	....	....	....	....	....	....	....	....	....	....	....	....
2001-02	Nebraska-Omaha	CCHA	41	24	21	45	92	....	....	....	....	....	....	....	....	....	....	....	....	....	....	....	....	....	....
	Houston Aeros	AHL	....	....	....	....	....	....	....	....	....	....	....	....	....	....	4	0	0	0	2	....	....	....	....
2002-03	Houston Aeros	AHL	65	6	5	11	45	....	....	....	....	....	....	....	....	....	14	1	2	3	23	....	....	....	....
2003-04	Houston Aeros	AHL	77	21	15	36	88	....	....	....	....	....	....	....	....	....	2	0	1	1	4	....	....	....	....
2004-05	Worcester IceCats	AHL	47	16	9	25	55	....	....	....	....	....	....	....	....	....	....	....	....	....	....	....	....	....	....
2005-06	**St. Louis**	**NHL**	**52**	**2**	**6**	**8**	**34**	**0**	**0**	**0**	**60**	**3.3**	**–16**	**4**	**25.0**	**8:47**	....	....	....	....	....	....	....	....	....
2006-07	**Boston**	**NHL**	**46**	**0**	**2**	**2**	**33**	**0**	**0**	**0**	**53**	**0.0**	**–8**	**3**	**33.3**	**7:04**	....	....	....	....	....	....	....	....	....
	Providence Bruins	AHL	22	4	7	11	27	....	....	....	....	....	....	....	....	....	13	4	3	7	17	....	....	....	....
2007-08	**Boston**	**NHL**	**1**	**0**	**0**	**0**	**0**	**0**	**0**	**0**	**0**	**0.0**	**0**	**0**	**0.0**	**7:57**	....	....	....	....	....	....	....	....	....
	Providence Bruins	AHL	71	29	31	60	59	....	....	....	....	....	....	....	....	....	5	3	4	7	4	....	....	....	....
	NHL Totals		**99**	**2**	**8**	**10**	**67**	**0**	**0**	**0**	**113**	**1.8**		**7**	**28.6**	**7:59**	....	....	....	....	....	....	....	....	....

CCHA First All-Star Team (2002) • NCAA West Second All-American Team (2002)

Signed to a PTO (tryout) contract by **Houston** (AHL), April 4, 2002. Signed as a free agent by **Minnesota**, August 20, 2002. Signed as a free agent by **Worcester** (AHL), September, 2004. Signed as a free agent by **St. Louis**, August 2, 2005. Signed as a free agent by **Boston**, July 21, 2006. Signed as a free agent by **Phoenix**, July 15, 2008.

HOLIK, Bobby

(HOH-leek, BAW-bee) **N.J.**

Center. Shoots right. 6'4", 230 lbs. Born, Jihlava, Czech., January 1, 1971. Hartford's 1st choice, 10th overall, in 1989 Entry Draft.

1987-88	Dukla Jihlava	Czech	31	5	9	14	16	....	....	....	....	....	....	....	....	....	....	....	....	....	....	....	....	....	....
1988-89	Dukla Jihlava	Czech	24	7	10	17	32	....	....	....	....	....	....	....	....	....	....	....	....	....	....	....	....	....	....
1989-90	Dukla Jihlava	Czech	42	15	26	41	....	....	....	....	....	....	....	....	....	....	....	....	....	....	....	....	....	....	....
1990-91	**Hartford**	**NHL**	**78**	**21**	**22**	**43**	**113**	**8**	**0**	**3**	**173**	**12.1**	**–3**	....	....	....	**6**	**0**	**0**	**0**	**7**	**0**	**0**	**0**	....
1991-92	**Hartford**	**NHL**	**76**	**21**	**24**	**45**	**44**	**1**	**0**	**2**	**207**	**10.1**	**4**	....	....	....	**7**	**0**	**1**	**1**	**6**	**0**	**0**	**0**	....
1992-93	**New Jersey**	**NHL**	**61**	**20**	**19**	**39**	**76**	**7**	**0**	**4**	**180**	**11.1**	**–6**	....	....	....	**5**	**1**	**1**	**2**	**6**	**0**	**0**	**0**	....
	Utica Devils	AHL	1	0	0	0	2	....	....	....	....	....	....	....	....	....	....	....	....	....	....	....	....	....	....
1993-94	**New Jersey**	**NHL**	**70**	**13**	**20**	**33**	**72**	**2**	**0**	**3**	**130**	**10.0**	**28**	....	....	....	**20**	**0**	**3**	**3**	**6**	**0**	**0**	**0**	....
1994-95♦	**New Jersey**	**NHL**	**48**	**10**	**10**	**20**	**18**	**0**	**0**	**2**	**84**	**11.9**	**9**	....	....	....	**20**	**4**	**4**	**8**	**22**	**2**	**0**	**1**	....
1995-96	**New Jersey**	**NHL**	**63**	**13**	**17**	**30**	**58**	**1**	**0**	**1**	**157**	**8.3**	**9**	....	....	....	....	....	....	....	....	....	....	....	....
1996-97	**New Jersey**	**NHL**	**82**	**23**	**39**	**62**	**54**	**5**	**0**	**6**	**192**	**12.0**	**24**	....	....	....	**10**	**2**	**3**	**5**	**4**	**1**	**0**	**0**	....
1997-98	**New Jersey**	**NHL**	**82**	**29**	**36**	**65**	**100**	**8**	**0**	**8**	**238**	**12.2**	**23**	....	....	....	**5**	**0**	**0**	**0**	**8**	**0**	**0**	**0**	....
1998-99	**New Jersey**	**NHL**	**78**	**27**	**37**	**64**	**119**	**5**	**0**	**8**	**253**	**10.7**	**16**	**1350**	**53.6**	**17:34**	**7**	**0**	**7**	**7**	**6**	**0**	**0**	**0**	**18:14**
99-2000♦	**New Jersey**	**NHL**	**79**	**23**	**23**	**46**	**106**	**7**	**0**	**4**	**257**	**8.9**	**7**	**1390**	**55.6**	**16:53**	**23**	**3**	**7**	**10**	**14**	**0**	**0**	**1**	**17:29**
2000-01	**New Jersey**	**NHL**	**80**	**15**	**35**	**50**	**97**	**3**	**0**	**3**	**206**	**7.3**	**19**	**1365**	**56.0**	**15:49**	**25**	**6**	**10**	**16**	**37**	**1**	**0**	**3**	**16:05**
2001-02	**New Jersey**	**NHL**	**81**	**25**	**29**	**54**	**97**	**6**	**0**	**3**	**270**	**9.3**	**7**	**1594**	**54.5**	**17:42**	**6**	**4**	**1**	**5**	**2**	**1**	**0**	**0**	**17:53**
2002-03	**NY Rangers**	**NHL**	**64**	**16**	**19**	**35**	**52**	**3**	**0**	**2**	**213**	**7.5**	**–1**	**1390**	**58.2**	**18:07**	....	....	....	....	....	....	....	....	....
2003-04	**NY Rangers**	**NHL**	**82**	**25**	**31**	**56**	**96**	**8**	**0**	**4**	**225**	**11.1**	**4**	**1664**	**54.2**	**18:34**	....	....	....	....	....	....	....	....	....
2004-05			DID NOT PLAY																						
2005-06	**Atlanta**	**NHL**	**64**	**15**	**18**	**33**	**79**	**5**	**0**	**0**	**151**	**9.9**	**–6**	**1385**	**55.7**	**17:31**	....	....	....	....	....	....	....	....	....
2006-07	**Atlanta**	**NHL**	**82**	**11**	**18**	**29**	**86**	**2**	**1**	**1**	**190**	**5.8**	**–3**	**1427**	**57.5**	**15:56**	**4**	**0**	**1**	**1**	**0**	**0**	**0**	**0**	**15:24**
2007-08	**Atlanta**	**NHL**	**82**	**15**	**19**	**34**	**90**	**3**	**0**	**3**	**140**	**10.7**	**–14**	**1502**	**58.4**	**15:58**	....	....	....	....	....	....	....	....	....
	NHL Totals		**1252**	**322**	**416**	**738**	**1357**	**74**	**1**	**57**	**3266**	**9.9**		**13067**	**55.9**	**17:05**	**138**	**20**	**38**	**58**	**118**	**5**	**0**	**5**	**16:56**

Played in NHL All-Star Game (1998, 1999)

Traded to **New Jersey** by **Hartford** with Hartford's 2nd round choice (Jay Pandolfo) in 1993 Entry Draft for Sean Burke and Eric Weinrich, August 28, 1992. Signed as a free agent by **NY Rangers**, July 1, 2002. Signed as a free agent by **Atlanta**, August 2, 2005. Signed as a free agent by **New Jersey**, July 1, 2008.

HOLLWEG, Ryan

(HOHL-wehg, RIGH-uhn) **TOR.**

Center. Shoots left. 5'11", 210 lbs. Born, Downey, CA, April 23, 1983. NY Rangers' 10th choice, 238th overall, in 2001 Entry Draft.

			Regular Season														Playoffs								
Season	Club	League	GP	G	A	Pts	PIM	PP	SH	GW	S	%	+/-	TF	F%	Min	GP	G	A	Pts	PIM	PP	SH	GW	Min
1998-99	Langley Hornets	BCHL	58	14	40	54	187	....	....	....	....	....	....	....	....	....	....	....	....	....	....	....	....	....	....
99-2000	Medicine Hat	WHL	54	19	27	46	107	....	....	....	....	....	....	....	....	....	....	....	....	....	....	....	....	....	....
2000-01	Medicine Hat	WHL	65	19	39	58	125	....	....	....	....	....	....	....	....	....	....	....	....	....	....	....	....	....	....
2001-02	Medicine Hat	WHL	58	30	40	70	121	....	....	....	....	....	....	....	....	....	....	....	....	....	....	....	....	....	....
	Hartford	AHL	8	1	1	2	2	....	....	....	....	....	....	....	....	....	9	0	2	2	19	....	....	....	....
2002-03	Medicine Hat	WHL	4	1	1	2	8	....	....	....	....	....	....	....	....	....	....	....	....	....	....	....	....	....	....
2003-04	Medicine Hat	WHL	52	25	32	57	117	....	....	....	....	....	....	....	....	....	20	6	9	15	22	....	....	....	....
2004-05	Hartford	AHL	73	8	6	14	239	....	....	....	....	....	....	....	....	....	6	1	0	1	9	....	....	....	....
2005-06	**NY Rangers**	**NHL**	**52**	**2**	**3**	**5**	**84**	**0**	**0**	**0**	**32**	**6.3**	**–3**	**19**	**57.9**	**7:15**	**4**	**0**	**1**	**1**	**19**	**0**	**0**	**0**	**10:26**
	Hartford	AHL	7	2	1	3	11	....	....	....	....	....	....	....	....	....	....	....	....	....	....	....	....	....	....
2006-07	**NY Rangers**	**NHL**	**78**	**1**	**2**	**3**	**131**	**0**	**0**	**0**	**63**	**1.6**	**–11**	**86**	**39.5**	**8:14**	**2**	**0**	**0**	**0**	**2**	**0**	**0**	**0**	**5:19**
2007-08	**NY Rangers**	**NHL**	**70**	**2**	**2**	**4**	**96**	**0**	**0**	**0**	**59**	**3.4**	**–12**	**39**	**46.2**	**8:18**	**8**	**0**	**0**	**0**	**2**	**0**	**0**	**0**	**4:50**
	NHL Totals		**200**	**5**	**7**	**12**	**311**	**0**	**0**	**0**	**154**	**3.2**		**144**	**43.8**	**8:00**	**14**	**0**	**1**	**1**	**23**	**0**	**0**	**0**	**6:30**

• Missed majority of 2002-03 season recovering from head injury suffered in game vs. Vancouver (WHL), October 8, 2002. Traded to **Toronto** by **NY Rangers** for Pittsburgh's 5th round choice (previously acquired) in 2009 Entry Draft, July 14, 2008.

HOLMQVIST, Michael

(HOHLM-kvihst, MIGH-kuhl)

Center. Shoots left. 6'3", 205 lbs. Born, Stockholm, Sweden, June 8, 1979. Anaheim's 1st choice, 18th overall, in 1997 Entry Draft.

Season	Club	League	GP	G	A	Pts	PIM	PP	SH	GW	S	%	+/-	TF	F%	Min	GP	G	A	Pts	PIM	PP	SH	GW	Min
1995-96	Djurgarden Jr.	Swe-Jr.	24	7	2	9	4	....	....	....	....	....	....	....	....	....	....	....	....	....	....	....	....	....	....
1996-97	Djurgarden Jr.	Swe-Jr.	39	29	35	64	110	....	....	....	....	....	....	....	....	....	....	....	....	....	....	....	....	....	....
	Djurgarden	Sweden	9	0	0	0	0	....	....	....	....	....	....	....	....	....	....	....	....	....	....	....	....	....	....
1997-98	Farjestad	Sweden	41	2	3	5	6	....	....	....	....	....	....	....	....	....	7	0	0	0	0	....	....	....	....
	Farjestad	EuroHL	5	2	2	4	2	....	....	....	....	....	....	....	....	....	....	....	....	....	....	....	....	....	....
1998-99	Farjestad Jr.	Swe-Jr.	2	2	2	4	2	....	....	....	....	....	....	....	....	....	....	....	....	....	....	....	....	....	....
	Farjestad	EuroHL	3	0	0	0	0	....	....	....	....	....	....	....	....	....	1	0	0	0	0	....	....	....	....
	Farjestad	Sweden	15	0	0	0	6	....	....	....	....	....	....	....	....	....	....	....	....	....	....	....	....	....	....
	Hammarby	Sweden-2	3	2	0	2	0	....	....	....	....	....	....	....	....	....	....	....	....	....	....	....	....	....	....
99-2000	TPS Turku	Finland	54	12	3	15	14	....	....	....	....	....	....	....	....	....	11	2	3	5	4	....	....	....	....
2000-01	TPS Turku	Finland	46	4	5	9	8	....	....	....	....	....	....	....	....	....	10	1	3	4	2	....	....	....	....
2001-02	TPS Turku	Finland	56	9	13	22	16	....	....	....	....	....	....	....	....	....	8	1	0	1	12	....	....	....	....
2002-03	TPS Turku	Finland	56	15	25	40	36	....	....	....	....	....	....	....	....	....	7	0	0	0	4	....	....	....	....
2003-04	**Anaheim**	**NHL**	**21**	**2**	**0**	**2**	**25**	**0**	**0**	**0**	**18**	**11.1**	**–6**	**16**	**31.3**	**8:24**	....	....	....	....	....	....	....	....	....
	Cincinnati	AHL	24	7	7	14	20	....	....	....	....	....	....	....	....	....	....	....	....	....	....	....	....	....	....
2004-05	Cincinnati	AHL	79	14	32	46	111	....	....	....	....	....	....	....	....	....	11	2	2	4	10	....	....	....	....
2005-06	**Chicago**	**NHL**	**72**	**10**	**10**	**20**	**16**	**2**	**0**	**1**	**106**	**9.4**	**–14**	**85**	**36.5**	**13:32**	....	....	....	....	....	....	....	....	....
2006-07	**Chicago**	**NHL**	**63**	**6**	**7**	**13**	**31**	**1**	**0**	**0**	**80**	**7.5**	**–5**	**161**	**44.7**	**13:47**	....	....	....	....	....	....	....	....	....
2007-08	Frolunda	Sweden	53	7	10	17	51	....	....	....	....	....	....	....	....	....	4	0	0	0	2	....	....	....	....
	NHL Totals		**156**	**18**	**17**	**35**	**72**	**3**	**0**	**1**	**204**	**8.8**		**262**	**41.2**	**12:57**	....	....	....	....	....	....	....	....	....

Traded to **Chicago** by **Anaheim** for Travis Moen, July 30, 2005.

HOLMSTROM, Tomas

(HOHLM-struhm, TAW-mas) **DET.**

Left wing. Shoots left. 6', 203 lbs. Born, Pitea, Sweden, January 23, 1973. Detroit's 9th choice, 257th overall, in 1994 Entry Draft.

Season	Club	League	GP	G	A	Pts	PIM	PP	SH	GW	S	%	+/-	TF	F%	Min	GP	G	A	Pts	PIM	PP	SH	GW	Min
1989-90	Pitea HC	Sweden-2	9	1	0	1	4	....	....	....	....	....	....	....	....	....	....	....	....	....	....	....	....	....	....
1990-91	Pitea HC	Sweden-2	26	5	4	9	16	....	....	....	....	....	....	....	....	....	....	....	....	....	....	....	....	....	....
1991-92	Pitea HC	Sweden-2	31	15	12	27	44	....	....	....	....	....	....	....	....	....	....	....	....	....	....	....	....	....	....
1992-93	Pitea HC	Sweden-2	32	17	15	32	30	....	....	....	....	....	....	....	....	....	....	....	....	....	....	....	....	....	....
1993-94	Bodens IK	Sweden-2	34	23	16	39	86	....	....	....	....	....	....	....	....	....	9	3	3	6	24	....	....	....	....
1994-95	Lulea HF	Sweden	40	14	14	28	56	....	....	....	....	....	....	....	....	....	8	1	2	3	20	....	....	....	....
1995-96	Lulea HF	Sweden	34	12	11	23	78	....	....	....	....	....	....	....	....	....	11	6	2	8	22	....	....	....	....
1996-97 ♦	**Detroit**	**NHL**	**47**	**6**	**3**	**9**	**33**	**3**	**0**	**0**	**53**	**11.3**	**–10**	....	....	....	**1**	**0**	**0**	**0**	**0**	**0**	**0**	**0**	....
	Adirondack	AHL	6	3	1	4	7	....	....	....	....	....	....	....	....	....	....	....	....	....	....	....	....	....	....
1997-98 ♦	**Detroit**	**NHL**	**57**	**5**	**17**	**22**	**44**	**1**	**0**	**1**	**48**	**10.4**	**6**	....	....	....	**22**	**7**	**12**	**19**	**16**	**2**	**0**	**0**	....
1998-99	**Detroit**	**NHL**	**82**	**13**	**21**	**34**	**69**	**5**	**0**	**4**	**100**	**13.0**	**–11**	**0**	**0.0**	**12:22**	**10**	**4**	**3**	**7**	**4**	**2**	**0**	**1**	**12:32**
99-2000	**Detroit**	**NHL**	**72**	**13**	**22**	**35**	**43**	**4**	**0**	**1**	**71**	**18.3**	**4**	**0**	**0.0**	**12:06**	**9**	**3**	**1**	**4**	**16**	**1**	**0**	**1**	**11:42**
2000-01	**Detroit**	**NHL**	**73**	**16**	**24**	**40**	**40**	**9**	**0**	**2**	**74**	**21.6**	**–12**	**2**	**50.0**	**11:41**	**6**	**1**	**3**	**4**	**8**	**1**	**0**	**0**	**14:23**
2001-02 ♦	**Detroit**	**NHL**	**69**	**8**	**18**	**26**	**58**	**6**	**0**	**1**	**79**	**10.1**	**–12**	**2**	**0.0**	**12:23**	**23**	**8**	**3**	**11**	**8**	**3**	**0**	**2**	**11:31**
	Sweden	Olympics	4	1	0	1	0	....	....	....	....	....	....	....	....	....	....	....	....	....	....	....	....	....	....
2002-03	**Detroit**	**NHL**	**74**	**20**	**20**	**40**	**62**	**12**	**0**	**2**	**109**	**18.3**	**11**	**2**	**0.0**	**12:28**	**4**	**1**	**1**	**2**	**4**	**1**	**0**	**0**	**14:37**
2003-04	**Detroit**	**NHL**	**67**	**15**	**15**	**30**	**38**	**6**	**0**	**0**	**74**	**20.3**	**8**	**3**	**0.0**	**12:23**	**12**	**2**	**2**	**4**	**10**	**1**	**0**	**1**	**11:27**
2004-05	Lulea HF	Sweden	47	14	16	30	50	....	....	....	....	....	....	....	....	....	4	0	0	0	18	....	....	....	....
2005-06	**Detroit**	**NHL**	**81**	**29**	**30**	**59**	**66**	**11**	**0**	**8**	**140**	**20.7**	**14**	**0**	**0.0**	**13:59**	**6**	**1**	**2**	**3**	**12**	**1**	**0**	**0**	**17:04**
	Sweden	Olympics	8	1	3	4	10	....	....	....	....	....	....	....	....	....	....	....	....	....	....	....	....	....	....
2006-07	**Detroit**	**NHL**	**77**	**30**	**22**	**52**	**58**	**13**	**0**	**5**	**176**	**17.0**	**13**	**0**	**0.0**	**15:13**	**15**	**5**	**3**	**8**	**14**	**4**	**0**	**1**	**16:15**
2007-08 ♦	**Detroit**	**NHL**	**59**	**20**	**20**	**40**	**58**	**11**	**0**	**5**	**137**	**14.6**	**9**	**1**	**0.0**	**17:33**	**21**	**4**	**8**	**12**	**26**	**1**	**0**	**0**	**17:10**
	NHL Totals		**758**	**175**	**212**	**387**	**569**	**81**	**0**	**29**	**1061**	**16.5**		**10**	**10.0**	**13:17**	**129**	**36**	**38**	**74**	**118**	**17**	**0**	**6**	**14:00**

Signed as a free agent by **Lulea** (Sweden), September 16, 2004.

HORCOFF, Shawn

(hohr-KAWF, SHAWN) **EDM.**

Center. Shoots left. 6'1", 208 lbs. Born, Trail, B.C., September 17, 1978. Edmonton's 3rd choice, 99th overall, in 1998 Entry Draft.

Season	Club	League	GP	G	A	Pts	PIM	PP	SH	GW	S	%	+/-	TF	F%	Min	GP	G	A	Pts	PIM	PP	SH	GW	Min
1994-95	Trail Smokies	RMJHL	47	50	46	96	26	....	....	....	....	....	....	....	....	....	....	....	....	....	....	....	....	....	....
1995-96	Chilliwack Chiefs	BCHL	58	49	96	*145	44	....	....	....	....	....	....	....	....	....	9	5	19	24	12	....	....	....	....
1996-97	Michigan State	CCHA	40	10	13	23	20	....	....	....	....	....	....	....	....	....	....	....	....	....	....	....	....	....	....
1997-98	Michigan State	CCHA	34	14	13	27	50	....	....	....	....	....	....	....	....	....	....	....	....	....	....	....	....	....	....
1998-99	Michigan State	CCHA	39	12	25	37	70	....	....	....	....	....	....	....	....	....	....	....	....	....	....	....	....	....	....
99-2000	Michigan State	CCHA	42	14	*51	*65	50	....	....	....	....	....	....	....	....	....	....	....	....	....	....	....	....	....	....
2000-01	**Edmonton**	**NHL**	**49**	**9**	**7**	**16**	**10**	**0**	**0**	**2**	**42**	**21.4**	**8**	**122**	**41.8**	**9:14**	**5**	**0**	**0**	**0**	**0**	**0**	**0**	**0**	**6:31**
	Hamilton	AHL	24	10	18	28	19	....	....	....	....	....	....	....	....	....	....	....	....	....	....	....	....	....	....
2001-02	**Edmonton**	**NHL**	**61**	**8**	**14**	**22**	**18**	**0**	**0**	**0**	**57**	**14.0**	**3**	**454**	**46.3**	**11:20**	....	....	....	....	....	....	....	....	....
	Hamilton	AHL	2	1	2	3	6	....	....	....	....	....	....	....	....	....	....	....	....	....	....	....	....	....	....
2002-03	**Edmonton**	**NHL**	**78**	**12**	**21**	**33**	**55**	**2**	**0**	**3**	**98**	**12.2**	**10**	**301**	**42.9**	**13:30**	**6**	**3**	**1**	**4**	**6**	**0**	**0**	**1**	**15:27**
2003-04	**Edmonton**	**NHL**	**80**	**15**	**25**	**40**	**73**	**0**	**2**	**3**	**110**	**13.6**	**0**	**1378**	**50.7**	**17:31**	....	....	....	....	....	....	....	....	....
2004-05	Mora IK	Sweden	50	19	27	46	117	....	....	....	....	....	....	....	....	....	....	....	....	....	....	....	....	....	....
2005-06	**Edmonton**	**NHL**	**79**	**22**	**51**	**73**	**85**	**3**	**3**	**5**	**167**	**13.2**	**0**	**1421**	**52.7**	**19:59**	**24**	**7**	**12**	**19**	**12**	**1**	**1**	**2**	**21:37**
2006-07	**Edmonton**	**NHL**	**80**	**16**	**35**	**51**	**56**	**5**	**0**	**5**	**168**	**9.5**	**–22**	**1422**	**50.6**	**20:50**	....	....	....	....	....	....	....	....	....
2007-08	**Edmonton**	**NHL**	**53**	**21**	**29**	**50**	**30**	**6**	**0**	**2**	**115**	**18.3**	**1**	**963**	**50.6**	**22:13**	....	....	....	....	....	....	....	....	....
	NHL Totals		**480**	**103**	**182**	**285**	**327**	**16**	**5**	**20**	**757**	**13.6**		**6061**	**50.2**	**16:42**	**35**	**10**	**13**	**23**	**18**	**1**	**1**	**3**	**18:24**

CCHA First All-Star Team (2000) • CCHA Player of the Year (2000) • NCAA West First All-American Team (2000)

Played in NHL All-Star Game (2008)

Signed as a free agent by **Mora** (Sweden), September 6, 2004.

HORDICHUK, Darcy

(HOHR-dih-chuhk, DAHR-see) **VAN.**

Left wing. Shoots left. 6'1", 215 lbs. Born, Kamsack, Sask., August 10, 1980. Atlanta's 9th choice, 180th overall, in 2000 Entry Draft.

Season	Club	League	GP	G	A	Pts	PIM	PP	SH	GW	S	%	+/-	TF	F%	Min	GP	G	A	Pts	PIM	PP	SH	GW	Min
1996-97	Yorkton Mallers	SMHL	57	6	15	21	230	....	....	....	....	....	....	....	....	....	....	....	....	....	....	....	....	....	....
	Calgary Hitmen	WHL	3	0	0	0	2	....	....	....	....	....	....	....	....	....	....	....	....	....	....	....	....	....	....
1997-98	Dauphin Kings	MJHL	58	12	21	33	279	....	....	....	....	....	....	....	....	....	....	....	....	....	....	....	....	....	....
1998-99	Saskatoon Blades	WHL	66	3	2	5	246	....	....	....	....	....	....	....	....	....	....	....	....	....	....	....	....	....	....
99-2000	Saskatoon Blades	WHL	63	6	8	14	269	....	....	....	....	....	....	....	....	....	11	4	2	6	43	....	....	....	....
2000-01	**Atlanta**	**NHL**	**11**	**0**	**0**	**0**	**38**	**0**	**0**	**0**	**6**	**0.0**	**–3**	**0**	**0.0**	**7:18**	....	....	....	....	....	....	....	....	....
	Orlando	IHL	69	7	3	10	*369	....	....	....	....	....	....	....	....	....	16	3	3	6	*41	....	....	....	....
2001-02	**Atlanta**	**NHL**	**33**	**1**	**1**	**2**	**127**	**0**	**0**	**0**	**8**	**12.5**	**–5**	**4**	**25.0**	**6:03**	....	....	....	....	....	....	....	....	....
	Chicago Wolves	AHL	34	5	4	9	127	....	....	....	....	....	....	....	....	....	....	....	....	....	....	....	....	....	....
	Phoenix	**NHL**	**1**	**0**	**0**	**0**	**14**	**0**	**0**	**0**	**0**	**0.0**	**0**	**0**	**0.0**	**7:18**	....	....	....	....	....	....	....	....	....

			Regular Season														Playoffs								
Season	Club	League	GP	G	A	Pts	PIM	PP	SH	GW	S	%	+/-	TF	F%	Min	GP	G	A	Pts	PIM	PP	SH	GW	Min
2002-03	**Phoenix**	**NHL**	**25**	**0**	**0**	**0**	**82**	**0**	**0**	**0**	**5**	**0.0**	**–1**	**0**	**0.0**	**4:47**	....	....	....	....	....	....	....	....	....
	Springfield	AHL	22	1	3	4	38	....	....	....	....	....	....	....	....	....	....	....	....	....	....	....	....	....	....
	Florida	**NHL**	**3**	**0**	**0**	**0**	**15**	**0**	**0**	**0**	**2**	**0.0**	**–1**	**0**	**0.0**	**9:45**	....	....	....	....	....	....	....	....	....
2003-04	**Florida**	**NHL**	**57**	**3**	**1**	**4**	**158**	**0**	**0**	**1**	**27**	**11.1**	**–10**	**4**	**50.0**	**6:46**	....	....	....	....	....	....	....	....	....
2004-05			DID NOT PLAY																						
2005-06	**Nashville**	**NHL**	**74**	**7**	**6**	**13**	**163**	**0**	**0**	**1**	**52**	**13.5**	**9**	**1**	**0.0**	**6:09**	....	....	....	....	....	....	....	....	....
2006-07	**Nashville**	**NHL**	**53**	**1**	**3**	**4**	**90**	**0**	**0**	**0**	**22**	**4.5**	**–2**	**0**	**0.0**	**4:48**	**2**	**0**	**0**	**0**	**0**	**0**	**0**	**0**	**3:38**
2007-08	**Nashville**	**NHL**	**45**	**1**	**2**	**3**	**60**	**0**	**0**	**1**	**18**	**5.6**	**–1**	**0**	**0.0**	**5:09**	**5**	**0**	**0**	**0**	**2**	**0**	**0**	**0**	**3:32**
	NHL Totals		**302**	**13**	**13**	**26**	**747**	**0**	**0**	**3**	**140**	**9.3**		**9**	**33.3**	**5:50**	**7**	**0**	**0**	**0**	**2**	**0**	**0**	**0**	**3:33**

Traded to **Phoenix** by **Atlanta** with Atlanta's 4th (Lance Monych) and 5th (John Zeiler) round choices in 2002 Entry Draft for Kiril Safronov, the rights to Ruslan Zainullin and Phoenix's 4th round choice (Patrick Dwyer) in 2002 Entry Draft, March 19, 2002. Traded to **Florida** by **Phoenix** with Phoenix's 2nd round choice (later traded to Tampa Bay – Tampa Bay selected Matt Smaby) in 2003 Entry Draft for Brad Ference, March 8, 2003. Traded to **Nashville** by **Florida** for Nashville's 4th round choice (Matt Duffy) in 2005 Entry Draft, July 27, 2005. Rights traded to **Carolina** by **Nashville** with Nashville's 5th round choice in 2010 Entry Draft for a 5th round choice in 2009 Entry Draft, June 19, 2008. Signed as a free agent by **Vancouver**, July 1, 2008.

HORTON, Nathan

(HOHR-tuhn, NAY-thuhn) **FLA.**

Center. Shoots right. 6'2", 229 lbs. Born, Welland, Ont., May 29, 1985. Florida's 1st choice, 3rd overall, in 2003 Entry Draft.

2000-01	Thorold	OHA-B	41	16	31	47	75	....	....	....	....	....	....	....	....	....	....	....	....	....	....	....	....	....	....
2001-02	Oshawa Generals	OHL	64	31	36	67	84	....	....	....	....	....	....	....	....	....	5	1	2	3	10	....	....	....	....
2002-03	Oshawa Generals	OHL	54	33	35	68	111	....	....	....	....	....	....	....	....	....	13	9	6	15	10	....	....	....	....
2003-04	**Florida**	**NHL**	**55**	**14**	**8**	**22**	**57**	**6**	**1**	**0**	**81**	**17.3**	**–5**	**270**	**41.9**	**13:20**	....	....	....	....	....	....	....	....	....
2004-05	San Antonio	AHL	21	5	4	9	21	....	....	....	....	....	....	....	....	....	....	....	....	....	....	....	....	....	....
2005-06	**Florida**	**NHL**	**71**	**28**	**19**	**47**	**89**	**3**	**0**	**1**	**162**	**17.3**	**8**	**24**	**45.8**	**16:53**	....	....	....	....	....	....	....	....	....
2006-07	**Florida**	**NHL**	**82**	**31**	**31**	**62**	**61**	**7**	**1**	**3**	**217**	**14.3**	**15**	**31**	**48.4**	**18:04**	....	....	....	....	....	....	....	....	....
2007-08	**Florida**	**NHL**	**82**	**27**	**35**	**62**	**85**	**9**	**0**	**3**	**212**	**12.7**	**15**	**73**	**39.7**	**18:44**	....	....	....	....	....	....	....	....	....
	NHL Totals		**290**	**100**	**93**	**193**	**292**	**25**	**2**	**7**	**672**	**14.9**		**398**	**42.2**	**17:04**	....	....	....	....	....	....	....	....	....

OHL All-Rookie Team (2002)

Signed as a free agent by **San Antonio** (AHL), October 28, 2004.

HOSSA, Marcel

(HOH-sa, MAHR-sehl)

Left wing. Shoots left. 6'3", 220 lbs. Born, Ilava, Czech., October 12, 1981. Montreal's 2nd choice, 16th overall, in 2000 Entry Draft.

1996-97	Dukla Trencin Jr.	Slovak-Jr.	45	30	21	51	30	....	....	....	....	....	....	....	....	....	....	....	....	....	....	....	....	....	....
1997-98	Dukla Trencin Jr.	Slovak-Jr.	39	11	38	49	44	....	....	....	....	....	....	....	....	....	....	....	....	....	....	....	....	....	....
1998-99	Portland	WHL	70	7	14	21	66	....	....	....	....	....	....	....	....	....	2	0	0	0	2	....	....	....	....
99-2000	Portland	WHL	60	24	29	53	58	....	....	....	....	....	....	....	....	....	....	....	....	....	....	....	....	....	....
2000-01	Portland	WHL	58	34	56	90	58	....	....	....	....	....	....	....	....	....	16	5	7	12	14	....	....	....	....
2001-02	**Montreal**	**NHL**	**10**	**3**	**1**	**4**	**2**	**0**	**0**	**0**	**20**	**15.0**	**2**	**0**	**0.0**	**11:09**	....	....	....	....	....	....	....	....	....
	Quebec Citadelles	AHL	50	17	15	32	24	....	....	....	....	....	....	....	....	....	3	0	0	0	4	....	....	....	....
2002-03	**Montreal**	**NHL**	**34**	**6**	**7**	**13**	**14**	**2**	**0**	**1**	**51**	**11.8**	**3**	**4**	**50.0**	**13:58**	....	....	....	....	....	....	....	....	....
	Hamilton	AHL	37	19	13	32	18	....	....	....	....	....	....	....	....	....	21	4	7	11	12	....	....	....	....
2003-04	**Montreal**	**NHL**	**15**	**1**	**1**	**2**	**8**	**0**	**0**	**0**	**19**	**5.3**	**–3**	**5**	**40.0**	**14:50**	....	....	....	....	....	....	....	....	....
	Hamilton	AHL	57	18	22	40	45	....	....	....	....	....	....	....	....	....	10	2	3	5	8	....	....	....	....
2004-05	Mora IK	Sweden	48	18	6	24	69	....	....	....	....	....	....	....	....	....	....	....	....	....	....	....	....	....	....
2005-06	**NY Rangers**	**NHL**	**64**	**10**	**6**	**16**	**28**	**3**	**0**	**0**	**105**	**9.5**	**–6**	**7**	**28.6**	**10:45**	**4**	**0**	**0**	**0**	**6**	**0**	**0**	**0**	**13:18**
	Slovakia	Olympics	6	0	0	0	0	....	....	....	....	....	....	....	....	....	....	....	....	....	....	....	....	....	....
2006-07	**NY Rangers**	**NHL**	**64**	**10**	**8**	**18**	**26**	**3**	**0**	**2**	**83**	**12.0**	**–4**	**18**	**16.7**	**12:27**	**10**	**2**	**2**	**4**	**4**	**0**	**0**	**0**	**15:58**
2007-08	**NY Rangers**	**NHL**	**36**	**1**	**7**	**8**	**24**	**0**	**0**	**0**	**54**	**1.9**	**8**	**5**	**20.0**	**14:36**	....	....	....	....	....	....	....	....	....
	Hartford	AHL	5	1	0	1	2	....	....	....	....	....	....	....	....	....	....	....	....	....	....	....	....	....	....
	Phoenix	**NHL**	**14**	**0**	**0**	**0**	**4**	**0**	**0**	**0**	**12**	**0.0**	**–6**	**10**	**20.0**	**11:39**	....	....	....	....	....	....	....	....	....
	NHL Totals		**237**	**31**	**30**	**61**	**106**	**8**	**0**	**3**	**344**	**9.0**		**49**	**24.5**	**12:35**	**14**	**2**	**2**	**4**	**10**	**0**	**0**	**0**	**15:12**

WHL West Second All-Star Team (2001)

Signed as a free agent by **Mora** (Sweden), September 25, 2004. Traded to **NY Rangers** by **Montreal** for Garth Murray, September 30, 2005. Traded to **Phoenix** by **NY Rangers** with Al Montoya for Fredrik Sjostrom, Josh Gratton, David LeNeveu and future considerations, February 26, 2008.

HOSSA, Marian

(HOH-sa, MAIR-ee-uhn) **DET.**

Right wing. Shoots left. 6'1", 210 lbs. Born, Stara Lubovna, Czech., January 12, 1979. Ottawa's 1st choice, 12th overall, in 1997 Entry Draft.

1995-96	Dukla Trencin Jr.	Slovak-Jr.	53	42	49	91	26	....	....	....	....	....	....	....	....	....	....	....	....	....	....	....	....	....	....
1996-97	Dukla Trencin	Slovakia	46	25	19	44	33	....	....	....	....	....	....	....	....	....	7	5	5	10	....	....	....	....	....
1997-98	Portland	WHL	53	45	40	85	50	....	....	....	....	....	....	....	....	....	16	13	6	19	6	....	....	....	....
	Ottawa	**NHL**	**7**	**0**	**1**	**1**	**0**	**0**	**0**	**0**	**10**	**0.0**	**–1**	....	....	....	....	....	....	....	....	....	....	....	....
1998-99	**Ottawa**	**NHL**	**60**	**15**	**15**	**30**	**37**	**1**	**0**	**2**	**124**	**12.1**	**18**	**4**	**25.0**	**13:59**	**4**	**0**	**2**	**2**	**4**	**0**	**0**	**0**	**16:46**
99-2000	**Ottawa**	**NHL**	**78**	**29**	**27**	**56**	**32**	**5**	**0**	**4**	**240**	**12.1**	**5**	**7**	**57.1**	**17:12**	**6**	**0**	**0**	**0**	**2**	**0**	**0**	**0**	**15:22**
2000-01	**Ottawa**	**NHL**	**81**	**32**	**43**	**75**	**44**	**11**	**2**	**7**	**249**	**12.9**	**19**	**14**	**42.9**	**18:01**	**4**	**1**	**1**	**2**	**4**	**0**	**0**	**0**	**19:02**
2001-02	Dukla Trencin	Slovakia	8	3	4	7	16	....	....	....	....	....	....	....	....	....	....	....	....	....	....	....	....	....	....
	Ottawa	**NHL**	**80**	**31**	**35**	**66**	**50**	**9**	**1**	**4**	**278**	**11.2**	**11**	**12**	**33.3**	**18:29**	**12**	**4**	**6**	**10**	**2**	**1**	**0**	**0**	**19:04**
	Slovakia	Olympics	2	4	2	6	0	....	....	....	....	....	....	....	....	....	....	....	....	....	....	....	....	....	....
2002-03	**Ottawa**	**NHL**	**80**	**45**	**35**	**80**	**34**	**14**	**0**	**10**	**229**	**19.7**	**8**	**19**	**36.8**	**18:31**	**18**	**5**	**11**	**16**	**6**	**3**	**0**	**1**	**18:41**
2003-04	**Ottawa**	**NHL**	**81**	**36**	**46**	**82**	**46**	**14**	**1**	**5**	**233**	**15.5**	**4**	**25**	**40.0**	**18:37**	**7**	**3**	**1**	**4**	**0**	**1**	**0**	**2**	**21:24**
2004-05	Mora IK	Sweden	24	18	14	32	22	....	....	....	....	....	....	....	....	....	....	....	....	....	....	....	....	....	....
	Dukla Trencin	Slovakia	25	22	20	42	38	....	....	....	....	....	....	....	....	....	5	4	5	9	14	....	....	....	....
2005-06	**Atlanta**	**NHL**	**80**	**39**	**53**	**92**	**67**	**14**	**7**	**7**	**341**	**11.4**	**17**	**15**	**26.7**	**21:41**	....	....	....	....	....	....	....	....	....
	Slovakia	Olympics	6	5	5	10	4	....	....	....	....	....	....	....	....	....	....	....	....	....	....	....	....	....	....
2006-07	**Atlanta**	**NHL**	**82**	**43**	**57**	**100**	**49**	**17**	**3**	**5**	**340**	**12.6**	**18**	**18**	**22.2**	**21:41**	**4**	**0**	**1**	**1**	**6**	**0**	**0**	**0**	**18:55**
2007-08	**Atlanta**	**NHL**	**60**	**26**	**30**	**56**	**30**	**8**	**2**	**4**	**229**	**11.4**	**–14**	**14**	**28.6**	**21:55**	....	....	....	....	....	....	....	....	....
	Pittsburgh	**NHL**	**12**	**3**	**7**	**10**	**6**	**0**	**0**	**0**	**35**	**8.6**	**0**	**1**	**0.0**	**18:34**	**20**	**12**	**14**	**26**	**12**	**5**	**0**	**2**	**21:00**
	NHL Totals		**701**	**299**	**349**	**648**	**395**	**93**	**16**	**48**	**2308**	**13.0**		**129**	**34.1**	**18:58**	**75**	**25**	**36**	**61**	**36**	**10**	**0**	**5**	**19:17**

WHL West First All-Star Team (1998) • WHL Rookie of the Year (1998) • Canadian Major Junior First All-Star Team (1998) • Memorial Cup Tournament All-Star Team (1998) • NHL All-Rookie Team (1999)

Played in NHL All-Star Game (2001, 2003, 2007, 2008)

Signed as a free agent by **Trencin** (Slovakia), September 16, 2004. Signed as a free agent by **Mora** (Sweden), November 11, 2004. Signed as a free agent by **Trencin** (Slovakia), January 31, 2005. Traded to **Atlanta** by **Ottawa** with Greg de Vries for Dany Heatley, August 23, 2005. Traded to **Pittsburgh** by **Atlanta** with Pascal Dupuis for Colby Armstrong, Erik Christensen, Angelo Esposito and Pittsburgh's 1st round choice (Daulton Leveille) in 2008 Entry Draft , February 26, 2008. Signed as a free agent by **Detroit**, July 2, 2008.

HUDLER, Jiri

(HOOD-luhr, YIH-ree) **DET.**

Center. Shoots left. 5'9", 182 lbs. Born, Olomouc, Czech., January 4, 1984. Detroit's 1st choice, 58th overall, in 2002 Entry Draft.

1998-99	HC Vsetin U17	CzR-U17	46	57	57	114	....	....	....	....	....	....	....	....	....	....	....	....	....	....	....	....	....	....	....
99-2000	HC Vsetin Jr.	CzRep-Jr.	53	29	31	60	75	....	....	....	....	....	....	....	....	....	....	....	....	....	....	....	....	....	....
	Vsetin	CzRep	2	0	1	1	0	....	....	....	....	....	....	....	....	....	....	....	....	....	....	....	....	....	....
2000-01	HC Vsetin Jr.	CzRep-Jr.	16	8	14	22	16	....	....	....	....	....	....	....	....	....	....	....	....	....	....	....	....	....	....
	HC Slovnaft Vsetin	CzRep	22	1	4	5	10	....	....	....	....	....	....	....	....	....	....	....	....	....	....	....	....	....	....
	HC Femax Havirov	CzRep	15	5	1	6	12	....	....	....	....	....	....	....	....	....	....	....	....	....	....	....	....	....	....
2001-02	HC Vsetin	CzRep	46	15	31	46	54	....	....	....	....	....	....	....	....	....	....	....	....	....	....	....	....	....	....
	Liberec	CzRep-2	13	9	7	16	10	....	....	....	....	....	....	....	....	....	....	....	....	....	....	....	....	....	....
	HC Olomouc	CzRep-3	1	0	2	2	4	....	....	....	....	....	....	....	....	....	....	....	....	....	....	....	....	....	....
2002-03	HC Vsetin	CzRep	30	19	27	46	22	....	....	....	....	....	....	....	....	....	....	....	....	....	....	....	....	....	....
	Ak Bars Kazan	Russia	11	1	5	6	12	....	....	....	....	....	....	....	....	....	1	0	0	0	0	....	....	....	....
2003-04	**Detroit**	**NHL**	**12**	**1**	**2**	**3**	**10**	**1**	**0**	**0**	**8**	**12.5**	**–1**	**50**	**30.0**	**8:10**	....	....	....	....	....	....	....	....	....
	Grand Rapids	AHL	57	17	32	49	46	....	....	....	....	....	....	....	....	....	4	1	5	6	2	....	....	....	....
2004-05	Grand Rapids	AHL	52	12	22	34	10	....	....	....	....	....	....	....	....	....	....	....	....	....	....	....	....	....	....
	HC Vsetin	CzRep	7	5	2	7	10	....	....	....	....	....	....	....	....	....	....	....	....	....	....	....	....	....	....
2005-06	**Detroit**	**NHL**	**4**	**0**	**0**	**0**	**2**	**0**	**0**	**0**	**3**	**0.0**	**0**	**0**	**0.0**	**7:13**	....	....	....	....	....	....	....	....	....
	Grand Rapids	AHL	76	36	61	97	56	....	....	....	....	....	....	....	....	....	16	6	16	22	20	....	....	....	....

			Regular Season														Playoffs								
Season	Club	League	GP	G	A	Pts	PIM	PP	SH	GW	S	%	+/-	TF	F%	Min	GP	G	A	Pts	PIM	PP	SH	GW	Min
2006-07	**Detroit**	**NHL**	**76**	**15**	**10**	**25**	**36**	**3**	**0**	**4**	**107**	**14.0**	**16**	**20**	**30.0**	**10:02**	**6**	**0**	**2**	**2**	**4**	**0**	**0**	**0**	**9:09**
2007-08 ♦	**Detroit**	**NHL**	**81**	**13**	**29**	**42**	**26**	**3**	**0**	**2**	**131**	**9.9**	**11**	**26**	**38.5**	**13:10**	**22**	**5**	**9**	**14**	**14**	**2**	**0**	**2**	**11:36**
	NHL Totals		**173**	**29**	**41**	**70**	**74**	**7**	**0**	**6**	**249**	**11.6**		**96**	**32.3**	**11:18**	**28**	**5**	**11**	**16**	**18**	**2**	**0**	**2**	**11:04**

AHL Second All-Star Team (2006)

Signed as a free agent by **Vsetin** (CzRep), December 2, 2004.

HUNT, Jamie

(HUHNT, JAY-mee)

Defense. Shoots left. 6'2", 200 lbs. Born, Calgary, Alta., April 20, 1984.

Season	Club	League	GP	G	A	Pts	PIM	PP	SH	GW	S	%	+/-	TF	F%	Min	GP	G	A	Pts	PIM	PP	SH	GW	Min
2002-03	Calgary Canucks	AJHL	63	8	20	28	35	....	....	....	....	....	....	....	....	....	....	....	....	....	....	....	....	....	....
2003-04	Mercyhurst	AH	27	3	16	19	4	....	....	....	....	....	....	....	....	....	....	....	....	....	....	....	....	....	....
2004-05	Mercyhurst	AH	38	5	12	17	36	....	....	....	....	....	....	....	....	....	....	....	....	....	....	....	....	....	....
2005-06	Mercyhurst	AH	33	12	33	45	49	....	....	....	....	....	....	....	....	....	....	....	....	....	....	....	....	....	....
2006-07	**Washington**	**NHL**	**1**	**0**	**0**	**0**	**0**	**0**	**0**	**0**	**0**	**0.0**	**–1**	**0**	**0.0**	**6:01**	....	....	....	....	....	....	....	....	....
	Hershey Bears	AHL	36	2	10	12	33	....	....	....	....	....	....	....	....	....	....	....	....	....	....	....	....	....	....
2007-08	Hershey Bears	AHL	60	4	9	13	30	....	....	....	....	....	....	....	....	....	4	0	0	0	0	....	....	....	....
	NHL Totals		**1**	**0**	**0**	**0**	**0**	**0**	**0**	**0**	**0**	**0.0**		**0**	**0.0**	**6:01**	....	....	....	....	....	....	....	....	....

AH All-Rookie Team (2004) • AH First All-Star Team (2006)

Signed as a free agent by **Washington**, March 31, 2006. • Missed majority of 2006-07 season recovering from wrist injury suffered in game vs. Philadelphia (AHL), January 24, 2007.

HUNTER, Trent

(HUHN-tuhr, TREHNT) **NYI**

Right wing. Shoots right. 6'3", 210 lbs. Born, Red Deer, Alta., July 5, 1980. Anaheim's 4th choice, 150th overall, in 1998 Entry Draft.

Season	Club	League	GP	G	A	Pts	PIM	PP	SH	GW	S	%	+/-	TF	F%	Min	GP	G	A	Pts	PIM	PP	SH	GW	Min
1996-97	Red Deer	AMHL	42	30	25	55	50	....	....	....	....	....	....	....	....	....	....	....	....	....	....	....	....	....	....
1997-98	Prince George	WHL	60	13	14	27	34	....	....	....	....	....	....	....	....	....	8	1	0	1	4	....	....	....	....
1998-99	Prince George	WHL	50	18	20	38	34	....	....	....	....	....	....	....	....	....	7	2	5	7	2	....	....	....	....
99-2000	Prince George	WHL	67	46	49	95	47	....	....	....	....	....	....	....	....	....	13	7	15	22	6	....	....	....	....
2000-01	Springfield	AHL	57	18	17	35	14	....	....	....	....	....	....	....	....	....	....	....	....	....	....	....	....	....	....
2001-02	Bridgeport	AHL	80	30	35	65	30	....	....	....	....	....	....	....	....	....	17	8	11	19	6	....	....	....	....
	NY Islanders	**NHL**	....	....	....	....	....	....	....	....	....	....	....	....	....	....	**4**	**1**	**1**	**2**	**2**	**0**	**0**	**0**	**11:13**
2002-03	**NY Islanders**	**NHL**	**8**	**0**	**4**	**4**	**4**	**0**	**0**	**0**	**19**	**0.0**	**5**	**1**	**0.0**	**12:13**	....	....	....	....	....	....	....	....	....
	Bridgeport	AHL	70	30	41	71	39	....	....	....	....	....	....	....	....	....	9	7	4	11	10	....	....	....	....
2003-04	**NY Islanders**	**NHL**	**77**	**25**	**26**	**51**	**16**	**4**	**0**	**7**	**187**	**13.4**	**23**	**19**	**36.8**	**15:39**	**5**	**0**	**0**	**0**	**4**	**0**	**0**	**0**	**11:38**
2004-05	Nykoping	Sweden-2	33	13	12	25	73	....	....	....	....	....	....	....	....	....	4	5	3	8	2	....	....	....	....
2005-06	**NY Islanders**	**NHL**	**82**	**16**	**19**	**35**	**34**	**5**	**0**	**3**	**221**	**7.2**	**–9**	**32**	**28.1**	**17:50**	....	....	....	....	....	....	....	....	....
2006-07	**NY Islanders**	**NHL**	**77**	**20**	**15**	**35**	**22**	**5**	**1**	**2**	**168**	**11.9**	**5**	**14**	**42.9**	**16:00**	**5**	**3**	**0**	**3**	**0**	**0**	**0**	**0**	**15:05**
2007-08	**NY Islanders**	**NHL**	**82**	**12**	**29**	**41**	**43**	**2**	**0**	**1**	**222**	**5.4**	**–17**	**29**	**20.7**	**18:13**	....	....	....	....	....	....	....	....	....
	NHL Totals		**326**	**73**	**93**	**166**	**119**	**16**	**1**	**13**	**817**	**8.9**		**95**	**29.5**	**16:50**	**14**	**4**	**1**	**5**	**6**	**0**	**0**	**0**	**12:45**

WHL West First All-Star Team (2000) • NHL All-Rookie Team (2004)

Traded to **NY Islanders** by **Anaheim** for Columbus' 4th round choice (previously acquired, Anaheim selected Jonas Ronnqvist) in 2000 Entry Draft, May 23, 2000. Signed as a free agent by **Nykoping** (Sweden-2), November 8, 2004.

HUNWICK, Matt

(HUHN-wihk, MAT) **BOS.**

Defense. Shoots left. 5'11", 193 lbs. Born, Warren, MI, May 21, 1985. Boston's 6th choice, 224th overall, in 2004 Entry Draft.

Season	Club	League	GP	G	A	Pts	PIM	PP	SH	GW	S	%	+/-	TF	F%	Min	GP	G	A	Pts	PIM	PP	SH	GW	Min
2001-02	USNTDP	U-17	14	3	4	7	6	....	....	....	....	....	....	....	....	....	....	....	....	....	....	....	....	....	....
	USNTDP	NAHL	29	2	1	3	30	....	....	....	....	....	....	....	....	....	....	....	....	....	....	....	....	....	....
2002-03	USNTDP	U-18	40	6	16	22	40	....	....	....	....	....	....	....	....	....	....	....	....	....	....	....	....	....	....
	USNTDP	NAHL	8	2	2	4	23	....	....	....	....	....	....	....	....	....	....	....	....	....	....	....	....	....	....
2003-04	U. of Michigan	CCHA	41	1	14	15	62	....	....	....	....	....	....	....	....	....	....	....	....	....	....	....	....	....	....
2004-05	U. of Michigan	CCHA	40	6	19	25	60	....	....	....	....	....	....	....	....	....	....	....	....	....	....	....	....	....	....
2005-06	U. of Michigan	CCHA	41	11	19	30	70	....	....	....	....	....	....	....	....	....	....	....	....	....	....	....	....	....	....
2006-07	U. of Michigan	CCHA	41	6	21	27	64	....	....	....	....	....	....	....	....	....	....	....	....	....	....	....	....	....	....
2007-08	**Boston**	**NHL**	**13**	**0**	**1**	**1**	**4**	**0**	**0**	**0**	**6**	**0.0**	**–1**	**0**	**0.0**	**10:36**	....	....	....	....	....	....	....	....	....
	Providence Bruins	AHL	55	2	21	23	49	....	....	....	....	....	....	....	....	....	10	0	5	5	8	....	....	....	....
	NHL Totals		**13**	**0**	**1**	**1**	**4**	**0**	**0**	**0**	**6**	**0.0**		**0**	**0.0**	**10:36**	....	....	....	....	....	....	....	....	....

CCHA All-Rookie Team (2004) • CCHA Second All-Star Team (2005, 2006) • CCHA First All-Star Team (2007) • NCAA West Second All-American Team (2007)

HUSELIUS, Kristian

(hoo-SAY-lee-uhs, KRIHST-yan) **CBJ**

Left wing. Shoots left. 6'1", 179 lbs. Born, Osterhaninge, Sweden, November 10, 1978. Florida's 2nd choice, 47th overall, in 1997 Entry Draft.

Season	Club	League	GP	G	A	Pts	PIM	PP	SH	GW	S	%	+/-	TF	F%	Min	GP	G	A	Pts	PIM	PP	SH	GW	Min
1994-95	Hammarby Jr.	Swe-Jr.	17	6	2	8	2	....	....	....	....	....	....	....	....	....	....	....	....	....	....	....	....	....	....
1995-96	Hammarby Jr.	Swe-Jr.	25	13	8	21	14	....	....	....	....	....	....	....	....	....	....	....	....	....	....	....	....	....	....
	Hammarby	Sweden-2	6	1	0	1	0	....	....	....	....	....	....	....	....	....	....	....	....	....	....	....	....	....	....
1996-97	Farjestad	Sweden	13	2	0	2	4	....	....	....	....	....	....	....	....	....	5	1	0	1	0	....	....	....	....
1997-98	Farjestad	Sweden	34	2	1	3	2	....	....	....	....	....	....	....	....	....	11	0	0	0	0	....	....	....	....
	Farjestad	EuroHL	5	2	3	5	0	....	....	....	....	....	....	....	....	....	....	....	....	....	....	....	....	....	....
1998-99	Farjestad	Sweden	28	4	4	8	4	....	....	....	....	....	....	....	....	....	....	....	....	....	....	....	....	....	....
	Farjestad	EuroHL	6	2	2	4	8	....	....	....	....	....	....	....	....	....	1	0	0	0	0	....	....	....	....
	V.Frolunda	Sweden	20	2	2	4	2	....	....	....	....	....	....	....	....	....	4	1	0	1	0	....	....	....	....
99-2000	V.Frolunda	Sweden	50	21	23	44	20	....	....	....	....	....	....	....	....	....	5	2	2	4	8	....	....	....	....
2000-01	V.Frolunda	Sweden	49	*32	*35	*67	26	....	....	....	....	....	....	....	....	....	5	4	5	9	14	....	....	....	....
2001-02	**Florida**	**NHL**	**79**	**23**	**22**	**45**	**14**	**6**	**1**	**3**	**169**	**13.6**	**–4**	**14**	**21.4**	**16:55**	....	....	....	....	....	....	....	....	....
2002-03	**Florida**	**NHL**	**78**	**20**	**23**	**43**	**20**	**3**	**0**	**3**	**187**	**10.7**	**–6**	**6**	**33.3**	**17:20**	....	....	....	....	....	....	....	....	....
2003-04	**Florida**	**NHL**	**76**	**10**	**21**	**31**	**24**	**2**	**0**	**2**	**168**	**6.0**	**–6**	**185**	**37.8**	**14:14**	....	....	....	....	....	....	....	....	....
2004-05	Linkopings HC	Sweden	34	14	*35	49	10	....	....	....	....	....	....	....	....	....	....	....	....	....	....	....	....	....	....
	Rapperswil	Swiss	....	....	....	....	....	....	....	....	....	....	....	....	....	....	4	1	3	4	2	....	....	....	....
2005-06	**Florida**	**NHL**	**24**	**5**	**3**	**8**	**4**	**2**	**0**	**0**	**57**	**8.8**	**–11**	**3**	**66.7**	**14:44**	....	....	....	....	....	....	....	....	....
	Calgary	**NHL**	**54**	**15**	**24**	**39**	**36**	**6**	**0**	**4**	**107**	**14.0**	**2**	**3**	**33.3**	**14:55**	**7**	**2**	**4**	**6**	**4**	**2**	**0**	**0**	**15:35**
2006-07	**Calgary**	**NHL**	**81**	**34**	**43**	**77**	**26**	**14**	**2**	**6**	**173**	**19.7**	**21**	**14**	**28.6**	**17:23**	**6**	**0**	**2**	**2**	**4**	**0**	**0**	**0**	**15:08**
2007-08	**Calgary**	**NHL**	**81**	**25**	**41**	**66**	**40**	**6**	**0**	**5**	**202**	**12.4**	**10**	**4**	**25.0**	**17:42**	**7**	**0**	**4**	**4**	**6**	**0**	**0**	**0**	**13:45**
	NHL Totals		**473**	**132**	**177**	**309**	**164**	**39**	**3**	**23**	**1063**	**12.4**		**229**	**36.2**	**16:26**	**20**	**2**	**10**	**12**	**14**	**2**	**0**	**0**	**14:49**

NHL All-Rookie Team (2002)

Signed as a free agent by **Linkopings** (Sweden), July 29, 2004. Signed as a free agent by **Rapperswil** (Swiss), February 23, 2005. Traded to **Calgary** by **Florida** for Steve Montador and Dustin Johner, December 2, 2005. Signed as a free agent by **Columbus**, July 2, 2008.

HUSKINS, Kent

(HUHS-kihnz, KEHNT) **ANA.**

Defense. Shoots left. 6'3", 209 lbs. Born, Ottawa, Ont., May 4, 1979. Chicago's 3rd choice, 156th overall, in 1998 Entry Draft.

Season	Club	League	GP	G	A	Pts	PIM	PP	SH	GW	S	%	+/-	TF	F%	Min	GP	G	A	Pts	PIM	PP	SH	GW	Min
1995-96	Kanata Valley	CJHL	49	6	21	27	18	....	....	....	....	....	....	....	....	....	....	....	....	....	....	....	....	....	....
1996-97	Kanata Valley	CJHL	53	11	36	47	89	....	....	....	....	....	....	....	....	....	....	....	....	....	....	....	....	....	....
1997-98	Clarkson Knights	ECAC	35	2	8	10	46	....	....	....	....	....	....	....	....	....	....	....	....	....	....	....	....	....	....
1998-99	Clarkson Knights	ECAC	37	5	11	16	28	....	....	....	....	....	....	....	....	....	....	....	....	....	....	....	....	....	....
99-2000	Clarkson Knights	ECAC	28	2	16	18	30	....	....	....	....	....	....	....	....	....	....	....	....	....	....	....	....	....	....
2000-01	Clarkson Knights	ECAC	35	6	28	34	22	....	....	....	....	....	....	....	....	....	....	....	....	....	....	....	....	....	....
2001-02	Norfolk Admirals	AHL	65	4	11	15	44	....	....	....	....	....	....	....	....	....	4	0	1	1	0	....	....	....	....
2002-03	Norfolk Admirals	AHL	80	5	22	27	48	....	....	....	....	....	....	....	....	....	9	2	2	4	4	....	....	....	....
2003-04	San Antonio	AHL	79	5	14	19	42	....	....	....	....	....	....	....	....	....	....	....	....	....	....	....	....	....	....
2004-05	Manitoba Moose	AHL	65	5	11	16	41	....	....	....	....	....	....	....	....	....	14	0	2	2	12	....	....	....	....
2005-06	Portland Pirates	AHL	80	8	23	31	64	....	....	....	....	....	....	....	....	....	18	3	6	9	14	....	....	....	....
2006-07 ♦	**Anaheim**	**NHL**	**33**	**0**	**3**	**3**	**14**	**0**	**0**	**0**	**16**	**0.0**	**–3**	**0**	**0.0**	**14:04**	**21**	**0**	**1**	**1**	**11**	**0**	**0**	**0**	**11:45**
	Portland Pirates	AHL	39	3	12	15	23	....	....	....	....	....	....	....	....	....	....	....	....	....	....	....	....	....	....
2007-08	**Anaheim**	**NHL**	**76**	**4**	**15**	**19**	**59**	**1**	**0**	**2**	**46**	**8.7**	**23**	**0**	**0.0**	**16:05**	**6**	**0**	**1**	**1**	**2**	**0**	**0**	**0**	**14:35**
	NHL Totals		**109**	**4**	**18**	**22**	**73**	**1**	**0**	**2**	**62**	**6.5**		**0**	**0.0**	**15:28**	**27**	**0**	**2**	**2**	**13**	**0**	**0**	**0**	**12:23**

ECAC First All-Star Team (2000, 2001) • NCAA East First All-American Team (2001)

Signed as a free agent by **Florida**, August 14, 2003. Signed as a free agent by **Manitoba** (AHL), September 16, 2004. Signed as a free agent by **Anaheim**, August 30, 2005.

HUSSEY, Matt

(HUH-see, MAT)

Center. Shoots left. 6'2", 212 lbs. Born, New Haven, CT, May 28, 1979. Pittsburgh's 10th choice, 254th overall, in 1998 Entry Draft.

Season	Club	League	GP	G	A	Pts	PIM	PP	SH	GW	S	%	+/-	TF	F%	Min	Playoffs GP	G	A	Pts	PIM	PP	SH	GW	Min
1996-97	Wayzata	High-MN	48	34	31	65	....	....	....	....	....	....	....	....	....	....	....	....	....	....	....	....	....	....	....
1997-98	Avon Old Farms	High-CT	26	26	23	49	20	....	....	....	....	....	....	....	....	....	....	....	....	....	....	....	....	....	....
1998-99	U. of Wisconsin	WCHA	37	10	5	15	18	....	....	....	....	....	....	....	....	....	....	....	....	....	....	....	....	....	....
99-2000	U. of Wisconsin	WCHA	35	5	11	16	8	....	....	....	....	....	....	....	....	....	....	....	....	....	....	....	....	....	....
2000-01	U. of Wisconsin	WCHA	40	9	11	20	24	....	....	....	....	....	....	....	....	....	....	....	....	....	....	....	....	....	....
2001-02	U. of Wisconsin	WCHA	39	18	15	33	16	....	....	....	....	....	....	....	....	....	....	....	....	....	....	....	....	....	....
2002-03	Wilkes-Barre	AHL	69	12	11	23	28	....	....	....	....	....	....	....	....	....	2	0	0	0	0	....	....	....	....
2003-04	**Pittsburgh**	**NHL**	**3**	**2**	**1**	**3**	**0**	**2**	**0**	**0**	**8**	**25.0**	**–1**	**0**	**0.0**	**13:35**	....	....	....	....	....	....	....	....	....
	Wilkes-Barre	AHL	55	2	1	3	6	....	....	....	....	....	....	....	....	....	6	2	2	4	0	....	....	....	....
2004-05	Wilkes-Barre	AHL	80	16	14	30	19	....	....	....	....	....	....	....	....	....	10	1	2	3	2	....	....	....	....
2005-06	**Pittsburgh**	**NHL**	**13**	**0**	**1**	**1**	**0**	**0**	**0**	**0**	**17**	**0.0**	**–5**	**63**	**38.1**	**10:17**	....	....	....	....	....	....	....	....	....
	Wilkes-Barre	AHL	65	21	30	51	34	....	....	....	....	....	....	....	....	....	9	1	0	1	0	....	....	....	....
2006-07	**Detroit**	**NHL**	**5**	**0**	**0**	**0**	**2**	**0**	**0**	**0**	**6**	**0.0**	**0**	**0**	**0.0**	**5:38**	....	....	....	....	....	....	....	....	....
	Grand Rapids	AHL	75	15	29	44	36	....	....	....	....	....	....	....	....	....	6	1	1	2	2	....	....	....	....
2007-08	Lake Erie	AHL	37	8	8	16	18	....	....	....	....	....	....	....	....	....	....	....	....	....	....	....	....	....	....
	Jokerit Helsinki	Finland	11	0	3	3	4	....	....	....	....	....	....	....	....	....	11	0	0	0	0	....	....	....	....
	NHL Totals		**21**	**2**	**2**	**4**	**2**	**2**	**0**	**0**	**31**	**6.5**		**63**	**38.1**	**9:39**	....	....	....	....	....	....	....	....	....

Signed as a free agent by **Detroit**, July 13, 2006. Signed as a free agent by **Colorado**, July 13, 2007. Signed as a free agent by **Jokerit Helsinki** (Finland), January 31, 2008.

HUTCHINSON, Andrew

(HUHT-chihn-suhn, AN-droo) **T.B.**

Defense. Shoots right. 6'2", 206 lbs. Born, Evanston, IL, March 24, 1980. Nashville's 4th choice, 54th overall, in 1999 Entry Draft.

Season	Club	League	GP	G	A	Pts	PIM	PP	SH	GW	S	%	+/-	TF	F%	Min	Playoffs GP	G	A	Pts	PIM	PP	SH	GW	Min
1996-97	Det. Caesars	MNHL	82	15	41	56	....	....	....	....	....	....	....	....	....	....	....	....	....	....	....	....	....	....	....
1997-98	USNTDP	U-18	27	3	11	14	35	....	....	....	....	....	....	....	....	....	....	....	....	....	....	....	....	....	....
	USNTDP	USHL	15	0	7	7	8	....	....	....	....	....	....	....	....	....	....	....	....	....	....	....	....	....	....
	USNTDP	NAHL	12	2	0	2	8	....	....	....	....	....	....	....	....	....	5	2	3	5	2	....	....	....	....
1998-99	Michigan State	CCHA	37	3	12	15	26	....	....	....	....	....	....	....	....	....	....	....	....	....	....	....	....	....	....
99-2000	Michigan State	CCHA	42	5	12	17	64	....	....	....	....	....	....	....	....	....	....	....	....	....	....	....	....	....	....
2000-01	Michigan State	CCHA	42	5	19	24	46	....	....	....	....	....	....	....	....	....	....	....	....	....	....	....	....	....	....
2001-02	Michigan State	CCHA	39	6	16	22	24	....	....	....	....	....	....	....	....	....	....	....	....	....	....	....	....	....	....
	Milwaukee	AHL	5	0	1	1	0	....	....	....	....	....	....	....	....	....	....	....	....	....	....	....	....	....	....
2002-03	Milwaukee	AHL	63	9	17	26	40	....	....	....	....	....	....	....	....	....	3	1	0	1	0	....	....	....	....
	Toledo Storm	ECHL	10	2	5	7	4	....	....	....	....	....	....	....	....	....	....	....	....	....	....	....	....	....	....
2003-04	**Nashville**	**NHL**	**18**	**4**	**4**	**8**	**4**	**2**	**0**	**1**	**24**	**16.7**	**1**	**0**	**0.0**	**16:43**	....	....	....	....	....	....	....	....	....
	Milwaukee	AHL	46	12	12	24	39	....	....	....	....	....	....	....	....	....	22	5	11	16	33	....	....	....	....
2004-05	Milwaukee	AHL	76	10	35	45	79	....	....	....	....	....	....	....	....	....	7	1	3	4	8	....	....	....	....
2005-06 ♦	**Carolina**	**NHL**	**36**	**3**	**8**	**11**	**18**	**2**	**0**	**0**	**33**	**9.1**	**–2**	**0**	**0.0**	**10:22**	....	....	....	....	....	....	....	....	....
2006-07	**Carolina**	**NHL**	**41**	**3**	**11**	**14**	**30**	**2**	**0**	**0**	**45**	**6.7**	**0**	**0**	**0.0**	**12:13**	....	....	....	....	....	....	....	....	....
2007-08	Hartford	AHL	67	18	46	64	66	....	....	....	....	....	....	....	....	....	5	2	2	4	4	....	....	....	....
	NHL Totals		**95**	**10**	**23**	**33**	**52**	**6**	**0**	**1**	**102**	**9.8**		**0**	**0.0**	**12:22**	....	....	....	....	....	....	....	....	....

CCHA Second All-Star Team (2001, 2002) • NCAA West Second All-American Team (2002) • AHL First All-Star Team (2008) • Eddie Shore Award (Outstanding Defenseman – AHL) (2008)

Traded to **Carolina** by **Nashville** for Phoenix's 3rd round choice (previously acquired, Nashville selected Teemu Laakso) in 2005 Entry Draft, July 29, 2005. Traded to **NY Rangers** by **Carolina** with Joe Barnes and Carolina's 3rd round choice (Evgeny Grachev) in 2008 Entry Draft for Matt Cullen, July 17, 2007. Signed as a free agent by **Tampa Bay**, July 9, 2008.

IGGULDEN, Mike

(IHG-gul-den, MIGHK) **NYI**

Right wing. Shoots right. 6'3", 215 lbs. Born, St. Catharines, Ont., November 9, 1982.

Season	Club	League	GP	G	A	Pts	PIM	PP	SH	GW	S	%	+/-	TF	F%	Min	Playoffs GP	G	A	Pts	PIM	PP	SH	GW	Min
2001-02	Cornell Big Red	ECAC	30	1	3	4	6	....	....	....	....	....	....	....	....	....	....	....	....	....	....	....	....	....	....
2002-03	Cornell Big Red	ECAC	15	0	2	2	19	....	....	....	....	....	....	....	....	....	....	....	....	....	....	....	....	....	....
2003-04	Cornell Big Red	ECAC	30	2	8	10	10	....	....	....	....	....	....	....	....	....	....	....	....	....	....	....	....	....	....
2004-05	Cornell Big Red	ECAC	35	10	8	18	8	....	....	....	....	....	....	....	....	....	....	....	....	....	....	....	....	....	....
	Rochester	AHL	6	1	0	1	7	....	....	....	....	....	....	....	....	....	....	....	....	....	....	....	....	....	....
2005-06	Cleveland Barons	AHL	77	22	26	48	57	....	....	....	....	....	....	....	....	....	....	....	....	....	....	....	....	....	....
2006-07	Worcester Sharks	AHL	73	30	27	57	55	....	....	....	....	....	....	....	....	....	6	3	3	6	0	....	....	....	....
2007-08	**San Jose**	**NHL**	**1**	**0**	**0**	**0**	**0**	**0**	**0**	**0**	**1**	**0.0**	**–1**	**0**	**0.0**	**6:40**	....	....	....	....	....	....	....	....	....
	Worcester Sharks	AHL	78	29	37	66	63	....	....	....	....	....	....	....	....	....	....	....	....	....	....	....	....	....	....
	NHL Totals		**1**	**0**	**0**	**0**	**0**	**0**	**0**	**0**	**1**	**0.0**		**0**	**0.0**	**6:40**	....	....	....	....	....	....	....	....	....

Signed to an ATO (tryout) contract by **Rochester** (AHL), April 5, 2004. Signed to a PTO (tryout) contract by **Cleveland** (AHL), September 19, 2005. Signed as a free agent by **San Jose**, January 16, 2006. Signed as a free agent by **NY Islanders**, July 3, 2008.

IGINLA, Jarome

(ih-GIHN-lah, jah-ROHM) **CGY.**

Right wing. Shoots right. 6'1", 207 lbs. Born, Edmonton, Alta., July 1, 1977. Dallas' 1st choice, 11th overall, in 1995 Entry Draft.

Season	Club	League	GP	G	A	Pts	PIM	PP	SH	GW	S	%	+/-	TF	F%	Min	Playoffs GP	G	A	Pts	PIM	PP	SH	GW	Min
1991-92	St. Albert Raiders	AMHL	36	26	30	56	22	....	....	....	....	....	....	....	....	....	....	....	....	....	....	....	....	....	....
1992-93	St. Albert Raiders	AMHL	36	34	53	*87	20	....	....	....	....	....	....	....	....	....	....	....	....	....	....	....	....	....	....
1993-94	Kamloops Blazers	WHL	48	6	23	29	33	....	....	....	....	....	....	....	....	....	19	3	6	9	10	....	....	....	....
1994-95	Kamloops Blazers	WHL	72	33	38	71	111	....	....	....	....	....	....	....	....	....	21	7	11	18	34	....	....	....	....
1995-96	Kamloops Blazers	WHL	63	63	73	136	120	....	....	....	....	....	....	....	....	....	16	16	13	29	44	....	....	....	....
	Calgary	**NHL**	....	....	....	....	....	....	....	....	....	....	....	....	....	....	**2**	**1**	**1**	**2**	**0**	**0**	**0**	**0**	....
1996-97	**Calgary**	**NHL**	**82**	**21**	**29**	**50**	**37**	**8**	**1**	**3**	**169**	**12.4**	**–4**				....	....	....	....	....	....	....	....	....
1997-98	**Calgary**	**NHL**	**70**	**13**	**19**	**32**	**29**	**0**	**2**	**1**	**154**	**8.4**	**–10**				....	....	....	....	....	....	....	....	....
1998-99	**Calgary**	**NHL**	**82**	**28**	**23**	**51**	**58**	**7**	**0**	**4**	**211**	**13.3**	**1**	**111**	**51.4**	**16:30**	....	....	....	....	....	....	....	....	....
99-2000	**Calgary**	**NHL**	**77**	**29**	**34**	**63**	**26**	**12**	**0**	**4**	**256**	**11.3**	**0**	**278**	**52.9**	**18:24**	....	....	....	....	....	....	....	....	....
2000-01	**Calgary**	**NHL**	**77**	**31**	**40**	**71**	**62**	**10**	**0**	**4**	**229**	**13.5**	**–2**	**638**	**51.7**	**19:58**	....	....	....	....	....	....	....	....	....
2001-02	**Calgary**	**NHL**	**82**	***52**	**44**	***96**	**77**	**16**	**1**	**7**	**311**	**16.7**	**27**	**308**	**55.2**	**22:22**	....	....	....	....	....	....	....	....	....
	Canada	Olympics	6	3	1	4	0	....	....	....	....	....	....	....	....	....	....	....	....	....	....	....	....	....	....
2002-03	**Calgary**	**NHL**	**75**	**35**	**32**	**67**	**49**	**11**	**3**	**6**	**316**	**11.1**	**–10**	**90**	**43.3**	**21:26**	....	....	....	....	....	....	....	....	....
2003-04	**Calgary**	**NHL**	**81**	***41**	**32**	**73**	**84**	**8**	**4**	**10**	**265**	**15.5**	**21**	**305**	**54.4**	**21:18**	**26**	***13**	**9**	**22**	**45**	**4**	**2**	**3**	**23:18**
2004-05			DID NOT PLAY																						
2005-06	**Calgary**	**NHL**	**82**	**35**	**32**	**67**	**86**	**17**	**1**	**6**	**293**	**11.9**	**5**	**541**	**54.2**	**21:42**	**7**	**5**	**3**	**8**	**11**	**1**	**1**	**1**	**24:14**
	Canada	Olympics	6	2	1	3	4	....	....	....	....	....	....	....	....	....	....	....	....	....	....	....	....	....	....
2006-07	**Calgary**	**NHL**	**70**	**39**	**55**	**94**	**40**	**13**	**1**	**7**	**264**	**14.8**	**12**	**406**	**53.0**	**22:04**	**6**	**2**	**2**	**4**	**12**	**0**	**0**	**1**	**23:45**
2007-08	**Calgary**	**NHL**	**82**	**50**	**48**	**98**	**83**	**15**	**0**	**9**	**338**	**14.8**	**27**	**445**	**55.1**	**21:26**	**7**	**4**	**5**	**9**	**2**	**3**	**0**	**0**	**22:43**
	NHL Totals		**860**	**374**	**388**	**762**	**631**	**117**	**13**	**61**	**2806**	**13.3**		**3122**	**53.2**	**20:33**	**48**	**25**	**20**	**45**	**70**	**8**	**3**	**5**	**23:25**

George Parsons Trophy (Memorial Cup Tournament - Most Sportsmanlike Player) (1995) • WHL West First All-Star Team (1996) • WHL Player of the Year (1996) • Canadian Major Junior First All-Star Team (1996) • NHL All-Rookie Team (1997) • NHL First All-Star Team (2002, 2008) • Maurice "Rocket" Richard Trophy (2002) • Art Ross Trophy (2002) • Lester B. Pearson Award (2002) • NHL Second All-Star Team (2004) • King Clancy Memorial Trophy (2004) • Maurice "Rocket" Richard Trophy (2004) (tied with Ilya Kovalchuk and Rick Nash)

Played in NHL All-Star Game (2002, 2003, 2004, 2008)

Traded to **Calgary** by **Dallas** with Corey Millen for Joe Nieuwendyk, December 19, 1995.

IMMONEN, Jarkko

(IH-moh-nihn, YAHR-koh) **NYR**

Center. Shoots right. 6', 210 lbs. Born, Rantasalmi, Finland, April 19, 1982. Toronto's 8th choice, 254th overall, in 2002 Entry Draft.

Season	Club	League	GP	G	A	Pts	PIM	PP	SH	GW	S	%	+/-	TF	F%	Min	Playoffs GP	G	A	Pts	PIM	PP	SH	GW	Min
1997-98	SaPKo Jr.	Fin-Jr.	14	8	12	20	0	....	....	....	....	....	....	....	....	....	....	....	....	....	....	....	....	....	....
1998-99	SaPKo Jr.	Fin-Jr.	12	6	10	16	14	....	....	....	....	....	....	....	....	....	....	....	....	....	....	....	....	....	....
	SaPKo Savonlinna	Finland-2	36	2	2	4	6	....	....	....	....	....	....	....	....	....	....	....	....	....	....	....	....	....	....
99-2000	SaPKo Jr.	Fin-Jr.	....	....	....	....	....	....	....	....	....	....	....	....	....	....	2	0	4	4	4	....	....	....	....
	SaPKo Savonlinna	Finland-2	42	18	16	34	34	....	....	....	....	....	....	....	....	....	....	....	....	....	....	....	....	....	....
2000-01	TuTo Turku Jr.	Fin-Jr.	1	0	1	1	0	....	....	....	....	....	....	....	....	....	1	0	0	0	2	....	....	....	....
	TuTo Turku	Finland-2	41	20	20	40	22	....	....	....	....	....	....	....	....	....	11	5	7	12	10	....	....	....	....
2001-02	Assat Pori	Finland	44	0	2	2	6	....	....	....	....	....	....	....	....	....	....	....	....	....	....	....	....	....	....
	Assat Pori Jr.	Fin-Jr.	....	....	....	....	....	....	....	....	....	....	....	....	....	....	8	5	1	6	10	....	....	....	....
2002-03	JYP Jyvaskyla	Finland	56	10	23	33	34	....	....	....	....	....	....	....	....	....	7	1	1	2	8	....	....	....	....
2003-04	JYP Jyvaskyla	Finland	52	23	26	49	28	....	....	....	....	....	....	....	....	....	2	0	0	0	0	....	....	....	....
2004-05	JYP Jyvaskyla	Finland	54	19	28	47	24	....	....	....	....	....	....	....	....	....	3	0	2	2	2	....	....	....	....

Season	Club	League	GP	G	A	Pts	PIM	PP	SH	GW	S	%	+/-	TF	F%	Min	GP	G	A	Pts	PIM	PP	SH	GW	Min
			Regular Season														Playoffs								
2005-06	**NY Rangers**	**NHL**	**6**	**2**	**0**	**2**	**0**	**1**	**0**	**0**	**8**	**25.0**	**–1**	**51**	**56.9**	**10:15**									
	Hartford	AHL	74	30	40	70	34										6	2	3	5	2				
2006-07	**NY Rangers**	**NHL**	**14**	**1**	**5**	**6**	**4**	**0**	**0**	**1**	**14**	**7.1**	**–2**	**108**	**56.5**	**10:22**									
	Hartford	AHL	54	20	26	46	30										7	2	6	8	2				
2007-08	JYP Jyvaskyla	Finland	54	26	37	63	54										6	1	8	9	8				
	SaiPa	Finland	56	19	19	38	44																		
	NHL Totals		**20**	**3**	**5**	**8**	**4**	**1**	**0**	**1**	**22**	**13.6**		**159**	**56.6**	**10:20**									

Traded to **NY Rangers** by **Toronto** with Maxim Kondratiev, Toronto's 1st round choice (later traded to Calgary - Calgary selected Kris Chucko) in 2004 Entry Draft and Toronto's 2nd round choice (Michael Sauer) in 2005 Entry Draft for Brian Leetch and Edmonton's 4th round choice (previously acquired, Toronto selected Roman Kukumberg) in 2004 Entry Draft, March 3, 2004.

ISBISTER, Brad

(IHZ-bihs-tuhr, BRAD)

Left wing. Shoots right. 6'4", 225 lbs. Born, Edmonton, Alta., May 7, 1977. Winnipeg's 4th choice, 67th overall, in 1995 Entry Draft.

Season	Club	League	GP	G	A	Pts	PIM	PP	SH	GW	S	%	+/-	TF	F%	Min	GP	G	A	Pts	PIM	PP	SH	GW	Min
1992-93	Calgary Canucks	ABHL	35	24	25	49	74																		
1993-94	Portland	WHL	64	7	10	17	45										10	0	2	2	0				
1994-95	Portland	WHL	67	16	20	36	123																		
1995-96	Portland	WHL	71	45	44	89	184										7	2	4	6	20				
1996-97	Portland	WHL	24	15	18	33	45										6	2	1	3	16				
	Springfield	AHL	7	3	1	4	14										9	1	2	3	10				
1997-98	**Phoenix**	**NHL**	**66**	**9**	**8**	**17**	**102**	**1**	**0**	**1**	**115**	**7.8**	**4**				**5**	**0**	**0**	**0**	**2**	**0**	**0**	**0**	
	Springfield	AHL	9	8	2	10	36																		
1998-99	**Phoenix**	**NHL**	**32**	**4**	**4**	**8**	**46**	**0**	**0**	**2**	**48**	**8.3**	**1**	**3**	**0.0**	**11:33**									
	Springfield	AHL	4	1	1	2	12																		
	Las Vegas	IHL	2	0	0	0	9																		
99-2000	**NY Islanders**	**NHL**	**64**	**22**	**20**	**42**	**100**	**9**	**0**	**1**	**135**	**16.3**	**–18**	**55**	**54.6**	**16:58**									
2000-01	**NY Islanders**	**NHL**	**51**	**18**	**14**	**32**	**59**	**7**	**1**	**4**	**129**	**14.0**	**–19**	**255**	**45.9**	**19:26**									
2001-02	**NY Islanders**	**NHL**	**79**	**17**	**21**	**38**	**113**	**4**	**0**	**2**	**142**	**12.0**	**1**	**71**	**45.1**	**15:18**	**3**	**1**	**1**	**2**	**17**	**1**	**0**	**1**	**12:33**
2002-03	**NY Islanders**	**NHL**	**53**	**10**	**13**	**23**	**34**	**2**	**0**	**2**	**90**	**11.1**	**–9**	**13**	**46.2**	**13:54**									
	Edmonton	**NHL**	**13**	**3**	**2**	**5**	**9**	**0**	**0**	**1**	**29**	**10.3**	**0**	**10**	**50.0**	**13:14**	**6**	**0**	**1**	**1**	**12**	**0**	**0**	**0**	**10:04**
2003-04	**Edmonton**	**NHL**	**51**	**10**	**8**	**18**	**54**	**1**	**0**	**2**	**80**	**12.5**	**–2**	**55**	**56.4**	**12:46**									
2004-05	Innsbruck	Austria	11	7	4	11	41										5	3	1	4	6				
2005-06	**Boston**	**NHL**	**58**	**6**	**17**	**23**	**46**	**1**	**0**	**0**	**112**	**5.4**	**–2**	**10**	**60.0**	**13:55**									
2006-07	Albany River Rats	AHL	9	3	5	8	54																		
	NY Rangers	**NHL**	**19**	**1**	**4**	**5**	**14**	**1**	**0**	**0**	**36**	**2.8**	**5**	**12**	**33.3**	**13:36**	**4**	**0**	**0**	**0**	**2**	**0**	**0**	**0**	**9:58**
	Hartford	AHL	34	12	8	20	22																		
2007-08	**Vancouver**	**NHL**	**55**	**6**	**5**	**11**	**38**	**0**	**0**	**1**	**71**	**8.5**	**–4**	**17**	**47.1**	**10:49**									
	NHL Totals		**541**	**106**	**116**	**222**	**615**	**26**	**1**	**16**	**987**	**10.7**		**501**	**47.7**	**14:29**	**18**	**1**	**2**	**3**	**33**	**1**	**0**	**1**	**10:36**

WHL West Second All-Star Team (1997)

Rights transferred to **Phoenix** after **Winnipeg** franchise relocated, July 1, 1996. Traded to **NY Islanders** by **Phoenix** with Phoenix's 3rd round choice (Brian Collins) in 1999 Entry Draft for Robert Reichel, NY Islanders' 3rd round choice (Jason Jaspers) in 1999 Entry Draft and Ottawa's 4th round choice (previously acquired, Phoenix selected Preston Mizzi) in 1999 Entry Draft, March 20, 1999. Traded to **Edmonton** by **NY Islanders** with Raffi Torres for Janne Niinimaa and Washington's 2nd round choice (previously acquired, NY Islanders selected Evgeni Tunik) in 2003 Entry Draft , March 11, 2003. Signed as a free agent by **Innsbruck** (Austria), February 12, 2005. Traded to **Boston** by **Edmonton** for Boston's 4th round choice (later traded back to Boston - later traded to San Jose - San Jose selected James Delory) in 2006 Entry Draft, August 1, 2005. Signed as a free agent by **Carolina**, August 30, 2006. Traded to **NY Rangers** by **Carolina** for Jakub Petruzalek and future considerations, November 21, 2006. Signed as a free agent by **Vancouver**, July 3, 2007.

IVANANS, Raitis

(ih-VAH-nehns, RIGH-this) **L.A.**

Left wing. Shoots left. 6'4", 263 lbs. Born, Riga, Latvia, January 3, 1979.

Season	Club	League	GP	G	A	Pts	PIM	PP	SH	GW	S	%	+/-	TF	F%	Min	GP	G	A	Pts	PIM	PP	SH	GW	Min
1997-98	Flint Generals	UHL	18	0	1	1	20																		
1998-99	Macon Whoopee	CHL	16	1	1	2	20																		
	Tulsa Oilers	CHL	32	2	7	9	39																		
99-2000	Pensacola	ECHL	59	3	7	10	146										2	0	0	0	0				
2000-01	Hershey Bears	AHL	2	0	0	0	0																		
	New Haven	UHL	66	4	10	14	270										8	1	0	1	4				
2001-02	Toledo Storm	ECHL	16	2	2	4	59																		
	Baton Rouge	ECHL	40	4	5	9	180																		
2002-03	Milwaukee	AHL	17	0	0	0	38										1	0	0	0	15				
	Rockford IceHogs	UHL	50	4	2	6	208																		
2003-04	Milwaukee	AHL	54	1	7	8	166										7	0	1	1	17				
	Rockford IceHogs	UHL	1	0	0	0	0																		
2004-05	Hamilton	AHL	75	2	5	7	259										2	0	1	1	0				
2005-06	**Montreal**	**NHL**	**4**	**0**	**0**	**0**	**9**	**0**	**0**	**0**	**0**	**0.0**	**–1**	**0**	**0.0**	**2:58**									
	Hamilton	AHL	43	2	0	2	120																		
2006-07	**Los Angeles**	**NHL**	**66**	**4**	**4**	**8**	**140**	**0**	**0**	**0**	**37**	**10.8**	**–12**	**1**	**0.0**	**6:59**									
2007-08	**Los Angeles**	**NHL**	**73**	**6**	**2**	**8**	**134**	**0**	**0**	**0**	**48**	**12.5**	**–10**	**0**	**0.0**	**7:30**									
	NHL Totals		**143**	**10**	**6**	**16**	**283**	**0**	**0**	**0**	**85**	**11.8**		**1**	**0.0**	**7:08**									

Signed as a free agent by **Montreal**, July 16, 2004. Signed as a free agent by **Los Angeles**, July 13, 2006.

JACKMAN, Barret

(JAK-man, BAIR-reht) **ST.L.**

Defense. Shoots left. 6', 203 lbs. Born, Trail, B.C., March 5, 1981. St. Louis' 1st choice, 17th overall, in 1999 Entry Draft.

Season	Club	League	GP	G	A	Pts	PIM	PP	SH	GW	S	%	+/-	TF	F%	Min	GP	G	A	Pts	PIM	PP	SH	GW	Min
1996-97	Beaver Valley	VIJHL	32	22	25	47	180																		
1997-98	Regina Pats	WHL	68	2	11	13	224										9	0	3	3	32				
1998-99	Regina Pats	WHL	70	8	36	44	259																		
99-2000	Regina Pats	WHL	53	9	37	46	175										6	1	1	2	19				
	Worcester IceCats	AHL															2	0	0	0	13				
2000-01	Regina Pats	WHL	43	9	27	36	138										6	0	3	3	8				
2001-02	**St. Louis**	**NHL**	**1**	**0**	**0**	**0**	**0**	**0**	**0**	**0**	**1**	**0.0**	**0**	**0**	**0.0**	**18:56**	**1**	**0**	**0**	**0**	**2**	**0**	**0**	**0**	**18:24**
	Worcester IceCats	AHL	75	2	12	14	266										3	0	1	1	4				
2002-03	**St. Louis**	**NHL**	**82**	**3**	**16**	**19**	**190**	**0**	**0**	**0**	**66**	**4.5**	**23**	**0**	**0.0**	**20:03**	**7**	**0**	**0**	**0**	**14**	**0**	**0**	**0**	**21:59**
2003-04	**St. Louis**	**NHL**	**15**	**1**	**2**	**3**	**41**	**0**	**0**	**0**	**11**	**9.1**	**–1**	**0**	**0.0**	**18:16**									
2004-05	Missouri	UHL	28	3	17	20	61										3	0	0	0	4				
2005-06	**St. Louis**	**NHL**	**63**	**4**	**6**	**10**	**156**	**0**	**0**	**2**	**56**	**7.1**	**–6**	**0**	**0.0**	**18:46**									
2006-07	**St. Louis**	**NHL**	**70**	**3**	**24**	**27**	**82**	**1**	**0**	**1**	**86**	**3.5**	**20**	**0**	**0.0**	**21:30**									
	Peoria Rivermen	AHL	1	0	0	0	0																		
2007-08	**St. Louis**	**NHL**	**78**	**2**	**14**	**16**	**93**	**1**	**0**	**0**	**80**	**2.5**	**–12**	**0**	**0.0**	**22:24**									
	NHL Totals		**309**	**13**	**62**	**75**	**562**	**2**	**0**	**3**	**300**	**4.3**		**0**	**0.0**	**20:37**	**8**	**0**	**0**	**0**	**16**	**0**	**0**	**0**	**21:32**

WHL East Second All-Star Team (2000) • AHL All-Rookie Team (2002) • NHL All-Rookie Team (2003) • Calder Memorial Trophy (2003)

• Missed majority of 2003-04 season recovering from shoulder injury suffered in game vs. Vancouver, October 22, 2003. Signed as a free agent by **Missouri** (UHL), February 3, 2005.

JACKMAN, Ric

(JAK-man, RIHK)

Defense. Shoots right. 6'2", 214 lbs. Born, Toronto, Ont., June 28, 1978. Dallas' 1st choice, 5th overall, in 1996 Entry Draft.

Season	Club	League	GP	G	A	Pts	PIM	PP	SH	GW	S	%	+/-	TF	F%	Min	GP	G	A	Pts	PIM	PP	SH	GW	Min
1993-94	Miss. Sens	MTHL	81	35	53	88	156																		
1994-95	Miss. Sens	MTHL	53	20	37	57	120																		
	Richmond Hill	MTJHL	10	2	9	11	16																		
1995-96	Sault Ste. Marie	OHL	66	13	29	42	97										4	1	0	1	15				
1996-97	Sault Ste. Marie	OHL	53	13	34	47	116										10	2	6	8	24				
1997-98	Sault Ste. Marie	OHL	60	33	40	73	111																		
	Michigan	IHL	14	1	5	6	10										4	0	0	0	10				
1998-99	Michigan	IHL	71	13	17	30	106										5	0	4	4	6				
99-2000	**Dallas**	**NHL**	**22**	**1**	**2**	**3**	**6**	**1**	**0**	**0**	**16**	**6.3**	**–1**	**0**	**0.0**	**8:06**									
	Michigan	IHL	50	3	16	19	51																		
2000-01	**Dallas**	**NHL**	**16**	**0**	**0**	**0**	**18**	**0**	**0**	**0**	**10**	**0.0**	**–6**	**0**	**0.0**	**8:51**									
	Utah Grizzlies	IHL	57	9	19	28	24																		
2001-02	**Boston**	**NHL**	**2**	**0**	**0**	**0**	**2**	**0**	**0**	**0**	**4**	**0.0**	**–1**	**0**	**0.0**	**13:26**									
	Providence Bruins	AHL	9	0	1	1	8										2	0	0	0	2				
2002-03	**Toronto**	**NHL**	**42**	**0**	**2**	**2**	**41**	**0**	**0**	**0**	**35**	**0.0**	**–10**	**0**	**0.0**	**13:59**									
	St. John's	AHL	8	2	6	8	24																		

			Regular Season														Playoffs								
Season	Club	League	GP	G	A	Pts	PIM	PP	SH	GW	S	%	+/-	TF	F%	Min	GP	G	A	Pts	PIM	PP	SH	GW	Min
2003-04	**Toronto**	**NHL**	**29**	**2**	**4**	**6**	**13**	**1**	**0**	**1**	**35**	**5.7**	**–11**	**0**	**0.0**	**18:00**	....	....	....	....	....	....	....	....	....
	Pittsburgh	**NHL**	**25**	**7**	**17**	**24**	**14**	**6**	**0**	**1**	**56**	**12.5**	**–5**	**0**	**0.0**	**24:14**	....	....	....	....	....	....	....	....	....
2004-05	Bjorkloven	Sweden-2	46	13	26	39	209	....	....	....	....	....	....	....	....	....	....	....	....	....	....	....	....	....	....
2005-06	**Pittsburgh**	**NHL**	**49**	**6**	**22**	**28**	**46**	**3**	**0**	**1**	**95**	**6.3**	**–20**	**0**	**0.0**	**18:21**	....	....	....	....	....	....	....	....	....
	Florida	**NHL**	**15**	**1**	**1**	**2**	**6**	**0**	**0**	**0**	**25**	**4.0**	**0**	**0**	**0.0**	**14:04**	....	....	....	....	....	....	....	....	....
2006-07	**Florida**	**NHL**	**7**	**1**	**0**	**1**	**10**	**0**	**0**	**1**	**13**	**7.7**	**–3**	**0**	**0.0**	**10:31**	....	....	....	....	....	....	....	....	....
	♦ **Anaheim**	**NHL**	**24**	**1**	**10**	**11**	**10**	**1**	**0**	**0**	**23**	**4.3**	**3**	**0**	**0.0**	**14:38**	**7**	**1**	**1**	**2**	**2**	**1**	**0**	**0**	**6:04**
2007-08	Salzburg	Austria	31	7	23	30	34	....	....	....	....	....	....	....	....	....	....	....	....	....	....	....	....	....	....
	Leksands IF	Sweden-2	8	1	5	6	10	....	....	....	....	....	....	....	....	....	10	4	5	9	10	....	....	....	....
	NHL Totals		**231**	**19**	**58**	**77**	**166**	**12**	**0**	**4**	**312**	**6.1**		**0**	**0.0**	**15:34**	**7**	**1**	**1**	**2**	**2**	**1**	**0**	**0**	**6:04**

OHL All-Rookie Team (1996) • OHL Second All-Star Team (1998)

Traded to **Boston** by **Dallas** for Cameron Mann, June 23, 2001. • Missed majority of 2001-02 season recovering from shoulder injury suffered in game vs. St. Louis, October 21, 2001. Traded to **Toronto** by **Boston** for the rights to Kris Vernarsky, May 13, 2002. Traded to **Pittsburgh** by **Toronto** for Drake Berehowsky, February 11, 2004. Signed as a free agent by **Bjorkloven** (Sweden-2), September 17, 2004. Traded to **Florida** by **Pittsburgh** for Petr Taticek, March 9, 2006. Traded to **Anaheim** by **Florida** for Anaheim's 6th round choice (Corey Syvret) in 2007 Entry Draft, January 3, 2007. Signed as a free agent by **Salzburg** (Austria), August 2, 2007.

JACKMAN, Tim

(JAK-man, TIHM) **NYI**

Right wing. Shoots right. 6'4", 210 lbs. Born, Minot, ND, November 14, 1981. Columbus' 2nd choice, 38th overall, in 2001 Entry Draft.

Season	Club	League	GP	G	A	Pts	PIM	PP	SH	GW	S	%	+/-	TF	F%	Min	GP	G	A	Pts	PIM	PP	SH	GW	Min
1998-99	Park Center	High-MN	22	22	22	44	....	....	....	....	....	....	....	....	....	....	....	....	....	....	....	....	....	....	....
99-2000	Park Center	High-MN	19	34	22	56	....	....	....	....	....	....	....	....	....	....	....	....	....	....	....	....	....	....	....
	Twin Cities	USHL	25	11	9	20	58	....	....	....	....	....	....	....	....	....	13	8	5	13	12	....	....	....	....
2000-01	Minnesota State	WCHA	37	11	14	25	92	....	....	....	....	....	....	....	....	....	....	....	....	....	....	....	....	....	....
2001-02	Minnesota State	WCHA	36	14	14	28	86	....	....	....	....	....	....	....	....	....	....	....	....	....	....	....	....	....	....
2002-03	Syracuse Crunch	AHL	77	9	7	16	48	....	....	....	....	....	....	....	....	....	....	....	....	....	....	....	....	....	....
2003-04	**Columbus**	**NHL**	**19**	**1**	**2**	**3**	**16**	**0**	**0**	**0**	**18**	**5.6**	**–7**	**1**	**100.0**	**9:56**	....	....	....	....	....	....	....	....	....
	Syracuse Crunch	AHL	64	23	13	36	61	....	....	....	....	....	....	....	....	....	7	2	3	5	12	....	....	....	....
2004-05	Syracuse Crunch	AHL	73	14	21	35	98	....	....	....	....	....	....	....	....	....	....	....	....	....	....	....	....	....	....
2005-06	**Phoenix**	**NHL**	**8**	**0**	**0**	**0**	**21**	**0**	**0**	**0**	**4**	**0.0**	**1**	**1**	**0.0**	**7:13**	....	....	....	....	....	....	....	....	....
	San Antonio	AHL	50	7	13	20	127	....	....	....	....	....	....	....	....	....	....	....	....	....	....	....	....	....	....
	Manchester	AHL	18	2	3	5	33	....	....	....	....	....	....	....	....	....	7	0	3	3	20	....	....	....	....
2006-07	**Los Angeles**	**NHL**	**5**	**0**	**0**	**0**	**10**	**0**	**0**	**0**	**3**	**0.0**	**–1**	**0**	**0.0**	**6:36**	....	....	....	....	....	....	....	....	....
	Manchester	AHL	69	19	14	33	143	....	....	....	....	....	....	....	....	....	16	3	3	6	26	....	....	....	....
2007-08	**NY Islanders**	**NHL**	**36**	**1**	**3**	**4**	**57**	**0**	**0**	**0**	**36**	**2.8**	**–3**	**2**	**100.0**	**6:37**	....	....	....	....	....	....	....	....	....
	Bridgeport	AHL	44	15	21	36	67	....	....	....	....	....	....	....	....	....	....	....	....	....	....	....	....	....	....
	NHL Totals		**68**	**2**	**5**	**7**	**104**	**0**	**0**	**0**	**61**	**3.3**		**4**	**75.0**	**7:36**	....	....	....	....	....	....	....	....	....

Traded to **Phoenix** by **Columbus** with Geoff Sanderson for Cale Hulse, Mike Rupp and Jason Chimera, October 8, 2005. Traded to **Los Angeles** by **Phoenix** for Yanick Lehoux, March 9, 2006. Signed as a free agent by **NY Islanders**, July 5, 2007.

JACQUES, Jean-Francois

(ZHAWK, ZHAWN-fran-SWUH) **EDM.**

Left wing. Shoots left. 6'4", 217 lbs. Born, Montreal, Que., April 29, 1985. Edmonton's 3rd choice, 68th overall, in 2003 Entry Draft.

Season	Club	League	GP	G	A	Pts	PIM	PP	SH	GW	S	%	+/-	TF	F%	Min	GP	G	A	Pts	PIM	PP	SH	GW	Min
2000-01	Cap-d-Madeleine	QAAA	39	22	13	35	28	....	....	....	....	....	....	....	....	....	10	5	8	13	14	....	....	....	....
2001-02	Baie-Comeau	QMJHL	66	10	14	24	136	....	....	....	....	....	....	....	....	....	5	1	0	1	2	....	....	....	....
2002-03	Baie-Comeau	QMJHL	67	12	21	33	123	....	....	....	....	....	....	....	....	....	12	4	2	6	13	....	....	....	....
2003-04	Baie-Comeau	QMJHL	59	20	24	44	70	....	....	....	....	....	....	....	....	....	4	1	0	1	4	....	....	....	....
2004-05	Baie-Comeau	QMJHL	69	36	42	78	56	....	....	....	....	....	....	....	....	....	6	3	5	8	6	....	....	....	....
	Edmonton	AHL	6	0	0	0	5	....	....	....	....	....	....	....	....	....	....	....	....	....	....	....	....	....	....
2005-06	**Edmonton**	**NHL**	**7**	**0**	**0**	**0**	**0**	**0**	**0**	**0**	**8**	**0.0**	**–3**	**0**	**0.0**	**6:43**	....	....	....	....	....	....	....	....	....
	Hamilton	AHL	65	24	19	43	131	....	....	....	....	....	....	....	....	....	....	....	....	....	....	....	....	....	....
2006-07	**Edmonton**	**NHL**	**37**	**0**	**0**	**0**	**33**	**0**	**0**	**0**	**23**	**0.0**	**–11**	**2**	**0.0**	**7:55**	....	....	....	....	....	....	....	....	....
	Wilkes-Barre	AHL	29	10	17	27	53	....	....	....	....	....	....	....	....	....	11	1	2	3	43	....	....	....	....
2007-08	**Edmonton**	**NHL**	**9**	**0**	**0**	**0**	**2**	**0**	**0**	**0**	**2**	**0.0**	**–3**	**0**	**0.0**	**6:10**	....	....	....	....	....	....	....	....	....
	Springfield	AHL	38	11	14	25	63	....	....	....	....	....	....	....	....	....	....	....	....	....	....	....	....	....	....
	NHL Totals		**53**	**0**	**0**	**0**	**35**	**0**	**0**	**0**	**33**	**0.0**		**2**	**0.0**	**7:27**	....	....	....	....	....	....	....	....	....

JAFFRAY, Jason

(JAF-ray, JAY-suhn) **VAN.**

Left wing. Shoots left. 6'1", 205 lbs. Born, Rimbey, Alta., June 30, 1981.

Season	Club	League	GP	G	A	Pts	PIM	PP	SH	GW	S	%	+/-	TF	F%	Min	GP	G	A	Pts	PIM	PP	SH	GW	Min
1997-98	Edmonton Ice	WHL	6	0	1	1	0	....	....	....	....	....	....	....	....	....	....	....	....	....	....	....	....	....	....
1998-99	Kootenay Ice	WHL	57	14	12	26	50	....	....	....	....	....	....	....	....	....	7	1	2	3	6	....	....	....	....
99-2000	Kootenay Ice	WHL	71	24	28	52	104	....	....	....	....	....	....	....	....	....	21	10	9	19	17	....	....	....	....
2000-01	Kootenay Ice	WHL	70	31	42	73	108	....	....	....	....	....	....	....	....	....	11	5	7	12	10	....	....	....	....
2001-02	Kootenay Ice	WHL	32	15	19	34	38	....	....	....	....	....	....	....	....	....	....	....	....	....	....	....	....	....	....
	Swift Current	WHL	41	23	26	49	44	....	....	....	....	....	....	....	....	....	12	4	5	9	25	....	....	....	....
2002-03	Norfolk Admirals	AHL	2	0	0	0	0	....	....	....	....	....	....	....	....	....	....	....	....	....	....	....	....	....	....
	Roanoke Express	ECHL	64	34	51	85	89	....	....	....	....	....	....	....	....	....	4	0	3	3	4	....	....	....	....
2003-04	Wilkes-Barre	AHL	5	0	1	1	0	....	....	....	....	....	....	....	....	....	....	....	....	....	....	....	....	....	....
	Wheeling Nailers	ECHL	54	37	37	74	81	....	....	....	....	....	....	....	....	....	2	1	1	2	2	....	....	....	....
2004-05	Cleveland Barons	AHL	30	10	6	16	23	....	....	....	....	....	....	....	....	....	....	....	....	....	....	....	....	....	....
	Manitoba Moose	AHL	14	4	4	8	6	....	....	....	....	....	....	....	....	....	1	0	0	0	0	....	....	....	....
	Wheeling Nailers	ECHL	23	6	6	12	22	....	....	....	....	....	....	....	....	....	....	....	....	....	....	....	....	....	....
2005-06	Manitoba Moose	AHL	73	12	35	47	58	....	....	....	....	....	....	....	....	....	13	6	1	7	11	....	....	....	....
2006-07	Manitoba Moose	AHL	77	35	46	81	75	....	....	....	....	....	....	....	....	....	13	6	7	13	6	....	....	....	....
2007-08	**Vancouver**	**NHL**	**19**	**2**	**4**	**6**	**19**	**1**	**0**	**1**	**15**	**13.3**	**4**	**176**	**47.7**	**12:35**	....	....	....	....	....	....	....	....	....
	Manitoba Moose	AHL	43	21	27	48	51	....	....	....	....	....	....	....	....	....	3	1	4	5	0	....	....	....	....
	NHL Totals		**19**	**2**	**4**	**6**	**19**	**1**	**0**	**1**	**15**	**13.3**		**176**	**47.7**	**12:35**	....	....	....	....	....	....	....	....	....

AHL Second All-Star Team (2007)

Signed as a free agent by **Vancouver**, July 3, 2007.

JAGR, Jaromir

(YAH-guhr, YAIR-oh-MEER)

Right wing. Shoots left. 6'3", 240 lbs. Born, Kladno, Czech., February 15, 1972. Pittsburgh's 1st choice, 5th overall, in 1990 Entry Draft.

Season	Club	League	GP	G	A	Pts	PIM	PP	SH	GW	S	%	+/-	TF	F%	Min	GP	G	A	Pts	PIM	PP	SH	GW	Min
1984-85	Kladno Jr.	Czech-Jr.	34	24	17	41	....	....	....	....	....	....	....	....	....	....	....	....	....	....	....	....	....	....	....
1985-86	Kladno Jr.	Czech-Jr.	36	41	29	70	....	....	....	....	....	....	....	....	....	....	....	....	....	....	....	....	....	....	....
1986-87	Kladno Jr.	Czech-Jr.	30	35	35	70	....	....	....	....	....	....	....	....	....	....	....	....	....	....	....	....	....	....	....
1987-88	Kladno Jr.	Czech-Jr.	35	57	27	84	....	....	....	....	....	....	....	....	....	....	....	....	....	....	....	....	....	....	....
1988-89	Kladno	Czech	29	3	3	6	4	....	....	....	....	....	....	....	....	....	10	5	7	12	0	....	....	....	....
1989-90	Poldi Kladno	Czech	42	22	28	50	....	....	....	....	....	....	....	....	....	....	9	*8	2	10	....	....	....	....	....
1990-91 ♦	**Pittsburgh**	**NHL**	**80**	**27**	**30**	**57**	**42**	**7**	**0**	**4**	**136**	**19.9**	**–4**	....	....	....	**24**	**3**	**10**	**13**	**6**	**1**	**0**	**1**	....
1991-92 ♦	**Pittsburgh**	**NHL**	**70**	**32**	**37**	**69**	**34**	**4**	**0**	**4**	**194**	**16.5**	**12**	....	....	....	**21**	**11**	**13**	**24**	**6**	**2**	**0**	**4**	....
1992-93	**Pittsburgh**	**NHL**	**81**	**34**	**60**	**94**	**61**	**10**	**1**	**9**	**242**	**14.0**	**30**	....	....	....	**12**	**5**	**4**	**9**	**23**	**1**	**0**	**1**	....
1993-94	**Pittsburgh**	**NHL**	**80**	**32**	**67**	**99**	**61**	**9**	**0**	**6**	**298**	**10.7**	**15**	....	....	....	**6**	**2**	**4**	**6**	**16**	**0**	**0**	**1**	....
1994-95	HC Kladno	CzRep	11	8	14	22	10	....	....	....	....	....	....	....	....	....	....	....	....	....	....	....	....	....	....
	HC Bolzano	Euroliga	5	8	8	16	4	....	....	....	....	....	....	....	....	....	....	....	....	....	....	....	....	....	....
	HC Bolzano	Italy	1	0	0	0	0	....	....	....	....	....	....	....	....	....	....	....	....	....	....	....	....	....	....
	Schalke	German-2	1	1	10	11	0	....	....	....	....	....	....	....	....	....	....	....	....	....	....	....	....	....	....
	Pittsburgh	**NHL**	**48**	**32**	**38**	***70**	**37**	**8**	**3**	**7**	**192**	**16.7**	**23**	....	....	....	**12**	**10**	**5**	**15**	**6**	**2**	**1**	**1**	....
1995-96	**Pittsburgh**	**NHL**	**82**	**62**	**87**	**149**	**96**	**20**	**1**	**12**	**403**	**15.4**	**31**	....	....	....	**18**	**11**	**12**	**23**	**18**	**5**	**1**	**1**	....
1996-97	**Pittsburgh**	**NHL**	**63**	**47**	**48**	**95**	**40**	**11**	**2**	**6**	**234**	**20.1**	**22**	....	....	....	**5**	**4**	**4**	**8**	**4**	**2**	**0**	**0**	....
1997-98	**Pittsburgh**	**NHL**	**77**	**35**	***67**	***102**	**64**	**7**	**0**	**8**	**262**	**13.4**	**17**	....	....	....	**6**	**4**	**5**	**9**	**2**	**1**	**0**	**0**	....
	Czech Republic	Olympics	6	1	4	5	2	....	....	....	....	....	....	....	....	....	....	....	....	....	....	....	....	....	....
1998-99	**Pittsburgh**	**NHL**	**81**	**44**	***83**	***127**	**66**	**10**	**1**	**7**	**343**	**12.8**	**17**	**4**	**50.0**	**25:51**	**9**	**5**	**7**	**12**	**16**	**1**	**0**	**1**	**25:32**
99-2000	**Pittsburgh**	**NHL**	**63**	**42**	**54**	***96**	**50**	**10**	**0**	**5**	**290**	**14.5**	**25**	**9**	**22.2**	**23:12**	**11**	**8**	**8**	**16**	**6**	**2**	**0**	**4**	**24:32**
2000-01	**Pittsburgh**	**NHL**	**81**	**52**	***69**	***121**	**42**	**14**	**1**	**10**	**317**	**16.4**	**19**	**2**	**0.0**	**23:19**	**16**	**2**	**10**	**12**	**18**	**2**	**0**	**0**	**22:15**
2001-02	**Washington**	**NHL**	**69**	**31**	**48**	**79**	**30**	**10**	**0**	**3**	**197**	**15.7**	**0**	**2**	**50.0**	**21:43**	....	....	....	....	....	....	....	....	....
	Czech Republic	Olympics	4	2	3	5	4	....	....	....	....	....	....	....	....	....	....	....	....	....	....	....	....	....	....
2002-03	**Washington**	**NHL**	**75**	**36**	**41**	**77**	**38**	**13**	**2**	**9**	**290**	**12.4**	**5**	**5**	**20.0**	**21:18**	**6**	**2**	**5**	**7**	**2**	**1**	**0**	**0**	**25:13**
2003-04	**Washington**	**NHL**	**46**	**16**	**29**	**45**	**26**	**6**	**0**	**1**	**159**	**10.1**	**–4**	**1**	**0.0**	**21:05**	....	....	....	....	....	....	....	....	....
	NY Rangers	**NHL**	**31**	**15**	**14**	**29**	**12**	**4**	**0**	**2**	**98**	**15.3**	**–1**	**0**	**0.0**	**20:45**	....	....	....	....	....	....	....	....	....

Season	Club	League	GP	G	A	Pts	PIM	PP	SH	GW	S	%	+/-	TF	F%	Min	GP	G	A	Pts	PIM	PP	SH	GW	Min
			Regular Season														Playoffs								
2004-05	HC Rabat Kladno	CzRep	17	11	17	28	16	....	....	....	....	....	....	....	....	....	....	....	....	....	....	....	....	....	....
	Avangard Omsk	Russia	32	16	22	38	63	....	....	....	....	....	....	....	....	....	11	4	*10	*14	22	....	....	....	....
2005-06	**NY Rangers**	**NHL**	**82**	**54**	**69**	**123**	**72**	**24**	**0**	**9**	**368**	**14.7**	**34**	**6**	**16.7**	**22:05**	**3**	**0**	**1**	**1**	**2**	**0**	**0**	**0**	**13:47**
	Czech Republic	Olympics	8	2	5	7	6	....	....	....	....	....	....	....	....	....	....	....	....	....	....	....	....	....	....
2006-07	**NY Rangers**	**NHL**	**82**	**30**	**66**	**96**	**78**	**7**	**0**	**5**	**324**	**9.3**	**26**	**6**	**16.7**	**21:46**	**10**	**5**	**6**	**11**	**12**	**2**	**0**	**0**	**22:07**
2007-08	**NY Rangers**	**NHL**	**82**	**25**	**46**	**71**	**58**	**7**	**0**	**5**	**249**	**10.0**	**8**	**3**	**33.3**	**20:28**	**10**	**5**	**10**	**15**	**12**	**2**	**0**	**1**	**19:54**
	NHL Totals		**1273**	**646**	**953**	**1599**	**907**	**181**	**11**	**112**	**4596**	**14.1**		**38**	**23.7**	**22:18**	**169**	**77**	**104**	**181**	**149**	**24**	**2**	**15**	**22:36**

NHL All-Rookie Team (1991) • NHL First All-Star Team (1995, 1996, 1998, 1999, 2000, 2001, 2006) • Art Ross Trophy (1995, 1998, 1999, 2000, 2001) • NHL Second All-Star Team (1997) • Lester B. Pearson Award (1999, 2000, 2006) • Hart Memorial Trophy (1999)

Played in NHL All-Star Game (1992, 1993, 1996, 1998, 1999, 2000, 2002, 2003, 2004)

Traded to **Washington** by **Pittsburgh** with Frantisek Kucera for Kris Beech, Michal Sivek, Ross Lupaschuk and future considerations, July 11, 2001. Traded to **NY Rangers** by **Washington** for Anson Carter, January 23, 2004. Signed as a free agent by **Kladno** (CzRep), September 17, 2004. Signed as a free agent by **Omsk** (Russia), November 7, 2004. Signed as a free agent by **Omsk** (Russia), July 4, 2008.

JAMES, Connor

(JAYMZ, KAW-nuhr) **PIT.**

Right wing. Shoots right. 5'10", 180 lbs. Born, Calgary, Alta., August 25, 1982. Los Angeles' 11th choice, 279th overall, in 2002 Entry Draft.

Season	Club	League	GP	G	A	Pts	PIM	PP	SH	GW	S	%	+/-	TF	F%	Min	GP	G	A	Pts	PIM	PP	SH	GW	Min
1998-99	Calgary Buffaloes	AMHL	36	33	53	86	20	....	....	....	....	....	....	....	....	....	....	....	....	....	....	....	....	....	....
99-2000	Calgary Royals	AJHL	64	36	57	93	41	....	....	....	....	....	....	....	....	....	....	....	....	....	....	....	....	....	....
2000-01	U. of Denver	WCHA	38	8	19	27	14	....	....	....	....	....	....	....	....	....	....	....	....	....	....	....	....	....	....
2001-02	U. of Denver	WCHA	41	16	26	42	18	....	....	....	....	....	....	....	....	....	....	....	....	....	....	....	....	....	....
2002-03	U. of Denver	WCHA	41	20	23	43	12	....	....	....	....	....	....	....	....	....	....	....	....	....	....	....	....	....	....
2003-04	U. of Denver	WCHA	40	13	25	38	16	....	....	....	....	....	....	....	....	....	....	....	....	....	....	....	....	....	....
2004-05	Bakersfield	ECHL	51	21	25	46	34	....	....	....	....	....	....	....	....	....	5	3	1	4	0	....	....	....	....
	Manchester	AHL	14	2	1	3	10	....	....	....	....	....	....	....	....	....	3	0	0	0	0	....	....	....	....
2005-06	**Los Angeles**	**NHL**	**2**	**0**	**0**	**0**	**0**	**0**	**0**	**0**	**1**	**0.0**	**–1**	**6**	**33.3**	**7:19**	....	....	....	....	....	....	....	....	....
	Manchester	AHL	77	17	25	42	43	....	....	....	....	....	....	....	....	....	7	0	0	0	2	....	....	....	....
2006-07	Wilkes-Barre	AHL	70	12	20	32	29	....	....	....	....	....	....	....	....	....	11	4	4	8	8	....	....	....	....
2007-08	**Pittsburgh**	**NHL**	**13**	**1**	**0**	**1**	**2**	**1**	**0**	**0**	**9**	**11.1**	**–2**	**0**	**0.0**	**7:26**	....	....	....	....	....	....	....	....	....
	Wilkes-Barre	AHL	64	9	28	37	30	....	....	....	....	....	....	....	....	....	23	8	5	13	6	....	....	....	....
	NHL Totals		**15**	**1**	**0**	**1**	**2**	**1**	**0**	**0**	**10**	**10.0**		**6**	**33.3**	**7:25**	....	....	....	....	....	....	....	....	....

NCAA Championship All-Tournament Team (2004)

Signed as a free agent by **Pittsburgh**, August 9, 2006.

JANCEVSKI, Dan

(jan-SEHV-skee, DAN) **DAL.**

Defense. Shoots left. 6'3", 218 lbs. Born, Windsor, Ont., June 15, 1981. Dallas' 2nd choice, 66th overall, in 1999 Entry Draft.

Season	Club	League	GP	G	A	Pts	PIM	PP	SH	GW	S	%	+/-	TF	F%	Min	GP	G	A	Pts	PIM	PP	SH	GW	Min
1995-96	Riverside Selects	Minor-ON	59	9	22	31	67	....	....	....	....	....	....	....	....	....	....	....	....	....	....	....	....	....	....
1996-97	Windsor Lions	Minor-ON	47	6	20	26	99	....	....	....	....	....	....	....	....	....	....	....	....	....	....	....	....	....	....
1997-98	Tecumseh	OHA-B	49	3	11	14	145	....	....	....	....	....	....	....	....	....	....	....	....	....	....	....	....	....	....
1998-99	London Knights	OHL	68	2	12	14	115	....	....	....	....	....	....	....	....	....	25	1	7	8	24	....	....	....	....
99-2000	London Knights	OHL	59	8	15	23	138	....	....	....	....	....	....	....	....	....	....	....	....	....	....	....	....	....	....
2000-01	London Knights	OHL	39	4	23	27	95	....	....	....	....	....	....	....	....	....	....	....	....	....	....	....	....	....	....
	Sudbury Wolves	OHL	31	3	14	17	42	....	....	....	....	....	....	....	....	....	12	0	9	9	17	....	....	....	....
2001-02	Utah Grizzlies	AHL	77	0	13	13	147	....	....	....	....	....	....	....	....	....	5	0	0	0	4	....	....	....	....
2002-03	Utah Grizzlies	AHL	76	1	10	11	172	....	....	....	....	....	....	....	....	....	2	0	1	1	12	....	....	....	....
2003-04	Utah Grizzlies	AHL	80	5	17	22	171	....	....	....	....	....	....	....	....	....	....	....	....	....	....	....	....	....	....
2004-05	Hamilton	AHL	80	6	20	26	163	....	....	....	....	....	....	....	....	....	4	0	0	0	2	....	....	....	....
2005-06	**Dallas**	**NHL**	**2**	**0**	**0**	**0**	**0**	**0**	**0**	**0**	**0**	**0.0**	**1**	**0**	**0.0**	**9:13**	....	....	....	....	....	....	....	....	....
	Iowa Stars	AHL	77	9	29	38	91	....	....	....	....	....	....	....	....	....	7	1	1	2	6	....	....	....	....
2006-07	Hamilton	AHL	80	7	24	31	87	....	....	....	....	....	....	....	....	....	22	3	11	14	16	....	....	....	....
2007-08	**Tampa Bay**	**NHL**	**2**	**0**	**0**	**0**	**2**	**0**	**0**	**0**	**0**	**0.0**	**–1**	**0**	**0.0**	**2:23**	....	....	....	....	....	....	....	....	....
	Norfolk Admirals	AHL	37	4	16	20	52	....	....	....	....	....	....	....	....	....	....	....	....	....	....	....	....	....	....
	Dallas	**NHL**	**2**	**0**	**0**	**0**	**0**	**0**	**0**	**0**	**3**	**0.0**	**0**	**0**	**0.0**	**9:19**	....	....	....	....	....	....	....	....	....
	Iowa Stars	AHL	33	3	7	10	36	....	....	....	....	....	....	....	....	....	....	....	....	....	....	....	....	....	....
	NHL Totals		**6**	**0**	**0**	**0**	**2**	**0**	**0**	**0**	**3**	**0.0**		**0**	**0.0**	**6:58**	....	....	....	....	....	....	....	....	....

Signed as a free agent by **Montreal**, July 13, 2006. Signed as a free agent by **Tampa Bay**, July 6, 2007. Traded to **Dallas** by **Tampa Bay** for Junior Lessard, January 15, 2008.

JANIK, Doug

(JAN-nihk, DUHG) **CHI.**

Defense. Shoots left. 6'2", 209 lbs. Born, Agawam, MA, March 26, 1980. Buffalo's 3rd choice, 55th overall, in 1999 Entry Draft.

Season	Club	League	GP	G	A	Pts	PIM	PP	SH	GW	S	%	+/-	TF	F%	Min	GP	G	A	Pts	PIM	PP	SH	GW	Min
1995-96	N.E. Jr. Whalers	EJHL	48	16	38	54	....	....	....	....	....	....	....	....	....	....	....	....	....	....	....	....	....	....	....
1996-97	N.E. Jr. Whalers	EJHL	39	12	24	36	22	....	....	....	....	....	....	....	....	....	11	5	9	14	10	....	....	....	....
1997-98	USNTDP	U-18	29	6	13	19	43	....	....	....	....	....	....	....	....	....	....	....	....	....	....	....	....	....	....
	USNTDP	USHL	19	1	6	7	34	....	....	....	....	....	....	....	....	....	....	....	....	....	....	....	....	....	....
	USNTDP	NAHL	10	0	4	4	10	....	....	....	....	....	....	....	....	....	7	1	3	4	18	....	....	....	....
1998-99	U. of Maine	H-East	35	3	13	16	44	....	....	....	....	....	....	....	....	....	....	....	....	....	....	....	....	....	....
99-2000	U. of Maine	H-East	36	6	14	20	54	....	....	....	....	....	....	....	....	....	....	....	....	....	....	....	....	....	....
2000-01	U. of Maine	H-East	39	3	15	18	52	....	....	....	....	....	....	....	....	....	....	....	....	....	....	....	....	....	....
2001-02	Rochester	AHL	80	6	17	23	100	....	....	....	....	....	....	....	....	....	2	0	0	0	0	....	....	....	....
2002-03	**Buffalo**	**NHL**	**6**	**0**	**0**	**0**	**2**	**0**	**0**	**0**	**1**	**0.0**	**1**	**0**	**0.0**	**7:42**	....	....	....	....	....	....	....	....	....
	Rochester	AHL	75	3	13	16	120	....	....	....	....	....	....	....	....	....	3	0	0	0	6	....	....	....	....
2003-04	**Buffalo**	**NHL**	**4**	**0**	**0**	**0**	**19**	**0**	**0**	**0**	**3**	**0.0**	**0**	**0**	**0.0**	**8:26**	....	....	....	....	....	....	....	....	....
	Rochester	AHL	74	2	14	16	109	....	....	....	....	....	....	....	....	....	16	1	2	3	22	....	....	....	....
2004-05	Rochester	AHL	76	2	10	12	196	....	....	....	....	....	....	....	....	....	9	0	2	2	10	....	....	....	....
2005-06	Rochester	AHL	71	5	19	24	161	....	....	....	....	....	....	....	....	....	....	....	....	....	....	....	....	....	....
	Buffalo	**NHL**	....	....	....	....	....	....	....	....	....	....	....	....	....	....	**5**	**1**	**0**	**1**	**2**	**0**	**0**	**0**	**10:30**
2006-07	**Tampa Bay**	**NHL**	**75**	**2**	**9**	**11**	**53**	**0**	**0**	**0**	**49**	**4.1**	**–11**	**0**	**0.0**	**14:28**	**1**	**0**	**0**	**0**	**0**	**0**	**0**	**0**	**3:42**
2007-08	**Tampa Bay**	**NHL**	**61**	**1**	**3**	**4**	**45**	**0**	**0**	**0**	**23**	**4.3**	**–3**	**0**	**0.0**	**9:20**	....	....	....	....	....	....	....	....	....
	NHL Totals		**146**	**3**	**12**	**15**	**119**	**0**	**0**	**0**	**76**	**3.9**		**0**	**0.0**	**11:53**	**6**	**1**	**0**	**1**	**2**	**0**	**0**	**0**	**9:22**

Signed as a free agent by **Tampa Bay**, July 6, 2006. Signed as a free agent by **Chicago**, July 15, 2008.

JANSSEN, Cam

(JAN-suhn, KAM) **ST.L.**

Right wing. Shoots right. 6', 210 lbs. Born, St. Louis, MO, April 15, 1984. New Jersey's 6th choice, 117th overall, in 2002 Entry Draft.

Season	Club	League	GP	G	A	Pts	PIM	PP	SH	GW	S	%	+/-	TF	F%	Min	GP	G	A	Pts	PIM	PP	SH	GW	Min
2000-01	St. Louis Jr. Blues	CSJHL	45	1	2	3	244	....	....	....	....	....	....	....	....	....	....	....	....	....	....	....	....	....	....
2001-02	Windsor Spitfires	OHL	64	5	17	22	*268	....	....	....	....	....	....	....	....	....	10	0	0	0	13	....	....	....	....
2002-03	Windsor Spitfires	OHL	50	1	12	13	211	....	....	....	....	....	....	....	....	....	7	0	1	1	22	....	....	....	....
2003-04	Windsor Spitfires	OHL	35	4	9	13	144	....	....	....	....	....	....	....	....	....	....	....	....	....	....	....	....	....	....
	Guelph Storm	OHL	29	7	4	11	125	....	....	....	....	....	....	....	....	....	22	3	3	6	49	....	....	....	....
2004-05	Albany River Rats	AHL	70	1	3	4	337	....	....	....	....	....	....	....	....	....	....	....	....	....	....	....	....	....	....
2005-06	**New Jersey**	**NHL**	**47**	**0**	**0**	**0**	**91**	**0**	**0**	**0**	**10**	**0.0**	**–3**	**2**	**100.0**	**4:44**	**9**	**0**	**0**	**0**	**26**	**0**	**0**	**0**	**3:43**
	Albany River Rats	AHL	26	1	3	4	117	....	....	....	....	....	....	....	....	....	....	....	....	....	....	....	....	....	....
2006-07	**New Jersey**	**NHL**	**48**	**1**	**0**	**1**	**114**	**0**	**0**	**0**	**9**	**11.1**	**–2**	**1**	**100.0**	**4:06**	....	....	....	....	....	....	....	....	....
	Lowell Devils	AHL	9	0	1	1	29	....	....	....	....	....	....	....	....	....	....	....	....	....	....	....	....	....	....
2007-08	**St. Louis**	**NHL**	**12**	**0**	**1**	**1**	**18**	**0**	**0**	**0**	**9**	**0.0**	**–1**	**0**	**0.0**	**7:07**	....	....	....	....	....	....	....	....	....
	Lowell Devils	AHL	3	0	0	0	4	....	....	....	....	....	....	....	....	....	....	....	....	....	....	....	....	....	....
	NHL Totals		**107**	**1**	**1**	**2**	**223**	**0**	**0**	**0**	**28**	**3.6**		**3**	**100.0**	**4:43**	**9**	**0**	**0**	**0**	**26**	**0**	**0**	**0**	**3:43**

Traded to **St. Louis** by **New Jersey** for Bryce Salvador, February 26, 2008.

JENSEN, Joe

(JEHN-suhn, JOH) **CAR.**

Center. Shoots left. 5'11", 180 lbs. Born, Maple Grove, MN, February 6, 1983. Pittsburgh's 10th choice, 232nd overall, in 2003 Entry Draft.

Season	Club	League	GP	G	A	Pts	PIM	PP	SH	GW	S	%	+/-	TF	F%	Min	GP	G	A	Pts	PIM	PP	SH	GW	Min
2000-01	Sioux City	USHL	56	14	20	34	59	....	....	....	....	....	....	....	....	....	8	2	4	6	12	....	....	....	....
2001-02	Sioux City	USHL	57	20	26	46	135	....	....	....	....	....	....	....	....	....	3	0	0	0	6	....	....	....	....
2002-03	St. Cloud State	WCHA	37	9	9	18	14	....	....	....	....	....	....	....	....	....	....	....	....	....	....	....	....	....	....
2003-04	St. Cloud State	WCHA	38	10	14	24	42	....	....	....	....	....	....	....	....	....	....	....	....	....	....	....	....	....	....
2004-05	St. Cloud State	WCHA	40	12	14	26	36	....	....	....	....	....	....	....	....	....	....	....	....	....	....	....	....	....	....
2005-06	St. Cloud State	WCHA	38	14	18	32	14	....	....	....	....	....	....	....	....	....	....	....	....	....	....	....	....	....	....

			Regular Season														Playoffs								
Season	Club	League	GP	G	A	Pts	PIM	PP	SH	GW	S	%	+/-	TF	F%	Min	GP	G	A	Pts	PIM	PP	SH	GW	Min
2006-07	Wilkes-Barre	AHL	26	6	5	11	16	....	....	....	....	....	....	....	....	....	7	2	1	3	6	....	....	....	....
	Wheeling Nailers	ECHL	28	11	18	29	45	....	....	....	....	....	....	....	....	....	....	....	....	....	....	....	....	....	....
2007-08	Wilkes-Barre	AHL	27	2	2	4	23	....	....	....	....	....	....	....	....	....	....	....	....	....	....	....	....	....	....
	Wheeling Nailers	ECHL	9	4	3	7	28	....	....	....	....	....	....	....	....	....	....	....	....	....	....	....	....	....	....
	Carolina	**NHL**	**6**	**1**	**0**	**1**	**2**	**0**	**0**	**1**	**6**	**16.7**	**1**	**14**	**42.9**	**6:30**	....	....	....	....	....	....	....	....	....
	Albany River Rats	AHL	24	8	3	11	27	....	....	....	....	....	....	....	....	....	7	1	0	1	8	....	....	....	....
	NHL Totals		**6**	**1**	**0**	**1**	**2**	**0**	**0**	**1**	**6**	**16.7**		**14**	**42.9**	**6:30**	....	....	....	....	....	....	....	....	....

Traded to **Carolina** by **Pittsburgh** for David Gove, January 31, 2008.

JILLSON, Jeff

(JIHL-suhn, JEHF)

Defense. Shoots right. 6'3", 215 lbs. Born, North Smithfield, RI, July 24, 1980. San Jose's 1st choice, 14th overall, in 1999 Entry Draft.

Season	Club	League	GP	G	A	Pts	PIM	PP	SH	GW	S	%	+/-	TF	F%	Min	GP	G	A	Pts	PIM	PP	SH	GW	Min
1995-96	Mount St. Charles	High-RI	15	8	7	15	15	....	....	....	....	....	....	....	....	....	5	1	1	2	4	....	....	....	....
1996-97	Mount St. Charles	High-RI	15	16	14	30	20	....	....	....	....	....	....	....	....	....	4	0	4	4	6	....	....	....	....
1997-98	Mount St. Charles	High-RI	15	10	13	23	32	....	....	....	....	....	....	....	....	....	5	4	5	9	6	....	....	....	....
1998-99	U. of Michigan	CCHA	38	5	19	24	71	....	....	....	....	....	....	....	....	....	....	....	....	....	....	....	....	....	....
99-2000	U. of Michigan	CCHA	38	8	26	34	115	....	....	....	....	....	....	....	....	....	....	....	....	....	....	....	....	....	....
2000-01	U. of Michigan	CCHA	43	10	20	30	74	....	....	....	....	....	....	....	....	....	....	....	....	....	....	....	....	....	....
2001-02	**San Jose**	**NHL**	**48**	**5**	**13**	**18**	**29**	**3**	**0**	**2**	**47**	**10.6**	**2**	**0**	**0.0**	**14:36**	**4**	**0**	**0**	**0**	**0**	**0**	**0**	**0**	**5:45**
	Cleveland Barons	AHL	27	2	13	15	45	....	....	....	....	....	....	....	....	....	....	....	....	....	....	....	....	....	....
2002-03	**San Jose**	**NHL**	**26**	**0**	**6**	**6**	**9**	**0**	**0**	**0**	**22**	**0.0**	**–7**	**0**	**0.0**	**13:45**	....	....	....	....	....	....	....	....	....
	Cleveland Barons	AHL	19	3	5	8	12	....	....	....	....	....	....	....	....	....	....	....	....	....	....	....	....	....	....
	Providence Bruins	AHL	30	4	11	15	26	....	....	....	....	....	....	....	....	....	4	0	2	2	8	....	....	....	....
2003-04	**Boston**	**NHL**	**50**	**4**	**10**	**14**	**35**	**1**	**0**	**1**	**80**	**5.0**	**–1**	**0**	**0.0**	**17:53**	....	....	....	....	....	....	....	....	....
	Buffalo	**NHL**	**14**	**0**	**3**	**3**	**19**	**0**	**0**	**0**	**35**	**0.0**	**–3**	**0**	**0.0**	**18:21**	....	....	....	....	....	....	....	....	....
2004-05	Rochester	AHL	78	12	17	29	46	....	....	....	....	....	....	....	....	....	9	1	1	2	12	....	....	....	....
2005-06	**Buffalo**	**NHL**	**2**	**0**	**0**	**0**	**4**	**0**	**0**	**0**	**1**	**0.0**	**0**	**0**	**0.0**	**14:40**	**4**	**0**	**0**	**0**	**0**	**0**	**0**	**0**	**11:41**
	Rochester	AHL	73	10	20	30	94	....	....	....	....	....	....	....	....	....	....	....	....	....	....	....	....	....	....
2006-07	Eisbaren Berlin	Germany	30	2	9	11	48	....	....	....	....	....	....	....	....	....	1	0	0	0	2	....	....	....	....
2007-08	Lake Erie	AHL	70	3	19	22	46	....	....	....	....	....	....	....	....	....	....	....	....	....	....	....	....	....	....
	NHL Totals		**140**	**9**	**32**	**41**	**96**	**4**	**0**	**3**	**185**	**4.9**		**0**	**0.0**	**15:59**	**8**	**0**	**0**	**0**	**0**	**0**	**0**	**0**	**8:43**

CCHA All-Rookie Team (1999) • CCHA First All-Star Team (2000, 2001) • NCAA West First All-American Team (2000) • NCAA West Second All-American Team (2001)

Traded to **Boston** by **San Jose** with Jeff Hackett for Kyle McLaren and Boston's 4th round choice (Torrey Mitchell) in 2004 Entry Draft, January 23, 2003. Traded to **San Jose** by **Boston** for Brad Boyes, March 9, 2004. Traded to **Buffalo** by **San Jose** with San Jose's compensatory 7th round choice (Andrew Orpik) in 2005 Entry Draft for Curtis Brown and Andy Delmore, March 9, 2004. Signed as a free agent by **Berlin** (Germany), October 25, 2006. Signed as a free agent by **Colorado**, July 17, 2007.

JOHANSSON, Magnus

(yoh-HAHN-suhn, MAG-nuhs)

Defense. Shoots left. 5'11", 180 lbs. Born, Linkoping, Sweden, September 4, 1973.

Season	Club	League	GP	G	A	Pts	PIM	PP	SH	GW	S	%	+/-	TF	F%	Min	GP	G	A	Pts	PIM	PP	SH	GW	Min
1997-98	V.Frolunda	Sweden	46	5	8	13	24	....	....	....	....	....	....	....	....	....	....	....	....	....	....	....	....	....	....
1998-99	V.Frolunda	Sweden	48	10	9	19	4	....	....	....	....	....	....	....	....	....	4	0	1	1	4	....	....	....	....
99-2000	V.Frolunda	Sweden	49	12	22	34	20	....	....	....	....	....	....	....	....	....	....	....	....	....	....	....	....	....	....
2000-01	V.Frolunda	Sweden	50	6	28	34	26	....	....	....	....	....	....	....	....	....	5	2	1	3	14	....	....	....	....
2001-02	V.Frolunda	Sweden	48	14	21	35	36	....	....	....	....	....	....	....	....	....	10	1	5	6	8	....	....	....	....
2002-03	V.Frolunda	Sweden	50	11	15	26	14	....	....	....	....	....	....	....	....	....	16	2	3	5	20	....	....	....	....
2003-04	Langnau	Swiss	48	4	21	25	36	....	....	....	....	....	....	....	....	....	....	....	....	....	....	....	....	....	....
2004-05	Linkopings HC	Sweden	47	9	25	34	26	....	....	....	....	....	....	....	....	....	6	3	0	3	0	....	....	....	....
2005-06	Linkopings HC	Sweden	50	11	11	22	30	....	....	....	....	....	....	....	....	....	13	2	1	3	10	....	....	....	....
2006-07	Linkopings HC	Sweden	52	8	28	36	46	....	....	....	....	....	....	....	....	....	....	....	....	....	....	....	....	....	....
2007-08	**Chicago**	**NHL**	**18**	**0**	**4**	**4**	**4**	**0**	**0**	**0**	**15**	**0.0**	**–5**	**0**	**0.0**	**14:39**	....	....	....	....	....	....	....	....	....
	Florida	**NHL**	**27**	**0**	**10**	**10**	**14**	**0**	**0**	**0**	**22**	**0.0**	**0**	**0**	**0.0**	**16:29**	....	....	....	....	....	....	....	....	....
	NHL Totals		**45**	**0**	**14**	**14**	**18**	**0**	**0**	**0**	**37**	**0.0**		**0**	**0.0**	**15:45**	....	....	....	....	....	....	....	....	....

Signed as a free agent by **Chicago**, June 4, 2007. Traded to **Florida** by **Chicago** for Florida's 7th round choice in 2009 Entry Draft, January 10, 2008.

JOHNSON, Aaron

(JAWN-suhn, AIR-ruhn) **CHI.**

Defense. Shoots left. 6'2", 211 lbs. Born, Port Hawkesbury, N.S., April 30, 1983. Columbus' 4th choice, 85th overall, in 2001 Entry Draft.

Season	Club	League	GP	G	A	Pts	PIM	PP	SH	GW	S	%	+/-	TF	F%	Min	GP	G	A	Pts	PIM	PP	SH	GW	Min
1998-99	Cape Breton	NSAHA	56	28	42	70	98	....	....	....	....	....	....	....	....	....	....	....	....	....	....	....	....	....	....
99-2000	Rimouski Oceanic	QMJHL	63	1	14	15	57	....	....	....	....	....	....	....	....	....	8	0	0	0	0	....	....	....	....
2000-01	Rimouski Oceanic	QMJHL	64	12	41	53	128	....	....	....	....	....	....	....	....	....	11	2	4	6	35	....	....	....	....
2001-02	Rimouski Oceanic	QMJHL	68	17	49	66	172	....	....	....	....	....	....	....	....	....	7	1	2	3	12	....	....	....	....
2002-03	Rimouski Oceanic	QMJHL	25	4	20	24	41	....	....	....	....	....	....	....	....	....	....	....	....	....	....	....	....	....	....
	Quebec Remparts	QMJHL	32	6	31	37	41	....	....	....	....	....	....	....	....	....	11	4	4	8	25	....	....	....	....
2003-04	**Columbus**	**NHL**	**29**	**2**	**6**	**8**	**32**	**0**	**0**	**1**	**33**	**6.1**	**–2**	**0**	**0.0**	**15:02**	....	....	....	....	....	....	....	....	....
	Syracuse Crunch	AHL	49	6	15	21	83	....	....	....	....	....	....	....	....	....	7	2	3	5	27	....	....	....	....
2004-05	Syracuse Crunch	AHL	77	6	17	23	140	....	....	....	....	....	....	....	....	....	....	....	....	....	....	....	....	....	....
2005-06	**Columbus**	**NHL**	**26**	**2**	**6**	**8**	**23**	**1**	**0**	**1**	**28**	**7.1**	**9**	**0**	**0.0**	**14:12**	....	....	....	....	....	....	....	....	....
	Syracuse Crunch	AHL	49	5	24	29	122	....	....	....	....	....	....	....	....	....	6	1	3	4	19	....	....	....	....
2006-07	**Columbus**	**NHL**	**61**	**3**	**7**	**10**	**38**	**0**	**0**	**0**	**52**	**5.8**	**–9**	**0**	**0.0**	**12:44**	....	....	....	....	....	....	....	....	....
2007-08	**NY Islanders**	**NHL**	**30**	**0**	**2**	**2**	**30**	**0**	**0**	**0**	**16**	**0.0**	**2**	**0**	**0.0**	**13:52**	....	....	....	....	....	....	....	....	....
	Bridgeport	AHL	2	0	0	0	0	....	....	....	....	....	....	....	....	....	....	....	....	....	....	....	....	....	....
	NHL Totals		**146**	**7**	**21**	**28**	**123**	**1**	**0**	**2**	**129**	**5.4**		**0**	**0.0**	**13:41**	....	....	....	....	....	....	....	....	....

Signed as a free agent by **NY Islanders**, July 12, 2007. • Missed majority of 2007-08 season recovering from recurring knee injury and as a healthy reserve. Signed as a free agent by **Chicago**, July 15, 2008.

JOHNSON, Erik

(JAWN-suhn, AIR-ihk) **ST.L.**

Defense. Shoots right. 6'4", 219 lbs. Born, Bloomington, MN, March 21, 1988. St. Louis' 1st choice, 1st overall, in 2006 Entry Draft.

Season	Club	League	GP	G	A	Pts	PIM	PP	SH	GW	S	%	+/-	TF	F%	Min	GP	G	A	Pts	PIM	PP	SH	GW	Min
2003-04	Holy Angels	High-MN	31	13	21	34		....	....	....	....	....	....	....	....	....	....	....	....	....	....	....	....	....	....
2004-05	USNTDP	U-17	26	5	9	14	14	....	....	....	....	....	....	....	....	....	....	....	....	....	....	....	....	....	....
	USNTDP	NAHL	31	6	6	12	12	....	....	....	....	....	....	....	....	....	....	....	....	....	....	....	....	....	....
2005-06	USNTDP	U-18	36	12	22	34	78	....	....	....	....	....	....	....	....	....	....	....	....	....	....	....	....	....	....
	USNTDP	NAHL	11	4	11	15	10	....	....	....	....	....	....	....	....	....	....	....	....	....	....	....	....	....	....
2006-07	U. of Minnesota	WCHA	41	4	20	24	50	....	....	....	....	....	....	....	....	....	....	....	....	....	....	....	....	....	....
2007-08	**St. Louis**	**NHL**	**69**	**5**	**28**	**33**	**28**	**4**	**0**	**3**	**105**	**4.8**	**–9**	**1**	**0.0**	**18:11**	....	....	....	....	....	....	....	....	....
	Peoria Rivermen	AHL	1	0	0	0	2	....	....	....	....	....	....	....	....	....	....	....	....	....	....	....	....	....	....
	NHL Totals		**69**	**5**	**28**	**33**	**28**	**4**	**0**	**3**	**105**	**4.8**		**1**	**0.0**	**18:11**	....	....	....	....	....	....	....	....	....

WCHA All-Rookie Team (2007)

JOHNSON, Jack

(JAWN-suhn, JAK) **L.A.**

Defense. Shoots left. 6'1", 212 lbs. Born, Indianapolis, IN, January 13, 1987. Carolina's 1st choice, 3rd overall, in 2005 Entry Draft.

Season	Club	League	GP	G	A	Pts	PIM	PP	SH	GW	S	%	+/-	TF	F%	Min	GP	G	A	Pts	PIM	PP	SH	GW	Min
2002-03	Shat.-St. Mary's	High-MN	48	15	27	42	....	....	....	....	....	....	....	....	....	....	....	....	....	....	....	....	....	....	....
2003-04	USNTDP	U-17	31	12	9	21	78	....	....	....	....	....	....	....	....	....	....	....	....	....	....	....	....	....	....
	USNTDP	NAHL	29	3	12	15	93	....	....	....	....	....	....	....	....	....	....	....	....	....	....	....	....	....	....
2004-05	USNTDP	U-18	26	5	9	14	86	....	....	....	....	....	....	....	....	....	....	....	....	....	....	....	....	....	....
	USNTDP	NAHL	12	7	10	17	57	....	....	....	....	....	....	....	....	....	....	....	....	....	....	....	....	....	....
2005-06	U. of Michigan	CCHA	38	10	22	32	*149	....	....	....	....	....	....	....	....	....	....	....	....	....	....	....	....	....	....
2006-07	U. of Michigan	CCHA	36	16	23	39	87	....	....	....	....	....	....	....	....	....	....	....	....	....	....	....	....	....	....
	Los Angeles	**NHL**	**5**	**0**	**0**	**0**	**18**	**0**	**0**	**0**	**5**	**0.0**	**–5**	**0**	**0.0**	**21:23**	....	....	....	....	....	....	....	....	....
2007-08	**Los Angeles**	**NHL**	**74**	**3**	**8**	**11**	**76**	**0**	**0**	**0**	**81**	**3.7**	**–19**	**5**	**60.0**	**21:42**	....	....	....	....	....	....	....	....	....
	NHL Totals		**79**	**3**	**8**	**11**	**94**	**0**	**0**	**0**	**86**	**3.5**		**5**	**60.0**	**21:41**	....	....	....	....	....	....	....	....	....

CCHA All-Rookie Team (2006) • CCHA First All-Star Team (2007) • NCAA West First All-American Team (2007)

Traded to **Los Angeles** by **Carolina** with Oleg Tverdovsky for Eric Belanger and Tim Gleason, September 29, 2006.

JOHNSON, Mike
(JAWN-suhn, MIGHK)

Right wing. Shoots right. 6'2", 202 lbs. Born, Scarborough, Ont., October 3, 1974.

			Regular Season														Playoffs								
Season	Club	League	GP	G	A	Pts	PIM	PP	SH	GW	S	%	+/-	TF	F%	Min	GP	G	A	Pts	PIM	PP	SH	GW	Min
1991-92	Hillcrest Summits	MTHL	45	43	66	109	....	....	....	....	....	....	....	....	....	....	20	10	19	29	....	....	....	....	....
1992-93	Aurora Eagles	MTJHL	48	25	40	65	18	....	....	....	....	....	....	....	....	....	7	7	15	22	....	....	....	....	....
1993-94	Bowling Green	CCHA	38	6	14	20	18	....	....	....	....	....	....	....	....	....	....	....	....	....	....	....	....	....	....
1994-95	Bowling Green	CCHA	37	16	33	49	35	....	....	....	....	....	....	....	....	....	....	....	....	....	....	....	....	....	....
1995-96	Bowling Green	CCHA	30	12	19	31	22	....	....	....	....	....	....	....	....	....	....	....	....	....	....	....	....	....	....
1996-97	Bowling Green	CCHA	38	30	32	62	46	....	....	....	....	....	....	....	....	....	....	....	....	....	....	....	....	....	....
	Toronto	**NHL**	**13**	**2**	**2**	**4**	**4**	**0**	**1**	**1**	**27**	**7.4**	**–2**	....	....	....	....	....	....	....	....	....	....	....	....
1997-98	**Toronto**	**NHL**	**82**	**15**	**32**	**47**	**24**	**5**	**0**	**0**	**143**	**10.5**	**–4**	....	....	....	....	....	....	....	....	....	....	....	....
1998-99	**Toronto**	**NHL**	**79**	**20**	**24**	**44**	**35**	**5**	**3**	**2**	**149**	**13.4**	**13**	**15**	**53.3**	**16:16**	**17**	**3**	**2**	**5**	**4**	**0**	**0**	**1**	**16:28**
99-2000	**Toronto**	**NHL**	**52**	**11**	**14**	**25**	**23**	**2**	**1**	**3**	**89**	**12.4**	**8**	**2**	**50.0**	**15:22**	....	....	....	....	....	....	....	....	....
	Tampa Bay	**NHL**	**28**	**10**	**12**	**22**	**4**	**4**	**0**	**0**	**43**	**23.3**	**–2**	**5**	**60.0**	**20:33**	....	....	....	....	....	....	....	....	....
2000-01	**Tampa Bay**	**NHL**	**64**	**11**	**27**	**38**	**38**	**3**	**1**	**0**	**107**	**10.3**	**–10**	**2**	**0.0**	**18:13**	....	....	....	....	....	....	....	....	....
	Phoenix	**NHL**	**12**	**2**	**3**	**5**	**4**	**1**	**0**	**0**	**17**	**11.8**	**0**	**0**	**0.0**	**12:12**	....	....	....	....	....	....	....	....	....
2001-02	**Phoenix**	**NHL**	**57**	**5**	**22**	**27**	**28**	**1**	**2**	**0**	**73**	**6.8**	**14**	**13**	**30.8**	**15:49**	**5**	**1**	**1**	**2**	**6**	**0**	**0**	**0**	**14:45**
2002-03	**Phoenix**	**NHL**	**82**	**23**	**40**	**63**	**47**	**8**	**0**	**3**	**178**	**12.9**	**9**	**34**	**50.0**	**19:39**	....	....	....	....	....	....	....	....	....
2003-04	**Phoenix**	**NHL**	**11**	**1**	**9**	**10**	**10**	**1**	**0**	**0**	**17**	**5.9**	**–1**	**2**	**50.0**	**19:50**	....	....	....	....	....	....	....	....	....
2004-05	Farjestad	Sweden	8	1	2	3	4	....	....	....	....	....	....	....	....	....	6	0	2	2	4	....	....	....	....
2005-06	**Phoenix**	**NHL**	**80**	**16**	**38**	**54**	**50**	**6**	**1**	**3**	**145**	**11.0**	**7**	**234**	**44.4**	**16:34**	....	....	....	....	....	....	....	....	....
2006-07	**Montreal**	**NHL**	**80**	**11**	**20**	**31**	**40**	**1**	**2**	**1**	**131**	**8.4**	**6**	**38**	**31.6**	**15:23**	....	....	....	....	....	....	....	....	....
2007-08	**St. Louis**	**NHL**	**21**	**2**	**3**	**5**	**8**	**0**	**0**	**0**	**21**	**9.5**	**–4**	**8**	**25.0**	**13:01**	....	....	....	....	....	....	....	....	....
	NHL Totals		**661**	**129**	**246**	**375**	**315**	**37**	**11**	**13**	**1140**	**11.3**		**353**	**43.1**	**16:50**	**22**	**4**	**3**	**7**	**10**	**0**	**0**	**1**	**16:05**

NHL All-Rookie Team (1998)

Signed as a free agent by **Toronto**, March 16, 1997. Traded to **Tampa Bay** by **Toronto** with Marek Posmyk and Toronto's 5th (Pavel Sedov) and 6th (Aaron Gionet) round choices in 2000 Entry Draft for Darcy Tucker and Tampa Bay's 4th round choice (Miguel Delisle) in 2000 Entry Draft, February 9, 2000. Traded to **Phoenix** by **Tampa Bay** with Paul Mara, Ruslan Zainullin and NY Islanders' 2nd round choice (previously acquired, Phoenix selected Matthew Spiller) in 2001 Entry Draft for Nikolai Khabibulin and Stan Neckar, March 5, 2001. • Missed majority of 2003-04 season recovering from shoulder injury suffered in game vs. Los Angeles, November 1, 2003. Signed as a free agent by **Farjestad** (Sweden), January 31, 2005. Traded to **Montreal** by **Phoenix** for Montreal's 4th round choice (Vladimir Ruzicka) in 2007 Entry Draft, July 12, 2006. Signed as a free agent by **St. Louis**, October 4, 2007.

JOHNSON, Ryan
(JAWN-suhn, RIGH-uhn) **VAN.**

Center. Shoots left. 6'1", 202 lbs. Born, Thunder Bay, Ont., June 14, 1976. Florida's 4th choice, 36th overall, in 1994 Entry Draft.

			Regular Season														Playoffs								
Season	Club	League	GP	G	A	Pts	PIM	PP	SH	GW	S	%	+/-	TF	F%	Min	GP	G	A	Pts	PIM	PP	SH	GW	Min
1992-93	Thunder Bay	TBAHA	60	25	33	58	....	....	....	....	....	....	....	....	....	....	....	....	....	....	....	....	....	....	....
1993-94	Thunder Bay	USHL	48	14	36	50	28	....	....	....	....	....	....	....	....	....	....	....	....	....	....	....	....	....	....
1994-95	North Dakota	WCHA	38	6	22	28	39	....	....	....	....	....	....	....	....	....	....	....	....	....	....	....	....	....	....
1995-96	North Dakota	WCHA	21	2	17	19	14	....	....	....	....	....	....	....	....	....	....	....	....	....	....	....	....	....	....
	Canada	Nat-Tm	28	5	12	17	14	....	....	....	....	....	....	....	....	....	....	....	....	....	....	....	....	....	....
1996-97	Carolina	AHL	79	18	24	42	28	....	....	....	....	....	....	....	....	....	....	....	....	....	....	....	....	....	....
1997-98	**Florida**	**NHL**	**10**	**0**	**2**	**2**	**0**	**0**	**0**	**0**	**6**	**0.0**	**–4**	....	....	....	....	....	....	....	....	....	....	....	....
	New Haven	AHL	64	19	48	67	12	....	....	....	....	....	....	....	....	....	3	0	1	1	0	....	....	....	....
1998-99	**Florida**	**NHL**	**1**	**1**	**0**	**1**	**0**	**0**	**0**	**0**	**1**	**100.0**	**0**	**16**	**37.5**	**15:26**	....	....	....	....	....	....	....	....	....
	New Haven	AHL	37	8	19	27	18	....	....	....	....	....	....	....	....	....	....	....	....	....	....	....	....	....	....
99-2000	**Florida**	**NHL**	**66**	**4**	**12**	**16**	**14**	**0**	**0**	**0**	**44**	**9.1**	**1**	**684**	**51.8**	**11:47**	....	....	....	....	....	....	....	....	....
	Tampa Bay	**NHL**	**14**	**0**	**2**	**2**	**2**	**0**	**0**	**0**	**5**	**0.0**	**–9**	**117**	**53.0**	**11:02**	....	....	....	....	....	....	....	....	....
2000-01	**Tampa Bay**	**NHL**	**80**	**7**	**14**	**21**	**44**	**1**	**0**	**0**	**71**	**9.9**	**–20**	**951**	**48.9**	**15:47**	....	....	....	....	....	....	....	....	....
2001-02	**Florida**	**NHL**	**29**	**1**	**3**	**4**	**10**	**0**	**0**	**0**	**24**	**4.2**	**–5**	**336**	**47.9**	**13:00**	....	....	....	....	....	....	....	....	....
2002-03	**Florida**	**NHL**	**58**	**2**	**5**	**7**	**26**	**0**	**0**	**0**	**54**	**3.7**	**–13**	**689**	**48.0**	**10:40**	....	....	....	....	....	....	....	....	....
	St. Louis	**NHL**	**17**	**0**	**0**	**0**	**12**	**0**	**0**	**0**	**13**	**0.0**	**0**	**180**	**51.7**	**10:34**	**6**	**0**	**2**	**2**	**6**	**0**	**0**	**0**	**8:14**
2003-04	**St. Louis**	**NHL**	**69**	**4**	**7**	**11**	**8**	**0**	**1**	**1**	**36**	**11.1**	**–2**	**537**	**53.6**	**9:54**	**3**	**0**	**0**	**0**	**0**	**0**	**0**	**0**	**6:11**
2004-05	Missouri	UHL	29	7	14	21	12	....	....	....	....	....	....	....	....	....	6	1	0	1	13	....	....	....	....
2005-06	**St. Louis**	**NHL**	**65**	**3**	**6**	**9**	**33**	**1**	**1**	**0**	**57**	**5.3**	**–21**	**569**	**55.9**	**11:24**	....	....	....	....	....	....	....	....	....
2006-07	**St. Louis**	**NHL**	**59**	**7**	**4**	**11**	**47**	**0**	**2**	**0**	**50**	**14.0**	**–7**	**525**	**55.4**	**12:21**	....	....	....	....	....	....	....	....	....
2007-08	**St. Louis**	**NHL**	**79**	**5**	**13**	**18**	**22**	**0**	**1**	**1**	**85**	**5.9**	**–2**	**803**	**54.6**	**14:22**	....	....	....	....	....	....	....	....	....
	NHL Totals		**547**	**34**	**68**	**102**	**218**	**2**	**5**	**2**	**446**	**7.6**		**5407**	**51.9**	**12:26**	**9**	**0**	**2**	**2**	**6**	**0**	**0**	**0**	**7:33**

Traded to **Tampa Bay** by **Florida** with Dwayne Hay for Mike Sillinger, March 14, 2000. Traded to **Florida** by **Tampa Bay** with Tampa Bay's 6th round choice (later traded back to Tampa Bay – Tampa Bay selected Doug O'Brien) in 2003 Entry Draft for Vaclav Prospal, July 10, 2001. • Missed majority of 2001-02 season recovering from head injury suffered in game vs. St. Louis, December 22, 2001. Claimed on waivers by **St. Louis** from **Florida**, February 19, 2003. Signed as a free agent by **Missouri** (UHL), February 3, 2005. Signed as a free agent by **Vancouver**, July 2, 2008.

JOHNSSON, Kim
(YAWN-suhn, KIHM) **MIN.**

Defense. Shoots left. 6'1", 193 lbs. Born, Malmo, Sweden, March 16, 1976. NY Rangers' 15th choice, 286th overall, in 1994 Entry Draft.

			Regular Season														Playoffs								
Season	Club	League	GP	G	A	Pts	PIM	PP	SH	GW	S	%	+/-	TF	F%	Min	GP	G	A	Pts	PIM	PP	SH	GW	Min
1993-94	Malmo IF Jr.	Swe-Jr.	14	5	3	8	14	....	....	....	....	....	....	....	....	....	....	....	....	....	....	....	....	....	....
	Malmo IF	Sweden	2	0	0	0	0	....	....	....	....	....	....	....	....	....	....	....	....	....	....	....	....	....	....
1994-95	Malmo IF Jr.	Swe-Jr.	29	6	15	21	40	....	....	....	....	....	....	....	....	....	....	....	....	....	....	....	....	....	....
	Malmo IF	Sweden	13	0	0	0	4	....	....	....	....	....	....	....	....	....	1	0	0	0	0	....	....	....	....
1995-96	Malmo IF	Sweden	38	2	0	2	30	....	....	....	....	....	....	....	....	....	4	0	1	1	8	....	....	....	....
1996-97	Malmo	Sweden	49	4	9	13	42	....	....	....	....	....	....	....	....	....	4	0	0	0	2	....	....	....	....
1997-98	Malmo	Sweden	45	5	9	14	29	....	....	....	....	....	....	....	....	....	....	....	....	....	....	....	....	....	....
1998-99	Malmo	Sweden	49	9	8	17	76	....	....	....	....	....	....	....	....	....	8	2	3	5	12	....	....	....	....
99-2000	**NY Rangers**	**NHL**	**76**	**6**	**15**	**21**	**46**	**1**	**0**	**1**	**101**	**5.9**	**–13**	**0**	**0.0**	**18:06**	....	....	....	....	....	....	....	....	....
2000-01	**NY Rangers**	**NHL**	**75**	**5**	**21**	**26**	**40**	**4**	**0**	**0**	**104**	**4.8**	**–3**	**0**	**0.0**	**21:16**	....	....	....	....	....	....	....	....	....
2001-02	**Philadelphia**	**NHL**	**82**	**11**	**30**	**41**	**42**	**5**	**0**	**1**	**150**	**7.3**	**12**	**0**	**0.0**	**23:02**	**5**	**0**	**0**	**0**	**2**	**0**	**0**	**0**	**22:48**
	Sweden	Olympics	4	1	1	2	0	....	....	....	....	....	....	....	....	....	....	....	....	....	....	....	....	....	....
2002-03	**Philadelphia**	**NHL**	**82**	**10**	**29**	**39**	**38**	**5**	**0**	**2**	**159**	**6.3**	**11**	**0**	**0.0**	**24:05**	**13**	**0**	**3**	**3**	**8**	**0**	**0**	**0**	**26:07**
2003-04	**Philadelphia**	**NHL**	**80**	**13**	**29**	**42**	**26**	**4**	**0**	**3**	**189**	**6.9**	**16**	**0**	**0.0**	**24:27**	**15**	**2**	**6**	**8**	**8**	**0**	**0**	**1**	**26:11**
2004-05	HC Ambri-Piotta	Swiss	24	4	10	14	61	....	....	....	....	....	....	....	....	....	....	....	....	....	....	....	....	....	....
2005-06	**Philadelphia**	**NHL**	**47**	**6**	**19**	**25**	**34**	**3**	**0**	**0**	**97**	**6.2**	**5**	**0**	**0.0**	**23:17**	....	....	....	....	....	....	....	....	....
	Sweden	Olympics	DID NOT PLAY																						
2006-07	**Minnesota**	**NHL**	**76**	**3**	**19**	**22**	**64**	**3**	**0**	**0**	**98**	**3.1**	**–4**	**0**	**0.0**	**23:33**	**4**	**0**	**0**	**0**	**2**	**0**	**0**	**0**	**23:06**
2007-08	**Minnesota**	**NHL**	**80**	**4**	**23**	**27**	**42**	**2**	**0**	**0**	**87**	**4.6**	**–4**	**0**	**0.0**	**23:27**	**6**	**0**	**1**	**1**	**18**	**0**	**0**	**0**	**28:08**
	NHL Totals		**598**	**58**	**185**	**243**	**332**	**27**	**0**	**7**	**985**	**5.9**		**0**	**0.0**	**22:40**	**43**	**2**	**10**	**12**	**38**	**0**	**0**	**1**	**25:45**

Traded to **Philadelphia** by **NY Rangers** with Jan Hlavac, Pavel Brendl and NY Rangers' 3rd round choice (Stefan Ruzicka) in 2003 Entry Draft for Eric Lindros, August 20, 2001. Signed as a free agent by **Ambri-Piotta** (Swiss), September 18, 2004. Signed as a free agent by **Minnesota**, July 1, 2006.

JOKINEN, Jussi
(YOH-kih-nihn, YEW-see) **T.B.**

Center. Shoots left. 5'11", 190 lbs. Born, Kalajoki, Finland, April 1, 1983. Dallas' 7th choice, 192nd overall, in 2001 Entry Draft.

			Regular Season														Playoffs								
Season	Club	League	GP	G	A	Pts	PIM	PP	SH	GW	S	%	+/-	TF	F%	Min	GP	G	A	Pts	PIM	PP	SH	GW	Min
99-2000	Karpat Oulu U18	Fin-U18	15	6	25	31	14	....	....	....	....	....	....	....	....	....	6	2	3	5	0	....	....	....	....
	Karpat Oulu Jr.	Fin-Jr.	28	4	7	11	14	....	....	....	....	....	....	....	....	....	....	....	....	....	....	....	....	....	....
2000-01	Karpat Oulu U18	Fin-U18	1	2	1	3	0	....	....	....	....	....	....	....	....	....	....	....	....	....	....	....	....	....	....
	Karpat Oulu Jr.	Fin-Jr.	41	18	31	49	69	....	....	....	....	....	....	....	....	....	6	2	1	3	0	....	....	....	....
2001-02	Karpat Oulu Jr.	Fin-Jr.	2	4	1	5	2	....	....	....	....	....	....	....	....	....	1	1	1	2	0	....	....	....	....
	Karpat Oulu	Finland	54	10	6	16	38	....	....	....	....	....	....	....	....	....	4	1	0	1	0	....	....	....	....
2002-03	Karpat Oulu	Finland	51	14	23	37	10	....	....	....	....	....	....	....	....	....	15	2	1	3	33	....	....	....	....
2003-04	Karpat Oulu	Finland	55	15	23	38	20	....	....	....	....	....	....	....	....	....	15	3	4	7	6	....	....	....	....
2004-05	Karpat Oulu	Finland	56	23	24	47	24	....	....	....	....	....	....	....	....	....	12	3	4	7	2	....	....	....	....
2005-06	**Dallas**	**NHL**	**81**	**17**	**38**	**55**	**30**	**8**	**0**	**2**	**107**	**15.9**	**2**	**23**	**30.4**	**13:34**	**5**	**2**	**1**	**3**	**0**	**1**	**0**	**0**	**13:40**
	Finland	Olympics	8	1	3	4	2	....	....	....	....	....	....	....	....	....	....	....	....	....	....	....	....	....	....
2006-07	**Dallas**	**NHL**	**82**	**14**	**34**	**48**	**18**	**6**	**0**	**1**	**121**	**11.6**	**8**	**278**	**52.2**	**13:54**	**4**	**0**	**1**	**1**	**0**	**0**	**0**	**0**	**13:22**
2007-08	**Dallas**	**NHL**	**52**	**14**	**14**	**28**	**14**	**5**	**0**	**2**	**93**	**15.1**	**2**	**295**	**53.2**	**12:44**	....	....	....	....	....	....	....	....	....
	Tampa Bay	**NHL**	**20**	**2**	**12**	**14**	**4**	**1**	**0**	**0**	**38**	**5.3**	**–16**	**46**	**45.7**	**18:57**	....	....	....	....	....	....	....	....	....
	NHL Totals		**235**	**47**	**98**	**145**	**66**	**20**	**0**	**5**	**359**	**13.1**		**642**	**51.4**	**13:57**	**9**	**2**	**2**	**4**	**0**	**1**	**0**	**0**	**13:32**

Traded to **Tampa Bay** by **Dallas** with Mike Smith, Jeff Halpern and Dallas' 4th round choice in 2009 Entry Draft for Brad Richards and Johan Holmqvist, February 26, 2008.

JOKINEN, Olli

(YOH-kih-nihn, OH-lee) **PHX.**

Center. Shoots left. 6'3", 214 lbs. Born, Kuopio, Finland, December 5, 1978. Los Angeles' 1st choice, 3rd overall, in 1997 Entry Draft.

			Regular Season														Playoffs								
Season	Club	League	GP	G	A	Pts	PIM	PP	SH	GW	S	%	+/-	TF	F%	Min	GP	G	A	Pts	PIM	PP	SH	GW	Min
1994-95	KalPa Kuopio U18	Fin-U18	30	22	28	50	92	....	....	....	....	....	....	....	....	....	....	....	....	....	....	....	....	....	....
	KalPa Kuopio Jr.	Fin-Jr.	6	0	1	1	6	....	....	....	....	....	....	....	....	....	....	....	....	....	....	....	....	....	....
1995-96	KalPa Kuopio U18	Fin-U18	9	9	13	22	4	....	....	....	....	....	....	....	....	....	....	....	....	....	....	....	....	....	....
	KalPa Kuopio Jr.	Fin-Jr.	25	20	14	34	47	....	....	....	....	....	....	....	....	....	7	4	4	8	20	....	....	....	....
	KalPa Kuopio	Finland	15	1	1	2	2	....	....	....	....	....	....	....	....	....	....	....	....	....	....	....	....	....	....
1996-97	HIFK Helsinki Jr.	Fin-Jr.	2	1	0	1	6	....	....	....	....	....	....	....	....	....	....	....	....	....	....	....	....	....	....
	HIFK Helsinki	Finland	50	14	27	41	88	....	....	....	....	....	....	....	....	....	....	....	....	....	....	....	....	....	....
1997-98	**Los Angeles**	**NHL**	**8**	**0**	**0**	**0**	**6**	**0**	**0**	**0**	**12**	**0.0**	**-5**	....	....	....	....	....	....	....	....	....	....	....	....
	HIFK Helsinki	Finland	30	11	28	39	32	....	....	....	....	....	....	....	....	....	9	7	2	9	2	....	....	....	....
1998-99	**Los Angeles**	**NHL**	**66**	**9**	**12**	**21**	**44**	**3**	**1**	**1**	**87**	**10.3**	**-10**	**779**	**43.9**	**14:42**	....	....	....	....	....	....	....	....	....
	Springfield	AHL	9	3	6	9	6	....	....	....	....	....	....	....	....	....	....	....	....	....	....	....	....	....	....
99-2000	**NY Islanders**	**NHL**	**82**	**11**	**10**	**21**	**80**	**1**	**2**	**3**	**138**	**8.0**	**0**	**841**	**46.1**	**16:15**	....	....	....	....	....	....	....	....	....
2000-01	**Florida**	**NHL**	**78**	**6**	**10**	**16**	**106**	**0**	**0**	**0**	**121**	**5.0**	**-22**	**638**	**42.3**	**13:23**	....	....	....	....	....	....	....	....	....
2001-02	**Florida**	**NHL**	**80**	**9**	**20**	**29**	**98**	**3**	**1**	**0**	**153**	**5.9**	**-16**	**1222**	**45.2**	**18:05**	....	....	....	....	....	....	....	....	....
	Finland	Olympics	4	2	1	3	0	....	....	....	....	....	....	....	....	....	....	....	....	....	....	....	....	....	....
2002-03	**Florida**	**NHL**	**81**	**36**	**29**	**65**	**79**	**13**	**3**	**6**	**240**	**15.0**	**-17**	**1925**	**46.7**	**22:02**	....	....	....	....	....	....	....	....	....
2003-04	**Florida**	**NHL**	**82**	**26**	**32**	**58**	**81**	**8**	**2**	**8**	**280**	**9.3**	**-16**	**1986**	**47.1**	**22:35**	....	....	....	....	....	....	....	....	....
2004-05	Kloten Flyers	Swiss	8	6	1	7	14	....	....	....	....	....	....	....	....	....	....	....	....	....	....	....	....	....	....
	Sodertalje SK	Sweden	23	13	9	22	52	....	....	....	....	....	....	....	....	....	....	....	....	....	....	....	....	....	....
	HIFK Helsinki	Finland	14	9	8	17	10	....	....	....	....	....	....	....	....	....	5	2	0	2	24	....	....	....	....
2005-06	**Florida**	**NHL**	**82**	**38**	**51**	**89**	**88**	**14**	**1**	**9**	**351**	**10.8**	**14**	**955**	**46.9**	**20:29**	....	....	....	....	....	....	....	....	....
	Finland	Olympics	8	6	2	8	2	....	....	....	....	....	....	....	....	....	....	....	....	....	....	....	....	....	....
2006-07	**Florida**	**NHL**	**82**	**39**	**52**	**91**	**78**	**9**	**1**	**8**	**351**	**11.1**	**18**	**1074**	**44.3**	**20:32**	....	....	....	....	....	....	....	....	....
2007-08	**Florida**	**NHL**	**82**	**34**	**37**	**71**	**67**	**18**	**0**	**5**	**341**	**10.0**	**-19**	**938**	**43.1**	**19:54**	....	....	....	....	....	....	....	....	....
	NHL Totals		**723**	**208**	**253**	**461**	**727**	**69**	**11**	**40**	**2074**	**10.0**		**10358**	**45.5**	**18:47**	....	....	....	....	....	....	....	....	....

Played in NHL All-Star Game (2003)

Traded to **NY Islanders** by **Los Angeles** with Josh Green, Mathieu Biron and Los Angeles' 1st round choice (Taylor Pyatt) in 1999 Entry Draft for Ziggy Palffy, Bryan Smolinski, Marcel Cousineau and New Jersey's 4th round choice (previously acquired, Los Angeles selected Daniel Johansson) in 1999 Entry Draft, June 20, 1999. Traded to **Florida** by **NY Islanders** with Roberto Luongo for Mark Parrish and Oleg Kvasha, June 24, 2000. Signed as a free agent by **Kloten** (Swiss), September 15, 2004. Signed as a free agent by **Sodertalje** (Sweden), November, 2004. Signed as a free agent by **HIFK Helsinki** (Finland), January 30, 2005.Traded to **Phoenix** by **Florida** for Keith Ballard, Nick Boynton and Ottawa's 2nd round choice (previously acquired, later traded back to Phoenix - Phoenix selected Jared Staal) in 2008 Entry Draft, June 20, 2008.

JONES, Blair

(JOHNZ, BLAYR) **T.B.**

Center. Shoots right. 6'3", 210 lbs. Born, Central Butte, Sask., September 27, 1986. Tampa Bay's 5th choice, 102nd overall, in 2005 Entry Draft.

Season	Club	League	GP	G	A	Pts	PIM	PP	SH	GW	S	%	+/-	TF	F%	Min	GP	G	A	Pts	PIM	PP	SH	GW	Min
2002-03	Bethune	SBHL	STATISTICS NOT AVAILABLE																						
	Red Deer Rebels	WHL	37	3	4	7	17	....	....	....	....	....	....	....	....	....	10	1	0	1	0	....	....	....	....
2003-04	Red Deer Rebels	WHL	72	9	22	31	55	....	....	....	....	....	....	....	....	....	19	1	5	6	24	....	....	....	....
2004-05	Red Deer Rebels	WHL	39	7	18	25	48	....	....	....	....	....	....	....	....	....	....	....	....	....	....	....	....	....	....
	Moose Jaw	WHL	29	7	18	25	30	....	....	....	....	....	....	....	....	....	5	2	5	7	8	....	....	....	....
2005-06	Moose Jaw	WHL	72	35	50	85	85	....	....	....	....	....	....	....	....	....	22	9	12	21	45	....	....	....	....
2006-07	**Tampa Bay**	**NHL**	**20**	**1**	**2**	**3**	**2**	**0**	**0**	**0**	**6**	**16.7**	**0**	**65**	**41.5**	**5:46**	....	....	....	....	....	....	....	....	....
	Springfield	AHL	45	5	16	21	36	....	....	....	....	....	....	....	....	....	....	....	....	....	....	....	....	....	....
2007-08	**Tampa Bay**	**NHL**	**4**	**0**	**0**	**0**	**0**	**0**	**0**	**0**	**1**	**0.0**	**0**	**8**	**12.5**	**1:55**	....	....	....	....	....	....	....	....	....
	Norfolk Admirals	AHL	75	14	28	42	50	....	....	....	....	....	....	....	....	....	....	....	....	....	....	....	....	....	....
	NHL Totals		**24**	**1**	**2**	**3**	**2**	**0**	**0**	**0**	**7**	**14.3**		**73**	**38.4**	**5:08**	....	....	....	....	....	....	....	....	....

WHL East Second All-Star Team (2006)

JONES, David

(JOHNZ, DAY-vihd) **COL.**

Right wing. Shoots right. 6'2", 220 lbs. Born, Guelph, Ont., August 10, 1984. Colorado's 8th choice, 288th overall, in 2003 Entry Draft.

Season	Club	League	GP	G	A	Pts	PIM	PP	SH	GW	S	%	+/-	TF	F%	Min	GP	G	A	Pts	PIM	PP	SH	GW	Min
2000-01	Port Coquitlam	PIJHL	40	18	11	29	33	....	....	....	....	....	....	....	....	....	....	....	....	....	....	....	....	....	....
2001-02	Coquitlam	BCHL	59	19	32	51	62	....	....	....	....	....	....	....	....	....	....	....	....	....	....	....	....	....	....
2002-03	Coquitlam	BCHL	35	9	19	28	55	....	....	....	....	....	....	....	....	....	7	2	6	8	8	....	....	....	....
2003-04	Coquitlam	BCHL	53	33	60	93	78	....	....	....	....	....	....	....	....	....	7	3	6	9	4	....	....	....	....
2004-05	Dartmouth	ECAC	34	9	5	14	26	....	....	....	....	....	....	....	....	....	....	....	....	....	....	....	....	....	....
2005-06	Dartmouth	ECAC	33	17	17	34	38	....	....	....	....	....	....	....	....	....	....	....	....	....	....	....	....	....	....
2006-07	Dartmouth	ECAC	33	18	26	*44	22	....	....	....	....	....	....	....	....	....	....	....	....	....	....	....	....	....	....
2007-08	**Colorado**	**NHL**	**27**	**2**	**4**	**6**	**8**	**1**	**0**	**0**	**37**	**5.4**	**-5**	**8**	**37.5**	**11:22**	**10**	**0**	**1**	**1**	**6**	**0**	**0**	**0**	**11:50**
	Lake Erie	AHL	45	14	16	30	16	....	....	....	....	....	....	....	....	....	....	....	....	....	....	....	....	....	....
	NHL Totals		**27**	**2**	**4**	**6**	**8**	**1**	**0**	**0**	**37**	**5.4**		**8**	**37.5**	**11:22**	**10**	**0**	**1**	**1**	**6**	**0**	**0**	**0**	**11:50**

ECAC Second All-Star Team (2006) • ECAC First All-Star Tearm (2007) • NCAA East First All-American Team (2007)

JONES, Matt

(JOHNZ, MAT) **PHX.**

Defense. Shoots left. 6', 215 lbs. Born, Downers Grove, IL, August 8, 1983. Phoenix's 5th choice, 80th overall, in 2002 Entry Draft.

Season	Club	League	GP	G	A	Pts	PIM	PP	SH	GW	S	%	+/-	TF	F%	Min	GP	G	A	Pts	PIM	PP	SH	GW	Min
99-2000	Green Bay	USHL	54	1	4	5	59	....	....	....	....	....	....	....	....	....	13	0	0	0	2	....	....	....	....
2000-01	Green Bay	USHL	52	3	10	13	58	....	....	....	....	....	....	....	....	....	4	0	0	0	2	....	....	....	....
2001-02	North Dakota	WCHA	37	2	5	7	20	....	....	....	....	....	....	....	....	....	....	....	....	....	....	....	....	....	....
2002-03	North Dakota	WCHA	39	1	6	7	26	....	....	....	....	....	....	....	....	....	....	....	....	....	....	....	....	....	....
2003-04	North Dakota	WCHA	41	7	14	21	40	....	....	....	....	....	....	....	....	....	....	....	....	....	....	....	....	....	....
2004-05	North Dakota	WCHA	45	6	11	17	66	....	....	....	....	....	....	....	....	....	....	....	....	....	....	....	....	....	....
2005-06	**Phoenix**	**NHL**	**16**	**0**	**2**	**2**	**14**	**0**	**0**	**0**	**10**	**0.0**	**-2**	**0**	**0.0**	**11:35**	....	....	....	....	....	....	....	....	....
	San Antonio	AHL	59	2	11	13	46	....	....	....	....	....	....	....	....	....	....	....	....	....	....	....	....	....	....
2006-07	**Phoenix**	**NHL**	**45**	**1**	**6**	**7**	**39**	**0**	**0**	**0**	**20**	**5.0**	**-12**	**0**	**0.0**	**16:23**	....	....	....	....	....	....	....	....	....
	San Antonio	AHL	24	0	2	2	23	....	....	....	....	....	....	....	....	....	....	....	....	....	....	....	....	....	....
2007-08	**Phoenix**	**NHL**	**45**	**0**	**2**	**2**	**10**	**0**	**0**	**0**	**25**	**0.0**	**-13**	**0**	**0.0**	**14:34**	....	....	....	....	....	....	....	....	....
	San Antonio	AHL	5	0	0	0	0	....	....	....	....	....	....	....	....	....	....	....	....	....	....	....	....	....	....
	NHL Totals		**106**	**1**	**10**	**11**	**63**	**0**	**0**	**0**	**55**	**1.8**		**0**	**0.0**	**14:53**	....	....	....	....	....	....	....	....	....

WCHA Second All-Star Team (2004)

JONES, Randy

(JOHNZ, RAN-dee) **PHI.**

Defense. Shoots left. 6'2", 200 lbs. Born, Quispamsis, N.B., July 23, 1981.

Season	Club	League	GP	G	A	Pts	PIM	PP	SH	GW	S	%	+/-	TF	F%	Min	GP	G	A	Pts	PIM	PP	SH	GW	Min
99-2000	Cobourg Cougars	OPJHL	44	20	36	56	51	....	....	....	....	....	....	....	....	....	....	....	....	....	....	....	....	....	....
2000-01	Cobourg Cougars	OPJHL	28	15	21	36	46	....	....	....	....	....	....	....	....	....	....	....	....	....	....	....	....	....	....
2001-02	Clarkson Knights	ECAC	34	9	11	20	32	....	....	....	....	....	....	....	....	....	....	....	....	....	....	....	....	....	....
2002-03	Clarkson Knights	ECAC	33	13	20	33	65	....	....	....	....	....	....	....	....	....	....	....	....	....	....	....	....	....	....
2003-04	**Philadelphia**	**NHL**	**5**	**0**	**0**	**0**	**0**	**0**	**0**	**0**	**5**	**0.0**	**1**	**0**	**0.0**	**12:00**	....	....	....	....	....	....	....	....	....
	Philadelphia	AHL	55	8	24	32	63	....	....	....	....	....	....	....	....	....	12	0	1	1	17	....	....	....	....
2004-05	Philadelphia	AHL	69	5	19	24	32	....	....	....	....	....	....	....	....	....	18	0	5	5	10	....	....	....	....
2005-06	**Philadelphia**	**NHL**	**28**	**0**	**8**	**8**	**16**	**0**	**0**	**0**	**21**	**0.0**	**-6**	**1**	**100.0**	**14:58**	....	....	....	....	....	....	....	....	....
	Philadelphia	AHL	21	2	3	5	53	....	....	....	....	....	....	....	....	....	....	....	....	....	....	....	....	....	....
2006-07	**Philadelphia**	**NHL**	**66**	**4**	**18**	**22**	**38**	**0**	**0**	**0**	**67**	**6.0**	**-14**	**1**	**0.0**	**16:06**	....	....	....	....	....	....	....	....	....
2007-08	**Philadelphia**	**NHL**	**71**	**5**	**26**	**31**	**58**	**1**	**0**	**0**	**103**	**4.9**	**8**	**0**	**0.0**	**19:24**	**16**	**0**	**2**	**2**	**4**	**0**	**0**	**0**	**21:24**
	NHL Totals		**170**	**9**	**52**	**61**	**112**	**1**	**0**	**0**	**196**	**4.6**		**2**	**50.0**	**17:10**	**16**	**0**	**2**	**2**	**4**	**0**	**0**	**0**	**21:24**

ECAC First All-Star Team (2003)

Signed as a free agent by **Philadelphia**, July 24, 2003.

JONSSON, Lars

(YAWN-suhn, LARZ)

Defense. Shoots left. 6'1", 205 lbs. Born, Borlange, Sweden, January 2, 1982. Boston's 1st choice, 7th overall, in 2000 Entry Draft.

Season	Club	League	Regular Season GP	G	A	Pts	PIM	PP	SH	GW	S	%	+/-	TF	F%	Min	Playoffs GP	G	A	Pts	PIM	PP	SH	GW	Min
1998-99	Leksands IF Jr.	Swe-Jr.	40	4	8	12	42	....	....	....	....	....	....	....	....	....	....	....	....	....	....	....	....	....	....
99-2000	Leksands IF Jr.	Swe-Jr.	34	16	22	38	50	....	....	....	....	....	....	....	....	....	2	0	0	0	0	....	....	....	....
	Leksands IF	Sweden	5	0	0	0	4	....	....	....	....	....	....	....	....	....	....	....	....	....	....	....	....	....	....
2000-01	Leksands IF Jr.	Swe-Jr.	7	1	3	4	6	....	....	....	....	....	....	....	....	....	....	....	....	....	....	....	....	....	....
	Leksands IF	Sweden	31	2	1	3	12	....	....	....	....	....	....	....	....	....	....	....	....	....	....	....	....	....	....
2001-02	Leksands IF Jr.	Swe-Jr.	3	2	1	3	4	....	....	....	....	....	....	....	....	....	1	0	0	0	0	....	....	....	....
	Leksands IF	Sweden-2	28	1	7	8	59	....	....	....	....	....	....	....	....	....	....	....	....	....	....	....	....	....	....
2002-03	Leksands IF	Sweden	21	0	0	0	12	....	....	....	....	....	....	....	....	....	5	0	0	0	2	....	....	....	....
	Bjorkloven	Sweden-2	9	3	4	7	10	....	....	....	....	....	....	....	....	....	....	....	....	....	....	....	....	....	....
	IFK Arboga IK	Sweden-2	4	0	0	0	4	....	....	....	....	....	....	....	....	....	....	....	....	....	....	....	....	....	....
2003-04	Leksands IF	Sweden	50	3	9	12	30	....	....	....	....	....	....	....	....	....	....	....	....	....	....	....	....	....	....
	Leksands IF	Sweden-Q	4	1	0	1	2	....	....	....	....	....	....	....	....	....	....	....	....	....	....	....	....	....	....
2004-05	Timra IK	Sweden	50	5	6	11	32	....	....	....	....	....	....	....	....	....	7	0	0	0	2	....	....	....	....
2005-06	HV 71 Jonkoping	Sweden	50	11	16	27	46	....	....	....	....	....	....	....	....	....	11	2	3	5	14	....	....	....	....
2006-07	**Philadelphia**	**NHL**	**8**	**0**	**2**	**2**	**6**	**0**	**0**	**0**	**4**	**0.0**	**–4**	**0**	**0.0**	**12:25**	....	....	....	....	....	....	....	....	....
	Philadelphia	AHL	40	4	11	15	26	....	....	....	....	....	....	....	....	....	....	....	....	....	....	....	....	....	....
2007-08	Philadelphia	AHL	44	5	13	18	18	....	....	....	....	....	....	....	....	....	7	1	4	5	6	....	....	....	....
	NHL Totals		**8**	**0**	**2**	**2**	**6**	**0**	**0**	**0**	**4**	**0.0**		**0**	**0.0**	**12:25**	....	....	....	....	....	....	....	....	....

Signed as a free agent by **Philadephia**, July 1, 2006.

JOVANOVSKI, Ed

(joh-van-OHV-skee, EHD) **PHX.**

Defense. Shoots left. 6'2", 210 lbs. Born, Windsor, Ont., June 26, 1976. Florida's 1st choice, 1st overall, in 1994 Entry Draft.

Season	Club	League	Regular Season GP	G	A	Pts	PIM	PP	SH	GW	S	%	+/-	TF	F%	Min	Playoffs GP	G	A	Pts	PIM	PP	SH	GW	Min
1991-92	Windsor	Minor-ON	50	25	40	65	88	....	....	....	....	....	....	....	....	....	....	....	....	....	....	....	....	....	....
1992-93	Windsor Bulldogs	OHA-B	48	7	46	53	88	....	....	....	....	....	....	....	....	....	....	....	....	....	....	....	....	....	....
1993-94	Windsor Spitfires	OHL	62	15	36	51	221	....	....	....	....	....	....	....	....	....	4	0	0	0	15	....	....	....	....
1994-95	Windsor Spitfires	OHL	50	23	42	65	198	....	....	....	....	....	....	....	....	....	9	2	7	9	39	....	....	....	....
1995-96	**Florida**	**NHL**	**70**	**10**	**11**	**21**	**137**	**2**	**0**	**2**	**116**	**8.6**	**–3**	....	....	....	**22**	**1**	**8**	**9**	**52**	**0**	**0**	**0**	....
1996-97	**Florida**	**NHL**	**61**	**7**	**16**	**23**	**172**	**3**	**0**	**1**	**80**	**8.8**	**–1**	....	....	....	**5**	**0**	**0**	**0**	**4**	**0**	**0**	**0**	....
1997-98	**Florida**	**NHL**	**81**	**9**	**14**	**23**	**158**	**2**	**1**	**3**	**142**	**6.3**	**–12**	....	....	....	....	....	....	....	....	....	....	....	....
1998-99	**Florida**	**NHL**	**41**	**3**	**13**	**16**	**82**	**1**	**0**	**1**	**68**	**4.4**	**–4**	**0**	**0.0**	**22:35**	....	....	....	....	....	....	....	....	....
	Vancouver	**NHL**	**31**	**2**	**9**	**11**	**44**	**0**	**0**	**0**	**41**	**4.9**	**–5**	**0**	**0.0**	**21:16**	....	....	....	....	....	....	....	....	....
99-2000	**Vancouver**	**NHL**	**75**	**5**	**21**	**26**	**54**	**1**	**0**	**1**	**109**	**4.6**	**–3**	**0**	**0.0**	**24:03**	....	....	....	....	....	....	....	....	....
2000-01	**Vancouver**	**NHL**	**79**	**12**	**35**	**47**	**102**	**4**	**0**	**2**	**193**	**6.2**	**–1**	**0**	**0.0**	**24:57**	**4**	**1**	**1**	**2**	**0**	**0**	**0**	**0**	**25:54**
2001-02	**Vancouver**	**NHL**	**82**	**17**	**31**	**48**	**101**	**7**	**1**	**3**	**202**	**8.4**	**–7**	**0**	**0.0**	**25:11**	**6**	**1**	**4**	**5**	**8**	**1**	**0**	**0**	**25:48**
	Canada	Olympics	6	0	3	3	4	....	....	....	....	....	....	....	....	....	....	....	....	....	....	....	....	....	....
2002-03	**Vancouver**	**NHL**	**67**	**6**	**40**	**46**	**113**	**2**	**0**	**1**	**145**	**4.1**	**19**	**0**	**0.0**	**24:15**	**14**	**7**	**1**	**8**	**22**	**4**	**1**	**2**	**23:40**
2003-04	**Vancouver**	**NHL**	**56**	**7**	**16**	**23**	**64**	**2**	**0**	**1**	**143**	**4.9**	**2**	**0**	**0.0**	**23:11**	**7**	**0**	**4**	**4**	**6**	**0**	**0**	**0**	**26:36**
2004-05			DID NOT PLAY																						
2005-06	**Vancouver**	**NHL**	**44**	**8**	**25**	**33**	**58**	**6**	**0**	**2**	**87**	**9.2**	**–8**	**0**	**0.0**	**24:26**	....	....	....	....	....	....	....	....	....
	Canada	Olympics	DID NOT PLAY – INJURED																						
2006-07	**Phoenix**	**NHL**	**54**	**11**	**18**	**29**	**63**	**6**	**0**	**1**	**135**	**8.1**	**–6**	**0**	**0.0**	**23:09**	....	....	....	....	....	....	....	....	....
2007-08	**Phoenix**	**NHL**	**80**	**12**	**39**	**51**	**73**	**8**	**0**	**2**	**240**	**5.0**	**–13**	**0**	**0.0**	**22:33**	....	....	....	....	....	....	....	....	....
	NHL Totals		**821**	**109**	**288**	**397**	**1221**	**44**	**2**	**20**	**1701**	**6.4**		**0**	**0.0**	**23:46**	**58**	**10**	**18**	**28**	**92**	**5**	**1**	**2**	**25:02**

OHL All-Rookie Team (1994) • OHL Second All-Star Team (1994) • OHL First All-Star Team (1995) • NHL All-Rookie Team (1996)

Played in NHL All-Star Game (2001, 2002, 2003, 2007, 2008)

Traded to **Vancouver** by **Florida** with Dave Gagner, Mike Brown, Kevin Weekes and Florida's 1st round choice (Nathan Smith) in 2000 Entry Draft for Pavel Bure, Bret Hedican, Brad Ference and Vancouver's 3rd round choice (Robert Fried) in 2000 Entry Draft, January 17, 1999. Signed as a free agent by **Phoenix**, July 1, 2006.

JURCINA, Milan

(YEWR-chee-nah, MEE-lan) **WSH.**

Defense. Shoots right. 6'4", 237 lbs. Born, Liptovsky Mikulas, Czech., June 7, 1983. Boston's 7th choice, 241st overall, in 2001 Entry Draft.

Season	Club	League	Regular Season GP	G	A	Pts	PIM	PP	SH	GW	S	%	+/-	TF	F%	Min	Playoffs GP	G	A	Pts	PIM	PP	SH	GW	Min
99-2000	L. Mikulas Jr.	Slovak-Jr.	STATISTICS NOT AVAILABLE																						
2000-01	Halifax	QMJHL	68	0	5	5	56	....	....	....	....	....	....	....	....	....	6	0	2	2	12	....	....	....	....
2001-02	Halifax	QMJHL	61	4	16	20	58	....	....	....	....	....	....	....	....	....	13	5	3	8	10	....	....	....	....
2002-03	Halifax	QMJHL	51	15	13	28	102	....	....	....	....	....	....	....	....	....	25	6	6	12	40	....	....	....	....
2003-04	Providence Bruins	AHL	73	5	12	17	52	....	....	....	....	....	....	....	....	....	2	0	1	1	2	....	....	....	....
2004-05	Providence Bruins	AHL	79	6	17	23	92	....	....	....	....	....	....	....	....	....	17	1	3	4	30	....	....	....	....
2005-06	**Boston**	**NHL**	**51**	**6**	**5**	**11**	**54**	**2**	**0**	**0**	**64**	**9.4**	**3**	**1**	**0.0**	**16:28**	....	....	....	....	....	....	....	....	....
	Providence Bruins	AHL	7	0	3	3	8	....	....	....	....	....	....	....	....	....	....	....	....	....	....	....	....	....	....
	Slovakia	Olympics	6	0	1	1	8	....	....	....	....	....	....	....	....	....	....	....	....	....	....	....	....	....	....
2006-07	**Boston**	**NHL**	**40**	**2**	**1**	**3**	**20**	**0**	**0**	**1**	**29**	**6.9**	**–5**	**0**	**0.0**	**10:42**	....	....	....	....	....	....	....	....	....
	Washington	**NHL**	**30**	**2**	**7**	**9**	**24**	**0**	**0**	**0**	**42**	**4.8**	**5**	**0**	**0.0**	**23:09**	....	....	....	....	....	....	....	....	....
2007-08	**Washington**	**NHL**	**75**	**1**	**8**	**9**	**30**	**1**	**0**	**0**	**58**	**1.7**	**4**	**0**	**0.0**	**16:38**	**7**	**0**	**0**	**0**	**6**	**0**	**0**	**0**	**16:26**
	NHL Totals		**196**	**11**	**21**	**32**	**128**	**3**	**0**	**1**	**193**	**5.7**		**1**	**0.0**	**16:23**	**7**	**0**	**0**	**0**	**6**	**0**	**0**	**0**	**16:26**

Traded to **Washington** by **Boston** for Washington's 4th round choice (later traded to Calgary - Calgary selected T.J. Brodie) in 2008 Entry Draft, February 1, 2007.

KABERLE, Frantisek

(KA-buhr-lay, FRAN-tih-sehk) **CAR.**

Defense. Shoots left. 6', 190 lbs. Born, Kladno, Czech., November 8, 1973. Los Angeles' 3rd choice, 76th overall, in 1999 Entry Draft.

Season	Club	League	Regular Season GP	G	A	Pts	PIM	PP	SH	GW	S	%	+/-	TF	F%	Min	Playoffs GP	G	A	Pts	PIM	PP	SH	GW	Min
1991-92	Poldi Kladno	Czech	37	1	4	5	8	....	....	....	....	....	....	....	....	....	8	0	1	1	0	....	....	....	....
1992-93	Poldi Kladno	Czech	40	4	5	9	....	....	....	....	....	....	....	....	....	....	9	2	4	6	....	....	....	....	....
1993-94	HC Kladno	CzRep	41	4	16	20	....	....	....	....	....	....	....	....	....	....	11	1	1	2	....	....	....	....	....
1994-95	HC Kladno	CzRep	40	7	17	24	20	....	....	....	....	....	....	....	....	....	8	0	3	3	12	....	....	....	....
1995-96	MoDo	Sweden	40	5	7	12	34	....	....	....	....	....	....	....	....	....	8	0	1	1	0	....	....	....	....
1996-97	MoDo	Sweden	50	3	11	14	28	....	....	....	....	....	....	....	....	....	....	....	....	....	....	....	....	....	....
1997-98	MoDo	Sweden	46	5	4	9	22	....	....	....	....	....	....	....	....	....	9	1	1	2	4	....	....	....	....
1998-99	MoDo	Sweden	45	15	18	33	4	....	....	....	....	....	....	....	....	....	13	2	5	7	8	....	....	....	....
99-2000	**Los Angeles**	**NHL**	**37**	**0**	**9**	**9**	**4**	**0**	**0**	**0**	**41**	**0.0**	**3**	**0**	**0.0**	**17:04**	....	....	....	....	....	....	....	....	....
	Long Beach	IHL	18	2	8	10	8	....	....	....	....	....	....	....	....	....	....	....	....	....	....	....	....	....	....
	Atlanta	**NHL**	**14**	**1**	**6**	**7**	**6**	**0**	**1**	**0**	**35**	**2.9**	**–13**	**0**	**0.0**	**24:39**	....	....	....	....	....	....	....	....	....
	Lowell	AHL	4	0	2	2	0	....	....	....	....	....	....	....	....	....	....	....	....	....	....	....	....	....	....
2000-01	**Atlanta**	**NHL**	**51**	**4**	**11**	**15**	**18**	**1**	**0**	**1**	**99**	**4.0**	**11**	**1**	**0.0**	**22:17**	....	....	....	....	....	....	....	....	....
2001-02	**Atlanta**	**NHL**	**61**	**5**	**20**	**25**	**24**	**1**	**0**	**0**	**82**	**6.1**	**–11**	**0**	**0.0**	**21:35**	....	....	....	....	....	....	....	....	....
2002-03	**Atlanta**	**NHL**	**79**	**7**	**19**	**26**	**32**	**3**	**1**	**2**	**105**	**6.7**	**–19**	**0**	**0.0**	**21:57**	....	....	....	....	....	....	....	....	....
2003-04	**Atlanta**	**NHL**	**67**	**3**	**26**	**29**	**30**	**2**	**0**	**1**	**94**	**3.2**	**2**	**2**	**50.0**	**23:20**	....	....	....	....	....	....	....	....	....
2004-05	HC Rabat Kladno	CzRep	22	5	11	16	34	....	....	....	....	....	....	....	....	....	....	....	....	....	....	....	....	....	....
	MODO	Sweden	8	2	2	4	0	....	....	....	....	....	....	....	....	....	6	1	0	1	27	....	....	....	....
2005-06 •	**Carolina**	**NHL**	**77**	**6**	**38**	**44**	**46**	**1**	**0**	**3**	**126**	**4.8**	**8**	**0**	**0.0**	**19:37**	**25**	**4**	**9**	**13**	**8**	**3**	**0**	**1**	**18:25**
	Czech Republic	Olympics	8	0	1	1	6	....	....	....	....	....	....	....	....	....	....	....	....	....	....	....	....	....	....
2006-07	**Carolina**	**NHL**	**27**	**2**	**6**	**8**	**20**	**1**	**0**	**1**	**33**	**6.1**	**8**	**0**	**0.0**	**15:32**	....	....	....	....	....	....	....	....	....
2007-08	**Carolina**	**NHL**	**80**	**0**	**22**	**22**	**30**	**0**	**0**	**0**	**89**	**0.0**	**–4**	**0**	**0.0**	**17:09**	....	....	....	....	....	....	....	....	....
	NHL Totals		**493**	**28**	**157**	**185**	**210**	**9**	**2**	**8**	**704**	**4.0**		**3**	**33.3**	**20:20**	**25**	**4**	**9**	**13**	**8**	**3**	**0**	**1**	**18:25**

Traded to **Atlanta** by **Los Angeles** with Donald Audette for Kelly Buchberger and Nelson Emerson, March 13, 2000. Signed as a free agent by **Carolina**, July 15, 2004. Signed as a free agent by **Kladno** (CzRep), September 17, 2004. Signed as a free agent by **MODO** (Sweden), January 31, 2005. • Missed majority of 2006-07 season recovering from off-season shoulder surgery.

KABERLE, Tomas

(KA-buhr-lay, TAW-mas) **TOR.**

Defense. Shoots left. 6'1", 198 lbs. Born, Rakovnik, Czech., March 2, 1978. Toronto's 13th choice, 204th overall, in 1996 Entry Draft.

Season	Club	League	Regular Season GP	G	A	Pts	PIM	PP	SH	GW	S	%	+/-	TF	F%	Min	Playoffs GP	G	A	Pts	PIM	PP	SH	GW	Min
1994-95	HC Kladno Jr.	CzRep-Jr.	37	7	10	17	....	....	....	....	....	....	....	....	....	....	....	....	....	....	....	....	....	....	....
	HC Kladno	CzRep	4	0	1	1	0	....	....	....	....	....	....	....	....	....	....	....	....	....	....	....	....	....	....
1995-96	Kladno Jr.	CzRep-Jr.	23	6	13	19	....	....	....	....	....	....	....	....	....	....	....	....	....	....	....	....	....	....	....
	HC Poldi Kladno	CzRep	23	0	1	1	2	....	....	....	....	....	....	....	....	....	2	0	0	0	0	....	....	....	....
1996-97	HC Poldi Kladno	CzRep	49	0	5	5	26	....	....	....	....	....	....	....	....	....	3	0	0	0	0	....	....	....	....
1997-98	Kladno	CzRep	47	4	19	23	12	....	....	....	....	....	....	....	....	....	....	....	....	....	....	....	....	....	....
	St. John's	AHL	2	0	0	0	0	....	....	....	....	....	....	....	....	....	....	....	....	....	....	....	....	....	....
1998-99	**Toronto**	**NHL**	**57**	**4**	**18**	**22**	**12**	**0**	**0**	**2**	**71**	**5.6**	**3**	**0**	**0.0**	**18:42**	**14**	**0**	**3**	**3**	**2**	**0**	**0**	**0**	**17:10**

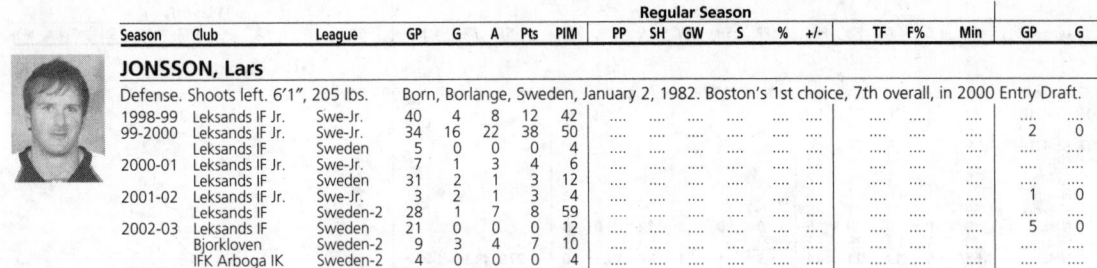

			Regular Season														Playoffs								
Season	Club	League	GP	G	A	Pts	PIM	PP	SH	GW	S	%	+/-	TF	F%	Min	GP	G	A	Pts	PIM	PP	SH	GW	Min
99-2000	Toronto	NHL	82	7	33	40	24	2	0	0	82	8.5	3	0	0.0	22:55	12	1	4	5	0	0	0	1	23:01
2000-01	Toronto	NHL	82	6	39	45	24	0	0	1	96	6.3	10	2	0.0	22:41	11	1	3	4	0	0	0	1	21:33
2001-02	Kladno	CzRep	9	1	7	8	4	....	....	....	....	....	....	....	....	....	....	....	....	....	....	....	....	....	....
	Toronto	NHL	69	10	29	39	2	5	0	3	85	11.8	5	2	100.0	25:00	20	2	8	10	16	0	0	0	28:40
	Czech Republic	Olympics	4	0	1	1	2	....	....	....	....	....	....	....	....	....	....	....	....	....	....	....	....	....	....
2002-03	Toronto	NHL	82	11	36	47	30	4	1	2	119	9.2	20	3	66.7	24:50	7	2	1	3	0	1	0	1	30:04
2003-04	Toronto	NHL	71	3	28	31	18	0	0	1	88	3.4	16	2	0.0	23:12	13	0	3	3	6	0	0	0	20:16
2004-05	HC Rabat Kladno	CzRep	49	8	31	39	38	....	....	....	....	....	....	....	....	....	7	1	0	1	0	....	....	....	....
2005-06	Toronto	NHL	82	9	58	67	46	6	0	2	163	5.5	–1	0	0.0	28:10	....	....	....	....	....	....	....	....	....
	Czech Republic	Olympics	8	2	2	4	2	....	....	....	....	....	....	....	....	....	....	....	....	....	....	....	....	....	....
2006-07	Toronto	NHL	74	11	47	58	20	2	0	1	128	8.6	3	0	0.0	25:52	....	....	....	....	....	....	....	....	....
2007-08	Toronto	NHL	82	8	45	53	22	6	0	1	155	5.2	–8	2	50.0	24:52	....	....	....	....	....	....	....	....	....
	NHL Totals		681	69	333	402	198	25	1	13	987	7.0		11	45.5	24:12	77	6	22	28	24	1	0	3	23:23

Played in NHL All-Star Game (2002, 2007, 2008)

Signed as a restricted free agent by **Kladno** (CzRep) with **Toronto** retaining NHL rights, September 29, 2001. Signed as a free agent by **Kladno** (CzRep), September 17, 2004.

KAIGORODOV, Alexei

(kay-goh-ROH-dahv, al-EHX-ay) **PHX.**

Center. Shoots left. 6'1", 194 lbs. Born, Magnitogorsk, USSR, July 29, 1983. Ottawa's 2nd choice, 47th overall, in 2002 Entry Draft.

1998-99	Magnitogorsk 2	Russia-4	10	6	4	10	2	....	....	....	....	....	....	....	....	....	....	....	....	....	....	....	....	....	....
99-2000	Magnitogorsk 2	Russia-3	19	2	3	5	8	....	....	....	....	....	....	....	....	....	....	....	....	....	....	....	....	....	....
2000-01	Magnitogorsk 2	Russia-3	45	12	30	42	26	....	....	....	....	....	....	....	....	....	....	....	....	....	....	....	....	....	....
2001-02	Magnitogorsk	Russia	46	4	12	16	20	....	....	....	....	....	....	....	....	....	9	0	3	3	2	....	....	....	....
2002-03	Magnitogorsk	Russia	46	8	14	22	20	....	....	....	....	....	....	....	....	....	3	0	1	1	0	....	....	....	....
2003-04	Magnitogorsk	Russia	49	4	12	16	24	....	....	....	....	....	....	....	....	....	14	2	2	4	4	....	....	....	....
2004-05	Magnitogorsk	Russia	57	15	34	49	40	....	....	....	....	....	....	....	....	....	5	0	3	3	2	....	....	....	....
2005-06	Magnitogorsk	Russia	50	9	21	30	42	....	....	....	....	....	....	....	....	....	11	0	1	1	6	....	....	....	....
2006-07	Ottawa	NHL	6	0	1	1	0	0	0	0	3	0.0	1	24	20.8	4:53	....	....	....	....	....	....	....	....	....
	Magnitogorsk	Russia	32	6	12	18	18	....	....	....	....	....	....	....	....	....	15	2	8	10	14	....	....	....	....
2007-08	Magnitogorsk	Russia	56	6	33	39	30	....	....	....	....	....	....	....	....	....	13	1	4	5	4	....	....	....	....
	NHL Totals		6	0	1	1	0	0	0	0	3	0.0		24	20.8	4:53	....	....	....	....	....	....	....	....	....

Traded to **Phoenix** by **Ottawa** for Mike Comrie, January 3, 2007.

KALETA, Patrick

(ka-LEH-tuh, PAT-rihk) **BUF.**

Right wing. Shoots right. 6', 195 lbs. Born, Buffalo, NY, June 8, 1986. Buffalo's 5th choice, 176th overall, in 2004 Entry Draft.

2002-03	Peterborough	OHL	67	7	9	16	67	....	....	....	....	....	....	....	....	....	7	0	0	0	6	....	....	....	....
2003-04	Peterborough	OHL	67	14	14	28	124	....	....	....	....	....	....	....	....	....	....	....	....	....	....	....	....	....	....
2004-05	Peterborough	OHL	62	24	28	52	146	....	....	....	....	....	....	....	....	....	14	3	3	6	30	....	....	....	....
2005-06	Peterborough	OHL	68	16	35	51	121	....	....	....	....	....	....	....	....	....	19	8	10	18	43	....	....	....	....
2006-07	Buffalo	NHL	7	0	2	2	21	0	0	0	6	0.0	3	0	0.0	6:49	....	....	....	....	....	....	....	....	....
	Rochester	AHL	58	5	10	15	133	....	....	....	....	....	....	....	....	....	5	0	0	0	12	....	....	....	....
2007-08	Buffalo	NHL	40	3	2	5	41	0	0	0	26	11.5	1	6	16.7	6:19	....	....	....	....	....	....	....	....	....
	Rochester	AHL	29	1	3	4	109	....	....	....	....	....	....	....	....	....	....	....	....	....	....	....	....	....	....
	NHL Totals		47	3	4	7	62	0	0	0	32	9.4		6	16.7	6:24	....	....	....	....	....	....	....	....	....

KALININ, Dmitri

(kah-LIHN-ihn, dih-MEE-tree) **NYR**

Defense. Shoots left. 6'3", 215 lbs. Born, Chelyabinsk, USSR, July 22, 1980. Buffalo's 1st choice, 18th overall, in 1998 Entry Draft.

1995-96	Chelyabinsk	CIS	20	0	3	3	10	....	....	....	....	....	....	....	....	....	....	....	....	....	....	....	....	....	....
1996-97	Yunior-T Kurgan	Russia-3	20	0	0	0	10	....	....	....	....	....	....	....	....	....	....	....	....	....	....	....	....	....	....
	Chelyabinsk	Russia	2	0	0	0	0	....	....	....	....	....	....	....	....	....	2	0	0	0	0	....	....	....	....
1997-98	Chelyabinsk	Russia	26	0	2	2	24	....	....	....	....	....	....	....	....	....	....	....	....	....	....	....	....	....	....
1998-99	Moncton Wildcats	QMJHL	39	7	18	25	44	....	....	....	....	....	....	....	....	....	4	1	1	2	0	....	....	....	....
	Rochester	AHL	3	0	1	1	14	....	....	....	....	....	....	....	....	....	7	0	0	0	6	....	....	....	....
99-2000	Buffalo	NHL	4	0	0	0	4	0	0	0	3	0.0	0	0	0.0	16:53	....	....	....	....	....	....	....	....	....
	Rochester	AHL	75	2	19	21	52	....	....	....	....	....	....	....	....	....	21	2	9	11	8	....	....	....	....
2000-01	Buffalo	NHL	79	4	18	22	38	2	0	0	88	4.5	–2	1	100.0	19:50	13	0	2	2	4	0	0	0	20:05
2001-02	Buffalo	NHL	58	2	11	13	26	0	0	0	67	3.0	–6	0	0.0	18:03	....	....	....	....	....	....	....	....	....
2002-03	Buffalo	NHL	65	8	13	21	57	3	1	0	83	9.6	–7	0	0.0	21:41	....	....	....	....	....	....	....	....	....
	Rochester	AHL	1	0	0	0	0	....	....	....	....	....	....	....	....	....	....	....	....	....	....	....	....	....	....
2003-04	Buffalo	NHL	77	10	24	34	42	2	1	4	118	8.5	0	0	0.0	23:06	....	....	....	....	....	....	....	....	....
2004-05	Magnitogorsk	Russia	48	2	8	10	14	....	....	....	....	....	....	....	....	....	5	0	0	0	2	....	....	....	....
2005-06	Buffalo	NHL	55	2	16	18	54	0	0	0	47	4.3	14	0	0.0	16:45	8	0	2	2	2	0	0	0	16:53
2006-07	Buffalo	NHL	82	7	22	29	36	0	1	0	86	8.1	19	1	100.0	19:31	16	2	3	5	14	0	0	0	18:11
2007-08	Buffalo	NHL	46	1	7	8	32	1	0	0	60	1.7	–7	0	0.0	17:20	....	....	....	....	....	....	....	....	....
	NHL Totals		466	34	111	145	289	8	3	4	552	6.2		2	100.0	19:43	37	2	7	9	20	0	0	0	18:34

AHL All-Rookie Team (2000)

Signed as a free agent by **Magnitogorsk** (Russia), September 25, 2004. Signed as a free agent by **NY Rangers**, July 3, 2008.

KALUS, Petr

(KAY-lihs, PEE-tuhr) **MIN.**

Left wing. Shoots left. 6'1", 201 lbs. Born, Ostrava, Czech., June 29, 1987. Boston's 2nd choice, 39th overall, in 2005 Entry Draft.

2002-03	HC Ostrava U17	CzR-U17	18	3	19	22	14	....	....	....	....	....	....	....	....	....	....	....	....	....	....	....	....	....	....
	HC Vitkovice U17	CzR-U17	10	3	1	4	37	....	....	....	....	....	....	....	....	....	....	....	....	....	....	....	....	....	....
	HC Vitkovice Jr.	CzRep-Jr.	11	0	0	0	4	....	....	....	....	....	....	....	....	....	....	....	....	....	....	....	....	....	....
2003-04	HC Vitkovice U17	CzR-U17	9	7	5	12	60	....	....	....	....	....	....	....	....	....	7	3	5	8	2	....	....	....	....
	HC Vitkovice Jr.	CzRep-Jr.	41	8	8	16	67	....	....	....	....	....	....	....	....	....	....	....	....	....	....	....	....	....	....
2004-05	HC Vitkovice Jr.	CzRep-Jr.	39	20	11	31	161	....	....	....	....	....	....	....	....	....	2	2	0	2	25	....	....	....	....
	Vitkovice	CzRep	1	0	0	0	0	....	....	....	....	....	....	....	....	....	....	....	....	....	....	....	....	....	....
2005-06	Regina Pats	WHL	60	36	22	58	87	....	....	....	....	....	....	....	....	....	6	4	1	5	6	....	....	....	....
2006-07	Boston	NHL	9	4	1	5	6	1	0	0	8	50.0	0	0	0.0	11:16	....	....	....	....	....	....	....	....	....
	Providence Bruins	AHL	43	13	17	30	110	....	....	....	....	....	....	....	....	....	9	1	0	1	12	....	....	....	....
2007-08	Houston Aeros	AHL	58	8	10	18	57	....	....	....	....	....	....	....	....	....	....	....	....	....	....	....	....	....	....
	NHL Totals		9	4	1	5	6	1	0	0	8	50.0		0	0.0	11:16	....	....	....	....	....	....	....	....	....

Traded to **Minnesota** by **Boston** with Boston's 4th round choice in 2009 Entry Draft for Manny Fernandez, July 1, 2007.

KANE, Boyd

(KAYN, BOID) **PHI.**

Left wing. Shoots left. 6'2", 220 lbs. Born, Swift Current, Sask., April 18, 1978. NY Rangers' 4th choice, 114th overall, in 1998 Entry Draft.

1994-95	Regina Pats	WHL	25	6	5	11	6	....	....	....	....	....	....	....	....	....	4	0	0	0	0	....	....	....	....
1995-96	Regina Pats	WHL	72	21	42	63	155	....	....	....	....	....	....	....	....	....	11	5	7	12	12	....	....	....	....
1996-97	Regina Pats	WHL	66	25	50	75	154	....	....	....	....	....	....	....	....	....	5	1	1	2	15	....	....	....	....
1997-98	Regina Pats	WHL	68	48	45	93	133	....	....	....	....	....	....	....	....	....	9	5	7	12	29	....	....	....	....
1998-99	Hartford	AHL	56	3	5	8	23	....	....	....	....	....	....	....	....	....	....	....	....	....	....	....	....	....	....
	Charlotte	ECHL	12	5	6	11	14	....	....	....	....	....	....	....	....	....	....	....	....	....	....	....	....	....	....
99-2000	Hartford	AHL	8	0	0	0	9	....	....	....	....	....	....	....	....	....	....	....	....	....	....	....	....	....	....
	Charlotte	ECHL	47	10	19	29	110	....	....	....	....	....	....	....	....	....	....	....	....	....	....	....	....	....	....
	Binghamton	UHL	3	0	2	2	4	....	....	....	....	....	....	....	....	....	1	0	0	0	0	....	....	....	....
2000-01	Charlotte	ECHL	12	9	8	17	6	....	....	....	....	....	....	....	....	....	....	....	....	....	....	....	....	....	....
	Hartford	AHL	56	11	17	28	81	....	....	....	....	....	....	....	....	....	5	2	0	2	2	....	....	....	....
2001-02	Hartford	AHL	78	17	22	39	193	....	....	....	....	....	....	....	....	....	10	1	2	3	50	....	....	....	....
2002-03	Springfield	AHL	72	15	22	37	121	....	....	....	....	....	....	....	....	....	6	3	1	4	8	....	....	....	....
2003-04	Philadelphia	NHL	7	0	0	0	7	0	0	0	6	0.0	–4	3	33.3	9:56	....	....	....	....	....	....	....	....	....
	Philadelphia	AHL	73	13	22	35	177	....	....	....	....	....	....	....	....	....	12	0	1	1	39	....	....	....	....
2004-05	Philadelphia	AHL	58	9	15	24	112	....	....	....	....	....	....	....	....	....	21	0	7	7	28	....	....	....	....
2005-06	Washington	NHL	5	0	1	1	2	0	0	0	1	0.0	1	0	0.0	4:04	....	....	....	....	....	....	....	....	....
	Hershey Bears	AHL	74	20	29	49	185	....	....	....	....	....	....	....	....	....	21	4	9	13	14	....	....	....	....

			Regular Season														Playoffs								
Season	Club	League	GP	G	A	Pts	PIM	PP	SH	GW	S	%	+/-	TF	F%	Min	GP	G	A	Pts	PIM	PP	SH	GW	Min
2006-07	Philadelphia	NHL	15	0	2	2	28	0	0	0	7	0.0	–4	4	25.0	6:58	....	....	....	....	....	....	....	....	....
	Philadelphia	AHL	57	10	22	32	98	....	....	....	....	....	....	....	....	....	....	....	....	....	....	....	....	....	....
2007-08	Philadelphia	AHL	57	18	26	44	102	....	....	....	....	....	....	....	....	....	12	4	4	8	25	....	....	....	....
	NHL Totals		27	0	3	3	37	0	0	0	14	0.0		7	28.6	7:12	....	....	....	....	....	....	....	....	....

• Re-entered NHL Entry Draft. Originally Pittsburgh's 3rd choice, 72nd overall, in 1996 Entry Draft.

Traded to **Tampa Bay** by **NY Rangers** for Gordie Dwyer, October 10, 2002. Signed as a free agent by **Philadelphia**, July 14, 2003. Signed as a free agent by **Washington**, August 12, 2005. Signed as a free agent by **Philadelphia**, July 13, 2006.

KANE, Patrick (KAYN, PAT-rihk) CHI.

Right wing. Shoots left. 5'10", 163 lbs. Born, Buffalo, NY, November 19, 1988. Chicago's 1st choice, 1st overall, in 2007 Entry Draft.

Season	Club	League	GP	G	A	Pts	PIM	PP	SH	GW	S	%	+/-	TF	F%	Min	GP	G	A	Pts	PIM	PP	SH	GW	Min
2003-04	Det. Honeybaked	MWEHL	70	83	77	160	....	....	....	....	....	....	....	....	....	....	....	....	....	....	....	....	....	....	....
2004-05	USNTDP	U-17	23	16	17	33	8	....	....	....	....	....	....	....	....	....	....	....	....	....	....	....	....	....	....
	USNTDP	NAHL	40	16	21	37	8	....	....	....	....	....	....	....	....	....	9	7	8	15	2	....	....	....	....
2005-06	USNTDP	U-18	43	35	33	68	10	....	....	....	....	....	....	....	....	....	....	....	....	....	....	....	....	....	....
	USNTDP	NAHL	15	17	17	34	12	....	....	....	....	....	....	....	....	....	....	....	....	....	....	....	....	....	....
2006-07	London Knights	OHL	58	62	83	*145	52	....	....	....	....	....	....	....	....	....	16	10	21	*31	16	....	....	....	....
2007-08	Chicago	NHL	82	21	51	72	52	7	0	4	191	11.0	–5	26	61.5	18:22	....	....	....	....	....	....	....	....	....
	NHL Totals		82	21	51	72	52	7	0	4	191	11.0		26	61.5	18:22	....	....	....	....	....	....	....	....	....

OHL All-Rookie Team (2007) • OHL First All-Star Team (2007) • OHL Rookie of the Year (2007) • Canadian Major Junior Rookie of the Year (2007) • NHL All-Rookie Team (2008) • Calder Memorial Trophy (2008)

KAPANEN, Niko (KA-pah-nehn, NEE-KOH)

Center. Shoots left. 5'9", 180 lbs. Born, Hameenlinna, Finland, April 29, 1978. Dallas' 5th choice, 173rd overall, in 1998 Entry Draft.

Season	Club	League	GP	G	A	Pts	PIM	PP	SH	GW	S	%	+/-	TF	F%	Min	GP	G	A	Pts	PIM	PP	SH	GW	Min
1993-94	HPK U18	Fin-U18	31	17	33	50	34	....	....	....	....	....	....	....	....	....	....	....	....	....	....	....	....	....	....
1994-95	HPK U18	Fin-U18	31	16	39	55	40	....	....	....	....	....	....	....	....	....	....	....	....	....	....	....	....	....	....
	HPK Jr.	Fin-Jr.	6	3	5	8	0	....	....	....	....	....	....	....	....	....	....	....	....	....	....	....	....	....	....
1995-96	HPK U18	Fin-U18	10	6	6	12	8	....	....	....	....	....	....	....	....	....	....	....	....	....	....	....	....	....	....
	HPK Jr.	Fin-Jr.	26	15	22	37	34	....	....	....	....	....	....	....	....	....	....	....	....	....	....	....	....	....	....
	HPK Hameenlinna	Finland	7	1	0	1	0	....	....	....	....	....	....	....	....	....	....	....	....	....	....	....	....	....	....
1996-97	HPK Jr.	Fin-Jr.	5	1	7	8	2	....	....	....	....	....	....	....	....	....	2	0	1	1	2	....	....	....	....
	HPK Hameenlinna	Finland	41	6	9	15	12	....	....	....	....	....	....	....	....	....	10	4	5	9	2	....	....	....	....
	HPK Hameenlinna	EuroHL	6	3	0	3	4	....	....	....	....	....	....	....	....	....	1	0	0	0	0	....	....	....	....
1997-98	HPK Jr.	Fin-Jr.	2	1	1	2	0	....	....	....	....	....	....	....	....	....	....	....	....	....	....	....	....	....	....
	HPK Hameenlinna	Finland	48	8	18	26	44	....	....	....	....	....	....	....	....	....	....	....	....	....	....	....	....	....	....
1998-99	HPK Jr.	Fin-Jr.	5	3	1	4	0	....	....	....	....	....	....	....	....	....	1	0	2	2	0	....	....	....	....
	HPK Hameenlinna	Finland	53	14	29	43	49	....	....	....	....	....	....	....	....	....	8	3	4	7	4	....	....	....	....
99-2000	HPK Hameenlinna	Finland	53	20	28	48	38	....	....	....	....	....	....	....	....	....	8	1	9	10	4	....	....	....	....
2000-01	TPS Turku	Finland	56	11	22	33	20	....	....	....	....	....	....	....	....	....	10	2	1	3	4	....	....	....	....
2001-02	Dallas	NHL	9	0	1	1	2	0	0	0	3	0.0	–1	59	40.7	9:44	....	....	....	....	....	....	....	....	....
	Utah Grizzlies	AHL	59	13	28	41	40	....	....	....	....	....	....	....	....	....	5	2	1	3	0	....	....	....	....
2002-03	Dallas	NHL	82	5	29	34	44	0	1	1	80	6.3	25	1111	47.5	14:39	12	4	3	7	12	0	1	0	16:03
2003-04	Dallas	NHL	67	1	5	6	16	0	0	0	57	1.8	–15	619	47.7	11:30	1	1	0	1	0	0	0	0	6:51
2004-05	EV Zug	Swiss	44	10	33	43	24	....	....	....	....	....	....	....	....	....	9	2	5	7	35	....	....	....	....
2005-06	Dallas	NHL	81	14	21	35	36	5	2	4	97	14.4	–10	798	49.9	14:13	5	0	1	1	10	0	0	0	14:52
	Finland	Olympics	8	2	1	3	2	....	....	....	....	....	....	....	....	....	....	....	....	....	....	....	....	....	....
2006-07	Atlanta	NHL	60	4	9	13	20	1	0	0	51	7.8	–12	527	54.1	10:45	....	....	....	....	....	....	....	....	....
	Phoenix	NHL	19	2	7	9	8	1	0	1	28	7.1	–11	279	54.1	17:36	....	....	....	....	....	....	....	....	....
2007-08	Phoenix	NHL	79	10	18	28	34	5	0	5	85	11.8	–1	806	52.1	13:49	....	....	....	....	....	....	....	....	....
	NHL Totals		397	36	90	126	160	12	3	11	401	9.0		4199	50.0	13:18	18	5	4	9	22	0	1	0	15:13

Signed as a free agent by **Zug** (Swiss), June 9, 2004. Traded to **Atlanta** by **Dallas** with Dallas' 7th round choice (Will O'Neill) in 2006 Entry Draft for Patrik Stefan and Jaroslav Modry, June 24, 2006. Claimed on waivers by **Phoenix** from **Atlanta**, February 27, 2007.

KAPANEN, Sami (KA-pah-nehn, SA-mee)

Right wing. Shoots left. 5'10", 185 lbs. Born, Vantaa, Finland, June 14, 1973. Hartford's 4th choice, 87th overall, in 1995 Entry Draft.

Season	Club	League	GP	G	A	Pts	PIM	PP	SH	GW	S	%	+/-	TF	F%	Min	GP	G	A	Pts	PIM	PP	SH	GW	Min
1989-90	KalPa Kuopio Jr.	Fin-Jr.	30	14	13	27	4	....	....	....	....	....	....	....	....	....	....	....	....	....	....	....	....	....	....
1990-91	KalPa Kuopio Jr.	Fin-Jr.	31	9	27	36	10	....	....	....	....	....	....	....	....	....	....	....	....	....	....	....	....	....	....
	KalPa Kuopio	Finland	14	1	2	3	2	....	....	....	....	....	....	....	....	....	8	2	1	3	2	....	....	....	....
1991-92	KalPa Kuopio Jr.	Fin-Jr.	8	1	3	4	12	....	....	....	....	....	....	....	....	....	....	....	....	....	....	....	....	....	....
	KalPa Kuopio	Finland	42	15	10	25	8	....	....	....	....	....	....	....	....	....	....	....	....	....	....	....	....	....	....
1992-93	KalPa Kuopio Jr.	Fin-Jr.	8	11	16	27	2	....	....	....	....	....	....	....	....	....	....	....	....	....	....	....	....	....	....
	KalPa Kuopio	Finland	37	4	17	21	12	....	....	....	....	....	....	....	....	....	....	....	....	....	....	....	....	....	....
1993-94	KalPa Kuopio	Finland	48	23	32	55	16	....	....	....	....	....	....	....	....	....	....	....	....	....	....	....	....	....	....
	Finland	Olympics	8	1	0	1	2	....	....	....	....	....	....	....	....	....	....	....	....	....	....	....	....	....	....
1994-95	HIFK Helsinki	Finland	49	14	28	42	42	....	....	....	....	....	....	....	....	....	3	0	0	0	0	....	....	....	....
1995-96	Hartford	NHL	35	5	4	9	6	0	0	0	46	10.9	0	....	....	....	....	....	....	....	....	....	....	....	....
	Springfield	AHL	28	14	17	31	4	....	....	....	....	....	....	....	....	....	3	1	2	3	0	....	....	....	....
1996-97	Hartford	NHL	45	13	12	25	2	3	0	2	82	15.9	6	....	....	....	....	....	....	....	....	....	....	....	....
1997-98	Carolina	NHL	81	26	37	63	16	4	0	5	190	13.7	9	....	....	....	....	....	....	....	....	....	....	....	....
	Finland	Olympics	6	0	1	1	0	....	....	....	....	....	....	....	....	....	....	....	....	....	....	....	....	....	....
1998-99	Carolina	NHL	81	24	35	59	10	5	0	7	254	9.4	–1	10	50.0	19:25	5	1	1	2	0	0	0	0	19:09
99-2000	Carolina	NHL	76	24	24	48	12	7	0	5	229	10.5	10	2	50.0	19:53	....	....	....	....	....	....	....	....	....
2000-01	Carolina	NHL	82	20	37	57	24	7	0	4	223	9.0	–12	6	16.7	18:56	6	2	3	5	0	1	0	0	20:13
2001-02	Carolina	NHL	77	27	42	69	23	11	0	4	248	10.9	9	7	14.3	20:38	23	1	8	9	6	0	0	0	20:03
	Finland	Olympics	4	1	2	3	4	....	....	....	....	....	....	....	....	....	....	....	....	....	....	....	....	....	....
2002-03	Carolina	NHL	43	6	12	18	12	3	0	1	108	5.6	–17	16	31.3	18:37	....	....	....	....	....	....	....	....	....
	Philadelphia	NHL	28	4	9	13	6	2	0	1	81	4.9	–1	5	40.0	19:21	13	4	3	7	6	2	0	0	20:12
2003-04	Philadelphia	NHL	74	12	18	30	14	0	1	2	149	8.1	9	18	44.4	16:31	18	3	7	10	6	0	1	1	17:41
2004-05	KalPa Kuopio	Finland-2	10	6	3	9	2	....	....	....	....	....	....	....	....	....	9	5	3	8	4	....	....	....	....
2005-06	Philadelphia	NHL	58	12	22	34	12	3	4	2	123	9.8	–9	43	39.5	18:04	6	0	0	0	2	0	0	0	20:19
2006-07	Philadelphia	NHL	77	11	14	25	22	1	2	1	129	8.5	–21	39	33.3	16:58	....	....	....	....	....	....	....	....	....
2007-08	Philadelphia	NHL	74	5	3	8	16	0	1	1	76	6.6	–12	31	41.9	13:19	16	2	0	2	2	0	0	0	10:47
	NHL Totals		831	189	269	458	175	46	8	35	1938	9.8		177	37.3	18:06	87	13	22	35	22	3	1	1	17:51

Played in NHL All-Star Game (2000, 2002)

Transferred to **Carolina** after **Hartford** franchise relocated, June 25, 1997. Traded to **Philadelphia** by **Carolina** with Ryan Bast for Pavel Brendl and Bruno St. Jacques, February 7, 2003. Signed as a free agent by **Kuopio** (Finland-2), November 17, 2004. • Officially announced his retirement, June 3, 2008.

KARIYA, Paul (kah-REE-ah, PAWL) ST.L.

Left wing. Shoots left. 5'10", 180 lbs. Born, Vancouver, B.C., October 16, 1974. Anaheim's 1st choice, 4th overall, in 1993 Entry Draft.

Season	Club	League	GP	G	A	Pts	PIM	PP	SH	GW	S	%	+/-	TF	F%	Min	GP	G	A	Pts	PIM	PP	SH	GW	Min
1990-91	Penticton	BCJHL	54	45	67	112	8	....	....	....	....	....	....	....	....	....	....	....	....	....	....	....	....	....	....
1991-92	Penticton	BCJHL	40	46	86	132	18	....	....	....	....	....	....	....	....	....	....	....	....	....	....	....	....	....	....
1992-93	U. of Maine	H-East	39	25	*75	*100	12	....	....	....	....	....	....	....	....	....	....	....	....	....	....	....	....	....	....
1993-94	U. of Maine	H-East	12	8	16	24	4	....	....	....	....	....	....	....	....	....	....	....	....	....	....	....	....	....	....
	Canada	Nat-Tm	23	7	34	41	2	....	....	....	....	....	....	....	....	....	....	....	....	....	....	....	....	....	....
	Canada	Olympics	8	3	4	7	2	....	....	....	....	....	....	....	....	....	....	....	....	....	....	....	....	....	....
1994-95	Anaheim	NHL	47	18	21	39	4	7	1	3	134	13.4	–17	....	....	....	....	....	....	....	....	....	....	....	....
1995-96	Anaheim	NHL	82	50	58	108	20	20	3	9	349	14.3	9	....	....	....	....	....	....	....	....	....	....	....	....
1996-97	Anaheim	NHL	69	44	55	99	6	15	3	10	340	12.9	36	....	....	....	11	7	6	13	4	4	0	1	....
1997-98	Anaheim	NHL	22	17	14	31	23	3	0	2	103	16.5	12	....	....	....	....	....	....	....	....	....	....	....	....
1998-99	Anaheim	NHL	82	39	62	101	40	11	2	4	429	9.1	17	91	48.4	25:32	3	1	3	4	0	0	0	0	26:03
99-2000	Anaheim	NHL	74	42	44	86	24	11	3	3	324	13.0	22	99	39.4	24:22	....	....	....	....	....	....	....	....	....
2000-01	Anaheim	NHL	66	33	34	67	20	18	3	3	230	14.3	–9	149	44.3	23:02	....	....	....	....	....	....	....	....	....
2001-02	Anaheim	NHL	82	32	25	57	28	11	0	8	289	11.1	–15	94	41.5	22:13	....	....	....	....	....	....	....	....	....
	Canada	Olympics	6	3	1	4	0	....	....	....	....	....	....	....	....	....	....	....	....	....	....	....	....	....	....
2002-03	Anaheim	NHL	82	25	56	81	48	11	1	2	257	9.7	–3	39	30.8	20:17	21	6	6	12	6	0	0	1	21:15
2003-04	Colorado	NHL	51	11	25	36	22	5	1	1	110	10.0	–5	18	27.8	18:37	1	0	1	1	0	0	0	0	16:00

			Regular Season														Playoffs								
Season	Club	League	GP	G	A	Pts	PIM	PP	SH	GW	S	%	+/-	TF	F%	Min	GP	G	A	Pts	PIM	PP	SH	GW	Min
2004-05			Did not play																						
2005-06	**Nashville**	**NHL**	82	31	54	85	40	14	0	3	245	12.7	–6	9	11.1	19:05	5	2	5	7	0	2	0	0	20:47
2006-07	**Nashville**	**NHL**	82	24	52	76	36	5	0	2	224	10.7	6	3	0.0	20:23	5	0	2	2	2	0	0	0	19:36
2007-08	**St. Louis**	**NHL**	82	16	49	65	50	5	0	1	223	7.2	–10	6	0.0	18:44	....	....	....	....	....	....	....	....	....
	NHL Totals		903	382	549	931	361	136	17	51	3257	11.7		508	40.6	21:25	46	16	23	39	12	6	0	2	21:12

Hockey East First All-Star Team (1993) • Hockey East Rookie of the Year (1993) • Hockey East Player of the Year (1993) • NCAA East First All-American Team (1993) • NCAA Championship All-Tournament Team (1993) • Hobey Baker Memorial Award (Top U.S. Collegiate Player) (1993) • NHL All-Rookie Team (1995) • Lady Byng Memorial Trophy (1996, 1997) • NHL First All-Star Team (1996, 1997, 1999) • NHL Second All-Star Team (2000, 2003)

Played in NHL All-Star Game (1996, 1997, 1999, 2000, 2001, 2002, 2003)

• Missed majority of 1997-98 season after failing to come to contract terms with **Anaheim** and recovering from head injury suffered in game vs. San Jose, February 1, 1998. Signed as a free agent by **Colorado**, July 3, 2003. Signed as a free agent by **Nashville**, August 5, 2005. Signed as a free agent by **St. Louis**, July 1, 2007.

KARLSSON, Andreas

(KARL-suhn, awn-DRAY-uhs)

Center. Shoots left. 6'4", 201 lbs. Born, Ludvika, Sweden, August 19, 1975. Calgary's 8th choice, 148th overall, in 1993 Entry Draft.

1992-93	Leksands IF	Sweden	13	0	0	0	6	....	....	....	....	....	....	....	....	....	....	....	....	....	....	....	....	....	....
1993-94	Leksands IF	Sweden	21	0	0	0	10	....	....	....	....	....	....	....	....	....	3	0	0	0	0	....	....	....	....
1994-95	Leksands IF Jr.	Swe-Jr.	3	3	3	6	0	....	....	....	....	....	....	....	....	....	....	....	....	....	....	....	....	....	....
	Leksands IF	Sweden	24	7	8	15	0	....	....	....	....	....	....	....	....	....	4	0	1	1	0	....	....	....	....
1995-96	Leksands IF Jr.	Swe-Jr.	2	4	1	5	6	....	....	....	....	....	....	....	....	....	....	....	....	....	....	....	....	....	....
	Leksands IF	Sweden	40	10	13	23	10	....	....	....	....	....	....	....	....	....	....	....	....	....	....	....	....	....	....
1996-97	Leksands IF	Sweden	49	13	11	24	39	....	....	....	....	....	....	....	....	....	9	2	0	2	2	....	....	....	....
1997-98	Leksands IF	Sweden	33	9	14	23	20	....	....	....	....	....	....	....	....	....	4	1	0	1	0	....	....	....	....
	Leksands IF	EuroHL	6	2	3	5	2	....	....	....	....	....	....	....	....	....	....	....	....	....	....	....	....	....	....
1998-99	Leksands IF	Sweden	49	18	15	33	18	....	....	....	....	....	....	....	....	....	4	1	0	1	6	....	....	....	....
	Leksands IF	EuroHL	6	1	3	4	2	....	....	....	....	....	....	....	....	....	2	1	1	2	2	....	....	....	....
99-2000	**Atlanta**	**NHL**	51	5	9	14	14	1	0	0	74	6.8	–17	552	46.7	13:00	....	....	....	....	....	....	....	....	....
	Orlando	IHL	18	5	5	10	6	....	....	....	....	....	....	....	....	....	....	....	....	....	....	....	....	....	....
2000-01	**Atlanta**	**NHL**	60	5	11	16	16	0	1	0	83	6.0	–2	743	48.6	12:54	....	....	....	....	....	....	....	....	....
2001-02	**Atlanta**	**NHL**	42	1	7	8	20	0	0	0	41	2.4	–8	386	45.1	12:30	....	....	....	....	....	....	....	....	....
	Chicago Wolves	AHL	16	6	14	20	11	....	....	....	....	....	....	....	....	....	23	7	14	21	6	....	....	....	....
2002-03	Chicago Wolves	AHL	41	12	20	32	16	....	....	....	....	....	....	....	....	....	9	1	3	4	4	....	....	....	....
2003-04	EHC Basel	Swiss	40	7	21	28	30	....	....	....	....	....	....	....	....	....	....	....	....	....	....	....	....	....	....
2004-05	HV 71 Jonkoping	Sweden	39	11	13	24	12	....	....	....	....	....	....	....	....	....	....	....	....	....	....	....	....	....	....
2005-06	HV 71 Jonkoping	Sweden	50	*26	29	*55	30	....	....	....	....	....	....	....	....	....	12	5	8	13	8	....	....	....	....
2006-07	**Tampa Bay**	**NHL**	53	3	6	9	12	0	0	1	25	12.0	–4	286	45.1	8:25	6	0	0	0	0	0	0	0	7:07
2007-08	**Tampa Bay**	**NHL**	58	2	2	4	10	0	0	1	31	6.5	–7	333	54.7	9:39	....	....	....	....	....	....	....	....	....
	NHL Totals		264	16	35	51	72	1	1	2	254	6.3		2300	48.0	11:15	6	0	0	0	0	0	0	0	7:07

Traded to **Atlanta** by **Calgary** for future considerations, June 25, 1999. Signed as a free agent by **Basel** (Swiss), July 18, 2003. Signed as a free agent by **Tampa Bay**, July 1, 2006.

KASPAR, Lukas

(kas-PAHR, LOO-kahsh) **S.J.**

Right wing. Shoots left. 6'2", 220 lbs. Born, Most, Czech., September 23, 1985. San Jose's 1st choice, 22nd overall, in 2004 Entry Draft.

2000-01	Litvinov U17	CzR-U17	48	27	19	46	64	....	....	....	....	....	....	....	....	....	6	2	3	5	0	....	....	....	....
2001-02	Litvinov U17	CzR-U17	48	35	41	76	143	....	....	....	....	....	....	....	....	....	2	1	1	2	0	....	....	....	....
2002-03	Litvinov Jr.	CzRep-Jr.	26	14	14	28	40	....	....	....	....	....	....	....	....	....	....	....	....	....	....	....	....	....	....
	Litvinov	CzRep	9	1	1	2	2	....	....	....	....	....	....	....	....	....	....	....	....	....	....	....	....	....	....
2003-04	Litvinov Jr.	CzRep-Jr.	23	21	14	35	56	....	....	....	....	....	....	....	....	....	1	0	0	0	0	....	....	....	....
	Litvinov	CzRep	37	4	2	6	10	....	....	....	....	....	....	....	....	....	....	....	....	....	....	....	....	....	....
	Usti n. L.	CzRep-2	1	1	0	1	0	....	....	....	....	....	....	....	....	....	....	....	....	....	....	....	....	....	....
	Most	CzRep-3	....	....	....	....	....	....	....	....	....	....	....	....	....	....	1	0	0	0	2	....	....	....	....
2004-05	Ottawa 67's	OHL	59	21	30	51	45	....	....	....	....	....	....	....	....	....	21	6	14	20	8	....	....	....	....
2005-06	Cleveland Barons	AHL	76	14	22	36	88	....	....	....	....	....	....	....	....	....	....	....	....	....	....	....	....	....	....
2006-07	Worcester Sharks	AHL	78	12	28	40	64	....	....	....	....	....	....	....	....	....	6	0	2	2	6	....	....	....	....
2007-08	**San Jose**	**NHL**	3	0	0	0	0	0	0	0	5	0.0	–2	1	0.0	12:15	....	....	....	....	....	....	....	....	....
	Worcester Sharks	AHL	73	17	24	41	44	....	....	....	....	....	....	....	....	....	....	....	....	....	....	....	....	....	....
	NHL Totals		3	0	0	0	0	0	0	0	5	0.0		1	0.0	12:15	....	....	....	....	....	....	....	....	....

KEITH, Duncan

(KEETH, DUHN-kuhn) **CHI.**

Defense. Shoots left. 6', 195 lbs. Born, Winnipeg, Man., July 16, 1983. Chicago's 2nd choice, 54th overall, in 2002 Entry Draft.

1998-99	Penticton	Minor-BC	44	51	57	108	45	....	....	....	....	....	....	....	....	....	....	....	....	....	....	....	....	....	....
99-2000	Penticton	BCHL	59	9	27	36	37	....	....	....	....	....	....	....	....	....	....	....	....	....	....	....	....	....	....
2000-01	Penticton	BCHL	60	18	64	82	61	....	....	....	....	....	....	....	....	....	9	4	6	10	18	....	....	....	....
2001-02	Michigan State	CCHA	41	3	12	15	18	....	....	....	....	....	....	....	....	....	....	....	....	....	....	....	....	....	....
2002-03	Michigan State	CCHA	15	3	6	9	8	....	....	....	....	....	....	....	....	....	....	....	....	....	....	....	....	....	....
	Kelowna Rockets	WHL	37	11	35	46	60	....	....	....	....	....	....	....	....	....	19	3	11	14	12	....	....	....	....
2003-04	Norfolk Admirals	AHL	75	7	18	25	44	....	....	....	....	....	....	....	....	....	8	1	1	2	6	....	....	....	....
2004-05	Norfolk Admirals	AHL	79	9	17	26	78	....	....	....	....	....	....	....	....	....	6	0	0	0	14	....	....	....	....
2005-06	**Chicago**	**NHL**	81	9	12	21	79	1	1	0	134	6.7	–11	0	0.0	23:26	....	....	....	....	....	....	....	....	....
2006-07	**Chicago**	**NHL**	82	2	29	31	76	0	0	0	122	1.6	0	0	0.0	23:36	....	....	....	....	....	....	....	....	....
2007-08	**Chicago**	**NHL**	82	12	20	32	56	1	1	0	148	8.1	30	0	0.0	25:34	....	....	....	....	....	....	....	....	....
	NHL Totals		245	23	61	84	211	2	2	0	404	5.7		0	0.0	24:12	....	....	....	....	....	....	....	....	....

Played in NHL All-Star Game (2008)

• Left **Michigan State** (CCHA) and signed as a free agent by **Kelowna** (WHL), December 27, 2002.

KEITH, Matt

(KEETH, MAT)

Right wing. Shoots right. 6'2", 200 lbs. Born, Edmonton, Alta., April 11, 1983. Chicago's 3rd choice, 59th overall, in 2001 Entry Draft.

1998-99	Banff Icemen	HJHL	Statistics not available																						
	Spokane Chiefs	WHL	7	1	0	1	4	....	....	....	....	....	....	....	....	....	....	....	....	....	....	....	....	....	....
99-2000	Spokane Chiefs	WHL	39	1	3	4	37	....	....	....	....	....	....	....	....	....	15	1	2	3	11	....	....	....	....
2000-01	Spokane Chiefs	WHL	33	13	14	27	63	....	....	....	....	....	....	....	....	....	12	1	3	4	14	....	....	....	....
2001-02	Spokane Chiefs	WHL	68	34	33	67	71	....	....	....	....	....	....	....	....	....	11	5	5	10	16	....	....	....	....
2002-03	Spokane Chiefs	WHL	7	2	2	4	11	....	....	....	....	....	....	....	....	....	....	....	....	....	....	....	....	....	....
	Red Deer Rebels	WHL	49	25	26	51	32	....	....	....	....	....	....	....	....	....	23	6	7	13	30	....	....	....	....
2003-04	**Chicago**	**NHL**	20	2	3	5	10	1	0	0	21	9.5	–5	2	100.0	11:58	....	....	....	....	....	....	....	....	....
	Norfolk Admirals	AHL	66	13	13	26	57	....	....	....	....	....	....	....	....	....	8	1	2	3	10	....	....	....	....
2004-05	Norfolk Admirals	AHL	80	18	31	49	74	....	....	....	....	....	....	....	....	....	6	0	1	1	0	....	....	....	....
2005-06	**Chicago**	**NHL**	2	0	0	0	0	0	0	0	6	0.0	0	0	0.0	11:42	....	....	....	....	....	....	....	....	....
	Norfolk Admirals	AHL	72	26	19	45	61	....	....	....	....	....	....	....	....	....	3	0	1	1	0	....	....	....	....
2006-07	**Chicago**	**NHL**	2	0	0	0	4	0	0	0	0	0.0	–2	0	0.0	9:33	....	....	....	....	....	....	....	....	....
	Norfolk Admirals	AHL	19	2	8	10	15	....	....	....	....	....	....	....	....	....	....	....	....	....	....	....	....	....	....
	Portland Pirates	AHL	44	10	12	22	22	....	....	....	....	....	....	....	....	....	....	....	....	....	....	....	....	....	....
2007-08	Portland Pirates	AHL	34	5	5	10	13	....	....	....	....	....	....	....	....	....	....	....	....	....	....	....	....	....	....
	NY Islanders	**NHL**	3	0	0	0	0	0	0	0	3	0.0	–1	0	0.0	10:41	....	....	....	....	....	....	....	....	....
	Bridgeport	AHL	42	8	9	17	22	....	....	....	....	....	....	....	....	....	....	....	....	....	....	....	....	....	....
	NHL Totals		27	2	3	5	14	1	0	0	30	6.7		2	100.0	11:37	....	....	....	....	....	....	....	....	....

• Missed majority of 2000-01 season recovering from shoulder injury suffered in game vs. Tri-City (WHL), September 22, 2000. Traded to **Anaheim** by **Chicago** with Sebastien Caron and Chris Durno for Pierre Parenteau and Bruno St. Jacques, December 28, 2006. Traded to **NY Islanders** by **Anaheim** for Darryl Bootland, January 9, 2008.

KELLY, Chris

(KEHL-lee, KRIHS) **OTT.**

Center/Left wing. Shoots left. 6', 195 lbs. Born, Toronto, Ont., November 11, 1980. Ottawa's 4th choice, 94th overall, in 1999 Entry Draft.

Season	Club	League	Regular Season														Playoffs								
			GP	G	A	Pts	PIM	PP	SH	GW	S	%	+/-	TF	F%	Min	GP	G	A	Pts	PIM	PP	SH	GW	Min
1995-96	Toronto Marlies	MTHL	42	25	45	70	25	....	....	....	....	....	....	....	....	....	....	....	....	....	....	....	....	....	....
1996-97	Aurora Tigers	MTJHL	49	14	20	34	11	....	....	....	....	....	....	....	....	....	....	....	....	....	....	....	....	....	....
1997-98	London Knights	OHL	54	15	14	29	4	....	....	....	....	....	....	....	....	....	16	4	5	9	12	....	....	....	....
1998-99	London Knights	OHL	68	36	41	77	60	....	....	....	....	....	....	....	....	....	25	9	17	26	22	....	....	....	....
99-2000	London Knights	OHL	63	29	43	72	57	....	....	....	....	....	....	....	....	....	....	....	....	....	....	....	....	....	....
2000-01	London Knights	OHL	31	21	34	55	46	....	....	....	....	....	....	....	....	....	....	....	....	....	....	....	....	....	....
	Sudbury Wolves	OHL	19	5	16	21	17	....	....	....	....	....	....	....	....	....	12	11	5	16	14	....	....	....	....
2001-02	Grand Rapids	AHL	31	3	3	6	20	....	....	....	....	....	....	....	....	....	5	1	1	2	5	....	....	....	....
	Muskegon Fury	UHL	4	1	2	3	0	....	....	....	....	....	....	....	....	....	....	....	....	....	....	....	....	....	....
2002-03	Binghamton	AHL	77	17	14	31	73	....	....	....	....	....	....	....	....	....	14	2	3	5	8	....	....	....	....
2003-04	**Ottawa**	**NHL**	**4**	**0**	**0**	**0**	**0**	**0**	**0**	**0**	**4**	**0.0**	**–2**	**5**	**40.0**	**9:29**	....	....	....	....	....	....	....	....	....
	Binghamton	AHL	54	15	19	34	40	....	....	....	....	....	....	....	....	....	2	0	0	0	4	....	....	....	....
2004-05	Binghamton	AHL	77	24	36	60	57	....	....	....	....	....	....	....	....	....	6	1	2	3	11	....	....	....	....
2005-06	**Ottawa**	**NHL**	**82**	**10**	**20**	**30**	**76**	**1**	**0**	**2**	**112**	**8.9**	**21**	**808**	**45.8**	**12:20**	**10**	**0**	**0**	**0**	**2**	**0**	**0**	**0**	**11:49**
2006-07	**Ottawa**	**NHL**	**82**	**15**	**23**	**38**	**40**	**1**	**2**	**0**	**131**	**11.5**	**28**	**564**	**49.8**	**15:18**	**20**	**3**	**4**	**7**	**4**	**0**	**0**	**0**	**15:28**
2007-08	**Ottawa**	**NHL**	**75**	**11**	**19**	**30**	**30**	**0**	**1**	**1**	**124**	**8.9**	**3**	**162**	**53.1**	**16:36**	....	....	....	....	....	....	....	....	....
	NHL Totals		**243**	**36**	**62**	**98**	**146**	**2**	**3**	**3**	**371**	**9.7**		**1539**	**48.0**	**14:36**	**30**	**3**	**4**	**7**	**6**	**0**	**0**	**0**	**14:15**

KELLY, Steve

(KEHL-lee, STEEV) **CBJ**

Center. Shoots left. 6'2", 205 lbs. Born, Vancouver, B.C., October 26, 1976. Edmonton's 1st choice, 6th overall, in 1995 Entry Draft.

Season	Club	League	Regular Season														Playoffs								
			GP	G	A	Pts	PIM	PP	SH	GW	S	%	+/-	TF	F%	Min	GP	G	A	Pts	PIM	PP	SH	GW	Min
1991-92	Westbank	Minor-BC	30	25	60	85	75	....	....	....	....	....	....	....	....	....	....	....	....	....	....	....	....	....	....
1992-93	Prince Albert	WHL	65	11	9	20	75	....	....	....	....	....	....	....	....	....	....	....	....	....	....	....	....	....	....
1993-94	Prince Albert	WHL	65	19	42	61	106	....	....	....	....	....	....	....	....	....	....	....	....	....	....	....	....	....	....
1994-95	Prince Albert	WHL	68	31	41	72	153	....	....	....	....	....	....	....	....	....	15	7	9	16	35	....	....	....	....
1995-96	Prince Albert	WHL	70	27	74	101	203	....	....	....	....	....	....	....	....	....	18	13	18	31	47	....	....	....	....
1996-97	**Edmonton**	**NHL**	**8**	**1**	**0**	**1**	**6**	**0**	**0**	**1**	**6**	**16.7**	**–1**	....	....	....	**6**	**0**	**0**	**0**	**2**	**0**	**0**	**0**	....
	Hamilton	AHL	48	9	29	38	111	....	....	....	....	....	....	....	....	....	11	3	3	6	24	....	....	....	....
1997-98	**Edmonton**	**NHL**	**19**	**0**	**2**	**2**	**8**	**0**	**0**	**0**	**5**	**0.0**	**–4**	....	....	....	....	....	....	....	....	....	....	....	....
	Hamilton	AHL	11	2	8	10	18	....	....	....	....	....	....	....	....	....	....	....	....	....	....	....	....	....	....
	Tampa Bay	**NHL**	**24**	**2**	**1**	**3**	**15**	**1**	**0**	**0**	**17**	**11.8**	**–9**	....	....	....	....	....	....	....	....	....	....	....	....
	Milwaukee	IHL	5	0	1	1	19	....	....	....	....	....	....	....	....	....	....	....	....	....	....	....	....	....	....
	Cleveland	IHL	5	1	1	2	29	....	....	....	....	....	....	....	....	....	1	0	1	1	0	....	....	....	....
1998-99	**Tampa Bay**	**NHL**	**34**	**1**	**3**	**4**	**27**	**0**	**0**	**1**	**15**	**6.7**	**–15**	**11**	**54.5**	**10:51**	....	....	....	....	....	....	....	....	....
	Cleveland	IHL	18	6	7	13	36	....	....	....	....	....	....	....	....	....	....	....	....	....	....	....	....	....	....
99-2000	Detroit Vipers	IHL	1	0	0	0	4	....	....	....	....	....	....	....	....	....	....	....	....	....	....	....	....	....	....
	♦ **New Jersey**	**NHL**	**1**	**0**	**0**	**0**	**0**	**0**	**0**	**0**	**0**	**0.0**	**0**	**0**	**0.0**	**4:28**	**10**	**0**	**0**	**0**	**4**	**0**	**0**	**0**	**11:32**
	Albany River Rats	AHL	76	21	36	57	131	....	....	....	....	....	....	....	....	....	3	1	1	2	2	....	....	....	....
2000-01	**New Jersey**	**NHL**	**24**	**2**	**2**	**4**	**21**	**0**	**0**	**0**	**18**	**11.1**	**0**	**87**	**48.3**	**9:58**	....	....	....	....	....	....	....	....	....
	Los Angeles	**NHL**	**11**	**1**	**0**	**1**	**4**	**0**	**0**	**0**	**4**	**25.0**	**0**	**51**	**39.2**	**6:44**	**8**	**0**	**0**	**0**	**2**	**0**	**0**	**0**	**5:23**
2001-02	**Los Angeles**	**NHL**	**8**	**0**	**1**	**1**	**2**	**0**	**0**	**0**	**0**	**0.0**	**–1**	**44**	**36.4**	**6:52**	**1**	**0**	**0**	**0**	**0**	**0**	**0**	**0**	**5:54**
	Manchester	AHL	49	10	21	31	88	....	....	....	....	....	....	....	....	....	5	1	8	9	4	....	....	....	....
2002-03	**Los Angeles**	**NHL**	**15**	**2**	**3**	**5**	**0**	**0**	**0**	**1**	**14**	**14.3**	**–6**	**133**	**42.9**	**12:29**	....	....	....	....	....	....	....	....	....
	Manchester	AHL	54	19	44	63	144	....	....	....	....	....	....	....	....	....	3	0	1	1	0	....	....	....	....
2003-04	**Los Angeles**	**NHL**	**3**	**0**	**0**	**0**	**0**	**0**	**0**	**0**	**5**	**0.0**	**0**	**30**	**43.3**	**10:30**	....	....	....	....	....	....	....	....	....
	Manchester	AHL	59	21	49	70	117	....	....	....	....	....	....	....	....	....	1	0	0	0	2	....	....	....	....
2004-05	Adler Mannheim	Germany	46	11	22	33	*210	....	....	....	....	....	....	....	....	....	12	1	4	5	*72	....	....	....	....
2005-06	Adler Mannheim	Germany	19	4	17	21	44	....	....	....	....	....	....	....	....	....	....	....	....	....	....	....	....	....	....
	Frankfurt Lions	Germany	22	6	14	20	119	....	....	....	....	....	....	....	....	....	....	....	....	....	....	....	....	....	....
2006-07	Frankfurt Lions	Germany	47	9	29	38	209	....	....	....	....	....	....	....	....	....	8	2	8	10	30	....	....	....	....
2007-08	**Minnesota**	**NHL**	**2**	**0**	**0**	**0**	**0**	**0**	**0**	**0**	**1**	**0.0**	**0**	**3**	**66.7**	**3:44**	....	....	....	....	....	....	....	....	....
	Houston Aeros	AHL	48	10	18	28	81	....	....	....	....	....	....	....	....	....	3	0	0	0	6	....	....	....	....
	NHL Totals		**149**	**9**	**12**	**21**	**83**	**1**	**0**	**3**	**85**	**10.6**		**359**	**43.5**	**9:53**	**25**	**0**	**0**	**0**	**8**	**0**	**0**	**0**	**8:39**

Traded to **Tampa Bay** by **Edmonton** with Bryan Marchment and Jason Bonsignore for Roman Hamrlik and Paul Comrie, December 30, 1997. Traded to **New Jersey** by **Tampa Bay** for New Jersey's 7th round choice (Brian Eklund) in 2000 Entry Draft, October 7, 1999. Traded to **Los Angeles** by **New Jersey** to complete transaction that sent Bob Corkum to New Jersey (February 23, 2001), February 27, 2001. • Spent majority of 2000-01 season with New Jersey and Los Angeles as a healthy reserve. Signed as a free agent by **Mannheim** (Germany), May 4, 2004. Signed as a free agent by **Minnesota**, July 2, 2007. Signed as a free agent by **Columbus**, July 16. 2008.

KENNEDY, Tyler

(KEH-nuh-dee, TIGH-luhr) **PIT.**

Center. Shoots right. 5'11", 183 lbs. Born, Sault Ste. Marie, Ont., July 15, 1986. Pittsburgh's 6th choice, 99th overall, in 2004 Entry Draft.

Season	Club	League	Regular Season														Playoffs								
			GP	G	A	Pts	PIM	PP	SH	GW	S	%	+/-	TF	F%	Min	GP	G	A	Pts	PIM	PP	SH	GW	Min
2002-03	Sault Ste. Marie	OHL	61	5	10	15	28	....	....	....	....	....	....	....	....	....	4	0	0	0	0	....	....	....	....
2003-04	Sault Ste. Marie	OHL	63	16	26	42	28	....	....	....	....	....	....	....	....	....	....	....	....	....	....	....	....	....	....
2004-05	Sault Ste. Marie	OHL	61	21	36	57	37	....	....	....	....	....	....	....	....	....	4	1	3	4	4	....	....	....	....
2005-06	Sault Ste. Marie	OHL	64	22	48	70	60	....	....	....	....	....	....	....	....	....	4	1	2	3	2	....	....	....	....
2006-07	Wilkes-Barre	AHL	40	12	25	37	20	....	....	....	....	....	....	....	....	....	....	....	....	....	....	....	....	....	....
2007-08	**Pittsburgh**	**NHL**	**55**	**10**	**9**	**19**	**35**	**1**	**0**	**4**	**104**	**9.6**	**2**	**8**	**25.0**	**12:13**	**20**	**0**	**4**	**4**	**13**	**0**	**0**	**0**	**10:18**
	Wilkes-Barre	AHL	10	5	4	9	10	....	....	....	....	....	....	....	....	....	....	....	....	....	....	....	....	....	....
	NHL Totals		**55**	**10**	**9**	**19**	**35**	**1**	**0**	**4**	**104**	**9.6**		**8**	**25.0**	**12:13**	**20**	**0**	**4**	**4**	**13**	**0**	**0**	**0**	**10:18**

KESLER, Ryan

(KEHZ-luhr, RIGH-uhn) **VAN.**

Center. Shoots right. 6'2", 205 lbs. Born, Livonia, MI, August 31, 1984. Vancouver's 1st choice, 23rd overall, in 2003 Entry Draft.

Season	Club	League	Regular Season														Playoffs								
			GP	G	A	Pts	PIM	PP	SH	GW	S	%	+/-	TF	F%	Min	GP	G	A	Pts	PIM	PP	SH	GW	Min
99-2000	Det. Honeybaked	MWEHL	72	44	73	117	....	....	....	....	....	....	....	....	....	....	....	....	....	....	....	....	....	....	....
2000-01	USNTDP	U-18	26	8	20	28	24	....	....	....	....	....	....	....	....	....	....	....	....	....	....	....	....	....	....
	USNTDP	NAHL	56	7	21	28	40	....	....	....	....	....	....	....	....	....	....	....	....	....	....	....	....	....	....
2001-02	USNTDP	U-18	46	11	33	44	23	....	....	....	....	....	....	....	....	....	....	....	....	....	....	....	....	....	....
	USNTDP	USHL	13	5	5	10	10	....	....	....	....	....	....	....	....	....	....	....	....	....	....	....	....	....	....
	USNTDP	NAHL	10	5	6	11	4	....	....	....	....	....	....	....	....	....	....	....	....	....	....	....	....	....	....
2002-03	Ohio State	CCHA	40	11	20	31	44	....	....	....	....	....	....	....	....	....	....	....	....	....	....	....	....	....	....
2003-04	**Vancouver**	**NHL**	**28**	**2**	**3**	**5**	**16**	**0**	**0**	**0**	**23**	**8.7**	**–2**	**194**	**40.2**	**10:42**	....	....	....	....	....	....	....	....	....
	Manitoba Moose	AHL	33	3	8	11	29	....	....	....	....	....	....	....	....	....	....	....	....	....	....	....	....	....	....
2004-05	Manitoba Moose	AHL	78	30	27	57	105	....	....	....	....	....	....	....	....	....	14	4	5	9	8	....	....	....	....
2005-06	**Vancouver**	**NHL**	**82**	**10**	**13**	**23**	**79**	**1**	**0**	**2**	**119**	**8.4**	**1**	**984**	**46.8**	**14:03**	....	....	....	....	....	....	....	....	....
2006-07	**Vancouver**	**NHL**	**48**	**6**	**10**	**16**	**40**	**0**	**0**	**0**	**88**	**6.8**	**1**	**690**	**46.1**	**16:26**	**1**	**0**	**0**	**0**	**0**	**0**	**0**	**0**	**27:51**
2007-08	**Vancouver**	**NHL**	**80**	**21**	**16**	**37**	**79**	**4**	**2**	**2**	**177**	**11.9**	**1**	**1358**	**53.0**	**19:03**	....	....	....	....	....	....	....	....	....
	NHL Totals		**238**	**39**	**42**	**81**	**214**	**5**	**2**	**4**	**407**	**9.6**		**3226**	**48.9**	**15:49**	**1**	**0**	**0**	**0**	**0**	**0**	**0**	**0**	**27:51**

KESSEL, Phil

(KEH-suhl, FIHL) **BOS.**

Center. Shoots right. 5'11", 180 lbs. Born, Madison, WI, October 2, 1987. Boston's 1st choice, 5th overall, in 2006 Entry Draft.

Season	Club	League	Regular Season														Playoffs								
			GP	G	A	Pts	PIM	PP	SH	GW	S	%	+/-	TF	F%	Min	GP	G	A	Pts	PIM	PP	SH	GW	Min
2003-04	USNTDP	U-17	32	31	18	49	8	....	....	....	....	....	....	....	....	....	....	....	....	....	....	....	....	....	....
	USNTDP	NAHL	30	21	12	33	18	....	....	....	....	....	....	....	....	....	....	....	....	....	....	....	....	....	....
2004-05	USNTDP	U-18	31	41	32	73	16	....	....	....	....	....	....	....	....	....	....	....	....	....	....	....	....	....	....
	USNTDP	NAHL	14	11	14	25	21	....	....	....	....	....	....	....	....	....	....	....	....	....	....	....	....	....	....
2005-06	U. of Minnesota	WCHA	39	18	33	51	28	....	....	....	....	....	....	....	....	....	....	....	....	....	....	....	....	....	....
2006-07	**Boston**	**NHL**	**70**	**11**	**18**	**29**	**12**	**1**	**0**	**0**	**170**	**6.5**	**–12**	**373**	**40.8**	**14:04**	....	....	....	....	....	....	....	....	....
	Providence Bruins	AHL	2	1	0	1	2	....	....	....	....	....	....	....	....	....	....	....	....	....	....	....	....	....	....
2007-08	**Boston**	**NHL**	**82**	**19**	**18**	**37**	**28**	**5**	**0**	**3**	**213**	**8.9**	**–6**	**326**	**42.3**	**15:14**	**4**	**3**	**1**	**4**	**2**	**1**	**0**	**0**	**14:31**
	NHL Totals		**152**	**30**	**36**	**66**	**40**	**6**	**0**	**3**	**383**	**7.8**		**699**	**41.5**	**14:41**	**4**	**3**	**1**	**4**	**2**	**1**	**0**	**0**	**14:31**

WCHA All-Rookie Team (2006) • WCHA Rookie of the Year (2006) • Bill Masterton Memorial Trophy (2007)

KILGER, Chad

(KIHL-guhr, CHAD) **FLA.**

Left wing. Shoots left. 6'4", 224 lbs. Born, Cornwall, Ont., November 27, 1976. Anaheim's 1st choice, 4th overall, in 1995 Entry Draft.

Season	Club	League	GP	G	A	Pts	PIM	PP	SH	GW	S	%	+/-	TF	F%	Min	GP	G	A	Pts	PIM	PP	SH	GW	Min
			Regular Season														Playoffs								
1992-93	Cornwall Colts	CJHL	55	30	36	66	26	....	....	....	....	....	....	....	....	....	6	0	0	0	0	....	....	....	....
1993-94	Kingston	OHL	66	17	35	52	23	....	....	....	....	....	....	....	....	....	6	7	2	9	8	....	....	....	....
1994-95	Kingston	OHL	65	42	53	95	95	....	....	....	....	....	....	....	....	....	6	5	2	7	10	....	....	....	....
1995-96	Anaheim	NHL	45	5	7	12	22	0	0	1	38	13.2	-2	....	....	....	....	....	....	....	....	....	....	....	....
	Winnipeg	NHL	29	2	3	5	12	0	0	0	19	10.5	-2	....	....	....	4	1	0	1	0	0	0	1	....
1996-97	Phoenix	NHL	24	4	3	7	13	1	0	0	30	13.3	-5	....	....	....	....	....	....	....	....	....	....	....	....
	Springfield	AHL	52	17	28	45	36	....	....	....	....	....	....	....	....	....	16	5	7	12	56	....	....	....	....
1997-98	Phoenix	NHL	10	0	1	1	4	0	0	0	9	0.0	-2	....	....	....	....	....	....	....	....	....	....	....	....
	Springfield	AHL	35	14	14	28	33	....	....	....	....	....	....	....	....	....	....	....	....	....	....	....	....	....	....
	Chicago	NHL	22	3	8	11	6	2	0	1	23	13.0	2	....	....	....	....	....	....	....	....	....	....	....	....
1998-99	Chicago	NHL	64	14	11	25	30	2	1	1	68	20.6	-1	488	56.6	14:03	....	....	....	....	....	....	....	....	....
	Edmonton	NHL	13	1	1	2	4	0	0	0	13	7.7	-3	82	53.7	11:22	4	0	0	0	4	0	0	0	12:59
99-2000	Edmonton	NHL	40	3	2	5	18	0	0	0	32	9.4	-6	269	48.0	8:33	3	0	0	0	0	0	0	0	8:01
	Hamilton	AHL	7	4	2	6	4	....	....	....	....	....	....	....	....	....	....	....	....	....	....	....	....	....	....
2000-01	Edmonton	NHL	34	5	2	7	17	1	0	0	28	17.9	-7	391	53.5	8:18	....	....	....	....	....	....	....	....	....
	Montreal	NHL	43	9	16	25	34	1	1	1	75	12.0	-1	319	52.4	17:57	....	....	....	....	....	....	....	....	....
2001-02	Montreal	NHL	75	8	15	23	27	0	1	2	87	9.2	-7	357	53.8	13:14	12	0	1	1	9	0	0	0	14:00
2002-03	Montreal	NHL	60	9	7	16	21	0	0	1	60	15.0	-4	208	46.6	10:42	....	....	....	....	....	....	....	....	....
2003-04	Montreal	NHL	36	2	2	4	14	0	0	0	29	6.9	2	95	48.4	10:26	....	....	....	....	....	....	....	....	....
	Hamilton	AHL	2	1	0	1	0	....	....	....	....	....	....	....	....	....	....	....	....	....	....	....	....	....	....
	Toronto	NHL	5	1	1	2	2	0	0	1	6	16.7	2	2	0.0	12:14	13	2	1	3	0	0	0	0	11:41
2004-05			DID NOT PLAY																						
2005-06	Toronto	NHL	79	17	11	28	63	1	1	2	103	16.5	-6	89	51.7	12:25	....	....	....	....	....	....	....	....	....
2006-07	Toronto	NHL	82	14	14	28	58	0	1	2	141	9.9	-5	198	46.0	14:30	....	....	....	....	....	....	....	....	....
2007-08	Toronto	NHL	53	10	7	17	18	0	0	0	74	13.5	1	70	48.6	11:38	....	....	....	....	....	....	....	....	....
	NHL Totals		714	107	111	218	363	8	5	12	835	12.8		2568	51.8	12:30	36	3	2	5	13	0	0	1	12:22

Traded to **Winnipeg** by **Anaheim** with Oleg Tverdovsky and Anaheim's 3rd round choice (Per-Anton Lundstrom) in 1996 Entry Draft for Teemu Selanne, Marc Chouinard and Winnipeg's 4th round choice (later traded to Toronto – later traded to Montreal – Montreal selected Kim Staal) in 1996 Entry Draft, February 7, 1996. Transferred to **Phoenix** after **Winnipeg** franchise relocated, July 1, 1996. Traded to **Chicago** by **Phoenix** with Jayson More for Keith Carney and Jim Cummins, March 4, 1998. Traded to **Edmonton** by **Chicago** with Daniel Cleary, Ethan Moreau and Christian Laflamme for Boris Mironov, Dean McAmmond and Jonas Elofsson, March 20, 1999. Traded to **Montreal** by **Edmonton** for Sergei Zholtok, December 18, 2000. Claimed on waivers by **Toronto** from **Montreal**, March 9, 2004. Traded to **Florida** by **Toronto** for Florida's 3rd round choice (later traded to St. Louis - St. Louis selected James Livingston) in 2008 Entry Draft, February 26, 2008. • Suspended indefinitely by **Florida** for failing to report to team, March 5, 2008.

KING, D.J.

(KIHNG, DEE-JAY) **ST.L.**

Center. Shoots left. 6'3", 228 lbs. Born, Meadow Lake, Sask., January 27, 1984. St. Louis' 6th choice, 191st overall, in 2002 Entry Draft.

Season	Club	League	GP	G	A	Pts	PIM	PP	SH	GW	S	%	+/-	TF	F%	Min	GP	G	A	Pts	PIM	PP	SH	GW	Min
2000-01	Beardy's	SMHL	52	30	28	58	120	....	....	....	....	....	....	....	....	....	....	....	....	....	....	....	....	....	....
2001-02	Lethbridge	WHL	65	10	14	24	104	....	....	....	....	....	....	....	....	....	....	....	....	....	....	....	....	....	....
2002-03	Lethbridge	WHL	55	15	17	32	139	....	....	....	....	....	....	....	....	....	....	....	....	....	....	....	....	....	....
2003-04	Lethbridge	WHL	35	8	15	23	102	....	....	....	....	....	....	....	....	....	....	....	....	....	....	....	....	....	....
	Kelowna Rockets	WHL	28	5	2	7	80	....	....	....	....	....	....	....	....	....	17	1	6	7	16	....	....	....	....
2004-05	Worcester IceCats	AHL	74	6	8	14	178	....	....	....	....	....	....	....	....	....	....	....	....	....	....	....	....	....	....
2005-06	Peoria Rivermen	AHL	67	5	6	11	160	....	....	....	....	....	....	....	....	....	2	0	0	0	2	....	....	....	....
	Alaska Aces	ECHL	5	0	4	4	4	....	....	....	....	....	....	....	....	....	....	....	....	....	....	....	....	....	....
2006-07	St. Louis	NHL	27	1	1	2	52	0	0	0	12	8.3	-3	2	50.0	5:31	....	....	....	....	....	....	....	....	....
	Peoria Rivermen	AHL	38	5	4	9	102	....	....	....	....	....	....	....	....	....	....	....	....	....	....	....	....	....	....
2007-08	St. Louis	NHL	61	3	3	6	100	0	0	1	36	8.3	-4	7	28.6	5:36	....	....	....	....	....	....	....	....	....
	NHL Totals		88	4	4	8	152	0	0	1	48	8.3		9	33.3	5:35	....	....	....	....	....	....	....	....	....

KING, Jason

(KIHNG, JAY-suhn)

Center. Shoots left. 6'1", 195 lbs. Born, Corner Brook, Nfld., September 14, 1981. Vancouver's 5th choice, 212th overall, in 2001 Entry Draft.

Season	Club	League	GP	G	A	Pts	PIM	PP	SH	GW	S	%	+/-	TF	F%	Min	GP	G	A	Pts	PIM	PP	SH	GW	Min
99-2000	Halifax	QMJHL	53	3	7	10	8	....	....	....	....	....	....	....	....	....	10	0	0	0	2	....	....	....	....
2000-01	Halifax	QMJHL	72	48	41	89	78	....	....	....	....	....	....	....	....	....	6	3	2	5	16	....	....	....	....
2001-02	Halifax	QMJHL	61	*63	36	99	39	....	....	....	....	....	....	....	....	....	13	9	8	17	13	....	....	....	....
2002-03	Vancouver	NHL	8	0	2	2	0	0	0	0	12	0.0	0	0	0.0	11:17	....	....	....	....	....	....	....	....	....
	Manitoba Moose	AHL	67	20	20	40	15	....	....	....	....	....	....	....	....	....	14	4	3	7	14	....	....	....	....
2003-04	Vancouver	NHL	47	12	9	21	8	6	0	1	107	11.2	0	3	66.7	12:43	1	0	0	0	0	0	0	0	6:21
	Manitoba Moose	AHL	29	12	11	23	6	....	....	....	....	....	....	....	....	....	....	....	....	....	....	....	....	....	....
2004-05	Manitoba Moose	AHL	59	26	27	53	22	....	....	....	....	....	....	....	....	....	....	....	....	....	....	....	....	....	....
2005-06	Manitoba Moose	AHL	36	20	14	34	34	....	....	....	....	....	....	....	....	....	13	3	4	7	8	....	....	....	....
2006-07	Skelleftea AIK HK	Sweden	55	15	4	19	20	....	....	....	....	....	....	....	....	....	....	....	....	....	....	....	....	....	....
	Skelleftea AIK HK	Sweden-Q	9	3	2	5	6	....	....	....	....	....	....	....	....	....	....	....	....	....	....	....	....	....	....
2007-08	Anaheim	NHL	4	0	0	0	0	0	0	0	2	0.0	-3	1	100.0	10:57	....	....	....	....	....	....	....	....	....
	Portland Pirates	AHL	65	29	30	59	42	....	....	....	....	....	....	....	....	....	13	6	3	9	12	....	....	....	....
	NHL Totals		59	12	11	23	8	6	0	1	121	9.9		4	75.0	12:24	1	0	0	0	0	0	0	0	6:21

QMJHL Second All-Star Team (2001)

• Missed majority of 2005-06 season recovering from head injury suffered in game vs. Grand Rapids (AHL), March 9, 2005. Traded to **Anaheim** by **Vancouver** for Ryan Shannon and future considerations, June 23, 2007. Signed as a free agent by **Skelleftea** (Sweden), September 13, 2006.

KLEE, Ken

(KLEE, KEHN) **ATL.**

Defense. Shoots right. 6', 210 lbs. Born, Indianapolis, IN, April 24, 1971. Washington's 11th choice, 177th overall, in 1990 Entry Draft.

Season	Club	League	GP	G	A	Pts	PIM	PP	SH	GW	S	%	+/-	TF	F%	Min	GP	G	A	Pts	PIM	PP	SH	GW	Min
1988-89	St. Mike's B's	OHA-B	40	9	23	32	64	....	....	....	....	....	....	....	....	....	27	5	12	17	54	....	....	....	....
1989-90	Bowling Green	CCHA	39	0	5	5	52	....	....	....	....	....	....	....	....	....	....	....	....	....	....	....	....	....	....
1990-91	Bowling Green	CCHA	37	7	28	35	50	....	....	....	....	....	....	....	....	....	....	....	....	....	....	....	....	....	....
1991-92	Bowling Green	CCHA	10	0	1	1	14	....	....	....	....	....	....	....	....	....	....	....	....	....	....	....	....	....	....
1992-93	Baltimore	AHL	77	4	14	18	93	....	....	....	....	....	....	....	....	....	7	0	1	1	15	....	....	....	....
1993-94	Portland Pirates	AHL	65	2	9	11	87	....	....	....	....	....	....	....	....	....	17	1	2	3	14	....	....	....	....
1994-95	Portland Pirates	AHL	49	5	7	12	89	....	....	....	....	....	....	....	....	....	....	....	....	....	....	....	....	....	....
	Washington	NHL	23	3	1	4	41	0	0	0	18	16.7	2	....	....	....	7	0	0	0	4	0	0	0	....
1995-96	Washington	NHL	66	8	3	11	60	0	1	2	76	10.5	-1	....	....	....	1	0	0	0	0	0	0	0	....
1996-97	Washington	NHL	80	3	8	11	115	0	0	2	108	2.8	-5	....	....	....	....	....	....	....	....	....	....	....	....
1997-98	Washington	NHL	51	4	2	6	46	0	0	1	44	9.1	-3	....	....	....	9	1	0	1	10	0	0	0	....
1998-99	Washington	NHL	78	7	13	20	80	0	0	1	132	5.3	-9	0	0.0	19:07	....	....	....	....	....	....	....	....	....
99-2000	Washington	NHL	80	7	13	20	79	0	0	2	113	6.2	8	0	0.0	20:29	5	0	1	1	10	0	0	0	21:38
2000-01	Washington	NHL	54	2	4	6	60	0	0	0	58	3.4	-5	0	0.0	17:15	6	0	1	1	8	0	0	0	13:47
2001-02	Washington	NHL	68	8	8	16	38	2	0	3	85	9.4	4	2	0.0	19:24	....	....	....	....	....	....	....	....	....
2002-03	Washington	NHL	70	1	16	17	89	0	0	0	67	1.5	22	0	0.0	21:49	6	0	0	0	6	0	0	0	23:11
2003-04	Toronto	NHL	66	4	25	29	36	3	0	1	85	4.7	-1	1	100.0	22:08	11	0	0	0	6	0	0	0	18:45
2004-05			DID NOT PLAY																						
2005-06	Toronto	NHL	56	3	12	15	66	1	0	1	65	4.6	-1	0	0.0	20:02	....	....	....	....	....	....	....	....	....
	New Jersey	NHL	18	0	0	0	14	0	0	0	5	0.0	-3	0	0.0	15:03	6	1	0	1	6	0	0	0	12:05
2006-07	Colorado	NHL	81	3	16	19	68	0	0	0	90	3.3	18	0	0.0	20:38	....	....	....	....	....	....	....	....	....
2007-08	Atlanta	NHL	72	1	9	10	60	0	0	0	56	1.8	-5	0	0.0	20:03	....	....	....	....	....	....	....	....	....
	NHL Totals		863	54	130	184	852	6	1	13	1002	5.4		3	33.3	20:01	51	2	2	4	50	0	0	0	17:54

Signed as a free agent by **Toronto**, September 27, 2003. Traded to **New Jersey** by **Toronto** for Aleksander Suglobov, March 8, 2006. Signed as a free agent by **Colorado**, July 24, 2006. Signed as a free agent by **Atlanta**, July 2, 2007.

KLEIN, Kevin — (KLIGHN, KEH-vihn) — NSH.

Defense. Shoots right. 6'1", 195 lbs. Born, Kitchener, Ont., December 13, 1984. Nashville's 3rd choice, 37th overall, in 2003 Entry Draft.

			Regular Season														Playoffs								
Season	Club	League	GP	G	A	Pts	PIM	PP	SH	GW	S	%	+/-	TF	F%	Min	GP	G	A	Pts	PIM	PP	SH	GW	Min
99-2000	Kitchener Midgets	Minor-ON	54	12	29	41	40																		
2000-01	St. Michael's	OHL	58	3	16	19	21										18	0	5	5	17				
2001-02	St. Michael's	OHL	68	5	22	27	35										15	2	7	9	12				
2002-03	St. Michael's	OHL	67	11	33	44	88										17	1	9	10	8				
2003-04	St. Michael's	OHL	5	0	1	1	2																		
	Guelph Storm	OHL	46	6	23	29	40										22	10	11	21	12				
2004-05	Milwaukee	AHL	65	4	12	16	22										7	0	0	0	11				
	Rockford IceHogs	UHL	3	2	1	3	0																		
2005-06	**Nashville**	**NHL**	2	0	0	0	0	0	0	0	0	0.0	−1	0	0.0	13:40									
	Milwaukee	AHL	76	10	33	43	31										21	3	7	10	31				
2006-07	**Nashville**	**NHL**	3	1	0	1	0	0	0	0	2	50.0	3	0	0.0	16:37									
	Milwaukee	AHL	70	5	15	20	67										4	1	0	1	0				
2007-08	**Nashville**	**NHL**	13	0	2	2	6	0	0	0	14	0.0	−3	0	0.0	14:24									
	Milwaukee	AHL	9	0	3	3	2																		
	NHL Totals		**18**	**1**	**2**	**3**	**6**	**0**	**0**	**0**	**16**	**6.3**		**0**	**0.0**	**14:41**									

KLEMM, Jon — (KLEHM, JAWN)

Defense. Shoots right. 6'2", 205 lbs. Born, Cranbrook, B.C., January 8, 1970.

1986-87	Cranbrook Colts	KIJHL	59	20	51	71	54																		
1987-88	Seattle	WHL	68	6	7	13	24																		
1988-89	Seattle	WHL	2	1	1	2	0																		
	Spokane Chiefs	WHL	66	6	34	40	42																		
1989-90	Spokane Chiefs	WHL	66	3	28	31	100										6	1	1	2	5				
1990-91	Spokane Chiefs	WHL	72	7	58	65	65										15	3	6	9	8				
1991-92	**Quebec**	**NHL**	4	0	1	1	0	0	0	0	2	0.0	2												
	Halifax Citadels	AHL	70	6	13	19	40																		
1992-93	Halifax Citadels	AHL	80	3	20	23	32																		
1993-94	**Quebec**	**NHL**	7	0	0	0	4	0	0	0	11	0.0	−1												
	Cornwall Aces	AHL	66	4	26	30	78										13	1	2	3	6				
1994-95	Cornwall Aces	AHL	65	6	13	19	84																		
	Quebec	**NHL**	4	1	0	1	2	0	0	0	5	20.0	3												
1995-96♦	**Colorado**	**NHL**	56	3	12	15	20	0	1	1	61	4.9	12				15	2	1	3	0	1	0	0	
1996-97	**Colorado**	**NHL**	80	9	15	24	37	1	2	1	103	8.7	12				17	1	1	2	6	0	0	0	
1997-98	**Colorado**	**NHL**	67	6	8	14	30	0	0	0	60	10.0	−3				4	0	0	0	0	0	0	0	
1998-99	**Colorado**	**NHL**	39	1	2	3	31	0	0	0	28	3.6	4	14	35.7	13:43	19	0	1	1	10	0	0	0	8:32
99-2000	**Colorado**	**NHL**	73	5	7	12	34	0	0	0	64	7.8	26	17	47.1	17:22	17	2	1	3	9	0	0	0	14:25
2000-01♦	**Colorado**	**NHL**	78	4	11	15	54	2	0	2	97	4.1	22	1	100.0	19:56	22	1	2	3	16	0	0	1	16:15
2001-02	**Chicago**	**NHL**	82	4	16	20	42	2	0	1	111	3.6	−3	1	0.0	23:50	5	0	1	1	4	0	0	0	21:58
2002-03	**Chicago**	**NHL**	70	2	14	16	44	1	0	1	74	2.7	−9	2	0.0	21:57									
2003-04	**Chicago**	**NHL**	19	0	1	1	20	0	0	0	19	0.0	6	0	0.0	21:21									
	Dallas	**NHL**	58	2	4	6	24	0	0	1	52	3.8	10	1	0.0	16:00									
2004-05				DID NOT PLAY																					
2005-06	**Dallas**	**NHL**	76	4	7	11	60	1	0	1	57	7.0	−3	2	50.0	16:56	5	1	0	1	0	0	0	0	15:44
2006-07	**Dallas**	**NHL**	38	1	2	3	24	0	0	0	25	4.0	0	0	0.0	13:03	1	0	0	0	2	0	0	0	13:47
2007-08	**Los Angeles**	**NHL**	22	0	0	0	10	0	0	0	6	0.0	−5	2	100.0	10:57									
	Manchester	AHL	41	0	6	6	38																		
	NHL Totals		**773**	**42**	**100**	**142**	**436**	**7**	**3**	**8**	**775**	**5.4**		**40**	**42.5**	**18:23**	**105**	**7**	**7**	**14**	**47**	**1**	**0**	**1**	**14:01**

WHL West Second All-Star Team (1991)

Signed as a free agent by **Quebec**, May 14, 1991. Transferred to **Colorado** after **Quebec** franchise relocated, June 21, 1995. • Missed majority of 1998-99 season recovering from knee injury suffered in game vs. Phoenix, November 10, 1998. Signed as a free agent by **Chicago**, July 1, 2001. Traded to **Dallas** by **Chicago** with NY Rangers' 4th round choice (previously acquired, Dallas selected Fredrik Naslund) in 2004 Entry Draft for Stephane Robidas and Dallas' 2nd round choice (Jakub Sindel) in 2004 Entry Draft, November 17, 2003. • Spent majority of 2006-07 season as a healthy reserve. Signed as a free agent by **Los Angeles**, August 20, 2007.

KLEPIS, Jakub — (KLEH-pihsh, YA-kuhb)

Center. Shoots right. 6'1", 198 lbs. Born, Prague, Czech., June 5, 1984. Ottawa's 1st choice, 16th overall, in 2002 Entry Draft.

99-2000	Slavia Jr.	CzRep-Jr.	48	14	26	40	30																		
2000-01	Slavia Jr.	CzRep-Jr.	52	21	25	46	82																		
2001-02	Portland	WHL	70	14	50	64	111										7	0	3	3	22				
2002-03	HC Slavia Praha	CzRep	38	2	6	8	22										4	0	0	0	6				
	Slavia Jr.	CzRep-Jr.	11	4	5	9	59										3	0	3	3	4				
2003-04	HC Slavia Praha	CzRep	44	4	9	13	43										17	5	3	8	10				
2004-05	Portland Pirates	AHL	78	13	14	27	76																		
2005-06	**Washington**	**NHL**	25	1	3	4	8	0	0	0	26	3.8	−11	22	40.9	7:25									
	Hershey Bears	AHL	54	11	20	31	49										15	2	6	8	4				
2006-07	**Washington**	**NHL**	41	3	7	10	28	0	0	0	38	7.9	−2	184	41.3	9:58									
	Hershey Bears	AHL	31	6	26	32	24										19	7	7	14	14				
2007-08	Hershey Bears	AHL	19	5	6	11	9																		
	HC Slavia Praha	CzRep	24	5	7	12	22										19	*10	7	17	24				
	NHL Totals		**66**	**4**	**10**	**14**	**36**	**0**	**0**	**0**	**64**	**6.3**		**206**	**41.3**	**9:00**									

Traded to **Buffalo** by **Ottawa** for Vaclav Varada and Buffalo's 5th round choice (Tim Cook) in 2003 Entry Draft, February 25, 2003. Traded to **Washington** by **Buffalo** for Mike Grier, March 9, 2004.

KLESLA, Rostislav — (KLEHS-luh, RAHS-tih-slav) — CBJ

Defense. Shoots left. 6'3", 220 lbs. Born, Novy Jicin, Czech., March 21, 1982. Columbus' 1st choice, 4th overall, in 2000 Entry Draft.

1997-98	HC Opava Jr.	CzRep-Jr.	38	11	18	29	87										8	2	2	4	0				
1998-99	Sioux City	USHL	54	4	12	16	100										5	2	0	2	2				
99-2000	Brampton	OHL	67	16	29	45	174										6	1	1	2	21				
2000-01	**Columbus**	**NHL**	8	2	0	2	6	0	0	0	10	20.0	−1	0	0.0	18:25									
	Brampton	OHL	45	18	36	54	59										9	2	9	11	26				
2001-02	**Columbus**	**NHL**	75	8	8	16	74	1	0	0	102	7.8	−6	0	0.0	18:52									
2002-03	**Columbus**	**NHL**	72	2	14	16	71	0	0	0	89	2.2	−22	0	0.0	18:45									
2003-04	**Columbus**	**NHL**	47	2	11	13	27	0	0	1	74	2.7	−16	0	0.0	18:19									
2004-05	HC Vsetin	CzRep	41	7	17	24	136																		
	HPK Hameenlinna	Finland	9	1	2	3	12										10	0	2	2	12				
2005-06	**Columbus**	**NHL**	51	6	13	19	75	2	0	1	84	7.1	−4	2	100.0	21:27									
2006-07	**Columbus**	**NHL**	75	9	13	22	105	2	0	0	159	5.7	−13	0	0.0	22:54									
2007-08	**Columbus**	**NHL**	82	6	12	18	60	3	0	1	130	4.6	7	5	80.0	23:13									
	NHL Totals		**410**	**35**	**71**	**106**	**418**	**8**	**0**	**3**	**648**	**5.4**		**7**	**85.7**	**20:42**									

OHL All-Rookie Team (2000) • Canadian Major Junior All-Rookie Team (2000) • OHL First All-Star Team (2001) • NHL All-Rookie Team (2002)

Signed as a free agent by **Vsetin** (CzRep), September 17, 2004. Signed as a free agent by **Hameenlinna** (Finland), January 29, 2005.

KNUBLE, Mike — (kuh-NOO-buhl, MIGHK) — PHI.

Right wing. Shoots right. 6'3", 230 lbs. Born, Toronto, Ont., July 4, 1972. Detroit's 4th choice, 76th overall, in 1991 Entry Draft.

1988-89	East Kentwood	High-MI	28	52	37	89	60																		
1989-90	East Kentwood	High-MI	29	63	40	103	40																		
1990-91	Kalamazoo	NAHL	36	18	24	42	30																		
1991-92	U. of Michigan	CCHA	43	7	8	15	48																		
1992-93	U. of Michigan	CCHA	39	26	16	42	57																		
1993-94	U. of Michigan	CCHA	41	32	26	58	71																		
1994-95	U. of Michigan	CCHA	34	*38	22	60	62																		
	Adirondack	AHL															3	0	0	0	0				
1995-96	Adirondack	AHL	80	22	23	45	59										3	1	0	1	0				
1996-97	**Detroit**	**NHL**	9	1	0	1	0	0	0	0	10	10.0	−1												
	Adirondack	AHL	68	28	35	63	54																		

Season	Club	League	GP	G	A	Pts	PIM	PP	SH	GW	S	%	+/-	TF	F%	Min	GP	G	A	Pts	PIM	PP	SH	GW	Min
			Regular Season														Playoffs								
1997-98 ♦	**Detroit**	**NHL**	**53**	**7**	**6**	**13**	**16**	**0**	**0**	**0**	**54**	**13.0**	**2**	....	....	....	**3**	**0**	**1**	**1**	**0**	**0**	**0**	**0**	....
1998-99	**NY Rangers**	**NHL**	**82**	**15**	**20**	**35**	**26**	**3**	**0**	**1**	**113**	**13.3**	**–7**	**1**	**100.0**	**14:52**	....	....	....	....	....	....	....	....	....
99-2000	**NY Rangers**	**NHL**	**59**	**9**	**5**	**14**	**18**	**1**	**0**	**1**	**50**	**18.0**	**–5**	**9**	**55.6**	**10:39**	....	....	....	....	....	....	....	....	....
	Boston	**NHL**	**14**	**3**	**3**	**6**	**8**	**1**	**0**	**1**	**28**	**10.7**	**–2**	**3**	**0.0**	**19:29**	....	....	....	....	....	....	....	....	....
2000-01	**Boston**	**NHL**	**82**	**7**	**13**	**20**	**37**	**0**	**1**	**1**	**92**	**7.6**	**0**	**115**	**31.3**	**10:34**	....	....	....	....	....	....	....	....	....
2001-02	**Boston**	**NHL**	**54**	**8**	**6**	**14**	**42**	**0**	**0**	**2**	**77**	**10.4**	**9**	**27**	**44.4**	**9:45**	**2**	**0**	**0**	**0**	**0**	**0**	**0**	**0**	**3:30**
2002-03	**Boston**	**NHL**	**75**	**30**	**29**	**59**	**45**	**9**	**0**	**4**	**185**	**16.2**	**18**	**34**	**44.1**	**17:24**	**5**	**0**	**2**	**2**	**2**	**0**	**0**	**0**	**17:35**
2003-04	**Boston**	**NHL**	**82**	**21**	**25**	**46**	**32**	**4**	**0**	**3**	**192**	**10.9**	**19**	**54**	**31.5**	**18:47**	**7**	**2**	**0**	**2**	**0**	**1**	**0**	**0**	**19:45**
2004-05	Linkopings HC	Sweden	49	*26	13	39	40	....	....	....	....	....	....	....	....	....	6	0	1	1	2	....	....	....	....
2005-06	**Philadelphia**	**NHL**	**82**	**34**	**31**	**65**	**80**	**13**	**2**	**6**	**217**	**15.7**	**25**	**161**	**32.3**	**20:21**	**6**	**1**	**3**	**4**	**8**	**0**	**0**	**0**	**19:17**
	United States	Olympics	6	1	1	2	4	....	....	....	....	....	....	....	....	....	....	....	....	....	....	....	....	....	....
2006-07	**Philadelphia**	**NHL**	**64**	**24**	**30**	**54**	**56**	**10**	**0**	**1**	**160**	**15.0**	**2**	**62**	**37.1**	**19:38**	....	....	....	....	....	....	....	....	....
2007-08	**Philadelphia**	**NHL**	**82**	**29**	**26**	**55**	**72**	**15**	**1**	**3**	**177**	**16.4**	**–3**	**25**	**40.0**	**18:55**	**12**	**3**	**4**	**7**	**6**	**0**	**0**	**1**	**18:34**
	NHL Totals		**738**	**188**	**194**	**382**	**432**	**56**	**4**	**23**	**1355**	**13.9**		**491**	**34.8**	**16:02**	**35**	**6**	**10**	**16**	**16**	**1**	**0**	**1**	**17:52**

CCHA Second All-Star Team (1994, 1995) • NCAA West Second All-American Team (1995)

Traded to **NY Rangers** by **Detroit** for NY Rangers' 2nd round choice (Tomas Kopecky) in 2000 Entry Draft, October 1, 1998. Traded to **Boston** by **NY Rangers** for Rob DiMaio, March 10, 2000. Signed as a free agent by **Philadelphia**, July 3, 2004. Signed as a free agent by **Linkopings** (Sweden), August 2, 2004.

KOBASEW, Chuck (KOH-buh-soo, CHUHK) BOS.

Center. Shoots left. 5'11", 192 lbs. Born, Vancouver, B.C., April 17, 1982. Calgary's 1st choice, 14th overall, in 2001 Entry Draft.

Season	Club	League	GP	G	A	Pts	PIM	PP	SH	GW	S	%	+/-	TF	F%	Min	GP	G	A	Pts	PIM	PP	SH	GW	Min
1997-98	Osoyoos Heat	KIJHL	6	2	2	4	2	....	....	....	....	....	....	....	....	....	....	....	....	....	....	....	....	....	....
1998-99	Osoyoos Heat	KIJHL	23	25	24	49	....	....	....	....	....	....	....	....	....	....	....	....	....	....	....	....	....	....	....
	Penticton	BCHL	30	11	17	28	18	....	....	....	....	....	....	....	....	....	....	....	....	....	....	....	....	....	....
99-2000	Penticton	BCHL	58	*54	52	106	83	....	....	....	....	....	....	....	....	....	....	....	....	....	....	....	....	....	....
2000-01	Boston College	H-East	43	27	22	49	38	....	....	....	....	....	....	....	....	....	....	....	....	....	....	....	....	....	....
2001-02	Kelowna Rockets	WHL	55	41	21	62	114	....	....	....	....	....	....	....	....	....	15	10	5	15	22	....	....	....	....
2002-03	**Calgary**	**NHL**	**23**	**4**	**2**	**6**	**8**	**1**	**0**	**1**	**29**	**13.8**	**–3**	**5**	**0.0**	**11:48**	....	....	....	....	....	....	....	....	....
	Saint John Flames	AHL	48	21	12	33	61	....	....	....	....	....	....	....	....	....	....	....	....	....	....	....	....	....	....
2003-04	**Calgary**	**NHL**	**70**	**6**	**11**	**17**	**51**	**3**	**0**	**0**	**78**	**7.7**	**–12**	**91**	**42.9**	**10:22**	**26**	**0**	**1**	**1**	**24**	**0**	**0**	**0**	**9:02**
2004-05	Lowell	AHL	79	38	37	75	110	....	....	....	....	....	....	....	....	....	11	6	3	9	27	....	....	....	....
2005-06	**Calgary**	**NHL**	**77**	**20**	**11**	**31**	**64**	**10**	**0**	**4**	**143**	**14.0**	**–10**	**47**	**25.5**	**12:16**	**7**	**1**	**0**	**1**	**0**	**0**	**0**	**1**	**12:29**
2006-07	**Calgary**	**NHL**	**40**	**4**	**13**	**17**	**37**	**1**	**0**	**1**	**69**	**5.8**	**7**	**26**	**30.8**	**13:13**	....	....	....	....	....	....	....	....	....
	Boston	**NHL**	**10**	**1**	**1**	**2**	**25**	**1**	**0**	**0**	**24**	**4.2**	**–6**	**6**	**16.7**	**18:51**	....	....	....	....	....	....	....	....	....
2007-08	**Boston**	**NHL**	**73**	**22**	**17**	**39**	**29**	**6**	**3**	**3**	**147**	**15.0**	**6**	**70**	**40.0**	**17:41**	....	....	....	....	....	....	....	....	....
	NHL Totals		**293**	**57**	**55**	**112**	**214**	**22**	**3**	**9**	**490**	**11.6**		**245**	**35.9**	**13:29**	**33**	**1**	**1**	**2**	**24**	**0**	**0**	**1**	**9:45**

Hockey East Second All-Star Team (2001) • Hockey East Rookie of the Year (2001) • NCAA Championship All-Tournament Team (2001) • NCAA Championship Tournament MVP (2001) • AHL First All-Star Team (2005)

• Left **Boston College** (Hockey East) and signed with **Kelowna** (WHL), August 13, 2001. Traded to **Boston** by **Calgary** with Andrew Ference for Brad Stuart, Wayne Primeau and Washington's 4th round choice (previously acquired, Calgary selected T.J. Brodie) in 2008 Entry Draft, February 10, 2007.

KOCI, David (KOH-chee, DAY-vihd) T.B.

Left wing. Shoots left. 6'6", 238 lbs. Born, Prague, Czech., May 12, 1981. Pittsburgh's 5th choice, 146th overall, in 2000 Entry Draft.

Season	Club	League	GP	G	A	Pts	PIM	PP	SH	GW	S	%	+/-	TF	F%	Min	GP	G	A	Pts	PIM	PP	SH	GW	Min
1997-98	Sparta Jr.	CzRep-Jr.	41	2	9	11	105	....	....	....	....	....	....	....	....	....	....	....	....	....	....	....	....	....	....
1998-99	Hvezda Praha Jr.	CzRep-Jr.	22	1	3	4	36	....	....	....	....	....	....	....	....	....	....	....	....	....	....	....	....	....	....
	Sparta Jr.	CzRep-Jr.	7	0	0	0	4	....	....	....	....	....	....	....	....	....	....	....	....	....	....	....	....	....	....
99-2000	Sparta Jr.	CzRep-Jr.	47	0	6	6	124	....	....	....	....	....	....	....	....	....	....	....	....	....	....	....	....	....	....
2000-01	Prince George	WHL	70	2	7	9	155	....	....	....	....	....	....	....	....	....	6	0	0	0	20	....	....	....	....
2001-02	Wilkes-Barre	AHL	26	1	3	4	98	....	....	....	....	....	....	....	....	....	....	....	....	....	....	....	....	....	....
	Wheeling Nailers	ECHL	33	2	4	6	105	....	....	....	....	....	....	....	....	....	....	....	....	....	....	....	....	....	....
2002-03	Wilkes-Barre	AHL	9	0	0	0	4	....	....	....	....	....	....	....	....	....	....	....	....	....	....	....	....	....	....
	Wheeling Nailers	ECHL	48	0	1	1	103	....	....	....	....	....	....	....	....	....	....	....	....	....	....	....	....	....	....
2003-04	Wilkes-Barre	AHL	78	1	7	8	298	....	....	....	....	....	....	....	....	....	10	0	0	0	24	....	....	....	....
2004-05	Wilkes-Barre	AHL	68	1	8	9	311	....	....	....	....	....	....	....	....	....	....	....	....	....	....	....	....	....	....
2005-06	Wilkes-Barre	AHL	13	0	0	0	59	....	....	....	....	....	....	....	....	....	....	....	....	....	....	....	....	....	....
2006-07	**Chicago**	**NHL**	**9**	**0**	**0**	**0**	**88**	**0**	**0**	**0**	**3**	**0.0**	**–3**	**0**	**0.0**	**4:44**	....	....	....	....	....	....	....	....	....
	Norfolk Admirals	AHL	44	0	1	1	223	....	....	....	....	....	....	....	....	....	....	....	....	....	....	....	....	....	....
2007-08	**Chicago**	**NHL**	**18**	**0**	**0**	**0**	**68**	**0**	**0**	**0**	**2**	**0.0**	**–4**	**0**	**0.0**	**3:38**	....	....	....	....	....	....	....	....	....
	Rockford IceHogs	AHL	7	0	0	0	25	....	....	....	....	....	....	....	....	....	....	....	....	....	....	....	....	....	....
	Norfolk Admirals	AHL	21	0	2	2	57	....	....	....	....	....	....	....	....	....	....	....	....	....	....	....	....	....	....
	NHL Totals		**27**	**0**	**0**	**0**	**156**	**0**	**0**	**0**	**5**	**0.0**		**0**	**0.0**	**4:00**	....	....	....	....	....	....	....	....	....

• Missed majority of 2005-06 season recovering from knee injury, November, 2006. Signed as a free agent by **Chicago**, July 17, 2006. Signed as a free agent by **Tampa Bay**, July 3, 2008.

KOISTINEN, Ville (KOIS-tih-nehn, VIHL-ee) NSH.

Defense. Shoots left. 5'11", 190 lbs. Born, Oulu, Finland, June 17, 1982.

Season	Club	League	GP	G	A	Pts	PIM	PP	SH	GW	S	%	+/-	TF	F%	Min	GP	G	A	Pts	PIM	PP	SH	GW	Min
1998-99	Ilves Tampere U18	Fin-U18	34	4	10	14	86	....	....	....	....	....	....	....	....	....	....	....	....	....	....	....	....	....	....
	Ilves Tampere Jr.	Fin-Jr.	1	0	0	0	2	....	....	....	....	....	....	....	....	....	....	....	....	....	....	....	....	....	....
99-2000	Ilves Tampere U18	Fin-U18	14	4	6	10	69	....	....	....	....	....	....	....	....	....	....	....	....	....	....	....	....	....	....
	Ilves Tampere Jr.	Fin-Jr.	34	4	2	6	40	....	....	....	....	....	....	....	....	....	....	....	....	....	....	....	....	....	....
2000-01	Ilves Tampere	Finland	6	0	0	0	0	....	....	....	....	....	....	....	....	....	5	0	1	1	0	....	....	....	....
	Ilves Tampere Jr.	Fin-Jr.	26	1	8	9	101	....	....	....	....	....	....	....	....	....	....	....	....	....	....	....	....	....	....
2001-02	Ilves Tampere	Finland	53	1	8	9	42	....	....	....	....	....	....	....	....	....	....	....	....	....	....	....	....	....	....
	Ilves Tampere Jr.	Fin-Jr.	6	2	2	4	16	....	....	....	....	....	....	....	....	....	....	....	....	....	....	....	....	....	....
2002-03	Ilves Tampere	Finland	18	4	1	5	8	....	....	....	....	....	....	....	....	....	....	....	....	....	....	....	....	....	....
	Ilves Tampere Jr.	Fin-Jr.	1	0	0	0	10	....	....	....	....	....	....	....	....	....	....	....	....	....	....	....	....	....	....
2003-04	Ilves Tampere	Finland	54	7	16	23	51	....	....	....	....	....	....	....	....	....	7	0	2	2	0	....	....	....	....
2004-05	Ilves Tampere	Finland	52	6	14	20	69	....	....	....	....	....	....	....	....	....	3	0	0	0	0	....	....	....	....
2005-06	Ilves Tampere	Finland	56	8	26	34	70	....	....	....	....	....	....	....	....	....	4	0	1	1	2	....	....	....	....
2006-07	Milwaukee	AHL	59	9	32	41	44	....	....	....	....	....	....	....	....	....	4	0	2	2	4	....	....	....	....
2007-08	**Nashville**	**NHL**	**48**	**4**	**13**	**17**	**18**	**2**	**0**	**1**	**60**	**6.7**	**13**	**0**	**0.0**	**16:48**	....	....	....	....	....	....	....	....	....
	NHL Totals		**48**	**4**	**13**	**17**	**18**	**2**	**0**	**1**	**60**	**6.7**		**0**	**0.0**	**16:48**	....	....	....	....	....	....	....	....	....

Signed as a free agent by **Nashville**, May 11, 2006.

KOIVU, Mikko (KOI-voo, MEE-koh) MIN.

Center. Shoots left. 6'2", 200 lbs. Born, Turku, Finland, March 12, 1983. Minnesota's 1st choice, 6th overall, in 2001 Entry Draft.

Season	Club	League	GP	G	A	Pts	PIM	PP	SH	GW	S	%	+/-	TF	F%	Min	GP	G	A	Pts	PIM	PP	SH	GW	Min
99-2000	TPS Turku U18	Fin-U18	11	4	9	13	18	....	....	....	....	....	....	....	....	....	....	....	....	....	....	....	....	....	....
	TPS Turku Jr.	Fin-Jr.	30	4	8	12	22	....	....	....	....	....	....	....	....	....	13	1	4	5	8	....	....	....	....
2000-01	TPS Turku U18	Fin-U18	....	....	....	....	....	....	....	....	....	....	....	....	....	....	7	2	10	12	2	....	....	....	....
	TPS Turku Jr.	Fin-Jr.	26	9	36	45	26	....	....	....	....	....	....	....	....	....	3	1	1	2	6	....	....	....	....
	TPS Turku	Finland	21	0	1	1	2	....	....	....	....	....	....	....	....	....	....	....	....	....	....	....	....	....	....
2001-02	TPS Turku Jr.	Fin-Jr.	2	0	1	1	12	....	....	....	....	....	....	....	....	....	....	....	....	....	....	....	....	....	....
	TPS Turku	Finland	48	4	3	7	34	....	....	....	....	....	....	....	....	....	8	0	3	3	4	....	....	....	....
2002-03	TPS Turku	Finland	37	7	13	20	20	....	....	....	....	....	....	....	....	....	7	2	2	4	6	....	....	....	....
2003-04	TPS Turku	Finland	45	6	24	30	36	....	....	....	....	....	....	....	....	....	13	1	7	8	8	....	....	....	....
2004-05	Houston Aeros	AHL	67	20	28	48	47	....	....	....	....	....	....	....	....	....	5	1	0	1	2	....	....	....	....
2005-06	**Minnesota**	**NHL**	**64**	**6**	**15**	**21**	**40**	**3**	**0**	**0**	**96**	**6.3**	**–9**	**724**	**47.4**	**13:17**	....	....	....	....	....	....	....	....	....
	Finland	Olympics	8	0	0	0	6	....	....	....	....	....	....	....	....	....	....	....	....	....	....	....	....	....	....
2006-07	**Minnesota**	**NHL**	**82**	**20**	**34**	**54**	**58**	**9**	**2**	**2**	**162**	**12.3**	**6**	**1165**	**50.9**	**17:29**	**5**	**1**	**0**	**1**	**4**	**0**	**0**	**0**	**17:43**
2007-08	**Minnesota**	**NHL**	**57**	**11**	**31**	**42**	**42**	**2**	**0**	**2**	**144**	**7.6**	**13**	**1032**	**52.5**	**20:53**	**6**	**4**	**1**	**5**	**4**	**0**	**1**	**0**	**21:56**
	NHL Totals		**203**	**37**	**80**	**117**	**140**	**14**	**2**	**4**	**402**	**9.2**		**2921**	**50.6**	**17:07**	**11**	**5**	**1**	**6**	**8**	**0**	**1**	**0**	**20:01**

KOIVU, Saku

(KOI-voo, SA-koo) **MTL.**

Center. Shoots left. 5'10", 187 lbs. Born, Turku, Finland, November 23, 1974. Montreal's 1st choice, 21st overall, in 1993 Entry Draft.

			Regular Season														Playoffs								
Season	Club	League	GP	G	A	Pts	PIM	PP	SH	GW	S	%	+/-	TF	F%	Min	GP	G	A	Pts	PIM	PP	SH	GW	Min
1990-91	TPS Turku U18	Fin-U18	24	20	28	48	26	....	....	....	....	....	....	....	....	....	....	....	....	....	....	....	....	....	....
	TPS Turku Jr.	Fin-Jr.	13	3	7	10	6	....	....	....	....	....	....	....	....	....	....	....	....	....	....	....	....	....	....
1991-92	TPS Turku U18	Fin-U18	12	3	7	10	6	....	....	....	....	....	....	....	....	....	....	....	....	....	....	....	....	....	....
	TPS Turku Jr.	Fin-Jr.	34	25	28	53	57	....	....	....	....	....	....	....	....	....	8	5	9	14	6	....	....	....	....
1992-93	TPS Turku	Finland	46	3	7	10	28	....	....	....	....	....	....	....	....	....	11	3	2	5	2	....	....	....	....
1993-94	TPS Turku	Finland	47	23	30	53	42	....	....	....	....	....	....	....	....	....	11	4	8	12	16	....	....	....	....
	Finland	Olympics	8	4	3	7	12	....	....	....	....	....	....	....	....	....	....	....	....	....	....	....	....	....	....
1994-95	TPS Turku	Finland	45	27	47	74	73	....	....	....	....	....	....	....	....	....	13	7	10	17	16	....	....	....	....
1995-96	**Montreal**	**NHL**	**82**	**20**	**25**	**45**	**40**	**8**	**3**	**2**	**136**	**14.7**	**–7**	....	....	....	**6**	**3**	**1**	**4**	**8**	**0**	**0**	**0**	....
1996-97	**Montreal**	**NHL**	**50**	**17**	**39**	**56**	**38**	**5**	**0**	**3**	**135**	**12.6**	**7**	....	....	....	**5**	**1**	**3**	**4**	**10**	**0**	**0**	**0**	....
1997-98	**Montreal**	**NHL**	**69**	**14**	**43**	**57**	**48**	**2**	**2**	**3**	**145**	**9.7**	**8**	....	....	....	**6**	**2**	**3**	**5**	**2**	**1**	**0**	**0**	....
	Finland	Olympics	6	2	8	10	4	....	....	....	....	....	....	....	....	....	....	....	....	....	....	....	....	....	....
1998-99	**Montreal**	**NHL**	**65**	**14**	**30**	**44**	**38**	**4**	**2**	**0**	**145**	**9.7**	**–7**	**1427**	**52.6**	**20:02**	....	....	....	....	....	....	....	....	....
99-2000	**Montreal**	**NHL**	**24**	**3**	**18**	**21**	**14**	**1**	**0**	**0**	**53**	**5.7**	**7**	**495**	**52.9**	**19:13**	....	....	....	....	....	....	....	....	....
2000-01	**Montreal**	**NHL**	**54**	**17**	**30**	**47**	**40**	**7**	**0**	**3**	**113**	**15.0**	**2**	**1092**	**47.6**	**21:23**	....	....	....	....	....	....	....	....	....
2001-02	**Montreal**	**NHL**	**3**	**0**	**2**	**2**	**0**	**0**	**0**	**0**	**2**	**0.0**	**0**	**13**	**61.5**	**13:57**	**12**	**4**	**6**	**10**	**4**	**1**	**0**	**1**	**15:54**
2002-03	**Montreal**	**NHL**	**82**	**21**	**50**	**71**	**72**	**5**	**1**	**5**	**147**	**14.3**	**5**	**1566**	**49.6**	**19:14**	....	....	....	....	....	....	....	....	....
2003-04	**Montreal**	**NHL**	**68**	**14**	**41**	**55**	**52**	**5**	**0**	**3**	**112**	**12.5**	**–5**	**1194**	**53.9**	**19:18**	**11**	**3**	**8**	**11**	**10**	**2**	**0**	**0**	**20:34**
2004-05	TPS Turku	Finland	20	8	8	16	28	....	....	....	....	....	....	....	....	....	6	3	2	5	30	....	....	....	....
2005-06	**Montreal**	**NHL**	**72**	**17**	**45**	**62**	**70**	**5**	**0**	**4**	**138**	**12.3**	**1**	**1412**	**53.8**	**18:31**	**3**	**0**	**2**	**2**	**2**	**0**	**0**	**0**	**14:24**
	Finland	Olympics	8	3	8	11	12	....	....	....	....	....	....	....	....	....	....	....	....	....	....	....	....	....	....
2006-07	**Montreal**	**NHL**	**81**	**22**	**53**	**75**	**74**	**11**	**1**	**4**	**154**	**14.3**	**–21**	**1453**	**54.9**	**18:07**	....	....	....	....	....	....	....	....	....
2007-08	**Montreal**	**NHL**	**77**	**16**	**40**	**56**	**93**	**8**	**0**	**3**	**150**	**10.7**	**–4**	**1341**	**52.3**	**18:07**	**7**	**3**	**6**	**9**	**4**	**2**	**0**	**0**	**19:33**
	NHL Totals		**727**	**175**	**416**	**591**	**579**	**61**	**9**	**30**	**1430**	**12.2**		**9993**	**52.2**	**19:06**	**50**	**16**	**29**	**45**	**40**	**6**	**0**	**1**	**18:06**

Bill Masterton Memorial Trophy (2002) • Olympic Tournament All-Star Team (2006) • King Clancy Memorial Trophy (2007)

Played in NHL All-Star Game (1998)

• Missed majority of 1999-2000 season recovering from shoulder injury suffered in game vs. NY Rangers, October 30, 1999. • Missed majority of 2001-02 season recovering from non-Hodgkin's lymphoma, September 6, 2001. Signed as a free agent by **Turku** (Finland), October 21, 2004.

KOLANOS, Krys

(koh-LA-nohs, KRIHS)

Center. Shoots right. 6'3", 206 lbs. Born, Calgary, Alta., July 27, 1981. Phoenix's 1st choice, 19th overall, in 2000 Entry Draft.

Season	Club	League	GP	G	A	Pts	PIM	PP	SH	GW	S	%	+/-	TF	F%	Min	GP	G	A	Pts	PIM	PP	SH	GW	Min
1996-97	Calgary Flames	AAHA	24	24	35	59	....	....	....	....	....	....	....	....	....	....	....	....	....	....	....	....	....	....	....
1997-98	Calgary Buffaloes	AMHL	34	34	43	77	29	....	....	....	....	....	....	....	....	....	....	....	....	....	....	....	....	....	....
1998-99	Calgary Royals	AJHL	58	43	67	110	98	....	....	....	....	....	....	....	....	....	....	....	....	....	....	....	....	....	....
99-2000	Boston College	H-East	42	16	16	32	48	....	....	....	....	....	....	....	....	....	....	....	....	....	....	....	....	....	....
2000-01	Boston College	H-East	41	25	25	50	54	....	....	....	....	....	....	....	....	....	....	....	....	....	....	....	....	....	....
2001-02	**Phoenix**	**NHL**	**57**	**11**	**11**	**22**	**48**	**0**	**0**	**5**	**81**	**13.6**	**6**	**703**	**46.4**	**13:05**	**2**	**0**	**0**	**0**	**6**	**0**	**0**	**0**	**11:12**
2002-03	**Phoenix**	**NHL**	**2**	**0**	**0**	**0**	**0**	**0**	**0**	**0**	**8**	**0.0**	**0**	**16**	**31.3**	**14:06**	....	....	....	....	....	....	....	....	....
2003-04	**Phoenix**	**NHL**	**41**	**4**	**6**	**10**	**24**	**1**	**0**	**1**	**61**	**6.6**	**–9**	**283**	**43.8**	**13:31**	....	....	....	....	....	....	....	....	....
	Springfield	AHL	32	10	11	21	38	....	....	....	....	....	....	....	....	....	....	....	....	....	....	....	....	....	....
2004-05	Blues Espoo	Finland	15	7	9	16	40	....	....	....	....	....	....	....	....	....	....	....	....	....	....	....	....	....	....
	Krefeld Pinguine	Germany	7	3	2	5	16	....	....	....	....	....	....	....	....	....	....	....	....	....	....	....	....	....	....
2005-06	**Phoenix**	**NHL**	**9**	**2**	**1**	**3**	**2**	**1**	**0**	**0**	**15**	**13.3**	**2**	**75**	**53.3**	**11:30**	....	....	....	....	....	....	....	....	....
	San Antonio	AHL	3	0	1	1	0	....	....	....	....	....	....	....	....	....	....	....	....	....	....	....	....	....	....
	Edmonton	**NHL**	**6**	**0**	**0**	**0**	**2**	**0**	**0**	**0**	**7**	**0.0**	**–1**	**32**	**50.0**	**7:39**	....	....	....	....	....	....	....	....	....
	Lowell	AHL	19	10	11	21	40	....	....	....	....	....	....	....	....	....	....	....	....	....	....	....	....	....	....
	Wilkes-Barre	AHL	18	10	8	18	19	....	....	....	....	....	....	....	....	....	11	2	0	2	16	....	....	....	....
2006-07	Grand Rapids	AHL	17	6	6	12	8	....	....	....	....	....	....	....	....	....	....	....	....	....	....	....	....	....	....
	Langnau	Swiss	14	2	9	11	48	....	....	....	....	....	....	....	....	....	....	....	....	....	....	....	....	....	....
	EV Zug	Swiss	....	....	....	....	....	....	....	....	....	....	....	....	....	....	8	6	0	6	8	....	....	....	....
2007-08	Quad City Flames	AHL	65	30	33	63	84	....	....	....	....	....	....	....	....	....	....	....	....	....	....	....	....	....	....
	NHL Totals		**115**	**17**	**18**	**35**	**76**	**2**	**0**	**6**	**172**	**9.9**		**1109**	**46.1**	**12:51**	**2**	**0**	**0**	**0**	**6**	**0**	**0**	**0**	**11:12**

Hockey East All-Rookie Team (2000) • Hockey East Second All-Star Team (2001) • NCAA East Second All-American Team (2001) • NCAA Championship All-Tournament Team (2001)

• Missed majority of 2002-03 season recovering from head injury suffered in game vs. Pittsburgh, March 20, 2002. Signed as a free agent by **Espoo** (Finland), October 25, 2004. Signed as a free agent by **Krefeld** (Germany), February 16, 2005. Claimed on waivers by **Edmonton** from **Phoenix**, November 11, 2005. Claimed on waivers by **Phoenix** from **Edmonton**, December 19, 2005. Traded to **Carolina** by **Phoenix** for Pavel Brendl, December 28, 2005. Traded to **Pittsburgh** by **Carolina** with Niklas Nordgren and Carolina's 2nd round choice (later traded to San Jose - later traded to Philadelphia - Philadelphia selected Kevin Marshall) in 2007 Entry Draft for Mark Recchi, March 9, 2006. Signed as a free agent by **Detroit**, July 15, 2006.

KOLNIK, Juraj

(KOHL-nihk, YUHR-ay)

Right wing. Shoots right. 5'10", 190 lbs. Born, Nitra, Czech., November 13, 1980. NY Islanders' 7th choice, 101st overall, in 1999 Entry Draft.

Season	Club	League	GP	G	A	Pts	PIM	PP	SH	GW	S	%	+/-	TF	F%	Min	GP	G	A	Pts	PIM	PP	SH	GW	Min
1997-98	Nitra Jr.	Slovak-Jr.	26	28	16	44	50	....	....	....	....	....	....	....	....	....	....	....	....	....	....	....	....	....	....
	Nitra	Slovakia	28	1	3	4	6	....	....	....	....	....	....	....	....	....	....	....	....	....	....	....	....	....	....
1998-99	Quebec Remparts	QMJHL	12	6	5	11	6	....	....	....	....	....	....	....	....	....	....	....	....	....	....	....	....	....	....
	Rimouski Oceanic	QMJHL	50	36	37	73	34	....	....	....	....	....	....	....	....	....	11	9	6	15	6	....	....	....	....
99-2000	Rimouski Oceanic	QMJHL	47	53	53	106	53	....	....	....	....	....	....	....	....	....	14	10	17	27	16	....	....	....	....
2000-01	**NY Islanders**	**NHL**	**29**	**4**	**3**	**7**	**12**	**0**	**0**	**0**	**38**	**10.5**	**–8**	**1**	**100.0**	**10:28**	....	....	....	....	....	....	....	....	....
	Lowell	AHL	25	2	6	8	18	....	....	....	....	....	....	....	....	....	....	....	....	....	....	....	....	....	....
	Springfield	AHL	29	15	20	35	20	....	....	....	....	....	....	....	....	....	....	....	....	....	....	....	....	....	....
2001-02	**NY Islanders**	**NHL**	**7**	**2**	**0**	**2**	**0**	**1**	**0**	**0**	**10**	**20.0**	**–2**	**1**	**0.0**	**7:57**	....	....	....	....	....	....	....	....	....
	Bridgeport	AHL	67	18	30	48	40	....	....	....	....	....	....	....	....	....	20	7	14	21	17	....	....	....	....
2002-03	**Florida**	**NHL**	**10**	**0**	**1**	**1**	**0**	**0**	**0**	**0**	**14**	**0.0**	**1**	**1**	**0.0**	**10:33**	....	....	....	....	....	....	....	....	....
	San Antonio	AHL	65	25	15	40	36	....	....	....	....	....	....	....	....	....	3	0	1	1	4	....	....	....	....
2003-04	**Florida**	**NHL**	**53**	**14**	**11**	**25**	**14**	**2**	**0**	**1**	**100**	**14.0**	**–7**	**25**	**64.0**	**16:05**	....	....	....	....	....	....	....	....	....
	San Antonio	AHL	15	2	14	16	21	....	....	....	....	....	....	....	....	....	....	....	....	....	....	....	....	....	....
2004-05	San Antonio	AHL	74	13	16	29	24	....	....	....	....	....	....	....	....	....	....	....	....	....	....	....	....	....	....
2005-06	**Florida**	**NHL**	**77**	**15**	**20**	**35**	**40**	**4**	**1**	**3**	**145**	**10.3**	**1**	**28**	**28.6**	**14:19**	....	....	....	....	....	....	....	....	....
2006-07	**Florida**	**NHL**	**64**	**11**	**14**	**25**	**18**	**0**	**0**	**1**	**113**	**9.7**	**2**	**5**	**40.0**	**12:05**	....	....	....	....	....	....	....	....	....
2007-08	Geneve	Swiss	50	21	*45	66	30	....	....	....	....	....	....	....	....	....	11	2	8	10	8	....	....	....	....
	NHL Totals		**240**	**46**	**49**	**95**	**84**	**7**	**1**	**5**	**420**	**11.0**		**61**	**44.3**	**13:18**	....	....	....	....	....	....	....	....	....

Memorial Cup Tournament All-Star Team (2000)

Traded to **Florida** by **NY Islanders** with NY Islanders' 9th round choice (later traded to San Jose – San Jose selected Carter Lee) in 2003 Entry Draft for Sven Butenschon, October 11, 2002. Signed as a free agent by **Geneve** (Swiss), August 6, 2007.

KOLTSOV, Konstantin

(kohlt-SAHV, KAWN-stan-tihn)

Right wing. Shoots left. 6', 206 lbs. Born, Minsk, USSR, April 17, 1981. Pittsburgh's 1st choice, 18th overall, in 1999 Entry Draft.

Season	Club	League	GP	G	A	Pts	PIM	PP	SH	GW	S	%	+/-	TF	F%	Min	GP	G	A	Pts	PIM	PP	SH	GW	Min
1997-98	Cherepovets 2	Russia-3	44	11	12	23	16	....	....	....	....	....	....	....	....	....	....	....	....	....	....	....	....	....	....
	Cherepovets	Russia	2	0	0	0	2	....	....	....	....	....	....	....	....	....	....	....	....	....	....	....	....	....	....
1998-99	Cherepovets 3	Russia-4	2	0	1	1	2	....	....	....	....	....	....	....	....	....	....	....	....	....	....	....	....	....	....
	Cherepovets 2	Russia-3	11	1	4	5	18	....	....	....	....	....	....	....	....	....	....	....	....	....	....	....	....	....	....
	Cherepovets	Russia	33	3	0	3	8	....	....	....	....	....	....	....	....	....	1	0	0	0	2	....	....	....	....
99-2000	Magnitogorsk	Russia	30	3	4	7	12	....	....	....	....	....	....	....	....	....	11	1	1	2	6	....	....	....	....
2000-01	Ak Bars Kazan	Russia	24	7	8	15	10	....	....	....	....	....	....	....	....	....	2	0	0	0	4	....	....	....	....
	Spartak 2	Russia-3	2	0	1	1	0	....	....	....	....	....	....	....	....	....	....	....	....	....	....	....	....	....	....
2001-02	Ak Bars Kazan	Russia	10	1	2	3	2	....	....	....	....	....	....	....	....	....	....	....	....	....	....	....	....	....	....
	Spartak Moscow	Russia	23	1	0	1	12	....	....	....	....	....	....	....	....	....	....	....	....	....	....	....	....	....	....
	Belarus	Olympics	2	0	0	0	0	....	....	....	....	....	....	....	....	....	....	....	....	....	....	....	....	....	....
2002-03	**Pittsburgh**	**NHL**	**2**	**0**	**0**	**0**	**0**	**0**	**0**	**0**	**4**	**0.0**	**–2**	**0**	**0.0**	**13:06**	....	....	....	....	....	....	....	....	....
	Wilkes-Barre	AHL	65	9	21	30	41	....	....	....	....	....	....	....	....	....	6	2	4	6	4	....	....	....	....
2003-04	**Pittsburgh**	**NHL**	**82**	**9**	**20**	**29**	**30**	**2**	**0**	**3**	**123**	**7.3**	**–30**	**12**	**33.3**	**15:21**	....	....	....	....	....	....	....	....	....
	Wilkes-Barre	AHL	....	....	....	....	....	....	....	....	....	....	....	....	....	....	24	6	11	17	18	....	....	....	....
2004-05	Dynamo Minsk	BelOpen	11	6	2	8	38	....	....	....	....	....	....	....	....	....	....	....	....	....	....	....	....	....	....
	Spartak Moscow	Russia	31	6	10	16	48	....	....	....	....	....	....	....	....	....	....	....	....	....	....	....	....	....	....
2005-06	**Pittsburgh**	**NHL**	**60**	**3**	**6**	**9**	**20**	**0**	**1**	**0**	**72**	**4.2**	**–10**	**14**	**21.4**	**13:15**	....	....	....	....	....	....	....	....	....
	Wilkes-Barre	AHL	18	7	5	12	13	....	....	....	....	....	....	....	....	....	....	....	....	....	....	....	....	....	....

			Regular Season														Playoffs								
Season	Club	League	GP	G	A	Pts	PIM	PP	SH	GW	S	%	+/-	TF	F%	Min	GP	G	A	Pts	PIM	PP	SH	GW	Min
2006-07	Ufa	Russia	54	15	11	26	45	....	....	....	....	....	....	....	....	....	8	1	1	2	2	....	....	....	....
2007-08	Ufa	Russia	36	12	9	21	27	....	....	....	....	....	....	....	....	....	15	3	1	4	4	....	....	....	....
	NHL Totals		**144**	**12**	**26**	**38**	**50**	**2**	**1**	**3**	**199**	**6.0**		**26**	**26.9**	**14:27**	....	....	....	....	....	....	....	....	....

Signed as a free agent by **Minsk** (BelOpen), September 15, 2004. Signed as a free agent by **Spartak Moscow** (Russia), November, 2004. Signed as a free agent by **Ufa** (Russia), August 17, 2006.

KOMISAREK, Mike

(koh-mih-SAIR-ehk, MIGHK) **MTL.**

Defense. Shoots right. 6'4", 240 lbs. Born, West Islip, NY, January 19, 1982. Montreal's 1st choice, 7th overall, in 2001 Entry Draft.

1998-99	N.E. Jr. Coyotes	EJHL	53	17	24	51	....	....	....	....	....	....	....	....	....	....	....	....	....	....	....	....	....	....	....
99-2000	USNTDP	U-18	6	0	0	0	12	....	....	....	....	....	....	....	....	....	....	....	....	....	....	....	....	....	....
	USNTDP	USHL	51	5	8	13	124	....	....	....	....	....	....	....	....	....	....	....	....	....	....	....	....	....	....
	USNTDP	NAHL	1	0	0	0	16	....	....	....	....	....	....	....	....	....	....	....	....	....	....	....	....	....	....
2000-01	U. of Michigan	CCHA	41	4	12	16	77	....	....	....	....	....	....	....	....	....	....	....	....	....	....	....	....	....	....
2001-02	U. of Michigan	CCHA	40	11	19	30	70	....	....	....	....	....	....	....	....	....	....	....	....	....	....	....	....	....	....
2002-03	**Montreal**	**NHL**	**21**	**0**	**1**	**1**	**28**	**0**	**0**	**0**	**26**	**0.0**	**–6**	**0**	**0.0**	**16:42**	....	....	....	....	....	....	....	....	....
	Hamilton	AHL	56	5	25	30	79	....	....	....	....	....	....	....	....	....	23	1	5	6	60	....	....	....	....
2003-04	**Montreal**	**NHL**	**46**	**0**	**4**	**4**	**34**	**0**	**0**	**0**	**40**	**0.0**	**4**	**0**	**0.0**	**12:00**	**7**	**0**	**0**	**0**	**8**	**0**	**0**	**0**	**14:09**
	Hamilton	AHL	18	2	7	9	47	....	....	....	....	....	....	....	....	....	....	....	....	....	....	....	....	....	....
2004-05	Hamilton	AHL	20	1	4	5	49	....	....	....	....	....	....	....	....	....	4	0	1	1	8	....	....	....	....
2005-06	**Montreal**	**NHL**	**71**	**2**	**4**	**6**	**116**	**0**	**0**	**0**	**66**	**3.0**	**–1**	**0**	**0.0**	**14:40**	**6**	**0**	**0**	**0**	**10**	**0**	**0**	**0**	**18:35**
2006-07	**Montreal**	**NHL**	**82**	**4**	**15**	**19**	**96**	**0**	**2**	**1**	**78**	**5.1**	**7**	**0**	**0.0**	**19:16**	....	....	....	....	....	....	....	....	....
2007-08	**Montreal**	**NHL**	**75**	**4**	**13**	**17**	**101**	**0**	**0**	**1**	**75**	**5.3**	**9**	**1**	**0.0**	**21:09**	**12**	**1**	**2**	**3**	**18**	**0**	**0**	**1**	**20:02**
	NHL Totals		**295**	**10**	**37**	**47**	**375**	**0**	**2**	**2**	**285**	**3.5**		**1**	**0.0**	**17:19**	**25**	**1**	**2**	**3**	**36**	**0**	**0**	**1**	**18:02**

CCHA First All-Star Team (2002) • NCAA West First All-American Team (2002) • AHL All-Rookie Team (2003)

KONDRATIEV, Maxim

(kohn-DRAT-yehv, max-EEM)

Defense. Shoots left. 6'1", 194 lbs. Born, Togliatti, USSR, January 20, 1983. Toronto's 7th choice, 168th overall, in 2001 Entry Draft.

99-2000	Lada Togliatti 2	Russia-3	16	0	2	2	6	....	....	....	....	....	....	....	....	....	....	....	....	....	....	....	....	....	....
	Lada Togliatti	Russia	20	1	1	2	....	....	....	....	....	....	....	....	....	....	....	....	....	....	....	....	....	....	....
2000-01	Lada Togliatti 2	Russia-3	STATISTICS NOT AVAILABLE																						
	CSK VVS Samara	Russia-2	18	2	1	3	24	....	....	....	....	....	....	....	....	....	....	....	....	....	....	....	....	....	....
2001-02	Lada Togliatti	Russia	43	3	3	6	32	....	....	....	....	....	....	....	....	....	4	0	0	0	0	....	....	....	....
2002-03	Lada Togliatti	Russia	47	2	3	5	56	....	....	....	....	....	....	....	....	....	10	0	0	0	6	....	....	....	....
2003-04	**Toronto**	**NHL**	**7**	**0**	**0**	**0**	**2**	**0**	**0**	**0**	**6**	**0.0**	**0**	**0**	**0.0**	**15:36**	....	....	....	....	....	....	....	....	....
	St. John's	AHL	18	3	5	8	10	....	....	....	....	....	....	....	....	....	....	....	....	....	....	....	....	....	....
	Lada Togliatti	Russia	29	2	3	5	85	....	....	....	....	....	....	....	....	....	6	0	0	0	16	....	....	....	....
2004-05	Hartford	AHL	13	1	4	5	8	....	....	....	....	....	....	....	....	....	....	....	....	....	....	....	....	....	....
	Lada Togliatti	Russia	32	2	4	6	65	....	....	....	....	....	....	....	....	....	5	0	2	2	0	....	....	....	....
2005-06	**NY Rangers**	**NHL**	**29**	**1**	**2**	**3**	**22**	**1**	**0**	**0**	**16**	**6.3**	**–2**	**0**	**0.0**	**16:17**	....	....	....	....	....	....	....	....	....
	Hartford	AHL	4	0	0	0	0	....	....	....	....	....	....	....	....	....	....	....	....	....	....	....	....	....	....
	Portland Pirates	AHL	37	4	13	17	19	....	....	....	....	....	....	....	....	....	13	5	9	14	12	....	....	....	....
2006-07	Lada Togliatti	Russia	51	3	16	19	144	....	....	....	....	....	....	....	....	....	3	1	0	1	2	....	....	....	....
2007-08	St. Petersburg	Russia	23	2	4	6	24	....	....	....	....	....	....	....	....	....	1	0	0	0	0	....	....	....	....
	Anaheim	**NHL**	**4**	**0**	**0**	**0**	**0**	**0**	**0**	**0**	**1**	**0.0**	**–2**	**0**	**0.0**	**7:31**	....	....	....	....	....	....	....	....	....
	NHL Totals		**40**	**1**	**2**	**3**	**24**	**1**	**0**	**0**	**23**	**4.3**		**0**	**0.0**	**15:17**	....	....	....	....	....	....	....	....	....

Assigned to **Togliatti** (Russia) by **Toronto**, December 16, 2003. Traded to **NY Rangers** by **Toronto** with Jarkko Immonen, Toronto's 1st round choice (later traded to Calgary - Calgary selected Kris Chucko) in 2004 Entry Draft and Toronto's 2nd round choice (Michael Sauer) in 2005 Entry Draft for Brian Leetch and Edmonton's 4th round choice (previously acquired, Toronto selected Roman Kukumberg) in 2004 Entry Draft, March 3, 2004. Signed as a free agent by **Togliatti** (Russia), November 11, 2004. Traded to **Anaheim** by **NY Rangers** for Petr Sykora and NY Rangers' 4th round choice (previously acquired, later traded to Washington - Washington selected Brett Bruneteau) in 2007 Entry Draft, January 8, 2006. Signed as a free agent by **Togliatti** (Russia), August 18, 2006.

KONOPKA, Zenon

(kuh-NOHP-kah, ZEH-nohn) **T.B.**

Center. Shoots left. 6'1", 213 lbs. Born, Niagara Falls, Ont., January 2, 1981.

1998-99	Ottawa 67's	OHL	56	7	8	15	62	....	....	....	....	....	....	....	....	....	7	0	0	0	2	....	....	....	....
99-2000	Ottawa 67's	OHL	59	8	11	19	107	....	....	....	....	....	....	....	....	....	11	1	2	3	8	....	....	....	....
2000-01	Ottawa 67's	OHL	66	20	45	65	120	....	....	....	....	....	....	....	....	....	20	7	13	20	47	....	....	....	....
2001-02	Ottawa 67's	OHL	61	18	68	86	100	....	....	....	....	....	....	....	....	....	13	8	6	14	49	....	....	....	....
2002-03	Wilkes-Barre	AHL	4	0	1	1	9	....	....	....	....	....	....	....	....	....	....	....	....	....	....	....	....	....	....
	Wheeling Nailers	ECHL	68	22	48	70	231	....	....	....	....	....	....	....	....	....	....	....	....	....	....	....	....	....	....
2003-04	Utah Grizzlies	AHL	43	7	4	11	198	....	....	....	....	....	....	....	....	....	....	....	....	....	....	....	....	....	....
	Idaho Steelheads	ECHL	23	6	22	28	82	....	....	....	....	....	....	....	....	....	17	9	8	17	30	....	....	....	....
2004-05	Cincinnati	AHL	75	17	29	46	212	....	....	....	....	....	....	....	....	....	12	3	3	6	26	....	....	....	....
2005-06	**Anaheim**	**NHL**	**23**	**4**	**3**	**7**	**48**	**2**	**0**	**0**	**18**	**22.2**	**–4**	**142**	**53.5**	**7:19**	....	....	....	....	....	....	....	....	....
	Portland Pirates	AHL	34	18	26	44	57	....	....	....	....	....	....	....	....	....	19	11	18	29	46	....	....	....	....
2006-07	Lada Togliatti	Russia	4	0	0	0	8	....	....	....	....	....	....	....	....	....	....	....	....	....	....	....	....	....	....
	Columbus	**NHL**	**6**	**0**	**0**	**0**	**20**	**0**	**0**	**0**	**2**	**0.0**	**–2**	**22**	**63.6**	**5:00**	....	....	....	....	....	....	....	....	....
	Portland Pirates	AHL	42	11	24	35	97	....	....	....	....	....	....	....	....	....	....	....	....	....	....	....	....	....	....
	Syracuse Crunch	AHL	20	9	11	20	70	....	....	....	....	....	....	....	....	....	....	....	....	....	....	....	....	....	....
2007-08	**Columbus**	**NHL**	**3**	**0**	**0**	**0**	**15**	**0**	**0**	**0**	**4**	**0.0**	**0**	**21**	**52.4**	**7:54**	....	....	....	....	....	....	....	....	....
	Syracuse Crunch	AHL	62	24	31	55	194	....	....	....	....	....	....	....	....	....	13	3	7	10	42	....	....	....	....
	NHL Totals		**32**	**4**	**3**	**7**	**83**	**2**	**0**	**0**	**24**	**16.7**		**185**	**54.6**	**6:56**	....	....	....	....	....	....	....	....	....

ECHL All-Rookie Team (2003)

Signed as a free agent by **Utah** (AHL), September 10, 2003. Signed as a free agent by **Anaheim**, September 1, 2004. Signed as a free agent by **Togliatti** (Russia), July 26, 2006. Traded to **Columbus** by **Anaheim** with Curtis Glencross and Anaheim's 7th round choice (Trent Vogelhuber) in 2007 Entry Draft for Mark Hartigan, Joe Motzko and Columbus' 4th round choice (Sebastian Stefaniszin) in 2007 Entry Draft, January 26, 2007. Signed as a free agent by **Tampa Bay**, July 10, 2008.

KONTIOLA, Petri

(KAWN-tee-oh-la, PEH-tree) **CHI.**

Center. Shoots right. 6', 197 lbs. Born, Seinajoki, Finland, October 4, 1984. Chicago's 12th choice, 196th overall, in 2004 Entry Draft.

2001-02	Tappara U18	Fin-U18	22	5	3	8	8	....	....	....	....	....	....	....	....	....	2	1	0	1	2	....	....	....	....
2002-03	Tappara Jr.	Fin-Jr.	36	7	10	17	12	....	....	....	....	....	....	....	....	....	8	3	3	6	0	....	....	....	....
2003-04	Suomi U20	Finland-2	6	1	1	2	4	....	....	....	....	....	....	....	....	....	....	....	....	....	....	....	....	....	....
	Tappara Jr.	Fin-Jr.	12	3	12	15	8	....	....	....	....	....	....	....	....	....	10	4	4	8	10	....	....	....	....
	Tappara Tampere	Finland	39	4	9	13	29	....	....	....	....	....	....	....	....	....	3	1	1	2	0	....	....	....	....
2004-05	Tappara Jr.	Fin-Jr.	1	1	0	1	0	....	....	....	....	....	....	....	....	....	....	....	....	....	....	....	....	....	....
	Tappara Tampere	Finland	54	8	17	25	24	....	....	....	....	....	....	....	....	....	8	2	2	4	2	....	....	....	....
2005-06	Tappara Tampere	Finland	56	9	*35	44	55	....	....	....	....	....	....	....	....	....	6	1	3	4	0	....	....	....	....
2006-07	Tappara Tampere	Finland	51	12	35	47	50	....	....	....	....	....	....	....	....	....	5	1	3	4	8	....	....	....	....
2007-08	**Chicago**	**NHL**	**12**	**0**	**5**	**5**	**6**	**0**	**0**	**0**	**13**	**0.0**	**5**	**45**	**68.9**	**14:33**	....	....	....	....	....	....	....	....	....
	Rockford IceHogs	AHL	66	18	50	68	32	....	....	....	....	....	....	....	....	....	12	5	5	10	4	....	....	....	....
	NHL Totals		**12**	**0**	**5**	**5**	**6**	**0**	**0**	**0**	**13**	**0.0**		**45**	**68.9**	**14:33**	....	....	....	....	....	....	....	....	....

KOPECKY, Tomas

(koh-PEHTS-kee, TAW-mahsh) **DET.**

Center. Shoots left. 6'3", 200 lbs. Born, Ilava, Czech., February 5, 1982. Detroit's 2nd choice, 38th overall, in 2000 Entry Draft.

1997-98	Dukla Trencin Jr.	Slovak-Jr.	41	19	22	41	....	....	....	....	....	....	....	....	....	....	....	....	....	....	....	....	....	....	....
1998-99	Dukla Trencin Jr.	Slovak-Jr.	44	13	16	29	18	....	....	....	....	....	....	....	....	....	....	....	....	....	....	....	....	....	....
99-2000	Dukla Trencin Jr.	Slovak-Jr.	14	8	9	17	36	....	....	....	....	....	....	....	....	....	....	....	....	....	....	....	....	....	....
	Dukla Trencin	Slovakia	52	3	4	7	24	....	....	....	....	....	....	....	....	....	5	0	0	0	0	....	....	....	....
2000-01	Lethbridge	WHL	49	22	28	50	52	....	....	....	....	....	....	....	....	....	5	1	1	2	6	....	....	....	....
	Cincinnati	AHL	1	0	0	0	0	....	....	....	....	....	....	....	....	....	....	....	....	....	....	....	....	....	....
2001-02	Lethbridge	WHL	60	34	42	76	94	....	....	....	....	....	....	....	....	....	4	2	1	3	15	....	....	....	....
	Cincinnati	AHL	2	1	1	2	6	....	....	....	....	....	....	....	....	....	2	0	0	0	0	....	....	....	....
2002-03	Grand Rapids	AHL	70	17	21	38	32	....	....	....	....	....	....	....	....	....	14	0	0	0	6	....	....	....	....
2003-04	Grand Rapids	AHL	48	6	6	12	28	....	....	....	....	....	....	....	....	....	1	0	0	0	2	....	....	....	....
2004-05	Grand Rapids	AHL	48	8	8	16	35	....	....	....	....	....	....	....	....	....	....	....	....	....	....	....	....	....	....
2005-06	**Detroit**	**NHL**	**1**	**0**	**0**	**0**	**2**	**0**	**0**	**0**	**1**	**0.0**	**1**	**0**	**0.0**	**9:41**	....	....	....	....	....	....	....	....	....
	Grand Rapids	AHL	77	32	37	69	108	....	....	....	....	....	....	....	....	....	16	3	4	7	25	....	....	....	....

			Regular Season														Playoffs								
Season	Club	League	GP	G	A	Pts	PIM	PP	SH	GW	S	%	+/-	TF	F%	Min	GP	G	A	Pts	PIM	PP	SH	GW	Min
2006-07	Detroit	NHL	26	1	0	1	22	0	0	0	27	3.7	–2	5	40.0	7:15	4	0	0	0	6	0	0	0	3:38
2007-08•	Detroit	NHL	77	5	7	12	43	0	0	1	87	5.7	2	109	40.4	9:37									
	NHL Totals		**104**	**6**	**7**	**13**	**67**	**0**	**0**	**1**	**115**	**5.2**		**114**	**40.4**	**9:02**	**4**	**0**	**0**	**0**	**6**	**0**	**0**	**0**	**3:38**

• Missed majority of 2006-07 season recovering from broken collarbone suffered in game vs. Chicago, December 14, 2006.

KOPITAR, Anze

(KOH-pih-tahr, AN-zee) **L.A.**

Center. Shoots left. 6'4", 221 lbs. Born, Jesenice, Yugoslavia, August 24, 1987. Los Angeles' 1st choice, 11th overall, in 2005 Entry Draft.

Season	Club	League	GP	G	A	Pts	PIM	PP	SH	GW	S	%	+/-	TF	F%	Min	GP	G	A	Pts	PIM	PP	SH	GW	Min
2002-03	Jesenice U18	Sloven-U18	14	38	38	76	10																		
	Jesenice Jr.	Sloven-Jr.	20	15	12	27	8																		
	Kranjska Gora	Slovenia	11	4	4	8	4																		
2003-04	Jesenice Jr.	Sloven-Jr.	25	32	28	60	16																		
	Kranjska Gora	Slovenia	21	14	11	25	10										4	1	1	2	0				
2004-05	Sodertalje SK U18	Swe-U18	1	1	2	3	0										1	0	0	0	2				
	Sodertalje SK Jr.	Swe-Jr.	30	28	21	49	26										2	1	1	2	0				
	Sodertalje SK	Sweden	5	0	0	0	0										10	0	0	0	0				
2005-06	Sodertalje SK	Sweden	47	8	12	20	28																		
	Sodertalje SK	Sweden-Q	10	7	4	11	6																		
2006-07	**Los Angeles**	**NHL**	**72**	**20**	**41**	**61**	**24**	**7**	**2**	**1**	**193**	**10.4**	**–12**	**1204**	**46.1**	**20:32**									
2007-08	**Los Angeles**	**NHL**	**82**	**32**	**45**	**77**	**22**	**12**	**2**	**3**	**201**	**15.9**	**–15**	**1150**	**49.2**	**20:41**									
	NHL Totals		**154**	**52**	**86**	**138**	**46**	**19**	**4**	**4**	**394**	**13.2**		**2354**	**47.6**	**20:37**									

Played in NHL All-Star Game (2008)

KORPIKOSKI, Lauri

(kohr-pih-KAWS-kee, LOW-ree) **NYR**

Left wing. Shoots left. 6'1", 195 lbs. Born, Turku, Finland, July 28, 1986. NY Rangers' 2nd choice, 19th overall, in 2004 Entry Draft.

Season	Club	League	GP	G	A	Pts	PIM	PP	SH	GW	S	%	+/-	TF	F%	Min	GP	G	A	Pts	PIM	PP	SH	GW	Min
2002-03	TPS Turku U18	Fin-U18	21	7	4	11	10																		
2003-04	TPS Turku U18	Fin-U18															4	5	3	8	16				
	TPS Turku Jr.	Fin-Jr.	36	12	8	20	20										4	0	2	2	4				
2004-05	TPS Turku Jr.	Fin-Jr.	3	3	0	3	0																		
	TPS Turku	Finland	41	0	6	6	12										6	1	0	1	0				
2005-06	TPS Turku Jr.	Fin-Jr.	1	1	0	1	2																		
	Suomi U20	Finland-2	3	1	3	4	0																		
	TPS Turku	Finland	51	3	4	7	16										2	0	1	1	0				
	Hartford	AHL	5	2	1	3	0										11	1	0	1	2				
2006-07	Hartford	AHL	78	11	27	38	23										7	0	0	0	0				
2007-08	Hartford	AHL	79	23	27	50	71										5	1	1	2	0				
	NY Rangers	**NHL**															**1**	**1**	**0**	**1**	**0**	**0**	**0**	**0**	**7:14**
	NHL Totals																**1**	**1**	**0**	**1**	**0**	**0**	**0**	**0**	**7:14**

KOSTITSYN, Andrei

(kaws-TIHT-sihn, AWN-dray) **MTL.**

Wing. Shoots left. 6', 201 lbs. Born, Novopolotsk, USSR, February 3, 1985. Montreal's 1st choice, 10th overall, in 2003 Entry Draft.

Season	Club	League	GP	G	A	Pts	PIM	PP	SH	GW	S	%	+/-	TF	F%	Min	GP	G	A	Pts	PIM	PP	SH	GW	Min
2000-01	Novopolotsk	Belarus	1	2	1	3	2																		
	Novopolotsk	EEHL	5	1	0	1	0																		
	Yunost Minsk	Belarus	3	1	4	5	8																		
	HC Vitebsk	Belarus	17	17	6	23	42																		
2001-02	Novopolotsk	Belarus	17	9	6	15	28																		
	Novopolotsk	EEHL	29	9	8	17	16																		
	Yunost Minsk	Belarus	6	2	0	2	8																		
2002-03	CSKA Moscow	Russia	6	0	0	0	2																		
	Voskresensk	Russia-2	2	1	1	2	0																		
	Yunost Minsk	Belarus	4	6	4	10	43																		
	CSKA Moscow 2	Russia-3	3	2	2	4	25																		
2003-04	CSKA Moscow 2	Russia-3	STATISTICS NOT AVAILABLE																						
	CSKA Moscow	Russia	12	0	1	1	2																		
	Yunost Minsk	Belarus	STATISTICS NOT AVAILABLE																						
2004-05	Hamilton	AHL	66	12	11	23	24										3	0	0	0	0				
2005-06	**Montreal**	**NHL**	**12**	**2**	**1**	**3**	**2**	**0**	**0**	**0**	**9**	**22.2**	**1**	**1**	**0.0**	**7:32**									
	Hamilton	AHL	64	18	29	47	76																		
2006-07	**Montreal**	**NHL**	**22**	**1**	**10**	**11**	**6**	**0**	**0**	**0**	**38**	**2.6**	**3**	**1**	**0.0**	**13:17**									
	Hamilton	AHL	50	21	31	52	50																		
2007-08	**Montreal**	**NHL**	**78**	**26**	**27**	**53**	**29**	**12**	**0**	**5**	**156**	**16.7**	**15**	**6**	**66.7**	**15:41**	**12**	**5**	**3**	**8**	**2**	**1**	**0**	**1**	**16:01**
	NHL Totals		**112**	**29**	**38**	**67**	**37**	**12**	**0**	**5**	**203**	**14.3**		**8**	**50.0**	**14:21**	**12**	**5**	**3**	**8**	**2**	**1**	**0**	**1**	**16:00**

KOSTITSYN, Sergei

(kaws-TIHT-sihn, SAIR-gay) **MTL.**

Left wing. Shoots left. 5'11", 196 lbs. Born, Novopolotsk, USSR, March 20, 1987. Montreal's 6th choice, 200th overall, in 2005 Entry Draft.

Season	Club	League	GP	G	A	Pts	PIM	PP	SH	GW	S	%	+/-	TF	F%	Min	GP	G	A	Pts	PIM	PP	SH	GW	Min
2003-04	HK Gomel	EEHL	6	0	1	1	0																		
	HK Gomel 2	EEHL-B	6	7	2	9	14																		
	Yunior Minsk	EEHL-B	STATISTICS NOT AVAILABLE																						
	Yunior Minsk	Belarus	3	0	0	0	0																		
	HK Gomel	Belarus	22	5	4	9	4										11	1	2	3	8				
2004-05	HK Gomel	BelOpen	40	4	10	14	24										4	2	0	2	12				
2005-06	London Knights	OHL	63	26	52	78	78										19	13	24	37	*44				
2006-07	London Knights	OHL	59	40	*91	131	76										16	9	12	21	39				
2007-08	**Montreal**	**NHL**	**52**	**9**	**18**	**27**	**51**	**3**	**1**	**0**	**49**	**18.4**	**9**	**23**	**34.8**	**14:21**	**12**	**3**	**5**	**8**	**14**	**0**	**0**	**0**	**15:09**
	Hamilton	AHL	22	6	16	22	18																		
	NHL Totals		**52**	**9**	**18**	**27**	**51**	**3**	**1**	**0**	**49**	**18.4**		**23**	**34.8**	**14:21**	**12**	**3**	**5**	**8**	**14**	**0**	**0**	**0**	**15:09**

KOSTOPOULOS, Tom

(kaw-STAWP-oh-lihs, TAWM) **MTL.**

Right wing. Shoots right. 6', 200 lbs. Born, Mississauga, Ont., January 24, 1979. Pittsburgh's 9th choice, 204th overall, in 1999 Entry Draft.

Season	Club	League	GP	G	A	Pts	PIM	PP	SH	GW	S	%	+/-	TF	F%	Min	GP	G	A	Pts	PIM	PP	SH	GW	Min
1995-96	Brampton	OPJHL	24	9	9	18	28																		
1996-97	London Knights	OHL	64	13	12	25	67																		
1997-98	London Knights	OHL	66	24	26	50	108										16	6	4	10	26				
1998-99	London Knights	OHL	66	27	60	87	114										25	19	16	35	32				
99-2000	Wilkes-Barre	AHL	76	26	32	58	121																		
2000-01	Wilkes-Barre	AHL	80	16	36	52	120										21	3	9	12	6				
2001-02	**Pittsburgh**	**NHL**	**11**	**1**	**2**	**3**	**9**	**0**	**0**	**0**	**8**	**12.5**	**–1**	**0**	**0.0**	**12:03**									
	Wilkes-Barre	AHL	70	27	26	53	112																		
2002-03	**Pittsburgh**	**NHL**	**8**	**0**	**1**	**1**	**0**	**0**	**0**	**0**	**6**	**0.0**	**–4**	**2**	**0.0**	**4:33**									
	Wilkes-Barre	AHL	71	21	42	63	131										6	1	2	3	7				
2003-04	**Pittsburgh**	**NHL**	**60**	**9**	**13**	**22**	**67**	**2**	**1**	**1**	**101**	**8.9**	**–14**	**10**	**30.0**	**14:26**									
	Wilkes-Barre	AHL	21	7	13	20	43										24	7	16	23	32				
2004-05	Manchester	AHL	64	25	46	71	99										6	0	7	7	10				
2005-06	**Los Angeles**	**NHL**	**76**	**8**	**14**	**22**	**100**	**0**	**0**	**1**	**74**	**10.8**	**–8**	**30**	**36.7**	**12:56**									
2006-07	**Los Angeles**	**NHL**	**76**	**7**	**15**	**22**	**73**	**0**	**0**	**0**	**90**	**7.8**	**–2**	**62**	**29.0**	**11:34**									
2007-08	**Montreal**	**NHL**	**67**	**7**	**6**	**13**	**113**	**0**	**3**	**1**	**98**	**7.1**	**–3**	**28**	**28.6**	**11:16**	**12**	**3**	**1**	**4**	**6**	**0**	**0**	**1**	**13:35**
	NHL Totals		**298**	**32**	**51**	**83**	**362**	**2**	**4**	**3**	**377**	**8.5**		**132**	**30.3**	**12:15**	**12**	**3**	**1**	**4**	**6**	**0**	**0**	**1**	**13:35**

Signed as a free agent by **Manchester** (AHL), July 12, 2004. Signed as a free agent by **Los Angeles**, August 1, 2005. Signed as a free agent by **Montreal**, July 4, 2007.

			Regular Season														Playoffs								
Season	Club	League	GP	G	A	Pts	PIM	PP	SH	GW	S	%	+/-	TF	F%	Min	GP	G	A	Pts	PIM	PP	SH	GW	Min

KOTALIK, Ales
(KOH-tahl-eek, ahl-EHSH) **BUF.**

Right wing. Shoots right. 6'2", 227 lbs. Born, Jindrichuv Hradec, Czech., December 23, 1978. Buffalo's 7th choice, 164th overall, in 1998 Entry Draft.

1993-94	C. Budejovice Jr.	CzRep-Jr.	28	12	12	24	....	....	....	....	....	....	....	....	....	....	....	....	....	....	....	....	....	....	....
1994-95	C. Budejovice Jr.	CzRep-Jr.	36	26	17	43	....	....	....	....	....	....	....	....	....	....	....	....	....	....	....	....	....	....	....
1995-96	C. Budejovice Jr.	CzRep-Jr.	28	6	7	13	....	....	....	....	....	....	....	....	....	....	....	....	....	....	....	....	....	....	....
1996-97	C. Budejovice Jr.	CzRep-Jr.	36	15	16	31	24	....	....	....	....	....	....	....	....	....	....	....	....	....	....	....	....	....	....
1997-98	C. Budejovice	CzRep	47	9	7	16	14	....	....	....	....	....	....	....	....	....	....	....	....	....	....	....	....	....	....
1998-99	C. Budejovice	CzRep	41	8	13	21	16	....	....	....	....	....	....	....	....	....	3	0	0	0	....	....	....	....	....
99-2000	C. Budejovice	CzRep	43	7	12	19	34	....	....	....	....	....	....	....	....	....	3	0	1	1	6	....	....	....	....
2000-01	C. Budejovice	CzRep	52	19	29	48	54	....	....	....	....	....	....	....	....	....	....	....	....	....	....	....	....	....	....
2001-02	**Buffalo**	**NHL**	**13**	**1**	**3**	**4**	**2**	**0**	**0**	**0**	**21**	**4.8**	**–1**	**11**	**27.3**	**12:35**	....	....	....	....	....	....	....	....	....
	Rochester	AHL	68	18	25	43	55	....	....	....	....	....	....	....	....	....	1	0	0	0	0	....	....	....	....
2002-03	**Buffalo**	**NHL**	**68**	**21**	**14**	**35**	**30**	**4**	**0**	**2**	**138**	**15.2**	**–2**	**37**	**51.4**	**15:15**	....	....	....	....	....	....	....	....	....
	Rochester	AHL	8	0	2	2	4	....	....	....	....	....	....	....	....	....	....	....	....	....	....	....	....	....	....
2003-04	**Buffalo**	**NHL**	**62**	**15**	**11**	**26**	**41**	**2**	**0**	**3**	**142**	**10.6**	**–1**	**14**	**50.0**	**15:11**	....	....	....	....	....	....	....	....	....
2004-05	Liberec	CzRep	25	8	8	16	46	....	....	....	....	....	....	....	....	....	12	2	5	7	12	....	....	....	....
2005-06	**Buffalo**	**NHL**	**82**	**25**	**37**	**62**	**62**	**10**	**0**	**5**	**261**	**9.6**	**–3**	**29**	**41.4**	**15:34**	**18**	**4**	**7**	**11**	**8**	**0**	**0**	**3**	**15:15**
	Czech Republic	Olympics	4	0	0	0	0	....	....	....	....	....	....	....	....	....	....	....	....	....	....	....	....	....	....
2006-07	**Buffalo**	**NHL**	**66**	**16**	**22**	**38**	**46**	**3**	**0**	**4**	**162**	**9.9**	**–5**	**35**	**48.6**	**14:31**	**16**	**2**	**2**	**4**	**8**	**0**	**0**	**0**	**12:29**
2007-08	**Buffalo**	**NHL**	**79**	**23**	**20**	**43**	**58**	**12**	**0**	**1**	**207**	**11.1**	**–5**	**220**	**44.6**	**15:21**	....	....	....	....	....	....	....	....	....
	NHL Totals		**370**	**101**	**107**	**208**	**239**	**31**	**0**	**15**	**931**	**10.8**		**346**	**45.1**	**15:06**	**34**	**6**	**9**	**15**	**16**	**0**	**0**	**3**	**13:57**

Signed as a free agent by **Liberec** (CzRep), September 6, 2004.

KOVALCHUK, Ilya
(koh-vuhl-CHUHK, IHL-yah) **ATL.**

Left wing. Shoots right. 6'1", 220 lbs. Born, Tver, USSR, April 15, 1983. Atlanta's 1st choice, 1st overall, in 2001 Entry Draft.

99-2000	Spartak Moscow	Russia-2	49	12	5	17	75	....	....	....	....	....	....	....	....	....	....	....	....	....	....	....	....	....	....
	Spartak 2	Russia-3	2	2	1	3	14	....	....	....	....	....	....	....	....	....	....	....	....	....	....	....	....	....	....
2000-01	Spartak Moscow	Russia	40	28	18	46	78	....	....	....	....	....	....	....	....	....	12	14	4	18	38	....	....	....	....
2001-02	**Atlanta**	**NHL**	**65**	**29**	**22**	**51**	**28**	**7**	**0**	**4**	**184**	**15.8**	**–19**	**6**	**16.7**	**18:32**	....	....	....	....	....	....	....	....	....
	Russia	Olympics	6	1	2	3	14	....	....	....	....	....	....	....	....	....	....	....	....	....	....	....	....	....	....
2002-03	**Atlanta**	**NHL**	**81**	**38**	**29**	**67**	**57**	**9**	**0**	**3**	**257**	**14.8**	**–24**	**15**	**40.0**	**19:27**	....	....	....	....	....	....	....	....	....
2003-04	**Atlanta**	**NHL**	**81**	***41**	**46**	**87**	**63**	**16**	**1**	**6**	**341**	**12.0**	**–10**	**28**	**32.1**	**23:41**	....	....	....	....	....	....	....	....	....
2004-05	Ak Bars Kazan	Russia	53	19	23	42	72	....	....	....	....	....	....	....	....	....	4	0	1	1	0	....	....	....	....
2005-06	**Atlanta**	**NHL**	**78**	**52**	**46**	**98**	**68**	**27**	**0**	**7**	**323**	**16.1**	**–6**	**47**	**40.4**	**22:23**	....	....	....	....	....	....	....	....	....
	Russia	Olympics	8	4	1	5	31	....	....	....	....	....	....	....	....	....	....	....	....	....	....	....	....	....	....
2006-07	**Atlanta**	**NHL**	**82**	**42**	**34**	**76**	**66**	**18**	**0**	**7**	**336**	**12.5**	**–2**	**66**	**39.4**	**21:32**	**4**	**1**	**1**	**2**	**19**	**0**	**0**	**0**	**18:42**
2007-08	**Atlanta**	**NHL**	**79**	**52**	**35**	**87**	**52**	**16**	**2**	**4**	**283**	**18.4**	**–12**	**32**	**43.8**	**21:30**	....	....	....	....	....	....	....	....	....
	NHL Totals		**466**	**254**	**212**	**466**	**334**	**93**	**3**	**31**	**1724**	**14.7**		**194**	**38.7**	**21:16**	**4**	**1**	**1**	**2**	**19**	**0**	**0**	**0**	**18:42**

NHL All-Rookie Team (2002) • NHL Second All-Star Team (2004) • Maurice "Rocket" Richard Trophy (2004) (tied with Jarome Iginla and Rick Nash)
Played in NHL All-Star Game (2004, 2008)
Signed as a free agent by **Kazan** (Russia) August 22, 2004.

KOVALEV, Alex
(koh-VAH-lehv, AL-ehx) **MTL.**

Right wing. Shoots left. 6'1", 224 lbs. Born, Togliatti, USSR, February 24, 1973. NY Rangers' 1st choice, 15th overall, in 1991 Entry Draft.

1989-90	Dynamo Moscow	USSR	1	0	0	0	0	....	....	....	....	....	....	....	....	....	....	....	....	....	....	....	....	....	....
1990-91	Dyn'o Moscow 2	USSR-3	21	16	....	....	....	....	....	....	....	....	....	....	....	....	....	....	....	....	....	....	....	....	....
	Dynamo Moscow	USSR	18	1	2	3	4	....	....	....	....	....	....	....	....	....	....	....	....	....	....	....	....	....	....
	Dynamo Moscow	Super-S	1	0	0	0	0	....	....	....	....	....	....	....	....	....	....	....	....	....	....	....	....	....	....
1991-92	Dynamo Moscow	CIS	33	16	9	25	20	....	....	....	....	....	....	....	....	....	....	....	....	....	....	....	....	....	....
	Dyn'o Moscow 2	CIS-3	4	5	0	5	12	....	....	....	....	....	....	....	....	....	....	....	....	....	....	....	....	....	....
	Russia	Olympics	8	1	2	3	14	....	....	....	....	....	....	....	....	....	....	....	....	....	....	....	....	....	....
1992-93	**NY Rangers**	**NHL**	**65**	**20**	**18**	**38**	**79**	**3**	**0**	**3**	**134**	**14.9**	**–10**	....	....	....	....	....	....	....	....	....	....	....	....
	Binghamton	AHL	13	13	11	24	35	....	....	....	....	....	....	....	....	....	9	3	5	8	14	....	....	....	....
1993-94♦	**NY Rangers**	**NHL**	**76**	**23**	**33**	**56**	**154**	**7**	**0**	**3**	**184**	**12.5**	**18**	....	....	....	**23**	**9**	**12**	**21**	**18**	**5**	**0**	**2**	....
1994-95	Lada Togliatti	CIS	12	8	8	16	49	....	....	....	....	....	....	....	....	....	....	....	....	....	....	....	....	....	....
	NY Rangers	**NHL**	**48**	**13**	**15**	**28**	**30**	**1**	**1**	**1**	**103**	**12.6**	**–6**	....	....	....	**10**	**4**	**7**	**11**	**10**	**0**	**0**	**0**	....
1995-96	**NY Rangers**	**NHL**	**81**	**24**	**34**	**58**	**98**	**8**	**1**	**7**	**206**	**11.7**	**5**	....	....	....	**11**	**3**	**4**	**7**	**14**	**0**	**0**	**1**	....
1996-97	**NY Rangers**	**NHL**	**45**	**13**	**22**	**35**	**42**	**1**	**0**	**0**	**110**	**11.8**	**11**	....	....	....	....	....	....	....	....	....	....	....	....
1997-98	**NY Rangers**	**NHL**	**73**	**23**	**30**	**53**	**44**	**8**	**0**	**3**	**173**	**13.3**	**–22**	....	....	....	....	....	....	....	....	....	....	....	....
1998-99	**NY Rangers**	**NHL**	**14**	**3**	**4**	**7**	**12**	**1**	**0**	**1**	**35**	**8.6**	**–6**	**18**	**44.4**	**19:53**	....	....	....	....	....	....	....	....	....
	Pittsburgh	**NHL**	**63**	**20**	**26**	**46**	**37**	**5**	**1**	**4**	**156**	**12.8**	**8**	**226**	**43.4**	**20:30**	**10**	**5**	**7**	**12**	**14**	**0**	**0**	**1**	**20:24**
99-2000	**Pittsburgh**	**NHL**	**82**	**26**	**40**	**66**	**94**	**9**	**2**	**4**	**254**	**10.2**	**–3**	**306**	**47.4**	**22:53**	**11**	**1**	**5**	**6**	**10**	**0**	**0**	**0**	**26:35**
2000-01	**Pittsburgh**	**NHL**	**79**	**44**	**51**	**95**	**96**	**12**	**2**	**9**	**307**	**14.3**	**12**	**255**	**40.0**	**23:35**	**18**	**5**	**5**	**10**	**16**	**1**	**0**	**0**	**20:57**
2001-02	**Pittsburgh**	**NHL**	**67**	**32**	**44**	**76**	**80**	**8**	**1**	**3**	**266**	**12.0**	**2**	**179**	**45.3**	**24:03**	....	....	....	....	....	....	....	....	....
	Russia	Olympics	6	3	1	4	4	....	....	....	....	....	....	....	....	....	....	....	....	....	....	....	....	....	....
2002-03	**Pittsburgh**	**NHL**	**54**	**27**	**37**	**64**	**50**	**8**	**0**	**1**	**212**	**12.7**	**–11**	**19**	**31.6**	**24:03**	....	....	....	....	....	....	....	....	....
	NY Rangers	**NHL**	**24**	**10**	**3**	**13**	**20**	**3**	**0**	**2**	**59**	**16.9**	**2**	**19**	**42.1**	**20:09**	....	....	....	....	....	....	....	....	....
2003-04	**NY Rangers**	**NHL**	**66**	**13**	**29**	**42**	**54**	**3**	**0**	**0**	**178**	**7.3**	**–5**	**29**	**48.3**	**19:37**	....	....	....	....	....	....	....	....	....
	Montreal	**NHL**	**12**	**1**	**2**	**3**	**12**	**0**	**0**	**1**	**29**	**3.4**	**–4**	**2**	**50.0**	**15:36**	**11**	**6**	**4**	**10**	**8**	**1**	**0**	**1**	**20:11**
2004-05	Ak Bars Kazan	Russia	35	10	12	22	80	....	....	....	....	....	....	....	....	....	4	0	0	0	8	....	....	....	....
2005-06	**Montreal**	**NHL**	**69**	**23**	**42**	**65**	**76**	**9**	**0**	**5**	**206**	**11.2**	**–1**	**47**	**48.9**	**19:28**	**6**	**4**	**3**	**7**	**4**	**1**	**0**	**0**	**19:21**
	Russia	Olympics	8	4	2	6	4	....	....	....	....	....	....	....	....	....	....	....	....	....	....	....	....	....	....
2006-07	**Montreal**	**NHL**	**73**	**18**	**29**	**47**	**78**	**8**	**0**	**5**	**197**	**9.1**	**–19**	**162**	**46.3**	**18:15**	....	....	....	....	....	....	....	....	....
2007-08	**Montreal**	**NHL**	**82**	**35**	**49**	**84**	**70**	**17**	**0**	**5**	**230**	**15.2**	**18**	**58**	**55.2**	**19:33**	**12**	**5**	**6**	**11**	**8**	**2**	**1**	**1**	**21:41**
	NHL Totals		**1073**	**368**	**508**	**876**	**1126**	**111**	**8**	**57**	**3039**	**12.1**		**1320**	**44.9**	**21:07**	**112**	**42**	**53**	**95**	**102**	**10**	**1**	**6**	**21:39**

NHL Second All-Star Team (2008)
Played in NHL All-Star Game (2001, 2003)
Traded to **Pittsburgh** by **NY Rangers** with Harry York for Petr Nedved, Chris Tamer and Sean Pronger, November 25, 1998. Traded to **NY Rangers** by **Pittsburgh** with Mike Wilson, Janne Laukkanen and Dan LaCouture for Joel Bouchard, Richard Lintner, Rico Fata and Mikael Samuelsson, February 10, 2003. Traded to **Montreal** by **NY Rangers** for Jozef Balej and Montreal's 2nd round choice (Bruce Graham) in 2004 Entry Draft, March 2, 2004. Signed as a free agent by **Kazan** (Russia), November 3, 2004.

KOZLOV, Viktor
(KAWZ-lahf, VIHK-tohr) **WSH.**

Center. Shoots right. 6'4", 224 lbs. Born, Togliatti, USSR, February 14, 1975. San Jose's 1st choice, 6th overall, in 1993 Entry Draft.

1990-91	Lada Togliatti	USSR-2	2	2	0	2	0	....	....	....	....	....	....	....	....	....	....	....	....	....	....	....	....	....	....
1991-92	Lada Togliatti	CIS	3	0	0	0	0	....	....	....	....	....	....	....	....	....	....	....	....	....	....	....	....	....	....
1992-93	Dynamo Moscow	CIS	30	6	5	11	4	....	....	....	....	....	....	....	....	....	10	3	0	3	0	....	....	....	....
1993-94	Dynamo Moscow	CIS	42	16	9	25	14	....	....	....	....	....	....	....	....	....	....	....	....	....	....	....	....	....	....
1994-95	Dynamo Moscow	CIS	3	1	1	2	2	....	....	....	....	....	....	....	....	....	....	....	....	....	....	....	....	....	....
	San Jose	**NHL**	**16**	**2**	**0**	**2**	**2**	**0**	**0**	**0**	**23**	**8.7**	**–5**	....	....	....	....	....	....	....	....	....	....	....	....
	Kansas City	IHL	4	1	1	2	0	....	....	....	....	....	....	....	....	....	13	4	5	9	12	....	....	....	....
1995-96	**San Jose**	**NHL**	**62**	**6**	**13**	**19**	**6**	**1**	**0**	**0**	**107**	**5.6**	**–15**	....	....	....	....	....	....	....	....	....	....	....	....
	Kansas City	IHL	15	4	7	11	12	....	....	....	....	....	....	....	....	....	....	....	....	....	....	....	....	....	....
1996-97	**San Jose**	**NHL**	**78**	**16**	**25**	**41**	**40**	**4**	**0**	**4**	**184**	**8.7**	**–16**	....	....	....	....	....	....	....	....	....	....	....	....
1997-98	**San Jose**	**NHL**	**18**	**5**	**2**	**7**	**2**	**2**	**0**	**0**	**51**	**9.8**	**–2**	....	....	....	....	....	....	....	....	....	....	....	....
	Florida	**NHL**	**46**	**12**	**11**	**23**	**14**	**3**	**2**	**0**	**114**	**10.5**	**–1**	....	....	....	....	....	....	....	....	....	....	....	....
1998-99	**Florida**	**NHL**	**65**	**16**	**35**	**51**	**24**	**5**	**1**	**1**	**209**	**7.7**	**13**	**985**	**41.2**	**19:03**	....	....	....	....	....	....	....	....	....
99-2000	**Florida**	**NHL**	**80**	**17**	**53**	**70**	**16**	**6**	**0**	**2**	**223**	**7.6**	**24**	**1616**	**42.9**	**19:27**	**4**	**0**	**1**	**1**	**0**	**0**	**0**	**0**	**16:06**
2000-01	**Florida**	**NHL**	**51**	**14**	**23**	**37**	**10**	**6**	**0**	**2**	**139**	**10.1**	**–4**	**817**	**41.6**	**18:23**	....	....	....	....	....	....	....	....	....
2001-02	**Florida**	**NHL**	**50**	**9**	**18**	**27**	**20**	**6**	**0**	**1**	**143**	**6.3**	**–16**	**840**	**43.1**	**19:54**	....	....	....	....	....	....	....	....	....
2002-03	**Florida**	**NHL**	**74**	**22**	**34**	**56**	**18**	**7**	**1**	**1**	**232**	**9.5**	**–8**	**404**	**42.8**	**22:35**	....	....	....	....	....	....	....	....	....
2003-04	**Florida**	**NHL**	**48**	**11**	**16**	**27**	**16**	**3**	**1**	**1**	**117**	**9.4**	**–4**	**200**	**49.0**	**19:30**	....	....	....	....	....	....	....	....	....
	New Jersey	**NHL**	**11**	**2**	**4**	**6**	**2**	**0**	**0**	**0**	**26**	**7.7**	**0**	**112**	**56.3**	**13:26**	**2**	**0**	**0**	**0**	**0**	**0**	**0**	**0**	**8:55**
2004-05	Lada Togliatti	Russia	52	15	22	37	22	....	....	....	....	....	....	....	....	....	10	3	3	6	6	....	....	....	....
2005-06	**New Jersey**	**NHL**	**69**	**12**	**13**	**25**	**16**	**2**	**0**	**1**	**122**	**9.8**	**0**	**185**	**47.0**	**13:32**	**3**	**0**	**0**	**0**	**0**	**0**	**0**	**0**	**14:05**
	Russia	Olympics	8	2	3	5	2	....	....	....	....	....	....	....	....	....	....	....	....	....	....	....	....	....	....

			Regular Season														Playoffs								
Season	Club	League	GP	G	A	Pts	PIM	PP	SH	GW	S	%	+/-	TF	F%	Min	GP	G	A	Pts	PIM	PP	SH	GW	Min
2006-07	**NY Islanders**	**NHL**	**81**	**25**	**26**	**51**	**28**	**5**	**0**	**4**	**165**	**15.2**	**12**	**462**	**39.0**	**16:25**	**5**	**0**	**2**	**2**	**2**	**0**	**0**	**0**	**16:34**
2007-08	**Washington**	**NHL**	**81**	**16**	**38**	**54**	**18**	**2**	**0**	**2**	**219**	**7.3**	**28**	**442**	**45.9**	**17:35**	**7**	**0**	**3**	**3**	**2**	**0**	**0**	**0**	**17:58**
	NHL Totals		**830**	**185**	**311**	**496**	**232**	**52**	**5**	**19**	**2074**	**8.9**		**6063**	**43.0**	**18:19**	**21**	**0**	**6**	**6**	**4**	**0**	**0**	**0**	**15:51**

Played in NHL All-Star Game (2000)

Traded to **Florida** by **San Jose** with Florida's 5th round choice (previously acquired, Florida selected Jaroslav Spacek) in 1998 Entry Draft for Dave Lowry and Florida's 1st round choice (later traded to Tampa Bay – Tampa Bay selected Vincent Lecavalier) in 1998 Entry Draft, November 13, 1997. Traded to **New Jersey** by **Florida** for Christian Berglund and Victor Uchevatov, March 1, 2004. Signed as a free agent by **Togliatti** (Russia), July 11, 2004. Signed as a free agent by **NY Islanders**, September 13, 2006. Signed as a free agent by **Washington**, July 1, 2007.

KOZLOV, Vyacheslav

(KAWZ-lahf, V'YTACH-ih-slav) **ATL.**

Left wing. Shoots left. 5'10", 190 lbs. Born, Voskresensk, USSR, May 3, 1972. Detroit's 2nd choice, 45th overall, in 1990 Entry Draft.

			Regular Season														Playoffs								
Season	Club	League	GP	G	A	Pts	PIM	PP	SH	GW	S	%	+/-	TF	F%	Min	GP	G	A	Pts	PIM	PP	SH	GW	Min
1987-88	Voskresensk	USSR	2	0	0	0	0	....	....	....	....	....	....	....	....	....	....	....	....	....	....	....	....	....	....
1988-89	Voskresensk	USSR	14	0	1	1	2	....	....	....	....	....	....	....	....	....	....	....	....	....	....	....	....	....	....
1989-90	Voskresensk	USSR	45	14	12	26	38	....	....	....	....	....	....	....	....	....	....	....	....	....	....	....	....	....	....
1990-91	Voskresensk	USSR	45	11	13	24	46	....	....	....	....	....	....	....	....	....	....	....	....	....	....	....	....	....	....
1991-92	CSKA Moscow	CIS	11	6	5	11	12	....	....	....	....	....	....	....	....	....	....	....	....	....	....	....	....	....	....
	Detroit	**NHL**	**7**	**0**	**2**	**2**	**2**	**0**	**0**	**0**	**9**	**0.0**	**–2**	....	....	....	....	....	....	....	....	....	....	....	....
1992-93	**Detroit**	**NHL**	**17**	**4**	**1**	**5**	**14**	**0**	**0**	**0**	**26**	**15.4**	**–1**	....	....	....	**4**	**0**	**2**	**2**	**2**	**0**	**0**	**0**	....
	Adirondack	AHL	45	23	36	59	54	....	....	....	....	....	....	....	....	....	4	1	1	2	4	....	....	....	....
1993-94	**Detroit**	**NHL**	**77**	**34**	**39**	**73**	**50**	**8**	**2**	**6**	**202**	**16.8**	**27**	....	....	....	**7**	**2**	**5**	**7**	**12**	**0**	**0**	**0**	....
	Adirondack	AHL	3	0	1	1	15	....	....	....	....	....	....	....	....	....	....	....	....	....	....	....	....	....	....
1994-95	CSKA Moscow	CIS	10	3	4	7	14	....	....	....	....	....	....	....	....	....	....	....	....	....	....	....	....	....	....
	Detroit	**NHL**	**46**	**13**	**20**	**33**	**45**	**5**	**0**	**3**	**97**	**13.4**	**12**	....	....	....	**18**	**9**	**7**	**16**	**10**	**1**	**0**	**4**	....
1995-96	**Detroit**	**NHL**	**82**	**36**	**37**	**73**	**70**	**9**	**0**	**7**	**237**	**15.2**	**33**	....	....	....	**19**	**5**	**7**	**12**	**10**	**2**	**0**	**1**	....
1996-97♦	**Detroit**	**NHL**	**75**	**23**	**22**	**45**	**46**	**3**	**0**	**6**	**211**	**10.9**	**21**	....	....	....	**20**	**8**	**5**	**13**	**14**	**4**	**0**	**2**	....
1997-98♦	**Detroit**	**NHL**	**80**	**25**	**27**	**52**	**46**	**6**	**0**	**1**	**221**	**11.3**	**14**	....	....	....	**22**	**6**	**8**	**14**	**10**	**1**	**0**	**4**	....
1998-99	**Detroit**	**NHL**	**79**	**29**	**29**	**58**	**45**	**6**	**1**	**4**	**209**	**13.9**	**10**	**38**	**36.8**	**16:02**	**10**	**6**	**1**	**7**	**4**	**3**	**0**	**0**	**14:44**
99-2000	**Detroit**	**NHL**	**72**	**18**	**18**	**36**	**28**	**4**	**0**	**3**	**165**	**10.9**	**11**	**28**	**35.7**	**15:30**	**8**	**2**	**1**	**3**	**12**	**1**	**0**	**1**	**12:20**
2000-01	**Detroit**	**NHL**	**72**	**20**	**18**	**38**	**30**	**4**	**0**	**5**	**187**	**10.7**	**9**	**51**	**47.1**	**14:43**	**6**	**4**	**1**	**5**	**2**	**2**	**0**	**0**	**16:27**
2001-02	**Buffalo**	**NHL**	**38**	**9**	**13**	**22**	**16**	**3**	**0**	**1**	**68**	**13.2**	**0**	**24**	**41.7**	**16:31**	....	....	....	....	....	....	....	....	....
2002-03	**Atlanta**	**NHL**	**79**	**21**	**49**	**70**	**66**	**9**	**1**	**2**	**185**	**11.4**	**–10**	**67**	**34.3**	**20:01**	....	....	....	....	....	....	....	....	....
2003-04	**Atlanta**	**NHL**	**76**	**20**	**32**	**52**	**74**	**6**	**0**	**1**	**191**	**10.5**	**–12**	**164**	**32.3**	**20:20**	....	....	....	....	....	....	....	....	....
2004-05	Voskresensk	Russia	38	12	18	30	69	....	....	....	....	....	....	....	....	....	....	....	....	....	....	....	....	....	....
	Ak Bars Kazan	Russia	8	2	4	6	0	....	....	....	....	....	....	....	....	....	4	1	0	1	8	....	....	....	....
2005-06	**Atlanta**	**NHL**	**82**	**25**	**46**	**71**	**33**	**8**	**0**	**1**	**206**	**12.1**	**14**	**317**	**39.8**	**17:47**	....	....	....	....	....	....	....	....	....
2006-07	**Atlanta**	**NHL**	**81**	**28**	**52**	**80**	**36**	**8**	**0**	**8**	**190**	**14.7**	**9**	**326**	**46.9**	**20:29**	**4**	**0**	**0**	**0**	**6**	**0**	**0**	**0**	**17:33**
2007-08	**Atlanta**	**NHL**	**82**	**17**	**24**	**41**	**26**	**5**	**0**	**4**	**161**	**10.6**	**–10**	**68**	**45.6**	**15:56**	....	....	....	....	....	....	....	....	....
	NHL Totals		**1045**	**322**	**429**	**751**	**627**	**84**	**4**	**52**	**2565**	**12.6**		**1083**	**41.0**	**17:35**	**118**	**42**	**37**	**79**	**82**	**14**	**0**	**12**	**14:49**

Traded to **Buffalo** by **Detroit** with Detroit's 1st round choice (later traded to Columbus – later traded to Atlanta – Atlanta selected Jim Slater) in 2002 Entry Draft for Dominik Hasek, July 1, 2001. • Missed majority of 2001-02 season recovering from Achilles tendon injury suffered in game vs. Columbus, December 31, 2001. Traded to **Atlanta** by **Buffalo** with Buffalo's 2nd round choice (later traded to Columbus – Columbus selected Joakim Lindstrom) in 2003 Entry Draft for Atlanta's 2nd round choice (later traded to Edmonton – Edmonton selected Jeff Deslauriers) in 2003 Entry Draft and Vancouver's 3rd round choice (previously acquired, Buffalo selected John Adams) in 2003 Entry Draft, June 22, 2002. Signed as a free agent by **Voskresensk** (Russia), September 15, 2004. Signed as a free agent by **Kazan** (Russia), February 17, 2005.

KRAJICEK, Lukas

(KRIGH-ee-chehk, LOO-kahsh) **VAN.**

Defense. Shoots left. 6'2", 200 lbs. Born, Prostejov, Czech., March 11, 1983. Florida's 2nd choice, 24th overall, in 2001 Entry Draft.

			Regular Season														Playoffs								
Season	Club	League	GP	G	A	Pts	PIM	PP	SH	GW	S	%	+/-	TF	F%	Min	GP	G	A	Pts	PIM	PP	SH	GW	Min
1998-99	HC ZPS Zlin Jr.	CzRep-Jr.	48	8	18	26	40	....	....	....	....	....	....	....	....	....	....	....	....	....	....	....	....	....	....
99-2000	Det. Compuware	NAHL	53	5	22	27	61	....	....	....	....	....	....	....	....	....	5	0	1	1	18	....	....	....	....
2000-01	Peterborough	OHL	61	8	27	35	53	....	....	....	....	....	....	....	....	....	7	0	5	5	0	....	....	....	....
2001-02	**Florida**	**NHL**	**5**	**0**	**0**	**0**	**0**	**0**	**0**	**0**	**3**	**0.0**	**0**	**0**	**0.0**	**13:23**	....	....	....	....	....	....	....	....	....
	Peterborough	OHL	55	10	32	42	56	....	....	....	....	....	....	....	....	....	6	0	5	5	6	....	....	....	....
2002-03	Peterborough	OHL	52	11	42	53	42	....	....	....	....	....	....	....	....	....	7	0	3	3	0	....	....	....	....
	San Antonio	AHL	3	0	1	1	0	....	....	....	....	....	....	....	....	....	3	0	0	0	0	....	....	....	....
2003-04	**Florida**	**NHL**	**18**	**1**	**6**	**7**	**12**	**1**	**0**	**0**	**16**	**6.3**	**–2**	**0**	**0.0**	**13:32**	....	....	....	....	....	....	....	....	....
	San Antonio	AHL	54	5	12	17	24	....	....	....	....	....	....	....	....	....	....	....	....	....	....	....	....	....	....
2004-05	San Antonio	AHL	78	2	22	24	57	....	....	....	....	....	....	....	....	....	....	....	....	....	....	....	....	....	....
2005-06	**Florida**	**NHL**	**67**	**2**	**14**	**16**	**50**	**2**	**0**	**0**	**89**	**2.2**	**1**	**0**	**0.0**	**18:30**	....	....	....	....	....	....	....	....	....
2006-07	**Vancouver**	**NHL**	**78**	**3**	**13**	**16**	**64**	**1**	**0**	**2**	**105**	**2.9**	**–4**	**0**	**0.0**	**18:31**	**12**	**0**	**2**	**2**	**12**	**0**	**0**	**0**	**18:50**
2007-08	**Vancouver**	**NHL**	**39**	**2**	**9**	**11**	**36**	**1**	**0**	**0**	**28**	**7.1**	**–3**	**0**	**0.0**	**18:10**	....	....	....	....	....	....	....	....	....
	NHL Totals		**207**	**8**	**42**	**50**	**162**	**5**	**0**	**2**	**241**	**3.3**		**0**	**0.0**	**17:53**	**12**	**0**	**2**	**2**	**12**	**0**	**0**	**0**	**18:50**

OHL All-Rookie Team (2001) • OHL First All-Star Team (2003)

Traded to **Vancouver** by **Florida** with Roberto Luongo and Florida's 6th round choice (Sergei Shirokov) in 2006 Entry Draft for Todd Bertuzzi, Bryan Allen and Alex Auld, June 23, 2006.

KREJCI, David

(KRIGH-chee, DAY-vihd) **BOS.**

Center. Shoots right. 6', 177 lbs. Born, Sternberk, Czech., April 28, 1986. Boston's 1st choice, 63rd overall, in 2004 Entry Draft.

			Regular Season														Playoffs								
Season	Club	League	GP	G	A	Pts	PIM	PP	SH	GW	S	%	+/-	TF	F%	Min	GP	G	A	Pts	PIM	PP	SH	GW	Min
2000-01	HC Olomouc U17	CzR-U17	26	2	6	8	4	....	....	....	....	....	....	....	....	....	3	1	1	2	0	....	....	....	....
2001-02	HC Trinec U17	CzR-U17	48	32	27	59	30	....	....	....	....	....	....	....	....	....	6	2	4	6	2	....	....	....	....
2002-03	HC Trinec U17	CzR-U17	22	12	24	36	42	....	....	....	....	....	....	....	....	....	....	....	....	....	....	....	....	....	....
	HC Trinec Jr.	CzRep-Jr.	12	4	5	9	2	....	....	....	....	....	....	....	....	....	12	5	5	10	8	....	....	....	....
2003-04	HC Kladno Jr.	CzRep-Jr.	50	23	37	60	37	....	....	....	....	....	....	....	....	....	7	3	6	9	4	....	....	....	....
2004-05	Gatineau	QMJHL	62	22	41	63	31	....	....	....	....	....	....	....	....	....	10	2	7	9	10	....	....	....	....
2005-06	Gatineau	QMJHL	55	27	54	81	54	....	....	....	....	....	....	....	....	....	17	10	22	32	24	....	....	....	....
2006-07	**Boston**	**NHL**	**6**	**0**	**0**	**0**	**2**	**0**	**0**	**0**	**2**	**0.0**	**–3**	**14**	**28.6**	**4:24**	....	....	....	....	....	....	....	....	....
	Providence Bruins	AHL	69	31	43	74	47	....	....	....	....	....	....	....	....	....	13	3	13	16	22	....	....	....	....
2007-08	**Boston**	**NHL**	**56**	**6**	**21**	**27**	**20**	**1**	**1**	**0**	**73**	**8.2**	**–3**	**635**	**48.2**	**14:55**	**7**	**1**	**4**	**5**	**2**	**1**	**0**	**0**	**19:09**
	Providence Bruins	AHL	25	7	21	28	19	....	....	....	....	....	....	....	....	....	....	....	....	....	....	....	....	....	....
	NHL Totals		**62**	**6**	**21**	**27**	**22**	**1**	**1**	**0**	**75**	**8.0**		**649**	**47.8**	**13:54**	**7**	**1**	**4**	**5**	**2**	**1**	**0**	**0**	**19:09**

KREPS, Kamil

(KREHPS, KA-mihl) **FLA.**

Center. Shoots right. 6'2", 194 lbs. Born, Litomerice, Czech., November 18, 1984. Florida's 3rd choice, 38th overall, in 2003 Entry Draft.

			Regular Season														Playoffs								
Season	Club	League	GP	G	A	Pts	PIM	PP	SH	GW	S	%	+/-	TF	F%	Min	GP	G	A	Pts	PIM	PP	SH	GW	Min
99-2000	Litvinov Jr.	CzRep-Jr.	48	18	16	34	10	....	....	....	....	....	....	....	....	....	....	....	....	....	....	....	....	....	....
2000-01	Litvinov Jr.	CzRep-Jr.	47	16	23	39	6	....	....	....	....	....	....	....	....	....	6	2	6	8	10	....	....	....	....
2001-02	Brampton	OHL	68	19	24	43	14	....	....	....	....	....	....	....	....	....	....	....	....	....	....	....	....	....	....
2002-03	Brampton	OHL	53	19	42	61	12	....	....	....	....	....	....	....	....	....	11	3	5	8	4	....	....	....	....
2003-04	Brampton	OHL	57	19	27	46	19	....	....	....	....	....	....	....	....	....	12	7	8	15	2	....	....	....	....
2004-05	San Antonio	AHL	58	5	6	11	11	....	....	....	....	....	....	....	....	....	....	....	....	....	....	....	....	....	....
	Texas Wildcatters	ECHL	12	5	6	11	6	....	....	....	....	....	....	....	....	....	....	....	....	....	....	....	....	....	....
2005-06	Rochester	AHL	61	13	19	32	20	....	....	....	....	....	....	....	....	....	....	....	....	....	....	....	....	....	....
2006-07	**Florida**	**NHL**	**14**	**1**	**1**	**2**	**6**	**0**	**0**	**0**	**20**	**5.0**	**–1**	**113**	**48.7**	**11:13**	....	....	....	....	....	....	....	....	....
	Rochester	AHL	50	14	21	35	16	....	....	....	....	....	....	....	....	....	6	1	0	1	0	....	....	....	....
2007-08	**Florida**	**NHL**	**76**	**8**	**17**	**25**	**29**	**1**	**0**	**2**	**99**	**8.1**	**10**	**763**	**53.9**	**12:59**	....	....	....	....	....	....	....	....	....
	Rochester	AHL	6	1	5	6	6	....	....	....	....	....	....	....	....	....	....	....	....	....	....	....	....	....	....
	NHL Totals		**90**	**9**	**18**	**27**	**35**	**1**	**0**	**2**	**119**	**7.6**		**876**	**53.2**	**12:42**	....	....	....	....	....	....	....	....	....

KROG, Jason

(KROHG, JAY-suhn) **VAN.**

Center. Shoots right. 5'11", 185 lbs. Born, Fernie, B.C., October 9, 1975.

			Regular Season														Playoffs								
Season	Club	League	GP	G	A	Pts	PIM	PP	SH	GW	S	%	+/-	TF	F%	Min	GP	G	A	Pts	PIM	PP	SH	GW	Min
1992-93	Chilliwack Chiefs	BCJHL	52	30	27	57	52	....	....	....	....	....	....	....	....	....	....	....	....	....	....	....	....	....	....
1993-94	Chilliwack Chiefs	BCJHL	42	19	36	55	20	....	....	....	....	....	....	....	....	....	....	....	....	....	....	....	....	....	....
1994-95	Chilliwack Chiefs	BCJHL	60	47	81	128	36	....	....	....	....	....	....	....	....	....	....	....	....	....	....	....	....	....	....
1995-96	New Hampshire	H-East	34	4	16	20	20	....	....	....	....	....	....	....	....	....	....	....	....	....	....	....	....	....	....
1996-97	New Hampshire	H-East	39	23	*44	*67	28	....	....	....	....	....	....	....	....	....	....	....	....	....	....	....	....	....	....
1997-98	New Hampshire	H-East	38	*33	33	66	44	....	....	....	....	....	....	....	....	....	....	....	....	....	....	....	....	....	....
1998-99	New Hampshire	H-East	41	*34	*51	*85	38	....	....	....	....	....	....	....	....	....	....	....	....	....	....	....	....	....	....
99-2000	**NY Islanders**	**NHL**	**17**	**2**	**4**	**6**	**6**	**1**	**0**	**0**	**22**	**9.1**	**–1**	**81**	**53.1**	**10:03**	....	....	....	....	....	....	....	....	....
	Lowell	AHL	45	6	21	27	22	....	....	....	....	....	....	....	....	....	....	....	....	....	....	....	....	....	....
	Providence Bruins	AHL	11	9	8	17	4	....	....	....	....	....	....	....	....	....	6	2	2	4	0	....	....	....	....

			Regular Season														Playoffs								
Season	Club	League	GP	G	A	Pts	PIM	PP	SH	GW	S	%	+/-	TF	F%	Min	GP	G	A	Pts	PIM	PP	SH	GW	Min
2000-01	**NY Islanders**	**NHL**	**9**	**0**	**3**	**3**	**0**	**0**	**0**	**0**	**7**	**0.0**	**4**	**60**	**48.3**	**10:32**	....	....	....	....	....	....	....	....	....
	Lowell	AHL	26	11	16	27	6	....	....	....	....	....	....	....	....	....	....	....	....	....	....	....	....	....	....
	Springfield	AHL	24	7	23	30	4	....	....	....	....	....	....	....	....	....	....	....	....	....	....	....	....	....	....
2001-02	**NY Islanders**	**NHL**	**2**	**0**	**0**	**0**	**0**	**0**	**0**	**0**	**0**	**0.0**	**0**	**13**	**46.2**	**6:40**	....	....	....	....	....	....	....	....	....
	Bridgeport	AHL	64	26	36	62	13	....	....	....	....	....	....	....	....	....	20	10	13	23	8	....	....	....	....
2002-03	**Anaheim**	**NHL**	**67**	**10**	**15**	**25**	**12**	**0**	**1**	**1**	**92**	**10.9**	**1**	**634**	**60.4**	**13:47**	**21**	**3**	**1**	**4**	**4**	**0**	**0**	**0**	**12:10**
	Cincinnati	AHL	9	3	4	7	6	....	....	....	....	....	....	....	....	....	....	....	....	....	....	....	....	....	....
2003-04	**Anaheim**	**NHL**	**80**	**6**	**12**	**18**	**16**	**1**	**0**	**1**	**111**	**5.4**	**–4**	**769**	**58.5**	**11:58**	....	....	....	....	....	....	....	....	....
2004-05	EC Villacher SV	Austria	48	27	33	60	38	....	....	....	....	....	....	....	....	....	3	0	1	1	4	....	....	....	....
2005-06	Geneve	Swiss	29	15	14	29	32	....	....	....	....	....	....	....	....	....	....	....	....	....	....	....	....	....	....
	Frolunda	Sweden	7	5	1	6	6	....	....	....	....	....	....	....	....	....	17	5	3	8	10	....	....	....	....
2006-07	**Atlanta**	**NHL**	**14**	**1**	**3**	**4**	**6**	**0**	**0**	**0**	**14**	**7.1**	**3**	**165**	**55.2**	**13:58**	....	....	....	....	....	....	....	....	....
	Chicago Wolves	AHL	44	26	54	80	20	....	....	....	....	....	....	....	....	....	15	5	14	19	17	....	....	....	....
	NY Rangers	**NHL**	**9**	**2**	**0**	**2**	**4**	**0**	**0**	**1**	**8**	**25.0**	**2**	**66**	**56.1**	**9:58**	....	....	....	....	....	....	....	....	....
2007-08	Chicago Wolves	AHL	80	*39	*73	*112	30	....	....	....	....	....	....	....	....	....	24	*12	*26	*38	2	....	....	....	....
	NHL Totals		**198**	**21**	**37**	**58**	**44**	**2**	**1**	**3**	**254**	**8.3**		**1788**	**58.1**	**12:21**	**21**	**3**	**1**	**4**	**4**	**0**	**0**	**0**	**12:10**

Hockey East First All-Star Team (1997, 1998, 1999) • NCAA East Second All-American Team (1997) • Hockey East Player of the Year (1999) • NCAA East First All-American Team (1999) • NCAA Championship All-Tournament Team (1999) • Hobey Baker Memorial Award (Top U.S. Collegiate Player) (1999) • AHL First All-Star Team (2008) • Willie Marshall Award (Top Goal-scorer – AHL) (2008) • John B. Sollenberger Trophy (Leading Scorer – AHL) (2008) • Les Cunningham Award (MVP – AHL) (2008)

Signed as a free agent by **NY Islanders**, May 14, 1999. Loaned to **Providence** (AHL) by **NY Islanders**, March 1, 2000. Signed as a free agent by **Anaheim**, July 17, 2002. Signed as a free agent by **Villacher** (Austria), August 24, 2004. Signed as a free agent by **Geneve** (Swiss), May 19, 2005. Signed as a free agent by **Frolunda** (Sweden), January 31, 2006. Signed as a free agent by **Atlanta**, July 4, 2006. Claimed on waivers by **NY Rangers** from **Atlanta**, January 12, 2007. Claimed on waivers by **Atlanta** from **NY Rangers**, February 27, 2007. Signed as a free agent by **Vancouver**, July 14, 2008.

KRONWALL, Niklas

(KRAWN-wahl, NIHK-luhs) **DET.**

Defense. Shoots left. 6', 189 lbs. Born, Stockholm, Sweden, January 12, 1981. Detroit's 1st choice, 29th overall, in 2000 Entry Draft.

1996-97	Djurgarden Jr.	Swe-Jr.	1	0	0	0	0	....	....	....	....	....	....	....	....	....	....	....	....	....	....	....	....	....	....
1997-98	Djurgarden Jr.	Swe-Jr.	27	4	3	7	71	....	....	....	....	....	....	....	....	....	2	0	0	0	2	....	....	....	....
1998-99	Huddinge IK	Sweden-2	14	0	1	1	10	....	....	....	....	....	....	....	....	....	....	....	....	....	....	....	....	....	....
	Huddinge IK Jr.	Swe-Jr.	2	0	0	0	6	....	....	....	....	....	....	....	....	....	....	....	....	....	....	....	....	....	....
99-2000	Djurgarden	Sweden	37	1	4	5	16	....	....	....	....	....	....	....	....	....	8	0	0	0	8	....	....	....	....
2000-01	Djurgarden	Sweden	31	1	9	10	32	....	....	....	....	....	....	....	....	....	15	0	1	1	8	....	....	....	....
2001-02	Djurgarden	Sweden	48	5	7	12	34	....	....	....	....	....	....	....	....	....	5	0	0	0	0	....	....	....	....
2002-03	Djurgarden	Sweden	50	5	13	18	46	....	....	....	....	....	....	....	....	....	12	3	2	5	18	....	....	....	....
2003-04	**Detroit**	**NHL**	**20**	**1**	**4**	**5**	**16**	**0**	**0**	**1**	**18**	**5.6**	**5**	**0**	**0.0**	**13:51**	....	....	....	....	....	....	....	....	....
	Grand Rapids	AHL	25	2	11	13	20	....	....	....	....	....	....	....	....	....	....	....	....	....	....	....	....	....	....
2004-05	Grand Rapids	AHL	76	13	40	53	53	....	....	....	....	....	....	....	....	....	....	....	....	....	....	....	....	....	....
2005-06	**Detroit**	**NHL**	**27**	**1**	**8**	**9**	**28**	**1**	**0**	**0**	**28**	**3.6**	**11**	**0**	**0.0**	**20:31**	**6**	**0**	**3**	**3**	**2**	**0**	**0**	**0**	**22:43**
	Grand Rapids	AHL	1	0	0	0	0	....	....	....	....	....	....	....	....	....	....	....	....	....	....	....	....	....	....
	Sweden	Olympics	2	1	1	2	8	....	....	....	....	....	....	....	....	....	....	....	....	....	....	....	....	....	....
2006-07	**Detroit**	**NHL**	**68**	**1**	**21**	**22**	**54**	**1**	**0**	**0**	**104**	**1.0**	**0**	**0**	**0.0**	**20:39**	....	....	....	....	....	....	....	....	....
2007-08♦	**Detroit**	**NHL**	**65**	**7**	**28**	**35**	**44**	**0**	**0**	**0**	**108**	**6.5**	**25**	**0**	**0.0**	**21:06**	**22**	**0**	**15**	**15**	**18**	**0**	**0**	**0**	**23:20**
	NHL Totals		**180**	**10**	**61**	**71**	**142**	**2**	**0**	**1**	**258**	**3.9**		**0**	**0.0**	**20:03**	**28**	**0**	**18**	**18**	**20**	**0**	**0**	**0**	**23:12**

AHL First All-Star Team (2005) • Eddie Shore Award (Outstanding Defenseman – AHL) (2005)

• Missed majority of 2005-06 season recovering from knee surgery.

KRONWALL, Staffan

(KRAWN-wahl, STAH-fuhn) **TOR.**

Defense. Shoots left. 6'3", 209 lbs. Born, Jarfalla, Sweden, September 10, 1982. Toronto's 9th choice, 285th overall, in 2002 Entry Draft.

99-2000	Huddinge IK Jr.	Swe-Jr.	34	2	0	2	38	....	....	....	....	....	....	....	....	....	....	....	....	....	....	....	....	....	....
	Huddinge IK U18	Swe-U18	7	0	3	3	0	....	....	....	....	....	....	....	....	....	....	....	....	....	....	....	....	....	....
2000-01	Huddinge IK Jr.	Swe-Jr.	23	6	1	7	16	....	....	....	....	....	....	....	....	....	....	....	....	....	....	....	....	....	....
	Huddinge IK	Sweden-3	1	0	0	0	0	....	....	....	....	....	....	....	....	....	....	....	....	....	....	....	....	....	....
2001-02	Huddinge IK	Sweden-2	42	4	7	11	30	....	....	....	....	....	....	....	....	....	....	....	....	....	....	....	....	....	....
	Huddinge IK Jr.	Swe-Jr.	1	0	0	0	0	....	....	....	....	....	....	....	....	....	4	2	1	3	27	....	....	....	....
2002-03	Djurgarden	Sweden	48	4	6	10	65	....	....	....	....	....	....	....	....	....	12	1	1	2	8	....	....	....	....
2003-04	Djurgarden	Sweden	44	1	5	6	54	....	....	....	....	....	....	....	....	....	4	0	1	1	2	....	....	....	....
2004-05	Brynas IF Gavle	Sweden	3	0	1	1	4	....	....	....	....	....	....	....	....	....	....	....	....	....	....	....	....	....	....
	Djurgarden Jr.	Swe-Jr.	5	2	4	6	0	....	....	....	....	....	....	....	....	....	....	....	....	....	....	....	....	....	....
	Djurgarden	Sweden	35	1	4	5	43	....	....	....	....	....	....	....	....	....	12	2	0	2	10	....	....	....	....
2005-06	**Toronto**	**NHL**	**34**	**0**	**1**	**1**	**14**	**0**	**0**	**0**	**18**	**0.0**	**–3**	**0**	**0.0**	**12:57**	....	....	....	....	....	....	....	....	....
	Toronto Marlies	AHL	16	1	10	11	12	....	....	....	....	....	....	....	....	....	4	0	2	2	2	....	....	....	....
2006-07	Toronto Marlies	AHL	47	3	14	17	32	....	....	....	....	....	....	....	....	....	....	....	....	....	....	....	....	....	....
2007-08	**Toronto**	**NHL**	**18**	**0**	**0**	**0**	**7**	**0**	**0**	**0**	**9**	**0.0**	**–2**	**0**	**0.0**	**11:07**	....	....	....	....	....	....	....	....	....
	Toronto Marlies	AHL	26	3	7	10	14	....	....	....	....	....	....	....	....	....	19	1	1	2	11	....	....	....	....
	NHL Totals		**52**	**0**	**1**	**1**	**21**	**0**	**0**	**0**	**27**	**0.0**		**0**	**0.0**	**12:19**	....	....	....	....	....	....	....	....	....

KUBA, Filip

(KOO-bah, FIHL-ihp) **T.B.**

Defense. Shoots left. 6'5", 225 lbs. Born, Ostrava, Czech., December 29, 1976. Florida's 8th choice, 192nd overall, in 1995 Entry Draft.

1994-95	HC Vitkovice Jr.	CzRep-Jr.	35	10	15	25	....	....	....	....	....	....	....	....	....	....	....	....	....	....	....	....	....	....	....
	HC Vitkovice	CzRep	....	....	....	....	....	....	....	....	....	....	....	....	....	....	4	0	0	0	2	....	....	....	....
1995-96	HC Vitkovice	CzRep	19	0	1	1	....	....	....	....	....	....	....	....	....	....	....	....	....	....	....	....	....	....	....
1996-97	Carolina	AHL	51	0	12	12	38	....	....	....	....	....	....	....	....	....	....	....	....	....	....	....	....	....	....
1997-98	New Haven	AHL	77	4	13	17	58	....	....	....	....	....	....	....	....	....	3	1	1	2	0	....	....	....	....
1998-99	**Florida**	**NHL**	**5**	**0**	**1**	**1**	**0**	**0**	**0**	**0**	**5**	**0.0**	**2**	**0**	**0.0**	**22:29**	....	....	....	....	....	....	....	....	....
	Kentucky	AHL	45	2	8	10	33	....	....	....	....	....	....	....	....	....	10	0	1	1	4	....	....	....	....
99-2000	**Florida**	**NHL**	**13**	**1**	**5**	**6**	**2**	**1**	**0**	**1**	**16**	**6.3**	**–3**	**0**	**0.0**	**13:52**	....	....	....	....	....	....	....	....	....
	Houston Aeros	IHL	27	3	6	9	13	....	....	....	....	....	....	....	....	....	11	1	2	3	4	....	....	....	....
2000-01	**Minnesota**	**NHL**	**75**	**9**	**21**	**30**	**28**	**4**	**0**	**4**	**141**	**6.4**	**–6**	**1**	**0.0**	**24:16**	....	....	....	....	....	....	....	....	....
2001-02	**Minnesota**	**NHL**	**62**	**5**	**19**	**24**	**32**	**3**	**0**	**1**	**101**	**5.0**	**–6**	**0**	**0.0**	**25:30**	....	....	....	....	....	....	....	....	....
2002-03	**Minnesota**	**NHL**	**78**	**8**	**21**	**29**	**29**	**4**	**2**	**1**	**129**	**6.2**	**0**	**1**	**0.0**	**23:56**	**18**	**3**	**5**	**8**	**24**	**3**	**0**	**0**	**26:46**
2003-04	**Minnesota**	**NHL**	**77**	**5**	**19**	**24**	**28**	**2**	**1**	**2**	**114**	**4.4**	**–7**	**2**	**0.0**	**24:06**	....	....	....	....	....	....	....	....	....
2004-05			DID NOT PLAY																						
2005-06	**Minnesota**	**NHL**	**65**	**6**	**19**	**25**	**44**	**1**	**1**	**1**	**69**	**8.7**	**0**	**2**	**0.0**	**21:46**	....	....	....	....	....	....	....	....	....
	Czech Republic	Olympics	8	1	0	1	0	....	....	....	....	....	....	....	....	....	....	....	....	....	....	....	....	....	....
2006-07	**Tampa Bay**	**NHL**	**81**	**15**	**22**	**37**	**36**	**5**	**1**	**2**	**106**	**14.2**	**–9**	**0**	**0.0**	**20:12**	**6**	**1**	**4**	**5**	**4**	**0**	**1**	**0**	**20:47**
2007-08	**Tampa Bay**	**NHL**	**75**	**6**	**25**	**31**	**40**	**2**	**0**	**0**	**113**	**5.3**	**–8**	**2**	**0.0**	**24:57**	....	....	....	....	....	....	....	....	....
	NHL Totals		**531**	**55**	**152**	**207**	**239**	**22**	**5**	**12**	**794**	**6.9**		**8**	**0.0**	**23:14**	**24**	**4**	**9**	**13**	**28**	**3**	**1**	**0**	**25:16**

Played in NHL All-Star Game (2004)

Traded to **Calgary** by **Florida** for Rocky Thompson, March 16, 2000. Claimed by **Minnesota** from **Calgary** in Expansion Draft, June 23, 2000. Signed as a free agent by **Tampa Bay**, July 1, 2006.

KUBINA, Pavel

(koo-BEE-nuh, PAH-vehl) **TOR.**

Defense. Shoots right. 6'4", 244 lbs. Born, Celadna, Czech., April 15, 1977. Tampa Bay's 6th choice, 179th overall, in 1996 Entry Draft.

1993-94	HC Vitkovice Jr.	CzRep-Jr.	35	4	3	7	....	....	....	....	....	....	....	....	....	....	....	....	....	....	....	....	....	....	....
	HC Vitkovice	CzRep	1	0	0	0	....	....	....	....	....	....	....	....	....	....	....	....	....	....	....	....	....	....	....
1994-95	HC Vitkovice Jr.	CzRep-Jr.	20	6	10	16	....	....	....	....	....	....	....	....	....	....	....	....	....	....	....	....	....	....	....
	HC Vitkovice	CzRep	8	2	0	2	10	....	....	....	....	....	....	....	....	....	4	0	0	0	0	....	....	....	....
1995-96	HC Vitkovice Jr.	CzRep-Jr.	16	5	10	15	....	....	....	....	....	....	....	....	....	....	....	....	....	....	....	....	....	....	....
	HC Vitkovice	CzRep	33	3	4	7	32	....	....	....	....	....	....	....	....	....	4	0	0	0	0	....	....	....	....
1996-97	HC Vitkovice	CzRep	1	0	0	0	0	....	....	....	....	....	....	....	....	....	....	....	....	....	....	....	....	....	....
	Moose Jaw	WHL	61	12	32	44	116	....	....	....	....	....	....	....	....	....	11	2	5	7	27	....	....	....	....
1997-98	**Tampa Bay**	**NHL**	**10**	**1**	**2**	**3**	**22**	**0**	**0**	**0**	**8**	**12.5**	**–1**				....	....	....	....	....	....	....	....	....
	Adirondack	AHL	55	4	8	12	86	....	....	....	....	....	....	....	....	....	1	1	0	1	14	....	....	....	....
1998-99	**Tampa Bay**	**NHL**	**68**	**9**	**12**	**21**	**80**	**3**	**1**	**1**	**119**	**7.6**	**–33**	**2**	**0.0**	**22:47**	....	....	....	....	....	....	....	....	....
	Cleveland	IHL	6	2	2	4	16	....	....	....	....	....	....	....	....	....	....	....	....	....	....	....	....	....	....
99-2000	**Tampa Bay**	**NHL**	**69**	**8**	**18**	**26**	**93**	**6**	**0**	**3**	**128**	**6.3**	**–19**	**0**	**0.0**	**22:32**	....	....	....	....	....	....	....	....	....
2000-01	**Tampa Bay**	**NHL**	**70**	**11**	**19**	**30**	**103**	**6**	**1**	**1**	**128**	**8.6**	**–14**	**2**	**0.0**	**24:06**	....	....	....	....	....	....	....	....	....

			Regular Season													Playoffs								
Season	Club	League	GP	G	A	Pts	PIM	PP	SH	GW	S	%	+/-	TF	F%	Min	GP	G	A	Pts	PIM	PP	SH	GW	Min
2001-02	Tampa Bay	NHL	82	11	23	34	106	5	2	3	189	5.8	–22	1	100.0	23:39	....	....	....	....	....	....	....	....	....
	Czech Republic	Olympics	4	0	1	1	0	....	....	....	....	....	....	....	....	....	....	....	....	....	....	....	....	....	....
2002-03	Tampa Bay	NHL	75	3	19	22	78	0	0	0	139	2.2	–7	1	0.0	21:24	11	0	0	0	12	0	0	0	24:52
2003-04♦	Tampa Bay	NHL	81	17	18	35	85	8	1	4	153	11.1	9	1	0.0	21:09	22	0	4	4	50	0	0	0	22:54
2004-05	Vitkovice	CzRep	28	6	5	11	46	....	....	....	....	....	....	....	....	....	12	4	6	10	34	....	....	....	....
2005-06	Tampa Bay	NHL	76	5	33	38	96	4	0	3	155	3.2	–12	2	0.0	22:25	5	1	1	2	26	1	0	0	20:09
	Czech Republic	Olympics	8	1	1	2	12	....	....	....	....	....	....	....	....	....	....	....	....	....	....	....	....	....	....
2006-07	Toronto	NHL	61	7	14	21	48	4	0	1	97	7.2	7	0	0.0	21:19	....	....	....	....	....	....	....	....	....
2007-08	Toronto	NHL	72	11	29	40	116	6	0	4	136	8.1	5	1	0.0	23:55	....	....	....	....	....	....	....	....	....
	NHL Totals		664	83	187	270	827	42	5	20	1252	6.6		10	10.0	22:36	38	1	5	6	88	1	0	0	23:06

Played in NHL All-Star Game (2004)

Signed as a free agent by **Vitkovice** (CzRep), September 17, 2004. Signed as a free agent by **Toronto**, July 1, 2006.

KUKKONEN, Lasse

(koo-KOH-nuhn, LAH-say) **PHI.**

Defense. Shoots left. 6'1", 190 lbs. Born, Oulu, Finland, September 18, 1981. Chicago's 4th choice, 151st overall, in 2003 Entry Draft.

Season	Club	League	GP	G	A	Pts	PIM	PP	SH	GW	S	%	+/-	TF	F%	Min	GP	G	A	Pts	PIM	PP	SH	GW	Min
1997-98	Karpat Oulu U18	Fin-U18	36	5	16	21	46	....	....	....	....	....	....	....	....	....	....	....	....	....	....	....	....	....	....
1998-99	Karpat Oulu U18	Fin-U18	2	1	2	3	0	....	....	....	....	....	....	....	....	....	....	....	....	....	....	....	....	....	....
	Karpat Oulu Jr.	Fin-Jr.	34	2	13	15	24	....	....	....	....	....	....	....	....	....	....	....	....	....	....	....	....	....	....
99-2000	Karpat Oulu Jr.	Fin-Jr.	27	9	11	20	26	....	....	....	....	....	....	....	....	....	....	....	....	....	....	....	....	....	....
	Karpat Oulu	Finland-2	22	0	4	4	14	....	....	....	....	....	....	....	....	....	....	....	....	....	....	....	....	....	....
2000-01	Karpat Oulu	Finland	47	1	5	6	46	....	....	....	....	....	....	....	....	....	9	0	2	2	4	....	....	....	....
2001-02	Karpat Oulu	Finland	55	2	6	8	42	....	....	....	....	....	....	....	....	....	4	0	3	3	4	....	....	....	....
	Karpat Oulu Jr.	Fin-Jr.	....	....	....	....	....	....	....	....	....	....	....	....	....	....	1	1	0	1	0	....	....	....	....
2002-03	Karpat Oulu	Finland	56	6	12	18	67	....	....	....	....	....	....	....	....	....	15	1	4	5	16	....	....	....	....
2003-04	Chicago	NHL	10	0	1	1	4	0	0	0	9	0.0	–2	0	0.0	13:37	....	....	....	....	....	....	....	....	....
	Norfolk Admirals	AHL	59	3	11	14	58	....	....	....	....	....	....	....	....	....	8	0	0	0	8	....	....	....	....
2004-05	Karpat Oulu	Finland	55	5	13	18	68	....	....	....	....	....	....	....	....	....	12	0	2	2	6	....	....	....	....
2005-06	Karpat Oulu	Finland	56	11	16	27	38	....	....	....	....	....	....	....	....	....	11	5	7	12	8	....	....	....	....
	Finland	Olympics	2	0	0	0	0	....	....	....	....	....	....	....	....	....	....	....	....	....	....	....	....	....	....
2006-07	Chicago	NHL	54	5	9	14	30	1	0	2	45	11.1	5	0	0.0	16:35	....	....	....	....	....	....	....	....	....
	Philadelphia	NHL	20	0	0	0	8	0	0	0	9	0.0	–1	0	0.0	18:29	....	....	....	....	....	....	....	....	....
2007-08	Philadelphia	NHL	53	1	4	5	38	0	0	0	31	3.2	3	0	0.0	15:44	14	0	2	2	6	0	0	0	15:22
	NHL Totals		137	6	14	20	80	1	0	2	94	6.4		0	0.0	16:19	14	0	2	2	6	0	0	0	15:22

Signed as a free agent by **Oulu** (Finland), September 11, 2004. Traded to **Philadelphia** by **Chicago** with Chicago's 3rd round choice (Garrett Klotz) in 2007 Entry Draft for Kyle Calder, February 26, 2007.

KUNITZ, Chris

(KOO-nihtz, KRIHS) **ANA.**

Left wing. Shoots left. 5'11", 195 lbs. Born, Regina, Sask., September 26, 1979.

Season	Club	League	GP	G	A	Pts	PIM	PP	SH	GW	S	%	+/-	TF	F%	Min	GP	G	A	Pts	PIM	PP	SH	GW	Min
1996-97	Yorkton Mallers	SMHL	64	38	38	76	233	....	....	....	....	....	....	....	....	....	....	....	....	....	....	....	....	....	....
1997-98	Melville	SJHL	STATISTICS NOT AVAILABLE					....	....	....	....	....	....	....	....	....	....	....	....	....	....	....	....	....	....
1998-99	Melville	SJHL	63	57	32	89	222	....	....	....	....	....	....	....	....	....	....	....	....	....	....	....	....	....	....
99-2000	Ferris State	CCHA	38	20	9	29	70	....	....	....	....	....	....	....	....	....	....	....	....	....	....	....	....	....	....
2000-01	Ferris State	CCHA	37	16	13	29	81	....	....	....	....	....	....	....	....	....	....	....	....	....	....	....	....	....	....
2001-02	Ferris State	CCHA	35	*28	10	38	68	....	....	....	....	....	....	....	....	....	....	....	....	....	....	....	....	....	....
2002-03	Ferris State	CCHA	42	*35	*44	*79	56	....	....	....	....	....	....	....	....	....	....	....	....	....	....	....	....	....	....
2003-04	Anaheim	NHL	21	0	6	6	12	0	0	0	31	0.0	1	7	14.3	9:07	....	....	....	....	....	....	....	....	....
	Cincinnati	AHL	59	19	25	44	101	....	....	....	....	....	....	....	....	....	9	3	2	5	24	....	....	....	....
2004-05	Cincinnati	AHL	54	22	17	39	71	....	....	....	....	....	....	....	....	....	12	1	7	8	20	....	....	....	....
2005-06	Atlanta	NHL	2	0	0	0	2	0	0	0	0	0.0	–3	0	0.0	5:43	....	....	....	....	....	....	....	....	....
	Anaheim	NHL	67	19	22	41	69	5	1	2	149	12.8	19	15	46.7	14:08	16	3	5	8	8	0	0	0	12:30
	Portland Pirates	AHL	5	0	4	4	12	....	....	....	....	....	....	....	....	....	....	....	....	....	....	....	....	....	....
2006-07♦	Anaheim	NHL	81	25	35	60	81	11	0	5	180	13.9	23	13	30.8	17:03	13	1	5	6	19	0	0	0	17:47
2007-08	Anaheim	NHL	82	21	29	50	80	7	1	6	196	10.7	8	49	32.7	16:54	6	0	2	2	8	0	0	0	18:30
	NHL Totals		253	65	92	157	244	23	2	13	556	11.7		84	33.3	15:29	35	4	12	16	35	0	0	0	15:30

CCHA First All-Star Team (2002, 2003) • CCHA Player of the Year (2003) • NCAA West First All-American Team (2003)

Signed as a free agent by **Anaheim**, April 1, 2003. Claimed on waivers by **Atlanta** from **Anaheim**, October 4, 2005. Claimed on waivers by **Anaheim** from **Atlanta**, October 18, 2005.

KWIATKOWSKI, Joel

(KWEE-at-KOW-skee, JOHL)

Defense. Shoots left. 6'2", 210 lbs. Born, Kindersley, Sask., March 22, 1977. Dallas' 7th choice, 194th overall, in 1996 Entry Draft.

Season	Club	League	GP	G	A	Pts	PIM	PP	SH	GW	S	%	+/-	TF	F%	Min	GP	G	A	Pts	PIM	PP	SH	GW	Min
1994-95	Tacoma Rockets	WHL	70	4	13	17	66	....	....	....	....	....	....	....	....	....	4	0	0	0	2	....	....	....	....
1995-96	Kelowna Rockets	WHL	40	6	17	23	85	....	....	....	....	....	....	....	....	....	....	....	....	....	....	....	....	....	....
	Prince George	WHL	32	6	11	17	48	....	....	....	....	....	....	....	....	....	....	....	....	....	....	....	....	....	....
1996-97	Prince George	WHL	72	15	37	52	94	....	....	....	....	....	....	....	....	....	15	4	2	6	24	....	....	....	....
1997-98	Prince George	WHL	62	21	43	64	65	....	....	....	....	....	....	....	....	....	11	3	6	9	6	....	....	....	....
1998-99	Cincinnati	AHL	80	12	21	33	48	....	....	....	....	....	....	....	....	....	3	2	0	2	0	....	....	....	....
99-2000	Cincinnati	AHL	70	4	22	26	28	....	....	....	....	....	....	....	....	....	....	....	....	....	....	....	....	....	....
2000-01	Ottawa	NHL	4	1	0	1	0	0	0	0	2	50.0	1	0	0.0	12:04	....	....	....	....	....	....	....	....	....
	Grand Rapids	IHL	77	4	17	21	58	....	....	....	....	....	....	....	....	....	10	1	0	1	4	....	....	....	....
2001-02	Ottawa	NHL	11	0	0	0	12	0	0	0	9	0.0	5	0	0.0	13:41	....	....	....	....	....	....	....	....	....
	Grand Rapids	AHL	65	8	21	29	94	....	....	....	....	....	....	....	....	....	5	1	2	3	12	....	....	....	....
2002-03	Ottawa	NHL	20	0	2	2	6	0	0	0	28	0.0	2	2	0.0	12:13	....	....	....	....	....	....	....	....	....
	Binghamton	AHL	1	0	0	0	2	....	....	....	....	....	....	....	....	....	....	....	....	....	....	....	....	....	....
	Washington	NHL	34	0	3	3	12	0	0	0	28	0.0	1	2	0.0	15:32	6	0	0	0	2	0	0	0	17:48
2003-04	Washington	NHL	80	6	6	12	89	2	0	0	90	6.7	–28	0	0.0	21:16	....	....	....	....	....	....	....	....	....
2004-05	San Antonio	AHL	64	13	19	32	76	....	....	....	....	....	....	....	....	....	....	....	....	....	....	....	....	....	....
	St. John's	AHL	17	7	6	13	16	....	....	....	....	....	....	....	....	....	5	0	4	4	23	....	....	....	....
2005-06	Florida	NHL	73	4	8	12	86	1	0	1	87	4.6	3	0	0.0	16:21	....	....	....	....	....	....	....	....	....
2006-07	Florida	NHL	41	5	5	10	20	1	0	2	46	10.9	–5	1	100.0	9:46	....	....	....	....	....	....	....	....	....
	Pittsburgh	NHL	1	0	0	0	0	0	0	0	0	0.0	–1	0	0.0	11:59	....	....	....	....	....	....	....	....	....
2007-08	Atlanta	NHL	18	0	5	5	20	0	0	0	24	0.0	–5	0	0.0	16:44	....	....	....	....	....	....	....	....	....
	Chicago Wolves	AHL	59	21	29	50	119	....	....	....	....	....	....	....	....	....	24	10	15	25	30	....	....	....	....
	NHL Totals		282	16	29	45	245	4	0	3	314	5.1		5	20.0	16:14	6	0	0	0	2	0	0	0	17:48

WHL West Second All-Star Team (1997) • WHL West First All-Star Team (1998) • AHL Second All-Star Team (2008)

Signed as a free agent by **Anaheim**, June 18, 1998. Traded to **Ottawa** by **Anaheim** for Patrick Traverse, June 12, 2000. Traded to **Washington** by **Ottawa** for Washington's 9th round choice (later traded back to Washington – Washington selected Mark Olafson) in 2003 Entry Draft, January 15, 2003. Signed as a free agent by **Florida**, July 16, 2004. Loaned to **St. John's** (AHL) by **Florida** (San Antonio-AHL) for cash, March 11, 2005. Traded to **Pittsburgh** by **Florida** for Florida's 4th round choice (previously acquired, Florida selected Matt Rust) in 2007 Entry Draft, February 27, 2007. Signed as a free agent by **Atlanta**, August 30, 2007.

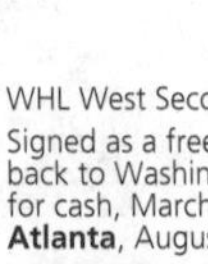

LAAKSONEN, Antti

(lah-AHK-soh-nehn, AN-tee)

Left wing. Shoots left. 6', 187 lbs. Born, Tammela, Finland, October 3, 1973. Boston's 10th choice, 191st overall, in 1997 Entry Draft.

Season	Club	League	GP	G	A	Pts	PIM	PP	SH	GW	S	%	+/-	TF	F%	Min	GP	G	A	Pts	PIM	PP	SH	GW	Min
1989-90	FoPS Forssa Jr.	Fin-Jr.	3	0	0	0	0	....	....	....	....	....	....	....	....	....	....	....	....	....	....	....	....	....	....
1990-91	FoPS Forssa Jr.	Fin-Jr.	STATISTICS NOT AVAILABLE					....	....	....	....	....	....	....	....	....	....	....	....	....	....	....	....	....	....
	FoPS Forssa	Finland-2	2	0	0	0	0	....	....	....	....	....	....	....	....	....	....	....	....	....	....	....	....	....	....
1991-92	FoPS Forssa Jr.	Fin-Jr.	24	19	23	42	22	....	....	....	....	....	....	....	....	....	....	....	....	....	....	....	....	....	....
	FoPS Forssa	Finland-2	41	16	15	31	8	....	....	....	....	....	....	....	....	....	....	....	....	....	....	....	....	....	....
1992-93	FoPS Forssa Jr.	Fin-Jr.	12	7	7	14	14	....	....	....	....	....	....	....	....	....	....	....	....	....	....	....	....	....	....
	FoPS Forssa	Finland-2	34	11	19	30	36	....	....	....	....	....	....	....	....	....	....	....	....	....	....	....	....	....	....
	HPK Jr.	Fin-Jr.	1	1	1	2	0	....	....	....	....	....	....	....	....	....	....	....	....	....	....	....	....	....	....
	HPK Hameenlinna	Finland	2	0	0	0	0	....	....	....	....	....	....	....	....	....	....	....	....	....	....	....	....	....	....
1993-94	U. of Denver	WCHA	36	12	9	21	38	....	....	....	....	....	....	....	....	....	....	....	....	....	....	....	....	....	....
1994-95	U. of Denver	WCHA	40	17	18	35	42	....	....	....	....	....	....	....	....	....	....	....	....	....	....	....	....	....	....
1995-96	U. of Denver	WCHA	39	25	28	53	71	....	....	....	....	....	....	....	....	....	....	....	....	....	....	....	....	....	....
1996-97	U. of Denver	WCHA	39	21	17	38	63	....	....	....	....	....	....	....	....	....	....	....	....	....	....	....	....	....	....
1997-98	Providence Bruins	AHL	38	3	2	5	14	....	....	....	....	....	....	....	....	....	....	....	....	....	....	....	....	....	....
	Charlotte	ECHL	15	4	3	7	12	....	....	....	....	....	....	....	....	....	6	0	3	3	0	....	....	....	....
1998-99	Boston	NHL	11	1	2	3	2	0	0	0	8	12.5	–1	0	0.0	9:20	....	....	....	....	....	....	....	....	....
	Providence Bruins	AHL	66	25	33	58	52	....	....	....	....	....	....	....	....	....	19	7	2	9	28	....	....	....	....

Season	Club	League	GP	G	A	Pts	PIM	PP	SH	GW	S	%	+/-	TF	F%	Min	GP	G	A	Pts	PIM	PP	SH	GW	Min
			Regular Season														Playoffs								
99-2000	Boston	NHL	27	6	3	9	2	0	0	1	23	26.1	3	3	66.7	7:50	....	....	....	....	....	....	....	....	....
	Providence Bruins	AHL	40	10	12	22	57	....	....	....	....	....	....	....	....	....	14	5	4	9	4	....	....	....	....
2000-01	Minnesota	NHL	82	12	16	28	24	0	2	1	129	9.3	–7	15	26.7	16:27	....	....	....	....	....	....	....	....	....
2001-02	Minnesota	NHL	82	16	17	33	22	0	0	1	104	15.4	–5	19	42.1	16:20	....	....	....	....	....	....	....	....	....
2002-03	Minnesota	NHL	82	15	16	31	26	1	2	4	106	14.2	4	51	29.4	15:55	16	1	3	4	4	0	0	0	16:34
2003-04	Minnesota	NHL	77	12	14	26	20	0	1	1	100	12.0	0	144	36.1	16:03	....	....	....	....	....	....	....	....	....
2004-05				DID NOT PLAY													....	....	....	....	....	....	....	....	....
2005-06	Colorado	NHL	81	16	18	34	40	0	2	4	141	11.3	–2	46	28.3	16:00	9	0	2	2	2	0	0	0	15:23
	Finland	Olympics	8	0	0	0	6	....	....	....	....	....	....	....	....	....	....	....	....	....	....	....	....	....	....
2006-07	Colorado	NHL	41	3	1	4	16	0	1	0	43	7.0	–3	13	7.7	10:41	....	....	....	....	....	....	....	....	....
	Albany River Rats	AHL	24	9	7	16	4	....	....	....	....	....	....	....	....	....	1	0	0	0	0	....	....	....	....
2007-08	Fribourg	Swiss	46	12	13	25	44	....	....	....	....	....	....	....	....	....	6	1	0	1	14	....	....	....	....
	NHL Totals		483	81	87	168	152	1	8	12	654	12.4		291	32.6	15:04	25	1	5	6	6	0	0	0	16:09

WCHA Second All-Star Team (1996)

Signed as a free agent by **Minnesota**, July 14, 2000. Signed as a free agent by **Colorado**, July 2, 2004. Signed as a free agent by **Fribourg** (Swiss), June 18, 2007.

LaCOUTURE, Dan
(LA-koo-TUHR, DAN)

Left wing. Shoots left. 6′2″, 215 lbs. Born, Hyannis, MA, April 18, 1977. NY Islanders' 2nd choice, 29th overall, in 1996 Entry Draft.

Season	Club	League	GP	G	A	Pts	PIM	PP	SH	GW	S	%	+/-	TF	F%	Min	GP	G	A	Pts	PIM	PP	SH	GW	Min
1992-93	Natick Redmen	High-MA	20	38	34	72	46	....	....	....	....	....	....	....	....	....	....	....	....	....	....	....	....	....	....
1993-94	Natick Redmen	High-MA	21	52	49	101	58	....	....	....	....	....	....	....	....	....	....	....	....	....	....	....	....	....	....
1994-95	Spring. Olympics	NEJHL	52	44	56	100	98	....	....	....	....	....	....	....	....	....	....	....	....	....	....	....	....	....	....
1995-96	Spring. Olympics	NEJHL	29	24	35	59	79	....	....	....	....	....	....	....	....	....	13	12	13	25	23	....	....	....	....
1996-97	Boston University	H-East	31	13	12	25	18	....	....	....	....	....	....	....	....	....	....	....	....	....	....	....	....	....	....
1997-98	Hamilton	AHL	77	15	10	25	31	....	....	....	....	....	....	....	....	....	5	1	0	1	0	....	....	....	....
1998-99	Edmonton	NHL	3	0	0	0	0	0	0	0	0	0.0	1	0	0.0	6:30	....	....	....	....	....	....	....	....	....
	Hamilton	AHL	72	17	14	31	73	....	....	....	....	....	....	....	....	....	9	2	1	3	2	....	....	....	....
99-2000	Edmonton	NHL	5	0	0	0	10	0	0	0	2	0.0	0	0	0.0	7:02	1	0	0	0	0	0	0	0	2:05
	Hamilton	AHL	70	23	17	40	85	....	....	....	....	....	....	....	....	....	6	2	1	3	0	....	....	....	....
2000-01	Edmonton	NHL	37	2	4	6	29	0	0	1	22	9.1	–2	5	20.0	7:06	....	....	....	....	....	....	....	....	....
	Pittsburgh	NHL	11	0	0	0	14	0	0	0	1	0.0	0	1	100.0	5:57	5	0	0	0	2	0	0	0	5:46
2001-02	Pittsburgh	NHL	82	6	11	17	71	0	1	0	77	7.8	–19	21	38.1	13:16	....	....	....	....	....	....	....	....	....
2002-03	Pittsburgh	NHL	44	2	2	4	72	0	0	0	30	6.7	–8	5	80.0	9:13	....	....	....	....	....	....	....	....	....
	NY Rangers	NHL	24	1	4	5	0	0	0	0	17	5.9	4	1	0.0	10:18	....	....	....	....	....	....	....	....	....
2003-04	NY Rangers	NHL	59	5	2	7	82	1	0	1	39	12.8	–13	8	50.0	9:29	....	....	....	....	....	....	....	....	....
2004-05	Providence Bruins	AHL	64	12	15	27	52	....	....	....	....	....	....	....	....	....	6	1	1	2	4	....	....	....	....
2005-06	HC Davos	Swiss	4	2	1	3	4	....	....	....	....	....	....	....	....	....	....	....	....	....	....	....	....	....	....
	Boston	NHL	55	2	2	4	53	0	1	0	37	5.4	–6	0	0.0	6:15	....	....	....	....	....	....	....	....	....
2006-07	New Jersey	NHL	6	0	0	0	7	0	0	0	0	0.0	0	0	0.0	4:57	....	....	....	....	....	....	....	....	....
	Lowell Devils	AHL	39	8	3	11	33	....	....	....	....	....	....	....	....	....	....	....	....	....	....	....	....	....	....
2007-08	HC Lugano	Swiss	15	1	1	2	18	....	....	....	....	....	....	....	....	....	....	....	....	....	....	....	....	....	....
	NHL Totals		326	18	25	43	338	1	2	2	225	8.0		41	43.9	9:23	6	0	0	0	2	0	0	0	5:09

Traded to **Edmonton** by **NY Islanders** for Mariusz Czerkawski, August 25, 1997. Traded to **Pittsburgh** by **Edmonton** for Sven Butenschon, March 13, 2001. Traded to **NY Rangers** by **Pittsburgh** with Mike Wilson, Alex Kovalev and Janne Laukkanen for Joel Bouchard, Richard Lintner, Rico Fata and Mikael Samuelsson, February 10, 2003. Signed to a PTO (tryout) contract by **Providence** (AHL), November 2, 2004. Signed as a free agent by **Boston**, November 24, 2005. Signed as a free agent by **New Jersey**, October 4, 2006. Signed as a free agent by **Anaheim**, July 18, 2007.

LADD, Andrew
(LAD, AN-droo) **CHI.**

Left wing. Shoots left. 6′2″, 201 lbs. Born, Maple Ridge, B.C., December 12, 1985. Carolina's 1st choice, 4th overall, in 2004 Entry Draft.

Season	Club	League	GP	G	A	Pts	PIM	PP	SH	GW	S	%	+/-	TF	F%	Min	GP	G	A	Pts	PIM	PP	SH	GW	Min
2000-01	Okanagan Chiefs	Minor-BC	6	4	8	12	10	....	....	....	....	....	....	....	....	....	....	....	....	....	....	....	....	....	....
2001-02	Port Coquitlam	Minor-BC	50	50	41	91	49	....	....	....	....	....	....	....	....	....	....	....	....	....	....	....	....	....	....
	Vancouver Giants	WHL	1	0	0	0	0	....	....	....	....	....	....	....	....	....	....	....	....	....	....	....	....	....	....
2002-03	Coquitlam	BCHL	58	15	40	55	61	....	....	....	....	....	....	....	....	....	....	....	....	....	....	....	....	....	....
2003-04	Calgary Hitmen	WHL	71	30	45	75	119	....	....	....	....	....	....	....	....	....	7	1	6	7	10	....	....	....	....
2004-05	Calgary Hitmen	WHL	65	19	26	45	167	....	....	....	....	....	....	....	....	....	12	7	4	11	18	....	....	....	....
2005-06♦	Carolina	NHL	29	6	5	11	4	3	0	0	43	14.0	0	0	0.0	11:10	17	2	3	5	4	0	0	1	9:27
	Lowell	AHL	25	11	8	19	28	....	....	....	....	....	....	....	....	....	....	....	....	....	....	....	....	....	....
2006-07	Carolina	NHL	65	11	10	21	46	2	0	3	109	10.1	1	1	0.0	11:12	....	....	....	....	....	....	....	....	....
2007-08	Carolina	NHL	43	9	9	18	31	0	0	1	76	11.8	9	5	60.0	11:45	....	....	....	....	....	....	....	....	....
	Albany River Rats	AHL	2	1	0	1	4	....	....	....	....	....	....	....	....	....	....	....	....	....	....	....	....	....	....
	Chicago	NHL	20	5	7	12	4	1	0	0	55	9.1	4	3	33.3	14:58	....	....	....	....	....	....	....	....	....
	NHL Totals		157	31	31	62	85	6	0	4	283	11.0		9	44.4	11:49	17	2	3	5	4	0	0	1	9:27

Traded to **Chicago** by **Carolina** for Tuomo Ruutu, February 26, 2008.

LAICH, Brooks
(LAYCH, BRUKS) **WSH.**

Center. Shoots left. 6′2″, 205 lbs. Born, Wawota, Sask., June 23, 1983. Ottawa's 7th choice, 193rd overall, in 2001 Entry Draft.

Season	Club	League	GP	G	A	Pts	PIM	PP	SH	GW	S	%	+/-	TF	F%	Min	GP	G	A	Pts	PIM	PP	SH	GW	Min
99-2000	Tisdale Trojans	SMHL	57	51	52	103	....	....	....	....	....	....	....	....	....	....	....	....	....	....	....	....	....	....	....
2000-01	Moose Jaw	WHL	71	9	21	30	28	....	....	....	....	....	....	....	....	....	4	0	0	0	5	....	....	....	....
2001-02	Moose Jaw	WHL	28	6	14	20	12	....	....	....	....	....	....	....	....	....	....	....	....	....	....	....	....	....	....
	Seattle	WHL	47	22	36	58	42	....	....	....	....	....	....	....	....	....	11	5	3	8	11	....	....	....	....
2002-03	Seattle	WHL	60	41	53	94	65	....	....	....	....	....	....	....	....	....	15	5	14	19	24	....	....	....	....
2003-04	Ottawa	NHL	1	0	0	0	2	0	0	0	1	0.0	0	7	42.9	9:34	....	....	....	....	....	....	....	....	....
	Binghamton	AHL	44	15	18	33	16	....	....	....	....	....	....	....	....	....	....	....	....	....	....	....	....	....	....
	Washington	NHL	4	0	1	1	0	0	0	0	2	0.0	–1	49	51.0	10:50	....	....	....	....	....	....	....	....	....
	Portland Pirates	AHL	22	1	3	4	12	....	....	....	....	....	....	....	....	....	6	0	0	0	0	....	....	....	....
2004-05	Portland Pirates	AHL	68	16	10	26	33	....	....	....	....	....	....	....	....	....	....	....	....	....	....	....	....	....	....
2005-06	Washington	NHL	73	7	14	21	26	1	0	1	118	5.9	–9	666	49.7	11:13	....	....	....	....	....	....	....	....	....
	Hershey Bears	AHL	10	7	6	13	8	....	....	....	....	....	....	....	....	....	21	8	7	15	29	....	....	....	....
2006-07	Washington	NHL	73	8	10	18	29	2	3	0	119	6.7	–2	563	51.9	13:36	....	....	....	....	....	....	....	....	....
2007-08	Washington	NHL	82	21	16	37	35	8	2	4	122	17.2	–3	596	47.2	14:03	7	1	5	6	4	0	0	0	18:37
	NHL Totals		233	36	41	77	92	11	5	5	362	9.9		1881	49.5	12:57	7	1	5	6	4	0	0	0	18:37

WHL West First All-Star Team (2003)

Traded to **Washington** by **Ottawa** with Ottawa's 2nd round choice (later traded to Colorado - Colorado selected Chris Durand) in 2005 Entry Draft for Peter Bondra, February 18, 2004.

LAING, Quintin
(LANG, QUIHN-tihn) **WSH.**

Left wing. Shoots left. 6′2″, 200 lbs. Born, Rosetown, Sask., June 8, 1979. Detroit's 3rd choice, 102nd overall, in 1997 Entry Draft.

Season	Club	League	GP	G	A	Pts	PIM	PP	SH	GW	S	%	+/-	TF	F%	Min	GP	G	A	Pts	PIM	PP	SH	GW	Min
1993-94	Delisle Contacts	SAHA	30	25	50	75	25	....	....	....	....	....	....	....	....	....	....	....	....	....	....	....	....	....	....
1994-95	Delisle Contacts	SAHA	30	30	45	75	15	....	....	....	....	....	....	....	....	....	....	....	....	....	....	....	....	....	....
1995-96	Sask. Contacts	SMHL	44	18	12	30	20	....	....	....	....	....	....	....	....	....	....	....	....	....	....	....	....	....	....
1996-97	Kelowna Rockets	WHL	63	13	24	37	54	....	....	....	....	....	....	....	....	....	1	0	0	0	0	....	....	....	....
1997-98	Kelowna Rockets	WHL	59	11	24	35	47	....	....	....	....	....	....	....	....	....	7	0	1	1	8	....	....	....	....
1998-99	Kelowna Rockets	WHL	70	11	10	21	107	....	....	....	....	....	....	....	....	....	6	3	0	3	0	....	....	....	....
99-2000	Kelowna Rockets	WHL	68	22	30	52	61	....	....	....	....	....	....	....	....	....	5	1	1	2	8	....	....	....	....
2000-01	Norfolk Admirals	AHL	10	0	1	1	10	....	....	....	....	....	....	....	....	....	....	....	....	....	....	....	....	....	....
	Jackson Bandits	ECHL	60	13	24	37	39	....	....	....	....	....	....	....	....	....	5	0	0	0	0	....	....	....	....
2001-02	Jackson Bandits	ECHL	16	4	6	10	12	....	....	....	....	....	....	....	....	....	....	....	....	....	....	....	....	....	....
	Norfolk Admirals	AHL	61	6	15	21	32	....	....	....	....	....	....	....	....	....	4	0	0	0	2	....	....	....	....
2002-03	Norfolk Admirals	AHL	69	5	12	17	33	....	....	....	....	....	....	....	....	....	8	2	2	4	0	....	....	....	....
2003-04	Chicago	NHL	3	0	1	1	0	0	0	0	3	0.0	1	0	0.0	11:57	....	....	....	....	....	....	....	....	....
	Norfolk Admirals	AHL	78	12	10	22	74	....	....	....	....	....	....	....	....	....	8	5	1	6	4	....	....	....	....
2004-05	Norfolk Admirals	AHL	66	10	13	23	54	....	....	....	....	....	....	....	....	....	4	0	0	0	0	....	....	....	....
2005-06	Norfolk Admirals	AHL	73	14	31	45	70	....	....	....	....	....	....	....	....	....	4	0	0	0	0	....	....	....	....
2006-07	Hershey Bears	AHL	75	15	28	43	44	....	....	....	....	....	....	....	....	....	19	2	5	7	21	....	....	....	....
2007-08	Washington	NHL	39	1	5	6	10	0	0	1	48	2.1	4	6	33.3	11:33	....	....	....	....	....	....	....	....	....
	Hershey Bears	AHL	20	2	6	8	28	....	....	....	....	....	....	....	....	....	....	....	....	....	....	....	....	....	....
	NHL Totals		42	1	6	7	10	0	0	1	51	2.0		6	33.3	11:35	....	....	....	....	....	....	....	....	....

Signed as a free agent by **Chicago**, June 4, 2003. Signed as a free agent by **Washington**, July 18, 2006.

LAMPMAN, Bryce

(LAMP-man, BRIGHS) **DAL.**

Defense. Shoots left. 6'1", 199 lbs. Born, Rochester, MN, August 31, 1982. NY Rangers' 4th choice, 113th overall, in 2001 Entry Draft.

			Regular Season														Playoffs								
Season	Club	League	GP	G	A	Pts	PIM	PP	SH	GW	S	%	+/-	TF	F%	Min	GP	G	A	Pts	PIM	PP	SH	GW	Min
1998-99	Rochester	USHL	53	3	8	11	33	....	....	....	....	....	....	....	....	....	....	....	....	....	....	....	....	....	....
99-2000	Rochester	USHL	10	0	0	0	14	....	....	....	....	....	....	....	....	....	....	....	....	....	....	....	....	....	....
	Omaha Lancers	USHL	11	1	2	3	38	....	....	....	....	....	....	....	....	....	4	0	0	0	0	....	....	....	....
2000-01	Omaha Lancers	USHL	55	10	11	21	77	....	....	....	....	....	....	....	....	....	12	1	4	5	12	....	....	....	....
2001-02	Nebraska-Omaha	CCHA	26	0	4	4	28	....	....	....	....	....	....	....	....	....	....	....	....	....	....	....	....	....	....
2002-03	Kamloops Blazers	WHL	29	1	17	18	32	....	....	....	....	....	....	....	....	....	....	....	....	....	....	....	....	....	....
	Hartford	AHL	45	0	6	6	32	....	....	....	....	....	....	....	....	....	2	0	1	1	0	....	....	....	....
2003-04	**NY Rangers**	**NHL**	**8**	**0**	**0**	**0**	**0**	**0**	**0**	**0**	**7**	**0.0**	**–4**	**0**	**0.0**	**19:34**	....	....	....	....	....	....	....	....	....
	Hartford	AHL	68	4	11	15	50	....	....	....	....	....	....	....	....	....	16	1	3	4	14	....	....	....	....
2004-05	Hartford	AHL	74	7	18	25	74	....	....	....	....	....	....	....	....	....	4	0	0	0	4	....	....	....	....
2005-06	**NY Rangers**	**NHL**	**1**	**0**	**0**	**0**	**2**	**0**	**0**	**0**	**1**	**0.0**	**–1**	**0**	**0.0**	**13:40**	....	....	....	....	....	....	....	....	....
	Hartford	AHL	11	2	3	5	16	....	....	....	....	....	....	....	....	....	....	....	....	....	....	....	....	....	....
2006-07	**NY Rangers**	**NHL**	**1**	**0**	**0**	**0**	**0**	**0**	**0**	**0**	**0**	**0.0**	**0**	**0**	**0.0**	**12:08**	....	....	....	....	....	....	....	....	....
	Hartford	AHL	60	6	19	25	62	....	....	....	....	....	....	....	....	....	7	2	0	2	2	....	....	....	....
2007-08	Norfolk Admirals	AHL	16	3	3	6	4	....	....	....	....	....	....	....	....	....	....	....	....	....	....	....	....	....	....
	Iowa Stars	AHL	53	4	11	15	32	....	....	....	....	....	....	....	....	....	....	....	....	....	....	....	....	....	....
	NHL Totals		**10**	**0**	**0**	**0**	**2**	**0**	**0**	**0**	**8**	**0.0**		**0**	**0.0**	**18:14**	....	....	....	....	....	....	....	....	....

• Left **University of Nebraska-Omaha** (CCHA) and signed as a free agent by **Kamloops** (WHL), August 1, 2002. • Missed majority of 2005-06 season recovering from shoulder injury. Rights traded to **Tampa Bay** by **NY Rangers** for the rights to Mitch Fritz, July 4, 2007. Traded to **Dallas** by **Tampa Bay** for Mario Scalzo, November 19, 2007.

LANG, Robert

(LANG, RAW-buhrt) **CHI.**

Center. Shoots right. 6'3", 216 lbs. Born, Teplice, Czech., December 19, 1970. Los Angeles' 6th choice, 133rd overall, in 1990 Entry Draft.

			Regular Season														Playoffs								
Season	Club	League	GP	G	A	Pts	PIM	PP	SH	GW	S	%	+/-	TF	F%	Min	GP	G	A	Pts	PIM	PP	SH	GW	Min
1988-89	CHZ Litvinov	Czech	7	3	2	5	0	....	....	....	....	....	....	....	....	....	....	....	....	....	....	....	....	....	....
1989-90	CHZ Litvinov	Czech	32	8	7	15	....	....	....	....	....	....	....	....	....	....	8	3	3	6	....	....	....	....	....
1990-91	HC CHZ Litvinov	Czech	56	26	26	52	38	....	....	....	....	....	....	....	....	....	....	....	....	....	....	....	....	....	....
1991-92	Litvinov	Czech	43	12	31	43	34	....	....	....	....	....	....	....	....	....	....	....	....	....	....	....	....	....	....
	Czechoslovakia	Olympics	8	5	8	13	8	....	....	....	....	....	....	....	....	....	....	....	....	....	....	....	....	....	....
1992-93	**Los Angeles**	**NHL**	**11**	**0**	**5**	**5**	**2**	**0**	**0**	**0**	**3**	**0.0**	**–3**	....	....	....	....	....	....	....	....	....	....	....	....
	Phoenix	IHL	38	9	21	30	20	....	....	....	....	....	....	....	....	....	....	....	....	....	....	....	....	....	....
1993-94	**Los Angeles**	**NHL**	**32**	**9**	**10**	**19**	**10**	**0**	**0**	**0**	**41**	**22.0**	**7**	....	....	....	....	....	....	....	....	....	....	....	....
	Phoenix	IHL	44	11	24	35	34	....	....	....	....	....	....	....	....	....	....	....	....	....	....	....	....	....	....
1994-95	Litvinov	CzRep	16	4	19	23	28	....	....	....	....	....	....	....	....	....	....	....	....	....	....	....	....	....	....
	Los Angeles	**NHL**	**36**	**4**	**8**	**12**	**4**	**0**	**0**	**0**	**38**	**10.5**	**–7**	....	....	....	....	....	....	....	....	....	....	....	....
1995-96	**Los Angeles**	**NHL**	**68**	**6**	**16**	**22**	**10**	**0**	**2**	**0**	**71**	**8.5**	**–15**	....	....	....	....	....	....	....	....	....	....	....	....
1996-97	HC Sparta Praha	CzRep	38	14	27	41	30	....	....	....	....	....	....	....	....	....	5	1	2	3	4	....	....	....	....
	HC Sparta Praha	EuroHL	4	2	2	4	0	....	....	....	....	....	....	....	....	....	4	2	1	3	2	....	....	....	....
1997-98	**Boston**	**NHL**	**3**	**0**	**0**	**0**	**2**	**0**	**0**	**0**	**2**	**0.0**	**1**	....	....	....	....	....	....	....	....	....	....	....	....
	Pittsburgh	**NHL**	**51**	**9**	**13**	**22**	**14**	**1**	**1**	**2**	**64**	**14.1**	**6**	....	....	....	**6**	**0**	**3**	**3**	**2**	**0**	**0**	**0**	....
	Czech Republic	Olympics	6	0	3	3	0	....	....	....	....	....	....	....	....	....	....	....	....	....	....	....	....	....	....
	Houston Aeros	IHL	9	1	7	8	4	....	....	....	....	....	....	....	....	....	....	....	....	....	....	....	....	....	....
1998-99	**Pittsburgh**	**NHL**	**72**	**21**	**23**	**44**	**24**	**7**	**0**	**3**	**137**	**15.3**	**–10**	**964**	**44.8**	**16:24**	**12**	**0**	**2**	**2**	**0**	**0**	**0**	**0**	**13:58**
99-2000	**Pittsburgh**	**NHL**	**78**	**23**	**42**	**65**	**14**	**13**	**0**	**5**	**142**	**16.2**	**–9**	**1433**	**50.7**	**19:22**	**11**	**3**	**3**	**6**	**0**	**2**	**0**	**0**	**21:42**
2000-01	**Pittsburgh**	**NHL**	**82**	**32**	**48**	**80**	**28**	**10**	**0**	**2**	**177**	**18.1**	**20**	**1348**	**43.9**	**20:24**	**16**	**4**	**4**	**8**	**4**	**0**	**0**	**0**	**19:21**
2001-02	**Pittsburgh**	**NHL**	**62**	**18**	**32**	**50**	**16**	**5**	**1**	**3**	**175**	**10.3**	**9**	**1172**	**46.3**	**22:56**	....	....	....	....	....	....	....	....	....
	Czech Republic	Olympics	4	1	2	3	2	....	....	....	....	....	....	....	....	....	....	....	....	....	....	....	....	....	....
2002-03	**Washington**	**NHL**	**82**	**22**	**47**	**69**	**22**	**10**	**0**	**2**	**146**	**15.1**	**12**	**1069**	**45.9**	**18:47**	**6**	**2**	**1**	**3**	**2**	**0**	**0**	**1**	**21:55**
2003-04	**Washington**	**NHL**	**63**	**29**	**45**	**74**	**24**	**10**	**0**	**2**	**149**	**19.5**	**2**	**744**	**44.1**	**21:46**	....	....	....	....	....	....	....	....	....
	Detroit	**NHL**	**6**	**1**	**4**	**5**	**0**	**0**	**0**	**1**	**14**	**7.1**	**2**	**96**	**57.3**	**16:20**	**12**	**4**	**5**	**9**	**6**	**0**	**0**	**0**	**18:10**
2004-05			DID NOT PLAY																						
2005-06	**Detroit**	**NHL**	**72**	**20**	**42**	**62**	**72**	**8**	**0**	**3**	**171**	**11.7**	**17**	**861**	**50.3**	**16:15**	**6**	**3**	**3**	**6**	**2**	**2**	**0**	**0**	**19:12**
	Czech Republic	Olympics	8	0	4	4	4	....	....	....	....	....	....	....	....	....	....	....	....	....	....	....	....	....	....
2006-07	**Detroit**	**NHL**	**81**	**19**	**33**	**52**	**66**	**6**	**0**	**4**	**166**	**11.4**	**12**	**812**	**49.4**	**16:49**	**18**	**2**	**6**	**8**	**8**	**0**	**0**	**0**	**15:10**
2007-08	**Chicago**	**NHL**	**76**	**21**	**33**	**54**	**50**	**7**	**0**	**3**	**172**	**12.2**	**9**	**1117**	**53.1**	**18:25**	....	....	....	....	....	....	....	....	....
	NHL Totals		**875**	**234**	**401**	**635**	**358**	**77**	**4**	**30**	**1668**	**14.0**		**9616**	**47.8**	**18:53**	**87**	**18**	**27**	**45**	**24**	**4**	**0**	**1**	**17:57**

Played in NHL All-Star Game (2004)

Signed as a free agent by **Pittsburgh**, September 2, 1997. Claimed by **Boston** from **Pittsburgh** in Waiver Draft, September 28, 1997. Claimed on waivers by **Pittsburgh** from **Boston**, October 25, 1997. Signed as a free agent by **Washington**, July 1, 2002. Traded to **Detroit** by **Washington** for Tomas Fleischmann, Detroit's 1st round choice (Mike Green) in 2004 Entry Draft and Detroit's 4th round choice (Luke Lynes) in 2006 Entry Draft, February 27, 2004. Signed as a free agent by **Chicago**, July 2, 2007.

LANGENBRUNNER, Jamie

(lan-gehn-BRUH-nuhr, JAY-mee) **N.J.**

Right wing. Shoots right. 6'1", 205 lbs. Born, Cloquet, MN, July 24, 1975. Dallas' 2nd choice, 35th overall, in 1993 Entry Draft.

			Regular Season														Playoffs								
Season	Club	League	GP	G	A	Pts	PIM	PP	SH	GW	S	%	+/-	TF	F%	Min	GP	G	A	Pts	PIM	PP	SH	GW	Min
1990-91	Cloquet	High-MN	20	6	16	22	8	....	....	....	....	....	....	....	....	....	....	....	....	....	....	....	....	....	....
1991-92	Cloquet	High-MN	23	16	23	39	24	....	....	....	....	....	....	....	....	....	....	....	....	....	....	....	....	....	....
1992-93	Cloquet	High-MN	27	27	62	89	18	....	....	....	....	....	....	....	....	....	....	....	....	....	....	....	....	....	....
1993-94	Peterborough	OHL	62	33	58	91	53	....	....	....	....	....	....	....	....	....	7	4	6	10	2	....	....	....	....
1994-95	Peterborough	OHL	62	42	57	99	84	....	....	....	....	....	....	....	....	....	11	8	14	22	12	....	....	....	....
	Dallas	**NHL**	**2**	**0**	**0**	**0**	**2**	**0**	**0**	**0**	**1**	**0.0**	**0**	....	....	....	....	....	....	....	....	....	....	....	....
	Kalamazoo Wings	IHL	....	....	....	....	....	....	....	....	....	....	....	....	....	....	11	1	3	4	2	....	....	....	....
1995-96	**Dallas**	**NHL**	**12**	**2**	**2**	**4**	**6**	**1**	**0**	**0**	**15**	**13.3**	**–2**	....	....	....	....	....	....	....	....	....	....	....	....
	Michigan	IHL	59	25	40	65	129	....	....	....	....	....	....	....	....	....	10	3	10	13	8	....	....	....	....
1996-97	**Dallas**	**NHL**	**76**	**13**	**26**	**39**	**51**	**3**	**0**	**3**	**112**	**11.6**	**–2**	....	....	....	**5**	**1**	**1**	**2**	**14**	**0**	**0**	**1**	....
1997-98	**Dallas**	**NHL**	**81**	**23**	**29**	**52**	**61**	**8**	**0**	**6**	**159**	**14.5**	**9**	....	....	....	**16**	**1**	**4**	**5**	**14**	**0**	**0**	**1**	....
	United States	Olympics	3	0	0	0	4	....	....	....	....	....	....	....	....	....	....	....	....	....	....	....	....	....	....
1998-99♦	**Dallas**	**NHL**	**75**	**12**	**33**	**45**	**62**	**4**	**0**	**1**	**145**	**8.3**	**10**	**217**	**46.1**	**15:51**	**23**	**10**	**7**	**17**	**16**	**4**	**0**	**3**	**17:43**
99-2000	**Dallas**	**NHL**	**65**	**18**	**21**	**39**	**68**	**4**	**2**	**6**	**153**	**11.8**	**16**	**40**	**50.0**	**17:33**	**15**	**1**	**7**	**8**	**18**	**1**	**0**	**0**	**15:28**
2000-01	**Dallas**	**NHL**	**53**	**12**	**18**	**30**	**57**	**3**	**2**	**4**	**104**	**11.5**	**4**	**316**	**45.3**	**16:30**	**10**	**2**	**2**	**4**	**6**	**0**	**0**	**1**	**19:26**
2001-02	**Dallas**	**NHL**	**68**	**10**	**16**	**26**	**54**	**0**	**1**	**2**	**132**	**7.6**	**–11**	**120**	**45.0**	**15:45**	....	....	....	....	....	....	....	....	....
	New Jersey	**NHL**	**14**	**3**	**3**	**6**	**23**	**0**	**0**	**2**	**31**	**9.7**	**2**	**2**	**50.0**	**15:27**	**5**	**0**	**1**	**1**	**8**	**0**	**0**	**0**	**14:57**
2002-03♦	**New Jersey**	**NHL**	**78**	**22**	**33**	**55**	**65**	**5**	**1**	**5**	**197**	**11.2**	**17**	**72**	**47.2**	**17:48**	**24**	***11**	**7**	***18**	**16**	**1**	**0**	**4**	**17:34**
2003-04	**New Jersey**	**NHL**	**53**	**10**	**16**	**26**	**43**	**1**	**2**	**2**	**130**	**7.7**	**9**	**31**	**51.6**	**16:01**	**5**	**0**	**2**	**2**	**2**	**0**	**0**	**0**	**15:04**
2004-05	ERC Ingolstadt	Germany	11	2	2	4	22	....	....	....	....	....	....	....	....	....	11	1	6	7	6	....	....	....	....
2005-06	**New Jersey**	**NHL**	**80**	**19**	**34**	**53**	**74**	**8**	**1**	**1**	**243**	**7.8**	**–1**	**41**	**43.9**	**18:36**	**9**	**3**	**10**	**13**	**16**	**1**	**0**	**1**	**19:46**
2006-07	**New Jersey**	**NHL**	**82**	**23**	**37**	**60**	**64**	**12**	**0**	**7**	**243**	**9.5**	**–9**	**23**	**34.8**	**18:33**	**11**	**2**	**6**	**8**	**7**	**1**	**0**	**1**	**19:16**
2007-08	**New Jersey**	**NHL**	**64**	**13**	**28**	**41**	**30**	**5**	**1**	**2**	**152**	**8.6**	**–1**	**18**	**55.6**	**18:18**	**5**	**0**	**4**	**4**	**4**	**0**	**0**	**0**	**18:30**
	NHL Totals		**803**	**180**	**296**	**476**	**660**	**54**	**10**	**41**	**1817**	**9.9**		**880**	**45.9**	**17:16**	**128**	**31**	**51**	**82**	**121**	**8**	**0**	**12**	**17:38**

Traded to **New Jersey** by **Dallas** with Joe Nieuwendyk for Jason Arnott, Randy McKay and New Jersey's 1st round choice (later traded to Columbus – later traded to Buffalo – Buffalo selected Dan Paille) in 2002 Entry Draft, March 19, 2002. Signed as a free agent by **Ingolstadt** (Germany), January 24, 2005.

LANGFELD, Josh

(LANG-fehld, JAWSH)

Right wing. Shoots right. 6'3", 216 lbs. Born, Fridley, MN, July 17, 1977. Ottawa's 3rd choice, 66th overall, in 1997 Entry Draft.

			Regular Season														Playoffs								
Season	Club	League	GP	G	A	Pts	PIM	PP	SH	GW	S	%	+/-	TF	F%	Min	GP	G	A	Pts	PIM	PP	SH	GW	Min
1995-96	Great Falls	AFHL	45	45	40	85	105	....	....	....	....	....	....	....	....	....	....	....	....	....	....	....	....	....	....
1996-97	Lincoln Stars	USHL	38	35	23	58	100	....	....	....	....	....	....	....	....	....	14	8	*13	*21	42	....	....	....	....
1997-98	U. of Michigan	CCHA	46	19	17	36	66	....	....	....	....	....	....	....	....	....	....	....	....	....	....	....	....	....	....
1998-99	U. of Michigan	CCHA	41	21	14	35	84	....	....	....	....	....	....	....	....	....	....	....	....	....	....	....	....	....	....
99-2000	U. of Michigan	CCHA	39	9	21	30	56	....	....	....	....	....	....	....	....	....	....	....	....	....	....	....	....	....	....
2000-01	U. of Michigan	CCHA	42	16	12	28	44	....	....	....	....	....	....	....	....	....	....	....	....	....	....	....	....	....	....
2001-02	**Ottawa**	**NHL**	**1**	**0**	**0**	**0**	**2**	**0**	**0**	**0**	**5**	**0.0**	**0**	**0**	**0.0**	**8:15**	....	....	....	....	....	....	....	....	....
	Grand Rapids	AHL	68	21	16	37	29	....	....	....	....	....	....	....	....	....	5	2	0	2	0	....	....	....	....
2002-03	**Ottawa**	**NHL**	**12**	**0**	**1**	**1**	**4**	**0**	**0**	**0**	**16**	**0.0**	**2**	**0**	**0.0**	**11:11**	....	....	....	....	....	....	....	....	....
	Binghamton	AHL	59	14	21	35	38	....	....	....	....	....	....	....	....	....	13	5	3	8	8	....	....	....	....
2003-04	**Ottawa**	**NHL**	**38**	**7**	**10**	**17**	**16**	**2**	**0**	**2**	**59**	**11.9**	**6**	**5**	**80.0**	**10:53**	....	....	....	....	....	....	....	....	....
	Binghamton	AHL	30	13	14	27	25	....	....	....	....	....	....	....	....	....	2	0	0	0	0	....	....	....	....
2004-05	Binghamton	AHL	74	32	25	57	75	....	....	....	....	....	....	....	....	....	6	2	2	4	2	....	....	....	....
2005-06	**San Jose**	**NHL**	**39**	**2**	**9**	**11**	**16**	**0**	**1**	**0**	**53**	**3.8**	**4**	**8**	**12.5**	**11:46**	....	....	....	....	....	....	....	....	....
	Boston	**NHL**	**18**	**0**	**1**	**1**	**10**	**0**	**0**	**0**	**32**	**0.0**	**–6**	**6**	**16.7**	**9:24**	....	....	....	....	....	....	....	....	....

Season	Club	League	Regular Season GP	G	A	Pts	PIM	PP	SH	GW	S	%	+/-	TF	F%	Min	Playoffs GP	G	A	Pts	PIM	PP	SH	GW	Min
2006-07	**Detroit**	**NHL**	33	0	2	2	12	0	0	0	37	0.0	2	1	100.0	5:33	....	....	....	....	....	....	....	....	....
	Grand Rapids	AHL	38	13	19	32	44	....	....	....	....	....	....	....	....	....	....	....	....	....	....	....	....	....	....
2007-08	**Nashville**	**NHL**	2	0	0	0	0	0	0	0	5	0.0	0	0	0.0	9:48	1	0	0	0	0	0	0	0	6:30
	Milwaukee	AHL	44	22	7	29	34	....	....	....	....	....	....	....	....	....	5	5	1	6	6	....	....	....	....
	NHL Totals		143	9	23	32	60	2	1	2	207	4.3		20	35.0	9:42	1	0	0	0	0	0	0	0	6:30

NCAA Championship All-Tournament Team (1998)

Signed as a free agent by **San Jose**, September 12, 2005. Claimed on waivers by **Boston** from **San Jose**, January 31, 2006. Signed as a free agent by **Detroit**, July 14, 2006. Signed as a free agent by **Nashville**, September 4, 2007.

LANGKOW, Daymond

(LANG-kow, DAY-muhn) **CGY.**

Center. Shoots left. 5'11", 181 lbs. Born, Edmonton, Alta., September 27, 1976. Tampa Bay's 1st choice, 5th overall, in 1995 Entry Draft.

Season	Club	League	GP	G	A	Pts	PIM	PP	SH	GW	S	%	+/-	TF	F%	Min	GP	G	A	Pts	PIM	PP	SH	GW	Min
1991-92	Edmonton Pats	AMHL	35	36	45	81	100	....	....	....	....	....	....	....	....	....	....	....	....	....	....	....	....	....	....
	Tri-City	WHL	1	0	0	0	0	....	....	....	....	....	....	....	....	....	....	....	....	....	....	....	....	....	....
1992-93	Tri-City	WHL	64	22	42	64	100	....	....	....	....	....	....	....	....	....	4	1	0	1	4	....	....	....	....
1993-94	Tri-City	WHL	61	40	43	83	174	....	....	....	....	....	....	....	....	....	4	2	2	4	15	....	....	....	....
1994-95	Tri-City	WHL	72	*67	73	*140	142	....	....	....	....	....	....	....	....	....	17	12	15	27	52	....	....	....	....
1995-96	Tri-City	WHL	48	30	61	91	103	....	....	....	....	....	....	....	....	....	11	14	13	27	20	....	....	....	....
	Tampa Bay	**NHL**	4	0	1	1	0	0	0	0	4	0.0	–1	....	....	....	....	....	....	....	....	....	....	....	....
1996-97	**Tampa Bay**	**NHL**	79	15	13	28	35	3	1	1	170	8.8	1	....	....	....	....	....	....	....	....	....	....	....	....
	Adirondack	AHL	2	1	1	2	0	....	....	....	....	....	....	....	....	....	....	....	....	....	....	....	....	....	....
1997-98	**Tampa Bay**	**NHL**	68	8	14	22	62	2	0	1	156	5.1	–9	....	....	....	....	....	....	....	....	....	....	....	....
1998-99	**Tampa Bay**	**NHL**	22	4	6	10	15	1	0	1	40	10.0	0	399	48.4	17:10	....	....	....	....	....	....	....	....	....
	Cleveland	IHL	4	1	1	2	18	....	....	....	....	....	....	....	....	....	....	....	....	....	....	....	....	....	....
	Philadelphia	**NHL**	56	10	13	23	24	3	1	1	109	9.2	–8	738	48.0	15:12	6	0	2	2	2	0	0	0	16:50
99-2000	**Philadelphia**	**NHL**	82	18	32	50	56	5	0	7	222	8.1	1	1263	45.1	16:57	16	5	5	10	23	1	1	2	20:03
2000-01	**Philadelphia**	**NHL**	71	13	41	54	50	3	0	2	190	6.8	12	1181	47.2	18:38	6	2	4	6	2	1	0	0	20:17
2001-02	**Phoenix**	**NHL**	80	27	35	62	36	6	3	2	171	15.8	18	1379	46.2	19:11	5	1	0	1	0	0	0	0	21:06
2002-03	**Phoenix**	**NHL**	82	20	32	52	56	4	2	2	196	10.2	20	1972	46.5	21:00	....	....	....	....	....	....	....	....	....
2003-04	**Phoenix**	**NHL**	81	21	31	52	40	4	1	2	174	12.1	4	1472	43.1	21:07	....	....	....	....	....	....	....	....	....
2004-05				DID NOT PLAY																					
2005-06	**Calgary**	**NHL**	82	25	34	59	46	11	0	7	171	14.6	2	1130	47.4	18:07	7	1	5	6	6	1	0	0	19:42
2006-07	**Calgary**	**NHL**	81	33	44	77	44	10	1	6	247	13.4	23	1173	45.9	20:07	6	2	2	4	4	2	0	1	20:06
2007-08	**Calgary**	**NHL**	80	30	35	65	19	14	1	4	201	14.9	16	817	43.7	18:50	7	3	2	5	0	2	0	0	18:21
	NHL Totals		868	224	331	555	483	66	10	36	2051	10.9		11524	45.9	18:52	53	14	20	34	37	7	1	3	19:33

WHL West First All-Star Team (1995) • Canadian Major Junior First All-Star Team (1995) • WHL West Second All-Star Team (1996)

Traded to **Philadelphia** by **Tampa Bay** with Mikael Renberg for Chris Gratton and Mike Sillinger, December 12, 1998. Traded to **Phoenix** by **Philadelphia** for Phoenix's 2nd round choice (later traded to Tampa Bay – later traded to San Jose – San Jose selected Dan Spang) in 2002 Entry Draft and Phoenix's 1st round choice (Jeff Carter) in 2003 Entry Draft, July 2, 2001. Traded to **Calgary** by **Phoenix** for Denis Gauthier and Oleg Saprykin, August 26, 2004.

LAPERRIERE, Ian

(luh-PAIR-ee-YAIR, EE-an) **COL.**

Right wing. Shoots right. 6'1", 200 lbs. Born, Montreal, Que., January 19, 1974. St. Louis' 6th choice, 158th overall, in 1992 Entry Draft.

Season	Club	League	GP	G	A	Pts	PIM	PP	SH	GW	S	%	+/-	TF	F%	Min	GP	G	A	Pts	PIM	PP	SH	GW	Min
1989-90	Mtl-Bourassa	QAAA	22	4	10	14	10	....	....	....	....	....	....	....	....	....	3	0	1	1	6	....	....	....	....
1990-91	Drummondville	QMJHL	65	19	29	48	117	....	....	....	....	....	....	....	....	....	14	2	9	11	48	....	....	....	....
1991-92	Drummondville	QMJHL	70	28	49	77	160	....	....	....	....	....	....	....	....	....	4	2	2	4	9	....	....	....	....
1992-93	Drummondville	QMJHL	60	44	*96	140	188	....	....	....	....	....	....	....	....	....	10	6	13	19	20	....	....	....	....
1993-94	Drummondville	QMJHL	62	41	72	113	150	....	....	....	....	....	....	....	....	....	9	4	6	10	35	....	....	....	....
	St. Louis	**NHL**	1	0	0	0	0	0	0	0	1	0.0	0	....	....	....	....	....	....	....	....	....	....	....	....
	Peoria Rivermen	IHL	....	....	....	....	....	....	....	....	....	....	....	....	....	....	5	1	3	4	2	....	....	....	....
1994-95	Peoria Rivermen	IHL	51	16	32	48	111	....	....	....	....	....	....	....	....	....	....	....	....	....	....	....	....	....	....
	St. Louis	**NHL**	37	13	14	27	85	1	0	1	53	24.5	12	....	....	....	7	0	4	4	21	0	0	0	....
1995-96	**St. Louis**	**NHL**	33	3	6	9	87	1	0	1	31	9.7	–4	....	....	....	....	....	....	....	....	....	....	....	....
	Worcester IceCats	AHL	3	2	1	3	22	....	....	....	....	....	....	....	....	....	....	....	....	....	....	....	....	....	....
	NY Rangers	**NHL**	28	1	2	3	53	0	0	0	21	4.8	–5	....	....	....	....	....	....	....	....	....	....	....	....
	Los Angeles	**NHL**	10	2	3	5	15	0	0	0	18	11.1	–2	....	....	....	....	....	....	....	....	....	....	....	....
1996-97	**Los Angeles**	**NHL**	62	8	15	23	102	0	1	2	84	9.5	–25	....	....	....	....	....	....	....	....	....	....	....	....
1997-98	**Los Angeles**	**NHL**	77	6	15	21	131	0	1	1	74	8.1	0	....	....	....	4	1	0	1	6	0	0	0	....
1998-99	**Los Angeles**	**NHL**	72	3	10	13	138	0	0	1	62	4.8	–5	643	47.3	11:47	....	....	....	....	....	....	....	....	....
99-2000	**Los Angeles**	**NHL**	79	9	13	22	185	0	0	1	87	10.3	–14	1111	53.7	13:15	4	0	0	0	2	0	0	0	10:22
2000-01	**Los Angeles**	**NHL**	79	8	10	18	141	0	0	0	60	13.3	5	297	51.9	12:02	13	1	2	3	12	0	0	0	14:01
2001-02	**Los Angeles**	**NHL**	81	8	14	22	125	0	0	3	89	9.0	5	134	49.3	13:45	7	0	1	1	9	0	0	0	14:18
2002-03	**Los Angeles**	**NHL**	73	7	12	19	122	1	1	1	85	8.2	–9	317	49.2	15:46	....	....	....	....	....	....	....	....	....
2003-04	**Los Angeles**	**NHL**	62	10	12	22	58	1	0	3	59	16.9	–4	446	54.0	15:50	....	....	....	....	....	....	....	....	....
2004-05				DID NOT PLAY																					
2005-06	**Colorado**	**NHL**	82	21	24	45	116	1	1	3	133	15.8	3	963	45.9	17:10	9	0	1	1	27	0	0	0	13:40
2006-07	**Colorado**	**NHL**	81	8	21	29	133	0	0	0	118	6.8	5	389	46.8	13:51	....	....	....	....	....	....	....	....	....
2007-08	**Colorado**	**NHL**	70	4	15	19	140	0	0	1	68	5.9	–5	141	45.4	13:39	10	1	1	2	19	0	0	0	12:54
	NHL Totals		927	111	186	297	1631	5	4	18	1043	10.6		4441	49.7	14:06	54	3	9	12	96	0	0	0	13:23

QMJHL Second All-Star Team (1993)

Traded to **NY Rangers** by **St. Louis** for Stephane Matteau, December 28, 1995. Traded to **Los Angeles** by **NY Rangers** with Ray Ferraro, Mattias Norstrom, Nathan LaFayette and NY Rangers' 4th round choice (Sean Blanchard) in 1997 Entry Draft for Marty McSorley, Jari Kurri and Shane Churla, March 14, 1996. Signed as a free agent by **Colorado**, July 2, 2004.

LAPIERRE, Maxim

(la-PEE-air, MAX-ihm) **MTL.**

Center. Shoots right. 6'2", 200 lbs. Born, St. Leonard, Que., March 29, 1985. Montreal's 3rd choice, 61st overall, in 2003 Entry Draft.

Season	Club	League	GP	G	A	Pts	PIM	PP	SH	GW	S	%	+/-	TF	F%	Min	GP	G	A	Pts	PIM	PP	SH	GW	Min
2001-02	Cap-d-Madeleine	QAAA	42	14	27	41	44	....	....	....	....	....	....	....	....	....	10	3	5	8	16	....	....	....	....
	Montreal Rocket	QMJHL	9	2	0	2	2	....	....	....	....	....	....	....	....	....	....	....	....	....	....	....	....	....	....
2002-03	Montreal Rocket	QMJHL	72	22	21	43	55	....	....	....	....	....	....	....	....	....	7	1	3	4	6	....	....	....	....
2003-04	PEI Rocket	QMJHL	67	25	36	61	138	....	....	....	....	....	....	....	....	....	11	7	2	9	14	....	....	....	....
2004-05	PEI Rocket	QMJHL	69	25	27	52	139	....	....	....	....	....	....	....	....	....	....	....	....	....	....	....	....	....	....
2005-06	**Montreal**	**NHL**	1	0	0	0	0	0	0	0	0	0.0	–1	2	50.0	3:04	....	....	....	....	....	....	....	....	....
	Hamilton	AHL	73	13	23	36	214	....	....	....	....	....	....	....	....	....	....	....	....	....	....	....	....	....	....
2006-07	**Montreal**	**NHL**	46	6	6	12	24	0	1	2	82	7.3	–7	425	45.2	11:25	....	....	....	....	....	....	....	....	....
	Hamilton	AHL	37	11	13	24	59	....	....	....	....	....	....	....	....	....	22	6	6	12	41	....	....	....	....
2007-08	**Montreal**	**NHL**	53	7	11	18	60	0	0	0	68	10.3	5	527	49.2	13:10	12	0	3	3	6	0	0	0	11:38
	Hamilton	AHL	19	7	7	14	63	....	....	....	....	....	....	....	....	....	....	....	....	....	....	....	....	....	....
	NHL Totals		100	13	17	30	84	0	1	2	150	8.7		954	47.4	12:16	12	0	3	3	6	0	0	0	11:38

LAPOINTE, Martin

(luh-POYNT, MAHR-tihn)

Right wing. Shoots right. 5'11", 215 lbs. Born, Ville St-Pierre, Que., September 12, 1973. Detroit's 1st choice, 10th overall, in 1991 Entry Draft.

Season	Club	League	GP	G	A	Pts	PIM	PP	SH	GW	S	%	+/-	TF	F%	Min	GP	G	A	Pts	PIM	PP	SH	GW	Min
1988-89	Lac St-Louis Lions	QAAA	42	39	45	84	46	....	....	....	....	....	....	....	....	....	3	6	2	8	4	....	....	....	....
1989-90	Laval Titan	QMJHL	65	42	54	96	77	....	....	....	....	....	....	....	....	....	14	8	17	25	54	....	....	....	....
1990-91	Laval Titan	QMJHL	64	44	54	98	66	....	....	....	....	....	....	....	....	....	13	7	14	21	26	....	....	....	....
1991-92	Laval Titan	QMJHL	31	25	30	55	84	....	....	....	....	....	....	....	....	....	10	4	10	14	32	....	....	....	....
	Detroit	**NHL**	4	0	1	1	5	0	0	0	2	0.0	2	....	....	....	3	0	1	1	4	0	0	0	....
	Adirondack	AHL	....	....	....	....	....	....	....	....	....	....	....	....	....	....	8	2	2	4	4	....	....	....	....
1992-93	Laval Titan	QMJHL	35	38	51	89	41	....	....	....	....	....	....	....	....	....	13	*13	*17	*30	22	....	....	....	....
	Detroit	**NHL**	3	0	0	0	0	0	0	0	2	0.0	–2	....	....	....	....	....	....	....	....	....	....	....	....
	Adirondack	AHL	8	1	2	3	9	....	....	....	....	....	....	....	....	....	....	....	....	....	....	....	....	....	....
1993-94	**Detroit**	**NHL**	50	8	8	16	55	2	0	0	45	17.8	7	....	....	....	4	0	0	0	6	0	0	0	....
	Adirondack	AHL	28	25	21	46	47	....	....	....	....	....	....	....	....	....	4	1	1	2	8	....	....	....	....
1994-95	Adirondack	AHL	39	29	16	45	80	....	....	....	....	....	....	....	....	....	....	....	....	....	....	....	....	....	....
	Detroit	**NHL**	39	4	6	10	73	0	0	1	46	8.7	1	....	....	....	2	0	1	1	8	0	0	0	....
1995-96	**Detroit**	**NHL**	58	6	3	9	93	1	0	0	76	7.9	0	....	....	....	11	1	2	3	12	0	0	0	....
1996-97 ♦	**Detroit**	**NHL**	78	16	17	33	167	5	1	1	149	10.7	–14	....	....	....	20	4	8	12	60	1	0	1	....
1997-98 ♦	**Detroit**	**NHL**	79	15	19	34	106	4	0	3	154	9.7	0	....	....	....	21	9	6	15	20	2	1	1	....
1998-99	**Detroit**	**NHL**	77	16	13	29	141	7	1	4	153	10.5	7	217	47.9	15:06	10	0	2	2	20	0	0	0	11:43
99-2000	**Detroit**	**NHL**	82	16	25	41	121	1	1	2	127	12.6	17	287	54.4	14:43	9	3	1	4	20	2	0	1	14:28

			Regular Season														Playoffs								
Season	Club	League	GP	G	A	Pts	PIM	PP	SH	GW	S	%	+/-	TF	F%	Min	GP	G	A	Pts	PIM	PP	SH	GW	Min
2000-01	**Detroit**	**NHL**	**82**	**27**	**30**	**57**	**127**	**13**	**0**	**8**	**181**	**14.9**	**3**	**461**	**53.2**	**16:06**	**6**	**0**	**1**	**1**	**8**	**0**	**0**	**0**	**16:53**
2001-02	**Boston**	**NHL**	**68**	**17**	**23**	**40**	**101**	**4**	**0**	**2**	**141**	**12.1**	**12**	**222**	**53.6**	**17:22**	**6**	**1**	**2**	**3**	**12**	**1**	**0**	**1**	**16:58**
2002-03	**Boston**	**NHL**	**59**	**8**	**10**	**18**	**87**	**1**	**0**	**1**	**110**	**7.3**	**–19**	**52**	**48.1**	**15:22**	**5**	**1**	**0**	**1**	**14**	**0**	**0**	**0**	**14:39**
2003-04	**Boston**	**NHL**	**78**	**15**	**10**	**25**	**67**	**9**	**0**	**2**	**136**	**11.0**	**–5**	**101**	**51.5**	**14:26**	**7**	**0**	**0**	**0**	**14**	**0**	**0**	**0**	**15:21**
2004-05			DID NOT PLAY																						
2005-06	**Chicago**	**NHL**	**82**	**14**	**17**	**31**	**106**	**6**	**0**	**3**	**135**	**10.4**	**–30**	**354**	**56.5**	**14:46**	....	....	....	....	....	....	....	....	....
2006-07	**Chicago**	**NHL**	**82**	**13**	**11**	**24**	**98**	**5**	**1**	**2**	**102**	**12.7**	**–14**	**341**	**52.8**	**13:59**	....	....	....	....	....	....	....	....	....
2007-08	**Chicago**	**NHL**	**52**	**3**	**4**	**7**	**47**	**0**	**0**	**0**	**39**	**7.7**	**–3**	**23**	**39.1**	**8:38**	....	....	....	....	....	....	....	....	....
	Ottawa	**NHL**	**18**	**3**	**3**	**6**	**23**	**1**	**0**	**0**	**24**	**12.5**	**–2**	**0**	**0.0**	**11:37**	**4**	**0**	**0**	**0**	**4**	**0**	**0**	**0**	**8:14**
	NHL Totals		**991**	**181**	**200**	**381**	**1417**	**59**	**4**	**29**	**1622**	**11.2**		**2058**	**53.0**	**14:35**	**108**	**19**	**24**	**43**	**202**	**6**	**1**	**4**	**14:08**

QMJHL First All-Star Team (1990, 1993) • QMJHL Offensive Rookie of the Year (1990) • QMJHL Second All-Star Team (1991) • Memorial Cup Tournament All-Star Team (1993)

Signed as a free agent by **Boston**, July 2, 2001. Signed as a free agent by **Chicago**, August 3, 2005. Traded to **Ottawa** by **Chicago** for Ottawa's 6th round choice (Ben Smith) in 2008 Entry Draft, February 26, 2008.

LARAQUE, Georges (luh-RAK, ZHAWRZH) MTL.

Right wing. Shoots right. 6'3", 243 lbs. Born, Montreal, Que., December 7, 1976. Edmonton's 2nd choice, 31st overall, in 1995 Entry Draft.

1991-92	Mtl-Bourassa	QAHA	28	20	20	40	30	....	....	....	....	....	....	....	....	....	....	....	....	....	....	....	....	....	....
1992-93	Mtl-Bourassa	QAAA	37	8	20	28	50	....	....	....	....	....	....	....	....	....	3	1	2	3	2	....	....	....	....
1993-94	St-Jean Lynx	QMJHL	70	11	11	22	142	....	....	....	....	....	....	....	....	....	4	0	0	0	7	....	....	....	....
1994-95	St-Jean Lynx	QMJHL	62	19	22	41	259	....	....	....	....	....	....	....	....	....	7	1	1	2	42	....	....	....	....
1995-96	Laval Titan	QMJHL	11	8	13	21	76	....	....	....	....	....	....	....	....	....	....	....	....	....	....	....	....	....	....
	St-Hyacinthe	QMJHL	8	3	4	7	59	....	....	....	....	....	....	....	....	....	....	....	....	....	....	....	....	....	....
	Granby	QMJHL	22	9	7	16	125	....	....	....	....	....	....	....	....	....	18	7	6	13	104	....	....	....	....
1996-97	Hamilton	AHL	73	14	20	34	179	....	....	....	....	....	....	....	....	....	15	1	3	4	12	....	....	....	....
1997-98	**Edmonton**	**NHL**	**11**	**0**	**0**	**0**	**59**	**0**	**0**	**0**	**4**	**0.0**	**–4**	....	....	....	....	....	....	....	....	....	....	....	....
	Hamilton	AHL	46	10	20	30	154	....	....	....	....	....	....	....	....	....	3	0	0	0	11	....	....	....	....
1998-99	**Edmonton**	**NHL**	**39**	**3**	**2**	**5**	**57**	**0**	**0**	**0**	**17**	**17.6**	**–1**	**0**	**0.0**	**5:31**	**4**	**0**	**0**	**0**	**2**	**0**	**0**	**0**	**7:35**
	Hamilton	AHL	25	6	8	14	93	....	....	....	....	....	....	....	....	....	....	....	....	....	....	....	....	....	....
99-2000	**Edmonton**	**NHL**	**76**	**8**	**8**	**16**	**123**	**0**	**0**	**0**	**56**	**14.3**	**5**	**0**	**0.0**	**8:28**	**5**	**0**	**1**	**1**	**6**	**0**	**0**	**0**	**9:14**
2000-01	**Edmonton**	**NHL**	**82**	**13**	**16**	**29**	**148**	**1**	**0**	**1**	**73**	**17.8**	**5**	**0**	**0.0**	**9:03**	**6**	**1**	**1**	**2**	**8**	**0**	**0**	**0**	**9:54**
2001-02	**Edmonton**	**NHL**	**80**	**5**	**14**	**19**	**157**	**1**	**0**	**1**	**95**	**5.3**	**6**	**0**	**0.0**	**9:48**	....	....	....	....	....	....	....	....	....
2002-03	**Edmonton**	**NHL**	**64**	**6**	**7**	**13**	**110**	**0**	**0**	**2**	**46**	**13.0**	**–4**	**0**	**0.0**	**9:15**	**6**	**1**	**3**	**4**	**4**	**0**	**0**	**0**	**12:11**
2003-04	**Edmonton**	**NHL**	**66**	**6**	**11**	**17**	**99**	**1**	**0**	**1**	**54**	**11.1**	**7**	**0**	**0.0**	**9:22**	....	....	....	....	....	....	....	....	....
2004-05	AIK Solna	Sweden-3	16	11	5	16	24	....	....	....	....	....	....	....	....	....	....	....	....	....	....	....	....	....	....
2005-06	**Edmonton**	**NHL**	**72**	**2**	**10**	**12**	**73**	**0**	**0**	**0**	**50**	**4.0**	**–5**	**3**	**33.3**	**6:35**	**15**	**1**	**1**	**2**	***44**	**0**	**0**	**0**	**5:31**
2006-07	**Phoenix**	**NHL**	**56**	**5**	**17**	**22**	**52**	**1**	**0**	**0**	**34**	**14.7**	**7**	**14**	**28.6**	**10:17**	....	....	....	....	....	....	....	....	....
	Pittsburgh	**NHL**	**17**	**0**	**2**	**2**	**18**	**0**	**0**	**0**	**10**	**0.0**	**–3**	**3**	**33.3**	**7:34**	**2**	**0**	**0**	**0**	**0**	**0**	**0**	**0**	**4:25**
2007-08	**Pittsburgh**	**NHL**	**71**	**4**	**9**	**13**	**141**	**0**	**0**	**2**	**29**	**13.8**	**0**	**1**	**0.0**	**7:42**	**15**	**1**	**2**	**3**	**4**	**0**	**0**	**0**	**6:02**
	NHL Totals		**634**	**52**	**96**	**148**	**1037**	**4**	**0**	**7**	**468**	**11.1**		**21**	**28.6**	**8:32**	**53**	**4**	**8**	**12**	**68**	**0**	**0**	**0**	**7:23**

Signed as a free agent by **Solna** (Sweden-3), January 31, 2005. Signed as a free agent by **Phoenix**, July 5, 2006. Traded to **Pittsburgh** by **Phoenix** for Daniel Carcillo and Pittsburgh's 3rd round choice (later traded to NY Rangers - NY Rangers selected Tomas Kundratek) in 2008 Entry Draft, February 27, 2007. Signed as a free agent by **Montreal**, July 3, 2008.

LARMAN, Drew (LAHR-man, DROO) FLA.

Center. Shoots right. 6'3", 195 lbs. Born, Canton, MI, May 15, 1985.

2002-03	Sarnia Sting	OHL	67	4	14	18	25	....	....	....	....	....	....	....	....	....	....	....	....	....	....	....	....	....	....
2003-04	Sarnia Sting	OHL	68	9	18	27	13	....	....	....	....	....	....	....	....	....	5	0	1	1	0	....	....	....	....
2004-05	Sarnia Sting	OHL	12	2	0	2	6	....	....	....	....	....	....	....	....	....	....	....	....	....	....	....	....	....	....
	London Knights	OHL	58	11	10	21	28	....	....	....	....	....	....	....	....	....	18	3	4	7	8	....	....	....	....
2005-06	Rochester	AHL	44	7	8	15	24	....	....	....	....	....	....	....	....	....	....	....	....	....	....	....	....	....	....
	Florida Everblades	ECHL	6	0	0	0	4	....	....	....	....	....	....	....	....	....	8	4	2	6	4	....	....	....	....
2006-07	**Florida**	**NHL**	**16**	**2**	**0**	**2**	**2**	**0**	**0**	**0**	**15**	**13.3**	**–3**	**97**	**46.4**	**7:23**	....	....	....	....	....	....	....	....	....
	Rochester	AHL	54	17	11	28	35	....	....	....	....	....	....	....	....	....	....	....	....	....	....	....	....	....	....
2007-08	**Florida**	**NHL**	**6**	**0**	**1**	**1**	**2**	**0**	**0**	**0**	**1**	**0.0**	**1**	**26**	**38.5**	**6:00**	....	....	....	....	....	....	....	....	....
	Rochester	AHL	54	10	12	22	44	....	....	....	....	....	....	....	....	....	....	....	....	....	....	....	....	....	....
	NHL Totals		**22**	**2**	**1**	**3**	**4**	**0**	**0**	**0**	**16**	**12.5**		**123**	**44.7**	**7:00**	....	....	....	....	....	....	....	....	....

Signed as a free agent by **Florida**, September 28, 2005.

LaROSE, Chad (lah-ROHZ, CHAD) CAR.

Right wing. Shoots right. 5'10", 181 lbs. Born, Fraser, MI, March 27, 1982.

99-2000	Sioux Falls	USHL	54	29	26	55	28	....	....	....	....	....	....	....	....	....	3	0	1	1	0	....	....	....	....
2000-01	Sioux Falls	USHL	24	11	22	33	50	....	....	....	....	....	....	....	....	....	....	....	....	....	....	....	....	....	....
	Plymouth Whalers	OHL	32	18	7	25	24	....	....	....	....	....	....	....	....	....	19	10	10	20	22	....	....	....	....
2001-02	Plymouth Whalers	OHL	53	32	27	59	40	....	....	....	....	....	....	....	....	....	6	3	4	7	16	....	....	....	....
2002-03	Plymouth Whalers	OHL	67	61	56	117	52	....	....	....	....	....	....	....	....	....	15	9	8	17	25	....	....	....	....
2003-04	Lowell	AHL	36	7	9	16	29	....	....	....	....	....	....	....	....	....	....	....	....	....	....	....	....	....	....
	Florida Everblades	ECHL	41	16	19	35	16	....	....	....	....	....	....	....	....	....	14	3	4	7	20	....	....	....	....
2004-05	Lowell	AHL	66	20	22	42	32	....	....	....	....	....	....	....	....	....	11	3	5	8	10	....	....	....	....
2005-06♦	**Carolina**	**NHL**	**49**	**1**	**12**	**13**	**35**	**0**	**0**	**1**	**62**	**1.6**	**7**	**5**	**40.0**	**10:35**	**21**	**0**	**1**	**1**	**10**	**0**	**0**	**0**	**8:58**
	Lowell	AHL	23	14	11	25	10	....	....	....	....	....	....	....	....	....	....	....	....	....	....	....	....	....	....
2006-07	**Carolina**	**NHL**	**80**	**6**	**12**	**18**	**10**	**0**	**2**	**0**	**94**	**6.4**	**–2**	**50**	**30.0**	**10:13**	....	....	....	....	....	....	....	....	....
2007-08	**Carolina**	**NHL**	**58**	**11**	**12**	**23**	**46**	**0**	**1**	**2**	**117**	**9.4**	**6**	**19**	**31.6**	**14:03**	....	....	....	....	....	....	....	....	....
	NHL Totals		**187**	**18**	**36**	**54**	**91**	**0**	**3**	**3**	**273**	**6.6**		**74**	**31.1**	**11:30**	**21**	**0**	**1**	**1**	**10**	**0**	**0**	**0**	**8:58**

OHL Second All-Star Team (2003)

Signed as a free agent by **Carolina**, August 6, 2003.

LAROSE, Cory (lah-ROHZ, KOH-ree) S.J.

Center. Shoots left. 6', 191 lbs. Born, Campbellton, N.B., May 14, 1975.

1993-94	Kimball Union	High-NH	21	18	11	29	14	....	....	....	....	....	....	....	....	....	....	....	....	....	....	....	....	....	....
1994-95	Langley Thunder	BCJHL	STATISTICS NOT AVAILABLE																						
1995-96	Langley Thunder	BCJHL	54	28	46	74	61	....	....	....	....	....	....	....	....	....	....	....	....	....	....	....	....	....	....
1996-97	U. of Maine	H-East	35	10	27	37	32	....	....	....	....	....	....	....	....	....	....	....	....	....	....	....	....	....	....
1997-98	U. of Maine	H-East	34	15	25	40	22	....	....	....	....	....	....	....	....	....	....	....	....	....	....	....	....	....	....
1998-99	U. of Maine	H-East	38	21	31	52	34	....	....	....	....	....	....	....	....	....	....	....	....	....	....	....	....	....	....
99-2000	U. of Maine	H-East	39	15	*36	51	45	....	....	....	....	....	....	....	....	....	....	....	....	....	....	....	....	....	....
2000-01	Cleveland	IHL	4	1	1	2	6	....	....	....	....	....	....	....	....	....	....	....	....	....	....	....	....	....	....
	Jackson Bandits	ECHL	63	21	32	53	73	....	....	....	....	....	....	....	....	....	5	2	2	4	12	....	....	....	....
2001-02	Houston Aeros	AHL	78	32	32	64	73	....	....	....	....	....	....	....	....	....	14	6	8	14	15	....	....	....	....
2002-03	Houston Aeros	AHL	58	18	38	56	57	....	....	....	....	....	....	....	....	....	....	....	....	....	....	....	....	....	....
	Hartford	AHL	24	9	10	19	20	....	....	....	....	....	....	....	....	....	2	0	1	1	0	....	....	....	....
2003-04	**NY Rangers**	**NHL**	**7**	**0**	**1**	**1**	**4**	**0**	**0**	**0**	**10**	**0.0**	**–2**	**40**	**47.5**	**11:27**	....	....	....	....	....	....	....	....	....
	Hartford	AHL	69	13	36	49	66	....	....	....	....	....	....	....	....	....	14	4	6	10	24	....	....	....	....
2004-05	Chicago Wolves	AHL	80	26	37	63	44	....	....	....	....	....	....	....	....	....	18	6	6	12	29	....	....	....	....
2005-06	Langnau	Swiss	42	17	14	31	76	....	....	....	....	....	....	....	....	....	6	4	3	7	6	....	....	....	....
2006-07	Chicago Wolves	AHL	63	22	61	83	75	....	....	....	....	....	....	....	....	....	15	3	4	7	21	....	....	....	....
2007-08	Ak Bars Kazan	Russia	4	0	0	0	0	....	....	....	....	....	....	....	....	....	....	....	....	....	....	....	....	....	....
	Lulea HF	Sweden	47	10	18	28	83	....	....	....	....	....	....	....	....	....	....	....	....	....	....	....	....	....	....
	NHL Totals		**7**	**0**	**1**	**1**	**4**	**0**	**0**	**0**	**10**	**0.0**		**40**	**47.5**	**11:27**	....	....	....	....	....	....	....	....	....

Hockey East First All-Star Team (2000) • NCAA East Second All-American Team (2000) • AHL All-Rookie Team (2002)

Signed as a free agent by **Minnesota**, May 10, 2000. Traded to **NY Rangers** by **Minnesota** for Jay Henderson, February 20, 2003. Signed as a free agent by **Atlanta**, July 14, 2004. Signed as a free agent by **Langnau** (Swiss), May 5, 2005. Signed as a free agent by **Atlanta**, June 21, 2006. Signed as a free agent by **San Jose**, July 15, 2008.

LARSEN, Brad

(LAR-suhn, BRAD) **ATL.**

Left wing. Shoots left. 6', 210 lbs. Born, Nakusp, B.C., June 28, 1977. Colorado's 5th choice, 87th overall, in 1997 Entry Draft.

Season	Club	League	GP	G	A	Pts	PIM	PP	SH	GW	S	%	+/-	TF	F%	Min	GP	G	A	Pts	PIM	PP	SH	GW	Min
			Regular Season														Playoffs								
1992-93	Nelson	RMJHL	42	31	37	68	164	....	....	....	....	....	....	....	....	....	....	....	....	....	....	....	....	....	....
1993-94	Swift Current	WHL	64	15	18	33	32	....	....	....	....	....	....	....	....	....	7	1	2	3	4	....	....	....	....
1994-95	Swift Current	WHL	62	24	33	57	73	....	....	....	....	....	....	....	....	....	6	0	1	1	2	....	....	....	....
1995-96	Swift Current	WHL	51	30	47	77	67	....	....	....	....	....	....	....	....	....	6	3	2	5	13	....	....	....	....
1996-97	Swift Current	WHL	61	36	46	82	61	....	....	....	....	....	....	....	....	....	....	....	....	....	....	....	....	....	....
1997-98	**Colorado**	**NHL**	**1**	**0**	**0**	**0**	**0**	**0**	**0**	**0**	**0**	**0.0**	**0**	....	....	....	....	....	....	....	....	....	....	....	....
	Hershey Bears	AHL	65	12	10	22	80	....	....	....	....	....	....	....	....	....	7	3	2	5	2	....	....	....	....
1998-99	Hershey Bears	AHL	18	3	4	7	11	....	....	....	....	....	....	....	....	....	5	0	1	1	6	....	....	....	....
99-2000	Hershey Bears	AHL	52	13	26	39	66	....	....	....	....	....	....	....	....	....	14	5	2	7	29	....	....	....	....
2000-01	**Colorado**	**NHL**	**9**	**0**	**0**	**0**	**0**	**0**	**0**	**0**	**3**	**0.0**	**1**	**14**	**57.1**	**9:17**	....	....	....	....	....	....	....	....	....
	Hershey Bears	AHL	67	21	25	46	93	....	....	....	....	....	....	....	....	....	10	1	3	4	6	....	....	....	....
2001-02	**Colorado**	**NHL**	**50**	**2**	**7**	**9**	**47**	**1**	**0**	**0**	**38**	**5.3**	**4**	**71**	**54.9**	**8:07**	**21**	**1**	**1**	**2**	**13**	**0**	**0**	**0**	**7:07**
2002-03	**Colorado**	**NHL**	**6**	**0**	**3**	**3**	**2**	**0**	**0**	**0**	**6**	**0.0**	**3**	**31**	**41.9**	**8:17**	....	....	....	....	....	....	....	....	....
	Hershey Bears	AHL	25	3	6	9	25	....	....	....	....	....	....	....	....	....	4	1	1	2	8	....	....	....	....
2003-04	**Colorado**	**NHL**	**26**	**2**	**2**	**4**	**11**	**0**	**0**	**0**	**17**	**11.8**	**2**	**9**	**44.4**	**7:41**	....	....	....	....	....	....	....	....	....
	Hershey Bears	AHL	21	4	13	17	40	....	....	....	....	....	....	....	....	....	....	....	....	....	....	....	....	....	....
	Atlanta	**NHL**	**6**	**0**	**0**	**0**	**2**	**0**	**0**	**0**	**6**	**0.0**	**–2**	**6**	**66.7**	**13:39**	....	....	....	....	....	....	....	....	....
2004-05	Chicago Wolves	AHL	75	26	23	49	112	....	....	....	....	....	....	....	....	....	18	4	7	11	22	....	....	....	....
2005-06	**Atlanta**	**NHL**	**62**	**7**	**8**	**15**	**21**	**0**	**3**	**1**	**48**	**14.6**	**–3**	**81**	**34.6**	**10:59**	....	....	....	....	....	....	....	....	....
	Chicago Wolves	AHL	6	1	0	1	8	....	....	....	....	....	....	....	....	....	....	....	....	....	....	....	....	....	....
2006-07	**Atlanta**	**NHL**	**72**	**7**	**6**	**13**	**39**	**0**	**2**	**0**	**61**	**11.5**	**–11**	**82**	**39.0**	**12:22**	**4**	**0**	**2**	**2**	**0**	**0**	**0**	**0**	**16:57**
2007-08	**Atlanta**	**NHL**	**62**	**1**	**3**	**4**	**12**	**0**	**0**	**0**	**35**	**2.9**	**–17**	**81**	**42.0**	**9:02**	....	....	....	....	....	....	....	....	....
	NHL Totals		**294**	**19**	**29**	**48**	**134**	**1**	**5**	**1**	**214**	**8.9**		**375**	**43.2**	**10:05**	**25**	**1**	**3**	**4**	**13**	**0**	**0**	**0**	**8:41**

• Re-entered NHL Entry Draft. Originally Ottawa's 3rd choice, 53rd overall, in 1995 Entry Draft.

WHL East Second All-Star Team (1997)

Rights traded to **Colorado** by **Ottawa** for Janne Laukkanen, January 26, 1996. • Missed majority of 1998-99 season recovering from abdominal injury suffered in game vs. Albany (AHL), November 20, 1998. • Missed majority of 2002-03 season recovering from groin (October 27, 2002 vs. Minnesota) and back (December 11, 2002 vs. Vancouver) injuries. Claimed on waivers by **Atlanta** from **Colorado**, February 25, 2004.

LASHOFF, Matt

(LASH-awf, MAT) **BOS.**

Defense. Shoots left. 6'2", 198 lbs. Born, Albany, NY, September 29, 1986. Boston's 1st choice, 22nd overall, in 2005 Entry Draft.

Season	Club	League	GP	G	A	Pts	PIM	PP	SH	GW	S	%	+/-	TF	F%	Min	GP	G	A	Pts	PIM	PP	SH	GW	Min
2002-03	USNTDP	U-17	16	1	3	4	14	....	....	....	....	....	....	....	....	....	....	....	....	....	....	....	....	....	....
	USNTDP	NAHL	46	2	5	7	53	....	....	....	....	....	....	....	....	....	....	....	....	....	....	....	....	....	....
2003-04	Kitchener Rangers	OHL	62	5	19	24	94	....	....	....	....	....	....	....	....	....	5	0	1	1	0	....	....	....	....
2004-05	Kitchener Rangers	OHL	44	4	18	22	44	....	....	....	....	....	....	....	....	....	13	0	3	3	18	....	....	....	....
2005-06	Kitchener Rangers	OHL	56	7	40	47	146	....	....	....	....	....	....	....	....	....	5	1	1	2	12	....	....	....	....
	Providence Bruins	AHL	7	1	1	2	6	....	....	....	....	....	....	....	....	....	6	0	0	0	6	....	....	....	....
2006-07	**Boston**	**NHL**	**12**	**0**	**2**	**2**	**12**	**0**	**0**	**0**	**8**	**0.0**	**–6**	**0**	**0.0**	**14:55**	....	....	....	....	....	....	....	....	....
	Providence Bruins	AHL	64	11	26	37	60	....	....	....	....	....	....	....	....	....	....	....	....	....	....	....	....	....	....
2007-08	**Boston**	**NHL**	**18**	**1**	**4**	**5**	**0**	**1**	**0**	**0**	**11**	**9.1**	**–2**	**0**	**0.0**	**13:35**	....	....	....	....	....	....	....	....	....
	Providence Bruins	AHL	60	9	27	36	79	....	....	....	....	....	....	....	....	....	9	0	4	4	6	....	....	....	....
	NHL Totals		**30**	**1**	**6**	**7**	**12**	**1**	**0**	**0**	**19**	**5.3**		**0**	**0.0**	**14:07**	....	....	....	....	....	....	....	....	....

AHL All-Rookie Team (2007)

LATENDRESSE, Guillaume

(lah-TEHN-drehs, GEE-OHM) **MTL.**

Right wing. Shoots left. 6'2", 222 lbs. Born, Ste-Catherine, Que., May 24, 1987. Montreal's 2nd choice, 45th overall, in 2005 Entry Draft.

Season	Club	League	GP	G	A	Pts	PIM	PP	SH	GW	S	%	+/-	TF	F%	Min	GP	G	A	Pts	PIM	PP	SH	GW	Min
2003-04	Drummondville	QMJHL	53	24	25	49	66	....	....	....	....	....	....	....	....	....	....	....	....	....	....	....	....	....	....
2004-05	Drummondville	QMJHL	65	29	49	78	76	....	....	....	....	....	....	....	....	....	6	6	4	10	7	....	....	....	....
2005-06	Drummondville	QMJHL	51	43	40	83	105	....	....	....	....	....	....	....	....	....	5	3	2	5	8	....	....	....	....
2006-07	**Montreal**	**NHL**	**80**	**16**	**13**	**29**	**47**	**5**	**0**	**3**	**121**	**13.2**	**–20**	**16**	**12.5**	**12:36**	....	....	....	....	....	....	....	....	....
2007-08	**Montreal**	**NHL**	**73**	**16**	**11**	**27**	**41**	**2**	**0**	**3**	**116**	**13.8**	**–2**	**8**	**25.0**	**12:15**	**8**	**0**	**1**	**1**	**19**	**0**	**0**	**0**	**10:43**
	NHL Totals		**153**	**32**	**24**	**56**	**88**	**7**	**0**	**6**	**237**	**13.5**		**24**	**16.7**	**12:26**	**8**	**0**	**1**	**1**	**19**	**0**	**0**	**0**	**10:43**

QMJHL All-Rookie Team (2004)

LaVALLEE, Jordan

(LA-VA-lee, JOHR-dahn) **ATL.**

Left wing. Shoots left. 6'3", 220 lbs. Born, Corvallis, OR, May 11, 1986. Atlanta's 5th choice, 116th overall, in 2005 Entry Draft.

Season	Club	League	GP	G	A	Pts	PIM	PP	SH	GW	S	%	+/-	TF	F%	Min	GP	G	A	Pts	PIM	PP	SH	GW	Min
2002-03	Quebec Remparts	QMJHL	55	3	6	9	54	....	....	....	....	....	....	....	....	....	11	0	1	1	0	....	....	....	....
2003-04	Quebec Remparts	QMJHL	69	11	16	27	111	....	....	....	....	....	....	....	....	....	5	2	0	2	6	....	....	....	....
2004-05	Quebec Remparts	QMJHL	64	40	26	66	108	....	....	....	....	....	....	....	....	....	13	5	2	7	26	....	....	....	....
2005-06	Quebec Remparts	QMJHL	37	18	19	37	34	....	....	....	....	....	....	....	....	....	23	7	8	15	30	....	....	....	....
2006-07	Chicago Wolves	AHL	79	16	18	34	90	....	....	....	....	....	....	....	....	....	14	7	1	8	8	....	....	....	....
2007-08	**Atlanta**	**NHL**	**2**	**1**	**1**	**2**	**0**	**0**	**0**	**0**	**1**	**100.0**	**2**	**0**	**0.0**	**11:28**	....	....	....	....	....	....	....	....	....
	Chicago Wolves	AHL	76	20	22	42	73	....	....	....	....	....	....	....	....	....	24	3	5	8	16	....	....	....	....
	NHL Totals		**2**	**1**	**1**	**2**	**0**	**0**	**0**	**0**	**1**	**100.0**		**0**	**0.0**	**11:28**	....	....	....	....	....	....	....	....	....

LEACH, Jay

(LEECH, JAY) **N.J.**

Defense. Shoots left. 6'4", 220 lbs. Born, Syracuse, NY, September 2, 1979. Phoenix's 5th choice, 115th overall, in 1998 Entry Draft.

Season	Club	League	GP	G	A	Pts	PIM	PP	SH	GW	S	%	+/-	TF	F%	Min	GP	G	A	Pts	PIM	PP	SH	GW	Min
1994-95	John Marshall	High-MN	10	0	0	0	14	....	....	....	....	....	....	....	....	....	....	....	....	....	....	....	....	....	....
1995-96	John Marshall	High-MN	11	1	2	3	8	....	....	....	....	....	....	....	....	....	4	0	0	0	0	....	....	....	....
	Capital District	Exhib.	53	3	8	11	33	....	....	....	....	....	....	....	....	....	....	....	....	....	....	....	....	....	....
1996-97	Capital District	Exhib.	57	8	50	58	140	....	....	....	....	....	....	....	....	....	....	....	....	....	....	....	....	....	....
1997-98	Providence	H-East	32	0	8	8	29	....	....	....	....	....	....	....	....	....	....	....	....	....	....	....	....	....	....
1998-99	Providence	H-East	33	1	8	9	42	....	....	....	....	....	....	....	....	....	....	....	....	....	....	....	....	....	....
99-2000	Providence	H-East	37	1	9	10	101	....	....	....	....	....	....	....	....	....	....	....	....	....	....	....	....	....	....
2000-01	Providence	H-East	40	4	21	25	104	....	....	....	....	....	....	....	....	....	....	....	....	....	....	....	....	....	....
2001-02	Mississippi	ECHL	70	3	13	16	116	....	....	....	....	....	....	....	....	....	10	1	1	2	8	....	....	....	....
2002-03	Springfield	AHL	9	0	0	0	0	....	....	....	....	....	....	....	....	....	....	....	....	....	....	....	....	....	....
	Augusta Lynx	ECHL	65	8	11	19	162	....	....	....	....	....	....	....	....	....	....	....	....	....	....	....	....	....	....
2003-04	Providence Bruins	AHL	3	0	0	0	4	....	....	....	....	....	....	....	....	....	....	....	....	....	....	....	....	....	....
	Long Beach	ECHL	3	0	1	1	4	....	....	....	....	....	....	....	....	....	....	....	....	....	....	....	....	....	....
	Bridgeport	AHL	23	0	1	1	33	....	....	....	....	....	....	....	....	....	....	....	....	....	....	....	....	....	....
	Trenton Titans	ECHL	31	2	11	13	45	....	....	....	....	....	....	....	....	....	7	0	1	1	10	....	....	....	....
2004-05	Providence Bruins	AHL	62	4	5	9	92	....	....	....	....	....	....	....	....	....	....	....	....	....	....	....	....	....	....
	Trenton Titans	ECHL	11	0	2	2	17	....	....	....	....	....	....	....	....	....	17	0	0	0	28	....	....	....	....
2005-06	**Boston**	**NHL**	**2**	**0**	**0**	**0**	**7**	**0**	**0**	**0**	**0**	**0.0**	**1**	**0**	**0.0**	**6:20**	....	....	....	....	....	....	....	....	....
	Providence Bruins	AHL	72	5	11	16	100	....	....	....	....	....	....	....	....	....	6	0	1	1	15	....	....	....	....
2006-07	Providence Bruins	AHL	73	2	5	7	128	....	....	....	....	....	....	....	....	....	13	0	4	4	13	....	....	....	....
2007-08	**Tampa Bay**	**NHL**	**2**	**0**	**0**	**0**	**0**	**0**	**0**	**0**	**0**	**0.0**	**–1**	**0**	**0.0**	**4:37**	....	....	....	....	....	....	....	....	....
	Norfolk Admirals	AHL	55	3	8	11	54	....	....	....	....	....	....	....	....	....	....	....	....	....	....	....	....	....	....
	Portland Pirates	AHL	20	3	6	9	30	....	....	....	....	....	....	....	....	....	18	1	0	1	7	....	....	....	....
	NHL Totals		**4**	**0**	**0**	**0**	**7**	**0**	**0**	**0**	**0**	**0.0**		**0**	**0.0**	**5:28**	....	....	....	....	....	....	....	....	....

Signed as a free agent by **Boston**, September 26, 2003. Signed as a free agent by **Tampa Bay**, July 3, 2007. Traded to **Anaheim** by **Tampa Bay** for Brandon Segal and Anaheim's 7th round choice (David Carle) in 2008 Entry Draft, February 26, 2008. Signed as a free agent by **New Jersey**, July 17, 2008.

LEAHY, Patrick
(LEH-hey, PAT-rihk)

Right wing. Shoots right. 6'3", 200 lbs. Born, Brighton, MA, June 9, 1979. NY Rangers' 5th choice, 122nd overall, in 1998 Entry Draft.

Season	Club	League	GP	G	A	Pts	PIM	PP	SH	GW	S	%	+/-	TF	F%	Min	Playoffs GP	G	A	Pts	PIM	PP	SH	GW	Min
1996-97	Bos. College High	High-MA	25	24	24	48	....	....	....	....	....	....	....	....	....	....	....	....	....	....	....	....	....	....	....
1997-98	Miami U.	CCHA	28	0	1	1	24	....	....	....	....	....	....	....	....	....	....	....	....	....	....	....	....	....	....
1998-99	Miami U.	CCHA	34	10	20	30	40	....	....	....	....	....	....	....	....	....	....	....	....	....	....	....	....	....	....
99-2000	Miami U.	CCHA	36	16	22	38	89	....	....	....	....	....	....	....	....	....	....	....	....	....	....	....	....	....	....
2000-01	Miami U.	CCHA	37	13	19	32	14	....	....	....	....	....	....	....	....	....	....	....	....	....	....	....	....	....	....
2001-02	Trenton Titans	ECHL	41	20	21	41	64	....	....	....	....	....	....	....	....	....	....	....	....	....	....	....	....	....	....
	Hershey Bears	AHL	9	1	2	3	8	....	....	....	....	....	....	....	....	....	....	....	....	....	....	....	....	....	....
	Portland Pirates	AHL	9	1	1	2	8	....	....	....	....	....	....	....	....	....	....	....	....	....	....	....	....	....	....
	Bridgeport	AHL	14	2	2	4	2	....	....	....	....	....	....	....	....	....	20	3	4	7	4	....	....	....	....
2002-03	Providence Bruins	AHL	66	20	23	43	63	....	....	....	....	....	....	....	....	....	4	1	0	1	18	....	....	....	....
2003-04	**Boston**	**NHL**	**6**	**0**	**0**	**0**	**0**	**0**	**0**	**0**	**2**	**0.0**	**1**	**0**	**0.0**	**5:27**	....	....	....	....	....	....	....	....	....
	Providence Bruins	AHL	55	14	16	30	37	....	....	....	....	....	....	....	....	....	2	0	0	0	0	....	....	....	....
2004-05	Providence Bruins	AHL	38	1	14	15	18	....	....	....	....	....	....	....	....	....	17	4	6	10	20	....	....	....	....
2005-06	**Boston**	**NHL**	**43**	**4**	**4**	**8**	**19**	**0**	**0**	**0**	**46**	**8.7**	**−2**	**12**	**58.3**	**9:06**	....	....	....	....	....	....	....	....	....
	Providence Bruins	AHL	4	1	2	3	4	....	....	....	....	....	....	....	....	....	....	....	....	....	....	....	....	....	....
2006-07	**Nashville**	**NHL**	**1**	**0**	**0**	**0**	**0**	**0**	**0**	**0**	**0**	**0.0**	**0**	**0**	**0.0**	**5:46**	....	....	....	....	....	....	....	....	....
	Milwaukee	AHL	52	10	21	31	30	....	....	....	....	....	....	....	....	....	3	1	1	2	2	....	....	....	....
2007-08	EHC Linz	Austria	44	20	25	45	44	....	....	....	....	....	....	....	....	....	....	....	....	....	....	....	....	....	....
	NHL Totals		**50**	**4**	**4**	**8**	**19**	**0**	**0**	**0**	**48**	**8.3**		**12**	**58.3**	**8:35**	....	....	....	....	....	....	....	....	....

Signed as a free agent by **Boston**, July 28, 2003. Signed as a free agent by **Nashville**, July 17, 2006. Signed as a free agent by **Linz** (Austria), September 4, 2007.

LEBDA, Brett
(LEHB-dah, BREHT) **DET.**

Defense. Shoots left. 5'9", 195 lbs. Born, Buffalo Grove, IL, January 15, 1982.

Season	Club	League	GP	G	A	Pts	PIM	PP	SH	GW	S	%	+/-	TF	F%	Min	Playoffs GP	G	A	Pts	PIM	PP	SH	GW	Min
1998-99	USNTDP	U-17	11	1	7	8	4	....	....	....	....	....	....	....	....	....	....	....	....	....	....	....	....	....	....
	USNTDP	USHL	3	0	0	0	0	....	....	....	....	....	....	....	....	....	....	....	....	....	....	....	....	....	....
	USNTDP	NAHL	52	11	17	28	56	....	....	....	....	....	....	....	....	....	....	....	....	....	....	....	....	....	....
99-2000	USNTDP	U-18	4	0	0	0	6	....	....	....	....	....	....	....	....	....	....	....	....	....	....	....	....	....	....
	USNTDP	USHL	22	6	7	13	28	....	....	....	....	....	....	....	....	....	....	....	....	....	....	....	....	....	....
2000-01	U. of Notre Dame	CCHA	39	7	19	26	109	....	....	....	....	....	....	....	....	....	....	....	....	....	....	....	....	....	....
2001-02	U. of Notre Dame	CCHA	34	6	8	14	54	....	....	....	....	....	....	....	....	....	....	....	....	....	....	....	....	....	....
2002-03	U. of Notre Dame	CCHA	40	7	14	21	48	....	....	....	....	....	....	....	....	....	....	....	....	....	....	....	....	....	....
2003-04	U. of Notre Dame	CCHA	39	6	18	24	42	....	....	....	....	....	....	....	....	....	....	....	....	....	....	....	....	....	....
	Grand Rapids	AHL	6	0	1	1	0	....	....	....	....	....	....	....	....	....	4	0	0	0	2	....	....	....	....
2004-05	Grand Rapids	AHL	80	2	10	12	34	....	....	....	....	....	....	....	....	....	....	....	....	....	....	....	....	....	....
2005-06	**Detroit**	**NHL**	**46**	**3**	**9**	**12**	**20**	**1**	**0**	**1**	**50**	**6.0**	**9**	**2**	**0.0**	**12:38**	**6**	**0**	**0**	**0**	**4**	**0**	**0**	**0**	**13:09**
	Grand Rapids	AHL	25	4	14	18	42	....	....	....	....	....	....	....	....	....	11	1	4	5	8	....	....	....	....
2006-07	**Detroit**	**NHL**	**74**	**5**	**13**	**18**	**61**	**1**	**0**	**2**	**107**	**4.7**	**16**	**0**	**0.0**	**14:54**	**12**	**0**	**2**	**2**	**8**	**0**	**0**	**0**	**16:23**
2007-08♦	**Detroit**	**NHL**	**78**	**3**	**11**	**14**	**48**	**0**	**0**	**1**	**110**	**2.7**	**−1**	**1**	**0.0**	**16:29**	**19**	**0**	**2**	**2**	**6**	**0**	**0**	**0**	**12:33**
	NHL Totals		**198**	**11**	**33**	**44**	**129**	**2**	**0**	**4**	**267**	**4.1**		**3**	**0.0**	**15:00**	**37**	**0**	**4**	**4**	**18**	**0**	**0**	**0**	**13:54**

CCHA All-Rookie Team (2001) • CCHA Second All-Star Team (2004)

Signed as a free agent by **Detroit**, April 1, 2004.

LECAVALIER, Vincent
(luh-KAV-uhl-YAY, VIHN-sihnt) **T.B.**

Center. Shoots left. 6'4", 219 lbs. Born, Ile Bizard, Que., April 21, 1980. Tampa Bay's 1st choice, 1st overall, in 1998 Entry Draft.

Season	Club	League	GP	G	A	Pts	PIM	PP	SH	GW	S	%	+/-	TF	F%	Min	Playoffs GP	G	A	Pts	PIM	PP	SH	GW	Min
1995-96	Notre Dame	SMHL	22	52	52	104	....	....	....	....	....	....	....	....	....	....	....	....	....	....	....	....	....	....	....
1996-97	Rimouski Oceanic	QMJHL	64	42	61	103	38	....	....	....	....	....	....	....	....	....	4	4	3	7	2	....	....	....	....
1997-98	Rimouski Oceanic	QMJHL	58	44	71	115	117	....	....	....	....	....	....	....	....	....	18	*15	*26	*41	46	....	....	....	....
1998-99	**Tampa Bay**	**NHL**	**82**	**13**	**15**	**28**	**23**	**2**	**0**	**2**	**125**	**10.4**	**−19**	**953**	**40.3**	**13:40**	....	....	....	....	....	....	....	....	....
99-2000	**Tampa Bay**	**NHL**	**80**	**25**	**42**	**67**	**43**	**6**	**0**	**3**	**166**	**15.1**	**−25**	**1288**	**44.4**	**19:18**	....	....	....	....	....	....	....	....	....
2000-01	**Tampa Bay**	**NHL**	**68**	**23**	**28**	**51**	**66**	**7**	**0**	**3**	**165**	**13.9**	**−26**	**1278**	**44.9**	**19:57**	....	....	....	....	....	....	....	....	....
2001-02	**Tampa Bay**	**NHL**	**76**	**20**	**17**	**37**	**61**	**5**	**0**	**3**	**164**	**12.2**	**−18**	**931**	**41.5**	**17:09**	....	....	....	....	....	....	....	....	....
2002-03	**Tampa Bay**	**NHL**	**80**	**33**	**45**	**78**	**39**	**11**	**2**	**3**	**274**	**12.0**	**0**	**1200**	**43.9**	**19:33**	**11**	**3**	**3**	**6**	**22**	**1**	**0**	**1**	**22:36**
2003-04♦	**Tampa Bay**	**NHL**	**81**	**32**	**34**	**66**	**52**	**5**	**2**	**6**	**242**	**13.2**	**23**	**1119**	**41.4**	**18:04**	**23**	**9**	**7**	**16**	**25**	**2**	**0**	**0**	**19:39**
2004-05	Ak Bars Kazan	Russia	30	7	9	16	78	....	....	....	....	....	....	....	....	....	4	1	0	1	6	....	....	....	....
2005-06	**Tampa Bay**	**NHL**	**80**	**35**	**40**	**75**	**90**	**13**	**2**	**7**	**309**	**11.3**	**0**	**1366**	**51.2**	**20:08**	**5**	**1**	**3**	**4**	**7**	**1**	**0**	**0**	**22:17**
	Canada	Olympics	6	0	3	3	16	....	....	....	....	....	....	....	....	....	....	....	....	....	....	....	....	....	....
2006-07	**Tampa Bay**	**NHL**	**82**	***52**	**56**	**108**	**44**	**16**	**5**	**7**	**339**	**15.3**	**2**	**1653**	**46.6**	**22:36**	**6**	**5**	**2**	**7**	**10**	**1**	**0**	**1**	**26:29**
2007-08	**Tampa Bay**	**NHL**	**81**	**40**	**52**	**92**	**89**	**10**	**1**	**7**	**318**	**12.6**	**−17**	**1671**	**48.8**	**22:57**	....	....	....	....	....	....	....	....	....
	NHL Totals		**710**	**273**	**329**	**602**	**507**	**75**	**12**	**41**	**2102**	**13.0**		**11459**	**45.3**	**19:15**	**45**	**18**	**15**	**33**	**64**	**5**	**0**	**2**	**21:34**

QMJHL All-Rookie Team (1997) • QMJHL Offensive Rookie of the Year (1997) • Canadian Major Junior Rookie of the Year (1997) • QMJHL First All-Star Team (1998) • Canadian Major Junior First All-Star Team (1998) • NHL Second All-Star Team (2007) • Maurice "Rocket" Richard Trophy (2007) • King Clancy Memorial Trophy (2008)

Played in NHL All-Star Game (2003, 2007, 2008)

Signed as a free agent by **Kazan** (Russia), November 4, 2004.

LEE, Brian
(LEE, BRIGH-uhn) **OTT.**

Defense. Shoots right. 6'2", 201 lbs. Born, Fargo, ND, March 26, 1987. Ottawa's 1st choice, 9th overall, in 2005 Entry Draft.

Season	Club	League	GP	G	A	Pts	PIM	PP	SH	GW	S	%	+/-	TF	F%	Min	Playoffs GP	G	A	Pts	PIM	PP	SH	GW	Min
2003-04	Moorhead Spuds	High-MN	29	10	38	48	....	....	....	....	....	....	....	....	....	....	....	....	....	....	....	....	....	....	....
2004-05	Moorhead Spuds	High-MN	25	12	26	38	....	....	....	....	....	....	....	....	....	....	....	....	....	....	....	....	....	....	....
	Lincoln Stars	USHL	12	0	3	3	4	....	....	....	....	....	....	....	....	....	4	2	3	5	2	....	....	....	....
2005-06	North Dakota	WCHA	44	4	23	27	44	....	....	....	....	....	....	....	....	....	....	....	....	....	....	....	....	....	....
2006-07	North Dakota	WCHA	38	2	24	26	69	....	....	....	....	....	....	....	....	....	....	....	....	....	....	....	....	....	....
2007-08	**Ottawa**	**NHL**	**6**	**0**	**1**	**1**	**4**	**0**	**0**	**0**	**6**	**0.0**	**1**	**0**	**0.0**	**16:49**	**4**	**0**	**0**	**0**	**2**	**0**	**0**	**0**	**14:31**
	Binghamton	AHL	55	3	22	25	51	....	....	....	....	....	....	....	....	....	....	....	....	....	....	....	....	....	....
	NHL Totals		**6**	**0**	**1**	**1**	**4**	**0**	**0**	**0**	**6**	**0.0**		**0**	**0.0**	**16:49**	**4**	**0**	**0**	**0**	**2**	**0**	**0**	**0**	**14:31**

WCHA All-Rookie Team (2006)

LEGWAND, David
(LEHG-wawnd, DAY-vihd) **NSH.**

Center. Shoots left. 6'2", 190 lbs. Born, Detroit, MI, August 17, 1980. Nashville's 1st choice, 2nd overall, in 1998 Entry Draft.

Season	Club	League	GP	G	A	Pts	PIM	PP	SH	GW	S	%	+/-	TF	F%	Min	Playoffs GP	G	A	Pts	PIM	PP	SH	GW	Min
1996-97	Det. Compuware	MNHL	44	21	41	62	58	....	....	....	....	....	....	....	....	....	....	....	....	....	....	....	....	....	....
1997-98	Plymouth Whalers	OHL	59	54	51	105	56	....	....	....	....	....	....	....	....	....	15	8	12	20	24	....	....	....	....
1998-99	Plymouth Whalers	OHL	55	31	49	80	65	....	....	....	....	....	....	....	....	....	11	3	8	11	8	....	....	....	....
	Nashville	**NHL**	**1**	**0**	**0**	**0**	**0**	**0**	**0**	**0**	**2**	**0.0**	**0**	**9**	**55.6**	**12:50**	....	....	....	....	....	....	....	....	....
99-2000	**Nashville**	**NHL**	**71**	**13**	**15**	**28**	**30**	**4**	**0**	**2**	**111**	**11.7**	**−6**	**637**	**41.6**	**14:43**	....	....	....	....	....	....	....	....	....
2000-01	**Nashville**	**NHL**	**81**	**13**	**28**	**41**	**38**	**3**	**0**	**3**	**172**	**7.6**	**1**	**888**	**40.3**	**15:14**	....	....	....	....	....	....	....	....	....
2001-02	**Nashville**	**NHL**	**63**	**11**	**19**	**30**	**54**	**1**	**1**	**1**	**121**	**9.1**	**1**	**843**	**40.5**	**16:25**	....	....	....	....	....	....	....	....	....
2002-03	**Nashville**	**NHL**	**64**	**17**	**31**	**48**	**34**	**3**	**1**	**4**	**167**	**10.2**	**−2**	**1095**	**46.6**	**19:14**	....	....	....	....	....	....	....	....	....
2003-04	**Nashville**	**NHL**	**82**	**18**	**29**	**47**	**46**	**5**	**1**	**5**	**165**	**10.9**	**9**	**1109**	**45.1**	**17:17**	**6**	**1**	**0**	**1**	**8**	**0**	**1**	**0**	**15:41**
2004-05	EHC Basel	Swiss-2	3	6	2	8	2	....	....	....	....	....	....	....	....	....	19	16	23	39	20	....	....	....	....
2005-06	**Nashville**	**NHL**	**44**	**7**	**19**	**26**	**34**	**0**	**0**	**5**	**109**	**6.4**	**3**	**580**	**44.7**	**16:50**	**5**	**0**	**1**	**1**	**8**	**0**	**0**	**0**	**17:21**
	Milwaukee	AHL	3	0	0	0	0	....	....	....	....	....	....	....	....	....	....	....	....	....	....	....	....	....	....
2006-07	**Nashville**	**NHL**	**78**	**27**	**36**	**63**	**44**	**3**	**1**	**7**	**153**	**17.6**	**23**	**1108**	**45.3**	**18:22**	**5**	**0**	**3**	**3**	**2**	**0**	**0**	**0**	**22:23**
2007-08	**Nashville**	**NHL**	**65**	**15**	**29**	**44**	**38**	**4**	**0**	**1**	**144**	**10.4**	**−4**	**700**	**43.6**	**18:01**	**3**	**1**	**0**	**1**	**2**	**0**	**0**	**0**	**18:15**
	NHL Totals		**549**	**121**	**206**	**327**	**318**	**23**	**4**	**28**	**1144**	**10.6**		**6969**	**43.7**	**16:58**	**19**	**2**	**4**	**6**	**20**	**0**	**1**	**0**	**18:18**

OHL All-Rookie Team (1998) • OHL First All-Star Team (1998) • OHL Rookie of the Year (1998) • OHL MVP (1998) • Canadian Major Junior Rookie of the Year (1998)

Signed as a free agent by **Basel** (Swiss-2), January 27, 2005.

LEHOUX, Yanick
(luh-HOO, YAH-nihk) **MTL.**

Center. Shoots right. 6'1", 200 lbs. Born, Montreal, Que., April 8, 1982. Los Angeles' 3rd choice, 86th overall, in 2000 Entry Draft.

			Regular Season														Playoffs								
Season	Club	League	GP	G	A	Pts	PIM	PP	SH	GW	S	%	+/-	TF	F%	Min	GP	G	A	Pts	PIM	PP	SH	GW	Min
1997-98	Cap-d-Madeleine	QAAA	42	29	50	79	26																		
1998-99	Baie-Comeau	QMJHL	63	10	20	30	31																		
99-2000	Baie-Comeau	QMJHL	67	31	61	92	14										6	1	2	3	2				
2000-01	Baie-Comeau	QMJHL	70	67	68	135	62										11	8	16	24	0				
2001-02	Baie-Comeau	QMJHL	66	56	69	125	63										5	5	4	9	0				
	Manchester	AHL															1	0	0	0	0				
2002-03	Manchester	AHL	78	16	21	37	26										1	0	0	0	0				
2003-04	Manchester	AHL	66	14	28	42	22										5	2	3	5	16				
2004-05	Manchester	AHL	38	23	31	54	16																		
2005-06	Geneve	Swiss	7	5	2	7	6																		
	EHC Basel	Swiss	4	0	2	2	4																		
	Phoenix	**NHL**	**3**	**1**	**0**	**1**	**2**	0	0	0	5	20.0	1	24	33.3	9:50									
	San Antonio	AHL	23	8	6	14	13																		
	Manchester	AHL	31	10	6	16	23																		
2006-07	**Phoenix**	**NHL**	**7**	**1**	**2**	**3**	**4**	1	0	0	10	10.0	–1	10	60.0	12:32									
	San Antonio	AHL	72	31	42	73	26																		
2007-08	San Antonio	AHL	7	1	3	4	2																		
	Mytischi	Russia	17	2	5	7	8																		
	NHL Totals		**10**	**2**	**2**	**4**	**6**	1	0	0	15	13.3		34	41.2	11:44									

QMJHL Second All-Star Team (2002)

Signed as a free agent by **Geneve** (Swiss), September 5 2005. Claimed on waivers by **Phoenix** from **Los Angeles**, November 5, 2005. Claimed on waivers by **Los Angeles** from **Phoenix**, November 25, 2005. Traded to **Phoenix** by **Los Angeles** for Tim Jackman, March 9, 2006. Signed as a free agent by **Mytischi** (Russia), November 10, 2007. Signed as a free agent by **Montreal**, July 25, 2008.

LEHTINEN, Jere
(LEH-tih-nehn, YUH-ree) **DAL.**

Right wing. Shoots right. 6', 192 lbs. Born, Espoo, Finland, June 24, 1973. Minnesota's 3rd choice, 88th overall, in 1992 Entry Draft.

			Regular Season														Playoffs								
Season	Club	League	GP	G	A	Pts	PIM	PP	SH	GW	S	%	+/-	TF	F%	Min	GP	G	A	Pts	PIM	PP	SH	GW	Min
1989-90	Kiekko-Espoo Jr.	Fin-Jr.	32	23	23	46	6										5	0	3	3	0				
1990-91	K-Espoo U18	Fin-U18	11	18	14	32	0																		
	Kiekko-Espoo Jr.	Fin-Jr.	10	8	6	14	4																		
	Kiekko-Espoo	Finland-2	32	15	9	24	12																		
1991-92	Kiekko-Espoo Jr.	Fin-Jr.	8	5	4	9	2																		
	Kiekko-Espoo	Finland-2	43	32	17	49	6										5	2	4	6	2				
1992-93	Kiekko-Espoo Jr.	Fin-Jr.	4	5	3	8	8																		
	Kiekko-Espoo	Finland	45	13	14	27	6																		
1993-94	TPS Turku	Finland	42	19	20	39	6										11	11	2	13	2				
	Finland	Olympics	8	3	0	3	0																		
1994-95	TPS Turku	Finland	39	19	23	42	33										13	8	6	14	4				
1995-96	**Dallas**	**NHL**	**57**	**6**	**22**	**28**	**16**	0	0	1	109	5.5	5												
	Michigan	IHL	1	1	0	1	0																		
1996-97	**Dallas**	**NHL**	**63**	**16**	**27**	**43**	**2**	3	1	2	134	11.9	26				7	2	2	4	0	0	0	0	
1997-98	**Dallas**	**NHL**	**72**	**23**	**19**	**42**	**20**	7	2	6	201	11.4	19				12	3	5	8	2	1	0	0	
	Finland	Olympics	6	4	2	6	2																		
1998-99♦	**Dallas**	**NHL**	**74**	**20**	**32**	**52**	**18**	7	1	2	173	11.6	29	9	33.3	19:36	23	10	3	13	2	1	1	0	21:09
99-2000	**Dallas**	**NHL**	**17**	**3**	**5**	**8**	**0**	0	0	1	29	10.3	1	0	0.0	17:31	13	1	5	6	2	0	0	0	21:15
2000-01	**Dallas**	**NHL**	**74**	**20**	**25**	**45**	**24**	7	0	1	148	13.5	14	7	28.6	19:17	10	1	0	1	2	0	0	0	20:13
2001-02	**Dallas**	**NHL**	**73**	**25**	**24**	**49**	**14**	7	1	4	198	12.6	27	18	22.2	19:50									
	Finland	Olympics	4	1	2	3	2																		
2002-03	**Dallas**	**NHL**	**80**	**31**	**17**	**48**	**20**	5	0	3	238	13.0	39	36	22.2	18:47	12	3	2	5	0	1	0	1	21:12
2003-04	**Dallas**	**NHL**	**58**	**13**	**13**	**26**	**20**	4	1	4	138	9.4	0	10	40.0	19:27	5	0	0	0	0	0	0	0	19:19
2004-05			DID NOT PLAY																						
2005-06	**Dallas**	**NHL**	**80**	**33**	**19**	**52**	**30**	14	1	6	216	15.3	9	28	21.4	18:42	5	3	1	4	0	1	0	0	22:10
	Finland	Olympics	8	3	5	8	0																		
2006-07	**Dallas**	**NHL**	**73**	**26**	**17**	**43**	**16**	11	1	5	194	13.4	5	36	13.9	19:26	7	0	0	0	2	0	0	0	24:02
2007-08	**Dallas**	**NHL**	**48**	**15**	**22**	**37**	**14**	9	0	1	118	12.7	9	11	9.1	18:55	14	4	4	8	2	3	0	0	20:34
	NHL Totals		**769**	**231**	**242**	**473**	**194**	74	8	36	1896	12.2		155	21.3	19:12	108	27	22	49	12	7	1	1	21:09

Frank J. Selke Trophy (1998, 1999, 2003)
Played in NHL All-Star Game (1998)

Rights transferred to **Dallas** after **Minnesota** franchise relocated, June 9, 1993. • Missed majority of 1999-2000 season recovering from leg injury suffered in game vs. Nashville, October 16, 1999.

LEHTONEN, Mikko
(LEH-tuh-nehn, MEE-koh)

Defense. Shoots left. 6'1", 194 lbs. Born, Oulu, Finland, June 12, 1978. Nashville's 9th choice, 271st overall, in 2001 Entry Draft.

			Regular Season														Playoffs								
Season	Club	League	GP	G	A	Pts	PIM	PP	SH	GW	S	%	+/-	TF	F%	Min	GP	G	A	Pts	PIM	PP	SH	GW	Min
1995-96	Karpat Oulu U18	Fin-U18	15	4	5	9	30																		
1996-97	Karpat Oulu Jr.	Fin-Jr.	35	6	19	25	82																		
1997-98	Karpat Oulu Jr.	Fin-Jr.	34	8	12	20	56																		
	Karpat Oulu U18	Fin-U18	11	5	7	12	31																		
1998-99	Karpat Oulu Jr.	Fin-Jr.	35	13	22	35	65																		
	Karpat Oulu	Finland-2	2	0	0	0	0																		
	Karpat Oulu U18	Fin-U18	13	6	14	20	14																		
99-2000	Karpat Oulu	Finland-2	45	5	10	15	26										6	0	0	0	4				
2000-01	Karpat Oulu	Finland	54	6	9	15	58										9	0	3	3	4				
2001-02	Karpat Oulu	Finland	55	8	11	19	32										4	1	1	2	4				
2002-03	Karpat Oulu	Finland	55	5	12	17	50										15	3	1	4	22				
2003-04	Karpat Oulu	Finland	53	5	13	18	62										12	2	4	6	8				
2004-05	Karpat Oulu	Finland	53	11	17	28	28										12	3	3	6	12				
2005-06	Karpat Oulu	Finland	43	6	8	14	46										10	2	2	4	12				
2006-07	**Nashville**	**NHL**	**15**	**1**	**2**	**3**	**8**	0	0	0	14	7.1	0	0	0.0	14:36									
	Milwaukee	AHL	35	4	8	12	28																		
	Rochester	AHL	21	1	8	9	10																		
2007-08	Karpat Oulu	Finland	48	8	25	33	34										15	4	5	9	12				
	NHL Totals		**15**	**1**	**2**	**3**	**8**	0	0	0	14	7.1		0	0.0	14:36									

Traded to **Buffalo** by **Nashville** for Buffalo's 4th round choice (Mark Santorelli) in 2007 Entry Draft, February 27, 2007. Signed as a free agent by **Oulu** (Finland), July 30, 2007.

LEOPOLD, Jordan
(LEE-oh-pohld, JOHR-dahn) **COL.**

Defense. Shoots left. 6'1", 200 lbs. Born, Golden Valley, MN, August 3, 1980. Anaheim's 1st choice, 44th overall, in 1999 Entry Draft.

			Regular Season														Playoffs								
Season	Club	League	GP	G	A	Pts	PIM	PP	SH	GW	S	%	+/-	TF	F%	Min	GP	G	A	Pts	PIM	PP	SH	GW	Min
1995-96	Armstrong	High-MN	19	11	14	25	30																		
1996-97	Armstrong	High-MN	30	24	36	60	....																		
1997-98	USNTDP	U-18	25	7	3	10	2																		
	USNTDP	USHL	19	2	4	6	6																		
	USNTDP	NAHL	16	2	5	7	8																		
1998-99	U. of Minnesota	WCHA	39	7	16	23	20																		
99-2000	U. of Minnesota	WCHA	39	6	18	24	20																		
2000-01	U. of Minnesota	WCHA	42	12	37	49	38																		
2001-02	U. of Minnesota	WCHA	44	20	28	48	28																		
2002-03	**Calgary**	**NHL**	**58**	**4**	**10**	**14**	**12**	3	0	0	78	5.1	–15	0	0.0	20:36									
	Saint John Flames	AHL	3	1	2	3	0																		
2003-04	**Calgary**	**NHL**	**82**	**9**	**24**	**33**	**24**	6	0	1	138	6.5	8	0	0.0	22:14	26	0	10	10	6	0	0	0	25:41
2004-05			DID NOT PLAY																						
2005-06	**Calgary**	**NHL**	**74**	**2**	**18**	**20**	**68**	2	0	1	87	2.3	6	0	0.0	22:20	7	0	1	1	4	0	0	0	19:13
	United States	Olympics	6	1	0	1	4																		

			Regular Season														Playoffs								
Season	Club	League	GP	G	A	Pts	PIM	PP	SH	GW	S	%	+/-	TF	F%	Min	GP	G	A	Pts	PIM	PP	SH	GW	Min
2006-07	Colorado	NHL	15	2	3	5	14	1	1	0	19	10.5	–4	0	0.0	19:47	....	....	....	....	....	....	....	....	....
2007-08	Colorado	NHL	43	5	8	13	20	2	0	1	35	14.3	5	0	0.0	15:59	7	0	3	3	0	0	0	0	17:00
	NHL Totals		272	22	63	85	138	14	1	3	357	6.2		0	0.0	20:47	40	0	14	14	10	0	0	0	23:02

WCHA All-Rookie Team (1999) • WCHA Second All-Star Team (2000) • WCHA First All-Star Team (2001, 2002) • NCAA West First All-American Team (2001) • Hobey Baker Memorial Award (Top U.S. Collegiate Player) (2002)

Traded to **Calgary** by **Anaheim** for Andrei Nazarov and Calgary's 2nd round choice (later traded to Phoenix – later traded back to Calgary – Calgary selected Andrei Taratukhin) in 2001 Entry Draft, September 26, 2000. Traded to **Colorado** by **Calgary** with Calgary's 2nd round choice (Codey Burki) in 2006 Entry Draft and Calgary's 2nd round choice (Trevor Cann) in 2007 Entry Draft for Alex Tanguay, June 24, 2006. • Missed majority of 2006-07 season recovering from off-season hernia surgery, groin injury and wrist injury suffered in game vs. Calgary, February 15, 2007.

LEPISTO, Sami

(LEH-pihs-toh, SA-mee) **WSH.**

Defense. Shoots left. 6'1", 195 lbs. Born, Espoo, Finland, October 17, 1984. Washington's 6th choice, 66th overall, in 2004 Entry Draft.

2001-02	Jokerit U18	Fin-U18	20	8	14	22	36	....	....	....	....	....	....	....	....	....	8	4	8	12	12	....	....	....	....
	Jokerit Helsinki Jr.	Fin-Jr.	14	0	5	5	2	....	....	....	....	....	....	....	....	....	....	....	....	....	....	....	....	....	....
2002-03	Jokerit Helsinki Jr.	Fin-Jr.	36	5	14	19	34	....	....	....	....	....	....	....	....	....	11	1	5	6	8	....	....	....	....
2003-04	Suomi U20	Finland-2	1	0	0	0	0	....	....	....	....	....	....	....	....	....	....	....	....	....	....	....	....	....	....
	Jokerit Helsinki	Finland	53	3	4	7	20	....	....	....	....	....	....	....	....	....	8	0	1	1	4	....	....	....	....
2004-05	Jokerit Helsinki	Finland	55	7	18	25	44	....	....	....	....	....	....	....	....	....	12	1	7	8	12	....	....	....	....
2005-06	Jokerit Helsinki	Finland	56	8	21	29	68	....	....	....	....	....	....	....	....	....	....	....	....	....	....	....	....	....	....
2006-07	Jokerit Helsinki	Finland	26	1	9	10	32	....	....	....	....	....	....	....	....	....	10	2	2	4	4	....	....	....	....
2007-08	Washington	NHL	7	0	1	1	12	0	0	0	8	0.0	–1	0	0.0	13:17	....	....	....	....	....	....	....	....	....
	Hershey Bears	AHL	55	4	41	45	51	....	....	....	....	....	....	....	....	....	5	0	1	1	4	....	....	....	....
	NHL Totals		7	0	1	1	12	0	0	0	8	0.0		0	0.0	13:17	....	....	....	....	....	....	....	....	....

LESSARD, Francis

(leh-SAHR, FRAN-sihs) **PHX.**

Right wing. Shoots right. 6'3", 225 lbs. Born, Montreal, Que., May 30, 1979. Carolina's 3rd choice, 80th overall, in 1997 Entry Draft.

1994-95	Laval-Laurentides	QAAA	1	0	0	0	0	....	....	....	....	....	....	....	....	....	....	....	....	....	....	....	....	....	....
1995-96	Laval-Laurentides	QAAA	41	5	7	12	73	....	....	....	....	....	....	....	....	....	13	1	3	4	....	....	....	....	....
1996-97	Val-d'Or Foreurs	QMJHL	66	1	9	10	287	....	....	....	....	....	....	....	....	....	....	....	....	....	....	....	....	....	....
1997-98	Val-d'Or Foreurs	QMJHL	63	3	20	23	338	....	....	....	....	....	....	....	....	....	19	1	6	7	*101	....	....	....	....
1998-99	Drummondville	QMJHL	53	12	36	48	295	....	....	....	....	....	....	....	....	....	....	....	....	....	....	....	....	....	....
99-2000	Philadelphia	AHL	78	4	8	12	416	....	....	....	....	....	....	....	....	....	5	0	1	1	7	....	....	....	....
2000-01	Philadelphia	AHL	64	3	7	10	330	....	....	....	....	....	....	....	....	....	10	0	0	0	33	....	....	....	....
2001-02	Philadelphia	AHL	60	0	6	6	251	....	....	....	....	....	....	....	....	....	....	....	....	....	....	....	....	....	....
	Atlanta	NHL	5	0	0	0	26	0	0	0	2	0.0	0	0	0.0	12:45	....	....	....	....	....	....	....	....	....
	Chicago Wolves	AHL	7	2	1	3	34	....	....	....	....	....	....	....	....	....	15	0	1	1	40	....	....	....	....
2002-03	Atlanta	NHL	18	0	2	2	61	0	0	0	7	0.0	1	0	0.0	5:40	....	....	....	....	....	....	....	....	....
	Chicago Wolves	AHL	50	2	5	7	194	....	....	....	....	....	....	....	....	....	1	0	0	0	0	....	....	....	....
2003-04	Atlanta	NHL	62	1	1	2	181	0	0	0	19	5.3	–5	1	0.0	4:28	....	....	....	....	....	....	....	....	....
2004-05		DID NOT PLAY																							
2005-06	Atlanta	NHL	6	0	0	0	0	0	0	0	0	0.0	–2	0	0.0	2:33	....	....	....	....	....	....	....	....	....
	Chicago Wolves	AHL	36	2	3	5	163	....	....	....	....	....	....	....	....	....	....	....	....	....	....	....	....	....	....
2006-07	Hartford	AHL	58	3	6	9	*309	....	....	....	....	....	....	....	....	....	....	....	....	....	....	....	....	....	....
2007-08	Hartford	AHL	14	4	1	5	49	....	....	....	....	....	....	....	....	....	....	....	....	....	....	....	....	....	....
	NHL Totals		91	1	3	4	268	0	0	0	28	3.6		1	0.0	5:02	....	....	....	....	....	....	....	....	....

Memorial Cup Tournament All-Star Team (1998)

Traded to **Philadelphia** by **Carolina** for Philadelphia's 8th round choice (Antti Jokella) in 1999 Entry Draft, May 25, 1999. Traded to **Atlanta** by **Philadelphia** for David Harlock and Atlanta's 3rd (later traded to Phoenix – Phoenix selected Tyler Redenbach) and 7th (later traded to San Jose – San Jose selected Joe Pavelski) round choices in 2003 Entry Draft, March 15, 2002. Signed as a free agent by **Phoenix**, July 31, 2008.

LESSARD, Junior

(leh-SAHR, JEW-nyuhr) **ATL.**

Right wing/Center. Shoots right. 5'11", 200 lbs. Born, St-Joseph-de-Beauce, Que., May 26, 1980.

99-2000	Portage Terriers	MJHL	60	60	48	108	61	....	....	....	....	....	....	....	....	....	....	....	....	....	....	....	....	....	....
2000-01	U. Minn-Duluth	WCHA	36	4	8	12	12	....	....	....	....	....	....	....	....	....	....	....	....	....	....	....	....	....	....
2001-02	U. Minn-Duluth	WCHA	39	17	13	30	50	....	....	....	....	....	....	....	....	....	....	....	....	....	....	....	....	....	....
2002-03	U. Minn-Duluth	WCHA	40	21	16	37	20	....	....	....	....	....	....	....	....	....	....	....	....	....	....	....	....	....	....
2003-04	U. Minn-Duluth	WCHA	45	*32	31	*63	34	....	....	....	....	....	....	....	....	....	....	....	....	....	....	....	....	....	....
2004-05	Houston Aeros	AHL	71	11	11	22	25	....	....	....	....	....	....	....	....	....	5	1	0	1	0	....	....	....	....
2005-06	Dallas	NHL	5	1	0	1	12	0	0	0	6	16.7	0	0	0.0	7:23	....	....	....	....	....	....	....	....	....
	Iowa Stars	AHL	66	26	31	57	30	....	....	....	....	....	....	....	....	....	7	3	4	7	4	....	....	....	....
2006-07	Dallas	NHL	1	1	0	1	0	1	0	0	3	33.3	1	0	0.0	11:56	....	....	....	....	....	....	....	....	....
	Iowa Stars	AHL	65	27	25	52	32	....	....	....	....	....	....	....	....	....	12	4	5	9	4	....	....	....	....
2007-08	Dallas	NHL	2	0	0	0	2	0	0	0	3	0.0	–1	0	0.0	12:05	....	....	....	....	....	....	....	....	....
	Iowa Stars	AHL	36	10	11	21	15	....	....	....	....	....	....	....	....	....	....	....	....	....	....	....	....	....	....
	Tampa Bay	NHL	19	1	1	2	9	0	0	0	18	5.6	–5	0	0.0	9:38	....	....	....	....	....	....	....	....	....
	Norfolk Admirals	AHL	19	6	9	15	4	....	....	....	....	....	....	....	....	....	....	....	....	....	....	....	....	....	....
	NHL Totals		27	3	1	4	23	1	0	0	30	10.0		0	0.0	9:29	....	....	....	....	....	....	....	....	....

WCHA First All-Star Team (2004) • WCHA Player of the Year (2004) • NCAA West First All-American Team (2004) • NCAA Championship All-Tournament Team (2004) • Hobey Baker Memorial Award (Top U.S. Collegiate Player) (2004)

Signed as a free agent by **Dallas**, April 15, 2004. Traded to **Tampa Bay** by **Dallas** for Dan Jancevski, January 15, 2008. Signed as a free agent by **Atlanta**, July 9, 2008.

LETANG, Kris

(leh-TANG, KRIHS) **PIT.**

Defense. Shoots right. 6', 201 lbs. Born, Montreal, Que., April 24, 1987. Pittsburgh's 3rd choice, 62nd overall, in 2005 Entry Draft.

2002-03	Antoine-Girouard	QAAA	42	2	10	12	34	....	....	....	....	....	....	....	....	....	....	....	....	....	....	....	....	....	....
2003-04	Antoine-Girouard	QAAA	39	12	41	53	94	....	....	....	....	....	....	....	....	....	13	7	9	16	38	....	....	....	....
2004-05	Val-d'Or Foreurs	QMJHL	70	13	19	32	79	....	....	....	....	....	....	....	....	....	....	....	....	....	....	....	....	....	....
2005-06	Val-d'Or Foreurs	QMJHL	60	25	43	68	156	....	....	....	....	....	....	....	....	....	5	1	5	6	20	....	....	....	....
2006-07	Pittsburgh	NHL	7	2	0	2	4	2	0	0	8	25.0	–3	0	0.0	11:33	....	....	....	....	....	....	....	....	....
	Val-d'Or Foreurs	QMJHL	40	14	38	52	74	....	....	....	....	....	....	....	....	....	19	12	19	31	48	....	....	....	....
	Wilkes-Barre	AHL	....	....	....	....	....	....	....	....	....	....	....	....	....	....	1	0	1	1	2	....	....	....	....
2007-08	Pittsburgh	NHL	63	6	11	17	23	1	0	3	68	8.8	–1	0	0.0	18:10	16	0	2	2	12	0	0	0	17:07
	Wilkes-Barre	AHL	10	1	6	7	4	....	....	....	....	....	....	....	....	....	....	....	....	....	....	....	....	....	....
	NHL Totals		70	8	11	19	27	3	0	3	76	10.5		0	0.0	17:30	16	0	2	2	12	0	0	0	17:07

QMJHL All-Rookie Team (2005) • Canadian Major Junior All-Rookie Team (2005) • QMJHL First All-Star Team (2006, 2007)

LETOWSKI, Trevor

(leh-TOW-skee, TREH-vuhr)

Right wing. Shoots right. 5'10", 180 lbs. Born, Thunder Bay, Ont., April 5, 1977. Phoenix's 6th choice, 174th overall, in 1996 Entry Draft.

1993-94	T. Bay Kings	TBMHL	64	41	60	101	48	....	....	....	....	....	....	....	....	....	....	....	....	....	....	....	....	....	....
1994-95	Sarnia Sting	OHL	66	22	19	41	33	....	....	....	....	....	....	....	....	....	4	0	1	1	9	....	....	....	....
1995-96	Sarnia Sting	OHL	66	36	63	99	66	....	....	....	....	....	....	....	....	....	10	9	5	14	10	....	....	....	....
1996-97	Sarnia Sting	OHL	55	35	73	108	51	....	....	....	....	....	....	....	....	....	12	9	12	21	20	....	....	....	....
1997-98	Springfield	AHL	75	11	20	31	26	....	....	....	....	....	....	....	....	....	4	1	0	1	2	....	....	....	....
1998-99	Phoenix	NHL	14	2	2	4	2	0	0	0	8	25.0	1	49	55.1	6:01	....	....	....	....	....	....	....	....	....
	Springfield	AHL	67	32	35	67	46	....	....	....	....	....	....	....	....	....	3	1	0	1	2	....	....	....	....
99-2000	Phoenix	NHL	82	19	20	39	20	3	4	3	125	15.2	2	692	47.7	16:03	5	1	1	2	4	0	0	0	15:52
2000-01	Phoenix	NHL	77	7	15	22	32	0	1	3	110	6.4	–2	726	46.1	16:20	....	....	....	....	....	....	....	....	....
2001-02	Phoenix	NHL	33	2	6	8	4	0	0	0	43	4.7	2	250	52.4	14:27	....	....	....	....	....	....	....	....	....
	Vancouver	NHL	42	7	10	17	15	1	0	0	65	10.8	2	111	44.1	12:47	6	0	1	1	8	0	0	0	11:50
2002-03	Vancouver	NHL	78	11	14	25	36	1	1	2	136	8.1	8	70	41.4	12:26	6	0	1	1	0	0	0	0	9:40
2003-04	Columbus	NHL	73	15	17	32	16	4	0	1	126	11.9	–12	146	43.8	16:19	....	....	....	....	....	....	....	....	....
2004-05	Fribourg	Swiss	9	4	5	9	6	....	....	....	....	....	....	....	....	....	11	7	9	16	8	....	....	....	....
2005-06	Columbus	NHL	81	10	18	28	36	1	1	1	135	7.4	–2	284	45.8	16:32	....	....	....	....	....	....	....	....	....

			Regular Season														Playoffs								
Season	Club	League	GP	G	A	Pts	PIM	PP	SH	GW	S	%	+/-	TF	F%	Min	GP	G	A	Pts	PIM	PP	SH	GW	Min
2006-07	**Carolina**	**NHL**	**61**	**2**	**6**	**8**	**18**	**0**	**0**	**0**	**69**	**2.9**	**–8**	**208**	**48.6**	**9:41**	....	....	....	....	....	....	....	....	....
2007-08	**Carolina**	**NHL**	**75**	**9**	**9**	**18**	**30**	**0**	**1**	**1**	**67**	**13.4**	**–10**	**602**	**44.7**	**10:16**	....	....	....	....	....	....	....	....	....
	NHL Totals		**616**	**84**	**117**	**201**	**209**	**10**	**8**	**11**	**884**	**9.5**		**3138**	**46.7**	**13:51**	**17**	**1**	**3**	**4**	**12**	**0**	**0**	**0**	**12:15**

Traded to **Vancouver** by **Phoenix** with Todd Warriner, Tyler Bouck and Phoenix's 3rd round choice (later traded back to Phoenix – Phoenix selected Dimitri Pestunov) in 2003 Entry Draft for Drake Berehowsky and Denis Pederson, December 28, 2001. Signed as a free agent by **Columbus**, July 3, 2003. Signed as a free agent by **Fribourg** (Swiss), January 7, 2005. Signed as a free agent by **Carolina**, July 6, 2006.

LIDSTROM, Nicklas

(LID-struhm, NIHK-luhs) **DET.**

Defense. Shoots left. 6'1", 189 lbs. Born, Vasteras, Sweden, April 28, 1970. Detroit's 3rd choice, 53rd overall, in 1989 Entry Draft.

1987-88	Vasteras	Sweden-2	3	0	0	0	0	....	....	....	....	....	....	....	....	....	5	0	0	0	6	....	....	....	....
1988-89	Vasteras IK	Sweden	34	1	6	7	4	....	....	....	....	....	....	....	....	....	5	0	2	2	0	....	....	....	....
1989-90	Vasteras IK	Sweden	39	8	8	16	14	....	....	....	....	....	....	....	....	....	2	0	1	1	2	....	....	....	....
1990-91	Vasteras IK	Sweden	38	4	19	23	2	....	....	....	....	....	....	....	....	....	4	0	0	0	4	....	....	....	....
1991-92	**Detroit**	**NHL**	**80**	**11**	**49**	**60**	**22**	**5**	**0**	**1**	**168**	**6.5**	**36**	....	....	....	**11**	**1**	**2**	**3**	**0**	**1**	**0**	**0**	....
1992-93	**Detroit**	**NHL**	**84**	**7**	**34**	**41**	**28**	**3**	**0**	**2**	**156**	**4.5**	**7**	....	....	....	**7**	**1**	**0**	**1**	**0**	**1**	**0**	**0**	....
1993-94	**Detroit**	**NHL**	**84**	**10**	**46**	**56**	**26**	**4**	**0**	**3**	**200**	**5.0**	**43**	....	....	....	**7**	**3**	**2**	**5**	**0**	**1**	**1**	**0**	....
1994-95	Vasteras IK	Sweden	13	2	10	12	4	....	....	....	....	....	....	....	....	....	....	....	....	....	....	....	....	....	....
	Detroit	**NHL**	**43**	**10**	**16**	**26**	**6**	**7**	**0**	**0**	**90**	**11.1**	**15**	....	....	....	**18**	**4**	**12**	**16**	**8**	**3**	**0**	**2**	....
1995-96	**Detroit**	**NHL**	**81**	**17**	**50**	**67**	**20**	**8**	**1**	**1**	**211**	**8.1**	**29**	....	....	....	**19**	**5**	**9**	**14**	**10**	**1**	**0**	**0**	....
1996-97◆	**Detroit**	**NHL**	**79**	**15**	**42**	**57**	**30**	**8**	**0**	**1**	**214**	**7.0**	**11**	....	....	....	**20**	**2**	**6**	**8**	**2**	**0**	**0**	**0**	....
1997-98◆	**Detroit**	**NHL**	**80**	**17**	**42**	**59**	**18**	**7**	**1**	**1**	**205**	**8.3**	**22**	....	....	....	**22**	**6**	**13**	**19**	**8**	**2**	**0**	**2**	....
	Sweden	Olympics	4	1	1	2	2	....	....	....	....	....	....	....	....	....	....	....	....	....	....	....	....	....	....
1998-99	**Detroit**	**NHL**	**81**	**14**	**43**	**57**	**14**	**6**	**2**	**3**	**205**	**6.8**	**14**	**0**	**0.0**	**26:31**	**10**	**2**	**9**	**11**	**4**	**2**	**0**	**0**	**30:21**
99-2000	**Detroit**	**NHL**	**81**	**20**	**53**	**73**	**18**	**9**	**4**	**3**	**218**	**9.2**	**19**	**0**	**0.0**	**28:45**	**9**	**2**	**4**	**6**	**4**	**1**	**0**	**0**	**30:28**
2000-01	**Detroit**	**NHL**	**82**	**15**	**56**	**71**	**18**	**8**	**0**	**0**	**272**	**5.5**	**9**	**0**	**0.0**	**28:27**	**6**	**1**	**7**	**8**	**0**	**0**	**0**	**0**	**29:17**
2001-02◆	**Detroit**	**NHL**	**78**	**9**	**50**	**59**	**20**	**6**	**0**	**0**	**215**	**4.2**	**13**	**0**	**0.0**	**28:49**	**23**	**5**	**11**	**16**	**2**	**2**	**1**	**2**	**31:10**
	Sweden	Olympics	4	1	5	6	0	....	....	....	....	....	....	....	....	....	....	....	....	....	....	....	....	....	....
2002-03	**Detroit**	**NHL**	**82**	**18**	**44**	**62**	**38**	**8**	**1**	**4**	**175**	**10.3**	**40**	**0**	**0.0**	**29:20**	**4**	**0**	**2**	**2**	**0**	**0**	**0**	**0**	**33:35**
2003-04	**Detroit**	**NHL**	**81**	**10**	**28**	**38**	**18**	**3**	**1**	**3**	**194**	**5.2**	**19**	**0**	**0.0**	**27:39**	**12**	**2**	**5**	**7**	**4**	**2**	**0**	**0**	**27:01**
2004-05			DID NOT PLAY																						
2005-06	**Detroit**	**NHL**	**80**	**16**	**64**	**80**	**50**	**9**	**0**	**2**	**243**	**6.6**	**21**	**0**	**0.0**	**28:07**	**6**	**1**	**1**	**2**	**2**	**1**	**0**	**1**	**31:55**
	Sweden	Olympics	8	2	4	6	2	....	....	....	....	....	....	....	....	....	....	....	....	....	....	....	....	....	....
2006-07	**Detroit**	**NHL**	**80**	**13**	**49**	**62**	**46**	**10**	**0**	**1**	**224**	**5.8**	**40**	**0**	**0.0**	**27:29**	**18**	**4**	**14**	**18**	**6**	**4**	**0**	**2**	**30:37**
2007-08◆	**Detroit**	**NHL**	**76**	**10**	**60**	**70**	**40**	**5**	**0**	**4**	**188**	**5.3**	**40**	**0**	**0.0**	**26:43**	**22**	**3**	**10**	**13**	**14**	**1**	**1**	**1**	**26:49**
	NHL Totals		**1252**	**212**	**726**	**938**	**412**	**106**	**10**	**29**	**3178**	**6.7**		**0**	**0.0**	**27:59**	**214**	**42**	**107**	**149**	**64**	**22**	**3**	**10**	**29:39**

NHL All-Rookie Team (1992) • NHL First All-Star Team (1998, 1999, 2000, 2001, 2002, 2003, 2006, 2007, 2008) • James Norris Memorial Trophy (2001, 2002, 2003, 2006, 2007, 2008) • Conn Smythe Trophy (2002) • Olympic Tournament All-Star Team (2006)

Played in NHL All-Star Game (1996, 1998, 1999, 2000, 2001, 2002, 2003, 2004, 2007, 2008)

LIFFITON, David

(LIH-fih-tuhn, DAY-vihd)

Defense. Shoots left. 6'2", 210 lbs. Born, Windsor, Ont., October 18, 1984. Colorado's 1st choice, 63rd overall, in 2003 Entry Draft.

2000-01	Aylmer Aces	OHA-B	51	1	9	10	51	....	....	....	....	....	....	....	....	....	....	....	....	....	....	....	....	....	....
2001-02	Plymouth Whalers	OHL	62	3	9	12	65	....	....	....	....	....	....	....	....	....	6	0	0	0	0	....	....	....	....
2002-03	Plymouth Whalers	OHL	64	5	11	16	139	....	....	....	....	....	....	....	....	....	18	1	3	4	29	....	....	....	....
2003-04	Plymouth Whalers	OHL	44	2	9	11	85	....	....	....	....	....	....	....	....	....	9	0	0	0	12	....	....	....	....
2004-05	Hartford	AHL	33	0	1	1	74	....	....	....	....	....	....	....	....	....	....	....	....	....	....	....	....	....	....
	Charlotte	ECHL	16	0	2	2	18	....	....	....	....	....	....	....	....	....	15	1	4	5	27	....	....	....	....
2005-06	**NY Rangers**	**NHL**	**1**	**0**	**0**	**0**	**2**	**0**	**0**	**0**	**0**	**0.0**	**0**	**0**	**0.0**	**8:42**	....	....	....	....	....	....	....	....	....
	Hartford	AHL	50	2	7	9	158	....	....	....	....	....	....	....	....	....	....	....	....	....	....	....	....	....	....
2006-07	**NY Rangers**	**NHL**	**2**	**0**	**0**	**0**	**7**	**0**	**0**	**0**	**2**	**0.0**	**1**	**0**	**0.0**	**11:31**	....	....	....	....	....	....	....	....	....
	Hartford	AHL	72	2	11	13	189	....	....	....	....	....	....	....	....	....	7	1	1	2	18	....	....	....	....
2007-08	Hartford	AHL	21	0	2	2	52	....	....	....	....	....	....	....	....	....	....	....	....	....	....	....	....	....	....
	NHL Totals		**3**	**0**	**0**	**0**	**9**	**0**	**0**	**0**	**2**	**0.0**		**0**	**0.0**	**10:35**	....	....	....	....	....	....	....	....	....

Traded to **NY Rangers** by **Colorado** with Chris McAllister and Florida's 2nd round choice (previously acquired, later traded back to Florida – Florida selected David Shantz) in 2004 Entry Draft for Matthew Barnaby and NY Rangers' 3rd round choice (Denis Parshin) in 2004 Entry Draft, March 8, 2004. • Missed majority of 2007-08 season recovering from post-concussion symptoms.

LILES, John-Michael

(LIGH-uhls, JAWN-MIGHK-uhl) **COL.**

Defense. Shoots left. 5'10", 185 lbs. Born, Indianapolis, IN, November 25, 1980. Colorado's 8th choice, 159th overall, in 2000 Entry Draft.

1997-98	USNTDP	U-17	15	0	6	6	4	....	....	....	....	....	....	....	....	....	....	....	....	....	....	....	....	....	....
	USNTDP	USHL	5	0	1	1	0	....	....	....	....	....	....	....	....	....	....	....	....	....	....	....	....	....	....
	USNTDP	NAHL	42	4	7	11	40	....	....	....	....	....	....	....	....	....	5	2	0	2	0	....	....	....	....
1998-99	USNTDP	USHL	46	4	14	18	47	....	....	....	....	....	....	....	....	....	....	....	....	....	....	....	....	....	....
	USNTDP	NAHL	13	2	5	7	6	....	....	....	....	....	....	....	....	....	....	....	....	....	....	....	....	....	....
99-2000	Michigan State	CCHA	40	8	20	28	26	....	....	....	....	....	....	....	....	....	....	....	....	....	....	....	....	....	....
2000-01	Michigan State	CCHA	42	7	18	25	28	....	....	....	....	....	....	....	....	....	....	....	....	....	....	....	....	....	....
2001-02	Michigan State	CCHA	41	13	22	35	18	....	....	....	....	....	....	....	....	....	....	....	....	....	....	....	....	....	....
2002-03	Michigan State	CCHA	39	16	34	50	46	....	....	....	....	....	....	....	....	....	....	....	....	....	....	....	....	....	....
	Hershey Bears	AHL	5	0	1	1	4	....	....	....	....	....	....	....	....	....	5	0	0	0	2	....	....	....	....
2003-04	**Colorado**	**NHL**	**79**	**10**	**24**	**34**	**28**	**2**	**0**	**1**	**115**	**8.7**	**7**	**0**	**0.0**	**16:14**	**11**	**0**	**1**	**1**	**4**	**0**	**0**	**0**	**16:41**
2004-05	Iserlohn Roosters	Germany	17	5	6	11	24	....	....	....	....	....	....	....	....	....	....	....	....	....	....	....	....	....	....
2005-06	**Colorado**	**NHL**	**82**	**14**	**35**	**49**	**44**	**6**	**0**	**1**	**154**	**9.1**	**5**	**1**	**100.0**	**18:31**	**9**	**1**	**2**	**3**	**6**	**1**	**0**	**0**	**17:35**
	United States	Olympics	6	0	2	2	2	....	....	....	....	....	....	....	....	....	....	....	....	....	....	....	....	....	....
2006-07	**Colorado**	**NHL**	**71**	**14**	**30**	**44**	**24**	**8**	**0**	**3**	**128**	**10.9**	**0**	**0**	**0.0**	**17:46**	....	....	....	....	....	....	....	....	....
2007-08	**Colorado**	**NHL**	**81**	**6**	**26**	**32**	**26**	**5**	**0**	**1**	**163**	**3.7**	**2**	**0**	**0.0**	**19:40**	**10**	**2**	**3**	**5**	**2**	**1**	**0**	**0**	**19:08**
	NHL Totals		**313**	**44**	**115**	**159**	**122**	**21**	**0**	**6**	**560**	**7.9**		**1**	**100.0**	**18:04**	**30**	**3**	**6**	**9**	**12**	**2**	**0**	**0**	**17:46**

CCHA Second All-Star Team (2001) • CCHA First All-Star Team (2002, 2003) • NCAA West Second All-American Team (2002) • NCAA West First All-American Team (2003) • NHL All-Rookie Team (2004)

Signed as a free agent by **Iserlohn** (Germany), December 29, 2004.

LILJA, Andreas

(LIHL-yuh, awn-DRAY-uhs) **DET.**

Defense. Shoots left. 6'3", 220 lbs. Born, Helsingborg, Sweden, July 13, 1975. Los Angeles' 2nd choice, 54th overall, in 2000 Entry Draft.

1993-94	Malmo IF Jr.	Swe-Jr.	14	3	7	10	38	....	....	....	....	....	....	....	....	....	....	....	....	....	....	....	....	....	....
1994-95	Malmo IF Jr.	Swe-Jr.	30	7	13	20	82	....	....	....	....	....	....	....	....	....	....	....	....	....	....	....	....	....	....
	Malmo IF	Sweden	3	0	0	0	2	....	....	....	....	....	....	....	....	....	....	....	....	....	....	....	....	....	....
1995-96	Malmo IF Jr.	Swe-Jr.	3	0	1	1	6	....	....	....	....	....	....	....	....	....	....	....	....	....	....	....	....	....	....
	Malmo IF	Sweden	40	1	5	6	63	....	....	....	....	....	....	....	....	....	5	0	1	1	2	....	....	....	....
1996-97	Malmo	Sweden	47	1	0	1	22	....	....	....	....	....	....	....	....	....	4	0	0	0	10	....	....	....	....
1997-98	Malmo	Sweden	10	0	0	0	0	....	....	....	....	....	....	....	....	....	....	....	....	....	....	....	....	....	....
	Mora IK	Sweden-2	13	1	4	5	30	....	....	....	....	....	....	....	....	....	4	1	0	1	14	....	....	....	....
1998-99	Malmo	Sweden	41	0	3	3	44	....	....	....	....	....	....	....	....	....	1	0	0	0	4	....	....	....	....
99-2000	Malmo	Sweden	49	8	11	19	88	....	....	....	....	....	....	....	....	....	6	0	0	0	8	....	....	....	....
2000-01	**Los Angeles**	**NHL**	**2**	**0**	**0**	**0**	**4**	**0**	**0**	**0**	**1**	**0.0**	**–2**	**0**	**0.0**	**12:22**	**1**	**0**	**0**	**0**	**0**	**0**	**0**	**0**	**6:56**
	Lowell	AHL	61	7	29	36	149	....	....	....	....	....	....	....	....	....	4	0	6	6	6	....	....	....	....
2001-02	**Los Angeles**	**NHL**	**26**	**1**	**4**	**5**	**22**	**1**	**0**	**0**	**12**	**8.3**	**3**	**0**	**0.0**	**11:27**	**5**	**0**	**0**	**0**	**6**	**0**	**0**	**0**	**10:26**
	Manchester	AHL	4	0	1	1	4	....	....	....	....	....	....	....	....	....	....	....	....	....	....	....	....	....	....
2002-03	**Los Angeles**	**NHL**	**17**	**0**	**3**	**3**	**14**	**0**	**0**	**0**	**13**	**0.0**	**5**	**0**	**0.0**	**20:04**	....	....	....	....	....	....	....	....	....
	Florida	**NHL**	**56**	**4**	**8**	**12**	**56**	**0**	**0**	**0**	**59**	**6.8**	**8**	**0**	**0.0**	**19:11**	....	....	....	....	....	....	....	....	....
2003-04	**Florida**	**NHL**	**79**	**3**	**4**	**7**	**90**	**0**	**0**	**0**	**79**	**3.8**	**–8**	**1**	**0.0**	**19:34**	....	....	....	....	....	....	....	....	....
2004-05	Mora IK	Sweden	44	3	8	11	67	....	....	....	....	....	....	....	....	....	....	....	....	....	....	....	....	....	....
	HC Ambri-Piotta	Swiss	....	....	....	....	....	....	....	....	....	....	....	....	....	....	5	0	2	2	6	....	....	....	....
2005-06	**Detroit**	**NHL**	**82**	**2**	**13**	**15**	**98**	**0**	**0**	**1**	**78**	**2.6**	**18**	**1**	**0.0**	**19:01**	**6**	**0**	**1**	**1**	**6**	**0**	**0**	**0**	**19:21**

			Regular Season														Playoffs								
Season	Club	League	GP	G	A	Pts	PIM	PP	SH	GW	S	%	+/-	TF	F%	Min	GP	G	A	Pts	PIM	PP	SH	GW	Min
2006-07	**Detroit**	**NHL**	**57**	**0**	**5**	**5**	**54**	**0**	**0**	**0**	**37**	**0.0**	**6**	**1**	**0.0**	**15:25**	**18**	**1**	**0**	**1**	**10**	**0**	**0**	**0**	**19:02**
2007-08 ♦	**Detroit**	**NHL**	**79**	**2**	**10**	**12**	**93**	**0**	**0**	**2**	**72**	**2.8**	**−2**	**1**	**0.0**	**18:14**	**12**	**0**	**1**	**1**	**16**	**0**	**0**	**0**	**14:05**
	NHL Totals		**398**	**12**	**47**	**59**	**431**	**1**	**0**	**3**	**351**	**3.4**		**4**	**0.0**	**17:59**	**42**	**1**	**2**	**3**	**38**	**0**	**0**	**0**	**16:21**

• Spent majority of 2001-02 season as a healthy reserve. Traded to **Florida** by **Los Angeles** with Jaroslav Bednar for Dmitry Yushkevich and Florida's 5th round choice (previously acquired, Los Angeles selected Brady Murray) in 2003 Entry Draft, November 26, 2002. Signed as a free agent by **Nashville**, July 26, 2004. Signed as a free agent by **Mora** (Sweden), September 15, 2004. Signed as a free agent by **Ambri-Piotta** (Swiss), February 25, 2005. Signed as a free agent by **Detroit**, August 24, 2005.

LINDEN, Trevor

(LIHND-duhn, TREH-vuhr)

Right wing. Shoots right. 6'4", 220 lbs. Born, Medicine Hat, Alta., April 11, 1970. Vancouver's 1st choice, 2nd overall, in 1988 Entry Draft.

1985-86	Medicine Hat	AMHL	40	14	22	36	14	....	....	....	....	....	....	....	....	....	....	....	....	....	....	....	....	....	....
	Medicine Hat	WHL	5	2	0	2	0	....	....	....	....	....	....	....	....	....	....	....	....	....	....	....	....	....	....
1986-87	Medicine Hat	WHL	72	14	22	36	59	....	....	....	....	....	....	....	....	....	20	5	4	9	17	....	....	....	....
1987-88	Medicine Hat	WHL	67	46	64	110	76	....	....	....	....	....	....	....	....	....	16	*13	12	25	19	....	....	....	....
1988-89	**Vancouver**	**NHL**	**80**	**30**	**29**	**59**	**41**	**10**	**1**	**2**	**186**	**16.1**	**−10**	....	....	....	**7**	**3**	**4**	**7**	**8**	**2**	**1**	**0**	....
1989-90	**Vancouver**	**NHL**	**73**	**21**	**30**	**51**	**43**	**6**	**2**	**3**	**171**	**12.3**	**−17**	....	....	....	....	....	....	....	....	....	....	....	....
1990-91	**Vancouver**	**NHL**	**80**	**33**	**37**	**70**	**65**	**16**	**2**	**4**	**229**	**14.4**	**−25**	....	....	....	**6**	**0**	**7**	**7**	**2**	**0**	**0**	**0**	....
1991-92	**Vancouver**	**NHL**	**80**	**31**	**44**	**75**	**101**	**6**	**1**	**6**	**201**	**15.4**	**3**	....	....	....	**13**	**4**	**8**	**12**	**6**	**2**	**0**	**1**	....
1992-93	**Vancouver**	**NHL**	**84**	**33**	**39**	**72**	**64**	**8**	**0**	**3**	**209**	**15.8**	**19**	....	....	....	**12**	**5**	**8**	**13**	**16**	**2**	**0**	**1**	....
1993-94	**Vancouver**	**NHL**	**84**	**32**	**29**	**61**	**73**	**10**	**2**	**3**	**234**	**13.7**	**6**	....	....	....	**24**	**12**	**13**	**25**	**18**	**5**	**1**	**1**	....
1994-95	**Vancouver**	**NHL**	**48**	**18**	**22**	**40**	**40**	**9**	**0**	**1**	**129**	**14.0**	**−5**	....	....	....	**11**	**2**	**6**	**8**	**12**	**1**	**0**	**0**	....
1995-96	**Vancouver**	**NHL**	**82**	**33**	**47**	**80**	**42**	**12**	**1**	**2**	**202**	**16.3**	**6**	....	....	....	**6**	**4**	**4**	**8**	**6**	**2**	**0**	**0**	....
1996-97	**Vancouver**	**NHL**	**49**	**9**	**31**	**40**	**27**	**2**	**2**	**2**	**84**	**10.7**	**5**	....	....	....	....	....	....	....	....	....	....	....	....
1997-98	**Vancouver**	**NHL**	**42**	**7**	**14**	**21**	**49**	**2**	**0**	**1**	**74**	**9.5**	**−13**	....	....	....	....	....	....	....	....	....	....	....	....
	NY Islanders	**NHL**	**25**	**10**	**7**	**17**	**33**	**3**	**2**	**1**	**59**	**16.9**	**−1**	....	....	....	....	....	....	....	....	....	....	....	....
	Canada	Olympics	6	1	0	1	10	....	....	....	....	....	....	....	....	....	....	....	....	....	....	....	....	....	....
1998-99	**NY Islanders**	**NHL**	**82**	**18**	**29**	**47**	**32**	**8**	**1**	**1**	**167**	**10.8**	**−14**	**261**	**50.2**	**21:29**	....	....	....	....	....	....	....	....	....
99-2000	**Montreal**	**NHL**	**50**	**13**	**17**	**30**	**34**	**4**	**0**	**3**	**87**	**14.9**	**−3**	**860**	**56.3**	**17:51**	....	....	....	....	....	....	....	....	....
2000-01	**Montreal**	**NHL**	**57**	**12**	**21**	**33**	**52**	**6**	**0**	**3**	**96**	**12.5**	**−2**	**1142**	**52.7**	**20:47**	....	....	....	....	....	....	....	....	....
	Washington	**NHL**	**12**	**3**	**1**	**4**	**8**	**0**	**0**	**0**	**30**	**10.0**	**2**	**75**	**60.0**	**18:03**	**6**	**0**	**4**	**4**	**14**	**0**	**0**	**0**	**22:41**
2001-02	**Washington**	**NHL**	**16**	**1**	**2**	**3**	**6**	**1**	**0**	**0**	**19**	**5.3**	**−2**	**71**	**49.3**	**16:06**	....	....	....	....	....	....	....	....	....
	Vancouver	**NHL**	**64**	**12**	**22**	**34**	**65**	**2**	**0**	**2**	**122**	**9.8**	**−3**	**1190**	**53.4**	**19:23**	**6**	**1**	**4**	**5**	**0**	**0**	**0**	**0**	**19:36**
2002-03	**Vancouver**	**NHL**	**71**	**19**	**22**	**41**	**30**	**4**	**1**	**1**	**116**	**16.4**	**−1**	**568**	**54.4**	**15:52**	**14**	**1**	**2**	**3**	**10**	**0**	**1**	**0**	**17:38**
2003-04	**Vancouver**	**NHL**	**82**	**14**	**22**	**36**	**26**	**4**	**0**	**1**	**97**	**14.4**	**−6**	**1285**	**55.8**	**16:17**	**7**	**0**	**0**	**0**	**6**	**0**	**0**	**0**	**18:29**
2004-05			DID NOT PLAY																						
2005-06	**Vancouver**	**NHL**	**82**	**7**	**9**	**16**	**15**	**1**	**1**	**0**	**55**	**12.7**	**3**	**668**	**49.6**	**11:20**	....	....	....	....	....	....	....	....	....
2006-07	**Vancouver**	**NHL**	**80**	**12**	**13**	**25**	**34**	**5**	**0**	**1**	**92**	**13.0**	**−6**	**211**	**50.7**	**12:20**	**12**	**2**	**5**	**7**	**6**	**1**	**0**	**2**	**17:15**
2007-08	**Vancouver**	**NHL**	**59**	**7**	**5**	**12**	**15**	**0**	**2**	**1**	**45**	**15.6**	**0**	**316**	**50.0**	**11:19**	....	....	....	....	....	....	....	....	....
	NHL Totals		**1382**	**375**	**492**	**867**	**895**	**119**	**18**	**41**	**2704**	**13.9**		**6647**	**53.5**	**16:11**	**124**	**34**	**65**	**99**	**104**	**15**	**3**	**5**	**18:36**

WHL East Second All-Star Team (1988) • Memorial Cup Tournament All-Star Team (1988) • NHL All-Rookie Team (1989) • King Clancy Memorial Trophy (1997)

Played in NHL All-Star Game (1991, 1992)

Traded to **NY Islanders** by **Vancouver** for Todd Bertuzzi, Bryan McCabe and NY Islanders' 3rd round choice (Jarkko Ruutu) in 1998 Entry Draft, February 6, 1998. Traded to **Montreal** by **NY Islanders** for Montreal's 1st round choice (Branislav Mezei) in 1999 Entry Draft, May 29, 1999. Traded to **Washington** by **Montreal** with Dainius Zubrus and New Jersey's 2nd round choice (previously acquired, later traded to Tampa Bay – Tampa Bay selected Andreas Holmqvist) in 2001 Entry Draft for Richard Zednik, Jan Bulis and Washington's 1st round choice (Alexander Perezhogin) in 2001 Entry Draft, March 13, 2001. Traded to **Vancouver** by **Washington** with NY Islanders' 2nd round choice (previously acquired, Vancouver selected Denis Grot) in 2002 Entry Draft for Vancouver's 1st round choice (Boyd Gordon) in 2002 Entry Draft and Vancouver's 3rd round choice (later traded to Edmonton – Edmonton selected Zachery Stortini) in 2003 Entry Draft, November 10, 2001. • Officially announced his retirement, June 11, 2008.

LINDSTROM, Joakim

(LIHND-struhm, YOH-ah-kihm) **ANA.**

Center. Shoots left. 6', 187 lbs. Born, Skelleftea, Sweden, December 5, 1983. Columbus' 2nd choice, 41st overall, in 2002 Entry Draft.

99-2000	MoDo U18	Swe-U18	17	6	*14	20	32	....	....	....	....	....	....	....	....	....	....	....	....	....	....	....	....	....	....
	Malmo Jr.	Swe-Jr.	10	4	4	8	2	....	....	....	....	....	....	....	....	....	....	....	....	....	....	....	....	....	....
2000-01	Malmo Jr.	Swe-Jr.	12	7	14	21	46	....	....	....	....	....	....	....	....	....	4	2	3	5	24	....	....	....	....
	MoDo	Sweden	10	2	3	5	2	....	....	....	....	....	....	....	....	....	7	0	1	1	0	....	....	....	....
2001-02	Malmo Jr.	Swe-Jr.	10	9	6	15	67	....	....	....	....	....	....	....	....	....	....	....	....	....	....	....	....	....	....
	IF Troja-Ljungby	Sweden-2	3	0	0	0	12	....	....	....	....	....	....	....	....	....	....	....	....	....	....	....	....	....	....
	MODO	Sweden	42	4	3	7	20	....	....	....	....	....	....	....	....	....	14	3	5	8	8	....	....	....	....
2002-03	MODO	Sweden	29	4	2	6	14	....	....	....	....	....	....	....	....	....	6	1	1	2	2	....	....	....	....
	Malmo Jr.	Swe-Jr.	2	5	1	6	8	....	....	....	....	....	....	....	....	....	....	....	....	....	....	....	....	....	....
	Ornskoldsviks SK	Sweden-2	2	1	1	2	4	....	....	....	....	....	....	....	....	....	....	....	....	....	....	....	....	....	....
2003-04	MODO	Sweden	15	0	2	2	0	....	....	....	....	....	....	....	....	....	....	....	....	....	....	....	....	....	....
	Sundsvall	Sweden-2	2	0	5	5	0	....	....	....	....	....	....	....	....	....	....	....	....	....	....	....	....	....	....
2004-05	MODO Jr.	Swe-Jr.	2	4	1	5	0	....	....	....	....	....	....	....	....	....	....	....	....	....	....	....	....	....	....
	MODO	Sweden	37	2	3	5	24	....	....	....	....	....	....	....	....	....	....	....	....	....	....	....	....	....	....
	Syracuse Crunch	AHL	13	4	4	8	0	....	....	....	....	....	....	....	....	....	....	....	....	....	....	....	....	....	....
2005-06	**Columbus**	**NHL**	**3**	**0**	**0**	**0**	**0**	**0**	**0**	**0**	**4**	**0.0**	**0**	**0**	**0.0**	**5:11**	....	....	....	....	....	....	....	....	....
	Syracuse Crunch	AHL	64	14	29	43	52	....	....	....	....	....	....	....	....	....	6	1	1	2	0	....	....	....	....
2006-07	**Columbus**	**NHL**	**9**	**1**	**0**	**1**	**4**	**0**	**0**	**0**	**9**	**11.1**	**−3**	**0**	**0.0**	**8:28**	....	....	....	....	....	....	....	....	....
	Syracuse Crunch	AHL	50	22	26	48	34	....	....	....	....	....	....	....	....	....	....	....	....	....	....	....	....	....	....
2007-08	**Columbus**	**NHL**	**25**	**3**	**4**	**7**	**14**	**2**	**0**	**1**	**25**	**12.0**	**0**	**7**	**28.6**	**9:26**	....	....	....	....	....	....	....	....	....
	Syracuse Crunch	AHL	49	25	35	60	68	....	....	....	....	....	....	....	....	....	13	4	3	7	6	....	....	....	....
	NHL Totals		**37**	**4**	**4**	**8**	**18**	**2**	**0**	**1**	**38**	**10.5**		**7**	**28.6**	**8:51**	....	....	....	....	....	....	....	....	....

Traded to **Anaheim** by **Columbus** for future considerations, July 15, 2008.

LING, David

(LIHNG, DAY-vihd)

Right wing. Shoots right. 5'10", 204 lbs. Born, Halifax, N.S., January 9, 1975. Quebec's 9th choice, 179th overall, in 1993 Entry Draft.

1991-92	Charlotwn Abbies	MJrHL	30	33	42	75	270	....	....	....	....	....	....	....	....	....	....	....	....	....	....	....	....	....	....
	St. Mike's B's	OHA-B	8	5	14	19	25	....	....	....	....	....	....	....	....	....	....	....	....	....	....	....	....	....	....
1992-93	Kingston	OHL	64	17	46	63	275	....	....	....	....	....	....	....	....	....	16	3	12	15	*72	....	....	....	....
1993-94	Kingston	OHL	61	37	40	77	*254	....	....	....	....	....	....	....	....	....	6	4	2	6	16	....	....	....	....
1994-95	Kingston	OHL	62	*61	74	135	136	....	....	....	....	....	....	....	....	....	6	7	8	15	12	....	....	....	....
1995-96	Saint John Flames	AHL	75	24	32	56	179	....	....	....	....	....	....	....	....	....	9	0	5	5	12	....	....	....	....
1996-97	Saint John Flames	AHL	5	0	2	2	19	....	....	....	....	....	....	....	....	....	....	....	....	....	....	....	....	....	....
	Montreal	**NHL**	**2**	**0**	**0**	**0**	**0**	**0**	**0**	**0**	**0**	**0.0**	**0**	....	....	....	....	....	....	....	....	....	....	....	....
	Fredericton	AHL	48	22	36	58	229	....	....	....	....	....	....	....	....	....	....	....	....	....	....	....	....	....	....
1997-98	**Montreal**	**NHL**	**1**	**0**	**0**	**0**	**0**	**0**	**0**	**0**	**1**	**0.0**	**−1**	....	....	....	....	....	....	....	....	....	....	....	....
	Fredericton	AHL	67	25	41	66	148	....	....	....	....	....	....	....	....	....	....	....	....	....	....	....	....	....	....
	Indianapolis Ice	IHL	12	8	6	14	30	....	....	....	....	....	....	....	....	....	5	4	1	5	31	....	....	....	....
1998-99	Kansas City	IHL	82	30	42	72	112	....	....	....	....	....	....	....	....	....	3	1	0	1	20	....	....	....	....
99-2000	Kansas City	IHL	82	35	48	83	210	....	....	....	....	....	....	....	....	....	....	....	....	....	....	....	....	....	....
2000-01	Utah Grizzlies	IHL	79	15	28	43	202	....	....	....	....	....	....	....	....	....	....	....	....	....	....	....	....	....	....
2001-02	**Columbus**	**NHL**	**5**	**0**	**0**	**0**	**7**	**0**	**0**	**0**	**5**	**0.0**	**−1**	**1**	**0.0**	**9:47**	....	....	....	....	....	....	....	....	....
	Syracuse Crunch	AHL	71	19	41	60	240	....	....	....	....	....	....	....	....	....	10	5	5	10	16	....	....	....	....
2002-03	**Columbus**	**NHL**	**35**	**3**	**2**	**5**	**86**	**0**	**0**	**0**	**37**	**8.1**	**−6**	**15**	**40.0**	**7:56**	....	....	....	....	....	....	....	....	....
	Syracuse Crunch	AHL	46	7	34	41	129	....	....	....	....	....	....	....	....	....	....	....	....	....	....	....	....	....	....
2003-04	**Columbus**	**NHL**	**50**	**1**	**2**	**3**	**98**	**0**	**0**	**0**	**45**	**2.2**	**−3**	**8**	**37.5**	**7:45**	....	....	....	....	....	....	....	....	....
	Syracuse Crunch	AHL	14	7	10	17	25	....	....	....	....	....	....	....	....	....	7	0	1	1	36	....	....	....	....
2004-05	St. John's	AHL	80	28	60	88	152	....	....	....	....	....	....	....	....	....	5	1	1	2	43	....	....	....	....
2005-06	Spartak Moscow	Russia	50	15	17	32	40	....	....	....	....	....	....	....	....	....	3	2	1	3	4	....	....	....	....
2006-07	Dynamo Moscow	Russia	42	10	16	26	91	....	....	....	....	....	....	....	....	....	3	1	1	2	4	....	....	....	....
2007-08	Toronto Marlies	AHL	71	17	42	59	179	....	....	....	....	....	....	....	....	....	17	3	11	14	18	....	....	....	....
	NHL Totals		**93**	**4**	**4**	**8**	**191**	**0**	**0**	**0**	**88**	**4.5**		**24**	**37.5**	**7:56**	....	....	....	....	....	....	....	....	....

OHL First All-Star Team (1995) • OHL MVP (1995) • Canadian Major Junior First All-Star Team (1995) • Canadian Major Junior Player of the Year (1995) • IHL First All-Star Team (2000)

Rights transferred to **Colorado** after **Quebec** franchise relocated, June 21, 1995. Traded to **Calgary** by **Colorado** with Colorado's 9th round choice (Steve Shirreffs) in 1995 Entry Draft for Calgary's 9th round choice (Chris George) in 1995 Entry Draft, July 7, 1995. Traded to **Montreal** by **Calgary** with Calgary's 6th round choice (Gordie Dwyer) in 1998 Entry Draft for Scott Fraser, October 24, 1996. Traded to **Chicago** by **Montreal** for Martin Gendron, March 14, 1998. Signed as a free agent by **Kansas City** (IHL) with Chicago retaining NHL rights, September 3, 1998. Traded to **Dallas** by **Chicago** for future considerations, August 11, 2000. Signed as a free agent by **Columbus**, July 7, 2001. Signed as a free agent by **Toronto**, July 29, 2004. Signed as a free agent by **Dynamo Moscow** (Russia), August 22, 2006. Signed as a free agent by **Toronto**, July 9, 2007.

LISIN, Enver

(LIH-sihn, EHN-vuhr) **PHX.**

Right wing. Shoots left. 6'2", 190 lbs. Born, Moscow, USSR, April 22, 1986. Phoenix's 3rd choice, 50th overall, in 2004 Entry Draft.

			Regular Season														Playoffs								
Season	Club	League	GP	G	A	Pts	PIM	PP	SH	GW	S	%	+/-	TF	F%	Min	GP	G	A	Pts	PIM	PP	SH	GW	Min
2001-02	Dyn'o Moscow 2	Russia-3	6	3	0	3	14	....	....	....	....	....	....	....	....	....	....	....	....	....	....	....	....	....	....
2002-03	Dyn'o Moscow 2	Russia-3	STATISTICS NOT AVAILABLE																						
2003-04	Dyn'o Moscow 2	Russia-3	STATISTICS NOT AVAILABLE																						
	Kristall Saratov	Russia-2	35	10	6	16	30	....	....	....	....	....	....	....	....	....	4	1	0	1	0	....	....	....	....
2004-05	Ak Bars Kazan 2	Russia-3	....	4	3	7	....	....	....	....	....	....	....	....	....	....	....	....	....	....	....	....	....	....	....
	Ak Bars Kazan	Russia	53	8	4	12	4	....	....	....	....	....	....	....	....	....	3	0	0	0	0	....	....	....	....
2005-06	Ak Bars Kazan	Russia	43	7	5	12	26	....	....	....	....	....	....	....	....	....	13	3	1	4	6	....	....	....	....
2006-07	**Phoenix**	**NHL**	**17**	**1**	**1**	**2**	**16**	**1**	**0**	**0**	**35**	**2.9**	**–18**	**7**	**28.6**	**15:02**	....	....	....	....	....	....	....	....	....
	San Antonio	AHL	2	2	0	2	4	....	....	....	....	....	....	....	....	....	....	....	....	....	....	....	....	....	....
	Ak Bars Kazan	Russia	20	6	2	8	18	....	....	....	....	....	....	....	....	....	1	0	0	0	0	....	....	....	....
2007-08	**Phoenix**	**NHL**	**13**	**4**	**1**	**5**	**6**	**1**	**0**	**0**	**27**	**14.8**	**–5**	**2**	**50.0**	**14:27**	....	....	....	....	....	....	....	....	....
	San Antonio	AHL	58	16	19	35	26	....	....	....	....	....	....	....	....	....	6	1	2	3	0	....	....	....	....
	NHL Totals		**30**	**5**	**2**	**7**	**22**	**2**	**0**	**0**	**62**	**8.1**		**9**	**33.3**	**14:47**	....	....	....	....	....	....	....	....	....

LITTLE, Bryan

(LIH-tuhl, BRIGH-uhn) **ATL.**

Center. Shoots right. 5'11", 200 lbs. Born, Edmonton, Alta., November 12, 1987. Atlanta's 1st choice, 12th overall, in 2006 Entry Draft.

Season	Club	League	GP	G	A	Pts	PIM	PP	SH	GW	S	%	+/-	TF	F%	Min	GP	G	A	Pts	PIM	PP	SH	GW	Min
2003-04	Barrie Colts	OHL	64	34	24	58	18	....	....	....	....	....	....	....	....	....	12	5	5	10	7	....	....	....	....
2004-05	Barrie Colts	OHL	62	36	32	68	34	....	....	....	....	....	....	....	....	....	4	5	1	6	2	....	....	....	....
2005-06	Barrie Colts	OHL	64	42	67	109	99	....	....	....	....	....	....	....	....	....	14	8	15	23	19	....	....	....	....
2006-07	Barrie Colts	OHL	57	41	66	107	77	....	....	....	....	....	....	....	....	....	8	4	5	9	8	....	....	....	....
	Chicago Wolves	AHL	....	....	....	....	....	....	....	....	....	....	....	....	....	....	2	0	0	0	0	....	....	....	....
2007-08	**Atlanta**	**NHL**	**48**	**6**	**10**	**16**	**18**	**2**	**0**	**1**	**76**	**7.9**	**–2**	**505**	**45.2**	**15:37**	....	....	....	....	....	....	....	....	....
	Chicago Wolves	AHL	34	9	16	25	10	....	....	....	....	....	....	....	....	....	24	8	5	13	10	....	....	....	....
	NHL Totals		**48**	**6**	**10**	**16**	**18**	**2**	**0**	**1**	**76**	**7.9**		**505**	**45.1**	**15:37**	....	....	....	....	....	....	....	....	....

OHL Second All-Star Team (2007)

LOCKE, Corey

(LAWK, KOH-ree) **MIN.**

Center. Shoots left. 5'9", 168 lbs. Born, Toronto, Ont., May 8, 1984. Montreal's 5th choice, 113th overall, in 2003 Entry Draft.

Season	Club	League	GP	G	A	Pts	PIM	PP	SH	GW	S	%	+/-	TF	F%	Min	GP	G	A	Pts	PIM	PP	SH	GW	Min
2000-01	Newmarket	OPJHL	49	34	51	85	16	....	....	....	....	....	....	....	....	....	16	10	12	22	14	....	....	....	....
2001-02	Ottawa 67's	OHL	55	18	25	43	18	....	....	....	....	....	....	....	....	....	13	6	7	13	10	....	....	....	....
2002-03	Ottawa 67's	OHL	66	*63	*88	*151	83	....	....	....	....	....	....	....	....	....	23	*19	19	*38	30	....	....	....	....
2003-04	Ottawa 67's	OHL	65	*51	67	*118	82	....	....	....	....	....	....	....	....	....	7	7	3	10	10	....	....	....	....
2004-05	Hamilton	AHL	78	16	27	43	20	....	....	....	....	....	....	....	....	....	4	0	0	0	2	....	....	....	....
2005-06	Hamilton	AHL	77	19	40	59	67	....	....	....	....	....	....	....	....	....	....	....	....	....	....	....	....	....	....
2006-07	Hamilton	AHL	80	20	35	55	54	....	....	....	....	....	....	....	....	....	22	*10	12	22	10	....	....	....	....
2007-08	**Montreal**	**NHL**	**1**	**0**	**0**	**0**	**0**	**0**	**0**	**0**	**1**	**0.0**	**–1**	**5**	**40.0**	**5:59**	....	....	....	....	....	....	....	....	....
	Hamilton	AHL	78	30	42	72	50	....	....	....	....	....	....	....	....	....	....	....	....	....	....	....	....	....	....
	NHL Totals		**1**	**0**	**0**	**0**	**0**	**0**	**0**	**0**	**1**	**0.0**		**5**	**40.0**	**5:59**	....	....	....	....	....	....	....	....	....

OHL First All-Star Team (2003, 2004) • OHL Player of the Year (2003, 2004) • Canadian Major Junior First All-Star Team (2003, 2004) • Canadian Major Junior Player of the Year (2003)

Traded to **Minnesota** by **Montreal** for Shawn Belle, July 11, 2008.

LOJEK, Martin

(LOI-yehk, MAHR-tihn)

Defense. Shoots right. 6'4", 220 lbs. Born, Brno, Czech., August 19, 1985. Florida's 5th choice, 105th overall, in 2003 Entry Draft.

Season	Club	League	GP	G	A	Pts	PIM	PP	SH	GW	S	%	+/-	TF	F%	Min	GP	G	A	Pts	PIM	PP	SH	GW	Min
2000-01	HC Pardubice Jr.	CzRep-Jr.	48	2	2	4	42	....	....	....	....	....	....	....	....	....	7	0	0	0	6	....	....	....	....
2001-02	HC Pardubice Jr.	CzRep-Jr.	40	2	4	6	24	....	....	....	....	....	....	....	....	....	7	1	0	1	2	....	....	....	....
2002-03	Brampton	OHL	65	1	13	14	47	....	....	....	....	....	....	....	....	....	11	0	1	1	6	....	....	....	....
2003-04	Brampton	OHL	68	3	17	20	37	....	....	....	....	....	....	....	....	....	12	0	4	4	2	....	....	....	....
2004-05	Brampton	OHL	58	1	12	13	58	....	....	....	....	....	....	....	....	....	6	0	0	0	6	....	....	....	....
2005-06	Rochester	AHL	15	1	1	2	16	....	....	....	....	....	....	....	....	....	....	....	....	....	....	....	....	....	....
	Florida Everblades	ECHL	45	3	11	14	40	....	....	....	....	....	....	....	....	....	2	0	0	0	0	....	....	....	....
2006-07	**Florida**	**NHL**	**3**	**0**	**1**	**1**	**0**	**0**	**0**	**0**	**0**	**0.0**	**2**	**0**	**0.0**	**8:23**	....	....	....	....	....	....	....	....	....
	Rochester	AHL	69	6	13	19	87	....	....	....	....	....	....	....	....	....	....	....	....	....	....	....	....	....	....
2007-08	**Florida**	**NHL**	**2**	**0**	**0**	**0**	**0**	**0**	**0**	**0**	**2**	**0.0**	**–1**	**0**	**0.0**	**6:08**	....	....	....	....	....	....	....	....	....
	Rochester	AHL	72	6	5	11	97	....	....	....	....	....	....	....	....	....	....	....	....	....	....	....	....	....	....
	NHL Totals		**5**	**0**	**1**	**1**	**0**	**0**	**0**	**0**	**2**	**0.0**		**0**	**0.0**	**7:29**	....	....	....	....	....	....	....	....	....

LOMBARDI, Matthew

(lawm-BAHR-dee, MA-thew) **CGY.**

Center. Shoots left. 6', 198 lbs. Born, Montreal, Que., March 18, 1982. Calgary's 3rd choice, 90th overall, in 2002 Entry Draft.

Season	Club	League	GP	G	A	Pts	PIM	PP	SH	GW	S	%	+/-	TF	F%	Min	GP	G	A	Pts	PIM	PP	SH	GW	Min
1997-98	Gatineau	QAAA	42	10	13	23	....	....	....	....	....	....	....	....	....	....	13	4	7	11	....	....	....	....	....
1998-99	Victoriaville Tigres	QMJHL	47	6	10	16	8	....	....	....	....	....	....	....	....	....	5	0	0	0	0	....	....	....	....
99-2000	Victoriaville Tigres	QMJHL	65	18	26	44	28	....	....	....	....	....	....	....	....	....	6	0	0	0	6	....	....	....	....
2000-01	Victoriaville Tigres	QMJHL	72	28	39	67	66	....	....	....	....	....	....	....	....	....	13	12	6	18	10	....	....	....	....
2001-02	Victoriaville Tigres	QMJHL	66	57	73	130	70	....	....	....	....	....	....	....	....	....	22	*17	18	35	18	....	....	....	....
2002-03	Saint John Flames	AHL	76	25	21	46	41	....	....	....	....	....	....	....	....	....	....	....	....	....	....	....	....	....	....
2003-04	**Calgary**	**NHL**	**79**	**16**	**13**	**29**	**32**	**3**	**2**	**4**	**130**	**12.3**	**4**	**992**	**47.9**	**14:26**	**13**	**1**	**5**	**6**	**4**	**0**	**0**	**1**	**14:46**
2004-05	Lowell	AHL	9	3	1	4	9	....	....	....	....	....	....	....	....	....	11	0	3	3	16	....	....	....	....
2005-06	**Calgary**	**NHL**	**55**	**6**	**20**	**26**	**48**	**1**	**2**	**2**	**72**	**8.3**	**–1**	**499**	**52.9**	**14:09**	**7**	**0**	**2**	**2**	**2**	**0**	**0**	**0**	**15:51**
	Omaha	AHL	1	1	1	2	0	....	....	....	....	....	....	....	....	....	....	....	....	....	....	....	....	....	....
2006-07	**Calgary**	**NHL**	**81**	**20**	**26**	**46**	**48**	**5**	**4**	**5**	**176**	**11.4**	**10**	**965**	**49.1**	**16:22**	**6**	**1**	**1**	**2**	**0**	**1**	**0**	**0**	**15:19**
2007-08	**Calgary**	**NHL**	**82**	**14**	**22**	**36**	**67**	**2**	**2**	**4**	**181**	**7.7**	**–6**	**955**	**47.6**	**17:19**	**7**	**0**	**0**	**0**	**4**	**0**	**0**	**0**	**17:14**
	NHL Totals		**297**	**56**	**81**	**137**	**195**	**11**	**10**	**15**	**559**	**10.0**		**3411**	**48.9**	**15:42**	**33**	**2**	**8**	**10**	**10**	**1**	**0**	**1**	**15:37**

• Re-entered NHL Entry Draft. Originally Edmonton's 7th choice, 215th overall, in 2000 Entry Draft.

Memorial Cup Tournament All-Star Team (2002) • Ed Chynoweth Trophy (Memorial Cup Tournament - Leading Scorer) (2002)

LUCIC, Milan

(LOO-chihtch, MEE-lan) **BOS.**

Left wing. Shoots left. 6'3", 228 lbs. Born, Vancouver, B.C., June 7, 1988. Boston's 3rd choice, 50th overall, in 2006 Entry Draft.

Season	Club	League	GP	G	A	Pts	PIM	PP	SH	GW	S	%	+/-	TF	F%	Min	GP	G	A	Pts	PIM	PP	SH	GW	Min
2004-05	Coquitlam	BCHL	50	9	14	23	100	....	....	....	....	....	....	....	....	....	....	....	....	....	....	....	....	....	....
	Vancouver Giants	WHL	1	0	0	0	2	....	....	....	....	....	....	....	....	....	2	0	0	0	0	....	....	....	....
2005-06	Vancouver Giants	WHL	62	9	10	19	149	....	....	....	....	....	....	....	....	....	18	3	4	7	23	....	....	....	....
2006-07	Vancouver Giants	WHL	70	30	38	68	147	....	....	....	....	....	....	....	....	....	22	7	12	19	26	....	....	....	....
2007-08	**Boston**	**NHL**	**77**	**8**	**19**	**27**	**89**	**1**	**0**	**4**	**88**	**9.1**	**–2**	**8**	**50.0**	**12:07**	**7**	**2**	**0**	**2**	**4**	**0**	**0**	**0**	**16:24**
	NHL Totals		**77**	**8**	**19**	**27**	**89**	**1**	**0**	**4**	**88**	**9.1**		**8**	**50.0**	**12:07**	**7**	**2**	**0**	**2**	**4**	**0**	**0**	**0**	**16:24**

Memorial Cup Tournament All-Star Team (2007) • Stafford Smythe Memorial Trophy (Memorial Cup Tournament - MVP) (2007)

LUKOWICH, Brad

(loo-KUH-which, BRAD) **S.J.**

Defense. Shoots left. 6'1", 201 lbs. Born, Cranbrook, B.C., August 12, 1976. NY Islanders' 4th choice, 90th overall, in 1994 Entry Draft.

Season	Club	League	GP	G	A	Pts	PIM	PP	SH	GW	S	%	+/-	TF	F%	Min	GP	G	A	Pts	PIM	PP	SH	GW	Min
1992-93	Cranbrook Colts	RMJHL	54	21	41	62	162	....	....	....	....	....	....	....	....	....	....	....	....	....	....	....	....	....	....
	Kamloops Blazers	WHL	1	0	0	0	0	....	....	....	....	....	....	....	....	....	....	....	....	....	....	....	....	....	....
1993-94	Kamloops Blazers	WHL	42	5	11	16	166	....	....	....	....	....	....	....	....	....	16	0	1	1	35	....	....	....	....
1994-95	Kamloops Blazers	WHL	63	10	35	45	125	....	....	....	....	....	....	....	....	....	18	0	7	7	21	....	....	....	....
1995-96	Kamloops Blazers	WHL	65	14	55	69	114	....	....	....	....	....	....	....	....	....	13	2	10	12	29	....	....	....	....
1996-97	Michigan	IHL	69	2	6	8	77	....	....	....	....	....	....	....	....	....	4	0	1	1	2	....	....	....	....
1997-98	**Dallas**	**NHL**	**4**	**0**	**1**	**1**	**2**	**0**	**0**	**0**	**2**	**0.0**	**–2**	....	....	....	....	....	....	....	....	....	....	....	....
	Michigan	IHL	60	6	27	33	104	....	....	....	....	....	....	....	....	....	4	0	4	4	14	....	....	....	....
1998-99	**Dallas**	**NHL**	**14**	**1**	**2**	**3**	**19**	**0**	**0**	**0**	**8**	**12.5**	**3**	**0**	**0.0**	**16:18**	**8**	**0**	**1**	**1**	**4**	**0**	**0**	**0**	**10:00**
	Michigan	IHL	67	8	21	29	95	....	....	....	....	....	....	....	....	....	....	....	....	....	....	....	....	....	....
99-2000	**Dallas**	**NHL**	**60**	**3**	**1**	**4**	**50**	**0**	**0**	**1**	**33**	**9.1**	**–14**	**1**	**0.0**	**11:44**	....	....	....	....	....	....	....	....	....
2000-01	**Dallas**	**NHL**	**80**	**4**	**10**	**14**	**76**	**0**	**0**	**2**	**43**	**9.3**	**28**	**1**	**100.0**	**14:48**	**10**	**1**	**0**	**1**	**4**	**0**	**0**	**0**	**17:28**
2001-02	**Dallas**	**NHL**	**66**	**1**	**6**	**7**	**40**	**0**	**0**	**0**	**56**	**1.8**	**–1**	**0**	**0.0**	**13:14**	....	....	....	....	....	....	....	....	....

			Regular Season														Playoffs								
Season	Club	League	GP	G	A	Pts	PIM	PP	SH	GW	S	%	+/-	TF	F%	Min	GP	G	A	Pts	PIM	PP	SH	GW	Min
2002-03	**Tampa Bay**	**NHL**	**70**	**1**	**14**	**15**	**46**	**0**	**0**	**0**	**52**	**1.9**	**4**	**1**	**0.0**	**17:34**	**9**	**0**	**1**	**1**	**2**	**0**	**0**	**0**	**17:48**
2003-04♦	**Tampa Bay**	**NHL**	**79**	**5**	**14**	**19**	**24**	**0**	**0**	**1**	**86**	**5.8**	**29**	**3**	**0.0**	**18:45**	**18**	**0**	**2**	**2**	**6**	**0**	**0**	**0**	**15:51**
2004-05	Fort Worth	CHL	16	3	5	8	33	....	....	....	....	....	....	....	....	....	....	....	....	....	....	....	....	....	....
2005-06	**NY Islanders**	**NHL**	**57**	**1**	**12**	**13**	**32**	**0**	**0**	**1**	**36**	**2.8**	**–3**	**0**	**0.0**	**19:15**	....	....	....	....	....	....	....	....	....
	New Jersey	**NHL**	**18**	**1**	**7**	**8**	**8**	**0**	**0**	**0**	**13**	**7.7**	**3**	**0**	**0.0**	**19:11**	**9**	**0**	**0**	**0**	**4**	**0**	**0**	**0**	**21:28**
2006-07	**New Jersey**	**NHL**	**75**	**4**	**8**	**12**	**36**	**0**	**1**	**2**	**50**	**8.0**	**1**	**0**	**0.0**	**20:13**	**11**	**0**	**1**	**1**	**2**	**0**	**0**	**0**	**19:57**
2007-08	**Tampa Bay**	**NHL**	**59**	**1**	**6**	**7**	**20**	**0**	**0**	**0**	**28**	**3.6**	**–15**	**0**	**0.0**	**16:36**	....	....	....	....	....	....	....	....	....
	NHL Totals		**582**	**22**	**81**	**103**	**353**	**0**	**1**	**7**	**407**	**5.4**		**6**	**16.7**	**16:41**	**65**	**1**	**5**	**6**	**22**	**0**	**0**	**0**	**17:07**

Traded to **Dallas** by **NY Islanders** for Dallas' 3rd round choice (Robert Schnabel) in 1997 Entry Draft, June 1, 1996. Traded to **Minnesota** by **Dallas** with Manny Fernandez for Minnesota's 3rd round choice (Joel Lundqvist) in 2000 Entry Draft and Minnesota's 4th round choice (later traded back to Minnesota – later traded to Los Angeles – Los Angeles selected Aaron Rome) in 2002 Entry Draft, June 12, 2000. Traded to **Dallas** by **Minnesota** with Minnesota's 3rd (Yared Hagos) and 9th (Dale Sullivan) round choices in 2001 Entry Draft for Aaron Gavey, Pavel Patera, Dallas' 8th round choice (Eric Johansson) in 2000 Entry Draft and Minnesota's 4th round choice (previously acquired, later traded to Los Angeles – Los Angeles selected Aaron Rome) in 2002 Entry Draft, June 25, 2000. Traded to **Tampa Bay** by **Dallas** with Dallas' 7th round choice (Jay Rosehill) in 2003 Entry Draft for Tampa Bay's 2nd round choice (previously acquired, later traded back to Tampa Bay – later traded to Dallas – Dallas selected Tobias Stephan) in 2002 Entry Draft, June 22, 2002. Signed as a free agent by **Fort Worth** (CHL), September 21, 2004. Signed as a free agent by **NY Islanders**, August 11, 2005. Traded to **New Jersey** by **NY Islanders** for New Jersey's 3rd round choice (later traded to Phoenix - Phoenix selected Jonas Ahnelov) in 2006 Entry Draft, March 9, 2006. Signed as a free agent by **Tampa Bay**, July 3, 2007. Traded to **San Jose** by **Tampa Bay** with Dan Boyle for Matt Carle, Ty Wishart, San Jose's 1st round choice in 2009 Entry Draft and San Jose's 4th round choice in 2010 Entry Draft, July 4, 2008.

LUNDIN, Mike

(LUHN-dihn, MIGHK) **T.B.**

Defense. Shoots left. 6'2", 188 lbs. Born, Burnsville, MN, September 24, 1984. Tampa Bay's 3rd choice, 102nd overall, in 2004 Entry Draft.

2002-03	Apple Valley	High-MN	27	8	20	27	....	....	....	....	....	....	....	....	....	....	....	....	....	....	....	....	....	....	....
2003-04	U. of Maine	H-East	44	3	16	19	34	....	....	....	....	....	....	....	....	....	....	....	....	....	....	....	....	....	....
2004-05	U. of Maine	H-East	40	1	13	14	2	....	....	....	....	....	....	....	....	....	....	....	....	....	....	....	....	....	....
2005-06	U. of Maine	H-East	36	3	13	16	4	....	....	....	....	....	....	....	....	....	....	....	....	....	....	....	....	....	....
2006-07	U. of Maine	H-East	40	6	14	20	2	....	....	....	....	....	....	....	....	....	....	....	....	....	....	....	....	....	....
2007-08	**Tampa Bay**	**NHL**	**81**	**0**	**6**	**6**	**16**	**0**	**0**	**0**	**33**	**0.0**	**3**	**0**	**0.0**	**13:48**	....	....	....	....	....	....	....	....	....
	NHL Totals		**81**	**0**	**6**	**6**	**16**	**0**	**0**	**0**	**33**	**0.0**		**0**	**0.0**	**13:48**	....	....	....	....	....	....	....	....	....

Hockey East Second All-Star Team (2007)

LUNDMARK, Jamie

(LUHND-mahrk, JAY-mee) **CGY.**

Center. Shoots right. 6', 200 lbs. Born, Edmonton, Alta., January 16, 1981. NY Rangers' 2nd choice, 9th overall, in 1999 Entry Draft.

1996-97	St. Albert Saints	AJHL	35	10	9	19	8	....	....	....	....	....	....	....	....	....	....	....	....	....	....	....	....	....	....
1997-98	St. Albert Saints	AJHL	57	33	58	91	171	....	....	....	....	....	....	....	....	....	19	13	18	31	5	....	....	....	....
1998-99	Moose Jaw	WHL	70	40	51	91	121	....	....	....	....	....	....	....	....	....	11	5	4	9	24	....	....	....	....
99-2000	Moose Jaw	WHL	37	21	27	48	33	....	....	....	....	....	....	....	....	....	....	....	....	....	....	....	....	....	....
2000-01	Seattle	WHL	52	35	42	77	49	....	....	....	....	....	....	....	....	....	9	4	4	8	16	....	....	....	....
2001-02	Hartford	AHL	79	27	32	59	56	....	....	....	....	....	....	....	....	....	10	3	4	7	16	....	....	....	....
2002-03	**NY Rangers**	**NHL**	**55**	**8**	**11**	**19**	**16**	**0**	**0**	**0**	**78**	**10.3**	**–3**	**62**	**43.6**	**12:04**	....	....	....	....	....	....	....	....	....
	Hartford	AHL	22	9	9	18	18	....	....	....	....	....	....	....	....	....	2	0	0	0	0	....	....	....	....
2003-04	**NY Rangers**	**NHL**	**56**	**2**	**8**	**10**	**33**	**0**	**0**	**1**	**68**	**2.9**	**–8**	**379**	**40.4**	**12:46**	....	....	....	....	....	....	....	....	....
2004-05	HC Forst Bolzano	Italy	14	9	9	18	22	....	....	....	....	....	....	....	....	....	....	....	....	....	....	....	....	....	....
	Hartford	AHL	64	14	27	41	146	....	....	....	....	....	....	....	....	....	6	2	4	6	8	....	....	....	....
2005-06	**NY Rangers**	**NHL**	**3**	**1**	**0**	**1**	**6**	**0**	**0**	**0**	**1**	**100.0**	**–2**	**2**	**0.0**	**9:49**	....	....	....	....	....	....	....	....	....
	Phoenix	**NHL**	**38**	**5**	**13**	**18**	**36**	**1**	**0**	**0**	**61**	**8.2**	**–1**	**366**	**58.7**	**12:37**	....	....	....	....	....	....	....	....	....
	San Antonio	AHL	4	1	2	3	2	....	....	....	....	....	....	....	....	....	....	....	....	....	....	....	....	....	....
	Calgary	**NHL**	**12**	**4**	**6**	**10**	**20**	**1**	**0**	**1**	**16**	**25.0**	**2**	**103**	**53.4**	**12:32**	**4**	**0**	**1**	**1**	**7**	**0**	**0**	**0**	**9:44**
2006-07	**Calgary**	**NHL**	**39**	**0**	**4**	**4**	**31**	**0**	**0**	**0**	**28**	**0.0**	**–4**	**233**	**55.4**	**8:37**	....	....	....	....	....	....	....	....	....
	Los Angeles	**NHL**	**29**	**7**	**2**	**9**	**25**	**0**	**0**	**0**	**53**	**13.2**	**–8**	**410**	**47.6**	**16:03**	....	....	....	....	....	....	....	....	....
2007-08	Dynamo Moscow	Russia	17	2	1	3	31	....	....	....	....	....	....	....	....	....	....	....	....	....	....	....	....	....	....
	Lake Erie	AHL	51	13	20	33	71	....	....	....	....	....	....	....	....	....	....	....	....	....	....	....	....	....	....
	NHL Totals		**232**	**27**	**44**	**71**	**167**	**2**	**0**	**2**	**305**	**8.9**		**1555**	**49.8**	**12:14**	**4**	**0**	**1**	**1**	**7**	**0**	**0**	**0**	**9:44**

WHL All-Rookie Team (1999) • WHL East Second All-Star Team (1999) • WHL West First All-Star Team (2001)

Signed as a free agent by **Bolzano** (Italy), September 21, 2004. Signed as a free agent by **Hartford** (AHL), November 16, 2004. Traded to **Phoenix** by **NY Rangers** for Jeff Taffe, October 18, 2005. Traded to **Calgary** by **Phoenix** for Calgary's 4th round choice (later traded to NY Islanders - NY Islanders selected Doug Rogers) in 2006 Entry Draft, March 9, 2006. Traded to **Los Angeles** by **Calgary** with Calgary's 4th round choice (Dwight King) in 2007 Entry Draft and Calgary's 2nd round choice (later traded back to Calgary - Calgary selected Mitch Wahl) in 2008 Entry Draft for Craig Conroy, January 29, 2007. Signed as a free agent by **Calgary**, July 16, 2008.

LUNDQVIST, Joel

(LUHND-kvihst, JOHL) **DAL.**

Center. Shoots left. 6'1", 194 lbs. Born, Are, Sweden, March 2, 1982. Dallas' 3rd choice, 68th overall, in 2000 Entry Draft.

1997-98	Rogle Jr.	Swe-Jr.	59	36	40	76	....	....	....	....	....	....	....	....	....	....	....	....	....	....	....	....	....	....	....
1998-99	V.Frolunda U18	Swe-U18	32	26	38	64	37	....	....	....	....	....	....	....	....	....	4	3	1	4	2	....	....	....	....
99-2000	V.Frolunda U18	Swe-U18	4	2	4	6	4	....	....	....	....	....	....	....	....	....	....	....	....	....	....	....	....	....	....
	V.Frolunda Jr.	Swe-Jr.	25	7	12	19	2	....	....	....	....	....	....	....	....	....	6	2	3	5	2	....	....	....	....
2000-01	V.Frolunda Jr.	Swe-Jr.	18	14	27	41	12	....	....	....	....	....	....	....	....	....	....	....	....	....	....	....	....	....	....
	Molndal	Sweden-2	26	18	13	31	22	....	....	....	....	....	....	....	....	....	....	....	....	....	....	....	....	....	....
	V.Frolunda	Sweden	9	0	0	0	0	....	....	....	....	....	....	....	....	....	....	....	....	....	....	....	....	....	....
2001-02	V.Frolunda	Sweden	46	12	14	26	28	....	....	....	....	....	....	....	....	....	10	1	3	4	8	....	....	....	....
	V.Frolunda Jr.	Swe-Jr.	....	....	....	....	....	....	....	....	....	....	....	....	....	....	1	0	0	0	0	....	....	....	....
2002-03	V.Frolunda	Sweden	50	17	20	37	113	....	....	....	....	....	....	....	....	....	16	6	3	9	12	....	....	....	....
2003-04	V.Frolunda	Sweden	49	9	14	23	48	....	....	....	....	....	....	....	....	....	10	2	2	4	8	....	....	....	....
2004-05	Frolunda	Sweden	50	7	12	19	38	....	....	....	....	....	....	....	....	....	13	2	5	7	57	....	....	....	....
2005-06	Frolunda	Sweden	49	10	22	32	87	....	....	....	....	....	....	....	....	....	17	3	4	7	34	....	....	....	....
2006-07	**Dallas**	**NHL**	**36**	**3**	**3**	**6**	**14**	**0**	**0**	**0**	**36**	**8.3**	**–5**	**91**	**62.6**	**11:20**	**7**	**2**	**0**	**2**	**6**	**0**	**0**	**0**	**13:58**
	Iowa Stars	AHL	40	16	22	38	30	....	....	....	....	....	....	....	....	....	9	6	4	10	10	....	....	....	....
2007-08	**Dallas**	**NHL**	**55**	**3**	**11**	**14**	**22**	**0**	**0**	**0**	**48**	**6.3**	**–3**	**224**	**47.8**	**10:52**	**18**	**2**	**5**	**7**	**8**	**0**	**0**	**1**	**14:07**
	Iowa Stars	AHL	8	2	4	6	2	....	....	....	....	....	....	....	....	....	....	....	....	....	....	....	....	....	....
	NHL Totals		**91**	**6**	**14**	**20**	**36**	**0**	**0**	**0**	**84**	**7.1**		**315**	**52.1**	**11:03**	**25**	**4**	**5**	**9**	**14**	**0**	**0**	**1**	**14:04**

LUPUL, Joffrey

(LOO-puhl, JAWF-ree) **PHI.**

Right wing. Shoots right. 6'1", 205 lbs. Born, Fort Saskatchewan, Alta., September 23, 1983. Anaheim's 1st choice, 7th overall, in 2002 Entry Draft.

1998-99	Ft. Saskatchewan	ABHL	36	40	50	90	40	....	....	....	....	....	....	....	....	....	....	....	....	....	....	....	....	....	....
99-2000	Ft. Saskatchewan	AMHL	34	43	30	*73	47	....	....	....	....	....	....	....	....	....	4	0	1	1	2	....	....	....	....
2000-01	Medicine Hat	WHL	69	30	26	56	39	....	....	....	....	....	....	....	....	....	22	3	6	9	2	....	....	....	....
2001-02	Medicine Hat	WHL	72	*56	50	106	95	....	....	....	....	....	....	....	....	....	....	....	....	....	....	....	....	....	....
2002-03	Medicine Hat	WHL	50	41	37	78	82	....	....	....	....	....	....	....	....	....	11	4	11	15	20	....	....	....	....
2003-04	**Anaheim**	**NHL**	**75**	**13**	**21**	**34**	**28**	**4**	**0**	**2**	**137**	**9.5**	**–6**	**11**	**9.1**	**13:37**	....	....	....	....	....	....	....	....	....
	Cincinnati	AHL	3	3	2	5	2	....	....	....	....	....	....	....	....	....	....	....	....	....	....	....	....	....	....
2004-05	Cincinnati	AHL	65	30	26	56	58	....	....	....	....	....	....	....	....	....	12	3	9	12	27	....	....	....	....
2005-06	**Anaheim**	**NHL**	**81**	**28**	**25**	**53**	**48**	**12**	**2**	**2**	**296**	**9.5**	**–13**	**101**	**37.6**	**16:38**	**16**	**9**	**2**	**11**	**31**	**1**	**0**	**1**	**16:43**
2006-07	**Edmonton**	**NHL**	**81**	**16**	**12**	**28**	**45**	**5**	**0**	**1**	**172**	**9.3**	**–29**	**14**	**35.7**	**15:36**	....	....	....	....	....	....	....	....	....
2007-08	**Philadelphia**	**NHL**	**56**	**20**	**26**	**46**	**35**	**7**	**0**	**3**	**176**	**11.4**	**2**	**4**	**75.0**	**18:13**	**17**	**4**	**6**	**10**	**2**	**2**	**0**	**1**	**16:13**
	NHL Totals		**293**	**77**	**84**	**161**	**156**	**28**	**2**	**8**	**781**	**9.9**		**130**	**36.2**	**15:52**	**33**	**13**	**8**	**21**	**33**	**3**	**0**	**2**	**16:28**

WHL East First All-Star Team (2002) • Canadian Major Junior First All-Star Team (2002)

Traded to **Edmonton** by **Anaheim** with Ladislav Smid, Anaheim's 1st round choice (later traded to Phoenix - Phoenix selected Nick Ross) in 2007 Entry Draft and Anaheim's 1st (Jordan Eberle) and 2nd (later traded to NY Islanders - NY Islanders selected Travis Hamonic) round choices in 2008 Entry Draft for Chris Pronger, July 3, 2006. Traded to **Philadelphia** by **Edmonton** with Jason Smith for Joni Pitkanen, Geoff Sanderson and Philadelphia's 3rd round choice in 2009 Entry Draft, July 1, 2007.

LYDMAN, Toni

(LEWD-man, TOH-nee) **BUF.**

Defense. Shoots left. 6'1", 204 lbs. Born, Lahti, Finland, September 25, 1977. Calgary's 5th choice, 89th overall, in 1996 Entry Draft.

1993-94	K-Reipas U18	Fin-U18	9	3	1	4	4	....	....	....	....	....	....	....	....	....	....	....	....	....	....	....	....	....	....
	K-Reipas Jr.	Fin-Jr.	1	0	0	0	0	....	....	....	....	....	....	....	....	....	....	....	....	....	....	....	....	....	....
1994-95	K-Reipas U18	Fin-U18	9	7	4	11	12	....	....	....	....	....	....	....	....	....	....	....	....	....	....	....	....	....	....
	K-Reipas Jr.	Fin-Jr.	26	6	4	10	10	....	....	....	....	....	....	....	....	....	....	....	....	....	....	....	....	....	....
1995-96	Reipas Lahti Jr.	Fin-Jr.	9	2	2	4	6	....	....	....	....	....	....	....	....	....	....	....	....	....	....	....	....	....	....
	Reipas Lahti	Finland-2	39	5	2	7	30	....	....	....	....	....	....	....	....	....	3	0	1	1	0	....	....	....	....

Season	Club	League	Regular Season GP	G	A	Pts	PIM	PP	SH	GW	S	%	+/-	TF	F%	Min	Playoffs GP	G	A	Pts	PIM	PP	SH	GW	Min
1996-97	Tappara Tampere	Finland	49	1	2	3	65	....	....	....	....	....	....	....	....	....	3	0	0	0	6	....	....	....	....
1997-98	Tappara Tampere	Finland	48	4	10	14	48	....	....	....	....	....	....	....	....	....	4	0	2	2	0	....	....	....	....
1998-99	HIFK Helsinki	Finland	42	4	7	11	36	....	....	....	....	....	....	....	....	....	11	0	3	3	2	....	....	....	....
	HIFK Helsinki	EuroHL	6	0	2	2	29	....	....	....	....	....	....	....	....	....	4	1	....	....	....	....	....	....	....
99-2000	HIFK Helsinki	Finland	46	4	18	22	36	....	....	....	....	....	....	....	....	....	9	0	4	4	6	....	....	....	....
2000-01	**Calgary**	**NHL**	62	3	16	19	30	1	0	0	80	3.8	–7	0	0.0	20:36	....	....	....	....	....	....	....	....	....
2001-02	**Calgary**	**NHL**	79	6	22	28	52	1	0	0	126	4.8	–8	0	0.0	21:10	....	....	....	....	....	....	....	....	....
2002-03	**Calgary**	**NHL**	81	6	20	26	28	3	0	0	143	4.2	–7	0	0.0	25:47	....	....	....	....	....	....	....	....	....
2003-04	**Calgary**	**NHL**	67	4	16	20	30	2	0	1	93	4.3	6	0	0.0	21:13	6	0	1	1	2	0	0	0	14:30
2004-05	HIFK Helsinki	Finland	8	1	2	3	2	....	....	....	....	....	....	....	....	....	5	0	3	3	0	....	....	....	....
2005-06	**Buffalo**	**NHL**	75	1	16	17	82	0	0	0	68	1.5	9	0	0.0	21:38	18	1	4	5	18	0	0	0	23:03
	Finland	Olympics	8	1	0	1	10	....	....	....	....	....	....	....	....	....	....	....	....	....	....	....	....	....	....
2006-07	**Buffalo**	**NHL**	67	2	17	19	55	0	0	1	44	4.5	10	0	0.0	20:36	16	2	2	4	14	0	0	0	23:41
2007-08	**Buffalo**	**NHL**	82	4	22	26	74	3	0	0	86	4.7	1	1	0.0	21:40	....	....	....	....	....	....	....	....	....
	NHL Totals		513	26	129	155	351	10	0	2	640	4.1		1	0.0	21:54	40	3	7	10	34	0	0	0	22:01

Signed as a free agent by **HIFK Helsinki** (Finland), January 31, 2005. Traded to **Buffalo** by **Calgary** for Buffalo's 3rd round choice (John Armstrong) in 2006 Entry Draft, August 25, 2005.

MacARTHUR, Clarke

(muh-KAR-thuhr, KLAHRK) **BUF.**

Left wing. Shoots left. 6', 195 lbs. Born, Lloydminster, Alta., April 6, 1985. Buffalo's 3rd choice, 74th overall, in 2003 Entry Draft.

Season	Club	League	GP	G	A	Pts	PIM	PP	SH	GW	S	%	+/-	TF	F%	Min	GP	G	A	Pts	PIM	PP	SH	GW	Min
99-2000	Lloydminster	CABHL	24	19	45	64	51	....	....	....	....	....	....	....	....	....	5	9	6	15	4	....	....	....	....
2000-01	Strathcona	AMBHL	38	36	63	99	44	....	....	....	....	....	....	....	....	....	8	6	2	8	10	....	....	....	....
2001-02	Drayton Valley	AJHL	61	22	40	62	33	....	....	....	....	....	....	....	....	....	16	5	8	13	34	....	....	....	....
2002-03	Medicine Hat	WHL	70	23	52	75	104	....	....	....	....	....	....	....	....	....	11	3	6	9	8	....	....	....	....
2003-04	Medicine Hat	WHL	62	35	40	75	93	....	....	....	....	....	....	....	....	....	20	8	10	18	16	....	....	....	....
2004-05	Medicine Hat	WHL	58	30	44	74	100	....	....	....	....	....	....	....	....	....	13	3	8	11	18	....	....	....	....
	Rochester	AHL	....	....	....	....	....	....	....	....	....	....	....	....	....	....	3	0	1	1	0	....	....	....	....
2005-06	Rochester	AHL	69	21	32	53	71	....	....	....	....	....	....	....	....	....	....	....	....	....	....	....	....	....	....
2006-07	**Buffalo**	**NHL**	19	3	4	7	4	0	0	0	16	18.8	4	50	46.0	8:54	....	....	....	....	....	....	....	....	....
	Rochester	AHL	51	21	42	63	57	....	....	....	....	....	....	....	....	....	6	2	4	6	4	....	....	....	....
2007-08	**Buffalo**	**NHL**	37	8	7	15	20	0	0	1	51	15.7	3	14	28.6	14:34	....	....	....	....	....	....	....	....	....
	Rochester	AHL	43	14	28	42	26	....	....	....	....	....	....	....	....	....	....	....	....	....	....	....	....	....	....
	NHL Totals		56	11	11	22	24	0	0	1	67	16.4		64	42.2	12:38	....	....	....	....	....	....	....	....	....

Memorial Cup Tournament All-Star Team (2004) • WHL East First All-Star Team (2005)

MacDONALD, Craig

(MAK-DAWN-uhld, KRAYG) **CBJ**

Left wing. Shoots left. 6'1", 201 lbs. Born, Antigonish, N.S., April 7, 1977. Hartford's 3rd choice, 88th overall, in 1996 Entry Draft.

Season	Club	League	GP	G	A	Pts	PIM	PP	SH	GW	S	%	+/-	TF	F%	Min	GP	G	A	Pts	PIM	PP	SH	GW	Min
1994-95	Lawrence	High-MA	30	25	52	77	10	....	....	....	....	....	....	....	....	....	....	....	....	....	....	....	....	....	....
1995-96	Harvard Crimson	ECAC	34	7	10	17	10	....	....	....	....	....	....	....	....	....	....	....	....	....	....	....	....	....	....
1996-97	Harvard Crimson	ECAC	32	6	10	16	20	....	....	....	....	....	....	....	....	....	....	....	....	....	....	....	....	....	....
1997-98	Canada	Nat-Tm	58	18	29	47	38	....	....	....	....	....	....	....	....	....	....	....	....	....	....	....	....	....	....
1998-99	**Carolina**	**NHL**	11	0	0	0	0	0	0	0	5	0.0	0	2	100.0	2:29	1	0	0	0	0	0	0	0	2:46
	New Haven	AHL	62	17	31	48	77	....	....	....	....	....	....	....	....	....	....	....	....	....	....	....	....	....	....
99-2000	Cincinnati	IHL	78	12	24	36	76	....	....	....	....	....	....	....	....	....	11	4	1	5	8	....	....	....	....
2000-01	Cincinnati	IHL	82	20	28	48	104	....	....	....	....	....	....	....	....	....	5	0	1	1	6	....	....	....	....
2001-02	**Carolina**	**NHL**	12	1	1	2	0	0	0	0	15	6.7	–1	19	47.4	10:11	4	0	0	0	2	0	0	0	4:42
	Lowell	AHL	64	19	22	41	61	....	....	....	....	....	....	....	....	....	....	....	....	....	....	....	....	....	....
2002-03	**Carolina**	**NHL**	35	1	3	4	20	0	0	0	43	2.3	–3	72	55.6	9:21	....	....	....	....	....	....	....	....	....
	Lowell	AHL	27	7	20	27	38	....	....	....	....	....	....	....	....	....	....	....	....	....	....	....	....	....	....
2003-04	**Florida**	**NHL**	34	0	3	3	25	0	0	0	42	0.0	–5	398	45.7	12:31	....	....	....	....	....	....	....	....	....
	San Antonio	AHL	2	0	0	0	4	....	....	....	....	....	....	....	....	....	....	....	....	....	....	....	....	....	....
	Boston	**NHL**	18	0	3	3	8	0	0	0	17	0.0	0	155	47.1	8:42	1	0	0	0	0	0	0	0	2:11
2004-05	Lowell	AHL	71	10	18	28	104	....	....	....	....	....	....	....	....	....	2	0	0	0	0	....	....	....	....
2005-06	**Calgary**	**NHL**	25	3	2	5	8	1	0	0	27	11.1	5	33	45.5	10:16	1	0	0	0	0	0	0	0	7:50
	Omaha	AHL	37	8	19	27	57	....	....	....	....	....	....	....	....	....	....	....	....	....	....	....	....	....	....
2006-07	**Chicago**	**NHL**	25	3	2	5	14	0	1	0	30	10.0	–2	178	47.8	11:12	....	....	....	....	....	....	....	....	....
	Norfolk Admirals	AHL	50	15	25	40	45	....	....	....	....	....	....	....	....	....	6	2	3	5	8	....	....	....	....
2007-08	**Tampa Bay**	**NHL**	65	2	9	11	16	0	0	0	84	2.4	–10	406	49.8	10:52	....	....	....	....	....	....	....	....	....
	Norfolk Admirals	AHL	7	3	8	11	8	....	....	....	....	....	....	....	....	....	....	....	....	....	....	....	....	....	....
	NHL Totals		225	10	23	33	91	1	1	0	263	3.8		1263	48.1	10:14	7	0	0	0	2	0	0	0	4:31

Rights transferred to **Carolina** after **Hartford** franchise relocated, June 25, 1997. Signed as a free agent by **Florida**, August 14, 2003. Claimed on waivers by **Boston** from **Florida**, January 20, 2004. Signed as a free agent by **Calgary**, August 11, 2005. Signed as a free agent by **Chicago**, August 1, 2006. Signed as a free agent by **Tampa Bay**, July 2, 2007. Signed as a free agent by **Columbus**, July 14, 2008.

MacKENZIE, Derek

(muh-KEHN-zee, DAIR-ihk) **CBJ**

Center. Shoots left. 5'10", 178 lbs. Born, Sudbury, Ont., June 11, 1981. Atlanta's 6th choice, 128th overall, in 1999 Entry Draft.

Season	Club	League	GP	G	A	Pts	PIM	PP	SH	GW	S	%	+/-	TF	F%	Min	GP	G	A	Pts	PIM	PP	SH	GW	Min
1996-97	Rayside-Balfour	NOJHA	40	23	32	55	40	....	....	....	....	....	....	....	....	....	....	....	....	....	....	....	....	....	....
1997-98	Sudbury Wolves	OHL	59	9	11	20	26	....	....	....	....	....	....	....	....	....	....	....	....	....	....	....	....	....	....
1998-99	Sudbury Wolves	OHL	68	22	65	87	74	....	....	....	....	....	....	....	....	....	4	2	4	6	2	....	....	....	....
99-2000	Sudbury Wolves	OHL	68	24	33	57	110	....	....	....	....	....	....	....	....	....	12	5	9	14	16	....	....	....	....
2000-01	Sudbury Wolves	OHL	62	40	49	89	89	....	....	....	....	....	....	....	....	....	12	6	8	14	16	....	....	....	....
2001-02	**Atlanta**	**NHL**	1	0	0	0	2	0	0	0	1	0.0	–1	16	56.3	13:51	....	....	....	....	....	....	....	....	....
	Chicago Wolves	AHL	68	13	12	25	80	....	....	....	....	....	....	....	....	....	25	4	2	6	20	....	....	....	....
2002-03	Chicago Wolves	AHL	80	14	18	32	97	....	....	....	....	....	....	....	....	....	9	0	0	0	4	....	....	....	....
2003-04	**Atlanta**	**NHL**	12	0	1	1	10	0	0	0	7	0.0	0	63	46.0	6:38	....	....	....	....	....	....	....	....	....
	Chicago Wolves	AHL	63	19	16	35	67	....	....	....	....	....	....	....	....	....	10	7	1	8	13	....	....	....	....
2004-05	Chicago Wolves	AHL	78	13	20	33	87	....	....	....	....	....	....	....	....	....	18	5	6	11	33	....	....	....	....
2005-06	**Atlanta**	**NHL**	11	0	1	1	8	0	0	0	11	0.0	0	59	55.9	6:33	....	....	....	....	....	....	....	....	....
	Chicago Wolves	AHL	36	10	12	22	48	....	....	....	....	....	....	....	....	....	....	....	....	....	....	....	....	....	....
2006-07	**Atlanta**	**NHL**	4	0	0	0	0	0	0	0	3	0.0	1	16	56.3	5:00	....	....	....	....	....	....	....	....	....
	Chicago Wolves	AHL	52	14	23	37	62	....	....	....	....	....	....	....	....	....	....	....	....	....	....	....	....	....	....
2007-08	**Columbus**	**NHL**	17	2	0	2	8	0	0	0	19	10.5	–2	73	34.3	7:47	....	....	....	....	....	....	....	....	....
	Syracuse Crunch	AHL	62	25	24	49	46	....	....	....	....	....	....	....	....	....	13	6	8	14	22	....	....	....	....
	NHL Totals		45	2	2	4	28	0	0	0	41	4.9		227	46.3	7:04	....	....	....	....	....	....	....	....	....

Signed as a free agent by **Columbus**, July 11, 2007.

MacLEAN, Don

(muh-KLAIN, DAWN)

Center. Shoots left. 6'2", 199 lbs. Born, Sydney, N.S., January 14, 1977. Los Angeles' 2nd choice, 33rd overall, in 1995 Entry Draft.

Season	Club	League	GP	G	A	Pts	PIM	PP	SH	GW	S	%	+/-	TF	F%	Min	GP	G	A	Pts	PIM	PP	SH	GW	Min
1992-93	Halifax Hawks	NSMHL	27	15	25	40	34	....	....	....	....	....	....	....	....	....	....	....	....	....	....	....	....	....	....
1993-94	Halifax Hawks	NSMHL	25	35	35	70	151	....	....	....	....	....	....	....	....	....	....	....	....	....	....	....	....	....	....
1994-95	Beauport	QMJHL	64	15	27	42	37	....	....	....	....	....	....	....	....	....	17	4	4	8	6	....	....	....	....
1995-96	Beauport	QMJHL	1	0	1	1	0	....	....	....	....	....	....	....	....	....	....	....	....	....	....	....	....	....	....
	Laval Titan	QMJHL	21	17	11	28	29	....	....	....	....	....	....	....	....	....	....	....	....	....	....	....	....	....	....
	Hull Olympiques	QMJHL	39	26	34	60	44	....	....	....	....	....	....	....	....	....	17	6	7	13	14	....	....	....	....
1996-97	Hull Olympiques	QMJHL	69	34	47	81	67	....	....	....	....	....	....	....	....	....	14	11	10	21	39	....	....	....	....
1997-98	**Los Angeles**	**NHL**	22	5	2	7	4	2	0	0	25	20.0	–1	....	....	....	....	....	....	....	....	....	....	....	....
	Fredericton	AHL	39	9	5	14	32	....	....	....	....	....	....	....	....	....	4	1	3	4	2	....	....	....	....
1998-99	Springfield	AHL	41	5	14	19	31	....	....	....	....	....	....	....	....	....	....	....	....	....	....	....	....	....	....
	Grand Rapids	IHL	28	6	13	19	8	....	....	....	....	....	....	....	....	....	....	....	....	....	....	....	....	....	....
99-2000	Lowell	AHL	40	11	17	28	18	....	....	....	....	....	....	....	....	....	....	....	....	....	....	....	....	....	....
	St. John's	AHL	21	14	12	26	8	....	....	....	....	....	....	....	....	....	....	....	....	....	....	....	....	....	....
2000-01	**Toronto**	**NHL**	3	0	1	1	2	0	0	0	2	0.0	–2	33	54.6	9:48	....	....	....	....	....	....	....	....	....
	St. John's	AHL	61	26	34	60	48	....	....	....	....	....	....	....	....	....	4	2	1	3	2	....	....	....	....
2001-02	St. John's	AHL	75	33	*54	*87	49	....	....	....	....	....	....	....	....	....	9	5	5	10	6	....	....	....	....
	Toronto	**NHL**	....	....	....	....	....	....	....	....	....	....	....	....	....	....	3	0	0	0	0	0	0	0	1:39
2002-03	Syracuse Crunch	AHL	17	9	9	18	6	....	....	....	....	....	....	....	....	....	....	....	....	....	....	....	....	....	....
2003-04	**Columbus**	**NHL**	4	1	0	1	0	0	0	0	10	10.0	–1	31	58.1	11:41	....	....	....	....	....	....	....	....	....
	Syracuse Crunch	AHL	77	27	41	68	45	....	....	....	....	....	....	....	....	....	7	0	3	3	4	....	....	....	....

			Regular Season														Playoffs								
Season	Club	League	GP	G	A	Pts	PIM	PP	SH	GW	S	%	+/-	TF	F%	Min	GP	G	A	Pts	PIM	PP	SH	GW	Min
2004-05	Blues Espoo	Finland	51	22	21	43	46	....	....	....	....	....	....	....	....	....	....	....	....	....	....	....	....	....	....
2005-06	**Detroit**	**NHL**	**3**	**1**	**1**	**2**	**0**	**1**	**0**	**1**	**3**	**33.3**	**2**	**13**	**61.5**	**12:45**	....	....	....	....	....	....	....	....	....
	Grand Rapids	AHL	76	*56	32	88	63	....	....	....	....	....	....	....	....	....	14	6	2	8	8	....	....	....	....
2006-07	**Phoenix**	**NHL**	**9**	**1**	**1**	**2**	**0**	**0**	**0**	**0**	**12**	**8.3**	**–4**	**2**	**50.0**	**12:38**	....	....	....	....	....	....	....	....	....
	San Antonio	AHL	66	33	28	61	51	....	....	....	....	....	....	....	....	....	....	....	....	....	....	....	....	....	....
2007-08	ZSC Lions Zurich	Swiss	11	4	1	5	16	....	....	....	....	....	....	....	....	....	....	....	....	....	....	....	....	....	....
	Salzburg	Austria	13	13	7	20	8	....	....	....	....	....	....	....	....	....	14	8	5	13	30	....	....	....	....
	NHL Totals		**41**	**8**	**5**	**13**	**6**	**3**	**0**	**1**	**52**	**15.4**		**79**	**57.0**	**12:00**	**3**	**0**	**0**	**0**	**0**	**0**	**0**	**0**	**1:39**

John P. Sollenberger Trophy (Leading Scorer – AHL) (2002) • AHL First All-Star Team (2006) • Willie Marshall Award (Top Goal-scorer - AHL) (2006) (tied with Denis Hamel) • Les Cunningham Plaque (MVP-AHL) (2006)

Traded to **Toronto** by **Los Angeles** for Craig Charron, February 23, 2000. Signed as a free agent by **Columbus**, July 17, 2002. • Missed majority of 2002-03 season recovering from neck surgery, September 16, 2002. Signed as a free agent by **Espoo** (Finland), July 2, 2004. Signed as a free agent by **Detroit**, August 24, 2005. Signed as a free agent by **Phoenix**, July 17, 2006. Signed as a free agent by **Zurich** (Swiss), July 16, 2007.

MADDEN, John

(MA-dehn, JAWN) **N.J.**

Center. Shoots left. 5'11", 190 lbs. Born, Barrie, Ont., May 4, 1973.

1989-90	Alliston Hornets	OHA-C	31	24	25	49	26	....	....	....	....	....	....	....	....	....	....	....	....	....	....	....	....	....	....
1990-91	Alliston Hornets	OHA-C	14	15	21	36	10	....	....	....	....	....	....	....	....	....	....	....	....	....	....	....	....	....	....
	Barrie Colts	OHA-B	1	0	0	0	0	....	....	....	....	....	....	....	....	....	....	....	....	....	....	....	....	....	....
1991-92	Barrie Colts	OHA-B	42	50	54	104	46	....	....	....	....	....	....	....	....	....	13	10	9	19	14	....	....	....	....
1992-93	Barrie Colts	COJHL	43	49	75	124	62	....	....	....	....	....	....	....	....	....	....	....	....	....	....	....	....	....	....
1993-94	U. of Michigan	CCHA	36	6	11	17	14	....	....	....	....	....	....	....	....	....	....	....	....	....	....	....	....	....	....
1994-95	U. of Michigan	CCHA	39	21	22	43	8	....	....	....	....	....	....	....	....	....	....	....	....	....	....	....	....	....	....
1995-96	U. of Michigan	CCHA	43	27	30	57	45	....	....	....	....	....	....	....	....	....	....	....	....	....	....	....	....	....	....
1996-97	U. of Michigan	CCHA	42	26	37	63	56	....	....	....	....	....	....	....	....	....	....	....	....	....	....	....	....	....	....
1997-98	Albany River Rats	AHL	74	20	36	56	40	....	....	....	....	....	....	....	....	....	13	3	13	16	14	....	....	....	....
1998-99	**New Jersey**	**NHL**	**4**	**0**	**1**	**1**	**0**	**0**	**0**	**0**	**4**	**0.0**	**–2**	**0**	**0.0**	**9:13**	....	....	....	....	....	....	....	....	....
	Albany River Rats	AHL	75	38	60	98	44	....	....	....	....	....	....	....	....	....	5	2	2	4	6	....	....	....	....
99-2000 ♦	**New Jersey**	**NHL**	**74**	**16**	**9**	**25**	**6**	**0**	**6**	**3**	**115**	**13.9**	**7**	**770**	**47.5**	**11:40**	**20**	**3**	**4**	**7**	**0**	**0**	**1**	**2**	**15:30**
2000-01	**New Jersey**	**NHL**	**80**	**23**	**15**	**38**	**12**	**0**	**3**	**4**	**163**	**14.1**	**24**	**974**	**46.6**	**15:35**	**25**	**4**	**3**	**7**	**6**	**0**	**0**	**0**	**15:15**
2001-02	**New Jersey**	**NHL**	**82**	**15**	**8**	**23**	**25**	**0**	**0**	**2**	**170**	**8.8**	**6**	**1001**	**47.0**	**15:36**	**6**	**0**	**0**	**0**	**0**	**0**	**0**	**0**	**17:25**
2002-03 ♦	**New Jersey**	**NHL**	**80**	**19**	**22**	**41**	**26**	**2**	**2**	**3**	**207**	**9.2**	**13**	**1502**	**50.9**	**18:18**	**24**	**6**	**10**	**16**	**2**	**2**	**1**	**1**	**19:38**
2003-04	**New Jersey**	**NHL**	**80**	**12**	**23**	**35**	**22**	**1**	**1**	**1**	**210**	**5.7**	**7**	**1377**	**53.3**	**17:17**	**5**	**0**	**0**	**0**	**0**	**0**	**0**	**0**	**14:51**
2004-05	HIFK Helsinki	Finland	3	0	0	0	0	....	....	....	....	....	....	....	....	....	....	....	....	....	....	....	....	....	....
2005-06	**New Jersey**	**NHL**	**82**	**16**	**20**	**36**	**36**	**0**	**1**	**0**	**194**	**8.2**	**–7**	**1613**	**51.5**	**18:59**	**9**	**4**	**1**	**5**	**8**	**0**	**2**	**0**	**18:56**
2006-07	**New Jersey**	**NHL**	**74**	**12**	**20**	**32**	**14**	**0**	**0**	**1**	**153**	**7.8**	**–7**	**1366**	**49.8**	**18:53**	**11**	**1**	**1**	**2**	**2**	**0**	**0**	**0**	**21:17**
2007-08	**New Jersey**	**NHL**	**80**	**20**	**23**	**43**	**26**	**3**	**3**	**3**	**185**	**10.8**	**1**	**1463**	**53.7**	**19:27**	**5**	**2**	**1**	**3**	**2**	**0**	**0**	**1**	**21:18**
	NHL Totals		**636**	**133**	**141**	**274**	**167**	**6**	**16**	**17**	**1401**	**9.5**		**10066**	**50.5**	**16:57**	**105**	**20**	**20**	**40**	**20**	**2**	**4**	**4**	**17:39**

CCHA First All-Star Team (1997) • NCAA West First All-American Team (1997) • Frank J. Selke Trophy (2001)

Signed as a free agent by **New Jersey**, June 26, 1997. Signed as a free agent by **HIFK Helsinki** (Finland), November 29, 2004.

MAIR, Adam

(MAIR, A-duhm) **BUF.**

Center. Shoots right. 6'1", 208 lbs. Born, Hamilton, Ont., February 15, 1979. Toronto's 2nd choice, 84th overall, in 1997 Entry Draft.

1994-95	Ohsweken	OHA-B	39	21	23	44	91	....	....	....	....	....	....	....	....	....	....	....	....	....	....	....	....	....	....
1995-96	Owen Sound	OHL	62	12	15	27	63	....	....	....	....	....	....	....	....	....	6	0	0	0	2	....	....	....	....
1996-97	Owen Sound	OHL	65	16	35	51	113	....	....	....	....	....	....	....	....	....	4	1	0	1	2	....	....	....	....
1997-98	Owen Sound	OHL	56	25	27	52	179	....	....	....	....	....	....	....	....	....	11	6	3	9	31	....	....	....	....
1998-99	Owen Sound	OHL	43	23	41	64	109	....	....	....	....	....	....	....	....	....	16	10	10	20	*47	....	....	....	....
	Toronto	**NHL**	....	....	....	....	....	....	....	....	....	....	....	....	....	....	**5**	**1**	**0**	**1**	**14**	**0**	**0**	**0**	**5:37**
	St. John's	AHL	....	....	....	....	....	....	....	....	....	....	....	....	....	....	3	1	0	1	6	....	....	....	....
99-2000	**Toronto**	**NHL**	**8**	**1**	**0**	**1**	**6**	**0**	**0**	**0**	**7**	**14.3**	**–1**	**9**	**33.3**	**11:33**	**5**	**0**	**0**	**0**	**8**	**0**	**0**	**0**	**10:15**
	St. John's	AHL	66	22	27	49	124	....	....	....	....	....	....	....	....	....	....	....	....	....	....	....	....	....	....
2000-01	**Toronto**	**NHL**	**16**	**0**	**2**	**2**	**14**	**0**	**0**	**0**	**17**	**0.0**	**3**	**56**	**51.8**	**9:01**	....	....	....	....	....	....	....	....	....
	St. John's	AHL	47	18	27	45	69	....	....	....	....	....	....	....	....	....	....	....	....	....	....	....	....	....	....
	Los Angeles	**NHL**	**10**	**0**	**0**	**0**	**6**	**0**	**0**	**0**	**5**	**0.0**	**–3**	**21**	**61.9**	**6:14**	....	....	....	....	....	....	....	....	....
2001-02	**Los Angeles**	**NHL**	**18**	**1**	**1**	**2**	**57**	**0**	**0**	**0**	**10**	**10.0**	**1**	**31**	**58.1**	**7:11**	....	....	....	....	....	....	....	....	....
	Manchester	AHL	27	10	9	19	48	....	....	....	....	....	....	....	....	....	5	5	1	6	10	....	....	....	....
2002-03	**Buffalo**	**NHL**	**79**	**6**	**11**	**17**	**146**	**0**	**1**	**1**	**83**	**7.2**	**–4**	**572**	**51.2**	**10:37**	....	....	....	....	....	....	....	....	....
2003-04	**Buffalo**	**NHL**	**81**	**6**	**14**	**20**	**146**	**1**	**0**	**1**	**82**	**7.3**	**–3**	**340**	**45.9**	**9:38**	....	....	....	....	....	....	....	....	....
2004-05			DID NOT PLAY																						
2005-06	**Buffalo**	**NHL**	**40**	**2**	**5**	**7**	**47**	**0**	**0**	**0**	**40**	**5.0**	**–2**	**12**	**41.7**	**7:59**	**3**	**0**	**0**	**0**	**0**	**0**	**0**	**0**	**9:17**
2006-07	**Buffalo**	**NHL**	**82**	**2**	**9**	**11**	**128**	**0**	**0**	**0**	**73**	**2.7**	**–1**	**130**	**46.2**	**7:33**	**16**	**1**	**4**	**5**	**10**	**0**	**0**	**0**	**7:33**
2007-08	**Buffalo**	**NHL**	**72**	**5**	**12**	**17**	**66**	**0**	**0**	**2**	**62**	**8.1**	**–2**	**361**	**45.4**	**8:52**	....	....	....	....	....	....	....	....	....
	NHL Totals		**406**	**23**	**54**	**77**	**616**	**1**	**1**	**4**	**379**	**6.1**		**1532**	**48.4**	**8:56**	**29**	**2**	**4**	**6**	**32**	**0**	**0**	**0**	**7:52**

Traded to **Los Angeles** by **Toronto** with Toronto's 2nd round choice (Michael Cammalleri) in 2001 Entry Draft for Aki Berg, March 13, 2001. Traded to **Buffalo** by **Los Angeles** with Los Angeles' 5th round choice (Thomas Morrow) in 2003 Entry Draft for Erik Rasmussen, July 24, 2002. • Missed majority of 2005-06 season recovering from groin (training camp) and head (January 12, 2006 vs. Phoenix) injuries.

MAKI, Tomi

(MA-kee, TAW-mee)

Right wing. Shoots left. 5'11", 187 lbs. Born, Helsinki, Finland, August 19, 1983. Calgary's 4th choice, 108th overall, in 2001 Entry Draft.

99-2000	Jokerit Helsinki Jr.	Fin-Jr.	33	6	1	7	12	....	....	....	....	....	....	....	....	....	3	0	0	0	0	....	....	....	....
2000-01	Jokerit U18	Fin-U18	10	4	10	14	4	....	....	....	....	....	....	....	....	....	6	4	3	7	0	....	....	....	....
	Jokerit Helsinki Jr.	Fin-Jr.	39	7	8	15	10	....	....	....	....	....	....	....	....	....	2	0	0	0	2	....	....	....	....
2001-02	Jokerit Helsinki Jr.	Fin-Jr.	29	12	13	25	12	....	....	....	....	....	....	....	....	....	1	0	0	0	2	....	....	....	....
	Kiekko-Vantaa	Finland-2	5	0	0	0	0	....	....	....	....	....	....	....	....	....	....	....	....	....	....	....	....	....	....
	Jokerit Helsinki	Finland	8	0	1	1	2	....	....	....	....	....	....	....	....	....	....	....	....	....	....	....	....	....	....
2002-03	Jokerit Helsinki Jr.	Fin-Jr.	14	4	4	8	12	....	....	....	....	....	....	....	....	....	11	3	3	6	4	....	....	....	....
	Kiekko-Vantaa	Finland-2	3	1	0	1	4	....	....	....	....	....	....	....	....	....	....	....	....	....	....	....	....	....	....
	Jokerit Helsinki	Finland	18	2	2	4	4	....	....	....	....	....	....	....	....	....	1	0	0	0	0	....	....	....	....
2003-04	Jokerit Helsinki	Finland	50	5	5	10	14	....	....	....	....	....	....	....	....	....	8	0	0	0	0	....	....	....	....
2004-05	Jokerit Helsinki	Finland	51	1	4	5	14	....	....	....	....	....	....	....	....	....	12	1	1	2	2	....	....	....	....
2005-06	Omaha	AHL	80	12	17	29	33	....	....	....	....	....	....	....	....	....	....	....	....	....	....	....	....	....	....
2006-07	**Calgary**	**NHL**	**1**	**0**	**0**	**0**	**0**	**0**	**0**	**0**	**0**	**0.0**	**0**	**0**	**0.0**	**10:56**	....	....	....	....	....	....	....	....	....
	Omaha	AHL	67	4	11	15	20	....	....	....	....	....	....	....	....	....	6	1	1	2	2	....	....	....	....
2007-08	Quad City Flames	AHL	78	8	5	13	38	....	....	....	....	....	....	....	....	....	....	....	....	....	....	....	....	....	....
	NHL Totals		**1**	**0**	**0**	**0**	**0**	**0**	**0**	**0**	**0**	**0.0**		**0**	**0.0**	**10:56**	....	....	....	....	....	....	....	....	....

MALHOTRA, Manny

(mal-HOH-truh, MAN-ee) **CBJ**

Center. Shoots left. 6'2", 217 lbs. Born, Mississauga, Ont., May 18, 1980. NY Rangers' 1st choice, 7th overall, in 1998 Entry Draft.

1995-96	Mississauga Reps	MTHL	54	27	44	71	62	....	....	....	....	....	....	....	....	....	....	....	....	....	....	....	....	....	....
1996-97	Guelph Storm	OHL	61	16	28	44	26	....	....	....	....	....	....	....	....	....	18	7	7	14	11	....	....	....	....
1997-98	Guelph Storm	OHL	57	16	35	51	29	....	....	....	....	....	....	....	....	....	12	7	6	13	8	....	....	....	....
1998-99	**NY Rangers**	**NHL**	**73**	**8**	**8**	**16**	**13**	**1**	**0**	**2**	**61**	**13.1**	**–2**	**588**	**43.9**	**8:36**	....	....	....	....	....	....	....	....	....
99-2000	**NY Rangers**	**NHL**	**27**	**0**	**0**	**0**	**4**	**0**	**0**	**0**	**18**	**0.0**	**–6**	**132**	**44.7**	**6:42**	....	....	....	....	....	....	....	....	....
	Guelph Storm	OHL	5	2	2	4	4	....	....	....	....	....	....	....	....	....	6	0	2	2	4	....	....	....	....
	Hartford	AHL	12	1	5	6	2	....	....	....	....	....	....	....	....	....	23	1	2	3	10	....	....	....	....
2000-01	**NY Rangers**	**NHL**	**50**	**4**	**8**	**12**	**31**	**0**	**0**	**2**	**46**	**8.7**	**–10**	**248**	**44.4**	**9:03**	....	....	....	....	....	....	....	....	....
	Hartford	AHL	28	5	6	11	69	....	....	....	....	....	....	....	....	....	5	0	0	0	0	....	....	....	....
2001-02	**NY Rangers**	**NHL**	**56**	**7**	**6**	**13**	**42**	**0**	**1**	**1**	**41**	**17.1**	**–1**	**310**	**42.9**	**10:14**	....	....	....	....	....	....	....	....	....
	Dallas	**NHL**	**16**	**1**	**0**	**1**	**5**	**0**	**0**	**0**	**19**	**5.3**	**–3**	**121**	**48.8**	**10:37**	....	....	....	....	....	....	....	....	....
2002-03	**Dallas**	**NHL**	**59**	**3**	**7**	**10**	**42**	**0**	**0**	**1**	**62**	**4.8**	**–2**	**447**	**47.0**	**9:22**	**5**	**1**	**0**	**1**	**0**	**0**	**0**	**0**	**8:13**
2003-04	**Dallas**	**NHL**	**9**	**0**	**0**	**0**	**4**	**0**	**0**	**0**	**4**	**0.0**	**–2**	**13**	**61.5**	**7:48**	....	....	....	....	....	....	....	....	....
	Columbus	**NHL**	**56**	**12**	**13**	**25**	**24**	**1**	**0**	**2**	**103**	**11.7**	**–5**	**840**	**53.8**	**14:47**	....	....	....	....	....	....	....	....	....
2004-05	Ljubljana	Slovenia	13	6	7	13	20	....	....	....	....	....	....	....	....	....	....	....	....	....	....	....	....	....	....
	Ljubljana	Interliga	13	7	7	14	16	....	....	....	....	....	....	....	....	....	....	....	....	....	....	....	....	....	....
	HV 71 Jonkoping	Sweden	20	5	2	7	16	....	....	....	....	....	....	....	....	....	....	....	....	....	....	....	....	....	....

Season	Club	League	GP	G	A	Pts	PIM	PP	SH	GW	S	%	+/-	TF	F%	Min	GP	G	A	Pts	PIM	PP	SH	GW	Min
					Regular Season												Playoffs								
2005-06	Columbus	NHL	58	10	21	31	41	1	1	0	102	9.8	1	827	56.4	16:21	....	....	....	....	....	....	....	....	....
2006-07	Columbus	NHL	82	9	16	25	76	2	0	3	109	8.3	–8	1127	55.1	14:48	....	....	....	....	....	....	....	....	....
2007-08	Columbus	NHL	71	11	18	29	34	2	0	2	112	9.8	–3	1158	59.0	16:28	....	....	....	....	....	....	....	....	....
	NHL Totals		557	65	97	162	316	7	2	13	677	9.6		5811	52.6	12:11	5	1	0	1	0	0	0	0	8:13

Memorial Cup Tournament All-Star Team (1998) • George Parsons Trophy (Memorial Cup Tournament - Most Sportsmanlike Player) (1998)

Traded to **Dallas** by **NY Rangers** with Barrett Heisten for Martin Rucinsky and Roman Lyashenko, March 12, 2002. Claimed on waivers by **Columbus** from **Dallas**, November 21, 2003. Signed as a free agent by **Ljubljana** (Slovenia), October 8, 2004. Signed as a free agent by **Jonkoping** (Sweden), December 20, 2004.

MALIK, Marek

(MAW-leck, MAIR-ehk)

Defense. Shoots left. 6'6", 235 lbs. Born, Ostrava, Czech., June 24, 1975. Hartford's 2nd choice, 72nd overall, in 1993 Entry Draft.

1992-93	TJ Vitkovice Jr.	Czech-Jr.	20	5	10	15	16	....	....	....	....	....	....	....	....	....	....	....	....	....	....	....	....	....	....
1993-94	HC Vitkovice	CzRep	38	3	3	6	0	....	....	....	....	....	....	....	....	....	3	0	1	1	0	....	....	....	....
1994-95	Springfield	AHL	58	11	30	41	91	....	....	....	....	....	....	....	....	....	....	....	....	....	....	....	....	....	....
	Hartford	**NHL**	**1**	**0**	**1**	**1**	**0**	**0**	**0**	**0**	**0**	**0.0**	**1**	....	....	....	....	....	....	....	....	....	....	....	....
1995-96	**Hartford**	**NHL**	**7**	**0**	**0**	**0**	**4**	**0**	**0**	**0**	**2**	**0.0**	**–3**	....	....	....	....	....	....	....	....	....	....	....	....
	Springfield	AHL	68	8	14	22	135	....	....	....	....	....	....	....	....	....	8	1	3	4	20	....	....	....	....
1996-97	**Hartford**	**NHL**	**47**	**1**	**5**	**6**	**50**	**0**	**0**	**1**	**33**	**3.0**	**5**	....	....	....	....	....	....	....	....	....	....	....	....
	Springfield	AHL	3	0	3	3	4	....	....	....	....	....	....	....	....	....	....	....	....	....	....	....	....	....	....
1997-98	Malmo	Sweden	37	1	5	6	21	....	....	....	....	....	....	....	....	....	....	....	....	....	....	....	....	....	....
1998-99	HC Vitkovice	CzRep	1	1	0	1	6	....	....	....	....	....	....	....	....	....	....	....	....	....	....	....	....	....	....
	Carolina	**NHL**	**52**	**2**	**9**	**11**	**36**	**1**	**0**	**0**	**36**	**5.6**	**–6**	**0**	**0.0**	**21:14**	**4**	**0**	**0**	**0**	**4**	**0**	**0**	**0**	**11:26**
	New Haven	AHL	21	2	8	10	28	....	....	....	....	....	....	....	....	....	....	....	....	....	....	....	....	....	....
99-2000	**Carolina**	**NHL**	**57**	**4**	**10**	**14**	**63**	**0**	**0**	**1**	**57**	**7.0**	**13**	**0**	**0.0**	**18:00**	....	....	....	....	....	....	....	....	....
2000-01	**Carolina**	**NHL**	**61**	**6**	**14**	**20**	**34**	**1**	**0**	**1**	**72**	**8.3**	**–4**	**0**	**0.0**	**19:36**	**3**	**0**	**0**	**0**	**6**	**0**	**0**	**0**	**19:37**
2001-02	**Carolina**	**NHL**	**82**	**4**	**19**	**23**	**88**	**0**	**0**	**0**	**91**	**4.4**	**8**	**0**	**0.0**	**20:29**	**23**	**0**	**3**	**3**	**18**	**0**	**0**	**0**	**18:09**
2002-03	**Carolina**	**NHL**	**10**	**0**	**2**	**2**	**16**	**0**	**0**	**0**	**9**	**0.0**	**–3**	**0**	**0.0**	**17:02**	....	....	....	....	....	....	....	....	....
	Vancouver	**NHL**	**69**	**7**	**11**	**18**	**52**	**1**	**1**	**2**	**68**	**10.3**	**23**	**1**	**0.0**	**18:06**	**14**	**1**	**1**	**2**	**10**	**1**	**0**	**0**	**16:06**
2003-04	**Vancouver**	**NHL**	**78**	**3**	**16**	**19**	**45**	**0**	**0**	**0**	**61**	**4.9**	**35**	**1**	**0.0**	**18:05**	**7**	**0**	**0**	**0**	**10**	**0**	**0**	**0**	**20:03**
2004-05	Vitkovice	CzRep	42	1	9	10	50	....	....	....	....	....	....	....	....	....	7	0	0	0	37	....	....	....	....
2005-06	**NY Rangers**	**NHL**	**74**	**2**	**16**	**18**	**78**	**0**	**0**	**2**	**70**	**2.9**	**28**	**0**	**0.0**	**20:26**	**4**	**0**	**1**	**1**	**6**	**0**	**0**	**0**	**20:43**
	Czech Republic	Olympics	8	0	0	0	8	....	....	....	....	....	....	....	....	....	....	....	....	....	....	....	....	....	....
2006-07	**NY Rangers**	**NHL**	**69**	**2**	**19**	**21**	**70**	**0**	**0**	**0**	**57**	**3.5**	**32**	**2**	**0.0**	**19:16**	**10**	**1**	**3**	**4**	**10**	**0**	**0**	**0**	**21:25**
2007-08	**NY Rangers**	**NHL**	**42**	**2**	**8**	**10**	**48**	**0**	**0**	**0**	**34**	**5.9**	**7**	**0**	**0.0**	**19:14**	....	....	....	....	....	....	....	....	....
	NHL Totals		**649**	**33**	**130**	**163**	**584**	**3**	**1**	**7**	**590**	**5.6**		**4**	**0.0**	**19:20**	**65**	**2**	**8**	**10**	**64**	**1**	**0**	**0**	**18:14**

Transferred to **Carolina** after **Hartford** franchise relocated, June 25, 1997. Traded to **Vancouver** by **Carolina** with Darren Langdon for Jan Hlavac and Harold Druken, November 1, 2002. Signed as a free agent by **Vitkovice** (CzRep), September 17, 2004. Signed as a free agent by **NY Rangers**, August 2, 2005.

MALKIN, Evgeni

(MAHL-kihn, ehv-GEH-nee) **PIT.**

Center. Shoots left. 6'3", 195 lbs. Born, Magnitogorsk, USSR, July 31, 1986. Pittsburgh's 1st choice, 2nd overall, in 2004 Entry Draft.

2003-04	Magnitogorsk 2	Russia-3	2	1	0	1	8	....	....	....	....	....	....	....	....	....	....	....	....	....	....	....	....	....	....
	Magnitogorsk	Russia	34	3	9	12	12	....	....	....	....	....	....	....	....	....	....	....	....	....	....	....	....	....	....
2004-05	Magnitogorsk 2	Russia-3	2	1	1	2	2	....	....	....	....	....	....	....	....	....	....	....	....	....	....	....	....	....	....
	Magnitogorsk	Russia	52	12	20	32	24	....	....	....	....	....	....	....	....	....	5	0	4	4	0	....	....	....	....
2005-06	Magnitogorsk	Russia	46	21	26	47	46	....	....	....	....	....	....	....	....	....	11	5	10	15	41	....	....	....	....
	Russia	Olympics	7	2	4	6	31	....	....	....	....	....	....	....	....	....	....	....	....	....	....	....	....	....	....
2006-07	**Pittsburgh**	**NHL**	**78**	**33**	**52**	**85**	**80**	**16**	**0**	**6**	**242**	**13.6**	**2**	**728**	**43.3**	**19:10**	**5**	**0**	**4**	**4**	**8**	**0**	**0**	**0**	**19:34**
2007-08	**Pittsburgh**	**NHL**	**82**	**47**	**59**	**106**	**78**	**17**	**0**	**5**	**272**	**17.3**	**16**	**890**	**39.3**	**21:19**	**20**	**10**	**12**	**22**	**24**	**5**	**1**	**3**	**20:48**
	NHL Totals		**160**	**80**	**111**	**191**	**158**	**33**	**0**	**11**	**514**	**15.6**		**1618**	**41.1**	**20:16**	**25**	**10**	**16**	**26**	**32**	**5**	**1**	**3**	**20:33**

NHL All-Rookie Team (2007) • Calder Memorial Trophy (2007) • NHL First All-Star Team (2008)

Played in NHL All-Star Game (2008)

MALMIVAARA, Olli

(mal-mih-VAH-ruh, OH-lee) **N.J.**

Defense. Shoots left. 6'7", 230 lbs. Born, Kajaani, Finland, March 13, 1982. Chicago's 6th choice, 117th overall, in 2000 Entry Draft.

1998-99	Jokerit U18	Fin-U18	35	1	8	9	10	....	....	....	....	....	....	....	....	....	7	0	0	0	2	....	....	....	....
99-2000	Jokerit U18	Fin-U18	14	6	6	12	14	....	....	....	....	....	....	....	....	....	1	0	0	0	2	....	....	....	....
	Jokerit U18	Fin-U18	27	3	3	6	12	....	....	....	....	....	....	....	....	....	12	0	2	2	2	....	....	....	....
2000-01	Jokerit Helsinki Jr.	Fin-Jr.	33	10	13	23	24	....	....	....	....	....	....	....	....	....	2	0	0	0	0	....	....	....	....
	Kiekko-Vantaa	Finland-2	4	1	0	1	2	....	....	....	....	....	....	....	....	....	....	....	....	....	....	....	....	....	....
	Jokerit Helsinki	Finland	5	0	0	0	2	....	....	....	....	....	....	....	....	....	....	....	....	....	....	....	....	....	....
2001-02	Jokerit Helsinki Jr.	Fin-Jr.	2	0	1	1	0	....	....	....	....	....	....	....	....	....	....	....	....	....	....	....	....	....	....
	Jokerit Helsinki	Finland	53	0	6	6	16	....	....	....	....	....	....	....	....	....	11	0	0	0	2	....	....	....	....
2002-03	Jokerit Helsinki Jr.	Fin-Jr.	1	0	0	0	0	....	....	....	....	....	....	....	....	....	....	....	....	....	....	....	....	....	....
	Kiekko-Vantaa	Finland-2	2	1	1	2	2	....	....	....	....	....	....	....	....	....	....	....	....	....	....	....	....	....	....
	Jokerit Helsinki	Finland	42	1	0	1	22	....	....	....	....	....	....	....	....	....	5	0	0	0	0	....	....	....	....
2003-04	Jokerit Helsinki	Finland	25	1	0	1	2	....	....	....	....	....	....	....	....	....	....	....	....	....	....	....	....	....	....
	SaiPa	Finland	11	1	0	1	6	....	....	....	....	....	....	....	....	....	....	....	....	....	....	....	....	....	....
2004-05	SaiPa	Finland	56	9	1	10	89	....	....	....	....	....	....	....	....	....	....	....	....	....	....	....	....	....	....
2005-06	SaiPa	Finland	54	11	9	20	134	....	....	....	....	....	....	....	....	....	8	1	0	1	12	....	....	....	....
2006-07	Lowell Devils	AHL	60	1	10	11	44	....	....	....	....	....	....	....	....	....	....	....	....	....	....	....	....	....	....
2007-08	**New Jersey**	**NHL**	**2**	**0**	**0**	**0**	**0**	**0**	**0**	**0**	**0**	**0.0**	**2**	**0**	**0.0**	**8:48**	....	....	....	....	....	....	....	....	....
	Lowell Devils	AHL	57	8	9	17	53	....	....	....	....	....	....	....	....	....	....	....	....	....	....	....	....	....	....
	NHL Totals		**2**	**0**	**0**	**0**	**0**	**0**	**0**	**0**	**0**	**0.0**		**0**	**0.0**	**8:48**	....	....	....	....	....	....	....	....	....

Signed as a free agent by **Jyvaskyla** (Finland), May 1, 2008.

MALONE, Ryan

(MA-lohn, RIGH-uhn) **T.B.**

Left wing. Shoots left. 6'4", 224 lbs. Born, Pittsburgh, PA, December 1, 1979. Pittsburgh's 5th choice, 115th overall, in 1999 Entry Draft.

1997-98	Shat.-St. Mary's	High-MN	50	41	44	85	69	....	....	....	....	....	....	....	....	....	....	....	....	....	....	....	....	....	....
1998-99	Omaha Lancers	USHL	51	14	22	36	81	....	....	....	....	....	....	....	....	....	12	2	4	6	23	....	....	....	....
99-2000	St. Cloud State	WCHA	38	9	21	30	68	....	....	....	....	....	....	....	....	....	....	....	....	....	....	....	....	....	....
2000-01	St. Cloud State	WCHA	36	7	18	25	52	....	....	....	....	....	....	....	....	....	....	....	....	....	....	....	....	....	....
2001-02	St. Cloud State	WCHA	41	24	25	49	76	....	....	....	....	....	....	....	....	....	....	....	....	....	....	....	....	....	....
2002-03	St. Cloud State	WCHA	27	16	20	36	85	....	....	....	....	....	....	....	....	....	....	....	....	....	....	....	....	....	....
	Wilkes-Barre	AHL	3	0	1	1	2	....	....	....	....	....	....	....	....	....	....	....	....	....	....	....	....	....	....
2003-04	**Pittsburgh**	**NHL**	**81**	**22**	**21**	**43**	**64**	**5**	**3**	**4**	**139**	**15.8**	**–23**	**230**	**27.4**	**18:54**	....	....	....	....	....	....	....	....	....
2004-05	Blues Espoo	Finland	9	2	1	3	36	....	....	....	....	....	....	....	....	....	....	....	....	....	....	....	....	....	....
	SV Renon	Italy	10	6	2	8	20	....	....	....	....	....	....	....	....	....	6	4	4	8	36	....	....	....	....
	HC Ambri-Piotta	Swiss						....	....	....	....	....	....	....	....	....	1	0	0	0	2	....	....	....	....
2005-06	**Pittsburgh**	**NHL**	**77**	**22**	**22**	**44**	**63**	**10**	**5**	**1**	**153**	**14.4**	**–22**	**728**	**39.6**	**18:06**	....	....	....	....	....	....	....	....	....
2006-07	**Pittsburgh**	**NHL**	**64**	**16**	**15**	**31**	**71**	**1**	**1**	**0**	**125**	**12.8**	**4**	**109**	**44.0**	**16:15**	**5**	**0**	**0**	**0**	**0**	**0**	**0**	**0**	**13:48**
2007-08	**Pittsburgh**	**NHL**	**77**	**27**	**24**	**51**	**103**	**11**	**2**	**6**	**159**	**17.0**	**14**	**38**	**31.6**	**19:05**	**20**	**6**	**10**	**16**	**25**	**3**	**0**	**2**	**18:43**
	NHL Totals		**299**	**87**	**82**	**169**	**301**	**27**	**11**	**11**	**576**	**15.1**		**1105**	**37.2**	**18:10**	**25**	**6**	**10**	**16**	**25**	**3**	**0**	**2**	**17:44**

NHL All-Rookie Team (2004)

Signed as a free agent by **Espoo** (Finland), September 29, 2004. Signed as a free agent by **Renon** (Italy), January 3, 2005. Signed as a free agent by **Ambri-Piotta** (Swiss), February 25, 2005. Rights traded to **Tampa Bay** by **Pittsburgh** with the rights to Gary Roberts for Tampa Bay's 3rd round choice in 2009 Entry Draft, June 28, 2008.

MALTBY, Kirk

(MAHLT-bee, KUHRK) **DET.**

Right wing. Shoots right. 6', 193 lbs. Born, Guelph, Ont., December 22, 1972. Edmonton's 4th choice, 65th overall, in 1992 Entry Draft.

1988-89	Cambridge	OHA-B	48	28	18	46	138	....	....	....	....	....	....	....	....	....	....	....	....	....	....	....	....	....	....
1989-90	Owen Sound	OHL	61	12	15	27	90	....	....	....	....	....	....	....	....	....	12	1	6	7	15	....	....	....	....
1990-91	Owen Sound	OHL	66	34	32	66	100	....	....	....	....	....	....	....	....	....	....	....	....	....	....	....	....	....	....
1991-92	Owen Sound	OHL	66	50	41	91	99	....	....	....	....	....	....	....	....	....	5	3	3	6	18	....	....	....	....
1992-93	Cape Breton	AHL	73	22	23	45	130	....	....	....	....	....	....	....	....	....	16	3	3	6	45	....	....	....	....
1993-94	**Edmonton**	**NHL**	**68**	**11**	**8**	**19**	**74**	**0**	**1**	**1**	**89**	**12.4**	**–2**	....	....	....	....	....	....	....	....	....	....	....	....
1994-95	**Edmonton**	**NHL**	**47**	**8**	**3**	**11**	**49**	**0**	**2**	**1**	**73**	**11.0**	**–11**	....	....	....	....	....	....	....	....	....	....	....	....

			Regular Season														Playoffs								
Season	Club	League	GP	G	A	Pts	PIM	PP	SH	GW	S	%	+/-	TF	F%	Min	GP	G	A	Pts	PIM	PP	SH	GW	Min
1995-96	Edmonton	NHL	49	2	6	8	61	0	0	1	51	3.9	−16	....	....	....	....	....	....	....	....	....	....	....	....
	Cape Breton	AHL	4	1	2	3	6	....	....	....	....	....	....	....	....	....	....	....	....	....	....	....	....	....	....
	Detroit	NHL	6	1	0	1	6	0	0	0	4	25.0	0	....	....	....	8	0	1	1	4	0	0	0	....
1996-97 ♦	Detroit	NHL	66	3	5	8	75	0	0	0	62	4.8	3	....	....	....	20	5	2	7	24	0	1	1	....
1997-98 ♦	Detroit	NHL	65	14	9	23	89	2	1	3	106	13.2	11	....	....	....	22	3	1	4	30	0	1	0	....
1998-99	Detroit	NHL	53	8	6	14	34	0	1	2	76	10.5	−6	10	40.0	13:13	10	1	0	1	8	0	0	1	11:32
99-2000	Detroit	NHL	41	6	8	14	24	0	2	1	71	8.5	1	2	50.0	13:30	8	0	1	1	4	0	0	0	13:45
2000-01	Detroit	NHL	79	12	7	19	22	1	3	3	119	10.1	16	14	35.7	14:17	6	0	0	0	6	0	0	0	15:23
2001-02 ♦	Detroit	NHL	82	9	15	24	40	0	1	5	108	8.3	15	38	47.4	13:23	23	3	3	6	32	0	2	0	16:34
2002-03	Detroit	NHL	82	14	23	37	91	0	4	1	116	12.1	17	43	37.2	16:10	4	0	0	0	4	0	0	0	17:18
2003-04	Detroit	NHL	79	14	19	33	80	1	4	4	123	11.4	24	30	43.3	16:16	12	1	3	4	11	0	0	0	17:34
2004-05			DID NOT PLAY																						
2005-06	Detroit	NHL	82	5	6	11	80	0	1	0	115	4.3	−9	22	50.0	13:44	6	2	1	3	4	0	0	1	13:02
2006-07	Detroit	NHL	82	6	5	11	50	0	0	0	113	5.3	−9	14	28.6	13:11	18	1	1	2	10	0	1	0	10:46
2007-08 ♦	Detroit	NHL	61	6	4	10	32	0	0	1	70	8.6	−8	7	42.9	12:04	12	0	1	1	10	0	0	0	9:47
	NHL Totals		942	119	124	243	807	4	20	23	1296	9.2		180	41.7	14:06	149	16	14	30	147	0	5	3	13:49

Traded to **Detroit** by **Edmonton** for Dan McGillis, March 20, 1996. • Missed majority of 1999-2000 season recovering from hernia injury suffered in game vs. Dallas, October 5, 1999.

MANCARI, Mark

(man-KAH-ree, MAHRK) **BUF.**

Right wing. Shoots right. 6'3", 220 lbs. Born, London, Ont., July 11, 1985. Buffalo's 6th choice, 207th overall, in 2004 Entry Draft.

2001-02	Ottawa 67's	OHL	34	3	3	6	10	....	....	....	....	....	....	....	....	....	2	0	1	1	0	....	....	....	....
2002-03	Ottawa 67's	OHL	61	8	11	19	20	....	....	....	....	....	....	....	....	....	11	2	1	3	2	....	....	....	....
2003-04	Ottawa 67's	OHL	67	29	36	65	56	....	....	....	....	....	....	....	....	....	7	5	3	8	11	....	....	....	....
2004-05	Ottawa 67's	OHL	64	36	32	68	86	....	....	....	....	....	....	....	....	....	21	*14	10	24	24	....	....	....	....
2005-06	Rochester	AHL	71	18	24	42	80	....	....	....	....	....	....	....	....	....	....	....	....	....	....	....	....	....	....
2006-07	Buffalo	NHL	3	0	1	1	2	0	0	0	1	0.0	−1	0	0.0	6:12	....	....	....	....	....	....	....	....	....
	Rochester	AHL	64	23	34	57	49	....	....	....	....	....	....	....	....	....	6	1	5	6	6	....	....	....	....
2007-08	Rochester	AHL	80	21	36	57	78	....	....	....	....	....	....	....	....	....	....	....	....	....	....	....	....	....	....
	NHL Totals		3	0	1	1	2	0	0	0	1	0.0		0	0.0	6:12	....	....	....	....	....	....	....	....	....

MANLOW, Eric

(MAN-low, AIR-ihk)

Center. Shoots left. 6', 180 lbs. Born, Belleville, Ont., April 7, 1975. Chicago's 2nd choice, 50th overall, in 1993 Entry Draft.

1990-91	Peterborough	Minor-ON	59	67	51	118	90	....	....	....	....	....	....	....	....	....	....	....	....	....	....	....	....	....	....
	Peterborough	OHA-B	1	0	0	0	0	....	....	....	....	....	....	....	....	....	....	....	....	....	....	....	....	....	....
1991-92	Kitchener Rangers	OHL	59	12	20	32	17	....	....	....	....	....	....	....	....	....	14	2	5	7	10	....	....	....	....
1992-93	Kitchener Rangers	OHL	53	26	21	47	31	....	....	....	....	....	....	....	....	....	4	0	1	1	2	....	....	....	....
1993-94	Kitchener Rangers	OHL	49	28	32	60	25	....	....	....	....	....	....	....	....	....	3	0	1	1	4	....	....	....	....
1994-95	Kitchener Rangers	OHL	44	25	29	54	26	....	....	....	....	....	....	....	....	....	....	....	....	....	....	....	....	....	....
	Detroit	OHL	16	4	16	20	11	....	....	....	....	....	....	....	....	....	21	11	10	21	18	....	....	....	....
1995-96	Indianapolis Ice	IHL	75	6	11	17	32	....	....	....	....	....	....	....	....	....	4	0	1	1	4	....	....	....	....
1996-97	Baltimore Bandits	AHL	36	6	6	12	13	....	....	....	....	....	....	....	....	....	3	0	0	0	0	....	....	....	....
	Columbus Chill	ECHL	32	18	18	36	20	....	....	....	....	....	....	....	....	....	....	....	....	....	....	....	....	....	....
1997-98	Indianapolis Ice	IHL	60	8	11	19	25	....	....	....	....	....	....	....	....	....	3	1	0	1	0	....	....	....	....
1998-99	Long Beach	IHL	51	9	19	28	30	....	....	....	....	....	....	....	....	....	8	0	0	0	8	....	....	....	....
	Florida Everblades	ECHL	18	8	15	23	11	....	....	....	....	....	....	....	....	....	....	....	....	....	....	....	....	....	....
99-2000	Florida Everblades	ECHL	26	14	24	38	24	....	....	....	....	....	....	....	....	....	....	....	....	....	....	....	....	....	....
	Providence Bruins	AHL	46	17	16	33	14	....	....	....	....	....	....	....	....	....	14	6	8	14	8	....	....	....	....
2000-01	Boston	NHL	8	0	1	1	2	0	0	0	3	0.0	0	61	50.8	7:26	....	....	....	....	....	....	....	....	....
	Providence Bruins	AHL	60	16	51	67	18	....	....	....	....	....	....	....	....	....	17	6	7	13	6	....	....	....	....
2001-02	Boston	NHL	3	0	0	0	0	0	0	0	2	0.0	0	16	31.3	6:05	....	....	....	....	....	....	....	....	....
	Providence Bruins	AHL	70	13	35	48	30	....	....	....	....	....	....	....	....	....	2	0	0	0	2	....	....	....	....
2002-03	NY Islanders	NHL	8	2	1	3	4	1	0	0	7	28.6	2	84	54.8	12:27	....	....	....	....	....	....	....	....	....
	Bridgeport	AHL	62	19	40	59	58	....	....	....	....	....	....	....	....	....	9	0	6	6	2	....	....	....	....
2003-04	NY Islanders	NHL	18	0	2	2	2	0	0	0	10	0.0	−2	178	53.9	10:13	....	....	....	....	....	....	....	....	....
	Bridgeport	AHL	40	8	27	35	16	....	....	....	....	....	....	....	....	....	1	0	0	0	2	....	....	....	....
2004-05	Grand Rapids	AHL	61	21	20	41	24	....	....	....	....	....	....	....	....	....	....	....	....	....	....	....	....	....	....
2005-06	Grand Rapids	AHL	80	25	47	72	44	....	....	....	....	....	....	....	....	....	16	3	3	6	12	....	....	....	....
2006-07	Hamilton	AHL	60	5	13	18	28	....	....	....	....	....	....	....	....	....	22	6	5	11	10	....	....	....	....
2007-08	Hamilton	AHL	76	12	18	30	30	....	....	....	....	....	....	....	....	....	....	....	....	....	....	....	....	....	....
	NHL Totals		37	2	4	6	8	1	0	0	22	9.1		339	52.5	9:46	....	....	....	....	....	....	....	....	....

Signed as a free agent by **Providence** (AHL), January 24, 2000. Signed as a free agent by **Boston**, July 11, 2000. Signed as a free agent by **NY Islanders**, July 21, 2002. Signed as a free agent by **Detroit**, July 21, 2004. Signed as a free agent by **Hamilton** (AHL), July 10, 2006.

MAPLETOFT, Justin

(MAP-uhl-tawft, JUHS-tihn)

Center. Shoots left. 6'1", 202 lbs. Born, Lloydminster, Sask., January 11, 1981. NY Islanders' 9th choice, 130th overall, in 1999 Entry Draft.

1996-97	Calgary Royals	AMHL	36	25	36	51	....	....	....	....	....	....	....	....	....	....	....	....	....	....	....	....	....	....	....
	Red Deer Rebels	WHL	2	0	0	0	0	....	....	....	....	....	....	....	....	....	....	....	....	....	....	....	....	....	....
1997-98	Red Deer Rebels	WHL	65	9	4	13	41	....	....	....	....	....	....	....	....	....	....	....	....	....	....	....	....	....	....
1998-99	Red Deer Rebels	WHL	72	24	22	46	81	....	....	....	....	....	....	....	....	....	....	....	....	....	....	....	....	....	....
99-2000	Red Deer Rebels	WHL	72	39	57	96	135	....	....	....	....	....	....	....	....	....	4	2	1	3	28	....	....	....	....
2000-01	Red Deer Rebels	WHL	70	43	*77	*120	111	....	....	....	....	....	....	....	....	....	22	13	*21	34	59	....	....	....	....
2001-02	Bridgeport	AHL	80	13	20	33	60	....	....	....	....	....	....	....	....	....	20	7	10	17	23	....	....	....	....
2002-03	NY Islanders	NHL	11	2	2	4	2	1	0	0	12	16.7	−1	138	41.3	12:17	2	0	0	0	0	0	0	0	7:23
	Bridgeport	AHL	63	13	26	39	47	....	....	....	....	....	....	....	....	....	7	1	2	3	6	....	....	....	....
2003-04	NY Islanders	NHL	27	1	4	5	6	0	0	0	15	6.7	−1	134	48.5	6:09	....	....	....	....	....	....	....	....	....
	Bridgeport	AHL	36	10	13	23	59	....	....	....	....	....	....	....	....	....	....	....	....	....	....	....	....	....	....
2004-05	Bridgeport	AHL	61	11	24	35	51	....	....	....	....	....	....	....	....	....	....	....	....	....	....	....	....	....	....
2005-06	Jokerit Helsinki	Finland	18	1	3	4	8	....	....	....	....	....	....	....	....	....	....	....	....	....	....	....	....	....	....
	Sodertalje SK	Sweden	31	14	7	21	34	....	....	....	....	....	....	....	....	....	....	....	....	....	....	....	....	....	....
	Sodertalje SK	Sweden-Q	10	1	5	6	8	....	....	....	....	....	....	....	....	....	....	....	....	....	....	....	....	....	....
2006-07	Nurnberg	Germany	10	2	3	5	2	....	....	....	....	....	....	....	....	....	13	2	4	6	10	....	....	....	....
2007-08	Binghamton	AHL	78	18	22	40	77	....	....	....	....	....	....	....	....	....	....	....	....	....	....	....	....	....	....
	NHL Totals		38	3	6	9	8	1	0	0	27	11.1		272	44.9	7:56	2	0	0	0	0	0	0	0	7:23

WHL East First All-Star Team (2000, 2001) • WHL Player of the Year (2001) • Canadian Major Junior First All-Star Team (2001)

Signed as a free agent by **Jokerit Helsinki** (Finland), September 6, 2005. Signed as a free agent by **Sodertalje** (Sweden), November 8, 2005. Signed as a free agent by **Nurnberg** (Germany), January 25, 2007. Signed as a free agent by **Ottawa**, August 10, 2007.

MARA, Paul

(MAIR-uh, PAWL) **NYR**

Defense. Shoots left. 6'4", 212 lbs. Born, Ridgewood, NJ, September 7, 1979. Tampa Bay's 1st choice, 7th overall, in 1997 Entry Draft.

1994-95	Belmont Hill	High-MA	28	5	17	22	28	....	....	....	....	....	....	....	....	....	....	....	....	....	....	....	....	....	....
1995-96	Belmont Hill	High-MA	28	18	20	38	40	....	....	....	....	....	....	....	....	....	....	....	....	....	....	....	....	....	....
1996-97	Sudbury Wolves	OHL	44	9	34	43	61	....	....	....	....	....	....	....	....	....	....	....	....	....	....	....	....	....	....
1997-98	Sudbury Wolves	OHL	25	8	18	26	79	....	....	....	....	....	....	....	....	....	....	....	....	....	....	....	....	....	....
	Plymouth Whalers	OHL	25	8	15	23	30	....	....	....	....	....	....	....	....	....	15	3	14	17	30	....	....	....	....
1998-99	Plymouth Whalers	OHL	52	13	41	54	95	....	....	....	....	....	....	....	....	....	11	5	7	12	28	....	....	....	....
	Tampa Bay	NHL	1	1	1	2	0	1	0	0	1	100.0	−3	0	0.0	19:34	....	....	....	....	....	....	....	....	....
99-2000	Tampa Bay	NHL	54	7	11	18	73	4	0	1	78	9.0	−27	0	0.0	22:13	....	....	....	....	....	....	....	....	....
	Detroit Vipers	IHL	15	3	5	8	22	....	....	....	....	....	....	....	....	....	....	....	....	....	....	....	....	....	....
2000-01	Tampa Bay	NHL	46	6	10	16	40	2	0	1	58	10.3	−17	0	0.0	23:06	....	....	....	....	....	....	....	....	....
	Detroit Vipers	IHL	10	3	3	6	22	....	....	....	....	....	....	....	....	....	....	....	....	....	....	....	....	....	....
	Phoenix	NHL	16	0	4	4	14	0	0	0	20	0.0	1	0	0.0	19:22	....	....	....	....	....	....	....	....	....
2001-02	Phoenix	NHL	75	7	17	24	58	2	0	0	112	6.3	−6	2	100.0	21:34	5	0	0	0	4	0	0	0	22:57
2002-03	Phoenix	NHL	73	10	15	25	78	1	0	0	95	10.5	−7	1	0.0	21:06	....	....	....	....	....	....	....	....	....
2003-04	Phoenix	NHL	81	6	36	42	48	1	0	0	140	4.3	−11	2	0.0	23:37	....	....	....	....	....	....	....	....	....
2004-05	Hannover	Germany	35	5	13	18	89	....	....	....	....	....	....	....	....	....	....	....	....	....	....	....	....	....	....
2005-06	Phoenix	NHL	78	15	32	47	70	8	0	0	157	9.6	−12	1	0.0	21:29	....	....	....	....	....	....	....	....	....

			Regular Season														Playoffs								
Season	Club	League	GP	G	A	Pts	PIM	PP	SH	GW	S	%	+/-	TF	F%	Min	GP	G	A	Pts	PIM	PP	SH	GW	Min
2006-07	Boston	NHL	59	3	15	18	95	0	0	0	60	5.0	–22	0	0.0	21:53	....	....	....	....	....	....	....	....	....
	NY Rangers	NHL	19	2	3	5	18	1	0	0	40	5.0	6	0	0.0	22:56	10	2	2	4	18	2	0	0	19:43
2007-08	NY Rangers	NHL	61	1	16	17	52	0	0	0	80	1.3	1	1	0.0	17:53	10	0	1	1	20	0	0	0	17:48
	NHL Totals		563	58	160	218	546	20	0	2	841	6.9		7	28.6	21:36	25	2	3	5	42	2	0	0	19:36

Traded to **Phoenix** by **Tampa Bay** with Mike Johnson, Ruslan Zainullin and NY Islanders' 2nd round choice (previously acquired, Phoenix selected Matthew Spiller) in 2001 Entry Draft for Nikolai Khabibulin and Stan Neckar, March 5, 2001. Signed as a free agent by **Hannover** (Germany), October 29, 2004. Traded to **Boston** by **Phoenix** with Phoenix's 3rd round choice (later traded to Anaheim - Anaheim selected Maxime Macenauer) in 2007 Entry Draft for Nick Boynton and Boston's 4th round choice (later traded to Toronto - Toronto selected Matt Frattin) in 2007 Entry Draft, June 26, 2006. Traded to **NY Rangers** by **Boston** for Aaron Ward, February 27, 2007.

MARCHANT, Todd

(mahr-SHAHNT, TAWD) **ANA.**

Center. Shoots left. 5'10", 180 lbs. Born, Buffalo, NY, August 12, 1973. NY Rangers' 8th choice, 164th overall, in 1993 Entry Draft.

1990-91	Niagara Scenics	NAHL	37	31	47	78	....	....	....	....	....	....	....	....	....	....	....	....	....	....	....	....	....	....	....
1991-92	Clarkson Knights	ECAC	32	20	12	32	32	....	....	....	....	....	....	....	....	....	....	....	....	....	....	....	....	....	....
1992-93	Clarkson Knights	ECAC	33	18	28	46	38	....	....	....	....	....	....	....	....	....	....	....	....	....	....	....	....	....	....
1993-94	United States	Nat-Tm	59	28	39	67	48	....	....	....	....	....	....	....	....	....	....	....	....	....	....	....	....	....	....
	United States	Olympics	8	1	1	2	6	....	....	....	....	....	....	....	....	....	....	....	....	....	....	....	....	....	....
	NY Rangers	**NHL**	**1**	**0**	**0**	**0**	**0**	**0**	**0**	**0**	**1**	**0.0**	**–1**	....	....	....	....	....	....	....	....	....	....	....	....
	Binghamton	AHL	8	2	7	9	6	....	....	....	....	....	....	....	....	....	....	....	....	....	....	....	....	....	....
	Edmonton	**NHL**	**3**	**0**	**1**	**1**	**2**	**0**	**0**	**0**	**5**	**0.0**	**–1**	....	....	....	....	....	....	....	....	....	....	....	....
	Cape Breton	AHL	3	1	4	5	2	....	....	....	....	....	....	....	....	....	5	1	1	2	0	....	....	....	....
1994-95	Cape Breton	AHL	38	22	25	47	25	....	....	....	....	....	....	....	....	....	....	....	....	....	....	....	....	....	....
	Edmonton	**NHL**	**45**	**13**	**14**	**27**	**32**	**3**	**2**	**2**	**95**	**13.7**	**–3**	....	....	....	....	....	....	....	....	....	....	....	....
1995-96	**Edmonton**	**NHL**	**81**	**19**	**19**	**38**	**66**	**2**	**3**	**2**	**221**	**8.6**	**–19**	....	....	....	....	....	....	....	....	....	....	....	....
1996-97	**Edmonton**	**NHL**	**79**	**14**	**19**	**33**	**44**	**0**	**4**	**3**	**202**	**6.9**	**11**	....	....	....	**12**	**4**	**2**	**6**	**12**	**0**	**3**	**1**	....
1997-98	**Edmonton**	**NHL**	**76**	**14**	**21**	**35**	**71**	**2**	**1**	**3**	**194**	**7.2**	**9**	....	....	....	**12**	**1**	**1**	**2**	**10**	**0**	**0**	**0**	....
1998-99	**Edmonton**	**NHL**	**82**	**14**	**22**	**36**	**65**	**3**	**1**	**2**	**183**	**7.7**	**3**	**1449**	**50.0**	**16:47**	**4**	**1**	**1**	**2**	**12**	**0**	**0**	**0**	**24:21**
99-2000	**Edmonton**	**NHL**	**82**	**17**	**23**	**40**	**70**	**0**	**1**	**0**	**170**	**10.0**	**7**	**1593**	**52.9**	**17:08**	**3**	**1**	**0**	**1**	**2**	**0**	**0**	**0**	**18:07**
2000-01	**Edmonton**	**NHL**	**71**	**13**	**26**	**39**	**51**	**0**	**4**	**2**	**113**	**11.5**	**1**	**1549**	**53.8**	**17:54**	**6**	**0**	**0**	**0**	**4**	**0**	**0**	**0**	**22:57**
2001-02	**Edmonton**	**NHL**	**82**	**12**	**22**	**34**	**41**	**0**	**3**	**1**	**124**	**9.7**	**7**	**1523**	**52.4**	**16:58**	....	....	....	....	....	....	....	....	....
2002-03	**Edmonton**	**NHL**	**77**	**20**	**40**	**60**	**48**	**7**	**1**	**3**	**146**	**13.7**	**13**	**1336**	**58.0**	**19:54**	**6**	**0**	**2**	**2**	**2**	**0**	**0**	**0**	**20:03**
2003-04	**Columbus**	**NHL**	**77**	**9**	**25**	**34**	**34**	**4**	**0**	**2**	**163**	**5.5**	**–17**	**1412**	**50.9**	**20:39**	....	....	....	....	....	....	....	....	....
2004-05			DID NOT PLAY																						
2005-06	**Columbus**	**NHL**	**18**	**3**	**6**	**9**	**20**	**0**	**0**	**0**	**42**	**7.1**	**–1**	**289**	**50.2**	**20:05**	....	....	....	....	....	....	....	....	....
	Anaheim	**NHL**	**61**	**6**	**19**	**25**	**46**	**0**	**0**	**0**	**90**	**6.7**	**3**	**743**	**51.7**	**16:25**	**16**	**3**	**10**	**13**	**14**	**0**	**0**	**0**	**17:34**
2006-07♦	**Anaheim**	**NHL**	**56**	**8**	**15**	**23**	**44**	**0**	**3**	**2**	**115**	**7.0**	**7**	**647**	**54.3**	**15:10**	**11**	**0**	**3**	**3**	**12**	**0**	**0**	**0**	**15:44**
2007-08	**Anaheim**	**NHL**	**75**	**9**	**7**	**16**	**48**	**0**	**0**	**0**	**93**	**9.7**	**–3**	**673**	**49.2**	**14:49**	**6**	**2**	**0**	**2**	**0**	**0**	**0**	**0**	**17:40**
	NHL Totals		**966**	**171**	**279**	**450**	**682**	**21**	**23**	**22**	**1957**	**8.7**		**11214**	**52.6**	**17:28**	**76**	**12**	**19**	**31**	**68**	**0**	**3**	**1**	**18:39**

ECAC Second All-Star Team (1993)

Traded to **Edmonton** by **NY Rangers** for Craig MacTavish, March 21, 1994. Signed as a free agent by **Columbus**, July 3, 2003. Claimed on waivers by **Anaheim** from **Columbus**, November 21, 2005.

MARKOV, Andrei

(MAHR-kahf, AHN-dray) **MTL.**

Defense. Shoots left. 6', 204 lbs. Born, Voskresensk, USSR, December 20, 1978. Montreal's 6th choice, 162nd overall, in 1998 Entry Draft.

1995-96	Voskresensk	CIS	38	0	0	0	14	....	....	....	....	....	....	....	....	....	....	....	....	....	....	....	....	....	....
1996-97	Voskresensk	Russia	43	8	4	12	32	....	....	....	....	....	....	....	....	....	2	1	1	2	0	....	....	....	....
1997-98	Voskresensk	Russia	43	10	5	15	83	....	....	....	....	....	....	....	....	....	....	....	....	....	....	....	....	....	....
1998-99	Dynamo Moscow	Russia	38	10	11	21	32	....	....	....	....	....	....	....	....	....	16	3	6	9	6	....	....	....	....
	Dynamo Moscow	EuroHL	12	7	5	12	12	....	....	....	....	....	....	....	....	....	6	2	2	4	4	....	....	....	....
99-2000	Dynamo Moscow	Russia	29	11	12	23	28	....	....	....	....	....	....	....	....	....	17	4	3	7	8	....	....	....	....
2000-01	**Montreal**	**NHL**	**63**	**6**	**17**	**23**	**18**	**2**	**0**	**0**	**82**	**7.3**	**–6**	**2**	**50.0**	**16:53**	....	....	....	....	....	....	....	....	....
	Quebec Citadelles	AHL	14	0	5	5	4	....	....	....	....	....	....	....	....	....	7	1	1	2	2	....	....	....	....
2001-02	**Montreal**	**NHL**	**56**	**5**	**19**	**24**	**24**	**2**	**0**	**1**	**73**	**6.8**	**–1**	**0**	**0.0**	**17:15**	**12**	**1**	**3**	**4**	**8**	**0**	**0**	**1**	**15:53**
	Quebec Citadelles	AHL	12	4	6	10	7	....	....	....	....	....	....	....	....	....	....	....	....	....	....	....	....	....	....
2002-03	**Montreal**	**NHL**	**79**	**13**	**24**	**37**	**34**	**3**	**0**	**2**	**159**	**8.2**	**13**	**1**	**0.0**	**23:17**	....	....	....	....	....	....	....	....	....
2003-04	**Montreal**	**NHL**	**69**	**6**	**22**	**28**	**20**	**2**	**0**	**0**	**105**	**5.7**	**–2**	**2**	**50.0**	**21:29**	**11**	**1**	**4**	**5**	**8**	**0**	**0**	**1**	**22:52**
2004-05	Dynamo Moscow	Russia	42	7	16	23	76	....	....	....	....	....	....	....	....	....	10	2	0	2	22	....	....	....	....
2005-06	**Montreal**	**NHL**	**67**	**10**	**36**	**46**	**74**	**6**	**1**	**1**	**88**	**11.4**	**13**	**1**	**0.0**	**23:33**	**6**	**0**	**1**	**1**	**4**	**0**	**0**	**0**	**25:29**
	Russia	Olympics	8	1	2	3	6	....	....	....	....	....	....	....	....	....	....	....	....	....	....	....	....	....	....
2006-07	**Montreal**	**NHL**	**77**	**6**	**43**	**49**	**56**	**5**	**0**	**2**	**128**	**4.7**	**2**	**1**	**0.0**	**24:29**	....	....	....	....	....	....	....	....	....
2007-08	**Montreal**	**NHL**	**82**	**16**	**42**	**58**	**63**	**10**	**1**	**2**	**145**	**11.0**	**1**	**0**	**0.0**	**24:58**	**12**	**1**	**3**	**4**	**8**	**0**	**0**	**0**	**24:54**
	NHL Totals		**493**	**62**	**203**	**265**	**289**	**30**	**2**	**8**	**780**	**7.9**		**7**	**28.6**	**22:02**	**41**	**3**	**11**	**14**	**28**	**0**	**0**	**2**	**21:48**

Played in NHL All-Star Game (2008)

Signed as a free agent by **Dynamo Moscow** (Russia), June 19, 2004.

MARKOV, Danny

(MAHR-kahf, DA-nee)

Defense. Shoots left. 6'1", 190 lbs. Born, Moscow, USSR, July 30, 1976. Toronto's 7th choice, 223rd overall, in 1995 Entry Draft.

1993-94	Spartak Moscow	CIS	13	1	0	1	6	....	....	....	....	....	....	....	....	....	1	0	0	0	0	....	....	....	....
1994-95	Spartak Moscow	CIS	39	0	1	1	36	....	....	....	....	....	....	....	....	....	....	....	....	....	....	....	....	....	....
1995-96	Spartak Moscow	CIS	38	2	0	2	12	....	....	....	....	....	....	....	....	....	2	0	0	0	2	....	....	....	....
1996-97	Spartak Moscow	Russia	39	3	6	9	41	....	....	....	....	....	....	....	....	....	....	....	....	....	....	....	....	....	....
	St. John's	AHL	10	2	4	6	18	....	....	....	....	....	....	....	....	....	11	2	6	8	14	....	....	....	....
1997-98	**Toronto**	**NHL**	**25**	**2**	**5**	**7**	**28**	**1**	**0**	**0**	**15**	**13.3**	**0**	....	....	....	....	....	....	....	....	....	....	....	....
	St. John's	AHL	52	3	23	26	124	....	....	....	....	....	....	....	....	....	2	0	1	1	0	....	....	....	....
1998-99	**Toronto**	**NHL**	**57**	**4**	**8**	**12**	**47**	**0**	**0**	**0**	**34**	**11.8**	**5**	**0**	**0.0**	**18:41**	**17**	**0**	**6**	**6**	**18**	**0**	**0**	**0**	**22:24**
99-2000	**Toronto**	**NHL**	**59**	**0**	**10**	**10**	**28**	**0**	**0**	**0**	**38**	**0.0**	**13**	**1**	**0.0**	**20:08**	**12**	**0**	**3**	**3**	**10**	**0**	**0**	**0**	**21:05**
2000-01	**Toronto**	**NHL**	**59**	**3**	**13**	**16**	**34**	**1**	**0**	**2**	**49**	**6.1**	**6**	**0**	**0.0**	**19:02**	**11**	**1**	**1**	**2**	**12**	**0**	**0**	**0**	**21:30**
2001-02	**Phoenix**	**NHL**	**72**	**6**	**30**	**36**	**67**	**4**	**0**	**1**	**103**	**5.8**	**–7**	**0**	**0.0**	**22:55**	....	....	....	....	....	....	....	....	....
	Russia	Olympics	5	0	1	1	0	....	....	....	....	....	....	....	....	....	....	....	....	....	....	....	....	....	....
2002-03	**Phoenix**	**NHL**	**64**	**4**	**16**	**20**	**36**	**2**	**0**	**0**	**105**	**3.8**	**2**	**0**	**0.0**	**23:16**	....	....	....	....	....	....	....	....	....
2003-04	**Carolina**	**NHL**	**44**	**4**	**10**	**14**	**37**	**2**	**0**	**1**	**73**	**5.5**	**–6**	**0**	**0.0**	**23:39**	....	....	....	....	....	....	....	....	....
	Philadelphia	**NHL**	**34**	**2**	**3**	**5**	**58**	**1**	**0**	**1**	**27**	**7.4**	**0**	**0**	**0.0**	**21:16**	**18**	**1**	**2**	**3**	**25**	**0**	**0**	**1**	**23:03**
2004-05	Vityaz Chekhov	Russia-2	26	5	7	12	16	....	....	....	....	....	....	....	....	....	12	0	3	3	6	....	....	....	....
2005-06	**Nashville**	**NHL**	**58**	**0**	**11**	**11**	**62**	**0**	**0**	**0**	**59**	**0.0**	**9**	**0**	**0.0**	**19:33**	**5**	**0**	**0**	**0**	**6**	**0**	**0**	**0**	**19:22**
	Russia	Olympics	8	0	2	2	4	....	....	....	....	....	....	....	....	....	....	....	....	....	....	....	....	....	....
2006-07	**Detroit**	**NHL**	**66**	**4**	**12**	**16**	**59**	**0**	**0**	**0**	**66**	**6.1**	**25**	**0**	**0.0**	**18:53**	**18**	**0**	**0**	**0**	**13**	**0**	**0**	**0**	**22:04**
2007-08	Dynamo Moscow	Russia	29	0	4	4	71	....	....	....	....	....	....	....	....	....	9	2	1	3	12	....	....	....	....
	NHL Totals		**538**	**29**	**118**	**147**	**456**	**11**	**0**	**5**	**569**	**5.1**		**1**	**0.0**	**20:47**	**81**	**2**	**12**	**14**	**84**	**0**	**0**	**1**	**21:58**

Traded to **Phoenix** by **Toronto** for Robert Reichel, Travis Green and Craig Mills, June 12, 2001. Traded to **Carolina** by **Phoenix** with Edmonton's 3rd round choice (previously acquired, later traded to NY Rangers - NY Rangers selected Billy Ryan) in 2004 Entry Draft for David Tanabe and Igor Knyazev, June 21, 2003. Traded to **Philadelphia** by **Carolina** for Justin Williams, January 20, 2004. Signed as a free agent by **Chekhov** (Russia-2), November 15, 2004. Traded to **Nashville** by **Philadelphia** for Nashville's 3rd round choice (later traded to Los Angeles - Los Angeles selected Bud Holloway) in 2006 Entry Draft, August 2, 2005. Signed as a free agent by **Detroit**, July 26, 2006. Signed as a free agent by **Dynamo Moscow** (Russia), October 26, 2007.

MARLEAU, Patrick

(mahr-LOH, PAT-rihk) **S.J.**

Center. Shoots left. 6'2", 220 lbs. Born, Aneroid, Sask., September 15, 1979. San Jose's 1st choice, 2nd overall, in 1997 Entry Draft.

1993-94	Swift Current	SMHL	53	72	95	167	....	....	....	....	....	....	....	....	....	....	....	....	....	....	....	....	....	....	....
1994-95	Swift Current	SMHL	31	30	22	52	18	....	....	....	....	....	....	....	....	....	....	....	....	....	....	....	....	....	....
1995-96	Seattle	WHL	72	32	42	74	22	....	....	....	....	....	....	....	....	....	5	3	4	7	4	....	....	....	....
1996-97	Seattle	WHL	71	51	74	125	37	....	....	....	....	....	....	....	....	....	15	7	16	23	12	....	....	....	....
1997-98	**San Jose**	**NHL**	**74**	**13**	**19**	**32**	**14**	**1**	**0**	**2**	**90**	**14.4**	**5**	....	....	....	**5**	**0**	**1**	**1**	**0**	**0**	**0**	**0**	....
1998-99	**San Jose**	**NHL**	**81**	**21**	**24**	**45**	**24**	**4**	**0**	**4**	**134**	**15.7**	**10**	**1121**	**43.4**	**15:11**	**6**	**2**	**1**	**3**	**4**	**2**	**0**	**0**	**11:08**
99-2000	**San Jose**	**NHL**	**81**	**17**	**23**	**40**	**36**	**3**	**0**	**3**	**161**	**10.6**	**–9**	**851**	**42.0**	**14:11**	**5**	**1**	**1**	**2**	**2**	**1**	**0**	**0**	**11:51**
2000-01	**San Jose**	**NHL**	**81**	**25**	**27**	**52**	**22**	**5**	**0**	**6**	**146**	**17.1**	**7**	**1088**	**44.8**	**16:17**	**6**	**2**	**0**	**2**	**4**	**0**	**0**	**0**	**14:50**
2001-02	**San Jose**	**NHL**	**79**	**21**	**23**	**44**	**40**	**3**	**0**	**5**	**121**	**17.4**	**9**	**897**	**47.3**	**14:04**	**12**	**6**	**5**	**11**	**6**	**1**	**0**	**3**	**15:50**
2002-03	**San Jose**	**NHL**	**82**	**28**	**29**	**57**	**33**	**8**	**1**	**3**	**172**	**16.3**	**–10**	**1403**	**47.3**	**18:31**	....	....	....	....	....	....	....	....	....
2003-04	**San Jose**	**NHL**	**80**	**28**	**29**	**57**	**24**	**9**	**0**	**5**	**220**	**12.7**	**–5**	**1014**	**41.6**	**18:12**	**17**	**8**	**4**	**12**	**6**	**4**	**1**	**2**	**19:16**
2004-05			DID NOT PLAY																						
2005-06	**San Jose**	**NHL**	**82**	**34**	**52**	**86**	**26**	**20**	**1**	**4**	**260**	**13.1**	**–12**	**1216**	**46.8**	**19:56**	**11**	**9**	**5**	**14**	**8**	**4**	**0**	**2**	**21:07**

			Regular Season														Playoffs								
Season	Club	League	GP	G	A	Pts	PIM	PP	SH	GW	S	%	+/-	TF	F%	Min	GP	G	A	Pts	PIM	PP	SH	GW	Min
2006-07	San Jose	NHL	77	32	46	78	33	14	0	9	180	17.8	9	693	50.5	18:34	11	3	3	6	2	1	0	1	18:59
2007-08	San Jose	NHL	78	19	29	48	33	7	0	2	185	10.3	−19	605	52.4	18:14	13	4	4	8	2	0	2	0	23:04
	NHL Totals		795	238	301	539	285	74	2	43	1669	14.3		8888	45.9	17:01	86	35	24	59	34	13	3	8	18:12

WHL West First All-Star Team (1997)
Played in NHL All-Star Game (2004, 2007)

MARSHALL, Grant

(MAR-shuhl, GRANT)

Right wing. Shoots right. 6'1", 200 lbs. Born, Mississauga, Ont., June 9, 1973. Toronto's 2nd choice, 23rd overall, in 1992 Entry Draft.

Season	Club	League	GP	G	A	Pts	PIM	PP	SH	GW	S	%	+/-	TF	F%	Min	GP	G	A	Pts	PIM	PP	SH	GW	Min
1989-90	Tor. Young Nats	MTHL	39	15	28	43	56	....	....	....	....	....	....	....	....	....	....	....	....	....	....	....	....	....	....
1990-91	Ottawa 67's	OHL	26	6	11	17	25	....	....	....	....	....	....	....	....	....	1	0	0	0	0	....	....	....	....
1991-92	Ottawa 67's	OHL	61	32	51	83	132	....	....	....	....	....	....	....	....	....	11	6	11	17	11	....	....	....	....
1992-93	Ottawa 67's	OHL	30	14	29	43	83	....	....	....	....	....	....	....	....	....	....	....	....	....	....	....	....	....	....
	Newmarket	OHL	31	11	25	36	89	....	....	....	....	....	....	....	....	....	7	4	7	11	20	....	....	....	....
	St. John's	AHL	2	0	0	0	0	....	....	....	....	....	....	....	....	....	2	0	0	0	2	....	....	....	....
1993-94	St. John's	AHL	67	11	29	40	155	....	....	....	....	....	....	....	....	....	11	1	5	6	17	....	....	....	....
1994-95	Kalamazoo Wings	IHL	61	17	29	46	96	....	....	....	....	....	....	....	....	....	16	9	3	12	27	....	....	....	....
	Dallas	**NHL**	**2**	**0**	**1**	**1**	**0**	**0**	**0**	**0**	**0**	**0.0**	**1**	....	....	....	....	....	....	....	....	....	....	....	....
1995-96	**Dallas**	**NHL**	**70**	**9**	**19**	**28**	**111**	**0**	**0**	**0**	**62**	**14.5**	**0**	....	....	....	....	....	....	....	....	....	....	....	....
1996-97	**Dallas**	**NHL**	**56**	**6**	**4**	**10**	**98**	**0**	**0**	**0**	**0**	**0.0**	**5**	....	....	....	**5**	**0**	**2**	**2**	**8**	**0**	**0**	**0**	....
1997-98	**Dallas**	**NHL**	**72**	**9**	**10**	**19**	**96**	**3**	**0**	**1**	**91**	**9.9**	**−2**	....	....	....	**17**	**0**	**2**	**2**	***47**	**0**	**0**	**0**	....
1998-99 ♦	**Dallas**	**NHL**	**82**	**13**	**18**	**31**	**85**	**2**	**0**	**4**	**112**	**11.6**	**1**	**2**	**50.0**	**12:39**	**14**	**0**	**3**	**3**	**20**	**0**	**0**	**0**	**11:42**
99-2000	**Dallas**	**NHL**	**45**	**2**	**6**	**8**	**38**	**1**	**0**	**0**	**43**	**4.7**	**−5**	**3**	**0.0**	**11:19**	**14**	**0**	**1**	**1**	**4**	**0**	**0**	**0**	**10:08**
2000-01	**Dallas**	**NHL**	**75**	**13**	**24**	**37**	**64**	**4**	**0**	**1**	**93**	**14.0**	**1**	**16**	**56.3**	**11:05**	**9**	**0**	**0**	**0**	**0**	**0**	**0**	**0**	**11:15**
2001-02	**Columbus**	**NHL**	**81**	**15**	**18**	**33**	**86**	**6**	**0**	**4**	**152**	**9.9**	**−20**	**28**	**39.3**	**15:27**	....	....	....	....	....	....	....	....	....
2002-03	**Columbus**	**NHL**	**66**	**8**	**20**	**28**	**71**	**3**	**0**	**2**	**96**	**8.3**	**−8**	**26**	**46.2**	**13:56**	....	....	....	....	....	....	....	....	....
	♦ **New Jersey**	**NHL**	**10**	**1**	**3**	**4**	**7**	**0**	**0**	**0**	**17**	**5.9**	**−3**	**1**	**100.0**	**11:38**	**24**	**6**	**2**	**8**	**8**	**2**	**0**	**1**	**14:30**
2003-04	**New Jersey**	**NHL**	**65**	**8**	**7**	**15**	**67**	**5**	**0**	**2**	**76**	**10.5**	**−9**	**5**	**40.0**	**12:53**	....	....	....	....	....	....	....	....	....
2004-05			DID NOT PLAY																						
2005-06	**New Jersey**	**NHL**	**76**	**8**	**17**	**25**	**70**	**4**	**0**	**3**	**89**	**9.0**	**−18**	**4**	**25.0**	**12:38**	**7**	**0**	**1**	**1**	**8**	**0**	**0**	**0**	**14:07**
2006-07	Lowell Devils	AHL	59	8	16	24	31	....	....	....	....	....	....	....	....	....	....	....	....	....	....	....	....	....	....
2007-08	Lowell Devils	AHL	66	5	32	37	24	....	....	....	....	....	....	....	....	....	....	....	....	....	....	....	....	....	....
	NHL Totals		**700**	**92**	**147**	**239**	**793**	**28**	**0**	**17**	**831**	**11.1**		**85**	**43.5**	**12:56**	**90**	**6**	**11**	**17**	**95**	**2**	**0**	**1**	**12:33**

• Missed majority of 1990-91 season recovering from neck injury suffered in game vs. Sudbury (OHL), December 4, 1990. Awarded to **Dallas** from **Toronto** with Peter Zezel as compensation for Toronto's signing of free agent Mike Craig, August 10, 1994. Traded to **Columbus** by **Dallas** for Columbus' 2nd round choice (Loui Eriksson) in 2003 Entry Draft, August 29, 2001. Traded to **New Jersey** by **Columbus** for New Jersey's 4th round choice (later traded to Carolina – later traded to Calgary – Calgary selected Kristopher Hogg) in 2004 Entry Draft, March 10, 2003.

MARTIN, Paul

(MAHR-tihn, PAWL) **N.J.**

Defense. Shoots left. 6'1", 195 lbs. Born, Minneapolis, MN, March 5, 1981. New Jersey's 5th choice, 62nd overall, in 2000 Entry Draft.

Season	Club	League	GP	G	A	Pts	PIM	PP	SH	GW	S	%	+/-	TF	F%	Min	GP	G	A	Pts	PIM	PP	SH	GW	Min
1998-99	Elk River Elks	High-MN	24	9	11	20	....	....	....	....	....	....	....	....	....	....	....	....	....	....	....	....	....	....	....
99-2000	Elk River Elks	High-MN	24	15	35	50	26	....	....	....	....	....	....	....	....	....	....	....	....	....	....	....	....	....	....
2000-01	U. of Minnesota	WCHA	38	3	17	20	8	....	....	....	....	....	....	....	....	....	....	....	....	....	....	....	....	....	....
2001-02	U. of Minnesota	WCHA	44	8	30	38	22	....	....	....	....	....	....	....	....	....	....	....	....	....	....	....	....	....	....
2002-03	U. of Minnesota	WCHA	45	9	30	39	32	....	....	....	....	....	....	....	....	....	....	....	....	....	....	....	....	....	....
2003-04	**New Jersey**	**NHL**	**70**	**6**	**18**	**24**	**4**	**2**	**0**	**2**	**82**	**7.3**	**12**	**0**	**0.0**	**20:08**	**5**	**1**	**1**	**2**	**4**	**1**	**0**	**0**	**23:40**
2004-05	Fribourg	Swiss	11	3	4	7	2	....	....	....	....	....	....	....	....	....	....	....	....	....	....	....	....	....	....
2005-06	**New Jersey**	**NHL**	**80**	**5**	**32**	**37**	**32**	**3**	**0**	**0**	**97**	**5.2**	**1**	**0**	**0.0**	**23:37**	**9**	**0**	**3**	**3**	**4**	**0**	**0**	**0**	**24:17**
	United States	Olympics	DID NOT PLAY																						
2006-07	**New Jersey**	**NHL**	**82**	**3**	**23**	**26**	**18**	**1**	**0**	**0**	**84**	**3.6**	**−9**	**0**	**0.0**	**25:13**	**11**	**0**	**4**	**4**	**6**	**0**	**0**	**0**	**25:09**
2007-08	**New Jersey**	**NHL**	**73**	**5**	**27**	**32**	**22**	**2**	**0**	**2**	**93**	**5.4**	**20**	**0**	**0.0**	**23:53**	**5**	**1**	**2**	**3**	**2**	**1**	**0**	**0**	**25:35**
	NHL Totals		**305**	**19**	**100**	**119**	**76**	**8**	**0**	**4**	**356**	**5.3**		**0**	**0.0**	**23:19**	**30**	**2**	**10**	**12**	**16**	**2**	**0**	**0**	**24:43**

Minnesota High School Player of the Year (1999) • WCHA All-Rookie Team (2001) • WCHA Second All-Star Team (2002, 2003) • NCAA West Second All-American Team (2003) • NCAA Championship All-Tournament Team (2003)

Signed as a free agent by **Fribourg** (Swiss), November 4, 2004.

MARTINEK, Radek

(MAHR-tih-nehk, RA-dehk) **NYI**

Defense. Shoots right. 5'11", 200 lbs. Born, Havlickuv Brod, Czech., August 31, 1976. NY Islanders' 12th choice, 228th overall, in 1999 Entry Draft.

Season	Club	League	GP	G	A	Pts	PIM	PP	SH	GW	S	%	+/-	TF	F%	Min	GP	G	A	Pts	PIM	PP	SH	GW	Min
1996-97	C. Budejovice	CzRep	52	3	5	8	40	....	....	....	....	....	....	....	....	....	5	0	1	1	2	....	....	....	....
	C. Budejovice	EuroHL	6	0	0	0	0	....	....	....	....	....	....	....	....	....	2	0	0	0	0	....	....	....	....
1997-98	C. Budejovice	CzRep	42	2	7	9	36	....	....	....	....	....	....	....	....	....	....	....	....	....	....	....	....	....	....
1998-99	C. Budejovice	CzRep	52	12	13	25	50	....	....	....	....	....	....	....	....	....	3	0	2	2	....	....	....	....	....
99-2000	C. Budejovice	CzRep	45	5	18	23	24	....	....	....	....	....	....	....	....	....	3	0	0	0	6	....	....	....	....
2000-01	C. Budejovice	CzRep	44	8	10	18	45	....	....	....	....	....	....	....	....	....	....	....	....	....	....	....	....	....	....
2001-02	**NY Islanders**	**NHL**	**23**	**1**	**4**	**5**	**16**	**0**	**0**	**1**	**25**	**4.0**	**5**	**0**	**0.0**	**21:07**	....	....	....	....	....	....	....	....	....
2002-03	**NY Islanders**	**NHL**	**66**	**2**	**11**	**13**	**26**	**0**	**0**	**1**	**67**	**3.0**	**15**	**0**	**0.0**	**17:15**	**4**	**0**	**0**	**0**	**4**	**0**	**0**	**0**	**10:16**
	Bridgeport	AHL	3	0	3	3	2	....	....	....	....	....	....	....	....	....	....	....	....	....	....	....	....	....	....
2003-04	**NY Islanders**	**NHL**	**47**	**4**	**3**	**7**	**43**	**0**	**0**	**1**	**48**	**8.3**	**−9**	**0**	**0.0**	**13:03**	**5**	**0**	**1**	**1**	**0**	**0**	**0**	**0**	**12:12**
2004-05	C. Budejovice	CzRep-2	30	12	18	30	80	....	....	....	....	....	....	....	....	....	12	2	3	5	6	....	....	....	....
2005-06	**NY Islanders**	**NHL**	**74**	**1**	**16**	**17**	**32**	**0**	**0**	**0**	**79**	**1.3**	**−9**	**1**	**0.0**	**18:16**	....	....	....	....	....	....	....	....	....
2006-07	**NY Islanders**	**NHL**	**43**	**2**	**15**	**17**	**40**	**0**	**0**	**0**	**44**	**4.5**	**19**	**1**	**100.0**	**19:54**	....	....	....	....	....	....	....	....	....
2007-08	**NY Islanders**	**NHL**	**69**	**0**	**15**	**15**	**40**	**0**	**0**	**0**	**98**	**0.0**	**−9**	**0**	**0.0**	**22:52**	....	....	....	....	....	....	....	....	....
	NHL Totals		**322**	**10**	**64**	**74**	**197**	**0**	**0**	**3**	**361**	**2.8**		**2**	**50.0**	**18:42**	**9**	**0**	**1**	**1**	**4**	**0**	**0**	**0**	**11:20**

• Missed majority of 2001-02 season recovering from knee injury suffered in game vs. NY Rangers, November 11, 2001. Signed as a free agent by **Ceske Budejovice** (CzRep-2), September 17, 2004.

MARTINS, Steve

(MAHR-tihns, STEEV)

Center. Shoots left. 5'9", 185 lbs. Born, Gatineau, Que., April 13, 1972. Hartford's 1st choice, 5th overall, in 1994 Supplemental Draft.

Season	Club	League	GP	G	A	Pts	PIM	PP	SH	GW	S	%	+/-	TF	F%	Min	GP	G	A	Pts	PIM	PP	SH	GW	Min
1988-89	L'Outaouais	QAAA	38	18	33	51	70	....	....	....	....	....	....	....	....	....	....	....	....	....	....	....	....	....	....
1989-90	Choate-Rosemary	High-CT	STATISTICS NOT AVAILABLE																						
1990-91	Choate-Rosemary	High-CT	STATISTICS NOT AVAILABLE																						
1991-92	Harvard Crimson	ECAC	20	13	14	27	26	....	....	....	....	....	....	....	....	....	....	....	....	....	....	....	....	....	....
1992-93	Harvard Crimson	ECAC	18	6	8	14	40	....	....	....	....	....	....	....	....	....	....	....	....	....	....	....	....	....	....
1993-94	Harvard Crimson	ECAC	32	25	35	60	*93	....	....	....	....	....	....	....	....	....	....	....	....	....	....	....	....	....	....
1994-95	Harvard Crimson	ECAC	28	15	23	38	93	....	....	....	....	....	....	....	....	....	....	....	....	....	....	....	....	....	....
1995-96	**Hartford**	**NHL**	**23**	**1**	**3**	**4**	**8**	**0**	**0**	**0**	**27**	**3.7**	**−3**	....	....	....	....	....	....	....	....	....	....	....	....
	Springfield	AHL	30	9	20	29	10	....	....	....	....	....	....	....	....	....	....	....	....	....	....	....	....	....	....
1996-97	**Hartford**	**NHL**	**2**	**0**	**1**	**1**	**0**	**0**	**0**	**0**	**2**	**0.0**	**0**	....	....	....	....	....	....	....	....	....	....	....	....
	Springfield	AHL	63	12	31	43	78	....	....	....	....	....	....	....	....	....	17	1	3	4	26	....	....	....	....
1997-98	**Carolina**	**NHL**	**3**	**0**	**0**	**0**	**0**	**0**	**0**	**0**	**0**	**0.0**	**0**	....	....	....	....	....	....	....	....	....	....	....	....
	Chicago Wolves	IHL	78	20	41	61	122	....	....	....	....	....	....	....	....	....	21	6	14	20	28	....	....	....	....
1998-99	**Ottawa**	**NHL**	**36**	**4**	**3**	**7**	**10**	**1**	**0**	**1**	**27**	**14.8**	**4**	**191**	**56.0**	**8:28**	....	....	....	....	....	....	....	....	....
	Detroit Vipers	IHL	4	1	6	7	16	....	....	....	....	....	....	....	....	....	....	....	....	....	....	....	....	....	....
99-2000	**Ottawa**	**NHL**	**2**	**1**	**0**	**1**	**0**	**0**	**0**	**0**	**3**	**33.3**	**−1**	**3**	**0.0**	**11:10**	....	....	....	....	....	....	....	....	....
	Tampa Bay	**NHL**	**57**	**5**	**7**	**12**	**37**	**0**	**1**	**1**	**62**	**8.1**	**−11**	**806**	**50.9**	**13:27**	....	....	....	....	....	....	....	....	....
2000-01	**Tampa Bay**	**NHL**	**20**	**1**	**1**	**2**	**13**	**0**	**0**	**0**	**18**	**5.6**	**−9**	**184**	**52.2**	**9:35**	....	....	....	....	....	....	....	....	....
	Detroit Vipers	IHL	8	5	4	9	4	....	....	....	....	....	....	....	....	....	....	....	....	....	....	....	....	....	....
	NY Islanders	**NHL**	**39**	**1**	**3**	**4**	**20**	**0**	**1**	**0**	**28**	**3.6**	**−7**	**302**	**58.0**	**9:41**	....	....	....	....	....	....	....	....	....
	Chicago Wolves	IHL	5	1	2	3	0	....	....	....	....	....	....	....	....	....	16	1	6	7	22	....	....	....	....
2001-02	**Ottawa**	**NHL**	**14**	**1**	**0**	**1**	**4**	**0**	**0**	**0**	**11**	**9.1**	**1**	**121**	**55.4**	**9:33**	**2**	**0**	**0**	**0**	**0**	**0**	**0**	**0**	**7:13**
	Grand Rapids	AHL	51	10	21	31	66	....	....	....	....	....	....	....	....	....	3	0	0	0	0	....	....	....	....
2002-03	**Ottawa**	**NHL**	**14**	**2**	**3**	**5**	**10**	**0**	**0**	**0**	**13**	**15.4**	**3**	**111**	**55.9**	**9:45**	....	....	....	....	....	....	....	....	....
	Binghamton	AHL	26	5	11	16	31	....	....	....	....	....	....	....	....	....	....	....	....	....	....	....	....	....	....
	St. Louis	**NHL**	**28**	**3**	**3**	**6**	**18**	**0**	**1**	**0**	**25**	**12.0**	**−8**	**369**	**54.7**	**13:38**	**2**	**0**	**1**	**1**	**0**	**0**	**0**	**0**	**9:23**
2003-04	**St. Louis**	**NHL**	**25**	**1**	**0**	**1**	**22**	**0**	**1**	**0**	**27**	**3.7**	**−7**	**172**	**61.1**	**10:29**	**1**	**0**	**0**	**0**	**0**	**0**	**0**	**0**	**5:29**
	Worcester IceCats	AHL	22	4	9	13	16	....	....	....	....	....	....	....	....	....	....	....	....	....	....	....	....	....	....
2004-05	JYP Jyvaskyla	Finland	54	13	12	25	66	....	....	....	....	....	....	....	....	....	3	0	0	0	4	....	....	....	....
2005-06	**Ottawa**	**NHL**	**4**	**1**	**1**	**2**	**0**	**0**	**0**	**0**	**6**	**16.7**	**2**	**23**	**47.8**	**7:50**	....	....	....	....	....	....	....	....	....
	Binghamton	AHL	76	22	58	80	80	....	....	....	....	....	....	....	....	....	....	....	....	....	....	....	....	....	....

			Regular Season														Playoffs								
Season	Club	League	GP	G	A	Pts	PIM	PP	SH	GW	S	%	+/-	TF	F%	Min	GP	G	A	Pts	PIM	PP	SH	GW	Min
2006-07	Chicago Wolves	AHL	48	13	26	39	49	....	....	....	....	....	....	....	....	....	....	....	....	....	....	....	....	....	....
2007-08	Chicago Wolves	AHL	76	17	40	57	78	....	....	....	....	....	....	....	....	....	22	2	7	9	30	....	....	....	....
	NHL Totals		**267**	**21**	**25**	**46**	**142**	**1**	**4**	**2**	**249**	**8.4**		**2282**	**54.1**	**10:55**	**5**	**0**	**1**	**1**	**0**	**0**	**0**	**0**	**7:44**

ECAC First All-Star Team (1994) • ECAC Player of the Year (1994) • NCAA East First All-American Team (1994) • NCAA Final Four All-Tournament Team (1994)

Transferred to **Carolina** after **Hartford** franchise relocated, June 25, 1997. Signed as a free agent by **Ottawa**, July 20, 1998. Claimed on waivers by **Tampa Bay** from **Ottawa**, October 29, 1999. Traded to **NY Islanders** by **Tampa Bay** for future considerations, January 3, 2001. Signed as a free agent by **Ottawa**, August 30, 2001. Claimed on waivers by **St. Louis** from **Ottawa**, January 15, 2003. Signed as a free agent by **Jyvaskyla** (Finland), September 7, 2004. Signed as a free agent by **Ottawa**, August 19, 2005.

MATTHIAS, Shawn

(muh-TIGH-uhs, SHAWN) **FLA.**

Center. Shoots left. 6'3", 211 lbs. Born, Mississauga, Ont., February 19, 1988. Detroit's 2nd choice, 47th overall, in 2006 Entry Draft.

Season	Club	League	GP	G	A	Pts	PIM	PP	SH	GW	S	%	+/-	TF	F%	Min	GP	G	A	Pts	PIM	PP	SH	GW	Min
2004-05	Belleville Bulls	OHL	37	1	1	2	15	....	....	....	....	....	....	....	....	....	3	0	0	0	0	....	....	....	....
2005-06	Belleville Bulls	OHL	67	13	21	34	42	....	....	....	....	....	....	....	....	....	6	3	0	3	2	....	....	....	....
2006-07	Belleville Bulls	OHL	64	38	35	73	61	....	....	....	....	....	....	....	....	....	15	13	5	18	10	....	....	....	....
2007-08	**Florida**	**NHL**	**4**	**2**	**0**	**2**	**2**	**1**	**0**	**0**	**5**	**40.0**	**–2**	**38**	**44.7**	**13:08**	....	....	....	....	....	....	....	....	....
	Belleville Bulls	OHL	53	32	47	79	50	....	....	....	....	....	....	....	....	....	1	1	0	1	0	....	....	....	....
	NHL Totals		**4**	**2**	**0**	**2**	**2**	**1**	**0**	**0**	**5**	**40.0**		**38**	**44.7**	**13:08**	....	....	....	....	....	....	....	....	....

Traded to **Florida** by **Detroit** with Detroit's 2nd round choice (later traded to Nashville - Nashville selected Nick Spaling) in 2007 Entry Draft for Todd Bertuzzi, February 27, 2007.

MATVICHUK, Richard

(MAT-vih-chuhk, RIH-chuhrd)

Defense. Shoots left. 6'3", 215 lbs. Born, Edmonton, Alta., February 5, 1973. Minnesota's 1st choice, 8th overall, in 1991 Entry Draft.

Season	Club	League	GP	G	A	Pts	PIM	PP	SH	GW	S	%	+/-	TF	F%	Min	GP	G	A	Pts	PIM	PP	SH	GW	Min
1988-89	Ft. Saskatchewan	AJHL	58	7	36	43	147	....	....	....	....	....	....	....	....	....	....	....	....	....	....	....	....	....	....
1989-90	Saskatoon Blades	WHL	56	8	24	32	126	....	....	....	....	....	....	....	....	....	10	2	8	10	16	....	....	....	....
1990-91	Saskatoon Blades	WHL	68	13	36	49	117	....	....	....	....	....	....	....	....	....	....	....	....	....	....	....	....	....	....
1991-92	Saskatoon Blades	WHL	58	14	40	54	126	....	....	....	....	....	....	....	....	....	22	1	9	10	61	....	....	....	....
1992-93	**Minnesota**	**NHL**	**53**	**2**	**3**	**5**	**26**	**1**	**0**	**0**	**51**	**3.9**	**–8**	....	....	....	....	....	....	....	....	....	....	....	....
	Kalamazoo Wings	IHL	3	0	1	1	6	....	....	....	....	....	....	....	....	....	....	....	....	....	....	....	....	....	....
1993-94	**Dallas**	**NHL**	**25**	**0**	**3**	**3**	**22**	**0**	**0**	**0**	**18**	**0.0**	**1**	....	....	....	**7**	**1**	**1**	**2**	**12**	**1**	**0**	**0**	....
	Kalamazoo Wings	IHL	43	8	17	25	84	....	....	....	....	....	....	....	....	....	....	....	....	....	....	....	....	....	....
1994-95	**Dallas**	**NHL**	**14**	**0**	**2**	**2**	**14**	**0**	**0**	**0**	**21**	**0.0**	**–7**	....	....	....	**5**	**0**	**2**	**2**	**4**	**0**	**0**	**0**	....
	Kalamazoo Wings	IHL	17	0	6	6	16	....	....	....	....	....	....	....	....	....	....	....	....	....	....	....	....	....	....
1995-96	**Dallas**	**NHL**	**73**	**6**	**16**	**22**	**71**	**0**	**0**	**1**	**81**	**7.4**	**4**	....	....	....	....	....	....	....	....	....	....	....	....
1996-97	**Dallas**	**NHL**	**57**	**5**	**7**	**12**	**87**	**0**	**2**	**0**	**83**	**6.0**	**1**	....	....	....	**7**	**0**	**1**	**1**	**20**	**0**	**0**	**0**	....
1997-98	**Dallas**	**NHL**	**74**	**3**	**15**	**18**	**63**	**0**	**0**	**0**	**71**	**4.2**	**7**	....	....	....	**16**	**1**	**1**	**2**	**14**	**0**	**0**	**0**	....
1998-99 ♦	**Dallas**	**NHL**	**64**	**3**	**9**	**12**	**51**	**1**	**0**	**0**	**54**	**5.6**	**23**	**0**	**0.0**	**21:19**	**22**	**1**	**5**	**6**	**20**	**0**	**0**	**0**	**22:40**
99-2000	**Dallas**	**NHL**	**70**	**4**	**21**	**25**	**42**	**0**	**0**	**1**	**73**	**5.5**	**7**	**0**	**0.0**	**24:27**	**23**	**2**	**5**	**7**	**14**	**0**	**0**	**0**	**25:51**
2000-01	**Dallas**	**NHL**	**78**	**4**	**16**	**20**	**62**	**2**	**0**	**1**	**85**	**4.7**	**5**	**1**	**100.0**	**22:53**	**10**	**0**	**0**	**0**	**14**	**0**	**0**	**0**	**22:43**
2001-02	**Dallas**	**NHL**	**82**	**9**	**12**	**21**	**52**	**4**	**0**	**2**	**109**	**8.3**	**11**	**1**	**0.0**	**23:47**	....	....	....	....	....	....	....	....	....
2002-03	**Dallas**	**NHL**	**68**	**1**	**5**	**6**	**58**	**0**	**0**	**1**	**59**	**1.7**	**1**	**3**	**0.0**	**19:23**	**12**	**0**	**3**	**3**	**8**	**0**	**0**	**0**	**19:55**
2003-04	**Dallas**	**NHL**	**75**	**1**	**20**	**21**	**36**	**0**	**0**	**1**	**85**	**1.2**	**0**	**2**	**50.0**	**21:50**	**5**	**0**	**1**	**1**	**8**	**0**	**0**	**0**	**22:15**
2004-05			DID NOT PLAY																						
2005-06	**New Jersey**	**NHL**	**62**	**1**	**10**	**11**	**40**	**0**	**0**	**0**	**43**	**2.3**	**2**	**0**	**0.0**	**18:13**	**7**	**0**	**0**	**0**	**4**	**0**	**0**	**0**	**16:41**
2006-07	**New Jersey**	**NHL**	**1**	**0**	**0**	**0**	**0**	**0**	**0**	**0**	**0**	**0.0**	**–1**	**0**	**0.0**	**12:45**	**9**	**0**	**0**	**0**	**10**	**0**	**0**	**0**	**19:11**
2007-08	Lowell Devils	AHL	42	1	3	4	40	....	....	....	....	....	....	....	....	....	....	....	....	....	....	....	....	....	....
	NHL Totals		**796**	**39**	**139**	**178**	**624**	**8**	**2**	**7**	**833**	**4.7**		**7**	**28.6**	**21:49**	**123**	**5**	**19**	**24**	**128**	**1**	**0**	**0**	**22:17**

WHL East First All-Star Team (1992)

Transferred to **Dallas** after **Minnesota** franchise relocated, June 9, 1993. Signed as a free agent by **New Jersey**, July 12, 2004. • Missed majority of 2006-07 season recovering from recurring back injury.

MAULDIN, Greg

(MAWL-dihn, GREHG) **OTT.**

Center. Shoots right. 5'10", 198 lbs. Born, Boston, MA, June 10, 1982. Columbus' 10th choice, 199th overall, in 2002 Entry Draft.

Season	Club	League	GP	G	A	Pts	PIM	PP	SH	GW	S	%	+/-	TF	F%	Min	GP	G	A	Pts	PIM	PP	SH	GW	Min
99-2000	Junior Bruins	EJHL	58	45	42	87	14	....	....	....	....	....	....	....	....	....	....	....	....	....	....	....	....	....	....
2000-01	Junior Bruins	EJHL	53	48	58	106	73	....	....	....	....	....	....	....	....	....	....	....	....	....	....	....	....	....	....
2001-02	Massachusetts	H-East	33	12	12	24	10	....	....	....	....	....	....	....	....	....	....	....	....	....	....	....	....	....	....
2002-03	Massachusetts	H-East	36	21	20	41	26	....	....	....	....	....	....	....	....	....	....	....	....	....	....	....	....	....	....
2003-04	Massachusetts	H-East	29	15	14	29	15	....	....	....	....	....	....	....	....	....	....	....	....	....	....	....	....	....	....
	Columbus	**NHL**	**6**	**0**	**0**	**0**	**4**	**0**	**0**	**0**	**6**	**0.0**	**–2**	**0**	**0.0**	**8:47**	....	....	....	....	....	....	....	....	....
	Syracuse Crunch	AHL	2	0	0	0	0	....	....	....	....	....	....	....	....	....	....	....	....	....	....	....	....	....	....
2004-05	Syracuse Crunch	AHL	66	7	20	27	49	....	....	....	....	....	....	....	....	....	1	0	0	0	0	....	....	....	....
2005-06	Syracuse Crunch	AHL	56	12	17	29	53	....	....	....	....	....	....	....	....	....	....	....	....	....	....	....	....	....	....
	Houston Aeros	AHL	11	1	3	4	0	....	....	....	....	....	....	....	....	....	8	1	1	2	2	....	....	....	....
2006-07	Bloomington	UHL	2	0	0	0	2	....	....	....	....	....	....	....	....	....	....	....	....	....	....	....	....	....	....
	Huddinge IK	Sweden-2	6	1	2	3	0	....	....	....	....	....	....	....	....	....	....	....	....	....	....	....	....	....	....
	IK Oskarshamn	Sweden-2	26	5	8	13	31	....	....	....	....	....	....	....	....	....	....	....	....	....	....	....	....	....	....
2007-08	Binghamton	AHL	71	15	18	33	37	....	....	....	....	....	....	....	....	....	....	....	....	....	....	....	....	....	....
	NHL Totals		**6**	**0**	**0**	**0**	**4**	**0**	**0**	**0**	**6**	**0.0**		**0**	**0.0**	**8:47**	....	....	....	....	....	....	....	....	....

EJHL First All-Star Team (2000, 2001) • EJHL MVP (2000)

Signed as a free agent by **Oskarshamn** (Sweden-2), October 23, 2006. Signed as a free agent by **Binghamton** (AHL), August 9, 2007. Signed as a free agent by **Ottawa**, July 7, 2008.

MAY, Brad

(MAY, BRAD) **ANA.**

Left wing. Shoots left. 6'1", 218 lbs. Born, Toronto, Ont., November 29, 1971. Buffalo's 1st choice, 14th overall, in 1990 Entry Draft.

Season	Club	League	GP	G	A	Pts	PIM	PP	SH	GW	S	%	+/-	TF	F%	Min	GP	G	A	Pts	PIM	PP	SH	GW	Min
1987-88	Markham	Minor-ON	31	22	37	59	58	....	....	....	....	....	....	....	....	....	....	....	....	....	....	....	....	....	....
	Markham	OHA-B	6	1	1	2	21	....	....	....	....	....	....	....	....	....	....	....	....	....	....	....	....	....	....
1988-89	Niagara Falls	OHL	65	8	14	22	304	....	....	....	....	....	....	....	....	....	17	0	1	1	55	....	....	....	....
1989-90	Niagara Falls	OHL	61	32	58	90	223	....	....	....	....	....	....	....	....	....	16	9	13	22	64	....	....	....	....
1990-91	Niagara Falls	OHL	34	37	32	69	93	....	....	....	....	....	....	....	....	....	14	11	14	25	53	....	....	....	....
1991-92	**Buffalo**	**NHL**	**69**	**11**	**6**	**17**	**309**	**1**	**0**	**3**	**82**	**13.4**	**–12**	....	....	....	**7**	**1**	**4**	**5**	**2**	**0**	**0**	**1**	....
1992-93	**Buffalo**	**NHL**	**82**	**13**	**13**	**26**	**242**	**0**	**0**	**1**	**114**	**11.4**	**3**	....	....	....	**8**	**1**	**1**	**2**	**14**	**0**	**0**	**1**	....
1993-94	**Buffalo**	**NHL**	**84**	**18**	**27**	**45**	**171**	**3**	**0**	**3**	**166**	**10.8**	**–6**	....	....	....	**7**	**0**	**2**	**2**	**9**	**0**	**0**	**0**	....
1994-95	**Buffalo**	**NHL**	**33**	**3**	**3**	**6**	**87**	**1**	**0**	**0**	**42**	**7.1**	**5**	....	....	....	**4**	**0**	**0**	**0**	**2**	**0**	**0**	**0**	....
1995-96	**Buffalo**	**NHL**	**79**	**15**	**29**	**44**	**295**	**3**	**0**	**4**	**168**	**8.9**	**6**	....	....	....	....	....	....	....	....	....	....	....	....
1996-97	**Buffalo**	**NHL**	**42**	**3**	**4**	**7**	**106**	**1**	**0**	**1**	**75**	**4.0**	**–8**	....	....	....	**10**	**1**	**1**	**2**	**32**	**0**	**0**	**0**	....
1997-98	**Buffalo**	**NHL**	**36**	**4**	**7**	**11**	**113**	**0**	**0**	**0**	**41**	**9.8**	**2**	....	....	....	....	....	....	....	....	....	....	....	....
	Vancouver	**NHL**	**27**	**9**	**3**	**12**	**41**	**4**	**0**	**2**	**56**	**16.1**	**0**	....	....	....	....	....	....	....	....	....	....	....	....
1998-99	**Vancouver**	**NHL**	**66**	**6**	**11**	**17**	**102**	**1**	**0**	**1**	**91**	**6.6**	**–14**	**8**	**12.5**	**13:04**	....	....	....	....	....	....	....	....	....
99-2000	**Vancouver**	**NHL**	**59**	**9**	**7**	**16**	**90**	**0**	**0**	**3**	**66**	**13.6**	**–2**	**3**	**0.0**	**10:24**	....	....	....	....	....	....	....	....	....
2000-01	**Phoenix**	**NHL**	**62**	**11**	**14**	**25**	**107**	**0**	**0**	**0**	**83**	**13.3**	**10**	**3**	**33.3**	**11:11**	....	....	....	....	....	....	....	....	....
2001-02	**Phoenix**	**NHL**	**72**	**10**	**12**	**22**	**95**	**1**	**0**	**3**	**105**	**9.5**	**11**	**3**	**0.0**	**12:04**	**5**	**0**	**0**	**0**	**0**	**0**	**0**	**0**	**10:19**
2002-03	**Phoenix**	**NHL**	**20**	**3**	**4**	**7**	**32**	**0**	**0**	**0**	**24**	**12.5**	**3**	**0**	**0.0**	**9:56**	....	....	....	....	....	....	....	....	....
	Vancouver	**NHL**	**3**	**0**	**0**	**0**	**10**	**0**	**0**	**0**	**1**	**0.0**	**1**	**0**	**0.0**	**7:48**	**14**	**0**	**0**	**0**	**15**	**0**	**0**	**0**	**7:25**
2003-04	**Vancouver**	**NHL**	**70**	**5**	**6**	**11**	**137**	**0**	**0**	**0**	**75**	**6.7**	**–2**	**8**	**50.0**	**8:56**	**6**	**1**	**0**	**1**	**6**	**0**	**0**	**0**	**7:07**
2004-05			DID NOT PLAY																						
2005-06	**Colorado**	**NHL**	**54**	**3**	**3**	**6**	**82**	**0**	**0**	**0**	**55**	**5.5**	**–14**	**6**	**33.3**	**8:23**	**3**	**0**	**0**	**0**	**0**	**0**	**0**	**0**	**9:21**
2006-07	**Colorado**	**NHL**	**10**	**0**	**3**	**3**	**8**	**0**	**0**	**0**	**11**	**0.0**	**0**	**0**	**0.0**	**11:28**	....	....	....	....	....	....	....	....	....
	♦ **Anaheim**	**NHL**	**14**	**0**	**1**	**1**	**13**	**0**	**0**	**0**	**11**	**0.0**	**–1**	**0**	**0.0**	**8:39**	**18**	**0**	**1**	**1**	**28**	**0**	**0**	**0**	**7:21**
2007-08	**Anaheim**	**NHL**	**61**	**3**	**1**	**4**	**53**	**0**	**0**	**2**	**34**	**8.8**	**2**	**3**	**0.0**	**6:37**	**6**	**0**	**0**	**0**	**4**	**0**	**0**	**0**	**6:56**
	NHL Totals		**943**	**126**	**154**	**280**	**2093**	**15**	**0**	**23**	**1300**	**9.7**		**34**	**23.5**	**10:08**	**88**	**4**	**9**	**13**	**112**	**0**	**0**	**2**	**7:42**

OHL Second All-Star Team (1990, 1991)

• Missed majority of 1990-91 season recovering from knee injury suffered at Team Canada Juniors evaluation camp, August 21, 1990. Traded to **Vancouver** by **Buffalo** with Buffalo's 3rd round choice (later traded to Tampa Bay – Tampa Bay selected Jimmie Olvestad) in 1999 Entry Draft for Geoff Sanderson, February 4, 1998. Traded to **Phoenix** by **Vancouver** for future considerations, June 24, 2000. • Missed majority of 2002-03 season recovering from shoulder injury suffered in pre-season game vs. Detroit, October 6, 2002. Traded to **Vancouver** by **Phoenix** for Phoenix's 3rd round choice (previously acquired, Phoenix selected Dimitri Pestunov) in 2003 Entry Draft, March 11, 2003. Signed as a free agent by **Colorado**, August 5, 2005. Traded to **Anaheim** by **Colorado** for Michael Wall, February 27, 2007. • Missed majority of 2006-07 season recovering from shoulder injury suffered in pre-season game vs. Detroit, September 25, 2006.

MAYERS, Jamal

(MAI-uhrz, JUH-MAHL) **TOR.**

Right wing. Shoots right. 6'1", 214 lbs. Born, Toronto, Ont., October 24, 1974. St. Louis' 3rd choice, 89th overall, in 1993 Entry Draft.

			Regular Season														Playoffs								
Season	Club	League	GP	G	A	Pts	PIM	PP	SH	GW	S	%	+/-	TF	F%	Min	GP	G	A	Pts	PIM	PP	SH	GW	Min
1990-91	Thornhill	MTJHL	44	12	24	36	78	....	....	....	....	....	....	....	....	....	....	....	....	....	....	....	....	....	....
1991-92	Thornhill	MTJHL	56	38	69	107	36	....	....	....	....	....	....	....	....	....	....	....	....	....	....	....	....	....	....
1992-93	Western Mich.	CCHA	38	8	17	25	26	....	....	....	....	....	....	....	....	....	....	....	....	....	....	....	....	....	....
1993-94	Western Mich.	CCHA	40	17	32	49	40	....	....	....	....	....	....	....	....	....	....	....	....	....	....	....	....	....	....
1994-95	Western Mich.	CCHA	39	13	32	45	40	....	....	....	....	....	....	....	....	....	....	....	....	....	....	....	....	....	....
1995-96	Western Mich.	CCHA	38	17	22	39	75	....	....	....	....	....	....	....	....	....	....	....	....	....	....	....	....	....	....
1996-97	**St. Louis**	**NHL**	**6**	**0**	**1**	**1**	**2**	**0**	**0**	**0**	**7**	**0.0**	**-3**	....	....	....	....	....	....	....	....	....	....	....	....
	Worcester IceCats	AHL	62	12	14	26	104	....	....	....	....	....	....	....	....	....	5	4	5	9	4	....	....	....	....
1997-98	Worcester IceCats	AHL	61	19	24	43	117	....	....	....	....	....	....	....	....	....	11	3	4	7	10	....	....	....	....
1998-99	**St. Louis**	**NHL**	**34**	**4**	**5**	**9**	**40**	**0**	**0**	**0**	**48**	**8.3**	**-3**	**2**	**50.0**	**8:08**	**11**	**0**	**1**	**1**	**8**	**0**	**0**	**0**	**8:34**
	Worcester IceCats	AHL	20	9	7	16	34	....	....	....	....	....	....	....	....	....	....	....	....	....	....	....	....	....	....
99-2000	**St. Louis**	**NHL**	**79**	**7**	**10**	**17**	**90**	**0**	**0**	**0**	**99**	**7.1**	**0**	**77**	**52.0**	**9:46**	**7**	**0**	**4**	**4**	**2**	**0**	**0**	**0**	**10:42**
2000-01	**St. Louis**	**NHL**	**77**	**8**	**13**	**21**	**117**	**0**	**0**	**0**	**132**	**6.1**	**-3**	**273**	**51.3**	**11:04**	**15**	**2**	**3**	**5**	**8**	**0**	**0**	**0**	**11:28**
2001-02	**St. Louis**	**NHL**	**77**	**9**	**8**	**17**	**99**	**0**	**1**	**0**	**105**	**8.6**	**9**	**761**	**52.6**	**11:36**	**10**	**3**	**0**	**3**	**2**	**0**	**0**	**2**	**11:14**
2002-03	**St. Louis**	**NHL**	**15**	**2**	**5**	**7**	**8**	**0**	**0**	**0**	**26**	**7.7**	**1**	**111**	**51.4**	**14:21**	....	....	....	....	....	....	....	....	....
2003-04	**St. Louis**	**NHL**	**80**	**6**	**5**	**11**	**91**	**0**	**1**	**3**	**130**	**4.6**	**-19**	**681**	**48.6**	**13:01**	**5**	**0**	**0**	**0**	**0**	**0**	**0**	**0**	**12:55**
2004-05	Hammarby	Sweden-2	19	9	13	22	36	....	....	....	....	....	....	....	....	....	....	....	....	....	....	....	....	....	....
	Missouri	UHL	13	5	2	7	68	....	....	....	....	....	....	....	....	....	....	....	....	....	....	....	....	....	....
2005-06	**St. Louis**	**NHL**	**67**	**15**	**11**	**26**	**129**	**0**	**2**	**1**	**111**	**13.5**	**-22**	**363**	**48.5**	**15:07**	....	....	....	....	....	....	....	....	....
2006-07	**St. Louis**	**NHL**	**80**	**8**	**14**	**22**	**89**	**0**	**2**	**0**	**129**	**6.2**	**-19**	**432**	**57.4**	**14:37**	....	....	....	....	....	....	....	....	....
2007-08	**St. Louis**	**NHL**	**80**	**12**	**15**	**27**	**91**	**0**	**1**	**3**	**153**	**7.8**	**-19**	**683**	**56.2**	**15:56**	....	....	....	....	....	....	....	....	....
	NHL Totals		**595**	**71**	**87**	**158**	**756**	**0**	**7**	**7**	**940**	**7.6**		**3383**	**52.5**	**12:45**	**48**	**5**	**8**	**13**	**20**	**0**	**0**	**2**	**10:47**

• Missed majority of 2002-03 season recovering from knee injury suffered in game vs. Calgary, November 16, 2002. Signed as a free agent by **Hammarby** (Sweden-2), November 16, 2004. Signed as a free agent by **Missouri** (UHL), March 11, 2005. Traded to **Toronto** by **St. Louis** for Florida's 3rd round choice (previously acquired, St. Louis selected James Livingston) in 2008 Entry Draft, June 19, 2008.

McAMMOND, Dean

(muhK-AM-uhnd, DEEN) **OTT.**

Center. Shoots left. 5'11", 195 lbs. Born, Grand Cache, Alta., June 15, 1973. Chicago's 1st choice, 22nd overall, in 1991 Entry Draft.

			Regular Season														Playoffs								
Season	Club	League	GP	G	A	Pts	PIM	PP	SH	GW	S	%	+/-	TF	F%	Min	GP	G	A	Pts	PIM	PP	SH	GW	Min
1988-89	St. Albert Raiders	AMHL	36	33	44	77	132	....	....	....	....	....	....	....	....	....	....	....	....	....	....	....	....	....	....
1989-90	Prince Albert	WHL	53	11	11	22	49	....	....	....	....	....	....	....	....	....	14	2	3	5	18	....	....	....	....
1990-91	Prince Albert	WHL	71	33	35	68	108	....	....	....	....	....	....	....	....	....	2	0	1	1	6	....	....	....	....
1991-92	Prince Albert	WHL	63	37	54	91	189	....	....	....	....	....	....	....	....	....	10	12	11	23	26	....	....	....	....
	Chicago	**NHL**	**5**	**0**	**2**	**2**	**0**	**0**	**0**	**0**	**4**	**0.0**	**-2**	....	....	....	**3**	**0**	**0**	**0**	**2**	**0**	**0**	**0**	
1992-93	Prince Albert	WHL	30	19	29	48	44	....	....	....	....	....	....	....	....	....	....	....	....	....	....	....	....	....	....
	Swift Current	WHL	18	10	13	23	24	....	....	....	....	....	....	....	....	....	17	*16	19	35	20	....	....	....	....
1993-94	**Edmonton**	**NHL**	**45**	**6**	**21**	**27**	**16**	**2**	**0**	**0**	**52**	**11.5**	**12**	....	....	....	....	....	....	....	....	....	....	....	....
	Cape Breton	AHL	28	9	12	21	38	....	....	....	....	....	....	....	....	....	....	....	....	....	....	....	....	....	....
1994-95	**Edmonton**	**NHL**	**6**	**0**	**0**	**0**	**0**	**0**	**0**	**0**	**3**	**0.0**	**-1**	....	....	....	....	....	....	....	....	....	....	....	....
1995-96	**Edmonton**	**NHL**	**53**	**15**	**15**	**30**	**23**	**4**	**0**	**0**	**79**	**19.0**	**6**	....	....	....	....	....	....	....	....	....	....	....	....
	Cape Breton	AHL	22	9	15	24	55	....	....	....	....	....	....	....	....	....	....	....	....	....	....	....	....	....	....
1996-97	**Edmonton**	**NHL**	**57**	**12**	**17**	**29**	**28**	**4**	**0**	**6**	**106**	**11.3**	**-15**	....	....	....	....	....	....	....	....	....	....	....	....
1997-98	**Edmonton**	**NHL**	**77**	**19**	**31**	**50**	**46**	**8**	**0**	**3**	**128**	**14.8**	**9**	....	....	....	**12**	**1**	**4**	**5**	**12**	**0**	**0**	**0**	
1998-99	**Edmonton**	**NHL**	**65**	**9**	**16**	**25**	**36**	**1**	**0**	**0**	**122**	**7.4**	**5**	**26**	**38.5**	**14:15**	....	....	....	....	....	....	....	....	....
	Chicago	**NHL**	**12**	**1**	**4**	**5**	**2**	**0**	**0**	**1**	**16**	**6.3**	**3**	**37**	**48.6**	**15:43**	....	....	....	....	....	....	....	....	....
99-2000	**Chicago**	**NHL**	**76**	**14**	**18**	**32**	**72**	**1**	**0**	**1**	**118**	**11.9**	**11**	**257**	**39.7**	**16:25**	....	....	....	....	....	....	....	....	....
2000-01	**Chicago**	**NHL**	**61**	**10**	**16**	**26**	**43**	**1**	**0**	**1**	**95**	**10.5**	**4**	**23**	**43.5**	**15:30**	....	....	....	....	....	....	....	....	....
	Philadelphia	**NHL**	**10**	**1**	**1**	**2**	**0**	**1**	**0**	**0**	**17**	**5.9**	**-1**	**65**	**46.2**	**12:00**	**4**	**0**	**0**	**0**	**2**	**0**	**0**	**0**	**9:25**
2001-02	**Calgary**	**NHL**	**73**	**21**	**30**	**51**	**60**	**7**	**0**	**4**	**152**	**13.8**	**2**	**143**	**55.2**	**18:56**	....	....	....	....	....	....	....	....	....
2002-03	**Colorado**	**NHL**	**41**	**10**	**8**	**18**	**10**	**2**	**0**	**2**	**72**	**13.9**	**1**	**9**	**55.6**	**14:24**	....	....	....	....	....	....	....	....	....
2003-04	**Calgary**	**NHL**	**64**	**17**	**13**	**30**	**18**	**4**	**1**	**5**	**101**	**16.8**	**9**	**768**	**49.1**	**16:52**	....	....	....	....	....	....	....	....	....
2004-05	Albany River Rats	AHL	79	19	42	61	72	....	....	....	....	....	....	....	....	....	....	....	....	....	....	....	....	....	....
2005-06	**St. Louis**	**NHL**	**78**	**15**	**22**	**37**	**32**	**4**	**0**	**0**	**116**	**12.9**	**-25**	**289**	**47.4**	**16:02**	....	....	....	....	....	....	....	....	....
2006-07	**Ottawa**	**NHL**	**81**	**14**	**15**	**29**	**28**	**0**	**2**	**1**	**86**	**16.3**	**11**	**677**	**44.2**	**11:08**	**18**	**5**	**3**	**8**	**11**	**0**	**1**	**1**	**11:27**
2007-08	**Ottawa**	**NHL**	**68**	**9**	**13**	**22**	**12**	**0**	**3**	**1**	**67**	**13.4**	**1**	**259**	**43.2**	**11:32**	**4**	**0**	**0**	**0**	**4**	**0**	**0**	**0**	**13:30**
	NHL Totals		**872**	**173**	**242**	**415**	**426**	**39**	**6**	**25**	**1334**	**13.0**		**2553**	**46.2**	**14:58**	**41**	**6**	**7**	**13**	**31**	**0**	**1**	**1**	**11:27**

Traded to **Edmonton** by **Chicago** with Igor Kravchuk for Joe Murphy, February 24, 1993. Traded to **Chicago** by **Edmonton** with Boris Mironov and Jonas Elofsson for Chad Kilger, Daniel Cleary, Ethan Moreau and Christian Laflamme, March 20, 1999. Traded to **Philadelphia** by **Chicago** for Philadelphia's 3rd round choice (later traded to Toronto – Toronto selected Nicolas Corbeil) in 2001 Entry Draft, March 13, 2001. Traded to **Calgary** by **Philadelphia** for Calgary's 4th round choice (Rosario Ruggeri) in 2002 Entry Draft, June 24, 2001. Traded to **Colorado** by **Calgary** with Derek Morris and Jeff Shantz for Chris Drury and Stephane Yelle, October 1, 2002. Traded to **Calgary** by **Colorado** for Calgary's 5th round choice (Mark McCutcheon) in 2003 Entry Draft, March 11, 2003. • Ruled ineligible to play remainder of 2002-03 season by NHL due to transaction violation by Calgary, March 15, 2003. Signed as a free agent by **New Jersey**, October 5, 2004. Signed as a free agent by **St. Louis**, August 9, 2005. Signed as a free agent by **Ottawa**, August 2, 2006.

McCABE, Bryan

(muh-KAYB, BRIGH-uhn) **TOR.**

Defense. Shoots left. 6'2", 220 lbs. Born, St. Catharines, Ont., June 8, 1975. NY Islanders' 2nd choice, 40th overall, in 1993 Entry Draft.

			Regular Season														Playoffs								
Season	Club	League	GP	G	A	Pts	PIM	PP	SH	GW	S	%	+/-	TF	F%	Min	GP	G	A	Pts	PIM	PP	SH	GW	Min
1990-91	Calgary Canucks	AMHL	33	14	34	48	55	....	....	....	....	....	....	....	....	....	....	....	....	....	....	....	....	....	....
1991-92	Medicine Hat	WHL	68	6	24	30	157	....	....	....	....	....	....	....	....	....	4	0	0	0	6	....	....	....	....
1992-93	Medicine Hat	WHL	14	0	13	13	83	....	....	....	....	....	....	....	....	....	....	....	....	....	....	....	....	....	....
	Spokane Chiefs	WHL	46	3	44	47	134	....	....	....	....	....	....	....	....	....	6	1	5	6	28	....	....	....	....
1993-94	Spokane Chiefs	WHL	64	22	62	84	218	....	....	....	....	....	....	....	....	....	3	0	4	4	4	....	....	....	....
1994-95	Spokane Chiefs	WHL	42	14	39	53	115	....	....	....	....	....	....	....	....	....	....	....	....	....	....	....	....	....	....
	Brandon	WHL	20	6	10	16	38	....	....	....	....	....	....	....	....	....	18	4	13	17	59	....	....	....	....
1995-96	**NY Islanders**	**NHL**	**82**	**7**	**16**	**23**	**156**	**3**	**0**	**1**	**130**	**5.4**	**-24**	....	....	....	....	....	....	....	....	....	....	....	....
1996-97	**NY Islanders**	**NHL**	**82**	**8**	**20**	**28**	**165**	**2**	**1**	**2**	**117**	**6.8**	**-2**	....	....	....	....	....	....	....	....	....	....	....	....
1997-98	**NY Islanders**	**NHL**	**56**	**3**	**9**	**12**	**145**	**1**	**0**	**0**	**81**	**3.7**	**9**	....	....	....	....	....	....	....	....	....	....	....	....
	Vancouver	**NHL**	**26**	**1**	**11**	**12**	**64**	**0**	**1**	**0**	**42**	**2.4**	**10**	....	....	....	....	....	....	....	....	....	....	....	....
1998-99	**Vancouver**	**NHL**	**69**	**7**	**14**	**21**	**120**	**1**	**2**	**0**	**98**	**7.1**	**-11**	**1**	**0.0**	**24:13**	....	....	....	....	....	....	....	....	....
99-2000	**Chicago**	**NHL**	**79**	**6**	**19**	**25**	**139**	**2**	**0**	**2**	**119**	**5.0**	**-8**	**1**	**0.0**	**23:23**	....	....	....	....	....	....	....	....	....
2000-01	**Toronto**	**NHL**	**82**	**5**	**24**	**29**	**123**	**3**	**0**	**2**	**159**	**3.1**	**16**	**0**	**0.0**	**23:49**	**11**	**2**	**3**	**5**	**16**	**1**	**0**	**0**	**23:56**
2001-02	**Toronto**	**NHL**	**82**	**17**	**26**	**43**	**129**	**8**	**0**	**1**	**157**	**10.8**	**16**	**1**	**0.0**	**24:34**	**20**	**5**	**5**	**10**	**30**	**3**	**0**	**1**	**29:33**
2002-03	**Toronto**	**NHL**	**75**	**6**	**18**	**24**	**135**	**3**	**0**	**1**	**149**	**4.0**	**9**	**1**	**0.0**	**23:39**	**7**	**0**	**3**	**3**	**10**	**0**	**0**	**1**	**27:28**
2003-04	**Toronto**	**NHL**	**75**	**16**	**37**	**53**	**86**	**8**	**0**	**2**	**168**	**9.5**	**22**	**2**	**50.0**	**25:44**	**13**	**3**	**5**	**8**	**14**	**2**	**0**	**0**	**28:47**
2004-05	HV 71 Jonkoping	Sweden	10	1	0	1	30	....	....	....	....	....	....	....	....	....	....	....	....	....	....	....	....	....	....
2005-06	**Toronto**	**NHL**	**73**	**19**	**49**	**68**	**116**	**13**	**0**	**6**	**207**	**9.2**	**-1**	**1**	**0.0**	**28:18**	....	....	....	....	....	....	....	....	....
	Canada	Olympics	6	0	0	0	18	....	....	....	....	....	....	....	....	....	....	....	....	....	....	....	....	....	....
2006-07	**Toronto**	**NHL**	**82**	**15**	**42**	**57**	**115**	**11**	**0**	**1**	**207**	**7.2**	**3**	**0**	**0.0**	**26:50**	....	....	....	....	....	....	....	....	....
2007-08	**Toronto**	**NHL**	**54**	**5**	**18**	**23**	**81**	**4**	**0**	**2**	**107**	**4.7**	**-2**	**0**	**0.0**	**25:55**	....	....	....	....	....	....	....	....	....
	NHL Totals		**917**	**115**	**303**	**418**	**1574**	**59**	**4**	**20**	**1741**	**6.6**		**7**	**14.3**	**25:07**	**51**	**10**	**16**	**26**	**70**	**6**	**0**	**1**	**27:51**

WHL West Second All-Star Team (1993) • WHL West First All-Star Team (1994) • WHL East First All-Star Team (1995) • Memorial Cup Tournament All-Star Team (1995) • NHL Second All-Star Team (2004)

Traded to **Vancouver** by **NY Islanders** with Todd Bertuzzi and NY Islanders' 3rd round choice (Jarkko Ruutu) in 1998 Entry Draft for Trevor Linden, February 6, 1998. Traded to **Chicago** by **Vancouver** with Vancouver's 1st round choice (Pavel Vorobiev) in 2000 Entry Draft for Chicago's 1st round choice (later traded to Tampa Bay – later traded to NY Rangers – NY Rangers selected Pavel Brendl) in 1999 Entry Draft, June 25, 1999. Traded to **Toronto** by **Chicago** for Alexander Karpovtsev and Toronto's 4th round choice (Vladimir Gusev) in 2001 Entry Draft, October 2, 2000. Signed as a free agent by **Jonkoping** (Sweden), October 29, 2004.

McCARTHY, Steve

(muh-KAHR-thee, STEEV)

Defense. Shoots left. 6'1", 210 lbs. Born, Trail, B.C., February 3, 1981. Chicago's 1st choice, 23rd overall, in 1999 Entry Draft.

			Regular Season														Playoffs								
Season	Club	League	GP	G	A	Pts	PIM	PP	SH	GW	S	%	+/-	TF	F%	Min	GP	G	A	Pts	PIM	PP	SH	GW	Min
1996-97	Trail	BCHL	57	25	52	77	81	....	....	....	....	....	....	....	....	....	....	....	....	....	....	....	....	....	....
	Edmonton Ice	WHL	2	0	0	0	0	....	....	....	....	....	....	....	....	....	....	....	....	....	....	....	....	....	....
1997-98	Edmonton Ice	WHL	58	11	29	40	59	....	....	....	....	....	....	....	....	....	....	....	....	....	....	....	....	....	....
1998-99	Kootenay Ice	WHL	57	19	33	52	79	....	....	....	....	....	....	....	....	....	6	0	5	5	8	....	....	....	....
99-2000	**Chicago**	**NHL**	**5**	**1**	**1**	**2**	**4**	**1**	**0**	**0**	**4**	**25.0**	**0**	**0**	**0.0**	**15:09**	....	....	....	....	....	....	....	....	....
	Kootenay Ice	WHL	37	13	23	36	36	....	....	....	....	....	....	....	....	....	....	....	....	....	....	....	....	....	....
2000-01	**Chicago**	**NHL**	**44**	**0**	**5**	**5**	**8**	**0**	**0**	**0**	**32**	**0.0**	**-7**	**0**	**0.0**	**14:47**	....	....	....	....	....	....	....	....	....
	Norfolk Admirals	AHL	7	0	4	4	2	....	....	....	....	....	....	....	....	....	....	....	....	....	....	....	....	....	....
2001-02	**Chicago**	**NHL**	**3**	**0**	**0**	**0**	**2**	**0**	**0**	**0**	**2**	**0.0**	**-1**	**0**	**0.0**	**11:48**	....	....	....	....	....	....	....	....	....
	Norfolk Admirals	AHL	77	7	21	28	37	....	....	....	....	....	....	....	....	....	2	0	3	3	2	....	....	....	....

			Regular Season														Playoffs								
Season	Club	League	GP	G	A	Pts	PIM	PP	SH	GW	S	%	+/-	TF	F%	Min	GP	G	A	Pts	PIM	PP	SH	GW	Min
2002-03	**Chicago**	**NHL**	**57**	**1**	**4**	**5**	**23**	**0**	**0**	**0**	**55**	**1.8**	**–1**	**0**	**0.0**	**16:25**	....	....	....	....	....	....	....	....	....
	Norfolk Admirals	AHL	19	1	6	7	14	....	....	....	....	....	....	....	....	....	9	0	4	4	0	....	....	....	....
2003-04	**Chicago**	**NHL**	**25**	**1**	**3**	**4**	**8**	**0**	**0**	**0**	**29**	**3.4**	**–9**	**0**	**0.0**	**19:21**	....	....	....	....	....	....	....	....	....
2004-05			Did not play																						
2005-06	**Vancouver**	**NHL**	**51**	**2**	**4**	**6**	**43**	**0**	**0**	**0**	**46**	**4.3**	**3**	**0**	**0.0**	**13:17**	....	....	....	....	....	....	....	....	....
	Atlanta	**NHL**	**16**	**7**	**3**	**10**	**8**	**2**	**0**	**0**	**20**	**35.0**	**0**	**0**	**0.0**	**16:44**	....	....	....	....	....	....	....	....	....
2006-07	**Atlanta**	**NHL**	**46**	**4**	**12**	**16**	**24**	**3**	**0**	**0**	**51**	**7.8**	**4**	**0**	**0.0**	**15:17**	....	....	....	....	....	....	....	....	....
2007-08	**Atlanta**	**NHL**	**55**	**1**	**6**	**7**	**48**	**0**	**0**	**0**	**41**	**2.4**	**–23**	**0**	**0.0**	**15:47**	....	....	....	....	....	....	....	....	....
	NHL Totals		**302**	**17**	**38**	**55**	**168**	**6**	**0**	**0**	**280**	**6.1**		**0**	**0.0**	**15:33**	....	....	....	....	....	....	....	....	....

• Missed majority of 2003-04 season recovering from groin injury suffered in game vs. Calgary, November 22, 2003. Traded to **Vancouver** by **Chicago** for Vancouver's 3rd round choice (Josh Unice) in 2007 Entry Draft, August 22, 2005. Traded to **Atlanta** by **Vancouver** for Atlanta's 4th round choice (later traded back to Atlanta - Atlanta selected Niklas Lucenius) in 2007 Entry Draft, March 9, 2006.

McCARTY, Darren

(muh-KAHR-tee, DAIR-ehn)

Right wing. Shoots right. 6'1", 210 lbs. Born, Burnaby, B.C., April 1, 1972. Detroit's 2nd choice, 46th overall, in 1992 Entry Draft.

Season	Club	League	GP	G	A	Pts	PIM	PP	SH	GW	S	%	+/-	TF	F%	Min	GP	G	A	Pts	PIM	PP	SH	GW	Min
1988-89	Peterborough	OHA-B	34	18	17	35	135	....	....	....	....	....	....	....	....	....	....	....	....	....	....	....	....	....	....
1989-90	Belleville Bulls	OHL	63	12	15	27	142	....	....	....	....	....	....	....	....	....	11	1	1	2	21	....	....	....	....
1990-91	Belleville Bulls	OHL	60	30	37	67	151	....	....	....	....	....	....	....	....	....	6	2	2	4	13	....	....	....	....
1991-92	Belleville Bulls	OHL	65	*55	72	127	177	....	....	....	....	....	....	....	....	....	5	1	4	5	13	....	....	....	....
1992-93	Adirondack	AHL	73	17	19	36	278	....	....	....	....	....	....	....	....	....	11	0	1	1	33	....	....	....	....
1993-94	**Detroit**	**NHL**	**67**	**9**	**17**	**26**	**181**	**0**	**0**	**2**	**81**	**11.1**	**12**	....	....	....	**7**	**2**	**2**	**4**	**8**	**0**	**0**	**0**	....
1994-95	**Detroit**	**NHL**	**31**	**5**	**8**	**13**	**88**	**1**	**0**	**2**	**27**	**18.5**	**5**	....	....	....	**18**	**3**	**2**	**5**	**14**	**0**	**0**	**0**	....
1995-96	**Detroit**	**NHL**	**63**	**15**	**14**	**29**	**158**	**8**	**0**	**1**	**102**	**14.7**	**14**	....	....	....	**19**	**3**	**2**	**5**	**20**	**0**	**0**	**1**	....
1996-97♦	**Detroit**	**NHL**	**68**	**19**	**30**	**49**	**126**	**5**	**0**	**6**	**171**	**11.1**	**14**	....	....	....	**20**	**3**	**4**	**7**	**34**	**0**	**0**	**2**	....
1997-98♦	**Detroit**	**NHL**	**71**	**15**	**22**	**37**	**157**	**5**	**1**	**2**	**166**	**9.0**	**0**	....	....	....	**22**	**3**	**8**	**11**	**34**	**0**	**0**	**1**	....
1998-99	**Detroit**	**NHL**	**69**	**14**	**26**	**40**	**108**	**6**	**0**	**1**	**140**	**10.0**	**10**	**15**	**33.3**	**17:04**	**10**	**1**	**1**	**2**	**23**	**0**	**0**	**0**	**13:04**
99-2000	**Detroit**	**NHL**	**24**	**6**	**6**	**12**	**48**	**0**	**0**	**1**	**40**	**15.0**	**1**	**1**	**0.0**	**13:40**	**9**	**0**	**1**	**1**	**12**	**0**	**0**	**0**	**14:09**
2000-01	**Detroit**	**NHL**	**72**	**12**	**10**	**22**	**123**	**1**	**1**	**3**	**118**	**10.2**	**–5**	**26**	**53.9**	**13:26**	**6**	**1**	**0**	**1**	**2**	**0**	**0**	**0**	**13:11**
2001-02♦	**Detroit**	**NHL**	**62**	**5**	**7**	**12**	**98**	**0**	**0**	**1**	**74**	**6.8**	**2**	**26**	**38.5**	**11:47**	**23**	**4**	**4**	**8**	**34**	**0**	**0**	**1**	**13:33**
2002-03	**Detroit**	**NHL**	**73**	**13**	**9**	**22**	**138**	**1**	**0**	**2**	**129**	**10.1**	**10**	**320**	**57.8**	**13:18**	**4**	**0**	**0**	**0**	**6**	**0**	**0**	**0**	**15:45**
2003-04	**Detroit**	**NHL**	**43**	**6**	**5**	**11**	**50**	**1**	**0**	**0**	**61**	**9.8**	**2**	**141**	**50.4**	**12:20**	**12**	**0**	**1**	**1**	**7**	**0**	**0**	**0**	**11:30**
2004-05			Did not play																						
2005-06	**Calgary**	**NHL**	**67**	**7**	**6**	**13**	**117**	**1**	**0**	**0**	**67**	**10.4**	**–1**	**234**	**50.0**	**11:43**	**7**	**2**	**0**	**2**	**15**	**0**	**0**	**1**	**9:50**
2006-07	**Calgary**	**NHL**	**32**	**0**	**0**	**0**	**58**	**0**	**0**	**0**	**15**	**0.0**	**–3**	**6**	**83.3**	**5:24**	....	....	....	....	....	....	....	....	....
2007-08	Flint Generals	IHL	11	3	3	6	30	....	....	....	....	....	....	....	....	....	....	....	....	....	....	....	....	....	....
	Grand Rapids	AHL	13	5	5	10	21	....	....	....	....	....	....	....	....	....	....	....	....	....	....	....	....	....	....
	♦ Detroit	**NHL**	**3**	**0**	**1**	**1**	**2**	**0**	**0**	**0**	**3**	**0.0**	**2**	**0**	**0.0**	**7:47**	**17**	**1**	**1**	**2**	**19**	**0**	**0**	**0**	**6:23**
	NHL Totals		**745**	**126**	**161**	**287**	**1452**	**29**	**2**	**21**	**1194**	**10.6**		**769**	**52.9**	**12:47**	**174**	**23**	**26**	**49**	**228**	**0**	**0**	**6**	**11:40**

OHL First All-Star Team (1992)

• Missed majority of 1999-2000 season recovering from hernia injury suffered in game vs. Dallas, November 10, 1999. Signed as a free agent by **Calgary**, August 2, 2005. • Missed majority of 2006-07 season recovering from recurring hernia injury. Signed as a free agent by **Flint** (IHL), January 9, 2008. Signed as a free agent by **Grand Rapids** (AHL), February 4, 2008. Signed as a free agent by **Detroit**, February 25, 2008.

McCLEMENT, Jay

(muh-KLEHM-ehnt, JAY) **ST.L.**

Center. Shoots left. 6'1", 201 lbs. Born, Kingston, Ont., March 2, 1983. St. Louis' 1st choice, 57th overall, in 2001 Entry Draft.

Season	Club	League	GP	G	A	Pts	PIM	PP	SH	GW	S	%	+/-	TF	F%	Min	GP	G	A	Pts	PIM	PP	SH	GW	Min
1997-98	Kingston	OPJHL	48	3	8	11	15	....	....	....	....	....	....	....	....	....	....	....	....	....	....	....	....	....	....
1998-99	Kingston	OPJHL	51	25	28	53	34	....	....	....	....	....	....	....	....	....	....	....	....	....	....	....	....	....	....
99-2000	Brampton	OHL	63	13	16	29	34	....	....	....	....	....	....	....	....	....	6	0	4	4	8	....	....	....	....
2000-01	Brampton	OHL	66	30	19	49	61	....	....	....	....	....	....	....	....	....	9	4	2	6	10	....	....	....	....
2001-02	Brampton	OHL	61	26	29	55	43	....	....	....	....	....	....	....	....	....	....	....	....	....	....	....	....	....	....
2002-03	Brampton	OHL	45	22	27	49	37	....	....	....	....	....	....	....	....	....	11	3	4	7	11	....	....	....	....
	Worcester IceCats	AHL	....	....	....	....	....	....	....	....	....	....	....	....	....	....	1	0	0	0	0	....	....	....	....
2003-04	Worcester IceCats	AHL	69	12	13	25	20	....	....	....	....	....	....	....	....	....	10	0	3	3	0	....	....	....	....
2004-05	Worcester IceCats	AHL	79	17	34	51	45	....	....	....	....	....	....	....	....	....	....	....	....	....	....	....	....	....	....
2005-06	**St. Louis**	**NHL**	**67**	**6**	**21**	**27**	**30**	**1**	**0**	**2**	**76**	**7.9**	**–23**	**691**	**46.9**	**13:56**	....	....	....	....	....	....	....	....	....
	Peoria Rivermen	AHL	11	4	5	9	4	....	....	....	....	....	....	....	....	....	4	0	2	2	2	....	....	....	....
2006-07	**St. Louis**	**NHL**	**81**	**8**	**28**	**36**	**55**	**0**	**0**	**0**	**104**	**7.7**	**3**	**839**	**52.7**	**13:53**	....	....	....	....	....	....	....	....	....
2007-08	**St. Louis**	**NHL**	**81**	**9**	**13**	**22**	**26**	**0**	**0**	**2**	**110**	**8.2**	**–17**	**700**	**52.3**	**13:55**	....	....	....	....	....	....	....	....	....
	NHL Totals		**229**	**23**	**62**	**85**	**111**	**1**	**0**	**4**	**290**	**7.9**		**2230**	**50.8**	**13:55**	....	....	....	....	....	....	....	....	....

McCORMICK, Cody

(muh-KOHR-mihk, KOH-dee) **COL.**

Center/Right wing. Shoots right. 6'3", 215 lbs. Born, London, Ont., April 18, 1983. Colorado's 5th choice, 144th overall, in 2001 Entry Draft.

Season	Club	League	GP	G	A	Pts	PIM	PP	SH	GW	S	%	+/-	TF	F%	Min	GP	G	A	Pts	PIM	PP	SH	GW	Min
1998-99	Elgin-Middlesex	MHAO	58	22	40	62	81	....	....	....	....	....	....	....	....	....	....	....	....	....	....	....	....	....	....
99-2000	Belleville Bulls	OHL	45	3	4	7	42	....	....	....	....	....	....	....	....	....	9	1	0	1	10	....	....	....	....
2000-01	Belleville Bulls	OHL	66	7	16	23	135	....	....	....	....	....	....	....	....	....	10	1	1	2	23	....	....	....	....
2001-02	Belleville Bulls	OHL	63	10	17	27	118	....	....	....	....	....	....	....	....	....	11	2	4	6	24	....	....	....	....
2002-03	Belleville Bulls	OHL	61	36	33	69	166	....	....	....	....	....	....	....	....	....	7	4	7	11	11	....	....	....	....
2003-04	**Colorado**	**NHL**	**44**	**2**	**3**	**5**	**73**	**0**	**0**	**1**	**33**	**6.1**	**–4**	**110**	**32.7**	**8:07**	....	....	....	....	....	....	....	....	....
	Hershey Bears	AHL	32	3	6	9	60	....	....	....	....	....	....	....	....	....	....	....	....	....	....	....	....	....	....
2004-05	Hershey Bears	AHL	40	5	6	11	68	....	....	....	....	....	....	....	....	....	....	....	....	....	....	....	....	....	....
2005-06	**Colorado**	**NHL**	**45**	**4**	**4**	**8**	**29**	**0**	**0**	**1**	**43**	**9.3**	**1**	**16**	**25.0**	**7:42**	....	....	....	....	....	....	....	....	....
	Lowell	AHL	13	1	6	7	34	....	....	....	....	....	....	....	....	....	....	....	....	....	....	....	....	....	....
2006-07	**Colorado**	**NHL**	**6**	**0**	**1**	**1**	**6**	**0**	**0**	**0**	**6**	**0.0**	**1**	**3**	**33.3**	**6:44**	....	....	....	....	....	....	....	....	....
	Albany River Rats	AHL	42	8	8	16	64	....	....	....	....	....	....	....	....	....	5	1	0	1	4	....	....	....	....
2007-08	**Colorado**	**NHL**	**40**	**2**	**2**	**4**	**50**	**0**	**0**	**1**	**45**	**4.4**	**5**	**17**	**35.3**	**10:58**	**4**	**0**	**1**	**1**	**7**	**0**	**0**	**0**	**11:53**
	Lake Erie	AHL	13	2	4	6	16	....	....	....	....	....	....	....	....	....	....	....	....	....	....	....	....	....	....
	NHL Totals		**135**	**8**	**10**	**18**	**158**	**0**	**0**	**3**	**127**	**6.3**		**146**	**32.2**	**8:46**	**4**	**0**	**1**	**1**	**7**	**0**	**0**	**0**	**11:53**

OHL First All-Star Team (2003)

McDONALD, Andy

(muhk-DAWN-uhld, AN-dee) **ST.L.**

Center. Shoots left. 5'11", 183 lbs. Born, Strathroy, Ont., August 25, 1977.

Season	Club	League	GP	G	A	Pts	PIM	PP	SH	GW	S	%	+/-	TF	F%	Min	GP	G	A	Pts	PIM	PP	SH	GW	Min
1993-94	Strathroy Rockets	OHA-B	7	2	2	4	0	....	....	....	....	....	....	....	....	....	....	....	....	....	....	....	....	....	....
1994-95	Strathroy Rockets	OHA-B	50	32	41	73	24	....	....	....	....	....	....	....	....	....	....	....	....	....	....	....	....	....	....
1995-96	Strathroy Rockets	OHA-B	52	31	56	87	103	....	....	....	....	....	....	....	....	....	....	....	....	....	....	....	....	....	....
1996-97	Colgate	ECAC	33	9	10	19	16	....	....	....	....	....	....	....	....	....	....	....	....	....	....	....	....	....	....
1997-98	Colgate	ECAC	35	13	19	32	26	....	....	....	....	....	....	....	....	....	....	....	....	....	....	....	....	....	....
1998-99	Colgate	ECAC	35	20	26	46	42	....	....	....	....	....	....	....	....	....	....	....	....	....	....	....	....	....	....
99-2000	Colgate	ECAC	34	25	*33	*58	49	....	....	....	....	....	....	....	....	....	....	....	....	....	....	....	....	....	....
2000-01	**Anaheim**	**NHL**	**16**	**1**	**0**	**1**	**6**	**0**	**0**	**0**	**21**	**4.8**	**0**	**139**	**48.9**	**11:11**	....	....	....	....	....	....	....	....	....
	Cincinnati	AHL	46	15	25	40	21	....	....	....	....	....	....	....	....	....	3	0	1	1	2	....	....	....	....
2001-02	**Anaheim**	**NHL**	**53**	**7**	**21**	**28**	**10**	**2**	**0**	**3**	**79**	**8.9**	**2**	**818**	**53.7**	**15:59**	....	....	....	....	....	....	....	....	....
	Cincinnati	AHL	21	7	25	32	6	....	....	....	....	....	....	....	....	....	....	....	....	....	....	....	....	....	....
2002-03	**Anaheim**	**NHL**	**46**	**10**	**11**	**21**	**14**	**3**	**0**	**1**	**92**	**10.9**	**–1**	**604**	**56.0**	**18:31**	....	....	....	....	....	....	....	....	....
2003-04	**Anaheim**	**NHL**	**79**	**9**	**21**	**30**	**24**	**2**	**1**	**1**	**162**	**5.6**	**–13**	**282**	**54.3**	**16:34**	....	....	....	....	....	....	....	....	....
2004-05	ERC Ingolstadt	Germany	36	13	17	30	26	....	....	....	....	....	....	....	....	....	10	5	2	7	35	....	....	....	....
2005-06	**Anaheim**	**NHL**	**82**	**34**	**51**	**85**	**32**	**13**	**0**	**7**	**229**	**14.8**	**24**	**1095**	**56.3**	**16:48**	**16**	**2**	**7**	**9**	**10**	**2**	**0**	**0**	**16:33**
2006-07♦	**Anaheim**	**NHL**	**82**	**27**	**51**	**78**	**46**	**8**	**0**	**3**	**252**	**10.7**	**16**	**908**	**55.4**	**17:35**	**21**	**10**	**4**	**14**	**10**	**5**	**0**	**0**	**18:37**
2007-08	**Anaheim**	**NHL**	**33**	**4**	**12**	**16**	**30**	**0**	**0**	**0**	**79**	**5.1**	**–4**	**392**	**55.4**	**16:41**	....	....	....	....	....	....	....	....	....
	St. Louis	**NHL**	**49**	**14**	**22**	**36**	**32**	**3**	**0**	**1**	**103**	**13.6**	**–17**	**556**	**55.8**	**18:40**	....	....	....	....	....	....	....	....	....
	NHL Totals		**440**	**106**	**189**	**295**	**194**	**31**	**1**	**16**	**1017**	**10.4**		**4794**	**55.2**	**16:59**	**37**	**12**	**11**	**23**	**20**	**7**	**0**	**0**	**17:44**

ECAC Second All-Star Team (1999) • ECAC First All-Star Team (2000) • ECAC Player of the Year (2000) • NCAA East First All-American Team (2000)

Played in NHL All-Star Game (2007)

Signed as a free agent by **Anaheim**, April 3, 2000. Signed as a free agent by **Ingolstadt** (Germany), September 17, 2004. Traded to **St. Louis** by **Anaheim** for Doug Weight, Michal Birner and St. Louis' 7th round choice (later traded to Los Angeles - later traded back to St. Louis - St. Louis selected Paul Karpowich) in 2008 Entry Draft, December 14, 2007.

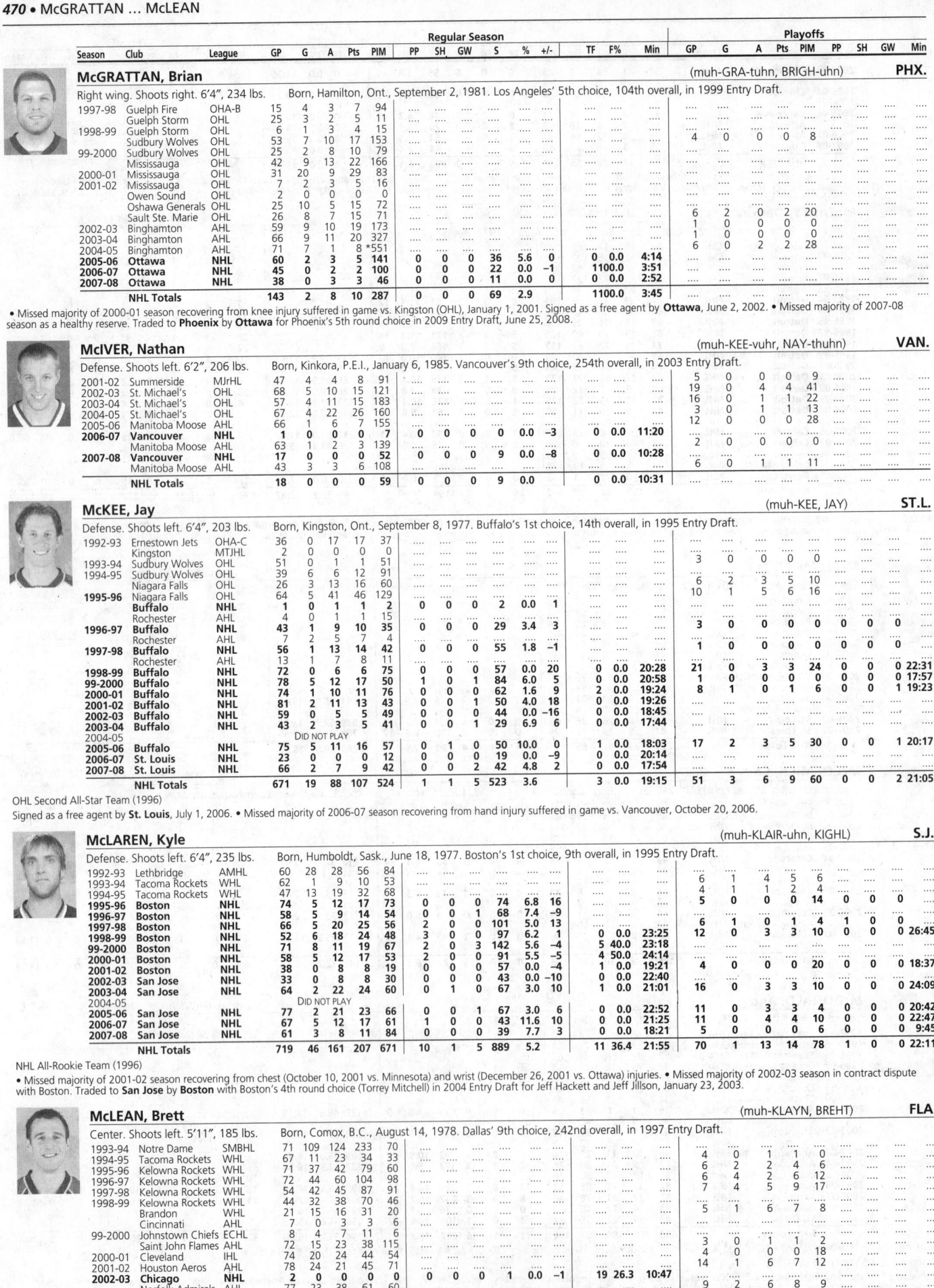

McGRATTAN, Brian (muh-GRA-tuhn, BRIGH-uhn) PHX.

Right wing. Shoots right. 6'4", 234 lbs. Born, Hamilton, Ont., September 2, 1981. Los Angeles' 5th choice, 104th overall, in 1999 Entry Draft.

			Regular Season														Playoffs								
Season	Club	League	GP	G	A	Pts	PIM	PP	SH	GW	S	%	+/-	TF	F%	Min	GP	G	A	Pts	PIM	PP	SH	GW	Min
1997-98	Guelph Fire	OHA-B	15	4	3	7	94	....	....	....	....	....	....	....	....	....	....	....	....	....	....	....	....	....	....
	Guelph Storm	OHL	25	3	2	5	11	....	....	....	....	....	....	....	....	....	....	....	....	....	....	....	....	....	....
1998-99	Guelph Storm	OHL	6	1	3	4	15	....	....	....	....	....	....	....	....	....	....	....	....	....	....	....	....	....	....
	Sudbury Wolves	OHL	53	7	10	17	153	....	....	....	....	....	....	....	....	....	4	0	0	0	8	....	....	....	....
99-2000	Sudbury Wolves	OHL	25	2	8	10	79	....	....	....	....	....	....	....	....	....	....	....	....	....	....	....	....	....	....
	Mississauga	OHL	42	9	13	22	166	....	....	....	....	....	....	....	....	....	....	....	....	....	....	....	....	....	....
2000-01	Mississauga	OHL	31	20	9	29	83	....	....	....	....	....	....	....	....	....	....	....	....	....	....	....	....	....	....
2001-02	Mississauga	OHL	7	2	3	5	16	....	....	....	....	....	....	....	....	....	....	....	....	....	....	....	....	....	....
	Owen Sound	OHL	2	0	0	0	0	....	....	....	....	....	....	....	....	....	....	....	....	....	....	....	....	....	....
	Oshawa Generals	OHL	25	10	5	15	72	....	....	....	....	....	....	....	....	....	....	....	....	....	....	....	....	....	....
	Sault Ste. Marie	OHL	26	8	7	15	71	....	....	....	....	....	....	....	....	....	6	2	0	2	20	....	....	....	....
2002-03	Binghamton	AHL	59	9	10	19	173	....	....	....	....	....	....	....	....	....	1	0	0	0	0	....	....	....	....
2003-04	Binghamton	AHL	66	9	11	20	327	....	....	....	....	....	....	....	....	....	1	0	0	0	0	....	....	....	....
2004-05	Binghamton	AHL	71	7	1	8	*551	....	....	....	....	....	....	....	....	....	6	0	2	2	28	....	....	....	....
2005-06	**Ottawa**	**NHL**	**60**	**2**	**3**	**5**	**141**	**0**	**0**	**0**	**36**	**5.6**	**0**	**0**	**0.0**	**4:14**	....	....	....	....	....	....	....	....	....
2006-07	**Ottawa**	**NHL**	**45**	**0**	**2**	**2**	**100**	**0**	**0**	**0**	**22**	**0.0**	**–1**	**1**	**100.0**	**3:51**	....	....	....	....	....	....	....	....	....
2007-08	**Ottawa**	**NHL**	**38**	**0**	**3**	**3**	**46**	**0**	**0**	**0**	**11**	**0.0**	**0**	**0**	**0.0**	**2:52**	....	....	....	....	....	....	....	....	....
	NHL Totals		**143**	**2**	**8**	**10**	**287**	**0**	**0**	**0**	**69**	**2.9**		**1**	**100.0**	**3:45**	....	....	....	....	....	....	....	....	....

• Missed majority of 2000-01 season recovering from knee injury suffered in game vs. Kingston (OHL), January 1, 2001. Signed as a free agent by **Ottawa**, June 2, 2002. • Missed majority of 2007-08 season as a healthy reserve. Traded to **Phoenix** by **Ottawa** for Phoenix's 5th round choice in 2009 Entry Draft, June 25, 2008.

McIVER, Nathan (muh-KEE-vuhr, NAY-thuhn) VAN.

Defense. Shoots left. 6'2", 206 lbs. Born, Kinkora, P.E.I., January 6, 1985. Vancouver's 9th choice, 254th overall, in 2003 Entry Draft.

Season	Club	League	GP	G	A	Pts	PIM	PP	SH	GW	S	%	+/-	TF	F%	Min	GP	G	A	Pts	PIM	PP	SH	GW	Min
2001-02	Summerside	MJrHL	47	4	4	8	91	....	....	....	....	....	....	....	....	....	5	0	0	0	9	....	....	....	....
2002-03	St. Michael's	OHL	68	5	10	15	121	....	....	....	....	....	....	....	....	....	19	0	4	4	41	....	....	....	....
2003-04	St. Michael's	OHL	57	4	11	15	183	....	....	....	....	....	....	....	....	....	16	0	1	1	22	....	....	....	....
2004-05	St. Michael's	OHL	67	4	22	26	160	....	....	....	....	....	....	....	....	....	3	0	1	1	13	....	....	....	....
2005-06	Manitoba Moose	AHL	66	1	6	7	155	....	....	....	....	....	....	....	....	....	12	0	0	0	28	....	....	....	....
2006-07	**Vancouver**	**NHL**	**1**	**0**	**0**	**0**	**7**	**0**	**0**	**0**	**0**	**0.0**	**–3**	**0**	**0.0**	**11:20**	....	....	....	....	....	....	....	....	....
	Manitoba Moose	AHL	63	1	2	3	139	....	....	....	....	....	....	....	....	....	2	0	0	0	0	....	....	....	....
2007-08	**Vancouver**	**NHL**	**17**	**0**	**0**	**0**	**52**	**0**	**0**	**0**	**9**	**0.0**	**–8**	**0**	**0.0**	**10:28**	....	....	....	....	....	....	....	....	....
	Manitoba Moose	AHL	43	3	3	6	108	....	....	....	....	....	....	....	....	....	6	0	1	1	11	....	....	....	....
	NHL Totals		**18**	**0**	**0**	**0**	**59**	**0**	**0**	**0**	**9**	**0.0**		**0**	**0.0**	**10:31**	....	....	....	....	....	....	....	....	....

McKEE, Jay (muh-KEE, JAY) ST.L.

Defense. Shoots left. 6'4", 203 lbs. Born, Kingston, Ont., September 8, 1977. Buffalo's 1st choice, 14th overall, in 1995 Entry Draft.

Season	Club	League	GP	G	A	Pts	PIM	PP	SH	GW	S	%	+/-	TF	F%	Min	GP	G	A	Pts	PIM	PP	SH	GW	Min
1992-93	Ernestown Jets	OHA-C	36	0	17	17	37	....	....	....	....	....	....	....	....	....	....	....	....	....	....	....	....	....	....
	Kingston	MTJHL	2	0	0	0	0	....	....	....	....	....	....	....	....	....	....	....	....	....	....	....	....	....	....
1993-94	Sudbury Wolves	OHL	51	0	1	1	51	....	....	....	....	....	....	....	....	....	3	0	0	0	0	....	....	....	....
1994-95	Sudbury Wolves	OHL	39	6	6	12	91	....	....	....	....	....	....	....	....	....	....	....	....	....	....	....	....	....	....
	Niagara Falls	OHL	26	3	13	16	60	....	....	....	....	....	....	....	....	....	6	2	3	5	10	....	....	....	....
1995-96	Niagara Falls	OHL	64	5	41	46	129	....	....	....	....	....	....	....	....	....	10	1	5	6	16	....	....	....	....
	Buffalo	**NHL**	**1**	**0**	**1**	**1**	**2**	**0**	**0**	**0**	**2**	**0.0**	**1**	....	....	....	....	....	....	....	....	....	....	....	....
	Rochester	AHL	4	0	1	1	15	....	....	....	....	....	....	....	....	....	....	....	....	....	....	....	....	....	....
1996-97	**Buffalo**	**NHL**	**43**	**1**	**9**	**10**	**35**	**0**	**0**	**0**	**29**	**3.4**	**3**	....	....	....	**3**	**0**	**0**	**0**	**0**	**0**	**0**	**0**	....
	Rochester	AHL	7	2	5	7	4	....	....	....	....	....	....	....	....	....	....	....	....	....	....	....	....	....	....
1997-98	**Buffalo**	**NHL**	**56**	**1**	**13**	**14**	**42**	**0**	**0**	**0**	**55**	**1.8**	**–1**	....	....	....	**1**	**0**	**0**	**0**	**0**	**0**	**0**	**0**	....
	Rochester	AHL	13	1	7	8	11	....	....	....	....	....	....	....	....	....	....	....	....	....	....	....	....	....	....
1998-99	**Buffalo**	**NHL**	**72**	**0**	**6**	**6**	**75**	**0**	**0**	**0**	**57**	**0.0**	**20**	**0**	**0.0**	**20:28**	**21**	**0**	**3**	**3**	**24**	**0**	**0**	**0**	**22:31**
99-2000	**Buffalo**	**NHL**	**78**	**5**	**12**	**17**	**50**	**1**	**0**	**1**	**84**	**6.0**	**5**	**0**	**0.0**	**20:58**	**1**	**0**	**0**	**0**	**0**	**0**	**0**	**0**	**17:57**
2000-01	**Buffalo**	**NHL**	**74**	**1**	**10**	**11**	**76**	**0**	**0**	**0**	**62**	**1.6**	**9**	**2**	**0.0**	**19:24**	**8**	**1**	**0**	**1**	**6**	**0**	**0**	**1**	**19:23**
2001-02	**Buffalo**	**NHL**	**81**	**2**	**11**	**13**	**43**	**0**	**0**	**1**	**50**	**4.0**	**18**	**0**	**0.0**	**19:26**	....	....	....	....	....	....	....	....	....
2002-03	**Buffalo**	**NHL**	**59**	**0**	**5**	**5**	**49**	**0**	**0**	**0**	**44**	**0.0**	**–16**	**0**	**0.0**	**18:45**	....	....	....	....	....	....	....	....	....
2003-04	**Buffalo**	**NHL**	**43**	**2**	**3**	**5**	**41**	**0**	**0**	**1**	**29**	**6.9**	**6**	**0**	**0.0**	**17:44**	....	....	....	....	....	....	....	....	....
2004-05			Did not play																						
2005-06	**Buffalo**	**NHL**	**75**	**5**	**11**	**16**	**57**	**0**	**1**	**0**	**50**	**10.0**	**0**	**1**	**0.0**	**18:03**	**17**	**2**	**3**	**5**	**30**	**0**	**0**	**1**	**20:17**
2006-07	**St. Louis**	**NHL**	**23**	**0**	**0**	**0**	**12**	**0**	**0**	**0**	**19**	**0.0**	**–9**	**0**	**0.0**	**20:14**	....	....	....	....	....	....	....	....	....
2007-08	**St. Louis**	**NHL**	**66**	**2**	**7**	**9**	**42**	**0**	**0**	**2**	**42**	**4.8**	**2**	**0**	**0.0**	**17:54**	....	....	....	....	....	....	....	....	....
	NHL Totals		**671**	**19**	**88**	**107**	**524**	**1**	**1**	**5**	**523**	**3.6**		**3**	**0.0**	**19:15**	**51**	**3**	**6**	**9**	**60**	**0**	**0**	**2**	**21:05**

OHL Second All-Star Team (1996)

Signed as a free agent by **St. Louis**, July 1, 2006. • Missed majority of 2006-07 season recovering from hand injury suffered in game vs. Vancouver, October 20, 2006.

McLAREN, Kyle (muh-KLAIR-uhn, KIGHL) S.J.

Defense. Shoots left. 6'4", 235 lbs. Born, Humboldt, Sask., June 18, 1977. Boston's 1st choice, 9th overall, in 1995 Entry Draft.

Season	Club	League	GP	G	A	Pts	PIM	PP	SH	GW	S	%	+/-	TF	F%	Min	GP	G	A	Pts	PIM	PP	SH	GW	Min
1992-93	Lethbridge	AMHL	60	28	28	56	84	....	....	....	....	....	....	....	....	....	....	....	....	....	....	....	....	....	....
1993-94	Tacoma Rockets	WHL	62	1	9	10	53	....	....	....	....	....	....	....	....	....	6	1	4	5	6	....	....	....	....
1994-95	Tacoma Rockets	WHL	47	13	19	32	68	....	....	....	....	....	....	....	....	....	4	1	1	2	4	....	....	....	....
1995-96	**Boston**	**NHL**	**74**	**5**	**12**	**17**	**73**	**0**	**0**	**0**	**74**	**6.8**	**16**	....	....	....	**5**	**0**	**0**	**0**	**14**	**0**	**0**	**0**	....
1996-97	**Boston**	**NHL**	**58**	**5**	**9**	**14**	**54**	**0**	**0**	**1**	**68**	**7.4**	**–9**	....	....	....	....	....	....	....	....	....	....	....	....
1997-98	**Boston**	**NHL**	**66**	**5**	**20**	**25**	**56**	**2**	**0**	**0**	**101**	**5.0**	**13**	....	....	....	**6**	**1**	**0**	**1**	**4**	**1**	**0**	**0**	....
1998-99	**Boston**	**NHL**	**52**	**6**	**18**	**24**	**48**	**3**	**0**	**0**	**97**	**6.2**	**1**	**0**	**0.0**	**23:25**	**12**	**0**	**3**	**3**	**10**	**0**	**0**	**0**	**26:45**
99-2000	**Boston**	**NHL**	**71**	**8**	**11**	**19**	**67**	**2**	**0**	**3**	**142**	**5.6**	**–4**	**5**	**40.0**	**23:18**	....	....	....	....	....	....	....	....	....
2000-01	**Boston**	**NHL**	**58**	**5**	**12**	**17**	**53**	**2**	**0**	**0**	**91**	**5.5**	**–5**	**4**	**50.0**	**24:14**	....	....	....	....	....	....	....	....	....
2001-02	**Boston**	**NHL**	**38**	**0**	**8**	**8**	**19**	**0**	**0**	**0**	**57**	**0.0**	**–4**	**1**	**0.0**	**19:21**	**4**	**0**	**0**	**0**	**20**	**0**	**0**	**0**	**18:37**
2002-03	**San Jose**	**NHL**	**33**	**0**	**8**	**8**	**30**	**0**	**0**	**0**	**43**	**0.0**	**–10**	**0**	**0.0**	**22:40**	....	....	....	....	....	....	....	....	....
2003-04	**San Jose**	**NHL**	**64**	**2**	**22**	**24**	**60**	**0**	**1**	**0**	**67**	**3.0**	**10**	**1**	**0.0**	**21:01**	**16**	**0**	**3**	**3**	**10**	**0**	**0**	**0**	**24:09**
2004-05			Did not play																						
2005-06	**San Jose**	**NHL**	**77**	**2**	**21**	**23**	**66**	**0**	**0**	**1**	**67**	**3.0**	**6**	**0**	**0.0**	**22:52**	**11**	**0**	**3**	**3**	**4**	**0**	**0**	**0**	**20:42**
2006-07	**San Jose**	**NHL**	**67**	**5**	**12**	**17**	**61**	**1**	**0**	**0**	**43**	**11.6**	**10**	**0**	**0.0**	**21:25**	**11**	**0**	**4**	**4**	**10**	**0**	**0**	**0**	**22:47**
2007-08	**San Jose**	**NHL**	**61**	**3**	**8**	**11**	**84**	**0**	**0**	**0**	**39**	**7.7**	**3**	**0**	**0.0**	**18:21**	**5**	**0**	**0**	**0**	**6**	**0**	**0**	**0**	**9:45**
	NHL Totals		**719**	**46**	**161**	**207**	**671**	**10**	**1**	**5**	**889**	**5.2**		**11**	**36.4**	**21:55**	**70**	**1**	**13**	**14**	**78**	**1**	**0**	**0**	**22:11**

NHL All-Rookie Team (1996)

• Missed majority of 2001-02 season recovering from chest (October 10, 2001 vs. Minnesota) and wrist (December 26, 2001 vs. Ottawa) injuries. • Missed majority of 2002-03 season in contract dispute with Boston. Traded to **San Jose** by **Boston** with Boston's 4th round choice (Torrey Mitchell) in 2004 Entry Draft for Jeff Hackett and Jeff Jillson, January 23, 2003.

McLEAN, Brett (muh-KLAYN, BREHT) FLA.

Center. Shoots left. 5'11", 185 lbs. Born, Comox, B.C., August 14, 1978. Dallas' 9th choice, 242nd overall, in 1997 Entry Draft.

Season	Club	League	GP	G	A	Pts	PIM	PP	SH	GW	S	%	+/-	TF	F%	Min	GP	G	A	Pts	PIM	PP	SH	GW	Min
1993-94	Notre Dame	SMBHL	71	109	124	233	70	....	....	....	....	....	....	....	....	....	....	....	....	....	....	....	....	....	....
1994-95	Tacoma Rockets	WHL	67	11	23	34	33	....	....	....	....	....	....	....	....	....	4	0	1	1	0	....	....	....	....
1995-96	Kelowna Rockets	WHL	71	37	42	79	60	....	....	....	....	....	....	....	....	....	6	2	2	4	6	....	....	....	....
1996-97	Kelowna Rockets	WHL	72	44	60	104	98	....	....	....	....	....	....	....	....	....	6	4	2	6	12	....	....	....	....
1997-98	Kelowna Rockets	WHL	54	42	45	87	91	....	....	....	....	....	....	....	....	....	7	4	5	9	17	....	....	....	....
1998-99	Kelowna Rockets	WHL	44	32	38	70	46	....	....	....	....	....	....	....	....	....	....	....	....	....	....	....	....	....	....
	Brandon	WHL	21	15	16	31	20	....	....	....	....	....	....	....	....	....	5	1	6	7	8	....	....	....	....
	Cincinnati	AHL	7	0	3	3	6	....	....	....	....	....	....	....	....	....	....	....	....	....	....	....	....	....	....
99-2000	Johnstown Chiefs	ECHL	8	4	7	11	6	....	....	....	....	....	....	....	....	....	....	....	....	....	....	....	....	....	....
	Saint John Flames	AHL	72	15	23	38	115	....	....	....	....	....	....	....	....	....	3	0	1	1	2	....	....	....	....
2000-01	Cleveland	IHL	74	20	24	44	54	....	....	....	....	....	....	....	....	....	4	0	0	0	18	....	....	....	....
2001-02	Houston Aeros	AHL	78	24	21	45	71	....	....	....	....	....	....	....	....	....	14	1	6	7	12	....	....	....	....
2002-03	**Chicago**	**NHL**	**2**	**0**	**0**	**0**	**0**	**0**	**0**	**0**	**1**	**0.0**	**–1**	**19**	**26.3**	**10:47**	....	....	....	....	....	....	....	....	....
	Norfolk Admirals	AHL	77	23	38	61	60	....	....	....	....	....	....	....	....	....	9	2	6	8	9	....	....	....	....
2003-04	**Chicago**	**NHL**	**76**	**11**	**20**	**31**	**54**	**5**	**1**	**0**	**125**	**8.8**	**–11**	**1135**	**51.1**	**17:33**	....	....	....	....	....	....	....	....	....
	Norfolk Admirals	AHL	4	3	3	6	6	....	....	....	....	....	....	....	....	....	....	....	....	....	....	....	....	....	....

			Regular Season														Playoffs								
Season	Club	League	GP	G	A	Pts	PIM	PP	SH	GW	S	%	+/-	TF	F%	Min	GP	G	A	Pts	PIM	PP	SH	GW	Min
2004-05	Malmo	Sweden	38	7	6	13	102	....	....	....	....	....	....	....	....	....	....	....	....	....	....	....	....	....	....
	Malmo	Sweden-Q	9	1	1	2	16	....	....	....	....	....	....	....	....	....	....	....	....	....	....	....	....	....	....
2005-06	**Colorado**	**NHL**	**82**	**9**	**31**	**40**	**51**	**1**	**0**	**0**	**115**	**7.8**	**–7**	**770**	**50.7**	**12:12**	**8**	**0**	**1**	**1**	**4**	**0**	**0**	**0**	**10:40**
2006-07	**Colorado**	**NHL**	**78**	**15**	**20**	**35**	**36**	**0**	**0**	**3**	**134**	**11.2**	**8**	**413**	**50.1**	**13:38**	....	....	....	....	....	....	....	....	....
2007-08	**Florida**	**NHL**	**67**	**14**	**23**	**37**	**34**	**3**	**1**	**1**	**140**	**10.0**	**–5**	**624**	**47.4**	**16:14**	....	....	....	....	....	....	....	....	....
	NHL Totals		**305**	**49**	**94**	**143**	**175**	**9**	**2**	**4**	**515**	**9.5**		**2961**	**49.9**	**14:47**	**8**	**0**	**1**	**1**	**4**	**0**	**0**	**0**	**10:40**

WHL West Second All-Star Team (1998)

Signed as a free agent by **Calgary**, September, 1999. Signed as a free agent by **Minnesota**, July 13, 2000. Signed as a free agent by **Chicago**, July 23, 2002. Signed as a free agent by **Colorado**, July 22, 2004. Signed as a free agent by **Malmo** (Sweden), September 24, 2004. Signed as a free agent by **Florida**, July 1, 2007.

McLEOD, Cody

(muh-KLOWD, KOH-dee) **COL.**

Left wing. Shoots left. 6'2", 210 lbs. Born, Binscarth, Man., June 26, 1984.

2001-02	Portland	WHL	47	10	3	13	86	....	....	....	....	....	....	....	....	....	5	0	0	0	0	....	....	....	....
2002-03	Portland	WHL	71	15	18	33	153	....	....	....	....	....	....	....	....	....	7	1	1	2	13	....	....	....	....
2003-04	Portland	WHL	69	13	18	31	227	....	....	....	....	....	....	....	....	....	5	2	2	4	6	....	....	....	....
2004-05	Portland	WHL	70	31	29	60	195	....	....	....	....	....	....	....	....	....	7	0	3	3	8	....	....	....	....
	Adirondack	UHL	1	0	0	0	0	....	....	....	....	....	....	....	....	....	5	0	0	0	11	....	....	....	....
2005-06	Lowell	AHL	33	4	5	9	87	....	....	....	....	....	....	....	....	....	....	....	....	....	....	....	....	....	....
	San Diego Gulls	ECHL	16	4	5	9	48	....	....	....	....	....	....	....	....	....	2	2	1	3	14	....	....	....	....
2006-07	Albany River Rats	AHL	73	11	8	19	180	....	....	....	....	....	....	....	....	....	5	0	0	0	4	....	....	....	....
2007-08	**Colorado**	**NHL**	**49**	**4**	**5**	**9**	**120**	**0**	**0**	**0**	**60**	**6.7**	**–6**	**3**	**0.0**	**10:07**	**10**	**1**	**1**	**2**	**26**	**0**	**0**	**0**	**12:23**
	Lake Erie	AHL	27	6	7	13	101	....	....	....	....	....	....	....	....	....	....	....	....	....	....	....	....	....	....
	NHL Totals		**49**	**4**	**5**	**9**	**120**	**0**	**0**	**0**	**60**	**6.7**		**3**	**0.0**	**10:07**	**10**	**1**	**1**	**2**	**26**	**0**	**0**	**0**	**12:23**

Signed as a free agent by **Colorado**, July 6, 2006.

MEECH, Derek

(MEECH, DAIR-ihk) **DET.**

Defense. Shoots left. 5'11", 197 lbs. Born, Winnipeg, Man., April 21, 1984. Detroit's 7th choice, 229th overall, in 2002 Entry Draft.

99-2000	Wpg. Warriors	MMMHL	36	15	40	55	24	....	....	....	....	....	....	....	....	....	....	....	....	....	....	....	....	....	....
	Red Deer Rebels	WHL	5	1	0	1	2	....	....	....	....	....	....	....	....	....	....	....	....	....	....	....	....	....	....
2000-01	Red Deer Rebels	WHL	60	2	7	9	40	....	....	....	....	....	....	....	....	....	22	0	0	0	9	....	....	....	....
2001-02	Red Deer Rebels	WHL	71	8	19	27	33	....	....	....	....	....	....	....	....	....	13	1	1	2	6	....	....	....	....
2002-03	Red Deer Rebels	WHL	65	6	16	22	53	....	....	....	....	....	....	....	....	....	12	1	1	2	12	....	....	....	....
2003-04	Red Deer Rebels	WHL	62	10	28	38	40	....	....	....	....	....	....	....	....	....	19	4	7	11	10	....	....	....	....
2004-05	Grand Rapids	AHL	78	6	8	14	40	....	....	....	....	....	....	....	....	....	....	....	....	....	....	....	....	....	....
2005-06	Grand Rapids	AHL	79	4	16	20	85	....	....	....	....	....	....	....	....	....	16	0	2	2	4	....	....	....	....
2006-07	**Detroit**	**NHL**	**4**	**0**	**0**	**0**	**2**	**0**	**0**	**0**	**3**	**0.0**	**1**	**0**	**0.0**	**5:47**	....	....	....	....	....	....	....	....	....
	Grand Rapids	AHL	67	6	23	29	40	....	....	....	....	....	....	....	....	....	7	0	1	1	4	....	....	....	....
2007-08	**Detroit**	**NHL**	**32**	**0**	**3**	**3**	**6**	**0**	**0**	**0**	**44**	**0.0**	**–5**	**0**	**0.0**	**12:08**	....	....	....	....	....	....	....	....	....
	Grand Rapids	AHL	6	1	1	2	0	....	....	....	....	....	....	....	....	....	....	....	....	....	....	....	....	....	....
	NHL Totals		**36**	**0**	**3**	**3**	**8**	**0**	**0**	**0**	**47**	**0.0**		**0**	**0.0**	**11:26**	....	....	....	....	....	....	....	....	....

WHL East Second All-Star Team (2004)

• Missed majority of 2007-08 season as a healthy reserve.

MELICHAR, Josef

(mehl-ee-KHAHR, YOH-sehf) **CAR.**

Defense. Shoots left. 6'2", 220 lbs. Born, Ceske Budejovice, Czech., January 20, 1979. Pittsburgh's 3rd choice, 71st overall, in 1997 Entry Draft.

1995-96	C. Budejovice Jr.	CzRep-Jr.	38	3	4	7	....	....	....	....	....	....	....	....	....	....	....	....	....	....	....	....	....	....	....
1996-97	C. Budejovice Jr.	CzRep-Jr.	41	2	3	5	10	....	....	....	....	....	....	....	....	....	....	....	....	....	....	....	....	....	....
1997-98	Tri-City	WHL	67	9	24	33	154	....	....	....	....	....	....	....	....	....	....	....	....	....	....	....	....	....	....
1998-99	Tri-City	WHL	65	8	28	36	125	....	....	....	....	....	....	....	....	....	11	1	0	1	15	....	....	....	....
99-2000	Wilkes-Barre	AHL	80	3	9	12	126	....	....	....	....	....	....	....	....	....	....	....	....	....	....	....	....	....	....
2000-01	**Pittsburgh**	**NHL**	**18**	**0**	**2**	**2**	**21**	**0**	**0**	**0**	**9**	**0.0**	**–5**	**0**	**0.0**	**14:54**	....	....	....	....	....	....	....	....	....
	Wilkes-Barre	AHL	46	2	5	7	69	....	....	....	....	....	....	....	....	....	21	0	5	5	6	....	....	....	....
2001-02	**Pittsburgh**	**NHL**	**60**	**0**	**3**	**3**	**68**	**0**	**0**	**0**	**46**	**0.0**	**–1**	**0**	**0.0**	**16:46**	....	....	....	....	....	....	....	....	....
2002-03	**Pittsburgh**	**NHL**	**8**	**0**	**0**	**0**	**2**	**0**	**0**	**0**	**6**	**0.0**	**–2**	**0**	**0.0**	**15:19**	....	....	....	....	....	....	....	....	....
2003-04	**Pittsburgh**	**NHL**	**82**	**3**	**5**	**8**	**62**	**0**	**0**	**0**	**78**	**3.8**	**–17**	**0**	**0.0**	**19:01**	....	....	....	....	....	....	....	....	....
2004-05	HC Sparta Praha	CzRep	13	0	4	4	8	....	....	....	....	....	....	....	....	....	5	0	0	0	6	....	....	....	....
2005-06	**Pittsburgh**	**NHL**	**72**	**3**	**12**	**15**	**66**	**0**	**1**	**0**	**53**	**5.7**	**–2**	**0**	**0.0**	**17:26**	....	....	....	....	....	....	....	....	....
2006-07	**Pittsburgh**	**NHL**	**70**	**1**	**11**	**12**	**44**	**0**	**0**	**0**	**57**	**1.8**	**1**	**0**	**0.0**	**18:49**	**5**	**0**	**0**	**0**	**2**	**0**	**0**	**0**	**17:21**
2007-08	C. Budejovice	CzRep	6	0	0	0	4	....	....	....	....	....	....	....	....	....	....	....	....	....	....	....	....	....	....
	Linkopings HC	Sweden	50	0	8	8	74	....	....	....	....	....	....	....	....	....	16	1	1	2	39	....	....	....	....
	NHL Totals		**310**	**7**	**33**	**40**	**263**	**0**	**1**	**0**	**249**	**2.8**		**0**	**0.0**	**17:50**	**5**	**0**	**0**	**0**	**2**	**0**	**0**	**0**	**17:21**

• Missed majority of 2002-03 season recovering from shoulder injury suffered in game vs. Boston, October 13, 2002. Signed as a free agent by **Sparta Praha** (CzRep), September 17, 2004. Signed as a free agent by **Linkoping** (Sweden), October 3, 2007. Signed as a free agent by **Carolina**, July 2, 2008.

MELIN, Bjorn

(MEH-lihn, b-YOHRN) **ANA.**

Right wing. Shoots right. 6'1", 205 lbs. Born, Jonkoping, Sweden, July 4, 1981. NY Islanders' 11th choice, 163rd overall, in 1999 Entry Draft.

1997-98	HV 71 Jr.	Swe-Jr.	8	0	3	3	2	....	....	....	....	....	....	....	....	....	....	....	....	....	....	....	....	....	....
1998-99	HV 71 Jr.	Swe-Jr.	30	12	7	19	50	....	....	....	....	....	....	....	....	....	....	....	....	....	....	....	....	....	....
99-2000	HV 71 Jr.	Swe-Jr.	24	19	16	35	70	....	....	....	....	....	....	....	....	....	....	....	....	....	....	....	....	....	....
	HV 71 Jonkoping	Sweden	23	3	0	3	2	....	....	....	....	....	....	....	....	....	5	0	0	0	0	....	....	....	....
2000-01	HV 71 Jr.	Swe-Jr.	10	6	5	11	66	....	....	....	....	....	....	....	....	....	....	....	....	....	....	....	....	....	....
	HV 71 Jonkoping	Sweden	43	2	1	3	26	....	....	....	....	....	....	....	....	....	....	....	....	....	....	....	....	....	....
2001-02	HV 71 Jonkoping	Sweden	50	7	9	16	40	....	....	....	....	....	....	....	....	....	8	0	0	0	6	....	....	....	....
2002-03	HV 71 Jonkoping	Sweden	48	7	9	16	44	....	....	....	....	....	....	....	....	....	7	0	2	2	6	....	....	....	....
2003-04	HV 71 Jonkoping	Sweden	47	7	11	18	28	....	....	....	....	....	....	....	....	....	19	4	8	12	10	....	....	....	....
2004-05	Malmo	Sweden	46	9	10	19	22	....	....	....	....	....	....	....	....	....	....	....	....	....	....	....	....	....	....
	Malmo	Sweden-Q	10	1	2	3	8	....	....	....	....	....	....	....	....	....	....	....	....	....	....	....	....	....	....
2005-06	HV 71 Jonkoping	Sweden	49	17	19	36	48	....	....	....	....	....	....	....	....	....	10	4	1	5	16	....	....	....	....
2006-07	**Anaheim**	**NHL**	**3**	**1**	**0**	**1**	**0**	**0**	**0**	**0**	**1**	**100.0**	**–1**	**0**	**0.0**	**7:19**	....	....	....	....	....	....	....	....	....
	Portland Pirates	AHL	59	8	14	22	28	....	....	....	....	....	....	....	....	....	....	....	....	....	....	....	....	....	....
2007-08	HV 71 Jonkoping	Sweden	40	9	10	19	32	....	....	....	....	....	....	....	....	....	12	0	3	3	4	....	....	....	....
	NHL Totals		**3**	**1**	**0**	**1**	**0**	**0**	**0**	**0**	**1**	**100.0**		**0**	**0.0**	**7:19**	....	....	....	....	....	....	....	....	....

Rights traded to **Anaheim** by **NY Islanders** with Ben Guite for Dave Roche, March 19, 2002.

MELOCHE, Eric

(muh-LAWSH, AIR-ihk)

Right wing. Shoots right. 5'10", 202 lbs. Born, Montreal, Que., May 1, 1976. Pittsburgh's 7th choice, 186th overall, in 1996 Entry Draft.

1994-95	Cornwall Colts	CJHL	40	7	15	22	51	....	....	....	....	....	....	....	....	....	....	....	....	....	....	....	....	....	....
1995-96	Cornwall Colts	CJHL	64	68	53	121	162	....	....	....	....	....	....	....	....	....	....	....	....	....	....	....	....	....	....
1996-97	Ohio State	CCHA	39	12	11	23	78	....	....	....	....	....	....	....	....	....	....	....	....	....	....	....	....	....	....
1997-98	Ohio State	CCHA	42	26	22	48	86	....	....	....	....	....	....	....	....	....	....	....	....	....	....	....	....	....	....
1998-99	Ohio State	CCHA	35	11	16	27	87	....	....	....	....	....	....	....	....	....	....	....	....	....	....	....	....	....	....
99-2000	Ohio State	CCHA	36	20	11	31	*138	....	....	....	....	....	....	....	....	....	....	....	....	....	....	....	....	....	....
2000-01	Wilkes-Barre	AHL	79	20	20	40	72	....	....	....	....	....	....	....	....	....	21	6	10	16	17	....	....	....	....
2001-02	**Pittsburgh**	**NHL**	**23**	**0**	**1**	**1**	**8**	**0**	**0**	**0**	**29**	**0.0**	**–7**	**4**	**0.0**	**10:10**	....	....	....	....	....	....	....	....	....
	Wilkes-Barre	AHL	55	13	14	27	91	....	....	....	....	....	....	....	....	....	....	....	....	....	....	....	....	....	....
2002-03	**Pittsburgh**	**NHL**	**13**	**5**	**1**	**6**	**4**	**2**	**0**	**1**	**34**	**14.7**	**–2**	**27**	**55.6**	**16:52**	....	....	....	....	....	....	....	....	....
	Wilkes-Barre	AHL	59	12	17	29	95	....	....	....	....	....	....	....	....	....	6	1	0	1	20	....	....	....	....
2003-04	**Pittsburgh**	**NHL**	**25**	**3**	**7**	**10**	**20**	**0**	**0**	**0**	**28**	**10.7**	**–6**	**92**	**39.1**	**14:47**	....	....	....	....	....	....	....	....	....
	Wilkes-Barre	AHL	56	16	26	42	49	....	....	....	....	....	....	....	....	....	23	9	6	15	14	....	....	....	....
2004-05	Philadelphia	AHL	63	6	11	17	102	....	....	....	....	....	....	....	....	....	17	3	2	5	18	....	....	....	....
2005-06	Philadelphia	AHL	10	1	2	3	16	....	....	....	....	....	....	....	....	....	....	....	....	....	....	....	....	....	....
	Norfolk Admirals	AHL	47	7	14	21	81	....	....	....	....	....	....	....	....	....	4	0	0	0	11	....	....	....	....

			Regular Season														Playoffs								
Season	Club	League	GP	G	A	Pts	PIM	PP	SH	GW	S	%	+/-	TF	F%	Min	GP	G	A	Pts	PIM	PP	SH	GW	Min
2006-07	**Philadelphia**	**NHL**	**13**	**1**	**2**	**3**	**4**	**1**	**0**	**0**	**12**	**8.3**	**–6**	**28**	**46.4**	**8:21**	....	....	....	....	....	....	....	....	....
	Philadelphia	AHL	49	11	13	24	82	....	....	....	....	....	....	....	....	....	....	....	....	....	....	....	....	....	....
2007-08	Straubing Tigers	Germany	54	17	23	40	125	....	....	....	....	....	....	....	....	....	....	....	....	....	....	....	....	....	....
	NHL Totals		**74**	**9**	**11**	**20**	**36**	**3**	**0**	**1**	**103**	**8.7**		**151**	**42.4**	**12:35**									

Signed as a free agent by **Philadelphia**, July 14, 2004. Traded to **Chicago** by **Philadelphia** with Patrick Sharp for Matt Ellison and Chicago's 3rd round choice (later traded to Montreal - Montereal selected Ryan White) in 2006 Entry Draft, December 5, 2005. Traded to **Philadelphia** by **Chicago** for Vaclav Pletka, August 2, 2006.

MESZAROS, Andrej (MEHT-zahr-ohsh, AWN-dray) OTT.

Defense. Shoots left. 6'2", 218 lbs. Born, Povazska Bystrica, Czech., October 13, 1985. Ottawa's 1st choice, 23rd overall, in 2004 Entry Draft.

2002-03	Dukla Trencin Jr.	Slovak-Jr.	33	6	10	16	12	....	....	....	....	....	....	....	....	....	....	....	....	....	....	....	....	....	....
	Dukla Trencin	Slovakia	23	0	1	1	4	....	....	....	....	....	....	....	....	....	....	....	....	....	....	....	....	....	....
2003-04	Dukla Trencin	Slovakia	44	3	3	6	8	....	....	....	....	....	....	....	....	....	14	3	1	4	2	....	....	....	....
	Dukla Trencin Jr.	Slovak-Jr.	5	2	2	4	0	....	....	....	....	....	....	....	....	....	....	....	....	....	....	....	....	....	....
2004-05	Vancouver Giants	WHL	59	11	30	41	94	....	....	....	....	....	....	....	....	....	6	1	3	4	14	....	....	....	....
2005-06	**Ottawa**	**NHL**	**82**	**10**	**29**	**39**	**61**	**5**	**0**	**2**	**137**	**7.3**	**34**	**1**	**0.0**	**18:11**	**10**	**1**	**0**	**1**	**18**	**0**	**0**	**0**	**17:50**
	Slovakia	Olympics	6	0	2	2	4	....	....	....	....	....	....	....	....	....	....	....	....	....	....	....	....	....	....
2006-07	**Ottawa**	**NHL**	**82**	**7**	**28**	**35**	**102**	**0**	**0**	**1**	**147**	**4.8**	**–15**	**0**	**0.0**	**21:41**	**20**	**1**	**6**	**7**	**12**	**0**	**0**	**0**	**20:29**
2007-08	**Ottawa**	**NHL**	**82**	**9**	**27**	**36**	**50**	**6**	**1**	**1**	**160**	**5.6**	**5**	**1**	**0.0**	**21:02**	**4**	**0**	**1**	**1**	**6**	**0**	**0**	**0**	**18:59**
	NHL Totals		**246**	**26**	**84**	**110**	**213**	**11**	**1**	**4**	**444**	**5.9**		**2**	**0.0**	**20:18**	**34**	**2**	**7**	**9**	**36**	**0**	**0**	**0**	**19:32**

WHL West Second All-Star Team (2005) • NHL All-Rookie Team (2006)

METHOT, Marc (meh-TOH, MAHRK) CBJ

Defense. Shoots left. 6'3", 224 lbs. Born, Ottawa, Ont., June 21, 1985. Columbus' 7th choice, 168th overall, in 2003 Entry Draft.

2001-02	Kanata Laser	CJHL	50	3	10	13	22	....	....	....	....	....	....	....	....	....	....	....	....	....	....	....	....	....	....
2002-03	London Knights	OHL	68	2	13	15	46	....	....	....	....	....	....	....	....	....	14	2	4	6	6	....	....	....	....
2003-04	London Knights	OHL	63	2	9	11	66	....	....	....	....	....	....	....	....	....	15	0	3	3	18	....	....	....	....
2004-05	London Knights	OHL	67	4	12	16	88	....	....	....	....	....	....	....	....	....	18	2	1	3	32	....	....	....	....
2005-06	Syracuse Crunch	AHL	70	1	12	13	75	....	....	....	....	....	....	....	....	....	5	0	0	0	8	....	....	....	....
2006-07	**Columbus**	**NHL**	**20**	**0**	**4**	**4**	**12**	**0**	**0**	**0**	**11**	**0.0**	**5**	**0**	**0.0**	**14:38**	....	....	....	....	....	....	....	....	....
	Syracuse Crunch	AHL	59	1	15	16	58	....	....	....	....	....	....	....	....	....	....	....	....	....	....	....	....	....	....
2007-08	**Columbus**	**NHL**	**9**	**0**	**0**	**0**	**8**	**0**	**0**	**0**	**9**	**0.0**	**–1**	**0**	**0.0**	**14:14**	....	....	....	....	....	....	....	....	....
	Syracuse Crunch	AHL	66	7	6	13	130	....	....	....	....	....	....	....	....	....	13	0	6	6	14	....	....	....	....
	NHL Totals		**29**	**0**	**4**	**4**	**20**	**0**	**0**	**0**	**20**	**0.0**		**0**	**0.0**	**14:30**	....	....	....	....	....	....	....	....	....

METROPOLIT, Glen (meh-troh-PAW-liht, GLEHN) PHI.

Center. Shoots right. 5'10", 193 lbs. Born, Toronto, Ont., June 25, 1974.

1992-93	Richmond Hill	MTJHL	43	27	36	63	36	....	....	....	....	....	....	....	....	....	....	....	....	....	....	....	....	....	....
1993-94	Richmond Hill	MTJHL	49	38	62	100	83	....	....	....	....	....	....	....	....	....	....	....	....	....	....	....	....	....	....
1994-95	Vernon Vipers	BCJHL	60	43	74	117	92	....	....	....	....	....	....	....	....	....	....	....	....	....	....	....	....	....	....
1995-96	Nashville Knights	ECHL	58	30	31	61	62	....	....	....	....	....	....	....	....	....	5	3	8	11	2	....	....	....	....
	Atlanta Knights	IHL	1	0	0	0	0	....	....	....	....	....	....	....	....	....	....	....	....	....	....	....	....	....	....
1996-97	Pensacola	ECHL	54	35	47	82	45	....	....	....	....	....	....	....	....	....	12	9	16	25	28	....	....	....	....
	Quebec Rafales	IHL	22	5	4	9	14	....	....	....	....	....	....	....	....	....	5	0	0	0	2	....	....	....	....
1997-98	Grand Rapids	IHL	79	20	35	55	90	....	....	....	....	....	....	....	....	....	3	1	1	2	0	....	....	....	....
1998-99	Grand Rapids	IHL	77	28	53	81	92	....	....	....	....	....	....	....	....	....	....	....	....	....	....	....	....	....	....
99-2000	**Washington**	**NHL**	**30**	**6**	**13**	**19**	**4**	**1**	**0**	**1**	**57**	**10.5**	**5**	**37**	**46.0**	**13:17**	**2**	**0**	**0**	**0**	**2**	**0**	**0**	**0**	**7:07**
	Portland Pirates	AHL	48	18	42	60	73	....	....	....	....	....	....	....	....	....	1	1	0	1	0	....	....	....	....
2000-01	**Washington**	**NHL**	**15**	**1**	**5**	**6**	**10**	**0**	**0**	**0**	**20**	**5.0**	**–2**	**3**	**33.3**	**11:50**	**1**	**0**	**0**	**0**	**0**	**0**	**0**	**0**	**7:03**
	Portland Pirates	AHL	51	25	42	67	59	....	....	....	....	....	....	....	....	....	....	....	....	....	....	....	....	....	....
2001-02	**Tampa Bay**	**NHL**	**2**	**0**	**0**	**0**	**0**	**0**	**0**	**0**	**1**	**0.0**	**–2**	**2**	**50.0**	**10:26**	....	....	....	....	....	....	....	....	....
	Washington	**NHL**	**33**	**1**	**16**	**17**	**6**	**0**	**0**	**0**	**51**	**2.0**	**3**	**145**	**49.7**	**14:24**	....	....	....	....	....	....	....	....	....
	Portland Pirates	AHL	32	17	22	39	20	....	....	....	....	....	....	....	....	....	....	....	....	....	....	....	....	....	....
2002-03	**Washington**	**NHL**	**23**	**2**	**3**	**5**	**6**	**0**	**0**	**1**	**22**	**9.1**	**4**	**99**	**49.5**	**10:07**	....	....	....	....	....	....	....	....	....
	Portland Pirates	AHL	33	7	23	30	23	....	....	....	....	....	....	....	....	....	3	1	1	2	0	....	....	....	....
2003-04	Jokerit Helsinki	Finland	55	15	35	50	77	....	....	....	....	....	....	....	....	....	7	6	1	7	33	....	....	....	....
2004-05	Jokerit Helsinki	Finland	51	16	31	47	42	....	....	....	....	....	....	....	....	....	12	5	6	11	20	....	....	....	....
2005-06	HC Lugano	Swiss	44	24	*39	*63	60	....	....	....	....	....	....	....	....	....	17	9	18	27	8	....	....	....	....
2006-07	**Atlanta**	**NHL**	**57**	**12**	**16**	**28**	**20**	**4**	**0**	**2**	**92**	**13.0**	**9**	**206**	**49.0**	**11:47**	....	....	....	....	....	....	....	....	....
	St. Louis	**NHL**	**20**	**2**	**3**	**5**	**14**	**1**	**0**	**0**	**31**	**6.5**	**0**	**154**	**50.0**	**12:58**	....	....	....	....	....	....	....	....	....
2007-08	**Boston**	**NHL**	**82**	**11**	**22**	**33**	**36**	**1**	**0**	**5**	**141**	**7.8**	**–3**	**1242**	**49.4**	**16:26**	**7**	**1**	**0**	**1**	**4**	**0**	**0**	**1**	**16:27**
	NHL Totals		**262**	**35**	**78**	**113**	**96**	**7**	**0**	**9**	**415**	**8.4**		**1888**	**49.3**	**13:40**	**10**	**1**	**0**	**1**	**6**	**0**	**0**	**1**	**13:39**

Signed as a free agent by **Washington**, July 19, 1999. Claimed by **Tampa Bay** from **Washington** in Waiver Draft, September 28, 2001. Claimed on waivers by **Washington** from **Tampa Bay**, October 20, 2001. Signed as a free agent by **Jokerit Helsinki** (Finland), April 22, 2003. Claimed by **Ottawa** from **Washington** in Waiver Draft, October 3, 2003. Signed as a free agent by **Atlanta**, July 3, 2006. Traded to **St. Louis** by **Atlanta** with Atlanta's 1st (later traded to Calgary - Calgary selected Mikael Backlund) and 3rd (Brett Sonne) round choices in 2007 Entry Draft and Atlanta's 1st (later traded back to Atlanta - Atlanta selected Zach Bogosian) and 2nd (Philip McRae) round choices in 2008 Entry Draft for Keith Tkachuk, February 25, 2007. Signed as a free agent by **Boston**, October 3, 2007. Signed as a free agent by **Philadelphia**, July 1, 2008.

MEYER, Freddy (MAY-uhr, FREHD) NYI

Defense. Shoots left. 5'10", 192 lbs. Born, Sanbornville, NH, January 4, 1981.

1996-97	Cardigan Mtn.	High-NH	STATISTICS NOT AVAILABLE																						
1997-98	USNTDP	NAHL	....	....	....	....	....	....	....	....	....	....	....	....	....	....	2	1	0	1	37	....	....	....	....
1998-99	USNTDP	U-18	6	1	4	5	8	....	....	....	....	....	....	....	....	....	....	....	....	....	....	....	....	....	....
	USNTDP	USHL	54	10	23	33	151	....	....	....	....	....	....	....	....	....	....	....	....	....	....	....	....	....	....
99-2000	USNTDP	USHL	28	3	8	11	60	....	....	....	....	....	....	....	....	....	....	....	....	....	....	....	....	....	....
	USNTDP	NAHL	3	0	2	2	0	....	....	....	....	....	....	....	....	....	....	....	....	....	....	....	....	....	....
	Boston University	H-East	25	1	11	12	52	....	....	....	....	....	....	....	....	....	....	....	....	....	....	....	....	....	....
2000-01	Boston University	H-East	28	6	13	19	82	....	....	....	....	....	....	....	....	....	....	....	....	....	....	....	....	....	....
2001-02	Boston University	H-East	37	5	15	20	78	....	....	....	....	....	....	....	....	....	....	....	....	....	....	....	....	....	....
2002-03	Boston University	H-East	36	5	16	21	76	....	....	....	....	....	....	....	....	....	....	....	....	....	....	....	....	....	....
2003-04	**Philadelphia**	**NHL**	**1**	**0**	**0**	**0**	**0**	**0**	**0**	**0**	**1**	**0.0**	**0**	**0**	**0.0**	**15:24**	....	....	....	....	....	....	....	....	....
	Philadelphia	AHL	59	14	14	28	50	....	....	....	....	....	....	....	....	....	12	0	3	3	8	....	....	....	....
2004-05	Philadelphia	AHL	59	6	9	15	71	....	....	....	....	....	....	....	....	....	21	3	9	12	34	....	....	....	....
2005-06	**Philadelphia**	**NHL**	**57**	**6**	**21**	**27**	**33**	**2**	**0**	**0**	**68**	**8.8**	**10**	**0**	**0.0**	**17:56**	**6**	**0**	**1**	**1**	**8**	**0**	**0**	**0**	**18:23**
	Philadelphia	AHL	11	3	3	6	22	....	....	....	....	....	....	....	....	....	....	....	....	....	....	....	....	....	....
2006-07	**Philadelphia**	**NHL**	**25**	**2**	**3**	**5**	**14**	**1**	**0**	**0**	**27**	**7.4**	**–4**	**0**	**0.0**	**18:36**	....	....	....	....	....	....	....	....	....
	NY Islanders	**NHL**	**35**	**0**	**3**	**3**	**24**	**0**	**0**	**0**	**14**	**0.0**	**0**	**0**	**0.0**	**16:39**	....	....	....	....	....	....	....	....	....
2007-08	**Phoenix**	**NHL**	**5**	**0**	**0**	**0**	**0**	**0**	**0**	**0**	**2**	**0.0**	**–4**	**0**	**0.0**	**6:43**	....	....	....	....	....	....	....	....	....
	San Antonio	AHL	8	0	2	2	12	....	....	....	....	....	....	....	....	....	....	....	....	....	....	....	....	....	....
	NY Islanders	**NHL**	**52**	**3**	**9**	**12**	**22**	**0**	**0**	**2**	**49**	**6.1**	**6**	**0**	**0.0**	**19:54**	....	....	....	....	....	....	....	....	....
	NHL Totals		**175**	**11**	**36**	**47**	**93**	**3**	**0**	**2**	**161**	**6.8**		**0**	**0.0**	**18:01**	**6**	**0**	**1**	**1**	**8**	**0**	**0**	**0**	**18:23**

Hockey East All-Rookie Team (2000) • Hockey East First All-Star Team (2003) • NCAA East First All-American Team (2003)

Signed as a free agent by **Philadelphia**, May 21, 2003. Traded to **NY Islanders** by **Philadelphia** with Philadelphia's 3rd round choice (Mark Katic) in 2007 Entry Draft for Alexei Zhitnik, December 16, 2006. Claimed on waivers by **Phoenix** from **NY Islanders**, October 8, 2007. Claimed on waivers by **NY Islanders** from **Phoenix**, November 10, 2007.

MEYER, Stefan (MAY-uhr, STEH-fan) FLA.

Left wing. Shoots left. 6'2", 194 lbs. Born, Medicine Hat, Alta., July 20, 1985. Florida's 4th choice, 55th overall, in 2003 Entry Draft.

2000-01	Notre Dame	SBHL	50	36	52	88	71	....	....	....	....	....	....	....	....	....	....	....	....	....	....	....	....	....	....
2001-02	Medicine Hat	WHL	67	18	22	40	48	....	....	....	....	....	....	....	....	....	....	....	....	....	....	....	....	....	....
2002-03	Medicine Hat	WHL	70	36	16	52	90	....	....	....	....	....	....	....	....	....	11	3	3	6	14	....	....	....	....
2003-04	Medicine Hat	WHL	72	34	41	75	69	....	....	....	....	....	....	....	....	....	19	7	10	17	27	....	....	....	....
2004-05	Medicine Hat	WHL	69	34	43	77	104	....	....	....	....	....	....	....	....	....	13	2	4	6	8	....	....	....	....
2005-06	Rochester	AHL	68	12	16	28	139	....	....	....	....	....	....	....	....	....	....	....	....	....	....	....	....	....	....
2006-07	Rochester	AHL	63	13	9	22	90	....	....	....	....	....	....	....	....	....	6	0	2	2	8	....	....	....	....

Season	Club	League	Regular Season														Playoffs								
			GP	G	A	Pts	PIM	PP	SH	GW	S	%	+/-	TF	F%	Min	GP	G	A	Pts	PIM	PP	SH	GW	Min
2007-08	**Florida**	**NHL**	**4**	**0**	**0**	**0**	**0**	**0**	**0**	**0**	**0**	**0.0**	**–1**	**6**	**50.0**	**2:26**	....	....	....	....	....	....	....	....	....
	Rochester	AHL	70	21	19	40	77	....	....	....	....	....	....	....	....	....	....	....	....	....	....	....	....	....	....
	NHL Totals		**4**	**0**	**0**	**0**	**0**	**0**	**0**	**0**	**0**	**0.0**		**6**	**50.0**	**2:26**	....	....	....	....	....	....	....	....	....

MEZEI, Branislav

(MEH-tzay, BRAN-ih-slav)

Defense. Shoots left. 6'4", 235 lbs. Born, Nitra, Czech., October 8, 1980. NY Islanders' 3rd choice, 10th overall, in 1999 Entry Draft.

1996-97	Nitra Jr.	Slovak-Jr.	40	8	17	25	42	....	....	....	....	....	....	....	....	....	....	....	....	....	....	....	....	....	....
1997-98	Belleville Bulls	OHL	53	3	5	8	58	....	....	....	....	....	....	....	....	....	8	0	2	2	8	....	....	....	....
1998-99	Belleville Bulls	OHL	60	5	18	23	90	....	....	....	....	....	....	....	....	....	18	0	4	4	29	....	....	....	....
99-2000	Belleville Bulls	OHL	58	7	21	28	99	....	....	....	....	....	....	....	....	....	6	0	3	3	10	....	....	....	....
2000-01	**NY Islanders**	**NHL**	**42**	**1**	**4**	**5**	**53**	**0**	**0**	**0**	**29**	**3.4**	**–5**	**0**	**0.0**	**14:48**	....	....	....	....	....	....	....	....	....
	Lowell	AHL	20	0	3	3	28	....	....	....	....	....	....	....	....	....	....	....	....	....	....	....	....	....	....
2001-02	**NY Islanders**	**NHL**	**24**	**0**	**2**	**2**	**12**	**0**	**0**	**0**	**4**	**0.0**	**2**	**0**	**0.0**	**8:28**	....	....	....	....	....	....	....	....	....
	Bridgeport	AHL	59	1	9	10	137	....	....	....	....	....	....	....	....	....	20	0	1	1	48	....	....	....	....
2002-03	**Florida**	**NHL**	**11**	**2**	**0**	**2**	**10**	**0**	**0**	**1**	**10**	**20.0**	**–2**	**0**	**0.0**	**18:22**	....	....	....	....	....	....	....	....	....
	San Antonio	AHL	1	0	0	0	0	....	....	....	....	....	....	....	....	....	3	0	0	0	0	....	....	....	....
2003-04	**Florida**	**NHL**	**45**	**0**	**7**	**7**	**80**	**0**	**0**	**0**	**26**	**0.0**	**–4**	**0**	**0.0**	**17:43**	....	....	....	....	....	....	....	....	....
2004-05	HC Ocelari Trinec	CzRep	41	1	2	3	68	....	....	....	....	....	....	....	....	....	....	....	....	....	....	....	....	....	....
	Dukla Trencin	Slovakia	10	1	1	2	16	....	....	....	....	....	....	....	....	....	12	1	2	3	38	....	....	....	....
2005-06	**Florida**	**NHL**	**16**	**0**	**1**	**1**	**37**	**0**	**0**	**0**	**13**	**0.0**	**3**	**0**	**0.0**	**19:17**	....	....	....	....	....	....	....	....	....
2006-07	**Florida**	**NHL**	**45**	**0**	**3**	**3**	**55**	**0**	**0**	**0**	**24**	**0.0**	**5**	**1**	**100.0**	**15:58**	....	....	....	....	....	....	....	....	....
2007-08	**Florida**	**NHL**	**57**	**2**	**2**	**4**	**64**	**0**	**0**	**0**	**38**	**5.3**	**–13**	**0**	**0.0**	**14:28**	....	....	....	....	....	....	....	....	....
	NHL Totals		**240**	**5**	**19**	**24**	**311**	**0**	**0**	**1**	**144**	**3.5**		**1**	**100.0**	**15:19**	....	....	....	....	....	....	....	....	....

OHL First All-Star Team (2000)

Traded to **Florida** by **NY Islanders** for Jason Wiemer, July 3, 2002. • Missed majority of 2002-03 season recovering from ankle (October 12, 2002 vs. Atlanta) and foot (January 1, 2003 vs. New Jersey) injuries. Signed as a free agent by **Trinec** (CzRep), September 25, 2004. Signed as a free agent by **Trencin** (Slovakia), January 30, 2005. • Missed remainder of 2005-06 season recovering from knee injury sufferd in game vs. NY Rangers, November 9, 2005.

MICHALEK, Milan

(mih-KHAL-ihk, MEE-lan) **S.J.**

Right wing. Shoots left. 6'2", 225 lbs. Born, Jindrichuv Hradec, Czech., December 7, 1984. San Jose's 1st choice, 6th overall, in 2003 Entry Draft.

99-2000	C. Budejovice Jr.	CzRep-Jr.	48	16	26	42	42	....	....	....	....	....	....	....	....	....	6	3	1	4	4	....	....	....	....
2000-01	C. Budejovice Jr.	CzRep-Jr.	30	10	13	23	30	....	....	....	....	....	....	....	....	....	4	1	3	4	2	....	....	....	....
	C. Budejovice	CzRep	5	0	0	0	0	....	....	....	....	....	....	....	....	....	....	....	....	....	....	....	....	....	....
2001-02	C. Budejovice	CzRep	47	6	11	17	12	....	....	....	....	....	....	....	....	....	....	....	....	....	....	....	....	....	....
	C. Budejovice Jr.	CzRep-Jr.	5	3	2	5	4	....	....	....	....	....	....	....	....	....	7	5	4	9	14	....	....	....	....
2002-03	C. Budejovice	CzRep	46	3	5	8	14	....	....	....	....	....	....	....	....	....	4	1	0	1	2	....	....	....	....
	Kladno	CzRep-2	....	....	....	....	....	....	....	....	....	....	....	....	....	....	6	2	2	4	16	....	....	....	....
2003-04	**San Jose**	**NHL**	**2**	**1**	**0**	**1**	**4**	**0**	**0**	**0**	**1**	**100.0**	**1**	**0**	**0.0**	**9:05**	....	....	....	....	....	....	....	....	....
	Cleveland Barons	AHL	7	2	2	4	4	....	....	....	....	....	....	....	....	....	....	....	....	....	....	....	....	....	....
2004-05			DID NOT PLAY																						
2005-06	**San Jose**	**NHL**	**81**	**17**	**18**	**35**	**45**	**4**	**0**	**2**	**159**	**10.7**	**1**	**4**	**0.0**	**15:46**	**9**	**1**	**4**	**5**	**8**	**1**	**0**	**0**	**15:11**
2006-07	**San Jose**	**NHL**	**78**	**26**	**40**	**66**	**36**	**11**	**0**	**9**	**191**	**13.6**	**17**	**11**	**18.2**	**16:46**	**11**	**4**	**2**	**6**	**4**	**0**	**0**	**1**	**18:50**
2007-08	**San Jose**	**NHL**	**79**	**24**	**31**	**55**	**47**	**5**	**1**	**8**	**233**	**10.3**	**19**	**10**	**60.0**	**18:05**	**13**	**4**	**0**	**4**	**4**	**1**	**0**	**1**	**17:34**
	NHL Totals		**240**	**68**	**89**	**157**	**132**	**20**	**1**	**19**	**584**	**11.6**		**25**	**32.0**	**16:48**	**33**	**9**	**6**	**15**	**16**	**2**	**0**	**2**	**17:20**

• Missed majority of 2003-04 season recovering from knee injury suffered in game vs. Calgary, October 11, 2003.

MICHALEK, Zbynek

(mih-KHAL-ihk, z'BIGH-nehk) **PHX.**

Defense. Shoots right. 6'1", 200 lbs. Born, Jindrichuv Hradec, Czech., December 23, 1982.

99-2000	Karlovy Vary Jr.	CzRep-Jr.	40	2	10	12	20	....	....	....	....	....	....	....	....	....	....	....	....	....	....	....	....	....	....
2000-01	Shawinigan	QMJHL	69	10	29	39	52	....	....	....	....	....	....	....	....	....	3	0	0	0	0	....	....	....	....
2001-02	Shawinigan	QMJHL	68	16	35	51	54	....	....	....	....	....	....	....	....	....	12	8	9	17	17	....	....	....	....
2002-03	Houston Aeros	AHL	62	4	10	14	26	....	....	....	....	....	....	....	....	....	23	1	1	2	6	....	....	....	....
2003-04	**Minnesota**	**NHL**	**22**	**1**	**1**	**2**	**4**	**0**	**0**	**0**	**17**	**5.9**	**–7**	**0**	**0.0**	**14:13**	....	....	....	....	....	....	....	....	....
	Houston Aeros	AHL	55	5	16	21	32	....	....	....	....	....	....	....	....	....	2	1	0	1	0	....	....	....	....
2004-05	Houston Aeros	AHL	76	7	17	24	48	....	....	....	....	....	....	....	....	....	5	1	2	3	4	....	....	....	....
2005-06	**Phoenix**	**NHL**	**82**	**9**	**15**	**24**	**62**	**5**	**0**	**2**	**105**	**8.6**	**4**	**0**	**0.0**	**22:50**	....	....	....	....	....	....	....	....	....
2006-07	**Phoenix**	**NHL**	**82**	**4**	**24**	**28**	**34**	**3**	**0**	**0**	**144**	**2.8**	**–20**	**1**	**100.0**	**23:40**	....	....	....	....	....	....	....	....	....
2007-08	**Phoenix**	**NHL**	**75**	**4**	**13**	**17**	**34**	**0**	**0**	**2**	**92**	**4.3**	**9**	**0**	**0.0**	**21:36**	....	....	....	....	....	....	....	....	....
	NHL Totals		**261**	**18**	**53**	**71**	**134**	**8**	**0**	**4**	**358**	**5.0**		**1**	**100.0**	**22:01**	....	....	....	....	....	....	....	....	....

Signed as a free agent by **Minnesota**, September 29, 2001. Traded to **Phoenix** by **Minnesota** for Erik Westrum and Dustin Wood, August 26, 2005.

MIETTINEN, Antti

(mih-EHT-tih-nehn, AN-tee) **MIN.**

Right wing. Shoots right. 6', 190 lbs. Born, Hameenlinna, Finland, July 3, 1980. Dallas' 10th choice, 224th overall, in 2000 Entry Draft.

1996-97	HPK U18	Fin-U18	36	24	29	53	34	....	....	....	....	....	....	....	....	....	....	....	....	....	....	....	....	....	....
1997-98	HPK U18	Fin-U18	34	13	28	41	63	....	....	....	....	....	....	....	....	....	....	....	....	....	....	....	....	....	....
	HPK Jr.	Fin-Jr.	8	1	0	1	2	....	....	....	....	....	....	....	....	....	....	....	....	....	....	....	....	....	....
1998-99	HPK Jr.	Fin-Jr.	35	17	22	39	28	....	....	....	....	....	....	....	....	....	3	2	3	5	2	....	....	....	....
	FPS Forssa	Finland-2	4	3	1	4	6	....	....	....	....	....	....	....	....	....	....	....	....	....	....	....	....	....	....
	HPK Hameenlinna	Finland	13	0	0	0	2	....	....	....	....	....	....	....	....	....	4	0	0	0	0	....	....	....	....
99-2000	HPK Jr.	Fin-Jr.	31	24	53	77	28	....	....	....	....	....	....	....	....	....	2	1	6	7	2	....	....	....	....
	HPK Hameenlinna	Finland	39	2	1	3	8	....	....	....	....	....	....	....	....	....	7	1	0	1	0	....	....	....	....
2000-01	HPK Jr.	Fin-Jr.	4	3	10	13	2	....	....	....	....	....	....	....	....	....	....	....	....	....	....	....	....	....	....
	HPK Hameenlinna	Finland	55	13	11	24	20	....	....	....	....	....	....	....	....	....	....	....	....	....	....	....	....	....	....
2001-02	HPK Hameenlinna	Finland	56	19	37	56	50	....	....	....	....	....	....	....	....	....	8	2	4	6	8	....	....	....	....
2002-03	HPK Hameenlinna	Finland	53	25	25	50	54	....	....	....	....	....	....	....	....	....	10	1	7	8	29	....	....	....	....
2003-04	**Dallas**	**NHL**	**16**	**1**	**0**	**1**	**0**	**0**	**0**	**1**	**17**	**5.9**	**–9**	**1**	**0.0**	**9:51**	....	....	....	....	....	....	....	....	....
	Utah Grizzlies	AHL	48	7	23	30	20	....	....	....	....	....	....	....	....	....	....	....	....	....	....	....	....	....	....
2004-05	Hamilton	AHL	35	8	20	28	21	....	....	....	....	....	....	....	....	....	4	1	1	2	6	....	....	....	....
2005-06	**Dallas**	**NHL**	**79**	**11**	**20**	**31**	**46**	**4**	**0**	**1**	**107**	**10.3**	**0**	**1**	**100.0**	**12:06**	**5**	**0**	**1**	**1**	**8**	**0**	**0**	**0**	**12:10**
2006-07	**Dallas**	**NHL**	**74**	**11**	**14**	**25**	**38**	**6**	**0**	**1**	**141**	**7.8**	**–5**	**11**	**18.2**	**14:20**	**4**	**1**	**1**	**2**	**2**	**0**	**0**	**0**	**12:16**
2007-08	**Dallas**	**NHL**	**69**	**15**	**19**	**34**	**34**	**5**	**0**	**3**	**136**	**11.0**	**4**	**23**	**60.9**	**13:59**	**15**	**1**	**1**	**2**	**0**	**0**	**0**	**0**	**9:33**
	NHL Totals		**238**	**38**	**53**	**91**	**118**	**15**	**0**	**6**	**401**	**9.5**		**36**	**47.2**	**13:11**	**24**	**2**	**3**	**5**	**10**	**0**	**0**	**0**	**10:33**

Signed as a free agent by **Minnesota**, July 3, 2008.

MIKHNOV, Alexei

(MIHKH-nahf, al-EHX-ay) **EDM.**

Left wing. Shoots left. 6'5", 200 lbs. Born, Kiev, USSR, August 31, 1982. Edmonton's 1st choice, 17th overall, in 2000 Entry Draft.

1997-98	Yaroslavl	Russia	6	0	0	0	0	....	....	....	....	....	....	....	....	....	....	....	....	....	....	....	....	....	....
1998-99	Yaroslavl 2	Russia-3	14	2	2	4	4	....	....	....	....	....	....	....	....	....	....	....	....	....	....	....	....	....	....
99-2000	Yaroslavl 2	Russia-3	53	24	17	41	10	....	....	....	....	....	....	....	....	....	....	....	....	....	....	....	....	....	....
2000-01	HK Moscow	Russia-2	4	0	0	0	2	....	....	....	....	....	....	....	....	....	....	....	....	....	....	....	....	....	....
	THK Tver	Russia-2	22	5	11	16	6	....	....	....	....	....	....	....	....	....	....	....	....	....	....	....	....	....	....
2001-02	Dyn'o Moscow 2	Russia-3	8	8	6	14	0	....	....	....	....	....	....	....	....	....	....	....	....	....	....	....	....	....	....
	Dynamo Moscow	Russia	35	2	1	3	4	....	....	....	....	....	....	....	....	....	3	0	0	0	2	....	....	....	....
	Ufa	Russia	1	0	0	0	0	....	....	....	....	....	....	....	....	....	....	....	....	....	....	....	....	....	....
2002-03	Sibir Novosibirsk	Russia	51	7	9	16	10	....	....	....	....	....	....	....	....	....	....	....	....	....	....	....	....	....	....
2003-04	Sibir Novosibirsk	Russia	58	14	8	22	22	....	....	....	....	....	....	....	....	....	....	....	....	....	....	....	....	....	....
2004-05	Sibir Novosibirsk	Russia	26	2	3	5	12	....	....	....	....	....	....	....	....	....	....	....	....	....	....	....	....	....	....
	Yaroslavl 2	Russia-3	2	1	0	1	0	....	....	....	....	....	....	....	....	....	....	....	....	....	....	....	....	....	....
	Yaroslavl	Russia	18	0	9	9	4	....	....	....	....	....	....	....	....	....	7	0	0	0	4	....	....	....	....
2005-06	Yaroslavl	Russia	40	14	7	21	18	....	....	....	....	....	....	....	....	....	11	4	4	8	4	....	....	....	....

Season	Club	League	GP	G	A	Pts	PIM	PP	SH	GW	S	%	+/-	TF	F%	Min	GP	G	A	Pts	PIM	PP	SH	GW	Min
			Regular Season														Playoffs								
2006-07	Edmonton	NHL	2	0	0	0	0	0	0	0	0	0.0	0	0	0.0	6:52	....	....	....	....	....	....	....	....	....
	Wilkes-Barre	AHL	27	6	12	18	22	....	....	....	....	....	....	....	....	....	....	....	....	....	....	....	....	....	....
	Yaroslavl	Russia	11	5	3	8	6	....	....	....	....	....	....	....	....	....	7	2	3	5	4	....	....	....	....
2007-08	Yaroslavl	Russia	52	14	20	34	50	....	....	....	....	....	....	....	....	....	16	3	5	8	14	....	....	....	....
	NHL Totals		2	0	0	0	0	0	0	0	0	0.0		0	0.0	6:52	....	....	....	....	....	....	....	....	....

MILLER, Aaron

(MIHL-luhr, AIR-ruhn)

Defense. Shoots right. 6'3", 210 lbs. Born, Buffalo, NY, August 11, 1971. NY Rangers' 6th choice, 88th overall, in 1989 Entry Draft.

Season	Club	League	GP	G	A	Pts	PIM	PP	SH	GW	S	%	+/-	TF	F%	Min	GP	G	A	Pts	PIM	PP	SH	GW	Min
1987-88	Niagara Scenics	NAHL	30	4	9	13	2	....	....	....	....	....	....	....	....	....	....	....	....	....	....	....	....	....	....
1988-89	Niagara Scenics	NAHL	59	24	38	62	60	....	....	....	....	....	....	....	....	....	....	....	....	....	....	....	....	....	....
1989-90	U. of Vermont	ECAC	31	1	15	16	24	....	....	....	....	....	....	....	....	....	....	....	....	....	....	....	....	....	....
1990-91	U. of Vermont	ECAC	30	3	7	10	22	....	....	....	....	....	....	....	....	....	....	....	....	....	....	....	....	....	....
1991-92	U. of Vermont	ECAC	31	3	16	19	28	....	....	....	....	....	....	....	....	....	....	....	....	....	....	....	....	....	....
1992-93	U. of Vermont	ECAC	30	4	13	17	16	....	....	....	....	....	....	....	....	....	....	....	....	....	....	....	....	....	....
1993-94	Quebec	NHL	1	0	0	0	0	0	0	0	0	0.0	−1	....	....	....	....	....	....	....	....	....	....	....	....
	Cornwall Aces	AHL	64	4	10	14	49	....	....	....	....	....	....	....	....	....	13	0	2	2	10	....	....	....	....
1994-95	Cornwall Aces	AHL	76	4	18	22	69	....	....	....	....	....	....	....	....	....	....	....	....	....	....	....	....	....	....
	Quebec	NHL	9	0	3	3	6	0	0	0	12	0.0	2	....	....	....	....	....	....	....	....	....	....	....	....
1995-96	Colorado	NHL	5	0	0	0	0	0	0	0	2	0.0	0	....	....	....	....	....	....	....	....	....	....	....	....
	Cornwall Aces	AHL	62	4	23	27	77	....	....	....	....	....	....	....	....	....	8	0	1	1	6	....	....	....	....
1996-97	Colorado	NHL	56	5	12	17	15	0	0	3	47	10.6	15	....	....	....	17	1	2	3	10	0	0	0	....
1997-98	Colorado	NHL	55	2	2	4	51	0	0	0	29	6.9	0	....	....	....	7	0	0	0	8	0	0	0	....
1998-99	Colorado	NHL	76	5	13	18	42	1	0	2	87	5.7	3	0	0.0	21:49	19	1	5	6	10	0	0	0	21:13
99-2000	Colorado	NHL	53	1	7	8	36	0	0	0	44	2.3	3	0	0.0	19:05	17	1	1	2	6	0	0	0	19:12
2000-01	Colorado	NHL	56	4	9	13	29	0	0	0	49	8.2	19	0	0.0	18:25	....	....	....	....	....	....	....	....	....
	Los Angeles	NHL	13	0	5	5	14	0	0	0	10	0.0	3	1	0.0	22:44	13	0	1	1	6	0	0	0	22:02
2001-02	Los Angeles	NHL	74	5	12	17	54	0	1	3	75	6.7	14	0	0.0	22:21	7	0	0	0	0	0	0	0	26:28
	United States	Olympics	6	0	0	0	4	....	....	....	....	....	....	....	....	....	....	....	....	....	....	....	....	....	....
2002-03	Los Angeles	NHL	49	1	5	6	24	0	0	0	34	2.9	−7	1	100.0	21:30	....	....	....	....	....	....	....	....	....
2003-04	Los Angeles	NHL	35	1	2	3	32	0	0	0	26	3.8	−3	0	0.0	19:00	....	....	....	....	....	....	....	....	....
2004-05			DID NOT PLAY																						
2005-06	Los Angeles	NHL	56	0	8	8	27	0	0	0	32	0.0	−6	1	100.0	18:26	....	....	....	....	....	....	....	....	....
2006-07	Los Angeles	NHL	82	0	8	8	60	0	0	0	56	0.0	−14	1	0.0	19:36	....	....	....	....	....	....	....	....	....
2007-08	Vancouver	NHL	57	1	8	9	32	0	0	1	27	3.7	−1	0	0.0	17:20	....	....	....	....	....	....	....	....	....
	NHL Totals		677	25	94	119	422	1	1	9	530	4.7		4	50.0	19:57	80	3	9	12	40	0	0	0	21:27

ECAC First All-Star Team (1993) • NCAA East Second All-American Team (1993)

Traded to **Quebec** by **NY Rangers** with NY Rangers' 5th round choice (Bill Lindsay) in 1991 Entry Draft for Joe Cirella, January 17, 1991. Transferred to **Colorado** after **Quebec** franchise relocated, June 21, 1995. Traded to **Los Angeles** by **Colorado** with Adam Deadmarsh, a player to be named later (Jared Aulin, March 22, 2001) and Colorado's 1st round choices in 2001 (Dave Steckel) and 2003 (Brian Boyle) Entry Drafts for Rob Blake and Steve Reinprecht, February 21, 2001. • Missed majority of 2003-04 season recovering from cervical injury suffered in game vs. Atlanta, December 10, 2003. Signed as a free agent by **Vancouver**, July 9, 2007.

MILLER, Drew

(MIHL-luhr, DROO) **ANA.**

Left wing. Shoots left. 6'2", 174 lbs. Born, Dover, NJ, February 17, 1984. Anaheim's 6th choice, 186th overall, in 2003 Entry Draft.

Season	Club	League	GP	G	A	Pts	PIM	PP	SH	GW	S	%	+/-	TF	F%	Min	GP	G	A	Pts	PIM	PP	SH	GW	Min
2000-01	Capital Centre	NAHL	37	4	3	7	22	....	....	....	....	....	....	....	....	....	....	....	....	....	....	....	....	....	....
2001-02	Capital Centre	NAHL	54	18	16	34	56	....	....	....	....	....	....	....	....	....	....	....	....	....	....	....	....	....	....
2002-03	Capital Centre	NAHL	11	10	9	19	....	....	....	....	....	....	....	....	....	....	....	....	....	....	....	....	....	....	....
	River City Lancers	USHL	49	14	11	25	22	....	....	....	....	....	....	....	....	....	11	5	4	9	6	....	....	....	....
2003-04	Michigan State	CCHA	41	4	6	10	39	....	....	....	....	....	....	....	....	....	....	....	....	....	....	....	....	....	....
2004-05	Michigan State	CCHA	40	17	16	33	20	....	....	....	....	....	....	....	....	....	....	....	....	....	....	....	....	....	....
2005-06	Michigan State	CCHA	44	18	25	43	30	....	....	....	....	....	....	....	....	....	....	....	....	....	....	....	....	....	....
2006-07	Portland Pirates	AHL	79	16	20	36	51	....	....	....	....	....	....	....	....	....	....	....	....	....	....	....	....	....	....
	◆ Anaheim	NHL	....	....	....	....	....	....	....	....	....	....	....	....	....	....	3	0	0	0	2	0	0	0	7:00
2007-08	Anaheim	NHL	26	2	3	5	6	0	0	0	30	6.7	−1	9	33.3	11:11	....	....	....	....	....	....	....	....	....
	Portland Pirates	AHL	31	16	20	36	12	....	....	....	....	....	....	....	....	....	16	1	7	8	12	....	....	....	....
	NHL Totals		26	2	3	5	6	0	0	0	30	6.7		9	33.3	11:11	3	0	0	0	2	0	0	0	7:00

MILLEY, Norm

(MIHL-lee, NOHR-man)

Right wing. Shoots right. 6', 211 lbs. Born, Toronto, Ont., February 14, 1980. Buffalo's 3rd choice, 47th overall, in 1998 Entry Draft.

Season	Club	League	GP	G	A	Pts	PIM	PP	SH	GW	S	%	+/-	TF	F%	Min	GP	G	A	Pts	PIM	PP	SH	GW	Min
1995-96	Tor. Red Wings	MTHL	42	42	36	78	....	....	....	....	....	....	....	....	....	....	....	....	....	....	....	....	....	....	....
	St. Mike's B's	OPJHL	5	2	1	3	0	....	....	....	....	....	....	....	....	....	....	....	....	....	....	....	....	....	....
1996-97	Sudbury Wolves	OHL	61	30	32	62	15	....	....	....	....	....	....	....	....	....	....	....	....	....	....	....	....	....	....
1997-98	Sudbury Wolves	OHL	62	33	41	74	48	....	....	....	....	....	....	....	....	....	10	0	1	1	4	....	....	....	....
1998-99	Sudbury Wolves	OHL	68	52	68	120	47	....	....	....	....	....	....	....	....	....	4	2	3	5	4	....	....	....	....
99-2000	Sudbury Wolves	OHL	68	*52	60	112	47	....	....	....	....	....	....	....	....	....	12	8	11	19	6	....	....	....	....
2000-01	Rochester	AHL	77	20	27	47	56	....	....	....	....	....	....	....	....	....	4	0	0	0	2	....	....	....	....
2001-02	Buffalo	NHL	5	0	1	1	0	0	0	0	10	0.0	0	1	0.0	13:12	....	....	....	....	....	....	....	....	....
	Rochester	AHL	74	20	18	38	20	....	....	....	....	....	....	....	....	....	2	0	3	3	6	....	....	....	....
2002-03	Buffalo	NHL	8	0	2	2	6	0	0	0	8	0.0	−2	2	50.0	10:41	....	....	....	....	....	....	....	....	....
	Rochester	AHL	67	16	32	48	39	....	....	....	....	....	....	....	....	....	3	2	0	2	2	....	....	....	....
2003-04	Buffalo	NHL	2	0	0	0	2	0	0	0	2	0.0	0	0	0.0	8:20	....	....	....	....	....	....	....	....	....
	Rochester	AHL	77	18	19	37	60	....	....	....	....	....	....	....	....	....	16	7	6	13	10	....	....	....	....
2004-05	Rochester	AHL	72	12	21	33	46	....	....	....	....	....	....	....	....	....	9	1	2	3	4	....	....	....	....
2005-06	Tampa Bay	NHL	14	2	1	3	4	1	0	0	12	16.7	−2	0	0.0	7:09	....	....	....	....	....	....	....	....	....
	Springfield	AHL	53	19	29	48	34	....	....	....	....	....	....	....	....	....	....	....	....	....	....	....	....	....	....
2006-07	Springfield	AHL	73	26	34	60	46	....	....	....	....	....	....	....	....	....	....	....	....	....	....	....	....	....	....
2007-08	Norfolk Admirals	AHL	56	18	28	46	30	....	....	....	....	....	....	....	....	....	....	....	....	....	....	....	....	....	....
	NHL Totals		29	2	4	6	12	1	0	0	32	6.3		3	33.3	9:15	....	....	....	....	....	....	....	....	....

OHL All-Rookie Team (1997) • OHL Second All-Star Team (1999) • OHL First All-Star Team (2000) • Canadian Major Junior First All-Star Team (2000)

Signed as a free agent by **Tampa Bay**, August 18, 2005.

MILROY, Duncan

(MIHL-roi, DUHN-kuhn)

Right wing. Shoots right. 6', 195 lbs. Born, Edmonton, Alta., February 8, 1983. Montreal's 3rd choice, 37th overall, in 2001 Entry Draft.

Season	Club	League	GP	G	A	Pts	PIM	PP	SH	GW	S	%	+/-	TF	F%	Min	GP	G	A	Pts	PIM	PP	SH	GW	Min
1998-99	Edm. Maple Leafs	AMHL	34	34	36	70	73	....	....	....	....	....	....	....	....	....	....	....	....	....	....	....	....	....	....
	Swift Current	WHL	3	0	0	0	0	....	....	....	....	....	....	....	....	....	....	....	....	....	....	....	....	....	....
99-2000	Swift Current	WHL	68	15	15	30	20	....	....	....	....	....	....	....	....	....	12	3	5	8	12	....	....	....	....
2000-01	Swift Current	WHL	68	38	54	92	51	....	....	....	....	....	....	....	....	....	19	9	12	21	6	....	....	....	....
2001-02	Swift Current	WHL	26	20	11	31	20	....	....	....	....	....	....	....	....	....	....	....	....	....	....	....	....	....	....
	Kootenay Ice	WHL	38	25	31	56	24	....	....	....	....	....	....	....	....	....	22	*17	*20	*37	26	....	....	....	....
2002-03	Kootenay Ice	WHL	61	34	44	78	40	....	....	....	....	....	....	....	....	....	11	5	3	8	8	....	....	....	....
2003-04	Hamilton	AHL	50	4	10	14	14	....	....	....	....	....	....	....	....	....	10	3	1	4	4	....	....	....	....
2004-05	Hamilton	AHL	76	15	18	33	18	....	....	....	....	....	....	....	....	....	3	0	0	0	2	....	....	....	....
2005-06	Hamilton	AHL	77	16	19	35	63	....	....	....	....	....	....	....	....	....	....	....	....	....	....	....	....	....	....
2006-07	Montreal	NHL	5	0	1	1	0	0	0	0	6	0.0	−2	1	0.0	12:56	....	....	....	....	....	....	....	....	....
	Hamilton	AHL	64	25	33	58	24	....	....	....	....	....	....	....	....	....	22	2	11	13	10	....	....	....	....
2007-08	Hamilton	AHL	79	15	24	39	37	....	....	....	....	....	....	....	....	....	....	....	....	....	....	....	....	....	....
	NHL Totals		5	0	1	1	0	0	0	0	6	0.0		1	0.0	12:56	....	....	....	....	....	....	....	....	....

Yanick Dupre Memorial Award (Outstanding Humanitarian Contribution - AHL) (2005)

MINARD, Chris

(mih-NAHRD, KRIHS) **PIT.**

Center. Shoots left. 6'1", 190 lbs. Born, Thompson, Man., November 18, 1981.

			Regular Season														Playoffs								
Season	Club	League	GP	G	A	Pts	PIM	PP	SH	GW	S	%	+/-	TF	F%	Min	GP	G	A	Pts	PIM	PP	SH	GW	Min
1997-98	Owen Sound	OHL	9	0	1	1	1	....	....	....	....	....	....	....	....	....	1	0	0	0	2	....	....	....	....
1998-99	Owen Sound	OHL	43	6	9	15	18	....	....	....	....	....	....	....	....	....	....	....	....	....	....	....	....	....	....
99-2000	Owen Sound	OHL	38	12	14	26	39	....	....	....	....	....	....	....	....	....	....	....	....	....	....	....	....	....	....
	St. Michael's	OHL	28	5	14	19	6	....	....	....	....	....	....	....	....	....	....	....	....	....	....	....	....	....	....
2000-01	St. Michael's	OHL	40	11	8	19	28	....	....	....	....	....	....	....	....	....	....	....	....	....	....	....	....	....	....
	Oshawa Generals	OHL	28	12	12	24	18	....	....	....	....	....	....	....	....	....	....	....	....	....	....	....	....	....	....
2001-02	Oshawa Generals	OHL	67	36	35	71	20	....	....	....	....	....	....	....	....	....	5	2	3	5	6	....	....	....	....
2002-03	Pensacola	ECHL	72	15	17	32	71	....	....	....	....	....	....	....	....	....	4	0	0	0	6	....	....	....	....
2003-04	San Angelo Saints	CHL	64	39	36	75	51	....	....	....	....	....	....	....	....	....	5	1	1	2	2	....	....	....	....
2004-05	Alaska Aces	ECHL	69	*49	29	78	54	....	....	....	....	....	....	....	....	....	15	4	4	8	12	....	....	....	....
	Milwaukee	AHL	1	0	0	0	0	....	....	....	....	....	....	....	....	....	....	....	....	....	....	....	....	....	....
2005-06	Albany River Rats	AHL	37	7	12	19	26	....	....	....	....	....	....	....	....	....	....	....	....	....	....	....	....	....	....
	Alaska Aces	ECHL	33	26	16	42	38	....	....	....	....	....	....	....	....	....	22	*14	5	19	*54	....	....	....	....
2006-07	Lowell Devils	AHL	65	32	17	49	30	....	....	....	....	....	....	....	....	....	....	....	....	....	....	....	....	....	....
2007-08	**Pittsburgh**	**NHL**	**15**	**1**	**1**	**2**	**10**	**0**	**0**	**0**	**9**	**11.1**	**–1**	**0**	**0.0**	**3:53**	....	....	....	....	....	....	....	....	....
	Wilkes-Barre	AHL	56	25	17	42	33	....	....	....	....	....	....	....	....	....	23	11	6	17	10	....	....	....	....
	NHL Totals		**15**	**1**	**1**	**2**	**10**	**0**	**0**	**0**	**9**	**11.1**		**0**	**0.0**	**3:53**	....	....	....	....	....	....	....	....	....

Signed as a free agent by **Albany** (AHL), August 16, 2005. Signed as a free agent by **Pittsburgh**, July 12, 2007.

MINK, Graham

(MIHNK, GRAY-uhm) **WSH.**

Center. Shoots right. 6'3", 220 lbs. Born, Stowe, VT, May 21, 1979.

Season	Club	League	GP	G	A	Pts	PIM	PP	SH	GW	S	%	+/-	TF	F%	Min	GP	G	A	Pts	PIM	PP	SH	GW	Min
1997-98	NMH School	High-MA	25	17	25	42		....	....	....	....	....	....	....	....	....	....	....	....	....	....	....	....	....	....
1998-99	U. of Vermont	ECAC	27	4	2	6	34	....	....	....	....	....	....	....	....	....	....	....	....	....	....	....	....	....	....
99-2000	U. of Vermont	ECAC	17	7	4	11	14	....	....	....	....	....	....	....	....	....	....	....	....	....	....	....	....	....	....
2000-01	U. of Vermont	ECAC	32	17	12	29	52	....	....	....	....	....	....	....	....	....	....	....	....	....	....	....	....	....	....
2001-02	Richmond	ECHL	29	8	9	17	78	....	....	....	....	....	....	....	....	....	....	....	....	....	....	....	....	....	....
	Portland Pirates	AHL	56	17	17	34	50	....	....	....	....	....	....	....	....	....	....	....	....	....	....	....	....	....	....
2002-03	Portland Pirates	AHL	71	22	15	37	115	....	....	....	....	....	....	....	....	....	....	....	....	....	....	....	....	....	....
2003-04	**Washington**	**NHL**	**2**	**0**	**0**	**0**	**2**	**0**	**0**	**0**	**0**	**0.0**	**–1**	**1**	**0.0**	**5:32**	....	....	....	....	....	....	....	....	....
	Portland Pirates	AHL	68	18	19	37	74	....	....	....	....	....	....	....	....	....	3	0	1	1	4	....	....	....	....
2004-05	Portland Pirates	AHL	63	18	21	39	86	....	....	....	....	....	....	....	....	....	....	....	....	....	....	....	....	....	....
2005-06	**Washington**	**NHL**	**3**	**0**	**0**	**0**	**0**	**0**	**0**	**0**	**1**	**0.0**	**0**	**0**	**0.0**	**5:32**	....	....	....	....	....	....	....	....	....
	Hershey Bears	AHL	43	21	19	40	50	....	....	....	....	....	....	....	....	....	21	8	13	21	29	....	....	....	....
2006-07	Worcester Sharks	AHL	61	31	32	63	52	....	....	....	....	....	....	....	....	....	6	1	5	6	8	....	....	....	....
2007-08	Worcester Sharks	AHL	71	24	31	55	67	....	....	....	....	....	....	....	....	....	....	....	....	....	....	....	....	....	....
	NHL Totals		**5**	**0**	**0**	**0**	**2**	**0**	**0**	**0**	**1**	**0.0**		**1**	**0.0**	**5:32**	....	....	....	....	....	....	....	....	....

Signed as a free agent by **Portland** (AHL), September 30, 2001. Signed as a free agent by **Washington**, April 9, 2002. Signed as a free agent by **San Jose**, July 14, 2006. Signed as a free agent by **Washington**, July 2, 2008.

MITCHELL, Torrey

(MIH-chuhl, TOH-ree) **S.J.**

Center. Shoots right. 5'11", 190 lbs. Born, Montreal, Que., January 30, 1985. San Jose's 3rd choice, 126th overall, in 2004 Entry Draft.

Season	Club	League	GP	G	A	Pts	PIM	PP	SH	GW	S	%	+/-	TF	F%	Min	GP	G	A	Pts	PIM	PP	SH	GW	Min
2002-03	Hotchkiss	High-CT	26	19	30	49	33	....	....	....	....	....	....	....	....	....	....	....	....	....	....	....	....	....	....
2003-04	Hotchkiss	High-CT	25	25	37	62	42	....	....	....	....	....	....	....	....	....	....	....	....	....	....	....	....	....	....
2004-05	U. of Vermont	ECAC	38	11	19	30	74	....	....	....	....	....	....	....	....	....	....	....	....	....	....	....	....	....	....
2005-06	U. of Vermont	H-East	38	12	28	40	34	....	....	....	....	....	....	....	....	....	....	....	....	....	....	....	....	....	....
2006-07	U. of Vermont	H-East	39	12	23	35	46	....	....	....	....	....	....	....	....	....	....	....	....	....	....	....	....	....	....
	Worcester Sharks	AHL	11	2	5	7	27	....	....	....	....	....	....	....	....	....	6	1	1	2	15	....	....	....	....
2007-08	**San Jose**	**NHL**	**82**	**10**	**10**	**20**	**50**	**1**	**2**	**0**	**110**	**9.1**	**–3**	**692**	**49.4**	**14:19**	**13**	**1**	**2**	**3**	**10**	**1**	**0**	**0**	**14:00**
	NHL Totals		**82**	**10**	**10**	**20**	**50**	**1**	**2**	**0**	**110**	**9.1**		**692**	**49.4**	**14:19**	**13**	**1**	**2**	**3**	**10**	**1**	**0**	**0**	**14:00**

ECAC All-Rookie Team (2005)

MITCHELL, Willie

(MIH-chuhl, WIHL-lee) **VAN.**

Defense. Shoots left. 6'3", 210 lbs. Born, Port McNeill, B.C., April 23, 1977. New Jersey's 12th choice, 199th overall, in 1996 Entry Draft.

Season	Club	League	GP	G	A	Pts	PIM	PP	SH	GW	S	%	+/-	TF	F%	Min	GP	G	A	Pts	PIM	PP	SH	GW	Min
1993-94	Notre Dame	SMHL	31	4	11	15	81	....	....	....	....	....	....	....	....	....	....	....	....	....	....	....	....	....	....
1994-95	Kelowna Spartans	BCHL	42	3	8	11	71	....	....	....	....	....	....	....	....	....	....	....	....	....	....	....	....	....	....
1995-96	Melfort Mustangs	SJHL	19	2	6	8	....	....	....	....	....	....	....	....	....	....	14	0	2	2	12	....	....	....	....
1996-97	Melfort Mustangs	SJHL	64	14	42	56	227	....	....	....	....	....	....	....	....	....	4	0	1	1	23	....	....	....	....
1997-98	Clarkson Knights	ECAC	34	9	17	26	105	....	....	....	....	....	....	....	....	....	....	....	....	....	....	....	....	....	....
1998-99	Clarkson Knights	ECAC	34	10	19	29	40	....	....	....	....	....	....	....	....	....	....	....	....	....	....	....	....	....	....
	Albany River Rats	AHL	6	1	3	4	29	....	....	....	....	....	....	....	....	....	....	....	....	....	....	....	....	....	....
99-2000	**New Jersey**	**NHL**	**2**	**0**	**0**	**0**	**0**	**0**	**0**	**0**	**2**	**0.0**	**1**	**0**	**0.0**	**16:04**	....	....	....	....	....	....	....	....	....
	Albany River Rats	AHL	63	5	14	19	71	....	....	....	....	....	....	....	....	....	5	1	2	3	4	....	....	....	....
2000-01	**New Jersey**	**NHL**	**16**	**0**	**2**	**2**	**29**	**0**	**0**	**0**	**14**	**0.0**	**0**	**0**	**0.0**	**14:52**	....	....	....	....	....	....	....	....	....
	Albany River Rats	AHL	41	3	13	16	94	....	....	....	....	....	....	....	....	....	....	....	....	....	....	....	....	....	....
	Minnesota	**NHL**	**17**	**1**	**7**	**8**	**11**	**0**	**0**	**0**	**16**	**6.3**	**4**	**0**	**0.0**	**20:49**	....	....	....	....	....	....	....	....	....
2001-02	**Minnesota**	**NHL**	**68**	**3**	**10**	**13**	**68**	**0**	**0**	**1**	**67**	**4.5**	**–16**	**0**	**0.0**	**21:25**	....	....	....	....	....	....	....	....	....
2002-03	**Minnesota**	**NHL**	**69**	**2**	**12**	**14**	**84**	**0**	**1**	**1**	**67**	**3.0**	**13**	**0**	**0.0**	**21:28**	**18**	**1**	**3**	**4**	**14**	**0**	**0**	**0**	**24:48**
2003-04	**Minnesota**	**NHL**	**70**	**1**	**13**	**14**	**83**	**0**	**0**	**0**	**58**	**1.7**	**12**	**2**	**50.0**	**22:36**	....	....	....	....	....	....	....	....	....
2004-05			DID NOT PLAY																						
2005-06	**Minnesota**	**NHL**	**64**	**2**	**6**	**8**	**87**	**0**	**0**	**0**	**48**	**4.2**	**15**	**0**	**0.0**	**20:52**	....	....	....	....	....	....	....	....	....
	Dallas	**NHL**	**16**	**0**	**2**	**2**	**26**	**0**	**0**	**0**	**10**	**0.0**	**4**	**0**	**0.0**	**20:46**	**5**	**0**	**0**	**0**	**2**	**0**	**0**	**0**	**23:21**
2006-07	**Vancouver**	**NHL**	**62**	**1**	**10**	**11**	**45**	**0**	**0**	**0**	**54**	**1.9**	**1**	**0**	**0.0**	**22:13**	**12**	**0**	**1**	**1**	**12**	**0**	**0**	**0**	**27:14**
2007-08	**Vancouver**	**NHL**	**72**	**2**	**10**	**12**	**81**	**0**	**0**	**1**	**65**	**3.1**	**6**	**0**	**0.0**	**23:12**	....	....	....	....	....	....	....	....	....
	NHL Totals		**456**	**12**	**72**	**84**	**514**	**0**	**1**	**3**	**401**	**3.0**		**2**	**50.0**	**21:37**	**35**	**1**	**4**	**5**	**28**	**0**	**0**	**0**	**25:26**

SJHL First All-Star Team (1997) • SJHL Top Defenseman Award (1997) • ECAC Second All-Star Team (1998) • ECAC Rookie of the Year (1998) (co-winner - Erik Cole) • ECAC First All-Star Team (1999) • NCAA East Second All-American Team (1999)

Traded to **Minnesota** by **New Jersey** for Sean O'Donnell, March 4, 2001. Traded to **Dallas** by **Minnesota** with Minnesota's 2nd round choice (Nico Saccheti) in 2007 Entry Draft for Martin Skoula and Shawn Belle, March 9, 2006. Signed as a free agent by **Vancouver**, July 1, 2006.

MODANO, Mike

(moh-DA-noh, MIGHK) **DAL.**

Center. Shoots left. 6'3", 210 lbs. Born, Livonia, MI, June 7, 1970. Minnesota's 1st choice, 1st overall, in 1988 Entry Draft.

Season	Club	League	GP	G	A	Pts	PIM	PP	SH	GW	S	%	+/-	TF	F%	Min	GP	G	A	Pts	PIM	PP	SH	GW	Min
1985-86	Det. Compuware	MNHL	69	66	65	131	32	....	....	....	....	....	....	....	....	....	....	....	....	....	....	....	....	....	....
1986-87	Prince Albert	WHL	70	32	30	62	96	....	....	....	....	....	....	....	....	....	8	1	4	5	4	....	....	....	....
1987-88	Prince Albert	WHL	65	47	80	127	80	....	....	....	....	....	....	....	....	....	9	7	11	18	18	....	....	....	....
1988-89	Prince Albert	WHL	41	39	66	105	74	....	....	....	....	....	....	....	....	....	....	....	....	....	....	....	....	....	....
	Minnesota	**NHL**	....	....	....	....	....	....	....	....	....	....	....	....	....	....	**2**	**0**	**0**	**0**	**0**	**0**	**0**	**0**	....
1989-90	**Minnesota**	**NHL**	**80**	**29**	**46**	**75**	**63**	**12**	**0**	**2**	**172**	**16.9**	**–7**	....	....	....	**7**	**1**	**1**	**2**	**12**	**0**	**0**	**0**	....
1990-91	**Minnesota**	**NHL**	**79**	**28**	**36**	**64**	**65**	**9**	**0**	**2**	**232**	**12.1**	**2**	....	....	....	**23**	**8**	**12**	**20**	**16**	**3**	**0**	**1**	....
1991-92	**Minnesota**	**NHL**	**76**	**33**	**44**	**77**	**46**	**5**	**0**	**8**	**256**	**12.9**	**–9**	....	....	....	**7**	**3**	**2**	**5**	**4**	**1**	**0**	**0**	....
1992-93	**Minnesota**	**NHL**	**82**	**33**	**60**	**93**	**83**	**9**	**0**	**7**	**307**	**10.7**	**–7**	....	....	....	....	....	....	....	....	....	....	....	....
1993-94	**Dallas**	**NHL**	**76**	**50**	**43**	**93**	**54**	**18**	**0**	**4**	**281**	**17.8**	**–8**	....	....	....	**9**	**7**	**3**	**10**	**16**	**2**	**0**	**2**	....
1994-95	**Dallas**	**NHL**	**30**	**12**	**17**	**29**	**8**	**4**	**1**	**0**	**100**	**12.0**	**7**	....	....	....	....	....	....	....	....	....	....	....	....
1995-96	**Dallas**	**NHL**	**78**	**36**	**45**	**81**	**63**	**8**	**4**	**4**	**320**	**11.3**	**–12**	....	....	....	....	....	....	....	....	....	....	....	....
1996-97	**Dallas**	**NHL**	**80**	**35**	**48**	**83**	**42**	**9**	**5**	**9**	**291**	**12.0**	**43**	....	....	....	**7**	**4**	**1**	**5**	**0**	**1**	**1**	**2**	....
1997-98	**Dallas**	**NHL**	**52**	**21**	**38**	**59**	**32**	**7**	**5**	**2**	**191**	**11.0**	**25**	....	....	....	**17**	**4**	**10**	**14**	**12**	**1**	**0**	**1**	....
	United States	Olympics	4	2	0	2	0	....	....	....	....	....	....	....	....	....	....	....	....	....	....	....	....	....	....
1998-99 ♦	**Dallas**	**NHL**	**77**	**34**	**47**	**81**	**44**	**6**	**4**	**7**	**224**	**15.2**	**29**	**1572**	**51.1**	**20:50**	**23**	**5**	***18**	**23**	**16**	**1**	**1**	**1**	**24:40**
99-2000	**Dallas**	**NHL**	**77**	**38**	**43**	**81**	**48**	**11**	**1**	**8**	**188**	**20.2**	**0**	**1763**	**51.4**	**22:55**	**23**	**10**	***13**	**23**	**10**	**4**	**0**	**2**	**25:26**
2000-01	**Dallas**	**NHL**	**81**	**33**	**51**	**84**	**52**	**8**	**3**	**7**	**208**	**15.9**	**26**	**1791**	**52.0**	**22:24**	**9**	**3**	**4**	**7**	**0**	**2**	**0**	**0**	**25:43**
2001-02	**Dallas**	**NHL**	**78**	**34**	**43**	**77**	**38**	**6**	**2**	**5**	**219**	**15.5**	**14**	**1710**	**53.7**	**22:27**	....	....	....	....	....	....	....	....	....
	United States	Olympics	6	0	*6	6	4	....	....	....	....	....	....	....	....	....	....	....	....	....	....	....	....	....	....
2002-03	**Dallas**	**NHL**	**79**	**28**	**57**	**85**	**30**	**5**	**2**	**6**	**193**	**14.5**	**34**	**1808**	**51.4**	**20:53**	**12**	**5**	**10**	**15**	**4**	**1**	**0**	**2**	**23:53**
2003-04	**Dallas**	**NHL**	**76**	**14**	**30**	**44**	**46**	**6**	**0**	**0**	**152**	**9.2**	**–21**	**1523**	**52.6**	**20:27**	**5**	**1**	**2**	**3**	**8**	**1**	**0**	**0**	**23:17**

			Regular Season														Playoffs								
Season	Club	League	GP	G	A	Pts	PIM	PP	SH	GW	S	%	+/-	TF	F%	Min	GP	G	A	Pts	PIM	PP	SH	GW	Min
2004-05			DID NOT PLAY																						
2005-06	**Dallas**	**NHL**	**78**	**27**	**50**	**77**	**58**	**12**	**1**	**4**	**207**	**13.0**	**23**	**1421**	**51.1**	**19:34**	**5**	**1**	**3**	**4**	**4**	**1**	**0**	**0**	**22:14**
	United States	Olympics	6	2	0	2	6	....	....	....	....	....	....	....	....	....	....	....	....	....	....	....	....	....	....
2006-07	**Dallas**	**NHL**	**59**	**22**	**21**	**43**	**34**	**9**	**0**	**7**	**141**	**15.6**	**9**	**918**	**52.2**	**18:24**	**7**	**1**	**1**	**2**	**4**	**1**	**0**	**1**	**26:14**
2007-08	**Dallas**	**NHL**	**82**	**21**	**36**	**57**	**48**	**5**	**1**	**4**	**200**	**10.5**	**–11**	**1145**	**49.2**	**19:14**	**18**	**5**	**7**	**12**	**22**	**5**	**0**	**3**	**19:42**
	NHL Totals		**1320**	**528**	**755**	**1283**	**854**	**149**	**29**	**86**	**3882**	**13.6**		**13651**	**51.7**	**20:51**	**174**	**58**	**87**	**145**	**128**	**24**	**2**	**15**	**23:53**

WHL East First All-Star Team (1989) • NHL All-Rookie Team (1990) • NHL Second All-Star Team (2000)

Played in NHL All-Star Game (1993, 1998, 1999, 2000, 2003, 2004)

Transferred to **Dallas** after **Minnesota** franchise relocated, June 9, 1993.

MODIN, Fredrik

(moh-DEEN, FREHD-rihk) **CBJ**

Left wing. Shoots left. 6'4", 217 lbs. Born, Sundsvall, Sweden, October 8, 1974. Toronto's 3rd choice, 64th overall, in 1994 Entry Draft.

1991-92	Sundsvall/Timra	Sweden-2	11	1	0	1	0	....	....	....	....	....	....	....	....	....	....	....	....	....	....	....	....	....	....
1992-93	Sundsvall/Timra	Sweden-2	30	5	7	12	12	....	....	....	....	....	....	....	....	....	5	1	0	1	0	....	....	....	....
1993-94	Sundsvall/Timra	Sweden-2	30	16	15	31	36	....	....	....	....	....	....	....	....	....	2	0	1	1	6	....	....	....	....
1994-95	Brynas IF Gavle	Sweden	38	9	10	19	33	....	....	....	....	....	....	....	....	....	14	4	4	8	6	....	....	....	....
1995-96	Brynas IF Gavle	Sweden	22	4	8	12	22	....	....	....	....	....	....	....	....	....	....	....	....	....	....	....	....	....	....
1996-97	**Toronto**	**NHL**	**76**	**6**	**7**	**13**	**24**	**0**	**0**	**0**	**85**	**7.1**	**–14**	....	....	....	....	....	....	....	....	....	....	....	....
1997-98	**Toronto**	**NHL**	**74**	**16**	**16**	**32**	**32**	**1**	**0**	**4**	**137**	**11.7**	**–5**	....	....	....	....	....	....	....	....	....	....	....	....
1998-99	**Toronto**	**NHL**	**67**	**16**	**15**	**31**	**35**	**1**	**0**	**3**	**108**	**14.8**	**14**	**2**	**50.0**	**13:34**	**8**	**0**	**0**	**0**	**6**	**0**	**0**	**0**	**9:50**
99-2000	**Tampa Bay**	**NHL**	**80**	**22**	**26**	**48**	**18**	**3**	**0**	**5**	**167**	**13.2**	**–26**	**6**	**50.0**	**15:32**	....	....	....	....	....	....	....	....	....
2000-01	**Tampa Bay**	**NHL**	**76**	**32**	**24**	**56**	**48**	**8**	**0**	**4**	**217**	**14.7**	**–1**	**21**	**42.9**	**17:15**	....	....	....	....	....	....	....	....	....
2001-02	**Tampa Bay**	**NHL**	**54**	**14**	**17**	**31**	**27**	**2**	**0**	**4**	**141**	**9.9**	**0**	**25**	**40.0**	**19:05**	....	....	....	....	....	....	....	....	....
2002-03	**Tampa Bay**	**NHL**	**76**	**17**	**23**	**40**	**43**	**2**	**1**	**4**	**179**	**9.5**	**7**	**35**	**28.6**	**17:35**	**11**	**2**	**0**	**2**	**18**	**0**	**0**	**0**	**19:18**
2003-04♦	**Tampa Bay**	**NHL**	**82**	**29**	**28**	**57**	**32**	**5**	**1**	**2**	**206**	**14.1**	**31**	**138**	**38.4**	**18:12**	**23**	**8**	**11**	**19**	**10**	**3**	**0**	**2**	**20:47**
2004-05	Timra IK	Sweden	43	12	24	36	58	....	....	....	....	....	....	....	....	....	7	1	1	2	8	....	....	....	....
2005-06	**Tampa Bay**	**NHL**	**77**	**31**	**23**	**54**	**56**	**12**	**1**	**4**	**221**	**14.0**	**5**	**171**	**51.5**	**19:35**	**5**	**0**	**0**	**0**	**6**	**0**	**0**	**0**	**18:46**
	Sweden	Olympics	8	2	1	3	6	....	....	....	....	....	....	....	....	....	....	....	....	....	....	....	....	....	....
2006-07	**Columbus**	**NHL**	**79**	**22**	**20**	**42**	**50**	**6**	**0**	**4**	**220**	**10.0**	**–3**	**508**	**46.5**	**19:07**	....	....	....	....	....	....	....	....	....
2007-08	**Columbus**	**NHL**	**23**	**6**	**6**	**12**	**20**	**2**	**0**	**1**	**41**	**14.6**	**1**	**103**	**44.7**	**16:51**	....	....	....	....	....	....	....	....	....
	NHL Totals		**764**	**211**	**205**	**416**	**385**	**42**	**3**	**35**	**1722**	**12.3**		**1009**	**45.2**	**17:28**	**47**	**10**	**11**	**21**	**40**	**3**	**0**	**2**	**18:21**

Played in NHL All-Star Game (2001)

Traded to **Tampa Bay** by **Toronto** for Cory Cross and Tampa Bay's 7th round choice (Ivan Kolozvary) in 2001 Entry Draft, October 1, 1999. Signed as a free agent by **Timra** (Sweden), October 5, 2004. Traded to **Columbus** by **Tampa Bay** with Fredrik Norrena for Marc Denis, June 30, 2006. • Missed majority of 2007-08 season recovering from shoulder injury suffered in game at Anaheim, November 1, 2007.

MODRY, Jaroslav

(MOH-dree, YAHR-roh-slav)

Defense. Shoots left. 6'2", 220 lbs. Born, Ceske Budejovice, Czech., February 27, 1971. New Jersey's 11th choice, 179th overall, in 1990 Entry Draft.

1987-88	C. Budejovice	Czech	3	0	0	0	0	....	....	....	....	....	....	....	....	....	....	....	....	....	....	....	....	....	....
1988-89	C. Budejovice	Czech	28	0	1	1	8	....	....	....	....	....	....	....	....	....	....	....	....	....	....	....	....	....	....
1989-90	C. Budejovice	Czech	41	2	2	4	....	....	....	....	....	....	....	....	....	....	....	....	....	....	....	....	....	....	....
1990-91	Dukla Trencin	Czech	33	1	9	10	6	....	....	....	....	....	....	....	....	....	....	....	....	....	....	....	....	....	....
1991-92	C. Budejovice	Czech-2	14	4	10	14	....	....	....	....	....	....	....	....	....	....	....	....	....	....	....	....	....	....	....
	Dukla Trencin	Czech	18	0	4	4	6	....	....	....	....	....	....	....	....	....	....	....	....	....	....	....	....	....	....
1992-93	Utica Devils	AHL	80	7	35	42	62	....	....	....	....	....	....	....	....	....	5	0	2	2	2	....	....	....	....
1993-94	**New Jersey**	**NHL**	**41**	**2**	**15**	**17**	**18**	**2**	**0**	**0**	**35**	**5.7**	**10**	....	....	....	....	....	....	....	....	....	....	....	....
	Albany River Rats	AHL	19	1	5	6	25	....	....	....	....	....	....	....	....	....	....	....	....	....	....	....	....	....	....
1994-95	C. Budejovice	CzRep	19	1	3	4	30	....	....	....	....	....	....	....	....	....	....	....	....	....	....	....	....	....	....
	New Jersey	**NHL**	**11**	**0**	**0**	**0**	**0**	**0**	**0**	**0**	**10**	**0.0**	**–1**	....	....	....	....	....	....	....	....	....	....	....	....
	Albany River Rats	AHL	18	5	6	11	14	....	....	....	....	....	....	....	....	....	14	3	3	6	4	....	....	....	....
1995-96	**Ottawa**	**NHL**	**64**	**4**	**14**	**18**	**38**	**1**	**0**	**1**	**89**	**4.5**	**–17**	....	....	....	....	....	....	....	....	....	....	....	....
	Los Angeles	**NHL**	**9**	**0**	**3**	**3**	**6**	**0**	**0**	**0**	**17**	**0.0**	**–4**	....	....	....	....	....	....	....	....	....	....	....	....
1996-97	**Los Angeles**	**NHL**	**30**	**3**	**3**	**6**	**25**	**1**	**1**	**0**	**32**	**9.4**	**–13**	....	....	....	....	....	....	....	....	....	....	....	....
	Phoenix	IHL	23	3	12	15	17	....	....	....	....	....	....	....	....	....	....	....	....	....	....	....	....	....	....
	Utah Grizzlies	IHL	11	1	4	5	20	....	....	....	....	....	....	....	....	....	7	0	1	1	6	....	....	....	....
1997-98	Utah Grizzlies	IHL	74	12	21	33	72	....	....	....	....	....	....	....	....	....	4	0	2	2	6	....	....	....	....
1998-99	**Los Angeles**	**NHL**	**5**	**0**	**1**	**1**	**0**	**0**	**0**	**0**	**11**	**0.0**	**1**	**0**	**0.0**	**26:00**	....	....	....	....	....	....	....	....	....
	Long Beach	IHL	64	6	29	35	44	....	....	....	....	....	....	....	....	....	8	4	2	6	4	....	....	....	....
99-2000	**Los Angeles**	**NHL**	**26**	**5**	**4**	**9**	**18**	**5**	**0**	**1**	**32**	**15.6**	**–2**	**0**	**0.0**	**19:13**	**2**	**0**	**0**	**0**	**2**	**0**	**0**	**0**	**16:48**
	Long Beach	IHL	11	2	4	6	8	....	....	....	....	....	....	....	....	....	....	....	....	....	....	....	....	....	....
2000-01	**Los Angeles**	**NHL**	**63**	**4**	**15**	**19**	**48**	**0**	**0**	**0**	**72**	**5.6**	**16**	**0**	**0.0**	**18:22**	**10**	**1**	**0**	**1**	**4**	**1**	**0**	**1**	**16:08**
2001-02	**Los Angeles**	**NHL**	**80**	**4**	**38**	**42**	**65**	**4**	**0**	**0**	**119**	**3.4**	**–4**	**0**	**0.0**	**19:31**	**7**	**0**	**2**	**2**	**0**	**0**	**0**	**0**	**21:26**
2002-03	**Los Angeles**	**NHL**	**82**	**13**	**25**	**38**	**68**	**8**	**0**	**1**	**205**	**6.3**	**–13**	**1**	**0.0**	**22:39**	....	....	....	....	....	....	....	....	....
2003-04	**Los Angeles**	**NHL**	**79**	**5**	**27**	**32**	**44**	**1**	**0**	**1**	**196**	**2.6**	**11**	**1**	**0.0**	**24:24**	....	....	....	....	....	....	....	....	....
2004-05	Liberec	CzRep	19	3	7	10	24	....	....	....	....	....	....	....	....	....	12	0	4	4	22	....	....	....	....
2005-06	**Atlanta**	**NHL**	**79**	**7**	**31**	**38**	**76**	**5**	**0**	**2**	**143**	**4.9**	**–9**	**0**	**0.0**	**20:48**	....	....	....	....	....	....	....	....	....
2006-07	**Dallas**	**NHL**	**57**	**1**	**9**	**10**	**32**	**0**	**0**	**0**	**60**	**1.7**	**10**	**1**	**0.0**	**17:30**	....	....	....	....	....	....	....	....	....
	Los Angeles	**NHL**	**19**	**0**	**8**	**8**	**22**	**0**	**0**	**0**	**29**	**0.0**	**1**	**0**	**0.0**	**22:57**	....	....	....	....	....	....	....	....	....
2007-08	**Los Angeles**	**NHL**	**61**	**1**	**5**	**6**	**42**	**0**	**0**	**0**	**39**	**2.6**	**2**	**1**	**0.0**	**18:35**	....	....	....	....	....	....	....	....	....
	Philadelphia	**NHL**	**19**	**0**	**3**	**3**	**8**	**0**	**0**	**0**	**17**	**0.0**	**–11**	**0**	**0.0**	**20:38**	**9**	**0**	**3**	**3**	**0**	**0**	**0**	**0**	**19:50**
	NHL Totals		**725**	**49**	**201**	**250**	**510**	**27**	**1**	**6**	**1106**	**4.4**		**4**	**0.0**	**20:35**	**28**	**1**	**5**	**6**	**6**	**1**	**0**	**1**	**18:42**

Played in NHL All-Star Game (2002)

Traded to **Ottawa** by **New Jersey** for Ottawa's 4th round choice (Alyn McCauley) in 1995 Entry Draft, July 8, 1995. Traded to **Los Angeles** by **Ottawa** with Ottawa's 8th round choice (Stephen Valiquette) in 1996 Entry Draft for Kevin Brown, March 20, 1996. Signed as a free agent by **Atlanta**, July 1, 2004. Signed as a free agent by **Liberec** (CzRep), October 20, 2004. Traded to **Dallas** by **Atlanta** with Patrik Stefan for Niko Kapanen and Dallas's 7th round choice (Will O'Neill) in 2006 Entry Draft, June 24, 2006. Traded to **Los Angeles** by **Dallas** with the rights to Johan Fransson, Dallas' 2nd (Oscar Moller) and 3rd (Bryan Cameron) round choices in 2007 Entry Draft and Dallas' 1st round choice (later traded to Phoenix - Phoenix selected Viktor Tikhonov) in 2008 Entry Draft for Mattias Norstrom, Konstantin Pushkarev and Los Angeles' 3rd (Sergei Korostin) and 4th (later traded to Columbus - Columbus selected Maxim Mayorov) round choices in 2007 Entry Draft, February 27, 2007. Traded to **Philadelphia** by **Los Angeles** for Philadelphia's 3rd round choice (Geordie Wudrick) in 2008 Entry Draft, February 19, 2008. Signed as a free agent by **Liberec**, July 31, 2008.

MOEN, Travis

(MOH-ehn, TRA-vihs) **ANA.**

Left wing. Shoots left. 6'2", 215 lbs. Born, Stewart Valley, Sask., April 6, 1982. Calgary's 6th choice, 155th overall, in 2000 Entry Draft.

1998-99	Swift Current	SMHL	STATISTICS NOT AVAILABLE																						
	Kelowna Rockets	WHL	4	0	0	0	0	....	....	....	....	....	....	....	....	....	....	....	....	....	....	....	....	....	....
99-2000	Kelowna Rockets	WHL	66	9	6	15	96	....	....	....	....	....	....	....	....	....	5	1	1	2	2	....	....	....	....
2000-01	Kelowna Rockets	WHL	40	8	8	16	106	....	....	....	....	....	....	....	....	....	....	....	....	....	....	....	....	....	....
2001-02	Kelowna Rockets	WHL	71	10	17	27	197	....	....	....	....	....	....	....	....	....	13	1	0	1	28	....	....	....	....
2002-03	Norfolk Admirals	AHL	42	1	2	3	62	....	....	....	....	....	....	....	....	....	9	0	0	0	20	....	....	....	....
2003-04	**Chicago**	**NHL**	**82**	**4**	**2**	**6**	**142**	**0**	**0**	**2**	**51**	**7.8**	**–17**	**19**	**15.8**	**10:57**	....	....	....	....	....	....	....	....	....
2004-05	Norfolk Admirals	AHL	79	8	12	20	187	....	....	....	....	....	....	....	....	....	6	0	1	1	6	....	....	....	....
2005-06	**Anaheim**	**NHL**	**39**	**4**	**1**	**5**	**72**	**0**	**0**	**0**	**28**	**14.3**	**–3**	**8**	**12.5**	**11:03**	**9**	**1**	**0**	**1**	**10**	**0**	**0**	**0**	**8:25**
2006-07♦	**Anaheim**	**NHL**	**82**	**11**	**10**	**21**	**101**	**0**	**0**	**0**	**124**	**8.9**	**–4**	**10**	**30.0**	**14:48**	**21**	**7**	**5**	**12**	**22**	**0**	**0**	**3**	**17:19**
2007-08	**Anaheim**	**NHL**	**77**	**3**	**5**	**8**	**81**	**0**	**1**	**1**	**98**	**3.1**	**–10**	**25**	**32.0**	**15:50**	**6**	**1**	**1**	**2**	**2**	**0**	**0**	**0**	**14:09**
	NHL Totals		**280**	**22**	**18**	**40**	**396**	**0**	**1**	**3**	**301**	**7.3**		**62**	**24.2**	**13:26**	**36**	**9**	**6**	**15**	**34**	**0**	**0**	**3**	**14:34**

Signed as a free agent by **Chicago**, October 21, 2002. Traded to **Anaheim** by **Chicago** for Michael Holmqvist, July 30, 2005. • Missed majority of 2005-06 season recovering from knee and shoulder injuries and as a healthy reserve.

MOJZIS, Tomas

(MOI-shihsh, TAW-mash) **MIN.**

Defense. Shoots left. 6'1", 192 lbs. Born, Kolin, Czech., May 2, 1982. Toronto's 11th choice, 246th overall, in 2001 Entry Draft.

99-2000	HC Pardubice Jr.	CzRep-Jr.	40	7	1	8	....	....	....	....	....	....	....	....	....	....	....	....	....	....	....	....	....	....	....
2000-01	Moose Jaw	WHL	72	11	25	36	115	....	....	....	....	....	....	....	....	....	4	0	1	1	8	....	....	....	....
2001-02	Moose Jaw	WHL	28	2	11	13	43	....	....	....	....	....	....	....	....	....	....	....	....	....	....	....	....	....	....
	Seattle	WHL	36	8	15	23	66	....	....	....	....	....	....	....	....	....	11	1	3	4	20	....	....	....	....
2002-03	Seattle	WHL	62	21	49	70	126	....	....	....	....	....	....	....	....	....	15	1	6	7	36	....	....	....	....
2003-04	Manitoba Moose	AHL	63	5	13	18	50	....	....	....	....	....	....	....	....	....	....	....	....	....	....	....	....	....	....
2004-05	Manitoba Moose	AHL	80	7	23	30	62	....	....	....	....	....	....	....	....	....	14	0	2	2	28	....	....	....	....

			Regular Season														Playoffs								
Season	Club	League	GP	G	A	Pts	PIM	PP	SH	GW	S	%	+/-	TF	F%	Min	GP	G	A	Pts	PIM	PP	SH	GW	Min
2005-06	**Vancouver**	**NHL**	**7**	**0**	**1**	**1**	**12**	**0**	**0**	**0**	**7**	**0.0**	**2**	**0**	**0.0**	**13:57**	....	....	....	....	....	....	....	....	....
	Manitoba Moose	AHL	37	5	13	18	52	....	....	....	....	....	....	....	....	....	....	....	....	....	....	....	....	....	....
	Peoria Rivermen	AHL	12	3	4	7	14	....	....	....	....	....	....	....	....	....	1	0	0	0	0	....	....	....	....
2006-07	**St. Louis**	**NHL**	**6**	**1**	**0**	**1**	**0**	**0**	**0**	**0**	**7**	**14.3**	**0**	**0**	**0.0**	**10:03**	....	....	....	....	....	....	....	....	....
	Peoria Rivermen	AHL	69	2	24	26	112	....	....	....	....	....	....	....	....	....	....	....	....	....	....	....	....	....	....
2007-08	Sibir Novosibirsk	Russia	28	2	2	4	38	....	....	....	....	....	....	....	....	....	....	....	....	....	....	....	....	....	....
	NHL Totals		**13**	**1**	**1**	**2**	**12**	**0**	**0**	**0**	**14**	**7.1**		**0**	**0.0**	**12:09**	....	....	....	....	....	....	....	....	....

WHL West First All-Star Team (2003) • Canadian Major Junior First All-Star Team (2003)

Traded to **Vancouver** by **Toronto** for Brad Leeb, September 4, 2002. Traded to **St. Louis** by **Vancouver** with Vancouver's 3rd round choice (later traded to New Jersey - New Jersey selected Vladimir Zharkov) in 2006 Entry Draft for Eric Weinrich, March 9, 2006. Signed as a free agent by **Novosibirsk** (Russia), May 21, 2007. Signed as a free agent by **Minesota**, July 7, 2008.

MONTADOR, Steve

(MAWN-tuh-dohr, STEEV) **ANA.**

Defense. Shoots right. 6', 205 lbs. Born, Vancouver, B.C., December 21, 1979.

1995-96	St. Mike's B's	OPJHL	46	3	16	19	145	....	....	....	....	....	....	....	....	....	7	1	2	3	10	....	....	....	....
1996-97	North Bay	OHL	63	7	28	35	129	....	....	....	....	....	....	....	....	....	....	....	....	....	....	....	....	....	....
1997-98	North Bay	OHL	37	5	16	21	54	....	....	....	....	....	....	....	....	....	....	....	....	....	....	....	....	....	....
	Erie Otters	OHL	26	3	17	20	35	....	....	....	....	....	....	....	....	....	7	1	1	2	9	....	....	....	....
1998-99	Erie Otters	OHL	61	9	33	42	114	....	....	....	....	....	....	....	....	....	5	0	2	2	4	....	....	....	....
99-2000	Peterborough	OHL	64	14	42	56	97	....	....	....	....	....	....	....	....	....	5	0	2	2	4	....	....	....	....
	Saint John Flames	AHL	....	....	....	....	....	....	....	....	....	....	....	....	....	....	2	0	0	0	0	....	....	....	....
2000-01	Saint John Flames	AHL	58	1	6	7	95	....	....	....	....	....	....	....	....	....	19	0	8	8	13	....	....	....	....
2001-02	**Calgary**	**NHL**	**11**	**1**	**2**	**3**	**26**	**0**	**0**	**0**	**10**	**10.0**	**–2**	**0**	**0.0**	**12:12**	....	....	....	....	....	....	....	....	....
	Saint John Flames	AHL	67	9	16	25	107	....	....	....	....	....	....	....	....	....	....	....	....	....	....	....	....	....	....
2002-03	**Calgary**	**NHL**	**50**	**1**	**1**	**2**	**114**	**0**	**0**	**0**	**64**	**1.6**	**–9**	**0**	**0.0**	**15:11**	....	....	....	....	....	....	....	....	....
	Saint John Flames	AHL	11	1	7	8	20	....	....	....	....	....	....	....	....	....	....	....	....	....	....	....	....	....	....
2003-04	**Calgary**	**NHL**	**26**	**1**	**2**	**3**	**50**	**0**	**0**	**1**	**31**	**3.2**	**–1**	**1**	**0.0**	**11:46**	**20**	**1**	**2**	**3**	**6**	**0**	**0**	**1**	**17:43**
2004-05	HC Mulhouse	France	15	1	7	8	69	....	....	....	....	....	....	....	....	....	....	....	....	....	....	....	....	....	....
2005-06	**Calgary**	**NHL**	**7**	**1**	**0**	**1**	**11**	**0**	**0**	**0**	**13**	**7.7**	**0**	**0**	**0.0**	**11:49**	....	....	....	....	....	....	....	....	....
	Florida	**NHL**	**51**	**1**	**5**	**6**	**68**	**0**	**0**	**0**	**42**	**2.4**	**4**	**0**	**0.0**	**14:04**	....	....	....	....	....	....	....	....	....
2006-07	**Florida**	**NHL**	**72**	**1**	**8**	**9**	**119**	**0**	**0**	**0**	**88**	**1.1**	**1**	**0**	**0.0**	**13:08**	....	....	....	....	....	....	....	....	....
2007-08	**Florida**	**NHL**	**73**	**8**	**15**	**23**	**73**	**2**	**0**	**0**	**96**	**8.3**	**1**	**0**	**0.0**	**11:39**	....	....	....	....	....	....	....	....	....
	NHL Totals		**290**	**14**	**33**	**47**	**461**	**2**	**0**	**1**	**344**	**4.1**		**1**	**0.0**	**13:05**	**20**	**1**	**2**	**3**	**6**	**0**	**0**	**1**	**17:43**

Signed as a free agent by **Calgary**, April 10, 2000. • Spent majority of 2003-04 season as a healthy reserve. Signed as a free agent by **Mulhouse** (France), September 17, 2004. Traded to **Florida** by **Calgary** with Dustin Johner for Kristian Huselius, December 2, 2005. Signed as a free agent by **Anaheim**, July 11, 2008.

MOORE, Dominic

(MOOR, DOHM-ihn-ihk) **TOR.**

Center. Shoots left. 6', 190 lbs. Born, Sarnia, Ont., August 3, 1980. NY Rangers' 2nd choice, 95th overall, in 2000 Entry Draft.

1996-97	Thornhill Islanders	MTJHL	29	4	6	10	48	....	....	....	....	....	....	....	....	....	1	0	1	1	0	....	....	....	....
1997-98	Aurora Tigers	OPJHL	51	10	15	25	16	....	....	....	....	....	....	....	....	....	....	....	....	....	....	....	....	....	....
1998-99	Aurora Tigers	OPJHL	51	34	53	87	70	....	....	....	....	....	....	....	....	....	....	....	....	....	....	....	....	....	....
99-2000	Harvard Crimson	ECAC	30	12	24	28	16	....	....	....	....	....	....	....	....	....	....	....	....	....	....	....	....	....	....
2000-01	Harvard Crimson	ECAC	32	15	28	43	40	....	....	....	....	....	....	....	....	....	....	....	....	....	....	....	....	....	....
2001-02	Harvard Crimson	ECAC	32	13	16	29	37	....	....	....	....	....	....	....	....	....	....	....	....	....	....	....	....	....	....
2002-03	Harvard Crimson	ECAC	34	*24	27	*51	30	....	....	....	....	....	....	....	....	....	....	....	....	....	....	....	....	....	....
2003-04	**NY Rangers**	**NHL**	**5**	**0**	**3**	**3**	**0**	**0**	**0**	**0**	**3**	**0.0**	**0**	**36**	**30.6**	**9:18**	....	....	....	....	....	....	....	....	....
	Hartford	AHL	70	14	25	39	60	....	....	....	....	....	....	....	....	....	16	3	3	6	8	....	....	....	....
2004-05	Hartford	AHL	78	19	31	50	78	....	....	....	....	....	....	....	....	....	6	1	1	2	4	....	....	....	....
2005-06	**NY Rangers**	**NHL**	**82**	**9**	**9**	**18**	**28**	**2**	**0**	**1**	**139**	**6.5**	**4**	**814**	**46.3**	**12:28**	**4**	**0**	**0**	**0**	**2**	**0**	**0**	**0**	**11:21**
2006-07	**Pittsburgh**	**NHL**	**59**	**6**	**9**	**15**	**46**	**0**	**0**	**0**	**100**	**6.0**	**1**	**678**	**51.6**	**13:04**	....	....	....	....	....	....	....	....	....
	Minnesota	**NHL**	**10**	**2**	**0**	**2**	**10**	**0**	**0**	**1**	**11**	**18.2**	**3**	**66**	**62.1**	**10:12**	....	....	....	....	....	....	....	....	....
2007-08	**Minnesota**	**NHL**	**30**	**1**	**2**	**3**	**10**	**0**	**0**	**0**	**28**	**3.6**	**–11**	**311**	**52.4**	**11:57**	....	....	....	....	....	....	....	....	....
	Toronto	**NHL**	**38**	**4**	**10**	**14**	**14**	**1**	**0**	**0**	**72**	**5.6**	**7**	**393**	**50.6**	**14:21**	....	....	....	....	....	....	....	....	....
	NHL Totals		**224**	**22**	**33**	**55**	**108**	**3**	**0**	**2**	**353**	**6.2**		**2298**	**49.7**	**12:42**	**4**	**0**	**0**	**0**	**2**	**0**	**0**	**0**	**11:21**

ECAC All-Rookie Team (2000) • ECAC Second All-Star Team (2001) • ECAC First All-Star Team (2003) • NCAA East First All-American Team (2003)

Traded to **Nashville** by **NY Rangers** for Adam Hall, July 19, 2006. Traded to **Pittsburgh** by **Nashville** with Libor Pivko for Pittsburgh's 3rd round choice (Ryan Thang) in 2007 Entry Draft, July 19, 2006. Traded to **Minnesota** by **Pittsburgh** for Minnesota's 3rd round choice (Casey Pierro-Zabotel) in 2007 Entry Draft, February 27, 2007. Claimed on waivers by **Toronto** from **Minnesota**, January 11, 2008.

MOORE, Greg

(MOOR, GREHG) **NYR**

Right wing. Shoots right. 6'1", 210 lbs. Born, Lisbon, ME, March 26, 1984. Calgary's 5th choice, 143rd overall, in 2003 Entry Draft.

99-2000	St. Dominic	High-ME	31	32	40	72	....	....	....	....	....	....	....	....	....	....	....	....	....	....	....	....	....	....	....
2000-01	USNTDP	U-17	13	4	6	10	1	....	....	....	....	....	....	....	....	....	....	....	....	....	....	....	....	....	....
	USNTDP	NAHL	56	8	12	20	22	....	....	....	....	....	....	....	....	....	....	....	....	....	....	....	....	....	....
2001-02	USNTDP	U-18	35	8	20	28	14	....	....	....	....	....	....	....	....	....	....	....	....	....	....	....	....	....	....
	USNTDP	USHL	12	2	2	4	4	....	....	....	....	....	....	....	....	....	....	....	....	....	....	....	....	....	....
	USNTDP	NAHL	6	3	2	5	2	....	....	....	....	....	....	....	....	....	....	....	....	....	....	....	....	....	....
2002-03	U. of Maine	H-East	33	9	7	16	10	....	....	....	....	....	....	....	....	....	....	....	....	....	....	....	....	....	....
2003-04	U. of Maine	H-East	39	15	8	23	44	....	....	....	....	....	....	....	....	....	....	....	....	....	....	....	....	....	....
2004-05	U. of Maine	H-East	40	14	9	23	16	....	....	....	....	....	....	....	....	....	....	....	....	....	....	....	....	....	....
2005-06	U. of Maine	H-East	42	28	17	45	47	....	....	....	....	....	....	....	....	....	....	....	....	....	....	....	....	....	....
	Hartford	AHL	2	1	1	2	2	....	....	....	....	....	....	....	....	....	13	2	5	7	6	....	....	....	....
2006-07	Hartford	AHL	79	8	17	25	41	....	....	....	....	....	....	....	....	....	7	0	1	1	4	....	....	....	....
2007-08	**NY Rangers**	**NHL**	**6**	**0**	**0**	**0**	**0**	**0**	**0**	**0**	**13**	**0.0**	**–2**	**8**	**37.5**	**11:49**	....	....	....	....	....	....	....	....	....
	Hartford	AHL	72	26	40	66	31	....	....	....	....	....	....	....	....	....	5	1	2	3	2	....	....	....	....
	NHL Totals		**6**	**0**	**0**	**0**	**0**	**0**	**0**	**0**	**13**	**0.0**		**8**	**37.5**	**11:49**	....	....	....	....	....	....	....	....	....

Hockey East First All-Star Team (2006) • NCAA East First All-American Team (2006)

Traded to **NY Rangers** by **Calgary** with Jamie McLennan and Blair Betts for Chris Simon and NY Rangers' 7th round choice (Matt Schneider) in 2004 Entry Draft, March 6, 2004.

MORAN, Brad

(moh-RAN, BRAD)

Center. Shoots left. 5'11", 187 lbs. Born, Abbotsford, B.C., March 20, 1979. Buffalo's 8th choice, 191st overall, in 1998 Entry Draft.

1994-95	Abbotsford	Minor-BC	56	66	93	159	40	....	....	....	....	....	....	....	....	....	....	....	....	....	....	....	....	....	....
1995-96	Calgary Hitmen	WHL	70	13	31	44	28	....	....	....	....	....	....	....	....	....	....	....	....	....	....	....	....	....	....
1996-97	Calgary Hitmen	WHL	72	30	36	66	61	....	....	....	....	....	....	....	....	....	....	....	....	....	....	....	....	....	....
1997-98	Calgary Hitmen	WHL	72	53	49	102	64	....	....	....	....	....	....	....	....	....	18	10	8	18	20	....	....	....	....
1998-99	Calgary Hitmen	WHL	71	60	58	118	96	....	....	....	....	....	....	....	....	....	21	17	*25	42	26	....	....	....	....
99-2000	Calgary Hitmen	WHL	72	48	*72	*120	84	....	....	....	....	....	....	....	....	....	13	7	15	22	18	....	....	....	....
2000-01	Syracuse Crunch	AHL	71	11	19	30	30	....	....	....	....	....	....	....	....	....	5	3	4	7	2	....	....	....	....
2001-02	**Columbus**	**NHL**	**3**	**0**	**0**	**0**	**0**	**0**	**0**	**0**	**2**	**0.0**	**0**	**22**	**40.9**	**7:39**	....	....	....	....	....	....	....	....	....
	Syracuse Crunch	AHL	64	25	24	49	51	....	....	....	....	....	....	....	....	....	10	5	8	13	2	....	....	....	....
2002-03	Syracuse Crunch	AHL	47	12	19	31	22	....	....	....	....	....	....	....	....	....	....	....	....	....	....	....	....	....	....
2003-04	**Columbus**	**NHL**	**2**	**1**	**1**	**2**	**2**	**0**	**0**	**0**	**4**	**25.0**	**–1**	**25**	**64.0**	**10:03**	....	....	....	....	....	....	....	....	....
	Syracuse Crunch	AHL	72	24	35	59	44	....	....	....	....	....	....	....	....	....	7	5	3	8	2	....	....	....	....
2004-05	Syracuse Crunch	AHL	80	26	46	72	70	....	....	....	....	....	....	....	....	....	....	....	....	....	....	....	....	....	....
2005-06	Langnau	Swiss	18	4	4	8	18	....	....	....	....	....	....	....	....	....	6	4	6	10	10	....	....	....	....
2006-07	**Vancouver**	**NHL**	**3**	**0**	**1**	**1**	**2**	**0**	**0**	**0**	**3**	**0.0**	**0**	**24**	**58.3**	**12:38**	....	....	....	....	....	....	....	....	....
	Manitoba Moose	AHL	69	25	47	72	52	....	....	....	....	....	....	....	....	....	13	5	6	11	12	....	....	....	....
2007-08	Manitoba Moose	AHL	74	22	55	77	44	....	....	....	....	....	....	....	....	....	6	1	4	5	4	....	....	....	....
	NHL Totals		**8**	**1**	**2**	**3**	**4**	**0**	**0**	**0**	**9**	**11.1**		**71**	**54.9**	**10:07**	....	....	....	....	....	....	....	....	....

WHL East First All-Star Team (1999, 2000) • WHL Player of the Year (2000)

Signed as a free agent by **Columbus**, June 5, 2000. Signed as a free agent by **Vancouver**, June 19, 2006.

			Regular Season														Playoffs								
Season	Club	League	GP	G	A	Pts	PIM	PP	SH	GW	S	%	+/-	TF	F%	Min	GP	G	A	Pts	PIM	PP	SH	GW	Min

MOREAU, Ethan
(moh-ROH, EE-than) **EDM.**

Left wing. Shoots left. 6'2", 220 lbs. Born, Huntsville, Ont., September 22, 1975. Chicago's 1st choice, 14th overall, in 1994 Entry Draft.

1990-91	Orillia Terriers	OHA-B	42	17	22	39	26	....	....	....	....	....	....	....	....	....	12	6	6	12	18	....	....	....	....
1991-92	Niagara Falls	OHL	62	20	35	55	39	....	....	....	....	....	....	....	....	....	17	4	6	10	4	....	....	....	....
1992-93	Niagara Falls	OHL	65	32	41	73	69	....	....	....	....	....	....	....	....	....	4	0	3	3	4	....	....	....	....
1993-94	Niagara Falls	OHL	59	44	54	98	100	....	....	....	....	....	....	....	....	....	....	....	....	....	....	....	....	....	....
1994-95	Niagara Falls	OHL	39	25	41	66	69	....	....	....	....	....	....	....	....	....	....	....	....	....	....	....	....	....	....
	Sudbury Wolves	OHL	23	13	17	30	22	....	....	....	....	....	....	....	....	....	18	6	12	18	26	....	....	....	....
1995-96	**Chicago**	**NHL**	**8**	**0**	**1**	**1**	**4**	**0**	**0**	**0**	**1**	**0.0**	**1**	....	....	....	....	....	....	....	....	....	....	....	....
	Indianapolis Ice	IHL	71	21	20	41	126	....	....	....	....	....	....	....	....	....	5	4	0	4	8	....	....	....	....
1996-97	**Chicago**	**NHL**	**82**	**15**	**16**	**31**	**123**	**0**	**0**	**1**	**114**	**13.2**	**13**	....	....	....	**6**	**1**	**0**	**1**	**9**	**0**	**0**	**0**	....
1997-98	**Chicago**	**NHL**	**54**	**9**	**9**	**18**	**73**	**2**	**0**	**0**	**87**	**10.3**	**0**	....	....	....	....	....	....	....	....	....	....	....	....
1998-99	**Chicago**	**NHL**	**66**	**9**	**6**	**15**	**84**	**0**	**0**	**1**	**80**	**11.3**	**–5**	**3**	**33.3**	**12:30**	....	....	....	....	....	....	....	....	....
	Edmonton	**NHL**	**14**	**1**	**5**	**6**	**8**	**0**	**0**	**1**	**16**	**6.3**	**2**	**1**	**0.0**	**11:47**	**4**	**0**	**3**	**3**	**6**	**0**	**0**	**0**	**17:26**
99-2000	**Edmonton**	**NHL**	**73**	**17**	**10**	**27**	**62**	**1**	**0**	**3**	**106**	**16.0**	**8**	**8**	**62.5**	**15:07**	**5**	**0**	**1**	**1**	**0**	**0**	**0**	**0**	**15:46**
2000-01	**Edmonton**	**NHL**	**68**	**9**	**10**	**19**	**90**	**0**	**1**	**3**	**97**	**9.3**	**–6**	**2**	**0.0**	**14:11**	**4**	**0**	**0**	**0**	**2**	**0**	**0**	**0**	**10:35**
2001-02	**Edmonton**	**NHL**	**80**	**11**	**5**	**16**	**81**	**0**	**2**	**1**	**129**	**8.5**	**4**	**11**	**54.6**	**12:43**	....	....	....	....	....	....	....	....	....
2002-03	**Edmonton**	**NHL**	**78**	**14**	**17**	**31**	**112**	**2**	**3**	**2**	**137**	**10.2**	**–7**	**25**	**12.0**	**13:30**	**6**	**0**	**1**	**1**	**16**	**0**	**0**	**0**	**12:23**
2003-04	**Edmonton**	**NHL**	**81**	**20**	**12**	**32**	**96**	**0**	**3**	**5**	**180**	**11.1**	**7**	**59**	**44.1**	**15:04**	....	....	....	....	....	....	....	....	....
2004-05	EC Villacher SV	Austria	16	10	6	16	73	....	....	....	....	....	....	....	....	....	3	4	0	4	0	....	....	....	....
2005-06	**Edmonton**	**NHL**	**74**	**11**	**16**	**27**	**87**	**2**	**4**	**4**	**151**	**7.3**	**6**	**29**	**48.3**	**15:59**	**21**	**2**	**1**	**3**	**19**	**0**	**0**	**0**	**14:35**
2006-07	**Edmonton**	**NHL**	**7**	**1**	**0**	**1**	**12**	**0**	**0**	**0**	**18**	**5.6**	**–4**	**20**	**50.0**	**15:08**	....	....	....	....	....	....	....	....	....
2007-08	**Edmonton**	**NHL**	**25**	**5**	**4**	**9**	**39**	**1**	**0**	**0**	**54**	**9.3**	**–4**	**23**	**43.5**	**15:55**	....	....	....	....	....	....	....	....	....
	NHL Totals		**710**	**122**	**111**	**233**	**871**	**8**	**13**	**21**	**1170**	**10.4**		**181**	**41.4**	**14:12**	**46**	**3**	**6**	**9**	**52**	**0**	**0**	**0**	**14:17**

OHL All-Rookie Team (1992)

Traded to **Edmonton** by **Chicago** with Daniel Cleary, Chad Kilger and Christian Laflamme for Boris Mironov, Dean McAmmond and Jonas Elofsson, March 20, 1999. Signed as a free agent by **Villacher** (Austria), December 20, 2004. • Missed majority of 2006-07 season recovering from shoulder injury suffered in game vs. Detroit, October 21, 2006. • Missed majority of 2007-08 season recovering from fractured left foot injury suffered in training camp.

MORGAN, Gavin
(MOHR-guhn, GA-vihn)

Center. Shoots right. 5'11", 191 lbs. Born, Scarborough, Ont., July 9, 1976.

1992-93	Wexford Raiders	MTJHL	3	0	1	1	0	....	....	....	....	....	....	....	....	....	....	....	....	....	....	....	....	....	....
1993-94	Wexford Raiders	MTJHL	49	18	32	50	91	....	....	....	....	....	....	....	....	....	....	....	....	....	....	....	....	....	....
1994-95	Wexford Raiders	MTJHL	49	26	39	65	170	....	....	....	....	....	....	....	....	....	....	....	....	....	....	....	....	....	....
1995-96	U. of Denver	WCHA	28	2	9	11	47	....	....	....	....	....	....	....	....	....	....	....	....	....	....	....	....	....	....
1996-97	U. of Denver	WCHA	41	8	15	23	46	....	....	....	....	....	....	....	....	....	....	....	....	....	....	....	....	....	....
1997-98	U. of Denver	WCHA	37	9	8	17	42	....	....	....	....	....	....	....	....	....	....	....	....	....	....	....	....	....	....
1998-99	U. of Denver	WCHA	40	13	16	29	85	....	....	....	....	....	....	....	....	....	....	....	....	....	....	....	....	....	....
99-2000	Idaho Steelheads	WCHL	54	17	33	50	150	....	....	....	....	....	....	....	....	....	3	0	3	3	4	....	....	....	....
	Long Beach	IHL	7	0	1	1	10	....	....	....	....	....	....	....	....	....	....	....	....	....	....	....	....	....	....
	Utah Grizzlies	IHL	10	0	2	2	4	....	....	....	....	....	....	....	....	....	2	1	0	1	2	....	....	....	....
2000-01	Utah Grizzlies	IHL	79	7	14	21	187	....	....	....	....	....	....	....	....	....	....	....	....	....	....	....	....	....	....
2001-02	Utah Grizzlies	AHL	76	8	24	32	249	....	....	....	....	....	....	....	....	....	5	0	1	1	2	....	....	....	....
2002-03	Utah Grizzlies	AHL	73	15	24	39	244	....	....	....	....	....	....	....	....	....	2	0	1	1	17	....	....	....	....
2003-04	**Dallas**	**NHL**	**6**	**0**	**0**	**0**	**21**	**0**	**0**	**0**	**7**	**0.0**	**0**	**20**	**70.0**	**5:49**	....	....	....	....	....	....	....	....	....
	Hershey Bears	AHL	67	10	23	33	152	....	....	....	....	....	....	....	....	....	....	....	....	....	....	....	....	....	....
2004-05	Hamilton	AHL	76	10	23	33	147	....	....	....	....	....	....	....	....	....	4	0	0	0	6	....	....	....	....
2005-06	EHC Basel	Swiss	10	1	3	4	38	....	....	....	....	....	....	....	....	....	....	....	....	....	....	....	....	....	....
	Peoria Rivermen	AHL	73	18	22	40	116	....	....	....	....	....	....	....	....	....	4	0	1	1	6	....	....	....	....
2006-07	Peoria Rivermen	AHL	54	4	15	19	93	....	....	....	....	....	....	....	....	....	....	....	....	....	....	....	....	....	....
2007-08	Rockford IceHogs	AHL	47	2	9	11	95	....	....	....	....	....	....	....	....	....	11	1	1	2	24	....	....	....	....
	NHL Totals		**6**	**0**	**0**	**0**	**21**	**0**	**0**	**0**	**7**	**0.0**		**20**	**70.0**	**5:49**	....	....	....	....	....	....	....	....	....

Signed as a free agent by **Idaho** (WCHL), August 25, 1999. Signed as a free agent by **Utah** (IHL), June 26, 2000. Signed as a free agent by **Dallas**, July 17, 2001. Signed as a free agent by **Montreal**, July 26, 2004. Signed as a free agent by **Basel** (Swiss), August 29, 2005.

MORGAN, Jason
(MOHR-guhn, JAY-suhn)

Center. Shoots left. 6'1", 200 lbs. Born, St. John's, Nfld., October 9, 1976. Los Angeles' 5th choice, 118th overall, in 1995 Entry Draft.

1992-93	Kitchener AA	Minor-ON	69	44	40	84	85	....	....	....	....	....	....	....	....	....	....	....	....	....	....	....	....	....	....
1993-94	Kitchener Rangers	OHL	65	6	15	21	16	....	....	....	....	....	....	....	....	....	5	1	0	1	0	....	....	....	....
1994-95	Kitchener Rangers	OHL	35	3	15	18	25	....	....	....	....	....	....	....	....	....	....	....	....	....	....	....	....	....	....
	Kingston	OHL	20	0	3	3	14	....	....	....	....	....	....	....	....	....	6	0	2	2	0	....	....	....	....
1995-96	Kingston	OHL	66	16	38	54	50	....	....	....	....	....	....	....	....	....	6	1	2	3	0	....	....	....	....
1996-97	**Los Angeles**	**NHL**	**3**	**0**	**0**	**0**	**0**	**0**	**0**	**0**	**4**	**0.0**	**–3**	....	....	....	....	....	....	....	....	....	....	....	....
	Phoenix	IHL	57	3	6	9	29	....	....	....	....	....	....	....	....	....	....	....	....	....	....	....	....	....	....
	Mississippi	ECHL	6	3	0	3	0	....	....	....	....	....	....	....	....	....	3	1	1	2	6	....	....	....	....
1997-98	**Los Angeles**	**NHL**	**11**	**1**	**0**	**1**	**4**	**0**	**0**	**0**	**5**	**20.0**	**–7**	....	....	....	....	....	....	....	....	....	....	....	....
	Springfield	AHL	58	13	22	35	66	....	....	....	....	....	....	....	....	....	3	1	0	1	18	....	....	....	....
1998-99	Long Beach	IHL	13	4	6	10	18	....	....	....	....	....	....	....	....	....	....	....	....	....	....	....	....	....	....
	Springfield	AHL	46	6	16	22	51	....	....	....	....	....	....	....	....	....	3	0	0	0	6	....	....	....	....
99-2000	Cincinnati	IHL	15	1	3	4	14	....	....	....	....	....	....	....	....	....	....	....	....	....	....	....	....	....	....
	Florida Everblades	ECHL	48	14	25	39	79	....	....	....	....	....	....	....	....	....	5	2	2	4	16	....	....	....	....
2000-01	Florida Everblades	ECHL	37	15	22	37	41	....	....	....	....	....	....	....	....	....	5	2	3	5	17	....	....	....	....
	Hamilton	AHL	11	2	0	2	10	....	....	....	....	....	....	....	....	....	....	....	....	....	....	....	....	....	....
	Springfield	AHL	16	1	4	5	19	....	....	....	....	....	....	....	....	....	....	....	....	....	....	....	....	....	....
	Saint John Flames	AHL	....	....	....	....	....	....	....	....	....	....	....	....	....	....	6	0	1	1	2	....	....	....	....
2001-02	Saint John Flames	AHL	76	17	20	37	69	....	....	....	....	....	....	....	....	....	....	....	....	....	....	....	....	....	....
2002-03	Saint John Flames	AHL	80	13	40	53	63	....	....	....	....	....	....	....	....	....	....	....	....	....	....	....	....	....	....
2003-04	**Calgary**	**NHL**	**13**	**0**	**2**	**2**	**2**	**0**	**0**	**0**	**14**	**0.0**	**1**	**98**	**44.9**	**9:45**	....	....	....	....	....	....	....	....	....
	Lowell	AHL	21	6	13	19	16	....	....	....	....	....	....	....	....	....	....	....	....	....	....	....	....	....	....
	Nashville	**NHL**	**6**	**0**	**2**	**2**	**2**	**0**	**0**	**0**	**6**	**0.0**	**0**	**15**	**73.3**	**10:06**	....	....	....	....	....	....	....	....	....
	Norfolk Admirals	AHL	19	6	8	14	16	....	....	....	....	....	....	....	....	....	8	0	1	1	10	....	....	....	....
2004-05	Norfolk Admirals	AHL	71	9	20	29	116	....	....	....	....	....	....	....	....	....	6	2	2	4	8	....	....	....	....
2005-06	**Chicago**	**NHL**	**7**	**1**	**1**	**2**	**6**	**0**	**0**	**0**	**6**	**16.7**	**1**	**52**	**55.8**	**10:06**	....	....	....	....	....	....	....	....	....
	Norfolk Admirals	AHL	51	8	31	39	58	....	....	....	....	....	....	....	....	....	....	....	....	....	....	....	....	....	....
2006-07	**Minnesota**	**NHL**	**4**	**0**	**0**	**0**	**4**	**0**	**0**	**0**	**0**	**0.0**	**–1**	**25**	**56.0**	**7:29**	....	....	....	....	....	....	....	....	....
	Houston Aeros	AHL	57	12	14	26	73	....	....	....	....	....	....	....	....	....	....	....	....	....	....	....	....	....	....
2007-08	Hershey Bears	AHL	74	19	25	44	99	....	....	....	....	....	....	....	....	....	4	0	3	3	9	....	....	....	....
	NHL Totals		**44**	**2**	**5**	**7**	**18**	**0**	**0**	**0**	**35**	**5.7**		**190**	**51.6**	**9:36**	....	....	....	....	....	....	....	....	....

Signed to a PTO (tryout) contract by **Saint John** (AHL), April 22, 2001. Signed as a free agent by **Saint John** (AHL), August 28, 2001. Signed as a free agent by **Calgary**, July 11, 2002. Claimed on waivers by **Nashville** from **Calgary**, December 31, 2003. Claimed on waivers by **Calgary** from **Nashville**, February 19, 2004. Traded to **Chicago** by **Calgary** with Calgary's 6th round choice (Joseph Fallon) in 2005 Entry Draft for Ville Nieminen, February 24, 2004. Signed as a free agent by **Minnesota**, July 17, 2006. Signed as a free agent by **Washington**, July 17, 2007.

MORMINA, Joey
(mohr-MEE-nah, JOH-ee) **PIT.**

Defense. Shoots left. 6'6", 220 lbs. Born, Montreal, Que., June 29, 1982. Philadelphia's 6th choice, 193rd overall, in 2002 Entry Draft.

2000-01	Holderness	High-NH	29	15	15	30	....	....	....	....	....	....	....	....	....	....	....	....	....	....	....	....	....	....	....
2001-02	Colgate	ECAC	34	2	13	15	28	....	....	....	....	....	....	....	....	....	....	....	....	....	....	....	....	....	....
2002-03	Colgate	ECAC	40	4	9	13	52	....	....	....	....	....	....	....	....	....	....	....	....	....	....	....	....	....	....
2003-04	Colgate	ECAC	28	2	10	12	26	....	....	....	....	....	....	....	....	....	....	....	....	....	....	....	....	....	....
2004-05	Colgate	ECAC	39	8	8	16	50	....	....	....	....	....	....	....	....	....	....	....	....	....	....	....	....	....	....
2005-06	Manchester	AHL	61	0	13	13	70	....	....	....	....	....	....	....	....	....	7	0	0	0	4	....	....	....	....
2006-07	Manchester	AHL	62	2	9	11	108	....	....	....	....	....	....	....	....	....	1	0	0	0	2	....	....	....	....
2007-08	**Carolina**	**NHL**	**1**	**0**	**0**	**0**	**0**	**0**	**0**	**0**	**1**	**0.0**	**0**	**0**	**0.0**	**7:45**	....	....	....	....	....	....	....	....	....
	Albany River Rats	AHL	77	4	9	13	96	....	....	....	....	....	....	....	....	....	7	0	0	0	4	....	....	....	....
	NHL Totals		**1**	**0**	**0**	**0**	**0**	**0**	**0**	**0**	**1**	**0.0**		**0**	**0.0**	**7:45**	....	....	....	....	....	....	....	....	....

Signed as a free agent by **Los Angeles**, August 24, 2005. Signed as a free agent by **Carolina**, July 2, 2007. Signed as a free agent by **Pittsburgh**, July 10, 2008.

MORRIS, Derek

(MOH-rihs, DAIR-ihk) **PHX.**

Defense. Shoots right. 6', 220 lbs. Born, Edmonton, Alta., August 24, 1978. Calgary's 1st choice, 13th overall, in 1996 Entry Draft.

			Regular Season														Playoffs								
Season	Club	League	GP	G	A	Pts	PIM	PP	SH	GW	S	%	+/-	TF	F%	Min	GP	G	A	Pts	PIM	PP	SH	GW	Min
1994-95	Red Deer Vipers	AMHL	31	6	35	41	74																		
1995-96	Regina Pats	WHL	67	8	44	52	70										11	1	7	8	26				
1996-97	Regina Pats	WHL	67	18	57	75	180										5	0	3	3	9				
	Saint John Flames	AHL	7	0	3	3	7										5	0	3	3	7				
1997-98	**Calgary**	**NHL**	**82**	**9**	**20**	**29**	**88**	**5**	**1**	**1**	**120**	**7.5**	**1**												
1998-99	**Calgary**	**NHL**	**71**	**7**	**27**	**34**	**73**	**3**	**0**	**2**	**150**	**4.7**	**4**	**0**	**0.0**	**20:44**									
99-2000	**Calgary**	**NHL**	**78**	**9**	**29**	**38**	**80**	**3**	**0**	**2**	**193**	**4.7**	**2**	**0**	**0.0**	**24:51**									
2000-01	**Calgary**	**NHL**	**51**	**5**	**23**	**28**	**56**	**3**	**1**	**4**	**142**	**3.5**	**–15**	**0**	**0.0**	**25:51**									
	Saint John Flames	AHL	3	1	2	3	2																		
2001-02	**Calgary**	**NHL**	**61**	**4**	**30**	**34**	**88**	**2**	**0**	**1**	**166**	**2.4**	**–4**	**1**	**100.0**	**24:40**									
2002-03	**Colorado**	**NHL**	**75**	**11**	**37**	**48**	**68**	**9**	**0**	**7**	**191**	**5.8**	**16**	**0**	**0.0**	**23:49**	**7**	**0**	**3**	**3**	**6**	**0**	**0**	**0**	**22:44**
2003-04	**Colorado**	**NHL**	**69**	**6**	**22**	**28**	**47**	**2**	**0**	**1**	**139**	**4.3**	**4**	**0**	**0.0**	**20:53**									
	Phoenix	**NHL**	**14**	**0**	**4**	**4**	**2**	**0**	**0**	**0**	**28**	**0.0**	**–5**	**0**	**0.0**	**25:02**									
2004-05			DID NOT PLAY																						
2005-06	**Phoenix**	**NHL**	**53**	**6**	**21**	**27**	**54**	**4**	**1**	**2**	**91**	**6.6**	**–7**	**1**	**0.0**	**20:52**									
2006-07	**Phoenix**	**NHL**	**82**	**6**	**19**	**25**	**115**	**2**	**0**	**1**	**129**	**4.7**	**–18**	**1**	**100.0**	**20:29**									
2007-08	**Phoenix**	**NHL**	**82**	**8**	**17**	**25**	**83**	**2**	**0**	**0**	**135**	**5.9**	**8**	**1**	**0.0**	**21:43**									
	NHL Totals		**718**	**71**	**249**	**320**	**754**	**35**	**3**	**21**	**1484**	**4.8**		**4**	**50.0**	**22:36**	**7**	**0**	**3**	**3**	**6**	**0**	**0**	**0**	**22:44**

WHL East First All-Star Team (1997) • NHL All-Rookie Team (1998)

Traded to **Colorado** by **Calgary** with Jeff Shantz and Dean McAmmond for Chris Drury and Stephane Yelle, October 1, 2002. Traded to **Phoenix** by **Colorado** with Keith Ballard for Ossi Vaananen, Chris Gratton and Phoenix's 2nd round choice (Paul Stastny) in 2005 Entry Draft, March 9, 2004.

MORRISON, Brendan

(MOHR-ih-suhn, BREHN-duhn) **ANA.**

Center. Shoots left. 5'11", 181 lbs. Born, Pitt Meadows, B.C., August 15, 1975. New Jersey's 3rd choice, 39th overall, in 1993 Entry Draft.

Season	Club	League	GP	G	A	Pts	PIM	PP	SH	GW	S	%	+/-	TF	F%	Min	GP	G	A	Pts	PIM	PP	SH	GW	Min
1990-91	Ridge Meadows	Minor-BC	77	126	127	253	88																		
1991-92	Ridge Meadows	Minor-BC	55	56	111	167	56																		
1992-93	Penticton	BCJHL	56	35	59	94	45																		
1993-94	U. of Michigan	CCHA	38	20	28	48	24										5	2	7	9	2				
1994-95	U. of Michigan	CCHA	39	23	*53	*76	42										5	1	11	12	6				
1995-96	U. of Michigan	CCHA	35	28	44	*72	41										7	6	9	15	4				
1996-97	U. of Michigan	CCHA	43	31	*57	*88	52										6	6	8	14	8				
1997-98	**New Jersey**	**NHL**	**11**	**5**	**4**	**9**	**0**	**0**	**0**	**1**	**19**	**26.3**	**3**				**3**	**0**	**1**	**1**	**0**	**0**	**0**	**0**	
	Albany River Rats	AHL	72	35	49	84	44										8	3	4	7	19				
1998-99	**New Jersey**	**NHL**	**76**	**13**	**33**	**46**	**18**	**5**	**0**	**2**	**111**	**11.7**	**–4**	**920**	**51.1**	**13:55**	**7**	**0**	**2**	**2**	**0**	**0**	**0**	**0**	**13:04**
99-2000	Trebic	CzRep-2	2	0	0	0	0																		
	Pardubice	CzRep	6	5	2	7	2																		
	New Jersey	**NHL**	**44**	**5**	**21**	**26**	**8**	**2**	**0**	**1**	**79**	**6.3**	**8**	**572**	**51.1**	**16:09**									
	Vancouver	**NHL**	**12**	**2**	**7**	**9**	**10**	**0**	**0**	**0**	**17**	**11.8**	**4**	**48**	**54.2**	**14:41**									
2000-01	**Vancouver**	**NHL**	**82**	**16**	**38**	**54**	**42**	**3**	**2**	**3**	**179**	**8.9**	**2**	**1685**	**50.1**	**18:22**	**4**	**1**	**2**	**3**	**0**	**1**	**0**	**0**	**20:50**
2001-02	**Vancouver**	**NHL**	**82**	**23**	**44**	**67**	**26**	**6**	**0**	**4**	**183**	**12.6**	**18**	**1307**	**49.9**	**19:21**	**6**	**0**	**2**	**2**	**6**	**0**	**0**	**0**	**19:44**
2002-03	**Vancouver**	**NHL**	**82**	**25**	**46**	**71**	**36**	**6**	**2**	**8**	**167**	**15.0**	**18**	**1585**	**48.3**	**21:13**	**14**	**4**	**7**	**11**	**18**	**1**	**0**	**1**	**20:18**
2003-04	**Vancouver**	**NHL**	**82**	**22**	**38**	**60**	**50**	**5**	**1**	**4**	**161**	**13.7**	**16**	**1486**	**51.0**	**20:08**	**7**	**2**	**3**	**5**	**8**	**1**	**0**	**1**	**22:00**
2004-05	Linkopings HC	Sweden	45	16	28	44	50										6	0	2	2	10				
2005-06	**Vancouver**	**NHL**	**82**	**19**	**37**	**56**	**84**	**8**	**0**	**5**	**156**	**12.2**	**–1**	**1328**	**50.5**	**19:31**									
2006-07	**Vancouver**	**NHL**	**82**	**20**	**31**	**51**	**60**	**6**	**2**	**3**	**139**	**14.4**	**–9**	**1230**	**50.8**	**17:57**	**12**	**1**	**3**	**4**	**6**	**0**	**0**	**0**	**23:09**
2007-08	**Vancouver**	**NHL**	**39**	**9**	**16**	**25**	**18**	**3**	**0**	**3**	**54**	**16.7**	**–3**	**370**	**45.1**	**15:23**									
	NHL Totals		**674**	**159**	**315**	**474**	**352**	**44**	**7**	**34**	**1265**	**12.6**		**10531**	**50.0**	**18:15**	**53**	**8**	**20**	**28**	**38**	**3**	**0**	**2**	**20:11**

CCHA Rookie of the Year (1994) • CCHA First All-Star Team (1995, 1996, 1997) • NCAA West First All-American Team (1995, 1996, 1997) • CCHA Player of the Year (1996, 1997) • NCAA Championship All-Tournament Team (1996) • NCAA Championship Tournament MVP (1996) • Hobey Baker Memorial Award (Top U.S. Collegiate Player) (1997) • AHL All-Rookie Team (1998)

Traded to **Vancouver** by **New Jersey** with Denis Pederson for Alexander Mogilny, March 14, 2000. Signed as a free agent by **Linkopings** (Sweden), September, 2004. Signed as a free agent by **Anaheim**, July 8, 2008.

MORRISONN, Shaone

(MOHR-ih-suhn, SHAWN) **WSH.**

Defense. Shoots left. 6'4", 212 lbs. Born, Vancouver, B.C., December 23, 1982. Boston's 1st choice, 19th overall, in 2001 Entry Draft.

Season	Club	League	GP	G	A	Pts	PIM	PP	SH	GW	S	%	+/-	TF	F%	Min	GP	G	A	Pts	PIM	PP	SH	GW	Min
1997-98	Vancouver T-Birds	Minor-BC	45	16	44	60	75																		
1998-99	South Surrey	BCHL	19	0	2	2	13																		
99-2000	Kamloops Blazers	WHL	57	1	6	7	80										4	0	0	0	6				
2000-01	Kamloops Blazers	WHL	61	13	25	38	132										4	0	0	0	6				
2001-02	Kamloops Blazers	WHL	61	11	26	37	106										4	0	2	2	2				
2002-03	**Boston**	**NHL**	**11**	**0**	**0**	**0**	**8**	**0**	**0**	**0**	**4**	**0.0**	**0**	**0**	**0.0**	**8:57**									
	Providence Bruins	AHL	60	5	16	21	103										4	0	0	0	6				
2003-04	**Boston**	**NHL**	**30**	**1**	**7**	**8**	**10**	**0**	**0**	**0**	**13**	**7.7**	**10**	**0**	**0.0**	**18:11**									
	Providence Bruins	AHL	18	0	2	2	16																		
	Washington	**NHL**	**3**	**0**	**0**	**0**	**0**	**0**	**0**	**0**	**1**	**0.0**	**0**	**0**	**0.0**	**18:52**									
	Portland Pirates	AHL	13	1	4	5	10										7	0	1	1	4				
2004-05	Portland Pirates	AHL	71	4	14	18	63																		
2005-06	**Washington**	**NHL**	**80**	**1**	**13**	**14**	**91**	**0**	**0**	**0**	**56**	**1.8**	**7**	**4**	**0.0**	**20:44**									
2006-07	**Washington**	**NHL**	**78**	**3**	**10**	**13**	**106**	**0**	**0**	**0**	**46**	**6.5**	**3**	**2**	**0.0**	**20:57**									
2007-08	**Washington**	**NHL**	**76**	**1**	**9**	**10**	**63**	**0**	**0**	**1**	**47**	**2.1**	**4**	**1**	**100.0**	**20:16**	**7**	**0**	**1**	**1**	**6**	**0**	**0**	**0**	**21:18**
	NHL Totals		**278**	**6**	**39**	**45**	**278**	**0**	**0**	**1**	**167**	**3.6**		**7**	**14.3**	**19:54**	**7**	**0**	**1**	**1**	**6**	**0**	**0**	**0**	**21:18**

Traded to **Washington** by **Boston** with Boston's 1st (Jeff Schultz) and 2nd (Michail Yunkov) round choices in 2004 Entry Draft for Sergei Gonchar, March 3, 2004.

MORROW, Brenden

(MOHR-roh, BREHN-duhn) **DAL.**

Left wing. Shoots left. 5'11", 205 lbs. Born, Carlyle, Sask., January 16, 1979. Dallas' 1st choice, 25th overall, in 1997 Entry Draft.

Season	Club	League	GP	G	A	Pts	PIM	PP	SH	GW	S	%	+/-	TF	F%	Min	GP	G	A	Pts	PIM	PP	SH	GW	Min
1994-95	Estevan	SMBHL	60	117	72	189	45																		
1995-96	Portland	WHL	65	13	12	25	61										7	0	0	0	8				
1996-97	Portland	WHL	71	39	49	88	178										6	2	1	3	4				
1997-98	Portland	WHL	68	34	52	86	184										16	10	8	18	65				
1998-99	Portland	WHL	61	41	44	85	248										4	0	4	4	18				
99-2000	**Dallas**	**NHL**	**64**	**14**	**19**	**33**	**81**	**3**	**0**	**3**	**113**	**12.4**	**8**	**25**	**48.0**	**15:51**	**21**	**2**	**4**	**6**	**22**	**1**	**0**	**0**	**15:04**
	Michigan	IHL	9	2	0	2	18																		
2000-01	**Dallas**	**NHL**	**82**	**20**	**24**	**44**	**128**	**7**	**0**	**6**	**121**	**16.5**	**18**	**22**	**45.5**	**15:29**	**10**	**0**	**3**	**3**	**12**	**0**	**0**	**0**	**17:00**
2001-02	**Dallas**	**NHL**	**72**	**17**	**18**	**35**	**109**	**4**	**0**	**3**	**102**	**16.7**	**12**	**39**	**41.0**	**16:52**									
2002-03	**Dallas**	**NHL**	**71**	**21**	**22**	**43**	**134**	**2**	**3**	**4**	**105**	**20.0**	**20**	**29**	**27.6**	**15:43**	**12**	**3**	**5**	**8**	**16**	**2**	**0**	**0**	**21:03**
2003-04	**Dallas**	**NHL**	**81**	**25**	**24**	**49**	**121**	**9**	**0**	**3**	**132**	**18.9**	**10**	**38**	**47.4**	**19:24**	**5**	**0**	**1**	**1**	**4**	**0**	**0**	**0**	**21:29**
2004-05	Oklahoma City	CHL	19	8	14	22	31																		
2005-06	**Dallas**	**NHL**	**81**	**23**	**42**	**65**	**183**	**8**	**1**	**4**	**146**	**15.8**	**30**	**32**	**37.5**	**19:15**	**5**	**1**	**5**	**6**	**6**	**0**	**0**	**0**	**21:57**
2006-07	**Dallas**	**NHL**	**40**	**16**	**15**	**31**	**33**	**8**	**0**	**3**	**101**	**15.8**	**–2**	**51**	**39.2**	**18:16**	**7**	**2**	**1**	**3**	**18**	**2**	**0**	**1**	**21:54**
2007-08	**Dallas**	**NHL**	**82**	**32**	**42**	**74**	**105**	**12**	**2**	**7**	**207**	**15.5**	**23**	**41**	**39.0**	**20:00**	**18**	**9**	**6**	**15**	**22**	**4**	**0**	**2**	**23:17**
	NHL Totals		**573**	**168**	**206**	**374**	**894**	**53**	**6**	**33**	**1027**	**16.4**		**277**	**40.4**	**17:39**	**78**	**17**	**25**	**42**	**100**	**9**	**0**	**3**	**19:36**

WHL West First All-Star Team (1999)

Signed as a free agent by **Oklahoma City** (CHL), October 19, 2004. • Missed majority of 2006-07 season recovering from groin (November 22, 2006 vs. Nashville) and right wrist (December 26, 2006 at Chicago) injuries.

MOSS, Dave

(MAWS, DAYV) **CGY.**

Left wing. Shoots left. 6'3", 200 lbs. Born, Dearborn, MI, December 28, 1981. Calgary's 9th choice, 220th overall, in 2001 Entry Draft.

Season	Club	League	GP	G	A	Pts	PIM	PP	SH	GW	S	%	+/-	TF	F%	Min	GP	G	A	Pts	PIM	PP	SH	GW	Min
99-2000	Catholic Central	High-MI	28	18	20	28	20																		
2000-01	St. Louis Jr. Blues	CSJHL	9	2	2	4	2																		
	Cedar Rapids	USHL	51	20	18	38	14										4	0	1	1	2				
2001-02	U. of Michigan	CCHA	43	4	9	13	10																		
2002-03	U. of Michigan	CCHA	43	14	17	31	37																		
2003-04	U. of Michigan	CCHA	38	8	12	20	18																		

			Regular Season														Playoffs								
Season	Club	League	GP	G	A	Pts	PIM	PP	SH	GW	S	%	+/-	TF	F%	Min	GP	G	A	Pts	PIM	PP	SH	GW	Min
2004-05	U. of Michigan	CCHA	38	10	20	30	26	....	....	....	....	....	....	....	....	....	....	....	....	....	....	....	....	....	....
2005-06	Omaha	AHL	63	21	27	48	28	....	....	....	....	....	....	....	....	....	....	....	....	....	....	....	....	....	....
2006-07	**Calgary**	**NHL**	**41**	**10**	**8**	**18**	**12**	**3**	**0**	**1**	**70**	**14.3**	**5**	**11**	**36.4**	**11:13**	**6**	**0**	**1**	**1**	**0**	**0**	**0**	**0**	**10:30**
	Omaha	AHL	28	9	12	21	22	....	....	....	....	....	....	....	....	....	....	....	....	....	....	....	....	....	....
2007-08	**Calgary**	**NHL**	**41**	**4**	**7**	**11**	**10**	**0**	**0**	**0**	**60**	**6.7**	**–4**	**17**	**41.2**	**12:24**	**5**	**1**	**1**	**2**	**4**	**0**	**0**	**0**	**10:20**
	NHL Totals		**82**	**14**	**15**	**29**	**22**	**3**	**0**	**1**	**130**	**10.8**		**28**	**39.3**	**11:48**	**11**	**1**	**2**	**3**	**4**	**0**	**0**	**0**	**10:25**

MOTTAU, Mike
(MAW-tuh, MIGHK) **N.J.**

Defense. Shoots left. 6', 190 lbs. Born, Quincy, MA, March 19, 1978. NY Rangers' 10th choice, 182nd overall, in 1997 Entry Draft.

Season	Club	League	GP	G	A	Pts	PIM	PP	SH	GW	S	%	+/-	TF	F%	Min	GP	G	A	Pts	PIM	PP	SH	GW	Min
1994-95	Thayer Academy	High-MA	29	7	19	26	....	....	....	....	....	....	....	....	....	....	....	....	....	....	....	....	....	....	....
1995-96	Thayer Academy	High-MA	31	6	20	26	14	....	....	....	....	....	....	....	....	....	....	....	....	....	....	....	....	....	....
1996-97	Boston College	H-East	38	5	18	23	77	....	....	....	....	....	....	....	....	....	....	....	....	....	....	....	....	....	....
1997-98	Boston College	H-East	40	13	36	49	50	....	....	....	....	....	....	....	....	....	....	....	....	....	....	....	....	....	....
1998-99	Boston College	H-East	43	3	39	42	44	....	....	....	....	....	....	....	....	....	....	....	....	....	....	....	....	....	....
99-2000	Boston College	H-East	42	6	37	43	61	....	....	....	....	....	....	....	....	....	....	....	....	....	....	....	....	....	....
2000-01	**NY Rangers**	**NHL**	**18**	**0**	**3**	**3**	**13**	**0**	**0**	**0**	**17**	**0.0**	**–6**	**0**	**0.0**	**15:18**	....	....	....	....	....	....	....	....	....
	Hartford	AHL	61	10	33	43	45	....	....	....	....	....	....	....	....	....	5	0	1	1	19	....	....	....	....
2001-02	**NY Rangers**	**NHL**	**1**	**0**	**0**	**0**	**0**	**0**	**0**	**0**	**0**	**0.0**	**0**	**0**	**0.0**	**6:20**	....	....	....	....	....	....	....	....	....
	Hartford	AHL	80	9	42	51	56	....	....	....	....	....	....	....	....	....	10	0	5	5	4	....	....	....	....
2002-03	Hartford	AHL	29	1	18	19	24	....	....	....	....	....	....	....	....	....	....	....	....	....	....	....	....	....	....
	Calgary	**NHL**	**4**	**0**	**0**	**0**	**0**	**0**	**0**	**0**	**0**	**0.0**	**–1**	**0**	**0.0**	**9:50**	....	....	....	....	....	....	....	....	....
	Saint John Flames	AHL	32	5	12	17	14	....	....	....	....	....	....	....	....	....	....	....	....	....	....	....	....	....	....
2003-04	Cincinnati	AHL	69	9	22	31	79	....	....	....	....	....	....	....	....	....	9	1	2	3	8	....	....	....	....
2004-05	Worcester IceCats	AHL	73	4	31	35	23	....	....	....	....	....	....	....	....	....	....	....	....	....	....	....	....	....	....
2005-06	Peoria Rivermen	AHL	76	8	48	56	81	....	....	....	....	....	....	....	....	....	4	0	1	1	6	....	....	....	....
2006-07	Lowell Devils	AHL	43	1	26	27	33	....	....	....	....	....	....	....	....	....	....	....	....	....	....	....	....	....	....
2007-08	**New Jersey**	**NHL**	**76**	**4**	**13**	**17**	**48**	**1**	**0**	**1**	**68**	**5.9**	**–11**	**0**	**0.0**	**20:39**	**5**	**1**	**0**	**1**	**0**	**0**	**0**	**0**	**21:24**
	NHL Totals		**99**	**4**	**16**	**20**	**61**	**1**	**0**	**1**	**85**	**4.7**		**0**	**0.0**	**19:06**	**5**	**1**	**0**	**1**	**0**	**0**	**0**	**0**	**21:24**

Hockey East First All-Star Team (1998, 2000) • NCAA East Second All-American Team (1998) • NCAA Championship All-Tournament Team (1998, 2000) • Hockey East Second All-Star Team (1999) • NCAA East First All-American Team (1999, 2000) • Hockey East Player of the Year (2000) (co-winner - Ty Conklin) • Hobey Baker Memorial Award (Top U.S. Collegiate Player) (2000) • AHL All-Rookie Team (2001)

Traded to **Calgary** by **NY Rangers** for Calgary's 6th round choice (Ivan Dornic) in 2003 Entry Draft and future considerations, January 22, 2003. Signed as a free agent by **Anaheim**, July 25, 2003. Signed as a free agent by **Worcester** (AHL), September 30, 2004. Signed as a free agent by **New Jersey**, July 17, 2006.

MOTZKO, Joe
(MAWTS-koh, JOH) **ATL.**

Right wing. Shoots right. 6', 185 lbs. Born, Bemidji, MN, March 14, 1980.

Season	Club	League	GP	G	A	Pts	PIM	PP	SH	GW	S	%	+/-	TF	F%	Min	GP	G	A	Pts	PIM	PP	SH	GW	Min
1997-98	Bemidji Jacks	High-MN	25	24	28	52	....	....	....	....	....	....	....	....	....	....	....	....	....	....	....	....	....	....	....
1998-99	Omaha Lancers	USHL	51	15	21	36	60	....	....	....	....	....	....	....	....	....	12	7	3	10	12	....	....	....	....
99-2000	St. Cloud State	WCHA	36	9	15	24	52	....	....	....	....	....	....	....	....	....	....	....	....	....	....	....	....	....	....
2000-01	St. Cloud State	WCHA	41	17	20	37	54	....	....	....	....	....	....	....	....	....	....	....	....	....	....	....	....	....	....
2001-02	St. Cloud State	WCHA	39	9	30	39	34	....	....	....	....	....	....	....	....	....	....	....	....	....	....	....	....	....	....
2002-03	St. Cloud State	WCHA	38	17	25	42	59	....	....	....	....	....	....	....	....	....	....	....	....	....	....	....	....	....	....
	Syracuse Crunch	AHL	2	0	0	0	0	....	....	....	....	....	....	....	....	....	....	....	....	....	....	....	....	....	....
2003-04	**Columbus**	**NHL**	**2**	**0**	**0**	**0**	**0**	**0**	**0**	**0**	**1**	**0.0**	**0**	**0**	**0.0**	**7:16**	....	....	....	....	....	....	....	....	....
	Syracuse Crunch	AHL	70	17	24	41	38	....	....	....	....	....	....	....	....	....	7	2	2	4	6	....	....	....	....
2004-05	Syracuse Crunch	AHL	79	28	38	66	72	....	....	....	....	....	....	....	....	....	....	....	....	....	....	....	....	....	....
2005-06	**Columbus**	**NHL**	**2**	**0**	**0**	**0**	**0**	**0**	**0**	**0**	**3**	**0.0**	**–2**	**1**	**0.0**	**10:35**	....	....	....	....	....	....	....	....	....
	Syracuse Crunch	AHL	61	27	34	61	54	....	....	....	....	....	....	....	....	....	3	0	0	0	0	....	....	....	....
2006-07	**Columbus**	**NHL**	**7**	**1**	**0**	**1**	**0**	**0**	**0**	**0**	**10**	**10.0**	**0**	**1**	**0.0**	**6:27**	....	....	....	....	....	....	....	....	....
	Syracuse Crunch	AHL	33	13	23	36	29	....	....	....	....	....	....	....	....	....	....	....	....	....	....	....	....	....	....
	Portland Pirates	AHL	34	15	14	29	20	....	....	....	....	....	....	....	....	....	....	....	....	....	....	....	....	....	....
	♦ Anaheim	**NHL**	....	....	....	....	....	....	....	....	....	....	....	....	....	....	**3**	**0**	**0**	**0**	**2**	**0**	**0**	**0**	**3:55**
2007-08	**Washington**	**NHL**	**8**	**2**	**2**	**4**	**0**	**0**	**0**	**0**	**10**	**20.0**	**1**	**3**	**0.0**	**12:27**	....	....	....	....	....	....	....	....	....
	Hershey Bears	AHL	48	21	27	48	44	....	....	....	....	....	....	....	....	....	....	....	....	....	....	....	....	....	....
	Chicago Wolves	AHL	24	6	16	22	16	....	....	....	....	....	....	....	....	....	16	2	9	11	12	....	....	....	....
	NHL Totals		**19**	**3**	**2**	**5**	**0**	**0**	**0**	**0**	**24**	**12.5**		**5**	**0.0**	**9:30**	**3**	**0**	**0**	**0**	**2**	**0**	**0**	**0**	**3:55**

Signed as a free agent by **Columbus**, May 15, 2003. Traded to **Anaheim** by **Columbus** with Mark Hartigan and Columbus' 4th round choice (Sebastian Stefaniszin) in 2007 Entry Draft for Zenon Konopka, Curtis Glencross and Anaheim's 7th round choice (Trent Vogelhuber) in 2007 Entry Draft, January 26, 2007. Signed as a free agent by **Washington**, July 9, 2007. Traded to **Atlanta** by **Washington** for Alexandre Giroux, February 26, 2008.

MOULSON, Matt
(MOWL-suhn, MAT) **L.A.**

Left wing. Shoots left. 6'1", 205 lbs. Born, North York, Ont., November 1, 1983. Pittsburgh's 11th choice, 263rd overall, in 2003 Entry Draft.

Season	Club	League	GP	G	A	Pts	PIM	PP	SH	GW	S	%	+/-	TF	F%	Min	GP	G	A	Pts	PIM	PP	SH	GW	Min
2001-02	Guelph	OHA-B	42	56	46	102	80	....	....	....	....	....	....	....	....	....	....	....	....	....	....	....	....	....	....
2002-03	Cornell Big Red	ECAC	33	13	10	23	22	....	....	....	....	....	....	....	....	....	....	....	....	....	....	....	....	....	....
2003-04	Cornell Big Red	ECAC	32	18	17	35	37	....	....	....	....	....	....	....	....	....	....	....	....	....	....	....	....	....	....
2004-05	Cornell Big Red	ECAC	34	22	20	42	33	....	....	....	....	....	....	....	....	....	....	....	....	....	....	....	....	....	....
2005-06	Cornell Big Red	ECAC	35	18	20	38	14	....	....	....	....	....	....	....	....	....	....	....	....	....	....	....	....	....	....
2006-07	Manchester	AHL	77	25	32	57	23	....	....	....	....	....	....	....	....	....	16	2	3	5	8	....	....	....	....
2007-08	**Los Angeles**	**NHL**	**22**	**5**	**4**	**9**	**4**	**0**	**0**	**0**	**35**	**14.3**	**2**	**4**	**25.0**	**12:05**	....	....	....	....	....	....	....	....	....
	Manchester	AHL	57	28	28	56	29	....	....	....	....	....	....	....	....	....	4	2	0	2	4	....	....	....	....
	NHL Totals		**22**	**5**	**4**	**9**	**4**	**0**	**0**	**0**	**35**	**14.3**		**4**	**25.0**	**12:05**	....	....	....	....	....	....	....	....	....

ECAC First All-Star Team (2005) • NCAA East Second All-American Team (2005) • ECAC Second All-Star Team (2006)

Signed as a free agent by **Los Angeles**, September 1, 2006.

MOWERS, Mark
(MAH-wuhrs, MAHRK)

Center. Shoots right. 5'11", 174 lbs. Born, Decatur, GA, February 16, 1974.

Season	Club	League	GP	G	A	Pts	PIM	PP	SH	GW	S	%	+/-	TF	F%	Min	GP	G	A	Pts	PIM	PP	SH	GW	Min
1992-93	Saginaw Jr. Gears	NAHL	39	31	39	70	....	....	....	....	....	....	....	....	....	....	....	....	....	....	....	....	....	....	....
1993-94	Dubuque	USHL	47	51	31	82	80	....	....	....	....	....	....	....	....	....	....	....	....	....	....	....	....	....	....
1994-95	New Hampshire	H-East	36	13	23	36	16	....	....	....	....	....	....	....	....	....	....	....	....	....	....	....	....	....	....
1995-96	New Hampshire	H-East	34	21	26	47	18	....	....	....	....	....	....	....	....	....	....	....	....	....	....	....	....	....	....
1996-97	New Hampshire	H-East	39	26	32	58	52	....	....	....	....	....	....	....	....	....	....	....	....	....	....	....	....	....	....
1997-98	New Hampshire	H-East	35	25	31	56	32	....	....	....	....	....	....	....	....	....	....	....	....	....	....	....	....	....	....
1998-99	**Nashville**	**NHL**	**30**	**0**	**6**	**6**	**4**	**0**	**0**	**0**	**24**	**0.0**	**–4**	**241**	**49.0**	**9:22**	....	....	....	....	....	....	....	....	....
	Milwaukee	IHL	51	14	22	36	24	....	....	....	....	....	....	....	....	....	1	0	0	0	0	....	....	....	....
99-2000	**Nashville**	**NHL**	**41**	**4**	**5**	**9**	**10**	**0**	**0**	**0**	**50**	**8.0**	**0**	**312**	**45.2**	**10:58**	....	....	....	....	....	....	....	....	....
	Milwaukee	IHL	23	11	15	26	34	....	....	....	....	....	....	....	....	....	....	....	....	....	....	....	....	....	....
2000-01	Milwaukee	IHL	63	25	25	50	54	....	....	....	....	....	....	....	....	....	5	1	2	3	2	....	....	....	....
2001-02	**Nashville**	**NHL**	**14**	**1**	**2**	**3**	**2**	**0**	**0**	**0**	**5**	**20.0**	**–2**	**24**	**33.3**	**8:31**	....	....	....	....	....	....	....	....	....
	Milwaukee	AHL	45	19	20	39	34	....	....	....	....	....	....	....	....	....	....	....	....	....	....	....	....	....	....
2002-03	Grand Rapids	AHL	78	34	47	81	47	....	....	....	....	....	....	....	....	....	15	3	4	7	4	....	....	....	....
2003-04	**Detroit**	**NHL**	**52**	**3**	**8**	**11**	**4**	**1**	**0**	**1**	**48**	**6.3**	**3**	**400**	**47.8**	**10:27**	....	....	....	....	....	....	....	....	....
	Grand Rapids	AHL	16	8	6	14	4	....	....	....	....	....	....	....	....	....	....	....	....	....	....	....	....	....	....
2004-05	Malmo	Sweden	9	2	0	2	0	....	....	....	....	....	....	....	....	....	....	....	....	....	....	....	....	....	....
	Fribourg	Swiss	3	2	0	2	0	....	....	....	....	....	....	....	....	....	9	9	8	17	12	....	....	....	....
2005-06	**Detroit**	**NHL**	**46**	**4**	**11**	**15**	**16**	**0**	**0**	**0**	**65**	**6.2**	**13**	**100**	**52.0**	**8:18**	**3**	**0**	**0**	**0**	**0**	**0**	**0**	**0**	**9:27**
2006-07	**Boston**	**NHL**	**78**	**5**	**12**	**17**	**26**	**0**	**0**	**0**	**60**	**8.3**	**–10**	**593**	**45.0**	**12:00**	....	....	....	....	....	....	....	....	....
2007-08	**Anaheim**	**NHL**	**17**	**1**	**0**	**1**	**8**	**0**	**0**	**0**	**6**	**16.7**	**0**	**45**	**48.9**	**9:02**	....	....	....	....	....	....	....	....	....
	SC Bern	Swiss	10	2	4	6	8	....	....	....	....	....	....	....	....	....	....	....	....	....	....	....	....	....	....
	NHL Totals		**278**	**18**	**44**	**62**	**70**	**1**	**1**	**1**	**258**	**7.0**		**1715**	**46.6**	**10:18**	**3**	**0**	**0**	**0**	**0**	**0**	**0**	**0**	**9:27**

Hockey East Rookie of the Year (1995) • Hockey East Second All-Star Team (1998) • NCAA East First All-American Team (1998) • Ken McKenzie Trophy (U.S. - Born Rookie of the Year – IHL) (1999) • AHL Second All-Star Team (2003)

Signed as a free agent by **Nashville**, June 11, 1998. Signed as a free agent by **Detroit**, August 5, 2002. Signed as a free agent by **Malmo** (Sweden), December 21, 2004. Signed as a free agent by **Fribourg** (Swiss), February 4, 2005. Signed as a free agent by **Boston**, July 6, 2006. Traded to **Anaheim** by **Boston** for Nathan Saunders and Brett Skinner, September 24, 2007. • Assigned to **Bern** (Swiss) by **Anaheim**, December 1, 2007. • Missed majority of 2007-08 season as a healthy reserve.

MUELLER, Peter

(MEW-luhr, PEE-tuhr) **PHX.**

Center. Shoots right. 6'2", 205 lbs. Born, Bloomington, MN, April 14, 1988. Phoenix's 1st choice, 8th overall, in 2006 Entry Draft.

			Regular Season														Playoffs								
Season	Club	League	GP	G	A	Pts	PIM	PP	SH	GW	S	%	+/-	TF	F%	Min	GP	G	A	Pts	PIM	PP	SH	GW	Min
2003-04	USNTDP	U-17	17	4	9	13	25	....	....	....	....	....	....	....	....	....	....	....	....	....	....	....	....	....	....
	USNTDP	NAHL	43	10	16	26	26	....	....	....	....	....	....	....	....	....	7	3	2	5	4	....	....	....	....
2004-05	USNTDP	U-18	43	27	27	64	75	....	....	....	....	....	....	....	....	....	....	....	....	....	....	....	....	....	....
	USNTDP	NAHL	14	11	13	24	16	....	....	....	....	....	....	....	....	....	....	....	....	....	....	....	....	....	....
2005-06	Everett Silvertips	WHL	52	26	32	58	44	....	....	....	....	....	....	....	....	....	15	7	6	13	10	....	....	....	....
2006-07	Everett Silvertips	WHL	51	21	57	78	45	....	....	....	....	....	....	....	....	....	12	7	9	16	12	....	....	....	....
2007-08	**Phoenix**	**NHL**	**81**	**22**	**32**	**54**	**32**	**7**	**0**	**3**	**201**	**10.9**	**-13**	**251**	**41.8**	**17:16**	....	....	....	....	....	....	....	....	....
	NHL Totals		**81**	**22**	**32**	**54**	**32**	**7**	**0**	**3**	**201**	**10.9**		**251**	**41.8**	**17:16**	....	....	....	....	....	....	....	....	....

WHL Rookie ot the Year (2006) • WHL West First All-Star Team (2007)

MUIR, Bryan

(MEWR, BRIGH-uhn)

Defense. Shoots left. 6'3", 224 lbs. Born, Winnipeg, Man., June 8, 1973.

Season	Club	League	GP	G	A	Pts	PIM	PP	SH	GW	S	%	+/-	TF	F%	Min	GP	G	A	Pts	PIM	PP	SH	GW	Min
1991-92	Wexford Raiders	MTJHL	44	3	19	22	35	....	....	....	....	....	....	....	....	....	....	....	....	....	....	....	....	....	....
1992-93	New Hampshire	H-East	26	1	2	3	24	....	....	....	....	....	....	....	....	....	....	....	....	....	....	....	....	....	....
1993-94	New Hampshire	H-East	40	0	4	4	48	....	....	....	....	....	....	....	....	....	....	....	....	....	....	....	....	....	....
1994-95	New Hampshire	H-East	28	9	9	18	46	....	....	....	....	....	....	....	....	....	....	....	....	....	....	....	....	....	....
1995-96	Canada	Nat-Tm	42	6	12	18	38	....	....	....	....	....	....	....	....	....	....	....	....	....	....	....	....	....	....
	Edmonton	**NHL**	**5**	**0**	**0**	**0**	**6**	**0**	**0**	**0**	**4**	**0.0**	**-4**	....	....	....	....	....	....	....	....	....	....	....	....
1996-97	Hamilton	AHL	75	8	16	24	80	....	....	....	....	....	....	....	....	....	14	0	5	5	12	....	....	....	....
	Edmonton	**NHL**	....	....	....	....	....	....	....	....	....	....	....	....	....	....	**5**	**0**	**0**	**0**	**4**	**0**	**0**	**0**	....
1997-98	**Edmonton**	**NHL**	**7**	**0**	**0**	**0**	**17**	**0**	**0**	**0**	**6**	**0.0**	**0**	....	....	....	....	....	....	....	....	....	....	....	....
	Hamilton	AHL	28	3	10	13	62	....	....	....	....	....	....	....	....	....	....	....	....	....	....	....	....	....	....
	Albany River Rats	AHL	41	3	10	13	67	....	....	....	....	....	....	....	....	....	13	3	0	3	12	....	....	....	....
1998-99	**New Jersey**	**NHL**	**1**	**0**	**0**	**0**	**0**	**0**	**0**	**0**	**4**	**0.0**	**0**	**0**	**0.0**	**9:54**	....	....	....	....	....	....	....	....	....
	Albany River Rats	AHL	10	0	0	0	29	....	....	....	....	....	....	....	....	....	....	....	....	....	....	....	....	....	....
	Chicago	**NHL**	**53**	**1**	**4**	**5**	**50**	**0**	**0**	**0**	**78**	**1.3**	**1**	**0**	**0.0**	**18:49**	....	....	....	....	....	....	....	....	....
	Portland Pirates	AHL	2	1	1	2	2	....	....	....	....	....	....	....	....	....	....	....	....	....	....	....	....	....	....
99-2000	**Chicago**	**NHL**	**11**	**2**	**3**	**5**	**13**	**0**	**1**	**0**	**19**	**10.5**	**-1**	**0**	**0.0**	**17:54**	....	....	....	....	....	....	....	....	....
	Tampa Bay	**NHL**	**30**	**1**	**1**	**2**	**32**	**0**	**0**	**0**	**32**	**3.1**	**-8**	**1**	**100.0**	**19:29**	....	....	....	....	....	....	....	....	....
2000-01	**Tampa Bay**	**NHL**	**10**	**0**	**3**	**3**	**15**	**0**	**0**	**0**	**14**	**0.0**	**-7**	**1**	**0.0**	**18:34**	....	....	....	....	....	....	....	....	....
	Detroit Vipers	IHL	21	5	7	12	36	....	....	....	....	....	....	....	....	....	....	....	....	....	....	....	....	....	....
	♦ **Colorado**	**NHL**	**8**	**0**	**0**	**0**	**4**	**0**	**0**	**0**	**3**	**0.0**	**0**	**0**	**0.0**	**8:14**	**3**	**0**	**0**	**0**	**0**	**0**	**0**	**0**	**3:15**
	Hershey Bears	AHL	26	5	8	13	50	....	....	....	....	....	....	....	....	....	....	....	....	....	....	....	....	....	....
2001-02	♦ **Colorado**	**NHL**	**22**	**1**	**1**	**2**	**9**	**0**	**0**	**0**	**26**	**3.8**	**1**	**0**	**0.0**	**10:20**	**21**	**0**	**0**	**0**	**2**	**0**	**0**	**0**	**5:39**
	Hershey Bears	AHL	59	10	16	26	133	....	....	....	....	....	....	....	....	....	....	....	....	....	....	....	....	....	....
2002-03	**Colorado**	**NHL**	**32**	**0**	**2**	**2**	**19**	**0**	**0**	**0**	**9**	**0.0**	**3**	**0**	**0.0**	**6:33**	....	....	....	....	....	....	....	....	....
	Hershey Bears	AHL	36	9	12	21	75	....	....	....	....	....	....	....	....	....	5	2	6	8	6	....	....	....	....
2003-04	**Los Angeles**	**NHL**	**2**	**0**	**1**	**1**	**2**	**0**	**0**	**0**	**2**	**0.0**	**1**	**0**	**0.0**	**17:56**	....	....	....	....	....	....	....	....	....
	Manchester	AHL	73	13	37	50	141	....	....	....	....	....	....	....	....	....	6	2	3	5	12	....	....	....	....
2004-05	MODO	Sweden	26	1	5	6	36	....	....	....	....	....	....	....	....	....	....	....	....	....	....	....	....	....	....
	Blues Espoo	Finland	11	1	0	1	30	....	....	....	....	....	....	....	....	....	....	....	....	....	....	....	....	....	....
2005-06	**Washington**	**NHL**	**72**	**8**	**18**	**26**	**72**	**4**	**0**	**0**	**136**	**5.9**	**-9**	**1**	**100.0**	**21:10**	....	....	....	....	....	....	....	....	....
2006-07	**Washington**	**NHL**	**26**	**3**	**4**	**7**	**42**	**0**	**0**	**1**	**28**	**10.7**	**3**	**0**	**0.0**	**14:37**	....	....	....	....	....	....	....	....	....
2007-08	Toronto Marlies	AHL	50	4	14	18	54	....	....	....	....	....	....	....	....	....	18	0	2	2	37	....	....	....	....
	NHL Totals		**279**	**16**	**37**	**53**	**281**	**4**	**1**	**1**	**361**	**4.4**		**3**	**66.7**	**16:33**	**29**	**0**	**0**	**0**	**6**	**0**	**0**	**0**	**5:21**

AHL First All-Star Team (2004)

Signed to five-game ATO (tryout) contract by **Edmonton**, February 29, 1996. Signed as a free agent by **Edmonton**, April 30, 1996. Traded to **New Jersey** by **Edmonton** with Jason Arnott for Valeri Zelepukin and Bill Guerin, January 4, 1998. Traded to **Chicago** by **New Jersey** for Chicago's 3rd round choice (Mike Rupp) in 2000 Entry Draft, November 13, 1998. Traded to **Tampa Bay** by **Chicago** with Reid Simpson for Michael Nylander, November 12, 1999. • Missed majority of 1999-2000 season recovering from leg injury suffered in game vs. Atlanta, November 17, 1999. Traded to **Colorado** by **Tampa Bay** for Colorado's 8th round choice (Dmitri Bezrukov) in 2001 Entry Draft, January 23, 2001. Signed as a free agent by **Los Angeles**, July 31, 2003. Signed as a free agent by **MODO** (Sweden), July 26, 2004. Signed as a free agent by **Espoo** (Finland), January 31, 2005. Signed as a free agent by **Washington**, August 30, 2005. • Missed majority of 2006-07 season recovering from foot injury and as a healthy reserve.

MURLEY, Matt

(MUHR-lee, MAT)

Left wing. Shoots left. 6'1", 206 lbs. Born, Troy, NY, December 17, 1979. Pittsburgh's 2nd choice, 51st overall, in 1999 Entry Draft.

Season	Club	League	GP	G	A	Pts	PIM	PP	SH	GW	S	%	+/-	TF	F%	Min	GP	G	A	Pts	PIM	PP	SH	GW	Min
1996-97	Syracuse	MTJHL	48	52	58	110	111	....	....	....	....	....	....	....	....	....	....	....	....	....	....	....	....	....	....
1997-98	Syracuse	MTJHL	49	56	70	126	103	....	....	....	....	....	....	....	....	....	....	....	....	....	....	....	....	....	....
1998-99	RPI Engineers	ECAC	36	17	32	49	32	....	....	....	....	....	....	....	....	....	....	....	....	....	....	....	....	....	....
99-2000	RPI Engineers	ECAC	35	9	29	38	42	....	....	....	....	....	....	....	....	....	....	....	....	....	....	....	....	....	....
2000-01	RPI Engineers	ECAC	34	*24	18	42	34	....	....	....	....	....	....	....	....	....	....	....	....	....	....	....	....	....	....
2001-02	RPI Engineers	ECAC	32	*24	22	46	26	....	....	....	....	....	....	....	....	....	....	....	....	....	....	....	....	....	....
2002-03	Wilkes-Barre	AHL	73	21	37	58	45	....	....	....	....	....	....	....	....	....	6	0	2	2	15	....	....	....	....
2003-04	**Pittsburgh**	**NHL**	**18**	**1**	**1**	**2**	**14**	**0**	**0**	**0**	**20**	**5.0**	**-6**	**2**	**50.0**	**11:49**	....	....	....	....	....	....	....	....	....
	Wilkes-Barre	AHL	63	10	26	36	69	....	....	....	....	....	....	....	....	....	24	7	6	13	17	....	....	....	....
2004-05	Wilkes-Barre	AHL	80	17	24	41	55	....	....	....	....	....	....	....	....	....	11	3	0	3	0	....	....	....	....
2005-06	**Pittsburgh**	**NHL**	**41**	**1**	**5**	**6**	**24**	**0**	**0**	**0**	**48**	**2.1**	**-9**	**11**	**36.4**	**11:29**	....	....	....	....	....	....	....	....	....
2006-07	Albany River Rats	AHL	61	23	32	55	18	....	....	....	....	....	....	....	....	....	5	1	5	6	8	....	....	....	....
2007-08	**Phoenix**	**NHL**	**3**	**0**	**1**	**1**	**0**	**0**	**0**	**0**	**3**	**0.0**	**1**	**3**	**66.7**	**11:44**	....	....	....	....	....	....	....	....	....
	San Antonio	AHL	76	21	41	62	43	....	....	....	....	....	....	....	....	....	7	2	2	4	0	....	....	....	....
	NHL Totals		**62**	**2**	**7**	**9**	**38**	**0**	**0**	**0**	**71**	**2.8**		**16**	**43.8**	**11:35**	....	....	....	....	....	....	....	....	....

ECAC First All-Star Team (2002)

Signed as a free agent by **Colorado**, July 12, 2006. Signed as a free agent by **Phoenix**, July 20, 2007.

MURPHY, Cory

(MUHR-fee, KOH-ree) **FLA.**

Defense. Shoots left. 5'10", 185 lbs. Born, Kanata, Ont., February 13, 1978.

Season	Club	League	GP	G	A	Pts	PIM	PP	SH	GW	S	%	+/-	TF	F%	Min	GP	G	A	Pts	PIM	PP	SH	GW	Min
1997-98	Colgate	ECAC	35	8	19	27	38	....	....	....	....	....	....	....	....	....	....	....	....	....	....	....	....	....	....
1998-99	Colgate	ECAC	34	3	23	26	26	....	....	....	....	....	....	....	....	....	....	....	....	....	....	....	....	....	....
99-2000	Colgate	ECAC	35	10	19	29	26	....	....	....	....	....	....	....	....	....	....	....	....	....	....	....	....	....	....
2000-01	Colgate	ECAC	34	7	22	29	34	....	....	....	....	....	....	....	....	....	....	....	....	....	....	....	....	....	....
2001-02	Blues Espoo	Finland	46	9	15	24	38	....	....	....	....	....	....	....	....	....	3	0	1	1	0	....	....	....	....
2002-03	Blues Espoo	Finland	45	11	4	15	49	....	....	....	....	....	....	....	....	....	7	1	0	1	2	....	....	....	....
2003-04	Ilves Tampere	Finland	56	18	26	44	22	....	....	....	....	....	....	....	....	....	7	1	2	3	2	....	....	....	....
2004-05	Ilves Tampere	Finland	56	12	23	35	36	....	....	....	....	....	....	....	....	....	7	1	3	4	18	....	....	....	....
2005-06	Fribourg	Swiss	44	13	22	35	52	....	....	....	....	....	....	....	....	....	....	....	....	....	....	....	....	....	....
2006-07	HIFK Helsinki	Finland	45	13	37	50	46	....	....	....	....	....	....	....	....	....	....	....	....	....	....	....	....	....	....
2007-08	**Florida**	**NHL**	**47**	**2**	**15**	**17**	**22**	**1**	**0**	**0**	**65**	**3.1**	**0**	**0**	**0.0**	**15:23**	....	....	....	....	....	....	....	....	....
	NHL Totals		**47**	**2**	**15**	**17**	**22**	**1**	**0**	**0**	**65**	**3.1**		**0**	**0.0**	**15:23**	....	....	....	....	....	....	....	....	....

Signed as a free agent by **Florida**, March 26, 2007.

MURPHY, Curtis

(MUHR-fee, KUHR-this)

Defense. Shoots right. 5'8", 185 lbs. Born, Kerrobert, Sask., December 3, 1975.

Season	Club	League	GP	G	A	Pts	PIM	PP	SH	GW	S	%	+/-	TF	F%	Min	GP	G	A	Pts	PIM	PP	SH	GW	Min
1993-94	Nipawin Hawks	SJHL	60	21	33	54	....	....	....	....	....	....	....	....	....	....	....	....	....	....	....	....	....	....	....
1994-95	North Dakota	WCHA	33	6	10	16	28	....	....	....	....	....	....	....	....	....	....	....	....	....	....	....	....	....	....
1995-96	North Dakota	WCHA	38	6	12	18	58	....	....	....	....	....	....	....	....	....	....	....	....	....	....	....	....	....	....
1996-97	North Dakota	WCHA	43	12	30	42	36	....	....	....	....	....	....	....	....	....	....	....	....	....	....	....	....	....	....
1997-98	North Dakota	WCHA	39	8	34	42	78	....	....	....	....	....	....	....	....	....	....	....	....	....	....	....	....	....	....
1998-99	Orlando	IHL	80	22	35	57	60	....	....	....	....	....	....	....	....	....	17	4	5	9	16	....	....	....	....
99-2000	Orlando	IHL	81	8	43	51	59	....	....	....	....	....	....	....	....	....	6	0	2	2	6	....	....	....	....
2000-01	Orlando	IHL	51	19	30	49	55	....	....	....	....	....	....	....	....	....	10	2	9	11	12	....	....	....	....
2001-02	Houston Aeros	AHL	80	12	35	47	75	....	....	....	....	....	....	....	....	....	14	2	4	6	10	....	....	....	....
2002-03	**Minnesota**	**NHL**	**1**	**0**	**0**	**0**	**0**	**0**	**0**	**0**	**0**	**0.0**	**0**	**0**	**0.0**	**8:56**	....	....	....	....	....	....	....	....	....
	Houston Aeros	AHL	80	23	31	54	63	....	....	....	....	....	....	....	....	....	23	2	7	9	22	....	....	....	....
2003-04	Milwaukee	AHL	79	17	36	53	51	....	....	....	....	....	....	....	....	....	22	4	8	12	12	....	....	....	....

			Regular Season														Playoffs								
Season	Club	League	GP	G	A	Pts	PIM	PP	SH	GW	S	%	+/-	TF	F%	Min	GP	G	A	Pts	PIM	PP	SH	GW	Min
2004-05	Yaroslavl	Russia	60	6	6	12	50	....	....	....	....	....	....	....	....	....	9	1	1	2	6	....	....	....	....
2005-06	Houston Aeros	AHL	80	14	53	67	76	....	....	....	....	....	....	....	....	....	8	0	4	4	4	....	....	....	....
2006-07	Houston Aeros	AHL	75	10	35	45	52	....	....	....	....	....	....	....	....	....	....	....	....	....	....	....	....	....	....
2007-08	Langnau	Swiss	50	7	20	27	56	....	....	....	....	....	....	....	....	....	7	2	3	5	14	....	....	....	....
	NHL Totals		**1**	**0**	**0**	**0**	**0**	**0**	**0**	**0**	**0**	**0.0**		**0**	**0.0**	**8:56**	....	....	....	....	....	....	....	....	....

WCHA First All-Star Team (1997, 1998) • NCAA West Second All-American Team (1997) • WCHA Player of the Year (1998) • NCAA West First All-American Team (1998) • IHL First All-Star Team (2001) • AHL First All-Star Team (2003, 2004, 2006) • Eddie Shore Award (Outstanding Defenseman – AHL) (2003, 2004)

Signed as a free agent by **Minnesota**, June 18, 2001. Traded to **Nashville** by **Minnesota** for Chris Bala, June 26, 2003. Signed as a free agent by **Yaroslavl** (Russia), May 28, 2004. Signed as a free agent by **Langnau** (Swiss), April 29, 2007.

MURRAY, Andrew

(MUHR-ree, AN-droo) **CBJ**

Center. Shoots left. 6'2", 216 lbs. Born, Selkirk, Man., November 6, 1981. Columbus' 11th choice, 242nd overall, in 2001 Entry Draft.

Season	Club	League	GP	G	A	Pts	PIM	PP	SH	GW	S	%	+/-	TF	F%	Min	GP	G	A	Pts	PIM	PP	SH	GW	Min
99-2000	Selkirk Steelers	MJHL	63	29	48	77	....	....	....	....	....	....	....	....	....	....	....	....	....	....	....	....	....	....	....
2000-01	Selkirk Steelers	MJHL	64	46	56	102	72	....	....	....	....	....	....	....	....	....	5	3	0	3	6	....	....	....	....
2001-02	Bemidji State	CHA	35	15	15	30	22	....	....	....	....	....	....	....	....	....	....	....	....	....	....	....	....	....	....
2002-03	Bemidji State	CHA	36	9	18	27	38	....	....	....	....	....	....	....	....	....	....	....	....	....	....	....	....	....	....
2003-04	Bemidji State	CHA	25	6	14	20	41	....	....	....	....	....	....	....	....	....	....	....	....	....	....	....	....	....	....
2004-05	Bemidji State	CHA	32	16	22	38	30	....	....	....	....	....	....	....	....	....	....	....	....	....	....	....	....	....	....
2005-06	Syracuse Crunch	AHL	77	13	16	29	73	....	....	....	....	....	....	....	....	....	6	0	1	1	17	....	....	....	....
2006-07	Syracuse Crunch	AHL	72	10	12	22	62	....	....	....	....	....	....	....	....	....	....	....	....	....	....	....	....	....	....
2007-08	**Columbus**	**NHL**	**39**	**6**	**4**	**10**	**12**	**0**	**0**	**0**	**45**	**13.3**	**0**	**32**	**46.9**	**11:42**	....	....	....	....	....	....	....	....	....
	Syracuse Crunch	AHL	34	13	2	15	15	....	....	....	....	....	....	....	....	....	....	....	....	....	....	....	....	....	....
	NHL Totals		**39**	**6**	**4**	**10**	**12**	**0**	**0**	**0**	**45**	**13.3**		**32**	**46.9**	**11:42**	....	....	....	....	....	....	....	....	....

CHA All-Rookie Team (2002)

MURRAY, Brady

(MUHR-ree, BRAY-dee) **L.A.**

Center. Shoots left. 5'9", 184 lbs. Born, Brandon, Man., August 17, 1984. Los Angeles' 6th choice, 152nd overall, in 2003 Entry Draft.

Season	Club	League	GP	G	A	Pts	PIM	PP	SH	GW	S	%	+/-	TF	F%	Min	GP	G	A	Pts	PIM	PP	SH	GW	Min
2001-02	Shat.-St. Mary's	High-MN	60	58	92	150	50	....	....	....	....	....	....	....	....	....	....	....	....	....	....	....	....	....	....
2002-03	Salmon Arm	BCHL	59	42	59	101	30	....	....	....	....	....	....	....	....	....	....	....	....	....	....	....	....	....	....
2003-04	North Dakota	WCHA	37	19	27	46	32	....	....	....	....	....	....	....	....	....	....	....	....	....	....	....	....	....	....
2004-05	North Dakota	WCHA	25	8	12	20	22	....	....	....	....	....	....	....	....	....	....	....	....	....	....	....	....	....	....
2005-06	Rapperswil	Swiss	36	3	9	12	28	....	....	....	....	....	....	....	....	....	10	3	2	5	10	....	....	....	....
2006-07	Rapperswil	Swiss	38	12	20	32	38	....	....	....	....	....	....	....	....	....	7	4	2	6	6	....	....	....	....
2007-08	**Los Angeles**	**NHL**	**4**	**1**	**0**	**1**	**6**	**0**	**0**	**0**	**2**	**50.0**	**–2**	**31**	**51.6**	**11:18**	....	....	....	....	....	....	....	....	....
	Manchester	AHL	58	14	13	27	50	....	....	....	....	....	....	....	....	....	4	1	0	1	2	....	....	....	....
	NHL Totals		**4**	**1**	**0**	**1**	**6**	**0**	**0**	**0**	**2**	**50.0**		**31**	**51.6**	**11:18**	....	....	....	....	....	....	....	....	....

WCHA All-Rookie Team (2004) • WCHA Rookie of the Year (2004)

MURRAY, Douglas

(MUHR-ree, DUHG-luhs) **S.J.**

Defense. Shoots left. 6'3", 240 lbs. Born, Bromma, Sweden, March 12, 1980. San Jose's 6th choice, 241st overall, in 1999 Entry Draft.

Season	Club	League	GP	G	A	Pts	PIM	PP	SH	GW	S	%	+/-	TF	F%	Min	GP	G	A	Pts	PIM	PP	SH	GW	Min
1998-99	NY Apple Core	EJHL	60	17	47	64	62	....	....	....	....	....	....	....	....	....	....	....	....	....	....	....	....	....	....
99-2000	Cornell Big Red	ECAC	32	3	6	9	38	....	....	....	....	....	....	....	....	....	....	....	....	....	....	....	....	....	....
2000-01	Cornell Big Red	ECAC	25	5	13	18	39	....	....	....	....	....	....	....	....	....	....	....	....	....	....	....	....	....	....
2001-02	Cornell Big Red	ECAC	35	11	21	32	67	....	....	....	....	....	....	....	....	....	....	....	....	....	....	....	....	....	....
2002-03	Cornell Big Red	ECAC	35	5	20	25	30	....	....	....	....	....	....	....	....	....	....	....	....	....	....	....	....	....	....
2003-04	Cleveland Barons	AHL	72	10	12	22	75	....	....	....	....	....	....	....	....	....	9	3	0	3	37	....	....	....	....
2004-05	Cleveland Barons	AHL	54	6	17	23	56	....	....	....	....	....	....	....	....	....	....	....	....	....	....	....	....	....	....
2005-06	**San Jose**	**NHL**	**34**	**0**	**1**	**1**	**27**	**0**	**0**	**0**	**21**	**0.0**	**3**	**0**	**0.0**	**13:53**	....	....	....	....	....	....	....	....	....
	Cleveland Barons	AHL	20	1	7	8	37	....	....	....	....	....	....	....	....	....	....	....	....	....	....	....	....	....	....
2006-07	**San Jose**	**NHL**	**35**	**0**	**3**	**3**	**31**	**0**	**0**	**0**	**18**	**0.0**	**0**	**0**	**0.0**	**10:46**	....	....	....	....	....	....	....	....	....
	Worcester Sharks	AHL	5	2	1	3	8	....	....	....	....	....	....	....	....	....	....	....	....	....	....	....	....	....	....
2007-08	**San Jose**	**NHL**	**66**	**1**	**9**	**10**	**98**	**0**	**0**	**0**	**48**	**2.1**	**20**	**2**	**50.0**	**17:28**	**13**	**1**	**1**	**2**	**2**	**0**	**0**	**0**	**18:09**
	NHL Totals		**135**	**1**	**13**	**14**	**156**	**0**	**0**	**0**	**87**	**1.1**		**2**	**50.0**	**14:50**	**13**	**1**	**1**	**2**	**2**	**0**	**0**	**0**	**18:09**

ECAC First All-Star Team (2002, 2003) • NCAA East First All-American Team (2003)
• Missed majority of 2006-07 season recovering from respiratory infection.

MURRAY, Garth

(MUHR-ree, GARTH) **PHX.**

Center. Shoots left. 6'2", 209 lbs. Born, Regina, Sask., September 17, 1982. NY Rangers' 3rd choice, 79th overall, in 2001 Entry Draft.

Season	Club	League	GP	G	A	Pts	PIM	PP	SH	GW	S	%	+/-	TF	F%	Min	GP	G	A	Pts	PIM	PP	SH	GW	Min
1997-98	Calgary Buffaloes	AMHL	56	26	34	60	110	....	....	....	....	....	....	....	....	....	....	....	....	....	....	....	....	....	....
	Regina Pats	WHL	4	0	0	0	2	....	....	....	....	....	....	....	....	....	2	0	0	0	0	....	....	....	....
1998-99	Regina Pats	WHL	60	3	5	8	101	....	....	....	....	....	....	....	....	....	....	....	....	....	....	....	....	....	....
99-2000	Regina Pats	WHL	68	14	26	40	155	....	....	....	....	....	....	....	....	....	7	1	1	2	7	....	....	....	....
2000-01	Regina Pats	WHL	72	28	16	44	183	....	....	....	....	....	....	....	....	....	6	1	1	2	10	....	....	....	....
2001-02	Regina Pats	WHL	62	33	30	63	154	....	....	....	....	....	....	....	....	....	6	2	3	5	9	....	....	....	....
	Hartford	AHL	4	0	0	0	0	....	....	....	....	....	....	....	....	....	9	1	3	4	6	....	....	....	....
2002-03	Hartford	AHL	64	10	14	24	121	....	....	....	....	....	....	....	....	....	2	0	0	0	6	....	....	....	....
2003-04	**NY Rangers**	**NHL**	**20**	**1**	**0**	**1**	**24**	**0**	**0**	**0**	**18**	**5.6**	**–5**	**5**	**20.0**	**9:16**	....	....	....	....	....	....	....	....	....
	Hartford	AHL	63	11	11	22	159	....	....	....	....	....	....	....	....	....	16	0	4	4	29	....	....	....	....
2004-05	Hartford	AHL	55	4	5	9	182	....	....	....	....	....	....	....	....	....	5	1	0	1	8	....	....	....	....
2005-06	**Montreal**	**NHL**	**36**	**5**	**1**	**6**	**44**	**0**	**0**	**1**	**25**	**20.0**	**–2**	**99**	**46.5**	**9:15**	**6**	**0**	**0**	**0**	**0**	**0**	**0**	**0**	**12:39**
	Hamilton	AHL	26	1	1	2	46	....	....	....	....	....	....	....	....	....	....	....	....	....	....	....	....	....	....
2006-07	**Montreal**	**NHL**	**43**	**2**	**1**	**3**	**32**	**0**	**0**	**0**	**28**	**7.1**	**–10**	**107**	**42.1**	**8:23**	....	....	....	....	....	....	....	....	....
2007-08	**Montreal**	**NHL**	**1**	**0**	**0**	**0**	**0**	**0**	**0**	**0**	**0**	**0.0**	**0**	**1**	**0.0**	**12:46**	....	....	....	....	....	....	....	....	....
	Florida	**NHL**	**6**	**0**	**0**	**0**	**19**	**0**	**0**	**0**	**3**	**0.0**	**0**	**2**	**0.0**	**5:09**	....	....	....	....	....	....	....	....	....
	NHL Totals		**106**	**8**	**2**	**10**	**119**	**0**	**0**	**1**	**74**	**10.8**		**214**	**43.0**	**8:42**	**6**	**0**	**0**	**0**	**0**	**0**	**0**	**0**	**12:39**

Traded to **Montreal** by **NY Rangers** for Marcel Hossa, September 30, 2005. Claimed off waivers by **Florida** from **Montreal**, November 13, 2007. Signed as a free agent by **Phoenix**, July 18, 2008.

MURRAY, Glen

(MUHR-ree, GLEHN)

Right wing. Shoots right. 6'3", 218 lbs. Born, Halifax, N.S., November 1, 1972. Boston's 1st choice, 18th overall, in 1991 Entry Draft.

Season	Club	League	GP	G	A	Pts	PIM	PP	SH	GW	S	%	+/-	TF	F%	Min	GP	G	A	Pts	PIM	PP	SH	GW	Min
1988-89	Bridgewater	NSMHL	45	50	56	106	62	....	....	....	....	....	....	....	....	....	....	....	....	....	....	....	....	....	....
1989-90	Sudbury Wolves	OHL	62	8	28	36	17	....	....	....	....	....	....	....	....	....	7	0	0	0	4	....	....	....	....
1990-91	Sudbury Wolves	OHL	66	27	38	65	82	....	....	....	....	....	....	....	....	....	5	8	4	12	10	....	....	....	....
1991-92	Sudbury Wolves	OHL	54	37	47	84	93	....	....	....	....	....	....	....	....	....	11	7	4	11	18	....	....	....	....
	Boston	**NHL**	**5**	**3**	**1**	**4**	**0**	**1**	**0**	**0**	**20**	**15.0**	**2**	....	....	....	**15**	**4**	**2**	**6**	**10**	**1**	**0**	**0**	....
1992-93	**Boston**	**NHL**	**27**	**3**	**4**	**7**	**8**	**2**	**0**	**1**	**28**	**10.7**	**–6**	....	....	....	....	....	....	....	....	....	....	....	....
	Providence Bruins	AHL	48	30	26	56	42	....	....	....	....	....	....	....	....	....	6	1	4	5	4	....	....	....	....
1993-94	**Boston**	**NHL**	**81**	**18**	**13**	**31**	**48**	**0**	**0**	**4**	**114**	**15.8**	**–1**	....	....	....	**13**	**4**	**5**	**9**	**14**	**0**	**0**	**0**	....
1994-95	**Boston**	**NHL**	**35**	**5**	**2**	**7**	**46**	**0**	**0**	**2**	**64**	**7.8**	**–11**	....	....	....	**2**	**0**	**0**	**0**	**2**	**0**	**0**	**0**	....
1995-96	**Pittsburgh**	**NHL**	**69**	**14**	**15**	**29**	**57**	**0**	**0**	**2**	**100**	**14.0**	**4**	....	....	....	**18**	**2**	**6**	**8**	**10**	**0**	**0**	**1**	....
1996-97	**Pittsburgh**	**NHL**	**66**	**11**	**11**	**22**	**24**	**3**	**0**	**1**	**127**	**8.7**	**–19**	....	....	....	....	....	....	....	....	....	....	....	....
	Los Angeles	**NHL**	**11**	**5**	**3**	**8**	**8**	**0**	**0**	**0**	**26**	**19.2**	**–2**	....	....	....	....	....	....	....	....	....	....	....	....
1997-98	**Los Angeles**	**NHL**	**81**	**29**	**31**	**60**	**54**	**7**	**3**	**7**	**193**	**15.0**	**6**	....	....	....	**4**	**2**	**0**	**2**	**6**	**0**	**0**	**0**	....
1998-99	**Los Angeles**	**NHL**	**61**	**16**	**15**	**31**	**36**	**3**	**3**	**3**	**173**	**9.2**	**–14**	**12**	**25.0**	**20:33**	....	....	....	....	....	....	....	....	....
99-2000	**Los Angeles**	**NHL**	**78**	**29**	**33**	**62**	**60**	**10**	**1**	**2**	**202**	**14.4**	**13**	**15**	**80.0**	**18:30**	**4**	**0**	**0**	**0**	**2**	**0**	**0**	**0**	**19:04**
2000-01	**Los Angeles**	**NHL**	**64**	**18**	**21**	**39**	**32**	**3**	**1**	**1**	**138**	**13.0**	**9**	**7**	**42.9**	**18:12**	**13**	**4**	**3**	**7**	**4**	**1**	**0**	**1**	**19:51**
2001-02	**Los Angeles**	**NHL**	**9**	**6**	**5**	**11**	**0**	**4**	**0**	**2**	**34**	**17.6**	**5**	**1**	**100.0**	**19:08**	....	....	....	....	....	....	....	....	....
	Boston	**NHL**	**73**	**35**	**25**	**60**	**40**	**5**	**0**	**7**	**212**	**16.5**	**26**	**39**	**23.1**	**19:50**	**6**	**1**	**4**	**5**	**4**	**0**	**0**	**0**	**18:02**
2002-03	**Boston**	**NHL**	**82**	**44**	**48**	**92**	**64**	**12**	**0**	**5**	**331**	**13.3**	**9**	**32**	**37.5**	**22:36**	**5**	**1**	**1**	**2**	**4**	**0**	**0**	**0**	**19:36**
2003-04	**Boston**	**NHL**	**81**	**32**	**28**	**60**	**56**	**11**	**0**	**9**	**260**	**12.3**	**17**	**53**	**35.9**	**20:56**	**7**	**2**	**1**	**3**	**8**	**0**	**0**	**1**	**19:57**
2004-05			DID NOT PLAY																						
2005-06	**Boston**	**NHL**	**64**	**24**	**29**	**53**	**52**	**6**	**1**	**3**	**195**	**12.3**	**–8**	**14**	**28.6**	**20:12**	....	....	....	....	....	....	....	....	....

			Regular Season														Playoffs								
Season	Club	League	GP	G	A	Pts	PIM	PP	SH	GW	S	%	+/-	TF	F%	Min	GP	G	A	Pts	PIM	PP	SH	GW	Min
2006-07	**Boston**	**NHL**	**59**	**28**	**17**	**45**	**44**	**12**	**0**	**4**	**201**	**13.9**	**–12**	**19**	**52.6**	**18:45**	....	....	....	....	....	....	....	....	....
2007-08	**Boston**	**NHL**	**63**	**17**	**13**	**30**	**50**	**7**	**0**	**2**	**158**	**10.8**	**–4**	**19**	**31.6**	**18:13**	**7**	**0**	**0**	**0**	**2**	**0**	**0**	**0**	**14:16**
	NHL Totals		**1009**	**337**	**314**	**651**	**679**	**86**	**9**	**55**	**2576**	**13.1**		**211**	**37.4**	**19:50**	**94**	**20**	**22**	**42**	**66**	**2**	**0**	**3**	**18:34**

Played in NHL All-Star Game (2003, 2004)

Traded to **Pittsburgh** by **Boston** with Bryan Smolinski and Boston's 3rd round choice (Boyd Kane) in 1996 Entry Draft for Kevin Stevens and Shawn McEachern, August 2, 1995. Traded to **Los Angeles** by **Pittsburgh** for Ed Olczyk, March 18, 1997. Traded to **Boston** by **Los Angeles** with Jozef Stumpel for Jason Allison and Mikko Eloranta, October 24, 2001.

MURRAY, Marty

(MUHR-ree, MAHR-tee)

Center. Shoots left. 5'9", 180 lbs. Born, Deloraine, Man., February 16, 1975. Calgary's 5th choice, 96th overall, in 1993 Entry Draft.

Season	Club	League	GP	G	A	Pts	PIM	PP	SH	GW	S	%	+/-	TF	F%	Min	GP	G	A	Pts	PIM	PP	SH	GW	Min
1990-91	S-W Cougars	MMMHL	36	46	47	93	50	....	....	....	....	....	....	....	....	....	....	....	....	....	....	....	....	....	....
1991-92	Brandon	WHL	68	20	36	56	22	....	....	....	....	....	....	....	....	....	....	....	....	....	....	....	....	....	....
1992-93	Brandon	WHL	67	29	65	94	50	....	....	....	....	....	....	....	....	....	4	1	3	4	0	....	....	....	....
1993-94	Brandon	WHL	64	43	71	114	33	....	....	....	....	....	....	....	....	....	14	6	14	20	14	....	....	....	....
1994-95	Brandon	WHL	65	40	*88	128	53	....	....	....	....	....	....	....	....	....	18	9	*20	29	16	....	....	....	....
1995-96	**Calgary**	**NHL**	**15**	**3**	**3**	**6**	**0**	**2**	**0**	**0**	**22**	**13.6**	**–4**	....	....	....	....	....	....	....	....	....	....	....	....
	Saint John Flames	AHL	58	25	31	56	20	....	....	....	....	....	....	....	....	....	14	2	4	6	4	....	....	....	....
1996-97	**Calgary**	**NHL**	**2**	**0**	**0**	**0**	**4**	**0**	**0**	**0**	**2**	**0.0**	**0**	....	....	....	....	....	....	....	....	....	....	....	....
	Saint John Flames	AHL	67	19	39	58	40	....	....	....	....	....	....	....	....	....	5	2	3	5	4	....	....	....	....
1997-98	**Calgary**	**NHL**	**2**	**0**	**0**	**0**	**2**	**0**	**0**	**0**	**2**	**0.0**	**1**	....	....	....	....	....	....	....	....	....	....	....	....
	Saint John Flames	AHL	41	10	30	40	16	....	....	....	....	....	....	....	....	....	21	10	10	20	12	....	....	....	....
1998-99	EC Villacher SV	Alpenliga	33	26	41	67	12	....	....	....	....	....	....	....	....	....	....	....	....	....	....	....	....	....	....
	EC Villacher SV	Austria	17	13	17	30	6	....	....	....	....	....	....	....	....	....	6	1	4	5	0	....	....	....	....
99-2000	Kolner Haie	Germany	56	12	47	59	28	....	....	....	....	....	....	....	....	....	10	4	3	7	2	....	....	....	....
2000-01	**Calgary**	**NHL**	**7**	**0**	**0**	**0**	**0**	**0**	**0**	**0**	**6**	**0.0**	**–2**	**88**	**55.7**	**14:28**	....	....	....	....	....	....	....	....	....
	Saint John Flames	AHL	56	24	52	76	36	....	....	....	....	....	....	....	....	....	19	4	16	20	18	....	....	....	....
2001-02	**Philadelphia**	**NHL**	**74**	**12**	**15**	**27**	**10**	**1**	**1**	**2**	**109**	**11.0**	**10**	**913**	**50.7**	**13:56**	**5**	**0**	**1**	**1**	**0**	**0**	**0**	**0**	**13:14**
	Philadelphia	AHL	3	0	3	3	2	....	....	....	....	....	....	....	....	....	....	....	....	....	....	....	....	....	....
2002-03	**Philadelphia**	**NHL**	**76**	**11**	**15**	**26**	**13**	**1**	**1**	**0**	**105**	**10.5**	**–1**	**472**	**55.1**	**12:22**	**4**	**0**	**0**	**0**	**4**	**0**	**0**	**0**	**11:01**
2003-04	**Carolina**	**NHL**	**66**	**5**	**7**	**12**	**8**	**0**	**0**	**0**	**56**	**8.9**	**6**	**229**	**52.8**	**11:49**	....	....	....	....	....	....	....	....	....
2004-05			DID NOT PLAY																						
2005-06	Hannover	Germany	24	7	15	22	16	....	....	....	....	....	....	....	....	....	9	4	3	7	35	....	....	....	....
2006-07	Philadelphia	AHL	11	2	13	15	4	....	....	....	....	....	....	....	....	....	....	....	....	....	....	....	....	....	....
	Los Angeles	**NHL**	**19**	**0**	**2**	**2**	**4**	**0**	**0**	**0**	**4**	**0.0**	**–5**	**139**	**46.8**	**9:32**	....	....	....	....	....	....	....	....	....
	Manchester	AHL	34	12	28	40	24	....	....	....	....	....	....	....	....	....	16	6	8	14	11	....	....	....	....
2007-08	HC Lugano	Swiss	49	7	25	32	22	....	....	....	....	....	....	....	....	....	5	2	3	5	0	....	....	....	....
	NHL Totals		**261**	**31**	**42**	**73**	**41**	**4**	**2**	**2**	**306**	**10.1**		**1841**	**52.0**	**12:32**	**9**	**0**	**1**	**1**	**4**	**0**	**0**	**0**	**12:15**

WHL East First All-Star Team (1994, 1995) • Canadian Major Junior Second All-Star Team (1994) • WHL Player of the Year (1995)

Signed as a free agent by **Philadelphia**, July 9, 2001. Traded to **Carolina** by **Philadelphia** for Carolina's 6th round choice (Frederik Cabana) in 2004 Entry Draft, June 22, 2003. Signed as a free agent by **Hannover** (Germany), August 16, 2005. Signed as a free agent by **Philadelphia**, June 15, 2006. Claimed on waivers by **Los Angeles** from **Philadelphia**, November 11, 2006. Signed as a free agent by **Lugano** (Swiss), May 27, 2007.

NAGY, Ladislav

(NA-gee, LA-dih-slahv)

Left wing. Shoots left. 5'11", 192 lbs. Born, Saca, Czech., June 1, 1979. St. Louis' 6th choice, 177th overall, in 1997 Entry Draft.

Season	Club	League	GP	G	A	Pts	PIM	PP	SH	GW	S	%	+/-	TF	F%	Min	GP	G	A	Pts	PIM	PP	SH	GW	Min
1995-96	HK Dragon Presov	Slovakia	11	6	5	11	....	....	....	....	....	....	....	....	....	....	....	....	....	....	....	....	....	....	....
1996-97	HC Kosice Jr.	Slovak-Jr.	45	29	30	59	105	....	....	....	....	....	....	....	....	....	....	....	....	....	....	....	....	....	....
1997-98	HC Kosice	Slovakia	29	19	15	34	41	....	....	....	....	....	....	....	....	....	11	2	4	6	6	....	....	....	....
1998-99	Halifax	QMJHL	63	71	55	126	148	....	....	....	....	....	....	....	....	....	5	3	3	6	18	....	....	....	....
	Worcester IceCats	AHL	....	....	....	....	....	....	....	....	....	....	....	....	....	....	3	2	2	4	0	....	....	....	....
99-2000	**St. Louis**	**NHL**	**11**	**2**	**4**	**6**	**2**	**1**	**0**	**0**	**15**	**13.3**	**2**	**6**	**33.3**	**12:19**	**6**	**1**	**1**	**2**	**0**	**0**	**0**	**0**	**13:29**
	Worcester IceCats	AHL	69	23	28	51	67	....	....	....	....	....	....	....	....	....	2	1	0	1	0	....	....	....	....
2000-01	**St. Louis**	**NHL**	**40**	**8**	**8**	**16**	**20**	**2**	**0**	**2**	**59**	**13.6**	**–2**	**28**	**50.0**	**13:03**	....	....	....	....	....	....	....	....	....
	Worcester IceCats	AHL	20	6	14	20	36	....	....	....	....	....	....	....	....	....	....	....	....	....	....	....	....	....	....
	Phoenix	**NHL**	**6**	**0**	**1**	**1**	**2**	**0**	**0**	**0**	**5**	**0.0**	**0**	**0**	**0.0**	**12:38**	....	....	....	....	....	....	....	....	....
2001-02	**Phoenix**	**NHL**	**74**	**23**	**19**	**42**	**50**	**5**	**0**	**5**	**187**	**12.3**	**6**	**17**	**47.1**	**15:04**	**5**	**0**	**0**	**0**	**21**	**0**	**0**	**0**	**15:45**
2002-03	HC Kosice	Slovakia	1	2	1	3	0	....	....	....	....	....	....	....	....	....	....	....	....	....	....	....	....	....	....
	Phoenix	**NHL**	**80**	**22**	**35**	**57**	**92**	**8**	**0**	**6**	**209**	**10.5**	**17**	**41**	**34.2**	**17:28**	....	....	....	....	....	....	....	....	....
2003-04	**Phoenix**	**NHL**	**55**	**24**	**28**	**52**	**46**	**11**	**0**	**6**	**160**	**15.0**	**11**	**33**	**42.4**	**18:10**	....	....	....	....	....	....	....	....	....
2004-05	HC Kosice	Slovakia	18	9	7	16	40	....	....	....	....	....	....	....	....	....	....	....	....	....	....	....	....	....	....
	Mora IK	Sweden	19	4	4	8	22	....	....	....	....	....	....	....	....	....	....	....	....	....	....	....	....	....	....
2005-06	**Phoenix**	**NHL**	**51**	**15**	**41**	**56**	**74**	**7**	**1**	**4**	**132**	**11.4**	**8**	**72**	**40.3**	**18:53**	....	....	....	....	....	....	....	....	....
2006-07	**Phoenix**	**NHL**	**55**	**8**	**33**	**41**	**48**	**2**	**0**	**0**	**113**	**7.1**	**–2**	**43**	**30.2**	**17:52**	....	....	....	....	....	....	....	....	....
	Dallas	**NHL**	**25**	**4**	**10**	**14**	**6**	**2**	**0**	**1**	**33**	**12.1**	**–3**	**5**	**20.0**	**16:08**	**7**	**1**	**1**	**2**	**2**	**0**	**0**	**0**	**18:53**
2007-08	**Los Angeles**	**NHL**	**38**	**9**	**17**	**26**	**18**	**2**	**0**	**1**	**78**	**11.5**	**–2**	**83**	**53.0**	**13:48**	....	....	....	....	....	....	....	....	....
	NHL Totals		**435**	**115**	**196**	**311**	**358**	**40**	**1**	**25**	**991**	**11.6**		**328**	**42.4**	**16:22**	**18**	**2**	**2**	**4**	**23**	**0**	**0**	**0**	**16:13**

Traded to **Phoenix** by **St. Louis** with Michal Handzus, the rights to Jeff Taffe and St. Louis' 1st round choice (Ben Eager) in 2002 Entry Draft for Keith Tkachuk, March 13, 2001. Signed as a free agent by **Kosice** (Slovakia), September 17, 2004. Signed as a free agent by **Mora** (Sweden), December 17, 2004. Traded to **Dallas** by **Phoenix** for Mathias Tjarnqvist and Dallas' 1st round choice (later traded to Edmonton - Edmonton selected Riley Nash) in 2007 Entry Draft, February 12, 2007. Signed as a free agent by **Los Angeles**, July 2, 2007.• Misssed majority of 2007-08 season with recurring neck injury.

NASH, Rick

(NASH, RIHK) **CBJ**

Left wing. Shoots left. 6'4", 218 lbs. Born, Brampton, Ont., June 16, 1984. Columbus' 1st choice, 1st overall, in 2002 Entry Draft.

Season	Club	League	GP	G	A	Pts	PIM	PP	SH	GW	S	%	+/-	TF	F%	Min	GP	G	A	Pts	PIM	PP	SH	GW	Min
99-2000	Tor. Marlboros	GTHL	34	61	54	115	34	....	....	....	....	....	....	....	....	....	....	....	....	....	....	....	....	....	....
2000-01	London Knights	OHL	58	31	35	66	56	....	....	....	....	....	....	....	....	....	4	3	3	6	8	....	....	....	....
2001-02	London Knights	OHL	54	32	40	72	88	....	....	....	....	....	....	....	....	....	12	10	9	19	21	....	....	....	....
2002-03	**Columbus**	**NHL**	**74**	**17**	**22**	**39**	**78**	**6**	**0**	**2**	**154**	**11.0**	**–27**	**14**	**35.7**	**13:57**	....	....	....	....	....	....	....	....	....
2003-04	**Columbus**	**NHL**	**80**	***41**	**16**	**57**	**87**	**19**	**0**	**7**	**269**	**15.2**	**–35**	**21**	**28.6**	**17:38**	....	....	....	....	....	....	....	....	....
2004-05	HC Davos	Swiss	44	26	20	46	83	....	....	....	....	....	....	....	....	....	15	9	2	11	26	....	....	....	....
2005-06	**Columbus**	**NHL**	**54**	**31**	**23**	**54**	**51**	**11**	**0**	**4**	**170**	**18.2**	**5**	**38**	**50.0**	**18:16**	....	....	....	....	....	....	....	....	....
	Canada	Olympics	6	0	1	1	10	....	....	....	....	....	....	....	....	....	....	....	....	....	....	....	....	....	....
2006-07	**Columbus**	**NHL**	**75**	**27**	**30**	**57**	**73**	**9**	**1**	**5**	**228**	**11.8**	**–8**	**143**	**42.7**	**19:12**	....	....	....	....	....	....	....	....	....
2007-08	**Columbus**	**NHL**	**80**	**38**	**31**	**69**	**95**	**10**	**4**	**6**	**329**	**11.6**	**2**	**44**	**31.8**	**20:29**	....	....	....	....	....	....	....	....	....
	NHL Totals		**363**	**154**	**122**	**276**	**384**	**55**	**5**	**24**	**1150**	**13.4**		**260**	**40.4**	**17:56**	....	....	....	....	....	....	....	....	....

OHL All-Rookie Team (2001) • OHL Rookie of the Year (2001) • CHL All-Rookie Team (2001) • NHL All-Rookie Team (2003) • Maurice "Rocket" Richard Trophy (2004) (tied with Jarome Iginla and Ilya Kovalchuk)

Played in NHL All-Star Game (2004, 2007, 2008)

Signed as a free agent by **Davos** (Swiss), August 3, 2004.

NASLUND, Markus

(NAZ-luhnd, MAHR-kuhs) **NYR**

Left wing. Shoots left. 6', 195 lbs. Born, Ornskoldsvik, Sweden, July 30, 1973. Pittsburgh's 1st choice, 16th overall, in 1991 Entry Draft.

Season	Club	League	GP	G	A	Pts	PIM	PP	SH	GW	S	%	+/-	TF	F%	Min	GP	G	A	Pts	PIM	PP	SH	GW	Min
1988-89	Ornskoldsviks IF	Sweden-3	14	7	6	13	....	....	....	....	....	....	....	....	....	....	....	....	....	....	....	....	....	....	....
1989-90	MoDo Jr.	Swe-Jr.	33	43	35	78	20	....	....	....	....	....	....	....	....	....	....	....	....	....	....	....	....	....	....
1990-91	MoDo	Sweden	32	10	9	19	14	....	....	....	....	....	....	....	....	....	....	....	....	....	....	....	....	....	....
1991-92	MoDo	Sweden	39	22	18	40	54	....	....	....	....	....	....	....	....	....	....	....	....	....	....	....	....	....	....
1992-93	MoDo Jr.	Swe-Jr.	2	4	1	5	2	....	....	....	....	....	....	....	....	....	....	....	....	....	....	....	....	....	....
	MoDo	Sweden	39	22	17	39	67	....	....	....	....	....	....	....	....	....	3	3	2	5	0	....	....	....	....
1993-94	**Pittsburgh**	**NHL**	**71**	**4**	**7**	**11**	**27**	**1**	**0**	**0**	**80**	**5.0**	**–3**	....	....	....	....	....	....	....	....	....	....	....	....
	Cleveland	IHL	5	1	6	7	4	....	....	....	....	....	....	....	....	....	....	....	....	....	....	....	....	....	....
1994-95	**Pittsburgh**	**NHL**	**14**	**2**	**2**	**4**	**2**	**0**	**0**	**0**	**13**	**15.4**	**0**	....	....	....	....	....	....	....	....	....	....	....	....
	Cleveland	IHL	7	3	4	7	6	....	....	....	....	....	....	....	....	....	4	1	3	4	8	....	....	....	....
1995-96	**Pittsburgh**	**NHL**	**66**	**19**	**33**	**52**	**36**	**3**	**0**	**4**	**125**	**15.2**	**17**	....	....	....	....	....	....	....	....	....	....	....	....
	Vancouver	**NHL**	**10**	**3**	**0**	**3**	**6**	**1**	**0**	**1**	**19**	**15.8**	**3**	....	....	....	**6**	**1**	**2**	**3**	**8**	**1**	**0**	**0**	....
1996-97	**Vancouver**	**NHL**	**78**	**21**	**20**	**41**	**30**	**4**	**0**	**4**	**120**	**17.5**	**–15**	....	....	....	....	....	....	....	....	....	....	....	....
1997-98	**Vancouver**	**NHL**	**76**	**14**	**20**	**34**	**56**	**2**	**1**	**0**	**106**	**13.2**	**5**	....	....	....	....	....	....	....	....	....	....	....	....
1998-99	**Vancouver**	**NHL**	**80**	**36**	**30**	**66**	**74**	**15**	**2**	**3**	**205**	**17.6**	**–13**	**14**	**57.1**	**19:57**	....	....	....	....	....	....	....	....	....
99-2000	**Vancouver**	**NHL**	**82**	**27**	**38**	**65**	**64**	**6**	**2**	**3**	**271**	**10.0**	**–5**	**13**	**46.2**	**20:13**	....	....	....	....	....	....	....	....	....
2000-01	**Vancouver**	**NHL**	**72**	**41**	**34**	**75**	**58**	**18**	**1**	**5**	**277**	**14.8**	**–2**	**6**	**50.0**	**19:03**	....	....	....	....	....	....	....	....	....

			Regular Season														Playoffs								
Season	Club	League	GP	G	A	Pts	PIM	PP	SH	GW	S	%	+/-	TF	F%	Min	GP	G	A	Pts	PIM	PP	SH	GW	Min
2001-02	**Vancouver**	**NHL**	**81**	**40**	**50**	**90**	**50**	**8**	**0**	**6**	**302**	**13.2**	**22**	**5**	**20.0**	**19:31**	**6**	**1**	**1**	**2**	**2**	**0**	**0**	**0**	**18:54**
	Sweden	Olympics	4	2	1	3	0																		
2002-03	**Vancouver**	**NHL**	**82**	**48**	**56**	**104**	**52**	**24**	**0**	**12**	**294**	**16.3**	**6**	**6**	**33.3**	**19:54**	**14**	**5**	**9**	**14**	**18**	**2**	**0**	**1**	**18:14**
2003-04	**Vancouver**	**NHL**	**78**	**35**	**49**	**84**	**58**	**5**	**0**	**6**	**296**	**11.8**	**24**	**14**	**35.7**	**19:23**	**7**	**2**	**7**	**9**	**2**	**2**	**0**	**0**	**19:21**
2004-05	MODO	Sweden	13	8	9	17	8										6	0	1	1	10				
2005-06	**Vancouver**	**NHL**	**81**	**32**	**47**	**79**	**66**	**13**	**0**	**2**	**264**	**12.1**	**–19**	**7**	**28.6**	**18:28**									
	Sweden	Olympics	DID NOT PLAY – INJURED																						
2006-07	**Vancouver**	**NHL**	**82**	**24**	**36**	**60**	**54**	**9**	**0**	**5**	**222**	**10.8**	**3**	**6**	**50.0**	**17:44**	**12**	**4**	**1**	**5**	**16**	**1**	**0**	**0**	**21:36**
2007-08	**Vancouver**	**NHL**	**82**	**25**	**30**	**55**	**46**	**9**	**0**	**2**	**237**	**10.5**	**–7**	**1**	**0.0**	**17:23**									
	NHL Totals		**1035**	**371**	**452**	**823**	**679**	**118**	**6**	**53**	**2831**	**13.1**		**72**	**41.7**	**19:04**	**45**	**13**	**20**	**33**	**46**	**6**	**0**	**1**	**19:34**

NHL First All-Star Team (2002, 2003, 2004) • Lester B. Pearson Award (2003)

Played in NHL All-Star Game (1999, 2001, 2002, 2003, 2004)

Traded to **Vancouver** by **Pittsburgh** for Alek Stojanov, March 20, 1996. Signed as a free agent by **MODO** (Sweden), December 20, 2004. Signed as a free agent by **NY Rangers**, July 3, 2008.

NASREDDINE, Alain

(NAS-ruh-deen, AL-eh)

Defense. Shoots left. 6'1", 204 lbs. Born, Montreal, Que., July 10, 1975. Florida's 8th choice, 135th overall, in 1993 Entry Draft.

Season	Club	League	GP	G	A	Pts	PIM	PP	SH	GW	S	%	+/-	TF	F%	Min	GP	G	A	Pts	PIM	PP	SH	GW	Min
1990-91	Mtl-Bourassa	QAAA	35	10	25	35	50																		
1991-92	Drummondville	QMJHL	61	1	9	10	78										4	0	0	0	17				
1992-93	Drummondville	QMJHL	64	0	14	14	137										10	0	1	1	36				
1993-94	Chicoutimi	QMJHL	60	3	24	27	218										26	2	10	12	118				
1994-95	Chicoutimi	QMJHL	67	8	31	39	342										13	3	5	8	40				
1995-96	Carolina Panthers	AHL	63	0	5	5	245																		
1996-97	Carolina	AHL	26	0	4	4	109																		
	Indianapolis Ice	IHL	49	0	2	2	248										4	1	1	2	27				
1997-98	Indianapolis Ice	IHL	75	1	12	13	258										5	0	2	2	12				
1998-99	**Chicago**	**NHL**	**7**	**0**	**0**	**0**	**19**	**0**	**0**	**0**	**2**	**0.0**	**–2**	**0**	**0.0**	**12:11**									
	Portland Pirates	AHL	7	0	1	1	36																		
	Montreal	**NHL**	**8**	**0**	**0**	**0**	**33**	**0**	**0**	**0**	**1**	**0.0**	**1**	**0**	**0.0**	**8:12**									
	Fredericton	AHL	38	0	10	10	108										15	0	3	3	39				
99-2000	Quebec Citadelles	AHL	59	1	6	7	178																		
	Hamilton	AHL	11	0	0	0	12										10	1	1	2	14				
2000-01	Hamilton	AHL	74	4	14	18	164																		
2001-02	Hamilton	AHL	79	7	10	17	154										12	1	3	4	22				
2002-03	**NY Islanders**	**NHL**	**3**	**0**	**0**	**0**	**2**	**0**	**0**	**0**	**0**	**0.0**	**0**	**0**	**0.0**	**12:11**									
	Bridgeport	AHL	67	3	9	12	114										9	0	0	0	27				
2003-04	Bridgeport	AHL	53	1	6	7	70																		
	Wilkes-Barre	AHL	17	1	1	2	16										24	1	0	1	48				
2004-05	Wilkes-Barre	AHL	75	3	15	18	129										11	0	1	1	18				
2005-06	**Pittsburgh**	**NHL**	**6**	**0**	**0**	**0**	**8**	**0**	**0**	**0**	**3**	**0.0**	**2**	**0**	**0.0**	**15:11**									
	Wilkes-Barre	AHL	71	0	12	12	71																		
2006-07	**Pittsburgh**	**NHL**	**44**	**1**	**4**	**5**	**18**	**0**	**0**	**0**	**29**	**3.4**	**12**	**0**	**0.0**	**15:47**									
	Wilkes-Barre	AHL	19	3	5	8	25																		
2007-08	**Pittsburgh**	**NHL**	**6**	**0**	**0**	**0**	**4**	**0**	**0**	**0**	**3**	**0.0**	**–4**	**0**	**0.0**	**12:53**									
	Wilkes-Barre	AHL	67	6	10	16	61										23	2	3	5	16				
	NHL Totals		**74**	**1**	**4**	**5**	**84**	**0**	**0**	**0**	**38**	**2.6**		**0**	**0.0**	**14:11**									

QMJHL Second All-Star Team (1995)

Traded to **Chicago** by **Florida** for Ivan Droppa, December 18, 1996. Traded to **Montreal** by **Chicago** with Jeff Hackett, Eric Weinrich and Tampa Bay's 4th round choice (previously acquired, Montreal selected Chris Dyment) in 1999 Entry Draft for Jocelyn Thibault, Dave Manson and Brad Brown, November 16, 1998. Traded to **Edmonton** by **Montreal** with Igor Ulanov for Christian Laflamme and Matthieu Descoteaux, March 9, 2000. Signed as a free agent by **NY Islanders**, September 6, 2002. Traded to **Pittsburgh** by **NY Islanders** for Steve Webb, March 8, 2004.

NEIL, Chris

(NEEL, KRIHS) **OTT.**

Right wing. Shoots right. 6'1", 214 lbs. Born, Markdale, Ont., June 18, 1979. Ottawa's 7th choice, 161st overall, in 1998 Entry Draft.

Season	Club	League	GP	G	A	Pts	PIM	PP	SH	GW	S	%	+/-	TF	F%	Min	GP	G	A	Pts	PIM	PP	SH	GW	Min
1995-96	Orangeville	OHA-B	43	15	15	30	50																		
1996-97	North Bay	OHL	65	13	16	29	150																		
1997-98	North Bay	OHL	59	26	29	55	231																		
1998-99	North Bay	OHL	66	26	46	72	215										4	1	0	1	15				
99-2000	Mobile Mysticks	ECHL	4	0	2	2	39																		
	Grand Rapids	IHL	51	9	10	19	301										8	0	2	2	24				
2000-01	Grand Rapids	IHL	78	15	21	36	354										10	2	2	4	22				
2001-02	**Ottawa**	**NHL**	**72**	**10**	**7**	**17**	**231**	**1**	**0**	**0**	**56**	**17.9**	**5**	**0**	**0.0**	**8:22**	**12**	**0**	**0**	**0**	**12**	**0**	**0**	**0**	**7:12**
2002-03	**Ottawa**	**NHL**	**68**	**6**	**4**	**10**	**147**	**0**	**0**	**0**	**62**	**9.7**	**8**	**5**	**60.0**	**7:40**	**15**	**1**	**0**	**1**	**24**	**0**	**0**	**0**	**7:57**
2003-04	**Ottawa**	**NHL**	**82**	**8**	**8**	**16**	**194**	**0**	**0**	**1**	**76**	**10.5**	**13**	**14**	**42.9**	**8:51**	**7**	**0**	**1**	**1**	**19**	**0**	**0**	**0**	**6:45**
2004-05	Binghamton	AHL	22	4	6	10	132										6	1	1	2	26				
2005-06	**Ottawa**	**NHL**	**79**	**16**	**17**	**33**	**204**	**8**	**0**	**0**	**126**	**12.7**	**9**	**9**	**22.2**	**12:18**	**10**	**1**	**0**	**1**	**14**	**0**	**0**	**0**	**6:58**
2006-07	**Ottawa**	**NHL**	**82**	**12**	**16**	**28**	**177**	**3**	**0**	**3**	**139**	**8.6**	**6**	**13**	**38.5**	**13:08**	**20**	**2**	**2**	**4**	**20**	**0**	**0**	**0**	**10:40**
2007-08	**Ottawa**	**NHL**	**68**	**6**	**14**	**20**	**199**	**0**	**0**	**1**	**78**	**7.7**	**–3**	**0**	**0.0**	**12:46**	**4**	**0**	**1**	**1**	**22**	**0**	**0**	**0**	**11:17**
	NHL Totals		**451**	**58**	**66**	**124**	**1152**	**12**	**0**	**5**	**537**	**10.8**		**41**	**39.0**	**10:34**	**68**	**4**	**4**	**8**	**111**	**0**	**0**	**0**	**8:33**

Signed as a free agent by **Binghamton** (AHL), March 2, 2005.

NEWBURY, Kris

(new-BUHR-ee, KRIHS) **TOR.**

Center. Shoots left. 5'10", 200 lbs. Born, Brampton, Ont., February 19, 1982. San Jose's 4th choice, 139th overall, in 2002 Entry Draft.

Season	Club	League	GP	G	A	Pts	PIM	PP	SH	GW	S	%	+/-	TF	F%	Min	GP	G	A	Pts	PIM	PP	SH	GW	Min
1996-97	Brampton	OPJHL	28	9	4	13	36																		
1997-98	Brampton	OPJHL	46	11	21	32	161																		
1998-99	Belleville Bulls	OHL	51	6	8	14	89																		
99-2000	Belleville Bulls	OHL	34	6	18	24	72																		
	Sarnia Sting	OHL	27	6	8	14	44										7	0	3	3	16				
2000-01	Sarnia Sting	OHL	64	28	30	58	126										4	1	3	4	20				
2001-02	Sarnia Sting	OHL	66	42	62	104	141										5	1	3	4	15				
2002-03	Sarnia Sting	OHL	64	34	58	92	149										6	4	4	8	16				
2003-04	St. John's	AHL	72	5	15	20	153																		
2004-05	St. John's	AHL	55	4	9	13	103										5	0	0	0	36				
	Pensacola	ECHL	6	2	4	6	20																		
2005-06	Toronto Marlies	AHL	74	22	37	59	215										5	0	1	1	12				
2006-07	**Toronto**	**NHL**	**15**	**2**	**2**	**4**	**26**	**0**	**0**	**0**	**30**	**6.7**	**4**	**20**	**45.0**	**7:42**									
	Toronto Marlies	AHL	37	12	24	36	87																		
2007-08	**Toronto**	**NHL**	**28**	**1**	**1**	**2**	**32**	**0**	**0**	**0**	**14**	**7.1**	**–7**	**55**	**40.0**	**4:22**									
	Toronto Marlies	AHL	54	16	27	43	101										19	4	9	13	*73				
	NHL Totals		**43**	**3**	**3**	**6**	**58**	**0**	**0**	**0**	**44**	**6.8**		**75**	**41.3**	**5:32**									

OHL Second All-Star Team (2002)

Signed as a free agent by **St. John's** (AHL), October 2, 2003. Signed as a free agent by **Toronto**, July 17, 2006.

NICHOL, Scott

(NIH-KOHL, SKAWT) **NSH.**

Center. Shoots right. 5'9", 175 lbs. Born, Edmonton, Alta., December 31, 1974. Buffalo's 9th choice, 272nd overall, in 1993 Entry Draft.

Season	Club	League	GP	G	A	Pts	PIM	PP	SH	GW	S	%	+/-	TF	F%	Min	GP	G	A	Pts	PIM	PP	SH	GW	Min
1991-92	Cgy. AAA Flames	AMHL	23	26	16	42	132																		
1992-93	Portland	WHL	67	31	33	64	146										16	8	8	16	41				
1993-94	Portland	WHL	65	40	53	93	144										10	3	8	11	16				
1994-95	Rochester	AHL	71	11	16	27	136										5	0	3	3	14				
1995-96	**Buffalo**	**NHL**	**2**	**0**	**0**	**0**	**10**	**0**	**0**	**0**	**4**	**0.0**	**0**												
	Rochester	AHL	62	14	18	32	170										19	7	6	13	36				
1996-97	Rochester	AHL	68	22	21	43	133										10	2	1	3	26				
1997-98	**Buffalo**	**NHL**	**3**	**0**	**0**	**0**	**4**	**0**	**0**	**0**	**5**	**0.0**	**0**												
	Rochester	AHL	35	13	7	20	113										17	0	6	6	18				
1998-99	Rochester	AHL	52	13	20	33	120																		
99-2000	Rochester	AHL	37	7	11	18	141										12	0	3	3	10				
2000-01	Detroit Vipers	IHL	67	7	24	31	198										11	1	1	2	12				
2001-02	**Calgary**	**NHL**	**60**	**8**	**9**	**17**	**107**	**2**	**1**	**0**	**49**	**16.3**	**–9**	**458**	**53.1**	**12:41**									

			Regular Season															Playoffs								
Season	Club	League	GP	G	A	Pts	PIM	PP	SH	GW	S	%	+/-	TF	F%	Min	GP	G	A	Pts	PIM	PP	SH	GW	Min
2002-03	Calgary	NHL	68	5	5	10	149	0	1	0	66	7.6	–7	357	58.3	10:47	....	....	....	....	....	....	....	....	....
2003-04	Chicago	NHL	75	7	11	18	145	0	0	1	112	6.3	–16	1178	57.4	15:46	....	....	....	....	....	....	....	....	....
2004-05	London Racers	Britain	16	7	12	19	86	....	....	....	....	....	....	....	....	....	....	....	....	....	....	....	....	....	....
2005-06	Nashville	NHL	34	3	3	6	79	0	1	0	32	9.4	3	242	58.3	10:30	3	0	0	0	2	0	0	0	7:45
	Milwaukee	AHL	6	3	5	8	18	....	....	....	....	....	....	....	....	....	....	....	....	....	....	....	....	....	....
2006-07	Nashville	NHL	59	7	6	13	79	1	1	2	58	12.1	7	623	58.0	12:32	5	0	0	0	17	0	0	0	10:22
2007-08	Nashville	NHL	73	10	8	18	72	0	2	1	101	9.9	12	738	59.8	13:16	2	0	0	0	0	0	0	0	7:31
	NHL Totals		374	40	42	82	645	3	6	4	427	9.4		3596	57.6	12:51	10	0	0	0	19	0	0	0	9:00

• Missed majority of 1999-2000 season recovering from knee injury suffered in game vs. Saint John (AHL), February 16, 2000. Signed as a free agent by **Calgary**, July 1, 2001. Signed as a free agent by **Chicago**, July 1, 2003. Signed as a free agent by **London** (Britain), October 26, 2004. Signed as a free agent by **Nashville**, August 6, 2005.

NIEDERMAYER, Rob

(NEE-duhr-MIGH-uhr, RAWB) **ANA.**

Center. Shoots left. 6'2", 200 lbs. Born, Cassiar, B.C., December 28, 1974. Florida's 1st choice, 5th overall, in 1993 Entry Draft.

1989-90	Cranbrook Blazers	Minor-BC	35	42	40	82	30	....	....	....	....	....	....	....	....	....	....	....	....	....	....	....	....	....	....
1990-91	Medicine Hat	WHL	71	24	26	50	8	....	....	....	....	....	....	....	....	....	12	3	7	10	2	....	....	....	....
1991-92	Medicine Hat	WHL	71	32	46	78	77	....	....	....	....	....	....	....	....	....	4	2	3	5	2	....	....	....	....
1992-93	Medicine Hat	WHL	52	43	34	77	67	....	....	....	....	....	....	....	....	....	....	....	....	....	....	....	....	....	....
1993-94	Florida	NHL	65	9	17	26	51	3	0	2	67	13.4	–11	....	....	....	....	....	....	....	....	....	....	....	....
1994-95	Medicine Hat	WHL	13	9	15	24	14	....	....	....	....	....	....	....	....	....	....	....	....	....	....	....	....	....	....
	Florida	NHL	48	4	6	10	36	1	0	0	58	6.9	–13	....	....	....	....	....	....	....	....	....	....	....	....
1995-96	Florida	NHL	82	26	35	61	107	11	0	6	155	16.8	1	....	....	....	22	5	3	8	12	2	0	2	....
1996-97	Florida	NHL	60	14	24	38	54	3	0	2	136	10.3	4	....	....	....	5	2	1	3	6	1	0	0	....
1997-98	Florida	NHL	33	8	7	15	41	5	0	2	64	12.5	–9	....	....	....	....	....	....	....	....	....	....	....	....
1998-99	Florida	NHL	82	18	33	51	50	6	1	3	142	12.7	–13	1895	47.1	21:17	....	....	....	....	....	....	....	....	....
99-2000	Florida	NHL	81	10	23	33	46	1	0	4	135	7.4	–5	1632	47.9	19:04	4	1	0	1	6	0	0	0	15:55
2000-01	Florida	NHL	67	12	20	32	50	3	1	0	115	10.4	–12	997	45.0	20:30	....	....	....	....	....	....	....	....	....
2001-02	Calgary	NHL	57	6	14	20	49	1	2	1	87	6.9	–15	777	48.4	18:01	....	....	....	....	....	....	....	....	....
2002-03	Calgary	NHL	54	8	10	18	42	2	0	1	104	7.7	–13	139	48.9	17:29	....	....	....	....	....	....	....	....	....
	Anaheim	NHL	12	2	2	4	15	1	0	0	21	9.5	3	14	42.9	15:21	21	3	7	10	18	0	2	0	23:35
2003-04	Anaheim	NHL	55	12	16	28	34	6	0	2	111	10.8	–6	45	64.4	19:28	....	....	....	....	....	....	....	....	....
2004-05	Ferencvaros	Hungary	5	2	1	3	14	....	....	....	....	....	....	....	....	....	....	....	....	....	....	....	....	....	....
2005-06	Anaheim	NHL	76	15	24	39	89	4	1	2	140	10.7	–5	447	45.6	17:52	16	1	3	4	10	1	0	0	19:36
2006-07♦	Anaheim	NHL	82	5	11	16	77	0	0	0	106	4.7	–8	76	40.8	16:39	21	5	5	10	39	0	1	1	18:35
2007-08	Anaheim	NHL	78	8	8	16	54	0	1	1	111	7.2	1	69	33.3	17:43	2	0	0	0	0	0	0	0	13:47
	NHL Totals		932	157	250	407	795	47	6	26	1552	10.1		6091	47.0	18:37	91	17	19	36	91	4	3	3	20:09

WHL East First All-Star Team (1993)

• Missed majority of 1997-98 season recovering from thumb (November 26, 1997 vs. Boston) and head (March 19, 1998 vs. Buffalo) injuries. Traded to **Calgary** by **Florida** with Philadelphia's 2nd round choice (previously acquired, Calgary selected Andrei Medvedev) in 2001 Entry Draft for Valeri Bure and Jason Wiemer, June 23, 2001. Traded to **Anaheim** by **Calgary** for Mike Commodore and Jean-Francois Damphousse, March 11, 2003. Signed as a free agent by **Ferencvaros** (Hungary), January 17, 2005.

NIEDERMAYER, Scott

(NEE-duhr-MIGH-uhr, SKAWT) **ANA.**

Defense. Shoots left. 6'1", 200 lbs. Born, Edmonton, Alta., August 31, 1973. New Jersey's 1st choice, 3rd overall, in 1991 Entry Draft.

1988-89	Cranbrook Blazers	Minor-BC	62	55	37	92	100	....	....	....	....	....	....	....	....	....	....	....	....	....	....	....	....	....	....
1989-90	Kamloops Blazers	WHL	64	14	55	69	64	....	....	....	....	....	....	....	....	....	17	2	14	16	35	....	....	....	....
1990-91	Kamloops Blazers	WHL	57	26	56	82	52	....	....	....	....	....	....	....	....	....	....	....	....	....	....	....	....	....	....
1991-92	Kamloops Blazers	WHL	35	7	32	39	61	....	....	....	....	....	....	....	....	....	17	9	14	23	28	....	....	....	....
	New Jersey	NHL	4	0	1	1	2	0	0	0	4	0.0	1	....	....	....	....	....	....	....	....	....	....	....	....
1992-93	New Jersey	NHL	80	11	29	40	47	5	0	0	131	8.4	8	....	....	....	5	0	3	3	2	0	0	0	....
1993-94	New Jersey	NHL	81	10	36	46	42	5	0	2	135	7.4	34	....	....	....	20	2	2	4	8	1	0	0	....
1994-95♦	New Jersey	NHL	48	4	15	19	18	4	0	0	52	7.7	19	....	....	....	20	4	7	11	10	2	0	1	....
1995-96	New Jersey	NHL	79	8	25	33	46	6	0	0	179	4.5	5	....	....	....	....	....	....	....	....	....	....	....	....
1996-97	New Jersey	NHL	81	5	30	35	64	3	0	3	159	3.1	–4	....	....	....	10	2	4	6	6	2	0	1	....
1997-98	New Jersey	NHL	81	14	43	57	27	11	0	1	175	8.0	5	....	....	....	6	0	2	2	4	0	0	0	....
1998-99	Utah Grizzlies	IHL	5	0	2	2	0	....	....	....	....	....	....	....	....	....	....	....	....	....	....	....	....	....	....
	New Jersey	NHL	72	11	35	46	26	1	1	3	161	6.8	16	13	15.4	24:40	7	1	3	4	18	1	0	0	25:30
99-2000♦	New Jersey	NHL	71	7	31	38	48	1	0	0	109	6.4	19	8	37.5	24:21	22	5	2	7	10	0	2	1	25:28
2000-01	New Jersey	NHL	57	6	29	35	22	1	0	5	87	6.9	14	5	0.0	23:19	21	0	6	6	14	0	0	0	23:53
2001-02	New Jersey	NHL	76	11	22	33	30	2	0	6	129	8.5	12	1	100.0	24:17	6	0	2	2	6	0	0	0	26:37
	Canada	Olympics	6	1	1	2	4	....	....	....	....	....	....	....	....	....	....	....	....	....	....	....	....	....	....
2002-03♦	New Jersey	NHL	81	11	28	39	62	3	0	3	164	6.7	23	1	0.0	24:30	24	2	*16	*18	16	1	0	0	26:07
2003-04	New Jersey	NHL	81	14	40	54	44	9	0	3	165	8.5	20	1	0.0	25:56	5	1	0	1	6	0	0	0	27:21
2004-05			Did not play																						
2005-06	Anaheim	NHL	82	13	50	63	96	9	0	3	181	7.2	8	7	28.6	25:30	16	2	9	11	14	1	1	1	28:54
	Canada	Olympics	Did not play – injured																						
2006-07♦	Anaheim	NHL	79	15	54	69	86	9	0	3	172	8.7	6	1	100.0	27:31	21	3	8	11	26	1	0	2	29:51
2007-08	Anaheim	NHL	48	8	17	25	16	7	0	3	87	9.2	–2	0	0.0	23:54	6	0	2	2	4	0	0	0	24:24
	NHL Totals		1101	148	485	633	676	76	1	35	2090	7.1		37	24.3	25:00	189	22	66	88	144	9	3	6	26:33

WHL West First All-Star Team (1991, 1992) • Canadian Major Junior Scholastic Player of the Year (1991) • Memorial Cup Tournament All-Star Team (1992) • Stafford Smythe Memorial Trophy (Memorial Cup Tournament - MVP) (1992) • NHL All-Rookie Team (1993) • NHL Second All-Star Team (1998) • NHL First All-Star Team (2004, 2006, 2007) • James Norris Memorial Trophy (2004) • Conn Smythe Trophy (2007)

Played in NHL All-Star Game (1998, 2001, 2004, 2008)

Signed to PTO (tryout) contract by **Utah** (IHL) with **New Jersey** retaining NHL rights, October 19, 1998. Signed as a free agent by **Anaheim**, August 4, 2005.

NIELSEN, Frans

(NEEL-sehn, FRAHNZ) **NYI**

Center. Shoots left. 5'11", 172 lbs. Born, Herning, Denmark, April 24, 1984. NY Islanders' 2nd choice, 87th overall, in 2002 Entry Draft.

99-2000	Herning IK Jr.	Den-Jr.	36	18	16	34	6	....	....	....	....	....	....	....	....	....	....	....	....	....	....	....	....	....	....
2000-01	Herning IK	Denmark	38	18	19	37	6	....	....	....	....	....	....	....	....	....	....	....	....	....	....	....	....	....	....
2001-02	Malmo	Sweden	20	0	1	1	0	....	....	....	....	....	....	....	....	....	....	....	....	....	....	....	....	....	....
	Malmo Jr.	Swe-Jr.	29	15	27	42	8	....	....	....	....	....	....	....	....	....	7	3	7	10	2	....	....	....	....
2002-03	Malmo	Sweden	47	3	6	9	10	....	....	....	....	....	....	....	....	....	....	....	....	....	....	....	....	....	....
	Malmo Jr.	Swe-Jr.	2	1	3	4	0	....	....	....	....	....	....	....	....	....	....	....	....	....	....	....	....	....	....
2003-04	Malmo	Sweden	50	9	7	16	28	....	....	....	....	....	....	....	....	....	....	....	....	....	....	....	....	....	....
	Malmo	Sweden-Q	10	3	5	8	2	....	....	....	....	....	....	....	....	....	....	....	....	....	....	....	....	....	....
2004-05	Malmo	Sweden	49	8	7	15	6	....	....	....	....	....	....	....	....	....	....	....	....	....	....	....	....	....	....
	Malmo	Sweden-Q	10	7	2	9	0	....	....	....	....	....	....	....	....	....	....	....	....	....	....	....	....	....	....
2005-06	Timra IK	Sweden	50	5	13	18	22	....	....	....	....	....	....	....	....	....	....	....	....	....	....	....	....	....	....
2006-07	NY Islanders	NHL	15	1	1	2	0	0	0	1	16	6.3	–2	53	45.3	5:13	....	....	....	....	....	....	....	....	....
	Bridgeport	AHL	54	20	24	44	10	....	....	....	....	....	....	....	....	....	....	....	....	....	....	....	....	....	....
2007-08	NY Islanders	NHL	16	2	1	3	0	0	0	0	17	11.8	1	111	48.7	8:42	....	....	....	....	....	....	....	....	....
	Bridgeport	AHL	48	10	28	38	18	....	....	....	....	....	....	....	....	....	....	....	....	....	....	....	....	....	....
	NHL Totals		31	3	2	5	0	0	0	1	33	9.1		164	47.6	7:01									

NIEMINEN, Ville

(nee-EHM-ih-nehn, VIHL-ee)

Left wing. Shoots left. 5'11", 200 lbs. Born, Tampere, Finland, April 6, 1977. Colorado's 4th choice, 78th overall, in 1997 Entry Draft.

1993-94	Tappara U18	Fin-U18	29	13	20	33	66	....	....	....	....	....	....	....	....	....	5	1	2	3	0	....	....	....	....
1994-95	Tappara U18	Fin-U18	15	14	18	32	68	....	....	....	....	....	....	....	....	....	7	2	16	18	22	....	....	....	....
	Tappara Jr.	Fin-Jr.	16	11	21	32	47	....	....	....	....	....	....	....	....	....	....	....	....	....	....	....	....	....	....
	Tappara Tampere	Finland	16	0	0	0	0	....	....	....	....	....	....	....	....	....	....	....	....	....	....	....	....	....	....
1995-96	Tappara Jr.	Fin-Jr.	20	20	23	43	63	....	....	....	....	....	....	....	....	....	....	....	....	....	....	....	....	....	....
	Tappara Tampere	Finland	4	0	1	1	8	....	....	....	....	....	....	....	....	....	....	....	....	....	....	....	....	....	....
	KooVee Tampere	Finland-2	7	2	1	3	4	....	....	....	....	....	....	....	....	....	....	....	....	....	....	....	....	....	....
1996-97	Tappara Jr.	Fin-Jr.	2	2	7	9	2	....	....	....	....	....	....	....	....	....	....	....	....	....	....	....	....	....	....
	Tappara Tampere	Finland	49	10	13	23	120	....	....	....	....	....	....	....	....	....	3	1	0	1	8	....	....	....	....
1997-98	Hershey Bears	AHL	74	14	22	36	85	....	....	....	....	....	....	....	....	....	....	....	....	....	....	....	....	....	....
1998-99	Hershey Bears	AHL	67	24	19	43	127	....	....	....	....	....	....	....	....	....	3	0	1	1	0	....	....	....	....

Season	Club	League	Regular Season GP	G	A	Pts	PIM	PP	SH	GW	S	%	+/-	TF	F%	Min	Playoffs GP	G	A	Pts	PIM	PP	SH	GW	Min
99-2000	**Colorado**	**NHL**	**1**	**0**	**0**	**0**	**0**	**0**	**0**	**0**	**2**	**0.0**	**0**	**0**	**0.0**	**10:12**	....	....	....	....	....	....	....	....	....
	Hershey Bears	AHL	74	21	30	51	54	....	....	....	....	....	....	....	....	....	9	2	4	6	6	....	....	....	....
2000-01 ♦	**Colorado**	**NHL**	**50**	**14**	**8**	**22**	**38**	**2**	**0**	**3**	**68**	**20.6**	**8**	**3**	**33.3**	**12:26**	**23**	**4**	**6**	**10**	**20**	**3**	**0**	**1**	**14:10**
	Hershey Bears	AHL	28	10	11	21	48	....	....	....	....	....	....	....	....	....	....	....	....	....	....	....	....	....	....
2001-02	**Colorado**	**NHL**	**53**	**10**	**14**	**24**	**30**	**1**	**0**	**5**	**72**	**13.9**	**1**	**8**	**62.5**	**12:41**	....	....	....	....	....	....	....	....	....
	Finland	Olympics	4	0	1	1	2	....	....	....	....	....	....	....	....	....	....	....	....	....	....	....	....	....	....
	Pittsburgh	**NHL**	**13**	**1**	**2**	**3**	**8**	**0**	**0**	**0**	**11**	**9.1**	**–2**	**0**	**0.0**	**16:10**	....	....	....	....	....	....	....	....	....
2002-03	**Pittsburgh**	**NHL**	**75**	**9**	**12**	**21**	**93**	**0**	**2**	**1**	**86**	**10.5**	**–25**	**46**	**52.2**	**14:08**	....	....	....	....	....	....	....	....	....
2003-04	**Chicago**	**NHL**	**60**	**2**	**11**	**13**	**40**	**1**	**0**	**0**	**56**	**3.6**	**–15**	**4**	**25.0**	**11:46**	....	....	....	....	....	....	....	....	....
	Calgary	**NHL**	**19**	**3**	**5**	**8**	**18**	**0**	**0**	**1**	**27**	**11.1**	**6**	**5**	**0.0**	**14:36**	**24**	**4**	**4**	**8**	**55**	**1**	**0**	**0**	**16:17**
2004-05	Tappara Tampere	Finland	26	14	13	27	32	....	....	....	....	....	....	....	....	....	8	2	4	6	12	....	....	....	....
2005-06	**NY Rangers**	**NHL**	**48**	**5**	**12**	**17**	**53**	**0**	**0**	**2**	**73**	**6.8**	**10**	**6**	**33.3**	**11:38**	....	....	....	....	....	....	....	....	....
	Finland	Olympics	8	0	1	1	4	....	....	....	....	....	....	....	....	....	....	....	....	....	....	....	....	....	....
	San Jose	**NHL**	**22**	**3**	**4**	**7**	**10**	**0**	**1**	**0**	**41**	**7.3**	**–3**	**3**	**33.3**	**15:23**	**11**	**0**	**2**	**2**	**24**	**0**	**0**	**0**	**15:39**
2006-07	**San Jose**	**NHL**	**30**	**1**	**1**	**2**	**14**	**0**	**0**	**0**	**30**	**3.3**	**–7**	**0**	**0.0**	**8:38**	....	....	....	....	....	....	....	....	....
	St. Louis	**NHL**	**14**	**0**	**0**	**0**	**29**	**0**	**0**	**0**	**13**	**0.0**	**–1**	**0**	**0.0**	**9:09**	....	....	....	....	....	....	....	....	....
2007-08	Malmo	Sweden-2	34	9	15	24	124	....	....	....	....	....	....	....	....	....	10	2	4	6	10	....	....	....	....
	NHL Totals		**385**	**48**	**69**	**117**	**333**	**4**	**3**	**12**	**479**	**10.0**		**75**	**45.3**	**12:35**	**58**	**8**	**12**	**20**	**99**	**4**	**0**	**1**	**15:19**

Traded to **Pittsburgh** by **Colorado** with Rick Berry for Darius Kasparaitis, March 19, 2002. Signed as a free agent by **Chicago**, July 29, 2003. Traded to **Calgary** by **Chicago** for Jason Morgan and Calgary's 6th round choice (Joseph Fallon) in 2005 Entry Draft, February 24, 2004. Signed as a free agent by **Tappara Tampere** (Finland), July 22, 2004. Signed as a free agent by **NY Rangers**, August 4, 2005. Traded to **San Jose** by **NY Rangers** for San Jose's 3rd round choice (later traded to Anaheim - Anaheim selected John DeGray) in 2006 Entry Draft, March 8, 2006. Traded to **St. Louis** by **San Jose** with Jay Barriball and New Jersey's 1st round choice (previously acquired, St. Louis selected David Perron) in 2007 Entry Draft for Bill Guerin, February 27, 2007.

NIKULIN, Alexander (nih-KOO-lihn, al-EHX-AN-duhr) OTT.

Center. Shoots left. 6'1", 205 lbs. Born, Moscow, USSR, August 25, 1985. Ottawa's 6th choice, 122nd overall, in 2004 Entry Draft.

Season	Club	League	GP	G	A	Pts	PIM	PP	SH	GW	S	%	+/-	TF	F%	Min	GP	G	A	Pts	PIM	PP	SH	GW	Min
2002-03	CSKA Moscow 2	Russia-3	46	22	14	36	....	....	....	....	....	....	....	....	....	....	....	....	....	....	....	....	....	....	....
2003-04	CSKA Moscow 2	Russia-3	47	21	20	41	46	....	....	....	....	....	....	....	....	....	....	....	....	....	....	....	....	....	....
2004-05	CSKA Moscow	Russia	16	3	3	6	0	....	....	....	....	....	....	....	....	....	....	....	....	....	....	....	....	....	....
2005-06	CSKA Moscow	Russia	51	10	12	22	22	....	....	....	....	....	....	....	....	....	7	1	0	1	2	....	....	....	....
2006-07	CSKA Moscow	Russia	33	5	11	16	8	....	....	....	....	....	....	....	....	....	12	4	2	6	4	....	....	....	....
2007-08	**Ottawa**	**NHL**	**2**	**0**	**0**	**0**	**0**	**0**	**0**	**0**	**0**	**0.0**	**–2**	**1**	**100.0**	**4:56**	....	....	....	....	....	....	....	....	....
	Binghamton	AHL	71	14	36	50	34	....	....	....	....	....	....	....	....	....	....	....	....	....	....	....	....	....	....
	NHL Totals		**2**	**0**	**0**	**0**	**0**	**0**	**0**	**0**	**0**	**0.0**		**1**	**100.0**	**4:56**	....	....	....	....	....	....	....	....	....

NILSON, Marcus (NIHL-suhn, MAHR-kuhs) CGY.

Left wing. Shoots right. 6'2", 189 lbs. Born, Balsta, Sweden, March 1, 1978. Florida's 1st choice, 20th overall, in 1996 Entry Draft.

Season	Club	League	GP	G	A	Pts	PIM	PP	SH	GW	S	%	+/-	TF	F%	Min	GP	G	A	Pts	PIM	PP	SH	GW	Min
1994-95	Djurgarden Jr.	Swe-Jr.	24	7	8	15	22	....	....	....	....	....	....	....	....	....	....	....	....	....	....	....	....	....	....
1995-96	Djurgarden Jr.	Swe-Jr.	25	19	17	36	46	....	....	....	....	....	....	....	....	....	2	1	1	2	12	....	....	....	....
	Djurgarden	Sweden	12	0	0	0	0	....	....	....	....	....	....	....	....	....	1	0	0	0	0	....	....	....	....
1996-97	Djurgarden	Sweden	37	0	3	3	33	....	....	....	....	....	....	....	....	....	4	0	0	0	0	....	....	....	....
1997-98	Djurgarden	Sweden	41	4	7	11	18	....	....	....	....	....	....	....	....	....	15	2	1	3	16	....	....	....	....
1998-99	**Florida**	**NHL**	**8**	**1**	**1**	**2**	**5**	**0**	**0**	**1**	**7**	**14.3**	**2**	**6**	**50.0**	**12:24**	....	....	....	....	....	....	....	....	....
	New Haven	AHL	69	8	25	33	10	....	....	....	....	....	....	....	....	....	....	....	....	....	....	....	....	....	....
99-2000	**Florida**	**NHL**	**9**	**0**	**2**	**2**	**2**	**0**	**0**	**0**	**6**	**0.0**	**2**	**14**	**64.3**	**7:56**	....	....	....	....	....	....	....	....	....
	Louisville Panthers	AHL	64	9	23	32	52	....	....	....	....	....	....	....	....	....	4	0	0	0	2	....	....	....	....
2000-01	**Florida**	**NHL**	**78**	**12**	**24**	**36**	**74**	**0**	**0**	**2**	**141**	**8.5**	**–3**	**169**	**40.8**	**15:46**	....	....	....	....	....	....	....	....	....
2001-02	**Florida**	**NHL**	**81**	**14**	**19**	**33**	**55**	**6**	**1**	**2**	**147**	**9.5**	**–14**	**539**	**43.8**	**16:31**	....	....	....	....	....	....	....	....	....
2002-03	**Florida**	**NHL**	**82**	**15**	**19**	**34**	**31**	**7**	**1**	**0**	**187**	**8.0**	**2**	**469**	**46.7**	**15:31**	....	....	....	....	....	....	....	....	....
2003-04	**Florida**	**NHL**	**69**	**6**	**13**	**19**	**26**	**1**	**1**	**1**	**110**	**5.5**	**–9**	**151**	**44.4**	**15:30**	....	....	....	....	....	....	....	....	....
	Calgary	**NHL**	**14**	**5**	**0**	**5**	**14**	**1**	**0**	**2**	**23**	**21.7**	**3**	**173**	**45.1**	**16:43**	**26**	**4**	**7**	**11**	**12**	**0**	**0**	**1**	**19:25**
2004-05	Djurgarden	Sweden	48	17	22	39	110	....	....	....	....	....	....	....	....	....	7	1	2	3	10	....	....	....	....
2005-06	**Calgary**	**NHL**	**70**	**6**	**11**	**17**	**32**	**2**	**0**	**2**	**83**	**7.2**	**13**	**392**	**45.4**	**14:50**	....	....	....	....	....	....	....	....	....
2006-07	**Calgary**	**NHL**	**63**	**5**	**10**	**15**	**27**	**0**	**0**	**1**	**69**	**7.2**	**7**	**119**	**31.9**	**13:07**	**6**	**0**	**0**	**0**	**2**	**0**	**0**	**0**	**13:32**
2007-08	**Calgary**	**NHL**	**47**	**3**	**2**	**5**	**4**	**0**	**0**	**0**	**47**	**6.4**	**2**	**41**	**51.2**	**9:49**	**2**	**0**	**0**	**0**	**0**	**0**	**0**	**0**	**4:50**
	NHL Totals		**521**	**67**	**101**	**168**	**270**	**17**	**3**	**11**	**820**	**8.2**		**2073**	**44.3**	**14:40**	**34**	**4**	**7**	**11**	**14**	**0**	**0**	**1**	**17:31**

Traded to **Calgary** by **Florida** for Calgary's 2nd round choice (David Booth) in 2004 Entry Draft, March 8, 2004. Signed as a free agent by **Djurgarden** (Sweden), September 16, 2004.

NILSSON, Robert (NIHL-suhn, RAW-buhrt) EDM.

Center. Shoots left. 5'11", 185 lbs. Born, Calgary, Alta., January 10, 1985. NY Islanders' 1st choice, 15th overall, in 2003 Entry Draft.

Season	Club	League	GP	G	A	Pts	PIM	PP	SH	GW	S	%	+/-	TF	F%	Min	GP	G	A	Pts	PIM	PP	SH	GW	Min
2000-01	Leksands IF Jr.	Swe-Jr.	23	14	28	42	26	....	....	....	....	....	....	....	....	....	2	0	0	0	2	....	....	....	....
	Leksands IF U18	Swe-U18	4	6	3	9	6	....	....	....	....	....	....	....	....	....	2	0	2	2	2	....	....	....	....
2001-02	Leksands IF Jr.	Swe-Jr.	21	13	18	31	24	....	....	....	....	....	....	....	....	....	5	0	5	5	8	....	....	....	....
	Leksands IF	Sweden-2	14	1	4	5	8	....	....	....	....	....	....	....	....	....	....	....	....	....	....	....	....	....	....
2002-03	Leksands IF	Sweden	41	8	13	21	10	....	....	....	....	....	....	....	....	....	5	0	1	1	2	....	....	....	....
	Leksands IF Jr.	Swe-Jr.	....	....	....	....	....	....	....	....	....	....	....	....	....	....	2	1	1	2	2	....	....	....	....
2003-04	Leksands IF Jr.	Swe-Jr.	4	2	8	10	4	....	....	....	....	....	....	....	....	....	....	....	....	....	....	....	....	....	....
	Leksands IF	Sweden	34	2	4	6	6	....	....	....	....	....	....	....	....	....	....	....	....	....	....	....	....	....	....
	Fribourg	Swiss	7	1	3	4	2	....	....	....	....	....	....	....	....	....	4	1	0	1	2	....	....	....	....
2004-05	Almtuna	Sweden-2	3	0	1	1	2	....	....	....	....	....	....	....	....	....	....	....	....	....	....	....	....	....	....
	Hammarby	Sweden-2	7	0	4	4	4	....	....	....	....	....	....	....	....	....	....	....	....	....	....	....	....	....	....
	Djurgarden Jr.	Swe-Jr.	8	8	4	12	12	....	....	....	....	....	....	....	....	....	....	....	....	....	....	....	....	....	....
	Djurgarden	Sweden	23	2	4	6	6	....	....	....	....	....	....	....	....	....	3	0	0	0	0	....	....	....	....
2005-06	**NY Islanders**	**NHL**	**53**	**6**	**14**	**20**	**26**	**1**	**0**	**1**	**70**	**8.6**	**–6**	**31**	**29.0**	**11:52**	....	....	....	....	....	....	....	....	....
	Bridgeport	AHL	29	8	20	28	12	....	....	....	....	....	....	....	....	....	7	1	4	5	0	....	....	....	....
2006-07	Bridgeport	AHL	50	12	34	46	34	....	....	....	....	....	....	....	....	....	....	....	....	....	....	....	....	....	....
	Edmonton	**NHL**	**4**	**1**	**0**	**1**	**4**	**0**	**0**	**0**	**8**	**12.5**	**–1**	**2**	**50.0**	**17:21**	....	....	....	....	....	....	....	....	....
	Wilkes-Barre	AHL	19	6	14	20	14	....	....	....	....	....	....	....	....	....	11	3	12	15	8	....	....	....	....
2007-08	**Edmonton**	**NHL**	**71**	**10**	**31**	**41**	**22**	**3**	**0**	**0**	**102**	**9.8**	**8**	**15**	**46.7**	**13:56**	....	....	....	....	....	....	....	....	....
	Springfield	AHL	5	2	2	4	4	....	....	....	....	....	....	....	....	....	....	....	....	....	....	....	....	....	....
	NHL Totals		**128**	**17**	**45**	**62**	**52**	**4**	**0**	**1**	**180**	**9.4**		**48**	**35.4**	**13:11**	....	....	....	....	....	....	....	....	....

Traded to **Edmonton** by **NY Islanders** with Ryan O'Marra and NY Islanders' 1st round choice (Alex Plante) in 2007 Entry Draft for Ryan Smyth, February 27, 2007.

NISKANEN, Matt (NIHS-kah-nehn, MAT) DAL.

Defense. Shoots right. 6', 194 lbs. Born, Virginia, MN, December 6, 1986. Dallas' 1st choice, 28th overall, in 2005 Entry Draft.

Season	Club	League	GP	G	A	Pts	PIM	PP	SH	GW	S	%	+/-	TF	F%	Min	GP	G	A	Pts	PIM	PP	SH	GW	Min
2003-04	Virginia	High-MN	....	24	37	61	....	....	....	....	....	....	....	....	....	....	....	....	....	....	....	....	....	....	....
2004-05	Virginia	High-MN	29	27	38	65	34	....	....	....	....	....	....	....	....	....	....	....	....	....	....	....	....	....	....
2005-06	U. Minn-Duluth	WCHA	38	1	13	14	40	....	....	....	....	....	....	....	....	....	....	....	....	....	....	....	....	....	....
2006-07	U. Minn-Duluth	WCHA	39	9	22	31	42	....	....	....	....	....	....	....	....	....	....	....	....	....	....	....	....	....	....
	Iowa Stars	AHL	13	0	3	3	6	....	....	....	....	....	....	....	....	....	12	2	5	7	10	....	....	....	....
2007-08	**Dallas**	**NHL**	**78**	**7**	**19**	**26**	**36**	**2**	**0**	**0**	**99**	**7.1**	**22**	**0**	**0.0**	**20:30**	**16**	**0**	**3**	**3**	**10**	**0**	**0**	**0**	**16:23**
	NHL Totals		**78**	**7**	**19**	**26**	**36**	**2**	**0**	**0**	**99**	**7.1**		**0**	**0.0**	**20:30**	**16**	**0**	**3**	**3**	**10**	**0**	**0**	**0**	**16:23**

WCHA First All-Star Team (2007)

NOKELAINEN, Petteri (noh-kuh-LAY-nehn, PEH-tuh-ree) BOS.

Center. Shoots right. 6'1", 195 lbs. Born, Imatra, Finland, January 16, 1986. NY Islanders' 1st choice, 16th overall, in 2004 Entry Draft.

Season	Club	League	GP	G	A	Pts	PIM	PP	SH	GW	S	%	+/-	TF	F%	Min	GP	G	A	Pts	PIM	PP	SH	GW	Min
2001-02	SaiPa U18	Fin-U18	6	2	1	3	14	....	....	....	....	....	....	....	....	....	....	....	....	....	....	....	....	....	....
2002-03	SaiPa U18	Fin-U18	10	3	8	11	18	....	....	....	....	....	....	....	....	....	....	....	....	....	....	....	....	....	....
	SaiPa Jr.	Fin-Jr.	28	7	4	11	28	....	....	....	....	....	....	....	....	....	3	1	0	1	4	....	....	....	....
	SaiPa	Finland	2	1	0	1	2	....	....	....	....	....	....	....	....	....	....	....	....	....	....	....	....	....	....
2003-04	Suomi U20	Finland-2	3	0	1	1	0	....	....	....	....	....	....	....	....	....	....	....	....	....	....	....	....	....	....
	SaiPa Jr.	Fin-Jr.	10	5	3	8	4	....	....	....	....	....	....	....	....	....	4	0	1	1	0	....	....	....	....
	SaiPa	Finland	40	4	4	8	16	....	....	....	....	....	....	....	....	....	....	....	....	....	....	....	....	....	....
2004-05	SaiPa	Finland	52	15	5	20	34	....	....	....	....	....	....	....	....	....	....	....	....	....	....	....	....	....	....
2005-06	**NY Islanders**	**NHL**	**15**	**1**	**1**	**2**	**4**	**0**	**0**	**1**	**13**	**7.7**	**–1**	**82**	**48.8**	**7:47**	....	....	....	....	....	....	....	....	....
2006-07	Bridgeport	AHL	60	6	10	16	51	....	....	....	....	....	....	....	....	....	....	....	....	....	....	....	....	....	....

			Regular Season														Playoffs								
Season	Club	League	GP	G	A	Pts	PIM	PP	SH	GW	S	%	+/-	TF	F%	Min	GP	G	A	Pts	PIM	PP	SH	GW	Min
2007-08	**Boston**	**NHL**	**57**	**7**	**3**	**10**	**19**	**0**	**0**	**1**	**40**	**17.5**	**0**	**288**	**52.8**	**8:16**	**7**	**0**	**2**	**2**	**4**	**0**	**0**	**0**	**12:38**
	Providence Bruins	AHL	8	3	5	8	4	....	....	....	....	....	....	....	....	....	6	4	1	5	0	....	....	....	....
	NHL Totals		**72**	**8**	**4**	**12**	**23**	**0**	**0**	**2**	**53**	**15.1**		**370**	**51.9**	**8:10**	**7**	**0**	**2**	**2**	**4**	**0**	**0**	**0**	**12:38**

• Missed majority of 2005-06 season recovering from knee injury suffered in game vs. Pittsburgh, November 3, 2005. Traded to **Boston** by **NY Islanders** for Ben Walter and future considerations, September 11, 2007.

NOLAN, Brandon

(NOH-lan, BRAN-duhn) **CAR.**

Center/Left wing. Shoots left. 5'10", 185 lbs. Born, Sault Ste. Marie, Ont., July 18, 1983. Vancouver's 3rd choice, 111th overall, in 2003 Entry Draft.

Season	Club	League	GP	G	A	Pts	PIM	PP	SH	GW	S	%	+/-	TF	F%	Min	GP	G	A	Pts	PIM	PP	SH	GW	Min
99-2000	St. Catharines	OHA-B	47	18	13	31	10	....	....	....	....	....	....	....	....	....	....	....	....	....	....	....	....	....	....
2000-01	Oshawa Generals	OHL	52	15	23	38	21	....	....	....	....	....	....	....	....	....	....	....	....	....	....	....	....	....	....
2001-02	Oshawa Generals	OHL	57	30	28	58	78	....	....	....	....	....	....	....	....	....	5	2	4	6	4	....	....	....	....
2002-03	Oshawa Generals	OHL	68	36	52	88	57	....	....	....	....	....	....	....	....	....	13	10	7	17	4	....	....	....	....
2003-04	Manitoba Moose	AHL	48	7	10	17	18	....	....	....	....	....	....	....	....	....	....	....	....	....	....	....	....	....	....
	Columbia Inferno	ECHL	19	5	10	15	38	....	....	....	....	....	....	....	....	....	3	0	1	1	17	....	....	....	....
2004-05	Manitoba Moose	AHL	48	4	8	12	16	....	....	....	....	....	....	....	....	....	....	....	....	....	....	....	....	....	....
2005-06	Manitoba Moose	AHL	18	3	8	11	10	....	....	....	....	....	....	....	....	....	....	....	....	....	....	....	....	....	....
	Columbia Inferno	ECHL	43	20	31	51	94	....	....	....	....	....	....	....	....	....	....	....	....	....	....	....	....	....	....
2006-07	Bridgeport	AHL	40	9	13	22	59	....	....	....	....	....	....	....	....	....	....	....	....	....	....	....	....	....	....
	Vaxjo Lakers HC	Sweden-2	19	6	10	16	44	....	....	....	....	....	....	....	....	....	....	....	....	....	....	....	....	....	....
2007-08	**Carolina**	**NHL**	**6**	**0**	**1**	**1**	**0**	**0**	**0**	**0**	**2**	**0.0**	**–2**	**0**	**0.0**	**7:15**	....	....	....	....	....	....	....	....	....
	Albany River Rats	AHL	48	22	26	48	72	....	....	....	....	....	....	....	....	....	....	....	....	....	....	....	....	....	....
	NHL Totals		**6**	**0**	**1**	**1**	**0**	**0**	**0**	**0**	**2**	**0.0**		**0**	**0.0**	**7:15**	....	....	....	....	....	....	....	....	....

• Re-entered NHL Entry Draft. Originally New Jersey's 6th choice, 72nd overall, in 2001 Entry Draft.

OHL Second All-Star Team (2003)

Signed as a free agent by **Carolina**, July 2, 2007.

NOLAN, Owen

(NOH-lan, OH-wehn) **MIN.**

Right wing. Shoots right. 6'1", 214 lbs. Born, Belfast, N.Ireland, February 12, 1972. Quebec's 1st choice, 1st overall, in 1990 Entry Draft.

Season	Club	League	GP	G	A	Pts	PIM	PP	SH	GW	S	%	+/-	TF	F%	Min	GP	G	A	Pts	PIM	PP	SH	GW	Min
1987-88	Thorold	Minor-ON	28	53	32	85	24	....	....	....	....	....	....	....	....	....	....	....	....	....	....	....	....	....	....
	Thorold	OHA-B	3	1	0	1	2	....	....	....	....	....	....	....	....	....	....	....	....	....	....	....	....	....	....
1988-89	Cornwall Royals	OHL	62	34	25	59	213	....	....	....	....	....	....	....	....	....	18	5	11	16	41	....	....	....	....
1989-90	Cornwall Royals	OHL	58	51	59	110	240	....	....	....	....	....	....	....	....	....	6	7	5	12	26	....	....	....	....
1990-91	**Quebec**	**NHL**	**59**	**3**	**10**	**13**	**109**	**0**	**0**	**0**	**54**	**5.6**	**–19**	....	....	....	....	....	....	....	....	....	....	....	....
	Halifax Citadels	AHL	6	4	4	8	11	....	....	....	....	....	....	....	....	....	....	....	....	....	....	....	....	....	....
1991-92	**Quebec**	**NHL**	**75**	**42**	**31**	**73**	**183**	**17**	**0**	**0**	**190**	**22.1**	**–9**	....	....	....	....	....	....	....	....	....	....	....	....
1992-93	**Quebec**	**NHL**	**73**	**36**	**41**	**77**	**185**	**15**	**0**	**4**	**241**	**14.9**	**–1**	....	....	....	**5**	**1**	**0**	**1**	**2**	**0**	**0**	**0**	....
1993-94	**Quebec**	**NHL**	**6**	**2**	**2**	**4**	**8**	**0**	**0**	**0**	**15**	**13.3**	**2**	....	....	....	....	....	....	....	....	....	....	....	....
1994-95	**Quebec**	**NHL**	**46**	**30**	**19**	**49**	**46**	**13**	**2**	**8**	**137**	**21.9**	**21**	....	....	....	**6**	**2**	**3**	**5**	**6**	**0**	**0**	**0**	....
1995-96	**Colorado**	**NHL**	**9**	**4**	**4**	**8**	**9**	**4**	**0**	**0**	**23**	**17.4**	**–3**	....	....	....	....	....	....	....	....	....	....	....	....
	San Jose	**NHL**	**72**	**29**	**32**	**61**	**137**	**12**	**1**	**2**	**184**	**15.8**	**–30**	....	....	....	....	....	....	....	....	....	....	....	....
1996-97	**San Jose**	**NHL**	**72**	**31**	**32**	**63**	**155**	**10**	**0**	**3**	**225**	**13.8**	**–19**	....	....	....	....	....	....	....	....	....	....	....	....
1997-98	**San Jose**	**NHL**	**75**	**14**	**27**	**41**	**144**	**3**	**1**	**1**	**192**	**7.3**	**–2**	....	....	....	**6**	**2**	**2**	**4**	**26**	**2**	**0**	**1**	....
1998-99	**San Jose**	**NHL**	**78**	**19**	**26**	**45**	**129**	**6**	**2**	**3**	**207**	**9.2**	**16**	**657**	**49.3**	**19:09**	**6**	**1**	**1**	**2**	**6**	**0**	**0**	**0**	**20:15**
99-2000	**San Jose**	**NHL**	**78**	**44**	**40**	**84**	**110**	**18**	**4**	**6**	**261**	**16.9**	**–1**	**357**	**50.7**	**21:07**	**10**	**8**	**2**	**10**	**6**	**2**	**2**	**3**	**22:14**
2000-01	**San Jose**	**NHL**	**57**	**24**	**25**	**49**	**75**	**10**	**1**	**4**	**191**	**12.6**	**0**	**407**	**46.9**	**21:49**	**6**	**1**	**1**	**2**	**8**	**0**	**0**	**1**	**22:45**
2001-02	**San Jose**	**NHL**	**75**	**23**	**43**	**66**	**93**	**8**	**2**	**2**	**217**	**10.6**	**7**	**545**	**47.0**	**19:23**	**12**	**3**	**6**	**9**	**8**	**0**	**0**	**0**	**19:46**
	Canada	Olympics	6	0	3	3	2	....	....	....	....	....	....	....	....	....	....	....	....	....	....	....	....	....	....
2002-03	**San Jose**	**NHL**	**61**	**22**	**20**	**42**	**91**	**8**	**3**	**4**	**192**	**11.5**	**–5**	**226**	**50.4**	**18:08**	....	....	....	....	....	....	....	....	....
	Toronto	**NHL**	**14**	**7**	**5**	**12**	**16**	**5**	**0**	**1**	**29**	**24.1**	**2**	**56**	**48.2**	**17:00**	**7**	**0**	**2**	**2**	**2**	**0**	**0**	**0**	**23:19**
2003-04	**Toronto**	**NHL**	**65**	**19**	**29**	**48**	**110**	**7**	**2**	**3**	**154**	**12.3**	**4**	**242**	**53.3**	**17:57**	....	....	....	....	....	....	....	....	....
2004-05			DID NOT PLAY																						
2005-06			DID NOT PLAY – INJURED																						
2006-07	**Phoenix**	**NHL**	**76**	**16**	**24**	**40**	**56**	**2**	**3**	**1**	**154**	**10.4**	**–2**	**238**	**52.5**	**15:25**	....	....	....	....	....	....	....	....	....
2007-08	**Calgary**	**NHL**	**77**	**16**	**16**	**32**	**71**	**1**	**1**	**3**	**163**	**9.8**	**6**	**346**	**52.3**	**16:33**	**7**	**3**	**2**	**5**	**2**	**0**	**0**	**2**	**19:11**
	NHL Totals		**1068**	**381**	**426**	**807**	**1727**	**139**	**22**	**45**	**2829**	**13.5**		**3074**	**49.7**	**18:35**	**65**	**21**	**19**	**40**	**66**	**4**	**2**	**7**	**21:09**

OHL Rookie of the Year (1989) • OHL First All-Star Team (1990)

Played in NHL All-Star Game (1992, 1996, 1997, 2000, 2002)

• Missed majority of 1993-94 season recovering from shoulder injury suffered in game vs. Tampa Bay, November 13, 1993. Transferred to **Colorado** after **Quebec** franchise relocated, June 21, 1995. Traded to **San Jose** by **Colorado** for Sandis Ozolinsh, October 26, 1995. Traded to **Toronto** by **San Jose** for Alyn McCauley, Brad Boyes and Toronto's 1st round choice (later traded to Boston – Boston selected Mark Stuart) in 2003 Entry Draft, March 5, 2003. • Missed entire 2005-06 seaon recovering from knee surgery, July, 2005. Signed as a free agent by **Phoenix**, August 16, 2006. Signed as a free agent by **Calgary**, July 3, 2007. Signed as a free agent by **Minnesota**, July 6, 2008.

NORDQVIST, Jonas

(NAWRD-kvihst, YOH-nuhs) **CHI.**

Center. Shoots left. 6'3", 202 lbs. Born, Leksand, Sweden, April 26, 1982. Chicago's 3rd choice, 49th overall, in 2000 Entry Draft.

Season	Club	League	GP	G	A	Pts	PIM	PP	SH	GW	S	%	+/-	TF	F%	Min	GP	G	A	Pts	PIM	PP	SH	GW	Min
1997-98	Leksands IF Jr.	Swe-Jr.	42	26	35	61	....	....	....	....	....	....	....	....	....	....	....	....	....	....	....	....	....	....	....
1998-99	Leksands IF Jr.	Swe-Jr.	32	14	25	39	....	....	....	....	....	....	....	....	....	....	....	....	....	....	....	....	....	....	....
99-2000	Leksands IF Jr.	Swe-Jr.	34	15	24	39	32	....	....	....	....	....	....	....	....	....	2	0	0	0	2	....	....	....	....
	Leksands IF	Sweden	3	0	0	0	0	....	....	....	....	....	....	....	....	....	....	....	....	....	....	....	....	....	....
	Leksands IF U18	Swe-U18	2	0	2	2	0	....	....	....	....	....	....	....	....	....	4	3	5	8	0	....	....	....	....
2000-01	Leksands IF Jr.	Swe-Jr.	10	6	13	19	6	....	....	....	....	....	....	....	....	....	5	1	6	7	2	....	....	....	....
	Leksands IF	Sweden	42	3	4	7	4	....	....	....	....	....	....	....	....	....	....	....	....	....	....	....	....	....	....
2001-02	Leksands IF Jr.	Swe-Jr.	8	14	7	21	6	....	....	....	....	....	....	....	....	....	1	0	1	1	0	....	....	....	....
	Leksands IF	Sweden-2	40	8	7	15	16	....	....	....	....	....	....	....	....	....	....	....	....	....	....	....	....	....	....
2002-03	Rogle	Sweden-2	27	12	19	32	4	....	....	....	....	....	....	....	....	....	....	....	....	....	....	....	....	....	....
2003-04	Lulea HF	Sweden	47	13	11	24	18	....	....	....	....	....	....	....	....	....	3	0	0	0	2	....	....	....	....
2004-05	Lulea HF	Sweden	49	16	16	32	12	....	....	....	....	....	....	....	....	....	4	1	1	2	0	....	....	....	....
2005-06	Lulea HF	Sweden	46	19	22	41	30	....	....	....	....	....	....	....	....	....	6	1	2	3	6	....	....	....	....
2006-07	**Chicago**	**NHL**	**3**	**0**	**2**	**2**	**2**	**0**	**0**	**0**	**2**	**0.0**	**1**	**27**	**29.6**	**13:55**	....	....	....	....	....	....	....	....	....
	Norfolk Admirals	AHL	65	15	26	41	18	....	....	....	....	....	....	....	....	....	6	3	4	7	0	....	....	....	....
2007-08	Frolunda	Sweden	45	9	19	28	37	....	....	....	....	....	....	....	....	....	7	0	2	2	6	....	....	....	....
	NHL Totals		**3**	**0**	**2**	**2**	**2**	**0**	**0**	**0**	**2**	**0.0**		**27**	**29.6**	**13:55**	....	....	....	....	....	....	....	....	....

NORSTROM, Mattias

(NOHR-struhm, mat-TEE-uhs)

Defense. Shoots left. 6'2", 210 lbs. Born, Stockholm, Sweden, January 2, 1972. NY Rangers' 2nd choice, 48th overall, in 1992 Entry Draft.

Season	Club	League	GP	G	A	Pts	PIM	PP	SH	GW	S	%	+/-	TF	F%	Min	GP	G	A	Pts	PIM	PP	SH	GW	Min
1990-91	Mora IK	Sweden-2	9	1	1	2	6	....	....	....	....	....	....	....	....	....	1	0	0	0	2	....	....	....	....
1991-92	AIK Solna	Sweden	39	4	3	7	28	....	....	....	....	....	....	....	....	....	3	0	2	2	2	....	....	....	....
1992-93	AIK Solna	Sweden	22	0	1	1	16	....	....	....	....	....	....	....	....	....	....	....	....	....	....	....	....	....	....
1993-94	**NY Rangers**	**NHL**	**9**	**0**	**2**	**2**	**6**	**0**	**0**	**0**	**3**	**0.0**	**0**	....	....	....	....	....	....	....	....	....	....	....	....
	Binghamton	AHL	55	1	9	10	70	....	....	....	....	....	....	....	....	....	....	....	....	....	....	....	....	....	....
1994-95	Binghamton	AHL	63	9	10	19	91	....	....	....	....	....	....	....	....	....	....	....	....	....	....	....	....	....	....
	NY Rangers	**NHL**	**9**	**0**	**3**	**3**	**2**	**0**	**0**	**0**	**4**	**0.0**	**2**	....	....	....	**3**	**0**	**0**	**0**	**0**	**0**	**0**	**0**	....
1995-96	**NY Rangers**	**NHL**	**25**	**2**	**1**	**3**	**22**	**0**	**0**	**0**	**17**	**11.8**	**5**	....	....	....	....	....	....	....	....	....	....	....	....
	Los Angeles	**NHL**	**11**	**0**	**1**	**1**	**18**	**0**	**0**	**0**	**17**	**0.0**	**–8**	....	....	....	....	....	....	....	....	....	....	....	....
1996-97	**Los Angeles**	**NHL**	**80**	**1**	**21**	**22**	**84**	**0**	**0**	**0**	**106**	**0.9**	**–4**	....	....	....	....	....	....	....	....	....	....	....	....
1997-98	**Los Angeles**	**NHL**	**73**	**1**	**12**	**13**	**90**	**0**	**0**	**0**	**61**	**1.6**	**14**	....	....	....	**4**	**0**	**0**	**0**	**2**	**0**	**0**	**0**	....
	Sweden	Olympics	4	0	1	1	2	....	....	....	....	....	....	....	....	....	....	....	....	....	....	....	....	....	....
1998-99	**Los Angeles**	**NHL**	**78**	**2**	**5**	**7**	**36**	**0**	**1**	**0**	**61**	**3.3**	**–10**	**1**	**0.0**	**20:20**	....	....	....	....	....	....	....	....	....
99-2000	**Los Angeles**	**NHL**	**82**	**1**	**13**	**14**	**66**	**0**	**0**	**0**	**62**	**1.6**	**22**	**0**	**0.0**	**21:49**	**4**	**0**	**0**	**0**	**6**	**0**	**0**	**0**	**21:36**
2000-01	**Los Angeles**	**NHL**	**82**	**0**	**18**	**18**	**60**	**0**	**0**	**0**	**59**	**0.0**	**10**	**2**	**0.0**	**21:50**	**13**	**0**	**2**	**2**	**18**	**0**	**0**	**0**	**23:16**
2001-02	**Los Angeles**	**NHL**	**79**	**2**	**9**	**11**	**38**	**0**	**0**	**0**	**42**	**4.8**	**–2**	**0**	**0.0**	**23:01**	**7**	**0**	**0**	**0**	**4**	**0**	**0**	**0**	**23:24**
	Sweden	Olympics	4	0	0	0	0	....	....	....	....	....	....	....	....	....	....	....	....	....	....	....	....	....	....
2002-03	**Los Angeles**	**NHL**	**82**	**0**	**6**	**6**	**49**	**0**	**0**	**0**	**63**	**0.0**	**0**	**1**	**100.0**	**21:30**	....	....	....	....	....	....	....	....	....
2003-04	**Los Angeles**	**NHL**	**74**	**1**	**13**	**14**	**44**	**0**	**0**	**0**	**65**	**1.5**	**–3**	**1**	**100.0**	**22:26**	....	....	....	....	....	....	....	....	....
2004-05	AIK Solna	Sweden-3	8	1	0	1	4	....	....	....	....	....	....	....	....	....	....	....	....	....	....	....	....	....	....
2005-06	**Los Angeles**	**NHL**	**77**	**4**	**23**	**27**	**58**	**2**	**1**	**1**	**83**	**4.8**	**–3**	**0**	**0.0**	**21:07**	....	....	....	....	....	....	....	....	....

			Regular Season														Playoffs								
Season	Club	League	GP	G	A	Pts	PIM	PP	SH	GW	S	%	+/-	TF	F%	Min	GP	G	A	Pts	PIM	PP	SH	GW	Min
2006-07	**Los Angeles**	**NHL**	**62**	**2**	**7**	**9**	**40**	**0**	**0**	**0**	**44**	**4.5**	**–20**	**4**	**25.0**	**20:55**									
	Dallas	**NHL**	**14**	**0**	**2**	**2**	**8**	**0**	**0**	**0**	**16**	**0.0**	**2**	**0**	**0.0**	**18:54**	**7**	**0**	**0**	**0**	**8**	**0**	**0**	**0**	**23:36**
2007-08	**Dallas**	**NHL**	**66**	**2**	**11**	**13**	**40**	**1**	**0**	**1**	**54**	**3.7**	**3**	**0**	**0.0**	**19:30**	**18**	**2**	**3**	**5**	**16**	**0**	**0**	**1**	**20:20**
	NHL Totals		**903**	**18**	**147**	**165**	**661**	**3**	**2**	**2**	**757**	**2.4**		**9**	**33.3**	**21:23**	**56**	**2**	**5**	**7**	**54**	**0**	**0**	**1**	**22:07**

Played in NHL All-Star Game (1999, 2004)

Traded to **Los Angeles** by **NY Rangers** with Ray Ferraro, Ian Laperriere, Nathan Lafayette and NY Rangers' 4th round choice (Sean Blanchard) in 1997 Entry Draft for Marty McSorley, Jari Kurri and Shane Churla, March 14, 1996. Signed as a free agent by **Solna** (Sweden-3), January 11, 2005. Traded to **Dallas** by **Los Angeles** with Konstantin Pushkarev and Los Angeles' 3rd (Sergei Korostin) and 4th (later traded to Columbus - Columbus selected Maxim Mayorov) round choices in 2007 Entry Draft for Jaroslav Modry, the rights to Johan Fransson, Dallas' 2nd (Oscar Moller) and 3rd (Bryan Cameron) round choices in 2007 Entry Draft and Dallas' 1st round choice (later traded to Phoenix - Phoenix selected Viktor Tikhonov) in 2008 Entry Draft, February 27, 2007.

NOVAK, Filip

(NOH-vak, FIHL-ihp)

Defense. Shoots left. 6'1", 198 lbs. Born, Ceske Budejovice, Czech., May 7, 1982. NY Rangers' 1st choice, 64th overall, in 2000 Entry Draft.

1998-99	C. Budejovice Jr.	CzRep-Jr.	68	8	10	18	34																		
99-2000	Regina Pats	WHL	47	7	32	39	70										7	1	4	5	5				
2000-01	Regina Pats	WHL	64	17	50	67	75										6	1	4	5	6				
2001-02	Regina Pats	WHL	60	12	46	58	125										6	2	2	4	19				
2002-03	San Antonio	AHL	57	10	17	27	79										1	0	0	0	0				
2003-04			DID NOT PLAY – INJURED																						
2004-05	San Antonio	AHL	71	1	12	13	84																		
2005-06	**Ottawa**	**NHL**	**11**	**0**	**0**	**0**	**4**	**0**	**0**	**0**	**5**	**0.0**	**–2**	**0**	**0.0**	**9:26**									
	Binghamton	AHL	64	8	44	52	58																		
2006-07	**Columbus**	**NHL**	**6**	**0**	**0**	**0**	**2**	**0**	**0**	**0**	**3**	**0.0**	**1**	**0**	**0.0**	**9:55**									
	Syracuse Crunch	AHL	67	5	32	37	92																		
2007-08	C. Budejovice	CzRep	45	2	2	4	50										12	0	0	0	29				
	HK 36 Skalica	Slovakia	37	4	1	5	14										4	0	0	0	0				
	NHL Totals		**17**	**0**	**0**	**0**	**6**	**0**	**0**	**0**	**8**	**0.0**		**0**	**0.0**	**9:36**									

WHL East Second All-Star Team (2001) • WHL East First All-Star Team (2002) • AHL All-Rookie Team (2003)

Traded to **Florida** by **NY Rangers** with Igor Ulanov, NY Rangers' 1st (later traded to Calgary – Calgary selected Eric Nystrom) and 2nd (Rob Globke) round choices in 2002 Entry Draft and NY Rangers' 4th round choice (later traded to Atlanta – Atlanta selected Guillaume Desbiens) in 2003 Entry Draft for Pavel Bure and Florida's 2nd round choice (Lee Falardeau) in 2002 Entry Draft, March 18, 2002. • Missed entire 2003-04 season recovering from ankle injury suffered in training camp, September 17, 2003. Traded to **Ottawa** by **Florida** for future considerations, October 5, 2005. Signed as a free agent by **Columbus**, August 13, 2006.

NOVOTNY, Jiri

(nuh-VAWT-nee, YIH-ree) **CBJ**

Center. Shoots right. 6'3", 209 lbs. Born, Pelhrimov, Czech., August 12, 1983. Buffalo's 1st choice, 22nd overall, in 2001 Entry Draft.

99-2000	C. Budejovice Jr.	CzRep-Jr.	36	11	10	21	6																		
	C. Budejovice U17	CzR-U17	11	5	7	12	4																		
	HC Slezan Opava	CzRep-2	17	2	2	4	6																		
2000-01	C. Budejovice Jr.	CzRep-Jr.	33	10	10	20	....																		
	Havl. Brod	CzRep-3	1	0	0	0	0																		
2001-02	C. Budejovice Jr.	CzRep-Jr.	7	4	4	8	4																		
	Jind. Hradec	CzRep-3	3	1	3	4	0																		
	C. Budejovice	CzRep	41	8	6	14	6																		
2002-03	Rochester	AHL	43	2	9	11	14										3	0	1	1	10				
2003-04	Rochester	AHL	48	1	14	15	16										13	0	1	1	10				
2004-05	Rochester	AHL	61	5	20	25	36										9	2	2	4	4				
2005-06	**Buffalo**	**NHL**	**14**	**2**	**1**	**3**	**0**	**0**	**1**	**0**	**15**	**13.3**	**–5**	**139**	**45.3**	**12:15**	**4**	**0**	**0**	**0**	**0**	**0**	**0**	**0**	**10:27**
	Rochester	AHL	66	17	37	54	40																		
2006-07	**Buffalo**	**NHL**	**50**	**6**	**7**	**13**	**26**	**0**	**0**	**0**	**60**	**10.0**	**–2**	**324**	**44.1**	**12:19**									
	Washington	**NHL**	**18**	**0**	**6**	**6**	**2**	**0**	**0**	**0**	**19**	**0.0**	**–2**	**202**	**51.5**	**14:36**									
2007-08	**Columbus**	**NHL**	**65**	**8**	**14**	**22**	**24**	**1**	**0**	**0**	**91**	**8.8**	**–10**	**791**	**47.4**	**17:43**									
	NHL Totals		**147**	**16**	**28**	**44**	**52**	**1**	**1**	**0**	**185**	**8.6**		**1456**	**47.0**	**14:59**	**4**	**0**	**0**	**0**	**0**	**0**	**0**	**0**	**10:27**

Traded to **Washington** by **Buffalo** with Buffalo's 1st round choice (later traded to San Jose - San Jose selected Nicholas Petrecki) in 2007 Entry Draft for Dainius Zubrus and Timo Helbling, February 27, 2007. Signed as a free agent by **Columbus**, July 3, 2007.

NUMMELIN, Petteri

(NOO-muh-lihn, PEH-tuh-ree)

Defense. Shoots left. 5'10", 188 lbs. Born, Turku, Finland, November 25, 1972. Columbus' 3rd choice, 133rd overall, in 2000 Entry Draft.

1988-89	TPS Turku U18	Fin-U18	9	4	10	14	12																		
	TPS Turku Jr.	Fin-Jr.	11	2	3	5	2																		
1989-90	TPS Turku Jr.	Fin-Jr.	33	6	14	20	45																		
1990-91	TPS Turku Jr.	Fin-Jr.	35	20	16	36	28																		
	Kiekko-67 Turku	Finland-2	2	0	2	2	4																		
1991-92	Kiekko-67 Jr.	Fin-Jr.	13	16	15	31	28																		
	Kiekko-67 Turku	Finland-2	41	12	24	36	36																		
1992-93	TPS Turku Jr.	Fin-Jr.	1	1	0	1	0																		
	TPS Turku	Finland	3	0	0	0	8																		
	Kiekko-67 Turku	Finland-2	28	14	15	29	18																		
	Reipas Lahti	Finland	14	3	4	7	18																		
	Reipas Lahti	Finland-Q	6	2	4	6	2																		
1993-94	TPS Turku	Finland	44	14	24	38	20										11	0	3	3	4				
1994-95	TPS Turku	Finland	48	10	17	27	32										11	4	3	7	0				
1995-96	V.Frolunda	Sweden	32	7	11	18	26										12	2	7	9	4				
1996-97	V.Frolunda	Sweden	44	20	14	34	39										2	0	1	1	0				
1997-98	HC Davos	Swiss	33	13	17	30	24										17	8	14	22	2				
1998-99	HC Davos	Swiss	44	11	42	53	22										4	0	2	2	2				
99-2000	HC Davos	Swiss	40	15	23	38	20										5	0	3	3	0				
2000-01	**Columbus**	**NHL**	**61**	**4**	**12**	**16**	**10**	**2**	**0**	**0**	**99**	**4.0**	**–11**	**1**	**0.0**	**17:14**									
2001-02	HC Lugano	Swiss	35	4	18	22	6										13	6	9	15	2				
2002-03	HC Lugano	Swiss	43	18	39	57	12										8	3	6	9	2				
2003-04	HC Lugano	Swiss	48	20	39	59	59										16	6	19	25	4				
2004-05	HC Lugano	Swiss	36	13	34	47	18										3	1	0	1	2				
2005-06	HC Lugano	Swiss	38	13	30	43	22										17	9	*20	*29	10				
	Finland	Olympics	8	0	2	2	2																		
2006-07	**Minnesota**	**NHL**	**51**	**3**	**17**	**20**	**22**	**0**	**0**	**0**	**69**	**4.3**	**–15**	**0**	**0.0**	**20:17**	**3**	**1**	**1**	**2**	**0**	**1**	**0**	**0**	**19:59**
2007-08	**Minnesota**	**NHL**	**27**	**2**	**7**	**9**	**2**	**1**	**0**	**1**	**31**	**6.5**	**–2**	**1**	**0.0**	**15:20**	**4**	**0**	**1**	**1**	**0**	**0**	**0**	**0**	**16:17**
	NHL Totals		**139**	**9**	**36**	**45**	**34**	**3**	**0**	**1**	**199**	**4.5**		**2**	**0.0**	**17:59**	**7**	**1**	**2**	**3**	**0**	**1**	**0**	**0**	**17:52**

Traded to **Atlanta** by **Columbus** with Chris Nielsen for Tomi Kallio and Pauli Levokari, December 2, 2002. Rights traded to **Minnesota** by **Atlanta** for Edmonton's 3rd round choice (previously acquired, Atlanta selected Spencer Machacek) in 2007 Entry Draft, June 14, 2006. • Missed majority of 2007-08 season due to recurring head/neck injury and as a healthy reserve.

NUMMINEN, Teppo

(NOO-mih-nehn, TEH-poh) **BUF.**

Defense. Shoots right. 6'2", 198 lbs. Born, Tampere, Finland, July 3, 1968. Winnipeg's 2nd choice, 29th overall, in 1986 Entry Draft.

1984-85	Whitby Lawmen	OJHL	16	3	9	12	0																		
1985-86	Tappara Jr.	Fin-Jr.	2	0	0	0	0										3	0	1	1	2				
	Tappara Tampere	Finland	31	2	4	6	6										8	0	0	0	0				
1986-87	Tappara Tampere	Finland	44	9	9	18	16										9	4	1	5	4				
1987-88	Tappara Tampere	Finland	40	10	10	20	29										10	6	6	12	6				
	Finland	Olympics	6	1	4	5	0																		
1988-89	**Winnipeg**	**NHL**	**69**	**1**	**14**	**15**	**36**	**0**	**1**	**0**	**85**	**1.2**	**–11**												
1989-90	**Winnipeg**	**NHL**	**79**	**11**	**32**	**43**	**20**	**1**	**0**	**1**	**105**	**10.5**	**–4**				**7**	**1**	**2**	**3**	**10**	**0**	**0**	**0**	
1990-91	**Winnipeg**	**NHL**	**80**	**8**	**25**	**33**	**28**	**3**	**0**	**0**	**151**	**5.3**	**–15**												
1991-92	**Winnipeg**	**NHL**	**80**	**5**	**34**	**39**	**32**	**4**	**0**	**1**	**143**	**3.5**	**15**				**7**	**0**	**0**	**0**	**0**	**0**	**0**	**0**	
1992-93	**Winnipeg**	**NHL**	**66**	**7**	**30**	**37**	**33**	**3**	**1**	**0**	**103**	**6.8**	**4**				**6**	**1**	**1**	**2**	**2**	**1**	**0**	**0**	
1993-94	**Winnipeg**	**NHL**	**57**	**5**	**18**	**23**	**28**	**4**	**0**	**1**	**89**	**5.6**	**–23**												
1994-95	TuTo Turku	Finland	12	3	8	11	4																		
	Winnipeg	**NHL**	**42**	**5**	**16**	**21**	**16**	**2**	**0**	**0**	**86**	**5.8**	**12**												
1995-96	**Winnipeg**	**NHL**	**74**	**11**	**43**	**54**	**22**	**6**	**0**	**3**	**165**	**6.7**	**–4**				**6**	**0**	**0**	**0**	**2**	**0**	**0**	**0**	
1996-97	**Phoenix**	**NHL**	**82**	**2**	**25**	**27**	**28**	**0**	**0**	**0**	**135**	**1.5**	**–3**				**7**	**3**	**3**	**6**	**0**	**1**	**0**	**1**	

			Regular Season														Playoffs								
Season	Club	League	GP	G	A	Pts	PIM	PP	SH	GW	S	%	+/-	TF	F%	Min	GP	G	A	Pts	PIM	PP	SH	GW	Min
1997-98	Phoenix	NHL	82	11	40	51	30	6	0	2	126	8.7	25	....	....	....	1	0	0	0	0	0	0	0	....
	Finland	Olympics	6	1	1	2	2	....	....	....	....	....	....	....	....	....	....	....	....	....	....	....	....	....	....
1998-99	Phoenix	NHL	82	10	30	40	30	1	0	0	156	6.4	3	2	0.0	24:26	7	2	1	3	4	2	0	0	26:09
99-2000	Phoenix	NHL	79	8	34	42	16	2	0	2	126	6.3	21	1	0.0	23:37	5	1	1	2	0	0	0	0	23:11
2000-01	Phoenix	NHL	72	5	26	31	36	1	0	2	109	4.6	9	0	0.0	24:28	....	....	....	....	....	....	....	....	....
2001-02	Phoenix	NHL	76	13	35	48	20	4	0	6	117	11.1	13	0	0.0	23:51	4	0	0	0	2	0	0	0	25:33
	Finland	Olympics	4	0	1	1	0	....	....	....	....	....	....	....	....	....	....	....	....	....	....	....	....	....	....
2002-03	Phoenix	NHL	78	6	24	30	30	2	0	1	108	5.6	0	0	0.0	23:51	....	....	....	....	....	....	....	....	....
2003-04	Dallas	NHL	62	3	14	17	18	0	0	0	83	3.6	–5	1	100.0	21:40	4	0	1	1	0	0	0	0	19:13
2004-05			DID NOT PLAY																						
2005-06	Buffalo	NHL	75	2	38	40	36	0	0	0	60	3.3	6	1	100.0	19:30	12	1	1	2	4	1	0	0	18:45
	Finland	Olympics	8	1	2	3	2	....	....	....	....	....	....	....	....	....	....	....	....	....	....	....	....	....	....
2006-07	Buffalo	NHL	79	2	27	29	32	0	0	0	69	2.9	17	0	0.0	20:48	16	0	4	4	4	0	0	0	19:33
2007-08	Buffalo	NHL	1	0	0	0	0	0	0	0	1	0.0	0	0	0.0	16:03	....	....	....	....	....	....	....	....	....
	NHL Totals		1315	115	505	620	491	39	2	19	2017	5.7		5	40.0	22:48	82	9	14	23	28	5	0	1	21:10

Played in NHL All-Star Game (1999, 2000, 2001)

Transferred to **Phoenix** after **Winnipeg** franchise relocated, July 1, 1996. Traded to **Dallas** by **Phoenix** for Mike Sillinger, July 22, 2003. Signed as a free agent by **Buffalo**, August 4, 2005. • Missed majority of 2007-08 recovering from open heart surgery, September 20, 2007.

NYCHOLAT, Lawrence

(NIH-koh-lat, LAW-rehnts) **OTT.**

Defense. Shoots left. 6', 200 lbs. Born, Calgary, Alta., May 7, 1979.

Season	Club	League	GP	G	A	Pts	PIM	PP	SH	GW	S	%	+/-	TF	F%	Min	GP	G	A	Pts	PIM	PP	SH	GW	Min
1995-96	Notre Dame	SMHL	42	10	36	46	66	....	....	....	....	....	....	....	....	....	....	....	....	....	....	....	....	....	....
1996-97	Swift Current	WHL	67	8	13	21	82	....	....	....	....	....	....	....	....	....	10	0	0	0	24	....	....	....	....
1997-98	Swift Current	WHL	71	13	35	48	108	....	....	....	....	....	....	....	....	....	1	0	0	0	0	....	....	....	....
1998-99	Swift Current	WHL	72	16	44	60	125	....	....	....	....	....	....	....	....	....	6	2	2	4	12	....	....	....	....
99-2000	Swift Current	WHL	70	22	58	80	92	....	....	....	....	....	....	....	....	....	2	0	0	0	0	....	....	....	....
2000-01	Jackson Bandits	ECHL	5	1	2	3	5	....	....	....	....	....	....	....	....	....	....	....	....	....	....	....	....	....	....
	Cleveland	IHL	42	3	7	10	69	....	....	....	....	....	....	....	....	....	4	0	0	0	2	....	....	....	....
2001-02	Houston Aeros	AHL	72	3	11	14	92	....	....	....	....	....	....	....	....	....	14	1	0	1	23	....	....	....	....
2002-03	Houston Aeros	AHL	66	11	28	39	155	....	....	....	....	....	....	....	....	....	....	....	....	....	....	....	....	....	....
	Hartford	AHL	15	2	9	11	6	....	....	....	....	....	....	....	....	....	2	2	0	2	0	....	....	....	....
2003-04	NY Rangers	NHL	9	0	0	0	6	0	0	0	6	0.0	–2	0	0.0	17:09	....	....	....	....	....	....	....	....	....
	Hartford	AHL	72	6	26	32	130	....	....	....	....	....	....	....	....	....	16	0	5	5	28	....	....	....	....
2004-05	Hartford	AHL	79	5	38	43	132	....	....	....	....	....	....	....	....	....	6	0	3	3	11	....	....	....	....
2005-06	Hershey Bears	AHL	73	13	44	57	94	....	....	....	....	....	....	....	....	....	16	2	12	14	12	....	....	....	....
2006-07	Washington	NHL	18	2	6	8	12	0	0	0	22	9.1	–3	0	0.0	20:32	....	....	....	....	....	....	....	....	....
	Hershey Bears	AHL	29	3	25	28	39	....	....	....	....	....	....	....	....	....	....	....	....	....	....	....	....	....	....
	Ottawa	NHL	1	0	0	0	0	0	0	0	3	0.0	0	0	0.0	12:48	....	....	....	....	....	....	....	....	....
2007-08	Ottawa	NHL	3	0	0	0	0	0	0	0	4	0.0	1	0	0.0	11:57	....	....	....	....	....	....	....	....	....
	Binghamton	AHL	77	12	37	49	74	....	....	....	....	....	....	....	....	....	....	....	....	....	....	....	....	....	....
	NHL Totals		31	2	6	8	18	0	0	0	35	5.7		0	0.0	18:28	....	....	....	....	....	....	....	....	....

AHL First All-Star Team (2008)

Signed as a free agent by **Minnesota**, August 31, 2000. Traded to **NY Rangers** by **Minnesota** for Johan Holmqvist, March 11, 2003. Signed as a free agent by **Washington**, August 9, 2005. Traded to **Ottawa** by **Washington** for Andy Hedlund and Ottawa's 6th round choice (Justin Taylor) in 2007 Entry Draft, February 26, 2007.

NYLANDER, Michael

(NEE-lan-duhr, MIGH-kuhl) **WSH.**

Center. Shoots left. 6'1", 195 lbs. Born, Stockholm, Sweden, October 3, 1972. Hartford's 4th choice, 59th overall, in 1991 Entry Draft.

Season	Club	League	GP	G	A	Pts	PIM	PP	SH	GW	S	%	+/-	TF	F%	Min	GP	G	A	Pts	PIM	PP	SH	GW	Min
1989-90	Huddinge IK	Sweden-2	31	7	15	22	4	....	....	....	....	....	....	....	....	....	5	3	0	3	0	....	....	....	....
1990-91	Huddinge IK	Sweden-2	33	14	20	34	10	....	....	....	....	....	....	....	....	....	2	0	0	0	0	....	....	....	....
1991-92	AIK Solna	Sweden	40	11	17	28	30	....	....	....	....	....	....	....	....	....	3	1	4	5	4	....	....	....	....
1992-93	Hartford	NHL	59	11	22	33	36	3	0	1	85	12.9	–7	....	....	....	....	....	....	....	....	....	....	....	....
	Springfield	AHL	....	....	....	....	....	....	....	....	....	....	....	....	....	....	3	3	3	6	2	....	....	....	....
1993-94	Hartford	NHL	58	11	33	44	24	4	0	1	74	14.9	–2	....	....	....	....	....	....	....	....	....	....	....	....
	Springfield	AHL	4	0	9	9	0	....	....	....	....	....	....	....	....	....	....	....	....	....	....	....	....	....	....
	Calgary	NHL	15	2	9	11	6	0	0	0	21	9.5	10	....	....	....	3	0	0	0	0	0	0	0	....
1994-95	JYP HT Jyvaskyla	Finland	16	11	19	30	63	....	....	....	....	....	....	....	....	....	....	....	....	....	....	....	....	....	....
	Calgary	NHL	6	0	1	1	2	0	0	0	2	0.0	1	....	....	....	6	0	6	6	2	0	0	0	....
1995-96	Calgary	NHL	73	17	38	55	20	4	0	6	163	10.4	0	....	....	....	4	0	0	0	0	0	0	0	....
1996-97	HC Lugano	Swiss	36	12	43	55	28	....	....	....	....	....	....	....	....	....	8	3	8	11	8	....	....	....	....
1997-98	Calgary	NHL	65	13	23	36	24	0	0	2	117	11.1	10	....	....	....	....	....	....	....	....	....	....	....	....
	Sweden	Olympics	4	0	0	0	6	....	....	....	....	....	....	....	....	....	....	....	....	....	....	....	....	....	....
1998-99	Calgary	NHL	9	2	3	5	2	1	0	0	7	28.6	1	25	60.0	11:10	....	....	....	....	....	....	....	....	....
	Tampa Bay	NHL	24	2	7	9	6	0	0	0	26	7.7	–10	75	44.0	13:29	....	....	....	....	....	....	....	....	....
99-2000	Tampa Bay	NHL	11	1	2	3	4	1	0	0	10	10.0	–3	35	57.1	10:32	....	....	....	....	....	....	....	....	....
	Chicago	NHL	66	23	28	51	26	4	0	2	112	20.5	9	561	46.9	16:39	....	....	....	....	....	....	....	....	....
2000-01	Chicago	NHL	82	25	39	64	32	4	0	5	176	14.2	7	1036	48.3	18:52	....	....	....	....	....	....	....	....	....
2001-02	Chicago	NHL	82	15	46	61	50	6	0	2	158	9.5	28	974	50.2	15:33	5	0	3	3	2	0	0	0	15:20
	Sweden	Olympics	4	1	2	3	0	....	....	....	....	....	....	....	....	....	....	....	....	....	....	....	....	....	....
2002-03	Chicago	NHL	9	0	4	4	4	0	0	0	20	0.0	0	86	48.8	15:19	....	....	....	....	....	....	....	....	....
	Washington	NHL	71	17	39	56	36	7	0	2	141	12.1	3	1005	47.4	18:41	6	3	2	5	8	1	0	1	16:45
2003-04	Washington	NHL	3	0	2	2	8	0	0	0	1	0.0	1	22	54.6	14:57	....	....	....	....	....	....	....	....	....
	Boston	NHL	15	1	11	12	14	0	0	1	29	3.4	3	128	46.1	15:43	6	3	3	6	0	0	0	0	18:57
2004-05	Karpat Oulu	Finland	23	5	15	20	22	....	....	....	....	....	....	....	....	....	....	....	....	....	....	....	....	....	....
	St. Petersburg	Russia	8	2	5	7	0	....	....	....	....	....	....	....	....	....	....	....	....	....	....	....	....	....	....
	Ak Bars Kazan	Russia	5	0	1	1	2	....	....	....	....	....	....	....	....	....	....	....	....	....	....	....	....	....	....
2005-06	NY Rangers	NHL	81	23	56	79	76	6	0	4	172	13.4	31	1143	46.5	19:20	4	0	1	1	0	0	0	0	20:33
2006-07	NY Rangers	NHL	79	26	57	83	42	14	0	4	193	13.5	12	1054	47.5	20:23	10	6	7	13	0	2	0	2	21:50
2007-08	Washington	NHL	40	11	26	37	24	5	0	1	77	14.3	–19	535	49.2	19:09	....	....	....	....	....	....	....	....	....
	NHL Totals		848	200	446	646	436	59	0	31	1584	12.6		6679	48.0	17:44	44	12	22	34	12	3	0	3	19:04

Traded to **Calgary** by **Hartford** with James Patrick and Zarley Zalapski for Gary Suter, Paul Ranheim and Ted Drury, March 10, 1994. • Missed majority of 1994-95 season recovering from wrist injury suffered in game vs. St. Louis, January 24, 1995. Traded to **Tampa Bay** by **Calgary** for Andrei Nazarov, January 19, 1999. Traded to **Chicago** by **Tampa Bay** for Bryan Muir and Reid Simpson, November 12, 1999. Traded to **Washington** by **Chicago** with Chicago's 3rd round choice (Stephen Werner) in 2003 Entry Draft and future considerations for Chris Simon and Andrei Nikolishin, November 1, 2002. • Missed majority of 2003-04 season recovering from leg injury suffered in practice, October 2, 2003. Traded to **Boston** by **Washington** for Boston's 4th round compensatory choice (Patrick McNeill) in 2005 Entry Draft and Boston's 2nd round choice (Francois Bouchard) in 2006 Entry Draft, March 4, 2004. Signed as a free agent by **NY Rangers**, August 10, 2004. Signed as a free agent by **Oulu** (Finland), September 25, 2004. Signed as a free agent by **St. Petersburg** (Russia), December 20, 2004. Signed as a free agent by **Kazan** (Russia), February 14, 2005. Signed as a free agent by **Washington**, July 2, 2007.

NYSTROM, Eric

(NIGH-stuhm, AIR-ihk) **CGY.**

Left wing. Shoots left. 6'1", 197 lbs. Born, Syosset, NY, February 14, 1983. Calgary's 1st choice, 10th overall, in 2002 Entry Draft.

Season	Club	League	GP	G	A	Pts	PIM	PP	SH	GW	S	%	+/-	TF	F%	Min	GP	G	A	Pts	PIM	PP	SH	GW	Min
99-2000	USNTDP	NAHL	55	7	16	23	57	....	....	....	....	....	....	....	....	....	3	0	0	0	0	....	....	....	....
2000-01	USNTDP	U-18	43	10	12	22	52	....	....	....	....	....	....	....	....	....	....	....	....	....	....	....	....	....	....
	USNTDP	USHL	23	5	5	10	50	....	....	....	....	....	....	....	....	....	....	....	....	....	....	....	....	....	....
2001-02	U. of Michigan	CCHA	40	18	13	31	42	....	....	....	....	....	....	....	....	....	....	....	....	....	....	....	....	....	....
2002-03	U. of Michigan	CCHA	39	15	11	26	24	....	....	....	....	....	....	....	....	....	....	....	....	....	....	....	....	....	....
2003-04	U. of Michigan	CCHA	43	10	12	22	50	....	....	....	....	....	....	....	....	....	....	....	....	....	....	....	....	....	....
2004-05	U. of Michigan	CCHA	38	13	19	32	33	....	....	....	....	....	....	....	....	....	....	....	....	....	....	....	....	....	....
2005-06	Calgary	NHL	2	0	0	0	0	0	0	0	0	0.0	–1	5	60.0	12:01	....	....	....	....	....	....	....	....	....
	Omaha	AHL	78	15	18	33	37	....	....	....	....	....	....	....	....	....	....	....	....	....	....	....	....	....	....
2006-07	Omaha	AHL	12	2	0	2	0	....	....	....	....	....	....	....	....	....	5	0	0	0	2	....	....	....	....
2007-08	Calgary	NHL	44	3	7	10	48	0	0	0	42	7.1	–5	14	50.0	11:30	7	0	0	0	2	0	0	0	7:39
	Quad City Flames	AHL	18	4	3	7	15	....	....	....	....	....	....	....	....	....	....	....	....	....	....	....	....	....	....
	NHL Totals		46	3	7	10	48	0	0	0	42	7.1		19	52.6	11:31	7	0	0	0	2	0	0	0	7:39

CCHA All-Rookie Team (2002)

• Missed majority of 2006-07 season recovering from shoulder injury.

O'BRIEN, Doug

(oh-BRIGH-uhn, DUHG)

Defense. Shoots left. 6'1", 200 lbs. Born, St. John's, Nfld., February 16, 1984. Tampa Bay's 4th choice, 192nd overall, in 2003 Entry Draft.

			Regular Season														Playoffs								
Season	Club	League	GP	G	A	Pts	PIM	PP	SH	GW	S	%	+/-	TF	F%	Min	GP	G	A	Pts	PIM	PP	SH	GW	Min
2000-01	Hull Olympiques	QMJHL	47	1	6	7	16										5	0	1	1	0				
2001-02	Hull Olympiques	QMJHL	46	1	5	6	36										12	0	0	0	14				
2002-03	Hull Olympiques	QMJHL	71	10	34	44	102										19	3	12	15	18				
2003-04	Gatineau	QMJHL	66	17	46	63	146										15	1	8	9	16				
2004-05	Springfield	AHL	74	4	13	17	76																		
	Johnstown Chiefs	ECHL	3	0	0	0	2																		
2005-06	**Tampa Bay**	**NHL**	**5**	**0**	**0**	**0**	**2**	**0**	**0**	**0**	**2**	**0.0**	**0**	**0**	**0.0**	**7:44**									
	Springfield	AHL	74	7	25	32	70																		
2006-07	Springfield	AHL	53	6	13	19	34																		
	Portland Pirates	AHL	22	0	6	6	19																		
2007-08	Lukko Rauma	Finland	39	5	4	9	51																		
	NHL Totals		**5**	**0**	**0**	**0**	**2**	**0**	**0**	**0**	**2**	**0.0**		**0**	**0.0**	**7:44**									

QMJHL First All-Star Team (2004) • Memorial Cup Tournament All-Star Team (2003, 2004) • Ed Chynoweth Trophy (Memorial Cup Tournament - Leading Scorer) (2004)

Traded to **Anaheim** by **Tampa Bay** for Joe Rullier, February 27, 2007.

O'BRIEN, Shane

(oh-BRIGH-uhn, SHAYN) **T.B.**

Defense. Shoots left. 6'3", 224 lbs. Born, Port Hope, Ont., August 9, 1983. Anaheim's 8th choice, 250th overall, in 2003 Entry Draft.

			Regular Season														Playoffs								
Season	Club	League	GP	G	A	Pts	PIM	PP	SH	GW	S	%	+/-	TF	F%	Min	GP	G	A	Pts	PIM	PP	SH	GW	Min
99-2000	Port Hope	OPJHL	47	6	27	33	110																		
2000-01	Kingston	OHL	61	2	12	14	89										4	0	1	1	6				
2001-02	Kingston	OHL	67	10	23	33	132										1	0	0	0	2				
2002-03	Kingston	OHL	28	8	15	23	100																		
	St. Michael's	OHL	34	8	11	19	108										19	4	10	14	*79				
2003-04	Cincinnati	AHL	60	2	8	10	163										9	0	2	2	20				
2004-05	Cincinnati	AHL	77	5	20	25	319										12	1	3	4	57				
2005-06	Portland Pirates	AHL	77	8	33	41	287										19	6	16	22	*81				
2006-07	**Anaheim**	**NHL**	**62**	**2**	**12**	**14**	**140**	**1**	**0**	**2**	**55**	**3.6**	**5**	**0**	**0.0**	**14:04**									
	Tampa Bay	**NHL**	**18**	**0**	**2**	**2**	**36**	**0**	**0**	**0**	**17**	**0.0**	**−8**	**0**	**0.0**	**18:08**	**6**	**0**	**0**	**0**	**12**	**0**	**0**	**0**	**17:12**
2007-08	**Tampa Bay**	**NHL**	**77**	**4**	**17**	**21**	**154**	**0**	**0**	**1**	**69**	**5.8**	**−2**	**0**	**0.0**	**21:13**									
	NHL Totals		**157**	**6**	**31**	**37**	**330**	**1**	**0**	**3**	**141**	**4.3**		**0**	**0.0**	**18:02**	**6**	**0**	**0**	**0**	**12**	**0**	**0**	**0**	**17:12**

Traded to **Tampa Bay** by **Anaheim** with Colorado's 3rd round choice (previously acquired, Tampa Bay selected Luca Cunti) in 2007 Entry Draft for Gerald Coleman and Tampa Bay's 1st round choice (later traded to Minnesota - Minnesota selected Colton Gillies) in 2007 Entry Draft, February 24, 2007.

O'BYRNE, Ryan

(oh-BUHRN, RIGH-uhn) **MTL.**

Defense. Shoots right. 6'6", 228 lbs. Born, Victoria, B.C., July 19, 1984. Montreal's 4th choice, 79th overall, in 2003 Entry Draft.

			Regular Season														Playoffs								
Season	Club	League	GP	G	A	Pts	PIM	PP	SH	GW	S	%	+/-	TF	F%	Min	GP	G	A	Pts	PIM	PP	SH	GW	Min
2001-02	Victoria Salsa	BCHL	52	2	9	11	91																		
2002-03	Victoria Salsa	BCHL	32	3	6	9	94																		
	Nanaimo Clippers	BCHL	9	2	4	6	24																		
2003-04	Cornell Big Red	ECAC	31	0	2	2	71																		
2004-05	Cornell Big Red	ECAC	33	3	7	10	68																		
2005-06	Cornell Big Red	ECAC	28	7	6	13	69																		
2006-07	Hamilton	AHL	80	0	12	12	129										22	2	5	7	32				
2007-08	**Montreal**	**NHL**	**33**	**1**	**6**	**7**	**45**	**0**	**0**	**0**	**10**	**10.0**	**7**	**0**	**0.0**	**13:24**	**4**	**0**	**0**	**0**	**0**	**0**	**0**	**0**	**10:46**
	Hamilton	AHL	20	2	6	8	49																		
	NHL Totals		**33**	**1**	**6**	**7**	**45**	**0**	**0**	**0**	**10**	**10.0**		**0**	**0.0**	**13:24**	**4**	**0**	**0**	**0**	**0**	**0**	**0**	**0**	**10:46**

O'DONNELL, Sean

(oh-DOHN-uhl, SHAWN) **ANA.**

Defense. Shoots left. 6'3", 234 lbs. Born, Ottawa, Ont., October 13, 1971. Buffalo's 6th choice, 123rd overall, in 1991 Entry Draft.

			Regular Season														Playoffs								
Season	Club	League	GP	G	A	Pts	PIM	PP	SH	GW	S	%	+/-	TF	F%	Min	GP	G	A	Pts	PIM	PP	SH	GW	Min
1987-88	Kanata Valley	CJHL	54	4	25	29	96																		
1988-89	Sudbury Wolves	OHL	56	1	9	10	49																		
1989-90	Sudbury Wolves	OHL	64	7	19	26	84										7	1	2	3	8				
1990-91	Sudbury Wolves	OHL	66	8	23	31	114										5	1	4	5	10				
1991-92	Rochester	AHL	73	4	9	13	193										16	1	2	3	21				
1992-93	Rochester	AHL	74	3	18	21	203										17	1	6	7	38				
1993-94	Rochester	AHL	64	2	10	12	242										4	0	1	1	21				
1994-95	Phoenix	IHL	61	2	18	20	132										9	0	1	1	21				
	Los Angeles	**NHL**	**15**	**0**	**2**	**2**	**49**	**0**	**0**	**0**	**12**	**0.0**	**−2**												
1995-96	**Los Angeles**	**NHL**	**71**	**2**	**5**	**7**	**127**	**0**	**0**	**0**	**65**	**3.1**	**3**												
1996-97	**Los Angeles**	**NHL**	**55**	**5**	**12**	**17**	**144**	**2**	**0**	**0**	**68**	**7.4**	**−13**												
1997-98	**Los Angeles**	**NHL**	**80**	**2**	**15**	**17**	**179**	**0**	**0**	**1**	**71**	**2.8**	**7**				**4**	**1**	**0**	**1**	**36**	**0**	**0**	**0**	
1998-99	**Los Angeles**	**NHL**	**80**	**1**	**13**	**14**	**186**	**0**	**0**	**0**	**64**	**1.6**	**1**	**0**	**0.0**	**19:10**									
99-2000	**Los Angeles**	**NHL**	**80**	**2**	**12**	**14**	**114**	**0**	**0**	**1**	**51**	**3.9**	**4**	**0**	**0.0**	**17:41**	**4**	**1**	**0**	**1**	**4**	**0**	**0**	**0**	**16:26**
2000-01	**Minnesota**	**NHL**	**63**	**4**	**12**	**16**	**128**	**1**	**0**	**2**	**58**	**6.9**	**−2**	**12**	**50.0**	**23:00**									
	New Jersey	**NHL**	**17**	**0**	**1**	**1**	**33**	**0**	**0**	**0**	**9**	**0.0**	**2**	**0**	**0.0**	**16:27**	**23**	**1**	**2**	**3**	**41**	**0**	**0**	**0**	**16:21**
2001-02	**Boston**	**NHL**	**80**	**3**	**22**	**25**	**89**	**1**	**0**	**2**	**112**	**2.7**	**27**	**0**	**0.0**	**24:50**	**6**	**0**	**2**	**2**	**4**	**0**	**0**	**0**	**24:58**
2002-03	**Boston**	**NHL**	**70**	**1**	**15**	**16**	**76**	**0**	**0**	**1**	**61**	**1.6**	**8**	**1**	**0.0**	**22:05**									
2003-04	**Boston**	**NHL**	**82**	**1**	**10**	**11**	**110**	**0**	**0**	**0**	**72**	**1.4**	**10**	**3**	**33.3**	**20:36**	**7**	**0**	**0**	**0**	**0**	**0**	**0**	**0**	**19:53**
2004-05			DID NOT PLAY																						
2005-06	**Phoenix**	**NHL**	**57**	**1**	**7**	**8**	**121**	**0**	**0**	**0**	**23**	**4.3**	**3**	**0**	**0.0**	**16:18**									
	Anaheim	**NHL**	**21**	**1**	**2**	**3**	**26**	**0**	**0**	**0**	**10**	**10.0**	**3**	**0**	**0.0**	**17:13**	**16**	**2**	**3**	**5**	**23**	**0**	**0**	**1**	**16:44**
2006-07♦	**Anaheim**	**NHL**	**79**	**2**	**15**	**17**	**92**	**0**	**0**	**1**	**47**	**4.3**	**9**	**1**	**0.0**	**19:55**	**21**	**0**	**2**	**2**	**10**	**0**	**0**	**0**	**20:20**
2007-08	**Anaheim**	**NHL**	**82**	**2**	**7**	**9**	**84**	**0**	**1**	**0**	**25**	**8.0**	**9**	**2**	**100.0**	**17:14**	**6**	**1**	**1**	**2**	**2**	**0**	**0**	**0**	**15:32**
	NHL Totals		**932**	**27**	**150**	**177**	**1558**	**4**	**1**	**8**	**748**	**3.6**		**19**	**47.4**	**19:56**	**87**	**6**	**10**	**16**	**120**	**0**	**0**	**1**	**18:18**

Traded to **Los Angeles** by **Buffalo** for Doug Houda, July 26, 1994. Claimed by **Minnesota** from **Los Angeles** in Expansion Draft, June 23, 2000. Traded to **New Jersey** by **Minnesota** for Willie Mitchell, March 4, 2001. Signed as a free agent by **Boston**, July 2, 2001. Signed as a free agent by **Phoenix**, July 6, 2004. Traded to **Anaheim** by **Phoenix** for Joel Perreault, March 9, 2006.

ODUYA, Johnny

(oh-DOO-yuh, JAW-nee) **N.J.**

Defense. Shoots left. 6', 200 lbs. Born, Stockholm, Sweden, October 1, 1981. Washington's 6th choice, 221st overall, in 2001 Entry Draft.

			Regular Season														Playoffs								
Season	Club	League	GP	G	A	Pts	PIM	PP	SH	GW	S	%	+/-	TF	F%	Min	GP	G	A	Pts	PIM	PP	SH	GW	Min
1996-97	Hammarby Jr.	Swe-Jr.	13	0	0	0																			
1997-98	Hammarby Jr.	Swe-Jr.	26	3	11	14	70																		
1998-99	Hammarby Jr.	Swe-Jr.	38	14	31	45	45																		
99-2000	Hammarby Jr.	Swe-Jr.	32	3	18	21	48										6	1	2	3	4				
	Hammarby	Sweden-2	1	0	0	0	0										1	0	0	0	0				
2000-01	Moncton Wildcats	QMJHL	44	11	38	49	147																		
	Victoriaville Tigres	QMJHL	24	3	16	19	112										13	4	9	13	10				
2001-02	Hammarby	Sweden-2	46	11	14	25	66										2	1	0	1	4				
2002-03	Hammarby	Sweden-2	48	15	25	40	200																		
2003-04	Djurgarden	Sweden	42	4	4	8	*173										4	0	0	0	6				
2004-05	Djurgarden	Sweden	49	2	4	6	139										12	0	2	2	39				
2005-06	Frolunda	Sweden	47	8	11	19	95										17	1	2	3	16				
2006-07	**New Jersey**	**NHL**	**76**	**2**	**9**	**11**	**61**	**0**	**0**	**0**	**55**	**3.6**	**−5**	**0**	**0.0**	**18:31**	**6**	**0**	**1**	**1**	**6**	**0**	**0**	**0**	**12:59**
2007-08	**New Jersey**	**NHL**	**75**	**6**	**20**	**26**	**46**	**2**	**0**	**0**	**63**	**9.5**	**27**	**0**	**0.0**	**19:02**	**5**	**0**	**1**	**1**	**6**	**0**	**0**	**0**	**20:40**
	NHL Totals		**151**	**8**	**29**	**37**	**107**	**2**	**0**	**0**	**118**	**6.8**		**0**	**0.0**	**18:46**	**11**	**0**	**2**	**2**	**12**	**0**	**0**	**0**	**16:28**

Signed as a free agent by **New Jersey**, July 24, 2006.

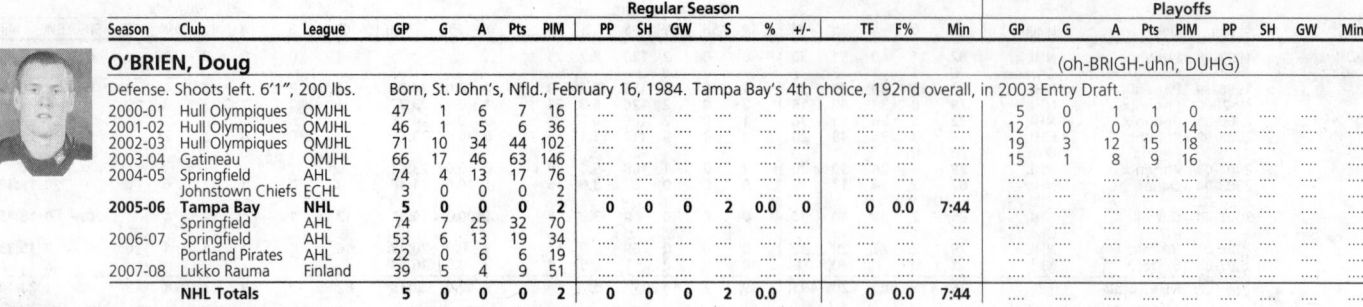

OHLUND, Mattias

(OH-luhnd, mat-TEE-uhs) **VAN.**

Defense. Shoots left. 6'2", 220 lbs. Born, Pitea, Sweden, September 9, 1976. Vancouver's 1st choice, 13th overall, in 1994 Entry Draft.

			Regular Season														Playoffs								
Season	Club	League	GP	G	A	Pts	PIM	PP	SH	GW	S	%	+/-	TF	F%	Min	GP	G	A	Pts	PIM	PP	SH	GW	Min
1992-93	Pitea HC	Sweden-2	22	0	6	6	16	....	....	....	....	....	....	....	....	....	....	....	....	....	....	....	....	....	....
1993-94	Pitea HC	Sweden-2	28	7	10	17	62	....	....	....	....	....	....	....	....	....	....	....	....	....	....	....	....	....	....
1994-95	Lulea HF	Sweden	34	6	10	16	34	....	....	....	....	....	....	....	....	....	9	4	0	4	16	....	....	....	....
1995-96	Lulea HF	Sweden	38	4	10	14	26	....	....	....	....	....	....	....	....	....	13	1	0	1	47	....	....	....	....
1996-97	Lulea HF	Sweden	47	7	9	16	38	....	....	....	....	....	....	....	....	....	10	1	2	3	8	....	....	....	....
	Lulea HF	EuroHL	6	0	3	3	0	....	....	....	....	....	....	....	....	....	....	....	....	....	....	....	....	....	....
1997-98	**Vancouver**	**NHL**	**77**	**7**	**23**	**30**	**76**	**1**	**0**	**0**	**172**	**4.1**	**3**	....	....	....	....	....	....	....	....	....	....	....	....
	Sweden	Olympics	4	0	1	1	4	....	....	....	....	....	....	....	....	....	....	....	....	....	....	....	....	....	....
1998-99	**Vancouver**	**NHL**	**74**	**9**	**26**	**35**	**83**	**2**	**1**	**1**	**129**	**7.0**	**–19**	**0**	**0.0**	**26:04**	....	....	....	....	....	....	....	....	....
99-2000	**Vancouver**	**NHL**	**42**	**4**	**16**	**20**	**24**	**2**	**1**	**1**	**63**	**6.3**	**6**	**0**	**0.0**	**27:41**	....	....	....	....	....	....	....	....	....
2000-01	**Vancouver**	**NHL**	**65**	**8**	**20**	**28**	**46**	**1**	**1**	**4**	**136**	**5.9**	**–16**	**0**	**0.0**	**25:00**	**4**	**1**	**3**	**4**	**6**	**1**	**0**	**0**	**26:32**
2001-02	**Vancouver**	**NHL**	**81**	**10**	**26**	**36**	**56**	**4**	**1**	**3**	**193**	**5.2**	**16**	**0**	**0.0**	**25:17**	**6**	**1**	**1**	**2**	**6**	**0**	**0**	**0**	**28:48**
	Sweden	Olympics	4	0	2	2	2	....	....	....	....	....	....	....	....	....	....	....	....	....	....	....	....	....	....
2002-03	**Vancouver**	**NHL**	**59**	**2**	**27**	**29**	**42**	**0**	**0**	**0**	**100**	**2.0**	**1**	**0**	**0.0**	**25:23**	**13**	**3**	**4**	**7**	**12**	**0**	**0**	**0**	**24:01**
2003-04	**Vancouver**	**NHL**	**82**	**14**	**20**	**34**	**73**	**5**	**0**	**3**	**129**	**10.9**	**14**	**0**	**0.0**	**25:47**	**7**	**1**	**4**	**5**	**13**	**0**	**0**	**1**	**27:25**
2004-05	Lulea HF	Sweden	2	1	0	1	4	....	....	....	....	....	....	....	....	....	....	....	....	....	....	....	....	....	....
2005-06	**Vancouver**	**NHL**	**78**	**13**	**20**	**33**	**92**	**8**	**1**	**2**	**183**	**7.1**	**–6**	**1**	**0.0**	**25:40**	....	....	....	....	....	....	....	....	....
	Sweden	Olympics	6	0	2	2	2	....	....	....	....	....	....	....	....	....	....	....	....	....	....	....	....	....	....
2006-07	**Vancouver**	**NHL**	**77**	**11**	**20**	**31**	**80**	**6**	**0**	**2**	**170**	**6.5**	**–3**	**1**	**0.0**	**24:47**	**12**	**2**	**5**	**7**	**12**	**1**	**0**	**0**	**28:18**
2007-08	**Vancouver**	**NHL**	**53**	**9**	**15**	**24**	**79**	**4**	**0**	**2**	**128**	**7.0**	**–1**	**0**	**0.0**	**23:46**	....	....	....	....	....	....	....	....	....
	NHL Totals		**688**	**87**	**213**	**300**	**651**	**33**	**5**	**18**	**1403**	**6.2**		**2**	**0.0**	**25:27**	**42**	**8**	**17**	**25**	**49**	**2**	**0**	**1**	**26:44**

NHL All-Rookie Team (1998)
Played in NHL All-Star Game (1999)
Signed as a free agent by **Lulea** (Sweden), December 21, 2004.

OKPOSO, Kyle

(awk-POH-soh, KIGHL) **NYI**

Right wing. Shoots right. 6'1", 200 lbs. Born, St. Paul, MN, April 16, 1988. NY Islanders' 1st choice, 7th overall, in 2006 Entry Draft.

Season	Club	League	GP	G	A	Pts	PIM	PP	SH	GW	S	%	+/-	TF	F%	Min	GP	G	A	Pts	PIM	PP	SH	GW	Min
2004-05	Shat.-St. Mary's	High-MN	65	47	45	92	72	....	....	....	....	....	....	....	....	....	....	....	....	....	....	....	....	....	....
2005-06	Des Moines	USHL	50	27	31	58	56	....	....	....	....	....	....	....	....	....	11	5	11	*16	8	....	....	....	....
2006-07	U. of Minnesota	WCHA	40	19	21	40	34	....	....	....	....	....	....	....	....	....	....	....	....	....	....	....	....	....	....
2007-08	U. of Minnesota	WCHA	18	7	4	11	6	....	....	....	....	....	....	....	....	....	....	....	....	....	....	....	....	....	....
	NY Islanders	**NHL**	**9**	**2**	**3**	**5**	**2**	**1**	**0**	**1**	**15**	**13.3**	**3**	**0**	**0.0**	**16:28**	....	....	....	....	....	....	....	....	....
	Bridgeport	AHL	35	9	19	28	12	....	....	....	....	....	....	....	....	....	....	....	....	....	....	....	....	....	....
	NHL Totals		**9**	**2**	**3**	**5**	**2**	**1**	**0**	**1**	**15**	**13.3**		**0**	**0.0**	**16:28**	....	....	....	....	....	....	....	....	....

USHL All-Rookie Team (2006) • USHL First All-Star Team (2006) • USHL Rookie of the Year (2006) • WCHA All-Rookie Team (2007) • WCHA Second All-Star Team (2007)

OLESZ, Rostislav

(OH-lehsh, RAHS-tih-slav) **FLA.**

Center. Shoots left. 6'1", 214 lbs. Born, Bilovec, Czech., October 10, 1985. Florida's 1st choice, 7th overall, in 2004 Entry Draft.

Season	Club	League	GP	G	A	Pts	PIM	PP	SH	GW	S	%	+/-	TF	F%	Min	GP	G	A	Pts	PIM	PP	SH	GW	Min
2000-01	HC Vitkovice Jr.	CzRep-Jr.	15	10	3	13	14	....	....	....	....	....	....	....	....	....	....	....	....	....	....	....	....	....	....
	HC Vitkovice	CzRep	3	0	1	1	0	....	....	....	....	....	....	....	....	....	....	....	....	....	....	....	....	....	....
2001-02	HC Vitkovice	CzRep	11	1	2	3	0	....	....	....	....	....	....	....	....	....	....	....	....	....	....	....	....	....	....
	HC Vitkovice Jr.	CzRep-Jr.	34	19	20	39	81	....	....	....	....	....	....	....	....	....	2	0	0	0	2	....	....	....	....
2002-03	HC Vitkovice Jr.	CzRep-Jr.	7	1	1	2	12	....	....	....	....	....	....	....	....	....	....	....	....	....	....	....	....	....	....
	HC Vitkovice	CzRep	40	6	3	9	41	....	....	....	....	....	....	....	....	....	5	0	0	0	2	....	....	....	....
	HC Slezan Opava	CzRep-2	1	0	0	0	0	....	....	....	....	....	....	....	....	....	....	....	....	....	....	....	....	....	....
2003-04	HC Vitkovice Jr.	CzRep-Jr.	3	2	0	2	0	....	....	....	....	....	....	....	....	....	....	....	....	....	....	....	....	....	....
	HC Vitkovice	CzRep	35	1	11	12	10	....	....	....	....	....	....	....	....	....	6	2	1	3	4	....	....	....	....
	HC Dukla Jihlava	CzRep-2	2	1	0	1	0	....	....	....	....	....	....	....	....	....	1	0	0	0	0	....	....	....	....
2004-05	HC Sparta Praha	CzRep	47	6	7	13	12	....	....	....	....	....	....	....	....	....	5	0	2	2	0	....	....	....	....
	Sparta Jr.	CzRep-Jr.	....	....	....	....	....	....	....	....	....	....	....	....	....	....	1	0	1	1	0	....	....	....	....
2005-06	**Florida**	**NHL**	**59**	**8**	**13**	**21**	**24**	**0**	**1**	**3**	**105**	**7.6**	**–4**	**10**	**30.0**	**14:52**	....	....	....	....	....	....	....	....	....
	Czech Republic	Olympics	8	0	0	0	2	....	....	....	....	....	....	....	....	....	....	....	....	....	....	....	....	....	....
2006-07	**Florida**	**NHL**	**75**	**11**	**19**	**30**	**28**	**2**	**0**	**2**	**164**	**6.7**	**2**	**12**	**58.3**	**15:30**	....	....	....	....	....	....	....	....	....
	Rochester	AHL	4	1	2	3	4	....	....	....	....	....	....	....	....	....	....	....	....	....	....	....	....	....	....
2007-08	**Florida**	**NHL**	**56**	**14**	**12**	**26**	**16**	**5**	**0**	**2**	**139**	**10.1**	**3**	**10**	**70.0**	**17:04**	....	....	....	....	....	....	....	....	....
	NHL Totals		**190**	**33**	**44**	**77**	**68**	**7**	**1**	**7**	**408**	**8.1**		**32**	**53.1**	**15:46**	....	....	....	....	....	....	....	....	....

ONDRUS, Ben

(AWN-druhs, BEHN) **TOR.**

Right wing. Shoots right. 6', 194 lbs. Born, Sherwood Park, Alta., June 25, 1982.

Season	Club	League	GP	G	A	Pts	PIM	PP	SH	GW	S	%	+/-	TF	F%	Min	GP	G	A	Pts	PIM	PP	SH	GW	Min
1997-98	Sherwood Park	AMBHL						....	....	....	....	....	....	....	....	....	....	....	....	....	....	....	....	....	....
1998-99	Swift Current	WHL	46	4	4	8	58	....	....	....	....	....	....	....	....	....	6	0	1	1	8	....	....	....	....
99-2000	Swift Current	WHL	67	14	15	29	138	....	....	....	....	....	....	....	....	....	12	1	0	1	22	....	....	....	....
2000-01	Swift Current	WHL	69	13	17	30	151	....	....	....	....	....	....	....	....	....	....	....	....	....	....	....	....	....	....
2001-02	Swift Current	WHL	67	30	41	71	153	....	....	....	....	....	....	....	....	....	12	4	3	7	18	....	....	....	....
2002-03	Swift Current	WHL	67	33	36	69	98	....	....	....	....	....	....	....	....	....	3	0	1	1	11	....	....	....	....
	Idaho Steelheads	WCHL	4	0	3	3	0	....	....	....	....	....	....	....	....	....	5	0	1	1	6	....	....	....	....
2003-04	St. John's	AHL	60	6	11	17	102	....	....	....	....	....	....	....	....	....	....	....	....	....	....	....	....	....	....
2004-05	St. John's	AHL	78	7	11	18	137	....	....	....	....	....	....	....	....	....	5	0	1	1	7	....	....	....	....
2005-06	**Toronto**	**NHL**	**22**	**0**	**0**	**0**	**18**	**0**	**0**	**0**	**17**	**0.0**	**–10**	**28**	**50.0**	**10:07**	....	....	....	....	....	....	....	....	....
	Toronto Marlies	AHL	53	12	17	29	104	....	....	....	....	....	....	....	....	....	5	1	2	3	4	....	....	....	....
2006-07	**Toronto**	**NHL**	**16**	**0**	**2**	**2**	**20**	**0**	**0**	**0**	**7**	**0.0**	**–5**	**9**	**44.4**	**4:54**	....	....	....	....	....	....	....	....	....
	Toronto Marlies	AHL	29	8	3	11	35	....	....	....	....	....	....	....	....	....	....	....	....	....	....	....	....	....	....
2007-08	**Toronto**	**NHL**	**3**	**0**	**0**	**0**	**5**	**0**	**0**	**0**	**4**	**0.0**	**–1**	**3**	**33.3**	**5:07**	....	....	....	....	....	....	....	....	....
	Toronto Marlies	AHL	59	14	12	26	63	....	....	....	....	....	....	....	....	....	19	1	5	6	14	....	....	....	....
	NHL Totals		**41**	**0**	**2**	**2**	**43**	**0**	**0**	**0**	**28**	**0.0**		**40**	**47.5**	**7:43**	....	....	....	....	....	....	....	....	....

Signed as a free agent by **Idaho** (WCHL), March 23, 2003. Signed as a free agent by **St. John's** (AHL), September 1, 2003. Signed as a free agent by **Toronto**, May 27, 2004.

O'NEILL, Jeff

(oh-NEEL, JEHF)

Right wing. Shoots right. 6'1", 195 lbs. Born, Richmond Hill, Ont., February 23, 1976. Hartford's 1st choice, 5th overall, in 1994 Entry Draft.

Season	Club	League	GP	G	A	Pts	PIM	PP	SH	GW	S	%	+/-	TF	F%	Min	GP	G	A	Pts	PIM	PP	SH	GW	Min
1990-91	Richmond Hill	Minor-ON	78	56	134	190	....	....	....	....	....	....	....	....	....	....	....	....	....	....	....	....	....	....	....
1991-92	Thornhill	MTJHL	43	27	*53	80	48	....	....	....	....	....	....	....	....	....	....	....	....	....	....	....	....	....	....
1992-93	Guelph Storm	OHL	65	32	47	79	88	....	....	....	....	....	....	....	....	....	5	2	2	4	6	....	....	....	....
1993-94	Guelph Storm	OHL	66	45	81	126	95	....	....	....	....	....	....	....	....	....	9	2	11	13	31	....	....	....	....
1994-95	Guelph Storm	OHL	57	43	81	124	56	....	....	....	....	....	....	....	....	....	14	8	18	26	34	....	....	....	....
1995-96	**Hartford**	**NHL**	**65**	**8**	**19**	**27**	**40**	**1**	**0**	**1**	**65**	**12.3**	**–3**	....	....	....	....	....	....	....	....	....	....	....	....
1996-97	**Hartford**	**NHL**	**72**	**14**	**16**	**30**	**40**	**2**	**1**	**2**	**101**	**13.9**	**–24**	....	....	....	....	....	....	....	....	....	....	....	....
	Springfield	AHL	1	0	0	0	0	....	....	....	....	....	....	....	....	....	....	....	....	....	....	....	....	....	....
1997-98	**Carolina**	**NHL**	**74**	**19**	**20**	**39**	**67**	**7**	**1**	**4**	**114**	**16.7**	**–8**	....	....	....	....	....	....	....	....	....	....	....	....
1998-99	**Carolina**	**NHL**	**75**	**16**	**15**	**31**	**66**	**4**	**0**	**2**	**121**	**13.2**	**3**	**941**	**45.6**	**16:44**	**6**	**0**	**1**	**1**	**0**	**0**	**0**	**0**	**19:25**
99-2000	**Carolina**	**NHL**	**80**	**25**	**38**	**63**	**72**	**4**	**0**	**7**	**189**	**13.2**	**–9**	**1337**	**49.5**	**19:20**	....	....	....	....	....	....	....	....	....
2000-01	**Carolina**	**NHL**	**82**	**41**	**26**	**67**	**106**	**17**	**0**	**5**	**242**	**16.9**	**–18**	**726**	**50.0**	**18:20**	**6**	**1**	**2**	**3**	**10**	**0**	**0**	**1**	**17:33**
2001-02	**Carolina**	**NHL**	**76**	**31**	**33**	**64**	**63**	**11**	**0**	**6**	**272**	**11.4**	**–5**	**831**	**56.7**	**19:44**	**22**	**8**	**5**	**13**	**27**	**3**	**0**	**1**	**19:00**
2002-03	**Carolina**	**NHL**	**82**	**30**	**31**	**61**	**38**	**11**	**0**	**7**	**316**	**9.5**	**–21**	**986**	**54.1**	**19:09**	....	....	....	....	....	....	....	....	....
2003-04	**Carolina**	**NHL**	**67**	**14**	**20**	**34**	**60**	**7**	**0**	**4**	**207**	**6.8**	**–12**	**660**	**57.6**	**17:29**	....	....	....	....	....	....	....	....	....
2004-05			DID NOT PLAY																						
2005-06	**Toronto**	**NHL**	**74**	**19**	**19**	**38**	**64**	**14**	**0**	**6**	**169**	**11.2**	**–19**	**45**	**51.1**	**12:39**	....	....	....	....	....	....	....	....	....
2006-07	**Toronto**	**NHL**	**74**	**20**	**22**	**42**	**54**	**6**	**0**	**3**	**165**	**12.1**	**1**	**249**	**57.8**	**13:43**	....	....	....	....	....	....	....	....	....

			Regular Season														Playoffs								
Season	Club	League	GP	G	A	Pts	PIM	PP	SH	GW	S	%	+/-	TF	F%	Min	GP	G	A	Pts	PIM	PP	SH	GW	Min
2007-08			DID NOT PLAY																						
	NHL Totals		**821**	**237**	**259**	**496**	**670**	**84**	**2**	**47**	**1961**	**12.1**		**5775**	**52.0**	**17:13**	**34**	**9**	**8**	**17**	**37**	**3**	**0**	**2**	**18:49**

OHL All-Rookie Team (1993) • OHL Rookie of the Year (1993) • OHL First All-Star Team (1995)

Played in NHL All-Star Game (2003)

Transferred to **Carolina** after **Hartford** franchise relocated, June 25, 1997. Traded to **Toronto** by **Carolina** for Toronto's 4th round choice (later traded to St. Louis - St. Louis selected Reto Berra) in 2006 Entry Draft, July 30, 2005.

ORPIK, Brooks (OHR-pihk, BRUKS) PIT.

Defense. Shoots left. 6'2", 219 lbs. Born, San Francisco, CA, September 26, 1980. Pittsburgh's 1st choice, 18th overall, in 2000 Entry Draft.

Season	Club	League	GP	G	A	Pts	PIM	PP	SH	GW	S	%	+/-	TF	F%	Min	GP	G	A	Pts	PIM	PP	SH	GW	Min
1996-97	Thayer Academy	High-MA	20	4	1	5	....	....	....	....	....	....	....	....	....	....	....	....	....	....	....	....	....	....	....
1997-98	Thayer Academy	High-MA	22	0	7	7	....	....	....	....	....	....	....	....	....	....	....	....	....	....	....	....	....	....	....
1998-99	Boston College	H-East	41	1	10	11	*96	....	....	....	....	....	....	....	....	....	....	....	....	....	....	....	....	....	....
99-2000	Boston College	H-East	38	1	9	10	102	....	....	....	....	....	....	....	....	....	....	....	....	....	....	....	....	....	....
2000-01	Boston College	H-East	40	0	20	20	*124	....	....	....	....	....	....	....	....	....	....	....	....	....	....	....	....	....	....
2001-02	Wilkes-Barre	AHL	78	2	18	20	99	....	....	....	....	....	....	....	....	....	....	....	....	....	....	....	....	....	....
2002-03	**Pittsburgh**	**NHL**	**6**	**0**	**0**	**0**	**2**	**0**	**0**	**0**	**2**	**0.0**	**–5**	**0**	**0.0**	**18:19**	....	....	....	....	....	....	....	....	....
	Wilkes-Barre	AHL	71	4	14	18	105	....	....	....	....	....	....	....	....	....	6	0	0	0	14	....	....	....	....
2003-04	**Pittsburgh**	**NHL**	**79**	**1**	**9**	**10**	**127**	**0**	**0**	**0**	**56**	**1.8**	**–36**	**0**	**0.0**	**18:25**	....	....	....	....	....	....	....	....	....
	Wilkes-Barre	AHL	3	0	0	0	2	....	....	....	....	....	....	....	....	....	24	0	4	4	53	....	....	....	....
2005-06	**Pittsburgh**	**NHL**	**64**	**2**	**7**	**9**	**124**	**0**	**0**	**0**	**32**	**6.3**	**–3**	**0**	**0.0**	**18:50**	....	....	....	....	....	....	....	....	....
2006-07	**Pittsburgh**	**NHL**	**70**	**0**	**6**	**6**	**82**	**0**	**0**	**0**	**59**	**0.0**	**4**	**0**	**0.0**	**16:37**	**5**	**0**	**0**	**0**	**8**	**0**	**0**	**0**	**15:43**
2007-08	**Pittsburgh**	**NHL**	**78**	**1**	**10**	**11**	**57**	**0**	**0**	**0**	**50**	**2.0**	**11**	**0**	**0.0**	**16:58**	**20**	**0**	**2**	**2**	**18**	**0**	**0**	**0**	**20:47**
	NHL Totals		**297**	**4**	**32**	**36**	**392**	**0**	**0**	**0**	**199**	**2.0**		**0**	**0.0**	**17:42**	**25**	**0**	**2**	**2**	**26**	**0**	**0**	**0**	**19:46**

ORR, Colton (OHR, KOHL-tuhn) NYR

Right wing. Shoots right. 6'3", 222 lbs. Born, Winnipeg, Man., March 3, 1982.

Season	Club	League	GP	G	A	Pts	PIM	PP	SH	GW	S	%	+/-	TF	F%	Min	GP	G	A	Pts	PIM	PP	SH	GW	Min
1998-99	St. Boniface	MJHL	STATISTICS NOT AVAILABLE																						
	Swift Current	WHL	2	0	0	0	0	....	....	....	....	....	....	....	....	....	....	....	....	....	....	....	....	....	....
99-2000	Swift Current	WHL	61	3	2	5	130	....	....	....	....	....	....	....	....	....	12	1	0	1	25	....	....	....	....
2000-01	Swift Current	WHL	19	0	4	4	67	....	....	....	....	....	....	....	....	....	....	....	....	....	....	....	....	....	....
	Kamloops Blazers	WHL	41	8	1	9	179	....	....	....	....	....	....	....	....	....	3	0	0	0	20	....	....	....	....
2001-02	Kamloops Blazers	WHL	1	0	0	0	7	....	....	....	....	....	....	....	....	....	2	0	0	0	2	....	....	....	....
2002-03	Kamloops Blazers	WHL	3	2	0	2	17	....	....	....	....	....	....	....	....	....	....	....	....	....	....	....	....	....	....
	Regina Pats	WHL	37	6	2	8	170	....	....	....	....	....	....	....	....	....	3	0	0	0	19	....	....	....	....
	Providence Bruins	AHL	1	0	0	0	7	....	....	....	....	....	....	....	....	....	....	....	....	....	....	....	....	....	....
2003-04	**Boston**	**NHL**	**1**	**0**	**0**	**0**	**0**	**0**	**0**	**0**	**0**	**0.0**	**–1**	**0**	**0.0**	**2:13**	....	....	....	....	....	....	....	....	....
	Providence Bruins	AHL	64	1	4	5	257	....	....	....	....	....	....	....	....	....	2	0	0	0	9	....	....	....	....
2004-05	Providence Bruins	AHL	61	1	6	7	279	....	....	....	....	....	....	....	....	....	17	1	0	1	44	....	....	....	....
2005-06	**Boston**	**NHL**	**20**	**0**	**0**	**0**	**27**	**0**	**0**	**0**	**1**	**0.0**	**0**	**0**	**0.0**	**1:49**	....	....	....	....	....	....	....	....	....
	NY Rangers	**NHL**	**15**	**0**	**1**	**1**	**44**	**0**	**0**	**0**	**0**	**0.0**	**1**	**0**	**0.0**	**4:19**	**1**	**0**	**0**	**0**	**2**	**0**	**0**	**0**	**4:17**
2006-07	**NY Rangers**	**NHL**	**53**	**2**	**1**	**3**	**126**	**0**	**0**	**1**	**23**	**8.7**	**–2**	**0**	**0.0**	**5:20**	**4**	**0**	**0**	**0**	**12**	**0**	**0**	**0**	**4:57**
2007-08	**NY Rangers**	**NHL**	**74**	**1**	**1**	**2**	**159**	**0**	**0**	**1**	**24**	**4.2**	**–13**	**2**	**50.0**	**7:49**	**2**	**0**	**0**	**0**	**0**	**0**	**0**	**0**	**4:26**
	NHL Totals		**163**	**3**	**3**	**6**	**356**	**0**	**0**	**2**	**48**	**6.3**		**2**	**50.0**	**5:55**	**7**	**0**	**0**	**0**	**14**	**0**	**0**	**0**	**4:42**

Signed as a free agent by **Boston**, September 19, 2001. • Missed majority of 2001-02 season recovering from wrist injury suffered in game vs. Red Deer (WHL), October 20, 2001. Claimed on waivers by **NY Rangers** from **Boston**, November 29, 2005.

ORTMEYER, Jed (OHRT-migh-uhr, JEHD) NSH.

Center. Shoots right. 6', 197 lbs. Born, Omaha, NE, September 3, 1978.

Season	Club	League	GP	G	A	Pts	PIM	PP	SH	GW	S	%	+/-	TF	F%	Min	GP	G	A	Pts	PIM	PP	SH	GW	Min
1997-98	Omaha Lancers	USHL	54	23	25	48	52	....	....	....	....	....	....	....	....	....	14	3	4	7	31	....	....	....	....
1998-99	Omaha Lancers	USHL	52	23	36	59	81	....	....	....	....	....	....	....	....	....	12	5	6	11	16	....	....	....	....
99-2000	U. of Michigan	CCHA	41	8	16	24	40	....	....	....	....	....	....	....	....	....	....	....	....	....	....	....	....	....	....
2000-01	U. of Michigan	CCHA	27	10	11	21	52	....	....	....	....	....	....	....	....	....	....	....	....	....	....	....	....	....	....
2001-02	U. of Michigan	CCHA	41	15	23	38	40	....	....	....	....	....	....	....	....	....	....	....	....	....	....	....	....	....	....
2002-03	U. of Michigan	CCHA	36	18	16	34	48	....	....	....	....	....	....	....	....	....	....	....	....	....	....	....	....	....	....
2003-04	**NY Rangers**	**NHL**	**58**	**2**	**4**	**6**	**16**	**0**	**0**	**0**	**48**	**4.2**	**–10**	**16**	**31.3**	**9:52**	....	....	....	....	....	....	....	....	....
	Hartford	AHL	13	2	8	10	4	....	....	....	....	....	....	....	....	....	16	5	2	7	6	....	....	....	....
2004-05	Hartford	AHL	61	7	20	27	63	....	....	....	....	....	....	....	....	....	6	0	1	1	4	....	....	....	....
2005-06	**NY Rangers**	**NHL**	**78**	**5**	**2**	**7**	**38**	**0**	**0**	**1**	**90**	**5.6**	**2**	**21**	**23.8**	**11:06**	**4**	**1**	**0**	**1**	**4**	**0**	**0**	**0**	**11:40**
2006-07	**NY Rangers**	**NHL**	**41**	**2**	**9**	**11**	**22**	**0**	**1**	**0**	**67**	**3.0**	**7**	**8**	**12.5**	**12:35**	**9**	**0**	**0**	**0**	**2**	**0**	**0**	**0**	**9:37**
	Hartford	AHL	8	1	3	4	6	....	....	....	....	....	....	....	....	....	....	....	....	....	....	....	....	....	....
2007-08	**Nashville**	**NHL**	**51**	**4**	**4**	**8**	**32**	**0**	**1**	**0**	**68**	**5.9**	**–8**	**12**	**50.0**	**12:27**	....	....	....	....	....	....	....	....	....
	NHL Totals		**228**	**13**	**19**	**32**	**108**	**0**	**2**	**1**	**273**	**4.8**		**57**	**29.8**	**11:21**	**13**	**1**	**0**	**1**	**6**	**0**	**0**	**0**	**10:15**

Signed as a free agent by **NY Rangers**, May 10, 2003. Signed as a free agent by **Nashville**, July 2, 2007.

O'SULLIVAN, Patrick (oh-SUHL-ih-van, PAT-rihk) L.A.

Center. Shoots left. 5'11", 190 lbs. Born, Winston Salem, NC, February 1, 1985. Minnesota's 2nd choice, 56th overall, in 2003 Entry Draft.

Season	Club	League	GP	G	A	Pts	PIM	PP	SH	GW	S	%	+/-	TF	F%	Min	GP	G	A	Pts	PIM	PP	SH	GW	Min
99-2000	Strathroy Rockets	OHA-B	45	6	13	19	53	....	....	....	....	....	....	....	....	....	....	....	....	....	....	....	....	....	....
2000-01	USNTDP	U-17	8	8	10	18	12	....	....	....	....	....	....	....	....	....	....	....	....	....	....	....	....	....	....
	USNTDP	NAHL	56	22	35	57	57	....	....	....	....	....	....	....	....	....	....	....	....	....	....	....	....	....	....
2001-02	Mississauga	OHL	68	34	58	92	61	....	....	....	....	....	....	....	....	....	....	....	....	....	....	....	....	....	....
	USNTDP	USHL	1	1	0	1	2	....	....	....	....	....	....	....	....	....	....	....	....	....	....	....	....	....	....
2002-03	Mississauga	OHL	56	40	41	81	57	....	....	....	....	....	....	....	....	....	5	2	9	11	18	....	....	....	....
2003-04	Mississauga	OHL	53	43	39	82	32	....	....	....	....	....	....	....	....	....	24	12	11	23	16	....	....	....	....
2004-05	Mississauga	OHL	57	31	59	90	63	....	....	....	....	....	....	....	....	....	5	0	4	4	6	....	....	....	....
2005-06	Houston Aeros	AHL	78	47	46	93	64	....	....	....	....	....	....	....	....	....	8	5	5	10	4	....	....	....	....
2006-07	**Los Angeles**	**NHL**	**44**	**5**	**14**	**19**	**14**	**2**	**0**	**1**	**92**	**5.4**	**–6**	**127**	**46.5**	**14:04**	....	....	....	....	....	....	....	....	....
	Manchester	AHL	41	18	21	39	12	....	....	....	....	....	....	....	....	....	16	8	9	17	10	....	....	....	....
2007-08	**Los Angeles**	**NHL**	**82**	**22**	**31**	**53**	**36**	**3**	**3**	**2**	**220**	**10.0**	**–8**	**461**	**44.0**	**18:42**	....	....	....	....	....	....	....	....	....
	NHL Totals		**126**	**27**	**45**	**72**	**50**	**5**	**3**	**3**	**312**	**8.7**		**588**	**44.6**	**17:05**	....	....	....	....	....	....	....	....	....

Canadian Major Junior Rookie of the Year (2002) • AHL All-Rookie Team (2006) • Dudley "Red" Garrett Memorial Trophy (Top Rookie - AHL) (2006)

Traded to **Los Angeles** by **Minnesota** with Edmonton's 1st round choice (previously acquired, Los Angeles selected Trevor Lewis) in 2006 Entry Draft for Pavol Demitra, June 24, 2006.

OTT, Steve (AWT, STEEV) DAL.

Center. Shoots left. 6', 193 lbs. Born, Summerside, P.E.I., August 19, 1982. Dallas' 1st choice, 25th overall, in 2000 Entry Draft.

Season	Club	League	GP	G	A	Pts	PIM	PP	SH	GW	S	%	+/-	TF	F%	Min	GP	G	A	Pts	PIM	PP	SH	GW	Min
1998-99	Leamington Flyers	OHA-B	48	14	30	44	110	....	....	....	....	....	....	....	....	....	....	....	....	....	....	....	....	....	....
99-2000	Windsor Spitfires	OHL	66	23	39	62	131	....	....	....	....	....	....	....	....	....	12	3	5	8	21	....	....	....	....
2000-01	Windsor Spitfires	OHL	55	50	37	87	164	....	....	....	....	....	....	....	....	....	9	3	8	11	27	....	....	....	....
2001-02	Windsor Spitfires	OHL	53	43	45	88	178	....	....	....	....	....	....	....	....	....	14	6	10	16	49	....	....	....	....
2002-03	**Dallas**	**NHL**	**26**	**3**	**4**	**7**	**31**	**0**	**0**	**0**	**25**	**12.0**	**6**	**4**	**50.0**	**8:46**	**1**	**0**	**0**	**0**	**0**	**0**	**0**	**0**	**6:57**
	Utah Grizzlies	AHL	40	9	11	20	98	....	....	....	....	....	....	....	....	....	....	....	....	....	....	....	....	....	....
2003-04	**Dallas**	**NHL**	**73**	**2**	**10**	**12**	**152**	**0**	**0**	**1**	**74**	**2.7**	**–2**	**59**	**49.2**	**10:14**	**4**	**1**	**0**	**1**	**0**	**0**	**0**	**1**	**6:55**
2004-05	Hamilton	AHL	67	18	21	39	279	....	....	....	....	....	....	....	....	....	4	0	0	0	20	....	....	....	....
2005-06	**Dallas**	**NHL**	**82**	**5**	**17**	**22**	**178**	**0**	**0**	**1**	**89**	**5.6**	**1**	**535**	**49.2**	**11:54**	**5**	**0**	**1**	**1**	**2**	**0**	**0**	**0**	**7:41**
2006-07	**Dallas**	**NHL**	**19**	**0**	**4**	**4**	**35**	**0**	**0**	**0**	**17**	**0.0**	**–4**	**39**	**59.0**	**9:11**	**6**	**0**	**0**	**0**	**8**	**0**	**0**	**0**	**6:43**
	Iowa Stars	AHL	3	0	0	0	8	....	....	....	....	....	....	....	....	....	....	....	....	....	....	....	....	....	....
2007-08	**Dallas**	**NHL**	**73**	**11**	**11**	**22**	**147**	**0**	**1**	**2**	**89**	**12.4**	**2**	**311**	**58.8**	**14:28**	**18**	**2**	**1**	**3**	**22**	**1**	**0**	**1**	**13:46**
	NHL Totals		**273**	**21**	**46**	**67**	**543**	**0**	**1**	**4**	**294**	**7.1**		**948**	**52.7**	**11:39**	**34**	**3**	**2**	**5**	**32**	**1**	**0**	**2**	**10:37**

OHL Second All-Star Team (2002)

• Missed majority of 2006-07 season recovering from ankle injury suffered in game vs. Los Angeles, October 28, 2006.

OUELLET, Michel
(oo-LEHT, mee-SHEHL) **T.B.**

Right wing. Shoots right. 6'1", 193 lbs. Born, Rimouski, Que., March 5, 1982. Pittsburgh's 4th choice, 124th overall, in 2000 Entry Draft.

Season	Club	League	GP	G	A	Pts	PIM	PP	SH	GW	S	%	+/-	TF	F%	Min	Playoffs GP	G	A	Pts	PIM	PP	SH	GW	Min
1997-98	Jonquiere Elites	QAAA	33	20	32	52	52																		
1998-99	Rimouski Oceanic	QMJHL	28	7	13	20	10										11	0	1	1	6				
99-2000	Rimouski Oceanic	QMJHL	72	36	53	89	38										14	4	5	9	14				
2000-01	Rimouski Oceanic	QMJHL	63	42	50	92	50										11	6	7	13	8				
2001-02	Rimouski Oceanic	QMJHL	61	40	58	98	66										7	3	6	9	4				
2002-03	Wilkes-Barre	AHL	4	0	2	2	0																		
	Wheeling Nailers	ECHL	55	20	26	46	40																		
2003-04	Wilkes-Barre	AHL	79	30	19	49	34										22	2	10	12	6				
2004-05	Wilkes-Barre	AHL	80	31	32	63	56										11	2	3	5	6				
2005-06	**Pittsburgh**	**NHL**	**50**	**16**	**16**	**32**	**16**	**11**	**0**	**0**	**87**	**18.4**	**–13**	**16**	**37.5**	**14:02**									
	Wilkes-Barre	AHL	19	10	20	30	12																		
2006-07	**Pittsburgh**	**NHL**	**73**	**19**	**29**	**48**	**30**	**11**	**0**	**2**	**148**	**12.8**	**–3**	**8**	**37.5**	**13:20**	**5**	**0**	**2**	**2**	**6**	**0**	**0**	**0**	**12:54**
2007-08	**Tampa Bay**	**NHL**	**64**	**17**	**19**	**36**	**12**	**5**	**0**	**0**	**132**	**12.9**	**11**	**42**	**45.2**	**13:38**									
	NHL Totals		**187**	**52**	**64**	**116**	**58**	**27**	**0**	**2**	**367**	**14.2**		**66**	**42.4**	**13:37**	**5**	**0**	**2**	**2**	**6**	**0**	**0**	**0**	**12:54**

AHL All-Rookie Team (2004)

Signed as a free agent by **Tampa Bay**, July 1, 2007.

OVECHKIN, Alex
(oh-VEHCH-kihn, AL-ehx) **WSH.**

Left wing. Shoots right. 6'2", 217 lbs. Born, Moscow, USSR, September 17, 1985. Washington's 1st choice, 1st overall, in 2004 Entry Draft.

Season	Club	League	GP	G	A	Pts	PIM	PP	SH	GW	S	%	+/-	TF	F%	Min	Playoffs GP	G	A	Pts	PIM	PP	SH	GW	Min
2001-02	Dyn'o Moscow 2	Russia-3	19	18	8	26	20																		
	Dynamo Moscow	Russia	22	2	2	4	4										3	0	0	0	0				
2002-03	Dynamo Moscow	Russia	40	8	7	15	28										5	0	0	0	2				
2003-04	Dynamo Moscow	Russia	53	13	11	24	40										3	0	0	0	2				
2004-05	Dynamo Moscow	Russia	37	13	13	26	32										10	2	4	6	31				
2005-06	**Washington**	**NHL**	**81**	**52**	**54**	**106**	**52**	**21**	**3**	**5**	**425**	**12.2**	**2**	**16**	**12.5**	**21:37**									
	Russia	Olympics	8	5	0	5	8																		
2006-07	**Washington**	**NHL**	**82**	**46**	**46**	**92**	**52**	**16**	**0**	**8**	**392**	**11.7**	**–19**	**17**	**47.1**	**21:23**									
2007-08	**Washington**	**NHL**	**82**	***65**	**47**	***112**	**40**	**22**	**0**	**11**	**446**	**14.6**	**28**	**18**	**38.9**	**23:06**	**7**	**4**	**5**	**9**	**0**	**1**	**0**	**2**	**24:03**
	NHL Totals		**245**	**163**	**147**	**310**	**144**	**59**	**3**	**24**	**1263**	**12.9**		**51**	**33.3**	**22:02**	**7**	**4**	**5**	**9**	**0**	**1**	**0**	**2**	**24:03**

Olympic Tournament All-Star Team (2006) • NHL All-Rookie Team (2006) • NHL First All-Star Team (2006, 2007, 2008) • Calder Memorial Trophy (2006) • Maurice "Rocket" Richard Trophy (2008) • Art Ross Trophy (2008) • Lester B. Pearson Trophy (2008) • Hart Trophy (2008)

Played in NHL All-Star Game (2007, 2008)

OZOLINSH, Sandis
(OH-zoh-LIHNCH, SAN-dihz)

Defense. Shoots left. 6'3", 215 lbs. Born, Riga, Latvia, August 3, 1972. San Jose's 3rd choice, 30th overall, in 1991 Entry Draft.

Season	Club	League	GP	G	A	Pts	PIM	PP	SH	GW	S	%	+/-	TF	F%	Min	Playoffs GP	G	A	Pts	PIM	PP	SH	GW	Min
1990-91	Dynamo Riga	USSR	44	0	3	3	51																		
	Riga 2	USSR-3	11	3																					
1991-92	Rigas Stars	CIS	30	6	0	6	42																		
	Kansas City	IHL	34	6	9	15	20										15	2	5	7	22				
1992-93	**San Jose**	**NHL**	**37**	**7**	**16**	**23**	**40**	**2**	**0**	**0**	**83**	**8.4**	**–9**												
1993-94	**San Jose**	**NHL**	**81**	**26**	**38**	**64**	**24**	**4**	**0**	**3**	**157**	**16.6**	**16**				**14**	**0**	**10**	**10**	**8**	**0**	**0**	**0**	
1994-95	**San Jose**	**NHL**	**48**	**9**	**16**	**25**	**30**	**3**	**1**	**2**	**83**	**10.8**	**–6**				**11**	**3**	**2**	**5**	**6**	**1**	**0**	**0**	
1995-96	San Francisco	IHL	2	1	0	1	0																		
	San Jose	**NHL**	**7**	**1**	**3**	**4**	**4**	**1**	**0**	**0**	**21**	**4.8**	**2**												
	♦ **Colorado**	**NHL**	**66**	**13**	**37**	**50**	**50**	**7**	**1**	**1**	**145**	**9.0**	**0**				**22**	**5**	**14**	**19**	**16**	**2**	**0**	**1**	
1996-97	**Colorado**	**NHL**	**80**	**23**	**45**	**68**	**88**	**13**	**0**	**4**	**232**	**9.9**	**4**				**17**	**4**	**13**	**17**	**24**	**2**	**0**	**1**	
1997-98	**Colorado**	**NHL**	**66**	**13**	**38**	**51**	**65**	**9**	**0**	**2**	**135**	**9.6**	**–12**				**7**	**0**	**7**	**7**	**14**	**0**	**0**	**0**	
1998-99	**Colorado**	**NHL**	**39**	**7**	**25**	**32**	**22**	**4**	**0**	**3**	**81**	**8.6**	**10**	**0**	**0.0**	**22:06**	**19**	**4**	**8**	**12**	**22**	**3**	**0**	**1**	**22:24**
99-2000	**Colorado**	**NHL**	**82**	**16**	**36**	**52**	**46**	**6**	**0**	**1**	**210**	**7.6**	**17**	**0**	**0.0**	**22:41**	**17**	**5**	**5**	**10**	**20**	**3**	**0**	**1**	**18:35**
2000-01	**Carolina**	**NHL**	**72**	**12**	**32**	**44**	**71**	**4**	**2**	**2**	**145**	**8.3**	**–25**	**0**	**0.0**	**22:12**	**6**	**0**	**2**	**2**	**5**	**0**	**0**	**0**	**19:04**
2001-02	**Carolina**	**NHL**	**46**	**4**	**19**	**23**	**34**	**1**	**0**	**0**	**71**	**5.6**	**–4**	**0**	**0.0**	**19:30**									
	Florida	**NHL**	**37**	**10**	**19**	**29**	**24**	**2**	**0**	**1**	**101**	**9.9**	**–3**	**0**	**0.0**	**30:30**									
	Latvia	Olympics	1	0	4	4	0																		
2002-03	**Florida**	**NHL**	**51**	**7**	**19**	**26**	**40**	**5**	**0**	**2**	**83**	**8.4**	**–16**	**0**	**0.0**	**28:23**									
	Anaheim	**NHL**	**31**	**5**	**13**	**18**	**16**	**1**	**0**	**1**	**54**	**9.3**	**10**	**0**	**0.0**	**22:08**	**21**	**2**	**6**	**8**	**10**	**0**	**0**	**1**	**23:37**
2003-04	**Anaheim**	**NHL**	**36**	**5**	**11**	**16**	**24**	**1**	**0**	**2**	**58**	**8.6**	**–7**	**0**	**0.0**	**19:57**									
2004-05			DID NOT PLAY																						
2005-06	**Anaheim**	**NHL**	**17**	**3**	**3**	**6**	**8**	**0**	**0**	**2**	**17**	**17.6**	**–4**	**0**	**0.0**	**17:45**									
	NY Rangers	**NHL**	**19**	**3**	**11**	**14**	**20**	**2**	**0**	**0**	**41**	**7.3**	**2**	**0**	**0.0**	**23:48**	**3**	**0**	**0**	**0**	**6**	**0**	**0**	**0**	**21:27**
	Latvia	Olympics	5	1	3	4	0																		
2006-07	**NY Rangers**	**NHL**	**21**	**0**	**3**	**3**	**8**	**0**	**0**	**0**	**15**	**0.0**	**–8**	**0**	**0.0**	**18:51**									
2007-08	Worcester Sharks	AHL	2	0	1	1	0																		
	San Jose	**NHL**	**39**	**3**	**13**	**16**	**24**	**2**	**0**	**0**	**39**	**7.7**	**–11**	**0**	**0.0**	**16:59**									
	NHL Totals		**875**	**167**	**397**	**564**	**638**	**67**	**4**	**26**	**1771**	**9.4**		**0**	**0.0**	**22:28**	**137**	**23**	**67**	**90**	**131**	**11**	**0**	**5**	**21:28**

NHL First All-Star Team (1997)

Played in NHL All-Star Game (1994, 1997, 1998, 2000, 2001, 2002, 2003)

• Missed majority of 1992-93 season recovering from knee injury suffered in game vs. Philadelphia, December 30, 1992. Traded to **Colorado** by **San Jose** for Owen Nolan, October 26, 1995. Traded to **Carolina** by **Colorado** with Columbus' 2nd round choice (previously acquired, Carolina selected Tomas Kurka) in 2000 Entry Draft for Nolan Pratt, Carolina's 1st (Vaclav Nedorost) and 2nd (Jared Aulin) round choices in 2000 Entry Draft and Philadelphia's 2nd round choice (previously acquired, Colorado selected Agris Saviels) in 2000 Entry Draft, June 24, 2000. Traded to **Florida** by **Carolina** with Byron Ritchie for Bret Hedican, Kevyn Adams and Tomas Malec, January 16, 2002. Traded to **Anaheim** by **Florida** with Lance Ward for Pavel Trnka, Matt Cullen and Anaheim's 4th round choice (James Pemberton) in 2003 Entry Draft, January 30, 2003. • Missed majority of 2003-04 season recovering from shoulder injury suffered in game vs. Colorado, December 19, 2003. Traded to **NY Rangers** by **Anaheim** for San Jose's 3rd round choice (previously acquired, Anaheim selected John DeGray) in 2006 Entry Draft, March 9, 2006. • Missed majority of 2006-07 season recovering from knee surgery (October 3, 2006) and a recurring knee injury. Signed as a free agent by **Worcester** (AHL), October 19, 2007. Signed as a free agent by **San Jose**, November 2, 2007.

PAETSCH, Nathan
(PASH, NAY-thuhn) **BUF.**

Defense. Shoots left. 6'1", 198 lbs. Born, Humboldt, Sask., March 30, 1983. Buffalo's 8th choice, 202nd overall, in 2003 Entry Draft.

Season	Club	League	GP	G	A	Pts	PIM	PP	SH	GW	S	%	+/-	TF	F%	Min	Playoffs GP	G	A	Pts	PIM	PP	SH	GW	Min
1998-99	Tisdale Trojans	SMHL	74	20	55	75	120																		
	Moose Jaw	WHL	2	0	0	0	0																		
99-2000	Moose Jaw	WHL	68	9	35	44	49										4	0	1	1	0				
2000-01	Moose Jaw	WHL	70	8	54	62	118										4	1	2	3	6				
2001-02	Moose Jaw	WHL	59	16	36	52	86										12	0	4	4	16				
2002-03	Moose Jaw	WHL	59	15	39	54	81										13	3	10	13	6				
2003-04	Rochester	AHL	54	5	5	10	49										16	1	1	2	28				
2004-05	Rochester	AHL	80	4	19	23	150										9	1	1	2	16				
2005-06	**Buffalo**	**NHL**	**1**	**0**	**1**	**1**	**0**	**0**	**0**	**0**	**0**	**0.0**	**–1**	**0**	**0.0**	**15:38**	**1**	**0**	**0**	**0**	**0**	**0**	**0**	**0**	**12:06**
	Rochester	AHL	72	11	39	50	90																		
2006-07	**Buffalo**	**NHL**	**63**	**2**	**22**	**24**	**50**	**0**	**0**	**0**	**62**	**3.2**	**10**	**0**	**0.0**	**15:15**									
2007-08	**Buffalo**	**NHL**	**59**	**2**	**7**	**9**	**27**	**0**	**0**	**0**	**49**	**4.1**	**3**	**0**	**0.0**	**13:38**									
	NHL Totals		**123**	**4**	**30**	**34**	**77**	**0**	**0**	**0**	**111**	**3.6**		**0**	**0.0**	**14:28**	**1**	**0**	**0**	**0**	**0**	**0**	**0**	**0**	**12:06**

• Re-entered NHL Entry Draft. Originally Washington's 1st choice, 58th overall, in 2001 Entry Draft.

WHL East Second All-Star Team (2003)

PAHLSSON, Samuel
(PAWL-suhn, SAM-ew-l) **ANA.**

Center. Shoots left. 6', 203 lbs. Born, Ange, Sweden, December 17, 1977. Colorado's 10th choice, 176th overall, in 1996 Entry Draft.

Season	Club	League	GP	G	A	Pts	PIM	PP	SH	GW	S	%	+/-	TF	F%	Min	Playoffs GP	G	A	Pts	PIM	PP	SH	GW	Min
1992-93	Ange IK	Sweden-4	9	0	0	0	0																		
1993-94	Ange IK	Sweden-4	STATISTICS NOT AVAILABLE																						
1994-95	MoDo	Sweden	1	0	0	0	0																		
1995-96	MoDo Jr.	Swe-Jr.	30	10	11	21	26																		
	MoDo	Sweden	36	1	3	4	8										4	0	0	0	0				
1996-97	MoDo	Sweden	49	8	9	17	83																		
	MoDo Jr.	Swe-Jr.	5	2	6	8	2																		
1997-98	MoDo	Sweden	23	6	11	17	24										9	3	0	3	6				

								Regular Season									Playoffs								
Season	Club	League	GP	G	A	Pts	PIM	PP	SH	GW	S	%	+/-	TF	F%	Min	GP	G	A	Pts	PIM	PP	SH	GW	Min
1998-99	MoDo	Sweden	50	17	17	34	44	....	....	....	....	....	....	....	....	....	13	3	3	6	10	....	....	....	....
99-2000	MoDo	Sweden	47	16	11	27	67	....	....	....	....	....	....	....	....	....	13	3	3	6	8	....	....	....	....
	MoDo	EuroHL	4	1	0	1	0	....	....	....	....	....	....	....	....	....	3	1	1	2	2	....	....	....	....
2000-01	**Boston**	**NHL**	17	1	1	2	6	0	0	0	13	7.7	–5	239	40.2	14:19	....	....	....	....	....	....	....	....	....
	Anaheim	**NHL**	59	3	4	7	14	1	1	1	46	6.5	–9	867	45.1	14:14	....	....	....	....	....	....	....	....	....
2001-02	**Anaheim**	**NHL**	80	6	14	20	26	1	1	0	99	6.1	–16	1201	49.8	16:24	....	....	....	....	....	....	....	....	....
2002-03	**Anaheim**	**NHL**	34	4	11	15	18	0	1	2	28	14.3	10	118	52.5	13:20	21	2	4	6	12	0	0	0	16:41
	Cincinnati	AHL	13	1	7	8	24	....	....	....	....	....	....	....	....	....	....	....	....	....	....	....	....	....	....
2003-04	**Anaheim**	**NHL**	82	8	14	22	52	1	0	2	134	6.0	–2	908	55.3	16:51	....	....	....	....	....	....	....	....	....
2004-05	Frolunda	Sweden	48	6	18	24	56	....	....	....	....	....	....	....	....	....	14	4	7	11	24	....	....	....	....
2005-06	**Anaheim**	**NHL**	82	11	10	21	34	0	3	1	116	9.5	–1	1517	52.8	16:30	16	2	3	5	18	0	0	2	17:06
	Sweden	Olympics	8	2	2	4	8	....	....	....	....	....	....	....	....	....	....	....	....	....	....	....	....	....	....
2006-07♦	**Anaheim**	**NHL**	82	8	18	26	42	0	0	1	111	7.2	–4	1523	52.7	17:22	21	3	9	12	20	0	0	2	19:25
2007-08	**Anaheim**	**NHL**	56	6	9	15	34	0	3	3	94	6.4	–2	1066	55.0	18:46	6	0	0	0	0	0	0	0	18:18
	NHL Totals		492	47	81	128	226	3	9	10	641	7.3		7439	51.6	16:23	64	7	16	23	50	0	0	4	17:50

Traded to **Boston** by **Colorado** with Brian Rolston, Martin Grenier and New Jersey's 1st round choice (previously acquired, Boston selected Martin Samuelsson) in 2000 Entry Draft for Raymond Bourque and Dave Andreychuk, March 6, 2000. Traded to **Anaheim** by **Boston** for Patrick Traverse and Andrei Nazarov, November 18, 2000. Signed as a free agent by **Frolunda** (Sweden), September, 2004.

PAILLE, Daniel

(PIGH-yay, DAN-yehl) **BUF.**

Left wing. Shoots left. 6', 197 lbs. Born, Welland, Ont., April 15, 1984. Buffalo's 2nd choice, 20th overall, in 2002 Entry Draft.

Season	Club	League	GP	G	A	Pts	PIM	PP	SH	GW	S	%	+/-	TF	F%	Min	GP	G	A	Pts	PIM	PP	SH	GW	Min
99-2000	Welland Cougars	OHA-B	42	14	17	31	19	....	....	....	....	....	....	....	....	....	16	16	16	32	....	....	....	....	....
2000-01	Guelph Storm	OHL	64	22	31	53	57	....	....	....	....	....	....	....	....	....	4	2	0	2	2	....	....	....	....
2001-02	Guelph Storm	OHL	62	27	30	57	54	....	....	....	....	....	....	....	....	....	9	5	2	7	9	....	....	....	....
2002-03	Guelph Storm	OHL	54	30	27	57	28	....	....	....	....	....	....	....	....	....	11	8	6	14	6	....	....	....	....
2003-04	Guelph Storm	OHL	59	37	43	80	63	....	....	....	....	....	....	....	....	....	22	9	9	18	14	....	....	....	....
2004-05	Rochester	AHL	79	14	15	29	54	....	....	....	....	....	....	....	....	....	9	2	2	4	6	....	....	....	....
2005-06	**Buffalo**	**NHL**	14	1	2	3	2	0	0	0	15	6.7	5	4	25.0	10:24	....	....	....	....	....	....	....	....	....
	Rochester	AHL	45	14	13	27	29	....	....	....	....	....	....	....	....	....	....	....	....	....	....	....	....	....	....
2006-07	**Buffalo**	**NHL**	29	3	8	11	18	0	0	0	45	6.7	5	6	33.3	12:47	1	0	0	0	0	0	0	0	4:52
	Rochester	AHL	29	7	14	21	12	....	....	....	....	....	....	....	....	....	....	....	....	....	....	....	....	....	....
2007-08	**Buffalo**	**NHL**	77	19	16	35	14	0	3	2	110	17.3	9	41	36.6	13:16	....	....	....	....	....	....	....	....	....
	NHL Totals		120	23	26	49	34	0	3	2	170	13.5		51	35.3	12:49	1	0	0	0	0	0	0	0	4:52

PANDOLFO, Jay

(pan-DAWL-foh, JAY) **N.J.**

Left wing. Shoots left. 6'1", 190 lbs. Born, Winchester, MA, December 27, 1974. New Jersey's 2nd choice, 32nd overall, in 1993 Entry Draft.

Season	Club	League	GP	G	A	Pts	PIM	PP	SH	GW	S	%	+/-	TF	F%	Min	GP	G	A	Pts	PIM	PP	SH	GW	Min
1989-90	Burlington	High-MA	23	33	30	63	18	....	....	....	....	....	....	....	....	....	....	....	....	....	....	....	....	....	....
1990-91	Burlington	High-MA	20	19	27	46	10	....	....	....	....	....	....	....	....	....	....	....	....	....	....	....	....	....	....
1991-92	Burlington	High-MA	20	35	34	69	14	....	....	....	....	....	....	....	....	....	....	....	....	....	....	....	....	....	....
1992-93	Boston University	H-East	37	16	22	38	16	....	....	....	....	....	....	....	....	....	....	....	....	....	....	....	....	....	....
1993-94	Boston University	H-East	37	17	25	42	27	....	....	....	....	....	....	....	....	....	....	....	....	....	....	....	....	....	....
1994-95	Boston University	H-East	20	7	13	20	6	....	....	....	....	....	....	....	....	....	....	....	....	....	....	....	....	....	....
1995-96	Boston University	H-East	39	*38	29	67	6	....	....	....	....	....	....	....	....	....	....	....	....	....	....	....	....	....	....
	Albany River Rats	AHL	5	3	1	4	0	....	....	....	....	....	....	....	....	....	3	0	0	0	0	....	....	....	....
1996-97	**New Jersey**	**NHL**	46	6	8	14	6	0	0	1	61	9.8	–1	....	....	....	6	0	1	1	0	0	0	0	....
	Albany River Rats	AHL	12	3	9	12	0	....	....	....	....	....	....	....	....	....	....	....	....	....	....	....	....	....	....
1997-98	**New Jersey**	**NHL**	23	1	3	4	4	0	0	0	23	4.3	–4	....	....	....	3	0	2	2	0	0	0	0	....
	Albany River Rats	AHL	51	18	19	37	24	....	....	....	....	....	....	....	....	....	....	....	....	....	....	....	....	....	....
1998-99	**New Jersey**	**NHL**	70	14	13	27	10	1	1	4	100	14.0	3	10	40.0	15:13	7	1	0	1	0	0	0	0	13:19
99-2000♦	**New Jersey**	**NHL**	71	7	8	15	4	0	0	0	86	8.1	0	19	47.4	13:25	23	0	5	5	0	0	0	0	15:35
2000-01	**New Jersey**	**NHL**	63	4	12	16	16	0	0	0	57	7.0	3	15	53.3	14:05	25	1	4	5	4	0	0	0	12:38
2001-02	**New Jersey**	**NHL**	65	4	10	14	15	0	1	0	72	5.6	12	12	41.7	13:59	6	0	0	0	0	0	0	0	16:11
2002-03♦	**New Jersey**	**NHL**	68	6	11	17	23	0	1	4	92	6.5	12	13	23.1	16:08	24	6	6	12	2	0	0	1	16:34
2003-04	**New Jersey**	**NHL**	82	13	13	26	14	1	2	4	140	9.3	5	25	44.0	16:00	5	0	0	0	0	0	0	0	13:41
2004-05	Salzburg	Austria	19	5	7	12	0	....	....	....	....	....	....	....	....	....	....	....	....	....	....	....	....	....	....
2005-06	**New Jersey**	**NHL**	82	10	10	20	16	0	0	0	116	8.6	2	13	30.8	18:03	9	1	4	5	0	0	1	1	18:37
2006-07	**New Jersey**	**NHL**	82	13	14	27	8	0	1	1	109	11.9	–5	16	6.3	18:37	11	1	0	1	4	0	0	0	19:39
2007-08	**New Jersey**	**NHL**	54	12	12	24	22	0	0	1	78	15.4	10	7	42.9	17:17	5	0	0	0	2	0	0	0	16:15
	NHL Totals		706	90	114	204	138	2	6	15	934	9.6		130	36.9	15:57	124	10	22	32	12	0	1	2	15:37

Hockey East First All-Star Team (1996) • Hockey East Player of the Year (1996) • NCAA East First All-American Team (1996)

Signed as a free agent by **Salzburg** (Austria), December 27, 2004.

PANDOLFO, Mike

(pan-DAWL-foh, MIGHK)

Left wing. Shoots left. 6'3", 225 lbs. Born, Winchester, MA, September 15, 1979. Buffalo's 5th choice, 77th overall, in 1998 Entry Draft.

Season	Club	League	GP	G	A	Pts	PIM	PP	SH	GW	S	%	+/-	TF	F%	Min	GP	G	A	Pts	PIM	PP	SH	GW	Min
1996-97	St. Sebastian's	High-MA	32	27	28	55	30	....	....	....	....	....	....	....	....	....	....	....	....	....	....	....	....	....	....
1997-98	St. Sebastian's	High-MA	28	29	23	52	18	....	....	....	....	....	....	....	....	....	....	....	....	....	....	....	....	....	....
1998-99	Boston University	H-East	34	13	4	17	26	....	....	....	....	....	....	....	....	....	....	....	....	....	....	....	....	....	....
99-2000	Boston University	H-East	41	13	10	23	37	....	....	....	....	....	....	....	....	....	....	....	....	....	....	....	....	....	....
2000-01	Boston University	H-East	37	16	13	29	30	....	....	....	....	....	....	....	....	....	....	....	....	....	....	....	....	....	....
2001-02	Boston University	H-East	38	22	18	40	22	....	....	....	....	....	....	....	....	....	....	....	....	....	....	....	....	....	....
2002-03	Syracuse Crunch	AHL	74	9	9	18	31	....	....	....	....	....	....	....	....	....	....	....	....	....	....	....	....	....	....
2003-04	**Columbus**	**NHL**	3	0	0	0	0	0	0	0	3	0.0	–2	0	0.0	8:18	....	....	....	....	....	....	....	....	....
	Syracuse Crunch	AHL	77	18	19	37	29	....	....	....	....	....	....	....	....	....	7	1	0	1	2	....	....	....	....
2004-05	Syracuse Crunch	AHL	62	8	8	16	18	....	....	....	....	....	....	....	....	....	....	....	....	....	....	....	....	....	....
2005-06	Binghamton	AHL	1	0	0	0	4	....	....	....	....	....	....	....	....	....	....	....	....	....	....	....	....	....	....
	Reading Royals	ECHL	23	14	11	25	8	....	....	....	....	....	....	....	....	....	....	....	....	....	....	....	....	....	....
	EHC Munchen	German-2	18	13	9	22	14	....	....	....	....	....	....	....	....	....	10	5	7	12	2	....	....	....	....
2006-07	Lowell Devils	AHL	24	4	5	9	4	....	....	....	....	....	....	....	....	....	....	....	....	....	....	....	....	....	....
	Trenton Titans	ECHL	48	36	31	67	10	....	....	....	....	....	....	....	....	....	1	0	0	0	0	....	....	....	....
2007-08	Lowell Devils	AHL	52	5	6	11	18	....	....	....	....	....	....	....	....	....	....	....	....	....	....	....	....	....	....
	NHL Totals		3	0	0	0	0	0	0	0	3	0.0		0	0.0	8:18	....	....	....	....	....	....	....	....	....

ECHL Second All-Star Team (2007)

Rights traded to **Columbus** by **Buffalo** with Detroit's 1st round choice (previously acquired, later traded to Atlanta – Atlanta selected Jim Slater) in 2002 Entry Draft for New Jersey's 1st round choice (previously acquired, Buffalo selected Dan Paille) in 2002 Entry Draft, June 22, 2002.

PARENT, Ryan

(PAIR-ehnt, RIGH-uhn) **PHI.**

Defense. Shoots left. 6'2", 205 lbs. Born, Prince Albert, Sask., March 17, 1987. Nashville's 1st choice, 18th overall, in 2005 Entry Draft.

Season	Club	League	GP	G	A	Pts	PIM	PP	SH	GW	S	%	+/-	TF	F%	Min	GP	G	A	Pts	PIM	PP	SH	GW	Min
2002-03	Waterloo Siskins	OHA-B	41	2	8	10	35	....	....	....	....	....	....	....	....	....	....	....	....	....	....	....	....	....	....
2003-04	Guelph Storm	OHL	58	1	5	6	18	....	....	....	....	....	....	....	....	....	22	0	0	0	2	....	....	....	....
2004-05	Guelph Storm	OHL	66	2	17	19	36	....	....	....	....	....	....	....	....	....	4	0	1	1	4	....	....	....	....
2005-06	Guelph Storm	OHL	60	4	17	21	122	....	....	....	....	....	....	....	....	....	15	1	4	5	24	....	....	....	....
	Milwaukee	AHL	....	....	....	....	....	....	....	....	....	....	....	....	....	....	10	0	0	0	4	....	....	....	....
2006-07	**Philadelphia**	**NHL**	1	0	0	0	0	0	0	0	1	0.0	0	0	0.0	14:10	....	....	....	....	....	....	....	....	....
	Philadelphia	AHL	6	1	0	1	4	....	....	....	....	....	....	....	....	....	....	....	....	....	....	....	....	....	....
	Guelph Storm	OHL	43	3	7	10	86	....	....	....	....	....	....	....	....	....	4	0	1	1	14	....	....	....	....
2007-08	**Philadelphia**	**NHL**	22	0	0	0	6	0	0	0	9	0.0	–4	0	0.0	14:59	4	0	1	1	0	0	0	0	16:36
	Philadelphia	AHL	53	1	7	8	42	....	....	....	....	....	....	....	....	....	....	....	....	....	....	....	....	....	....
	NHL Totals		23	0	0	0	6	0	0	0	10	0.0		0	0.0	14:57	4	0	1	1	0	0	0	0	16:35

OHL Second All-Star Team (2006, 2007)

Traded to **Philadelphia** by **Nashville** with Scottie Upshall and Nashville's 1st (later traded back to Nashville - Nashville selected Jonathon Blum) and 3rd (later traded to Washington - Washington selected Phil Desimone) round choices in 2007 Entry Draft for Peter Forsberg, February 15, 2007.

			Regular Season														Playoffs								
Season	Club	League	GP	G	A	Pts	PIM	PP	SH	GW	S	%	+/-	TF	F%	Min	GP	G	A	Pts	PIM	PP	SH	GW	Min

PARENTEAU, Pierre

(pair-ehn-TOH, PEE-air) **NYR**

Left wing. Shoots right. 5'11", 195 lbs. Born, Hull, Que., March 24, 1983. Anaheim's 11th choice, 264th overall, in 2001 Entry Draft.

Season	Club	League	GP	G	A	Pts	PIM	PP	SH	GW	S	%	+/-	TF	F%	Min	GP	G	A	Pts	PIM	PP	SH	GW	Min
99-2000	Charles-Lemoyne	QAAA	40	25	40	65	18	....	....	....	....	....	....	....	....	....	16	4	9	13	8	....	....	....	....
2000-01	Moncton Wildcats	QMJHL	45	10	19	29	38	....	....	....	....	....	....	....	....	....	....	....	....	....	....	....	....	....	....
	Chicoutimi	QMJHL	28	10	13	23	14	....	....	....	....	....	....	....	....	....	7	4	7	11	2	....	....	....	....
2001-02	Chicoutimi	QMJHL	68	51	67	118	120	....	....	....	....	....	....	....	....	....	4	3	1	4	10	....	....	....	....
2002-03	Chicoutimi	QMJHL	31	20	35	55	56	....	....	....	....	....	....	....	....	....	....	....	....	....	....	....	....	....	....
	Sherbrooke	QMJHL	28	13	35	48	84	....	....	....	....	....	....	....	....	....	12	8	11	19	6	....	....	....	....
2003-04	Cincinnati	AHL	66	14	16	30	20	....	....	....	....	....	....	....	....	....	7	1	2	3	6	....	....	....	....
2004-05	Cincinnati	AHL	76	17	24	41	58	....	....	....	....	....	....	....	....	....	9	2	0	2	8	....	....	....	....
2005-06	Portland Pirates	AHL	56	22	27	49	42	....	....	....	....	....	....	....	....	....	19	5	17	22	24	....	....	....	....
	Augusta Lynx	ECHL	2	0	1	1	0	....	....	....	....	....	....	....	....	....	....	....	....	....	....	....	....	....	....
2006-07	Portland Pirates	AHL	28	15	13	28	35	....	....	....	....	....	....	....	....	....	....	....	....	....	....	....	....	....	....
	Chicago	**NHL**	**5**	**0**	**1**	**1**	**2**	**0**	**0**	**0**	**7**	**0.0**	**–1**	**2**	**50.0**	**11:05**	....	....	....	....	....	....	....	....	....
	Norfolk Admirals	AHL	40	15	36	51	12	....	....	....	....	....	....	....	....	....	6	2	1	3	2	....	....	....	....
2007-08	Hartford	AHL	75	34	47	81	81	....	....	....	....	....	....	....	....	....	5	3	2	5	13	....	....	....	....
	NHL Totals		**5**	**0**	**1**	**1**	**2**	**0**	**0**	**0**	**7**	**0.0**		**2**	**50.0**	**11:05**	....	....	....	....	....	....	....	....	....

AHL Second All-Star Team (2008)

Traded to **Chicago** by **Anaheim** with Bruno St. Jacques for Sebastien Caron, Matt Keith and Chris Durno, December 28, 2006. Traded to **NY Rangers** by **Chicago** for future considerations, October 11, 2007.

PARISE, Zach

(pah-REE-say, ZAK) **N.J.**

Left wing. Shoots left. 5'11", 190 lbs. Born, Minneapolis, MN, July 28, 1984. New Jersey's 1st choice, 17th overall, in 2003 Entry Draft.

Season	Club	League	GP	G	A	Pts	PIM	PP	SH	GW	S	%	+/-	TF	F%	Min	GP	G	A	Pts	PIM	PP	SH	GW	Min
2000-01	Shat.-St. Mary's	High-MN	58	69	93	162		....	....	....	....	....	....	....	....	....	....	....	....	....	....	....	....	....	....
2001-02	Shat.-St. Mary's	High-MN	67	77	101	178	58	....	....	....	....	....	....	....	....	....	....	....	....	....	....	....	....	....	....
	USNTDP	U-18	12	7	7	14	6	....	....	....	....	....	....	....	....	....	....	....	....	....	....	....	....	....	....
2002-03	North Dakota	WCHA	39	26	35	61	34	....	....	....	....	....	....	....	....	....	....	....	....	....	....	....	....	....	....
2003-04	North Dakota	WCHA	37	23	32	55	24	....	....	....	....	....	....	....	....	....	....	....	....	....	....	....	....	....	....
2004-05	Albany River Rats	AHL	73	18	40	58	56	....	....	....	....	....	....	....	....	....	....	....	....	....	....	....	....	....	....
2005-06	**New Jersey**	**NHL**	**81**	**14**	**18**	**32**	**28**	**2**	**0**	**5**	**133**	**10.5**	**–1**	**162**	**42.6**	**13:08**	**9**	**1**	**2**	**3**	**2**	**0**	**0**	**0**	**15:03**
2006-07	**New Jersey**	**NHL**	**82**	**31**	**31**	**62**	**30**	**9**	**0**	**7**	**247**	**12.6**	**–3**	**52**	**44.2**	**17:32**	**11**	**7**	**3**	**10**	**8**	**2**	**0**	**1**	**19:08**
2007-08	**New Jersey**	**NHL**	**81**	**32**	**33**	**65**	**25**	**10**	**1**	**8**	**266**	**12.0**	**13**	**104**	**48.1**	**18:04**	**5**	**1**	**4**	**5**	**2**	**1**	**0**	**0**	**18:29**
	NHL Totals		**244**	**77**	**82**	**159**	**83**	**21**	**1**	**20**	**646**	**11.9**		**318**	**44.7**	**16:15**	**25**	**9**	**9**	**18**	**12**	**3**	**0**	**1**	**17:32**

WCHA All-Rookie Team (2003) • WCHA First All-Star Team (2004) • NCAA West First All-American Team (2004)

PARK, Richard

(PAHRK, RIH-chuhrd) **NYI**

Right wing. Shoots right. 5'11", 190 lbs. Born, Seoul, South Korea, May 27, 1976. Pittsburgh's 2nd choice, 50th overall, in 1994 Entry Draft.

Season	Club	League	GP	G	A	Pts	PIM	PP	SH	GW	S	%	+/-	TF	F%	Min	GP	G	A	Pts	PIM	PP	SH	GW	Min
1991-92	Tor. Young Nats	MTHL	76	49	58	107	91	....	....	....	....	....	....	....	....	....	....	....	....	....	....	....	....	....	....
1992-93	Belleville Bulls	OHL	66	23	38	61	38	....	....	....	....	....	....	....	....	....	5	0	0	0	14	....	....	....	....
1993-94	Belleville Bulls	OHL	59	27	49	76	70	....	....	....	....	....	....	....	....	....	12	3	5	8	18	....	....	....	....
1994-95	Belleville Bulls	OHL	45	28	51	79	35	....	....	....	....	....	....	....	....	....	16	9	18	27	12	....	....	....	....
	Pittsburgh	**NHL**	**1**	**0**	**1**	**1**	**2**	**0**	**0**	**0**	**4**	**0.0**	**1**	....	....	....	**3**	**0**	**0**	**0**	**2**	**0**	**0**	**0**	....
1995-96	Belleville Bulls	OHL	6	7	6	13	2	....	....	....	....	....	....	....	....	....	14	18	12	30	10	....	....	....	....
	Pittsburgh	**NHL**	**56**	**4**	**6**	**10**	**36**	**0**	**1**	**1**	**62**	**6.5**	**3**	....	....	....	**1**	**0**	**0**	**0**	**0**	**0**	**0**	**0**	....
1996-97	**Pittsburgh**	**NHL**	**1**	**0**	**0**	**0**	**0**	**0**	**0**	**0**	**1**	**0.0**	**–1**	....	....	....	....	....	....	....	....	....	....	....	....
	Cleveland	IHL	50	12	15	27	30	....	....	....	....	....	....	....	....	....	....	....	....	....	....	....	....	....	....
	Anaheim	**NHL**	**11**	**1**	**1**	**2**	**10**	**0**	**0**	**0**	**9**	**11.1**	**0**	....	....	....	**11**	**0**	**1**	**1**	**2**	**0**	**0**	**0**	....
1997-98	**Anaheim**	**NHL**	**15**	**0**	**2**	**2**	**8**	**0**	**0**	**0**	**14**	**0.0**	**–3**	....	....	....	....	....	....	....	....	....	....	....	....
	Cincinnati	AHL	56	17	26	43	36	....	....	....	....	....	....	....	....	....	....	....	....	....	....	....	....	....	....
1998-99	**Philadelphia**	**NHL**	**7**	**0**	**0**	**0**	**0**	**0**	**0**	**0**	**5**	**0.0**	**–1**	**15**	**53.3**	**9:21**	....	....	....	....	....	....	....	....	....
	Philadelphia	AHL	75	41	42	83	33	....	....	....	....	....	....	....	....	....	16	9	6	15	4	....	....	....	....
99-2000	Utah Grizzlies	IHL	82	28	32	60	36	....	....	....	....	....	....	....	....	....	5	1	0	1	0	....	....	....	....
2000-01	Cleveland	IHL	75	27	21	48	29	....	....	....	....	....	....	....	....	....	4	0	2	2	4	....	....	....	....
2001-02	**Minnesota**	**NHL**	**63**	**10**	**15**	**25**	**10**	**2**	**1**	**2**	**115**	**8.7**	**–1**	**79**	**41.8**	**16:28**	....	....	....	....	....	....	....	....	....
	Houston Aeros	AHL	13	4	10	14	6	....	....	....	....	....	....	....	....	....	....	....	....	....	....	....	....	....	....
2002-03	**Minnesota**	**NHL**	**81**	**14**	**10**	**24**	**16**	**2**	**2**	**3**	**149**	**9.4**	**–3**	**178**	**48.9**	**16:36**	**18**	**3**	**3**	**6**	**4**	**0**	**0**	**1**	**17:03**
2003-04	**Minnesota**	**NHL**	**73**	**13**	**12**	**25**	**28**	**4**	**0**	**1**	**142**	**9.2**	**0**	**379**	**40.1**	**16:30**	....	....	....	....	....	....	....	....	....
2004-05	Malmo	Sweden	9	1	3	4	4	....	....	....	....	....	....	....	....	....	....	....	....	....	....	....	....	....	....
	Langnau	Swiss	10	3	0	3	8	....	....	....	....	....	....	....	....	....	6	4	1	5	6	....	....	....	....
2005-06	**Vancouver**	**NHL**	**60**	**8**	**10**	**18**	**29**	**0**	**1**	**2**	**97**	**8.2**	**–2**	**26**	**26.9**	**11:00**	....	....	....	....	....	....	....	....	....
2006-07	**NY Islanders**	**NHL**	**82**	**10**	**16**	**26**	**33**	**0**	**2**	**2**	**93**	**10.8**	**4**	**218**	**39.0**	**11:39**	**5**	**0**	**1**	**1**	**2**	**0**	**0**	**0**	**9:16**
2007-08	**NY Islanders**	**NHL**	**82**	**12**	**20**	**32**	**20**	**1**	**4**	**2**	**132**	**9.1**	**–4**	**626**	**50.2**	**15:14**	....	....	....	....	....	....	....	....	....
	NHL Totals		**532**	**72**	**93**	**165**	**192**	**9**	**11**	**13**	**823**	**8.7**		**1521**	**45.1**	**14:33**	**38**	**3**	**5**	**8**	**10**	**0**	**0**	**1**	**15:22**

OHL All-Rookie Team (1993) • AHL Second All-Star Team (1999)

Traded to **Anaheim** by **Pittsburgh** for Roman Oksiuta, March 18, 1997. Signed as a free agent by **Philadelphia**, August 24, 1998. Signed as a free agent by **Utah** (IHL), September 22, 1999. Signed as a free agent by **Minnesota**, June 6, 2000. Signed as a free agent by **Malmo** (Sweden), November 8, 2004. Signed as a free agent by **Langnau** (Swiss), January 4, 2005. Signed as a free agent by **Vancouver**, August 8, 2005. Signed as a free agent by **NY Islanders**, October 2, 2006.

PARKER, Scott

(PAR-kuhr, SKAWT) **COL.**

Right wing. Shoots right. 6'5", 240 lbs. Born, Hanford, CA, January 29, 1978. Colorado's 4th choice, 20th overall, in 1998 Entry Draft.

Season	Club	League	GP	G	A	Pts	PIM	PP	SH	GW	S	%	+/-	TF	F%	Min	GP	G	A	Pts	PIM	PP	SH	GW	Min
1993-94	Alaska Arctic Ice	AAHL	34	8	12	20	86	....	....	....	....	....	....	....	....	....	....	....	....	....	....	....	....	....	....
1994-95	Spokane Braves	KIJHL	43	7	21	28	128	....	....	....	....	....	....	....	....	....	....	....	....	....	....	....	....	....	....
1995-96	Kelowna Rockets	WHL	64	3	4	7	159	....	....	....	....	....	....	....	....	....	6	0	0	0	12	....	....	....	....
1996-97	Kelowna Rockets	WHL	68	18	8	26	*330	....	....	....	....	....	....	....	....	....	6	0	2	2	4	....	....	....	....
1997-98	Kelowna Rockets	WHL	71	30	22	52	243	....	....	....	....	....	....	....	....	....	7	6	0	6	23	....	....	....	....
1998-99	**Colorado**	**NHL**	**27**	**0**	**0**	**0**	**71**	**0**	**0**	**0**	**3**	**0.0**	**–3**	**1**	**0.0**	**1:37**	....	....	....	....	....	....	....	....	....
	Hershey Bears	AHL	32	4	3	7	143	....	....	....	....	....	....	....	....	....	4	0	0	0	6	....	....	....	....
99-2000	Hershey Bears	AHL	68	12	7	19	206	....	....	....	....	....	....	....	....	....	11	1	1	2	56	....	....	....	....
2000-01♦	**Colorado**	**NHL**	**69**	**2**	**3**	**5**	**155**	**0**	**0**	**1**	**35**	**5.7**	**–2**	**2**	**0.0**	**5:42**	**4**	**0**	**0**	**0**	**2**	**0**	**0**	**0**	**2:12**
2001-02	**Colorado**	**NHL**	**63**	**1**	**4**	**5**	**154**	**0**	**0**	**0**	**32**	**3.1**	**0**	**0**	**0.0**	**5:50**	....	....	....	....	....	....	....	....	....
2002-03	**Colorado**	**NHL**	**43**	**1**	**3**	**4**	**82**	**0**	**0**	**0**	**20**	**5.0**	**6**	**0**	**0.0**	**6:15**	**1**	**0**	**0**	**0**	**2**	**0**	**0**	**0**	**1:44**
2003-04	**San Jose**	**NHL**	**50**	**1**	**3**	**4**	**101**	**0**	**0**	**0**	**20**	**5.0**	**0**	**5**	**40.0**	**6:37**	....	....	....	....	....	....	....	....	....
2004-05		DID NOT PLAY																							
2005-06	**San Jose**	**NHL**	**10**	**1**	**0**	**1**	**38**	**0**	**0**	**0**	**6**	**16.7**	**3**	**0**	**0.0**	**5:39**	....	....	....	....	....	....	....	....	....
2006-07	**San Jose**	**NHL**	**11**	**0**	**0**	**0**	**22**	**0**	**0**	**0**	**3**	**0.0**	**0**	**1**	**0.0**	**5:03**	....	....	....	....	....	....	....	....	....
	Colorado	**NHL**	**10**	**1**	**1**	**2**	**6**	**0**	**0**	**0**	**2**	**50.0**	**0**	**1**	**0.0**	**5:35**	....	....	....	....	....	....	....	....	....
2007-08	**Colorado**	**NHL**	**25**	**0**	**0**	**0**	**70**	**0**	**0**	**0**	**5**	**0.0**	**0**	**0**	**0.0**	**3:42**	....	....	....	....	....	....	....	....	....
	NHL Totals		**308**	**7**	**14**	**21**	**699**	**0**	**0**	**1**	**126**	**5.6**		**10**	**20.0**	**5:24**	**5**	**0**	**0**	**0**	**4**	**0**	**0**	**0**	**2:06**

• Re-entered NHL Entry Draft. Originally New Jersey's 6th choice, 63rd overall, in 1996 Entry Draft.

Traded to **San Jose** by **Colorado** for Colorado's 5th round choice (previously acquired, Colorado selected Brad Richardson) in 2003 Entry Draft, June 21, 2003. • Missed majority of 2005-06 season recovering from facial (pre-season) and head (November 21, 2005 at Edmonton) injuries. Traded to **Colorado** by **San Jose** for Colorado's 6th round choice (later traded back to Colorado - Colorado selected Jonas Holos) in 2008 Entry Draft, February 27, 2007. • Missed majority of 2006-07 season recovering from back and ankle injuries. • Missed majority of 2007-08 season as a healthy reserve.

PARRISH, Mark

(PAIR-ihsh, MAHRK)

Right wing. Shoots right. 5'11", 199 lbs. Born, Bloomington, MN, February 2, 1977. Colorado's 3rd choice, 79th overall, in 1996 Entry Draft.

Season	Club	League	GP	G	A	Pts	PIM	PP	SH	GW	S	%	+/-	TF	F%	Min	GP	G	A	Pts	PIM	PP	SH	GW	Min
1994-95	Jefferson Jaguars	High-MN	27	40	20	60	42	....	....	....	....	....	....	....	....	....	....	....	....	....	....	....	....	....	....
1995-96	St. Cloud State	WCHA	39	15	13	28	30	....	....	....	....	....	....	....	....	....	....	....	....	....	....	....	....	....	....
1996-97	St. Cloud State	WCHA	35	*27	15	42	60	....	....	....	....	....	....	....	....	....	....	....	....	....	....	....	....	....	....
1997-98	Seattle	WHL	54	54	38	92	29	....	....	....	....	....	....	....	....	....	5	2	3	5	2	....	....	....	....
	New Haven	AHL	1	1	0	1	2	....	....	....	....	....	....	....	....	....	....	....	....	....	....	....	....	....	....
1998-99	**Florida**	**NHL**	**73**	**24**	**13**	**37**	**25**	**5**	**0**	**5**	**129**	**18.6**	**–6**	**1**	**0.0**	**13:59**	....	....	....	....	....	....	....	....	....
	New Haven	AHL	2	1	0	1	0	....	....	....	....	....	....	....	....	....	....	....	....	....	....	....	....	....	....
99-2000	**Florida**	**NHL**	**81**	**26**	**18**	**44**	**39**	**6**	**0**	**3**	**152**	**17.1**	**1**	**8**	**75.0**	**14:04**	**4**	**0**	**1**	**1**	**0**	**0**	**0**	**0**	**12:37**
2000-01	**NY Islanders**	**NHL**	**70**	**17**	**13**	**30**	**28**	**6**	**0**	**3**	**123**	**13.8**	**–27**	**3**	**33.3**	**15:27**	....	....	....	....	....	....	....	....	....

			Regular Season														Playoffs								
Season	Club	League	GP	G	A	Pts	PIM	PP	SH	GW	S	%	+/-	TF	F%	Min	GP	G	A	Pts	PIM	PP	SH	GW	Min
2001-02	**NY Islanders**	**NHL**	**78**	**30**	**30**	**60**	**32**	**9**	**1**	**6**	**162**	**18.5**	**10**	**10**	**40.0**	**16:48**	**7**	**2**	**1**	**3**	**6**	**2**	**0**	**0**	**17:27**
2002-03	**NY Islanders**	**NHL**	**81**	**23**	**25**	**48**	**28**	**9**	**0**	**5**	**147**	**15.6**	**–11**	**9**	**44.4**	**16:12**	**5**	**1**	**0**	**1**	**4**	**1**	**0**	**0**	**16:02**
2003-04	**NY Islanders**	**NHL**	**59**	**24**	**11**	**35**	**18**	**6**	**0**	**6**	**105**	**22.9**	**8**	**5**	**20.0**	**17:20**	**5**	**1**	**2**	**3**	**0**	**0**	**0**	**0**	**20:35**
2004-05			Did not play																						
2005-06	**NY Islanders**	**NHL**	**57**	**24**	**17**	**41**	**16**	**13**	**0**	**5**	**102**	**23.5**	**–14**	**12**	**16.7**	**19:34**	....	....	....	....	....	....	....	....	....
	Los Angeles	**NHL**	**19**	**5**	**3**	**8**	**4**	**3**	**0**	**0**	**35**	**14.3**	**–9**	**0**	**0.0**	**15:29**	....	....	....	....	....	....	....	....	....
	United States	Olympics	6	0	0	0	4	....	....	....	....	....	....	....	....	....	....	....	....	....	....	....	....	....	....
2006-07	**Minnesota**	**NHL**	**76**	**19**	**20**	**39**	**18**	**5**	**0**	**4**	**141**	**13.5**	**9**	**13**	**30.8**	**14:20**	**5**	**1**	**0**	**1**	**0**	**0**	**0**	**0**	**15:46**
2007-08	**Minnesota**	**NHL**	**66**	**16**	**14**	**30**	**16**	**7**	**0**	**0**	**95**	**16.8**	**2**	**10**	**40.0**	**14:56**	**1**	**0**	**0**	**0**	**0**	**0**	**0**	**0**	**5:04**
	NHL Totals		**660**	**208**	**164**	**372**	**224**	**69**	**1**	**37**	**1191**	**17.5**		**71**	**36.6**	**15:43**	**27**	**5**	**4**	**9**	**10**	**3**	**0**	**0**	**16:17**

NCAA West Second All-American Team (1997) • WHL West First All-Star Team (1998)

Played in NHL All-Star Game (2002)

Rights traded to **Florida** by **Colorado** with Anaheim's 3rd round choice (previously acquired, Florida selected Lance Ward) in 1998 Entry Draft for Tom Fitzgerald, March 24, 1998. Traded to **NY Islanders** by **Florida** with Oleg Kvasha for Roberto Luongo and Olli Jokinen, June 24, 2000. Traded to **Los Angeles** by **NY Islanders** with Brent Sopel for Denis Grebeshkov and Jeff Tambellini, March 8, 2006. Signed as a free agent by **Minnesota**, July 1, 2006.

PARROS, George (PAIR-ohs, JOHRJ) ANA.

Right wing. Shoots right. 6'5", 229 lbs. Born, Washington, PA, December 29, 1979. Los Angeles' 9th choice, 222nd overall, in 1999 Entry Draft.

Season	Club	League	GP	G	A	Pts	PIM	PP	SH	GW	S	%	+/-	TF	F%	Min	GP	G	A	Pts	PIM	PP	SH	GW	Min
1996-97	Delbarton	High-NJ	14	15	8	23	....	....	....	....	....	....	....	....	....	....	....	....	....	....	....	....	....	....	....
1997-98	Delbarton	High-NJ	15	22	17	39	....	....	....	....	....	....	....	....	....	....	....	....	....	....	....	....	....	....	....
1998-99	Chicago Freeze	NAHL	54	30	20	50	126	....	....	....	....	....	....	....	....	....	....	....	....	....	....	....	....	....	....
99-2000	Princeton	ECAC	27	4	2	6	14	....	....	....	....	....	....	....	....	....	....	....	....	....	....	....	....	....	....
2000-01	Princeton	ECAC	31	7	10	17	38	....	....	....	....	....	....	....	....	....	....	....	....	....	....	....	....	....	....
2001-02	Princeton	ECAC	31	9	13	22	36	....	....	....	....	....	....	....	....	....	....	....	....	....	....	....	....	....	....
2002-03	Princeton	ECAC	22	0	7	7	29	....	....	....	....	....	....	....	....	....	....	....	....	....	....	....	....	....	....
	Manchester	AHL	9	0	1	1	7	....	....	....	....	....	....	....	....	....	....	....	....	....	....	....	....	....	....
2003-04	Manchester	AHL	57	3	6	9	126	....	....	....	....	....	....	....	....	....	5	0	0	0	4	....	....	....	....
2004-05	Manchester	AHL	67	14	8	22	247	....	....	....	....	....	....	....	....	....	6	1	1	2	27	....	....	....	....
	Reading Royals	ECHL	3	0	0	0	9	....	....	....	....	....	....	....	....	....	....	....	....	....	....	....	....	....	....
2005-06	**Los Angeles**	**NHL**	**55**	**2**	**3**	**5**	**138**	**0**	**0**	**0**	**23**	**8.7**	**1**	**1**	**0.0**	**4:56**	....	....	....	....	....	....	....	....	....
2006-07	**Colorado**	**NHL**	**2**	**0**	**0**	**0**	**0**	**0**	**0**	**0**	**1**	**0.0**	**–1**	**0**	**0.0**	**3:33**	....	....	....	....	....	....	....	....	....
	♦ Anaheim	**NHL**	**32**	**1**	**0**	**1**	**102**	**0**	**0**	**0**	**18**	**5.6**	**–2**	**0**	**0.0**	**5:09**	**5**	**0**	**0**	**0**	**10**	**0**	**0**	**0**	**3:49**
2007-08	**Anaheim**	**NHL**	**69**	**1**	**4**	**5**	**183**	**0**	**0**	**0**	**30**	**3.3**	**3**	**10**	**30.0**	**5:57**	**1**	**0**	**0**	**0**	**0**	**0**	**0**	**0**	**2:42**
	NHL Totals		**158**	**4**	**7**	**11**	**423**	**0**	**0**	**0**	**72**	**5.6**		**11**	**27.3**	**5:24**	**6**	**0**	**0**	**0**	**10**	**0**	**0**	**0**	**3:38**

Claimed on waivers by **Colorado** from **Los Angeles**, October 3, 2006. Traded to **Anaheim** by **Colorado** with Colorado's 3rd round choice (later traded to Tampa Bay - Tampa Bay selected Luca Cunti) in 2007 Entry Draft for Atlanta's 2nd round choice (previously acquired, Colorado selected T.J. Galiardi) in 2007 Entry Draft and Anaheim's 3rd round choice (later traded to San Jose - San Jose selected Tyson Sexsmith) in 2007 Entry Draft, November 13, 2006. • Missed majority of 2006-07 season recovering from a shoulder injury and as a healthy reserve.

PAVELSKI, Joe (pah-VEHL-skee, JOH) S.J.

Center. Shoots left. 5'11", 195 lbs. Born, Plover, WI, July 11, 1984. San Jose's 7th choice, 205th overall, in 2003 Entry Draft.

Season	Club	League	GP	G	A	Pts	PIM	PP	SH	GW	S	%	+/-	TF	F%	Min	GP	G	A	Pts	PIM	PP	SH	GW	Min
2002-03	Waterloo	USHL	60	36	33	69	32	....	....	....	....	....	....	....	....	....	7	5	7	12	8	....	....	....	....
2003-04	Waterloo	USHL	54	21	31	52	58	....	....	....	....	....	....	....	....	....	12	6	6	12	10	....	....	....	....
2004-05	U. of Wisconsin	WCHA	41	16	29	45	26	....	....	....	....	....	....	....	....	....	....	....	....	....	....	....	....	....	....
2005-06	U. of Wisconsin	WCHA	43	23	33	56	34	....	....	....	....	....	....	....	....	....	....	....	....	....	....	....	....	....	....
2006-07	**San Jose**	**NHL**	**46**	**14**	**14**	**28**	**18**	**5**	**0**	**3**	**111**	**12.6**	**4**	**389**	**48.6**	**15:02**	**6**	**1**	**0**	**1**	**0**	**0**	**0**	**0**	**10:27**
	Worcester Sharks	AHL	16	8	18	26	8	....	....	....	....	....	....	....	....	....	....	....	....	....	....	....	....	....	....
2007-08	**San Jose**	**NHL**	**82**	**19**	**21**	**40**	**28**	**8**	**1**	**4**	**207**	**9.2**	**1**	**501**	**53.5**	**14:07**	**13**	**5**	**4**	**9**	**0**	**2**	**0**	**3**	**22:03**
	NHL Totals		**128**	**33**	**35**	**68**	**46**	**13**	**1**	**7**	**318**	**10.4**		**890**	**51.3**	**14:26**	**19**	**6**	**4**	**10**	**0**	**2**	**0**	**3**	**18:23**

USHL All-Rookie Team (2003) • USHL First All-Star Team (2003) • USHL Rookie of the Year (2003) • WCHA All-Rookie Team (2005) • WCHA Second All-Star Team (2006) • NCAA West Second All-American Team (2006)

PAYER, Serge (pie-YAY, SAIRZH)

Center. Shoots left. 6', 191 lbs. Born, Rockland, Ont., May 7, 1979.

Season	Club	League	GP	G	A	Pts	PIM	PP	SH	GW	S	%	+/-	TF	F%	Min	GP	G	A	Pts	PIM	PP	SH	GW	Min
1994-95	Cumberland Colts	ODMHA	42	37	46	83	55	....	....	....	....	....	....	....	....	....	....	....	....	....	....	....	....	....	....
1995-96	Kitchener Rangers	OHL	66	8	16	24	18	....	....	....	....	....	....	....	....	....	12	0	2	2	2	....	....	....	....
1996-97	Kitchener Rangers	OHL	63	7	16	23	27	....	....	....	....	....	....	....	....	....	13	1	3	4	2	....	....	....	....
1997-98	Kitchener Rangers	OHL	44	20	21	41	51	....	....	....	....	....	....	....	....	....	6	3	0	3	7	....	....	....	....
1998-99	Kitchener Rangers	OHL	40	18	19	37	22	....	....	....	....	....	....	....	....	....	....	....	....	....	....	....	....	....	....
99-2000	Kitchener Rangers	OHL	44	10	26	36	53	....	....	....	....	....	....	....	....	....	5	0	3	3	6	....	....	....	....
2000-01	**Florida**	**NHL**	**43**	**5**	**1**	**6**	**21**	**0**	**1**	**0**	**34**	**14.7**	**0**	**97**	**42.3**	**7:27**	....	....	....	....	....	....	....	....	....
	Louisville Panthers	AHL	32	6	6	12	15	....	....	....	....	....	....	....	....	....	....	....	....	....	....	....	....	....	....
2001-02	Utah Grizzlies	AHL	20	6	2	8	9	....	....	....	....	....	....	....	....	....	....	....	....	....	....	....	....	....	....
2002-03	San Antonio	AHL	78	10	31	41	30	....	....	....	....	....	....	....	....	....	1	0	0	0	2	....	....	....	....
2003-04	**Ottawa**	**NHL**	**5**	**0**	**1**	**1**	**2**	**0**	**0**	**0**	**2**	**0.0**	**1**	**43**	**46.5**	**10:30**	....	....	....	....	....	....	....	....	....
	Binghamton	AHL	67	14	20	34	91	....	....	....	....	....	....	....	....	....	2	0	0	0	0	....	....	....	....
2004-05	San Antonio	AHL	3	1	1	2	4	....	....	....	....	....	....	....	....	....	....	....	....	....	....	....	....	....	....
2005-06	**Florida**	**NHL**	**71**	**2**	**4**	**6**	**26**	**0**	**0**	**0**	**70**	**2.9**	**–7**	**543**	**47.5**	**9:53**	....	....	....	....	....	....	....	....	....
2006-07	**Ottawa**	**NHL**	**5**	**0**	**0**	**0**	**0**	**0**	**0**	**0**	**4**	**0.0**	**–1**	**13**	**61.5**	**7:01**	....	....	....	....	....	....	....	....	....
	Binghamton	AHL	43	6	12	18	31	....	....	....	....	....	....	....	....	....	....	....	....	....	....	....	....	....	....
2007-08	Houston Aeros	AHL	66	11	20	31	57	....	....	....	....	....	....	....	....	....	5	0	1	1	4	....	....	....	....
	NHL Totals		**124**	**7**	**6**	**13**	**49**	**0**	**1**	**0**	**110**	**6.4**		**696**	**47.0**	**8:57**	....	....	....	....	....	....	....	....	....

Signed as a free agent by **Florida**, September 30, 1997. • Missed majority of 2001-02 season recovering from back injury suffered in training camp, September, 2001. Traded to **Ottawa** by **Florida** for Ottawa's 9th round choice (Luke Beaverson) in 2004 Entry Draft, September 10, 2003. Signed as a free agent by **Florida**, July 23, 2004. Signed as a free agent by **Ottawa**, August 2, 2006. Signed as a free agent by **Minnesota**, August 20, 2007.

PECA, Michael (PEH-kuh, MIGH-kuhl) CBJ

Center. Shoots right. 5'11", 183 lbs. Born, Toronto, Ont., March 26, 1974. Vancouver's 2nd choice, 40th overall, in 1992 Entry Draft.

Season	Club	League	GP	G	A	Pts	PIM	PP	SH	GW	S	%	+/-	TF	F%	Min	GP	G	A	Pts	PIM	PP	SH	GW	Min
1989-90	Tor. Red Wings	MTHL	39	42	53	95	40	....	....	....	....	....	....	....	....	....	....	....	....	....	....	....	....	....	....
1990-91	Sudbury Wolves	OHL	62	14	27	41	24	....	....	....	....	....	....	....	....	....	5	1	0	1	7	....	....	....	....
1991-92	Sudbury Wolves	OHL	39	16	34	50	61	....	....	....	....	....	....	....	....	....	....	....	....	....	....	....	....	....	....
	Ottawa 67's	OHL	27	8	17	25	32	....	....	....	....	....	....	....	....	....	11	6	10	16	6	....	....	....	....
1992-93	Ottawa 67's	OHL	55	38	64	102	80	....	....	....	....	....	....	....	....	....	....	....	....	....	....	....	....	....	....
	Hamilton	AHL	9	6	3	9	11	....	....	....	....	....	....	....	....	....	....	....	....	....	....	....	....	....	....
1993-94	Ottawa 67's	OHL	55	50	63	113	101	....	....	....	....	....	....	....	....	....	17	7	22	29	30	....	....	....	....
	Vancouver	**NHL**	**4**	**0**	**0**	**0**	**2**	**0**	**0**	**0**	**5**	**0.0**	**–1**	....	....	....	....	....	....	....	....	....	....	....	....
1994-95	Syracuse Crunch	AHL	35	10	24	34	75	....	....	....	....	....	....	....	....	....	....	....	....	....	....	....	....	....	....
	Vancouver	**NHL**	**33**	**6**	**6**	**12**	**30**	**2**	**0**	**1**	**46**	**13.0**	**–6**	....	....	....	**5**	**0**	**1**	**1**	**8**	**0**	**0**	**0**	....
1995-96	**Buffalo**	**NHL**	**68**	**11**	**20**	**31**	**67**	**4**	**3**	**1**	**109**	**10.1**	**–1**	....	....	....	....	....	....	....	....	....	....	....	....
1996-97	**Buffalo**	**NHL**	**79**	**20**	**29**	**49**	**80**	**5**	**6**	**4**	**137**	**14.6**	**26**	....	....	....	**10**	**0**	**2**	**2**	**8**	**0**	**0**	**0**	....
1997-98	**Buffalo**	**NHL**	**61**	**18**	**22**	**40**	**57**	**6**	**5**	**1**	**132**	**13.6**	**12**	....	....	....	**13**	**3**	**2**	**5**	**8**	**0**	**0**	**1**	....
1998-99	**Buffalo**	**NHL**	**82**	**27**	**29**	**56**	**81**	**10**	**0**	**8**	**199**	**13.6**	**7**	**1855**	**49.4**	**20:44**	**21**	**5**	**8**	**13**	**18**	**2**	**1**	**0**	**22:28**
99-2000	**Buffalo**	**NHL**	**73**	**20**	**21**	**41**	**67**	**2**	**0**	**3**	**144**	**13.9**	**6**	**1604**	**48.6**	**19:57**	**5**	**0**	**1**	**1**	**4**	**0**	**0**	**0**	**18:42**
2000-01			Did not play																						
2001-02	**NY Islanders**	**NHL**	**80**	**25**	**35**	**60**	**62**	**3**	**6**	**5**	**168**	**14.9**	**19**	**1804**	**52.4**	**20:14**	**5**	**1**	**0**	**1**	**2**	**0**	**0**	**0**	**16:15**
	Canada	Olympics	6	0	2	2	2	....	....	....	....	....	....	....	....	....	....	....	....	....	....	....	....	....	....
2002-03	**NY Islanders**	**NHL**	**66**	**13**	**29**	**42**	**43**	**4**	**2**	**2**	**117**	**11.1**	**–4**	**1315**	**53.0**	**18:57**	**5**	**0**	**0**	**0**	**4**	**0**	**0**	**0**	**20:10**
2003-04	**NY Islanders**	**NHL**	**76**	**11**	**29**	**40**	**71**	**0**	**1**	**0**	**117**	**9.4**	**17**	**1674**	**53.1**	**19:02**	**5**	**0**	**0**	**0**	**6**	**0**	**0**	**0**	**23:01**
2004-05			Did not play																						
2005-06	**Edmonton**	**NHL**	**71**	**9**	**14**	**23**	**56**	**2**	**2**	**1**	**108**	**8.3**	**–4**	**1048**	**54.9**	**16:39**	**24**	**6**	**5**	**11**	**20**	**0**	**1**	**1**	**19:06**

			Regular Season														Playoffs								
Season	Club	League	GP	G	A	Pts	PIM	PP	SH	GW	S	%	+/-	TF	F%	Min	GP	G	A	Pts	PIM	PP	SH	GW	Min
2006-07	Toronto	NHL	35	4	11	15	60	0	0	2	42	9.5	2	615	49.9	17:25									
2007-08	Columbus	NHL	65	8	26	34	64	3	0	3	86	9.3	–1	1084	52.7	18:34									
	NHL Totals		793	172	271	443	740	41	25	31	1410	12.2		10999	51.6	19:06	93	15	19	34	78	2	2	2	20:19

Frank J. Selke Trophy (1997, 2002)

Traded to **Buffalo** by **Vancouver** with Mike Wilson and Vancouver's 1st round choice (Jay McKee) in 1995 Entry Draft for Alexander Mogilny and Buffalo's 5th round choice (Todd Norman) in 1995 Entry Draft, July 8, 1995. • Missed entire 2000-01 season after failing to come to contract terms with **Buffalo**. Rights traded to **NY Islanders** by **Buffalo** for Tim Connolly and Taylor Pyatt, June 24, 2001. Traded to **Edmonton** by **NY Islanders** for Mike York and Edmonton's 4th round choice (later traded to Colorado - Colorado selected Kevin Montgomery) in 2006 Entry Draft, August 3, 2005. Signed as a free agent by **Toronto**, July 18, 2006. • Missed remainder of 2006-07 season recovering from leg injury suffered in game vs. Chicago, December 22, 2006. Signed as a free agent by **Columbus**, August 21, 2007.

PECKHAM, Theo (PEHK-uhm, THEE-oh) EDM.

Defense. Shoots left. 6'2", 223 lbs. Born, Richmond Hill, Ont., November 10, 1987. Edmonton's 2nd choice, 75th overall, in 2006 Entry Draft.

Season	Club	League	GP	G	A	Pts	PIM	PP	SH	GW	S	%	+/-	TF	F%	Min	GP	G	A	Pts	PIM	PP	SH	GW	Min
2003-04	North York	OPJHL	29	1	4	5	46																		
2004-05	Owen Sound	OHL	61	1	9	10	209										8	0	0	0	8				
2005-06	Owen Sound	OHL	67	6	9	15	236										11	1	6	7	32				
2006-07	Owen Sound	OHL	53	10	25	35	173										4	0	1	1	0				
2007-08	**Edmonton**	**NHL**	**1**	**0**	**0**	**0**	**2**	**0**	**0**	**0**	**0**	**0.0**	**0**	**0**	**0.0**	**13:22**									
	Springfield	AHL	59	6	7	13	174																		
	NHL Totals		**1**	**0**	**0**	**0**	**2**	**0**	**0**	**0**	**0**	**0.0**		**0**	**0.0**	**13:22**									

PELLETIER, Pascal (PEHL-tyay, pas-KAL) CHI.

Right wing. Shoots right. 5'11", 197 lbs. Born, Labrador City, Nfld., June 16, 1983.

Season	Club	League	GP	G	A	Pts	PIM	PP	SH	GW	S	%	+/-	TF	F%	Min	GP	G	A	Pts	PIM	PP	SH	GW	Min
2000-01	Baie-Comeau	QMJHL	70	15	44	59	176										11	2	11	13	6				
2001-02	Baie-Comeau	QMJHL	56	12	25	37	115										5	3	4	7	0				
2002-03	Baie-Comeau	QMJHL	67	46	55	101	113										12	5	7	12	14				
2003-04	Shawinigan	QMJHL	64	39	52	91	85										11	3	9	12	20				
2004-05	Louisiana	ECHL	61	10	28	38	75																		
	Gwinnett	ECHL	6	0	1	1	2										5	0	2	2	2				
2005-06	Providence Bruins	AHL	53	20	26	46	42										6	2	4	6	23				
	Gwinnett	ECHL	21	18	12	30	18																		
2006-07	Providence Bruins	AHL	80	14	35	49	60										13	5	4	9	16				
2007-08	**Boston**	**NHL**	**6**	**0**	**0**	**0**	**0**	**0**	**0**	**0**	**8**	**0.0**	**–2**	**1**	**100.0**	**11:04**									
	Providence Bruins	AHL	73	37	38	75	66										10	6	6	12	4				
	NHL Totals		**6**	**0**	**0**	**0**	**0**	**0**	**0**	**0**	**8**	**0.0**		**1**	**100.0**	**11:04**									

AHL First All-Star Team (2008)

Signed as a free agent by **Boston**, August 7, 2006. Traded to **Chicago** by **Boston** for Martin St. Pierre, July 24, 2008.

PELLEY, Rod (PEHL-lee, RAWD) N.J.

Center. Shoots left. 6', 200 lbs. Born, Kitimat, B.C., September 1, 1984.

Season	Club	League	GP	G	A	Pts	PIM	PP	SH	GW	S	%	+/-	TF	F%	Min	GP	G	A	Pts	PIM	PP	SH	GW	Min
2002-03	Ohio State	CCHA	43	8	3	11	26																		
2003-04	Ohio State	CCHA	42	10	12	22	38																		
2004-05	Ohio State	CCHA	41	22	19	41	54																		
2005-06	Ohio State	CCHA	39	7	7	14	42																		
2006-07	**New Jersey**	**NHL**	**9**	**0**	**0**	**0**	**0**	**0**	**0**	**0**	**8**	**0.0**	**–3**	**98**	**40.8**	**11:00**									
	Lowell Devils	AHL	65	17	12	29	35																		
2007-08	**New Jersey**	**NHL**	**58**	**2**	**4**	**6**	**19**	**0**	**0**	**1**	**59**	**3.4**	**–3**	**321**	**46.7**	**9:19**									
	Lowell Devils	AHL	11	2	1	3	18																		
	NHL Totals		**67**	**2**	**4**	**6**	**19**	**0**	**0**	**1**	**67**	**3.0**		**419**	**45.3**	**9:32**									

CCHA Second All-Star Team (2005)

Signed as a free agent by **New Jersey**, July 24, 2006.

PELTONEN, Ville (PEHL-TOH-nen, VIHL-ee) FLA.

Left wing. Shoots left. 5'11", 182 lbs. Born, Vantaa, Finland, May 24, 1973. San Jose's 4th choice, 58th overall, in 1993 Entry Draft.

Season	Club	League	GP	G	A	Pts	PIM	PP	SH	GW	S	%	+/-	TF	F%	Min	GP	G	A	Pts	PIM	PP	SH	GW	Min
1989-90	HIFK Helsinki U18	Fin-U18	24	21	24	45	14																		
1990-91	HIFK Helsinki Jr.	Fin-Jr.	36	21	16	37	16										7	2	3	5	10				
1991-92	HIFK Helsinki Jr.	Fin-Jr.	37	28	23	51	28										4	0	2	2	0				
	HIFK Helsinki	Finland	6	0	0	0	0																		
1992-93	HIFK Helsinki Jr.	Fin-Jr.	2	4	2	6	4																		
	HIFK Helsinki	Finland	46	13	24	37	16										4	0	2	2	2				
1993-94	HIFK Helsinki	Finland	43	16	22	38	14										3	0	0	0	2				
	Finland	Olympics	8	4	3	7	0																		
1994-95	HIFK Helsinki	Finland	45	20	16	36	16										3	0	0	0	0				
1995-96	**San Jose**	**NHL**	**31**	**2**	**11**	**13**	**14**	**0**	**0**	**0**	**58**	**3.4**	**–7**												
	Kansas City	IHL	29	5	13	18	8																		
1996-97	**San Jose**	**NHL**	**28**	**2**	**3**	**5**	**0**	**1**	**0**	**0**	**35**	**5.7**	**–8**												
	Kentucky	AHL	40	22	30	52	21																		
1997-98	V.Frolunda	Sweden	45	22	29	51	44										7	4	2	6	0				
	Finland	Olympics	6	2	1	3	6																		
1998-99	**Nashville**	**NHL**	**14**	**5**	**5**	**10**	**2**	**1**	**0**	**0**	**31**	**16.1**	**1**	**0**	**0.0**	**15:54**									
99-2000	**Nashville**	**NHL**	**79**	**6**	**22**	**28**	**22**	**2**	**0**	**2**	**125**	**4.8**	**–1**	**1**	**100.0**	**14:41**									
2000-01	**Nashville**	**NHL**	**23**	**3**	**1**	**4**	**2**	**0**	**0**	**0**	**38**	**7.9**	**–7**	**2**	**0.0**	**11:40**									
	Milwaukee	IHL	53	27	33	60	26										5	2	1	3	6				
2001-02	Jokerit Helsinki	Finland	30	11	18	29	8																		
2002-03	Jokerit Helsinki	Finland	49	23	19	42	14										10	4	6	10	0				
2003-04	HC Lugano	Swiss	48	28	44	72	14										16	4	7	11	8				
2004-05	HC Lugano	Swiss	44	24	33	57	16										5	0	3	3	2				
2005-06	HC Lugano	Swiss	39	22	25	47	22										17	*12	12	24	8				
	Finland	Olympics	8	4	5	9	6																		
2006-07	**Florida**	**NHL**	**72**	**17**	**20**	**37**	**28**	**4**	**0**	**0**	**145**	**11.7**	**7**	**35**	**31.4**	**16:25**									
2007-08	**Florida**	**NHL**	**56**	**5**	**15**	**20**	**20**	**1**	**0**	**0**	**108**	**4.6**	**–2**	**16**	**18.8**	**15:49**									
	NHL Totals		**303**	**40**	**77**	**117**	**88**	**9**	**0**	**2**	**540**	**7.4**		**54**	**27.8**	**15:14**									

IHL Second All-Star Team (2001)

Traded to **Nashville** by **San Jose** for Nashville's 5th round choice (later traded to Phoenix – Phoenix selected Josh Blackburn) in 1998 Entry Draft, June 26, 1998. • Missed majority of 1998-99 season recovering from shoulder surgery, December 10, 1998. Signed as a free agent by **Jokerit Helsinki** (Finland), April 26, 2001. Signed as a free agent by **Lugano** (Swiss), April 9, 2003. Signed as a free agent by **Florida**, June 15, 2006.

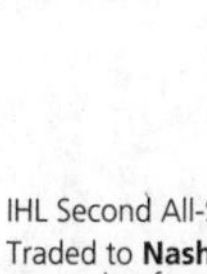

PENNER, Dustin (PEH-nuhr, DUHS-tihn) EDM.

Left wing. Shoots left. 6'4", 245 lbs. Born, Winkler, Man., September 28, 1982.

Season	Club	League	GP	G	A	Pts	PIM	PP	SH	GW	S	%	+/-	TF	F%	Min	GP	G	A	Pts	PIM	PP	SH	GW	Min
2001-02	MSU - Bottineau	NJCAA	23	20	12	32	30																		
2002-03	U. of Maine	H-East	DID NOT PLAY – FRESHMAN																						
2003-04	U. of Maine	H-East	43	11	12	23	52																		
2004-05	Cincinnati	AHL	77	10	18	28	82										9	2	3	5	13				
2005-06	**Anaheim**	**NHL**	**19**	**4**	**3**	**7**	**14**	**2**	**0**	**1**	**46**	**8.7**	**3**	**1**	**0.0**	**11:58**	**13**	**3**	**6**	**9**	**12**	**0**	**0**	**0**	**13:16**
	Portland Pirates	AHL	57	39	45	84	68										5	4	3	7	0				
2006-07♦	**Anaheim**	**NHL**	**82**	**29**	**16**	**45**	**58**	**9**	**0**	**5**	**204**	**14.2**	**–2**	**58**	**46.6**	**13:59**	**21**	**3**	**5**	**8**	**2**	**0**	**0**	**2**	**14:05**
2007-08	**Edmonton**	**NHL**	**82**	**23**	**24**	**47**	**45**	**13**	**0**	**4**	**201**	**11.4**	**–12**	**189**	**55.0**	**17:12**									
	NHL Totals		**183**	**56**	**43**	**99**	**117**	**24**	**0**	**10**	**451**	**12.4**		**248**	**52.8**	**15:13**	**34**	**6**	**11**	**17**	**14**	**0**	**0**	**2**	**13:46**

NCAA Championship All-Tournament Team (2004) • AHL Second All-Star Team (2006)

Signed as a free agent by **Anaheim**, May 12, 2004. Signed as a free agent by **Edmonton**, August 2, 2007.

			Regular Season														Playoffs								
Season	Club	League	GP	G	A	Pts	PIM	PP	SH	GW	S	%	+/-	TF	F%	Min	GP	G	A	Pts	PIM	PP	SH	GW	Min

PEREZHOGIN, Alexander

(pehr-eh-ZHOI-gihn, al-EHX-AN-duhr)

Left wing. Shoots left. 6', 205 lbs. Born, Ust-Kamenogorsk, USSR, August 10, 1983. Montreal's 2nd choice, 25th overall, in 2001 Entry Draft.

Season	Club	League	GP	G	A	Pts	PIM	PP	SH	GW	S	%	+/-	TF	F%	Min	GP	G	A	Pts	PIM	PP	SH	GW	Min
1998-99	Omsk 2	Russia-4	10	3	4	7	0	....	....	....	....	....	....	....	....	....	....	....	....	....	....	....	....	....	....
99-2000	Omsk 2	Russia-3	22	12	11	23	12	....	....	....	....	....	....	....	....	....	....	....	....	....	....	....	....	....	....
	Avangard Omsk	Russia	1	0	0	0	0	....	....	....	....	....	....	....	....	....	....	....	....	....	....	....	....	....	....
2000-01	Omsk 2	Russia-3	41	47	24	71	40	....	....	....	....	....	....	....	....	....	....	....	....	....	....	....	....	....	....
	Avangard Omsk	Russia	....	....	....	....	....	....	....	....	....	....	....	....	....	....	1	0	0	0	0	....	....	....	....
2001-02	Avangard Omsk	Russia	4	1	0	1	4	....	....	....	....	....	....	....	....	....	....	....	....	....	....	....	....	....	....
	Mostovik Kurgan	Russia-2	19	14	10	24	10	....	....	....	....	....	....	....	....	....	....	....	....	....	....	....	....	....	....
2002-03	Avangard Omsk	Russia	48	15	6	21	28	....	....	....	....	....	....	....	....	....	8	0	2	2	4	....	....	....	....
2003-04	Hamilton	AHL	77	23	27	50	52	....	....	....	....	....	....	....	....	....	5	3	3	6	16	....	....	....	....
2004-05	Avangard Omsk	Russia	43	15	18	33	18	....	....	....	....	....	....	....	....	....	11	3	2	5	8	....	....	....	....
2005-06	**Montreal**	**NHL**	**67**	**9**	**10**	**19**	**38**	**3**	**0**	**2**	**109**	**8.3**	**5**	**6**	**33.3**	**10:08**	**6**	**1**	**1**	**2**	**4**	**0**	**0**	**0**	**13:42**
	Hamilton	AHL	11	0	2	2	8	....	....	....	....	....	....	....	....	....	....	....	....	....	....	....	....	....	....
2006-07	**Montreal**	**NHL**	**61**	**6**	**9**	**15**	**48**	**1**	**0**	**1**	**103**	**5.8**	**11**	**7**	**0.0**	**11:51**	....	....	....	....	....	....	....	....	....
2007-08	Ufa	Russia	50	21	20	41	42	....	....	....	....	....	....	....	....	....	16	3	2	5	14	....	....	....	....
	NHL Totals		**128**	**15**	**19**	**34**	**86**	**4**	**0**	**3**	**212**	**7.1**		**13**	**15.4**	**10:57**	**6**	**1**	**1**	**2**	**4**	**0**	**0**	**0**	**13:42**

PERRAULT, Joel

(pair-OH, JOHL) **PHX.**

Center. Shoots right. 6'1", 197 lbs. Born, Montreal, Que., April 6, 1983. Anaheim's 7th choice, 137th overall, in 2001 Entry Draft.

Season	Club	League	GP	G	A	Pts	PIM	PP	SH	GW	S	%	+/-	TF	F%	Min	GP	G	A	Pts	PIM	PP	SH	GW	Min
99-2000	Antoine-Girouard	QAAA	19	4	7	11	6	....	....	....	....	....	....	....	....	....	....	....	....	....	....	....	....	....	....
2000-01	Baie-Comeau	QMJHL	68	10	14	24	46	....	....	....	....	....	....	....	....	....	11	1	1	2	10	....	....	....	....
2001-02	Baie-Comeau	QMJHL	57	18	44	62	96	....	....	....	....	....	....	....	....	....	5	2	0	2	6	....	....	....	....
2002-03	Baie-Comeau	QMJHL	70	51	65	*116	93	....	....	....	....	....	....	....	....	....	12	3	7	10	14	....	....	....	....
2003-04	Cincinnati	AHL	65	14	14	28	38	....	....	....	....	....	....	....	....	....	9	1	1	2	2	....	....	....	....
2004-05	Cincinnati	AHL	51	9	19	28	40	....	....	....	....	....	....	....	....	....	....	....	....	....	....	....	....	....	....
2005-06	Portland Pirates	AHL	25	12	12	24	20	....	....	....	....	....	....	....	....	....	....	....	....	....	....	....	....	....	....
	Phoenix	**NHL**	**5**	**1**	**1**	**2**	**2**	**0**	**0**	**0**	**7**	**14.3**	**0**	**47**	**34.0**	**11:29**	....	....	....	....	....	....	....	....	....
	San Antonio	AHL	12	1	6	7	4	....	....	....	....	....	....	....	....	....	....	....	....	....	....	....	....	....	....
2006-07	**Phoenix**	**NHL**	**15**	**1**	**2**	**3**	**14**	**0**	**0**	**0**	**18**	**9.1**	**–3**	**109**	**82.6**	**11:29**	....	....	....	....	....	....	....	....	....
	St. Louis	**NHL**	**11**	**0**	**0**	**0**	**0**	**0**	**0**	**0**	**13**	**0.0**	**–4**	**20**	**25.0**	**8:19**	....	....	....	....	....	....	....	....	....
	Peoria Rivermen	AHL	2	0	2	2	7	....	....	....	....	....	....	....	....	....	....	....	....	....	....	....	....	....	....
	San Antonio	AHL	21	10	4	14	8	....	....	....	....	....	....	....	....	....	....	....	....	....	....	....	....	....	....
2007-08	**Phoenix**	**NHL**	**49**	**7**	**10**	**17**	**48**	**3**	**0**	**2**	**87**	**8.0**	**–11**	**599**	**49.1**	**14:26**	....	....	....	....	....	....	....	....	....
	San Antonio	AHL	28	14	13	27	36	....	....	....	....	....	....	....	....	....	....	....	....	....	....	....	....	....	....
	NHL Totals		**80**	**9**	**13**	**22**	**64**	**3**	**0**	**2**	**125**	**7.2**		**775**	**52.3**	**12:51**	....	....	....	....	....	....	....	....	....

QMJHL First All-Star Team (2003) • Canadian Major Junior First All-Star Team (2003)

Traded to **Phoenix** by **Anaheim** for Sean O'Donnell, March 9, 2006. Claimed on waivers by **St. Louis** from **Phoenix**, October 31, 2006. Claimed on waivers by **Phoenix** from **St. Louis**, December 19, 2006.

PERREAULT, Yanic

(pair-OH, YAH-nihk)

Center. Shoots left. 5'11", 185 lbs. Born, Sherbrooke, Que., April 4, 1971. Toronto's 1st choice, 47th overall, in 1991 Entry Draft.

Season	Club	League	GP	G	A	Pts	PIM	PP	SH	GW	S	%	+/-	TF	F%	Min	GP	G	A	Pts	PIM	PP	SH	GW	Min
1987-88	Montreal L'est	QAAA	42	*70	57	*127	14	....	....	....	....	....	....	....	....	....	8	12	10	22	6	....	....	....	....
1988-89	Trois-Rivieres	QMJHL	70	53	55	108	48	....	....	....	....	....	....	....	....	....	....	....	....	....	....	....	....	....	....
1989-90	Trois-Rivieres	QMJHL	63	51	63	114	75	....	....	....	....	....	....	....	....	....	7	6	5	11	19	....	....	....	....
1990-91	Trois-Rivieres	QMJHL	67	*87	98	*185	103	....	....	....	....	....	....	....	....	....	6	4	7	11	6	....	....	....	....
1991-92	St. John's	AHL	62	38	38	76	19	....	....	....	....	....	....	....	....	....	16	7	8	15	4	....	....	....	....
1992-93	St. John's	AHL	79	49	46	95	56	....	....	....	....	....	....	....	....	....	9	4	5	9	2	....	....	....	....
1993-94	**Toronto**	**NHL**	**13**	**3**	**3**	**6**	**0**	**2**	**0**	**0**	**24**	**12.5**	**1**	....	....	....	....	....	....	....	....	....	....	....	....
	St. John's	AHL	62	45	60	105	38	....	....	....	....	....	....	....	....	....	11	*12	6	18	14	....	....	....	....
1994-95	Phoenix	IHL	68	51	48	99	52	....	....	....	....	....	....	....	....	....	....	....	....	....	....	....	....	....	....
	Los Angeles	**NHL**	**26**	**2**	**5**	**7**	**20**	**0**	**0**	**1**	**43**	**4.7**	**3**	....	....	....	....	....	....	....	....	....	....	....	....
1995-96	**Los Angeles**	**NHL**	**78**	**25**	**24**	**49**	**16**	**8**	**3**	**7**	**175**	**14.3**	**–11**	....	....	....	....	....	....	....	....	....	....	....	....
1996-97	**Los Angeles**	**NHL**	**41**	**11**	**14**	**25**	**20**	**1**	**1**	**0**	**98**	**11.2**	**0**	....	....	....	....	....	....	....	....	....	....	....	....
1997-98	**Los Angeles**	**NHL**	**79**	**28**	**20**	**48**	**32**	**3**	**2**	**3**	**206**	**13.6**	**6**	....	....	....	**4**	**1**	**2**	**3**	**6**	**1**	**0**	**0**	....
1998-99	**Los Angeles**	**NHL**	**64**	**10**	**17**	**27**	**30**	**2**	**2**	**1**	**113**	**8.8**	**–3**	**1024**	**56.5**	**15:24**	....	....	....	....	....	....	....	....	....
	Toronto	**NHL**	**12**	**7**	**8**	**15**	**12**	**2**	**1**	**2**	**28**	**25.0**	**10**	**164**	**62.8**	**13:20**	**17**	**3**	**6**	**9**	**6**	**0**	**0**	**2**	**15:55**
99-2000	**Toronto**	**NHL**	**58**	**18**	**27**	**45**	**22**	**5**	**0**	**4**	**114**	**15.8**	**3**	**987**	**61.8**	**15:18**	**1**	**0**	**1**	**1**	**0**	**0**	**0**	**0**	**12:56**
2000-01	**Toronto**	**NHL**	**76**	**24**	**28**	**52**	**52**	**5**	**0**	**2**	**134**	**17.9**	**0**	**1055**	**62.7**	**14:01**	**11**	**2**	**3**	**5**	**4**	**1**	**0**	**1**	**12:20**
2001-02	**Montreal**	**NHL**	**82**	**27**	**29**	**56**	**40**	**6**	**0**	**7**	**156**	**17.3**	**–3**	**1485**	**61.3**	**16:47**	**11**	**3**	**5**	**8**	**0**	**2**	**0**	**1**	**13:05**
2002-03	**Montreal**	**NHL**	**73**	**24**	**22**	**46**	**30**	**7**	**0**	**4**	**145**	**16.6**	**–11**	**1156**	**62.9**	**16:05**	....	....	....	....	....	....	....	....	....
2003-04	**Montreal**	**NHL**	**69**	**16**	**15**	**31**	**40**	**5**	**0**	**3**	**114**	**14.0**	**–10**	**861**	**65.2**	**13:46**	**9**	**2**	**2**	**4**	**0**	**0**	**0**	**1**	**12:29**
2004-05			Did not play																						
2005-06	**Nashville**	**NHL**	**69**	**22**	**35**	**57**	**30**	**10**	**0**	**2**	**145**	**15.2**	**–3**	**899**	**62.2**	**14:57**	**1**	**0**	**0**	**0**	**2**	**0**	**0**	**0**	**10:09**
2006-07	**Phoenix**	**NHL**	**49**	**19**	**14**	**33**	**30**	**7**	**0**	**5**	**101**	**18.8**	**–2**	**666**	**62.6**	**17:35**	....	....	....	....	....	....	....	....	....
	Toronto	**NHL**	**17**	**2**	**3**	**5**	**4**	**0**	**0**	**0**	**24**	**8.3**	**1**	**140**	**63.6**	**9:42**	....	....	....	....	....	....	....	....	....
2007-08	**Chicago**	**NHL**	**53**	**9**	**5**	**14**	**24**	**0**	**0**	**0**	**58**	**15.5**	**–1**	**457**	**64.3**	**11:30**	....	....	....	....	....	....	....	....	....
	NHL Totals		**859**	**247**	**269**	**516**	**402**	**63**	**9**	**41**	**1678**	**14.7**		**8894**	**62.0**	**14:54**	**54**	**11**	**19**	**30**	**18**	**4**	**0**	**5**	**13:43**

QMJHL All-Rookie Team (1989) • QMJHL Offensive Rookie of the Year (1989) • Canadian Major Junior Rookie of the Year (1989) • QMJHL First All-Star Team (1991) • QMJHL MVP (1991)

Played in NHL All-Star Game (2007)

Traded to **Los Angeles** by **Toronto** for Los Angeles' 4th round choice (later traded to Philadelphia – later traded back to Los Angeles – Los Angeles selected Mikael Simons) in 1996 Entry Draft, July 11, 1994. Traded to **Toronto** by **Los Angeles** for Jason Podollan and Toronto's 3rd round choice (Cory Campbell) in 1999 Entry Draft, March 23, 1999. Signed as a free agent by **Montreal**, July 4, 2001. Signed as a free agent by **Nashville**, October 3, 2005. Signed as a free agent by **Phoenix**, October 29, 2006. Traded to **Toronto** by **Phoenix** with Phoenix's 5th round choice (Joel Champagne) in 2008 Entry Draft for Brendan Bell and Toronto's 2nd round choice (later traded to Nashville - Nashville selected Roman Josi) in 2008 Entry Draft, February 27, 2007. Signed as a free agent by **Chicago**, July 1, 2007.

PERRIN, Eric

(peh-REHN, AIR-ihk) **ATL.**

Center. Shoots left. 5'9", 180 lbs. Born, Laval, Que., November 1, 1975.

Season	Club	League	GP	G	A	Pts	PIM	PP	SH	GW	S	%	+/-	TF	F%	Min	GP	G	A	Pts	PIM	PP	SH	GW	Min
1991-92	Laval-Laurentides	QAAA	42	41	50	91	....	....	....	....	....	....	....	....	....	....	12	7	16	23	....	....	....	....	....
1992-93	Laval College	CEGEP	Statistics not available																						
1993-94	U. of Vermont	ECAC	32	24	21	45	34	....	....	....	....	....	....	....	....	....	....	....	....	....	....	....	....	....	....
1994-95	U. of Vermont	ECAC	35	28	39	67	38	....	....	....	....	....	....	....	....	....	....	....	....	....	....	....	....	....	....
1995-96	U. of Vermont	ECAC	38	29	56	85	38	....	....	....	....	....	....	....	....	....	....	....	....	....	....	....	....	....	....
1996-97	U. of Vermont	ECAC	36	26	33	59	40	....	....	....	....	....	....	....	....	....	....	....	....	....	....	....	....	....	....
1997-98	Cleveland	IHL	69	12	31	43	34	....	....	....	....	....	....	....	....	....	....	....	....	....	....	....	....	....	....
	Quebec Rafales	IHL	13	2	12	14	4	....	....	....	....	....	....	....	....	....	....	....	....	....	....	....	....	....	....
1998-99	Kansas City	IHL	82	24	37	61	71	....	....	....	....	....	....	....	....	....	3	0	0	0	0	....	....	....	....
99-2000	Kansas City	IHL	21	3	15	18	16	....	....	....	....	....	....	....	....	....	....	....	....	....	....	....	....	....	....
2000-01	Jokerit Helsinki	Finland	6	1	1	2	4	....	....	....	....	....	....	....	....	....	....	....	....	....	....	....	....	....	....
	Assat Pori	Finland	43	15	23	38	70	....	....	....	....	....	....	....	....	....	....	....	....	....	....	....	....	....	....
2001-02	Assat Pori	Finland	45	13	13	26	16	....	....	....	....	....	....	....	....	....	....	....	....	....	....	....	....	....	....
	HPK Hameenlinna	Finland	12	5	10	15	4	....	....	....	....	....	....	....	....	....	8	2	4	6	6	....	....	....	....
2002-03	JYP Jyvaskyla	Finland	56	18	28	46	36	....	....	....	....	....	....	....	....	....	7	4	6	10	8	....	....	....	....
2003-04♦	**Tampa Bay**	**NHL**	**4**	**0**	**0**	**0**	**0**	**0**	**0**	**0**	**3**	**0.0**	**–1**	**30**	**60.0**	**8:32**	**12**	**0**	**1**	**1**	**6**	**0**	**0**	**0**	**5:20**
	Hershey Bears	AHL	71	21	54	75	49	....	....	....	....	....	....	....	....	....	....	....	....	....	....	....	....	....	....
2004-05	Hershey Bears	AHL	80	24	49	73	46	....	....	....	....	....	....	....	....	....	....	....	....	....	....	....	....	....	....
2005-06	SC Bern	Swiss	44	13	25	38	28	....	....	....	....	....	....	....	....	....	6	2	4	6	8	....	....	....	....
2006-07	**Tampa Bay**	**NHL**	**82**	**13**	**23**	**36**	**30**	**2**	**1**	**0**	**151**	**8.6**	**–7**	**407**	**50.9**	**17:00**	**6**	**1**	**1**	**2**	**2**	**0**	**0**	**0**	**12:32**
2007-08	**Atlanta**	**NHL**	**81**	**12**	**33**	**45**	**26**	**2**	**2**	**0**	**121**	**9.9**	**–5**	**717**	**53.0**	**17:50**	....	....	....	....	....	....	....	....	....
	NHL Totals		**167**	**25**	**56**	**81**	**56**	**4**	**3**	**0**	**275**	**9.1**		**1154**	**52.4**	**17:12**	**18**	**1**	**2**	**3**	**8**	**0**	**0**	**0**	**7:44**

ECAC All-Rookie Team (1994) • ECAC Rookie of the Year (1994) • ECAC First All-Star Team (1995, 1996) • ECAC Player of the Year (1996) • NCAA East First All-American Team (1996) • AHL First All-Star Team (2004)

Signed as a free agent by **Tampa Bay**, June 19, 2003. Signed as a free agent by **Bern** (Swiss), August 22, 2005. Signed as a free agent by **Atlanta**, July 1, 2007.

PERRON, David
(peh-RAWN, DAY-vihd) **ST.L.**

Left wing. Shoots right. 6', 180 lbs. Born, Sherbrooke, Que., May 28, 1988. St. Louis' 3rd choice, 26th overall, in 2007 Entry Draft.

			Regular Season														Playoffs								
Season	Club	League	GP	G	A	Pts	PIM	PP	SH	GW	S	%	+/-	TF	F%	Min	GP	G	A	Pts	PIM	PP	SH	GW	Min
2005-06	St-Jerome	QJHL	51	24	45	69	92	....	....	....	....	....	....	....	....	....	8	4	5	9	8	....	....	....	....
2006-07	Lewiston	QMJHL	70	39	44	83	75	....	....	....	....	....	....	....	....	....	17	12	16	28	22	....	....	....	....
2007-08	**St. Louis**	**NHL**	**62**	**13**	**14**	**27**	**38**	**3**	**0**	**1**	**68**	**19.1**	**16**	**14**	**35.7**	**12:33**	....	....	....	....	....	....	....	....	....
	NHL Totals		**62**	**13**	**14**	**27**	**38**	**3**	**0**	**1**	**68**	**19.1**		**14**	**35.7**	**12:33**	....	....	....	....	....	....	....	....	....

PERROTT, Nathan
(pair-OH, NAY-thuhn)

Right wing. Shoots right. 6', 225 lbs. Born, Owen Sound, Ont., December 8, 1976. New Jersey's 2nd choice, 44th overall, in 1995 Entry Draft.

Season	Club	League	GP	G	A	Pts	PIM	PP	SH	GW	S	%	+/-	TF	F%	Min	GP	G	A	Pts	PIM	PP	SH	GW	Min
1992-93	Walkerton	OHA-C	25	6	13	19	45	....	....	....	....	....	....	....	....	....	....	....	....	....	....	....	....	....	....
1993-94	St. Mary's Lincolns	OHA-B	41	11	26	37	249	....	....	....	....	....	....	....	....	....	....	....	....	....	....	....	....	....	....
1994-95	Oshawa Generals	OHL	63	18	28	46	233	....	....	....	....	....	....	....	....	....	2	1	1	2	9	....	....	....	....
1995-96	Oshawa Generals	OHL	59	30	32	62	158	....	....	....	....	....	....	....	....	....	5	2	3	5	8	....	....	....	....
	Albany River Rats	AHL	4	0	0	0	12	....	....	....	....	....	....	....	....	....	....	....	....	....	....	....	....	....	....
1996-97	Oshawa Generals	OHL	5	1	0	1	17	....	....	....	....	....	....	....	....	....	....	....	....	....	....	....	....	....	....
	Sault Ste. Marie	OHL	37	18	23	41	120	....	....	....	....	....	....	....	....	....	11	5	5	10	60	....	....	....	....
1997-98	Indianapolis Ice	IHL	31	4	3	7	76	....	....	....	....	....	....	....	....	....	....	....	....	....	....	....	....	....	....
	Jacksonville	ECHL	30	6	8	14	135	....	....	....	....	....	....	....	....	....	....	....	....	....	....	....	....	....	....
1998-99	Indianapolis Ice	IHL	72	14	11	25	307	....	....	....	....	....	....	....	....	....	7	3	1	4	45	....	....	....	....
99-2000	Cleveland	IHL	65	12	9	21	248	....	....	....	....	....	....	....	....	....	9	2	1	3	19	....	....	....	....
2000-01	Norfolk Admirals	AHL	73	11	17	28	268	....	....	....	....	....	....	....	....	....	9	2	0	2	18	....	....	....	....
2001-02	Norfolk Admirals	AHL	2	0	0	0	5	....	....	....	....	....	....	....	....	....	....	....	....	....	....	....	....	....	....
	Nashville	**NHL**	**22**	**1**	**2**	**3**	**74**	**0**	**0**	**1**	**7**	**14.3**	**–1**	**1**	**0.0**	**4:55**	....	....	....	....	....	....	....	....	....
	Milwaukee	AHL	56	6	10	16	190	....	....	....	....	....	....	....	....	....	....	....	....	....	....	....	....	....	....
2002-03	**Nashville**	**NHL**	**1**	**0**	**0**	**0**	**5**	**0**	**0**	**0**	**0**	**0.0**	**0**	**0**	**0.0**	**4:13**	....	....	....	....	....	....	....	....	....
	Milwaukee	AHL	27	1	2	3	106	....	....	....	....	....	....	....	....	....	....	....	....	....	....	....	....	....	....
	St. John's	AHL	36	7	8	15	97	....	....	....	....	....	....	....	....	....	....	....	....	....	....	....	....	....	....
2003-04	**Toronto**	**NHL**	**40**	**1**	**2**	**3**	**116**	**0**	**0**	**0**	**47**	**2.1**	**–1**	**5**	**20.0**	**7:40**	....	....	....	....	....	....	....	....	....
2004-05	St. John's	AHL	60	16	12	28	276	....	....	....	....	....	....	....	....	....	2	0	0	0	6	....	....	....	....
2005-06	**Toronto**	**NHL**	**3**	**0**	**0**	**0**	**2**	**0**	**0**	**0**	**2**	**0.0**	**–5**	**0**	**0.0**	**9:07**	....	....	....	....	....	....	....	....	....
	Dallas	**NHL**	**23**	**2**	**1**	**3**	**54**	**0**	**0**	**1**	**17**	**11.8**	**2**	**3**	**33.3**	**5:02**	....	....	....	....	....	....	....	....	....
2006-07	Toronto Marlies	AHL	4	0	0	0	19	....	....	....	....	....	....	....	....	....	....	....	....	....	....	....	....	....	....
2007-08	Toronto Marlies	AHL	4	0	0	0	12	....	....	....	....	....	....	....	....	....	....	....	....	....	....	....	....	....	....
	Vityaz Chekhov	Russia	15	0	1	1	98	....	....	....	....	....	....	....	....	....	....	....	....	....	....	....	....	....	....
	NHL Totals		**89**	**4**	**5**	**9**	**251**	**0**	**0**	**2**	**73**	**5.5**		**9**	**22.2**	**6:19**	....	....	....	....	....	....	....	....	....

Signed as a free agent by **Chicago**, August 27, 1997. Traded to **Nashville** by **Chicago** for future considerations, October 9, 2001. Traded to **Toronto** by **Nashville** for Bob Wren, December 31, 2002. • Missed majority of 2003-04 season as a healthy reserve. Traded to **Dallas** by **Toronto** for Dallas' 6th round choice (Leo Komarov) in 2006 Entry Draft, November 6, 2005. Signed as a free agent by **Toronto** (AHL), October 15, 2006. Signed as a free agent by **Vityaz Chekhov** (Russia), January 7, 2008.

PERRY, Corey
(PAIR-ee, KOH-ree) **ANA.**

Right wing. Shoots right. 6'3", 209 lbs. Born, Peterborough, Ont., May 16, 1985. Anaheim's 2nd choice, 28th overall, in 2003 Entry Draft.

Season	Club	League	GP	G	A	Pts	PIM	PP	SH	GW	S	%	+/-	TF	F%	Min	GP	G	A	Pts	PIM	PP	SH	GW	Min
2000-01	Peterborough	Minor-ON	64	69	46	115	20	....	....	....	....	....	....	....	....	....	3	3	0	3	0	....	....	....	....
2001-02	London Knights	OHL	67	28	31	59	56	....	....	....	....	....	....	....	....	....	12	2	3	5	30	....	....	....	....
2002-03	London Knights	OHL	67	25	*53	78	145	....	....	....	....	....	....	....	....	....	14	7	16	23	27	....	....	....	....
2003-04	London Knights	OHL	66	40	*73	113	98	....	....	....	....	....	....	....	....	....	15	7	15	22	20	....	....	....	....
	Cincinnati	AHL	....	....	....	....	....	....	....	....	....	....	....	....	....	....	3	1	1	2	4	....	....	....	....
2004-05	London Knights	OHL	60	*47	*83	*130	117	....	....	....	....	....	....	....	....	....	18	11	*27	*38	46	....	....	....	....
2005-06	**Anaheim**	**NHL**	**56**	**13**	**12**	**25**	**50**	**4**	**0**	**2**	**98**	**13.3**	**1**	**11**	**27.3**	**11:34**	**11**	**0**	**3**	**3**	**16**	**0**	**0**	**0**	**9:33**
	Portland Pirates	AHL	19	16	18	34	32	....	....	....	....	....	....	....	....	....	1	1	0	1	0	....	....	....	....
2006-07♦	**Anaheim**	**NHL**	**82**	**17**	**27**	**44**	**55**	**4**	**0**	**3**	**194**	**8.8**	**12**	**21**	**42.9**	**12:28**	**21**	**6**	**9**	**15**	**37**	**1**	**0**	**1**	**16:30**
2007-08	**Anaheim**	**NHL**	**70**	**29**	**25**	**54**	**108**	**11**	**0**	**4**	**200**	**14.5**	**12**	**16**	**18.8**	**17:57**	**3**	**2**	**1**	**3**	**8**	**0**	**0**	**0**	**14:55**
	NHL Totals		**208**	**59**	**64**	**123**	**213**	**19**	**0**	**9**	**492**	**12.0**		**48**	**31.3**	**14:04**	**35**	**8**	**13**	**21**	**61**	**1**	**0**	**1**	**14:11**

OHL First All-Star Team (2004, 2005) • Canadian Major Junior First All-Star Team (2005) • Memorial Cup Tournament All-Star Team (2005) • Stafford Smythe Memorial Trophy (Memorial Cup Tournament - MVP) (2005)

Played in NHL All-Star Game (2008)

PETERS, Andrew
(PEE-tuhrz, AN-droo) **BUF.**

Left wing. Shoots left. 6'4", 226 lbs. Born, St. Catharines, Ont., May 5, 1980. Buffalo's 2nd choice, 34th overall, in 1998 Entry Draft.

Season	Club	League	GP	G	A	Pts	PIM	PP	SH	GW	S	%	+/-	TF	F%	Min	GP	G	A	Pts	PIM	PP	SH	GW	Min
1996-97	Georgetown	OPJHL	46	11	16	27	65	....	....	....	....	....	....	....	....	....	....	....	....	....	....	....	....	....	....
1997-98	Oshawa Generals	OHL	60	11	7	18	220	....	....	....	....	....	....	....	....	....	7	2	0	2	19	....	....	....	....
1998-99	Oshawa Generals	OHL	54	14	10	24	137	....	....	....	....	....	....	....	....	....	15	2	7	9	36	....	....	....	....
99-2000	Kitchener Rangers	OHL	42	6	13	19	95	....	....	....	....	....	....	....	....	....	4	0	1	1	14	....	....	....	....
2000-01	Rochester	AHL	49	0	4	4	118	....	....	....	....	....	....	....	....	....	....	....	....	....	....	....	....	....	....
2001-02	Rochester	AHL	67	4	1	5	*388	....	....	....	....	....	....	....	....	....	....	....	....	....	....	....	....	....	....
2002-03	Rochester	AHL	57	3	0	3	223	....	....	....	....	....	....	....	....	....	3	0	0	0	24	....	....	....	....
2003-04	**Buffalo**	**NHL**	**42**	**2**	**0**	**2**	**151**	**0**	**0**	**0**	**19**	**10.5**	**–3**	**2**	**0.0**	**4:10**	....	....	....	....	....	....	....	....	....
2004-05	Bodens IK	Sweden-2	22	2	4	6	195	....	....	....	....	....	....	....	....	....	....	....	....	....	....	....	....	....	....
2005-06	**Buffalo**	**NHL**	**28**	**0**	**0**	**0**	**100**	**0**	**0**	**0**	**6**	**0.0**	**–2**	**2**	**100.0**	**3:16**	....	....	....	....	....	....	....	....	....
2006-07	**Buffalo**	**NHL**	**58**	**1**	**1**	**2**	**125**	**0**	**0**	**0**	**19**	**5.3**	**–1**	**0**	**0.0**	**3:46**	....	....	....	....	....	....	....	....	....
2007-08	**Buffalo**	**NHL**	**44**	**1**	**1**	**2**	**100**	**0**	**0**	**0**	**18**	**5.6**	**–4**	**1**	**0.0**	**3:09**	....	....	....	....	....	....	....	....	....
	NHL Totals		**172**	**4**	**2**	**6**	**476**	**0**	**0**	**0**	**62**	**6.5**		**5**	**40.0**	**3:38**	....	....	....	....	....	....	....	....	....

Signed as a free agent by **Bodens** (Sweden-2), August 20, 2004.

PETERSEN, Toby
(PEE-tuhr-suhn, TOH-bee) **DAL.**

Center. Shoots left. 5'10", 197 lbs. Born, Minneapolis, MN, October 27, 1978. Pittsburgh's 9th choice, 244th overall, in 1998 Entry Draft.

Season	Club	League	GP	G	A	Pts	PIM	PP	SH	GW	S	%	+/-	TF	F%	Min	GP	G	A	Pts	PIM	PP	SH	GW	Min
1995-96	Jefferson Jaguars	High-MN	25	29	30	59	....	....	....	....	....	....	....	....	....	....	....	....	....	....	....	....	....	....	....
1996-97	Colorado College	WCHA	40	17	21	38	18	....	....	....	....	....	....	....	....	....	....	....	....	....	....	....	....	....	....
1997-98	Colorado College	WCHA	40	16	17	33	34	....	....	....	....	....	....	....	....	....	....	....	....	....	....	....	....	....	....
1998-99	Colorado College	WCHA	21	12	12	24	2	....	....	....	....	....	....	....	....	....	....	....	....	....	....	....	....	....	....
99-2000	Colorado College	WCHA	37	14	19	33	8	....	....	....	....	....	....	....	....	....	....	....	....	....	....	....	....	....	....
2000-01	**Pittsburgh**	**NHL**	**12**	**2**	**6**	**8**	**4**	**0**	**0**	**1**	**25**	**8.0**	**3**	**39**	**35.9**	**13:22**	....	....	....	....	....	....	....	....	....
	Wilkes-Barre	AHL	73	26	41	67	22	....	....	....	....	....	....	....	....	....	21	7	6	13	4	....	....	....	....
2001-02	**Pittsburgh**	**NHL**	**79**	**8**	**10**	**18**	**4**	**1**	**1**	**0**	**116**	**6.9**	**–15**	**338**	**45.6**	**12:16**	....	....	....	....	....	....	....	....	....
2002-03	Wilkes-Barre	AHL	80	31	35	66	24	....	....	....	....	....	....	....	....	....	6	1	3	4	4	....	....	....	....
2003-04	Wilkes-Barre	AHL	62	15	29	44	4	....	....	....	....	....	....	....	....	....	21	2	10	12	12	....	....	....	....
2004-05	Edmonton	AHL	78	14	15	29	21	....	....	....	....	....	....	....	....	....	....	....	....	....	....	....	....	....	....
2005-06	**Edmonton**	**NHL**	....	....	....	....	....	....	....	....	....	....	....	....	....	....	**2**	**1**	**0**	**1**	**0**	**0**	**0**	**0**	**6:23**
	Iowa Stars	AHL	79	26	47	73	48	....	....	....	....	....	....	....	....	....	7	2	4	6	2	....	....	....	....
2006-07	**Edmonton**	**NHL**	**64**	**6**	**9**	**15**	**4**	**0**	**2**	**1**	**92**	**6.5**	**–18**	**214**	**48.1**	**13:40**	....	....	....	....	....	....	....	....	....
	Iowa Stars	AHL	7	2	6	8	0	....	....	....	....	....	....	....	....	....	....	....	....	....	....	....	....	....	....
2007-08	**Dallas**	**NHL**	**8**	**0**	**3**	**3**	**4**	**0**	**0**	**0**	**6**	**0.0**	**0**	**44**	**50.0**	**7:50**	**16**	**0**	**0**	**0**	**2**	**0**	**0**	**0**	**9:45**
	Iowa Stars	AHL	63	21	30	51	24	....	....	....	....	....	....	....	....	....	....	....	....	....	....	....	....	....	....
	NHL Totals		**163**	**16**	**28**	**44**	**16**	**1**	**3**	**2**	**239**	**6.7**		**635**	**46.1**	**12:41**	**18**	**1**	**0**	**1**	**2**	**0**	**0**	**0**	**9:23**

WCHA All-Rookie Team (1997) • AHL All-Rookie Team (2001)

Signed as a free agent by **Edmonton**, July 30, 2004. Signed as a free agent by **Dallas**, July 6, 2007.

PETIOT, Richard

(PEH-tee-awt, RIH-chuhrd) **TOR.**

Defense. Shoots left. 6'2", 190 lbs. Born, Daysland, Alta., August 20, 1982. Los Angeles' 6th choice, 116th overall, in 2001 Entry Draft.

			Regular Season														Playoffs								
Season	Club	League	GP	G	A	Pts	PIM	PP	SH	GW	S	%	+/-	TF	F%	Min	GP	G	A	Pts	PIM	PP	SH	GW	Min
2000-01	Camrose Kodiaks	AJHL	55	8	16	24	81	....	....	....	....	....	....	....	....	....	8	2	1	3	8	....	....	....	....
2001-02	Colorado College	WCHA	39	4	6	10	35	....	....	....	....	....	....	....	....	....	....	....	....	....	....	....	....	....	....
2002-03	Colorado College	WCHA	38	1	6	7	86	....	....	....	....	....	....	....	....	....	....	....	....	....	....	....	....	....	....
2003-04	Colorado College	WCHA	39	3	5	8	61	....	....	....	....	....	....	....	....	....	....	....	....	....	....	....	....	....	....
2004-05	Colorado College	WCHA	26	3	5	8	42	....	....	....	....	....	....	....	....	....	....	....	....	....	....	....	....	....	....
2005-06	**Los Angeles**	**NHL**	**2**	**0**	**0**	**0**	**2**	**0**	**0**	**0**	**1**	**0.0**	**–2**	**0**	**0.0**	**4:47**	....	....	....	....	....	....	....	....	....
	Manchester	AHL	63	4	10	14	52	....	....	....	....	....	....	....	....	....	7	1	0	1	6	....	....	....	....
2006-07	Manchester	AHL	13	1	1	2	25	....	....	....	....	....	....	....	....	....	2	0	0	0	2	....	....	....	....
2007-08	Manchester	AHL	40	2	5	7	56	....	....	....	....	....	....	....	....	....	....	....	....	....	....	....	....	....	....
	NHL Totals		**2**	**0**	**0**	**0**	**2**	**0**	**0**	**0**	**1**	**0.0**		**0**	**0.0**	**4:47**	....	....	....	....	....	....	....	....	....

AJHL All-Rookie Team (2001) • AJHL South Second All-Star Team (2001)

• Missed majority of 2006-07 season recovering from knee injury suffered in rookie training camp and resulting surgery, October 6, 2006. Signed as a free agent by **Toronto**, July 15, 2008.

PETROVICKY, Ronald

(PEHT-roh-vih-kee, RAW-nohld)

Right wing. Shoots right. 5'11", 190 lbs. Born, Zilina, Czech., February 15, 1977. Calgary's 9th choice, 228th overall, in 1996 Entry Draft.

Season	Club	League	GP	G	A	Pts	PIM	PP	SH	GW	S	%	+/-	TF	F%	Min	GP	G	A	Pts	PIM	PP	SH	GW	Min
1993-94	Dukla Trencin Jr.	Slovak-Jr.	36	28	27	55	42	....	....	....	....	....	....	....	....	....	....	....	....	....	....	....	....	....	....
	Dukla Trencin	Slovakia	1	0	0	0	0	....	....	....	....	....	....	....	....	....	....	....	....	....	....	....	....	....	....
1994-95	Tri-City	WHL	39	4	11	15	86	....	....	....	....	....	....	....	....	....	....	....	....	....	....	....	....	....	....
	Prince George	WHL	21	4	6	10	37	....	....	....	....	....	....	....	....	....	....	....	....	....	....	....	....	....	....
1995-96	Prince George	WHL	39	19	21	40	61	....	....	....	....	....	....	....	....	....	....	....	....	....	....	....	....	....	....
1996-97	Prince George	WHL	72	32	37	69	119	....	....	....	....	....	....	....	....	....	15	4	9	13	31	....	....	....	....
1997-98	Regina Pats	WHL	71	64	49	113	168	....	....	....	....	....	....	....	....	....	9	2	4	6	11	....	....	....	....
1998-99	Saint John Flames	AHL	78	12	21	33	114	....	....	....	....	....	....	....	....	....	7	1	2	3	19	....	....	....	....
99-2000	Saint John Flames	AHL	67	23	33	56	131	....	....	....	....	....	....	....	....	....	3	1	1	2	6	....	....	....	....
2000-01	**Calgary**	**NHL**	**30**	**4**	**5**	**9**	**54**	**1**	**0**	**1**	**30**	**13.3**	**0**	**7**	**42.9**	**11:33**	....	....	....	....	....	....	....	....	....
2001-02	**Calgary**	**NHL**	**77**	**5**	**7**	**12**	**85**	**1**	**0**	**1**	**78**	**6.4**	**0**	**28**	**46.4**	**11:42**	....	....	....	....	....	....	....	....	....
2002-03	**NY Rangers**	**NHL**	**66**	**5**	**9**	**14**	**77**	**2**	**1**	**1**	**65**	**7.7**	**–12**	**52**	**42.3**	**12:25**	....	....	....	....	....	....	....	....	....
2003-04	**Atlanta**	**NHL**	**78**	**16**	**15**	**31**	**123**	**0**	**0**	**1**	**102**	**15.7**	**–9**	**27**	**40.7**	**14:16**	....	....	....	....	....	....	....	....	....
2004-05	MsHK SKP Zilina	Slovakia	34	10	9	19	34	....	....	....	....	....	....	....	....	....	....	....	....	....	....	....	....	....	....
	Brynas IF Gavle	Sweden	10	0	5	5	27	....	....	....	....	....	....	....	....	....	....	....	....	....	....	....	....	....	....
	Brynas IF Gavle	Sweden-Q	9	0	2	2	0	....	....	....	....	....	....	....	....	....	....	....	....	....	....	....	....	....	....
2005-06	**Atlanta**	**NHL**	**60**	**8**	**12**	**20**	**62**	**2**	**0**	**2**	**70**	**11.4**	**–8**	**25**	**52.0**	**11:53**	....	....	....	....	....	....	....	....	....
	Slovakia	Olympics	6	1	0	1	2	....	....	....	....	....	....	....	....	....	....	....	....	....	....	....	....	....	....
2006-07	**Pittsburgh**	**NHL**	**31**	**3**	**3**	**6**	**28**	**0**	**0**	**1**	**27**	**11.1**	**4**	**4**	**50.0**	**8:20**	**3**	**0**	**0**	**0**	**2**	**0**	**0**	**0**	**5:10**
	Wilkes-Barre	AHL	4	0	0	0	4	....	....	....	....	....	....	....	....	....	....	....	....	....	....	....	....	....	....
2007-08	Dukla Trencin	Slovakia	2	0	1	1	2	....	....	....	....	....	....	....	....	....	....	....	....	....	....	....	....	....	....
	MODO	Sweden	18	1	1	2	10	....	....	....	....	....	....	....	....	....	....	....	....	....	....	....	....	....	....
	EV Zug	Swiss	10	0	0	0	35	....	....	....	....	....	....	....	....	....	7	0	0	0	8	....	....	....	....
	NHL Totals		**342**	**41**	**51**	**92**	**429**	**6**	**1**	**7**	**372**	**11.0**		**143**	**44.8**	**12:08**	**3**	**0**	**0**	**0**	**2**	**0**	**0**	**0**	**5:10**

WHL East Second All-Star Team (1998)

• Missed majority of 2000-01 season recovering from wrist injury suffered in game vs. Detroit, October 5, 2000. Claimed by **NY Rangers** from **Calgary** in Waiver Draft, October 4, 2002. Claimed by **Atlanta** from **NY Rangers** in Waiver Draft, October 3, 2003. Signed as a free agent by **Zilina** (Slovakia), September 17, 2004. Signed as a free agent by **Gavle** (Sweden), January 23, 2005. Signed as a free agent by **Pittsburgh**, July 24, 2006. • Missed majority of 2006-07 season recovering from pre-season hip surgery.

PETTINGER, Matt

(PEH-tihn-juhr, MAT) **VAN.**

Left wing. Shoots left. 6'1", 205 lbs. Born, Edmonton, Alta., October 22, 1980. Washington's 2nd choice, 43rd overall, in 2000 Entry Draft.

Season	Club	League	GP	G	A	Pts	PIM	PP	SH	GW	S	%	+/-	TF	F%	Min	GP	G	A	Pts	PIM	PP	SH	GW	Min
1994-95	Victoria Racquet	Minor-BC	55	52	48	100	41	....	....	....	....	....	....	....	....	....	....	....	....	....	....	....	....	....	....
1995-96	Victoria Racquet	Minor-BC	60	80	65	145	45	....	....	....	....	....	....	....	....	....	....	....	....	....	....	....	....	....	....
1996-97	Victoria Salsa	BCHL	49	22	14	36	31	....	....	....	....	....	....	....	....	....	....	....	....	....	....	....	....	....	....
1997-98	Victoria Salsa	BCHL	55	22	20	42	56	....	....	....	....	....	....	....	....	....	7	5	1	6	8	....	....	....	....
1998-99	U. of Denver	WCHA	33	6	14	20	44	....	....	....	....	....	....	....	....	....	....	....	....	....	....	....	....	....	....
99-2000	U. of Denver	WCHA	19	2	6	8	49	....	....	....	....	....	....	....	....	....	....	....	....	....	....	....	....	....	....
	Calgary Hitmen	WHL	27	14	6	20	41	....	....	....	....	....	....	....	....	....	11	2	6	8	30	....	....	....	....
2000-01	**Washington**	**NHL**	**10**	**0**	**0**	**0**	**2**	**0**	**0**	**0**	**6**	**0.0**	**–1**	**2**	**50.0**	**7:47**	....	....	....	....	....	....	....	....	....
	Portland Pirates	AHL	64	19	17	36	92	....	....	....	....	....	....	....	....	....	2	0	0	0	4	....	....	....	....
2001-02	**Washington**	**NHL**	**61**	**7**	**3**	**10**	**44**	**1**	**0**	**1**	**73**	**9.6**	**–8**	**5**	**20.0**	**9:39**	....	....	....	....	....	....	....	....	....
	Portland Pirates	AHL	9	3	3	6	24	....	....	....	....	....	....	....	....	....	....	....	....	....	....	....	....	....	....
2002-03	**Washington**	**NHL**	**1**	**0**	**0**	**0**	**0**	**0**	**0**	**0**	**0**	**0.0**	**0**	**1**	**0.0**	**3:30**	....	....	....	....	....	....	....	....	....
	Portland Pirates	AHL	69	14	13	27	72	....	....	....	....	....	....	....	....	....	3	0	2	2	2	....	....	....	....
2003-04	**Washington**	**NHL**	**71**	**7**	**5**	**12**	**37**	**1**	**0**	**1**	**92**	**7.6**	**–9**	**18**	**44.4**	**11:25**	....	....	....	....	....	....	....	....	....
2004-05	Ljubljana	Slovenia	1	0	1	1	0	....	....	....	....	....	....	....	....	....	....	....	....	....	....	....	....	....	....
	Ljubljana	Interliga	7	2	4	6	41	....	....	....	....	....	....	....	....	....	....	....	....	....	....	....	....	....	....
2005-06	**Washington**	**NHL**	**71**	**20**	**18**	**38**	**39**	**4**	**5**	**2**	**134**	**14.9**	**–2**	**39**	**12.8**	**15:29**	....	....	....	....	....	....	....	....	....
2006-07	**Washington**	**NHL**	**64**	**16**	**16**	**32**	**22**	**4**	**3**	**2**	**111**	**14.4**	**–13**	**23**	**30.4**	**16:53**	....	....	....	....	....	....	....	....	....
2007-08	**Washington**	**NHL**	**56**	**2**	**5**	**7**	**25**	**1**	**0**	**1**	**98**	**2.0**	**–11**	**12**	**58.3**	**14:43**	....	....	....	....	....	....	....	....	....
	Vancouver	**NHL**	**20**	**4**	**2**	**6**	**11**	**0**	**0**	**2**	**29**	**13.8**	**0**	**7**	**57.1**	**13:10**	....	....	....	....	....	....	....	....	....
	NHL Totals		**354**	**56**	**49**	**105**	**180**	**11**	**8**	**9**	**543**	**10.3**		**107**	**30.8**	**13:25**	....	....	....	....	....	....	....	....	....

• Left **University of Denver** (WCHA) and signed as a free agent with **Calgary** (WHL), January 10, 2000. Signed as a free agent by **Ljubljana** (Slovenia), December 6, 2004. Traded to **Vancouver** by **Washington** for Matt Cooke, February 26, 2008.

PEVERLEY, Rich

(PEH-vuhr-lee, RIHTCH) **NSH.**

Center. Shoots right. 6', 185 lbs. Born, Guelph, Ont., July 8, 1982.

Season	Club	League	GP	G	A	Pts	PIM	PP	SH	GW	S	%	+/-	TF	F%	Min	GP	G	A	Pts	PIM	PP	SH	GW	Min
2000-01	St. Lawrence	ECAC	29	2	4	6	4	....	....	....	....	....	....	....	....	....	....	....	....	....	....	....	....	....	....
2001-02	St. Lawrence	ECAC	34	10	21	31	18	....	....	....	....	....	....	....	....	....	....	....	....	....	....	....	....	....	....
2002-03	St. Lawrence	ECAC	34	15	23	38	12	....	....	....	....	....	....	....	....	....	....	....	....	....	....	....	....	....	....
2003-04	St. Lawrence	ECAC	41	17	25	42	34	....	....	....	....	....	....	....	....	....	....	....	....	....	....	....	....	....	....
2004-05	Portland Pirates	AHL	1	0	0	0	0	....	....	....	....	....	....	....	....	....	....	....	....	....	....	....	....	....	....
	South Carolina	ECHL	69	30	28	58	72	....	....	....	....	....	....	....	....	....	4	2	2	4	6	....	....	....	....
2005-06	Milwaukee	AHL	65	12	34	46	44	....	....	....	....	....	....	....	....	....	21	2	9	11	18	....	....	....	....
	Reading Royals	ECHL	11	4	11	15	4	....	....	....	....	....	....	....	....	....	....	....	....	....	....	....	....	....	....
2006-07	**Nashville**	**NHL**	**13**	**0**	**1**	**1**	**0**	**0**	**0**	**0**	**9**	**0.0**	**–1**	**45**	**48.9**	**7:31**	....	....	....	....	....	....	....	....	....
	Milwaukee	AHL	66	30	38	68	62	....	....	....	....	....	....	....	....	....	4	1	2	3	8	....	....	....	....
2007-08	Milwaukee	AHL	45	14	40	54	50	....	....	....	....	....	....	....	....	....	3	1	0	1	0	....	....	....	....
	Nashville	**NHL**	**33**	**5**	**5**	**10**	**8**	**0**	**0**	**2**	**43**	**11.6**	**4**	**132**	**46.2**	**10:20**	**6**	**0**	**2**	**2**	**0**	**0**	**0**	**0**	**8:52**
	NHL Totals		**46**	**5**	**6**	**11**	**8**	**0**	**0**	**2**	**52**	**9.6**		**177**	**46.9**	**9:32**	**6**	**0**	**2**	**2**	**0**	**0**	**0**	**0**	**8:52**

Signed as a free agent by **Nashville**, January 18, 2007.

PHANEUF, Dion

(fah-NOOF, DEE-awn) **CGY.**

Defense. Shoots left. 6'3", 214 lbs. Born, Edmonton, Alta., April 10, 1985. Calgary's 1st choice, 9th overall, in 2003 Entry Draft.

Season	Club	League	GP	G	A	Pts	PIM	PP	SH	GW	S	%	+/-	TF	F%	Min	GP	G	A	Pts	PIM	PP	SH	GW	Min
2000-01	Southgate Lions	AMBHL	35	15	50	65	208	....	....	....	....	....	....	....	....	....	4	3	4	7	15	....	....	....	....
2001-02	Red Deer Rebels	WHL	67	5	12	17	170	....	....	....	....	....	....	....	....	....	21	0	2	2	14	....	....	....	....
2002-03	Red Deer Rebels	WHL	71	16	14	30	185	....	....	....	....	....	....	....	....	....	23	7	7	14	34	....	....	....	....
2003-04	Red Deer Rebels	WHL	62	19	24	43	126	....	....	....	....	....	....	....	....	....	19	2	9	11	30	....	....	....	....
2004-05	Red Deer Rebels	WHL	55	24	32	56	73	....	....	....	....	....	....	....	....	....	7	1	4	5	12	....	....	....	....
2005-06	**Calgary**	**NHL**	**82**	**20**	**29**	**49**	**93**	**16**	**0**	**7**	**242**	**8.3**	**5**	**0**	**0.0**	**21:44**	**7**	**1**	**0**	**1**	**7**	**1**	**0**	**0**	**18:37**
2006-07	**Calgary**	**NHL**	**79**	**17**	**33**	**50**	**98**	**13**	**0**	**4**	**230**	**7.4**	**10**	**0**	**0.0**	**25:40**	**6**	**1**	**0**	**1**	**7**	**1**	**0**	**0**	**26:24**
2007-08	**Calgary**	**NHL**	**82**	**17**	**43**	**60**	**182**	**10**	**1**	**4**	**263**	**6.5**	**12**	**0**	**0.0**	**26:25**	**7**	**3**	**4**	**7**	**4**	**1**	**0**	**0**	**27:07**
	NHL Totals		**243**	**54**	**105**	**159**	**373**	**39**	**1**	**15**	**735**	**7.3**		**0**	**0.0**	**24:35**	**20**	**5**	**4**	**9**	**18**	**3**	**0**	**0**	**23:55**

WHL East First All-Star Team (2004, 2005) • WHL Defenseman of the Year (2004, 2005) • Canadian Major Junior First All-Star Team (2004, 2005) • NHL All-Rookie Team (2006) • NHL First All-Star Team (2008)

Played in NHL All-Star Game (2007, 2008)

Season	Club	League	Regular Season GP	G	A	Pts	PIM	PP	SH	GW	S	%	+/-	TF	F%	Min	Playoffs GP	G	A	Pts	PIM	PP	SH	GW	Min

PHILLIPS, Chris

(FIHL-ihps, KRIHS) **OTT.**

Defense. Shoots left. 6'3", 219 lbs. Born, Calgary, Alta., March 9, 1978. Ottawa's 1st choice, 1st overall, in 1996 Entry Draft.

1993-94	Fort McMurray	AJHL	56	6	16	22	72	....	....	....	....	....	....	....	....	....	10	0	3	3	16	....	....	....	....
1994-95	Fort McMurray	AJHL	48	16	32	48	127	....	....	....	....	....	....	....	....	....	11	4	2	6	10	....	....	....	....
1995-96	Prince Albert	WHL	61	10	30	40	97	....	....	....	....	....	....	....	....	....	18	2	12	14	30	....	....	....	....
1996-97	Prince Albert	WHL	32	3	23	26	58	....	....	....	....	....	....	....	....	....	....	....	....	....	....	....	....	....	....
	Lethbridge	WHL	26	4	18	22	28	....	....	....	....	....	....	....	....	....	19	4	*21	25	20	....	....	....	....
1997-98	**Ottawa**	**NHL**	**72**	**5**	**11**	**16**	**38**	**2**	**0**	**2**	**107**	**4.7**	**2**	....	....	....	**11**	**0**	**2**	**2**	**2**	**0**	**0**	**0**	....
1998-99	**Ottawa**	**NHL**	**34**	**3**	**3**	**6**	**32**	**2**	**0**	**0**	**51**	**5.9**	**–5**	**0**	**0.0**	**18:06**	**3**	**0**	**0**	**0**	**0**	**0**	**0**	**0**	**13:50**
99-2000	**Ottawa**	**NHL**	**65**	**5**	**14**	**19**	**39**	**0**	**0**	**1**	**96**	**5.2**	**12**	**0**	**0.0**	**16:50**	**6**	**0**	**1**	**1**	**4**	**0**	**0**	**0**	**18:17**
2000-01	**Ottawa**	**NHL**	**73**	**2**	**12**	**14**	**31**	**2**	**0**	**0**	**77**	**2.6**	**8**	**1**	**0.0**	**21:28**	**1**	**1**	**0**	**1**	**0**	**0**	**0**	**0**	**20:52**
2001-02	**Ottawa**	**NHL**	**63**	**6**	**16**	**22**	**29**	**1**	**0**	**1**	**103**	**5.8**	**5**	**0**	**0.0**	**19:31**	**12**	**0**	**0**	**0**	**12**	**0**	**0**	**0**	**21:44**
2002-03	**Ottawa**	**NHL**	**78**	**3**	**16**	**19**	**71**	**2**	**0**	**1**	**97**	**3.1**	**7**	**0**	**0.0**	**20:13**	**18**	**2**	**4**	**6**	**12**	**0**	**0**	**1**	**21:36**
2003-04	**Ottawa**	**NHL**	**82**	**7**	**16**	**23**	**46**	**0**	**0**	**1**	**93**	**7.5**	**15**	**1**	**100.0**	**20:50**	**7**	**1**	**0**	**1**	**12**	**1**	**0**	**0**	**20:26**
2004-05	Brynas IF Gavle	Sweden	27	5	3	8	45	....	....	....	....	....	....	....	....	....	....	....	....	....	....	....	....	....	....
	Brynas IF Gavle	Sweden-Q	9	1	2	3	2	....	....	....	....	....	....	....	....	....	....	....	....	....	....	....	....	....	....
2005-06	**Ottawa**	**NHL**	**69**	**1**	**18**	**19**	**90**	**0**	**0**	**0**	**79**	**1.3**	**19**	**0**	**0.0**	**20:52**	**9**	**2**	**0**	**2**	**6**	**0**	**0**	**0**	**21:41**
2006-07	**Ottawa**	**NHL**	**82**	**8**	**18**	**26**	**80**	**0**	**1**	**3**	**94**	**8.5**	**36**	**2**	**0.0**	**22:22**	**20**	**0**	**0**	**0**	**24**	**0**	**0**	**0**	**23:11**
2007-08	**Ottawa**	**NHL**	**81**	**5**	**13**	**18**	**56**	**1**	**0**	**1**	**80**	**6.3**	**15**	**1**	**0.0**	**22:29**	**4**	**0**	**0**	**0**	**4**	**0**	**0**	**0**	**22:00**
	NHL Totals		**699**	**45**	**137**	**182**	**512**	**10**	**1**	**10**	**877**	**5.1**		**5**	**20.0**	**20:33**	**91**	**6**	**7**	**13**	**76**	**1**	**0**	**1**	**21:24**

WHL Rookie of the Year (1996) • WHL East First All-Star Team (1997) • Canadian Major Junior First All-Star Team (1997) • Memorial Cup Tournament All-Star Team (1997)

• Missed majority of 1998-99 season recovering from ankle injury suffered in game vs. Buffalo, December 30, 1998. Signed as a free agent by **Gavle** (Sweden), November 2, 2004.

PICARD, Alexandre

(pee-KAR, al-ehx-AHN-druh) **T.B.**

Defense. Shoots left. 6'2", 220 lbs. Born, Gatineau, Que., July 5, 1985. Philadelphia's 5th choice, 85th overall, in 2003 Entry Draft.

2000-01	Gatineau	QAAA	42	6	15	21	38	....	....	....	....	....	....	....	....	....	11	0	1	1	8	....	....	....	....
2001-02	Halifax	QMJHL	59	2	12	14	28	....	....	....	....	....	....	....	....	....	13	2	3	5	6	....	....	....	....
2002-03	Halifax	QMJHL	71	4	30	34	64	....	....	....	....	....	....	....	....	....	25	1	5	6	14	....	....	....	....
2003-04	Cape Breton	QMJHL	57	10	26	36	44	....	....	....	....	....	....	....	....	....	5	0	0	0	0	....	....	....	....
2004-05	Halifax	QMJHL	68	15	23	38	46	....	....	....	....	....	....	....	....	....	13	1	5	6	14	....	....	....	....
	Philadelphia	AHL	....	....	....	....	....	....	....	....	....	....	....	....	....	....	2	0	0	0	0	....	....	....	....
2005-06	**Philadelphia**	**NHL**	**6**	**0**	**0**	**0**	**4**	**0**	**0**	**0**	**9**	**0.0**	**–2**	**0**	**0.0**	**9:33**	....	....	....	....	....	....	....	....	....
	Philadelphia	AHL	75	7	26	33	82	....	....	....	....	....	....	....	....	....	....	....	....	....	....	....	....	....	....
2006-07	**Philadelphia**	**NHL**	**62**	**3**	**19**	**22**	**17**	**1**	**0**	**0**	**56**	**5.4**	**–19**	**0**	**0.0**	**18:29**	....	....	....	....	....	....	....	....	....
	Philadelphia	AHL	6	1	2	3	2	....	....	....	....	....	....	....	....	....	....	....	....	....	....	....	....	....	....
2007-08	**Philadelphia**	**NHL**	**4**	**0**	**0**	**0**	**2**	**0**	**0**	**0**	**3**	**0.0**	**–3**	**0**	**0.0**	**13:02**	....	....	....	....	....	....	....	....	....
	Philadelphia	AHL	53	8	30	38	31	....	....	....	....	....	....	....	....	....	....	....	....	....	....	....	....	....	....
	Tampa Bay	**NHL**	**20**	**3**	**3**	**6**	**8**	**1**	**0**	**1**	**21**	**14.3**	**–9**	**0**	**0.0**	**21:54**	....	....	....	....	....	....	....	....	....
	Norfolk Admirals	AHL	1	0	0	0	0	....	....	....	....	....	....	....	....	....	....	....	....	....	....	....	....	....	....
	NHL Totals		**92**	**6**	**22**	**28**	**31**	**2**	**0**	**1**	**89**	**6.7**		**0**	**0.0**	**18:24**	....	....	....	....	....	....	....	....	....

QMJHL Second All-Star Team (2005)

Traded to **Tampa Bay** by **Philadelphia** for Vaclav Prospal and future considerations, February 25, 2008.

PICARD, Alexandre

(pee-KAR, al-ehx-AHN-druh) **CBJ**

Left wing. Shoots left. 6'2", 194 lbs. Born, Les Saules, Que., October 9, 1985. Columbus' 1st choice, 8th overall, in 2004 Entry Draft.

2000-01	St-Francois	QAAA	5	1	1	2	0	....	....	....	....	....	....	....	....	....	....	....	....	....	....	....	....	....	....
2001-02	St-Francois	QAAA	41	21	30	51	48	....	....	....	....	....	....	....	....	....	8	2	7	9	8	....	....	....	....
	Sherbrooke	QMJHL	6	0	3	3	0	....	....	....	....	....	....	....	....	....	....	....	....	....	....	....	....	....	....
2002-03	Sherbrooke	QMJHL	66	14	15	29	41	....	....	....	....	....	....	....	....	....	12	4	0	4	10	....	....	....	....
2003-04	Lewiston	QMJHL	69	39	41	80	88	....	....	....	....	....	....	....	....	....	7	7	4	11	6	....	....	....	....
2004-05	Lewiston	QMJHL	65	40	45	85	160	....	....	....	....	....	....	....	....	....	8	5	2	7	18	....	....	....	....
2005-06	**Columbus**	**NHL**	**17**	**0**	**0**	**0**	**14**	**0**	**0**	**0**	**10**	**0.0**	**–2**	**3**	**33.3**	**9:09**	....	....	....	....	....	....	....	....	....
	Syracuse Crunch	AHL	45	15	15	30	54	....	....	....	....	....	....	....	....	....	6	1	0	1	19	....	....	....	....
2006-07	**Columbus**	**NHL**	**23**	**0**	**1**	**1**	**6**	**0**	**0**	**0**	**20**	**0.0**	**–3**	**0**	**0.0**	**7:49**	....	....	....	....	....	....	....	....	....
	Syracuse Crunch	AHL	48	11	18	29	73	....	....	....	....	....	....	....	....	....	....	....	....	....	....	....	....	....	....
2007-08	**Columbus**	**NHL**	**3**	**0**	**0**	**0**	**2**	**0**	**0**	**0**	**1**	**0.0**	**0**	**0**	**0.0**	**6:46**	....	....	....	....	....	....	....	....	....
	Syracuse Crunch	AHL	50	7	13	20	116	....	....	....	....	....	....	....	....	....	13	2	1	3	14	....	....	....	....
	NHL Totals		**43**	**0**	**1**	**1**	**22**	**0**	**0**	**0**	**31**	**0.0**		**3**	**33.3**	**8:16**	....	....	....	....	....	....	....	....	....

QMJHL Second All-Star Team (2004)

PIHLMAN, Tuomas

(PIHL-mahn, TAWH-muhs) **N.J.**

Left wing. Shoots left. 6'2", 215 lbs. Born, Espoo, Finland, November 13, 1982. New Jersey's 3rd choice, 48th overall, in 2001 Entry Draft.

1997-98	JYP Jyvaskyla U18	Fin-U18	30	2	5	7	18	....	....	....	....	....	....	....	....	....	4	1	3	4	6	....	....	....	....
1998-99	JYP Jyvaskyla U18	Fin-U18	35	21	20	41	64	....	....	....	....	....	....	....	....	....	6	1	1	2	12	....	....	....	....
99-2000	JYP Jyvaskyla U18	Fin-U18	3	3	0	3	0	....	....	....	....	....	....	....	....	....	....	....	....	....	....	....	....	....	....
	JYP Jyvaskyla Jr.	Fin-Jr.	20	4	4	8	54	....	....	....	....	....	....	....	....	....	4	0	0	0	8	....	....	....	....
	JYP Jyvaskyla	Finland	17	0	0	0	18	....	....	....	....	....	....	....	....	....	....	....	....	....	....	....	....	....	....
2000-01	JYP Jyvaskyla Jr.	Fin-Jr.	1	1	0	1	2	....	....	....	....	....	....	....	....	....	6	2	4	6	4	....	....	....	....
	JYP Jyvaskyla	Finland	47	3	6	9	59	....	....	....	....	....	....	....	....	....	....	....	....	....	....	....	....	....	....
2001-02	JYP Jyvaskyla Jr.	Fin-Jr.	3	1	1	2	4	....	....	....	....	....	....	....	....	....	....	....	....	....	....	....	....	....	....
	JYP Jyvaskyla	Finland	44	9	2	11	95	....	....	....	....	....	....	....	....	....	....	....	....	....	....	....	....	....	....
2002-03	JYP Jyvaskyla	Finland	53	19	15	34	58	....	....	....	....	....	....	....	....	....	1	0	0	0	0	....	....	....	....
2003-04	**New Jersey**	**NHL**	**2**	**0**	**0**	**0**	**2**	**0**	**0**	**0**	**1**	**0.0**	**0**	**0**	**0.0**	**6:56**	....	....	....	....	....	....	....	....	....
	Albany River Rats	AHL	73	10	19	29	59	....	....	....	....	....	....	....	....	....	....	....	....	....	....	....	....	....	....
2004-05	Albany River Rats	AHL	68	9	13	22	48	....	....	....	....	....	....	....	....	....	....	....	....	....	....	....	....	....	....
2005-06	**New Jersey**	**NHL**	**11**	**1**	**1**	**2**	**10**	**0**	**0**	**0**	**14**	**7.1**	**–1**	**22**	**40.9**	**10:04**	....	....	....	....	....	....	....	....	....
	Albany River Rats	AHL	63	12	15	27	64	....	....	....	....	....	....	....	....	....	....	....	....	....	....	....	....	....	....
2006-07	**New Jersey**	**NHL**	**2**	**0**	**0**	**0**	**0**	**0**	**0**	**0**	**0**	**0.0**	**0**	**0**	**0.0**	**6:32**	....	....	....	....	....	....	....	....	....
	Lowell Devils	AHL	67	8	18	26	34	....	....	....	....	....	....	....	....	....	....	....	....	....	....	....	....	....	....
2007-08	JYP Jyvaskyla	Finland	56	20	29	49	58	....	....	....	....	....	....	....	....	....	6	4	0	4	10	....	....	....	....
	NHL Totals		**15**	**1**	**1**	**2**	**12**	**0**	**0**	**0**	**15**	**6.7**		**22**	**40.9**	**9:11**	....	....	....	....	....	....	....	....	....

PIHLSTROM, Antti

(PIHL-stuhm, AN-tee) **NSH.**

Left wing. Shoots left. 5'10", 181 lbs. Born, Vanntaa, Finland, October 22, 1984.

2001-02	Jokerit U18	Fin-U18	26	15	14	29	41	....	....	....	....	....	....	....	....	....	8	0	5	5	18	....	....	....	....
	Jokerit Helsinki Jr.	Fin-Jr.	1	0	0	0	0	....	....	....	....	....	....	....	....	....	....	....	....	....	....	....	....	....	....
2002-03	Blues Espoo Jr.	Fin-Jr.	36	10	16	26	38	....	....	....	....	....	....	....	....	....	10	1	1	2	8	....	....	....	....
2003-04	Blues Espoo Jr.	Fin-Jr.	23	9	19	28	42	....	....	....	....	....	....	....	....	....	1	0	2	2	0	....	....	....	....
	Suomi U20	Finland-2	4	0	1	1	2	....	....	....	....	....	....	....	....	....	....	....	....	....	....	....	....	....	....
	Blues Espoo	Finland	49	1	3	4	18	....	....	....	....	....	....	....	....	....	9	0	0	0	0	....	....	....	....
2004-05	Blues Espoo	Finland	53	4	3	7	30	....	....	....	....	....	....	....	....	....	....	....	....	....	....	....	....	....	....
	Blues Espoo Jr.	Fin-Jr.	11	7	3	10	36	....	....	....	....	....	....	....	....	....	7	0	2	2	26	....	....	....	....
2005-06	SaiPa	Finland	54	10	11	21	60	....	....	....	....	....	....	....	....	....	8	1	0	1	2	....	....	....	....
2006-07	HPK Hameenlinna	Finland	56	16	23	39	63	....	....	....	....	....	....	....	....	....	9	3	5	8	4	....	....	....	....
2007-08	**Nashville**	**NHL**	**1**	**0**	**0**	**0**	**0**	**0**	**0**	**0**	**1**	**0.0**	**–1**	**0**	**0.0**	**9:08**	....	....	....	....	....	....	....	....	....
	Milwaukee	AHL	78	27	18	45	62	....	....	....	....	....	....	....	....	....	6	1	0	1	8	....	....	....	....
	NHL Totals		**1**	**0**	**0**	**0**	**0**	**0**	**0**	**0**	**1**	**0.0**		**0**	**0.0**	**9:08**	....	....	....	....	....	....	....	....	....

Signed as a free agent by **Nashville**, June 1, 2007.

								Regular Season									Playoffs								
Season	Club	League	GP	G	A	Pts	PIM	PP	SH	GW	S	%	+/-	TF	F%	Min	GP	G	A	Pts	PIM	PP	SH	GW	Min

PILAR, Karel

(PEE-lahr, KAH-rehl)

Defense. Shoots right. 6'3", 210 lbs. Born, Prague, Czech., December 23, 1977. Toronto's 2nd choice, 39th overall, in 2001 Entry Draft.

Season	Club	League	GP	G	A	Pts	PIM	PP	SH	GW	S	%	+/-	TF	F%	Min	GP	G	A	Pts	PIM	PP	SH	GW	Min
99-2000	Litvinov	CzRep	49	2	12	14	61	....	....	....	....	....	....	....	....	....	7	0	0	0	4	....	....	....	....
2000-01	Litvinov	CzRep	52	12	26	38	52	....	....	....	....	....	....	....	....	....	4	1	1	2	25	....	....	....	....
2001-02	**Toronto**	**NHL**	**23**	**1**	**3**	**4**	**8**	**0**	**0**	**0**	**32**	**3.1**	**3**	**0**	**0.0**	**16:03**	**11**	**0**	**4**	**4**	**12**	**0**	**0**	**0**	**17:47**
	St. John's	AHL	52	10	14	24	26	....	....	....	....	....	....	....	....	....	....	....	....	....	....	....	....	....	....
2002-03	**Toronto**	**NHL**	**17**	**3**	**4**	**7**	**12**	**1**	**0**	**1**	**22**	**13.6**	**–7**	**0**	**0.0**	**18:29**	....	....	....	....	....	....	....	....	....
	St. John's	AHL	7	2	5	7	28	....	....	....	....	....	....	....	....	....	....	....	....	....	....	....	....	....	....
2003-04	**Toronto**	**NHL**	**50**	**2**	**17**	**19**	**22**	**1**	**0**	**1**	**74**	**2.7**	**2**	**0**	**0.0**	**18:03**	**1**	**1**	**0**	**1**	**0**	**0**	**0**	**0**	**20:48**
	St. John's	AHL	6	3	4	7	6	....	....	....	....	....	....	....	....	....	....	....	....	....	....	....	....	....	....
2004-05	HC Sparta Praha	CzRep	52	13	15	28	70	....	....	....	....	....	....	....	....	....	....	....	....	....	....	....	....	....	....
2005-06	HC Sparta Praha	CzRep	6	0	1	1	20	....	....	....	....	....	....	....	....	....	14	3	3	6	45	....	....	....	....
2006-07	Toronto Marlies	AHL	10	2	5	7	6	....	....	....	....	....	....	....	....	....	....	....	....	....	....	....	....	....	....
	HC Sparta Praha	CzRep	....	....	....	....	....	....	....	....	....	....	....	....	....	....	1	0	0	0	2	....	....	....	....
2007-08	Chicago Wolves	AHL	45	2	24	26	48	....	....	....	....	....	....	....	....	....	3	0	0	0	6	....	....	....	....
	NHL Totals		**90**	**6**	**24**	**30**	**42**	**2**	**0**	**2**	**128**	**4.7**		**0**	**0.0**	**17:38**	**12**	**1**	**4**	**5**	**12**	**0**	**0**	**0**	**18:02**

• Missed remainder of 2002-03 season, the start of 2003-04 season and the majority of the 2005-06 and 2006-07 seasons after being diagnosed with a heart condition, January, 2003. Signed as a free agent by **Sparta** (CzRep), August 9, 2004. Signed as a free agent by **Atlanta**, August 8, 2007. Claimed on waivers by **Chicago** from **Atlanta**, September 27, 2007. Claimed on waivers by **Atlanta** from **Chicago**, October 2, 2007.

PINEAULT, Adam

(pih-NOH, A-duhm) **CBJ**

Right wing. Shoots right. 6'1", 211 lbs. Born, Holyoke, MA, May 23, 1986. Columbus' 2nd choice, 46th overall, in 2004 Entry Draft.

Season	Club	League	GP	G	A	Pts	PIM	PP	SH	GW	S	%	+/-	TF	F%	Min	GP	G	A	Pts	PIM	PP	SH	GW	Min
2000-01	Junior Bruins	EJHL	57	30	35	65	56	....	....	....	....	....	....	....	....	....	....	....	....	....	....	....	....	....	....
2001-02	USNTDP	U-17	20	5	4	9	14	....	....	....	....	....	....	....	....	....	....	....	....	....	....	....	....	....	....
	USNTDP	NAHL	38	11	4	15	11	....	....	....	....	....	....	....	....	....	....	....	....	....	....	....	....	....	....
2002-03	USNTDP	U-17	43	13	15	28	76	....	....	....	....	....	....	....	....	....	....	....	....	....	....	....	....	....	....
	USNTDP	U-18	4	4	3	7	6	....	....	....	....	....	....	....	....	....	....	....	....	....	....	....	....	....	....
	USNTDP	NAHL	9	5	4	9	13	....	....	....	....	....	....	....	....	....	....	....	....	....	....	....	....	....	....
2003-04	Boston College	H-East	30	4	4	8	32	....	....	....	....	....	....	....	....	....	....	....	....	....	....	....	....	....	....
2004-05	Moncton Wildcats	QMJHL	61	26	20	46	64	....	....	....	....	....	....	....	....	....	12	2	6	8	18	....	....	....	....
2005-06	Moncton Wildcats	QMJHL	55	29	30	59	94	....	....	....	....	....	....	....	....	....	21	14	8	22	25	....	....	....	....
2006-07	Syracuse Crunch	AHL	57	12	16	28	66	....	....	....	....	....	....	....	....	....	....	....	....	....	....	....	....	....	....
2007-08	**Columbus**	**NHL**	**3**	**0**	**0**	**0**	**0**	**0**	**0**	**0**	**5**	**0.0**	**–2**	**1**	**0.0**	**11:03**	....	....	....	....	....	....	....	....	....
	Syracuse Crunch	AHL	74	21	27	48	64	....	....	....	....	....	....	....	....	....	8	0	2	2	2	....	....	....	....
	NHL Totals		**3**	**0**	**0**	**0**	**0**	**0**	**0**	**0**	**5**	**0.0**		**1**	**0.0**	**11:03**	....	....	....	....	....	....	....	....	....

Memorial Cup Tournament All-Star Team (2006)

PISANI, Fernando

(pih-ZAN-ee, FUHR-nan-DOH) **EDM.**

Right wing. Shoots left. 6'1", 205 lbs. Born, Edmonton, Alta., December 27, 1976. Edmonton's 9th choice, 195th overall, in 1996 Entry Draft.

Season	Club	League	GP	G	A	Pts	PIM	PP	SH	GW	S	%	+/-	TF	F%	Min	GP	G	A	Pts	PIM	PP	SH	GW	Min
1993-94	St. Albert Saints	AJHL	50	6	21	27	24	....	....	....	....	....	....	....	....	....	....	....	....	....	....	....	....	....	....
1994-95	Bonnyville	AJHL	16	4	34	37	97	....	....	....	....	....	....	....	....	....	....	....	....	....	....	....	....	....	....
	St. Albert Saints	AJHL	40	26	21	47	16	....	....	....	....	....	....	....	....	....	....	....	....	....	....	....	....	....	....
1995-96	St. Albert Saints	AJHL	58	40	63	103	134	....	....	....	....	....	....	....	....	....	18	7	22	29	28	....	....	....	....
1996-97	Providence	H-East	35	12	18	30	36	....	....	....	....	....	....	....	....	....	....	....	....	....	....	....	....	....	....
1997-98	Providence	H-East	36	16	18	34	20	....	....	....	....	....	....	....	....	....	....	....	....	....	....	....	....	....	....
1998-99	Providence	H-East	38	14	37	51	42	....	....	....	....	....	....	....	....	....	....	....	....	....	....	....	....	....	....
99-2000	Providence	H-East	38	14	24	38	56	....	....	....	....	....	....	....	....	....	....	....	....	....	....	....	....	....	....
2000-01	Hamilton	AHL	52	12	13	25	28	....	....	....	....	....	....	....	....	....	....	....	....	....	....	....	....	....	....
2001-02	Hamilton	AHL	79	26	34	60	60	....	....	....	....	....	....	....	....	....	15	4	6	10	4	....	....	....	....
2002-03	**Edmonton**	**NHL**	**35**	**8**	**5**	**13**	**10**	**0**	**1**	**0**	**32**	**25.0**	**9**	**1**	**100.0**	**10:43**	**6**	**1**	**0**	**1**	**2**	**0**	**0**	**0**	**13:48**
	Hamilton	AHL	41	17	15	32	24	....	....	....	....	....	....	....	....	....	....	....	....	....	....	....	....	....	....
2003-04	**Edmonton**	**NHL**	**76**	**16**	**14**	**30**	**46**	**4**	**1**	**1**	**99**	**16.2**	**14**	**10**	**20.0**	**12:46**	....	....	....	....	....	....	....	....	....
2004-05	Langnau	Swiss	7	1	3	4	0	....	....	....	....	....	....	....	....	....	....	....	....	....	....	....	....	....	....
	Asiago	Italy	12	1	5	6	6	....	....	....	....	....	....	....	....	....	9	4	6	10	0	....	....	....	....
2005-06	**Edmonton**	**NHL**	**80**	**18**	**19**	**37**	**42**	**4**	**1**	**2**	**131**	**13.7**	**5**	**35**	**22.9**	**13:51**	**24**	***14**	**4**	**18**	**10**	**3**	**1**	**5**	**17:12**
2006-07	**Edmonton**	**NHL**	**77**	**14**	**14**	**28**	**40**	**2**	**1**	**0**	**142**	**9.9**	**–1**	**20**	**40.0**	**16:54**	....	....	....	....	....	....	....	....	....
2007-08	**Edmonton**	**NHL**	**56**	**13**	**9**	**22**	**28**	**4**	**0**	**3**	**96**	**13.5**	**–5**	**7**	**28.6**	**16:32**	....	....	....	....	....	....	....	....	....
	NHL Totals		**324**	**69**	**61**	**130**	**166**	**14**	**4**	**6**	**500**	**13.8**		**73**	**28.8**	**14:27**	**30**	**15**	**4**	**19**	**12**	**3**	**1**	**5**	**16:31**

Signed as a free agent by **Langnau** (Swiss), October 24, 2004. Signed as a free agent by **Asiago** (Italy), December 23, 2004.

PISKULA, Joe

(PIHS-koo-luh, JOH) **L.A.**

Defense. Shoots left. 6'3", 216 lbs. Born, Antigo, WI, July 5, 1984.

Season	Club	League	GP	G	A	Pts	PIM	PP	SH	GW	S	%	+/-	TF	F%	Min	GP	G	A	Pts	PIM	PP	SH	GW	Min
2002-03	Chicago Steel	USHL	13	0	0	0	18	....	....	....	....	....	....	....	....	....	....	....	....	....	....	....	....	....	....
	Des Moines	USHL	32	2	6	8	18	....	....	....	....	....	....	....	....	....	4	0	1	1	4	....	....	....	....
2003-04	Des Moines	USHL	58	2	4	6	68	....	....	....	....	....	....	....	....	....	3	0	1	1	0	....	....	....	....
2004-05	U. of Wisconsin	WCHA	40	0	6	6	24	....	....	....	....	....	....	....	....	....	....	....	....	....	....	....	....	....	....
2005-06	U. of Wisconsin	WCHA	34	2	9	11	22	....	....	....	....	....	....	....	....	....	....	....	....	....	....	....	....	....	....
2006-07	U. of Wisconsin	WCHA	38	1	4	5	34	....	....	....	....	....	....	....	....	....	....	....	....	....	....	....	....	....	....
	Los Angeles	**NHL**	**5**	**0**	**0**	**0**	**6**	**0**	**0**	**0**	**4**	**0.0**	**–3**	**0**	**0.0**	**9:59**	....	....	....	....	....	....	....	....	....
2007-08	Manchester	AHL	55	0	7	7	57	....	....	....	....	....	....	....	....	....	4	0	0	0	4	....	....	....	....
	NHL Totals		**5**	**0**	**0**	**0**	**6**	**0**	**0**	**0**	**4**	**0.0**		**0**	**0.0**	**9:59**	....	....	....	....	....	....	....	....	....

Signed as a free agent by **Los Angeles**, March 21, 2007.

PITKANEN, Joni

(PIHT-ka-nuhn, YOH-nee) **CAR.**

Defense. Shoots left. 6'3", 214 lbs. Born, Oulu, Finland, September 19, 1983. Philadelphia's 1st choice, 4th overall, in 2002 Entry Draft.

Season	Club	League	GP	G	A	Pts	PIM	PP	SH	GW	S	%	+/-	TF	F%	Min	GP	G	A	Pts	PIM	PP	SH	GW	Min
1998-99	Karpat Oulu U18	Fin-U18	30	1	5	6	12	....	....	....	....	....	....	....	....	....	....	....	....	....	....	....	....	....	....
99-2000	Karpat Oulu U18	Fin-U18	36	12	14	26	26	....	....	....	....	....	....	....	....	....	6	1	4	5	2	....	....	....	....
	Karpat Oulu Jr.	Fin-Jr.	2	0	0	0	0	....	....	....	....	....	....	....	....	....	....	....	....	....	....	....	....	....	....
2000-01	Karpat Oulu Jr.	Fin-Jr.	24	6	11	17	77	....	....	....	....	....	....	....	....	....	....	....	....	....	....	....	....	....	....
	Karpat Oulu	Finland	21	0	0	0	10	....	....	....	....	....	....	....	....	....	2	0	0	0	2	....	....	....	....
2001-02	Karpat Oulu Jr.	Fin-Jr.	....	....	....	....	....	....	....	....	....	....	....	....	....	....	1	0	0	0	0	....	....	....	....
	Karpat Oulu	Finland	49	4	15	19	65	....	....	....	....	....	....	....	....	....	4	0	0	0	12	....	....	....	....
2002-03	Karpat Oulu	Finland	35	5	15	20	38	....	....	....	....	....	....	....	....	....	....	....	....	....	....	....	....	....	....
2003-04	**Philadelphia**	**NHL**	**71**	**8**	**19**	**27**	**44**	**5**	**0**	**2**	**133**	**6.0**	**15**	**0**	**0.0**	**16:35**	**15**	**0**	**3**	**3**	**6**	**0**	**0**	**0**	**12:13**
2004-05	Philadelphia	AHL	76	6	35	41	105	....	....	....	....	....	....	....	....	....	21	3	4	7	16	....	....	....	....
2005-06	**Philadelphia**	**NHL**	**58**	**13**	**33**	**46**	**78**	**5**	**0**	**3**	**118**	**11.0**	**22**	**0**	**0.0**	**23:43**	**6**	**0**	**2**	**2**	**2**	**0**	**0**	**0**	**24:12**
	Finland	Olympics	DID NOT PLAY – INJURED																						
2006-07	**Philadelphia**	**NHL**	**77**	**4**	**39**	**43**	**88**	**1**	**0**	**0**	**137**	**2.9**	**–25**	**0**	**0.0**	**24:33**	....	....	....	....	....	....	....	....	....
2007-08	**Edmonton**	**NHL**	**63**	**8**	**18**	**26**	**56**	**1**	**1**	**1**	**101**	**7.9**	**–5**	**0**	**0.0**	**24:07**	....	....	....	....	....	....	....	....	....
	NHL Totals		**269**	**33**	**109**	**142**	**266**	**12**	**1**	**6**	**489**	**6.7**		**0**	**0.0**	**22:10**	**21**	**0**	**5**	**5**	**8**	**0**	**0**	**0**	**15:39**

NHL All-Rookie Team (2004)

Traded to **Edmonton** by **Philadelphia** with Geoff Sanderson and Philadelphia's 3rd round choice in 2009 Entry Draft for Jason Smith and Joffrey Lupul, July 1, 2007. Traded to **Carolina** by **Edmonton** for Erik Cole, July 1, 2008.

PLATT, Geoff

(PLAT, JEHF)

Center. Shoots left. 5'9", 175 lbs. Born, Toronto, Ont., July 10, 1985.

Season	Club	League	GP	G	A	Pts	PIM	PP	SH	GW	S	%	+/-	TF	F%	Min	GP	G	A	Pts	PIM	PP	SH	GW	Min
2000-01	St. Mike's B's	OPJHL	6	2	0	2	4	....	....	....	....	....	....	....	....	....	....	....	....	....	....	....	....	....	....
2001-02	North Bay	OHL	63	4	6	10	34	....	....	....	....	....	....	....	....	....	5	0	0	0	6	....	....	....	....
2002-03	Saginaw Spirit	OHL	62	32	22	54	81	....	....	....	....	....	....	....	....	....	....	....	....	....	....	....	....	....	....
2003-04	Saginaw Spirit	OHL	27	7	13	20	49	....	....	....	....	....	....	....	....	....	....	....	....	....	....	....	....	....	....
	Erie Otters	OHL	28	18	11	29	22	....	....	....	....	....	....	....	....	....	9	9	1	10	22	....	....	....	....
2004-05	Erie Otters	OHL	68	45	34	79	84	....	....	....	....	....	....	....	....	....	6	2	3	5	16	....	....	....	....
	Atlantic City	ECHL	2	0	2	2	0	....	....	....	....	....	....	....	....	....	3	0	0	0	0	....	....	....	....

			Regular Season														Playoffs								
Season	Club	League	GP	G	A	Pts	PIM	PP	SH	GW	S	%	+/-	TF	F%	Min	GP	G	A	Pts	PIM	PP	SH	GW	Min
2005-06	Syracuse Crunch	AHL	66	31	34	65	58										6	3	0	3	6				
	Columbus	**NHL**	**15**	**0**	**5**	**5**	**16**	**0**	**0**	**0**	**29**	**0.0**	**–4**	**53**	**45.3**	**11:12**									
2006-07	**Columbus**	**NHL**	**26**	**4**	**5**	**9**	**10**	**0**	**0**	**0**	**40**	**10.0**	**1**	**168**	**56.6**	**10:04**									
	Syracuse Crunch	AHL	53	28	21	49	59																		
2007-08	Syracuse Crunch	AHL	15	4	3	7	6																		
	Anaheim	**NHL**	**5**	**0**	**0**	**0**	**2**	**0**	**0**	**0**	**4**	**0.0**	**2**	**7**	**28.6**	**11:17**									
	Portland Pirates	AHL	60	28	30	58	49										18	8	9	17	24				
	NHL Totals		**46**	**4**	**10**	**14**	**28**	**0**	**0**	**0**	**73**	**5.5**		**228**	**53.1**	**10:34**									

Signed as a free agent by **Syracuse** (AHL), September 23, 2005. Signed as a free agent by **Columbus**, November 25, 2005. Traded to **Anaheim** by **Columbus** for Aaron Rome and Clay Wilson, November 15, 2007.

PLEKANEC, Tomas

(pleh-KA-nyehts, TAW-mahsh) **MTL.**

Left wing. Shoots left. 5'10", 194 lbs. Born, Kladno, Czech., October 31, 1982. Montreal's 4th choice, 71st overall, in 2001 Entry Draft.

1996-97	Kladno U17	CzR-U17	13	1	3	4																			
1997-98	HC Kladno U17	CzR-U17	45	38	26	64																			
1998-99	HC Kladno Jr.	CzRep-Jr.	53	22	20	42																			
99-2000	HC Kladno Jr.	CzRep-Jr.	43	14	16	30																			
	Kralupy	CzRep-3	6	2	2	4	2																		
	HC CKD Slany	CzRep-3	3	0	1	1	6																		
2000-01	Kladno	CzRep	47	9	9	18	24																		
	HC Kladno Jr.	CzRep-Jr.	9	6	4	10	4																		
2001-02	Kladno	CzRep	48	7	16	23	28																		
	BK Mlada Boleslav	CzRep-3	6	6	3	9	14																		
	Kladno	CzRep-Q	5	0	1	1	0																		
2002-03	Hamilton	AHL	77	19	27	46	74										13	3	2	5	8				
2003-04	**Montreal**	**NHL**	**2**	**0**	**0**	**0**	**0**	**0**	**0**	**0**	**0**	**0.0**	**0**	**11**	**45.5**	**9:02**									
	Hamilton	AHL	74	23	43	66	90										10	2	5	7	6				
2004-05	Hamilton	AHL	80	29	35	64	68										4	2	4	6	6				
2005-06	**Montreal**	**NHL**	**67**	**9**	**20**	**29**	**32**	**1**	**0**	**0**	**99**	**9.1**	**4**	**708**	**50.3**	**13:15**	**6**	**0**	**4**	**4**	**6**	**0**	**0**	**0**	**18:00**
	Hamilton	AHL	2	0	0	0	2																		
2006-07	**Montreal**	**NHL**	**81**	**20**	**27**	**47**	**36**	**5**	**2**	**1**	**150**	**13.3**	**10**	**1159**	**48.3**	**15:59**									
2007-08	**Montreal**	**NHL**	**81**	**29**	**40**	**69**	**42**	**12**	**2**	**6**	**186**	**15.6**	**15**	**1381**	**49.5**	**18:05**	**12**	**4**	**5**	**9**	**2**	**2**	**0**	**0**	**18:02**
	NHL Totals		**231**	**58**	**87**	**145**	**110**	**18**	**4**	**7**	**435**	**13.3**		**3259**	**49.2**	**15:52**	**18**	**4**	**9**	**13**	**8**	**2**	**0**	**0**	**18:01**

PLIHAL, Tomas

(PLEE-hahl, TAW-mahsh) **S.J.**

Center. Shoots left. 6'1", 200 lbs. Born, Frydlant, Czech., March 28, 1983. San Jose's 4th choice, 140th overall, in 2001 Entry Draft.

99-2000	Liberec U17	CzR-U17	38	22	14	36																			
	Liberec Jr.	CzRep-Jr.	2	0	0	0	0																		
2000-01	HC Liberec U17	CzR-U17	18	3	5	8																			
	HC Liberec Jr.	CzRep-Jr.	33	16	12	28																			
2001-02	Kootenay Ice	WHL	72	32	54	86	28										22	4	10	14	14				
2002-03	Kootenay Ice	WHL	67	35	42	77	113										11	2	4	6	18				
2003-04	Cleveland Barons	AHL	51	4	12	16	16										6	0	3	3	2				
2004-05	Cleveland Barons	AHL	62	17	11	28	26																		
2005-06	Cleveland Barons	AHL	74	11	19	30	53																		
2006-07	**San Jose**	**NHL**	**3**	**0**	**0**	**0**	**0**	**0**	**0**	**0**	**10**	**0.0**	**0**	**8**	**75.0**	**9:44**									
	Worcester Sharks	AHL	47	6	9	15	28																		
2007-08	**San Jose**	**NHL**	**22**	**2**	**1**	**3**	**4**	**0**	**0**	**0**	**34**	**5.9**	**4**	**19**	**26.3**	**10:50**	**4**	**0**	**0**	**0**	**0**	**0**	**0**	**0**	**13:16**
	Worcester Sharks	AHL	22	5	7	12	12																		
	NHL Totals		**25**	**2**	**1**	**3**	**4**	**0**	**0**	**0**	**44**	**4.5**		**27**	**40.7**	**10:42**	**4**	**0**	**0**	**0**	**0**	**0**	**0**	**0**	**13:16**

George Parsons Trophy (Memorial Cup Tournament - Most Sportsmanlike Player) (2002)

POCK, Thomas

(PAWK, TAW-muhs) **NYR**

Defense. Shoots left. 6'1", 210 lbs. Born, Klagenfurt, Austria, December 2, 1981.

1998-99	Klagenfurt Jr.	Austria-Jr.	31	0	0	0	2																		
99-2000	Klagenfurter AC	Austria	15	3	8	11	14																		
	Klagenfurt	Alpenliga	33	4	11	15	48																		
2000-01	Massachusetts	H-East	33	6	6	12	59																		
2001-02	Massachusetts	H-East	23	5	7	12	26																		
	Austria	Nat-Tm	10	1	2	3	4																		
	Austria	Olympics	4	0	0	0	2																		
2002-03	Massachusetts	H-East	37	17	20	37	46																		
2003-04	Massachusetts	H-East	37	16	25	41	48																		
	NY Rangers	**NHL**	**6**	**2**	**2**	**4**	**0**	**0**	**0**	**0**	**8**	**25.0**	**–4**	**0**	**0.0**	**18:38**									
2004-05	Hartford	AHL	50	1	5	6	55										6	0	1	1	8				
	Charlotte	ECHL	3	0	2	2	2																		
2005-06	**NY Rangers**	**NHL**	**8**	**1**	**1**	**2**	**4**	**0**	**0**	**0**	**15**	**6.7**	**–3**	**0**	**0.0**	**15:10**									
	Hartford	AHL	67	15	46	61	99										6	0	3	3	15				
2006-07	**NY Rangers**	**NHL**	**44**	**4**	**4**	**8**	**16**	**0**	**0**	**0**	**76**	**5.3**	**–4**	**0**	**0.0**	**16:14**	**4**	**0**	**3**	**3**	**4**	**0**	**0**	**0**	**13:29**
	Hartford	AHL	4	0	1	1	2																		
2007-08	**NY Rangers**	**NHL**	**1**	**0**	**0**	**0**	**0**	**0**	**0**	**0**	**2**	**0.0**	**–2**	**0**	**0.0**	**18:53**									
	Hartford	AHL	74	7	37	44	63										5	0	0	0	8				
	NHL Totals		**59**	**7**	**7**	**14**	**20**	**0**	**0**	**0**	**101**	**6.9**		**0**	**0.0**	**16:22**	**4**	**0**	**3**	**3**	**4**	**0**	**0**	**0**	**13:29**

Hockey East Second All-Star Team (2003) • Hockey East First All-Star Team (2004) • NCAA East First All-American Team (2004) • AHL Second All-Star Team (2006)

Signed as a free agent by **NY Rangers**, March 23, 2004.

POHL, John

(PAWL, JAWN)

Center. Shoots right. 6'1", 196 lbs. Born, Rochester, MN, June 29, 1979. St. Louis' 8th choice, 255th overall, in 1998 Entry Draft.

1997-98	Red Wing High	High-MN	28	30	77	107	18																		
	Twin Cities	USHL	10	5	3	8	10																		
1998-99	U. of Minnesota	WCHA	42	7	10	17	18																		
99-2000	U. of Minnesota	WCHA	41	18	41	59	26																		
2000-01	U. of Minnesota	WCHA	38	19	26	45	24																		
2001-02	U. of Minnesota	WCHA	44	27	*52	*79	26																		
2002-03	Worcester IceCats	AHL	58	26	32	58	34										3	0	1	1	6				
2003-04	**St. Louis**	**NHL**	**1**	**0**	**0**	**0**	**0**	**0**	**0**	**0**	**1**	**0.0**	**–2**	**9**	**55.6**	**8:18**									
	Worcester IceCats	AHL	65	16	25	41	65										3	0	1	1	2				
2004-05	Worcester IceCats	AHL	13	3	6	9	2																		
2005-06	**Toronto**	**NHL**	**7**	**3**	**1**	**4**	**4**	**1**	**0**	**0**	**17**	**17.6**	**2**	**41**	**53.7**	**12:47**									
	Toronto Marlies	AHL	60	36	39	75	42										5	1	5	6	10				
2006-07	**Toronto**	**NHL**	**74**	**13**	**16**	**29**	**10**	**3**	**0**	**1**	**105**	**12.4**	**–4**	**553**	**53.4**	**11:21**									
2007-08	**Toronto**	**NHL**	**33**	**1**	**4**	**5**	**10**	**0**	**0**	**1**	**23**	**4.3**	**–4**	**94**	**43.6**	**7:06**									
	NHL Totals		**115**	**17**	**21**	**38**	**24**	**4**	**0**	**2**	**146**	**11.6**		**697**	**52.1**	**10:11**									

WCHA Second All-Star Team (2000) • WCHA First All-Star Team (2002) • NCAA Championship All-Tournament Team (2002)

Traded to **Toronto** by **St. Louis** for future considerations, August 24, 2005.

POLAK, Roman

(POH-lahk, ROH-muhn) **ST.L.**

Defense. Shoots right. 6'1", 198 lbs. Born, Ostrava, Czech., April 28, 1986. St. Louis' 6th choice, 180th overall, in 2004 Entry Draft.

2001-02	HC Ostrava Jr.	CzRep-Jr.	46	4	9	13	84																		
2002-03	HC Ostrava Jr.	CzRep-Jr.	32	3	12	15	34																		
2003-04	HC Vitkovice Jr.	CzRep-Jr.	52	4	8	12	48																		
2004-05	Kootenay Ice	WHL	65	5	18	23	85										9	0	0	0	6				
2005-06	HC Vitkovice Jr.	CzRep-Jr.	1	0	0	0	4																		
	Vitkovice	CzRep	37	0	1	1	16										6	0	0	0	6				

			Regular Season														Playoffs								
Season	Club	League	GP	G	A	Pts	PIM	PP	SH	GW	S	%	+/-	TF	F%	Min	GP	G	A	Pts	PIM	PP	SH	GW	Min
2006-07	**St. Louis**	**NHL**	**19**	**0**	**0**	**0**	**6**	**0**	**0**	**0**	**13**	**0.0**	**–3**	**0**	**0.0**	**13:38**									
	Peoria Rivermen	AHL	53	4	8	12	66																		
2007-08	**St. Louis**	**NHL**	**6**	**0**	**1**	**1**	**0**	**0**	**0**	**0**	**2**	**0.0**	**1**	**0**	**0.0**	**11:32**									
	Peoria Rivermen	AHL	34	0	7	7	33																		
	NHL Totals		**25**	**0**	**1**	**1**	**6**	**0**	**0**	**0**	**15**	**0.0**		**0**	**0.0**	**13:08**									

POLAK, Vojtech

(POH-lahk, VOI-tehk) **DAL.**

Left wing. Shoots left. 5'11", 180 lbs. Born, Ostrov nad Ohri, Czech., June 27, 1985. Dallas' 2nd choice, 36th overall, in 2003 Entry Draft.

Season	Club	League	GP	G	A	Pts	PIM	PP	SH	GW	S	%	+/-	TF	F%	Min	GP	G	A	Pts	PIM	PP	SH	GW	Min
99-2000	Karlovy Vary Jr.	CzRep-Jr.	49	17	23	40	48																		
2000-01	Karlovy Vary Jr.	CzRep-Jr.	47	36	33	69	38																		
	Karlovy Vary	CzRep	2	0	0	0	0																		
2001-02	Karlovy Vary Jr.	CzRep-Jr.	37	11	14	25	26																		
	Karlovy Vary	CzRep	9	1	1	2	2																		
2002-03	Karlovy Vary	CzRep	41	7	9	16	51																		
	Karlovy Vary Jr.	CzRep-Jr.	6	3	7	10	18																		
2003-04	HC Sparta Praha	CzRep	1	1	0	1	0																		
	Karlovy Vary	CzRep	44	0	8	8	42																		
	Karlovy Vary Jr.	CzRep-Jr.	5	8	4	12	2																		
2004-05	Jihlava Jr.	CzRep-Jr.	5	4	1	5	6																		
	HC Dukla Jihlava	CzRep	16	1	2	3	12																		
	Karlovy Vary Jr.	CzRep-Jr.	3	5	5	10	6																		
	SK Kadan	CzRep-2	7	1	2	3	39																		
	Karlovy Vary	CzRep	26	1	5	6	4																		
2005-06	**Dallas**	**NHL**	**3**	**0**	**0**	**0**	**0**	**0**	**0**	**0**	**3**	**0.0**	**–1**	**2**	**50.0**	**6:31**									
	Iowa Stars	AHL	60	12	22	34	41										3	0	1	1	0				
2006-07	**Dallas**	**NHL**	**2**	**0**	**0**	**0**	**0**	**0**	**0**	**0**	**2**	**0.0**	**–1**	**0**	**0.0**	**7:43**									
	Iowa Stars	AHL	67	17	28	45	48										7	1	0	1	8				
2007-08	Iowa Stars	AHL	35	6	10	16	18																		
	Karlovy Vary	CzRep	5	1	0	1	4										19	1	3	4	8				
	NHL Totals		**5**	**0**	**0**	**0**	**0**	**0**	**0**	**0**	**5**	**0.0**		**2**	**50.0**	**7:00**									

POMINVILLE, Jason

(paw-MIHN-vihl, JAY-suhn) **BUF.**

Right wing. Shoots right. 6', 186 lbs. Born, Repentigny, Que., November 30, 1982. Buffalo's 4th choice, 55th overall, in 2001 Entry Draft.

Season	Club	League	GP	G	A	Pts	PIM	PP	SH	GW	S	%	+/-	TF	F%	Min	GP	G	A	Pts	PIM	PP	SH	GW	Min
1997-98	Cap-d-Madeleine	QAAA	13	3	7	10	....																		
1998-99	Cap-d-Madeleine	QAAA	41	18	38	56	16										7	2	7	9	0				
	Shawinigan	QMJHL	2	0	0	0	0																		
99-2000	Shawinigan	QMJHL	60	4	17	21	12										13	2	3	5	0				
2000-01	Shawinigan	QMJHL	71	46	67	113	24										10	6	6	12	0				
2001-02	Shawinigan	QMJHL	66	57	64	121	32										2	0	0	0	0				
2002-03	Rochester	AHL	73	13	21	34	16										3	1	1	2	0				
2003-04	**Buffalo**	**NHL**	**1**	**0**	**0**	**0**	**0**	**0**	**0**	**0**	**3**	**0.0**	**0**	**0**	**0.0**	**14:22**									
	Rochester	AHL	66	34	30	64	30										16	9	10	19	6				
2004-05	Rochester	AHL	78	30	38	68	43																		
2005-06	**Buffalo**	**NHL**	**57**	**18**	**12**	**30**	**22**	**10**	**2**	**2**	**124**	**14.5**	**–4**	**5**	**20.0**	**14:07**	**18**	**5**	**5**	**10**	**8**	**0**	**1**	**1**	**12:11**
	Rochester	AHL	18	19	7	26	11																		
2006-07	**Buffalo**	**NHL**	**82**	**34**	**34**	**68**	**30**	**2**	**2**	**5**	**212**	**16.0**	**25**	**14**	**42.9**	**17:25**	**16**	**4**	**6**	**10**	**0**	**0**	**0**	**0**	**17:54**
2007-08	**Buffalo**	**NHL**	**82**	**27**	**53**	**80**	**20**	**2**	**1**	**1**	**232**	**11.6**	**16**	**67**	**37.3**	**19:58**									
	NHL Totals		**222**	**79**	**99**	**178**	**72**	**14**	**5**	**8**	**571**	**13.8**		**86**	**37.2**	**17:30**	**34**	**9**	**11**	**20**	**8**	**0**	**1**	**1**	**14:52**

QMJHL First All-Star Team (2002)

PONIKAROVSKY, Alexei

(poh-nih-kahr-OHV-skee, al-EHX-ay) **TOR.**

Left wing. Shoots left. 6'4", 220 lbs. Born, Kiev, USSR, April 9, 1980. Toronto's 4th choice, 87th overall, in 1998 Entry Draft.

Season	Club	League	GP	G	A	Pts	PIM	PP	SH	GW	S	%	+/-	TF	F%	Min	GP	G	A	Pts	PIM	PP	SH	GW	Min
1996-97	Dyn'o Moscow 2	Russia-3	60	12	15	27	30																		
	Dyn'o Moscow 2	Russia-3	2	0	0	0	2																		
1997-98	Dynamo Moscow	Russia	24	1	2	3	30																		
1998-99	Krylja Sovetov	Russia	13	2	1	3	2																		
	Dynamo Moscow	Russia	....	....	....	....	....										3	0	0	0	2				
99-2000	THK Tver	Russia-2	29	8	14	22	26																		
	Dynamo Moscow	Russia	19	1	0	1	8										1	0	0	0	0				
	Dynamo Moscow	EuroHL	2	0	2	2	0																		
2000-01	**Toronto**	**NHL**	**22**	**1**	**3**	**4**	**14**	**0**	**0**	**0**	**21**	**4.8**	**–1**	**7**	**28.6**	**8:32**									
	St. John's	AHL	49	12	24	36	44										4	0	0	0	4				
2001-02	**Toronto**	**NHL**	**8**	**2**	**0**	**2**	**0**	**0**	**0**	**1**	**8**	**25.0**	**2**	**2**	**50.0**	**8:03**	**10**	**0**	**0**	**0**	**4**	**0**	**0**	**0**	**8:15**
	St. John's	AHL	72	21	27	48	74										5	2	1	3	8				
	Ukraine	Olympics	4	1	1	2	6																		
2002-03	**Toronto**	**NHL**	**13**	**0**	**3**	**3**	**11**	**0**	**0**	**0**	**13**	**0.0**	**4**	**4**	**25.0**	**10:43**									
	St. John's	AHL	63	24	22	46	68																		
2003-04	**Toronto**	**NHL**	**73**	**9**	**19**	**28**	**44**	**1**	**0**	**2**	**110**	**8.2**	**14**	**20**	**30.0**	**11:36**	**13**	**1**	**3**	**4**	**8**	**0**	**0**	**1**	**14:20**
2004-05	Voskresensk	Russia	19	1	5	6	16																		
2005-06	**Toronto**	**NHL**	**81**	**21**	**17**	**38**	**68**	**2**	**4**	**3**	**157**	**13.4**	**15**	**13**	**30.8**	**14:06**									
2006-07	**Toronto**	**NHL**	**71**	**21**	**24**	**45**	**63**	**6**	**0**	**1**	**198**	**10.6**	**8**	**4**	**25.0**	**17:06**									
2007-08	**Toronto**	**NHL**	**66**	**18**	**17**	**35**	**36**	**1**	**0**	**1**	**150**	**12.0**	**3**	**4**	**25.0**	**15:58**									
	NHL Totals		**334**	**72**	**83**	**155**	**236**	**10**	**4**	**8**	**657**	**11.0**		**54**	**29.6**	**13:55**	**23**	**1**	**3**	**4**	**12**	**0**	**0**	**1**	**11:42**

Signed as a free agent by **Voskresensk** (Russia), November 13, 2004.

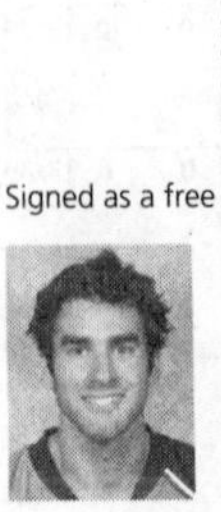

POPOVIC, Mark

(poh-PUH-vihk, MAHRK)

Defense. Shoots left. 6'1", 210 lbs. Born, Stoney Creek, Ont., October 11, 1982. Anaheim's 2nd choice, 35th overall, in 2001 Entry Draft.

Season	Club	League	GP	G	A	Pts	PIM	PP	SH	GW	S	%	+/-	TF	F%	Min	GP	G	A	Pts	PIM	PP	SH	GW	Min
1997-98	Mississauga	OPJHL	51	10	16	26	32																		
1998-99	St. Michael's	OHL	60	6	26	32	46																		
99-2000	St. Michael's	OHL	68	11	29	40	68																		
2000-01	St. Michael's	OHL	61	7	35	42	54										18	3	5	8	22				
2001-02	St. Michael's	OHL	58	12	29	41	42										15	1	11	12	10				
2002-03	Cincinnati	AHL	73	3	21	24	46																		
2003-04	**Anaheim**	**NHL**	**1**	**0**	**0**	**0**	**0**	**0**	**0**	**0**	**1**	**0.0**	**0**	**0**	**0.0**	**13:48**									
	Cincinnati	AHL	74	4	10	14	63										9	1	2	3	4				
2004-05	Cincinnati	AHL	74	1	17	18	47										11	2	3	5	6				
2005-06	**Atlanta**	**NHL**	**7**	**0**	**0**	**0**	**0**	**0**	**0**	**0**	**6**	**0.0**	**–5**	**0**	**0.0**	**11:04**									
	Chicago Wolves	AHL	73	12	26	38	51																		
2006-07	**Atlanta**	**NHL**	**3**	**0**	**1**	**1**	**0**	**0**	**0**	**0**	**1**	**0.0**	**1**	**0**	**0.0**	**10:15**									
	Chicago Wolves	AHL	65	16	24	40	51										15	3	6	9	4				
2007-08	**Atlanta**	**NHL**	**33**	**0**	**2**	**2**	**10**	**0**	**0**	**0**	**25**	**0.0**	**–4**	**0**	**0.0**	**14:28**									
	NHL Totals		**44**	**0**	**3**	**3**	**10**	**0**	**0**	**0**	**33**	**0.0**		**0**	**0.0**	**13:38**									

OHL First All-Star Team (2002)
Traded to **Atlanta** by **Anaheim** for Kip Brennan, August 23, 2005.

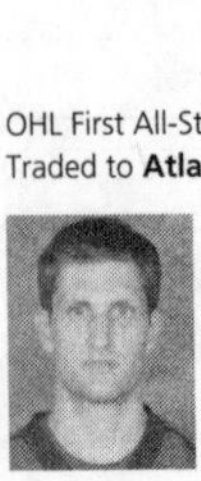

POTHIER, Brian

(POH-thee-uhr, BRIGH-uhn) **WSH.**

Defense. Shoots right. 6', 200 lbs. Born, New Bedford, MA, April 15, 1977.

Season	Club	League	GP	G	A	Pts	PIM	PP	SH	GW	S	%	+/-	TF	F%	Min	GP	G	A	Pts	PIM	PP	SH	GW	Min
1995-96	NMH School	High-MA	27	11	22	33	36																		
1996-97	RPI Engineers	ECAC	34	1	11	12	42																		
1997-98	RPI Engineers	ECAC	35	2	9	11	28																		
1998-99	RPI Engineers	ECAC	37	5	13	18	36																		
99-2000	RPI Engineers	ECAC	36	9	24	33	44																		
2000-01	**Atlanta**	**NHL**	**3**	**0**	**0**	**0**	**2**	**0**	**0**	**0**	**0**	**0.0**	**4**	**0**	**0.0**	**20:38**									
	Orlando	IHL	76	12	29	41	69										16	3	5	8	11				

Season	Club	League	GP	G	A	Pts	PIM	PP	SH	GW	S	%	+/-	TF	F%	Min	GP	G	A	Pts	PIM	PP	SH	GW	Min
			Regular Season														Playoffs								
2001-02	**Atlanta**	**NHL**	**33**	**3**	**6**	**9**	**22**	**1**	**0**	**1**	**65**	**4.6**	**–19**	**0**	**0.0**	**21:41**									
	Chicago Wolves	AHL	39	6	13	19	30																		
2002-03	**Ottawa**	**NHL**	**14**	**2**	**4**	**6**	**6**	**0**	**0**	**1**	**23**	**8.7**	**11**	**0**	**0.0**	**15:23**	**1**	**0**	**0**	**0**	**2**	**0**	**0**	**0**	**13:11**
	Binghamton	AHL	68	7	40	47	58										8	2	8	10	4				
2003-04	**Ottawa**	**NHL**	**55**	**2**	**6**	**8**	**24**	**1**	**0**	**1**	**78**	**2.6**	**6**	**0**	**0.0**	**16:43**	**7**	**0**	**0**	**0**	**6**	**0**	**0**	**0**	**17:15**
2004-05	Binghamton	AHL	77	12	36	48	64										6	0	1	1	6				
2005-06	**Ottawa**	**NHL**	**77**	**5**	**30**	**35**	**59**	**3**	**0**	**0**	**133**	**3.8**	**29**	**0**	**0.0**	**16:46**	**8**	**2**	**1**	**3**	**2**	**0**	**0**	**0**	**15:02**
2006-07	**Washington**	**NHL**	**72**	**3**	**25**	**28**	**44**	**2**	**0**	**0**	**118**	**2.5**	**–11**	**0**	**0.0**	**23:59**									
2007-08	**Washington**	**NHL**	**38**	**5**	**9**	**14**	**20**	**1**	**0**	**1**	**65**	**7.7**	**5**	**0**	**0.0**	**18:42**									
	NHL Totals		**292**	**20**	**80**	**100**	**177**	**8**	**0**	**4**	**482**	**4.1**		**0**	**0.0**	**19:19**	**16**	**2**	**1**	**3**	**10**	**0**	**0**	**0**	**15:53**

ECAC Second All-Star Team (2000) • ECAC All-Tournament Team (2000) • NCAA East Second All-American Team (2000) • Ken McKenzie Trophy (U.S. - Born Rookie of the Year – IHL) (2001) • Garry F. Longman Memorial Trophy (Rookie of the Year – IHL) (2001) • AHL Second All-Star Team (2003, 2005)

Signed as a free agent by **Atlanta**, March 27, 2000. Traded to **Ottawa** by **Atlanta** for Shawn McEachern and Ottawa's 6th round choice (Dan Turple) in 2004 Entry Draft, June 29, 2002. Signed as a free agent by **Washington**, July 1, 2006.

POTI, Tom

(POH-tee, TAWM) **WSH.**

Defense. Shoots left. 6'3", 210 lbs. Born, Worcester, MA, March 22, 1977. Edmonton's 4th choice, 59th overall, in 1996 Entry Draft.

Season	Club	League	GP	G	A	Pts	PIM	PP	SH	GW	S	%	+/-	TF	F%	Min	GP	G	A	Pts	PIM	PP	SH	GW	Min
1992-93	St. Peter's Marian	High-MA	55	25	46	71																			
1993-94	Cushing	High-MA	30	10	35	45																			
1994-95	Cushing	High-MA	36	17	54	71	35																		
	Central-Mass	MBAHL	8	8	10	18																			
1995-96	Cushing	High-MA	29	14	59	73	18																		
1996-97	Boston University	H-East	38	4	17	21	54																		
1997-98	Boston University	H-East	38	13	29	42	60																		
1998-99	**Edmonton**	**NHL**	**73**	**5**	**16**	**21**	**42**	**2**	**0**	**3**	**94**	**5.3**	**10**	**0**	**0.0**	**19:33**	**4**	**0**	**1**	**1**	**2**	**0**	**0**	**0**	**28:02**
99-2000	**Edmonton**	**NHL**	**76**	**9**	**26**	**35**	**65**	**2**	**1**	**1**	**125**	**7.2**	**8**	**0**	**0.0**	**24:10**	**5**	**0**	**1**	**1**	**0**	**0**	**0**	**0**	**23:53**
2000-01	**Edmonton**	**NHL**	**81**	**12**	**20**	**32**	**60**	**6**	**0**	**3**	**161**	**7.5**	**–4**	**0**	**0.0**	**22:44**	**6**	**0**	**2**	**2**	**2**	**0**	**0**	**0**	**20:25**
2001-02	**Edmonton**	**NHL**	**55**	**1**	**16**	**17**	**42**	**1**	**0**	**0**	**100**	**1.0**	**–6**	**0**	**0.0**	**24:32**									
	United States	Olympics	6	0	1	1	4																		
	NY Rangers	**NHL**	**11**	**1**	**7**	**8**	**2**	**1**	**0**	**1**	**9**	**11.1**	**–4**	**0**	**0.0**	**21:45**									
2002-03	**NY Rangers**	**NHL**	**80**	**11**	**37**	**48**	**58**	**3**	**0**	**2**	**148**	**7.4**	**–6**	**0**	**0.0**	**24:43**									
2003-04	**NY Rangers**	**NHL**	**67**	**10**	**14**	**24**	**47**	**4**	**0**	**5**	**124**	**8.1**	**–1**	**0**	**0.0**	**22:28**									
2004-05			DID NOT PLAY																						
2005-06	**NY Rangers**	**NHL**	**73**	**3**	**20**	**23**	**70**	**2**	**0**	**2**	**122**	**2.5**	**16**	**4**	**25.0**	**20:46**	**4**	**0**	**0**	**0**	**2**	**0**	**0**	**0**	**19:39**
2006-07	**NY Islanders**	**NHL**	**78**	**6**	**38**	**44**	**74**	**6**	**0**	**1**	**134**	**4.5**	**–1**	**0**	**0.0**	**25:43**	**5**	**0**	**3**	**3**	**6**	**0**	**0**	**0**	**27:34**
2007-08	**Washington**	**NHL**	**71**	**2**	**27**	**29**	**46**	**0**	**0**	**0**	**99**	**2.0**	**9**	**0**	**0.0**	**23:29**	**7**	**0**	**1**	**1**	**8**	**0**	**0**	**0**	**24:01**
	NHL Totals		**665**	**60**	**221**	**281**	**506**	**27**	**1**	**18**	**1116**	**5.4**		**4**	**25.0**	**23:06**	**31**	**0**	**8**	**8**	**20**	**0**	**0**	**0**	**23:50**

NCAA Championship All-Tournament Team (1997) • Hockey East First All-Star Team (1998) • NCAA East First All-American Team (1998) • NHL All-Rookie Team (1999)

Played in NHL All-Star Game (2003)

Traded to **NY Rangers** by **Edmonton** with Rem Murray for Mike York and NY Rangers' 4th round choice (Ivan Koltsov) in 2002 Entry Draft, March 19, 2002. Signed as a free agent by **NY Islanders**, July 8, 2006. Signed as a free agent by **Washington**, July 1, 2007.

POTULNY, Ryan

(poh-TUHL-nee, RIGH-uhn) **EDM.**

Center. Shoots left. 6', 190 lbs. Born, Grand Forks, ND, September 5, 1984. Philadelphia's 6th choice, 87th overall, in 2003 Entry Draft.

Season	Club	League	GP	G	A	Pts	PIM	PP	SH	GW	S	%	+/-	TF	F%	Min	GP	G	A	Pts	PIM	PP	SH	GW	Min
2001-02	Lincoln Stars	USHL	60	23	34	57	65										4	0	1	1	2				
2002-03	Lincoln Stars	USHL	54	35	*43	*78	18										10	6	*11	*17	8				
2003-04	U. of Minnesota	WCHA	15	6	8	14	10																		
2004-05	U. of Minnesota	WCHA	44	24	17	41	20																		
2005-06	U. of Minnesota	WCHA	41	*38	25	*63	31																		
	Philadelphia	**NHL**	**2**	**0**	**1**	**1**	**0**	**0**	**0**	**0**	**0**	**0.0**	**1**	**9**	**44.4**	**6:09**									
2006-07	**Philadelphia**	**NHL**	**35**	**7**	**5**	**12**	**22**	**0**	**0**	**2**	**56**	**12.5**	**1**	**278**	**43.5**	**11:00**									
	Philadelphia	AHL	30	12	14	26	34																		
2007-08	**Philadelphia**	**NHL**	**7**	**0**	**1**	**1**	**4**	**0**	**0**	**0**	**5**	**0.0**	**0**	**32**	**43.8**	**6:30**									
	Philadelphia	AHL	58	21	26	47	51										12	3	5	8	10				
	NHL Totals		**44**	**7**	**7**	**14**	**26**	**0**	**0**	**2**	**61**	**11.5**		**319**	**43.6**	**10:04**									

USHL First All-Star Team (2003) • USHL Player of the Year (2003) • USA Hockey Junior Player of the Year (2003) • WCHA First All-Star Team (2006) • NCAA West First All-American Team (2006)

• Missed majority of 2003-04 season recovering from knee injury suffered in game vs. North Dakota (WCHA), November 7, 2003. Traded to **Edmonton** by **Philadelphia** for Danny Syvret, June 6, 2008.

POULIOT, Benoit

(POO-lee-oh, BEHN-wah) **MIN.**

Left wing. Shoots left. 6'3", 199 lbs. Born, Alfred, Alfred, September 29, 1986. Minnesota's 1st choice, 4th overall, in 2005 Entry Draft.

Season	Club	League	GP	G	A	Pts	PIM	PP	SH	GW	S	%	+/-	TF	F%	Min	GP	G	A	Pts	PIM	PP	SH	GW	Min
2002-03	Clarence Beavers	OHA-B	38	13	17	30	86										5	0	2	2	8				
	Hawkesbury	CJHL	1	1	0	1	0																		
2003-04	Hawkesbury	CJHL	45	21	21	42	85										6	3	7	10	10				
	Sudbury Wolves	OHL	4	2	2	4	0										4	2	1	3	0				
2004-05	Sudbury Wolves	OHL	67	29	38	67	102										12	6	8	14	20				
2005-06	Sudbury Wolves	OHL	51	35	30	65	141										8	8	3	11	16				
	Houston Aeros	AHL															2	0	0	0	2				
2006-07	**Minnesota**	**NHL**	**3**	**0**	**0**	**0**	**0**	**0**	**0**	**0**	**1**	**0.0**	**–1**	**2**	**0.0**	**6:58**									
	Houston Aeros	AHL	67	19	17	36	109																		
2007-08	**Minnesota**	**NHL**	**11**	**2**	**1**	**3**	**0**	**0**	**0**	**0**	**10**	**20.0**	**–1**	**65**	**40.0**	**8:49**	**1**	**0**	**0**	**0**	**0**	**0**	**0**	**0**	**10:16**
	Houston Aeros	AHL	46	10	14	24	67										3	0	0	0	2				
	NHL Totals		**14**	**2**	**1**	**3**	**0**	**0**	**0**	**0**	**11**	**18.2**		**67**	**38.8**	**8:26**	**1**	**0**	**0**	**0**	**0**	**0**	**0**	**0**	**10:16**

OHL First All-Star Team (2005) • OHL Rookie of the Year (2005) • Canadian Major Junior All-Rookie Team (2005) • Canadian Major Junior Rookie of the Year (2005)

POULIOT, Marc-Antoine

(POO-lee-awt, MAHRK-AN-twahn) **EDM.**

Center. Shoots right. 6'1", 195 lbs. Born, Quebec City, Que., May 22, 1985. Edmonton's 1st choice, 22nd overall, in 2003 Entry Draft.

Season	Club	League	GP	G	A	Pts	PIM	PP	SH	GW	S	%	+/-	TF	F%	Min	GP	G	A	Pts	PIM	PP	SH	GW	Min
2000-01	Ste-Foy	QAAA	38	16	39	55	52										16	8	12	20	16				
2001-02	Rimouski Oceanic	QMJHL	28	9	14	23	32										5	0	0	0	4				
2002-03	Rimouski Oceanic	QMJHL	65	32	41	73	100																		
2003-04	Rimouski Oceanic	QMJHL	42	25	33	58	62										9	5	7	12	12				
2004-05	Rimouski Oceanic	QMJHL	70	45	69	114	83										13	4	15	19	8				
2005-06	**Edmonton**	**NHL**	**8**	**1**	**0**	**1**	**0**	**0**	**0**	**0**	**5**	**20.0**	**1**	**56**	**55.4**	**8:30**									
	Hamilton	AHL	65	15	31	46	63																		
2006-07	**Edmonton**	**NHL**	**46**	**4**	**7**	**11**	**18**	**0**	**0**	**0**	**73**	**5.5**	**–2**	**353**	**48.7**	**13:03**									
	Wilkes-Barre	AHL	33	14	17	31	20										11	5	5	10	4				
2007-08	**Edmonton**	**NHL**	**24**	**1**	**6**	**7**	**12**	**0**	**0**	**0**	**32**	**3.1**	**–1**	**44**	**47.7**	**10:20**									
	Springfield	AHL	55	21	26	47	47																		
	NHL Totals		**78**	**6**	**13**	**19**	**30**	**0**	**0**	**0**	**110**	**5.5**		**453**	**49.4**	**11:45**									

QMJHL First All-Star Team (2005) • George Parsons Trophy (Memorial Cup Tournament - Most Sportsmanlike Player) (2005)

PRATT, Nolan

(PRAT, NOH-luhn)

Defense. Shoots left. 6'3", 207 lbs. Born, Fort McMurray, Alta., August 14, 1975. Hartford's 4th choice, 115th overall, in 1993 Entry Draft.

Season	Club	League	GP	G	A	Pts	PIM	PP	SH	GW	S	%	+/-	TF	F%	Min	GP	G	A	Pts	PIM	PP	SH	GW	Min
1991-92	Bonnyville	AJHL	33	3	7	10	57																		
	Portland	WHL	22	2	9	11	13										6	1	3	4	12				
1992-93	Portland	WHL	70	4	19	23	97										16	2	7	9	31				
1993-94	Portland	WHL	72	4	32	36	105										10	1	2	3	14				
1994-95	Portland	WHL	72	6	37	43	196										9	1	6	7	10				
1995-96	Springfield	AHL	62	2	6	8	72										2	0	0	0	0				
	Richmond	ECHL	4	1	0	1	2																		
1996-97	**Hartford**	**NHL**	**9**	**0**	**2**	**2**	**6**	**0**	**0**	**0**	**4**	**0.0**	**0**												
	Springfield	AHL	66	1	18	19	127										17	0	3	3	18				
1997-98	**Carolina**	**NHL**	**23**	**0**	**2**	**2**	**44**	**0**	**0**	**0**	**11**	**0.0**	**–2**												
	New Haven	AHL	54	3	15	18	135																		

			Regular Season														Playoffs								
Season	Club	League	GP	G	A	Pts	PIM	PP	SH	GW	S	%	+/-	TF	F%	Min	GP	G	A	Pts	PIM	PP	SH	GW	Min
1998-99	**Carolina**	**NHL**	**61**	**1**	**14**	**15**	**95**	**0**	**0**	**1**	**46**	**2.2**	**15**	**0**	**0.0**	**16:45**	**3**	**0**	**0**	**0**	**2**	**0**	**0**	**0**	**19:58**
99-2000	**Carolina**	**NHL**	**64**	**3**	**1**	**4**	**90**	**0**	**0**	**1**	**47**	**6.4**	**-22**	**0**	**0.0**	**19:10**	....	....	....	....	....	....	....	....	....
2000-01	**Colorado**	**NHL**	**46**	**1**	**2**	**3**	**40**	**0**	**0**	**1**	**26**	**3.8**	**2**	**1**	**0.0**	**9:50**	....	....	....	....	....	....	....	....	....
2001-02	**Tampa Bay**	**NHL**	**46**	**0**	**3**	**3**	**51**	**0**	**0**	**0**	**38**	**0.0**	**-4**	**1**	**0.0**	**18:25**	....	....	....	....	....	....	....	....	....
2002-03	**Tampa Bay**	**NHL**	**67**	**1**	**7**	**8**	**35**	**0**	**0**	**0**	**38**	**2.6**	**-6**	**0**	**0.0**	**17:34**	**4**	**0**	**1**	**1**	**0**	**0**	**0**	**0**	**21:01**
2003-04♦	**Tampa Bay**	**NHL**	**58**	**1**	**3**	**4**	**42**	**0**	**0**	**0**	**35**	**2.9**	**11**	**0**	**0.0**	**16:25**	**20**	**0**	**0**	**0**	**8**	**0**	**0**	**0**	**18:06**
2004-05	EV Duisburg	German-2	10	2	2	4	14	....	....	....	....	....	....	....	....	....	12	0	3	3	10	....	....	....	....
2005-06	**Tampa Bay**	**NHL**	**82**	**0**	**9**	**9**	**60**	**0**	**0**	**0**	**26**	**0.0**	**7**	**0**	**0.0**	**17:59**	**5**	**0**	**0**	**0**	**7**	**0**	**0**	**0**	**15:30**
2006-07	**Tampa Bay**	**NHL**	**81**	**1**	**7**	**8**	**44**	**0**	**0**	**0**	**30**	**3.3**	**0**	**1**	**0.0**	**15:47**	**6**	**0**	**0**	**0**	**5**	**0**	**0**	**0**	**14:32**
2007-08	**Buffalo**	**NHL**	**55**	**1**	**6**	**7**	**30**	**0**	**0**	**0**	**21**	**4.8**	**1**	**0**	**0.0**	**13:31**	....	....	....	....	....	....	....	....	....
	NHL Totals		**592**	**9**	**56**	**65**	**537**	**0**	**0**	**3**	**322**	**2.8**		**3**	**0.0**	**16:23**	**38**	**0**	**1**	**1**	**22**	**0**	**0**	**0**	**17:39**

Transferred to **Carolina** after **Hartford** franchise relocated, June 25, 1997. Traded to **Colorado** by **Carolina** with Carolina's 1st (Vaclav Nedorost) and 2nd (Jared Aulin) round choices in 2000 Entry Draft and Philadelphia's 2nd round choice (previously acquired, Colorado selected Agris Saviels) in 2000 Entry Draft for Sandis Ozolinsh and Columbus' 2nd round choice (previously acquired, Carolina selected Tomas Kurka) in 2000 Entry Draft, June 24, 2000. Traded to **Tampa Bay** by **Colorado** for Los Angeles' 6th round choice (previously acquired, Colorado selected Scott Horvath) in 2001 Entry Draft, June 24, 2001. Signed as a free agent by **Duisburg** (German-2), January 15, 2005. Signed as a free agent by **Buffalo**, November 1, 2007.

PREISSING, Tom

(PREH-sihng, TAWM) **L.A.**

Defense. Shoots right. 6', 198 lbs. Born, Arlington Heights, IL, December 3, 1978.

1997-98	Green Bay	USHL	56	8	13	21	30	....	....	....	....	....	....	....	....	....	4	0	2	2	2	....	....	....	....
1998-99	Green Bay	USHL	53	18	37	55	40	....	....	....	....	....	....	....	....	....	6	3	6	9	2	....	....	....	....
99-2000	Colorado College	WCHA	36	4	14	18	20	....	....	....	....	....	....	....	....	....	....	....	....	....	....	....	....	....	....
2000-01	Colorado College	WCHA	33	6	18	24	26	....	....	....	....	....	....	....	....	....	....	....	....	....	....	....	....	....	....
2001-02	Colorado College	WCHA	43	6	26	32	42	....	....	....	....	....	....	....	....	....	....	....	....	....	....	....	....	....	....
2002-03	Colorado College	WCHA	42	23	29	52	16	....	....	....	....	....	....	....	....	....	....	....	....	....	....	....	....	....	....
2003-04	**San Jose**	**NHL**	**69**	**2**	**17**	**19**	**12**	**2**	**0**	**1**	**89**	**2.2**	**8**	**0**	**0.0**	**18:12**	**11**	**0**	**1**	**1**	**0**	**0**	**0**	**0**	**12:49**
2004-05	Krefeld Pinguine	Germany	33	1	6	7	32	....	....	....	....	....	....	....	....	....	....	....	....	....	....	....	....	....	....
2005-06	**San Jose**	**NHL**	**74**	**11**	**32**	**43**	**26**	**2**	**0**	**2**	**131**	**8.4**	**17**	**1**	**0.0**	**20:30**	**11**	**1**	**6**	**7**	**4**	**0**	**0**	**0**	**23:50**
2006-07	**Ottawa**	**NHL**	**80**	**7**	**31**	**38**	**18**	**3**	**0**	**0**	**94**	**7.4**	**40**	**0**	**0.0**	**15:15**	**20**	**2**	**5**	**7**	**10**	**1**	**0**	**1**	**15:02**
2007-08	**Los Angeles**	**NHL**	**77**	**8**	**16**	**24**	**16**	**6**	**0**	**1**	**93**	**8.6**	**-6**	**9**	**22.2**	**17:53**	....	....	....	....	....	....	....	....	....
	NHL Totals		**300**	**28**	**96**	**124**	**72**	**13**	**0**	**4**	**407**	**6.9**		**10**	**20.0**	**17:54**	**42**	**3**	**12**	**15**	**14**	**1**	**0**	**1**	**16:45**

WCHA First All-Star Team (2003) • NCAA West First All-American Team (2003)

Signed as a free agent by **San Jose**, April 4, 2003. Signed as a free agent by **Krefeld** (Germany), November 15, 2004. Traded to **Chicago** by **San Jose** with Josh Hennessy for Mark Bell, July 9, 2006. Traded to **Ottawa** by **Chicago** with Josh Hennessy, Michal Barinka and Chicago's 2nd round choice (Patrick Wiercioch) in 2008 Entry Draft for Martin Havlat and Bryan Smolinski, July 10, 2006. Signed as a free agent by **Los Angeles**, July 2, 2007.

PRIMEAU, Wayne

(PREE-moh, WAYN) **CGY.**

Center. Shoots left. 6'4", 225 lbs. Born, Scarborough, Ont., June 4, 1976. Buffalo's 1st choice, 17th overall, in 1994 Entry Draft.

1991-92	Whitby Flyers	Minor-ON	63	36	50	86	96	....	....	....	....	....	....	....	....	....	....	....	....	....	....	....	....	....	....
1992-93	Owen Sound	OHL	66	10	27	37	108	....	....	....	....	....	....	....	....	....	8	1	4	5	0	....	....	....	....
1993-94	Owen Sound	OHL	65	25	50	75	75	....	....	....	....	....	....	....	....	....	9	1	6	7	8	....	....	....	....
1994-95	Owen Sound	OHL	66	34	62	96	84	....	....	....	....	....	....	....	....	....	10	4	9	13	15	....	....	....	....
	Buffalo	**NHL**	**1**	**1**	**0**	**1**	**0**	**0**	**0**	**1**	**2**	**50.0**	**-2**	....	....	....	....	....	....	....	....	....	....	....	....
1995-96	Owen Sound	OHL	28	15	29	44	52	....	....	....	....	....	....	....	....	....	....	....	....	....	....	....	....	....	....
	Oshawa Generals	OHL	24	12	13	25	33	....	....	....	....	....	....	....	....	....	3	2	3	5	2	....	....	....	....
	Buffalo	**NHL**	**2**	**0**	**0**	**0**	**0**	**0**	**0**	**0**	**0**	**0.0**	**0**	....	....	....	....	....	....	....	....	....	....	....	....
	Rochester	AHL	8	2	3	5	6	....	....	....	....	....	....	....	....	....	17	3	1	4	11	....	....	....	....
1996-97	**Buffalo**	**NHL**	**45**	**2**	**4**	**6**	**64**	**1**	**0**	**0**	**25**	**8.0**	**-2**	....	....	....	**9**	**0**	**0**	**0**	**6**	**0**	**0**	**0**	....
	Rochester	AHL	24	9	5	14	27	....	....	....	....	....	....	....	....	....	1	0	0	0	0	....	....	....	....
1997-98	**Buffalo**	**NHL**	**69**	**6**	**6**	**12**	**87**	**2**	**0**	**1**	**51**	**11.8**	**9**	....	....	....	**14**	**1**	**3**	**4**	**6**	**0**	**0**	**0**	....
1998-99	**Buffalo**	**NHL**	**67**	**5**	**8**	**13**	**38**	**0**	**0**	**0**	**55**	**9.1**	**-6**	**529**	**48.6**	**10:19**	**19**	**3**	**4**	**7**	**6**	**1**	**0**	**0**	**13:29**
99-2000	**Buffalo**	**NHL**	**41**	**5**	**7**	**12**	**38**	**2**	**0**	**1**	**40**	**12.5**	**-8**	**430**	**45.6**	**11:03**	....	....	....	....	....	....	....	....	....
	Tampa Bay	**NHL**	**17**	**2**	**3**	**5**	**25**	**0**	**0**	**0**	**35**	**5.7**	**-4**	**290**	**45.5**	**14:21**	....	....	....	....	....	....	....	....	....
2000-01	**Tampa Bay**	**NHL**	**47**	**2**	**13**	**15**	**77**	**0**	**0**	**0**	**47**	**4.3**	**-17**	**630**	**52.2**	**14:11**	....	....	....	....	....	....	....	....	....
	Pittsburgh	**NHL**	**28**	**1**	**6**	**7**	**54**	**0**	**0**	**0**	**30**	**3.3**	**0**	**318**	**51.3**	**12:45**	**18**	**1**	**3**	**4**	**2**	**0**	**0**	**0**	**15:06**
2001-02	**Pittsburgh**	**NHL**	**33**	**3**	**7**	**10**	**18**	**0**	**1**	**0**	**28**	**10.7**	**-1**	**519**	**53.2**	**12:38**	....	....	....	....	....	....	....	....	....
2002-03	**Pittsburgh**	**NHL**	**70**	**5**	**11**	**16**	**55**	**1**	**0**	**0**	**101**	**5.0**	**-30**	**1240**	**50.4**	**16:17**	....	....	....	....	....	....	....	....	....
	San Jose	**NHL**	**7**	**1**	**1**	**2**	**0**	**0**	**0**	**0**	**13**	**7.7**	**2**	**98**	**45.9**	**15:59**	....	....	....	....	....	....	....	....	....
2003-04	**San Jose**	**NHL**	**72**	**9**	**20**	**29**	**90**	**0**	**1**	**1**	**142**	**6.3**	**4**	**867**	**46.6**	**15:28**	**17**	**1**	**2**	**3**	**4**	**0**	**0**	**0**	**15:41**
2004-05			DID NOT PLAY																						
2005-06	**San Jose**	**NHL**	**21**	**5**	**3**	**8**	**17**	**1**	**1**	**1**	**35**	**14.3**	**-6**	**194**	**41.8**	**13:55**	....	....	....	....	....	....	....	....	....
	Boston	**NHL**	**50**	**6**	**8**	**14**	**40**	**0**	**0**	**0**	**66**	**9.1**	**-10**	**749**	**49.8**	**17:16**	....	....	....	....	....	....	....	....	....
2006-07	**Boston**	**NHL**	**51**	**7**	**8**	**15**	**75**	**2**	**1**	**1**	**72**	**9.7**	**-15**	**652**	**50.5**	**15:05**	....	....	....	....	....	....	....	....	....
	Calgary	**NHL**	**27**	**3**	**4**	**7**	**36**	**0**	**1**	**2**	**35**	**8.6**	**-2**	**199**	**46.2**	**10:38**	**6**	**0**	**2**	**2**	**14**	**0**	**0**	**0**	**13:29**
2007-08	**Calgary**	**NHL**	**43**	**3**	**7**	**10**	**26**	**0**	**0**	**0**	**39**	**7.7**	**-3**	**94**	**54.3**	**11:03**	**7**	**1**	**0**	**1**	**4**	**0**	**0**	**0**	**10:35**
	NHL Totals		**691**	**66**	**116**	**182**	**740**	**9**	**5**	**8**	**816**	**8.1**		**6809**	**49.2**	**13:44**	**90**	**7**	**14**	**21**	**42**	**1**	**0**	**0**	**14:11**

Traded to **Tampa Bay** by **Buffalo** with Cory Sarich, Brian Holzinger and Buffalo's 3rd round choice (Alexander Kharitonov) in 2000 Entry Draft for Chris Gratton and Tampa Bay's 2nd round choice (Derek Roy) in 2001 Entry Draft, March 9, 2000. Traded to **Pittsburgh** by **Tampa Bay** for Matthew Barnaby, February 1, 2001. • Missed majority of 2001-02 season recovering from knee injury suffered in game vs. Buffalo, January 8, 2002. Traded to **San Jose** by **Pittsburgh** for Matt Bradley, March 11, 2003. Traded to **Boston** by **San Jose** with Brad Stuart and Marco Sturm for Joe Thornton, November 30, 2005. Traded to **Calgary** by **Boston** with Brad Stuart and Washington's 4th round choice (previously acquired, Calgary selected T.J. Brodie) in 2008 Entry Draft for Andrew Ference and Chuck Kobasew, February 10, 2007.

PRINTZ, David

(PRIHNTS, DAY-vihd)

Defense. Shoots left. 6'5", 220 lbs. Born, Stockholm, Sweden, July 24, 1980. Philadelphia's 9th choice, 225th overall, in 2001 Entry Draft.

1996-97	AIK Solna Jr.	Swe-Jr.	1	0	0	0	0	....	....	....	....	....	....	....	....	....	....	....	....	....	....	....	....	....	....
1997-98	AIK Solna Jr.	Swe-Jr.	8	0	0	0	6	....	....	....	....	....	....	....	....	....	....	....	....	....	....	....	....	....	....
1998-99	AIK Solna Jr.	Swe-Jr.	23	1	0	1	14	....	....	....	....	....	....	....	....	....	....	....	....	....	....	....	....	....	....
99-2000	AIK Solna Jr.	Swe-Jr.	36	8	4	12	53	....	....	....	....	....	....	....	....	....	....	....	....	....	....	....	....	....	....
2000-01	Great Falls	AWHL	54	13	23	36	93	....	....	....	....	....	....	....	....	....	13	3	5	8	16	....	....	....	....
2001-02	AIK Solna Jr.	Swe-Jr.	8	2	3	5	20	....	....	....	....	....	....	....	....	....	....	....	....	....	....	....	....	....	....
	AIK Solna	Sweden	37	3	2	5	59	....	....	....	....	....	....	....	....	....	....	....	....	....	....	....	....	....	....
	AIK Solna	Sweden-Q	10	0	0	0	12	....	....	....	....	....	....	....	....	....	....	....	....	....	....	....	....	....	....
2002-03	HPK Hameenlinna	Finland	17	1	0	1	10	....	....	....	....	....	....	....	....	....	....	....	....	....	....	....	....	....	....
	Ilves Tampere	Finland	25	1	2	3	10	....	....	....	....	....	....	....	....	....	....	....	....	....	....	....	....	....	....
2003-04	AIK Solna	Sweden-2	51	2	9	11	60	....	....	....	....	....	....	....	....	....	5	2	0	2	4	....	....	....	....
2004-05	Philadelphia	AHL	50	1	5	6	66	....	....	....	....	....	....	....	....	....	1	0	0	0	0	....	....	....	....
	Trenton Titans	ECHL	2	0	1	1	0	....	....	....	....	....	....	....	....	....	....	....	....	....	....	....	....	....	....
2005-06	**Philadelphia**	**NHL**	**1**	**0**	**0**	**0**	**0**	**0**	**0**	**0**	**0**	**0.0**	**0**	**0**	**0.0**	**5:45**	....	....	....	....	....	....	....	....	....
	Philadelphia	AHL	80	6	14	20	135	....	....	....	....	....	....	....	....	....	....	....	....	....	....	....	....	....	....
2006-07	**Philadelphia**	**NHL**	**12**	**0**	**0**	**0**	**4**	**0**	**0**	**0**	**1**	**0.0**	**-3**	**0**	**0.0**	**6:33**	....	....	....	....	....	....	....	....	....
	Philadelphia	AHL	62	4	12	16	73	....	....	....	....	....	....	....	....	....	....	....	....	....	....	....	....	....	....
2007-08	Djurgarden	Sweden	54	6	9	15	71	....	....	....	....	....	....	....	....	....	5	0	1	1	4	....	....	....	....
	NHL Totals		**13**	**0**	**0**	**0**	**4**	**0**	**0**	**0**	**1**	**0.0**		**0**	**0.0**	**6:29**	....	....	....	....	....	....	....	....	....

Signed as a free agent by **Djurgarden** (Sweden), June 4, 2007.

PRONGER, Chris

(PRAWN-guhr, KRIHS) **ANA.**

Defense. Shoots left. 6'6", 213 lbs. Born, Dryden, Ont., October 10, 1974. Hartford's 1st choice, 2nd overall, in 1993 Entry Draft.

1990-91	Stratford Cullitons	OHA-B	48	15	37	52	132	....	....	....	....	....	....	....	....	....	....	....	....	....	....	....	....	....	....
1991-92	Peterborough	OHL	63	17	45	62	90	....	....	....	....	....	....	....	....	....	10	1	8	9	28	....	....	....	....
1992-93	Peterborough	OHL	61	15	62	77	108	....	....	....	....	....	....	....	....	....	21	15	25	40	51	....	....	....	....
1993-94	**Hartford**	**NHL**	**81**	**5**	**25**	**30**	**113**	**2**	**0**	**0**	**174**	**2.9**	**-3**	....	....	....	....	....	....	....	....	....	....	....	....
1994-95	**Hartford**	**NHL**	**43**	**5**	**9**	**14**	**54**	**3**	**0**	**1**	**94**	**5.3**	**-12**	....	....	....	....	....	....	....	....	....	....	....	....
1995-96	**St. Louis**	**NHL**	**78**	**7**	**18**	**25**	**110**	**3**	**1**	**1**	**138**	**5.1**	**-18**	....	....	....	**13**	**1**	**5**	**6**	**16**	**0**	**0**	**0**	....
1996-97	**St. Louis**	**NHL**	**79**	**11**	**24**	**35**	**143**	**4**	**0**	**0**	**147**	**7.5**	**15**	....	....	....	**6**	**1**	**1**	**2**	**22**	**0**	**0**	**0**	....
1997-98	**St. Louis**	**NHL**	**81**	**9**	**27**	**36**	**180**	**1**	**0**	**2**	**145**	**6.2**	**47**	....	....	....	**10**	**1**	**9**	**10**	**26**	**0**	**0**	**0**	....
	Canada	Olympics	6	0	0	0	4	....	....	....	....	....	....	....	....	....	....	....	....	....	....	....	....	....	....
1998-99	**St. Louis**	**NHL**	**67**	**13**	**33**	**46**	**113**	**8**	**0**	**0**	**172**	**7.6**	**3**	**0**	**0.0**	**30:36**	**13**	**1**	**4**	**5**	**28**	**1**	**0**	**0**	**35:53**

			Regular Season														Playoffs								
Season	Club	League	GP	G	A	Pts	PIM	PP	SH	GW	S	%	+/-	TF	F%	Min	GP	G	A	Pts	PIM	PP	SH	GW	Min
99-2000	**St. Louis**	**NHL**	79	14	48	62	92	8	0	3	192	7.3	52	1	0.0	30:14	7	3	4	7	32	2	0	2	30:14
2000-01	**St. Louis**	**NHL**	51	8	39	47	75	4	0	0	121	6.6	21	0	0.0	27:45	15	1	7	8	32	0	0	0	33:50
2001-02	**St. Louis**	**NHL**	78	7	40	47	120	4	1	3	204	3.4	23	0	0.0	29:28	9	1	7	8	24	0	0	0	27:51
	Canada	Olympics	6	0	1	1	2	....	....	....	....	....	....	....	....	....	....	....	....	....	....	....	....	....	....
2002-03	**St. Louis**	**NHL**	5	1	3	4	10	0	0	0	11	9.1	−2	1	0.0	21:39	7	1	3	4	14	0	0	0	24:36
2003-04	**St. Louis**	**NHL**	80	14	40	54	88	7	0	3	203	6.9	−1	2	0.0	27:28	5	0	1	1	16	0	0	0	27:54
2004-05			DID NOT PLAY																						
2005-06	**Edmonton**	**NHL**	80	12	44	56	74	10	0	3	155	7.7	2	1	0.0	27:59	24	5	16	21	26	3	0	0	30:57
	Canada	Olympics	6	1	2	3	16	....	....	....	....	....	....	....	....	....	....	....	....	....	....	....	....	....	....
2006-07 ♦	**Anaheim**	**NHL**	66	13	46	59	69	8	0	2	166	7.8	27	4	25.0	27:06	19	3	12	15	26	1	0	0	30:11
2007-08	**Anaheim**	**NHL**	72	12	31	43	128	8	0	4	182	6.6	−1	7	57.1	26:00	6	2	3	5	12	2	0	1	24:14
	NHL Totals		940	131	427	558	1369	70	2	22	2104	6.2		16	31.3	28:18	134	20	72	92	274	9	0	3	30:34

OHL All-Rookie Team (1992) • OHL First All-Star Team (1993) • Canadian Major Junior First All-Star Team (1993) • Canadian Major Junior Defenseman of the Year (1993) • NHL All-Rookie Team (1994) • NHL Second All-Star Team (1998, 2004, 2007) • Bud Ice Plus/Minus Award (1998) • NHL First All-Star Team (2000) • Bud Light Plus/Minus Award (2000) • James Norris Memorial Trophy (2000) • Hart Memorial Trophy (2000)

Played in NHL All-Star Game (1999, 2000, 2002, 2004, 2008)

Traded to **St. Louis** by **Hartford** for Brendan Shanahan, July 27, 1995. • Missed majority of 2002-03 season recovering from wrist and knee surgery, September 10, 2002. Traded to **Edmonton** by **St. Louis** for Eric Brewer, Doug Lynch and Jeff Woywitka, August 2, 2005. Traded to **Anaheim** by **Edmonton** for Joffrey Lupul, Ladislav Smid, Anaheim's 1st round choice (later traded to Phoenix - Phoenix selected Nick Ross) in 2007 Entry Draft and Anaheim's 1st (Jordan Eberle) and 2nd (later traded to NY Islanders - NY Islanders selected Travis Hamonic) round choices in 2008 Entry Draft, July 3, 2006.

PROSPAL, Vaclav

(PRAWS-puhl, VAT-slav) **T.B.**

Center. Shoots left. 6'2", 198 lbs. Born, Ceske Budejovice, Czech., February 17, 1975. Philadelphia's 2nd choice, 71st overall, in 1993 Entry Draft.

Season	Club	League	GP	G	A	Pts	PIM	PP	SH	GW	S	%	+/-	TF	F%	Min	GP	G	A	Pts	PIM	PP	SH	GW	Min
1991-92	C. Budejovice Jr.	Czech-Jr.	36	16	16	32	12	....	....	....	....	....	....	....	....	....	....	....	....	....	....	....	....	....	....
1992-93	C. Budejovice Jr.	Czech-Jr.	32	26	31	57	24	....	....	....	....	....	....	....	....	....	....	....	....	....	....	....	....	....	....
1993-94	Hershey Bears	AHL	55	14	21	35	38	....	....	....	....	....	....	....	....	....	2	0	0	0	2	....	....	....	....
1994-95	Hershey Bears	AHL	69	13	32	45	36	....	....	....	....	....	....	....	....	....	2	1	0	1	4	....	....	....	....
1995-96	Hershey Bears	AHL	68	15	36	51	59	....	....	....	....	....	....	....	....	....	5	2	4	6	2	....	....	....	....
1996-97	**Philadelphia**	**NHL**	18	5	10	15	4	0	0	0	35	14.3	3	....	....	....	5	1	3	4	4	0	0	0	....
	Philadelphia	AHL	63	32	63	95	70	....	....	....	....	....	....	....	....	....	....	....	....	....	....	....	....	....	....
1997-98	**Philadelphia**	**NHL**	41	5	13	18	17	4	0	0	60	8.3	−10	....	....	....	....	....	....	....	....	....	....	....	....
	Ottawa	**NHL**	15	1	6	7	4	0	0	0	28	3.6	−1	....	....	....	6	0	0	0	0	0	0	0	....
1998-99	**Ottawa**	**NHL**	79	10	26	36	58	2	0	3	114	8.8	8	997	56.2	13:03	4	0	0	0	0	0	0	0	12:37
99-2000	**Ottawa**	**NHL**	79	22	33	55	40	5	0	4	204	10.8	−2	1331	49.6	16:26	6	0	4	4	4	0	0	0	17:40
2000-01	**Ottawa**	**NHL**	40	1	12	13	12	0	0	0	68	1.5	1	501	50.1	12:57	....	....	....	....	....	....	....	....	....
	Florida	**NHL**	34	4	12	16	10	1	0	0	68	5.9	−2	487	54.6	16:36	....	....	....	....	....	....	....	....	....
2001-02	**Tampa Bay**	**NHL**	81	18	37	55	38	7	0	2	166	10.8	−11	555	52.8	17:31	....	....	....	....	....	....	....	....	....
2002-03	**Tampa Bay**	**NHL**	80	22	57	79	53	9	0	4	134	16.4	9	161	51.6	18:39	11	4	2	6	8	2	0	0	21:15
2003-04	**Anaheim**	**NHL**	82	19	35	54	54	7	0	4	185	10.3	−9	45	46.7	18:37	....	....	....	....	....	....	....	....	....
2004-05	C. Budejovice	CzRep-2	39	28	60	88	82	....	....	....	....	....	....	....	....	....	16	15	15	30	32	....	....	....	....
2005-06	**Tampa Bay**	**NHL**	81	25	55	80	50	10	0	3	236	10.6	−3	267	45.3	19:10	5	0	2	2	0	0	0	0	15:56
	Czech Republic	Olympics	8	4	2	6	2	....	....	....	....	....	....	....	....	....	....	....	....	....	....	....	....	....	....
2006-07	**Tampa Bay**	**NHL**	82	14	41	55	36	2	0	1	219	6.4	−24	124	52.4	19:04	6	1	4	5	4	0	0	1	22:19
2007-08	**Tampa Bay**	**NHL**	62	29	28	57	39	9	0	4	175	16.6	−7	176	54.6	20:00	....	....	....	....	....	....	....	....	....
	Philadelphia	**NHL**	18	4	10	14	6	1	0	1	40	10.0	7	86	58.1	17:15	17	3	10	13	6	1	0	0	16:49
	NHL Totals		792	179	375	554	421	57	0	26	1732	10.3		4730	52.1	17:26	60	9	25	34	26	3	0	1	18:09

AHL First All-Star Team (1997)

Traded to **Ottawa** by **Philadelphia** with Pat Falloon and Dallas' 2nd round choice (previously acquired, Ottawa selected Chris Bala) in 1998 Entry Draft for Alexandre Daigle, January 17, 1998. Traded to **Florida** by **Ottawa** for future considerations, January 20, 2001. Traded to **Tampa Bay** by **Florida** for Ryan Johnson and Tampa Bay's 6th round choice (later traded back to Tampa Bay – Tampa Bay selected Doug O'Brien) in 2003 Entry Draft, July 10, 2001. Signed as a free agent by **Anaheim**, July 17, 2003. Traded to **Tampa Bay** by **Anaheim** for Tampa Bay's 2nd round choice (Brendan Mikkelson) in 2005 Entry Draft, August 16, 2004. Signed as a free agent by **Ceske Budejovice** (CzRep-2), September 17, 2004. Traded to **Philadelphia** by **Tampa Bay** for Alexandere Picard and future considerations, February 25, 2008. Traded to **Tampa Bay** by **Philadelphia** for Nashville's 7th round choice (previously acquired, Philadelphia selected Joacim Eriksson) in 2008 Entry Draft and future considerations, June 18, 2008.

PRUCHA, Petr

(PROO-khah, PEE-tuhr) **NYR**

Right wing. Shoots right. 6', 175 lbs. Born, Chrudim, Czech., September 14, 1982. NY Rangers' 8th choice, 240th overall, in 2002 Entry Draft.

Season	Club	League	GP	G	A	Pts	PIM	PP	SH	GW	S	%	+/-	TF	F%	Min	GP	G	A	Pts	PIM	PP	SH	GW	Min
99-2000	HC Chrudim Jr.	CzRep-Jr.	43	35	27	62	62	....	....	....	....	....	....	....	....	....	....	....	....	....	....	....	....	....	....
2000-01	HC Pardubice Jr.	CzRep-Jr.	54	39	22	61	18	....	....	....	....	....	....	....	....	....	....	....	....	....	....	....	....	....	....
2001-02	HC Pardubice Jr.	CzRep-Jr.	28	38	28	66	18	....	....	....	....	....	....	....	....	....	3	2	6	8	0	....	....	....	....
	Sumperk	CzRep-2	8	6	4	10	0	....	....	....	....	....	....	....	....	....	....	....	....	....	....	....	....	....	....
	Sumperk	CzRep-Q	5	5	3	8	0	....	....	....	....	....	....	....	....	....	....	....	....	....	....	....	....	....	....
	Pardubice	CzRep	20	1	1	2	2	....	....	....	....	....	....	....	....	....	5	0	0	0	0	....	....	....	....
2002-03	Pardubice	CzRep	49	7	9	16	12	....	....	....	....	....	....	....	....	....	17	2	6	8	8	....	....	....	....
	HC Pardubice Jr.	CzRep-Jr.	4	5	4	9	25	....	....	....	....	....	....	....	....	....	....	....	....	....	....	....	....	....	....
	Hr. Kralove	CzRep-2	11	3	5	8	35	....	....	....	....	....	....	....	....	....	....	....	....	....	....	....	....	....	....
2003-04	Pardubice	CzRep	48	11	13	24	24	....	....	....	....	....	....	....	....	....	7	4	3	7	2	....	....	....	....
	Hr. Kralove	CzRep-2	3	1	0	1	25	....	....	....	....	....	....	....	....	....	....	....	....	....	....	....	....	....	....
2004-05	Pardubice	CzRep	47	7	10	17	24	....	....	....	....	....	....	....	....	....	16	6	7	13	2	....	....	....	....
2005-06	**NY Rangers**	**NHL**	68	30	17	47	32	16	0	2	130	23.1	3	150	52.0	13:42	4	1	0	1	0	1	0	0	14:13
	Hartford	AHL	2	2	1	3	0	....	....	....	....	....	....	....	....	....	....	....	....	....	....	....	....	....	....
2006-07	**NY Rangers**	**NHL**	79	22	18	40	30	8	0	2	136	16.2	−7	70	50.0	13:00	10	0	1	1	4	0	0	0	13:35
2007-08	**NY Rangers**	**NHL**	62	7	10	17	22	2	0	1	89	7.9	3	3	66.7	11:38	3	0	0	0	0	0	0	0	8:13
	NHL Totals		209	59	45	104	84	26	0	5	355	16.6		223	51.6	12:49	17	1	1	2	4	1	0	0	12:47

PRUST, Brandon

(PROOST, BRAN-duhn) **CGY.**

Center/Left wing. Shoots left. 5'11", 195 lbs. Born, London, Ont., March 16, 1984. Calgary's 2nd choice, 70th overall, in 2004 Entry Draft.

Season	Club	League	GP	G	A	Pts	PIM	PP	SH	GW	S	%	+/-	TF	F%	Min	GP	G	A	Pts	PIM	PP	SH	GW	Min
2001-02	London Nationals	OHA-B	52	17	35	52	38	....	....	....	....	....	....	....	....	....	....	....	....	....	....	....	....	....	....
2002-03	London Knights	OHL	65	12	17	29	94	....	....	....	....	....	....	....	....	....	14	2	1	3	21	....	....	....	....
2003-04	London Knights	OHL	64	19	33	52	269	....	....	....	....	....	....	....	....	....	15	7	13	20	33	....	....	....	....
2004-05	London Knights	OHL	48	10	20	30	174	....	....	....	....	....	....	....	....	....	15	3	5	8	*71	....	....	....	....
2005-06	Omaha	AHL	79	12	14	26	294	....	....	....	....	....	....	....	....	....	....	....	....	....	....	....	....	....	....
2006-07	**Calgary**	**NHL**	10	0	0	0	25	0	0	0	1	0.0	1	0	0.0	6:03	....	....	....	....	....	....	....	....	....
	Omaha	AHL	63	17	10	27	211	....	....	....	....	....	....	....	....	....	6	0	3	3	20	....	....	....	....
2007-08	Quad City Flames	AHL	79	10	27	37	248	....	....	....	....	....	....	....	....	....	....	....	....	....	....	....	....	....	....
	NHL Totals		10	0	0	0	25	0	0	0	1	0.0		0	0.0	6:03	....	....	....	....	....	....	....	....	....

PURCELL, Teddy

(puhr-SHEL, THE-dee) **L.A.**

Right wing. Shoots right. 6'3", 197 lbs. Born, St. Johns, Nfld., September 8, 1985.

Season	Club	League	GP	G	A	Pts	PIM	PP	SH	GW	S	%	+/-	TF	F%	Min	GP	G	A	Pts	PIM	PP	SH	GW	Min
2003-04	Notre Dame	SJHL	51	21	25	46	8	....	....	....	....	....	....	....	....	....	....	....	....	....	....	....	....	....	....
2004-05	Cedar Rapids	USHL	58	20	47	67	22	....	....	....	....	....	....	....	....	....	11	5	9	14	4	....	....	....	....
2005-06	Cedar Rapids	USHL	55	19	52	71	14	....	....	....	....	....	....	....	....	....	8	3	8	11	4	....	....	....	....
2006-07	U. of Maine	H-East	40	16	27	43	34	....	....	....	....	....	....	....	....	....	....	....	....	....	....	....	....	....	....
2007-08	**Los Angeles**	**NHL**	10	1	2	3	0	0	0	0	10	10.0	2	0	0.0	11:59	....	....	....	....	....	....	....	....	....
	Manchester	AHL	67	25	58	83	34	....	....	....	....	....	....	....	....	....	4	0	3	3	0	....	....	....	....
	NHL Totals		10	1	2	3	0	0	0	0	10	10.0		0	0.0	11:59	....	....	....	....	....	....	....	....	....

AHL First All-Star Team (2008)

Signed as a free agent by **Los Angeles**, April 27, 2007.

PURINTON, Dale

(PUHR-ihn-TUHN, DAYL)

Defense. Shoots left. 6'3", 228 lbs. Born, Fort Wayne, IN, October 11, 1976. NY Rangers' 5th choice, 117th overall, in 1995 Entry Draft.

			Regular Season														Playoffs								
Season	Club	League	GP	G	A	Pts	PIM	PP	SH	GW	S	%	+/-	TF	F%	Min	GP	G	A	Pts	PIM	PP	SH	GW	Min
1992-93	Moose Jaw	SMHL	34	1	16	17	107	....	....	....	....	....	....	....	....	....	....	....	....	....	....	....	....	....	....
	Moose Jaw	WHL	2	0	0	0	2	....	....	....	....	....	....	....	....	....	....	....	....	....	....	....	....	....	....
1993-94	Vernon Vipers	BCJHL	42	1	6	7	194	....	....	....	....	....	....	....	....	....	....	....	....	....	....	....	....	....	....
1994-95	Tacoma Rockets	WHL	65	0	8	8	291	....	....	....	....	....	....	....	....	....	3	0	0	0	13	....	....	....	....
1995-96	Kelowna Rockets	WHL	22	1	4	5	88	....	....	....	....	....	....	....	....	....	....	....	....	....	....	....	....	....	....
	Lethbridge	WHL	37	3	6	9	144	....	....	....	....	....	....	....	....	....	4	1	1	2	25	....	....	....	....
1996-97	Lethbridge	WHL	51	6	26	32	254	....	....	....	....	....	....	....	....	....	18	3	5	8	*88	....	....	....	....
1997-98	Hartford	AHL	17	0	0	0	95	....	....	....	....	....	....	....	....	....	....	....	....	....	....	....	....	....	....
	Charlotte	ECHL	34	3	5	8	186	....	....	....	....	....	....	....	....	....	....	....	....	....	....	....	....	....	....
1998-99	Hartford	AHL	45	1	3	4	306	....	....	....	....	....	....	....	....	....	7	0	2	2	24	....	....	....	....
99-2000	**NY Rangers**	**NHL**	**1**	**0**	**0**	**0**	**7**	**0**	**0**	**0**	**1**	**0.0**	**-1**	**0**	**0.0**	**12:45**	....	....	....	....	....	....	....	....	....
	Hartford	AHL	62	4	4	8	415	....	....	....	....	....	....	....	....	....	23	0	3	3	*87	....	....	....	....
2000-01	**NY Rangers**	**NHL**	**42**	**0**	**2**	**2**	**180**	**0**	**0**	**0**	**13**	**0.0**	**5**	**0**	**0.0**	**9:33**	....	....	....	....	....	....	....	....	....
	Hartford	AHL	11	0	1	1	75	....	....	....	....	....	....	....	....	....	....	....	....	....	....	....	....	....	....
2001-02	**NY Rangers**	**NHL**	**40**	**0**	**4**	**4**	**113**	**0**	**0**	**0**	**11**	**0.0**	**4**	**0**	**0.0**	**7:37**	....	....	....	....	....	....	....	....	....
2002-03	**NY Rangers**	**NHL**	**58**	**3**	**9**	**12**	**161**	**0**	**0**	**0**	**50**	**6.0**	**-2**	**0**	**0.0**	**15:02**	....	....	....	....	....	....	....	....	....
2003-04	**NY Rangers**	**NHL**	**40**	**1**	**1**	**2**	**117**	**0**	**0**	**0**	**31**	**3.2**	**-9**	**0**	**0.0**	**12:47**	....	....	....	....	....	....	....	....	....
2004-05	Victoria	ECHL	25	3	9	12	192	....	....	....	....	....	....	....	....	....	....	....	....	....	....	....	....	....	....
2005-06	Hartford	AHL	25	3	3	6	109	....	....	....	....	....	....	....	....	....	10	0	2	2	45	....	....	....	....
2006-07	Hartford	AHL	55	3	7	10	240	....	....	....	....	....	....	....	....	....	5	0	1	1	29	....	....	....	....
2007-08	Lake Erie	AHL	35	0	4	4	193	....	....	....	....	....	....	....	....	....	....	....	....	....	....	....	....	....	....
	NHL Totals		**181**	**4**	**16**	**20**	**578**	**0**	**0**	**0**	**106**	**3.8**		**0**	**0.0**	**11:37**	....	....	....	....	....	....	....	....	....

• Missed majority of 2003-04 season as a healthy reserve. Signed as a free agent by **Victoria** (ECHL), December 3, 2004. • Missed majority of 2005-06 season recovering from knee (November 6, 2005 at Springfield - AHL) and finger (January 3, 2006 in practice) injuries. Signed as a free agent by **Colorado**, July 17, 2007.

PUSHKAREV, Konstantin

(puhsh-KAR-ehv, KAWN-stan-tihn) **DAL.**

Right wing. Shoots left. 6', 180 lbs. Born, Ust-Kamenogorsk, USSR, February 12, 1985. Los Angeles' 4th choice, 44th overall, in 2003 Entry Draft.

			Regular Season														Playoffs								
Season	Club	League	GP	G	A	Pts	PIM	PP	SH	GW	S	%	+/-	TF	F%	Min	GP	G	A	Pts	PIM	PP	SH	GW	Min
2002-03	Ust-Kam'gorsk 2	Russia-3	STATISTICS NOT AVAILABLE																						
	Ust-Kamenogorsk	Russia-2	4	0	0	0	4	....	....	....	....	....	....	....	....	....	....	....	....	....	....	....	....	....	....
2003-04	Omsk 2	Russia-3	34	17	11	28	64	....	....	....	....	....	....	....	....	....	....	....	....	....	....	....	....	....	....
	Avangard Omsk	Russia	5	1	0	1	0	....	....	....	....	....	....	....	....	....	....	....	....	....	....	....	....	....	....
2004-05	Avangard Omsk	Russia	1	0	0	0	0	....	....	....	....	....	....	....	....	....	....	....	....	....	....	....	....	....	....
	Calgary Hitmen	WHL	69	22	30	52	50	....	....	....	....	....	....	....	....	....	12	2	5	7	4	....	....	....	....
2005-06	**Los Angeles**	**NHL**	**1**	**0**	**1**	**1**	**0**	**0**	**0**	**0**	**0**	**0.0**	**0**	**0**	**0.0**	**9:33**	....	....	....	....	....	....	....	....	....
	Manchester	AHL	77	19	19	38	95	....	....	....	....	....	....	....	....	....	7	1	1	2	4	....	....	....	....
2006-07	**Los Angeles**	**NHL**	**16**	**2**	**2**	**4**	**8**	**0**	**0**	**0**	**10**	**20.0**	**-2**	**1**	**0.0**	**9:10**	....	....	....	....	....	....	....	....	....
	Manchester	AHL	35	4	11	15	29	....	....	....	....	....	....	....	....	....	....	....	....	....	....	....	....	....	....
	Iowa Stars	AHL	15	2	5	7	25	....	....	....	....	....	....	....	....	....	12	1	4	5	18	....	....	....	....
2007-08	Iowa Stars	AHL	49	13	27	40	52	....	....	....	....	....	....	....	....	....	....	....	....	....	....	....	....	....	....
	CSKA Moscow	Russia	5	0	1	1	2	....	....	....	....	....	....	....	....	....	....	....	....	....	....	....	....	....	....
	NHL Totals		**17**	**2**	**3**	**5**	**8**	**0**	**0**	**0**	**10**	**20.0**		**1**	**0.0**	**9:12**	....	....	....	....	....	....	....	....	....

Traded to **Dallas** by **Los Angeles** with Mattias Norstrom and Los Angeles' 3rd (Sergei Korostin) and 4th (later traded to Columbus - Columbus selected Maxim Mayorov) round choices in 2007 Entry Draft for Jaroslav Modry, the rights to Johan Fransson, Dallas' 2nd (Oscar Moller) and 3rd (Bryan Cameron) round choices in 2007 Entry Draft and Dallas' 1st round choice (later traded to Phoenix - Phoenix selected Viktor Tikhonov) in 2008 Entry Draft , February 27, 2007.

PYATT, Taylor

(PIGH-at, TAY-luhr) **VAN.**

Left wing. Shoots left. 6'4", 230 lbs. Born, Thunder Bay, Ont., August 19, 1981. NY Islanders' 2nd choice, 8th overall, in 1999 Entry Draft.

			Regular Season														Playoffs								
Season	Club	League	GP	G	A	Pts	PIM	PP	SH	GW	S	%	+/-	TF	F%	Min	GP	G	A	Pts	PIM	PP	SH	GW	Min
1996-97	Thunder Bay	TBAHA	60	52	61	113	72	....	....	....	....	....	....	....	....	....	....	....	....	....	....	....	....	....	....
1997-98	Sudbury Wolves	OHL	58	14	17	31	104	....	....	....	....	....	....	....	....	....	10	3	1	4	8	....	....	....	....
1998-99	Sudbury Wolves	OHL	68	37	38	75	95	....	....	....	....	....	....	....	....	....	4	0	4	4	6	....	....	....	....
99-2000	Sudbury Wolves	OHL	68	40	49	89	98	....	....	....	....	....	....	....	....	....	12	8	7	15	25	....	....	....	....
2000-01	**NY Islanders**	**NHL**	**78**	**4**	**14**	**18**	**39**	**1**	**0**	**2**	**86**	**4.7**	**-17**	**1**	**0.0**	**12:14**	....	....	....	....	....	....	....	....	....
2001-02	**Buffalo**	**NHL**	**48**	**10**	**10**	**20**	**35**	**0**	**0**	**0**	**61**	**16.4**	**4**	**0**	**0.0**	**13:30**	....	....	....	....	....	....	....	....	....
	Rochester	AHL	27	6	4	10	36	....	....	....	....	....	....	....	....	....	....	....	....	....	....	....	....	....	....
2002-03	**Buffalo**	**NHL**	**78**	**14**	**14**	**28**	**38**	**2**	**0**	**0**	**110**	**12.7**	**-8**	**8**	**25.0**	**14:06**	....	....	....	....	....	....	....	....	....
2003-04	**Buffalo**	**NHL**	**63**	**8**	**12**	**20**	**25**	**1**	**2**	**4**	**98**	**8.2**	**-7**	**19**	**26.3**	**15:36**	....	....	....	....	....	....	....	....	....
2004-05	Hammarby	Sweden-2	24	11	9	20	20	....	....	....	....	....	....	....	....	....	....	....	....	....	....	....	....	....	....
2005-06	**Buffalo**	**NHL**	**41**	**6**	**6**	**12**	**33**	**0**	**0**	**1**	**62**	**9.7**	**-1**	**11**	**18.2**	**11:14**	**14**	**0**	**5**	**5**	**10**	**0**	**0**	**0**	**11:08**
2006-07	**Vancouver**	**NHL**	**76**	**23**	**14**	**37**	**42**	**9**	**0**	**4**	**150**	**15.3**	**5**	**4**	**0.0**	**13:58**	**12**	**2**	**4**	**6**	**6**	**0**	**0**	**1**	**18:02**
2007-08	**Vancouver**	**NHL**	**79**	**16**	**21**	**37**	**60**	**7**	**0**	**2**	**167**	**9.6**	**9**	**36**	**33.3**	**15:47**	....	....	....	....	....	....	....	....	....
	NHL Totals		**463**	**81**	**91**	**172**	**272**	**20**	**2**	**13**	**734**	**11.0**		**79**	**26.6**	**13:56**	**26**	**2**	**9**	**11**	**16**	**0**	**0**	**1**	**14:19**

OHL First All-Star Team (2000)

Traded to **Buffalo** by **NY Islanders** with Tim Connolly for Michael Peca, June 24, 2001. Signed as a free agent by **Hammarby** (Sweden-2), November 16, 2004. Rights traded to **Vancouver** by **Buffalo** for Vancouver's 4th round choice (later traded to Calgary - Calgary selected Keith Aulie) in 2007 Entry Draft, July 14, 2006.

QUINCEY, Kyle

(KWIHN-see, KIGHL) **DET.**

Defense. Shoots left. 6'1", 207 lbs. Born, Kitchener, Ont., August 12, 1985. Detroit's 2nd choice, 132nd overall, in 2003 Entry Draft.

			Regular Season														Playoffs								
Season	Club	League	GP	G	A	Pts	PIM	PP	SH	GW	S	%	+/-	TF	F%	Min	GP	G	A	Pts	PIM	PP	SH	GW	Min
2001-02	Mississauga	OPJHL	27	5	14	19	31	....	....	....	....	....	....	....	....	....	....	....	....	....	....	....	....	....	....
2002-03	London Knights	OHL	66	6	12	18	77	....	....	....	....	....	....	....	....	....	14	3	4	7	11	....	....	....	....
2003-04	London Knights	OHL	3	0	2	2	4	....	....	....	....	....	....	....	....	....	....	....	....	....	....	....	....	....	....
	Mississauga	OHL	61	14	23	37	135	....	....	....	....	....	....	....	....	....	24	3	13	16	32	....	....	....	....
2004-05	Mississauga	OHL	59	15	31	46	111	....	....	....	....	....	....	....	....	....	5	0	3	3	4	....	....	....	....
2005-06	**Detroit**	**NHL**	**1**	**0**	**0**	**0**	**0**	**0**	**0**	**0**	**1**	**0.0**	**0**	**0**	**0.0**	**11:37**	....	....	....	....	....	....	....	....	....
	Grand Rapids	AHL	70	7	26	33	107	....	....	....	....	....	....	....	....	....	16	0	1	1	27	....	....	....	....
2006-07	**Detroit**	**NHL**	**6**	**1**	**0**	**1**	**0**	**0**	**0**	**0**	**7**	**14.3**	**0**	**0**	**0.0**	**11:26**	**13**	**0**	**0**	**0**	**2**	**0**	**0**	**0**	**8:11**
	Grand Rapids	AHL	65	4	18	22	126	....	....	....	....	....	....	....	....	....	2	0	0	0	0	....	....	....	....
2007-08	**Detroit**	**NHL**	**6**	**0**	**0**	**0**	**4**	**0**	**0**	**0**	**5**	**0.0**	**-3**	**0**	**0.0**	**13:58**	....	....	....	....	....	....	....	....	....
	Grand Rapids	AHL	66	5	15	20	149	....	....	....	....	....	....	....	....	....	....	....	....	....	....	....	....	....	....
	NHL Totals		**13**	**1**	**0**	**1**	**4**	**0**	**0**	**0**	**13**	**7.7**		**0**	**0.0**	**12:37**	**13**	**0**	**0**	**0**	**2**	**0**	**0**	**0**	**8:11**

OHL Second All-Star Team (2005)

QUINT, Deron

(KWIHNT, DAIR-uhn)

Defense. Shoots left. 6'2", 219 lbs. Born, Durham, NH, March 12, 1976. Winnipeg's 1st choice, 30th overall, in 1994 Entry Draft.

			Regular Season														Playoffs								
Season	Club	League	GP	G	A	Pts	PIM	PP	SH	GW	S	%	+/-	TF	F%	Min	GP	G	A	Pts	PIM	PP	SH	GW	Min
1990-91	Cardigan Mtn.	High-NH	31	67	54	121	....	....	....	....	....	....	....	....	....	....	....	....	....	....	....	....	....	....	....
1991-92	Cardigan Mtn.	High-NH	21	111	58	169	....	....	....	....	....	....	....	....	....	....	....	....	....	....	....	....	....	....	....
1992-93	Tabor	High-MA	28	15	26	41	30	....	....	....	....	....	....	....	....	....	1	0	2	2	0	....	....	....	....
1993-94	Seattle	WHL	63	15	29	44	47	....	....	....	....	....	....	....	....	....	9	4	12	16	8	....	....	....	....
1994-95	Seattle	WHL	65	29	60	89	82	....	....	....	....	....	....	....	....	....	3	1	2	3	6	....	....	....	....
1995-96	**Winnipeg**	**NHL**	**51**	**5**	**13**	**18**	**22**	**2**	**0**	**0**	**97**	**5.2**	**-2**	....	....	....	....	....	....	....	....	....	....	....	....
	Springfield	AHL	11	2	3	5	4	....	....	....	....	....	....	....	....	....	10	2	3	5	6	....	....	....	....
	Seattle	WHL	....	....	....	....	....	....	....	....	....	....	....	....	....	....	5	4	1	5	6	....	....	....	....
1996-97	**Phoenix**	**NHL**	**27**	**3**	**11**	**14**	**4**	**1**	**0**	**0**	**63**	**4.8**	**-4**	....	....	....	**7**	**0**	**2**	**2**	**0**	**0**	**0**	**0**	
	Springfield	AHL	43	6	18	24	20	....	....	....	....	....	....	....	....	....	12	2	7	9	4	....	....	....	....
1997-98	**Phoenix**	**NHL**	**32**	**4**	**7**	**11**	**16**	**1**	**0**	**1**	**61**	**6.6**	**-6**	....	....	....	....	....	....	....	....	....	....	....	....
	Springfield	AHL	8	1	7	8	10	....	....	....	....	....	....	....	....	....	1	0	0	0	0	....	....	....	....
1998-99	**Phoenix**	**NHL**	**60**	**5**	**8**	**13**	**20**	**2**	**0**	**0**	**94**	**5.3**	**-10**	**0**	**0.0**	**16:12**	....	....	....	....	....	....	....	....	....
99-2000	**Phoenix**	**NHL**	**50**	**3**	**7**	**10**	**22**	**0**	**0**	**1**	**88**	**3.4**	**0**	**0**	**0.0**	**16:39**	....	....	....	....	....	....	....	....	....
	New Jersey	**NHL**	**4**	**1**	**0**	**1**	**2**	**0**	**0**	**0**	**6**	**16.7**	**-2**	**0**	**0.0**	**16:26**	....	....	....	....	....	....	....	....	....
2000-01	**Columbus**	**NHL**	**57**	**7**	**16**	**23**	**16**	**3**	**0**	**0**	**148**	**4.7**	**-19**	**1**	**100.0**	**24:06**	....	....	....	....	....	....	....	....	....
	Syracuse Crunch	AHL	21	5	15	20	30	....	....	....	....	....	....	....	....	....	....	....	....	....	....	....	....	....	....
2001-02	**Columbus**	**NHL**	**75**	**7**	**18**	**25**	**26**	**3**	**0**	**1**	**169**	**4.1**	**-34**	**0**	**0.0**	**22:01**	....	....	....	....	....	....	....	....	....
2002-03	Springfield	AHL	4	1	2	3	4	....	....	....	....	....	....	....	....	....	....	....	....	....	....	....	....	....	....
	Phoenix	**NHL**	**51**	**7**	**10**	**17**	**20**	**2**	**0**	**0**	**85**	**8.2**	**-5**	**0**	**0.0**	**15:51**	....	....	....	....	....	....	....	....	....

			Regular Season														Playoffs								
Season	Club	League	GP	G	A	Pts	PIM	PP	SH	GW	S	%	+/-	TF	F%	Min	GP	G	A	Pts	PIM	PP	SH	GW	Min
2003-04	Chicago	NHL	51	4	7	11	18	2	0	0	72	5.6	–26	0	0.0	18:08	....	....	....	....	....	....	....	....	....
2004-05	HC Forst Bolzano	Italy	14	5	11	16	10	....	....	....	....	....	....	....	....	....	9	4	5	9	12	....	....	....	....
2005-06	Kloten Flyers	Swiss	16	5	10	15	6	....	....	....	....	....	....	....	....	....	....	....	....	....	....	....	....	....	....
	Eisbaren Berlin	Germany	31	5	7	12	26	....	....	....	....	....	....	....	....	....	11	4	7	11	6	....	....	....	....
2006-07	NY Islanders	NHL	5	0	0	0	0	0	0	0	2	0.0	0	0	0.0	10:34	....	....	....	....	....	....	....	....	....
	Eisbaren Berlin	Germany	52	18	28	46	34	....	....	....	....	....	....	....	....	....	3	1	0	1	12	....	....	....	....
2007-08	Eisbaren Berlin	Germany	56	21	30	51	28	....	....	....	....	....	....	....	....	....	14	6	3	9	4	....	....	....	....
	NHL Totals		463	46	97	143	166	16	0	3	885	5.2		1	100.0	18:56	7	0	2	2	0	0	0	0	....

WHL West First All-Star Team (1995)

Transferred to **Phoenix** after **Winnipeg** franchise relocated, July 1, 1996. Traded to **New Jersey** by **Phoenix** with Phoenix's 3rd round choice (later traded back to Phoenix – Phoenix selected Beat Forster) in 2001 Entry Draft for Lyle Odelein, March 7, 2000. Traded to **Columbus** by **New Jersey** to complete transaction that sent Krzysztof Oliwa to Columbus (June 12, 2000) and Turner Stevenson to New Jersey (June 23, 2000), June 23, 2000. Signed to a PTO (tryout) contract by **Springfield** (AHL), October 16, 2002. Signed as a free agent by **Phoenix**, October 26, 2002. Signed as a free agent by **Chicago**, August 5, 2003. Signed as a free agent by **Bolzano** (Italy), December 20, 2004. Signed as a free agent by **Kloten** (Swiss), May 21, 2005. Signed as a free agent by **Berlin** (Germany), November 11, 2005. Signed as a free agent by **NY Islanders**, March 31, 2007.

RACHUNEK, Karel

(ra-KHOO-nehk, KAH-rehl)

Defense. Shoots right. 6'2", 220 lbs. Born, Gottwaldov/Zlin, Czech., August 27, 1979. Ottawa's 8th choice, 229th overall, in 1997 Entry Draft.

Season	Club	League	GP	G	A	Pts	PIM	PP	SH	GW	S	%	+/-	TF	F%	Min	GP	G	A	Pts	PIM	PP	SH	GW	Min
1995-96	AC ZPS Zlin Jr.	CzRep-Jr.	38	8	11	19	....	....	....	....	....	....	....	....	....	....	....	....	....	....	....	....	....	....	....
1996-97	AC ZPS Zlin Jr.	CzRep-Jr.	27	2	11	13	....	....	....	....	....	....	....	....	....	....	....	....	....	....	....	....	....	....	....
1997-98	Zlin	CzRep	27	1	2	3	16	....	....	....	....	....	....	....	....	....	....	....	....	....	....	....	....	....	....
1998-99	Zlin	CzRep	39	3	9	12	88	....	....	....	....	....	....	....	....	....	6	0	0	0	....	....	....	....	....
99-2000	Ottawa	NHL	6	0	0	0	2	0	0	0	3	0.0	0	0	0.0	8:03	....	....	....	....	....	....	....	....	....
	Grand Rapids	IHL	62	6	20	26	64	....	....	....	....	....	....	....	....	....	9	0	5	5	6	....	....	....	....
2000-01	Ottawa	NHL	71	3	30	33	60	3	0	0	77	3.9	17	0	0.0	20:54	3	0	0	0	0	0	0	0	22:38
2001-02	Ottawa	NHL	51	3	15	18	24	1	0	2	55	5.5	7	2	0.0	19:19	....	....	....	....	....	....	....	....	....
2002-03	Yaroslavl	Russia	9	3	0	3	8	....	....	....	....	....	....	....	....	....	....	....	....	....	....	....	....	....	....
	Ottawa	NHL	58	4	25	29	30	3	0	1	110	3.6	23	3	33.3	21:46	17	1	3	4	14	0	0	0	23:14
	Binghamton	AHL	6	0	2	2	10	....	....	....	....	....	....	....	....	....	....	....	....	....	....	....	....	....	....
2003-04	Ottawa	NHL	60	1	16	17	29	0	0	0	99	1.0	17	0	0.0	19:43	....	....	....	....	....	....	....	....	....
	NY Rangers	NHL	12	1	3	4	4	1	0	0	21	4.8	–9	0	0.0	19:04	....	....	....	....	....	....	....	....	....
2004-05	Znojmo	CzRep	21	5	6	11	55	....	....	....	....	....	....	....	....	....	....	....	....	....	....	....	....	....	....
	Yaroslavl	Russia	27	6	8	14	69	....	....	....	....	....	....	....	....	....	9	2	0	2	6	....	....	....	....
2005-06	Yaroslavl	Russia	45	11	16	27	73	....	....	....	....	....	....	....	....	....	2	0	0	0	29	....	....	....	....
2006-07	NY Rangers	NHL	66	6	20	26	38	4	1	1	99	6.1	–9	0	0.0	19:23	6	0	4	4	2	0	0	0	18:22
2007-08	New Jersey	NHL	47	4	9	13	40	0	0	0	68	5.9	3	0	0.0	19:23	....	....	....	....	....	....	....	....	....
	NHL Totals		371	22	118	140	227	12	1	4	532	4.1		5	20.0	19:54	26	1	7	8	16	0	0	0	22:03

Traded to **NY Rangers** by **Ottawa** with Alexandre Giroux for Greg De Vries, March 9, 2004. Signed as a free agent by **Znojmo** (CzRep), September 6, 2004. Signed as a free agent by **Yaroslavl** (Russia), November 1, 2004. Signed as a free agent by **New Jersey**, July 3, 2007.

RADIVOJEVIC, Branko

(ra-dih-VOI-uh-vihch, BRAN-koh)

Right wing. Shoots right. 6', 208 lbs. Born, Piestany, Czech., November 24, 1980. Colorado's 3rd choice, 93rd overall, in 1999 Entry Draft.

Season	Club	League	GP	G	A	Pts	PIM	PP	SH	GW	S	%	+/-	TF	F%	Min	GP	G	A	Pts	PIM	PP	SH	GW	Min
1997-98	Dukla Trencin Jr.	Slovak-Jr.	52	30	31	61	50	....	....	....	....	....	....	....	....	....	....	....	....	....	....	....	....	....	....
	Dukla Trencin	Slovakia	1	0	0	0	2	....	....	....	....	....	....	....	....	....	....	....	....	....	....	....	....	....	....
1998-99	Belleville Bulls	OHL	68	20	38	58	61	....	....	....	....	....	....	....	....	....	21	7	17	24	18	....	....	....	....
99-2000	Belleville Bulls	OHL	59	23	49	72	86	....	....	....	....	....	....	....	....	....	16	5	8	13	32	....	....	....	....
2000-01	Belleville Bulls	OHL	61	34	70	104	77	....	....	....	....	....	....	....	....	....	10	6	10	16	18	....	....	....	....
2001-02	Phoenix	NHL	18	4	2	6	4	0	0	1	19	21.1	1	0	0.0	9:22	1	0	0	0	2	0	0	0	8:07
	Springfield	AHL	62	18	21	39	64	....	....	....	....	....	....	....	....	....	....	....	....	....	....	....	....	....	....
2002-03	Phoenix	NHL	79	12	15	27	63	1	0	3	109	11.0	–2	20	40.0	13:18	....	....	....	....	....	....	....	....	....
2003-04	Phoenix	NHL	53	9	14	23	36	2	1	2	83	10.8	–5	30	30.0	16:27	....	....	....	....	....	....	....	....	....
	Philadelphia	NHL	24	1	8	9	36	0	0	0	24	4.2	0	11	54.6	10:28	18	1	1	2	32	0	0	0	9:56
2004-05	HC Vsetin	CzRep	31	7	11	18	114	....	....	....	....	....	....	....	....	....	....	....	....	....	....	....	....	....	....
	Lulea HF	Sweden	10	6	5	11	8	....	....	....	....	....	....	....	....	....	4	0	0	0	44	....	....	....	....
2005-06	Philadelphia	NHL	64	8	6	14	44	1	0	1	84	9.5	–6	14	42.9	12:46	5	1	0	1	0	0	0	0	10:34
2006-07	Minnesota	NHL	82	11	13	24	21	4	0	3	116	9.5	–9	18	50.0	12:59	5	0	0	0	2	0	0	0	14:14
2007-08	Minnesota	NHL	73	7	10	17	48	1	0	3	91	7.7	–14	39	38.5	14:55	2	0	0	0	0	0	0	0	14:35
	NHL Totals		393	52	68	120	252	9	1	13	526	9.9		132	40.2	13:31	31	2	1	3	36	0	0	0	10:58

OHL First All-Star Team (2001)

Signed as a free agent by **Phoenix**, June 19, 2001. Traded to **Philadelphia** by **Phoenix** with Sean Burke and Ben Eager for Mike Comrie, February 9, 2004. Signed as a free agent by **Vsetin** (CzRep), September 17, 2004. Signed as a free agent by **Lulea** (Sweden), January 27, 2005. Signed as a free agent by **Minnesota**, July 6, 2006.

RADULOV, Alexander

(ra-DEW-lahf, al-EHX-AN-duhr) **NSH.**

Right wing. Shoots left. 6'1", 188 lbs. Born, Nizhny Tagil, USSR, July 5, 1986. Nashville's 1st choice, 15th overall, in 2004 Entry Draft.

Season	Club	League	GP	G	A	Pts	PIM	PP	SH	GW	S	%	+/-	TF	F%	Min	GP	G	A	Pts	PIM	PP	SH	GW	Min
2002-03	Dyn'o Moscow 2	Russia-3	STATISTICS NOT AVAILABLE																						
2003-04	Dyn'o Moscow 2	Russia-3	STATISTICS NOT AVAILABLE																						
	THK Tver	Russia-2	42	15	16	31	102	....	....	....	....	....	....	....	....	....	....	....	....	....	....	....	....	....	....
	Dynamo Moscow	Russia	1	0	0	0	2	....	....	....	....	....	....	....	....	....	....	....	....	....	....	....	....	....	....
2004-05	Quebec Remparts	QMJHL	65	32	43	75	64	....	....	....	....	....	....	....	....	....	13	6	5	11	15	....	....	....	....
2005-06	Quebec Remparts	QMJHL	62	61	*91	*152	101	....	....	....	....	....	....	....	....	....	23	21	*34	*55	30	....	....	....	....
2006-07	Nashville	NHL	64	18	19	37	26	5	0	4	96	18.8	19	0	0.0	11:38	4	3	1	4	19	0	0	0	13:10
	Milwaukee	AHL	11	6	12	18	26	....	....	....	....	....	....	....	....	....	....	....	....	....	....	....	....	....	....
2007-08	Nashville	NHL	81	26	32	58	44	4	0	2	183	14.2	7	1	0.0	16:24	6	2	2	4	6	1	0	0	15:59
	NHL Totals		145	44	51	95	70	9	0	6	279	15.8		1	0.0	14:18	10	5	3	8	25	1	0	0	14:51

QMJHL All-Rookie Team (2005) • QMJHL First All-Star Team (2006) • QMJHL Player of the Year (2006) • Canadian Major Junior First All-Star Team (2006) • Canadian Major Junior Player of the Year (2006) • Memorial Cup Tournament All-Star Team (2006) • Stafford Smythe Memorial Trophy (Memorial Cup Tournament - MVP) (2006)

RAFALSKI, Brian

(ra-FAWL-skee, BRIGH-uhn) **DET.**

Defense. Shoots right. 5'10", 191 lbs. Born, Dearborn, MI, September 28, 1973.

Season	Club	League	GP	G	A	Pts	PIM	PP	SH	GW	S	%	+/-	TF	F%	Min	GP	G	A	Pts	PIM	PP	SH	GW	Min
1990-91	Madison Capitols	USHL	47	12	11	23	28	....	....	....	....	....	....	....	....	....	....	....	....	....	....	....	....	....	....
1991-92	U. of Wisconsin	WCHA	34	3	14	17	34	....	....	....	....	....	....	....	....	....	....	....	....	....	....	....	....	....	....
1992-93	U. of Wisconsin	WCHA	32	0	13	13	10	....	....	....	....	....	....	....	....	....	....	....	....	....	....	....	....	....	....
1993-94	U. of Wisconsin	WCHA	37	6	17	23	26	....	....	....	....	....	....	....	....	....	....	....	....	....	....	....	....	....	....
1994-95	U. of Wisconsin	WCHA	43	11	34	45	48	....	....	....	....	....	....	....	....	....	....	....	....	....	....	....	....	....	....
1995-96	Brynas IF Gavle	Sweden	40	4	14	18	26	....	....	....	....	....	....	....	....	....	9	0	1	1	2	....	....	....	....
1996-97	HPK Hameenlinna	Finland	49	11	24	35	26	....	....	....	....	....	....	....	....	....	10	6	5	11	4	....	....	....	....
1997-98	HIFK Helsinki	Finland	40	13	10	23	20	....	....	....	....	....	....	....	....	....	9	5	6	11	0	....	....	....	....
1998-99	HIFK Helsinki	Finland	53	19	34	53	18	....	....	....	....	....	....	....	....	....	11	5	*9	*14	4	....	....	....	....
	HIFK Helsinki	EuroHL	6	4	6	10	10	....	....	....	....	....	....	....	....	....	4	1	0	1	2	....	....	....	....
99-2000 ♦	New Jersey	NHL	75	5	27	32	28	1	0	1	128	3.9	21	1	0.0	18:51	23	2	6	8	8	0	0	1	21:25
2000-01	New Jersey	NHL	78	9	43	52	26	6	0	1	142	6.3	36	2	100.0	21:41	25	7	11	18	7	1	0	3	22:08
2001-02	New Jersey	NHL	76	7	40	47	18	2	0	4	125	5.6	15	0	0.0	22:08	6	3	2	5	4	3	0	0	21:45
	United States	Olympics	6	1	2	3	2	....	....	....	....	....	....	....	....	....	....	....	....	....	....	....	....	....	....
2002-03 ♦	New Jersey	NHL	79	3	37	40	14	2	0	0	178	1.7	18	1	0.0	23:09	23	2	9	11	8	2	0	0	25:46
2003-04	New Jersey	NHL	69	6	30	36	24	2	0	1	130	4.6	6	0	0.0	22:48	5	0	1	1	0	0	0	0	22:22
2004-05			DID NOT PLAY																						
2005-06	New Jersey	NHL	82	6	43	49	36	3	0	2	126	4.8	0	1	0.0	25:32	9	1	8	9	2	1	0	0	27:26
	United States	Olympics	5	0	2	2	0	....	....	....	....	....	....	....	....	....	....	....	....	....	....	....	....	....	....
2006-07	New Jersey	NHL	82	8	47	55	34	3	1	4	148	5.4	4	0	0.0	25:29	11	2	6	8	8	2	0	0	22:54
2007-08 ♦	Detroit	NHL	73	13	42	55	34	10	0	1	175	7.4	27	0	0.0	24:04	22	4	10	14	12	2	0	0	24:53
	NHL Totals		614	57	309	366	214	29	1	14	1152	4.9		5	40.0	23:01	124	21	53	74	49	11	0	4	23:36

WCHA First All-Star Team (1995) • NCAA West First All-American Team (1995) • NHL All-Rookie Team (2000)

Played in NHL All-Star Game (2004, 2007)

Signed as a free agent by **New Jersey**, June 18, 1999. Signed as a free agent by **Detroit**, July 1, 2007.

			Regular Season														Playoffs								
Season	Club	League	GP	G	A	Pts	PIM	PP	SH	GW	S	%	+/-	TF	F%	Min	GP	G	A	Pts	PIM	PP	SH	GW	Min

RAMHOLT, Tim

(RAM-hohlt, TIHM) **PHI.**

Defense. Shoots left. 6'1", 194 lbs. Born, Zurich, Switz., November 2, 1984. Calgary's 2nd choice, 39th overall, in 2003 Entry Draft.

Season	Club	League	GP	G	A	Pts	PIM	PP	SH	GW	S	%	+/-	TF	F%	Min	GP	G	A	Pts	PIM	PP	SH	GW	Min
99-2000	Zurich/Kusn Jr.	Swiss-Jr.	35	2	9	11	26	....	....	....	....	....	....	....	....	....	4	0	2	2	4	....	....	....	....
	Grasshopper	Swiss-2	2	0	0	0	0	....	....	....	....	....	....	....	....	....	....	....	....	....	....	....	....	....	....
2000-01	GC Zurich	Swiss-2	37	0	2	2	38	....	....	....	....	....	....	....	....	....	3	0	0	0	4	....	....	....	....
	GC Zurich Jr.	Swiss-Jr.	17	3	6	9	10	....	....	....	....	....	....	....	....	....	....	....	....	....	....	....	....	....	....
2001-02	ZSC Lions Zurich	Swiss	37	3	0	3	14	....	....	....	....	....	....	....	....	....	17	0	3	3	2	....	....	....	....
	GCK/ZSC Zurich Jr.	Swiss-Jr.		5	2	2	4	4	....	....	....	....	....	....	....	....	....	....	....	....	....	....	....	....	....
....																									
	GC Zurich	Swiss-2	3	0	0	0	0	....	....	....	....	....	....	....	....	....	....	....	....	....	....	....	....	....	....
2002-03	ZSC Lions Zurich	Swiss	30	2	0	2	12	....	....	....	....	....	....	....	....	....	9	0	1	1	0	....	....	....	....
	GC Zurich	Swiss-2	12	0	4	4	6	....	....	....	....	....	....	....	....	....	....	....	....	....	....	....	....	....	....
2003-04	Cape Breton	QMJHL	51	9	27	36	26	....	....	....	....	....	....	....	....	....	5	0	1	1	4	....	....	....	....
2004-05	ZSC Lions Zurich	Swiss	41	1	3	4	38	....	....	....	....	....	....	....	....	....	15	0	0	0	10	....	....	....	....
2005-06	Kloten Flyers	Swiss	42	0	1	1	48	....	....	....	....	....	....	....	....	....	11	0	1	1	8	....	....	....	....
•2006-07	Omaha	AHL	67	2	10	12	61	....	....	....	....	....	....	....	....	....	6	0	1	1	10	....	....	....	....
2007-08	**Calgary**	**NHL**	**1**	**0**	**0**	**0**	**0**	**0**	**0**	**0**	**0**	**0.0**	**–1**	**0**	**0.0**	**0:45**	....	....	....	....	....	....	....	....	....
	Quad City Flames	AHL	77	4	20	24	73	....	....	....	....	....	....	....	....	....	....	....	....	....	....	....	....	....	....
	NHL Totals		**1**	**0**	**0**	**0**	**0**	**0**	**0**	**0**	**0**	**0.0**		**0**	**0.0**	**0:45**	....	....	....	....	....	....	....	....	....

Traded to **Philadelphia** by **Calgary** for Kyle Greentree, June 30, 2008.

RANGER, Paul

(RAIN-juhr, PAWL) **T.B.**

Defense. Shoots left. 6'3", 208 lbs. Born, Whitby, Ont., September 12, 1984. Tampa Bay's 7th choice, 183rd overall, in 2002 Entry Draft.

Season	Club	League	GP	G	A	Pts	PIM	PP	SH	GW	S	%	+/-	TF	F%	Min	GP	G	A	Pts	PIM	PP	SH	GW	Min
2000-01	Oshawa Generals	OHL	32	0	1	1	2	....	....	....	....	....	....	....	....	....	....	....	....	....	....	....	....	....	....
2001-02	Oshawa Generals	OHL	62	0	9	9	49	....	....	....	....	....	....	....	....	....	5	0	0	0	4	....	....	....	....
2002-03	Oshawa Generals	OHL	68	10	28	38	70	....	....	....	....	....	....	....	....	....	13	0	3	3	10	....	....	....	....
2003-04	Oshawa Generals	OHL	62	12	31	43	72	....	....	....	....	....	....	....	....	....	7	0	1	1	10	....	....	....	....
2004-05	Springfield	AHL	69	3	8	11	46	....	....	....	....	....	....	....	....	....	....	....	....	....	....	....	....	....	....
2005-06	**Tampa Bay**	**NHL**	**76**	**1**	**17**	**18**	**58**	**0**	**0**	**1**	**73**	**1.4**	**5**	**0**	**0.0**	**17:07**	**5**	**2**	**4**	**6**	**0**	**1**	**0**	**0**	**21:43**
	Springfield	AHL	1	1	2	3	0	....	....	....	....	....	....	....	....	....	....	....	....	....	....	....	....	....	....
2006-07	**Tampa Bay**	**NHL**	**72**	**4**	**24**	**28**	**42**	**0**	**0**	**2**	**90**	**4.4**	**5**	**0**	**0.0**	**20:19**	**6**	**0**	**1**	**1**	**4**	**0**	**0**	**0**	**21:22**
2007-08	**Tampa Bay**	**NHL**	**72**	**10**	**21**	**31**	**56**	**0**	**1**	**0**	**105**	**9.5**	**–13**	**0**	**0.0**	**25:13**	....	....	....	....	....	....	....	....	....
	NHL Totals		**220**	**15**	**62**	**77**	**156**	**0**	**1**	**3**	**268**	**5.6**		**0**	**0.0**	**20:49**	**11**	**2**	**5**	**7**	**4**	**1**	**0**	**0**	**21:31**

RASMUSSEN, Erik

(RAS-moo-suhn, AIR-ihk)

Left wing/Center. Shoots left. 6'1", 215 lbs. Born, Minneapolis, MN, March 28, 1977. Buffalo's 1st choice, 7th overall, in 1996 Entry Draft.

Season	Club	League	GP	G	A	Pts	PIM	PP	SH	GW	S	%	+/-	TF	F%	Min	GP	G	A	Pts	PIM	PP	SH	GW	Min
1992-93	St. Louis Park	High-MN	23	16	24	40	50	....	....	....	....	....	....	....	....	....	....	....	....	....	....	....	....	....	....
1993-94	St. Louis Park	High-MN	18	25	18	43	80	....	....	....	....	....	....	....	....	....	....	....	....	....	....	....	....	....	....
1994-95	St. Louis Park	High-MN	23	19	33	52	80	....	....	....	....	....	....	....	....	....	....	....	....	....	....	....	....	....	....
1995-96	U. of Minnesota	WCHA	40	16	32	48	55	....	....	....	....	....	....	....	....	....	....	....	....	....	....	....	....	....	....
1996-97	U. of Minnesota	WCHA	34	15	12	27	*123	....	....	....	....	....	....	....	....	....	....	....	....	....	....	....	....	....	....
1997-98	**Buffalo**	**NHL**	**21**	**2**	**3**	**5**	**14**	**0**	**0**	**0**	**28**	**7.1**	**2**	....	....	....	....	....	....	....	....	....	....	....	....
	Rochester	AHL	53	9	14	23	83	....	....	....	....	....	....	....	....	....	1	0	0	0	5	....	....	....	....
1998-99	**Buffalo**	**NHL**	**42**	**3**	**7**	**10**	**37**	**0**	**0**	**0**	**40**	**7.5**	**6**	**67**	**40.3**	**12:22**	**21**	**2**	**4**	**6**	**18**	**0**	**0**	**1**	**12:51**
	Rochester	AHL	37	12	14	26	47	....	....	....	....	....	....	....	....	....	....	....	....	....	....	....	....	....	....
99-2000	**Buffalo**	**NHL**	**67**	**8**	**6**	**14**	**43**	**0**	**0**	**2**	**76**	**10.5**	**1**	**130**	**44.6**	**11:27**	**3**	**0**	**0**	**0**	**4**	**0**	**0**	**0**	**8:59**
2000-01	**Buffalo**	**NHL**	**82**	**12**	**19**	**31**	**51**	**1**	**0**	**3**	**95**	**12.6**	**0**	**565**	**43.7**	**13:47**	**3**	**0**	**1**	**1**	**0**	**0**	**0**	**0**	**16:26**
2001-02	**Buffalo**	**NHL**	**69**	**8**	**11**	**19**	**34**	**0**	**0**	**2**	**89**	**9.0**	**–1**	**236**	**39.8**	**13:03**	....	....	....	....	....	....	....	....	....
2002-03	**Los Angeles**	**NHL**	**57**	**4**	**12**	**16**	**28**	**0**	**0**	**1**	**75**	**5.3**	**–1**	**278**	**44.6**	**13:39**	....	....	....	....	....	....	....	....	....
2003-04	**New Jersey**	**NHL**	**69**	**7**	**6**	**13**	**41**	**0**	**0**	**0**	**68**	**10.3**	**5**	**423**	**44.4**	**11:34**	**5**	**0**	**2**	**2**	**2**	**0**	**0**	**0**	**14:44**
2004-05			DID NOT PLAY																						
2005-06	**New Jersey**	**NHL**	**67**	**5**	**5**	**10**	**32**	**1**	**0**	**0**	**45**	**11.1**	**–4**	**230**	**37.4**	**7:04**	**9**	**0**	**0**	**0**	**8**	**0**	**0**	**0**	**6:44**
2006-07	**New Jersey**	**NHL**	**71**	**3**	**7**	**10**	**25**	**0**	**0**	**0**	**80**	**3.8**	**–3**	**52**	**48.1**	**9:28**	**11**	**0**	**0**	**0**	**14**	**0**	**0**	**0**	**5:21**
2007-08	Lowell Devils	AHL	26	2	3	5	14	....	....	....	....	....	....	....	....	....	....	....	....	....	....	....	....	....	....
	NHL Totals		**545**	**52**	**76**	**128**	**305**	**2**	**0**	**8**	**596**	**8.7**		**1981**	**42.9**	**11:31**	**52**	**2**	**7**	**9**	**46**	**0**	**0**	**1**	**10:22**

Minnesota High School - Player of the Year (1995)

Traded to **Los Angeles** by **Buffalo** for Adam Mair and Los Angeles' 5th round choice (Thomas Morrow) in 2003 Entry Draft, July 24, 2002. Signed as a free agent by **New Jersey**, July 25, 2003.

RATHJE, Mike

(RATH-jee, MIGHK) **PHI.**

Defense. Shoots left. 6'5", 235 lbs. Born, Mannville, Alta., May 11, 1974. San Jose's 1st choice, 3rd overall, in 1992 Entry Draft.

Season	Club	League	GP	G	A	Pts	PIM	PP	SH	GW	S	%	+/-	TF	F%	Min	GP	G	A	Pts	PIM	PP	SH	GW	Min
1989-90	Sherwood Park	AMHL	33	6	11	17	30	....	....	....	....	....	....	....	....	....	6	1	1	2	2	....	....	....	....
1990-91	Medicine Hat	WHL	64	1	16	17	28	....	....	....	....	....	....	....	....	....	12	0	4	4	2	....	....	....	....
1991-92	Medicine Hat	WHL	67	11	23	34	99	....	....	....	....	....	....	....	....	....	4	0	1	1	2	....	....	....	....
1992-93	Medicine Hat	WHL	57	12	37	49	103	....	....	....	....	....	....	....	....	....	10	3	3	6	12	....	....	....	....
	Kansas City	IHL	....	....	....	....	....	....	....	....	....	....	....	....	....	....	5	0	0	0	12	....	....	....	....
1993-94	**San Jose**	**NHL**	**47**	**1**	**9**	**10**	**59**	**1**	**0**	**0**	**30**	**3.3**	**–9**	....	....	....	**1**	**0**	**0**	**0**	**0**	**0**	**0**	**0**	....
	Kansas City	IHL	6	0	2	2	0	....	....	....	....	....	....	....	....	....	....	....	....	....	....	....	....	....	....
1994-95	Kansas City	IHL	6	0	1	1	7	....	....	....	....	....	....	....	....	....	....	....	....	....	....	....	....	....	....
	San Jose	**NHL**	**42**	**2**	**7**	**9**	**29**	**0**	**0**	**0**	**38**	**5.3**	**–1**	....	....	....	**11**	**5**	**2**	**7**	**4**	**5**	**0**	**0**	....
1995-96	**San Jose**	**NHL**	**27**	**0**	**7**	**7**	**14**	**0**	**0**	**0**	**26**	**0.0**	**–16**	....	....	....	....	....	....	....	....	....	....	....	....
	Kansas City	IHL	36	6	11	17	34	....	....	....	....	....	....	....	....	....	....	....	....	....	....	....	....	....	....
1996-97	**San Jose**	**NHL**	**31**	**0**	**8**	**8**	**21**	**0**	**0**	**0**	**22**	**0.0**	**–1**	....	....	....	....	....	....	....	....	....	....	....	....
1997-98	**San Jose**	**NHL**	**81**	**3**	**12**	**15**	**59**	**1**	**0**	**0**	**61**	**4.9**	**–4**	....	....	....	**6**	**1**	**0**	**1**	**6**	**1**	**0**	**0**	....
1998-99	**San Jose**	**NHL**	**82**	**5**	**9**	**14**	**36**	**2**	**0**	**1**	**67**	**7.5**	**15**	**0**	**0.0**	**20:07**	**6**	**0**	**0**	**0**	**4**	**0**	**0**	**0**	**22:08**
99-2000	**San Jose**	**NHL**	**66**	**2**	**14**	**16**	**31**	**0**	**0**	**0**	**46**	**4.3**	**–2**	**0**	**0.0**	**22:11**	**12**	**1**	**3**	**4**	**8**	**0**	**0**	**0**	**21:32**
2000-01	**San Jose**	**NHL**	**81**	**0**	**11**	**11**	**48**	**0**	**0**	**0**	**89**	**0.0**	**7**	**0**	**0.0**	**22:20**	**6**	**0**	**1**	**1**	**4**	**0**	**0**	**0**	**24:20**
2001-02	**San Jose**	**NHL**	**52**	**5**	**12**	**17**	**48**	**4**	**0**	**0**	**56**	**8.9**	**23**	**0**	**0.0**	**21:31**	**12**	**1**	**3**	**4**	**6**	**1**	**0**	**0**	**23:29**
2002-03	**San Jose**	**NHL**	**82**	**7**	**22**	**29**	**48**	**3**	**0**	**1**	**147**	**4.8**	**–19**	**1**	**0.0**	**24:07**	....	....	....	....	....	....	....	....	....
2003-04	**San Jose**	**NHL**	**80**	**2**	**17**	**19**	**46**	**0**	**1**	**0**	**105**	**1.9**	**18**	**0**	**0.0**	**23:27**	**17**	**1**	**5**	**6**	**13**	**0**	**0**	**0**	**23:26**
2004-05			DID NOT PLAY																						
2005-06	**Philadelphia**	**NHL**	**79**	**3**	**21**	**24**	**46**	**1**	**1**	**1**	**55**	**5.5**	**22**	**0**	**0.0**	**20:08**	**6**	**0**	**0**	**0**	**6**	**0**	**0**	**0**	**16:27**
2006-07	**Philadelphia**	**NHL**	**18**	**0**	**1**	**1**	**6**	**0**	**0**	**0**	**13**	**0.0**	**–7**	**0**	**0.0**	**20:49**	....	....	....	....	....	....	....	....	....
2007-08	**Philadelphia**	**NHL**	DID NOT PLAY – INJURED																						
	NHL Totals		**768**	**30**	**150**	**180**	**491**	**12**	**2**	**3**	**755**	**4.0**		**1**	**0.0**	**21:58**	**77**	**9**	**14**	**23**	**51**	**7**	**0**	**0**	**22:18**

WHL East Second All-Star Team (1992, 1993)

• Missed majority of 1996-97 season recovering from groin injury suffered in game vs. Dallas, November 8, 1996. Signed as a free agent by **Philadelphia**, August 2, 2005. • Missed majority of 2006-07 season recovering from recurring back injury. • Missed entire 2007-08 season recovering from groin injury.

RAYMOND, Mason

(RAY-muhnd, MAY-sohn) **VAN.**

Left wing. Shoots left. 6', 182 lbs. Born, Cochrane, Alta., September 17, 1985. Vancouver's 2nd choice, 51st overall, in 2005 Entry Draft.

Season	Club	League	GP	G	A	Pts	PIM	PP	SH	GW	S	%	+/-	TF	F%	Min	GP	G	A	Pts	PIM	PP	SH	GW	Min
2003-04	Camrose Kodiaks	AJHL	....	27	35	62	....	....	....	....	....	....	....	....	....	....	....	....	....	....	....	....	....	....	....
2004-05	Camrose Kodiaks	AJHL	55	*41	41	82	80	....	....	....	....	....	....	....	....	....	15	8	*12	20	....	....	....	....	....
2005-06	U. Minn-Duluth	WCHA	40	11	17	28	30	....	....	....	....	....	....	....	....	....	....	....	....	....	....	....	....	....	....
2006-07	U. Minn-Duluth	WCHA	39	14	32	46	45	....	....	....	....	....	....	....	....	....	....	....	....	....	....	....	....	....	....
	Manitoba Moose	AHL	11	2	2	4	6	....	....	....	....	....	....	....	....	....	13	0	1	1	0	....	....	....	....
2007-08	**Vancouver**	**NHL**	**49**	**9**	**12**	**21**	**2**	**1**	**0**	**0**	**80**	**11.3**	**1**	**63**	**38.1**	**12:31**	....	....	....	....	....	....	....	....	....
	Manitoba Moose	AHL	20	7	10	17	6	....	....	....	....	....	....	....	....	....	....	....	....	....	....	....	....	....	....
	NHL Totals		**49**	**9**	**12**	**21**	**2**	**1**	**0**	**0**	**80**	**11.3**		**63**	**38.1**	**12:31**	....	....	....	....	....	....	....	....	....

AJHL MVP (2005) • WCHA All-Rookie Team (2006) • WCHA First All-Star Team (2007)

REASONER, Marty

(REE-suh-nuhr, MAHR-tee) **ATL.**

Center. Shoots left. 6'1", 202 lbs. Born, Honeoye Falls, NY, February 26, 1977. St. Louis' 1st choice, 14th overall, in 1996 Entry Draft.

			Regular Season														Playoffs								
Season	Club	League	GP	G	A	Pts	PIM	PP	SH	GW	S	%	+/-	TF	F%	Min	GP	G	A	Pts	PIM	PP	SH	GW	Min
1993-94	Deerfield	High-MA	22	27	25	52	....	....	....	....	....	....	....	....	....	....	....	....	....	....	....	....	....	....	....
1994-95	Deerfield	High-MA	26	25	32	57	14	....	....	....	....	....	....	....	....	....	....	....	....	....	....	....	....	....	....
1995-96	Boston College	H-East	34	16	29	45	32	....	....	....	....	....	....	....	....	....	....	....	....	....	....	....	....	....	....
1996-97	Boston College	H-East	35	20	24	44	31	....	....	....	....	....	....	....	....	....	....	....	....	....	....	....	....	....	....
1997-98	Boston College	H-East	42	*33	40	*73	56	....	....	....	....	....	....	....	....	....	....	....	....	....	....	....	....	....	....
1998-99	**St. Louis**	**NHL**	**22**	**3**	**7**	**10**	**8**	**1**	**0**	**0**	**33**	**9.1**	**2**	**224**	**53.6**	**13:55**	....	....	....	....	....	....	....	....	....
	Worcester IceCats	AHL	44	17	22	39	24	....	....	....	....	....	....	....	....	....	4	2	1	3	6	....	....	....	....
99-2000	**St. Louis**	**NHL**	**32**	**10**	**14**	**24**	**20**	**3**	**0**	**0**	**51**	**19.6**	**9**	**379**	**49.6**	**15:20**	**7**	**2**	**1**	**3**	**4**	**1**	**0**	**0**	**13:12**
	Worcester IceCats	AHL	44	23	28	51	39	....	....	....	....	....	....	....	....	....	....	....	....	....	....	....	....	....	....
2000-01	**St. Louis**	**NHL**	**41**	**4**	**9**	**13**	**14**	**0**	**0**	**0**	**65**	**6.2**	**–5**	**454**	**53.1**	**14:00**	**10**	**3**	**1**	**4**	**0**	**0**	**0**	**1**	**12:21**
	Worcester IceCats	AHL	34	17	18	35	25	....	....	....	....	....	....	....	....	....	....	....	....	....	....	....	....	....	....
2001-02	**Edmonton**	**NHL**	**52**	**6**	**5**	**11**	**41**	**3**	**0**	**2**	**66**	**9.1**	**0**	**470**	**55.5**	**11:44**	....	....	....	....	....	....	....	....	....
2002-03	**Edmonton**	**NHL**	**70**	**11**	**20**	**31**	**28**	**2**	**2**	**0**	**102**	**10.8**	**19**	**968**	**53.5**	**14:50**	**6**	**1**	**0**	**1**	**2**	**1**	**0**	**0**	**14:22**
	Hamilton	AHL	2	0	2	2	2	....	....	....	....	....	....	....	....	....	....	....	....	....	....	....	....	....	....
2003-04	**Edmonton**	**NHL**	**17**	**2**	**6**	**8**	**10**	**0**	**1**	**0**	**28**	**7.1**	**5**	**321**	**52.7**	**16:30**	....	....	....	....	....	....	....	....	....
2004-05	Salzburg	Austria	11	5	4	9	12	....	....	....	....	....	....	....	....	....	....	....	....	....	....	....	....	....	....
2005-06	**Edmonton**	**NHL**	**58**	**9**	**17**	**26**	**20**	**5**	**0**	**1**	**63**	**14.3**	**–12**	**524**	**52.5**	**12:45**	....	....	....	....	....	....	....	....	....
	Boston	**NHL**	**19**	**2**	**6**	**8**	**8**	**1**	**0**	**0**	**39**	**5.1**	**–2**	**227**	**46.7**	**15:09**	....	....	....	....	....	....	....	....	....
2006-07	**Edmonton**	**NHL**	**72**	**6**	**14**	**20**	**60**	**0**	**0**	**1**	**84**	**7.1**	**–15**	**765**	**54.6**	**13:52**	....	....	....	....	....	....	....	....	....
2007-08	**Edmonton**	**NHL**	**82**	**11**	**14**	**25**	**50**	**0**	**0**	**0**	**113**	**9.7**	**–17**	**906**	**52.8**	**14:58**	....	....	....	....	....	....	....	....	....
	NHL Totals		**465**	**64**	**112**	**176**	**259**	**15**	**3**	**4**	**644**	**9.9**		**5238**	**53.0**	**14:06**	**23**	**6**	**2**	**8**	**6**	**2**	**0**	**1**	**13:08**

Hockey East Rookie of the Year (1996) • Hockey East First All-Star Team (1997, 1998) • NCAA East First All-American Team (1998) • NCAA Championship All-Tournament Team (1998)

Traded to **Edmonton** by **St. Louis** with Jochen Hecht and Jan Horacek for Doug Weight and Michel Riesen, July 1, 2001. • Missed majority of 2003-04 season recovering from ankle (November 8, 2003 vs. Toronto) and knee (January 13, 2004 vs. Florida) injuries. Signed as a free agent by **Salzburg** (Austria), January 30, 2005. Traded to **Boston** by **Edmonton** with Yan Stastny and Edmonton's 2nd round choice (Milan Lucic) in 2006 Entry Draft for Sergei Samsonov, March 9, 2006. Signed as a free agent by **Edmonton**, July 4, 2006. Signed as a free agent by **Atlanta**, July 17, 2008.

RECCHI, Mark

(REH-kee, MAHRK) **T.B.**

Right wing. Shoots left. 5'10", 195 lbs. Born, Kamloops, B.C., February 1, 1968. Pittsburgh's 4th choice, 67th overall, in 1988 Entry Draft.

			Regular Season														Playoffs								
Season	Club	League	GP	G	A	Pts	PIM	PP	SH	GW	S	%	+/-	TF	F%	Min	GP	G	A	Pts	PIM	PP	SH	GW	Min
1984-85	Langley Eagles	BCJHL	51	26	39	65	39	....	....	....	....	....	....	....	....	....	....	....	....	....	....	....	....	....	....
	New Westminster	WHL	4	1	0	1	0	....	....	....	....	....	....	....	....	....	....	....	....	....	....	....	....	....	....
1985-86	New Westminster	WHL	72	21	40	61	55	....	....	....	....	....	....	....	....	....	....	....	....	....	....	....	....	....	....
1986-87	Kamloops Chiefs	WHL	40	26	50	76	63	....	....	....	....	....	....	....	....	....	13	3	16	19	17	....	....	....	....
1987-88	Kamloops Chiefs	WHL	62	61	*93	154	75	....	....	....	....	....	....	....	....	....	17	10	*21	*31	18	....	....	....	....
1988-89	**Pittsburgh**	**NHL**	**15**	**1**	**1**	**2**	**0**	**0**	**0**	**0**	**11**	**9.1**	**–2**	....	....	....	....	....	....	....	....	....	....	....	....
	Muskegon	IHL	63	50	49	99	86	....	....	....	....	....	....	....	....	....	14	7	*14	*21	28	....	....	....	....
1989-90	**Pittsburgh**	**NHL**	**74**	**30**	**37**	**67**	**44**	**6**	**2**	**4**	**143**	**21.0**	**6**	....	....	....	....	....	....	....	....	....	....	....	....
	Muskegon	IHL	4	7	4	11	2	....	....	....	....	....	....	....	....	....	....	....	....	....	....	....	....	....	....
1990-91 ◆	**Pittsburgh**	**NHL**	**78**	**40**	**73**	**113**	**48**	**12**	**0**	**9**	**184**	**21.7**	**0**	....	....	....	**24**	**10**	**24**	**34**	**33**	**5**	**0**	**2**	....
1991-92	**Pittsburgh**	**NHL**	**58**	**33**	**37**	**70**	**78**	**16**	**1**	**4**	**156**	**21.2**	**–16**	....	....	....	....	....	....	....	....	....	....	....	....
	Philadelphia	**NHL**	**22**	**10**	**17**	**27**	**18**	**4**	**0**	**1**	**54**	**18.5**	**–5**	....	....	....	....	....	....	....	....	....	....	....	....
1992-93	**Philadelphia**	**NHL**	**84**	**53**	**70**	**123**	**95**	**15**	**4**	**6**	**274**	**19.3**	**1**	....	....	....	....	....	....	....	....	....	....	....	....
1993-94	**Philadelphia**	**NHL**	**84**	**40**	**67**	**107**	**46**	**11**	**0**	**5**	**217**	**18.4**	**–2**	....	....	....	....	....	....	....	....	....	....	....	....
1994-95	**Philadelphia**	**NHL**	**10**	**2**	**3**	**5**	**12**	**1**	**0**	**2**	**17**	**11.8**	**–6**	....	....	....	....	....	....	....	....	....	....	....	....
	Montreal	**NHL**	**39**	**14**	**29**	**43**	**16**	**8**	**0**	**1**	**104**	**13.5**	**–3**	....	....	....	....	....	....	....	....	....	....	....	....
1995-96	**Montreal**	**NHL**	**82**	**28**	**50**	**78**	**69**	**11**	**2**	**6**	**191**	**14.7**	**20**	....	....	....	**6**	**3**	**3**	**6**	**0**	**3**	**0**	**0**	....
1996-97	**Montreal**	**NHL**	**82**	**34**	**46**	**80**	**58**	**7**	**2**	**3**	**202**	**16.8**	**–1**	....	....	....	**5**	**4**	**2**	**6**	**2**	**0**	**0**	**0**	....
1997-98	**Montreal**	**NHL**	**82**	**32**	**42**	**74**	**51**	**9**	**1**	**6**	**216**	**14.8**	**11**	....	....	....	**10**	**4**	**8**	**12**	**6**	**0**	**0**	**2**	....
	Canada	Olympics	5	0	2	2	0	....	....	....	....	....	....	....	....	....	....	....	....	....	....	....	....	....	....
1998-99	**Montreal**	**NHL**	**61**	**12**	**35**	**47**	**28**	**3**	**0**	**2**	**152**	**7.9**	**–4**	**239**	**44.8**	**20:37**	....	....	....	....	....	....	....	....	....
	Philadelphia	**NHL**	**10**	**4**	**2**	**6**	**6**	**0**	**0**	**0**	**19**	**21.1**	**–3**	**4**	**25.0**	**19:30**	**6**	**0**	**1**	**1**	**2**	**0**	**0**	**0**	**19:35**
99-2000	**Philadelphia**	**NHL**	**82**	**28**	***63**	**91**	**50**	**7**	**1**	**5**	**223**	**12.6**	**20**	**353**	**49.6**	**21:43**	**18**	**6**	**12**	**18**	**6**	**2**	**0**	**1**	**23:10**
2000-01	**Philadelphia**	**NHL**	**69**	**27**	**50**	**77**	**33**	**7**	**1**	**8**	**191**	**14.1**	**15**	**138**	**42.8**	**21:40**	**6**	**2**	**2**	**4**	**2**	**1**	**0**	**1**	**23:01**
2001-02	**Philadelphia**	**NHL**	**80**	**22**	**42**	**64**	**46**	**7**	**2**	**4**	**205**	**10.7**	**5**	**82**	**53.7**	**20:40**	**4**	**0**	**0**	**0**	**2**	**0**	**0**	**0**	**21:10**
2002-03	**Philadelphia**	**NHL**	**79**	**20**	**32**	**52**	**35**	**8**	**1**	**3**	**171**	**11.7**	**0**	**168**	**52.4**	**18:50**	**13**	**7**	**3**	**10**	**2**	**1**	**0**	**1**	**18:00**
2003-04	**Philadelphia**	**NHL**	**82**	**26**	**49**	**75**	**47**	**14**	**1**	**5**	**167**	**15.6**	**18**	**298**	**52.4**	**17:12**	**18**	**4**	**2**	**6**	**4**	**2**	**0**	**0**	**16:46**
2004-05			DID NOT PLAY																						
2005-06	**Pittsburgh**	**NHL**	**63**	**24**	**33**	**57**	**56**	**11**	**0**	**2**	**164**	**14.6**	**–28**	**387**	**48.3**	**21:17**	....	....	....	....	....	....	....	....	....
	◆ **Carolina**	**NHL**	**20**	**4**	**3**	**7**	**12**	**2**	**0**	**1**	**35**	**11.4**	**–8**	**6**	**33.3**	**17:37**	**25**	**7**	**9**	**16**	**18**	**2**	**0**	**2**	**16:34**
2006-07	**Pittsburgh**	**NHL**	**82**	**24**	**44**	**68**	**62**	**14**	**0**	**3**	**190**	**12.6**	**1**	**26**	**46.2**	**19:42**	**5**	**0**	**4**	**4**	**0**	**0**	**0**	**0**	**19:09**
2007-08	**Pittsburgh**	**NHL**	**19**	**2**	**6**	**8**	**12**	**2**	**0**	**0**	**36**	**5.6**	**–2**	**9**	**44.4**	**16:25**	....	....	....	....	....	....	....	....	....
	Atlanta	**NHL**	**53**	**12**	**28**	**40**	**20**	**5**	**0**	**0**	**85**	**14.1**	**–16**	**49**	**46.9**	**18:23**	....	....	....	....	....	....	....	....	....
	NHL Totals		**1410**	**522**	**859**	**1381**	**942**	**180**	**18**	**80**	**3407**	**15.3**		**1759**	**48.8**	**19:49**	**140**	**47**	**70**	**117**	**77**	**16**	**0**	**9**	**18:59**

WHL West First All-Star Team (1988) • IHL Second All-Star Team (1989) • NHL Second All-Star Team (1992)

Played in NHL All-Star Game (1991, 1993, 1994, 1997, 1998, 1999, 2000)

Traded to **Philadelphia** by **Pittsburgh** with Brian Benning and Los Angeles' 1st round choice (previously acquired, Philadelphia selected Jason Bowen) in 1992 Entry Draft for Rick Tocchet, Kjell Samuelsson, Ken Wregget and Philadelphia's 3rd round choice (Dave Roche) in 1993 Entry Draft, February 19, 1992. Traded to **Montreal** by **Philadelphia** with Philadelphia's 3rd round choice (Martin Hohenberger) in 1995 Entry Draft for Eric Desjardins, Gilbert Dionne and John LeClair, February 9, 1995. Traded to **Philadelphia** by **Montreal** for Danius Zubrus, Philadelphia's 2nd round choice (Matt Carkner) in 1999 Entry Draft and NY Islanders' 6th round choice (previously acquired, Montreal selected Scott Selig) in 2000 Entry Draft, March 10, 1999. Signed as a free agent by **Pittsburgh**, July 9, 2004. Traded to **Carolina** by **Pittsburgh** for Niklas Nordgren, Krys Kolanos and Carolina's 2nd round choice (later traded to San Jose - later traded to Philadelphia - Philadelphia selected Kevin Marshall) in 2007 Entry Draft, March 9, 2006. Signed as a free agent by **Pittsburgh**, July 25, 2006. Claimed on waivers by **Atlanta** from **Pittsburgh**, December 8, 2007. Signed as a free agent by **Tampa Bay**, July 8, 2008.

REDDEN, Wade

(REH-duhn, WAYD) **NYR**

Defense. Shoots left. 6'2", 209 lbs. Born, Lloydminster, Sask., June 12, 1977. NY Islanders' 1st choice, 2nd overall, in 1995 Entry Draft.

			Regular Season														Playoffs								
Season	Club	League	GP	G	A	Pts	PIM	PP	SH	GW	S	%	+/-	TF	F%	Min	GP	G	A	Pts	PIM	PP	SH	GW	Min
1992-93	Lloydminster	AJHL	34	4	11	15	64	....	....	....	....	....	....	....	....	....	....	....	....	....	....	....	....	....	....
1993-94	Brandon	WHL	63	4	35	39	98	....	....	....	....	....	....	....	....	....	14	2	4	6	10	....	....	....	....
1994-95	Brandon	WHL	64	14	46	60	83	....	....	....	....	....	....	....	....	....	18	5	10	15	8	....	....	....	....
1995-96	Brandon	WHL	51	9	45	54	55	....	....	....	....	....	....	....	....	....	19	5	10	15	19	....	....	....	....
1996-97	**Ottawa**	**NHL**	**82**	**6**	**24**	**30**	**41**	**2**	**0**	**1**	**102**	**5.9**	**1**	....	....	....	**7**	**1**	**3**	**4**	**2**	**0**	**0**	**0**	....
1997-98	**Ottawa**	**NHL**	**80**	**8**	**14**	**22**	**27**	**3**	**0**	**2**	**103**	**7.8**	**17**	....	....	....	**9**	**0**	**2**	**2**	**2**	**0**	**0**	**0**	....
1998-99	**Ottawa**	**NHL**	**72**	**8**	**21**	**29**	**54**	**3**	**0**	**1**	**127**	**6.3**	**7**	**0**	**0.0**	**23:27**	**4**	**1**	**2**	**3**	**2**	**1**	**0**	**0**	**26:39**
99-2000	**Ottawa**	**NHL**	**81**	**10**	**26**	**36**	**49**	**3**	**0**	**2**	**163**	**6.1**	**–1**	**0**	**0.0**	**23:43**	....	....	....	....	....	....	....	....	....
2000-01	**Ottawa**	**NHL**	**78**	**10**	**37**	**47**	**49**	**4**	**0**	**0**	**159**	**6.3**	**22**	**0**	**0.0**	**25:17**	**4**	**0**	**0**	**0**	**0**	**0**	**0**	**0**	**27:29**
2001-02	**Ottawa**	**NHL**	**79**	**9**	**25**	**34**	**48**	**4**	**1**	**1**	**156**	**5.8**	**22**	**1**	**0.0**	**25:06**	**12**	**3**	**2**	**5**	**6**	**1**	**0**	**1**	**27:56**
2002-03	**Ottawa**	**NHL**	**76**	**10**	**35**	**45**	**70**	**4**	**0**	**3**	**154**	**6.5**	**23**	**0**	**0.0**	**25:24**	**18**	**1**	**8**	**9**	**10**	**0**	**0**	**1**	**25:28**
2003-04	**Ottawa**	**NHL**	**81**	**17**	**26**	**43**	**65**	**12**	**0**	**3**	**175**	**9.7**	**21**	**0**	**0.0**	**24:54**	**7**	**1**	**0**	**1**	**2**	**1**	**0**	**0**	**26:47**
2004-05			DID NOT PLAY																						
2005-06	**Ottawa**	**NHL**	**65**	**10**	**40**	**50**	**63**	**8**	**0**	**4**	**153**	**6.5**	**35**	**1**	**100.0**	**23:28**	**9**	**2**	**8**	**10**	**10**	**2**	**0**	**1**	**25:06**
	Canada	Olympics	6	1	0	1	0	....	....	....	....	....	....	....	....	....	....	....	....	....	....	....	....	....	....
2006-07	**Ottawa**	**NHL**	**64**	**7**	**29**	**36**	**50**	**4**	**0**	**3**	**122**	**5.7**	**1**	**0**	**0.0**	**22:54**	**20**	**3**	**7**	**10**	**10**	**3**	**0**	**1**	**23:37**
2007-08	**Ottawa**	**NHL**	**80**	**6**	**32**	**38**	**60**	**4**	**0**	**1**	**136**	**4.4**	**11**	**0**	**0.0**	**22:13**	**4**	**0**	**1**	**1**	**11**	**0**	**0**	**0**	**19:21**
	NHL Totals		**838**	**101**	**309**	**410**	**576**	**51**	**1**	**21**	**1550**	**6.5**		**2**	**50.0**	**24:05**	**94**	**12**	**33**	**45**	**55**	**8**	**0**	**4**	**25:18**

WHL Rookie of the Year (1994) • WHL East Second All-Star Team (1995) • WHL East First All-Star Team (1996) • Memorial Cup Tournament All-Star Team (1996)

Played in NHL All-Star Game (2002)

Traded to **Ottawa** by **NY Islanders** with Damian Rhodes for Don Beaupre, Martin Straka and Bryan Berard, January 23, 1996. Signed as a free agent by **NY Rangers**, July 1, 2008.

REDDOX, Liam

(REH-dawks, LEE-uhm) **EDM.**

Left wing. Shoots left. 5'10", 180 lbs. Born, East York, Ont., January 27, 1986. Edmonton's 5th choice, 112th overall, in 2004 Entry Draft.

			Regular Season														Playoffs								
Season	Club	League	GP	G	A	Pts	PIM	PP	SH	GW	S	%	+/-	TF	F%	Min	GP	G	A	Pts	PIM	PP	SH	GW	Min
2002-03	Wellington Dukes	OPJHL	45	32	32	64	29	....	....	....	....	....	....	....	....	....	....	....	....	....	....	....	....	....	....
	Peterborough	OHL	4	0	0	0	0	....	....	....	....	....	....	....	....	....	....	....	....	....	....	....	....	....	....
2003-04	Peterborough	OHL	68	31	33	64	24	....	....	....	....	....	....	....	....	....	....	....	....	....	....	....	....	....	....
2004-05	Peterborough	OHL	68	36	46	82	38	....	....	....	....	....	....	....	....	....	14	3	10	13	10	....	....	....	....
2005-06	Peterborough	OHL	68	19	45	64	74	....	....	....	....	....	....	....	....	....	19	5	9	14	20	....	....	....	....
2006-07	Stockton Thunder	ECHL	70	8	18	26	49	....	....	....	....	....	....	....	....	....	6	2	1	3	4	....	....	....	....

			Regular Season														Playoffs								
Season	Club	League	GP	G	A	Pts	PIM	PP	SH	GW	S	%	+/-	TF	F%	Min	GP	G	A	Pts	PIM	PP	SH	GW	Min
2007-08	**Edmonton**	**NHL**	**1**	**0**	**0**	**0**	**0**	**0**	**0**	**0**	**1**	**0.0**	**–1**	**0**	**0.0**	**5:55**	....	....	....	....	....	....	....	....	....
	Springfield	AHL	65	16	28	44	48	....	....	....	....	....	....	....	....	....	....	....	....	....	....	....	....	....	....
	NHL Totals		**1**	**0**	**0**	**0**	**0**	**0**	**0**	**0**	**1**	**0.0**		**0**	**0.0**	**5:55**	....	....	....	....	....	....	....	....	....

OHL All-Rookie Team (2004)

REGEHR, Richie (reh-GEER, RIH-chee)

Defense. Shoots right. 6', 190 lbs. Born, Bundung, Indonesia, January 17, 1983.

99-2000	Kelowna Rockets	WHL	50	6	8	14	22	....	....	....	....	....	....	....	....	....	5	0	1	1	0	....	....	....	....
2000-01	Kelowna Rockets	WHL	71	10	27	37	68	....	....	....	....	....	....	....	....	....	6	0	1	1	4	....	....	....	....
2001-02	Kelowna Rockets	WHL	15	1	9	10	12	....	....	....	....	....	....	....	....	....	....	....	....	....	....	....	....	....	....
	Portland	WHL	37	7	27	34	50	....	....	....	....	....	....	....	....	....	7	2	5	7	8	....	....	....	....
2002-03	Portland	WHL	67	16	45	61	115	....	....	....	....	....	....	....	....	....	7	2	2	4	8	....	....	....	....
2003-04	Portland	WHL	65	9	34	43	88	....	....	....	....	....	....	....	....	....	5	0	1	1	6	....	....	....	....
2004-05	Lowell	AHL	64	9	16	25	60	....	....	....	....	....	....	....	....	....	11	1	6	7	2	....	....	....	....
2005-06	**Calgary**	**NHL**	**14**	**0**	**2**	**2**	**6**	**0**	**0**	**0**	**12**	**0.0**	**0**	**0**	**0.0**	**11:21**	....	....	....	....	....	....	....	....	....
	Omaha	AHL	48	7	23	30	56	....	....	....	....	....	....	....	....	....	....	....	....	....	....	....	....	....	....
2006-07	**Calgary**	**NHL**	**6**	**1**	**1**	**2**	**0**	**1**	**0**	**0**	**4**	**25.0**	**–1**	**0**	**0.0**	**8:44**	....	....	....	....	....	....	....	....	....
	Omaha	AHL	22	5	9	14	37	....	....	....	....	....	....	....	....	....	....	....	....	....	....	....	....	....	....
2007-08	Frankfurt Lions	Germany	44	21	20	41	62	....	....	....	....	....	....	....	....	....	10	3	3	6	14	....	....	....	....
	NHL Totals		**20**	**1**	**3**	**4**	**6**	**1**	**0**	**0**	**16**	**6.3**		**0**	**0.0**	**10:34**	....	....	....	....	....	....	....	....	....

Signed as a free agent by **Calgary**, July 6, 2004. • Missed majority of 2006-07 season recovering from concussion suffered in game vs. Vancouver, December 27, 2006. Signed as a free agent by **Frankfurt** (Germany), July 16, 2007.

REGEHR, Robyn (reh-GEER, RAW-bihn) CGY.

Defense. Shoots left. 6'3", 225 lbs. Born, Recife, Brazil, April 19, 1980. Colorado's 3rd choice, 19th overall, in 1998 Entry Draft.

1995-96	Prince Albert	SMHL	59	8	24	32	157	....	....	....	....	....	....	....	....	....	....	....	....	....	....	....	....	....	....
1996-97	Kamloops Blazers	WHL	64	4	19	23	96	....	....	....	....	....	....	....	....	....	5	0	1	1	18	....	....	....	....
1997-98	Kamloops Blazers	WHL	65	4	10	14	120	....	....	....	....	....	....	....	....	....	5	0	3	3	8	....	....	....	....
1998-99	Kamloops Blazers	WHL	54	12	20	32	130	....	....	....	....	....	....	....	....	....	12	1	4	5	21	....	....	....	....
99-2000	**Calgary**	**NHL**	**57**	**5**	**7**	**12**	**46**	**2**	**0**	**0**	**64**	**7.8**	**–2**	**0**	**0.0**	**18:24**	....	....	....	....	....	....	....	....	....
	Saint John Flames	AHL	5	0	0	0	0	....	....	....	....	....	....	....	....	....	....	....	....	....	....	....	....	....	....
2000-01	**Calgary**	**NHL**	**71**	**1**	**3**	**4**	**70**	**0**	**0**	**0**	**62**	**1.6**	**–7**	**1**	**0.0**	**19:43**	....	....	....	....	....	....	....	....	....
2001-02	**Calgary**	**NHL**	**77**	**2**	**6**	**8**	**93**	**0**	**0**	**0**	**82**	**2.4**	**–24**	**0**	**0.0**	**20:54**	....	....	....	....	....	....	....	....	....
2002-03	**Calgary**	**NHL**	**76**	**0**	**12**	**12**	**87**	**0**	**0**	**0**	**109**	**0.0**	**–9**	**1**	**100.0**	**22:45**	....	....	....	....	....	....	....	....	....
2003-04	**Calgary**	**NHL**	**82**	**4**	**14**	**18**	**74**	**2**	**0**	**1**	**106**	**3.8**	**14**	**2**	**50.0**	**22:21**	**26**	**2**	**7**	**9**	**20**	**0**	**0**	**0**	**26:27**
2004-05			DID NOT PLAY																						
2005-06	**Calgary**	**NHL**	**68**	**6**	**20**	**26**	**67**	**5**	**0**	**2**	**89**	**6.7**	**6**	**1**	**100.0**	**23:08**	**7**	**1**	**3**	**4**	**6**	**1**	**0**	**0**	**22:22**
	Canada	Olympics	6	0	1	1	2	....	....	....	....	....	....	....	....	....	....	....	....	....	....	....	....	....	....
2006-07	**Calgary**	**NHL**	**78**	**2**	**19**	**21**	**75**	**0**	**0**	**0**	**66**	**3.0**	**27**	**1**	**0.0**	**21:55**	**1**	**0**	**0**	**0**	**0**	**0**	**0**	**0**	**11:15**
2007-08	**Calgary**	**NHL**	**82**	**5**	**15**	**20**	**79**	**1**	**1**	**0**	**93**	**5.4**	**11**	**0**	**0.0**	**21:20**	**7**	**0**	**2**	**2**	**2**	**0**	**0**	**0**	**21:50**
	NHL Totals		**591**	**25**	**96**	**121**	**591**	**10**	**1**	**3**	**671**	**3.7**		**6**	**50.0**	**21:24**	**41**	**3**	**12**	**15**	**28**	**1**	**0**	**0**	**24:36**

WHL West First All-Star Team (1999)

Traded to **Calgary** by **Colorado** with Rene Corbet, Wade Belak and Colorado's 2nd round compensatory choice (Jarret Stoll) in 2000 Entry Draft for Theoren Fleury and Chris Dingman, February 28, 1999.

REGIER, Steve (reh-GEER, STEEV) ST.L.

Left wing. Shoots left. 6'4", 194 lbs. Born, Edmonton, Alta., August 31, 1984. NY Islanders' 5th choice, 148th overall, in 2004 Entry Draft.

2000-01	Leduc Oil Kings	AMHL	35	22	39	61	135	....	....	....	....	....	....	....	....	....	....	....	....	....	....	....	....	....	....
2001-02	Medicine Hat	WHL	59	1	4	5	31	....	....	....	....	....	....	....	....	....	....	....	....	....	....	....	....	....	....
2002-03	Medicine Hat	WHL	61	11	10	21	114	....	....	....	....	....	....	....	....	....	11	2	2	4	20	....	....	....	....
2003-04	Medicine Hat	WHL	72	25	35	60	111	....	....	....	....	....	....	....	....	....	18	5	11	16	20	....	....	....	....
2004-05	Bridgeport	AHL	75	7	15	22	43	....	....	....	....	....	....	....	....	....	....	....	....	....	....	....	....	....	....
2005-06	**NY Islanders**	**NHL**	**9**	**0**	**0**	**0**	**0**	**0**	**0**	**0**	**4**	**0.0**	**–1**	**0**	**0.0**	**6:02**	....	....	....	....	....	....	....	....	....
	Bridgeport	AHL	73	16	21	37	54	....	....	....	....	....	....	....	....	....	7	0	2	2	6	....	....	....	....
2006-07	**NY Islanders**	**NHL**	**1**	**0**	**0**	**0**	**0**	**0**	**0**	**0**	**0**	**0.0**	**0**	**0**	**0.0**	**4:41**	....	....	....	....	....	....	....	....	....
	Bridgeport	AHL	77	19	27	46	77	....	....	....	....	....	....	....	....	....	....	....	....	....	....	....	....	....	....
2007-08	**NY Islanders**	**NHL**	**8**	**0**	**0**	**0**	**4**	**0**	**0**	**0**	**7**	**0.0**	**–1**	**1**	**0.0**	**7:59**	....	....	....	....	....	....	....	....	....
	Bridgeport	AHL	65	19	25	44	60	....	....	....	....	....	....	....	....	....	....	....	....	....	....	....	....	....	....
	NHL Totals		**18**	**0**	**0**	**0**	**4**	**0**	**0**	**0**	**11**	**0.0**		**1**	**0.0**	**6:50**	....	....	....	....	....	....	....	....	....

Signed as a free agent by **St. Louis**, July 15, 2008.

REICH, Jeremy (REECH, JAIR-eh-mee) BOS.

Left wing. Shoots left. 6'1", 203 lbs. Born, Craik, Sask., February 11, 1979. Chicago's 3rd choice, 39th overall, in 1997 Entry Draft.

1993-94	Pilote Butte	SAHA	80	70	65	135	120	....	....	....	....	....	....	....	....	....	....	....	....	....	....	....	....	....	....
1994-95	Sask. Contacts	SMHL	35	13	20	33	81	....	....	....	....	....	....	....	....	....	....	....	....	....	....	....	....	....	....
1995-96	Seattle	WHL	65	11	11	22	88	....	....	....	....	....	....	....	....	....	5	0	1	1	10	....	....	....	....
1996-97	Seattle	WHL	62	19	31	50	134	....	....	....	....	....	....	....	....	....	15	2	5	7	36	....	....	....	....
1997-98	Seattle	WHL	43	24	23	47	121	....	....	....	....	....	....	....	....	....	....	....	....	....	....	....	....	....	....
	Swift Current	WHL	22	8	8	16	47	....	....	....	....	....	....	....	....	....	12	5	6	11	37	....	....	....	....
1998-99	Swift Current	WHL	67	21	28	49	220	....	....	....	....	....	....	....	....	....	6	0	3	3	26	....	....	....	....
99-2000	Swift Current	WHL	72	33	58	91	167	....	....	....	....	....	....	....	....	....	12	2	10	12	19	....	....	....	....
2000-01	Syracuse Crunch	AHL	56	6	9	15	108	....	....	....	....	....	....	....	....	....	5	0	0	0	6	....	....	....	....
2001-02	Syracuse Crunch	AHL	59	9	7	16	178	....	....	....	....	....	....	....	....	....	10	4	0	4	16	....	....	....	....
2002-03	Syracuse Crunch	AHL	78	14	13	27	195	....	....	....	....	....	....	....	....	....	....	....	....	....	....	....	....	....	....
2003-04	**Columbus**	**NHL**	**9**	**0**	**1**	**1**	**20**	**0**	**0**	**0**	**3**	**0.0**	**–3**	**0**	**0.0**	**7:38**	....	....	....	....	....	....	....	....	....
	Syracuse Crunch	AHL	72	14	37	51	150	....	....	....	....	....	....	....	....	....	6	1	1	2	13	....	....	....	....
2004-05	Syracuse Crunch	AHL	50	4	5	9	189	....	....	....	....	....	....	....	....	....	....	....	....	....	....	....	....	....	....
	Houston Aeros	AHL	18	3	4	7	34	....	....	....	....	....	....	....	....	....	5	0	1	1	28	....	....	....	....
2005-06	Providence Bruins	AHL	77	8	15	23	235	....	....	....	....	....	....	....	....	....	6	0	0	0	27	....	....	....	....
2006-07	**Boston**	**NHL**	**32**	**0**	**1**	**1**	**63**	**0**	**0**	**0**	**27**	**0.0**	**–10**	**4**	**25.0**	**8:14**	....	....	....	....	....	....	....	....	....
	Providence Bruins	AHL	46	4	7	11	105	....	....	....	....	....	....	....	....	....	....	....	....	....	....	....	....	....	....
2007-08	**Boston**	**NHL**	**58**	**2**	**2**	**4**	**78**	**0**	**0**	**1**	**39**	**5.1**	**–5**	**31**	**48.4**	**8:15**	**4**	**0**	**0**	**0**	**8**	**0**	**0**	**0**	**10:27**
	NHL Totals		**99**	**2**	**4**	**6**	**161**	**0**	**0**	**1**	**69**	**2.9**		**35**	**45.7**	**8:12**	**4**	**0**	**0**	**0**	**8**	**0**	**0**	**0**	**10:27**

Signed as a free agent by **Columbus**, May 17, 2000. Loaned to **Houston** (AHL) by **Syracuse** (AHL) for the loan of Jason Beckett, March 10, 2005. Signed as a free agent by **Boston**, September 7, 2005.

REID, Brandon (REED, BRAN-duhn)

Center. Shoots right. 5'8", 185 lbs. Born, Kirkland, Que., March 9, 1981. Vancouver's 5th choice, 208th overall, in 2000 Entry Draft.

1996-97	Lac St-Louis Lions	QAAA	44	17	34	51	....	....	....	....	....	....	....	....	....	....	7	2	3	5	....	....	....	....	....
1997-98	Halifax	QMJHL	67	13	21	36	6	....	....	....	....	....	....	....	....	....	5	1	0	1	15	....	....	....	....
1998-99	Halifax	QMJHL	70	32	25	57	33	....	....	....	....	....	....	....	....	....	5	2	2	4	0	....	....	....	....
99-2000	Halifax	QMJHL	62	44	80	124	10	....	....	....	....	....	....	....	....	....	10	7	11	18	4	....	....	....	....
2000-01	Val-d'Or Foreurs	QMJHL	57	45	81	126	18	....	....	....	....	....	....	....	....	....	21	13	29	42	14	....	....	....	....
2001-02	Manitoba Moose	AHL	60	18	19	37	6	....	....	....	....	....	....	....	....	....	7	0	3	3	0	....	....	....	....
2002-03	**Vancouver**	**NHL**	**7**	**2**	**3**	**5**	**0**	**0**	**0**	**0**	**15**	**13.3**	**4**	**69**	**55.1**	**9:47**	**9**	**0**	**1**	**1**	**0**	**0**	**0**	**0**	**9:36**
	Manitoba Moose	AHL	73	18	36	54	18	....	....	....	....	....	....	....	....	....	1	1	1	2	0	....	....	....	....
2003-04	**Vancouver**	**NHL**	**3**	**0**	**1**	**1**	**0**	**0**	**0**	**0**	**2**	**0.0**	**1**	**38**	**47.4**	**9:21**	....	....	....	....	....	....	....	....	....
	Manitoba Moose	AHL	73	19	39	58	20	....	....	....	....	....	....	....	....	....	....	....	....	....	....	....	....	....	....
2004-05	Hamburg Freezers	Germany	45	18	29	47	41	....	....	....	....	....	....	....	....	....	6	0	3	3	4	....	....	....	....
2005-06	Rapperswil	Swiss	44	16	18	34	14	....	....	....	....	....	....	....	....	....	12	4	7	11	14	....	....	....	....

			Regular Season														Playoffs								
Season	Club	League	GP	G	A	Pts	PIM	PP	SH	GW	S	%	+/-	TF	F%	Min	GP	G	A	Pts	PIM	PP	SH	GW	Min
2006-07	**Vancouver**	**NHL**	**3**	**0**	**0**	**0**	**0**	**0**	**0**	**0**	**8**	**0.0**	**–1**	**7**	**42.9**	**11:43**	**1**	**0**	**1**	**1**	**0**	**0**	**0**	**0**	**11:06**
	Manitoba Moose	AHL	53	15	17	32	19	....	....	....	....	....	....	....	....	....	10	2	3	5	4	....	....	....	....
2007-08	Dusseldorf	Germany	56	12	28	40	8	....	....	....	....	....	....	....	....	....	13	7	4	11	4	....	....	....	....
	NHL Totals		**13**	**2**	**4**	**6**	**0**	**0**	**0**	**0**	**25**	**8.0**		**114**	**51.8**	**10:08**	**10**	**0**	**2**	**2**	**0**	**0**	**0**	**0**	**9:45**

QMJHL Second All-Star Team (2000) • George Parsons Trophy (Memorial Cup Tournament - Most Sportsmanlike Player) (2000, 2001) • QMJHL First All-Star Team (2001) • Canadian Major Junior - Sportsman of the Year (2001)

Signed as a free agent by **Hamburg** (Germany), July 7, 2004. Signed as a free agent by **Rapperswil** (Swiss), April 1, 2005. Signed as a free agent by **Dusseldorf** (Germany), May 29, 2007.

REID, Darren

(REED, DAIR-ehn)

Right wing. Shoots right. 6'2", 205 lbs. Born, Lac La Biche, Alta., May 8, 1983. Tampa Bay's 11th choice, 256th overall, in 2002 Entry Draft.

Season	Club	League	GP	G	A	Pts	PIM	PP	SH	GW	S	%	+/-	TF	F%	Min	GP	G	A	Pts	PIM	PP	SH	GW	Min
2000-01	Drayton Valley	AJHL	55	8	18	26	116	....	....	....	....	....	....	....	....	....	....	....	....	....	....	....	....	....	....
2001-02	Drayton Valley	AJHL	31	9	12	21	195	....	....	....	....	....	....	....	....	....	....	....	....	....	....	....	....	....	....
	Medicine Hat	WHL	37	8	9	17	70	....	....	....	....	....	....	....	....	....	....	....	....	....	....	....	....	....	....
2002-03	Medicine Hat	WHL	63	14	30	44	163	....	....	....	....	....	....	....	....	....	11	5	0	5	19	....	....	....	....
2003-04	Medicine Hat	WHL	67	33	48	81	194	....	....	....	....	....	....	....	....	....	20	*13	8	21	31	....	....	....	....
2004-05	Springfield	AHL	56	3	19	22	99	....	....	....	....	....	....	....	....	....	....	....	....	....	....	....	....	....	....
2005-06	**Tampa Bay**	**NHL**	**7**	**0**	**1**	**1**	**0**	**0**	**0**	**0**	**3**	**0.0**	**–2**	**0**	**0.0**	**5:41**	....	....	....	....	....	....	....	....	....
	Springfield	AHL	50	8	9	17	59	....	....	....	....	....	....	....	....	....	....	....	....	....	....	....	....	....	....
2006-07	Springfield	AHL	10	1	0	1	5	....	....	....	....	....	....	....	....	....	....	....	....	....	....	....	....	....	....
	Philadelphia	**NHL**	**14**	**0**	**0**	**0**	**18**	**0**	**0**	**0**	**8**	**0.0**	**–7**	**1**	**100.0**	**8:11**	....	....	....	....	....	....	....	....	....
	Philadelphia	AHL	43	16	14	30	20	....	....	....	....	....	....	....	....	....	....	....	....	....	....	....	....	....	....
2007-08	Philadelphia	AHL	41	8	13	21	37	....	....	....	....	....	....	....	....	....	9	1	2	3	0	....	....	....	....
	NHL Totals		**21**	**0**	**1**	**1**	**18**	**0**	**0**	**0**	**11**	**0.0**		**1**	**100.0**	**7:21**	....	....	....	....	....	....	....	....	....

Traded to **Philadelphia** by **Tampa Bay** for Daniel Corso, November 9, 2006.

REINPRECHT, Steve

(REIGHN-prehkt, STEEV) **PHX.**

Center. Shoots left. 6', 191 lbs. Born, Edmonton, Alta., May 7, 1976.

Season	Club	League	GP	G	A	Pts	PIM	PP	SH	GW	S	%	+/-	TF	F%	Min	GP	G	A	Pts	PIM	PP	SH	GW	Min
1993-94	Edmonton SSAC	AMHL	71	48	77	125	....	....	....	....	....	....	....	....	....	....	....	....	....	....	....	....	....	....	....
1994-95	St. Albert Saints	AJHL	56	35	44	79	14	....	....	....	....	....	....	....	....	....	....	....	....	....	....	....	....	....	....
1995-96	St. Albert Saints	AJHL	39	24	33	57	16	....	....	....	....	....	....	....	....	....	....	....	....	....	....	....	....	....	....
1996-97	U. of Wisconsin	WCHA	38	11	9	20	12	....	....	....	....	....	....	....	....	....	....	....	....	....	....	....	....	....	....
1997-98	U. of Wisconsin	WCHA	41	19	24	43	18	....	....	....	....	....	....	....	....	....	....	....	....	....	....	....	....	....	....
1998-99	U. of Wisconsin	WCHA	38	16	17	33	14	....	....	....	....	....	....	....	....	....	....	....	....	....	....	....	....	....	....
99-2000	U. of Wisconsin	WCHA	37	26	40	*66	14	....	....	....	....	....	....	....	....	....	....	....	....	....	....	....	....	....	....
	Los Angeles	**NHL**	**1**	**0**	**0**	**0**	**2**	**0**	**0**	**0**	**0**	**0.0**	**0**	**6**	**50.0**	**6:01**	....	....	....	....	....	....	....	....	....
2000-01	**Los Angeles**	**NHL**	**59**	**12**	**17**	**29**	**12**	**3**	**2**	**3**	**72**	**16.7**	**11**	**676**	**41.4**	**12:39**	....	....	....	....	....	....	....	....	....
	♦ Colorado	**NHL**	**21**	**3**	**4**	**7**	**2**	**0**	**0**	**0**	**28**	**10.7**	**–1**	**209**	**51.2**	**15:38**	**22**	**2**	**3**	**5**	**2**	**0**	**0**	**0**	**12:09**
2001-02	**Colorado**	**NHL**	**67**	**19**	**27**	**46**	**18**	**4**	**0**	**3**	**111**	**17.1**	**14**	**413**	**52.1**	**16:32**	**21**	**7**	**5**	**12**	**8**	**0**	**0**	**2**	**16:23**
2002-03	**Colorado**	**NHL**	**77**	**18**	**33**	**51**	**18**	**2**	**1**	**1**	**146**	**12.3**	**–6**	**928**	**46.4**	**17:22**	**7**	**1**	**2**	**3**	**0**	**0**	**0**	**0**	**15:32**
2003-04	**Calgary**	**NHL**	**44**	**7**	**22**	**29**	**4**	**3**	**0**	**1**	**68**	**10.3**	**1**	**120**	**40.0**	**17:05**	....	....	....	....	....	....	....	....	....
2004-05	HC Mulhouse	France	22	20	27	47	6	....	....	....	....	....	....	....	....	....	10	7	6	13	2	....	....	....	....
2005-06	**Calgary**	**NHL**	**52**	**10**	**19**	**29**	**24**	**5**	**0**	**1**	**72**	**13.9**	**10**	**340**	**49.4**	**14:49**	....	....	....	....	....	....	....	....	....
	Phoenix	**NHL**	**28**	**12**	**11**	**23**	**8**	**4**	**1**	**2**	**58**	**20.7**	**1**	**526**	**47.3**	**19:06**	....	....	....	....	....	....	....	....	....
2006-07	**Phoenix**	**NHL**	**49**	**9**	**24**	**33**	**28**	**2**	**0**	**1**	**71**	**12.7**	**–3**	**537**	**52.3**	**15:40**	....	....	....	....	....	....	....	....	....
2007-08	**Phoenix**	**NHL**	**81**	**16**	**30**	**46**	**26**	**5**	**1**	**0**	**105**	**15.2**	**–3**	**1020**	**50.6**	**15:42**	....	....	....	....	....	....	....	....	....
	NHL Totals		**479**	**106**	**187**	**293**	**142**	**28**	**5**	**12**	**731**	**14.5**		**4775**	**48.1**	**15:55**	**50**	**10**	**10**	**20**	**10**	**0**	**0**	**2**	**14:24**

WCHA Second All-Star Team (1998) • WCHA First All-Star Team (2000) • WCHA Player of the Year (2000) • NCAA West First All-American Team (2000)

Signed as a free agent by **Los Angeles**, March 31, 2000. Traded to **Colorado** by **Los Angeles** with Rob Blake for Adam Deadmarsh, Aaron Miller, a player to be named later (Jared Aulin, March 22, 2001) and Colorado's 1st round choices in 2001 (Dave Steckel) and 2003 (Brian Boyle) Entry Drafts, February 21, 2001. Traded to **Buffalo** by **Colorado** for Keith Ballard, July 3, 2003. Traded to **Calgary** by **Buffalo** with Rhett Warrener for Chris Drury and Steve Begin, July 3, 2003. Signed as a free agent by **Mulhouse** (France), September 28, 2004. Traded to **Phoenix** by **Calgary** with Philippe Sauve for Brian Boucher and Mike Leclerc, February 2, 2006.

REITZ, Erik

(REETZ, AIR-ihk) **MIN.**

Defense. Shoots right. 6'1", 215 lbs. Born, Detroit, MI, July 29, 1982. Minnesota's 5th choice, 170th overall, in 2000 Entry Draft.

Season	Club	League	GP	G	A	Pts	PIM	PP	SH	GW	S	%	+/-	TF	F%	Min	GP	G	A	Pts	PIM	PP	SH	GW	Min
1998-99	Leamington Flyers	OHA-B	50	5	10	15	80	....	....	....	....	....	....	....	....	....	....	....	....	....	....	....	....	....	....
99-2000	Barrie Colts	OHL	63	2	10	12	85	....	....	....	....	....	....	....	....	....	25	0	5	5	44	....	....	....	....
2000-01	Barrie Colts	OHL	68	5	21	26	178	....	....	....	....	....	....	....	....	....	5	1	0	1	21	....	....	....	....
2001-02	Barrie Colts	OHL	61	13	27	40	153	....	....	....	....	....	....	....	....	....	20	4	16	20	40	....	....	....	....
2002-03	Houston Aeros	AHL	62	6	13	19	112	....	....	....	....	....	....	....	....	....	11	0	3	3	31	....	....	....	....
2003-04	Houston Aeros	AHL	69	5	19	24	148	....	....	....	....	....	....	....	....	....	2	0	0	0	0	....	....	....	....
2004-05	Houston Aeros	AHL	38	2	12	14	91	....	....	....	....	....	....	....	....	....	....	....	....	....	....	....	....	....	....
2005-06	**Minnesota**	**NHL**	**5**	**0**	**0**	**0**	**4**	**0**	**0**	**0**	**0**	**0.0**	**–2**	**0**	**0.0**	**13:09**	....	....	....	....	....	....	....	....	....
	Houston Aeros	AHL	72	5	23	28	139	....	....	....	....	....	....	....	....	....	8	0	5	5	20	....	....	....	....
2006-07	**Minnesota**	**NHL**	**1**	**0**	**0**	**0**	**0**	**0**	**0**	**0**	**0**	**0.0**	**1**	**0**	**0.0**	**10:36**	....	....	....	....	....	....	....	....	....
	Houston Aeros	AHL	73	9	25	34	132	....	....	....	....	....	....	....	....	....	....	....	....	....	....	....	....	....	....
2007-08	Houston Aeros	AHL	49	8	26	34	99	....	....	....	....	....	....	....	....	....	3	0	0	0	2	....	....	....	....
	Minnesota	**NHL**	....	....	....	....	....	....	....	....	....	....	....	....	....	....	**2**	**0**	**0**	**0**	**0**	**0**	**0**	**0**	**6:18**
	NHL Totals		**6**	**0**	**0**	**0**	**4**	**0**	**0**	**0**	**0**	**0.0**		**0**	**0.0**	**12:44**	**2**	**0**	**0**	**0**	**0**	**0**	**0**	**0**	**6:18**

Memorial Cup Tournament All-Star Team (2000) • OHL First All-Star Team (2002)

• Missed majority of 2004-05 season recovering from elbow injury suffered in game vs. Milwaukee (AHL), February 5, 2005.

RHEAUME, Pascal

(RAY-awm, pas-KAL) **N.J.**

Center. Shoots left. 6'1", 210 lbs. Born, Quebec City, Que., June 21, 1973.

Season	Club	League	GP	G	A	Pts	PIM	PP	SH	GW	S	%	+/-	TF	F%	Min	GP	G	A	Pts	PIM	PP	SH	GW	Min
1990-91	Ste-Foy	QAAA	37	20	38	58	25	....	....	....	....	....	....	....	....	....	7	7	1	8	6	....	....	....	....
1991-92	Trois-Rivieres	QMJHL	65	17	20	37	84	....	....	....	....	....	....	....	....	....	14	5	4	9	23	....	....	....	....
1992-93	Sherbrooke	QMJHL	65	28	34	62	88	....	....	....	....	....	....	....	....	....	14	6	5	11	31	....	....	....	....
1993-94	Albany River Rats	AHL	55	17	18	35	43	....	....	....	....	....	....	....	....	....	5	0	1	1	0	....	....	....	....
1994-95	Albany River Rats	AHL	78	19	25	44	46	....	....	....	....	....	....	....	....	....	14	3	6	9	19	....	....	....	....
1995-96	Albany River Rats	AHL	68	26	42	68	50	....	....	....	....	....	....	....	....	....	4	1	2	3	2	....	....	....	....
1996-97	**New Jersey**	**NHL**	**2**	**1**	**0**	**1**	**0**	**0**	**0**	**0**	**5**	**20.0**	**1**	....	....	....	....	....	....	....	....	....	....	....	....
	Albany River Rats	AHL	51	22	23	45	40	....	....	....	....	....	....	....	....	....	16	2	8	10	16	....	....	....	....
1997-98	**St. Louis**	**NHL**	**48**	**6**	**9**	**15**	**35**	**1**	**0**	**0**	**45**	**13.3**	**4**	....	....	....	**10**	**1**	**3**	**4**	**8**	**1**	**0**	**0**	....
1998-99	**St. Louis**	**NHL**	**60**	**9**	**18**	**27**	**24**	**2**	**0**	**0**	**85**	**10.6**	**10**	**21**	**71.4**	**13:19**	**5**	**1**	**0**	**1**	**4**	**0**	**0**	**0**	**11:36**
99-2000	**St. Louis**	**NHL**	**7**	**1**	**1**	**2**	**6**	**0**	**0**	**0**	**5**	**20.0**	**–2**	**2**	**0.0**	**10:08**	....	....	....	....	....	....	....	....	....
	Worcester IceCats	AHL	7	1	1	2	4	....	....	....	....	....	....	....	....	....	....	....	....	....	....	....	....	....	....
2000-01	**St. Louis**	**NHL**	**8**	**2**	**0**	**2**	**5**	**2**	**0**	**0**	**16**	**12.5**	**–1**	**7**	**42.9**	**11:56**	**3**	**0**	**1**	**1**	**0**	**0**	**0**	**0**	**11:30**
	Worcester IceCats	AHL	56	23	35	58	63	....	....	....	....	....	....	....	....	....	11	2	4	6	2	....	....	....	....
2001-02	**Chicago**	**NHL**	**19**	**0**	**2**	**2**	**4**	**0**	**0**	**0**	**19**	**0.0**	**–1**	**165**	**51.5**	**9:22**	....	....	....	....	....	....	....	....	....
	Atlanta	**NHL**	**42**	**11**	**9**	**20**	**25**	**6**	**0**	**2**	**61**	**18.0**	**–3**	**510**	**45.9**	**14:27**	....	....	....	....	....	....	....	....	....
2002-03	**Atlanta**	**NHL**	**56**	**4**	**9**	**13**	**24**	**0**	**2**	**1**	**70**	**5.7**	**–8**	**602**	**46.8**	**12:17**	....	....	....	....	....	....	....	....	....
	♦ New Jersey	**NHL**	**21**	**4**	**1**	**5**	**8**	**0**	**1**	**1**	**23**	**17.4**	**3**	**248**	**51.6**	**11:50**	**24**	**1**	**2**	**3**	**13**	**0**	**0**	**0**	**13:32**
2003-04	**NY Rangers**	**NHL**	**17**	**0**	**0**	**0**	**5**	**0**	**0**	**0**	**15**	**0.0**	**–3**	**46**	**56.5**	**10:02**	....	....	....	....	....	....	....	....	....
	Hartford	AHL	3	1	0	1	0	....	....	....	....	....	....	....	....	....	....	....	....	....	....	....	....	....	....
	St. Louis	**NHL**	**25**	**1**	**3**	**4**	**4**	**0**	**0**	**0**	**23**	**4.3**	**–3**	**26**	**38.5**	**10:19**	**3**	**0**	**0**	**0**	**2**	**0**	**0**	**0**	**6:55**
2004-05	Albany River Rats	AHL	78	24	25	49	85	....	....	....	....	....	....	....	....	....	....	....	....	....	....	....	....	....	....
2005-06	**New Jersey**	**NHL**	**12**	**0**	**0**	**0**	**4**	**0**	**0**	**0**	**11**	**0.0**	**–6**	**81**	**42.0**	**9:15**	....	....	....	....	....	....	....	....	....
	Albany River Rats	AHL	9	2	0	2	9	....	....	....	....	....	....	....	....	....	....	....	....	....	....	....	....	....	....
	Phoenix	**NHL**	**1**	**0**	**0**	**0**	**0**	**0**	**0**	**0**	**0**	**0.0**	**–1**	**3**	**66.7**	**6:10**	....	....	....	....	....	....	....	....	....
	San Antonio	AHL	47	13	13	26	35	....	....	....	....	....	....	....	....	....	....	....	....	....	....	....	....	....	....

			Regular Season														Playoffs								
Season	Club	League	GP	G	A	Pts	PIM	PP	SH	GW	S	%	+/-	TF	F%	Min	GP	G	A	Pts	PIM	PP	SH	GW	Min
2006-07	San Antonio	AHL	79	15	32	47	63	....	....	....	....	....	....	....	....	....	....	....	....	....	....	....	....	....	....
2007-08	Vienna Capitals	Austria	35	11	18	29	30	....	....	....	....	....	....	....	....	....	7	1	1	2	33	....	....	....	....
	NHL Totals		**318**	**39**	**52**	**91**	**144**	**11**	**3**	**4**	**378**	**10.3**		**1711**	**47.9**	**12:04**	**45**	**3**	**6**	**9**	**27**	**1**	**0**	**0**	**12:31**

Signed as a free agent by **New Jersey**, October 1, 1993. Claimed by **St. Louis** from **New Jersey** in Waiver Draft, September 28, 1997. • Missed majority of 1999-2000 season recovering from shoulder surgery, August, 1999. Signed as a free agent by **Chicago**, July 31, 2001. Claimed on waivers by **Atlanta** from **Chicago**, November 14, 2001. Traded to **New Jersey** by **Atlanta** for future considerations, February 24, 2003. Signed as a free agent by **NY Rangers**, October 22, 2003. Claimed on waivers by **St. Louis** from **NY Rangers**, January 29, 2004. Signed as a free agent by **New Jersey**, August 13, 2004. Traded to **Phoenix** by **New Jersey** with Ray Schultz and Steven Spencer for Brad Ference, November 25, 2005. Signed as a free agent by **Vienna** (Austria), August 21, 2007. Signed as a free agent by **Lowell** (AHL), August 5, 2008.

RIBEIRO, Mike (rih-BAIR-roh, MIGHK) DAL.

Center. Shoots left. 6', 175 lbs. Born, Montreal, Que., February 10, 1980. Montreal's 2nd choice, 45th overall, in 1998 Entry Draft.

Season	Club	League	GP	G	A	Pts	PIM	PP	SH	GW	S	%	+/-	TF	F%	Min	GP	G	A	Pts	PIM	PP	SH	GW	Min
1996-97	Mtl-Bourassa	QAAA	43	32	57	89	48	....	....	....	....	....	....	....	....	....	16	15	23	38	14	....	....	....	....
1997-98	Rouyn-Noranda	QMJHL	67	40	*85	125	55	....	....	....	....	....	....	....	....	....	6	3	1	4	0	....	....	....	....
1998-99	Rouyn-Noranda	QMJHL	69	*67	*100	*167	137	....	....	....	....	....	....	....	....	....	11	5	11	16	12	....	....	....	....
	Fredericton	AHL	....	....	....	....	....	....	....	....	....	....	....	....	....	....	5	0	1	1	2	....	....	....	....
99-2000	**Montreal**	**NHL**	**19**	**1**	**1**	**2**	**2**	**1**	**0**	**0**	**18**	**5.6**	**–6**	**95**	**34.7**	**10:40**	....	....	....	....	....	....	....	....	....
	Quebec Citadelles	AHL	3	0	0	0	2	....	....	....	....	....	....	....	....	....	....	....	....	....	....	....	....	....	....
	Rouyn-Noranda	QMJHL	2	1	3	4	0	....	....	....	....	....	....	....	....	....	....	....	....	....	....	....	....	....	....
	Quebec Remparts	QMJHL	21	17	28	45	30	....	....	....	....	....	....	....	....	....	11	3	20	23	38	....	....	....	....
2000-01	**Montreal**	**NHL**	**2**	**0**	**0**	**0**	**2**	**0**	**0**	**0**	**3**	**0.0**	**0**	**11**	**18.2**	**10:38**	....	....	....	....	....	....	....	....	....
	Quebec Citadelles	AHL	74	26	40	66	44	....	....	....	....	....	....	....	....	....	9	1	5	6	23	....	....	....	....
2001-02	**Montreal**	**NHL**	**43**	**8**	**10**	**18**	**12**	**3**	**0**	**0**	**48**	**16.7**	**–11**	**141**	**44.0**	**13:55**	....	....	....	....	....	....	....	....	....
	Quebec Citadelles	AHL	23	9	14	23	36	....	....	....	....	....	....	....	....	....	3	0	3	3	0	....	....	....	....
2002-03	**Montreal**	**NHL**	**52**	**5**	**12**	**17**	**6**	**2**	**0**	**0**	**57**	**8.8**	**–3**	**358**	**50.3**	**11:07**	....	....	....	....	....	....	....	....	....
	Hamilton	AHL	3	0	1	1	0	....	....	....	....	....	....	....	....	....	....	....	....	....	....	....	....	....	....
2003-04	**Montreal**	**NHL**	**81**	**20**	**45**	**65**	**34**	**7**	**0**	**5**	**103**	**19.4**	**15**	**913**	**44.8**	**17:05**	**11**	**2**	**1**	**3**	**18**	**0**	**0**	**0**	**16:31**
2004-05	Blues Espoo	Finland	17	8	9	17	4	....	....	....	....	....	....	....	....	....	....	....	....	....	....	....	....	....	....
2005-06	**Montreal**	**NHL**	**79**	**16**	**35**	**51**	**36**	**8**	**0**	**2**	**130**	**12.3**	**–6**	**843**	**44.7**	**16:35**	**6**	**0**	**2**	**2**	**0**	**0**	**0**	**0**	**18:22**
2006-07	**Dallas**	**NHL**	**81**	**18**	**41**	**59**	**22**	**6**	**0**	**3**	**111**	**16.2**	**3**	**678**	**46.6**	**14:56**	**7**	**0**	**3**	**3**	**4**	**0**	**0**	**0**	**18:28**
2007-08	**Dallas**	**NHL**	**76**	**27**	**56**	**83**	**46**	**7**	**0**	**5**	**107**	**25.2**	**21**	**883**	**45.0**	**18:26**	**18**	**3**	**14**	**17**	**16**	**0**	**0**	**0**	**21:45**
	NHL Totals		**433**	**95**	**200**	**295**	**160**	**34**	**0**	**15**	**577**	**16.5**		**3922**	**45.3**	**15:29**	**42**	**5**	**20**	**25**	**38**	**0**	**0**	**0**	**19:21**

QMJHL Second All-Star Team (1998) • QMJHL First All-Star Team (1999) • Canadian Major Junior First All-Star Team (1999)

Played in NHL All-Star Game (2008)

Signed as a free agent by **Espoo** (Finland), January 17, 2005. Traded to **Dallas** by **Montreal** with Montreal's 6th round choice (Matthew Tassone) in 2008 Entry Draft for Janne Niinimaa and Dallas' 5th round choice (Andrew Conboy) in 2007 Entry Draft, September 30, 2006.

RICHARDS, Brad (RIH-chards, BRAD) DAL.

Center. Shoots left. 6', 192 lbs. Born, Murray Harbour, P.E.I., May 2, 1980. Tampa Bay's 2nd choice, 64th overall, in 1998 Entry Draft.

Season	Club	League	GP	G	A	Pts	PIM	PP	SH	GW	S	%	+/-	TF	F%	Min	GP	G	A	Pts	PIM	PP	SH	GW	Min
1996-97	Notre Dame	SJHL	63	39	48	87	73	....	....	....	....	....	....	....	....	....	....	....	....	....	....	....	....	....	....
1997-98	Rimouski Oceanic	QMJHL	68	33	82	115	44	....	....	....	....	....	....	....	....	....	19	8	24	32	2	....	....	....	....
1998-99	Rimouski Oceanic	QMJHL	59	39	92	131	55	....	....	....	....	....	....	....	....	....	11	9	12	21	6	....	....	....	....
99-2000	Rimouski Oceanic	QMJHL	63	*71	*115	*186	69	....	....	....	....	....	....	....	....	....	12	13	*24	*37	16	....	....	....	....
2000-01	**Tampa Bay**	**NHL**	**82**	**21**	**41**	**62**	**14**	**7**	**0**	**3**	**179**	**11.7**	**–10**	**955**	**41.4**	**16:54**	....	....	....	....	....	....	....	....	....
2001-02	**Tampa Bay**	**NHL**	**82**	**20**	**42**	**62**	**13**	**5**	**0**	**0**	**251**	**8.0**	**–18**	**911**	**41.2**	**19:48**	....	....	....	....	....	....	....	....	....
2002-03	**Tampa Bay**	**NHL**	**80**	**17**	**57**	**74**	**24**	**4**	**0**	**2**	**277**	**6.1**	**3**	**1007**	**47.5**	**19:56**	**11**	**0**	**5**	**5**	**12**	**0**	**0**	**0**	**22:21**
2003-04♦	**Tampa Bay**	**NHL**	**82**	**26**	**53**	**79**	**12**	**5**	**1**	**6**	**244**	**10.7**	**14**	**1167**	**46.7**	**20:26**	**23**	**12**	**14**	***26**	**4**	**7**	**0**	**7**	**23:28**
2004-05	Ak Bars Kazan	Russia	6	2	5	7	16	....	....	....	....	....	....	....	....	....	....	....	....	....	....	....	....	....	....
2005-06	**Tampa Bay**	**NHL**	**82**	**23**	**68**	**91**	**32**	**7**	**4**	**0**	**282**	**8.2**	**0**	**1288**	**50.2**	**22:45**	**5**	**3**	**5**	**8**	**6**	**0**	**0**	**0**	**24:11**
	Canada	Olympics	6	2	2	4	6	....	....	....	....	....	....	....	....	....	....	....	....	....	....	....	....	....	....
2006-07	**Tampa Bay**	**NHL**	**82**	**25**	**45**	**70**	**23**	**12**	**1**	**3**	**272**	**9.2**	**–19**	**1580**	**51.4**	**24:07**	**6**	**3**	**5**	**8**	**6**	**2**	**0**	**0**	**25:39**
2007-08	**Tampa Bay**	**NHL**	**62**	**18**	**33**	**51**	**15**	**9**	**1**	**4**	**228**	**7.9**	**–25**	**944**	**48.1**	**24:17**	....	....	....	....	....	....	....	....	....
	Dallas	**NHL**	**12**	**2**	**9**	**11**	**0**	**0**	**1**	**0**	**21**	**9.5**	**–2**	**130**	**56.2**	**19:15**	**18**	**3**	**12**	**15**	**8**	**0**	**0**	**0**	**21:06**
	NHL Totals		**564**	**152**	**348**	**500**	**133**	**49**	**8**	**18**	**1754**	**8.7**		**7982**	**47.3**	**21:02**	**63**	**21**	**41**	**62**	**36**	**9**	**0**	**7**	**22:52**

QMJHL First All-Star Team (2000) • Canadian Major Junior First All-Star Team (2000) • Canadian Major Junior Player of the Year (2000) • Memorial Cup Tournament All-Star Team (2000) • Stafford Smythe Memorial Trophy (Memorial Cup Tournament - MVP) (2000) • NHL All-Rookie Team (2001) • Lady Byng Memorial Trophy (2004) • Conn Smythe Trophy (2004)

Signed as a free agent by **Kazan** (Russia), November 8, 2004. Traded to **Dallas** by **Tampa Bay** with Johan Holmqvist for Mike Smith, Jussi Jokinen, Jeff Halpern and Dallas' 4th round choice in 2009 Entry Draft, February 26, 2008.

RICHARDS, Mike (RIH-chards, MIGHK) PHI.

Center. Shoots left. 5'11", 195 lbs. Born, Kenora, Ont., February 11, 1985. Philadelphia's 2nd choice, 24th overall, in 2003 Entry Draft.

Season	Club	League	GP	G	A	Pts	PIM	PP	SH	GW	S	%	+/-	TF	F%	Min	GP	G	A	Pts	PIM	PP	SH	GW	Min
2000-01	Kenora Stars	NOHA	85	76	73	149	20	....	....	....	....	....	....	....	....	....	....	....	....	....	....	....	....	....	....
2001-02	Kitchener Rangers	OHL	65	20	38	58	52	....	....	....	....	....	....	....	....	....	4	0	1	1	6	....	....	....	....
2002-03	Kitchener Rangers	OHL	67	37	50	87	99	....	....	....	....	....	....	....	....	....	21	9	18	27	24	....	....	....	....
2003-04	Kitchener Rangers	OHL	58	36	53	89	82	....	....	....	....	....	....	....	....	....	1	0	0	0	0	....	....	....	....
2004-05	Kitchener Rangers	OHL	43	22	36	58	75	....	....	....	....	....	....	....	....	....	15	11	17	28	36	....	....	....	....
	Philadelphia	AHL	....	....	....	....	....	....	....	....	....	....	....	....	....	....	14	7	8	15	28	....	....	....	....
2005-06	**Philadelphia**	**NHL**	**79**	**11**	**23**	**34**	**65**	**1**	**3**	**1**	**168**	**6.5**	**6**	**914**	**45.7**	**15:23**	**6**	**0**	**1**	**1**	**0**	**0**	**0**	**0**	**15:41**
2006-07	**Philadelphia**	**NHL**	**59**	**10**	**22**	**32**	**52**	**1**	**4**	**3**	**130**	**7.7**	**–12**	**978**	**47.8**	**17:50**	....	....	....	....	....	....	....	....	....
2007-08	**Philadelphia**	**NHL**	**73**	**28**	**47**	**75**	**76**	**8**	**5**	**6**	**212**	**13.2**	**14**	**1381**	**50.5**	**21:31**	**17**	**7**	**7**	**14**	**10**	**1**	**2**	**0**	**20:55**
	NHL Totals		**211**	**49**	**92**	**141**	**193**	**10**	**12**	**10**	**510**	**9.6**		**3273**	**48.4**	**18:11**	**23**	**7**	**8**	**15**	**10**	**1**	**2**	**0**	**19:33**

Memorial Cup Tournament All-Star Team (2003) • OHL Second All-Star Team (2005)

Played in NHL All-Star Game (2008)

RICHARDSON, Brad (RIH-chard-suhn, BRAD) L.A.

Center. Shoots left. 5'11", 185 lbs. Born, Belleville, Ont., February 4, 1985. Colorado's 4th choice, 163rd overall, in 2003 Entry Draft.

Season	Club	League	GP	G	A	Pts	PIM	PP	SH	GW	S	%	+/-	TF	F%	Min	GP	G	A	Pts	PIM	PP	SH	GW	Min
2001-02	Owen Sound	OHL	58	12	21	33	20	....	....	....	....	....	....	....	....	....	....	....	....	....	....	....	....	....	....
2002-03	Owen Sound	OHL	67	27	40	67	54	....	....	....	....	....	....	....	....	....	4	1	1	2	10	....	....	....	....
2003-04	Owen Sound	OHL	15	7	9	16	4	....	....	....	....	....	....	....	....	....	....	....	....	....	....	....	....	....	....
2004-05	Owen Sound	OHL	68	41	56	97	60	....	....	....	....	....	....	....	....	....	8	6	4	10	8	....	....	....	....
2005-06	**Colorado**	**NHL**	**41**	**3**	**10**	**13**	**12**	**1**	**0**	**0**	**51**	**5.9**	**0**	**305**	**41.0**	**10:44**	**9**	**1**	**0**	**1**	**6**	**0**	**0**	**0**	**11:41**
	Lowell	AHL	29	4	13	17	20	....	....	....	....	....	....	....	....	....	....	....	....	....	....	....	....	....	....
2006-07	**Colorado**	**NHL**	**73**	**14**	**8**	**22**	**28**	**0**	**3**	**3**	**129**	**10.9**	**4**	**358**	**40.8**	**13:10**	....	....	....	....	....	....	....	....	....
	Albany River Rats	AHL	3	0	1	1	2	....	....	....	....	....	....	....	....	....	....	....	....	....	....	....	....	....	....
2007-08	**Colorado**	**NHL**	**22**	**2**	**3**	**5**	**8**	**0**	**0**	**0**	**32**	**6.3**	**–3**	**60**	**43.3**	**13:29**	....	....	....	....	....	....	....	....	....
	Lake Erie	AHL	38	14	26	40	18	....	....	....	....	....	....	....	....	....	....	....	....	....	....	....	....	....	....
	NHL Totals		**136**	**19**	**21**	**40**	**48**	**1**	**3**	**3**	**212**	**9.0**		**723**	**41.1**	**12:29**	**9**	**1**	**0**	**1**	**6**	**0**	**0**	**0**	**11:41**

Traded to **Los Angeles** by **Colorado** for Detroit's 2nd round choice (previously acquired, Colorado selected Peter Delmas) in 2008 Entry Draft, June 20, 2008.

RICHARDSON, Luke (RIH-chard-suhn, LEWK)

Defense. Shoots left. 6'3", 208 lbs. Born, Ottawa, Ont., March 26, 1969. Toronto's 1st choice, 7th overall, in 1987 Entry Draft.

Season	Club	League	GP	G	A	Pts	PIM	PP	SH	GW	S	%	+/-	TF	F%	Min	GP	G	A	Pts	PIM	PP	SH	GW	Min
1984-85	Ottawa Knights	Minor-ON	35	5	26	31	72	....	....	....	....	....	....	....	....	....	....	....	....	....	....	....	....	....	....
1985-86	Peterborough	OHL	63	6	18	24	57	....	....	....	....	....	....	....	....	....	16	2	1	3	50	....	....	....	....
1986-87	Peterborough	OHL	59	13	32	45	70	....	....	....	....	....	....	....	....	....	12	0	5	5	24	....	....	....	....
1987-88	**Toronto**	**NHL**	**78**	**4**	**6**	**10**	**90**	**0**	**0**	**0**	**49**	**8.2**	**–25**	....	....	....	**2**	**0**	**0**	**0**	**0**	**0**	**0**	**0**	....
1988-89	**Toronto**	**NHL**	**55**	**2**	**7**	**9**	**106**	**0**	**0**	**0**	**59**	**3.4**	**–15**	....	....	....	....	....	....	....	....	....	....	....	....
1989-90	**Toronto**	**NHL**	**67**	**4**	**14**	**18**	**122**	**0**	**0**	**0**	**80**	**5.0**	**–1**	....	....	....	**5**	**0**	**0**	**0**	**22**	**0**	**0**	**0**	....
1990-91	**Toronto**	**NHL**	**78**	**1**	**9**	**10**	**238**	**0**	**0**	**0**	**68**	**1.5**	**–28**	....	....	....	....	....	....	....	....	....	....	....	....
1991-92	**Edmonton**	**NHL**	**75**	**2**	**19**	**21**	**118**	**0**	**0**	**0**	**85**	**2.4**	**–9**	....	....	....	**16**	**0**	**5**	**5**	**45**	**0**	**0**	**0**	....
1992-93	**Edmonton**	**NHL**	**82**	**3**	**10**	**13**	**142**	**0**	**2**	**0**	**78**	**3.8**	**–18**	....	....	....	....	....	....	....	....	....	....	....	....
1993-94	**Edmonton**	**NHL**	**69**	**2**	**6**	**8**	**131**	**0**	**0**	**0**	**92**	**2.2**	**–13**	....	....	....	....	....	....	....	....	....	....	....	....
1994-95	**Edmonton**	**NHL**	**46**	**3**	**10**	**13**	**40**	**1**	**1**	**1**	**51**	**5.9**	**–6**	....	....	....	....	....	....	....	....	....	....	....	....
1995-96	**Edmonton**	**NHL**	**82**	**2**	**9**	**11**	**108**	**0**	**0**	**0**	**61**	**3.3**	**–27**	....	....	....	....	....	....	....	....	....	....	....	....
1996-97	**Edmonton**	**NHL**	**82**	**1**	**11**	**12**	**91**	**0**	**0**	**0**	**67**	**1.5**	**9**	....	....	....	**12**	**0**	**2**	**2**	**14**	**0**	**0**	**0**	....

Season	Club	League	Regular Season														Playoffs								
			GP	G	A	Pts	PIM	PP	SH	GW	S	%	+/-	TF	F%	Min	GP	G	A	Pts	PIM	PP	SH	GW	Min
1997-98	Philadelphia	NHL	81	2	3	5	139	2	0	0	57	3.5	7	....	....	....	5	0	0	0	0	0	0	0	....
1998-99	Philadelphia	NHL	78	0	6	6	106	0	0	0	49	0.0	–3	0	0.0	16:33	....	....	....	....	....	....	....	....	....
99-2000	Philadelphia	NHL	74	2	5	7	140	0	0	1	50	4.0	14	0	0.0	16:11	18	0	1	1	41	0	0	0	21:58
2000-01	Philadelphia	NHL	82	2	6	8	131	0	1	0	75	2.7	23	1	0.0	20:42	6	0	0	0	4	0	0	0	24:39
2001-02	Philadelphia	NHL	72	1	8	9	102	0	0	0	65	1.5	18	0	0.0	18:17	5	0	0	0	4	0	0	0	19:18
2002-03	Columbus	NHL	82	0	13	13	73	0	0	0	56	0.0	–16	2	50.0	23:32	....	....	....	....	....	....	....	....	....
2003-04	Columbus	NHL	64	1	5	6	48	0	0	1	34	2.9	–11	0	0.0	20:07	....	....	....	....	....	....	....	....	....
2004-05			DID NOT PLAY																						
2005-06	Columbus	NHL	44	1	6	7	30	0	0	0	24	4.2	–18	0	0.0	15:15	....	....	....	....	....	....	....	....	....
	Toronto	NHL	21	0	3	3	41	0	0	0	16	0.0	–1	0	0.0	18:48	....	....	....	....	....	....	....	....	....
2006-07	Tampa Bay	NHL	27	0	3	3	16	0	0	0	3	0.0	3	0	0.0	7:07	....	....	....	....	....	....	....	....	....
2007-08	Ottawa	NHL	76	2	7	9	41	0	0	0	41	4.9	1	0	0.0	12:19	....	....	....	....	....	....	....	....	....
	NHL Totals		1415	35	166	201	2053	3	4	3	1160	3.0		3	33.3	17:36	69	0	8	8	130	0	0	0	22:04

Traded to **Edmonton** by **Toronto** with Vincent Damphousse, Peter Ing and Scott Thornton for Grant Fuhr, Glenn Anderson and Craig Berube, September 19, 1991. Signed as a free agent by **Philadelphia**, July 23, 1997. Signed as a free agent by **Columbus**, July 4, 2002. Traded to **Toronto** by **Columbus** for Toronto's 5th round choice (Nick Sucharski) in 2006 Entry Draft, March 8, 2006. Signed as a free agent by **Tampa Bay**, July 11, 2006. • Missed majority of 2006-07 season as a healthy reserve. Signed as a free agent by **Ottawa**, August 8, 2007.

RICHMOND, Danny

(RIHCH-muhnd, DA-nee) **PIT.**

Defense. Shoots left. 6', 192 lbs. Born, Chicago, IL, August 1, 1984. Carolina's 2nd choice, 31st overall, in 2003 Entry Draft.

Season	Club	League	GP	G	A	Pts	PIM	PP	SH	GW	S	%	+/-	TF	F%	Min	GP	G	A	Pts	PIM	PP	SH	GW	Min
2000-01	Team Illinois	MWEHL	79	25	40	65	....	....	....	....	....	....	....	....	....	....	....	....	....	....	....	....	....	....	....
2001-02	Chicago Steel	USHL	56	8	45	53	129	....	....	....	....	....	....	....	....	....	4	0	4	4	20	....	....	....	....
2002-03	U. of Michigan	CCHA	43	3	19	22	48	....	....	....	....	....	....	....	....	....	....	....	....	....	....	....	....	....	....
2003-04	London Knights	OHL	59	13	22	35	92	....	....	....	....	....	....	....	....	....	15	5	6	11	10	....	....	....	....
2004-05	Lowell	AHL	63	4	9	13	139	....	....	....	....	....	....	....	....	....	6	0	2	2	8	....	....	....	....
2005-06	Carolina	NHL	10	0	1	1	7	0	0	0	7	0.0	–3	0	0.0	9:00	....	....	....	....	....	....	....	....	....
	Lowell	AHL	32	4	11	15	60	....	....	....	....	....	....	....	....	....	....	....	....	....	....	....	....	....	....
	Chicago	NHL	10	0	0	0	18	0	0	0	6	0.0	–3	0	0.0	13:36	....	....	....	....	....	....	....	....	....
	Norfolk Admirals	AHL	31	4	8	12	42	....	....	....	....	....	....	....	....	....	3	0	1	1	2	....	....	....	....
2006-07	Chicago	NHL	22	0	2	2	48	0	0	0	13	0.0	–1	0	0.0	12:20	....	....	....	....	....	....	....	....	....
	Norfolk Admirals	AHL	57	10	24	34	144	....	....	....	....	....	....	....	....	....	6	0	0	0	8	....	....	....	....
2007-08	Chicago	NHL	7	0	0	0	2	0	0	0	2	0.0	–5	0	0.0	9:24	....	....	....	....	....	....	....	....	....
	Rockford IceHogs	AHL	40	2	12	14	156	....	....	....	....	....	....	....	....	....	....	....	....	....	....	....	....	....	....
	NHL Totals		49	0	3	3	75	0	0	0	28	0.0		0	0.0	11:29	....	....	....	....	....	....	....	....	....

USHL All-Rookie Team (2002) • USHL First All-Star Team (2002) • USHL Rookie of the Year (2002) • CCHA All-Rookie Team (2003)

Left **University of Michigan** (CCHA) and signed with **London** (OHL), June 6, 2003. Traded to **Chicago** by **Carolina** with Columbus' 4th round choice (previously acquired, later traded to Toronto - Toronto selected James Reimer) in 2006 Entry Draft for Anton Babchuk and Chicago's 4th round choice (later traded to St. Louis - St. Louis selected Cade Fairchild) in 2007 Entry Draft, January 20, 2006. Traded to **Pittsburgh** by **Chicago** for Tim Brent, July 17, 2008.

RISSMILLER, Patrick

(RIGHZ-mih-luhr, PAT-rihk) **NYR**

Left wing. Shoots left. 6'4", 220 lbs. Born, Belmont, MA, October 26, 1978.

Season	Club	League	GP	G	A	Pts	PIM	PP	SH	GW	S	%	+/-	TF	F%	Min	GP	G	A	Pts	PIM	PP	SH	GW	Min
1997-98	The Hill School	High-PA	STATISTICS NOT AVAILABLE																						
1998-99	Holy Cross	MAAC	34	13	28	41	23	....	....	....	....	....	....	....	....	....	....	....	....	....	....	....	....	....	....
99-2000	Holy Cross	MAAC	35	10	17	27	22	....	....	....	....	....	....	....	....	....	....	....	....	....	....	....	....	....	....
2000-01	Holy Cross	MAAC	29	14	15	29	40	....	....	....	....	....	....	....	....	....	....	....	....	....	....	....	....	....	....
2001-02	Holy Cross	MAAC	33	16	*30	*46	31	....	....	....	....	....	....	....	....	....	....	....	....	....	....	....	....	....	....
2002-03	Cleveland Barons	AHL	72	14	26	40	24	....	....	....	....	....	....	....	....	....	....	....	....	....	....	....	....	....	....
	Cincinnati	ECHL	2	2	2	4	0	....	....	....	....	....	....	....	....	....	....	....	....	....	....	....	....	....	....
2003-04	San Jose	NHL	4	0	0	0	0	0	0	0	2	0.0	0	26	53.9	7:07	....	....	....	....	....	....	....	....	....
	Cleveland Barons	AHL	75	14	31	45	66	....	....	....	....	....	....	....	....	....	9	0	1	1	8	....	....	....	....
2004-05	Cleveland Barons	AHL	69	21	23	44	50	....	....	....	....	....	....	....	....	....	....	....	....	....	....	....	....	....	....
2005-06	San Jose	NHL	18	3	3	6	8	1	0	1	26	11.5	1	3	0.0	9:22	11	2	1	3	6	0	0	0	8:06
	Cleveland Barons	AHL	68	15	37	52	30	....	....	....	....	....	....	....	....	....	....	....	....	....	....	....	....	....	....
2006-07	San Jose	NHL	79	7	15	22	22	1	0	0	100	7.0	1	25	36.0	12:10	11	1	3	4	0	0	0	1	12:40
2007-08	San Jose	NHL	79	8	9	17	30	0	0	2	119	6.7	–8	214	50.9	13:10	8	0	0	0	4	0	0	0	11:25
	NHL Totals		180	18	27	45	60	2	0	3	247	7.3		268	49.3	12:13	30	3	4	7	10	0	0	1	10:40

MAAC All-Rookie Team (1999) • MAAC First All-Star Team (2002) • MAAC Offensive Player of the Year (2002)

Signed as a free agent by **Cleveland** (AHL), September 23, 2002. Signed as a free agent by **San Jose**, June 30, 2003. Signed as a free agent by **NY Rangers**, July 1, 2008.

RITA, Jani

(REETA, YAH-nee) **PIT.**

Left wing. Shoots left. 6'1", 206 lbs. Born, Helsinki, Finland, July 25, 1981. Edmonton's 1st choice, 13th overall, in 1999 Entry Draft.

Season	Club	League	GP	G	A	Pts	PIM	PP	SH	GW	S	%	+/-	TF	F%	Min	GP	G	A	Pts	PIM	PP	SH	GW	Min
1995-96	Jokerit U18	Fin-U18	5	0	0	0	0	....	....	....	....	....	....	....	....	....	....	....	....	....	....	....	....	....	....
1996-97	Jokerit U18	Fin-U18	27	22	7	29	4	....	....	....	....	....	....	....	....	....	....	....	....	....	....	....	....	....	....
	Jokerit Helsinki Jr.	Fin-Jr.	3	0	0	0	0	....	....	....	....	....	....	....	....	....	....	....	....	....	....	....	....	....	....
1997-98	Jokerit U18	Fin-U18	7	7	4	11	2	....	....	....	....	....	....	....	....	....	....	....	....	....	....	....	....	....	....
	Jokerit Helsinki Jr.	Fin-Jr.	36	15	9	24	2	....	....	....	....	....	....	....	....	....	8	4	1	5	0	....	....	....	....
	Jokerit Helsinki	Finland	....	....	....	....	....	....	....	....	....	....	....	....	....	....	1	0	0	0	0	....	....	....	....
1998-99	Jokerit Helsinki Jr.	Fin-Jr.	20	9	13	22	8	....	....	....	....	....	....	....	....	....	6	1	1	2	8	....	....	....	....
	Jokerit Helsinki	Finland	41	3	2	5	39	....	....	....	....	....	....	....	....	....	....	....	....	....	....	....	....	....	....
	Jokerit Helsinki	EuroHL	3	0	0	0	0	....	....	....	....	....	....	....	....	....	....	....	....	....	....	....	....	....	....
99-2000	Jokerit Helsinki Jr.	Fin-Jr.	1	1	0	1	0	....	....	....	....	....	....	....	....	....	....	....	....	....	....	....	....	....	....
	Jokerit Helsinki	Finland	49	6	3	9	10	....	....	....	....	....	....	....	....	....	11	1	0	1	0	....	....	....	....
2000-01	Jokerit Helsinki Jr.	Fin-Jr.	3	3	2	5	0	....	....	....	....	....	....	....	....	....	....	....	....	....	....	....	....	....	....
	Jokerit Helsinki	Finland	50	5	10	15	18	....	....	....	....	....	....	....	....	....	5	0	0	0	2	....	....	....	....
2001-02	Edmonton	NHL	1	0	0	0	0	0	0	0	0	0.0	0	0	0.0	6:09	....	....	....	....	....	....	....	....	....
	Hamilton	AHL	76	25	17	42	32	....	....	....	....	....	....	....	....	....	15	8	4	12	0	....	....	....	....
2002-03	Edmonton	NHL	12	3	1	4	0	0	0	0	18	16.7	2	1	0.0	9:32	....	....	....	....	....	....	....	....	....
	Hamilton	AHL	64	21	27	48	18	....	....	....	....	....	....	....	....	....	23	3	4	7	2	....	....	....	....
2003-04	Edmonton	NHL	2	0	0	0	0	0	0	0	1	0.0	0	0	0.0	4:34	....	....	....	....	....	....	....	....	....
	Toronto	AHL	64	17	24	41	18	....	....	....	....	....	....	....	....	....	1	1	0	1	0	....	....	....	....
2004-05	HPK Hameenlinna	Finland	56	21	18	39	12	....	....	....	....	....	....	....	....	....	10	7	4	11	4	....	....	....	....
2005-06	Edmonton	NHL	21	3	0	3	6	0	0	0	13	23.1	0	2	0.0	6:46	....	....	....	....	....	....	....	....	....
	Pittsburgh	NHL	30	3	4	7	4	0	0	0	36	8.3	–6	104	45.2	10:06	....	....	....	....	....	....	....	....	....
2006-07	Jokerit Helsinki	Finland	56	*32	20	52	28	....	....	....	....	....	....	....	....	....	10	6	1	7	2	....	....	....	....
2007-08	Jokerit Helsinki	Finland	37	10	10	20	16	....	....	....	....	....	....	....	....	....	14	6	4	10	0	....	....	....	....
	NHL Totals		66	9	5	14	10	0	0	0	68	13.2		107	43.9	8:42	....	....	....	....	....	....	....	....	....

Signed as a free agent by **Hameenlinna** (Finland), August 17, 2004. Traded to **Pittsburgh** by **Edmonton** with Cory Cross for Dick Tarnstrom, January 26, 2006.

RITCHIE, Byron

(RIHT-chee, BIGH-rohn)

Center. Shoots left. 5'10", 190 lbs. Born, Burnaby, B.C., April 24, 1977. Hartford's 6th choice, 165th overall, in 1995 Entry Draft.

Season	Club	League	GP	G	A	Pts	PIM	PP	SH	GW	S	%	+/-	TF	F%	Min	GP	G	A	Pts	PIM	PP	SH	GW	Min
1992-93	North Delta	Minor-BC	60	102	151	253	147	....	....	....	....	....	....	....	....	....	....	....	....	....	....	....	....	....	....
1993-94	Lethbridge	WHL	44	4	11	15	44	....	....	....	....	....	....	....	....	....	6	0	0	0	14	....	....	....	....
1994-95	Lethbridge	WHL	58	22	28	50	132	....	....	....	....	....	....	....	....	....	....	....	....	....	....	....	....	....	....
1995-96	Lethbridge	WHL	66	55	51	106	163	....	....	....	....	....	....	....	....	....	4	0	2	2	4	....	....	....	....
	Springfield	AHL	6	2	1	3	4	....	....	....	....	....	....	....	....	....	8	0	3	3	0	....	....	....	....
1996-97	Lethbridge	WHL	63	50	76	126	115	....	....	....	....	....	....	....	....	....	18	*16	12	*28	28	....	....	....	....
1997-98	New Haven	AHL	65	13	18	31	97	....	....	....	....	....	....	....	....	....	....	....	....	....	....	....	....	....	....
1998-99	Carolina	NHL	3	0	0	0	0	0	0	0	0	0.0	0	5	20.0	3:25	....	....	....	....	....	....	....	....	....
	New Haven	AHL	66	24	33	57	139	....	....	....	....	....	....	....	....	....	....	....	....	....	....	....	....	....	....
99-2000	Carolina	NHL	26	0	2	2	17	0	0	0	13	0.0	–10	155	49.7	7:24	....	....	....	....	....	....	....	....	....
	Cincinnati	IHL	34	8	13	21	81	....	....	....	....	....	....	....	....	....	10	1	6	7	32	....	....	....	....
2000-01	Cincinnati	IHL	77	31	35	66	166	....	....	....	....	....	....	....	....	....	5	3	2	5	10	....	....	....	....
2001-02	Carolina	NHL	4	0	0	0	2	0	0	0	5	0.0	0	9	44.4	11:30	....	....	....	....	....	....	....	....	....
	Lowell	AHL	43	25	30	55	38	....	....	....	....	....	....	....	....	....	....	....	....	....	....	....	....	....	....
	Florida	NHL	31	5	6	11	34	2	0	0	55	9.1	–2	324	50.9	12:26	....	....	....	....	....	....	....	....	....
2002-03	Florida	NHL	30	0	3	3	19	0	0	0	29	0.0	–4	251	48.2	9:18	....	....	....	....	....	....	....	....	....
	San Antonio	AHL	26	3	14	17	68	....	....	....	....	....	....	....	....	....	3	1	0	1	0	....	....	....	....

			Regular Season														Playoffs								
Season	Club	League	GP	G	A	Pts	PIM	PP	SH	GW	S	%	+/-	TF	F%	Min	GP	G	A	Pts	PIM	PP	SH	GW	Min
2003-04	Florida	NHL	50	5	6	11	84	0	0	2	65	7.7	-10	168	48.8	13:54	....	....	....	....	....	....	....	....	....
2004-05	Rogle	Sweden-2	30	17	16	33	111	....	....	....	....	....	....	....	....	....	2	0	0	0	4	....	....	....	....
2005-06	Calgary	NHL	45	4	2	6	69	0	0	0	34	11.8	-2	313	52.4	9:52	7	0	0	0	0	0	0	0	9:15
2006-07	Calgary	NHL	64	8	6	14	68	0	1	0	46	17.4	3	282	50.0	9:46	1	0	0	0	10	0	0	0	4:41
2007-08	Vancouver	NHL	71	3	8	11	80	0	0	0	73	4.1	-10	515	50.9	12:19	....	....	....	....	....	....	....	....	....
	NHL Totals		324	25	33	58	373	2	1	2	320	7.8		2022	50.3	10:58	8	0	0	0	10	0	0	0	8:41

WHL East Second All-Star Team (1996, 1997) • Memorial Cup Tournament All-Star Team (1997)

Rights transferred to **Carolina** after **Hartford** franchise relocated, June 25, 1997. Traded to **Florida** by **Carolina** with Sandis Ozolinsh for Bret Hedican, Kevyn Adams and Tomas Malec, January 16, 2002. Signed as a free agent by **Calgary**, July 2, 2004. Signed as a free agent by **Rogle** (Sweden-2) September 25, 2004. Signed as a free agent by **Vancouver**, July 3, 2007.

RITOLA, Mattias (RIH-toh-lah, mat-TEE-uhs) DET.

Right wing. Shoots left. 6', 192 lbs. Born, Borlange, Sweden, March 14, 1987. Detroit's 4th choice, 103rd overall, in 2005 Entry Draft.

Season	Club	League	GP	G	A	Pts	PIM	PP	SH	GW	S	%	+/-	TF	F%	Min	GP	G	A	Pts	PIM	PP	SH	GW	Min
2003-04	V.Frolunda U18	Swe-U18	11	4	11	15	35	....	....	....	....	....	....	....	....	....	7	2	7	9	12	....	....	....	....
	V.Frolunda Jr.	Swe-Jr.	24	7	4	11	8	....	....	....	....	....	....	....	....	....	5	0	1	1	0	....	....	....	....
2004-05	Frolunda Jr.	Swe-Jr.	9	2	6	8	6	....	....	....	....	....	....	....	....	....	....	....	....	....	....	....	....	....	....
	Leksands IF U18	Swe-U18	STATISTICS NOT AVAILABLE																						
	Leksands IF Jr.	Swe-Jr.	18	8	10	18	14	....	....	....	....	....	....	....	....	....	5	1	1	2	2	....	....	....	....
2005-06	Leksands IF Jr.	Swe-Jr.	14	4	2	6	16	....	....	....	....	....	....	....	....	....	....	....	....	....	....	....	....	....	....
	Leksands IF	Sweden	30	0	3	3	10	....	....	....	....	....	....	....	....	....	....	....	....	....	....	....	....	....	....
	Leksands IF	Sweden-Q	8	0	0	0	4	....	....	....	....	....	....	....	....	....	....	....	....	....	....	....	....	....	....
2006-07	Leksands IF Jr.	Swe-Jr.	12	5	7	12	16	....	....	....	....	....	....	....	....	....	....	....	....	....	....	....	....	....	....
	Leksands IF	Sweden-2	23	1	4	5	4	....	....	....	....	....	....	....	....	....	....	....	....	....	....	....	....	....	....
	IFK Arboga IK	Sweden-2	3	1	0	1	2	....	....	....	....	....	....	....	....	....	....	....	....	....	....	....	....	....	....
	Borlange HF	Sweden-3	11	4	6	10	14	....	....	....	....	....	....	....	....	....	....	....	....	....	....	....	....	....	....
2007-08	Detroit	NHL	2	0	1	1	0	0	0	0	2	0.0	0	0	0.0	5:47	....	....	....	....	....	....	....	....	....
	Grand Rapids	AHL	72	7	15	22	62	....	....	....	....	....	....	....	....	....	....	....	....	....	....	....	....	....	....
	NHL Totals		2	0	1	1	0	0	0	0	2	0.0		0	0.0	5:47	....	....	....	....	....	....	....	....	....

RIVERS, Jamie (RIH-vuhrs, JAY-mee)

Defense. Shoots left. 6'1", 206 lbs. Born, Ottawa, Ont., March 16, 1975. St. Louis' 2nd choice, 63rd overall, in 1993 Entry Draft.

Season	Club	League	GP	G	A	Pts	PIM	PP	SH	GW	S	%	+/-	TF	F%	Min	GP	G	A	Pts	PIM	PP	SH	GW	Min
1989-90	Ottawa South	ODMHA	50	26	46	72	46	....	....	....	....	....	....	....	....	....	....	....	....	....	....	....	....	....	....
1990-91	Ott. Jr. Senators	CJHL	55	4	30	34	74	....	....	....	....	....	....	....	....	....	....	....	....	....	....	....	....	....	....
1991-92	Sudbury Wolves	OHL	55	3	13	16	20	....	....	....	....	....	....	....	....	....	8	0	0	0	0	....	....	....	....
1992-93	Sudbury Wolves	OHL	62	12	43	55	20	....	....	....	....	....	....	....	....	....	14	7	19	26	4	....	....	....	....
1993-94	Sudbury Wolves	OHL	65	32	*89	121	58	....	....	....	....	....	....	....	....	....	10	1	9	10	14	....	....	....	....
1994-95	Sudbury Wolves	OHL	46	9	56	65	30	....	....	....	....	....	....	....	....	....	18	7	26	33	22	....	....	....	....
1995-96	St. Louis	NHL	3	0	0	0	2	0	0	0	5	0.0	-1	....	....	....	....	....	....	....	....	....	....	....	....
	Worcester IceCats	AHL	75	7	45	52	130	....	....	....	....	....	....	....	....	....	4	0	1	1	4	....	....	....	....
1996-97	St. Louis	NHL	15	2	5	7	6	1	0	0	9	22.2	-4	....	....	....	....	....	....	....	....	....	....	....	....
	Worcester IceCats	AHL	63	8	35	43	83	....	....	....	....	....	....	....	....	....	5	1	2	3	14	....	....	....	....
1997-98	St. Louis	NHL	59	2	4	6	36	1	0	1	53	3.8	5	....	....	....	....	....	....	....	....	....	....	....	....
1998-99	St. Louis	NHL	76	2	5	7	47	1	0	0	78	2.6	-3	0	0.0	14:10	9	1	1	2	2	1	0	1	6:29
99-2000	NY Islanders	NHL	75	1	16	17	84	1	0	0	95	1.1	-4	0	0.0	19:39	....	....	....	....	....	....	....	....	....
2000-01	Ottawa	NHL	45	2	4	6	44	0	0	0	41	4.9	6	0	0.0	14:01	1	0	0	0	4	0	0	0	12:45
	Grand Rapids	IHL	2	0	0	0	2	....	....	....	....	....	....	....	....	....	....	....	....	....	....	....	....	....	....
2001-02	Ottawa	NHL	2	0	0	0	4	0	0	0	3	0.0	-3	0	0.0	11:37	....	....	....	....	....	....	....	....	....
	Boston	NHL	64	4	2	6	45	1	0	1	48	8.3	6	39	33.3	8:27	3	0	0	0	0	0	0	0	4:57
2002-03	Florida	NHL	1	0	0	0	2	0	0	0	2	0.0	-2	0	0.0	18:27	....	....	....	....	....	....	....	....	....
	San Antonio	AHL	50	6	19	25	68	....	....	....	....	....	....	....	....	....	3	0	1	1	10	....	....	....	....
2003-04	Detroit	NHL	50	3	4	7	41	0	0	0	31	9.7	9	1	0.0	10:14	2	0	0	0	2	0	0	0	5:40
	Grand Rapids	AHL	2	0	0	0	4	....	....	....	....	....	....	....	....	....	....	....	....	....	....	....	....	....	....
2004-05	Hershey Bears	AHL	50	7	13	20	46	....	....	....	....	....	....	....	....	....	....	....	....	....	....	....	....	....	....
2005-06	Detroit	NHL	15	0	1	1	12	0	0	0	4	0.0	0	0	0.0	8:51	....	....	....	....	....	....	....	....	....
	Phoenix	NHL	18	0	5	5	26	0	0	0	32	0.0	2	0	0.0	20:06	....	....	....	....	....	....	....	....	....
2006-07	St. Louis	NHL	31	1	3	4	36	1	0	0	17	5.9	-7	0	0.0	14:11	....	....	....	....	....	....	....	....	....
	Peoria Rivermen	AHL	30	4	19	23	24	....	....	....	....	....	....	....	....	....	....	....	....	....	....	....	....	....	....
2007-08	Spartak Moscow	Russia	19	0	3	3	42	....	....	....	....	....	....	....	....	....	4	0	0	0	8	....	....	....	....
	NHL Totals		454	17	49	66	385	6	0	2	418	4.1		40	32.5	13:49	15	1	1	2	8	1	0	1	6:29

OHL First All-Star Team (1994) • Canadian Major Junior Second All-Star Team (1994) • OHL Second All-Star Team (1995) • AHL Second All-Star Team (1997)

Claimed by **NY Islanders** from **St. Louis** in Waiver Draft, September 27, 1999. Signed as a free agent by **Ottawa**, November 30, 2000. Claimed on waivers by **Boston** from **Ottawa**, October 13, 2001. Signed as a free agent by **San Antonio** (AHL), November 2, 2002. Signed as a free agent by **Florida**, December 16, 2002. Signed as a free agent by **Detroit**, July 29, 2003. Signed as a free agent by **Hershey** (AHL), November 3, 2004. Traded to **Phoenix** by **Detroit** for Phoenix's 7th round choice (Nick Oslund) in 2006 Entry Draft, March 9, 2006. • Missed majority of 2005-06 season as a healthy reserve. Signed as a free agent by **St. Louis**, August 18, 2006. Signed as a free agent by **Montreal**, July 5, 2007.

RIVET, Craig (rih-VAY, KRAYG) BUF.

Defense. Shoots right. 6'2", 210 lbs. Born, North Bay, Ont., September 13, 1974. Montreal's 4th choice, 68th overall, in 1992 Entry Draft.

Season	Club	League	GP	G	A	Pts	PIM	PP	SH	GW	S	%	+/-	TF	F%	Min	GP	G	A	Pts	PIM	PP	SH	GW	Min
1990-91	Barrie Colts	OHA-B	42	9	17	26	55	....	....	....	....	....	....	....	....	....	....	....	....	....	....	....	....	....	....
1991-92	Kingston	OHL	66	5	21	26	97	....	....	....	....	....	....	....	....	....	....	....	....	....	....	....	....	....	....
1992-93	Kingston	OHL	64	19	55	74	117	....	....	....	....	....	....	....	....	....	16	5	7	12	39	....	....	....	....
1993-94	Kingston	OHL	61	12	52	64	100	....	....	....	....	....	....	....	....	....	6	0	3	3	6	....	....	....	....
	Fredericton	AHL	4	0	2	2	2	....	....	....	....	....	....	....	....	....	....	....	....	....	....	....	....	....	....
1994-95	Fredericton	AHL	78	5	27	32	126	....	....	....	....	....	....	....	....	....	12	0	4	4	17	....	....	....	....
	Montreal	NHL	5	0	1	1	5	0	0	0	2	0.0	2	....	....	....	....	....	....	....	....	....	....	....	....
1995-96	Montreal	NHL	19	1	4	5	54	0	0	0	9	11.1	4	....	....	....	....	....	....	....	....	....	....	....	....
	Fredericton	AHL	49	5	18	23	189	....	....	....	....	....	....	....	....	....	6	0	0	0	12	....	....	....	....
1996-97	Montreal	NHL	35	0	4	4	54	0	0	0	24	0.0	7	....	....	....	5	0	1	1	14	0	0	0	....
	Fredericton	AHL	23	3	12	15	99	....	....	....	....	....	....	....	....	....	....	....	....	....	....	....	....	....	....
1997-98	Montreal	NHL	61	0	2	2	93	0	0	0	26	0.0	-3	....	....	....	5	0	0	0	2	0	0	0	....
1998-99	Montreal	NHL	66	2	8	10	66	0	0	0	39	5.1	-3	0	0.0	14:20	....	....	....	....	....	....	....	....	....
99-2000	Montreal	NHL	61	3	14	17	76	0	0	1	71	4.2	11	0	0.0	19:03	....	....	....	....	....	....	....	....	....
2000-01	Montreal	NHL	26	1	2	3	36	0	0	0	22	4.5	-8	0	0.0	19:04	....	....	....	....	....	....	....	....	....
2001-02	Montreal	NHL	82	8	17	25	76	0	0	0	90	8.9	1	1	0.0	19:00	12	0	3	3	4	0	0	0	21:26
2002-03	Montreal	NHL	82	7	15	22	71	3	0	2	118	5.9	1	0	0.0	22:00	....	....	....	....	....	....	....	....	....
2003-04	Montreal	NHL	80	4	8	12	98	2	0	1	96	4.2	-1	0	0.0	19:28	11	1	4	5	2	1	0	0	24:07
2004-05	TPS Turku	Finland	18	3	1	4	28	....	....	....	....	....	....	....	....	....	6	0	0	0	39	....	....	....	....
2005-06	Montreal	NHL	82	7	27	34	109	5	0	1	122	5.7	-5	2	0.0	22:27	6	0	2	2	2	0	0	0	24:09
2006-07	Montreal	NHL	54	6	10	16	57	2	0	0	58	10.3	-7	0	0.0	21:04	....	....	....	....	....	....	....	....	....
	San Jose	NHL	17	1	7	8	12	0	0	0	31	3.2	8	0	0.0	23:31	11	2	3	5	18	1	0	0	25:18
2007-08	San Jose	NHL	74	5	30	35	104	2	0	0	105	4.8	3	0	0.0	21:12	13	0	6	6	16	0	0	0	23:01
	NHL Totals		744	45	149	194	911	14	0	5	813	5.5		3	0.0	19:59	63	3	19	22	58	2	0	0	23:29

• Missed majority of 2000-01 season recovering from shoulder injury suffered in game vs. Vancouver, October 30, 2000. Signed as a free agent by **Turku** (Finland), January 11, 2005. Traded to **San Jose** by **Montreal** with Montreal's 5th round choice (Julien Demers) in 2008 Entry Draft for Josh Gorges and San Jose's 1st round choice (Max Pacioretty) in 2007 Entry Draft, February 25, 2007. Traded to **Buffalo** by **San Jose** with San Jose's 7th round choice in 2010 Entry Draft for Buffalo's 2nd round choice in 2009 Entry Draft and Buffalo's 2nd round choice in 2010 Entry Draft, July 4, 2008.

ROBERTS, Gary (RAW-buhrts, GAIR-ree) T.B.

Left wing. Shoots left. 6'2", 215 lbs. Born, North York, Ont., May 23, 1966. Calgary's 1st choice, 12th overall, in 1984 Entry Draft.

Season	Club	League	GP	G	A	Pts	PIM	PP	SH	GW	S	%	+/-	TF	F%	Min	GP	G	A	Pts	PIM	PP	SH	GW	Min
1980-81	Hamilton Kilty B's	OHA-B	3	0	1	1	0	....	....	....	....	....	....	....	....	....	....	....	....	....	....	....	....	....	....
1981-82	Whitby	Minor-ON	44	55	31	86	133	....	....	....	....	....	....	....	....	....	....	....	....	....	....	....	....	....	....
1982-83	Ottawa 67's	OHL	53	12	8	20	83	....	....	....	....	....	....	....	....	....	5	1	0	1	19	....	....	....	....
1983-84	Ottawa 67's	OHL	48	27	30	57	144	....	....	....	....	....	....	....	....	....	13	10	7	17	62	....	....	....	....
1984-85	Ottawa 67's	OHL	59	44	62	106	186	....	....	....	....	....	....	....	....	....	5	2	8	10	10	....	....	....	....
	Moncton	AHL	7	4	2	6	7	....	....	....	....	....	....	....	....	....	....	....	....	....	....	....	....	....	....
1985-86	Ottawa 67's	OHL	24	26	25	51	83	....	....	....	....	....	....	....	....	....	....	....	....	....	....	....	....	....	....
	Guelph Platers	OHL	23	18	15	33	65	....	....	....	....	....	....	....	....	....	20	18	13	31	43	....	....	....	....
1986-87	Calgary	NHL	32	5	10	15	85	0	0	0	38	13.2	6	....	....	....	2	0	0	0	4	0	0	0	....
	Moncton	AHL	38	20	18	38	72	....	....	....	....	....	....	....	....	....	....	....	....	....	....	....	....	....	....
1987-88	Calgary	NHL	74	13	15	28	282	0	0	1	118	11.0	24	....	....	....	9	2	3	5	29	0	0	0	....

			Regular Season														Playoffs								
Season	Club	League	GP	G	A	Pts	PIM	PP	SH	GW	S	%	+/-	TF	F%	Min	GP	G	A	Pts	PIM	PP	SH	GW	Min
1988-89 ♦	**Calgary**	**NHL**	**71**	**22**	**16**	**38**	**250**	**0**	**1**	**2**	**123**	**17.9**	**32**	....	....	....	**22**	**5**	**7**	**12**	**57**	**0**	**0**	**0**	....
1989-90	**Calgary**	**NHL**	**78**	**39**	**33**	**72**	**222**	**5**	**0**	**5**	**175**	**22.3**	**31**	....	....	....	**6**	**2**	**5**	**7**	**41**	**0**	**0**	**0**	....
1990-91	**Calgary**	**NHL**	**80**	**22**	**31**	**53**	**252**	**0**	**0**	**3**	**132**	**16.7**	**15**	....	....	....	**7**	**1**	**3**	**4**	**18**	**0**	**0**	**0**	....
1991-92	**Calgary**	**NHL**	**76**	**53**	**37**	**90**	**207**	**15**	**0**	**2**	**196**	**27.0**	**32**	....	....	....	....	....	....	....	....	....	....	....	....
1992-93	**Calgary**	**NHL**	**58**	**38**	**41**	**79**	**172**	**8**	**3**	**4**	**166**	**22.9**	**32**	....	....	....	**5**	**1**	**6**	**7**	**43**	**1**	**0**	**0**	....
1993-94	**Calgary**	**NHL**	**73**	**41**	**43**	**84**	**145**	**12**	**3**	**5**	**202**	**20.3**	**37**	....	....	....	**7**	**2**	**6**	**8**	**24**	**1**	**0**	**1**	....
1994-95	**Calgary**	**NHL**	**8**	**2**	**2**	**4**	**43**	**2**	**0**	**0**	**20**	**10.0**	**1**	....	....	....	....	....	....	....	....	....	....	....	....
1995-96	**Calgary**	**NHL**	**35**	**22**	**20**	**42**	**78**	**9**	**0**	**5**	**84**	**26.2**	**15**	....	....	....	....	....	....	....	....	....	....	....	....
1996-97	**Calgary**	**NHL**	DID NOT PLAY – INJURED														....	....	....	....	....	....	....	....	....
1997-98	**Carolina**	**NHL**	**61**	**20**	**29**	**49**	**103**	**4**	**0**	**2**	**106**	**18.9**	**3**	....	....	....	....	....	....	....	....	....	....	....	....
1998-99	**Carolina**	**NHL**	**77**	**14**	**28**	**42**	**178**	**1**	**1**	**4**	**138**	**10.1**	**2**	**15**	**46.7**	**19:36**	**6**	**1**	**1**	**2**	**8**	**0**	**0**	**0**	**21:01**
99-2000	**Carolina**	**NHL**	**69**	**23**	**30**	**53**	**62**	**12**	**0**	**1**	**150**	**15.3**	**–10**	**7**	**28.6**	**18:31**	....	....	....	....	....	....	....	....	....
2000-01	**Toronto**	**NHL**	**82**	**29**	**24**	**53**	**109**	**8**	**2**	**3**	**138**	**21.0**	**16**	**13**	**46.2**	**17:08**	**11**	**2**	**9**	**11**	**0**	**0**	**0**	**0**	**19:49**
2001-02	**Toronto**	**NHL**	**69**	**21**	**27**	**48**	**63**	**6**	**2**	**2**	**122**	**17.2**	**–4**	**6**	**33.3**	**17:23**	**19**	**7**	**12**	**19**	**56**	**3**	**0**	**1**	**19:28**
2002-03	**Toronto**	**NHL**	**14**	**5**	**3**	**8**	**10**	**3**	**0**	**0**	**22**	**22.7**	**–2**	**4**	**50.0**	**15:35**	**7**	**1**	**1**	**2**	**8**	**0**	**0**	**0**	**21:04**
2003-04	**Toronto**	**NHL**	**72**	**28**	**20**	**48**	**84**	**11**	**1**	**7**	**124**	**22.6**	**9**	**12**	**33.3**	**17:33**	**13**	**4**	**4**	**8**	**10**	**2**	**0**	**1**	**17:45**
2004-05			DID NOT PLAY																						
2005-06	**Florida**	**NHL**	**58**	**14**	**26**	**40**	**51**	**4**	**0**	**1**	**122**	**11.5**	**4**	**19**	**31.6**	**16:45**	....	....	....	....	....	....	....	....	....
2006-07	**Florida**	**NHL**	**50**	**13**	**16**	**29**	**71**	**2**	**0**	**3**	**94**	**13.8**	**5**	**28**	**60.7**	**17:05**	....	....	....	....	....	....	....	....	....
	Pittsburgh	**NHL**	**19**	**7**	**6**	**13**	**26**	**4**	**0**	**1**	**31**	**22.6**	**–5**	**3**	**66.7**	**15:47**	**5**	**2**	**2**	**4**	**2**	**1**	**0**	**0**	**17:07**
2007-08	**Pittsburgh**	**NHL**	**38**	**3**	**12**	**15**	**40**	**1**	**0**	**0**	**41**	**7.3**	**–3**	**7**	**71.4**	**13:20**	**11**	**2**	**2**	**4**	**32**	**1**	**0**	**1**	**10:16**
	NHL Totals		**1194**	**434**	**469**	**903**	**2533**	**107**	**13**	**51**	**2342**	**18.5**		**114**	**46.5**	**17:21**	**130**	**32**	**61**	**93**	**332**	**9**	**0**	**4**	**17:55**

OHL Second All-Star Team (1985, 1986) • Bill Masterton Memorial Trophy (1996)

Played in NHL All-Star Game (1992, 1993, 2004)

• Missed remainder of 1994-95 season and majority of 1995-96 season recovering from neck injury suffered in game vs. Toronto, February 4, 1995. • Missed remainder of 1995-96 season and entire 1996-97 season recovering from neck injury suffered in game vs. Vancouver, April 3, 1996. Traded to **Carolina** by **Calgary** with Trevor Kidd for Andrew Cassels and Jean-Sebastien Giguere, August 25, 1997. Signed as a free agent by **Toronto**, July 4, 2000. • Missed majority of 2002-03 season recovering from off-season shoulder surgery, August 13, 2002. Signed as a free agent by **Florida**, August 1, 2005. Traded to **Pittsburgh** by **Florida** for Noah Welch, February 27, 2007. Rights traded to **Tampa Bay** by **Pittsburgh** with the rights to Ryan Malone for Tampa Bay's 3rd round choice in 2009 Entry Draft, June 28, 2008.

ROBIDAS, Stephane

(ROH-bih-dah, STEH-fan) **DAL.**

Defense. Shoots right. 5'11", 190 lbs. Born, Sherbrooke, Que., March 3, 1977. Montreal's 7th choice, 164th overall, in 1995 Entry Draft.

1992-93	Magog	QAAA	41	3	12	15	16	....	....	....	....	....	....	....	....	....	5	1	1	2	2	....	....	....	....
1993-94	Shawinigan	QMJHL	67	3	18	21	33	....	....	....	....	....	....	....	....	....	1	0	0	0	0	....	....	....	....
1994-95	Shawinigan	QMJHL	71	13	56	69	44	....	....	....	....	....	....	....	....	....	15	7	12	19	4	....	....	....	....
1995-96	Shawinigan	QMJHL	67	23	56	79	53	....	....	....	....	....	....	....	....	....	6	1	5	6	10	....	....	....	....
1996-97	Shawinigan	QMJHL	67	24	51	75	59	....	....	....	....	....	....	....	....	....	7	4	6	10	14	....	....	....	....
1997-98	Fredericton	AHL	79	10	21	31	50	....	....	....	....	....	....	....	....	....	4	0	2	2	0	....	....	....	....
1998-99	Fredericton	AHL	79	8	33	41	59	....	....	....	....	....	....	....	....	....	15	1	5	6	10	....	....	....	....
99-2000	**Montreal**	**NHL**	**1**	**0**	**0**	**0**	**0**	**0**	**0**	**0**	**0**	**0.0**	**0**	**0**	**0.0**	**15:54**	....	....	....	....	....	....	....	....	....
	Quebec Citadelles	AHL	76	14	31	45	36	....	....	....	....	....	....	....	....	....	3	0	1	1	0	....	....	....	....
2000-01	**Montreal**	**NHL**	**65**	**6**	**6**	**12**	**14**	**1**	**0**	**0**	**77**	**7.8**	**0**	**1**	**100.0**	**20:44**	....	....	....	....	....	....	....	....	....
2001-02	**Montreal**	**NHL**	**56**	**1**	**10**	**11**	**14**	**1**	**0**	**0**	**68**	**1.5**	**–25**	**3**	**33.3**	**18:58**	....	....	....	....	....	....	....	....	....
2002-03	**Dallas**	**NHL**	**76**	**3**	**7**	**10**	**35**	**0**	**0**	**1**	**47**	**6.4**	**15**	**1**	**100.0**	**12:54**	**2**	**0**	**0**	**0**	**4**	**0**	**0**	**0**	**13:07**
2003-04	**Dallas**	**NHL**	**14**	**1**	**0**	**1**	**8**	**1**	**0**	**0**	**8**	**12.5**	**–2**	**1**	**100.0**	**12:57**	**12**	**0**	**1**	**1**	**20**	**0**	**0**	**0**	**13:54**
	Chicago	**NHL**	**45**	**2**	**10**	**12**	**33**	**0**	**1**	**1**	**55**	**3.6**	**6**	**0**	**0.0**	**20:56**	....	....	....	....	....	....	....	....	....
2004-05	Frankfurt Lions	Germany	51	15	32	47	64	....	....	....	....	....	....	....	....	....	6	1	2	3	6	....	....	....	....
2005-06	**Dallas**	**NHL**	**75**	**5**	**15**	**20**	**67**	**1**	**1**	**0**	**95**	**5.3**	**15**	**0**	**0.0**	**16:59**	**5**	**0**	**2**	**2**	**4**	**0**	**0**	**0**	**16:42**
2006-07	**Dallas**	**NHL**	**75**	**0**	**17**	**17**	**86**	**0**	**0**	**0**	**106**	**0.0**	**–1**	**0**	**0.0**	**18:04**	**7**	**0**	**1**	**1**	**2**	**0**	**0**	**0**	**19:02**
2007-08	**Dallas**	**NHL**	**82**	**9**	**17**	**26**	**85**	**7**	**0**	**2**	**153**	**5.9**	**0**	**0**	**0.0**	**20:39**	**18**	**3**	**8**	**11**	**12**	**3**	**0**	**0**	**25:31**
	NHL Totals		**489**	**27**	**82**	**109**	**342**	**11**	**2**	**4**	**609**	**4.4**		**6**	**66.7**	**18:06**	**44**	**3**	**12**	**15**	**42**	**3**	**0**	**0**	**19:45**

QMJHL First All-Star Team (1996, 1997)

Claimed by **Atlanta** from **Montreal** in Waiver Draft, October 4, 2002. Traded to **Dallas** by **Atlanta** for future considerations, October 4, 2002. Traded to **Chicago** by **Dallas** with Dallas' 2nd round choice (Jakub Sindel) in 2004 Entry Draft for Jon Klemm and NY Rangers' 4th round choice (previously acquired, Dallas selected Fredrik Naslund) in 2004 Entry Draft, November 17, 2003. Signed as a free agent by **Frankfurt** (Germany), September 17, 2004. Signed as a free agent by **Dallas**, August 6, 2005.

ROBINSON, Nathan

(RAW-bihn-suhn, NAY-thuhn) **BOS.**

Center. Shoots left. 5'9", 181 lbs. Born, Scarborough, Ont., December 31, 1981.

1998-99	Belleville Bulls	OHL	50	11	8	19	23	....	....	....	....	....	....	....	....	....	21	4	4	8	14	....	....	....	....
99-2000	Belleville Bulls	OHL	61	19	18	37	45	....	....	....	....	....	....	....	....	....	15	3	4	7	10	....	....	....	....
2000-01	Belleville Bulls	OHL	66	32	37	69	57	....	....	....	....	....	....	....	....	....	10	6	10	16	7	....	....	....	....
2001-02	Belleville Bulls	OHL	67	47	63	*110	74	....	....	....	....	....	....	....	....	....	11	8	6	14	10	....	....	....	....
2002-03	Toledo Storm	ECHL	9	5	9	14	29	....	....	....	....	....	....	....	....	....	....	....	....	....	....	....	....	....	....
	Grand Rapids	AHL	53	3	14	17	24	....	....	....	....	....	....	....	....	....	8	0	3	3	0	....	....	....	....
2003-04	**Detroit**	**NHL**	**5**	**0**	**0**	**0**	**2**	**0**	**0**	**0**	**5**	**0.0**	**–1**	**0**	**0.0**	**6:01**	....	....	....	....	....	....	....	....	....
	Grand Rapids	AHL	69	24	26	50	41	....	....	....	....	....	....	....	....	....	3	0	0	0	2	....	....	....	....
2004-05	Grand Rapids	AHL	50	8	16	24	10	....	....	....	....	....	....	....	....	....	....	....	....	....	....	....	....	....	....
	Syracuse Crunch	AHL	19	6	14	20	18	....	....	....	....	....	....	....	....	....	....	....	....	....	....	....	....	....	....
2005-06	**Boston**	**NHL**	**2**	**0**	**0**	**0**	**0**	**0**	**0**	**0**	**1**	**0.0**	**0**	**0**	**0.0**	**3:32**	....	....	....	....	....	....	....	....	....
	Providence Bruins	AHL	70	29	31	60	55	....	....	....	....	....	....	....	....	....	6	4	5	9	2	....	....	....	....
2006-07	Adler Mannheim	Germany	50	15	29	44	34	....	....	....	....	....	....	....	....	....	11	4	7	11	26	....	....	....	....
2007-08	Eisbaren Berlin	Germany	56	14	40	54	62	....	....	....	....	....	....	....	....	....	13	4	*11	*15	29	....	....	....	....
	NHL Totals		**7**	**0**	**0**	**0**	**2**	**0**	**0**	**0**	**6**	**0.0**		**0**	**0.0**	**5:18**	....	....	....	....	....	....	....	....	....

OHL First All-Star Team (2002) • Canadian Major Junior First All-Star Team (2002)

Signed as a free agent by **Detroit**, October 12, 2002. Loaned to **Syracuse** (AHL) by **Grand Rapids** (AHL) for loan of Jeff Panzer, March 11, 2005. Signed as a free agent by **Boston**, August 15, 2005.

ROBITAILLE, Louis

(ROH-buh-tigh, LOO-ee)

Left wing. Shoots left. 6'1", 192 lbs. Born, Montreal, Que., March 16, 1982.

99-2000	Montreal Rocket	QMJHL	71	3	21	24	266	....	....	....	....	....	....	....	....	....	5	1	1	2	18	....	....	....	....
2000-01	Montreal Rocket	QMJHL	69	2	10	12	269	....	....	....	....	....	....	....	....	....	....	....	....	....	....	....	....	....	....
2001-02	Montreal Rocket	QMJHL	71	3	28	31	294	....	....	....	....	....	....	....	....	....	7	3	0	3	241	....	....	....	....
2002-03	Montreal Rocket	QMJHL	60	7	23	30	191	....	....	....	....	....	....	....	....	....	7	0	10	10	12	....	....	....	....
2003-04	Portland Pirates	AHL	58	1	5	6	103	....	....	....	....	....	....	....	....	....	5	1	0	1	17	....	....	....	....
	Quad City	UHL	2	0	1	1	10	....	....	....	....	....	....	....	....	....	....	....	....	....	....	....	....	....	....
2004-05	Portland Pirates	AHL	59	2	3	5	186	....	....	....	....	....	....	....	....	....	....	....	....	....	....	....	....	....	....
2005-06	**Washington**	**NHL**	**2**	**0**	**0**	**0**	**5**	**0**	**0**	**0**	**0**	**0.0**	**–1**	**0**	**0.0**	**4:42**	....	....	....	....	....	....	....	....	....
	Hershey Bears	AHL	65	7	12	19	334	....	....	....	....	....	....	....	....	....	21	0	2	2	64	....	....	....	....
2006-07	Hershey Bears	AHL	67	6	8	14	254	....	....	....	....	....	....	....	....	....	13	0	1	1	30	....	....	....	....
2007-08	Hershey Bears	AHL	68	4	8	12	*350	....	....	....	....	....	....	....	....	....	5	0	0	0	30	....	....	....	....
	NHL Totals		**2**	**0**	**0**	**0**	**5**	**0**	**0**	**0**	**0**	**0.0**		**0**	**0.0**	**4:42**	....	....	....	....	....	....	....	....	....

Signed as a free agent by **Washington**, August 24, 2004.

ROBITAILLE, Randy

(ROH-buh-tigh, RAN-dee)

Center. Shoots left. 5'11", 200 lbs. Born, Ottawa, Ont., October 12, 1975.

1993-94	Ott. Jr. Senators	CJHL	57	33	55	88	31	....	....	....	....	....	....	....	....	....	....	....	....	....	....	....	....	....	....
1994-95	Ott. Jr. Senators	CJHL	54	48	77	*125	111	....	....	....	....	....	....	....	....	....	....	....	....	....	....	....	....	....	....
1995-96	Miami U.	CCHA	36	14	31	45	26	....	....	....	....	....	....	....	....	....	....	....	....	....	....	....	....	....	....
1996-97	Miami U.	CCHA	39	27	34	61	44	....	....	....	....	....	....	....	....	....	....	....	....	....	....	....	....	....	....
	Boston	**NHL**	**1**	**0**	**0**	**0**	**0**	**0**	**0**	**0**	**0**	**0.0**	**0**	....	....	....	....	....	....	....	....	....	....	....	....
1997-98	**Boston**	**NHL**	**4**	**0**	**0**	**0**	**0**	**0**	**0**	**0**	**5**	**0.0**	**–2**	....	....	....	....	....	....	....	....	....	....	....	....
	Providence Bruins	AHL	48	15	29	44	16	....	....	....	....	....	....	....	....	....	....	....	....	....	....	....	....	....	....
1998-99	**Boston**	**NHL**	**4**	**0**	**2**	**2**	**0**	**0**	**0**	**0**	**5**	**0.0**	**–1**	**24**	**25.0**	**10:11**	**1**	**0**	**0**	**0**	**0**	**0**	**0**	**0**	**7:14**
	Providence Bruins	AHL	74	28	*74	102	34	....	....	....	....	....	....	....	....	....	19	6	*14	20	20	....	....	....	....
99-2000	**Nashville**	**NHL**	**69**	**11**	**14**	**25**	**10**	**2**	**0**	**1**	**113**	**9.7**	**–13**	**528**	**51.5**	**12:52**	....	....	....	....	....	....	....	....	....

			Regular Season														Playoffs								
Season	Club	League	GP	G	A	Pts	PIM	PP	SH	GW	S	%	+/-	TF	F%	Min	GP	G	A	Pts	PIM	PP	SH	GW	Min
2000-01	**Nashville**	**NHL**	**62**	**9**	**17**	**26**	**12**	**5**	**0**	**0**	**121**	**7.4**	**–11**	**481**	**48.4**	**14:10**									
	Milwaukee	IHL	19	10	23	33	4																		
2001-02	**Los Angeles**	**NHL**	**18**	**4**	**3**	**7**	**17**	**2**	**0**	**0**	**30**	**13.3**	**–9**	**60**	**65.0**	**12:54**									
	Manchester	AHL	6	7	3	10	0																		
	Pittsburgh	**NHL**	**40**	**10**	**20**	**30**	**16**	**3**	**0**	**1**	**91**	**11.0**	**–14**	**599**	**51.4**	**18:08**									
2002-03	**Pittsburgh**	**NHL**	**41**	**5**	**12**	**17**	**8**	**1**	**0**	**2**	**61**	**8.2**	**5**	**429**	**55.9**	**13:58**									
	NY Islanders	**NHL**	**10**	**1**	**2**	**3**	**2**	**1**	**0**	**0**	**8**	**12.5**	**0**	**68**	**48.5**	**12:28**	**5**	**1**	**1**	**2**	**0**	**1**	**0**	**0**	**13:03**
2003-04	**Atlanta**	**NHL**	**69**	**11**	**26**	**37**	**20**	**5**	**0**	**2**	**121**	**9.1**	**–12**	**1069**	**50.2**	**15:51**									
2004-05	ZSC Lions Zurich	Swiss	36	22	*45	*67	56										15	2	16	18	10				
2005-06	**Minnesota**	**NHL**	**67**	**12**	**28**	**40**	**54**	**7**	**0**	**2**	**112**	**10.7**	**–5**	**381**	**51.4**	**14:44**									
2006-07	**Philadelphia**	**NHL**	**28**	**5**	**12**	**17**	**22**	**2**	**0**	**0**	**46**	**10.9**	**–4**	**280**	**53.6**	**14:34**									
	NY Islanders	**NHL**	**50**	**6**	**17**	**23**	**22**	**1**	**0**	**1**	**74**	**8.1**	**–2**	**519**	**53.2**	**13:54**	**5**	**0**	**2**	**2**	**8**	**0**	**0**	**0**	**14:12**
2007-08	Yaroslavl	Russia	14	3	5	8	10																		
	Ottawa	**NHL**	**68**	**10**	**19**	**29**	**18**	**1**	**0**	**1**	**99**	**10.1**	**4**	**142**	**57.8**	**13:34**	**2**	**0**	**1**	**1**	**0**	**0**	**0**	**0**	**11:33**
	NHL Totals		**531**	**84**	**172**	**256**	**201**	**30**	**0**	**10**	**886**	**9.5**		**4580**	**51.8**	**14:23**	**13**	**1**	**4**	**5**	**8**	**1**	**0**	**0**	**12:49**

CCHA First All-Star Team (1997) • NCAA West First All-American Team (1997) • AHL First All-Star Team (1999) • Les Cunningham Award (MVP – AHL) (1999)

Signed as a free agent by **Boston**, March 27, 1997. Traded to **Atlanta** by **Boston** for Peter Ferraro, June 25, 1999. Traded to **Nashville** by **Atlanta** for Denny Lambert, August 16, 1999. Signed as a free agent by **Los Angeles**, July 6, 2001. Claimed on waivers by **Pittsburgh** from **Los Angeles**, January 4, 2002. Traded to **NY Islanders** by **Pittsburgh** for Philadelphia's 5th round choice (previously acquired, Pittsburgh selected Evgeni Isakov) in 2003 Entry Draft, March 9, 2003. Signed as a free agent by **Atlanta**, August 12, 2003. Signed as a free agent by **Zurich** (Swiss), April 26, 2004. Signed as a free agent by **Nashville**, August 19, 2005. Claimed on waivers by **Minnesota** from **Nashville**, October 4, 2005. Signed as a free agent by **Philadelphia**, July 4, 2006. Traded to **NY Islanders** by **Philadelphia** with Philadelphia's 5th round choice (Matthew Martin) in 2008 Entry Draft for Mike York, December 20, 2006. Signed as a free agent by **Yaroslavl** (Russia), May 18, 2007. Signed as a free agent by **Ottawa**, October 16, 2007.

ROCHE, Travis

(ROHSH, TRA-vihs)

Defense. Shoots right. 6'1", 200 lbs. Born, Grand Cache, Alta., June 17, 1978.

1996-97	Trail	BCHL	49	17	40	57	159																		
1997-98	Trail	BCHL	38	11	31	42	104										11	0	8	8	21				
1998-99	North Dakota	WCHA	DID NOT PLAY – FRESHMAN																						
99-2000	North Dakota	WCHA	42	6	22	28	60																		
2000-01	North Dakota	WCHA	42	11	38	49	42																		
	Minnesota	**NHL**	**1**	**0**	**0**	**0**	**0**	**0**	**0**	**0**	**0**	**0.0**	**0**	**0**	**0.0**	**15:22**									
2001-02	**Minnesota**	**NHL**	**4**	**0**	**0**	**0**	**2**	**0**	**0**	**0**	**1**	**0.0**	**–1**	**0**	**0.0**	**12:30**									
	Houston Aeros	AHL	60	13	21	34	107										12	2	3	5	6				
2002-03	Houston Aeros	AHL	65	14	34	48	42										23	3	5	8	26				
2003-04	**Minnesota**	**NHL**	**5**	**0**	**1**	**1**	**0**	**0**	**0**	**0**	**5**	**0.0**	**–3**	**0**	**0.0**	**16:07**									
	Houston Aeros	AHL	60	8	30	38	18										2	0	0	0	2				
2004-05	Chicago Wolves	AHL	73	12	38	50	59										18	1	6	7	18				
2005-06	Chicago Wolves	AHL	59	8	31	39	73																		
2006-07	**Phoenix**	**NHL**	**50**	**6**	**13**	**19**	**22**	**2**	**0**	**1**	**32**	**18.8**	**2**	**0**	**0.0**	**17:01**									
	San Antonio	AHL	17	1	8	9	16																		
2007-08	San Antonio	AHL	71	6	35	41	65										5	0	2	2	8				
	NHL Totals		**60**	**6**	**14**	**20**	**24**	**2**	**0**	**1**	**38**	**15.8**		**0**	**0.0**	**16:37**									

BCHL Second All-Star Team (1997) • BCHL Rookie of the Year Award (1997) • BCHL Playoff MVP Award (1997) • BCHL First All-Star Team (1998) • BCHL Best Defenseman Award (1998) • WCHA All-Rookie Team (2000) • WCHA First All-Star Team (2001) • NCAA West First All-American Team (2001) • NCAA Championship All-Tournament Team (2001) • Yanick Dupre Memorial Award (Outstanding Humanitarian Contribution - AHL) (2002) • AHL First All-Star Team (2005)

Signed as a free agent by **Minnesota**, April 8, 2001. Signed as a free agent by **Atlanta**, July 14, 2004. Signed as a free agent by **Phoenix**, July 20, 2006.

ROENICK, Jeremy

(ROH-nihk, JAIR-eh-mee) **S.J.**

Center. Shoots right. 6'1", 205 lbs. Born, Boston, MA, January 17, 1970. Chicago's 1st choice, 8th overall, in 1988 Entry Draft.

1986-87	Thayer Academy	High-MA	24	31	34	65																			
1987-88	Thayer Academy	High-MA	24	34	50	84																			
1988-89	Hull Olympiques	QMJHL	28	34	36	70	14																		
	Chicago	**NHL**	**20**	**9**	**9**	**18**	**4**	**2**	**0**	**0**	**52**	**17.3**	**4**				**10**	**1**	**3**	**4**	**7**	**1**	**0**	**1**	
1989-90	**Chicago**	**NHL**	**78**	**26**	**40**	**66**	**54**	**6**	**0**	**4**	**173**	**15.0**	**2**				**20**	**11**	**7**	**18**	**8**	**4**	**0**	**1**	
1990-91	**Chicago**	**NHL**	**79**	**41**	**53**	**94**	**80**	**15**	**4**	**10**	**194**	**21.1**	**38**				**6**	**3**	**5**	**8**	**4**	**1**	**0**	**1**	
1991-92	**Chicago**	**NHL**	**80**	**53**	**50**	**103**	**98**	**22**	**3**	**13**	**234**	**22.6**	**23**				**18**	**12**	**10**	**22**	**12**	**4**	**0**	**3**	
1992-93	**Chicago**	**NHL**	**84**	**50**	**57**	**107**	**86**	**22**	**3**	**3**	**255**	**19.6**	**15**				**4**	**1**	**2**	**3**	**2**	**0**	**0**	**0**	
1993-94	**Chicago**	**NHL**	**84**	**46**	**61**	**107**	**125**	**24**	**5**	**5**	**281**	**16.4**	**21**				**6**	**1**	**6**	**7**	**2**	**0**	**0**	**1**	
1994-95	Kolner Haie	Germany	3	3	1	4	2																		
	Chicago	**NHL**	**33**	**10**	**24**	**34**	**14**	**5**	**0**	**1**	**93**	**10.8**	**5**				**8**	**1**	**2**	**3**	**16**	**0**	**0**	**0**	
1995-96	**Chicago**	**NHL**	**66**	**32**	**35**	**67**	**109**	**12**	**4**	**2**	**171**	**18.7**	**9**				**10**	**5**	**7**	**12**	**2**	**1**	**0**	**1**	
1996-97	**Phoenix**	**NHL**	**72**	**29**	**40**	**69**	**115**	**10**	**3**	**7**	**228**	**12.7**	**–7**				**6**	**2**	**4**	**6**	**4**	**0**	**0**	**0**	
1997-98	**Phoenix**	**NHL**	**79**	**24**	**32**	**56**	**103**	**6**	**1**	**3**	**182**	**13.2**	**5**				**6**	**5**	**3**	**8**	**4**	**2**	**2**	**2**	
	United States	Olympics	4	0	1	1	6																		
1998-99	**Phoenix**	**NHL**	**78**	**24**	**48**	**72**	**130**	**4**	**0**	**3**	**203**	**11.8**	**7**	**956**	**47.6**	**20:10**	**1**	**0**	**0**	**0**	**0**	**0**	**0**	**0**	**26:55**
99-2000	**Phoenix**	**NHL**	**75**	**34**	**44**	**78**	**102**	**6**	**3**	**12**	**192**	**17.7**	**11**	**925**	**50.1**	**20:51**	**5**	**2**	**2**	**4**	**10**	**1**	**0**	**0**	**19:46**
2000-01	**Phoenix**	**NHL**	**80**	**30**	**46**	**76**	**114**	**13**	**0**	**7**	**192**	**15.6**	**–1**	**888**	**49.1**	**21:00**									
2001-02	**Philadelphia**	**NHL**	**75**	**21**	**46**	**67**	**74**	**5**	**0**	**3**	**167**	**12.6**	**32**	**1329**	**49.1**	**18:14**	**5**	**0**	**0**	**0**	**14**	**0**	**0**	**0**	**18:41**
	United States	Olympics	6	1	4	5	2																		
2002-03	**Philadelphia**	**NHL**	**79**	**27**	**32**	**59**	**75**	**8**	**1**	**6**	**197**	**13.7**	**20**	**1088**	**53.0**	**18:48**	**13**	**3**	**5**	**8**	**8**	**0**	**0**	**1**	**21:07**
2003-04	**Philadelphia**	**NHL**	**62**	**19**	**28**	**47**	**62**	**10**	**1**	**1**	**128**	**14.8**	**1**	**846**	**51.5**	**17:37**	**18**	**4**	**9**	**13**	**8**	**2**	**0**	**1**	**18:05**
2004-05			DID NOT PLAY																						
2005-06	**Los Angeles**	**NHL**	**58**	**9**	**13**	**22**	**36**	**2**	**0**	**1**	**111**	**8.1**	**–5**	**536**	**49.4**	**17:22**									
2006-07	**Phoenix**	**NHL**	**70**	**11**	**17**	**28**	**32**	**4**	**0**	**1**	**89**	**12.4**	**–18**	**595**	**51.4**	**13:54**									
2007-08	**San Jose**	**NHL**	**69**	**14**	**19**	**33**	**26**	**7**	**0**	**10**	**89**	**15.7**	**–8**	**188**	**44.2**	**13:45**	**12**	**2**	**3**	**5**	**2**	**1**	**0**	**0**	**14:30**
	NHL Totals		**1321**	**509**	**694**	**1203**	**1439**	**183**	**28**	**92**	**3231**	**15.8**		**7351**	**50.0**	**18:06**	**148**	**53**	**68**	**121**	**103**	**17**	**2**	**12**	**18:23**

QMJHL Second All-Star Team (1989)

Played in NHL All-Star Game (1991, 1992, 1993, 1994, 1999, 2000, 2002, 2003, 2004)

Traded to **Phoenix** by **Chicago** for Alex Zhamnov, Craig Mills and Phoenix's 1st round choice (Ty Jones) in 1997 Entry Draft, August 16, 1996. Signed as a free agent by **Philadelphia**, July 2, 2001. Traded to **Los Angeles** by **Philadelphia** with Nashville's 3rd round choice (previously acquired, Los Angeles selected Bud Holloway) in 2006 Entry Draft for future considerations, August 4, 2005. Signed as a free agent by **Phoenix**, July 4, 2006. Signed as a free agent by **San Jose**, September 4, 2007.

ROLSTON, Brian

(ROHL-stuhn, BRIGH-uhn) **N.J.**

Center/Right wing. Shoots left. 6'2", 210 lbs. Born, Flint, MI, February 21, 1973. New Jersey's 2nd choice, 11th overall, in 1991 Entry Draft.

1989-90	Det. Compuware	NAHL	40	36	37	73	57																		
1990-91	Det. Compuware	NAHL	36	49	46	95	14																		
1991-92	Lake Superior	CCHA	37	14	23	37	14																		
1992-93	Lake Superior	CCHA	39	33	31	64	20																		
1993-94	United States	Nat-Tm	41	20	28	48	36																		
	United States	Olympics	8	7	0	7	8																		
	Albany River Rats	AHL	17	5	5	10	8										5	1	2	3	0				
1994-95	Albany River Rats	AHL	18	9	11	20	10																		
	♦ **New Jersey**	**NHL**	**40**	**7**	**11**	**18**	**17**	**2**	**0**	**3**	**92**	**7.6**	**5**				**6**	**2**	**1**	**3**	**4**	**1**	**0**	**0**	
1995-96	**New Jersey**	**NHL**	**58**	**13**	**11**	**24**	**8**	**3**	**1**	**4**	**139**	**9.4**	**9**												
1996-97	**New Jersey**	**NHL**	**81**	**18**	**27**	**45**	**20**	**2**	**2**	**3**	**237**	**7.6**	**6**				**10**	**4**	**1**	**5**	**6**	**1**	**2**	**0**	
1997-98	**New Jersey**	**NHL**	**76**	**16**	**14**	**30**	**16**	**0**	**2**	**1**	**185**	**8.6**	**7**				**6**	**1**	**0**	**1**	**2**	**0**	**1**	**0**	
1998-99	**New Jersey**	**NHL**	**82**	**24**	**33**	**57**	**14**	**5**	**5**	**3**	**210**	**11.4**	**11**	**51**	**45.1**	**18:49**	**7**	**1**	**0**	**1**	**2**	**0**	**1**	**0**	**17:36**
99-2000	**New Jersey**	**NHL**	**11**	**3**	**1**	**4**	**0**	**1**	**0**	**2**	**33**	**9.1**	**–2**	**37**	**37.8**	**19:09**									
	Colorado	**NHL**	**50**	**8**	**10**	**18**	**12**	**1**	**0**	**3**	**107**	**7.5**	**–6**	**65**	**41.5**	**16:18**									
	Boston	**NHL**	**16**	**5**	**4**	**9**	**6**	**3**	**0**	**1**	**66**	**7.6**	**–4**	**265**	**41.1**	**22:13**									
2000-01	**Boston**	**NHL**	**77**	**19**	**39**	**58**	**28**	**5**	**0**	**4**	**286**	**6.6**	**6**	**666**	**45.7**	**19:19**									
2001-02	**Boston**	**NHL**	**82**	**31**	**31**	**62**	**30**	**6**	**9**	**7**	**331**	**9.4**	**11**	**1289**	**46.6**	**20:24**	**6**	**4**	**1**	**5**	**0**	**1**	**1**	**0**	**20:37**
	United States	Olympics	6	0	3	3	0																		
2002-03	**Boston**	**NHL**	**81**	**27**	**32**	**59**	**32**	**6**	**5**	**5**	**281**	**9.6**	**1**	**1148**	**47.6**	**20:28**	**5**	**0**	**2**	**2**	**0**	**0**	**0**	**0**	**18:39**
2003-04	**Boston**	**NHL**	**82**	**19**	**29**	**48**	**40**	**3**	**2**	**3**	**257**	**7.4**	**9**	**1205**	**50.7**	**19:38**	**7**	**1**	**0**	**1**	**8**	**0**	**0**	**0**	**16:33**
2004-05			DID NOT PLAY																						
2005-06	**Minnesota**	**NHL**	**82**	**34**	**45**	**79**	**50**	**15**	**5**	**7**	**293**	**11.6**	**14**	**403**	**46.4**	**20:21**									
	United States	Olympics	6	3	1	4	4																		

			Regular Season														Playoffs								
Season	Club	League	GP	G	A	Pts	PIM	PP	SH	GW	S	%	+/-	TF	F%	Min	GP	G	A	Pts	PIM	PP	SH	GW	Min
2006-07	**Minnesota**	**NHL**	**78**	**31**	**33**	**64**	**46**	**13**	**1**	**6**	**305**	**10.2**	**6**	**295**	**45.4**	**21:16**	**5**	**1**	**1**	**2**	**4**	**0**	**0**	**0**	**20:25**
2007-08	**Minnesota**	**NHL**	**81**	**31**	**28**	**59**	**53**	**11**	**1**	**8**	**289**	**10.7**	**–1**	**165**	**40.6**	**20:04**	**6**	**2**	**4**	**6**	**8**	**0**	**1**	**0**	**22:27**
	NHL Totals		**977**	**286**	**348**	**634**	**372**	**76**	**33**	**60**	**3111**	**9.2**		**5589**	**46.9**	**19:49**	**58**	**16**	**10**	**26**	**34**	**3**	**6**	**0**	**19:15**

NCAA Championship All-Tournament Team (1992, 1993) • CCHA First All-Star Team (1993) • NCAA West Second All-American Team (1993)

Played in NHL All-Star Game (2007)

Traded to **Colorado** by **New Jersey** with New Jersey's 1st round choice (later traded to Boston – Boston selected Martin Samuelsson) in 2000 Entry Draft for Claude Lemieux and Colorado's 1st (David Hale) and 2nd (Matt DeMarchi) round choices in 2000 Entry Draft, November 3, 1999. Traded to **Boston** by **Colorado** with Martin Grenier, Samuel Pahlsson and New Jersey's 1st round choice (previously acquired, Boston selected Martin Samuelsson) in 2000 Entry Draft for Raymond Bourque and Dave Andreychuk, March 6, 2000. Signed as a free agent by **Minnesota**, July 8, 2004. Rights traded to **Tampa Bay** by **Minnesota** for future considerations, June 29, 2008. Signed as a free agent by **New Jersey**, July 1, 2008.

ROME, Aaron
(ROHM, AIR-ruhn) **CBJ**

Defense. Shoots left. 6'1", 204 lbs. Born, Nesbitt, Man., September 27, 1983. Los Angeles' 4th choice, 104th overall, in 2002 Entry Draft.

1998-99	Sask. Contacts	SMHL	STATISTICS NOT AVAILABLE																						
	Saskatoon Blades	WHL	1	0	0	0	0	....	....	....	....	....	....	....	....	....	....	....	....	....	....	....	....	....	....
99-2000	Saskatoon Blades	WHL	47	0	6	6	22	....	....	....	....	....	....	....	....	....	1	0	0	0	0	....	....	....	....
2000-01	Saskatoon Blades	WHL	3	0	0	0	2	....	....	....	....	....	....	....	....	....	....	....	....	....	....	....	....	....	....
	Kootenay Ice	WHL	53	2	8	10	43	....	....	....	....	....	....	....	....	....	11	1	3	4	6	....	....	....	....
2001-02	Kootenay Ice	WHL	33	4	13	17	55	....	....	....	....	....	....	....	....	....	....	....	....	....	....	....	....	....	....
	Swift Current	WHL	37	3	11	14	113	....	....	....	....	....	....	....	....	....	10	1	4	5	23	....	....	....	....
2002-03	Swift Current	WHL	61	12	44	56	201	....	....	....	....	....	....	....	....	....	4	1	0	1	20	....	....	....	....
2003-04	Swift Current	WHL	41	7	26	33	122	....	....	....	....	....	....	....	....	....	....	....	....	....	....	....	....	....	....
	Moose Jaw	WHL	28	3	16	19	88	....	....	....	....	....	....	....	....	....	8	0	6	6	17	....	....	....	....
2004-05	Cincinnati	AHL	75	2	14	16	130	....	....	....	....	....	....	....	....	....	12	3	3	6	33	....	....	....	....
2005-06	Portland Pirates	AHL	64	5	19	24	87	....	....	....	....	....	....	....	....	....	18	1	4	5	33	....	....	....	....
2006-07♦	**Anaheim**	**NHL**	**1**	**0**	**0**	**0**	**0**	**0**	**0**	**0**	**1**	**0.0**	**–1**	**0**	**0.0**	**14:31**	**1**	**0**	**0**	**0**	**0**	**0**	**0**	**0**	**11:01**
	Portland Pirates	AHL	76	8	17	25	139	....	....	....	....	....	....	....	....	....	....	....	....	....	....	....	....	....	....
2007-08	**Columbus**	**NHL**	**17**	**1**	**1**	**2**	**33**	**0**	**0**	**0**	**15**	**6.7**	**–4**	**0**	**0.0**	**18:11**	....	....	....	....	....	....	....	....	....
	Portland Pirates	AHL	14	2	3	5	31	....	....	....	....	....	....	....	....	....	....	....	....	....	....	....	....	....	....
	Syracuse Crunch	AHL	41	3	21	24	126	....	....	....	....	....	....	....	....	....	....	....	....	....	....	....	....	....	....
	NHL Totals		**18**	**1**	**1**	**2**	**33**	**0**	**0**	**0**	**16**	**6.3**		**0**	**0.0**	**17:59**	**1**	**0**	**0**	**0**	**0**	**0**	**0**	**0**	**11:01**

WHL East Second All-Star Team (2004)

Signed as a free agent by **Anaheim**, June 7, 2004. Traded to **Columbus** by **Anaheim** with Clay Wilson for Geoff Platt, November 15, 2007.

ROURKE, Allan
(RAWRK, AL-lan)

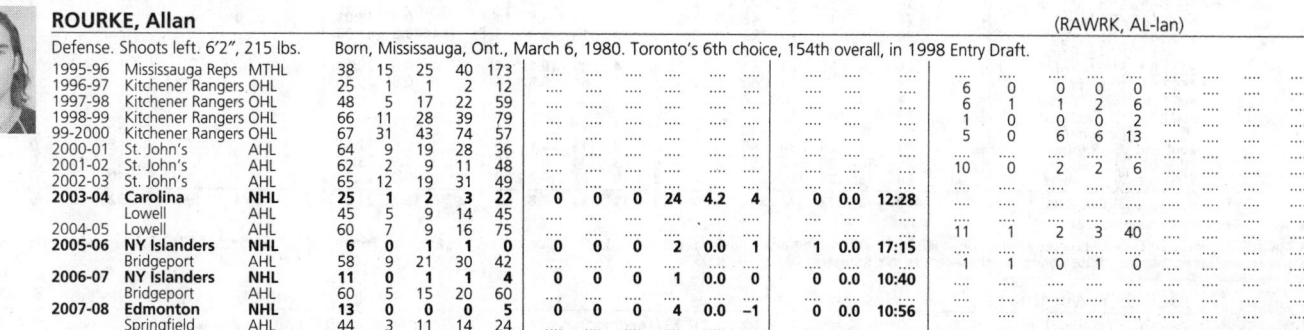

Defense. Shoots left. 6'2", 215 lbs. Born, Mississauga, Ont., March 6, 1980. Toronto's 6th choice, 154th overall, in 1998 Entry Draft.

1995-96	Mississauga Reps	MTHL	38	15	25	40	173	....	....	....	....	....	....	....	....	....	....	....	....	....	....	....	....	....	....
1996-97	Kitchener Rangers	OHL	25	1	1	2	12	....	....	....	....	....	....	....	....	....	6	0	0	0	0	....	....	....	....
1997-98	Kitchener Rangers	OHL	48	5	17	22	59	....	....	....	....	....	....	....	....	....	6	1	1	2	6	....	....	....	....
1998-99	Kitchener Rangers	OHL	66	11	28	39	79	....	....	....	....	....	....	....	....	....	1	0	0	0	2	....	....	....	....
99-2000	Kitchener Rangers	OHL	67	31	43	74	57	....	....	....	....	....	....	....	....	....	5	0	6	6	13	....	....	....	....
2000-01	St. John's	AHL	64	9	19	28	36	....	....	....	....	....	....	....	....	....	....	....	....	....	....	....	....	....	....
2001-02	St. John's	AHL	62	2	9	11	48	....	....	....	....	....	....	....	....	....	10	0	2	2	6	....	....	....	....
2002-03	St. John's	AHL	65	12	19	31	49	....	....	....	....	....	....	....	....	....	....	....	....	....	....	....	....	....	....
2003-04	**Carolina**	**NHL**	**25**	**1**	**2**	**3**	**22**	**0**	**0**	**0**	**24**	**4.2**	**4**	**0**	**0.0**	**12:28**	....	....	....	....	....	....	....	....	....
	Lowell	AHL	45	5	9	14	45	....	....	....	....	....	....	....	....	....	....	....	....	....	....	....	....	....	....
2004-05	Lowell	AHL	60	7	9	16	75	....	....	....	....	....	....	....	....	....	11	1	2	3	40	....	....	....	....
2005-06	**NY Islanders**	**NHL**	**6**	**0**	**1**	**1**	**0**	**0**	**0**	**0**	**2**	**0.0**	**1**	**1**	**0.0**	**17:15**	....	....	....	....	....	....	....	....	....
	Bridgeport	AHL	58	9	21	30	42	....	....	....	....	....	....	....	....	....	1	1	0	1	0	....	....	....	....
2006-07	**NY Islanders**	**NHL**	**11**	**0**	**1**	**1**	**4**	**0**	**0**	**0**	**1**	**0.0**	**0**	**0**	**0.0**	**10:40**	....	....	....	....	....	....	....	....	....
	Bridgeport	AHL	60	5	15	20	60	....	....	....	....	....	....	....	....	....	....	....	....	....	....	....	....	....	....
2007-08	**Edmonton**	**NHL**	**13**	**0**	**0**	**0**	**5**	**0**	**0**	**0**	**4**	**0.0**	**–1**	**0**	**0.0**	**10:56**	....	....	....	....	....	....	....	....	....
	Springfield	AHL	44	3	11	14	24	....	....	....	....	....	....	....	....	....	....	....	....	....	....	....	....	....	....
	NHL Totals		**55**	**1**	**4**	**5**	**31**	**0**	**0**	**0**	**31**	**3.2**		**1**	**0.0**	**12:16**	....	....	....	....	....	....	....	....	....

OHL Second All-Star Team (2000)

Traded to **Carolina** by **Toronto** for Harold Druken, May 29, 2003. Signed as a free agent by **NY Islanders**, August 12, 2005. Traded to **Edmonton** by **NY Islanders** with Edmonton's 3rd round choice (previously acquired, later traded to Anaheim - later traded back to NY Islanders - NY Islanders selected Kiril Petrov) in 2008 Entry Draft for Anaheim's 2nd round choice (previously acquired, NY Islanders selected Travis Hamonic) in 2008 Entry Draft, July 5, 2007. Signed as a free agent by **Ingolstadt** (Germany), July 15, 2008.

ROY, Andre
(WAH, AWN-dray) **CGY.**

Right wing. Shoots left. 6'3", 202 lbs. Born, Port Chester, NY, February 8, 1975. Boston's 5th choice, 151st overall, in 1994 Entry Draft.

1992-93	Nord Selects	QAHA	STATISTICS NOT AVAILABLE																						
1993-94	Goulbourn Royals	OHA-C	9	9	13	22	98	....	....	....	....	....	....	....	....	....	....	....	....	....	....	....	....	....	....
	Beauport	QMJHL	33	6	7	13	125	....	....	....	....	....	....	....	....	....	....	....	....	....	....	....	....	....	....
	Chicoutimi	QMJHL	32	4	14	18	152	....	....	....	....	....	....	....	....	....	25	3	6	9	94	....	....	....	....
1994-95	Chicoutimi	QMJHL	20	15	8	23	90	....	....	....	....	....	....	....	....	....	....	....	....	....	....	....	....	....	....
	Drummondville	QMJHL	34	18	13	31	233	....	....	....	....	....	....	....	....	....	4	2	0	2	34	....	....	....	....
1995-96	**Boston**	**NHL**	**3**	**0**	**0**	**0**	**0**	**0**	**0**	**0**	**0**	**0.0**	**0**	....	....	....	....	....	....	....	....	....	....	....	....
	Providence Bruins	AHL	58	7	8	15	167	....	....	....	....	....	....	....	....	....	1	0	0	0	10	....	....	....	....
1996-97	**Boston**	**NHL**	**10**	**0**	**2**	**2**	**12**	**0**	**0**	**0**	**12**	**0.0**	**–5**	....	....	....	....	....	....	....	....	....	....	....	....
	Providence Bruins	AHL	50	17	11	28	234	....	....	....	....	....	....	....	....	....	....	....	....	....	....	....	....	....	....
1997-98	Providence Bruins	AHL	36	3	11	14	154	....	....	....	....	....	....	....	....	....	....	....	....	....	....	....	....	....	....
	Charlotte	ECHL	27	10	8	18	132	....	....	....	....	....	....	....	....	....	7	2	3	5	34	....	....	....	....
1998-99	Fort Wayne	IHL	65	15	6	21	*395	....	....	....	....	....	....	....	....	....	2	0	0	0	11	....	....	....	....
99-2000	**Ottawa**	**NHL**	**73**	**4**	**3**	**7**	**145**	**0**	**0**	**1**	**39**	**10.3**	**3**	**3**	**33.3**	**6:29**	**5**	**0**	**0**	**0**	**2**	**0**	**0**	**0**	**5:54**
2000-01	**Ottawa**	**NHL**	**64**	**3**	**5**	**8**	**169**	**0**	**0**	**0**	**33**	**9.1**	**1**	**2**	**50.0**	**4:36**	**2**	**0**	**0**	**0**	**16**	**0**	**0**	**0**	**4:16**
2001-02	**Ottawa**	**NHL**	**56**	**6**	**8**	**14**	**148**	**0**	**0**	**0**	**60**	**10.0**	**3**	**1**	**100.0**	**8:23**	....	....	....	....	....	....	....	....	....
	Tampa Bay	**NHL**	**9**	**1**	**1**	**2**	**63**	**0**	**0**	**0**	**6**	**16.7**	**–5**	**0**	**0.0**	**8:58**	....	....	....	....	....	....	....	....	....
2002-03	**Tampa Bay**	**NHL**	**62**	**10**	**7**	**17**	**119**	**0**	**0**	**2**	**85**	**11.8**	**0**	**7**	**57.1**	**10:46**	**5**	**0**	**1**	**1**	**2**	**0**	**0**	**0**	**12:31**
2003-04♦	**Tampa Bay**	**NHL**	**33**	**1**	**1**	**2**	**78**	**0**	**0**	**0**	**24**	**4.2**	**–5**	**2**	**50.0**	**7:52**	**21**	**1**	**2**	**3**	**61**	**0**	**0**	**1**	**6:11**
2004-05			DID NOT PLAY																						
2005-06	**Pittsburgh**	**NHL**	**42**	**2**	**1**	**3**	**116**	**0**	**0**	**1**	**11**	**18.2**	**–3**	**1**	**100.0**	**5:03**	....	....	....	....	....	....	....	....	....
2006-07	**Pittsburgh**	**NHL**	**5**	**0**	**0**	**0**	**12**	**0**	**0**	**0**	**1**	**0.0**	**–1**	**1**	**0.0**	**3:12**	....	....	....	....	....	....	....	....	....
	Tampa Bay	**NHL**	**51**	**1**	**2**	**3**	**116**	**0**	**0**	**0**	**14**	**7.1**	**–3**	**2**	**0.0**	**4:35**	**6**	**0**	**0**	**0**	**17**	**0**	**0**	**0**	**2:31**
2007-08	**Tampa Bay**	**NHL**	**63**	**4**	**3**	**7**	**108**	**0**	**0**	**0**	**38**	**10.5**	**–1**	**0**	**0.0**	**5:28**	....	....	....	....	....	....	....	....	....
	NHL Totals		**471**	**32**	**33**	**65**	**1086**	**0**	**0**	**4**	**323**	**9.9**		**19**	**47.4**	**6:40**	**39**	**1**	**3**	**4**	**98**	**0**	**0**	**1**	**6:18**

Signed as a free agent by **Ottawa**, April 28, 1999. Traded to **Tampa Bay** by **Ottawa** with Ottawa's 6th round choice (Paul Ranger) in 2002 Entry Draft for Juha Ylonen, March 15, 2002. • Missed majority of 2003-04 season as a healthy reserve. Signed as a free agent by **Pittsburgh**, August 4, 2005. Claimed on waivers by **Tampa Bay** from **Pittsburgh**, December 2, 2006. Signed as a free agent by **Calgary**, July 21, 2008.

ROY, Derek
(ROI, DAIR-ihk) **BUF.**

Center. Shoots left. 5'9", 188 lbs. Born, Ottawa, Ont., May 4, 1983. Buffalo's 2nd choice, 32nd overall, in 2001 Entry Draft.

1998-99	Ontario East	Minor-ON	34	61	31	92	42	....	....	....	....	....	....	....	....	....	....	....	....	....	....	....	....	....	....
99-2000	Kitchener Rangers	OHL	66	34	53	87	44	....	....	....	....	....	....	....	....	....	5	4	1	5	6	....	....	....	....
2000-01	Kitchener Rangers	OHL	65	42	39	81	114	....	....	....	....	....	....	....	....	....	....	....	....	....	....	....	....	....	....
2001-02	Kitchener Rangers	OHL	62	43	46	89	92	....	....	....	....	....	....	....	....	....	4	1	2	3	2	....	....	....	....
2002-03	Kitchener Rangers	OHL	49	28	50	78	73	....	....	....	....	....	....	....	....	....	21	9	*23	32	14	....	....	....	....
2003-04	**Buffalo**	**NHL**	**49**	**9**	**10**	**19**	**12**	**1**	**0**	**4**	**71**	**12.7**	**–8**	**715**	**47.4**	**15:19**	....	....	....	....	....	....	....	....	....
	Rochester	AHL	26	10	16	26	20	....	....	....	....	....	....	....	....	....	16	6	8	14	18	....	....	....	....
2004-05	Rochester	AHL	67	16	45	61	60	....	....	....	....	....	....	....	....	....	9	6	5	11	6	....	....	....	....
2005-06	**Buffalo**	**NHL**	**70**	**18**	**28**	**46**	**57**	**5**	**1**	**1**	**151**	**11.9**	**1**	**807**	**48.0**	**17:02**	**18**	**5**	**10**	**15**	**16**	**1**	**1**	**0**	**17:03**
	Rochester	AHL	8	7	13	20	10	....	....	....	....	....	....	....	....	....	....	....	....	....	....	....	....	....	....

			Regular Season														Playoffs								
Season	Club	League	GP	G	A	Pts	PIM	PP	SH	GW	S	%	+/-	TF	F%	Min	GP	G	A	Pts	PIM	PP	SH	GW	Min
2006-07	**Buffalo**	**NHL**	**75**	**21**	**42**	**63**	**60**	**6**	**1**	**3**	**130**	**16.2**	**37**	**1129**	**48.5**	**18:28**	**16**	**2**	**5**	**7**	**14**	**0**	**0**	**0**	**18:03**
2007-08	**Buffalo**	**NHL**	**78**	**32**	**49**	**81**	**46**	**6**	**3**	**4**	**218**	**14.7**	**13**	**1393**	**51.2**	**20:58**	....	....	....	....	....	....	....	....	....
	NHL Totals		**272**	**80**	**129**	**209**	**175**	**18**	**5**	**12**	**570**	**14.0**		**4044**	**49.1**	**18:15**	**34**	**7**	**15**	**22**	**30**	**1**	**1**	**0**	**17:31**

OHL All-Rookie Team (2000) • OHL Rookie of the Year (2000) • CHL All-Rookie Team (2000) • CHL Plus/Minus Award (2000) • CHL Most Sportsmanlike Player (2000) • Memorial Cup Tournament All-Star Team (2003) • Stafford Smythe Memorial Trophy (Memorial Cup Tournament - MVP) (2003)

ROY, Mathieu

(WAH, MA-tyew) **EDM.**

Defense. Shoots right. 6'2", 210 lbs. Born, St-Georges, Que., August 10, 1983. Edmonton's 10th choice, 215th overall, in 2003 Entry Draft.

1998-99	Levis	QAAA	11	4	1	5	16	....	....	....	....	....	....	....	....	....	....	....	....	....	....	....	....	....	....
99-2000	Levis	QAAA	24	3	4	7	88	....	....	....	....	....	....	....	....	....	6	1	1	2	22	....	....	....	....
	Val-d'Or Foreurs	QMJHL	48	1	4	5	66	....	....	....	....	....	....	....	....	....	....	....	....	....	....	....	....	....	....
2000-01	Val-d'Or Foreurs	QMJHL	30	0	7	7	60	....	....	....	....	....	....	....	....	....	17	0	0	0	4	....	....	....	....
2001-02	Val-d'Or Foreurs	QMJHL	53	7	26	33	103	....	....	....	....	....	....	....	....	....	7	0	2	2	19	....	....	....	....
2002-03	Val-d'Or Foreurs	QMJHL	52	11	21	32	164	....	....	....	....	....	....	....	....	....	7	1	0	1	8	....	....	....	....
2003-04	Toronto	AHL	30	0	2	2	46	....	....	....	....	....	....	....	....	....	....	....	....	....	....	....	....	....	....
	Columbus	ECHL	10	1	2	3	13	....	....	....	....	....	....	....	....	....	....	....	....	....	....	....	....	....	....
2004-05	Edmonton	AHL	51	3	22	25	68	....	....	....	....	....	....	....	....	....	....	....	....	....	....	....	....	....	....
2005-06	**Edmonton**	**NHL**	**1**	**0**	**0**	**0**	**0**	**0**	**0**	**0**	**0**	**0.0**	**–1**	**0**	**0.0**	**13:00**	....	....	....	....	....	....	....	....	....
	Hamilton	AHL	50	3	16	19	82	....	....	....	....	....	....	....	....	....	....	....	....	....	....	....	....	....	....
2006-07	**Edmonton**	**NHL**	**16**	**2**	**0**	**2**	**30**	**0**	**0**	**0**	**18**	**11.1**	**–7**	**0**	**0.0**	**14:06**	....	....	....	....	....	....	....	....	....
	Hamilton	AHL	31	6	12	18	40	....	....	....	....	....	....	....	....	....	....	....	....	....	....	....	....	....	....
2007-08	**Edmonton**	**NHL**	**13**	**0**	**1**	**1**	**27**	**0**	**0**	**0**	**8**	**0.0**	**0**	**0**	**0.0**	**10:23**	....	....	....	....	....	....	....	....	....
	Springfield	AHL	20	2	8	10	34	....	....	....	....	....	....	....	....	....	....	....	....	....	....	....	....	....	....
	NHL Totals		**30**	**2**	**1**	**3**	**57**	**0**	**0**	**0**	**26**	**7.7**		**0**	**0.0**	**12:28**	....	....	....	....	....	....	....	....	....

• Missed majority of 2007-08 season recovering from shoulder injury and as a healthy reserve.

ROZSIVAL, Michal

(roh-ZIH-vahl, MEE-khahl) **NYR**

Defense. Shoots right. 6'2", 210 lbs. Born, Vlasim, Czech., September 3, 1978. Pittsburgh's 5th choice, 105th overall, in 1996 Entry Draft.

1994-95	Jihlava Jr.	CzRep-Jr.	31	8	13	21	....	....	....	....	....	....	....	....	....	....	....	....	....	....	....	....	....	....	....
1995-96	HC Dukla Jihlava	CzRep	36	3	4	7	....	....	....	....	....	....	....	....	....	....	....	....	....	....	....	....	....	....	....
1996-97	Swift Current	WHL	63	8	31	39	80	....	....	....	....	....	....	....	....	....	10	0	6	6	15	....	....	....	....
1997-98	Swift Current	WHL	71	14	55	69	122	....	....	....	....	....	....	....	....	....	12	0	5	5	33	....	....	....	....
1998-99	Syracuse Crunch	AHL	49	3	22	25	72	....	....	....	....	....	....	....	....	....	....	....	....	....	....	....	....	....	....
99-2000	**Pittsburgh**	**NHL**	**75**	**4**	**17**	**21**	**48**	**1**	**0**	**1**	**73**	**5.5**	**11**	**1**	**0.0**	**19:01**	**2**	**0**	**0**	**0**	**4**	**0**	**0**	**0**	**30:56**
2000-01	**Pittsburgh**	**NHL**	**30**	**1**	**4**	**5**	**26**	**0**	**0**	**0**	**17**	**5.9**	**3**	**1**	**100.0**	**17:06**	....	....	....	....	....	....	....	....	....
	Wilkes-Barre	AHL	29	8	8	16	32	....	....	....	....	....	....	....	....	....	21	3	*19	22	23	....	....	....	....
2001-02	**Pittsburgh**	**NHL**	**79**	**9**	**20**	**29**	**47**	**4**	**0**	**4**	**89**	**10.1**	**–6**	**0**	**0.0**	**20:01**	....	....	....	....	....	....	....	....	....
2002-03	**Pittsburgh**	**NHL**	**53**	**4**	**6**	**10**	**40**	**1**	**0**	**0**	**61**	**6.6**	**–5**	**0**	**0.0**	**20:25**	....	....	....	....	....	....	....	....	....
2003-04	Wilkes-Barre	AHL	1	0	0	0	2	....	....	....	....	....	....	....	....	....	....	....	....	....	....	....	....	....	....
2004-05	HC Ocelari Trinec	CzRep	35	1	10	11	40	....	....	....	....	....	....	....	....	....	....	....	....	....	....	....	....	....	....
	Pardubice	CzRep	16	1	3	4	30	....	....	....	....	....	....	....	....	....	16	1	2	3	34	....	....	....	....
2005-06	**NY Rangers**	**NHL**	**82**	**5**	**25**	**30**	**90**	**3**	**0**	**3**	**115**	**4.3**	**35**	**1**	**0.0**	**22:27**	**4**	**0**	**1**	**1**	**8**	**0**	**0**	**0**	**24:31**
2006-07	**NY Rangers**	**NHL**	**80**	**10**	**30**	**40**	**52**	**7**	**0**	**3**	**104**	**9.6**	**10**	**3**	**0.0**	**23:46**	**10**	**3**	**4**	**7**	**10**	**2**	**0**	**1**	**24:45**
2007-08	**NY Rangers**	**NHL**	**80**	**13**	**25**	**38**	**80**	**6**	**2**	**0**	**127**	**10.2**	**0**	**0**	**0.0**	**24:33**	**10**	**1**	**5**	**6**	**10**	**0**	**0**	**0**	**25:05**
	NHL Totals		**479**	**46**	**127**	**173**	**383**	**22**	**2**	**11**	**586**	**7.8**		**6**	**16.7**	**21:31**	**26**	**4**	**10**	**14**	**32**	**2**	**0**	**1**	**25:19**

WHL East First All-Star Team (1998)

• Missed majority of 2003-04 season recovering from knee injury suffered in training camp, September 18, 2003. Signed as a free agent by **Trinec** (CzRep), September 17, 2004. Signed as a free agent by **Pardubice** (CzRep), January, 2005. Signed as a free agent by **NY Rangers**, August 29, 2005.

RUCINSKY, Martin

(roo-CHIHN-skee, MAHR-tihn)

Left wing. Shoots left. 6'1", 205 lbs. Born, Most, Czech., March 11, 1971. Edmonton's 2nd choice, 20th overall, in 1991 Entry Draft.

1988-89	CHZ Litvinov	Czech	3	1	0	1	2	....	....	....	....	....	....	....	....	....	....	....	....	....	....	....	....	....	....
1989-90	CHZ Litvinov	Czech	39	12	6	18	....	....	....	....	....	....	....	....	....	....	8	5	3	8	....	....	....	....	....
1990-91	HC CHZ Litvinov	Czech	56	24	20	44	69	....	....	....	....	....	....	....	....	....	....	....	....	....	....	....	....	....	....
1991-92	**Edmonton**	**NHL**	**2**	**0**	**0**	**0**	**0**	**0**	**0**	**0**	**1**	**0.0**	**–3**	....	....	....	....	....	....	....	....	....	....	....	....
	Cape Breton	AHL	35	11	12	23	34	....	....	....	....	....	....	....	....	....	....	....	....	....	....	....	....	....	....
	Quebec	**NHL**	**4**	**1**	**1**	**2**	**2**	**0**	**0**	**0**	**4**	**25.0**	**1**	....	....	....	....	....	....	....	....	....	....	....	....
	Halifax Citadels	AHL	7	1	1	2	6	....	....	....	....	....	....	....	....	....	....	....	....	....	....	....	....	....	....
1992-93	**Quebec**	**NHL**	**77**	**18**	**30**	**48**	**51**	**4**	**0**	**1**	**133**	**13.5**	**16**	....	....	....	**6**	**1**	**1**	**2**	**4**	**1**	**0**	**0**	....
1993-94	**Quebec**	**NHL**	**60**	**9**	**23**	**32**	**58**	**4**	**0**	**1**	**96**	**9.4**	**4**	....	....	....	....	....	....	....	....	....	....	....	....
1994-95	Litvinov	CzRep	13	12	10	22	54	....	....	....	....	....	....	....	....	....	....	....	....	....	....	....	....	....	....
	Quebec	**NHL**	**20**	**3**	**6**	**9**	**14**	**0**	**0**	**0**	**32**	**9.4**	**5**	....	....	....	....	....	....	....	....	....	....	....	....
1995-96	HC Petra Vsetin	CzRep	1	1	1	2	0	....	....	....	....	....	....	....	....	....	....	....	....	....	....	....	....	....	....
	Colorado	**NHL**	**22**	**4**	**11**	**15**	**14**	**0**	**0**	**1**	**39**	**10.3**	**10**	....	....	....	....	....	....	....	....	....	....	....	....
	Montreal	**NHL**	**56**	**25**	**35**	**60**	**54**	**9**	**2**	**3**	**142**	**17.6**	**8**	....	....	....	....	....	....	....	....	....	....	....	....
1996-97	**Montreal**	**NHL**	**70**	**28**	**27**	**55**	**62**	**6**	**3**	**3**	**172**	**16.3**	**1**	....	....	....	**5**	**0**	**0**	**0**	**4**	**0**	**0**	**0**	....
1997-98	**Montreal**	**NHL**	**78**	**21**	**32**	**53**	**84**	**5**	**3**	**3**	**192**	**10.9**	**13**	....	....	....	**10**	**3**	**0**	**3**	**4**	**1**	**0**	**0**	....
	Czech Republic	Olympics	6	3	1	4	4	....	....	....	....	....	....	....	....	....	....	....	....	....	....	....	....	....	....
1998-99	Litvinov	CzRep	3	2	2	4	0	....	....	....	....	....	....	....	....	....	....	....	....	....	....	....	....	....	....
	Montreal	**NHL**	**73**	**17**	**17**	**34**	**50**	**5**	**0**	**1**	**180**	**9.4**	**–25**	**12**	**50.0**	**18:12**	....	....	....	....	....	....	....	....	....
99-2000	**Montreal**	**NHL**	**80**	**25**	**24**	**49**	**70**	**7**	**1**	**4**	**242**	**10.3**	**1**	**31**	**54.8**	**18:54**	....	....	....	....	....	....	....	....	....
2000-01	**Montreal**	**NHL**	**57**	**16**	**22**	**38**	**66**	**5**	**1**	**4**	**141**	**11.3**	**–5**	**5**	**40.0**	**19:11**	....	....	....	....	....	....	....	....	....
2001-02	**Montreal**	**NHL**	**18**	**2**	**6**	**8**	**12**	**1**	**0**	**0**	**41**	**4.9**	**–1**	**5**	**80.0**	**16:15**	....	....	....	....	....	....	....	....	....
	Dallas	**NHL**	**42**	**6**	**11**	**17**	**24**	**2**	**0**	**1**	**63**	**9.5**	**3**	**7**	**57.1**	**14:33**	....	....	....	....	....	....	....	....	....
	Czech Republic	Olympics	4	0	3	3	2	....	....	....	....	....	....	....	....	....	....	....	....	....	....	....	....	....	....
	NY Rangers	**NHL**	**15**	**3**	**10**	**13**	**6**	**0**	**0**	**1**	**24**	**12.5**	**6**	**3**	**33.3**	**16:39**	....	....	....	....	....	....	....	....	....
2002-03	Litvinov	CzRep	2	1	0	1	2	....	....	....	....	....	....	....	....	....	....	....	....	....	....	....	....	....	....
	St. Louis	**NHL**	**61**	**16**	**14**	**30**	**38**	**4**	**4**	**3**	**135**	**11.9**	**–1**	**19**	**57.9**	**16:55**	**7**	**4**	**2**	**6**	**4**	**0**	**0**	**0**	**16:52**
2003-04	**NY Rangers**	**NHL**	**69**	**13**	**29**	**42**	**62**	**0**	**1**	**2**	**161**	**8.1**	**13**	**14**	**14.3**	**18:51**	....	....	....	....	....	....	....	....	....
	Vancouver	**NHL**	**13**	**1**	**2**	**3**	**10**	**0**	**0**	**0**	**45**	**2.2**	**2**	**2**	**0.0**	**19:03**	**7**	**1**	**1**	**2**	**6**	**1**	**0**	**0**	**17:02**
2004-05	Litvinov	CzRep	38	15	26	41	87	....	....	....	....	....	....	....	....	....	....	....	....	....	....	....	....	....	....
2005-06	**NY Rangers**	**NHL**	**52**	**16**	**39**	**55**	**56**	**4**	**0**	**4**	**152**	**10.5**	**10**	**44**	**34.1**	**18:25**	**2**	**0**	**1**	**1**	**2**	**0**	**0**	**0**	**13:29**
	Czech Republic	Olympics	8	1	3	4	0	....	....	....	....	....	....	....	....	....	....	....	....	....	....	....	....	....	....
2006-07	**St. Louis**	**NHL**	**52**	**12**	**21**	**33**	**48**	**4**	**0**	**3**	**96**	**12.5**	**–3**	**14**	**21.4**	**16:43**	....	....	....	....	....	....	....	....	....
2007-08	**St. Louis**	**NHL**	**40**	**5**	**11**	**16**	**40**	**1**	**0**	**0**	**67**	**7.5**	**–9**	**13**	**53.9**	**15:01**	....	....	....	....	....	....	....	....	....
	NHL Totals		**961**	**241**	**371**	**612**	**821**	**61**	**15**	**35**	**2158**	**11.2**		**169**	**42.6**	**17:39**	**37**	**9**	**5**	**14**	**24**	**3**	**0**	**0**	**16:31**

Played in NHL All-Star Game (2000)

Traded to **Quebec** by **Edmonton** for Ron Tugnutt and Brad Zavisha, March 10, 1992. Transferred to **Colorado** after **Quebec** franchise relocated, June 21, 1995. Traded to **Montreal** by **Colorado** with Andrei Kovalenko and Jocelyn Thibault for Patrick Roy and Mike Keane, December 6, 1995. Traded to **Dallas** by **Montreal** with Benoit Brunet for Donald Audette and Shaun Van Allen, November 21, 2001. Traded to **NY Rangers** by **Dallas** with Roman Lyashenko for Manny Malhotra and Barrett Heisten, March 12, 2002. Signed as a free agent by **St. Louis**, October 30, 2002. Signed as a free agent by **NY Rangers**, August 28, 2003. Traded to **Vancouver** by **NY Rangers** for R.J. Umberger and Martin Grenier, March 9, 2004. Signed as a free agent by **Litvinov** (CzRep), August 20, 2004. Signed as a free agent by **NY Rangers**, August 3, 2005. Signed as a free agent by **St. Louis**, August 2, 2006. Signed as a free agent by **Sparta Praha** (CzRep), July 23, 2008.

RUPP, Mike

(RUHP, MIGHK) **N.J.**

Center. Shoots left. 6'5", 230 lbs. Born, Cleveland, OH, January 13, 1980. New Jersey's 7th choice, 76th overall, in 2000 Entry Draft.

1996-97	St. Edward's	High-OH	20	26	24	50	....	....	....	....	....	....	....	....	....	....	....	....	....	....	....	....	....	....	....
1997-98	Windsor Spitfires	OHL	38	9	8	17	60	....	....	....	....	....	....	....	....	....	....	....	....	....	....	....	....	....	....
	Erie Otters	OHL	26	7	3	10	57	....	....	....	....	....	....	....	....	....	7	3	1	4	6	....	....	....	....
1998-99	Erie Otters	OHL	63	22	25	47	102	....	....	....	....	....	....	....	....	....	5	0	2	2	25	....	....	....	....
99-2000	Erie Otters	OHL	58	32	21	53	134	....	....	....	....	....	....	....	....	....	13	5	5	10	22	....	....	....	....
2000-01	Albany River Rats	AHL	71	10	10	20	63	....	....	....	....	....	....	....	....	....	....	....	....	....	....	....	....	....	....
2001-02	Albany River Rats	AHL	78	13	17	30	90	....	....	....	....	....	....	....	....	....	....	....	....	....	....	....	....	....	....
2002-03 ♦	**New Jersey**	**NHL**	**26**	**5**	**3**	**8**	**21**	**2**	**0**	**3**	**34**	**14.7**	**0**	**150**	**44.7**	**11:39**	**4**	**1**	**3**	**4**	**0**	**0**	**0**	**1**	**11:28**
	Albany River Rats	AHL	47	8	11	19	74	....	....	....	....	....	....	....	....	....	....	....	....	....	....	....	....	....	....
2003-04	**New Jersey**	**NHL**	**51**	**6**	**5**	**11**	**41**	**1**	**0**	**1**	**64**	**9.4**	**–1**	**386**	**47.9**	**10:38**	....	....	....	....	....	....	....	....	....
	Phoenix	**NHL**	**6**	**0**	**1**	**1**	**6**	**0**	**0**	**0**	**12**	**0.0**	**–3**	**94**	**57.5**	**16:59**	....	....	....	....	....	....	....	....	....

Season	Club	League	GP	G	A	Pts	PIM	PP	SH	GW	S	%	+/-	TF	F%	Min	GP	G	A	Pts	PIM	PP	SH	GW	Min
								Regular Season									Playoffs								
2004-05	Danbury Trashers	UHL	14	5	5	10	30	....	....	....	....	....	....	....	....	....	11	3	4	7	38	....	....	....	....
2005-06	**Phoenix**	**NHL**	**1**	**0**	**0**	**0**	**0**	**0**	**0**	**0**	**1**	**0.0**	**0**	**1**	**0.0**	**6:30**	....	....	....	....	....	....	....	....	....
	Columbus	**NHL**	**39**	**4**	**2**	**6**	**58**	**0**	**0**	**0**	**38**	**10.5**	**–3**	**264**	**48.1**	**9:04**	....	....	....	....	....	....	....	....	....
	Syracuse Crunch	AHL	3	1	2	3	12	....	....	....	....	....	....	....	....	....	....	....	....	....	....	....	....	....	....
2006-07	**New Jersey**	**NHL**	**76**	**6**	**3**	**9**	**92**	**0**	**0**	**1**	**60**	**10.0**	**–10**	**33**	**45.5**	**6:27**	**9**	**0**	**1**	**1**	**7**	**0**	**0**	**0**	**2:46**
2007-08	**New Jersey**	**NHL**	**64**	**3**	**6**	**9**	**58**	**1**	**0**	**0**	**69**	**4.3**	**–8**	**155**	**48.4**	**8:04**	**5**	**0**	**1**	**1**	**2**	**0**	**0**	**0**	**7:48**
	NHL Totals		**263**	**24**	**20**	**44**	**276**	**4**	**0**	**5**	**278**	**8.6**		**1083**	**48.3**	**8:48**	**18**	**1**	**5**	**6**	**9**	**0**	**0**	**1**	**6:06**

• Re-entered NHL Entry Draft. Originally NY Islanders' 1st choice, 9th overall, in 1998 Entry Draft.

Traded to **Phoenix** by **New Jersey** with New Jersey's 2nd round choice (later traded to Edmonton – Edmonton selected Geoff Paukovich) in 2004 Entry Draft for Jan Hrdina, March 5, 2004. Signed as a free agent by **Danbury** (UHL), February 10, 2005. Traded to **Columbus** by **Phoenix** with Cale Hulse and Jason Chimera for Geoff Sanderson and Tim Jackman, October 8, 2005. Signed as a free agent by **New Jersey**, July 10, 2006.

RUSSELL, Kris

(RUH-sehl, KRIHS) **CBJ**

Defense. Shoots left. 5'10", 180 lbs. Born, Caroline, Alta., May 2, 1987. Columbus' 3rd choice, 67th overall, in 2005 Entry Draft.

Season	Club	League	GP	G	A	Pts	PIM	PP	SH	GW	S	%	+/-	TF	F%	Min	GP	G	A	Pts	PIM	PP	SH	GW	Min
2003-04	Medicine Hat	WHL	55	4	15	19	30	....	....	....	....	....	....	....	....	....	20	3	2	5	4	....	....	....	....
2004-05	Medicine Hat	WHL	72	26	35	61	37	....	....	....	....	....	....	....	....	....	10	2	1	3	4	....	....	....	....
2005-06	Medicine Hat	WHL	55	14	33	47	18	....	....	....	....	....	....	....	....	....	13	4	8	12	11	....	....	....	....
2006-07	Medicine Hat	WHL	59	32	37	69	56	....	....	....	....	....	....	....	....	....	23	4	15	19	24	....	....	....	....
2007-08	**Columbus**	**NHL**	**67**	**2**	**8**	**10**	**14**	**1**	**0**	**1**	**90**	**2.2**	**–12**	**0**	**0.0**	**14:47**	....	....	....	....	....	....	....	....	....
	NHL Totals		**67**	**2**	**8**	**10**	**14**	**1**	**0**	**1**	**90**	**2.2**		**0**	**0.0**	**14:47**	....	....	....	....	....	....	....	....	....

WHL East Second All-Star Team (2005) • WHL East First All-Star Team (2006, 2007) • WHL Defenseman of the Year (2006) • Canadian Major Junior Sportsman of the Year (2006) • WHL Player of the Year (2007) • Canadian Major Junior Defenseman of the Year (2007)

RUUTU, Jarkko

(ROO-too, YAHR-koh) **OTT.**

Right wing. Shoots left. 6', 200 lbs. Born, Vantaa, Finland, August 23, 1975. Vancouver's 3rd choice, 68th overall, in 1998 Entry Draft.

Season	Club	League	GP	G	A	Pts	PIM	PP	SH	GW	S	%	+/-	TF	F%	Min	GP	G	A	Pts	PIM	PP	SH	GW	Min
1991-92	HIFK Helsinki Jr.	Fin-Jr.	1	0	0	0	0	....	....	....	....	....	....	....	....	....	....	....	....	....	....	....	....	....	....
1992-93	HIFK Helsinki U18	Fin-U18	33	26	21	47	53	....	....	....	....	....	....	....	....	....	....	....	....	....	....	....	....	....	....
	HIFK Helsinki Jr.	Fin-Jr.	1	0	0	0	0	....	....	....	....	....	....	....	....	....	....	....	....	....	....	....	....	....	....
1993-94	HIFK Helsinki Jr.	Fin-Jr.	19	9	12	21	44	....	....	....	....	....	....	....	....	....	....	....	....	....	....	....	....	....	....
1994-95	HIFK Helsinki Jr.	Fin-Jr.	35	26	22	48	117	....	....	....	....	....	....	....	....	....	....	....	....	....	....	....	....	....	....
1995-96	Michigan Tech	WCHA	39	12	10	22	96	....	....	....	....	....	....	....	....	....	....	....	....	....	....	....	....	....	....
1996-97	HIFK Helsinki	Finland	48	11	10	21	155	....	....	....	....	....	....	....	....	....	....	....	....	....	....	....	....	....	....
1997-98	HIFK Helsinki	Finland	37	10	10	20	166	....	....	....	....	....	....	....	....	....	9	7	4	11	10	....	....	....	....
1998-99	HIFK Helsinki	Finland	25	10	4	14	136	....	....	....	....	....	....	....	....	....	9	0	2	2	43	....	....	....	....
	HIFK Helsinki	EuroHL	5	1	2	3	8	....	....	....	....	....	....	....	....	....	....	....	....	....	....	....	....	....	....
99-2000	**Vancouver**	**NHL**	**8**	**0**	**1**	**1**	**6**	**0**	**0**	**0**	**4**	**0.0**	**–1**	**0**	**0.0**	**8:47**	....	....	....	....	....	....	....	....	....
	Syracuse Crunch	AHL	65	26	32	58	164	....	....	....	....	....	....	....	....	....	4	3	1	4	8	....	....	....	....
2000-01	**Vancouver**	**NHL**	**21**	**3**	**3**	**6**	**32**	**0**	**1**	**0**	**23**	**13.0**	**1**	**0**	**0.0**	**10:39**	**4**	**0**	**1**	**1**	**8**	**0**	**0**	**0**	**10:18**
	Kansas City	IHL	46	11	18	29	111	....	....	....	....	....	....	....	....	....	....	....	....	....	....	....	....	....	....
2001-02	**Vancouver**	**NHL**	**49**	**2**	**7**	**9**	**74**	**0**	**0**	**0**	**37**	**5.4**	**–1**	**5**	**0.0**	**10:11**	**1**	**0**	**0**	**0**	**0**	**0**	**0**	**0**	**8:53**
	Finland	Olympics	4	0	0	0	4	....	....	....	....	....	....	....	....	....	....	....	....	....	....	....	....	....	....
2002-03	**Vancouver**	**NHL**	**36**	**2**	**2**	**4**	**66**	**0**	**0**	**1**	**36**	**5.6**	**–7**	**6**	**16.7**	**8:58**	**13**	**0**	**2**	**2**	**14**	**0**	**0**	**0**	**11:59**
2003-04	**Vancouver**	**NHL**	**71**	**6**	**8**	**14**	**133**	**1**	**0**	**0**	**70**	**8.6**	**–13**	**20**	**30.0**	**11:29**	**6**	**1**	**0**	**1**	**10**	**0**	**0**	**0**	**9:13**
2004-05	HIFK Helsinki	Finland	50	10	18	28	215	....	....	....	....	....	....	....	....	....	3	0	0	0	41	....	....	....	....
2005-06	**Vancouver**	**NHL**	**82**	**10**	**7**	**17**	**142**	**2**	**0**	**2**	**85**	**11.8**	**1**	**11**	**0.0**	**11:42**	....	....	....	....	....	....	....	....	....
	Finland	Olympics	8	0	0	0	31	....	....	....	....	....	....	....	....	....	....	....	....	....	....	....	....	....	....
2006-07	**Pittsburgh**	**NHL**	**81**	**7**	**9**	**16**	**125**	**0**	**0**	**2**	**63**	**11.1**	**0**	**3**	**100.0**	**9:20**	**5**	**0**	**0**	**0**	**10**	**0**	**0**	**0**	**6:38**
2007-08	**Pittsburgh**	**NHL**	**71**	**6**	**10**	**16**	**138**	**0**	**1**	**1**	**55**	**10.9**	**3**	**10**	**40.0**	**10:12**	**20**	**2**	**1**	**3**	**26**	**0**	**0**	**1**	**10:37**
	NHL Totals		**419**	**36**	**47**	**83**	**716**	**3**	**2**	**6**	**373**	**9.7**		**55**	**25.5**	**10:26**	**49**	**3**	**4**	**7**	**68**	**0**	**0**	**1**	**10:20**

• Missed majority of 2002-03 season as a healthy reserve. Signed as a free agent by **HIFK Helsinki** (Finland), September 23, 2004. Signed as a free agent by **Pittsburgh**, July 4, 2006. Signed as a free agent by **Ottawa**, July 2, 2008.

RUUTU, Tuomo

(ROO-too, TOO-oh-moh) **CAR.**

Center/Left wing. Shoots left. 6', 200 lbs. Born, Vantaa, Finland, February 16, 1983. Chicago's 1st choice, 9th overall, in 2001 Entry Draft.

Season	Club	League	GP	G	A	Pts	PIM	PP	SH	GW	S	%	+/-	TF	F%	Min	GP	G	A	Pts	PIM	PP	SH	GW	Min
1998-99	HIFK Helsinki U18	Fin-U18	25	9	11	20	88	....	....	....	....	....	....	....	....	....	2	1	1	2	2	....	....	....	....
99-2000	HIFK Helsinki U18	Fin-U18	5	0	3	3	12	....	....	....	....	....	....	....	....	....	3	1	2	3	2	....	....	....	....
	HIFK Helsinki Jr.	Fin-Jr.	35	11	16	27	32	....	....	....	....	....	....	....	....	....	3	0	1	1	4	....	....	....	....
	HIFK Helsinki	Finland	1	0	0	0	2	....	....	....	....	....	....	....	....	....	....	....	....	....	....	....	....	....	....
2000-01	Jokerit Helsinki Jr.	Fin-Jr.	2	1	0	1	0	....	....	....	....	....	....	....	....	....	....	....	....	....	....	....	....	....	....
	Jokerit Helsinki	Finland	47	11	11	22	94	....	....	....	....	....	....	....	....	....	5	0	0	0	4	....	....	....	....
2001-02	Jokerit Helsinki	Finland	51	7	16	23	69	....	....	....	....	....	....	....	....	....	10	0	6	6	29	....	....	....	....
2002-03	HIFK Helsinki	Finland	30	12	15	27	24	....	....	....	....	....	....	....	....	....	....	....	....	....	....	....	....	....	....
2003-04	**Chicago**	**NHL**	**82**	**23**	**21**	**44**	**58**	**10**	**0**	**3**	**174**	**13.2**	**–31**	**317**	**46.4**	**16:24**	....	....	....	....	....	....	....	....	....
2004-05			DID NOT PLAY																						
2005-06	**Chicago**	**NHL**	**15**	**2**	**3**	**5**	**31**	**1**	**0**	**0**	**30**	**6.7**	**–7**	**90**	**46.7**	**14:43**	....	....	....	....	....	....	....	....	....
2006-07	**Chicago**	**NHL**	**71**	**17**	**21**	**38**	**95**	**1**	**0**	**1**	**115**	**14.8**	**4**	**347**	**42.7**	**17:21**	....	....	....	....	....	....	....	....	....
2007-08	**Chicago**	**NHL**	**60**	**6**	**15**	**21**	**75**	**1**	**0**	**1**	**71**	**8.5**	**3**	**49**	**53.1**	**15:35**	....	....	....	....	....	....	....	....	....
	Carolina	**NHL**	**17**	**4**	**7**	**11**	**16**	**3**	**0**	**0**	**29**	**13.8**	**1**	**17**	**11.8**	**17:01**	....	....	....	....	....	....	....	....	....
	NHL Totals		**245**	**52**	**67**	**119**	**275**	**16**	**0**	**5**	**419**	**12.4**		**820**	**44.5**	**16:25**	....	....	....	....	....	....	....	....	....

• Missed majority of 2005-06 season recovering from back (October 15, 2005 at San Jose) and ankle (January 8, 2006 vs. Nashville) injuries. Traded to **Carolina** by **Chicago** for Andrew Ladd, February 26, 2008.

RUZICKA, Stefan

(roo-ZHEECH-kuh, STEH-fan) **PHI.**

Right wing. Shoots right. 6', 205 lbs. Born, Nitra, Czech., February 17, 1985. Philadelphia's 4th choice, 81st overall, in 2003 Entry Draft.

Season	Club	League	GP	G	A	Pts	PIM	PP	SH	GW	S	%	+/-	TF	F%	Min	GP	G	A	Pts	PIM	PP	SH	GW	Min
2000-01	Nitra Jr.	Slovak-Jr.	38	30	15	45	....	....	....	....	....	....	....	....	....	....	....	....	....	....	....	....	....	....	....
2001-02	HKM Nitra Jr.	Slovak-Jr.	29	27	25	52	....	....	....	....	....	....	....	....	....	....	....	....	....	....	....	....	....	....	....
	HKM Nitra	Slovakia	19	0	5	5	29	....	....	....	....	....	....	....	....	....	....	....	....	....	....	....	....	....	....
2002-03	HKM Nitra Jr.	Slovak-Jr.	30	18	22	40	64	....	....	....	....	....	....	....	....	....	....	....	....	....	....	....	....	....	....
	HKM Nitra	Slovak-2	17	5	7	12	4	....	....	....	....	....	....	....	....	....	....	....	....	....	....	....	....	....	....
2003-04	Owen Sound	OHL	62	34	38	72	63	....	....	....	....	....	....	....	....	....	7	1	6	7	8	....	....	....	....
	Philadelphia	AHL	2	0	0	0	0	....	....	....	....	....	....	....	....	....	3	1	0	1	2	....	....	....	....
2004-05	Owen Sound	OHL	62	37	33	70	61	....	....	....	....	....	....	....	....	....	8	3	3	6	14	....	....	....	....
2005-06	**Philadelphia**	**NHL**	**1**	**0**	**0**	**0**	**2**	**0**	**0**	**0**	**1**	**0.0**	**0**	**1**	**0.0**	**4:48**	....	....	....	....	....	....	....	....	....
	Philadelphia	AHL	73	16	32	48	88	....	....	....	....	....	....	....	....	....	....	....	....	....	....	....	....	....	....
2006-07	**Philadelphia**	**NHL**	**40**	**3**	**10**	**13**	**18**	**1**	**0**	**0**	**75**	**4.0**	**–6**	**3**	**0.0**	**12:44**	....	....	....	....	....	....	....	....	....
	Philadelphia	AHL	32	16	11	27	29	....	....	....	....	....	....	....	....	....	....	....	....	....	....	....	....	....	....
2007-08	**Philadelphia**	**NHL**	**14**	**1**	**3**	**4**	**27**	**0**	**0**	**0**	**10**	**10.0**	**5**	**5**	**0.0**	**8:40**	....	....	....	....	....	....	....	....	....
	Philadelphia	AHL	59	19	31	50	105	....	....	....	....	....	....	....	....	....	12	4	9	13	30	....	....	....	....
	NHL Totals		**55**	**4**	**13**	**17**	**47**	**1**	**0**	**0**	**86**	**4.7**		**9**	**0.0**	**11:33**	....	....	....	....	....	....	....	....	....

OHL All-Rookie Team (2004) • OHL Second All-Star Team (2004)

RYAN, Bobby

(RIGH-uhn, BAW-bee) **ANA.**

Right wing. Shoots right. 6'2", 218 lbs. Born, Cherry Hill, NJ, March 17, 1987. Anaheim's 1st choice, 2nd overall, in 2005 Entry Draft.

Season	Club	League	GP	G	A	Pts	PIM	PP	SH	GW	S	%	+/-	TF	F%	Min	GP	G	A	Pts	PIM	PP	SH	GW	Min
2003-04	Owen Sound	OHL	65	22	17	39	52	....	....	....	....	....	....	....	....	....	7	1	2	3	2	....	....	....	....
2004-05	Owen Sound	OHL	62	37	52	89	51	....	....	....	....	....	....	....	....	....	8	2	7	9	8	....	....	....	....
2005-06	Owen Sound	OHL	59	31	64	95	44	....	....	....	....	....	....	....	....	....	11	5	7	12	14	....	....	....	....
	Portland Pirates	AHL	....	....	....	....	....	....	....	....	....	....	....	....	....	....	19	1	7	8	22	....	....	....	....
2006-07	Owen Sound	OHL	63	43	59	102	63	....	....	....	....	....	....	....	....	....	4	1	1	2	2	....	....	....	....
	Portland Pirates	AHL	8	3	6	9	6	....	....	....	....	....	....	....	....	....	....	....	....	....	....	....	....	....	....
2007-08	**Anaheim**	**NHL**	**23**	**5**	**5**	**10**	**6**	**3**	**0**	**0**	**37**	**13.5**	**–1**	**1**	**100.0**	**11:16**	**2**	**0**	**0**	**0**	**2**	**0**	**0**	**0**	**11:09**
	Portland Pirates	AHL	48	21	28	49	38	....	....	....	....	....	....	....	....	....	16	8	12	20	18	....	....	....	....
	NHL Totals		**23**	**5**	**5**	**10**	**6**	**3**	**0**	**0**	**37**	**13.5**		**1**	**100.0**	**11:16**	**2**	**0**	**0**	**0**	**2**	**0**	**0**	**0**	**11:09**

OHL First All-Star Team (2005)

RYAN, Matt

(RIGH-uhn, MAT)

Center. Shoots right. 5'11", 185 lbs. Born, Sharon, Ont., November 12, 1983.

Season	Club	League	GP	G	A	Pts	PIM	PP	SH	GW	S	%	+/-	TF	F%	Min	Playoffs GP	G	A	Pts	PIM	PP	SH	GW	Min
			Regular Season														Playoffs								
2001-02	Niagara University	CHA	32	7	12	19	32	....	....	....	....	....	....	....	....	....	....	....	....	....	....	....	....	....	....
2002-03	Niagara University	CHA	9	6	2	8	14	....	....	....	....	....	....	....	....	....	....	....	....	....	....	....	....	....	....
	Guelph Storm	OHL	48	14	11	25	34	....	....	....	....	....	....	....	....	....	11	2	7	9	0	....	....	....	....
2003-04	Guelph Storm	OHL	68	42	35	77	63	....	....	....	....	....	....	....	....	....	22	8	11	19	24	....	....	....	....
2004-05	Manchester	AHL	77	9	15	24	59	....	....	....	....	....	....	....	....	....	6	0	1	1	4	....	....	....	....
2005-06	**Los Angeles**	**NHL**	**12**	**0**	**1**	**1**	**2**	**0**	**0**	**0**	**8**	**0.0**	**–4**	**64**	**45.3**	**6:07**	....	....	....	....	....	....	....	....	....
	Manchester	AHL	68	12	12	24	79	....	....	....	....	....	....	....	....	....	7	1	1	2	8	....	....	....	....
2006-07	Manchester	AHL	56	8	16	24	50	....	....	....	....	....	....	....	....	....	16	3	5	8	13	....	....	....	....
2007-08	Manchester	AHL	65	8	6	14	74	....	....	....	....	....	....	....	....	....	4	0	1	1	2	....	....	....	....
	NHL Totals		**12**	**0**	**1**	**1**	**2**	**0**	**0**	**0**	**8**	**0.0**		**64**	**45.3**	**6:07**	....	....	....	....	....	....	....	....	....

Signed as a free agent by **Los Angeles**, August 2, 2004.

RYAN, Michael

(RIGH-uhn, MIGH-kuhl)

Center. Shoots left. 6'1", 188 lbs. Born, Boston, MA, May 16, 1980. Dallas' 1st choice, 32nd overall, in 1999 Entry Draft.

Season	Club	League	GP	G	A	Pts	PIM	PP	SH	GW	S	%	+/-	TF	F%	Min	Playoffs GP	G	A	Pts	PIM	PP	SH	GW	Min
1997-98	Bos. College High	High-MA	23	22	14	36	28	....	....	....	....	....	....	....	....	....	....	....	....	....	....	....	....	....	....
1998-99	Bos. College High	High-MA	21	20	24	44	22	....	....	....	....	....	....	....	....	....	....	....	....	....	....	....	....	....	....
99-2000	Northeastern	H-East	32	4	9	13	47	....	....	....	....	....	....	....	....	....	....	....	....	....	....	....	....	....	....
2000-01	Northeastern	H-East	33	17	12	29	52	....	....	....	....	....	....	....	....	....	....	....	....	....	....	....	....	....	....
2001-02	Northeastern	H-East	36	24	15	39	54	....	....	....	....	....	....	....	....	....	....	....	....	....	....	....	....	....	....
2002-03	Northeastern	H-East	34	18	14	32	30	....	....	....	....	....	....	....	....	....	....	....	....	....	....	....	....	....	....
2003-04	Rochester	AHL	45	3	9	12	31	....	....	....	....	....	....	....	....	....	....	....	....	....	....	....	....	....	....
2004-05	Rochester	AHL	59	11	11	22	20	....	....	....	....	....	....	....	....	....	5	0	1	1	4	....	....	....	....
2005-06	Rochester	AHL	56	15	22	37	70	....	....	....	....	....	....	....	....	....	....	....	....	....	....	....	....	....	....
2006-07	**Buffalo**	**NHL**	**19**	**3**	**2**	**5**	**2**	**0**	**1**	**0**	**34**	**8.8**	**–8**	**2**	**0.0**	**13:40**	....	....	....	....	....	....	....	....	....
	Rochester	AHL	50	28	23	51	68	....	....	....	....	....	....	....	....	....	6	4	0	4	4	....	....	....	....
2007-08	**Buffalo**	**NHL**	**46**	**4**	**4**	**8**	**30**	**0**	**0**	**0**	**60**	**6.7**	**–4**	**2**	**0.0**	**9:53**	....	....	....	....	....	....	....	....	....
	NHL Totals		**65**	**7**	**6**	**13**	**32**	**0**	**1**	**0**	**94**	**7.4**		**4**	**0.0**	**10:59**	....	....	....	....	....	....	....	....	....

Traded to **Buffalo** by **Dallas** with Dallas's 2nd round choice (Branislav Fabry) in 2003 Entry Draft for Stu Barnes, March 10, 2003.

RYAN, Prestin

(RIGH-uhn, PREH-stuhn)

Defense. Shoots left. 6', 190 lbs. Born, Arcola, Sask., June 29, 1980.

Season	Club	League	GP	G	A	Pts	PIM	PP	SH	GW	S	%	+/-	TF	F%	Min	Playoffs GP	G	A	Pts	PIM	PP	SH	GW	Min
2000-01	U. of Maine	H-East	DID NOT PLAY – FRESHMAN																						
2001-02	U. of Maine	H-East	39	6	9	15	*91	....	....	....	....	....	....	....	....	....	....	....	....	....	....	....	....	....	....
2002-03	U. of Maine	H-East	37	1	8	9	*120	....	....	....	....	....	....	....	....	....	....	....	....	....	....	....	....	....	....
2003-04	U. of Maine	H-East	43	4	18	22	*148	....	....	....	....	....	....	....	....	....	....	....	....	....	....	....	....	....	....
	Syracuse Crunch	AHL	....	....	....	....	....	....	....	....	....	....	....	....	....	....	3	0	0	0	2	....	....	....	....
2004-05	Syracuse Crunch	AHL	59	3	6	9	161	....	....	....	....	....	....	....	....	....	....	....	....	....	....	....	....	....	....
2005-06	**Vancouver**	**NHL**	**1**	**0**	**0**	**0**	**2**	**0**	**0**	**0**	**0**	**0.0**	**–1**	**0**	**0.0**	**7:30**	....	....	....	....	....	....	....	....	....
	Manitoba Moose	AHL	64	11	12	23	63	....	....	....	....	....	....	....	....	....	13	1	1	2	25	....	....	....	....
2006-07	Manitoba Moose	AHL	58	5	16	21	125	....	....	....	....	....	....	....	....	....	13	2	3	5	33	....	....	....	....
2007-08	Rockford IceHogs	AHL	44	7	17	24	117	....	....	....	....	....	....	....	....	....	....	....	....	....	....	....	....	....	....
	NHL Totals		**1**	**0**	**0**	**0**	**2**	**0**	**0**	**0**	**0**	**0.0**		**0**	**0.0**	**7:30**	....	....	....	....	....	....	....	....	....

Hockey East Second All-Star Team (2004) • NCAA East Second All-American Team (2004) • NCAA Championship All-Tournament Team (2004)

Signed as a free agent by **Columbus**, April 12, 2004. Signed as a free agent by **Vancouver**, August 18, 2005. Signed as a free agent by **Chicago**, July 27, 2007.

RYCROFT, Mark

(RIGH-krawft, MAHRK)

Right wing. Shoots right. 6', 192 lbs. Born, Penticton, B.C., July 12, 1978.

Season	Club	League	GP	G	A	Pts	PIM	PP	SH	GW	S	%	+/-	TF	F%	Min	Playoffs GP	G	A	Pts	PIM	PP	SH	GW	Min
1993-94	Penticton Ice	Minor-BC	60	47	65	112	100	....	....	....	....	....	....	....	....	....	....	....	....	....	....	....	....	....	....
1994-95	Penticton Ice	Minor-BC	43	33	43	76	90	....	....	....	....	....	....	....	....	....	....	....	....	....	....	....	....	....	....
1995-96	Nanaimo Clippers	BCHL	60	17	28	45	28	....	....	....	....	....	....	....	....	....	....	....	....	....	....	....	....	....	....
1996-97	Nanaimo Clippers	BCHL	58	32	35	67	79	....	....	....	....	....	....	....	....	....	....	....	....	....	....	....	....	....	....
1997-98	U. of Denver	WCHA	35	15	17	32	28	....	....	....	....	....	....	....	....	....	....	....	....	....	....	....	....	....	....
1998-99	U. of Denver	WCHA	41	19	18	37	36	....	....	....	....	....	....	....	....	....	....	....	....	....	....	....	....	....	....
99-2000	U. of Denver	WCHA	41	17	17	34	87	....	....	....	....	....	....	....	....	....	....	....	....	....	....	....	....	....	....
2000-01	Worcester IceCats	AHL	71	24	26	50	68	....	....	....	....	....	....	....	....	....	11	2	5	7	4	....	....	....	....
2001-02	**St. Louis**	**NHL**	**9**	**0**	**3**	**3**	**4**	**0**	**0**	**0**	**14**	**0.0**	**0**	**1**	**0.0**	**9:50**	....	....	....	....	....	....	....	....	....
	Worcester IceCats	AHL	66	12	19	31	68	....	....	....	....	....	....	....	....	....	3	0	1	1	0	....	....	....	....
2002-03	Worcester IceCats	AHL	45	8	18	26	35	....	....	....	....	....	....	....	....	....	1	0	0	0	0	....	....	....	....
2003-04	**St. Louis**	**NHL**	**71**	**9**	**12**	**21**	**32**	**0**	**0**	**0**	**110**	**8.2**	**2**	**11**	**63.6**	**14:23**	**3**	**0**	**0**	**0**	**2**	**0**	**0**	**0**	**9:41**
2004-05	HC Briancon	France	13	8	8	16	18	....	....	....	....	....	....	....	....	....	4	2	1	3	0	....	....	....	....
2005-06	**St. Louis**	**NHL**	**80**	**6**	**4**	**10**	**46**	**0**	**1**	**2**	**77**	**7.8**	**–14**	**23**	**34.8**	**10:27**	....	....	....	....	....	....	....	....	....
2006-07	**Colorado**	**NHL**	**66**	**6**	**6**	**12**	**31**	**0**	**0**	**2**	**74**	**8.1**	**3**	**36**	**50.0**	**9:25**	....	....	....	....	....	....	....	....	....
2007-08	Lake Erie	AHL	30	1	6	7	17	....	....	....	....	....	....	....	....	....	....	....	....	....	....	....	....	....	....
	Syracuse Crunch	AHL	34	3	10	13	10	....	....	....	....	....	....	....	....	....	13	2	2	4	4	....	....	....	....
	NHL Totals		**226**	**21**	**25**	**46**	**113**	**0**	**1**	**4**	**275**	**7.6**		**71**	**46.5**	**11:22**	**3**	**0**	**0**	**0**	**2**	**0**	**0**	**0**	**9:41**

WCHA All-Rookie Team (1998)

Signed as a free agent by **St. Louis**, May 15, 2000. Signed as a free agent by **Briancon** (France), November 9, 2004. Signed as a free agent by **Colorado**, July 12, 2006. Traded to **Columbus** by **Colorado** for Darcy Campbell and Phillipe Dupuis, January 22, 2008.

RYDER, Michael

(RIGH-duhr, MIGH-kuhl) **BOS.**

Right wing. Shoots right. 6', 186 lbs. Born, Bonavista, Nfld., March 31, 1980. Montreal's 9th choice, 216th overall, in 1998 Entry Draft.

Season	Club	League	GP	G	A	Pts	PIM	PP	SH	GW	S	%	+/-	TF	F%	Min	Playoffs GP	G	A	Pts	PIM	PP	SH	GW	Min
1996-97	Bonavista Saints	NFAHA	23	31	17	48	....	....	....	....	....	....	....	....	....	....	....	....	....	....	....	....	....	....	....
1997-98	Hull Olympiques	QMJHL	69	34	28	62	41	....	....	....	....	....	....	....	....	....	10	4	2	6	4	....	....	....	....
1998-99	Hull Olympiques	QMJHL	69	44	43	87	65	....	....	....	....	....	....	....	....	....	23	*20	16	36	39	....	....	....	....
99-2000	Hull Olympiques	QMJHL	63	50	58	108	50	....	....	....	....	....	....	....	....	....	15	11	17	28	28	....	....	....	....
2000-01	Tallahassee	ECHL	5	4	5	9	6	....	....	....	....	....	....	....	....	....	....	....	....	....	....	....	....	....	....
	Quebec Citadelles	AHL	61	6	9	15	14	....	....	....	....	....	....	....	....	....	....	....	....	....	....	....	....	....	....
2001-02	Mississippi	ECHL	20	14	13	27	2	....	....	....	....	....	....	....	....	....	....	....	....	....	....	....	....	....	....
	Quebec Citadelles	AHL	50	11	17	28	9	....	....	....	....	....	....	....	....	....	3	0	1	1	2	....	....	....	....
2002-03	Hamilton	AHL	69	34	33	67	43	....	....	....	....	....	....	....	....	....	23	11	6	17	8	....	....	....	....
2003-04	**Montreal**	**NHL**	**81**	**25**	**38**	**63**	**26**	**10**	**0**	**4**	**215**	**11.6**	**10**	**25**	**24.0**	**16:00**	**11**	**1**	**2**	**3**	**4**	**0**	**0**	**0**	**16:52**
2004-05	Leksands IF	Sweden-2	42	34	27	61	32	....	....	....	....	....	....	....	....	....	....	....	....	....	....	....	....	....	....
2005-06	**Montreal**	**NHL**	**81**	**30**	**25**	**55**	**40**	**18**	**0**	**6**	**243**	**12.3**	**–5**	**17**	**52.9**	**16:10**	**6**	**2**	**3**	**5**	**0**	**1**	**0**	**1**	**16:09**
2006-07	**Montreal**	**NHL**	**82**	**30**	**28**	**58**	**60**	**17**	**2**	**3**	**221**	**13.6**	**–25**	**28**	**42.9**	**16:17**	....	....	....	....	....	....	....	....	....
2007-08	**Montreal**	**NHL**	**70**	**14**	**17**	**31**	**30**	**1**	**0**	**2**	**134**	**10.4**	**–4**	**19**	**26.3**	**13:15**	**4**	**0**	**0**	**0**	**2**	**0**	**0**	**0**	**10:46**
	NHL Totals		**314**	**99**	**108**	**207**	**156**	**46**	**2**	**15**	**813**	**12.2**		**89**	**36.0**	**15:30**	**21**	**3**	**5**	**8**	**6**	**1**	**0**	**1**	**15:30**

NHL All-Rookie Team (2004)

Signed as a free agent by **Leksands** (Sweden-2), September 19, 2004. Signed as a free agent by **Boston**, July 1, 2008.

RYPIEN, Rick

(RIH-pihn, RIHK) **VAN.**

Center. Shoots right. 5'11", 184 lbs. Born, Coleman, Alta, May 16, 1984.

Season	Club	League	GP	G	A	Pts	PIM	PP	SH	GW	S	%	+/-	TF	F%	Min	Playoffs GP	G	A	Pts	PIM	PP	SH	GW	Min
2001-02	Crowsnest Pass	AJHL	57	12	10	22	143	....	....	....	....	....	....	....	....	....	....	....	....	....	....	....	....	....	....
	Regina Pats	WHL	1	0	0	0	0	....	....	....	....	....	....	....	....	....	....	....	....	....	....	....	....	....	....
2002-03	Regina Pats	WHL	50	6	12	18	159	....	....	....	....	....	....	....	....	....	5	1	1	2	21	....	....	....	....
2003-04	Regina Pats	WHL	65	19	26	45	186	....	....	....	....	....	....	....	....	....	4	0	1	1	18	....	....	....	....
2004-05	Regina Pats	WHL	63	22	29	51	148	....	....	....	....	....	....	....	....	....	....	....	....	....	....	....	....	....	....
	Manitoba Moose	AHL	8	1	1	2	5	....	....	....	....	....	....	....	....	....	14	0	0	0	35	....	....	....	....
2005-06	Manitoba Moose	AHL	49	9	6	15	122	....	....	....	....	....	....	....	....	....	13	1	1	2	22	....	....	....	....
	Vancouver	**NHL**	**5**	**1**	**0**	**1**	**4**	**0**	**0**	**0**	**6**	**16.7**	**1**	**22**	**36.4**	**6:19**	....	....	....	....	....	....	....	....	....

			Regular Season														Playoffs								
Season	Club	League	GP	G	A	Pts	PIM	PP	SH	GW	S	%	+/-	TF	F%	Min	GP	G	A	Pts	PIM	PP	SH	GW	Min
2006-07	**Vancouver**	**NHL**	2	0	0	0	5	0	0	0	0	0.0	0	6	66.7	4:46	....	....	....	....	....	....	....	....	....
	Manitoba Moose	AHL	14	3	3	6	35	....	....	....	....	....	....	....	....	....	....	....	....	....	....	....	....	....	....
2007-08	**Vancouver**	**NHL**	22	1	2	3	41	0	0	0	8	12.5	–5	106	41.5	8:07	....	....	....	....	....	....	....	....	....
	Manitoba Moose	AHL	34	3	11	14	81	....	....	....	....	....	....	....	....	....	6	0	0	0	10	....	....	....	....
	NHL Totals		29	2	2	4	50	0	0	0	14	14.3		134	41.8	7:34	....	....	....	....	....	....	....	....	....

Signed to an ATO (tryout) contract by **Manitoba** (AHL), March 22, 2005. Signed as a free agent by **Vancouver**, November 9, 2005. • Missed majority of 2006-07 season recovering from recurring groin injury.

RYZNAR, Jason

(RIHZ-nuhr, JAY-suhn)

Left wing. Shoots left. 6′4″, 205 lbs. Born, Anchorage, AK, February 19, 1983. New Jersey's 3rd choice, 64th overall, in 2002 Entry Draft.

Season	Club	League	GP	G	A	Pts	PIM	PP	SH	GW	S	%	+/-	TF	F%	Min	GP	G	A	Pts	PIM	PP	SH	GW	Min
99-2000	USNTDP	NAHL	52	5	10	15	22	....	....	....	....	....	....	....	....	....	3	1	1	2	4	....	....	....	....
2000-01	USNTDP	U-18	42	11	14	25	71	....	....	....	....	....	....	....	....	....	....	....	....	....	....	....	....	....	....
	USNTDP	USHL	24	4	3	7	31	....	....	....	....	....	....	....	....	....	....	....	....	....	....	....	....	....	....
2001-02	U. of Michigan	CCHA	40	9	7	16	22	....	....	....	....	....	....	....	....	....	....	....	....	....	....	....	....	....	....
2002-03	U. of Michigan	CCHA	34	7	9	16	24	....	....	....	....	....	....	....	....	....	....	....	....	....	....	....	....	....	....
2003-04	U. of Michigan	CCHA	36	6	11	17	28	....	....	....	....	....	....	....	....	....	....	....	....	....	....	....	....	....	....
2004-05	U. of Michigan	CCHA	36	6	17	23	46	....	....	....	....	....	....	....	....	....	....	....	....	....	....	....	....	....	....
2005-06	**New Jersey**	**NHL**	8	0	0	0	2	0	0	0	1	0.0	–1	0	0.0	5:19	....	....	....	....	....	....	....	....	....
	Albany River Rats	AHL	59	7	18	25	52	....	....	....	....	....	....	....	....	....	....	....	....	....	....	....	....	....	....
2006-07	Lowell Devils	AHL	55	5	5	10	25	....	....	....	....	....	....	....	....	....	....	....	....	....	....	....	....	....	....
2007-08	Lowell Devils	AHL	55	10	8	18	38	....	....	....	....	....	....	....	....	....	....	....	....	....	....	....	....	....	....
	NHL Totals		8	0	0	0	2	0	0	0	1	0.0		0	0.0	5:19	....	....	....	....	....	....	....	....	....

ST. JACQUES, Bruno

(SAINT ZHAWK, BROO-noh)

Defense. Shoots left. 6′2″, 216 lbs. Born, Montreal, Que., August 22, 1980. Philadelphia's 12th choice, 253rd overall, in 1998 Entry Draft.

Season	Club	League	GP	G	A	Pts	PIM	PP	SH	GW	S	%	+/-	TF	F%	Min	GP	G	A	Pts	PIM	PP	SH	GW	Min
1996-97	Mtl-Bourassa	QAAA	40	5	8	13	....	....	....	....	....	....	....	....	....	....	16	0	7	7	....	....	....	....	....
1997-98	Baie-Comeau	QMJHL	63	1	11	12	140	....	....	....	....	....	....	....	....	....	....	....	....	....	....	....	....	....	....
1998-99	Baie-Comeau	QMJHL	49	8	13	21	85	....	....	....	....	....	....	....	....	....	....	....	....	....	....	....	....	....	....
99-2000	Baie-Comeau	QMJHL	60	8	28	36	120	....	....	....	....	....	....	....	....	....	6	0	2	2	10	....	....	....	....
	Philadelphia	AHL	3	0	1	1	0	....	....	....	....	....	....	....	....	....	1	0	0	0	0	....	....	....	....
2000-01	Philadelphia	AHL	45	1	16	17	83	....	....	....	....	....	....	....	....	....	10	1	0	1	16	....	....	....	....
2001-02	**Philadelphia**	**NHL**	7	0	0	0	2	0	0	0	4	0.0	4	0	0.0	13:51	....	....	....	....	....	....	....	....	....
	Philadelphia	AHL	55	3	11	14	59	....	....	....	....	....	....	....	....	....	4	0	0	0	0	....	....	....	....
2002-03	**Philadelphia**	**NHL**	6	0	0	0	2	0	0	0	5	0.0	–1	0	0.0	14:35	....	....	....	....	....	....	....	....	....
	Philadelphia	AHL	30	0	7	7	46	....	....	....	....	....	....	....	....	....	....	....	....	....	....	....	....	....	....
	Carolina	**NHL**	18	2	5	7	12	0	0	0	14	14.3	–3	0	0.0	18:15	....	....	....	....	....	....	....	....	....
	Lowell	AHL	8	1	1	2	8	....	....	....	....	....	....	....	....	....	....	....	....	....	....	....	....	....	....
2003-04	**Carolina**	**NHL**	35	0	2	2	31	0	0	0	16	0.0	–7	0	0.0	11:50	....	....	....	....	....	....	....	....	....
	Lowell	AHL	6	0	0	0	8	....	....	....	....	....	....	....	....	....	....	....	....	....	....	....	....	....	....
2004-05	Lowell	AHL	68	2	12	14	60	....	....	....	....	....	....	....	....	....	11	1	4	5	4	....	....	....	....
2005-06	**Anaheim**	**NHL**	1	1	0	1	0	0	0	0	2	50.0	1	0	0.0	13:53	....	....	....	....	....	....	....	....	....
	Portland Pirates	AHL	60	6	19	25	55	....	....	....	....	....	....	....	....	....	14	3	4	7	18	....	....	....	....
2006-07	Portland Pirates	AHL	25	1	8	9	26	....	....	....	....	....	....	....	....	....	....	....	....	....	....	....	....	....	....
	Norfolk Admirals	AHL	37	4	8	12	33	....	....	....	....	....	....	....	....	....	6	0	2	2	10	....	....	....	....
2007-08	Syracuse Crunch	AHL	13	0	8	8	16	....	....	....	....	....	....	....	....	....	....	....	....	....	....	....	....	....	....
	Portland Pirates	AHL	48	8	12	20	49	....	....	....	....	....	....	....	....	....	6	0	3	3	17	....	....	....	....
	NHL Totals		67	3	7	10	47	0	0	0	41	7.3		0	0.0	14:03	....	....	....	....	....	....	....	....	....

Traded to **Carolina** by **Philadelphia** with Pavel Brendl for Sami Kapanen and Ryan Bast, February 7, 2003. • Missed majority of 2003-04 season recovering from abdominal injury suffered in game vs. Philadelphia, November 28, 2003. Traded to **Anaheim** by **Carolina** for Craig Adams, October 3, 2005. Traded to **Chicago** by **Anaheim** with Pierre Parenteau for Sebastien Caron, Matt Keith and Chris Durno, December 28, 2006. Signed as a free agent by **Syracuse** (AHL), October 4, 2007. Traded to **Portland** (AHL) by **Syracuse** (AHL) for future considerations, November 15, 2007. Signed as a free agent by **Anaheim**, December 10, 2007.

ST. LOUIS, Martin

(SAINT loo-EE, mahr-TEHN) **T.B.**

Right wing. Shoots left. 5′9″, 177 lbs. Born, Laval, Que., June 18, 1975.

Season	Club	League	GP	G	A	Pts	PIM	PP	SH	GW	S	%	+/-	TF	F%	Min	GP	G	A	Pts	PIM	PP	SH	GW	Min
1991-92	Laval-Laurentides	QAAA	42	29	*74	*103	38	....	....	....	....	....	....	....	....	....	12	7	15	22	16	....	....	....	....
1992-93	Hawkesbury	CJHL	31	37	50	87	70	....	....	....	....	....	....	....	....	....	....	....	....	....	....	....	....	....	....
1993-94	U. of Vermont	ECAC	33	15	36	51	24	....	....	....	....	....	....	....	....	....	....	....	....	....	....	....	....	....	....
1994-95	U. of Vermont	ECAC	35	23	48	71	36	....	....	....	....	....	....	....	....	....	....	....	....	....	....	....	....	....	....
1995-96	U. of Vermont	ECAC	35	29	56	85	38	....	....	....	....	....	....	....	....	....	....	....	....	....	....	....	....	....	....
1996-97	U. of Vermont	ECAC	36	24	*36	60	65	....	....	....	....	....	....	....	....	....	....	....	....	....	....	....	....	....	....
1997-98	Cleveland	IHL	56	16	34	50	24	....	....	....	....	....	....	....	....	....	....	....	....	....	....	....	....	....	....
	Saint John Flames	AHL	25	15	11	26	20	....	....	....	....	....	....	....	....	....	20	5	15	20	16	....	....	....	....
1998-99	**Calgary**	**NHL**	13	1	1	2	10	0	0	0	14	7.1	–2	0	0.0	8:15	....	....	....	....	....	....	....	....	....
	Saint John Flames	AHL	53	28	34	62	30	....	....	....	....	....	....	....	....	....	7	4	4	8	2	....	....	....	....
99-2000	**Calgary**	**NHL**	56	3	15	18	22	0	0	1	73	4.1	–5	3	0.0	14:41	....	....	....	....	....	....	....	....	....
	Saint John Flames	AHL	17	15	11	26	14	....	....	....	....	....	....	....	....	....	....	....	....	....	....	....	....	....	....
2000-01	**Tampa Bay**	**NHL**	78	18	22	40	12	3	3	4	141	12.8	–4	48	41.7	15:14	....	....	....	....	....	....	....	....	....
2001-02	**Tampa Bay**	**NHL**	53	16	19	35	20	6	1	2	105	15.2	4	33	39.4	18:41	....	....	....	....	....	....	....	....	....
2002-03	**Tampa Bay**	**NHL**	82	33	37	70	32	12	3	5	201	16.4	10	37	37.8	19:43	11	7	5	12	0	1	2	3	22:21
2003-04♦	**Tampa Bay**	**NHL**	82	38	*56	*94	24	8	8	7	212	17.9	35	24	33.3	20:35	23	9	*15	24	14	3	1	3	22:52
2004-05	Lausanne HC	Swiss	23	9	16	25	16	....	....	....	....	....	....	....	....	....	....	....	....	....	....	....	....	....	....
2005-06	**Tampa Bay**	**NHL**	80	31	30	61	38	9	3	7	221	14.0	–3	13	23.1	20:59	5	4	0	4	2	1	0	1	22:53
	Canada	Olympics	6	2	1	3	0	....	....	....	....	....	....	....	....	....	....	....	....	....	....	....	....	....	....
2006-07	**Tampa Bay**	**NHL**	82	43	59	102	28	14	5	7	273	15.8	7	20	35.0	24:09	6	3	5	8	8	1	0	0	28:07
2007-08	**Tampa Bay**	**NHL**	82	25	58	83	26	10	2	5	241	10.4	–23	12	25.0	24:17	....	....	....	....	....	....	....	....	....
	NHL Totals		608	208	297	505	212	62	25	38	1481	14.0		190	35.8	19:50	45	23	25	48	24	6	3	7	23:27

ECAC First All-Star Team (1995, 1996, 1997) • ECAC Player of the Year (1995) • NCAA East First All-American Team (1995, 1996, 1997) • NCAA Championship All-Tournament Team (1996) • NHL First All-Star Team (2004) • Art Ross Trophy (2004) • Lester B. Pearson Award (2004) • Hart Memorial Trophy (2004) • NHL Second All-Star Team (2007)

Played in NHL All-Star Game (2003, 2004, 2007, 2008)

Signed as a free agent by **Calgary**, February 19, 1998. Signed as a free agent by **Tampa Bay**, July 31, 2000. Signed as a free agent by **Lausanne** (Swiss), November 4, 2004.

ST. PIERRE, Martin

(SAINT PEE-aihr, mahr-TEHN) **BOS.**

Center. Shoots left. 5′9″, 185 lbs. Born, Ottawa, Ont., August 11, 1983.

Season	Club	League	GP	G	A	Pts	PIM	PP	SH	GW	S	%	+/-	TF	F%	Min	GP	G	A	Pts	PIM	PP	SH	GW	Min
2000-01	Guelph Storm	OHL	68	20	49	69	40	....	....	....	....	....	....	....	....	....	4	0	0	0	4	....	....	....	....
2001-02	Guelph Storm	OHL	66	32	53	85	68	....	....	....	....	....	....	....	....	....	9	3	9	12	12	....	....	....	....
2002-03	Guelph Storm	OHL	55	11	45	56	74	....	....	....	....	....	....	....	....	....	11	5	11	16	4	....	....	....	....
2003-04	Guelph Storm	OHL	68	45	65	110	95	....	....	....	....	....	....	....	....	....	22	8	*27	*35	20	....	....	....	....
2004-05	Greenville	ECHL	45	14	39	53	55	....	....	....	....	....	....	....	....	....	7	2	5	7	6	....	....	....	....
	Edmonton	AHL	18	4	3	7	8	....	....	....	....	....	....	....	....	....	....	....	....	....	....	....	....	....	....
2005-06	**Chicago**	**NHL**	2	0	0	0	0	0	0	0	1	0.0	–1	15	33.3	12:02	....	....	....	....	....	....	....	....	....
	Norfolk Admirals	AHL	77	23	50	73	98	....	....	....	....	....	....	....	....	....	4	0	3	3	2	....	....	....	....
2006-07	**Chicago**	**NHL**	14	1	3	4	8	1	0	0	13	7.7	–3	129	48.1	12:29	....	....	....	....	....	....	....	....	....
	Norfolk Admirals	AHL	65	27	72	99	100	....	....	....	....	....	....	....	....	....	6	0	1	1	6	....	....	....	....
2007-08	Mytischi	Russia	14	1	6	7	16	....	....	....	....	....	....	....	....	....	....	....	....	....	....	....	....	....	....
	Chicago	**NHL**	5	0	0	0	0	0	0	0	2	0.0	–3	59	55.9	15:17	....	....	....	....	....	....	....	....	....
	Rockford IceHogs	AHL	69	21	67	88	80	....	....	....	....	....	....	....	....	....	12	2	12	14	12	....	....	....	....
	NHL Totals		21	1	3	4	8	1	0	0	16	6.3		203	49.3	13:06	....	....	....	....	....	....	....	....	....

AHL All-Rookie Team (2006) • AHL First All-Star Team (2007) • AHL Second All-Star Team (2008)

Signed as a free agent by **Chicago**, November 3, 2005. Signed as a free agent by **Mytischi** (Russia), June 22, 2007. Traded to **Boston** by **Chicago** for Pascal Pelletier, July 24, 2008.

SAKIC, Joe

(SAK-ihk, JOH) **COL.**

Center. Shoots left. 5'11", 195 lbs. Born, Burnaby, B.C., July 7, 1969. Quebec's 2nd choice, 15th overall, in 1987 Entry Draft.

			Regular Season														Playoffs								
Season	Club	League	GP	G	A	Pts	PIM	PP	SH	GW	S	%	+/-	TF	F%	Min	GP	G	A	Pts	PIM	PP	SH	GW	Min
1985-86	Burnaby	Minor-BC	80	83	73	156	96	....	....	....	....	....	....	....	....	....	....	....	....	....	....	....	....	....	....
	Lethbridge	WHL	3	0	0	0	0	....	....	....	....	....	....	....	....	....	....	....	....	....	....	....	....	....	....
1986-87	Swift Current	WHL	72	60	73	133	31	....	....	....	....	....	....	....	....	....	4	0	1	1	0	....	....	....	....
1987-88	Swift Current	WHL	64	*78	82	*160	64	....	....	....	....	....	....	....	....	....	10	11	13	24	12	....	....	....	....
1988-89	**Quebec**	**NHL**	**70**	**23**	**39**	**62**	**24**	**10**	**0**	**2**	**148**	**15.5**	**–36**	....	....	....	....	....	....	....	....	....	....	....	....
1989-90	**Quebec**	**NHL**	**80**	**39**	**63**	**102**	**27**	**8**	**1**	**2**	**234**	**16.7**	**–40**	....	....	....	....	....	....	....	....	....	....	....	....
1990-91	**Quebec**	**NHL**	**80**	**48**	**61**	**109**	**24**	**12**	**3**	**7**	**245**	**19.6**	**–26**	....	....	....	....	....	....	....	....	....	....	....	....
1991-92	**Quebec**	**NHL**	**69**	**29**	**65**	**94**	**20**	**6**	**3**	**1**	**217**	**13.4**	**5**	....	....	....	....	....	....	....	....	....	....	....	....
1992-93	**Quebec**	**NHL**	**78**	**48**	**57**	**105**	**40**	**20**	**2**	**4**	**264**	**18.2**	**–3**	....	....	....	**6**	**3**	**3**	**6**	**2**	**1**	**0**	**0**	....
1993-94	**Quebec**	**NHL**	**84**	**28**	**64**	**92**	**18**	**10**	**1**	**9**	**279**	**10.0**	**–8**	....	....	....	....	....	....	....	....	....	....	....	....
1994-95	**Quebec**	**NHL**	**47**	**19**	**43**	**62**	**30**	**3**	**2**	**5**	**157**	**12.1**	**7**	....	....	....	**6**	**4**	**1**	**5**	**0**	**1**	**1**	**1**	....
1995-96♦	**Colorado**	**NHL**	**82**	**51**	**69**	**120**	**44**	**17**	**6**	**7**	**339**	**15.0**	**14**	....	....	....	**22**	***18**	**16**	***34**	**14**	**6**	**0**	**6**	....
1996-97	**Colorado**	**NHL**	**65**	**22**	**52**	**74**	**34**	**10**	**2**	**5**	**261**	**8.4**	**–10**	....	....	....	**17**	**8**	***17**	**25**	**14**	**3**	**0**	**0**	....
1997-98	**Colorado**	**NHL**	**64**	**27**	**36**	**63**	**50**	**12**	**1**	**2**	**254**	**10.6**	**0**	....	....	....	**6**	**2**	**3**	**5**	**6**	**0**	**1**	**2**	....
	Canada	Olympics	4	1	2	3	4	....	....	....	....	....	....	....	....	....	....	....	....	....	....	....	....	....	....
1998-99	**Colorado**	**NHL**	**73**	**41**	**55**	**96**	**29**	**12**	**5**	**6**	**255**	**16.1**	**23**	**1723**	**51.4**	**25:35**	**19**	**6**	**13**	**19**	**8**	**1**	**1**	**1**	**25:01**
99-2000	**Colorado**	**NHL**	**60**	**28**	**53**	**81**	**28**	**5**	**1**	**5**	**242**	**11.6**	**30**	**1392**	**53.8**	**23:16**	**17**	**2**	**7**	**9**	**8**	**2**	**0**	**0**	**23:50**
2000-01♦	**Colorado**	**NHL**	**82**	**54**	**64**	**118**	**30**	**19**	**3**	**12**	**332**	**16.3**	**45**	**2292**	**53.0**	**23:01**	**21**	***13**	**13**	***26**	**6**	**5**	**0**	**3**	**21:33**
2001-02	**Colorado**	**NHL**	**82**	**26**	**53**	**79**	**18**	**9**	**1**	**4**	**260**	**10.0**	**12**	**2148**	**52.2**	**22:01**	**21**	**9**	**10**	**19**	**4**	**4**	**0**	**1**	**22:44**
	Canada	Olympics	6	4	3	7	0	....	....	....	....	....	....	....	....	....	....	....	....	....	....	....	....	....	....
2002-03	**Colorado**	**NHL**	**58**	**26**	**32**	**58**	**24**	**8**	**0**	**1**	**190**	**13.7**	**4**	**1359**	**50.8**	**21:12**	**7**	**6**	**3**	**9**	**2**	**2**	**0**	**1**	**22:29**
2003-04	**Colorado**	**NHL**	**81**	**33**	**54**	**87**	**42**	**13**	**1**	**3**	**253**	**13.0**	**11**	**1705**	**52.6**	**20:16**	**11**	**7**	**5**	**12**	**8**	**1**	**1**	**2**	**21:15**
2004-05			DID NOT PLAY																						
2005-06	**Colorado**	**NHL**	**82**	**32**	**55**	**87**	**60**	**10**	**0**	**6**	**263**	**12.2**	**10**	**1669**	**52.5**	**19:55**	**9**	**4**	**5**	**9**	**6**	**1**	**0**	**1**	**21:38**
	Canada	Olympics	6	1	2	3	0	....	....	....	....	....	....	....	....	....	....	....	....	....	....	....	....	....	....
2006-07	**Colorado**	**NHL**	**82**	**36**	**64**	**100**	**46**	**16**	**0**	**4**	**258**	**14.0**	**2**	**1368**	**53.1**	**20:11**	....	....	....	....	....	....	....	....	....
2007-08	**Colorado**	**NHL**	**44**	**13**	**27**	**40**	**20**	**5**	**0**	**1**	**124**	**10.5**	**–4**	**586**	**50.5**	**19:59**	**10**	**2**	**8**	**10**	**0**	**0**	**0**	**1**	**19:07**
	NHL Totals		**1363**	**623**	**1006**	**1629**	**608**	**205**	**32**	**86**	**4575**	**13.6**		**14242**	**52.4**	**21:44**	**172**	**84**	**104**	**188**	**78**	**27**	**4**	**19**	**22:30**

WHL East Second All-Star Team (1987) • WHL East Rookie of the Year (1987) • WHL East Player of the Year (1987) • WHL East First All-Star Team (1988) • WHL Player of the Year (1988) • Canadian Major Junior Player of the Year (1988) • Conn Smythe Trophy (1996) • NHL First All-Star Team (2001, 2002, 2004) • Bud Light Plus/Minus Award (2001) (tied with Patrik Elias) • Lady Byng Memorial Trophy (2001) • Lester B. Pearson Award (2001) • Hart Memorial Trophy (2001) • Olympic Tournament MVP (2002)

Played in NHL All-Star Game (1990, 1991, 1992, 1993, 1994, 1996, 1998, 2000, 2001, 2002, 2004, 2007)

Transferred to **Colorado** after **Quebec** franchise relocated, June 21, 1995.

SALEI, Ruslan

(sah-LAY, roos-LAHN) **COL.**

Defense. Shoots left. 6'1", 212 lbs. Born, Minsk, USSR, November 2, 1974. Anaheim's 1st choice, 9th overall, in 1996 Entry Draft.

			Regular Season														Playoffs								
Season	Club	League	GP	G	A	Pts	PIM	PP	SH	GW	S	%	+/-	TF	F%	Min	GP	G	A	Pts	PIM	PP	SH	GW	Min
1992-93	Dynamo Moscow	CIS	9	1	0	1	10	....	....	....	....	....	....	....	....	....	....	....	....	....	....	....	....	....	....
1993-94	Tivali Minsk	CIS	39	2	3	5	50	....	....	....	....	....	....	....	....	....	....	....	....	....	....	....	....	....	....
1994-95	Tivali Minsk	CIS	51	4	2	6	44	....	....	....	....	....	....	....	....	....	....	....	....	....	....	....	....	....	....
1995-96	Las Vegas	IHL	76	7	23	30	123	....	....	....	....	....	....	....	....	....	15	3	7	10	18	....	....	....	....
1996-97	**Anaheim**	**NHL**	**30**	**0**	**1**	**1**	**37**	**0**	**0**	**0**	**14**	**0.0**	**–8**	....	....	....	....	....	....	....	....	....	....	....	....
	Baltimore Bandits	AHL	12	1	4	5	12	....	....	....	....	....	....	....	....	....	....	....	....	....	....	....	....	....	....
	Las Vegas	IHL	8	0	2	2	24	....	....	....	....	....	....	....	....	....	3	2	1	3	6	....	....	....	....
1997-98	**Anaheim**	**NHL**	**66**	**5**	**10**	**15**	**70**	**1**	**0**	**0**	**104**	**4.8**	**7**	....	....	....	....	....	....	....	....	....	....	....	....
	Cincinnati	AHL	6	3	6	9	14	....	....	....	....	....	....	....	....	....	....	....	....	....	....	....	....	....	....
	Belarus	Olympics	7	1	0	1	4	....	....	....	....	....	....	....	....	....	....	....	....	....	....	....	....	....	....
1998-99	**Anaheim**	**NHL**	**74**	**2**	**14**	**16**	**65**	**1**	**0**	**0**	**123**	**1.6**	**1**	**0**	**0.0**	**22:03**	**3**	**0**	**0**	**0**	**4**	**0**	**0**	**0**	**15:40**
99-2000	**Anaheim**	**NHL**	**71**	**5**	**5**	**10**	**94**	**1**	**0**	**0**	**116**	**4.3**	**3**	**0**	**0.0**	**20:21**	....	....	....	....	....	....	....	....	....
2000-01	**Anaheim**	**NHL**	**50**	**1**	**5**	**6**	**70**	**0**	**0**	**0**	**73**	**1.4**	**–14**	**0**	**0.0**	**20:40**	....	....	....	....	....	....	....	....	....
2001-02	**Anaheim**	**NHL**	**82**	**4**	**7**	**11**	**97**	**0**	**0**	**1**	**96**	**4.2**	**–10**	**0**	**0.0**	**21:25**	....	....	....	....	....	....	....	....	....
	Belarus	Olympics	6	2	1	3	4	....	....	....	....	....	....	....	....	....	....	....	....	....	....	....	....	....	....
2002-03	**Anaheim**	**NHL**	**61**	**4**	**8**	**12**	**78**	**0**	**0**	**0**	**93**	**4.3**	**2**	**0**	**0.0**	**21:53**	**21**	**2**	**3**	**5**	**26**	**0**	**0**	**1**	**26:05**
2003-04	**Anaheim**	**NHL**	**82**	**4**	**11**	**15**	**110**	**0**	**1**	**2**	**145**	**2.8**	**–1**	**0**	**0.0**	**23:42**	....	....	....	....	....	....	....	....	....
2004-05	Ak Bars Kazan	Russia	35	8	12	20	36	....	....	....	....	....	....	....	....	....	4	0	0	0	2	....	....	....	....
2005-06	**Anaheim**	**NHL**	**78**	**1**	**18**	**19**	**114**	**0**	**0**	**0**	**108**	**0.9**	**17**	**2**	**100.0**	**22:31**	**16**	**3**	**2**	**5**	**18**	**0**	**0**	**1**	**22:08**
2006-07	**Florida**	**NHL**	**82**	**6**	**26**	**32**	**102**	**2**	**0**	**0**	**148**	**4.1**	**–13**	**0**	**0.0**	**23:20**	....	....	....	....	....	....	....	....	....
2007-08	**Florida**	**NHL**	**65**	**3**	**20**	**23**	**75**	**1**	**0**	**0**	**81**	**3.7**	**–5**	**1**	**0.0**	**23:17**	....	....	....	....	....	....	....	....	....
	Colorado	**NHL**	**17**	**3**	**4**	**7**	**23**	**0**	**0**	**1**	**30**	**10.0**	**1**	**0**	**0.0**	**19:17**	**10**	**1**	**4**	**5**	**4**	**1**	**0**	**0**	**20:52**
	NHL Totals		**758**	**38**	**129**	**167**	**935**	**6**	**1**	**4**	**1131**	**3.4**		**3**	**66.7**	**22:08**	**50**	**6**	**9**	**15**	**52**	**1**	**0**	**2**	**23:09**

Signed as a free agent by **Kazan** (Russia), October 20, 2004. Signed as a free agent by **Florida**, July 2, 2006. Traded to **Colorado** by **Florida** for Karlis Skrastins and Colorado's 3rd round choice (Adam Comrie) in 2008 Entry Draft, February 26, 2008.

SALMELAINEN, Tony

(sal-meh-LIGH-nehn, TOH-nee)

Left wing. Shoots right. 5'9", 185 lbs. Born, Espoo, Finland, August 8, 1981. Edmonton's 3rd choice, 41st overall, in 1999 Entry Draft.

			Regular Season														Playoffs								
Season	Club	League	GP	G	A	Pts	PIM	PP	SH	GW	S	%	+/-	TF	F%	Min	GP	G	A	Pts	PIM	PP	SH	GW	Min
1996-97	K-Espoo U18	Fin-U18	30	8	5	13	38	....	....	....	....	....	....	....	....	....	....	....	....	....	....	....	....	....	....
1997-98	K-Espoo U18	Fin-U18	5	2	2	4	10	....	....	....	....	....	....	....	....	....	....	....	....	....	....	....	....	....	....
	HIFK Helsinki U18	Fin-U18	28	23	16	39	30	....	....	....	....	....	....	....	....	....	....	....	....	....	....	....	....	....	....
	HIFK Helsinki Jr.	Fin-Jr.	5	0	0	0	0	....	....	....	....	....	....	....	....	....	....	....	....	....	....	....	....	....	....
1998-99	HIFK Helsinki U18	Fin-U18	6	5	4	9	16	....	....	....	....	....	....	....	....	....	2	1	2	3	12	....	....	....	....
	HIFK Helsinki Jr.	Fin-Jr.	31	23	18	41	55	....	....	....	....	....	....	....	....	....	....	....	....	....	....	....	....	....	....
99-2000	HIFK Helsinki Jr.	Fin-Jr.	1	0	1	1	0	....	....	....	....	....	....	....	....	....	....	....	....	....	....	....	....	....	....
	HIFK Helsinki	Finland	1	1	0	1	0	....	....	....	....	....	....	....	....	....	....	....	....	....	....	....	....	....	....
	HIFK Helsinki	EuroHL	1	0	0	0	0	....	....	....	....	....	....	....	....	....	....	....	....	....	....	....	....	....	....
2000-01	HIFK Helsinki Jr.	Fin-Jr.	3	3	3	6	0	....	....	....	....	....	....	....	....	....	....	....	....	....	....	....	....	....	....
	HIFK Helsinki	Finland	19	1	0	1	6	....	....	....	....	....	....	....	....	....	....	....	....	....	....	....	....	....	....
	Ilves Tampere Jr.	Fin-Jr.	3	1	2	3	2	....	....	....	....	....	....	....	....	....	....	....	....	....	....	....	....	....	....
	Ilves Tampere	Finland	26	3	10	13	4	....	....	....	....	....	....	....	....	....	3	0	0	0	0	....	....	....	....
2001-02	Ilves Tampere Jr.	Fin-Jr.	2	6	0	6	0	....	....	....	....	....	....	....	....	....	....	....	....	....	....	....	....	....	....
	Ilves Tampere	Finland	49	10	9	19	32	....	....	....	....	....	....	....	....	....	3	0	0	0	2	....	....	....	....
2002-03	Hamilton	AHL	67	14	19	33	14	....	....	....	....	....	....	....	....	....	17	6	8	14	0	....	....	....	....
2003-04	**Edmonton**	**NHL**	**13**	**0**	**1**	**1**	**4**	**0**	**0**	**0**	**17**	**0.0**	**–1**	**0**	**0.0**	**9:39**	....	....	....	....	....	....	....	....	....
	Toronto	AHL	58	19	25	44	27	....	....	....	....	....	....	....	....	....	3	0	1	1	0	....	....	....	....
2004-05	Edmonton	AHL	76	22	24	46	26	....	....	....	....	....	....	....	....	....	....	....	....	....	....	....	....	....	....
2005-06	HIFK Helsinki	Finland	53	*27	28	*55	63	....	....	....	....	....	....	....	....	....	12	4	2	6	36	....	....	....	....
2006-07	**Chicago**	**NHL**	**57**	**6**	**11**	**17**	**26**	**0**	**0**	**1**	**54**	**11.1**	**–3**	**1**	**0.0**	**9:52**	....	....	....	....	....	....	....	....	....
2007-08	Toronto Marlies	AHL	2	2	0	2	0	....	....	....	....	....	....	....	....	....	....	....	....	....	....	....	....	....	....
	Yaroslavl	Russia	29	3	4	7	2	....	....	....	....	....	....	....	....	....	16	0	0	0	6	....	....	....	....
	NHL Totals		**70**	**6**	**12**	**18**	**30**	**0**	**0**	**1**	**71**	**8.5**		**1**	**0.0**	**9:50**	....	....	....	....	....	....	....	....	....

Traded to **Chicago** by **Edmonton** for Jaroslav Spacek, January 26, 2006. Traded to **Montreal** by **Chicago** with Jassen Cullimore for Sergei Samsonov, June 16, 2007.Signed as a free agent by **Toronto**, August 31, 2007. Signed as a free agent by **Yaroslavl** (Russia), November 5, 2007.

SALO, Sami

(SA-loh, SA-mee) **VAN.**

Defense. Shoots right. 6'3", 215 lbs. Born, Turku, Finland, September 2, 1974. Ottawa's 7th choice, 239th overall, in 1996 Entry Draft.

			Regular Season														Playoffs								
Season	Club	League	GP	G	A	Pts	PIM	PP	SH	GW	S	%	+/-	TF	F%	Min	GP	G	A	Pts	PIM	PP	SH	GW	Min
1991-92	Kiekko-67 Jr.	Fin-Jr.	23	4	5	9	26	....	....	....	....	....	....	....	....	....	....	....	....	....	....	....	....	....	....
1992-93	Kiekko-67 Jr.	Fin-Jr.	21	9	4	13	4	....	....	....	....	....	....	....	....	....	....	....	....	....	....	....	....	....	....
1993-94	TPS Turku Jr.	Fin-Jr.	36	7	13	20	16	....	....	....	....	....	....	....	....	....	7	0	1	1	10	....	....	....	....
1994-95	TPS Turku Jr.	Fin-Jr.	14	1	3	4	6	....	....	....	....	....	....	....	....	....	....	....	....	....	....	....	....	....	....
	Kiekko-67 Turku	Finland-2	19	4	2	6	4	....	....	....	....	....	....	....	....	....	....	....	....	....	....	....	....	....	....
	TPS Turku	Finland	7	1	2	3	6	....	....	....	....	....	....	....	....	....	1	0	0	0	0	....	....	....	....
1995-96	TPS Turku	Finland	47	7	14	21	32	....	....	....	....	....	....	....	....	....	11	1	3	4	8	....	....	....	....
1996-97	TPS Turku	Finland	48	9	6	15	10	....	....	....	....	....	....	....	....	....	10	2	3	5	4	....	....	....	....
	TPS Turku	EuroHL	6	0	2	2	6	....	....	....	....	....	....	....	....	....	2	0	0	0	2	....	....	....	....
1997-98	Jokerit Helsinki	Finland	35	3	5	8	24	....	....	....	....	....	....	....	....	....	8	0	1	1	2	....	....	....	....
	Jokerit Helsinki	EuroHL	6	1	1	2	2	....	....	....	....	....	....	....	....	....	....	....	....	....	....	....	....	....	....

Season	Club	League	Regular Season GP	G	A	Pts	PIM	PP	SH	GW	S	%	+/-	TF	F%	Min	Playoffs GP	G	A	Pts	PIM	PP	SH	GW	Min
1998-99	Ottawa	NHL	61	7	12	19	24	2	0	1	106	6.6	20	0	0.0	19:42	4	0	0	0	0	0	0	0	21:32
	Detroit Vipers	IHL	5	0	2	2	0	....	....	....	....	....	....	....	....	....	....	....	....	....	....	....	....	....	....
99-2000	Ottawa	NHL	37	6	8	14	2	3	0	1	85	7.1	6	0	0.0	20:18	6	1	1	2	0	1	0	0	24:11
2000-01	Ottawa	NHL	31	2	16	18	10	1	0	0	61	3.3	9	0	0.0	19:44	4	0	0	0	0	0	0	0	22:30
2001-02	Ottawa	NHL	66	4	14	18	14	1	1	2	122	3.3	1	0	0.0	19:52	12	2	1	3	4	0	0	0	20:23
	Finland	Olympics	4	0	0	0	0	....	....	....	....	....	....	....	....	....	....	....	....	....	....	....	....	....	....
2002-03	Vancouver	NHL	79	9	21	30	10	4	0	1	126	7.1	9	0	0.0	20:08	12	1	3	4	0	0	0	0	20:52
2003-04	Vancouver	NHL	74	7	19	26	22	5	0	2	143	4.9	8	1	100.0	22:14	7	1	2	3	2	1	0	0	22:59
2004-05	Frolunda	Sweden	41	6	8	14	18	....	....	....	....	....	....	....	....	....	14	1	6	7	2	....	....	....	....
2005-06	Vancouver	NHL	59	10	23	33	38	9	0	2	140	7.1	9	0	0.0	24:30	....	....	....	....	....	....	....	....	....
	Finland	Olympics	6	1	3	4	0	....	....	....	....	....	....	....	....	....	....	....	....	....	....	....	....	....	....
2006-07	Vancouver	NHL	67	14	23	37	26	5	0	6	143	9.8	21	0	0.0	21:27	10	0	1	1	4	0	0	0	25:53
2007-08	Vancouver	NHL	63	8	17	25	38	6	0	1	122	6.6	8	0	0.0	23:39	....	....	....	....	....	....	....	....	....
	NHL Totals		537	67	153	220	184	36	1	16	1048	6.4		1	100.0	21:23	55	5	8	13	10	2	0	0	22:28

NHL All-Rookie Team (1999)

• Missed majority of 1999-2000 season recovering from wrist injury suffered in game vs. Philadelphia, November 28, 1999. • Missed majority of 2000-01 season recovering from shoulder injury suffered in game vs. Atlanta, December 14, 2000. Traded to **Vancouver** by **Ottawa** for Peter Schaefer, September 21, 2002. Signed as a free agent by **Frolunda** (Sweden), September 24, 2004.

SALVADOR, Bryce

(SAL-vuh-dohr, BRIGHS) **N.J.**

Defense. Shoots left. 6'2", 220 lbs. Born, Brandon, Man., February 11, 1976. Tampa Bay's 6th choice, 138th overall, in 1994 Entry Draft.

Season	Club	League	GP	G	A	Pts	PIM	PP	SH	GW	S	%	+/-	TF	F%	Min	GP	G	A	Pts	PIM	PP	SH	GW	Min
1991-92	Brandon	MAHA	52	6	23	29	38	....	....	....	....	....	....	....	....	....	....	....	....	....	....	....	....	....	....
1992-93	Lethbridge	WHL	64	1	4	5	29	....	....	....	....	....	....	....	....	....	4	0	0	0	0	....	....	....	....
1993-94	Lethbridge	WHL	61	4	14	18	36	....	....	....	....	....	....	....	....	....	9	0	1	1	2	....	....	....	....
1994-95	Lethbridge	WHL	67	1	9	10	88	....	....	....	....	....	....	....	....	....	....	....	....	....	....	....	....	....	....
1995-96	Lethbridge	WHL	56	4	12	16	75	....	....	....	....	....	....	....	....	....	3	0	1	1	2	....	....	....	....
1996-97	Lethbridge	WHL	63	8	32	40	81	....	....	....	....	....	....	....	....	....	19	0	7	7	14	....	....	....	....
1997-98	Worcester IceCats	AHL	46	2	8	10	74	....	....	....	....	....	....	....	....	....	11	0	1	1	45	....	....	....	....
1998-99	Worcester IceCats	AHL	69	5	13	18	129	....	....	....	....	....	....	....	....	....	4	0	1	1	2	....	....	....	....
99-2000	Worcester IceCats	AHL	55	0	13	13	53	....	....	....	....	....	....	....	....	....	9	0	1	1	2	....	....	....	....
2000-01	St. Louis	NHL	75	2	8	10	69	0	0	1	60	3.3	–4	1	0.0	16:38	14	2	0	2	18	0	0	1	14:41
2001-02	St. Louis	NHL	66	5	7	12	78	1	0	2	37	13.5	3	0	0.0	16:55	10	0	1	1	4	0	0	0	12:34
2002-03	St. Louis	NHL	71	2	8	10	95	1	0	0	73	2.7	7	0	0.0	18:57	7	0	0	0	2	0	0	0	17:17
2003-04	St. Louis	NHL	69	3	5	8	47	0	0	1	60	5.0	–4	0	0.0	17:29	5	0	0	0	2	0	0	0	14:31
	Worcester IceCats	AHL	2	0	1	1	0	....	....	....	....	....	....	....	....	....	....	....	....	....	....	....	....	....	....
2004-05	Missouri	UHL	7	0	0	0	16	....	....	....	....	....	....	....	....	....	3	0	0	0	0	....	....	....	....
2005-06	St. Louis	NHL	46	1	4	5	26	0	0	0	23	4.3	–24	1	0.0	19:48	....	....	....	....	....	....	....	....	....
2006-07	St. Louis	NHL	64	2	5	7	55	0	0	0	40	5.0	–5	0	0.0	19:44	....	....	....	....	....	....	....	....	....
2007-08	St. Louis	NHL	56	1	10	11	43	0	0	1	29	3.4	12	1	0.0	19:38	....	....	....	....	....	....	....	....	....
	New Jersey	NHL	8	0	0	0	11	0	0	0	0	0.0	0	0	0.0	20:54	5	1	0	1	2	0	0	0	17:55
	NHL Totals		455	16	47	63	424	2	0	5	322	5.0		3	0.0	18:22	41	3	1	4	28	0	0	1	14:59

Signed as a free agent by **St. Louis**, December 16, 1996. Signed as a free agent by **Missouri** (UHL), March 11, 2005. Traded to **New Jersey** by **St. Louis** for Cam Janssen, February 26, 2008.

SAMSONOV, Sergei

(sam-SAWN-nahf, SAIR-gay) **CAR.**

Left wing. Shoots right. 5'8", 188 lbs. Born, Moscow, USSR, October 27, 1978. Boston's 2nd choice, 8th overall, in 1997 Entry Draft.

Season	Club	League	GP	G	A	Pts	PIM	PP	SH	GW	S	%	+/-	TF	F%	Min	GP	G	A	Pts	PIM	PP	SH	GW	Min
1994-95	CSKA Moscow 2	CIS-2	50	110	72	182	....	....	....	....	....	....	....	....	....	....	....	....	....	....	....	....	....	....	....
	CSKA Moscow	CIS	13	2	2	4	14	....	....	....	....	....	....	....	....	....	2	0	0	0	0	....	....	....	....
1995-96	CSKA Moscow	CIS	51	21	17	38	12	....	....	....	....	....	....	....	....	....	3	1	1	2	4	....	....	....	....
1996-97	Detroit Vipers	IHL	73	29	35	64	18	....	....	....	....	....	....	....	....	....	19	8	4	12	12	....	....	....	....
1997-98	Boston	NHL	81	22	25	47	8	7	0	3	159	13.8	9	....	....	....	6	2	5	7	0	0	0	1	....
1998-99	Boston	NHL	79	25	26	51	18	6	0	8	160	15.6	–6	0	0.0	16:23	11	3	1	4	0	0	0	0	16:11
99-2000	Boston	NHL	77	19	26	45	4	6	0	3	145	13.1	–6	3	0.0	16:32	....	....	....	....	....	....	....	....	....
2000-01	Boston	NHL	82	29	46	75	18	3	0	3	215	13.5	6	14	42.9	19:23	....	....	....	....	....	....	....	....	....
2001-02	Boston	NHL	74	29	41	70	27	3	0	4	192	15.1	21	1	0.0	18:47	6	2	2	4	0	0	0	0	17:41
	Russia	Olympics	6	1	2	3	4	....	....	....	....	....	....	....	....	....	....	....	....	....	....	....	....	....	....
2002-03	Boston	NHL	8	5	6	11	2	1	0	3	23	21.7	8	0	0.0	20:20	5	0	2	2	0	0	0	0	17:07
2003-04	Boston	NHL	58	17	23	40	4	3	0	5	132	12.9	12	4	25.0	17:27	7	2	5	7	0	0	0	0	17:18
2004-05	Dynamo Moscow	Russia	3	1	0	1	0	....	....	....	....	....	....	....	....	....	3	1	2	3	0	....	....	....	....
2005-06	Boston	NHL	55	18	19	37	22	6	0	1	107	16.8	–3	1	100.0	16:53	....	....	....	....	....	....	....	....	....
	Edmonton	NHL	19	5	11	16	6	4	0	0	36	13.9	0	2	0.0	15:26	24	4	11	15	14	1	0	0	14:30
2006-07	Montreal	NHL	63	9	17	26	10	0	0	0	114	7.9	–4	14	14.3	13:59	....	....	....	....	....	....	....	....	....
2007-08	Chicago	NHL	23	0	4	4	6	0	0	0	38	0.0	–7	1	0.0	12:21	....	....	....	....	....	....	....	....	....
	Rockford IceHogs	AHL	2	1	0	1	0	....	....	....	....	....	....	....	....	....	....	....	....	....	....	....	....	....	....
	Carolina	NHL	38	14	18	32	10	3	0	2	71	19.7	6	2	0.0	18:02	....	....	....	....	....	....	....	....	....
	NHL Totals		657	192	262	454	135	42	0	32	1392	13.8		42	23.8	17:00	59	13	26	39	14	1	0	1	15:50

Garry F. Longman Memorial Trophy (Rookie of the Year – IHL) (1997) • NHL All-Rookie Team (1998) • Calder Memorial Trophy (1998)

Played in NHL All-Star Game (2001)

• Missed majority of 2002-03 season recovering from wrist injury suffered in game vs. Columbus, October 18, 2002. Signed as a free agent by **Dynamo Moscow** (Russia), February 2, 2005. Traded to **Edmonton** by **Boston** for Marty Reasoner, Yan Stastny and Edmonton's 2nd round choice (Milan Lucic) in 2006 Entry Draft, March 9, 2006. Signed as a free agent by **Montreal**, July 12, 2006. Traded to **Chicago** by **Montreal** for Jassen Cullimore and Tony Salmelainen, June 16, 2007. Claimed on waivers by **Carolina** from **Chicago**, January 8, 2008.

SAMUELSSON, Martin

(SAM-yuhl-suhn, MAHR-tihn) **BOS.**

Right wing. Shoots left. 6'2", 210 lbs. Born, Upplands-Vasby, Sweden, January 25, 1982. Boston's 2nd choice, 27th overall, in 2000 Entry Draft.

Season	Club	League	GP	G	A	Pts	PIM	PP	SH	GW	S	%	+/-	TF	F%	Min	GP	G	A	Pts	PIM	PP	SH	GW	Min
1996-97	Hammarby Jr.	Swe-Jr.	6	1	1	2	0	....	....	....	....	....	....	....	....	....	....	....	....	....	....	....	....	....	....
1997-98	Hammarby Jr.	Swe-Jr.	20	13	12	25	....	....	....	....	....	....	....	....	....	....	....	....	....	....	....	....	....	....	....
	Hammarby	Sweden-2	2	0	0	0	0	....	....	....	....	....	....	....	....	....	....	....	....	....	....	....	....	....	....
1998-99	Malmo Jr.	Swe-Jr.	31	18	13	31	10	....	....	....	....	....	....	....	....	....	....	....	....	....	....	....	....	....	....
99-2000	MoDo U18	Swe-U18	6	3	0	3	4	....	....	....	....	....	....	....	....	....	....	....	....	....	....	....	....	....	....
	Malmo Jr.	Swe-Jr.	19	9	8	17	18	....	....	....	....	....	....	....	....	....	2	1	0	1	2	....	....	....	....
2000-01	Hammarby	Sweden-2	24	13	4	17	8	....	....	....	....	....	....	....	....	....	5	0	0	0	2	....	....	....	....
	Hammarby Jr.	Swe-Jr.	1	0	1	1	0	....	....	....	....	....	....	....	....	....	....	....	....	....	....	....	....	....	....
2001-02	Hammarby Jr.	Swe-Jr.	2	5	2	7	2	....	....	....	....	....	....	....	....	....	....	....	....	....	....	....	....	....	....
	Hammarby	Sweden-2	44	13	10	23	45	....	....	....	....	....	....	....	....	....	2	0	0	0	2	....	....	....	....
2002-03	Boston	NHL	8	0	1	1	2	0	0	0	3	0.0	–1	0	0.0	11:42	....	....	....	....	....	....	....	....	....
	Providence Bruins	AHL	64	24	15	39	34	....	....	....	....	....	....	....	....	....	4	0	0	0	0	....	....	....	....
2003-04	Boston	NHL	6	0	0	0	0	0	0	0	7	0.0	–1	1	0.0	5:38	....	....	....	....	....	....	....	....	....
	Providence Bruins	AHL	56	1	9	10	15	....	....	....	....	....	....	....	....	....	1	0	0	0	0	....	....	....	....
2004-05	Providence Bruins	AHL	64	7	10	17	35	....	....	....	....	....	....	....	....	....	10	1	0	1	6	....	....	....	....
2005-06	Linkopings HC	Sweden	44	3	4	7	45	....	....	....	....	....	....	....	....	....	8	0	0	0	29	....	....	....	....
2006-07	Linkopings HC	Sweden	33	4	2	6	14	....	....	....	....	....	....	....	....	....	15	0	1	1	8	....	....	....	....
2007-08	Malmo	Sweden-2	41	4	4	8	76	....	....	....	....	....	....	....	....	....	3	0	0	0	0	....	....	....	....
	NHL Totals		14	0	1	1	2	0	0	0	10	0.0		1	0.0	9:06	....	....	....	....	....	....	....	....	....

SAMUELSSON, Mikael

(SAM-yuhl-suhn, MIH-kigh-ehl) **DET.**

Right wing. Shoots right. 6'2", 213 lbs. Born, Mariefred, Sweden, December 23, 1976. San Jose's 7th choice, 145th overall, in 1998 Entry Draft.

Season	Club	League	GP	G	A	Pts	PIM	PP	SH	GW	S	%	+/-	TF	F%	Min	GP	G	A	Pts	PIM	PP	SH	GW	Min
1994-95	Sodertalje SK Jr.	Swe-Jr.	30	8	6	14	12	....	....	....	....	....	....	....	....	....	....	....	....	....	....	....	....	....	....
1995-96	Sodertalje SK Jr.	Swe-Jr.	22	13	12	25	20	....	....	....	....	....	....	....	....	....	....	....	....	....	....	....	....	....	....
	Sodertalje SK	Sweden-2	18	5	1	6	0	....	....	....	....	....	....	....	....	....	4	0	0	0	0	....	....	....	....
1996-97	Sodertalje SK Jr.	Swe-Jr.	2	2	1	3	....	....	....	....	....	....	....	....	....	....	....	....	....	....	....	....	....	....	....
	Sodertalje SK	Sweden	29	3	2	5	10	....	....	....	....	....	....	....	....	....	10	0	0	0	4	....	....	....	....
1997-98	Nykoping	Sweden-2	10	5	1	6	14	....	....	....	....	....	....	....	....	....	....	....	....	....	....	....	....	....	....
	Sodertalje SK	Sweden	41	11	9	20	66	....	....	....	....	....	....	....	....	....	....	....	....	....	....	....	....	....	....
1998-99	Sodertalje SK	Sweden-2	18	13	10	23	26	....	....	....	....	....	....	....	....	....	10	2	2	4	12	....	....	....	....
	V.Frolunda	Sweden	27	0	5	5	10	....	....	....	....	....	....	....	....	....	....	....	....	....	....	....	....	....	....
99-2000	Brynas IF Gavle	Sweden	40	4	3	7	76	....	....	....	....	....	....	....	....	....	11	7	2	9	6	....	....	....	....
	Brynas IF Gavle	EuroHL	4	0	2	2	4	....	....	....	....	....	....	....	....	....	....	....	....	....	....	....	....	....	....

			Regular Season														Playoffs								
Season	Club	League	GP	G	A	Pts	PIM	PP	SH	GW	S	%	+/-	TF	F%	Min	GP	G	A	Pts	PIM	PP	SH	GW	Min
2000-01	**San Jose**	**NHL**	**4**	**0**	**0**	**0**	**0**	**0**	**0**	**0**	**3**	**0.0**	**0**	**0**	**0.0**	**4:41**	....	....	....	....	....	....	....	....	....
	Kentucky	AHL	66	32	46	78	58	....	....	....	....	....	....	....	....	....	3	1	0	1	0	....	....	....	....
2001-02	**NY Rangers**	**NHL**	**67**	**6**	**10**	**16**	**23**	**1**	**2**	**1**	**94**	**6.4**	**10**	**5**	**40.0**	**11:52**	....	....	....	....	....	....	....	....	....
	Hartford	AHL	8	3	6	9	12	....	....	....	....	....	....	....	....	....	....	....	....	....	....	....	....	....	....
2002-03	**NY Rangers**	**NHL**	**58**	**8**	**14**	**22**	**32**	**1**	**1**	**2**	**118**	**6.8**	**0**	**35**	**42.9**	**15:32**	....	....	....	....	....	....	....	....	....
	Pittsburgh	**NHL**	**22**	**2**	**0**	**2**	**8**	**1**	**0**	**0**	**36**	**5.6**	**–21**	**8**	**75.0**	**14:04**	....	....	....	....	....	....	....	....	....
2003-04	**Florida**	**NHL**	**37**	**3**	**6**	**9**	**35**	**0**	**0**	**1**	**50**	**6.0**	**0**	**28**	**28.6**	**12:15**	....	....	....	....	....	....	....	....	....
2004-05	Geneve	Swiss	12	2	4	6	14	....	....	....	....	....	....	....	....	....	....	....	....	....	....	....	....	....	....
	Sodertalje SK	Sweden	29	7	13	20	45	....	....	....	....	....	....	....	....	....	10	3	3	6	24	....	....	....	....
2005-06	Rapperswil	Swiss	1	0	0	0	0	....	....	....	....	....	....	....	....	....	....	....	....	....	....	....	....	....	....
	Detroit	**NHL**	**71**	**23**	**22**	**45**	**42**	**7**	**0**	**3**	**187**	**12.3**	**27**	**11**	**27.3**	**13:31**	**6**	**0**	**1**	**1**	**6**	**0**	**0**	**0**	**15:33**
	Sweden	Olympics	8	1	3	4	2	....	....	....	....	....	....	....	....	....	....	....	....	....	....	....	....	....	....
2006-07	**Detroit**	**NHL**	**53**	**14**	**20**	**34**	**28**	**6**	**0**	**2**	**189**	**7.4**	**1**	**3**	**66.7**	**15:09**	**18**	**3**	**8**	**11**	**14**	**1**	**0**	**1**	**15:27**
2007-08♦	**Detroit**	**NHL**	**73**	**11**	**29**	**40**	**26**	**3**	**0**	**1**	**249**	**4.4**	**21**	**14**	**42.9**	**16:16**	**22**	**5**	**8**	**13**	**8**	**0**	**0**	**1**	**15:56**
	NHL Totals		**385**	**67**	**101**	**168**	**194**	**19**	**3**	**10**	**926**	**7.2**		**104**	**40.4**	**14:06**	**46**	**8**	**17**	**25**	**28**	**1**	**0**	**2**	**15:41**

Traded to **NY Rangers** by **San Jose** with Christian Gosselin for Adam Graves and future considerations, June 24, 2001. Traded to **Pittsburgh** by **NY Rangers** with Joel Bouchard, Richard Lintner and Rico Fata for Mike Wilson, Alex Kovalev, Janne Laukkanen and Dan LaCouture, February 10, 2003. Traded to **Florida** by **Pittsburgh** with Pittsburgh's 1st round choice (Nathan Horton) and 2nd round compensatory choice (Stefan Meyer) in 2003 Entry Draft for Florida's 1st (Marc-Andre Fleury) and 3rd (Daniel Carcillo) round choices in 2003 Entry Draft, June 21, 2003. • Missed majority of 2003-04 season recovering from jaw (November 21, 2003 vs. Washington) and hand (January 21, 2004 vs. Columbus) injuries. Signed as a free agent by **Geneve** (Swiss), September 8, 2004. Signed as a free agent by **Sodertalje** (Sweden), October 26, 2004. Signed as a free agent by **Detroit**, September 17, 2005.

SANDERSON, Geoff

(SAN-duhr-sohn, JEHF)

Left wing. Shoots left. 6', 190 lbs. Born, Hay River, N.W.T., February 1, 1972. Hartford's 2nd choice, 36th overall, in 1990 Entry Draft.

Season	Club	League	GP	G	A	Pts	PIM	PP	SH	GW	S	%	+/-	TF	F%	Min	GP	G	A	Pts	PIM	PP	SH	GW	Min
1987-88	St. Albert Royals	AMHL	45	65	55	120	175	....	....	....	....	....	....	....	....	....	....	....	....	....	....	....	....	....	....
1988-89	Swift Current	WHL	58	17	11	28	16	....	....	....	....	....	....	....	....	....	12	3	5	8	6	....	....	....	....
1989-90	Swift Current	WHL	70	32	62	94	56	....	....	....	....	....	....	....	....	....	4	1	4	5	8	....	....	....	....
1990-91	Swift Current	WHL	70	62	50	112	57	....	....	....	....	....	....	....	....	....	3	1	2	3	4	....	....	....	....
	Hartford	**NHL**	**2**	**1**	**0**	**1**	**0**	**0**	**0**	**0**	**2**	**50.0**	**–2**	....	....	....	**3**	**0**	**0**	**0**	**0**	**0**	**0**	**0**	....
	Springfield	AHL	....	....	....	....	....	....	....	....	....	....	....	....	....	....	1	0	0	0	2	....	....	....	....
1991-92	**Hartford**	**NHL**	**64**	**13**	**18**	**31**	**18**	**2**	**0**	**1**	**98**	**13.3**	**5**	....	....	....	**7**	**1**	**0**	**1**	**2**	**0**	**0**	**0**	....
1992-93	**Hartford**	**NHL**	**82**	**46**	**43**	**89**	**28**	**21**	**2**	**4**	**271**	**17.0**	**–21**	....	....	....	....	....	....	....	....	....	....	....	....
1993-94	**Hartford**	**NHL**	**82**	**41**	**26**	**67**	**42**	**15**	**1**	**6**	**266**	**15.4**	**–13**	....	....	....	....	....	....	....	....	....	....	....	....
1994-95	HPK Hameenlinna	Finland	12	6	4	10	24	....	....	....	....	....	....	....	....	....	....	....	....	....	....	....	....	....	....
	Hartford	**NHL**	**46**	**18**	**14**	**32**	**24**	**4**	**0**	**4**	**170**	**10.6**	**–10**	....	....	....	....	....	....	....	....	....	....	....	....
1995-96	**Hartford**	**NHL**	**81**	**34**	**31**	**65**	**40**	**6**	**0**	**7**	**314**	**10.8**	**0**	....	....	....	....	....	....	....	....	....	....	....	....
1996-97	**Hartford**	**NHL**	**82**	**36**	**31**	**67**	**29**	**12**	**1**	**4**	**297**	**12.1**	**–9**	....	....	....	....	....	....	....	....	....	....	....	....
1997-98	**Carolina**	**NHL**	**40**	**7**	**10**	**17**	**14**	**2**	**0**	**0**	**96**	**7.3**	**–4**	....	....	....	....	....	....	....	....	....	....	....	....
	Vancouver	**NHL**	**9**	**0**	**3**	**3**	**4**	**0**	**0**	**0**	**29**	**0.0**	**–1**	....	....	....	....	....	....	....	....	....	....	....	....
	Buffalo	**NHL**	**26**	**4**	**5**	**9**	**20**	**0**	**0**	**2**	**72**	**5.6**	**6**	....	....	....	**14**	**3**	**1**	**4**	**4**	**1**	**0**	**1**	....
1998-99	**Buffalo**	**NHL**	**75**	**12**	**18**	**30**	**22**	**1**	**0**	**1**	**155**	**7.7**	**8**	**4**	**50.0**	**12:55**	**19**	**4**	**6**	**10**	**14**	**0**	**0**	**1**	**13:52**
99-2000	**Buffalo**	**NHL**	**67**	**13**	**13**	**26**	**22**	**4**	**0**	**3**	**136**	**9.6**	**4**	**3**	**100.0**	**12:54**	**5**	**0**	**2**	**2**	**8**	**0**	**0**	**0**	**12:16**
2000-01	**Columbus**	**NHL**	**68**	**30**	**26**	**56**	**46**	**9**	**0**	**7**	**199**	**15.1**	**4**	**726**	**49.0**	**16:37**	....	....	....	....	....	....	....	....	....
2001-02	**Columbus**	**NHL**	**42**	**11**	**5**	**16**	**12**	**5**	**0**	**2**	**112**	**9.8**	**–15**	**322**	**42.9**	**16:50**	....	....	....	....	....	....	....	....	....
2002-03	**Columbus**	**NHL**	**82**	**34**	**33**	**67**	**34**	**15**	**2**	**2**	**286**	**11.9**	**–4**	**96**	**41.7**	**18:44**	....	....	....	....	....	....	....	....	....
2003-04	**Columbus**	**NHL**	**67**	**13**	**16**	**29**	**34**	**5**	**0**	**1**	**191**	**6.8**	**–9**	**102**	**47.1**	**16:20**	....	....	....	....	....	....	....	....	....
	Vancouver	**NHL**	**13**	**3**	**4**	**7**	**4**	**1**	**0**	**1**	**36**	**8.3**	**–1**	**14**	**21.4**	**14:46**	**7**	**1**	**1**	**2**	**4**	**0**	**0**	**0**	**12:54**
2004-05	Geneve	Swiss	9	4	1	5	29	....	....	....	....	....	....	....	....	....	....	....	....	....	....	....	....	....	....
2005-06	**Columbus**	**NHL**	**2**	**0**	**0**	**0**	**0**	**0**	**0**	**0**	**7**	**0.0**	**–1**	**1**	**0.0**	**10:54**	....	....	....	....	....	....	....	....	....
	Phoenix	**NHL**	**75**	**25**	**21**	**46**	**58**	**11**	**1**	**1**	**152**	**16.4**	**–14**	**359**	**51.0**	**13:47**	....	....	....	....	....	....	....	....	....
2006-07	**Philadelphia**	**NHL**	**58**	**11**	**18**	**29**	**44**	**3**	**0**	**2**	**143**	**7.7**	**–16**	**163**	**41.7**	**13:59**	....	....	....	....	....	....	....	....	....
2007-08	**Edmonton**	**NHL**	**41**	**3**	**10**	**13**	**16**	**0**	**0**	**0**	**40**	**7.5**	**–7**	**23**	**52.2**	**10:09**	....	....	....	....	....	....	....	....	....
	NHL Totals		**1104**	**355**	**345**	**700**	**511**	**116**	**7**	**48**	**3072**	**11.6**		**1813**	**47.0**	**14:52**	**55**	**9**	**10**	**19**	**32**	**1**	**0**	**2**	**13:23**

Played in NHL All-Star Game (1994, 1997)

Transferred to **Carolina** after **Hartford** franchise relocated, June 25, 1997. Traded to **Vancouver** by **Carolina** with Sean Burke and Enrico Ciccone for Kirk McLean and Martin Gelinas, January 3, 1998. Traded to **Buffalo** by **Vancouver** for Brad May and Buffalo's 3rd round choice (later traded to Tampa Bay – Tampa Bay selected Jimmie Olvestad) in 1999 Entry Draft, February 4, 1998. Claimed by **Columbus** from **Buffalo** in Expansion Draft, June 23, 2000. Traded to **Vancouver** by **Columbus** for Vancouver's 3rd round choice (Daniel Lacosta) in 2004 Entry Draft, March 9, 2004. Claimed on waivers by **Columbus** from **Vancouver**, June 28, 2004. Signed as a free agent by **Geneve** (Swiss), January 5, 2005. Traded to **Phoenix** by **Columbus** with Tim Jackman for Cale Hulse, Mike Rupp and Jason Chimera, October 8, 2005. Signed as a free agent by **Philadelphia**, July 19, 2006. Traded to **Edmonton** by **Philadelphia** with Joni Pitkanen and Philadelphia's 3rd round choice in 2009 Entry Draft for Jason Smith and Joffrey Lupul, July 1, 2007.

SANTALA, Tommi

(SAHN-tah-luh, TAW-mee)

Center. Shoots right. 6'3", 210 lbs. Born, Helsinki, Finland, June 27, 1979. Atlanta's 10th choice, 245th overall, in 1999 Entry Draft.

Season	Club	League	GP	G	A	Pts	PIM	PP	SH	GW	S	%	+/-	TF	F%	Min	GP	G	A	Pts	PIM	PP	SH	GW	Min
1995-96	Jokerit U18	Fin-U18	25	8	4	12	12	....	....	....	....	....	....	....	....	....	6	1	2	3	4	....	....	....	....
1996-97	Jokerit U18	Fin-U18	30	13	19	32	64	....	....	....	....	....	....	....	....	....	....	....	....	....	....	....	....	....	....
	Jokerit Helsinki Jr.	Fin-Jr.	20	0	2	2	10	....	....	....	....	....	....	....	....	....	5	0	0	0	0	....	....	....	....
1997-98	Jokerit Helsinki Jr.	Fin-Jr.	36	10	28	38	48	....	....	....	....	....	....	....	....	....	8	0	1	1	4	....	....	....	....
1998-99	Jokerit Helsinki Jr.	Fin-Jr.	30	20	24	44	20	....	....	....	....	....	....	....	....	....	8	1	3	4	22	....	....	....	....
	Jokerit Helsinki	Finland	30	0	0	0	14	....	....	....	....	....	....	....	....	....	3	0	0	0	0	....	....	....	....
99-2000	Jokerit Helsinki Jr.	Fin-Jr.	5	6	4	10	4	....	....	....	....	....	....	....	....	....	....	....	....	....	....	....	....	....	....
	Jokerit Helsinki	Finland	14	0	1	1	2	....	....	....	....	....	....	....	....	....	....	....	....	....	....	....	....	....	....
	HPK Jr.	Fin-Jr.	6	7	3	10	4	....	....	....	....	....	....	....	....	....	....	....	....	....	....	....	....	....	....
	HPK Hameenlinna	Finland	38	8	19	27	63	....	....	....	....	....	....	....	....	....	8	3	4	7	10	....	....	....	....
2000-01	HPK Hameenlinna	Finland	56	16	24	40	90	....	....	....	....	....	....	....	....	....	....	....	....	....	....	....	....	....	....
2001-02	HPK Hameenlinna	Finland	17	6	16	22	14	....	....	....	....	....	....	....	....	....	....	....	....	....	....	....	....	....	....
2002-03	HPK Hameenlinna	Finland	50	13	38	51	92	....	....	....	....	....	....	....	....	....	13	6	6	12	18	....	....	....	....
2003-04	**Atlanta**	**NHL**	**33**	**1**	**2**	**3**	**22**	**0**	**0**	**1**	**23**	**4.3**	**–7**	**252**	**51.2**	**10:08**	....	....	....	....	....	....	....	....	....
	Chicago Wolves	AHL	50	15	22	37	34	....	....	....	....	....	....	....	....	....	10	1	6	7	31	....	....	....	....
2004-05	Chicago Wolves	AHL	67	8	40	48	83	....	....	....	....	....	....	....	....	....	18	5	6	11	42	....	....	....	....
2005-06	Jokerit Helsinki	Finland	43	9	23	32	80	....	....	....	....	....	....	....	....	....	....	....	....	....	....	....	....	....	....
2006-07	**Vancouver**	**NHL**	**30**	**1**	**5**	**6**	**24**	**0**	**0**	**0**	**20**	**5.0**	**0**	**139**	**56.8**	**7:22**	**1**	**0**	**0**	**0**	**0**	**0**	**0**	**0**	**2:16**
	Manitoba Moose	AHL	6	0	3	3	8	....	....	....	....	....	....	....	....	....	....	....	....	....	....	....	....	....	....
2007-08	Jokerit Helsinki	Finland	56	28	30	58	82	....	....	....	....	....	....	....	....	....	13	4	12	16	18	....	....	....	....
	NHL Totals		**63**	**2**	**7**	**9**	**46**	**0**	**0**	**1**	**43**	**4.7**		**391**	**53.2**	**8:49**	**1**	**0**	**0**	**0**	**0**	**0**	**0**	**0**	**2:16**

Assigned to **Jokerit Helsinki** (Finland) by **Atlanta**, October 5, 2005. Traded to **Vancouver** by **Atlanta** with Atlanta's 5th round choice (Charles-Antoine Messier) in 2007 Entry Draft for Atlanta's 4th round choice (previously acquired, Atlanta selected Niklas Lucenius) in 2007 Entry Draft, June 14, 2006. • Missed majority of 2006-07 season recovering from knee injury suffered in game at Vancouver, December 8, 2006. Signed as a free agent by **Jokerit Helsinki** (Finland), September 5, 2007.

SAPRYKIN, Oleg

(sah-PRIH-kihn, OH-lehg)

Left wing. Shoots left. 6'1", 190 lbs. Born, Moscow, USSR, February 12, 1981. Calgary's 1st choice, 11th overall, in 1999 Entry Draft.

Season	Club	League	GP	G	A	Pts	PIM	PP	SH	GW	S	%	+/-	TF	F%	Min	GP	G	A	Pts	PIM	PP	SH	GW	Min
1997-98	HK CSKA Moscow	Russia-Q	15	0	3	3	6	....	....	....	....	....	....	....	....	....	....	....	....	....	....	....	....	....	....
	HK CSKA Moscow	Russia	20	0	2	2	8	....	....	....	....	....	....	....	....	....	....	....	....	....	....	....	....	....	....
1998-99	Seattle	WHL	66	47	46	93	107	....	....	....	....	....	....	....	....	....	11	5	11	16	36	....	....	....	....
99-2000	**Calgary**	**NHL**	**4**	**0**	**1**	**1**	**2**	**0**	**0**	**0**	**2**	**0.0**	**–4**	**0**	**0.0**	**12:35**	....	....	....	....	....	....	....	....	....
	Seattle	WHL	48	30	36	66	91	....	....	....	....	....	....	....	....	....	6	3	3	6	37	....	....	....	....
2000-01	**Calgary**	**NHL**	**59**	**9**	**14**	**23**	**43**	**2**	**0**	**0**	**95**	**9.5**	**4**	**2**	**50.0**	**12:10**	....	....	....	....	....	....	....	....	....
2001-02	**Calgary**	**NHL**	**3**	**0**	**0**	**0**	**0**	**0**	**0**	**0**	**9**	**0.0**	**–2**	**0**	**0.0**	**13:25**	....	....	....	....	....	....	....	....	....
	Saint John Flames	AHL	52	5	19	24	53	....	....	....	....	....	....	....	....	....	....	....	....	....	....	....	....	....	....
2002-03	**Calgary**	**NHL**	**52**	**8**	**15**	**23**	**46**	**1**	**0**	**1**	**116**	**6.9**	**5**	**1**	**0.0**	**11:53**	....	....	....	....	....	....	....	....	....
	Saint John Flames	AHL	21	12	9	21	22	....	....	....	....	....	....	....	....	....	....	....	....	....	....	....	....	....	....
2003-04	**Calgary**	**NHL**	**69**	**12**	**17**	**29**	**41**	**4**	**0**	**0**	**151**	**7.9**	**1**	**13**	**23.1**	**13:48**	**26**	**3**	**3**	**6**	**14**	**1**	**0**	**1**	**14:01**
2004-05	CSKA Moscow	Russia	40	15	8	23	105	....	....	....	....	....	....	....	....	....	....	....	....	....	....	....	....	....	....
2005-06	**Phoenix**	**NHL**	**67**	**11**	**14**	**25**	**50**	**3**	**0**	**1**	**126**	**8.7**	**–16**	**18**	**38.9**	**13:42**	....	....	....	....	....	....	....	....	....

			Regular Season														Playoffs								
Season	Club	League	GP	G	A	Pts	PIM	PP	SH	GW	S	%	+/-	TF	F%	Min	GP	G	A	Pts	PIM	PP	SH	GW	Min
2006-07	**Phoenix**	**NHL**	**59**	**14**	**20**	**34**	**54**	**2**	**0**	**2**	**135**	**10.4**	**8**	**16**	**12.5**	**13:29**	....	....	....	....	....	....	....	....	....
	Ottawa	**NHL**	**12**	**1**	**1**	**2**	**4**	**0**	**0**	**0**	**15**	**6.7**	**–3**	**2**	**100.0**	**7:25**	**15**	**1**	**1**	**2**	**4**	**0**	**0**	**1**	**7:31**
2007-08	CSKA Moscow	Russia	57	29	20	49	119	....	....	....	....	....	....	....	....	....	6	1	1	2	24	....	....	....	....
	NHL Totals		**325**	**55**	**82**	**137**	**240**	**12**	**0**	**4**	**649**	**8.5**		**52**	**28.8**	**12:52**	**41**	**4**	**4**	**8**	**18**	**1**	**0**	**2**	**11:38**

WHL West Second All-Star Team (1999, 2000)

Traded to **Phoenix** by **Calgary** with Denis Gauthier for Daymond Langkow, August 26, 2004. Signed as a free agent by **CSKA Moscow** (Russia), September 25, 2004. Traded to **Ottawa** by **Phoenix** with Phoenix's 7th round choice (Torrie Jung) in 2007 Entry Draft for Ottawa's 2nd round choice (later traded to Anaheim - Anaheim selected Jared Staal) in 2008 Entry Draft, February 27, 2007. Signed as a free agent by **CSKA Moscow** (Russia), July 30, 2007.

SARICH, Cory (SAHR-ihch, KOH-ree) CGY.

Defense. Shoots right. 6'4", 207 lbs. Born, Saskatoon, Sask., August 16, 1978. Buffalo's 2nd choice, 27th overall, in 1996 Entry Draft.

Season	Club	League	GP	G	A	Pts	PIM	PP	SH	GW	S	%	+/-	TF	F%	Min	GP	G	A	Pts	PIM	PP	SH	GW	Min
1994-95	Sask. Contacts	SMHL	31	5	22	27	99	....	....	....	....	....	....	....	....	....	....	....	....	....	....	....	....	....	....
	Saskatoon Blades	WHL	6	0	0	0	4	....	....	....	....	....	....	....	....	....	3	0	1	1	0	....	....	....	....
1995-96	Saskatoon Blades	WHL	59	5	18	23	54	....	....	....	....	....	....	....	....	....	3	0	0	0	4	....	....	....	....
1996-97	Saskatoon Blades	WHL	58	6	27	33	158	....	....	....	....	....	....	....	....	....	....	....	....	....	....	....	....	....	....
1997-98	Saskatoon Blades	WHL	33	5	24	29	90	....	....	....	....	....	....	....	....	....	....	....	....	....	....	....	....	....	....
	Seattle	WHL	13	3	16	19	47	....	....	....	....	....	....	....	....	....	....	....	....	....	....	....	....	....	....
1998-99	**Buffalo**	**NHL**	**4**	**0**	**0**	**0**	**0**	**0**	**0**	**0**	**2**	**0.0**	**3**	**0**	**0.0**	**13:11**	....	....	....	....	....	....	....	....	....
	Rochester	AHL	77	3	26	29	82	....	....	....	....	....	....	....	....	....	20	2	4	6	14	....	....	....	....
99-2000	**Buffalo**	**NHL**	**42**	**0**	**4**	**4**	**35**	**0**	**0**	**0**	**49**	**0.0**	**2**	**0**	**0.0**	**17:42**	....	....	....	....	....	....	....	....	....
	Rochester	AHL	15	0	6	6	44	....	....	....	....	....	....	....	....	....	....	....	....	....	....	....	....	....	....
	Tampa Bay	**NHL**	**17**	**0**	**2**	**2**	**42**	**0**	**0**	**0**	**20**	**0.0**	**–8**	**0**	**0.0**	**20:42**	....	....	....	....	....	....	....	....	....
2000-01	**Tampa Bay**	**NHL**	**73**	**1**	**8**	**9**	**106**	**0**	**0**	**1**	**66**	**1.5**	**–25**	**3**	**0.0**	**18:44**	....	....	....	....	....	....	....	....	....
	Detroit Vipers	IHL	3	0	2	2	2	....	....	....	....	....	....	....	....	....	....	....	....	....	....	....	....	....	....
2001-02	**Tampa Bay**	**NHL**	**72**	**0**	**11**	**11**	**105**	**0**	**0**	**0**	**55**	**0.0**	**–4**	**2**	**50.0**	**16:06**	....	....	....	....	....	....	....	....	....
	Springfield	AHL	2	0	0	0	0	....	....	....	....	....	....	....	....	....	....	....	....	....	....	....	....	....	....
2002-03	**Tampa Bay**	**NHL**	**82**	**5**	**9**	**14**	**63**	**0**	**0**	**2**	**79**	**6.3**	**–3**	**3**	**0.0**	**19:36**	**11**	**0**	**2**	**2**	**6**	**0**	**0**	**0**	**21:18**
2003-04♦	**Tampa Bay**	**NHL**	**82**	**3**	**16**	**19**	**89**	**0**	**1**	**1**	**93**	**3.2**	**5**	**1**	**0.0**	**18:31**	**23**	**0**	**2**	**2**	**25**	**0**	**0**	**0**	**19:11**
2004-05			DID NOT PLAY																						
2005-06	**Tampa Bay**	**NHL**	**82**	**1**	**14**	**15**	**79**	**0**	**0**	**0**	**88**	**1.1**	**–2**	**0**	**0.0**	**18:34**	**5**	**0**	**1**	**1**	**4**	**0**	**0**	**0**	**15:46**
2006-07	**Tampa Bay**	**NHL**	**82**	**0**	**15**	**15**	**70**	**0**	**0**	**0**	**64**	**0.0**	**–6**	**1**	**0.0**	**18:07**	**6**	**0**	**0**	**0**	**2**	**0**	**0**	**0**	**16:37**
2007-08	**Calgary**	**NHL**	**80**	**2**	**5**	**7**	**135**	**0**	**0**	**0**	**57**	**3.5**	**2**	**0**	**0.0**	**18:49**	**7**	**0**	**1**	**1**	**4**	**0**	**0**	**0**	**19:35**
	NHL Totals		**616**	**12**	**84**	**96**	**724**	**0**	**1**	**4**	**573**	**2.1**		**10**	**10.0**	**18:22**	**52**	**0**	**6**	**6**	**41**	**0**	**0**	**0**	**19:04**

WHL West Second All-Star Team (1998) • AHL All-Rookie Team (1999)

Traded to **Tampa Bay** by **Buffalo** with Wayne Primeau, Brian Holzinger and Buffalo's 3rd round choice (Alexander Kharitonov) in 2000 Entry Draft for Chris Gratton and Tampa Bay's 2nd round choice (Derek Roy) in 2001 Entry Draft, March 9, 2000. Signed as a free agent by **Calgary**, July 1, 2007.

SATAN, Miroslav (shuh-TAN, MEER-oh-slav) PIT.

Left wing. Shoots left. 6'3", 191 lbs. Born, Topolcany, Czech., October 22, 1974. Edmonton's 6th choice, 111th overall, in 1993 Entry Draft.

Season	Club	League	GP	G	A	Pts	PIM	PP	SH	GW	S	%	+/-	TF	F%	Min	GP	G	A	Pts	PIM	PP	SH	GW	Min
1991-92	Topolcany Jr.	Czech-Jr.	31	30	22	52	....	....	....	....	....	....	....	....	....	....	....	....	....	....	....	....	....	....	....
	VTJ Topolcany	Czech-2	9	2	1	3	6	....	....	....	....	....	....	....	....	....	....	....	....	....	....	....	....	....	....
1992-93	Dukla Trencin	Czech	38	11	6	17	....	....	....	....	....	....	....	....	....	....	....	....	....	....	....	....	....	....	....
1993-94	Dukla Trencin	Slovakia	30	32	16	48	16	....	....	....	....	....	....	....	....	....	....	....	....	....	....	....	....	....	....
	Slovakia	Olympics	8	*9	0	9	0	....	....	....	....	....	....	....	....	....	....	....	....	....	....	....	....	....	....
1994-95	Cape Breton	AHL	25	24	16	40	15	....	....	....	....	....	....	....	....	....	....	....	....	....	....	....	....	....	....
	Detroit Vipers	IHL	8	1	3	4	4	....	....	....	....	....	....	....	....	....	....	....	....	....	....	....	....	....	....
	San Diego Gulls	IHL	6	0	2	2	6	....	....	....	....	....	....	....	....	....	....	....	....	....	....	....	....	....	....
1995-96	**Edmonton**	**NHL**	**62**	**18**	**17**	**35**	**22**	**6**	**0**	**4**	**113**	**15.9**	**0**	....	....	....	....	....	....	....	....	....	....	....	....
1996-97	**Edmonton**	**NHL**	**64**	**17**	**11**	**28**	**22**	**5**	**0**	**2**	**90**	**18.9**	**–4**	....	....	....	....	....	....	....	....	....	....	....	....
	Buffalo	**NHL**	**12**	**8**	**2**	**10**	**4**	**2**	**0**	**1**	**29**	**27.6**	**1**	....	....	....	**7**	**0**	**0**	**0**	**0**	**0**	**0**	**0**	....
1997-98	**Buffalo**	**NHL**	**79**	**22**	**24**	**46**	**34**	**9**	**0**	**4**	**139**	**15.8**	**2**	....	....	....	**14**	**5**	**4**	**9**	**4**	**4**	**0**	**1**	....
1998-99	**Buffalo**	**NHL**	**81**	**40**	**26**	**66**	**44**	**13**	**3**	**6**	**208**	**19.2**	**24**	**9**	**55.6**	**20:49**	**12**	**3**	**5**	**8**	**2**	**1**	**0**	**1**	**21:18**
99-2000	Dukla Trencin	Slovakia	3	2	8	10	2	....	....	....	....	....	....	....	....	....	....	....	....	....	....	....	....	....	....
	Buffalo	**NHL**	**81**	**33**	**34**	**67**	**32**	**5**	**3**	**5**	**265**	**12.5**	**16**	**7**	**14.3**	**20:35**	**5**	**3**	**2**	**5**	**0**	**0**	**0**	**0**	**19:52**
2000-01	**Buffalo**	**NHL**	**82**	**29**	**33**	**62**	**36**	**8**	**2**	**4**	**206**	**14.1**	**5**	**11**	**36.4**	**19:56**	**13**	**3**	**10**	**13**	**8**	**1**	**0**	**0**	**21:18**
2001-02	**Buffalo**	**NHL**	**82**	**37**	**36**	**73**	**33**	**15**	**5**	**5**	**267**	**13.9**	**14**	**4**	**50.0**	**21:10**	....	....	....	....	....	....	....	....	....
	Slovakia	Olympics	2	0	1	1	0	....	....	....	....	....	....	....	....	....	....	....	....	....	....	....	....	....	....
2002-03	**Buffalo**	**NHL**	**79**	**26**	**49**	**75**	**20**	**11**	**1**	**3**	**240**	**10.8**	**–3**	**10**	**20.0**	**21:23**	....	....	....	....	....	....	....	....	....
2003-04	Bratislava	Slovakia	7	6	4	10	41	....	....	....	....	....	....	....	....	....	....	....	....	....	....	....	....	....	....
	Buffalo	**NHL**	**82**	**29**	**28**	**57**	**30**	**11**	**1**	**5**	**206**	**14.1**	**–15**	**9**	**22.2**	**20:02**	....	....	....	....	....	....	....	....	....
2004-05	Bratislava	Slovakia	18	11	9	20	14	....	....	....	....	....	....	....	....	....	18	*15	7	*22	16	....	....	....	....
2005-06	**NY Islanders**	**NHL**	**82**	**35**	**31**	**66**	**54**	**17**	**0**	**2**	**253**	**13.8**	**–8**	**342**	**53.2**	**19:10**	....	....	....	....	....	....	....	....	....
	Slovakia	Olympics	6	0	2	2	2	....	....	....	....	....	....	....	....	....	....	....	....	....	....	....	....	....	....
2006-07	**NY Islanders**	**NHL**	**81**	**27**	**32**	**59**	**46**	**7**	**1**	**2**	**216**	**12.5**	**–12**	**164**	**55.5**	**18:35**	**5**	**1**	**2**	**3**	**0**	**0**	**0**	**0**	**15:15**
2007-08	**NY Islanders**	**NHL**	**80**	**16**	**25**	**41**	**39**	**5**	**0**	**4**	**171**	**9.4**	**–11**	**38**	**50.0**	**18:19**	....	....	....	....	....	....	....	....	....
	NHL Totals		**947**	**337**	**348**	**685**	**416**	**114**	**16**	**47**	**2403**	**14.0**		**594**	**51.9**	**20:00**	**56**	**15**	**23**	**38**	**14**	**6**	**0**	**2**	**20:14**

Played in NHL All-Star Game (2000, 2003)

Traded to **Buffalo** by **Edmonton** for Barrie Moore and Craig Millar, March 18, 1997. Signed as a free agent by **Bratislava** (Slovakia), December 29, 2004. Signed as a free agent by **NY Islanders**, August 3, 2005. Signed as a free agent by **Pittsburgh**, July 3, 2008.

SAUER, Kurt (SAW-uhr, KUHRT) PHX.

Defense. Shoots left. 6'4", 220 lbs. Born, St. Cloud, MN, January 16, 1981. Colorado's 5th choice, 88th overall, in 2000 Entry Draft.

Season	Club	League	GP	G	A	Pts	PIM	PP	SH	GW	S	%	+/-	TF	F%	Min	GP	G	A	Pts	PIM	PP	SH	GW	Min
1998-99	North Iowa	USHL	52	1	4	5	67	....	....	....	....	....	....	....	....	....	....	....	....	....	....	....	....	....	....
99-2000	Spokane Chiefs	WHL	71	3	12	15	48	....	....	....	....	....	....	....	....	....	15	2	1	3	8	....	....	....	....
2000-01	Spokane Chiefs	WHL	48	5	10	15	85	....	....	....	....	....	....	....	....	....	3	1	0	1	2	....	....	....	....
2001-02	Spokane Chiefs	WHL	61	4	20	24	73	....	....	....	....	....	....	....	....	....	11	0	3	3	12	....	....	....	....
2002-03	**Anaheim**	**NHL**	**80**	**1**	**2**	**3**	**74**	**0**	**0**	**0**	**50**	**2.0**	**–23**	**0**	**0.0**	**18:33**	**21**	**1**	**1**	**2**	**6**	**0**	**1**	**1**	**20:45**
2003-04	**Anaheim**	**NHL**	**55**	**1**	**4**	**5**	**32**	**0**	**0**	**0**	**32**	**3.1**	**–8**	**0**	**0.0**	**16:54**	....	....	....	....	....	....	....	....	....
	Colorado	**NHL**	**14**	**0**	**1**	**1**	**19**	**0**	**0**	**0**	**12**	**0.0**	**–3**	**0**	**0.0**	**15:04**	**3**	**0**	**0**	**0**	**0**	**0**	**0**	**0**	**11:56**
2004-05			DID NOT PLAY																						
2005-06	**Colorado**	**NHL**	**37**	**1**	**4**	**5**	**24**	**0**	**0**	**0**	**19**	**5.3**	**5**	**0**	**0.0**	**12:48**	**9**	**0**	**0**	**0**	**4**	**0**	**0**	**0**	**8:39**
	Lowell	AHL	4	0	0	0	0	....	....	....	....	....	....	....	....	....	....	....	....	....	....	....	....	....	....
2006-07	**Colorado**	**NHL**	**48**	**0**	**6**	**6**	**24**	**0**	**0**	**0**	**29**	**0.0**	**–3**	**0**	**0.0**	**18:20**	....	....	....	....	....	....	....	....	....
2007-08	**Colorado**	**NHL**	**54**	**1**	**5**	**6**	**41**	**0**	**0**	**0**	**28**	**3.6**	**17**	**0**	**0.0**	**18:41**	**10**	**1**	**0**	**1**	**8**	**0**	**0**	**0**	**19:23**
	NHL Totals		**288**	**4**	**22**	**26**	**214**	**0**	**0**	**0**	**170**	**2.4**		**0**	**0.0**	**17:19**	**43**	**2**	**1**	**3**	**18**	**0**	**1**	**1**	**17:17**

WHL West First All-Star Team (2002)

Signed as a free agent by **Anaheim**, July 6, 2002. Traded to **Colorado** by **Anaheim** with Anaheim's 4th round choice (Raymond Macias) in 2005 Entry Draft for Martin Skoula, February 21, 2004. Signed as a free agent by **Phoenix**, July 1, 2008.

SAVARD, Marc (sa-VAHR, MAHRK) BOS.

Center. Shoots left. 5'10", 191 lbs. Born, Ottawa, Ont., July 17, 1977. NY Rangers' 3rd choice, 91st overall, in 1995 Entry Draft.

Season	Club	League	GP	G	A	Pts	PIM	PP	SH	GW	S	%	+/-	TF	F%	Min	GP	G	A	Pts	PIM	PP	SH	GW	Min
1992-93	Metcalfe Jets	OHA-B	36	*44	55	*99	38	....	....	....	....	....	....	....	....	....	....	....	....	....	....	....	....	....	....
1993-94	Oshawa Generals	OHL	61	18	39	57	20	....	....	....	....	....	....	....	....	....	5	4	3	7	8	....	....	....	....
1994-95	Oshawa Generals	OHL	66	43	96	*139	78	....	....	....	....	....	....	....	....	....	7	5	6	11	8	....	....	....	....
1995-96	Oshawa Generals	OHL	48	28	59	87	77	....	....	....	....	....	....	....	....	....	5	4	5	9	6	....	....	....	....
1996-97	Oshawa Generals	OHL	64	43	*87	*130	94	....	....	....	....	....	....	....	....	....	18	13	*24	*37	20	....	....	....	....
1997-98	**NY Rangers**	**NHL**	**28**	**1**	**5**	**6**	**4**	**0**	**0**	**0**	**32**	**3.1**	**–4**	....	....	....	....	....	....	....	....	....	....	....	....
	Hartford	AHL	58	21	53	74	66	....	....	....	....	....	....	....	....	....	15	8	19	27	24	....	....	....	....
1998-99	**NY Rangers**	**NHL**	**70**	**9**	**36**	**45**	**38**	**4**	**0**	**1**	**116**	**7.8**	**–7**	**956**	**48.4**	**14:35**	....	....	....	....	....	....	....	....	....
	Hartford	AHL	9	3	10	13	16	....	....	....	....	....	....	....	....	....	7	1	12	13	16	....	....	....	....
99-2000	**Calgary**	**NHL**	**78**	**22**	**31**	**53**	**56**	**4**	**0**	**3**	**184**	**12.0**	**–2**	**1021**	**49.6**	**16:36**	....	....	....	....	....	....	....	....	....
2000-01	**Calgary**	**NHL**	**77**	**23**	**42**	**65**	**46**	**10**	**1**	**5**	**197**	**11.7**	**–12**	**1050**	**53.1**	**19:13**	....	....	....	....	....	....	....	....	....
2001-02	**Calgary**	**NHL**	**56**	**14**	**19**	**33**	**48**	**7**	**0**	**3**	**140**	**10.0**	**–18**	**577**	**54.8**	**17:20**	....	....	....	....	....	....	....	....	....
2002-03	**Calgary**	**NHL**	**10**	**1**	**2**	**3**	**8**	**0**	**0**	**0**	**21**	**4.8**	**–3**	**89**	**52.8**	**14:41**	....	....	....	....	....	....	....	....	....
	Atlanta	**NHL**	**57**	**16**	**31**	**47**	**77**	**6**	**0**	**4**	**127**	**12.6**	**–11**	**1247**	**50.9**	**19:50**	....	....	....	....	....	....	....	....	....

			Regular Season														Playoffs								
Season	Club	League	GP	G	A	Pts	PIM	PP	SH	GW	S	%	+/-	TF	F%	Min	GP	G	A	Pts	PIM	PP	SH	GW	Min
2003-04	**Atlanta**	**NHL**	**45**	**19**	**33**	**52**	**85**	**6**	**1**	**3**	**133**	**14.3**	**-8**	**1083**	**49.9**	**22:19**	....	....	....	....	....	....	....	....	....
2004-05	HC Thurgau	Swiss-2	13	9	19	28	10	....	....	....	....	....	....	....	....	....	....	....	....	....	....	....	....	....	....
	SC Bern	Swiss	5	1	2	3	0	....	....	....	....	....	....	....	....	....	....	....	....	....	....	....	....	....	....
2005-06	**Atlanta**	**NHL**	**82**	**28**	**69**	**97**	**100**	**14**	**1**	**4**	**212**	**13.2**	**7**	**1529**	**51.6**	**20:30**	....	....	....	....	....	....	....	....	....
2006-07	**Boston**	**NHL**	**82**	**22**	**74**	**96**	**96**	**10**	**1**	**3**	**221**	**10.0**	**-19**	**1420**	**50.1**	**20:13**	....	....	....	....	....	....	....	....	....
2007-08	**Boston**	**NHL**	**74**	**15**	**63**	**78**	**66**	**4**	**0**	**2**	**196**	**7.7**	**3**	**1555**	**51.6**	**20:31**	**7**	**1**	**5**	**6**	**6**	**0**	**0**	**1**	**17:06**
	NHL Totals		**659**	**170**	**405**	**575**	**624**	**65**	**4**	**28**	**1579**	**10.8**		**10527**	**51.0**	**18:52**	**7**	**1**	**5**	**6**	**6**	**0**	**0**	**1**	**17:06**

OHL Second All-Star Team (1995)

Played in NHL All-Star Game (2008)

Traded to **Calgary** by **NY Rangers** with NY Rangers 1st round choice (Oleg Saprykin) in 1999 Entry Draft for the rights to Jan Hlavac and Calgary's 1st (Jamie Lundmark) and 3rd (later traded back to Calgary – Calgary selected Craig Andersson) round choices in 1999 Entry Draft, June 26, 1999. Traded to **Atlanta** by **Calgary** for Ruslan Zainullin, November 15, 2002. Signed as a free agent by **Thurgau** (Swiss-2), October 11, 2004. Signed as a free agent by **Bern** (Swiss), November 23, 2004. Signed as a free agent by **Boston**, July 1, 2006.

SCATCHARD, Dave

(SKAT-chuhrd, DAYV)

Center. Shoots right. 6'3", 220 lbs. Born, Hinton, Alta., February 20, 1976. Vancouver's 3rd choice, 42nd overall, in 1994 Entry Draft.

1991-92	Salmon Arm	Minor-BC	65	98	100	198	167	....	....	....	....	....	....	....	....	....	....	....	....	....	....	....	....	....	....
1992-93	Kimberley	RMJHL	51	20	23	43	61	....	....	....	....	....	....	....	....	....	....	....	....	....	....	....	....	....	....
1993-94	Portland	WHL	47	9	11	20	46	....	....	....	....	....	....	....	....	....	10	2	1	3	4	....	....	....	....
1994-95	Portland	WHL	71	20	30	50	148	....	....	....	....	....	....	....	....	....	8	0	3	3	21	....	....	....	....
1995-96	Portland	WHL	59	19	28	47	146	....	....	....	....	....	....	....	....	....	7	1	8	9	14	....	....	....	....
	Syracuse Crunch	AHL	1	0	0	0	0	....	....	....	....	....	....	....	....	....	15	2	5	7	29	....	....	....	....
1996-97	Syracuse Crunch	AHL	26	8	7	15	65	....	....	....	....	....	....	....	....	....	....	....	....	....	....	....	....	....	....
1997-98	**Vancouver**	**NHL**	**76**	**13**	**11**	**24**	**165**	**0**	**0**	**1**	**85**	**15.3**	**-4**	....	....	....	....	....	....	....	....	....	....	....	....
1998-99	**Vancouver**	**NHL**	**82**	**13**	**13**	**26**	**140**	**0**	**2**	**2**	**130**	**10.0**	**-12**	**1007**	**56.3**	**13:46**	....	....	....	....	....	....	....	....	....
99-2000	**Vancouver**	**NHL**	**21**	**0**	**4**	**4**	**24**	**0**	**0**	**0**	**25**	**0.0**	**-3**	**190**	**59.5**	**10:12**	....	....	....	....	....	....	....	....	....
	NY Islanders	**NHL**	**44**	**12**	**14**	**26**	**93**	**0**	**1**	**1**	**103**	**11.7**	**0**	**710**	**55.8**	**13:42**	....	....	....	....	....	....	....	....	....
2000-01	**NY Islanders**	**NHL**	**81**	**21**	**24**	**45**	**114**	**4**	**0**	**5**	**176**	**11.9**	**-9**	**1322**	**55.1**	**16:50**	....	....	....	....	....	....	....	....	....
2001-02	**NY Islanders**	**NHL**	**80**	**12**	**15**	**27**	**111**	**3**	**1**	**4**	**117**	**10.3**	**-4**	**788**	**53.8**	**12:31**	**7**	**1**	**1**	**2**	**22**	**0**	**0**	**0**	**12:38**
2002-03	**NY Islanders**	**NHL**	**81**	**27**	**18**	**45**	**108**	**5**	**0**	**2**	**165**	**16.4**	**9**	**1147**	**52.7**	**14:30**	**5**	**1**	**0**	**1**	**6**	**0**	**0**	**1**	**15:58**
2003-04	**NY Islanders**	**NHL**	**61**	**9**	**16**	**25**	**78**	**1**	**1**	**1**	**111**	**8.1**	**12**	**1052**	**52.7**	**16:13**	**5**	**0**	**1**	**1**	**6**	**0**	**0**	**0**	**16:18**
2004-05			DID NOT PLAY																						
2005-06	**Boston**	**NHL**	**16**	**4**	**6**	**10**	**28**	**1**	**0**	**0**	**40**	**10.0**	**-2**	**272**	**54.8**	**16:56**	....	....	....	....	....	....	....	....	....
	Phoenix	**NHL**	**47**	**11**	**12**	**23**	**84**	**4**	**0**	**3**	**81**	**13.6**	**-11**	**594**	**53.2**	**14:44**	....	....	....	....	....	....	....	....	....
2006-07	**Phoenix**	**NHL**	**46**	**3**	**5**	**8**	**72**	**0**	**0**	**1**	**77**	**3.9**	**-18**	**385**	**52.5**	**13:31**	....	....	....	....	....	....	....	....	....
2007-08	Hartford	AHL	3	0	1	1	0	....	....	....	....	....	....	....	....	....	....	....	....	....	....	....	....	....	....
	Milwaukee	AHL	8	1	2	3	14	....	....	....	....	....	....	....	....	....	....	....	....	....	....	....	....	....	....
	NHL Totals		**635**	**125**	**138**	**263**	**1017**	**18**	**5**	**20**	**1110**	**11.3**		**7467**	**54.3**	**14:25**	**17**	**2**	**2**	**4**	**34**	**0**	**0**	**1**	**14:41**

Traded to **NY Islanders** by **Vancouver** with Kevin Weekes and Bill Muckalt for Felix Potvin, NY Islanders' 2nd round compensatory choice (later traded to New Jersey – New Jersey selected Teemu Laine) in 2000 Entry Draft and NY Islanders' 3rd round choice (Thatcher Bell) in 2000 Entry Draft, December 19, 1999. Signed as a free agent by **Boston**, August 2, 2005. Traded to **Phoenix** by **Boston** for David Tanabe, November 18, 2005. Signed to a PTO (tryout) contract by **Hartford** (AHL), October 17, 2007.

SCHAEFER, Peter

(SHAY-fuhr, PEE-tuhr) **BOS.**

Left wing. Shoots left. 6'1", 200 lbs. Born, Regina, Sask., July 12, 1977. Vancouver's 3rd choice, 66th overall, in 1995 Entry Draft.

1993-94	Yorkton Mallers	SMHL	32	27	14	41	133	....	....	....	....	....	....	....	....	....	....	....	....	....	....	....	....	....	....
	Brandon	WHL	2	1	0	1	0	....	....	....	....	....	....	....	....	....	....	....	....	....	....	....	....	....	....
1994-95	Brandon	WHL	68	27	32	59	34	....	....	....	....	....	....	....	....	....	18	5	3	8	18	....	....	....	....
1995-96	Brandon	WHL	69	47	61	108	53	....	....	....	....	....	....	....	....	....	19	10	13	23	5	....	....	....	....
1996-97	Brandon	WHL	61	49	74	123	85	....	....	....	....	....	....	....	....	....	6	1	4	5	4	....	....	....	....
	Syracuse Crunch	AHL	5	0	3	3	0	....	....	....	....	....	....	....	....	....	3	1	3	4	14	....	....	....	....
1997-98	Syracuse Crunch	AHL	73	19	44	63	41	....	....	....	....	....	....	....	....	....	5	2	1	3	2	....	....	....	....
1998-99	**Vancouver**	**NHL**	**25**	**4**	**4**	**8**	**8**	**1**	**0**	**1**	**24**	**16.7**	**-1**	**6**	**0.0**	**13:21**	....	....	....	....	....	....	....	....	....
	Syracuse Crunch	AHL	41	10	19	29	66	....	....	....	....	....	....	....	....	....	....	....	....	....	....	....	....	....	....
99-2000	**Vancouver**	**NHL**	**71**	**16**	**15**	**31**	**20**	**2**	**2**	**4**	**101**	**15.8**	**0**	**21**	**19.1**	**15:28**	....	....	....	....	....	....	....	....	....
	Syracuse Crunch	AHL	2	0	0	0	2	....	....	....	....	....	....	....	....	....	....	....	....	....	....	....	....	....	....
2000-01	**Vancouver**	**NHL**	**82**	**16**	**20**	**36**	**22**	**3**	**4**	**2**	**163**	**9.8**	**4**	**25**	**32.0**	**16:18**	**3**	**0**	**0**	**0**	**0**	**0**	**0**	**0**	**13:08**
2001-02	TPS Turku	Finland	33	16	15	31	93	....	....	....	....	....	....	....	....	....	8	1	2	3	2	....	....	....	....
2002-03	**Ottawa**	**NHL**	**75**	**6**	**17**	**23**	**32**	**0**	**0**	**1**	**93**	**6.5**	**11**	**44**	**20.5**	**14:59**	**16**	**2**	**3**	**5**	**6**	**0**	**1**	**0**	**11:51**
2003-04	**Ottawa**	**NHL**	**81**	**15**	**24**	**39**	**26**	**2**	**2**	**3**	**112**	**13.4**	**22**	**39**	**23.1**	**15:36**	**7**	**0**	**2**	**2**	**4**	**0**	**0**	**0**	**14:25**
2004-05	HC Forst Bolzano	Italy	15	11	14	25	10	....	....	....	....	....	....	....	....	....	10	1	7	8	12	....	....	....	....
2005-06	**Ottawa**	**NHL**	**82**	**20**	**30**	**50**	**40**	**4**	**4**	**2**	**137**	**14.6**	**16**	**27**	**37.0**	**15:49**	**10**	**2**	**5**	**7**	**14**	**0**	**0**	**0**	**16:39**
2006-07	**Ottawa**	**NHL**	**77**	**12**	**34**	**46**	**32**	**5**	**0**	**2**	**132**	**9.1**	**7**	**7**	**28.6**	**16:44**	**20**	**1**	**5**	**6**	**10**	**0**	**0**	**0**	**14:32**
2007-08	**Boston**	**NHL**	**63**	**9**	**17**	**26**	**18**	**0**	**0**	**0**	**91**	**9.9**	**4**	**7**	**42.9**	**14:58**	**7**	**1**	**3**	**4**	**0**	**0**	**0**	**0**	**12:50**
	NHL Totals		**556**	**98**	**161**	**259**	**198**	**17**	**12**	**15**	**853**	**11.5**		**176**	**25.6**	**15:37**	**63**	**6**	**18**	**24**	**34**	**0**	**1**	**0**	**13:55**

WHL East First All-Star Team (1996, 1997) • WHL Player of the Year (1997) • Canadian Major Junior First All-Star Team (1997)

Signed as a free agent by **Turku** (Finland), October 18, 2001. Traded to **Ottawa** by **Vancouver** for Sami Salo, September 21, 2002. Signed as a free agent by **Bolzano** (Italy), November 30, 2004. Traded to **Boston** by **Ottawa** for Shean Donovan, July 17, 2007.

SCHNEIDER, Mathieu

(SHNIGH-duhr, MA-thew) **ANA.**

Defense. Shoots left. 5'11", 195 lbs. Born, New York, NY, June 12, 1969. Montreal's 4th choice, 44th overall, in 1987 Entry Draft.

1985-86	Mount St. Charles	High-RI	19	3	27	30	....	....	....	....	....	....	....	....	....	....	....	....	....	....	....	....	....	....	....
1986-87	Cornwall Royals	OHL	63	7	29	36	75	....	....	....	....	....	....	....	....	....	5	0	0	0	22	....	....	....	....
1987-88	Cornwall Royals	OHL	48	21	40	61	83	....	....	....	....	....	....	....	....	....	11	2	6	8	14	....	....	....	....
	Montreal	**NHL**	**4**	**0**	**0**	**0**	**2**	**0**	**0**	**0**	**2**	**0.0**	**-1**	....	....	....	....	....	....	....	....	....	....	....	....
	Sherbrooke	AHL	....	....	....	....	....	....	....	....	....	....	....	....	....	....	3	0	3	3	12	....	....	....	....
1988-89	Cornwall Royals	OHL	59	16	57	73	96	....	....	....	....	....	....	....	....	....	18	7	20	27	30	....	....	....	....
1989-90	**Montreal**	**NHL**	**44**	**7**	**14**	**21**	**25**	**5**	**0**	**1**	**84**	**8.3**	**2**	....	....	....	**9**	**1**	**3**	**4**	**31**	**1**	**0**	**0**	....
	Sherbrooke	AHL	28	6	13	19	20	....	....	....	....	....	....	....	....	....	....	....	....	....	....	....	....	....	....
1990-91	**Montreal**	**NHL**	**69**	**10**	**20**	**30**	**63**	**5**	**0**	**3**	**164**	**6.1**	**7**	....	....	....	**13**	**2**	**7**	**9**	**18**	**1**	**0**	**0**	....
1991-92	**Montreal**	**NHL**	**78**	**8**	**24**	**32**	**72**	**2**	**0**	**1**	**194**	**4.1**	**10**	....	....	....	**10**	**1**	**4**	**5**	**6**	**1**	**0**	**0**	....
1992-93♦	**Montreal**	**NHL**	**60**	**13**	**31**	**44**	**91**	**3**	**0**	**2**	**169**	**7.7**	**8**	....	....	....	**11**	**1**	**2**	**3**	**16**	**0**	**0**	**0**	....
1993-94	**Montreal**	**NHL**	**75**	**20**	**32**	**52**	**62**	**11**	**0**	**4**	**193**	**10.4**	**15**	....	....	....	**1**	**0**	**0**	**0**	**0**	**0**	**0**	**0**	....
1994-95	**Montreal**	**NHL**	**30**	**5**	**15**	**20**	**49**	**2**	**0**	**0**	**82**	**6.1**	**-3**	....	....	....	....	....	....	....	....	....	....	....	....
	NY Islanders	**NHL**	**13**	**3**	**6**	**9**	**30**	**1**	**0**	**2**	**36**	**8.3**	**-5**	....	....	....	....	....	....	....	....	....	....	....	....
1995-96	**NY Islanders**	**NHL**	**65**	**11**	**36**	**47**	**93**	**7**	**0**	**1**	**155**	**7.1**	**-18**	....	....	....	....	....	....	....	....	....	....	....	....
	Toronto	**NHL**	**13**	**2**	**5**	**7**	**10**	**0**	**0**	**0**	**36**	**5.6**	**-2**	....	....	....	**6**	**0**	**4**	**4**	**8**	**0**	**0**	**0**	....
1996-97	**Toronto**	**NHL**	**26**	**5**	**7**	**12**	**20**	**1**	**0**	**1**	**63**	**7.9**	**3**	....	....	....	....	....	....	....	....	....	....	....	....
1997-98	**Toronto**	**NHL**	**76**	**11**	**26**	**37**	**44**	**4**	**1**	**1**	**181**	**6.1**	**-12**	....	....	....	....	....	....	....	....	....	....	....	....
	United States	Olympics	4	0	0	0	6	....	....	....	....	....	....	....	....	....	....	....	....	....	....	....	....	....	....
1998-99	**NY Rangers**	**NHL**	**75**	**10**	**24**	**34**	**71**	**5**	**0**	**2**	**159**	**6.3**	**-19**	**0**	**0.0**	**24:35**	....	....	....	....	....	....	....	....	....
99-2000	**NY Rangers**	**NHL**	**80**	**10**	**20**	**30**	**78**	**3**	**0**	**1**	**228**	**4.4**	**-6**	**0**	**0.0**	**22:31**	....	....	....	....	....	....	....	....	....
2000-01	**Los Angeles**	**NHL**	**73**	**16**	**35**	**51**	**56**	**7**	**1**	**2**	**183**	**8.7**	**0**	**0**	**0.0**	**23:04**	**13**	**0**	**9**	**9**	**10**	**0**	**0**	**0**	**25:51**
2001-02	**Los Angeles**	**NHL**	**55**	**7**	**23**	**30**	**68**	**4**	**0**	**0**	**123**	**5.7**	**3**	**0**	**0.0**	**22:25**	**7**	**0**	**1**	**1**	**18**	**0**	**0**	**0**	**22:52**
2002-03	**Los Angeles**	**NHL**	**65**	**14**	**29**	**43**	**57**	**10**	**0**	**1**	**162**	**8.6**	**0**	**0**	**0.0**	**22:20**	....	....	....	....	....	....	....	....	....
	Detroit	**NHL**	**13**	**2**	**5**	**7**	**16**	**1**	**0**	**0**	**37**	**5.4**	**2**	**0**	**0.0**	**22:42**	**4**	**0**	**0**	**0**	**6**	**0**	**0**	**0**	**28:16**
2003-04	**Detroit**	**NHL**	**78**	**14**	**32**	**46**	**56**	**4**	**1**	**4**	**165**	**8.5**	**22**	**4**	**0.0**	**24:29**	**12**	**1**	**2**	**3**	**8**	**1**	**0**	**1**	**26:30**
2004-05			DID NOT PLAY																						
2005-06	**Detroit**	**NHL**	**72**	**21**	**38**	**59**	**86**	**11**	**0**	**4**	**188**	**11.2**	**33**	**4**	**25.0**	**24:31**	**6**	**1**	**7**	**8**	**6**	**0**	**0**	**0**	**26:44**
	United States	Olympics	6	1	2	3	16	....	....	....	....	....	....	....	....	....	....	....	....	....	....	....	....	....	....

			Regular Season														Playoffs								
Season	Club	League	GP	G	A	Pts	PIM	PP	SH	GW	S	%	+/-	TF	F%	Min	GP	G	A	Pts	PIM	PP	SH	GW	Min
2006-07	**Detroit**	**NHL**	68	11	41	52	66	2	1	2	184	6.0	12	0	0.0	23:35	11	2	4	6	16	1	0	1	23:35
2007-08	**Anaheim**	**NHL**	65	12	27	39	50	5	0	2	139	8.6	22	0	0.0	22:18	6	1	0	1	8	0	0	0	20:29
	NHL Totals		1197	212	490	702	1165	93	4	34	2927	7.2		8	12.5	23:21	109	10	43	53	151	5	0	2	24:55

OHL First All-Star Team (1988, 1989)

Played in NHL All-Star Game (1996, 2003)

Traded to **NY Islanders** by **Montreal** with Kirk Muller and Craig Darby for Pierre Turgeon and Vladimir Malakhov, April 5, 1995. Traded to **Toronto** by **NY Islanders** with Wendel Clark and D.J. Smith for Darby Hendrickson, Sean Haggerty, Kenny Jonsson and Toronto's 1st round choice (Roberto Luongo) in 1997 Entry Draft, March 13, 1996. • Missed majority of 1996-97 season recovering from groin injury suffered in game vs. St. Louis, December 27, 1996. Rights traded to **NY Rangers** by **Toronto** for Alexander Karpovtsev and NY Rangers' 4th round choice (Mirko Murovic) in 1999 Entry Draft, October 14, 1998. Claimed by **Columbus** from **NY Rangers** in Expansion Draft, June 23, 2000. Signed as a free agent by **Los Angeles**, August 14, 2000. Traded to **Detroit** by **Los Angeles** for Sean Avery, Maxim Kuznetsov, Detroit's 1st round choice (Jeff Tambellini) in 2003 Entry Draft and Detroit's 2nd round choice (later traded to Boston – Boston selected Martins Karsums) in 2004 Entry Draft, March 11, 2003. Signed as a free agent by **Anaheim**, July 1, 2007.

SCHREMP, Rob (SHREHMP, RAWB) EDM.

Center. Shoots left. 5'11", 200 lbs. Born, Syracuse, NY, July 1, 1986. Edmonton's 2nd choice, 25th overall, in 2004 Entry Draft.

Season	Club	League	GP	G	A	Pts	PIM	PP	SH	GW	S	%	+/-	TF	F%	Min	GP	G	A	Pts	PIM	PP	SH	GW	Min
2000-01	Syracuse	OPJHL	49	32	46	78	....	....	....	....	....	....	....	....	....	....	....	....	....	....	....	....	....	....	....
2001-02	Syracuse	OPJHL	47	41	47	88	93	....	....	....	....	....	....	....	....	....	1	1	2	3	0	....	....	....	....
2002-03	Mississauga	OHL	65	26	48	74	25	....	....	....	....	....	....	....	....	....	2	1	0	1	0	....	....	....	....
2003-04	USNTDP	U-18	2	0	0	0	8	....	....	....	....	....	....	....	....	....	....	....	....	....	....	....	....	....	....
	Mississauga	OHL	3	2	4	6	0	....	....	....	....	....	....	....	....	....	....	....	....	....	....	....	....	....	....
	London Knights	OHL	60	28	41	69	18	....	....	....	....	....	....	....	....	....	15	7	6	13	2	....	....	....	....
2004-05	London Knights	OHL	62	41	49	90	54	....	....	....	....	....	....	....	....	....	18	13	16	29	16	....	....	....	....
2005-06	London Knights	OHL	57	*57	*88	*145	74	....	....	....	....	....	....	....	....	....	19	10	*37	*47	35	....	....	....	....
2006-07	**Edmonton**	**NHL**	1	0	0	0	0	0	0	0	2	0.0	0	12	50.0	13:50	....	....	....	....	....	....	....	....	....
	Wilkes-Barre	AHL	69	17	36	53	36	....	....	....	....	....	....	....	....	....	....	....	....	....	....	....	....	....	....
2007-08	**Edmonton**	**NHL**	2	0	0	0	0	0	0	0	3	0.0	–1	1	0.0	6:57	....	....	....	....	....	....	....	....	....
	Springfield	AHL	78	23	53	76	64	....	....	....	....	....	....	....	....	....	....	....	....	....	....	....	....	....	....
	NHL Totals		3	0	0	0	0	0	0	0	5	0.0		13	46.2	9:15	....	....	....	....	....	....	....	....	....

OHL All-Rookie Team (2003) • OHL Rookie of the Year (2003) • OHL First All-Star Team (2006)

SCHUBERT, Christoph (SHOO-buhrt, KRIHS-tawf) OTT.

Defense. Shoots left. 6'3", 229 lbs. Born, Munich, West Germany, February 5, 1982. Ottawa's 5th choice, 127th overall, in 2001 Entry Draft.

Season	Club	League	GP	G	A	Pts	PIM	PP	SH	GW	S	%	+/-	TF	F%	Min	GP	G	A	Pts	PIM	PP	SH	GW	Min
1998-99	EV Landshut Jr.	Ger-Jr.	28	15	20	35	77	....	....	....	....	....	....	....	....	....	....	....	....	....	....	....	....	....	....
99-2000	EV Landshut Jr.	Ger-Jr.	11	14	11	25	51	....	....	....	....	....	....	....	....	....	....	....	....	....	....	....	....	....	....
	EV Landshut	German-3	55	7	5	12	68	....	....	....	....	....	....	....	....	....	....	....	....	....	....	....	....	....	....
2000-01	Munchen Barons	Germany	55	6	3	9	80	....	....	....	....	....	....	....	....	....	10	0	2	2	27	....	....	....	....
2001-02	Munchen Barons	Germany	50	5	11	16	125	....	....	....	....	....	....	....	....	....	9	3	4	7	32	....	....	....	....
2002-03	Binghamton	AHL	70	2	8	10	102	....	....	....	....	....	....	....	....	....	8	0	1	1	2	....	....	....	....
2003-04	Binghamton	AHL	70	2	10	12	69	....	....	....	....	....	....	....	....	....	1	0	0	0	0	....	....	....	....
2004-05	Binghamton	AHL	76	10	22	32	110	....	....	....	....	....	....	....	....	....	6	2	2	4	20	....	....	....	....
2005-06	**Ottawa**	**NHL**	56	4	6	10	48	0	1	0	72	5.6	4	5	0.0	11:06	7	0	1	1	4	0	0	0	7:53
	Germany	Olympics	5	0	1	1	2	....	....	....	....	....	....	....	....	....	....	....	....	....	....	....	....	....	....
2006-07	**Ottawa**	**NHL**	80	8	17	25	56	1	0	1	97	8.2	30	1	0.0	11:13	20	0	1	1	22	0	0	0	9:10
2007-08	**Ottawa**	**NHL**	82	8	16	24	64	1	0	0	137	5.8	7	4	25.0	13:34	4	0	0	0	8	0	0	0	11:58
	NHL Totals		218	20	39	59	168	2	1	1	306	6.5		10	10.0	12:04	31	0	2	2	34	0	0	0	9:14

SCHULTZ, Jeff (SHUHLTZ, JEHF) WSH.

Defense. Shoots left. 6'6", 221 lbs. Born, Calgary, Alta., February 25, 1986. Washington's 2nd choice, 27th overall, in 2004 Entry Draft.

Season	Club	League	GP	G	A	Pts	PIM	PP	SH	GW	S	%	+/-	TF	F%	Min	GP	G	A	Pts	PIM	PP	SH	GW	Min
2000-01	Calgary Hawks	CBHL	27	7	8	15	20	....	....	....	....	....	....	....	....	....	....	....	....	....	....	....	....	....	....
2001-02	Calgary Rangers	CBHL	27	5	18	23	42	....	....	....	....	....	....	....	....	....	....	....	....	....	....	....	....	....	....
2002-03	Calgary Hitmen	WHL	50	2	1	3	4	....	....	....	....	....	....	....	....	....	4	0	0	0	0	....	....	....	....
2003-04	Calgary Hitmen	WHL	72	11	24	35	33	....	....	....	....	....	....	....	....	....	7	1	1	2	0	....	....	....	....
2004-05	Calgary Hitmen	WHL	72	2	27	29	31	....	....	....	....	....	....	....	....	....	12	2	1	3	6	....	....	....	....
2005-06	Calgary Hitmen	WHL	68	7	33	40	36	....	....	....	....	....	....	....	....	....	13	4	6	10	6	....	....	....	....
	Hershey Bears	AHL	....	....	....	....	....	....	....	....	....	....	....	....	....	....	7	1	3	4	4	....	....	....	....
2006-07	**Washington**	**NHL**	38	0	3	3	16	0	0	0	22	0.0	5	0	0.0	18:13	....	....	....	....	....	....	....	....	....
	Hershey Bears	AHL	44	2	10	12	39	....	....	....	....	....	....	....	....	....	19	0	1	1	18	....	....	....	....
2007-08	**Washington**	**NHL**	72	5	13	18	28	0	0	0	36	13.9	12	1	100.0	18:05	2	0	0	0	2	0	0	0	10:25
	Hershey Bears	AHL	1	0	0	0	0	....	....	....	....	....	....	....	....	....	....	....	....	....	....	....	....	....	....
	NHL Totals		110	5	16	21	44	0	0	0	58	8.6		1	100.0	18:08	2	0	0	0	2	0	0	0	10:25

WHL East Second All-Star Team (2006)

SCHULTZ, Jesse (SHUHLTZ, JEH-see) MIN.

Right wing. Shoots right. 6'1", 195 lbs. Born, Strasbourg, Sask., September 28, 1982.

Season	Club	League	GP	G	A	Pts	PIM	PP	SH	GW	S	%	+/-	TF	F%	Min	GP	G	A	Pts	PIM	PP	SH	GW	Min
99-2000	Tri-City	WHL	62	10	6	16	34	....	....	....	....	....	....	....	....	....	4	1	1	2	2	....	....	....	....
2000-01	Tri-City	WHL	30	5	8	13	16	....	....	....	....	....	....	....	....	....	....	....	....	....	....	....	....	....	....
	Prince Albert	WHL	35	14	18	32	14	....	....	....	....	....	....	....	....	....	....	....	....	....	....	....	....	....	....
2001-02	Prince Albert	WHL	45	18	24	42	16	....	....	....	....	....	....	....	....	....	....	....	....	....	....	....	....	....	....
	Kelowna Rockets	WHL	28	10	12	22	14	....	....	....	....	....	....	....	....	....	....	....	....	....	....	....	....	....	....
2002-03	Kelowna Rockets	WHL	72	53	51	104	47	....	....	....	....	....	....	....	....	....	19	*12	16	*28	21	....	....	....	....
2003-04	Manitoba Moose	AHL	2	0	1	1	0	....	....	....	....	....	....	....	....	....	....	....	....	....	....	....	....	....	....
	Columbia Inferno	ECHL	52	27	21	48	72	....	....	....	....	....	....	....	....	....	4	1	2	3	2	....	....	....	....
2004-05	Manitoba Moose	AHL	70	9	15	24	33	....	....	....	....	....	....	....	....	....	14	3	2	5	2	....	....	....	....
2005-06	Manitoba Moose	AHL	80	37	30	67	63	....	....	....	....	....	....	....	....	....	13	5	7	12	10	....	....	....	....
2006-07	**Vancouver**	**NHL**	2	0	0	0	0	0	0	0	6	0.0	0	0	0.0	10:09	....	....	....	....	....	....	....	....	....
	Manitoba Moose	AHL	67	18	21	39	35	....	....	....	....	....	....	....	....	....	7	0	0	0	2	....	....	....	....
2007-08	Chicago Wolves	AHL	80	26	40	66	43	....	....	....	....	....	....	....	....	....	24	8	6	14	18	....	....	....	....
	NHL Totals		2	0	0	0	0	0	0	0	6	0.0		0	0.0	10:09	....	....	....	....	....	....	....	....	....

WHL West First All-Star Team (2003)

Signed as a free agent by **Vancouver**, July 31, 2003. Traded to **Atlanta** by **Vancouver** for Jim Sharrow, June 23, 2007. Signed as a free agent by **Minnesota**, July 6, 2008.

SCHULTZ, Nick (SHUHLTZ, NIHK) MIN.

Defense. Shoots left. 6'1", 200 lbs. Born, Strasbourg, Sask., August 25, 1982. Minnesota's 2nd choice, 33rd overall, in 2000 Entry Draft.

Season	Club	League	GP	G	A	Pts	PIM	PP	SH	GW	S	%	+/-	TF	F%	Min	GP	G	A	Pts	PIM	PP	SH	GW	Min
1997-98	Yorkton Mallers	SMHL	59	10	30	40	74	....	....	....	....	....	....	....	....	....	....	....	....	....	....	....	....	....	....
1998-99	Prince Albert	WHL	58	5	18	23	37	....	....	....	....	....	....	....	....	....	14	0	7	7	0	....	....	....	....
99-2000	Prince Albert	WHL	72	11	33	44	38	....	....	....	....	....	....	....	....	....	6	0	3	3	2	....	....	....	....
2000-01	Prince Albert	WHL	59	17	30	47	120	....	....	....	....	....	....	....	....	....	....	....	....	....	....	....	....	....	....
	Cleveland	IHL	4	1	1	2	2	....	....	....	....	....	....	....	....	....	3	0	1	1	0	....	....	....	....
2001-02	**Minnesota**	**NHL**	52	4	6	10	14	1	0	1	47	8.5	0	0	0.0	16:08	....	....	....	....	....	....	....	....	....
	Houston Aeros	AHL	....	....	....	....	....	....	....	....	....	....	....	....	....	....	14	1	5	6	2	....	....	....	....
2002-03	**Minnesota**	**NHL**	75	3	7	10	23	0	0	1	70	4.3	11	0	0.0	18:28	18	0	1	1	10	0	0	0	19:39
2003-04	**Minnesota**	**NHL**	79	6	10	16	16	1	0	0	72	8.3	12	0	0.0	20:19	....	....	....	....	....	....	....	....	....
2004-05	Kassel Huskies	Germany	46	7	15	22	26	....	....	....	....	....	....	....	....	....	7	0	4	4	6	....	....	....	....
2005-06	**Minnesota**	**NHL**	79	2	12	14	43	0	0	0	45	4.4	2	0	0.0	17:58	....	....	....	....	....	....	....	....	....
2006-07	**Minnesota**	**NHL**	82	2	10	12	42	0	0	1	69	2.9	0	0	0.0	20:13	5	0	1	1	0	0	0	0	18:06
2007-08	**Minnesota**	**NHL**	81	2	13	15	42	0	0	0	52	3.8	9	0	0.0	20:10	1	0	0	0	0	0	0	0	16:11
	NHL Totals		448	19	58	77	180	2	0	3	355	5.4		0	0.0	19:04	24	0	2	2	10	0	0	0	19:11

Signed as a free agent by **Kassel** (Germany), September 24, 2004.

SCUDERI, Rob

(SKUD-uh-ree, RAWB) **PIT.**

Defense. Shoots left. 6', 218 lbs. Born, Syosset, NY, December 30, 1978. Pittsburgh's 5th choice, 134th overall, in 1998 Entry Draft.

			Regular Season														Playoffs								
Season	Club	League	GP	G	A	Pts	PIM	PP	SH	GW	S	%	+/-	TF	F%	Min	GP	G	A	Pts	PIM	PP	SH	GW	Min
1995-96	NY Apple Core	MtJHL	76	18	60	78	....	....	....	....	....	....	....	....	....	....	....	....	....	....	....	....	....	....	....
1996-97	NY Apple Core	MtJHL	82	42	70	112	64	....	....	....	....	....	....	....	....	....	....	....	....	....	....	....	....	....	....
1997-98	Boston College	H-East	42	0	24	24	12	....	....	....	....	....	....	....	....	....	....	....	....	....	....	....	....	....	....
1998-99	Boston College	H-East	41	2	8	10	20	....	....	....	....	....	....	....	....	....	....	....	....	....	....	....	....	....	....
99-2000	Boston College	H-East	42	1	12	13	22	....	....	....	....	....	....	....	....	....	....	....	....	....	....	....	....	....	....
2000-01	Boston College	H-East	43	4	19	23	42	....	....	....	....	....	....	....	....	....	....	....	....	....	....	....	....	....	....
2001-02	Wilkes-Barre	AHL	75	1	22	23	66	....	....	....	....	....	....	....	....	....	....	....	....	....	....	....	....	....	....
2002-03	Wilkes-Barre	AHL	74	4	17	21	44	....	....	....	....	....	....	....	....	....	6	0	1	1	4	....	....	....	....
2003-04	**Pittsburgh**	**NHL**	**13**	**1**	**2**	**3**	**4**	**0**	**0**	**0**	**4**	**25.0**	**2**	**0**	**0.0**	**20:06**	....	....	....	....	....	....	....	....	....
	Wilkes-Barre	AHL	64	1	15	16	54	....	....	....	....	....	....	....	....	....	24	0	3	3	14	....	....	....	....
2004-05	Wilkes-Barre	AHL	79	2	18	20	34	....	....	....	....	....	....	....	....	....	11	2	1	3	2	....	....	....	....
2005-06	**Pittsburgh**	**NHL**	**57**	**0**	**4**	**4**	**36**	**0**	**0**	**0**	**28**	**0.0**	**-18**	**0**	**0.0**	**20:15**	....	....	....	....	....	....	....	....	....
	Wilkes-Barre	AHL	13	0	8	8	8	....	....	....	....	....	....	....	....	....	....	....	....	....	....	....	....	....	....
2006-07	**Pittsburgh**	**NHL**	**78**	**1**	**10**	**11**	**28**	**0**	**0**	**0**	**31**	**3.2**	**3**	**0**	**0.0**	**18:49**	**5**	**0**	**0**	**0**	**2**	**0**	**0**	**0**	**17:14**
2007-08	**Pittsburgh**	**NHL**	**71**	**0**	**5**	**5**	**26**	**0**	**0**	**0**	**28**	**0.0**	**3**	**0**	**0.0**	**18:45**	**20**	**0**	**3**	**3**	**2**	**0**	**0**	**0**	**19:02**
	NHL Totals		**219**	**2**	**21**	**23**	**94**	**0**	**0**	**0**	**91**	**2.2**		**0**	**0.0**	**19:14**	**25**	**0**	**3**	**3**	**4**	**0**	**0**	**0**	**18:40**

NCAA Championship All-Tournament Team (2001)

SEABROOK, Brent

(SEE-bruk, BREHNT) **CHI.**

Defense. Shoots right. 6'3", 220 lbs. Born, Richmond, B.C., April 20, 1985. Chicago's 1st choice, 14th overall, in 2003 Entry Draft.

Season	Club	League	GP	G	A	Pts	PIM	PP	SH	GW	S	%	+/-	TF	F%	Min	GP	G	A	Pts	PIM	PP	SH	GW	Min
2000-01	Delta Ice Hawks	PIJHL	54	16	26	42	55	....	....	....	....	....	....	....	....	....	....	....	....	....	....	....	....	....	....
	Lethbridge	WHL	4	0	0	0	0	....	....	....	....	....	....	....	....	....	....	....	....	....	....	....	....	....	....
2001-02	Lethbridge	WHL	67	6	33	39	70	....	....	....	....	....	....	....	....	....	4	1	1	2	2	....	....	....	....
2002-03	Lethbridge	WHL	69	9	33	42	113	....	....	....	....	....	....	....	....	....	....	....	....	....	....	....	....	....	....
2003-04	Lethbridge	WHL	61	12	29	41	107	....	....	....	....	....	....	....	....	....	....	....	....	....	....	....	....	....	....
2004-05	Lethbridge	WHL	63	12	42	54	107	....	....	....	....	....	....	....	....	....	5	1	2	3	10	....	....	....	....
	Norfolk Admirals	AHL	3	0	0	0	2	....	....	....	....	....	....	....	....	....	6	0	1	1	6	....	....	....	....
2005-06	**Chicago**	**NHL**	**69**	**5**	**27**	**32**	**60**	**1**	**0**	**2**	**114**	**4.4**	**5**	**0**	**0.0**	**20:02**	....	....	....	....	....	....	....	....	....
2006-07	**Chicago**	**NHL**	**81**	**4**	**20**	**24**	**104**	**0**	**0**	**0**	**144**	**2.8**	**-6**	**2**	**50.0**	**20:46**	....	....	....	....	....	....	....	....	....
2007-08	**Chicago**	**NHL**	**82**	**9**	**23**	**32**	**90**	**4**	**0**	**2**	**152**	**5.9**	**13**	**1**	**0.0**	**21:30**	....	....	....	....	....	....	....	....	....
	NHL Totals		**232**	**18**	**70**	**88**	**254**	**5**	**0**	**4**	**410**	**4.4**		**3**	**33.3**	**20:48**	....	....	....	....	....	....	....	....	....

WHL East Second All-Star Team (2005)

SEDIN, Daniel

(suh-DEEN, DAN-yehl) **VAN.**

Left wing. Shoots left. 6'1", 185 lbs. Born, Ornskoldsvik, Sweden, September 26, 1980. Vancouver's 1st choice, 2nd overall, in 1999 Entry Draft.

Season	Club	League	GP	G	A	Pts	PIM	PP	SH	GW	S	%	+/-	TF	F%	Min	GP	G	A	Pts	PIM	PP	SH	GW	Min
1997-98	Malmo Jr.	Swe-Jr.	4	3	3	6	4	....	....	....	....	....	....	....	....	....	....	....	....	....	....	....	....	....	....
	MoDo Jr.	Swe-Jr.	26	26	14	40	....	....	....	....	....	....	....	....	....	....	....	....	....	....	....	....	....	....	....
	MoDo	Sweden	45	4	8	12	26	....	....	....	....	....	....	....	....	....	9	0	0	0	2	....	....	....	....
1998-99	MoDo	Sweden	50	21	21	42	20	....	....	....	....	....	....	....	....	....	13	4	8	12	14	....	....	....	....
99-2000	MoDo	Sweden	50	19	26	45	28	....	....	....	....	....	....	....	....	....	13	*8	6	14	18	....	....	....	....
	MoDo	EuroHL	4	3	3	6	0	....	....	....	....	....	....	....	....	....	2	0	0	0	0	....	....	....	....
2000-01	**Vancouver**	**NHL**	**75**	**20**	**14**	**34**	**24**	**10**	**0**	**3**	**127**	**15.7**	**-3**	**10**	**60.0**	**13:00**	**4**	**1**	**2**	**3**	**0**	**0**	**0**	**0**	**16:15**
2001-02	**Vancouver**	**NHL**	**79**	**9**	**23**	**32**	**32**	**4**	**0**	**2**	**117**	**7.7**	**1**	**18**	**33.3**	**12:22**	**6**	**0**	**1**	**1**	**0**	**0**	**0**	**0**	**10:44**
2002-03	**Vancouver**	**NHL**	**79**	**14**	**17**	**31**	**34**	**4**	**0**	**2**	**134**	**10.4**	**8**	**24**	**45.8**	**12:26**	**14**	**1**	**5**	**6**	**8**	**1**	**0**	**1**	**12:23**
2003-04	**Vancouver**	**NHL**	**82**	**18**	**36**	**54**	**18**	**1**	**0**	**3**	**153**	**11.8**	**18**	**71**	**47.9**	**13:33**	**7**	**1**	**2**	**3**	**0**	**1**	**0**	**0**	**16:03**
2004-05	MODO	Sweden	49	13	20	33	40	....	....	....	....	....	....	....	....	....	6	0	3	3	6	....	....	....	....
2005-06	**Vancouver**	**NHL**	**82**	**22**	**49**	**71**	**34**	**11**	**0**	**4**	**204**	**10.8**	**7**	**49**	**42.9**	**16:40**	....	....	....	....	....	....	....	....	....
	Sweden	Olympics	8	1	3	4	2	....	....	....	....	....	....	....	....	....	....	....	....	....	....	....	....	....	....
2006-07	**Vancouver**	**NHL**	**81**	**36**	**48**	**84**	**36**	**16**	**0**	**8**	**236**	**15.3**	**19**	**44**	**22.7**	**18:04**	**12**	**2**	**3**	**5**	**4**	**0**	**0**	**0**	**21:31**
2007-08	**Vancouver**	**NHL**	**82**	**29**	**45**	**74**	**50**	**12**	**0**	**7**	**247**	**11.7**	**6**	**38**	**44.7**	**19:03**	....	....	....	....	....	....	....	....	....
	NHL Totals		**560**	**148**	**232**	**380**	**228**	**58**	**0**	**29**	**1218**	**12.2**		**254**	**41.3**	**15:04**	**43**	**5**	**13**	**18**	**12**	**2**	**0**	**1**	**15:40**

Signed as a free agent by **MODO** (Sweden), September 18, 2004.

SEDIN, Henrik

(suh-DEEN, HEHN-rihk) **VAN.**

Center. Shoots left. 6'2", 190 lbs. Born, Ornskoldsvik, Sweden, September 26, 1980. Vancouver's 2nd choice, 3rd overall, in 1999 Entry Draft.

Season	Club	League	GP	G	A	Pts	PIM	PP	SH	GW	S	%	+/-	TF	F%	Min	GP	G	A	Pts	PIM	PP	SH	GW	Min
1997-98	Malmo Jr.	Swe-Jr.	8	4	7	11	6	....	....	....	....	....	....	....	....	....	....	....	....	....	....	....	....	....	....
	MoDo Jr.	Swe-Jr.	26	14	22	36	....	....	....	....	....	....	....	....	....	....	....	....	....	....	....	....	....	....	....
	MoDo	Sweden	39	1	4	5	8	....	....	....	....	....	....	....	....	....	7	0	0	0	0	....	....	....	....
1998-99	MoDo	Sweden	49	12	22	34	32	....	....	....	....	....	....	....	....	....	13	2	8	10	6	....	....	....	....
99-2000	MoDo	Sweden	50	9	38	47	22	....	....	....	....	....	....	....	....	....	13	5	9	14	2	....	....	....	....
2000-01	**Vancouver**	**NHL**	**82**	**9**	**20**	**29**	**38**	**2**	**0**	**1**	**98**	**9.2**	**-2**	**1020**	**44.1**	**13:31**	**4**	**0**	**4**	**4**	**0**	**0**	**0**	**0**	**16:31**
2001-02	**Vancouver**	**NHL**	**82**	**16**	**20**	**36**	**36**	**3**	**0**	**1**	**78**	**20.5**	**9**	**785**	**47.4**	**12:48**	**6**	**3**	**0**	**3**	**0**	**0**	**0**	**1**	**11:55**
2002-03	**Vancouver**	**NHL**	**78**	**8**	**31**	**39**	**38**	**4**	**1**	**1**	**81**	**9.9**	**9**	**995**	**48.2**	**13:58**	**14**	**3**	**2**	**5**	**8**	**1**	**0**	**0**	**13:01**
2003-04	**Vancouver**	**NHL**	**76**	**11**	**31**	**42**	**32**	**2**	**0**	**2**	**99**	**11.1**	**23**	**961**	**50.0**	**14:02**	**7**	**2**	**2**	**4**	**2**	**2**	**0**	**0**	**16:02**
2004-05	MODO	Sweden	44	14	22	36	50	....	....	....	....	....	....	....	....	....	6	1	3	4	6	....	....	....	....
2005-06	**Vancouver**	**NHL**	**82**	**18**	**57**	**75**	**56**	**5**	**1**	**0**	**113**	**15.9**	**11**	**1238**	**50.7**	**16:54**	....	....	....	....	....	....	....	....	....
	Sweden	Olympics	8	3	1	4	2	....	....	....	....	....	....	....	....	....	....	....	....	....	....	....	....	....	....
2006-07	**Vancouver**	**NHL**	**82**	**10**	**71**	**81**	**66**	**1**	**0**	**2**	**134**	**7.5**	**19**	**1220**	**52.5**	**18:26**	**12**	**2**	**2**	**4**	**14**	**1**	**0**	**1**	**22:12**
2007-08	**Vancouver**	**NHL**	**82**	**15**	**61**	**76**	**56**	**4**	**1**	**2**	**141**	**10.6**	**6**	**1369**	**47.0**	**19:31**	....	....	....	....	....	....	....	....	....
	NHL Totals		**564**	**87**	**291**	**378**	**322**	**21**	**3**	**9**	**744**	**11.7**		**7588**	**48.7**	**15:38**	**43**	**10**	**10**	**20**	**24**	**4**	**0**	**2**	**16:15**

Played in NHL All-Star Game (2008)

Signed as a free agent by **MODO** (Sweden), September 18, 2004.

SEIDENBERG, Dennis

(SIGH-dehn-buhrg, DEH-nihs) **CAR.**

Defense. Shoots left. 6'1", 210 lbs. Born, Schwenningen, West Germany, July 18, 1981. Philadelphia's 6th choice, 172nd overall, in 2001 Entry Draft.

Season	Club	League	GP	G	A	Pts	PIM	PP	SH	GW	S	%	+/-	TF	F%	Min	GP	G	A	Pts	PIM	PP	SH	GW	Min
99-2000	Mannheim Jr.	Ger-Jr.	52	12	28	40	28	....	....	....	....	....	....	....	....	....	....	....	....	....	....	....	....	....	....
	Adler Mannheim	Germany	3	0	0	0	0	....	....	....	....	....	....	....	....	....	....	....	....	....	....	....	....	....	....
2000-01	Mannheim Jr.	Ger-Jr.	9	3	8	11	20	....	....	....	....	....	....	....	....	....	....	....	....	....	....	....	....	....	....
	Adler Mannheim	Germany	55	2	5	7	6	....	....	....	....	....	....	....	....	....	12	0	1	1	10	....	....	....	....
2001-02	Adler Mannheim	Germany	55	7	13	20	56	....	....	....	....	....	....	....	....	....	8	0	0	0	2	....	....	....	....
2002-03	**Philadelphia**	**NHL**	**58**	**4**	**9**	**13**	**20**	**1**	**0**	**0**	**123**	**3.3**	**8**	**1**	**0.0**	**16:50**	....	....	....	....	....	....	....	....	....
	Philadelphia	AHL	19	5	6	11	17	....	....	....	....	....	....	....	....	....	....	....	....	....	....	....	....	....	....
2003-04	**Philadelphia**	**NHL**	**5**	**0**	**0**	**0**	**2**	**0**	**0**	**0**	**14**	**0.0**	**-4**	**0**	**0.0**	**17:20**	**3**	**0**	**0**	**0**	**0**	**0**	**0**	**0**	**7:36**
	Philadelphia	AHL	33	7	12	19	31	....	....	....	....	....	....	....	....	....	9	2	2	4	4	....	....	....	....
2004-05	Philadelphia	AHL	79	13	28	41	47	....	....	....	....	....	....	....	....	....	18	2	8	10	19	....	....	....	....
2005-06	**Philadelphia**	**NHL**	**29**	**2**	**5**	**7**	**4**	**1**	**0**	**0**	**34**	**5.9**	**-4**	**1**	**0.0**	**14:22**	....	....	....	....	....	....	....	....	....
	Phoenix	**NHL**	**34**	**1**	**10**	**11**	**14**	**1**	**0**	**0**	**49**	**2.0**	**-9**	**0**	**0.0**	**19:13**	....	....	....	....	....	....	....	....	....
	Germany	Olympics	5	0	0	0	6	....	....	....	....	....	....	....	....	....	....	....	....	....	....	....	....	....	....
2006-07	**Phoenix**	**NHL**	**32**	**1**	**1**	**2**	**16**	**0**	**0**	**0**	**36**	**2.8**	**-4**	**0**	**0.0**	**14:43**	....	....	....	....	....	....	....	....	....
	Carolina	**NHL**	**20**	**1**	**5**	**6**	**2**	**0**	**0**	**0**	**47**	**2.1**	**-12**	**0**	**0.0**	**18:29**	....	....	....	....	....	....	....	....	....
2007-08	**Carolina**	**NHL**	**47**	**0**	**15**	**15**	**18**	**0**	**0**	**0**	**80**	**0.0**	**6**	**1**	**100.0**	**18:50**	....	....	....	....	....	....	....	....	....
	NHL Totals		**225**	**9**	**45**	**54**	**76**	**3**	**0**	**0**	**383**	**2.3**		**3**	**33.3**	**17:09**	**3**	**0**	**0**	**0**	**0**	**0**	**0**	**0**	**7:36**

• Missed majority of 2003-04 season recovering from leg injury suffered in game vs. Edmonton, January 10, 2004. Traded to **Phoenix** by **Philadelphia** with Philadelphia's 4th round choice (later traded to NY Islanders - NY Islanders selected Tomas Marcinko) in 2006 Entry Draft for Petr Nedved and Phoenix's 4th round choice (Joonas Lehtivuori) in 2006 Entry Draft, January 20, 2006. Traded to **Carolina** by **Phoenix** for Kevyn Adams, January 8, 2007.

Season	Club	League	Regular Season GP	G	A	Pts	PIM	PP	SH	GW	S	%	+/-	TF	F%	Min	Playoffs GP	G	A	Pts	PIM	PP	SH	GW	Min

SEKERA, Andrej

(SEH-kuhr-ah, AWN-dray) **BUF.**

Defense. Shoots left. 6', 199 lbs. Born, Bojnice, Czech., June 8, 1986. Buffalo's 3rd choice, 71st overall, in 2004 Entry Draft.

2001-02	Dukla Trencin Jr.	Slovak-Jr.	52	5	10	15	10	....	....	....	....	....	....	....	....	....	....	....	....	....	....	....	....	....	....
2002-03	Dukla Trencin Jr.	Slovak-Jr.	48	9	15	24	20	....	....	....	....	....	....	....	....	....	....	....	....	....	....	....	....	....	....
2003-04	Dukla Trencin Jr.	Slovak-Jr.	42	5	12	17	40	....	....	....	....	....	....	....	....	....	2	0	1	1	4	....	....	....	....
	Dukla Trencin	Slovakia	3	0	0	0	2	....	....	....	....	....	....	....	....	....	....	....	....	....	....	....	....	....	....
	Dukla Trencin U18	Svk-U18	5	0	0	0	0	....	....	....	....	....	....	....	....	....	....	....	....	....	....	....	....	....	....
2004-05	Owen Sound	OHL	51	7	21	28	18	....	....	....	....	....	....	....	....	....	6	0	4	4	4	....	....	....	....
2005-06	Owen Sound	OHL	51	21	34	55	54	....	....	....	....	....	....	....	....	....	11	5	8	13	9	....	....	....	....
2006-07	**Buffalo**	**NHL**	**2**	**0**	**0**	**0**	**2**	**0**	**0**	**0**	**0**	**0.0**	**1**	**0**	**0.0**	**7:31**	....	....	....	....	....	....	....	....	....
	Rochester	AHL	54	3	16	19	28	....	....	....	....	....	....	....	....	....	....	....	....	....	....	....	....	....	....
2007-08	**Buffalo**	**NHL**	**37**	**2**	**6**	**8**	**16**	**0**	**0**	**1**	**28**	**7.1**	**5**	**0**	**0.0**	**19:37**	....	....	....	....	....	....	....	....	....
	Rochester	AHL	40	2	15	17	22	....	....	....	....	....	....	....	....	....	....	....	....	....	....	....	....	....	....
	NHL Totals		**39**	**2**	**6**	**8**	**18**	**0**	**0**	**1**	**28**	**7.1**		**0**	**0.0**	**19:00**	....	....	....	....	....	....	....	....	....

OHL All-Rookie Team (2005) • OHL First All-Star Team (2006)

SELANNE, Teemu

(seh-LAH-nee, TEE-moo)

Right wing. Shoots right. 6', 204 lbs. Born, Helsinki, Finland, July 3, 1970. Winnipeg's 1st choice, 10th overall, in 1988 Entry Draft.

1986-87	Jokerit U18	Fin-U18	....	....	....	....	....	....	....	....	....	....	....	....	....	....	7	10	3	13	2	....	....	....	....
	Jokerit Helsinki Jr.	Fin-Jr.	33	10	12	22	8	....	....	....	....	....	....	....	....	....	....	....	....	....	....	....	....	....	....
1987-88	Jokerit Helsinki Jr.	Fin-Jr.	33	43	23	66	18	....	....	....	....	....	....	....	....	....	5	4	3	7	2	....	....	....	....
	Jokerit Helsinki	Finland-2	5	1	1	2	0	....	....	....	....	....	....	....	....	....	....	....	....	....	....	....	....	....	....
1988-89	PvUK Lahti Jr.	Fin-Jr.	3	3	1	4	2	....	....	....	....	....	....	....	....	....	....	....	....	....	....	....	....	....	....
	Jokerit Helsinki Jr.	Fin-Jr.	3	8	8	16	4	....	....	....	....	....	....	....	....	....	....	....	....	....	....	....	....	....	....
	Jokerit Helsinki	Finland-2	35	36	33	69	14	....	....	....	....	....	....	....	....	....	5	7	3	10	4	....	....	....	....
1989-90	Jokerit Helsinki	Finland	11	4	8	12	0	....	....	....	....	....	....	....	....	....	....	....	....	....	....	....	....	....	....
1990-91	Jokerit Helsinki Jr.	Fin-Jr.	4	3	2	5	10	....	....	....	....	....	....	....	....	....	....	....	....	....	....	....	....	....	....
	Jokerit Helsinki	Finland	42	33	25	58	12	....	....	....	....	....	....	....	....	....	....	....	....	....	....	....	....	....	....
1991-92	Jokerit Helsinki	Finland	44	39	23	62	20	....	....	....	....	....	....	....	....	....	10	10	7	17	18	....	....	....	....
	Finland	Olympics	8	7	4	11	6	....	....	....	....	....	....	....	....	....	....	....	....	....	....	....	....	....	....
1992-93	**Winnipeg**	**NHL**	**84**	***76**	**56**	**132**	**45**	**24**	**0**	**7**	**387**	**19.6**	**8**	....	....	....	**6**	**4**	**2**	**6**	**2**	**2**	**0**	**2**	....
1993-94	**Winnipeg**	**NHL**	**51**	**25**	**29**	**54**	**22**	**11**	**0**	**2**	**191**	**13.1**	**–23**	....	....	....	....	....	....	....	....	....	....	....	....
1994-95	Jokerit Helsinki	Finland	20	7	12	19	6	....	....	....	....	....	....	....	....	....	....	....	....	....	....	....	....	....	....
	Winnipeg	**NHL**	**45**	**22**	**26**	**48**	**2**	**8**	**2**	**1**	**167**	**13.2**	**1**	....	....	....	....	....	....	....	....	....	....	....	....
1995-96	**Winnipeg**	**NHL**	**51**	**24**	**48**	**72**	**18**	**6**	**1**	**4**	**163**	**14.7**	**3**	....	....	....	....	....	....	....	....	....	....	....	....
	Anaheim	**NHL**	**28**	**16**	**20**	**36**	**4**	**3**	**0**	**1**	**104**	**15.4**	**2**	....	....	....	....	....	....	....	....	....	....	....	....
1996-97	**Anaheim**	**NHL**	**78**	**51**	**58**	**109**	**34**	**11**	**1**	**8**	**273**	**18.7**	**28**	....	....	....	**11**	**7**	**3**	**10**	**4**	**3**	**0**	**1**	....
1997-98	**Anaheim**	**NHL**	**73**	***52**	**34**	**86**	**30**	**10**	**1**	**10**	**268**	**19.4**	**12**	....	....	....	....	....	....	....	....	....	....	....	....
	Finland	Olympics	5	4	6	10	8	....	....	....	....	....	....	....	....	....	....	....	....	....	....	....	....	....	....
1998-99	**Anaheim**	**NHL**	**75**	***47**	**60**	**107**	**30**	**25**	**0**	**7**	**281**	**16.7**	**18**	**5**	**20.0**	**22:47**	**4**	**2**	**2**	**4**	**2**	**1**	**0**	**0**	**22:23**
99-2000	**Anaheim**	**NHL**	**79**	**33**	**52**	**85**	**12**	**8**	**0**	**6**	**236**	**14.0**	**6**	**13**	**23.1**	**22:44**	....	....	....	....	....	....	....	....	....
2000-01	**Anaheim**	**NHL**	**61**	**26**	**33**	**59**	**36**	**10**	**0**	**5**	**202**	**12.9**	**–8**	**4**	**50.0**	**21:51**	....	....	....	....	....	....	....	....	....
	San Jose	**NHL**	**12**	**7**	**6**	**13**	**0**	**2**	**0**	**2**	**31**	**22.6**	**1**	**4**	**75.0**	**18:14**	**6**	**0**	**2**	**2**	**2**	**0**	**0**	**0**	**17:13**
2001-02	**San Jose**	**NHL**	**82**	**29**	**25**	**54**	**40**	**9**	**1**	**8**	**202**	**14.4**	**–11**	**12**	**25.0**	**16:58**	**12**	**5**	**3**	**8**	**2**	**2**	**0**	**1**	**16:51**
	Finland	Olympics	4	3	0	3	2	....	....	....	....	....	....	....	....	....	....	....	....	....	....	....	....	....	....
2002-03	**San Jose**	**NHL**	**82**	**28**	**36**	**64**	**30**	**7**	**0**	**5**	**253**	**11.1**	**–6**	**107**	**42.1**	**19:14**	....	....	....	....	....	....	....	....	....
2003-04	**Colorado**	**NHL**	**78**	**16**	**16**	**32**	**32**	**6**	**1**	**4**	**182**	**8.8**	**2**	**80**	**43.8**	**16:10**	**10**	**0**	**3**	**3**	**2**	**0**	**0**	**0**	**12:53**
2004-05			DID NOT PLAY																						
2005-06	**Anaheim**	**NHL**	**80**	**40**	**50**	**90**	**44**	**18**	**0**	**5**	**267**	**15.0**	**28**	**209**	**41.6**	**17:48**	**16**	**6**	**8**	**14**	**6**	**1**	**0**	**2**	**17:56**
	Finland	Olympics	8	6	5	11	4	....	....	....	....	....	....	....	....	....	....	....	....	....	....	....	....	....	....
2006-07♦	**Anaheim**	**NHL**	**82**	**48**	**46**	**94**	**82**	**25**	**0**	**10**	**257**	**18.7**	**26**	**351**	**50.7**	**17:42**	**21**	**5**	**10**	**15**	**10**	**0**	**0**	**2**	**19:08**
2007-08	**Anaheim**	**NHL**	**26**	**12**	**11**	**23**	**8**	**7**	**0**	**2**	**87**	**13.8**	**5**	**67**	**50.8**	**18:07**	**6**	**2**	**2**	**4**	**6**	**2**	**0**	**1**	**19:35**
	NHL Totals		**1067**	**552**	**606**	**1158**	**469**	**190**	**7**	**87**	**3551**	**15.5**		**852**	**45.9**	**19:14**	**92**	**31**	**35**	**66**	**36**	**11**	**0**	**9**	**17:44**

NHL All-Rookie Team (1993) • NHL First All-Star Team (1993, 1997) • Calder Memorial Trophy (1993) • NHL Second All-Star Team (1998, 1999) • Maurice "Rocket" Richard Trophy (1999) • Olympic Tournament All-Star Team (2006) • Best Forward - Olympic Tournament (2006) • Bill Masterton Memorial Trophy (2006)

Played in NHL All-Star Game (1993, 1994, 1996, 1997, 1998, 1999, 2000, 2002, 2003, 2007)

• Missed majority of 1989-90 season recovering from leg injury suffered in game vs. HIFK Helsinki (Finland), October 19, 1989. Traded to **Anaheim** by **Winnipeg** with Marc Chouinard and Winnipeg's 4th round choice (later traded to Toronto – later traded to Montreal – Montreal selected Kim Staal) in 1996 Entry Draft for Chad Kilger, Oleg Tverdovsky and Anaheim's 3rd round choice (Per-Anton Lundstrom) in 1996 Entry Draft, February 7, 1996. Traded to **San Jose** by **Anaheim** for Jeff Friesen, Steve Shields and San Jose's 2nd round choice (later traded to Dallas – Dallas selected Vojtech Polak) in 2003 Entry Draft, March 5, 2001. Signed as a free agent by **Colorado**, July 3, 2003. Signed as a free agent by **Anaheim**, August 22, 2005. • Missed majority of 2007-08 season contemplating retirement.

SEMENOV, Alexei

(seh-MEH-nahv, al-EHX-ay) **S.J.**

Defense. Shoots left. 6'6", 235 lbs. Born, Murmansk, USSR, April 10, 1981. Edmonton's 2nd choice, 36th overall, in 1999 Entry Draft.

1997-98	Krylja Sovetov 2	Russia-3	52	1	2	3	48	....	....	....	....	....	....	....	....	....	....	....	....	....	....	....	....	....	....
1998-99	St. Petersburg 2	Russia-4	19	0	1	1	20	....	....	....	....	....	....	....	....	....	....	....	....	....	....	....	....	....	....
	Sudbury Wolves	OHL	28	0	3	3	28	....	....	....	....	....	....	....	....	....	2	0	0	0	4	....	....	....	....
99-2000	Sudbury Wolves	OHL	65	9	35	44	135	....	....	....	....	....	....	....	....	....	12	1	3	4	23	....	....	....	....
	Hamilton	AHL	....	....	....	....	....	....	....	....	....	....	....	....	....	....	3	0	0	0	0	....	....	....	....
2000-01	Sudbury Wolves	OHL	65	21	42	63	106	....	....	....	....	....	....	....	....	....	12	4	13	17	17	....	....	....	....
2001-02	Hamilton	AHL	78	5	11	16	67	....	....	....	....	....	....	....	....	....	....	....	....	....	....	....	....	....	....
2002-03	**Edmonton**	**NHL**	**46**	**1**	**6**	**7**	**58**	**0**	**0**	**0**	**33**	**3.0**	**–7**	**0**	**0.0**	**19:41**	**6**	**0**	**0**	**0**	**0**	**0**	**0**	**0**	**13:05**
	Hamilton	AHL	37	4	3	7	45	....	....	....	....	....	....	....	....	....	....	....	....	....	....	....	....	....	....
2003-04	**Edmonton**	**NHL**	**46**	**2**	**3**	**5**	**32**	**1**	**0**	**0**	**36**	**5.6**	**8**	**0**	**0.0**	**17:16**	....	....	....	....	....	....	....	....	....
2004-05	St. Petersburg	Russia	50	0	8	8	26	....	....	....	....	....	....	....	....	....	....	....	....	....	....	....	....	....	....
2005-06	Yaroslavl	Russia	2	0	1	1	2	....	....	....	....	....	....	....	....	....	....	....	....	....	....	....	....	....	....
	Edmonton	**NHL**	**11**	**1**	**1**	**2**	**17**	**0**	**0**	**0**	**3**	**33.3**	**–3**	**0**	**0.0**	**10:49**	....	....	....	....	....	....	....	....	....
	Florida	**NHL**	**16**	**1**	**1**	**2**	**21**	**1**	**0**	**0**	**13**	**7.7**	**–1**	**0**	**0.0**	**12:33**	....	....	....	....	....	....	....	....	....
	Rochester	AHL	3	0	0	0	7	....	....	....	....	....	....	....	....	....	....	....	....	....	....	....	....	....	....
2006-07	**Florida**	**NHL**	**23**	**0**	**5**	**5**	**28**	**0**	**0**	**0**	**23**	**0.0**	**9**	**1**	**0.0**	**12:22**	....	....	....	....	....	....	....	....	....
	Rochester	AHL	4	0	0	0	6	....	....	....	....	....	....	....	....	....	....	....	....	....	....	....	....	....	....
	Ufa	Russia	20	1	2	3	32	....	....	....	....	....	....	....	....	....	....	....	....	....	....	....	....	....	....
2007-08	**San Jose**	**NHL**	**22**	**1**	**3**	**4**	**36**	**1**	**0**	**0**	**23**	**4.3**	**–8**	**0**	**0.0**	**15:15**	**2**	**0**	**0**	**0**	**2**	**0**	**0**	**0**	**11:15**
	NHL Totals		**164**	**6**	**19**	**25**	**192**	**3**	**0**	**0**	**131**	**4.6**		**1**	**0.0**	**16:06**	**8**	**0**	**0**	**0**	**2**	**0**	**0**	**0**	**12:37**

OHL First All-Star Team (2001)

Signed as a free agent by **St. Petersburg** (Russia), July 30, 2004. Traded to **Florida** by **Edmonton** for Florida's 5th round choice (Bryan Pitton) in 2006 Entry Draft, November 19, 2005. Signed as a free agent by **San Jose**, July 27, 2007.

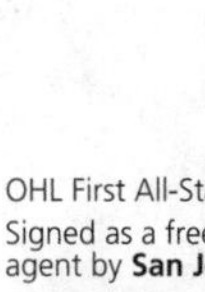

SEMIN, Alexander

(SEH-min, al-EHX-AN-duhr) **WSH.**

Left wing. Shoots left. 6'2", 205 lbs. Born, Krasnoyarsk, USSR, March 3, 1984. Washington's 2nd choice, 13th overall, in 2002 Entry Draft.

2001-02	Chelyabinsk	Russia-2	46	13	8	21	52	....	....	....	....	....	....	....	....	....	2	2	0	2	0	....	....	....	....
2002-03	Lada Togliatti	Russia	47	10	7	17	36	....	....	....	....	....	....	....	....	....	10	*5	3	8	10	....	....	....	....
2003-04	**Washington**	**NHL**	**52**	**10**	**12**	**22**	**36**	**4**	**0**	**2**	**92**	**10.9**	**–2**	**6**	**50.0**	**12:37**	....	....	....	....	....	....	....	....	....
	Portland Pirates	AHL	4	3	1	4	6	....	....	....	....	....	....	....	....	....	7	4	7	11	19	....	....	....	....
2004-05	Lada Togliatti	Russia	50	19	11	30	56	....	....	....	....	....	....	....	....	....	10	1	1	2	0	....	....	....	....
2005-06	Lada Togliatti	Russia	16	5	4	9	52	....	....	....	....	....	....	....	....	....	....	....	....	....	....	....	....	....	....
	Mytischi	Russia	26	3	7	10	24	....	....	....	....	....	....	....	....	....	8	3	2	5	6	....	....	....	....
2006-07	**Washington**	**NHL**	**77**	**38**	**35**	**73**	**90**	**17**	**0**	**6**	**243**	**15.6**	**–7**	**44**	**27.3**	**18:24**	....	....	....	....	....	....	....	....	....
2007-08	**Washington**	**NHL**	**63**	**26**	**16**	**42**	**54**	**10**	**0**	**2**	**185**	**14.1**	**–18**	**11**	**36.4**	**16:55**	**7**	**3**	**5**	**8**	**8**	**2**	**0**	**1**	**19:45**
	NHL Totals		**192**	**74**	**63**	**137**	**180**	**31**	**0**	**10**	**520**	**14.2**		**61**	**31.1**	**16:21**	**7**	**3**	**5**	**8**	**8**	**2**	**0**	**1**	**19:45**

Signed as a free agent by **Togliatti** (Russia), September 25, 2004. • Suspended by **Washington** for failing to report to **Portland** (AHL), September 28, 2004. Signed as a free agent by **Mytischi** (Russia), November 22, 2005.

Regular Season | Playoffs

SESTITO, Tom

(sehs-TEE-toh, TAWM) **CBJ**

Left wing. Shoots left. 6'5", 226 lbs. Born, Utica, NY, September 28, 1987. Columbus' 3rd choice, 85th overall, in 2006 Entry Draft.

Season	Club	League	GP	G	A	Pts	PIM	PP	SH	GW	S	%	+/-	TF	F%	Min	GP	G	A	Pts	PIM	PP	SH	GW	Min
2003-04	Syracuse Jr. Stars	EmJHL	31	13	16	29	137										6	5	6	11	32				
2004-05	Plymouth Whalers	OHL	35	1	3	4	88																		
2005-06	Plymouth Whalers	OHL	57	10	10	20	176										13	5	2	7	29				
2006-07	Plymouth Whalers	OHL	60	42	22	64	135										19	11	6	17	57				
2007-08	**Columbus**	**NHL**	**1**	**0**	**0**	**0**	**17**	**0**	**0**	**0**	**0**	**0.0**	**0**	**0**	**0.0**	**4:36**									
	Syracuse Crunch	AHL	66	7	16	23	202										9	3	0	3	57				
	NHL Totals		**1**	**0**	**0**	**0**	**17**	**0**	**0**	**0**	**0**	**0.0**		**0**	**0.0**	**4:36**									

SETOGUCHI, Devin

(SEHT-oh-GOO-chee, DEH-vihn) **S.J.**

Right wing. Shoots right. 6', 205 lbs. Born, Taber, Alta., January 1, 1987. San Jose's 1st choice, 8th overall, in 2005 Entry Draft.

Season	Club	League	GP	G	A	Pts	PIM	PP	SH	GW	S	%	+/-	TF	F%	Min	GP	G	A	Pts	PIM	PP	SH	GW	Min
2003-04	Saskatoon Blades	WHL	66	13	18	31	53																		
2004-05	Saskatoon Blades	WHL	69	33	31	64	34										4	0	1	1	0				
2005-06	Saskatoon Blades	WHL	65	36	47	83	69										10	8	4	12	8				
2006-07	Prince George	WHL	55	36	29	65	55										15	*11	10	21	24				
2007-08	**San Jose**	**NHL**	**44**	**11**	**6**	**17**	**8**	**3**	**0**	**2**	**105**	**10.5**	**6**	**17**	**64.7**	**14:15**	**9**	**1**	**1**	**2**	**2**	**0**	**0**	**0**	**10:25**
	Worcester Sharks	AHL	23	8	11	19	25																		
	NHL Totals		**44**	**11**	**6**	**17**	**8**	**3**	**0**	**2**	**105**	**10.5**		**17**	**64.7**	**14:15**	**9**	**1**	**1**	**2**	**2**	**0**	**0**	**0**	**10:25**

WHL East Second All-Star Team (2006)

SHANAHAN, Brendan

(SHA-na-HAN, BREHN-duhn)

Left wing. Shoots right. 6'3", 220 lbs. Born, Mimico, Ont., January 23, 1969. New Jersey's 1st choice, 2nd overall, in 1987 Entry Draft.

Season	Club	League	GP	G	A	Pts	PIM	PP	SH	GW	S	%	+/-	TF	F%	Min	GP	G	A	Pts	PIM	PP	SH	GW	Min
1984-85	Mississauga Reps	MTHL	36	20	21	41	26																		
	Dixie Beehives	OJHL	1	0	0	0	0																		
1985-86	London Knights	OHL	59	28	34	62	70										5	5	5	10	5				
1986-87	London Knights	OHL	56	39	53	92	92																		
1987-88	**New Jersey**	**NHL**	**65**	**7**	**19**	**26**	**131**	**2**	**0**	**2**	**72**	**9.7**	**–20**				**12**	**2**	**1**	**3**	**44**	**1**	**0**	**0**	
1988-89	**New Jersey**	**NHL**	**68**	**22**	**28**	**50**	**115**	**9**	**0**	**0**	**152**	**14.5**	**2**												
1989-90	**New Jersey**	**NHL**	**73**	**30**	**42**	**72**	**137**	**8**	**0**	**5**	**196**	**15.3**	**15**				**6**	**3**	**3**	**6**	**20**	**1**	**0**	**1**	
1990-91	**New Jersey**	**NHL**	**75**	**29**	**37**	**66**	**141**	**7**	**0**	**2**	**195**	**14.9**	**4**				**7**	**3**	**5**	**8**	**12**	**2**	**0**	**0**	
1991-92	**St. Louis**	**NHL**	**80**	**33**	**36**	**69**	**171**	**13**	**0**	**2**	**215**	**15.3**	**–3**				**6**	**2**	**3**	**5**	**14**	**1**	**0**	**0**	
1992-93	**St. Louis**	**NHL**	**71**	**51**	**43**	**94**	**174**	**18**	**0**	**8**	**232**	**22.0**	**10**				**11**	**4**	**3**	**7**	**18**	**2**	**0**	**0**	
1993-94	**St. Louis**	**NHL**	**81**	**52**	**50**	**102**	**211**	**15**	**7**	**8**	**397**	**13.1**	**–9**				**4**	**2**	**5**	**7**	**4**	**0**	**0**	**0**	
1994-95	Dusseldorfer EG	Germany	3	5	3	8	4																		
	St. Louis	**NHL**	**45**	**20**	**21**	**41**	**136**	**6**	**2**	**6**	**153**	**13.1**	**7**				**5**	**4**	**5**	**9**	**14**	**1**	**0**	**1**	
1995-96	**Hartford**	**NHL**	**74**	**44**	**34**	**78**	**125**	**17**	**2**	**6**	**280**	**15.7**	**2**												
1996-97	**Hartford**	**NHL**	**2**	**1**	**0**	**1**	**0**	**0**	**1**	**0**	**13**	**7.7**	**1**												
	♦ **Detroit**	**NHL**	**79**	**46**	**41**	**87**	**131**	**20**	**2**	**7**	**323**	**14.2**	**31**				**20**	**9**	**8**	**17**	**43**	**2**	**0**	**2**	
1997-98	♦ **Detroit**	**NHL**	**75**	**28**	**29**	**57**	**154**	**15**	**1**	**9**	**266**	**10.5**	**6**				**20**	**5**	**4**	**9**	**22**	**3**	**0**	**2**	
	Canada	Olympics	6	2	0	2	0																		
1998-99	**Detroit**	**NHL**	**81**	**31**	**27**	**58**	**123**	**5**	**0**	**5**	**288**	**10.8**	**2**	**18**	**44.4**	**17:31**	**10**	**3**	**7**	**10**	**6**	**1**	**0**	**1**	**18:31**
99-2000	**Detroit**	**NHL**	**78**	**41**	**37**	**78**	**105**	**13**	**1**	**9**	**283**	**14.5**	**24**	**24**	**50.0**	**18:35**	**9**	**3**	**2**	**5**	**10**	**0**	**0**	**0**	**17:36**
2000-01	**Detroit**	**NHL**	**81**	**31**	**45**	**76**	**81**	**15**	**1**	**7**	**278**	**11.2**	**9**	**115**	**43.5**	**18:22**	**2**	**2**	**2**	**4**	**0**	**0**	**0**	**1**	**21:02**
2001-02	♦ **Detroit**	**NHL**	**80**	**37**	**38**	**75**	**118**	**12**	**3**	**7**	**277**	**13.4**	**23**	**70**	**47.1**	**18:55**	**23**	**8**	**11**	**19**	**20**	**1**	**0**	**2**	**19:06**
	Canada	Olympics	6	0	1	1	0																		
2002-03	**Detroit**	**NHL**	**78**	**30**	**38**	**68**	**103**	**13**	**0**	**6**	**260**	**11.5**	**5**	**28**	**60.7**	**18:38**	**4**	**1**	**1**	**2**	**4**	**1**	**0**	**0**	**22:03**
2003-04	**Detroit**	**NHL**	**82**	**25**	**28**	**53**	**117**	**8**	**0**	**7**	**280**	**8.9**	**15**	**32**	**46.9**	**18:05**	**12**	**1**	**5**	**6**	**20**	**0**	**1**	**0**	**16:49**
2004-05			Did not play																						
2005-06	**Detroit**	**NHL**	**82**	**40**	**41**	**81**	**105**	**14**	**0**	**6**	**289**	**13.8**	**29**	**26**	**50.0**	**16:35**	**6**	**1**	**1**	**2**	**6**	**0**	**0**	**0**	**18:54**
2006-07	**NY Rangers**	**NHL**	**67**	**29**	**33**	**62**	**47**	**14**	**3**	**3**	**295**	**9.8**	**2**	**281**	**48.0**	**19:49**	**10**	**5**	**2**	**7**	**12**	**3**	**0**	**2**	**19:00**
2007-08	**NY Rangers**	**NHL**	**73**	**23**	**23**	**46**	**35**	**11**	**0**	**3**	**265**	**8.7**	**–2**	**8**	**75.0**	**18:31**	**10**	**1**	**4**	**5**	**8**	**0**	**0**	**0**	**17:05**
	NHL Totals		**1490**	**650**	**690**	**1340**	**2460**	**235**	**23**	**108**	**5009**	**13.0**		**602**	**48.0**	**18:18**	**177**	**59**	**72**	**131**	**277**	**19**	**1**	**12**	**18:29**

NHL First All-Star Team (1994, 2000) • NHL Second All-Star Team (2002) • King Clancy Memorial Trophy (2003)

Played in NHL All-Star Game (1994, 1996, 1997, 1998, 1999, 2000, 2002, 2007)

Signed as a free agent by **St. Louis**, July 25, 1991. Traded to **Hartford** by **St. Louis** for Chris Pronger, July 27, 1995. Traded to **Detroit** by **Hartford** with Brian Glynn for Paul Coffey, Keith Primeau and Detroit's 1st round choice (Nikos Tselios) in 1997 Entry Draft, October 9, 1996. Signed as a free agent by **NY Rangers**, July 9, 2006.

SHANNON, Ryan

(SHA-nuhn, RIGH-uhn) **VAN.**

Center. Shoots right. 5'9", 173 lbs. Born, Darien, CT, March 2, 1983.

Season	Club	League	GP	G	A	Pts	PIM	PP	SH	GW	S	%	+/-	TF	F%	Min	GP	G	A	Pts	PIM	PP	SH	GW	Min
2001-02	Boston College	H-East	38	8	17	25	12																		
2002-03	Boston College	H-East	36	14	24	38	4																		
2003-04	Boston College	H-East	42	15	27	42	22																		
2004-05	Boston College	H-East	38	14	31	45	22																		
	Cincinnati	AHL	4	1	0	1	2																		
2005-06	Portland Pirates	AHL	71	27	59	86	44										19	11	11	22	8				
2006-07	♦ **Anaheim**	**NHL**	**53**	**2**	**9**	**11**	**10**	**0**	**0**	**0**	**77**	**2.6**	**–2**	**25**	**52.0**	**10:39**	**11**	**0**	**0**	**0**	**6**	**0**	**0**	**0**	**4:04**
	Portland Pirates	AHL	14	2	7	9	12																		
2007-08	**Vancouver**	**NHL**	**27**	**5**	**8**	**13**	**24**	**4**	**0**	**0**	**34**	**14.7**	**–1**	**82**	**39.0**	**12:53**									
	Manitoba Moose	AHL	13	1	7	8	10																		
	NHL Totals		**80**	**7**	**17**	**24**	**34**	**4**	**0**	**0**	**111**	**6.3**		**107**	**42.1**	**11:24**	**11**	**0**	**0**	**0**	**6**	**0**	**0**	**0**	**4:04**

Hockey East First All-Star Team (2004) • NCAA East Second All-American Team (2004) • AHL All-Rookie Team (2006)

Signed as a free agent by **Anaheim**, November 28, 2005. Traded to **Vancouver** by **Anaheim** for Jason King and future considerations, June 23, 2007.

SHARP, Patrick

(SHAHRP, PAT-rihk) **CHI.**

Center. Shoots right. 6'1", 197 lbs. Born, Thunder Bay, Ont., December 27, 1981. Philadelphia's 2nd choice, 95th overall, in 2001 Entry Draft.

Season	Club	League	GP	G	A	Pts	PIM	PP	SH	GW	S	%	+/-	TF	F%	Min	GP	G	A	Pts	PIM	PP	SH	GW	Min
1998-99	Thunder Bay	USHL	55	19	24	43	48										3	1	1	2	0				
99-2000	Thunder Bay	USHL	56	20	35	55	41																		
2000-01	U. of Vermont	ECAC	34	12	15	27	36																		
2001-02	U. of Vermont	ECAC	31	13	13	26	50																		
2002-03	**Philadelphia**	**NHL**	**3**	**0**	**0**	**0**	**2**	**0**	**0**	**0**	**3**	**0.0**	**0**	**7**	**42.9**	**5:59**									
	Philadelphia	AHL	53	14	19	33	39																		
2003-04	**Philadelphia**	**NHL**	**41**	**5**	**2**	**7**	**55**	**0**	**0**	**1**	**44**	**11.4**	**–3**	**272**	**46.7**	**9:56**	**12**	**1**	**0**	**1**	**2**	**0**	**0**	**0**	**6:12**
	Philadelphia	AHL	35	15	14	29	45										1	2	0	2	0				
2004-05	Philadelphia	AHL	75	23	29	52	80										21	8	13	*21	20				
2005-06	**Philadelphia**	**NHL**	**22**	**5**	**3**	**8**	**10**	**1**	**0**	**3**	**33**	**15.2**	**4**	**38**	**52.6**	**7:43**									
	Chicago	**NHL**	**50**	**9**	**14**	**23**	**36**	**0**	**1**	**2**	**111**	**8.1**	**1**	**664**	**48.0**	**16:19**									
2006-07	**Chicago**	**NHL**	**80**	**20**	**15**	**35**	**74**	**5**	**3**	**1**	**160**	**12.5**	**–15**	**1008**	**46.5**	**17:04**									
2007-08	**Chicago**	**NHL**	**80**	**36**	**26**	**62**	**55**	**9**	**7**	**7**	**209**	**17.2**	**23**	**594**	**51.4**	**18:47**									
	NHL Totals		**276**	**75**	**60**	**135**	**232**	**15**	**11**	**14**	**560**	**13.4**		**2583**	**48.1**	**15:30**	**12**	**1**	**0**	**1**	**2**	**0**	**0**	**0**	**6:12**

Traded to **Chicago** by **Philadelphia** with Eric Meloche for Matt Ellison and Chicago's 3rd round choice (later traded to Montreal - Montreal selected Ryan White) in 2006 Entry Draft, December 5, 2005.

SHELLEY, Jody

(SHEH-lee, JOH-dee) **S.J.**

Left wing. Shoots left. 6'4", 230 lbs. Born, Thompson, Man., February 7, 1976.

Season	Club	League	GP	G	A	Pts	PIM	PP	SH	GW	S	%	+/-	TF	F%	Min	GP	G	A	Pts	PIM	PP	SH	GW	Min
1994-95	Halifax	QMJHL	72	10	12	22	194										7	0	1	1	12				
1995-96	Halifax	QMJHL	50	13	19	32	319										6	0	2	2	36				
1996-97	Halifax	QMJHL	58	25	19	44	*448										17	6	6	12	*123				
1997-98	Dalhousie	AUAA	19	6	11	17	145																		
	Saint John Flames	AHL	18	1	1	2	50																		
1998-99	Saint John Flames	AHL	8	0	0	0	46																		
	Johnstown Chiefs	ECHL	52	12	17	29	325																		

			Regular Season														Playoffs								
Season	Club	League	GP	G	A	Pts	PIM	PP	SH	GW	S	%	+/-	TF	F%	Min	GP	G	A	Pts	PIM	PP	SH	GW	Min
99-2000	Johnstown Chiefs	ECHL	36	9	17	26	256	....	....	....	....	....	....	....	....	....	....	....	....	....	....	....	....	....	....
	Saint John Flames	AHL	22	1	4	5	93	....	....	....	....	....	....	....	....	....	3	0	0	0	2	....	....	....	....
2000-01	Syracuse Crunch	AHL	69	1	7	8	*357	....	....	....	....	....	....	....	....	....	5	0	0	0	21	....	....	....	....
	Columbus	**NHL**	**1**	**0**	**0**	**0**	**10**	**0**	**0**	**0**	**0**	**0.0**	**0**	**0**	**0.0**	**1:33**	....	....	....	....	....	....	....	....	....
2001-02	**Columbus**	**NHL**	**52**	**3**	**3**	**6**	**206**	**0**	**0**	**0**	**35**	**8.6**	**1**	**0**	**0.0**	**6:32**	....	....	....	....	....	....	....	....	....
	Syracuse Crunch	AHL	22	3	5	8	165	....	....	....	....	....	....	....	....	....	....	....	....	....	....	....	....	....	....
2002-03	**Columbus**	**NHL**	**68**	**1**	**4**	**5**	***249**	**0**	**0**	**0**	**39**	**2.6**	**–5**	**1**	**0.0**	**6:08**	....	....	....	....	....	....	....	....	....
2003-04	**Columbus**	**NHL**	**76**	**3**	**3**	**6**	**228**	**1**	**0**	**0**	**62**	**4.8**	**–10**	**3**	**0.0**	**7:14**	....	....	....	....	....	....	....	....	....
2004-05	JYP Jyvaskyla	Finland	11	0	1	1	20	....	....	....	....	....	....	....	....	....	3	0	0	0	25	....	....	....	....
2005-06	**Columbus**	**NHL**	**80**	**3**	**7**	**10**	**163**	**0**	**0**	**1**	**39**	**7.7**	**–4**	**7**	**14.3**	**5:58**	....	....	....	....	....	....	....	....	....
2006-07	**Columbus**	**NHL**	**72**	**1**	**1**	**2**	**125**	**0**	**0**	**0**	**32**	**3.1**	**–6**	**2**	**0.0**	**4:52**	....	....	....	....	....	....	....	....	....
2007-08	**Columbus**	**NHL**	**31**	**0**	**0**	**0**	**44**	**0**	**0**	**0**	**10**	**0.0**	**–2**	**1**	**0.0**	**4:20**	....	....	....	....	....	....	....	....	....
	San Jose	**NHL**	**31**	**1**	**6**	**7**	**91**	**0**	**0**	**0**	**31**	**3.2**	**–2**	**1**	**0.0**	**7:24**	**6**	**0**	**0**	**0**	**2**	**0**	**0**	**0**	**3:16**
	NHL Totals		**411**	**12**	**24**	**36**	**1116**	**1**	**0**	**1**	**248**	**4.8**		**15**	**6.7**	**6:05**	**6**	**0**	**0**	**0**	**2**	**0**	**0**	**0**	**3:16**

Signed as a free agent by **Calgary**, September 1, 1998. Signed as a free agent by **Syracuse** (AHL), September 15, 2000. Signed as a free agent by **Columbus**, January 31, 2001. Signed as a free agent by **Jyvaskyla** (Finland), January 17, 2005. Traded to **San Jose** by **Columbus** for San Jose's 6th round choice in 2009 Entry Draft, January 29, 2008.

SHEPPARD, James

(sheh-PUHRD, JAYMZ) **MIN.**

Center. Shoots left. 6'2", 210 lbs. Born, Halifax, N.S., April 25, 1988. Minnesota's 1st choice, 9th overall, in 2006 Entry Draft.

Season	Club	League	GP	G	A	Pts	PIM	PP	SH	GW	S	%	+/-	TF	F%	Min	GP	G	A	Pts	PIM	PP	SH	GW	Min
2003-04	Dartmouth	NSMHL	61	38	54	92	46	....	....	....	....	....	....	....	....	....	....	....	....	....	....	....	....	....	....
2004-05	Cape Breton	QMJHL	65	14	31	45	40	....	....	....	....	....	....	....	....	....	5	1	3	4	2	....	....	....	....
2005-06	Cape Breton	QMJHL	66	30	54	84	78	....	....	....	....	....	....	....	....	....	9	2	5	7	12	....	....	....	....
2006-07	Cape Breton	QMJHL	56	33	63	96	62	....	....	....	....	....	....	....	....	....	16	8	12	20	14	....	....	....	....
2007-08	**Minnesota**	**NHL**	**78**	**4**	**15**	**19**	**29**	**0**	**0**	**1**	**57**	**7.0**	**0**	**655**	**41.5**	**10:37**	**6**	**0**	**1**	**1**	**4**	**0**	**0**	**0**	**10:37**
	NHL Totals		**78**	**4**	**15**	**19**	**29**	**0**	**0**	**1**	**57**	**7.0**		**655**	**41.5**	**10:37**	**6**	**0**	**1**	**1**	**4**	**0**	**0**	**0**	**10:37**

QMJHL Second All-Star Team (2007)

SIGALET, Jonathan

(SIH-ga-leht, JAWN-ah-thuhn) **CBJ**

Defense. Shoots left. 6'1", 185 lbs. Born, Vancouver, B.C., February 12, 1986. Boston's 4th choice, 100th overall, in 2005 Entry Draft.

Season	Club	League	GP	G	A	Pts	PIM	PP	SH	GW	S	%	+/-	TF	F%	Min	GP	G	A	Pts	PIM	PP	SH	GW	Min
2002-03	Salmon Arm	BCHL	52	13	39	52	34	....	....	....	....	....	....	....	....	....	....	....	....	....	....	....	....	....	....
2003-04	Bowling Green	CCHA	37	3	12	15	26	....	....	....	....	....	....	....	....	....	....	....	....	....	....	....	....	....	....
2004-05	Bowling Green	CCHA	35	3	13	16	36	....	....	....	....	....	....	....	....	....	....	....	....	....	....	....	....	....	....
2005-06	Providence Bruins	AHL	75	9	27	36	59	....	....	....	....	....	....	....	....	....	6	2	1	3	9	....	....	....	....
2006-07	**Boston**	**NHL**	**1**	**0**	**0**	**0**	**4**	**0**	**0**	**0**	**1**	**0.0**	**–2**	**0**	**0.0**	**14:41**	....	....	....	....	....	....	....	....	....
	Providence Bruins	AHL	50	9	13	22	37	....	....	....	....	....	....	....	....	....	....	....	....	....	....	....	....	....	....
2007-08	Providence Bruins	AHL	74	3	20	23	58	....	....	....	....	....	....	....	....	....	10	0	3	3	12	....	....	....	....
	NHL Totals		**1**	**0**	**0**	**0**	**4**	**0**	**0**	**0**	**1**	**0.0**		**0**	**0.0**	**14:41**	....	....	....	....	....	....	....	....	....

Traded to **Columbus** by **Boston** for Matt Marquardt, May 27, 2008.

SILLINGER, Mike

(SIHL-ihn-juhr, MIGHK) **NYI**

Center. Shoots right. 5'11", 198 lbs. Born, Regina, Sask., June 29, 1971. Detroit's 1st choice, 11th overall, in 1989 Entry Draft.

Season	Club	League	GP	G	A	Pts	PIM	PP	SH	GW	S	%	+/-	TF	F%	Min	GP	G	A	Pts	PIM	PP	SH	GW	Min
1986-87	Regina Kings	SMHL	31	83	51	134	....	....	....	....	....	....	....	....	....	....	....	....	....	....	....	....	....	....	....
1987-88	Regina Pats	WHL	67	18	25	43	17	....	....	....	....	....	....	....	....	....	4	2	2	4	0	....	....	....	....
1988-89	Regina Pats	WHL	72	53	78	131	52	....	....	....	....	....	....	....	....	....	....	....	....	....	....	....	....	....	....
1989-90	Regina Pats	WHL	70	57	72	129	41	....	....	....	....	....	....	....	....	....	11	12	10	22	2	....	....	....	....
	Adirondack	AHL	....	....	....	....	....	....	....	....	....	....	....	....	....	....	1	0	0	0	0	....	....	....	....
1990-91	Regina Pats	WHL	57	50	66	116	42	....	....	....	....	....	....	....	....	....	8	6	9	15	4	....	....	....	....
	Detroit	**NHL**	**3**	**0**	**1**	**1**	**0**	**0**	**0**	**0**	**6**	**0.0**	**–2**	....	....	....	**3**	**0**	**1**	**1**	**0**	**0**	**0**	**0**	....
1991-92	Adirondack	AHL	64	25	41	66	26	....	....	....	....	....	....	....	....	....	15	9	*19	*28	12	....	....	....	....
	Detroit	**NHL**	....	....	....	....	....	....	....	....	....	....	....	....	....	....	**8**	**2**	**2**	**4**	**2**	**0**	**0**	**0**	....
1992-93	**Detroit**	**NHL**	**51**	**4**	**17**	**21**	**16**	**0**	**0**	**0**	**47**	**8.5**	**0**	....	....	....	....	....	....	....	....	....	....	....	....
	Adirondack	AHL	15	10	20	30	31	....	....	....	....	....	....	....	....	....	11	5	13	18	10	....	....	....	....
1993-94	**Detroit**	**NHL**	**62**	**8**	**21**	**29**	**10**	**0**	**1**	**1**	**91**	**8.8**	**2**	....	....	....	....	....	....	....	....	....	....	....	....
1994-95	CE Wien	Austria	13	13	14	27	10	....	....	....	....	....	....	....	....	....	....	....	....	....	....	....	....	....	....
	Detroit	**NHL**	**13**	**2**	**6**	**8**	**2**	**0**	**0**	**0**	**11**	**18.2**	**3**	....	....	....	....	....	....	....	....	....	....	....	....
	Anaheim	**NHL**	**15**	**2**	**5**	**7**	**6**	**2**	**0**	**0**	**28**	**7.1**	**1**	....	....	....	....	....	....	....	....	....	....	....	....
1995-96	**Anaheim**	**NHL**	**62**	**13**	**21**	**34**	**32**	**7**	**0**	**2**	**143**	**9.1**	**–20**	....	....	....	....	....	....	....	....	....	....	....	....
	Vancouver	**NHL**	**12**	**1**	**3**	**4**	**6**	**0**	**1**	**0**	**16**	**6.3**	**2**	....	....	....	**6**	**0**	**0**	**0**	**2**	**0**	**0**	**0**	....
1996-97	**Vancouver**	**NHL**	**78**	**17**	**20**	**37**	**25**	**3**	**3**	**2**	**112**	**15.2**	**–3**	....	....	....	....	....	....	....	....	....	....	....	....
1997-98	**Vancouver**	**NHL**	**48**	**10**	**9**	**19**	**34**	**1**	**2**	**1**	**56**	**17.9**	**–14**	....	....	....	....	....	....	....	....	....	....	....	....
	Philadelphia	**NHL**	**27**	**11**	**11**	**22**	**16**	**1**	**2**	**0**	**40**	**27.5**	**3**	....	....	....	**3**	**1**	**0**	**1**	**0**	**0**	**0**	**0**	....
1998-99	**Philadelphia**	**NHL**	**25**	**0**	**3**	**3**	**8**	**0**	**0**	**0**	**23**	**0.0**	**–9**	**229**	**62.9**	**10:42**	....	....	....	....	....	....	....	....	....
	Tampa Bay	**NHL**	**54**	**8**	**2**	**10**	**28**	**0**	**2**	**0**	**69**	**11.6**	**–20**	**320**	**57.8**	**13:57**	....	....	....	....	....	....	....	....	....
99-2000	**Tampa Bay**	**NHL**	**67**	**19**	**25**	**44**	**86**	**6**	**3**	**1**	**126**	**15.1**	**–29**	**493**	**56.0**	**19:42**	....	....	....	....	....	....	....	....	....
	Florida	**NHL**	**13**	**4**	**4**	**8**	**16**	**2**	**0**	**1**	**20**	**20.0**	**–1**	**248**	**61.3**	**19:33**	**4**	**2**	**1**	**3**	**2**	**0**	**0**	**0**	**20:24**
2000-01	**Florida**	**NHL**	**55**	**13**	**21**	**34**	**44**	**1**	**0**	**2**	**100**	**13.0**	**–12**	**1028**	**59.7**	**18:52**	....	....	....	....	....	....	....	....	....
	Ottawa	**NHL**	**13**	**3**	**4**	**7**	**4**	**0**	**0**	**0**	**19**	**15.8**	**1**	**215**	**63.3**	**14:31**	**4**	**0**	**0**	**0**	**2**	**0**	**0**	**0**	**13:40**
2001-02	**Columbus**	**NHL**	**80**	**20**	**23**	**43**	**54**	**8**	**0**	**5**	**150**	**13.3**	**–35**	**2024**	**57.0**	**20:51**	....	....	....	....	....	....	....	....	....
2002-03	**Columbus**	**NHL**	**75**	**18**	**25**	**43**	**52**	**9**	**3**	**3**	**128**	**14.1**	**–21**	**1490**	**56.5**	**19:08**	....	....	....	....	....	....	....	....	....
2003-04	**Phoenix**	**NHL**	**60**	**8**	**6**	**14**	**54**	**0**	**1**	**0**	**66**	**12.1**	**–14**	**771**	**56.3**	**15:22**	....	....	....	....	....	....	....	....	....
	St. Louis	**NHL**	**16**	**5**	**5**	**10**	**14**	**0**	**1**	**0**	**40**	**12.5**	**4**	**351**	**57.8**	**20:08**	**5**	**3**	**1**	**4**	**6**	**0**	**1**	**0**	**22:17**
2004-05		DID NOT PLAY																							
2005-06	**St. Louis**	**NHL**	**48**	**22**	**19**	**41**	**49**	**11**	**1**	**1**	**131**	**16.8**	**–17**	**797**	**55.3**	**19:41**	....	....	....	....	....	....	....	....	....
	Nashville	**NHL**	**31**	**10**	**12**	**22**	**14**	**3**	**0**	**1**	**80**	**12.5**	**0**	**542**	**56.6**	**18:34**	**5**	**2**	**1**	**3**	**12**	**1**	**0**	**0**	**17:09**
2006-07	**NY Islanders**	**NHL**	**82**	**26**	**33**	**59**	**46**	**11**	**2**	**3**	**152**	**17.1**	**5**	**1708**	**58.8**	**19:19**	**5**	**1**	**1**	**2**	**2**	**1**	**0**	**0**	**20:49**
2007-08	**NY Islanders**	**NHL**	**52**	**14**	**12**	**26**	**28**	**3**	**2**	**2**	**94**	**14.9**	**–10**	**1027**	**56.3**	**18:36**	....	....	....	....	....	....	....	....	....
	NHL Totals		**1042**	**238**	**308**	**546**	**644**	**68**	**24**	**25**	**1748**	**13.6**		**11243**	**57.5**	**18:15**	**43**	**11**	**7**	**18**	**28**	**2**	**1**	**0**	**19:01**

WHL East Second All-Star Team (1990) • WHL East First All-Star Team (1991)

Traded to **Anaheim** by **Detroit** with Jason York for Stu Grimson, Mark Ferner and Anaheim's 6th round choice (Magnus Nilsson) in 1996 Entry Draft, April 4, 1995. Traded to **Vancouver** by **Anaheim** for Roman Oksiuta, March 15, 1996. Traded to **Philadelphia** by **Vancouver** for Philadelphia's 5th round choice (later traded back to Philadelphia – Philadelphia selected Garrett Prosofsky) in 1998 Entry Draft, February 5, 1998. Traded to **Tampa Bay** by **Philadelphia** with Chris Gratton for Mikael Renberg and Daymond Langkow, December 12, 1998. Traded to **Florida** by **Tampa Bay** for Ryan Johnson and Dwayne Hay, March 14, 2000. Traded to **Ottawa** by **Florida** for future considerations, March 13, 2001. Signed as a free agent by **Columbus**, July 7, 2001. Traded to **Dallas** by **Columbus** with Columbus' 2nd round choice (Johan Fransson) in 2004 Entry Draft for Darryl Sydor, July 22, 2003. Traded to **Phoenix** by **Dallas** with future considerations for Teppo Numminen, July 22, 2003. Traded to **St. Louis** by **Phoenix** for Brent Johnson, March 4, 2004. Traded to **Nashville** by **St. Louis** for Timofei Shishkanov, January 30, 2006. Signed as a free agent by **NY Islanders**, July 2, 2006.

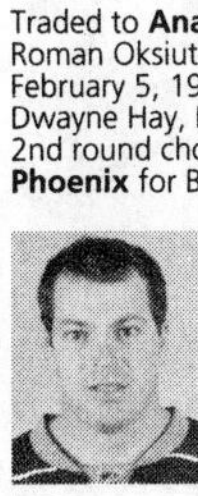

SIM, Jon

(SIHM, JAWN) **NYI**

Left wing. Shoots left. 5'10", 195 lbs. Born, New Glasgow, N.S., September 29, 1977. Dallas' 2nd choice, 70th overall, in 1996 Entry Draft.

Season	Club	League	GP	G	A	Pts	PIM	PP	SH	GW	S	%	+/-	TF	F%	Min	GP	G	A	Pts	PIM	PP	SH	GW	Min
1994-95	Laval Titan	QMJHL	9	0	1	1	6	....	....	....	....	....	....	....	....	....	....	....	....	....	....	....	....	....	....
	Sarnia Sting	OHL	25	9	12	21	19	....	....	....	....	....	....	....	....	....	4	3	2	5	2	....	....	....	....
1995-96	Sarnia Sting	OHL	63	56	46	102	130	....	....	....	....	....	....	....	....	....	10	8	7	15	26	....	....	....	....
1996-97	Sarnia Sting	OHL	64	*56	39	95	109	....	....	....	....	....	....	....	....	....	12	9	5	14	32	....	....	....	....
1997-98	Sarnia Sting	OHL	59	44	50	94	95	....	....	....	....	....	....	....	....	....	5	1	4	5	14	....	....	....	....
1998-99♦	**Dallas**	**NHL**	**7**	**1**	**0**	**1**	**12**	**0**	**0**	**0**	**8**	**12.5**	**1**	**6**	**50.0**	**11:26**	**4**	**0**	**0**	**0**	**0**	**0**	**0**	**0**	**6:27**
	Michigan	IHL	68	24	27	51	91	....	....	....	....	....	....	....	....	....	5	3	1	4	18	....	....	....	....
99-2000	**Dallas**	**NHL**	**25**	**5**	**3**	**8**	**10**	**2**	**0**	**1**	**44**	**11.4**	**4**	**4**	**75.0**	**10:51**	**7**	**1**	**0**	**1**	**6**	**0**	**0**	**0**	**11:11**
	Michigan	IHL	35	14	16	30	65	....	....	....	....	....	....	....	....	....	....	....	....	....	....	....	....	....	....
2000-01	**Dallas**	**NHL**	**15**	**0**	**3**	**3**	**6**	**0**	**0**	**0**	**18**	**0.0**	**–2**	**1**	**100.0**	**8:47**	....	....	....	....	....	....	....	....	....
	Utah Grizzlies	IHL	39	16	13	29	44	....	....	....	....	....	....	....	....	....	....	....	....	....	....	....	....	....	....
2001-02	**Dallas**	**NHL**	**26**	**3**	**0**	**3**	**10**	**1**	**0**	**0**	**43**	**7.0**	**–3**	**3**	**0.0**	**9:30**	....	....	....	....	....	....	....	....	....
	Utah Grizzlies	AHL	31	21	6	27	63	....	....	....	....	....	....	....	....	....	....	....	....	....	....	....	....	....	....
2002-03	**Dallas**	**NHL**	**4**	**0**	**0**	**0**	**0**	**0**	**0**	**0**	**7**	**0.0**	**–1**	**2**	**50.0**	**9:10**	....	....	....	....	....	....	....	....	....
	Utah Grizzlies	AHL	42	16	31	47	85	....	....	....	....	....	....	....	....	....	....	....	....	....	....	....	....	....	....
	Nashville	**NHL**	**4**	**1**	**0**	**1**	**0**	**0**	**0**	**0**	**3**	**33.3**	**0**	**14**	**35.7**	**9:18**	....	....	....	....	....	....	....	....	....
	Los Angeles	**NHL**	**14**	**0**	**2**	**2**	**19**	**0**	**0**	**0**	**29**	**0.0**	**–3**	**3**	**33.3**	**12:05**	....	....	....	....	....	....	....	....	....
2003-04	**Los Angeles**	**NHL**	**48**	**6**	**7**	**13**	**27**	**0**	**0**	**1**	**73**	**8.2**	**0**	**19**	**31.6**	**10:01**	....	....	....	....	....	....	....	....	....
	Pittsburgh	**NHL**	**15**	**2**	**3**	**5**	**6**	**0**	**0**	**1**	**27**	**7.4**	**–4**	**0**	**0.0**	**13:39**	....	....	....	....	....	....	....	....	....

Season	Club	League	GP	G	A	Pts	PIM	PP	SH	GW	S	%	+/-	TF	F%	Min	GP	G	A	Pts	PIM	PP	SH	GW	Min
			Regular Season														Playoffs								
2004-05	Utah Grizzlies	AHL	10	2	2	4	12																		
	Philadelphia	AHL	63	35	26	61	66										21	*10	7	17	44				
2005-06	**Philadelphia**	**NHL**	39	7	7	14	28	4	0	2	80	8.8	–6	1	0.0	10:59									
	Florida	**NHL**	33	10	8	18	26	4	0	3	92	10.9	–1	0	0.0	12:28									
2006-07	**Atlanta**	**NHL**	77	17	12	29	60	2	0	1	141	12.1	–1	9	22.2	11:45	4	0	0	0	0	0	0	0	5:29
2007-08	**NY Islanders**	**NHL**	2	0	1	1	2	0	0	0	8	0.0	–1	0	0.0	14:19									
	NHL Totals		309	52	46	98	206	13	0	9	573	9.1		62	35.5	11:06	15	1	0	1	6	0	0	0	8:24

OHL Second All-Star Team (1998)

Traded to **Nashville** by **Dallas** for Bubba Berenzweig and future considerations, February 17, 2003. Claimed on waivers by **Los Angeles** from **Nashville**, March 8, 2003. Claimed on waivers by **Pittsburgh** from **Los Angeles**, March 4, 2004. Signed as a free agent by **Phoenix**, September 2, 2004. Loaned to **Philadelphia** (AHL) by **Phoenix** (Utah - AHL) for the loan of Peter White, November 14, 2004. Signed as a free agent by **Philadelphia**, August 2, 2005. Traded to **Florida** by **Philadelphia** for Florida's 6th round choice (Patrick Maroon) in 2007 Entry Draft, January 23, 2006. Signed as a free agent by **Atlanta**, July 14, 2006. Signed as a free agent by **NY Islanders**, July 1, 2007.

SIMON, Ben

(SIGH-mohn, BEHN)

Left wing. Shoots left. 6', 195 lbs. Born, Shaker Heights, OH, June 14, 1978. Chicago's 5th choice, 110th overall, in 1997 Entry Draft.

Season	Club	League	GP	G	A	Pts	PIM	PP	SH	GW	S	%	+/-	TF	F%	Min	GP	G	A	Pts	PIM	PP	SH	GW	Min
1992-93	Shaker Heights	High-OH	25	15	21	36																			
1993-94	Shaker Heights	High-OH	24	45	41	86																			
1994-95	Shaker Heights	High-OH	25	61	68	129																			
1995-96	Cleveland Barons	NAHL	45	38	33	71											5	7	13	20					
1996-97	U. of Notre Dame	CCHA	30	4	15	19	79																		
1997-98	U. of Notre Dame	CCHA	37	9	28	37	91																		
1998-99	U. of Notre Dame	CCHA	37	18	24	42	65																		
99-2000	U. of Notre Dame	CCHA	40	13	19	32	53																		
2000-01	Orlando	IHL	77	8	12	20	47										16	6	5	11	20				
2001-02	**Atlanta**	**NHL**	6	0	0	0	6	0	0	0	7	0.0	1	32	40.6	9:20									
	Chicago Wolves	AHL	74	11	23	34	56										25	2	3	5	24				
2002-03	**Atlanta**	**NHL**	10	0	1	1	9	0	0	0	7	0.0	0	54	31.5	9:25									
	Chicago Wolves	AHL	69	15	17	32	78										9	0	0	0	6				
2003-04	Milwaukee	AHL	18	1	3	4	6																		
	Atlanta	**NHL**	52	3	0	3	28	0	0	0	30	10.0	–10	203	33.0	6:05									
2004-05	Chicago Wolves	AHL	53	11	10	21	58										18	1	5	6	44				
2005-06	**Columbus**	**NHL**	13	0	0	0	4	0	0	0	7	0.0	–4	53	24.5	5:38									
	Syracuse Crunch	AHL	66	13	24	37	88										3	0	1	1	2				
2006-07	Syracuse Crunch	AHL	56	9	12	21	77																		
	Grand Rapids	AHL	21	4	5	9	28										7	0	0	0	9				
2007-08	Springfield	AHL	80	12	10	22	88																		
	NHL Totals		81	3	1	4	47	0	0	0	51	5.9		342	32.2	6:40									

CCHA Second All-Star Team (1999)

Rights traded to **Atlanta** by **Chicago** for Atlanta's 9th round choice (Peter Flache) in 2000 Entry Draft, June 25, 2000. Signed as a free agent by **Nashville**, July 14, 2003. Traded to **Atlanta** by **Nashville** with Tomas Kloucek for Simon Gamache and Kirill Safronov, December 2, 2003. Signed as a free agent by **Columbus**, August 11, 2005.

SIMON, Chris

(SIGH-mohn, KRIHS)

Left wing. Shoots left. 6'3", 233 lbs. Born, Wawa, Ont., January 30, 1972. Philadelphia's 2nd choice, 25th overall, in 1990 Entry Draft.

Season	Club	League	GP	G	A	Pts	PIM	PP	SH	GW	S	%	+/-	TF	F%	Min	GP	G	A	Pts	PIM	PP	SH	GW	Min
1986-87	Wawa Flyers	NOHA	36	12	20	32	108																		
1987-88	Soo Thunderbirds	NOHA	55	42	36	78	172																		
1988-89	Ottawa 67's	OHL	36	4	2	6	31																		
1989-90	Ottawa 67's	OHL	57	36	38	74	146										3	2	1	3	4				
1990-91	Ottawa 67's	OHL	20	16	6	22	69										17	5	9	14	59				
1991-92	Ottawa 67's	OHL	2	1	1	2	24																		
	Sault Ste. Marie	OHL	31	19	25	44	143										11	5	8	13	49				
1992-93	**Quebec**	**NHL**	16	1	1	2	67	0	0	1	15	6.7	–2				5	0	0	0	26	0	0	0	
	Halifax Citadels	AHL	36	12	6	18	131																		
1993-94	**Quebec**	**NHL**	37	4	4	8	132	0	0	1	39	10.3	–2												
1994-95	**Quebec**	**NHL**	29	3	9	12	106	0	0	0	33	9.1	14				6	1	1	2	19	0	0	1	
1995-96♦	**Colorado**	**NHL**	64	16	18	34	250	4	0	1	105	15.2	10				12	1	2	3	11	0	0	0	
1996-97	**Washington**	**NHL**	42	9	13	22	165	3	0	1	89	10.1	–1												
1997-98	**Washington**	**NHL**	28	7	10	17	38	4	0	1	71	9.9	–1				18	1	0	1	26	0	0	0	
1998-99	**Washington**	**NHL**	23	3	7	10	48	0	0	0	29	10.3	–4	2	50.0	12:08									
99-2000	**Washington**	**NHL**	75	29	20	49	146	7	0	5	201	14.4	11	7	28.6	15:32	4	2	0	2	24	0	0	0	18:07
2000-01	**Washington**	**NHL**	60	10	10	20	109	4	0	2	123	8.1	–12	3	33.3	14:34	6	0	1	1	4	0	0	0	9:55
2001-02	**Washington**	**NHL**	82	14	17	31	137	1	0	1	121	11.6	–8	7	28.6	12:11									
2002-03	**Washington**	**NHL**	10	0	2	2	23	0	0	0	16	0.0	–3	0	0.0	8:53									
	Chicago	**NHL**	61	12	6	18	125	2	0	2	72	16.7	–4	5	20.0	11:06									
2003-04	**NY Rangers**	**NHL**	65	14	9	23	225	3	0	0	116	12.1	14	3	0.0	11:56									
	Calgary	**NHL**	13	3	2	5	25	1	0	0	31	9.7	1	2	100.0	16:38	16	5	2	7	*74	4	0	1	15:06
2004-05	DID NOT PLAY																								
2005-06	**Calgary**	**NHL**	72	8	14	22	94	2	0	3	76	10.5	0	17	47.1	10:26	6	0	1	1	7	0	0	0	10:12
2006-07	**NY Islanders**	**NHL**	67	10	17	27	75	2	0	0	82	12.2	17	44	47.7	11:00									
2007-08	**NY Islanders**	**NHL**	28	1	2	3	43	0	0	0	18	5.6	–1	1	100.0	6:59									
	Minnesota	**NHL**	10	0	0	0	16	0	0	0	9	0.0	–1	1	100.0	7:44	2	0	0	0	0	0	0	0	6:54
	NHL Totals		782	144	161	305	1824	33	0	18	1246	11.6		92	43.5	12:05	75	10	7	17	191	4	0	2	13:12

• Missed majority of 1990-91 season recovering from shoulder surgery, October, 1990. Traded to **Quebec** by **Philadelphia** with Philadelphia's 1st round choice (later traded to Toronto – later traded to Washington – Washington selected Nolan Baumgartner) in 1994 Entry Draft to complete transaction that sent Eric Lindros to Philadelphia (June 30, 1992), July 21, 1992. Transferred to **Colorado** after **Quebec** franchise relocated, June 21, 1995. Traded to **Washington** by **Colorado** with Curtis Leschyshyn for Keith Jones and Washington's 1st (Scott Parker) and 4th (later traded back to Washington – Washington selected Krys Barch) round choices in 1998 Entry Drarft, November 2, 1996. Traded to **Chicago** by **Washington** with Andrei Nikolishin for Michael Nylander, Chicago's 3rd round choice (Stephen Werner) in 2003 Entry Draft and future considerations, November 1, 2002. Signed as a free agent by **NY Rangers**, July 25, 2003. Traded to **Calgary** by **NY Rangers** with NY Rangers' 7th round choice (Matt Schneider) in 2004 Entry Draft for Jamie McLennan, Blair Betts and Greg Moore, March 6, 2004. Signed as a free agent by **NY Islanders**, July 11, 2006. Traded to **Minnesota** by **NY Islanders** for Minnesota's 6th round choice (Justin DiBenedetto) in 2008 Entry Draft, February 26, 2008. Signed as a free agent by **Vityaz Chekhov** (Russia). May 17, 2008.

SIMPSON, Todd

(SIHMP-suhn, TAWD)

Defense. Shoots left. 6'3", 218 lbs. Born, North Vancouver, B.C., May 28, 1973.

Season	Club	League	GP	G	A	Pts	PIM	PP	SH	GW	S	%	+/-	TF	F%	Min	GP	G	A	Pts	PIM	PP	SH	GW	Min
1991-92	Brown U.	ECAC	18	1	4	5	38																		
1992-93	Tri-City	WHL	69	5	18	23	196										4	0	0	0	13				
1993-94	Tri-City	WHL	12	2	3	5	32																		
	Saskatoon Blades	WHL	51	7	19	26	175										16	1	5	6	42				
1994-95	Saint John Flames	AHL	80	3	10	13	321										5	0	0	0	4				
1995-96	**Calgary**	**NHL**	6	0	0	0	32	0	0	0	3	0.0	0												
	Saint John Flames	AHL	66	4	13	17	277										16	2	3	5	32				
1996-97	**Calgary**	**NHL**	82	1	13	14	208	0	0	0	85	1.2	–14												
1997-98	**Calgary**	**NHL**	53	1	5	6	109	0	0	1	51	2.0	–10												
1998-99	**Calgary**	**NHL**	73	2	8	10	151	0	0	0	52	3.8	18	1	100.0	17:19									
99-2000	**Florida**	**NHL**	82	1	6	7	202	0	0	0	50	2.0	5	0	0.0	16:35	4	0	0	0	4	0	0	0	15:24
2000-01	**Florida**	**NHL**	25	1	3	4	74	0	0	1	26	3.8	0	0	0.0	16:29									
	Phoenix	**NHL**	13	0	1	1	12	0	0	0	9	0.0	–4	0	0.0	13:56									
2001-02	**Phoenix**	**NHL**	67	2	13	15	152	0	0	0	51	3.9	20	0	0.0	17:20	5	0	2	2	6	0	0	0	18:30
2002-03	**Phoenix**	**NHL**	66	2	7	9	135	0	0	0	67	3.0	7	0	0.0	16:59									
2003-04	**Anaheim**	**NHL**	46	4	3	7	105	0	0	0	42	9.5	–6	0	0.0	14:18									
	Ottawa	**NHL**	16	0	1	1	47	0	0	0	10	0.0	–1	1	0.0	14:21									
2004-05	Herning Blue Fox	Denmark	7	2	3	5	35										16	3	5	8	82				
2005-06	**Chicago**	**NHL**	45	0	3	3	116	0	0	0	25	0.0	–2	2	0.0	13:05									
	Montreal	**NHL**	6	0	0	0	14	0	0	0	6	0.0	0	0	0.0	15:59									
2006-07	Hannover Scorp.	Germany	45	1	9	10	174										6	0	0	0	49				
	NHL Totals		580	14	63	77	1357	0	0	2	477	2.9		4	25.0	16:06	9	0	2	2	10	0	0	0	17:07

Signed as free agent by **Calgary**, July 6, 1994. Traded to **Florida** by **Calgary** for Bill Lindsay, September 30, 1999. • Missed majority of 2000-01 season recovering from head injury suffered in game vs. NY Islanders, December 6, 2000. Traded to **Phoenix** by **Florida** for Phoenix's 2nd round choice (later traded to New Jersey – New Jersey selected Tuomas Pihlman) in 2001 Entry Draft, March 13, 2001. Claimed by **Anaheim** from **Phoenix** in Waiver Draft, October 3, 2003. Traded to **Ottawa** by **Anaheim** for Petr Schastlivy, February 4, 2004. Signed as a free agent by **Herning** (Denmark), December 16, 2004. Signed as a free agent by **Chicago**, August 23, 2005. Traded to **Montreal** by **Chicago** for Montreal's 6th round choice (Chris Auger) in 2006 Entry Draft, March 9, 2006.

SJOSTROM, Fredrik
(SHAW-strahm, FREHD-rihk) **NYR**

Right wing. Shoots left. 6'1", 217 lbs. Born, Fargelanda, Sweden, May 6, 1983. Phoenix's 1st choice, 11th overall, in 2001 Entry Draft.

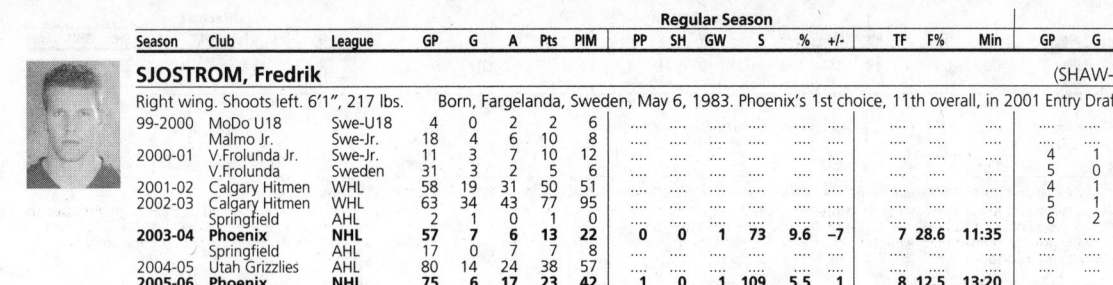

			Regular Season														Playoffs								
Season	Club	League	GP	G	A	Pts	PIM	PP	SH	GW	S	%	+/-	TF	F%	Min	GP	G	A	Pts	PIM	PP	SH	GW	Min
99-2000	MoDo U18	Swe-U18	4	0	2	2	6																		
	Malmo Jr.	Swe-Jr.	18	4	6	10	8																		
2000-01	V.Frolunda Jr.	Swe-Jr.	11	3	7	10	12										4	1	2	3	6				
	V.Frolunda	Sweden	31	3	2	5	6										5	0	0	0	2				
2001-02	Calgary Hitmen	WHL	58	19	31	50	51										4	1	1	2	8				
2002-03	Calgary Hitmen	WHL	63	34	43	77	95										5	1	3	4	4				
	Springfield	AHL	2	1	0	1	0										6	2	0	2	12				
2003-04	Phoenix	NHL	57	7	6	13	22	0	0	1	73	9.6	-7	7	28.6	11:35									
	Springfield	AHL	17	0	7	7	8																		
2004-05	Utah Grizzlies	AHL	80	14	24	38	57																		
2005-06	Phoenix	NHL	75	6	17	23	42	1	0	1	109	5.5	1	8	12.5	13:20									
2006-07	Phoenix	NHL	78	9	9	18	48	2	0	1	125	7.2	-11	15	13.3	14:07									
2007-08	Phoenix	NHL	51	10	9	19	14	2	2	1	84	11.9	-2	33	18.2	13:33									
	NY Rangers	NHL	18	2	0	2	8	0	0	1	26	7.7	0	3	0.0	8:05	10	0	1	1	2	0	0	0	6:28
	NHL Totals		279	34	41	75	134	5	2	5	417	8.2		66	16.7	12:54	10	0	1	1	2	0	0	0	6:28

Traded to **NY Rangers** by **Phoenix** with Josh Gratton, David LeNeveu and future considerations for Al Montoya and Marcel Hossa, February 26, 2008.

SKILLE, Jack
(SKIH-lee, JAK) **CHI.**

Right wing. Shoots right. 6'1", 198 lbs. Born, Madison, WI, May 19, 1987. Chicago's 1st choice, 7th overall, in 2005 Entry Draft.

Season	Club	League	GP	G	A	Pts	PIM	PP	SH	GW	S	%	+/-	TF	F%	Min	GP	G	A	Pts	PIM	PP	SH	GW	Min
2003-04	USNTDP	U-17	33	14	10	24	30																		
	USNTDP	NAHL	28	11	9	20	31																		
2004-05	USNTDP	U-18	26	9	11	20	36																		
	USNTDP	NAHL	16	6	11	17	20																		
2005-06	U. of Wisconsin	WCHA	41	13	8	21	37																		
2006-07	U. of Wisconsin	WCHA	26	8	10	18	12																		
	Norfolk Admirals	AHL	9	4	4	8	0										3	0	0	0	2				
2007-08	Chicago	NHL	16	3	2	5	0	0	0	0	23	13.0	1	4	50.0	11:59									
	Rockford IceHogs	AHL	59	16	18	34	44										12	2	1	3	6				
	NHL Totals		16	3	2	5	0	0	0	0	23	13.0		4	50.0	11:59									

SKOULA, Martin
(SHKOO-la, MAHR-tihn) **MIN.**

Defense. Shoots left. 6'3", 226 lbs. Born, Litomerice, Czech., October 28, 1979. Colorado's 2nd choice, 17th overall, in 1998 Entry Draft.

Season	Club	League	GP	G	A	Pts	PIM	PP	SH	GW	S	%	+/-	TF	F%	Min	GP	G	A	Pts	PIM	PP	SH	GW	Min
1995-96	Litvinov Jr.	CzRep-Jr.	38	0	4	4																			
	Litvinov	CzRep															1	0	0	0	0				
1996-97	Litvinov Jr.	CzRep-Jr.	38	2	9	11																			
	Litvinov	CzRep	1	0	0	0	0																		
1997-98	Barrie Colts	OHL	66	8	36	44	36										6	1	3	4	4				
1998-99	Barrie Colts	OHL	67	13	46	59	46										12	3	10	13	13				
	Hershey Bears	AHL															1	0	0	0	0				
99-2000	Colorado	NHL	80	3	13	16	20	2	0	0	66	4.5	5	0	0.0	18:15	17	0	2	2	4	0	0	0	18:45
2000-01 ♦	Colorado	NHL	82	8	17	25	38	3	0	2	108	7.4	8	1	100.0	20:41	23	1	4	5	8	0	0	0	11:59
2001-02	Colorado	NHL	82	10	21	31	42	5	0	1	100	10.0	-3	0	0.0	22:18	21	0	6	6	2	0	0	0	14:37
	Czech Republic	Olympics	4	0	0	0	0																		
2002-03	Colorado	NHL	81	4	21	25	68	2	0	0	93	4.3	11	1	100.0	18:27	7	0	1	1	4	0	0	0	11:05
2003-04	Colorado	NHL	58	2	14	16	30	0	0	0	54	3.7	2	0	0.0	17:21									
	Anaheim	NHL	21	2	7	9	2	1	0	0	30	6.7	3	1	0.0	21:14									
2004-05	Litvinov	CzRep	47	4	15	19	101										6	0	0	0	6				
2005-06	Dallas	NHL	61	4	11	15	36	3	0	1	78	5.1	6	0	0.0	18:41									
	Minnesota	NHL	17	1	5	6	10	0	0	0	14	7.1	0	0	0.0	20:49									
2006-07	Minnesota	NHL	81	0	15	15	36	0	0	0	91	0.0	9	0	0.0	20:14	5	0	0	0	4	0	0	0	19:02
2007-08	Minnesota	NHL	80	3	8	11	26	0	0	1	63	4.8	-16	0	0.0	20:29	6	0	0	0	0	0	0	0	26:41
	NHL Totals		643	37	132	169	308	16	0	5	697	5.3		3	66.7	19:45	79	1	13	14	22	0	0	0	15:37

OHL All-Rookie Team (1998) • OHL Second All-Star Team (1999)

Traded to **Anaheim** by **Colorado** for Kurt Sauer and Anaheim's 4th round choice (Raymond Macias) in 2005 Entry Draft, February 21, 2004. Signed as a free agent by **Litvinov** (CzRep), September 17, 2004. Signed as a free agent by **Dallas**, August 3, 2005. Traded to **Minnesota** by **Dallas** with Shawn Belle for Willie Mitchell and Minnesota's 2nd round choice (Nico Sacchetti) in 2007 Entry Draft, March 8, 2006.

SKRASTINS, Karlis
(SKRAS-tihnz, KAR-lihs) **FLA.**

Defense. Shoots left. 6'1", 210 lbs. Born, Riga, Latvia, July 9, 1974. Nashville's 8th choice, 230th overall, in 1998 Entry Draft.

Season	Club	League	GP	G	A	Pts	PIM	PP	SH	GW	S	%	+/-	TF	F%	Min	GP	G	A	Pts	PIM	PP	SH	GW	Min
1992-93	Pardaugava Riga	CIS	40	3	5	8	16										2	0	0	0	0				
1993-94	Pardaugava Riga	CIS	42	7	5	12	18										2	1	0	1	4				
1994-95	Pardaugava Riga	CIS	52	4	14	18	69																		
1995-96	TPS Turku	Finland	50	4	11	15	32										11	2	2	4	10				
1996-97	TPS Turku	Finland	50	2	8	10	20										12	0	4	4	2				
	TPS Turku	EuroHL	6	0	1	1	4										4	0	0	0	14				
1997-98	TPS Turku	Finland	48	4	15	19	67										4	0	0	0	0				
	TPS Turku	EuroHL	6	0	1	1	6																		
1998-99	Nashville	NHL	2	0	1	1	0	0	0	0	0	0.0	0	0	0.0	11:47									
	Milwaukee	IHL	75	8	36	44	47										2	0	1	1	2				
99-2000	Nashville	NHL	59	5	6	11	20	1	0	2	51	9.8	-7	0	0.0	20:51									
	Milwaukee	IHL	19	3	8	11	10																		
2000-01	Nashville	NHL	82	1	11	12	30	0	0	1	66	1.5	-12	0	0.0	19:12									
2001-02	Nashville	NHL	82	4	13	17	36	0	0	1	84	4.8	-12	0	0.0	20:29									
	Latvia	Olympics	1	0	0	0	0																		
2002-03	Nashville	NHL	82	3	10	13	44	0	1	0	86	3.5	-18	0	0.0	20:17									
2003-04	Colorado	NHL	82	5	8	13	26	0	1	1	102	4.9	18	0	0.0	21:49	11	0	2	2	2	0	0	0	23:07
2004-05	HK Riga 2000	Latvia	4	0	4	4	0										9	3	10	13	33				
	HK Riga 2000	BelOpen	34	8	17	25	30										3	0	0	0	25				
2005-06	Colorado	NHL	82	3	11	14	65	0	2	0	58	5.2	-7	0	0.0	21:49	9	0	1	1	10	0	0	0	23:24
	Latvia	Olympics	5	0	1	1	0																		
2006-07	Colorado	NHL	68	0	11	11	30	0	0	0	65	0.0	0	0	0.0	21:14									
2007-08	Colorado	NHL	43	1	3	4	20	0	0	0	34	2.9	-2	0	0.0	18:02									
	Florida	NHL	17	1	0	1	12	0	0	1	11	9.1	-9	0	0.0	20:03									
	NHL Totals		599	23	74	97	283	1	4	6	557	4.1		0	0.0	20:33	20	0	3	3	12	0	0	0	23:15

Traded to **Colorado** by **Nashville** for Colorado's 3rd round choice (later traded to Ottawa – Ottawa selected Peter Regin Jensen) in 2004 Entry Draft, June 30, 2003. Signed as a free agent by **Riga** (Latvia), September 25, 2004. Traded to **Florida** by **Colorado** with Colorado's 3rd round choice (Adam Comrie) in 2008 Entry Draft for Ruslan Salei, February 26, 2008.

SLATER, Jim
(SLAY-tuhr, JIHM) **ATL.**

Center. Shoots left. 6', 195 lbs. Born, Petoskey, MI, December 9, 1982. Atlanta's 2nd choice, 30th overall, in 2002 Entry Draft.

Season	Club	League	GP	G	A	Pts	PIM	PP	SH	GW	S	%	+/-	TF	F%	Min	GP	G	A	Pts	PIM	PP	SH	GW	Min
1998-99	USNTDP	U-18	3	0	1	1	0																		
	Cleveland Barons	NAHL	50	13	20	33	58										2	0	0	0	2				
99-2000	Cleveland Barons	NAHL	56	35	50	85	129										3	1	3	4	4				
2000-01	Cleveland Barons	NAHL	48	27	37	64	122										6	6	6	12	6				
2001-02	Michigan State	CCHA	37	11	21	32	50																		
2002-03	Michigan State	CCHA	37	18	26	44	26																		
2003-04	Michigan State	CCHA	42	19	29	*48	38																		
2004-05	Michigan State	CCHA	41	16	32	48	30																		
2005-06	Atlanta	NHL	71	10	10	20	46	1	0	0	108	9.3	1	287	56.5	10:06									
	Chicago Wolves	AHL	4	0	2	2	2																		
2006-07	Atlanta	NHL	74	5	14	19	62	0	0	2	90	5.6	8	373	54.4	10:14	4	0	0	0	2	0	0	0	5:10

Season	Club	League	GP	G	A	Pts	PIM	PP	SH	GW	S	%	+/-	TF	F%	Min	GP	G	A	Pts	PIM	PP	SH	GW	Min
		Regular Season															Playoffs								
2007-08	**Atlanta**	**NHL**	**69**	**8**	**5**	**13**	**41**	**0**	**2**	**0**	**95**	**8.4**	**–10**	**367**	**52.0**	**10:24**	....	....	....	....	....	....	....	....	....
	Chicago Wolves	AHL	3	0	0	0	0	....	....	....	....	....	....	....	....	....	....	....	....	....	....	....	....	....	....
	NHL Totals		**214**	**23**	**29**	**52**	**149**	**1**	**2**	**2**	**293**	**7.8**		**1027**	**54.1**	**10:14**	**4**	**0**	**0**	**0**	**2**	**0**	**0**	**0**	**5:10**

CCHA All-Rookie Team (2002) • CCHA First All-Star Team (2003, 2004) • NCAA West Second All-American Team (2004)

SMABY, Matt (SMA-bee, MAT) T.B.

Defense. Shoots left. 6'5", 222 lbs. Born, Minneapolis, MN, October 14, 1984. Tampa Bay's 2nd choice, 41st overall, in 2003 Entry Draft.

Season	Club	League	GP	G	A	Pts	PIM	PP	SH	GW	S	%	+/-	TF	F%	Min	GP	G	A	Pts	PIM	PP	SH	GW	Min
2001-02	Shat.-St. Mary's	High-MN	65	7	18	25	134	....	....	....	....	....	....	....	....	....	....	....	....	....	....	....	....	....	....
2002-03	Shat.-St. Mary's	High-MN	57	3	20	23	114	....	....	....	....	....	....	....	....	....	....	....	....	....	....	....	....	....	....
2003-04	North Dakota	WCHA	39	1	6	7	81	....	....	....	....	....	....	....	....	....	....	....	....	....	....	....	....	....	....
2004-05	North Dakota	WCHA	44	1	2	3	86	....	....	....	....	....	....	....	....	....	....	....	....	....	....	....	....	....	....
2005-06	North Dakota	WCHA	46	4	15	19	*113	....	....	....	....	....	....	....	....	....	....	....	....	....	....	....	....	....	....
2006-07	Springfield	AHL	66	2	14	16	43	....	....	....	....	....	....	....	....	....	....	....	....	....	....	....	....	....	....
2007-08	**Tampa Bay**	**NHL**	**14**	**0**	**0**	**0**	**12**	**0**	**0**	**0**	**7**	**0.0**	**–6**	**0**	**0.0**	**12:08**	....	....	....	....	....	....	....	....	....
	Norfolk Admirals	AHL	58	1	5	6	66	....	....	....	....	....	....	....	....	....	....	....	....	....	....	....	....	....	....
	NHL Totals		**14**	**0**	**0**	**0**	**12**	**0**	**0**	**0**	**7**	**0.0**		**0**	**0.0**	**12:08**	....	....	....	....	....	....	....	....	....

SMID, Ladislav (SHMIHD, LA-dih-slahv) EDM.

Defense. Shoots left. 6'3", 226 lbs. Born, Frydlant V Cechach, Czech., February 1, 1986. Anaheim's 1st choice, 9th overall, in 2004 Entry Draft.

Season	Club	League	GP	G	A	Pts	PIM	PP	SH	GW	S	%	+/-	TF	F%	Min	GP	G	A	Pts	PIM	PP	SH	GW	Min
2001-02	HC Liberec Jr.	CzRep-Jr.	43	6	10	16	87	....	....	....	....	....	....	....	....	....	....	....	....	....	....	....	....	....	....
2002-03	HC Liberec Jr.	CzRep-Jr.	32	1	14	15	12	....	....	....	....	....	....	....	....	....	8	2	1	3	31	....	....	....	....
	Liberec	CzRep	4	0	0	0	0	....	....	....	....	....	....	....	....	....	....	....	....	....	....	....	....	....	....
2003-04	HC Liberec Jr.	CzRep-Jr.	14	4	10	14	38	....	....	....	....	....	....	....	....	....	2	1	0	1	6	....	....	....	....
	Liberec	CzRep	45	1	1	2	51	....	....	....	....	....	....	....	....	....	....	....	....	....	....	....	....	....	....
	Beroun	CzRep-2	....	....	....	....	....	....	....	....	....	....	....	....	....	....	3	1	1	2	4	....	....	....	....
2004-05	HC Liberec Jr.	CzRep-Jr.	3	0	1	1	4	....	....	....	....	....	....	....	....	....	....	....	....	....	....	....	....	....	....
	Liberec	CzRep	39	1	3	4	14	....	....	....	....	....	....	....	....	....	12	0	0	0	6	....	....	....	....
2005-06	Portland Pirates	AHL	71	3	25	28	48	....	....	....	....	....	....	....	....	....	16	0	1	1	16	....	....	....	....
2006-07	**Edmonton**	**NHL**	**77**	**3**	**7**	**10**	**37**	**0**	**0**	**0**	**53**	**5.7**	**–16**	**0**	**0.0**	**19:14**	....	....	....	....	....	....	....	....	....
2007-08	**Edmonton**	**NHL**	**65**	**0**	**4**	**4**	**58**	**0**	**0**	**0**	**45**	**0.0**	**–15**	**0**	**0.0**	**17:52**	....	....	....	....	....	....	....	....	....
	Springfield	AHL	8	1	4	5	15	....	....	....	....	....	....	....	....	....	....	....	....	....	....	....	....	....	....
	NHL Totals		**142**	**3**	**11**	**14**	**95**	**0**	**0**	**0**	**98**	**3.1**		**0**	**0.0**	**18:36**	....	....	....	....	....	....	....	....	....

Traded to **Edmonton** by **Anaheim** with Joffrey Lupul, Anaheim's 1st round choice (later traded to Phoenix - Phoenix selected Nick Ross) in 2007 Entry Draft and Anaheim's 1st (Jordan Eberle) and 2nd (later traded to NY Islanders - NY Islanders selected Travis Hamonic) round choices in 2008 Entry Draft for Chris Pronger, July 3, 2006.

SMITH, Dan (SMIHTH, DAN)

Defense. Shoots left. 6'2", 200 lbs. Born, Fernie, B.C., October 19, 1976. Colorado's 7th choice, 181st overall, in 1995 Entry Draft.

Season	Club	League	GP	G	A	Pts	PIM	PP	SH	GW	S	%	+/-	TF	F%	Min	GP	G	A	Pts	PIM	PP	SH	GW	Min
1994-95	U.B.C.	CWUAA	28	1	3	4	26	....	....	....	....	....	....	....	....	....	....	....	....	....	....	....	....	....	....
1995-96	Tri-City	WHL	58	1	21	22	70	....	....	....	....	....	....	....	....	....	11	1	3	4	14	....	....	....	....
1996-97	Tri-City	WHL	72	5	19	24	174	....	....	....	....	....	....	....	....	....	....	....	....	....	....	....	....	....	....
	Hershey Bears	AHL	8	0	1	1	6	....	....	....	....	....	....	....	....	....	15	0	1	1	25	....	....	....	....
1997-98	Hershey Bears	AHL	50	1	2	3	71	....	....	....	....	....	....	....	....	....	6	0	0	0	4	....	....	....	....
1998-99	**Colorado**	**NHL**	**12**	**0**	**0**	**0**	**9**	**0**	**0**	**0**	**6**	**0.0**	**5**	**0**	**0.0**	**12:14**	....	....	....	....	....	....	....	....	....
	Hershey Bears	AHL	54	5	7	12	72	....	....	....	....	....	....	....	....	....	5	0	1	1	0	....	....	....	....
99-2000	**Colorado**	**NHL**	**3**	**0**	**0**	**0**	**0**	**0**	**0**	**0**	**0**	**0.0**	**2**	**0**	**0.0**	**11:03**	....	....	....	....	....	....	....	....	....
	Hershey Bears	AHL	49	7	15	22	56	....	....	....	....	....	....	....	....	....	....	....	....	....	....	....	....	....	....
2000-01	Hershey Bears	AHL	58	2	12	14	34	....	....	....	....	....	....	....	....	....	12	0	1	1	4	....	....	....	....
2001-02	Colorado	WCHL	12	0	2	2	16	....	....	....	....	....	....	....	....	....	....	....	....	....	....	....	....	....	....
	Lukko Rauma	Finland	32	1	2	3	18	....	....	....	....	....	....	....	....	....	....	....	....	....	....	....	....	....	....
2002-03	Springfield	AHL	69	1	14	15	53	....	....	....	....	....	....	....	....	....	6	0	2	2	0	....	....	....	....
2003-04	Toronto	AHL	66	4	9	13	41	....	....	....	....	....	....	....	....	....	....	....	....	....	....	....	....	....	....
2004-05	Edmonton	AHL	72	5	10	15	72	....	....	....	....	....	....	....	....	....	....	....	....	....	....	....	....	....	....
2005-06	**Edmonton**	**NHL**	**7**	**0**	**0**	**0**	**7**	**0**	**0**	**0**	**1**	**0.0**	**1**	**0**	**0.0**	**11:21**	....	....	....	....	....	....	....	....	....
	Hamilton	AHL	69	0	15	15	61	....	....	....	....	....	....	....	....	....	....	....	....	....	....	....	....	....	....
2006-07	Grand Rapids	AHL	80	1	10	11	97	....	....	....	....	....	....	....	....	....	7	0	1	1	8	....	....	....	....
2007-08	Syracuse Crunch	AHL	77	1	6	7	73	....	....	....	....	....	....	....	....	....	10	0	1	1	17	....	....	....	....
	NHL Totals		**22**	**0**	**0**	**0**	**16**	**0**	**0**	**0**	**7**	**0.0**		**0**	**0.0**	**11:47**	....	....	....	....	....	....	....	....	....

Signed as a free agent by **Colorado** (WCHL), October 26, 2001. Signed as a free agent by **Rauma** (Finland) after receiving release from Colorado (WCHL), November 21, 2001. Signed as a free agent by **Edmonton**, August 21, 2003. Signed as a free agent by **Detroit**, July 13, 2006. Signed as a free agent by **Columbus**, July 11, 2007.

SMITH, Jason (SMIHTH, JAY-suhn) OTT.

Defense. Shoots right. 6'3", 215 lbs. Born, Calgary, Alta., November 2, 1973. New Jersey's 1st choice, 18th overall, in 1992 Entry Draft.

Season	Club	League	GP	G	A	Pts	PIM	PP	SH	GW	S	%	+/-	TF	F%	Min	GP	G	A	Pts	PIM	PP	SH	GW	Min
1990-91	Calgary Canucks	AJHL	45	3	15	18	69	....	....	....	....	....	....	....	....	....	....	....	....	....	....	....	....	....	....
	Regina Pats	WHL	2	0	0	0	7	....	....	....	....	....	....	....	....	....	4	0	0	0	2	....	....	....	....
1991-92	Regina Pats	WHL	62	9	29	38	138	....	....	....	....	....	....	....	....	....	....	....	....	....	....	....	....	....	....
1992-93	Regina Pats	WHL	64	14	52	66	175	....	....	....	....	....	....	....	....	....	13	4	8	12	39	....	....	....	....
	Utica Devils	AHL	....	....	....	....	....	....	....	....	....	....	....	....	....	....	1	0	0	0	2	....	....	....	....
1993-94	**New Jersey**	**NHL**	**41**	**0**	**5**	**5**	**43**	**0**	**0**	**0**	**47**	**0.0**	**7**	....	....	....	**6**	**0**	**0**	**0**	**7**	**0**	**0**	**0**	....
	Albany River Rats	AHL	20	6	3	9	31	....	....	....	....	....	....	....	....	....	....	....	....	....	....	....	....	....	....
1994-95	Albany River Rats	AHL	7	0	2	2	15	....	....	....	....	....	....	....	....	....	11	2	2	4	19	....	....	....	....
	New Jersey	**NHL**	**2**	**0**	**0**	**0**	**0**	**0**	**0**	**0**	**5**	**0.0**	**–3**	....	....	....	....	....	....	....	....	....	....	....	....
1995-96	**New Jersey**	**NHL**	**64**	**2**	**1**	**3**	**86**	**0**	**0**	**0**	**52**	**3.8**	**5**	....	....	....	....	....	....	....	....	....	....	....	....
1996-97	**New Jersey**	**NHL**	**57**	**1**	**2**	**3**	**38**	**0**	**0**	**0**	**48**	**2.1**	**–8**	....	....	....	....	....	....	....	....	....	....	....	....
	Toronto	**NHL**	**21**	**0**	**5**	**5**	**16**	**0**	**0**	**0**	**26**	**0.0**	**–4**	....	....	....	....	....	....	....	....	....	....	....	....
1997-98	**Toronto**	**NHL**	**81**	**3**	**13**	**16**	**100**	**0**	**0**	**0**	**97**	**3.1**	**–5**	....	....	....	....	....	....	....	....	....	....	....	....
1998-99	**Toronto**	**NHL**	**60**	**2**	**11**	**13**	**40**	**0**	**0**	**0**	**53**	**3.8**	**–9**	**0**	**0.0**	**17:31**	....	....	....	....	....	....	....	....	....
	Edmonton	**NHL**	**12**	**1**	**1**	**2**	**11**	**0**	**0**	**0**	**15**	**6.7**	**0**	**0**	**0.0**	**20:26**	**4**	**0**	**1**	**1**	**4**	**0**	**0**	**0**	**26:29**
99-2000	**Edmonton**	**NHL**	**80**	**3**	**11**	**14**	**60**	**0**	**0**	**1**	**96**	**3.1**	**16**	**1**	**100.0**	**21:15**	**5**	**0**	**1**	**1**	**4**	**0**	**0**	**0**	**21:56**
2000-01	**Edmonton**	**NHL**	**82**	**5**	**15**	**20**	**120**	**1**	**1**	**0**	**140**	**3.6**	**14**	**1**	**0.0**	**21:40**	**6**	**0**	**2**	**2**	**6**	**0**	**0**	**0**	**25:27**
2001-02	**Edmonton**	**NHL**	**74**	**5**	**13**	**18**	**103**	**0**	**1**	**1**	**85**	**5.9**	**14**	**0**	**0.0**	**21:00**	....	....	....	....	....	....	....	....	....
2002-03	**Edmonton**	**NHL**	**68**	**4**	**8**	**12**	**64**	**0**	**0**	**1**	**93**	**4.3**	**5**	**0**	**0.0**	**21:46**	**6**	**0**	**0**	**0**	**19**	**0**	**0**	**0**	**21:17**
2003-04	**Edmonton**	**NHL**	**68**	**7**	**12**	**19**	**98**	**0**	**1**	**1**	**84**	**8.3**	**13**	**2**	**50.0**	**21:22**	....	....	....	....	....	....	....	....	....
2004-05			DID NOT PLAY																						
2005-06	**Edmonton**	**NHL**	**76**	**4**	**13**	**17**	**84**	**0**	**0**	**0**	**79**	**5.1**	**1**	**0**	**0.0**	**19:39**	**24**	**1**	**4**	**5**	**16**	**0**	**0**	**1**	**22:29**
2006-07	**Edmonton**	**NHL**	**82**	**2**	**9**	**11**	**103**	**0**	**0**	**1**	**61**	**3.3**	**–13**	**1**	**0.0**	**21:08**	....	....	....	....	....	....	....	....	....
2007-08	**Philadelphia**	**NHL**	**77**	**1**	**9**	**10**	**86**	**0**	**0**	**0**	**58**	**1.7**	**–4**	**1**	**100.0**	**17:56**	**17**	**0**	**2**	**2**	**4**	**0**	**0**	**0**	**16:42**
	NHL Totals		**945**	**40**	**128**	**168**	**1052**	**1**	**3**	**5**	**1039**	**3.8**		**6**	**33.3**	**20:25**	**68**	**1**	**10**	**11**	**60**	**0**	**0**	**1**	**21:17**

WHL East First All-Star Team (1993) • Canadian Major Junior First All-Star Team (1993)

• Missed majority of 1994-95 season recovering from knee injury suffered in practice, November 5, 1994. Traded to **Toronto** by **New Jersey** with Steve Sullivan and the rights to Alyn McCauley for Doug Gilmour, Dave Ellett and New Jersey's 4th round choice (previously acquired, New Jersey selected Andre Lakos) in 1999 Entry Draft, February 25, 1997. Traded to **Edmonton** by **Toronto** for Edmonton's 4th round choice (Jonathon Zion) in 1999 Entry Draft and Edmonton's 2nd round choice (Kris Vernarsky) in 2000 Entry Draft, March 23, 1999. Traded to **Philadelphia** by **Edmonton** with Joffrey Lupul for Joni Pitkanen, Geoff Sanderson and Philadelphia's 3rd round choice in 2009 Entry Draft, July 1, 2007. Signed as a free agent by **Ottawa**, July 8, 2008.

SMITH, Mark (SMIHTH, MAHRK)

Center. Shoots left. 5'10", 200 lbs. Born, Edmonton, Alta., October 24, 1977. San Jose's 7th choice, 219th overall, in 1997 Entry Draft.

Season	Club	League	GP	G	A	Pts	PIM	PP	SH	GW	S	%	+/-	TF	F%	Min	GP	G	A	Pts	PIM	PP	SH	GW	Min
1993-94	Nipawin Hawks	SJHL	62	14	12	26	44	....	....	....	....	....	....	....	....	....	....	....	....	....	....	....	....	....	....
1994-95	Lethbridge	WHL	49	3	4	7	25	....	....	....	....	....	....	....	....	....	....	....	....	....	....	....	....	....	....
1995-96	Lethbridge	WHL	71	11	24	35	59	....	....	....	....	....	....	....	....	....	4	2	0	2	2	....	....	....	....
1996-97	Lethbridge	WHL	62	19	38	57	125	....	....	....	....	....	....	....	....	....	19	7	13	20	51	....	....	....	....
1997-98	Lethbridge	WHL	70	42	67	109	206	....	....	....	....	....	....	....	....	....	3	0	2	2	18	....	....	....	....
	Kentucky	AHL	2	0	0	0	0	....	....	....	....	....	....	....	....	....	....	....	....	....	....	....	....	....	....
1998-99	Kentucky	AHL	78	18	21	39	101	....	....	....	....	....	....	....	....	....	12	2	7	9	16	....	....	....	....
99-2000	Kentucky	AHL	79	21	45	66	153	....	....	....	....	....	....	....	....	....	9	0	5	5	22	....	....	....	....
2000-01	**San Jose**	**NHL**	**42**	**2**	**2**	**4**	**51**	**0**	**0**	**0**	**39**	**5.1**	**2**	**308**	**52.9**	**8:48**	....	....	....	....	....	....	....	....	....
	Kentucky	AHL	6	2	6	8	23	....	....	....	....	....	....	....	....	....	....	....	....	....	....	....	....	....	....

			Regular Season														Playoffs								
Season	Club	League	GP	G	A	Pts	PIM	PP	SH	GW	S	%	+/-	TF	F%	Min	GP	G	A	Pts	PIM	PP	SH	GW	Min
2001-02	**San Jose**	**NHL**	**49**	**3**	**3**	**6**	**72**	**0**	**0**	**1**	**40**	**7.5**	**-1**	**368**	**54.1**	**8:03**	....	....	....	....	....	....	....	....	....
2002-03	**San Jose**	**NHL**	**75**	**4**	**11**	**15**	**64**	**0**	**0**	**0**	**68**	**5.9**	**1**	**632**	**57.0**	**9:21**	....	....	....	....	....	....	....	....	....
2003-04	**San Jose**	**NHL**	**36**	**1**	**3**	**4**	**72**	**0**	**0**	**0**	**31**	**3.2**	**-5**	**207**	**50.2**	**8:22**	**10**	**1**	**0**	**1**	**11**	**0**	**0**	**1**	**7:44**
2004-05	Victoria	ECHL	20	6	9	15	41	....	....	....	....	....	....	....	....	....	....	....	....	....	....	....	....	....	....
2005-06	**San Jose**	**NHL**	**80**	**9**	**15**	**24**	**97**	**2**	**1**	**1**	**100**	**9.0**	**3**	**514**	**52.0**	**12:03**	**11**	**3**	**0**	**3**	**6**	**1**	**0**	**0**	**13:21**
2006-07	**San Jose**	**NHL**	**41**	**3**	**10**	**13**	**42**	**2**	**0**	**0**	**38**	**7.9**	**-4**	**79**	**59.5**	**10:25**	**3**	**0**	**0**	**0**	**4**	**0**	**0**	**0**	**8:28**
2007-08	**Calgary**	**NHL**	**54**	**1**	**3**	**4**	**59**	**0**	**0**	**0**	**27**	**3.7**	**-6**	**57**	**54.4**	**5:56**	....	....	....	....	....	....	....	....	....
	NHL Totals		**377**	**23**	**47**	**70**	**457**	**4**	**1**	**2**	**343**	**6.7**		**2165**	**54.1**	**9:13**	**24**	**4**	**0**	**4**	**21**	**1**	**0**	**1**	**10:24**

WHL East Second All-Star Team (1998)

• Missed majority of 2003-04 season as a healthy reserve. Signed as a free agent by **Victoria** (ECHL), January 21, 2005. Signed as a free agent by **Calgary**, September 29, 2007.

SMITH, Nathan (SMIHTH, NAY-thun) COL.

Center. Shoots left. 6'2", 206 lbs. Born, Edmonton, Alta., February 9, 1982. Vancouver's 1st choice, 23rd overall, in 2000 Entry Draft.

Season	Club	League	GP	G	A	Pts	PIM	PP	SH	GW	S	%	+/-	TF	F%	Min	GP	G	A	Pts	PIM	PP	SH	GW	Min
1997-98	Sherwood Park	AMHL	35	15	13	28	24	....	....	....	....	....	....	....	....	....	....	....	....	....	....	....	....	....	....
1998-99	Swift Current	WHL	47	5	8	13	26	....	....	....	....	....	....	....	....	....	....	....	....	....	....	....	....	....	....
99-2000	Swift Current	WHL	70	21	28	49	72	....	....	....	....	....	....	....	....	....	12	1	6	7	4	....	....	....	....
2000-01	Swift Current	WHL	67	28	62	90	78	....	....	....	....	....	....	....	....	....	19	4	3	7	20	....	....	....	....
2001-02	Swift Current	WHL	47	22	38	60	52	....	....	....	....	....	....	....	....	....	12	3	6	9	18	....	....	....	....
2002-03	Manitoba Moose	AHL	53	9	8	17	30	....	....	....	....	....	....	....	....	....	14	1	3	4	25	....	....	....	....
2003-04	**Vancouver**	**NHL**	**2**	**0**	**0**	**0**	**0**	**0**	**0**	**0**	**1**	**0.0**	**-1**	**12**	**33.3**	**5:16**	....	....	....	....	....	....	....	....	....
	Manitoba Moose	AHL	76	4	16	20	71	....	....	....	....	....	....	....	....	....	....	....	....	....	....	....	....	....	....
2004-05	Manitoba Moose	AHL	72	7	9	16	67	....	....	....	....	....	....	....	....	....	14	2	4	6	20	....	....	....	....
2005-06	**Vancouver**	**NHL**	**1**	**0**	**0**	**0**	**0**	**0**	**0**	**0**	**2**	**0.0**	**0**	**9**	**33.3**	**10:52**	....	....	....	....	....	....	....	....	....
	Manitoba Moose	AHL	20	5	4	9	57	....	....	....	....	....	....	....	....	....	....	....	....	....	....	....	....	....	....
2006-07	**Vancouver**	**NHL**	**1**	**0**	**0**	**0**	**0**	**0**	**0**	**0**	**0**	**0.0**	**0**	**9**	**66.7**	**8:45**	**4**	**0**	**0**	**0**	**0**	**0**	**0**	**0**	**6:57**
	Manitoba Moose	AHL	72	19	21	40	76	....	....	....	....	....	....	....	....	....	6	0	1	1	12	....	....	....	....
2007-08	**Pittsburgh**	**NHL**	**13**	**0**	**0**	**0**	**2**	**0**	**0**	**0**	**3**	**0.0**	**0**	**75**	**53.3**	**7:41**	....	....	....	....	....	....	....	....	....
	Wilkes-Barre	AHL	68	22	28	50	61	....	....	....	....	....	....	....	....	....	22	7	11	18	40	....	....	....	....
	NHL Totals		**17**	**0**	**0**	**0**	**2**	**0**	**0**	**0**	**6**	**0.0**		**105**	**50.5**	**7:39**	**4**	**0**	**0**	**0**	**0**	**0**	**0**	**0**	**6:57**

• Missed remainder of 2005-06 season recovering from knee injury suffered in game vs. Cleveland (AHL), November 27, 2005. Signed as a free agent by **Pittsburgh**, July 12, 2007. Signed as a free agent by **Colorado**, July 14, 2008.

SMITH, Wyatt (SMIHTH, WIGH-uht) T.B.

Center. Shoots left. 5'11", 205 lbs. Born, Thief River Falls, MN, February 13, 1977. Phoenix's 6th choice, 233rd overall, in 1997 Entry Draft.

Season	Club	League	GP	G	A	Pts	PIM	PP	SH	GW	S	%	+/-	TF	F%	Min	GP	G	A	Pts	PIM	PP	SH	GW	Min
1994-95	Warroad Warriors	High-MN	28	29	31	60	28	....	....	....	....	....	....	....	....	....	....	....	....	....	....	....	....	....	....
1995-96	U. of Minnesota	WCHA	32	4	5	9	32	....	....	....	....	....	....	....	....	....	....	....	....	....	....	....	....	....	....
1996-97	U. of Minnesota	WCHA	38	16	14	30	44	....	....	....	....	....	....	....	....	....	....	....	....	....	....	....	....	....	....
1997-98	U. of Minnesota	WCHA	39	24	23	47	62	....	....	....	....	....	....	....	....	....	....	....	....	....	....	....	....	....	....
1998-99	U. of Minnesota	WCHA	43	23	20	43	37	....	....	....	....	....	....	....	....	....	....	....	....	....	....	....	....	....	....
99-2000	**Phoenix**	**NHL**	**2**	**0**	**0**	**0**	**0**	**0**	**0**	**0**	**0**	**0.0**	**-2**	**20**	**30.0**	**11:39**	....	....	....	....	....	....	....	....	....
	Springfield	AHL	60	14	26	40	26	....	....	....	....	....	....	....	....	....	5	2	3	5	13	....	....	....	....
2000-01	**Phoenix**	**NHL**	**42**	**3**	**7**	**10**	**13**	**0**	**1**	**0**	**40**	**7.5**	**7**	**335**	**40.9**	**12:20**	....	....	....	....	....	....	....	....	....
	Springfield	AHL	18	5	7	12	11	....	....	....	....	....	....	....	....	....	....	....	....	....	....	....	....	....	....
2001-02	**Phoenix**	**NHL**	**10**	**0**	**0**	**0**	**0**	**0**	**0**	**0**	**4**	**0.0**	**-5**	**81**	**48.2**	**10:36**	....	....	....	....	....	....	....	....	....
	Springfield	AHL	69	23	32	55	69	....	....	....	....	....	....	....	....	....	....	....	....	....	....	....	....	....	....
2002-03	**Nashville**	**NHL**	**11**	**1**	**0**	**1**	**0**	**0**	**0**	**0**	**8**	**12.5**	**-1**	**123**	**49.6**	**11:56**	....	....	....	....	....	....	....	....	....
	Milwaukee	AHL	56	24	27	51	89	....	....	....	....	....	....	....	....	....	4	1	0	1	2	....	....	....	....
2003-04	**Nashville**	**NHL**	**18**	**3**	**1**	**4**	**2**	**0**	**1**	**0**	**21**	**14.3**	**2**	**193**	**57.0**	**10:22**	....	....	....	....	....	....	....	....	....
	Milwaukee	AHL	40	9	7	16	40	....	....	....	....	....	....	....	....	....	22	5	7	12	25	....	....	....	....
2004-05	Milwaukee	AHL	69	19	28	47	89	....	....	....	....	....	....	....	....	....	7	1	4	5	10	....	....	....	....
2005-06	**NY Islanders**	**NHL**	**42**	**0**	**8**	**8**	**26**	**0**	**0**	**0**	**37**	**0.0**	**-7**	**384**	**48.4**	**11:14**	....	....	....	....	....	....	....	....	....
	Bridgeport	AHL	39	13	16	29	40	....	....	....	....	....	....	....	....	....	....	....	....	....	....	....	....	....	....
2006-07	**Minnesota**	**NHL**	**61**	**3**	**3**	**6**	**16**	**1**	**0**	**0**	**44**	**6.8**	**-8**	**508**	**43.5**	**9:31**	**4**	**0**	**0**	**0**	**0**	**0**	**0**	**0**	**11:02**
	Houston Aeros	AHL	12	4	3	7	12	....	....	....	....	....	....	....	....	....	....	....	....	....	....	....	....	....	....
2007-08	**Colorado**	**NHL**	**25**	**0**	**3**	**3**	**8**	**0**	**0**	**0**	**25**	**0.0**	**-4**	**108**	**50.9**	**11:38**	**1**	**0**	**0**	**0**	**0**	**0**	**0**	**0**	**10:47**
	Lake Erie	AHL	40	17	18	35	34	....	....	....	....	....	....	....	....	....	....	....	....	....	....	....	....	....	....
	NHL Totals		**211**	**10**	**22**	**32**	**65**	**1**	**2**	**0**	**179**	**5.6**		**1752**	**46.5**	**10:56**	**5**	**0**	**0**	**0**	**0**	**0**	**0**	**0**	**10:59**

Signed as a free agent by **Nashville**, July 15, 2002. Signed as a free agent by **NY Islanders**, August 10, 2005. Signed as a free agent by **Minnesota**, July 19, 2006. Signed as a free agent by **Colorado** , August 20, 2007. Signed as a free agent by **Tampa Bay**, July 3, 2008.

SMITHSON, Jerred (SMIHTH-suhn, JEHR-rehd) NSH.

Center. Shoots right. 6'3", 194 lbs. Born, Vernon, B.C., February 4, 1979.

Season	Club	League	GP	G	A	Pts	PIM	PP	SH	GW	S	%	+/-	TF	F%	Min	GP	G	A	Pts	PIM	PP	SH	GW	Min
1994-95	Vernon	Minor-BC	64	39	46	85	120	....	....	....	....	....	....	....	....	....	....	....	....	....	....	....	....	....	....
1995-96	Calgary Hitmen	WHL	60	4	2	6	16	....	....	....	....	....	....	....	....	....	....	....	....	....	....	....	....	....	....
1996-97	Calgary Hitmen	WHL	65	3	6	9	49	....	....	....	....	....	....	....	....	....	....	....	....	....	....	....	....	....	....
1997-98	Calgary Hitmen	WHL	65	12	9	21	65	....	....	....	....	....	....	....	....	....	18	0	2	2	25	....	....	....	....
1998-99	Calgary Hitmen	WHL	63	14	22	36	108	....	....	....	....	....	....	....	....	....	21	3	7	10	17	....	....	....	....
99-2000	Calgary Hitmen	WHL	66	14	25	39	111	....	....	....	....	....	....	....	....	....	10	1	1	2	16	....	....	....	....
2000-01	Lowell	AHL	24	1	1	2	10	....	....	....	....	....	....	....	....	....	4	0	0	0	2	....	....	....	....
	Trenton Titans	ECHL	3	0	1	1	2	....	....	....	....	....	....	....	....	....	....	....	....	....	....	....	....	....	....
2001-02	Manchester	AHL	78	5	13	18	45	....	....	....	....	....	....	....	....	....	5	0	1	1	4	....	....	....	....
2002-03	**Los Angeles**	**NHL**	**22**	**0**	**2**	**2**	**21**	**0**	**0**	**0**	**9**	**0.0**	**-5**	**175**	**48.0**	**8:50**	....	....	....	....	....	....	....	....	....
	Manchester	AHL	38	4	21	25	60	....	....	....	....	....	....	....	....	....	3	0	0	0	4	....	....	....	....
2003-04	**Los Angeles**	**NHL**	**8**	**0**	**1**	**1**	**4**	**0**	**0**	**0**	**2**	**0.0**	**0**	**86**	**64.0**	**10:39**	....	....	....	....	....	....	....	....	....
	Manchester	AHL	66	7	13	20	51	....	....	....	....	....	....	....	....	....	6	0	1	1	10	....	....	....	....
2004-05	Milwaukee	AHL	80	11	11	22	92	....	....	....	....	....	....	....	....	....	5	0	0	0	4	....	....	....	....
2005-06	**Nashville**	**NHL**	**66**	**5**	**9**	**14**	**54**	**0**	**0**	**1**	**50**	**10.0**	**9**	**613**	**54.3**	**11:50**	**3**	**0**	**0**	**0**	**4**	**0**	**0**	**0**	**9:26**
	Milwaukee	AHL	8	0	0	0	12	....	....	....	....	....	....	....	....	....	....	....	....	....	....	....	....	....	....
2006-07	**Nashville**	**NHL**	**64**	**5**	**7**	**12**	**42**	**1**	**1**	**2**	**47**	**10.6**	**-8**	**420**	**56.4**	**11:03**	**5**	**0**	**0**	**0**	**17**	**0**	**0**	**0**	**11:30**
2007-08	**Nashville**	**NHL**	**81**	**7**	**9**	**16**	**50**	**0**	**2**	**2**	**61**	**11.5**	**-9**	**572**	**52.1**	**12:05**	**6**	**0**	**0**	**0**	**2**	**0**	**0**	**0**	**11:52**
	NHL Totals		**241**	**17**	**28**	**45**	**171**	**1**	**3**	**5**	**169**	**10.1**		**1866**	**54.0**	**11:24**	**14**	**0**	**0**	**0**	**23**	**0**	**0**	**0**	**11:13**

Signed as a free agent by **Los Angeles**, February 18, 2000. Signed as a free agent by **Nashville**, July 22, 2004.

SMOLINSKI, Bryan (smoh-LIHN-skee, BRIGH-uhn)

Center. Shoots right. 6'1", 203 lbs. Born, Toledo, OH, December 27, 1971. Boston's 1st choice, 21st overall, in 1990 Entry Draft.

Season	Club	League	GP	G	A	Pts	PIM	PP	SH	GW	S	%	+/-	TF	F%	Min	GP	G	A	Pts	PIM	PP	SH	GW	Min
1987-88	Det. Caesars	MNHL	80	43	77	120	....	....	....	....	....	....	....	....	....	....	....	....	....	....	....	....	....	....	....
1988-89	Stratford Cullitons	OHA-B	46	32	62	94	132	....	....	....	....	....	....	....	....	....	....	....	....	....	....	....	....	....	....
1989-90	Michigan State	CCHA	35	9	13	22	34	....	....	....	....	....	....	....	....	....	....	....	....	....	....	....	....	....	....
1990-91	Michigan State	CCHA	35	9	12	21	24	....	....	....	....	....	....	....	....	....	....	....	....	....	....	....	....	....	....
1991-92	Michigan State	CCHA	41	28	33	61	55	....	....	....	....	....	....	....	....	....	....	....	....	....	....	....	....	....	....
1992-93	Michigan State	CCHA	40	31	37	*68	93	....	....	....	....	....	....	....	....	....	....	....	....	....	....	....	....	....	....
	Boston	**NHL**	**9**	**1**	**3**	**4**	**0**	**0**	**0**	**0**	**10**	**10.0**	**3**	....	....	....	**4**	**1**	**0**	**1**	**2**	**0**	**0**	**0**	....
1993-94	**Boston**	**NHL**	**83**	**31**	**20**	**51**	**82**	**4**	**3**	**5**	**179**	**17.3**	**4**	....	....	....	**13**	**5**	**4**	**9**	**4**	**2**	**0**	**0**	....
1994-95	**Boston**	**NHL**	**44**	**18**	**13**	**31**	**31**	**6**	**0**	**5**	**121**	**14.9**	**-3**	....	....	....	**5**	**0**	**1**	**1**	**4**	**0**	**0**	**0**	....
1995-96	**Pittsburgh**	**NHL**	**81**	**24**	**40**	**64**	**69**	**8**	**2**	**1**	**229**	**10.5**	**6**	....	....	....	**18**	**5**	**4**	**9**	**10**	**0**	**0**	**1**	....
1996-97	Detroit Vipers	IHL	6	5	7	12	10	....	....	....	....	....	....	....	....	....	....	....	....	....	....	....	....	....	....
	NY Islanders	**NHL**	**64**	**28**	**28**	**56**	**25**	**9**	**0**	**1**	**183**	**15.3**	**9**	....	....	....	....	....	....	....	....	....	....	....	....
1997-98	**NY Islanders**	**NHL**	**81**	**13**	**30**	**43**	**34**	**3**	**0**	**4**	**203**	**6.4**	**-16**	....	....	....	....	....	....	....	....	....	....	....	....
1998-99	**NY Islanders**	**NHL**	**82**	**16**	**24**	**40**	**49**	**7**	**0**	**3**	**223**	**7.2**	**-7**	**1011**	**48.3**	**19:19**	....	....	....	....	....	....	....	....	....
99-2000	**Los Angeles**	**NHL**	**79**	**20**	**36**	**56**	**48**	**2**	**0**	**0**	**160**	**12.5**	**2**	**1545**	**50.9**	**18:35**	**4**	**0**	**0**	**0**	**2**	**0**	**0**	**0**	**18:22**
2000-01	**Los Angeles**	**NHL**	**78**	**27**	**32**	**59**	**40**	**5**	**3**	**5**	**183**	**14.8**	**10**	**952**	**48.7**	**18:32**	**13**	**1**	**5**	**6**	**14**	**0**	**0**	**0**	**20:35**
2001-02	**Los Angeles**	**NHL**	**80**	**13**	**25**	**38**	**56**	**4**	**1**	**0**	**187**	**7.0**	**7**	**1316**	**45.7**	**19:23**	**7**	**2**	**0**	**2**	**2**	**1**	**0**	**0**	**18:15**
2002-03	**Los Angeles**	**NHL**	**58**	**18**	**20**	**38**	**18**	**6**	**1**	**8**	**150**	**12.0**	**-1**	**831**	**46.3**	**19:02**	....	....	....	....	....	....	....	....	....
	Ottawa	**NHL**	**10**	**3**	**5**	**8**	**2**	**0**	**0**	**0**	**26**	**11.5**	**1**	**127**	**46.5**	**15:42**	**18**	**2**	**7**	**9**	**6**	**0**	**0**	**0**	**15:21**
2003-04	**Ottawa**	**NHL**	**80**	**19**	**27**	**46**	**49**	**4**	**0**	**3**	**182**	**10.4**	**22**	**880**	**44.7**	**16:39**	**7**	**1**	**1**	**2**	**4**	**0**	**0**	**0**	**16:04**
2004-05	Motor City	UHL	21	9	23	32	18	....	....	....	....	....	....	....	....	....	....	....	....	....	....	....	....	....	....

			Regular Season														Playoffs								
Season	Club	League	GP	G	A	Pts	PIM	PP	SH	GW	S	%	+/-	TF	F%	Min	GP	G	A	Pts	PIM	PP	SH	GW	Min
2005-06	**Ottawa**	**NHL**	**81**	**17**	**31**	**48**	**46**	**4**	**0**	**5**	**178**	**9.6**	**8**	**1039**	**49.8**	**14:48**	**10**	**3**	**3**	**6**	**2**	**1**	**0**	**0**	**12:34**
2006-07	**Chicago**	**NHL**	**62**	**14**	**23**	**37**	**29**	**4**	**3**	**3**	**122**	**11.5**	**10**	**911**	**51.0**	**18:36**	....	....	....	....	....	....	....	....	....
	Vancouver	**NHL**	**20**	**4**	**3**	**7**	**8**	**2**	**1**	**0**	**41**	**9.8**	**–3**	**301**	**48.5**	**16:06**	**12**	**2**	**2**	**4**	**8**	**0**	**0**	**0**	**18:39**
2007-08	**Montreal**	**NHL**	**64**	**8**	**17**	**25**	**20**	**1**	**0**	**2**	**89**	**9.0**	**–6**	**738**	**51.8**	**13:08**	**12**	**1**	**2**	**3**	**2**	**0**	**0**	**0**	**14:32**
	NHL Totals		**1056**	**274**	**377**	**651**	**606**	**69**	**14**	**45**	**2466**	**11.1**		**9651**	**48.6**	**17:31**	**123**	**23**	**29**	**52**	**60**	**4**	**0**	**1**	**16:39**

CCHA First All-Star Team (1993) • NCAA West First All-American Team (1993)

Traded to **Pittsburgh** by **Boston** with Glen Murray and Boston's 3rd round choice (Boyd Kane) in 1996 Entry Draft for Kevin Stevens and Shawn McEachern, August 2, 1995. Traded to **NY Islanders** by **Pittsburgh** for Darius Kasparaitis and Andreas Johansson, November 17, 1996. Traded to **Los Angeles** by **NY Islanders** with Ziggy Palffy, Marcel Cousineau and New Jersey's 4th round choice (previously acquired, Los Angeles selected Daniel Johansson) in 1999 Entry Draft for Olli Jokinen, Josh Green, Mathieu Biron and Los Angeles' 1st round choice (Taylor Pyatt) in 1999 Entry Draft, June 20, 1999. Traded to **Ottawa** by **Los Angeles** for the rights to Tim Gleason, March 11, 2003. Signed as a free agent by **Motor City** (UHL), February 11, 2005. Traded to **Chicago** by **Ottawa** with Martin Havlat for Tom Preissing, Josh Hennessy, Michal Barinka and Chicago's 2nd round choice (Patrick Wiercioch) 2008 Entry Draft, July 10, 2006. Traded to **Vancouver** by **Chicago** for Vancouver's 2nd round choice (Akim Aliu) in 2007 Entry Draft, February 26, 2007. Signed as a free agent by **Montreal**, July 2, 2007.

SMYTH, Ryan

(SMIHTH, RIGH-uhn) **COL.**

Left wing. Shoots left. 6'1", 190 lbs. Born, Banff, Alta., February 21, 1976. Edmonton's 2nd choice, 6th overall, in 1994 Entry Draft.

Season	Club	League	GP	G	A	Pts	PIM	PP	SH	GW	S	%	+/-	TF	F%	Min	GP	G	A	Pts	PIM	PP	SH	GW	Min
1990-91	Banff Blazers	ABHL	25	100	50	150	....	....	....	....	....	....	....	....	....	....	....	....	....	....	....	....	....	....	....
	Lethbridge	AMHL	34	8	21	29	....	....	....	....	....	....	....	....	....	....	....	....	....	....	....	....	....	....	....
1991-92	Caronport	SMHL	35	55	61	116	98	....	....	....	....	....	....	....	....	....	....	....	....	....	....	....	....	....	....
	Moose Jaw	WHL	2	0	0	0	0	....	....	....	....	....	....	....	....	....	....	....	....	....	....	....	....	....	....
1992-93	Moose Jaw	WHL	64	19	14	33	59	....	....	....	....	....	....	....	....	....	....	....	....	....	....	....	....	....	....
1993-94	Moose Jaw	WHL	72	50	55	105	88	....	....	....	....	....	....	....	....	....	....	....	....	....	....	....	....	....	....
1994-95	Moose Jaw	WHL	50	41	45	86	66	....	....	....	....	....	....	....	....	....	10	6	9	15	22	....	....	....	....
	Edmonton	**NHL**	**3**	**0**	**0**	**0**	**0**	**0**	**0**	**0**	**2**	**0.0**	**–1**	....	....	....	....	....	....	....	....	....	....	....	....
1995-96	**Edmonton**	**NHL**	**48**	**2**	**9**	**11**	**28**	**1**	**0**	**0**	**65**	**3.1**	**–10**	....	....	....	....	....	....	....	....	....	....	....	....
	Cape Breton	AHL	9	6	5	11	4	....	....	....	....	....	....	....	....	....	....	....	....	....	....	....	....	....	....
1996-97	**Edmonton**	**NHL**	**82**	**39**	**22**	**61**	**76**	**20**	**0**	**4**	**265**	**14.7**	**–7**	....	....	....	**12**	**5**	**5**	**10**	**12**	**1**	**0**	**2**	....
1997-98	**Edmonton**	**NHL**	**65**	**20**	**13**	**33**	**44**	**10**	**0**	**2**	**205**	**9.8**	**–24**	....	....	....	**12**	**1**	**3**	**4**	**16**	**1**	**0**	**0**	....
1998-99	**Edmonton**	**NHL**	**71**	**13**	**18**	**31**	**62**	**6**	**0**	**2**	**161**	**8.1**	**0**	**5**	**20.0**	**14:26**	**3**	**3**	**0**	**3**	**0**	**2**	**0**	**0**	**24:35**
99-2000	**Edmonton**	**NHL**	**82**	**28**	**26**	**54**	**58**	**11**	**0**	**4**	**238**	**11.8**	**–2**	**24**	**54.2**	**19:12**	**5**	**1**	**0**	**1**	**6**	**0**	**1**	**0**	**19:18**
2000-01	**Edmonton**	**NHL**	**82**	**31**	**39**	**70**	**58**	**11**	**0**	**6**	**245**	**12.7**	**10**	**17**	**35.3**	**19:58**	**6**	**3**	**4**	**7**	**4**	**0**	**0**	**0**	**24:46**
2001-02	**Edmonton**	**NHL**	**61**	**15**	**35**	**50**	**48**	**7**	**1**	**5**	**150**	**10.0**	**7**	**12**	**41.7**	**19:27**	....	....	....	....	....	....	....	....	....
	Canada	Olympics	6	0	1	1	0	....	....	....	....	....	....	....	....	....	....	....	....	....	....	....	....	....	....
2002-03	**Edmonton**	**NHL**	**66**	**27**	**34**	**61**	**67**	**10**	**0**	**3**	**199**	**13.6**	**5**	**42**	**42.9**	**19:21**	**6**	**2**	**0**	**2**	**16**	**0**	**1**	**0**	**17:39**
2003-04	**Edmonton**	**NHL**	**82**	**23**	**36**	**59**	**70**	**8**	**2**	**6**	**245**	**9.4**	**11**	**484**	**47.1**	**19:39**	....	....	....	....	....	....	....	....	....
2004-05				DID NOT PLAY																					
2005-06	**Edmonton**	**NHL**	**75**	**36**	**30**	**66**	**58**	**19**	**2**	**3**	**230**	**15.7**	**–5**	**159**	**47.8**	**20:13**	**24**	**7**	**9**	**16**	**22**	**4**	**0**	**1**	**21:27**
	Canada	Olympics	6	0	1	1	4	....	....	....	....	....	....	....	....	....	....	....	....	....	....	....	....	....	....
2006-07	**Edmonton**	**NHL**	**53**	**31**	**22**	**53**	**38**	**14**	**1**	**5**	**161**	**19.3**	**2**	**63**	**47.6**	**20:09**	....	....	....	....	....	....	....	....	....
	NY Islanders	**NHL**	**18**	**5**	**10**	**15**	**14**	**1**	**0**	**0**	**49**	**10.2**	**0**	**9**	**22.2**	**22:26**	**5**	**1**	**3**	**4**	**4**	**0**	**0**	**0**	**22:42**
2007-08	**Colorado**	**NHL**	**55**	**14**	**23**	**37**	**50**	**2**	**0**	**3**	**168**	**8.3**	**–4**	**33**	**39.4**	**19:37**	**8**	**2**	**3**	**5**	**2**	**1**	**0**	**1**	**17:29**
	NHL Totals		**843**	**284**	**317**	**601**	**671**	**120**	**6**	**43**	**2383**	**11.9**		**848**	**46.2**	**19:11**	**81**	**25**	**27**	**52**	**82**	**9**	**2**	**4**	**20:56**

WHL East Second All-Star Team (1995)

Played in NHL All-Star Game (2007)

Traded to **NY Islanders** by **Edmonton** for Ryan O'Marra, Robert Nilsson and NY Islanders' 1st round choice (Alex Plante) in 2007 Entry Draft, February 27, 2007. Signed as a free agent by **Colorado**, July 1, 2007.

SOBOTKA, Vladimir

(soh-BAWT-kah, vla-DIH-meer) **BOS.**

Center. Shoots left. 5'11", 193 lbs. Born, Trebic, Czech., July 2, 1987. Boston's 5th choice, 106th overall, in 2005 Entry Draft.

Season	Club	League	GP	G	A	Pts	PIM	PP	SH	GW	S	%	+/-	TF	F%	Min	GP	G	A	Pts	PIM	PP	SH	GW	Min
2002-03	Slavia U17	CzR-U17	46	16	24	40	48	....	....	....	....	....	....	....	....	....	8	1	1	2	29	....	....	....	....
2003-04	Slavia U17	CzR-U17	35	24	41	65	109	....	....	....	....	....	....	....	....	....	7	7	12	19	8	....	....	....	....
	Slavia Jr.	CzRep-Jr.	18	6	6	12	16	....	....	....	....	....	....	....	....	....	....	....	....	....	....	....	....	....	....
	HC Slavia Praha	CzRep	1	0	0	0	0	....	....	....	....	....	....	....	....	....	....	....	....	....	....	....	....	....	....
2004-05	Slavia Jr.	CzRep-Jr.	27	12	21	33	93	....	....	....	....	....	....	....	....	....	....	....	....	....	....	....	....	....	....
	HC Slavia Praha	CzRep	18	0	1	1	8	....	....	....	....	....	....	....	....	....	....	....	....	....	....	....	....	....	....
	Havl. Brod	CzRep-3	7	3	0	3	31	....	....	....	....	....	....	....	....	....	7	1	5	6	0	....	....	....	....
2005-06	Slavia Jr.	CzRep-Jr.	8	10	4	14	42	....	....	....	....	....	....	....	....	....	....	....	....	....	....	....	....	....	....
	HC Slavia Praha	CzRep	33	1	9	10	28	....	....	....	....	....	....	....	....	....	11	2	3	5	10	....	....	....	....
2006-07	HC Slavia Praha	CzRep	33	7	6	13	38	....	....	....	....	....	....	....	....	....	....	....	....	....	....	....	....	....	....
2007-08	**Boston**	**NHL**	**48**	**1**	**6**	**7**	**24**	**0**	**0**	**1**	**40**	**2.5**	**1**	**247**	**48.6**	**8:50**	**6**	**2**	**0**	**2**	**0**	**0**	**0**	**0**	**8:37**
	Providence Bruins	AHL	18	10	10	20	37	....	....	....	....	....	....	....	....	....	6	0	4	4	0	....	....	....	....
	NHL Totals		**48**	**1**	**6**	**7**	**24**	**0**	**0**	**1**	**40**	**2.5**		**247**	**48.6**	**8:50**	**6**	**2**	**0**	**2**	**0**	**0**	**0**	**0**	**8:37**

SOPEL, Brent

(SOH-puhl, BREHNT) **CHI.**

Defense. Shoots right. 6'2", 205 lbs. Born, Calgary, Alta., January 7, 1977. Vancouver's 6th choice, 144th overall, in 1995 Entry Draft.

Season	Club	League	GP	G	A	Pts	PIM	PP	SH	GW	S	%	+/-	TF	F%	Min	GP	G	A	Pts	PIM	PP	SH	GW	Min
1992-93	Sask. Legion	SMHL	36	7	17	24	95	....	....	....	....	....	....	....	....	....	....	....	....	....	....	....	....	....	....
1993-94	Saskatoon Blazers	SMHL	34	9	30	39	180	....	....	....	....	....	....	....	....	....	....	....	....	....	....	....	....	....	....
	Saskatoon Blades	WHL	11	2	2	4	2	....	....	....	....	....	....	....	....	....	....	....	....	....	....	....	....	....	....
1994-95	Saskatoon Blades	WHL	22	1	10	11	31	....	....	....	....	....	....	....	....	....	....	....	....	....	....	....	....	....	....
	Swift Current	WHL	41	4	19	23	50	....	....	....	....	....	....	....	....	....	3	0	3	3	0	....	....	....	....
1995-96	Swift Current	WHL	71	13	48	61	87	....	....	....	....	....	....	....	....	....	6	1	2	3	4	....	....	....	....
	Syracuse Crunch	AHL	1	0	0	0	0	....	....	....	....	....	....	....	....	....	....	....	....	....	....	....	....	....	....
1996-97	Swift Current	WHL	62	15	41	56	109	....	....	....	....	....	....	....	....	....	10	5	11	16	32	....	....	....	....
	Syracuse Crunch	AHL	2	0	0	0	0	....	....	....	....	....	....	....	....	....	3	0	0	0	0	....	....	....	....
1997-98	Syracuse Crunch	AHL	76	10	33	43	70	....	....	....	....	....	....	....	....	....	5	0	7	7	12	....	....	....	....
1998-99	**Vancouver**	**NHL**	**5**	**1**	**0**	**1**	**4**	**1**	**0**	**0**	**5**	**20.0**	**–1**	**0**	**0.0**	**11:58**	....	....	....	....	....	....	....	....	....
	Syracuse Crunch	AHL	53	10	21	31	59	....	....	....	....	....	....	....	....	....	....	....	....	....	....	....	....	....	....
99-2000	**Vancouver**	**NHL**	**18**	**2**	**4**	**6**	**12**	**0**	**0**	**1**	**11**	**18.2**	**9**	**0**	**0.0**	**10:31**	....	....	....	....	....	....	....	....	....
	Syracuse Crunch	AHL	50	6	25	31	67	....	....	....	....	....	....	....	....	....	4	0	2	2	8	....	....	....	....
2000-01	**Vancouver**	**NHL**	**52**	**4**	**10**	**14**	**10**	**0**	**0**	**1**	**57**	**7.0**	**4**	**0**	**0.0**	**16:01**	**4**	**0**	**0**	**0**	**2**	**0**	**0**	**0**	**19:05**
	Kansas City	IHL	4	0	1	1	0	....	....	....	....	....	....	....	....	....	....	....	....	....	....	....	....	....	....
2001-02	**Vancouver**	**NHL**	**66**	**8**	**17**	**25**	**44**	**1**	**0**	**3**	**116**	**6.9**	**21**	**0**	**0.0**	**19:01**	**6**	**0**	**2**	**2**	**2**	**0**	**0**	**0**	**24:45**
2002-03	**Vancouver**	**NHL**	**81**	**7**	**30**	**37**	**23**	**6**	**0**	**1**	**167**	**4.2**	**–15**	**0**	**0.0**	**21:42**	**14**	**2**	**6**	**8**	**4**	**1**	**0**	**1**	**22:33**
2003-04	**Vancouver**	**NHL**	**80**	**10**	**32**	**42**	**36**	**6**	**0**	**2**	**173**	**5.8**	**11**	**0**	**0.0**	**21:56**	**7**	**0**	**1**	**1**	**0**	**0**	**0**	**0**	**23:55**
2004-05				DID NOT PLAY																					
2005-06	**NY Islanders**	**NHL**	**57**	**2**	**25**	**27**	**64**	**2**	**0**	**0**	**121**	**1.7**	**–9**	**0**	**0.0**	**23:35**	....	....	....	....	....	....	....	....	....
	Los Angeles	**NHL**	**11**	**0**	**1**	**1**	**6**	**0**	**0**	**0**	**12**	**0.0**	**–4**	**0**	**0.0**	**22:02**	....	....	....	....	....	....	....	....	....
2006-07	**Los Angeles**	**NHL**	**44**	**4**	**19**	**23**	**14**	**2**	**0**	**2**	**104**	**3.8**	**2**	**3**	**33.3**	**21:06**	....	....	....	....	....	....	....	....	....
	Vancouver	**NHL**	**20**	**1**	**4**	**5**	**10**	**0**	**0**	**0**	**27**	**3.7**	**0**	**0**	**0.0**	**18:25**	**11**	**0**	**0**	**0**	**2**	**0**	**0**	**0**	**19:44**
2007-08	**Chicago**	**NHL**	**58**	**1**	**19**	**20**	**28**	**0**	**0**	**0**	**56**	**1.8**	**9**	**0**	**0.0**	**20:18**	....	....	....	....	....	....	....	....	....
	NHL Totals		**492**	**40**	**161**	**201**	**251**	**18**	**0**	**10**	**849**	**4.7**		**3**	**33.3**	**20:09**	**42**	**2**	**9**	**11**	**10**	**1**	**0**	**1**	**22:02**

Traded to **NY Islanders** by **Vancouver** for NY Islanders' 2nd round choice (later traded to Anaheim - Anaheim selected Bryce Swan) in 2006 Entry Draft, August 3, 2005. Traded to **Los Angeles** by **NY Islanders** with Mark Parrish for Denis Grebeshkov and Jeff Tambellini, March 8, 2006. Traded to **Vancouver** by **Los Angeles** for Anaheim's 2nd round choice (previously acquired, Los Angeles selected Wayne Simmonds) in 2007 Entry Draft and and Vancouver's 4th round choice (later traded to Buffalo - Buffalo selected Justin Jokinen) in 2008 Entry Draft, February 26, 2006. Signed as a free agent by **Chicago**, October 3, 2007.

SOURAY, Sheldon

(SOO-ray, SHEHL-duhn) **EDM.**

Defense. Shoots left. 6'4", 233 lbs. Born, Elk Point, Alta., July 13, 1976. New Jersey's 3rd choice, 71st overall, in 1994 Entry Draft.

Season	Club	League	GP	G	A	Pts	PIM	PP	SH	GW	S	%	+/-	TF	F%	Min	GP	G	A	Pts	PIM	PP	SH	GW	Min
1990-91	Bonnyville Sabres	AAHA	30	15	20	35	100	....	....	....	....	....	....	....	....	....	....	....	....	....	....	....	....	....	....
1991-92	Quesnel	Minor-BC	20	5	15	20	200	....	....	....	....	....	....	....	....	....	....	....	....	....	....	....	....	....	....
	Alberta Cycle	AMHL	11	0	5	5	67	....	....	....	....	....	....	....	....	....	....	....	....	....	....	....	....	....	....
1992-93	Ft. Saskatchewan	AJHL	35	0	12	12	125	....	....	....	....	....	....	....	....	....	....	....	....	....	....	....	....	....	....
	Tri-City	WHL	2	0	0	0	0	....	....	....	....	....	....	....	....	....	....	....	....	....	....	....	....	....	....
1993-94	Tri-City	WHL	42	3	6	9	122	....	....	....	....	....	....	....	....	....	....	....	....	....	....	....	....	....	....
1994-95	Tri-City	WHL	40	2	24	26	140	....	....	....	....	....	....	....	....	....	....	....	....	....	....	....	....	....	....
	Prince George	WHL	11	2	3	5	23	....	....	....	....	....	....	....	....	....	....	....	....	....	....	....	....	....	....
	Albany River Rats	AHL	7	0	2	2	8	....	....	....	....	....	....	....	....	....	....	....	....	....	....	....	....	....	....

			Regular Season														Playoffs								
Season	Club	League	GP	G	A	Pts	PIM	PP	SH	GW	S	%	+/-	TF	F%	Min	GP	G	A	Pts	PIM	PP	SH	GW	Min
1995-96	Prince George	WHL	32	9	18	27	91	....	....	....	....	....	....	....	....	....	....	....	....	....	....	....	....	....	....
	Kelowna Rockets	WHL	27	7	20	27	94	....	....	....	....	....	....	....	....	....	6	0	5	5	2	....	....	....	....
	Albany River Rats	AHL	6	0	2	2	12	....	....	....	....	....	....	....	....	....	4	0	1	1	4	....	....	....	....
1996-97	Albany River Rats	AHL	70	2	11	13	160	....	....	....	....	....	....	....	....	....	16	2	3	5	47	....	....	....	....
1997-98	**New Jersey**	**NHL**	**60**	**3**	**7**	**10**	**85**	**0**	**0**	**1**	**74**	**4.1**	**18**	....	....	....	**3**	**0**	**1**	**1**	**2**	**0**	**0**	**0**	....
	Albany River Rats	AHL	6	0	0	0	8	....	....	....	....	....	....	....	....	....	....	....	....	....	....	....	....	....	....
1998-99	**New Jersey**	**NHL**	**70**	**1**	**7**	**8**	**110**	**0**	**0**	**0**	**101**	**1.0**	**5**	**0**	**0.0**	**14:56**	**2**	**0**	**1**	**1**	**0**	**0**	**0**	**0**	**12:57**
99-2000	**New Jersey**	**NHL**	**52**	**0**	**8**	**8**	**70**	**0**	**0**	**0**	**74**	**0.0**	**–6**	**0**	**0.0**	**17:12**	....	....	....	....	....	....	....	....	....
	Montreal	**NHL**	**19**	**3**	**0**	**3**	**44**	**0**	**0**	**0**	**39**	**7.7**	**7**	**0**	**0.0**	**19:18**	....	....	....	....	....	....	....	....	....
2000-01	**Montreal**	**NHL**	**52**	**3**	**8**	**11**	**95**	**0**	**0**	**2**	**103**	**2.9**	**–11**	**0**	**0.0**	**20:36**	....	....	....	....	....	....	....	....	....
2001-02	**Montreal**	**NHL**	**34**	**3**	**5**	**8**	**62**	**1**	**0**	**0**	**56**	**5.4**	**–5**	**1**	**100.0**	**18:11**	**12**	**0**	**1**	**1**	**16**	**0**	**0**	**0**	**19:01**
2002-03	**Montreal**	**NHL**	DID NOT PLAY – INJURED																						
2003-04	**Montreal**	**NHL**	**63**	**15**	**20**	**35**	**104**	**6**	**1**	**3**	**186**	**8.1**	**4**	**0**	**0.0**	**23:26**	**11**	**0**	**2**	**2**	**39**	**0**	**0**	**0**	**23:55**
2004-05	Farjestad	Sweden	39	9	8	17	117	....	....	....	....	....	....	....	....	....	15	1	6	7	77	....	....	....	....
2005-06	**Montreal**	**NHL**	**75**	**12**	**27**	**39**	**116**	**7**	**1**	**0**	**202**	**5.9**	**–11**	**0**	**0.0**	**22:15**	**6**	**3**	**2**	**5**	**8**	**2**	**0**	**0**	**18:47**
2006-07	**Montreal**	**NHL**	**81**	**26**	**38**	**64**	**135**	**19**	**1**	**6**	**224**	**11.6**	**–28**	**2**	**100.0**	**23:11**	....	....	....	....	....	....	....	....	....
2007-08	**Edmonton**	**NHL**	**26**	**3**	**7**	**10**	**36**	**2**	**0**	**1**	**71**	**4.2**	**–7**	**0**	**0.0**	**24:21**	....	....	....	....	....	....	....	....	....
	NHL Totals		**532**	**69**	**127**	**196**	**857**	**35**	**3**	**13**	**1130**	**6.1**		**3**	**100.0**	**20:27**	**34**	**3**	**7**	**10**	**65**	**2**	**0**	**0**	**20:19**

WHL West Second All-Star Team (1996)

Played in NHL All-Star Game (2004, 2007)

Traded to **Montreal** by **New Jersey** with Josh DeWolf and New Jersey's 2nd round choice (later traded to Washington – later traded to Tampa Bay – Tampa Bay selected Andreas Holmqvist) in 2001 Entry Draft for Vladimir Malakhov, March 1, 2000. • Missed remainder of 2001-02 season and entire 2002-03 season recovering from wrist injury suffered in game vs. Tampa Bay, November 17, 2001. Signed as a free agent by **Farjestad** (Sweden), September 22, 2004. Signed as a free agent by **Edmonton**, July 12, 2007. • Missed majority of 2007-08 season recovering from shoulder injury suffered in game at Vancouver, October 13, 2007 and resulting surgery, February 8, 2008.

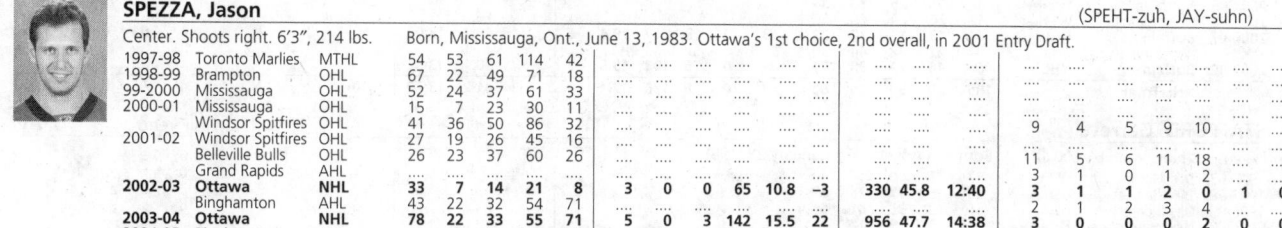

SPACEK, Jaroslav

(SPAH-chehk, YAHR-roh-slav) **BUF.**

Defense. Shoots left. 5'11", 204 lbs. Born, Rokycany, Czech., February 11, 1974. Florida's 5th choice, 117th overall, in 1998 Entry Draft.

Season	Club	League	GP	G	A	Pts	PIM	PP	SH	GW	S	%	+/-	TF	F%	Min	GP	G	A	Pts	PIM	PP	SH	GW	Min
1992-93	HC Skoda Plzen	Czech	16	1	3	4	....	....	....	....	....	....	....	....	....	....	....	....	....	....	....	....	....	....	....
1993-94	HC Skoda Plzen	CzRep	34	2	6	8	....	....	....	....	....	....	....	....	....	....	....	....	....	....	....	....	....	....	....
1994-95	Plzen	CzRep	38	4	8	12	14	....	....	....	....	....	....	....	....	....	3	1	0	1	2	....	....	....	....
1995-96	HC ZKZ Plzen	CzRep	40	3	10	13	42	....	....	....	....	....	....	....	....	....	3	0	1	1	4	....	....	....	....
1996-97	HC ZKZ Plzen	CzRep	52	9	29	38	44	....	....	....	....	....	....	....	....	....	....	....	....	....	....	....	....	....	....
1997-98	Farjestad	Sweden	45	10	16	26	63	....	....	....	....	....	....	....	....	....	12	2	5	7	14	....	....	....	....
	Farjestad	EuroHL	6	2	3	5	2	....	....	....	....	....	....	....	....	....	....	....	....	....	....	....	....	....	....
1998-99	**Florida**	**NHL**	**63**	**3**	**12**	**15**	**28**	**2**	**1**	**0**	**92**	**3.3**	**15**	**1**	**100.0**	**19:27**	....	....	....	....	....	....	....	....	....
	New Haven	AHL	14	4	8	12	15	....	....	....	....	....	....	....	....	....	....	....	....	....	....	....	....	....	....
99-2000	**Florida**	**NHL**	**82**	**10**	**26**	**36**	**53**	**4**	**0**	**1**	**111**	**9.0**	**7**	**1**	**0.0**	**22:40**	**4**	**0**	**0**	**0**	**0**	**0**	**0**	**0**	**20:29**
2000-01	**Florida**	**NHL**	**12**	**2**	**1**	**3**	**8**	**1**	**0**	**0**	**21**	**9.5**	**–4**	**0**	**0.0**	**19:12**	....	....	....	....	....	....	....	....	....
	Chicago	**NHL**	**50**	**5**	**18**	**23**	**20**	**2**	**0**	**1**	**85**	**5.9**	**7**	**0**	**0.0**	**21:31**	....	....	....	....	....	....	....	....	....
2001-02	**Chicago**	**NHL**	**60**	**3**	**10**	**13**	**29**	**0**	**0**	**1**	**64**	**4.7**	**5**	**0**	**0.0**	**16:25**	....	....	....	....	....	....	....	....	....
	Czech Republic	Olympics	4	0	0	0	0	....	....	....	....	....	....	....	....	....	....	....	....	....	....	....	....	....	....
	Columbus	**NHL**	**14**	**2**	**3**	**5**	**24**	**1**	**1**	**1**	**29**	**6.9**	**–9**	**0**	**0.0**	**23:35**	....	....	....	....	....	....	....	....	....
2002-03	**Columbus**	**NHL**	**81**	**9**	**36**	**45**	**70**	**5**	**0**	**1**	**166**	**5.4**	**–23**	**0**	**0.0**	**24:47**	....	....	....	....	....	....	....	....	....
2003-04	**Columbus**	**NHL**	**58**	**5**	**17**	**22**	**45**	**2**	**1**	**2**	**108**	**4.6**	**–13**	**0**	**0.0**	**23:26**	....	....	....	....	....	....	....	....	....
2004-05	Plzen	CzRep	30	3	8	11	26	....	....	....	....	....	....	....	....	....	....	....	....	....	....	....	....	....	....
	HC Slavia Praha	CzRep	17	4	9	13	29	....	....	....	....	....	....	....	....	....	7	0	2	2	8	....	....	....	....
2005-06	**Chicago**	**NHL**	**45**	**7**	**17**	**24**	**72**	**1**	**0**	**0**	**80**	**8.8**	**8**	**0**	**0.0**	**23:00**	....	....	....	....	....	....	....	....	....
	Edmonton	**NHL**	**31**	**5**	**14**	**19**	**24**	**3**	**0**	**0**	**70**	**7.1**	**3**	**0**	**0.0**	**24:37**	**24**	**3**	**11**	**14**	**24**	**2**	**0**	**0**	**25:53**
2006-07	**Buffalo**	**NHL**	**65**	**5**	**16**	**21**	**62**	**1**	**0**	**2**	**78**	**6.4**	**20**	**0**	**0.0**	**19:09**	**16**	**0**	**0**	**0**	**10**	**0**	**0**	**0**	**14:39**
2007-08	**Buffalo**	**NHL**	**60**	**9**	**23**	**32**	**42**	**7**	**0**	**1**	**95**	**9.5**	**7**	**0**	**0.0**	**22:59**	....	....	....	....	....	....	....	....	....
	NHL Totals		**621**	**65**	**193**	**258**	**477**	**29**	**3**	**10**	**999**	**6.5**		**2**	**50.0**	**21:44**	**44**	**3**	**11**	**14**	**34**	**2**	**0**	**0**	**21:18**

Traded to **Chicago** by **Florida** for Anders Eriksson, November 6, 2000. Traded to **Columbus** by **Chicago** with Chicago's 2nd round choice (Dan Fritsche) in 2003 Entry Draft for Lyle Odelein, March 19, 2002. Signed as a free agent by **Plzen** (CzRep), September 17, 2004. Signed as a free agent by **Slavia Praha** (CzRep), January 4, 2005. Signed as a free agent by **Chicago**, August 3, 2005. Traded to **Edmonton** by **Chicago** for Tony Salmelainen, January 26, 2006. Signed as a free agent by **Buffalo**, July 5, 2006.

SPEZZA, Jason

(SPEHT-zuh, JAY-suhn) **OTT.**

Center. Shoots right. 6'3", 214 lbs. Born, Mississauga, Ont., June 13, 1983. Ottawa's 1st choice, 2nd overall, in 2001 Entry Draft.

Season	Club	League	GP	G	A	Pts	PIM	PP	SH	GW	S	%	+/-	TF	F%	Min	GP	G	A	Pts	PIM	PP	SH	GW	Min
1997-98	Toronto Marlies	MTHL	54	53	61	114	42	....	....	....	....	....	....	....	....	....	....	....	....	....	....	....	....	....	....
1998-99	Brampton	OHL	67	22	49	71	18	....	....	....	....	....	....	....	....	....	....	....	....	....	....	....	....	....	....
99-2000	Mississauga	OHL	52	24	37	61	33	....	....	....	....	....	....	....	....	....	....	....	....	....	....	....	....	....	....
2000-01	Mississauga	OHL	15	7	23	30	11	....	....	....	....	....	....	....	....	....	....	....	....	....	....	....	....	....	....
	Windsor Spitfires	OHL	41	36	50	86	32	....	....	....	....	....	....	....	....	....	9	4	5	9	10	....	....	....	....
2001-02	Windsor Spitfires	OHL	27	19	26	45	16	....	....	....	....	....	....	....	....	....	....	....	....	....	....	....	....	....	....
	Belleville Bulls	OHL	26	23	37	60	26	....	....	....	....	....	....	....	....	....	11	5	6	11	18	....	....	....	....
	Grand Rapids	AHL	....	....	....	....	....	....	....	....	....	....	....	....	....	....	3	1	0	1	2	....	....	....	....
2002-03	**Ottawa**	**NHL**	**33**	**7**	**14**	**21**	**8**	**3**	**0**	**0**	**65**	**10.8**	**–3**	**330**	**45.8**	**12:40**	**3**	**1**	**1**	**2**	**0**	**1**	**0**	**0**	**11:34**
	Binghamton	AHL	43	22	32	54	71	....	....	....	....	....	....	....	....	....	2	1	2	3	4	....	....	....	....
2003-04	**Ottawa**	**NHL**	**78**	**22**	**33**	**55**	**71**	**5**	**0**	**3**	**142**	**15.5**	**22**	**956**	**47.7**	**14:38**	**3**	**0**	**0**	**0**	**2**	**0**	**0**	**0**	**9:44**
2004-05	Binghamton	AHL	80	32	*85	*117	50	....	....	....	....	....	....	....	....	....	6	1	3	4	6	....	....	....	....
2005-06	**Ottawa**	**NHL**	**68**	**19**	**71**	**90**	**33**	**7**	**0**	**5**	**156**	**12.2**	**23**	**1220**	**52.6**	**19:00**	**10**	**5**	**9**	**14**	**2**	**3**	**0**	**1**	**17:59**
2006-07	**Ottawa**	**NHL**	**67**	**34**	**53**	**87**	**45**	**13**	**1**	**5**	**162**	**21.0**	**19**	**1261**	**53.0**	**19:17**	**20**	**7**	***15**	***22**	**10**	**3**	**0**	**0**	**20:58**
2007-08	**Ottawa**	**NHL**	**76**	**34**	**58**	**92**	**66**	**11**	**0**	**6**	**210**	**16.2**	**26**	**1445**	**50.5**	**20:40**	**4**	**0**	**1**	**1**	**0**	**0**	**0**	**0**	**19:45**
	NHL Totals		**322**	**116**	**229**	**345**	**223**	**39**	**1**	**19**	**735**	**15.8**		**5212**	**50.8**	**17:45**	**40**	**13**	**26**	**39**	**14**	**7**	**0**	**1**	**18:33**

OHL All-Rookie Team (1999) • AHL All-Rookie Team (2003) • AHL First All-Star Team (2005) • John P. Sollenberger Trophy (Top Scorer - AHL) (2005) • Les Cunningham Award (MVP – AHL) (2005)

Played in NHL All-Star Game (2008)

SPILLER, Matthew

(SPIHL-uhr, MA-thew) **N.J.**

Defense. Shoots left. 6'5", 235 lbs. Born, Daysland, Alta., February 7, 1983. Phoenix's 2nd choice, 31st overall, in 2001 Entry Draft.

Season	Club	League	GP	G	A	Pts	PIM	PP	SH	GW	S	%	+/-	TF	F%	Min	GP	G	A	Pts	PIM	PP	SH	GW	Min
1998-99	East Central Chill	AMBHL	36	8	19	27	140	....	....	....	....	....	....	....	....	....	....	....	....	....	....	....	....	....	....
99-2000	Seattle	WHL	60	1	10	11	108	....	....	....	....	....	....	....	....	....	7	0	0	0	25	....	....	....	....
2000-01	Seattle	WHL	71	4	7	11	174	....	....	....	....	....	....	....	....	....	....	....	....	....	....	....	....	....	....
2001-02	Seattle	WHL	72	8	23	31	168	....	....	....	....	....	....	....	....	....	1	0	0	0	4	....	....	....	....
2002-03	Seattle	WHL	68	11	24	35	198	....	....	....	....	....	....	....	....	....	15	2	7	9	36	....	....	....	....
2003-04	**Phoenix**	**NHL**	**51**	**0**	**0**	**0**	**54**	**0**	**0**	**0**	**22**	**0.0**	**–11**	**0**	**0.0**	**10:42**	....	....	....	....	....	....	....	....	....
	Springfield	AHL	21	1	2	3	32	....	....	....	....	....	....	....	....	....	....	....	....	....	....	....	....	....	....
2004-05	Utah Grizzlies	AHL	79	4	7	11	160	....	....	....	....	....	....	....	....	....	....	....	....	....	....	....	....	....	....
2005-06	**Phoenix**	**NHL**	**8**	**0**	**1**	**1**	**13**	**0**	**0**	**0**	**3**	**0.0**	**–1**	**0**	**0.0**	**10:30**	....	....	....	....	....	....	....	....	....
	San Antonio	AHL	69	2	7	9	167	....	....	....	....	....	....	....	....	....	....	....	....	....	....	....	....	....	....
2006-07	San Antonio	AHL	80	1	7	8	187	....	....	....	....	....	....	....	....	....	....	....	....	....	....	....	....	....	....
2007-08	**NY Islanders**	**NHL**	**9**	**0**	**1**	**1**	**7**	**0**	**0**	**0**	**6**	**0.0**	**–2**	**0**	**0.0**	**19:47**	....	....	....	....	....	....	....	....	....
	Bridgeport	AHL	75	1	6	7	177	....	....	....	....	....	....	....	....	....	....	....	....	....	....	....	....	....	....
	NHL Totals		**68**	**0**	**2**	**2**	**74**	**0**	**0**	**0**	**31**	**0.0**		**0**	**0.0**	**11:53**	....	....	....	....	....	....	....	....	....

Signed as a free agent by **NY Islanders**, July 3, 2007. Signed as a free agent by **New Jersey**, July, 2008.

SPRUKTS, Janis

(SPRUKTS, YAN-ish) **FLA.**

Center. Shoots left. 6'3", 235 lbs. Born, Riga, Latvia, January 31, 1982. Florida's 7th choice, 234th overall, in 2000 Entry Draft.

Season	Club	League	GP	G	A	Pts	PIM	PP	SH	GW	S	%	+/-	TF	F%	Min	GP	G	A	Pts	PIM	PP	SH	GW	Min
99-2000	Lukko Rauma Jr.	Fin-Jr.	26	2	5	7	6	....	....	....	....	....	....	....	....	....	3	0	0	0	0	....	....	....	....
	HC Essamika Jr.	EEHL-2	2	4	4	8	0	....	....	....	....	....	....	....	....	....	....	....	....	....	....	....	....	....	....
2000-01	Lukko Rauma Jr.	Fin-Jr.	36	15	22	37	24	....	....	....	....	....	....	....	....	....	3	0	0	0	0	....	....	....	....
	Lukko Rauma	Finland	9	0	0	0	2	....	....	....	....	....	....	....	....	....	....	....	....	....	....	....	....	....	....
2001-02	Acadie-Bathurst	QMJHL	63	35	44	79	46	....	....	....	....	....	....	....	....	....	16	14	8	22	12	....	....	....	....
2002-03	Sport Vaasa	Finland-2	21	5	6	11	8	....	....	....	....	....	....	....	....	....	....	....	....	....	....	....	....	....	....
	Acadie-Bathurst	QMJHL	30	9	29	38	12	....	....	....	....	....	....	....	....	....	11	3	5	8	0	....	....	....	....
2003-04	ASK Ogre	Latvia	5	2	4	6	0	....	....	....	....	....	....	....	....	....	....	....	....	....	....	....	....	....	....
	Odense IK	Denmark	2	0	1	1	2	....	....	....	....	....	....	....	....	....	....	....	....	....	....	....	....	....	....

			Regular Season														Playoffs								
Season	Club	League	GP	G	A	Pts	PIM	PP	SH	GW	S	%	+/-	TF	F%	Min	GP	G	A	Pts	PIM	PP	SH	GW	Min
2004-05	HK Riga 2000	BelOpen	21	7	9	16	10	....	....	....	....	....	....	....	....	....	3	0	0	0	2	....	....	....	....
	HK Riga 2000	Latvia	3	2	3	5	0	....	....	....	....	....	....	....	....	....	9	3	4	7	2	....	....	....	....
2005-06	HPK Hameenlinna	Finland	35	18	10	28	14	....	....	....	....	....	....	....	....	....	13	3	4	7	14	....	....	....	....
2006-07	**Florida**	**NHL**	13	1	2	3	2	0	0	0	10	10.0	1	61	44.3	6:19	....	....	....	....	....	....	....	....	....
	Rochester	AHL	58	18	41	59	60	....	....	....	....	....	....	....	....	....	6	1	3	4	4	....	....	....	....
2007-08	Lukko Rauma	Finland	53	12	17	29	20	....	....	....	....	....	....	....	....	....	3	0	1	1	0	....	....	....	....
	NHL Totals		13	1	2	3	2	0	0	0	10	10.0		61	44.3	6:19	....	....	....	....	....	....	....	....	....

• Released by **Vaasa** (Finland-2) and returned to **Acadie-Bathurst** (QMJHL), January 3, 2003.

STAAL, Eric
(STAHL, AIR-ihk) **CAR.**

Center. Shoots left. 6'4", 205 lbs. Born, Thunder Bay, Ont., October 29, 1984. Carolina's 1st choice, 2nd overall, in 2003 Entry Draft.

Season	Club	League	GP	G	A	Pts	PIM	PP	SH	GW	S	%	+/-	TF	F%	Min	GP	G	A	Pts	PIM	PP	SH	GW	Min
99-2000	Thunder Bay	Exhib.	7	4	8	12	0	....	....	....	....	....	....	....	....	....	....	....	....	....	....	....	....	....	....
2000-01	Peterborough	OHL	63	19	30	49	23	....	....	....	....	....	....	....	....	....	7	2	5	7	4	....	....	....	....
2001-02	Peterborough	OHL	56	23	39	62	40	....	....	....	....	....	....	....	....	....	6	3	6	9	10	....	....	....	....
2002-03	Peterborough	OHL	66	39	59	98	36	....	....	....	....	....	....	....	....	....	7	9	5	14	6	....	....	....	....
2003-04	**Carolina**	**NHL**	81	11	20	31	40	2	1	3	164	6.7	-6	669	43.1	16:40	....	....	....	....	....	....	....	....	....
2004-05	Lowell	AHL	77	26	51	77	88	....	....	....	....	....	....	....	....	....	11	2	8	10	12	....	....	....	....
2005-06♦	**Carolina**	**NHL**	82	45	55	100	81	19	4	4	279	16.1	-8	1309	42.6	19:39	25	9	*19	*28	8	7	0	1	19:48
2006-07	**Carolina**	**NHL**	82	30	40	70	68	12	1	1	288	10.4	-6	1238	45.2	20:08	....	....	....	....	....	....	....	....	....
2007-08	**Carolina**	**NHL**	82	38	44	82	50	14	0	7	310	12.3	-2	1708	44.9	21:38	....	....	....	....	....	....	....	....	....
	NHL Totals		327	124	159	283	239	47	6	15	1041	11.9		4924	44.1	19:32	25	9	19	28	8	7	0	1	19:48

OHL Second All-Star Team (2003) • Canadian Major Junior First All-Star Team (2003) • NHL Second All-Star Team (2006)
Played in NHL All-Star Game (2007, 2008)

STAAL, Jordan
(STAHL, JOHR-dahn) **PIT.**

Center. Shoots left. 6'4", 220 lbs. Born, Thunder Bay, Ont., September 10, 1988. Pittsburgh's 1st choice, 2nd overall, in 2006 Entry Draft.

Season	Club	League	GP	G	A	Pts	PIM	PP	SH	GW	S	%	+/-	TF	F%	Min	GP	G	A	Pts	PIM	PP	SH	GW	Min
2004-05	Peterborough	OHL	66	9	19	28	29	....	....	....	....	....	....	....	....	....	14	5	5	10	16	....	....	....	....
2005-06	Peterborough	OHL	68	28	40	68	69	....	....	....	....	....	....	....	....	....	19	10	6	16	16	....	....	....	....
2006-07	**Pittsburgh**	**NHL**	81	29	13	42	24	4	7	4	131	22.1	16	383	37.1	14:56	5	3	0	3	2	0	0	0	16:00
2007-08	**Pittsburgh**	**NHL**	82	12	16	28	55	3	0	4	183	6.6	-5	1202	42.2	18:16	20	6	1	7	14	1	0	1	18:16
	NHL Totals		163	41	29	70	79	7	7	8	314	13.1		1585	40.9	16:37	25	9	1	10	16	1	0	1	17:49

NHL All-Rookie Team (2007)

STAAL, Marc
(STAHL, MAHRK) **NYR**

Defense. Shoots left. 6'4", 210 lbs. Born, Thunder Bay, Ont., January 13, 1987. NY Rangers' 1st choice, 12th overall, in 2005 Entry Draft.

Season	Club	League	GP	G	A	Pts	PIM	PP	SH	GW	S	%	+/-	TF	F%	Min	GP	G	A	Pts	PIM	PP	SH	GW	Min
2003-04	Sudbury Wolves	OHL	61	1	13	14	34	....	....	....	....	....	....	....	....	....	7	1	2	3	2	....	....	....	....
2004-05	Sudbury Wolves	OHL	65	6	20	26	53	....	....	....	....	....	....	....	....	....	12	0	4	4	15	....	....	....	....
2005-06	Sudbury Wolves	OHL	57	11	38	49	60	....	....	....	....	....	....	....	....	....	10	0	8	8	8	....	....	....	....
	Hartford	AHL	....	....	....	....	....	....	....	....	....	....	....	....	....	....	12	0	2	2	8	....	....	....	....
2006-07	Sudbury Wolves	OHL	53	5	29	34	68	....	....	....	....	....	....	....	....	....	21	5	15	20	22	....	....	....	....
2007-08	**NY Rangers**	**NHL**	80	2	8	10	42	0	0	0	78	2.6	2	0	0.0	18:48	10	1	2	3	8	0	0	1	22:21
	NHL Totals		80	2	8	10	42	0	0	0	78	2.6		0	0.0	18:48	10	1	2	3	8	0	0	1	22:21

OHL First All-Star Team (2006, 2007)

STAFFORD, Drew
(STA-fuhrd, DROO) **BUF.**

Right wing. Shoots right. 6'2", 213 lbs. Born, Milwaukee, WI, October 30, 1985. Buffalo's 1st choice, 13th overall, in 2004 Entry Draft.

Season	Club	League	GP	G	A	Pts	PIM	PP	SH	GW	S	%	+/-	TF	F%	Min	GP	G	A	Pts	PIM	PP	SH	GW	Min
2001-02	Shat.-St. Mary's	High-MN	45	35	53	88	30	....	....	....	....	....	....	....	....	....	....	....	....	....	....	....	....	....	....
2002-03	Shat.-St. Mary's	High-MN	65	49	67	116	....	....	....	....	....	....	....	....	....	....	....	....	....	....	....	....	....	....	....
2003-04	North Dakota	WCHA	36	11	21	32	30	....	....	....	....	....	....	....	....	....	....	....	....	....	....	....	....	....	....
2004-05	North Dakota	WCHA	42	13	25	38	34	....	....	....	....	....	....	....	....	....	....	....	....	....	....	....	....	....	....
2005-06	North Dakota	WCHA	42	24	24	48	63	....	....	....	....	....	....	....	....	....	....	....	....	....	....	....	....	....	....
2006-07	**Buffalo**	**NHL**	41	13	14	27	33	3	0	3	67	19.4	5	13	46.2	13:08	10	2	2	4	4	0	0	0	11:52
	Rochester	AHL	34	22	22	44	30	....	....	....	....	....	....	....	....	....	....	....	....	....	....	....	....	....	....
2007-08	**Buffalo**	**NHL**	64	16	22	38	51	1	0	5	103	15.5	3	21	38.1	13:32	....	....	....	....	....	....	....	....	....
	NHL Totals		105	29	36	65	84	4	0	8	170	17.1		34	41.2	13:23	10	2	2	4	4	0	0	0	11:52

STAFFORD, Garrett
(STA-fuhrd, GAIR-reht) **DAL.**

Defense. Shoots right. 6', 200 lbs. Born, Los Angeles, CA, January 28, 1980.

Season	Club	League	GP	G	A	Pts	PIM	PP	SH	GW	S	%	+/-	TF	F%	Min	GP	G	A	Pts	PIM	PP	SH	GW	Min
1996-97	Des Moines	USHL	37	1	10	11	40	....	....	....	....	....	....	....	....	....	5	0	0	0	0	....	....	....	....
1997-98	Des Moines	USHL	53	6	17	23	89	....	....	....	....	....	....	....	....	....	12	1	3	4	42	....	....	....	....
1998-99	Des Moines	USHL	56	8	33	41	54	....	....	....	....	....	....	....	....	....	13	2	2	4	18	....	....	....	....
99-2000	New Hampshire	H-East	38	3	9	12	28	....	....	....	....	....	....	....	....	....	....	....	....	....	....	....	....	....	....
2000-01	New Hampshire	H-East	37	5	21	26	44	....	....	....	....	....	....	....	....	....	....	....	....	....	....	....	....	....	....
2001-02	New Hampshire	H-East	36	5	22	27	42	....	....	....	....	....	....	....	....	....	....	....	....	....	....	....	....	....	....
2002-03	New Hampshire	H-East	23	1	15	16	24	....	....	....	....	....	....	....	....	....	....	....	....	....	....	....	....	....	....
2003-04	Cleveland Barons	AHL	73	12	34	46	71	....	....	....	....	....	....	....	....	....	6	0	0	0	6	....	....	....	....
2004-05	Cleveland Barons	AHL	68	6	18	24	55	....	....	....	....	....	....	....	....	....	....	....	....	....	....	....	....	....	....
2005-06	Cleveland Barons	AHL	80	11	28	39	86	....	....	....	....	....	....	....	....	....	....	....	....	....	....	....	....	....	....
2006-07	Worcester Sharks	AHL	77	11	30	41	58	....	....	....	....	....	....	....	....	....	6	0	3	3	2	....	....	....	....
2007-08	**Detroit**	**NHL**	2	0	0	0	0	0	0	0	1	0.0	0	0	0.0	6:45	....	....	....	....	....	....	....	....	....
	Grand Rapids	AHL	69	11	33	44	36	....	....	....	....	....	....	....	....	....	....	....	....	....	....	....	....	....	....
	NHL Totals		2	0	0	0	0	0	0	0	1	0.0		0	0.0	6:45	....	....	....	....	....	....	....	....	....

Hockey East Second All-Star Team (2002) • AHL All-Rookie Team (2004) • AHL Second All-Star Team (2004)
Signed as a free agent by **Cleveland** (AHL), October 10, 2003. Signed as a free agent by **San Jose**, December 9, 2003. Signed as a free agent by **Detroit**, July 16, 2007. Signed as a free agent by **Dallas**, July 3, 2008.

STAIOS, Steve
(STAY-ohs, STEEV) **EDM.**

Defense. Shoots right. 6'1", 200 lbs. Born, Hamilton, Ont., July 28, 1973. St. Louis' 1st choice, 27th overall, in 1991 Entry Draft.

Season	Club	League	GP	G	A	Pts	PIM	PP	SH	GW	S	%	+/-	TF	F%	Min	GP	G	A	Pts	PIM	PP	SH	GW	Min
1988-89	Hamilton Huskies	Minor-ON	58	13	39	52	78	....	....	....	....	....	....	....	....	....	....	....	....	....	....	....	....	....	....
1989-90	Hamilton Kilty B's	OHA-B	40	9	27	36	66	....	....	....	....	....	....	....	....	....	....	....	....	....	....	....	....	....	....
1990-91	Niagara Falls	OHL	66	17	29	46	115	....	....	....	....	....	....	....	....	....	12	2	3	5	10	....	....	....	....
1991-92	Niagara Falls	OHL	65	11	42	53	122	....	....	....	....	....	....	....	....	....	17	7	8	15	27	....	....	....	....
1992-93	Niagara Falls	OHL	12	4	14	18	30	....	....	....	....	....	....	....	....	....	....	....	....	....	....	....	....	....	....
	Sudbury Wolves	OHL	53	13	44	57	67	....	....	....	....	....	....	....	....	....	11	5	6	11	22	....	....	....	....
1993-94	Peoria Rivermen	IHL	38	3	9	12	42	....	....	....	....	....	....	....	....	....	....	....	....	....	....	....	....	....	....
1994-95	Peoria Rivermen	IHL	60	3	13	16	64	....	....	....	....	....	....	....	....	....	6	0	0	0	10	....	....	....	....
1995-96	Peoria Rivermen	IHL	6	0	1	1	14	....	....	....	....	....	....	....	....	....	....	....	....	....	....	....	....	....	....
	Worcester IceCats	AHL	57	1	11	12	114	....	....	....	....	....	....	....	....	....	....	....	....	....	....	....	....	....	....
	Boston	**NHL**	12	0	0	0	4	0	0	0	4	0.0	-5	....	....	....	3	0	0	0	0	0	0	0	....
	Providence Bruins	AHL	7	1	4	5	8	....	....	....	....	....	....	....	....	....	....	....	....	....	....	....	....	....	....
1996-97	**Boston**	**NHL**	54	3	8	11	71	0	0	0	56	5.4	-26	....	....	....	....	....	....	....	....	....	....	....	....
	Vancouver	**NHL**	9	0	6	6	20	0	0	0	10	0.0	2	....	....	....	....	....	....	....	....	....	....	....	....
1997-98	**Vancouver**	**NHL**	77	3	4	7	134	0	0	1	45	6.7	-3	....	....	....	....	....	....	....	....	....	....	....	....
1998-99	**Vancouver**	**NHL**	57	0	2	2	54	0	0	0	33	0.0	-12	4	25.0	6:53	....	....	....	....	....	....	....	....	....
99-2000	**Atlanta**	**NHL**	27	2	3	5	66	0	0	0	38	5.3	-5	2	50.0	13:01	....	....	....	....	....	....	....	....	....
2000-01	**Atlanta**	**NHL**	70	9	13	22	137	4	0	0	156	5.8	-23	1	0.0	21:45	....	....	....	....	....	....	....	....	....
2001-02	**Edmonton**	**NHL**	73	5	5	10	108	0	0	1	101	5.0	10	0	0.0	18:05	....	....	....	....	....	....	....	....	....
2002-03	**Edmonton**	**NHL**	76	5	21	26	96	1	3	0	126	4.0	13	1	0.0	22:17	6	0	0	0	4	0	0	0	23:27
2003-04	**Edmonton**	**NHL**	82	6	22	28	86	1	0	1	153	3.9	17	0	0.0	23:03	....	....	....	....	....	....	....	....	....
2004-05	Lulea HF	Sweden	7	2	1	3	12	....	....	....	....	....	....	....	....	....	....	....	....	....	....	....	....	....	....
2005-06	**Edmonton**	**NHL**	82	8	20	28	84	1	0	1	140	5.7	10	0	0.0	20:53	24	1	5	6	28	1	0	0	21:31

Season	Club	League	GP	G	A	Pts	PIM	PP	SH	GW	S	%	+/-	TF	F%	Min	GP	G	A	Pts	PIM	PP	SH	GW	Min
			Regular Season														Playoffs								
2006-07	**Edmonton**	**NHL**	**58**	**2**	**15**	**17**	**97**	**0**	**0**	**0**	**71**	**2.8**	**–5**	**0**	**0.0**	**21:23**	....	....	....	....	....	....	....	....	....
2007-08	**Edmonton**	**NHL**	**82**	**7**	**9**	**16**	**121**	**1**	**0**	**0**	**73**	**9.6**	**–14**	**1**	**100.0**	**22:01**	....	....	....	....	....	....	....	....	....
	NHL Totals		**759**	**50**	**128**	**178**	**1078**	**8**	**3**	**4**	**1006**	**5.0**		**9**	**33.3**	**19:39**	**33**	**1**	**5**	**6**	**32**	**1**	**0**	**0**	**21:54**

Traded to **Boston** by **St. Louis** with Kevin Sawyer for Steve Leach, March 8, 1996. Claimed on waivers by **Vancouver** from **Boston**, March 18, 1997. Claimed by **Atlanta** from **Vancouver** in Expansion Draft, June 25, 1999. • Missed majority of 1999-2000 season recovering from knee injury suffered in game vs. Colorado, October 23, 1999. Traded to **New Jersey** by **Atlanta** for New Jersey's 9th round choice (Simon Gamache) in 2000 Entry Draft, June 12, 2000. Traded to **Atlanta** by **New Jersey** for future considerations, July 10, 2000. Signed as a free agent by **Edmonton**, July 12, 2001. Signed as a free agent by **Lulea** (Sweden), January 28, 2005.

STAJAN, Matt

(STAY-juhn, MAHT) **TOR.**

Center. Shoots left. 6'1", 200 lbs. Born, Mississauga, Ont., December 19, 1983. Toronto's 2nd choice, 57th overall, in 2002 Entry Draft.

Season	Club	League	GP	G	A	Pts	PIM	PP	SH	GW	S	%	+/-	TF	F%	Min	GP	G	A	Pts	PIM	PP	SH	GW	Min
99-2000	Miss. Senators	GTHL	STATISTICS NOT AVAILABLE																						
2000-01	Belleville Bulls	OHL	57	9	18	27	27	....	....	....	....	....	....	....	....	....	7	1	6	7	5	....	....	....	....
2001-02	Belleville Bulls	OHL	68	33	52	85	50	....	....	....	....	....	....	....	....	....	11	3	8	11	14	....	....	....	....
2002-03	Belleville Bulls	OHL	57	34	60	94	75	....	....	....	....	....	....	....	....	....	7	5	8	13	16	....	....	....	....
	St. John's	AHL	1	0	1	1	0	....	....	....	....	....	....	....	....	....	....	....	....	....	....	....	....	....	....
	Toronto	**NHL**	**1**	**1**	**0**	**1**	**0**	**0**	**0**	**0**	**1**	**100.0**	**1**	**12**	**33.3**	**11:00**	....	....	....	....	....	....	....	....	....
2003-04	**Toronto**	**NHL**	**69**	**14**	**13**	**27**	**22**	**0**	**0**	**0**	**63**	**22.2**	**7**	**450**	**38.9**	**11:00**	**3**	**0**	**0**	**0**	**2**	**0**	**0**	**0**	**11:13**
2004-05	St. John's	AHL	80	23	43	66	43	....	....	....	....	....	....	....	....	....	5	2	2	4	6	....	....	....	....
2005-06	**Toronto**	**NHL**	**80**	**15**	**12**	**27**	**50**	**3**	**4**	**5**	**83**	**18.1**	**5**	**373**	**44.5**	**11:38**	....	....	....	....	....	....	....	....	....
2006-07	**Toronto**	**NHL**	**82**	**10**	**29**	**39**	**44**	**1**	**1**	**1**	**132**	**7.6**	**3**	**985**	**46.1**	**16:09**	....	....	....	....	....	....	....	....	....
2007-08	**Toronto**	**NHL**	**82**	**16**	**17**	**33**	**47**	**2**	**1**	**3**	**127**	**12.6**	**–11**	**1293**	**47.6**	**18:54**	....	....	....	....	....	....	....	....	....
	NHL Totals		**314**	**56**	**71**	**127**	**163**	**6**	**6**	**9**	**406**	**13.8**		**3113**	**45.4**	**14:34**	**3**	**0**	**0**	**0**	**2**	**0**	**0**	**0**	**11:13**

• Scored a goal in his first NHL game (April 5, 2003 vs. Ottawa).

STASTNY, Paul

(STAS-nee, PAWL) **COL.**

Center. Shoots left. 6', 205 lbs. Born, Quebec City, Que., December 27, 1985. Colorado's 2nd choice, 44th overall, in 2005 Entry Draft.

Season	Club	League	GP	G	A	Pts	PIM	PP	SH	GW	S	%	+/-	TF	F%	Min	GP	G	A	Pts	PIM	PP	SH	GW	Min
2003-04	River City Lancers	USHL	56	30	*47	77	46	....	....	....	....	....	....	....	....	....	3	1	2	3	0	....	....	....	....
2004-05	U. of Denver	WCHA	42	17	28	45	30	....	....	....	....	....	....	....	....	....	....	....	....	....	....	....	....	....	....
2005-06	U. of Denver	WCHA	39	19	34	53	79	....	....	....	....	....	....	....	....	....	....	....	....	....	....	....	....	....	....
2006-07	**Colorado**	**NHL**	**82**	**28**	**50**	**78**	**42**	**11**	**0**	**6**	**185**	**15.1**	**4**	**1226**	**48.5**	**18:10**	....	....	....	....	....	....	....	....	....
2007-08	**Colorado**	**NHL**	**66**	**24**	**47**	**71**	**24**	**3**	**0**	**4**	**138**	**17.4**	**22**	**1101**	**51.0**	**21:05**	**9**	**2**	**1**	**3**	**6**	**0**	**0**	**1**	**19:56**
	NHL Totals		**148**	**52**	**97**	**149**	**66**	**14**	**0**	**10**	**323**	**16.1**		**2327**	**49.6**	**19:28**	**9**	**2**	**1**	**3**	**6**	**0**	**0**	**1**	**19:56**

WCHA All-Rookie Team (2005) • WCHA Rookie of the Year (2005) • NCAA Championship All-Tournament Team (2005) • WCHA First All-Star Team (2006) • NCAA West Second All-American Team (2006) • NHL All-Rookie Team (2007)

STASTNY, Yan

(STAS-nee, YAHN) **ST.L.**

Center. Shoots left. 5'10", 191 lbs. Born, Quebec City, Que., September 30, 1982. Boston's 6th choice, 259th overall, in 2002 Entry Draft.

Season	Club	League	GP	G	A	Pts	PIM	PP	SH	GW	S	%	+/-	TF	F%	Min	GP	G	A	Pts	PIM	PP	SH	GW	Min
99-2000	St. Louis Sting	NAHL	45	12	23	35	77	....	....	....	....	....	....	....	....	....	....	....	....	....	....	....	....	....	....
2000-01	St. Louis Jr. Blues	CSJHL	6	0	2	2	23	....	....	....	....	....	....	....	....	....	....	....	....	....	....	....	....	....	....
	Omaha Lancers	USHL	44	17	14	31	101	....	....	....	....	....	....	....	....	....	11	6	6	12	12	....	....	....	....
2001-02	U. of Notre Dame	CCHA	33	6	11	17	38	....	....	....	....	....	....	....	....	....	....	....	....	....	....	....	....	....	....
2002-03	U. of Notre Dame	CCHA	39	14	9	23	44	....	....	....	....	....	....	....	....	....	....	....	....	....	....	....	....	....	....
2003-04	Nurnberg	Germany	44	9	20	29	83	....	....	....	....	....	....	....	....	....	6	0	1	1	6	....	....	....	....
2004-05	Nurnberg	Germany	51	24	30	54	60	....	....	....	....	....	....	....	....	....	6	2	1	3	8	....	....	....	....
2005-06	**Edmonton**	**NHL**	**3**	**0**	**0**	**0**	**0**	**0**	**0**	**0**	**1**	**0.0**	**–2**	**17**	**41.2**	**6:53**	....	....	....	....	....	....	....	....	....
	Iowa Stars	AHL	51	14	17	31	42	....	....	....	....	....	....	....	....	....	....	....	....	....	....	....	....	....	....
	Boston	**NHL**	**17**	**1**	**3**	**4**	**10**	**0**	**0**	**0**	**13**	**7.7**	**–2**	**122**	**42.6**	**10:16**	....	....	....	....	....	....	....	....	....
	Providence Bruins	AHL	....	....	....	....	....	....	....	....	....	....	....	....	....	....	6	0	5	5	12	....	....	....	....
2006-07	**Boston**	**NHL**	**21**	**0**	**2**	**2**	**19**	**0**	**0**	**0**	**7**	**0.0**	**–3**	**51**	**45.1**	**7:28**	....	....	....	....	....	....	....	....	....
	Providence Bruins	AHL	11	3	9	12	12	....	....	....	....	....	....	....	....	....	....	....	....	....	....	....	....	....	....
	Peoria Rivermen	AHL	39	11	17	28	35	....	....	....	....	....	....	....	....	....	....	....	....	....	....	....	....	....	....
2007-08	**St. Louis**	**NHL**	**12**	**1**	**1**	**2**	**9**	**0**	**0**	**0**	**10**	**10.0**	**0**	**61**	**44.3**	**10:59**	....	....	....	....	....	....	....	....	....
	Peoria Rivermen	AHL	43	13	11	24	69	....	....	....	....	....	....	....	....	....	....	....	....	....	....	....	....	....	....
	NHL Totals		**53**	**2**	**6**	**8**	**38**	**0**	**0**	**0**	**31**	**6.5**		**251**	**43.4**	**9:08**	....	....	....	....	....	....	....	....	....

Signed as a free agent by **Nurnberg** (Germany), September 18, 2003. Traded to **Edmonton** by **Boston** for Boston's 4th round choice (previously acquired, later traded to San Jose - San Jose selected James Delory) in 2006 Entry Draft, August 30, 2005. Traded to **Boston** by **Edmonton** with Marty Reasoner and Edmonton's 2nd round choice (Milan Lucic) in 2006 Entry Draft for Sergei Samsonov, March 9, 2006. Traded to **St. Louis** by **Boston** for St. Louis' 5th round choice (Denis Reul) in 2007 Entry Draft, January 16, 2006.

STECKEL, David

(STEH-kuhl, DAY-vihd) **WSH.**

Center. Shoots left. 6'5", 218 lbs. Born, Westbend, WI, March 15, 1982. Los Angeles' 2nd choice, 30th overall, in 2001 Entry Draft.

Season	Club	League	GP	G	A	Pts	PIM	PP	SH	GW	S	%	+/-	TF	F%	Min	GP	G	A	Pts	PIM	PP	SH	GW	Min
1998-99	USNTDP	USHL	2	0	0	0	2	....	....	....	....	....	....	....	....	....	....	....	....	....	....	....	....	....	....
	USNTDP	NAHL	51	3	14	17	18	....	....	....	....	....	....	....	....	....	....	....	....	....	....	....	....	....	....
99-2000	USNTDP	U-18	6	2	5	7	14	....	....	....	....	....	....	....	....	....	....	....	....	....	....	....	....	....	....
	USNTDP	USHL	52	13	13	26	94	....	....	....	....	....	....	....	....	....	....	....	....	....	....	....	....	....	....
2000-01	Ohio State	CCHA	33	17	18	35	80	....	....	....	....	....	....	....	....	....	....	....	....	....	....	....	....	....	....
2001-02	Ohio State	CCHA	36	6	16	22	75	....	....	....	....	....	....	....	....	....	....	....	....	....	....	....	....	....	....
2002-03	Ohio State	CCHA	36	10	8	18	50	....	....	....	....	....	....	....	....	....	....	....	....	....	....	....	....	....	....
2003-04	Ohio State	CCHA	41	17	13	30	44	....	....	....	....	....	....	....	....	....	....	....	....	....	....	....	....	....	....
2004-05	Manchester	AHL	63	10	7	17	26	....	....	....	....	....	....	....	....	....	6	1	1	2	4	....	....	....	....
2005-06	**Washington**	**NHL**	**7**	**0**	**0**	**0**	**0**	**0**	**0**	**0**	**6**	**0.0**	**1**	**48**	**35.4**	**7:39**	....	....	....	....	....	....	....	....	....
	Hershey Bears	AHL	74	14	20	34	58	....	....	....	....	....	....	....	....	....	21	10	5	15	20	....	....	....	....
2006-07	**Washington**	**NHL**	**5**	**0**	**0**	**0**	**2**	**0**	**0**	**0**	**4**	**0.0**	**–2**	**43**	**65.1**	**12:26**	....	....	....	....	....	....	....	....	....
	Hershey Bears	AHL	71	30	31	61	46	....	....	....	....	....	....	....	....	....	19	6	9	15	16	....	....	....	....
2007-08	**Washington**	**NHL**	**67**	**5**	**7**	**12**	**34**	**0**	**0**	**1**	**66**	**7.6**	**1**	**900**	**56.3**	**13:34**	**7**	**1**	**1**	**2**	**4**	**0**	**0**	**0**	**14:23**
	NHL Totals		**79**	**5**	**7**	**12**	**36**	**0**	**0**	**1**	**76**	**6.6**		**991**	**55.7**	**12:58**	**7**	**1**	**1**	**2**	**4**	**0**	**0**	**0**	**14:23**

CCHA All-Rookie Team (2001)

Signed as a free agent by **Washington**, August 25, 2005.

STEEN, Alex

(STEEN, AL-ehx) **TOR.**

Center. Shoots left. 6'1", 205 lbs. Born, Winnipeg, Man., March 1, 1984. Toronto's 1st choice, 24th overall, in 2002 Entry Draft.

Season	Club	League	GP	G	A	Pts	PIM	PP	SH	GW	S	%	+/-	TF	F%	Min	GP	G	A	Pts	PIM	PP	SH	GW	Min
99-2000	V.Frolunda Jr.	Swe-Jr.	8	5	7	12	0	....	....	....	....	....	....	....	....	....	....	....	....	....	....	....	....	....	....
	V.Frolunda U18	Swe-U18	14	3	5	8	16	....	....	....	....	....	....	....	....	....	....	....	....	....	....	....	....	....	....
2000-01	V.Frolunda Jr.	Swe-Jr.	23	11	12	23	15	....	....	....	....	....	....	....	....	....	3	1	0	1	2	....	....	....	....
	V.Frolunda U18	Swe-U18	6	3	3	6	9	....	....	....	....	....	....	....	....	....	....	....	....	....	....	....	....	....	....
2001-02	V.Frolunda Jr.	Swe-Jr.	23	21	17	38	47	....	....	....	....	....	....	....	....	....	2	1	1	2	2	....	....	....	....
	V.Frolunda	Sweden	26	0	3	3	14	....	....	....	....	....	....	....	....	....	10	1	2	3	0	....	....	....	....
2002-03	V.Frolunda	Sweden	45	5	10	15	18	....	....	....	....	....	....	....	....	....	16	2	3	5	4	....	....	....	....
	V.Frolunda Jr.	Swe-Jr.	2	0	2	2	0	....	....	....	....	....	....	....	....	....	....	....	....	....	....	....	....	....	....
2003-04	V.Frolunda	Sweden	48	10	14	24	50	....	....	....	....	....	....	....	....	....	10	4	6	10	14	....	....	....	....
2004-05	MODO	Sweden	50	9	8	17	26	....	....	....	....	....	....	....	....	....	6	1	0	1	4	....	....	....	....
2005-06	**Toronto**	**NHL**	**75**	**18**	**27**	**45**	**42**	**9**	**1**	**3**	**176**	**10.2**	**–9**	**29**	**24.1**	**17:37**	....	....	....	....	....	....	....	....	....
2006-07	**Toronto**	**NHL**	**82**	**15**	**20**	**35**	**26**	**4**	**0**	**5**	**192**	**7.8**	**5**	**44**	**34.1**	**15:42**	....	....	....	....	....	....	....	....	....
2007-08	**Toronto**	**NHL**	**76**	**15**	**27**	**42**	**32**	**2**	**1**	**2**	**169**	**8.9**	**0**	**179**	**33.0**	**18:05**	....	....	....	....	....	....	....	....	....
	NHL Totals		**233**	**48**	**74**	**122**	**100**	**15**	**2**	**10**	**537**	**8.9**		**252**	**32.1**	**17:06**	....	....	....	....	....	....	....	....	....

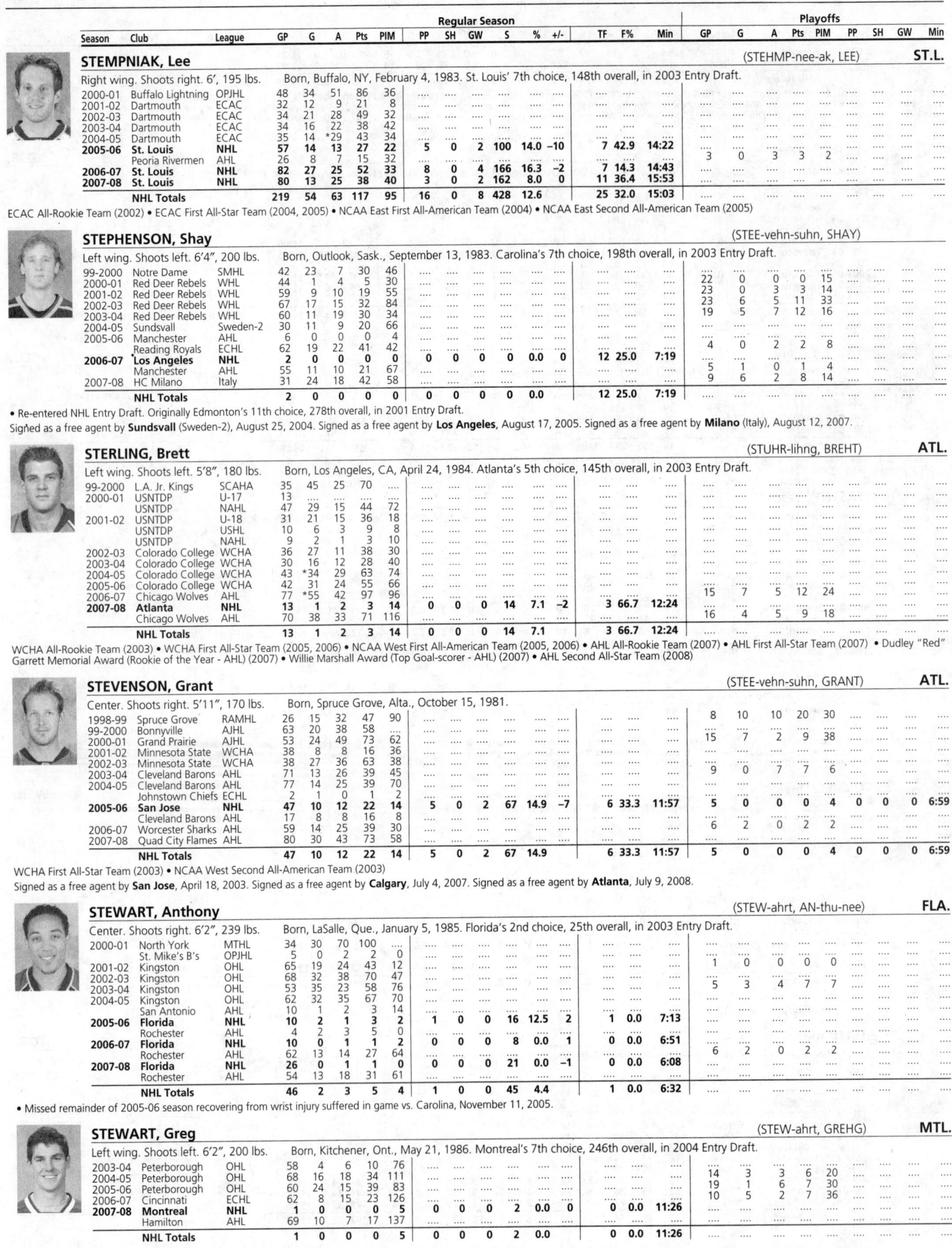

			Regular Season														Playoffs								
Season	Club	League	GP	G	A	Pts	PIM	PP	SH	GW	S	%	+/-	TF	F%	Min	GP	G	A	Pts	PIM	PP	SH	GW	Min

STEMPNIAK, Lee

(STEHMP-nee-ak, LEE) **ST.L.**

Right wing. Shoots right. 6', 195 lbs. Born, Buffalo, NY, February 4, 1983. St. Louis' 7th choice, 148th overall, in 2003 Entry Draft.

2000-01	Buffalo Lightning	OPJHL	48	34	51	86	36	....	....	....	....	....	....	....	....	....	....	....	....	....	....	....	....	....	....
2001-02	Dartmouth	ECAC	32	12	9	21	8	....	....	....	....	....	....	....	....	....	....	....	....	....	....	....	....	....	....
2002-03	Dartmouth	ECAC	34	21	28	49	32	....	....	....	....	....	....	....	....	....	....	....	....	....	....	....	....	....	....
2003-04	Dartmouth	ECAC	34	16	22	38	42	....	....	....	....	....	....	....	....	....	....	....	....	....	....	....	....	....	....
2004-05	Dartmouth	ECAC	35	14	*29	43	34	....	....	....	....	....	....	....	....	....	....	....	....	....	....	....	....	....	....
2005-06	**St. Louis**	**NHL**	**57**	**14**	**13**	**27**	**22**	**5**	**0**	**2**	**100**	**14.0**	**–10**	**7**	**42.9**	**14:22**	....	....	....	....	....	....	....	....	....
	Peoria Rivermen	AHL	26	8	7	15	32	....	....	....	....	....	....	....	....	....	3	0	3	3	2	....	....	....	....
2006-07	**St. Louis**	**NHL**	**82**	**27**	**25**	**52**	**33**	**8**	**0**	**4**	**166**	**16.3**	**–2**	**7**	**14.3**	**14:43**	....	....	....	....	....	....	....	....	....
2007-08	**St. Louis**	**NHL**	**80**	**13**	**25**	**38**	**40**	**3**	**0**	**2**	**162**	**8.0**	**0**	**11**	**36.4**	**15:53**	....	....	....	....	....	....	....	....	....
	NHL Totals		**219**	**54**	**63**	**117**	**95**	**16**	**0**	**8**	**428**	**12.6**		**25**	**32.0**	**15:03**	....	....	....	....	....	....	....	....	....

ECAC All-Rookie Team (2002) • ECAC First All-Star Team (2004, 2005) • NCAA East First All-American Team (2004) • NCAA East Second All-American Team (2005)

STEPHENSON, Shay

(STEE-vehn-suhn, SHAY)

Left wing. Shoots left. 6'4", 200 lbs. Born, Outlook, Sask., September 13, 1983. Carolina's 7th choice, 198th overall, in 2003 Entry Draft.

99-2000	Notre Dame	SMHL	42	23	7	30	46	....	....	....	....	....	....	....	....	....	....	....	....	....	....	....	....	....	....
2000-01	Red Deer Rebels	WHL	44	1	4	5	30	....	....	....	....	....	....	....	....	....	22	0	0	0	15	....	....	....	....
2001-02	Red Deer Rebels	WHL	59	9	10	19	55	....	....	....	....	....	....	....	....	....	23	0	3	3	14	....	....	....	....
2002-03	Red Deer Rebels	WHL	67	17	15	32	84	....	....	....	....	....	....	....	....	....	23	6	5	11	33	....	....	....	....
2003-04	Red Deer Rebels	WHL	60	11	19	30	34	....	....	....	....	....	....	....	....	....	19	5	7	12	16	....	....	....	....
2004-05	Sundsvall	Sweden-2	30	11	9	20	66	....	....	....	....	....	....	....	....	....	....	....	....	....	....	....	....	....	....
2005-06	Manchester	AHL	6	0	0	0	4	....	....	....	....	....	....	....	....	....	....	....	....	....	....	....	....	....	....
	Reading Royals	ECHL	62	19	22	41	42	....	....	....	....	....	....	....	....	....	4	0	2	2	8	....	....	....	....
2006-07	**• Los Angeles**	**NHL**	**2**	**0**	**0**	**0**	**0**	**0**	**0**	**0**	**0**	**0.0**	**0**	**12**	**25.0**	**7:19**	....	....	....	....	....	....	....	....	....
	Manchester	AHL	55	11	10	21	67	....	....	....	....	....	....	....	....	....	5	1	0	1	4	....	....	....	....
2007-08	HC Milano	Italy	31	24	18	42	58	....	....	....	....	....	....	....	....	....	9	6	2	8	14	....	....	....	....
	NHL Totals		**2**	**0**	**0**	**0**	**0**	**0**	**0**	**0**	**0**	**0.0**		**12**	**25.0**	**7:19**	....	....	....	....	....	....	....	....	....

• Re-entered NHL Entry Draft. Originally Edmonton's 11th choice, 278th overall, in 2001 Entry Draft.
Signed as a free agent by **Sundsvall** (Sweden-2), August 25, 2004. Signed as a free agent by **Los Angeles**, August 17, 2005. Signed as a free agent by **Milano** (Italy), August 12, 2007.

STERLING, Brett

(STUHR-lihng, BREHT) **ATL.**

Left wing. Shoots left. 5'8", 180 lbs. Born, Los Angeles, CA, April 24, 1984. Atlanta's 5th choice, 145th overall, in 2003 Entry Draft.

99-2000	L.A. Jr. Kings	SCAHA	35	45	25	70	....	....	....	....	....	....	....	....	....	....	....	....	....	....	....	....	....	....	....
2000-01	USNTDP	U-17	13	....	....	....	....	....	....	....	....	....	....	....	....	....	....	....	....	....	....	....	....	....	....
	USNTDP	NAHL	47	29	15	44	72	....	....	....	....	....	....	....	....	....	....	....	....	....	....	....	....	....	....
2001-02	USNTDP	U-18	31	21	15	36	18	....	....	....	....	....	....	....	....	....	....	....	....	....	....	....	....	....	....
	USNTDP	USHL	10	6	3	9	8	....	....	....	....	....	....	....	....	....	....	....	....	....	....	....	....	....	....
	USNTDP	NAHL	9	2	1	3	10	....	....	....	....	....	....	....	....	....	....	....	....	....	....	....	....	....	....
2002-03	Colorado College	WCHA	36	27	11	38	30	....	....	....	....	....	....	....	....	....	....	....	....	....	....	....	....	....	....
2003-04	Colorado College	WCHA	30	16	12	28	40	....	....	....	....	....	....	....	....	....	....	....	....	....	....	....	....	....	....
2004-05	Colorado College	WCHA	43	*34	29	63	74	....	....	....	....	....	....	....	....	....	....	....	....	....	....	....	....	....	....
2005-06	Colorado College	WCHA	42	31	24	55	66	....	....	....	....	....	....	....	....	....	....	....	....	....	....	....	....	....	....
2006-07	Chicago Wolves	AHL	77	*55	42	97	96	....	....	....	....	....	....	....	....	....	15	7	5	12	24	....	....	....	....
2007-08	**Atlanta**	**NHL**	**13**	**1**	**2**	**3**	**14**	**0**	**0**	**0**	**14**	**7.1**	**–2**	**3**	**66.7**	**12:24**	....	....	....	....	....	....	....	....	....
	Chicago Wolves	AHL	70	38	33	71	116	....	....	....	....	....	....	....	....	....	16	4	5	9	18	....	....	....	....
	NHL Totals		**13**	**1**	**2**	**3**	**14**	**0**	**0**	**0**	**14**	**7.1**		**3**	**66.7**	**12:24**	....	....	....	....	....	....	....	....	....

WCHA All-Rookie Team (2003) • WCHA First All-Star Team (2005, 2006) • NCAA West First All-American Team (2005, 2006) • AHL All-Rookie Team (2007) • AHL First All-Star Team (2007) • Dudley "Red" Garrett Memorial Award (Rookie of the Year - AHL) (2007) • Willie Marshall Award (Top Goal-scorer - AHL) (2007) • AHL Second All-Star Team (2008)

STEVENSON, Grant

(STEE-vehn-suhn, GRANT) **ATL.**

Center. Shoots right. 5'11", 170 lbs. Born, Spruce Grove, Alta., October 15, 1981.

1998-99	Spruce Grove	RAMHL	26	15	32	47	90	....	....	....	....	....	....	....	....	....	8	10	10	20	30	....	....	....	....
99-2000	Bonnyville	AJHL	63	20	38	58	....	....	....	....	....	....	....	....	....	....	....	....	....	....	....	....	....	....	....
2000-01	Grand Prairie	AJHL	53	24	49	73	62	....	....	....	....	....	....	....	....	....	15	7	2	9	38	....	....	....	....
2001-02	Minnesota State	WCHA	38	8	8	16	36	....	....	....	....	....	....	....	....	....	....	....	....	....	....	....	....	....	....
2002-03	Minnesota State	WCHA	38	27	36	63	38	....	....	....	....	....	....	....	....	....	....	....	....	....	....	....	....	....	....
2003-04	Cleveland Barons	AHL	71	13	26	39	45	....	....	....	....	....	....	....	....	....	9	0	7	7	6	....	....	....	....
2004-05	Cleveland Barons	AHL	77	14	25	39	70	....	....	....	....	....	....	....	....	....	....	....	....	....	....	....	....	....	....
	Johnstown Chiefs	ECHL	2	1	0	1	2	....	....	....	....	....	....	....	....	....	....	....	....	....	....	....	....	....	....
2005-06	**San Jose**	**NHL**	**47**	**10**	**12**	**22**	**14**	**5**	**0**	**2**	**67**	**14.9**	**–7**	**6**	**33.3**	**11:57**	**5**	**0**	**0**	**0**	**4**	**0**	**0**	**0**	**6:59**
	Cleveland Barons	AHL	17	8	8	16	8	....	....	....	....	....	....	....	....	....	....	....	....	....	....	....	....	....	....
2006-07	Worcester Sharks	AHL	59	14	25	39	30	....	....	....	....	....	....	....	....	....	6	2	0	2	2	....	....	....	....
2007-08	Quad City Flames	AHL	80	30	43	73	58	....	....	....	....	....	....	....	....	....	....	....	....	....	....	....	....	....	....
	NHL Totals		**47**	**10**	**12**	**22**	**14**	**5**	**0**	**2**	**67**	**14.9**		**6**	**33.3**	**11:57**	**5**	**0**	**0**	**0**	**4**	**0**	**0**	**0**	**6:59**

WCHA First All-Star Team (2003) • NCAA West Second All-American Team (2003)
Signed as a free agent by **San Jose**, April 18, 2003. Signed as a free agent by **Calgary**, July 4, 2007. Signed as a free agent by **Atlanta**, July 9, 2008.

STEWART, Anthony

(STEW-ahrt, AN-thu-nee) **FLA.**

Center. Shoots right. 6'2", 239 lbs. Born, LaSalle, Que., January 5, 1985. Florida's 2nd choice, 25th overall, in 2003 Entry Draft.

2000-01	North York	MTHL	34	30	70	100	....	....	....	....	....	....	....	....	....	....	....	....	....	....	....	....	....	....	....
	St. Mike's B's	OPJHL	5	0	2	2	0	....	....	....	....	....	....	....	....	....	....	....	....	....	....	....	....	....	....
2001-02	Kingston	OHL	65	19	24	43	12	....	....	....	....	....	....	....	....	....	1	0	0	0	0	....	....	....	....
2002-03	Kingston	OHL	68	32	38	70	47	....	....	....	....	....	....	....	....	....	....	....	....	....	....	....	....	....	....
2003-04	Kingston	OHL	53	35	23	58	76	....	....	....	....	....	....	....	....	....	5	3	4	7	7	....	....	....	....
2004-05	Kingston	OHL	62	32	35	67	70	....	....	....	....	....	....	....	....	....	....	....	....	....	....	....	....	....	....
	San Antonio	AHL	10	1	2	3	14	....	....	....	....	....	....	....	....	....	....	....	....	....	....	....	....	....	....
2005-06	**Florida**	**NHL**	**10**	**2**	**1**	**3**	**2**	**1**	**0**	**0**	**16**	**12.5**	**2**	**1**	**0.0**	**7:13**	....	....	....	....	....	....	....	....	....
	Rochester	AHL	4	2	3	5	0	....	....	....	....	....	....	....	....	....	....	....	....	....	....	....	....	....	....
2006-07	**Florida**	**NHL**	**10**	**0**	**1**	**1**	**2**	**0**	**0**	**0**	**8**	**0.0**	**1**	**0**	**0.0**	**6:51**	....	....	....	....	....	....	....	....	....
	Rochester	AHL	62	13	14	27	64	....	....	....	....	....	....	....	....	....	6	2	0	2	2	....	....	....	....
2007-08	**Florida**	**NHL**	**26**	**0**	**1**	**1**	**0**	**0**	**0**	**0**	**21**	**0.0**	**–1**	**0**	**0.0**	**6:08**	....	....	....	....	....	....	....	....	....
	Rochester	AHL	54	13	18	31	61	....	....	....	....	....	....	....	....	....	....	....	....	....	....	....	....	....	....
	NHL Totals		**46**	**2**	**3**	**5**	**4**	**1**	**0**	**0**	**45**	**4.4**		**1**	**0.0**	**6:32**	....	....	....	....	....	....	....	....	....

• Missed remainder of 2005-06 season recovering from wrist injury suffered in game vs. Carolina, November 11, 2005.

STEWART, Greg

(STEW-ahrt, GREHG) **MTL.**

Left wing. Shoots left. 6'2", 200 lbs. Born, Kitchener, Ont., May 21, 1986. Montreal's 7th choice, 246th overall, in 2004 Entry Draft.

2003-04	Peterborough	OHL	58	4	6	10	76	....	....	....	....	....	....	....	....	....	....	....	....	....	....	....	....	....	....
2004-05	Peterborough	OHL	68	16	18	34	111	....	....	....	....	....	....	....	....	....	14	3	3	6	20	....	....	....	....
2005-06	Peterborough	OHL	60	24	15	39	83	....	....	....	....	....	....	....	....	....	19	1	6	7	30	....	....	....	....
2006-07	Cincinnati	ECHL	62	8	15	23	126	....	....	....	....	....	....	....	....	....	10	5	2	7	36	....	....	....	....
2007-08	**Montreal**	**NHL**	**1**	**0**	**0**	**0**	**5**	**0**	**0**	**0**	**2**	**0.0**	**0**	**0**	**0.0**	**11:26**	....	....	....	....	....	....	....	....	....
	Hamilton	AHL	69	10	7	17	137	....	....	....	....	....	....	....	....	....	....	....	....	....	....	....	....	....	....
	NHL Totals		**1**	**0**	**0**	**0**	**5**	**0**	**0**	**0**	**2**	**0.0**		**0**	**0.0**	**11:26**	....	....	....	....	....	....	....	....	....

STEWART, Karl

(STEW-ahrt, KAHRL)

Left wing. Shoots left. 5'11", 185 lbs. Born, Aurora, Ont., June 30, 1983.

			Regular Season														Playoffs								
Season	Club	League	GP	G	A	Pts	PIM	PP	SH	GW	S	%	+/-	TF	F%	Min	GP	G	A	Pts	PIM	PP	SH	GW	Min
99-2000	Thornhill Rattlers	OPJHL	49	15	19	34	61	....	....	....	....	....	....	....	....	....	....	....	....	....	....	....	....	....	....
2000-01	Plymouth Whalers	OHL	68	9	14	23	87	....	....	....	....	....	....	....	....	....	19	3	4	7	14	....	....	....	....
2001-02	Plymouth Whalers	OHL	65	20	23	43	104	....	....	....	....	....	....	....	....	....	6	0	2	2	21	....	....	....	....
2002-03	Plymouth Whalers	OHL	68	35	50	85	120	....	....	....	....	....	....	....	....	....	17	7	10	17	31	....	....	....	....
2003-04	**Atlanta**	**NHL**	**5**	**0**	**1**	**1**	**4**	**0**	**0**	**0**	**2**	**0.0**	**0**	**10**	**10.0**	**4:27**	....	....	....	....	....	....	....	....	....
	Chicago Wolves	AHL	72	10	32	42	186	....	....	....	....	....	....	....	....	....	10	2	3	5	29	....	....	....	....
2004-05	Chicago Wolves	AHL	77	16	8	24	226	....	....	....	....	....	....	....	....	....	12	4	2	6	32	....	....	....	....
2005-06	**Atlanta**	**NHL**	**8**	**0**	**0**	**0**	**15**	**0**	**0**	**0**	**6**	**0.0**	**–3**	**3**	**100.0**	**5:40**	....	....	....	....	....	....	....	....	....
	Chicago Wolves	AHL	71	22	18	40	184	....	....	....	....	....	....	....	....	....	....	....	....	....	....	....	....	....	....
2006-07	**Pittsburgh**	**NHL**	**3**	**0**	**0**	**0**	**2**	**0**	**0**	**0**	**0**	**0.0**	**–1**	**1**	**100.0**	**3:23**	....	....	....	....	....	....	....	....	....
	Chicago	**NHL**	**37**	**2**	**3**	**5**	**43**	**0**	**1**	**0**	**19**	**10.5**	**–2**	**2**	**50.0**	**9:22**	....	....	....	....	....	....	....	....	....
	Tampa Bay	**NHL**	**7**	**0**	**0**	**0**	**2**	**0**	**0**	**0**	**2**	**0.0**	**–2**	**0**	**0.0**	**7:10**	....	....	....	....	....	....	....	....	....
2007-08	**Tampa Bay**	**NHL**	**9**	**0**	**0**	**0**	**2**	**0**	**0**	**0**	**2**	**0.0**	**–2**	**0**	**0.0**	**4:06**	....	....	....	....	....	....	....	....	....
	Norfolk Admirals	AHL	62	14	13	27	96	....	....	....	....	....	....	....	....	....	....	....	....	....	....	....	....	....	....
	NHL Totals		**69**	**2**	**4**	**6**	**68**	**0**	**1**	**0**	**31**	**6.5**		**16**	**37.5**	**7:25**	....	....	....	....	....	....	....	....	....

Signed as a free agent by **Atlanta**, September 28, 2001. Traded to **Anaheim** by **Atlanta** with Atlanta's 2nd round choice (later traded to Colorado - Colorado selected T.J. Galiardi) in 2007 Entry Draft and future considerations for Vitaly Vishnevski, August 17, 2006. Claimed on waivers by **Pittsburgh** from **Anaheim**, September 27, 2006. Claimed on waivers by **Chicago** from **Pittsburgh**, October 26, 2006. Traded to **Tampa Bay** by **Chicago** with Florida's 6th round choice (previously acquired, Tampa Bay selected Luke Witkowski) in 2008 Entry Draft for Nikita Alexeev, February 27, 2007.

STILLMAN, Cory

(STIHL-mahn, KOHR-ee) **FLA.**

Left wing. Shoots left. 6', 200 lbs. Born, Peterborough, Ont., December 20, 1973. Calgary's 1st choice, 6th overall, in 1992 Entry Draft.

Season	Club	League	GP	G	A	Pts	PIM	PP	SH	GW	S	%	+/-	TF	F%	Min	GP	G	A	Pts	PIM	PP	SH	GW	Min
1989-90	Peterborough	OHA-B	41	30	*54	84	76	....	....	....	....	....	....	....	....	....	....	....	....	....	....	....	....	....	....
1990-91	Windsor Spitfires	OHL	64	31	70	101	31	....	....	....	....	....	....	....	....	....	11	3	6	9	8	....	....	....	....
1991-92	Windsor Spitfires	OHL	53	29	61	90	59	....	....	....	....	....	....	....	....	....	7	2	4	6	8	....	....	....	....
1992-93	Peterborough	OHL	61	25	55	80	55	....	....	....	....	....	....	....	....	....	18	3	8	11	18	....	....	....	....
1993-94	Saint John Flames	AHL	79	35	48	83	52	....	....	....	....	....	....	....	....	....	7	2	4	6	16	....	....	....	....
1994-95	Saint John Flames	AHL	63	28	53	81	70	....	....	....	....	....	....	....	....	....	5	0	2	2	2	....	....	....	....
	Calgary	**NHL**	**10**	**0**	**2**	**2**	**2**	**0**	**0**	**0**	**7**	**0.0**	**1**	....	....	....	....	....	....	....	....	....	....	....	....
1995-96	**Calgary**	**NHL**	**74**	**16**	**19**	**35**	**41**	**4**	**1**	**3**	**132**	**12.1**	**–5**	....	....	....	**2**	**1**	**1**	**2**	**0**	**0**	**0**	**0**	....
1996-97	**Calgary**	**NHL**	**58**	**6**	**20**	**26**	**14**	**2**	**0**	**0**	**112**	**5.4**	**–6**	....	....	....	....	....	....	....	....	....	....	....	....
1997-98	**Calgary**	**NHL**	**72**	**27**	**22**	**49**	**40**	**9**	**4**	**1**	**178**	**15.2**	**–9**	....	....	....	....	....	....	....	....	....	....	....	....
1998-99	**Calgary**	**NHL**	**76**	**27**	**30**	**57**	**38**	**9**	**3**	**5**	**175**	**15.4**	**7**	**535**	**46.5**	**16:19**	....	....	....	....	....	....	....	....	....
99-2000	**Calgary**	**NHL**	**37**	**12**	**9**	**21**	**12**	**6**	**0**	**3**	**59**	**20.3**	**–9**	**283**	**54.4**	**17:45**	....	....	....	....	....	....	....	....	....
2000-01	**Calgary**	**NHL**	**66**	**21**	**24**	**45**	**45**	**7**	**0**	**4**	**148**	**14.2**	**–6**	**346**	**43.9**	**18:50**	....	....	....	....	....	....	....	....	....
	St. Louis	**NHL**	**12**	**3**	**4**	**7**	**6**	**3**	**0**	**0**	**26**	**11.5**	**–2**	**36**	**61.1**	**18:37**	**15**	**3**	**5**	**8**	**8**	**1**	**0**	**1**	**14:58**
2001-02	**St. Louis**	**NHL**	**80**	**23**	**22**	**45**	**36**	**6**	**0**	**4**	**140**	**16.4**	**8**	**196**	**46.4**	**15:03**	**9**	**0**	**2**	**2**	**2**	**0**	**0**	**0**	**12:46**
2002-03	**St. Louis**	**NHL**	**79**	**24**	**43**	**67**	**56**	**6**	**0**	**4**	**157**	**15.3**	**12**	**266**	**41.7**	**18:20**	**6**	**2**	**2**	**4**	**2**	**2**	**0**	**1**	**18:05**
2003-04♦	**Tampa Bay**	**NHL**	**81**	**25**	**55**	**80**	**36**	**11**	**1**	**6**	**178**	**14.0**	**18**	**38**	**31.6**	**19:32**	**21**	**2**	**5**	**7**	**15**	**0**	**1**	**0**	**17:22**
2004-05			DID NOT PLAY																						
2005-06♦	**Carolina**	**NHL**	**72**	**21**	**55**	**76**	**32**	**10**	**0**	**3**	**177**	**11.9**	**–9**	**11**	**27.3**	**18:40**	**25**	**9**	**17**	**26**	**14**	**4**	**0**	**3**	**18:42**
2006-07	**Carolina**	**NHL**	**43**	**5**	**22**	**27**	**24**	**1**	**0**	**0**	**85**	**5.9**	**–8**	**7**	**28.6**	**17:25**	....	....	....	....	....	....	....	....	....
2007-08	**Carolina**	**NHL**	**55**	**21**	**25**	**46**	**14**	**10**	**0**	**6**	**124**	**16.9**	**–7**	**11**	**54.6**	**19:53**	....	....	....	....	....	....	....	....	....
	Ottawa	**NHL**	**24**	**3**	**16**	**19**	**10**	**1**	**0**	**0**	**42**	**7.1**	**–8**	**6**	**16.7**	**16:54**	**4**	**2**	**0**	**2**	**2**	**1**	**0**	**0**	**18:26**
	NHL Totals		**839**	**234**	**368**	**602**	**406**	**85**	**9**	**39**	**1740**	**13.4**		**1735**	**46.3**	**17:54**	**82**	**19**	**32**	**51**	**43**	**8**	**1**	**5**	**16:55**

OHL Rookie of the Year (1991)

• Missed majority of 1999-2000 season recovering from shoulder injury suffered in game vs. Philadelphia, December 27, 1999. Traded to **St. Louis by Calgary** for Craig Conroy and St. Louis' 7th round choice (David Moss) in 2001 Entry Draft, March 13, 2001. Traded to **Tampa Bay** by **St. Louis** for Tampa Bay's 2nd round choice (David Backes) in 2003 Entry Draft, June 21, 2003. Signed as a free agent by **Carolina**, August 2, 2005. Traded to **Ottawa** by **Carolina** with Mike Commodore for Joe Corvo and Patrick Eaves, February 11, 2008. Signed as a free agent by **Florida**, July 1, 2008.

STOLL, Jarret

(STOHL, JEHR-eht) **L.A.**

Center. Shoots right. 6'1", 210 lbs. Born, Melville, Sask., June 25, 1982. Edmonton's 3rd choice, 36th overall, in 2002 Entry Draft.

Season	Club	League	GP	G	A	Pts	PIM	PP	SH	GW	S	%	+/-	TF	F%	Min	GP	G	A	Pts	PIM	PP	SH	GW	Min
1997-98	Saskatoon Blazers	SMHL	44	45	44	*89	78	....	....	....	....	....	....	....	....	....	....	....	....	....	....	....	....	....	....
	Edmonton Ice	WHL	8	2	3	5	4	....	....	....	....	....	....	....	....	....	....	....	....	....	....	....	....	....	....
1998-99	Kootenay Ice	WHL	57	13	21	34	38	....	....	....	....	....	....	....	....	....	4	0	0	0	2	....	....	....	....
99-2000	Kootenay Ice	WHL	71	37	38	75	64	....	....	....	....	....	....	....	....	....	20	7	9	16	24	....	....	....	....
2000-01	Kootenay Ice	WHL	62	40	66	106	105	....	....	....	....	....	....	....	....	....	11	5	9	14	22	....	....	....	....
2001-02	Kootenay Ice	WHL	47	32	34	66	64	....	....	....	....	....	....	....	....	....	22	6	14	20	35	....	....	....	....
2002-03	**Edmonton**	**NHL**	**4**	**0**	**1**	**1**	**0**	**0**	**0**	**0**	**5**	**0.0**	**–3**	**30**	**63.3**	**7:44**	....	....	....	....	....	....	....	....	....
	Hamilton	AHL	76	21	33	54	86	....	....	....	....	....	....	....	....	....	23	5	8	13	25	....	....	....	....
2003-04	**Edmonton**	**NHL**	**68**	**10**	**11**	**21**	**42**	**1**	**1**	**2**	**107**	**9.3**	**8**	**1019**	**54.1**	**13:54**	....	....	....	....	....	....	....	....	....
2004-05	Edmonton	AHL	66	21	17	38	92	....	....	....	....	....	....	....	....	....	....	....	....	....	....	....	....	....	....
2005-06	**Edmonton**	**NHL**	**82**	**22**	**46**	**68**	**74**	**11**	**1**	**4**	**243**	**9.1**	**4**	**1348**	**56.8**	**18:23**	**24**	**4**	**6**	**10**	**24**	**2**	**0**	**1**	**17:06**
2006-07	**Edmonton**	**NHL**	**51**	**13**	**26**	**39**	**48**	**6**	**1**	**2**	**115**	**11.3**	**2**	**901**	**55.6**	**18:12**	....	....	....	....	....	....	....	....	....
2007-08	**Edmonton**	**NHL**	**81**	**14**	**22**	**36**	**74**	**8**	**3**	**1**	**187**	**7.5**	**–23**	**1229**	**55.1**	**17:56**	....	....	....	....	....	....	....	....	....
	NHL Totals		**286**	**59**	**106**	**165**	**238**	**26**	**6**	**9**	**657**	**9.0**		**4527**	**55.5**	**17:00**	**24**	**4**	**6**	**10**	**24**	**2**	**0**	**1**	**17:06**

• Re-entered NHL Entry Draft. Originally Calgary's 3rd choice, 46th overall, in 2000 Entry Draft.

WHL East First All-Star Team (2001) • Canadian Major Junior First All-Star Team (2001) • WHL West First All-Star Team (2002)

Traded to **Los Angeles** by **Edmonton** with Matt Greene for Lubomir Visnovsky, June 29, 2008.

STONE, Ryan

(STOHN, RIGH-uhn) **PIT.**

Center. Shoots left. 6'2", 207 lbs. Born, Calgary, Alta., March 20, 1985. Pittsburgh's 2nd choice, 32nd overall, in 2003 Entry Draft.

Season	Club	League	GP	G	A	Pts	PIM	PP	SH	GW	S	%	+/-	TF	F%	Min	GP	G	A	Pts	PIM	PP	SH	GW	Min
2000-01	Cgy. North Stars	AMHL	34	37	28	55	90	....	....	....	....	....	....	....	....	....	....	....	....	....	....	....	....	....	....
2001-02	Brandon	WHL	65	11	27	38	128	....	....	....	....	....	....	....	....	....	19	0	3	3	39	....	....	....	....
2002-03	Brandon	WHL	54	14	31	45	158	....	....	....	....	....	....	....	....	....	12	4	2	6	20	....	....	....	....
2003-04	Brandon	WHL	50	20	38	58	125	....	....	....	....	....	....	....	....	....	11	1	3	4	24	....	....	....	....
2004-05	Brandon	WHL	70	33	*66	99	127	....	....	....	....	....	....	....	....	....	24	4	*23	27	48	....	....	....	....
2005-06	Wilkes-Barre	AHL	75	14	22	36	109	....	....	....	....	....	....	....	....	....	11	4	7	11	12	....	....	....	....
2006-07	Wilkes-Barre	AHL	41	7	26	33	86	....	....	....	....	....	....	....	....	....	10	2	3	5	21	....	....	....	....
2007-08	**Pittsburgh**	**NHL**	**6**	**0**	**1**	**1**	**5**	**0**	**0**	**0**	**3**	**0.0**	**–1**	**5**	**60.0**	**6:25**	....	....	....	....	....	....	....	....	....
	Wilkes-Barre	AHL	65	11	28	39	129	....	....	....	....	....	....	....	....	....	23	5	12	17	33	....	....	....	....
	NHL Totals		**6**	**0**	**1**	**1**	**5**	**0**	**0**	**0**	**3**	**0.0**		**5**	**60.0**	**6:25**	....	....	....	....	....	....	....	....	....

WHL East First All-Star Team (2005)

STORTINI, Zack

(stohr-TEE-nee, ZAK) **EDM.**

Right wing. Shoots right. 6'4", 220 lbs. Born, Elliot Lake, Ont., September 11, 1985. Edmonton's 5th choice, 94th overall, in 2003 Entry Draft.

Season	Club	League	GP	G	A	Pts	PIM	PP	SH	GW	S	%	+/-	TF	F%	Min	GP	G	A	Pts	PIM	PP	SH	GW	Min
2000-01	Newmarket	OPJHL	34	3	10	13	68	....	....	....	....	....	....	....	....	....	....	....	....	....	....	....	....	....	....
2001-02	Sudbury Wolves	OHL	65	8	6	14	187	....	....	....	....	....	....	....	....	....	5	1	0	1	24	....	....	....	....
2002-03	Sudbury Wolves	OHL	62	13	16	29	222	....	....	....	....	....	....	....	....	....	....	....	....	....	....	....	....	....	....
2003-04	Sudbury Wolves	OHL	62	21	16	37	151	....	....	....	....	....	....	....	....	....	7	1	1	2	14	....	....	....	....
	Toronto	AHL	2	0	0	0	7	....	....	....	....	....	....	....	....	....	3	0	0	0	4	....	....	....	....
2004-05	Sudbury Wolves	OHL	58	13	27	40	186	....	....	....	....	....	....	....	....	....	12	2	5	7	27	....	....	....	....
2005-06	Iowa Stars	AHL	27	2	1	3	108	....	....	....	....	....	....	....	....	....	....	....	....	....	....	....	....	....	....
	Milwaukee	AHL	37	0	7	7	153	....	....	....	....	....	....	....	....	....	....	....	....	....	....	....	....	....	....
2006-07	**Edmonton**	**NHL**	**29**	**1**	**0**	**1**	**105**	**0**	**0**	**0**	**17**	**5.9**	**–7**	**3**	**100.0**	**7:09**	....	....	....	....	....	....	....	....	....
	Hamilton	AHL	47	9	6	15	195	....	....	....	....	....	....	....	....	....	22	3	0	3	*56	....	....	....	....
2007-08	**Edmonton**	**NHL**	**66**	**3**	**9**	**12**	**201**	**0**	**0**	**0**	**38**	**7.9**	**3**	**7**	**42.9**	**8:10**	....	....	....	....	....	....	....	....	....
	Springfield	AHL	4	3	2	5	21	....	....	....	....	....	....	....	....	....	....	....	....	....	....	....	....	....	....
	NHL Totals		**95**	**4**	**9**	**13**	**306**	**0**	**0**	**0**	**55**	**7.3**		**10**	**60.0**	**7:52**	....	....	....	....	....	....	....	....	....

STRAKA, Martin

(STRAH-kuh, MAHR-tihn)

Center. Shoots left. 5'9", 180 lbs. Born, Plzen, Czech., September 3, 1972. Pittsburgh's 1st choice, 19th overall, in 1992 Entry Draft.

			Regular Season														Playoffs								
Season	Club	League	GP	G	A	Pts	PIM	PP	SH	GW	S	%	+/-	TF	F%	Min	GP	G	A	Pts	PIM	PP	SH	GW	Min
1989-90	Skoda Plzen	Czech	1	0	3	3	....	....	....	....	....	....	....	....	....	....	....	....	....	....	....	....	....	....	....
1990-91	HC Skoda Plzen	Czech	47	7	24	31	6	....	....	....	....	....	....	....	....	....	....	....	....	....	....	....	....	....	....
1991-92	HC Skoda Plzen	Czech	50	27	28	55	20	....	....	....	....	....	....	....	....	....	....	....	....	....	....	....	....	....	....
1992-93	**Pittsburgh**	**NHL**	**42**	**3**	**13**	**16**	**29**	**0**	**0**	**1**	**28**	**10.7**	**2**	....	....	....	**11**	**2**	**1**	**3**	**2**	**0**	**0**	**0**	....
	Cleveland	IHL	4	4	3	7	0	....	....	....	....	....	....	....	....	....	....	....	....	....	....	....	....	....	....
1993-94	**Pittsburgh**	**NHL**	**84**	**30**	**34**	**64**	**24**	**2**	**0**	**6**	**130**	**23.1**	**24**	....	....	....	**6**	**1**	**0**	**1**	**2**	**0**	**0**	**0**	....
1994-95	Plzen	CzRep	19	10	11	21	18	....	....	....	....	....	....	....	....	....	....	....	....	....	....	....	....	....	....
	Pittsburgh	**NHL**	**31**	**4**	**12**	**16**	**16**	**0**	**0**	**0**	**36**	**11.1**	**0**	....	....	....	....	....	....	....	....	....	....	....	....
	Ottawa	**NHL**	**6**	**1**	**1**	**2**	**0**	**0**	**0**	**0**	**13**	**7.7**	**–1**	....	....	....	....	....	....	....	....	....	....	....	....
1995-96	**Ottawa**	**NHL**	**43**	**9**	**16**	**25**	**29**	**5**	**0**	**1**	**63**	**14.3**	**–14**	....	....	....	....	....	....	....	....	....	....	....	....
	NY Islanders	**NHL**	**22**	**2**	**10**	**12**	**6**	**0**	**0**	**0**	**18**	**11.1**	**–6**	....	....	....	....	....	....	....	....	....	....	....	....
	Florida	**NHL**	**12**	**2**	**4**	**6**	**6**	**1**	**0**	**0**	**17**	**11.8**	**1**	....	....	....	**13**	**2**	**2**	**4**	**2**	**0**	**0**	**0**	....
1996-97	**Florida**	**NHL**	**55**	**7**	**22**	**29**	**12**	**2**	**0**	**1**	**94**	**7.4**	**9**	....	....	....	**4**	**0**	**0**	**0**	**0**	**0**	**0**	**0**	....
1997-98	**Pittsburgh**	**NHL**	**75**	**19**	**23**	**42**	**28**	**4**	**3**	**4**	**117**	**16.2**	**–1**	....	....	....	**6**	**2**	**0**	**2**	**2**	**0**	**1**	**0**	....
	Czech Republic	Olympics	6	1	2	3	0	....	....	....	....	....	....	....	....	....	....	....	....	....	....	....	....	....	....
1998-99	**Pittsburgh**	**NHL**	**80**	**35**	**48**	**83**	**26**	**5**	**4**	**4**	**177**	**19.8**	**12**	**845**	**43.6**	**23:35**	**13**	**6**	**9**	**15**	**6**	**1**	**0**	**0**	**25:00**
99-2000	**Pittsburgh**	**NHL**	**71**	**20**	**39**	**59**	**26**	**3**	**1**	**2**	**146**	**13.7**	**24**	**651**	**42.9**	**23:58**	**11**	**3**	**9**	**12**	**10**	**1**	**0**	**0**	**24:27**
2000-01	**Pittsburgh**	**NHL**	**82**	**27**	**68**	**95**	**38**	**7**	**1**	**4**	**185**	**14.6**	**19**	**331**	**43.2**	**23:01**	**18**	**5**	**8**	**13**	**8**	**3**	**0**	**2**	**21:24**
2001-02	**Pittsburgh**	**NHL**	**13**	**5**	**4**	**9**	**0**	**1**	**0**	**1**	**33**	**15.2**	**3**	**5**	**60.0**	**18:00**	....	....	....	....	....	....	....	....	....
2002-03	**Pittsburgh**	**NHL**	**60**	**18**	**28**	**46**	**12**	**7**	**0**	**4**	**136**	**13.2**	**–18**	**115**	**45.2**	**20:37**	....	....	....	....	....	....	....	....	....
2003-04	**Pittsburgh**	**NHL**	**22**	**4**	**8**	**12**	**16**	**1**	**0**	**0**	**34**	**11.8**	**–16**	**121**	**38.8**	**21:32**	....	....	....	....	....	....	....	....	....
	Los Angeles	**NHL**	**32**	**6**	**8**	**14**	**4**	**1**	**1**	**0**	**34**	**17.6**	**–9**	**66**	**48.5**	**16:47**	....	....	....	....	....	....	....	....	....
2004-05	Plzen	CzRep	45	16	18	34	76	....	....	....	....	....	....	....	....	....	....	....	....	....	....	....	....	....	....
2005-06	**NY Rangers**	**NHL**	**82**	**22**	**54**	**76**	**42**	**4**	**0**	**4**	**171**	**12.9**	**17**	**237**	**39.7**	**19:09**	**4**	**0**	**0**	**0**	**2**	**0**	**0**	**0**	**20:30**
	Czech Republic	Olympics	8	2	6	8	6	....	....	....	....	....	....	....	....	....	....	....	....	....	....	....	....	....	....
2006-07	**NY Rangers**	**NHL**	**77**	**29**	**41**	**70**	**24**	**8**	**0**	**6**	**165**	**17.6**	**16**	**213**	**40.4**	**19:57**	**10**	**2**	**8**	**10**	**2**	**1**	**0**	**0**	**19:48**
2007-08	**NY Rangers**	**NHL**	**65**	**14**	**27**	**41**	**22**	**3**	**1**	**2**	**116**	**12.1**	**5**	**19**	**36.8**	**18:37**	**10**	**3**	**7**	**10**	**16**	**1**	**0**	**0**	**19:57**
	NHL Totals		**954**	**257**	**460**	**717**	**360**	**54**	**11**	**40**	**1713**	**15.0**		**2603**	**42.7**	**21:01**	**106**	**26**	**44**	**70**	**52**	**7**	**1**	**2**	**22:06**

Czechoslovakian First All-Star Team (1992)

Played in NHL All-Star Game (1999)

Traded to **Ottawa** by **Pittsburgh** for Troy Murray and Norm Maciver, April 7, 1995. Traded to **NY Islanders** by **Ottawa** with Don Beaupre and Bryan Berard for Damian Rhodes and Wade Redden, January 23, 1996. Claimed on waivers by **Florida** from **NY Islanders**, March 15, 1996. Signed as a free agent by **Pittsburgh**, August 6, 1997. • Missed majority of 2001-02 season recovering from leg injury suffered in game vs. Florida, October 28, 2001. Traded to **Los Angeles** by **Pittsburgh** for Martin Strbak and Sergei Anshakov, November 30, 2003. Signed as a free agent by **Plzen** (CzRep), September 17, 2004. Signed as a free agent by **NY Rangers**, August 2, 2005. Signed as a free agent by **Plzen** (CzRep), July 10, 2008.

STRALMAN, Anton

(STROHL-muhn, AN-tawn) **TOR.**

Defense. Shoots right. 6'1", 200 lbs. Born, Tibro, Sweden, August 1, 1986. Toronto's 5th choice, 216th overall, in 2005 Entry Draft.

			Regular Season														Playoffs								
Season	Club	League	GP	G	A	Pts	PIM	PP	SH	GW	S	%	+/-	TF	F%	Min	GP	G	A	Pts	PIM	PP	SH	GW	Min
2002-03	Skovde IK Jr.	Swe-Jr.	46	20	9	29	38	....	....	....	....	....	....	....	....	....	....	....	....	....	....	....	....	....	....
2003-04	Skovde IK	Sweden-3	27	4	8	12	18	....	....	....	....	....	....	....	....	....	....	....	....	....	....	....	....	....	....
2004-05	Skovde IK	Sweden-2	50	10	11	21	40	....	....	....	....	....	....	....	....	....	....	....	....	....	....	....	....	....	....
2005-06	Timra IK	Sweden	45	1	4	5	28	....	....	....	....	....	....	....	....	....	....	....	....	....	....	....	....	....	....
	Timra IK Jr.	Swe-Jr.	....	....	....	....	....	....	....	....	....	....	....	....	....	....	3	0	0	0	4	....	....	....	....
2006-07	Timra IK	Sweden	53	10	11	21	34	....	....	....	....	....	....	....	....	....	7	1	3	4	10	....	....	....	....
2007-08	**Toronto**	**NHL**	**50**	**3**	**6**	**9**	**18**	**0**	**0**	**0**	**40**	**7.5**	**–10**	**0**	**0.0**	**12:49**	....	....	....	....	....	....	....	....	....
	Toronto Marlies	AHL	21	0	11	11	22	....	....	....	....	....	....	....	....	....	....	....	....	....	....	....	....	....	....
	NHL Totals		**50**	**3**	**6**	**9**	**18**	**0**	**0**	**0**	**40**	**7.5**		**0**	**0.0**	**12:49**	....	....	....	....	....	....	....	....	....

STREIT, Mark

(STREET, MAHRK) **NYI**

Defense. Shoots left. 6', 197 lbs. Born, Englisberg, Switz., December 11, 1977. Montreal's 8th choice, 262nd overall, in 2004 Entry Draft.

			Regular Season														Playoffs								
Season	Club	League	GP	G	A	Pts	PIM	PP	SH	GW	S	%	+/-	TF	F%	Min	GP	G	A	Pts	PIM	PP	SH	GW	Min
1995-96	Fribourg	Swiss	34	2	2	4	6	....	....	....	....	....	....	....	....	....	4	0	0	0	2	....	....	....	....
1996-97	HC Davos	Swiss	46	2	9	11	18	....	....	....	....	....	....	....	....	....	6	0	0	0	0	....	....	....	....
1997-98	HC Ambri-Piotta	Swiss	2	0	0	0	0	....	....	....	....	....	....	....	....	....	....	....	....	....	....	....	....	....	....
	HC Davos	Swiss	38	4	10	14	14	....	....	....	....	....	....	....	....	....	18	1	5	6	20	....	....	....	....
1998-99	HC Davos	Swiss	44	7	18	25	42	....	....	....	....	....	....	....	....	....	6	3	3	6	8	....	....	....	....
99-2000	Springfield	AHL	43	3	12	15	18	....	....	....	....	....	....	....	....	....	5	0	0	0	2	....	....	....	....
	Utah Grizzlies	IHL	1	0	1	1	2	....	....	....	....	....	....	....	....	....	....	....	....	....	....	....	....	....	....
	Tallahassee	ECHL	14	0	5	5	16	....	....	....	....	....	....	....	....	....	....	....	....	....	....	....	....	....	....
2000-01	ZSC Lions Zurich	Swiss	44	5	11	16	48	....	....	....	....	....	....	....	....	....	16	2	5	7	37	....	....	....	....
2001-02	ZSC Lions Zurich	Swiss	28	6	17	23	36	....	....	....	....	....	....	....	....	....	16	0	6	6	14	....	....	....	....
	Switzerland	Olympics	4	1	1	2	0	....	....	....	....	....	....	....	....	....	....	....	....	....	....	....	....	....	....
2002-03	ZSC Lions Zurich	Swiss	37	4	19	23	62	....	....	....	....	....	....	....	....	....	12	1	7	8	2	....	....	....	....
2003-04	ZSC Lions Zurich	Swiss	48	12	24	36	78	....	....	....	....	....	....	....	....	....	13	5	2	7	14	....	....	....	....
2004-05	ZSC Lions Zurich	Swiss	44	14	29	43	46	....	....	....	....	....	....	....	....	....	15	4	11	15	20	....	....	....	....
2005-06	**Montreal**	**NHL**	**48**	**2**	**9**	**11**	**28**	**2**	**0**	**0**	**52**	**3.8**	**–6**	**1**	**0.0**	**14:36**	**1**	**0**	**0**	**0**	**0**	**0**	**0**	**0**	**3:29**
	Switzerland	Olympics	6	2	1	3	6	....	....	....	....	....	....	....	....	....	....	....	....	....	....	....	....	....	....
2006-07	**Montreal**	**NHL**	**76**	**10**	**26**	**36**	**14**	**2**	**1**	**1**	**102**	**9.8**	**–5**	**12**	**33.3**	**14:01**	....	....	....	....	....	....	....	....	....
2007-08	**Montreal**	**NHL**	**81**	**13**	**49**	**62**	**28**	**7**	**0**	**3**	**165**	**7.9**	**–6**	**1**	**0.0**	**17:31**	**11**	**1**	**3**	**4**	**8**	**0**	**0**	**0**	**14:48**
	NHL Totals		**205**	**25**	**84**	**109**	**70**	**11**	**1**	**4**	**319**	**7.8**		**14**	**28.6**	**15:32**	**12**	**1**	**3**	**4**	**8**	**0**	**0**	**0**	**13:51**

Signed as a free agent by **NY Islanders**, July 1, 2008.

STRUDWICK, Jason

(STRUHD-wihk, JAY-suhn) **EDM.**

Defense. Shoots left. 6'4", 225 lbs. Born, Edmonton, Alta., July 17, 1975. NY Islanders' 3rd choice, 63rd overall, in 1994 Entry Draft.

			Regular Season														Playoffs								
Season	Club	League	GP	G	A	Pts	PIM	PP	SH	GW	S	%	+/-	TF	F%	Min	GP	G	A	Pts	PIM	PP	SH	GW	Min
1991-92	Edmonton Legion	AMHL	35	3	8	11	67	....	....	....	....	....	....	....	....	....	....	....	....	....	....	....	....	....	....
1992-93	Edmonton Pats	AMHL	33	8	20	28	135	....	....	....	....	....	....	....	....	....	....	....	....	....	....	....	....	....	....
1993-94	Kamloops Blazers	WHL	61	6	8	14	118	....	....	....	....	....	....	....	....	....	19	0	4	4	24	....	....	....	....
1994-95	Kamloops Blazers	WHL	72	3	11	14	183	....	....	....	....	....	....	....	....	....	21	1	1	2	39	....	....	....	....
1995-96	**NY Islanders**	**NHL**	**1**	**0**	**0**	**0**	**7**	**0**	**0**	**0**	**0**	**0.0**	**0**	....	....	....	....	....	....	....	....	....	....	....	....
	Worcester IceCats	AHL	60	2	7	9	119	....	....	....	....	....	....	....	....	....	4	0	1	1	0	....	....	....	....
1996-97	Kentucky	AHL	80	1	9	10	198	....	....	....	....	....	....	....	....	....	4	0	0	0	0	....	....	....	....
1997-98	**NY Islanders**	**NHL**	**17**	**0**	**1**	**1**	**36**	**0**	**0**	**0**	**3**	**0.0**	**1**	....	....	....	....	....	....	....	....	....	....	....	....
	Kentucky	AHL	39	3	1	4	87	....	....	....	....	....	....	....	....	....	....	....	....	....	....	....	....	....	....
	Vancouver	**NHL**	**11**	**0**	**1**	**1**	**29**	**0**	**0**	**0**	**5**	**0.0**	**–3**	....	....	....	....	....	....	....	....	....	....	....	....
	Syracuse Crunch	AHL	....	....	....	....	....	....	....	....	....	....	....	....	....	....	3	0	0	0	6	....	....	....	....
1998-99	**Vancouver**	**NHL**	**65**	**0**	**3**	**3**	**114**	**0**	**0**	**0**	**25**	**0.0**	**–19**	**0**	**0.0**	**12:49**	....	....	....	....	....	....	....	....	....
99-2000	**Vancouver**	**NHL**	**63**	**1**	**3**	**4**	**64**	**0**	**0**	**0**	**18**	**5.6**	**–13**	**0**	**0.0**	**15:12**	....	....	....	....	....	....	....	....	....
2000-01	**Vancouver**	**NHL**	**60**	**1**	**4**	**5**	**64**	**0**	**0**	**1**	**21**	**4.8**	**16**	**0**	**0.0**	**9:59**	**2**	**0**	**0**	**0**	**0**	**0**	**0**	**0**	**2:15**
2001-02	**Vancouver**	**NHL**	**44**	**2**	**4**	**6**	**96**	**0**	**0**	**0**	**13**	**15.4**	**4**	**0**	**0.0**	**9:45**	....	....	....	....	....	....	....	....	....
2002-03	**Chicago**	**NHL**	**48**	**2**	**3**	**5**	**87**	**0**	**0**	**0**	**19**	**10.5**	**–4**	**3**	**0.0**	**8:32**	....	....	....	....	....	....	....	....	....
2003-04	**Chicago**	**NHL**	**54**	**1**	**3**	**4**	**73**	**0**	**0**	**0**	**32**	**3.1**	**–16**	**1**	**0.0**	**14:55**	....	....	....	....	....	....	....	....	....
2004-05	Ferencvaros	Hungary	6	1	2	3	8	....	....	....	....	....	....	....	....	....	....	....	....	....	....	....	....	....	....
2005-06	**NY Rangers**	**NHL**	**65**	**3**	**4**	**7**	**66**	**0**	**0**	**0**	**31**	**9.7**	**–10**	**3**	**33.3**	**15:31**	**3**	**0**	**0**	**0**	**0**	**0**	**0**	**0**	**13:35**
2006-07	**NY Rangers**	**NHL**	**8**	**0**	**0**	**0**	**2**	**0**	**0**	**0**	**3**	**0.0**	**0**	**0**	**0.0**	**13:40**	....	....	....	....	....	....	....	....	....
	HC Lugano	Swiss	34	2	3	5	28	....	....	....	....	....	....	....	....	....	6	0	0	0	4	....	....	....	....
2007-08	**NY Rangers**	**NHL**	**52**	**1**	**1**	**2**	**40**	**0**	**0**	**1**	**21**	**4.8**	**0**	**0**	**0.0**	**12:57**	**2**	**0**	**0**	**0**	**0**	**0**	**0**	**0**	**9:41**
	NHL Totals		**488**	**11**	**27**	**38**	**678**	**0**	**0**	**2**	**191**	**5.8**		**7**	**14.3**	**12:41**	**7**	**0**	**0**	**0**	**0**	**0**	**0**	**0**	**9:14**

Traded to **Vancouver** by **NY Islanders** for Gino Odjick, March 23, 1998. Signed as a free agent by **Chicago**, July 15, 2002. Signed as a free agent by **NY Rangers**, July 20, 2004. Signed as a free agent by **Ferencvaros** (Hungary), January 17, 2005. Signed as a free agent by **Edmonton**, July 10, 2008.

STUART, Brad

(STEW-ahrt, BRAD) **DET.**

Defense. Shoots left. 6'2", 213 lbs. Born, Rocky Mountain House, Alta., November 6, 1979. San Jose's 1st choice, 3rd overall, in 1998 Entry Draft.

			Regular Season														Playoffs								
Season	Club	League	GP	G	A	Pts	PIM	PP	SH	GW	S	%	+/-	TF	F%	Min	GP	G	A	Pts	PIM	PP	SH	GW	Min
1995-96	Red Deer	AMHL	35	12	25	37	83																		
	Regina Pats	WHL	3	0	0	0	0																		
1996-97	Regina Pats	WHL	57	7	36	43	58										5	0	4	4	14				
1997-98	Regina Pats	WHL	72	20	45	65	82										9	3	4	7	10				
1998-99	Regina Pats	WHL	29	10	19	29	43																		
	Calgary Hitmen	WHL	30	11	22	33	26										21	8	15	23	59				
99-2000	**San Jose**	**NHL**	**82**	**10**	**26**	**36**	**32**	**5**	**1**	**3**	**133**	**7.5**	**3**	**0**	**0.0**	**20:24**	**12**	**1**	**0**	**1**	**6**	**1**	**0**	**0**	**16:30**
2000-01	**San Jose**	**NHL**	**77**	**5**	**18**	**23**	**56**	**1**	**0**	**2**	**119**	**4.2**	**10**	**0**	**0.0**	**20:06**	**5**	**1**	**0**	**1**	**0**	**0**	**0**	**0**	**20:19**
2001-02	**San Jose**	**NHL**	**82**	**6**	**23**	**29**	**39**	**2**	**0**	**2**	**96**	**6.3**	**13**	**0**	**0.0**	**21:41**	**12**	**0**	**3**	**3**	**8**	**0**	**0**	**0**	**19:42**
2002-03	**San Jose**	**NHL**	**36**	**4**	**10**	**14**	**46**	**2**	**0**	**1**	**63**	**6.3**	**–6**	**0**	**0.0**	**20:53**									
2003-04	**San Jose**	**NHL**	**77**	**9**	**30**	**39**	**34**	**5**	**0**	**0**	**129**	**7.0**	**9**	**0**	**0.0**	**22:09**	**17**	**1**	**5**	**6**	**13**	**0**	**0**	**0**	**23:23**
2004-05			DID NOT PLAY																						
2005-06	**San Jose**	**NHL**	**23**	**2**	**10**	**12**	**14**	**1**	**0**	**0**	**41**	**4.9**	**–2**	**0**	**0.0**	**23:15**									
	Boston	**NHL**	**55**	**10**	**21**	**31**	**38**	**6**	**0**	**2**	**122**	**8.2**	**–6**	**0**	**0.0**	**25:40**									
2006-07	**Boston**	**NHL**	**48**	**7**	**10**	**17**	**26**	**1**	**0**	**2**	**74**	**9.5**	**–22**	**0**	**0.0**	**22:55**									
	Calgary	**NHL**	**27**	**0**	**5**	**5**	**18**	**0**	**0**	**0**	**35**	**0.0**	**12**	**0**	**0.0**	**22:48**	**6**	**0**	**1**	**1**	**6**	**0**	**0**	**0**	**25:16**
2007-08	**Los Angeles**	**NHL**	**63**	**5**	**16**	**21**	**67**	**2**	**0**	**1**	**111**	**4.5**	**–16**	**4**	**0.0**	**21:13**									
	♦ Detroit	**NHL**	**9**	**1**	**1**	**2**	**2**	**0**	**0**	**0**	**21**	**4.8**	**6**	**0**	**0.0**	**20:46**	**21**	**1**	**6**	**7**	**14**	**0**	**0**	**1**	**21:40**
	NHL Totals		**579**	**59**	**170**	**229**	**372**	**25**	**1**	**13**	**944**	**6.3**		**4**	**0.0**	**21:50**	**73**	**4**	**15**	**19**	**47**	**1**	**0**	**1**	**21:06**

WHL East Second All-Star Team (1998) • WHL East First All-Star Team (1999) • Canadian Major Junior First All-Star Team (1999) • Canadian Major Junior Defenseman of the Year (1999) • NHL All-Rookie Team (2000)

• Missed majority of 2002-03 season recovering from ankle (January 4, 2003 vs. Los Angeles) and head (February 21, 2003 vs. Columbus) injuries. Traded to **Boston** by **San Jose** with Marco Sturm and Wayne Primeau for Joe Thornton, November 30, 2005. Traded to **Calgary** by **Boston** with Wayne Primeau and Washington's 4th round choice (previously acquired, Calgary selected T.J. Brodie) in 2008 Entry Draft for Andrew Ference and Chuck Kobasew, February 10, 2007. Signed as a free agent by **Los Angeles**, July 3, 2007. Traded to **Detroit** by **Los Angeles** for Detroit's 2nd round choice (later traded to Colorado - Colorado selected Peter Delmas) in 2008 Entry Draft and Detroit's 4th round choice in 2009 Entry Draft, February 26, 2008.

STUART, Colin

(STEW-ahrt, KAW-lihn) **ATL.**

Left wing. Shoots left. 6'2", 205 lbs. Born, Rochester, MN, July 8, 1982. Atlanta's 5th choice, 135th overall, in 2001 Entry Draft.

Season	Club	League	GP	G	A	Pts	PIM	PP	SH	GW	S	%	+/-	TF	F%	Min	GP	G	A	Pts	PIM	PP	SH	GW	Min
1998-99	Roch. Lourdes	High-MN	23	22	32	54																			
99-2000	Lincoln Stars	USHL	53	18	19	37	38										9	1	3	4	2				
2000-01	Colorado College	WCHA	41	2	7	9	26																		
2001-02	Colorado College	WCHA	43	13	9	22	34																		
2002-03	Colorado College	WCHA	42	13	11	24	56																		
2003-04	Colorado College	WCHA	30	10	12	22	38																		
2004-05	Chicago Wolves	AHL	39	3	2	5	12																		
	Gwinnett	ECHL	5	1	3	4	4																		
2005-06	Chicago Wolves	AHL	78	13	14	27	65																		
2006-07	Chicago Wolves	AHL	67	18	11	29	75										15	2	5	7	10				
2007-08	**Atlanta**	**NHL**	**18**	**3**	**2**	**5**	**6**	**0**	**1**	**1**	**19**	**15.8**	**2**	**7**	**57.1**	**12:20**									
	Chicago Wolves	AHL	58	8	8	16	45										24	3	3	6	18				
	NHL Totals		**18**	**3**	**2**	**5**	**6**	**0**	**1**	**1**	**19**	**15.8**		**7**	**57.1**	**12:20**									

STUART, Mark

(STEW-ahrt, MAHRK) **BOS.**

Defense. Shoots left. 6'2", 213 lbs. Born, Rochester, MN, April 27, 1984. Boston's 1st choice, 21st overall, in 2003 Entry Draft.

Season	Club	League	GP	G	A	Pts	PIM	PP	SH	GW	S	%	+/-	TF	F%	Min	GP	G	A	Pts	PIM	PP	SH	GW	Min
99-2000	Roch. Lourdes	High-MN	28	19	22	41																			
2000-01	USNTDP	U-17	12	1	5	6	6																		
	USNTDP	NAHL	52	2	11	13	114																		
2001-02	USNTDP	U-18	40	9	9	18																			
	USNTDP	USHL	12	0	1	1	25																		
	USNTDP	NAHL	9	0	1	1	18																		
2002-03	Colorado College	WCHA	38	3	17	20	81																		
2003-04	Colorado College	WCHA	37	4	11	15	100																		
2004-05	Colorado College	WCHA	43	5	14	19	94																		
2005-06	**Boston**	**NHL**	**17**	**1**	**1**	**2**	**10**	**0**	**0**	**0**	**9**	**11.1**	**–1**	**0**	**0.0**	**17:46**									
	Providence Bruins	AHL	60	4	3	7	76										6	0	0	0	25				
2006-07	**Boston**	**NHL**	**15**	**0**	**1**	**1**	**14**	**0**	**0**	**0**	**4**	**0.0**	**7**	**0**	**0.0**	**10:23**									
	Providence Bruins	AHL	49	4	16	20	62										3	0	1	1	9				
2007-08	**Boston**	**NHL**	**82**	**4**	**4**	**8**	**81**	**0**	**0**	**1**	**60**	**6.7**	**2**	**0**	**0.0**	**15:22**	**7**	**0**	**1**	**1**	**8**	**0**	**0**	**0**	**16:00**
	NHL Totals		**114**	**5**	**6**	**11**	**105**	**0**	**0**	**1**	**73**	**6.8**		**0**	**0.0**	**15:05**	**7**	**0**	**1**	**1**	**8**	**0**	**0**	**0**	**16:00**

WCHA All-Rookie Team (2003) • WCHA Second All-Star Team (2005) • NCAA West First All-American Team (2005)

STUMPEL, Jozef

(STUM-puhl, JOH-zehf)

Center. Shoots right. 6'3", 222 lbs. Born, Nitra, Czech., July 20, 1972. Boston's 2nd choice, 40th overall, in 1991 Entry Draft.

Season	Club	League	GP	G	A	Pts	PIM	PP	SH	GW	S	%	+/-	TF	F%	Min	GP	G	A	Pts	PIM	PP	SH	GW	Min
1989-90	Plastika Nitra	Czech-2	38	12	11	23																			
1990-91	AC Nitra	Czech	49	23	22	45	14																		
1991-92	Kolner EC	Germany	33	19	18	37	35										4	1	1	2	0				
	Boston	**NHL**	**4**	**1**	**0**	**1**	**0**	**0**	**0**	**0**	**3**	**33.3**	**1**												
1992-93	**Boston**	**NHL**	**13**	**1**	**3**	**4**	**4**	**0**	**0**	**0**	**8**	**12.5**	**–3**												
	Providence Bruins	AHL	56	31	61	92	26										6	4	4	8	0				
1993-94	**Boston**	**NHL**	**59**	**8**	**15**	**23**	**14**	**0**	**0**	**1**	**62**	**12.9**	**4**				**13**	**1**	**7**	**8**	**4**	**0**	**0**	**0**	
	Providence Bruins	AHL	17	5	12	17	4																		
1994-95	Kolner Haie	Germany	25	16	23	39	18																		
	Boston	**NHL**	**44**	**5**	**13**	**18**	**8**	**1**	**0**	**2**	**46**	**10.9**	**4**				**5**	**0**	**0**	**0**	**0**	**0**	**0**	**0**	
1995-96	**Boston**	**NHL**	**76**	**18**	**36**	**54**	**14**	**5**	**0**	**2**	**158**	**11.4**	**–8**				**5**	**1**	**2**	**3**	**0**	**0**	**0**	**0**	
1996-97	**Boston**	**NHL**	**78**	**21**	**55**	**76**	**14**	**6**	**0**	**1**	**168**	**12.5**	**–22**												
1997-98	**Los Angeles**	**NHL**	**77**	**21**	**58**	**79**	**53**	**4**	**0**	**2**	**162**	**13.0**	**17**				**4**	**1**	**2**	**3**	**2**	**0**	**0**	**0**	
1998-99	**Los Angeles**	**NHL**	**64**	**13**	**21**	**34**	**10**	**1**	**0**	**1**	**131**	**9.9**	**–18**	**1484**	**54.0**	**19:44**									
99-2000	**Los Angeles**	**NHL**	**57**	**17**	**41**	**58**	**10**	**3**	**0**	**7**	**126**	**13.5**	**23**	**1088**	**50.6**	**19:16**	**4**	**0**	**4**	**4**	**8**	**0**	**0**	**0**	**21:06**
2000-01	Bratislava	Slovakia	9	2	4	6	16																		
	Los Angeles	**NHL**	**63**	**16**	**39**	**55**	**14**	**9**	**0**	**6**	**95**	**16.8**	**20**	**1278**	**52.7**	**19:35**	**13**	**3**	**5**	**8**	**10**	**2**	**0**	**1**	**21:56**
2001-02	**Los Angeles**	**NHL**	**9**	**1**	**3**	**4**	**4**	**0**	**0**	**0**	**7**	**14.3**	**1**	**164**	**48.2**	**20:06**									
	Boston	**NHL**	**72**	**7**	**47**	**54**	**14**	**1**	**0**	**3**	**93**	**7.5**	**21**	**1346**	**49.7**	**18:36**	**6**	**0**	**2**	**2**	**0**	**0**	**0**	**0**	**16:43**
	Slovakia	Olympics	2	2	1	3	0																		
2002-03	**Boston**	**NHL**	**78**	**14**	**37**	**51**	**12**	**4**	**0**	**2**	**110**	**12.7**	**0**	**1601**	**54.7**	**18:27**	**5**	**0**	**2**	**2**	**0**	**0**	**0**	**0**	**17:31**
2003-04	**Los Angeles**	**NHL**	**64**	**8**	**29**	**37**	**16**	**4**	**0**	**0**	**78**	**10.3**	**5**	**1105**	**49.3**	**18:46**									
2004-05	HC Slavia Praha	CzRep	52	13	26	39	41										7	4	2	6	10				
2005-06	**Florida**	**NHL**	**74**	**15**	**37**	**52**	**26**	**3**	**1**	**1**	**115**	**13.0**	**11**	**916**	**49.1**	**17:47**									
	Slovakia	Olympics	3	0	0	0	0																		
2006-07	**Florida**	**NHL**	**73**	**23**	**34**	**57**	**22**	**9**	**2**	**4**	**131**	**17.6**	**2**	**986**	**50.5**	**19:07**									
2007-08	**Florida**	**NHL**	**52**	**7**	**13**	**20**	**10**	**3**	**0**	**1**	**64**	**10.9**	**–11**	**643**	**51.2**	**17:22**									
	NHL Totals		**957**	**196**	**481**	**677**	**245**	**53**	**3**	**33**	**1557**	**12.6**		**10611**	**51.6**	**18:46**	**55**	**6**	**24**	**30**	**24**	**2**	**0**	**1**	**19:55**

Traded to **Los Angeles** by **Boston** with Sandy Moger and Boston's 4th round choice (later traded to New Jersey – New Jersey selected Pierre Dagenais) in 1998 Entry Draft for Dmitri Kristich and Byron Dafoe, August 29, 1997. Traded to **Boston** by **Los Angeles** with Glen Murray for Jason Allison and Mikko Eloranta, October 24, 2001. Traded to **Los Angeles** by **Boston** with Boston's 7th round choice (later traded to Nashville – Nashville selected Miroslav Hanuljak) in 2003 Entry Draft for Philadelphia's 4th round choice (previously acquired, Boston selected Patrick Valcak) in 2003 Entry Draft and Detroit's 2nd round choice (previously acquired, Boston selected Martins Karsums) in 2004 Entry Draft, June 22, 2003. Signed as a free agent by **Slavia Praha** (CzRep), August 28, 2004. Signed as a free agent by **Florida**, August 17, 2005.

STURM, Marco

(STURHM, MAHR-koh) **BOS.**

Left wing. Shoots left. 6', 194 lbs. Born, Dingolfing, West Germany, September 8, 1978. San Jose's 2nd choice, 21st overall, in 1996 Entry Draft.

			Regular Season														Playoffs								
Season	Club	League	GP	G	A	Pts	PIM	PP	SH	GW	S	%	+/-	TF	F%	Min	GP	G	A	Pts	PIM	PP	SH	GW	Min
1995-96	EV Landshut	Germany	47	12	20	32	50	....	....	....	....	....	....	....	....	....	11	1	3	4	18	....	....	....	....
1996-97	EV Landshut	Germany	46	16	27	43	40	....	....	....	....	....	....	....	....	....	7	1	4	5	6	....	....	....	....
1997-98	**San Jose**	**NHL**	**74**	**10**	**20**	**30**	**40**	**2**	**0**	**3**	**118**	**8.5**	**−2**	....	....	....	**2**	**0**	**0**	**0**	**0**	**0**	**0**	**0**	....
	Germany	Olympics	2	0	0	0	0	....	....	....	....	....	....	....	....	....	....	....	....	....	....	....	....	....	....
1998-99	**San Jose**	**NHL**	**78**	**16**	**22**	**38**	**52**	**3**	**2**	**3**	**140**	**11.4**	**7**	**576**	**45.0**	**15:23**	**6**	**2**	**2**	**4**	**4**	**0**	**0**	**1**	**14:16**
99-2000	**San Jose**	**NHL**	**74**	**12**	**15**	**27**	**22**	**2**	**4**	**3**	**120**	**10.0**	**4**	**183**	**45.4**	**14:07**	**12**	**1**	**3**	**4**	**6**	**0**	**0**	**0**	**13:00**
2000-01	**San Jose**	**NHL**	**81**	**14**	**18**	**32**	**28**	**2**	**3**	**5**	**153**	**9.2**	**9**	**517**	**40.2**	**16:06**	**6**	**0**	**2**	**2**	**0**	**0**	**0**	**0**	**18:18**
2001-02	**San Jose**	**NHL**	**77**	**21**	**20**	**41**	**32**	**4**	**3**	**5**	**174**	**12.1**	**23**	**105**	**47.6**	**15:39**	**12**	**3**	**2**	**5**	**2**	**0**	**0**	**0**	**15:33**
	Germany	Olympics	5	0	1	1	0	....	....	....	....	....	....	....	....	....	....	....	....	....	....	....	....	....	....
2002-03	**San Jose**	**NHL**	**82**	**28**	**20**	**48**	**16**	**6**	**0**	**2**	**208**	**13.5**	**9**	**83**	**48.2**	**16:31**	....	....	....	....	....	....	....	....	....
2003-04	**San Jose**	**NHL**	**64**	**21**	**20**	**41**	**36**	**10**	**2**	**6**	**158**	**13.3**	**0**	**7**	**42.9**	**16:25**	....	....	....	....	....	....	....	....	....
2004-05	ERC Ingolstadt	Germany	45	22	16	38	56	....	....	....	....	....	....	....	....	....	11	3	4	7	12	....	....	....	....
2005-06	**San Jose**	**NHL**	**23**	**6**	**10**	**16**	**16**	**3**	**0**	**0**	**48**	**12.5**	**−8**	**9**	**44.4**	**17:28**	....	....	....	....	....	....	....	....	....
	Boston	**NHL**	**51**	**23**	**20**	**43**	**32**	**5**	**0**	**6**	**132**	**17.4**	**14**	**3**	**33.3**	**18:44**	....	....	....	....	....	....	....	....	....
2006-07	**Boston**	**NHL**	**76**	**27**	**17**	**44**	**46**	**10**	**2**	**1**	**224**	**12.1**	**−24**	**13**	**61.5**	**18:36**	....	....	....	....	....	....	....	....	....
2007-08	**Boston**	**NHL**	**80**	**27**	**29**	**56**	**40**	**10**	**1**	**5**	**229**	**11.8**	**11**	**34**	**29.4**	**18:00**	**7**	**2**	**2**	**4**	**6**	**0**	**1**	**1**	**18:20**
	NHL Totals		**760**	**205**	**211**	**416**	**360**	**57**	**17**	**39**	**1704**	**12.0**		**1530**	**43.5**	**16:34**	**45**	**8**	**11**	**19**	**18**	**0**	**1**	**2**	**15:29**

Played in NHL All-Star Game (1999)

Signed as a free agent by **Ingolstadt** (Germany), August 8, 2004. Traded to **Boston** by **San Jose** with Brad Stuart and Wayne Primeau for Joe Thornton, November 30, 2005.

SULLIVAN, Steve

(SUHL-ih-vuhn, STEEV) **NSH.**

Right wing. Shoots right. 5'8", 165 lbs. Born, Timmins, Ont., July 6, 1974. New Jersey's 10th choice, 233rd overall, in 1994 Entry Draft.

			Regular Season														Playoffs								
Season	Club	League	GP	G	A	Pts	PIM	PP	SH	GW	S	%	+/-	TF	F%	Min	GP	G	A	Pts	PIM	PP	SH	GW	Min
1991-92	Timmins	NOJHA	47	66	55	121	141	....	....	....	....	....	....	....	....	....	....	....	....	....	....	....	....	....	....
1992-93	Sault Ste. Marie	OHL	62	36	27	63	44	....	....	....	....	....	....	....	....	....	16	3	8	11	18	....	....	....	....
1993-94	Sault Ste. Marie	OHL	63	51	62	113	82	....	....	....	....	....	....	....	....	....	14	9	16	25	22	....	....	....	....
1994-95	Albany River Rats	AHL	75	31	50	81	124	....	....	....	....	....	....	....	....	....	14	4	7	11	10	....	....	....	....
1995-96	**New Jersey**	**NHL**	**16**	**5**	**4**	**9**	**8**	**2**	**0**	**1**	**23**	**21.7**	**3**	....	....	....	....	....	....	....	....	....	....	....	....
	Albany River Rats	AHL	53	33	42	75	127	....	....	....	....	....	....	....	....	....	4	3	0	3	6	....	....	....	....
1996-97	**New Jersey**	**NHL**	**33**	**8**	**14**	**22**	**14**	**2**	**0**	**2**	**63**	**12.7**	**9**	....	....	....	....	....	....	....	....	....	....	....	....
	Albany River Rats	AHL	15	8	7	15	16	....	....	....	....	....	....	....	....	....	....	....	....	....	....	....	....	....	....
	Toronto	**NHL**	**21**	**5**	**11**	**16**	**23**	**1**	**0**	**1**	**45**	**11.1**	**5**	....	....	....	....	....	....	....	....	....	....	....	....
1997-98	**Toronto**	**NHL**	**63**	**10**	**18**	**28**	**40**	**1**	**0**	**1**	**112**	**8.9**	**−8**	....	....	....	....	....	....	....	....	....	....	....	....
1998-99	**Toronto**	**NHL**	**63**	**20**	**20**	**40**	**28**	**4**	**0**	**5**	**110**	**18.2**	**12**	**685**	**44.4**	**14:12**	**13**	**3**	**3**	**6**	**14**	**2**	**0**	**0**	**16:20**
99-2000	**Toronto**	**NHL**	**7**	**0**	**1**	**1**	**4**	**0**	**0**	**0**	**11**	**0.0**	**−1**	**47**	**48.9**	**11:52**	....	....	....	....	....	....	....	....	....
	Chicago	**NHL**	**73**	**22**	**42**	**64**	**52**	**2**	**1**	**6**	**169**	**13.0**	**20**	**692**	**48.0**	**18:05**	....	....	....	....	....	....	....	....	....
2000-01	**Chicago**	**NHL**	**81**	**34**	**41**	**75**	**54**	**6**	**8**	**3**	**204**	**16.7**	**3**	**649**	**42.4**	**20:32**	....	....	....	....	....	....	....	....	....
2001-02	**Chicago**	**NHL**	**78**	**21**	**39**	**60**	**67**	**3**	**0**	**8**	**155**	**13.5**	**23**	**758**	**48.9**	**19:10**	**5**	**1**	**0**	**1**	**2**	**0**	**0**	**0**	**18:04**
2002-03	**Chicago**	**NHL**	**82**	**26**	**35**	**61**	**42**	**4**	**2**	**3**	**190**	**13.7**	**15**	**382**	**46.1**	**19:15**	....	....	....	....	....	....	....	....	....
2003-04	**Chicago**	**NHL**	**56**	**15**	**28**	**43**	**36**	**4**	**2**	**4**	**140**	**10.7**	**−7**	**103**	**44.7**	**21:19**	....	....	....	....	....	....	....	....	....
	Nashville	**NHL**	**24**	**9**	**21**	**30**	**12**	**7**	**0**	**0**	**78**	**11.5**	**8**	**124**	**43.6**	**20:02**	**6**	**1**	**1**	**2**	**6**	**0**	**0**	**1**	**18:58**
2004-05			DID NOT PLAY																						
2005-06	**Nashville**	**NHL**	**69**	**31**	**37**	**68**	**50**	**13**	**4**	**5**	**192**	**16.1**	**2**	**42**	**52.4**	**19:06**	**5**	**0**	**2**	**2**	**0**	**0**	**0**	**0**	**17:02**
2006-07	**Nashville**	**NHL**	**57**	**22**	**38**	**60**	**20**	**6**	**3**	**4**	**122**	**18.0**	**16**	**39**	**38.5**	**19:25**	....	....	....	....	....	....	....	....	....
2007-08	**Nashville**	**NHL**	DID NOT PLAY – INJURED																						
	NHL Totals		**723**	**228**	**349**	**577**	**450**	**55**	**20**	**43**	**1614**	**14.1**		**3521**	**46.0**	**18:52**	**29**	**5**	**6**	**11**	**22**	**2**	**0**	**1**	**17:18**

AHL First All-Star Team (1996)

Traded to **Toronto** by **New Jersey** with Jason Smith and the rights to Alyn McCauley for Doug Gilmour, Dave Ellett and New Jersey's 3rd round choice (previously acquired, New Jersey selected Andre Lakos) in 1999 Entry Draft, February 25, 1997. Claimed on waivers by **Chicago** from **Toronto**, October 23, 1999. Traded to **Nashville** by **Chicago** for Nashville's 2nd round choices in 2004 (Ryan Garlock) and 2005 (Michael Blunden) Entry Drafts, February 16, 2004. • Missed remainder of 2006-07 season and entire 2007-08 season recovering from back injury, suffered in game vs. Montreal, February 22, 2006..

SUNDIN, Mats

(suhn-DEEN, MATS)

Center. Shoots right. 6'5", 231 lbs. Born, Bromma, Sweden, February 13, 1971. Quebec's 1st choice, 1st overall, in 1989 Entry Draft.

			Regular Season														Playoffs								
Season	Club	League	GP	G	A	Pts	PIM	PP	SH	GW	S	%	+/-	TF	F%	Min	GP	G	A	Pts	PIM	PP	SH	GW	Min
1988-89	Nacka HK	Sweden-2	25	10	8	18	18	....	....	....	....	....	....	....	....	....	....	....	....	....	....	....	....	....	....
1989-90	Djurgarden	Sweden	34	10	8	18	16	....	....	....	....	....	....	....	....	....	8	7	0	7	4	....	....	....	....
1990-91	**Quebec**	**NHL**	**80**	**23**	**36**	**59**	**58**	**4**	**0**	**0**	**155**	**14.8**	**−24**	....	....	....	....	....	....	....	....	....	....	....	....
1991-92	**Quebec**	**NHL**	**80**	**33**	**43**	**76**	**103**	**8**	**2**	**2**	**231**	**14.3**	**−19**	....	....	....	....	....	....	....	....	....	....	....	....
1992-93	**Quebec**	**NHL**	**80**	**47**	**67**	**114**	**96**	**13**	**4**	**9**	**215**	**21.9**	**21**	....	....	....	**6**	**3**	**1**	**4**	**6**	**1**	**0**	**0**	....
1993-94	**Quebec**	**NHL**	**84**	**32**	**53**	**85**	**60**	**6**	**2**	**4**	**226**	**14.2**	**1**	....	....	....	....	....	....	....	....	....	....	....	....
1994-95	Djurgarden	Sweden	12	7	2	9	14	....	....	....	....	....	....	....	....	....	....	....	....	....	....	....	....	....	....
	Toronto	**NHL**	**47**	**23**	**24**	**47**	**14**	**9**	**0**	**4**	**173**	**13.3**	**−5**	....	....	....	**7**	**5**	**4**	**9**	**4**	**2**	**0**	**1**	....
1995-96	**Toronto**	**NHL**	**76**	**33**	**50**	**83**	**46**	**7**	**6**	**7**	**301**	**11.0**	**8**	....	....	....	**6**	**3**	**1**	**4**	**4**	**2**	**0**	**1**	....
1996-97	**Toronto**	**NHL**	**82**	**41**	**53**	**94**	**59**	**7**	**4**	**8**	**281**	**14.6**	**6**	....	....	....	....	....	....	....	....	....	....	....	....
1997-98	**Toronto**	**NHL**	**82**	**33**	**41**	**74**	**49**	**9**	**1**	**5**	**219**	**15.1**	**−3**	....	....	....	....	....	....	....	....	....	....	....	....
	Sweden	Olympics	4	3	0	3	4	....	....	....	....	....	....	....	....	....	....	....	....	....	....	....	....	....	....
1998-99	**Toronto**	**NHL**	**82**	**31**	**52**	**83**	**58**	**4**	**0**	**6**	**209**	**14.8**	**22**	**1993**	**57.3**	**20:41**	**17**	**8**	**8**	**16**	**16**	**3**	**0**	**2**	**22:46**
99-2000	**Toronto**	**NHL**	**73**	**32**	**41**	**73**	**46**	**10**	**2**	**7**	**184**	**17.4**	**16**	**1619**	**50.8**	**20:11**	**12**	**3**	**5**	**8**	**10**	**0**	**0**	**1**	**21:27**
2000-01	**Toronto**	**NHL**	**82**	**28**	**46**	**74**	**76**	**9**	**0**	**6**	**226**	**12.4**	**15**	**1870**	**56.6**	**19:21**	**11**	**6**	**7**	**13**	**14**	**2**	**1**	**1**	**20:12**
2001-02	**Toronto**	**NHL**	**82**	**41**	**39**	**80**	**94**	**10**	**2**	**9**	**262**	**15.6**	**6**	**1812**	**57.5**	**19:20**	**8**	**2**	**5**	**7**	**4**	**0**	**0**	**0**	**20:07**
	Sweden	Olympics	4	5	4	*9	10	....	....	....	....	....	....	....	....	....	....	....	....	....	....	....	....	....	....
2002-03	**Toronto**	**NHL**	**75**	**37**	**35**	**72**	**58**	**16**	**3**	**8**	**223**	**16.6**	**1**	**1774**	**56.1**	**20:15**	**7**	**1**	**3**	**4**	**6**	**1**	**0**	**0**	**24:17**
2003-04	**Toronto**	**NHL**	**81**	**31**	**44**	**75**	**52**	**11**	**1**	**10**	**226**	**13.7**	**11**	**1705**	**53.0**	**19:52**	**9**	**4**	**5**	**9**	**8**	**0**	**0**	**1**	**18:24**
2004-05			DID NOT PLAY																						
2005-06	**Toronto**	**NHL**	**70**	**31**	**47**	**78**	**58**	**16**	**2**	**2**	**220**	**14.1**	**7**	**1557**	**54.0**	**19:59**	....	....	....	....	....	....	....	....	....
	Sweden	Olympics	8	3	5	8	4	....	....	....	....	....	....	....	....	....	....	....	....	....	....	....	....	....	....
2006-07	**Toronto**	**NHL**	**75**	**27**	**49**	**76**	**62**	**6**	**1**	**3**	**321**	**8.4**	**−2**	**1790**	**55.2**	**20:28**	....	....	....	....	....	....	....	....	....
2007-08	**Toronto**	**NHL**	**74**	**32**	**46**	**78**	**76**	**10**	**1**	**4**	**259**	**12.4**	**17**	**1713**	**55.2**	**20:04**	....	....	....	....	....	....	....	....	....
	NHL Totals		**1305**	**555**	**766**	**1321**	**1065**	**155**	**31**	**94**	**3931**	**14.1**		**15833**	**55.2**	**20:01**	**83**	**35**	**39**	**74**	**72**	**11**	**1**	**7**	**21:18**

NHL Second All-Star Team (2002, 2004)

Played in NHL All-Star Game (1996, 1997, 1998, 1999, 2000, 2001, 2002, 2004)

Traded to **Toronto** by **Quebec** with Garth Butcher, Todd Warriner and Philadelphia's 1st round choice (previously acquired, later traded to Washington – Washington selected Nolan Baumgartner) in 1994 Entry Draft for Wendel Clark, Sylvain Lefebvre, Landon Wilson and Toronto's 1st round choice (Jeffrey Kealty) in 1994 Entry Draft, June 28, 1994.

SUTER, Ryan

(SOO-tuhr, RIGH-uhn) **NSH.**

Defense. Shoots left. 6'1", 196 lbs. Born, Madison, WI, January 21, 1985. Nashville's 1st choice, 7th overall, in 2003 Entry Draft.

			Regular Season														Playoffs								
Season	Club	League	GP	G	A	Pts	PIM	PP	SH	GW	S	%	+/-	TF	F%	Min	GP	G	A	Pts	PIM	PP	SH	GW	Min
2000-01	Culver Academy	High-IN	26	13	32	45	....	....	....	....	....	....	....	....	....	....	....	....	....	....	....	....	....	....	....
2001-02	USNTDP	U-17	8	2	11	13	21	....	....	....	....	....	....	....	....	....	....	....	....	....	....	....	....	....	....
	USNTDP	U-18	27	4	10	14	6	....	....	....	....	....	....	....	....	....	....	....	....	....	....	....	....	....	....
	USNTDP	NAHL	35	2	10	12	75	....	....	....	....	....	....	....	....	....	....	....	....	....	....	....	....	....	....
2002-03	USNTDP	NAHL	9	2	5	7	12	....	....	....	....	....	....	....	....	....	....	....	....	....	....	....	....	....	....
	USNTDP	U-18	42	7	17	24	124	....	....	....	....	....	....	....	....	....	....	....	....	....	....	....	....	....	....
2003-04	U. of Wisconsin	WCHA	39	3	16	19	93	....	....	....	....	....	....	....	....	....	....	....	....	....	....	....	....	....	....
2004-05	Milwaukee	AHL	63	7	16	23	70	....	....	....	....	....	....	....	....	....	7	1	5	6	16	....	....	....	....
2005-06	**Nashville**	**NHL**	**71**	**1**	**15**	**16**	**66**	**0**	**0**	**0**	**84**	**1.2**	**7**	**0**	**0.0**	**17:21**	....	....	....	....	....	....	....	....	....
2006-07	**Nashville**	**NHL**	**82**	**8**	**16**	**24**	**54**	**1**	**0**	**0**	**87**	**9.2**	**10**	**0**	**0.0**	**20:09**	**5**	**1**	**0**	**1**	**8**	**0**	**0**	**0**	**23:19**
2007-08	**Nashville**	**NHL**	**76**	**7**	**24**	**31**	**71**	**1**	**0**	**1**	**138**	**5.1**	**3**	**0**	**0.0**	**20:35**	**6**	**1**	**1**	**2**	**4**	**0**	**0**	**0**	**21:12**
	NHL Totals		**229**	**16**	**55**	**71**	**191**	**2**	**0**	**1**	**309**	**5.2**		**0**	**0.0**	**19:26**	**11**	**2**	**1**	**3**	**12**	**0**	**0**	**0**	**22:10**

WCHA All-Rookie Team (2004)

SUTHERBY, Brian
(SUH-thur-bee, BRIGH-uhn) **ANA.**

Center. Shoots left. 6'3", 210 lbs. Born, Edmonton, Alta., March 1, 1982. Washington's 1st choice, 26th overall, in 2000 Entry Draft.

			Regular Season														Playoffs								
Season	Club	League	GP	G	A	Pts	PIM	PP	SH	GW	S	%	+/-	TF	F%	Min	GP	G	A	Pts	PIM	PP	SH	GW	Min
1997-98	CAC Cement	AMHL	36	36	23	59	60	....	....	....	....	....	....	....	....	....	....	....	....	....	....	....	....	....	....
1998-99	Moose Jaw	WHL	66	9	12	21	47	....	....	....	....	....	....	....	....	....	11	0	1	1	0	....	....	....	....
99-2000	Moose Jaw	WHL	47	18	17	35	102	....	....	....	....	....	....	....	....	....	4	1	1	2	12	....	....	....	....
2000-01	Moose Jaw	WHL	59	34	43	77	138	....	....	....	....	....	....	....	....	....	4	2	1	3	10	....	....	....	....
2001-02	**Washington**	**NHL**	**7**	**0**	**0**	**0**	**2**	**0**	**0**	**0**	**3**	**0.0**	**–3**	**39**	**35.9**	**7:17**	....	....	....	....	....	....	....	....	....
	Moose Jaw	WHL	36	18	27	45	75	....	....	....	....	....	....	....	....	....	12	7	5	12	33	....	....	....	....
2002-03	**Washington**	**NHL**	**72**	**2**	**9**	**11**	**93**	**0**	**0**	**0**	**38**	**5.3**	**7**	**288**	**43.8**	**9:44**	**5**	**0**	**0**	**0**	**10**	**0**	**0**	**0**	**4:10**
	Portland Pirates	AHL	5	0	5	5	11	....	....	....	....	....	....	....	....	....	....	....	....	....	....	....	....	....	....
2003-04	**Washington**	**NHL**	**30**	**2**	**0**	**2**	**28**	**0**	**0**	**0**	**24**	**8.3**	**–5**	**116**	**41.4**	**10:15**	....	....	....	....	....	....	....	....	....
	Portland Pirates	AHL	6	2	4	6	16	....	....	....	....	....	....	....	....	....	....	....	....	....	....	....	....	....	....
2004-05	Portland Pirates	AHL	53	10	19	29	115	....	....	....	....	....	....	....	....	....	....	....	....	....	....	....	....	....	....
2005-06	**Washington**	**NHL**	**76**	**14**	**16**	**30**	**73**	**0**	**2**	**0**	**85**	**16.5**	**–17**	**904**	**48.7**	**13:44**	....	....	....	....	....	....	....	....	....
2006-07	**Washington**	**NHL**	**69**	**7**	**10**	**17**	**78**	**1**	**0**	**0**	**87**	**8.0**	**–9**	**762**	**50.1**	**13:41**	....	....	....	....	....	....	....	....	....
2007-08	**Washington**	**NHL**	**5**	**1**	**0**	**1**	**7**	**0**	**0**	**0**	**3**	**33.3**	**–2**	**23**	**52.2**	**6:49**	....	....	....	....	....	....	....	....	....
	Anaheim	**NHL**	**45**	**0**	**1**	**1**	**57**	**0**	**0**	**0**	**46**	**0.0**	**–2**	**255**	**45.5**	**8:47**	**5**	**0**	**0**	**0**	**2**	**0**	**0**	**0**	**5:29**
	NHL Totals		**304**	**26**	**36**	**62**	**338**	**1**	**2**	**0**	**286**	**9.1**		**2387**	**47.7**	**11:26**	**10**	**0**	**0**	**0**	**12**	**0**	**0**	**0**	**4:49**

• Missed majority of 2003-04 season recovering from groin injury suffered in game vs. St. Louis, October 18, 2003. Traded to **Anaheim** by **Washington** for Anaheim's 2nd round choice in 2009 Entry Draft, November 19, 2007.

SUTTON, Andy
(SUH-tuhn, AN-dee) **NYI**

Defense. Shoots left. 6'6", 245 lbs. Born, Kingston, Ont., March 10, 1975.

			Regular Season														Playoffs								
Season	Club	League	GP	G	A	Pts	PIM	PP	SH	GW	S	%	+/-	TF	F%	Min	GP	G	A	Pts	PIM	PP	SH	GW	Min
1991-92	Gananoque	OHA-B	36	11	9	20		....	....	....	....	....	....	....	....	....	14	9	21	30	....	....	....	....	....
1992-93	Gananoque	OHA-B	38	14	9	23	....	....	....	....	....	....	....	....	....	....	12	16	13	29	....	....	....	....	....
1993-94	St. Mike's B's	MTJHL	48	17	23	40	161	....	....	....	....	....	....	....	....	....	3	0	0	0	20	....	....	....	....
1994-95	Michigan Tech	WCHA	19	2	1	3	42	....	....	....	....	....	....	....	....	....	....	....	....	....	....	....	....	....	....
1995-96	Michigan Tech	WCHA	33	2	2	4	58	....	....	....	....	....	....	....	....	....	....	....	....	....	....	....	....	....	....
1996-97	Michigan Tech	WCHA	32	2	7	9	73	....	....	....	....	....	....	....	....	....	....	....	....	....	....	....	....	....	....
1997-98	Michigan Tech	WCHA	38	16	24	40	97	....	....	....	....	....	....	....	....	....	....	....	....	....	....	....	....	....	....
	Kentucky	AHL	7	0	0	0	33	....	....	....	....	....	....	....	....	....	....	....	....	....	....	....	....	....	....
1998-99	**San Jose**	**NHL**	**31**	**0**	**3**	**3**	**65**	**0**	**0**	**0**	**24**	**0.0**	**–4**	**0**	**0.0**	**12:58**	....	....	....	....	....	....	....	....	....
	Kentucky	AHL	21	5	10	15	53	....	....	....	....	....	....	....	....	....	5	0	0	0	23	....	....	....	....
99-2000	**San Jose**	**NHL**	**40**	**1**	**1**	**2**	**80**	**0**	**0**	**0**	**29**	**3.4**	**–5**	**0**	**0.0**	**12:57**	....	....	....	....	....	....	....	....	....
	Kentucky	AHL	3	0	1	1	0	....	....	....	....	....	....	....	....	....	....	....	....	....	....	....	....	....	....
2000-01	**Minnesota**	**NHL**	**69**	**3**	**4**	**7**	**131**	**2**	**0**	**0**	**64**	**4.7**	**–11**	**3**	**33.3**	**12:55**	....	....	....	....	....	....	....	....	....
2001-02	**Minnesota**	**NHL**	**19**	**2**	**4**	**6**	**35**	**1**	**0**	**0**	**21**	**9.5**	**–4**	**2**	**0.0**	**10:57**	....	....	....	....	....	....	....	....	....
	Atlanta	**NHL**	**24**	**0**	**4**	**4**	**46**	**0**	**0**	**0**	**20**	**0.0**	**0**	**0**	**0.0**	**15:25**	....	....	....	....	....	....	....	....	....
2002-03	**Atlanta**	**NHL**	**53**	**3**	**18**	**21**	**114**	**1**	**1**	**0**	**65**	**4.6**	**–8**	**3**	**33.3**	**18:00**	....	....	....	....	....	....	....	....	....
2003-04	**Atlanta**	**NHL**	**65**	**8**	**13**	**21**	**94**	**7**	**1**	**1**	**102**	**7.8**	**0**	**1**	**0.0**	**23:21**	....	....	....	....	....	....	....	....	....
2004-05	GCK Lions Zurich	Swiss-2	18	8	18	26	58	....	....	....	....	....	....	....	....	....	6	2	4	6	16	....	....	....	....
	ZSC Lions Zurich	Swiss	8	2	2	4	32	....	....	....	....	....	....	....	....	....	1	0	1	1	2	....	....	....	....
2005-06	**Atlanta**	**NHL**	**76**	**8**	**17**	**25**	**144**	**2**	**1**	**3**	**86**	**9.3**	**13**	**1**	**0.0**	**21:05**	....	....	....	....	....	....	....	....	....
2006-07	**Atlanta**	**NHL**	**55**	**2**	**14**	**16**	**76**	**0**	**1**	**0**	**51**	**3.9**	**6**	**0**	**0.0**	**19:28**	**4**	**0**	**0**	**0**	**10**	**0**	**0**	**0**	**17:34**
2007-08	**NY Islanders**	**NHL**	**58**	**1**	**7**	**8**	**86**	**0**	**0**	**1**	**57**	**1.8**	**–6**	**0**	**0.0**	**18:10**	....	....	....	....	....	....	....	....	....
	NHL Totals		**490**	**28**	**85**	**113**	**871**	**13**	**4**	**5**	**519**	**5.4**		**10**	**20.0**	**17:31**	**4**	**0**	**0**	**0**	**10**	**0**	**0**	**0**	**17:34**

WCHA Second All-Star Team (1998)

Signed as a free agent by **San Jose**, March 20, 1998. Traded to **Minnesota** by **San Jose** with San Jose's 7th round choice (Peter Bartos) in 2000 Entry Draft and San Jose's 3rd round choice (later traded to Atlanta – later traded to Pittsburgh – later traded to Columbus – Columbus selected Aaron Johnson) in 2001 Entry Draft for Minnesota's 8th round choice (later traded to Calgary – Calgary selected Joe Campbell) in 2001 Entry Draft and future considerations, June 12, 2000. Traded to **Atlanta** by **Minnesota** for Hnat Domenichelli, January 22, 2002. Signed as a free agent by **GCK Zurich** (Swiss-2), September 24, 2004. Loaned to **ZSC Zurich** (Swiss) by **GCK Zurich** (Swiss-2), February 22, 2005. Signed as a free agent by **NY Islanders**, August 10, 2007.

SVATOS, Marek
(SVA-tohs, MAIR-ehk) **COL.**

Right wing. Shoots right. 5'10", 185 lbs. Born, Kosice, Czech., June 17, 1982. Colorado's 10th choice, 227th overall, in 2001 Entry Draft.

			Regular Season														Playoffs								
Season	Club	League	GP	G	A	Pts	PIM	PP	SH	GW	S	%	+/-	TF	F%	Min	GP	G	A	Pts	PIM	PP	SH	GW	Min
99-2000	HC VSZ Kosice Jr.	Slovak-Jr.	39	43	30	73	28	....	....	....	....	....	....	....	....	....	....	....	....	....	....	....	....	....	....
	HC VSZ Kosice	Slovakia	19	2	2	4	0	....	....	....	....	....	....	....	....	....	....	....	....	....	....	....	....	....	....
2000-01	Kootenay Ice	WHL	39	23	18	41	47	....	....	....	....	....	....	....	....	....	11	7	2	9	26	....	....	....	....
2001-02	Kootenay Ice	WHL	53	38	39	77	58	....	....	....	....	....	....	....	....	....	21	12	6	18	40	....	....	....	....
2002-03	Hershey Bears	AHL	30	9	4	13	10	....	....	....	....	....	....	....	....	....	....	....	....	....	....	....	....	....	....
2003-04	**Colorado**	**NHL**	**4**	**2**	**0**	**2**	**0**	**1**	**0**	**1**	**6**	**33.3**	**1**	**0**	**0.0**	**10:18**	**11**	**1**	**5**	**6**	**2**	**0**	**0**	**1**	**12:29**
2004-05	Hershey Bears	AHL	72	18	28	46	69	....	....	....	....	....	....	....	....	....	....	....	....	....	....	....	....	....	....
2005-06	**Colorado**	**NHL**	**61**	**32**	**18**	**50**	**60**	**12**	**0**	**9**	**165**	**19.4**	**0**	**5**	**20.0**	**13:45**	....	....	....	....	....	....	....	....	....
	Slovakia	Olympics	6	0	0	0	0	....	....	....	....	....	....	....	....	....	....	....	....	....	....	....	....	....	....
2006-07	**Colorado**	**NHL**	**66**	**15**	**15**	**30**	**46**	**8**	**0**	**2**	**179**	**8.4**	**1**	**1**	**100.0**	**12:30**	....	....	....	....	....	....	....	....	....
2007-08	**Colorado**	**NHL**	**62**	**26**	**11**	**37**	**32**	**3**	**0**	**6**	**140**	**18.6**	**13**	**3**	**33.3**	**13:39**	....	....	....	....	....	....	....	....	....
	NHL Totals		**193**	**75**	**44**	**119**	**138**	**24**	**0**	**18**	**490**	**15.3**		**9**	**33.3**	**13:13**	**11**	**1**	**5**	**6**	**2**	**0**	**0**	**1**	**12:29**

WHL West Second All-Star Team (2002)

• Missed majority of 2002-03 season recovering from shoulder injury that required surgery, January 28, 2003. • Missed majority of 2003-04 season recovering from shoulder injury suffered in game vs. St. Louis, October 12, 2003.

SVITOV, Alexander
(SVEE-tawf, al-EHX-AN-duhr) **CBJ**

Center. Shoots left. 6'3", 228 lbs. Born, Omsk, USSR, November 3, 1982. Tampa Bay's 1st choice, 3rd overall, in 2001 Entry Draft.

			Regular Season														Playoffs								
Season	Club	League	GP	G	A	Pts	PIM	PP	SH	GW	S	%	+/-	TF	F%	Min	GP	G	A	Pts	PIM	PP	SH	GW	Min
1997-98	Novokuznetsk 2	Russia-3	4	0	0	0	0	....	....	....	....	....	....	....	....	....	....	....	....	....	....	....	....	....	....
1998-99	Omsk 2	Russia-4	27	15	8	23	20	....	....	....	....	....	....	....	....	....	....	....	....	....	....	....	....	....	....
	Avangard Omsk	Russia	....	....	....	....	....	....	....	....	....	....	....	....	....	....	1	0	0	0	0	....	....	....	....
99-2000	Omsk 2	Russia-3	14	13	9	22	62	....	....	....	....	....	....	....	....	....	....	....	....	....	....	....	....	....	....
	Avangard Omsk	Russia	18	3	3	6	45	....	....	....	....	....	....	....	....	....	6	1	0	1	16	....	....	....	....
2000-01	Avangard Omsk	Russia	39	8	6	14	115	....	....	....	....	....	....	....	....	....	14	2	1	3	34	....	....	....	....
2001-02	CSKA Moscow 2	Russia-3	2	1	0	1	2	....	....	....	....	....	....	....	....	....	....	....	....	....	....	....	....	....	....
	Avangard Omsk	Russia	2	0	1	1	2	....	....	....	....	....	....	....	....	....	....	....	....	....	....	....	....	....	....
2002-03	**Tampa Bay**	**NHL**	**63**	**4**	**4**	**8**	**58**	**1**	**0**	**0**	**69**	**5.8**	**–4**	**395**	**42.8**	**8:50**	**7**	**0**	**0**	**0**	**6**	**0**	**0**	**0**	**7:19**
	Springfield	AHL	11	4	5	9	17	....	....	....	....	....	....	....	....	....	....	....	....	....	....	....	....	....	....
2003-04	**Tampa Bay**	**NHL**	**11**	**0**	**3**	**3**	**4**	**0**	**0**	**0**	**16**	**0.0**	**0**	**79**	**58.2**	**9:18**	....	....	....	....	....	....	....	....	....
	Hamilton	AHL	30	9	9	18	79	....	....	....	....	....	....	....	....	....	....	....	....	....	....	....	....	....	....
	Columbus	**NHL**	**29**	**2**	**6**	**8**	**16**	**0**	**0**	**0**	**36**	**5.6**	**–8**	**293**	**43.0**	**12:39**	....	....	....	....	....	....	....	....	....
2004-05	Syracuse Crunch	AHL	69	19	23	42	200	....	....	....	....	....	....	....	....	....	....	....	....	....	....	....	....	....	....
2005-06	Avangard Omsk	Russia	32	3	6	9	142	....	....	....	....	....	....	....	....	....	13	4	1	5	10	....	....	....	....
2006-07	**Columbus**	**NHL**	**76**	**7**	**11**	**18**	**145**	**1**	**0**	**2**	**83**	**8.4**	**–10**	**928**	**50.9**	**13:47**	....	....	....	....	....	....	....	....	....
2007-08	Avangard Omsk	Russia	54	10	11	21	140	....	....	....	....	....	....	....	....	....	4	0	3	3	10	....	....	....	....
	NHL Totals		**179**	**13**	**24**	**37**	**223**	**2**	**0**	**2**	**204**	**6.4**		**1695**	**48.0**	**11:35**	**7**	**0**	**0**	**0**	**6**	**0**	**0**	**0**	**7:19**

Traded to **Columbus** by **Tampa Bay** with Tampa Bay's 3rd round choice (later traded to Calgary – Calgary selected Dustin Boyd) in 2004 Entry Draft for Darryl Sydor and Columbus' 4th round choice (Mike Lundin) in 2004 Entry Draft, January 27, 2004. Signed as a free agent by **Omsk** (Russia), August 17, 2007.

SYDOR, Darryl
(sih-DOHR, DAIR-uhl) **PIT.**

Defense. Shoots left. 6'1", 211 lbs. Born, Edmonton, Alta., May 13, 1972. Los Angeles' 1st choice, 7th overall, in 1990 Entry Draft.

			Regular Season														Playoffs								
Season	Club	League	GP	G	A	Pts	PIM	PP	SH	GW	S	%	+/-	TF	F%	Min	GP	G	A	Pts	PIM	PP	SH	GW	Min
1985-86	Genstar Cement	AAHA	34	20	17	37	60	....	....	....	....	....	....	....	....	....	....	....	....	....	....	....	....	....	....
1986-87	Genstar Cement	AAHA	36	15	20	35	60	....	....	....	....	....	....	....	....	....	....	....	....	....	....	....	....	....	....
1987-88	Edmonton Mets	AJHL	38	10	11	21	54	....	....	....	....	....	....	....	....	....	....	....	....	....	....	....	....	....	....
1988-89	Kamloops Blazers	WHL	65	12	14	26	86	....	....	....	....	....	....	....	....	....	15	1	4	5	19	....	....	....	....
1989-90	Kamloops Blazers	WHL	67	29	66	95	129	....	....	....	....	....	....	....	....	....	17	2	9	11	28	....	....	....	....
1990-91	Kamloops Blazers	WHL	66	27	78	105	88	....	....	....	....	....	....	....	....	....	12	3	*22	25	10	....	....	....	....
1991-92	Kamloops Blazers	WHL	29	9	39	48	33	....	....	....	....	....	....	....	....	....	17	3	15	18	18	....	....	....	....
	Los Angeles	**NHL**	**18**	**1**	**5**	**6**	**22**	**0**	**0**	**0**	**18**	**5.6**	**–3**	....	....	....	....	....	....	....	....	....	....	....	....
1992-93	**Los Angeles**	**NHL**	**80**	**6**	**23**	**29**	**63**	**0**	**0**	**1**	**112**	**5.4**	**–2**	....	....	....	**24**	**3**	**8**	**11**	**16**	**2**	**0**	**0**	....
1993-94	**Los Angeles**	**NHL**	**84**	**8**	**27**	**35**	**94**	**1**	**0**	**0**	**146**	**5.5**	**–9**	....	....	....	....	....	....	....	....	....	....	....	....

Season	Club	League	Regular Season														Playoffs								
			GP	G	A	Pts	PIM	PP	SH	GW	S	%	+/-	TF	F%	Min	GP	G	A	Pts	PIM	PP	SH	GW	Min
1994-95	**Los Angeles**	**NHL**	**48**	**4**	**19**	**23**	**36**	**3**	**0**	**0**	**96**	**4.2**	**–2**	....	....	....	....	....	....	....	....	....	....	....	....
1995-96	**Los Angeles**	**NHL**	**58**	**1**	**11**	**12**	**34**	**1**	**0**	**0**	**84**	**1.2**	**–11**	....	....	....	....	....	....	....	....	....	....	....	....
	Dallas	**NHL**	**26**	**2**	**6**	**8**	**41**	**1**	**0**	**0**	**33**	**6.1**	**–1**	....	....	....	....	....	....	....	....	....	....	....	....
1996-97	**Dallas**	**NHL**	**82**	**8**	**40**	**48**	**51**	**2**	**0**	**2**	**142**	**5.6**	**37**	....	....	....	**7**	**0**	**2**	**2**	**0**	**0**	**0**	**0**	....
1997-98	**Dallas**	**NHL**	**79**	**11**	**35**	**46**	**51**	**4**	**1**	**1**	**166**	**6.6**	**17**	....	....	....	**17**	**0**	**5**	**5**	**14**	**0**	**0**	**0**	....
1998-99 ♦	**Dallas**	**NHL**	**74**	**14**	**34**	**48**	**50**	**9**	**0**	**2**	**163**	**8.6**	**–1**	**1**	**100.0**	**21:16**	**23**	**3**	**9**	**12**	**16**	**1**	**0**	**1**	**22:20**
99-2000	**Dallas**	**NHL**	**74**	**8**	**26**	**34**	**32**	**5**	**0**	**1**	**132**	**6.1**	**6**	**1**	**0.0**	**23:09**	**23**	**1**	**6**	**7**	**6**	**0**	**0**	**0**	**20:48**
2000-01	**Dallas**	**NHL**	**81**	**10**	**37**	**47**	**34**	**8**	**0**	**1**	**140**	**7.1**	**5**	**1**	**0.0**	**21:25**	**10**	**1**	**3**	**4**	**0**	**1**	**0**	**0**	**22:42**
2001-02	**Dallas**	**NHL**	**78**	**4**	**29**	**33**	**50**	**2**	**0**	**0**	**183**	**2.2**	**3**	**0**	**0.0**	**21:07**	....	....	....	....	....	....	....	....	....
2002-03	**Dallas**	**NHL**	**81**	**5**	**31**	**36**	**40**	**2**	**0**	**1**	**132**	**3.8**	**22**	**0**	**0.0**	**18:19**	**12**	**0**	**6**	**6**	**6**	**0**	**0**	**0**	**19:14**
2003-04	**Columbus**	**NHL**	**49**	**2**	**13**	**15**	**26**	**1**	**0**	**0**	**80**	**2.5**	**–19**	**1**	**0.0**	**21:54**	....	....	....	....	....	....	....	....	....
	♦ **Tampa Bay**	**NHL**	**31**	**1**	**6**	**7**	**6**	**0**	**0**	**0**	**42**	**2.4**	**3**	**0**	**0.0**	**19:06**	**23**	**0**	**6**	**6**	**9**	**0**	**0**	**0**	**21:50**
2004-05			DID NOT PLAY																						
2005-06	**Tampa Bay**	**NHL**	**80**	**4**	**19**	**23**	**30**	**1**	**0**	**0**	**64**	**6.3**	**–18**	**1**	**0.0**	**19:06**	**5**	**0**	**1**	**1**	**0**	**0**	**0**	**0**	**17:54**
2006-07	**Dallas**	**NHL**	**74**	**5**	**16**	**21**	**36**	**2**	**0**	**1**	**75**	**6.7**	**–4**	**0**	**0.0**	**20:09**	**7**	**1**	**1**	**2**	**4**	**0**	**0**	**0**	**23:19**
2007-08	**Pittsburgh**	**NHL**	**74**	**1**	**12**	**13**	**26**	**1**	**0**	**0**	**59**	**1.7**	**1**	**0**	**0.0**	**17:33**	**4**	**0**	**0**	**0**	**2**	**0**	**0**	**0**	**16:20**
	NHL Totals		**1171**	**95**	**389**	**484**	**722**	**43**	**1**	**10**	**1867**	**5.1**		**5**	**20.0**	**20:19**	**155**	**9**	**47**	**56**	**73**	**4**	**0**	**1**	**21:13**

WHL West First All-Star Team (1990, 1991, 1992)

Played in NHL All-Star Game (1998, 1999)

Traded to **Dallas** by **Los Angeles** with Los Angeles' 5th round choice (Ryan Christie) in 1996 Entry Draft for Shane Churla and Doug Zmolek, February 17, 1996. Traded to **Columbus** by **Dallas** for Mike Sillinger and Columbus' 2nd round choice (Johan Fransson) in 2004 Entry Draft, July 22, 2003. Traded to **Tampa Bay** by **Columbus** with Columbus' 4th round choice (Mike Lundin) in 2004 Entry Draft for Alexander Svitov and Tampa Bay's 3rd round choice (later traded to Calgary – Calgary selected Dustin Boyd) in 2004 Entry Draft, January 27, 2004. Traded to **Dallas** by **Tampa Bay** for Dallas' 4th round choice (later traded to Ottawa - Ottawa selected Derek Grant) in 2008 Entry Draft, July 2, 2006. Signed as a free agent by **Pittsburgh**, July 2, 2007.

SYKORA, Petr

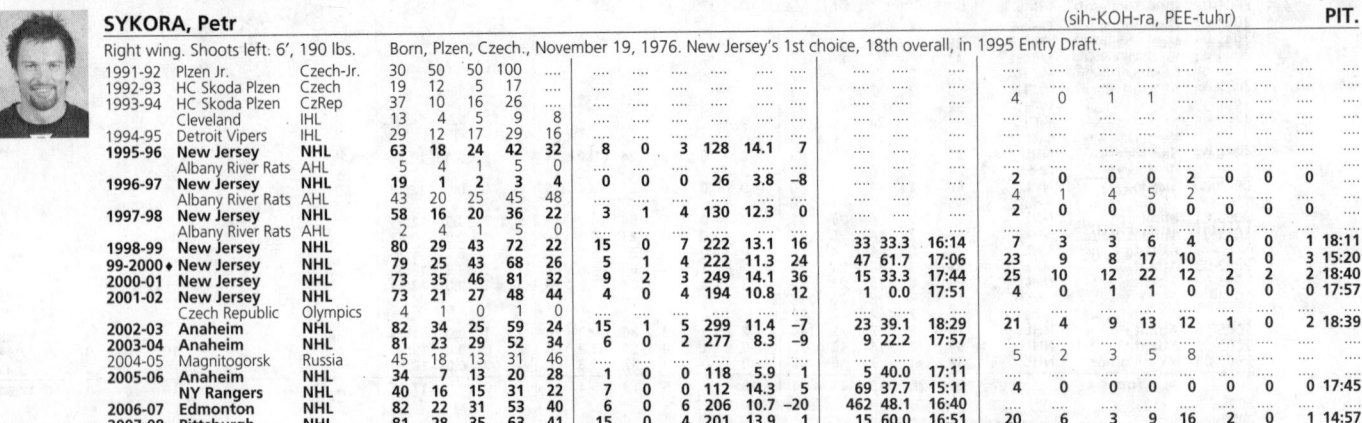

(sih-KOH-ra, PEE-tuhr) **PIT.**

Right wing. Shoots left. 6', 190 lbs. Born, Plzen, Czech., November 19, 1976. New Jersey's 1st choice, 18th overall, in 1995 Entry Draft.

1991-92	Plzen Jr.	Czech-Jr.	30	50	50	100	....	....	....	....	....	....	....	....	....	....	....	....	....	....	....	....	....	....	....
1992-93	HC Skoda Plzen	Czech	19	12	5	17	....	....	....	....	....	....	....	....	....	....	....	....	....	....	....	....	....	....	....
1993-94	HC Skoda Plzen	CzRep	37	10	16	26	....	....	....	....	....	....	....	....	....	....	4	0	1	1	....	....	....	....	....
	Cleveland	IHL	13	4	5	9	8	....	....	....	....	....	....	....	....	....	....	....	....	....	....	....	....	....	....
1994-95	Detroit Vipers	IHL	29	12	17	29	16	....	....	....	....	....	....	....	....	....	....	....	....	....	....	....	....	....	....
1995-96	**New Jersey**	**NHL**	**63**	**18**	**24**	**42**	**32**	**8**	**0**	**3**	**128**	**14.1**	**7**	....	....	....	....	....	....	....	....	....	....	....	....
	Albany River Rats	AHL	5	4	1	5	0	....	....	....	....	....	....	....	....	....	....	....	....	....	....	....	....	....	....
1996-97	**New Jersey**	**NHL**	**19**	**1**	**2**	**3**	**4**	**0**	**0**	**0**	**26**	**3.8**	**–8**	....	....	....	**2**	**0**	**0**	**0**	**2**	**0**	**0**	**0**	....
	Albany River Rats	AHL	43	20	25	45	48	....	....	....	....	....	....	....	....	....	4	1	4	5	2	....	....	....	....
1997-98	**New Jersey**	**NHL**	**58**	**16**	**20**	**36**	**22**	**3**	**1**	**4**	**130**	**12.3**	**0**	....	....	....	**2**	**0**	**0**	**0**	**0**	**0**	**0**	**0**	....
	Albany River Rats	AHL	2	4	1	5	0	....	....	....	....	....	....	....	....	....	....	....	....	....	....	....	....	....	....
1998-99	**New Jersey**	**NHL**	**80**	**29**	**43**	**72**	**22**	**15**	**0**	**7**	**222**	**13.1**	**16**	**33**	**33.3**	**16:14**	**7**	**3**	**3**	**6**	**4**	**0**	**0**	**1**	**18:11**
99-2000 ♦	**New Jersey**	**NHL**	**79**	**25**	**43**	**68**	**26**	**5**	**1**	**4**	**222**	**11.3**	**24**	**47**	**61.7**	**17:06**	**23**	**9**	**8**	**17**	**10**	**1**	**0**	**3**	**15:20**
2000-01	**New Jersey**	**NHL**	**73**	**35**	**46**	**81**	**32**	**9**	**2**	**3**	**249**	**14.1**	**36**	**15**	**33.3**	**17:44**	**25**	**10**	**12**	**22**	**12**	**2**	**2**	**2**	**18:40**
2001-02	**New Jersey**	**NHL**	**73**	**21**	**27**	**48**	**44**	**4**	**0**	**4**	**194**	**10.8**	**12**	**1**	**0.0**	**17:51**	**4**	**0**	**1**	**1**	**0**	**0**	**0**	**0**	**17:57**
	Czech Republic	Olympics	4	1	0	1	0	....	....	....	....	....	....	....	....	....	....	....	....	....	....	....	....	....	....
2002-03	**Anaheim**	**NHL**	**82**	**34**	**25**	**59**	**24**	**15**	**1**	**5**	**299**	**11.4**	**–7**	**23**	**39.1**	**18:29**	**21**	**4**	**9**	**13**	**12**	**1**	**0**	**2**	**18:39**
2003-04	**Anaheim**	**NHL**	**81**	**23**	**29**	**52**	**34**	**6**	**0**	**2**	**277**	**8.3**	**–9**	**9**	**22.2**	**17:57**	....	....	....	....	....	....	....	....	....
2004-05	Magnitogorsk	Russia	45	18	13	31	46	....	....	....	....	....	....	....	....	....	5	2	3	5	8	....	....	....	....
2005-06	**Anaheim**	**NHL**	**34**	**7**	**13**	**20**	**28**	**1**	**0**	**0**	**118**	**5.9**	**1**	**5**	**40.0**	**17:11**	....	....	....	....	....	....	....	....	....
	NY Rangers	**NHL**	**40**	**16**	**15**	**31**	**22**	**7**	**0**	**0**	**112**	**14.3**	**5**	**69**	**37.7**	**15:11**	**4**	**0**	**0**	**0**	**0**	**0**	**0**	**0**	**17:45**
2006-07	**Edmonton**	**NHL**	**82**	**22**	**31**	**53**	**40**	**6**	**0**	**6**	**206**	**10.7**	**–20**	**462**	**48.1**	**16:40**	....	....	....	....	....	....	....	....	....
2007-08	**Pittsburgh**	**NHL**	**81**	**28**	**35**	**63**	**41**	**15**	**0**	**4**	**201**	**13.9**	**1**	**15**	**60.0**	**16:51**	**20**	**6**	**3**	**9**	**16**	**2**	**0**	**1**	**14:57**
	NHL Totals		**845**	**275**	**353**	**628**	**371**	**94**	**5**	**42**	**2384**	**11.5**		**679**	**46.1**	**17:13**	**108**	**32**	**36**	**68**	**56**	**6**	**2**	**9**	**17:07**

NHL All-Rookie Team (1996)

Traded to **Anaheim** by **New Jersey** with Mike Commodore, Jean-Francois Damphousse and Igor Pohanka for Jeff Friesen, Oleg Tverdovsky and Maxim Balmochnykh, July 6, 2002. Signed as a free agent by **Magnitogorsk** (Russia), August 12, 2004. Traded to **NY Rangers** by **Anaheim** with NY Rangers' 4th round choice (previously acquired, later traded to Washington - Washington selected Brett Bruneteau) in 2007 Entry Draft for Maxim Kondratiev, January 8, 2006. Signed as a free agent by **Edmonton**, August 11, 2006. Signed as a free agent by **Pittsburgh**, July 2, 2007.

SYVRET, Danny

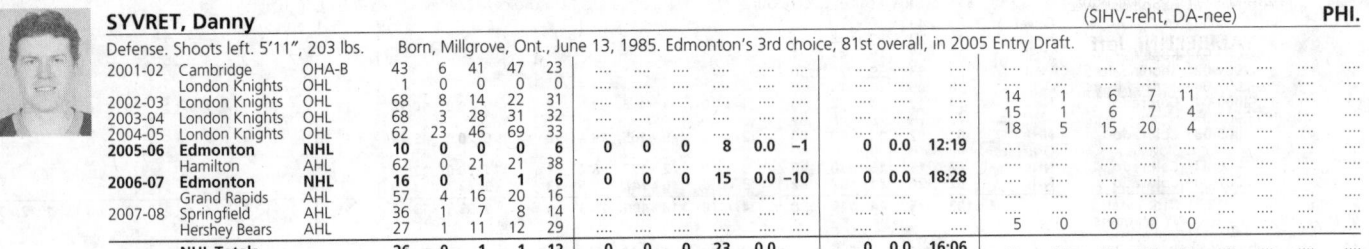

(SIHV-reht, DA-nee) **PHI.**

Defense. Shoots left. 5'11", 203 lbs. Born, Millgrove, Ont., June 13, 1985. Edmonton's 3rd choice, 81st overall, in 2005 Entry Draft.

2001-02	Cambridge	OHA-B	43	6	41	47	23	....	....	....	....	....	....	....	....	....	....	....	....	....	....	....	....	....	....
	London Knights	OHL	1	0	0	0	0	....	....	....	....	....	....	....	....	....	....	....	....	....	....	....	....	....	....
2002-03	London Knights	OHL	68	8	14	22	31	....	....	....	....	....	....	....	....	....	14	1	6	7	11	....	....	....	....
2003-04	London Knights	OHL	68	3	28	31	32	....	....	....	....	....	....	....	....	....	15	1	6	7	4	....	....	....	....
2004-05	London Knights	OHL	62	23	46	69	33	....	....	....	....	....	....	....	....	....	18	5	15	20	4	....	....	....	....
2005-06	**Edmonton**	**NHL**	**10**	**0**	**0**	**0**	**6**	**0**	**0**	**0**	**8**	**0.0**	**–1**	**0**	**0.0**	**12:19**	....	....	....	....	....	....	....	....	....
	Hamilton	AHL	62	0	21	21	38	....	....	....	....	....	....	....	....	....	....	....	....	....	....	....	....	....	....
2006-07	**Edmonton**	**NHL**	**16**	**0**	**1**	**1**	**6**	**0**	**0**	**0**	**15**	**0.0**	**–10**	**0**	**0.0**	**18:28**	....	....	....	....	....	....	....	....	....
	Grand Rapids	AHL	57	4	16	20	16	....	....	....	....	....	....	....	....	....	....	....	....	....	....	....	....	....	....
2007-08	Springfield	AHL	36	1	7	8	14	....	....	....	....	....	....	....	....	....	....	....	....	....	....	....	....	....	....
	Hershey Bears	AHL	27	1	11	12	29	....	....	....	....	....	....	....	....	....	5	0	0	0	0	....	....	....	....
	NHL Totals		**26**	**0**	**1**	**1**	**12**	**0**	**0**	**0**	**23**	**0.0**		**0**	**0.0**	**16:06**	....	....	....	....	....	....	....	....	....

OHL First All-Star Team (2005) • Canadian Major Junior Defenseman of the Year (2005) • Canadian Major Junior First All-Star Team (2005) • Memorial Cup Tournament All-Star Team (2005)

Traded to **Philadelphia** by **Edmonton** for Ryan Potulny, June 6, 2008.

TAFFE, Jeff

(TAYF, JEHF) **PIT.**

Center. Shoots left. 6'3", 207 lbs. Born, Hastings, MN, February 19, 1981. St. Louis' 1st choice, 30th overall, in 2000 Entry Draft.

1996-97	Hastings Huskies	High-MN	25	21	37	58	....	....	....	....	....	....	....	....	....	....	....	....	....	....	....	....	....	....	....
1997-98	Hastings Huskies	High-MN	28	37	29	66	....	....	....	....	....	....	....	....	....	....	....	....	....	....	....	....	....	....	....
1998-99	Hastings Huskies	High-MN	28	39	51	90	....	....	....	....	....	....	....	....	....	....	....	....	....	....	....	....	....	....	....
	Rochester	USHL	17	12	9	21	26	....	....	....	....	....	....	....	....	....	....	....	....	....	....	....	....	....	....
99-2000	U. of Minnesota	WCHA	39	10	10	20	22	....	....	....	....	....	....	....	....	....	....	....	....	....	....	....	....	....	....
2000-01	U. of Minnesota	WCHA	38	12	23	35	56	....	....	....	....	....	....	....	....	....	....	....	....	....	....	....	....	....	....
2001-02	U. of Minnesota	WCHA	43	34	24	58	86	....	....	....	....	....	....	....	....	....	....	....	....	....	....	....	....	....	....
2002-03	**Phoenix**	**NHL**	**20**	**3**	**1**	**4**	**4**	**1**	**0**	**1**	**18**	**16.7**	**–4**	**113**	**29.2**	**11:34**	....	....	....	....	....	....	....	....	....
	Springfield	AHL	57	23	26	49	44	....	....	....	....	....	....	....	....	....	5	0	3	3	8	....	....	....	....
2003-04	**Phoenix**	**NHL**	**59**	**8**	**10**	**18**	**20**	**5**	**0**	**0**	**67**	**11.9**	**–8**	**219**	**43.4**	**11:02**	....	....	....	....	....	....	....	....	....
	Springfield	AHL	15	10	6	16	19	....	....	....	....	....	....	....	....	....	....	....	....	....	....	....	....	....	....
2004-05	Utah Grizzlies	AHL	27	9	10	19	35	....	....	....	....	....	....	....	....	....	....	....	....	....	....	....	....	....	....
2005-06	**NY Rangers**	**NHL**	**2**	**0**	**0**	**0**	**0**	**0**	**0**	**0**	**1**	**0.0**	**0**	**0**	**0.0**	**3:49**	....	....	....	....	....	....	....	....	....
	Hartford	AHL	36	6	16	22	34	....	....	....	....	....	....	....	....	....	....	....	....	....	....	....	....	....	....
	Phoenix	**NHL**	**2**	**0**	**0**	**0**	**0**	**0**	**0**	**0**	**2**	**0.0**	**0**	**1**	**100.0**	**9:06**	....	....	....	....	....	....	....	....	....
	San Antonio	AHL	33	5	6	11	29	....	....	....	....	....	....	....	....	....	....	....	....	....	....	....	....	....	....
2006-07	**Phoenix**	**NHL**	**17**	**4**	**2**	**6**	**2**	**1**	**0**	**0**	**34**	**11.8**	**–7**	**64**	**39.1**	**14:12**	....	....	....	....	....	....	....	....	....
	San Antonio	AHL	59	20	20	40	22	....	....	....	....	....	....	....	....	....	....	....	....	....	....	....	....	....	....
2007-08	**Pittsburgh**	**NHL**	**45**	**5**	**7**	**12**	**8**	**1**	**0**	**1**	**56**	**8.9**	**2**	**152**	**48.7**	**9:35**	....	....	....	....	....	....	....	....	....
	Wilkes-Barre	AHL	27	11	10	21	22	....	....	....	....	....	....	....	....	....	....	....	....	....	....	....	....	....	....
	NHL Totals		**145**	**20**	**20**	**40**	**34**	**8**	**0**	**2**	**178**	**11.2**		**549**	**41.5**	**10:54**	....	....	....	....	....	....	....	....	....

Rights traded to **Phoenix** by **St. Louis** with Michal Handzus, Ladislav Nagy and St. Louis' 1st round choice (Ben Eager) in 2002 Entry Draft for Keith Tkachuk, March 13, 2001. Traded to **NY Rangers** by **Phoenix** for Jamie Lundmark, October 18, 2005. Traded to **Phoenix** by **NY Rangers** for Martin Sonnenberg, January 24, 2006. Signed as a free agent by **Pittsburgh**, July 13, 2007.

TALBOT, Maxime
(TAL-buht, max-EEM) **PIT.**

Center. Shoots left. 5'11", 190 lbs. Born, Lemoyne, Que., February 11, 1984. Pittsburgh's 9th choice, 234th overall, in 2002 Entry Draft.

			Regular Season														Playoffs								
Season	Club	League	GP	G	A	Pts	PIM	PP	SH	GW	S	%	+/-	TF	F%	Min	GP	G	A	Pts	PIM	PP	SH	GW	Min
99-2000	Antoine-Girouard	QAAA	42	19	21	40	32	....	....	....	....	....	....	....	....	....	7	3	6	9	0	....	....	....	....
2000-01	Rouyn-Noranda	QMJHL	40	9	15	24	78	....	....	....	....	....	....	....	....	....	....	....	....	....	....	....	....	....	....
	Hull Olympiques	QMJHL	24	6	7	13	60	....	....	....	....	....	....	....	....	....	5	1	0	1	2	....	....	....	....
2001-02	Hull Olympiques	QMJHL	65	24	36	60	174	....	....	....	....	....	....	....	....	....	12	4	6	10	51	....	....	....	....
2002-03	Hull Olympiques	QMJHL	69	46	58	104	130	....	....	....	....	....	....	....	....	....	20	14	*30	*44	33	....	....	....	....
2003-04	Gatineau	QMJHL	51	25	73	98	41	....	....	....	....	....	....	....	....	....	15	*11	*16	*27	0	....	....	....	....
2004-05	Wilkes-Barre	AHL	75	7	12	19	62	....	....	....	....	....	....	....	....	....	11	0	1	1	22	....	....	....	....
2005-06	**Pittsburgh**	**NHL**	**48**	**5**	**3**	**8**	**59**	**0**	**2**	**1**	**45**	**11.1**	**-12**	**473**	**42.9**	**10:58**	....	....	....	....	....	....	....	....	....
	Wilkes-Barre	AHL	42	12	20	32	80	....	....	....	....	....	....	....	....	....	11	3	6	9	16	....	....	....	....
2006-07	**Pittsburgh**	**NHL**	**75**	**13**	**11**	**24**	**53**	**0**	**4**	**4**	**88**	**14.8**	**-2**	**903**	**44.4**	**13:54**	**5**	**0**	**1**	**1**	**7**	**0**	**0**	**0**	**15:51**
	Wilkes-Barre	AHL	5	4	0	4	2	....	....	....	....	....	....	....	....	....	....	....	....	....	....	....	....	....	....
2007-08	**Pittsburgh**	**NHL**	**63**	**12**	**14**	**26**	**53**	**0**	**2**	**1**	**80**	**15.0**	**8**	**513**	**45.0**	**15:28**	**17**	**3**	**6**	**9**	**36**	**0**	**0**	**1**	**14:27**
	NHL Totals		**186**	**30**	**28**	**58**	**165**	**0**	**8**	**6**	**213**	**14.1**		**1889**	**44.2**	**13:40**	**22**	**3**	**7**	**10**	**43**	**0**	**0**	**1**	**14:46**

QMJHL Second All-Star Team (2003, 2004)

TALLACKSON, Barry
(TAL-ak-suhn, BAIR-ee) **N.J.**

Right wing. Shoots right. 6'5", 215 lbs. Born, Grafton, ND, April 14, 1983. New Jersey's 2nd choice, 53rd overall, in 2002 Entry Draft.

			Regular Season														Playoffs								
Season	Club	League	GP	G	A	Pts	PIM	PP	SH	GW	S	%	+/-	TF	F%	Min	GP	G	A	Pts	PIM	PP	SH	GW	Min
99-2000	USNTDP	NAHL	53	14	6	20	90	....	....	....	....	....	....	....	....	....	3	1	0	1	8	....	....	....	....
2000-01	USNTDP	U-18	40	16	17	33	45	....	....	....	....	....	....	....	....	....	....	....	....	....	....	....	....	....	....
	USNTDP	USHL	23	7	7	14	32	....	....	....	....	....	....	....	....	....	....	....	....	....	....	....	....	....	....
2001-02	U. of Minnesota	WCHA	44	13	10	23	44	....	....	....	....	....	....	....	....	....	....	....	....	....	....	....	....	....	....
2002-03	U. of Minnesota	WCHA	32	9	14	23	18	....	....	....	....	....	....	....	....	....	....	....	....	....	....	....	....	....	....
2003-04	U. of Minnesota	WCHA	44	10	15	25	46	....	....	....	....	....	....	....	....	....	....	....	....	....	....	....	....	....	....
2004-05	U. of Minnesota	WCHA	36	11	8	19	54	....	....	....	....	....	....	....	....	....	....	....	....	....	....	....	....	....	....
	Albany River Rats	AHL	4	1	1	2	0	....	....	....	....	....	....	....	....	....	....	....	....	....	....	....	....	....	....
2005-06	**New Jersey**	**NHL**	**10**	**1**	**1**	**2**	**2**	**0**	**0**	**0**	**11**	**9.1**	**-2**	**2**	**0.0**	**8:04**	....	....	....	....	....	....	....	....	....
	Albany River Rats	AHL	60	14	23	37	62	....	....	....	....	....	....	....	....	....	....	....	....	....	....	....	....	....	....
2006-07	**New Jersey**	**NHL**	**3**	**0**	**0**	**0**	**0**	**0**	**0**	**0**	**3**	**0.0**	**-1**	**0**	**0.0**	**12:06**	....	....	....	....	....	....	....	....	....
	Lowell Devils	AHL	58	10	24	34	33	....	....	....	....	....	....	....	....	....	....	....	....	....	....	....	....	....	....
2007-08	**New Jersey**	**NHL**	**3**	**0**	**0**	**0**	**0**	**0**	**0**	**0**	**0**	**0.0**	**0**	**0**	**0.0**	**7:03**	....	....	....	....	....	....	....	....	....
	Lowell Devils	AHL	63	22	23	45	54	....	....	....	....	....	....	....	....	....	....	....	....	....	....	....	....	....	....
	NHL Totals		**16**	**1**	**1**	**2**	**2**	**0**	**0**	**0**	**14**	**7.1**		**2**	**0.0**	**8:38**	....	....	....	....	....	....	....	....	....

TALLINDER, Henrik
(tah-LIHN-duhr, HEHN-rihk) **BUF.**

Defense. Shoots left. 6'3", 214 lbs. Born, Stockholm, Sweden, January 10, 1979. Buffalo's 2nd choice, 48th overall, in 1997 Entry Draft.

			Regular Season														Playoffs								
Season	Club	League	GP	G	A	Pts	PIM	PP	SH	GW	S	%	+/-	TF	F%	Min	GP	G	A	Pts	PIM	PP	SH	GW	Min
1996-97	AIK Solna Jr.	Swe-Jr.	40	4	13	17	55	....	....	....	....	....	....	....	....	....	....	....	....	....	....	....	....	....	....
	AIK Solna	Sweden	1	0	0	0	0	....	....	....	....	....	....	....	....	....	....	....	....	....	....	....	....	....	....
1997-98	AIK Solna	Sweden	34	0	0	0	26	....	....	....	....	....	....	....	....	....	....	....	....	....	....	....	....	....	....
1998-99	AIK Solna	Sweden	36	0	0	0	30	....	....	....	....	....	....	....	....	....	....	....	....	....	....	....	....	....	....
99-2000	AIK Solna	Sweden	50	0	2	2	59	....	....	....	....	....	....	....	....	....	....	....	....	....	....	....	....	....	....
2000-01	TPS Turku	Finland	56	5	9	14	62	....	....	....	....	....	....	....	....	....	10	2	1	3	8	....	....	....	....
2001-02	**Buffalo**	**NHL**	**2**	**0**	**0**	**0**	**0**	**0**	**0**	**0**	**4**	**0.0**	**-1**	**0**	**0.0**	**18:10**	....	....	....	....	....	....	....	....	....
	Rochester	AHL	73	6	14	20	26	....	....	....	....	....	....	....	....	....	2	0	0	0	0	....	....	....	....
2002-03	**Buffalo**	**NHL**	**46**	**3**	**10**	**13**	**28**	**1**	**0**	**0**	**37**	**8.1**	**-3**	**0**	**0.0**	**19:53**	....	....	....	....	....	....	....	....	....
2003-04	**Buffalo**	**NHL**	**72**	**1**	**9**	**10**	**26**	**0**	**0**	**0**	**63**	**1.6**	**5**	**1**	**0.0**	**18:23**	....	....	....	....	....	....	....	....	....
2004-05	Linkopings HC	Sweden	44	6	10	16	63	....	....	....	....	....	....	....	....	....	....	....	....	....	....	....	....	....	....
	SC Bern	Swiss	....	....	....	....	....	....	....	....	....	....	....	....	....	....	10	1	1	2	4	....	....	....	....
2005-06	**Buffalo**	**NHL**	**82**	**6**	**15**	**21**	**74**	**0**	**1**	**1**	**79**	**7.6**	**10**	**0**	**0.0**	**20:21**	**14**	**2**	**6**	**8**	**16**	**0**	**0**	**0**	**22:16**
2006-07	**Buffalo**	**NHL**	**47**	**4**	**10**	**14**	**34**	**0**	**0**	**0**	**34**	**11.8**	**19**	**1**	**0.0**	**21:07**	**16**	**0**	**2**	**2**	**10**	**0**	**0**	**0**	**23:40**
2007-08	**Buffalo**	**NHL**	**71**	**1**	**17**	**18**	**48**	**0**	**0**	**0**	**70**	**1.4**	**5**	**0**	**0.0**	**21:02**	....	....	....	....	....	....	....	....	....
	NHL Totals		**320**	**15**	**61**	**76**	**210**	**1**	**1**	**1**	**287**	**5.2**		**2**	**0.0**	**20:05**	**30**	**2**	**8**	**10**	**26**	**0**	**0**	**0**	**23:01**

Signed as a free agent by **Linkopings** (Sweden), September 9, 2004. Signed as a free agent by **Bern** (Swiss), February 22, 2005.

TAMBELLINI, Jeff
(tam-buh-LEE-nee, JEHF) **NYI**

Left wing. Shoots left. 5'11", 186 lbs. Born, Calgary, Alta., April 13, 1984. Los Angeles' 3rd choice, 27th overall, in 2003 Entry Draft.

			Regular Season														Playoffs								
Season	Club	League	GP	G	A	Pts	PIM	PP	SH	GW	S	%	+/-	TF	F%	Min	GP	G	A	Pts	PIM	PP	SH	GW	Min
99-2000	Port Coquitlam	PIJHL	41	30	34	64	....	....	....	....	....	....	....	....	....	....	....	....	....	....	....	....	....	....	....
2000-01	Chilliwack Chiefs	BCHL	54	21	30	51	13	....	....	....	....	....	....	....	....	....	....	....	....	....	....	....	....	....	....
2001-02	Chilliwack Chiefs	BCHL	34	46	71	117	23	....	....	....	....	....	....	....	....	....	29	27	27	54	....	....	....	....	....
2002-03	U. of Michigan	CCHA	43	26	19	45	24	....	....	....	....	....	....	....	....	....	....	....	....	....	....	....	....	....	....
2003-04	U. of Michigan	CCHA	39	15	12	27	18	....	....	....	....	....	....	....	....	....	....	....	....	....	....	....	....	....	....
2004-05	U. of Michigan	CCHA	42	*24	33	*57	32	....	....	....	....	....	....	....	....	....	....	....	....	....	....	....	....	....	....
2005-06	**Los Angeles**	**NHL**	**4**	**0**	**0**	**0**	**2**	**0**	**0**	**0**	**6**	**0.0**	**-1**	**1**	**0.0**	**9:23**	....	....	....	....	....	....	....	....	....
	Manchester	AHL	56	25	31	56	26	....	....	....	....	....	....	....	....	....	....	....	....	....	....	....	....	....	....
	NY Islanders	**NHL**	**21**	**1**	**3**	**4**	**8**	**0**	**0**	**0**	**11**	**9.1**	**2**	**3**	**33.3**	**9:54**	....	....	....	....	....	....	....	....	....
	Bridgeport	AHL	....	....	....	....	....	....	....	....	....	....	....	....	....	....	7	1	2	3	2	....	....	....	....
2006-07	**NY Islanders**	**NHL**	**23**	**2**	**7**	**9**	**6**	**0**	**0**	**0**	**20**	**10.0**	**6**	**1**	**0.0**	**7:14**	....	....	....	....	....	....	....	....	....
	Bridgeport	AHL	50	30	29	59	46	....	....	....	....	....	....	....	....	....	....	....	....	....	....	....	....	....	....
2007-08	**NY Islanders**	**NHL**	**31**	**1**	**3**	**4**	**8**	**0**	**0**	**0**	**43**	**2.3**	**-9**	**0**	**0.0**	**10:25**	....	....	....	....	....	....	....	....	....
	Bridgeport	AHL	57	38	38	76	38	....	....	....	....	....	....	....	....	....	....	....	....	....	....	....	....	....	....
	NHL Totals		**79**	**4**	**13**	**17**	**24**	**0**	**0**	**0**	**80**	**5.0**		**5**	**20.0**	**9:18**	....	....	....	....	....	....	....	....	....

CCHA All-Rookie Team (2003) • CCHA Second All-Star Team (2003) • CCHA Rookie of the Year (2003) • CCHA First All-Star Team (2005) • NCAA West Second All-American Team (2005)
Traded to **NY Islanders** by **Los Angeles** with Denis Grebeshkov for Mark Parrish and Brent Sopel, March 8, 2006.

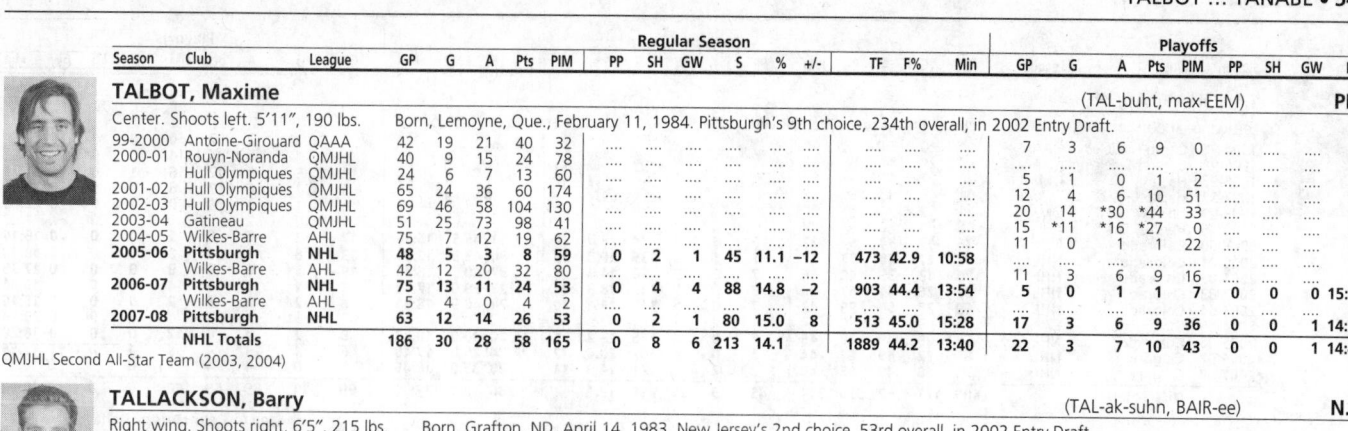

TANABE, David
(tuh-NA-bee, DAY-vihd)

Defense. Shoots right. 6'1", 212 lbs. Born, White Bear Lake, MN, July 19, 1980. Carolina's 1st choice, 16th overall, in 1999 Entry Draft.

			Regular Season														Playoffs								
Season	Club	League	GP	G	A	Pts	PIM	PP	SH	GW	S	%	+/-	TF	F%	Min	GP	G	A	Pts	PIM	PP	SH	GW	Min
1996-97	Hill-Murray	High-MN	28	12	14	26	....	....	....	....	....	....	....	....	....	....	....	....	....	....	....	....	....	....	....
1997-98	USNTDP	U-18	33	4	15	19	48	....	....	....	....	....	....	....	....	....	....	....	....	....	....	....	....	....	....
	USNTDP	USHL	21	1	3	4	18	....	....	....	....	....	....	....	....	....	....	....	....	....	....	....	....	....	....
	USNTDP	NAHL	12	1	2	3	10	....	....	....	....	....	....	....	....	....	....	....	....	....	....	....	....	....	....
1998-99	U. of Wisconsin	WCHA	35	10	12	22	44	....	....	....	....	....	....	....	....	....	7	2	1	3	20	....	....	....	....
99-2000	**Carolina**	**NHL**	**31**	**4**	**0**	**4**	**14**	**3**	**0**	**0**	**28**	**14.3**	**-4**	**0**	**0.0**	**12:53**	....	....	....	....	....	....	....	....	....
	Cincinnati	IHL	32	0	13	13	14	....	....	....	....	....	....	....	....	....	11	1	4	5	6	....	....	....	....
2000-01	**Carolina**	**NHL**	**74**	**7**	**22**	**29**	**42**	**5**	**0**	**1**	**130**	**5.4**	**-9**	**0**	**0.0**	**17:55**	**6**	**2**	**0**	**2**	**12**	**2**	**0**	**0**	**20:47**
2001-02	**Carolina**	**NHL**	**78**	**1**	**15**	**16**	**35**	**0**	**0**	**0**	**113**	**0.9**	**-13**	**0**	**0.0**	**18:27**	**1**	**0**	**1**	**1**	**0**	**0**	**0**	**0**	**7:31**
2002-03	**Carolina**	**NHL**	**68**	**3**	**10**	**13**	**24**	**2**	**0**	**0**	**104**	**2.9**	**-27**	**0**	**0.0**	**18:12**	....	....	....	....	....	....	....	....	....
2003-04	**Phoenix**	**NHL**	**45**	**5**	**7**	**12**	**22**	**2**	**0**	**2**	**88**	**5.7**	**4**	**0**	**0.0**	**23:02**	....	....	....	....	....	....	....	....	....
2004-05	Rapperswil	Swiss	8	4	5	9	4	....	....	....	....	....	....	....	....	....	....	....	....	....	....	....	....	....	....
	Kloten Flyers	Swiss	20	3	7	10	18	....	....	....	....	....	....	....	....	....	5	1	4	5	8	....	....	....	....
2005-06	**Phoenix**	**NHL**	**21**	**0**	**4**	**4**	**8**	**0**	**0**	**0**	**21**	**0.0**	**-5**	**0**	**0.0**	**21:08**	....	....	....	....	....	....	....	....	....
	Boston	**NHL**	**54**	**4**	**12**	**16**	**48**	**0**	**0**	**1**	**82**	**4.9**	**0**	**0**	**0.0**	**20:08**	....	....	....	....	....	....	....	....	....
2006-07	**Carolina**	**NHL**	**60**	**5**	**12**	**17**	**44**	**2**	**0**	**0**	**83**	**6.0**	**5**	**0**	**0.0**	**17:48**	....	....	....	....	....	....	....	....	....
2007-08	**Carolina**	**NHL**	**18**	**1**	**2**	**3**	**8**	**0**	**0**	**0**	**12**	**8.3**	**2**	**0**	**0.0**	**11:59**	....	....	....	....	....	....	....	....	....
	NHL Totals		**449**	**30**	**84**	**114**	**245**	**14**	**0**	**4**	**661**	**4.5**		**0**	**0.0**	**18:23**	**7**	**2**	**1**	**3**	**12**	**2**	**0**	**0**	**18:53**

WCHA All-Rookie Team (1999)

Traded to **Phoenix** by **Carolina** with Igor Knyazev for Danny Markov and Edmonton's 3rd round choice (previously acquired, later traded to NY Rangers - NY Rangers selected Billy Ryan) in 2004 Entry Draft, June 21, 2003. Signed as a free agent by **Rapperswil** (Swiss), October 21, 2004. Signed as a free agent by **Kloten** (Swiss), November 29, 2004. Traded to **Boston** by **Phoenix** for Dave Scatchard, November 18, 2005. Signed as a free agent by **Carolina**, August 29, 2006. • Missed majority of 2007-08 season recovering from concussion suffered in game at Toronto, December 18, 2007.

TANGUAY, Alex

(TAN-guay, AL-ehx) **MTL.**

Left wing. Shoots left. 6'1", 189 lbs. Born, Ste-Justine, Que., November 21, 1979. Colorado's 1st choice, 12th overall, in 1998 Entry Draft.

			Regular Season														Playoffs								
Season	Club	League	GP	G	A	Pts	PIM	PP	SH	GW	S	%	+/-	TF	F%	Min	GP	G	A	Pts	PIM	PP	SH	GW	Min
1994-95	Cap-d-Madeleine	QAAA	1	0	1	1	0	....	....	....	....	....	....	....	....	....	....	....	....	....	....	....	....	....	....
1995-96	Cap-d-Madeleine	QAAA	44	29	34	63	64	....	....	....	....	....	....	....	....	....	5	2	4	6	14	....	....	....	....
1996-97	Halifax	QMJHL	70	27	41	68	60	....	....	....	....	....	....	....	....	....	12	5	8	13	8	....	....	....	....
1997-98	Halifax	QMJHL	51	47	38	85	32	....	....	....	....	....	....	....	....	....	5	7	6	13	4	....	....	....	....
1998-99	Halifax	QMJHL	31	27	34	61	30	....	....	....	....	....	....	....	....	....	5	1	2	3	2	....	....	....	....
	Hershey Bears	AHL	5	1	2	3	2	....	....	....	....	....	....	....	....	....	5	0	2	2	0	....	....	....	....
99-2000	**Colorado**	**NHL**	**76**	**17**	**34**	**51**	**22**	**5**	**0**	**3**	**74**	**23.0**	**6**	**11**	**45.5**	**15:38**	**17**	**2**	**1**	**3**	**2**	**1**	**0**	**1**	**10:49**
2000-01 ♦	**Colorado**	**NHL**	**82**	**27**	**50**	**77**	**37**	**7**	**1**	**3**	**135**	**20.0**	**35**	**30**	**43.3**	**17:51**	**23**	**6**	**15**	**21**	**8**	**1**	**0**	**2**	**19:18**
2001-02	**Colorado**	**NHL**	**70**	**13**	**35**	**48**	**36**	**7**	**0**	**2**	**90**	**14.4**	**8**	**37**	**40.5**	**18:20**	**19**	**5**	**8**	**13**	**0**	**3**	**0**	**0**	**17:25**
2002-03	**Colorado**	**NHL**	**82**	**26**	**41**	**67**	**36**	**3**	**0**	**5**	**142**	**18.3**	**34**	**123**	**39.0**	**17:48**	**7**	**1**	**2**	**3**	**4**	**0**	**0**	**1**	**19:06**
2003-04	**Colorado**	**NHL**	**69**	**25**	**54**	**79**	**42**	**7**	**0**	**5**	**117**	**21.4**	**30**	**71**	**40.9**	**18:21**	**8**	**2**	**2**	**4**	**2**	**1**	**0**	**1**	**15:46**
2004-05	HC Lugano	Swiss	6	3	3	6	4	....	....	....	....	....	....	....	....	....	....	....	....	....	....	....	....	....	....
2005-06	**Colorado**	**NHL**	**71**	**29**	**49**	**78**	**46**	**8**	**0**	**4**	**125**	**23.2**	**8**	**20**	**30.0**	**18:22**	**9**	**2**	**4**	**6**	**12**	**0**	**0**	**1**	**18:20**
2006-07	**Calgary**	**NHL**	**81**	**22**	**59**	**81**	**44**	**5**	**0**	**0**	**107**	**20.6**	**12**	**24**	**25.0**	**17:40**	**6**	**1**	**3**	**4**	**8**	**1**	**0**	**0**	**17:56**
2007-08	**Calgary**	**NHL**	**78**	**18**	**40**	**58**	**48**	**3**	**2**	**3**	**121**	**14.9**	**11**	**20**	**35.0**	**18:46**	**7**	**0**	**4**	**4**	**4**	**0**	**0**	**0**	**18:15**
	NHL Totals		**609**	**177**	**362**	**539**	**311**	**45**	**3**	**25**	**911**	**19.4**		**336**	**38.4**	**17:50**	**96**	**19**	**39**	**58**	**40**	**7**	**0**	**6**	**16:52**

QMJHL All-Rookie Team (1997)

Played in NHL All-Star Game (2004)

Signed as a free agent by **Lugano** (Swiss), October 7, 2004. Traded to **Calgary** by **Colorado** for Jordan Leopold, Calgary's 2nd round choice (Codey Burki) in 2006 Entry Draft and Calgary's 2nd round choice (Trevor Cann) in 2007 Entry Draft, June 24, 2006. Traded to **Montreal** by **Calgary** with Calgary's 5th round choice (Maxim Trunev) in 2008 Entry Draft for Montreal's 1st round choice (Greg Nemisz) in 2008 Entry Draft and Montreal's 2nd round choice in 2009 Entry Draft, June 20, 2008.

TARNASKY, Nick

(tahr-NAS-kee, NIHK) **T.B.**

Center. Shoots left. 6'2", 224 lbs. Born, Rocky Mtn. House, Alta., November 25, 1984. Tampa Bay's 11th choice, 287th overall, in 2003 Entry Draft.

			Regular Season														Playoffs								
Season	Club	League	GP	G	A	Pts	PIM	PP	SH	GW	S	%	+/-	TF	F%	Min	GP	G	A	Pts	PIM	PP	SH	GW	Min
99-2000	Leduc Oil Kings	AMBHL	36	21	11	32	59	....	....	....	....	....	....	....	....	....	....	....	....	....	....	....	....	....	....
2000-01	Leduc Oil Kings	AMHL	35	39	29	68	95	....	....	....	....	....	....	....	....	....	....	....	....	....	....	....	....	....	....
2001-02	Drayton Valley	AJHL	20	7	4	11	10	....	....	....	....	....	....	....	....	....	....	....	....	....	....	....	....	....	....
	Vancouver Giants	WHL	10	1	0	1	5	....	....	....	....	....	....	....	....	....	....	....	....	....	....	....	....	....	....
2002-03	Kelowna Rockets	WHL	39	4	12	16	39	....	....	....	....	....	....	....	....	....	....	....	....	....	....	....	....	....	....
	Lethbridge	WHL	30	5	8	13	45	....	....	....	....	....	....	....	....	....	....	....	....	....	....	....	....	....	....
2003-04	Lethbridge	WHL	71	26	23	49	108	....	....	....	....	....	....	....	....	....	....	....	....	....	....	....	....	....	....
2004-05	Springfield	AHL	80	7	10	17	176	....	....	....	....	....	....	....	....	....	....	....	....	....	....	....	....	....	....
2005-06	**Tampa Bay**	**NHL**	**12**	**0**	**1**	**1**	**4**	**0**	**0**	**0**	**9**	**0.0**	**–3**	**15**	**40.0**	**4:40**	....	....	....	....	....	....	....	....	....
	Springfield	AHL	68	14	9	23	100	....	....	....	....	....	....	....	....	....	....	....	....	....	....	....	....	....	....
2006-07	**Tampa Bay**	**NHL**	**77**	**5**	**4**	**9**	**80**	**0**	**0**	**1**	**41**	**12.2**	**–6**	**13**	**30.8**	**6:30**	**6**	**0**	**0**	**0**	**10**	**0**	**0**	**0**	**6:13**
2007-08	**Tampa Bay**	**NHL**	**80**	**6**	**4**	**10**	**78**	**1**	**0**	**1**	**91**	**6.6**	**–15**	**9**	**44.4**	**8:15**	....	....	....	....	....	....	....	....	....
	NHL Totals		**169**	**11**	**9**	**20**	**162**	**1**	**0**	**2**	**141**	**7.8**		**37**	**37.8**	**7:12**	**6**	**0**	**0**	**0**	**10**	**0**	**0**	**0**	**6:13**

TARNSTROM, Dick

(TAHRN-struhm, DIHK)

Defense. Shoots left. 6'1", 205 lbs. Born, Sundbyberg, Sweden, January 20, 1975. NY Islanders' 12th choice, 272nd overall, in 1994 Entry Draft.

			Regular Season														Playoffs								
Season	Club	League	GP	G	A	Pts	PIM	PP	SH	GW	S	%	+/-	TF	F%	Min	GP	G	A	Pts	PIM	PP	SH	GW	Min
1992-93	AIK Solna	Sweden	3	0	0	0	0	....	....	....	....	....	....	....	....	....	....	....	....	....	....	....	....	....	....
1993-94	AIK Solna	Sweden-2	33	1	4	5	....	....	....	....	....	....	....	....	....	....	....	....	....	....	....	....	....	....	....
1994-95	AIK Solna	Sweden	37	8	4	12	26	....	....	....	....	....	....	....	....	....	....	....	....	....	....	....	....	....	....
1995-96	AIK Solna	Sweden	40	0	5	5	32	....	....	....	....	....	....	....	....	....	....	....	....	....	....	....	....	....	....
1996-97	AIK Solna	Sweden	49	5	3	8	38	....	....	....	....	....	....	....	....	....	7	0	1	1	6	....	....	....	....
1997-98	AIK Solna	Sweden	45	2	12	14	30	....	....	....	....	....	....	....	....	....	....	....	....	....	....	....	....	....	....
1998-99	AIK Solna	Sweden	47	9	14	23	36	....	....	....	....	....	....	....	....	....	....	....	....	....	....	....	....	....	....
99-2000	AIK Solna	Sweden	42	7	15	22	20	....	....	....	....	....	....	....	....	....	....	....	....	....	....	....	....	....	....
2000-01	AIK Solna	Sweden	50	10	18	28	28	....	....	....	....	....	....	....	....	....	5	0	0	0	8	....	....	....	....
2001-02	**NY Islanders**	**NHL**	**62**	**3**	**16**	**19**	**38**	**0**	**0**	**0**	**59**	**5.1**	**–12**	**0**	**0.0**	**17:39**	**5**	**0**	**0**	**0**	**2**	**0**	**0**	**0**	**7:13**
	Bridgeport	AHL	9	0	2	2	2	....	....	....	....	....	....	....	....	....	....	....	....	....	....	....	....	....	....
2002-03	**Pittsburgh**	**NHL**	**61**	**7**	**34**	**41**	**50**	**3**	**0**	**0**	**115**	**6.1**	**–11**	**0**	**0.0**	**23:54**	....	....	....	....	....	....	....	....	....
2003-04	**Pittsburgh**	**NHL**	**80**	**16**	**36**	**52**	**38**	**12**	**0**	**0**	**158**	**10.1**	**–37**	**0**	**0.0**	**24:03**	....	....	....	....	....	....	....	....	....
2004-05	Sodertalje SK	Sweden	50	7	18	25	46	....	....	....	....	....	....	....	....	....	9	1	0	1	6	....	....	....	....
2005-06	**Pittsburgh**	**NHL**	**33**	**5**	**5**	**10**	**52**	**4**	**0**	**0**	**40**	**12.5**	**–10**	**1**	**100.0**	**16:54**	....	....	....	....	....	....	....	....	....
	Edmonton	**NHL**	**22**	**1**	**3**	**4**	**24**	**0**	**0**	**0**	**20**	**5.0**	**–5**	**0**	**0.0**	**16:58**	**12**	**0**	**2**	**2**	**10**	**0**	**0**	**0**	**14:00**
2006-07	HC Lugano	Swiss	44	3	26	29	90	....	....	....	....	....	....	....	....	....	5	1	6	7	8	....	....	....	....
2007-08	**Edmonton**	**NHL**	**29**	**1**	**4**	**5**	**40**	**0**	**0**	**0**	**22**	**4.5**	**–6**	**0**	**0.0**	**19:35**	....	....	....	....	....	....	....	....	....
	Columbus	**NHL**	**19**	**2**	**7**	**9**	**12**	**1**	**0**	**0**	**22**	**9.1**	**–5**	**0**	**0.0**	**19:03**	....	....	....	....	....	....	....	....	....
	NHL Totals		**306**	**35**	**105**	**140**	**254**	**20**	**0**	**0**	**436**	**8.0**		**1**	**100.0**	**20:43**	**17**	**0**	**2**	**2**	**12**	**0**	**0**	**0**	**12:00**

Claimed on waivers by **Pittsburgh** from **NY Islanders**, August 6, 2002. Signed as a free agent by **Sodertalje** (Sweden), August 9, 2004. Traded to **Edmonton** by **Pittsburgh** for Jani Rita and Cory Cross, January 26, 2006. Signed as a free agent by **Lugano** (Swiss), August 16, 2006. Signed as a free agent by **Edmonton**, July 1, 2007. Traded to **Columbus** by **Edmonton** for Curtis Glencross, February 1, 2008.

TENKRAT, Petr

(TEHN-krat, PEE-tuhr)

Right wing. Shoots right. 6', 183 lbs. Born, Kladno, Czech., May 31, 1977. Anaheim's 6th choice, 230th overall, in 1999 Entry Draft.

			Regular Season														Playoffs								
Season	Club	League	GP	G	A	Pts	PIM	PP	SH	GW	S	%	+/-	TF	F%	Min	GP	G	A	Pts	PIM	PP	SH	GW	Min
1994-95	HC Kladno	CzRep	1	0	0	0	0	....	....	....	....	....	....	....	....	....	....	....	....	....	....	....	....	....	....
1995-96	HC Poldi Kladno	CzRep	20	0	4	4	4	....	....	....	....	....	....	....	....	....	3	0	1	1	0	....	....	....	....
1996-97	HC Poldi Kladno	CzRep	43	5	9	14	6	....	....	....	....	....	....	....	....	....	3	0	1	1	0	....	....	....	....
1997-98	Kladno	CzRep	52	9	10	19	24	....	....	....	....	....	....	....	....	....	....	....	....	....	....	....	....	....	....
1998-99	Kladno	CzRep	50	21	14	35	32	....	....	....	....	....	....	....	....	....	....	....	....	....	....	....	....	....	....
99-2000	HPK Hameenlinna	Finland	32	20	9	29	31	....	....	....	....	....	....	....	....	....	....	....	....	....	....	....	....	....	....
	Ilves Tampere	Finland	22	15	5	20	44	....	....	....	....	....	....	....	....	....	3	1	1	2	14	....	....	....	....
2000-01	**Anaheim**	**NHL**	**46**	**5**	**9**	**14**	**16**	**0**	**0**	**2**	**79**	**6.3**	**–11**	**0**	**0.0**	**12:48**	....	....	....	....	....	....	....	....	....
	Cincinnati	AHL	25	9	9	18	24	....	....	....	....	....	....	....	....	....	4	3	2	5	0	....	....	....	....
2001-02	**Anaheim**	**NHL**	**9**	**0**	**0**	**0**	**6**	**0**	**0**	**0**	**13**	**0.0**	**–6**	**1**	**0.0**	**11:47**	....	....	....	....	....	....	....	....	....
	Cincinnati	AHL	3	2	3	5	2	....	....	....	....	....	....	....	....	....	....	....	....	....	....	....	....	....	....
	Nashville	**NHL**	**58**	**8**	**16**	**24**	**28**	**0**	**1**	**2**	**82**	**9.8**	**–4**	**7**	**28.6**	**12:00**	....	....	....	....	....	....	....	....	....
	Milwaukee	AHL	4	0	0	0	2	....	....	....	....	....	....	....	....	....	....	....	....	....	....	....	....	....	....
2002-03	Karpat Oulu	Finland	51	21	19	40	60	....	....	....	....	....	....	....	....	....	14	4	2	6	6	....	....	....	....
2003-04	Voskresensk	Russia	19	0	2	2	18	....	....	....	....	....	....	....	....	....	....	....	....	....	....	....	....	....	....
	Karpat Oulu	Finland	35	22	15	37	30	....	....	....	....	....	....	....	....	....	15	3	7	10	*45	....	....	....	....
2004-05	Karpat Oulu	Finland	53	18	20	38	46	....	....	....	....	....	....	....	....	....	12	*7	4	11	6	....	....	....	....
2005-06	Karpat Oulu	Finland	36	10	21	31	22	....	....	....	....	....	....	....	....	....	11	*6	3	9	18	....	....	....	....
2006-07	**Boston**	**NHL**	**64**	**9**	**5**	**14**	**34**	**2**	**0**	**1**	**82**	**11.0**	**–16**	**15**	**33.3**	**12:31**	....	....	....	....	....	....	....	....	....
	Providence Bruins	AHL	7	2	7	9	6	....	....	....	....	....	....	....	....	....	....	....	....	....	....	....	....	....	....
2007-08	Kladno	CzRep	13	4	5	9	18	....	....	....	....	....	....	....	....	....	....	....	....	....	....	....	....	....	....
	Timra IK	Sweden	42	10	12	22	72	....	....	....	....	....	....	....	....	....	11	4	3	7	10	....	....	....	....
	NHL Totals		**177**	**22**	**30**	**52**	**84**	**2**	**1**	**5**	**256**	**8.6**		**23**	**30.4**	**12:23**	....	....	....	....	....	....	....	....	....

Traded to **Nashville** by **Anaheim** for Patrick Kjellberg, November 1, 2001. Claimed by **Florida** from **Nashville** in Waiver Draft, October 4, 2002. Traded to **Columbus** by **Florida** for Mathieu Biron, October 4, 2002. Signed as a free agent by **Oulu** (Finland), May 15, 2002. Claimed by **Toronto** from **Columbus** in Waiver Draft, October 3, 2003. Traded to **Boston** by **Toronto** for Boston's 7th round choice (later traded to Phoenix - Phoenix selected Chris Frank) in 2006 Entry Draft, June 15, 2006. Signed as a free agent by **Timra** (Sweden), June 18, 2007.

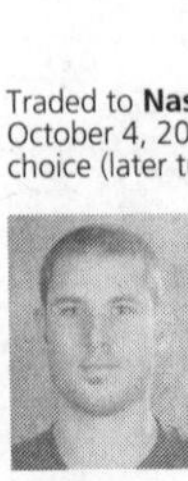

TENUTE, Joey

(teh-NOOT, JOH-ee)

Center. Shoots left. 5'9", 188 lbs. Born, Hamilton, Ont., April 2, 1983. New Jersey's 6th choice, 261st overall, in 2003 Entry Draft.

			Regular Season														Playoffs								
Season	Club	League	GP	G	A	Pts	PIM	PP	SH	GW	S	%	+/-	TF	F%	Min	GP	G	A	Pts	PIM	PP	SH	GW	Min
99-2000	Georgetown	OPJHL	47	27	43	70	34	....	....	....	....	....	....	....	....	....	....	....	....	....	....	....	....	....	....
2000-01	Barrie Colts	OHL	61	13	18	31	38	....	....	....	....	....	....	....	....	....	5	1	1	2	10	....	....	....	....
2001-02	Barrie Colts	OHL	66	19	31	50	76	....	....	....	....	....	....	....	....	....	20	7	7	14	28	....	....	....	....
2002-03	Sarnia Sting	OHL	68	41	71	112	75	....	....	....	....	....	....	....	....	....	3	1	2	3	0	....	....	....	....
2003-04	Sarnia Sting	OHL	58	22	56	78	70	....	....	....	....	....	....	....	....	....	3	2	2	4	17	....	....	....	....
2004-05	South Carolina	ECHL	68	34	41	75	102	....	....	....	....	....	....	....	....	....	4	2	1	3	0	....	....	....	....
2005-06	**Washington**	**NHL**	**1**	**0**	**0**	**0**	**0**	**0**	**0**	**0**	**1**	**0.0**	**0**	**4**	**25.0**	**7:21**	....	....	....	....	....	....	....	....	....
	Hershey Bears	AHL	61	20	30	50	60	....	....	....	....	....	....	....	....	....	19	2	3	5	12	....	....	....	....

			Regular Season														Playoffs								
Season	Club	League	GP	G	A	Pts	PIM	PP	SH	GW	S	%	+/-	TF	F%	Min	GP	G	A	Pts	PIM	PP	SH	GW	Min
2006-07	Hershey Bears	AHL	68	28	39	67	58	....	....	....	....	....	....	....	....	....	9	4	1	5	8	....	....	....	....
2007-08	San Antonio	AHL	78	21	28	49	72	....	....	....	....	....	....	....	....	....	7	2	0	2	2	....	....	....	....
	NHL Totals		**1**	**0**	**0**	**0**	**0**	**0**	**0**	**0**	**1**	**0.0**		**4**	**25.0**	**7:21**	....	....	....	....	....	....	....	....	....

ECHL All-Rookie Team (2005) • ECHL Second All-Star Team (2005) • ECHL Rookie of the Year (2005)

Signed as a free agent by **Washington**, November 21, 2005. Signed as a free agent by **Phoenix**, July 9, 2007.

THOMAS, Bill

(TAW-mas, BIHL) **PIT.**

Right wing. Shoots right. 6'1", 191 lbs. Born, Pittsburgh, PA, June 20, 1983.

2002-03	Tri-City Storm	USHL	60	29	21	50	20	....	....	....	....	....	....	....	....	....	3	0	3	3	4	....	....	....	....
2003-04	Tri-City Storm	USHL	60	31	38	69	30	....	....	....	....	....	....	....	....	....	11	*9	7	*16	4	....	....	....	....
2004-05	Nebraska-Omaha	CCHA	39	19	26	45	12	....	....	....	....	....	....	....	....	....	....	....	....	....	....	....	....	....	....
2005-06	Nebraska-Omaha	CCHA	41	*27	23	50	43	....	....	....	....	....	....	....	....	....	....	....	....	....	....	....	....	....	....
	Phoenix	**NHL**	**9**	**1**	**2**	**3**	**8**	**1**	**0**	**0**	**15**	**6.7**	**–2**	**2**	**50.0**	**13:30**	....	....	....	....	....	....	....	....	....
2006-07	**Phoenix**	**NHL**	**24**	**8**	**6**	**14**	**2**	**4**	**0**	**1**	**60**	**13.3**	**–6**	**0**	**0.0**	**13:29**	....	....	....	....	....	....	....	....	....
	San Antonio	AHL	47	13	20	33	20	....	....	....	....	....	....	....	....	....	....	....	....	....	....	....	....	....	....
2007-08	**Phoenix**	**NHL**	**7**	**0**	**0**	**0**	**0**	**0**	**0**	**0**	**9**	**0.0**	**–2**	**0**	**0.0**	**13:08**	....	....	....	....	....	....	....	....	....
	San Antonio	AHL	75	24	28	52	40	....	....	....	....	....	....	....	....	....	7	1	2	3	0	....	....	....	....
	NHL Totals		**40**	**9**	**8**	**17**	**10**	**5**	**0**	**1**	**84**	**10.7**		**2**	**50.0**	**13:26**	....	....	....	....	....	....	....	....	....

CCHA All-Rookie Team (2005) • CCHA Rookie of the Year (2005) • CCHA Second All-Star Team (2005) • CCHA First All-Star Team (2006)

Signed as a free agent by **Phoenix**. March 27, 2006. Signed as a free agent by **Pittsburgh**. July 15, 2008.

THOMPSON, Nate

(TAWM-suhn, NAYT) **BOS.**

Center. Shoots left. 6', 206 lbs. Born, Anchorage, AK, October 5, 1984. Boston's 8th choice, 183rd overall, in 2003 Entry Draft.

2001-02	Seattle	WHL	69	13	26	39	42	....	....	....	....	....	....	....	....	....	11	1	3	4	13	....	....	....	....
2002-03	Seattle	WHL	61	10	24	34	48	....	....	....	....	....	....	....	....	....	15	5	4	9	6	....	....	....	....
2003-04	Seattle	WHL	65	13	23	36	24	....	....	....	....	....	....	....	....	....	....	....	....	....	....	....	....	....	....
2004-05	Seattle	WHL	58	19	15	34	39	....	....	....	....	....	....	....	....	....	12	1	2	3	2	....	....	....	....
	Providence Bruins	AHL	....	....	....	....	....	....	....	....	....	....	....	....	....	....	11	0	1	1	6	....	....	....	....
2005-06	Providence Bruins	AHL	74	8	10	18	58	....	....	....	....	....	....	....	....	....	3	0	0	0	10	....	....	....	....
2006-07	**Boston**	**NHL**	**4**	**0**	**0**	**0**	**0**	**0**	**0**	**0**	**5**	**0.0**	**0**	**10**	**40.0**	**4:46**	....	....	....	....	....	....	....	....	....
	Providence Bruins	AHL	67	8	15	23	74	....	....	....	....	....	....	....	....	....	13	0	2	2	9	....	....	....	....
2007-08	Providence Bruins	AHL	75	19	20	39	83	....	....	....	....	....	....	....	....	....	10	2	3	5	4	....	....	....	....
	NHL Totals		**4**	**0**	**0**	**0**	**0**	**0**	**0**	**0**	**5**	**0.0**		**10**	**40.0**	**4:46**	....	....	....	....	....	....	....	....	....

THORBURN, Chris

(THOHR-buhrn, KRIHS) **ATL.**

Center. Shoots right. 6'3", 225 lbs. Born, Sault Ste. Marie, Ont., June 3, 1983. Buffalo's 3rd choice, 50th overall, in 2001 Entry Draft.

1998-99	Elliot Lake Vikings	NOJHA	40	21	12	33	28	....	....	....	....	....	....	....	....	....	....	....	....	....	....	....	....	....	....
99-2000	North Bay	OHL	56	12	8	20	33	....	....	....	....	....	....	....	....	....	6	0	2	2	0	....	....	....	....
2000-01	North Bay	OHL	66	22	32	54	64	....	....	....	....	....	....	....	....	....	4	0	1	1	9	....	....	....	....
2001-02	North Bay	OHL	67	15	43	58	112	....	....	....	....	....	....	....	....	....	5	1	2	3	8	....	....	....	....
2002-03	Saginaw Spirit	OHL	37	19	19	38	68	....	....	....	....	....	....	....	....	....	....	....	....	....	....	....	....	....	....
	Plymouth Whalers	OHL	27	11	22	33	56	....	....	....	....	....	....	....	....	....	18	11	9	20	10	....	....	....	....
2003-04	Rochester	AHL	58	6	16	22	77	....	....	....	....	....	....	....	....	....	16	3	2	5	18	....	....	....	....
2004-05	Rochester	AHL	73	12	17	29	185	....	....	....	....	....	....	....	....	....	4	0	1	1	2	....	....	....	....
2005-06	**Buffalo**	**NHL**	**2**	**0**	**1**	**1**	**7**	**0**	**0**	**0**	**1**	**0.0**	**–1**	**1**	**0.0**	**6:52**	....	....	....	....	....	....	....	....	....
	Rochester	AHL	77	23	27	50	134	....	....	....	....	....	....	....	....	....	....	....	....	....	....	....	....	....	....
2006-07	**Pittsburgh**	**NHL**	**39**	**3**	**2**	**5**	**69**	**0**	**0**	**1**	**40**	**7.5**	**1**	**8**	**25.0**	**7:54**	....	....	....	....	....	....	....	....	....
	Wilkes-Barre	AHL	3	0	1	1	2	....	....	....	....	....	....	....	....	....	....	....	....	....	....	....	....	....	....
2007-08	**Atlanta**	**NHL**	**73**	**5**	**13**	**18**	**92**	**0**	**0**	**1**	**72**	**6.9**	**–4**	**20**	**60.0**	**8:56**	....	....	....	....	....	....	....	....	....
	NHL Totals		**114**	**8**	**16**	**24**	**168**	**0**	**0**	**2**	**113**	**7.1**		**29**	**48.3**	**8:33**	....	....	....	....	....	....	....	....	....

Claimed on waivers by **Pittsburgh** from **Buffalo**, October 3, 2006. Traded to **Atlanta** by **Pittsburgh** for NY Rangers' 3rd round choice (previously acquired, Pittsburgh selected Robert Bortuzzo) in 2007 Entry Draft, June 22, 2007.

THORESEN, Patrick

(THOR-eh-sehn, PAT-rihk)

Center. Shoots left. 5'11", 188 lbs. Born, Oslo, Norway, November 8, 1983.

99-2000	Storhamar	Norway	25	1	8	9	4	....	....	....	....	....	....	....	....	....	....	....	....	....	....	....	....	....	....
2000-01	Storhamar	Norway	40	18	27	45	24	....	....	....	....	....	....	....	....	....	....	....	....	....	....	....	....	....	....
2001-02	Moncton Wildcats	QMJHL	60	30	43	73	50	....	....	....	....	....	....	....	....	....	....	....	....	....	....	....	....	....	....
2002-03	Baie-Comeau	QMJHL	71	33	*75	108	57	....	....	....	....	....	....	....	....	....	12	2	8	10	8	....	....	....	....
2003-04	Morrums GoIS IK	Sweden-2	38	19	22	41	40	....	....	....	....	....	....	....	....	....	....	....	....	....	....	....	....	....	....
	Djurgarden	Sweden	3	0	0	0	2	....	....	....	....	....	....	....	....	....	....	....	....	....	....	....	....	....	....
2004-05	Djurgarden	Sweden	30	10	7	17	33	....	....	....	....	....	....	....	....	....	12	2	2	4	29	....	....	....	....
2005-06	Djurgarden	Sweden	50	17	19	36	44	....	....	....	....	....	....	....	....	....	....	....	....	....	....	....	....	....	....
	Salzburg	Austria	....	....	....	....	....	....	....	....	....	....	....	....	....	....	9	4	7	11	12	....	....	....	....
2006-07	**Edmonton**	**NHL**	**68**	**4**	**12**	**16**	**52**	**0**	**1**	**2**	**73**	**5.5**	**–1**	**82**	**51.2**	**11:25**	....	....	....	....	....	....	....	....	....
	Wilkes-Barre	AHL	5	1	5	6	4	....	....	....	....	....	....	....	....	....	....	....	....	....	....	....	....	....	....
2007-08	**Edmonton**	**NHL**	**17**	**2**	**1**	**3**	**6**	**0**	**0**	**0**	**18**	**11.1**	**–4**	**19**	**52.6**	**10:43**	....	....	....	....	....	....	....	....	....
	Springfield	AHL	29	13	13	26	13	....	....	....	....	....	....	....	....	....	....	....	....	....	....	....	....	....	....
	Philadelphia	**NHL**	**21**	**0**	**5**	**5**	**8**	**0**	**0**	**0**	**21**	**0.0**	**–6**	**81**	**38.3**	**12:36**	**14**	**0**	**2**	**2**	**4**	**0**	**0**	**0**	**9:22**
	NHL Totals		**106**	**6**	**18**	**24**	**66**	**0**	**1**	**2**	**112**	**5.4**		**182**	**45.6**	**11:32**	**14**	**0**	**2**	**2**	**4**	**0**	**0**	**0**	**9:22**

Signed as a free agent by **Edmonton**, June 12, 2006. Claimed on waivers by **Philadelphia** from **Edmonton**, February 22, 2008. Signed as a free agent by **Lugano** (Swiss), July 14, 2008.

THORNTON, Joe

(THOHRN-tuhn, JOH) **S.J.**

Center. Shoots left. 6'4", 235 lbs. Born, London, Ont., July 2, 1979. Boston's 1st choice, 1st overall, in 1997 Entry Draft.

1993-94	Elgin-Middlesex	Minor-ON	67	*83	*85	*168	45	....	....	....	....	....	....	....	....	....	....	....	....	....	....	....	....	....	....
	St. Thomas Stars	OHA-B	6	2	6	8	2	....	....	....	....	....	....	....	....	....	....	....	....	....	....	....	....	....	....
1994-95	St. Thomas Stars	OHA-B	50	40	64	104	53	....	....	....	....	....	....	....	....	....	....	....	....	....	....	....	....	....	....
1995-96	Sault Ste. Marie	OHL	66	30	46	76	53	....	....	....	....	....	....	....	....	....	4	1	1	2	11	....	....	....	....
1996-97	Sault Ste. Marie	OHL	59	41	81	122	123	....	....	....	....	....	....	....	....	....	11	11	8	19	24	....	....	....	....
1997-98	**Boston**	**NHL**	**55**	**3**	**4**	**7**	**19**	**0**	**0**	**1**	**33**	**9.1**	**–6**	....	....	....	**6**	**0**	**0**	**0**	**9**	**0**	**0**	**0**	....
1998-99	**Boston**	**NHL**	**81**	**16**	**25**	**41**	**69**	**7**	**0**	**1**	**128**	**12.5**	**3**	**1073**	**48.7**	**15:21**	**11**	**3**	**6**	**9**	**4**	**2**	**0**	**2**	**19:52**
99-2000	**Boston**	**NHL**	**81**	**23**	**37**	**60**	**82**	**5**	**0**	**3**	**171**	**13.5**	**–5**	**1861**	**49.5**	**21:18**	....	....	....	....	....	....	....	....	....
2000-01	**Boston**	**NHL**	**72**	**37**	**34**	**71**	**107**	**19**	**1**	**5**	**181**	**20.4**	**–4**	**1651**	**52.1**	**21:45**	....	....	....	....	....	....	....	....	....
2001-02	**Boston**	**NHL**	**66**	**22**	**46**	**68**	**127**	**6**	**0**	**5**	**152**	**14.5**	**7**	**1341**	**49.1**	**19:59**	**6**	**2**	**4**	**6**	**10**	**0**	**0**	**0**	**21:09**
2002-03	**Boston**	**NHL**	**77**	**36**	**65**	**101**	**109**	**12**	**2**	**4**	**196**	**18.4**	**12**	**1766**	**49.5**	**22:33**	**5**	**1**	**2**	**3**	**4**	**1**	**0**	**0**	**20:13**
2003-04	**Boston**	**NHL**	**77**	**23**	**50**	**73**	**98**	**4**	**0**	**6**	**187**	**12.3**	**18**	**1671**	**56.3**	**21:38**	**7**	**0**	**0**	**0**	**14**	**0**	**0**	**0**	**21:30**
2004-05	HC Davos	Swiss	40	10	44	54	80	....	....	....	....	....	....	....	....	....	14	4	*20	*24	29	....	....	....	....
2005-06	**Boston**	**NHL**	**23**	**9**	***24**	***33**	**6**	**3**	**0**	**2**	**60**	**15.0**	**0**	**511**	**52.3**	**21:33**	....	....	....	....	....	....	....	....	....
	San Jose	**NHL**	**58**	**20**	***72**	***92**	**55**	**8**	**0**	**4**	**135**	**14.8**	**31**	**1287**	**50.9**	**21:15**	**11**	**2**	**7**	**9**	**12**	**1**	**0**	**1**	**25:09**
	Canada	Olympics	6	1	2	3	0	....	....	....	....	....	....	....	....	....	....	....	....	....	....	....	....	....	....
2006-07	**San Jose**	**NHL**	**82**	**22**	***92**	**114**	**44**	**10**	**0**	**5**	**213**	**10.3**	**24**	**1522**	**51.1**	**20:19**	**11**	**1**	**10**	**11**	**10**	**0**	**0**	**0**	**22:00**
2007-08	**San Jose**	**NHL**	**82**	**29**	***67**	**96**	**59**	**11**	**0**	**5**	**178**	**16.3**	**18**	**1485**	**52.9**	**21:24**	**13**	**2**	**8**	**10**	**2**	**1**	**0**	**1**	**24:42**
	NHL Totals		**754**	**240**	**516**	**756**	**775**	**85**	**3**	**41**	**1634**	**14.7**		**14168**	**51.3**	**20:36**	**70**	**11**	**37**	**48**	**65**	**5**	**0**	**4**	**22:27**

OHL All-Rookie Team (1996) • OHL Rookie of the Year (1996) • Canadian Major Junior Rookie of the Year (1996) • OHL Second All-Star Team (1997) • NHL Second All-Star Team (2003, 2008) • NHL First All-Star Team (2006) • Art Ross Trophy (2006) • Hart Memorial Trophy (2006)

Played in NHL All-Star Game (2002, 2003, 2004, 2007, 2008)

Signed as a free agent by **Davos** (Swiss), July 8, 2004. Traded to **San Jose** by **Boston** for Brad Stuart, Marco Sturm and Wayne Primeau, November 30, 2005.

THORNTON, Scott

(THOHRN-tuhn, SKAWT)

Left wing. Shoots left. 6'3", 220 lbs. Born, London, Ont., January 9, 1971. Toronto's 1st choice, 3rd overall, in 1989 Entry Draft.

			Regular Season														Playoffs								
Season	Club	League	GP	G	A	Pts	PIM	PP	SH	GW	S	%	+/-	TF	F%	Min	GP	G	A	Pts	PIM	PP	SH	GW	Min
1986-87	London	OHA-B	31	10	7	17	10	....	....	....	....	....	....	....	....	....	....	....	....	....	....	....	....	....	....
1987-88	Belleville Bulls	OHL	62	11	19	30	54	....	....	....	....	....	....	....	....	....	6	0	1	1	2	....	....	....	....
1988-89	Belleville Bulls	OHL	59	28	34	62	103	....	....	....	....	....	....	....	....	....	5	1	1	2	6	....	....	....	....
1989-90	Belleville Bulls	OHL	47	21	28	49	91	....	....	....	....	....	....	....	....	....	11	2	10	12	15	....	....	....	....
1990-91	Belleville Bulls	OHL	3	2	1	3	2	....	....	....	....	....	....	....	....	....	6	0	7	7	14	....	....	....	....
	Toronto	**NHL**	**33**	**1**	**3**	**4**	**30**	**0**	**0**	**0**	**31**	**3.2**	**–15**	....	....	....	....	....	....	....	....	....	....	....	....
	Newmarket Saints	AHL	5	1	0	1	4	....	....	....	....	....	....	....	....	....	....	....	....	....	....	....	....	....	....
1991-92	**Edmonton**	**NHL**	**15**	**0**	**1**	**1**	**43**	**0**	**0**	**0**	**11**	**0.0**	**–6**	....	....	....	**1**	**0**	**0**	**0**	**0**	**0**	**0**	**0**	....
	Cape Breton	AHL	49	9	14	23	40	....	....	....	....	....	....	....	....	....	5	1	0	1	8	....	....	....	....
1992-93	**Edmonton**	**NHL**	**9**	**0**	**1**	**1**	**0**	**0**	**0**	**0**	**7**	**0.0**	**–4**	....	....	....	....	....	....	....	....	....	....	....	....
	Cape Breton	AHL	58	23	27	50	102	....	....	....	....	....	....	....	....	....	16	1	2	3	35	....	....	....	....
1993-94	**Edmonton**	**NHL**	**61**	**4**	**7**	**11**	**104**	**0**	**0**	**0**	**65**	**6.2**	**–15**	....	....	....	....	....	....	....	....	....	....	....	....
	Cape Breton	AHL	2	1	1	2	31	....	....	....	....	....	....	....	....	....	....	....	....	....	....	....	....	....	....
1994-95	**Edmonton**	**NHL**	**47**	**10**	**12**	**22**	**89**	**0**	**1**	**1**	**69**	**14.5**	**–4**	....	....	....	....	....	....	....	....	....	....	....	....
1995-96	**Edmonton**	**NHL**	**77**	**9**	**9**	**18**	**149**	**0**	**2**	**3**	**95**	**9.5**	**–25**	....	....	....	....	....	....	....	....	....	....	....	....
1996-97	**Montreal**	**NHL**	**73**	**10**	**10**	**20**	**128**	**1**	**1**	**1**	**110**	**9.1**	**–19**	....	....	....	**5**	**1**	**0**	**1**	**2**	**0**	**0**	**0**	....
1997-98	**Montreal**	**NHL**	**67**	**6**	**9**	**15**	**158**	**1**	**0**	**1**	**51**	**11.8**	**0**	....	....	....	**9**	**0**	**2**	**2**	**10**	**0**	**0**	**0**	....
1998-99	**Montreal**	**NHL**	**47**	**7**	**4**	**11**	**87**	**1**	**0**	**1**	**56**	**12.5**	**–2**	**466**	**52.8**	**12:24**	....	....	....	....	....	....	....	....	....
99-2000	**Montreal**	**NHL**	**35**	**2**	**3**	**5**	**70**	**0**	**0**	**1**	**36**	**5.6**	**–7**	**253**	**51.8**	**12:40**	....	....	....	....	....	....	....	....	....
	Dallas	**NHL**	**30**	**6**	**3**	**9**	**38**	**1**	**0**	**0**	**47**	**12.8**	**–5**	**14**	**14.3**	**13:03**	**23**	**2**	**7**	**9**	**28**	**0**	**0**	**1**	**14:11**
2000-01	**San Jose**	**NHL**	**73**	**19**	**17**	**36**	**114**	**4**	**0**	**1**	**159**	**11.9**	**4**	**29**	**41.4**	**13:54**	**6**	**3**	**0**	**3**	**8**	**0**	**0**	**1**	**15:50**
2001-02	**San Jose**	**NHL**	**77**	**26**	**16**	**42**	**116**	**6**	**0**	**5**	**144**	**18.1**	**11**	**18**	**61.1**	**13:31**	**12**	**3**	**3**	**6**	**6**	**0**	**0**	**0**	**15:52**
2002-03	**San Jose**	**NHL**	**41**	**9**	**12**	**21**	**41**	**4**	**0**	**1**	**64**	**14.1**	**–7**	**6**	**50.0**	**13:53**	....	....	....	....	....	....	....	....	....
2003-04	**San Jose**	**NHL**	**80**	**13**	**14**	**27**	**84**	**1**	**0**	**1**	**127**	**10.2**	**–6**	**27**	**40.7**	**13:57**	**12**	**2**	**2**	**4**	**22**	**0**	**0**	**0**	**12:31**
2004-05	Sodertalje SK	Sweden	12	2	5	7	10	....	....	....	....	....	....	....	....	....	10	0	3	3	27	....	....	....	....
2005-06	**San Jose**	**NHL**	**71**	**10**	**11**	**21**	**84**	**1**	**0**	**2**	**122**	**8.2**	**–8**	**28**	**35.7**	**13:19**	**11**	**2**	**0**	**2**	**6**	**0**	**0**	**0**	**11:18**
2006-07	**Los Angeles**	**NHL**	**58**	**7**	**6**	**13**	**85**	**0**	**1**	**0**	**65**	**10.8**	**–15**	**145**	**57.9**	**12:24**	....	....	....	....	....	....	....	....	....
2007-08	**Los Angeles**	**NHL**	**47**	**5**	**3**	**8**	**39**	**0**	**0**	**1**	**35**	**14.3**	**1**	**40**	**45.0**	**8:48**	....	....	....	....	....	....	....	....	....
	NHL Totals		**941**	**144**	**141**	**285**	**1459**	**20**	**5**	**19**	**1294**	**11.1**		**1026**	**51.5**	**12:57**	**79**	**13**	**14**	**27**	**82**	**0**	**0**	**2**	**13:51**

Traded to **Edmonton** by **Toronto** with Vincent Damphousse, Peter Ing and Luke Richardson for Grant Fuhr, Glenn Anderson and Craig Berube, September 19, 1991. Traded to **Montreal** by **Edmonton** for Andrei Kovalenko, September 6, 1996. Traded to **Dallas** by **Montreal** for Juha Lind, January 22, 2000. Signed as a free agent by **San Jose**, July 1, 2000. • Missed majority of 2002-03 season recovering from shoulder (October 7, 2002 in training camp) and head (February 21, 2003 vs. Columbus) injuries. Signed as a free agent by **Sodertalje** (Sweden), January 13, 2005. Signed as a free agent by **Los Angeles**, July 1, 2006.

THORNTON, Shawn

(THOHRN-tohn, SHAWN) **BOS.**

Right wing. Shoots right. 6'2", 217 lbs. Born, Oshawa, Ont., July 23, 1977. Toronto's 6th choice, 190th overall, in 1997 Entry Draft.

			Regular Season														Playoffs								
Season	Club	League	GP	G	A	Pts	PIM	PP	SH	GW	S	%	+/-	TF	F%	Min	GP	G	A	Pts	PIM	PP	SH	GW	Min
1995-96	Peterborough	OHL	63	4	10	14	192	....	....	....	....	....	....	....	....	....	24	3	0	3	25	....	....	....	....
1996-97	Peterborough	OHL	61	19	10	29	204	....	....	....	....	....	....	....	....	....	11	2	4	6	20	....	....	....	....
1997-98	St. John's	AHL	59	0	3	3	225	....	....	....	....	....	....	....	....	....	....	....	....	....	....	....	....	....	....
1998-99	St. John's	AHL	78	8	11	19	354	....	....	....	....	....	....	....	....	....	5	0	0	0	9	....	....	....	....
99-2000	St. John's	AHL	60	4	12	16	316	....	....	....	....	....	....	....	....	....	....	....	....	....	....	....	....	....	....
2000-01	St. John's	AHL	79	5	12	17	320	....	....	....	....	....	....	....	....	....	3	1	2	3	2	....	....	....	....
2001-02	Norfolk Admirals	AHL	70	8	14	22	281	....	....	....	....	....	....	....	....	....	4	0	0	0	4	....	....	....	....
2002-03	**Chicago**	**NHL**	**13**	**1**	**1**	**2**	**31**	**0**	**0**	**0**	**15**	**6.7**	**–4**	**3**	**66.7**	**8:30**	....	....	....	....	....	....	....	....	....
	Norfolk Admirals	AHL	50	11	2	13	213	....	....	....	....	....	....	....	....	....	9	0	2	2	28	....	....	....	....
2003-04	**Chicago**	**NHL**	**8**	**1**	**0**	**1**	**23**	**0**	**0**	**0**	**14**	**7.1**	**2**	**19**	**42.1**	**11:14**	....	....	....	....	....	....	....	....	....
	Norfolk Admirals	AHL	64	6	11	17	259	....	....	....	....	....	....	....	....	....	8	1	1	2	6	....	....	....	....
2004-05	Norfolk Admirals	AHL	71	5	9	14	253	....	....	....	....	....	....	....	....	....	6	0	0	0	8	....	....	....	....
2005-06	**Chicago**	**NHL**	**10**	**0**	**0**	**0**	**16**	**0**	**0**	**0**	**16**	**0.0**	**–5**	**17**	**58.8**	**7:18**	....	....	....	....	....	....	....	....	....
	Norfolk Admirals	AHL	59	10	22	32	192	....	....	....	....	....	....	....	....	....	4	0	0	0	35	....	....	....	....
2006-07 ♦	**Anaheim**	**NHL**	**48**	**2**	**7**	**9**	**88**	**0**	**0**	**0**	**60**	**3.3**	**3**	**8**	**25.0**	**8:26**	**15**	**0**	**0**	**0**	**19**	**0**	**0**	**0**	**3:58**
	Portland Pirates	AHL	15	4	4	8	55	....	....	....	....	....	....	....	....	....	....	....	....	....	....	....	....	....	....
2007-08	**Boston**	**NHL**	**58**	**4**	**3**	**7**	**74**	**0**	**0**	**1**	**65**	**6.2**	**–1**	**7**	**28.6**	**7:24**	**7**	**0**	**0**	**0**	**6**	**0**	**0**	**0**	**8:04**
	NHL Totals		**137**	**8**	**11**	**19**	**232**	**0**	**0**	**1**	**170**	**4.7**		**54**	**44.4**	**8:05**	**22**	**0**	**0**	**0**	**25**	**0**	**0**	**0**	**5:16**

Traded to **Chicago** by **Toronto** for Marty Wilford, September 30, 2001. Signed as a free agent by **Anaheim**, July 14, 2006. Signed as a free agent by **Boston**, July 1, 2007.

TIMONEN, Jussi

(TEEM-oh-nehn, YEW-see)

Defense. Shoots left. 6', 200 lbs. Born, Kuopio, Finland, June 29, 1983. Philadelphia's 3rd choice, 146th overall, in 2001 Entry Draft.

			Regular Season														Playoffs								
Season	Club	League	GP	G	A	Pts	PIM	PP	SH	GW	S	%	+/-	TF	F%	Min	GP	G	A	Pts	PIM	PP	SH	GW	Min
99-2000	KalPa Kuopio U18	Fin-U18	14	3	2	5	10	....	....	....	....	....	....	....	....	....	....	....	....	....	....	....	....	....	....
	KalPa Kuopio Jr.	Fin-Jr.	19	1	0	1	6	....	....	....	....	....	....	....	....	....	4	0	0	0	4	....	....	....	....
2000-01	KalPa Kuopio U18	Fin-U18	4	1	4	5	10	....	....	....	....	....	....	....	....	....	....	....	....	....	....	....	....	....	....
	KalPa Kuopio Jr.	Fin-Jr.	38	6	7	13	22	....	....	....	....	....	....	....	....	....	....	....	....	....	....	....	....	....	....
	KalPa Kuopio	Finland-3	7	0	1	1	2	....	....	....	....	....	....	....	....	....	2	1	0	1	0	....	....	....	....
2001-02	KalPa Kuopio Jr.	Fin-Jr.	10	1	1	2	10	....	....	....	....	....	....	....	....	....	....	....	....	....	....	....	....	....	....
	KalPa Kuopio	Finland-2	41	3	8	11	10	....	....	....	....	....	....	....	....	....	8	0	2	2	0	....	....	....	....
2002-03	TPS Turku Jr.	Fin-Jr.	2	0	0	0	0	....	....	....	....	....	....	....	....	....	....	....	....	....	....	....	....	....	....
	TuTo Turku	Finland-2	3	0	0	0	0	....	....	....	....	....	....	....	....	....	....	....	....	....	....	....	....	....	....
	TPS Turku	Finland	39	1	0	1	10	....	....	....	....	....	....	....	....	....	7	0	2	2	4	....	....	....	....
2003-04	TPS Turku	Finland	20	0	0	0	4	....	....	....	....	....	....	....	....	....	....	....	....	....	....	....	....	....	....
	Jukurit Mikkeli	Finland-2	25	7	9	16	10	....	....	....	....	....	....	....	....	....	13	0	4	4	0	....	....	....	....
2004-05	SaiPa	Finland	54	1	5	6	53	....	....	....	....	....	....	....	....	....	....	....	....	....	....	....	....	....	....
2005-06	SaiPa	Finland	52	0	7	7	30	....	....	....	....	....	....	....	....	....	8	1	0	1	27	....	....	....	....
2006-07	**Philadelphia**	**NHL**	**14**	**0**	**4**	**4**	**6**	**0**	**0**	**0**	**8**	**0.0**	**–10**	**0**	**0.0**	**14:11**	....	....	....	....	....	....	....	....	....
	Philadelphia	AHL	46	2	15	17	18	....	....	....	....	....	....	....	....	....	....	....	....	....	....	....	....	....	....
2007-08	Philadelphia	AHL	14	0	7	7	14	....	....	....	....	....	....	....	....	....	....	....	....	....	....	....	....	....	....
	Iowa Stars	AHL	33	0	11	11	12	....	....	....	....	....	....	....	....	....	....	....	....	....	....	....	....	....	....
	NHL Totals		**14**	**0**	**4**	**4**	**6**	**0**	**0**	**0**	**8**	**0.0**		**0**	**0.0**	**14:11**	....	....	....	....	....	....	....	....	....

Traded to **Dallas** by **Philadelphia** for future considerations, December 10, 2007.

TIMONEN, Kimmo

(TEEM-oh-nehn, KEE-moh) **PHI.**

Defense. Shoots left. 5'10", 194 lbs. Born, Kuopio, Finland, March 18, 1975. Los Angeles' 11th choice, 250th overall, in 1993 Entry Draft.

			Regular Season														Playoffs								
Season	Club	League	GP	G	A	Pts	PIM	PP	SH	GW	S	%	+/-	TF	F%	Min	GP	G	A	Pts	PIM	PP	SH	GW	Min
1990-91	KalPa Kuopio Jr.	Fin-Jr.	4	0	1	1	2	....	....	....	....	....	....	....	....	....	....	....	....	....	....	....	....	....	....
1991-92	KalPa Kuopio Jr.	Fin-Jr.	32	7	10	17	4	....	....	....	....	....	....	....	....	....	....	....	....	....	....	....	....	....	....
	KalPa Kuopio	Finland	5	0	0	0	0	....	....	....	....	....	....	....	....	....	....	....	....	....	....	....	....	....	....
1992-93	KalPa Kuopio U18	Fin-U18	3	0	5	5	0	....	....	....	....	....	....	....	....	....	....	....	....	....	....	....	....	....	....
	KalPa Kuopio Jr.	Fin-Jr.	16	9	15	24	10	....	....	....	....	....	....	....	....	....	....	....	....	....	....	....	....	....	....
	KalPa Kuopio	Finland	33	0	2	2	4	....	....	....	....	....	....	....	....	....	....	....	....	....	....	....	....	....	....
1993-94	KalPa Kuopio Jr.	Fin-Jr.	5	4	7	11	0	....	....	....	....	....	....	....	....	....	....	....	....	....	....	....	....	....	....
	KalPa Kuopio	Finland	46	6	7	13	55	....	....	....	....	....	....	....	....	....	....	....	....	....	....	....	....	....	....
1994-95	TPS Turku Jr.	Fin-Jr.	1	0	0	0	0	....	....	....	....	....	....	....	....	....	....	....	....	....	....	....	....	....	....
	TPS Turku	Finland	45	3	4	7	10	....	....	....	....	....	....	....	....	....	13	0	1	1	6	....	....	....	....
1995-96	TPS Turku	Finland	48	3	21	24	22	....	....	....	....	....	....	....	....	....	9	1	2	3	12	....	....	....	....
1996-97	TPS Turku	Finland	50	10	14	24	18	....	....	....	....	....	....	....	....	....	12	2	7	9	6	....	....	....	....
	TPS Turku	EuroHL	6	1	0	1	27	....	....	....	....	....	....	....	....	....	4	0	1	1	0	....	....	....	....
1997-98	HIFK Helsinki	Finland	45	10	15	25	24	....	....	....	....	....	....	....	....	....	9	3	4	7	8	....	....	....	....
	Finland	Olympics	6	0	1	1	2	....	....	....	....	....	....	....	....	....	....	....	....	....	....	....	....	....	....
1998-99	**Nashville**	**NHL**	**50**	**4**	**8**	**12**	**30**	**1**	**0**	**0**	**75**	**5.3**	**–4**	**0**	**0.0**	**19:04**	....	....	....	....	....	....	....	....	....
	Milwaukee	IHL	29	2	13	15	22	....	....	....	....	....	....	....	....	....	....	....	....	....	....	....	....	....	....
99-2000	**Nashville**	**NHL**	**51**	**8**	**25**	**33**	**26**	**2**	**1**	**2**	**97**	**8.2**	**–5**	**0**	**0.0**	**21:06**	....	....	....	....	....	....	....	....	....
2000-01	**Nashville**	**NHL**	**82**	**12**	**13**	**25**	**50**	**6**	**0**	**3**	**151**	**7.9**	**–6**	**2**	**50.0**	**23:11**	....	....	....	....	....	....	....	....	....
2001-02	**Nashville**	**NHL**	**82**	**13**	**29**	**42**	**28**	**9**	**0**	**1**	**154**	**8.4**	**2**	**0**	**0.0**	**24:12**	....	....	....	....	....	....	....	....	....
	Finland	Olympics	4	0	1	1	2	....	....	....	....	....	....	....	....	....	....	....	....	....	....	....	....	....	....
2002-03	**Nashville**	**NHL**	**72**	**6**	**34**	**40**	**46**	**4**	**0**	**0**	**144**	**4.2**	**–3**	**0**	**0.0**	**22:25**	....	....	....	....	....	....	....	....	....
2003-04	**Nashville**	**NHL**	**77**	**12**	**32**	**44**	**52**	**8**	**0**	**1**	**180**	**6.7**	**–7**	**1**	**0.0**	**23:52**	**6**	**0**	**0**	**0**	**10**	**0**	**0**	**0**	**24:16**

			Regular Season														Playoffs								
Season	Club	League	GP	G	A	Pts	PIM	PP	SH	GW	S	%	+/-	TF	F%	Min	GP	G	A	Pts	PIM	PP	SH	GW	Min
2004-05	HC Lugano	Swiss	3	0	1	1	0	....	....	....	....	....	....	....	....	....	....	....	....	....	....	....	....	....	....
	Brynas IF Gavle	Sweden	10	5	3	8	8	....	....	....	....	....	....	....	....	....	....	....	....	....	....	....	....	....	....
	KalPa Kuopio	Finland-2	12	4	13	17	6	....	....	....	....	....	....	....	....	....	8	3	7	10	4	....	....	....	....
2005-06	**Nashville**	**NHL**	**79**	**11**	**39**	**50**	**74**	**8**	**0**	**1**	**156**	**7.1**	**–3**	**5**	**80.0**	**22:26**	**5**	**1**	**3**	**4**	**4**	**0**	**1**	**0**	**24:42**
	Finland	Olympics	8	1	4	5	2	....	....	....	....	....	....	....	....	....	....	....	....	....	....	....	....	....	....
2006-07	**Nashville**	**NHL**	**80**	**13**	**42**	**55**	**42**	**8**	**0**	**2**	**121**	**10.7**	**20**	**1**	**0.0**	**21:51**	**5**	**0**	**2**	**2**	**4**	**0**	**0**	**0**	**24:33**
2007-08	**Philadelphia**	**NHL**	**80**	**8**	**36**	**44**	**50**	**3**	**1**	**1**	**125**	**6.4**	**0**	**0**	**0.0**	**23:35**	**13**	**0**	**6**	**6**	**8**	**0**	**0**	**0**	**24:41**
	NHL Totals		**653**	**87**	**258**	**345**	**398**	**49**	**2**	**11**	**1203**	**7.2**		**9**	**55.6**	**22:37**	**29**	**1**	**11**	**12**	**26**	**0**	**1**	**0**	**24:34**

Olympic Tournament All-Star Team (2006)

Played in NHL All-Star Game (2004, 2007, 2008)

Traded to **Nashville** by **Los Angeles** with Jan Vopat for future considerations, June 26, 1998. Signed as a free agent by **Lugano** (Swiss), October 31, 2004. Signed as a free agent by **Gavle** (Sweden), November 8, 2004. Signed as a free agent by **Kuopio** (Finland-2), January 3, 2005. Traded to **Philadelphia** by **Nashville** with Scott Hartnell for Nashville's 1st round choice (previously acquired, Nashville selected Jonathon Blum) in 2007 Entry Draft, June 18, 2007.

TJARNQVIST, Daniel

(T'YAHRN-kvihst, DAN-yehl) **COL.**

Defense. Shoots left. 6'2", 200 lbs. Born, Umea, Sweden, October 14, 1976. Florida's 5th choice, 88th overall, in 1995 Entry Draft.

			Regular Season														Playoffs								
Season	Club	League	GP	G	A	Pts	PIM	PP	SH	GW	S	%	+/-	TF	F%	Min	GP	G	A	Pts	PIM	PP	SH	GW	Min
1992-93	Rogle Jr.	Swe-Jr.	7	1	0	1	0	....	....	....	....	....	....	....	....	....	....	....	....	....	....	....	....	....	....
1993-94	Rogle U18	Swe-U18	STATISTICS NOT AVAILABLE																						
1994-95	Rogle	Sweden	18	0	1	1	2	....	....	....	....	....	....	....	....	....	....	....	....	....	....	....	....	....	....
	Rogle	Sweden-Q	15	2	3	5	0	....	....	....	....	....	....	....	....	....	....	....	....	....	....	....	....	....	....
1995-96	Rogle	Sweden	22	1	7	8	6	....	....	....	....	....	....	....	....	....	....	....	....	....	....	....	....	....	....
1996-97	Jokerit Helsinki	Finland	44	3	8	11	4	....	....	....	....	....	....	....	....	....	9	0	3	3	4	....	....	....	....
	Jokerit Helsinki	EuroHL	6	1	1	2	2	....	....	....	....	....	....	....	....	....	....	....	....	....	....	....	....	....	....
1997-98	Djurgarden	Sweden	40	5	9	14	12	....	....	....	....	....	....	....	....	....	15	1	1	2	2	....	....	....	....
1998-99	Djurgarden	Sweden	40	4	3	7	16	....	....	....	....	....	....	....	....	....	4	0	0	0	2	....	....	....	....
99-2000	Djurgarden	Sweden	42	3	16	19	8	....	....	....	....	....	....	....	....	....	5	0	0	0	2	....	....	....	....
2000-01	Djurgarden	Sweden	45	9	17	26	26	....	....	....	....	....	....	....	....	....	16	6	5	11	2	....	....	....	....
2001-02	**Atlanta**	**NHL**	**75**	**2**	**16**	**18**	**14**	**1**	**0**	**0**	**68**	**2.9**	**–22**	**4**	**25.0**	**21:32**	....	....	....	....	....	....	....	....	....
2002-03	**Atlanta**	**NHL**	**75**	**3**	**12**	**15**	**26**	**1**	**0**	**0**	**65**	**4.6**	**–20**	**3**	**66.7**	**21:53**	....	....	....	....	....	....	....	....	....
2003-04	**Atlanta**	**NHL**	**68**	**5**	**15**	**20**	**20**	**0**	**2**	**1**	**65**	**7.7**	**–4**	**4**	**25.0**	**22:17**	....	....	....	....	....	....	....	....	....
2004-05	Djurgarden	Sweden	49	12	12	24	30	....	....	....	....	....	....	....	....	....	12	2	5	7	10	....	....	....	....
2005-06	**Minnesota**	**NHL**	**60**	**3**	**15**	**18**	**32**	**3**	**0**	**1**	**54**	**5.6**	**–11**	**0**	**0.0**	**19:46**	....	....	....	....	....	....	....	....	....
	Sweden	Olympics	8	2	1	3	4	....	....	....	....	....	....	....	....	....	....	....	....	....	....	....	....	....	....
2006-07	**Edmonton**	**NHL**	**37**	**3**	**12**	**15**	**30**	**2**	**0**	**0**	**33**	**9.1**	**3**	**0**	**0.0**	**22:42**	....	....	....	....	....	....	....	....	....
2007-08	Yaroslavl	Russia	18	1	2	3	14	....	....	....	....	....	....	....	....	....	8	0	4	4	4	....	....	....	....
	NHL Totals		**315**	**16**	**70**	**86**	**122**	**7**	**2**	**2**	**285**	**5.6**		**11**	**36.4**	**21:35**	....	....	....	....	....	....	....	....	....

Traded to **Atlanta** by **Florida** with Gord Murphy, Herbert Vasiljevs and Ottawa's 6th round choice (previously acquired, later traded to Dallas – Dallas selected Justin Cox) in 1999 Entry Draft for Trevor Kidd, June 25, 1999. Signed as a free agent by **Djurgarden** (Sweden), September 16, 2004. Signed as a free agent by **Minnesota**, August 15, 2005. Signed as a free agent by **Edmonton**, July 6, 2006. • Missed majority of 2006-07 season recovering from recurring groin injury. Signed as a free agent by **Kazan** (Russia), August 23, 2007. Signed as a free agent by **Colorado**, July 3, 2008.

TJARNQVIST, Mathias

(T'YAHRN-kvihst, MAT-ee-uhs)

Right wing. Shoots left. 6'2", 196 lbs. Born, Umea, Sweden, April 15, 1979. Dallas' 3rd choice, 96th overall, in 1999 Entry Draft.

			Regular Season														Playoffs								
Season	Club	League	GP	G	A	Pts	PIM	PP	SH	GW	S	%	+/-	TF	F%	Min	GP	G	A	Pts	PIM	PP	SH	GW	Min
1995-96	Rogle Jr.	Swe-Jr.	4	2	0	2	0	....	....	....	....	....	....	....	....	....	....	....	....	....	....	....	....	....	....
1996-97	Rogle Jr.	Swe-Jr.	18	5	8	13	....	....	....	....	....	....	....	....	....	....	....	....	....	....	....	....	....	....	....
	Rogle	Sweden-2	15	1	4	5	4	....	....	....	....	....	....	....	....	....	....	....	....	....	....	....	....	....	....
1997-98	Rogle	Sweden-2	31	12	11	23	30	....	....	....	....	....	....	....	....	....	4	2	0	2	6	....	....	....	....
1998-99	Rogle	Sweden-2	34	18	16	34	44	....	....	....	....	....	....	....	....	....	5	4	1	5	4	....	....	....	....
99-2000	Djurgarden	Sweden	50	12	12	24	20	....	....	....	....	....	....	....	....	....	13	3	2	5	16	....	....	....	....
2000-01	Djurgarden	Sweden	47	11	8	19	53	....	....	....	....	....	....	....	....	....	16	1	2	3	6	....	....	....	....
2001-02	Djurgarden	Sweden	6	0	1	1	4	....	....	....	....	....	....	....	....	....	2	0	0	0	2	....	....	....	....
2002-03	Djurgarden	Sweden	38	11	13	24	30	....	....	....	....	....	....	....	....	....	9	4	1	5	12	....	....	....	....
2003-04	**Dallas**	**NHL**	**18**	**1**	**1**	**2**	**2**	**0**	**0**	**1**	**11**	**9.1**	**–6**	**4**	**25.0**	**9:43**	....	....	....	....	....	....	....	....	....
	Utah Grizzlies	AHL	60	15	13	28	51	....	....	....	....	....	....	....	....	....	....	....	....	....	....	....	....	....	....
2004-05	HV 71 Jonkoping	Sweden	46	8	9	17	18	....	....	....	....	....	....	....	....	....	....	....	....	....	....	....	....	....	....
2005-06	**Dallas**	**NHL**	**33**	**2**	**4**	**6**	**18**	**0**	**0**	**0**	**36**	**5.6**	**4**	**4**	**75.0**	**8:10**	....	....	....	....	....	....	....	....	....
	Iowa Stars	AHL	34	17	12	29	28	....	....	....	....	....	....	....	....	....	1	0	0	0	0	....	....	....	....
2006-07	**Dallas**	**NHL**	**18**	**1**	**3**	**4**	**4**	**0**	**0**	**0**	**13**	**7.7**	**–3**	**7**	**42.9**	**9:15**	....	....	....	....	....	....	....	....	....
	Iowa Stars	AHL	2	1	1	2	0	....	....	....	....	....	....	....	....	....	....	....	....	....	....	....	....	....	....
	Phoenix	**NHL**	**26**	**5**	**4**	**9**	**2**	**0**	**1**	**0**	**31**	**16.1**	**–2**	**11**	**54.6**	**14:50**	....	....	....	....	....	....	....	....	....
2007-08	**Phoenix**	**NHL**	**78**	**4**	**7**	**11**	**34**	**0**	**0**	**0**	**90**	**4.4**	**–1**	**46**	**32.6**	**13:39**	....	....	....	....	....	....	....	....	....
	NHL Totals		**173**	**13**	**19**	**32**	**60**	**0**	**1**	**1**	**181**	**7.2**		**72**	**38.9**	**11:55**	....	....	....	....	....	....	....	....	....

Signed as a free agent by **Jonkoping** (Sweden), August 30, 2004. Traded to **Phoenix** by **Dallas** with Dallas' 1st round choice (later traded to Edmonton - Edmonton selected Riley Nash) in 2007 Entry Draft for Ladislav Nagy, February 12, 2007.

TKACHUK, Keith

(kuh-CHUK, KEETH) **ST.L.**

Left wing. Shoots left. 6'2", 232 lbs. Born, Melrose, MA, March 28, 1972. Winnipeg's 1st choice, 19th overall, in 1990 Entry Draft.

			Regular Season														Playoffs								
Season	Club	League	GP	G	A	Pts	PIM	PP	SH	GW	S	%	+/-	TF	F%	Min	GP	G	A	Pts	PIM	PP	SH	GW	Min
1988-89	Malden Cath.	High-MA	21	30	16	46	....	....	....	....	....	....	....	....	....	....	....	....	....	....	....	....	....	....	....
1989-90	Malden Cath.	High-MA	6	12	14	26	....	....	....	....	....	....	....	....	....	....	....	....	....	....	....	....	....	....	....
1990-91	Boston University	H-East	36	17	23	40	70	....	....	....	....	....	....	....	....	....	....	....	....	....	....	....	....	....	....
1991-92	United States	Nat-Tm	45	10	10	20	141	....	....	....	....	....	....	....	....	....	....	....	....	....	....	....	....	....	....
	United States	Olympics	8	1	1	2	12	....	....	....	....	....	....	....	....	....	....	....	....	....	....	....	....	....	....
	Winnipeg	**NHL**	**17**	**3**	**5**	**8**	**28**	**2**	**0**	**0**	**22**	**13.6**	**0**	....	....	....	**7**	**3**	**0**	**3**	**30**	**0**	**0**	**0**	....
1992-93	**Winnipeg**	**NHL**	**83**	**28**	**23**	**51**	**201**	**12**	**0**	**2**	**199**	**14.1**	**–13**	....	....	....	**6**	**4**	**0**	**4**	**14**	**1**	**0**	**0**	....
1993-94	**Winnipeg**	**NHL**	**84**	**41**	**40**	**81**	**255**	**22**	**3**	**3**	**218**	**18.8**	**–12**	....	....	....	....	....	....	....	....	....	....	....	....
1994-95	**Winnipeg**	**NHL**	**48**	**22**	**29**	**51**	**152**	**7**	**2**	**2**	**129**	**17.1**	**–4**	....	....	....	....	....	....	....	....	....	....	....	....
1995-96	**Winnipeg**	**NHL**	**76**	**50**	**48**	**98**	**156**	**20**	**2**	**6**	**249**	**20.1**	**11**	....	....	....	**6**	**1**	**2**	**3**	**22**	**0**	**0**	**0**	....
1996-97	**Phoenix**	**NHL**	**81**	***52**	**34**	**86**	**228**	**9**	**2**	**7**	**296**	**17.6**	**–1**	....	....	....	**7**	**6**	**0**	**6**	**7**	**2**	**0**	**0**	....
1997-98	**Phoenix**	**NHL**	**69**	**40**	**26**	**66**	**147**	**11**	**0**	**8**	**232**	**17.2**	**9**	....	....	....	**6**	**3**	**3**	**6**	**10**	**0**	**0**	**0**	....
	United States	Olympics	4	0	2	2	6	....	....	....	....	....	....	....	....	....	....	....	....	....	....	....	....	....	....
1998-99	**Phoenix**	**NHL**	**68**	**36**	**32**	**68**	**151**	**11**	**2**	**7**	**258**	**14.0**	**22**	**770**	**47.7**	**20:59**	**7**	**1**	**3**	**4**	**13**	**1**	**0**	**0**	**25:09**
99-2000	**Phoenix**	**NHL**	**50**	**22**	**21**	**43**	**82**	**5**	**1**	**1**	**183**	**12.0**	**7**	**500**	**50.4**	**19:21**	**5**	**1**	**1**	**2**	**4**	**1**	**0**	**0**	**18:46**
2000-01	**Phoenix**	**NHL**	**64**	**29**	**42**	**71**	**108**	**15**	**0**	**4**	**230**	**12.6**	**6**	**646**	**51.9**	**20:11**	....	....	....	....	....	....	....	....	....
	St. Louis	**NHL**	**12**	**6**	**2**	**8**	**14**	**2**	**0**	**1**	**41**	**14.6**	**–3**	**87**	**54.0**	**19:39**	**15**	**2**	**7**	**9**	**20**	**2**	**0**	**1**	**19:17**
2001-02	**St. Louis**	**NHL**	**73**	**38**	**37**	**75**	**117**	**13**	**0**	**7**	**244**	**15.6**	**21**	**88**	**43.2**	**19:38**	**10**	**5**	**5**	**10**	**18**	**1**	**0**	**0**	**19:24**
	United States	Olympics	5	2	0	2	2	....	....	....	....	....	....	....	....	....	....	....	....	....	....	....	....	....	....
2002-03	**St. Louis**	**NHL**	**56**	**31**	**24**	**55**	**139**	**14**	**0**	**5**	**185**	**16.8**	**1**	**346**	**55.8**	**19:16**	**7**	**1**	**3**	**4**	**14**	**0**	**0**	**0**	**19:22**
2003-04	**St. Louis**	**NHL**	**75**	**33**	**38**	**71**	**83**	**18**	**0**	**8**	**233**	**14.2**	**8**	**410**	**49.5**	**19:39**	**5**	**0**	**2**	**2**	**10**	**0**	**0**	**0**	**19:18**
2004-05			DID NOT PLAY																						
2005-06	**St. Louis**	**NHL**	**41**	**15**	**21**	**36**	**46**	**10**	**0**	**1**	**133**	**11.3**	**–15**	**250**	**50.4**	**19:27**	....	....	....	....	....	....	....	....	....
	United States	Olympics	6	0	0	0	8	....	....	....	....	....	....	....	....	....	....	....	....	....	....	....	....	....	....
2006-07	**St. Louis**	**NHL**	**61**	**20**	**23**	**43**	**92**	**8**	**0**	**1**	**160**	**12.5**	**3**	**678**	**49.4**	**17:26**	....	....	....	....	....	....	....	....	....
	Atlanta	**NHL**	**18**	**7**	**8**	**15**	**34**	**2**	**0**	**3**	**36**	**19.4**	**8**	**348**	**52.9**	**17:41**	**4**	**1**	**2**	**3**	**12**	**0**	**0**	**0**	**16:33**
2007-08	**St. Louis**	**NHL**	**79**	**27**	**31**	**58**	**69**	**12**	**1**	**1**	**177**	**15.3**	**–2**	**1118**	**49.4**	**16:51**	....	....	....	....	....	....	....	....	....
	NHL Totals		**1055**	**500**	**484**	**984**	**2102**	**193**	**13**	**67**	**3225**	**15.5**		**5241**	**50.2**	**19:07**	**85**	**28**	**28**	**56**	**174**	**8**	**0**	**1**	**19:50**

NHL Second All-Star Team (1995, 1998)

Played in NHL All-Star Game (1997, 1998, 1999, 2004)

Transferred to **Phoenix** after **Winnipeg** franchise relocated, July 1, 1996. Traded to **St. Louis** by **Phoenix** for Michal Handzus, Ladislav Nagy, the rights to Jeff Taffe and St. Louis' 1st round choice (Ben Eager) in 2002 Entry Draft, March 13, 2001. Traded to **Atlanta** by **St. Louis** for Glen Metropolit, Atlanta's 1st (later traded to Calgary - Calgary selected Mikael Backlund) and 3rd (Brett Sonne) round choices in 2007 Entry Draft, and Atlanta's 1st (later traded back to Atlanta - Atlanta selected Zach Bogosian) and 2nd (Philip McRae) round choices in 2008 Entry Draft, February 25, 2007. Traded to **St. Louis** by **Atlanta** with future considerations for Atlanta's 1st round choice (previously acquired, Atlanta selected Zach Bogosian) in 2008 Entry Draft, June 26, 2007.

Season	Club	League	Regular Season GP	G	A	Pts	PIM	PP	SH	GW	S	%	+/-	TF	F%	Min	Playoffs GP	G	A	Pts	PIM	PP	SH	GW	Min

TLUSTY, Jiri

(T'LOO-stee, YIH-ree) **TOR.**

Center. Shoots left. 6', 209 lbs. Born, Slany, Czech., March 16, 1988. Toronto's 1st choice, 13th overall, in 2006 Entry Draft.

Season	Club	League	GP	G	A	Pts	PIM	PP	SH	GW	S	%	+/-	TF	F%	Min	GP	G	A	Pts	PIM	PP	SH	GW	Min
2001-02	HC Kladno U17	CzR-U17	1	0	0	0	0	....	....	....	....	....	....	....	....	....	....	....	....	....	....	....	....	....	....
2002-03	HC Kladno U17	CzR-U17	48	28	17	45	22	....	....	....	....	....	....	....	....	....	10	5	4	9	12	....	....	....	....
2003-04	HC Kladno U17	CzR-U17	1	0	0	0	2	....	....	....	....	....	....	....	....	....	1	0	0	0	2	....	....	....	....
	HC Kladno Jr.	CzRep-Jr.	51	10	3	13	12	....	....	....	....	....	....	....	....	....	1	0	0	0	0	....	....	....	....
2004-05	HC Kladno Jr.	CzRep-Jr.	42	15	12	27	54	....	....	....	....	....	....	....	....	....	10	2	2	4	8	....	....	....	....
2005-06	HC Kladno Jr.	CzRep-Jr.	6	4	2	6	2	....	....	....	....	....	....	....	....	....	6	7	6	13	6	....	....	....	....
	HC Rabat Kladno	CzRep	44	7	3	10	51	....	....	....	....	....	....	....	....	....	....	....	....	....	....	....	....	....	....
2006-07	Sault Ste. Marie	OHL	37	13	21	34	28	....	....	....	....	....	....	....	....	....	13	9	8	17	14	....	....	....	....
	Toronto Marlies	AHL	6	3	1	4	4	....	....	....	....	....	....	....	....	....	....	....	....	....	....	....	....	....	....
2007-08	**Toronto**	**NHL**	**58**	**10**	**6**	**16**	**14**	**2**	**0**	**2**	**69**	**14.5**	**–12**	**2**	**50.0**	**10:55**	....	....	....	....	....	....	....	....	....
	Toronto Marlies	AHL	14	7	11	18	8	....	....	....	....	....	....	....	....	....	19	2	8	10	8	....	....	....	....
	NHL Totals		**58**	**10**	**6**	**16**	**14**	**2**	**0**	**2**	**69**	**14.5**		**2**	**50.0**	**10:55**	....	....	....	....	....	....	....	....	....

TOEWS, Jonathan

(TAYVES, JAWN-ah-thuhn) **CHI.**

Center. Shoots left. 6'2", 203 lbs. Born, Winnipeg, Man., April 29, 1988. Chicago's 1st choice, 3rd overall, in 2006 Entry Draft.

Season	Club	League	GP	G	A	Pts	PIM	PP	SH	GW	S	%	+/-	TF	F%	Min	GP	G	A	Pts	PIM	PP	SH	GW	Min
2004-05	Shat.-St. Mary's	High-MN	64	48	62	110	38	....	....	....	....	....	....	....	....	....	....	....	....	....	....	....	....	....	....
2005-06	North Dakota	WCHA	42	22	17	39	22	....	....	....	....	....	....	....	....	....	....	....	....	....	....	....	....	....	....
2006-07	North Dakota	WCHA	34	18	28	46	10	....	....	....	....	....	....	....	....	....	....	....	....	....	....	....	....	....	....
2007-08	**Chicago**	**NHL**	**64**	**24**	**30**	**54**	**44**	**7**	**0**	**4**	**144**	**16.7**	**11**	**956**	**53.2**	**18:40**	....	....	....	....	....	....	....	....	....
	NHL Totals		**64**	**24**	**30**	**54**	**44**	**7**	**0**	**4**	**144**	**16.7**		**956**	**53.2**	**18:40**	....	....	....	....	....	....	....	....	....

WCHA Second All-Star Team (2007) • NCAA West First All-American Team (2007) • NHL All-Rookie Team (2008)

TOLLEFSEN, Ole-Kristian

(TOHL-uhf-suhn, OH-lay-KRIHS-tyahn) **CBJ**

Defense. Shoots left. 6'2", 211 lbs. Born, Oslo, Norway, March 29, 1984. Columbus' 3rd choice, 65th overall, in 2002 Entry Draft.

Season	Club	League	GP	G	A	Pts	PIM	PP	SH	GW	S	%	+/-	TF	F%	Min	GP	G	A	Pts	PIM	PP	SH	GW	Min
2000-01	Lillehammer IK	Norway	4	0	0	0	2	....	....	....	....	....	....	....	....	....	....	....	....	....	....	....	....	....	....
2001-02	Lillehammer IK	Norway	37	1	5	6	63	....	....	....	....	....	....	....	....	....	6	1	1	2	10	....	....	....	....
	Lillehammer IK	Nor-Jr.	....	....	....	....	....	....	....	....	....	....	....	....	....	....	1	0	2	2	4	....	....	....	....
2002-03	Brandon	WHL	43	6	14	20	73	....	....	....	....	....	....	....	....	....	17	0	2	2	38	....	....	....	....
2003-04	Brandon	WHL	53	3	27	30	94	....	....	....	....	....	....	....	....	....	11	0	4	4	15	....	....	....	....
2004-05	Syracuse Crunch	AHL	64	0	3	3	115	....	....	....	....	....	....	....	....	....	....	....	....	....	....	....	....	....	....
	Dayton Bombers	ECHL	2	0	0	0	0	....	....	....	....	....	....	....	....	....	....	....	....	....	....	....	....	....	....
2005-06	**Columbus**	**NHL**	**5**	**0**	**0**	**0**	**2**	**0**	**0**	**0**	**3**	**0.0**	**–2**	**0**	**0.0**	**16:18**	....	....	....	....	....	....	....	....	....
	Syracuse Crunch	AHL	58	2	16	18	155	....	....	....	....	....	....	....	....	....	1	0	0	0	6	....	....	....	....
2006-07	**Columbus**	**NHL**	**70**	**2**	**3**	**5**	**123**	**1**	**0**	**0**	**39**	**5.1**	**2**	**0**	**0.0**	**14:14**	....	....	....	....	....	....	....	....	....
2007-08	**Columbus**	**NHL**	**51**	**2**	**2**	**4**	**111**	**0**	**1**	**0**	**21**	**9.5**	**–3**	**0**	**0.0**	**12:18**	....	....	....	....	....	....	....	....	....
	NHL Totals		**126**	**4**	**5**	**9**	**236**	**1**	**1**	**0**	**63**	**6.3**		**0**	**0.0**	**13:32**	....	....	....	....	....	....	....	....	....

TOLPEKO, Denis

(tohl-PEH-koh, DEH-nihs) **PHI.**

Right wing. Shoots left. 6'1", 190 lbs. Born, Moscow, USSR, January 29, 1985.

Season	Club	League	GP	G	A	Pts	PIM	PP	SH	GW	S	%	+/-	TF	F%	Min	GP	G	A	Pts	PIM	PP	SH	GW	Min
2003-04	Seattle	WHL	72	13	16	29	63	....	....	....	....	....	....	....	....	....	....	....	....	....	....	....	....	....	....
2004-05	Seattle	WHL	54	13	18	31	48	....	....	....	....	....	....	....	....	....	12	1	0	1	10	....	....	....	....
2005-06	Regina Pats	WHL	53	20	31	51	66	....	....	....	....	....	....	....	....	....	6	0	4	4	16	....	....	....	....
2006-07	Philadelphia	AHL	58	11	19	30	58	....	....	....	....	....	....	....	....	....	....	....	....	....	....	....	....	....	....
2007-08	**Philadelphia**	**NHL**	**26**	**1**	**5**	**6**	**24**	**0**	**0**	**0**	**24**	**4.2**	**–4**	**0**	**0.0**	**8:17**	....	....	....	....	....	....	....	....	....
	Philadelphia	AHL	24	8	9	17	26	....	....	....	....	....	....	....	....	....	....	....	....	....	....	....	....	....	....
	NHL Totals		**26**	**1**	**5**	**6**	**24**	**0**	**0**	**0**	**24**	**4.2**		**0**	**0.0**	**8:17**	....	....	....	....	....	....	....	....	....

Signed as a free agent by **Philadelphia**, July 5, 2006.

TOOTOO, Jordin

(TOO-TOO, JOHR-dahn) **NSH.**

Right wing. Shoots right. 5'9", 194 lbs. Born, Churchill, Man., February 2, 1983. Nashville's 6th choice, 98th overall, in 2001 Entry Draft.

Season	Club	League	GP	G	A	Pts	PIM	PP	SH	GW	S	%	+/-	TF	F%	Min	GP	G	A	Pts	PIM	PP	SH	GW	Min
1997-98	Spruce Grove	AMBHL	STATISTICS NOT AVAILABLE																						
1998-99	OCN Blizzard	MJHL	47	16	21	37	251	....	....	....	....	....	....	....	....	....	....	....	....	....	....	....	....	....	....
99-2000	Brandon	WHL	45	6	10	16	214	....	....	....	....	....	....	....	....	....	....	....	....	....	....	....	....	....	....
2000-01	Brandon	WHL	60	20	28	48	172	....	....	....	....	....	....	....	....	....	6	2	4	6	18	....	....	....	....
2001-02	Brandon	WHL	64	32	39	71	272	....	....	....	....	....	....	....	....	....	16	4	3	7	*58	....	....	....	....
2002-03	Brandon	WHL	51	35	39	74	216	....	....	....	....	....	....	....	....	....	17	6	3	9	49	....	....	....	....
2003-04	**Nashville**	**NHL**	**70**	**4**	**4**	**8**	**137**	**2**	**0**	**0**	**92**	**4.3**	**–6**	**18**	**55.6**	**8:29**	**5**	**0**	**0**	**0**	**4**	**0**	**0**	**0**	**5:09**
2004-05	Milwaukee	AHL	59	10	12	22	266	....	....	....	....	....	....	....	....	....	6	0	0	0	41	....	....	....	....
2005-06	**Nashville**	**NHL**	**34**	**4**	**6**	**10**	**55**	**0**	**0**	**0**	**61**	**6.6**	**9**	**17**	**70.6**	**9:15**	**3**	**0**	**0**	**0**	**0**	**0**	**0**	**0**	**4:04**
	Milwaukee	AHL	41	13	14	27	133	....	....	....	....	....	....	....	....	....	15	9	2	11	35	....	....	....	....
2006-07	**Nashville**	**NHL**	**65**	**3**	**6**	**9**	**116**	**0**	**0**	**0**	**77**	**3.9**	**–11**	**12**	**33.3**	**8:24**	**4**	**0**	**1**	**1**	**21**	**0**	**0**	**0**	**9:32**
2007-08	**Nashville**	**NHL**	**63**	**11**	**7**	**18**	**100**	**0**	**0**	**1**	**98**	**11.2**	**–8**	**4**	**50.0**	**9:54**	**6**	**2**	**0**	**2**	**4**	**0**	**0**	**0**	**12:31**
	NHL Totals		**232**	**22**	**23**	**45**	**408**	**2**	**0**	**1**	**328**	**6.7**		**51**	**54.9**	**8:58**	**18**	**2**	**1**	**3**	**29**	**0**	**0**	**0**	**8:24**

WHL East First All-Star Team (2003)

TORRES, Raffi

(TOHR-ehz, RA-fee) **CBJ**

Left wing. Shoots left. 6', 215 lbs. Born, Toronto, Ont., October 8, 1981. NY Islanders' 2nd choice, 5th overall, in 2000 Entry Draft.

Season	Club	League	GP	G	A	Pts	PIM	PP	SH	GW	S	%	+/-	TF	F%	Min	GP	G	A	Pts	PIM	PP	SH	GW	Min
1997-98	Thornhill Rattlers	MTJHL	46	17	16	33	90	....	....	....	....	....	....	....	....	....	....	....	....	....	....	....	....	....	....
1998-99	Brampton	OHL	62	35	27	62	32	....	....	....	....	....	....	....	....	....	6	5	2	7	23	....	....	....	....
99-2000	Brampton	OHL	68	43	48	91	40	....	....	....	....	....	....	....	....	....	8	7	4	11	19	....	....	....	....
2000-01	Brampton	OHL	55	33	37	70	76	....	....	....	....	....	....	....	....	....	....	....	....	....	....	....	....	....	....
2001-02	**NY Islanders**	**NHL**	**14**	**0**	**1**	**1**	**6**	**0**	**0**	**0**	**9**	**0.0**	**2**	**0**	**0.0**	**7:35**	....	....	....	....	....	....	....	....	....
	Bridgeport	AHL	59	20	10	30	45	....	....	....	....	....	....	....	....	....	20	8	9	17	26	....	....	....	....
2002-03	**NY Islanders**	**NHL**	**17**	**0**	**5**	**5**	**10**	**0**	**0**	**0**	**12**	**0.0**	**0**	**4**	**25.0**	**7:40**	....	....	....	....	....	....	....	....	....
	Bridgeport	AHL	49	17	15	32	54	....	....	....	....	....	....	....	....	....	....	....	....	....	....	....	....	....	....
	Hamilton	AHL	11	1	7	8	14	....	....	....	....	....	....	....	....	....	23	6	1	7	29	....	....	....	....
2003-04	**Edmonton**	**NHL**	**80**	**20**	**14**	**34**	**65**	**5**	**0**	**3**	**136**	**14.7**	**12**	**21**	**28.6**	**12:38**	....	....	....	....	....	....	....	....	....
2004-05	Edmonton	AHL	67	21	25	46	165	....	....	....	....	....	....	....	....	....	....	....	....	....	....	....	....	....	....
2005-06	**Edmonton**	**NHL**	**82**	**27**	**14**	**41**	**50**	**6**	**0**	**3**	**164**	**16.5**	**4**	**60**	**41.7**	**13:24**	**22**	**4**	**7**	**11**	**16**	**1**	**0**	**1**	**13:15**
2006-07	**Edmonton**	**NHL**	**82**	**15**	**19**	**34**	**88**	**1**	**0**	**0**	**154**	**9.7**	**–7**	**50**	**44.0**	**14:19**	....	....	....	....	....	....	....	....	....
2007-08	**Edmonton**	**NHL**	**32**	**5**	**6**	**11**	**36**	**1**	**0**	**2**	**87**	**5.7**	**–4**	**20**	**65.0**	**17:01**	....	....	....	....	....	....	....	....	....
	NHL Totals		**307**	**67**	**59**	**126**	**255**	**13**	**0**	**8**	**562**	**11.9**		**155**	**43.2**	**13:14**	**22**	**4**	**7**	**11**	**16**	**1**	**0**	**1**	**13:15**

OHL All-Rookie Team (1999) • OHL Second All-Star Team (2000, 2001)

Traded to **Edmonton** by **NY Islanders** with Brad Isbister for Janne Niinimaa and Washington's 2nd round choice (previously acquired, NY Islanders selected Evgeni Tunik) in 2003 Entry Draft, March 11, 2003. • Missed majority of 2007-08 season recovering from knee injury suffered in game vs. Detroit, December 15, 2007. Traded to **Columbus** by **Edmonton** for Gilbert Brule, July 1, 2008.

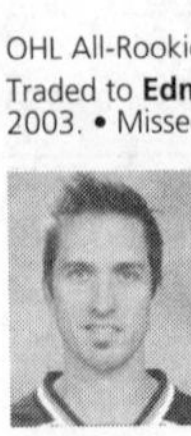

TRAVERSE, Patrick

(tra-VAIRZ, PAT-rihk)

Defense. Shoots left. 6'4", 207 lbs. Born, Montreal, Que., March 14, 1974. Ottawa's 3rd choice, 50th overall, in 1992 Entry Draft.

Season	Club	League	GP	G	A	Pts	PIM	PP	SH	GW	S	%	+/-	TF	F%	Min	GP	G	A	Pts	PIM	PP	SH	GW	Min
1990-91	Mtl-Bourassa	QAAA	42	4	19	23	10	....	....	....	....	....	....	....	....	....	5	0	3	3	2	....	....	....	....
1991-92	Shawinigan	QMJHL	59	3	11	14	12	....	....	....	....	....	....	....	....	....	10	0	0	0	4	....	....	....	....
1992-93	Shawinigan	QMJHL	53	5	24	29	24	....	....	....	....	....	....	....	....	....	....	....	....	....	....	....	....	....	....
	St-Jean Lynx	QMJHL	15	1	6	7	0	....	....	....	....	....	....	....	....	....	4	0	1	1	2	....	....	....	....
	New Haven	AHL	2	0	0	0	2	....	....	....	....	....	....	....	....	....	....	....	....	....	....	....	....	....	....
1993-94	St-Jean Lynx	QMJHL	66	15	37	52	30	....	....	....	....	....	....	....	....	....	5	0	4	4	4	....	....	....	....
	P.E.I. Senators	AHL	3	0	1	1	2	....	....	....	....	....	....	....	....	....	....	....	....	....	....	....	....	....	....
1994-95	P.E.I. Senators	AHL	70	5	13	18	19	....	....	....	....	....	....	....	....	....	7	0	2	2	0	....	....	....	....
1995-96	**Ottawa**	**NHL**	**5**	**0**	**0**	**0**	**2**	**0**	**0**	**0**	**2**	**0.0**	**–1**	....	....	....	....	....	....	....	....	....	....	....	....
	P.E.I. Senators	AHL	55	4	21	25	32	....	....	....	....	....	....	....	....	....	5	1	2	3	2	....	....	....	....

			Regular Season														Playoffs								
Season	Club	League	GP	G	A	Pts	PIM	PP	SH	GW	S	%	+/-	TF	F%	Min	GP	G	A	Pts	PIM	PP	SH	GW	Min
1996-97	Worcester IceCats	AHL	24	0	4	4	23	....	....	....	....	....	....	....	....	....	....	....	....	....	....	....	....	....	....
	Grand Rapids	IHL	10	2	1	3	10	....	....	....	....	....	....	....	....	....	2	0	1	1	2	....	....	....	....
1997-98	Hershey Bears	AHL	71	14	15	29	67	....	....	....	....	....	....	....	....	....	7	1	3	4	4	....	....	....	....
1998-99	**Ottawa**	**NHL**	**46**	**1**	**9**	**10**	**22**	**0**	**0**	**0**	**35**	**2.9**	**12**	**0**	**0.0**	**14:56**	....	....	....	....	....	....	....	....	....
99-2000	**Ottawa**	**NHL**	**66**	**6**	**17**	**23**	**21**	**1**	**0**	**0**	**73**	**8.2**	**17**	**0**	**0.0**	**18:43**	**6**	**0**	**0**	**0**	**2**	**0**	**0**	**0**	**17:50**
2000-01	**Anaheim**	**NHL**	**15**	**1**	**0**	**1**	**6**	**0**	**0**	**0**	**7**	**14.3**	**–6**	**0**	**0.0**	**17:19**	....	....	....	....	....	....	....	....	....
	Boston	**NHL**	**37**	**2**	**6**	**8**	**14**	**1**	**0**	**1**	**39**	**5.1**	**4**	**0**	**0.0**	**16:38**	....	....	....	....	....	....	....	....	....
	Montreal	**NHL**	**19**	**2**	**3**	**5**	**10**	**0**	**0**	**0**	**16**	**12.5**	**–8**	**0**	**0.0**	**21:36**	....	....	....	....	....	....	....	....	....
2001-02	**Montreal**	**NHL**	**25**	**2**	**3**	**5**	**14**	**2**	**0**	**0**	**24**	**8.3**	**–7**	**0**	**0.0**	**18:14**	....	....	....	....	....	....	....	....	....
	Quebec Citadelles	AHL	4	0	2	2	4	....	....	....	....	....	....	....	....	....	....	....	....	....	....	....	....	....	....
2002-03	**Montreal**	**NHL**	**65**	**0**	**13**	**13**	**24**	**0**	**0**	**0**	**63**	**0.0**	**–9**	**0**	**0.0**	**20:12**	....	....	....	....	....	....	....	....	....
2003-04	Hamilton	AHL	80	5	21	26	31	....	....	....	....	....	....	....	....	....	10	1	2	3	0	....	....	....	....
2004-05	Houston Aeros	AHL	72	6	9	15	28	....	....	....	....	....	....	....	....	....	5	0	0	0	2	....	....	....	....
2005-06	**Dallas**	**NHL**	**1**	**0**	**0**	**0**	**0**	**0**	**0**	**0**	**1**	**0.0**	**0**	**0**	**0.0**	**11:27**	....	....	....	....	....	....	....	....	....
	Iowa Stars	AHL	40	3	21	24	16	....	....	....	....	....	....	....	....	....	7	1	2	3	2	....	....	....	....
2006-07	Hamilton	AHL	26	1	4	5	10	....	....	....	....	....	....	....	....	....	....	....	....	....	....	....	....	....	....
	Worcester Sharks	AHL	54	5	17	22	14	....	....	....	....	....	....	....	....	....	6	0	2	2	2	....	....	....	....
2007-08	Worcester Sharks	AHL	65	6	19	25	52	....	....	....	....	....	....	....	....	....	....	....	....	....	....	....	....	....	....
	NHL Totals		**279**	**14**	**51**	**65**	**113**	**4**	**0**	**1**	**260**	**5.4**		**0**	**0.0**	**18:12**	**6**	**0**	**0**	**0**	**2**	**0**	**0**	**0**	**17:50**

Traded to **Anaheim** by **Ottawa** for Joel Kwiatkowski, June 12, 2000. Traded to **Boston** by **Anaheim** with Andrei Nazarov for Samuel Pahlsson, November 18, 2000. Traded to **Montreal** by **Boston** for Eric Weinrich, February 21, 2001. • Missed majority of 2001-02 season recovering from knee (November 3, 2001 vs. Calgary) and head (January 10, 2002 vs. NY Islanders) injuries. Signed as a free agent by **Dallas**, September 9, 2004. Signed as a free agent by **San Jose**, July 10, 2006. Claimed on waivers by **Montreal** from **San Jose**, September 28, 2006. Traded to **San Jose** by **Montreal** for Mathieu Biron, December 15, 2006.

TREMBLAY, Yannick

(TRAHM-blay, YA-nihk)

Defense. Shoots right. 6'2", 200 lbs. Born, Pointe-aux-Trembles, Que., November 15, 1975. Toronto's 4th choice, 145th overall, in 1995 Entry Draft.

Season	Club	League	GP	G	A	Pts	PIM	PP	SH	GW	S	%	+/-	TF	F%	Min	GP	G	A	Pts	PIM	PP	SH	GW	Min
1991-92	Mtl-Bourassa	QAAA	35	2	5	7	55	....	....	....	....	....	....	....	....	....	8	0	4	4	2	....	....	....	....
1992-93	Mtl-Bourassa	CEGEP	21	2	5	7	10	....	....	....	....	....	....	....	....	....	3	0	0	0	2	....	....	....	....
1993-94	St. Thomas U.	AUAA	25	2	3	5	10	....	....	....	....	....	....	....	....	....	....	....	....	....	....	....	....	....	....
1994-95	Beauport	QMJHL	70	10	32	42	22	....	....	....	....	....	....	....	....	....	17	6	8	14	6	....	....	....	....
1995-96	Beauport	QMJHL	61	12	33	45	42	....	....	....	....	....	....	....	....	....	20	3	16	19	18	....	....	....	....
	St. John's	AHL	3	0	1	1	0	....	....	....	....	....	....	....	....	....	....	....	....	....	....	....	....	....	....
1996-97	**Toronto**	**NHL**	**5**	**0**	**0**	**0**	**0**	**0**	**0**	**0**	**2**	**0.0**	**–4**	....	....	....	....	....	....	....	....	....	....	....	....
	St. John's	AHL	67	7	25	32	34	....	....	....	....	....	....	....	....	....	11	2	9	11	0	....	....	....	....
1997-98	**Toronto**	**NHL**	**38**	**2**	**4**	**6**	**6**	**1**	**0**	**0**	**45**	**4.4**	**–6**	....	....	....	....	....	....	....	....	....	....	....	....
	St. John's	AHL	17	3	7	10	4	....	....	....	....	....	....	....	....	....	4	0	1	1	5	....	....	....	....
1998-99	**Toronto**	**NHL**	**35**	**2**	**7**	**9**	**16**	**0**	**0**	**0**	**37**	**5.4**	**0**	**0**	**0.0**	**17:39**	....	....	....	....	....	....	....	....	....
99-2000	**Atlanta**	**NHL**	**75**	**10**	**21**	**31**	**22**	**4**	**1**	**2**	**139**	**7.2**	**–42**	**3**	**0.0**	**19:27**	....	....	....	....	....	....	....	....	....
2000-01	**Atlanta**	**NHL**	**46**	**4**	**8**	**12**	**30**	**1**	**0**	**1**	**102**	**3.9**	**–6**	**1**	**100.0**	**20:27**	....	....	....	....	....	....	....	....	....
2001-02	**Atlanta**	**NHL**	**66**	**9**	**15**	**24**	**47**	**1**	**0**	**1**	**115**	**7.8**	**–15**	**0**	**0.0**	**21:50**	....	....	....	....	....	....	....	....	....
2002-03	**Atlanta**	**NHL**	**75**	**8**	**22**	**30**	**32**	**5**	**0**	**1**	**151**	**5.3**	**–27**	**1**	**0.0**	**21:45**	....	....	....	....	....	....	....	....	....
2003-04	**Atlanta**	**NHL**	**38**	**2**	**8**	**10**	**13**	**1**	**0**	**1**	**47**	**4.3**	**–13**	**2**	**50.0**	**21:36**	....	....	....	....	....	....	....	....	....
2004-05	Sherbrooke	QNAHL	36	26	25	51	40	....	....	....	....	....	....	....	....	....	....	....	....	....	....	....	....	....	....
	Adler Mannheim	Germany	14	1	4	5	16	....	....	....	....	....	....	....	....	....	14	2	6	8	6	....	....	....	....
2005-06	Adler Mannheim	Germany	46	11	17	28	44	....	....	....	....	....	....	....	....	....	....	....	....	....	....	....	....	....	....
2006-07	**Vancouver**	**NHL**	**12**	**1**	**2**	**3**	**12**	**1**	**0**	**0**	**30**	**3.3**	**–6**	**0**	**0.0**	**12:44**	....	....	....	....	....	....	....	....	....
	Manitoba Moose	AHL	45	12	21	33	40	....	....	....	....	....	....	....	....	....	12	3	7	10	11	....	....	....	....
2007-08	HC Lugano	Swiss	46	8	21	29	34	....	....	....	....	....	....	....	....	....	4	0	5	5	6	....	....	....	....
	NHL Totals		**390**	**38**	**87**	**125**	**178**	**14**	**1**	**6**	**668**	**5.7**		**7**	**28.6**	**20:21**	....	....	....	....	....	....	....	....	....

Claimed by **Atlanta** from **Toronto** in Expansion Draft, June 25, 1999. • Missed majority of 2003-04 season recovering from foot (November 15, 2003 vs. Philadelphia) and hip (January 30, 2004 vs. Toronto) injuries. Signed as a free agent by **Sherbrooke** (QNAHL), November 16, 2004. Signed as a free agent by **Mannheim** (Germany), January 13, 2005. Signed as a free agent by **Vancouver**, July 28, 2006. Signed as a free agent by **Lugano** (Swiss), July 18, 2007.

TRUDEL, Jean-Guy

(TROO-dehl, zhawn-gee)

Left wing. Shoots left. 5'11", 202 lbs. Born, Sudbury, Ont., October 18, 1975.

Season	Club	League	GP	G	A	Pts	PIM	PP	SH	GW	S	%	+/-	TF	F%	Min	GP	G	A	Pts	PIM	PP	SH	GW	Min
1991-92	Beauport	QMJHL	35	5	7	12	20	....	....	....	....	....	....	....	....	....	....	....	....	....	....	....	....	....	....
1992-93	Beauport	QMJHL	56	1	4	5	20	....	....	....	....	....	....	....	....	....	....	....	....	....	....	....	....	....	....
	Verdun	QMJHL	10	1	0	1	0	....	....	....	....	....	....	....	....	....	2	0	0	0	5	....	....	....	....
1993-94			Did Not Play																						
1994-95	Hull Olympiques	QMJHL	54	29	42	71	76	....	....	....	....	....	....	....	....	....	19	4	13	17	25	....	....	....	....
1995-96	Hull Olympiques	QMJHL	70	50	71	121	96	....	....	....	....	....	....	....	....	....	17	11	18	29	8	....	....	....	....
1996-97	Quad City	ColHL	5	8	7	15	4	....	....	....	....	....	....	....	....	....	....	....	....	....	....	....	....	....	....
	Chicago Wolves	IHL	6	1	2	3	2	....	....	....	....	....	....	....	....	....	....	....	....	....	....	....	....	....	....
	San Antonio	IHL	12	1	5	6	4	....	....	....	....	....	....	....	....	....	....	....	....	....	....	....	....	....	....
	Peoria Rivermen	ECHL	37	25	29	54	47	....	....	....	....	....	....	....	....	....	9	9	10	19	22	....	....	....	....
1997-98	Peoria Rivermen	ECHL	62	39	74	113	147	....	....	....	....	....	....	....	....	....	3	0	0	0	2	....	....	....	....
1998-99	Kansas City	IHL	76	24	25	49	66	....	....	....	....	....	....	....	....	....	3	1	0	1	0	....	....	....	....
99-2000	**Phoenix**	**NHL**	**1**	**0**	**0**	**0**	**0**	**0**	**0**	**0**	**0**	**0.0**	**–1**	**0**	**0.0**	**4:33**	....	....	....	....	....	....	....	....	....
	Springfield	AHL	72	34	39	73	80	....	....	....	....	....	....	....	....	....	3	0	1	1	4	....	....	....	....
2000-01	Springfield	AHL	80	34	65	99	89	....	....	....	....	....	....	....	....	....	....	....	....	....	....	....	....	....	....
2001-02	**Phoenix**	**NHL**	**3**	**0**	**0**	**0**	**2**	**0**	**0**	**0**	**1**	**0.0**	**0**	**0**	**0.0**	**8:42**	....	....	....	....	....	....	....	....	....
	Springfield	AHL	76	22	48	70	83	....	....	....	....	....	....	....	....	....	....	....	....	....	....	....	....	....	....
2002-03	**Minnesota**	**NHL**	**1**	**0**	**0**	**0**	**2**	**0**	**0**	**0**	**0**	**0.0**	**0**	**0**	**0.0**	**5:37**	....	....	....	....	....	....	....	....	....
	Houston Aeros	AHL	79	31	54	85	85	....	....	....	....	....	....	....	....	....	23	7	9	16	22	....	....	....	....
2003-04	HC Ambri-Piotta	Swiss	47	29	39	68	64	....	....	....	....	....	....	....	....	....	7	4	4	8	14	....	....	....	....
2004-05	HC Ambri-Piotta	Swiss	42	23	35	58	105	....	....	....	....	....	....	....	....	....	....	....	....	....	....	....	....	....	....
2005-06	HC Ambri-Piotta	Swiss	44	24	35	59	50	....	....	....	....	....	....	....	....	....	7	4	4	8	12	....	....	....	....
2006-07	HC Ambri-Piotta	Swiss	44	27	26	53	38	....	....	....	....	....	....	....	....	....	7	5	4	9	12	....	....	....	....
2007-08	Peoria Rivermen	AHL	78	23	44	67	56	....	....	....	....	....	....	....	....	....	....	....	....	....	....	....	....	....	....
	NHL Totals		**5**	**0**	**0**	**0**	**4**	**0**	**0**	**0**	**1**	**0.0**		**0**	**0.0**	**7:15**	....	....	....	....	....	....	....	....	....

QMJHL Second All-Star Team (1996) • ECHL First All-Star Team (1998) • AHL Second All-Star Team (2000, 2002) • AHL First All-Star Team (2001, 2003)

• Sat out 1993-94 season to regain eligibility for U.S. College scholarship. Signed as a free agent by **Phoenix**, July 17, 1999. Signed as a free agent by **Minnesota**, July 16, 2002. Signed as a free agent by **Ambri-Piotta** (Swiss), April 3, 2003. Signed as a free agent by **St. Louis**, June 19, 2007.

TUCKER, Darcy

(TUH-kuhr, DAHR-see) **COL.**

Right wing. Shoots left. 5'10", 178 lbs. Born, Castor, Alta., March 15, 1975. Montreal's 8th choice, 151st overall, in 1993 Entry Draft.

Season	Club	League	GP	G	A	Pts	PIM	PP	SH	GW	S	%	+/-	TF	F%	Min	GP	G	A	Pts	PIM	PP	SH	GW	Min
1990-91	Red Deer	AMHL	47	70	90	160	48	....	....	....	....	....	....	....	....	....	....	....	....	....	....	....	....	....	....
1991-92	Kamloops Blazers	WHL	26	3	10	13	32	....	....	....	....	....	....	....	....	....	9	0	1	1	16	....	....	....	....
1992-93	Kamloops Blazers	WHL	67	31	58	89	155	....	....	....	....	....	....	....	....	....	13	7	6	13	34	....	....	....	....
1993-94	Kamloops Blazers	WHL	66	52	88	140	143	....	....	....	....	....	....	....	....	....	19	9	*18	*27	43	....	....	....	....
1994-95	Kamloops Blazers	WHL	64	64	73	137	94	....	....	....	....	....	....	....	....	....	21	*16	15	*31	19	....	....	....	....
1995-96	**Montreal**	**NHL**	**3**	**0**	**0**	**0**	**0**	**0**	**0**	**0**	**1**	**0.0**	**–1**	....	....	....	....	....	....	....	....	....	....	....	....
	Fredericton	AHL	74	29	64	93	174	....	....	....	....	....	....	....	....	....	7	7	3	10	14	....	....	....	....
1996-97	**Montreal**	**NHL**	**73**	**7**	**13**	**20**	**110**	**1**	**0**	**3**	**62**	**11.3**	**–5**	....	....	....	**4**	**0**	**0**	**0**	**0**	**0**	**0**	**0**	....
1997-98	**Montreal**	**NHL**	**39**	**1**	**5**	**6**	**57**	**0**	**0**	**0**	**19**	**5.3**	**–6**	....	....	....	....	....	....	....	....	....	....	....	....
	Tampa Bay	**NHL**	**35**	**6**	**8**	**14**	**89**	**1**	**1**	**0**	**44**	**13.6**	**–8**	....	....	....	....	....	....	....	....	....	....	....	....
1998-99	**Tampa Bay**	**NHL**	**82**	**21**	**22**	**43**	**176**	**8**	**2**	**3**	**178**	**11.8**	**–34**	**1470**	**45.6**	**19:24**	....	....	....	....	....	....	....	....	....
99-2000	**Tampa Bay**	**NHL**	**50**	**14**	**20**	**34**	**108**	**1**	**0**	**2**	**98**	**14.3**	**–15**	**152**	**48.7**	**19:58**	....	....	....	....	....	....	....	....	....
	Toronto	**NHL**	**27**	**7**	**10**	**17**	**55**	**0**	**2**	**3**	**40**	**17.5**	**3**	**11**	**54.6**	**16:41**	**12**	**4**	**2**	**6**	**15**	**1**	**0**	**2**	**17:23**
2000-01	**Toronto**	**NHL**	**82**	**16**	**21**	**37**	**141**	**2**	**0**	**4**	**122**	**13.1**	**6**	**413**	**47.0**	**16:09**	**11**	**0**	**2**	**2**	**6**	**0**	**0**	**0**	**13:59**
2001-02	**Toronto**	**NHL**	**77**	**24**	**35**	**59**	**92**	**7**	**0**	**5**	**124**	**19.4**	**24**	**138**	**43.5**	**16:59**	**17**	**4**	**4**	**8**	**38**	**1**	**0**	**1**	**16:50**
2002-03	**Toronto**	**NHL**	**77**	**10**	**26**	**36**	**119**	**4**	**1**	**2**	**108**	**9.3**	**–7**	**68**	**45.6**	**15:21**	**6**	**0**	**3**	**3**	**6**	**0**	**0**	**0**	**21:07**
2003-04	**Toronto**	**NHL**	**64**	**21**	**11**	**32**	**68**	**8**	**1**	**2**	**146**	**14.4**	**4**	**136**	**50.7**	**17:50**	**12**	**2**	**0**	**2**	**14**	**1**	**0**	**0**	**13:54**
2004-05			Did Not Play																						
2005-06	**Toronto**	**NHL**	**74**	**28**	**33**	**61**	**100**	**18**	**0**	**4**	**189**	**14.8**	**–12**	**29**	**58.6**	**17:38**	....	....	....	....	....	....	....	....	....

			Regular Season														Playoffs								
Season	Club	League	GP	G	A	Pts	PIM	PP	SH	GW	S	%	+/-	TF	F%	Min	GP	G	A	Pts	PIM	PP	SH	GW	Min
2006-07	Toronto	NHL	56	24	19	43	81	15	0	6	143	16.8	–11	15	40.0	17:47									
2007-08	Toronto	NHL	74	18	16	34	100	7	0	3	152	11.8	–8	25	52.0	16:26									
	NHL Totals		813	197	239	436	1296	72	7	37	1426	13.8		2457	46.4	17:22	62	10	11	21	79	3	0	3	16:15

WHL West First All-Star Team (1994, 1995) • Canadian Major Junior First All-Star Team (1994) • Memorial Cup Tournament All-Star Team (1994, 1995) • Stafford Smythe Memorial Trophy (Memorial Cup Tournament MVP) (1994) • Dudley "Red" Garrett Memorial Award (Rookie of the Year – AHL) (1996)

Traded to **Tampa Bay** by **Montreal** with Stephane Richer and David Wilkie for Patrick Poulin, Mick Vukota and Igor Ulanov, January 15, 1998. Traded to **Toronto** by **Tampa Bay** with Tampa Bay's 4th round choice (Miguel Delisle) in 2000 Entry Draft for Mike Johnson, Marek Posmyk and Toronto's 5th (Pavel Sedov) and 6th (Aaron Gionet) round choices in 2000 Entry Draft, February 9, 2000. Signed as a free agent by **Colorado**, July 1, 2008.

TUKONEN, Lauri

(too-KOH-nehn, LOW-ree) **DAL.**

Right wing. Shoots right. 6'2", 200 lbs. Born, Hyvinkaa, Finland, September 1, 1986. Los Angeles' 1st choice, 11th overall, in 2004 Entry Draft.

Season	Club	League	GP	G	A	Pts	PIM	PP	SH	GW	S	%	+/-	TF	F%	Min	GP	G	A	Pts	PIM	PP	SH	GW	Min
2001-02	Ahmat Jr.	Fin-Jr.	2	4	0	4	2																		
	Ahmat Hyvinkaa	Finland-2	24	7	4	11	6																		
	HC Sunne	Sweden-3	2	4	0	4	2																		
2002-03	Ahmat Jr.	Fin-Jr.	4	3	1	4	2																		
	Ahmat Hyvinkaa	Finland-2	12	2	2	4	2																		
	Blues Espoo Jr.	Fin-Jr.	17	6	6	12	18										5	0	0	0	10				
2003-04	Suomi U20	Finland-2	6	0	0	0	6																		
	Blues Espoo Jr.	Fin-Jr.	14	14	9	23	4																		
	Blues Espoo	Finland	35	3	3	6	16										7	0	0	0	0				
2004-05	Blues Espoo Jr.	Fin-Jr.	2	0	0	0	2																		
	Blues Espoo	Finland	43	5	5	10	10																		
2005-06	Manchester	AHL	62	14	22	36	20																		
2006-07	Los Angeles	NHL	4	0	0	0	0	0	0	0	1	0.0	–2	0	0.0	6:33									
	Manchester	AHL	61	13	19	32	30										6	0	3	3	0				
2007-08	Los Angeles	NHL	1	0	0	0	0	0	0	0	1	0.0	0	0	0.0	9:48									
	Manchester	AHL	62	9	26	35	24										2	0	0	0	0				
	NHL Totals		5	0	0	0	0	0	0	0	2	0.0		0	0.0	7:12									

Traded to **Dallas** by **Los Angeles** for Richard Clune, July 21, 2008.

TURRIS, Kyle

(TUH-rihs, KIGHL) **PHX.**

Center. Shoots right. 6'1", 180 lbs. Born, New Westminster, B.C., August 14, 1989. Phoenix's 1st choice, 3rd overall, in 2007 Entry Draft.

Season	Club	League	GP	G	A	Pts	PIM	PP	SH	GW	S	%	+/-	TF	F%	Min	GP	G	A	Pts	PIM	PP	SH	GW	Min
2004-05	Grandview	Minor-BC	30	13	20	33											12	3	6	9					
2005-06	Burnaby Express	BCHL	57	36	36	72	32										20	10	13	23	6				
2006-07	Burnaby Express	BCHL	53	66	55	121	83										14	12	14	26	16				
2007-08	U. of Wisconsin	WCHA	36	11	24	35	38																		
	Phoenix	NHL	3	0	1	1	2	0	0	0	11	0.0	–5	42	40.5	19:45									
	NHL Totals		3	0	1	1	2	0	0	0	11	0.0		42	40.5	19:45									

WCHA All-Rookie Team (2008)

TYUTIN, Fedor

(T'YOO-tihn, feh-DUHR) **CBJ**

Defense. Shoots left. 6'3", 210 lbs. Born, Izhevsk, USSR, July 19, 1983. NY Rangers' 2nd choice, 40th overall, in 2001 Entry Draft.

Season	Club	League	GP	G	A	Pts	PIM	PP	SH	GW	S	%	+/-	TF	F%	Min	GP	G	A	Pts	PIM	PP	SH	GW	Min
1998-99	Magnitogorsk 2	Russia-4	7	0	1	1	2																		
99-2000	Izhstal Izhevsk 2	Russia-3	38	11	8	19	68																		
	Izhstal Izhevsk	Russia-2	10	0	1	1	12																		
2000-01	St. Petersburg	Russia	34	2	4	6	20																		
2001-02	Guelph Storm	OHL	53	19	40	59	54										9	2	8	10	8				
2002-03	St. Petersburg	Russia	10	1	1	2	16																		
	Ak Bars Kazan	Russia	10	0	0	0	8										5	0	0	0	4				
2003-04	NY Rangers	NHL	25	2	5	7	14	0	1	0	33	6.1	–4	1	0.0	20:08									
	Hartford	AHL	43	5	9	14	50										16	0	5	5	18				
2004-05	Hartford	AHL	13	2	1	3	10																		
	St. Petersburg	Russia	35	5	3	8	24																		
2005-06	NY Rangers	NHL	77	6	19	25	58	4	0	2	102	5.9	1	1	0.0	20:33	4	0	1	1	0	0	0	0	17:50
	Russia	Olympics	8	0	1	1	4																		
2006-07	NY Rangers	NHL	66	2	12	14	44	1	1	0	75	2.7	–8	1	0.0	20:02	10	0	5	5	8	0	0	0	19:30
2007-08	NY Rangers	NHL	82	5	15	20	43	1	0	0	131	3.8	5	0	0.0	20:27	10	0	3	3	4	0	0	0	19:52
	NHL Totals		250	15	51	66	159	6	2	2	341	4.4		3	0.0	20:20	24	0	9	9	12	0	0	0	19:22

Signed as a free agent by **St. Petersburg** (Russia), November 11, 2004. Traded to **Columbus** by **NY Rangers** with Christian Backman for Nikolai Zherdev and Dan Fritsche, July 2, 2008.

UMBERGER, R.J.

(UHM-buhr-guhr, AHR-JAY) **CBJ**

Center. Shoots left. 6'2", 200 lbs. Born, Pittsburgh, PA, May 3, 1982. Vancouver's 1st choice, 16th overall, in 2001 Entry Draft.

Season	Club	League	GP	G	A	Pts	PIM	PP	SH	GW	S	%	+/-	TF	F%	Min	GP	G	A	Pts	PIM	PP	SH	GW	Min
1997-98	Plum Mustangs	High-PA	26	*60	*56	*116																			
1998-99	USNTDP	USHL	5	2	2	4	0																		
	USNTDP	NAHL	50	21	21	42	32																		
99-2000	USNTDP	U-18	6	1	0	1	2																		
	USNTDP	USHL	57	33	35	68	20																		
2000-01	Ohio State	CCHA	32	14	23	37	18																		
2001-02	Ohio State	CCHA	37	18	21	39	31																		
2002-03	Ohio State	CCHA	43	26	27	53	16																		
2003-04			DID NOT PLAY																						
2004-05	Philadelphia	AHL	80	21	44	65	36										21	3	7	10	12				
2005-06	Philadelphia	NHL	73	20	18	38	18	5	0	2	138	14.5	9	163	50.3	13:14	5	1	0	1	2	0	0	0	11:15
	Philadelphia	AHL	8	3	7	10	8																		
2006-07	Philadelphia	NHL	81	16	12	28	41	2	2	1	134	11.9	–32	535	44.5	14:32									
2007-08	Philadelphia	NHL	74	13	37	50	19	4	0	3	173	7.5	0	117	38.5	17:52	17	10	5	15	10	1	0	2	16:51
	NHL Totals		228	49	67	116	78	11	2	6	445	11.0		815	44.8	15:12	22	11	5	16	12	1	0	2	15:35

CCHA All-Rookie Team (2001) • CCHA Rookie of the Year (2001) • CCHA First All-Star Team (2003) • NCAA West Second All-American Team (2003)

• Missed entire 2003-04 season due to a contract dispute. Traded to **NY Rangers** by **Vancouver** with Martin Grenier for Martin Rucinsky, March 9, 2004. Signed as a free agent by **Philadelphia**, June 16, 2004. Traded to **Columbus** by **Philadelphia** with Philadelphia's 4th round choice (Drew Olson) in 2008 Entry Draft for Colorado's 1st round choice (previously acquired, Philadelphia selected Luca Sbisa) in 2008 Entry Draft and Columbus's 3rd round choice (Marc-Andre Bourdon) in 2008 Entry Draft, June 20, 2008.

UPSHALL, Scottie

(UHP-shuhl, SKAW-tee) **PHI.**

Left wing. Shoots left. 6', 197 lbs. Born, Fort McMurray, Alta., October 7, 1983. Nashville's 1st choice, 6th overall, in 2002 Entry Draft.

Season	Club	League	GP	G	A	Pts	PIM	PP	SH	GW	S	%	+/-	TF	F%	Min	GP	G	A	Pts	PIM	PP	SH	GW	Min
1998-99	Fort McMurray	AMHL	28	62	40	102	100																		
99-2000	Fort McMurray	AJHL	52	26	26	52	65																		
2000-01	Kamloops Blazers	WHL	70	42	45	87	111										4	0	2	2	10				
2001-02	Kamloops Blazers	WHL	61	32	51	83	139										4	1	2	3	21				
2002-03	Nashville	NHL	8	1	0	1	0	0	0	0	6	16.7	2	2	0.0	8:42									
	Kamloops Blazers	WHL	42	25	31	56	111										6	0	2	2	34				
	Milwaukee	AHL	2	1	0	1	2										6	0	0	0	2				
2003-04	Nashville	NHL	7	0	1	1	0	0	0	0	6	0.0	–2	8	37.5	9:11									
	Milwaukee	AHL	31	13	11	24	42										8	3	0	3	4				
2004-05	Milwaukee	AHL	62	19	27	46	108										5	2	2	4	8				
2005-06	Nashville	NHL	48	8	16	24	34	1	0	2	72	11.1	14	11	45.5	10:26	2	0	0	0	0	0	0	0	11:57
	Milwaukee	AHL	23	17	16	33	44										14	6	10	16	20				

			Regular Season														Playoffs								
Season	Club	League	GP	G	A	Pts	PIM	PP	SH	GW	S	%	+/-	TF	F%	Min	GP	G	A	Pts	PIM	PP	SH	GW	Min
2006-07	**Nashville**	**NHL**	**14**	**2**	**1**	**3**	**18**	**0**	**0**	**2**	**27**	**7.4**	**–1**	**0**	**0.0**	**10:28**	....	....	....	....	....	....	....	....	....
	Milwaukee	AHL	5	0	1	1	6	....	....	....	....	....	....	....	....	....	....	....	....	....	....	....	....	....	....
	Philadelphia	**NHL**	**18**	**6**	**7**	**13**	**8**	**1**	**1**	**2**	**60**	**10.0**	**4**	**18**	**44.4**	**18:05**	....	....	....	....	....	....	....	....	....
2007-08	**Philadelphia**	**NHL**	**61**	**14**	**16**	**30**	**74**	**3**	**0**	**1**	**128**	**10.9**	**2**	**7**	**28.6**	**13:20**	**17**	**3**	**4**	**7**	***44**	**1**	**0**	**1**	**13:57**
	NHL Totals		**156**	**31**	**41**	**72**	**134**	**5**	**1**	**7**	**299**	**10.4**		**46**	**39.1**	**12:18**	**19**	**3**	**4**	**7**	**44**	**1**	**0**	**1**	**13:44**

WHL All-Rookie Team (2001) • WHL Rookie of the Year (2001) • CHL All-Rookie Team (2001) • Canadian Major Junior Rookie of the Year (2001) • WHL West Second All-Star Team (2002)

• Missed majority of 2003-04 season recovering from knee injury suffered in game vs. Phoenix, December 22, 2003. Traded to **Philadelphia** by **Nashville** with Ryan Parent and Nashville's 1st (later traded back to Nashville - Nashville selected Jonathon Blum) and 3rd (later traded to Washington - Washington selected Phil Desimone) round choices in 2007 Entry Draft for Peter Forsberg, February 15, 2007.

VAANANEN, Ossi

(VAN-ih-nehn, AW-see) **PHI.**

Defense. Shoots left. 6'4", 215 lbs. Born, Vantaa, Finland, August 18, 1980. Phoenix's 2nd choice, 43rd overall, in 1998 Entry Draft.

1995-96	Jokerit U18	Fin-U18	8	0	0	0	2	....	....	....	....	....	....	....	....	....	2	0	0	0	0	....	....	....	....
1996-97	Jokerit U18	Fin-U18	18	1	2	3	43	....	....	....	....	....	....	....	....	....	....	....	....	....	....	....	....	....	....
	Jokerit Helsinki Jr.	Fin-Jr.	1	0	0	0	0	....	....	....	....	....	....	....	....	....	....	....	....	....	....	....	....	....	....
1997-98	Jokerit U18	Fin-U18	7	3	3	6	8	....	....	....	....	....	....	....	....	....	....	....	....	....	....	....	....	....	....
	Jokerit Helsinki Jr.	Fin-Jr.	31	0	6	6	24	....	....	....	....	....	....	....	....	....	7	0	2	2	16	....	....	....	....
1998-99	Jokerit Helsinki Jr.	Fin-Jr.	12	1	6	7	16	....	....	....	....	....	....	....	....	....	6	1	0	1	12	....	....	....	....
	Jokerit Helsinki	Finland	48	0	1	1	42	....	....	....	....	....	....	....	....	....	3	0	1	1	2	....	....	....	....
	Jokerit Helsinki	EuroHL	5	0	0	0	2	....	....	....	....	....	....	....	....	....	1	0	1	1	2	....	....	....	....
99-2000	Jokerit Helsinki	Finland	49	1	6	7	46	....	....	....	....	....	....	....	....	....	11	1	1	2	2	....	....	....	....
2000-01	**Phoenix**	**NHL**	**81**	**4**	**12**	**16**	**90**	**0**	**0**	**2**	**69**	**5.8**	**9**	**0**	**0.0**	**19:09**	....	....	....	....	....	....	....	....	....
2001-02	**Phoenix**	**NHL**	**76**	**2**	**12**	**14**	**74**	**0**	**1**	**0**	**41**	**4.9**	**6**	**0**	**0.0**	**20:13**	**5**	**0**	**0**	**0**	**6**	**0**	**0**	**0**	**20:33**
	Finland	Olympics	2	0	1	1	0	....	....	....	....	....	....	....	....	....	....	....	....	....	....	....	....	....	....
2002-03	**Phoenix**	**NHL**	**67**	**2**	**7**	**9**	**82**	**0**	**0**	**0**	**49**	**4.1**	**1**	**0**	**0.0**	**19:15**	....	....	....	....	....	....	....	....	....
2003-04	**Phoenix**	**NHL**	**67**	**2**	**4**	**6**	**87**	**0**	**0**	**1**	**39**	**5.1**	**–10**	**0**	**0.0**	**19:21**	....	....	....	....	....	....	....	....	....
	Colorado	**NHL**	**12**	**0**	**0**	**0**	**2**	**0**	**0**	**0**	**6**	**0.0**	**–4**	**0**	**0.0**	**18:36**	**11**	**0**	**1**	**1**	**18**	**0**	**0**	**0**	**22:06**
2004-05	Jokerit Helsinki	Finland	28	2	2	4	30	....	....	....	....	....	....	....	....	....	12	0	0	0	26	....	....	....	....
2005-06	**Colorado**	**NHL**	**53**	**0**	**4**	**4**	**56**	**0**	**0**	**0**	**34**	**0.0**	**10**	**1**	**0.0**	**13:34**	**1**	**0**	**0**	**0**	**0**	**0**	**0**	**0**	**13:58**
2006-07	**Colorado**	**NHL**	**74**	**2**	**6**	**8**	**69**	**0**	**0**	**1**	**32**	**6.3**	**6**	**0**	**0.0**	**14:20**	....	....	....	....	....	....	....	....	....
2007-08	Djurgarden	Sweden	45	7	8	15	102	....	....	....	....	....	....	....	....	....	5	0	0	0	2	....	....	....	....
	NHL Totals		**430**	**12**	**45**	**57**	**460**	**0**	**1**	**4**	**270**	**4.4**		**1**	**0.0**	**17:51**	**17**	**0**	**1**	**1**	**24**	**0**	**0**	**0**	**21:10**

Traded to **Colorado** by **Phoenix** with Chris Gratton and Phoenix's 2nd round choice (Paul Stastny) in 2005 Entry Draft for Derek Morris and Keith Ballard, March 9, 2004. Signed as a free agent by **Jokerit Helsinki** (Finland), December 1, 2004. Signed as a free agent by **Philadelphia**, July 1, 2008.

VALABIK, Boris

(vuh-LA-bihk, BOHR-ihs) **ATL.**

Defense. Shoots left. 6'7", 240 lbs. Born, Nitra, Czech., February 14, 1986. Atlanta's 1st choice, 10th overall, in 2004 Entry Draft.

2002-03	HKM Nitra Jr.	Slovak-Jr.	46	2	12	14	145	....	....	....	....	....	....	....	....	....	....	....	....	....	....	....	....	....	....
2003-04	Kitchener Rangers	OHL	68	3	13	16	278	....	....	....	....	....	....	....	....	....	5	0	0	0	8	....	....	....	....
2004-05	Kitchener Rangers	OHL	43	0	4	4	231	....	....	....	....	....	....	....	....	....	15	0	0	0	56	....	....	....	....
2005-06	Kitchener Rangers	OHL	52	1	9	10	216	....	....	....	....	....	....	....	....	....	5	0	2	2	14	....	....	....	....
2006-07	Chicago Wolves	AHL	50	2	7	9	184	....	....	....	....	....	....	....	....	....	8	0	1	1	37	....	....	....	....
2007-08	**Atlanta**	**NHL**	**7**	**0**	**0**	**0**	**42**	**0**	**0**	**0**	**5**	**0.0**	**–2**	**0**	**0.0**	**16:42**	....	....	....	....	....	....	....	....	....
	Chicago Wolves	AHL	58	1	7	8	229	....	....	....	....	....	....	....	....	....	24	3	1	4	71	....	....	....	....
	NHL Totals		**7**	**0**	**0**	**0**	**42**	**0**	**0**	**0**	**5**	**0.0**		**0**	**0.0**	**16:42**	....	....	....	....	....	....	....	....	....

OHL All-Rookie Team (2004) • Canadian Major Junior All-Rookie Team (2004)

VANDERMEER, Jim

(VAN-duhr-meer, JIHM) **CGY.**

Defense. Shoots left. 6'1", 208 lbs. Born, Caroline, Alta., February 21, 1980.

1997-98	Red Deer	AMHL	26	4	8	12	51	....	....	....	....	....	....	....	....	....	....	....	....	....	....	....	....	....	....
	Red Deer Rebels	WHL	35	0	3	3	55	....	....	....	....	....	....	....	....	....	2	0	0	0	0	....	....	....	....
1998-99	Red Deer Rebels	WHL	70	5	23	28	258	....	....	....	....	....	....	....	....	....	9	0	1	1	24	....	....	....	....
99-2000	Red Deer Rebels	WHL	71	8	30	38	221	....	....	....	....	....	....	....	....	....	4	0	1	1	16	....	....	....	....
2000-01	Red Deer Rebels	WHL	72	21	44	65	180	....	....	....	....	....	....	....	....	....	22	3	13	16	43	....	....	....	....
2001-02	Philadelphia	AHL	74	1	13	14	88	....	....	....	....	....	....	....	....	....	5	0	2	2	14	....	....	....	....
2002-03	**Philadelphia**	**NHL**	**24**	**2**	**1**	**3**	**27**	**0**	**0**	**0**	**22**	**9.1**	**9**	**0**	**0.0**	**13:42**	**8**	**0**	**1**	**1**	**9**	**0**	**0**	**0**	**12:42**
	Philadelphia	AHL	48	4	8	12	122	....	....	....	....	....	....	....	....	....	....	....	....	....	....	....	....	....	....
2003-04	**Philadelphia**	**NHL**	**23**	**3**	**2**	**5**	**25**	**0**	**0**	**1**	**24**	**12.5**	**–5**	**0**	**0.0**	**15:47**	....	....	....	....	....	....	....	....	....
	Philadelphia	AHL	26	1	6	7	120	....	....	....	....	....	....	....	....	....	....	....	....	....	....	....	....	....	....
	Chicago	**NHL**	**23**	**2**	**10**	**12**	**58**	**1**	**1**	**0**	**37**	**5.4**	**–6**	**1**	**100.0**	**22:03**	....	....	....	....	....	....	....	....	....
2004-05	Norfolk Admirals	AHL	52	3	10	13	164	....	....	....	....	....	....	....	....	....	....	....	....	....	....	....	....	....	....
2005-06	**Chicago**	**NHL**	**76**	**6**	**18**	**24**	**116**	**2**	**0**	**1**	**93**	**6.5**	**–2**	**1**	**100.0**	**21:47**	....	....	....	....	....	....	....	....	....
2006-07	**Chicago**	**NHL**	**46**	**1**	**6**	**7**	**53**	**0**	**0**	**0**	**50**	**2.0**	**–3**	**0**	**0.0**	**17:50**	....	....	....	....	....	....	....	....	....
2007-08	**Chicago**	**NHL**	**26**	**2**	**7**	**9**	**44**	**1**	**0**	**0**	**23**	**8.7**	**3**	**0**	**0.0**	**19:37**	....	....	....	....	....	....	....	....	....
	Philadelphia	**NHL**	**28**	**1**	**5**	**6**	**27**	**1**	**0**	**0**	**26**	**3.8**	**–1**	**0**	**0.0**	**19:34**	....	....	....	....	....	....	....	....	....
	Calgary	**NHL**	**21**	**0**	**2**	**2**	**39**	**0**	**0**	**0**	**23**	**0.0**	**4**	**0**	**0.0**	**19:44**	**7**	**0**	**0**	**0**	**4**	**0**	**0**	**0**	**16:18**
	NHL Totals		**267**	**17**	**51**	**68**	**389**	**5**	**1**	**2**	**298**	**5.7**		**2**	**100.0**	**19:17**	**15**	**0**	**1**	**1**	**13**	**0**	**0**	**0**	**14:23**

WHL East First All-Star Team (2001) • Canadian Major Junior Humanitarian Player of the Year (2001)

Signed as a free agent by **Philadelphia**, December 21, 2000. Traded to **Chicago** by **Philadelphia** with the rights to Colin Fraser and Los Angeles' 2nd round choice (previously acquired, Chicago selected Bryan Bickell) in 2004 Entry Draft for Alex Zhamnov and Washington's 4th round choice (previously acquired, Philadelphia selected R.J. Anderson) in 2004 Entry Draft, February 19, 2004. Traded to **Philadelphia** by **Chicago** for Ben Eager, December 18, 2007. Traded to **Calgary** by **Philadelphia** for Calgary's 3rd round choice in 2009 Entry Draft, February 20, 2008.

VANDERMEER, Peter

(VAN-duhr-meer, PEE-tuhr) **CGY.**

Left wing. Shoots left. 6', 210 lbs. Born, Caroline, Alta., October 14, 1975.

1992-93	Red Deer	AMHL	34	26	30	56	172	....	....	....	....	....	....	....	....	....	....	....	....	....	....	....	....	....	....
	Red Deer Rebels	WHL	2	0	0	0	2	....	....	....	....	....	....	....	....	....	....	....	....	....	....	....	....	....	....
1993-94	Red Deer Rebels	WHL	54	4	9	13	170	....	....	....	....	....	....	....	....	....	....	....	....	....	....	....	....	....	....
1994-95	Red Deer Rebels	WHL	61	16	16	32	218	....	....	....	....	....	....	....	....	....	....	....	....	....	....	....	....	....	....
1995-96	Red Deer Rebels	WHL	63	21	40	61	207	....	....	....	....	....	....	....	....	....	....	....	....	....	....	....	....	....	....
1996-97	Columbus Chill	ECHL	30	6	11	17	195	....	....	....	....	....	....	....	....	....	....	....	....	....	....	....	....	....	....
1997-98	Columbus Chill	ECHL	20	4	7	11	78	....	....	....	....	....	....	....	....	....	7	2	1	3	26	....	....	....	....
	Richmond	ECHL	18	2	5	7	165	....	....	....	....	....	....	....	....	....	....	....	....	....	....	....	....	....	....
	Rochester	AHL	30	4	2	6	140	....	....	....	....	....	....	....	....	....	....	....	....	....	....	....	....	....	....
1998-99	Rochester	AHL	2	1	0	1	16	....	....	....	....	....	....	....	....	....	4	1	0	1	13	....	....	....	....
	Binghamton	UHL	62	15	21	36	*390	....	....	....	....	....	....	....	....	....	16	1	0	1	38	....	....	....	....
99-2000	Wilkes-Barre	AHL	4	0	0	0	7	....	....	....	....	....	....	....	....	....	5	2	2	4	0	....	....	....	....
	Richmond	ECHL	58	31	25	56	*457	....	....	....	....	....	....	....	....	....	....	....	....	....	....	....	....	....	....
	Providence Bruins	AHL	....	....	....	....	....	....	....	....	....	....	....	....	....	....	3	0	1	1	20	....	....	....	....
2000-01	Providence Bruins	AHL	62	19	18	37	240	....	....	....	....	....	....	....	....	....	9	0	3	3	2	....	....	....	....
2001-02	Philadelphia	AHL	61	5	1	6	313	....	....	....	....	....	....	....	....	....	4	0	0	0	16	....	....	....	....
	Trenton Titans	ECHL	2	0	1	1	2	....	....	....	....	....	....	....	....	....	5	0	0	0	8	....	....	....	....
2002-03	Philadelphia	AHL	77	5	8	13	335	....	....	....	....	....	....	....	....	....	....	....	....	....	....	....	....	....	....
2003-04	Philadelphia	AHL	71	5	8	13	*398	....	....	....	....	....	....	....	....	....	....	....	....	....	....	....	....	....	....
2004-05	Grand Rapids	AHL	73	4	13	17	310	....	....	....	....	....	....	....	....	....	12	1	0	1	29	....	....	....	....
2005-06	Hamilton	AHL	67	6	6	12	276	....	....	....	....	....	....	....	....	....	....	....	....	....	....	....	....	....	....
2006-07	Hershey Bears	AHL	26	2	5	7	129	....	....	....	....	....	....	....	....	....	....	....	....	....	....	....	....	....	....
2007-08	San Antonio	AHL	38	2	6	8	332	....	....	....	....	....	....	....	....	....	2	0	0	0	0	....	....	....	....
	Phoenix	**NHL**	**2**	**0**	**0**	**0**	**0**	**0**	**0**	**0**	**0**	**0.0**	**0**	**0**	**0.0**	**7:33**	....	....	....	....	....	....	....	....	....
	NHL Totals		**2**	**0**	**0**	**0**	**0**	**0**	**0**	**0**	**0**	**0.0**		**0**	**0.0**	**7:33**	....	....	....	....	....	....	....	....	....

Signed as a free agent by **Philadelphia**, July 6, 2001. Signed as a free agent by **Detroit**, August 16, 2004. Signed as a free agent by **Montreal**, August 2, 2005. Signed as a free agent by **Washington**, July 21, 2006. Signed as a free agent by **San Antonio** (AHL), August 16, 2007. Signed as a free agent by **Phoenix**, February 8, 2008. Signed as a free agent by **Calgary**, July 2, 2008.

VANEK, Thomas
(VAH-NEHK, TAW-muhs) **BUF.**

Left wing. Shoots right. 6'2", 208 lbs. Born, Vienna, Austria, January 19, 1984. Buffalo's 1st choice, 5th overall, in 2003 Entry Draft.

Season	Club	League	GP	G	A	Pts	PIM	PP	SH	GW	S	%	+/-	TF	F%	Min	PO GP	PO G	PO A	PO Pts	PO PIM	PO PP	PO SH	PO GW	PO Min
99-2000	Sioux Falls	USHL	35	15	18	33	12	....	....	....	....	....	....	....	....	....	3	0	1	1	0	....	....	....	....
2000-01	Sioux Falls	USHL	20	19	10	29	15	....	....	....	....	....	....	....	....	....	8	5	4	9	2	....	....	....	....
2001-02	Sioux Falls	USHL	53	46	45	91	54	....	....	....	....	....	....	....	....	....	3	0	0	0	9	....	....	....	....
2002-03	U. of Minnesota	WCHA	45	31	31	62	60	....	....	....	....	....	....	....	....	....	....	....	....	....	....	....	....	....	....
2003-04	U. of Minnesota	WCHA	38	26	25	51	72	....	....	....	....	....	....	....	....	....	....	....	....	....	....	....	....	....	....
2004-05	Rochester	AHL	74	42	26	68	62	....	....	....	....	....	....	....	....	....	5	2	3	5	10	....	....	....	....
2005-06	**Buffalo**	**NHL**	**81**	**25**	**23**	**48**	**72**	**11**	**0**	**4**	**204**	**12.3**	**-11**	**23**	**21.7**	**14:44**	**10**	**2**	**0**	**2**	**6**	**2**	**0**	**0**	**10:45**
2006-07	**Buffalo**	**NHL**	**82**	**43**	**41**	**84**	**40**	**15**	**0**	**5**	**237**	**18.1**	**47**	**39**	**28.2**	**16:47**	**16**	**6**	**4**	**10**	**10**	**1**	**0**	**2**	**16:27**
2007-08	**Buffalo**	**NHL**	**82**	**36**	**28**	**64**	**64**	**19**	**0**	**9**	**240**	**15.0**	**-5**	**13**	**46.2**	**16:51**	....	....	....	....	....	....	....	....	....
	NHL Totals		**245**	**104**	**92**	**196**	**176**	**45**	**0**	**18**	**681**	**15.3**		**75**	**29.3**	**16:08**	**26**	**8**	**4**	**12**	**16**	**3**	**0**	**2**	**14:15**

USHL First All-Star Team (2002) • USHL MVP (2002) • WCHA All-Rookie Team (2003) • WCHA Second All-Star Team (2003, 2004) • WCHA Rookie of the Year (2003) • NCAA Championship All-Tournament Team (2003) • NCAA Championship Tournament - MVP (2003) • NCAA West Second All-American Team (2004) • AHL All-Rookie Team (2005) • NHL Second All-Star Team (2007)

VAN RYN, Mike
(VAN RIHN, MIGHK) **FLA.**

Defense. Shoots right. 6'1", 198 lbs. Born, London, Ont., May 14, 1979. New Jersey's 1st choice, 26th overall, in 1998 Entry Draft.

Season	Club	League	GP	G	A	Pts	PIM	PP	SH	GW	S	%	+/-	TF	F%	Min	PO GP	PO G	PO A	PO Pts	PO PIM	PO PP	PO SH	PO GW	PO Min
1995-96	London Nationals	OHA-B	44	9	14	23	24	....	....	....	....	....	....	....	....	....	....	....	....	....	....	....	....	....	....
1996-97	London Nationals	OHA-B	46	14	31	45	32	....	....	....	....	....	....	....	....	....	....	....	....	....	....	....	....	....	....
1997-98	U. of Michigan	CCHA	38	4	14	18	44	....	....	....	....	....	....	....	....	....	....	....	....	....	....	....	....	....	....
1998-99	U. of Michigan	CCHA	37	10	13	23	52	....	....	....	....	....	....	....	....	....	....	....	....	....	....	....	....	....	....
99-2000	Sarnia Sting	OHL	61	6	35	41	34	....	....	....	....	....	....	....	....	....	7	0	5	5	4	....	....	....	....
2000-01	**St. Louis**	**NHL**	**1**	**0**	**0**	**0**	**0**	**0**	**0**	**0**	**1**	**0.0**	**-2**	**0**	**0.0**	**13:43**	....	....	....	....	....	....	....	....	....
	Worcester IceCats	AHL	37	3	10	13	12	....	....	....	....	....	....	....	....	....	7	1	1	2	2	....	....	....	....
2001-02	**St. Louis**	**NHL**	**48**	**2**	**8**	**10**	**18**	**0**	**0**	**1**	**52**	**3.8**	**10**	**0**	**0.0**	**16:23**	**9**	**0**	**0**	**0**	**0**	**0**	**0**	**0**	**16:04**
	Worcester IceCats	AHL	24	2	7	9	17	....	....	....	....	....	....	....	....	....	....	....	....	....	....	....	....	....	....
2002-03	**St. Louis**	**NHL**	**20**	**0**	**3**	**3**	**8**	**0**	**0**	**0**	**21**	**0.0**	**3**	**0**	**0.0**	**15:04**	....	....	....	....	....	....	....	....	....
	Worcester IceCats	AHL	33	2	8	10	16	....	....	....	....	....	....	....	....	....	....	....	....	....	....	....	....	....	....
	San Antonio	AHL	11	0	3	3	20	....	....	....	....	....	....	....	....	....	3	0	0	0	0	....	....	....	....
2003-04	**Florida**	**NHL**	**79**	**13**	**24**	**37**	**52**	**6**	**1**	**0**	**136**	**9.6**	**-16**	**3**	**33.3**	**24:26**	....	....	....	....	....	....	....	....	....
2004-05			DID NOT PLAY																						
2005-06	**Florida**	**NHL**	**80**	**8**	**29**	**37**	**90**	**3**	**0**	**2**	**154**	**5.2**	**15**	**0**	**0.0**	**22:36**	....	....	....	....	....	....	....	....	....
2006-07	**Florida**	**NHL**	**78**	**4**	**25**	**29**	**64**	**1**	**0**	**0**	**121**	**3.3**	**-5**	**1**	**0.0**	**21:08**	....	....	....	....	....	....	....	....	....
2007-08	**Florida**	**NHL**	**20**	**0**	**2**	**2**	**14**	**0**	**0**	**0**	**16**	**0.0**	**-2**	**0**	**0.0**	**17:49**	....	....	....	....	....	....	....	....	....
	NHL Totals		**326**	**27**	**91**	**118**	**246**	**10**	**1**	**3**	**501**	**5.4**		**4**	**25.0**	**21:00**	**9**	**0**	**0**	**0**	**0**	**0**	**0**	**0**	**16:04**

OHA-B First All-Star Team (1997)

Signed as a free agent by **St. Louis**, June 30, 2000. • Missed majority of 2000-01 season recovering from shoulder injury suffered in game vs. Phoenix, October 5, 2000. Traded to **Florida** by **St. Louis** for Valeri Bure and Florida's 5th round choice (Nikita Nikitin) in 2004 Entry Draft, March 11, 2003. • Missed majority of 2007-08 season recovering from off-season wrist surgery and recurring complications.

VASICEK, Josef
(VAS-ih-chehk, YOH-zehf)

Center. Shoots left. 6'5", 214 lbs. Born, Havlickuv Brod, Czech., September 12, 1980. Carolina's 4th choice, 91st overall, in 1998 Entry Draft.

Season	Club	League	GP	G	A	Pts	PIM	PP	SH	GW	S	%	+/-	TF	F%	Min	PO GP	PO G	PO A	PO Pts	PO PIM	PO PP	PO SH	PO GW	PO Min
1995-96	Havl. Brod U17	CzR-U17	36	25	25	50	....	....	....	....	....	....	....	....	....	....	....	....	....	....	....	....	....	....	....
1996-97	Slavia U17	CzR-U17	37	20	40	60	....	....	....	....	....	....	....	....	....	....	....	....	....	....	....	....	....	....	....
1997-98	Slavia Jr.	CzRep-Jr.	34	13	20	33	....	....	....	....	....	....	....	....	....	....	....	....	....	....	....	....	....	....	....
1998-99	Sault Ste. Marie	OHL	66	21	35	56	30	....	....	....	....	....	....	....	....	....	5	3	0	3	10	....	....	....	....
99-2000	Sault Ste. Marie	OHL	54	26	46	72	49	....	....	....	....	....	....	....	....	....	17	5	15	20	8	....	....	....	....
2000-01	**Carolina**	**NHL**	**76**	**8**	**13**	**21**	**53**	**1**	**0**	**0**	**103**	**7.8**	**-8**	**786**	**46.6**	**11:49**	**6**	**2**	**0**	**2**	**0**	**0**	**0**	**0**	**13:56**
	Cincinnati	IHL	....	....	....	....	....	....	....	....	....	....	....	....	....	....	3	0	0	0	0	....	....	....	....
2001-02	**Carolina**	**NHL**	**78**	**14**	**17**	**31**	**53**	**3**	**0**	**3**	**117**	**12.0**	**-7**	**878**	**48.3**	**14:11**	**23**	**3**	**2**	**5**	**12**	**0**	**0**	**1**	**14:50**
2002-03	**Carolina**	**NHL**	**57**	**10**	**10**	**20**	**33**	**4**	**0**	**1**	**87**	**11.5**	**-19**	**652**	**49.5**	**15:57**	....	....	....	....	....	....	....	....	....
2003-04	**Carolina**	**NHL**	**82**	**19**	**26**	**45**	**60**	**6**	**0**	**5**	**161**	**11.8**	**-3**	**262**	**48.9**	**17:06**	....	....	....	....	....	....	....	....	....
2004-05	HC Slavia Praha	CzRep	52	20	23	43	42	....	....	....	....	....	....	....	....	....	7	1	6	7	10	....	....	....	....
2005-06♦	**Carolina**	**NHL**	**23**	**4**	**5**	**9**	**8**	**0**	**0**	**0**	**41**	**9.8**	**3**	**46**	**60.9**	**15:23**	**8**	**0**	**0**	**0**	**2**	**0**	**0**	**0**	**10:04**
2006-07	**Nashville**	**NHL**	**38**	**4**	**9**	**13**	**29**	**0**	**0**	**0**	**47**	**8.5**	**1**	**307**	**49.8**	**13:11**	....	....	....	....	....	....	....	....	....
	Carolina	**NHL**	**25**	**2**	**7**	**9**	**22**	**0**	**0**	**0**	**30**	**6.7**	**-6**	**292**	**51.4**	**13:42**	....	....	....	....	....	....	....	....	....
2007-08	**NY Islanders**	**NHL**	**81**	**16**	**19**	**35**	**53**	**0**	**2**	**2**	**126**	**12.7**	**1**	**1105**	**55.7**	**15:51**	....	....	....	....	....	....	....	....	....
	NHL Totals		**460**	**77**	**106**	**183**	**311**	**14**	**2**	**11**	**712**	**10.8**		**4328**	**50.5**	**14:47**	**37**	**5**	**2**	**7**	**14**	**0**	**0**	**1**	**13:39**

Signed as a free agent by **Slavia Praha** (CzRep), September 17, 2004. • Missed majority of 2005-06 season recovering from knee injury sufferd in game at Florida, November 11, 2005. Traded to **Nashville** by **Carolina** for Scott Walker, July 18, 2006. Traded to **Carolina** by **Nashville** for Eric Belanger, February 9, 2007. Signed as a free agent by **NY Islanders**, August 15, 2007.

VEILLEUX, Stephane
(VAY-oo, STEH-fan) **MIN.**

Left wing. Shoots left. 6', 190 lbs. Born, Beauceville, Que., November 16, 1981. Minnesota's 4th choice, 93rd overall, in 2001 Entry Draft.

Season	Club	League	GP	G	A	Pts	PIM	PP	SH	GW	S	%	+/-	TF	F%	Min	PO GP	PO G	PO A	PO Pts	PO PIM	PO PP	PO SH	PO GW	PO Min
1997-98	Beauce-Amiante	QAAA	21	20	17	37	....	....	....	....	....	....	....	....	....	....	....	....	....	....	....	....	....	....	....
	Levis-Lauzon	QAAA	14	3	5	8	....	....	....	....	....	....	....	....	....	....	1	0	0	0	0	....	....	....	....
1998-99	Victoriaville Tigres	QMJHL	65	6	13	19	35	....	....	....	....	....	....	....	....	....	6	1	3	4	2	....	....	....	....
99-2000	Victoriaville Tigres	QMJHL	22	1	4	5	17	....	....	....	....	....	....	....	....	....	....	....	....	....	....	....	....	....	....
	Val-d'Or Foreurs	QMJHL	50	14	28	42	100	....	....	....	....	....	....	....	....	....	....	....	....	....	....	....	....	....	....
2000-01	Val-d'Or Foreurs	QMJHL	68	48	67	115	90	....	....	....	....	....	....	....	....	....	21	15	18	33	42	....	....	....	....
2001-02	Houston Aeros	AHL	77	13	22	35	113	....	....	....	....	....	....	....	....	....	14	2	4	6	20	....	....	....	....
2002-03	**Minnesota**	**NHL**	**38**	**3**	**2**	**5**	**23**	**1**	**0**	**0**	**52**	**5.8**	**-6**	**13**	**7.7**	**12:08**	....	....	....	....	....	....	....	....	....
	Houston Aeros	AHL	29	8	4	12	43	....	....	....	....	....	....	....	....	....	23	7	11	18	12	....	....	....	....
2003-04	**Minnesota**	**NHL**	**19**	**2**	**8**	**10**	**20**	**1**	**1**	**1**	**37**	**5.4**	**0**	**10**	**40.0**	**14:20**	....	....	....	....	....	....	....	....	....
	Houston Aeros	AHL	64	13	25	38	66	....	....	....	....	....	....	....	....	....	2	1	1	2	2	....	....	....	....
2004-05	Houston Aeros	AHL	59	15	24	39	35	....	....	....	....	....	....	....	....	....	....	....	....	....	....	....	....	....	....
2005-06	**Minnesota**	**NHL**	**71**	**7**	**9**	**16**	**63**	**0**	**0**	**1**	**87**	**8.0**	**-13**	**33**	**33.3**	**12:58**	....	....	....	....	....	....	....	....	....
2006-07	**Minnesota**	**NHL**	**75**	**7**	**11**	**18**	**47**	**0**	**0**	**1**	**84**	**8.3**	**3**	**32**	**21.9**	**12:17**	**5**	**0**	**0**	**0**	**4**	**0**	**0**	**0**	**12:40**
2007-08	**Minnesota**	**NHL**	**77**	**11**	**7**	**18**	**61**	**0**	**0**	**0**	**136**	**8.1**	**-13**	**45**	**37.8**	**14:32**	**6**	**0**	**0**	**0**	**27**	**0**	**0**	**0**	**15:43**
	NHL Totals		**280**	**30**	**37**	**67**	**214**	**2**	**1**	**3**	**396**	**7.6**		**133**	**30.1**	**13:12**	**11**	**0**	**0**	**0**	**31**	**0**	**0**	**0**	**14:20**

VERMETTE, Antoine
(vuhr-MEHT, AN-twuhn) **OTT.**

Center. Shoots left. 6'1", 200 lbs. Born, St-Agapit, Que., July 20, 1982. Ottawa's 3rd choice, 55th overall, in 2000 Entry Draft.

Season	Club	League	GP	G	A	Pts	PIM	PP	SH	GW	S	%	+/-	TF	F%	Min	PO GP	PO G	PO A	PO Pts	PO PIM	PO PP	PO SH	PO GW	PO Min
1997-98	Quebec Select	QAHA	19	11	20	31	36	....	....	....	....	....	....	....	....	....	....	....	....	....	....	....	....	....	....
	Levis-Lauzon	QAAA	8	1	1	2	4	....	....	....	....	....	....	....	....	....	1	0	0	0	0	....	....	....	....
1998-99	Quebec Remparts	QMJHL	57	9	17	26	32	....	....	....	....	....	....	....	....	....	13	0	0	0	2	....	....	....	....
99-2000	Victoriaville Tigres	QMJHL	71	30	41	71	87	....	....	....	....	....	....	....	....	....	6	0	1	1	6	....	....	....	....
2000-01	Victoriaville Tigres	QMJHL	71	57	62	119	102	....	....	....	....	....	....	....	....	....	9	4	6	10	14	....	....	....	....
2001-02	Victoriaville Tigres	QMJHL	4	0	2	2	6	....	....	....	....	....	....	....	....	....	22	10	16	26	10	....	....	....	....
2002-03	Binghamton	AHL	80	34	28	62	57	....	....	....	....	....	....	....	....	....	14	2	9	11	10	....	....	....	....
2003-04	**Ottawa**	**NHL**	**57**	**7**	**7**	**14**	**16**	**0**	**1**	**0**	**63**	**11.1**	**5**	**100**	**44.0**	**11:59**	**4**	**0**	**1**	**1**	**4**	**0**	**0**	**0**	**11:35**
	Binghamton	AHL	3	0	0	0	6	....	....	....	....	....	....	....	....	....	....	....	....	....	....	....	....	....	....
2004-05	Binghamton	AHL	78	28	45	73	36	....	....	....	....	....	....	....	....	....	6	1	4	5	10	....	....	....	....
2005-06	**Ottawa**	**NHL**	**82**	**21**	**12**	**33**	**44**	**1**	**6**	**4**	**123**	**17.1**	**17**	**537**	**57.9**	**12:35**	**10**	**2**	**0**	**2**	**4**	**0**	**0**	**1**	**15:00**
2006-07	**Ottawa**	**NHL**	**77**	**19**	**20**	**39**	**52**	**2**	**3**	**2**	**151**	**12.6**	**-2**	**834**	**53.0**	**15:42**	**20**	**2**	**3**	**5**	**6**	**0**	**0**	**0**	**16:20**
2007-08	**Ottawa**	**NHL**	**81**	**24**	**29**	**53**	**51**	**4**	**3**	**3**	**175**	**13.7**	**3**	**1217**	**56.7**	**17:35**	**4**	**0**	**0**	**0**	**4**	**0**	**0**	**0**	**20:33**
	NHL Totals		**297**	**71**	**68**	**139**	**163**	**7**	**13**	**9**	**512**	**13.9**		**2688**	**55.3**	**14:38**	**38**	**4**	**4**	**8**	**18**	**0**	**0**	**1**	**15:56**

AHL All-Rookie Team (2003)

• Missed majority of 2001-02 season recovering from neck injury suffered at Team Canada Jr. Selection Camp, June 3, 2001.

VERSTEEG, Kris

(vuhr-STEEG, KRIHS) **CHI.**

Right wing. Shoots right. 5'10", 179 lbs. Born, Lethbridge, Alta., May 13, 1986. Boston's 4th choice, 134th overall, in 2004 Entry Draft.

			Regular Season														Playoffs								
Season	Club	League	GP	G	A	Pts	PIM	PP	SH	GW	S	%	+/-	TF	F%	Min	GP	G	A	Pts	PIM	PP	SH	GW	Min
2002-03	Lethbridge	WHL	57	8	10	18	32																		
2003-04	Lethbridge	WHL	68	16	33	49	85																		
2004-05	Lethbridge	WHL	68	22	30	52	68										5	0	1	1	4				
2005-06	Kamloops Blazers	WHL	14	6	6	12	24																		
	Red Deer Rebels	WHL	57	10	26	36	103																		
	Providence Bruins	AHL	13	2	4	6	13										3	0	0	0	6				
2006-07	Providence Bruins	AHL	43	22	27	49	19																		
	Norfolk Admirals	AHL	27	4	19	23	20										2	0	0	0	2				
2007-08	**Chicago**	**NHL**	**13**	**2**	**2**	**4**	**6**	**0**	**0**	**0**	**21**	**9.5**	**–1**	**3**	**66.7**	**15:52**									
	Rockford IceHogs	AHL	56	18	31	49	174										12	6	5	11	6				
	NHL Totals		**13**	**2**	**2**	**4**	**6**	**0**	**0**	**0**	**21**	**9.5**		**3**	**66.7**	**15:52**									

Traded to **Chicago** by **Boston** with future considerations for Brandon Bochenski, February 3, 2007.

VIGIER, J.P.

(vih-ZHAY, JAY-pee)

Right wing. Shoots right. 6', 200 lbs. Born, Notre Dame de Lourdes, Man., September 11, 1976.

Season	Club	League	GP	G	A	Pts	PIM	PP	SH	GW	S	%	+/-	TF	F%	Min	GP	G	A	Pts	PIM	PP	SH	GW	Min
1995-96	Portage Terriers	MJHL	56	32	49	81																			
1996-97	Northern Mich.	WCHA	36	10	14	24	54																		
1997-98	Northern Mich.	CCHA	36	12	15	27	60																		
1998-99	Northern Mich.	CCHA	42	21	18	39	80																		
99-2000	Northern Mich.	CCHA	39	18	17	35	72																		
	Orlando	IHL	3	1	0	1	0																		
2000-01	**Atlanta**	**NHL**	**2**	**0**	**0**	**0**	**0**	**0**	**0**	**0**	**1**	**0.0**	**–2**	**1**	**100.0**	**9:56**									
	Orlando	IHL	78	23	17	40	66										16	6	6	12	14				
2001-02	**Atlanta**	**NHL**	**15**	**4**	**1**	**5**	**4**	**0**	**0**	**0**	**18**	**22.2**	**–5**	**3**	**66.7**	**13:13**									
	Chicago Wolves	AHL	62	25	16	41	26										21	7	7	14	20				
2002-03	**Atlanta**	**NHL**	**13**	**0**	**0**	**0**	**4**	**0**	**0**	**0**	**21**	**0.0**	**–13**	**1**	**0.0**	**14:07**									
	Chicago Wolves	AHL	63	29	27	56	54										9	3	1	4	4				
2003-04	**Atlanta**	**NHL**	**70**	**10**	**8**	**18**	**22**	**2**	**2**	**3**	**110**	**9.1**	**–18**	**53**	**47.2**	**14:36**									
2004-05	Chicago Wolves	AHL	76	29	41	70	56										18	5	6	11	19				
2005-06	**Atlanta**	**NHL**	**41**	**4**	**6**	**10**	**40**	**1**	**1**	**0**	**53**	**7.5**	**–4**	**70**	**24.3**	**14:21**									
2006-07	**Atlanta**	**NHL**	**72**	**5**	**8**	**13**	**27**	**0**	**0**	**0**	**83**	**6.0**	**0**	**32**	**31.3**	**11:00**									
2007-08	Geneve	Swiss	46	15	20	35	46										12	7	6	13	10				
	NHL Totals		**213**	**23**	**23**	**46**	**97**	**3**	**3**	**3**	**286**	**8.0**		**160**	**34.4**	**13:10**									

CCHA Second All-Star Team (1999) • CCHA All-Tournament Team (1999) • AHL Second All-Star Team (2005)

Signed as a free agent by **Atlanta**, April 20, 2000. Signed as a free agent by **Geneve** (Swiss), August 3, 2007.

VISHNEVSKI, Vitaly

(vihsh-NEHV-skee, vih-TAL-ee) **N.J.**

Defense. Shoots left. 6'2", 215 lbs. Born, Kharkov, USSR, March 18, 1980. Anaheim's 1st choice, 5th overall, in 1998 Entry Draft.

Season	Club	League	GP	G	A	Pts	PIM	PP	SH	GW	S	%	+/-	TF	F%	Min	GP	G	A	Pts	PIM	PP	SH	GW	Min
1995-96	Yaroslavl 2	CIS-2	40	4	4	8	20																		
1996-97	Yaroslavl 2	Russia-3	45	0	2	2	30																		
1997-98	Yaroslavl 2	Russia-2	47	8	9	17	164																		
1998-99	Yaroslavl	Russia	34	3	4	7	38										10	0	0	0	4				
99-2000	**Anaheim**	**NHL**	**31**	**1**	**1**	**2**	**26**	**1**	**0**	**0**	**17**	**5.9**	**0**	**0**	**0.0**	**16:38**									
	Cincinnati	AHL	35	1	3	4	45																		
2000-01	**Anaheim**	**NHL**	**76**	**1**	**10**	**11**	**99**	**0**	**0**	**0**	**49**	**2.0**	**–1**	**0**	**0.0**	**19:14**									
2001-02	**Anaheim**	**NHL**	**74**	**0**	**3**	**3**	**60**	**0**	**0**	**0**	**54**	**0.0**	**–10**	**0**	**0.0**	**17:36**									
2002-03	**Anaheim**	**NHL**	**80**	**2**	**6**	**8**	**76**	**0**	**1**	**0**	**65**	**3.1**	**–8**	**0**	**0.0**	**14:10**	**21**	**0**	**1**	**1**	**6**	**0**	**0**	**0**	**10:02**
2003-04	**Anaheim**	**NHL**	**73**	**6**	**10**	**16**	**51**	**0**	**0**	**0**	**86**	**7.0**	**0**	**0**	**0.0**	**17:10**									
2004-05	Voskresensk	Russia	51	7	17	24	92																		
2005-06	**Anaheim**	**NHL**	**82**	**1**	**7**	**8**	**91**	**0**	**0**	**0**	**90**	**1.1**	**8**	**1**	**100.0**	**16:26**	**16**	**0**	**4**	**4**	**10**	**0**	**0**	**0**	**13:41**
	Russia	Olympics	8	0	1	1	4																		
2006-07	**Atlanta**	**NHL**	**52**	**3**	**9**	**12**	**31**	**0**	**0**	**0**	**41**	**7.3**	**–5**	**0**	**0.0**	**19:18**									
	Nashville	**NHL**	**15**	**0**	**1**	**1**	**10**	**0**	**0**	**0**	**6**	**0.0**	**1**	**0**	**0.0**	**10:02**									
2007-08	**New Jersey**	**NHL**	**69**	**2**	**5**	**7**	**50**	**0**	**0**	**0**	**48**	**4.2**	**–12**	**0**	**0.0**	**15:32**	**3**	**0**	**0**	**0**	**2**	**0**	**0**	**0**	**13:29**
	NHL Totals		**552**	**16**	**52**	**68**	**494**	**1**	**1**	**0**	**456**	**3.5**		**1**	**100.0**	**16:44**	**40**	**0**	**5**	**5**	**18**	**0**	**0**	**0**	**11:45**

Signed as a free agent by **Voskresensk** (Russia), August 25, 2004. Traded to **Atlanta** by **Anaheim** for Karl Stewart, Atlanta's 2nd round choice (later traded to Colorado - Colorado selected T.J. Galiardi) in 2007 Entry Draft and future considerations, August 17, 2006. Traded to **Nashville** by **Atlanta** for Eric Belanger, February 10, 2007. Signed as a free agent by **New Jersey**, July 10, 2007.

VISNOVSKY, Lubomir

(vihsh-NAWV-skee, LOO-boh-mihr) **EDM.**

Defense. Shoots left. 5'10", 188 lbs. Born, Topolcany, Czech., August 11, 1976. Los Angeles' 4th choice, 118th overall, in 2000 Entry Draft.

Season	Club	League	GP	G	A	Pts	PIM	PP	SH	GW	S	%	+/-	TF	F%	Min	GP	G	A	Pts	PIM	PP	SH	GW	Min
1994-95	Bratislava	Slovakia	36	11	12	23	10										9	1	3	4	2				
1995-96	Bratislava	Slovakia	35	8	6	14	22										13	1	5	6	2				
1996-97	Bratislava	Slovakia	44	11	12	23											2	0	1	1					
	Bratislava	EuroHL	6	3	1	4	2										2	0	0	0	6				
1997-98	Bratislava	Slovakia	36	7	9	16	16										11	2	4	6	8				
	Bratislava	EuroHL	6	1	0	1	4																		
	Slovakia	Olympics	3	0	0	0	2																		
1998-99	Bratislava	Slovakia	40	9	10	19	31										10	5	5	10	0				
	Bratislava	EuroHL	6	0	3	3	4																		
99-2000	Bratislava	Slovakia	52	21	24	45	38										8	5	3	8	16				
2000-01	**Los Angeles**	**NHL**	**81**	**7**	**32**	**39**	**36**	**3**	**0**	**3**	**105**	**6.7**	**16**	**0**	**0.0**	**16:58**	**8**	**0**	**0**	**0**	**0**	**0**	**0**	**0**	**13:57**
2001-02	**Los Angeles**	**NHL**	**72**	**4**	**17**	**21**	**14**	**1**	**0**	**2**	**95**	**4.2**	**–5**	**0**	**0.0**	**16:15**	**4**	**0**	**1**	**1**	**0**	**0**	**0**	**0**	**8:22**
	Slovakia	Olympics	3	1	2	3	0																		
2002-03	**Los Angeles**	**NHL**	**57**	**8**	**16**	**24**	**28**	**1**	**0**	**1**	**85**	**9.4**	**2**	**0**	**0.0**	**19:20**									
2003-04	**Los Angeles**	**NHL**	**58**	**8**	**21**	**29**	**26**	**5**	**0**	**0**	**114**	**7.0**	**8**	**0**	**0.0**	**24:02**									
2004-05	Bratislava	Slovakia	43	13	25	38	40										14	2	10	12	10				
2005-06	**Los Angeles**	**NHL**	**80**	**17**	**50**	**67**	**50**	**10**	**0**	**3**	**152**	**11.2**	**7**	**1**	**100.0**	**23:16**									
	Slovakia	Olympics	6	1	1	2	0																		
2006-07	**Los Angeles**	**NHL**	**69**	**18**	**40**	**58**	**26**	**8**	**0**	**0**	**159**	**11.3**	**1**	**6**	**33.3**	**24:27**									
2007-08	**Los Angeles**	**NHL**	**82**	**8**	**33**	**41**	**34**	**3**	**0**	**1**	**153**	**5.2**	**–18**	**8**	**12.5**	**23:00**									
	NHL Totals		**499**	**70**	**209**	**279**	**214**	**31**	**0**	**10**	**863**	**8.1**		**15**	**26.7**	**21:00**	**12**	**0**	**1**	**1**	**0**	**0**	**0**	**0**	**12:05**

NHL All-Rookie Team (2001)

Played in NHL All-Star Game (2007)

Signed as a free agent by **Bratislava** (Slovakia), September 27, 2004. Traded to **Edmonton** by **Los Angeles** for Jarret Stoll and Matt Greene, June 29, 2008.

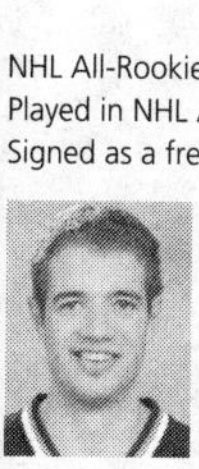

VLASIC, Marc-Edouard

(vih-LASH-ihc, MAHRK-EHD-wahrd) **S.J.**

Defense. Shoots left. 6'1", 200 lbs. Born, Montreal, Que., March 30, 1987. San Jose's 2nd choice, 35th overall, in 2005 Entry Draft.

Season	Club	League	GP	G	A	Pts	PIM	PP	SH	GW	S	%	+/-	TF	F%	Min	GP	G	A	Pts	PIM	PP	SH	GW	Min
2003-04	Quebec Remparts	QMJHL	41	1	9	10	4										5	0	1	1	0				
2004-05	Quebec Remparts	QMJHL	70	5	25	30	33										13	2	7	9	2				
2005-06	Quebec Remparts	QMJHL	66	16	57	73	57										23	5	24	29	10				
2006-07	**San Jose**	**NHL**	**81**	**3**	**23**	**26**	**18**	**2**	**0**	**0**	**66**	**4.5**	**13**	**0**	**0.0**	**22:12**	**11**	**0**	**1**	**1**	**2**	**0**	**0**	**0**	**22:52**
2007-08	**San Jose**	**NHL**	**82**	**2**	**12**	**14**	**24**	**1**	**0**	**0**	**72**	**2.8**	**–12**	**0**	**0.0**	**21:37**	**13**	**0**	**1**	**1**	**0**	**0**	**0**	**0**	**24:39**
	Worcester Sharks	AHL	1	0	2	2	0																		
	NHL Totals		**163**	**5**	**35**	**40**	**42**	**3**	**0**	**0**	**138**	**3.6**		**0**	**0.0**	**21:54**	**24**	**0**	**2**	**2**	**2**	**0**	**0**	**0**	**23:50**

NHL All-Rookie Team (2007)

VOLCHENKOV, Anton

(vohl-chen-KAHF, AN-tawn) **OTT.**

Defense. Shoots left. 6'1", 232 lbs. Born, Moscow, USSR, February 25, 1982. Ottawa's 1st choice, 21st overall, in 2000 Entry Draft.

			Regular Season														Playoffs								
Season	Club	League	GP	G	A	Pts	PIM	PP	SH	GW	S	%	+/-	TF	F%	Min	GP	G	A	Pts	PIM	PP	SH	GW	Min
99-2000	HK Moscow 2	Russia-3	6	0	1	1	10	....	....	....	....	....	....	....	....	....	....	....	....	....	....	....	....	....	....
	HK Moscow	Russia-2	30	2	9	11	36	....	....	....	....	....	....	....	....	....	....	....	....	....	....	....	....	....	....
2000-01	Krylja Sovetov	Russia-2	34	3	4	7	56	....	....	....	....	....	....	....	....	....	....	....	....	....	....	....	....	....	....
2001-02	Krylja Sovetov 2	Russia-3	1	0	0	0	0	....	....	....	....	....	....	....	....	....	....	....	....	....	....	....	....	....	....
	Krylja Sovetov	Russia	47	4	16	20	50	....	....	....	....	....	....	....	....	....	3	0	0	0	29	....	....	....	....
2002-03	**Ottawa**	**NHL**	**57**	**3**	**13**	**16**	**40**	**0**	**0**	**0**	**75**	**4.0**	**–4**	**0**	**0.0**	**15:30**	**17**	**1**	**1**	**2**	**4**	**0**	**0**	**1**	**13:31**
2003-04	**Ottawa**	**NHL**	**19**	**1**	**2**	**3**	**8**	**0**	**0**	**0**	**15**	**6.7**	**1**	**0**	**0.0**	**13:04**	**5**	**0**	**0**	**0**	**6**	**0**	**0**	**0**	**11:52**
2004-05	Binghamton	AHL	69	10	35	45	62	....	....	....	....	....	....	....	....	....	6	0	3	3	0	....	....	....	....
2005-06	**Ottawa**	**NHL**	**75**	**4**	**13**	**17**	**53**	**0**	**0**	**0**	**82**	**4.9**	**21**	**0**	**0.0**	**18:03**	**9**	**0**	**4**	**4**	**8**	**0**	**0**	**0**	**13:53**
	Russia	Olympics	8	0	0	0	2	....	....	....	....	....	....	....	....	....	....	....	....	....	....	....	....	....	....
2006-07	**Ottawa**	**NHL**	**78**	**1**	**18**	**19**	**67**	**0**	**0**	**0**	**85**	**1.2**	**37**	**0**	**0.0**	**21:17**	**20**	**2**	**4**	**6**	**24**	**0**	**0**	**1**	**23:19**
2007-08	**Ottawa**	**NHL**	**67**	**1**	**14**	**15**	**55**	**0**	**0**	**1**	**71**	**1.4**	**14**	**0**	**0.0**	**20:31**	**4**	**0**	**1**	**1**	**2**	**0**	**0**	**0**	**17:11**
	NHL Totals		**296**	**10**	**60**	**70**	**223**	**0**	**0**	**1**	**328**	**3.0**		**0**	**0.0**	**18:39**	**55**	**3**	**10**	**13**	**44**	**0**	**0**	**2**	**17:16**

• Missed majority of 2003-04 season recovering from shoulder injury suffered in game vs. Boston, December 8, 2003.

VOROBIEV, Pavel

(voh-roh-BEE-ehf, PAH-vehl) **CHI.**

Right wing. Shoots right. 6', 195 lbs. Born, Karaganda, USSR, May 5, 1982. Chicago's 2nd choice, 11th overall, in 2000 Entry Draft.

			Regular Season														Playoffs								
Season	Club	League	GP	G	A	Pts	PIM	PP	SH	GW	S	%	+/-	TF	F%	Min	GP	G	A	Pts	PIM	PP	SH	GW	Min
1996-97	Molot Perm 2	Russia-3	2	0	0	0	0	....	....	....	....	....	....	....	....	....	....	....	....	....	....	....	....	....	....
1997-98	Yaroslavl 2	Russia-2	16	2	0	2	6	....	....	....	....	....	....	....	....	....	....	....	....	....	....	....	....	....	....
1998-99	Yaroslavl 2	Russia-3	17	0	1	1	0	....	....	....	....	....	....	....	....	....	....	....	....	....	....	....	....	....	....
99-2000	Yaroslavl 2	Russia-3	40	19	15	34	20	....	....	....	....	....	....	....	....	....	....	....	....	....	....	....	....	....	....
	Yaroslavl	Russia	8	2	0	2	4	....	....	....	....	....	....	....	....	....	10	2	2	4	0	....	....	....	....
2000-01	Yaroslavl	Russia	36	8	8	16	28	....	....	....	....	....	....	....	....	....	10	4	1	5	8	....	....	....	....
2001-02	Yaroslavl	Russia	9	3	2	5	6	....	....	....	....	....	....	....	....	....	7	0	0	0	4	....	....	....	....
2002-03	Yaroslavl	Russia	44	10	18	28	10	....	....	....	....	....	....	....	....	....	7	0	1	1	2	....	....	....	....
2003-04	**Chicago**	**NHL**	**18**	**1**	**3**	**4**	**4**	**1**	**0**	**1**	**20**	**5.0**	**1**	**0**	**0.0**	**12:48**	....	....	....	....	....	....	....	....	....
	Norfolk Admirals	AHL	57	13	16	29	8	....	....	....	....	....	....	....	....	....	4	0	0	0	0	....	....	....	....
2004-05	Norfolk Admirals	AHL	79	19	25	44	48	....	....	....	....	....	....	....	....	....	6	2	1	3	4	....	....	....	....
2005-06	**Chicago**	**NHL**	**39**	**9**	**12**	**21**	**34**	**2**	**0**	**0**	**87**	**10.3**	**–2**	**8**	**37.5**	**14:18**	....	....	....	....	....	....	....	....	....
	Norfolk Admirals	AHL	32	9	16	25	23	....	....	....	....	....	....	....	....	....	4	1	2	3	0	....	....	....	....
2006-07	Mytischi	Russia	41	8	11	19	24	....	....	....	....	....	....	....	....	....	9	0	2	2	4	....	....	....	....
2007-08	Spartak Moscow	Russia	56	13	14	27	18	....	....	....	....	....	....	....	....	....	5	0	2	2	6	....	....	....	....
	NHL Totals		**57**	**10**	**15**	**25**	**38**	**3**	**0**	**1**	**107**	**9.3**		**8**	**37.5**	**13:50**	....	....	....	....	....	....	....	....	....

VOROS, Aaron

(VOH-ruhs, AIR-ruhn) **NYR**

Center. Shoots left. 6'3", 202 lbs. Born, Vancouver, B.C., July 2, 1981. New Jersey's 10th choice, 229th overall, in 2001 Entry Draft.

			Regular Season														Playoffs								
Season	Club	League	GP	G	A	Pts	PIM	PP	SH	GW	S	%	+/-	TF	F%	Min	GP	G	A	Pts	PIM	PP	SH	GW	Min
99-2000	Victoria Salsa	BCHL	58	14	21	35	285	....	....	....	....	....	....	....	....	....	....	....	....	....	....	....	....	....	....
2000-01	Victoria Salsa	BCHL	57	34	34	68	196	....	....	....	....	....	....	....	....	....	30	16	15	31	....	....	....	....	....
2001-02	Alaska	CCHA	37	18	12	30	*101	....	....	....	....	....	....	....	....	....	....	....	....	....	....	....	....	....	....
2002-03	Alaska	CCHA	16	2	5	7	42	....	....	....	....	....	....	....	....	....	....	....	....	....	....	....	....	....	....
2003-04	Alaska	CCHA	36	16	8	24	*132	....	....	....	....	....	....	....	....	....	....	....	....	....	....	....	....	....	....
	Albany River Rats	AHL	9	2	1	3	14	....	....	....	....	....	....	....	....	....	....	....	....	....	....	....	....	....	....
2004-05	Albany River Rats	AHL	71	11	17	28	220	....	....	....	....	....	....	....	....	....	....	....	....	....	....	....	....	....	....
2005-06	Albany River Rats	AHL	73	16	14	30	180	....	....	....	....	....	....	....	....	....	....	....	....	....	....	....	....	....	....
2006-07	Lowell Devils	AHL	39	9	8	17	111	....	....	....	....	....	....	....	....	....	....	....	....	....	....	....	....	....	....
	Houston Aeros	AHL	19	2	3	5	58	....	....	....	....	....	....	....	....	....	....	....	....	....	....	....	....	....	....
2007-08	**Minnesota**	**NHL**	**55**	**7**	**7**	**14**	**141**	**0**	**0**	**1**	**52**	**13.5**	**–7**	**15**	**20.0**	**9:11**	**5**	**1**	**0**	**1**	**16**	**0**	**0**	**0**	**10:39**
	Houston Aeros	AHL	12	4	4	8	46	....	....	....	....	....	....	....	....	....	....	....	....	....	....	....	....	....	....
	NHL Totals		**55**	**7**	**7**	**14**	**141**	**0**	**0**	**1**	**52**	**13.5**		**15**	**20.0**	**9:11**	**5**	**1**	**0**	**1**	**16**	**0**	**0**	**0**	**10:39**

CCHA All-Rookie Team (2002)

• Missed majority of 2002-03 season recovering from leg surgery, January 30, 2003. Traded to **Minnesota** by **New Jersey** for Minnesota's 7th round choice (Jean-Sebastien Berube) in 2008 Entry Draft, February 28, 2007. Signed as a free agent by **NY Rangers**, July 1, 2008.

VRBATA, Radim

(vuhr-BA-tuh, RA-dihm) **T.B.**

Right wing. Shoots right. 6'1", 190 lbs. Born, Mlada Boleslav, Czech., June 13, 1981. Colorado's 10th choice, 212th overall, in 1999 Entry Draft.

			Regular Season														Playoffs								
Season	Club	League	GP	G	A	Pts	PIM	PP	SH	GW	S	%	+/-	TF	F%	Min	GP	G	A	Pts	PIM	PP	SH	GW	Min
1997-98	Ml. Boleslav Jr.	CzRep-Jr.	35	42	31	73	4	....	....	....	....	....	....	....	....	....	....	....	....	....	....	....	....	....	....
1998-99	Hull Olympiques	QMJHL	54	22	38	60	16	....	....	....	....	....	....	....	....	....	23	6	13	19	6	....	....	....	....
99-2000	Hull Olympiques	QMJHL	58	29	45	74	26	....	....	....	....	....	....	....	....	....	15	3	9	12	8	....	....	....	....
2000-01	Shawinigan	QMJHL	55	56	64	120	67	....	....	....	....	....	....	....	....	....	10	4	7	11	4	....	....	....	....
	Hershey Bears	AHL	....	....	....	....	....	....	....	....	....	....	....	....	....	....	1	0	1	1	2	....	....	....	....
2001-02	**Colorado**	**NHL**	**52**	**18**	**12**	**30**	**14**	**6**	**0**	**3**	**112**	**16.1**	**7**	**8**	**37.5**	**14:32**	**9**	**0**	**0**	**0**	**0**	**0**	**0**	**0**	**13:05**
	Hershey Bears	AHL	20	8	14	22	8	....	....	....	....	....	....	....	....	....	....	....	....	....	....	....	....	....	....
2002-03	**Colorado**	**NHL**	**66**	**11**	**19**	**30**	**16**	**3**	**0**	**4**	**171**	**6.4**	**0**	**14**	**50.0**	**13:55**	....	....	....	....	....	....	....	....	....
	Carolina	**NHL**	**10**	**5**	**0**	**5**	**2**	**3**	**0**	**0**	**44**	**11.4**	**–7**	**15**	**46.7**	**19:00**	....	....	....	....	....	....	....	....	....
2003-04	**Carolina**	**NHL**	**80**	**12**	**13**	**25**	**24**	**4**	**0**	**2**	**195**	**6.2**	**–10**	**21**	**38.1**	**13:42**	....	....	....	....	....	....	....	....	....
2004-05	Liberec	CzRep	45	18	21	39	91	....	....	....	....	....	....	....	....	....	12	3	2	5	0	....	....	....	....
2005-06	**Carolina**	**NHL**	**16**	**2**	**3**	**5**	**6**	**1**	**0**	**0**	**38**	**5.3**	**0**	**3**	**33.3**	**12:37**	....	....	....	....	....	....	....	....	....
	Chicago	**NHL**	**45**	**13**	**21**	**34**	**16**	**5**	**0**	**0**	**147**	**8.8**	**4**	**6**	**50.0**	**15:43**	....	....	....	....	....	....	....	....	....
2006-07	**Chicago**	**NHL**	**77**	**14**	**27**	**41**	**26**	**5**	**0**	**2**	**215**	**6.5**	**–4**	**12**	**33.3**	**16:53**	....	....	....	....	....	....	....	....	....
2007-08	**Phoenix**	**NHL**	**76**	**27**	**29**	**56**	**14**	**7**	**3**	**5**	**246**	**11.0**	**6**	**19**	**36.8**	**18:12**	....	....	....	....	....	....	....	....	....
	NHL Totals		**422**	**102**	**124**	**226**	**118**	**34**	**3**	**16**	**1168**	**8.7**		**98**	**40.8**	**15:32**	**9**	**0**	**0**	**0**	**0**	**0**	**0**	**0**	**13:05**

QMJHL First All-Star Team (2001)

Traded to **Carolina** by **Colorado** for Bates Battaglia, March 11, 2003. Signed as a free agent by **Liberec** (CzRep), September 4, 2004. Traded to **Chicago** by **Carolina** for Chicago's 4th round choice (later traded to St. Louis - St. Louis selected Cade Fairchild) in 2007 Entry Draft, December 29, 2005. Traded to **Phoenix** by **Chicago** for Kevyn Adams, August 11, 2007. Signed as a free agent by **Tampa Bay**, July 1, 2008.

VYBORNY, David

(vih-BOHR-nee, DAY-vihd)

Right wing. Shoots left. 5'10", 181 lbs. Born, Jihlava, Czech., January 22, 1975. Edmonton's 3rd choice, 33rd overall, in 1993 Entry Draft.

			Regular Season														Playoffs								
Season	Club	League	GP	G	A	Pts	PIM	PP	SH	GW	S	%	+/-	TF	F%	Min	GP	G	A	Pts	PIM	PP	SH	GW	Min
1991-92	HC Sparta Praha	Czech	32	6	9	15	2	....	....	....	....	....	....	....	....	....	....	....	....	....	....	....	....	....	....
1992-93	HC Sparta Praha	Czech	52	20	24	44	....	....	....	....	....	....	....	....	....	....	....	....	....	....	....	....	....	....	....
1993-94	HC Sparta Praha	CzRep	44	15	20	35	0	....	....	....	....	....	....	....	....	....	6	4	7	11	0	....	....	....	....
1994-95	Cape Breton	AHL	76	23	38	61	30	....	....	....	....	....	....	....	....	....	....	....	....	....	....	....	....	....	....
1995-96	HC Sparta Praha	CzRep	40	12	18	30	....	....	....	....	....	....	....	....	....	....	12	6	5	11	....	....	....	....	....
1996-97	HC Sparta Praha	CzRep	47	20	29	49	14	....	....	....	....	....	....	....	....	....	10	7	7	14	6	....	....	....	....
1997-98	MoDo	Sweden	45	16	21	37	34	....	....	....	....	....	....	....	....	....	9	0	2	2	2	....	....	....	....
1998-99	HC Sparta Praha	CzRep	52	24	*46	*70	22	....	....	....	....	....	....	....	....	....	8	1	3	4	....	....	....	....	....
99-2000	HC Sparta Praha	CzRep	50	25	38	63	30	....	....	....	....	....	....	....	....	....	9	3	*8	*11	4	....	....	....	....
2000-01	**Columbus**	**NHL**	**79**	**13**	**19**	**32**	**22**	**5**	**0**	**1**	**125**	**10.4**	**–9**	**36**	**44.4**	**15:25**	....	....	....	....	....	....	....	....	....
2001-02	**Columbus**	**NHL**	**75**	**13**	**18**	**31**	**6**	**6**	**0**	**2**	**103**	**12.6**	**–14**	**25**	**44.0**	**15:27**	....	....	....	....	....	....	....	....	....
2002-03	**Columbus**	**NHL**	**79**	**20**	**26**	**46**	**16**	**4**	**1**	**4**	**125**	**16.0**	**12**	**46**	**32.6**	**16:20**	....	....	....	....	....	....	....	....	....
2003-04	**Columbus**	**NHL**	**82**	**22**	**31**	**53**	**40**	**8**	**4**	**2**	**158**	**13.9**	**–26**	**97**	**21.7**	**20:23**	....	....	....	....	....	....	....	....	....
2004-05	HC Sparta Praha	CzRep	51	12	34	46	10	....	....	....	....	....	....	....	....	....	5	2	5	7	4	....	....	....	....
2005-06	**Columbus**	**NHL**	**80**	**22**	**43**	**65**	**50**	**5**	**2**	**6**	**145**	**15.2**	**–9**	**292**	**30.1**	**20:41**	....	....	....	....	....	....	....	....	....
	Czech Republic	Olympics	8	1	3	4	0	....	....	....	....	....	....	....	....	....	....	....	....	....	....	....	....	....	....
2006-07	**Columbus**	**NHL**	**82**	**16**	**48**	**64**	**60**	**6**	**0**	**2**	**158**	**10.1**	**6**	**269**	**37.9**	**20:20**	....	....	....	....	....	....	....	....	....
2007-08	**Columbus**	**NHL**	**66**	**7**	**19**	**26**	**34**	**2**	**0**	**0**	**106**	**6.6**	**–8**	**57**	**36.8**	**15:29**	....	....	....	....	....	....	....	....	....
	NHL Totals		**543**	**113**	**204**	**317**	**228**	**36**	**7**	**17**	**920**	**12.3**		**822**	**33.3**	**17:50**	....	....	....	....	....	....	....	....	....

Signed as a free agent by **Columbus**, June 8, 2000. Signed as a free agent by **Sparta Praha** (CzRep), August 9, 2004.

WAGNER, Steve

(WAG-nuhr, STEEV) **ST.L.**

Defense. Shoots left. 6'2", 190 lbs. Born, Grand Rapids, MN, March 6, 1984.

			Regular Season														Playoffs								
Season	Club	League	GP	G	A	Pts	PIM	PP	SH	GW	S	%	+/-	TF	F%	Min	GP	G	A	Pts	PIM	PP	SH	GW	Min
2002-03	Des Moines	USHL	14	0	1	1	17	....	....	....	....	....	....	....	....	....	....	....	....	....	....	....	....	....	....
	Tri-City Storm	USHL	27	0	5	5	52	....	....	....	....	....	....	....	....	....	3	1	0	1	0	....	....	....	....
2003-04	Tri-City Storm	USHL	43	3	19	22	52	....	....	....	....	....	....	....	....	....	9	0	4	4	13	....	....	....	....
2004-05	Minnesota State	WCHA	37	1	9	10	40	....	....	....	....	....	....	....	....	....	....	....	....	....	....	....	....	....	....
2005-06	Minnesota State	WCHA	38	5	11	16	53	....	....	....	....	....	....	....	....	....	....	....	....	....	....	....	....	....	....
2006-07	Minnesota State	WCHA	38	6	23	29	63	....	....	....	....	....	....	....	....	....	....	....	....	....	....	....	....	....	....
	Peoria Rivermen	AHL	14	1	2	3	8	....	....	....	....	....	....	....	....	....	....	....	....	....	....	....	....	....	....
2007-08	**St. Louis**	**NHL**	**24**	**2**	**6**	**8**	**8**	**1**	**0**	**0**	**25**	**8.0**	**–4**	**0**	**0.0**	**18:29**	....	....	....	....	....	....	....	....	....
	Peoria Rivermen	AHL	23	5	7	12	16	....	....	....	....	....	....	....	....	....	....	....	....	....	....	....	....	....	....
	NHL Totals		**24**	**2**	**6**	**8**	**8**	**1**	**0**	**0**	**25**	**8.0**		**0**	**0.0**	**18:29**	....	....	....	....	....	....	....	....	....

Signed as a free agent by **St. Louis**, March 20, 2007.

WALKER, Matt

(WAH-kuhr, MAT) **CHI.**

Defense. Shoots right. 6'3", 213 lbs. Born, Beaverlodge, Alta., April 7, 1980. St. Louis' 3rd choice, 83rd overall, in 1998 Entry Draft.

Season	Club	League	GP	G	A	Pts	PIM	PP	SH	GW	S	%	+/-	TF	F%	Min	GP	G	A	Pts	PIM	PP	SH	GW	Min
1996-97	Grand Prairie	AAHA	68	22	62	74	186	....	....	....	....	....	....	....	....	....	....	....	....	....	....	....	....	....	....
1997-98	Portland	WHL	64	2	13	15	124	....	....	....	....	....	....	....	....	....	16	0	0	0	21	....	....	....	....
1998-99	Portland	WHL	64	1	10	11	151	....	....	....	....	....	....	....	....	....	4	0	1	1	6	....	....	....	....
99-2000	Portland	WHL	38	2	7	9	97	....	....	....	....	....	....	....	....	....	....	....	....	....	....	....	....	....	....
	Kootenay Ice	WHL	31	4	19	23	53	....	....	....	....	....	....	....	....	....	21	5	13	18	24	....	....	....	....
2000-01	Worcester IceCats	AHL	61	4	8	12	131	....	....	....	....	....	....	....	....	....	11	0	0	0	6	....	....	....	....
	Peoria Rivermen	ECHL	8	1	0	1	70	....	....	....	....	....	....	....	....	....	....	....	....	....	....	....	....	....	....
2001-02	Worcester IceCats	AHL	49	2	11	13	164	....	....	....	....	....	....	....	....	....	3	0	0	0	8	....	....	....	....
2002-03	**St. Louis**	**NHL**	**16**	**0**	**1**	**1**	**38**	**0**	**0**	**0**	**13**	**0.0**	**0**	**1**	**100.0**	**11:09**	....	....	....	....	....	....	....	....	....
	Worcester IceCats	AHL	40	1	8	9	58	....	....	....	....	....	....	....	....	....	....	....	....	....	....	....	....	....	....
2003-04	**St. Louis**	**NHL**	**14**	**0**	**1**	**1**	**25**	**0**	**0**	**0**	**8**	**0.0**	**0**	**0**	**0.0**	**11:23**	**4**	**0**	**0**	**0**	**0**	**0**	**0**	**0**	**9:43**
	Worcester IceCats	AHL	4	0	1	1	7	....	....	....	....	....	....	....	....	....	....	....	....	....	....	....	....	....	....
2004-05	Worcester IceCats	AHL	20	2	4	6	44	....	....	....	....	....	....	....	....	....	....	....	....	....	....	....	....	....	....
2005-06	**St. Louis**	**NHL**	**54**	**0**	**2**	**2**	**79**	**0**	**0**	**0**	**59**	**0.0**	**–7**	**0**	**0.0**	**14:15**	....	....	....	....	....	....	....	....	....
2006-07	**St. Louis**	**NHL**	**48**	**0**	**5**	**5**	**72**	**0**	**0**	**0**	**34**	**0.0**	**7**	**0**	**0.0**	**15:15**	....	....	....	....	....	....	....	....	....
	Peoria Rivermen	AHL	2	0	1	1	0	....	....	....	....	....	....	....	....	....	....	....	....	....	....	....	....	....	....
2007-08	**St. Louis**	**NHL**	**43**	**1**	**1**	**2**	**61**	**0**	**0**	**0**	**47**	**2.1**	**–3**	**0**	**0.0**	**15:54**	....	....	....	....	....	....	....	....	....
	NHL Totals		**175**	**1**	**10**	**11**	**275**	**0**	**0**	**0**	**161**	**0.6**		**1**	**100.0**	**14:25**	**4**	**0**	**0**	**0**	**0**	**0**	**0**	**0**	**9:43**

• Missed majority of 2003-04 season recovering from groin injury suffered in training camp, September 23, 2003. Signed as a free agent by **Chicago**, July 7, 2008.

WALKER, Scott

(WAH-kuhr, SKAWT) **CAR.**

Right wing. Shoots right. 5'10", 196 lbs. Born, Cambridge, Ont., July 19, 1973. Vancouver's 4th choice, 124th overall, in 1993 Entry Draft.

Season	Club	League	GP	G	A	Pts	PIM	PP	SH	GW	S	%	+/-	TF	F%	Min	GP	G	A	Pts	PIM	PP	SH	GW	Min
1989-90	Kitchener	OHA-B	6	0	5	5	4	....	....	....	....	....	....	....	....	....	....	....	....	....	....	....	....	....	....
	Cambridge	OHA-B	27	7	22	29	87	....	....	....	....	....	....	....	....	....	....	....	....	....	....	....	....	....	....
1990-91	Cambridge	OHA-B	45	10	27	37	241	....	....	....	....	....	....	....	....	....	....	....	....	....	....	....	....	....	....
1991-92	Owen Sound	OHL	53	7	31	38	128	....	....	....	....	....	....	....	....	....	5	0	7	7	8	....	....	....	....
1992-93	Owen Sound	OHL	57	23	68	91	110	....	....	....	....	....	....	....	....	....	8	1	5	6	16	....	....	....	....
1993-94	Hamilton	AHL	77	10	29	39	272	....	....	....	....	....	....	....	....	....	4	0	1	1	25	....	....	....	....
1994-95	Syracuse Crunch	AHL	74	14	38	52	334	....	....	....	....	....	....	....	....	....	....	....	....	....	....	....	....	....	....
	Vancouver	**NHL**	**11**	**0**	**1**	**1**	**33**	**0**	**0**	**0**	**8**	**0.0**	**0**	....	....	....	....	....	....	....	....	....	....	....	....
1995-96	**Vancouver**	**NHL**	**63**	**4**	**8**	**12**	**137**	**0**	**1**	**1**	**45**	**8.9**	**–7**	....	....	....	....	....	....	....	....	....	....	....	....
	Syracuse Crunch	AHL	15	3	12	15	52	....	....	....	....	....	....	....	....	....	16	9	8	17	39	....	....	....	....
1996-97	**Vancouver**	**NHL**	**64**	**3**	**15**	**18**	**132**	**0**	**0**	**0**	**55**	**5.5**	**2**	....	....	....	....	....	....	....	....	....	....	....	....
1997-98	**Vancouver**	**NHL**	**59**	**3**	**10**	**13**	**164**	**0**	**1**	**1**	**40**	**7.5**	**–8**	....	....	....	....	....	....	....	....	....	....	....	....
1998-99	**Nashville**	**NHL**	**71**	**15**	**25**	**40**	**103**	**0**	**1**	**2**	**96**	**15.6**	**0**	**265**	**48.3**	**16:21**	....	....	....	....	....	....	....	....	....
99-2000	**Nashville**	**NHL**	**69**	**7**	**21**	**28**	**90**	**0**	**1**	**0**	**98**	**7.1**	**–16**	**30**	**36.7**	**15:49**	....	....	....	....	....	....	....	....	....
2000-01	**Nashville**	**NHL**	**74**	**25**	**29**	**54**	**66**	**9**	**3**	**1**	**159**	**15.7**	**–2**	**541**	**51.4**	**19:17**	....	....	....	....	....	....	....	....	....
2001-02	**Nashville**	**NHL**	**28**	**4**	**5**	**9**	**18**	**1**	**0**	**0**	**46**	**8.7**	**–13**	**149**	**38.9**	**18:38**	....	....	....	....	....	....	....	....	....
2002-03	**Nashville**	**NHL**	**60**	**15**	**18**	**33**	**58**	**7**	**0**	**5**	**124**	**12.1**	**2**	**336**	**49.1**	**19:50**	....	....	....	....	....	....	....	....	....
2003-04	**Nashville**	**NHL**	**75**	**25**	**42**	**67**	**94**	**9**	**3**	**3**	**157**	**15.9**	**4**	**367**	**41.4**	**20:03**	**6**	**0**	**1**	**1**	**6**	**0**	**0**	**0**	**20:10**
2004-05	Cambridge	OHA-Sr.	5	2	6	8	4	....	....	....	....	....	....	....	....	....	....	....	....	....	....	....	....	....	....
	Dundas	OHA-Sr.	3	3	2	5	8	....	....	....	....	....	....	....	....	....	....	....	....	....	....	....	....	....	....
2005-06	**Nashville**	**NHL**	**33**	**5**	**11**	**16**	**36**	**1**	**0**	**0**	**57**	**8.8**	**2**	**87**	**44.8**	**17:23**	**5**	**0**	**0**	**0**	**6**	**0**	**0**	**0**	**16:01**
2006-07	**Carolina**	**NHL**	**81**	**21**	**30**	**51**	**45**	**6**	**0**	**6**	**183**	**11.5**	**–10**	**95**	**42.1**	**16:10**	....	....	....	....	....	....	....	....	....
2007-08	**Carolina**	**NHL**	**58**	**14**	**18**	**32**	**115**	**4**	**2**	**4**	**122**	**11.5**	**–3**	**48**	**43.8**	**16:37**	....	....	....	....	....	....	....	....	....
	NHL Totals		**746**	**141**	**233**	**374**	**1091**	**37**	**12**	**23**	**1190**	**11.8**		**1918**	**46.5**	**17:45**	**11**	**0**	**1**	**1**	**12**	**0**	**0**	**0**	**18:16**

OHL Second All-Star Team (1993)

Claimed by **Nashville** from **Vancouver** in Expansion Draft, June 26, 1998. Signed as a free agent by **Cambridge** (OHA-Sr.), October 21, 2004. Signed as a free agent by **Dundas** (OHA-Sr.), February 10, 2005. • Missed majority of 2005-06 season recovering from sports hernia (October 25, 2005 vs. Chicago) and wrist (February 6, 2006 at Dallas) injuries. Traded to **Carolina** by **Nashville** for Josef Vasicek, July 18, 2006.

WALLIN, Niclas

(WAHL-ihn, NIHK-luhs) **CAR.**

Defense. Shoots left. 6'3", 220 lbs. Born, Boden, Sweden, February 20, 1975. Carolina's 3rd choice, 97th overall, in 2000 Entry Draft.

Season	Club	League	GP	G	A	Pts	PIM	PP	SH	GW	S	%	+/-	TF	F%	Min	GP	G	A	Pts	PIM	PP	SH	GW	Min
1994-95	Bodens IK	Swe-Jr.	30	2	13	15	125	....	....	....	....	....	....	....	....	....	....	....	....	....	....	....	....	....	....
	Bodens IK	Sweden-2	13	0	0	0	0	....	....	....	....	....	....	....	....	....	2	0	0	0	0	....	....	....	....
1995-96	Bodens IK	Swe-Jr.	2	2	2	4	0	....	....	....	....	....	....	....	....	....	....	....	....	....	....	....	....	....	....
	Bodens IK	Sweden-2	30	2	7	9	26	....	....	....	....	....	....	....	....	....	2	0	1	1	2	....	....	....	....
1996-97	Brynas IF Gavle	Sweden	47	1	1	2	14	....	....	....	....	....	....	....	....	....	....	....	....	....	....	....	....	....	....
1997-98	Brynas IF Gavle	Sweden	44	2	3	5	57	....	....	....	....	....	....	....	....	....	3	0	1	1	4	....	....	....	....
1998-99	Brynas IF Gavle	Sweden	46	2	4	6	52	....	....	....	....	....	....	....	....	....	14	0	1	1	8	....	....	....	....
99-2000	Brynas IF Gavle	Sweden	48	7	9	16	73	....	....	....	....	....	....	....	....	....	11	2	1	3	14	....	....	....	....
	Brynas IF Gavle	EuroHL	5	1	1	2	10	....	....	....	....	....	....	....	....	....	....	....	....	....	....	....	....	....	....
2000-01	**Carolina**	**NHL**	**37**	**2**	**3**	**5**	**21**	**0**	**0**	**0**	**19**	**10.5**	**–11**	**0**	**0.0**	**14:57**	**3**	**0**	**0**	**0**	**2**	**0**	**0**	**0**	**19:10**
	Cincinnati	IHL	8	1	2	3	4	....	....	....	....	....	....	....	....	....	3	0	0	0	2	....	....	....	....
2001-02	**Carolina**	**NHL**	**52**	**1**	**2**	**3**	**36**	**0**	**0**	**0**	**33**	**3.0**	**1**	**0**	**0.0**	**12:12**	**23**	**2**	**1**	**3**	**12**	**0**	**0**	**2**	**15:26**
2002-03	**Carolina**	**NHL**	**77**	**2**	**8**	**10**	**71**	**0**	**0**	**2**	**69**	**2.9**	**–19**	**0**	**0.0**	**16:12**	....	....	....	....	....	....	....	....	....
2003-04	**Carolina**	**NHL**	**57**	**3**	**7**	**10**	**51**	**0**	**0**	**0**	**74**	**4.1**	**–8**	**0**	**0.0**	**18:40**	....	....	....	....	....	....	....	....	....
2004-05	Lulea HF	Sweden	39	6	7	13	89	....	....	....	....	....	....	....	....	....	3	0	1	1	6	....	....	....	....
2005-06 ♦	**Carolina**	**NHL**	**50**	**4**	**4**	**8**	**42**	**0**	**0**	**0**	**44**	**9.1**	**2**	**0**	**0.0**	**16:50**	**25**	**1**	**4**	**5**	**14**	**0**	**0**	**1**	**16:39**
2006-07	**Carolina**	**NHL**	**67**	**2**	**8**	**10**	**48**	**0**	**0**	**0**	**76**	**2.6**	**–2**	**0**	**0.0**	**18:33**	....	....	....	....	....	....	....	....	....
2007-08	**Carolina**	**NHL**	**66**	**2**	**6**	**8**	**54**	**0**	**0**	**0**	**60**	**3.3**	**–18**	**1**	**0.0**	**18:08**	....	....	....	....	....	....	....	....	....
	NHL Totals		**406**	**16**	**38**	**54**	**323**	**0**	**0**	**2**	**375**	**4.3**		**1**	**0.0**	**16:42**	**51**	**3**	**5**	**8**	**28**	**0**	**0**	**3**	**16:15**

Signed as a free agent by **Lulea** (Sweden), September 19, 2004.

WALLIN, Rickard

(WAHL-ihn, RIH-kahrd)

Center. Shoots left. 6'2", 185 lbs. Born, Stockholm, Sweden, April 19, 1980. Phoenix's 8th choice, 160th overall, in 1998 Entry Draft.

Season	Club	League	GP	G	A	Pts	PIM	PP	SH	GW	S	%	+/-	TF	F%	Min	GP	G	A	Pts	PIM	PP	SH	GW	Min
1996-97	Vasteras IK Jr.	Swe-Jr.	26	3	3	6	....	....	....	....	....	....	....	....	....	....	....	....	....	....	....	....	....	....	....
1997-98	Farjestad Jr.	Swe-Jr.	29	20	30	50	32	....	....	....	....	....	....	....	....	....	2	1	1	2	2	....	....	....	....
1998-99	Farjestad Jr.	Swe-Jr.	21	11	15	26	30	....	....	....	....	....	....	....	....	....	....	....	....	....	....	....	....	....	....
	Farjestad	Sweden	5	0	0	0	0	....	....	....	....	....	....	....	....	....	....	....	....	....	....	....	....	....	....
99-2000	IF Troja-Ljungby	Sweden-2	46	15	22	37	54	....	....	....	....	....	....	....	....	....	....	....	....	....	....	....	....	....	....
2000-01	Farjestad	Sweden	47	9	22	31	24	....	....	....	....	....	....	....	....	....	16	11	3	14	4	....	....	....	....
2001-02	Farjestad	Sweden	50	12	31	43	56	....	....	....	....	....	....	....	....	....	10	4	9	13	8	....	....	....	....
2002-03	**Minnesota**	**NHL**	**4**	**1**	**0**	**1**	**0**	**0**	**0**	**1**	**1**	**100.0**	**1**	**28**	**53.6**	**7:44**	....	....	....	....	....	....	....	....	....
	Houston Aeros	AHL	52	13	22	35	70	....	....	....	....	....	....	....	....	....	23	4	11	15	22	....	....	....	....
2003-04	**Minnesota**	**NHL**	**15**	**5**	**4**	**9**	**14**	**3**	**0**	**1**	**16**	**31.3**	**1**	**189**	**45.5**	**14:20**	....	....	....	....	....	....	....	....	....
	Houston Aeros	AHL	47	14	18	32	36	....	....	....	....	....	....	....	....	....	2	0	0	0	2	....	....	....	....
2004-05	Houston Aeros	AHL	79	12	31	43	61	....	....	....	....	....	....	....	....	....	5	1	0	1	29	....	....	....	....

			Regular Season														Playoffs								
Season	Club	League	GP	G	A	Pts	PIM	PP	SH	GW	S	%	+/-	TF	F%	Min	GP	G	A	Pts	PIM	PP	SH	GW	Min
2005-06	Farjestad	Sweden	50	11	19	30	82	....	....	....	....	....	....	....	....	....	18	6	3	9	28	....	....	....	....
2006-07	HC Lugano	Swiss	44	14	35	49	87	....	....	....	....	....	....	....	....	....	6	3	3	6	16	....	....	....	....
2007-08	Farjestad	Sweden	55	17	23	40	54	....	....	....	....	....	....	....	....	....	12	1	5	6	18	....	....	....	....
	NHL Totals		**19**	**6**	**4**	**10**	**14**	**3**	**0**	**2**	**17**	**35.3**		**217**	**46.5**	**12:56**	....	....	....	....	....	....	....	....	....

Rights traded to **Minnesota** by **Phoenix** for Joe Juneau, June 23, 2000. Reassigned to **Farjestad** (Sweden) by **Minnesota**, September 22, 2005. Signed as a free agent by **Lugano** (Swiss), July 23, 2006.

WALSER, Derrick

(WAHL-zuhr, DAIR-ihk)

Defense. Shoots left. 5'10", 190 lbs. Born, New Glasgow, N.S., May 12, 1978.

Season	Club	League	GP	G	A	Pts	PIM	PP	SH	GW	S	%	+/-	TF	F%	Min	GP	G	A	Pts	PIM	PP	SH	GW	Min
1994-95	Beauport	QMJHL	48	4	18	22	34	....	....	....	....	....	....	....	....	....	12	2	5	7	2	....	....	....	....
1995-96	Beauport	QMJHL	69	9	31	40	56	....	....	....	....	....	....	....	....	....	20	2	11	13	16	....	....	....	....
1996-97	Beauport	QMJHL	37	13	25	38	26	....	....	....	....	....	....	....	....	....	....	....	....	....	....	....	....	....	....
	Rimouski Oceanic	QMJHL	31	15	30	45	44	....	....	....	....	....	....	....	....	....	4	2	2	4	6	....	....	....	....
1997-98	Rimouski Oceanic	QMJHL	70	41	69	110	135	....	....	....	....	....	....	....	....	....	18	10	*26	36	49	....	....	....	....
1998-99	Saint John Flames	AHL	40	3	7	10	24	....	....	....	....	....	....	....	....	....	....	....	....	....	....	....	....	....	....
	Johnstown Chiefs	ECHL	24	8	12	20	29	....	....	....	....	....	....	....	....	....	....	....	....	....	....	....	....	....	....
99-2000	Saint John Flames	AHL	14	2	3	5	10	....	....	....	....	....	....	....	....	....	....	....	....	....	....	....	....	....	....
	Johnstown Chiefs	ECHL	54	17	26	43	104	....	....	....	....	....	....	....	....	....	7	3	3	6	8	....	....	....	....
2000-01	Saint John Flames	AHL	76	19	36	55	36	....	....	....	....	....	....	....	....	....	19	7	9	16	14	....	....	....	....
2001-02	**Columbus**	**NHL**	**2**	**1**	**0**	**1**	**0**	**0**	**0**	**0**	**2**	**50.0**	**–2**	**0**	**0.0**	**16:18**	....	....	....	....	....	....	....	....	....
	Syracuse Crunch	AHL	73	23	38	61	70	....	....	....	....	....	....	....	....	....	10	1	5	6	12	....	....	....	....
2002-03	**Columbus**	**NHL**	**53**	**4**	**13**	**17**	**34**	**3**	**0**	**2**	**86**	**4.7**	**–9**	**1**	**100.0**	**14:52**	....	....	....	....	....	....	....	....	....
	Syracuse Crunch	AHL	28	7	14	21	30	....	....	....	....	....	....	....	....	....	....	....	....	....	....	....	....	....	....
2003-04	**Columbus**	**NHL**	**27**	**1**	**8**	**9**	**22**	**1**	**0**	**0**	**35**	**2.9**	**–6**	**0**	**0.0**	**18:23**	....	....	....	....	....	....	....	....	....
	Syracuse Crunch	AHL	48	10	26	36	82	....	....	....	....	....	....	....	....	....	3	1	1	2	4	....	....	....	....
2004-05	Eisbaren Berlin	Germany	50	9	14	23	143	....	....	....	....	....	....	....	....	....	12	4	4	8	20	....	....	....	....
2005-06	Eisbaren Berlin	Germany	48	19	24	43	120	....	....	....	....	....	....	....	....	....	11	6	1	7	20	....	....	....	....
2006-07	Albany River Rats	AHL	6	0	1	1	4	....	....	....	....	....	....	....	....	....	....	....	....	....	....	....	....	....	....
	Columbus	**NHL**	**9**	**2**	**0**	**2**	**0**	**2**	**0**	**0**	**10**	**20.0**	**–1**	**0**	**0.0**	**12:14**	....	....	....	....	....	....	....	....	....
	Syracuse Crunch	AHL	49	9	27	36	59	....	....	....	....	....	....	....	....	....	....	....	....	....	....	....	....	....	....
2007-08	Toronto Marlies	AHL	77	16	29	45	82	....	....	....	....	....	....	....	....	....	17	2	5	7	30	....	....	....	....
	NHL Totals		**91**	**8**	**21**	**29**	**56**	**6**	**0**	**2**	**133**	**6.0**		**1**	**100.0**	**15:41**	....	....	....	....	....	....	....	....	....

QMJHL First All-Star Team (1997, 1998) • Emile Bouchard Trophy (Top Defenseman – QMJHL) (1998) • Canadian Major Junior First All-Star Team (1998) • Canadian Major Junior Defenseman of the Year (1998)

Signed as a free agent by **Calgary**, October 16, 1998. Signed as a free agent by **Columbus**, September 17, 2001. Signed as a free agent by **Berlin** (Germany), May 13, 2004. Rights traded to **Carolina** by **Columbus** with Columbus' 4th round choice (later traded to Toronto - Toronto selected James Reimer) in 2006 Entry Draft for Carolina's 4th round choice (Jared Boll) in 2005 Entry Draft, July 30, 2005. Traded to **Columbus** by **Carolina** for Mark Flood, November 29, 2006. Signed a free agent by **Toronto**, July 18, 2007.

WALTER, Ben

(WAHL-tuhr, BEHN) **NYI**

Center. Shoots left. 6'1", 195 lbs. Born, Beaconsfield, Que., May 11, 1984. Boston's 5th choice, 160th overall, in 2004 Entry Draft.

Season	Club	League	GP	G	A	Pts	PIM	PP	SH	GW	S	%	+/-	TF	F%	Min	GP	G	A	Pts	PIM	PP	SH	GW	Min
2000-01	Langley Hornets	BCHL	50	8	22	30	19	....	....	....	....	....	....	....	....	....	....	....	....	....	....	....	....	....	....
2001-02	Langley Hornets	BCHL	50	29	47	76	29	....	....	....	....	....	....	....	....	....	....	....	....	....	....	....	....	....	....
2002-03	U. Mass-Lowell	H-East	35	5	12	17	12	....	....	....	....	....	....	....	....	....	....	....	....	....	....	....	....	....	....
2003-04	U. Mass-Lowell	H-East	36	18	16	34	18	....	....	....	....	....	....	....	....	....	....	....	....	....	....	....	....	....	....
2004-05	U. Mass-Lowell	H-East	36	*26	13	39	28	....	....	....	....	....	....	....	....	....	....	....	....	....	....	....	....	....	....
2005-06	**Boston**	**NHL**	**6**	**0**	**0**	**0**	**4**	**0**	**0**	**0**	**6**	**0.0**	**2**	**32**	**53.1**	**11:49**	....	....	....	....	....	....	....	....	....
	Providence Bruins	AHL	62	16	25	41	33	....	....	....	....	....	....	....	....	....	3	2	0	2	2	....	....	....	....
2006-07	**Boston**	**NHL**	**4**	**0**	**0**	**0**	**0**	**0**	**0**	**0**	**0**	**0.0**	**0**	**24**	**41.7**	**6:11**	....	....	....	....	....	....	....	....	....
	Providence Bruins	AHL	73	24	43	67	58	....	....	....	....	....	....	....	....	....	13	4	4	8	6	....	....	....	....
2007-08	**NY Islanders**	**NHL**	**8**	**1**	**0**	**1**	**0**	**1**	**0**	**0**	**6**	**16.7**	**–1**	**33**	**30.3**	**6:05**	....	....	....	....	....	....	....	....	....
	Bridgeport	AHL	68	20	46	66	31	....	....	....	....	....	....	....	....	....	....	....	....	....	....	....	....	....	....
	NHL Totals		**18**	**1**	**0**	**1**	**4**	**1**	**0**	**0**	**12**	**8.3**		**89**	**41.6**	**8:01**	....	....	....	....	....	....	....	....	....

Hockey East Second All-Star Team (2005)

Traded to **NY Islanders** by **Boston** with future considerations for Petteri Nokelainen, September 11, 2007.

WALZ, Wes

(WAHLZ, WEHS)

Center. Shoots right. 5'10", 189 lbs. Born, Calgary, Alta., May 15, 1970. Boston's 3rd choice, 57th overall, in 1989 Entry Draft.

Season	Club	League	GP	G	A	Pts	PIM	PP	SH	GW	S	%	+/-	TF	F%	Min	GP	G	A	Pts	PIM	PP	SH	GW	Min
1987-88	Cgy. North Stars	AMHL	35	47	52	99	72	....	....	....	....	....	....	....	....	....	....	....	....	....	....	....	....	....	....
	Prince Albert	WHL	1	1	1	2	0	....	....	....	....	....	....	....	....	....	....	....	....	....	....	....	....	....	....
1988-89	Lethbridge	WHL	63	29	75	104	32	....	....	....	....	....	....	....	....	....	8	1	5	6	6	....	....	....	....
1989-90	Lethbridge	WHL	56	54	86	140	69	....	....	....	....	....	....	....	....	....	19	13	*24	*37	33	....	....	....	....
	Boston	**NHL**	**2**	**1**	**1**	**2**	**0**	**1**	**0**	**0**	**1**	**100.0**	**–1**	....	....	....	....	....	....	....	....	....	....	....	....
1990-91	**Boston**	**NHL**	**56**	**8**	**8**	**16**	**32**	**1**	**0**	**1**	**57**	**14.0**	**–14**	....	....	....	**2**	**0**	**0**	**0**	**0**	**0**	**0**	**0**	....
	Maine Mariners	AHL	20	8	12	20	19	....	....	....	....	....	....	....	....	....	2	0	0	0	21	....	....	....	....
1991-92	**Boston**	**NHL**	**15**	**0**	**3**	**3**	**12**	**0**	**0**	**0**	**17**	**0.0**	**–3**	....	....	....	....	....	....	....	....	....	....	....	....
	Maine Mariners	AHL	21	13	11	24	38	....	....	....	....	....	....	....	....	....	....	....	....	....	....	....	....	....	....
	Philadelphia	**NHL**	**2**	**1**	**0**	**1**	**0**	**0**	**0**	**1**	**2**	**50.0**	**1**	....	....	....	....	....	....	....	....	....	....	....	....
	Hershey Bears	AHL	41	13	28	41	37	....	....	....	....	....	....	....	....	....	6	1	2	3	0	....	....	....	....
1992-93	Hershey Bears	AHL	78	35	45	80	106	....	....	....	....	....	....	....	....	....	....	....	....	....	....	....	....	....	....
1993-94	**Calgary**	**NHL**	**53**	**11**	**27**	**38**	**16**	**1**	**0**	**0**	**79**	**13.9**	**20**	....	....	....	**6**	**3**	**0**	**3**	**2**	**0**	**0**	**0**	....
	Saint John Flames	AHL	15	6	6	12	14	....	....	....	....	....	....	....	....	....	....	....	....	....	....	....	....	....	....
1994-95	**Calgary**	**NHL**	**39**	**6**	**12**	**18**	**11**	**4**	**0**	**1**	**73**	**8.2**	**7**	....	....	....	**1**	**0**	**0**	**0**	**0**	**0**	**0**	**0**	....
1995-96	**Detroit**	**NHL**	**2**	**0**	**0**	**0**	**0**	**0**	**0**	**0**	**2**	**0.0**	**0**	....	....	....	....	....	....	....	....	....	....	....	....
	Adirondack	AHL	38	20	35	55	58	....	....	....	....	....	....	....	....	....	....	....	....	....	....	....	....	....	....
1996-97	EV Zug	Swiss	41	24	22	46	67	....	....	....	....	....	....	....	....	....	9	5	1	6	39	....	....	....	....
1997-98	EV Zug	Swiss	38	18	34	52	32	....	....	....	....	....	....	....	....	....	20	*16	*12	*28	18	....	....	....	....
	EV Zug	EuroHL	5	1	3	4	10	....	....	....	....	....	....	....	....	....	....	....	....	....	....	....	....	....	....
1998-99	EV Zug	Swiss	42	22	27	49	75	....	....	....	....	....	....	....	....	....	10	3	9	12	2	....	....	....	....
	EV Zug	EuroHL	6	7	5	12	4	....	....	....	....	....	....	....	....	....	2	0	0	0	12	....	....	....	....
99-2000	Long Beach	IHL	6	4	3	7	8	....	....	....	....	....	....	....	....	....	....	....	....	....	....	....	....	....	....
	HC Lugano	Swiss	13	7	11	18	14	....	....	....	....	....	....	....	....	....	5	3	4	7	4	....	....	....	....
2000-01	**Minnesota**	**NHL**	**82**	**18**	**12**	**30**	**37**	**0**	**7**	**3**	**152**	**11.8**	**–8**	**1533**	**47.2**	**16:45**	....	....	....	....	....	....	....	....	....
2001-02	**Minnesota**	**NHL**	**64**	**10**	**20**	**30**	**43**	**0**	**2**	**5**	**97**	**10.3**	**0**	**1231**	**44.8**	**16:42**	....	....	....	....	....	....	....	....	....
2002-03	**Minnesota**	**NHL**	**80**	**13**	**19**	**32**	**63**	**0**	**0**	**4**	**115**	**11.3**	**11**	**1505**	**50.4**	**15:56**	**18**	**7**	**6**	**13**	**14**	**0**	**2**	**2**	**17:24**
2003-04	**Minnesota**	**NHL**	**57**	**12**	**13**	**25**	**32**	**0**	**3**	**2**	**70**	**17.1**	**5**	**909**	**46.3**	**16:18**	....	....	....	....	....	....	....	....	....
2004-05			DID NOT PLAY																						
2005-06	**Minnesota**	**NHL**	**82**	**19**	**18**	**37**	**61**	**1**	**1**	**0**	**127**	**15.0**	**7**	**1119**	**46.9**	**15:54**	....	....	....	....	....	....	....	....	....
2006-07	**Minnesota**	**NHL**	**62**	**9**	**15**	**24**	**30**	**0**	**1**	**1**	**77**	**11.7**	**3**	**786**	**47.2**	**14:53**	**5**	**0**	**1**	**1**	**4**	**0**	**0**	**0**	**11:50**
2007-08	**Minnesota**	**NHL**	**11**	**1**	**3**	**4**	**6**	**0**	**0**	**0**	**9**	**11.1**	**–5**	**135**	**45.9**	**13:48**	....	....	....	....	....	....	....	....	....
	NHL Totals		**607**	**109**	**151**	**260**	**343**	**8**	**14**	**18**	**878**	**12.4**		**7218**	**47.3**	**16:02**	**32**	**10**	**7**	**17**	**20**	**0**	**2**	**2**	**16:12**

WHL Rookie of the Year (1989) • WHL East First All-Star Team (1990)

Traded to **Philadelphia** by **Boston** with Garry Galley and Boston's 3rd round choice (Milos Holan) in 1993 Entry Draft for Gord Murphy, Brian Dobbin, Philadelphia's 3rd round choice (Sergei Zholtok) in 1992 Entry Draft and Philadelphia's 4th round choice (Charles Paquette) in 1993 Entry Draft, January 2, 1992. Signed as a free agent by **Calgary**, August 26, 1993. Signed as a free agent by **Detroit**, September 6, 1995. Signed as a free agent by **Long Beach** (IHL), October 12, 1999. Signed as a free agent by **Minnesota**, June 28, 2000. • Officially announced his retirement December 1, 2007.

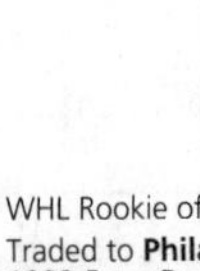

WANVIG, Kyle

(WEHN-vihg, KIGHL)

Right wing. Shoots right. 6'2", 210 lbs. Born, Calgary, Alta., January 29, 1981. Minnesota's 2nd choice, 36th overall, in 2001 Entry Draft.

Season	Club	League	GP	G	A	Pts	PIM	PP	SH	GW	S	%	+/-	TF	F%	Min	GP	G	A	Pts	PIM	PP	SH	GW	Min
1996-97	Calgary Blazers	AMHL	26	31	48	79	85	....	....	....	....	....	....	....	....	....	....	....	....	....	....	....	....	....	....
1997-98	Edmonton Ice	WHL	62	17	12	29	69	....	....	....	....	....	....	....	....	....	....	....	....	....	....	....	....	....	....
1998-99	Kootenay Ice	WHL	71	12	20	32	119	....	....	....	....	....	....	....	....	....	7	1	3	4	18	....	....	....	....
99-2000	Kootenay Ice	WHL	6	2	2	4	12	....	....	....	....	....	....	....	....	....	....	....	....	....	....	....	....	....	....
	Red Deer Rebels	WHL	58	21	18	39	123	....	....	....	....	....	....	....	....	....	4	1	0	1	4	....	....	....	....
2000-01	Red Deer Rebels	WHL	69	55	46	101	202	....	....	....	....	....	....	....	....	....	22	10	12	22	47	....	....	....	....
2001-02	Houston Aeros	AHL	34	6	7	13	43	....	....	....	....	....	....	....	....	....	9	0	1	1	23	....	....	....	....
2002-03	**Minnesota**	**NHL**	**7**	**1**	**0**	**1**	**13**	**0**	**0**	**0**	**5**	**20.0**	**0**	**1**	**100.0**	**9:14**	....	....	....	....	....	....	....	....	....
	Houston Aeros	AHL	57	13	16	29	137	....	....	....	....	....	....	....	....	....	21	6	4	10	27	....	....	....	....

			Regular Season														Playoffs								
Season	Club	League	GP	G	A	Pts	PIM	PP	SH	GW	S	%	+/-	TF	F%	Min	GP	G	A	Pts	PIM	PP	SH	GW	Min
2003-04	**Minnesota**	**NHL**	**6**	**0**	**1**	**1**	**10**	**0**	**0**	**0**	**16**	**0.0**	**–2**	**4**	**75.0**	**13:48**									
	Houston Aeros	AHL	72	25	16	41	147										2	0	1	1	0				
2004-05	Houston Aeros	AHL	76	13	17	30	158										5	1	2	3	8				
2005-06	**Minnesota**	**NHL**	**51**	**4**	**8**	**12**	**64**	**1**	**0**	**0**	**55**	**7.3**	**–8**	**26**	**46.2**	**10:39**									
2006-07	Chicago Wolves	AHL	26	10	11	21	61																		
	Tampa Bay	**NHL**	**4**	**0**	**0**	**0**	**0**	**0**	**0**	**0**	**0**	**0.0**	**0**	**0**	**0.0**	**5:12**									
	Springfield	AHL	23	11	7	18	40																		
2007-08	**Tampa Bay**	**NHL**	**7**	**1**	**0**	**1**	**7**	**0**	**0**	**1**	**10**	**10.0**	**–1**	**1**	**100.0**	**10:09**									
	Norfolk Admirals	AHL	62	23	33	56	110																		
	NHL Totals		**75**	**6**	**9**	**15**	**94**	**1**	**0**	**1**	**86**	**7.0**		**32**	**53.1**	**10:26**									

• Re-entered NHL Entry Draft. Originally Boston's 3rd choice, 89th overall, in 1999 Entry Draft.
WHL East Second All-Star Team (2001) • Memorial Cup Tournament All-Star Team (2001) • Stafford Smythe Memorial Trophy (Memorial Cup Tournament - MVP) (2001)
• Missed majority of 2001-02 season recovering from ankle injury suffered in game vs. Grand Rapids (AHL), December 30, 2001. Signed as a free agent by **Atlanta**, July 18, 2006. Traded to **Tampa Bay** by **Atlanta** with Stephen Baby for Andy Delmore and Andre Deveaux, February 1, 2007.

WARD, Aaron (WOHRD, AIR-ruhn) BOS.

Defense. Shoots right. 6'2", 209 lbs. Born, Windsor, Ont., January 17, 1973. Winnipeg's 1st choice, 5th overall, in 1991 Entry Draft.

Season	Club	League	GP	G	A	Pts	PIM	PP	SH	GW	S	%	+/-	TF	F%	Min	GP	G	A	Pts	PIM	PP	SH	GW	Min
1988-89	Nepean Raiders	CJHL	54	1	14	15	40																		
1989-90	Nepean Raiders	CJHL	52	6	33	39	85																		
1990-91	U. of Michigan	CCHA	46	8	11	19	126																		
1991-92	U. of Michigan	CCHA	42	7	12	19	64																		
1992-93	U. of Michigan	CCHA	30	5	8	13	73																		
1993-94	**Detroit**	**NHL**	**5**	**1**	**0**	**1**	**4**	**0**	**0**	**0**	**3**	**33.3**	**2**												
	Adirondack	AHL	58	4	12	16	87										9	2	6	8	6				
1994-95	Adirondack	AHL	76	11	24	35	87										4	0	1	1	0				
	Detroit	**NHL**	**1**	**0**	**1**	**1**	**2**	**0**	**0**	**0**	**0**	**0.0**	**1**												
1995-96	Adirondack	AHL	74	5	10	15	133										3	0	0	0	6				
1996-97♦	**Detroit**	**NHL**	**49**	**2**	**5**	**7**	**52**	**0**	**0**	**0**	**40**	**5.0**	**–9**				**19**	**0**	**0**	**0**	**17**	**0**	**0**	**0**	
1997-98♦	**Detroit**	**NHL**	**52**	**5**	**5**	**10**	**47**	**0**	**0**	**1**	**47**	**10.6**	**–1**												
1998-99	**Detroit**	**NHL**	**60**	**3**	**8**	**11**	**52**	**0**	**0**	**0**	**46**	**6.5**	**–5**	**0**	**0.0**	**13:55**	**8**	**0**	**1**	**1**	**8**	**0**	**0**	**0**	**10:15**
99-2000	**Detroit**	**NHL**	**36**	**1**	**3**	**4**	**24**	**0**	**0**	**0**	**25**	**4.0**	**–4**	**0**	**0.0**	**12:36**	**3**	**0**	**0**	**0**	**0**	**0**	**0**	**0**	**7:36**
2000-01	**Detroit**	**NHL**	**73**	**4**	**5**	**9**	**57**	**0**	**0**	**1**	**48**	**8.3**	**–4**	**0**	**0.0**	**17:00**									
2001-02	**Carolina**	**NHL**	**79**	**3**	**11**	**14**	**74**	**0**	**0**	**2**	**69**	**4.3**	**0**	**1**	**100.0**	**19:40**	**23**	**1**	**1**	**2**	**22**	**0**	**0**	**0**	**21:12**
2002-03	**Carolina**	**NHL**	**77**	**3**	**6**	**9**	**90**	**0**	**0**	**1**	**66**	**4.5**	**–23**	**0**	**0.0**	**18:43**									
2003-04	**Carolina**	**NHL**	**49**	**3**	**5**	**8**	**37**	**2**	**0**	**0**	**51**	**5.9**	**1**	**0**	**0.0**	**17:52**									
2004-05	ERC Ingolstadt	Germany	8	0	3	3	16										11	1	1	2	16				
2005-06♦	**Carolina**	**NHL**	**71**	**6**	**19**	**25**	**62**	**0**	**0**	**1**	**60**	**10.0**	**2**	**1**	**0.0**	**19:07**	**25**	**2**	**3**	**5**	**18**	**0**	**0**	**0**	**21:42**
2006-07	**NY Rangers**	**NHL**	**60**	**3**	**10**	**13**	**57**	**0**	**0**	**0**	**45**	**6.7**	**–3**	**0**	**0.0**	**19:42**									
	Boston	**NHL**	**20**	**1**	**2**	**3**	**18**	**0**	**0**	**0**	**17**	**5.9**	**–8**	**0**	**0.0**	**21:36**									
2007-08	**Boston**	**NHL**	**65**	**5**	**8**	**13**	**54**	**0**	**0**	**3**	**68**	**7.4**	**9**	**0**	**0.0**	**20:45**	**6**	**0**	**1**	**1**	**6**	**0**	**0**	**0**	**22:20**
	NHL Totals		**697**	**40**	**88**	**128**	**630**	**2**	**0**	**9**	**585**	**6.8**		**2**	**50.0**	**18:10**	**84**	**3**	**6**	**9**	**71**	**0**	**0**	**0**	**19:31**

Traded to **Detroit** by **Winnipeg** with Toronto's 4th round choice (previously acquired, Detroit selected John Jakopin) in 1993 Entry Draft for Paul Ysebaert and future considerations (Alan Kerr, June 18, 1993), June 11, 1993. • Missed majority of 1999-2000 season recovering from shoulder injury suffered in game vs. Vancouver, January 19, 2000. Traded to **Carolina** by **Detroit** for Carolina's 2nd round choice (Jiri Hudler) in 2002 Entry Draft, July 9, 2001. Signed as a free agent by **Ingolstadt** (Germany), February 15, 2005. Signed as a free agent by **NY Rangers**, July 3, 2006. Traded to **Boston** by **NY Rangers** for Paul Mara, February 27, 2007.

WARD, Jason (WOHRD, JAY-suhn) T.B.

Right wing. Shoots right. 6'2", 208 lbs. Born, Chapleau, Ont., January 16, 1979. Montreal's 1st choice, 11th overall, in 1997 Entry Draft.

Season	Club	League	GP	G	A	Pts	PIM	PP	SH	GW	S	%	+/-	TF	F%	Min	GP	G	A	Pts	PIM	PP	SH	GW	Min
1994-95	Oshawa	OHA-B	47	30	31	61	75																		
1995-96	Niagara Falls	OHL	64	15	35	50	139										10	6	4	10	23				
1996-97	Erie Otters	OHL	58	25	39	64	137										5	1	2	3	2				
1997-98	Erie Otters	OHL	21	7	9	16	42																		
	Windsor Spitfires	OHL	26	19	27	46	34																		
	Fredericton	AHL	7	1	0	1	2										1	0	0	0	2				
1998-99	Windsor Spitfires	OHL	12	8	11	19	25																		
	Plymouth Whalers	OHL	23	14	13	27	28										11	6	8	14	12				
	Fredericton	AHL															10	4	2	6	22				
99-2000	**Montreal**	**NHL**	**32**	**2**	**1**	**3**	**10**	**1**	**0**	**0**	**24**	**8.3**	**–1**	**86**	**44.2**	**9:10**									
	Quebec Citadelles	AHL	40	14	12	26	30										3	2	1	3	4				
2000-01	**Montreal**	**NHL**	**12**	**0**	**0**	**0**	**12**	**0**	**0**	**0**	**4**	**0.0**	**3**	**2**	**50.0**	**8:16**									
	Quebec Citadelles	AHL	23	7	12	19	69																		
2001-02	Quebec Citadelles	AHL	78	24	33	57	128										3	0	0	0	2				
2002-03	**Montreal**	**NHL**	**8**	**3**	**2**	**5**	**0**	**0**	**0**	**0**	**10**	**30.0**	**3**	**6**	**50.0**	**11:17**									
	Hamilton	AHL	69	31	41	72	78										23	*12	9	*21	20				
2003-04	**Montreal**	**NHL**	**53**	**5**	**7**	**12**	**21**	**2**	**0**	**1**	**56**	**8.9**	**3**	**98**	**41.8**	**12:39**	**5**	**0**	**2**	**2**	**2**	**0**	**0**	**0**	**15:39**
	Hamilton	AHL	2	0	3	3	17																		
2004-05	Hamilton	AHL	77	20	34	54	66										4	2	1	3	2				
2005-06	**NY Rangers**	**NHL**	**81**	**10**	**18**	**28**	**44**	**0**	**2**	**1**	**125**	**8.0**	**–4**	**153**	**47.7**	**13:12**	**1**	**0**	**0**	**0**	**2**	**0**	**0**	**0**	**2:39**
2006-07	**NY Rangers**	**NHL**	**46**	**4**	**6**	**10**	**26**	**0**	**1**	**1**	**68**	**5.9**	**–3**	**191**	**41.9**	**12:19**									
	Los Angeles	**NHL**	**7**	**0**	**1**	**1**	**4**	**0**	**0**	**0**	**2**	**0.0**	**–1**	**7**	**14.3**	**4:51**									
	Tampa Bay	**NHL**	**17**	**4**	**4**	**8**	**10**	**0**	**0**	**0**	**38**	**10.5**	**–11**	**16**	**37.5**	**16:38**	**6**	**0**	**1**	**1**	**6**	**0**	**0**	**0**	**20:03**
2007-08	**Tampa Bay**	**NHL**	**79**	**8**	**6**	**14**	**42**	**1**	**1**	**0**	**85**	**9.4**	**–18**	**45**	**40.0**	**12:33**									
	NHL Totals		**335**	**36**	**45**	**81**	**169**	**4**	**4**	**3**	**412**	**8.7**		**604**	**43.2**	**12:14**	**12**	**0**	**3**	**3**	**10**	**0**	**0**	**0**	**16:46**

AHL First All-Star Team (2003) • Les Cunningham Award (MVP – AHL) (2003)
• Missed majority of 2000-01 season recovering from knee injury suffered in game vs. Carolina, January 16, 2001. Signed as a free agent by **Hamilton** (AHL), October 19, 2004. Signed as a free agent by **NY Rangers**, August 4, 2005. Traded to **Los Angeles** by **NY Rangers** with Jan Marek, Marc-Andre Cliche and NY Rangers' 3rd round choice (later traded to Buffalo - Buffalo selected Corey Fienhage) in 2008 Entry Draft for Sean Avery and John Seymour, February 5, 2007. Traded to **Tampa Bay** by **Los Angeles** for Tampa Bay's 5th round choice (Joshua Turnbull) in 2007 Entry Draft, February 27, 2007.

WARD, Joel (WOHRD, JOHL) NSH.

Right wing. Shoots right. 6'2", 205 lbs. Born, Toronto, Ont., December 2, 1980.

Season	Club	League	GP	G	A	Pts	PIM	PP	SH	GW	S	%	+/-	TF	F%	Min	GP	G	A	Pts	PIM	PP	SH	GW	Min
1997-98	Owen Sound	OHL	47	8	4	12	14										11	1	1	2	5				
1998-99	Owen Sound	OHL	58	19	16	35	23										16	2	4	6	0				
99-2000	Owen Sound	OHL	63	23	20	43	51																		
2000-01	Owen Sound	OHL	67	26	36	62	45										5	2	4	6	4				
	Long Beach	WCHL															8	0	0	0	0				
2001-02	U. of P.E.I.	CIS	22	13	14	27	16																		
2002-03	U. of P.E.I.	CIS	19	11	15	26	24																		
2003-04	U. of P.E.I.	CIS	27	14	24	38	42																		
2004-05	U. of P.E.I.	CIS	28	16	28	44	42																		
2005-06	Houston Aeros	AHL	66	8	14	22	34										8	4	2	6	4				
2006-07	**Minnesota**	**NHL**	**11**	**0**	**1**	**1**	**0**	**0**	**0**	**0**	**12**	**0.0**	**0**	**1**	**0.0**	**7:42**									
	Houston Aeros	AHL	64	9	14	23	45																		
2007-08	Houston Aeros	AHL	79	21	20	41	47										4	0	2	2	0				
	NHL Totals		**11**	**0**	**1**	**1**	**0**	**0**	**0**	**0**	**12**	**0.0**		**1**	**0.0**	**7:42**									

Signed as a free agent by **Houston** (AHL), December 4, 2005. Signed as a free agent by **Minnesota**, September 27, 2006. Signed as a free agent by **Nashville**, July 14, 2008.

WARRENER, Rhett (WAHR-ihn-uhr, REHT) CGY.

Defense. Shoots right. 6'1", 203 lbs. Born, Shaunavon, Sask., January 27, 1976. Florida's 2nd choice, 27th overall, in 1994 Entry Draft.

Season	Club	League	GP	G	A	Pts	PIM	PP	SH	GW	S	%	+/-	TF	F%	Min	GP	G	A	Pts	PIM	PP	SH	GW	Min
1991-92	Saskatoon Blazers	SMHL	33	6	5	11	71																		
	Saskatoon Blades	WHL	2	0	0	0	0																		
1992-93	Saskatoon Blades	WHL	68	2	17	19	100										9	0	0	0	14				
1993-94	Saskatoon Blades	WHL	61	7	19	26	131										16	0	5	5	33				
1994-95	Saskatoon Blades	WHL	66	13	26	39	137										10	0	3	3	6				
1995-96	**Florida**	**NHL**	**28**	**0**	**3**	**3**	**46**	**0**	**0**	**0**	**19**	**0.0**	**4**				**21**	**0**	**1**	**1**	**0**	**0**	**0**	**0**	
	Carolina Panthers	AHL	9	0	0	0	4																		
1996-97	**Florida**	**NHL**	**62**	**4**	**9**	**13**	**88**	**1**	**0**	**1**	**58**	**6.9**	**20**				**5**	**0**	**0**	**0**	**0**	**0**	**0**	**0**	

			Regular Season														Playoffs								
Season	Club	League	GP	G	A	Pts	PIM	PP	SH	GW	S	%	+/-	TF	F%	Min	GP	G	A	Pts	PIM	PP	SH	GW	Min
1997-98	Florida	NHL	79	0	4	4	99	0	0	0	66	0.0	–16	....	....	....	....	....	....	....	....	....	....	....	....
1998-99	Florida	NHL	48	0	7	7	64	0	0	0	33	0.0	–1	0	0.0	19:01	....	....	....	....	....	....	....	....	....
	Buffalo	NHL	13	1	0	1	20	0	0	0	11	9.1	3	0	0.0	18:13	20	1	3	4	32	0	0	0	22:08
99-2000	Buffalo	NHL	61	0	3	3	89	0	0	0	68	0.0	18	0	0.0	19:51	5	0	0	0	2	0	0	0	21:42
2000-01	Buffalo	NHL	77	3	16	19	78	0	0	2	103	2.9	10	0	0.0	20:24	13	0	2	2	4	0	0	0	22:37
2001-02	Buffalo	NHL	65	5	5	10	113	0	0	1	66	7.6	15	0	0.0	19:39	....	....	....	....	....	....	....	....	....
2002-03	Buffalo	NHL	50	0	9	9	63	0	0	0	47	0.0	1	0	0.0	18:14	....	....	....	....	....	....	....	....	....
2003-04	Calgary	NHL	77	3	14	17	97	0	1	1	82	3.7	8	1	0.0	19:52	24	0	1	1	6	0	0	0	24:06
2004-05			DID NOT PLAY																						
2005-06	Calgary	NHL	61	3	3	6	54	0	1	0	40	7.5	7	0	0.0	19:12	7	0	0	0	14	0	0	0	19:56
2006-07	Calgary	NHL	62	4	6	10	67	1	1	1	31	12.9	6	0	0.0	17:08	6	0	0	0	10	0	0	0	21:15
2007-08	Calgary	NHL	31	1	3	4	21	0	0	0	15	6.7	–2	1	0.0	13:26	....	....	....	....	....	....	....	....	....
	NHL Totals		**714**	**24**	**82**	**106**	**899**	**2**	**3**	**6**	**639**	**3.8**		**2**	**0.0**	**18:54**	**101**	**1**	**7**	**8**	**68**	**0**	**0**	**0**	**22:32**

Traded to **Buffalo** by **Florida** with Florida's 5th round choice (Ryan Miller) in 1999 Entry Draft for Mike Wilson, March 23, 1999. Traded to **Calgary** by **Buffalo** with Steve Reinprecht for Chris Drury and Steve Begin, July 3, 2003. • Missed majority of 2007-08 season recovering from leg and foot injuries.

WEAVER, Mike (WEE-vuhr, MIGHK) ST.L.

Defense. Shoots right. 5'9", 182 lbs. Born, Bramalea, Ont., May 2, 1978.

Season	Club	League	GP	G	A	Pts	PIM	PP	SH	GW	S	%	+/-	TF	F%	Min	GP	G	A	Pts	PIM	PP	SH	GW	Min
1995-96	Bramalea Blues	OPJHL	48	10	39	49	103	....	....	....	....	....	....	....	....	....	....	....	....	....	....	....	....	....	....
1996-97	Michigan State	CCHA	39	0	7	7	46	....	....	....	....	....	....	....	....	....	....	....	....	....	....	....	....	....	....
1997-98	Michigan State	CCHA	44	4	22	26	68	....	....	....	....	....	....	....	....	....	....	....	....	....	....	....	....	....	....
1998-99	Michigan State	CCHA	42	1	6	7	54	....	....	....	....	....	....	....	....	....	....	....	....	....	....	....	....	....	....
99-2000	Michigan State	CCHA	26	0	7	7	20	....	....	....	....	....	....	....	....	....	....	....	....	....	....	....	....	....	....
2000-01	Orlando	IHL	68	0	8	8	34	....	....	....	....	....	....	....	....	....	16	0	2	2	8	....	....	....	....
2001-02	**Atlanta**	**NHL**	**16**	**0**	**1**	**1**	**10**	**0**	**0**	**0**	**9**	**0.0**	**0**	**0**	**0.0**	**13:54**	....	....	....	....	....	....	....	....	....
	Chicago Wolves	AHL	58	2	8	10	67	....	....	....	....	....	....	....	....	....	25	1	3	4	21	....	....	....	....
2002-03	**Atlanta**	**NHL**	**40**	**0**	**5**	**5**	**20**	**0**	**0**	**0**	**21**	**0.0**	**–5**	**0**	**0.0**	**18:38**	....	....	....	....	....	....	....	....	....
	Chicago Wolves	AHL	33	2	2	4	32	....	....	....	....	....	....	....	....	....	9	0	3	3	4	....	....	....	....
2003-04	**Atlanta**	**NHL**	**1**	**0**	**0**	**0**	**0**	**0**	**0**	**0**	**0**	**0.0**	**–1**	**0**	**0.0**	**8:28**	....	....	....	....	....	....	....	....	....
	Chicago Wolves	AHL	78	3	14	17	89	....	....	....	....	....	....	....	....	....	9	2	2	4	20	....	....	....	....
2004-05	Manchester	AHL	79	1	22	23	61	....	....	....	....	....	....	....	....	....	6	0	1	1	0	....	....	....	....
2005-06	**Los Angeles**	**NHL**	**53**	**0**	**9**	**9**	**14**	**0**	**0**	**0**	**21**	**0.0**	**–3**	**0**	**0.0**	**15:03**	....	....	....	....	....	....	....	....	....
2006-07	**Los Angeles**	**NHL**	**39**	**3**	**6**	**9**	**16**	**1**	**0**	**1**	**22**	**13.6**	**–4**	**3**	**66.7**	**15:20**	....	....	....	....	....	....	....	....	....
	Manchester	AHL	7	1	3	4	2	....	....	....	....	....	....	....	....	....	....	....	....	....	....	....	....	....	....
2007-08	**Vancouver**	**NHL**	**55**	**0**	**1**	**1**	**33**	**0**	**0**	**0**	**33**	**0.0**	**1**	**1**	**0.0**	**14:02**	....	....	....	....	....	....	....	....	....
	NHL Totals		**204**	**3**	**22**	**25**	**93**	**1**	**0**	**1**	**106**	**2.8**		**4**	**50.0**	**15:24**	....	....	....	....	....	....	....	....	....

OPJHL Defenseman of the Year (1996) • CCHA All-Tournament Team (1997) • CCHA First All-Star Team (1999, 2000) • CCHA Best Defensive Defenseman Award (1999, 2000) • NCAA West Second All-American Team (1999, 2000)

Signed as a free agent by **Atlanta**, June 15, 2000. Signed as a free agent by **Los Angeles**, July 16, 2004. Signed as a free agent by **Pittsburgh**, August 8, 2007. Claimed on waivers by **Vancouver** from **Pittsburgh**, October 2, 2007. Signed as a free agent by **St. Louis**, July 10, 2008.

WEBER, Mike (WEH-buhr, MIGHK) BUF.

Defense. Shoots left. 6'2", 214 lbs. Born, Pittsburgh, PA, December 16, 1987. Buffalo's 3rd choice, 57th overall, in 2006 Entry Draft.

Season	Club	League	GP	G	A	Pts	PIM	PP	SH	GW	S	%	+/-	TF	F%	Min	GP	G	A	Pts	PIM	PP	SH	GW	Min
2002-03	Jr. Penguins	EmJHL	28	4	11	15	109	....	....	....	....	....	....	....	....	....	3	0	0	0	20	....	....	....	....
2003-04	Windsor Spitfires	OHL	65	0	2	2	49	....	....	....	....	....	....	....	....	....	....	....	....	....	....	....	....	....	....
2004-05	Windsor Spitfires	OHL	68	2	6	8	132	....	....	....	....	....	....	....	....	....	11	0	1	1	18	....	....	....	....
2005-06	Windsor Spitfires	OHL	68	5	21	26	181	....	....	....	....	....	....	....	....	....	7	0	0	0	12	....	....	....	....
2006-07	Windsor Spitfires	OHL	30	3	16	19	86	....	....	....	....	....	....	....	....	....	....	....	....	....	....	....	....	....	....
	Barrie Colts	OHL	30	3	12	15	86	....	....	....	....	....	....	....	....	....	7	0	6	6	10	....	....	....	....
2007-08	**Buffalo**	**NHL**	**16**	**0**	**3**	**3**	**14**	**0**	**0**	**0**	**12**	**0.0**	**12**	**0**	**0.0**	**16:41**	....	....	....	....	....	....	....	....	....
	Rochester	AHL	59	1	13	14	178	....	....	....	....	....	....	....	....	....	....	....	....	....	....	....	....	....	....
	NHL Totals		**16**	**0**	**3**	**3**	**14**	**0**	**0**	**0**	**12**	**0.0**		**0**	**0.0**	**16:41**	....	....	....	....	....	....	....	....	....

WEBER, Shea (WEH-buhr, SHAY) NSH.

Defense. Shoots right. 6'3", 213 lbs. Born, Sicamous, B.C., August 14, 1985. Nashville's 4th choice, 49th overall, in 2003 Entry Draft.

Season	Club	League	GP	G	A	Pts	PIM	PP	SH	GW	S	%	+/-	TF	F%	Min	GP	G	A	Pts	PIM	PP	SH	GW	Min
2001-02	Sicamous Eagles	KIJHL	47	9	33	42	87	....	....	....	....	....	....	....	....	....	....	....	....	....	....	....	....	....	....
	Kelowna Rockets	WHL	5	0	0	0	0	....	....	....	....	....	....	....	....	....	....	....	....	....	....	....	....	....	....
2002-03	Kelowna Rockets	WHL	70	2	16	18	167	....	....	....	....	....	....	....	....	....	19	1	4	5	26	....	....	....	....
2003-04	Kelowna Rockets	WHL	60	12	20	32	126	....	....	....	....	....	....	....	....	....	17	3	14	17	16	....	....	....	....
2004-05	Kelowna Rockets	WHL	55	12	29	41	95	....	....	....	....	....	....	....	....	....	18	9	8	17	25	....	....	....	....
2005-06	**Nashville**	**NHL**	**28**	**2**	**8**	**10**	**42**	**2**	**0**	**1**	**46**	**4.3**	**8**	**0**	**0.0**	**17:00**	**4**	**2**	**0**	**2**	**8**	**1**	**0**	**0**	**14:12**
	Milwaukee	AHL	46	12	15	27	49	....	....	....	....	....	....	....	....	....	14	6	5	11	16	....	....	....	....
2006-07	**Nashville**	**NHL**	**79**	**17**	**23**	**40**	**60**	**6**	**0**	**2**	**152**	**11.2**	**13**	**0**	**0.0**	**19:23**	**5**	**0**	**3**	**3**	**2**	**0**	**0**	**0**	**21:41**
2007-08	**Nashville**	**NHL**	**54**	**6**	**14**	**20**	**49**	**5**	**0**	**2**	**152**	**3.9**	**–6**	**0**	**0.0**	**19:30**	**6**	**1**	**3**	**4**	**6**	**0**	**0**	**0**	**19:30**
	NHL Totals		**161**	**25**	**45**	**70**	**151**	**13**	**0**	**5**	**350**	**7.1**		**0**	**0.0**	**19:01**	**15**	**3**	**6**	**9**	**16**	**1**	**0**	**0**	**18:49**

WHL West Second All-Star Team (2004) • Memorial Cup Tournament All-Star Team (2004) • WHL West First All-Star Team (2005)

WEIGHT, Doug (WAYT, DUHG) NYI

Center. Shoots left. 5'11", 196 lbs. Born, Warren, MI, January 21, 1971. NY Rangers' 2nd choice, 34th overall, in 1990 Entry Draft.

Season	Club	League	GP	G	A	Pts	PIM	PP	SH	GW	S	%	+/-	TF	F%	Min	GP	G	A	Pts	PIM	PP	SH	GW	Min
1988-89	Bloomfield Jets	NAHL	34	26	53	79	105	....	....	....	....	....	....	....	....	....	....	....	....	....	....	....	....	....	....
1989-90	Lake Superior	CCHA	46	21	48	69	44	....	....	....	....	....	....	....	....	....	....	....	....	....	....	....	....	....	....
1990-91	Lake Superior	CCHA	42	29	46	75	86	....	....	....	....	....	....	....	....	....	....	....	....	....	....	....	....	....	....
	NY Rangers	**NHL**	....	....	....	....	....	....	....	....	....	....	....	....	....	....	**1**	**0**	**0**	**0**	**0**	**0**	**0**	**0**	....
1991-92	**NY Rangers**	**NHL**	**53**	**8**	**22**	**30**	**23**	**0**	**0**	**2**	**72**	**11.1**	**–3**	....	....	....	**7**	**2**	**2**	**4**	**0**	**1**	**0**	**0**	....
	Binghamton	AHL	9	3	14	17	2	....	....	....	....	....	....	....	....	....	4	1	4	5	6	....	....	....	....
1992-93	**NY Rangers**	**NHL**	**65**	**15**	**25**	**40**	**55**	**3**	**0**	**1**	**90**	**16.7**	**4**	....	....	....	....	....	....	....	....	....	....	....	....
	Edmonton	**NHL**	**13**	**2**	**6**	**8**	**10**	**0**	**0**	**0**	**35**	**5.7**	**–2**	....	....	....	....	....	....	....	....	....	....	....	....
1993-94	**Edmonton**	**NHL**	**84**	**24**	**50**	**74**	**47**	**4**	**1**	**1**	**188**	**12.8**	**–22**	....	....	....	....	....	....	....	....	....	....	....	....
1994-95	Rosenheim	Germany	8	2	3	5	18	....	....	....	....	....	....	....	....	....	....	....	....	....	....	....	....	....	....
	Edmonton	**NHL**	**48**	**7**	**33**	**40**	**69**	**1**	**0**	**1**	**104**	**6.7**	**–17**	....	....	....	....	....	....	....	....	....	....	....	....
1995-96	**Edmonton**	**NHL**	**82**	**25**	**79**	**104**	**95**	**9**	**0**	**2**	**204**	**12.3**	**–19**	....	....	....	....	....	....	....	....	....	....	....	....
1996-97	**Edmonton**	**NHL**	**80**	**21**	**61**	**82**	**80**	**4**	**0**	**2**	**235**	**8.9**	**1**	....	....	....	**12**	**3**	**8**	**11**	**8**	**0**	**0**	**0**	....
1997-98	**Edmonton**	**NHL**	**79**	**26**	**44**	**70**	**69**	**9**	**0**	**4**	**205**	**12.7**	**1**	....	....	....	**12**	**2**	**7**	**9**	**14**	**2**	**0**	**1**	....
	United States	Olympics	4	0	2	2	2	....	....	....	....	....	....	....	....	....	....	....	....	....	....	....	....	....	....
1998-99	**Edmonton**	**NHL**	**43**	**6**	**31**	**37**	**12**	**1**	**0**	**0**	**79**	**7.6**	**–8**	**853**	**49.5**	**19:51**	**4**	**1**	**1**	**2**	**15**	**0**	**0**	**0**	**14:43**
99-2000	**Edmonton**	**NHL**	**77**	**21**	**51**	**72**	**54**	**3**	**1**	**4**	**167**	**12.6**	**6**	**1588**	**50.4**	**20:35**	**5**	**3**	**2**	**5**	**4**	**2**	**0**	**1**	**21:05**
2000-01	**Edmonton**	**NHL**	**82**	**25**	**65**	**90**	**91**	**8**	**0**	**3**	**188**	**13.3**	**12**	**1514**	**51.3**	**22:08**	**6**	**1**	**5**	**6**	**17**	**0**	**0**	**0**	**22:45**
2001-02	**St. Louis**	**NHL**	**61**	**15**	**34**	**49**	**40**	**3**	**0**	**1**	**131**	**11.5**	**20**	**1123**	**49.2**	**19:48**	**10**	**1**	**1**	**2**	**4**	**1**	**0**	**1**	**16:26**
	United States	Olympics	6	0	3	3	4	....	....	....	....	....	....	....	....	....	....	....	....	....	....	....	....	....	....
2002-03	**St. Louis**	**NHL**	**70**	**15**	**52**	**67**	**52**	**7**	**0**	**3**	**182**	**8.2**	**–6**	**1048**	**50.4**	**20:23**	**7**	**5**	**8**	**13**	**2**	**5**	**0**	**1**	**22:26**
2003-04	**St. Louis**	**NHL**	**75**	**14**	**51**	**65**	**37**	**6**	**0**	**5**	**198**	**7.1**	**–3**	**1115**	**50.4**	**20:25**	**5**	**2**	**1**	**3**	**6**	**1**	**1**	**0**	**19:24**
2004-05	Frankfurt Lions	Germany	7	6	9	15	26	....	....	....	....	....	....	....	....	....	11	2	10	12	8	....	....	....	....
2005-06	**St. Louis**	**NHL**	**47**	**11**	**33**	**44**	**50**	**7**	**0**	**1**	**123**	**8.9**	**–11**	**638**	**49.8**	**22:17**	....	....	....	....	....	....	....	....	....
	♦ **Carolina**	**NHL**	**23**	**4**	**9**	**13**	**25**	**2**	**0**	**0**	**52**	**7.7**	**–6**	**256**	**46.1**	**17:35**	**23**	**3**	**13**	**16**	**20**	**2**	**0**	**0**	**15:27**
	United States	Olympics	6	0	3	3	4	....	....	....	....	....	....	....	....	....	....	....	....	....	....	....	....	....	....
2006-07	**St. Louis**	**NHL**	**82**	**16**	**43**	**59**	**56**	**5**	**0**	**3**	**123**	**13.0**	**10**	**1025**	**47.7**	**18:17**	....	....	....	....	....	....	....	....	....

			Regular Season														Playoffs								
Season	Club	League	GP	G	A	Pts	PIM	PP	SH	GW	S	%	+/-	TF	F%	Min	GP	G	A	Pts	PIM	PP	SH	GW	Min
2007-08	St. Louis	NHL	29	4	7	11	12	0	0	0	47	8.5	4	289	49.5	16:11	....	....	....	....	....	....	....	....	....
	Anaheim	NHL	38	6	8	14	20	2	0	1	49	12.2	0	325	45.2	13:25	5	0	1	1	4	0	0	0	7:39
	NHL Totals		1131	265	704	969	897	74	2	34	2472	10.7	–	9774	49.7	19:42	97	23	49	72	94	14	1	4	17:07

CCHA First All-Star Team (1991) • NCAA West Second All-American Team (1991)

Played in NHL All-Star Game (1996, 1998, 2001, 2003)

Traded to **Edmonton** by **NY Rangers** for Esa Tikkanen, March 17, 1993. Traded to **St. Louis** by **Edmonton** with Michel Riesen for Marty Reasoner, Jochen Hecht and Jan Horacek, July 1, 2001. Signed as a free agent by **Frankfurt** (Germany), February 11, 2005. Traded to **Carolina** by **St. Louis** with Erkki Rajamaki for Jesse Boulerice, Mike Zigomanis, the rights to Magnus Kahnberg, Carolina's 1st round choice (later traded to New Jersey - New Jersey selected Matthew Corrente) in 2006 Entry Draft, Toronto's 4th round choice (previously acquired, St. Louis selected Reto Berra) in 2006 Entry Draft and Chicago's 4th round choice (previously acquired, St. Louis selected Cade Fairchild) in 2007 Entry Draft, January 30, 2006. Signed as a free agent by **St. Louis**, July 2, 2006. Traded to **Anaheim** by **St. Louis** with Michal Birner and St. Louis' 7th round choice (later traded to Los Angeles - later traded back to St. Louis - St. Louis selected Paul Karpowich) in 2008 Entry Draft for Andy McDonald, December 14, 2007. Signed as a free agent by **NY Islanders**, July 2, 2008.

WEINHANDL, Mattias

(WIGHN-han-duhl, mat-TEE-uhs)

Right wing. Shoots right. 6', 183 lbs. Born, Ljungby, Sweden, June 1, 1980. NY Islanders' 5th choice, 78th overall, in 1999 Entry Draft.

1995-96	Troja Jr.	Swe-Jr.	28	38	40	78	....	....	....	....	....	....	....	....	....	....	....	....	....	....	....	....	....	....	....
1996-97	Troja Jr.	Swe-Jr.	48	61	69	130	46	....	....	....	....	....	....	....	....	....	....	....	....	....	....	....	....	....	....
1997-98	IF Troja-Ljungby	Sweden-2	28	3	2	5	2	....	....	....	....	....	....	....	....	....	5	0	0	0	2	....	....	....	....
1998-99	IF Troja-Ljungby	Sweden-2	38	20	20	40	30	....	....	....	....	....	....	....	....	....	5	4	3	7	4	....	....	....	....
99-2000	Malmo Jr.	Swe-Jr.	1	2	2	4	2	....	....	....	....	....	....	....	....	....	....	....	....	....	....	....	....	....	....
	MoDo	Sweden	32	15	9	24	6	....	....	....	....	....	....	....	....	....	13	5	3	8	8	....	....	....	....
2000-01	MoDo	Sweden	48	16	16	32	14	....	....	....	....	....	....	....	....	....	6	1	3	4	6	....	....	....	....
2001-02	MODO	Sweden	50	18	16	34	10	....	....	....	....	....	....	....	....	....	14	4	*11	*15	4	....	....	....	....
2002-03	**NY Islanders**	**NHL**	**47**	**6**	**17**	**23**	**10**	**1**	**0**	**0**	**66**	**9.1**	**–2**	**5**	**60.0**	**13:52**	....	....	....	....	....	....	....	....	....
	Bridgeport	AHL	23	9	12	21	14	....	....	....	....	....	....	....	....	....	....	....	....	....	....	....	....	....	....
2003-04	**NY Islanders**	**NHL**	**55**	**8**	**12**	**20**	**26**	**4**	**0**	**2**	**49**	**16.3**	**9**	**6**	**33.3**	**12:20**	**5**	**0**	**0**	**0**	**2**	**0**	**0**	**0**	**13:07**
	Bridgeport	AHL	10	3	6	9	10	....	....	....	....	....	....	....	....	....	....	....	....	....	....	....	....	....	....
2004-05	MODO	Sweden	50	*26	20	46	18	....	....	....	....	....	....	....	....	....	6	0	0	0	4	....	....	....	....
2005-06	**NY Islanders**	**NHL**	**53**	**2**	**4**	**6**	**14**	**0**	**0**	**0**	**40**	**5.0**	**–4**	**10**	**40.0**	**7:36**	....	....	....	....	....	....	....	....	....
	Minnesota	**NHL**	**15**	**2**	**3**	**5**	**10**	**0**	**0**	**0**	**17**	**11.8**	**0**	**11**	**27.3**	**14:43**	....	....	....	....	....	....	....	....	....
2006-07	**Minnesota**	**NHL**	**12**	**1**	**1**	**2**	**10**	**0**	**0**	**0**	**3**	**33.3**	**–2**	**1**	**0.0**	**6:28**	....	....	....	....	....	....	....	....	....
	Houston Aeros	AHL	48	18	27	45	20	....	....	....	....	....	....	....	....	....	....	....	....	....	....	....	....	....	....
2007-08	Linkopings HC	Sweden	54	*35	27	62	69	....	....	....	....	....	....	....	....	....	16	7	10	17	8	....	....	....	....
	NHL Totals		**182**	**19**	**37**	**56**	**70**	**5**	**0**	**2**	**175**	**10.9**		**33**	**36.4**	**11:10**	**5**	**0**	**0**	**0**	**2**	**0**	**0**	**0**	**13:07**

Signed as a free agent by **MODO** (Sweden), September 18, 2004. Claimed on waivers by **Minnesota** from **NY Islanders**, March 4, 2006.

WEISS, Stephen

(WIGHS, STEE-vehn) **FLA.**

Center. Shoots left. 5'11", 185 lbs. Born, Toronto, Ont., April 3, 1983. Florida's 1st choice, 4th overall, in 2001 Entry Draft.

1997-98	Tor. Young Nats	MTHL	48	51	58	109	....	....	....	....	....	....	....	....	....	....	....	....	....	....	....	....	....	....	....
1998-99	North York	OPJHL	35	15	22	37	10	....	....	....	....	....	....	....	....	....	....	....	....	....	....	....	....	....	....
99-2000	Plymouth Whalers	OHL	64	24	42	66	35	....	....	....	....	....	....	....	....	....	23	8	18	26	18	....	....	....	....
2000-01	Plymouth Whalers	OHL	62	40	47	87	45	....	....	....	....	....	....	....	....	....	18	7	16	23	10	....	....	....	....
2001-02	**Florida**	**NHL**	**7**	**1**	**1**	**2**	**0**	**1**	**0**	**0**	**15**	**6.7**	**0**	**107**	**52.3**	**16:14**	....	....	....	....	....	....	....	....	....
	Plymouth Whalers	OHL	46	25	45	70	69	....	....	....	....	....	....	....	....	....	6	2	7	9	13	....	....	....	....
2002-03	**Florida**	**NHL**	**77**	**6**	**15**	**21**	**17**	**0**	**0**	**2**	**87**	**6.9**	**–13**	**1065**	**46.3**	**14:17**	....	....	....	....	....	....	....	....	....
2003-04	**Florida**	**NHL**	**50**	**12**	**17**	**29**	**10**	**3**	**0**	**2**	**82**	**14.6**	**–10**	**799**	**44.9**	**17:42**	....	....	....	....	....	....	....	....	....
	San Antonio	AHL	10	6	3	9	14	....	....	....	....	....	....	....	....	....	....	....	....	....	....	....	....	....	....
2004-05	San Antonio	AHL	62	15	23	38	38	....	....	....	....	....	....	....	....	....	....	....	....	....	....	....	....	....	....
	Chicago Wolves	AHL	18	7	9	16	12	....	....	....	....	....	....	....	....	....	18	2	7	9	17	....	....	....	....
2005-06	**Florida**	**NHL**	**41**	**9**	**12**	**21**	**22**	**5**	**0**	**1**	**74**	**12.2**	**–2**	**514**	**49.6**	**15:15**	....	....	....	....	....	....	....	....	....
2006-07	**Florida**	**NHL**	**74**	**20**	**28**	**48**	**28**	**10**	**0**	**1**	**176**	**11.4**	**–1**	**1182**	**45.9**	**17:07**	....	....	....	....	....	....	....	....	....
2007-08	**Florida**	**NHL**	**74**	**13**	**29**	**42**	**40**	**4**	**0**	**4**	**132**	**9.8**	**14**	**1198**	**51.2**	**17:35**	....	....	....	....	....	....	....	....	....
	NHL Totals		**323**	**61**	**102**	**163**	**117**	**23**	**0**	**10**	**566**	**10.8**		**4865**	**47.7**	**16:23**	....	....	....	....	....	....	....	....	....

OHL All-Rookie Team (2000)

Loaned to **Chicago** (AHL) by **San Antonio** (AHL) for cash, March 8, 2005.

WELCH, Noah

(WEHLCH, NOH-uh) **FLA.**

Defense. Shoots left. 6'4", 218 lbs. Born, Brighton, MA, August 26, 1982. Pittsburgh's 2nd choice, 54th overall, in 2001 Entry Draft.

99-2000	St. Sebastian's	High-MA	26	4	11	15	35	....	....	....	....	....	....	....	....	....	....	....	....	....	....	....	....	....	....
	Eastern-Mass	MBAHL	4	0	3	3	6	....	....	....	....	....	....	....	....	....	....	....	....	....	....	....	....	....	....
2000-01	St. Sebastian's	High-MA	30	11	20	31	37	....	....	....	....	....	....	....	....	....	....	....	....	....	....	....	....	....	....
2001-02	Harvard Crimson	ECAC	27	5	6	11	56	....	....	....	....	....	....	....	....	....	....	....	....	....	....	....	....	....	....
2002-03	Harvard Crimson	ECAC	34	6	22	28	70	....	....	....	....	....	....	....	....	....	....	....	....	....	....	....	....	....	....
2003-04	Harvard Crimson	ECAC	34	6	13	19	58	....	....	....	....	....	....	....	....	....	....	....	....	....	....	....	....	....	....
2004-05	Harvard Crimson	ECAC	34	6	12	18	*86	....	....	....	....	....	....	....	....	....	....	....	....	....	....	....	....	....	....
2005-06	**Pittsburgh**	**NHL**	**5**	**1**	**3**	**4**	**2**	**0**	**0**	**0**	**5**	**20.0**	**0**	**0**	**0.0**	**17:24**	....	....	....	....	....	....	....	....	....
	Wilkes-Barre	AHL	77	9	20	29	99	....	....	....	....	....	....	....	....	....	11	1	0	1	18	....	....	....	....
2006-07	**Pittsburgh**	**NHL**	**22**	**1**	**1**	**2**	**22**	**0**	**0**	**0**	**14**	**7.1**	**1**	**0**	**0.0**	**13:34**	....	....	....	....	....	....	....	....	....
	Wilkes-Barre	AHL	27	5	16	21	24	....	....	....	....	....	....	....	....	....	....	....	....	....	....	....	....	....	....
	Florida	**NHL**	**2**	**1**	**0**	**1**	**2**	**0**	**0**	**0**	**4**	**25.0**	**3**	**0**	**0.0**	**18:08**	....	....	....	....	....	....	....	....	....
	Rochester	AHL	11	2	4	6	21	....	....	....	....	....	....	....	....	....	6	0	2	2	12	....	....	....	....
2007-08	**Florida**	**NHL**	**4**	**0**	**0**	**0**	**7**	**0**	**0**	**0**	**0**	**0.0**	**1**	**0**	**0.0**	**8:04**	....	....	....	....	....	....	....	....	....
	NHL Totals		**33**	**3**	**4**	**7**	**33**	**0**	**0**	**0**	**23**	**13.0**		**0**	**0.0**	**13:45**	....	....	....	....	....	....	....	....	....

ECAC All-Rookie Team (2002) • ECAC Second All-Star Team (2002, 2003) • NCAA East Second All-American Team (2003) • ECAC First All-Star Team (2005) • NCAA East First All-American Team (2005)

Traded to **Florida** by **Pittsburgh** for Gary Roberts, February 27, 2007. • Missed remainder of 2007-08 season recovering from shoulder injury suffered in game at Montreal, October 16, 2007.

WELLER, Craig

(WEHL-uhr, KRAIG) **MIN.**

Right wing. Shoots right. 6'4", 220 lbs. Born, Calgary, Alta., January 17, 1981. St. Louis' 6th choice, 167th overall, in 2000 Entry Draft.

1997-98	Cgy. AAA Flames	AMHL	33	2	10	12	65	....	....	....	....	....	....	....	....	....	3	0	1	1	2	....	....	....	....
1998-99	Calgary Canucks	AJHL	49	4	14	18	80	....	....	....	....	....	....	....	....	....	13	0	1	1	10	....	....	....	....
99-2000	Calgary Canucks	AJHL	53	3	14	17	100	....	....	....	....	....	....	....	....	....	4	0	0	0	4	....	....	....	....
2000-01	U. Minn-Duluth	WCHA	6	0	1	1	0	....	....	....	....	....	....	....	....	....	....	....	....	....	....	....	....	....	....
	Kootenay Ice	WHL	30	1	5	6	40	....	....	....	....	....	....	....	....	....	11	0	2	2	26	....	....	....	....
2001-02	Kootenay Ice	WHL	69	5	13	18	127	....	....	....	....	....	....	....	....	....	22	3	7	10	27	....	....	....	....
2002-03	Hartford	AHL	11	0	0	0	8	....	....	....	....	....	....	....	....	....	2	0	0	0	0	....	....	....	....
	Charlotte	ECHL	48	3	11	14	84	....	....	....	....	....	....	....	....	....	....	....	....	....	....	....	....	....	....
2003-04	Hartford	AHL	68	5	9	14	86	....	....	....	....	....	....	....	....	....	16	2	2	4	30	....	....	....	....
2004-05	Hartford	AHL	76	10	9	19	182	....	....	....	....	....	....	....	....	....	6	0	1	1	6	....	....	....	....
2005-06	Hartford	AHL	80	12	21	33	152	....	....	....	....	....	....	....	....	....	13	2	3	5	44	....	....	....	....
2006-07	Hartford	AHL	56	11	6	17	96	....	....	....	....	....	....	....	....	....	4	0	0	0	4	....	....	....	....
2007-08	**Phoenix**	**NHL**	**59**	**3**	**8**	**11**	**80**	**0**	**0**	**1**	**72**	**4.2**	**–7**	**2**	**0.0**	**10:23**	....	....	....	....	....	....	....	....	....
	NHL Totals		**59**	**3**	**8**	**11**	**80**	**0**	**0**	**1**	**72**	**4.2**		**2**	**0.0**	**10:23**	....	....	....	....	....	....	....	....	....

WHL West Second All-Star Team (2002)

• Left **University of Minnesota-Duluth** (WCHA) and signed as a free agent by **Kootenay** (WHL), January 7, 2001. Signed as a free agent by **NY Rangers**, July 11, 2002. Signed as a free agent by **Phoenix**, July 19, 2007. Signed as a free agent by **Minnesota**, July 1, 2008.

WELLWOOD, Kyle

(WEHL-wud, KIGHL) **VAN.**

Center. Shoots right. 5'10", 180 lbs. Born, Windsor, Ont., May 16, 1983. Toronto's 6th choice, 134th overall, in 2001 Entry Draft.

1998-99	Tecumseh	OHA-B	51	22	41	63	12	....	....	....	....	....	....	....	....	....	....	....	....	....	....	....	....	....	....
99-2000	Belleville Bulls	OHL	65	14	37	51	14	....	....	....	....	....	....	....	....	....	16	3	7	10	6	....	....	....	....
2000-01	Belleville Bulls	OHL	68	35	*83	*118	24	....	....	....	....	....	....	....	....	....	10	3	16	19	4	....	....	....	....
2001-02	Belleville Bulls	OHL	28	16	24	40	4	....	....	....	....	....	....	....	....	....	....	....	....	....	....	....	....	....	....
	Windsor Spitfires	OHL	26	14	21	35	0	....	....	....	....	....	....	....	....	....	16	12	12	24	0	....	....	....	....
2002-03	Windsor Spitfires	OHL	57	41	59	100	0	....	....	....	....	....	....	....	....	....	7	5	9	14	0	....	....	....	....

Season	Club	League	Regular Season														Playoffs								
			GP	G	A	Pts	PIM	PP	SH	GW	S	%	+/-	TF	F%	Min	GP	G	A	Pts	PIM	PP	SH	GW	Min
2003-04	Toronto	NHL	1	0	0	0	0	0	0	0	1	0.0	−1	13	30.8	7:56	....	....	....	....	....	....	....	....	....
	St. John's	AHL	76	20	35	55	6	....	....	....	....	....	....	....	....	....	....	....	....	....	....	....	....	....	....
2004-05	St. John's	AHL	80	38	49	87	20	....	....	....	....	....	....	....	....	....	5	2	2	4	2	....	....	....	....
2005-06	Toronto	NHL	81	11	34	45	14	3	0	0	117	9.4	0	593	56.3	12:47	....	....	....	....	....	....	....	....	....
2006-07	Toronto	NHL	48	12	30	42	0	7	0	2	99	12.1	3	291	56.4	16:38	....	....	....	....	....	....	....	....	....
2007-08	Toronto	NHL	59	8	13	21	0	5	0	1	57	14.0	−12	325	54.8	12:39	....	....	....	....	....	....	....	....	....
	NHL Totals		189	31	77	108	14	15	0	3	274	11.3		1222	55.6	13:41	....	....	....	....	....	....	....	....	....

OHL First All-Star Team (2001) • Canadian Major Junior Sportsman of the Year (2003)

Claimed on waivers by **Vancouver** from **Toronto**, June 25, 2008.

WESLEY, Glen

(WEH-slee, GLEHN)

Defense. Shoots left. 6'1", 207 lbs. Born, Red Deer, Alta., October 2, 1968. Boston's 1st choice, 3rd overall, in 1987 Entry Draft.

Season	Club	League	GP	G	A	Pts	PIM	PP	SH	GW	S	%	+/-	TF	F%	Min	GP	G	A	Pts	PIM	PP	SH	GW	Min
1983-84	Red Deer Rustlers	AJHL	57	9	20	29	40	....	....	....	....	....	....	....	....	....	....	....	....	....	....	....	....	....	....
	Portland	WHL	3	1	2	3	0	....	....	....	....	....	....	....	....	....	....	....	....	....	....	....	....	....	....
1984-85	Portland	WHL	67	16	52	68	76	....	....	....	....	....	....	....	....	....	6	1	6	7	8	....	....	....	....
1985-86	Portland	WHL	69	16	75	91	96	....	....	....	....	....	....	....	....	....	15	3	11	14	29	....	....	....	....
1986-87	Portland	WHL	63	16	46	62	72	....	....	....	....	....	....	....	....	....	20	8	18	26	27	....	....	....	....
1987-88	Boston	NHL	79	7	30	37	69	1	2	0	158	4.4	21	....	....	....	23	6	8	14	22	4	1	0	....
1988-89	Boston	NHL	77	19	35	54	61	8	1	1	181	10.5	23	....	....	....	10	0	2	2	4	0	0	0	....
1989-90	Boston	NHL	78	9	27	36	48	5	0	4	166	5.4	6	....	....	....	21	2	6	8	36	0	0	1	....
1990-91	Boston	NHL	80	11	32	43	78	5	1	1	199	5.5	0	....	....	....	19	2	9	11	19	2	0	0	....
1991-92	Boston	NHL	78	9	37	46	54	4	0	1	211	4.3	−9	....	....	....	15	2	4	6	16	0	0	0	....
1992-93	Boston	NHL	64	8	25	33	47	4	1	0	183	4.4	−2	....	....	....	4	0	0	0	0	0	0	0	....
1993-94	Boston	NHL	81	14	44	58	64	6	1	1	265	5.3	1	....	....	....	13	3	3	6	12	1	0	0	....
1994-95	Hartford	NHL	48	2	14	16	50	1	0	1	125	1.6	−6	....	....	....	....	....	....	....	....	....	....	....	....
1995-96	Hartford	NHL	68	8	16	24	88	6	0	1	129	6.2	−9	....	....	....	....	....	....	....	....	....	....	....	....
1996-97	Hartford	NHL	68	6	26	32	40	3	1	0	126	4.8	0	....	....	....	....	....	....	....	....	....	....	....	....
1997-98	Carolina	NHL	82	6	19	25	36	1	0	1	121	5.0	7	....	....	....	....	....	....	....	....	....	....	....	....
1998-99	Carolina	NHL	74	7	17	24	44	0	0	2	112	6.3	14	1	0.0	22:31	6	0	0	0	2	0	0	0	28:21
99-2000	Carolina	NHL	78	7	15	22	38	1	0	0	99	7.1	−4	0	0.0	21:32	....	....	....	....	....	....	....	....	....
2000-01	Carolina	NHL	71	5	16	21	42	3	0	0	92	5.4	−2	0	0.0	22:21	6	0	0	0	0	0	0	0	22:07
2001-02	Carolina	NHL	77	5	13	18	56	1	0	0	88	5.7	−8	0	0.0	20:13	22	0	2	2	12	0	0	0	21:04
2002-03	Carolina	NHL	63	1	7	8	40	1	0	0	72	1.4	−5	0	0.0	21:24	....	....	....	....	....	....	....	....	....
	Toronto	NHL	7	0	3	3	4	0	0	0	5	0.0	3	0	0.0	20:41	5	0	1	1	2	0	0	0	27:39
2003-04	Carolina	NHL	74	0	6	6	32	0	0	0	82	0.0	18	0	0.0	21:22	....	....	....	....	....	....	....	....	....
2004-05			DID NOT PLAY																						
2005-06 ♦	Carolina	NHL	64	2	8	10	46	0	0	0	28	7.1	10	0	0.0	15:28	25	0	2	2	16	0	0	0	16:10
2006-07	Carolina	NHL	68	1	12	13	56	0	1	1	51	2.0	11	0	0.0	15:35	....	....	....	....	....	....	....	....	....
2007-08	Carolina	NHL	78	1	7	8	52	0	0	1	63	1.6	−3	0	0.0	16:06	....	....	....	....	....	....	....	....	....
	NHL Totals		1457	128	409	537	1045	50	8	15	2556	5.0		1	0.0	19:41	169	15	37	52	141	7	1	1	20:27

WHL West First All-Star Team (1986, 1987) • NHL All-Rookie Team (1988)

Played in NHL All-Star Game (1989)

Traded to **Hartford** by **Boston** for Hartford's 1st round choices in 1995 (Kyle McLaren), 1996 (Johnathan Aitken) and 1997 (Sergei Samsonov) Entry Drafts, August 26, 1994. Transferred to **Carolina** after **Hartford** franchise relocated, June 25, 1997. Traded to **Toronto** by **Carolina** for Toronto's 2nd round choice (later traded to Columbus – Columbus selected Kyle Wharton) in 2004 Entry Draft, March 9, 2003. Signed as a free agent by **Carolina**, July 8, 2003. • Officially announced his retirement, June 5, 2008.

WESTCOTT, Duvie

(WEST-koht, DOO-vee)

Defense. Shoots right. 5'11", 197 lbs. Born, Winnipeg, Man., October 30, 1977.

Season	Club	League	GP	G	A	Pts	PIM	PP	SH	GW	S	%	+/-	TF	F%	Min	GP	G	A	Pts	PIM	PP	SH	GW	Min
1996-97	Winnipeg South	MJHL	52	12	47	59	....	....	....	....	....	....	....	....	....	....	....	....	....	....	....	....	....	....	....
1997-98	Alaska Anchorage	WCHA	25	3	5	8	43	....	....	....	....	....	....	....	....	....	....	....	....	....	....	....	....	....	....
	Omaha Lancers	USHL	12	3	3	6	31	....	....	....	....	....	....	....	....	....	14	0	8	8	84	....	....	....	....
1998-99	St. Cloud State	WCHA	DID NOT PLAY – TRANSFERRED COLLEGES																						
99-2000	St. Cloud State	WCHA	36	1	18	19	67	....	....	....	....	....	....	....	....	....	....	....	....	....	....	....	....	....	....
2000-01	St. Cloud State	WCHA	38	10	24	34	116	....	....	....	....	....	....	....	....	....	....	....	....	....	....	....	....	....	....
2001-02	Columbus	NHL	4	0	0	0	2	0	0	0	3	0.0	−2	0	0.0	15:08	....	....	....	....	....	....	....	....	....
	Syracuse Crunch	AHL	68	4	29	33	99	....	....	....	....	....	....	....	....	....	10	0	1	1	12	....	....	....	....
2002-03	Columbus	NHL	39	0	7	7	77	0	0	0	27	0.0	−3	0	0.0	18:41	....	....	....	....	....	....	....	....	....
	Syracuse Crunch	AHL	22	1	10	11	54	....	....	....	....	....	....	....	....	....	....	....	....	....	....	....	....	....	....
2003-04	Columbus	NHL	34	0	7	7	39	0	0	0	43	0.0	−15	0	0.0	21:11	....	....	....	....	....	....	....	....	....
2004-05	JYP Jyvaskyla	Finland	46	11	7	18	106	....	....	....	....	....	....	....	....	....	1	2	0	2	25	....	....	....	....
2005-06	Columbus	NHL	78	6	22	28	133	1	1	0	113	5.3	1	0	0.0	22:34	....	....	....	....	....	....	....	....	....
2006-07	Columbus	NHL	23	4	6	10	18	2	0	1	34	11.8	−13	0	0.0	22:09	....	....	....	....	....	....	....	....	....
2007-08	Columbus	NHL	23	1	3	4	30	1	0	0	27	3.7	−10	0	0.0	16:25	....	....	....	....	....	....	....	....	....
	Syracuse Crunch	AHL	37	4	23	27	77	....	....	....	....	....	....	....	....	....	13	2	4	6	10	....	....	....	....
	NHL Totals		201	11	45	56	299	4	1	1	247	4.5		0	0.0	20:41	....	....	....	....	....	....	....	....	....

WCHA Second All-Star Team (2001)

Signed as a free agent by **Columbus**, May 10, 2001. • Missed majority of 2003-04 season recovering from ankle (October 13, 2003 vs. Vancouver) and hand (January 31, 2004 vs. Minnesota) injuries. Signed as a free agent by **Jyvaskyla** (Finland), September 30, 2004. • Missed majority of 2006-07 season recovering from finger (November 3, 2006 vs. Calgary) and head (January 6, 2007 vs. San Jose) injuries.

WESTRUM, Erik

(WEHST-ruhm, AIR-ihk)

Center. Shoots left. 6', 204 lbs. Born, Minneapolis, MN, July 26, 1979. Phoenix's 9th choice, 187th overall, in 1998 Entry Draft.

Season	Club	League	GP	G	A	Pts	PIM	PP	SH	GW	S	%	+/-	TF	F%	Min	GP	G	A	Pts	PIM	PP	SH	GW	Min
1995/97	Apple Valley	High-MN	78	56	84	140	....	....	....	....	....	....	....	....	....	....	....	....	....	....	....	....	....	....	....
1997-98	U. of Minnesota	WCHA	39	6	12	18	43	....	....	....	....	....	....	....	....	....	....	....	....	....	....	....	....	....	....
1998-99	U. of Minnesota	WCHA	41	10	26	36	81	....	....	....	....	....	....	....	....	....	....	....	....	....	....	....	....	....	....
99-2000	U. of Minnesota	WCHA	39	27	26	53	99	....	....	....	....	....	....	....	....	....	....	....	....	....	....	....	....	....	....
2000-01	U. of Minnesota	WCHA	42	26	35	61	84	....	....	....	....	....	....	....	....	....	....	....	....	....	....	....	....	....	....
2001-02	Springfield	AHL	73	13	29	42	116	....	....	....	....	....	....	....	....	....	....	....	....	....	....	....	....	....	....
2002-03	Springfield	AHL	70	10	22	32	65	....	....	....	....	....	....	....	....	....	6	0	4	4	6	....	....	....	....
2003-04	Phoenix	NHL	15	1	1	2	20	0	0	0	29	3.4	−3	106	39.6	16:00	....	....	....	....	....	....	....	....	....
	Springfield	AHL	56	14	18	32	91	....	....	....	....	....	....	....	....	....	....	....	....	....	....	....	....	....	....
2004-05	Utah Grizzlies	AHL	80	18	15	33	117	....	....	....	....	....	....	....	....	....	....	....	....	....	....	....	....	....	....
2005-06	Minnesota	NHL	10	0	1	1	2	0	0	0	16	0.0	−1	68	38.2	10:48	....	....	....	....	....	....	....	....	....
	Houston Aeros	AHL	71	34	64	98	138	....	....	....	....	....	....	....	....	....	8	1	7	8	20	....	....	....	....
2006-07	Toronto	NHL	2	0	0	0	0	0	0	0	0	0.0	0	5	40.0	3:31	....	....	....	....	....	....	....	....	....
	Toronto Marlies	AHL	70	23	34	57	135	....	....	....	....	....	....	....	....	....	....	....	....	....	....	....	....	....	....
2007-08	HC Ambri-Piotta	Swiss	50	*33	39	*72	102	....	....	....	....	....	....	....	....	....	7	3	6	9	*71	....	....	....	....
	NHL Totals		27	1	2	3	22	0	0	0	45	2.2		179	39.1	13:09	....	....	....	....	....	....	....	....	....

WCHA Second All-Star Team (2001) • AHL First All-Star Team (2006)

• Statistics for **Apple Valley** (High-MN) are career totals for 1995-1997 seasons. Traded to **Minnesota** by **Phoenix** with Dustin Wood for Zbynek Michalek, August 26, 2005. Signed as a free agent by **Toronto**, July 13, 2006.

WHITE, Colin

(WIGHT, KAW-lihn) **N.J.**

Defense. Shoots left. 6'4", 220 lbs. Born, New Glasgow, N.S., December 12, 1977. New Jersey's 5th choice, 49th overall, in 1996 Entry Draft.

Season	Club	League	GP	G	A	Pts	PIM	PP	SH	GW	S	%	+/-	TF	F%	Min	GP	G	A	Pts	PIM	PP	SH	GW	Min
1994-95	Laval Titan	QMJHL	7	0	1	1	32	....	....	....	....	....	....	....	....	....	....	....	....	....	....	....	....	....	....
	Hull Olympiques	QMJHL	5	0	1	1	4	....	....	....	....	....	....	....	....	....	12	0	0	0	23	....	....	....	....
1995-96	Hull Olympiques	QMJHL	62	2	8	10	303	....	....	....	....	....	....	....	....	....	18	0	4	4	42	....	....	....	....
1996-97	Hull Olympiques	QMJHL	63	3	12	15	297	....	....	....	....	....	....	....	....	....	14	3	12	15	65	....	....	....	....
1997-98	Albany River Rats	AHL	76	3	13	16	235	....	....	....	....	....	....	....	....	....	13	0	0	0	55	....	....	....	....
1998-99	Albany River Rats	AHL	77	2	12	14	265	....	....	....	....	....	....	....	....	....	5	0	1	1	8	....	....	....	....
99-2000 ♦	New Jersey	NHL	21	2	1	3	40	0	0	1	29	6.9	3	0	0.0	14:45	23	1	5	6	18	0	0	1	14:25
	Albany River Rats	AHL	52	5	21	26	176	....	....	....	....	....	....	....	....	....	....	....	....	....	....	....	....	....	....
2000-01	New Jersey	NHL	82	1	19	20	155	0	0	1	114	0.9	32	0	0.0	19:06	25	0	3	3	42	0	0	0	16:45
2001-02	New Jersey	NHL	73	2	3	5	133	0	0	0	81	2.5	6	0	0.0	20:06	6	0	0	0	2	0	0	0	21:50
2002-03 ♦	New Jersey	NHL	72	5	8	13	98	0	0	1	81	6.2	19	0	0.0	19:41	24	0	5	5	29	0	0	0	22:02

			Regular Season														Playoffs								
Season	Club	League	GP	G	A	Pts	PIM	PP	SH	GW	S	%	+/-	TF	F%	Min	GP	G	A	Pts	PIM	PP	SH	GW	Min
2003-04	**New Jersey**	**NHL**	75	2	11	13	96	0	0	0	61	3.3	10	0	0.0	21:02	5	0	0	0	4	0	0	0	19:40
2004-05			DID NOT PLAY																						
2005-06	**New Jersey**	**NHL**	73	3	14	17	91	1	0	1	60	5.0	–2	0	0.0	21:48	4	0	0	0	4	0	0	0	17:39
2006-07	**New Jersey**	**NHL**	69	0	8	8	69	0	0	0	47	0.0	–8	0	0.0	22:28	7	0	0	0	6	0	0	0	21:16
2007-08	**New Jersey**	**NHL**	57	2	8	10	26	0	0	1	27	7.4	–5	0	0.0	19:40	5	0	0	0	6	0	0	0	20:27
	NHL Totals		**522**	**17**	**72**	**89**	**708**	**1**	**0**	**5**	**500**	**3.4**		**0**	**0.0**	**20:18**	**99**	**1**	**13**	**14**	**111**	**0**	**0**	**1**	**18:29**

QMJHL All-Rookie Team (1996) • NHL All-Rookie Team (2001)

WHITE, Ian
(WIGHT, EE-an) **TOR.**

Defense. Shoots right. 5'10", 185 lbs. Born, Steinbach, Man., June 4, 1984. Toronto's 6th choice, 191st overall, in 2002 Entry Draft.

99-2000	Eastman Selects	MAHA	32	29	33	62	36	....	....	....	....	....	....	....	....	....	....	....	....	....	....	....	....	....	....
2000-01	Swift Current	WHL	69	12	31	43	24	....	....	....	....	....	....	....	....	....	....	....	....	....	....	....	....	....	....
2001-02	Swift Current	WHL	70	32	47	79	40	....	....	....	....	....	....	....	....	....	12	4	5	9	12	....	....	....	....
2002-03	Swift Current	WHL	64	24	44	68	44	....	....	....	....	....	....	....	....	....	4	0	4	4	0	....	....	....	....
2003-04	Swift Current	WHL	43	9	23	32	32	....	....	....	....	....	....	....	....	....	5	1	3	4	8	....	....	....	....
	St. John's	AHL	8	0	4	4	2	....	....	....	....	....	....	....	....	....	....	....	....	....	....	....	....	....	....
2004-05	St. John's	AHL	78	4	22	26	54	....	....	....	....	....	....	....	....	....	5	0	2	2	2	....	....	....	....
2005-06	**Toronto**	**NHL**	12	1	5	6	10	0	0	0	21	4.8	2	0	0.0	19:07	....	....	....	....	....	....	....	....	....
	Toronto Marlies	AHL	59	7	30	37	42	....	....	....	....	....	....	....	....	....	5	1	4	5	4	....	....	....	....
2006-07	**Toronto**	**NHL**	76	3	23	26	40	1	0	1	138	2.2	8	0	0.0	18:32	....	....	....	....	....	....	....	....	....
2007-08	**Toronto**	**NHL**	81	5	16	21	44	0	0	2	116	4.3	–9	0	0.0	18:48	....	....	....	....	....	....	....	....	....
	NHL Totals		**169**	**9**	**44**	**53**	**94**	**1**	**0**	**3**	**275**	**3.3**		**0**	**0.0**	**18:42**	....	....	....	....	....	....	....	....	....

WHL East Second All-Star Team (2002) • WHL East First All-Star Team (2003)

WHITE, Todd
(WIGHT, TAWD) **ATL.**

Center. Shoots left. 5'10", 195 lbs. Born, Kanata, Ont., May 21, 1975.

1990-91	Powassan	NOJHA	38	34	38	72	118	....	....	....	....	....	....	....	....	....	....	....	....	....	....	....	....	....	....
1991-92	Kanata Valley	CJHL	55	39	49	88	30	....	....	....	....	....	....	....	....	....	....	....	....	....	....	....	....	....	....
1992-93	Kanata Valley	CJHL	49	51	87	138	46	....	....	....	....	....	....	....	....	....	....	....	....	....	....	....	....	....	....
1993-94	Clarkson Knights	ECAC	33	10	12	22	28	....	....	....	....	....	....	....	....	....	....	....	....	....	....	....	....	....	....
1994-95	Clarkson Knights	ECAC	34	13	16	29	44	....	....	....	....	....	....	....	....	....	....	....	....	....	....	....	....	....	....
1995-96	Clarkson Knights	ECAC	38	29	43	72	36	....	....	....	....	....	....	....	....	....	....	....	....	....	....	....	....	....	....
1996-97	Clarkson Knights	ECAC	37	*38	*36	*74	22	....	....	....	....	....	....	....	....	....	....	....	....	....	....	....	....	....	....
1997-98	**Chicago**	**NHL**	7	1	0	1	2	0	0	0	3	33.3	0	....	....	....	....	....	....	....	....	....	....	....	....
	Indianapolis Ice	IHL	65	46	36	82	28	....	....	....	....	....	....	....	....	....	5	2	3	5	4	....	....	....	....
1998-99	**Chicago**	**NHL**	35	5	8	13	20	2	0	0	43	11.6	–1	452	46.0	13:39	....	....	....	....	....	....	....	....	....
	Chicago Wolves	IHL	25	11	13	24	8	....	....	....	....	....	....	....	....	....	10	1	4	5	8	....	....	....	....
99-2000	**Chicago**	**NHL**	1	0	0	0	0	0	0	0	0	0.0	0	9	55.6	13:02	....	....	....	....	....	....	....	....	....
	Cleveland	IHL	42	21	30	51	32	....	....	....	....	....	....	....	....	....	....	....	....	....	....	....	....	....	....
	Philadelphia	**NHL**	3	1	0	1	0	0	0	0	4	25.0	–1	25	40.0	10:29	....	....	....	....	....	....	....	....	....
	Philadelphia	AHL	32	19	24	43	12	....	....	....	....	....	....	....	....	....	5	2	1	3	8	....	....	....	....
2000-01	**Ottawa**	**NHL**	16	4	1	5	4	0	0	0	12	33.3	5	133	57.1	8:33	2	0	0	0	0	0	0	0	7:29
	Grand Rapids	IHL	64	22	32	54	20	....	....	....	....	....	....	....	....	....	10	4	4	8	10	....	....	....	....
2001-02	**Ottawa**	**NHL**	81	20	30	50	24	4	0	1	147	13.6	12	1508	50.5	18:22	12	2	2	4	6	0	0	0	18:57
2002-03	**Ottawa**	**NHL**	80	25	35	60	28	8	1	5	144	17.4	19	1396	50.5	17:58	18	5	1	6	6	1	1	2	16:59
2003-04	**Ottawa**	**NHL**	53	9	20	29	22	1	1	2	98	9.2	12	879	52.0	17:32	7	1	0	1	4	0	0	0	18:04
2004-05	Sodertalje SK	Sweden	1	0	1	1	4	....	....	....	....	....	....	....	....	....	....	....	....	....	....	....	....	....	....
2005-06	**Minnesota**	**NHL**	61	19	21	40	18	5	0	0	109	17.4	–1	886	49.1	17:12	....	....	....	....	....	....	....	....	....
2006-07	**Minnesota**	**NHL**	77	13	31	44	24	6	1	1	162	8.0	8	1051	49.2	17:13	4	0	0	0	0	0	0	0	14:18
2007-08	**Atlanta**	**NHL**	74	14	23	37	36	6	1	4	111	12.6	–12	1166	46.6	18:26	....	....	....	....	....	....	....	....	....
	NHL Totals		**488**	**111**	**169**	**280**	**178**	**32**	**4**	**13**	**833**	**13.3**		**7505**	**49.5**	**17:09**	**43**	**8**	**3**	**11**	**16**	**1**	**1**	**2**	**17:01**

ECAC Second All-Star Team (1996) • NCAA East Second All-American Team (1996) • ECAC First All-Star Team (1997) • ECAC Player of the Year (1997) • NCAA East First All-American Team (1997) • Garry F. Longman Memorial Trophy (Rookie of the Year – IHL) (1998)

Signed as a free agent by **Chicago**, August 27, 1997. Traded to **Philadelphia** by **Chicago** for future considerations, January 26, 2000. Signed as a free agent by **Ottawa**, July 12, 2000. Signed as a free agent by **Sodertalje** (Sweden), December 21, 2004. Traded to **Minnesota** by **Ottawa** for Colorado's 4th round choice (previously acquired, Ottawa selected Cody Bass) in 2005 Entry Draft, July 30, 2005. Signed as a free agent by **Atlanta**, July 1, 2007.

WHITFIELD, Trent
(WHIHT-feeld, TREHNT) **ST.L.**

Center. Shoots left. 5'11", 209 lbs. Born, Estevan, Sask., June 17, 1977. Boston's 5th choice, 100th overall, in 1996 Entry Draft.

1993-94	Saskatoon Blazers	SMHL	36	26	22	48	42	....	....	....	....	....	....	....	....	....	....	....	....	....	....	....	....	....	....
	Spokane Chiefs	WHL	5	1	1	2	0	....	....	....	....	....	....	....	....	....	....	....	....	....	....	....	....	....	....
1994-95	Spokane Chiefs	WHL	48	8	17	25	26	....	....	....	....	....	....	....	....	....	11	7	6	13	5	....	....	....	....
1995-96	Spokane Chiefs	WHL	72	33	51	84	75	....	....	....	....	....	....	....	....	....	18	8	10	18	10	....	....	....	....
1996-97	Spokane Chiefs	WHL	58	34	42	76	74	....	....	....	....	....	....	....	....	....	9	5	7	12	10	....	....	....	....
1997-98	Spokane Chiefs	WHL	65	38	44	82	97	....	....	....	....	....	....	....	....	....	18	9	10	19	15	....	....	....	....
1998-99	Portland Pirates	AHL	50	10	8	18	20	....	....	....	....	....	....	....	....	....	....	....	....	....	....	....	....	....	....
	Hampton Roads	ECHL	19	13	12	25	12	....	....	....	....	....	....	....	....	....	4	2	0	2	14	....	....	....	....
99-2000	Portland Pirates	AHL	79	18	35	53	52	....	....	....	....	....	....	....	....	....	3	1	1	2	2	....	....	....	....
	Washington	**NHL**	....	....	....	....	....	....	....	....	....	....	....	....	....	....	3	0	0	0	0	0	0	0	5:47
2000-01	**Washington**	**NHL**	61	2	4	6	35	0	0	0	47	4.3	3	520	51.9	9:39	5	0	0	0	2	0	0	0	7:07
	Portland Pirates	AHL	19	9	11	20	27	....	....	....	....	....	....	....	....	....	....	....	....	....	....	....	....	....	....
2001-02	**Washington**	**NHL**	24	0	1	1	28	0	0	0	15	0.0	–3	189	54.0	7:06	....	....	....	....	....	....	....	....	....
	Portland Pirates	AHL	10	4	4	8	8	....	....	....	....	....	....	....	....	....	....	....	....	....	....	....	....	....	....
	NY Rangers	**NHL**	1	0	0	0	0	0	0	0	0	0.0	1	18	50.0	12:44	....	....	....	....	....	....	....	....	....
	Portland Pirates	AHL	24	10	16	26	16	....	....	....	....	....	....	....	....	....	....	....	....	....	....	....	....	....	....
2002-03	**Washington**	**NHL**	14	1	1	2	6	0	0	1	4	25.0	1	124	57.3	8:30	6	0	0	0	10	0	0	0	11:01
	Portland Pirates	AHL	64	27	34	61	42	....	....	....	....	....	....	....	....	....	....	....	....	....	....	....	....	....	....
2003-04	**Washington**	**NHL**	44	6	5	11	14	0	1	2	38	15.8	–2	598	55.4	12:48	....	....	....	....	....	....	....	....	....
	Portland Pirates	AHL	24	8	7	15	22	....	....	....	....	....	....	....	....	....	....	....	....	....	....	....	....	....	....
2004-05	Portland Pirates	AHL	67	17	38	55	75	....	....	....	....	....	....	....	....	....	....	....	....	....	....	....	....	....	....
2005-06	**St. Louis**	**NHL**	30	2	5	7	14	1	0	0	41	4.9	–3	330	54.6	11:56	....	....	....	....	....	....	....	....	....
	Peoria Rivermen	AHL	41	19	34	53	18	....	....	....	....	....	....	....	....	....	....	....	....	....	....	....	....	....	....
2006-07	Peoria Rivermen	AHL	79	33	45	78	70	....	....	....	....	....	....	....	....	....	....	....	....	....	....	....	....	....	....
2007-08	Peoria Rivermen	AHL	80	22	30	52	51	....	....	....	....	....	....	....	....	....	....	....	....	....	....	....	....	....	....
	NHL Totals		**174**	**11**	**16**	**27**	**97**	**1**	**1**	**3**	**145**	**7.6**		**1779**	**54.1**	**10:25**	**14**	**0**	**0**	**0**	**12**	**0**	**0**	**0**	**8:30**

WHL West First All-Star Team (1997) • WHL West Second All-Star Team (1998)

Signed as a free agent by **Washington**, September 1, 1998. Claimed on waivers by **NY Rangers** from **Washington**, January 16, 2002. Claimed on waivers by **Washington** from **NY Rangers**, February 1, 2002. Signed as a free agent by **St. Louis**, August 2, 2005.

WHITNEY, Ray
(WHIHT-nee, RAY) **CAR.**

Left wing. Shoots right. 5'10", 180 lbs. Born, Fort Saskatchewan, Alta., May 8, 1972. San Jose's 2nd choice, 23rd overall, in 1991 Entry Draft.

1987-88	Ft. Saskatchewan	AMHL	71	80	155	235	119	....	....	....	....	....	....	....	....	....	....	....	....	....	....	....	....	....	....
1988-89	Spokane Chiefs	WHL	71	17	33	50	16	....	....	....	....	....	....	....	....	....	....	....	....	....	....	....	....	....	....
1989-90	Spokane Chiefs	WHL	71	57	56	113	50	....	....	....	....	....	....	....	....	....	6	3	4	7	6	....	....	....	....
1990-91	Spokane Chiefs	WHL	72	67	118	*185	36	....	....	....	....	....	....	....	....	....	15	13	18	*31	12	....	....	....	....
1991-92	Kolner EC	Germany	10	3	6	9	4	....	....	....	....	....	....	....	....	....	....	....	....	....	....	....	....	....	....
	Canada	Nat-Tm	5	1	0	1	6	....	....	....	....	....	....	....	....	....	....	....	....	....	....	....	....	....	....
	San Jose	**NHL**	2	0	3	3	0	0	0	0	4	0.0	–1	....	....	....	....	....	....	....	....	....	....	....	....
	San Diego Gulls	IHL	63	36	54	90	12	....	....	....	....	....	....	....	....	....	4	0	0	0	0	....	....	....	....
1992-93	**San Jose**	**NHL**	26	4	6	10	4	1	0	0	24	16.7	–14	....	....	....	....	....	....	....	....	....	....	....	....
	Kansas City	IHL	46	20	33	53	14	....	....	....	....	....	....	....	....	....	12	5	7	12	2	....	....	....	....
1993-94	**San Jose**	**NHL**	61	14	26	40	14	1	0	0	82	17.1	2	....	....	....	14	0	4	4	8	0	0	0	....
1994-95	**San Jose**	**NHL**	39	13	12	25	14	4	0	1	67	19.4	–7	....	....	....	11	4	4	8	2	0	0	1	....
1995-96	**San Jose**	**NHL**	60	17	24	41	16	4	2	2	106	16.0	–23	....	....	....	....	....	....	....	....	....	....	....	....

			Regular Season														Playoffs								
Season	Club	League	GP	G	A	Pts	PIM	PP	SH	GW	S	%	+/-	TF	F%	Min	GP	G	A	Pts	PIM	PP	SH	GW	Min
1996-97	San Jose	NHL	12	0	2	2	4	0	0	0	24	0.0	–6	....	....	....	....	....	....	....	....	....	....	....	....
	Kentucky	AHL	9	1	7	8	2	....	....	....	....	....	....	....	....	....	....	....	....	....	....	....	....	....	....
	Utah Grizzlies	IHL	43	13	35	48	34	....	....	....	....	....	....	....	....	....	7	3	1	4	6	....	....	....	....
1997-98	Edmonton	NHL	9	1	3	4	0	0	0	0	19	5.3	–1	....	....	....	....	....	....	....	....	....	....	....	....
	Florida	NHL	68	32	29	61	28	12	0	2	156	20.5	10	....	....	....	....	....	....	....	....	....	....	....	....
1998-99	Florida	NHL	81	26	38	64	18	7	0	6	193	13.5	–3	144	43.8	18:20	....	....	....	....	....	....	....	....	....
99-2000	Florida	NHL	81	29	42	71	35	5	0	3	198	14.6	16	198	49.0	18:41	4	1	0	1	4	0	0	0	18:13
2000-01	Florida	NHL	43	10	21	31	28	5	0	0	117	8.5	–16	38	39.5	17:41	....	....	....	....	....	....	....	....	....
	Columbus	NHL	3	0	3	3	2	0	0	0	3	0.0	–1	19	36.8	20:17	....	....	....	....	....	....	....	....	....
2001-02	Columbus	NHL	67	21	40	61	12	6	0	3	210	10.0	–22	21	47.6	20:13	....	....	....	....	....	....	....	....	....
2002-03	Columbus	NHL	81	24	52	76	22	8	2	2	235	10.2	–26	29	44.8	21:00	....	....	....	....	....	....	....	....	....
2003-04	Detroit	NHL	67	14	29	43	22	3	1	4	119	11.8	7	18	38.9	16:24	12	1	3	4	4	0	0	1	11:56
2004-05		DID NOT PLAY																							
2005-06♦	Carolina	NHL	63	17	38	55	42	12	0	2	147	11.6	0	13	38.5	17:11	24	9	6	15	14	5	0	1	14:07
2006-07	Carolina	NHL	81	32	51	83	46	6	0	6	215	14.9	–5	7	28.6	18:42	....	....	....	....	....	....	....	....	....
2007-08	Carolina	NHL	66	25	36	61	30	6	0	4	204	12.3	–6	5	60.0	18:56	....	....	....	....	....	....	....	....	....
	NHL Totals		910	279	455	734	337	80	5	35	2123	13.1		492	45.1	18:41	65	15	17	32	32	5	0	3	13:52

WHL West First All-Star Team (1991) • WHL Player of the Year (1991) • Memorial Cup Tournament All-Star Team (1991) • George Parsons Trophy (Memorial Cup Tournament - Most Sportsmanlike Player) (1991)

Played in NHL All-Star Game (2000, 2003)

Signed as a free agent by **Edmonton**, October 1, 1997. Claimed on waivers by **Florida** from **Edmonton**, November 6, 1997. Traded to **Columbus** by **Florida** with future considerations for Kevyn Adams and Columbus's 4th round choice (Michael Woodford) in 2001 Entry Draft, March 13, 2001. Signed as a free agent by **Detroit**, July 30, 2003. Signed as a free agent by **Carolina**, August 7, 2005.

WHITNEY, Ryan

(WHIHT-nee, RIGH-uhn) **PIT.**

Defense. Shoots left. 6'4", 219 lbs. Born, Boston, MA, February 19, 1983. Pittsburgh's 1st choice, 5th overall, in 2002 Entry Draft.

Season	Club	League	GP	G	A	Pts	PIM	PP	SH	GW	S	%	+/-	TF	F%	Min	GP	G	A	Pts	PIM	PP	SH	GW	Min
99-2000	Thayer Academy	High-MA	22	5	33	38	....	....	....	....	....	....	....	....	....	....	....	....	....	....	....	....	....	....	....
2000-01	USNTDP	U-18	40	7	23	30	64	....	....	....	....	....	....	....	....	....	....	....	....	....	....	....	....	....	....
	USNTDP	USHL	20	2	8	10	22	....	....	....	....	....	....	....	....	....	....	....	....	....	....	....	....	....	....
2001-02	Boston University	H-East	35	4	17	21	46	....	....	....	....	....	....	....	....	....	....	....	....	....	....	....	....	....	....
2002-03	Boston University	H-East	34	3	10	13	48	....	....	....	....	....	....	....	....	....	....	....	....	....	....	....	....	....	....
2003-04	Boston University	H-East	38	9	16	25	56	....	....	....	....	....	....	....	....	....	....	....	....	....	....	....	....	....	....
	Wilkes-Barre	AHL	....	....	....	....	....	....	....	....	....	....	....	....	....	....	20	1	9	10	6	....	....	....	....
2004-05	Wilkes-Barre	AHL	80	6	35	41	101	....	....	....	....	....	....	....	....	....	11	2	7	9	12	....	....	....	....
2005-06	Pittsburgh	NHL	68	6	32	38	85	2	0	1	113	5.3	–7	1	0.0	23:50	....	....	....	....	....	....	....	....	....
	Wilkes-Barre	AHL	9	5	9	14	6	....	....	....	....	....	....	....	....	....	11	1	4	5	8	....	....	....	....
2006-07	Pittsburgh	NHL	81	14	45	59	77	9	0	2	129	10.9	9	5	20.0	23:56	5	1	1	2	6	1	0	0	22:51
2007-08	Pittsburgh	NHL	76	12	28	40	45	7	1	1	119	10.1	–2	0	0.0	22:27	20	1	5	6	25	1	0	0	20:46
	NHL Totals		225	32	105	137	207	18	1	4	361	8.9		6	16.7	23:24	25	2	6	8	31	2	0	0	21:11

Hockey East All-Rookie Team (2002)

WIDEMAN, Dennis

(WIGHD-muhn, DEH-nihs) **BOS.**

Defense. Shoots right. 6', 196 lbs. Born, Kitchener, Ont., March 20, 1983. Buffalo's 9th choice, 241st overall, in 2002 Entry Draft.

Season	Club	League	GP	G	A	Pts	PIM	PP	SH	GW	S	%	+/-	TF	F%	Min	GP	G	A	Pts	PIM	PP	SH	GW	Min
1998-99	Elmira	OHA-B	47	18	30	48	142	....	....	....	....	....	....	....	....	....	....	....	....	....	....	....	....	....	....
99-2000	Sudbury Wolves	OHL	63	10	26	36	64	....	....	....	....	....	....	....	....	....	12	1	2	3	22	....	....	....	....
2000-01	Sudbury Wolves	OHL	25	7	11	18	37	....	....	....	....	....	....	....	....	....	....	....	....	....	....	....	....	....	....
	London Knights	OHL	24	8	8	16	38	....	....	....	....	....	....	....	....	....	5	0	4	4	6	....	....	....	....
2001-02	London Knights	OHL	65	27	42	69	141	....	....	....	....	....	....	....	....	....	12	4	9	13	26	....	....	....	....
2002-03	London Knights	OHL	55	20	27	47	83	....	....	....	....	....	....	....	....	....	14	6	6	12	10	....	....	....	....
2003-04	London Knights	OHL	60	24	41	65	85	....	....	....	....	....	....	....	....	....	15	7	10	17	17	....	....	....	....
2004-05	Worcester IceCats	AHL	79	13	30	43	65	....	....	....	....	....	....	....	....	....	....	....	....	....	....	....	....	....	....
2005-06	St. Louis	NHL	67	8	16	24	83	5	1	1	150	5.3	–31	1	0.0	21:41	....	....	....	....	....	....	....	....	....
	Peoria Rivermen	AHL	12	2	4	6	31	....	....	....	....	....	....	....	....	....	....	....	....	....	....	....	....	....	....
2006-07	St. Louis	NHL	55	5	17	22	44	4	0	1	94	5.3	–7	0	0.0	20:12	....	....	....	....	....	....	....	....	....
	Boston	NHL	20	1	2	3	27	0	0	0	28	3.6	–3	1	0.0	17:20	....	....	....	....	....	....	....	....	....
2007-08	Boston	NHL	81	13	23	36	70	9	0	1	171	7.6	11	0	0.0	25:09	6	0	3	3	0	0	0	0	24:21
	NHL Totals		223	27	58	85	224	18	1	3	443	6.1		2	0.0	22:11	6	0	3	3	0	0	0	0	24:21

OHL First All-Star Team (2004)

Signed as a free agent by **St. Louis**, June 30, 2004. Traded to **Boston** by **St. Louis** for Brad Boyes, February 27, 2007.

WILLIAMS, Jason

(WIHL-yuhms, JAY-suhn) **ATL.**

Center. Shoots right. 5'11", 195 lbs. Born, London, Ont., August 11, 1980.

Season	Club	League	GP	G	A	Pts	PIM	PP	SH	GW	S	%	+/-	TF	F%	Min	GP	G	A	Pts	PIM	PP	SH	GW	Min
1995-96	Mount Brydges	OHA-D	36	31	28	59	18	....	....	....	....	....	....	....	....	....	....	....	....	....	....	....	....	....	....
1996-97	Peterborough	OHL	60	4	8	12	8	....	....	....	....	....	....	....	....	....	10	1	0	1	2	....	....	....	....
1997-98	Peterborough	OHL	55	8	27	35	31	....	....	....	....	....	....	....	....	....	4	0	1	1	2	....	....	....	....
1998-99	Peterborough	OHL	68	26	48	74	42	....	....	....	....	....	....	....	....	....	5	1	2	3	2	....	....	....	....
99-2000	Peterborough	OHL	66	36	37	75	64	....	....	....	....	....	....	....	....	....	5	2	1	3	2	....	....	....	....
2000-01	Detroit	NHL	5	0	3	3	2	0	0	0	7	0.0	1	56	39.3	12:24	2	0	0	0	0	0	0	0	11:45
	Cincinnati	AHL	76	24	45	69	48	....	....	....	....	....	....	....	....	....	1	0	0	0	2	....	....	....	....
2001-02♦	Detroit	NHL	25	8	2	10	4	4	0	0	32	25.0	2	208	47.6	10:50	9	0	0	0	2	0	0	0	6:12
	Cincinnati	AHL	52	23	27	50	27	....	....	....	....	....	....	....	....	....	3	0	1	1	6	....	....	....	....
2002-03	Detroit	NHL	16	3	3	6	2	1	0	0	20	15.0	3	78	51.3	10:43	....	....	....	....	....	....	....	....	....
	Grand Rapids	AHL	45	23	22	45	18	....	....	....	....	....	....	....	....	....	15	1	7	8	16	....	....	....	....
2003-04	Detroit	NHL	49	6	7	13	15	0	0	0	44	13.6	1	315	49.2	9:27	3	0	0	0	2	0	0	0	6:11
2004-05	Assat Pori	Finland	43	26	17	43	52	....	....	....	....	....	....	....	....	....	2	1	1	2	4	....	....	....	....
2005-06	Detroit	NHL	80	21	37	58	26	6	0	4	177	11.9	4	29	55.2	14:55	6	1	1	2	6	0	0	0	18:10
2006-07	Detroit	NHL	58	11	15	26	24	3	0	2	111	9.9	7	11	45.5	14:26	....	....	....	....	....	....	....	....	....
	Chicago	NHL	20	4	2	6	20	2	1	0	38	10.5	–6	193	42.5	18:17	....	....	....	....	....	....	....	....	....
2007-08	Chicago	NHL	43	13	23	36	22	6	0	4	101	12.9	–2	15	60.0	16:35	....	....	....	....	....	....	....	....	....
	NHL Totals		296	66	92	158	115	22	1	10	530	12.5		905	47.3	13:46	20	1	1	2	10	0	0	0	10:20

Signed as a free agent by **Detroit**, September 18, 2000. Signed as a free agent by **Pori** (Finland), October 18, 2004. Traded to **Chicago** by **Detroit** for Kyle Calder, February 26, 2007. Signed as a free agent by **Atlanta**, July 14, 2008.

WILLIAMS, Jeremy

(WIHL-yuhms, JAIR-eh-mee) **TOR.**

Center. Shoots right. 5'11", 190 lbs. Born, Regina, Sask., January 26, 1984. Toronto's 5th choice, 220th overall, in 2003 Entry Draft.

Season	Club	League	GP	G	A	Pts	PIM	PP	SH	GW	S	%	+/-	TF	F%	Min	GP	G	A	Pts	PIM	PP	SH	GW	Min
2001-02	Swift Current	SMMHL	24	18	23	41	64	....	....	....	....	....	....	....	....	....	....	....	....	....	....	....	....	....	....
	Swift Current	WHL	32	6	7	13	30	....	....	....	....	....	....	....	....	....	12	1	0	1	4	....	....	....	....
2002-03	Swift Current	WHL	72	41	52	93	117	....	....	....	....	....	....	....	....	....	4	1	0	1	6	....	....	....	....
2003-04	Swift Current	WHL	68	*52	49	101	82	....	....	....	....	....	....	....	....	....	5	2	1	3	12	....	....	....	....
	St. John's	AHL	4	0	2	2	0	....	....	....	....	....	....	....	....	....	....	....	....	....	....	....	....	....	....
2004-05	St. John's	AHL	75	16	20	36	24	....	....	....	....	....	....	....	....	....	5	0	0	0	0	....	....	....	....
2005-06	Toronto	NHL	1	1	0	1	0	0	0	0	1	100.0	0	0	0.0	9:31	....	....	....	....	....	....	....	....	....
	Toronto Marlies	AHL	55	23	33	56	62	....	....	....	....	....	....	....	....	....	5	1	0	1	6	....	....	....	....
2006-07	Toronto	NHL	1	1	0	1	0	0	0	0	3	33.3	1	1	0.0	7:18	....	....	....	....	....	....	....	....	....
	Toronto Marlies	AHL	23	6	9	15	27	....	....	....	....	....	....	....	....	....	....	....	....	....	....	....	....	....	....
2007-08	Toronto	NHL	18	2	0	2	4	0	0	0	16	12.5	–3	4	0.0	7:20	....	....	....	....	....	....	....	....	....
	Toronto Marlies	AHL	49	18	15	33	36	....	....	....	....	....	....	....	....	....	....	....	....	....	....	....	....	....	....
	NHL Totals		20	4	0	4	4	0	0	0	20	20.0		5	0.0	7:27	....	....	....	....	....	....	....	....	....

WHL East First All-Star Team (2004) • Canadian Major Junior First All-Star Team (2004)

WILLIAMS, Justin
(WIHL-yuhms, JUHS-tihn) **CAR.**

Right wing. Shoots right. 6'1", 195 lbs. Born, Cobourg, Ont., October 4, 1981. Philadelphia's 1st choice, 28th overall, in 2000 Entry Draft.

Season	Club	League	GP	G	A	Pts	PIM	PP	SH	GW	S	%	+/-	TF	F%	Min	GP	G	A	Pts	PIM	PP	SH	GW	Min
			Regular Season														Playoffs								
1997-98	Colborne Colts	OHA-C	36	32	35	67	26																		
	Cobourg Cougars	OPJHL	17	0	3	3	5																		
1998-99	Plymouth Whalers	OHL	47	4	8	12	28										7	1	2	3	0				
99-2000	Plymouth Whalers	OHL	68	37	46	83	46										23	*14	16	*30	10				
2000-01	**Philadelphia**	**NHL**	**63**	**12**	**13**	**25**	**22**	**0**	**0**	**0**	**99**	**12.1**	**6**	**13**	**53.9**	**12:31**									
2001-02	**Philadelphia**	**NHL**	**75**	**17**	**23**	**40**	**32**	**0**	**0**	**1**	**162**	**10.5**	**11**	**16**	**25.0**	**14:27**	**5**	**0**	**0**	**0**	**4**	**0**	**0**	**0**	**16:42**
2002-03	**Philadelphia**	**NHL**	**41**	**8**	**16**	**24**	**22**	**0**	**0**	**2**	**105**	**7.6**	**15**	**16**	**50.0**	**15:57**	**12**	**1**	**5**	**6**	**8**	**0**	**0**	**1**	**14:11**
2003-04	**Philadelphia**	**NHL**	**47**	**6**	**20**	**26**	**32**	**3**	**0**	**1**	**107**	**5.6**	**10**	**38**	**31.6**	**15:30**									
	Carolina	**NHL**	**32**	**5**	**13**	**18**	**32**	**1**	**0**	**0**	**96**	**5.2**	**2**	**25**	**36.0**	**18:52**									
2004-05	Lulea HF	Sweden	49	14	18	32	61										4	0	1	1	29				
2005-06♦	**Carolina**	**NHL**	**82**	**31**	**45**	**76**	**60**	**8**	**4**	**4**	**255**	**12.2**	**1**	**17**	**29.4**	**21:08**	**25**	**7**	**11**	**18**	**34**	**0**	**1**	**1**	**21:36**
2006-07	**Carolina**	**NHL**	**82**	**33**	**34**	**67**	**73**	**12**	**2**	**8**	**258**	**12.8**	**-11**	**24**	**37.5**	**20:51**									
2007-08	**Carolina**	**NHL**	**37**	**9**	**21**	**30**	**43**	**2**	**0**	**0**	**106**	**8.5**	**2**	**13**	**38.5**	**19:18**									
	NHL Totals		**459**	**121**	**185**	**306**	**316**	**26**	**6**	**16**	**1188**	**10.2**		**162**	**36.4**	**17:28**	**42**	**8**	**16**	**24**	**46**	**0**	**1**	**2**	**18:54**

Played in NHL All-Star Game (2007)

• Missed majority of 2002-03 season recovering from shoulder (November 15, 2002 vs. Carolina) and knee (January 18, 2003 vs. Tampa Bay) injuries. Traded to **Carolina** by **Philadelphia** for Danny Markov, January 20, 2004. Signed as a free agent by **Lulea** (Sweden), September 21, 2004. • Missed majority of 2007-08 season recovering from knee injury suffered in game at Florida, December 20, 2007.

WILLSIE, Brian
(WIHL-see, BRIGH-uhn) **COL.**

Right wing. Shoots right. 6'1", 202 lbs. Born, London, Ont., March 16, 1978. Colorado's 7th choice, 146th overall, in 1996 Entry Draft.

Season	Club	League	GP	G	A	Pts	PIM	PP	SH	GW	S	%	+/-	TF	F%	Min	GP	G	A	Pts	PIM	PP	SH	GW	Min
1993-94	Belmont Bombers	OHA-D	13	9	5	14	14																		
1994-95	St. Thomas Stars	OHA-B	45	35	47	82	47																		
1995-96	Guelph Storm	OHL	65	13	21	34	18										16	4	2	6	6				
1996-97	Guelph Storm	OHL	64	37	31	68	37										18	15	4	19	10				
1997-98	Guelph Storm	OHL	57	45	31	76	41										12	9	5	14	18				
1998-99	Hershey Bears	AHL	72	19	10	29	28										3	1	0	1	0				
99-2000	**Colorado**	**NHL**	**1**	**0**	**0**	**0**	**0**	**0**	**0**	**0**	**1**	**0.0**	**0**	**0**	**0.0**	**8:16**									
	Hershey Bears	AHL	78	20	39	59	44										12	2	6	8	8				
2000-01	Hershey Bears	AHL	48	18	23	41	20										12	7	2	9	14				
2001-02	**Colorado**	**NHL**	**56**	**7**	**7**	**14**	**14**	**2**	**0**	**1**	**66**	**10.6**	**4**	**8**	**12.5**	**11:24**	**4**	**0**	**1**	**1**	**2**	**0**	**0**	**0**	**11:54**
2002-03	**Colorado**	**NHL**	**12**	**0**	**1**	**1**	**15**	**0**	**0**	**0**	**12**	**0.0**	**0**	**7**	**14.3**	**9:36**	**6**	**1**	**0**	**1**	**2**	**0**	**0**	**1**	**10:48**
	Hershey Bears	AHL	59	29	28	57	49																		
2003-04	**Washington**	**NHL**	**49**	**10**	**5**	**15**	**18**	**1**	**1**	**1**	**85**	**11.8**	**-7**	**46**	**34.8**	**12:42**									
2004-05	Ljubljana	Slovenia	2	0	3	3	4																		
	Ljubljana	Interliga	12	7	6	13	34																		
	Portland Pirates	AHL	53	23	17	40	47																		
2005-06	**Washington**	**NHL**	**82**	**19**	**22**	**41**	**77**	**8**	**1**	**2**	**185**	**10.3**	**-19**	**52**	**51.9**	**16:40**									
2006-07	**Los Angeles**	**NHL**	**81**	**11**	**10**	**21**	**49**	**2**	**0**	**1**	**131**	**8.4**	**-20**	**201**	**45.3**	**13:23**									
2007-08	**Los Angeles**	**NHL**	**53**	**4**	**8**	**12**	**30**	**0**	**0**	**0**	**62**	**6.5**	**-8**	**24**	**58.3**	**10:38**									
	NHL Totals		**334**	**51**	**53**	**104**	**203**	**13**	**2**	**5**	**542**	**9.4**		**338**	**44.4**	**13:10**	**10**	**1**	**1**	**2**	**4**	**0**	**0**	**1**	**11:14**

OHL First All-Star Team (1998)

Claimed by **Washington** from **Colorado** in Waiver Draft, October 3, 2003. Signed as a free agent by **Ljubljana** (Slovenia), October 8, 2004. Signed as a free agent by **Portland** (AHL), December 15, 2004. Signed as a free agent by **Los Angeles**, July 4, 2006. Signed as a free agent by **Colorado**, July 15, 2008.

WILSON, Clay
(WIHL-suhn, KLAY) **CBJ**

Defense. Shoots left. 6', 195 lbs. Born, Sturgeon Lake, MN, April 5, 1983.

Season	Club	League	GP	G	A	Pts	PIM	PP	SH	GW	S	%	+/-	TF	F%	Min	GP	G	A	Pts	PIM	PP	SH	GW	Min
2001-02	Michigan Tech	WCHA	38	4	8	12	18																		
2002-03	Michigan Tech	WCHA	38	8	17	25	37																		
2003-04	Michigan Tech	WCHA	37	2	11	13	22																		
2004-05	Michigan Tech	WCHA	35	3	4	7	42																		
	Muskegon Fury	UHL	14	3	3	6	2										17	0	2	2	8				
2005-06	Muskegon Fury	UHL	13	3	9	12	9																		
	Grand Rapids	AHL	60	10	27	37	40										16	0	3	3	8				
2006-07	Portland Pirates	AHL	79	9	34	43	52																		
2007-08	Portland Pirates	AHL	14	3	5	8	6																		
	Columbus	**NHL**	**7**	**1**	**1**	**2**	**2**	**0**	**0**	**0**	**12**	**8.3**	**3**	**0**	**0.0**	**16:55**									
	Syracuse Crunch	AHL	57	11	28	39	29										13	2	5	7	4				
	NHL Totals		**7**	**1**	**1**	**2**	**2**	**0**	**0**	**0**	**12**	**8.3**		**0**	**0.0**	**16:55**									

Signed as a free agent by **Anaheim**, July 11, 2006. Traded to **Columbus** by **Anaheim** with Aaron Rome for Geoff Platt, November 15, 2007.

WILSON, Landon
(WIHL-suhn, LAN-duhn) **DAL.**

Right wing. Shoots right. 6'3", 226 lbs. Born, St. Louis, MO, March 13, 1975. Toronto's 2nd choice, 19th overall, in 1993 Entry Draft.

Season	Club	League	GP	G	A	Pts	PIM	PP	SH	GW	S	%	+/-	TF	F%	Min	GP	G	A	Pts	PIM	PP	SH	GW	Min
1991-92	California	WSJHL	38	50	42	92	135																		
1992-93	Dubuque	USHL	43	29	36	65	284																		
1993-94	North Dakota	WCHA	35	18	15	33	*147																		
1994-95	North Dakota	WCHA	31	7	16	23	141																		
	Cornwall Aces	AHL	8	4	4	8	25										13	3	4	7	68				
1995-96	**Colorado**	**NHL**	**7**	**1**	**0**	**1**	**6**	**0**	**0**	**0**	**6**	**16.7**	**3**												
	Cornwall Aces	AHL	53	21	13	34	154										8	1	3	4	22				
1996-97	**Colorado**	**NHL**	**9**	**1**	**2**	**3**	**23**	**0**	**0**	**0**	**7**	**14.3**	**1**												
	Boston	**NHL**	**40**	**7**	**10**	**17**	**49**	**0**	**0**	**0**	**76**	**9.2**	**-6**												
	Providence Bruins	AHL	2	2	1	3	2										10	3	4	7	16				
1997-98	**Boston**	**NHL**	**28**	**1**	**5**	**6**	**7**	**0**	**0**	**0**	**26**	**3.8**	**3**				**1**	**0**	**0**	**0**	**0**	**0**	**0**	**0**	
	Providence Bruins	AHL	42	18	10	28	146																		
1998-99	**Boston**	**NHL**	**22**	**3**	**3**	**6**	**17**	**0**	**0**	**0**	**32**	**9.4**	**0**	**3**	**0.0**	**10:04**	**8**	**1**	**1**	**2**	**8**	**1**	**0**	**1**	**13:41**
	Providence Bruins	AHL	48	31	22	53	89										11	7	1	8	19				
99-2000	**Boston**	**NHL**	**40**	**1**	**3**	**4**	**18**	**0**	**0**	**0**	**67**	**1.5**	**-6**	**14**	**42.9**	**10:09**									
	Providence Bruins	AHL	17	5	5	10	45										9	2	3	5	38				
2000-01	**Phoenix**	**NHL**	**70**	**18**	**13**	**31**	**92**	**2**	**0**	**3**	**123**	**14.6**	**3**	**13**	**46.2**	**11:26**									
2001-02	**Phoenix**	**NHL**	**47**	**7**	**12**	**19**	**46**	**1**	**0**	**0**	**100**	**7.0**	**4**	**15**	**53.3**	**12:51**	**4**	**0**	**0**	**0**	**12**	**0**	**0**	**0**	**12:03**
	Springfield	AHL	2	2	1	3	2																		
2002-03	**Phoenix**	**NHL**	**31**	**6**	**8**	**14**	**26**	**0**	**0**	**3**	**92**	**6.5**	**1**	**35**	**54.3**	**12:11**									
2003-04	**Phoenix**	**NHL**	**35**	**1**	**3**	**4**	**16**	**0**	**0**	**0**	**41**	**2.4**	**-3**	**44**	**31.8**	**9:51**									
	Pittsburgh	**NHL**	**19**	**5**	**1**	**6**	**31**	**2**	**0**	**0**	**35**	**14.3**	**0**	**2**	**0.0**	**11:21**									
2004-05	Blues Espoo	Finland	37	8	11	19	80																		
2005-06	HC Davos	Swiss	36	27	14	41	142										11	5	3	8	40				
2006-07	HC Lugano	Swiss	35	20	11	31	67										6	3	2	5	12				
2007-08	HC Lugano	Swiss	30	13	7	20	67										3	4	0	4	2				
	NHL Totals		**348**	**51**	**60**	**111**	**331**	**5**	**0**	**6**	**605**	**8.4**		**126**	**42.1**	**11:15**	**13**	**1**	**1**	**2**	**20**	**1**	**0**	**1**	**13:08**

WCHA Rookie of the Year (1994) • AHL First All-Star Team (1999)

Traded to **Quebec** by **Toronto** with Wendel Clark, Sylvain Lefebvre and Toronto's 1st round choice (Jeffrey Kealty) in 1994 Entry Draft for Mats Sundin, Garth Butcher, Todd Warriner and Philadelphia's 1st round choice (previously acquired, later traded to Washington – Washington selected Nolan Baumgartner) in 1994 Entry Draft, June 28, 1994. Transferred to **Colorado** after **Quebec** franchise relocated, June 21, 1995. Traded to **Boston** by **Colorado** with Anders Myrvold for Boston's 1st round choice (Robyn Regehr) in 1998 Entry Draft, November 22, 1996. Signed as a free agent by **Phoenix**, July 7, 2000. • Missed majority of 2002-03 season recovering from eye injury suffered in game vs. Washington, December 13, 2002. Traded to **Pittsburgh** by **Phoenix** for future considerations, February 22, 2004. Signed as a free agent by **Espoo** (Finland), June 23, 2004. Signed as a free agent by **Davos** (Swiss), August 31, 2005. Signed as a free agent by **Lugano** (Swiss), July 17, 2006. Signed as a free agent by **Dallas**, July 3, 2008.

WINCHESTER, Brad
(WIHN-chehst-uhr, BRAD) **ST.L.**

Center/left wing. Shoots left. 6'5", 228 lbs. Born, Madison, WI, March 1, 1981. Edmonton's 2nd choice, 35th overall, in 2000 Entry Draft.

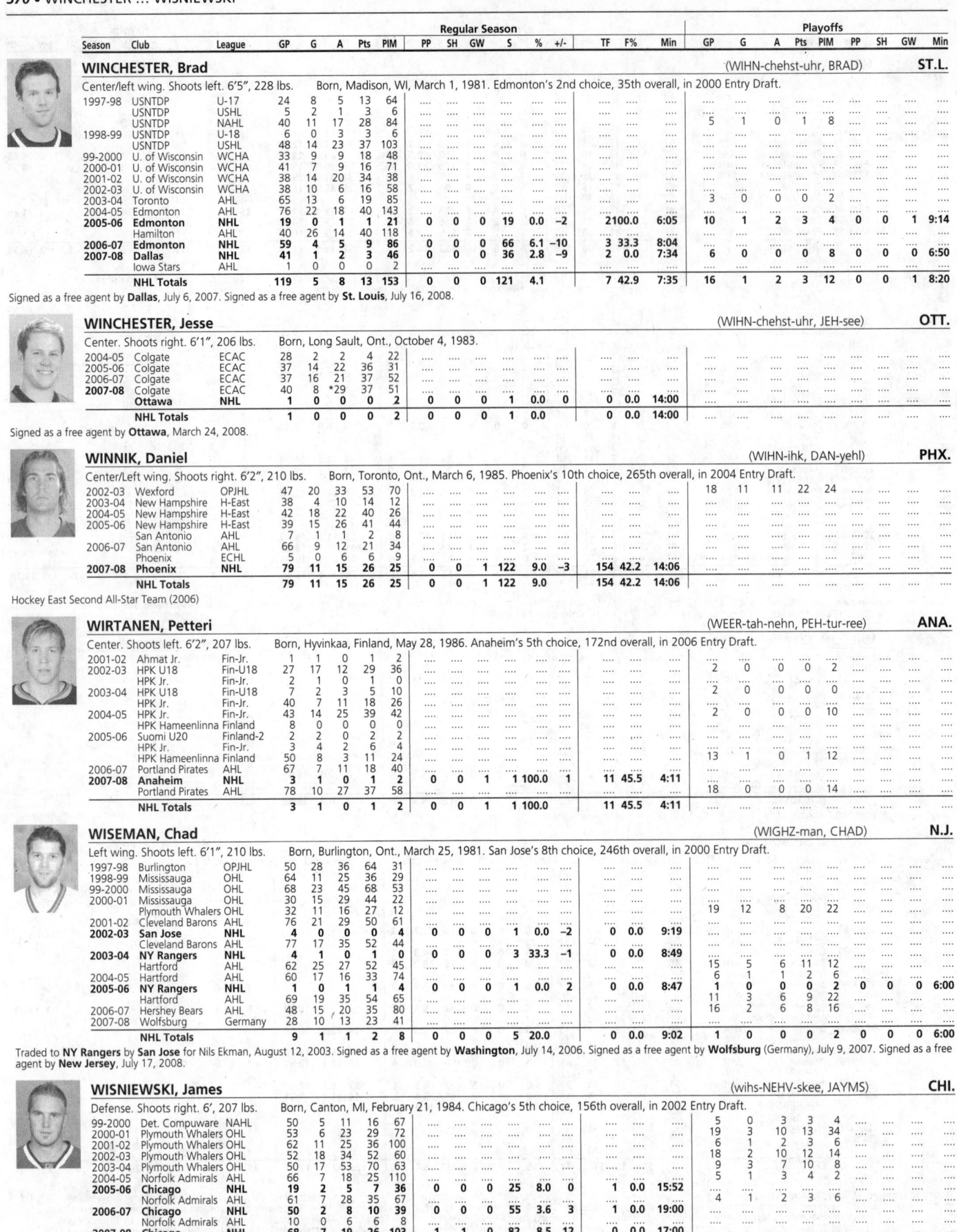

			Regular Season														Playoffs								
Season	Club	League	GP	G	A	Pts	PIM	PP	SH	GW	S	%	+/-	TF	F%	Min	GP	G	A	Pts	PIM	PP	SH	GW	Min
1997-98	USNTDP	U-17	24	8	5	13	64	....	....	....	....	....	....	....	....	....	....	....	....	....	....	....	....	....	....
	USNTDP	USHL	5	2	1	3	6	....	....	....	....	....	....	....	....	....	....	....	....	....	....	....	....	....	....
	USNTDP	NAHL	40	11	17	28	84	....	....	....	....	....	....	....	....	....	5	1	0	1	8	....	....	....	....
1998-99	USNTDP	U-18	6	0	3	3	6	....	....	....	....	....	....	....	....	....	....	....	....	....	....	....	....	....	....
	USNTDP	USHL	48	14	23	37	103	....	....	....	....	....	....	....	....	....	....	....	....	....	....	....	....	....	....
99-2000	U. of Wisconsin	WCHA	33	9	9	18	48	....	....	....	....	....	....	....	....	....	....	....	....	....	....	....	....	....	....
2000-01	U. of Wisconsin	WCHA	41	7	9	16	71	....	....	....	....	....	....	....	....	....	....	....	....	....	....	....	....	....	....
2001-02	U. of Wisconsin	WCHA	38	14	20	34	38	....	....	....	....	....	....	....	....	....	....	....	....	....	....	....	....	....	....
2002-03	U. of Wisconsin	WCHA	38	10	6	16	58	....	....	....	....	....	....	....	....	....	....	....	....	....	....	....	....	....	....
2003-04	Toronto	AHL	65	13	6	19	85	....	....	....	....	....	....	....	....	....	3	0	0	0	2	....	....	....	....
2004-05	Edmonton	AHL	76	22	18	40	143	....	....	....	....	....	....	....	....	....	....	....	....	....	....	....	....	....	....
2005-06	**Edmonton**	**NHL**	**19**	**0**	**1**	**1**	**21**	**0**	**0**	**0**	**19**	**0.0**	**-2**	**2**	**100.0**	**6:05**	**10**	**1**	**2**	**3**	**4**	**0**	**0**	**1**	**9:14**
	Hamilton	AHL	40	26	14	40	118	....	....	....	....	....	....	....	....	....	....	....	....	....	....	....	....	....	....
2006-07	**Edmonton**	**NHL**	**59**	**4**	**5**	**9**	**86**	**0**	**0**	**0**	**66**	**6.1**	**-10**	**3**	**33.3**	**8:04**	....	....	....	....	....	....	....	....	....
2007-08	**Dallas**	**NHL**	**41**	**1**	**2**	**3**	**46**	**0**	**0**	**0**	**36**	**2.8**	**-9**	**2**	**0.0**	**7:34**	**6**	**0**	**0**	**0**	**8**	**0**	**0**	**0**	**6:50**
	Iowa Stars	AHL	1	0	0	0	2	....	....	....	....	....	....	....	....	....	....	....	....	....	....	....	....	....	....
	NHL Totals		**119**	**5**	**8**	**13**	**153**	**0**	**0**	**0**	**121**	**4.1**		**7**	**42.9**	**7:35**	**16**	**1**	**2**	**3**	**12**	**0**	**0**	**1**	**8:20**

Signed as a free agent by **Dallas**, July 6, 2007. Signed as a free agent by **St. Louis**, July 16, 2008.

WINCHESTER, Jesse
(WIHN-chehst-uhr, JEH-see) **OTT.**

Center. Shoots right. 6'1", 206 lbs. Born, Long Sault, Ont., October 4, 1983.

Season	Club	League	GP	G	A	Pts	PIM	PP	SH	GW	S	%	+/-	TF	F%	Min	GP	G	A	Pts	PIM	PP	SH	GW	Min
2004-05	Colgate	ECAC	28	2	2	4	22	....	....	....	....	....	....	....	....	....	....	....	....	....	....	....	....	....	....
2005-06	Colgate	ECAC	37	14	22	36	31	....	....	....	....	....	....	....	....	....	....	....	....	....	....	....	....	....	....
2006-07	Colgate	ECAC	37	16	21	37	52	....	....	....	....	....	....	....	....	....	....	....	....	....	....	....	....	....	....
2007-08	Colgate	ECAC	40	8	*29	37	51	....	....	....	....	....	....	....	....	....	....	....	....	....	....	....	....	....	....
	Ottawa	**NHL**	**1**	**0**	**0**	**0**	**2**	**0**	**0**	**0**	**1**	**0.0**	**0**	**0**	**0.0**	**14:00**	....	....	....	....	....	....	....	....	....
	NHL Totals		**1**	**0**	**0**	**0**	**2**	**0**	**0**	**0**	**1**	**0.0**		**0**	**0.0**	**14:00**	....	....	....	....	....	....	....	....	....

Signed as a free agent by **Ottawa**, March 24, 2008.

WINNIK, Daniel
(WIHN-ihk, DAN-yehl) **PHX.**

Center/Left wing. Shoots right. 6'2", 210 lbs. Born, Toronto, Ont., March 6, 1985. Phoenix's 10th choice, 265th overall, in 2004 Entry Draft.

Season	Club	League	GP	G	A	Pts	PIM	PP	SH	GW	S	%	+/-	TF	F%	Min	GP	G	A	Pts	PIM	PP	SH	GW	Min
2002-03	Wexford	OPJHL	47	20	33	53	70	....	....	....	....	....	....	....	....	....	18	11	11	22	24	....	....	....	....
2003-04	New Hampshire	H-East	38	4	10	14	12	....	....	....	....	....	....	....	....	....	....	....	....	....	....	....	....	....	....
2004-05	New Hampshire	H-East	42	18	22	40	26	....	....	....	....	....	....	....	....	....	....	....	....	....	....	....	....	....	....
2005-06	New Hampshire	H-East	39	15	26	41	44	....	....	....	....	....	....	....	....	....	....	....	....	....	....	....	....	....	....
	San Antonio	AHL	7	1	1	2	8	....	....	....	....	....	....	....	....	....	....	....	....	....	....	....	....	....	....
2006-07	San Antonio	AHL	66	9	12	21	34	....	....	....	....	....	....	....	....	....	....	....	....	....	....	....	....	....	....
	Phoenix	ECHL	5	0	6	6	9	....	....	....	....	....	....	....	....	....	....	....	....	....	....	....	....	....	....
2007-08	**Phoenix**	**NHL**	**79**	**11**	**15**	**26**	**25**	**0**	**0**	**1**	**122**	**9.0**	**-3**	**154**	**42.2**	**14:06**	....	....	....	....	....	....	....	....	....
	NHL Totals		**79**	**11**	**15**	**26**	**25**	**0**	**0**	**1**	**122**	**9.0**		**154**	**42.2**	**14:06**	....	....	....	....	....	....	....	....	....

Hockey East Second All-Star Team (2006)

WIRTANEN, Petteri
(WEER-tah-nehn, PEH-tur-ree) **ANA.**

Center. Shoots left. 6'2", 207 lbs. Born, Hyvinkaa, Finland, May 28, 1986. Anaheim's 5th choice, 172nd overall, in 2006 Entry Draft.

Season	Club	League	GP	G	A	Pts	PIM	PP	SH	GW	S	%	+/-	TF	F%	Min	GP	G	A	Pts	PIM	PP	SH	GW	Min
2001-02	Ahmat Jr.	Fin-Jr.	1	1	0	1	2	....	....	....	....	....	....	....	....	....	....	....	....	....	....	....	....	....	....
2002-03	HPK U18	Fin-U18	27	17	12	29	36	....	....	....	....	....	....	....	....	....	2	0	0	0	2	....	....	....	....
	HPK Jr.	Fin-Jr.	2	1	0	1	0	....	....	....	....	....	....	....	....	....	....	....	....	....	....	....	....	....	....
2003-04	HPK U18	Fin-U18	7	2	3	5	10	....	....	....	....	....	....	....	....	....	2	0	0	0	0	....	....	....	....
	HPK Jr.	Fin-Jr.	40	7	11	18	26	....	....	....	....	....	....	....	....	....	....	....	....	....	....	....	....	....	....
2004-05	HPK Jr.	Fin-Jr.	43	14	25	39	42	....	....	....	....	....	....	....	....	....	2	0	0	0	10	....	....	....	....
	HPK Hameenlinna	Finland	8	0	0	0	0	....	....	....	....	....	....	....	....	....	....	....	....	....	....	....	....	....	....
2005-06	Suomi U20	Finland-2	2	2	0	2	2	....	....	....	....	....	....	....	....	....	....	....	....	....	....	....	....	....	....
	HPK Jr.	Fin-Jr.	3	4	2	6	4	....	....	....	....	....	....	....	....	....	....	....	....	....	....	....	....	....	....
	HPK Hameenlinna	Finland	50	8	3	11	24	....	....	....	....	....	....	....	....	....	13	1	0	1	12	....	....	....	....
2006-07	Portland Pirates	AHL	67	7	11	18	40	....	....	....	....	....	....	....	....	....	....	....	....	....	....	....	....	....	....
2007-08	**Anaheim**	**NHL**	**3**	**1**	**0**	**1**	**2**	**0**	**0**	**1**	**1**	**100.0**	**1**	**11**	**45.5**	**4:11**	....	....	....	....	....	....	....	....	....
	Portland Pirates	AHL	78	10	27	37	58	....	....	....	....	....	....	....	....	....	18	0	0	0	14	....	....	....	....
	NHL Totals		**3**	**1**	**0**	**1**	**2**	**0**	**0**	**1**	**1**	**100.0**		**11**	**45.5**	**4:11**	....	....	....	....	....	....	....	....	....

WISEMAN, Chad
(WIGHZ-man, CHAD) **N.J.**

Left wing. Shoots left. 6'1", 210 lbs. Born, Burlington, Ont., March 25, 1981. San Jose's 8th choice, 246th overall, in 2000 Entry Draft.

Season	Club	League	GP	G	A	Pts	PIM	PP	SH	GW	S	%	+/-	TF	F%	Min	GP	G	A	Pts	PIM	PP	SH	GW	Min
1997-98	Burlington	OPJHL	50	28	36	64	31	....	....	....	....	....	....	....	....	....	....	....	....	....	....	....	....	....	....
1998-99	Mississauga	OHL	64	11	25	36	29	....	....	....	....	....	....	....	....	....	....	....	....	....	....	....	....	....	....
99-2000	Mississauga	OHL	68	23	45	68	53	....	....	....	....	....	....	....	....	....	....	....	....	....	....	....	....	....	....
2000-01	Mississauga	OHL	30	15	29	44	22	....	....	....	....	....	....	....	....	....	....	....	....	....	....	....	....	....	....
	Plymouth Whalers	OHL	32	11	16	27	12	....	....	....	....	....	....	....	....	....	19	12	8	20	22	....	....	....	....
2001-02	Cleveland Barons	AHL	76	21	29	50	61	....	....	....	....	....	....	....	....	....	....	....	....	....	....	....	....	....	....
2002-03	**San Jose**	**NHL**	**4**	**0**	**0**	**0**	**4**	**0**	**0**	**0**	**1**	**0.0**	**-2**	**0**	**0.0**	**9:19**	....	....	....	....	....	....	....	....	....
	Cleveland Barons	AHL	77	17	35	52	44	....	....	....	....	....	....	....	....	....	....	....	....	....	....	....	....	....	....
2003-04	**NY Rangers**	**NHL**	**4**	**1**	**0**	**1**	**0**	**0**	**0**	**0**	**3**	**33.3**	**-1**	**0**	**0.0**	**8:49**	....	....	....	....	....	....	....	....	....
	Hartford	AHL	62	25	27	52	45	....	....	....	....	....	....	....	....	....	15	5	6	11	12	....	....	....	....
2004-05	Hartford	AHL	60	17	16	33	74	....	....	....	....	....	....	....	....	....	6	1	1	2	6	....	....	....	....
2005-06	**NY Rangers**	**NHL**	**1**	**0**	**1**	**1**	**4**	**0**	**0**	**0**	**1**	**0.0**	**2**	**0**	**0.0**	**8:47**	**1**	**0**	**0**	**0**	**2**	**0**	**0**	**0**	**6:00**
	Hartford	AHL	69	19	35	54	65	....	....	....	....	....	....	....	....	....	11	3	6	9	22	....	....	....	....
2006-07	Hershey Bears	AHL	48	15	20	35	80	....	....	....	....	....	....	....	....	....	16	2	6	8	16	....	....	....	....
2007-08	Wolfsburg	Germany	28	10	13	23	41	....	....	....	....	....	....	....	....	....	....	....	....	....	....	....	....	....	....
	NHL Totals		**9**	**1**	**1**	**2**	**8**	**0**	**0**	**0**	**5**	**20.0**		**0**	**0.0**	**9:02**	**1**	**0**	**0**	**0**	**2**	**0**	**0**	**0**	**6:00**

Traded to **NY Rangers** by **San Jose** for Nils Ekman, August 12, 2003. Signed as a free agent by **Washington**, July 14, 2006. Signed as a free agent by **Wolfsburg** (Germany), July 9, 2007. Signed as a free agent by **New Jersey**, July 17, 2008.

WISNIEWSKI, James
(wihs-NEHV-skee, JAYMS) **CHI.**

Defense. Shoots right. 6', 207 lbs. Born, Canton, MI, February 21, 1984. Chicago's 5th choice, 156th overall, in 2002 Entry Draft.

Season	Club	League	GP	G	A	Pts	PIM	PP	SH	GW	S	%	+/-	TF	F%	Min	GP	G	A	Pts	PIM	PP	SH	GW	Min
99-2000	Det. Compuware	NAHL	50	5	11	16	67	....	....	....	....	....	....	....	....	....	5	0	3	3	4	....	....	....	....
2000-01	Plymouth Whalers	OHL	53	6	23	29	72	....	....	....	....	....	....	....	....	....	19	3	10	13	34	....	....	....	....
2001-02	Plymouth Whalers	OHL	62	11	25	36	100	....	....	....	....	....	....	....	....	....	6	1	2	3	6	....	....	....	....
2002-03	Plymouth Whalers	OHL	52	18	34	52	60	....	....	....	....	....	....	....	....	....	18	2	10	12	14	....	....	....	....
2003-04	Plymouth Whalers	OHL	50	17	53	70	63	....	....	....	....	....	....	....	....	....	9	3	7	10	8	....	....	....	....
2004-05	Norfolk Admirals	AHL	66	7	18	25	110	....	....	....	....	....	....	....	....	....	5	1	3	4	2	....	....	....	....
2005-06	**Chicago**	**NHL**	**19**	**2**	**5**	**7**	**36**	**0**	**0**	**0**	**25**	**8.0**	**0**	**1**	**0.0**	**15:52**	....	....	....	....	....	....	....	....	....
	Norfolk Admirals	AHL	61	7	28	35	67	....	....	....	....	....	....	....	....	....	4	1	2	3	6	....	....	....	....
2006-07	**Chicago**	**NHL**	**50**	**2**	**8**	**10**	**39**	**0**	**0**	**0**	**55**	**3.6**	**3**	**1**	**0.0**	**19:00**	....	....	....	....	....	....	....	....	....
	Norfolk Admirals	AHL	10	0	6	6	8	....	....	....	....	....	....	....	....	....	....	....	....	....	....	....	....	....	....
2007-08	**Chicago**	**NHL**	**68**	**7**	**19**	**26**	**103**	**1**	**1**	**0**	**82**	**8.5**	**12**	**0**	**0.0**	**17:00**	....	....	....	....	....	....	....	....	....
	NHL Totals		**137**	**11**	**32**	**43**	**178**	**1**	**1**	**0**	**162**	**6.8**		**2**	**0.0**	**17:34**	....	....	....	....	....	....	....	....	....

OHL First All-Star Team (2004) • OHL Defenseman of the Year (2004) • Canadian Major Junior First All-Star Team (2004) • Canadian Major Junior Defenseman of the Year (2004)

Season	Club	League	Regular Season GP	G	A	Pts	PIM	PP	SH	GW	S	%	+/-	TF	F%	Min	Playoffs GP	G	A	Pts	PIM	PP	SH	GW	Min

WITT, Brendan

(WIHT, BREHN-duhn) **NYI**

Defense. Shoots left. 6'2", 223 lbs. Born, Humboldt, Sask., February 20, 1975. Washington's 1st choice, 11th overall, in 1993 Entry Draft.

Season	Club	League	GP	G	A	Pts	PIM	PP	SH	GW	S	%	+/-	TF	F%	Min	GP	G	A	Pts	PIM	PP	SH	GW	Min
1990-91	Saskatoon Blazers	SMHL	31	5	13	18	42																		
	Seattle	WHL															1	0	0	0	0				
1991-92	Seattle	WHL	67	3	9	12	212										15	1	1	2	84				
1992-93	Seattle	WHL	70	2	26	28	239										5	1	2	3	30				
1993-94	Seattle	WHL	56	8	31	39	235										9	3	8	11	23				
1994-95			DID NOT PLAY																						
1995-96	**Washington**	**NHL**	**48**	**2**	**3**	**5**	**85**	**0**	**0**	**1**	**44**	**4.5**	**–4**												
1996-97	**Washington**	**NHL**	**44**	**3**	**2**	**5**	**88**	**0**	**0**	**0**	**41**	**7.3**	**–20**												
	Portland Pirates	AHL	30	2	4	6	56										5	1	0	1	30				
1997-98	**Washington**	**NHL**	**64**	**1**	**7**	**8**	**112**	**0**	**0**	**0**	**68**	**1.5**	**–11**				**16**	**1**	**0**	**1**	**14**	**0**	**0**	**0**	
1998-99	**Washington**	**NHL**	**54**	**2**	**5**	**7**	**87**	**0**	**0**	**0**	**51**	**3.9**	**–6**	**0**	**0.0**	**15:50**									
99-2000	**Washington**	**NHL**	**77**	**1**	**7**	**8**	**114**	**0**	**0**	**0**	**64**	**1.6**	**5**	**2**	**50.0**	**20:56**	**3**	**0**	**0**	**0**	**0**	**0**	**0**	**0**	**20:52**
2000-01	**Washington**	**NHL**	**72**	**3**	**3**	**6**	**101**	**0**	**0**	**0**	**87**	**3.4**	**2**	**1**	**100.0**	**20:41**	**6**	**2**	**0**	**2**	**12**	**1**	**0**	**0**	**20:50**
2001-02	**Washington**	**NHL**	**68**	**3**	**7**	**10**	**78**	**0**	**0**	**0**	**81**	**3.7**	**–1**	**1**	**100.0**	**20:03**									
2002-03	**Washington**	**NHL**	**69**	**2**	**9**	**11**	**106**	**0**	**0**	**0**	**80**	**2.5**	**12**	**0**	**0.0**	**20:55**	**6**	**1**	**0**	**1**	**0**	**0**	**0**	**0**	**23:33**
2003-04	**Washington**	**NHL**	**72**	**2**	**10**	**12**	**123**	**0**	**0**	**0**	**91**	**2.2**	**–22**	**3**	**66.7**	**22:48**									
2004-05	Bracknell Bees	Britain-2	3	1	4	5	0																		
2005-06	**Washington**	**NHL**	**58**	**1**	**10**	**11**	**141**	**0**	**0**	**0**	**62**	**1.6**	**–5**	**0**	**0.0**	**21:41**									
	Nashville	**NHL**	**17**	**0**	**3**	**3**	**68**	**0**	**0**	**0**	**13**	**0.0**	**5**	**0**	**0.0**	**17:29**	**5**	**0**	**0**	**0**	**12**	**0**	**0**	**0**	**17:07**
2006-07	**NY Islanders**	**NHL**	**81**	**1**	**13**	**14**	**131**	**0**	**0**	**0**	**75**	**1.3**	**14**	**0**	**0.0**	**21:39**	**5**	**0**	**1**	**1**	**6**	**0**	**0**	**0**	**20:06**
2007-08	**NY Islanders**	**NHL**	**59**	**2**	**5**	**7**	**51**	**0**	**0**	**0**	**58**	**3.4**	**–8**	**0**	**0.0**	**21:46**									
	NHL Totals		**783**	**23**	**84**	**107**	**1285**	**0**	**0**	**1**	**815**	**2.8**		**7**	**71.4**	**20:44**	**41**	**4**	**1**	**5**	**44**	**1**	**0**	**0**	**20:36**

WHL West First All-Star Team (1993, 1994) • Canadian Major Junior First All-Star Team (1994)

• Missed entire 1994-95 season after failing to come to contract terms with **Washington**. Signed as a free agent by **Bracknell** (Britain-2), December 21, 2004. Traded to **Nashville** by **Washington** for Kris Beech and Nashville's 1st round choice (Simeon Varlamov) in 2006 Entry Draft, March 9, 2006. Signed as a free agent by **NY Islanders**, July 3, 2006.

WOLSKI, Wojtek

(WOHL-skee, VOI-tehk) **COL.**

Left wing. Shoots left. 6'3", 200 lbs. Born, Zabrze, Poland, February 24, 1986. Colorado's 1st choice, 21st overall, in 2004 Entry Draft.

Season	Club	League	GP	G	A	Pts	PIM	PP	SH	GW	S	%	+/-	TF	F%	Min	GP	G	A	Pts	PIM	PP	SH	GW	Min
2001-02	St. Mike's B's	OPJHL	33	16	33	49	40																		
2002-03	Brampton	OHL	64	25	32	57	26										11	5	0	5	6				
2003-04	Brampton	OHL	66	29	41	70	30										12	5	3	8	8				
2004-05	Brampton	OHL	67	29	44	73	41										6	2	5	7	6				
2005-06	**Colorado**	**NHL**	**9**	**2**	**4**	**6**	**4**	**2**	**0**	**0**	**9**	**22.2**	**–5**	**4**	**0.0**	**9:44**	**8**	**1**	**3**	**4**	**2**	**0**	**0**	**0**	**12:06**
	Brampton	OHL	56	47	81	128	46										11	7	11	18	4				
2006-07	**Colorado**	**NHL**	**76**	**22**	**28**	**50**	**14**	**7**	**0**	**2**	**165**	**13.3**	**2**	**3**	**100.0**	**15:31**									
2007-08	**Colorado**	**NHL**	**77**	**18**	**30**	**48**	**14**	**4**	**0**	**6**	**158**	**11.4**	**10**	**48**	**50.0**	**15:56**	**7**	**2**	**3**	**5**	**2**	**1**	**0**	**1**	**13:15**
	NHL Totals		**162**	**42**	**62**	**104**	**32**	**13**	**0**	**8**	**332**	**12.7**		**55**	**49.1**	**15:24**	**15**	**3**	**6**	**9**	**4**	**1**	**0**	**1**	**12:38**

OHL First All-Star Team (2004) • OHL Second All-Star Team (2006)

WOTTON, Mark

(WAH-tuhn, MAHRK)

Defense. Shoots left. 6'1", 195 lbs. Born, Foxwarren, Man., November 16, 1973. Vancouver's 11th choice, 237th overall, in 1992 Entry Draft.

Season	Club	League	GP	G	A	Pts	PIM	PP	SH	GW	S	%	+/-	TF	F%	Min	GP	G	A	Pts	PIM	PP	SH	GW	Min
1988-89	Foxwarren Blades	MAHA	60	10	30	40	70																		
1989-90	Saskatoon Blades	WHL	51	2	3	5	31										7	1	1	2	15				
1990-91	Saskatoon Blades	WHL	45	4	11	15	37																		
1991-92	Saskatoon Blades	WHL	64	11	25	36	62										21	2	6	8	22				
1992-93	Saskatoon Blades	WHL	71	15	51	66	90										9	6	5	11	18				
1993-94	Saskatoon Blades	WHL	65	12	34	46	108										16	3	12	15	32				
1994-95	Syracuse Crunch	AHL	75	12	29	41	50																		
	Vancouver	**NHL**	**1**	**0**	**0**	**0**	**0**	**0**	**0**	**0**	**2**	**0.0**	**1**				**5**	**0**	**0**	**0**	**4**	**0**	**0**	**0**	
1995-96	Syracuse Crunch	AHL	80	10	35	45	96										15	1	12	13	20				
1996-97	**Vancouver**	**NHL**	**36**	**3**	**6**	**9**	**19**	**0**	**1**	**0**	**41**	**7.3**	**8**												
	Syracuse Crunch	AHL	27	2	8	10	25										2	0	0	0	4				
1997-98	**Vancouver**	**NHL**	**5**	**0**	**0**	**0**	**6**	**0**	**0**	**0**	**3**	**0.0**	**–2**												
	Syracuse Crunch	AHL	56	12	21	33	80										5	0	0	0	12				
1998-99	Syracuse Crunch	AHL	72	4	31	35	74																		
99-2000	Michigan	IHL	70	3	7	10	72																		
2000-01	**Dallas**	**NHL**	**1**	**0**	**0**	**0**	**0**	**0**	**0**	**0**	**0**	**0.0**	**0**	**0**	**0.0**	**13:45**									
	Utah Grizzlies	IHL	63	2	2	4	64																		
2001-02	Utah Grizzlies	AHL	57	9	18	27	68										4	0	1	1	6				
2002-03	Utah Grizzlies	AHL	69	8	26	34	68										2	0	0	0	2				
2003-04	Utah Grizzlies	AHL	23	1	3	4	25																		
2004-05	St. Petersburg	Russia	50	3	4	7	36																		
2005-06	Hershey Bears	AHL	69	7	19	26	58										14	0	4	4	6				
2006-07	Bridgeport	AHL	78	9	24	33	56																		
2007-08	Bridgeport	AHL	69	2	18	20	54																		
	NHL Totals		**43**	**3**	**6**	**9**	**25**	**0**	**1**	**0**	**46**	**6.5**		**0**	**0.0**	**13:45**	**5**	**0**	**0**	**0**	**4**	**0**	**0**	**0**	

WHL East Second All-Star Team (1994)

Signed as a free agent by **Dallas**, July 9, 1999. • Missed majority of 2003-04 season recovering from knee injury suffered in game vs. Cincinnati (AHL), December 6, 2003. Signed as a free agent by **St. Petersburg** (Russia), July 9, 2004. Signed as a free agent by **Washington**, August 17, 2005. Signed as a free agent by **NY Islanders**, July 27, 2006.

WOYWITKA, Jeff

(WOI-wiht-ka, JEHF) **ST.L.**

Defense. Shoots left. 6'2", 217 lbs. Born, Vermilion, Alta., September 1, 1983. Philadelphia's 1st choice, 27th overall, in 2001 Entry Draft.

Season	Club	League	GP	G	A	Pts	PIM	PP	SH	GW	S	%	+/-	TF	F%	Min	GP	G	A	Pts	PIM	PP	SH	GW	Min
1998-99	Wainwright	AAHA	26	7	15	22	60																		
99-2000	Red Deer Rebels	WHL	67	4	12	16	40										4	0	3	3	2				
2000-01	Red Deer Rebels	WHL	72	7	28	35	113										22	2	8	10	25				
2001-02	Red Deer Rebels	WHL	72	14	23	37	109										23	2	10	12	22				
2002-03	Red Deer Rebels	WHL	57	16	36	52	65										23	1	9	10	25				
2003-04	Philadelphia	AHL	29	0	6	6	51																		
	Toronto	AHL	53	4	18	22	41										3	0	0	0	2				
2004-05	Edmonton	AHL	80	6	20	26	84																		
2005-06	**St. Louis**	**NHL**	**26**	**0**	**2**	**2**	**25**	**0**	**0**	**0**	**23**	**0.0**	**–12**	**0**	**0.0**	**10:38**									
	Peoria Rivermen	AHL	53	1	14	15	58										4	0	0	0	4				
2006-07	**St. Louis**	**NHL**	**34**	**1**	**6**	**7**	**12**	**0**	**0**	**0**	**28**	**3.6**	**4**	**0**	**0.0**	**14:45**									
	Peoria Rivermen	AHL	41	0	18	18	20																		
2007-08	**St. Louis**	**NHL**	**27**	**2**	**6**	**8**	**12**	**0**	**0**	**0**	**25**	**8.0**	**2**	**0**	**0.0**	**16:04**									
	Peoria Rivermen	AHL	52	10	20	30	35																		
	NHL Totals		**87**	**3**	**14**	**17**	**49**	**0**	**0**	**0**	**76**	**3.9**		**0**	**0.0**	**13:56**									

WHL East Second All-Star Team (2002) • WHL East First All-Star Team (2003)

Traded to **Edmonton** by **Philadelphia** with Philadelphia's 1st round choice (Rob Schremp) in 2004 Entry Draft and Philadelphia's 3rd round choice (Danny Syvret) in 2005 Entry Draft for Mike Comrie, December 16, 2003. Traded to **St. Louis** by **Edmonton** with Eric Brewer and Doug Lynch for Chris Pronger, August 2, 2005.

WOZNIEWSKI, Andy

(wuhz-NYOO-skee, AN-dee) **ST.L.**

Defense. Shoots left. 6'5", 225 lbs. Born, Buffalo Grove, IL, May 25, 1980.

Season	Club	League	GP	G	A	Pts	PIM	PP	SH	GW	S	%	+/-	TF	F%	Min	GP	G	A	Pts	PIM	PP	SH	GW	Min
99-2000	U. Mass-Lowell	H-East	17	1	1	2	8																		
2000-01	Texas Tornado	NAHL	54	10	34	44	98										8	2	7	9	12				
2001-02	U. of Wisconsin	WCHA	39	3	13	16	54																		
2002-03	U. of Wisconsin	WCHA	33	1	7	8	47																		
2003-04	U. of Wisconsin	WCHA	43	6	8	14	*104																		
	St. John's	AHL	3	0	1	1	0																		

			Regular Season														Playoffs								
Season	Club	League	GP	G	A	Pts	PIM	PP	SH	GW	S	%	+/-	TF	F%	Min	GP	G	A	Pts	PIM	PP	SH	GW	Min
2004-05	St. John's	AHL	28	1	4	5	20	....	....	....	....	....	....	....	....	....	....	....	....	....	....	....	....	....	....
2005-06	**Toronto**	**NHL**	**13**	**0**	**1**	**1**	**13**	**0**	**0**	**0**	**6**	**0.0**	**–8**	**0**	**0.0**	**17:55**	....	....	....	....	....	....	....	....	....
	Toronto Marlies	AHL	31	4	11	15	42	....	....	....	....	....	....	....	....	....	....	....	....	....	....	....	....	....	....
2006-07	**Toronto**	**NHL**	**15**	**0**	**2**	**2**	**14**	**0**	**0**	**0**	**10**	**0.0**	**–1**	**0**	**0.0**	**13:55**	....	....	....	....	....	....	....	....	....
	Toronto Marlies	AHL	5	0	3	3	8	....	....	....	....	....	....	....	....	....	....	....	....	....	....	....	....	....	....
2007-08	**Toronto**	**NHL**	**48**	**2**	**7**	**9**	**54**	**0**	**0**	**0**	**34**	**5.9**	**5**	**0**	**0.0**	**14:10**	....	....	....	....	....	....	....	....	....
	Toronto Marlies	AHL	33	7	10	17	26	....	....	....	....	....	....	....	....	....	19	4	5	9	14	....	....	....	....
	NHL Totals		**76**	**2**	**10**	**12**	**81**	**0**	**0**	**0**	**50**	**4.0**		**0**	**0.0**	**14:46**	....	....	....	....	....	....	....	....	....

Signed as a free agent by **Toronto**, May 27, 2004. • Missed majority of 2006-07 season recovering from shoulder surgery, October 10, 2006. Signed as a free agent by **St. Louis**, July 17, 2008.

YANDLE, Keith

(Yan-duhl, KEETH) **PHX.**

Defense. Shoots left. 6'2", 195 lbs. Born, Boston, MA, September 9, 1986. Phoenix's 3rd choice, 105th overall, in 2005 Entry Draft.

Season	Club	League	GP	G	A	Pts	PIM	PP	SH	GW	S	%	+/-	TF	F%	Min	GP	G	A	Pts	PIM	PP	SH	GW	Min
2004-05	Cushing	High-MA	34	14	40	54	52	....	....	....	....	....	....	....	....	....	....	....	....	....	....	....	....	....	....
2005-06	Moncton Wildcats	QMJHL	66	25	59	84	109	....	....	....	....	....	....	....	....	....	21	6	14	20	36	....	....	....	....
2006-07	**Phoenix**	**NHL**	**7**	**0**	**2**	**2**	**8**	**0**	**0**	**0**	**10**	**0.0**	**0**	**0**	**0.0**	**20:10**	....	....	....	....	....	....	....	....	....
	San Antonio	AHL	69	6	27	33	97	....	....	....	....	....	....	....	....	....	....	....	....	....	....	....	....	....	....
2007-08	**Phoenix**	**NHL**	**43**	**5**	**7**	**12**	**14**	**4**	**0**	**0**	**72**	**6.9**	**–12**	**0**	**0.0**	**14:04**	....	....	....	....	....	....	....	....	....
	San Antonio	AHL	30	1	14	15	80	....	....	....	....	....	....	....	....	....	5	0	0	0	8	....	....	....	....
	NHL Totals		**50**	**5**	**9**	**14**	**22**	**4**	**0**	**0**	**82**	**6.1**		**0**	**0.0**	**14:56**	....	....	....	....	....	....	....	....	....

QMJHL First All-Star Team (2006) • Canadian Major Junior Defenseman of the Year (2006)

YASHIN, Alexei

(YAH-shin, al-EHX-ay)

Center. Shoots right. 6'3", 225 lbs. Born, Sverdlovsk, USSR, November 5, 1973. Ottawa's 1st choice, 2nd overall, in 1992 Entry Draft.

Season	Club	League	GP	G	A	Pts	PIM	PP	SH	GW	S	%	+/-	TF	F%	Min	GP	G	A	Pts	PIM	PP	SH	GW	Min
1989-90	Luch Sverdlovsk	USSR-2	STATISTICS NOT AVAILABLE																						
1990-91	Sverdlovsk	USSR	26	2	1	3	10	....	....	....	....	....	....	....	....	....	....	....	....	....	....	....	....	....	....
	Sverdlovsk	USSR-Q	12	1	1	2	12	....	....	....	....	....	....	....	....	....	....	....	....	....	....	....	....	....	....
1991-92	Dynamo Moscow	CIS	35	7	5	12	19	....	....	....	....	....	....	....	....	....	....	....	....	....	....	....	....	....	....
	Dyn'o Moscow 2	CIS-3	6	6	2	8	8	....	....	....	....	....	....	....	....	....	....	....	....	....	....	....	....	....	....
1992-93	Dynamo Moscow	CIS	27	10	12	22	18	....	....	....	....	....	....	....	....	....	10	7	3	10	18	....	....	....	....
1993-94	**Ottawa**	**NHL**	**83**	**30**	**49**	**79**	**22**	**11**	**2**	**3**	**232**	**12.9**	**–49**	....	....	....	....	....	....	....	....	....	....	....	....
1994-95	Las Vegas	IHL	24	15	20	35	32	....	....	....	....	....	....	....	....	....	....	....	....	....	....	....	....	....	....
	Ottawa	**NHL**	**47**	**21**	**23**	**44**	**20**	**11**	**0**	**1**	**154**	**13.6**	**–20**	....	....	....	....	....	....	....	....	....	....	....	....
1995-96	CSKA Moscow	CIS	4	2	2	4	4	....	....	....	....	....	....	....	....	....	....	....	....	....	....	....	....	....	....
	Ottawa	**NHL**	**46**	**15**	**24**	**39**	**28**	**8**	**0**	**1**	**143**	**10.5**	**–15**	....	....	....	....	....	....	....	....	....	....	....	....
1996-97	**Ottawa**	**NHL**	**82**	**35**	**40**	**75**	**44**	**10**	**0**	**5**	**291**	**12.0**	**–7**	....	....	....	**7**	**1**	**5**	**6**	**2**	**1**	**0**	**0**	....
1997-98	**Ottawa**	**NHL**	**82**	**33**	**39**	**72**	**24**	**5**	**0**	**6**	**291**	**11.3**	**6**	....	....	....	**11**	**5**	**3**	**8**	**8**	**3**	**0**	**2**	....
	Russia	Olympics	6	3	3	6	0	....	....	....	....	....	....	....	....	....	....	....	....	....	....	....	....	....	....
1998-99	**Ottawa**	**NHL**	**82**	**44**	**50**	**94**	**54**	**19**	**0**	**5**	**337**	**13.1**	**16**	**1428**	**41.9**	**22:05**	**4**	**0**	**0**	**0**	**10**	**0**	**0**	**0**	**26:06**
99-2000	**Ottawa**	**NHL**	DID NOT PLAY – SUSPENDED																						
2000-01	**Ottawa**	**NHL**	**82**	**40**	**48**	**88**	**30**	**13**	**2**	**10**	**263**	**15.2**	**10**	**1414**	**43.1**	**20:24**	**4**	**0**	**1**	**1**	**0**	**0**	**0**	**0**	**24:54**
2001-02	**NY Islanders**	**NHL**	**78**	**32**	**43**	**75**	**25**	**15**	**0**	**5**	**239**	**13.4**	**–3**	**828**	**46.7**	**20:37**	**7**	**3**	**4**	**7**	**2**	**1**	**0**	**0**	**21:54**
	Russia	Olympics	6	1	1	2	0	....	....	....	....	....	....	....	....	....	....	....	....	....	....	....	....	....	....
2002-03	**NY Islanders**	**NHL**	**81**	**26**	**39**	**65**	**32**	**14**	**0**	**7**	**274**	**9.5**	**–12**	**1074**	**47.2**	**18:32**	**5**	**2**	**2**	**4**	**2**	**0**	**0**	**0**	**21:06**
2003-04	**NY Islanders**	**NHL**	**47**	**15**	**19**	**34**	**10**	**3**	**0**	**1**	**148**	**10.1**	**–1**	**603**	**42.8**	**17:19**	**5**	**0**	**1**	**1**	**0**	**0**	**0**	**0**	**15:33**
2004-05	Yaroslavl	Russia	10	3	3	6	14	....	....	....	....	....	....	....	....	....	9	3	7	10	10	....	....	....	....
2005-06	**NY Islanders**	**NHL**	**82**	**28**	**38**	**66**	**68**	**10**	**0**	**2**	**253**	**11.1**	**–14**	**1116**	**50.2**	**18:30**	....	....	....	....	....	....	....	....	....
	Russia	Olympics	8	1	3	4	4	....	....	....	....	....	....	....	....	....	....	....	....	....	....	....	....	....	....
2006-07	**NY Islanders**	**NHL**	**58**	**18**	**32**	**50**	**44**	**5**	**0**	**3**	**203**	**8.9**	**6**	**527**	**45.9**	**17:04**	**5**	**0**	**0**	**0**	**0**	**0**	**0**	**0**	**11:45**
2007-08	Yaroslavl	Russia	56	16	27	43	63	....	....	....	....	....	....	....	....	....	16	8	6	*14	16	....	....	....	....
	NHL Totals		**850**	**337**	**444**	**781**	**401**	**124**	**4**	**49**	**2828**	**11.9**		**6990**	**45.2**	**19:26**	**48**	**11**	**16**	**27**	**24**	**5**	**0**	**2**	**19:59**

NHL Second All-Star Team (1999)
Played in NHL All-Star Game (1994, 1999, 2002)

• Suspended for entire 1999-2000 season by **Ottawa** for refusing to report to team, November 9, 1999. Traded to **NY Islanders** by **Ottawa** for Bill Muckalt, Zdeno Chara and NY Islanders' 1st round choice (Jason Spezza) in 2001 Entry Draft, June 23, 2001. Signed as a free agent by **Yaroslavl** (Russia), February 14, 2005. Signed as a free agent by **Yaroslavl** (Russia), July 20, 2007.

YELLE, Stephane

(YEHL, STEH-fan)

Center. Shoots left. 6'2", 182 lbs. Born, Ottawa, Ont., May 9, 1974. New Jersey's 9th choice, 186th overall, in 1992 Entry Draft.

Season	Club	League	GP	G	A	Pts	PIM	PP	SH	GW	S	%	+/-	TF	F%	Min	GP	G	A	Pts	PIM	PP	SH	GW	Min
1990-91	Cumberland	OHA-B	33	20	30	50	16	....	....	....	....	....	....	....	....	....	....	....	....	....	....	....	....	....	....
1991-92	Oshawa Generals	OHL	55	12	14	26	20	....	....	....	....	....	....	....	....	....	7	2	0	2	2	....	....	....	....
1992-93	Oshawa Generals	OHL	66	24	50	74	20	....	....	....	....	....	....	....	....	....	10	2	4	6	4	....	....	....	....
1993-94	Oshawa Generals	OHL	66	35	69	104	22	....	....	....	....	....	....	....	....	....	5	1	7	8	2	....	....	....	....
1994-95	Cornwall Aces	AHL	40	18	15	33	22	....	....	....	....	....	....	....	....	....	13	7	7	14	8	....	....	....	....
1995-96♦	**Colorado**	**NHL**	**71**	**13**	**14**	**27**	**30**	**0**	**2**	**1**	**93**	**14.0**	**15**	....	....	....	**22**	**1**	**4**	**5**	**8**	**0**	**1**	**0**	....
1996-97	**Colorado**	**NHL**	**79**	**9**	**17**	**26**	**38**	**0**	**1**	**1**	**89**	**10.1**	**1**	....	....	....	**12**	**1**	**6**	**7**	**2**	**0**	**0**	**0**	....
1997-98	**Colorado**	**NHL**	**81**	**7**	**15**	**22**	**48**	**0**	**1**	**0**	**93**	**7.5**	**–10**	....	....	....	**7**	**1**	**0**	**1**	**12**	**0**	**0**	**0**	....
1998-99	**Colorado**	**NHL**	**72**	**8**	**7**	**15**	**40**	**1**	**0**	**0**	**99**	**8.1**	**–8**	**1201**	**51.2**	**15:15**	**10**	**0**	**1**	**1**	**6**	**0**	**0**	**0**	**15:13**
99-2000	**Colorado**	**NHL**	**79**	**8**	**14**	**22**	**28**	**0**	**1**	**1**	**90**	**8.9**	**9**	**1294**	**52.2**	**15:51**	**17**	**1**	**2**	**3**	**4**	**0**	**0**	**0**	**15:38**
2000-01♦	**Colorado**	**NHL**	**50**	**4**	**10**	**14**	**20**	**0**	**1**	**0**	**54**	**7.4**	**–3**	**736**	**56.4**	**14:28**	**23**	**1**	**2**	**3**	**8**	**0**	**0**	**1**	**13:52**
2001-02	**Colorado**	**NHL**	**73**	**5**	**12**	**17**	**48**	**0**	**1**	**1**	**71**	**7.0**	**1**	**1036**	**51.8**	**14:02**	**20**	**0**	**2**	**2**	**14**	**0**	**0**	**0**	**13:26**
2002-03	**Calgary**	**NHL**	**82**	**10**	**15**	**25**	**50**	**3**	**0**	**3**	**121**	**8.3**	**–10**	**1494**	**53.4**	**18:06**	....	....	....	....	....	....	....	....	....
2003-04	**Calgary**	**NHL**	**53**	**4**	**13**	**17**	**24**	**1**	**0**	**0**	**76**	**5.3**	**1**	**996**	**56.6**	**15:48**	**23**	**3**	**3**	**6**	**16**	**0**	**1**	**1**	**17:04**
2004-05			DID NOT PLAY																						
2005-06	**Calgary**	**NHL**	**74**	**4**	**14**	**18**	**48**	**1**	**1**	**1**	**93**	**4.3**	**10**	**1072**	**55.4**	**14:27**	**7**	**1**	**0**	**1**	**8**	**0**	**0**	**0**	**15:28**
2006-07	**Calgary**	**NHL**	**56**	**10**	**14**	**24**	**32**	**1**	**1**	**1**	**55**	**18.2**	**5**	**808**	**50.4**	**14:37**	**6**	**0**	**0**	**0**	**2**	**0**	**0**	**0**	**15:13**
2007-08	**Calgary**	**NHL**	**74**	**3**	**9**	**12**	**20**	**0**	**1**	**0**	**62**	**4.8**	**–4**	**381**	**49.9**	**11:57**	**7**	**2**	**0**	**2**	**6**	**0**	**0**	**1**	**14:35**
	NHL Totals		**844**	**85**	**154**	**239**	**426**	**7**	**10**	**9**	**996**	**8.5**		**9018**	**53.2**	**15:00**	**154**	**11**	**20**	**31**	**86**	**0**	**2**	**3**	**15:03**

Traded to **Quebec** by **New Jersey** with New Jersey's 11th round choice (Steven Low) in 1994 Entry Draft for Quebec's 11th round choice (Mike Hanson) in 1994 Entry Draft, June 1, 1994. Transferred to **Colorado** after **Quebec** franchise relocated, June 21, 1995. Traded to **Calgary** by **Colorado** with Chris Drury for Derek Morris, Jeff Shantz and Dean McAmmond, October 1, 2002.

YONKMAN, Nolan

(YAWNK-man, NOH-luhn)

Defense. Shoots right. 6'6", 245 lbs. Born, Punnichy, Sask., April 1, 1981. Washington's 5th choice, 37th overall, in 1999 Entry Draft.

Season	Club	League	GP	G	A	Pts	PIM	PP	SH	GW	S	%	+/-	TF	F%	Min	GP	G	A	Pts	PIM	PP	SH	GW	Min
1996-97	Naicam Vikings	SAHA	64	15	23	38	36	....	....	....	....	....	....	....	....	....	....	....	....	....	....	....	....	....	....
	Kelowna Rockets	WHL	4	0	0	0	0	....	....	....	....	....	....	....	....	....	....	....	....	....	....	....	....	....	....
1997-98	Kelowna Rockets	WHL	65	0	2	2	36	....	....	....	....	....	....	....	....	....	7	0	0	0	2	....	....	....	....
1998-99	Kelowna Rockets	WHL	61	1	6	7	129	....	....	....	....	....	....	....	....	....	6	0	0	0	6	....	....	....	....
99-2000	Kelowna Rockets	WHL	71	5	7	12	153	....	....	....	....	....	....	....	....	....	5	0	0	0	8	....	....	....	....
2000-01	Kelowna Rockets	WHL	7	0	1	1	19	....	....	....	....	....	....	....	....	....	....	....	....	....	....	....	....	....	....
	Brandon	WHL	51	6	10	16	94	....	....	....	....	....	....	....	....	....	6	0	1	1	12	....	....	....	....
2001-02	**Washington**	**NHL**	**11**	**1**	**0**	**1**	**4**	**0**	**0**	**0**	**7**	**14.3**	**3**	**0**	**0.0**	**12:44**	....	....	....	....	....	....	....	....	....
	Portland Pirates	AHL	59	4	3	7	116	....	....	....	....	....	....	....	....	....	....	....	....	....	....	....	....	....	....
2002-03	Portland Pirates	AHL	24	1	4	5	40	....	....	....	....	....	....	....	....	....	3	0	1	1	2	....	....	....	....
2003-04	**Washington**	**NHL**	**1**	**0**	**0**	**0**	**0**	**0**	**0**	**0**	**0**	**0.0**	**0**	**0**	**0.0**	**5:00**	....	....	....	....	....	....	....	....	....
	Portland Pirates	AHL	4	0	0	0	11	....	....	....	....	....	....	....	....	....	....	....	....	....	....	....	....	....	....
2004-05	Portland Pirates	AHL	32	0	3	3	68	....	....	....	....	....	....	....	....	....	....	....	....	....	....	....	....	....	....
2005-06	**Washington**	**NHL**	**38**	**0**	**7**	**7**	**86**	**0**	**0**	**0**	**14**	**0.0**	**1**	**0**	**0.0**	**8:13**	....	....	....	....	....	....	....	....	....
	Hershey Bears	AHL	6	0	0	0	15	....	....	....	....	....	....	....	....	....	....	....	....	....	....	....	....	....	....
2006-07	Milwaukee	AHL	77	3	10	13	113	....	....	....	....	....	....	....	....	....	4	0	0	0	2	....	....	....	....
2007-08	Milwaukee	AHL	69	0	7	7	103	....	....	....	....	....	....	....	....	....	6	0	1	1	18	....	....	....	....
	NHL Totals		**50**	**1**	**7**	**8**	**90**	**0**	**0**	**0**	**21**	**4.8**		**0**	**0.0**	**9:09**	....	....	....	....	....	....	....	....	....

• Missed majority of 2002-03 season recovering from abdominal injury suffered in training camp, September 25, 2002. • Missed majority of 2003-04 and 2004-05 seasons recovering from knee injury suffered in game vs. Worcester (AHL), October 23, 2003. Signed as a free agent by **Nashville**, July 17, 2006.

YORK, Mike — (YOHRK, MIGHK) — CBJ

Left wing. Shoots right. 5'10", 185 lbs. Born, Waterford, MI, January 3, 1978. NY Rangers' 7th choice, 136th overall, in 1997 Entry Draft.

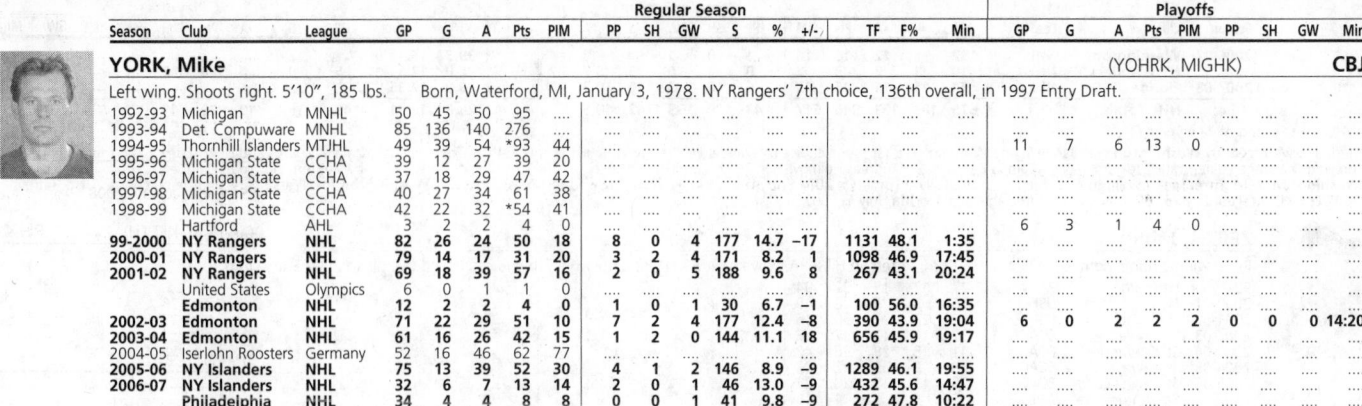

			Regular Season														Playoffs								
Season	Club	League	GP	G	A	Pts	PIM	PP	SH	GW	S	%	+/-	TF	F%	Min	GP	G	A	Pts	PIM	PP	SH	GW	Min
1992-93	Michigan	MNHL	50	45	50	95	....	....	....	....	....	....	....	....	....	....	....	....	....	....	....	....	....	....	....
1993-94	Det. Compuware	MNHL	85	136	140	276	....	....	....	....	....	....	....	....	....	....	....	....	....	....	....	....	....	....	....
1994-95	Thornhill Islanders	MTJHL	49	39	54	*93	44	....	....	....	....	....	....	....	....	....	11	7	6	13	0	....	....	....	....
1995-96	Michigan State	CCHA	39	12	27	39	20	....	....	....	....	....	....	....	....	....	....	....	....	....	....	....	....	....	....
1996-97	Michigan State	CCHA	37	18	29	47	42	....	....	....	....	....	....	....	....	....	....	....	....	....	....	....	....	....	....
1997-98	Michigan State	CCHA	40	27	34	61	38	....	....	....	....	....	....	....	....	....	....	....	....	....	....	....	....	....	....
1998-99	Michigan State	CCHA	42	22	32	*54	41	....	....	....	....	....	....	....	....	....	....	....	....	....	....	....	....	....	....
	Hartford	AHL	3	2	2	4	0	....	....	....	....	....	....	....	....	....	6	3	1	4	0	....	....	....	....
99-2000	**NY Rangers**	**NHL**	**82**	**26**	**24**	**50**	**18**	**8**	**0**	**4**	**177**	**14.7**	**–17**	**1131**	**48.1**	**1:35**	....	....	....	....	....	....	....	....	....
2000-01	**NY Rangers**	**NHL**	**79**	**14**	**17**	**31**	**20**	**3**	**2**	**4**	**171**	**8.2**	**1**	**1098**	**46.9**	**17:45**	....	....	....	....	....	....	....	....	....
2001-02	**NY Rangers**	**NHL**	**69**	**18**	**39**	**57**	**16**	**2**	**0**	**5**	**188**	**9.6**	**8**	**267**	**43.1**	**20:24**	....	....	....	....	....	....	....	....	....
	United States	Olympics	6	0	1	1	0	....	....	....	....	....	....	....	....	....	....	....	....	....	....	....	....	....	....
	Edmonton	**NHL**	**12**	**2**	**2**	**4**	**0**	**1**	**0**	**1**	**30**	**6.7**	**–1**	**100**	**56.0**	**16:35**	....	....	....	....	....	....	....	....	....
2002-03	**Edmonton**	**NHL**	**71**	**22**	**29**	**51**	**10**	**7**	**2**	**4**	**177**	**12.4**	**–8**	**390**	**43.9**	**19:04**	**6**	**0**	**2**	**2**	**2**	**0**	**0**	**0**	**14:20**
2003-04	**Edmonton**	**NHL**	**61**	**16**	**26**	**42**	**15**	**1**	**2**	**0**	**144**	**11.1**	**18**	**656**	**45.9**	**19:17**	....	....	....	....	....	....	....	....	....
2004-05	Iserlohn Roosters	Germany	52	16	46	62	77	....	....	....	....	....	....	....	....	....	....	....	....	....	....	....	....	....	....
2005-06	**NY Islanders**	**NHL**	**75**	**13**	**39**	**52**	**30**	**4**	**1**	**2**	**146**	**8.9**	**–9**	**1289**	**46.1**	**19:55**	....	....	....	....	....	....	....	....	....
2006-07	**NY Islanders**	**NHL**	**32**	**6**	**7**	**13**	**14**	**2**	**0**	**1**	**46**	**13.0**	**–9**	**432**	**45.6**	**14:47**	....	....	....	....	....	....	....	....	....
	Philadelphia	**NHL**	**34**	**4**	**4**	**8**	**8**	**0**	**0**	**1**	**41**	**9.8**	**–9**	**272**	**47.8**	**10:22**	....	....	....	....	....	....	....	....	....
2007-08	**Phoenix**	**NHL**	**63**	**6**	**8**	**14**	**4**	**4**	**0**	**1**	**85**	**7.1**	**–8**	**205**	**50.7**	**11:59**	....	....	....	....	....	....	....	....	....
	NHL Totals		**578**	**127**	**195**	**322**	**135**	**32**	**7**	**23**	**1205**	**10.5**		**5840**	**46.7**	**15:08**	**6**	**0**	**2**	**2**	**2**	**0**	**0**	**0**	**14:20**

CCHA Second All-Star Team (1998) • NCAA West First All-American Team (1998, 1999) • CCHA First All-Star Team (1999) • CCHA Player of the Year (1999) • NHL All-Rookie Team (2000)

Played in NHL All-Star Game (2002)

Traded to **Edmonton** by **NY Rangers** with NY Rangers' 4th round choice (Ivan Koltsov) in 2002 Entry Draft for Tom Poti and Rem Murray, March 19, 2002. Signed as a free agent by **Iserlohn** (Germany), February 25, 2005. Traded to **NY Islanders** by **Edmonton** with Edmonton's 4th round choice (later traded to Colorado - Colorado selected Kevin Montgomery) in 2006 Entry Draft for Michael Peca, August 3, 2005. Traded to **Philadelphia** by **NY Islanders** for Randy Robitaille and Philadelphia's 5th round choice (Matthew Martin) in 2008 Entry Draft, December 20, 2006. Signed as a free agent by **Phoenix**, July 9, 2007. Signed as a free agent by **Columbus**, July 25, 2008.

YOUNG, Bryan — (YUHNG, BRIGH-uhn) — EDM.

Defense. Shoots left. 6'1", 191 lbs. Born, Kitchener, Ont., August 6, 1986. Edmonton's 6th choice, 146th overall, in 2004 Entry Draft.

Season	Club	League	GP	G	A	Pts	PIM	PP	SH	GW	S	%	+/-	TF	F%	Min	GP	G	A	Pts	PIM	PP	SH	GW	Min
2002-03	Lindsay Muskies	OPJHL	47	1	9	10	56	....	....	....	....	....	....	....	....	....	....	....	....	....	....	....	....	....	....
	Peterborough	OHL	2	0	0	0	0	....	....	....	....	....	....	....	....	....	....	....	....	....	....	....	....	....	....
2003-04	Peterborough	OHL	60	0	8	8	63	....	....	....	....	....	....	....	....	....	....	....	....	....	....	....	....	....	....
2004-05	Peterborough	OHL	60	1	11	12	44	....	....	....	....	....	....	....	....	....	14	0	1	1	10	....	....	....	....
2005-06	Peterborough	OHL	64	0	10	10	113	....	....	....	....	....	....	....	....	....	19	0	0	0	37	....	....	....	....
2006-07	**Edmonton**	**NHL**	**15**	**0**	**0**	**0**	**10**	**0**	**0**	**0**	**2**	**0.0**	**–8**	**0**	**0.0**	**10:06**	....	....	....	....	....	....	....	....	....
	Milwaukee	AHL	22	0	0	0	6	....	....	....	....	....	....	....	....	....	....	....	....	....	....	....	....	....	....
	Stockton Thunder	ECHL	17	0	4	4	24	....	....	....	....	....	....	....	....	....	....	....	....	....	....	....	....	....	....
	Wilkes-Barre	AHL	10	0	1	1	2	....	....	....	....	....	....	....	....	....	4	0	1	1	2	....	....	....	....
2007-08	**Edmonton**	**NHL**	**2**	**0**	**0**	**0**	**0**	**0**	**0**	**0**	**0**	**0.0**	**–1**	**0**	**0.0**	**2:08**	....	....	....	....	....	....	....	....	....
	Springfield	AHL	74	0	7	7	62	....	....	....	....	....	....	....	....	....	....	....	....	....	....	....	....	....	....
	NHL Totals		**17**	**0**	**0**	**0**	**10**	**0**	**0**	**0**	**2**	**0.0**		**0**	**0.0**	**9:10**	....	....	....	....	....	....	....	....	....

ZAJAC, Travis — (ZAY-jak, TRA-vihs) — N.J.

Center. Shoots right. 6'2", 200 lbs. Born, Winnipeg, Man., May 13, 1985. New Jersey's 1st choice, 20th overall, in 2004 Entry Draft.

Season	Club	League	GP	G	A	Pts	PIM	PP	SH	GW	S	%	+/-	TF	F%	Min	GP	G	A	Pts	PIM	PP	SH	GW	Min
2002-03	Salmon Arm	BCHL	59	16	36	52	27	....	....	....	....	....	....	....	....	....	11	2	4	6	6	....	....	....	....
2003-04	Salmon Arm	BCHL	59	43	69	112	110	....	....	....	....	....	....	....	....	....	14	10	13	23	10	....	....	....	....
2004-05	North Dakota	WCHA	45	20	19	39	16	....	....	....	....	....	....	....	....	....	....	....	....	....	....	....	....	....	....
2005-06	North Dakota	WCHA	46	18	29	47	20	....	....	....	....	....	....	....	....	....	....	....	....	....	....	....	....	....	....
	Albany River Rats	AHL	2	0	1	1	2	....	....	....	....	....	....	....	....	....	....	....	....	....	....	....	....	....	....
2006-07	**New Jersey**	**NHL**	**80**	**17**	**25**	**42**	**16**	**6**	**0**	**2**	**134**	**12.7**	**1**	**904**	**46.9**	**16:03**	**11**	**1**	**4**	**5**	**4**	**0**	**0**	**0**	**16:22**
2007-08	**New Jersey**	**NHL**	**82**	**14**	**20**	**34**	**31**	**5**	**0**	**1**	**155**	**9.0**	**–11**	**1032**	**51.2**	**16:44**	**5**	**0**	**1**	**1**	**4**	**0**	**0**	**0**	**13:35**
	NHL Totals		**162**	**31**	**45**	**76**	**47**	**11**	**0**	**3**	**289**	**10.7**		**1936**	**49.2**	**16:24**	**16**	**1**	**5**	**6**	**8**	**0**	**0**	**0**	**15:30**

WCHA All-Rookie Team (2005) • NCAA Championship All-Tournament Team (2005)

ZANON, Greg — (ZA-nuhn, GREHG) — NSH.

Defense. Shoots left. 5'11", 211 lbs. Born, Burnaby, B.C., June 5, 1980. Ottawa's 6th choice, 156th overall, in 2000 Entry Draft.

Season	Club	League	GP	G	A	Pts	PIM	PP	SH	GW	S	%	+/-	TF	F%	Min	GP	G	A	Pts	PIM	PP	SH	GW	Min
1995-96	Burnaby Beavers	Minor-BC	49	16	27	43	142	....	....	....	....	....	....	....	....	....	....	....	....	....	....	....	....	....	....
1996-97	Victoria Salsa	BCHL	53	4	13	17	124	....	....	....	....	....	....	....	....	....	....	....	....	....	....	....	....	....	....
1997-98	Victoria Salsa	BCHL	59	11	21	32	108	....	....	....	....	....	....	....	....	....	7	0	2	2	10	....	....	....	....
1998-99	South Surrey	BCHL	59	17	54	71	154	....	....	....	....	....	....	....	....	....	....	....	....	....	....	....	....	....	....
99-2000	Nebraska-Omaha	CCHA	42	3	26	29	56	....	....	....	....	....	....	....	....	....	....	....	....	....	....	....	....	....	....
2000-01	Nebraska-Omaha	CCHA	39	12	16	28	64	....	....	....	....	....	....	....	....	....	....	....	....	....	....	....	....	....	....
2001-02	Nebraska-Omaha	CCHA	41	9	16	25	54	....	....	....	....	....	....	....	....	....	....	....	....	....	....	....	....	....	....
2002-03	Nebraska-Omaha	CCHA	32	6	19	25	44	....	....	....	....	....	....	....	....	....	....	....	....	....	....	....	....	....	....
2003-04	Milwaukee	AHL	62	4	12	16	59	....	....	....	....	....	....	....	....	....	22	2	6	8	31	....	....	....	....
2004-05	Milwaukee	AHL	80	2	17	19	59	....	....	....	....	....	....	....	....	....	7	0	1	1	10	....	....	....	....
2005-06	**Nashville**	**NHL**	**4**	**0**	**2**	**2**	**6**	**0**	**0**	**0**	**3**	**0.0**	**0**	**0**	**0.0**	**17:19**	....	....	....	....	....	....	....	....	....
	Milwaukee	AHL	71	8	27	35	55	....	....	....	....	....	....	....	....	....	21	1	7	8	24	....	....	....	....
2006-07	**Nashville**	**NHL**	**66**	**3**	**5**	**8**	**32**	**0**	**0**	**0**	**43**	**7.0**	**16**	**0**	**0.0**	**17:20**	**5**	**0**	**2**	**2**	**2**	**0**	**0**	**0**	**20:44**
	Milwaukee	AHL	2	0	2	2	0	....	....	....	....	....	....	....	....	....	....	....	....	....	....	....	....	....	....
2007-08	**Nashville**	**NHL**	**78**	**0**	**5**	**5**	**24**	**0**	**0**	**0**	**38**	**0.0**	**–5**	**0**	**0.0**	**18:28**	**6**	**0**	**2**	**2**	**4**	**0**	**0**	**0**	**18:45**
	NHL Totals		**148**	**3**	**12**	**15**	**62**	**0**	**0**	**0**	**84**	**3.6**		**0**	**0.0**	**17:56**	**11**	**0**	**4**	**4**	**6**	**0**	**0**	**0**	**19:39**

CCHA First All-Star Team (2001) • NCAA West Second All-American Team (2001, 2002) • CCHA Second All-Star Team (2002)

Signed as a free agent by **Nashville**, July 9, 2004.

ZEDNIK, Richard — (ZEHD-nihk, RIH-chuhrd) — FLA.

Right wing. Shoots left. 6', 200 lbs. Born, Banska Bystrica, Czech., January 6, 1976. Washington's 10th choice, 249th overall, in 1994 Entry Draft.

Season	Club	League	GP	G	A	Pts	PIM	PP	SH	GW	S	%	+/-	TF	F%	Min	GP	G	A	Pts	PIM	PP	SH	GW	Min
1993-94	B. Bystrica	Slovak-2	25	3	6	9	....	....	....	....	....	....	....	....	....	....	....	....	....	....	....	....	....	....	....
1994-95	Portland	WHL	65	35	51	86	89	....	....	....	....	....	....	....	....	....	9	5	5	10	20	....	....	....	....
1995-96	Portland	WHL	61	44	37	81	154	....	....	....	....	....	....	....	....	....	7	8	4	12	23	....	....	....	....
	Washington	**NHL**	**1**	**0**	**0**	**0**	**0**	**0**	**0**	**0**	**0**	**0.0**	**0**	....	....	....	....	....	....	....	....	....	....	....	....
	Portland Pirates	AHL	1	1	1	2	0	....	....	....	....	....	....	....	....	....	21	4	5	9	26	....	....	....	....
1996-97	**Washington**	**NHL**	**11**	**2**	**1**	**3**	**4**	**1**	**0**	**0**	**21**	**9.5**	**–5**	....	....	....	....	....	....	....	....	....	....	....	....
	Portland Pirates	AHL	56	15	20	35	70	....	....	....	....	....	....	....	....	....	5	1	0	1	6	....	....	....	....
1997-98	**Washington**	**NHL**	**65**	**17**	**9**	**26**	**28**	**2**	**0**	**2**	**148**	**11.5**	**–2**	....	....	....	**17**	**7**	**3**	**10**	**16**	**2**	**0**	**0**	....
1998-99	**Washington**	**NHL**	**49**	**9**	**8**	**17**	**50**	**1**	**0**	**2**	**115**	**7.8**	**–6**	**2**	**0.0**	**15:08**	....	....	....	....	....	....	....	....	....
99-2000	**Washington**	**NHL**	**69**	**19**	**16**	**35**	**54**	**1**	**0**	**2**	**179**	**10.6**	**6**	**1**	**100.0**	**15:34**	**5**	**0**	**0**	**0**	**5**	**0**	**0**	**0**	**16:57**
2000-01	**Washington**	**NHL**	**62**	**16**	**19**	**35**	**61**	**4**	**0**	**3**	**155**	**10.3**	**–2**	**1**	**0.0**	**15:32**	....	....	....	....	....	....	....	....	....
	Montreal	**NHL**	**12**	**3**	**6**	**9**	**10**	**1**	**0**	**0**	**23**	**13.0**	**–2**	**0**	**0.0**	**18:29**	....	....	....	....	....	....	....	....	....
2001-02	**Montreal**	**NHL**	**82**	**22**	**22**	**44**	**59**	**4**	**0**	**3**	**249**	**8.8**	**–3**	**10**	**30.0**	**17:39**	**4**	**4**	**4**	**8**	**6**	**2**	**0**	**0**	**21:19**
2002-03	**Montreal**	**NHL**	**80**	**31**	**19**	**50**	**79**	**9**	**0**	**2**	**250**	**12.4**	**4**	**10**	**30.0**	**18:25**	....	....	....	....	....	....	....	....	....
2003-04	**Montreal**	**NHL**	**81**	**26**	**24**	**50**	**63**	**7**	**0**	**9**	**218**	**11.9**	**5**	**6**	**50.0**	**17:30**	**11**	**3**	**3**	**6**	**2**	**0**	**0**	**1**	**18:52**
2004-05	HKm Zvolen	Slovakia	36	15	19	34	56	....	....	....	....	....	....	....	....	....	17	9	10	19	12	....	....	....	....
2005-06	**Montreal**	**NHL**	**67**	**16**	**14**	**30**	**48**	**6**	**0**	**4**	**161**	**9.9**	**–2**	**6**	**16.7**	**15:46**	**6**	**2**	**0**	**2**	**4**	**1**	**0**	**0**	**15:13**
	Slovakia	Olympics	6	1	0	1	12	....	....	....	....	....	....	....	....	....	....	....	....	....	....	....	....	....	....

			Regular Season														Playoffs								
Season	Club	League	GP	G	A	Pts	PIM	PP	SH	GW	S	%	+/-	TF	F%	Min	GP	G	A	Pts	PIM	PP	SH	GW	Min
2006-07	Washington	NHL	32	6	12	18	16	1	0	1	68	8.8	–4	3	33.3	15:42	....	....	....	....	....	....	....	....	....
	NY Islanders	NHL	10	1	2	3	2	0	0	0	15	6.7	–2	1	0.0	12:51	5	0	0	0	8	0	0	0	10:45
2007-08	Florida	NHL	54	15	11	26	43	6	0	5	140	10.7	–5	2	0.0	17:35	....	....	....	....	....	....	....	....	....
	NHL Totals		**675**	**183**	**163**	**346**	**517**	**43**	**0**	**33**	**1742**	**10.5**		**42**	**28.6**	**16:41**	**48**	**16**	**10**	**26**	**41**	**5**	**0**	**1**	**16:51**

WHL West Second All-Star Team (1996)

Traded to **Montreal** by **Washington** with Jan Bulis and Washington's 1st round choice (Alexander Perezhogin) in 2001 Entry Draft for Trevor Linden, Dainius Zubrus and New Jersey's 2nd round choice (previously acquired, later traded to Tampa Bay – Tampa Bay selected Andreas Holmqvist) in 2001 Entry Draft, March 13, 2001. Signed as a free agent by **Zvolen** (Slovakia), October 7, 2004. Traded to **Washington** by **Montreal** for Wahington's 3rd round choice (Olivier Fortier) in 2007 Entry Draft, July 12, 2006. Traded to **NY Islanders** by **Washington** for NY Islanders' 2nd round choice (Theo Ruth) in 2007 Entry Draft, February 26, 2007. Signed as a free agent by **Florida**, July 1, 2007.

ZEILER, John (ZIGH-luhr, JAWN) L.A.

Right wing. Shoots right. 6', 203 lbs. Born, Jefferson Hills, PA, November 21, 1982. Phoenix's 7th choice, 132nd overall, in 2002 Entry Draft.

Season	Club	League	GP	G	A	Pts	PIM	PP	SH	GW	S	%	+/-	TF	F%	Min	GP	G	A	Pts	PIM	PP	SH	GW	Min
99-2000	Pittsburgh	PAHA	27	17	15	32	94	....	....	....	....	....	....	....	....	....	....	....	....	....	....	....	....	....	....
2000-01	Sioux City	USHL	56	8	20	28	45	....	....	....	....	....	....	....	....	....	2	0	0	0	26	....	....	....	....
2001-02	Sioux City	USHL	60	23	27	50	116	....	....	....	....	....	....	....	....	....	12	2	3	5	25	....	....	....	....
2002-03	St. Lawrence	ECAC	37	10	17	27	28	....	....	....	....	....	....	....	....	....	....	....	....	....	....	....	....	....	....
2003-04	St. Lawrence	ECAC	41	8	*28	36	42	....	....	....	....	....	....	....	....	....	....	....	....	....	....	....	....	....	....
2004-05	St. Lawrence	ECAC	38	9	23	32	42	....	....	....	....	....	....	....	....	....	....	....	....	....	....	....	....	....	....
2005-06	St. Lawrence	ECAC	28	13	15	28	28	....	....	....	....	....	....	....	....	....	....	....	....	....	....	....	....	....	....
	San Antonio	AHL	8	0	1	1	10	....	....	....	....	....	....	....	....	....	....	....	....	....	....	....	....	....	....
	Lubbock	CHL	4	2	0	2	16	....	....	....	....	....	....	....	....	....	....	....	....	....	....	....	....	....	....
2006-07	Manchester	AHL	56	12	16	28	70	....	....	....	....	....	....	....	....	....	16	3	2	5	14	....	....	....	....
	Los Angeles	**NHL**	**23**	**1**	**2**	**3**	**22**	**0**	**0**	**0**	**12**	**8.3**	**–2**	**22**	**40.9**	**8:36**	....	....	....	....	....	....	....	....	....
2007-08	**Los Angeles**	**NHL**	**36**	**0**	**1**	**1**	**23**	**0**	**0**	**0**	**18**	**0.0**	**–6**	**31**	**38.7**	**8:29**	....	....	....	....	....	....	....	....	....
	Manchester	AHL	45	6	5	11	40	....	....	....	....	....	....	....	....	....	4	0	2	2	8	....	....	....	....
	NHL Totals		**59**	**1**	**3**	**4**	**45**	**0**	**0**	**0**	**30**	**3.3**		**53**	**39.6**	**8:32**	....	....	....	....	....	....	....	....	....

ECAC All-Rookie Team (2003)

Signed as a free agent by **San Antonio** (AHL), March 18, 2006. Signed as a free agent by **Los Angeles**, February 17, 2007.

ZETTERBERG, Henrik (ZEH-tuhr-buhrg, HEHN-rihk) DET.

Left wing. Shoots left. 5'11", 195 lbs. Born, Njurunda, Sweden, October 9, 1980. Detroit's 4th choice, 210th overall, in 1999 Entry Draft.

Season	Club	League	GP	G	A	Pts	PIM	PP	SH	GW	S	%	+/-	TF	F%	Min	GP	G	A	Pts	PIM	PP	SH	GW	Min
1997-98	Timra IK Jr.	Swe-Jr.	18	9	5	14	4	....	....	....	....	....	....	....	....	....	....	....	....	....	....	....	....	....	....
	Timra IK	Sweden-2	16	1	2	3	4	....	....	....	....	....	....	....	....	....	4	0	1	1	0	....	....	....	....
1998-99	Timra IK	Sweden-2	37	15	13	28	2	....	....	....	....	....	....	....	....	....	4	2	1	3	2	....	....	....	....
99-2000	Timra IK	Sweden-2	32	20	14	34	20	....	....	....	....	....	....	....	....	....	10	10	4	14	4	....	....	....	....
2000-01	Timra IK	Sweden	47	15	31	46	24	....	....	....	....	....	....	....	....	....	....	....	....	....	....	....	....	....	....
2001-02	Timra IK	Sweden	48	10	22	32	20	....	....	....	....	....	....	....	....	....	....	....	....	....	....	....	....	....	....
	Sweden	Olympics	4	0	1	1	0	....	....	....	....	....	....	....	....	....	....	....	....	....	....	....	....	....	....
2002-03	**Detroit**	**NHL**	**79**	**22**	**22**	**44**	**8**	**5**	**1**	**4**	**135**	**16.3**	**6**	**401**	**46.1**	**16:19**	**4**	**1**	**0**	**1**	**0**	**0**	**0**	**0**	**18:19**
2003-04	**Detroit**	**NHL**	**61**	**15**	**28**	**43**	**14**	**7**	**1**	**2**	**137**	**10.9**	**15**	**627**	**45.6**	**18:15**	**12**	**2**	**2**	**4**	**4**	**0**	**0**	**0**	**17:17**
2004-05	Timra IK	Sweden	50	19	31	*50	24	....	....	....	....	....	....	....	....	....	7	6	2	8	2	....	....	....	....
2005-06	**Detroit**	**NHL**	**77**	**39**	**46**	**85**	**30**	**17**	**1**	**9**	**270**	**14.4**	**29**	**583**	**50.3**	**18:57**	**6**	**6**	**0**	**6**	**2**	**4**	**0**	**0**	**21:43**
	Sweden	Olympics	8	3	3	6	0	....	....	....	....	....	....	....	....	....	....	....	....	....	....	....	....	....	....
2006-07	**Detroit**	**NHL**	**63**	**33**	**35**	**68**	**36**	**11**	**1**	**10**	**224**	**14.7**	**26**	**888**	**52.5**	**20:50**	**18**	**6**	**8**	**14**	**12**	**3**	**0**	**1**	**22:45**
2007-08♦	**Detroit**	**NHL**	**75**	**43**	**49**	**92**	**34**	**16**	**1**	**7**	**358**	**12.0**	**30**	**1210**	**55.0**	**22:04**	**22**	***13**	**14**	***27**	**16**	**4**	**2**	**4**	**22:36**
	NHL Totals		**355**	**152**	**180**	**332**	**122**	**56**	**5**	**32**	**1124**	**13.5**		**3709**	**51.1**	**19:14**	**62**	**28**	**24**	**52**	**34**	**11**	**2**	**5**	**21:15**

Swedish Elite League Rookie of the Year (2001) • NHL All-Rookie Team (2003) • NHL Second All-Star Team (2008) • Conn Smythe Trophy (2008)

Signed as a free agent by **Timra** (Sweden), September 20, 2004.

ZHERDEV, Nikolai (ZHAIR-dehv, NIH-koh-ligh) NYR

Wing. Shoots right. 6'2", 205 lbs. Born, Kiev, USSR, November 5, 1984. Columbus' 1st choice, 4th overall, in 2003 Entry Draft.

Season	Club	League	GP	G	A	Pts	PIM	PP	SH	GW	S	%	+/-	TF	F%	Min	GP	G	A	Pts	PIM	PP	SH	GW	Min
99-2000	Elektrostal 2	Russia-3	21	10	7	17	26	....	....	....	....	....	....	....	....	....	7	0	0	0	0	....	....	....	....
2000-01	Elektrostal	Russia-2	18	5	8	13	12	....	....	....	....	....	....	....	....	....	....	....	....	....	....	....	....	....	....
	Russia	Exhib.	17	10	11	21	17	....	....	....	....	....	....	....	....	....	....	....	....	....	....	....	....	....	....
2001-02	Elektrostal	Russia-2	53	13	15	28	62	....	....	....	....	....	....	....	....	....	....	....	....	....	....	....	....	....	....
	Elektrostal 2	Russia-3	1	1	0	1	4	....	....	....	....	....	....	....	....	....	....	....	....	....	....	....	....	....	....
2002-03	CSKA Moscow	Russia	44	12	12	24	34	....	....	....	....	....	....	....	....	....	....	....	....	....	....	....	....	....	....
2003-04	CSKA Moscow	Russia	20	2	2	4	14	....	....	....	....	....	....	....	....	....	....	....	....	....	....	....	....	....	....
	Columbus	**NHL**	**57**	**13**	**21**	**34**	**54**	**5**	**0**	**1**	**137**	**9.5**	**–11**	**9**	**11.1**	**16:11**	....	....	....	....	....	....	....	....	....
2004-05	CSKA Moscow	Russia	51	19	21	40	62	....	....	....	....	....	....	....	....	....	....	....	....	....	....	....	....	....	....
2005-06	**Columbus**	**NHL**	**73**	**27**	**27**	**54**	**50**	**10**	**0**	**0**	**194**	**13.9**	**–13**	**20**	**10.0**	**17:36**	....	....	....	....	....	....	....	....	....
	Syracuse Crunch	AHL	2	1	0	1	0	....	....	....	....	....	....	....	....	....	....	....	....	....	....	....	....	....	....
2006-07	Mytischi	Russia	8	2	4	6	10	....	....	....	....	....	....	....	....	....	....	....	....	....	....	....	....	....	....
	Columbus	**NHL**	**71**	**10**	**22**	**32**	**26**	**3**	**0**	**2**	**164**	**6.1**	**–19**	**17**	**23.5**	**16:13**	....	....	....	....	....	....	....	....	....
2007-08	**Columbus**	**NHL**	**82**	**26**	**35**	**61**	**34**	**7**	**0**	**3**	**254**	**10.2**	**–9**	**29**	**41.4**	**19:22**	....	....	....	....	....	....	....	....	....
	NHL Totals		**283**	**76**	**105**	**181**	**164**	**25**	**0**	**6**	**749**	**10.1**		**75**	**25.3**	**17:29**	....	....	....	....	....	....	....	....	....

Signed as a free agent by **CSKA Moscow** (Russia), July 27, 2004. Signed as a free agent by **Mystichi** (Russia), July 20, 2006. Traded to **NY Rangers** by **Columbus** with Dan Fritsche for Fedor Tyutin and Christian Backman, July 2, 2008.

ZHITNIK, Alexei (ZHIHT-nihk, al-EHX-ay)

Defense. Shoots left. 5'11", 225 lbs. Born, Kiev, USSR, October 10, 1972. Los Angeles' 3rd choice, 81st overall, in 1991 Entry Draft.

Season	Club	League	GP	G	A	Pts	PIM	PP	SH	GW	S	%	+/-	TF	F%	Min	GP	G	A	Pts	PIM	PP	SH	GW	Min
1989-90	Sokol Kiev	USSR	31	3	4	7	16	....	....	....	....	....	....	....	....	....	....	....	....	....	....	....	....	....	....
1990-91	Sokol Kiev	USSR	46	1	4	5	46	....	....	....	....	....	....	....	....	....	....	....	....	....	....	....	....	....	....
	ShVSM Kiev	USSR-3	1	0	....	....	....	....	....	....	....	....	....	....	....	....	....	....	....	....	....	....	....	....	....
1991-92	CSKA Moscow	CIS	44	2	7	9	52	....	....	....	....	....	....	....	....	....	....	....	....	....	....	....	....	....	....
	Russia	Olympics	8	1	0	1	0	....	....	....	....	....	....	....	....	....	....	....	....	....	....	....	....	....	....
1992-93	**Los Angeles**	**NHL**	**78**	**12**	**36**	**48**	**80**	**5**	**0**	**2**	**136**	**8.8**	**–3**	....	....	....	**24**	**3**	**9**	**12**	**26**	**2**	**0**	**1**	....
1993-94	**Los Angeles**	**NHL**	**81**	**12**	**40**	**52**	**101**	**11**	**0**	**1**	**227**	**5.3**	**–11**	....	....	....	....	....	....	....	....	....	....	....	....
1994-95	**Los Angeles**	**NHL**	**11**	**2**	**5**	**7**	**27**	**2**	**0**	**0**	**33**	**6.1**	**–3**	....	....	....	....	....	....	....	....	....	....	....	....
	Buffalo	**NHL**	**21**	**2**	**5**	**7**	**34**	**1**	**0**	**0**	**33**	**6.1**	**–3**	....	....	....	**5**	**0**	**1**	**1**	**14**	**0**	**0**	**0**	....
1995-96	**Buffalo**	**NHL**	**80**	**6**	**30**	**36**	**58**	**5**	**0**	**0**	**193**	**3.1**	**–25**	....	....	....	....	....	....	....	....	....	....	....	....
1996-97	**Buffalo**	**NHL**	**80**	**7**	**28**	**35**	**95**	**3**	**1**	**0**	**170**	**4.1**	**10**	....	....	....	**12**	**1**	**0**	**1**	**16**	**0**	**0**	**0**	....
1997-98	**Buffalo**	**NHL**	**78**	**15**	**30**	**45**	**102**	**2**	**3**	**3**	**191**	**7.9**	**19**	....	....	....	**15**	**0**	**3**	**3**	**36**	**0**	**0**	**0**	....
	Russia	Olympics	6	0	2	2	2	....	....	....	....	....	....	....	....	....	....	....	....	....	....	....	....	....	....
1998-99	**Buffalo**	**NHL**	**81**	**7**	**26**	**33**	**96**	**3**	**1**	**2**	**185**	**3.8**	**–6**	**0**	**0.0**	**25:39**	**21**	**4**	**11**	**15**	***52**	**4**	**0**	**2**	**27:07**
99-2000	**Buffalo**	**NHL**	**74**	**2**	**11**	**13**	**95**	**1**	**0**	**0**	**139**	**1.4**	**–6**	**0**	**0.0**	**24:48**	**4**	**0**	**0**	**0**	**8**	**0**	**0**	**0**	**25:50**
2000-01	**Buffalo**	**NHL**	**78**	**8**	**29**	**37**	**75**	**5**	**0**	**1**	**149**	**5.4**	**–3**	**0**	**0.0**	**24:15**	**13**	**1**	**6**	**7**	**12**	**0**	**0**	**0**	**25:38**
2001-02	**Buffalo**	**NHL**	**82**	**1**	**33**	**34**	**80**	**1**	**0**	**0**	**150**	**0.7**	**–1**	**0**	**0.0**	**25:36**	....	....	....	....	....	....	....	....	....
2002-03	**Buffalo**	**NHL**	**70**	**3**	**18**	**21**	**85**	**0**	**0**	**1**	**138**	**2.2**	**–5**	**1**	**0.0**	**26:33**	....	....	....	....	....	....	....	....	....
2003-04	**Buffalo**	**NHL**	**68**	**4**	**24**	**28**	**102**	**2**	**0**	**0**	**134**	**3.0**	**–13**	**0**	**0.0**	**25:01**	....	....	....	....	....	....	....	....	....
2004-05	Ak Bars Kazan	Russia	23	1	8	9	30	....	....	....	....	....	....	....	....	....	4	0	0	0	2	....	....	....	....
2005-06	**NY Islanders**	**NHL**	**59**	**5**	**24**	**29**	**88**	**3**	**0**	**0**	**99**	**5.1**	**4**	**0**	**0.0**	**24:30**	....	....	....	....	....	....	....	....	....

			Regular Season														Playoffs								
Season	Club	League	GP	G	A	Pts	PIM	PP	SH	GW	S	%	+/-	TF	F%	Min	GP	G	A	Pts	PIM	PP	SH	GW	Min
2006-07	**NY Islanders**	**NHL**	**30**	**2**	**9**	**11**	**40**	**0**	**0**	**1**	**49**	**4.1**	**13**	**1**	**100.0**	**21:37**	....	....	....	....	....	....	....	....	....
	Philadelphia	**NHL**	**31**	**3**	**10**	**13**	**38**	**1**	**0**	**0**	**61**	**4.9**	**–16**	**1**	**0.0**	**25:30**	....	....	....	....	....	....	....	....	....
	Atlanta	**NHL**	**18**	**2**	**12**	**14**	**14**	**2**	**0**	**1**	**22**	**9.1**	**4**	**0**	**0.0**	**25:49**	**4**	**0**	**0**	**0**	**4**	**0**	**0**	**0**	**25:21**
2007-08	**Atlanta**	**NHL**	**65**	**3**	**5**	**8**	**58**	**0**	**0**	**1**	**79**	**3.8**	**–8**	**0**	**0.0**	**19:01**	....	....	....	....	....	....	....	....	....
	NHL Totals		**1085**	**96**	**375**	**471**	**1268**	**47**	**5**	**13**	**2188**	**4.4**		**3**	**33.3**	**24:28**	**98**	**9**	**30**	**39**	**168**	**6**	**0**	**3**	**26:22**

Played in NHL All-Star Game (1999, 2002)

Traded to **Buffalo** by **Los Angeles** with Robb Stauber, Charlie Huddy and Los Angeles' 5th round choice (Marian Menhart) in 1995 Entry Draft for Philippe Boucher, Denis Tsygurov and Grant Fuhr, February 14, 1995. Signed as a free agent by **Kazan** (Russia), December 6, 2004. Signed as a free agent by **NY Islanders**, August 2, 2005. Traded to **Philadelphia** by **NY Islanders** for Freddy Meyer and Philadelphia's 3rd round choice (Mark Katic) in 2007 Entry Draft, December 16, 2006. Traded to **Atlanta** by **Philadelphia** for Braydon Coburn, February 24, 2007.

ZIDLICKY, Marek

(zihd-LIH-kee, MAIR-ehk) **MIN.**

Defense. Shoots right. 5'11", 190 lbs. Born, Most, Czech., February 3, 1977. NY Rangers' 6th choice, 176th overall, in 2001 Entry Draft.

Season	Club	League	GP	G	A	Pts	PIM	PP	SH	GW	S	%	+/-	TF	F%	Min	GP	G	A	Pts	PIM	PP	SH	GW	Min
1994-95	HC Kladno	CzRep	30	2	2	4	38	....	....	....	....	....	....	....	....	....	11	1	1	2	10	....	....	....	....
1995-96	HC Poldi Kladno	CzRep	37	4	5	9	74	....	....	....	....	....	....	....	....	....	7	1	1	2	8	....	....	....	....
1996-97	HC Poldi Kladno	CzRep	49	5	16	21	60	....	....	....	....	....	....	....	....	....	2	0	0	0	0	....	....	....	....
1997-98	Kladno	CzRep	51	2	13	15	121	....	....	....	....	....	....	....	....	....	....	....	....	....	....	....	....	....	....
1998-99	Kladno	CzRep	50	10	12	22	94	....	....	....	....	....	....	....	....	....	....	....	....	....	....	....	....	....	....
99-2000	HIFK Helsinki	Finland	47	4	16	20	66	....	....	....	....	....	....	....	....	....	9	3	2	5	24	....	....	....	....
	HIFK Helsinki	EuroHL	4	2	2	4	10	....	....	....	....	....	....	....	....	....	1	0	0	0	0	....	....	....	....
2000-01	HIFK Helsinki	Finland	51	12	25	37	146	....	....	....	....	....	....	....	....	....	5	0	1	1	6	....	....	....	....
2001-02	HIFK Helsinki	Finland	56	11	29	40	107	....	....	....	....	....	....	....	....	....	....	....	....	....	....	....	....	....	....
2002-03	HIFK Helsinki	Finland	54	10	37	47	79	....	....	....	....	....	....	....	....	....	4	0	0	0	4	....	....	....	....
2003-04	**Nashville**	**NHL**	**82**	**14**	**39**	**53**	**82**	**9**	**0**	**4**	**143**	**9.8**	**–16**	**0**	**0.0**	**20:02**	**1**	**0**	**0**	**0**	**0**	**0**	**0**	**0**	**2:16**
2004-05	HIFK Helsinki	Finland	49	11	20	31	91	....	....	....	....	....	....	....	....	....	5	0	3	3	14	....	....	....	....
2005-06	**Nashville**	**NHL**	**67**	**12**	**37**	**49**	**82**	**10**	**0**	**1**	**113**	**10.6**	**8**	**0**	**0.0**	**20:04**	**2**	**0**	**1**	**1**	**2**	**0**	**0**	**0**	**15:19**
	Czech Republic	Olympics	7	4	1	5	16	....	....	....	....	....	....	....	....	....	....	....	....	....	....	....	....	....	....
2006-07	**Nashville**	**NHL**	**79**	**4**	**26**	**30**	**72**	**2**	**0**	**1**	**114**	**3.5**	**8**	**0**	**0.0**	**19:43**	**5**	**0**	**2**	**2**	**4**	**0**	**0**	**0**	**19:19**
2007-08	**Nashville**	**NHL**	**79**	**5**	**38**	**43**	**63**	**4**	**0**	**0**	**122**	**4.1**	**–5**	**0**	**0.0**	**20:50**	**6**	**0**	**3**	**3**	**8**	**0**	**0**	**0**	**19:04**
	NHL Totals		**307**	**35**	**140**	**175**	**299**	**25**	**0**	**6**	**492**	**7.1**		**0**	**0.0**	**20:10**	**14**	**0**	**6**	**6**	**14**	**0**	**0**	**0**	**17:25**

Traded to **Nashville** by **NY Rangers** with Rem Murray and Tomas Kloucek for Mike Dunham, December 12, 2002. Signed as a free agent by **HIFK Helsinki** (Finland), September 17, 2004. Traded to **Minnesota** by **Nashville** for Ryan Jones and Minnesota's 2nd round choice in 2009 Entry Draft, July 1, 2008.

ZIGOMANIS, Mike

(zih-goh-MAN-ihs, MIGHK) **PHX.**

Center. Shoots right. 6'1", 200 lbs. Born, Toronto, Ont., January 17, 1981. Carolina's 2nd choice, 46th overall, in 2001 Entry Draft.

Season	Club	League	GP	G	A	Pts	PIM	PP	SH	GW	S	%	+/-	TF	F%	Min	GP	G	A	Pts	PIM	PP	SH	GW	Min
1996-97	Wexford Raiders	MTHL	40	37	48	85	23	....	....	....	....	....	....	....	....	....	....	....	....	....	....	....	....	....	....
	Wexford Raiders	MTJHL	8	2	5	7	2	....	....	....	....	....	....	....	....	....	....	....	....	....	....	....	....	....	....
1997-98	Kingston	OHL	62	23	51	74	30	....	....	....	....	....	....	....	....	....	12	1	6	7	2	....	....	....	....
1998-99	Kingston	OHL	67	29	56	85	36	....	....	....	....	....	....	....	....	....	5	1	7	8	2	....	....	....	....
99-2000	Kingston	OHL	59	40	54	94	49	....	....	....	....	....	....	....	....	....	5	0	4	4	0	....	....	....	....
2000-01	Kingston	OHL	52	40	37	77	44	....	....	....	....	....	....	....	....	....	....	....	....	....	....	....	....	....	....
2001-02	Lowell	AHL	79	18	30	48	24	....	....	....	....	....	....	....	....	....	5	1	1	2	2	....	....	....	....
2002-03	**Carolina**	**NHL**	**19**	**2**	**1**	**3**	**0**	**1**	**1**	**0**	**19**	**10.5**	**–4**	**147**	**59.2**	**9:43**	....	....	....	....	....	....	....	....	....
	Lowell	AHL	38	13	18	31	19	....	....	....	....	....	....	....	....	....	....	....	....	....	....	....	....	....	....
2003-04	**Carolina**	**NHL**	**17**	**0**	**3**	**3**	**2**	**0**	**0**	**0**	**13**	**0.0**	**–1**	**108**	**53.7**	**8:37**	....	....	....	....	....	....	....	....	....
	Lowell	AHL	61	17	35	52	56	....	....	....	....	....	....	....	....	....	....	....	....	....	....	....	....	....	....
2004-05	Lowell	AHL	76	29	31	60	71	....	....	....	....	....	....	....	....	....	11	4	7	11	8	....	....	....	....
2005-06	**Carolina**	**NHL**	**21**	**1**	**0**	**1**	**4**	**0**	**0**	**0**	**16**	**6.3**	**1**	**72**	**50.0**	**9:25**	....	....	....	....	....	....	....	....	....
	Lowell	AHL	11	6	7	13	19	....	....	....	....	....	....	....	....	....	....	....	....	....	....	....	....	....	....
	St. Louis	**NHL**	**2**	**0**	**0**	**0**	**0**	**0**	**0**	**0**	**1**	**0.0**	**0**	**1**	**100.0**	**7:39**	....	....	....	....	....	....	....	....	....
	Peoria Rivermen	AHL	28	10	18	28	16	....	....	....	....	....	....	....	....	....	4	2	4	6	6	....	....	....	....
2006-07	**Phoenix**	**NHL**	**75**	**14**	**9**	**23**	**46**	**2**	**1**	**0**	**142**	**9.9**	**–8**	**1010**	**56.2**	**14:53**	....	....	....	....	....	....	....	....	....
2007-08	**Phoenix**	**NHL**	**33**	**2**	**1**	**3**	**6**	**0**	**0**	**0**	**35**	**5.7**	**–7**	**328**	**59.8**	**12:24**	....	....	....	....	....	....	....	....	....
	San Antonio	AHL	27	10	15	25	14	....	....	....	....	....	....	....	....	....	7	0	5	5	10	....	....	....	....
	NHL Totals		**167**	**19**	**14**	**33**	**58**	**3**	**2**	**0**	**226**	**8.4**		**1666**	**56.8**	**12:24**	....	....	....	....	....	....	....	....	....

• Re-entered NHL Entry Draft. Originally Buffalo's 4th choice, 64th overall, in 1999 Entry Draft.

Traded to **St. Louis** by **Carolina** with Jesse Boulerice, the rights to Magnus Kahnberg, Carolina's 1st round choice (later traded to New Jersey - New Jersey selected Matthew Corrente) in 2006 Entry Draft, Toronto's 4th round choice (previously acquired, St. Louis selected Reto Berra) in 2006 Entry Draft and Chicago's 4th round choice (previously acquired, St. Louis selected Cade Fairchild) in 2007 Entry Draft for Doug Weight and Erkki Rajamaki, January 30, 2006. Signed as a free agent by **Phoenix**, July 21, 2006.

ZINGER, Dwayne

(ZIHN-guhr, DWAYN)

Defense. Shoots left. 6'4", 216 lbs. Born, Coronation, Alta., July 5, 1976.

Season	Club	League	GP	G	A	Pts	PIM	PP	SH	GW	S	%	+/-	TF	F%	Min	GP	G	A	Pts	PIM	PP	SH	GW	Min
1995-96	Melville	SJHL	64	7	17	24	....	....	....	....	....	....	....	....	....	....	....	....	....	....	....	....	....	....	....
1996-97	Alaska	CCHA	32	1	5	6	45	....	....	....	....	....	....	....	....	....	....	....	....	....	....	....	....	....	....
1997-98	Alaska	CCHA	32	1	3	4	91	....	....	....	....	....	....	....	....	....	....	....	....	....	....	....	....	....	....
1998-99	Alaska	CCHA	33	4	14	18	42	....	....	....	....	....	....	....	....	....	....	....	....	....	....	....	....	....	....
99-2000	Alaska	CCHA	34	10	4	14	34	....	....	....	....	....	....	....	....	....	....	....	....	....	....	....	....	....	....
	Cincinnati	AHL	13	0	2	2	33	....	....	....	....	....	....	....	....	....	....	....	....	....	....	....	....	....	....
2000-01	Cincinnati	AHL	68	6	9	15	120	....	....	....	....	....	....	....	....	....	4	1	1	2	2	....	....	....	....
2001-02	Cincinnati	AHL	67	6	13	19	156	....	....	....	....	....	....	....	....	....	3	0	1	1	2	....	....	....	....
2002-03	Portland Pirates	AHL	65	1	7	8	67	....	....	....	....	....	....	....	....	....	3	0	0	0	2	....	....	....	....
2003-04	**Washington**	**NHL**	**7**	**0**	**1**	**1**	**9**	**0**	**0**	**0**	**0**	**0.0**	**2**	**0**	**0.0**	**5:24**	....	....	....	....	....	....	....	....	....
	Portland Pirates	AHL	68	6	10	16	49	....	....	....	....	....	....	....	....	....	7	0	0	0	16	....	....	....	....
2004-05	Portland Pirates	AHL	58	0	4	4	118	....	....	....	....	....	....	....	....	....	....	....	....	....	....	....	....	....	....
2005-06	Hershey Bears	AHL	30	0	0	0	74	....	....	....	....	....	....	....	....	....	....	....	....	....	....	....	....	....	....
	San Antonio	AHL	35	1	2	3	68	....	....	....	....	....	....	....	....	....	....	....	....	....	....	....	....	....	....
2006-07	Providence Bruins	AHL	78	3	15	18	100	....	....	....	....	....	....	....	....	....	12	1	1	2	13	....	....	....	....
2007-08	Providence Bruins	AHL	53	0	8	8	83	....	....	....	....	....	....	....	....	....	6	0	0	0	0	....	....	....	....
	NHL Totals		**7**	**0**	**1**	**1**	**9**	**0**	**0**	**0**	**0**	**0.0**		**0**	**0.0**	**5:24**	....	....	....	....	....	....	....	....	....

SJHL First All-Star Team (1996)

Signed as a free agent by **Detroit**, March 13, 2000. Signed as a free agent by **Washington**, July 9, 2002. Traded to **Phoenix** by **Washington** for Doug Doull, February 3, 2006.

ZINOVJEV, Sergei

(zih-NOH-vee-ehv, SAIR-gay) **BOS.**

Center/Left wing. Shoots left. 5'10", 185 lbs. Born, Novokuznetsk, USSR, March 4, 1980. Boston's 6th choice, 73rd overall, in 2000 Entry Draft.

Season	Club	League	GP	G	A	Pts	PIM	PP	SH	GW	S	%	+/-	TF	F%	Min	GP	G	A	Pts	PIM	PP	SH	GW	Min
1995-96	Novokuznetsk 2	CIS-2	10	1	0	1	2	....	....	....	....	....	....	....	....	....	....	....	....	....	....	....	....	....	....
1996-97	Novokuznetsk 2	Russia-3	29	2	1	3	8	....	....	....	....	....	....	....	....	....	....	....	....	....	....	....	....	....	....
1997-98	Novokuznetsk 2	Russia-3	40	7	7	14	36	....	....	....	....	....	....	....	....	....	....	....	....	....	....	....	....	....	....
	Novokuznetsk 2	Russia-3	2	1	0	1	0	....	....	....	....	....	....	....	....	....	....	....	....	....	....	....	....	....	....
1998-99	Novokuznetsk 2	Russia-4	4	0	1	1	8	....	....	....	....	....	....	....	....	....	....	....	....	....	....	....	....	....	....
	Magnitogorsk	Russia	31	2	4	6	14	....	....	....	....	....	....	....	....	....	3	0	0	0	0	....	....	....	....
99-2000	Magnitogorsk	Russia	28	0	2	2	16	....	....	....	....	....	....	....	....	....	....	....	....	....	....	....	....	....	....
2000-01	Yaroslavl	Russia	27	2	10	12	36	....	....	....	....	....	....	....	....	....	....	....	....	....	....	....	....	....	....
	Ufa	Russia	8	4	5	9	6	....	....	....	....	....	....	....	....	....	....	....	....	....	....	....	....	....	....
2001-02	Spartak Moscow	Russia	51	12	18	30	43	....	....	....	....	....	....	....	....	....	....	....	....	....	....	....	....	....	....
2002-03	Ak Bars Kazan	Russia	47	14	17	31	50	....	....	....	....	....	....	....	....	....	5	1	1	2	6	....	....	....	....
2003-04	**Boston**	**NHL**	**10**	**0**	**1**	**1**	**2**	**0**	**0**	**0**	**8**	**0.0**	**1**	**72**	**41.7**	**9:48**	....	....	....	....	....	....	....	....	....
	Providence Bruins	AHL	4	1	2	3	0	....	....	....	....	....	....	....	....	....	....	....	....	....	....	....	....	....	....
	Ak Bars Kazan	Russia	27	5	9	14	75	....	....	....	....	....	....	....	....	....	8	0	1	1	12	....	....	....	....
2004-05	Ak Bars Kazan	Russia	54	17	21	38	82	....	....	....	....	....	....	....	....	....	4	1	0	1	12	....	....	....	....
2005-06	Ak Bars Kazan	Russia	43	15	20	35	58	....	....	....	....	....	....	....	....	....	13	9	8	17	26	....	....	....	....

			Regular Season														Playoffs								
Season	Club	League	GP	G	A	Pts	PIM	PP	SH	GW	S	%	+/-	TF	F%	Min	GP	G	A	Pts	PIM	PP	SH	GW	Min
2006-07	Ak Bars Kazan	Russia	41	19	35	54	103	....	....	....	....	....	....	....	....	....	16	7	10	*17	20	....	....	....	....
2007-08	Ak Bars Kazan	Russia	37	9	21	30	53	....	....	....	....	....	....	....	....	....	10	4	7	11	16	....	....	....	....
	NHL Totals		**10**	**0**	**1**	**1**	**2**	**0**	**0**	**0**	**8**	**0.0**		**72**	**41.7**	**9:48**	....	....	....	....	....	....	....	....	....

Signed as a free agent by **Kazan** (Russia), December 9, 2003.

ZIZKA, Tomas
(ZHIHZH-kuh, TAW-mahsh) **L.A.**

Defense. Shoots left. 6'1", 198 lbs. Born, Sternberk, Czech., October 10, 1979. Los Angeles' 6th choice, 163rd overall, in 1998 Entry Draft.

1994-95	AC ZPS Zlin Jr.	CzRep-Jr.	39	1	10	11	....	....	....	....	....	....	....	....	....	....	....	....	....	....	....	....	....	....	....
1995-96	AC ZPS Zlin Jr.	CzRep-Jr.	47	2	8	10	....	....	....	....	....	....	....	....	....	....	....	....	....	....	....	....	....	....	....
1996-97	AC ZPS Zlin Jr.	CzRep-Jr.	14	1	0	1	....	....	....	....	....	....	....	....	....	....	....	....	....	....	....	....	....	....	....
1997-98	HC ZPS Zlin Jr.	CzRep-Jr.	11	3	4	7	....	....	....	....	....	....	....	....	....	....	....	....	....	....	....	....	....	....	....
	Zlin	CzRep	33	0	3	3	2	....	....	....	....	....	....	....	....	....	....	....	....	....	....	....	....	....	....
1998-99	Zlin	CzRep	44	3	7	10	14	....	....	....	....	....	....	....	....	....	11	1	2	3	....	....	....	....	....
99-2000	Zlin	CzRep	46	4	6	10	30	....	....	....	....	....	....	....	....	....	4	1	0	1	4	....	....	....	....
2000-01	Zlin	CzRep	43	2	11	13	16	....	....	....	....	....	....	....	....	....	6	0	0	0	6	....	....	....	....
2001-02	Manchester	AHL	58	4	17	21	22	....	....	....	....	....	....	....	....	....	4	1	0	1	14	....	....	....	....
2002-03	**Los Angeles**	**NHL**	**10**	**0**	**3**	**3**	**4**	**0**	**0**	**0**	**12**	**0.0**	**–4**	**0**	**0.0**	**15:24**	....	....	....	....	....	....	....	....	....
	Manchester	AHL	61	13	30	43	50	....	....	....	....	....	....	....	....	....	3	0	2	2	2	....	....	....	....
2003-04	**Los Angeles**	**NHL**	**15**	**2**	**3**	**5**	**12**	**1**	**0**	**0**	**24**	**8.3**	**–4**	**0**	**0.0**	**16:54**	....	....	....	....	....	....	....	....	....
	Manchester	AHL	58	4	24	28	31	....	....	....	....	....	....	....	....	....	5	0	3	3	10	....	....	....	....
2004-05	Spartak Moscow	Russia	23	0	3	3	32	....	....	....	....	....	....	....	....	....	....	....	....	....	....	....	....	....	....
	HC Slavia Praha	CzRep	26	2	4	6	26	....	....	....	....	....	....	....	....	....	2	0	0	0	2	....	....	....	....
2005-06	HC Slavia Praha	CzRep	52	6	9	15	48	....	....	....	....	....	....	....	....	....	14	1	2	3	31	....	....	....	....
2006-07	HC Slavia Praha	CzRep	38	4	5	9	54	....	....	....	....	....	....	....	....	....	6	1	2	3	10	....	....	....	....
2007-08	HC Slavia Praha	CzRep	48	5	9	14	76	....	....	....	....	....	....	....	....	....	19	2	1	3	28	....	....	....	....
	NHL Totals		**25**	**2**	**6**	**8**	**16**	**1**	**0**	**0**	**36**	**5.6**		**0**	**0.0**	**16:18**	....	....	....	....	....	....	....	....	....

Signed as a free agent by **Spartak Moscow** (Russia), August 31, 2004. Signed as a free agent by **Slavia Praha** (CzRep), November, 2004.

ZUBOV, Ilya
(ZOO-bahf, IHL-yah) **OTT.**

Center. Shoots left. 5'11", 211 lbs. Born, Chelyabinsk, USSR, February 14, 1987. Ottawa's 4th choice, 98th overall, in 2005 Entry Draft.

2003-04	Chelyabinsk	Russia-2	33	7	7	14	16	....	....	....	....	....	....	....	....	....	8	2	1	3	2	....	....	....	....
2004-05	Chelyabinsk	Russia-2	40	9	8	17	36	....	....	....	....	....	....	....	....	....	....	....	....	....	....	....	....	....	....
	Chelyabinsk 2	Russia-3	1	0	0	0	0	....	....	....	....	....	....	....	....	....	....	....	....	....	....	....	....	....	....
2005-06	Spartak 2	Russia-3	1	0	1	1	4	....	....	....	....	....	....	....	....	....	....	....	....	....	....	....	....	....	....
	Spartak Moscow	Russia	43	4	8	12	12	....	....	....	....	....	....	....	....	....	3	2	2	4	0	....	....	....	....
2006-07	Mytischi	Russia	16	1	1	2	4	....	....	....	....	....	....	....	....	....	....	....	....	....	....	....	....	....	....
	Ufa	Russia	26	3	7	10	4	....	....	....	....	....	....	....	....	....	8	2	3	5	2	....	....	....	....
2007-08	**Ottawa**	**NHL**	**1**	**0**	**0**	**0**	**0**	**0**	**0**	**0**	**0**	**0.0**	**0**	**5**	**40.0**	**14:38**	....	....	....	....	....	....	....	....	....
	Binghamton	AHL	74	15	23	38	18	....	....	....	....	....	....	....	....	....	....	....	....	....	....	....	....	....	....
	NHL Totals		**1**	**0**	**0**	**0**	**0**	**0**	**0**	**0**	**0**	**0.0**		**5**	**40.0**	**14:38**	....	....	....	....	....	....	....	....	....

ZUBOV, Sergei
(ZOO-bahf, SAIR-gay) **DAL.**

Defense. Shoots right. 6'1", 198 lbs. Born, Moscow, USSR, July 22, 1970. NY Rangers' 6th choice, 85th overall, in 1990 Entry Draft.

1988-89	CSKA Moscow	USSR	29	1	4	5	10	....	....	....	....	....	....	....	....	....	....	....	....	....	....	....	....	....	....
1989-90	CSKA Moscow	USSR	48	6	2	8	16	....	....	....	....	....	....	....	....	....	....	....	....	....	....	....	....	....	....
1990-91	CSKA Moscow	USSR	41	6	5	11	12	....	....	....	....	....	....	....	....	....	....	....	....	....	....	....	....	....	....
	CSKA Moscow	Super-S	7	0	1	1	0	....	....	....	....	....	....	....	....	....	....	....	....	....	....	....	....	....	....
1991-92	CSKA Moscow	CIS	44	4	7	11	8	....	....	....	....	....	....	....	....	....	....	....	....	....	....	....	....	....	....
	Russia	Olympics	8	0	1	1	0	....	....	....	....	....	....	....	....	....	....	....	....	....	....	....	....	....	....
1992-93	CSKA Moscow	CIS	1	0	1	1	0	....	....	....	....	....	....	....	....	....	....	....	....	....	....	....	....	....	....
	NY Rangers	**NHL**	**49**	**8**	**23**	**31**	**4**	**3**	**0**	**0**	**93**	**8.6**	**–1**	....	....	....	....	....	....	....	....	....	....	....	....
	Binghamton	AHL	30	7	29	36	14	....	....	....	....	....	....	....	....	....	11	5	5	10	2	....	....	....	....
1993-94♦	**NY Rangers**	**NHL**	**78**	**12**	**77**	**89**	**39**	**9**	**0**	**1**	**222**	**5.4**	**20**	....	....	....	**22**	**5**	**14**	**19**	**0**	**2**	**0**	**0**	....
	Binghamton	AHL	2	1	2	3	0	....	....	....	....	....	....	....	....	....	....	....	....	....	....	....	....	....	....
1994-95	**NY Rangers**	**NHL**	**38**	**10**	**26**	**36**	**18**	**6**	**0**	**0**	**116**	**8.6**	**–2**	....	....	....	**10**	**3**	**8**	**11**	**2**	**1**	**0**	**0**	....
1995-96	**Pittsburgh**	**NHL**	**64**	**11**	**55**	**66**	**22**	**3**	**2**	**1**	**141**	**7.8**	**28**	....	....	....	**18**	**1**	**14**	**15**	**26**	**1**	**0**	**0**	....
1996-97	**Dallas**	**NHL**	**78**	**13**	**30**	**43**	**24**	**1**	**0**	**3**	**133**	**9.8**	**19**	....	....	....	**7**	**0**	**3**	**3**	**2**	**0**	**0**	**0**	....
1997-98	**Dallas**	**NHL**	**73**	**10**	**47**	**57**	**16**	**5**	**1**	**2**	**148**	**6.8**	**16**	....	....	....	**17**	**4**	**5**	**9**	**2**	**3**	**0**	**1**	....
1998-99♦	**Dallas**	**NHL**	**81**	**10**	**41**	**51**	**20**	**5**	**0**	**3**	**155**	**6.5**	**9**	**0**	**0.0**	**24:14**	**23**	**1**	**12**	**13**	**4**	**0**	**0**	**0**	**30:16**
99-2000	**Dallas**	**NHL**	**77**	**9**	**33**	**42**	**18**	**3**	**1**	**3**	**179**	**5.0**	**–2**	**0**	**0.0**	**28:50**	**18**	**2**	**7**	**9**	**6**	**1**	**1**	**0**	**26:28**
2000-01	**Dallas**	**NHL**	**79**	**10**	**41**	**51**	**24**	**6**	**0**	**1**	**173**	**5.8**	**22**	**0**	**0.0**	**26:37**	**10**	**1**	**5**	**6**	**4**	**0**	**0**	**0**	**30:37**
2001-02	**Dallas**	**NHL**	**80**	**12**	**32**	**44**	**22**	**8**	**0**	**2**	**198**	**6.1**	**–4**	**0**	**0.0**	**26:46**	....	....	....	....	....	....	....	....	....
2002-03	**Dallas**	**NHL**	**82**	**11**	**44**	**55**	**26**	**8**	**0**	**2**	**158**	**7.0**	**21**	**0**	**0.0**	**25:50**	**12**	**4**	**10**	**14**	**4**	**2**	**0**	**0**	**30:45**
2003-04	**Dallas**	**NHL**	**77**	**7**	**35**	**42**	**20**	**4**	**1**	**1**	**154**	**4.5**	**0**	**0**	**0.0**	**25:50**	**5**	**1**	**1**	**2**	**0**	**1**	**0**	**0**	**28:01**
2004-05			DID NOT PLAY																						
2005-06	**Dallas**	**NHL**	**78**	**13**	**58**	**71**	**46**	**9**	**0**	**0**	**141**	**9.2**	**20**	**0**	**0.0**	**26:27**	**5**	**1**	**5**	**6**	**6**	**1**	**0**	**0**	**29:42**
2006-07	**Dallas**	**NHL**	**78**	**12**	**42**	**54**	**26**	**9**	**0**	**3**	**156**	**7.7**	**0**	**1**	**100.0**	**25:57**	**6**	**0**	**4**	**4**	**2**	**0**	**0**	**0**	**30:51**
2007-08	**Dallas**	**NHL**	**46**	**4**	**31**	**35**	**12**	**2**	**0**	**0**	**84**	**4.8**	**6**	**0**	**0.0**	**25:42**	**11**	**1**	**5**	**6**	**4**	**1**	**0**	**0**	**26:01**
	NHL Totals		**1058**	**152**	**615**	**767**	**337**	**81**	**5**	**22**	**2251**	**6.8**		**1**	**100.0**	**26:16**	**164**	**24**	**93**	**117**	**62**	**13**	**1**	**1**	**28:58**

NHL Second All-Star Team (2006)
Played in NHL All-Star Game (1998, 1999, 2000)
Traded to **Pittsburgh** by **NY Rangers** with Petr Nedved for Luc Robitaille and Ulf Samuelsson, August 31, 1995. Traded to **Dallas** by **Pittsburgh** for Kevin Hatcher, June 22, 1996.

ZUBRUS, Dainius
(ZOO-bruhs, DAYN-ihs) **N.J.**

Center. Shoots left. 6'5", 225 lbs. Born, Elektrenai, USSR, June 16, 1978. Philadelphia's 1st choice, 15th overall, in 1996 Entry Draft.

1995-96	Pembroke	CJHL	28	19	13	32	73	....	....	....	....	....	....	....	....	....	....	....	....	....	....	....	....	....	....
	Caledon	MTJHL	7	3	7	10	2	....	....	....	....	....	....	....	....	....	17	11	12	23	4	....	....	....	....
1996-97	**Philadelphia**	**NHL**	**68**	**8**	**13**	**21**	**22**	**1**	**0**	**2**	**71**	**11.3**	**3**	....	....	....	**19**	**5**	**4**	**9**	**12**	**1**	**0**	**1**	....
1997-98	**Philadelphia**	**NHL**	**69**	**8**	**25**	**33**	**42**	**1**	**0**	**5**	**101**	**7.9**	**29**	....	....	....	**5**	**0**	**1**	**1**	**2**	**0**	**0**	**0**	....
1998-99	**Philadelphia**	**NHL**	**63**	**3**	**5**	**8**	**25**	**0**	**1**	**0**	**49**	**6.1**	**–5**	**29**	**51.7**	**11:00**	....	....	....	....	....	....	....	....	....
	Montreal	**NHL**	**17**	**3**	**5**	**8**	**4**	**0**	**0**	**1**	**31**	**9.7**	**–3**	**2**	**50.0**	**16:53**	....	....	....	....	....	....	....	....	....
99-2000	**Montreal**	**NHL**	**73**	**14**	**28**	**42**	**54**	**3**	**0**	**1**	**139**	**10.1**	**–1**	**212**	**39.2**	**17:37**	....	....	....	....	....	....	....	....	....
2000-01	**Montreal**	**NHL**	**49**	**12**	**12**	**24**	**30**	**3**	**0**	**0**	**70**	**17.1**	**–7**	**190**	**41.1**	**18:30**	....	....	....	....	....	....	....	....	....
	Washington	**NHL**	**12**	**1**	**1**	**2**	**7**	**1**	**0**	**0**	**13**	**7.7**	**–4**	**0**	**0.0**	**13:05**	**6**	**0**	**0**	**0**	**2**	**0**	**0**	**0**	**17:24**
2001-02	**Washington**	**NHL**	**71**	**17**	**26**	**43**	**38**	**4**	**0**	**3**	**138**	**12.3**	**5**	**131**	**37.4**	**18:52**	....	....	....	....	....	....	....	....	....
2002-03	**Washington**	**NHL**	**63**	**13**	**22**	**35**	**43**	**2**	**0**	**0**	**104**	**12.5**	**15**	**565**	**50.3**	**16:26**	**6**	**2**	**2**	**4**	**4**	**1**	**0**	**0**	**21:30**
2003-04	**Washington**	**NHL**	**54**	**12**	**15**	**27**	**38**	**6**	**1**	**2**	**115**	**10.4**	**–16**	**916**	**48.0**	**19:32**	....	....	....	....	....	....	....	....	....
2004-05	Lada Togliatti	Russia	42	8	11	19	85	....	....	....	....	....	....	....	....	....	10	3	1	4	22	....	....	....	....
2005-06	**Washington**	**NHL**	**71**	**23**	**34**	**57**	**84**	**13**	**0**	**5**	**181**	**12.7**	**3**	**1118**	**50.3**	**20:22**	....	....	....	....	....	....	....	....	....
2006-07	**Washington**	**NHL**	**60**	**20**	**32**	**52**	**50**	**9**	**0**	**4**	**127**	**15.7**	**–16**	**1096**	**49.7**	**19:51**	....	....	....	....	....	....	....	....	....
	Buffalo	**NHL**	**19**	**4**	**4**	**8**	**12**	**1**	**0**	**0**	**31**	**12.9**	**–3**	**69**	**39.1**	**18:22**	**15**	**0**	**8**	**8**	**8**	**0**	**0**	**0**	**18:38**
2007-08	**New Jersey**	**NHL**	**82**	**13**	**25**	**38**	**38**	**4**	**0**	**2**	**128**	**10.2**	**2**	**144**	**55.6**	**15:42**	**5**	**0**	**1**	**1**	**8**	**0**	**0**	**0**	**16:18**
	NHL Totals		**771**	**151**	**247**	**398**	**487**	**48**	**2**	**25**	**1298**	**11.6**		**4472**	**48.4**	**17:24**	**56**	**7**	**16**	**23**	**36**	**2**	**0**	**1**	**18:35**

Traded to **Montreal** by **Philadelphia** with Philadelphia's 2nd round choice (Matt Carkner) in 1999 Entry Draft and NY Islanders' 6th round choice (previously acquired, Montreal selected Scott Selig) in 2000 Entry Draft for Mark Recchi, March 10, 1999. Traded to **Washington** by **Montreal** with Trevor Linden and New Jersey's 2nd round choice (previously acquired, later traded to Tampa Bay – Tampa Bay selected Andreas Holmqvist) in 2001 Entry Draft for Richard Zednik, Jan Bulis and Washington's 1st round choice (Alexander Perezhogin) in 2001 Entry Draft, March 13, 2001. Signed as a free agent by **Togliatti** (Russia), July 1, 2004. Traded to **Buffalo** by **Washington** with Timo Helbling for Jiri Novotny and Buffalo's 1st round choice (later traded to San Jose - San Jose selected Nicholas Petrecki) in 2007 Entry Draft, February 27, 2007. Signed as a free agent by **New Jersey**, July 3, 2007.

ZYUZIN, Andrei

(ZYOO-zin, AWN-dray)

Defense. Shoots left. 6'1", 208 lbs. Born, Ufa, USSR, January 21, 1978. San Jose's 1st choice, 2nd overall, in 1996 Entry Draft.

			Regular Season														Playoffs								
Season	Club	League	GP	G	A	Pts	PIM	PP	SH	GW	S	%	+/-	TF	F%	Min	GP	G	A	Pts	PIM	PP	SH	GW	Min
1994-95	Ufa	CIS	30	3	0	3	16	....	....	....	....	....	....	....	....	....	....	....	....	....	....	....	....	....	....
1995-96	Ufa	CIS	41	6	3	9	24	....	....	....	....	....	....	....	....	....	....	....	....	....	....	....	....	....	....
1996-97	Ufa	Russia	32	7	10	17	28	....	....	....	....	....	....	....	....	....	7	1	1	2	4	....	....	....	....
1997-98	**San Jose**	**NHL**	**56**	**6**	**7**	**13**	**66**	**2**	**0**	**2**	**72**	**8.3**	**8**	....	....	....	**6**	**1**	**0**	**1**	**14**	**0**	**0**	**1**	....
	Kentucky	AHL	17	4	5	9	28	....	....	....	....	....	....	....	....	....	....	....	....	....	....	....	....	....	....
1998-99	**San Jose**	**NHL**	**25**	**3**	**1**	**4**	**38**	**2**	**0**	**0**	**44**	**6.8**	**5**	**0**	**0.0**	**15:56**	....	....	....	....	....	....	....	....	....
	Kentucky	AHL	23	2	12	14	42	....	....	....	....	....	....	....	....	....	....	....	....	....	....	....	....	....	....
99-2000	**Tampa Bay**	**NHL**	**34**	**2**	**9**	**11**	**33**	**0**	**0**	**0**	**47**	**4.3**	**–11**	**0**	**0.0**	**20:28**	....	....	....	....	....	....	....	....	....
2000-01	**Tampa Bay**	**NHL**	**64**	**4**	**16**	**20**	**76**	**2**	**1**	**1**	**92**	**4.3**	**–8**	**0**	**0.0**	**18:39**	....	....	....	....	....	....	....	....	....
	Detroit Vipers	IHL	2	0	1	1	0	....	....	....	....	....	....	....	....	....	....	....	....	....	....	....	....	....	....
2001-02	**Tampa Bay**	**NHL**	**9**	**0**	**2**	**2**	**6**	**0**	**0**	**0**	**14**	**0.0**	**–6**	**0**	**0.0**	**19:41**	....	....	....	....	....	....	....	....	....
	New Jersey	**NHL**	**38**	**1**	**2**	**3**	**25**	**1**	**0**	**0**	**47**	**2.1**	**1**	**0**	**0.0**	**15:04**	....	....	....	....	....	....	....	....	....
	Albany River Rats	AHL	3	0	1	1	2	....	....	....	....	....	....	....	....	....	....	....	....	....	....	....	....	....	....
2002-03	**New Jersey**	**NHL**	**1**	**0**	**1**	**1**	**2**	**0**	**0**	**0**	**0**	**0.0**	**–1**	**0**	**0.0**	**20:03**	....	....	....	....	....	....	....	....	....
	Minnesota	**NHL**	**66**	**4**	**12**	**16**	**34**	**2**	**0**	**0**	**113**	**3.5**	**–7**	**4**	**25.0**	**21:38**	**18**	**0**	**1**	**1**	**14**	**0**	**0**	**0**	**23:07**
2003-04	**Minnesota**	**NHL**	**65**	**8**	**13**	**21**	**48**	**4**	**0**	**1**	**104**	**7.7**	**4**	**0**	**0.0**	**20:22**	....	....	....	....	....	....	....	....	....
2004-05	Ufa	Russia	14	2	1	3	6	....	....	....	....	....	....	....	....	....	....	....	....	....	....	....	....	....	....
	Cherepovets	Russia	10	2	1	3	8	....	....	....	....	....	....	....	....	....	....	....	....	....	....	....	....	....	....
2005-06	**Minnesota**	**NHL**	**57**	**7**	**11**	**18**	**50**	**4**	**0**	**1**	**80**	**8.8**	**–12**	**2**	**50.0**	**18:53**	....	....	....	....	....	....	....	....	....
2006-07	**Calgary**	**NHL**	**49**	**1**	**5**	**6**	**30**	**0**	**0**	**0**	**36**	**2.8**	**–2**	**0**	**0.0**	**13:49**	**5**	**1**	**0**	**1**	**2**	**0**	**1**	**0**	**15:51**
2007-08	**Chicago**	**NHL**	**32**	**2**	**3**	**5**	**38**	**1**	**0**	**0**	**34**	**5.9**	**–11**	**0**	**0.0**	**14:58**	....	....	....	....	....	....	....	....	....
	NHL Totals		**496**	**38**	**82**	**120**	**446**	**18**	**1**	**5**	**683**	**5.6**		**6**	**33.3**	**18:17**	**29**	**2**	**1**	**3**	**30**	**0**	**1**	**1**	**21:32**

• Suspended for remainder of 1998-99 season by **San Jose** for leaving team without permission, April 1, 1999. Traded to **Tampa Bay** by **San Jose** with Bill Houlder, Shawn Burr and Steve Guolla for Niklas Sundstrom and NY Rangers' 3rd round choice (previously acquired, later traded to Chicago – Chicago selected Igor Radulov) in 2000 Entry Draft, August 4, 1999. • Missed majority of 1999-2000 season recovering from shoulder injury suffered in game vs. NY Islanders, January 13, 2000. Traded to **New Jersey** by **Tampa Bay** for Josef Boumedienne, Sascha Goc and the rights to Anton But, November 9, 2001. Claimed on waivers by **Minnesota** from **New Jersey**, November 2, 2002. Signed as a free agent by **Ufa** (Russia), September 25, 2004. Signed as a free agent by **Cherepovets** (Russia), December 20, 2004. Signed as a free agent by **Calgary**, July 1, 2006. Traded to **Chicago** by **Calgary** with Steve Marr for Adrian Aucoin and Chicago's 7th round choice (C. J. Severyn) in 2007 Entry Draft, June 22, 2007.
• Missed majority of 2007-08 season with backside muscle and groin injuries

NHL Goaltenders

Craig Anderson | Jean-Sebastien Aubin | Alex Auld | Jason Bacashihua | Niklas Backstrom | Jonathan Bernier | Martin Biron | Brian Boucher | Martin Brodeur | Ilya Bryzgalov

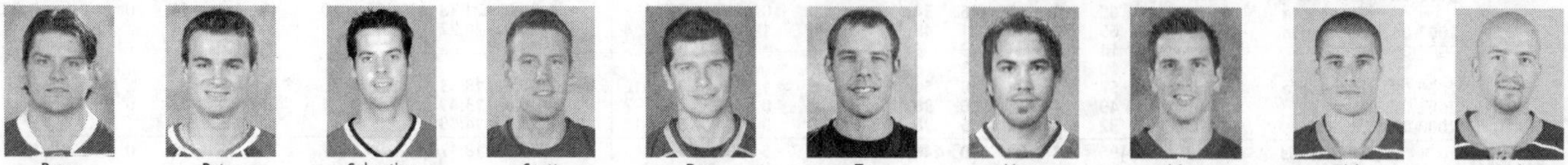

Barry Brust | Peter Budaj | Sebastian Caron | Scott Clemmensen | Dan Cloutier | Ty Conklin | Yann Danis | Marc Denis | Rick DiPietro | Wade Dubielewicz

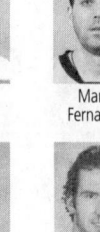

Dan Ellis | Ray Emery | Erik Ersberg | Robert Esche | Manny Fernandez | Wade Flaherty | Marc-Andre Fleury | Yutaka Fukufuji | Michael Garnett | Mathieu Garon

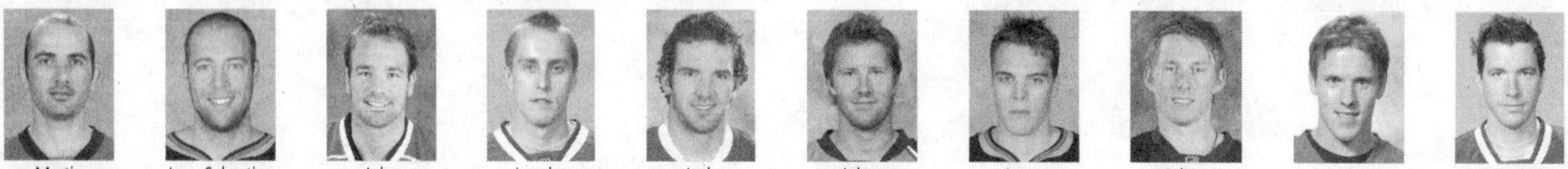

Martin Gerber | Jean-Sebastien Giguere | John Grahame | Jaroslav Halak | Josh Harding | Johan Hedberg | Jonas Hiller | Johan Holmqvist | James Howard | Cristobal Huet

Brent Johnson | Curtis Joseph | Nikolai Khabibulin | Miikka Kiprusoff | Olaf Kolzig | Jason Labarbera | Patrick Lalime | Pascal Leclaire | Manny Legace | Kari Lehtonen

Michael Leighton | David LeNeveu | Henrik Lundqvist | Roberto Luongo | Joey MacDonald | Jussi Markkanen | Chris Mason | Curtis McElhinney | Ryan Miller | Mike Morrison

Evgeni Nabokov | Antero Niittymaki | Fredrik Norrena | Chris Osgood | Dimitri Patzold | Ondrej Pavelec | Jean-Marc Pelletier | Carey Price | Karri Ramo | Tuukka Rask

Andrew Raycroft | Dwayne Roloson | Dany Sabourin | Curtis Sanford | Philippe Sauve | Nolan Schaefer | Marek Schwarz | Mike Smith | Mikael Tellqvist | Jose Theodore

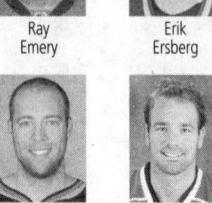

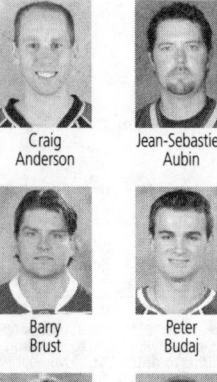

Jocelyn Thibault | Tim Thomas | Hannu Toivonen | Vesa Toskala | Marty Turco | Steve Valiquette | Tomas Vokoun | Michael Wall | Cam Ward | Kevin Weekes

2008-09 Goaltender Register

Note: The 2008-09 Goaltender Register lists all active NHL goaltenders, every goaltender drafted in the 2008 Entry Draft, goaltenders on NHL Reserve Lists and other goaltenders.

Trades and roster changes are current as of August 21, 2008.

To calculate a goaltender's goals-against per game average **(Avg)**, divide goals against **(GA)** by minutes played **(Mins)** and multiply this result by **60**.

Abbreviations: GP – games played; **W** – wins; **L** – losses; **O/T** – overtime losses/ties; **Mins** – minutes played; **GA** – goals against; **SO** – shutouts; **Avg** – goals-against-per-game average; ***** – league-leading total ♦ – member of Stanley Cup-winning team.

NHL Player Register begins on page 344.

Prospect Register begins on page 273.

League Abbreviations are listed on page 654.

AEBISCHER, David (A-bih-shuhr, DAY-vihd)

Goaltender. Catches left. 6'1", 185 lbs. Born, Fribourg, Switz., February 7, 1978.
(Colorado's 7th choice, 161st overall, in 1997 Entry Draft).

			Regular Season								Playoffs						
Season	Club	League	GP	W	L	O/T	Mins	GA	SO	Avg	GP	W	L	Mins	GA	SO	Avg
1996-97	Fribourg	Swiss	10	....	....	....	577	34	0	3.54	3	1	2	184	13	0	4.24
1997-98	Chesapeake	ECHL	17	5	7	2	930	52	0	3.35	....	....	....	....	....	....	....
	Wheeling Nailers	ECHL	10	5	3	1	564	30	1	3.19	....	....	....	....	....	....	....
	Hershey Bears	AHL	2	0	0	1	79	5	0	3.76	....	....	....	....	....	....	....
	Fribourg	Swiss	1	1	0	0	60	1	0	1.00	4	....	....	240	17	....	4.25
1998-99	Hershey Bears	AHL	38	17	10	5	1932	79	2	2.45	3	1	2	152	6	0	2.37
99-2000	Hershey Bears	AHL	58	29	23	2	3259	180	1	3.31	14	7	6	788	40	2	3.05
2000-01 ♦	**Colorado**	**NHL**	**26**	**12**	**7**	**3**	**1393**	**52**	**3**	**2.24**	**1**	**0**	**0**	**1**	**0**	**0**	**0.00**
2001-02	**Colorado**	**NHL**	**21**	**13**	**6**	**0**	**1184**	**37**	**2**	**1.88**	**1**	**0**	**0**	**34**	**1**	**0**	**1.76**
	Switzerland	Olympics	2	1	0	0	81	6	0	4.43	....	....	....	....	....	....	....
2002-03	**Colorado**	**NHL**	**22**	**7**	**12**	**0**	**1235**	**50**	**1**	**2.43**	....	....	....	....	....	....	....
2003-04	**Colorado**	**NHL**	**62**	**32**	**19**	**9**	**3703**	**129**	**4**	**2.09**	**11**	**6**	**5**	**662**	**23**	**1**	**2.08**
2004-05	HC Lugano	Swiss	18	12	2	3	1019	41	0	2.41	4	1	3	240	10	0	2.50
	EHC Chur	Swiss-2	....	....	....	....	....	....	....	....	2	....	....	130	4	0	1.84
2005-06	**Colorado**	**NHL**	**43**	**25**	**14**	**2**	**2477**	**123**	**3**	**2.98**	....	....	....	....	....	....	....
	Switzerland	Olympics	4	....	....	....	200	7	0	2.10	....	....	....	....	....	....	....
	Montreal	**NHL**	**7**	**4**	**3**	**0**	**418**	**26**	**0**	**3.73**	....	....	....	....	....	....	....
2006-07	**Montreal**	**NHL**	**32**	**13**	**12**	**3**	**1760**	**93**	**0**	**3.17**	....	....	....	....	....	....	....
2007-08	**Phoenix**	**NHL**	**1**	**0**	**1**	**0**	**60**	**3**	**0**	**3.00**	....	....	....	....	....	....	....
	San Antonio	AHL	5	2	3	0	302	13	0	2.58	....	....	....	....	....	....	....
	HC Lugano	Swiss	26	12	14	0	1576	69	2	2.63	5	4	1	301	14	0	2.79
	NHL Totals		**214**	**106**	**74**	**17**	**12230**	**513**	**13**	**2.52**	**13**	**6**	**5**	**697**	**24**	**1**	**2.07**

Signed as a free agent by **Lugano** (Swiss), September 17, 2004. Traded to **Montreal** by **Colorado** for Jose Theodore, March 8, 2006. Signed as a free agent by **Phoenix**, July 19, 2007. Loaned to **Lugano** (Swiss) by **Phoenix**, November 23, 2007.

AKERLUND, Magnus (AK-uhr-luhnd, MAG-nuhs) CAR.

Goaltender. Catches right. 6'1", 183 lbs. Born, Osby, Sweden, April 25, 1986.
(Carolina's 5th choice, 137th overall, in 2004 Entry Draft).

			Regular Season								Playoffs						
Season	Club	League	GP	W	L	O/T	Mins	GA	SO	Avg	GP	W	L	Mins	GA	SO	Avg
2002-03	HV 71 Jr.	Swe-Jr.	18	....	....	....	861	44	1	3.07	2	....	....	80	6	0	4.50
2003-04	HV 71 Jr.	Swe-Jr.	26	....	....	....	1556	85	1	3.28	2	....	....	119	10	0	5.04
2004-05	HV 71 Jr.	Swe-Jr.	19	....	....	....	1096	48	1	2.63	....	....	....	....	....	....	....
	HV 71 Jonkoping	Sweden	3	....	....	....	185	9	0	2.92	....	....	....	....	....	....	....
	Skovde IK	Sweden-2	22	....	....	....	1290	55	1	2.56	....	....	....	....	....	....	....
2005-06	HV 71 Jr.	Swe-Jr.	4	....	....	....	214	17	0	4.76	....	....	....	....	....	....	....
	Nykoping	Sweden-2	21	....	....	....	1236	67	0	3.25	....	....	....	....	....	....	....
2006-07	Skovde IK	Sweden-3	38	....	....	....	2293	91	6	2.38	....	....	....	....	....	....	....
	HV 71 Jonkoping	Sweden	1	....	....	....	65	1	0	0.92	....	....	....	....	....	....	....
2007-08	Timra IK	Sweden	9	....	....	....	512	25	1	2.93	....	....	....	....	....	....	....
	Sundsvall	Sweden-2	5	....	....	....	305	16	0	3.15	....	....	....	....	....	....	....

ALLEN, Jake (A-lehn, JAYK) ST.L.

Goaltender. Catches left. 6'2", 175 lbs. Born, Fredericton, N. B., August 7, 1990.
(St. Louis' 3rd choice, 34th overall, in 2008 Entry Draft).

			Regular Season								Playoffs						
Season	Club	League	GP	W	L	O/T	Mins	GA	SO	Avg	GP	W	L	Mins	GA	SO	Avg
2006-07	Fredericton	NBPEI					STATISTICS NOT AVAILABLE										
2007-08	St. John's	QMJHL	30	9	12	....	1507	79	2	3.14	4	2	1	128	8	0	3.74

ANDERSON, Craig (AN-duhr-suhn, KRAYG) FLA.

Goaltender. Catches left. 6'2", 180 lbs. Born, Park Ridge, IL, May 21, 1981.
(Chicago's 4th choice, 73rd overall, in 2001 Entry Draft).

			Regular Season								Playoffs						
Season	Club	League	GP	W	L	O/T	Mins	GA	SO	Avg	GP	W	L	Mins	GA	SO	Avg
1997-98	Chicago Jets	MEHL	50	....	....	....	2991	143	2	2.86	....	....	....	....	....	....	....
1998-99	Chicago Freeze	NAHL	14	11	3	0	840	40	0	2.56	....	....	....	....	....	....	....
	Guelph Storm	OHL	21	12	5	1	1006	52	1	3.10	3	0	2	114	9	0	4.74
99-2000	Guelph Storm	OHL	38	12	17	2	1955	117	0	3.59	3	0	1	110	5	0	2.73
2000-01	Guelph Storm	OHL	59	30	19	9	3555	156	3	2.63	4	0	4	240	17	0	4.25
2001-02	Norfolk Admirals	AHL	28	9	13	4	1568	77	2	2.95	1	0	1	21	1	0	2.83
2002-03	**Chicago**	**NHL**	**6**	**0**	**3**	**2**	**270**	**18**	**0**	**4.00**	....	....	....	....	....	....	....
	Norfolk Admirals	AHL	32	15	11	5	1795	58	4	1.94	5	2	3	345	15	0	2.61
2003-04	**Chicago**	**NHL**	**21**	**6**	**14**	**0**	**1205**	**57**	**1**	**2.84**	....	....	....	....	....	....	....
	Norfolk Admirals	AHL	37	17	20	0	2108	74	3	2.11	5	2	3	327	10	0	1.84
2004-05	Norfolk Admirals	AHL	15	9	4	1	886	27	2	1.83	6	2	4	356	14	0	2.36
2005-06	**Chicago**	**NHL**	**29**	**6**	**12**	**4**	**1554**	**86**	**1**	**3.32**	....	....	....	....	....	....	....
2006-07	**Florida**	**NHL**	**5**	**1**	**1**	**1**	**217**	**8**	**0**	**2.21**	....	....	....	....	....	....	....
	Rochester	AHL	34	23	10	1	2060	88	1	2.56	6	2	4	376	18	0	2.87
2007-08	**Florida**	**NHL**	**17**	**8**	**6**	**1**	**935**	**35**	**2**	**2.25**	....	....	....	....	....	....	....
	NHL Totals		**78**	**21**	**36**	**8**	**4181**	**204**	**4**	**2.93**	....	....	....	....	....	....	....

• Re-entered NHL Entry Draft. Originally Calgary's 3rd choice, 77th overall, in 1999 Entry Draft.

OHL First All-Star Team (2001)

Claimed on waivers by **Boston** from **Chicago**, January 19, 2006. Claimed on waivers by **St. Louis** from **Boston**, January 31, 2006. Claimed on waivers by **Chicago** from **St. Louis**, February 3, 2006. Traded to **Florida** by **Chicago** for Florida's 6th round choice (later traded to Tampa Bay - Tampa Bay selected Luke Witkowski) in 2008 Entry Draft, June 24, 2006.

AUBIN, Jean-Sebastien , (oh-BEHN, ZHAWN-suh-BAS-tee-yeh)

Goaltender. Catches right. 5'11", 180 lbs. Born, Montreal, Que., July 19, 1977.
(Pittsburgh's 2nd choice, 76th overall, in 1995 Entry Draft).

			Regular Season								Playoffs						
Season	Club	League	GP	W	L	O/T	Mins	GA	SO	Avg	GP	W	L	Mins	GA	SO	Avg
1993-94	Montreal-Bourassa	QAAA	27	14	13	0	1524	96	1	3.74	4	1	3	222	19	0	5.14
1994-95	Sherbrooke	QMJHL	27	13	10	1	1287	73	1	3.40	3	1	2	185	11	0	3.57
1995-96	Sherbrooke	QMJHL	40	18	14	2	2140	127	0	3.57	4	1	3	238	23	0	5.55
1996-97	Sherbrooke	QMJHL	4	3	1	0	249	8	0	1.93	1	0	1	60	4	0	4.00
	Moncton Wildcats	QMJHL	22	9	12	0	1252	67	1	3.21	....	....	....	....	....	....	....
	Laval Titan	QMJHL	11	2	6	1	532	41	0	4.62	....	....	....	....	....	....	....
1997-98	Syracuse Crunch	AHL	8	2	4	1	380	26	0	4.10	....	....	....	....	....	....	....
	Dayton Bombers	ECHL	21	15	2	2	1177	59	1	3.01	3	1	1	142	4	0	1.69
1998-99	**Pittsburgh**	**NHL**	**17**	**4**	**3**	**6**	**756**	**28**	**2**	**2.22**	....	....	....	....	....	....	....
	Kansas City Blades	IHL	13	5	7	1	751	41	0	3.28	....	....	....	....	....	....	....
99-2000	**Pittsburgh**	**NHL**	**51**	**23**	**21**	**3**	**2789**	**120**	**2**	**2.58**	....	....	....	....	....	....	....
	Wilkes-Barre	AHL	11	2	8	0	538	39	0	4.35	....	....	....	....	....	....	....
2000-01	**Pittsburgh**	**NHL**	**36**	**20**	**14**	**1**	**2050**	**107**	**0**	**3.13**	**1**	**0**	**0**	**1**	**0**	**0**	**0.00**
2001-02	**Pittsburgh**	**NHL**	**21**	**3**	**12**	**1**	**1094**	**65**	**0**	**3.56**	....	....	....	....	....	....	....
2002-03	**Pittsburgh**	**NHL**	**21**	**6**	**13**	**0**	**1132**	**59**	**1**	**3.13**	....	....	....	....	....	....	....
	Wilkes-Barre	AHL	16	8	6	1	919	29	3	1.89	6	3	3	356	12	0	2.02
2003-04	**Pittsburgh**	**NHL**	**22**	**7**	**9**	**0**	**1067**	**53**	**1**	**2.98**	....	....	....	....	....	....	....
	Wilkes-Barre	AHL	13	4	5	2	670	31	0	2.78	....	....	....	....	....	....	....
2004-05	St. John's	AHL	23	12	9	0	1336	64	3	2.87	1	0	0	47	1	0	1.27
2005-06	**Toronto**	**NHL**	**11**	**9**	**0**	**2**	**677**	**25**	**1**	**2.22**	....	....	....	....	....	....	....
	Toronto Marlies	AHL	46	19	18	2	2491	126	2	3.03	5	1	4	359	17	0	2.84
2006-07	**Toronto**	**NHL**	**20**	**3**	**5**	**2**	**804**	**46**	**0**	**3.43**	....	....	....	....	....	....	....
2007-08	**Los Angeles**	**NHL**	**19**	**5**	**6**	**1**	**828**	**44**	**0**	**3.19**	....	....	....	....	....	....	....
	Manchester	AHL	1	0	0	0	9	4	0	27.69	....	....	....	....	....	....	....
	Portland Pirates	AHL	11	6	4	0	645	18	3	1.67	12	9	3	757	29	0	2.30
	NHL Totals		**218**	**80**	**83**	**16**	**11197**	**547**	**7**	**2.93**	**1**	**0**	**0**	**1**	**0**	**0**	**0.00**

Signed to a PTO (tryout) contract by **St. John's** (AHL), November 13, 2004. Signed as a free agent by **Toronto**, August 18, 2005. Signed as a free agent by **Los Angeles**, August 28, 2007. Traded to **Anaheim** by **Los Angeles** for St. Louis' 7th round choice (previously acquired, later traded back to St. Louis - St. Louis selected Paul Karpowich) in 2008 Entry Draft, February 26, 2008.

AULD, Alex (AWLD, AL-ehx) OTT.

Goaltender. Catches left. 6'5", 221 lbs. Born, Cold Lake, Alta., January 7, 1981.
(Florida's 2nd choice, 40th overall, in 1999 Entry Draft).

			Regular Season								Playoffs						
Season	Club	League	GP	W	L	O/T	Mins	GA	SO	Avg	GP	W	L	Mins	GA	SO	Avg
1996-97	Thunder Bay Kings	TBMHL	35	....	....	....	2100	46	10	1.35	....	....	....	....	....	....	....
1997-98	Sturgeon Falls Lynx	NOJHA	11	4	6	0	611	46	0	4.52	....	....	....	....	....	....	....
	North Bay	OHL	6	0	4	0	206	17	0	4.95	....	....	....	....	....	....	....
1998-99	North Bay	OHL	37	9	20	1	1894	106	1	3.36	3	0	3	170	10	0	3.53
99-2000	North Bay	OHL	55	21	26	6	3047	167	2	3.29	6	2	4	374	12	0	*1.93
2000-01	North Bay	OHL	40	22	11	5	2319	98	1	2.54	4	0	4	240	15	0	3.75
2001-02	**Vancouver**	**NHL**	**1**	**1**	**0**	**0**	**60**	**2**	**0**	**2.00**	....	....	....	....	....	....	....
	Columbia Inferno	ECHL	6	3	1	2	375	12	0	1.92	....	....	....	....	....	....	....
	Manitoba Moose	AHL	21	11	9	0	1104	65	1	3.53	1	0	0	20	0	0	0.00
2002-03	**Vancouver**	**NHL**	**7**	**3**	**3**	**0**	**382**	**10**	**1**	**1.57**	**1**	**0**	**0**	**20**	**1**	**0**	**3.00**
	Manitoba Moose	AHL	37	15	19	3	2209	97	3	2.64	....	....	....	....	....	....	....
2003-04	**Vancouver**	**NHL**	**6**	**2**	**2**	**2**	**349**	**12**	**0**	**2.06**	**3**	**1**	**2**	**222**	**9**	**0**	**2.43**
	Manitoba Moose	AHL	40	18	16	4	2329	99	4	2.55	....	....	....	....	....	....	....
2004-05	Manitoba Moose	AHL	50	25	18	4	2764	118	2	2.56	3	0	2	128	7	0	3.29
2005-06	**Vancouver**	**NHL**	**67**	**33**	**26**	**6**	**3859**	**189**	**0**	**2.94**	....	....	....	....	....	....	....
2006-07	**Florida**	**NHL**	**27**	**7**	**13**	**5**	**1471**	**82**	**1**	**3.34**	....	....	....	....	....	....	....

2007-08	Phoenix	NHL	9	3	6	0	509	30	1	3.54	....	....	....	....	....	....	....
	San Antonio	AHL	2	1	1	0	119	5	1	2.53	....	....	....	....	....	....	....
	Boston	NHL	23	9	7	5	1213	47	2	2.32	....	....	....	....	....	....	....
	NHL Totals		140	58	57	18	7843	372	5	2.85	4	1	2	242	10	0	2.48

Rights traded to **Vancouver** by **Florida** for Vancouver's 2nd round compensatory choice (later traded to New Jersey – New Jersey selected Tuomas Pihlman) in 2001 Entry Draft and Vancouver's 3rd round choice (later traded to Atlanta – later traded to Buffalo – Buffalo selected John Adams) in 2002 Entry Draft, May 31, 2001. Traded to **Florida** by **Vancouver** with Todd Bertuzzi and Bryan Allen for Roberto Luongo, Lukas Krajicek and Florida's 6th round choice (Sergei Shirokov) in 2006 Entry Draft, June 23, 2006. Signed as a free agent by **Phoenix**, August 13, 2007. Traded to **Boston** by **Phoenix** for Nick DiCasmirro and Boston's 5th round choice in 2009 Entry Draft, December 6, 2007. Signed as a free agent by **Ottawa**, July 1, 2008.

BACASHIHUA, Jason (buh-KAH-shoo-wuh, JAY-suhn) COL.

Goaltender. Catches left. 5'11", 177 lbs. Born, Garden City, MI, September 20, 1982.
(Dallas' 1st choice, 26th overall, in 2001 Entry Draft).

			Regular Season								Playoffs						
Season	Club	League	GP	W	L	O/T	Mins	GA	SO	Avg	GP	W	L	Mins	GA	SO	Avg
99-2000	Chicago Freeze	NAHL	41	20	19	2	2432	118	2	2.91	2	0	2	103	12	0	6.97
2000-01	Chicago Freeze	NAHL	39	24	14	0	2246	121	1	3.23	3	1	2	190	12	0	3.79
2001-02	Plymouth Whalers	OHL	46	26	12	7	2688	105	*5	2.34	6	2	4	360	15	0	2.50
	Utah Grizzlies	AHL	1	0	1	0	61	3	0	2.97	....	....	....	....	....	....	....
2002-03	Utah Grizzlies	AHL	39	18	18	2	2245	118	3	3.15	1	0	1	59	2	0	2.05
2003-04	Utah Grizzlies	AHL	39	13	19	5	2234	99	3	2.66	....	....	....	....	....	....	....
2004-05	Worcester IceCats	AHL	35	18	13	1	1909	80	2	2.51	....	....	....	....	....	....	....
2005-06	St. Louis	NHL	19	4	10	1	966	52	0	3.23	....	....	....	....	....	....	....
	Peoria Rivermen	AHL	15	9	4	0	820	36	2	2.63	....	....	....	....	....	....	....
2006-07	St. Louis	NHL	19	3	7	3	894	47	0	3.15	....	....	....	....	....	....	....
	Peoria Rivermen	AHL	20	5	10	4	1139	55	1	2.90	....	....	....	....	....	....	....
2007-08	Peoria Rivermen	AHL	4	1	3	0	208	11	0	3.17	....	....	....	....	....	....	....
	Johnstown Chiefs	ECHL	1	1	0	0	65	4	0	3.70	....	....	....	....	....	....	....
	Lake Erie Monsters	AHL	19	5	11	2	1074	60	1	3.35	....	....	....	....	....	....	....
	NHL Totals		38	7	17	4	1860	99	0	3.19	....	....	....	....	....	....	....

Traded to **St. Louis** by **Dallas** for the rights to Shawn Belle, June 25, 2004. Traded to **Colorado** by **St. Louis** for future considerations, November 8, 2007.

BACHMAN, Richard (BAWK-mahn, RIH-chuhrd) DAL.

Goaltender. Catches left. 5'11", 160 lbs. Born, Salt Lake City, UT, July 25, 1987.
(Dallas' 3rd choice, 120th overall, in 2006 Entry Draft).

			Regular Season								Playoffs						
Season	Club	League	GP	W	L	O/T	Mins	GA	SO	Avg	GP	W	L	Mins	GA	SO	Avg
2004-05	Cushing	High-MA	28	....	....	....	1498	53	3	1.89	....	....	....	....	....	....	....
	Boston Jr. Bruins	EmJHL	25	....	....	....	....	....	....	....	....	....	....	....	....	....	....
2005-06	Cushing	High-MA	30	....	....	....	1598	60	4	2.25	....	....	....	....	....	....	....
	Boston Jr. Bruins	EmJHL	....	31	1	2	....	....	....	1.69	....	....	....	....	....	....	....
2006-07	Chicago Steel	USHL	7	2	5	0	359	29	0	4.85	....	....	....	....	....	....	....
	Cedar Rapids	USHL	26	14	10	2	1565	78	4	2.99	6	4	1	329	7	*2	*1.28
2007-08	Colorado College	WCHA	35	25	9	1	2103	65	4	1.85	....	....	....	....	....	....	....

WCHA All-Rookie Team (2008) • WCHA First All-Star Team (2008) • WCHA Rookie of the Year (2008) • WCHA Player of the Year (2008) • NCAA West First All-American Team (2008)

BACKSTROM, Niklas (BAK-struhm, NIHK-luhs) MIN.

Goaltender. Catches left. 6'1", 196 lbs. Born, Helsinki, Finland, February 13, 1978.

			Regular Season								Playoffs						
Season	Club	League	GP	W	L	O/T	Mins	GA	SO	Avg	GP	W	L	Mins	GA	SO	Avg
1994-95	HIFK Helsinki U18	Fin-U18					Statistics not available										
1995-96	HIFK Helsinki U18	Fin-U18	12	....	....	....	699	44	....	3.77	4	....	....	203	9	....	2.66
1996-97	HIFK Helsinki Jr.	Fin-Jr.	21	....	....	....	1243	57	....	2.75	....	....	....	....	....	....	....
	PiTa Helsinki	Finland-2	8	....	....	....	390	24	....	3.69	....	....	....	....	....	....	....
	HIFK Helsinki	Finland	2	0	0	0	30	3	0	5.85	....	....	....	....	....	....	....
1997-98	HIFK Helsinki Jr.	Fin-Jr.	14	7	7	0	847	42	....	2.98	....	....	....	....	....	....	....
	Hermes Kokkola	Finland-2	9	4	3	1	468	23	1	2.95	....	....	....	....	....	....	....
1998-99	HIFK Helsinki	Finland	16	9	5	1	923	26	1	*1.69	....	....	....	....	....	....	....
	HIFK Helsinki Jr.	Fin-Jr.	15	7	7	1	898	45	1	3.01	....	....	....	....	....	....	....
99-2000	HIFK Helsinki	Finland	4	0	4	0	155	17	0	6.58	....	....	....	....	....	....	....
	FPS Forssa	Finland-2	22	13	8	1	1320	50	1	2.27	3	1	2	178	8	0	2.69
2000-01	SaiPa	Finland	49	22	24	3	2826	120	2	2.55	....	....	....	....	....	....	....
2001-02	AIK Solna	Sweden	40	....	....	....	2186	111	1	3.05	....	....	....	....	....	....	....
	AIK Solna	Sweden-Q	9	....	....	....	543	20	0	2.21	....	....	....	....	....	....	....
2002-03	Karpat Oulu	Finland	36	16	8	9	2136	77	4	2.16	*15	7	8	*990	33	1	2.00
2003-04	Karpat Oulu	Finland	43	24	8	0	2572	87	7	2.03	*15	*9	6	*927	36	1	2.33
2004-05	Karpat Oulu	Finland	47	27	10	10	2819	102	7	2.17	*12	*10	2	720	15	*3	*1.25
2005-06	Karpat Oulu	Finland	51	*32	9	10	3077	86	*10	*1.68	4	3	1	195	6	0	1.84
2006-07	Minnesota	NHL	41	23	8	6	2227	73	5	*1.97	5	1	4	297	11	0	2.22
2007-08	Minnesota	NHL	58	33	13	8	3409	131	4	2.31	6	2	4	361	17	0	2.83
	NHL Totals		99	56	21	14	5636	204	9	2.17	11	3	8	658	28	0	2.55

William M. Jennings Trophy (2007) (shared with Manny Fernandez) • MBNA Roger Crozier Saving Grace Award (2007)

Signed as a free agent by **Minnesota**, June 1, 2006.

BARULIN, Konstantin (bah-ROO-lihn, KAWN-stan-tihn) ST.L.

Goaltender. Catches left. 6', 180 lbs. Born, Karaganda, USSR, September 4, 1984.
(St. Louis' 3rd choice, 84th overall, in 2003 Entry Draft).

			Regular Season								Playoffs						
Season	Club	League	GP	W	L	O/T	Mins	GA	SO	Avg	GP	W	L	Mins	GA	SO	Avg
2001-02	Gazovik Tyumen	Russia-2	4	....	....	....	190	15	0	4.73	....	....	....	....	....	....	....
2002-03	Gazovik Tyumen	Russia-2	41	....	....	....	2361	67	5	1.70	....	....	....	....	....	....	....
2003-04	Gazovik Tyumen	Russia-2	11	....	....	....	663	24	....	2.17	....	....	....	....	....	....	....
	SKA St. Petersburg	Russia	1	....	....	....	1	0	0	0.00	....	....	....	....	....	....	....
	St. Petersburg 2	Russia-3	11	....	....	....	668	24	1	2.15	....	....	....	....	....	....	....
2004-05	Gazovik Tyumen	Russia-2	30	....	....	....	1773	59	6	2.00	3	....	....	136	9	0	3.97
2005-06	Spartak Moscow	Russia	36	....	....	....	2102	75	2	2.14	2	....	....	104	4	0	2.30
2006-07	Mytischi	Russia	26	....	....	....	1249	45	1	2.16	1	....	....	48	3	0	3.76
2007-08	Mytischi	Russia	11	....	....	....	434	20	0	2.77	....	....	....	....	....	....	....

BECKFORD-TSEU, Chris (BEHK-fuhrd-TSEW, KRIHS) FLA.

Goaltender. Catches left. 6'2", 201 lbs. Born, Toronto, Ont., June 22, 1984.
(St. Louis' 8th choice, 159th overall, in 2003 Entry Draft).

			Regular Season								Playoffs						
Season	Club	League	GP	W	L	O/T	Mins	GA	SO	Avg	GP	W	L	Mins	GA	SO	Avg
2000-01	St. Mike's B's	OPJHL	25	9	15	1	1506	119	1	4.75	4	1	3	240	10	0	2.50
2001-02	Oshawa	OPJHL					Statistics not available										
	Guelph Storm	OHL	5	2	0	0	207	16	0	4.64	....	....	....	....	....	....	....
	Oshawa Generals	OHL	7	2	3	0	341	19	0	3.34	5	1	4	310	16	0	3.10
2002-03	Oshawa Generals	OHL	54	25	26	2	2978	157	4	3.16	13	6	7	727	48	1	3.96
2003-04	Oshawa Generals	OHL	9	1	5	2	495	28	0	3.39	....	....	....	....	....	....	....
	Kingston	OHL	40	16	19	2	2226	121	3	3.26	5	1	4	303	18	0	3.56
2004-05	Worcester IceCats	AHL	1	0	0	0	29	0	0	0.00	....	....	....	....	....	....	....
	Peoria Rivermen	ECHL	29	11	12	3	1594	72	1	2.71	....	....	....	....	....	....	....
2005-06	Peoria Rivermen	AHL	16	7	5	1	737	38	0	3.10	4	0	4	238	15	0	3.78
	Alaska Aces	ECHL	19	16	1	2	1152	36	2	1.87	12	8	4	795	27	*3	*2.04
2006-07	Peoria Rivermen	AHL	29	12	11	4	1654	75	1	2.72	....	....	....	....	....	....	....
	Alaska Aces	ECHL	7	7	0	0	426	9	2	1.27	....	....	....	....	....	....	....
2007-08	St. Louis	NHL	1	0	0	0	27	1	0	2.22	....	....	....	....	....	....	....
	Peoria Rivermen	AHL	34	15	14	2	1871	82	1	2.63	....	....	....	....	....	....	....
	Alaska Aces	ECHL	16	12	4	0	921	36	1	2.34	2	0	2	98	7	0	4.27
	NHL Totals		1	0	0	0	27	1	0	2.22	....	....	....	....	....	....	....

Signed as a free agent by **Florida**, July 3, 2008.

BELFOUR, Ed (BEHL-fohr, EHD)

Goaltender. Catches left. 5'11", 202 lbs. Born, Carman, Man., April 21, 1965.

			Regular Season								Playoffs						
Season	Club	League	GP	W	L	O/T	Mins	GA	SO	Avg	GP	W	L	Mins	GA	SO	Avg
1983-84	Winkler Flyers	MJHL	14	....	....	....	818	68	0	4.99	....	....	....	....	....	....	....
1984-85	Winkler Flyers	MJHL	34	....	....	....	1973	145	1	4.41	7	3	4	528	41	0	4.66
1985-86	Winkler Flyers	MJHL	33	....	....	....	1943	124	1	3.83	....	....	....	....	....	....	....
1986-87	North Dakota	WCHA	34	29	4	0	2049	81	3	2.37	....	....	....	....	....	....	....
1987-88	Saginaw Hawks	IHL	61	32	25	0	*3446	183	3	3.19	9	4	5	561	33	0	3.53
1988-89	Chicago	NHL	23	4	12	3	1148	74	0	3.87	....	....	....	....	....	....	....
	Saginaw Hawks	IHL	29	12	10	0	1760	92	0	3.14	5	2	3	298	14	0	2.82
1989-90	Canada	Nat-Tm	33	13	12	6	1808	93	0	3.09	....	....	....	....	....	....	....
	Chicago	NHL	....	....	....	....	....	....	....	....	9	4	2	409	17	0	2.49
1990-91	Chicago	NHL	*74	*43	19	7	*4127	170	4	*2.47	6	2	4	295	20	0	4.07
1991-92	Chicago	NHL	52	21	18	10	2928	132	*5	2.70	18	12	4	949	39	1	*2.47
1992-93	Chicago	NHL	*71	41	18	11	*4106	177	*7	2.59	4	0	4	249	13	0	3.13
1993-94	Chicago	NHL	70	37	24	6	3998	178	*7	2.67	6	2	4	360	15	0	2.50
1994-95	Chicago	NHL	42	22	15	3	2450	93	*5	2.28	16	9	7	1014	37	1	2.19
1995-96	Chicago	NHL	50	22	17	10	2956	135	1	2.74	9	6	3	666	23	1	*2.07
1996-97	Chicago	NHL	33	11	15	6	1966	88	1	2.69	....	....	....	....	....	....	....
	San Jose	NHL	13	3	9	0	757	43	1	3.41	....	....	....	....	....	....	....
1997-98	Dallas	NHL	61	37	12	10	3581	112	9	*1.88	17	10	7	1039	31	1	*1.79
1998-99 ♦	Dallas	NHL	61	35	15	9	3536	117	5	1.99	*23	*16	7	*1544	43	*3	*1.67
99-2000	Dallas	NHL	62	32	21	7	3620	127	4	2.10	*23	14	9	1443	45	*4	1.87
2000-01	Dallas	NHL	63	35	20	7	3687	144	8	2.34	10	4	6	671	25	0	2.24
2001-02	Dallas	NHL	60	21	27	11	3467	153	1	2.65	....	....	....	....	....	....	....
	Canada	Olympics					Did not play – spare goaltender										
2002-03	Toronto	NHL	62	37	20	5	3738	141	7	2.26	7	3	4	532	24	0	2.71
2003-04	Toronto	NHL	59	34	19	6	3444	122	10	2.13	13	6	7	774	27	3	2.09
2004-05								Did not play									
2005-06	Toronto	NHL	49	22	22	4	2897	159	0	3.29	....	....	....	....	....	....	....
2006-07	Florida	NHL	58	27	17	10	3289	152	1	2.77	....	....	....	....	....	....	....
2007-08	Leksands IF	Sweden-2	29	....	....	....	1715	58	7	2.03	....	....	....	....	....	....	....
	NHL Totals		963	484	320	125	55695	2317	76	2.50	161	88	68	9945	359	14	2.17

WCHA First All-Star Team (1987) • NCAA Championship All-Tournament Team (1987) • IHL First All-Star Team (1988) • Garry F. Longman Memorial Trophy (Rookie of the Year – IHL) (1988) (co-winner - John Cullen) • NHL All-Rookie Team (1991) • NHL First All-Star Team (1991, 1993) • Trico Goaltender Award (1991) • Calder Memorial Trophy (1991) • William M. Jennings Trophy (1991, 1993, 1995) • Vezina Trophy (1991, 1993) • NHL Second All-Star Team (1995) • William M. Jennings Trophy (1999) (shared with Roman Turek) • MBNA Roger Crozier Saving Grace Award (2000)

Played in NHL All-Star Game (1992, 1993, 1996, 1998, 1999)

Signed as a free agent by **Chicago**, September 25, 1987. Traded to **San Jose** by **Chicago** for Chris Terreri, Ulf Dahlen and Michal Sykora, January 25, 1997. Signed as a free agent by **Dallas**, July 2, 1997. Traded to **Nashville** by **Dallas** with Cameron Mann for David Gosselin and Nashville's 5th round choice (Eero Kilpelainen) in 2003 Entry Draft, June 29, 2002. Signed as a free agent by **Toronto**, July 2, 2002. Signed as a free agent by **Florida**, July 25, 2006. Signed as a free agent by **Leksands** (Sweden-2), August 28, 2007.

BENNETT, Brett (BEHN-neht, BREHT) PHX.

Goaltender. Catches left. 6'1", 185 lbs. Born, Buffalo, NY, March 8, 1988.
(Phoenix's 4th choice, 130th overall, in 2006 Entry Draft).

			Regular Season								Playoffs						
Season	Club	League	GP	W	L	O/T	Mins	GA	SO	Avg	GP	W	L	Mins	GA	SO	Avg
2003-04	Det. Honeybaked	MWEHL	31	....	....	....	....	....	....	....	....	....	....	....	....	....	....
2004-05	USNTDP	U-17	14	10	6	1	930	41	0	2.65	....	....	....	....	....	....	....
	USNTDP	NAHL	23	10	7	1	1217	56	1	2.76	10	7	3	598	20	3	2.01
2005-06	USNTDP	U-18	12	7	2	0	593	24	0	2.43	....	....	....	....	....	....	....
	USNTDP	NAHL	5	3	0	0	238	5	0	1.26	....	....	....	....	....	....	....
2006-07	Boston University	H-East	1	1	0	0	60	1	0	1.00	....	....	....	....	....	....	....
2007-08	Boston University	H-East	31	16	10	3	1780	78	*3	2.63	....	....	....	....	....	....	....

BERKHOEL, Adam (BUHRK-uhl, A-duhm) DET.

Goaltender. Catches left. 5'11", 185 lbs. Born, St. Paul, MN, May 16, 1981.
(Chicago's 12th choice, 240th overall, in 2000 Entry Draft).

			Regular Season								Playoffs						
Season	Club	League	GP	W	L	O/T	Mins	GA	SO	Avg	GP	W	L	Mins	GA	SO	Avg
99-2000	Twin Cities	USHL	49	25	15	7	2848	129	0	2.72	13	7	6	797	43	0	3.24
2000-01	U. of Denver	WCHA	15	7	6	1	745	38	1	3.06	....	....	....	....	....	....	....
2001-02	U. of Denver	WCHA	18	12	4	1	1026	40	1	2.34	....	....	....	....	....	....	....
2002-03	U. of Denver	WCHA	26	12	6	4	1436	55	3	*2.30	....	....	....	....	....	....	....
2003-04	U. of Denver	WCHA	39	24	11	4	2225	91	*7	2.45	....	....	....	....	....	....	....
2004-05	Chicago Wolves	AHL	1	0	1	0	59	4	0	4.04	....	....	....	....	....	....	....
	Gwinnett	ECHL	24	9	10	5	1458	59	2	2.43	7	4	1	353	9	0	*1.53
2005-06	Atlanta	NHL	9	2	4	1	473	30	0	3.81	....	....	....	....	....	....	....
	Chicago Wolves	AHL	11	3	6	0	526	32	0	3.65	....	....	....	....	....	....	....
	Gwinnett	ECHL	15	10	4	1	902	41	1	2.73	9	6	3	551	30	0	3.27
2006-07	Rochester	AHL	6	2	3	0	316	17	0	3.22	....	....	....	....	....	....	....
	Dayton Bombers	ECHL	43	23	17	3	2584	105	5	2.44	*22	12	10	1385	59	*3	2.56
2007-08	Grand Rapids	AHL	31	10	14	4	1697	83	1	2.93	....	....	....	....	....	....	....
	NHL Totals		9	2	4	1	473	30	0	3.81	....	....	....	....	....	....	....

USHL All-Rookie Team (2000) • USHL Second All-Star Team (2000) • NCAA Championship All-Tournament Team (2004) • NCAA Championship Tournament MVP (2004) • ECHL First All-Star Team (2007)

Traded to **Atlanta** by **Chicago** for Atlanta's 7th round choice (Adam Hobson) in 2005 Entry Draft, June 27, 2004. Signed as a free agent by **Detroit**, July 3, 2007.

BERNIER, Jonathan (BAIRN-yay, JAWN-ah-thuhn) L.A.

Goaltender. Catches left. 6', 186 lbs. Born, Laval, Que., August 7, 1988.
(Los Angeles' 1st choice, 11th overall, in 2006 Entry Draft).

			Regular Season								Playoffs						
Season	Club	League	GP	W	L	O/T	Mins	GA	SO	Avg	GP	W	L	Mins	GA	SO	Avg
2003-04	Laval Regents	QAAA	27	16	4	0	1329	62	2	2.80	3	1	2	180	5	0	1.70
2004-05	Lewiston	QMJHL	23	7	12	3	1353	67	0	2.97	1	0	0	20	0	0	0.00
2005-06	Lewiston	QMJHL	54	27	26	0	3241	146	2	2.70	6	2	4	359	17	1	2.84
2006-07	Lewiston	QMJHL	37	26	10	....	2186	94	2	2.58	17	*16	1	1025	40	1	2.34

							Regular Season							Playoffs			
2007-08	**Los Angeles**	**NHL**	**4**	**1**	**3**	**0**	**238**	**16**	**0**	**4.03**	....	....	....	....	....	....	....
	Lewiston	QMJHL	34	18	15	....	2024	92	0	2.73	6	2	4	348	17	0	2.93
	Manchester	AHL	3	1	1	1	184	5	0	1.63	3	0	3	195	9	0	2.76
	NHL Totals		**4**	**1**	**3**	**0**	**238**	**16**	**0**	**4.03**	....	....	....	....	....	....	....

QMJHL Second All-Star Team (2007)

BERRA, Reto (BAIR-ruh, REH-toh) ST.L.

Goaltender. Catches left. 6'4", 189 lbs. Born, Bulach, Switz., January 3, 1987.
(St. Louis' 6th choice, 106th overall, in 2006 Entry Draft).

							Regular Season							Playoffs			
Season	Club	League	GP	W	L	O/T	Mins	GA	SO	Avg	GP	W	L	Mins	GA	SO	Avg
2004-05	GCK Zurich Jr.	Swiss-Jr.	22	....	....	....	....	....	....	....	....	....	....	....	....	....	....
	GCK Lions Zurich	Swiss-2	3	....	....	....	180	12	0	4.00	....	....	....	....	....	....	....
	EHC Dubendorf	Swiss-3					STATISTICS NOT AVAILABLE										
2005-06	GCK Zurich Jr.	Swiss-Jr.	23	....	....	....	....	....	....	....	....	....	....	....	....	....	....
	GCK Lions Zurich	Swiss-2	15	....	....	....	835	51	1	3.56	....	....	....	....	....	....	....
	ZSC Lions Zurich	Swiss	2	0	1	0	90	6	0	3.99	....	....	....	....	....	....	....
2006-07	Switzerland U20	Swiss-2	3	0	3	0	179	13	0	4.69	....	....	....	....	....	....	....
	GCK Lions Zurich	Swiss-2	6	4	2	0	359	18	0	3.01	....	....	....	....	....	....	....
	ZSC Lions Zurich	Swiss	2	1	0	0	78	4	0	3.08	4	0	3	188	9	0	2.87
2007-08	HC Davos	Swiss	16	9	7	0	966	44	0	2.73	....	....	....	....	....	....	....

BESKOROWANY, Tyler (behs-koor-WAH-nee, TIGH-luhr) DAL.

Goaltender. Catches left. 6'4", 203 lbs. Born, Sudbury, Ont., April 28, 1990.
(Dallas' 1st choice, 59th overall, in 2008 Entry Draft).

							Regular Season							Playoffs			
Season	Club	League	GP	W	L	O/T	Mins	GA	SO	Avg	GP	W	L	Mins	GA	SO	Avg
2006-07	Valley East Cobras	GNML	32	....	....	....	1443	80	1	3.33	7	....	....	410	22	2	3.22
2007-08	Owen Sound	OHL	35	12	19	3	2021	136	0	4.04	....	....	....	....	....	....	....

BIRON, Martin (BEE-rawn, MAHR-tihn) PHI.

Goaltender. Catches left. 6'3", 163 lbs. Born, Lac-St-Charles, Que., August 15, 1977.
(Buffalo's 2nd choice, 16th overall, in 1995 Entry Draft).

							Regular Season							Playoffs			
Season	Club	League	GP	W	L	O/T	Mins	GA	SO	Avg	GP	W	L	Mins	GA	SO	Avg
1993-94	Trois-Rivieres	QAAA	23	14	8	1	1412	80	1	3.40	2	1	1	112	7	0	3.73
1994-95	Beauport Harfangs	QMJHL	56	29	16	9	3193	132	3	*2.48	16	8	7	900	37	*4	2.47
1995-96	Beauport Harfangs	QMJHL	55	29	17	7	3201	152	1	2.85	*19	*12	7	1134	64	0	3.39
	Buffalo	**NHL**	**3**	**0**	**2**	**0**	**119**	**10**	**0**	**5.04**	....	....	....	....	....	....	....
1996-97	Beauport Harfangs	QMJHL	18	6	9	1	928	61	1	3.94	....	....	....	....	....	....	....
	Hull Olympiques	QMJHL	16	11	4	1	974	43	2	2.65	6	3	1	325	19	0	3.51
1997-98	South Carolina	ECHL	2	0	1	1	86	3	0	2.09	....	....	....	....	....	....	....
	Rochester	AHL	41	14	18	6	2312	113	*5	2.93	4	1	3	239	16	0	4.01
1998-99	**Buffalo**	**NHL**	**6**	**1**	**2**	**1**	**281**	**10**	**0**	**2.14**	....	....	....	....	....	....	....
	Rochester	AHL	52	36	13	3	3129	108	*6	*2.07	*20	12	8	1167	42	1	*2.16
99-2000	**Buffalo**	**NHL**	**41**	**19**	**18**	**2**	**2229**	**90**	**5**	**2.42**	....	....	....	....	....	....	....
	Rochester	AHL	6	6	0	0	344	12	1	2.09	....	....	....	....	....	....	....
2000-01	**Buffalo**	**NHL**	**18**	**7**	**7**	**1**	**918**	**39**	**2**	**2.55**	....	....	....	....	....	....	....
	Rochester	AHL	4	3	1	0	239	4	1	1.00	....	....	....	....	....	....	....
2001-02	**Buffalo**	**NHL**	**72**	**31**	**28**	**10**	**4085**	**151**	**4**	**2.22**	....	....	....	....	....	....	....
2002-03	**Buffalo**	**NHL**	**54**	**17**	**28**	**6**	**3170**	**135**	**4**	**2.56**	....	....	....	....	....	....	....
2003-04	**Buffalo**	**NHL**	**52**	**26**	**18**	**5**	**2972**	**125**	**2**	**2.52**	....	....	....	....	....	....	....
2004-05								DID NOT PLAY									
2005-06	**Buffalo**	**NHL**	**35**	**21**	**8**	**3**	**1934**	**93**	**1**	**2.89**	....	....	....	....	....	....	....
2006-07	**Buffalo**	**NHL**	**19**	**12**	**4**	**1**	**1066**	**54**	**0**	**3.04**	....	....	....	....	....	....	....
	Philadelphia	**NHL**	**16**	**6**	**8**	**2**	**935**	**47**	**0**	**3.02**	....	....	....	....	....	....	....
2007-08	**Philadelphia**	**NHL**	**62**	**30**	**20**	**9**	**3539**	**153**	**5**	**2.59**	**17**	**9**	**8**	**1049**	**52**	**1**	**2.97**
	NHL Totals		**378**	**170**	**143**	**40**	**21248**	**907**	**23**	**2.56**	**17**	**9**	**8**	**1049**	**52**	**1**	**2.97**

QMJHL All-Rookie Team (1995) • Canadian Major Junior First All-Star Team (1995) • Canadian Major Junior Goaltender of the Year (1995) • AHL First All-Star Team (1999) • Harry "Hap" Holmes Memorial Award (fewest goals against – AHL) (1999) (shared with Tom Draper) • Aldege "Baz" Bastien Memorial Award (Outstanding Goaltender – AHL) (1999)

Traded to **Philadelphia** by **Buffalo** for Philadelphia's 2nd round choice (T.J. Brennan) in 2007 Entry Draft, February 27, 2007.

BISHOP, Ben (BIH-shuhp, BEHN) ST.L.

Goaltender. Catches left. 6'5", 205 lbs. Born, Denver, CO, November 21, 1986.
(St. Louis' 3rd choice, 85th overall, in 2005 Entry Draft).

							Regular Season							Playoffs			
Season	Club	League	GP	W	L	O/T	Mins	GA	SO	Avg	GP	W	L	Mins	GA	SO	Avg
2003-04	St.L. AAA Blues	MAHL	11	8	1	2	660	19	1	1.73	....	....	....	....	....	....	....
	St.L. AAA Blues	Exhib.	26	15	7	4	1480	62	3	2.51	....	....	....	....	....	....	....
2004-05	Texas Tornado	NAHL	45	*35	8	0	2577	83	5	1.93	*11	*9	2	*660	30	0	2.73
2005-06	University of Maine	H-East	31	21	8	2	1788	68	0	2.28	....	....	....	....	....	....	....
2006-07	University of Maine	H-East	34	21	9	2	1907	68	3	2.14	....	....	....	....	....	....	....
2007-08	University of Maine	H-East	34	13	18	3	1972	80	2	2.43	....	....	....	....	....	....	....
	Peoria Rivermen	AHL	5	2	2	1	302	12	0	2.38	....	....	....	....	....	....	....

Hockey East All-Rookie Team (2006) • Hockey East Second All-Star Team (2008)

BJURLING, Bjorn (b-YUHR-lihng, b-YOHRN) EDM.

Goaltender. Catches left. 6', 205 lbs. Born, Stockholm, Sweden, August 21, 1979.
(Edmonton's 10th choice, 274th overall, in 2004 Entry Draft).

							Regular Season							Playoffs			
Season	Club	League	GP	W	L	O/T	Mins	GA	SO	Avg	GP	W	L	Mins	GA	SO	Avg
2000-01	Bodens IK	Sweden-2	32	....	....	....	1914	80	0	2.51	6	....	....	398	16	1	2.41
2001-02	Bodens IK	Sweden-2	43	....	....	....	2568	128	2	2.99	9	....	....	508	36	0	4.25
2002-03	Bodens IK	Sweden-2	3	....	....	....	179	7	1	2.35	....	....	....	....	....	....	....
	Djurgarden	Sweden	15	....	....	....	571	21	2	2.21	....	....	....	....	....	....	....
2003-04	Djurgarden	Sweden	45	....	....	....	2601	100	4	2.31	2	....	....	100	15	0	9.00
2004-05	Djurgarden	Sweden	24	....	....	....	1441	61	1	2.54	....	....	....	....	....	....	....
2005-06	Salzburg	Austria	23	....	....	....	1367	78	1	3.42	....	....	....	....	....	....	....
	Geneve	Swiss	7	2	2	2	430	24	1	3.35	....	....	....	....	....	....	....
2006-07	Valerengen IF Oslo	Norway	35	....	....	....	2027	69	5	2.04	15	....	....	907	32	1	2.11
2007-08	Sodertalje SK	Sweden	30	....	....	....	1752	70	2	2.40	....	....	....	....	....	....	....

BOUCHER, Brian (BOO-shay, BRIGH-uhn) S.J.

Goaltender. Catches left. 6'2", 198 lbs. Born, Woonsocket, RI, January 2, 1977.
(Philadelphia's 1st choice, 22nd overall, in 1995 Entry Draft).

							Regular Season							Playoffs			
Season	Club	League	GP	W	L	O/T	Mins	GA	SO	Avg	GP	W	L	Mins	GA	SO	Avg
1993-94	Mount St. Charles	High-RI	15	*14	0	1	*504	*8	*9	*0.57	4	*4	0	*180	*6	*1	*1.20
1994-95	Wexford Raiders	MTJHL	8	....	....	....	425	23	0	3.25	....	....	....	....	....	....	....
	Tri-City Americans	WHL	35	17	11	2	1969	108	1	3.29	13	6	5	795	50	0	3.77
1995-96	Tri-City Americans	WHL	55	33	19	2	3183	181	1	3.41	11	6	5	653	37	*2	3.40
1996-97	Tri-City Americans	WHL	41	10	24	6	2458	149	1	3.64	....	....	....	....	....	....	....
1997-98	Philadelphia	AHL	34	16	12	3	1901	101	0	3.19	2	0	0	30	1	0	1.95
1998-99	Philadelphia	AHL	36	20	8	5	2061	89	2	2.59	16	9	7	947	45	0	2.85
99-2000	**Philadelphia**	**NHL**	**35**	**20**	**10**	**3**	**2038**	**65**	**4**	***1.91**	**18**	**11**	**7**	**1183**	**40**	**1**	**2.03**
	Philadelphia	AHL	1	0	0	1	65	3	0	2.77	....	....	....	....	....	....	....
2000-01	**Philadelphia**	**NHL**	**27**	**8**	**12**	**5**	**1470**	**80**	**1**	**3.27**	**1**	**0**	**0**	**37**	**3**	**0**	**4.86**
2001-02	**Philadelphia**	**NHL**	**41**	**18**	**16**	**4**	**2295**	**92**	**2**	**2.41**	**2**	**0**	**1**	**88**	**2**	**0**	**1.36**
2002-03	**Phoenix**	**NHL**	**45**	**15**	**20**	**8**	**2544**	**128**	**0**	**3.02**	....	....	....	....	....	....	....
2003-04	**Phoenix**	**NHL**	**40**	**10**	**19**	**10**	**2364**	**108**	**5**	**2.74**	....	....	....	....	....	....	....
2004-05	HV 71 Jonkoping	Sweden	4	....	....	....	235	13	0	3.32	....	....	....	....	....	....	....
2005-06	**Phoenix**	**NHL**	**11**	**3**	**6**	**0**	**512**	**33**	**0**	**3.87**	....	....	....	....	....	....	....
	San Antonio	AHL	6	2	3	0	345	8	0	1.39	....	....	....	....	....	....	....
	Calgary	**NHL**	**3**	**1**	**2**	**0**	**182**	**15**	**0**	**4.95**	....	....	....	....	....	....	....
2006-07	**Chicago**	**NHL**	**15**	**1**	**10**	**3**	**827**	**45**	**1**	**3.26**	....	....	....	....	....	....	....
	Columbus	**NHL**	**3**	**1**	**1**	**0**	**142**	**9**	**0**	**3.80**	....	....	....	....	....	....	....
2007-08	Philadelphia	AHL	42	23	16	1	2288	94	4	2.47	....	....	....	....	....	....	....
	San Jose	**NHL**	**5**	**3**	**1**	**1**	**238**	**7**	**1**	**1.76**	**1**	**0**	**0**	**2**	**0**	**0**	**0.00**
	NHL Totals		**225**	**80**	**97**	**34**	**12612**	**582**	**14**	**2.77**	**22**	**11**	**8**	**1310**	**45**	**1**	**2.06**

WHL West Second All-Star Team (1996) • WHL West First All-Star Team (1997) • WHL Goaltender of the Year (1997) • NHL All-Rookie Team (2000)

Traded to **Phoenix** by **Philadelphia** with Nashville's 3rd round choice (previously acquired, Phoenix selected Joe Callahan) in 2002 Entry Draft for Michal Handzus and Robert Esche, June 12, 2002. Signed as a free agent by **Jonkoping** (Sweden), October 20, 2004. Traded to **Calgary** by **Phoenix** with Mike Leclerc for Steve Reinprecht and Philippe Sauve, February 2, 2006. Signed as a free agent by **Chicago**, September 24, 2006. Claimed on waivers by **Columbus** from **Chicago**, February 27, 2007. Signed as a free agent by **Philadelphia** (AHL), July 23, 2007. Signed as a free agent by **San Jose**, February 26, 2008.

BOUTIN, Jonathan (boo-TEHN, JAWN-ah-thuhn)

Goaltender. Catches left. 6'1", 200 lbs. Born, Granby, Que., March 28, 1985.
(Tampa Bay's 3rd choice, 96th overall, in 2003 Entry Draft).

							Regular Season							Playoffs			
Season	Club	League	GP	W	L	O/T	Mins	GA	SO	Avg	GP	W	L	Mins	GA	SO	Avg
2001-02	Fort Saskatchewan	AJHL					STATISTICS NOT AVAILABLE										
	Halifax	QMJHL	11	4	1	1	459	18	0	2.35	2	0	0	15	0	0	0.00
2002-03	Halifax	QMJHL	47	22	11	2	2190	106	4	2.90	1	0	0	27	0	0	0.00
2003-04	PEI Rocket	QMJHL	30	13	12	2	1612	80	1	2.98	11	6	5	672	23	0	2.06
2004-05	PEI Rocket	QMJHL	32	15	14	2	1814	98	1	3.24	....	....	....	....	....	....	....
	Quebec Remparts	QMJHL	10	4	5	0	534	30	0	3.37	10	5	4	558	30	*1	3.22
2005-06	Springfield Falcons	AHL	22	8	12	2	1266	67	1	3.18	....	....	....	....	....	....	....
	Johnstown Chiefs	ECHL	19	8	9	2	1145	56	2	2.93	3	1	2	170	10	0	3.53
2006-07	Springfield Falcons	AHL	37	9	17	1	1660	91	1	3.29	....	....	....	....	....	....	....
	Johnstown Chiefs	ECHL	2	0	2	0	117	6	0	3.07	....	....	....	....	....	....	....
2007-08	Norfolk Admirals	AHL	38	13	18	3	2070	114	2	3.31	....	....	....	....	....	....	....

BRODEUR, Martin (broh-DUHR, MAHR-tihn) N.J.

Goaltender. Catches left. 6'2", 215 lbs. Born, Montreal, Que., May 6, 1972.
(New Jersey's 1st choice, 20th overall, in 1990 Entry Draft).

							Regular Season							Playoffs			
Season	Club	League	GP	W	L	O/T	Mins	GA	SO	Avg	GP	W	L	Mins	GA	SO	Avg
1988-89	Montreal-Bourassa	QAAA	27	13	12	1	1580	98	0	3.72	3	0	3	210	14	0	3.99
1989-90	St-Hyacinthe Laser	QMJHL	42	23	13	2	2333	156	0	4.01	12	5	7	678	46	0	4.07
1990-91	St-Hyacinthe Laser	QMJHL	52	22	24	4	2946	162	2	3.30	4	0	4	232	16	0	4.14
1991-92	St-Hyacinthe Laser	QMJHL	48	27	16	4	2846	161	2	3.39	5	2	3	317	14	0	2.65
	New Jersey	**NHL**	**4**	**2**	**1**	**0**	**179**	**10**	**0**	**3.35**	**1**	**0**	**1**	**32**	**3**	**0**	**5.63**
1992-93	Utica Devils	AHL	32	14	13	5	1952	131	0	4.03	4	1	3	258	18	0	4.19
1993-94	**New Jersey**	**NHL**	**47**	**27**	**11**	**8**	**2625**	**105**	**3**	**2.40**	**17**	**8**	**9**	**1171**	**38**	**1**	**1.95**
1994-95 ♦	**New Jersey**	**NHL**	**40**	**19**	**11**	**6**	**2184**	**89**	**3**	**2.45**	***20**	***16**	**4**	***1222**	**34**	***3**	***1.67**
1995-96	**New Jersey**	**NHL**	**77**	**34**	**30**	**12**	***4433**	**173**	**6**	**2.34**	....	....	....	....	....	....	....
1996-97	**New Jersey**	**NHL**	**67**	**37**	**14**	**13**	**3838**	**120**	***10**	***1.88**	**10**	**5**	**5**	**659**	**19**	**2**	***1.73**
1997-98	**New Jersey**	**NHL**	**70**	***43**	**17**	**8**	**4128**	**130**	**10**	**1.89**	**6**	**2**	**4**	**366**	**12**	**0**	**1.97**
1998-99	**New Jersey**	**NHL**	***70**	***39**	**21**	**10**	***4239**	**162**	**4**	**2.29**	**7**	**3**	**4**	**425**	**20**	**0**	**2.82**
99-2000 ♦	**New Jersey**	**NHL**	**72**	***43**	**20**	**8**	**4312**	**161**	**6**	**2.24**	***23**	***16**	**7**	***1450**	**39**	**2**	***1.61**
2000-01	**New Jersey**	**NHL**	**72**	***42**	**17**	**11**	**4297**	**166**	**9**	**2.32**	***25**	**15**	**10**	***1505**	**52**	***4**	**2.07**
2001-02	**New Jersey**	**NHL**	***73**	**38**	**26**	**9**	***4347**	**156**	**4**	**2.15**	**6**	**2**	**4**	**381**	**9**	**1**	**1.42**
	Canada	Olympics	5	*4	0	1	300	9	0	*1.80	....	....	....	....	....	....	....
2002-03 ♦	**New Jersey**	**NHL**	**73**	***41**	**23**	**9**	**4374**	**147**	***9**	**2.02**	***24**	***16**	**8**	***1491**	**41**	***7**	**1.65**
2003-04	**New Jersey**	**NHL**	***75**	***38**	**26**	**11**	***4555**	**154**	***11**	**2.03**	**5**	**1**	**4**	**298**	**13**	**0**	**2.62**
2004-05								DID NOT PLAY									
2005-06	**New Jersey**	**NHL**	**73**	***43**	**23**	**7**	**4365**	**187**	**5**	**2.57**	**9**	**5**	**4**	**533**	**20**	**1**	**2.25**
	Canada	Olympics	4	2	2	0	239	8	0	2.01	....	....	....	....	....	....	....
2006-07	**New Jersey**	**NHL**	***78**	***48**	**23**	**7**	***4697**	**171**	***12**	**2.18**	**11**	**5**	**6**	**688**	**28**	**1**	**2.44**
2007-08	**New Jersey**	**NHL**	***77**	**44**	**27**	**6**	***4635**	**168**	**4**	**2.17**	**5**	**1**	**4**	**301**	**16**	**0**	**3.19**
	NHL Totals		**968**	**538**	**290**	**125**	**57208**	**2099**	**96**	**2.20**	**169**	**95**	**74**	**10522**	**344**	**22**	**1.96**

QMJHL All-Rookie Team (1990) • QMJHL Second All-Star Team (1992) • NHL All-Rookie Team (1994) • Calder Memorial Trophy (1994) • NHL Second All-Star Team (1997, 1998, 2006, 2008) • William M. Jennings Trophy (1997) (shared with Mike Dunham) • William M. Jennings Trophy (1998, 2004) • NHL First All-Star Team (2003, 2004, 2007) • William M. Jennings Trophy (2003) (tied with Roman Cechmanek/Robert Esche) • Vezina Trophy (2003, 2004, 2007, 2008)

Played in NHL All-Star Game (1996, 1997, 1998, 1999, 2000, 2001, 2003, 2004, 2007)

• Scored a goal in playoffs vs. Montreal, April 17, 1997.

BRODEUR, Mike (broh-DUHR, MIGHK)

Goaltender. Catches left. 6'2", 171 lbs. Born, Calgary, Alta., March 30, 1983.
(Chicago's 7th choice, 211th overall, in 2003 Entry Draft).

							Regular Season							Playoffs			
Season	Club	League	GP	W	L	O/T	Mins	GA	SO	Avg	GP	W	L	Mins	GA	SO	Avg
2000-01	Cgy. AAA Flames	AMHL	21	11	8	3	1231	54	1	2.63	10	6	4	620	31	0	3.00
2001-02	Camrose Kodiaks	AJHL	24	13	9	1	1299	65	1	2.91	....	....	....	....	....	....	....
2002-03	Camrose Kodiaks	AJHL	48	28	16	2	2570	113	2	2.64	21	16	5	1378	48	4	2.09
2003-04	Moose Jaw	WHL	41	23	12	5	2385	84	5	2.11	10	6	4	624	18	1	*1.73
2004-05	Norfolk Admirals	AHL	1	0	1	0	39	4	0	6.17	....	....	....	....	....	....	....
	Greenville Grrrowl	ECHL	35	19	15	1	2081	93	2	2.68	5	2	3	302	10	1	1.98
2005-06	Greenville Grrrowl	ECHL	24	14	8	2	1466	63	1	2.58	....	....	....	....	....	....	....
2006-07	Norfolk Admirals	AHL	10	4	3	0	495	28	0	3.39	1	0	0	8	2	0	14.17
	Augusta Lynx	ECHL	2	2	0	0	120	4	1	2.00	....	....	....	....	....	....	....
	Toledo Storm	ECHL	5	3	2	0	300	10	2	2.00	....	....	....	....	....	....	....
2007-08	Rockford IceHogs	AHL	8	2	3	0	341	16	0	2.81	....	....	....	....	....	....	....
	Pensacola Ice Pilots	ECHL	26	10	9	5	1504	71	1	2.83	....	....	....	....	....	....	....

BROWN, David (BROWN, DAY-vihd) PIT.

Goaltender. Catches left. 6', 185 lbs. Born, Stoney Creek, Ont., February 11, 1985.
(Pittsburgh's 11th choice, 228th overall, in 2004 Entry Draft).

							Regular Season							Playoffs			
Season	Club	League	GP	W	L	O/T	Mins	GA	SO	Avg	GP	W	L	Mins	GA	SO	Avg
2002-03	Hamilton Kilty B's	OPJHL	35	....	....	....	....	....	....	3.11	....	....	....	....	....	....	....
2003-04	U. of Notre Dame	CCHA	26	14	7	3	1445	56	5	2.32	....	....	....	....	....	....	....
2004-05	U. of Notre Dame	CCHA	15	2	10	1	767	55	0	4.30	....	....	....	....	....	....	....
2005-06	U. of Notre Dame	CCHA	31	9	15	4	1724	71	0	2.47	....	....	....	....	....	....	....
2006-07	U. of Notre Dame	CCHA	39	*30	6	3	2390	63	*6	*1.58	....	....	....	....	....	....	....
2007-08	Wilkes-Barre	AHL	19	9	7	1	1050	41	0	2.34	1	0	0	20	1	0	3.00
	Wheeling Nailers	ECHL	13	6	6	1	707	39	0	3.31	....	....	....	....	....	....	....

CCHA First All-Star Team (2007) • CCHA Player of the Year (2007) • NCAA West First All-American Team (2007)

BROWN, Mike (BROWN, MIGHK)

Goaltender. Catches left. 6', 203 lbs. Born, Syracuse, NY, March 4, 1985.
(Boston's 7th choice, 153rd overall, in 2003 Entry Draft).

			Regular Season								Playoffs						
Season	Club	League	GP	W	L	O/T	Mins	GA	SO	Avg	GP	W	L	Mins	GA	SO	Avg
2001-02	Baldwinsville Bees	High-NY	7	....	....	....	420	8	4	0.86	5	3	2	300	6	1	1.20
2002-03	Saginaw Spirit	OHL	39	8	23	3	2186	134	0	3.68	....	....	....	....	....	....	....
2003-04	Saginaw Spirit	OHL	51	14	32	3	2886	156	4	3.24	....	....	....	....	....	....	....
2004-05	Saginaw Spirit	OHL	26	7	17	1	1482	91	0	3.68	....	....	....	....	....	....	....
	Owen Sound	OHL	33	17	11	4	1956	81	3	2.48	8	4	4	485	19	*2	2.35
2005-06	Providence Bruins	AHL	2	0	0	0	42	2	0	2.87	....	....	....	....	....	....	....
	South Carolina	ECHL	3	0	1	2	188	15	0	4.79	....	....	....	....	....	....	....
	Dayton Bombers	ECHL	18	4	12	2	1050	64	0	3.66	....	....	....	....	....	....	....
2006-07	Providence Bruins	AHL	1	0	0	0	20	0	0	0.00	....	....	....	....	....	....	....
	Long Beach	ECHL	43	15	21	2	2283	124	1	3.26	....	....	....	....	....	....	....
2007-08	Providence Bruins	AHL	9	6	2	0	460	22	0	2.87	....	....	....	....	....	....	....
	Johnstown Chiefs	ECHL	6	0	6	0	336	23	0	4.11	....	....	....	....	....	....	....
	Alaska Aces	ECHL	15	9	4	0	796	33	0	2.49	....	....	....	....	....	....	....

BRUST, Barry (BRUHST, BAIR-ree) MIN.

Goaltender. Catches left. 6'2", 235 lbs. Born, Swan River, Man., August 8, 1983.
(Minnesota's 4th choice, 73rd overall, in 2002 Entry Draft).

			Regular Season								Playoffs						
Season	Club	League	GP	W	L	O/T	Mins	GA	SO	Avg	GP	W	L	Mins	GA	SO	Avg
99-2000	Swan Valley	MJHL	19	10	9	0	1140	67	0	3.50	....	....	....	....	....	....	....
2000-01	Spokane Chiefs	WHL	16	4	6	1	777	42	0	3.24	....	....	....	....	....	....	....
2001-02	Spokane Chiefs	WHL	60	28	21	10	3540	152	1	2.58	11	6	5	677	23	0	2.04
2002-03	Spokane Chiefs	WHL	*59	22	31	4	*3385	194	0	3.44	11	4	7	722	37	0	3.07
2003-04	Spokane Chiefs	WHL	27	10	13	2	1505	75	0	2.99	....	....	....	....	....	....	....
	Calgary Hitmen	WHL	25	12	8	3	1448	54	2	2.24	7	3	4	457	15	2	1.97
2004-05	Reading Royals	ECHL	42	27	9	4	2413	79	4	1.96	8	4	4	481	14	2	1.74
2005-06	Manchester	AHL	35	19	14	1	1971	89	2	2.71	5	2	2	279	17	1	3.66
	Reading Royals	ECHL	6	3	3	0	361	18	0	3.00	....	....	....	....	....	....	....
2006-07	**Los Angeles**	**NHL**	**11**	**2**	**4**	**1**	**486**	**30**	**0**	**3.70**	....	....	....	....	....	....	....
	Manchester	AHL	18	9	7	0	951	38	2	2.40	5	2	1	199	6	0	1.81
2007-08	Houston Aeros	AHL	43	24	16	3	2380	90	4	2.27	3	1	2	202	6	1	1.78
	NHL Totals		**11**	**2**	**4**	**1**	**486**	**30**	**0**	**3.70**	....	....	....	....	....	....	....

WHL West First All-Star Team (2002) • Harry "Hap" Holmes Memorial Award (fewest goals against – AHL) (2008) (shared with Nolan Schaefer)

Signed as a free agent by **Los Angeles**, June 10, 2004. Signed as a free agent by **Minnesota**, July 6, 2008.

BRYZGALOV, Ilya (breez-GAH-lahf, IHL-yah) PHX.

Goaltender. Catches left. 6'3", 210 lbs. Born, Togliatti, USSR, June 22, 1980.
(Anaheim's 2nd choice, 44th overall, in 2000 Entry Draft).

			Regular Season								Playoffs						
Season	Club	League	GP	W	L	O/T	Mins	GA	SO	Avg	GP	W	L	Mins	GA	SO	Avg
1996-97	Lada Togliatti 2	Russia-3	5	....	....	....	....	....	....	....	....	....	....	....	....	....	....
1997-98	Lada Togliatti 2	Russia-3	8	....	....	....	....	28	....	....	....	....	....	....	....	....	....
1998-99	Lada Togliatti 2	Russia-4	20	....	....	....	....	43	....	....	....	....	....	....	....	....	....
99-2000	Spartak Moscow	Russia-2	10	....	....	....	500	21	....	2.52	....	....	....	....	....	....	....
	Lada Togliatti 2	Russia-3	2	....	....	....	....	5	....	....	....	....	....	....	....	....	....
	Lada Togliatti	Russia	14	....	....	....	796	18	3	1.36	7	....	....	407	10	1	1.47
2000-01	Lada Togliatti	Russia	34	....	....	....	1992	61	8	1.84	5	....	....	249	8	0	1.93
2001-02	**Anaheim**	**NHL**	**1**	**0**	**0**	**0**	**32**	**1**	**0**	**1.88**	....	....	....	....	....	....	....
	Cincinnati	AHL	45	20	16	4	2399	99	4	2.48	....	....	....	....	....	....	....
	Russia	Olympics				DID NOT PLAY – SPARE GOALTENDER											
2002-03	Cincinnati	AHL	54	12	26	9	3020	142	1	2.82	....	....	....	....	....	....	....
2003-04	**Anaheim**	**NHL**	**1**	**1**	**0**	**0**	**60**	**2**	**0**	**2.00**	....	....	....	....	....	....	....
	Cincinnati	AHL	*64	27	25	10	*3748	145	6	2.32	9	5	4	536	27	1	3.02
2004-05	Cincinnati	AHL	36	17	13	1	2007	87	4	2.60	7	3	3	314	13	0	2.48
2005-06	**Anaheim**	**NHL**	**31**	**13**	**12**	**1**	**1575**	**66**	**1**	**2.51**	**11**	**6**	**4**	**659**	**16**	***3**	***1.46**
	Russia	Olympics	1	0	1	0	60	5	0	5.00	....	....	....	....	....	....	....
2006-07 ♦	**Anaheim**	**NHL**	**27**	**10**	**8**	**6**	**1509**	**62**	**1**	**2.47**	**5**	**3**	**1**	**267**	**10**	**0**	**2.25**
2007-08	**Anaheim**	**NHL**	**9**	**2**	**3**	**1**	**447**	**19**	**0**	**2.55**	....	....	....	....	....	....	....
	Phoenix	**NHL**	**55**	**26**	**22**	**5**	**3167**	**128**	**3**	**2.43**	....	....	....	....	....	....	....
	NHL Totals		**124**	**52**	**45**	**13**	**6790**	**278**	**5**	**2.46**	**16**	**9**	**5**	**926**	**26**	**3**	**1.68**

Claimed on waivers by **Phoenix** from **Anaheim**, November 17, 2007.

BUDAJ, Peter (BOO-digh, PEE-tuhr) COL.

Goaltender. Catches left. 6'1", 200 lbs. Born, Banska Bystrica, Czech., September 18, 1982.
(Colorado's 1st choice, 63rd overall, in 2001 Entry Draft).

			Regular Season								Playoffs						
Season	Club	League	GP	W	L	O/T	Mins	GA	SO	Avg	GP	W	L	Mins	GA	SO	Avg
99-2000	St. Michael's	OHL	34	6	18	1	1676	112	1	4.01	....	....	....	....	....	....	....
2000-01	St. Michael's	OHL	37	17	12	3	1996	95	3	2.86	11	6	4	621	26	1	2.51
2001-02	St. Michael's	OHL	42	26	9	5	2329	89	2	*2.29	12	5	6	620	34	*1	3.29
2002-03	Hershey Bears	AHL	28	10	10	2	1467	65	2	2.66	1	0	0	6	2	0	20.81
2003-04	Hershey Bears	AHL	46	17	20	6	2574	120	3	2.80	....	....	....	....	....	....	....
2004-05	Hershey Bears	AHL	59	29	25	2	3356	148	5	2.65	....	....	....	....	....	....	....
2005-06	**Colorado**	**NHL**	**34**	**14**	**10**	**6**	**1803**	**86**	**2**	**2.86**	....	....	....	....	....	....	....
	Slovakia	Olympics	3	2	1	0	179	6	0	2.01	....	....	....	....	....	....	....
2006-07	**Colorado**	**NHL**	**57**	**31**	**16**	**6**	**3199**	**143**	**3**	**2.68**	....	....	....	....	....	....	....
2007-08	**Colorado**	**NHL**	**35**	**16**	**10**	**4**	**1912**	**82**	**0**	**2.57**	**3**	**0**	**0**	**108**	**6**	**0**	**3.33**
	NHL Totals		**126**	**61**	**36**	**16**	**6914**	**311**	**5**	**2.70**	**3**	**0**	**0**	**108**	**6**	**0**	**3.33**

OHL Second All-Star Team (2002)

CANN, Trevor (KAN, TREH-vuhr) COL.

Goaltender. Catches left. 5'11", 199 lbs. Born, Oakville, Ont., March 30, 1989.
(Colorado's 3rd choice, 49th overall, in 2007 Entry Draft).

			Regular Season								Playoffs						
Season	Club	League	GP	W	L	O/T	Mins	GA	SO	Avg	GP	W	L	Mins	GA	SO	Avg
2005-06	Peterborough	OHL	20	16	2	0	1176	52	1	2.65	1	0	0	35	3	0	5.14
2006-07	Peterborough	OHL	*62	23	32	5	3565	219	0	3.69	....	....	....	....	....	....	....
2007-08	Peterborough	OHL	51	20	28	3	2976	178	2	3.59	5	1	4	317	21	0	3.98

CARON, Sebastien (KAIR-aw, suh-BAS-tee-yeh)

Goaltender. Catches left. 6'1", 170 lbs. Born, Amqui, Que., June 25, 1980.
(Pittsburgh's 4th choice, 86th overall, in 1999 Entry Draft).

			Regular Season								Playoffs						
Season	Club	League	GP	W	L	O/T	Mins	GA	SO	Avg	GP	W	L	Mins	GA	SO	Avg
1997-98	TGV Pentagone	QAHA	17	....	....	....	762	48	1	2.84	....	....	....	....	....	....	....
1998-99	Rimouski Oceanic	QMJHL	30	13	10	3	1570	85	0	3.25	2	1	0	68	0	0	0.00
99-2000	Rimouski Oceanic	QMJHL	54	*38	11	3	3040	179	1	3.53	14	*12	2	828	50	0	3.62
2000-01	Wilkes-Barre	AHL	30	12	14	3	1746	103	4	3.54	....	....	....	....	....	....	....
2001-02	Wilkes-Barre	AHL	46	14	22	8	2671	139	1	3.12	....	....	....	....	....	....	....
2002-03	**Pittsburgh**	**NHL**	**24**	**7**	**14**	**2**	**1408**	**62**	**2**	**2.64**	....	....	....	....	....	....	....
	Wilkes-Barre	AHL	27	12	14	1	1561	81	1	3.11	....	....	....	....	....	....	....
2003-04	**Pittsburgh**	**NHL**	**40**	**9**	**24**	**5**	**2213**	**138**	**1**	**3.74**	....	....	....	....	....	....	....
	Wilkes-Barre	AHL	14	7	3	4	811	26	2	1.92	7	3	4	395	23	0	3.50
2004-05	Saguenay Fjord	QNAHL					STATISTICS NOT AVAILABLE										
2005-06	**Pittsburgh**	**NHL**	**26**	**8**	**9**	**5**	**1312**	**87**	**1**	**3.98**	....	....	....	....	....	....	....
	Wilkes-Barre	AHL	6	3	3	0	357	7	2	1.18	....	....	....	....	....	....	....
2006-07	**Chicago**	**NHL**	**1**	**1**	**0**	**0**	**60**	**1**	**0**	**1.00**	....	....	....	....	....	....	....
	Norfolk Admirals	AHL	9	4	4	0	506	34	0	4.03	....	....	....	....	....	....	....
	Anaheim	**NHL**	**1**	**0**	**0**	**0**	**28**	**1**	**0**	**2.14**	....	....	....	....	....	....	....
	Portland Pirates	AHL	17	7	6	4	1025	40	0	2.34	....	....	....	....	....	....	....
2007-08	Fribourg	Swiss	48	24	24	0	2851	144	5	3.03	7	4	3	437	21	0	2.88
	NHL Totals		**92**	**25**	**47**	**12**	**5021**	**289**	**4**	**3.45**	....	....	....	....	....	....	....

Memorial Cup Tournament All-Star Team (2000) • Hap Emms Memorial Trophy (Memorial Cup Tournament - Top Goaltender) (2000) • NHL All-Rookie Team (2003)

Signed as a free agent by **Saguenay** (QNAHL), September 21, 2004. Signed as a free agent by **Chicago**, August 8, 2006. Traded to **Anaheim** by **Chicago** with Matt Keith and Chris Durno for Pierre Parenteau and Bruno St. Jacques, December 28, 2006. Signed as a free agent by **Fribourg** (Swiss), June 21, 2007.

CARROZZI, Christopher (ka-ROH-zee, KRIHS-toh-fuhr) ATL.

Goaltender. Catches left. 6'3", 185 lbs. Born, Ottawa, Ont., March 2, 1990.
(Atlanta's 6th choice, 154th overall, in 2008 Entry Draft).

			Regular Season								Playoffs						
Season	Club	League	GP	W	L	O/T	Mins	GA	SO	Avg	GP	W	L	Mins	GA	SO	Avg
2005-06	Nepean Raiders	Minor-ON	23	....	....	....	....	42	4	1.82	....	....	....	....	....	....	....
2006-07	St. Michael's	OHL	25	6	7	2	1130	81	0	4.30	....	....	....	....	....	....	....
2007-08	St. Michael's	OHL	47	25	18	2	2505	115	*4	2.75	4	0	4	240	18	0	4.50

CARUSO, Dave (kah-ROO-soh, DAYV) N.J.

Goaltender. Catches left. 6'1", 210 lbs. Born, Queens, NY, June 18, 1982.

			Regular Season								Playoffs						
Season	Club	League	GP	W	L	O/T	Mins	GA	SO	Avg	GP	W	L	Mins	GA	SO	Avg
2002-03	Ohio State	CCHA	8	5	2	0	460	12	2	1.56	....	....	....	....	....	....	....
2003-04	Ohio State	CCHA	14	9	3	0	762	25	2	*1.97	....	....	....	....	....	....	....
2004-05	Ohio State	CCHA	38	25	9	4	2272	81	2	2.14	....	....	....	....	....	....	....
2005-06	Ohio State	CCHA	36	13	18	5	2146	77	*5	2.15	....	....	....	....	....	....	....
2006-07	Chicago Wolves	AHL	1	1	0	0	36	4	0	6.75	....	....	....	....	....	....	....
	Gwinnett	ECHL	38	23	11	4	2297	120	1	3.13	3	1	2	200	9	0	2.71
2007-08	Lowell Devils	AHL	16	7	8	0	930	51	0	3.29	....	....	....	....	....	....	....
	Trenton Devils	ECHL	34	13	16	4	1972	85	2	2.59	....	....	....	....	....	....	....

Signed as a free agent by **Atlanta**, July 6, 2006. Signed as a free agent by **New Jersey**, August 10, 2007.

CASSIVI, Frederic (KASS-ih-vee, FREHD-uhr-ihk)

Goaltender. Catches left. 6'4", 220 lbs. Born, Sorel, Que., June 12, 1975.
(Ottawa's 7th choice, 210th overall, in 1994 Entry Draft).

			Regular Season								Playoffs						
Season	Club	League	GP	W	L	O/T	Mins	GA	SO	Avg	GP	W	L	Mins	GA	SO	Avg
1991-92	Abitibi Forestiers	QAAA	22	5	17	0	1320	106	0	4.84	3	1	2	180	15	0	5.06
1992-93							STATISTICS NOT AVAILABLE										
1993-94	St-Hyacinthe Laser	QMJHL	35	15	13	3	1751	127	1	4.35	....	....	....	....	....	....	....
1994-95	Halifax	QMJHL	24	9	12	1	1362	105	0	4.63	....	....	....	....	....	....	....
	St-Jean Lynx	QMJHL	19	12	6	0	1021	55	1	3.23	5	2	3	258	18	0	4.19
1995-96	Thunder Bay	ColHL	12	6	4	2	715	51	0	4.28	....	....	....	....	....	....	....
	P.E.I. Senators	AHL	41	20	14	3	2347	128	1	3.27	5	2	3	317	24	0	4.54
1996-97	Syracuse Crunch	AHL	55	23	22	8	3069	164	2	3.21	1	0	1	60	3	0	3.01
1997-98	Worcester IceCats	AHL	45	20	22	2	2593	140	1	3.24	6	3	3	326	18	0	3.31
1998-99	Cincinnati	IHL	44	21	17	2	2418	123	1	3.05	3	1	2	139	6	0	2.59
99-2000	Hershey Bears	AHL	31	14	9	3	1554	78	1	3.01	2	0	1	63	5	0	4.75
2000-01	Hershey Bears	AHL	49	17	24	3	2620	124	2	2.84	9	7	2	564	14	1	*1.49
2001-02	Hershey Bears	AHL	21	6	10	4	1201	50	0	2.50	....	....	....	....	....	....	....
	Atlanta	**NHL**	**6**	**2**	**3**	**0**	**307**	**17**	**0**	**3.32**	....	....	....	....	....	....	....
	Chicago Wolves	AHL	12	6	2	1	625	26	0	2.50	5	2	2	264	11	0	2.50
2002-03	**Atlanta**	**NHL**	**2**	**1**	**1**	**0**	**123**	**11**	**0**	**5.37**	....	....	....	....	....	....	....
	Chicago Wolves	AHL	21	10	8	1	1171	62	0	3.18	2	0	2	90	3	0	2.00
2003-04	Chicago Wolves	AHL	34	15	12	5	1911	82	1	2.57	....	....	....	....	....	....	....
2004-05	Cincinnati	AHL	46	25	18	2	2549	88	*10	2.07	8	2	4	444	21	0	2.84
2005-06	**Washington**	**NHL**	**1**	**0**	**1**	**0**	**59**	**4**	**0**	**4.07**	....	....	....	....	....	....	....
	Hershey Bears	AHL	*61	*34	19	6	*3538	153	3	2.59	*21	*16	5	*1316	46	*4	2.10
2006-07	**Washington**	**NHL**	**4**	**0**	**1**	**1**	**139**	**6**	**0**	**2.59**	....	....	....	....	....	....	....
	Hershey Bears	AHL	39	22	10	5	2286	90	3	2.36	19	13	6	1169	51	1	2.62
2007-08	Hershey Bears	AHL	45	20	20	4	2594	138	0	3.19	5	1	3	284	19	0	4.02
	NHL Totals		**13**	**3**	**6**	**1**	**628**	**38**	**0**	**3.63**	....	....	....	....	....	....	....

Jack A. Butterfield Trophy (Playoff MVP - AHL) (2006)

Signed as a free agent by **Colorado**, August 17, 1999. Traded to **Atlanta** by **Colorado** for Brett Clark, January 24, 2002. Signed as a free agent by **Cincinnati** (AHL), September 28, 2004. Signed as a free agent by **Washington**, August 11, 2005.

CHEVERIE, Marc (she-VEH-ree, MAHRK) FLA.

Goaltender. Catches left. 6'3", 183 lbs. Born, Cole Harbour, N.S., February 22, 1987.
(Florida's 6th choice, 193rd overall, in 2006 Entry Draft).

			Regular Season								Playoffs						
Season	Club	League	GP	W	L	O/T	Mins	GA	SO	Avg	GP	W	L	Mins	GA	SO	Avg
2003-04	Dartmouth	NSMHL	....	19	4	2	1521	76	1	2.99	....	....	....	....	....	....	....
2004-05	Notre Dame	SMHL	25	....	....	....	....	....	....	2.25	....	....	....	....	....	....	....
2005-06	Nanaimo Clippers	BCHL	46	23	9	0	2032	86	4	2.54	....	....	....	....	....	....	....
2006-07	Nanaimo Clippers	BCHL	34	21	9	2	2015	104	3	3.10	....	....	....	....	....	....	....
2007-08	U. of Denver	WCHA	5	1	0	0	141	4	0	1.70	....	....	....	....	....	....	....

CLARK, Morgan (KLAHRK, MOHR-guhn) VAN.

Goaltender. Catches left. 5'11", 160 lbs. Born, Toronto, Ont., February 17, 1990.
(Vancouver's 5th choice, 191st overall, in 2008 Entry Draft).

			Regular Season								Playoffs						
Season	Club	League	GP	W	L	O/T	Mins	GA	SO	Avg	GP	W	L	Mins	GA	SO	Avg
2006-07	Red Deer Rebels	WHL	21	9	5	2	1015	55	1	3.25	....	....	....	....	....	....	....
2007-08	Red Deer Rebels	WHL	47	10	30	0	2513	155	1	3.70	....	....	....	....	....	....	....

CLEMMENSEN, Scott (KLEH-mehn-sehn, SKAWT) N.J.

Goaltender. Catches left. 6'3", 205 lbs. Born, Des Moines, IA, July 23, 1977.
(New Jersey's 7th choice, 215th overall, in 1997 Entry Draft).

			Regular Season								Playoffs						
Season	Club	League	GP	W	L	O/T	Mins	GA	SO	Avg	GP	W	L	Mins	GA	SO	Avg
1995-96	Dubuque	USHL	20	10	7	1	1082	62	0	3.44	....	....	....	....	....	....	....
1996-97	Des Moines	USHL	36	22	9	2	2042	111	1	3.26	4	1	2	200	9	1	2.70
1997-98	Boston College	H-East	37	24	9	4	2205	102	*4	2.78	....	....	....	....	....	....	....
1998-99	Boston College	H-East	*42	26	12	4	*2507	120	1	2.87	....	....	....	....	....	....	....
99-2000	Boston College	H-East	29	19	7	0	1610	59	*5	2.20	....	....	....	....	....	....	....
2000-01	Boston College	H-East	*39	*30	7	2	*2312	82	3	2.13	....	....	....	....	....	....	....
2001-02	**New Jersey**	**NHL**	**2**	**0**	**0**	**0**	**20**	**1**	**0**	**3.00**	....	....	....	....	....	....	....
	Albany River Rats	AHL	29	5	19	4	1677	92	0	3.29	....	....	....	....	....	....	....
2002-03	Albany River Rats	AHL	47	12	24	8	2694	119	1	2.65	....	....	....	....	....	....	....
2003-04	**New Jersey**	**NHL**	**4**	**3**	**1**	**0**	**238**	**4**	**2**	**1.01**	....	....	....	....	....	....	....
	Albany River Rats	AHL	22	5	12	4	1309	67	0	3.07	....	....	....	....	....	....	....

2004-05	Albany River Rats	AHL	46	13	25	5	2645	124	2	2.81	....	....	....	....	....	....	....
2005-06	**New Jersey**	**NHL**	**13**	**3**	**4**	**2**	**627**	**35**	**0**	**3.35**	**1**	**0**	**0**	**7**	**0**	**0**	**0.00**
	Albany River Rats	AHL	1	0	1	0	59	5	0	5.05	....	....	....	....	....	....	....
2006-07	**New Jersey**	**NHL**	**6**	**1**	**1**	**2**	**305**	**16**	**0**	**3.15**	....	....	....	....	....	....	....
	Lowell Devils	AHL	1	1	0	0	60	0	1	0.00	....	....	....	....	....	....	....
2007-08	**Toronto**	**NHL**	**3**	**1**	**1**	**0**	**154**	**10**	**0**	**3.90**	....	....	....	....	....	....	....
	Toronto Marlies	AHL	40	23	14	2	2363	96	1	2.44	17	8	9	992	50	0	3.02
	NHL Totals		**28**	**8**	**7**	**4**	**1344**	**66**	**2**	**2.95**	**1**	**0**	**0**	**7**	**0**	**0**	**0.00**

NCAA Championship All-Tournament Team (2001)

Signed as a free agent by **Toronto**, July 6, 2007. Signed as a free agent by **New Jersey**, July 10, 2008.

CLOUTIER, Dan (KLOO-tyay, DAN)

Goaltender. Catches left. 6'1", 195 lbs. Born, Mont-Laurier, Que., April 22, 1976.
(NY Rangers' 1st choice, 26th overall, in 1994 Entry Draft).

			Regular Season								Playoffs						
Season	**Club**	**League**	**GP**	**W**	**L**	**O/T**	**Mins**	**GA**	**SO**	**Avg**	**GP**	**W**	**L**	**Mins**	**GA**	**SO**	**Avg**
1991-92	St. Thomas Stars	OJHL-B	14	....	....	....	823	80	0	5.83	....	....	....	....	....	....	....
1992-93	Timmins	NOJHA	5	4	0	0	255	10	0	2.35	....	....	....	....	....	....	....
	Sault Ste. Marie	OHL	12	4	6	0	572	44	0	4.62	4	1	2	231	12	0	3.12
1993-94	Sault Ste. Marie	OHL	55	28	14	6	2934	174	*2	3.56	14	*10	4	833	52	0	3.75
1994-95	Sault Ste. Marie	OHL	45	15	26	2	2518	185	1	4.41	....	....	....	....	....	....	....
1995-96	Sault Ste. Marie	OHL	13	9	3	0	641	43	0	4.02	....	....	....	....	....	....	....
	Guelph Storm	OHL	17	12	2	2	1004	35	2	2.09	16	11	5	993	52	*2	3.14
1996-97	Binghamton	AHL	60	23	28	8	3367	199	3	3.55	4	1	3	236	13	0	3.31
1997-98	**NY Rangers**	**NHL**	**12**	**4**	**5**	**1**	**551**	**23**	**0**	**2.50**	....	....	....	....	....	....	....
	Hartford Wolf Pack	AHL	24	12	8	3	1417	62	0	2.63	8	5	3	478	24	0	3.01
1998-99	**NY Rangers**	**NHL**	**22**	**6**	**8**	**3**	**1097**	**49**	**0**	**2.68**	....	....	....	....	....	....	....
99-2000	**Tampa Bay**	**NHL**	**52**	**9**	**30**	**3**	**2492**	**145**	**0**	**3.49**	....	....	....	....	....	....	....
2000-01	**Tampa Bay**	**NHL**	**24**	**3**	**13**	**3**	**1005**	**59**	**1**	**3.52**	....	....	....	....	....	....	....
	Detroit Vipers	IHL	1	0	1	0	59	3	0	3.05	....	....	....	....	....	....	....
	Vancouver	**NHL**	**16**	**4**	**6**	**5**	**914**	**37**	**0**	**2.43**	**2**	**0**	**2**	**117**	**9**	**0**	**4.62**
2001-02	**Vancouver**	**NHL**	**62**	**31**	**22**	**5**	**3502**	**142**	**7**	**2.43**	**6**	**2**	**3**	**273**	**16**	**0**	**3.52**
2002-03	**Vancouver**	**NHL**	**57**	**33**	**16**	**7**	**3376**	**136**	**2**	**2.42**	**14**	**7**	**7**	**833**	**45**	**0**	**3.24**
2003-04	**Vancouver**	**NHL**	**60**	**33**	**21**	**6**	**3539**	**134**	**5**	**2.27**	**3**	**1**	**1**	**138**	**5**	**0**	**2.17**
2004-05	Klagenfurter AC	Austria	13	7	0	5	772	25	1	1.94	10	6	4	590	27	1	2.75
2005-06	**Vancouver**	**NHL**	**13**	**8**	**3**	**1**	**681**	**36**	**0**	**3.17**	....	....	....	....	....	....	....
2006-07	**Los Angeles**	**NHL**	**24**	**6**	**14**	**2**	**1281**	**85**	**0**	**3.98**	....	....	....	....	....	....	....
2007-08	**Los Angeles**	**NHL**	**9**	**2**	**4**	**1**	**489**	**28**	**0**	**3.44**	....	....	....	....	....	....	....
	Manchester	AHL	14	4	9	0	719	42	0	3.50	....	....	....	....	....	....	....
	NHL Totals		**351**	**139**	**142**	**37**	**18927**	**874**	**15**	**2.77**	**25**	**10**	**13**	**1361**	**75**	**0**	**3.31**

OHL Second All-Star Team (1996) • AHL All-Rookie Team (1997)

Traded to **Tampa Bay** by **NY Rangers** with Niklas Sundstrom and NY Rangers' 1st (Nikita Alexeev) and 3rd (later traded to San Jose – later traded to Chicago – Chicago selected Igor Radulov) round choices in 2000 Entry Draft for Chicago's 1st round choice (previously acquired, NY Rangers selected Pavel Brendl) in 1999 Entry Draft, June 26, 1999. Traded to **Vancouver** by **Tampa Bay** for Adrian Aucoin and Vancouver's 2nd round choice (Alexander Polushin) in 2001 Entry Draft, February 7, 2001. Signed as a free agent by **Klagenfurter** (Austria), January 20, 2005. Traded to **Los Angeles** by **Vancouver** for Los Angeles' 2nd round choice (Taylor Ellington) in 2007 Entry Draft and Los Angeles' 3rd round choice in 2009 Entry Draft, July 5, 2006.

COLEMAN, Gerald (KOHL-man, JAIR-uhld)

Goaltender. Catches left. 6'4", 214 lbs. Born, Romeoville, IL, April 3, 1985.
(Tampa Bay's 5th choice, 224th overall, in 2003 Entry Draft).

			Regular Season								Playoffs						
Season	**Club**	**League**	**GP**	**W**	**L**	**O/T**	**Mins**	**GA**	**SO**	**Avg**	**GP**	**W**	**L**	**Mins**	**GA**	**SO**	**Avg**
99-2000	Chicago	MEHL	26	....	....	....	1560	65	0	2.50	....	....	....	....	....	....	....
2000-01	USNTDP	U-17	9	3	0	4	527	26	0	2.96	....	....	....	....	....	....	....
	USNTDP	NAHL	36	8	23	1	1859	132	0	4.26	....	....	....	....	....	....	....
2001-02	USNTDP	U-18	13	8	1	3	667	38	1	3.42	....	....	....	....	....	....	....
	USNTDP	USHL	2	1	1	0	76	4	0	3.15	....	....	....	....	....	....	....
	USNTDP	NAHL	22	5	14	2	1263	75	0	3.56	....	....	....	....	....	....	....
2002-03	London Knights	OHL	26	6	9	3	1074	59	1	3.30	....	....	....	....	....	....	....
2003-04	London Knights	OHL	33	24	8	0	1852	68	*5	2.20	8	5	2	442	19	1	2.58
2004-05	London Knights	OHL	38	*32	2	2	2224	63	*8	*1.70	8	7	1	455	13	0	*1.71
2005-06	**Tampa Bay**	**NHL**	**2**	**0**	**0**	**1**	**43**	**2**	**0**	**2.79**	....	....	....	....	....	....	....
	Springfield Falcons	AHL	43	14	21	3	2413	156	2	3.88	....	....	....	....	....	....	....
2006-07	Springfield Falcons	AHL	3	2	1	0	179	6	0	2.01	....	....	....	....	....	....	....
	Johnstown Chiefs	ECHL	17	7	9	0	914	52	0	3.41	....	....	....	....	....	....	....
	Portland Pirates	AHL	11	4	5	0	603	29	0	2.89	....	....	....	....	....	....	....
2007-08	Portland Pirates	AHL	18	8	7	1	968	47	2	2.91	1	0	0	39	4	0	6.09
	Augusta Lynx	ECHL	9	2	5	0	500	22	0	2.64	....	....	....	....	....	....	....
	NHL Totals		**2**	**0**	**0**	**1**	**43**	**2**	**0**	**2.79**	....	....	....	....	....	....	....

Traded to **Anaheim** by **Tampa Bay** with Tampa Bay's 1st round choice (later traded to Minnesota - Minnesota selected Colton Gillies) in 2007 Entry Draft for Shane O'Brien and Colorado's 3rd round choice (previously acquired, Tampa Bay selected Luca Cunti) in 2007 Entry Draft, February 24, 2007.

CONKLIN, Ty (KAWN-klihn, TIGH) DET.

Goaltender. Catches left. 6', 184 lbs. Born, Anchorage, AK, March 30, 1976.

			Regular Season								Playoffs						
Season	**Club**	**League**	**GP**	**W**	**L**	**O/T**	**Mins**	**GA**	**SO**	**Avg**	**GP**	**W**	**L**	**Mins**	**GA**	**SO**	**Avg**
1995-96	Green Bay	USHL	30	....	....	....	1727	82	1	2.85	....	....	....	....	....	....	....
1996-97	Alaska Anchorage	WCHA					DID NOT PLAY – FRESHMAN										
	Green Bay	USHL	30	19	7	1	1609	86	1	3.21	17	8	9	980	56	1	3.43
1997-98	New Hampshire	H-East					DID NOT PLAY – TRANSFERRED COLLEGES										
1998-99	New Hampshire	H-East	22	18	3	1	1338	41	0	*1.84	....	....	....	....	....	....	....
99-2000	New Hampshire	H-East	*37	*22	8	6	*2194	91	2	2.49	....	....	....	....	....	....	....
2000-01	New Hampshire	H-East	34	17	12	5	2048	70	*5	*2.05	....	....	....	....	....	....	....
2001-02	**Edmonton**	**NHL**	**4**	**2**	**0**	**0**	**148**	**4**	**0**	**1.62**	....	....	....	....	....	....	....
	Hamilton Bulldogs	AHL	37	13	12	8	2043	89	1	2.61	7	4	2	416	18	0	2.60
2002-03	Hamilton Bulldogs	AHL	38	19	13	3	2140	91	4	2.55	17	9	6	1024	38	1	2.23
2003-04	**Edmonton**	**NHL**	**38**	**17**	**14**	**4**	**2086**	**84**	**1**	**2.42**	....	....	....	....	....	....	....
2004-05	Wolfsburg	Germany	11	....	....	....	623	31	0	2.99	7	....	....	414	11	2	1.59
2005-06	**Edmonton**	**NHL**	**18**	**8**	**5**	**1**	**922**	**43**	**1**	**2.80**	**1**	**0**	**1**	**6**	**1**	**0**	**10.00**
	Hamilton Bulldogs	AHL	3	1	2	0	152	8	0	3.17	....	....	....	....	....	....	....
	Hartford Wolf Pack	AHL	2	1	0	1	130	5	0	2.31	....	....	....	....	....	....	....
2006-07	**Columbus**	**NHL**	**11**	**2**	**3**	**2**	**491**	**27**	**0**	**3.30**	....	....	....	....	....	....	....
	Syracuse Crunch	AHL	19	3	12	3	1085	60	0	3.32	....	....	....	....	....	....	....
	Buffalo	**NHL**	**5**	**1**	**2**	**0**	**227**	**13**	**0**	**3.44**	....	....	....	....	....	....	....
2007-08	**Pittsburgh**	**NHL**	**33**	**18**	**8**	**5**	**1866**	**78**	**2**	**2.51**	....	....	....	....	....	....	....
	Wilkes-Barre	AHL	18	11	7	0	1058	39	2	2.21	....	....	....	....	....	....	....
	NHL Totals		**109**	**48**	**32**	**12**	**5740**	**249**	**4**	**2.60**	**1**	**0**	**1**	**6**	**1**	**0**	**10.00**

USHL Second All-Star Team (1996) • Hockey East All-Rookie Team (1999) • Hockey East Second All-Star Team (1999) • Hockey East First All-Star Team (2000, 2001) • Hockey East Player of the Year (2000) (co-winner - Mike Mottau) • NCAA East Second All-American Team (2000) • NCAA East First All-American Team (2001)

• Left **Alaska-Anchorage** (WCHA) and returned to **Green Bay** (USHL), November 14, 1996. Signed as a free agent by **Edmonton**, April 18, 2001. Signed as a free agent by **Wolfsburg** (Germany), January 25, 2005. Loaned to **Hartford** (AHL) by **Edmonton**, March 8, 2006. Signed as a free agent by **Columbus**, July 6, 2006. Traded to **Buffalo** by **Columbus** for Buffalo's 5th round choice (later traded to Dallas - Dallas selected Michael Neal) in 2007 Entry Draft, February 27, 2007. Signed as a free agent by **Pittsburgh**, July 19, 2007. Signed as a free agent by **Detroit**, July 1, 2008.

COURCHAINE, Adam (KOOR-shayn, A-duhm) BOS.

Goaltender. Catches left. 6'2", 181 lbs. Born, Calgary, Alta., February 20, 1989.

			Regular Season								Playoffs						
Season	**Club**	**League**	**GP**	**W**	**L**	**O/T**	**Mins**	**GA**	**SO**	**Avg**	**GP**	**W**	**L**	**Mins**	**GA**	**SO**	**Avg**
2006-07	Orleans Blues	CJHL	39	19	11	5	2285	119	1	3.12	6	2	2	372	16	0	2.58
2007-08	Ottawa 67's	OHL	48	17	25	4	2813	152	2	3.24	4	0	4	158	12	0	4.56
	Providence Bruins	AHL	3	2	0	0	144	4	0	1.67	....	....	....	....	....	....	....

Signed as a free agent by **Boston**, September 30, 2007.

COUSINEAU, Marco (KOO-zih-noh, MAHR-koh) ANA.

Goaltender. Catches left. 6', 195 lbs. Born, St.Lazare, Que., November 9, 1989.
(Anaheim's 6th choice, 83rd overall, in 2008 Entry Draft).

			Regular Season								Playoffs						
Season	**Club**	**League**	**GP**	**W**	**L**	**O/T**	**Mins**	**GA**	**SO**	**Avg**	**GP**	**W**	**L**	**Mins**	**GA**	**SO**	**Avg**
2006-07	Baie-Comeau	QMJHL	23	4	12	....	1015	71	0	4.20	1	0	0	10	2	0	11.88
2007-08	Baie-Comeau	QMJHL	58	34	19	....	3227	151	4	2.81	5	1	4	305	11	0	*2.17

QMJHL Second All-Star Team (2008)

CRAWFORD, Corey (KRAW-fohrd, KOH-ree) CHI.

Goaltender. Catches left. 6'2", 183 lbs. Born, Montreal, Que., December 31, 1984.
(Chicago's 2nd choice, 52nd overall, in 2003 Entry Draft).

			Regular Season								Playoffs						
Season	**Club**	**League**	**GP**	**W**	**L**	**O/T**	**Mins**	**GA**	**SO**	**Avg**	**GP**	**W**	**L**	**Mins**	**GA**	**SO**	**Avg**
2000-01	Gatineau Intrepide	QAAA	21	17	3	1	1260	40	2	1.92	....	....	....	....	....	....	....
2001-02	Moncton Wildcats	QMJHL	38	9	20	3	1863	116	1	3.74	....	....	....	....	....	....	....
2002-03	Moncton Wildcats	QMJHL	50	24	17	6	2855	130	2	2.73	6	2	3	303	20	0	3.97
2003-04	Moncton Wildcats	QMJHL	54	*35	15	3	3019	132	2	2.62	*20	*13	6	*1170	42	0	2.15
2004-05	Moncton Wildcats	QMJHL	51	28	16	6	2942	121	*6	2.47	12	6	6	725	33	*1	2.73
2005-06	**Chicago**	**NHL**	**2**	**0**	**0**	**1**	**86**	**5**	**0**	**3.49**	....	....	....	....	....	....	....
	Norfolk Admirals	AHL	48	22	23	1	2734	134	1	2.94	1	0	0	17	1	0	3.49
2006-07	Norfolk Admirals	AHL	60	38	20	2	3467	164	1	2.84	6	2	4	363	20	0	3.31
2007-08	**Chicago**	**NHL**	**5**	**1**	**2**	**0**	**224**	**8**	**1**	**2.14**	....	....	....	....	....	....	....
	Rockford IceHogs	AHL	55	29	19	5	3028	143	3	2.83	12	7	5	741	27	0	2.19
	NHL Totals		**7**	**1**	**2**	**1**	**310**	**13**	**1**	**2.52**	....	....	....	....	....	....	....

QMJHL Second All-Star Team (2004, 2005)

CURRY, John (KUH-ree, JAWN) PIT.

Goaltender. Catches left. 5'11", 185 lbs. Born, Shorewood, MN, February 27, 1984.

			Regular Season								Playoffs						
Season	**Club**	**League**	**GP**	**W**	**L**	**O/T**	**Mins**	**GA**	**SO**	**Avg**	**GP**	**W**	**L**	**Mins**	**GA**	**SO**	**Avg**
2003-04	Boston University	H-East	1	0	0	0	5	0	0	0.00	....	....	....	....	....	....	....
2004-05	Boston University	H-East	33	18	11	3	1950	64	3	1.97	....	....	....	....	....	....	....
2005-06	Boston University	H-East	37	24	8	4	2166	81	3	2.24	....	....	....	....	....	....	....
2006-07	Boston University	H-East	36	17	10	8	2154	72	7	2.01	....	....	....	....	....	....	....
2007-08	Wilkes-Barre	AHL	40	24	12	3	2343	87	3	2.23	23	14	9	1358	64	1	2.83
	Las Vegas	ECHL	6	4	1	0	342	16	0	2.81	....	....	....	....	....	....	....
	Wheeling Nailers	ECHL	1	0	1	0	60	4	0	4.00	....	....	....	....	....	....	....

NCAA East Second All-American Team (2006) • NCAA East First All-American Team (2007)

Signed as a free agent by **Pittsburgh**, July 13, 2007.

DAIGNEAULT, Maxime (DAYN-yoh, max-EEM)

Goaltender. Catches left. 6'3", 202 lbs. Born, St-Jacques-le-Mineur, Que., January 23, 1984.
(Washington's 4th choice, 59th overall, in 2002 Entry Draft).

			Regular Season								Playoffs						
Season	**Club**	**League**	**GP**	**W**	**L**	**O/T**	**Mins**	**GA**	**SO**	**Avg**	**GP**	**W**	**L**	**Mins**	**GA**	**SO**	**Avg**
99-2000	Magog	QAAA	19	12	3	3	1108	53	3	2.87	18	12	5	945	42	1	2.67
2000-01	Val-d'Or Foreurs	QMJHL	28	14	8	1	1386	82	0	3.55	10	8	1	504	21	0	2.50
2001-02	Val-d'Or Foreurs	QMJHL	61	25	27	5	3270	184	3	3.38	7	3	4	431	23	0	3.20
2002-03	Val-d'Or Foreurs	QMJHL	48	23	18	3	2694	138	2	3.07	8	4	3	487	23	1	2.83
2003-04	Val-d'Or Foreurs	QMJHL	57	23	22	9	3250	158	2	2.92	7	3	4	416	16	0	2.31
2004-05	Portland Pirates	AHL	11	3	2	1	474	23	0	2.91	....	....	....	....	....	....	....
	South Carolina	ECHL	21	11	6	1	1172	59	1	3.02	....	....	....	....	....	....	....
2005-06	South Carolina	ECHL	38	16	12	9	2172	117	1	3.23	....	....	....	....	....	....	....
	Hershey Bears	AHL	3	0	1	2	190	7	0	2.21	....	....	....	....	....	....	....
2006-07	Hershey Bears	AHL	33	23	6	0	1815	80	3	2.64	....	....	....	....	....	....	....
2007-08	Milwaukee	AHL	9	4	5	0	474	20	2	2.53	....	....	....	....	....	....	....
	Cincinnati	ECHL	14	11	3	0	826	36	1	2.62	7	5	1	390	18	0	2.77

Memorial Cup Tournament All-Star Team (2002) • Hap Emms Memorial Trophy (Memorial Cup Tournament - Top Goaltender) (2002)

DAKERS, Taylor (DAK-uhrs, TAY-luhr) S.J.

Goaltender. Catches left. 6'1", 175 lbs. Born, Richmond, B.C., September 14, 1986.
(San Jose's 4th choice, 140th overall, in 2005 Entry Draft).

			Regular Season								Playoffs						
Season	**Club**	**League**	**GP**	**W**	**L**	**O/T**	**Mins**	**GA**	**SO**	**Avg**	**GP**	**W**	**L**	**Mins**	**GA**	**SO**	**Avg**
2002-03	Columbia Valley	KIJHL	37	....	....	....	2077	93	4	2.68	....	....	....	....	....	....	....
2003-04	Kootenay Ice	WHL	19	6	10	0	856	48	1	3.36	....	....	....	....	....	....	....
2004-05	Kootenay Ice	WHL	23	13	7	2	1303	44	4	2.03	....	....	....	....	....	....	....
2005-06	Kootenay Ice	WHL	47	30	15	1	2671	94	8	2.11	6	2	4	378	23	0	3.65
2006-07	Kootenay Ice	WHL	48	33	10	4	2831	102	5	2.16	7	3	4	429	18	1	2.52
2007-08	Worcester Sharks	AHL	22	7	11	1	1226	64	0	3.13	....	....	....	....	....	....	....
	Phoenix	ECHL	15	6	7	2	899	35	0	2.34	....	....	....	....	....	....	....

WHL East Second All-Star Team (2007)

DANIS, Yann (DA-nihs, YAN) NYI

Goaltender. Catches left. 6', 181 lbs. Born, Lafontaine, Que., June 21, 1981.

			Regular Season								Playoffs						
Season	**Club**	**League**	**GP**	**W**	**L**	**O/T**	**Mins**	**GA**	**SO**	**Avg**	**GP**	**W**	**L**	**Mins**	**GA**	**SO**	**Avg**
99-2000	St-Jerome	QJHL					STATISTICS NOT AVAILABLE										
	Cornwall Colts	CJHL	26	....	....	....	1367	71	0	3.12	....	....	....	....	....	....	....
2000-01	Brown U.	ECAC	12	2	8	1	667	40	0	3.60	....	....	....	....	....	....	....
2001-02	Brown U.	ECAC	24	11	10	2	1451	45	3	1.86	....	....	....	....	....	....	....
2002-03	Brown U.	ECAC	*34	15	14	5	*2074	80	5	2.31	....	....	....	....	....	....	....

2003-04	Brown U.	ECAC	30	15	11	4	1821	55	*5	*1.81	....	....	....	....	....	....	....
	Hamilton Bulldogs	AHL	2	2	0	0	120	3	1	1.50	1	0	0	12	0	0	0.00
2004-05	Hamilton Bulldogs	AHL	53	28	17	6	3075	120	5	2.34	4	0	4	237	13	0	3.29
2005-06	**Montreal**	**NHL**	**6**	**3**	**2**	**0**	**312**	**14**	**1**	**2.69**	....	....	....	....	....	....	....
	Hamilton Bulldogs	AHL	39	17	17	3	2242	111	0	2.97	....	....	....	....	....	....	....
2006-07	Hamilton Bulldogs	AHL	44	23	14	5	2540	119	1	2.81	1	1	0	54	1	0	1.12
2007-08	Hamilton Bulldogs	AHL	38	11	19	4	2064	113	0	3.28	....	....	....	....	....	....	....
	NHL Totals		**6**	**3**	**2**	**0**	**312**	**14**	**1**	**2.69**	....	....	....	....	....	....	....

ECAC Second All-Star Team (2002, 2003) • ECAC First All-Star Team (2004) • ECAC Goaltender of the Year (2004) • ECAC Player of the Year (2004) • NCAA East First All-American Team (2004)

Signed as a free agent by **Montreal**, March 19, 2004. Signed as a free agent by **NY Islanders**, July 2, 2008.

DARLING, Scott (DAHR-lihng, SKAWT) PHX.

Goaltender. Catches left. 6'6", 190 lbs. Born, Lemont, IL, December 22, 1988.
(Phoenix's 7th choice, 153rd overall, in 2007 Entry Draft).

			Regular Season								Playoffs						
Season	**Club**	**League**	**GP**	**W**	**L**	**O/T**	**Mins**	**GA**	**SO**	**Avg**	**GP**	**W**	**L**	**Mins**	**GA**	**SO**	**Avg**
2005-06	Chicago	MWEHL	2	0	2	0	120	10	0	5.00	....	....	....	....	....	....	....
	North Iowa	NAHL	8	2	4	0	405	28	0	4.15	....	....	....	....	....	....	....
2006-07	Capital District	EJHL	22	9	9	3	1243	70	1	3.38	....	....	....	....	....	....	....
	North Iowa	NAHL	1	0	0	0	15	3	0	12.00	....	....	....	....	....	....	....
2007-08	Indiana Ice	USHL	42	27	10	2	2391	121	1	3.04	3	1	2	179	11	0	3.69

• Signed Letter of Intent to attend **University of Maine** (Hockey East) in fall of 2008.

DEKANICH, Mark (deh-KAN-ihch, MAHRK) NSH.

Goaltender. Catches left. 6'2", 196 lbs. Born, N. Vancouver, B.C., May 10, 1986.
(Nashville's 3rd choice, 146th overall, in 2006 Entry Draft).

			Regular Season								Playoffs						
Season	**Club**	**League**	**GP**	**W**	**L**	**O/T**	**Mins**	**GA**	**SO**	**Avg**	**GP**	**W**	**L**	**Mins**	**GA**	**SO**	**Avg**
2003-04	Coquitlam Express	BCHL	30	13	15	1	1647	89	2	3.24	....	....	....	....	....	....	....
2004-05	Colgate	ECAC	5	1	1	0	162	5	0	1.85	....	....	....	....	....	....	....
2005-06	Colgate	ECAC	36	18	11	6	2126	81	4	2.29	....	....	....	....	....	....	....
2006-07	Colgate	ECAC	36	15	17	4	2136	83	1	2.33	....	....	....	....	....	....	....
2007-08	Colgate	ECAC	*41	18	16	6	*2389	86	*6	2.16	....	....	....	....	....	....	....

ECAC First All-Star Team (2006) • ECAC Second All-Star Team (2007)

DELMAS, Peter (DEHL-mas, PEE-tuhr) COL.

Goaltender. Catches left. 6'2", 169 lbs. Born, Alliston, Ont., February 16, 1990.
(Colorado's 2nd choice, 61st overall, in 2008 Entry Draft).

			Regular Season								Playoffs						
Season	**Club**	**League**	**GP**	**W**	**L**	**O/T**	**Mins**	**GA**	**SO**	**Avg**	**GP**	**W**	**L**	**Mins**	**GA**	**SO**	**Avg**
2006-07	Lewiston	QMJHL	34	23	10	....	1983	93	3	2.81	....	....	....	....	....	....	....
2007-08	Lewiston	QMJHL	34	17	17	....	1987	94	0	2.84	....	....	....	....	....	....	....

DENIS, Marc (deh-NEE, MAHRK) MTL.

Goaltender. Catches left. 6'1", 193 lbs. Born, Montreal, Que., August 1, 1977.
(Colorado's 1st choice, 25th overall, in 1995 Entry Draft).

			Regular Season								Playoffs						
Season	**Club**	**League**	**GP**	**W**	**L**	**O/T**	**Mins**	**GA**	**SO**	**Avg**	**GP**	**W**	**L**	**Mins**	**GA**	**SO**	**Avg**
1992-93	Montreal-Bourassa	QAAA	26	....	....	....	1559	74	5	2.87	....	....	....	....	....	....	....
1993-94	Trois-Rivieres	QAAA	36	10	22	3	2093	158	0	4.53	4	1	3	249	20	0	4.83
1994-95	Chicoutimi	QMJHL	32	17	9	1	1688	98	0	3.48	6	4	2	372	19	1	3.06
1995-96	Chicoutimi	QMJHL	51	23	21	4	2951	157	2	3.19	16	8	8	957	69	0	4.33
1996-97	Chicoutimi	QMJHL	41	22	15	2	2323	104	4	*2.69	*21	*11	10	*1229	70	*1	3.42
	Colorado	**NHL**	**1**	**0**	**1**	**0**	**60**	**3**	**0**	**3.00**	....	....	....	....	....	....	....
	Hershey Bears	AHL	....	....	....	....	....	....	....	....	4	1	0	56	1	0	1.08
1997-98	Hershey Bears	AHL	47	17	23	4	2588	125	1	2.90	6	3	3	346	15	0	2.59
1998-99	**Colorado**	**NHL**	**4**	**1**	**1**	**1**	**217**	**9**	**0**	**2.49**	....	....	....	....	....	....	....
	Hershey Bears	AHL	52	20	23	5	2908	137	4	2.83	3	1	1	143	7	0	2.93
99-2000	**Colorado**	**NHL**	**23**	**9**	**8**	**3**	**1203**	**51**	**3**	**2.54**	....	....	....	....	....	....	....
2000-01	**Columbus**	**NHL**	**32**	**6**	**20**	**4**	**1830**	**99**	**0**	**3.25**	....	....	....	....	....	....	....
2001-02	**Columbus**	**NHL**	**42**	**9**	**24**	**5**	**2335**	**121**	**1**	**3.11**	....	....	....	....	....	....	....
2002-03	**Columbus**	**NHL**	***77**	**27**	**41**	**8**	***4511**	**232**	**5**	**3.09**	....	....	....	....	....	....	....
2003-04	**Columbus**	**NHL**	**66**	**21**	**36**	**7**	**3796**	**162**	**5**	**2.56**	....	....	....	....	....	....	....
2004-05							DID NOT PLAY										
2005-06	**Columbus**	**NHL**	**49**	**21**	**25**	**1**	**2786**	**151**	**1**	**3.25**	....	....	....	....	....	....	....
2006-07	**Tampa Bay**	**NHL**	**44**	**17**	**18**	**2**	**2353**	**125**	**1**	**3.19**	....	....	....	....	....	....	....
2007-08	**Tampa Bay**	**NHL**	**10**	**1**	**5**	**0**	**415**	**28**	**0**	**4.05**	....	....	....	....	....	....	....
	Norfolk Admirals	AHL	32	11	17	2	1832	89	1	2.91	....	....	....	....	....	....	....
	NHL Totals		**348**	**112**	**179**	**31**	**19506**	**981**	**16**	**3.02**	....	....	....	....	....	....	....

QMJHL First All-Star Team (1997) • Canadian Major Junior First All-Star Team (1997) • Canadian Major Junior Goaltender of the Year (1997)

Traded to **Columbus** by **Colorado** for Columbus' 2nd round choice (later traded to Carolina – Carolina selected Tomas Kurka) in 2000 Entry Draft, June 7, 2000. Traded to **Tampa Bay** by **Columbus** for Fredrik Modin and Fredrik Norrena, June 30, 2006. Signed as a free agent by **Montreal**, July 3, 2008.

DENNIS, Adam (DEH-nihs, A-duhm) BUF.

Goaltender. Catches left. 5'11", 182 lbs. Born, Toronto, Ont., February 8, 1985.
(Buffalo's 6th choice, 182nd overall, in 2005 Entry Draft).

			Regular Season								Playoffs						
Season	**Club**	**League**	**GP**	**W**	**L**	**O/T**	**Mins**	**GA**	**SO**	**Avg**	**GP**	**W**	**L**	**Mins**	**GA**	**SO**	**Avg**
2002-03	Guelph Storm	OHL	18	6	7	1	846	45	0	3.19	....	....	....	....	....	....	....
2003-04	Guelph Storm	OHL	46	*33	10	2	2662	111	3	2.50	20	*15	5	1205	40	1	*1.99
2004-05	Guelph Storm	OHL	23	5	11	6	1372	57	3	2.49	....	....	....	....	....	....	....
	London Knights	OHL	16	12	4	0	920	23	3	1.50	11	9	1	629	22	*2	2.10
2005-06	London Knights	OHL	57	*44	9	4	*3444	162	1	2.82	18	12	6	1090	59	0	3.25
2006-07	Rochester	AHL	35	18	17	0	2068	115	1	3.34	....	....	....	....	....	....	....
2007-08	Rochester	AHL	46	17	26	2	2601	138	3	3.18	....	....	....	....	....	....	....

OHL First All-Star Team (2005, 2006) • Memorial Cup Tournament All-Star Team (2005) • Hap Emms Memorial Trophy (Memorial Cup Tournament - Top Goaltender) (2005)

DESERRES, Jacob (deh-SAIR, JAY-kawb) PHI.

Goaltender. Catches left. 6'2", 195 lbs. Born, East York, Ont., March 18, 1990.
(Philadelphia's 3rd choice, 84th overall, in 2008 Entry Draft).

			Regular Season								Playoffs						
Season	**Club**	**League**	**GP**	**W**	**L**	**O/T**	**Mins**	**GA**	**SO**	**Avg**	**GP**	**W**	**L**	**Mins**	**GA**	**SO**	**Avg**
2005-06	Calgary Buffaloes	AMHL	21	11	7	3	1246	55	....	2.65	11	9	2	698	19	....	1.63
	Seattle	WHL	3	3	0	0	183	5	0	1.64	....	....	....	....	....	....	....
2006-07	Seattle	WHL	20	7	9	2	1076	50	3	2.79	2	0	0	31	4	0	7.67
2007-08	Seattle	WHL	34	20	11	0	1972	75	3	2.28	5	1	2	208	10	0	2.88

DESJARDINS, Cedric (deh-ZHAHR-dai, sEH-DRIHK) MTL.

Goaltender. Catches left. 6', 183 lbs. Born, Edmunston, NB, September 30, 1985.

			Regular Season								Playoffs						
Season	**Club**	**League**	**GP**	**W**	**L**	**O/T**	**Mins**	**GA**	**SO**	**Avg**	**GP**	**W**	**L**	**Mins**	**GA**	**SO**	**Avg**
2002-03	Coaticook	QJHL					STATISTICS NOT AVAILABLE										
	Rimouski Oceanic	QMJHL	23	1	19	0	1239	109	0	5.28	....	....	....	....	....	....	....
2003-04	Rimouski Oceanic	QMJHL	20	8	11	0	1119	72	0	3.86	1	0	0	14	0	0	0.00
2004-05	Rimouski Oceanic	QMJHL	44	*30	7	4	2439	120	2	2.95	13	*12	1	*767	34	*1	2.66
2005-06	Quebec Remparts	QMJHL	41	28	10	0	2254	111	*5	2.95	*23	14	9	*1413	60	1	2.55
2006-07	Cincinnati	ECHL	45	24	19	1	2648	112	4	2.54	....	....	....	....	....	....	....
	Hamilton Bulldogs	AHL	3	0	2	0	142	7	0	2.96	....	....	....	....	....	....	....
2007-08	Hamilton Bulldogs	AHL	12	4	3	2	572	29	0	3.04	....	....	....	....	....	....	....
	Cincinnati	ECHL	22	16	4	2	1285	41	*5	1.91	16	11	4	947	29	1	*1.83

Memorial Cup Tournament All-Star Team (2006) • Hap Emms Memorial Trophy (Memorial Cup Tournament - Top Goaltender) (2006) • ECHL All-Rookie-Team (2007)

Signed as a free agent by **Hamilton** (AHL), July 26, 2006. Signed as a free agent by **Montreal**, July 3, 2008.

DiPIETRO, Rick (dee-pee-EHT-roh, RIHK) NYI

Goaltender. Catches right. 6'1", 210 lbs. Born, Winthrop, MA, September 19, 1981.
(NY Islanders' 1st choice, 1st overall, in 2000 Entry Draft).

			Regular Season								Playoffs						
Season	**Club**	**League**	**GP**	**W**	**L**	**O/T**	**Mins**	**GA**	**SO**	**Avg**	**GP**	**W**	**L**	**Mins**	**GA**	**SO**	**Avg**
1997-98	USNTDP	U-17	10	6	4	0	800	31	0	2.33	....	....	....	....	....	....	....
	USNTDP	USHL	3	0	2	0	117	8	0	4.09	....	....	....	....	....	....	....
	USNTDP	NAHL	30	13	12	0	1602	85	1	3.18	3	2	1	179	7	1	2.35
1998-99	USNTDP	U-18	16	9	5	1	1027	46	....	2.69	....	....	....	....	....	....	....
	USNTDP	USHL	30	22	6	1	1733	67	3	2.32	....	....	....	....	....	....	....
99-2000	Boston University	H-East	29	18	5	5	1790	73	2	2.45	....	....	....	....	....	....	....
2000-01	**NY Islanders**	**NHL**	**20**	**3**	**15**	**1**	**1083**	**63**	**0**	**3.49**	....	....	....	....	....	....	....
	Chicago Wolves	IHL	14	4	5	2	778	44	0	3.39	....	....	....	....	....	....	....
2001-02	Bridgeport	AHL	59	*30	22	7	3472	134	4	2.32	20	12	8	*1270	45	*3	2.13
2002-03	**NY Islanders**	**NHL**	**10**	**2**	**5**	**2**	**585**	**29**	**0**	**2.97**	**1**	**0**	**0**	**15**	**0**	**0**	**0.00**
	Bridgeport	AHL	34	16	10	8	2044	73	3	2.14	5	2	3	299	10	1	2.01
2003-04	**NY Islanders**	**NHL**	**50**	**23**	**18**	**5**	**2844**	**112**	**5**	**2.36**	**5**	**1**	**4**	**303**	**11**	**1**	**2.18**
	Bridgeport	AHL	2	0	2	0	119	3	0	1.51	....	....	....	....	....	....	....
2004-05								DID NOT PLAY									
2005-06	**NY Islanders**	**NHL**	**63**	**30**	**24**	**5**	**3572**	**180**	**1**	**3.02**	....	....	....	....	....	....	....
	United States	Olympics	4	1	3	0	237	9	0	2.28	....	....	....	....	....	....	....
2006-07	**NY Islanders**	**NHL**	**62**	**32**	**19**	**9**	**3627**	**156**	**5**	**2.58**	**4**	**1**	**3**	**236**	**13**	**0**	**3.31**
2007-08	**NY Islanders**	**NHL**	**63**	**26**	**28**	**7**	**3707**	**174**	**3**	**2.82**	....	....	....	....	....	....	....
	NHL Totals		**268**	**116**	**109**	**29**	**15418**	**714**	**14**	**2.78**	**10**	**2**	**7**	**554**	**24**	**1**	**2.60**

Hockey East Second All-Star Team (2000) • Hockey East Rookie of the Year (2000)

Played in NHL All-Star Game (2008)

DOYLE, Frank (DOIL, FRANK)

Goaltender. Catches left. 6'1", 185 lbs. Born, Guelph, Ont., September 8, 1980.

			Regular Season								Playoffs						
Season	**Club**	**League**	**GP**	**W**	**L**	**O/T**	**Mins**	**GA**	**SO**	**Avg**	**GP**	**W**	**L**	**Mins**	**GA**	**SO**	**Avg**
2000-01	Cambridge	OHA-B	32	....	....	....	....	....	4	2.94	....	....	....	....	....	....	....
2001-02	University of Maine	H-East					DID NOT PLAY – FRESHMAN										
2002-03	University of Maine	H-East	21	10	4	5	1180	42	2	*2.14	....	....	....	....	....	....	....
2003-04	University of Maine	H-East	23	19	4	0	1325	40	5	1.81	....	....	....	....	....	....	....
2004-05	Utah Grizzlies	AHL	1	0	1	0	20	3	0	9.00	....	....	....	....	....	....	....
	Idaho Steelheads	ECHL	52	*32	13	4	2938	106	4	2.16	3	1	2	169	12	0	4.26
2005-06	Albany River Rats	AHL	58	21	33	3	3413	176	1	3.09	....	....	....	....	....	....	....
2006-07	Lowell Devils	AHL	49	20	24	4	2907	124	1	2.56	....	....	....	....	....	....	....
2007-08	Lowell Devils	AHL	48	14	29	4	2793	142	1	3.05	....	....	....	....	....	....	....

Signed as a free agent by **New Jersey**, August 12, 2005.

DROUIN-DESLAURIERS, Jeff (droo-EHN-duh-LAW-ree-yay, JEHF) EDM.

Goaltender. Catches right. 6'4", 189 lbs. Born, St-Jean-Richelieu, Que., May 15, 1984.
(Edmonton's 2nd choice, 31st overall, in 2002 Entry Draft).

			Regular Season								Playoffs						
Season	**Club**	**League**	**GP**	**W**	**L**	**O/T**	**Mins**	**GA**	**SO**	**Avg**	**GP**	**W**	**L**	**Mins**	**GA**	**SO**	**Avg**
2000-01	Gatineau Intrepide	QAAA	22	10	9	2	1194	61	2	3.07	2	1	0	125	6	0	2.89
2001-02	Chicoutimi	QMJHL	51	28	20	1	2909	170	1	3.51	4	0	3	197	20	0	6.11
2002-03	Chicoutimi	QMJHL	54	18	24	1	2582	164	0	3.81	4	0	4	240	15	0	9.00
2003-04	Chicoutimi	QMJHL	50	21	20	6	2701	129	1	2.87	18	10	8	956	50	1	3.14
2004-05	Edmonton	AHL	22	6	13	2	1258	62	0	2.96	....	....	....	....	....	....	....
	Greenville Grrrowl	ECHL	11	7	3	1	673	26	1	2.32	....	....	....	....	....	....	....
2005-06	Hamilton Bulldogs	AHL	13	4	7	0	666	35	0	3.15	....	....	....	....	....	....	....
	Greenville Grrrowl	ECHL	6	2	4	0	335	17	0	3.05	....	....	....	....	....	....	....
2006-07	Wilkes-Barre	AHL	40	22	12	3	2231	92	4	2.47	....	....	....	....	....	....	....
2007-08	Springfield Falcons	AHL	57	26	23	5	3045	147	0	2.90	....	....	....	....	....	....	....

QMJHL All-Rookie Team (2002)

DUBIELEWICZ, Wade (DOO-bih-wihtz, WAYD)

Goaltender. Catches left. 5'10", 185 lbs. Born, Invermere, B.C., January 30, 1978.

			Regular Season								Playoffs						
Season	**Club**	**League**	**GP**	**W**	**L**	**O/T**	**Mins**	**GA**	**SO**	**Avg**	**GP**	**W**	**L**	**Mins**	**GA**	**SO**	**Avg**
1997-98	Trail Smoke Eaters	BCHL	41	....	....	....	2225	118	0	3.18	....	....	....	....	....	....	....
1998-99	Trail Smoke Eaters	BCHL					STATISTICS NOT AVAILABLE										
	Chilliwack Chiefs	BCHL	14	10	4	0	834	....	0	....	....	....	....	....	....	....	....
99-2000	U. of Denver	WCHA	13	3	5	1	596	27	1	2.72	....	....	....	....	....	....	....
2000-01	U. of Denver	WCHA	29	12	9	3	1542	59	2	2.30	....	....	....	....	....	....	....
2001-02	U. of Denver	WCHA	24	20	4	0	1431	41	2	*1.72	....	....	....	....	....	....	....
2002-03	U. of Denver	WCHA	19	9	8	2	1060	43	3	2.43	....	....	....	....	....	....	....
2003-04	**NY Islanders**	**NHL**	**2**	**1**	**0**	**1**	**105**	**3**	**0**	**1.71**	....	....	....	....	....	....	....
	Bridgeport	AHL	33	20	8	5	1959	45	9	*1.38	3	2	1	181	11	0	3.64
2004-05	Bridgeport	AHL	43	18	23	1	2539	113	1	2.67	....	....	....	....	....	....	....
2005-06	**NY Islanders**	**NHL**	**7**	**2**	**3**	**0**	**310**	**15**	**0**	**2.90**	....	....	....	....	....	....	....
	Bridgeport	AHL	46	20	21	2	2575	134	3	3.12	7	3	4	435	16	0	2.21
2006-07	**NY Islanders**	**NHL**	**8**	**4**	**1**	**0**	**379**	**13**	**0**	**2.06**	**1**	**0**	**1**	**59**	**4**	**0**	**4.07**
	Bridgeport	AHL	40	22	12	5	2405	108	2	2.69	....	....	....	....	....	....	....
2007-08	**NY Islanders**	**NHL**	**20**	**9**	**9**	**1**	**1132**	**51**	**0**	**2.70**	....	....	....	....	....	....	....
	Bridgeport	AHL	2	1	1	0	124	5	0	2.42	....	....	....	....	....	....	....
	NHL Totals		**37**	**16**	**13**	**2**	**1926**	**82**	**0**	**2.55**	**1**	**0**	**1**	**59**	**4**	**0**	**4.07**

WCHA Second All-Star Team (2001, 2003) • WCHA First All-Star Team (2002) • AHL All-Rookie Team (2004) • AHL Second All-Star Team (2004) • Dudley "Red" Garrett Memorial Award (Rookie of the Year - AHL) (2004) • Harry "Hap" Holmes Memorial Award (fewest goals against - AHL) (2004) (shared with Dieter Kochan)

Signed as a free agent by **NY Islanders**, May 25, 2003.

DUBNYK, Devan (DUHN-nihk, DEH-vuhn) EDM.

Goaltender. Catches left. 6'5", 194 lbs. Born, Regina, Sask., May 4, 1986.
(Edmonton's 1st choice, 14th overall, in 2004 Entry Draft).

			Regular Season								Playoffs						
Season	Club	League	GP	W	L	O/T	Mins	GA	SO	Avg	GP	W	L	Mins	GA	SO	Avg
2000-01	Calgary Bruins	CBHL	14	....	....	....	815	39	2	3.10	....	....	....	....	....	....	....
2001-02	Titaanit Kotka Jr.	Fin-Jr.	5	5	0	0	300	7	....	1.40	....	....	....	....	....	....	....
	Calgary Bruins	CBHL	18	7	9	2	1105	68	1	3.69	....	....	....	....	....	....	....
	Kamloops Blazers	WHL	3	1	1	0	143	13	0	5.45	....	....	....	....	....	....	....
2002-03	Kamloops Blazers	WHL	26	12	8	1	1279	68	2	3.19	....	....	....	....	....	....	....
2003-04	Kamloops Blazers	WHL	44	20	18	5	2533	106	6	2.51	4	1	3	245	12	0	2.94
2004-05	Kamloops Blazers	WHL	*65	23	34	7	3699	166	6	2.69	6	2	4	363	22	0	3.64
2005-06	Kamloops Blazers	WHL	54	27	26	1	3207	136	1	2.54	....	....	....	....	....	....	....
2006-07	Wilkes-Barre	AHL	4	2	1	0	204	10	0	2.94	....	....	....	....	....	....	....
	Stockton Thunder	ECHL	43	24	11	7	2529	108	2	2.56	6	2	4	395	18	0	2.73
2007-08	Springfield Falcons	AHL	33	9	17	0	1772	92	0	3.12	....	....	....	....	....	....	....

Canadian Major Junior Scholastic Player of the Year (2004)

DUCHESNE, Jeremy (DOO-shayn, JAIR-eh-mee) PHI.

Goaltender. Catches left. 6', 218 lbs. Born, Silver Spring, MD, October 17, 1986.
(Philadelphia's 3rd choice, 119th overall, in 2005 Entry Draft).

			Regular Season								Playoffs						
Season	Club	League	GP	W	L	O/T	Mins	GA	SO	Avg	GP	W	L	Mins	GA	SO	Avg
2002-03	St-Francois Blizzard	QAAA	26	7	11	5	1341	75	0	3.35	....	....	....	....	....	....	....
2003-04	Victoriaville Tigres	QMJHL	17	3	8	1	870	60	0	4.14	....	....	....	....	....	....	....
2004-05	Victoriaville Tigres	QMJHL	15	2	9	0	711	41	2	*3.46	....	....	....	....	....	....	....
	Halifax	QMJHL	18	12	0	2	921	23	3	*1.50	12	8	4	723	33	*1	2.74
2005-06	Halifax	QMJHL	55	25	29	0	3175	185	4	3.50	11	5	6	626	34	1	3.26
2006-07	Halifax	QMJHL	28	12	15	....	1580	97	1	3.68	....	....	....	....	....	....	....
	Val-d'Or Foreurs	QMJHL	24	13	10	....	1356	66	1	2.92	*18	11	7	*1157	56	0	2.90
2007-08	Philadelphia	AHL	2	1	0	0	80	6	0	4.50	....	....	....	....	....	....	....
	Dayton Bombers	ECHL	31	13	13	5	1838	91	1	2.97	....	....	....	....	....	....	....

DUNN, Dan (DUHN, DAN) WSH.

Goaltender. Catches left. 6'5", 200 lbs. Born, Oshawa, Ont., June 20, 1988.
(Washington's 7th choice, 154th overall, in 2007 Entry Draft).

			Regular Season								Playoffs						
Season	Club	League	GP	W	L	O/T	Mins	GA	SO	Avg	GP	W	L	Mins	GA	SO	Avg
2005-06	Oshawa	OPJHL	10	2	4	2	494	29	1	3.52	....	....	....	....	....	....	....
	Cobourg Cougars	OPJHL	6	0	5	0	277	33	0	7.14	....	....	....	....	....	....	....
2006-07	Wellington Dukes	OPJHL	27	19	4	2	1546	50	2	1.94	....	....	....	....	....	....	....
2007-08	St. Cloud State	WCHA	9	3	2	2	433	19	0	2.63	....	....	....	....	....	....	....

EHELECHNER, Patrick (eh-heh-LEHCH-nuhr, PAT-rihk) PIT.

Goaltender. Catches left. 6'2", 169 lbs. Born, Rosenheim, West Germany, September 23, 1984.
(San Jose's 5th choice, 139th overall, in 2003 Entry Draft).

			Regular Season								Playoffs						
Season	Club	League	GP	W	L	O/T	Mins	GA	SO	Avg	GP	W	L	Mins	GA	SO	Avg
2000-01	Jung. Mannheim	German-4	40	....	....	....	2423	171	2	4.23	....	....	....	....	....	....	....
2001-02	EV Landshut	German-3	2	....	....	....	130	6	0	2.77	....	....	....	....	....	....	....
	Hannover	Germany	8	....	....	....	475	24	0	3.03	....	....	....	....	....	....	....
2002-03	ESC Wedemark	German-4					STATISTICS NOT AVAILABLE										
	Hannover	Germany	4	....	....	....	162	16	0	5.90	....	....	....	....	....	....	....
2003-04	Sudbury Wolves	OHL	56	22	26	6	3089	148	3	2.87	7	2	4	390	14	2	2.15
2004-05	Sudbury Wolves	OHL	51	23	21	4	2997	128	3	2.56	10	4	5	497	29	0	3.50
2005-06	Adler Mannheim	Germany	1	....	....	....	59	5	0	5.02	....	....	....	....	....	....	....
	Fuchse Duisburg	Germany	26	....	....	....	1243	75	2	3.62	....	....	....	....	....	....	....
2006-07	Fuchse Duisburg	Germany	6	....	....	....	244	28	0	6.89	....	....	....	....	....	....	....
2007-08	Nurnberg	Germany	15	10	4	0	820	37	0	2.71	2	0	0	17	1	0	3.57

OHL Second All-Star Team (2004)

Signed as a free agent by **Mannheim** (Germany), April 25, 2005. Traded to **Pittsburgh** by **San Jose** with Nils Ekman for Carolina's 2nd round choice (previously acquired, later traded to Philadelphia - Philadelphia selected Kevin Marshall) in 2007 Entry Draft, July 20, 2006.

EIDSNESS, Bradley (IGHD-nehz, BRAD-lee) BUF.

Goaltender. Catches left. 5'11", 182 lbs. Born, Chestermere, Alta., June 2, 1989.
(Buffalo's 4th choice, 139th overall, in 2007 Entry Draft).

			Regular Season								Playoffs						
Season	Club	League	GP	W	L	O/T	Mins	GA	SO	Avg	GP	W	L	Mins	GA	SO	Avg
2005-06	Okotoks Oilers	AJHL	4	3	1	0	238	4	2	1.01	....	....	....	....	....	....	....
	Strathmore	AMHL	18	12	4	2	1046	45	....	2.58	8	5	3	512	14	....	1.64
2006-07	Okotoks Oilers	AJHL	48	24	18	2	2658	127	4	2.87	....	....	....	....	....	....	....
2007-08	Okotoks Oilers	AJHL	....	29	4	4	2264	80	3	2.12	9	4	5	547	25	0	2.74

ELLIOTT, Brian (EHL-lee-awt, BRIGH-uhn) OTT.

Goaltender. Catches left. 6'2", 200 lbs. Born, Newmarket, Ont., April 9, 1985.
(Ottawa's 9th choice, 291st overall, in 2003 Entry Draft).

			Regular Season								Playoffs						
Season	Club	League	GP	W	L	O/T	Mins	GA	SO	Avg	GP	W	L	Mins	GA	SO	Avg
2002-03	Ajax Axemen	OPJHL	39	....	....	....	2097	135	0	3.86	....	....	....	....	....	....	....
2003-04	U. of Wisconsin	WCHA	6	3	3	0	336	12	0	2.14	....	....	....	....	....	....	....
2004-05	U. of Wisconsin	WCHA	9	6	2	1	467	9	3	1.16	....	....	....	....	....	....	....
2005-06	U. of Wisconsin	WCHA	35	*27	5	3	2128	55	*8	*1.55	....	....	....	....	....	....	....
2006-07	U. of Wisconsin	WCHA	36	15	17	2	2053	72	*5	2.10	....	....	....	....	....	....	....
	Binghamton	AHL	8	3	4	0	425	30	0	4.24	....	....	....	....	....	....	....
2007-08	**Ottawa**	**NHL**	**1**	**1**	**0**	**0**	**60**	**1**	**0**	**1.00**	....	....	....	....	....	....	....
	Binghamton	AHL	44	18	19	1	2394	112	2	2.81	....	....	....	....	....	....	....
	NHL Totals		**1**	**1**	**0**	**0**	**60**	**1**	**0**	**1.00**	....	....	....	....	....	....	....

WCHA Second All-Star Team (2006, 2007) • NCAA West First All-American Team (2006) • NCAA Championship All-Tournament Team (2006)

ELLIS, Dan (EHL-ihs, DAN) NSH.

Goaltender. Catches left. 6', 185 lbs. Born, Orangeville, Ont., June 19, 1980.
(Dallas' 2nd choice, 60th overall, in 2000 Entry Draft).

			Regular Season								Playoffs						
Season	Club	League	GP	W	L	O/T	Mins	GA	SO	Avg	GP	W	L	Mins	GA	SO	Avg
1998-99	Newmarket	OPJHL	28	24	3	1	1670	63	3	2.25	....	....	....	....	....	....	....
99-2000	Omaha Lancers	USHL	55	*34	16	4	*3274	123	*11	*2.25	4	1	3	238	10	0	2.52
2000-01	Nebraska-Omaha	CCHA	40	21	14	3	2285	95	2	2.49	....	....	....	....	....	....	....
2001-02	Nebraska-Omaha	CCHA	40	20	15	4	2405	97	3	2.42	....	....	....	....	....	....	....
2002-03	Nebraska-Omaha	CCHA	39	11	21	5	2211	117	3	3.18	....	....	....	....	....	....	....
2003-04	**Dallas**	**NHL**	**1**	**1**	**0**	**0**	**60**	**3**	**0**	**3.00**	....	....	....	....	....	....	....
	Utah Grizzlies	AHL	20	5	14	0	1130	55	2	2.92	....	....	....	....	....	....	....
	Idaho Steelheads	ECHL	23	13	8	1	1334	57	2	2.56	*16	*13	3	*966	30	*3	*1.86
2004-05	Hamilton Bulldogs	AHL	31	10	19	0	1774	82	1	2.77	....	....	....	....	....	....	....
2005-06	Iowa Stars	AHL	34	16	13	1	1857	86	2	2.78	....	....	....	....	....	....	....
2006-07	Iowa Stars	AHL	55	30	21	1	3194	148	4	2.78	12	6	6	679	35	0	3.09
2007-08	**Nashville**	**NHL**	**44**	**23**	**10**	**3**	**2229**	**87**	**6**	**2.34**	**6**	**2**	**4**	**357**	**15**	**0**	**2.52**
	NHL Totals		**45**	**24**	**10**	**3**	**2289**	**90**	**6**	**2.36**	**6**	**2**	**4**	**357**	**15**	**0**	**2.52**

USHL First All-Star Team (2000) • USHL Goaltender of the Year (2000) • USHL Player of the Year (2000) • CCHA Second All-Star Team (2002) • ECHL Playoff MVP (2004)

Signed as a free agent by **Nashville**, July 5, 2007.

ELLIS, Julien (EHL-ihs, JEW-lee-ehn) VAN.

Goaltender. Catches left. 6', 186 lbs. Born, Sorel, Que., January 27, 1986.
(Vancouver's 5th choice, 189th overall, in 2004 Entry Draft).

			Regular Season								Playoffs						
Season	Club	League	GP	W	L	O/T	Mins	GA	SO	Avg	GP	W	L	Mins	GA	SO	Avg
2001-02	Antoine-Girouard	QAAA	22	16	2	1	1227	55	2	2.69	....	....	....	....	....	....	....
2002-03	Antoine-Girouard	QAAA	16	11	4	1	966	29	4	1.80	....	....	....	....	....	....	....
	Shawinigan	QMJHL	7	2	3	0	365	21	0	3.45	....	....	....	....	....	....	....
2003-04	Shawinigan	QMJHL	*59	32	18	2	*3287	156	1	2.85	10	3	6	569	33	0	3.48
2004-05	Shawinigan	QMJHL	*59	27	21	11	*3480	140	4	2.41	4	0	3	175	10	0	3.43
2005-06	Shawinigan	QMJHL	48	27	19	0	2680	154	3	3.45	7	4	3	412	18	*2	2.62
2006-07	Manitoba Moose	AHL	8	1	7	0	463	26	0	3.37	....	....	....	....	....	....	....
	Victoria	ECHL	37	21	14	2	2190	117	1	3.21	4	1	3	213	15	0	4.23
2007-08	Manitoba Moose	AHL	1	0	0	0	40	1	0	1.50	....	....	....	....	....	....	....
	Victoria	ECHL	42	24	11	5	2412	128	2	3.18	3	1	1	136	9	0	3.97

QMJHL All-Rookie Team (2004) • QMJHL First All-Star Team (2005)

EMERY, Ray (EH-muhr-ee, RAY)

Goaltender. Catches left. 6'2", 196 lbs. Born, Cayuga, Ont., September 28, 1982.
(Ottawa's 4th choice, 99th overall, in 2001 Entry Draft).

			Regular Season								Playoffs						
Season	Club	League	GP	W	L	O/T	Mins	GA	SO	Avg	GP	W	L	Mins	GA	SO	Avg
1998-99	Dunnville Terriers	OJHL-C	22	3	19	0	1320	140	0	6.37	....	....	....	....	....	....	....
99-2000	Welland Cougars	OHA-B	23	13	10	1	1323	62	1	2.68	....	....	....	....	....	....	....
	Sault Ste. Marie	OHL	16	9	3	0	716	36	1	3.02	15	8	7	883	33	*3	2.24
2000-01	Sault Ste. Marie	OHL	52	18	29	2	2938	174	1	3.55	....	....	....	....	....	....	....
2001-02	Sault Ste. Marie	OHL	*59	*33	17	9	*3477	158	4	2.73	6	2	4	360	19	*1	3.17
2002-03	**Ottawa**	**NHL**	**3**	**1**	**0**	**0**	**85**	**2**	**0**	**1.41**	....	....	....	....	....	....	....
	Binghamton	AHL	50	27	17	6	2924	118	*7	2.42	14	8	6	848	40	*2	2.83
2003-04	**Ottawa**	**NHL**	**3**	**2**	**0**	**0**	**126**	**5**	**0**	**2.38**	....	....	....	....	....	....	....
	Binghamton	AHL	53	21	23	7	3109	128	3	2.47	2	0	2	120	6	0	3.01
2004-05	Binghamton	AHL	51	28	18	5	2993	132	0	2.65	6	2	4	409	14	0	2.05
2005-06	**Ottawa**	**NHL**	**39**	**23**	**11**	**4**	**2168**	**102**	**3**	**2.82**	**10**	**5**	**5**	**604**	**29**	**0**	**2.88**
2006-07	**Ottawa**	**NHL**	**58**	**33**	**16**	**6**	**3351**	**138**	**5**	**2.47**	***20**	***13**	**7**	***1249**	**47**	***3**	**2.26**
2007-08	**Ottawa**	**NHL**	**31**	**12**	**13**	**4**	**1689**	**88**	**0**	**3.13**	....	....	....	....	....	....	....
	Binghamton	AHL	2	1	1	0	120	6	0	3.00	....	....	....	....	....	....	....
	NHL Totals		**134**	**71**	**40**	**14**	**7419**	**335**	**8**	**2.71**	**30**	**18**	**12**	**1853**	**76**	**3**	**2.46**

OHL First All-Star Team (2002) • Canadian Major Junior First All-Star Team (2002) • Canadian Major Junior Goaltender of the Year (2002) • AHL All-Rookie Team (2003)

Signed as a free agent by **Mytischi** (KHL), July 9, 2008.

ENGREN, Atte (EHN-grehn, AH-tay) NSH.

Goaltender. Catches left. 6'1", 194 lbs. Born, Rauma, Finland, February 19, 1988.
(Nashville's 9th choice, 204th overall, in 2007 Entry Draft).

			Regular Season								Playoffs						
Season	Club	League	GP	W	L	O/T	Mins	GA	SO	Avg	GP	W	L	Mins	GA	SO	Avg
2004-05	Lukko Rauma U18	Fin-U18	10	....	....	....	603	22	0	2.19	....	....	....	....	....	....	....
2005-06	Lukko Rauma U18	Fin-U18	16	....	....	....	966	44	0	2.73	....	....	....	....	....	....	....
	Lukko Rauma Jr.	Fin-Jr.	11	....	....	....	637	30	0	2.83	9	....	....	509	27	0	3.18
2006-07	Lukko Rauma Jr.	Fin-Jr.	38	....	....	....	2277	115	1	3.03	....	....	....	....	....	....	....
	Suomi U20	Finland-2	2	....	....	....	100	7	0	4.20	....	....	....	....	....	....	....
2007-08	Hokki Kajaani	Finland-2	1	0	0	0	15	4	0	15.70	....	....	....	....	....	....	....
	Lukko Rauma	Finland	1	0	1	0	59	3	0	3.04	....	....	....	....	....	....	....
	Lukko Rauma Jr.	Fin-Jr.	31	14	13	0	1791	89	1	2.98	2	2	0	120	3	0	1.50

ENO, Nick (EE-noh, NIHK) BUF.

Goaltender. Catches left. 6'1", 190 lbs. Born, Howell, MI, February 12, 1989.
(Buffalo's 7th choice, 187th overall, in 2007 Entry Draft).

			Regular Season								Playoffs						
Season	Club	League	GP	W	L	O/T	Mins	GA	SO	Avg	GP	W	L	Mins	GA	SO	Avg
2005-06	Howell	High-MI	25	....	....	....	1020	52	5	2.29	....	....	....	....	....	....	....
2006-07	Green Mountain	EJHL	25	9	14	2	1398	84	1	3.60	....	....	....	....	....	....	....
2007-08	Bowling Green	CCHA	22	12	10	0	1269	59	0	2.79	....	....	....	....	....	....	....

CCHA All-Rookie Team (2008)

ENROTH, Jhonas (EHN-rawth, YOH-nuhs) BUF.

Goaltender. Catches left. 5'10", 174 lbs. Born, Stockholm, Sweden, June 25, 1988.
(Buffalo's 2nd choice, 46th overall, in 2006 Entry Draft).

			Regular Season								Playoffs						
Season	Club	League	GP	W	L	O/T	Mins	GA	SO	Avg	GP	W	L	Mins	GA	SO	Avg
2003-04	Huddinge IK U18	Swe-U18	6	....	....	....	324	15	0	2.77	....	....	....	....	....	....	....
2004-05	Huddinge IK Jr.	Swe-Jr.	19	....	....	....	1144	49	3	2.57	3	....	....	186	6	1	1.93
	Huddinge IK U18	Swe-U18	2	....	....	....	125	5	0	2.40	....	....	....	....	....	....	....
	Huddinge IK	Sweden-2	2	....	....	....	51	6	0	6.95	....	....	....	....	....	....	....
2005-06	Sodertalje SK Jr.	Swe-Jr.	39	....	....	....	2378	86	1	2.17	4	....	....	243	9	0	2.22
	Sodertalje SK U18	Swe-U18	2	....	....	....	120	5	0	2.50	....	....	....	....	....	....	....
2006-07	Sodertalje SK Jr.	Swe-Jr.	3	....	....	....	180	4	0	1.33	....	....	....	....	....	....	....
	Sodertalje SK	Sweden-2	33	....	....	....	1938	57	3	1.76	....	....	....	....	....	....	....
2007-08	Sodertalje SK Jr.	Swe-Jr.	1	....	....	....	59	4	0	4.05	....	....	....	....	....	....	....
	Sodertalje SK	Sweden	27	....	....	....	1578	56	2	*2.13	....	....	....	....	....	....	....

ERIKSSON, Joacim (AIR-ihk-suhn, YOH-a-kihm) PHI.

Goaltender. Catches right. 6'1", 189 lbs. Born, Gavle, Sweden, April 9, 1990.
(Philadelphia's 5th choice, 196th overall, in 2008 Entry Draft).

			Regular Season								Playoffs						
Season	Club	League	GP	W	L	O/T	Mins	GA	SO	Avg	GP	W	L	Mins	GA	SO	Avg
2006-07	Valbo AIF Jr.	Swe-Jr.	18	....	....	....	1072	55	....	3.08	....	....	....	....	....	....	....
	Valbo AIF	Sweden-3	1	....	....	....	34	2	0	3.51	....	....	....	....	....	....	....
2007-08	Brynas U18	Swe-U18	9	....	....	....	545	21	2	2.31	5	....	....	296	7	2	1.42
	Brynas IF Gavle Jr.	Swe-Jr.	16	....	....	....	960	53	0	3.31	7	....	....	426	13	1	1.83
	Valbo HC	Sweden-3	2	....	....	....	123	8	0	3.91	....	....	....	....	....	....	....

ERSBERG, Erik (AIRZ-buhrg, AIR-ihk) L.A.

Goaltender. Catches left. 6', 182 lbs. Born, Sala, Sweden, March 8, 1982.

			Regular Season								Playoffs						
Season	Club	League	GP	W	L	O/T	Mins	GA	SO	Avg	GP	W	L	Mins	GA	SO	Avg
99-2000	Vasteras IK U18	Swe-U18	1	....	....	....	60	2	0	2.00	2	....	....	119	10	0	5.02
	Vasteras IK Jr.	Swe-Jr.	16	....	....	....	885	36	0	2.44	....	....	....	....	....	....	....
2000-01	Vasteras	Sweden-4	33	....	....	....	....	....	....	1.48	....	....	....	....	....	....	....
2001-02	Vasteras Jr.	Swe-Jr.	....	....	....	....	....	....	....	....	2	....	....	118	11	0	5.61
	Vasteras	Sweden-3	37	....	....	....	....	....	....	....	....	....	....	....	....	....	....
2002-03	Vasteras	Sweden-2	32	....	....	....	1920	91	1	2.84	....	....	....	....	....	....	....

2003-04	Vasteras	Sweden-2	32	....	....	....	1850	79	3	2.56	....	....	....	....	....	....	....
2004-05	Vasteras	Sweden-2	37	....	....	....	2189	76	3	2.08	5	....	....	308	8	2	1.56
2005-06	VIK Vasteras HK	Sweden-2	2	....	....	....	118	4	0	2.02	....	....	....	....	....	....	....
	HV 71 Jonkoping	Sweden	10	....	....	....	602	18	2	1.79	2	....	....	79	4	0	3.05
	HV 71 Jr.	Swe-Jr.	1	....	....	....	60	1	0	1.00	....	....	....	....	....	....	....
2006-07	HV 71 Jonkoping	Sweden	41	....	....	....	2455	98	4	2.39	14	....	....	834	39	0	2.81
2007-08	**Los Angeles**	**NHL**	**14**	**6**	**5**	**3**	**799**	**33**	**2**	**2.48**	....	....	....	....	....	....	....
	Manchester	AHL	30	10	13	2	1540	75	1	2.92	....	....	....	....	....	....	....
	NHL Totals		**14**	**6**	**5**	**3**	**799**	**33**	**2**	**2.48**	....	....	....	....	....	....	....

Signed as a free agent by **Los Angeles**, May 31, 2007.

ESCHE, Robert (EHSH, RAW-buhrt)

Goaltender. Catches left. 6'1", 210 lbs. Born, Whitesboro, NY, January 22, 1978.
(Phoenix's 5th choice, 139th overall, in 1996 Entry Draft).

			Regular Season								Playoffs						
Season	Club	League	GP	W	L	O/T	Mins	GA	SO	Avg	GP	W	L	Mins	GA	SO	Avg
1994-95	Gloucester	CJHL	20	10	6	0	1034	70	0	4.06	....	....	....	....	....	....	....
1995-96	Detroit Jr. Whalers	OHL	23	13	6	0	1219	76	1	3.74	3	0	2	105	4	0	2.29
1996-97	Detroit Jr. Whalers	OHL	58	24	28	2	3241	206	2	3.81	5	1	4	317	19	0	3.60
1997-98	Plymouth Whalers	OHL	48	29	13	4	2810	135	3	2.88	15	8	7	869	45	0	3.11
1998-99	**Phoenix**	**NHL**	**3**	**0**	**1**	**0**	**130**	**7**	**0**	**3.23**	....	....	....	....	....	....	....
	Springfield Falcons	AHL	55	24	20	6	2957	138	1	2.80	1	0	1	60	4	0	4.02
99-2000	**Phoenix**	**NHL**	**8**	**2**	**5**	**0**	**408**	**23**	**0**	**3.38**	....	....	....	....	....	....	....
	Houston Aeros	IHL	7	4	2	1	419	16	2	2.29	....	....	....	....	....	....	....
	Springfield Falcons	AHL	21	9	9	2	1207	61	2	3.03	3	1	2	180	12	0	4.01
2000-01	**Phoenix**	**NHL**	**25**	**10**	**8**	**4**	**1350**	**68**	**2**	**3.02**	....	....	....	....	....	....	....
2001-02	**Phoenix**	**NHL**	**22**	**6**	**10**	**2**	**1145**	**52**	**1**	**2.72**	....	....	....	....	....	....	....
	Springfield Falcons	AHL	1	1	0	0	60	0	1	0.00	....	....	....	....	....	....	....
2002-03	**Philadelphia**	**NHL**	**30**	**12**	**9**	**3**	**1638**	**60**	**2**	**2.20**	**1**	**0**	**0**	**30**	**1**	**0**	**2.00**
2003-04	**Philadelphia**	**NHL**	**40**	**21**	**11**	**7**	**2322**	**79**	**3**	**2.04**	**18**	**11**	**7**	**1061**	**41**	**1**	**2.32**
2004-05							Did not play										
2005-06	**Philadelphia**	**NHL**	**40**	**22**	**11**	**5**	**2286**	**113**	**1**	**2.97**	**6**	**2**	**4**	**314**	**22**	**0**	**4.20**
	United States	Olympics	1	0	1	0	59	5	0	5.10	....	....	....	....	....	....	....
2006-07	**Philadelphia**	**NHL**	**18**	**5**	**9**	**1**	**860**	**62**	**1**	**4.33**	....	....	....	....	....	....	....
2007-08	Ak Bars Kazan	Russia	18	....	....	....	1095	34	3	1.86	10	....	....	609	25	1	2.46
	NHL Totals		**186**	**78**	**64**	**22**	**10139**	**464**	**10**	**2.75**	**25**	**13**	**11**	**1405**	**64**	**1**	**2.73**

OHL Second All-Star Team (1998) • AHL All-Rookie Team (1999) • William M. Jennings Trophy (2003) (shared with Roman Cechmanek) (tied with Martin Brodeur)

Traded to **Philadelphia** by **Phoenix** with Michal Handzus for Brian Boucher and Nashville's 3rd round choice (previously acquired, Phoenix selected Joe Callahan) in 2002 Entry Draft, June 12, 2002. Signed as a free agent by **Kazan** (Russia), October 18, 2007.

FALLON, Joseph (FA-lohn, JOH-sehf) CHI.

Goaltender. Catches left. 6'3", 203 lbs. Born, Bemidji, MN, February 1, 1985.
(Chicago's 9th choice, 167th overall, in 2005 Entry Draft).

			Regular Season								Playoffs						
Season	Club	League	GP	W	L	O/T	Mins	GA	SO	Avg	GP	W	L	Mins	GA	SO	Avg
2001-02	Rochester	USHL	27	7	16	1	1484	93	0	3.76	....	....	....	....	....	....	....
2002-03	Cedar Rapids	USHL	42	20	15	6	2495	108	2	2.60	7	3	4	426	21	0	2.96
2003-04	Cedar Rapids	USHL	42	25	13	2	2370	108	4	2.73	4	1	3	237	9	0	2.28
2004-05	U. of Vermont	ECAC	32	17	10	4	1932	63	5	1.96	....	....	....	....	....	....	....
2005-06	U. of Vermont	H-East	33	14	14	5	1931	65	6	2.02	....	....	....	....	....	....	....
2006-07	U. of Vermont	H-East	34	17	14	3	1997	62	6	*1.86	....	....	....	....	....	....	....
2007-08	U. of Vermont	H-East	33	15	13	5	1942	77	*3	2.38	....	....	....	....	....	....	....

ECAC All-Rookie Team (2005) • ECAC Rookie of the Year (2005)

FERNANDEZ, Manny (fuhr-NAN-dehz, MAN-ee) BOS.

Goaltender. Catches left. 6'1", 207 lbs. Born, Etobicoke, Ont., August 27, 1974.
(Quebec's 4th choice, 52nd overall, in 1992 Entry Draft).

			Regular Season								Playoffs						
Season	Club	League	GP	W	L	O/T	Mins	GA	SO	Avg	GP	W	L	Mins	GA	SO	Avg
1990-91	Lac St-Louis Lions	QAAA	20	13	5	0	1176	69	*3	3.52	3	2	1	181	12	0	3.98
1991-92	Laval Titan	QMJHL	31	14	13	2	1593	99	1	3.73	9	3	5	468	39	0	5.00
1992-93	Laval Titan	QMJHL	43	26	14	2	2347	141	1	3.60	13	*12	1	818	42	0	3.08
1993-94	Laval Titan	QMJHL	51	29	14	1	2776	143	*5	3.09	19	14	5	1116	49	*1	*2.63
1994-95	Kalamazoo Wings	IHL	46	21	10	9	2470	115	2	2.79	14	10	2	753	34	1	2.71
	Dallas	**NHL**	**1**	**0**	**1**	**0**	**59**	**3**	**0**	**3.05**	....	....	....	....	....	....	....
1995-96	**Dallas**	**NHL**	**5**	**0**	**1**	**1**	**249**	**19**	**0**	**4.58**	....	....	....	....	....	....	....
	Michigan K-Wings	IHL	47	22	15	9	2664	133	*4	3.00	6	5	1	372	14	0	*2.26
1996-97	Michigan K-Wings	IHL	48	20	24	2	2720	142	2	3.13	4	1	3	277	15	0	3.25
1997-98	**Dallas**	**NHL**	**2**	**1**	**0**	**0**	**69**	**2**	**0**	**1.74**	**1**	**0**	**0**	**2**	**0**	**0**	**0.00**
	Michigan K-Wings	IHL	55	27	17	5	3022	139	5	2.76	2	0	2	88	7	0	4.73
1998-99	**Dallas**	**NHL**	**1**	**0**	**1**	**0**	**60**	**2**	**0**	**2.00**	....	....	....	....	....	....	....
	Houston Aeros	IHL	50	34	6	9	2949	116	2	2.36	*19	*11	8	*1126	49	1	2.61
99-2000	**Dallas**	**NHL**	**24**	**11**	**8**	**3**	**1353**	**48**	**1**	**2.13**	**1**	**0**	**0**	**17**	**1**	**0**	**3.53**
2000-01	**Minnesota**	**NHL**	**42**	**19**	**17**	**4**	**2461**	**92**	**4**	**2.24**	....	....	....	....	....	....	....
2001-02	**Minnesota**	**NHL**	**44**	**12**	**24**	**5**	**2463**	**125**	**1**	**3.05**	....	....	....	....	....	....	....
2002-03	**Minnesota**	**NHL**	**35**	**19**	**13**	**2**	**1979**	**74**	**2**	**2.24**	**9**	**3**	**4**	**552**	**18**	**0**	**1.96**
2003-04	**Minnesota**	**NHL**	**37**	**11**	**14**	**9**	**2166**	**90**	**2**	**2.49**	....	....	....	....	....	....	....
2004-05	Lulea HF	Sweden	19	....	....	....	1083	50	2	2.77	3	....	....	159	13	0	4.90
2005-06	**Minnesota**	**NHL**	**58**	**30**	**18**	**7**	**3411**	**130**	**1**	**2.29**	....	....	....	....	....	....	....
2006-07	**Minnesota**	**NHL**	**44**	**22**	**16**	**1**	**2422**	**103**	**2**	**2.55**	....	....	....	....	....	....	....
2007-08	**Boston**	**NHL**	**4**	**2**	**2**	**0**	**244**	**16**	**1**	**3.93**	....	....	....	....	....	....	....
	NHL Totals		**297**	**127**	**115**	**32**	**16936**	**704**	**14**	**2.49**	**11**	**3**	**4**	**571**	**19**	**0**	**2.00**

QMJHL First All-Star Team (1994) • QMJHL MVP (1994) • IHL Second All-Star Team (1995) • William M. Jennings Trophy (2007) (shared with Niklas Backstrom)

Rights traded to **Dallas** by **Quebec** for Tommy Sjodin and Dallas' 3rd round choice (Chris Drury) in 1994 Entry Draft, February 13, 1994. Traded to **Minnesota** by **Dallas** with Brad Lukowich for Minnesota's 3rd round choice (Joel Lundqvist) in 2000 Entry Draft and Minnesota's 4th round choice (later traded back to Minnesota – later traded to Los Angeles – Los Angeles selected Aaron Rome) in 2002 Entry Draft, June 12, 2000. Signed as a free agent by **Lulea** (Sweden), December 18, 2004. Traded to **Boston** by **Minnesota** for Petr Kalus and Boston's 4th round choice in 2009 Entry Draft, July 1, 2007. • Missed majority of 2007-08 season recovering from back and knee injuries.

FISHER, Glenn (FIH-shuhr, GLEHN) EDM.

Goaltender. Catches left. 6'1", 190 lbs. Born, Edmonton, Alta., April 25, 1983.
(Edmonton's 9th choice, 148th overall, in 2002 Entry Draft).

			Regular Season								Playoffs						
Season	Club	League	GP	W	L	O/T	Mins	GA	SO	Avg	GP	W	L	Mins	GA	SO	Avg
99-2000	Edm. Maple Leafs	AMBHL	16	9	5	2	944	62	0	3.94	....	....	....	....	....	....	....
2000-01	Edm. Maple Leafs	AMHL	19	6	9	3	1116	77	0	4.14	....	....	....	....	....	....	....
2001-02	Fort Saskatchewan	AJHL	47	14	26	2	2649	196	2	4.44	3	0	3	180	14	0	4.67
2002-03	Fort Saskatchewan	AJHL	51	17	27	6	2885	202	0	4.20	....	....	....	....	....	....	....
2003-04	U. of Denver	WCHA	9	3	1	1	436	26	0	3.58	....	....	....	....	....	....	....
2004-05	U. of Denver	WCHA	22	14	5	1	1247	59	0	2.84	....	....	....	....	....	....	....
2005-06	U. of Denver	WCHA	21	9	7	2	1102	50	1	2.72	....	....	....	....	....	....	....
2006-07	U. of Denver	WCHA	24	13	9	2	1394	54	3	2.32	....	....	....	....	....	....	....
2007-08	Springfield Falcons	AHL	1	0	0	0	10	3	0	18.88	....	....	....	....	....	....	....
	Stockton Thunder	ECHL	38	14	19	2	2074	116	2	3.36	....	....	....	....	....	....	....

FLAHERTY, Wade (FLAY-uhr-tee, WAYD)

Goaltender. Catches left. 6', 171 lbs. Born, Terrace, B.C., January 11, 1968.
(Buffalo's 10th choice, 181st overall, in 1988 Entry Draft).

			Regular Season								Playoffs						
Season	Club	League	GP	W	L	O/T	Mins	GA	SO	Avg	GP	W	L	Mins	GA	SO	Avg
1984-85	Kelowna Wings	WHL	1	0	0	0	55	5	0	5.45	....	....	....	....	....	....	....
1985-86	Seattle	WHL	9	1	3	0	271	36	0	7.97	....	....	....	....	....	....	....
	Spokane Chiefs	WHL	5	0	3	0	161	21	0	7.83	....	....	....	....	....	....	....
1986-87	Nanaimo Clippers	BCJHL	15	....	....	....	830	53	0	3.83	....	....	....	....	....	....	....
	Victoria Cougars	WHL	3	0	2	0	127	16	0	7.56	....	....	....	....	....	....	....
1987-88	Victoria Cougars	WHL	36	20	15	0	2052	135	0	3.95	5	2	3	300	18	0	3.60
1988-89	Victoria Cougars	WHL	42	21	19	0	2408	180	4	4.49	....	....	....	....	....	....	....
1989-90	Greensboro	ECHL	27	12	10	0	1308	96	0	4.40	....	....	....	....	....	....	....
1990-91	Kansas City Blades	IHL	*56	16	31	4	2990	224	0	4.49	....	....	....	....	....	....	....
1991-92	**San Jose**	**NHL**	**3**	**0**	**3**	**0**	**178**	**13**	**0**	**4.38**	....	....	....	....	....	....	....
	Kansas City Blades	IHL	43	26	14	3	2603	140	1	3.23	1	0	0	1	0	0	0.00
1992-93	**San Jose**	**NHL**	**1**	**0**	**1**	**0**	**60**	**5**	**0**	**5.00**	....	....	....	....	....	....	....
	Kansas City Blades	IHL	*61	*34	19	7	*3642	195	2	3.21	*12	6	6	733	34	*1	2.78
1993-94	Kansas City Blades	IHL	*60	32	19	9	*3564	202	0	3.40	....	....	....	....	....	....	....
1994-95	**San Jose**	**NHL**	**18**	**5**	**6**	**1**	**852**	**44**	**1**	**3.10**	**7**	**2**	**3**	**377**	**31**	**0**	**4.93**
1995-96	**San Jose**	**NHL**	**24**	**3**	**12**	**1**	**1137**	**92**	**0**	**4.85**	....	....	....	....	....	....	....
1996-97	**San Jose**	**NHL**	**7**	**2**	**4**	**0**	**359**	**31**	**0**	**5.18**	....	....	....	....	....	....	....
	Kentucky	AHL	19	8	6	2	1032	54	1	3.14	3	1	2	200	11	0	3.30
1997-98	**NY Islanders**	**NHL**	**16**	**4**	**4**	**3**	**694**	**23**	**3**	**1.99**	....	....	....	....	....	....	....
	Utah Grizzlies	IHL	24	16	5	3	1341	40	3	1.79	....	....	....	....	....	....	....
1998-99	**NY Islanders**	**NHL**	**20**	**5**	**11**	**2**	**1048**	**53**	**0**	**3.03**	....	....	....	....	....	....	....
	Lowell	AHL	5	1	3	1	305	16	0	3.15	....	....	....	....	....	....	....
99-2000	**NY Islanders**	**NHL**	**4**	**0**	**1**	**1**	**182**	**7**	**0**	**2.31**	....	....	....	....	....	....	....
2000-01	**NY Islanders**	**NHL**	**20**	**6**	**10**	**0**	**1017**	**56**	**1**	**3.30**	....	....	....	....	....	....	....
	Tampa Bay	**NHL**	**2**	**0**	**2**	**0**	**118**	**8**	**0**	**4.07**	....	....	....	....	....	....	....
2001-02	**Florida**	**NHL**	**4**	**2**	**1**	**1**	**245**	**12**	**0**	**2.94**	....	....	....	....	....	....	....
	Utah Grizzlies	AHL	45	22	13	5	2351	92	2	2.35	5	2	3	312	11	0	2.12
2002-03	**Nashville**	**NHL**	**1**	**0**	**1**	**0**	**51**	**4**	**0**	**4.71**	....	....	....	....	....	....	....
	San Antonio	AHL	30	11	13	5	1791	86	1	2.88	....	....	....	....	....	....	....
2003-04	Milwaukee	AHL	36	21	12	3	2146	78	3	2.18	*21	*16	5	*1371	44	1	1.93
2004-05	Manitoba Moose	AHL	36	19	10	3	2010	78	4	2.33	12	8	4	720	29	2	2.42
2005-06	Manitoba Moose	AHL	49	26	17	4	2822	113	*6	2.40	12	7	5	675	23	0	*2.04
2006-07	Manitoba Moose	AHL	32	17	9	2	1735	70	2	2.42	3	2	1	166	5	0	1.81
2007-08	Rockford IceHogs	AHL	31	13	8	1	1486	63	2	2.54	....	....	....	....	....	....	....
	NHL Totals		**120**	**27**	**56**	**9**	**5941**	**348**	**5**	**3.51**	**7**	**2**	**3**	**377**	**31**	**0**	**4.93**

WHL West Second All-Star Team (1988) • ECHL Playoff MVP (1990) • James Norris Memorial Trophy (fewest goals against – IHL) (1992) (shared with Arturs Irbe) • IHL Second All-Star Team (1993, 1994) • Jack A. Butterfield Trophy (Playoff MVP - AHL) (2004) • AHL Second All-Star Team (2006)

Signed as a free agent by **San Jose**, September 3, 1991. Signed as a free agent by **NY Islanders**, July 22, 1997. Traded to **Tampa Bay** by **NY Islanders** for future considerations, February 16, 2001. Signed as a free agent by **Florida**, August 2, 2001. Traded to **Nashville** by **Florida** for Pascal Trepanier, March 9, 2003. Signed as a free agent by **Vancouver**, July 7, 2004. Signed as a free agent by **Chicago**, July 27, 2007.

FLEURY, Marc-Andre (fluh-REE, MAHRK-AWN-dray) PIT.

Goaltender. Catches left. 6'2", 180 lbs. Born, Sorel, Que., November 28, 1984.
(Pittsburgh's 1st choice, 1st overall, in 2003 Entry Draft).

			Regular Season								Playoffs						
Season	Club	League	GP	W	L	O/T	Mins	GA	SO	Avg	GP	W	L	Mins	GA	SO	Avg
99-2000	Charles-Lemoyne	QAAA	15	4	9	0	780	36	1	2.77	....	....	....	....	....	....	....
2000-01	Cape Breton	QMJHL	35	12	13	2	1705	115	0	4.05	2	0	1	32	4	0	7.50
2001-02	Cape Breton	QMJHL	55	26	14	8	3043	141	2	2.78	16	9	7	1003	55	0	3.29
2002-03	Cape Breton	QMJHL	51	17	24	6	2889	162	2	3.36	4	0	4	228	17	0	4.47
2003-04	**Pittsburgh**	**NHL**	**21**	**4**	**14**	**2**	**1154**	**70**	**1**	**3.64**	....	....	....	....	....	....	....
	Cape Breton	QMJHL	10	8	1	1	606	20	0	1.98	4	1	3	251	13	0	3.10
	Wilkes-Barre	AHL	....	....	....	....	....	....	....	....	2	0	1	92	6	0	3.90
2004-05	Wilkes-Barre	AHL	54	26	19	4	3029	127	5	2.52	4	0	2	151	11	0	4.36
2005-06	**Pittsburgh**	**NHL**	**50**	**13**	**27**	**6**	**2809**	**152**	**1**	**3.25**	....	....	....	....	....	....	....
	Wilkes-Barre	AHL	12	10	2	0	727	19	0	1.57	5	2	3	311	18	0	3.48
2006-07	**Pittsburgh**	**NHL**	**67**	**40**	**16**	**9**	**3905**	**184**	**5**	**2.83**	**5**	**1**	**4**	**287**	**18**	**0**	**3.76**
2007-08	**Pittsburgh**	**NHL**	**35**	**19**	**10**	**2**	**1857**	**72**	**4**	**2.33**	***20**	***14**	**6**	***1251**	**41**	***3**	**1.97**
	Wilkes-Barre	AHL	5	3	2	0	297	7	0	1.42	....	....	....	....	....	....	....
	NHL Totals		**173**	**76**	**67**	**19**	**9725**	**478**	**11**	**2.95**	**25**	**15**	**10**	**1538**	**59**	**3**	**2.30**

QMJHL Second All-Star Team (2003)

FOSTER, Brian (FAW-stuhr, BRIGH-uhn) FLA.

Goaltender. Catches left. 6'1", 155 lbs. Born, Pembroke, NH, February 4, 1987.
(Florida's 6th choice, 161st overall, in 2005 Entry Draft).

			Regular Season								Playoffs						
Season	Club	League	GP	W	L	O/T	Mins	GA	SO	Avg	GP	W	L	Mins	GA	SO	Avg
2003-04	N.H. Jr. Monarchs	EJHL					Statistics not available										
2004-05	N.H. Jr. Monarchs	EJHL	41	30	6	4	2339	....	3	2.51	....	....	....	....	....	....	....
2005-06	Des Moines	USHL	26	12	9	3	1516	71	0	2.81	1	0	0	12	0	0	0.00
2006-07	New Hampshire	H-East	7	2	2	0	298	11	2	2.21	....	....	....	....	....	....	....
2007-08	New Hampshire	H-East	6	2	2	2	372	19	0	3.06	....	....	....	....	....	....	....

FRAZEE, Jeff (FRAY-zee, JEHF) N.J.

Goaltender. Catches left. 6', 195 lbs. Born, Edina, MN, May 13, 1987.
(New Jersey's 2nd choice, 38th overall, in 2005 Entry Draft).

			Regular Season								Playoffs						
Season	Club	League	GP	W	L	O/T	Mins	GA	SO	Avg	GP	W	L	Mins	GA	SO	Avg
2001-02	Holy Angels	High-MN	6	6	0	0	....	....	....	....	....	....	....	....	....	....	....
2002-03	Holy Angels	High-MN	16	14	1	1	....	....	....	....	....	....	....	....	....	....	....
2003-04	USNTDP	U-17	16	9	3	0	781	31	....	2.38	....	....	....	....	....	....	....
	USNTDP	NAHL	25	14	8	3	1463	71	3	2.91	....	....	....	....	....	....	....
2004-05	USNTDP	U-18	24	....	....	....	1309	59	3	2.71	....	....	....	....	....	....	....
	USNTDP	NAHL	9	8	1	0	500	18	1	2.16	....	....	....	....	....	....	....
2005-06	U. of Minnesota	WCHA	12	6	3	2	660	26	2	2.36	....	....	....	....	....	....	....
2006-07	U. of Minnesota	WCHA	20	14	3	1	1148	45	1	2.35	....	....	....	....	....	....	....
2007-08	U. of Minnesota	WCHA	14	6	7	0	798	39	1	2.93	....	....	....	....	....	....	....
	Lowell Devils	AHL	1	0	1	0	40	3	0	4.50	....	....	....	....	....	....	....

FUKUFUJI, Yutaka (foo-koo-FOO-jee, yoo-TA-ka)

Goaltender. Catches left. 6'1", 180 lbs. Born, Tokyo, Japan, September 17, 1982.
(Los Angeles' 9th choice, 238th overall, in 2004 Entry Draft).

			Regular Season								Playoffs						
Season	Club	League	GP	W	L	O/T	Mins	GA	SO	Avg	GP	W	L	Mins	GA	SO	Avg
2003-04	Kokudo Toyko	AsianHL	7	....	....	....	420	13	....	1.86	....	....	....	....	....	....	....
	Kokudo Toyko	Japan	7	....	....	....	430	12	....	1.67	....	....	....	....	....	....	....
2004-05	Bakersfield	ECHL	44	27	9	5	2517	104	3	2.48	....	....	....	....	....	....	....
2005-06	Manchester	AHL	2	1	1	0	120	6	0	3.00	....	....	....	....	....	....	....
	Reading Royals	ECHL	29	15	9	4	1691	82	1	2.91	4	1	2	196	11	0	3.36
2006-07	**Los Angeles**	**NHL**	**4**	**0**	**3**	**0**	**96**	**7**	**0**	**4.38**	....	....	....	....	....	....	....
	Manchester	AHL	5	3	1	0	261	4	1	0.92	1	0	0	0	0	0	0.00
	Reading Royals	ECHL	28	13	10	0	1522	75	1	2.96	....	....	....	....	....	....	....

2007-08	Bakersfield	ECHL	46	18	18	1	2427	137	1	3.39	6	2	2	372	22	0	3.55
	NHL Totals		**4**	**0**	**3**	**0**	**96**	**7**	**0**	**4.38**	....	....	....	....	....	....	....

GAIDUCHENKO, Sergei (gay-doo-CHEHN-koh, SAIR-gay) FLA.

Goaltender. Catches left. 6'5", 222 lbs. Born, Kiev, USSR, June 6, 1989.
(Florida's 8th choice, 202nd overall, in 2007 Entry Draft).

			Regular Season								Playoffs						
Season	Club	League	GP	W	L	O/T	Mins	GA	SO	Avg	GP	W	L	Mins	GA	SO	Avg
2006-07	Yaroslavl 2	Russia-3	23	....	....	....	1180	57	3	2.90	....	....	....	....	....	....	....
2007-08	Novokuznetsk 2	Russia-3	2	....	....	....	....	5	....	....	....	....	....	....	....	....	....
	Novokuznetsk	Russia	11	....	....	....	533	27	0	3.04	....	....	....	....	....	....	....

GARNETT, Michael (gahr-NEHT, MIGH-kuhl)

Goaltender. Catches left. 6'1", 205 lbs. Born, Saskatoon, Sask., November 25, 1982.
(Atlanta's 2nd choice, 80th overall, in 2001 Entry Draft).

			Regular Season								Playoffs						
Season	Club	League	GP	W	L	O/T	Mins	GA	SO	Avg	GP	W	L	Mins	GA	SO	Avg
1997-98	Sask. Contacts	SMHL	3	1	1	0	82	8	0	5.85	....	....	....	....	....	....	....
1998-99	Sask. Contacts	SMHL					STATISTICS NOT AVAILABLE										
99-2000	Kindersley Klippers	SJHL	36	....	....	....	2067	140	1	3.57	....	....	....	....	....	....	....
	Red Deer Rebels	WHL	1	0	0	0	14	0	0	0.00	1	0	1	65	2	0	1.85
2000-01	Red Deer Rebels	WHL	21	14	5	1	1133	39	3	2.07	....	....	....	....	....	....	....
	Saskatoon Blades	WHL	28	7	17	2	1501	83	1	3.32	....	....	....	....	....	....	....
2001-02	Saskatoon Blades	WHL	*67	27	34	4	*3738	205	2	3.29	7	3	4	450	15	0	2.00
2002-03	Greenville Grrrowl	ECHL	38	16	15	3	2092	119	0	3.41	3	1	2	178	13	0	4.38
	Chicago Wolves	AHL	2	0	1	0	33	2	0	3.64	....	....	....	....	....	....	....
2003-04	Chicago Wolves	AHL	13	7	3	2	731	32	0	2.63	....	....	....	....	....	....	....
	Gwinnett	ECHL	33	21	10	2	1936	69	4	2.14	12	7	5	770	34	0	2.65
2004-05	Chicago Wolves	AHL	24	11	9	0	1321	63	1	2.86	2	2	0	119	3	0	1.51
2005-06	**Atlanta**	**NHL**	**24**	**10**	**7**	**4**	**1271**	**73**	**2**	**3.45**	....	....	....	....	....	....	....
	Chicago Wolves	AHL	35	15	12	4	1892	106	1	3.36	....	....	....	....	....	....	....
2006-07	Chicago Wolves	AHL	42	23	15	1	2380	120	2	3.03	11	8	3	675	28	1	2.49
2007-08	Nizhnekamsk	Russia	50	....	....	....	2676	110	3	2.47	5	....	....	234	16	0	4.10
	NHL Totals		**24**	**10**	**7**	**4**	**1271**	**73**	**2**	**3.45**	....	....	....	....	....	....	....

Signed as a free agent by **Nizhnekamsk** (Russia), July 13, 2007.

GARON, Mathieu (gah-ROHN, MA-tyew) EDM.

Goaltender. Catches right. 6'2", 207 lbs. Born, Chandler, Que., January 9, 1978.
(Montreal's 2nd choice, 44th overall, in 1996 Entry Draft).

			Regular Season								Playoffs						
Season	Club	League	GP	W	L	O/T	Mins	GA	SO	Avg	GP	W	L	Mins	GA	SO	Avg
1993-94	Jonquiere Elites	QAAA	17	0	13	0	834	88	0	6.33	....	....	....	....	....	....	....
1994-95	Jonquiere Elites	QAAA	27	13	13	1	1554	94	0	3.63	9	6	2	467	26	0	3.34
1995-96	Victoriaville Tigres	QMJHL	51	18	27	0	2709	189	1	4.19	12	7	4	676	38	1	3.39
1996-97	Victoriaville Tigres	QMJHL	53	29	18	3	3032	150	*6	2.97	6	2	4	330	23	0	4.18
1997-98	Victoriaville Tigres	QMJHL	47	27	18	2	2802	125	5	2.68	6	2	4	345	22	0	3.82
1998-99	Fredericton	AHL	40	14	22	2	2222	114	3	3.08	6	1	1	208	12	0	3.47
99-2000	Quebec Citadelles	AHL	53	17	28	3	2884	149	2	3.10	1	0	0	20	3	0	8.82
2000-01	**Montreal**	**NHL**	**11**	**4**	**5**	**1**	**589**	**24**	**2**	**2.44**	....	....	....	....	....	....	....
	Quebec Citadelles	AHL	31	16	13	1	1768	86	1	2.92	8	4	4	459	22	1	2.88
2001-02	**Montreal**	**NHL**	**5**	**1**	**4**	**0**	**261**	**19**	**0**	**4.37**	....	....	....	....	....	....	....
	Quebec Citadelles	AHL	50	21	15	12	2988	136	2	2.73	3	0	3	198	12	0	3.63
2002-03	**Montreal**	**NHL**	**8**	**3**	**5**	**0**	**482**	**16**	**2**	**1.99**	....	....	....	....	....	....	....
	Hamilton Bulldogs	AHL	20	15	2	2	1150	34	4	1.77	....	....	....	....	....	....	....
2003-04	**Montreal**	**NHL**	**19**	**8**	**6**	**2**	**1003**	**38**	**0**	**2.27**	**1**	**0**	**0**	**12**	**0**	**0**	**0.00**
2004-05	Manchester	AHL	52	32	14	4	2969	105	8	2.12	6	2	4	285	17	0	3.58
2005-06	**Los Angeles**	**NHL**	**63**	**31**	**26**	**3**	**3446**	**185**	**4**	**3.22**	....	....	....	....	....	....	....
2006-07	**Los Angeles**	**NHL**	**32**	**13**	**10**	**6**	**1779**	**79**	**2**	**2.66**	....	....	....	....	....	....	....
2007-08	**Edmonton**	**NHL**	**47**	**26**	**18**	**1**	**2658**	**118**	**4**	**2.66**	....	....	....	....	....	....	....
	NHL Totals		**185**	**86**	**74**	**13**	**10218**	**479**	**14**	**2.81**	**1**	**0**	**0**	**12**	**0**	**0**	**0.00**

QMJHL All-Rookie Team (1996) • QMJHL Defensive Rookie of the Year (1996) • QMJHL First All-Star Team (1998) • Canadian Major Junior First All-Star Team (1998) • Canadian Major Junior Goaltender of the Year (1998)

Traded to **Los Angeles** by **Montreal** with San Jose's 3rd round choice (previously acquired, Los Angeles selected Paul Baier) in 2004 Entry Draft for Radek Bonk and Cristobal Huet, June 26, 2004. Signed as a free agent by **Edmonton**, July 3, 2007.

GERBER, Martin (GUHR-buhr, MAHR-tihn) OTT.

Goaltender. Catches left. 5'11", 201 lbs. Born, Burgdorf, Switz., September 3, 1974.
(Anaheim's 10th choice, 232nd overall, in 2001 Entry Draft).

			Regular Season								Playoffs						
Season	Club	League	GP	W	L	O/T	Mins	GA	SO	Avg	GP	W	L	Mins	GA	SO	Avg
1996-97	SC Langnau	Swiss-2	38	....	....	....	2286	121	0	3.18	8	....	....	488	29	0	3.57
1997-98	SC Langnau	Swiss-2	40	....	....	....	2430	141	2	3.48	16	....	....	961	42	0	2.62
1998-99	SC Langnau	Swiss	42	....	....	....	2521	203	1	4.83	11	....	....	664	50	0	4.52
99-2000	SC Langnau	Swiss	44	....	....	....	2652	161	3	3.64	6	....	....	360	13	*2	*2.17
2000-01	SCL Tigers Langnau	Swiss	*44	....	....	....	2671	114	3	2.56	5	....	....	319	7	1	1.32
2001-02	Farjestad	Sweden	44	....	....	....	2664	87	*4	*1.96	*10	....	....	*657	18	*2	*1.64
	Switzerland	Olympics	3	1	1	1	158	4	0	1.52	....	....	....	....	....	....	....
2002-03	**Anaheim**	**NHL**	**22**	**6**	**11**	**3**	**1203**	**39**	**1**	**1.95**	**2**	**0**	**0**	**20**	**1**	**0**	**3.00**
	Cincinnati	AHL	1	1	0	0	60	2	0	2.00	....	....	....	....	....	....	....
2003-04	**Anaheim**	**NHL**	**32**	**11**	**12**	**4**	**1698**	**64**	**2**	**2.26**	....	....	....	....	....	....	....
2004-05	SCL Tigers Langnau	Swiss	20	6	10	4	1220	59	0	2.90	....	....	....	....	....	....	....
	Farjestad	Sweden	30	20	6	4	1827	58	4	1.90	*15	9	6	*900	36	1	2.40
2005-06 ♦	**Carolina**	**NHL**	**60**	**38**	**14**	**6**	**3493**	**162**	**3**	**2.78**	**6**	**1**	**1**	**221**	**13**	**1**	**3.53**
	Switzerland	Olympics	3	....	....	....	160	11	1	4.13	....	....	....	....	....	....	....
2006-07	**Ottawa**	**NHL**	**29**	**15**	**9**	**3**	**1599**	**74**	**1**	**2.78**	....	....	....	....	....	....	....
2007-08	**Ottawa**	**NHL**	**57**	**30**	**18**	**4**	**3197**	**145**	**2**	**2.72**	**4**	**0**	**4**	**238**	**14**	**0**	**3.53**
	NHL Totals		**200**	**100**	**64**	**20**	**11190**	**484**	**9**	**2.60**	**12**	**1**	**5**	**479**	**28**	**1**	**3.51**

• Scored a goal in playoffs vs. Martigny (Swiss-2), February 27, 1997. Traded to **Carolina** by **Anaheim** for Tomas Malec and Carolina's 3rd round choice (Kyle Klubertanz) in 2004 Entry Draft, June 18, 2004. Signed as a free agent by **Langnau** (Swiss), September 17, 2004. Signed as a free agent by **Farjestad** (Sweden), November 7, 2004. Signed as a free agent by **Ottawa**, July 1, 2006.

GIGUERE, Jean-Sebastien (zhih-GAIR, ZHAWN-suh-BAS-tee-yehn) ANA.

Goaltender. Catches left. 6'1", 201 lbs. Born, Montreal, Que., May 16, 1977.
(Hartford's 1st choice, 13th overall, in 1995 Entry Draft).

			Regular Season								Playoffs						
Season	Club	League	GP	W	L	O/T	Mins	GA	SO	Avg	GP	W	L	Mins	GA	SO	Avg
1992-93	Laval-Laurentides	QAAA	25	12	11	2	1498	76	0	3.02	11	6	5	654	38	0	3.49
1993-94	Verdun	QMJHL	25	13	5	2	1234	66	1	3.21	....	....	....	....	....	....	....
1994-95	Halifax	QMJHL	47	14	27	5	2755	181	2	3.94	7	3	4	417	17	1	*2.45
1995-96	Halifax	QMJHL	55	26	23	2	3230	185	1	3.44	6	1	5	354	24	0	4.07
1996-97	**Hartford**	**NHL**	**8**	**1**	**4**	**0**	**394**	**24**	**0**	**3.65**	....	....	....	....	....	....	....
	Halifax	QMJHL	50	28	19	3	3014	170	2	3.38	16	9	7	954	58	0	3.65
1997-98	Saint John Flames	AHL	31	16	10	3	1758	72	2	2.46	10	5	3	536	27	0	3.02
1998-99	**Calgary**	**NHL**	**15**	**6**	**7**	**1**	**860**	**46**	**0**	**3.21**	....	....	....	....	....	....	....
	Saint John Flames	AHL	39	18	16	3	2145	123	3	3.44	7	3	2	304	21	0	4.14
99-2000	**Calgary**	**NHL**	**7**	**1**	**3**	**1**	**330**	**15**	**0**	**2.73**	....	....	....	....	....	....	....
	Saint John Flames	AHL	41	17	17	3	2243	114	0	3.05	3	0	3	178	9	0	3.03
2000-01	**Anaheim**	**NHL**	**34**	**11**	**17**	**5**	**2031**	**87**	**4**	**2.57**	....	....	....	....	....	....	....
	Cincinnati	AHL	23	12	7	2	1306	53	0	2.43	....	....	....	....	....	....	....
2001-02	**Anaheim**	**NHL**	**53**	**20**	**25**	**6**	**3127**	**111**	**4**	**2.13**	....	....	....	....	....	....	....
2002-03	**Anaheim**	**NHL**	**65**	**34**	**22**	**6**	**3775**	**145**	**8**	**2.30**	**21**	**15**	**6**	**1407**	**38**	**5**	***1.62**
2003-04	**Anaheim**	**NHL**	**55**	**17**	**31**	**6**	**3210**	**140**	**3**	**2.62**	....	....	....	....	....	....	....
2004-05	Hamburg Freezers	Germany	6	....	....	....	301	12	0	2.39	2	....	....	100	7	0	4.20
2005-06	**Anaheim**	**NHL**	**60**	**30**	**15**	**11**	**3381**	**150**	**2**	**2.66**	**6**	**3**	**3**	**318**	**18**	**0**	**3.40**
2006-07 ♦	**Anaheim**	**NHL**	**56**	**36**	**10**	**8**	**3245**	**122**	**4**	**2.26**	**18**	***13**	**4**	**1067**	**35**	**1**	**1.97**
2007-08	**Anaheim**	**NHL**	**58**	**35**	**17**	**6**	**3310**	**117**	**4**	**2.12**	**6**	**2**	**4**	**358**	**19**	**0**	**3.18**
	NHL Totals		**411**	**191**	**151**	**50**	**23663**	**957**	**29**	**2.43**	**51**	**33**	**17**	**3150**	**110**	**6**	**2.10**

QMJHL Second All-Star Team (1997) • AHL All-Rookie Team (1998) • Harry "Hap" Holmes Memorial Award (fewest goals against – AHL) (1998) (shared with Tyler Moss) • Conn Smythe Trophy (2003)

Transferred to **Carolina** after **Hartford** franchise relocated, June 25, 1997. Traded to **Calgary** by **Carolina** with Andrew Cassels for Gary Roberts and Trevor Kidd, August 25, 1997. Traded to **Anaheim** by **Calgary** for Anaheim's 2nd round choice (later traded to Washington – Washington selected Matt Pettinger) in 2000 Entry Draft, June 10, 2000. Signed as a free agent by **Hamburg** (Germany), January 31, 2005.

GISTEDT, Joel (GIHZ-tehd, JOHL) PHX.

Goaltender. Catches left. 5'11", 176 lbs. Born, Uddevalla, Sweden, December 7, 1987.
(Phoenix's 4th choice, 36th overall, in 2007 Entry Draft).

			Regular Season								Playoffs						
Season	Club	League	GP	W	L	O/T	Mins	GA	SO	Avg	GP	W	L	Mins	GA	SO	Avg
2003-04	V.Frolunda U18	Swe-U18	21	....	....	....	1258	49	1	2.34	7	....	....	422	11	2	1.57
2004-05	Frolunda U18	Swe-U18	2	....	....	....	120	6	0	3.00	6	....	....	366	14	1	2.30
	Frolunda Jr.	Swe-Jr.	8	....	....	....	485	14	0	1.73	....	....	....	....	....	....	....
2005-06	Frolunda Jr.	Swe-Jr.	32	....	....	....	1926	76	5	2.37	7	....	....	434	18	0	2.49
	Frolunda	Sweden	3	....	....	....	181	5	1	1.66	....	....	....	....	....	....	....
2006-07	Frolunda Jr.	Swe-Jr.	2	....	....	....	120	3	1	1.50	8	....	....	484	15	0	1.86
	Frolunda	Sweden	35	....	....	....	2050	88	2	2.58	....	....	....	....	....	....	....
2007-08	Frolunda Jr.	Swe-Jr.	5	....	....	....	303	7	0	1.38	....	....	....	....	....	....	....
	Frolunda	Sweden	11	....	....	....	578	37	0	3.84	....	....	....	....	....	....	....

GLASS, Jeff (GLAS, JEHF) OTT.

Goaltender. Catches left. 6'3", 206 lbs. Born, Calgary, Alta., November 19, 1985.
(Ottawa's 5th choice, 89th overall, in 2004 Entry Draft).

			Regular Season								Playoffs						
Season	Club	League	GP	W	L	O/T	Mins	GA	SO	Avg	GP	W	L	Mins	GA	SO	Avg
2001-02	Crowsnest Pass	AJHL	34	....	....	....	1802	126	0	4.20	....	....	....	....	....	....	....
2002-03	Kootenay Ice	WHL	35	15	16	3	1884	77	4	2.45	9	4	5	643	23	0	2.15
2003-04	Kootenay Ice	WHL	57	26	20	6	3263	128	5	2.35	4	0	4	239	14	0	3.51
2004-05	Kootenay Ice	WHL	51	34	11	5	3061	90	8	1.76	16	10	6	1027	39	0	2.28
2005-06	Binghamton	AHL	6	1	4	0	312	20	0	3.85	....	....	....	....	....	....	....
	Charlotte Checkers	ECHL	39	19	15	4	2221	119	2	3.22	3	1	2	178	11	0	3.71
2006-07	Binghamton	AHL	43	9	24	2	2174	149	1	4.11	....	....	....	....	....	....	....
2007-08	Binghamton	AHL	45	15	20	4	2313	111	2	2.88	....	....	....	....	....	....	....

WHL West First All-Star Team (2005) • WHL Goaltender of the Year (2005) • Canadian Major Junior First All-Star Team (2005) • Canadian Major Junior Goaltender of the Year (2005)

GOEHRING, Karl (GAIR-ihng, KAHRL)

Goaltender. Catches left. 5'8", 160 lbs. Born, Apple Valley, MN, August 23, 1978.

			Regular Season								Playoffs						
Season	Club	League	GP	W	L	O/T	Mins	GA	SO	Avg	GP	W	L	Mins	GA	SO	Avg
1996-97	Fargo-Moorhead	USHL	32	13	18	1	1909	79	*4	*2.48	5	2	3	251	15	1	3.58
1997-98	North Dakota	WCHA	27	23	3	1	1504	57	1	*2.27	....	....	....	....	....	....	....
1998-99	North Dakota	WCHA	31	22	5	2	1774	71	3	2.40	....	....	....	....	....	....	....
99-2000	North Dakota	WCHA	30	19	6	4	1747	55	*8	*1.89	....	....	....	....	....	....	....
2000-01	North Dakota	WCHA	30	16	6	6	1662	66	*3	2.38	....	....	....	....	....	....	....
2001-02	Syracuse Crunch	AHL	15	5	6	3	891	37	1	2.49	....	....	....	....	....	....	....
	Dayton Bombers	ECHL	23	11	9	3	1393	52	2	2.24	*14	9	5	*866	35	1	2.43
2002-03	Syracuse Crunch	AHL	49	18	21	4	2608	116	4	2.67	....	....	....	....	....	....	....
2003-04	Syracuse Crunch	AHL	38	17	14	6	2234	97	1	2.60	5	2	2	295	16	0	3.26
2004-05	Syracuse Crunch	AHL	49	23	22	0	2788	128	3	2.75	....	....	....	....	....	....	....
2005-06	Jokerit Helsinki	Finland	19	5	10	3	1076	57	2	3.18	....	....	....	....	....	....	....
	San Antonio	AHL	23	4	16	1	1250	65	1	3.12	....	....	....	....	....	....	....
2006-07	Milwaukee	AHL	44	22	15	4	2524	113	1	2.69	....	....	....	....	....	....	....
2007-08	Wilkes-Barre	AHL	2	0	1	0	85	3	0	2.11	....	....	....	....	....	....	....
	Norfolk Admirals	AHL	1	0	0	0	25	3	0	7.30	....	....	....	....	....	....	....
	Syracuse Crunch	AHL	26	15	8	2	1471	52	2	2.12	13	7	6	829	33	0	2.39

WCHA First All-Star Team (1998, 2000) • WCHA Rookie of the Year (1998) • NCAA West First All-American Team (1998, 2000) • WCHA Second All-Star Team (1999)

Signed as a free agent by **Columbus**, May 7, 2001. Signed as a free agent by **Jokerit Helsinki** (Finland), September 16, 2005. Signed as a free agent by **Nashville**, July 17, 2006. Signed as a free agent by **Wilkes-Barre/Scranton** (AHL), October 3, 2007.

GRAHAME, John (GRAY-uhm, JAWN)

Goaltender. Catches left. 6'3", 220 lbs. Born, Denver, CO, August 31, 1975.
(Boston's 7th choice, 229th overall, in 1994 Entry Draft).

			Regular Season								Playoffs						
Season	Club	League	GP	W	L	O/T	Mins	GA	SO	Avg	GP	W	L	Mins	GA	SO	Avg
1993-94	Sioux City	USHL	20	....	....	....	1200	73	0	3.70	....	....	....	....	....	....	....
1994-95	Lake Superior State	CCHA	28	16	7	3	1616	75	2	2.79	....	....	....	....	....	....	....
1995-96	Lake Superior State	CCHA	29	21	4	2	1558	66	2	2.54	....	....	....	....	....	....	....
1996-97	Lake Superior State	CCHA	37	19	13	4	2197	134	3	3.66	....	....	....	....	....	....	....
1997-98	Providence Bruins	AHL	55	15	31	4	3053	164	3	3.22	....	....	....	....	....	....	....
1998-99	Providence Bruins	AHL	48	*37	9	1	2771	134	3	2.90	19	*15	4	*1209	48	1	2.38
99-2000	**Boston**	**NHL**	**24**	**7**	**10**	**5**	**1344**	**55**	**2**	**2.46**	....	....	....	....	....	....	....
	Providence Bruins	AHL	27	11	13	2	1528	86	1	3.38	13	10	3	839	35	0	2.50
2000-01	**Boston**	**NHL**	**10**	**3**	**4**	**0**	**471**	**28**	**0**	**3.57**	....	....	....	....	....	....	....
	Providence Bruins	AHL	16	4	7	3	893	47	0	3.16	17	8	9	1043	46	2	2.65
2001-02	**Boston**	**NHL**	**19**	**8**	**7**	**2**	**1079**	**52**	**1**	**2.89**	....	....	....	....	....	....	....
2002-03	**Boston**	**NHL**	**23**	**11**	**9**	**2**	**1352**	**61**	**1**	**2.71**	....	....	....	....	....	....	....
	Tampa Bay	**NHL**	**17**	**6**	**5**	**4**	**914**	**34**	**2**	**2.23**	**1**	**0**	**1**	**111**	**2**	**0**	**1.08**
2003-04 ♦	**Tampa Bay**	**NHL**	**29**	**18**	**9**	**1**	**1688**	**58**	**1**	**2.06**	**1**	**0**	**0**	**34**	**2**	**0**	**3.53**
2004-05							DID NOT PLAY										
2005-06	**Tampa Bay**	**NHL**	**57**	**29**	**22**	**1**	**3152**	**161**	**5**	**3.06**	**4**	**1**	**3**	**188**	**15**	**0**	**4.79**
	United States	Olympics	1	0	0	1	60	3	0	3.00	....	....	....	....	....	....	....
2006-07	**Carolina**	**NHL**	**28**	**10**	**13**	**2**	**1515**	**72**	**0**	**2.85**	....	....	....	....	....	....	....
2007-08	**Carolina**	**NHL**	**17**	**5**	**7**	**1**	**848**	**53**	**0**	**3.75**	....	....	....	....	....	....	....
	Albany River Rats	AHL	7	4	3	0	415	21	0	3.04	....	....	....	....	....	....	....
	NHL Totals		**224**	**97**	**86**	**18**	**12363**	**574**	**12**	**2.79**	**6**	**1**	**4**	**333**	**19**	**0**	**3.42**

Traded to **Tampa Bay** by **Boston** for Tampa Bay's 4th round choice (later traded to San Jose – San Jose selected Jason Churchill) in 2004 Entry Draft, January 13, 2003. Signed as a free agent by **Carolina**, July 1, 2006. Signed as a free agent by **Omsk** (Russia), May 17, 2008.

GREISS, Thomas (GRIGHS, TAW-muhs) S.J.

Goaltender. Catches left. 6'1", 200 lbs. Born, Straubing, West Germany, January 29, 1986.
(San Jose's 2nd choice, 94th overall, in 2004 Entry Draft).

			Regular Season								Playoffs						
Season	Club	League	GP	W	L	O/T	Mins	GA	SO	Avg	GP	W	L	Mins	GA	SO	Avg
2001-02	EV Fussen Jr.	Ger-Jr.					STATISTICS NOT AVAILABLE										
2002-03	Koln Jr.	Ger-Jr.	25	....	....	....	1613	58	0	2.16	3	1	2	180	8	1	2.67
2003-04	Koln Jr.	Ger-Jr.	24	....	....	....	1286	56	....	2.61	....	....	....	....	....	....	....
	Kolner Haie	Germany	1	....	....	....	20	4	0	12.00	....	....	....	....	....	....	....
2004-05	Kolner Haie	Germany	8	....	....	....	459	16	0	2.09	....	....	....	....	....	....	....
	Regensburg	German-2	1	....	....	....	60	2	0	2.00	2	....	....	56	2	0	2.14
2005-06	Kolner Haie	Germany	27	....	....	....	1560	64	1	2.46	9	....	....	533	27	*1	3.04
	Germany	Olympics	1	0	1	0	60	5	0	5.00	....	....	....	....	....	....	....
2006-07	Worcester Sharks	AHL	43	26	15	2	2555	111	0	2.61	3	0	3	172	12	0	4.18
	Fresno Falcons	ECHL	3	1	2	0	180	7	0	2.34	....	....	....	....	....	....	....
2007-08	**San Jose**	**NHL**	**3**	**0**	**1**	**1**	**129**	**7**	**0**	**3.26**	....	....	....	....	....	....	....
	Worcester Sharks	AHL	41	18	21	2	2424	125	0	3.09	....	....	....	....	....	....	....
	NHL Totals		**3**	**0**	**1**	**1**	**129**	**7**	**0**	**3.26**	....	....	....	....	....	....	....

GRUMET-MORRIS, Dov (groo-MAY-MAW-rihs, DAWV)

Goaltender. Catches left. 6'2", 205 lbs. Born, Evanston, IL, February 28, 1982.
(Philadelphia's 4th choice, 161st overall, in 2002 Entry Draft).

			Regular Season								Playoffs						
Season	Club	League	GP	W	L	O/T	Mins	GA	SO	Avg	GP	W	L	Mins	GA	SO	Avg
2000-01	Danville Wings	NAHL	27	19	5	2	1547	57	3	2.21	5	2	2	300	17	0	3.40
2001-02	Harvard Crimson	ECAC	21	10	8	1	1226	58	1	2.84	....	....	....	....	....	....	....
2002-03	Harvard Crimson	ECAC	29	18	9	2	1741	69	1	2.38	....	....	....	....	....	....	....
2003-04	Harvard Crimson	ECAC	33	16	14	3	1933	76	3	2.36	....	....	....	....	....	....	....
2004-05	Harvard Crimson	ECAC	31	19	9	3	1911	52	6	1.63	....	....	....	....	....	....	....
2005-06	San Antonio	AHL	1	0	1	0	60	7	0	7.04	....	....	....	....	....	....	....
	Laredo Bucks	CHL	25	18	5	2	1477	50	3	*2.03	10	*8	2	644	21	*1	1.96
2006-07	Portland Pirates	AHL	11	1	6	3	594	30	1	3.03	....	....	....	....	....	....	....
	Hamilton Bulldogs	AHL	2	1	0	1	125	2	1	0.96	....	....	....	....	....	....	....
	Manitoba Moose	AHL	4	2	1	1	245	5	2	1.23	....	....	....	....	....	....	....
	Cincinnati	ECHL	22	11	8	3	1341	62	0	2.78	....	....	....	....	....	....	....
2007-08	Milwaukee	AHL	9	4	4	0	511	23	0	2.70	1	0	0	20	0	0	0.00
	Cincinnati	ECHL	26	20	3	1	1496	59	0	2.37	....	....	....	....	....	....	....

ECAC Second All-Star Team (2005) • NCAA East Second All-American Team (2005)

Signed as a free agent by **Nashville**, July 2, 2007.

HALAK, Jaroslav (HAH-lak, YAHR-roh-slav) MTL.

Goaltender. Catches left. 5'11", 182 lbs. Born, Bratislava, Czech., May 13, 1985.
(Montreal's 11th choice, 271st overall, in 2003 Entry Draft).

			Regular Season								Playoffs						
Season	Club	League	GP	W	L	O/T	Mins	GA	SO	Avg	GP	W	L	Mins	GA	SO	Avg
2001-02	Bratislava Jr.	Slovak-Jr.	22	....	....	....	1257	41	0	1.96	6	6	0	353	7	2	1.19
2002-03	Bratislava Jr.	Slovak-Jr.	20	13	3	3	1200	41	1	2.02	....	....	....	....	....	....	....
2003-04	Bratislava Jr.	Slovak-Jr.	29	....	....	....	1694	51	....	1.81	....	....	....	....	....	....	....
	HK 91 Senica	Slovak-2	21	....	....	....	1240	54	....	2.61	....	....	....	....	....	....	....
	Bratislava	Slovakia	12	....	....	....	650	18	0	1.66	1	....	....	45	6	0	8.00
2004-05	Lewiston	QMJHL	47	24	17	4	2697	125	4	2.78	8	4	4	460	27	0	3.52
2005-06	Hamilton Bulldogs	AHL	13	7	6	0	786	30	3	2.29	....	....	....	....	....	....	....
	Long Beach	ECHL	20	11	4	2	1026	35	2	2.05	4	2	2	252	13	0	3.10
2006-07	**Montreal**	**NHL**	**16**	**10**	**6**	**0**	**912**	**44**	**2**	**2.89**	....	....	....	....	....	....	....
	Hamilton Bulldogs	AHL	28	16	11	0	1618	54	6	*2.00	....	....	....	....	....	....	....
2007-08	**Montreal**	**NHL**	**6**	**2**	**1**	**1**	**285**	**10**	**1**	**2.11**	**2**	**0**	**1**	**77**	**3**	**0**	**2.34**
	Hamilton Bulldogs	AHL	28	15	10	2	1630	57	2	2.10	....	....	....	....	....	....	....
	NHL Totals		**22**	**12**	**7**	**1**	**1197**	**54**	**3**	**2.71**	**2**	**0**	**1**	**77**	**3**	**0**	**2.34**

AHL All-Rookie Team (2007)

HARDING, Josh (HAHR-dihng, JAWSH) MIN.

Goaltender. Catches right. 6'1", 197 lbs. Born, Regina, Sask., June 18, 1984.
(Minnesota's 2nd choice, 38th overall, in 2002 Entry Draft).

			Regular Season								Playoffs						
Season	Club	League	GP	W	L	O/T	Mins	GA	SO	Avg	GP	W	L	Mins	GA	SO	Avg
2000-01	Reg. Pat Cdns.	SMHL	36	17	13	0	2106	96	2	2.75	3	1	2	170	11	0	3.88
2001-02	Regina Pats	WHL	42	27	13	1	2389	95	*4	2.39	6	2	4	325	16	0	2.95
2002-03	Regina Pats	WHL	57	18	24	13	*3385	155	3	2.75	5	1	4	321	13	0	2.43
2003-04	Regina Pats	WHL	28	12	14	2	1665	67	2	2.41	....	....	....	....	....	....	....
	Brandon	WHL	27	13	11	3	1612	65	5	2.42	11	5	6	660	36	0	3.27
2004-05	Houston Aeros	AHL	42	21	16	3	2388	80	4	2.01	2	0	2	119	8	0	4.03
2005-06	**Minnesota**	**NHL**	**3**	**2**	**1**	**0**	**185**	**8**	**1**	**2.59**	....	....	....	....	....	....	....
	Houston Aeros	AHL	38	29	8	0	2215	99	2	2.68	8	4	4	476	30	0	3.79
2006-07	**Minnesota**	**NHL**	**7**	**3**	**2**	**1**	**361**	**7**	**1**	**1.16**	....	....	....	....	....	....	....
	Houston Aeros	AHL	38	17	16	4	2270	94	1	2.48	....	....	....	....	....	....	....
2007-08	**Minnesota**	**NHL**	**29**	**11**	**15**	**2**	**1571**	**77**	**1**	**2.94**	**1**	**0**	**0**	**20**	**0**	**0**	**0.00**
	NHL Totals		**39**	**16**	**18**	**3**	**2117**	**92**	**3**	**2.61**	**1**	**0**	**0**	**20**	**0**	**0**	**0.00**

WHL East Second All-Star Team (2002) • WHL East First All-Star Team (2003) • WHL Goaltender of the Year (2003) • WHL Player of the Year (2003)

HASEK, Dominik (HAH-shihk, DOHM-ihn-ihk)

Goaltender. Catches left. 6'1", 166 lbs. Born, Pardubice, Czech., January 29, 1965.
(Chicago's 11th choice, 207th overall, in 1983 Entry Draft).

			Regular Season								Playoffs						
Season	Club	League	GP	W	L	O/T	Mins	GA	SO	Avg	GP	W	L	Mins	GA	SO	Avg
1981-82	Tesla Pardubice	Czech	12	....	....	....	661	34	....	3.09	....	....	....	....	....	....	....
1982-83	Tesla Pardubice	Czech	42	....	....	....	2358	105	....	2.67	....	....	....	....	....	....	....
1983-84	Tesla Pardubice	Czech	40	....	....	....	2304	108	....	2.81	....	....	....	....	....	....	....
1984-85	Tesla Pardubice	Czech	42	....	....	....	2419	131	....	3.25	....	....	....	....	....	....	....
1985-86	Tesla Pardubice	Czech	45	....	....	....	2689	138	....	3.08	....	....	....	....	....	....	....
1986-87	Tesla Pardubice	Czech	43	....	....	....	2515	103	....	2.46	....	....	....	....	....	....	....
1987-88	Tesla Pardubice	Czech	31	....	....	....	1862	93	....	3.00	....	....	....	....	....	....	....
	Czechoslovakia	Olympics	5	3	2	0	217	18	1	4.98	....	....	....	....	....	....	....
1988-89	Tesla Pardubice	Czech	42	....	....	....	2507	114	....	2.73	....	....	....	....	....	....	....
1989-90	Dukla Jihlava	Czech	40	....	....	....	2251	80	....	2.13	....	....	....	....	....	....	....
1990-91	**Chicago**	**NHL**	**5**	**3**	**0**	**1**	**195**	**8**	**0**	**2.46**	**3**	**0**	**0**	**69**	**3**	**0**	**2.61**
	Indianapolis Ice	IHL	33	20	11	1	1903	80	*5	*2.52	1	1	0	60	3	0	3.00
1991-92	**Chicago**	**NHL**	**20**	**10**	**4**	**1**	**1014**	**44**	**1**	**2.60**	**3**	**0**	**2**	**158**	**8**	**0**	**3.04**
	Indianapolis Ice	IHL	20	7	10	3	1162	69	1	3.56	....	....	....	....	....	....	....
1992-93	**Buffalo**	**NHL**	**28**	**11**	**10**	**4**	**1429**	**75**	**0**	**3.15**	**1**	**1**	**0**	**45**	**1**	**0**	**1.33**
1993-94	**Buffalo**	**NHL**	**58**	**30**	**20**	**6**	**3358**	**109**	***7**	***1.95**	**7**	**3**	**4**	**484**	**13**	**2**	***1.61**
1994-95	HC Pardubice	CzRep	2	1	0	1	124	6	0	2.90	....	....	....	....	....	....	....
	Buffalo	**NHL**	**41**	**19**	**14**	**7**	**2416**	**85**	***5**	***2.11**	**5**	**1**	**4**	**309**	**18**	**0**	**3.50**
1995-96	**Buffalo**	**NHL**	**59**	**22**	**30**	**6**	**3417**	**161**	**2**	**2.83**	....	....	....	....	....	....	....
1996-97	**Buffalo**	**NHL**	**67**	**37**	**20**	**10**	**4037**	**153**	**5**	**2.27**	**3**	**1**	**1**	**153**	**5**	**0**	**1.96**
1997-98	**Buffalo**	**NHL**	***72**	**33**	**23**	**13**	***4220**	**147**	***13**	**2.09**	**15**	**10**	**5**	**948**	**32**	**1**	**2.03**
	Czech Republic	Olympics	6	*5	1	0	*369	6	*2	*0.97	....	....	....	....	....	....	....
1998-99	**Buffalo**	**NHL**	**64**	**30**	**18**	**14**	**3817**	**119**	**9**	**1.87**	**19**	**13**	**6**	**1217**	**36**	**2**	**1.77**
99-2000	**Buffalo**	**NHL**	**35**	**15**	**11**	**6**	**2066**	**76**	**3**	**2.21**	**5**	**1**	**4**	**301**	**12**	**0**	**2.39**
2000-01	**Buffalo**	**NHL**	**67**	**37**	**24**	**4**	**3904**	**137**	***11**	**2.11**	**13**	**7**	**6**	**833**	**29**	**1**	**2.09**
2001-02 ♦	**Detroit**	**NHL**	**65**	***41**	**15**	**8**	**3872**	**140**	**5**	**2.17**	***23**	***16**	**7**	***1455**	**45**	***6**	**1.86**
	Czech Republic	Olympics	4	1	2	1	239	8	0	2.01	....	....	....	....	....	....	....
2002-03							OUT OF HOCKEY – RETIRED										
2003-04	**Detroit**	**NHL**	**14**	**8**	**3**	**2**	**817**	**30**	**2**	**2.20**	....	....	....	....	....	....	....
2004-05							DID NOT PLAY										
2005-06	**Ottawa**	**NHL**	**43**	**28**	**10**	**4**	**2584**	**90**	**5**	**2.09**	....	....	....	....	....	....	....
	Czech Republic	Olympics	1	0	0	0	9	0	0	0.00	....	....	....	....	....	....	....
2006-07	**Detroit**	**NHL**	**56**	**38**	**11**	**6**	**3341**	**114**	**8**	**2.05**	**18**	**10**	**8**	**1140**	**34**	**2**	**1.79**
2007-08 ♦	**Detroit**	**NHL**	**41**	**27**	**10**	**3**	**2350**	**84**	**5**	**2.14**	**4**	**2**	**2**	**206**	**10**	**0**	**2.91**
	NHL Totals		**735**	**389**	**223**	**95**	**42837**	**1572**	**81**	**2.20**	**119**	**65**	**49**	**7318**	**246**	**14**	**2.02**

Czechoslovakian Goaltender of the Year (1986, 1987, 1988, 1989, 1990) • Czechoslovakian Player of the Year (1987, 1989, 1990) • Czechoslovakian First All-Star Team (1988, 1989, 1990) • IHL First All-Star Team (1991) • NHL All-Rookie Team (1992) • NHL First All-Star Team (1994, 1995, 1997, 1998, 1999, 2001) • William M. Jennings Trophy (1994) (shared with Grant Fuhr) • Vezina Trophy (1994, 1995, 1997, 1998, 1999, 2001) • Lester B. Pearson Award (1997, 1998) • Hart Memorial Trophy (1997, 1998) • William M. Jennings Trophy (2001) • William M. Jennings Trophy (2008) (shared with Chris Osgood)

Played in NHL All-Star Game (1996, 1997, 1998, 1999, 2001, 2002)

Traded to **Buffalo** by **Chicago** for Stephane Beauregard and Buffalo's 4th round choice (Eric Daze) in 1993 Entry Draft, August 7, 1992. Traded to **Detroit** by **Buffalo** for Vyacheslav Kozlov, Detroit's 1st round choice (later traded to Columbus – later traded to Atlanta – Atlanta selected Jim Slater) in 2002 Entry Draft, July 1, 2001. • Officially announced his retirement, June 25, 2002. • **Detroit** picked up the option on his contract, July 1, 2003. • Missed majority of 2003-04 season recovering from groin injury suffered in game vs. St. Louis, October 29, 2003. Signed as a free agent by **Ottawa**, July 6, 2004. Signed as a free agent by **Detroit**, July 31, 2006. • Officially announced his retirement, June 9, 2008.

HAUSER, Adam (HOW-suhr, A-duhm)

Goaltender. Catches left. 6'2", 195 lbs. Born, Bovey, MN, May 27, 1980.
(Edmonton's 4th choice, 81st overall, in 1999 Entry Draft).

			Regular Season								Playoffs						
Season	Club	League	GP	W	L	O/T	Mins	GA	SO	Avg	GP	W	L	Mins	GA	SO	Avg
1996-97	Greenway Raiders	High-MN	25	....	....	....	1496	63	0	2.54	....	....	....	....	....	....	....
1997-98	USNTDP	U-18	19	9	5	4	1138	44	1	2.32	....	....	....	....	....	....	....
	USNTDP	USHL	13	5	4	3	668	39	1	3.50	....	....	....	....	....	....	....
	USNTDP	NAHL	5	4	1	0	304	11	1	2.17	1	1	0	60	0	1	0.00
1998-99	U. of Minnesota	WCHA	*40	14	18	8	*2350	136	3	3.47	....	....	....	....	....	....	....
99-2000	U. of Minnesota	WCHA	36	20	14	2	2114	104	1	2.95	....	....	....	....	....	....	....
2000-01	U. of Minnesota	WCHA	40	*26	12	2	2366	101	*3	2.56	....	....	....	....	....	....	....
2001-02	U. of Minnesota	WCHA	35	*23	6	4	2003	80	1	2.40	....	....	....	....	....	....	....
2002-03	Providence Bruins	AHL	1	0	0	1	64	3	0	2.80	....	....	....	....	....	....	....
	Jackson Bandits	ECHL	34	20	9	4	2021	83	*5	2.46	....	....	....	....	....	....	....
2003-04	Manchester	AHL	43	20	15	7	2536	82	7	1.94	4	2	2	286	9	2	1.89
	Reading Royals	ECHL	4	3	0	1	245	7	1	1.71	....	....	....	....	....	....	....
2004-05	Manchester	AHL	32	19	11	0	1867	60	5	1.93	2	0	0	70	2	0	1.71
2005-06	**Los Angeles**	**NHL**	**1**	**0**	**0**	**0**	**51**	**6**	**0**	**7.06**	....	....	....	....	....	....	....
	Manchester	AHL	45	22	17	2	2600	111	3	2.56	3	1	2	177	9	0	3.05
2006-07	Kolner Haie	Germany	40	....	....	....	2427	95	4	2.35	9	....	....	554	29	1	3.14
2007-08	Adler Mannheim	Germany	51	31	19	0	2950	141	1	2.87	4	1	3	351	14	0	2.39
	NHL Totals		**1**	**0**	**0**	**0**	**51**	**6**	**0**	**7.06**	....	....	....	....	....	....	....

NCAA Championship All-Tournament Team (2002) • ECHL All-Rookie Team (2003)

Signed as a free agent by **Manchester** (AHL), August 19, 2003. Signed as a free agent by **Los Angeles**, July 8, 2004. Signed as a free agent by **Kolner** (Germany), July 9, 2006.

HEDBERG, Johan (HEHD-buhrg, YOH-han) ATL.

Goaltender. Catches left. 6', 185 lbs. Born, Leksand, Sweden, May 5, 1973.
(Philadelphia's 8th choice, 218th overall, in 1994 Entry Draft).

			Regular Season								Playoffs						
Season	Club	League	GP	W	L	O/T	Mins	GA	SO	Avg	GP	W	L	Mins	GA	SO	Avg
1992-93	Leksands IF	Sweden	10	....	....	....	600	24	....	2.40	....	....	....	....	....	....	....
1993-94	Leksands IF	Sweden	17	....	....	....	1020	48	....	2.82	....	....	....	....	....	....	....
1994-95	Leksands IF	Sweden	17	....	....	....	986	58	....	3.53	....	....	....	....	....	....	....
1995-96	Leksands IF	Sweden	34	....	....	....	2013	95	....	2.83	4	....	....	240	13	....	3.25
1996-97	Leksands IF	Sweden	38	....	....	....	2260	95	3	2.52	8	....	....	581	18	1	1.86
1997-98	Detroit Vipers	IHL	16	7	2	2	726	32	1	2.64	....	....	....	....	....	....	....
	Baton Rouge	ECHL	2	1	1	0	100	7	0	4.20	....	....	....	....	....	....	....
	Manitoba Moose	IHL	14	8	4	1	745	32	1	2.58	2	0	2	105	6	0	3.40
	Sweden	Olympics					DID NOT PLAY – SPARE GOALTENDER										
1998-99	Leksands IF	Sweden	*48	....	....	....	*2940	140	0	2.86	4	....	....	255	15	0	3.53
99-2000	Kentucky	AHL	33	18	9	5	1973	88	3	2.68	5	3	2	311	10	1	1.93
2000-01	Manitoba Moose	IHL	46	23	13	7	2697	115	1	2.56	....	....	....	....	....	....	....
	Pittsburgh	**NHL**	**9**	**7**	**1**	**1**	**545**	**24**	**0**	**2.64**	**18**	**9**	**9**	**1123**	**43**	**2**	**2.30**
2001-02	**Pittsburgh**	**NHL**	**66**	**25**	**34**	**7**	**3877**	**178**	**6**	**2.75**	....	....	....	....	....	....	....
	Sweden	Olympics	1	1	0	0	60	1	0	1.00	....	....	....	....	....	....	....
2002-03	**Pittsburgh**	**NHL**	**41**	**14**	**22**	**4**	**2410**	**126**	**1**	**3.14**	....	....	....	....	....	....	....
2003-04	**Vancouver**	**NHL**	**21**	**8**	**6**	**2**	**1098**	**46**	**3**	**2.51**	**2**	**1**	**1**	**98**	**4**	**0**	**2.45**
	Manitoba Moose	AHL	2	0	2	0	125	9	0	4.32	....	....	....	....	....	....	....
2004-05	Leksands IF	Sweden-2	21	....	....	....	1274	45	1	2.12	....	....	....	....	....	....	....
2005-06	**Dallas**	**NHL**	**19**	**12**	**4**	**1**	**1079**	**48**	**0**	**2.67**	....	....	....	....	....	....	....
2006-07	**Atlanta**	**NHL**	**21**	**9**	**4**	**2**	**1057**	**51**	**0**	**2.89**	**2**	**0**	**2**	**117**	**5**	**0**	**2.56**
2007-08	**Atlanta**	**NHL**	**36**	**14**	**15**	**3**	**1927**	**111**	**1**	**3.46**	....	....	....	....	....	....	....
	NHL Totals		**213**	**89**	**86**	**20**	**11993**	**584**	**11**	**2.92**	**22**	**10**	**12**	**1338**	**52**	**2**	**2.33**

Rights traded to **San Jose** by **Philadelphia** for San Jose's 7th round choice (Pavel Kasparik) in 1999 Entry Draft, August 6, 1998. Traded to **Pittsburgh** by **San Jose** with Bobby Dollas for Jeff Norton, March 12, 2001. Traded to **Vancouver** by **Pittsburgh** for Vancouver's 2nd round choice (Alex Goligoski) in 2004 Entry Draft, August 25, 2003. Signed as a free agent by **Leksands** (Sweden-2), August 1, 2004. Signed as a free agent by **Dallas**, August 5, 2005. Signed as a free agent by **Atlanta**, July 1, 2006.

HELENIUS, Riku (heh-lehn-NEE-uhs, REE-koo) T.B.

Goaltender. Catches left. 6'3", 202 lbs. Born, Palkane, Finland, March 1, 1988.
(Tampa Bay's 1st choice, 15th overall, in 2006 Entry Draft).

			Regular Season								Playoffs						
Season	Club	League	GP	W	L	O/T	Mins	GA	SO	Avg	GP	W	L	Mins	GA	SO	Avg
2004-05	Ilves Tampere U18	Fin-U18	16	....	....	....	903	30	3	1.99	5	....	....	295	15	0	3.05
	Ilves Tampere Jr.	Fin-Jr.	2	....	....	....	86	4	0	2.77	....	....	....	....	....	....	....
2005-06	Suomi U20	Finland-2	1	....	....	....	60	3	0	3.00	....	....	....	....	....	....	....
	Ilves Tampere U18	Fin-U18	2	....	....	....	120	2	0	1.00	5	....	....	300	13	0	2.60
	Ilves Tampere Jr.	Fin-Jr.	26	....	....	....	1565	70	4	2.68	2	....	....	135	7	0	3.11
2006-07	Ilves Tampere Jr.	Fin-Jr.	2	2	0	0	120	4	0	2.00	....	....	....	....	....	....	....
2007-08	Seattle	WHL	41	22	12	6	2358	95	3	2.42	9	4	5	534	24	0	2.70

HILLER, Jonas (HIHL-uhr, YOH-nuhs) ANA.

Goaltender. Catches right. 6'2", 196 lbs. Born, Felben Wellhausen, Switz., February 12, 1982.

			Regular Season								Playoffs						
Season	Club	League	GP	W	L	O/T	Mins	GA	SO	Avg	GP	W	L	Mins	GA	SO	Avg
2000-01	HC Davos	Swiss	1	0	0	0	9	0	0	0.00	....	....	....	....	....	....	....

2001-02	HC Davos	Swiss					DID NOT PLAY										
2002-03	HC Davos	Swiss					DID NOT PLAY										
2003-04	Chaux-de-Fonds	Swiss-2	1	0	1	0	60	4	0	4.00	....	....	....	....	....	....	....
	Lausanne HC	Swiss	21	....	....	....	1161	64	1	3.31	....	....	....	....	....	....	....
	Lausanne HC	Swiss-Q	....	....	....	....	....	....	....	....	4	4	0	251	7	0	1.67
2004-05	HC Davos	Swiss	43	26	12	4	2519	95	8	2.26	15	12	3	932	34	0	2.19
2005-06	HC Davos	Swiss	44	23	16	5	2676	110	3	2.47	15	9	6	900	45	1	3.00
2006-07	HC Davos	Swiss	44	28	16	0	2656	115	3	2.60	19	12	7	1138	39	3	2.05
2007-08	**Anaheim**	**NHL**	**23**	**10**	**7**	**1**	**1223**	**42**	**0**	**2.06**	....	....	....	....	....	....	....
	Portland Pirates	AHL	6	3	2	1	370	13	0	2.11	....	....	....	....	....	....	....
	NHL Totals		**23**	**10**	**7**	**1**	**1223**	**42**	**0**	**2.06**	....	....	....	....	....	....	....

Signed as a free agent by **Anaheim**, May 25, 2007.

HOLMQVIST, Johan (HOHLM-kvihst, YOH-han)

Goaltender. Catches left. 6'3", 198 lbs. Born, Tolfta, Sweden, May 24, 1978.
(NY Rangers' 9th choice, 175th overall, in 1997 Entry Draft).

			Regular Season								Playoffs						
Season	**Club**	**League**	**GP**	**W**	**L**	**O/T**	**Mins**	**GA**	**SO**	**Avg**	**GP**	**W**	**L**	**Mins**	**GA**	**SO**	**Avg**
1996-97	Brynas IF Gavle	Sweden	2	0	0	0	80	4	0	3.00	....	....	....	....	....	....	....
1997-98	Brynas IF Gavle	Sweden	33	....	....	....	1897	82	....	2.59	3	0	3	180	14	....	4.67
1998-99	Brynas IF Gavle	Sweden	41	....	....	....	2383	111	4	2.79	*14	9	5	*855	34	0	2.39
99-2000	Brynas IF Gavle	Sweden	41	....	....	....	2402	104	4	2.60	11	....	....	671	30	1	2.68
2000-01	**NY Rangers**	**NHL**	**2**	**0**	**2**	**0**	**119**	**10**	**0**	**5.04**	....	....	....	....	....	....	....
	Hartford Wolf Pack	AHL	43	19	14	4	2305	111	2	2.89	5	2	3	314	13	0	2.48
2001-02	**NY Rangers**	**NHL**	**1**	**0**	**0**	**0**	**9**	**0**	**0**	**0.00**	....	....	....	....	....	....	....
	Hartford Wolf Pack	AHL	48	26	12	6	2734	140	1	3.07	4	1	2	163	12	0	4.41
2002-03	**NY Rangers**	**NHL**	**1**	**0**	**1**	**0**	**39**	**2**	**0**	**3.08**	....	....	....	....	....	....	....
	Hartford Wolf Pack	AHL	35	14	13	5	1904	84	2	2.65	....	....	....	....	....	....	....
	Charlotte Checkers	ECHL	1	1	0	0	60	2	0	2.00	....	....	....	....	....	....	....
	Houston Aeros	AHL	8	5	3	0	479	23	1	2.88	*23	*15	8	*1499	50	1	2.00
2003-04	Houston Aeros	AHL	59	23	27	7	3467	148	4	2.56	....	....	....	....	....	....	....
2004-05	Brynas IF Gavle	Sweden	42	....	....	....	2445	138	1	3.39	....	....	....	....	....	....	....
2005-06	Brynas IF Gavle	Sweden	26	....	....	....	1539	50	3	*1.95	4	....	....	194	13	0	4.02
2006-07	**Tampa Bay**	**NHL**	**48**	**27**	**15**	**3**	**2548**	**121**	**1**	**2.85**	**6**	**2**	**4**	**370**	**18**	**0**	**2.92**
2007-08	**Tampa Bay**	**NHL**	**45**	**20**	**16**	**6**	**2469**	**124**	**2**	**3.01**	....	....	....	....	....	....	....
	Dallas	**NHL**	**2**	**1**	**0**	**0**	**80**	**5**	**0**	**3.75**	....	....	....	....	....	....	....
	NHL Totals		**99**	**48**	**34**	**9**	**5264**	**262**	**3**	**2.99**	**6**	**2**	**4**	**370**	**18**	**0**	**2.92**

Jack A. Butterfield Trophy (Playoff MVP – AHL) (2003)

Traded to **Minnesota** by **NY Rangers** for Lawrence Nycholat, March 11, 2003. Signed as a free agent by **Gavle** (Sweden), July 29, 2004. Signed as a free agent by **Tampa Bay**, June 1, 2006. Traded to **Dallas** by **Tampa Bay** with Brad Richards for Mike Smith, Jussi Jokinen, Jeff Halpern and Dallas' 4th round choice in 2009 Entry Draft, February 26, 2008.

HOLT, Chris (HOHLT, KRIHS)

Goaltender. Catches left. 6'3", 221 lbs. Born, Vancouver, B.C., June 5, 1985.
(NY Rangers' 8th choice, 180th overall, in 2003 Entry Draft).

			Regular Season								Playoffs						
Season	**Club**	**League**	**GP**	**W**	**L**	**O/T**	**Mins**	**GA**	**SO**	**Avg**	**GP**	**W**	**L**	**Mins**	**GA**	**SO**	**Avg**
2001-02	Billings Bulls	AWHL	24	13	7	1	1184	59	2	2.99	....	....	....	....	....	....	....
2002-03	USNTDP	U-18	27	7	12	2	1519	81	1	3.20	....	....	....	....	....	....	....
	USNTDP	NAHL	5	2	3	0	255	14	0	3.30	....	....	....	....	....	....	....
2003-04	Nebraska-Omaha	CCHA	27	5	17	2	1499	81	0	3.24	....	....	....	....	....	....	....
2004-05	Nebraska-Omaha	CCHA	37	19	14	4	2190	106	1	2.90	....	....	....	....	....	....	....
2005-06	**NY Rangers**	**NHL**	**1**	**0**	**0**	**0**	**10**	**0**	**0**	**0.00**	....	....	....	....	....	....	....
	Hartford Wolf Pack	AHL	9	3	2	1	459	31	0	4.06	8	4	4	487	24	0	2.96
	Charlotte Checkers	ECHL	23	7	11	1	1229	84	0	4.10	....	....	....	....	....	....	....
2006-07	Hartford Wolf Pack	AHL	6	2	1	0	240	8	0	2.00	1	0	0	26	1	0	2.28
	Charlotte Checkers	ECHL	45	24	18	2	2650	139	1	3.15	4	2	2	223	11	0	2.97
2007-08	Hartford Wolf Pack	AHL	9	5	3	0	447	18	0	2.42	....	....	....	....	....	....	....
	Charlotte Checkers	ECHL	32	15	13	2	1808	82	3	2.72	3	0	3	179	10	0	3.35
	NHL Totals		**1**	**0**	**0**	**0**	**10**	**0**	**0**	**0.00**	....	....	....	....	....	....	....

HOLTBY, Braden (HOHLT-bee, BRAY-duhn) WSH.

Goaltender. Catches left. 6'1", 202 lbs. Born, Lloydminster, Sask., September 16, 1989.
(Washington's 5th choice, 93rd overall, in 2008 Entry Draft).

			Regular Season								Playoffs						
Season	**Club**	**League**	**GP**	**W**	**L**	**O/T**	**Mins**	**GA**	**SO**	**Avg**	**GP**	**W**	**L**	**Mins**	**GA**	**SO**	**Avg**
2005-06	Saskatoon Blazers	SMHL					STATISTICS NOT AVAILABLE										
	Saskatoon Blades	WHL	1	0	1	0	59	4	0	4.07	....	....	....	....	....	....	....
2006-07	Saskatoon Blades	WHL	51	17	29	3	2725	146	0	3.21	....	....	....	....	....	....	....
2007-08	Saskatoon Blades	WHL	*64	25	29	0	3632	172	1	2.84	....	....	....	....	....	....	....

HOULE, Martin (HOOL, MAHR-tihn)

Goaltender. Catches left. 5'11", 185 lbs. Born, Montreal, Que., February 12, 1985.
(Philadelphia's 8th choice, 232nd overall, in 2004 Entry Draft).

			Regular Season								Playoffs						
Season	**Club**	**League**	**GP**	**W**	**L**	**O/T**	**Mins**	**GA**	**SO**	**Avg**	**GP**	**W**	**L**	**Mins**	**GA**	**SO**	**Avg**
2001-02	Antoine-Girouard	QAAA	23	17	4	2	1309	45	1	2.06	....	....	....	....	....	....	....
	Cape Breton	QMJHL	1	1	0	0	38	0	0	0.00	....	....	....	....	....	....	....
2002-03	Cape Breton	QMJHL	30	4	18	3	1450	98	0	4.06	1	0	0	11	0	0	0.00
2003-04	Cape Breton	QMJHL	51	34	15	1	2951	114	3	2.32	1	0	1	59	4	0	4.10
2004-05	Cape Breton	QMJHL	56	26	18	5	3108	130	*6	2.51	4	1	3	246	10	0	*2.44
2005-06	Philadelphia	AHL	40	18	18	1	2153	91	2	2.54	....	....	....	....	....	....	....
	Trenton Titans	ECHL	7	4	3	0	429	15	1	2.10	....	....	....	....	....	....	....
2006-07	**Philadelphia**	**NHL**	**1**	**0**	**0**	**0**	**2**	**1**	**0**	**30.00**	....	....	....	....	....	....	....
	Philadelphia	AHL	37	12	17	2	1879	104	0	3.32	....	....	....	....	....	....	....
2007-08	Philadelphia	AHL	10	2	5	0	442	21	1	2.85	....	....	....	....	....	....	....
	Wheeling Nailers	ECHL	26	5	13	3	1318	82	0	3.73	....	....	....	....	....	....	....
	NHL Totals		**1**	**0**	**0**	**0**	**2**	**1**	**0**	**30.00**	....	....	....	....	....	....	....

QMJHL First All-Star Team (2004)

HOVINEN, Niko (HOH-vih-nehn, NEE-KOH) MIN.

Goaltender. Catches left. 6'6", 208 lbs. Born, Helsinki, Finland, March 16, 1988.
(Minnesota's 5th choice, 132nd overall, in 2006 Entry Draft).

			Regular Season								Playoffs						
Season	**Club**	**League**	**GP**	**W**	**L**	**O/T**	**Mins**	**GA**	**SO**	**Avg**	**GP**	**W**	**L**	**Mins**	**GA**	**SO**	**Avg**
2004-05	Jokerit U18	Fin-U18	20	....	....	....	1166	38	3	1.95	4	....	....	246	9	1	2.20
	Jokerit Helsinki Jr.	Fin-Jr.	4	....	....	....	242	13	0	3.21	....	....	....	....	....	....	....
2005-06	Jokerit Helsinki Jr.	Fin-Jr.	26	....	....	....	1480	77	0	3.12	....	....	....	....	....	....	....
	Jokerit U18	Fin-U18	11	....	....	....	637	34	1	3.20	4	....	....	232	14	1	3.62
	Suomi U20	Finland-2	1	....	....	....	60	4	0	4.00	....	....	....	....	....	....	....
2006-07	Jokerit Helsinki Jr.	Fin-Jr.	27	13	10	0	1641	74	1	2.71	5	2	3	303	12	1	2.38
	Suomi U20	Finland-2	6	1	2	0	329	18	0	3.28	....	....	....	....	....	....	....
	Jokerit Helsinki	Finland	1	0	1	0	60	4	0	4.00	....	....	....	....	....	....	....
2007-08	Suomi U20	Finland-2	3	2	1	0	180	12	0	4.00	....	....	....	....	....	....	....
	Jokerit Helsinki	Finland	4	0	1	0	125	12	0	5.78	....	....	....	....	....	....	....
	Jokerit Helsinki Jr.	Fin-Jr.	22	13	8	0	1272	58	2	2.74	3	1	2	182	14	0	4.62

HOWARD, James (HOW-uhrd, JAYMZ) DET.

Goaltender. Catches left. 6', 218 lbs. Born, Syracuse, NY, March 26, 1984.
(Detroit's 1st choice, 64th overall, in 2003 Entry Draft).

			Regular Season								Playoffs						
Season	**Club**	**League**	**GP**	**W**	**L**	**O/T**	**Mins**	**GA**	**SO**	**Avg**	**GP**	**W**	**L**	**Mins**	**GA**	**SO**	**Avg**
2001-02	USNTDP	U-18	19	15	4	1	1170	37	4	1.90	....	....	....	....	....	....	....
	USNTDP	USHL	8	4	3	0	425	14	0	1.98	....	....	....	....	....	....	....
	USNTDP	NAHL	8	3	4	0	381	25	0	3.93	....	....	....	....	....	....	....
2002-03	University of Maine	H-East	21	14	6	0	1151	47	3	2.45	....	....	....	....	....	....	....
2003-04	University of Maine	H-East	23	14	4	3	1364	27	*6	*1.19	....	....	....	....	....	....	....
2004-05	University of Maine	H-East	*39	*19	13	7	*2310	74	*6	1.92	....	....	....	....	....	....	....
2005-06	**Detroit**	**NHL**	**4**	**1**	**2**	**0**	**201**	**10**	**0**	**2.99**	....	....	....	....	....	....	....
	Grand Rapids	AHL	38	27	6	2	2140	92	2	2.58	13	5	7	763	44	0	3.46
2006-07	Grand Rapids	AHL	49	21	21	3	2776	125	6	2.70	7	3	4	434	14	0	1.93
2007-08	**Detroit**	**NHL**	**4**	**0**	**2**	**0**	**197**	**7**	**0**	**2.13**	....	....	....	....	....	....	....
	Grand Rapids	AHL	54	21	28	2	3097	146	2	2.83	....	....	....	....	....	....	....
	NHL Totals		**8**	**1**	**4**	**0**	**398**	**17**	**0**	**2.56**	....	....	....	....	....	....	....

Hockey East All-Rookie Team (2003) • Hockey East Rookie of the Year (2003) • Hockey East First All-Star Team (2004) • NCAA East Second All-American Team (2004) • AHL All-Rookie Team (2006)

HUET, Cristobal (hew-AY, KRIHS-toh-bahl) CHI.

Goaltender. Catches left. 6'1", 204 lbs. Born, St. Martin d'Heres, France, September 3, 1975.
(Los Angeles' 9th choice, 214th overall, in 2001 Entry Draft).

			Regular Season								Playoffs						
Season	**Club**	**League**	**GP**	**W**	**L**	**O/T**	**Mins**	**GA**	**SO**	**Avg**	**GP**	**W**	**L**	**Mins**	**GA**	**SO**	**Avg**
1997-98	CSG Grenoble	France					STATISTICS NOT AVAILABLE										
	France	Olympics	2	1	1	0	120	5	0	2.50	....	....	....	....	....	....	....
1998-99	HC Lugano	Swiss	21	....	....	....	1275	58	1	2.73	10	....	....	628	18	1	*1.72
99-2000	HC Lugano	Swiss	31	....	....	....	1886	50	*8	*1.59	13	....	....	783	29	0	2.22
2000-01	HC Lugano	Swiss	39	....	....	....	2365	77	*6	*1.95	*18	....	....	*1141	39	2	2.05
2001-02	HC Lugano	Swiss	39	....	....	....	2313	107	*4	2.78	1	0	1	60	3	0	3.00
	France	Olympics	3	0	2	1	179	10	0	3.36	....	....	....	....	....	....	....
2002-03	**Los Angeles**	**NHL**	**12**	**4**	**4**	**1**	**541**	**21**	**1**	**2.33**	....	....	....	....	....	....	....
	Manchester	AHL	30	16	8	5	1784	68	1	2.29	1	0	1	30	4	0	8.08
2003-04	**Los Angeles**	**NHL**	**41**	**10**	**16**	**10**	**2199**	**89**	**3**	**2.43**	....	....	....	....	....	....	....
2004-05	Adler Mannheim	Germany	36	....	....	....	2001	93	1	2.79	*14	....	....	*850	40	2	2.82
2005-06	**Montreal**	**NHL**	**36**	**18**	**11**	**4**	**2103**	**77**	**7**	**2.20**	**6**	**2**	**4**	**386**	**15**	**0**	**2.33**
	Hamilton Bulldogs	AHL	4	0	4	0	237	15	0	3.79	....	....	....	....	....	....	....
2006-07	**Montreal**	**NHL**	**42**	**19**	**16**	**3**	**2286**	**107**	**2**	**2.81**	....	....	....	....	....	....	....
2007-08	**Montreal**	**NHL**	**39**	**21**	**12**	**6**	**2278**	**97**	**2**	**2.55**	....	....	....	....	....	....	....
	Washington	**NHL**	**13**	**11**	**2**	**0**	**771**	**21**	**2**	**1.63**	**7**	**3**	**4**	**451**	**22**	**0**	**2.93**
	NHL Totals		**183**	**83**	**61**	**24**	**10178**	**412**	**17**	**2.43**	**13**	**5**	**8**	**837**	**37**	**0**	**2.65**

Played in NHL All-Star Game (2007)

Traded to **Montreal** by **Los Angeles** with Radek Bonk for Mathieu Garon and San Jose's 3rd round choice (previously acquired, Los Angeles selected Piaul Baier) in 2004 Entry Draft, June 26, 2004. Signed as a free agent by **Mannheim** (Germany), September 14, 2004. Traded to **Washington** by **Montreal** for Anaheim's 2nd round choice (previously acquired) in 2009 Entry Draft, February 26, 2008. Signed as a free agent by **Chicago**, July 1, 2008.

HUTCHINSON, Michael (HUH-chihn-suhn, MIGH-kuhl) BOS.

Goaltender. Catches right. 6'3", 185 lbs. Born, Barrie, Ont., March 2, 1990.
(Boston's 3rd choice, 77th overall, in 2008 Entry Draft).

			Regular Season								Playoffs						
Season	**Club**	**League**	**GP**	**W**	**L**	**O/T**	**Mins**	**GA**	**SO**	**Avg**	**GP**	**W**	**L**	**Mins**	**GA**	**SO**	**Avg**
2006-07	Orangeville	OPJHL	8	1	4	0	289	24	0	4.99	....	....	....	....	....	....	....
	Barrie Colts	OHL	14	8	3	0	768	27	0	2.11	1	1	0	45	1	0	1.33
2007-08	Barrie Colts	OHL	32	12	15	4	1826	92	1	3.02	8	4	4	500	22	1	2.64

IRVING, Leland (UHR-vihng, LEE-land) CGY.

Goaltender. Catches left. 6', 180 lbs. Born, Barrhead, Alta., April 11, 1988.
(Calgary's 1st choice, 26th overall, in 2006 Entry Draft).

			Regular Season								Playoffs						
Season	**Club**	**League**	**GP**	**W**	**L**	**O/T**	**Mins**	**GA**	**SO**	**Avg**	**GP**	**W**	**L**	**Mins**	**GA**	**SO**	**Avg**
2002-03	Spruce Grove	AMBHL	....	11	11	4	1559	94	....	3.62	....	....	....	....	....	....	....
2003-04	Spruce Grove	RAMHL	19	....	....	....	1017	44	1	2.60	....	....	....	....	....	....	....
	Everett Silvertips	WHL	1	0	0	0	8	0	0	0.00	....	....	....	....	....	....	....
2004-05	Everett Silvertips	WHL	23	9	8	1	1132	34	2	1.80	....	....	....	....	....	....	....
2005-06	Everett Silvertips	WHL	*67	37	22	4	*3791	121	4	1.92	12	8	4	747	21	3	1.69
2006-07	Everett Silvertips	WHL	48	34	9	3	2802	87	*11	1.86	12	6	5	639	30	0	2.82
2007-08	Everett Silvertips	WHL	56	27	24	0	3258	133	4	2.45	3	0	3	139	10	0	4.32

WHL West Second All-Star Team (2006, 2007)

JOHNSON, Brent (JAWN-suhn, BREHNT) WSH.

Goaltender. Catches left. 6'3", 210 lbs. Born, Farmington, MI, March 12, 1977.
(Colorado's 5th choice, 129th overall, in 1995 Entry Draft).

			Regular Season								Playoffs						
Season	**Club**	**League**	**GP**	**W**	**L**	**O/T**	**Mins**	**GA**	**SO**	**Avg**	**GP**	**W**	**L**	**Mins**	**GA**	**SO**	**Avg**
1993-94	Det. Compuware	NAHL	18	....	....	....	1024	49	1	3.52	....	....	....	....	....	....	....
1994-95	Owen Sound	OHL	18	3	9	1	904	75	0	4.98	....	....	....	....	....	....	....
1995-96	Owen Sound	OHL	58	24	28	1	3211	243	1	4.54	6	2	4	371	29	0	4.69
1996-97	Owen Sound	OHL	50	20	28	1	2798	201	1	4.31	4	0	4	253	24	0	5.69
1997-98	Worcester IceCats	AHL	42	14	15	7	2240	119	0	3.19	6	3	2	332	19	0	3.43
1998-99	**St. Louis**	**NHL**	**6**	**3**	**2**	**0**	**286**	**10**	**0**	**2.10**	....	....	....	....	....	....	....
	Worcester IceCats	AHL	49	22	22	4	2925	146	2	2.99	4	1	3	238	12	0	3.02
99-2000	Worcester IceCats	AHL	58	24	27	5	3319	161	3	2.91	9	4	5	561	23	1	2.46
2000-01	**St. Louis**	**NHL**	**31**	**19**	**9**	**2**	**1744**	**63**	**4**	**2.17**	**2**	**0**	**1**	**62**	**2**	**0**	**1.94**
2001-02	**St. Louis**	**NHL**	**58**	**34**	**20**	**4**	**3491**	**127**	**5**	**2.18**	**10**	**5**	**5**	**590**	**18**	**3**	**1.83**
2002-03	**St. Louis**	**NHL**	**38**	**16**	**13**	**5**	**2042**	**84**	**2**	**2.47**	....	....	....	....	....	....	....
	Worcester IceCats	AHL	2	0	1	1	125	8	0	3.84	....	....	....	....	....	....	....
2003-04	**St. Louis**	**NHL**	**10**	**4**	**3**	**1**	**493**	**20**	**1**	**2.43**	....	....	....	....	....	....	....
	Worcester IceCats	AHL	8	2	2	2	365	14	0	2.30	....	....	....	....	....	....	....
	Phoenix	**NHL**	**8**	**1**	**6**	**1**	**486**	**21**	**0**	**2.59**	....	....	....	....	....	....	....
2004-05							DID NOT PLAY										
2005-06	**Washington**	**NHL**	**26**	**9**	**12**	**1**	**1413**	**81**	**1**	**3.44**	....	....	....	....	....	....	....
2006-07	**Washington**	**NHL**	**30**	**6**	**15**	**7**	**1644**	**99**	**0**	**3.61**	....	....	....	....	....	....	....
2007-08	**Washington**	**NHL**	**19**	**7**	**8**	**2**	**1032**	**46**	**0**	**2.67**	....	....	....	....	....	....	....
	Hershey Bears	AHL	1	0	1	0	59	3	0	3.04	....	....	....	....	....	....	....
	NHL Totals		**226**	**99**	**88**	**23**	**12631**	**551**	**13**	**2.62**	**12**	**5**	**6**	**652**	**20**	**3**	**1.84**

Traded to **St. Louis** by **Colorado** for San Jose's 3rd round choice (previously acquired, Colorado selected Rick Berry) in 1997 Entry Draft, May 30, 1997. Traded to **Phoenix** by **St. Louis** for Mike Sillinger, March 4, 2004. Signed as a free agent by **Vancouver**, September 1, 2005. Claimed on waivers by **Washington** from **Vancouver**, October 4, 2005.

JOHNSON, Chad (JAWN-suhn, CHAD) PIT.

Goaltender. Catches left. 6'2", 175 lbs. Born, Calgary, Alta., June 10, 1986.
(Pittsburgh's 4th choice, 125th overall, in 2006 Entry Draft).

			Regular Season								Playoffs						
Season	**Club**	**League**	**GP**	**W**	**L**	**O/T**	**Mins**	**GA**	**SO**	**Avg**	**GP**	**W**	**L**	**Mins**	**GA**	**SO**	**Avg**
2002-03	Calgary Buffaloes	AMHL	....	8	8	2	1145	62	....	3.25	1	0	1	60	3	0	3.00
2003-04	Brooks Bandits	AJHL	31	6	20	3	1782	117	0	3.94	....	....	....	....	....	....	....

							Regular Season							Playoffs			
2004-05	Brooks Bandits	AJHL	43	25	16	2	2505	109	2	2.61	119	4	5	493			
2005-06	Alaska	CCHA	18	6	7	4	985	42	0	2.56							
2006-07	Alaska	CCHA	19	5	6	2	1002	52	1	3.11							
2007-08	Alaska	CCHA	7	0	6	0	357	20	0	3.36							

JOSEPH, Curtis (JOH-sehf, KUHR-tihs) TOR.

Goaltender. Catches left. 5'11", 193 lbs. Born, Keswick, Ont., April 29, 1967.

			Regular Season								Playoffs						
Season	Club	League	GP	W	L	O/T	Mins	GA	SO	Avg	GP	W	L	Mins	GA	SO	Avg
1984-85	King City Dukes	OHA-B	18				947	76	0	4.82							
	Newmarket Flyers	OPJHL	2	1	1	0	120	16	0	8.00							
1985-86	Richmond Hill	OPJHL	33	12	18	0	1716	156	1	5.45							
1986-87	Richmond Hill	OPJHL	30	14	7	6	1764	128	1	4.35							
1987-88	Notre Dame	SJHL	36	25	4	7	2174	94	1	2.59							
1988-89	U. of Wisconsin	WCHA	38	21	11	5	2267	94	1	2.49							
1989-90	**St. Louis**	**NHL**	**15**	**9**	**5**	**1**	**852**	**48**	**0**	**3.38**	**6**	**4**	**1**	**327**	**18**	**0**	**3.30**
	Peoria Rivermen	IHL	23	10	8	2	1241	80	0	3.87							
1990-91	**St. Louis**	**NHL**	**30**	**16**	**10**	**2**	**1710**	**89**	**0**	**3.12**							
1991-92	**St. Louis**	**NHL**	**60**	**27**	**20**	**10**	**3494**	**175**	**2**	**3.01**	**6**	**2**	**4**	**379**	**23**	**0**	**3.64**
1992-93	**St. Louis**	**NHL**	**68**	**29**	**28**	**9**	**3890**	**196**	**1**	**3.02**	**11**	**7**	**4**	**715**	**27**	***2**	**2.27**
1993-94	**St. Louis**	**NHL**	**71**	**36**	**23**	**11**	**4127**	**213**	**1**	**3.10**	**4**	**0**	**4**	**246**	**15**	**0**	**3.66**
1994-95	**St. Louis**	**NHL**	**36**	**20**	**10**	**1**	**1914**	**89**	**1**	**2.79**	**7**	**3**	**3**	**392**	**24**	**0**	**3.67**
1995-96	Las Vegas Thunder	IHL	15	12	2	1	874	29	1	1.99							
	Edmonton	**NHL**	**34**	**15**	**16**	**2**	**1936**	**111**	**0**	**3.44**							
1996-97	**Edmonton**	**NHL**	**72**	**32**	**29**	**9**	**4100**	**200**	**6**	**2.93**	**12**	**5**	**7**	**767**	**36**	**2**	**2.82**
1997-98	**Edmonton**	**NHL**	**71**	**29**	**31**	**9**	**4132**	**181**	**8**	**2.63**	**12**	**5**	**7**	**716**	**23**	**3**	**1.93**
1998-99	**Toronto**	**NHL**	**67**	**35**	**24**	**7**	**4001**	**171**	**3**	**2.56**	**17**	**9**	**8**	**1011**	**41**	**1**	**2.43**
99-2000	**Toronto**	**NHL**	**63**	**36**	**20**	**7**	**3801**	**158**	**4**	**2.49**	**12**	**6**	**6**	**729**	**25**	**1**	**2.06**
2000-01	**Toronto**	**NHL**	**68**	**33**	**27**	**8**	**4100**	**163**	**6**	**2.39**	**11**	**7**	**4**	**685**	**24**	**3**	**2.10**
2001-02	**Toronto**	**NHL**	**51**	**29**	**17**	**5**	**3065**	**114**	**4**	**2.23**	**20**	**10**	**10**	**1253**	**48**	**3**	**2.30**
	Canada	Olympics	1	0	1	0	60	5	0	5.00							
2002-03	**Detroit**	**NHL**	**61**	**34**	**19**	**6**	**3566**	**148**	**5**	**2.49**	**4**	**0**	**4**	**289**	**10**	**0**	**2.08**
2003-04	**Detroit**	**NHL**	**31**	**16**	**10**	**3**	**1708**	**68**	**2**	**2.39**	**9**	**4**	**4**	**518**	**12**	**1**	***1.39**
	Grand Rapids	AHL	1	1	0	0	60	1	0	1.00							
2004-05							DID NOT PLAY										
2005-06	**Phoenix**	**NHL**	**60**	**32**	**21**	**3**	**3424**	**166**	**4**	**2.91**							
2006-07	**Phoenix**	**NHL**	**55**	**18**	**31**	**2**	**2993**	**159**	**4**	**3.19**							
2007-08	**Calgary**	**NHL**	**9**	**3**	**2**	**0**	**400**	**17**	**0**	**2.55**	**2**	**1**	**0**	**79**	**1**	**0**	**0.76**
	NHL Totals		**922**	**449**	**343**	**95**	**53213**	**2466**	**51**	**2.78**	**133**	**63**	**66**	**8106**	**327**	**16**	**2.42**

WCHA First All-Star Team (1989) • WCHA Freshman of the Year (1989) • WCHA Most Valuable Player (1989) • NCAA West Second All-American Team (1989) • King Clancy Memorial Trophy (2000)

Played in NHL All-Star Game (1994, 2000)

Signed as a free agent by **St. Louis**, June 16, 1989. Traded to **Edmonton** by **St. Louis** with the rights to Mike Grier for St. Louis' 1st round choices (previously acquired) in 1996 (Marty Reasoner) and 1997 (later traded to Los Angeles – Los Angeles selected Matt Zultek) Entry Drafts, August 4, 1995. Signed as a free agent by **Toronto**, July 15, 1998. Traded to **Calgary** by **Toronto** for Calgary's 3rd round choice (later traded to Minnesota – Minnesota selected Danny Irmen) in 2003 Entry Draft and future considerations, June 30, 2002. Signed as a free agent by **Detroit**, July 2, 2002. Signed as a free agent by **Phoenix**, August 17, 2005. Signed as a free agent by **Calgary**, January 17, 2008. Signed as a free agent by **Toronto**, July 1, 2008.

JUNG, Torrie (YUHNG, TOHR-ee) T.B.

Goaltender. Catches left. 6'2", 170 lbs. Born, Nanaimo, B.C., January 21, 1989.
(Tampa Bay's 7th choice, 183rd overall, in 2007 Entry Draft).

			Regular Season								Playoffs						
Season	Club	League	GP	W	L	O/T	Mins	GA	SO	Avg	GP	W	L	Mins	GA	SO	Avg
2004-05	Saanich Braves	VIJHL	17				1002	58	0	3.47							
	Nanaimo Clippers	BCHL	1	0	0	0	2	0	0	0.00							
2005-06	Cowichan Valley	BCHL	18	5	11	0	1051	69	0	3.94	1	0	1	44	5	0	6.82
2006-07	Kelowna Rockets	WHL	33	8	15	7	1874	108	1	3.46							
2007-08	Kelowna Rockets	WHL	33	13	12	5	1842	86	0	2.80	1	0	0	47	3	0	3.83

KANGAS, Alex (KANG-uhs, AL-ehx) ATL.

Goaltender. Catches left. 6'1", 175 lbs. Born, Rochester, NY, May 28, 1987.
(Atlanta's 4th choice, 135th overall, in 2006 Entry Draft).

			Regular Season								Playoffs						
Season	Club	League	GP	W	L	O/T	Mins	GA	SO	Avg	GP	W	L	Mins	GA	SO	Avg
2001-02	Rochester Century	High-MN	3	3	0	0		3	2	1.00							
2002-03	Rochester Century	High-MN	27	17	9	0		50	6	1.76							
2003-04	Rochester Century	High-MN	28	15	12	1		59	3	2.08							
2004-05	Rochester Century	High-MN	30	23	4	3		55	7	1.86							
2005-06	Sioux Falls	USHL	29	20	6	3	1733	62	3	2.15	6	4	2	359	17	0	2.84
2006-07	Indiana Ice	USHL	46	19	19	5	2467	136	1	3.31	7	6	1	434	18	0	2.49
2007-08	U. of Minnesota	WCHA	31	12	10	9	1967	65	0	1.98							

USHL All-Rookie Team (2006)

KARPOWICH, Paul (KAHR-puh-wihch, PAWL) ST.L.

Goaltender. Catches left. 6', 160 lbs. Born, Thunder Bay, Ont., October 25, 1988.
(St. Louis' 10th choice, 185th overall, in 2008 Entry Draft).

			Regular Season								Playoffs						
Season	Club	League	GP	W	L	O/T	Mins	GA	SO	Avg	GP	W	L	Mins	GA	SO	Avg
2004-05	Thunder Bay Kings	Minor-ON	38	25	7	3	2057	103	2	3.00							
2005-06	Thunder Bay Kings	Minor-ON	42	29	8	3	2280	91	6	2.39							
2006-07	Brooks Bandits	AJHL	18	6	6	2	1010	59	0	3.51	2	1	0	92	8	0	5.21
2007-08	Wellington Dukes	OPJHL	22	15	3	2	1202	43	3	2.15	13	9	4	771	35	1	2.72

• Signed Letter of Intent to attend **Clarkson University** (ECAC) in fall of 2008.

KEETLEY, Matt (KEET-lee, MAT) CGY.

Goaltender. Catches right. 6'1", 194 lbs. Born, Medicine Hat, Alta., April 27, 1986.
(Calgary's 6th choice, 158th overall, in 2005 Entry Draft).

			Regular Season								Playoffs						
Season	Club	League	GP	W	L	O/T	Mins	GA	SO	Avg	GP	W	L	Mins	GA	SO	Avg
2003-04	Medicine Hat	AMHL		7	4	2	813	48		3.54							
	Medicine Hat	WHL	3	0	1	0	72	5	0	4.17	2	0	0	15	1	0	4.00
2004-05	Medicine Hat	WHL	32	21	5	3	1846	51	6	*1.66	3	1	0	103	8	0	4.66
2005-06	Medicine Hat	WHL	62	*42	13	6	3741	130	6	2.09	13	9	4	864	30	0	2.08
2006-07	Medicine Hat	WHL	55	*42	11	1	3258	119	6	2.19	*23	*16	7	*1407	51	*4	2.18
2007-08	**Calgary**	**NHL**	**1**	**0**	**0**	**0**	**9**	**0**	**0**	**0.00**							
	Quad City Flames	AHL	26	10	8	3	1393	54	1	2.33							
	NHL Totals		**1**	**0**	**0**	**0**	**9**	**0**	**0**	**0.00**							

WHL East Second All-Star Team (2006) • WHL East First All-Star Team (2007) • Memorial Cup Tournament All-Star Team (2007) • Hap Emms Memorial Trophy (Memorial Cup Tournament - Top Goaltender) (2007)

KHABIBULIN, Nikolai (khah-bee-BOO-lihn, NIH-koh-ligh) CHI.

Goaltender. Catches left. 6'1", 208 lbs. Born, Sverdlovsk, USSR, January 13, 1973.
(Winnipeg's 8th choice, 204th overall, in 1992 Entry Draft).

			Regular Season								Playoffs						
Season	Club	League	GP	W	L	O/T	Mins	GA	SO	Avg	GP	W	L	Mins	GA	SO	Avg
1988-89	Sverdlovsk	USSR	1				3	0	0	0.00							
1989-90	Luch Sverdlovsk	USSR-2					STATISTICS NOT AVAILABLE										
1990-91	Nizhny Tagil	USSR-3	10														
	Sverdlovsk	USSR-Q	2					7									
1991-92	CSKA Moscow 2	CIS-3	11														
	CSKA Moscow	CIS	2				34	2	0	3.53							
	Russia	Olympics					DID NOT PLAY – SPARE GOALTENDER										
1992-93	CSKA Moscow	CIS	13				491	27		3.29							
	Serov	CIS-2	18														
1993-94	CSKA Moscow	CIS	46				2625	116		2.65							
	Russian Penguins	IHL	12	2	7	2	639	47	0	4.41							
1994-95	Springfield Indians	AHL	23	9	9	3	1240	80	0	3.87							
	Winnipeg	**NHL**	**26**	**8**	**9**	**4**	**1339**	**76**	**0**	**3.41**							
1995-96	**Winnipeg**	**NHL**	**53**	**26**	**20**	**3**	**2914**	**152**	**2**	**3.13**	**6**	**2**	**4**	**359**	**19**	**0**	**3.18**
1996-97	**Phoenix**	**NHL**	**72**	**30**	**33**	**6**	**4091**	**193**	**7**	**2.83**	**7**	**3**	**4**	**426**	**15**	**1**	**2.11**
1997-98	**Phoenix**	**NHL**	**70**	**30**	**28**	**10**	**4026**	**184**	**4**	**2.74**	**4**	**2**	**1**	**185**	**13**	**0**	**4.22**
1998-99	**Phoenix**	**NHL**	**63**	**32**	**23**	**7**	**3657**	**130**	**8**	**2.13**	**7**	**3**	**4**	**449**	**18**	**0**	**2.41**
99-2000	Long Beach	IHL	33	21	11	1	1936	59	5	*1.83	5	2	3	321	15	0	2.81
2000-01	**Tampa Bay**	**NHL**	**2**	**1**	**1**	**0**	**123**	**6**	**0**	**2.93**							
2001-02	**Tampa Bay**	**NHL**	**70**	**24**	**32**	**10**	**3896**	**153**	**7**	**2.36**							
	Russia	Olympics	6	3	2	1	*359	14	*1	2.34							
2002-03	**Tampa Bay**	**NHL**	**65**	**30**	**22**	**11**	**3787**	**156**	**4**	**2.47**	**10**	**5**	**5**	**644**	**26**	**0**	**2.42**
2003-04 ♦	**Tampa Bay**	**NHL**	**55**	**28**	**19**	**7**	**3274**	**127**	**3**	**2.33**	**23**	***16**	**7**	**1401**	**40**	***5**	**1.71**
2004-05	Ak Bars Kazan	Russia	24				1457	40	5	1.65	2			118	6	0	3.04
2005-06	**Chicago**	**NHL**	**50**	**17**	**26**	**6**	**2815**	**157**	**0**	**3.35**							
	Russia	Olympics					DID NOT PLAY – INJURED										
2006-07	**Chicago**	**NHL**	**60**	**25**	**26**	**5**	**3425**	**163**	**1**	**2.86**							
2007-08	**Chicago**	**NHL**	**50**	**23**	**20**	**6**	**2892**	**127**	**2**	**2.63**							
	NHL Totals		**636**	**274**	**259**	**75**	**36239**	**1624**	**38**	**2.69**	**57**	**31**	**25**	**3464**	**131**	**6**	**2.27**

James Gatschene Memorial Trophy (MVP – IHL) (2000) (co-winner - Frederic Chabot)

Played in NHL All-Star Game (1998, 1999, 2002, 2003)

Transferred to **Phoenix** after **Winnipeg** franchise relocated, July 1, 1996. • Missed entire 1999-2000 NHL season and majority of 2000-01 season after failing to come to contract terms with **Phoenix**. Signed as a free agent by **Long Beach** (IHL) with **Phoenix** retaining NHL rights, January 14, 2000. Traded to **Tampa Bay** by **Phoenix** with Stan Neckar for Mike Johnson, Paul Mara, Ruslan Zainullin and NY Islanders' 2nd round choice (previously acquired, Phoenix selected Matthew Spiller) in 2001 Entry Draft, March 5, 2001. Signed as a free agent by **Kazan** (Russia), November 8, 2004. Signed as a free agent by **Chicago**, August 5, 2005.

KHUDOBIN, Anton (khuh-DAW-bihn, AN-tawn) MIN.

Goaltender. Catches left. 5'11", 176 lbs. Born, Ust-Kamenogorsk, USSR, May 7, 1986.
(Minnesota's 11th choice, 206th overall, in 2004 Entry Draft).

			Regular Season								Playoffs						
Season	Club	League	GP	W	L	O/T	Mins	GA	SO	Avg	GP	W	L	Mins	GA	SO	Avg
2003-04	Magnitogorsk 2	Russia-3	38					80									
2004-05	Magnitogorsk	Russia	4				133	0	1	0.00							
	Magnitogorsk 2	Russia-3	27					52									
2005-06	Saskatoon Blades	WHL	44	23	13	3	2362	114	4	2.90	10	4	6	685	32	0	2.80
2006-07	Magnitogorsk	Russia	16				618	28	0	2.72	3			26	1	0	2.30
2007-08	Houston Aeros	AHL	12	2	2	1	482	16	1	1.99							
	Texas Wildcatters	ECHL	27	20	1	4	1549	51	3	1.98	9	5	2	547	20	1	2.19

ECHL First All-Star Team (2008) • ECHL Goalie of the Year (2008)

KILLEEN, Patrick (kih-LEEN, PAT-rihk) PIT.

Goaltender. Catches left. 6'4", 194 lbs. Born, Almonte, Ont., April 15, 1990.
(Pittsburgh's 3rd choice, 180th overall, in 2008 Entry Draft).

			Regular Season								Playoffs						
Season	Club	League	GP	W	L	O/T	Mins	GA	SO	Avg	GP	W	L	Mins	GA	SO	Avg
2006-07	Ottawa Jr. Sens	CJHL	7	5	1	0	376	20	0	3.19							
	Brampton Battalion	OHL	8	1	3	0	304	29	0	5.72							
2007-08	Brampton Battalion	OHL	34	20	9	2	1959	90	1	2.76							

KIPRUSOFF, Miikka (KIHP-roo-sawf, MEE-kah) CGY.

Goaltender. Catches left. 6'1", 184 lbs. Born, Turku, Finland, October 26, 1976.
(San Jose's 5th choice, 116th overall, in 1995 Entry Draft).

			Regular Season								Playoffs						
Season	Club	League	GP	W	L	O/T	Mins	GA	SO	Avg	GP	W	L	Mins	GA	SO	Avg
1993-94	TPS Turku Jr.	Fin-Jr.	35	20	9	5	2101	100	0	2.85	6	3	3	369	26	0	4.23
1994-95	TPS Turku Jr.	Fin-Jr.	31	13	14	4	1896	92	2	2.91							
	Kiekko-67 Turku	Finland-2	1	0	1	0	60	6	0	6.00							
	TPS Turku	Finland	4	3	1	0	240	12	0	3.00	2	2	0	120	7	0	3.50
1995-96	TPS Turku Jr.	Fin-Jr.	3	1	2	0	180	9	0	3.00							
	Kiekko-67 Turku	Finland-2	5	5	0	0	300	7	1	1.40							
	TPS Turku	Finland	12	5	3	1	550	38	0	4.14	3	0	1	113	4	0	2.12
1996-97	AIK Solna	Sweden	42				2440	93	3	2.29	7			420	22	0	3.14
1997-98	AIK Solna	Sweden	43				2517	111	1	2.65							
	AIK Solna	Sweden-Q	9				540	15	2	1.67							
1998-99	TPS Turku	Finland	39	26	6	6	2259	70	4	1.86	10	9	1	580	15	3	1.55
99-2000	Kentucky	AHL	47	23	19	4	2759	114	3	2.48	5	1	3	239	13	0	3.27
2000-01	**San Jose**	**NHL**	**5**	**2**	**1**	**0**	**154**	**5**	**0**	**1.95**	**3**	**1**	**1**	**149**	**5**	**0**	**2.01**
	Kentucky	AHL	36	19	9	6	2038	76	2	2.24							
2001-02	**San Jose**	**NHL**	**20**	**7**	**6**	**3**	**1037**	**43**	**2**	**2.49**	**1**	**0**	**0**	**8**	**0**	**0**	**0.00**
	Cleveland Barons	AHL	4	4	0	0	242	7	0	1.73							
2002-03	**San Jose**	**NHL**	**22**	**5**	**14**	**0**	**1199**	**65**	**1**	**3.25**							
2003-04	**Calgary**	**NHL**	**38**	**24**	**10**	**4**	**2301**	**65**	**4**	***1.69**	***26**	**15**	**11**	***1655**	**51**	***5**	**1.85**
2004-05	Timra IK	Sweden	46				2719	97	5	2.14	6			356	13	0	2.19
2005-06	**Calgary**	**NHL**	**74**	**42**	**20**	**11**	***4380**	**151**	***10**	***2.07**	**7**	**3**	**4**	**428**	**16**	**0**	**2.24**
	Finland	Olympics					DID NOT PLAY – INJURED										
2006-07	**Calgary**	**NHL**	**74**	**40**	**24**	**9**	**4419**	**181**	**7**	**2.46**	**6**	**2**	**4**	**384**	**18**	**0**	**2.81**
2007-08	**Calgary**	**NHL**	**76**	**39**	**26**	**10**	**4398**	**197**	**2**	**2.69**	**7**	**2**	**4**	**336**	**18**	**1**	**3.21**
	NHL Totals		**309**	**159**	**101**	**37**	**17888**	**707**	**26**	**2.37**	**50**	**23**	**24**	**2960**	**108**	**6**	**2.19**

NHL First All-Star Team (2006) • Vezina Trophy (2006)

Played in NHL All-Star Game (2007)

Traded to **Calgary** by **San Jose** for Calgary's 2nd round choice (Marc-Edouard Vlasic) in 2005 Entry Draft, November 16, 2003. Signed as a free agent by **Timra** (Sweden), September 20, 2004.

KOLZIG, Olaf (KOHL-zihg, OH-lahf) T.B.

Goaltender. Catches left. 6'3", 224 lbs. Born, Johannesburg, South Africa, April 6, 1970.
(Washington's 1st choice, 19th overall, in 1989 Entry Draft).

			Regular Season								Playoffs						
Season	Club	League	GP	W	L	O/T	Mins	GA	SO	Avg	GP	W	L	Mins	GA	SO	Avg
1986-87	Abbotsford Pilots	Minor-BC	17	5	9	0	857	81	0	5.67							
1987-88	New Westminster	WHL	15	6	5	0	650	48	1	4.43	3	0	3	149	11	0	4.43
1988-89	Tri-City Americans	WHL	30	16	10	2	1671	97	1	*3.48							
1989-90	**Washington**	**NHL**	**2**	**0**	**2**	**0**	**120**	**12**	**0**	**6.00**							
	Tri-City Americans	WHL	48	21	18	3	2504	187	1	4.48	6	4	0	318	27	0	5.09

1990-91	Baltimore Skipjacks	AHL	26	10	12	1	1367	72	0	3.16	....	....	....	....	....	....	....
	Hampton Roads	ECHL	21	11	9	1	1248	71	2	3.41	3	1	2	180	14	0	4.66
1991-92	Baltimore Skipjacks	AHL	28	5	17	2	1503	105	1	4.19	....	....	....	....	....	....	....
	Hampton Roads	ECHL	14	11	3	0	847	41	0	2.90	....	....	....	....	....	....	....
1992-93	**Washington**	**NHL**	**1**	**0**	**0**	**0**	**20**	**2**	**0**	**6.00**	....	....	....	....	....	....	....
	Rochester	AHL	49	25	16	4	2737	168	0	3.68	*17	9	8	*1040	61	0	3.52
1993-94	**Washington**	**NHL**	**7**	**0**	**3**	**0**	**224**	**20**	**0**	**5.36**	....	....	....	....	....	....	....
	Portland Pirates	AHL	29	16	8	5	1725	88	3	3.06	17	*12	5	1035	44	0	*2.55
1994-95	**Washington**	**NHL**	**14**	**2**	**8**	**2**	**724**	**30**	**0**	**2.49**	**2**	**1**	**0**	**44**	**1**	**0**	**1.36**
	Portland Pirates	AHL	2	1	0	1	125	3	0	1.44	....	....	....	....	....	....	....
1995-96	**Washington**	**NHL**	**18**	**4**	**8**	**2**	**897**	**46**	**0**	**3.08**	**5**	**2**	**3**	**341**	**11**	**0**	***1.94**
	Portland Pirates	AHL	5	5	0	0	300	7	1	1.40	....	....	....	....	....	....	....
1996-97	**Washington**	**NHL**	**29**	**8**	**15**	**4**	**1645**	**71**	**2**	**2.59**	....	....	....	....	....	....	....
1997-98	**Washington**	**NHL**	**64**	**33**	**18**	**10**	**3788**	**139**	**5**	**2.20**	**21**	**12**	**9**	**1351**	**44**	***4**	**1.95**
	Germany	Olympics	2	2	0	0	120	2	1	1.00	....	....	....	....	....	....	....
1998-99	**Washington**	**NHL**	**64**	**26**	**31**	**3**	**3586**	**154**	**4**	**2.58**	....	....	....	....	....	....	....
99-2000	**Washington**	**NHL**	**73**	**41**	**20**	**11**	***4371**	**163**	**5**	**2.24**	**5**	**1**	**4**	**284**	**16**	**0**	**3.38**
2000-01	**Washington**	**NHL**	**72**	**37**	**26**	**8**	**4279**	**177**	**5**	**2.48**	**6**	**2**	**4**	**375**	**14**	**1**	**2.24**
2001-02	**Washington**	**NHL**	**71**	**31**	**29**	**8**	**4131**	**192**	**6**	**2.79**	....	....	....	....	....	....	....
2002-03	**Washington**	**NHL**	**66**	**33**	**25**	**6**	**3894**	**156**	**4**	**2.40**	**6**	**2**	**4**	**404**	**14**	**1**	**2.08**
2003-04	**Washington**	**NHL**	**63**	**19**	**35**	**9**	**3738**	**180**	**2**	**2.89**	....	....	....	....	....	....	....
2004-05	Eisbaren Berlin	Germany	8	....	....	....	452	19	2	2.52	....	....	....	....	....	....	....
2005-06	**Washington**	**NHL**	**59**	**20**	**28**	**11**	**3506**	**206**	**0**	**3.53**	....	....	....	....	....	....	....
	Germany	Olympics	3	0	1	2	179	8	0	2.68	....	....	....	....	....	....	....
2006-07	**Washington**	**NHL**	**54**	**22**	**24**	**6**	**3184**	**159**	**1**	**3.00**	....	....	....	....	....	....	....
2007-08	**Washington**	**NHL**	**54**	**25**	**21**	**6**	**3154**	**153**	**1**	**2.91**	....	....	....	....	....	....	....
	NHL Totals		**711**	**301**	**293**	**86**	**41261**	**1860**	**35**	**2.70**	**45**	**20**	**24**	**2799**	**100**	**6**	**2.14**

WHL West Second All-Star Team (1989) • Harry ''Hap'' Holmes Memorial Award (fewest goals against – AHL) (1994) (shared with Byron Dafoe) • Jack A. Butterfield Trophy (Playoff MVP – AHL) (1994) • NHL First All-Star Team (2000) • Vezina Trophy (2000) • King Clancy Memorial Trophy (2006)

Played in NHL All-Star Game (1998, 2000)

• Scored a goal while with Tri-City (WHL), November 29, 1989. Signed as a free agent by **Berlin** (Germany), February 2, 2005. Signed as a free agent by **Tampa Bay**, July 1, 2008.

KOSHECHKIN, Vasily (KOH-shech-kihn, va-SEE-lee) T.B.

Goaltender. Catches left. 6'6", 210 lbs. Born, Togliatti, USSR, March 27, 1983.
(Tampa Bay's 9th choice, 233rd overall, in 2002 Entry Draft).

			Regular Season								Playoffs						
Season	**Club**	**League**	**GP**	**W**	**L**	**O/T**	**Mins**	**GA**	**SO**	**Avg**	**GP**	**W**	**L**	**Mins**	**GA**	**SO**	**Avg**
1998-99	Lada Togliatti 2	Russia-4	8	....	....	....	....	8	....	....	....	....	....	....	....	....	....
99-2000	Lada Togliatti 2	Russia-3	18	....	....	....	....	20	....	....	....	....	....	....	....	....	....
2000-01	Lada Togliatti 2	Russia-3	Statistics not available														
2001-02	Lada Togliatti 2	Russia-3	Statistics not available														
2002-03	Lada Togliatti 2	Russia-3	Statistics not available														
	Kirovo-Chepetsk	Russia-2	10	....	....	....	613	14	3	1.37	....	....	....	....	....	....	....
	Almetjevsk	Russia-2	14	....	....	....	675	29	1	2.58	....	....	....	....	....	....	....
2003-04	Lada Togliatti 2	Russia-3	13	....	....	....	....	19	1	....	3	....	....	....	....	....	....
	Lada Togliatti	Russia	8	....	....	....	247	10	0	2.43	1	....	....	40	3	0	4.50
2004-05	Lada Togliatti	Russia	4	....	....	....	121	5	0	2.47	....	....	....	....	....	....	....
	Lada Togliatti	Russia	4	....	....	....	121	5	0	2.47	....	....	....	....	....	....	....
2005-06	Lada Togliatti	Russia	41	....	....	....	2375	63	9	1.59	8	....	....	474	20	1	2.53
2006-07	Lada Togliatti	Russia	42	....	....	....	2430	82	5	2.02	3	....	....	179	13	0	4.35
2007-08	Ak Bars Kazan	Russia	19	....	....	....	990	45	0	2.73	....	....	....	....	....	....	....

KOVAR, Jakub (KOH-vahr, YA-kuhb) PHI.

Goaltender. Catches left. 6', 193 lbs. Born, Pisek, Czech., July 19, 1988.
(Philadelphia's 7th choice, 109th overall, in 2006 Entry Draft).

			Regular Season								Playoffs						
Season	**Club**	**League**	**GP**	**W**	**L**	**O/T**	**Mins**	**GA**	**SO**	**Avg**	**GP**	**W**	**L**	**Mins**	**GA**	**SO**	**Avg**
2004-05	IHC Pisek U17	CzR-U17	40	....	....	....	2298	137	4	3.58	....	....	....	....	....	....	....
2005-06	C. Budejovice Jr.	CzRep-Jr.	19	....	....	....	1048	39	2	2.23	5	....	....	304	8	0	1.58
2006-07	C. Budejovice Jr.	CzRep-Jr.	38	....	....	....	2231	77	3	2.07	3	....	....	160	16	0	6.00
2007-08	Oshawa Generals	OHL	16	12	3	0	917	48	0	3.14	....	....	....	....	....	....	....
	Windsor Spitfires	OHL	20	14	3	3	1194	68	1	3.42	4	1	2	188	13	0	4.15

KRAHN, Brent (KRAWN, BREHNT)

Goaltender. Catches left. 6'5", 220 lbs. Born, Winnipeg, Man., April 2, 1982.
(Calgary's 1st choice, 9th overall, in 2000 Entry Draft).

			Regular Season								Playoffs						
Season	**Club**	**League**	**GP**	**W**	**L**	**O/T**	**Mins**	**GA**	**SO**	**Avg**	**GP**	**W**	**L**	**Mins**	**GA**	**SO**	**Avg**
1997-98	Pembina Valley	MMMHL	22	20	0	1	1265	40	3	1.90	2	2	0	120	2	1	1.00
1998-99	Pembina Valley	MMMHL	13	10	3	0	770	30	2	2.34	....	....	....	....	....	....	....
99-2000	Calgary Hitmen	WHL	39	33	6	0	2315	92	4	2.38	5	2	2	266	13	0	2.93
2000-01	Calgary Hitmen	WHL	37	22	10	3	2087	104	1	2.99	....	....	....	....	....	....	....
2001-02	Calgary Hitmen	WHL	18	8	6	2	1033	61	0	3.54	2	1	1	119	6	0	3.03
2002-03	Calgary Hitmen	WHL	23	11	10	2	1343	72	2	3.22	....	....	....	....	....	....	....
	Seattle	WHL	5	5	0	0	302	9	2	1.79	15	9	6	960	38	2	2.38
2003-04	San Antonio	AHL	14	3	7	1	715	41	0	3.44	....	....	....	....	....	....	....
	Lowell	AHL	7	2	3	0	344	15	0	2.62	....	....	....	....	....	....	....
	Las Vegas	ECHL	14	7	5	2	828	36	0	2.61	....	....	....	....	....	....	....
2004-05	Lowell	AHL	35	20	11	2	1998	83	6	2.49	1	0	0	1	0	0	0.00
2005-06	Omaha	AHL	57	26	20	9	3241	135	3	2.50	....	....	....	....	....	....	....
2006-07	Omaha	AHL	28	14	12	0	1564	63	2	2.42	1	0	1	59	3	0	3.06
2007-08	Quad City Flames	AHL	14	6	6	2	795	33	0	2.49	....	....	....	....	....	....	....

LaBARBERA, Jason (lah-BAR-buhr-uh, JAY-suhn) L.A.

Goaltender. Catches left. 6'3", 235 lbs. Born, Burnaby, B.C., January 18, 1980.
(NY Rangers' 3rd choice, 66th overall, in 1998 Entry Draft).

			Regular Season								Playoffs						
Season	**Club**	**League**	**GP**	**W**	**L**	**O/T**	**Mins**	**GA**	**SO**	**Avg**	**GP**	**W**	**L**	**Mins**	**GA**	**SO**	**Avg**
1995-96	Prince George	Minor-BC	31	....	....	....	1860	83	0	2.68	....	....	....	....	....	....	....
1996-97	Tri-City Americans	WHL	2	1	0	0	63	4	0	3.81	....	....	....	....	....	....	....
	Portland	WHL	9	5	1	1	443	18	0	2.44	....	....	....	....	....	....	....
1997-98	Portland	WHL	23	18	4	0	1305	72	1	3.31	....	....	....	....	....	....	....
1998-99	Portland	WHL	51	18	23	9	2991	170	4	3.41	4	0	4	252	19	0	4.52
99-2000	Portland	WHL	34	8	24	2	2005	123	1	3.68	....	....	....	....	....	....	....
	Spokane Chiefs	WHL	21	12	6	2	1146	50	0	2.62	9	6	1	435	18	1	2.48
2000-01	**NY Rangers**	**NHL**	**1**	**0**	**0**	**0**	**10**	**0**	**0**	**0.00**	....	....	....	....	....	....	....
	Hartford Wolf Pack	AHL	4	1	1	0	156	12	0	4.61	....	....	....	....	....	....	....
	Charlotte Checkers	ECHL	35	18	10	7	2100	112	1	3.20	2	1	1	143	5	0	2.09
2001-02	Hartford Wolf Pack	AHL	20	7	11	1	1058	55	0	3.12	....	....	....	....	....	....	....
	Charlotte Checkers	ECHL	13	9	3	1	744	29	0	2.34	4	2	2	212	12	0	3.39
2002-03	Hartford Wolf Pack	AHL	46	18	17	6	2452	105	2	2.57	2	0	2	117	6	0	3.07
2003-04	**NY Rangers**	**NHL**	**4**	**1**	**2**	**0**	**198**	**16**	**0**	**4.85**	....	....	....	....	....	....	....
	Hartford Wolf Pack	AHL	59	34	9	9	3393	90	*13	1.59	16	11	5	1043	30	*3	*1.73
2004-05	Hartford Wolf Pack	AHL	53	31	16	2	2937	90	6	1.84	4	1	3	238	9	0	2.27
2005-06	**Los Angeles**	**NHL**	**29**	**11**	**9**	**2**	**1433**	**69**	**1**	**2.89**	....	....	....	....	....	....	....
	Manchester	AHL	3	1	1	1	185	10	0	3.25	....	....	....	....	....	....	....
2006-07	Manchester	AHL	*62	*39	20	1	*3619	133	*7	2.21	13	6	7	824	38	1	2.77
2007-08	**Los Angeles**	**NHL**	**45**	**17**	**23**	**2**	**2421**	**121**	**1**	**3.00**	....	....	....	....	....	....	....
	NHL Totals		**79**	**29**	**34**	**4**	**4062**	**206**	**2**	**3.04**	....	....	....	....	....	....	....

AHL First All-Star Team (2004, 2007) • Aldege "Baz" Bastien Memorial Award (Outstanding Goaltender - AHL) (2004, 2007) • Les Cunningham Award (MVP - AHL) (2004) • Harry "Hap" Holmes Memorial Trophy (fewest goals against - AHL) (shared with Steve Valiquette) (2005) • Harry "Hap" Holmes Memorial Trophy (fewest goals against - AHL) (2007)

Signed as a free agent by **Los Angeles**, August 2, 2005.

LACASSE, Loic (luh-KAS, LOIK) MTL.

Goaltender. Catches left. 6'3", 178 lbs. Born, Granby, Que., April 23, 1986.
(Montreal's 5th choice, 181st overall, in 2004 Entry Draft).

			Regular Season								Playoffs						
Season	**Club**	**League**	**GP**	**W**	**L**	**O/T**	**Mins**	**GA**	**SO**	**Avg**	**GP**	**W**	**L**	**Mins**	**GA**	**SO**	**Avg**
2002-03	Antoine-Girouard	QAAA	24	22	1	1	1453	50	1	2.07	....	....	....	....	....	....	....
2003-04	Baie-Comeau	QMJHL	41	9	15	4	1758	117	0	3.99	4	0	4	172	16	0	5.57
2004-05	Baie-Comeau	QMJHL	39	10	22	2	2001	138	1	4.14	2	0	1	54	2	0	2.21
2005-06	Baie-Comeau	QMJHL	27	10	12	0	1394	94	1	4.05	....	....	....	....	....	....	....
	Drummondville	QMJHL	6	2	3	0	272	18	0	3.97	5	3	2	280	13	0	2.78
2006-07	Oshawa Generals	OHL	33	16	12	5	1964	129	3	3.94	9	3	5	523	43	0	4.93
2007-08	Bloomington	IHL	47	18	17	5	2558	138	1	3.24	....	....	....	....	....	....	....

LACOSTA, Dan (luh-KAWS-tah, DAN) CBJ

Goaltender. Catches left. 6'2", 194 lbs. Born, Labrador City, Nfld., March 28, 1986.
(Columbus' 4th choice, 93rd overall, in 2004 Entry Draft).

			Regular Season								Playoffs						
Season	**Club**	**League**	**GP**	**W**	**L**	**O/T**	**Mins**	**GA**	**SO**	**Avg**	**GP**	**W**	**L**	**Mins**	**GA**	**SO**	**Avg**
2001-02	Wellington Dukes	OPJHL	24	19	2	3	1377	44	2	*1.92	....	....	....	....	....	....	....
2002-03	Owen Sound	OHL	28	8	10	3	1321	82	0	3.72	....	....	....	....	....	....	....
2003-04	Owen Sound	OHL	37	17	10	1	1810	82	4	2.72	....	....	....	....	....	....	....
2004-05	Owen Sound	OHL	25	15	7	2	1423	70	0	2.95	....	....	....	....	....	....	....
	Barrie Colts	OHL	21	10	5	2	1054	48	1	2.73	5	1	2	215	11	0	3.07
2005-06	Barrie Colts	OHL	*59	36	17	4	3340	142	6	2.55	11	5	5	654	34	0	3.12
2006-07	Syracuse Crunch	AHL	19	5	7	1	852	40	3	2.82	....	....	....	....	....	....	....
	Dayton Bombers	ECHL	10	3	5	1	556	32	0	3.45	....	....	....	....	....	....	....
2007-08	**Columbus**	**NHL**	**1**	**0**	**0**	**0**	**13**	**0**	**0**	**0.00**	....	....	....	....	....	....	....
	Syracuse Crunch	AHL	15	9	2	3	848	30	1	2.12	....	....	....	....	....	....	....
	Elmira Jackals	ECHL	14	7	4	1	754	27	0	2.15	....	....	....	....	....	....	....
	NHL Totals		**1**	**0**	**0**	**0**	**13**	**0**	**0**	**0.00**	....	....	....	....	....	....	....

LAFLEUR, Antoine (lah-FLEWR, AN-twuhn) NYR

Goaltender. Catches left. 6'5", 195 lbs. Born, Gatineau, Que., December 12, 1988.
(NY Rangers' 2nd choice, 48th overall, in 2007 Entry Draft).

			Regular Season								Playoffs						
Season	**Club**	**League**	**GP**	**W**	**L**	**O/T**	**Mins**	**GA**	**SO**	**Avg**	**GP**	**W**	**L**	**Mins**	**GA**	**SO**	**Avg**
2005-06	PEI Rocket	QMJHL	18	2	7	0	710	56	0	4.73	2	0	0	9	0	0	0.00
2006-07	PEI Rocket	QMJHL	49	27	19	....	2708	134	3	2.97	7	3	4	430	30	0	4.19
2007-08	PEI Rocket	QMJHL	39	14	19	....	1993	140	0	4.21	3	0	3	148	17	0	6.89

LALANDE, Kevin (lah-LAWND, KEH-vihn) CGY.

Goaltender. Catches left. 6', 180 lbs. Born, Kingston, Ont., February 19, 1987.
(Calgary's 5th choice, 128th overall, in 2005 Entry Draft).

			Regular Season								Playoffs						
Season	**Club**	**League**	**GP**	**W**	**L**	**O/T**	**Mins**	**GA**	**SO**	**Avg**	**GP**	**W**	**L**	**Mins**	**GA**	**SO**	**Avg**
2003-04	Hawkesbury	CJHL	35	....	....	....	2010	105	3	3.13	6	....	....	286	19	0	3.99
	Belleville Bulls	OHL	3	1	2	0	133	15	0	6.77	....	....	....	....	....	....	....
2004-05	Belleville Bulls	OHL	30	15	11	3	1797	79	1	2.64	2	0	2	120	8	0	4.00
2005-06	Belleville Bulls	OHL	50	24	17	5	2789	143	3	3.08	....	....	....	....	....	....	....
2006-07	Belleville Bulls	OHL	48	27	17	3	2772	139	3	3.01	15	10	5	989	42	*1	2.55
2007-08	Quad City Flames	AHL	7	2	3	0	360	20	0	3.34	....	....	....	....	....	....	....
	Las Vegas	ECHL	27	17	5	4	1607	55	3	2.05	*20	*13	6	1142	48	3	2.52

LALIME, Patrick (lah-LEEM, PAT-rihk) BUF.

Goaltender. Catches left. 6'3", 189 lbs. Born, St-Bonaventure, Que., July 7, 1974.
(Pittsburgh's 6th choice, 156th overall, in 1993 Entry Draft).

			Regular Season								Playoffs						
Season	**Club**	**League**	**GP**	**W**	**L**	**O/T**	**Mins**	**GA**	**SO**	**Avg**	**GP**	**W**	**L**	**Mins**	**GA**	**SO**	**Avg**
1990-91	Abitibi Forestiers	QAAA	26	9	17	0	1595	151	0	5.81	....	....	....	....	....	....	....
1991-92	Shawinigan	QMJHL	6	....	....	....	272	25	0	5.50	....	....	....	....	....	....	....
1992-93	Shawinigan	QMJHL	44	10	24	4	2467	192	0	4.67	....	....	....	....	....	....	....
1993-94	Shawinigan	QMJHL	48	22	20	0	2733	192	1	4.22	5	1	3	223	25	0	6.73
1994-95	Hampton Roads	ECHL	26	15	7	3	1470	82	2	3.35	....	....	....	....	....	....	....
	Cleveland	IHL	23	7	10	4	1230	91	0	4.44	....	....	....	....	....	....	....
1995-96	Cleveland	IHL	41	20	12	7	2314	149	0	3.86	....	....	....	....	....	....	....
1996-97	**Pittsburgh**	**NHL**	**39**	**21**	**12**	**2**	**2058**	**101**	**3**	**2.94**	....	....	....	....	....	....	....
	Cleveland	IHL	14	6	6	2	834	45	1	3.24	....	....	....	....	....	....	....
1997-98	Grand Rapids	IHL	31	10	10	9	1749	76	2	2.61	1	0	1	77	4	0	3.11
1998-99	Kansas City Blades	IHL	*66	*39	20	4	*3789	190	2	3.01	3	1	2	179	6	1	2.01
99-2000	**Ottawa**	**NHL**	**38**	**19**	**14**	**3**	**2038**	**79**	**3**	**2.33**	....	....	....	....	....	....	....
2000-01	**Ottawa**	**NHL**	**60**	**36**	**19**	**5**	**3607**	**141**	**7**	**2.35**	**4**	**0**	**4**	**251**	**10**	**0**	**2.39**
2001-02	**Ottawa**	**NHL**	**61**	**27**	**24**	**8**	**3583**	**148**	**7**	**2.48**	**12**	**7**	**5**	**778**	**18**	**4**	***1.39**
2002-03	**Ottawa**	**NHL**	**67**	**39**	**20**	**7**	**3943**	**142**	**8**	**2.16**	**18**	**11**	**7**	**1122**	**34**	**1**	**1.82**
2003-04	**Ottawa**	**NHL**	**57**	**25**	**23**	**7**	**3324**	**127**	**5**	**2.29**	**7**	**3**	**4**	**398**	**13**	**0**	**1.96**
2004-05			Did not play														
2005-06	**St. Louis**	**NHL**	**31**	**4**	**18**	**8**	**1699**	**103**	**0**	**3.64**	....	....	....	....	....	....	....
	Peoria Rivermen	AHL	14	6	6	1	798	38	1	2.86	....	....	....	....	....	....	....
2006-07	**Chicago**	**NHL**	**12**	**4**	**6**	**1**	**645**	**33**	**1**	**3.07**	....	....	....	....	....	....	....
	Norfolk Admirals	AHL	4	3	1	0	241	10	0	2.49	....	....	....	....	....	....	....
2007-08	**Chicago**	**NHL**	**32**	**16**	**12**	**2**	**1828**	**86**	**1**	**2.82**	....	....	....	....	....	....	....
	NHL Totals		**397**	**191**	**148**	**43**	**22725**	**960**	**35**	**2.53**	**41**	**21**	**20**	**2549**	**75**	**5**	**1.77**

NHL All-Rookie Team (1997) • IHL First All-Star Team (1999)

Played in NHL All-Star Game (2003)

Rights traded to **Anaheim** by **Pittsburgh** for Sean Pronger, March 24, 1998. Traded to **Ottawa** by **Anaheim** for Ted Donato and the rights to Antti-Jussi Niemi, June 18, 1999. Traded to **St. Louis** by **Ottawa** for St. Louis' 4th round choice (Ilja Zubov) in 2005 Entry Draft, June 27, 2004. Signed as a free agent by **Chicago**, July 1, 2006. Signed as a free agent by **Buffalo**, July 1, 2008.

LARSSON, Daniel (LAR-suhn, DAN-yehl) DET.

Goaltender. Catches left. 6', 170 lbs. Born, Boden, Sweden, February 7, 1986.
(Detroit's 4th choice, 92nd overall, in 2006 Entry Draft).

			Regular Season								Playoffs						
Season	**Club**	**League**	**GP**	**W**	**L**	**O/T**	**Mins**	**GA**	**SO**	**Avg**	**GP**	**W**	**L**	**Mins**	**GA**	**SO**	**Avg**
2002-03	Lulea HF U18	Swe-U18	12	....	....	....	731	50	0	4.10	....	....	....	....	....	....	....
2003-04	Lulea HF Jr.	Swe-Jr.	4	....	....	....	239	12	0	3.01	....	....	....	....	....	....	....
	Bodens IK	Sweden-2	1	....	....	....	20	1	0	3.00	....	....	....	....	....	....	....
2004-05	Bodens IK	Sweden-2	28	....	....	....	1514	97	1	3.84	....	....	....	....	....	....	....
2005-06	Hammarby Jr.	Swe-Jr.	9	....	....	....	548	24	1	2.63	....	....	....	....	....	....	....
	Hammarby	Sweden-2	36	....	....	....	2001	90	0	2.70	....	....	....	....	....	....	....
2006-07	Djurgarden	Sweden	24	....	....	....	1259	53	3	2.53	....	....	....	....	....	....	....
2007-08	Djurgarden	Sweden	46	....	....	....	2721	104	6	2.29	5	....	....	295	13	0	2.64

LECLAIRE, Pascal (luh-KLAIR, pas-KAL) CBJ

Goaltender. Catches left. 6'2", 200 lbs. Born, Repentigny, Que., November 7, 1982.
(Columbus' 1st choice, 8th overall, in 2001 Entry Draft).

			Regular Season								Playoffs						
Season	Club	League	GP	W	L	O/T	Mins	GA	SO	Avg	GP	W	L	Mins	GA	SO	Avg
1997-98	Cap-d-Madeleine	QAAA	26	6	17	3	1580	127	0	4.90	....	....	....	....	....	....	....
1998-99	Halifax	QMJHL	33	19	11	1	1828	96	2	3.15	1	0	0	17	2	0	7.06
99-2000	Halifax	QMJHL	31	16	8	4	1729	103	1	3.57	5	1	2	198	12	0	3.65
2000-01	Halifax	QMJHL	35	14	16	5	2111	126	1	3.58	2	0	2	109	10	0	5.49
2001-02	Montreal Rocket	QMJHL	45	15	23	4	2513	138	1	3.29	7	3	4	441	15	0	*2.04
2002-03	Syracuse Crunch	AHL	36	8	21	3	1886	112	0	3.56	....	....	....	....	....	....	....
2003-04	**Columbus**	**NHL**	**2**	**0**	**2**	**0**	**119**	**7**	**0**	**3.53**	....	....	....	....	....	....	....
	Syracuse Crunch	AHL	44	21	16	3	2447	125	2	3.06	3	1	2	142	12	0	5.07
2004-05	Syracuse Crunch	AHL	14	5	6	3	845	33	2	2.34	....	....	....	....	....	....	....
2005-06	**Columbus**	**NHL**	**33**	**11**	**15**	**3**	**1804**	**97**	**0**	**3.23**	....	....	....	....	....	....	....
	Syracuse Crunch	AHL	7	3	3	0	340	16	1	2.82	5	2	3	288	11	1	2.29
2006-07	**Columbus**	**NHL**	**24**	**6**	**15**	**2**	**1315**	**65**	**1**	**2.97**	....	....	....	....	....	....	....
2007-08	**Columbus**	**NHL**	**54**	**24**	**17**	**6**	**2986**	**112**	**9**	**2.25**	....	....	....	....	....	....	....
	NHL Totals		**113**	**41**	**49**	**11**	**6224**	**281**	**10**	**2.71**	....	....	....	....	....	....	....

LEGACE, Manny (LEH-gah-see, MAN-ee) ST.L.

Goaltender. Catches left. 5'10", 200 lbs. Born, Toronto, Ont., February 4, 1973.
(Hartford's 5th choice, 188th overall, in 1993 Entry Draft).

			Regular Season								Playoffs						
Season	Club	League	GP	W	L	O/T	Mins	GA	SO	Avg	GP	W	L	Mins	GA	SO	Avg
1987-88	Alliston Hornets	OJHL-C	16	7	9	0	960	83	0	5.17	....	....	....	....	....	....	....
1988-89	Vaughan Raiders	MTJHL	23	....	....	....	1303	92	1	4.24	....	....	....	....	....	....	....
1989-90	Vaughan Raiders	MTJHL	21	8	11	1	1180	89	1	4.53	....	....	....	....	....	....	....
	Thornhill	OHA-B	8	3	3	2	480	30	0	3.75	....	....	....	....	....	....	....
1990-91	Niagara Falls	OHL	30	13	11	2	1515	107	0	4.24	4	1	1	119	10	0	5.04
1991-92	Niagara Falls	OHL	43	21	16	3	2384	143	0	3.60	14	8	5	791	56	0	4.25
1992-93	Niagara Falls	OHL	48	22	19	3	2630	171	0	3.90	4	0	4	240	18	0	4.50
1993-94	Canada	Nat-Tm	16	8	6	0	859	36	2	2.51	....	....	....	....	....	....	....
1994-95	Springfield Indians	AHL	39	12	17	6	2169	128	2	3.54	....	....	....	....	....	....	....
1995-96	Springfield Falcons	AHL	37	20	12	4	2196	83	*5	*2.27	4	1	3	220	18	0	4.91
1996-97	Springfield Falcons	AHL	36	17	14	5	2119	107	1	3.03	12	9	3	745	25	*2	2.01
	Richmond	ECHL	3	2	1	0	157	8	0	3.05	....	....	....	....	....	....	....
1997-98	Springfield Falcons	AHL	6	4	2	0	345	16	0	2.78	....	....	....	....	....	....	....
	Las Vegas Thunder	IHL	41	18	16	4	2106	111	1	3.16	4	1	3	237	16	0	4.05
1998-99	**Los Angeles**	**NHL**	**17**	**2**	**9**	**2**	**899**	**39**	**0**	**2.60**	....	....	....	....	....	....	....
	Long Beach	IHL	33	22	8	1	1796	67	2	2.24	6	4	2	338	9	0	*1.60
99-2000	**Detroit**	**NHL**	**4**	**4**	**0**	**0**	**240**	**11**	**0**	**2.75**	....	....	....	....	....	....	....
	Manitoba Moose	IHL	42	17	18	5	2409	104	2	2.59	2	0	2	141	7	0	2.97
2000-01	**Detroit**	**NHL**	**39**	**24**	**5**	**5**	**2136**	**73**	**2**	**2.05**	....	....	....	....	....	....	....
2001-02 ◆	**Detroit**	**NHL**	**20**	**10**	**6**	**2**	**1117**	**45**	**1**	**2.42**	**1**	**0**	**0**	**11**	**1**	**0**	**5.45**
2002-03	**Detroit**	**NHL**	**25**	**14**	**5**	**4**	**1406**	**51**	**0**	**2.18**	....	....	....	....	....	....	....
2003-04	**Detroit**	**NHL**	**41**	**23**	**10**	**5**	**2325**	**82**	**3**	**2.12**	**4**	**2**	**2**	**220**	**8**	**0**	**2.18**
2004-05	Voskresensk	Russia	2	....	....	....	89	10	0	6.73	....	....	....	....	....	....	....
2005-06	**Detroit**	**NHL**	**51**	**37**	**8**	**3**	**2905**	**106**	**7**	**2.19**	**6**	**2**	**4**	**408**	**18**	**0**	**2.65**
	Grand Rapids	AHL	1	1	0	0	60	2	0	2.00	....	....	....	....	....	....	....
2006-07	**St. Louis**	**NHL**	**45**	**23**	**15**	**5**	**2522**	**109**	**5**	**2.59**	....	....	....	....	....	....	....
2007-08	**St. Louis**	**NHL**	**66**	**27**	**25**	**8**	**3666**	**147**	**5**	**2.41**	....	....	....	....	....	....	....
	NHL Totals		**308**	**164**	**83**	**34**	**17216**	**663**	**23**	**2.31**	**11**	**4**	**6**	**639**	**27**	**0**	**2.54**

OHL First All-Star Team (1993) • AHL First All-Star Team (1996) • Harry ''Hap'' Holmes Memorial Award (fewest goals against – AHL) (1996) (shared with Scott Langkow) • Aldege "Baz" Bastien Memorial Award (Outstanding Goaltender – AHL) (1996)

Played in NHL All-Star Game (2008)

Rights transferred to **Carolina** after **Hartford** franchise relocated, June 25, 1997. Traded to **Los Angeles** by **Carolina** for future considerations, July 31, 1998. Signed as a free agent by **Detroit**, August 9, 1999. Claimed on waivers by **Vancouver** from **Detroit**, September 30, 1999. Claimed on waivers by **Detroit** from **Vancouver**, October 13, 1999. Signed as a free agent by **Voskresensk** (Russia), December 20, 2004. Signed as a free agent by **St. Louis**, August 8, 2006.

LEHTONEN, Kari (LEH-tuh-nehn, KAH-ree) ATL.

Goaltender. Catches left. 6'4", 205 lbs. Born, Helsinki, Finland, November 16, 1983.
(Atlanta's 1st choice, 2nd overall, in 2002 Entry Draft).

			Regular Season								Playoffs						
Season	Club	League	GP	W	L	O/T	Mins	GA	SO	Avg	GP	W	L	Mins	GA	SO	Avg
1998-99	Jokerit U18	Fin-U18	2	....	....	....	....	....	....	....	4	2	2	240	7	0	1.75
99-2000	Jokerit Helsinki Jr.	Fin-Jr.	33	21	9	3	1974	86	2	2.61	12	9	3	758	14	4	1.11
2000-01	Jokerit U18	Fin-U18	....	....	....	....	....	....	....	....	6	....	....	....	....	....	....
	Jokerit Helsinki Jr.	Fin-Jr.	31	20	9	1	1799	71	3	2.37	1	0	1	54	4	0	4.44
	Jokerit Helsinki	Finland	4	3	1	0	189	6	0	1.90	....	....	....	....	....	....	....
2001-02	Jokerit Helsinki Jr.	Fin-Jr.	6	5	1	0	360	11	1	1.83	....	....	....	....	....	....	....
	Jokerit Helsinki	Finland	23	13	5	2	1242	37	4	1.79	11	8	2	623	18	3	1.73
2002-03	Jokerit Helsinki	Finland	45	23	14	6	2634	87	5	1.98	10	6	4	626	17	2	1.63
2003-04	**Atlanta**	**NHL**	**4**	**4**	**0**	**0**	**240**	**5**	**1**	**1.25**	....	....	....	....	....	....	....
	Chicago Wolves	AHL	39	20	14	2	2192	88	3	2.41	10	6	4	663	23	1	2.08
2004-05	Chicago Wolves	AHL	57	38	17	2	3378	128	5	2.27	16	10	6	983	28	2	*1.71
2005-06	**Atlanta**	**NHL**	**38**	**20**	**15**	**0**	**2166**	**106**	**2**	**2.94**	....	....	....	....	....	....	....
2006-07	**Atlanta**	**NHL**	**68**	**34**	**24**	**9**	**3934**	**183**	**4**	**2.79**	**2**	**0**	**2**	**118**	**11**	**0**	**5.59**
2007-08	**Atlanta**	**NHL**	**48**	**17**	**22**	**5**	**2707**	**131**	**4**	**2.90**	....	....	....	....	....	....	....
	Chicago Wolves	AHL	2	2	0	0	124	4	0	1.93	....	....	....	....	....	....	....
	NHL Totals		**158**	**75**	**61**	**14**	**9047**	**425**	**11**	**2.82**	**2**	**0**	**2**	**118**	**11**	**0**	**5.59**

AHL Second All-Star Team (2005)

LEIGHTON, Michael (LAY-tohn, MIGH-kuhl) CAR.

Goaltender. Catches left. 6'3", 186 lbs. Born, Petrolia, Ont., May 19, 1981.
(Chicago's 5th choice, 165th overall, in 1999 Entry Draft).

			Regular Season								Playoffs						
Season	Club	League	GP	W	L	O/T	Mins	GA	SO	Avg	GP	W	L	Mins	GA	SO	Avg
1997-98	Petrolia Jets	OHA-B	30	....	....	....	1583	87	2	3.30	....	....	....	....	....	....	....
1998-99	Windsor Spitfires	OHL	28	4	17	2	1389	112	0	4.84	3	0	1	80	10	0	7.50
99-2000	Windsor Spitfires	OHL	42	17	17	2	2272	118	1	3.12	12	5	6	616	32	0	3.12
2000-01	Windsor Spitfires	OHL	54	32	13	5	3035	138	2	2.73	9	4	5	519	27	1	3.12
2001-02	Norfolk Admirals	AHL	52	27	16	8	3114	111	6	2.14	4	1	2	238	8	0	2.02
2002-03	**Chicago**	**NHL**	**8**	**2**	**3**	**2**	**447**	**21**	**1**	**2.82**	....	....	....	....	....	....	....
	Norfolk Admirals	AHL	36	18	13	5	2184	91	4	2.50	4	3	1	240	7	1	1.75
2003-04	**Chicago**	**NHL**	**34**	**6**	**18**	**8**	**1988**	**99**	**2**	**2.99**	....	....	....	....	....	....	....
	Norfolk Admirals	AHL	18	10	7	1	1081	33	1	1.83	4	2	1	212	2	2	0.57
2004-05	Norfolk Admirals	AHL	41	20	16	3	2319	78	7	2.02	....	....	....	....	....	....	....
2005-06	Rochester	AHL	40	15	22	1	2318	124	2	3.21	....	....	....	....	....	....	....
2006-07	Portland Pirates	AHL	16	8	6	1	962	37	2	2.31	....	....	....	....	....	....	....
	Nashville	**NHL**	**1**	**0**	**0**	**0**	**20**	**2**	**0**	**6.00**	....	....	....	....	....	....	....
	Philadelphia	**NHL**	**4**	**2**	**2**	**0**	**195**	**12**	**0**	**3.69**	....	....	....	....	....	....	....
	Philadelphia	AHL	5	2	0	2	270	7	0	1.56	....	....	....	....	....	....	....
2007-08	**Carolina**	**NHL**	**3**	**1**	**1**	**0**	**158**	**7**	**0**	**2.66**	....	....	....	....	....	....	....
	Albany River Rats	AHL	58	28	25	4	3451	121	*7	2.10	7	3	4	510	10	*2	*1.18
	NHL Totals		**50**	**11**	**24**	**10**	**2808**	**141**	**3**	**3.01**	....	....	....	....	....	....	....

AHL All-Rookie Team (2002) • AHL First All-Star Team (2008) • Aldege "Baz" Bastien Memorial Award (Outstanding Goaltender – AHL) (2008)

Traded to **Buffalo** by **Chicago** for Milan Bartovic, October 4, 2005. Signed as a free agent by **Anaheim**, July 13, 2006. Claimed on waivers by **Nashville** from **Anaheim**, November 27, 2006. Claimed on waivers by **Philadelphia** from **Nashville**, January 11, 2007. Claimed on waivers by **Montreal** from **Philadelphia**, February 27, 2007. Traded to **Carolina** by **Montreal** for Carolina's 7th round choice (Scott Kishel) in 2007 Entry Draft, June 23, 2007.

LeNEVEU, David (LEH-neh-voo, DAY-vihd) ANA.

Goaltender. Catches left. 6'1", 187 lbs. Born, Fernie, B.C., May 23, 1983.
(Phoenix's 3rd choice, 46th overall, in 2002 Entry Draft).

			Regular Season								Playoffs						
Season	Club	League	GP	W	L	O/T	Mins	GA	SO	Avg	GP	W	L	Mins	GA	SO	Avg
99-2000	Fernie Ghostriders	AWHL	22	15	2	0	1140	48	0	2.49	....	....	....	....	....	....	....
2000-01	Nanaimo Clippers	BCHL	41	....	....	....	2330	127	6	3.29	....	....	....	....	....	....	....
2001-02	Cornell Big Red	ECAC	14	11	2	1	842	21	2	*1.50	....	....	....	....	....	....	....
2002-03	Cornell Big Red	ECAC	32	*28	3	1	1946	39	*9	*1.20	....	....	....	....	....	....	....
2003-04	Springfield Falcons	AHL	38	16	19	3	2217	102	1	2.76	....	....	....	....	....	....	....
2004-05	Utah Grizzlies	AHL	48	11	32	3	2702	132	0	2.93	....	....	....	....	....	....	....
2005-06	**Phoenix**	**NHL**	**15**	**3**	**8**	**2**	**814**	**44**	**0**	**3.24**	....	....	....	....	....	....	....
	San Antonio	AHL	28	10	16	2	1646	80	2	2.92	....	....	....	....	....	....	....
2006-07	**Phoenix**	**NHL**	**6**	**2**	**1**	**0**	**233**	**15**	**0**	**3.86**	....	....	....	....	....	....	....
	San Antonio	AHL	37	13	20	2	2101	104	2	2.97	....	....	....	....	....	....	....
2007-08	San Antonio	AHL	21	9	7	3	1172	52	1	2,66	....	....	....	....	....	....	....
	Hartford Wolf Pack	AHL	13	8	3	2	786	24	1	1.83	4	1	3	266	11	0	2.48
	NHL Totals		**21**	**5**	**9**	**2**	**1047**	**59**	**0**	**3.38**	....	....	....	....	....	....	....

ECAC All-Rookie Team (2002) • ECAC First All-Star Team (2003) • ECAC Goaltender of the Year (2003) • ECAC Player of the Year (2003) (co-winner - Christopher Higgins) • NCAA East First All-American Team (2003)

Traded to **NY Rangers** by **Phoenix** with Fredrik Sjostrom, Josh Gratton and future considerations for Al Montoya and Marcel Hossa, February 26, 2008. Signed as a free agent by **Anaheim**, July 7, 2008.

LEVASSEUR, Jean-Philippe (leh-VAH-soor, ZHAWN-fihl-EEP) ANA.

Goaltender. Catches right. 6'1", 205 lbs. Born, Victoriaville, Que., January 15, 1987.
(Anaheim's 6th choice, 197th overall, in 2005 Entry Draft).

			Regular Season								Playoffs						
Season	Club	League	GP	W	L	O/T	Mins	GA	SO	Avg	GP	W	L	Mins	GA	SO	Avg
2002-03	Magog	QAAA	28	15	10	1	1563	71	3	2.73	....	....	....	....	....	....	....
2003-04	Magog	QAAA	24	12	11	2	1424	86	0	3.62	13	7	5	762	35	0	2.80
	Rouyn-Noranda	QMJHL	3	0	2	1	184	14	0	4.57	....	....	....	....	....	....	....
2004-05	Rouyn-Noranda	QMJHL	29	8	14	3	1393	89	0	3.83	3	0	0	48	3	0	3.76
2005-06	Rouyn-Noranda	QMJHL	58	*35	19	0	3125	178	2	3.42	5	1	4	297	16	0	3.23
2006-07	Rouyn-Noranda	QMJHL	58	*31	21	....	3118	182	1	3.50	15	8	6	852	51	0	3.59
2007-08	Portland Pirates	AHL	10	4	5	1	600	25	1	2.50	....	....	....	....	....	....	....
	Augusta Lynx	ECHL	29	10	11	2	1527	76	1	2.99	1	0	1	59	2	0	2.02

LINDBACK, Anders (LIHND-bak, AN-duhrs) NSH.

Goaltender. Catches left. 6'6", 198 lbs. Born, Gavle, Sweden, May 3, 1988.
(Nashville's 7th choice, 207th overall, in 2008 Entry Draft).

			Regular Season								Playoffs						
Season	Club	League	GP	W	L	O/T	Mins	GA	SO	Avg	GP	W	L	Mins	GA	SO	Avg
2003-04	Brynas U18	Swe-U18	3	....	....	....	178	13	0	4.38	....	....	....	....	....	....	....
2004-05	Brynas U18	Swe-U18	49	....	....	....	2940	108	7	2.20	....	....	....	....	....	....	....
2005-06	Brynas U18	Swe-U18	11	....	....	....	666	36	2	3.24	....	....	....	....	....	....	....
	Brynas IF Gavle Jr.	Swe-Jr.	5	....	....	....	257	7	2	1.64	....	....	....	....	....	....	....
2006-07	Brynas IF Gavle Jr.	Swe-Jr.	36	....	....	....	2143	81	5	2.27	3	....	....	180	6	0	2.00
2007-08	Almtuna	Sweden-2	18	....	....	....	1034	53	0	3.07	....	....	....	....	....	....	....

LUNDQVIST, Henrik (LUHND-kvihst, HEHN-rihk) NYR

Goaltender. Catches left. 6'1", 195 lbs. Born, Are, Sweden, March 2, 1982.
(NY Rangers' 7th choice, 205th overall, in 2000 Entry Draft).

			Regular Season								Playoffs						
Season	Club	League	GP	W	L	O/T	Mins	GA	SO	Avg	GP	W	L	Mins	GA	SO	Avg
1998-99	V.Frolunda Jr.	Swe-Jr.	35	....	....	....	2100	95	0	2.73	....	....	....	....	....	....	....
99-2000	V.Frolunda Jr.	Swe-Jr.	30	....	....	....	1726	73	0	2.54	5	4	1	300	7	2	1.40
2000-01	V.Frolunda U18	Swe-U18	2	....	....	....	120	5	0	2.50	3	2	1	182	5	0	1.62
	V.Frolunda Jr.	Swe-Jr.	19	....	....	....	1140	50	2	2.64	....	....	....	....	....	....	....
	IF Molndal Hockey	Sweden-2	7	....	....	....	420	29	0	4.22	....	....	....	....	....	....	....
	V.Frolunda	Sweden	4	....	....	....	190	11	0	3.47	....	....	....	....	....	....	....
2001-02	V.Frolunda	Sweden	20	....	....	....	1152	52	2	2.71	8	8	0	489	18	*2	2.21
	V.Frolunda Jr.	Swe-Jr.	1	1	0	0	60	4	0	4.00	....	....	....	....	....	....	....
2002-03	V.Frolunda	Sweden	28	....	....	....	1650	40	*6	*1.45	12	....	....	739	26	*2	2.11
	V.Frolunda Jr.	Swe-Jr.	1	1	0	0	60	4	0	4.00	....	....	....	....	....	....	....
2003-04	V.Frolunda	Sweden	*48	....	....	....	*2897	105	7	2.17	10	....	....	610	20	0	1.97
2004-05	Frolunda	Sweden	44	*33	8	3	2642	79	*6	*1.79	*14	*12	2	854	15	*6	*1.05
2005-06	**NY Rangers**	**NHL**	**53**	**30**	**12**	**9**	**3112**	**116**	**2**	**2.24**	**3**	**0**	**3**	**177**	**13**	**0**	**4.41**
	Sweden	Olympics	6	5	1	0	360	14	0	2.33	....	....	....	....	....	....	....
2006-07	**NY Rangers**	**NHL**	**70**	**37**	**22**	**8**	**4109**	**160**	**5**	**2.34**	**10**	**6**	**4**	**637**	**22**	**1**	**2.07**
2007-08	**NY Rangers**	**NHL**	**72**	**37**	**24**	**10**	**4305**	**160**	***10**	**2.23**	**10**	**5**	**5**	**608**	**26**	**1**	**2.57**
	NHL Totals		**195**	**104**	**58**	**27**	**11526**	**436**	**17**	**2.27**	**23**	**11**	**12**	**1422**	**61**	**2**	**2.57**

NHL All-Rookie Team (2006)

LUONGO, Roberto (loo-WAHN-goh, roh-BUHR-toh) VAN.

Goaltender. Catches left. 6'3", 205 lbs. Born, Montreal, Que., April 4, 1979.
(NY Islanders' 1st choice, 4th overall, in 1997 Entry Draft).

			Regular Season								Playoffs						
Season	Club	League	GP	W	L	O/T	Mins	GA	SO	Avg	GP	W	L	Mins	GA	SO	Avg
1994-95	Montreal-Bourassa	QAAA	25	10	14	0	1465	94	0	3.85	....	....	....	....	....	....	....
1995-96	Val-d'Or Foreurs	QMJHL	23	6	11	4	1201	74	0	3.70	3	0	1	68	5	0	4.41
1996-97	Val-d'Or Foreurs	QMJHL	60	32	22	2	3305	171	2	3.10	13	8	5	777	44	0	3.40
1997-98	Val-d'Or Foreurs	QMJHL	54	27	20	5	3046	157	*7	3.09	*17	*14	3	*1019	37	*2	*2.18
1998-99	Val-d'Or Foreurs	QMJHL	21	6	10	2	1176	77	1	3.93	....	....	....	....	....	....	....
	Acadie-Bathurst	QMJHL	22	14	7	1	1340	74	0	3.31	*23	*16	6	*1400	64	0	2.74
99-2000	**NY Islanders**	**NHL**	**24**	**7**	**14**	**1**	**1292**	**70**	**1**	**3.25**	....	....	....	....	....	....	....
	Lowell	AHL	26	10	12	4	1517	74	1	2.93	6	3	3	359	18	0	3.01
2000-01	**Florida**	**NHL**	**47**	**12**	**24**	**7**	**2628**	**107**	**5**	**2.44**	....	....	....	....	....	....	....
	Louisville Panthers	AHL	3	1	2	0	178	10	0	3.38	....	....	....	....	....	....	....
2001-02	**Florida**	**NHL**	**58**	**16**	**33**	**4**	**3030**	**140**	**4**	**2.77**	....	....	....	....	....	....	....
2002-03	**Florida**	**NHL**	**65**	**20**	**34**	**7**	**3627**	**164**	**6**	**2.71**	....	....	....	....	....	....	....
2003-04	**Florida**	**NHL**	**72**	**25**	**33**	**14**	**4252**	**172**	**7**	**2.43**	....	....	....	....	....	....	....
2004-05							DID NOT PLAY										
2005-06	**Florida**	**NHL**	***75**	**35**	**30**	**9**	**4305**	**213**	**4**	**2.97**	....	....	....	....	....	....	....
	Canada	Olympics	2	1	1	0	119	3	0	1.51	....	....	....	....	....	....	....
2006-07	**Vancouver**	**NHL**	**76**	**47**	**22**	**6**	**4490**	**171**	**5**	**2.29**	**12**	**5**	**7**	**847**	**25**	**0**	**1.77**

2007-08	**Vancouver**	**NHL**	**73**	**35**	**29**	**9**	**4233**	**168**	**6**	**2.38**	....	....	....	....	....	....	....
	NHL Totals		**490**	**197**	**219**	**57**	**27857**	**1205**	**38**	**2.60**	**12**	**5**	**7**	**847**	**25**	**0**	**1.77**

NHL Second All-Star Team (2004, 2007)

Played in NHL All-Star Game (2004, 2007)

Traded to **Florida** by **NY Islanders** with Olli Jokinen for Mark Parrish and Oleg Kvasha, June 24, 2000. Traded to **Vancouver** by **Florida** with Lukas Krajicek and Florida's 6th round choice (Sergei Shirokov) in 2006 Entry Draft for Todd Bertuzzi, Bryan Allen and Alex Auld, June 23, 2006.

MacDONALD, Joey (MAK-DAWN-uhld, JOH-ee) NYI

Goaltender. Catches left. 6', 197 lbs. Born, Pictou, N.S., February 7, 1980.

			Regular Season								Playoffs						
Season	Club	League	GP	W	L	O/T	Mins	GA	SO	Avg	GP	W	L	Mins	GA	SO	Avg
1997-98	Halifax	QMJHL	17	3	12	0	815	54	0	3.97	3	1	2	140	15	0	6.43
1998-99	Peterborough	OHL	47	22	15	2	2483	123	3	2.97	3	0	2	145	13	0	5.38
99-2000	Peterborough	OHL	48	20	15	6	2641	125	2	2.84	5	1	4	280	16	1	3.43
2000-01	Peterborough	OHL	57	25	21	7	3284	161	1	2.94	7	3	4	425	18	0	2.54
2001-02	Toledo Storm	ECHL	38	12	15	7	2084	100	1	2.88	....	....	....	....	....	....	....
2002-03	Grand Rapids	AHL	25	14	6	0	1337	49	3	2.20	1	0	0	8	1	0	7.95
2003-04	Grand Rapids	AHL	39	22	12	3	2249	74	6	1.97	1	0	1	40	4	0	6.04
2004-05	Grand Rapids	AHL	*66	34	29	2	*3755	143	5	2.29	....	....	....	....	....	....	....
2005-06	Grand Rapids	AHL	32	17	9	2	1745	91	2	3.13	....	....	....	....	....	....	....
	Toledo Storm	ECHL	1	1	0	0	60	1	0	1.00	....	....	....	....	....	....	....
2006-07	**Detroit**	**NHL**	**8**	**1**	**5**	**1**	**468**	**27**	**0**	**3.46**	....	....	....	....	....	....	....
	Grand Rapids	AHL	2	1	1	0	123	6	0	2.93	....	....	....	....	....	....	....
	Boston	**NHL**	**7**	**2**	**2**	**1**	**358**	**16**	**0**	**2.68**	....	....	....	....	....	....	....
2007-08	**NY Islanders**	**NHL**	**2**	**0**	**1**	**1**	**120**	**6**	**0**	**3.00**	....	....	....	....	....	....	....
	Bridgeport	AHL	38	16	19	2	2266	109	2	2.89	....	....	....	....	....	....	....
	NHL Totals		**17**	**3**	**8**	**3**	**946**	**49**	**0**	**3.11**	....	....	....	....	....	....	....

Harry "Hap" Holmes Memorial Award (fewest goals against – AHL) (2003) (shared with Marc Lamothe)

Signed as a free agent by **Detroit**, December 21, 2001. Claimed on waivers by **Boston** from **Detroit**, February 24, 2007. Signed as a free agent by **NY Islanders**, July 7, 2007.

MACHESNEY, Daren (muh-KEHS-nee, DAIR-ehn) WSH.

Goaltender. Catches left. 6', 182 lbs. Born, Hamilton, Ont., December 13, 1986.
(Washington's 5th choice, 143rd overall, in 2005 Entry Draft).

			Regular Season								Playoffs						
Season	Club	League	GP	W	L	O/T	Mins	GA	SO	Avg	GP	W	L	Mins	GA	SO	Avg
2003-04	Newmarket	OPJHL	32	....	....	....	1868	82	1	2.63	....	....	....	....	....	....	....
	Brampton Battalion	OHL	5	3	2	0	300	15	0	3.00	....	....	....	....	....	....	....
2004-05	Brampton Battalion	OHL	38	16	13	6	2166	99	1	2.74	5	2	3	331	15	0	2.72
2005-06	Brampton Battalion	OHL	49	28	17	3	2830	143	3	3.03	11	5	6	633	32	0	3.03
2006-07	Hershey Bears	AHL	10	3	3	1	377	20	0	3.18	....	....	....	....	....	....	....
	South Carolina	ECHL	15	5	8	2	836	46	1	3.30	....	....	....	....	....	....	....
2007-08	Hershey Bears	AHL	38	22	10	2	2139	91	1	2.55	2	0	1	21	3	0	8.54

OHL All-Rookie Team (2005)

MacINTYRE, Drew (MAK-ihn-tighr, DROO) NSH.

Goaltender. Catches left. 6'2", 185 lbs. Born, Charlottetown, P.E.I., June 24, 1983.
(Detroit's 2nd choice, 121st overall, in 2001 Entry Draft).

			Regular Season								Playoffs						
Season	Club	League	GP	W	L	O/T	Mins	GA	SO	Avg	GP	W	L	Mins	GA	SO	Avg
1998-99	Trenton Sting	OPJHL	20	....	....	....	1173	71	2	3.63	....	....	....	....	....	....	....
99-2000	Sherbrooke	QMJHL	24	10	7	2	1253	67	0	3.21	....	....	....	....	....	....	....
2000-01	Sherbrooke	QMJHL	48	17	22	3	2552	139	4	3.27	4	0	4	238	19	0	4.78
2001-02	Sherbrooke	QMJHL	55	15	34	3	3028	201	1	3.98	....	....	....	....	....	....	....
2002-03	Sherbrooke	QMJHL	*61	31	24	5	*3515	161	2	2.75	12	5	7	767	52	0	4.07
2003-04	Toledo Storm	ECHL	11	6	4	0	574	25	0	2.61	....	....	....	....	....	....	....
2004-05	Grand Rapids	AHL	24	7	8	0	1049	47	1	2.69	....	....	....	....	....	....	....
	Toledo Storm	ECHL	2	0	1	0	87	6	0	4.12	....	....	....	....	....	....	....
2005-06	Grand Rapids	AHL	13	8	4	0	681	33	0	2.91	5	3	1	260	7	0	1.62
	Toledo Storm	ECHL	33	24	7	2	1981	68	2	*2.06	6	5	1	360	12	0	2.00
2006-07	Manitoba Moose	AHL	41	24	12	2	2290	83	3	2.17	11	4	6	633	21	1	1.99
2007-08	**Vancouver**	**NHL**	**2**	**0**	**1**	**0**	**61**	**3**	**0**	**2.95**	....	....	....	....	....	....	....
	Manitoba Moose	AHL	46	25	18	2	2736	106	2	2.32	1	1	0	31	2	0	3.93
	NHL Totals		**2**	**0**	**1**	**0**	**61**	**3**	**0**	**2.95**	....	....	....	....	....	....	....

AHL Second All-Star Team (2008)

• Missed majority of 2003-04 season recovering from thigh injury suffered in practice, December 27, 2003. Traded to **Vancouver** by **Detroit** for future considerations, September 12, 2006. Signed as a free agent by **Nashville**, July 1, 2008.

MANNINO, Peter (ma-NEE-noh, PE-tuhr) NYI

Goaltender. Catches . 6', 200 lbs. Born, Farmington Hills, MI, February 17, 1984.

			Regular Season								Playoffs						
Season	Club	League	GP	W	L	O/T	Mins	GA	SO	Avg	GP	W	L	Mins	GA	SO	Avg
2001-02	Pittsburgh Forge	NAHL	11	....	....	....	....	....	....	....	....	....	....	....	....	....	....
2002-03	Pittsburgh Forge	NAHL	45	....	....	....	....	....	....	....	....	....	....	....	....	....	....
2003-04	Tri-City Storm	USHL	38	26	7	0	1988	70	5	2.11	....	....	....	....	....	....	....
2004-05	U. of Denver	WCHA	21	16	4	1	1224	46	5	2.25	....	....	....	....	....	....	....
2005-06	U. of Denver	WCHA	22	12	8	1	1241	56	1	2.71	....	....	....	....	....	....	....
2006-07	U. of Denver	WCHA	18	8	6	2	1021	39	3	2.29	....	....	....	....	....	....	....
2007-08	U. of Denver	WCHA	40	25	14	1	2302	87	*6	2.27	....	....	....	....	....	....	....

Signed as a free agent by **NY Islanders**, July 3, 2008.

MANZATO, Daniel (man-ZA-toh, DAN-yehl) CAR.

Goaltender. Catches left. 6', 178 lbs. Born, Fribourg, Switz., January 17, 1984.
(Carolina's 3rd choice, 160th overall, in 2002 Entry Draft).

			Regular Season								Playoffs						
Season	Club	League	GP	W	L	O/T	Mins	GA	SO	Avg	GP	W	L	Mins	GA	SO	Avg
2000-01	Fribourg Jr.	Swiss-Jr.	36	....	....	....	2160	32	6	0.91	....	....	....	....	....	....	....
2001-02	Victoriaville Tigres	QMJHL	36	20	8	2	1894	102	0	3.23	6	3	0	249	17	0	4.09
2002-03	Victoriaville Tigres	QMJHL	48	23	18	5	2756	155	3	3.37	3	0	3	125	11	0	5.27
2003-04	Victoriaville Tigres	QMJHL	23	7	13	0	1170	78	0	4.00	....	....	....	....	....	....	....
	Kloten Flyers	Swiss	15	....	....	....	912	39	1	2.57	....	....	....	....	....	....	....
2004-05	HC Ambri-Piotta	Swiss	25	....	....	....	1446	65	1	2.70	....	....	....	....	....	....	....
2005-06	EHC Basel	Swiss	41	18	14	9	2449	107	*5	2.62	5	1	4	280	22	0	4.71
2006-07	EHC Basel	Swiss	43	13	30	0	2590	157	1	3.64	13	7	6	795	41	2	3.09
2007-08	Albany River Rats	AHL	1	0	1	0	59	5	0	5.07	....	....	....	....	....	....	....
	Charlotte Checkers	ECHL	2	2	0	0	120	4	0	2.00	....	....	....	....	....	....	....
	Las Vegas	ECHL	33	22	5	6	1985	79	3	2.39	2	1	0	97	4	0	2.48

Signed as a free agent by **Kloten** (Swiss), January 5, 2004, following release by **Victoriaville** (QMJHL), January 4, 2004. Signed as a free agent by **Ambri-Piotta** (Swiss), August 5, 2004. Signed as a free agent by **Basel** (Swiss), August, 2005.

MARKKANEN, Jussi (MAHR-kah-nehn, YEW-see)

Goaltender. Catches left. 6', 182 lbs. Born, Imatra, Finland, May 8, 1975.
(Edmonton's 5th choice, 133rd overall, in 2001 Entry Draft).

			Regular Season								Playoffs						
Season	Club	League	GP	W	L	O/T	Mins	GA	SO	Avg	GP	W	L	Mins	GA	SO	Avg
1991-92	SaiPa Jr.	Fin-Jr.	6	3	3	0	360	25	0	4.16	....	....	....	....	....	....	....
1992-93	SaiPa Jr.	Fin-Jr.	7	....	....	....	367	28	0	4.58	....	....	....	....	....	....	....
	SaiPa	Finland-2	16	6	6	2	798	60	0	4.51	....	....	....	....	....	....	....
1993-94	SaiPa Jr.	Fin-Jr.	4	....	....	....	....	....	....	2.26	....	....	....	....	....	....	....
	SaiPa	Finland-2	30	....	....	....	1726	97	....	3.37	....	....	....	....	....	....	....
1994-95	SaiPa	Finland-2	36	....	....	....	2067	95	....	2.76	10	6	4	621	33	0	3.19
1995-96	Tappara Jr.	Fin-Jr.	5	....	....	....	298	21	....	4.23	....	....	....	....	....	....	....
	Tappara Tampere	Finland	23	11	8	2	1239	59	1	2.86	....	....	....	....	....	....	....
1996-97	SaiPa	Finland	41	9	24	7	2340	132	0	3.38	....	....	....	....	....	....	....
1997-98	SaiPa	Finland	48	21	20	5	2870	138	4	2.88	3	0	3	164	11	0	4.02
1998-99	SaiPa	Finland	45	21	19	4	2633	105	4	2.39	7	3	3	366	21	0	3.44
99-2000	SaiPa	Finland	48	14	23	9	2794	150	2	3.24	....	....	....	....	....	....	....
2000-01	Tappara Tampere	Finland	52	30	17	4	3076	107	9	2.09	10	7	3	608	18	1	1.78
2001-02	**Edmonton**	**NHL**	**14**	**6**	**4**	**2**	**784**	**24**	**2**	**1.84**	....	....	....	....	....	....	....
	Hamilton Bulldogs	AHL	4	2	2	0	239	9	0	2.26	....	....	....	....	....	....	....
	Finland	Olympics					DID NOT PLAY										
2002-03	**Edmonton**	**NHL**	**22**	**7**	**8**	**3**	**1180**	**51**	**3**	**2.59**	**1**	**0**	**0**	**14**	**1**	**0**	**4.29**
2003-04	**NY Rangers**	**NHL**	**26**	**8**	**12**	**1**	**1244**	**53**	**2**	**2.56**	....	....	....	....	....	....	....
	Edmonton	**NHL**	**7**	**2**	**2**	**2**	**394**	**12**	**0**	**1.83**	....	....	....	....	....	....	....
2004-05	Lada Togliatti	Russia	54	....	....	....	3157	63	11	1.20	10	....	....	627	15	1	1.44
2005-06	**Edmonton**	**NHL**	**37**	**15**	**12**	**6**	**2016**	**105**	**0**	**3.13**	**6**	**3**	**3**	**360**	**13**	**1**	**2.17**
2006-07	**Edmonton**	**NHL**	**22**	**5**	**9**	**1**	**992**	**52**	**0**	**3.15**	....	....	....	....	....	....	....
2007-08	Jokerit Helsinki	Finland	50	26	11	12	2939	114	4	2.33	1	0	0	20	1	0	3.00
	NHL Totals		**128**	**43**	**47**	**15**	**6610**	**297**	**7**	**2.70**	**7**	**3**	**3**	**374**	**14**	**1**	**2.25**

Traded to **NY Rangers** by **Edmonton** with Edmonton's 4th round choice (later traded to Toronto – Toronto selected Roman Kukumberg) for Brian Leetch, June 30, 2003. Traded to **Edmonton** by **NY Rangers** with Petr Nedved for Steve Valiquette, Dwight Helminen and Edmonton's 2nd round compensatory choice (Dane Byers) in 2004 Entry Draft, March 3, 2004. Signed as a free agent by **Togliatti** (Russia), September 25, 2004. Signed as a free agent by **Jokerit** (Finland), July 30, 2007.

MARKSTROM, Jacob (MAHRK-struhm, JAY-kawb) FLA.

Goaltender. Catches left. 6'3", 178 lbs. Born, Gavle, Sweden, January 31, 1990.
(Florida's 1st choice, 31st overall, in 2008 Entry Draft).

			Regular Season								Playoffs						
Season	Club	League	GP	W	L	O/T	Mins	GA	SO	Avg	GP	W	L	Mins	GA	SO	Avg
2006-07	Brynas U18	Swe-U18	13	....	....	....	789	27	0	2.05	3	....	....	193	6	1	1.86
	Brynas IF Gavle Jr.	Swe-Jr.	1	....	....	....	65	3	0	2.77	1	....	....	25	4	0	9.76
2007-08	Brynas U18	Swe-U18	1	....	....	....	60	3	0	3.00	....	....	....	....	....	....	....
	Brynas IF Gavle Jr.	Swe-Jr.	22	....	....	....	1320	44	2	2.00	....	....	....	....	....	....	....
	Brynas IF Gavle	Sweden	7	....	....	....	423	22	0	3.12	....	....	....	....	....	....	....
	Brynas IF Gavle	Sweden-Q	9	....	....	....	505	15	2	1.78	....	....	....	....	....	....	....

MASON, Chris (MAY-sohn, KRIHS) ST.L.

Goaltender. Catches left. 6', 195 lbs. Born, Red Deer, Alta., April 20, 1976.
(New Jersey's 7th choice, 122nd overall, in 1995 Entry Draft).

			Regular Season								Playoffs						
Season	Club	League	GP	W	L	O/T	Mins	GA	SO	Avg	GP	W	L	Mins	GA	SO	Avg
1992-93	Red Deer	AMHL	20	....	....	....	1280	76	0	3.35	....	....	....	....	....	....	....
1993-94	Victoria Cougars	WHL	5	1	4	0	237	27	0	6.84	....	....	....	....	....	....	....
1994-95	Prince George	WHL	44	8	30	1	2288	192	1	5.03	....	....	....	....	....	....	....
1995-96	Prince George	WHL	59	16	37	1	3289	236	1	4.31	....	....	....	....	....	....	....
1996-97	Prince George	WHL	50	19	24	4	2851	172	2	3.62	15	9	6	938	44	*1	2.81
1997-98	Cincinnati	AHL	47	13	19	7	2368	136	0	3.45	....	....	....	....	....	....	....
1998-99	**Nashville**	**NHL**	**3**	**0**	**0**	**0**	**69**	**6**	**0**	**5.22**	....	....	....	....	....	....	....
	Milwaukee	IHL	34	15	12	6	1901	92	1	2.90	....	....	....	....	....	....	....
99-2000	Milwaukee	IHL	53	20	21	8	2952	137	2	2.78	3	1	2	252	11	0	2.62
2000-01	**Nashville**	**NHL**	**1**	**0**	**1**	**0**	**59**	**2**	**0**	**2.03**	....	....	....	....	....	....	....
	Milwaukee	IHL	37	17	14	5	2226	87	5	2.35	4	1	3	239	12	0	3.02
2001-02	Milwaukee	AHL	48	17	21	7	2755	116	2	2.53	....	....	....	....	....	....	....
2002-03	San Antonio	AHL	50	25	18	6	2914	122	1	2.51	3	0	3	195	9	0	2.77
2003-04	**Nashville**	**NHL**	**17**	**4**	**4**	**1**	**744**	**27**	**1**	**2.18**	....	....	....	....	....	....	....
	Milwaukee	AHL	1	1	0	0	60	2	0	2.00	....	....	....	....	....	....	....
2004-05	Valerengen IF Oslo	Norway	20	....	....	....	1204	36	1	1.79	11	....	....	657	22	1	2.01
2005-06	**Nashville**	**NHL**	**23**	**12**	**5**	**1**	**1227**	**52**	**2**	**2.54**	**5**	**1**	**4**	**296**	**17**	**0**	**3.45**
2006-07	**Nashville**	**NHL**	**40**	**24**	**11**	**4**	**2342**	**93**	**5**	**2.38**	....	....	....	....	....	....	....
2007-08	**Nashville**	**NHL**	**51**	**18**	**22**	**6**	**2692**	**130**	**4**	**2.90**	....	....	....	....	....	....	....
	NHL Totals		**135**	**58**	**43**	**12**	**7133**	**310**	**12**	**2.61**	**5**	**1**	**4**	**296**	**17**	**0**	**3.45**

Signed as a free agent by **Anaheim**, June 27, 1997. Traded to **Nashville** by **Anaheim** with Marc Moro for Dominic Roussel, October 5, 1998. Signed as a free agent by **Florida**, August 20, 2002. Claimed by **Nashville** from **Florida** in Waiver Draft, October 3, 2003. Signed as a free agent by **Oslo** (Norway), November 30, 2004. Traded to **St. Louis** by **Nashville** for NY Rangers' 4th round choice (previously acquired, later traded back to NY Rangers - NY Rangers selected Dale Weise) in 2008 Entry Draft, June 20, 2008.

MASON, Steve (MAY-sohn, STEEV) CBJ

Goaltender. Catches right. 6'4", 202 lbs. Born, Oakville, Ont., May 29, 1988.
(Columbus' 2nd choice, 69th overall, in 2006 Entry Draft).

			Regular Season								Playoffs						
Season	Club	League	GP	W	L	O/T	Mins	GA	SO	Avg	GP	W	L	Mins	GA	SO	Avg
2004-05	Grimsby	OJHL-C	45	....	....	....	2800	....	6	1.75	....	....	....	....	....	....	....
2005-06	Petrolia Jets	OJHL-B	9	6	3	0	521	....	1	2.53	....	....	....	....	....	....	....
	London Knights	OHL	12	5	3	0	497	22	0	2.66	4	0	1	150	7	0	2.80
2006-07	London Knights	OHL	*62	*45	13	4	*3733	199	2	3.20	16	9	7	931	54	0	3.48
2007-08	London Knights	OHL	26	19	4	3	1569	73	2	2.79	....	....	....	....	....	....	....
	Kitchener Rangers	OHL	16	13	3	0	961	33	1	2.06	5	5	0	313	10	1	1.92

OHL First All-Star Team (2007) • OHL Second All-Star Team (2008)

McCOLLUM, Thomas (muk-KAWL-uhm, TAW-muhs) DET.

Goaltender. Catches left. 6'2", 205 lbs. Born, Amherst, NY, December 7, 1989.
(Detroit's 1st choice, 30th overall, in 2008 Entry Draft).

			Regular Season								Playoffs						
Season	Club	League	GP	W	L	O/T	Mins	GA	SO	Avg	GP	W	L	Mins	GA	SO	Avg
2005-06	Wheatfield Blades	EmJHL	24	2	19	3	1448	109	1	4.52	....	....	....	....	....	....	....
2006-07	Guelph Storm	OHL	55	26	18	10	3158	126	*5	2.39	4	0	4	233	17	0	4.38
2007-08	Guelph Storm	OHL	51	25	17	6	2978	124	*4	2.50	10	5	5	596	19	1	1.91

McELHINNEY, Curtis (MAK-IHL-ehn-ee, KUHR-this) CGY.

Goaltender. Catches left. 6'1", 193 lbs. Born, London, Ont., May 23, 1983.
(Calgary's 9th choice, 176th overall, in 2002 Entry Draft).

			Regular Season								Playoffs						
Season	Club	League	GP	W	L	O/T	Mins	GA	SO	Avg	GP	W	L	Mins	GA	SO	Avg
2000-01	Notre Dame	SJHL					STATISTICS NOT AVAILABLE										
2001-02	Colorado College	WCHA	9	6	0	1	441	15	1	2.04	....	....	....	....	....	....	....
2002-03	Colorado College	WCHA	*37	*25	6	5	*2147	85	*4	2.37	....	....	....	....	....	....	....
2003-04	Colorado College	WCHA	19	10	6	1	1015	41	2	2.42	....	....	....	....	....	....	....
2004-05	Colorado College	WCHA	26	*21	4	1	1550	58	2	2.24	....	....	....	....	....	....	....

2005-06	Omaha	AHL	33	9	14	2	1621	68	3	2.52	....	....	....	....	....	....	....
2006-07	Omaha	AHL	57	35	17	1	3181	113	*7	2.13	5	2	3	311	11	0	2.12
2007-08	**Calgary**	**NHL**	**5**	**0**	**2**	**0**	**150**	**5**	**0**	**2.00**	....	....	....	....	....	....	....
	Quad City Flames	AHL	41	20	18	2	2320	88	3	2.28	....	....	....	....	....	....	....
	NHL Totals		**5**	**0**	**2**	**0**	**150**	**5**	**0**	**2.00**	....	....	....	....	....	....	....

WCHA First All-Star Team (2003, 2005) • NCAA West Second All-American Team (2003) • NCAA West First All-American Team (2005) • AHL Second All-Star Team (2007)

McGANN, Pat (muh-GAN, PAT) DAL.

Goaltender. Catches right. 5'11", 160 lbs. Born, Evergreen Park, IL, January 27, 1987.
(Dallas' 7th choice, 223rd overall, in 2005 Entry Draft).

			Regular Season								Playoffs						
Season	Club	League	GP	W	L	O/T	Mins	GA	SO	Avg	GP	W	L	Mins	GA	SO	Avg
2003-04	Chicago Chill	MAHL	31	14	16	1	....	....	....	3.40	....	....	....	....	....	....	....
2004-05	Team Illinois	MWEHL	50	31	18	1	....	91	5	2.21	....	....	....	....	....	....	....
2005-06	Cedar Rapids	USHL	17	5	8	3	998	49	1	2.95	....	....	....	....	....	....	....
2006-07	Cedar Rapids	USHL	6	3	3	0	357	22	0	3.70	....	....	....	....	....	....	....
	Chicago Steel	USHL	17	2	14	1	935	67	0	4.30	....	....	....	....	....	....	....
2007-08	Quinnipiac	ECAC	8	2	1	0	242	19	0	4.72	....	....	....	....	....	....	....

McKENNA, Mike (mih-KEHN-ah, MIGHK)

Goaltender. Catches right. 6'3", 195 lbs. Born, St. Louis, MO, April 11, 1983.
(Nashville's 4th choice, 172nd overall, in 2002 Entry Draft).

			Regular Season								Playoffs						
Season	Club	League	GP	W	L	O/T	Mins	GA	SO	Avg	GP	W	L	Mins	GA	SO	Avg
2001-02	St. Lawrence	ECAC	20	7	10	1	1121	59	0	3.16	....	....	....	....	....	....	....
2002-03	St. Lawrence	ECAC	15	1	7	2	618	38	0	3.69	....	....	....	....	....	....	....
2003-04	St. Lawrence	ECAC	27	9	10	3	1475	60	3	2.44	....	....	....	....	....	....	....
2004-05	St. Lawrence	ECAC	35	15	17	2	2022	92	3	2.73	....	....	....	....	....	....	....
2005-06	Norfolk Admirals	AHL	7	4	2	1	388	25	0	3.86	....	....	....	....	....	....	....
	Las Vegas	ECHL	25	19	2	1	1383	49	1	2.13	4	1	1	173	9	0	3.12
2006-07	Las Vegas	ECHL	38	27	4	7	2258	83	5	*2.21	6	3	3	358	15	0	2.51
	Milwaukee	AHL	1	0	0	0	11	3	0	15.72	....	....	....	....	....	....	....
	Omaha	AHL	2	0	1	0	96	6	0	3.74	....	....	....	....	....	....	....
2007-08	Portland Pirates	AHL	41	24	13	1	2269	103	3	2.72	6	2	4	320	18	0	3.38

ECHL Second All-Star Team (2007)

MENSATOR, Lukas (MEHN-suh-tohr, LOO-kahsh) VAN.

Goaltender. Catches left. 5'8", 180 lbs. Born, Sokolov, Czech., August 18, 1984.
(Vancouver's 4th choice, 83rd overall, in 2002 Entry Draft).

			Regular Season								Playoffs						
Season	Club	League	GP	W	L	O/T	Mins	GA	SO	Avg	GP	W	L	Mins	GA	SO	Avg
99-2000	Karlovy Vary U17	CzR-U17	42	....	....	....	2406	160	0	3.99	....	....	....	....	....	....	....
	Karlovy Vary Jr.	CzRep-Jr.	1	1	0	0	60	3	0	3.00	....	....	....	....	....	....	....
2000-01	Karlovy Vary U17	CzR-U17	6	....	....	....	360	15	0	2.50	....	....	....	....	....	....	....
	Karlovy Vary Jr.	CzRep-Jr.	19	....	....	....	1085	60	0	3.32	....	....	....	....	....	....	....
2001-02	Karlovy Vary Jr.	CzRep-Jr.	31	....	....	....	1809	93	0	3.08	9	....	....	459	17	0	2.22
	Banik CHZ Sokolov	CzRep-3	3	....	....	....	180	12	0	4.00	....	....	....	....	....	....	....
2002-03	Ottawa 67's	OHL	42	26	8	5	2395	122	0	3.06	*23	13	8	*1381	63	*2	2.74
2003-04	Ottawa 67's	OHL	50	18	22	7	2924	162	0	3.32	7	3	4	447	23	0	3.09
2004-05	Karlovy Vary	CzRep	13	....	....	....	686	34	1	2.97	....	....	....	....	....	....	....
	IHC Pisek	CzRep-2	14	....	....	....	808	41	1	3.04	....	....	....	....	....	....	....
	BK Mlada Boleslav	CzRep-2	17	....	....	....	991	34	4	2.06	7	....	....	393	17	1	2.60
2005-06	Karlovy Vary	CzRep	36	....	....	....	1981	69	5	2.09	....	....	....	....	....	....	....
	SK Kadan	CzRep-2	1	....	....	....	49	5	0	6.12	....	....	....	....	....	....	....
2006-07	Karlovy Vary	CzRep	22	....	....	....	1166	47	1	2.42	....	....	....	....	....	....	....
2007-08	Karlovy Vary	CzRep	38	....	....	....	2254	94	3	2.50	*19	....	....	*1149	47	2	2.45

Signed as a free agent by **Karlovy Vary** (CzRep), May 17, 2004.

MILLER, Ryan (MIHL-luhr, RIGH-uhn) BUF.

Goaltender. Catches left. 6'2", 175 lbs. Born, East Lansing, MI, July 17, 1980.
(Buffalo's 7th choice, 138th overall, in 1999 Entry Draft).

			Regular Season								Playoffs						
Season	Club	League	GP	W	L	O/T	Mins	GA	SO	Avg	GP	W	L	Mins	GA	SO	Avg
1997-98	Soo Indians	NAHL	37	21	14	0	2113	82	3	2.33	2	0	2	158	7	0	2.66
1998-99	Soo Indians	NAHL	47	31	14	1	2711	104	8	2.30	4	2	2	218	10	1	2.76
99-2000	Michigan State	CCHA	26	16	5	3	1525	39	*8	*1.53	....	....	....	....	....	....	....
2000-01	Michigan State	CCHA	40	*31	5	4	2447	54	*10	*1.32	....	....	....	....	....	....	....
2001-02	Michigan State	CCHA	40	26	9	5	2411	71	*8	*1.77	....	....	....	....	....	....	....
2002-03	**Buffalo**	**NHL**	**15**	**6**	**8**	**1**	**912**	**40**	**1**	**2.63**	....	....	....	....	....	....	....
	Rochester	AHL	47	23	18	5	2817	110	2	2.34	3	1	2	190	13	0	4.11
2003-04	**Buffalo**	**NHL**	**3**	**0**	**3**	**0**	**178**	**15**	**0**	**5.06**	....	....	....	....	....	....	....
	Rochester	AHL	60	27	25	7	3579	132	5	2.21	14	7	7	857	26	2	1.82
2004-05	Rochester	AHL	63	*41	17	4	3741	153	8	2.45	9	5	4	547	24	0	2.63
2005-06	**Buffalo**	**NHL**	**48**	**30**	**14**	**3**	**2862**	**124**	**1**	**2.60**	**18**	**11**	**7**	**1123**	**48**	**1**	**2.56**
	Rochester	AHL	2	1	1	0	120	5	0	2.50	....	....	....	....	....	....	....
2006-07	**Buffalo**	**NHL**	**63**	**40**	**16**	**6**	**3692**	**168**	**2**	**2.73**	**16**	**9**	**7**	**1029**	**38**	**0**	**2.22**
2007-08	**Buffalo**	**NHL**	**76**	**36**	**27**	**10**	**4474**	**197**	**3**	**2.64**	....	....	....	....	....	....	....
	NHL Totals		**205**	**112**	**68**	**20**	**12118**	**544**	**7**	**2.69**	**34**	**20**	**14**	**2152**	**86**	**1**	**2.40**

CCHA Second All-Star Team (2000) • CCHA First All-Star Team (2001, 2002) • NCAA West First All-American Team (2001, 2002) • CCHA Player of the Year (2001, 2002) • Hobey Baker Memorial Award (Top U.S. Collegiate Player) (2001) • AHL First All-Star Team (2005) • Aldege "Baz" Bastien Memorial Award (Outstanding Goaltender – AHL) (2005)

Played in NHL All-Star Game (2007)

MISSIAEN, Jason (MIHS-ee-ehn, JAY-suhn) MTL.

Goaltender. Catches left. 6'8", 193 lbs. Born, Chatham, Ont., April 25, 1990.
(Montreal's 3rd choice, 116th overall, in 2008 Entry Draft).

			Regular Season								Playoffs						
Season	Club	League	GP	W	L	O/T	Mins	GA	SO	Avg	GP	W	L	Mins	GA	SO	Avg
2004-05	Dresden Kings	OHA-C	16	11	4	1	919	47	1	3.07	....	....	....	....	....	....	....
2005-06	Dresden Kings	OHA-C	26	13	8	2	1560	76	1	2.93	....	....	....	....	....	....	....
2006-07	Peterborough	OHL	12	1	7	0	559	48	0	5.15	....	....	....	....	....	....	....
2007-08	Peterborough	OHL	22	8	8	1	1134	62	1	3.28	....	....	....	....	....	....	....

MODIG, Mattias (moh-DIHG, MA-tee-uhs) ANA.

Goaltender. Catches left. 6', 171 lbs. Born, Lulea, Sweden, April 1, 1987.
(Anaheim's 7th choice, 121st overall, in 2007 Entry Draft).

			Regular Season								Playoffs						
Season	Club	League	GP	W	L	O/T	Mins	GA	SO	Avg	GP	W	L	Mins	GA	SO	Avg
2002-03	Lulea HF U18	Swe-U18	2	....	....	....	120	4	0	2.00	....	....	....	....	....	....	....
2003-04	Lulea HF U18	Swe-U18	14	....	....	....	854	30	2	2.11	7	....	....	449	14	0	1.87
	Lulea HF Jr.	Swe-Jr.	2	....	....	....	66	2	0	1.81	....	....	....	....	....	....	....
2004-05	Lulea HF U18	Swe-U18	2	....	....	....	120	4	0	2.00	....	....	....	....	....	....	....
	Lulea HF Jr.	Swe-Jr.	14	....	....	....	819	42	2	3.08	5	....	....	306	16	0	3.14
2005-06	Lulea HF Jr.	Swe-Jr.	19	....	....	....	1154	42	1	2.18	3	....	....	175	10	0	3.43
	Lulea HF	Sweden	2	....	....	....	66	3	0	2.74	....	....	....	....	....	....	....
2006-07	Lulea HF Jr.	Swe-Jr.	2	....	....	....	120	7	0	3.50	....	....	....	....	....	....	....
	Lulea HF	Sweden	32	....	....	....	1636	69	1	2.53	1	....	....	20	1	0	3.00
2007-08	Lulea HF Jr.	Swe-Jr.	5	....	....	....	297	14	0	2.83	....	....	....	....	....	....	....
	Lulea HF	Sweden	13	....	....	....	696	41	1	3.53	....	....	....	....	....	....	....

MOLE, Mike (MOHL, MIGHK)

Goaltender. Catches right. 6', 183 lbs. Born, Orleans, Ont., October 12, 1982.

			Regular Season								Playoffs						
Season	Club	League	GP	W	L	O/T	Mins	GA	SO	Avg	GP	W	L	Mins	GA	SO	Avg
99-2000	Mississauga	OHL	37	5	28	0	2007	173	0	5.17	....	....	....	....	....	....	....
2000-01	Mississauga	OHL	45	2	35	4	2435	219	0	5.40	....	....	....	....	....	....	....
2001-02	Mississauga	OHL	23	5	15	2	1342	96	0	4.29	....	....	....	....	....	....	....
	Belleville Bulls	OHL	26	20	4	2	1575	66	2	2.51	11	6	5	685	25	1	2.19
2002-03	Belleville Bulls	OHL	54	25	23	5	3138	153	1	2.93	7	3	4	400	21	0	3.15
	Lowell	AHL	1	0	0	0	20	4	0	12.00	....	....	....	....	....	....	....
2003-04	St. FX University	AUAA	22	16	3	2	1301	54	3	2.49	....	....	....	....	....	....	....
2004-05	St. FX University	AUAA	25	10	11	4	1496	58	3	2.33	....	....	....	....	....	....	....
2005-06	Phoenix	ECHL	48	15	27	3	2617	142	2	3.26	....	....	....	....	....	....	....
	San Diego Gulls	ECHL	9	4	3	2	549	24	0	2.62	....	....	....	....	....	....	....
2006-07	Bridgeport	AHL	15	3	8	0	762	41	0	3.23	....	....	....	....	....	....	....
	Pensacola Ice Pilots	ECHL	39	13	18	3	2189	144	0	3.95	....	....	....	....	....	....	....
2007-08	Utah Grizzlies	ECHL	37	18	13	5	2208	121	0	3.29	8	3	1	410	18	1	2.64

Signed as a free agent by **NY Islanders**, October 5, 2006.

MONTOYA, Al (mawn-TOI-uh, AL) PHX.

Goaltender. Catches left. 6'2", 193 lbs. Born, Chicago, IL, February 13, 1985.
(NY Rangers' 1st choice, 6th overall, in 2004 Entry Draft).

			Regular Season								Playoffs						
Season	Club	League	GP	W	L	O/T	Mins	GA	SO	Avg	GP	W	L	Mins	GA	SO	Avg
99-2000	Loyola Academy	High-MN	28	12	13	3	1685	56	1	2.01	....	....	....	....	....	....	....
2000-01	Texas Tornado	NAHL	15	10	3	0	780	38	0	2.92	1	1	0	60	2	0	2.00
	United States	Nat-Tm	2	2	0	0	120	4	0	2.00	....	....	....	....	....	....	....
2001-02	USNTDP	U-17	10	5	5	0	570	24	0	2.53	....	....	....	....	....	....	....
	USNTDP	NAHL	24	6	11	4	1344	79	0	3.53	....	....	....	....	....	....	....
2002-03	U. of Michigan	CCHA	*43	*30	10	3	*2547	99	4	2.33	....	....	....	....	....	....	....
2003-04	U. of Michigan	CCHA	*40	*26	12	2	*2340	87	6	2.23	....	....	....	....	....	....	....
2004-05	U. of Michigan	CCHA	*40	*30	7	3	*2359	99	3	2.52	....	....	....	....	....	....	....
2005-06	Hartford Wolf Pack	AHL	40	23	9	1	2094	91	2	2.61	5	2	1	257	8	1	1.87
	Charlotte Checkers	ECHL	2	1	1	0	123	8	0	3.92	....	....	....	....	....	....	....
2006-07	Hartford Wolf Pack	AHL	48	27	17	0	2556	98	6	2.30	7	3	4	391	20	1	3.07
2007-08	Hartford Wolf Pack	AHL	31	16	8	3	1704	72	0	2.54	....	....	....	....	....	....	....
	San Antonio	AHL	14	8	6	0	789	34	1	2.59	1	0	1	59	4	0	4.04

CCHA All-Rookie Team (2003) • NCAA West Second All-American Team (2004)

Traded to **Phoenix** by **NY Rangers** with Marcel Hossa for Fredrik Sjostrom, Josh Gratton, David LeNeveu and future considerations, February 26, 2008.

MORRISON, Mike (MOHR-ih-suhn, MIGHK)

Goaltender. Catches right. 6'3", 194 lbs. Born, Medford, MA, July 11, 1979.
(Edmonton's 8th choice, 186th overall, in 1998 Entry Draft).

			Regular Season								Playoffs						
Season	Club	League	GP	W	L	O/T	Mins	GA	SO	Avg	GP	W	L	Mins	GA	SO	Avg
1997-98	Exeter	High-NH	27	15	11	2	1632	64	1	2.35	....	....	....	....	....	....	....
1998-99	University of Maine	H-East	11	3	0	1	347	10	1	1.73	....	....	....	....	....	....	....
99-2000	University of Maine	H-East	12	7	2	1	608	27	1	2.67	....	....	....	....	....	....	....
2000-01	University of Maine	H-East	10	2	3	3	490	16	1	1.96	....	....	....	....	....	....	....
2001-02	University of Maine	H-East	30	20	3	4	1645	60	2	2.19	....	....	....	....	....	....	....
2002-03	Columbus	ECHL	38	9	18	6	1948	113	1	3.48	....	....	....	....	....	....	....
2003-04	Toronto	AHL	27	12	8	2	1309	55	3	2.52	....	....	....	....	....	....	....
2004-05	Edmonton	AHL	14	2	5	5	728	21	2	1.73	....	....	....	....	....	....	....
	Greenville Grrrowl	ECHL	26	13	10	2	1576	72	1	2.74	3	1	1	150	9	0	3.61
2005-06	**Edmonton**	**NHL**	**21**	**10**	**4**	**2**	**892**	**42**	**0**	**2.83**	....	....	....	....	....	....	....
	Greenville Grrrowl	ECHL	9	7	2	0	548	20	0	2.19	....	....	....	....	....	....	....
	Ottawa	**NHL**	**4**	**1**	**0**	**1**	**207**	**12**	**0**	**3.48**	....	....	....	....	....	....	....
2006-07	**Phoenix**	**NHL**	**4**	**0**	**3**	**0**	**127**	**13**	**0**	**6.14**	....	....	....	....	....	....	....
	San Antonio	AHL	2	0	1	0	60	11	0	11.01	....	....	....	....	....	....	....
	Phoenix	ECHL	27	9	12	3	1423	80	1	3.37	....	....	....	....	....	....	....
2007-08	Bridgeport	AHL	43	23	17	1	2445	114	5	2.80	....	....	....	....	....	....	....
	NHL Totals		**29**	**11**	**7**	**3**	**1226**	**67**	**0**	**3.28**	....	....	....	....	....	....	....

Hockey East First All-Star Team (2002)

Claimed on waivers by **Ottawa** from **Edmonton**, March 9, 2006. Signed as a free agent by **Phoenix**, July 2, 2006.

MUNCE, Ryan (MUNTS, RIGH-uhn)

Goaltender. Catches left. 6'2", 180 lbs. Born, Mississauga, Ont., April 16, 1985.
(Los Angeles' 5th choice, 82nd overall, in 2003 Entry Draft).

			Regular Season								Playoffs						
Season	Club	League	GP	W	L	O/T	Mins	GA	SO	Avg	GP	W	L	Mins	GA	SO	Avg
2002-03	Sarnia Sting	OHL	27	15	7	0	1410	62	3	2.64	4	1	1	149	8	1	3.22
2003-04	Sarnia Sting	OHL	54	28	21	4	3160	158	2	3.00	5	1	4	298	17	0	3.42
2004-05	Sarnia Sting	OHL	55	12	32	6	3090	163	0	3.17	....	....	....	....	....	....	....
2005-06	Bakersfield	ECHL	55	30	18	5	*3234	150	2	2.78	11	5	5	642	36	0	3.36
2006-07	Reading Royals	ECHL	17	5	6	4	837	46	0	3.30	....	....	....	....	....	....	....
	Johnstown Chiefs	ECHL	14	6	3	1	652	28	0	2.58	1	0	1	59	4	0	4.08
2007-08	Norfolk Admirals	AHL	10	3	6	0	502	25	0	2.99	....	....	....	....	....	....	....
	Mississippi	ECHL	35	19	16	0	2067	97	3	2.82	4	1	3	242	16	0	3.97

Traded to **Tampa Bay** by **Los Angeles** for Tampa Bay's 4th round choice (later traded to San Jose - San Jose selected Samuel Groulx) in 2008 Entry Draft, January 20, 2007.

MUNRO, Adam (muhn-ROH, A-duhm)

Goaltender. Catches left. 6'2", 219 lbs. Born, St. George, Ont., November 12, 1982.
(Chicago's 1st choice, 29th overall, in 2001 Entry Draft).

			Regular Season								Playoffs						
Season	Club	League	GP	W	L	O/T	Mins	GA	SO	Avg	GP	W	L	Mins	GA	SO	Avg
1997-98	Brantford Classics	Minor-ON	15	13	2	0	660	20	*4	*1.36	....	....	....	....	....	....	....
1998-99	Brant County	OJHL-B	10	....	....	....	348	30	0	5.17	....	....	....	....	....	....	....
	Bowmanville	OPJHL	14	....	....	....	816	50	0	3.68	....	....	....	....	....	....	....
	Erie Otters	OHL	1	0	0	0	1	0	0	0.00	....	....	....	....	....	....	....
99-2000	Bowmanville	OPJHL	2	2	0	0	125	5	0	2.40	....	....	....	....	....	....	....
	Erie Otters	OHL	22	8	7	1	948	48	1	3.04	1	0	0	5	1	0	12.00
2000-01	Erie Otters	OHL	41	26	6	6	2283	88	*4	2.31	10	6	2	509	27	1	3.18
2001-02	Erie Otters	OHL	43	24	13	1	2277	128	3	3.37	6	4	2	361	17	0	2.83
2002-03	Erie Otters	OHL	8	2	6	0	426	24	1	3.38	....	....	....	....	....	....	....
	Sault Ste. Marie	OHL	42	20	20	2	2494	160	1	3.85	4	0	4	240	12	0	3.00
2003-04	**Chicago**	**NHL**	**7**	**1**	**5**	**1**	**426**	**26**	**0**	**3.66**	....	....	....	....	....	....	....
	Norfolk Admirals	AHL	12	5	4	1	695	26	0	2.24	....	....	....	....	....	....	....
	Gwinnett	ECHL	6	4	1	1	370	17	0	2.76	1	0	1	60	2	0	2.01
2004-05	Norfolk Admirals	AHL	30	14	10	2	1595	66	4	2.48	....	....	....	....	....	....	....
	Atlantic City	ECHL	5	2	2	1	272	9	0	1.99	....	....	....	....	....	....	....
2005-06	**Chicago**	**NHL**	**10**	**3**	**5**	**2**	**501**	**25**	**1**	**2.99**	....	....	....	....	....	....	....
	Norfolk Admirals	AHL	28	17	8	1	1612	73	1	2.72	4	0	4	239	15	0	3.77
2006-07	Fribourg	Swiss	41	12	28	0	2488	149	0	3.59	....	....	....	....	....	....	....

2007-08	Syracuse Crunch	AHL	25	13	9	1	1414	57	2	2.42	1	0	0	20	4	0	12.04
	NHL Totals		**17**	**4**	**10**	**3**	**927**	**51**	**1**	**3.30**	....	....	....	....	....	....	....

Signed as a free agent by **Fribourg** (Swiss), July 7, 2006. Signed as a free agent by **Syracuse** (AHL), July 23, 2007.

MUNROE, Scott (muhn-ROH, SKAWT) PHI.

Goaltender. Catches left. 6'2", 210 lbs. Born, Moose Jaw, Sask., January 20, 1982.

			Regular Season								Playoffs						
Season	Club	League	GP	W	L	O/T	Mins	GA	SO	Avg	GP	W	L	Mins	GA	SO	Avg
2002-03	AL-Huntsville	CHA	20	11	6	1	1049	49	1	2.80	....	....	....	....	....	....	....
2003-04	AL-Huntsville	CHA	17	5	9	1	891	47	0	3.16	....	....	....	....	....	....	....
2004-05	AL-Huntsville	CHA	31	16	10	4	1805	69	3	2.29	....	....	....	....	....	....	....
2005-06	AL-Huntsville	CHA	31	17	11	2	1813	91	0	3.01	....	....	....	....	....	....	....
	Philadelphia	AHL	2	0	2	0	119	7	0	3.54	....	....	....	....	....	....	....
2006-07	Philadelphia	AHL	40	15	19	2	2298	117	2	3.05	....	....	....	....	....	....	....
2007-08	Philadelphia	AHL	36	18	8	2	1779	68	4	2.29	12	5	7	784	29	*2	2.22

CHA All-Rookie Team (2003) • CHA Rookie of the Year (2003)

Signed as a free agent by **Philadelphia** (AHL), March 18, 2006.

MURPHY, Mike (MUHR-phee, MIGHK) CAR.

Goaltender. Catches left. 5'11", 161 lbs. Born, Kingston, Ont., January 15, 1989.
(Carolina's 4th choice, 165th overall, in 2008 Entry Draft).

			Regular Season								Playoffs						
Season	Club	League	GP	W	L	O/T	Mins	GA	SO	Avg	GP	W	L	Mins	GA	SO	Avg
2005-06	Kingston	OPJHL	33	16	13	2	....	102	3	3.30	4	0	3	174	19	0	6.55
	Belleville Bulls	OHL	3	1	1	0	93	9	0	5.81	....	....	....	....	....	....	....
2006-07	Belleville Bulls	OHL	18	8	6	2	995	61	0	3.68	....	....	....	....	....	....	....
2007-08	Belleville Bulls	OHL	49	36	7	4	2942	110	3	*2.24	*19	*14	4	*1085	42	1	2.32

OHL First All-Star Team (2008) • Canadian Major Junior Second All-Star Team (2008)

NABOKOV, Evgeni (na-BAW-kahv, ehv-GEH-nee) S.J.

Goaltender. Catches left. 6', 200 lbs. Born, Ust-Kamenogorsk, USSR, July 25, 1975.
(San Jose's 9th choice, 219th overall, in 1994 Entry Draft).

			Regular Season								Playoffs						
Season	Club	League	GP	W	L	O/T	Mins	GA	SO	Avg	GP	W	L	Mins	GA	SO	Avg
1991-92	Ust-Kamenogorsk	CIS	1	....	....	....	20	1	0	3.00	....	....	....	....	....	....	....
1992-93	Ust-Kam'gorsk 2	CIS-2	19	....	....	....	....	....	....	....	....	....	....	....	....	....	....
	Ust-Kamenogorsk	CIS	4	....	....	....	109	5	0	2.75	....	....	....	....	....	....	....
1993-94	Ust-Kamenogorsk	CIS	11	....	....	....	539	29	....	3.23	....	....	....	....	....	....	....
1994-95	Dynamo Moscow	CIS	24	....	....	....	1326	40	3	1.81	13	....	....	806	30	2	2.23
1995-96	Dynamo Moscow	CIS	39	....	....	....	2008	67	5	2.00	....	....	....	....	....	....	....
1996-97	Dynamo Moscow	Russia	27	....	....	....	1588	56	2	2.11	4	....	....	255	12	0	2.82
	Dynamo Moscow 2	Russia-3	1	....	....	....	....	2	....	....	....	....	....	....	....	....	....
1997-98	Kentucky	AHL	33	10	21	2	1866	122	0	3.92	1	0	0	23	1	0	2.59
1998-99	Kentucky	AHL	43	26	14	1	2429	106	5	2.62	11	6	5	599	30	*2	3.00
99-2000	**San Jose**	**NHL**	**11**	**2**	**2**	**1**	**414**	**15**	**1**	**2.17**	**1**	**0**	**0**	**20**	**0**	**0**	**0.00**
	Kentucky	AHL	2	1	1	0	120	3	1	1.50	....	....	....	....	....	....	....
	Cleveland	IHL	20	12	4	3	1164	52	0	2.68	....	....	....	....	....	....	....
2000-01	**San Jose**	**NHL**	**66**	**32**	**21**	**7**	**3700**	**135**	**6**	**2.19**	**4**	**1**	**3**	**218**	**10**	**1**	**2.75**
2001-02	**San Jose**	**NHL**	**67**	**37**	**24**	**5**	**3901**	**149**	**7**	**2.29**	**12**	**7**	**5**	**712**	**31**	**0**	**2.61**
2002-03	**San Jose**	**NHL**	**55**	**19**	**28**	**8**	**3227**	**146**	**3**	**2.71**	....	....	....	....	....	....	....
2003-04	**San Jose**	**NHL**	**59**	**31**	**19**	**8**	**3456**	**127**	**9**	**2.20**	**17**	**10**	**7**	**1052**	**30**	**3**	**1.71**
2004-05	Magnitogorsk	Russia	14	....	....	....	808	27	3	2.00	5	....	....	307	13	0	2.53
2005-06	**San Jose**	**NHL**	**45**	**16**	**19**	**7**	**2575**	**133**	**1**	**3.10**	**1**	**0**	**0**	**12**	**1**	**0**	**5.00**
	Russia	Olympics	7	....	....	....	359	8	3	1.34	....	....	....	....	....	....	....
2006-07	**San Jose**	**NHL**	**50**	**25**	**16**	**4**	**2778**	**106**	**7**	**2.29**	**11**	**6**	**5**	**701**	**26**	**1**	**2.23**
2007-08	**San Jose**	**NHL**	***77**	***46**	**21**	**8**	**4561**	**163**	**6**	**2.14**	**13**	**6**	**7**	**853**	**31**	**1**	**2.18**
	NHL Totals		**430**	**208**	**150**	**48**	**24612**	**974**	**40**	**2.37**	**59**	**30**	**27**	**3568**	**129**	**6**	**2.17**

NHL All-Rookie Team (2001) • Calder Memorial Trophy (2001) • NHL First All-Star Team (2008)

Played in NHL All-Star Game (2001, 2008)

• Scored a goal vs. Vancouver, March 10, 2002. Signed as a free agent by **Magnitogorsk** (Russia), December 2, 2004.

NEUVIRTH, Michal (NOI-vihrt, MEE-khahl) WSH.

Goaltender. Catches left. 6'1", 190 lbs. Born, Usti nad Labem, Czech., March 23, 1988.
(Washington's 3rd choice, 34th overall, in 2006 Entry Draft).

			Regular Season								Playoffs						
Season	Club	League	GP	W	L	O/T	Mins	GA	SO	Avg	GP	W	L	Mins	GA	SO	Avg
2003-04	Sparta U17	CzR-U17	55	....	....	....	3137	96	5	1.84	3	....	....	180	13	0	4.33
2004-05	Sparta U17	CzR-U17	20	....	....	....	1178	49	3	2.50	8	....	....	482	17	0	2.12
	Sparta Jr.	CzRep-Jr.	10	....	....	....	501	20	1	2.40	....	....	....	....	....	....	....
2005-06	Sparta Jr.	CzRep-Jr.	42	....	....	....	2516	82	5	1.96	3	....	....	179	9	0	3.02
2006-07	Plymouth Whalers	OHL	41	26	8	4	2223	86	4	2.32	18	14	4	1080	44	0	2.44
2007-08	Plymouth Whalers	OHL	10	5	4	1	600	26	0	2.60	....	....	....	....	....	....	....
	Windsor Spitfires	OHL	8	6	1	1	482	17	0	2.12	....	....	....	....	....	....	....
	Oshawa Generals	OHL	15	6	2	6	844	57	0	4.05	9	7	2	507	21	0	2.49

OHL Second All-Star Team (2007)

NIEMI, Antti (nee-YEH-mee, AN-tee) CHI.

Goaltender. Catches left. 6'1", 200 lbs. Born, Vantaa, Finland, August 29, 1983.

			Regular Season								Playoffs						
Season	Club	League	GP	W	L	O/T	Mins	GA	SO	Avg	GP	W	L	Mins	GA	SO	Avg
2000-01	Kiekko-Vantaa Jr.	Fin-Jr.	4	....	....	....	....	....	....	6.86	....	....	....	....	....	....	....
2001-02	Kiekko-Vantaa	Finland-2	24	....	....	....	....	....	....	....	3	....	....	....	....	....	....
2002-03	Kiekko-Vantaa	Finland-2	....	....	....	....	364	16	0	2.63	....	....	....	....	....	....	....
2003-04	Kiekko-Vantaa Jr.	Fin-Jr.	19	....	....	....	1095	58	2	3.18	....	....	....	....	....	....	....
	Kiekko-Vantaa	Finland-2	19	....	....	....	1048	47	1	2.52	3	....	....	187	13	0	4.17
2004-05	Kiekko-Vantaa	Finland-2	38	....	....	....	2261	95	1	2.52	3	....	....	187	13	0	4.17
2005-06	Pelicans Lahti	Finland	40	12	17	8	2263	103	3	2.73	....	....	....	....	....	....	....
2006-07	Pelicans Lahti	Finland	48	18	21	7	2780	119	3	2.57	6	2	4	371	9	1	1.46
2007-08	Pelicans Lahti	Finland	49	26	14	6	2778	109	4	2.35	6	2	3	327	21	0	3.85

Signed as a free agent by **Chicago**, May 5, 2008.

NIITTYMAKI, Antero (nih-tih-MA-kee, AN-tehr-oh) PHI.

Goaltender. Catches left. 6'1", 215 lbs. Born, Turku, Finland, June 18, 1980.
(Philadelphia's 7th choice, 168th overall, in 1998 Entry Draft).

			Regular Season								Playoffs						
Season	Club	League	GP	W	L	O/T	Mins	GA	SO	Avg	GP	W	L	Mins	GA	SO	Avg
1997-98	TPS Turku U18	Fin-U18	12	....	....	....	....	....	....	....	1	1	0	60	1	0	1.00
	TPS Turku Jr.	Fin-Jr.	19	10	8	1	1131	34	....	1.80	4	3	1	220	7	0	1.91
1998-99	TPS Turku Jr.	Fin-Jr.	35	27	8	0	2095	60	3	1.72	6	3	3	362	14	0	2.32
99-2000	TPS Turku Jr.	Fin-Jr.	1	1	0	0	60	1	0	1.00	1	0	1	60	5	0	5.00
	TPS Turku	Finland	32	23	6	3	1899	68	3	2.15	8	6	2	453	13	0	1.72
2000-01	TPS Turku Jr.	Fin-Jr.	....	....	....	....	....	....	....	....	2	1	1	120	4	1	2.00
	TPS Turku	Finland	21	10	5	1	1112	46	2	2.48	....	....	....	....	....	....	....
2001-02	TPS Turku	Finland	27	16	8	1	1498	46	3	1.84	4	2	2	295	11	0	2.24
2002-03	Philadelphia	AHL	40	14	21	2	2283	98	0	2.58	....	....	....	....	....	....	....
2003-04	**Philadelphia**	**NHL**	**3**	**3**	**0**	**0**	**180**	**3**	**0**	**1.00**	....	....	....	....	....	....	....
	Philadelphia	AHL	49	24	13	6	2728	92	7	2.02	12	6	6	796	24	0	1.81
2004-05	Philadelphia	AHL	58	33	21	4	3453	119	6	2.07	*21	*15	5	*1269	37	*3	1.75
2005-06	**Philadelphia**	**NHL**	**46**	**23**	**15**	**6**	**2690**	**133**	**2**	**2.97**	**2**	**0**	**0**	**73**	**5**	**0**	**4.11**
	Finland	Olympics	6	5	1	0	359	8	3	1.34	....	....	....	....	....	....	....
2006-07	**Philadelphia**	**NHL**	**52**	**9**	**29**	**9**	**2943**	**166**	**0**	**3.38**	....	....	....	....	....	....	....
2007-08	**Philadelphia**	**NHL**	**28**	**12**	**9**	**2**	**1424**	**69**	**1**	**2.91**	....	....	....	....	....	....	....
	NHL Totals		**129**	**47**	**53**	**17**	**7237**	**371**	**3**	**3.08**	**2**	**0**	**0**	**73**	**5**	**0**	**4.11**

Jack A. Butterfield Trophy (Playoff MVP – AHL) (2005) • Olympic Tournament All-Star Team (2006) • Best Goaltender - Olympic Tournament (2006) • MVP - Olympic Tournament (2006)

NORRENA, Fredrik (noh-REH-nah, FREHD-rihk) CBJ

Goaltender. Catches left. 6', 189 lbs. Born, Pietarsaari, Finland, November 29, 1973.
(Tampa Bay's 8th choice, 213th overall, in 2002 Entry Draft).

			Regular Season								Playoffs						
Season	Club	League	GP	W	L	O/T	Mins	GA	SO	Avg	GP	W	L	Mins	GA	SO	Avg
1989-90	LIFK Leppalahti	Finland-3	36	....	....	....	....	....	....	....	....	....	....	....	....	....	....
1990-91	LIFK Leppalahti	Finland-3	36	....	....	....	....	....	....	....	....	....	....	....	....	....	....
1991-92	LIFK Leppalahti	Finland-3	35	....	....	....	....	....	....	....	....	....	....	....	....	....	....
1992-93	TPS Turku Jr.	Fin-Jr.	25	15	9	1	1449	74	1	3.06	5	....	....	307	11	1	2.14
	TPS Turku	Finland	2	0	1	0	30	1	0	2.00	....	....	....	....	....	....	....
1993-94	TPS Turku Jr.	Fin-Jr.	2	0	1	0	80	5	0	3.75	1	0	1	58	4	0	4.10
	TPS Turku	Finland	10	3	3	0	387	19	0	2.94	....	....	....	....	....	....	....
	Kiekko-67 Turku	Finland-2	15	7	7	1	884	43	2	2.92	....	....	....	....	....	....	....
1994-95	TPS Turku	Finland	22	14	6	2	1328	60	1	2.71	11	7	4	666	27	1	2.43
	Kiekko-67 Turku	Finland-2	15	....	....	....	828	34	0	2.46	....	....	....	....	....	....	....
1995-96	TPS Turku	Finland	26	14	8	3	1539	68	0	2.65	....	....	....	....	....	....	....
1996-97	Kiekko-67 Turku	Finland-2	12	....	....	....	725	36	0	2.98	....	....	....	....	....	....	....
	AIK Solna	Sweden	5	....	....	....	274	21	1	4.60	....	....	....	....	....	....	....
1997-98	Lukko Rauma	Finland	37	12	19	4	2174	105	0	2.90	....	....	....	....	....	....	....
1998-99	TPS Turku	Finland	20	11	4	1	1010	35	2	2.08	1	0	0	20	2	0	6.00
99-2000	TPS Turku	Finland	21	15	4	0	1175	35	2	1.79	4	3	0	234	10	0	2.56
	TuTo Turku	Finland-2	2	1	1	0	118	7	0	3.54	....	....	....	....	....	....	....
2000-01	TPS Turku	Finland	39	26	10	3	2266	66	6	1.75	10	9	1	603	13	2	1.29
2001-02	TPS Turku	Finland	32	14	11	5	1878	62	2	1.98	4	1	3	256	7	1	1.64
2002-03	V.Frolunda	Sweden	23	....	....	....	1386	56	1	2.42	4	....	....	288	6	1	1.25
2003-04	Linkopings HC	Sweden	40	....	....	....	2414	68	9	1.69	3	....	....	176	6	0	2.05
2004-05	Linkopings HC	Sweden	43	....	....	....	2522	78	5	1.86	6	....	....	383	13	0	2.03
2005-06	Linkopings HC	Sweden	36	....	....	....	2170	78	4	2.16	11	....	....	693	22	2	*1.90
	Finland	Olympics	2	2	0	0	120	0	2	0.00	....	....	....	....	....	....	....
2006-07	**Columbus**	**NHL**	**55**	**24**	**23**	**3**	**2952**	**137**	**3**	**2.78**	....	....	....	....	....	....	....
2007-08	**Columbus**	**NHL**	**37**	**10**	**19**	**6**	**1960**	**89**	**2**	**2.72**	....	....	....	....	....	....	....
	NHL Totals		**92**	**34**	**42**	**9**	**4912**	**226**	**5**	**2.76**	....	....	....	....	....	....	....

Traded to **Columbus** by **Tampa Bay** with Fredrik Modin for Marc Denis, June 30, 2006.

O'KEEFE, Mitchell (oh-KEEF, MIH-chuhl) OTT.

Goaltender. Catches left. 6'2", 218 lbs. Born, Almonte, Ont., March 29, 1984.

			Regular Season								Playoffs						
Season	Club	League	GP	W	L	O/T	Mins	GA	SO	Avg	GP	W	L	Mins	GA	SO	Avg
2005-06	Ferris State	CCHA	33	14	12	7	1970	88	2	2.68	....	....	....	....	....	....	....
2006-07	Ferris State	CCHA	29	7	19	3	1682	85	1	3.03	....	....	....	....	....	....	....
2007-08	Ferris State	CCHA	24	10	8	5	1422	54	3	2.28	....	....	....	....	....	....	....
	Iowa Stars	AHL	2	0	1	0	76	3	0	2.35	....	....	....	....	....	....	....

Signed as a free agent by **Ottawa**, July 11, 2008.

OSGOOD, Chris (AWS-gud, KRIHS) DET.

Goaltender. Catches left. 5'10", 178 lbs. Born, Peace River, Alta., November 26, 1972.
(Detroit's 3rd choice, 54th overall, in 1991 Entry Draft).

			Regular Season								Playoffs						
Season	Club	League	GP	W	L	O/T	Mins	GA	SO	Avg	GP	W	L	Mins	GA	SO	Avg
1988-89	Medicine Hat	AMHL	26	....	....	....	1441	88	0	3.66	....	....	....	....	....	....	....
1989-90	Medicine Hat	WHL	57	24	28	2	3094	228	0	4.42	3	0	3	173	17	0	5.91
1990-91	Medicine Hat	WHL	46	23	18	3	2630	173	2	3.95	12	7	5	712	42	0	3.54
1991-92	Medicine Hat	WHL	15	10	3	0	819	44	0	3.22	....	....	....	....	....	....	....
	Brandon	WHL	16	3	10	1	890	60	1	4.04	....	....	....	....	....	....	....
	Seattle	WHL	21	12	7	1	1217	65	1	3.20	15	9	6	904	51	0	3.38
1992-93	Adirondack	AHL	45	19	19	4	2438	159	0	3.91	1	0	1	59	2	0	2.03
1993-94	**Detroit**	**NHL**	**41**	**23**	**8**	**5**	**2206**	**105**	**2**	**2.86**	**6**	**3**	**2**	**307**	**12**	**1**	**2.35**
	Adirondack	AHL	4	3	1	0	239	13	0	3.26	....	....	....	....	....	....	....
1994-95	**Detroit**	**NHL**	**19**	**14**	**5**	**0**	**1087**	**41**	**1**	**2.26**	**2**	**0**	**0**	**68**	**2**	**0**	**1.76**
	Adirondack	AHL	2	1	1	0	120	6	0	3.00	....	....	....	....	....	....	....
1995-96	**Detroit**	**NHL**	**50**	***39**	**6**	**5**	**2933**	**106**	**5**	**2.17**	**15**	**8**	**7**	**936**	**33**	**2**	**2.12**
1996-97 ♦	**Detroit**	**NHL**	**47**	**23**	**13**	**9**	**2769**	**106**	**6**	**2.30**	**2**	**0**	**0**	**47**	**2**	**0**	**2.55**
1997-98 ♦	**Detroit**	**NHL**	**64**	**33**	**20**	**11**	**3807**	**140**	**6**	**2.21**	***22**	***16**	**6**	***1361**	**48**	**2**	**2.12**
1998-99	**Detroit**	**NHL**	**63**	**34**	**25**	**4**	**3691**	**149**	**3**	**2.42**	**6**	**4**	**2**	**358**	**14**	**1**	**2.35**
99-2000	**Detroit**	**NHL**	**53**	**30**	**14**	**8**	**3148**	**126**	**6**	**2.40**	**9**	**5**	**4**	**547**	**18**	**2**	**1.97**
2000-01	**Detroit**	**NHL**	**52**	**25**	**19**	**4**	**2834**	**127**	**1**	**2.69**	**6**	**2**	**4**	**365**	**15**	**1**	**2.47**
2001-02	**NY Islanders**	**NHL**	**66**	**32**	**25**	**6**	**3743**	**156**	**4**	**2.50**	**7**	**3**	**4**	**392**	**17**	**0**	**2.60**
2002-03	**NY Islanders**	**NHL**	**37**	**17**	**14**	**4**	**1993**	**97**	**2**	**2.92**	....	....	....	....	....	....	....
	St. Louis	**NHL**	**9**	**4**	**3**	**2**	**532**	**27**	**2**	**3.05**	**7**	**3**	**4**	**417**	**17**	**1**	**2.45**
2003-04	**St. Louis**	**NHL**	**67**	**31**	**25**	**8**	**3861**	**144**	**3**	**2.24**	**5**	**1**	**4**	**287**	**12**	**0**	**2.51**
2004-05							DID NOT PLAY										
2005-06	**Detroit**	**NHL**	**32**	**20**	**6**	**5**	**1846**	**85**	**2**	**2.76**	....	....	....	....	....	....	....
	Grand Rapids	AHL	3	2	1	0	180	10	0	3.34	....	....	....	....	....	....	....
2006-07	**Detroit**	**NHL**	**21**	**11**	**3**	**6**	**1161**	**46**	**0**	**2.38**	....	....	....	....	....	....	....
2007-08 ♦	**Detroit**	**NHL**	**43**	**27**	**9**	**4**	**2409**	**84**	**4**	***2.09**	**19**	***14**	**4**	**1160**	**30**	***3**	***1.55**
	NHL Totals		**664**	**363**	**195**	**81**	**38020**	**1539**	**47**	**2.43**	**106**	**59**	**41**	**6245**	**220**	**13**	**2.11**

WHL East Second All-Star Team (1991) • NHL Second All-Star Team (1996) • William M. Jennings Trophy (1996) (shared with Mike Vernon) • William M. Jennings Trophy (2008) (shared with Dominik Hasek)

Played in NHL All-Star Game (1996, 2008)

• Scored a goal while with Medicine Hat (WHL), January 3, 1991. • Scored a goal vs. Hartford, March 6, 1996. Claimed by **NY Islanders** from **Detroit** in Waiver Draft, September 28, 2001. Traded to **St. Louis** by **NY Islanders** with NY Islanders' 3rd round choice (Konstantin Barulin) in 2003 Entry Draft for Justin Papineau and St. Louis' 2nd round choice (Jeremy Colliton) in 2003 Entry Draft, March 11, 2003. Signed as a free agent by **Detroit**, August 8, 2005.

PALMER, Joe (PAHL-muhr, JOH) CHI.

Goaltender. Catches left. 6'1", 205 lbs. Born, Yorkville, NY, February 19, 1988.
(Chicago's 6th choice, 96th overall, in 2006 Entry Draft).

			Regular Season								Playoffs						
Season	Club	League	GP	W	L	O/T	Mins	GA	SO	Avg	GP	W	L	Mins	GA	SO	Avg
2003-04	Syracuse Jr. Stars	EmJHL	31	....	....	....	1147	69	1	3.61	6	....	....	368	19	0	3.10
	USNTDP	U-17	1	0	0	0	11	2	0	10.91	....	....	....	....	....	....	....
2004-05	USNTDP	U-17	8	6	1	1	495	22	0	2.67	....	....	....	....	....	....	....
	USNTDP	NAHL	19	10	8	1	1020	56	0	3.29	....	....	....	....	....	....	....
2005-06	USNTDP	U-18	33	16	14	3	1900	99	0	3.13	....	....	....	....	....	....	....
	USNTDP	NAHL	14	13	1	0	776	22	1	1.70	....	....	....	....	....	....	....
2006-07	Ohio State	CCHA	34	15	15	4	1968	97	1	2.96	....	....	....	....	....	....	....
2007-08	Ohio State	CCHA	34	10	19	4	1980	103	1	3.12	....	....	....	....	....	....	....

PATTERSON, Kent (PA-tuhr-suhn, KEHNT) COL.

Goaltender. Catches left. 6', 184 lbs. Born, St. Louis Park, MI, September 15, 1989.
(Colorado's 6th choice, 113th overall, in 2007 Entry Draft).

			Regular Season								Playoffs						
Season	Club	League	GP	W	L	O/T	Mins	GA	SO	Avg	GP	W	L	Mins	GA	SO	Avg
2004-05	Blake Bears	High-MN	14	9	4	1	673	27	....	2.05	....	....	....	....	....	....	....
2005-06	Blake Bears	High-MN	25	14	8	2	1249	66	....	2.70	....	....	....	....	....	....	....
2006-07	Cedar Rapids	USHL	29	20	5	3	1710	83	2	2.91	1	0	1	41	6	0	8.78
2007-08	Cedar Rapids	USHL	20	10	6	1	1110	46	1	2.49	....	....	....	....	....	....	....

PATZOLD, Dimitri (PATZ-ohld, dih-MEE-tree)

Goaltender. Catches left. 6', 195 lbs. Born, Ust-Kamenogorsk, USSR, February 3, 1983.
(San Jose's 3rd choice, 107th overall, in 2001 Entry Draft).

			Regular Season								Playoffs						
Season	Club	League	GP	W	L	O/T	Mins	GA	SO	Avg	GP	W	L	Mins	GA	SO	Avg
99-2000	Kolner EC Jr.	Ger-Jr.	38	....	....	....	2131	73	0	2.06	....	....	....	....	....	....	....
	Kolner Haie 2	German-5	16	....	....	....	896	58	0	3.88	....	....	....	....	....	....	....
2000-01	EV Duisburg	German-3	6	....	....	....	360	17	0	2.83	....	....	....	....	....	....	....
	Erding Jets	German-2	24	....	....	....	1378	89	0	3.88	....	....	....	....	....	....	....
2001-02	Kolner Haie	Germany	7	....	....	....	260	16	0	3.69	....	....	....	....	....	....	....
	EV Duisburg	German-2	6	....	....	....	360	17	0	2.83	....	....	....	....	....	....	....
2002-03	Adler Mannheim	Germany	15	....	....	....	817	35	0	2.57	2	....	....	34	2	0	3.53
2003-04	Cleveland Barons	AHL	27	10	15	0	1457	70	3	2.88	....	....	....	....	....	....	....
	Johnstown Chiefs	ECHL	8	7	0	0	443	20	0	2.71	1	0	1	59	2	0	2.02
2004-05	Cleveland Barons	AHL	41	18	16	5	2418	104	1	2.58	....	....	....	....	....	....	....
2005-06	Cleveland Barons	AHL	33	10	21	0	1876	124	0	3.97	....	....	....	....	....	....	....
2006-07	Worcester Sharks	AHL	24	10	8	3	1378	77	0	3.35	4	2	1	256	8	0	1.87
	Fresno Falcons	ECHL	4	2	2	0	239	8	0	2.01	....	....	....	....	....	....	....
2007-08	**San Jose**	**NHL**	**3**	**0**	**0**	**0**	**44**	**4**	**0**	**5.45**	....	....	....	....	....	....	....
	Worcester Sharks	AHL	21	7	10	3	1184	56	1	2.84	....	....	....	....	....	....	....
	NHL Totals		**3**	**0**	**0**	**0**	**44**	**4**	**0**	**5.45**	....	....	....	....	....	....	....

PAVELEC, Ondrej (pah-vah-LEK, AWN-dray) ATL.

Goaltender. Catches left. 6'2", 200 lbs. Born, Kladno, Czech., August 31, 1987.
(Atlanta's 2nd choice, 41st overall, in 2005 Entry Draft).

			Regular Season								Playoffs						
Season	Club	League	GP	W	L	O/T	Mins	GA	SO	Avg	GP	W	L	Mins	GA	SO	Avg
2003-04	HC Kladno U17	CzR-U17	38	....	....	....	2079	77	3	2.22	2	....	....	67	7	0	6.27
2004-05	HC Kladno Jr.	CzRep-Jr.	39	....	....	....	2218	85	7	2.30	10	....	....	587	24	1	2.45
	HK LEV Slany	CzRep-3	1	....	....	....	60	4	0	4.00	....	....	....	....	....	....	....
2005-06	Cape Breton	QMJHL	47	27	18	0	2578	108	3	2.51	9	4	5	507	19	0	*2.25
2006-07	Cape Breton	QMJHL	43	28	11	....	2335	98	1	*2.52	16	11	5	970	37	*2	*2.29
2007-08	**Atlanta**	**NHL**	**7**	**3**	**3**	**0**	**347**	**18**	**0**	**3.11**	....	....	....	....	....	....	....
	Chicago Wolves	AHL	52	33	16	3	3033	140	2	2.77	*24	*16	8	*1438	56	*2	2.34
	NHL Totals		**7**	**3**	**3**	**0**	**347**	**18**	**0**	**3.11**	....	....	....	....	....	....	....

QMJHL All-Rookie Team (2006) • QMJHL First All-Star Team (2006, 2007) • QMJHL Defensive Rookie of the Year (2006)

PECHURSKI, Alexander (puh-CHUHR-skee, al-ehx-AN-duhr) PIT.

Goaltender. Catches left. 6', 187 lbs. Born, Magnitogorsk, USSR, June 4, 1990.
(Pittsburgh's 2nd choice, 150th overall, in 2008 Entry Draft).

			Regular Season								Playoffs						
Season	Club	League	GP	W	L	O/T	Mins	GA	SO	Avg	GP	W	L	Mins	GA	SO	Avg
2007-08	Magnitogorsk 2	Russia-3	27	....	....	....	....	62	....	....	....	....	....	....	....	....	....
	Magnitogorsk	Russia	1	....	....	....	1	0	0	0.00	....	....	....	....	....	....	....

PELLETIER, Jean-Marc (PEHL-tyay, ZHAWN-MAHRK)

Goaltender. Catches left. 6'3", 209 lbs. Born, Atlanta, GA, March 4, 1978.
(Philadelphia's 1st choice, 30th overall, in 1997 Entry Draft).

			Regular Season								Playoffs						
Season	Club	League	GP	W	L	O/T	Mins	GA	SO	Avg	GP	W	L	Mins	GA	SO	Avg
1993-94	Richelieu Riverains	QAAA	24	14	8	2	1440	91	0	3.79	2	1	0	104	11	0	6.32
1994-95	Richelieu Riverains	QAAA	21	15	6	0	1260	71	0	3.36	2	1	1	153	11	0	4.32
1995-96	Cornell Big Red	ECAC	5	1	2	0	179	15	0	5.03	....	....	....	....	....	....	....
1996-97	Cornell Big Red	ECAC	11	5	2	3	679	28	1	2.47	....	....	....	....	....	....	....
1997-98	Rimouski Oceanic	QMJHL	34	17	11	3	1913	118	0	3.70	16	11	3	895	51	1	3.42
1998-99	**Philadelphia**	**NHL**	**1**	**0**	**1**	**0**	**60**	**5**	**0**	**5.00**	....	....	....	....	....	....	....
	Philadelphia	AHL	47	25	16	4	2636	122	2	2.78	1	0	0	27	0	0	0.00
99-2000	Philadelphia	AHL	24	14	10	0	1405	58	3	2.48	....	....	....	....	....	....	....
	Cincinnati	IHL	22	14	4	2	1278	52	2	2.44	3	1	1	160	8	1	3.00
2000-01	Cincinnati	IHL	39	18	14	5	2261	119	2	3.16	5	1	4	318	15	0	2.83
2001-02	Lowell	AHL	40	21	12	4	2284	98	2	2.57	5	2	3	298	13	0	2.62
2002-03	Lowell	AHL	17	6	10	0	861	51	1	3.55	....	....	....	....	....	....	....
	Phoenix	**NHL**	**2**	**0**	**2**	**0**	**119**	**6**	**0**	**3.03**	....	....	....	....	....	....	....
	Springfield Falcons	AHL	24	12	7	4	1391	55	2	2.37	6	3	3	368	16	1	2.61
2003-04	**Phoenix**	**NHL**	**4**	**1**	**1**	**0**	**175**	**12**	**0**	**4.11**	....	....	....	....	....	....	....
	Springfield Falcons	AHL	43	10	24	5	2433	109	2	2.69	....	....	....	....	....	....	....
2004-05	Utah Grizzlies	AHL	23	6	12	1	1231	77	0	3.75	....	....	....	....	....	....	....
	Springfield Falcons	AHL	13	2	10	1	715	35	0	2.94	....	....	....	....	....	....	....
2005-06	Rochester	AHL	39	21	15	1	2198	120	0	3.28	....	....	....	....	....	....	....
2006-07	Rochester	AHL	4	4	0	0	244	10	0	2.46	....	....	....	....	....	....	....
	Adler Mannheim	Germany	19	....	....	....	1129	49	0	2.60	11	....	....	674	24	1	*2.14
2007-08	Hamburg Freezers	Germany	41	17	23	0	2397	113	1	2.83	1	0	1	63	4	0	3.83
	NHL Totals		**7**	**1**	**4**	**0**	**354**	**23**	**0**	**3.90**	....	....	....	....	....	....	....

Traded to **Carolina** by **Philadelphia** with Rod Brind'Amour and Philadelphia's 2nd round choice (later traded to Colorado – Colorado selected Argis Saviels) in 2000 Entry Draft for Keith Primeau and Carolina's 5th round choice (later traded to NY Islanders – NY Islanders selected Kristofer Ottosson) in 2000 Entry Draft, January 23, 2000. Traded to **Phoenix** by **Carolina** for Patrick DesRochers, December 31, 2002. Signed as a free agent by **Florida**, August 19, 2005.

PETERS, Justin (PEE-tuhrz, JUHS-tihn) CAR.

Goaltender. Catches left. 6'1", 209 lbs. Born, Blyth, Ont., August 30, 1986.
(Carolina's 2nd choice, 38th overall, in 2004 Entry Draft).

			Regular Season								Playoffs						
Season	Club	League	GP	W	L	O/T	Mins	GA	SO	Avg	GP	W	L	Mins	GA	SO	Avg
2001-02	Huron-Perth	Minor-ON	17	11	2	4	810	32	1	1.89	13	9	4	285	30	1	2.31
2002-03	St. Michael's	OHL	23	6	10	1	1052	54	0	3.08	7	1	0	126	4	0	1.90
2003-04	St. Michael's	OHL	53	30	16	6	3149	139	4	2.65	18	10	8	1109	37	4	2.00
2004-05	St. Michael's	OHL	58	23	23	5	3150	146	3	2.78	10	4	4	524	25	0	2.86
2005-06	St. Michael's	OHL	20	10	6	3	1174	75	0	3.83	....	....	....	....	....	....	....
	Plymouth Whalers	OHL	35	19	15	1	2073	95	1	2.75	13	6	7	789	42	0	3.19
2006-07	Albany River Rats	AHL	34	10	18	0	1765	96	1	3.26	....	....	....	....	....	....	....
	Florida Everblades	ECHL	1	0	0	1	65	6	0	5.54	....	....	....	....	....	....	....
2007-08	Albany River Rats	AHL	11	7	3	0	645	29	0	2.70	....	....	....	....	....	....	....
	Florida Everblades	ECHL	31	18	10	2	1846	79	1	2.57	....	....	....	....	....	....	....

PHILLIPS, Brad (FIHL-ihps , BRAD) PHI.

Goaltender. Catches left. 6'2", 163 lbs. Born, Allen Park, MI, April 22, 1989.
(Philadelphia's 7th choice, 182nd overall, in 2007 Entry Draft).

			Regular Season								Playoffs						
Season	Club	League	GP	W	L	O/T	Mins	GA	SO	Avg	GP	W	L	Mins	GA	SO	Avg
2004-05	Det. Honeybaked	MWEHL	38	32	3	3	....	50	10	1.32	....	....	....	....	....	....	....
2005-06	USNTDP	U-17	13	8	5	0	610	28	....	2.75	....	....	....	....	....	....	....
	USNTDP	NAHL	21	12	6	3	1261	51	0	2.43	4	1	3	254	12	0	2.83
2006-07	USNTDP	U-18	12	7	1	2	706	29	0	2.46	....	....	....	....	....	....	....
	USNTDP	NAHL	11	8	3	0	660	24	2	2.18	1	0	1	60	3	0	3.00
2007-08	U. of Notre Dame	CCHA	5	4	1	0	275	7	1	1.53	....	....	....	....	....	....	....

PICKARD, Chet (PIH-kuhrd, CHEHT) NSH.

Goaltender. Catches left. 6'2", 220 lbs. Born, Moncton, N. B., November 29, 1989.
(Nashville's 2nd choice, 18th overall, in 2008 Entry Draft).

			Regular Season								Playoffs						
Season	Club	League	GP	W	L	O/T	Mins	GA	SO	Avg	GP	W	L	Mins	GA	SO	Avg
2004-05	Wpg. Monarchs	MMHL	22	....	....	....	1264	55	2	2.61	....	....	....	....	....	....	....
2005-06	Tri-City Americans	WHL	26	9	9	1	1270	62	3	2.93	....	....	....	....	....	....	....
2006-07	Tri-City Americans	WHL	29	17	10	1	1577	75	1	2.85	1	0	0	20	1	0	3.00
2007-08	Tri-City Americans	WHL	*64	*46	12	0	*3779	146	2	2.32	16	11	5	1010	30	*3	1.78

WHL West First All-Star Team (2008) • WHL Goaltender of the Year (2008) • Canadian Major Junior First All-Star Team (2008) • Canadian Major Junior Goaltender of the Year (2008)

PIELMEIER, Timo (PEEL-migh-uhr, TEE-moh) S.J.

Goaltender. Catches left. 5'11", 175 lbs. Born, Deggendorf, West Germany, July 7, 1989.
(San Jose's 3rd choice, 83rd overall, in 2007 Entry Draft).

			Regular Season								Playoffs						
Season	Club	League	GP	W	L	O/T	Mins	GA	SO	Avg	GP	W	L	Mins	GA	SO	Avg
2004-05	Mannheimer ERC	German-5	1	....	....	....	....	....	....	8.15	....	....	....	....	....	....	....
	Mannheim Jr.	Ger-Jr.	10	....	....	....	568	33	....	3.49	....	....	....	....	....	....	....
2005-06	Koln Jr.	Ger-Jr.	8	....	....	....	459	52	....	6.79	2	....	....	100	17	....	10.20
2006-07	Koln Jr.	Ger-Jr.	20	....	....	....	1159	77	....	3.99	6	....	....	370	17	....	2.76
2007-08	St. John's	QMJHL	50	23	26	....	2719	133	1	2.94	5	0	3	231	22	0	5.71

PITTON, Bryan (PIH-tuhn, BRIGH-uhn) EDM.

Goaltender. Catches left. 6'2", 176 lbs. Born, Mississauga, Ont., January 26, 1988.
(Edmonton's 3rd choice, 133rd overall, in 2006 Entry Draft).

			Regular Season								Playoffs						
Season	Club	League	GP	W	L	O/T	Mins	GA	SO	Avg	GP	W	L	Mins	GA	SO	Avg
2004-05	Wellington Dukes	OPJHL	....	24	7	3	....	....	2	2.93	....	....	....	....	....	....	....
2005-06	Brampton Battalion	OHL	24	16	4	0	1293	74	0	3.43	2	0	0	45	5	0	6.67
2006-07	Brampton Battalion	OHL	61	26	29	4	3494	208	0	3.57	4	0	4	270	15	0	3.33
2007-08	Brampton Battalion	OHL	39	22	13	2	2153	91	*4	2.54	5	1	4	333	10	0	*1.80
	Springfield Falcons	AHL	1	0	0	0	12	1	0	4.88	....	....	....	....	....	....	....

PLANTE, Tyler (PLAWNT, TIGH-luhr) FLA.

Goaltender. Catches left. 6'3", 191 lbs. Born, Milwaukee, WI, April 16, 1987.
(Florida's 2nd choice, 32nd overall, in 2005 Entry Draft).

			Regular Season								Playoffs						
Season	Club	League	GP	W	L	O/T	Mins	GA	SO	Avg	GP	W	L	Mins	GA	SO	Avg
2003-04	Brandon	WHL	2	0	0	1	58	2	0	2.07	....	....	....	....	....	....	....
2004-05	Brandon	WHL	48	34	11	2	2833	122	6	2.58	*24	*13	11	*1408	69	0	2.94
2005-06	Brandon	WHL	60	25	24	9	3414	189	2	3.32	6	2	4	360	18	0	3.00
2006-07	Brandon	WHL	54	30	14	9	3215	145	4	2.71	11	6	5	659	37	0	3.37
2007-08	Rochester	AHL	25	6	16	1	1451	86	0	3.56	....	....	....	....	....	....	....
	Florida Everblades	ECHL	10	4	5	1	598	28	1	2.81	....	....	....	....	....	....	....

WHL Rookie of the Year (2005) • Canadian Major Junior All-Rookie Team (2005)

POGGE, Justin (POH-gee, JUHS-tihn) TOR.

Goaltender. Catches left. 6'3", 200 lbs. Born, Ft. McMurray, Alta., April 22, 1986.
(Toronto's 1st choice, 90th overall, in 2004 Entry Draft).

			Regular Season								Playoffs						
Season	Club	League	GP	W	L	O/T	Mins	GA	SO	Avg	GP	W	L	Mins	GA	SO	Avg
2002-03	Summerland Sting	KIJHL	30	....	....	....	1761	91	0	3.13	....	....	....	....	....	....	....
2003-04	Prince George	WHL	44	17	18	2	2271	107	3	2.83	....	....	....	....	....	....	....
2004-05	Prince George	WHL	24	10	9	2	1198	56	4	2.80	....	....	....	....	....	....	....
	Calgary Hitmen	WHL	29	14	12	3	1727	66	2	2.29	12	7	5	742	24	1	1.94
2005-06	Calgary Hitmen	WHL	54	38	10	6	3237	93	*11	*1.72	13	7	6	802	34	2	2.54
2006-07	Toronto Marlies	AHL	48	19	25	2	2812	142	3	3.03	....	....	....	....	....	....	....
2007-08	Toronto Marlies	AHL	41	26	10	4	2415	94	4	2.34	4	1	1	172	6	0	2.09

WHL East First All-Star Team (2006) • WHL Goaltender of the Year (2006) • WHL Player of the Year (2006) • Canadian Major Junior Goaltender of the Year (2006)

POPPERLE, Tomas (PAW-puhr-lay, TAW-mahsh)

Goaltender. Catches left. 6'1", 187 lbs. Born, Broumov, Czech., October 10, 1984.
(Columbus' 5th choice, 131st overall, in 2005 Entry Draft).

			Regular Season								Playoffs						
Season	Club	League	GP	W	L	O/T	Mins	GA	SO	Avg	GP	W	L	Mins	GA	SO	Avg
2001-02	Sparta Jr.	CzRep-Jr.	29	....	....	....	1653	65	2	2.36	5	....	....	320	15	0	2.81
2002-03	Sparta Jr.	CzRep-Jr.	28	....	....	....	1500	52	2	2.08	....	....	....	....	....	....	....
2003-04	Sparta Jr.	CzRep-Jr.	30	....	....	....	1778	60	4	2.02	....	....	....	....	....	....	....
	HC Pribram	CzRep-3	2	....	....	....	60	2	0	2.00	....	....	....	....	....	....	....
	Beroun	CzRep-2	5	....	....	....	305	7	0	1.38	2	....	....	120	4	0	2.00
	HC Sparta Praha	CzRep	....	....	....	....	....	....	....	....	1	....	....	11	0	0	0.00
2004-05	Beroun	CzRep-2	16	....	....	....	966	29	1	1.80	2	....	....	120	5	0	2.50
	HC Sparta Praha	CzRep	25	....	....	....	1325	35	4	*1.58	2	....	....	12	4	0	20.00
2005-06	Eisbaren Berlin	Germany	31	....	....	....	1845	67	3	2.18	11	....	....	655	23	1	2.11
2006-07	**Columbus**	**NHL**	**2**	**0**	**0**	**0**	**45**	**1**	**0**	**1.33**	....	....	....	....	....	....	....
	Syracuse Crunch	AHL	49	25	19	4	2833	135	4	2.86	....	....	....	....	....	....	....
2007-08	Syracuse Crunch	AHL	17	7	8	0	890	44	1	2.97	....	....	....	....	....	....	....
	NHL Totals		**2**	**0**	**0**	**0**	**45**	**1**	**0**	**1.33**	....	....	....	....	....	....	....

POULIN, Kevin (POO-lihn, KEH-vihn) NYI

Goaltender. Catches left. 6'2", 210 lbs. Born, Montreal, Que., April 12, 1990.
(NY Islanders' 10th choice, 126th overall, in 2008 Entry Draft).

			Regular Season								Playoffs						
Season	Club	League	GP	W	L	O/T	Mins	GA	SO	Avg	GP	W	L	Mins	GA	SO	Avg
2005-06	C.C. Lemoyne	QAAA	27	13	8	2	1440	71	1	2.96	7	4	3	373	16	1	2.57
2006-07	Victoriaville Tigres	QMJHL	24	10	6	....	1220	68	0	3.34	2	0	0	42	5	0	7.20
2007-08	Victoriaville Tigres	QMJHL	52	18	24	....	2734	168	0	3.69	6	2	4	279	27	0	5.80

PRICE, Carey (PRIGHS, KAIR-ee) MTL.

Goaltender. Catches left. 6'3", 226 lbs. Born, Vancouver, B.C., August 16, 1987.
(Montreal's 1st choice, 5th overall, in 2005 Entry Draft).

			Regular Season								Playoffs						
Season	Club	League	GP	W	L	O/T	Mins	GA	SO	Avg	GP	W	L	Mins	GA	SO	Avg
2002-03	Williams Lake	Minor-BC	18	....	....	....	1050	48	1	2.70	....	....	....	....	....	....	....
	Tri-City Americans	WHL	1	0	0	0	20	2	0	6.00	....	....	....	....	....	....	....
2003-04	Tri-City Americans	WHL	28	8	9	3	1363	54	1	2.38	8	5	3	470	19	0	2.43
2004-05	Tri-City Americans	WHL	63	24	31	8	3712	145	8	2.34	5	1	4	325	12	0	2.22
2005-06	Tri-City Americans	WHL	55	21	25	6	3072	147	3	2.87	5	1	4	302	12	0	2.38
2006-07	Tri-City Americans	WHL	46	30	13	1	2722	111	3	2.45	6	2	4	348	17	0	2.93
	Hamilton Bulldogs	AHL	2	1	1	0	117	3	0	1.53	*22	*15	6	*1314	45	*2	2.06
2007-08	**Montreal**	**NHL**	**41**	**24**	**12**	**3**	**2413**	**103**	**3**	**2.56**	**11**	**5**	**6**	**648**	**30**	**2**	**2.78**
	Hamilton Bulldogs	AHL	10	6	4	0	581	26	1	2.69	....	....	....	....	....	....	....
	NHL Totals		**41**	**24**	**12**	**3**	**2413**	**103**	**3**	**2.56**	**11**	**5**	**6**	**648**	**30**	**2**	**2.78**

WHL West First All-Star Team (2007) • Canadian Major Junior Goaltender of the Year (2007) • Jack A. Butterfield Trophy (Playoff MVP - AHL) (2007) • NHL All-Rookie Team (2008)

QUICK, Jonathan (KWIHK, JAWN-ah-thuhn) L.A.

Goaltender. Catches left. 6'1", 206 lbs. Born, Milford, CT, January 21, 1986.
(Los Angeles' 4th choice, 72nd overall, in 2005 Entry Draft).

			Regular Season								Playoffs						
Season	Club	League	GP	W	L	O/T	Mins	GA	SO	Avg	GP	W	L	Mins	GA	SO	Avg
2002-03	Avon Old Farms	High-CT	13	8	5	0	780	38	0	2.92	....	....	....	....	....	....	....
2003-04	Avon Old Farms	High-CT	21	20	1	0	1260	26	2	1.71	....	....	....	....	....	....	....
2004-05	Avon Old Farms	High-CT	27	25	2	0	1413	1.14	9	1.14	....	....	....	....	....	....	....
2005-06	Massachusetts	H-East	17	4	10	1	905	45	0	2.98	....	....	....	....	....	....	....
2006-07	Massachusetts	H-East	37	19	12	5	2224	80	3	2.16	....	....	....	....	....	....	....
2007-08	**Los Angeles**	**NHL**	**3**	**1**	**2**	**0**	**141**	**9**	**0**	**3.83**	....	....	....	....	....	....	....
	Manchester	AHL	19	11	8	0	1085	42	3	2.32	1	0	1	59	1	0	1.02
	Reading Royals	ECHL	38	23	11	3	2257	105	1	2.79	....	....	....	....	....	....	....
	NHL Totals		**3**	**1**	**2**	**0**	**141**	**9**	**0**	**3.83**	....	....	....	....	....	....	....

Hockey East Second All-Star Team (2007) • NCAA East Second All-American Team (2007)

RAMO, Karri (RAH-moh, KAH-ree) T.B.

Goaltender. Catches left. 6'2", 201 lbs. Born, Asikkala, Finland, July 1, 1986.
(Tampa Bay's 7th choice, 191st overall, in 2004 Entry Draft).

			Regular Season								Playoffs						
Season	Club	League	GP	W	L	O/T	Mins	GA	SO	Avg	GP	W	L	Mins	GA	SO	Avg
2002-03	K-Reipas U18	Fin-U18	19	12	3	2	1013	47	0	2.78	4	2	2	182	11	0	3.62
2003-04	Pelicans Lahti U18	Fin-U18	3	3	0	0	180	7	0	2.33	5	2	2	268	10	0	2.24
	Pelicans Lahti Jr.	Fin-Jr.	18	5	9	2	960	53	0	3.31	2	2	0	120	1	1	0.50
	Pelicans Lahti	Finland	3	0	2	0	138	10	0	4.34	....	....	....	....	....	....	....
2004-05	Pelicans Lahti Jr.	Fin-Jr.	21	10	5	6	1269	36	6	1.70	4	1	3	206	16	0	4.66
	Pelicans Lahti	Finland	26	4	12	4	1267	84	1	3.98	....	....	....	....	....	....	....
2005-06	Haukat Jarvenpaa	Finland-2	1	....	....	....	60	5	0	5.00	....	....	....	....	....	....	....
	Suomi U20	Finland-2	3	....	....	....	183	12	0	3.93	....	....	....	....	....	....	....
	HPK Hameenlinna	Finland	24	7	8	7	1359	49	2	2.16	3	2	1	204	5	1	1.46
2006-07	**Tampa Bay**	**NHL**	**2**	**0**	**0**	**0**	**70**	**4**	**0**	**3.43**	....	....	....	....	....	....	....
	Springfield Falcons	AHL	45	15	24	1	2432	127	1	3.13	....	....	....	....	....	....	....
2007-08	**Tampa Bay**	**NHL**	**22**	**7**	**11**	**3**	**1269**	**64**	**0**	**3.03**	....	....	....	....	....	....	....
	Norfolk Admirals	AHL	6	2	4	0	342	19	0	3.33	....	....	....	....	....	....	....
	NHL Totals		**24**	**7**	**11**	**3**	**1339**	**68**	**0**	**3.05**	....	....	....	....	....	....	....

RASK, Tuukka (RASK, TU-kah) BOS.

Goaltender. Catches left. 6'2", 171 lbs. Born, Savonlinna, Finland, March 10, 1987.
(Toronto's 1st choice, 21st overall, in 2005 Entry Draft).

			Regular Season								Playoffs						
Season	Club	League	GP	W	L	O/T	Mins	GA	SO	Avg	GP	W	L	Mins	GA	SO	Avg
2003-04	Ilves Tampere U18	Fin-U18	9	4	3	2	533	25	0	2.81	....	....	....	....	....	....	....
	Ilves Tampere Jr.	Fin-Jr.	30	12	10	7	1767	65	2	2.21	3	1	2	178	6	0	2.02
2004-05	Ilves Tampere Jr.	Fin-Jr.	26	17	3	4	1517	47	2	1.86	10	9	1	619	9	6	0.87
	Ilves Tampere	Finland	4	0	1	1	201	15	0	4.46	....	....	....	....	....	....	....
2005-06	Ilves Tampere Jr.	Fin-Jr.	1	....	....	....	60	2	0	2.00	....	....	....	....	....	....	....
	Suomi U20	Finland-2	3	....	....	....	179	6	0	2.01	....	....	....	....	....	....	....
	Ilves Tampere	Finland	30	12	8	7	1724	60	2	2.09	3	0	3	180	7	0	2.33
2006-07	Suomi U20	Finland-2	1	0	1	0	58	4	0	4.14	....	....	....	....	....	....	....
	Ilves Tampere	Finland	49	18	18	10	2872	114	3	2.38	7	2	5	397	20	0	3.02
2007-08	**Boston**	**NHL**	**4**	**2**	**1**	**1**	**184**	**10**	**0**	**3.26**	....	....	....	....	....	....	....
	Providence Bruins	AHL	45	27	13	2	2570	100	1	2.33	10	6	4	605	22	*2	2.18
	NHL Totals		**4**	**2**	**1**	**1**	**184**	**10**	**0**	**3.26**	....	....	....	....	....	....	....

Traded to **Boston** by **Toronto** for Andrew Raycroft, June 24, 2006.

RAYCROFT, Andrew (RAY-krawft, AN-droo) COL.

Goaltender. Catches left. 6', 185 lbs. Born, Belleville, Ont., May 4, 1980.
(Boston's 4th choice, 135th overall, in 1998 Entry Draft).

			Regular Season								Playoffs						
Season	Club	League	GP	W	L	O/T	Mins	GA	SO	Avg	GP	W	L	Mins	GA	SO	Avg
1996-97	Wellington Dukes	MTJHL	27	....	....	....	1402	92	0	3.94	....	....	....	....	....	....	....
1997-98	Sudbury Wolves	OHL	33	8	16	5	1802	125	0	4.16	2	0	1	89	8	0	5.39
1998-99	Sudbury Wolves	OHL	45	17	22	5	2528	173	1	4.11	3	0	2	96	13	0	8.13
99-2000	Kingston	OHL	*61	33	20	5	3340	191	0	3.43	5	1	4	300	21	0	4.20
2000-01	**Boston**	**NHL**	**15**	**4**	**6**	**0**	**649**	**32**	**0**	**2.96**	....	....	....	....	....	....	....
	Providence Bruins	AHL	26	8	14	4	1459	82	1	3.37	....	....	....	....	....	....	....
2001-02	**Boston**	**NHL**	**1**	**0**	**0**	**1**	**65**	**3**	**0**	**2.77**	....	....	....	....	....	....	....
	Providence Bruins	AHL	56	25	24	6	3317	142	4	2.57	2	0	2	119	5	0	2.52
2002-03	**Boston**	**NHL**	**5**	**2**	**3**	**0**	**300**	**12**	**0**	**2.40**	....	....	....	....	....	....	....
	Providence Bruins	AHL	39	23	10	3	2255	94	1	2.50	4	1	3	264	6	1	*1.36
2003-04	**Boston**	**NHL**	**57**	**29**	**18**	**9**	**3420**	**117**	**3**	**2.05**	**7**	**3**	**4**	**447**	**16**	**1**	**2.15**
2004-05	Tappara Tampere	Finland	11	4	5	2	657	32	1	2.92	3	0	2	104	11	0	6.36
2005-06	**Boston**	**NHL**	**30**	**8**	**19**	**2**	**1619**	**100**	**0**	**3.71**	....	....	....	....	....	....	....
	Providence Bruins	AHL	1	1	0	0	64	3	0	2.80	....	....	....	....	....	....	....
2006-07	**Toronto**	**NHL**	**72**	**37**	**25**	**9**	**4108**	**205**	**2**	**2.99**	....	....	....	....	....	....	....
2007-08	**Toronto**	**NHL**	**19**	**2**	**9**	**5**	**965**	**63**	**1**	**3.92**	....	....	....	....	....	....	....
	NHL Totals		**199**	**82**	**80**	**26**	**11126**	**532**	**6**	**2.87**	**7**	**3**	**4**	**447**	**16**	**1**	**2.15**

OHL First All-Star Team (2000) • Canadian Major Junior First All-Star Team (2000) • Canadian Major Junior Goaltender of the Year (2000) • NHL All-Rookie Team (2004) • Calder Memorial Trophy (2004)

Signed as a free agent by **Tappara Tampere** (Finland), January 17, 2005. Traded to **Toronto** by **Boston** for Tuukka Rask, June 24, 2006. Signed as a free agent by **Colorado**, July 1, 2008.

REGAN, Kevin (REE-guhn, KEH-vihn) BOS.

Goaltender. Catches left. 6'1", 190 lbs. Born, Boston, MA, July 25, 1984.
(Boston's 10th choice, 277th overall, in 2003 Entry Draft).

			Regular Season								Playoffs						
Season	Club	League	GP	W	L	O/T	Mins	GA	SO	Avg	GP	W	L	Mins	GA	SO	Avg
2001-02	St. Sebastian's	High-MA	31	27	4	0	1860	56	0	1.91	....	....	....	....	....	....	....
	USNTDP	U-18	1	0	0	0	12	0	0	0.00	....	....	....	....	....	....	....
	South Boston	USHA	3	3	0	0	158	8	0	2.58	....	....	....	....	....	....	....
2002-03	St. Sebastian's	High-MA	28	....	....	....	1215	47	4	1.81	....	....	....	....	....	....	....
2003-04	Waterloo	USHL	50	*28	19	1	0	111	*6	2.37	*12	*9	3	*735	19	*1	*1.55
2004-05	New Hampshire	H-East	23	15	4	2	1276	50	0	2.35	....	....	....	....	....	....	....
2005-06	New Hampshire	H-East	23	8	8	5	1299	57	3	2.63	....	....	....	....	....	....	....
2006-07	New Hampshire	H-East	35	24	9	2	2066	71	3	2.06	....	....	....	....	....	....	....
2007-08	New Hampshire	H-East	32	23	8	1	1958	72	*3	2.21	....	....	....	....	....	....	....
	Providence Bruins	AHL	1	1	0	0	60	0	1	0.00	....	....	....	....	....	....	....

Hockey East All-Rookie Team (2005) (co-winners - Cory Schneider and Peter Vetri) • Hockey East First All-Star Team (2008) • Hockey East Player of the Year (2008) • NCAA East First All-American Team (2008)

REIMER, James (RIGH-muhr, JAYMZ) TOR.

Goaltender. Catches left. 6'2", 208 lbs. Born, Winnipeg, Man., March 15, 1988.
(Toronto's 3rd choice, 99th overall, in 2006 Entry Draft).

			Regular Season								Playoffs						
Season	Club	League	GP	W	L	O/T	Mins	GA	SO	Avg	GP	W	L	Mins	GA	SO	Avg
2003-04	Interlake Lightning	MMHL	27	6	5	2	863	41	1	2.85	....	....	....	....	....	....	....
2004-05	Interlake Lightning	MMHL	37	19	6	2	1646	58	4	2.11	435	26	0	3.59	....	....	....
2005-06	Red Deer Rebels	WHL	34	7	18	3	1709	80	0	2.81	....	....	....	....	....	....	....
2006-07	Red Deer Rebels	WHL	60	26	23	7	3339	148	3	2.66	7	3	4	417	27	0	3.88
2007-08	Red Deer Rebels	WHL	30	8	15	0	1668	76	1	2.73	....	....	....	....	....	....	....

RIDDERWALL, Stefan (RIH-duhr-vahl, STEH-fan) NYI

Goaltender. Catches left. 6'1", 189 lbs. Born, Stockholm, Sweden, March 5, 1988.
(NY Islanders' 12th choice, 173rd overall, in 2006 Entry Draft).

			Regular Season								Playoffs						
Season	Club	League	GP	W	L	O/T	Mins	GA	SO	Avg	GP	W	L	Mins	GA	SO	Avg
2003-04	Huddinge IK U18	Swe-U18	7	....	....	....	345	31	0	5.38	....	....	....	....	....	....	....
2004-05	Djurgarden U18	Swe-U18	3	....	....	....	154	8	0	3.10	4	....	....	234	11	0	2.81
	Djurgarden Jr.	Swe-Jr.	16	....	....	....	972	51	0	3.15	....	....	....	....	....	....	....
2005-06	Djurgarden Jr.	Swe-Jr.	18	....	....	....	1073	43	3	2.40	4	....	....	242	13	1	3.22
	Djurgarden	Sweden	1	....	....	....	4	0	0	0.00	....	....	....	....	....	....	....
2006-07	Djurgarden Jr.	Swe-Jr.	28	....	....	....	1690	50	4	1.78	7	....	....	417	10	1	1.44
2007-08	Nykoping	Sweden-2	1	....	....	....	58	5	0	5.14	....	....	....	....	....	....	....
	Almtuna	Sweden-2	3	....	....	....	182	10	0	3.29	....	....	....	....	....	....	....
	Djurgarden	Sweden	11	....	....	....	605	27	0	2.68	....	....	....	....	....	....	....
	Djurgarden Jr.	Swe-Jr.	8	....	....	....	479	14	1	1.75	4	....	....	254	7	0	1.65

RINNE, Pekka (RIH-neh, PEH-kuh) NSH.

Goaltender. Catches left. 6'5", 207 lbs. Born, Kempele, Finland, November 3, 1982.
(Nashville's 10th choice, 258th overall, in 2004 Entry Draft).

			Regular Season								Playoffs						
Season	Club	League	GP	W	L	O/T	Mins	GA	SO	Avg	GP	W	L	Mins	GA	SO	Avg
2000-01	Karpat Oulu Jr.	Fin-Jr.	20	9	4	5	1148	63	0	3.29	....	....	....	....	....	....	....
2001-02	Karpat Oulu Jr.	Fin-Jr.	30	19	7	3	1724	61	3	2.12	3	1	2	184	10	1	3.26
2002-03	Karpat Oulu Jr.	Fin-Jr.	25	14	8	3	1479	48	5	1.95	4	1	3	238	7	0	1.76
	Karpat Oulu	Finland	1	0	1	0	60	7	0	7.00	....	....	....	....	....	....	....
2003-04	Karpat Oulu	Finland	14	5	4	4	824	41	0	2.99	2	1	0	22	0	0	0.00
	Hokki Kajaani	Finland-2	8	5	2	1	463	16	2	2.07	....	....	....	....	....	....	....
2004-05	Karpat Oulu	Finland	10	8	0	1	571	16	0	1.68	....	....	....	....	....	....	....
2005-06	**Nashville**	**NHL**	**2**	**1**	**1**	**0**	**63**	**4**	**0**	**3.81**	....	....	....	....	....	....	....
	Milwaukee	AHL	51	30	18	2	2960	139	2	2.82	14	10	4	734	35	3	2.86
2006-07	Milwaukee	AHL	29	15	7	6	1670	65	3	2.34	4	0	4	247	12	0	2.91
2007-08	**Nashville**	**NHL**	**1**	**0**	**0**	**0**	**29**	**0**	**0**	**0.00**	....	....	....	....	....	....	....
	Milwaukee	AHL	*65	*36	24	3	*3840	158	5	2.47	6	2	4	358	15	1	2.51
	NHL Totals		**3**	**1**	**1**	**0**	**92**	**4**	**0**	**2.61**	....	....	....	....	....	....	....

ROLLHEISER, Grant (rohl-HIGH-zuhr, GRANT) TOR.

Goaltender. Catches left. 6'4", 195 lbs. Born, Chilliwak, B.C., July 24, 1989.
(Toronto's 7th choice, 158th overall, in 2008 Entry Draft).

			Regular Season								Playoffs						
Season	Club	League	GP	W	L	O/T	Mins	GA	SO	Avg	GP	W	L	Mins	GA	SO	Avg
2006-07	Nelson Leafs	KIJHL	35	25	8	0	1990	110	2	3.32	15	9	6	907	35	2	2.31
2007-08	Trail Smoke Eaters	BCHL	46	19	26	0	2557	136	2	3.19	3	0	3	159	13	0	4.90

• Signed Letter of Intent to attend **Boston University** (Hockey East) in fall of 2008.

ROLOSON, Dwayne (ROH-loh-suhn, DWAYN) EDM.

Goaltender. Catches left. 6'1", 180 lbs. Born, Simcoe, Ont., October 12, 1969.

			Regular Season								Playoffs						
Season	Club	League	GP	W	L	O/T	Mins	GA	SO	Avg	GP	W	L	Mins	GA	SO	Avg
1984-85	Simcoe Penguins	OJHL-C	3	....	....	....	100	21	0	12.60	....	....	....	....	....	....	....
1985-86	Simcoe Rams	OJHL-C	1	....	....	....	60	6	0	6.00	....	....	....	....	....	....	....
1986-87	Norwich	OJHL-C	19	....	....	....	1091	55	0	*3.03	....	....	....	....	....	....	....
1987-88	Belleville Bobcats	OJHL-B	21	9	6	1	1070	60	*2	3.36	....	....	....	....	....	....	....
1988-89	Thorold	OJHL-B	27	15	6	4	1490	82	0	3.30	....	....	....	....	....	....	....
1989-90	Thorold	OHA-B	30	18	8	1	1683	108	0	3.85	....	....	....	....	....	....	....
1990-91	U. Mass-Lowell	H-East	15	5	9	0	823	63	0	4.59	....	....	....	....	....	....	....
1991-92	U. Mass-Lowell	H-East	12	3	8	0	660	52	0	4.73	....	....	....	....	....	....	....
1992-93	U. Mass-Lowell	H-East	*39	20	17	2	*2342	150	0	3.84	....	....	....	....	....	....	....
1993-94	U. Mass-Lowell	H-East	*40	*23	10	7	*2305	106	0	2.76	....	....	....	....	....	....	....
1994-95	Saint John Flames	AHL	46	16	21	8	2734	156	1	3.42	5	1	4	298	13	0	2.61
1995-96	Saint John Flames	AHL	67	*33	22	11	4026	190	1	2.83	16	10	6	1027	49	1	2.86
1996-97	**Calgary**	**NHL**	**31**	**9**	**14**	**3**	**1618**	**78**	**1**	**2.89**	....	....	....	....	....	....	....
	Saint John Flames	AHL	8	6	2	0	481	22	1	2.75	....	....	....	....	....	....	....
1997-98	**Calgary**	**NHL**	**39**	**11**	**16**	**8**	**2205**	**110**	**0**	**2.99**	....	....	....	....	....	....	....
	Saint John Flames	AHL	4	3	0	1	245	8	0	1.96	....	....	....	....	....	....	....
1998-99	**Buffalo**	**NHL**	**18**	**6**	**8**	**2**	**911**	**42**	**1**	**2.77**	**4**	**1**	**1**	**139**	**10**	**0**	**4.32**
	Rochester	AHL	2	2	0	0	120	4	0	2.00	....	....	....	....	....	....	....
99-2000	**Buffalo**	**NHL**	**14**	**1**	**7**	**3**	**677**	**32**	**0**	**2.84**	....	....	....	....	....	....	....
2000-01	Worcester IceCats	AHL	52	*32	15	5	*3127	113	*6	*2.17	11	6	5	697	23	1	1.98
2001-02	**Minnesota**	**NHL**	**45**	**14**	**20**	**7**	**2506**	**112**	**5**	**2.68**	....	....	....	....	....	....	....
2002-03	**Minnesota**	**NHL**	**50**	**23**	**16**	**8**	**2945**	**98**	**4**	**2.00**	**11**	**5**	**6**	**579**	**25**	**0**	**2.59**
2003-04	**Minnesota**	**NHL**	**48**	**19**	**18**	**11**	**2847**	**89**	**5**	**1.88**	....	....	....	....	....	....	....
2004-05	Lukko Rauma	Finland	34	20	10	4	2048	70	4	2.05	9	4	5	512	18	2	2.11
2005-06	**Minnesota**	**NHL**	**24**	**6**	**17**	**1**	**1361**	**68**	**1**	**3.00**	....	....	....	....	....	....	....
	Edmonton	**NHL**	**19**	**8**	**7**	**4**	**1163**	**47**	**1**	**2.42**	**18**	**12**	**5**	**1160**	**45**	**1**	**2.33**
2006-07	**Edmonton**	**NHL**	**68**	**27**	**34**	**6**	**3932**	**180**	**4**	**2.75**	....	....	....	....	....	....	....
2007-08	**Edmonton**	**NHL**	**43**	**15**	**17**	**5**	**2340**	**119**	**0**	**3.05**	....	....	....	....	....	....	....
	NHL Totals		**399**	**139**	**174**	**58**	**22505**	**975**	**22**	**2.60**	**33**	**18**	**12**	**1878**	**80**	**1**	**2.56**

Hockey East First All-Star Team (1994) • Hockey East Player of the Year (1994) • NCAA East First All-American Team (1994) • AHL First All-Star Team (2001) • Aldege "Baz" Bastien Memorial Award (Outstanding Goaltender – AHL) (2001) • MBNA/Mastercard Roger Crozier Saving Grace Award (2004)

Played in NHL All-Star Game (2004)

Signed as a free agent by **Calgary**, July 4, 1994. Signed as a free agent by **Buffalo**, July 15, 1998. Claimed by **Columbus** from **Buffalo** in Expansion Draft, June 23, 2000. Signed as a free agent by **St. Louis**, July 14, 2000. Signed as a free agent by **Minnesota**, July 2, 2001. Signed as a free agent by **Rauma** (Finland), October 18, 2004. Traded to **Edmonton** by **Minnesota** for Edmonton's 1st round choice (later traded to Los Angeles - Los Angeles selected Trevor Lewis) in 2006 Entry Draft and Edmonton's 3rd round chocie (later traded to Atlanta - Atlanta selected Spencer Machacek) in 2007 Entry Draft, March 8, 2006.

ROWAT, Linden (ROH-wat, LIHND-dehn) L.A.

Goaltender. Catches left. 6'1", 177 lbs. Born, Cochrane, Alta., June 27, 1989.
(Los Angeles' 7th choice, 124th overall, in 2007 Entry Draft).

			Regular Season								Playoffs						
Season	Club	League	GP	W	L	O/T	Mins	GA	SO	Avg	GP	W	L	Mins	GA	SO	Avg
2005-06	Regina Pats	WHL	26	8	9	2	1248	65	1	3.13	....	....	....	....	....	....	....
2006-07	Regina Pats	WHL	52	25	18	7	2948	141	4	2.87	10	4	6	624	33	1	3.17
2007-08	Regina Pats	WHL	57	33	15	0	3244	145	3	2.68	6	2	4	345	21	0	3.65

WHL East First All-Star Team (2008)

SABOURIN, Dany (SA-boo-rihn, DA-nee) PIT.

Goaltender. Catches left. 6'4", 200 lbs. Born, Val-d'Or, Que., September 2, 1980.
(Calgary's 5th choice, 108th overall, in 1998 Entry Draft).

			Regular Season								Playoffs						
Season	Club	League	GP	W	L	O/T	Mins	GA	SO	Avg	GP	W	L	Mins	GA	SO	Avg
1996-97	Amos Forestiers	QAAA	24	6	16	0	1440	107	0	4.48	....	....	....	....	....	....	....
1997-98	Sherbrooke	QMJHL	37	15	15	2	1906	128	1	4.03	....	....	....	....	....	....	....
1998-99	Sherbrooke	QMJHL	30	8	13	2	1477	102	1	4.14	1	0	1	49	2	0	2.45
	Saint John Flames	AHL	....	....	....	....	....	....	....	....	1	0	1	57	4	0	4.19
99-2000	Sherbrooke	QMJHL	55	25	22	5	3067	181	1	3.54	5	1	4	324	18	0	3.33
2000-01	Saint John Flames	AHL	1	1	0	0	40	0	0	0.00	....	....	....	....	....	....	....
	Johnstown Chiefs	ECHL	19	4	9	1	903	56	0	3.72	1	0	0	40	2	0	3.00
2001-02	Johnstown Chiefs	ECHL	27	14	10	1	1539	84	0	3.28	3	0	2	137	5	0	2.18
2002-03	Saint John Flames	AHL	41	15	17	4	2220	100	4	2.70	....	....	....	....	....	....	....
2003-04	**Calgary**	**NHL**	**4**	**0**	**3**	**0**	**169**	**10**	**0**	**3.55**	....	....	....	....	....	....	....
	Lowell	AHL	14	5	7	2	821	39	0	2.85	....	....	....	....	....	....	....
	Las Vegas	ECHL	10	6	3	1	613	24	0	2.35	1	0	1	58	2	0	2.07
2004-05	Wilkes-Barre	AHL	20	8	8	2	1029	38	1	2.22	....	....	....	....	....	....	....
	Wheeling Nailers	ECHL	27	19	6	1	1579	44	5	*1.67	....	....	....	....	....	....	....
2005-06	**Pittsburgh**	**NHL**	**1**	**0**	**1**	**0**	**21**	**4**	**0**	**11.43**	....	....	....	....	....	....	....
	Wilkes-Barre	AHL	49	30	14	4	2943	111	4	*2.26	6	2	4	362	13	1	2.15
2006-07	**Vancouver**	**NHL**	**9**	**2**	**4**	**1**	**480**	**21**	**0**	**2.63**	**2**	**0**	**0**	**14**	**1**	**0**	**4.29**
	Manitoba Moose	AHL	2	1	1	0	119	4	1	2.01	....	....	....	....	....	....	....
2007-08	**Pittsburgh**	**NHL**	**24**	**10**	**9**	**1**	**1242**	**57**	**2**	**2.75**	....	....	....	....	....	....	....
	NHL Totals		**38**	**12**	**17**	**2**	**1912**	**92**	**2**	**2.89**	**2**	**0**	**0**	**14**	**1**	**0**	**4.29**

AHL First All-Star Team (2006) • Aldege "Baz" Bastien Memorial Award (Outstanding Goaltender – AHL) (2006)

Signed as a free agent by **Pittsburgh**, August 10, 2005. Claimed on waivers by **Vancouver** from **Pittsburgh**, October 4, 2006. Signed as a free agent by **Pittsburgh**, July 1, 2007.

SANFORD, Curtis (SAN-fohrd, KUHR-this) VAN.

Goaltender. Catches left. 5'10", 187 lbs. Born, Owen Sound, Ont., October 5, 1979.

			Regular Season								Playoffs						
Season	Club	League	GP	W	L	O/T	Mins	GA	SO	Avg	GP	W	L	Mins	GA	SO	Avg
1994-95	Wiarton Wolves	OJHL-C	18	....	....	....	949	98	0	6.20	....	....	....	....	....	....	....
1995-96	Collingwood	OJHL	21	....	....	....	2128	74	0	3.54	....	....	....	....	....	....	....
1996-97	Owen Sound	OHL	19	4	8	1	847	77	0	5.45	....	....	....	....	....	....	....
	Owen Sound	OJHL-B	6	....	....	....	360	28	0	4.68	....	....	....	....	....	....	....
1997-98	Owen Sound	OHL	30	13	10	2	1542	114	1	4.44	9	4	4	456	30	1	3.95
1998-99	Owen Sound	OHL	56	30	16	5	2998	191	2	3.82	16	9	7	960	58	0	3.63
99-2000	Owen Sound	OHL	53	18	26	6	3124	198	1	3.80	....	....	....	....	....	....	....
	Missouri	UHL	6	3	1	0	237	6	0	1.52	....	....	....	....	....	....	....
2000-01	Worcester IceCats	AHL	5	3	0	1	237	16	0	4.06	....	....	....	....	....	....	....
	Peoria Rivermen	ECHL	27	15	7	4	1511	48	3	*1.91	14	9	4	813	28	*2	2.07
2001-02	Worcester IceCats	AHL	9	5	4	0	537	22	0	2.46	....	....	....	....	....	....	....
	Peoria Rivermen	ECHL	24	13	8	2	1418	58	1	2.45	....	....	....	....	....	....	....
2002-03	**St. Louis**	**NHL**	**8**	**5**	**1**	**0**	**397**	**13**	**1**	**1.96**	....	....	....	....	....	....	....
	Worcester IceCats	AHL	41	18	14	8	2317	93	3	2.41	3	0	3	179	8	0	2.68
2003-04	Worcester IceCats	AHL	43	20	16	3	2367	84	5	2.13	9	4	5	569	24	0	2.53
2004-05	Worcester IceCats	AHL	50	19	25	2	2743	123	2	2.69	....	....	....	....	....	....	....
2005-06	**St. Louis**	**NHL**	**34**	**13**	**13**	**5**	**1830**	**81**	**3**	**2.66**	....	....	....	....	....	....	....
	Peoria Rivermen	AHL	6	4	2	0	358	11	2	1.84	....	....	....	....	....	....	....
2006-07	**St. Louis**	**NHL**	**31**	**8**	**12**	**5**	**1492**	**79**	**0**	**3.18**	....	....	....	....	....	....	....
	Peoria Rivermen	AHL	2	1	1	0	119	5	0	2.52	....	....	....	....	....	....	....
2007-08	**Vancouver**	**NHL**	**16**	**4**	**3**	**1**	**679**	**32**	**0**	**2.83**	....	....	....	....	....	....	....
	NHL Totals		**89**	**30**	**29**	**11**	**4398**	**205**	**4**	**2.80**	....	....	....	....	....	....	....

ECHL Second All-Star Team (2001)

Signed as a free agent by **St. Louis**, October 1, 2000. Signed as a free agent by **Vancouver**, July 2, 2007.

SATERI, Harri (SA-teh-ree, HAR-ree) S.J.

Goaltender. Catches left. 6'1", 190 lbs. Born, Toijala, Finland, December 29, 1989.
(San Jose's 3rd choice, 106th overall, in 2008 Entry Draft).

			Regular Season								Playoffs						
Season	Club	League	GP	W	L	O/T	Mins	GA	SO	Avg	GP	W	L	Mins	GA	SO	Avg
2005-06	HPK U18	Fin-U18	27	....	....	....	1515	66	5	2.61	2	....	....	118	10	0	5.08
	HPK Jr.	Fin-Jr.	1	....	....	....	50	3	0	3.60	....	....	....	....	....	....	....
2006-07	Tappara U18	Fin-U18	2	....	....	....	119	4	0	2.02	....	....	....	....	....	....	....
	Tappara Jr.	Fin-Jr.	23	....	....	....	1346	59	2	2.63	10	....	....	614	31	0	3.03
2007-08	Tappara Jr.	Fin-Jr.	34	13	17	0	2048	102	1	2.99	3	0	3	178	8	0	2.70

SAUER, Billy (SAW-uhr, BIHL-lee) COL.

Goaltender. Catches left. 6'2", 180 lbs. Born, Rochester, NY, January 6, 1988.
(Colorado's 5th choice, 201st overall, in 2006 Entry Draft).

			Regular Season								Playoffs						
Season	Club	League	GP	W	L	O/T	Mins	GA	SO	Avg	GP	W	L	Mins	GA	SO	Avg
2004-05	Chicago Steel	USHL	30	12	12	2	1592	81	2	3.05	....	....	....	....	....	....	....
2005-06	U. of Michigan	CCHA	23	11	6	4	1281	65	1	3.04	....	....	....	....	....	....	....
2006-07	U. of Michigan	CCHA	40	25	14	1	2354	119	1	3.03	....	....	....	....	....	....	....
2007-08	U. of Michigan	CCHA	38	30	4	3	2272	74	*4	1.95	....	....	....	....	....	....	....

SAUVE, Philippe (SOH-vay, fihl-EEP)

Goaltender. Catches left. 6', 188 lbs. Born, Buffalo, NY, February 27, 1980.
(Colorado's 6th choice, 38th overall, in 1998 Entry Draft).

			Regular Season								Playoffs						
Season	Club	League	GP	W	L	O/T	Mins	GA	SO	Avg	GP	W	L	Mins	GA	SO	Avg
1995-96	Laval-Laurentides	QAAA	25	9	10	0	1184	87	1	4.11	15	7	8	900	54	0	3.58
1996-97	Rimouski Oceanic	QMJHL	26	11	9	2	1334	84	0	3.78	1	0	0	14	3	0	12.90
1997-98	Rimouski Oceanic	QMJHL	40	23	16	0	2326	131	1	3.38	7	0	5	262	33	0	7.55
1998-99	Rimouski Oceanic	QMJHL	44	16	19	4	2401	155	0	3.87	11	6	4	595	30	*1	3.03
99-2000	Drummondville	QMJHL	28	12	12	2	1526	106	0	4.17	....	....	....	....	....	....	....
	Hull Olympiques	QMJHL	17	9	7	1	992	57	0	3.45	12	6	6	735	47	0	3.84
2000-01	Hershey Bears	AHL	42	17	18	1	2182	100	3	2.75	3	0	3	218	10	0	2.75
2001-02	Hershey Bears	AHL	55	25	20	6	3130	111	6	2.13	8	3	5	486	21	0	2.59
2002-03	Hershey Bears	AHL	*60	26	20	12	3394	134	5	2.37	5	2	3	295	14	0	2.85
2003-04	**Colorado**	**NHL**	**17**	**7**	**7**	**3**	**986**	**50**	**0**	**3.04**	....	....	....	....	....	....	....
	Hershey Bears	AHL	10	3	7	0	578	25	2	2.59	....	....	....	....	....	....	....
2004-05	Mississippi	ECHL	21	13	4	4	1298	56	2	2.59	4	1	3	227	16	0	4.23
2005-06	**Calgary**	**NHL**	**8**	**3**	**3**	**0**	**402**	**22**	**0**	**3.28**	....	....	....	....	....	....	....
	Phoenix	**NHL**	**5**	**0**	**4**	**0**	**187**	**17**	**0**	**5.45**	....	....	....	....	....	....	....
2006-07	San Antonio	AHL	10	4	5	0	536	34	0	3.80	....	....	....	....	....	....	....
	Boston	**NHL**	**2**	**0**	**0**	**0**	**41**	**4**	**0**	**5.85**	....	....	....	....	....	....	....
	Providence Bruins	AHL	23	10	11	1	1292	61	1	2.83	....	....	....	....	....	....	....
	Hamilton Bulldogs	AHL	6	2	3	0	325	13	1	2.40	....	....	....	....	....	....	....
2007-08	Iowa Stars	AHL	12	5	5	0	550	39	0	4.25	....	....	....	....	....	....	....
	Hamburg Freezers	Germany	13	9	4	0	783	38	0	2.91	7	3	4	382	30	0	4.71
	NHL Totals		**32**	**10**	**14**	**3**	**1616**	**93**	**0**	**3.45**	....	....	....	....	....	....	....

Canadian Major Junior Humanitarian Player of the Year (1999)

Signed as a free agent by **Mississippi** (ECHL), January 27, 2005. Traded to **Calgary** by **Colorado** for future considerations, August 9, 2005. Traded to **Phoenix** by **Calgary** with Steve Reinprecht for Brian Boucher and Mike Leclerc, February 2, 2006. Traded to **Boston** by **Phoenix** for Tyler Redenbach, November 14, 2006. Signed as a free agent by **Hamburg** (Germany), January 22, 2008.

SCHAEFER, Nolan (SHAY-fuhr, NOH-luhn) MIN.

Goaltender. Catches right. 6'2", 195 lbs. Born, Yellow Grass, Sask., January 15, 1980.
(San Jose's 4th choice, 166th overall, in 2000 Entry Draft).

			Regular Season								Playoffs						
Season	Club	League	GP	W	L	O/T	Mins	GA	SO	Avg	GP	W	L	Mins	GA	SO	Avg
1996-97	Yorkton Mallers	SMHL	36	....	....	....	1854	132	0	4.27	....	....	....	....	....	....	....
1997-98	Yorkton Mallers	SMHL	5	....	....	....	239	17	0	4.25	....	....	....	....	....	....	....
	Nipawin Hawks	SJHL	21	12	4	3	1080	42	*3	*2.33	....	....	....	....	....	....	....
1998-99	Nipawin Hawks	SJHL	46	....	....	....	2478	165	0	3.60	....	....	....	....	....	....	....
99-2000	Providence College	H-East	14	6	5	1	778	42	0	3.24	....	....	....	....	....	....	....
2000-01	Providence College	H-East	25	15	8	2	1529	63	3	2.47	....	....	....	....	....	....	....
2001-02	Providence College	H-East	*35	11	18	5	*2062	113	0	3.29	....	....	....	....	....	....	....
2002-03	Providence College	H-East	25	13	8	2	1440	71	0	2.96	....	....	....	....	....	....	....
2003-04	Cleveland Barons	AHL	27	14	9	3	1592	62	2	2.34	9	4	5	573	24	0	2.51
	Fresno Falcons	ECHL	12	5	5	0	654	34	1	3.12	....	....	....	....	....	....	....
2004-05	Cleveland Barons	AHL	43	17	23	1	2418	110	3	2.73	....	....	....	....	....	....	....
2005-06	**San Jose**	**NHL**	**7**	**5**	**1**	**0**	**352**	**11**	**1**	**1.88**	....	....	....	....	....	....	....
	Cleveland Barons	AHL	36	12	21	2	2058	118	2	3.44	....	....	....	....	....	....	....
2006-07	Worcester Sharks	AHL	16	5	8	3	921	43	0	2.80	....	....	....	....	....	....	....
	Hershey Bears	AHL	3	0	3	0	162	10	0	3.70	....	....	....	....	....	....	....
	Wilkes-Barre	AHL	15	9	5	0	804	30	1	2.24	11	5	6	699	32	0	2.75
2007-08	Houston Aeros	AHL	34	19	13	0	1980	68	6	*2.06	2	0	2	117	4	0	2.05
	NHL Totals		**7**	**5**	**1**	**0**	**352**	**11**	**1**	**1.88**	....	....	....	....	....	....	....

Hockey East Second All-Star Team (2001) • NCAA East Second All-American Team (2001)Harry "Hap" Holmes Memorial Award (fewest goals against – AHL) (2008) (shared with Barry Brust)

Traded to **Pittsburgh** by **San Jose** for Pittsburgh's 7th round choice (Justin Braun) in 2007 Entry Draft, February 27, 2007. Signed as a free agent by **Minnesota**, July 3, 2007.

SCHNEIDER, Cory (SHNIGH-duhr, KOHR-ee) VAN.

Goaltender. Catches left. 6'2", 202 lbs. Born, Marblehead, MA, March 18, 1986.
(Vancouver's 1st choice, 26th overall, in 2004 Entry Draft).

			Regular Season								Playoffs						
Season	Club	League	GP	W	L	O/T	Mins	GA	SO	Avg	GP	W	L	Mins	GA	SO	Avg
2002-03	Andover	High-MA	23	13	7	2	1385	39	3	1.69	....	....	....	....	....	....	....
2003-04	Andover	High-MA	24	17	5	2	1336	32	6	1.42	....	....	....	....	....	....	....
	USNTDP	U-18	10	9	1	0	559	15	1	1.61	....	....	....	....	....	....	....
	USNTDP	NAHL	2	2	0	0	120	6	0	3.00	....	....	....	....	....	....	....
2004-05	Boston College	H-East	18	13	1	4	1102	35	1	1.90	....	....	....	....	....	....	....
2005-06	Boston College	H-East	*39	*24	13	2	*2362	83	*8	2.11	....	....	....	....	....	....	....
2006-07	Boston College	H-East	*42	*29	12	1	*2517	90	6	2.15	....	....	....	....	....	....	....
2007-08	Manitoba Moose	AHL	36	21	12	2	2054	78	3	2.28	6	1	4	375	12	0	1.92

Hockey East All-Rookie Team (2005) (co-winners - Kevin Regan and Peter Vetri) • Hockey East Second All-Star Team (2006) • NCAA East First All-American Team (2006)

SCHWARZ, Marek (SHWAHRTS, MAIR-ehk) ST.L.

Goaltender. Catches right. 6', 180 lbs. Born, Mlada Boleslav, Czech., April 1, 1986.
(St. Louis' 1st choice, 17th overall, in 2004 Entry Draft).

			Regular Season								Playoffs						
Season	Club	League	GP	W	L	O/T	Mins	GA	SO	Avg	GP	W	L	Mins	GA	SO	Avg
2000-01	Ml. Boleslav Jr.	CzRep-Jr.	45	....	....	....	1969	154	0	4.69	....	....	....	....	....	....	....
2001-02	Sparta Jr.	CzRep-Jr.	46	....	....	....	2692	86	9	1.92	6	....	....	368	16	0	2.61
2002-03	Sparta Jr.	CzRep-Jr.	34	....	....	....	1778	57	3	1.92	2	....	....	120	5	0	2.50
	HC Sparta Praha	CzRep	1	....	....	....	1	0	0	0.00	....	....	....	....	....	....	....
2003-04	Sparta Jr.	CzRep-Jr.	7	....	....	....	352	14	2	2.39	....	....	....	....	....	....	....
	Plzen	CzRep	10	....	....	....	603	33	0	3.28	....	....	....	....	....	....	....
	HC Sparta Praha	CzRep	8	....	....	....	335	20	0	3.58	....	....	....	....	....	....	....
	HC Ocelari Trinec	CzRep	5	....	....	....	280	12	0	2.57	....	....	....	....	....	....	....
	BK Mlada Boleslav	CzRep-2	1	....	....	....	63	6	0	5.71	....	....	....	....	....	....	....
2004-05	Vancouver Giants	WHL	56	26	24	4	3304	147	2	2.67	6	2	4	378	18	0	2.86
2005-06	Sparta Jr.	CzRep-Jr.	3	....	....	....	178	5	0	1.69	....	....	....	....	....	....	....
	HC Sparta Praha	CzRep	15	....	....	....	746	32	1	2.57	1	....	....	1	0	0	0.00
	Beroun	CzRep-2	4	....	....	....	229	17	0	4.45	....	....	....	....	....	....	....
2006-07	**St. Louis**	**NHL**	**2**	**0**	**1**	**0**	**60**	**3**	**0**	**3.00**	....	....	....	....	....	....	....
	Peoria Rivermen	AHL	34	19	13	0	1912	88	1	2.76	....	....	....	....	....	....	....
2007-08	**St. Louis**	**NHL**	**2**	**0**	**1**	**0**	**50**	**6**	**0**	**7.20**	....	....	....	....	....	....	....
	Peoria Rivermen	AHL	33	14	14	2	1808	84	0	2.79	....	....	....	....	....	....	....
	Alaska Aces	ECHL	6	6	0	0	375	13	0	2.08	8	5	2	468	25	0	3.21
	NHL Totals		**4**	**0**	**2**	**0**	**110**	**9**	**0**	**4.91**	....	....	....	....	....	....	....

SEXSMITH, Tyson (SEHX-smihth, TIGH-suhn) S.J.

Goaltender. Catches left. 6', 204 lbs. Born, Calgary, Alta., March 19, 1989.
(San Jose's 4th choice, 91st overall, in 2007 Entry Draft).

			Regular Season								Playoffs						
Season	Club	League	GP	W	L	O/T	Mins	GA	SO	Avg	GP	W	L	Mins	GA	SO	Avg
2004-05	Olds Grizzlys	AJHL	STATISTICS NOT AVAILABLE														
	Medicine Hat	WHL	1	0	0	0	5	0	0	0.00	....	....	....	....	....	....	....
	Vancouver Giants	WHL	2	1	0	0	80	4	0	3.00	....	....	....	....	....	....	....
2005-06	Vancouver Giants	WHL	11	6	3	1	547	21	1	2.30	....	....	....	....	....	....	....
2006-07	Vancouver Giants	WHL	51	31	12	8	3047	91	10	*1.79	22	14	7	1339	40	*4	*1.79
2007-08	Vancouver Giants	WHL	62	43	11	0	3678	116	*9	*1.89	10	6	4	658	20	0	1.82

WHL West Second All-Star Team (2008)

SHANTZ, David (SHAWNTS, DAY-vihd) FLA.

Goaltender. Catches left. 6'1", 202 lbs. Born, Burlington, Ont., May 5, 1986.
(Florida's 2nd choice, 37th overall, in 2004 Entry Draft).

			Regular Season								Playoffs						
Season	Club	League	GP	W	L	O/T	Mins	GA	SO	Avg	GP	W	L	Mins	GA	SO	Avg
2002-03	Thorold	OJHL-B	36	30	3	3	2107	63	8	1.79	....	....	....	....	....	....	....
2003-04	Mississauga	OHL	43	21	18	3	2483	120	1	2.90	*24	12	12	*1449	49	*5	2.03
2004-05	Mississauga	OHL	27	10	11	3	1524	72	0	2.83	2	0	1	80	2	0	1.50
2005-06	Peterborough	OHL	49	31	14	3	2946	141	2	2.87	*19	*16	3	*1239	54	1	2.62
2006-07	Rochester	AHL	2	1	1	0	120	9	0	4.51	....	....	....	....	....	....	....
	Florida Everblades	ECHL	23	13	7	1	1338	66	0	2.96	1	0	0	20	1	0	3.00
2007-08	Rochester	AHL	14	1	10	1	780	53	0	4.07	....	....	....	....	....	....	....
	Florida Everblades	ECHL	20	11	5	3	1101	47	0	2.56	2	0	1	77	3	0	2.33

OHL All-Rookie Team (2004) • Canadian Major Junior All-Rookie Team (2004)

SIGALET, Jordan
(SIH-ga-leht, JOHR-dahn)

Goaltender. Catches left. 6'1", 180 lbs. Born, New Westminster, B.C., February 19, 1981.
(Boston's 6th choice, 209th overall, in 2001 Entry Draft).

			Regular Season								Playoffs						
Season	Club	League	GP	W	L	O/T	Mins	GA	SO	Avg	GP	W	L	Mins	GA	SO	Avg
99-2000	Victoria Salsa	BCHL	33				1980	108	0	3.28							
2000-01	Victoria Salsa	BCHL	48	23	22	0	2820	142	0	3.03	18	12	5	1060	143	0	2.62
2001-02	Bowling Green	CCHA	13	2	6	2	657	38	0	3.47							
2002-03	Bowling Green	CCHA	20	6	11	2	1208	66	1	3.28							
2003-04	Bowling Green	CCHA	37	10	17	9	2210	101	2	2.74							
2004-05	Bowling Green	CCHA	32	16	12	3	1849	89	1	2.89							
2005-06	**Boston**	**NHL**	**1**	**0**	**0**	**0**	**1**	**0**	**0**	**0.00**							
	Providence Bruins	AHL	37	19	11	2	1955	83	1	2.55	3	0	2	159	10	0	3.77
2006-07	Providence Bruins	AHL	25	15	5	2	1332	53	3	2.39	2	0	0	32	0	0	0.00
2007-08	Providence Bruins	AHL	19	12	5	1	1049	44	0	2.52	2	0	0	21	0	0	0.00
	NHL Totals		**1**	**0**	**0**	**0**	**1**	**0**	**0**	**0.00**							

CCHA First All-Star Team (2004) • CCHA Second All-Star Team (2005) • Fred T. Hunt Memorial Award (Sportsmanship – AHL) (2008)

SMITH, Jason
(SMIHTH, JAY-suhn) **N.J.**

Goaltender. Catches left. 6'1", 195 lbs. Born, St-Lambert, Que., July 17, 1985.
(New Jersey's 5th choice, 197th overall, in 2003 Entry Draft).

			Regular Season								Playoffs						
Season	Club	League	GP	W	L	O/T	Mins	GA	SO	Avg	GP	W	L	Mins	GA	SO	Avg
2002-03	Lennoxville	QJHL	29	22	4	1	1622	62	3	2.29	14	11	3	816	34	1	2.52
2003-04	Sacred Heart	AH	5	1	4	0	302	19	0	3.78							
2004-05	Sacred Heart	AH	8	3	5	0	493	31	0	3.77							
2005-06	Sacred Heart	AH	30	18	11	1	1793	67	1	*2.24							
2006-07	Sacred Heart	AH	28	16	9	3	1703	79	1	2.78							
2007-08	Trenton Devils	ECHL	35	13	18	3	2071	108	2	3.13							

AH First All-Star Team (2007)

SMITH, Jeremy
(SMIHTH, JAIR-eh-mee) **NSH.**

Goaltender. Catches left. 6', 168 lbs. Born, Dearborn, MI, April 13, 1989.
(Nashville's 2nd choice, 54th overall, in 2007 Entry Draft).

			Regular Season								Playoffs						
Season	Club	League	GP	W	L	O/T	Mins	GA	SO	Avg	GP	W	L	Mins	GA	SO	Avg
2005-06	Det. Compuware	MWEHL	13	5	6	0	696	31	0	2.67							
	Det. Compuware	Exhib.	3	2	1	0	178	8	0	2.70							
	Plymouth Whalers	OHL	5	0	2	0	111	11	0	5.95							
2006-07	Plymouth Whalers	OHL	34	23	6	1	1901	82	4	2.59	3	2	0	149	8	0	3.22
2007-08	Plymouth Whalers	OHL	40	23	13	4	2431	116	3	2.86	4	0	4	224	29	0	7.77

SMITH, Mike
(SMIHTH, MIGHK) **T.B.**

Goaltender. Catches left. 6'3", 211 lbs. Born, Kingston, Ont., March 22, 1982.
(Dallas' 5th choice, 161st overall, in 2001 Entry Draft).

			Regular Season								Playoffs						
Season	Club	League	GP	W	L	O/T	Mins	GA	SO	Avg	GP	W	L	Mins	GA	SO	Avg
1998-99	Kingston	OPJHL	16				905	53	0	3.51							
99-2000	Kingston	OHL	15	4	5	0	666	42	0	3.78							
2000-01	Kingston	OHL	3	0	0	2	136	8	0	3.53							
	Sudbury Wolves	OHL	43	22	13	7	2571	108	3	2.52	12	7	5	735	26	2	*2.12
2001-02	Sudbury Wolves	OHL	53	19	28	5	3082	157	3	3.06	5	1	4	302	15	0	2.98
2002-03	Lexington	ECHL	27	11	10	4	1553	66	1	2.55	2	0	1	93	8	0	5.14
	Utah Grizzlies	AHL	11	5	5	0	614	33	0	3.23							
2003-04	Utah Grizzlies	AHL	21	8	11	0	1186	56	2	2.83							
2004-05	Houston Aeros	AHL	45	19	17	3	2408	97	5	2.42	3	1	2	181	4	0	1.33
2005-06	Iowa Stars	AHL	50	25	19	6	2998	125	3	2.50	7	3	4	417	19	0	2.74
2006-07	**Dallas**	**NHL**	**23**	**12**	**5**	**2**	**1213**	**45**	**3**	**2.23**							
2007-08	**Dallas**	**NHL**	**21**	**12**	**9**	**0**	**1172**	**48**	**2**	**2.46**							
	Tampa Bay	**NHL**	**13**	**3**	**10**	**0**	**774**	**36**	**1**	**2.79**							
	NHL Totals		**57**	**27**	**24**	**2**	**3159**	**129**	**6**	**2.45**							

NHL All-Rookie Team (2007)

Traded to **Tampa Bay** by **Dallas** with Jussi Jokinen, Jeff Halpern and Dallas' 4th round choice in 2009 Entry Draft for Brad Richards and Johan Holmqvist, February 26, 2008.

SPRATT, James
(SPRAT, JAYMZ) **CGY.**

Goaltender. Catches left. 6'1", 185 lbs. Born, Detroit, MI, November 10, 1985.
(Calgary's 9th choice, 213th overall, in 2004 Entry Draft).

			Regular Season								Playoffs						
Season	Club	League	GP	W	L	O/T	Mins	GA	SO	Avg	GP	W	L	Mins	GA	SO	Avg
2002-03	Sioux City	USHL	18	6	6	2	905	49	0	3.25							
2003-04	Sioux City	USHL	34	19	6	5	1922	75	3	2.34	7	4	3	468	19	0	2.44
2004-05	Sioux City	USHL	42	24	11	3	2328	109	2	2.81	*13	*8	5	*752	32	*1	2.55
2005-06	Bowling Green	CCHA	16	4	10	1	923	67	0	4.36							
2006-07	Bowling Green	CCHA	31	6	22	1	1730	105	0	3.64							
2007-08	Bowling Green	CCHA	19	6	11	0	1052	54	0	3.08							

STALOCK, Alex
(STAY-lahk, AL-ehx) **S.J.**

Goaltender. Catches left. 5'11", 170 lbs. Born, St. Paul, MN, July 28, 1987.
(San Jose's 3rd choice, 112th overall, in 2005 Entry Draft).

			Regular Season								Playoffs						
Season	Club	League	GP	W	L	O/T	Mins	GA	SO	Avg	GP	W	L	Mins	GA	SO	Avg
2003-04	South St. Paul	High-MN	31	23	7	1				2.20							
2004-05	Cedar Rapids	USHL	32	19	9	3	1801	82	1	2.73	9	7	2	582	14	*1	*1.44
2005-06	Cedar Rapids	USHL	44	*28	13	3	2641	112	4	2.54	8	3	5	472	25	0	3.18
2006-07	U. Minn-Duluth	WCHA	23	5	14	3	1364	76	1	3.34							
2007-08	U. Minn-Duluth	WCHA	36	13	17	6	2170	85	3	2.35							

USHL Playoff MVP (2005) • USHL First All-Star Team (2006) • WCHA All-Rookie Team (2007)

STEFANISZIN, Sebastian
(steh-fan-IHSH-ihn, suh-BAS-tee-yeh **ANA.**

Goaltender. Catches left. 6', 190 lbs. Born, Berlin, East Germany, July 22, 1987.
(Anaheim's 6th choice, 98th overall, in 2007 Entry Draft).

			Regular Season								Playoffs						
Season	Club	League	GP	W	L	O/T	Mins	GA	SO	Avg	GP	W	L	Mins	GA	SO	Avg
2002-03	Eisb. Jrs. Berl. Jr.	Ger-Jr.	12														
2003-04	Eisb. Jrs. Berl. Jr.	Ger-Jr.	23							2.87	3						5.45
2004-05	Eisb. Jrs. Berlin	German-3	4				183	10	1	3.28							
	Eisb. Jrs. Berl. Jr.	Ger-Jr.	20				1048	55	1	3.15	4			240	21	0	5.25
2005-06	Eisbaren Berlin	Germany	3				175	11	0	3.77							
	Eisb. Jrs. Berlin	German-3	16				818	57	0	4.18							
	Hamburg Freezers	Germany	4				240	8	0	2.00							
2006-07	Eisbaren Berlin	Germany	2				39	3	0	4.59							
	Eisb. Jrs. Berlin	German-3	36				2005	130	1	3.89	2			120	11	0	5.50
2007-08	Essen	German-2	10	0	5	0	492	37	0	4.51							
	Iserlohn Roosters	Germany	9	1	6	0	467	35	0	4.50							

STEPHAN, Tobias
(STEH-fan, toh-BUY-uhs) **DAL.**

Goaltender. Catches left. 6'2", 180 lbs. Born, Zurich, Switz., January 21, 1984.
(Dallas' 3rd choice, 34th overall, in 2002 Entry Draft).

			Regular Season								Playoffs						
Season	Club	League	GP	W	L	O/T	Mins	GA	SO	Avg	GP	W	L	Mins	GA	SO	Avg
2000-01	Kloten Flyers Jr.	Swiss-Jr.	STATISTICS NOT AVAILABLE														
2001-02	EHC Chur	Swiss	23				1396	80	0	3.44	10			604	39	0	3.87
2002-03	Kloten Flyers	Swiss	*44				2670	125	2	2.81	5			292	20	0	4.11
2003-04	Kloten Flyers	Swiss	26				1547	61	5	2.37							
2004-05	Kloten Flyers	Swiss	*44				2580	123	4	2.86	5			301	11	0	2.19
2005-06	Kloten Flyers	Swiss	*44	16	19	8	2663	125	*5	2.82	11	5	6	683	34	0	2.98
2006-07	Iowa Stars	AHL	27	10	15	0	1396	67	1	2.88	2	0	0	52	3	0	3.46
2007-08	**Dallas**	**NHL**	**1**	**0**	**0**	**1**	**61**	**2**	**0**	**1.97**							
	Iowa Stars	AHL	60	27	25	2	3329	147	6	2.65							
	NHL Totals		**1**	**0**	**0**	**1**	**61**	**2**	**0**	**1.97**							

TAYLOR, Daniel
(TAY-luhr, DAN-yehl) **L.A.**

Goaltender. Catches left. 5'11", 179 lbs. Born, Plymouth, England, April 28, 1986.
(Los Angeles' 8th choice, 221st overall, in 2004 Entry Draft).

			Regular Season								Playoffs						
Season	Club	League	GP	W	L	O/T	Mins	GA	SO	Avg	GP	W	L	Mins	GA	SO	Avg
2002-03	Cumberland Grads	CJHL	23	13	3	1	1009	41	1	2.44	6	3	3	432	17	0	2.36
2003-04	Guelph Storm	OHL	26	16	4	3	1462	66	0	2.71	3	1	1	159	9	0	3.40
2004-05	Guelph Storm	OHL	31	13	14	3	1821	80	2	2.64	1	0	1	59	4	0	4.07
2005-06	Kingston	OHL	57	32	15	6	3319	172	3	3.11							
2006-07	Bakersfield	ECHL	17	7	7	2	969	70	0	4.33							
	Wheeling Nailers	ECHL	1	0	0	1	62	4	0	3.86							
	Texas Wildcatters	ECHL	2	0	1	0	74	2	0	1.61							
2007-08	**Los Angeles**	**NHL**	**1**	**0**	**0**	**0**	**20**	**2**	**0**	**6.00**							
	Manchester	AHL	23	13	5	2	1275	51	4	2.40							
	Reading Royals	ECHL	5	3	0	0	182	8	0	2.63	13	7	6	815	38	1	2.80
	NHL Totals		**1**	**0**	**0**	**0**	**20**	**2**	**0**	**6.00**							

TELLQVIST, Mikael
(TEHL-kvihst, MIGH-kuhl) **PHX.**

Goaltender. Catches left. 5'11", 185 lbs. Born, Sundbyberg, Sweden, September 19, 1979.
(Toronto's 3rd choice, 70th overall, in 2000 Entry Draft).

			Regular Season								Playoffs						
Season	Club	League	GP	W	L	O/T	Mins	GA	SO	Avg	GP	W	L	Mins	GA	SO	Avg
1997-98	Djurgarden Jr.	Swe-Jr.	23				1380	55		2.39	2	0	2	120	8	0	4.00
1998-99	Djurgarden	Sweden	3	1	2	0	124	8	0	3.87	4			240	11	0	2.75
	Djurgarden	EuroHL	3	2	1	0	180	8		2.33							
99-2000	Huddinge IK	Sweden-2	11	4	7	0	660	33		3.30							
	Djurgarden	Sweden	30				1909	66	2	*2.07	*13			*814	21	*3	*1.55
2000-01	Djurgarden	Sweden	43				2622	91	*5	*2.08	*16			*1006	45	*1	2.68
2001-02	St. John's	AHL	28	8	11	6	1521	79	0	3.12	1	1	0	15	0	0	0.00
	Sweden	Olympics	DID NOT PLAY – SPARE GOALTENDER														
2002-03	**Toronto**	**NHL**	**3**	**1**	**1**	**0**	**86**	**4**	**0**	**2.79**							
	St. John's	AHL	47	17	25	3	2651	148	1	3.35							
2003-04	**Toronto**	**NHL**	**11**	**5**	**3**	**2**	**647**	**31**	**0**	**2.87**							
	St. John's	AHL	23	10	11	1	1343	59	1	2.64							
2004-05	St. John's	AHL	45	24	16	4	2600	115	0	2.65	5	1	4	253	15	0	3.56
2005-06	**Toronto**	**NHL**	**25**	**10**	**11**	**2**	**1399**	**73**	**2**	**3.13**							
	Sweden	Olympics	1	0	1	0	60	3	0	3.00							
2006-07	**Toronto**	**NHL**	**1**	**0**	**1**	**0**	**59**	**2**	**0**	**2.03**							
	Toronto Marlies	AHL	3	2	1	0	182	12	0	3.95							
	Phoenix	**NHL**	**30**	**11**	**11**	**3**	**1591**	**90**	**2**	**3.39**							
2007-08	**Phoenix**	**NHL**	**22**	**9**	**8**	**2**	**1224**	**56**	**2**	**2.75**							
	NHL Totals		**92**	**36**	**35**	**9**	**5006**	**256**	**6**	**3.07**							

Traded to **Phoenix** by **Toronto** for Tyson Nash and Boston's 4th round choice (previously acquired, Toronto selected Matt Frattin) in 2007 Entry Draft, November 28, 2006.

TESLAK, Michael
(TEHZ-lak, MIGH-kuhl) **PHI.**

Goaltender. Catches left. 6'2", 192 lbs. Born, Fernie, B.C., December 2, 1985.

			Regular Season								Playoffs						
Season	Club	League	GP	W	L	O/T	Mins	GA	SO	Avg	GP	W	L	Mins	GA	SO	Avg
2003-04	Alberni Valley	BCHL	22	8	11	0	1139	77	0	4.05							
2004-05	Prince George	BCHL	33	21	9	0	1920	79	1	2.47							
2005-06	Michigan Tech	WCHA	26	7	14	4	1437	88	0	3.68							
2006-07	Michigan Tech	WCHA	22	11	8	3	1259	42	4	2.00							
2007-08	Michigan Tech	WCHA	25	8	11	4	1389	51	1	2.20							
	Philadelphia	AHL	5	2	2	0	236	10	0	2.54	1	0	0	27	3	0	6.55

Signed as a free agent by **Philadelphia**, March 18, 2008.

THEODORE, Jose
(THEE-uh-dohr, joh-SAY) **WSH.**

Goaltender. Catches right. 5'11", 182 lbs. Born, Laval, Que., September 13, 1976.
(Montreal's 2nd choice, 44th overall, in 1994 Entry Draft).

			Regular Season								Playoffs						
Season	Club	League	GP	W	L	O/T	Mins	GA	SO	Avg	GP	W	L	Mins	GA	SO	Avg
1990-91	Richelieu	QAHA	42				2520	80	0	1.90							
1991-92	Richelieu Riverains	QAAA	24	9	13	2	1440	96	0	3.99	5	2	3	295	26	0	5.28
1992-93	St-Jean Lynx	QMJHL	34	12	16	2	1776	112	0	3.78	3	0	2	175	11	0	3.77
1993-94	St-Jean Lynx	QMJHL	57	20	29	6	3225	194	0	3.61	5	1	4	296	18	0	3.65
1994-95	Hull Olympiques	QMJHL	*58	*32	22	2	*3348	193	5	3.46	*21	*15	6	*1263	59	*1	2.80
	Fredericton	AHL									1	0	1	60	3	0	3.00
1995-96	**Montreal**	**NHL**	**1**	**0**	**0**	**0**	**9**	**1**	**0**	**6.67**							
	Hull Olympiques	QMJHL	48	33	11	2	2807	158	0	3.38	5	2	3	299	20	0	4.01
1996-97	**Montreal**	**NHL**	**16**	**5**	**6**	**2**	**821**	**53**	**0**	**3.87**	**2**	**1**	**1**	**168**	**7**	**0**	**2.50**
	Fredericton	AHL	26	12	12	0	1469	87	0	3.55							
1997-98	Fredericton	AHL	53	20	23	8	3053	145	2	2.85	4	1	3	237	13	0	3.28
	Montreal	**NHL**									**3**	**0**	**1**	**120**	**1**	**0**	**0.50**
1998-99	**Montreal**	**NHL**	**18**	**4**	**12**	**0**	**913**	**50**	**1**	**3.29**							
	Fredericton	AHL	27	12	13	2	1609	77	2	2.87	13	8	5	694	35	1	3.03
99-2000	**Montreal**	**NHL**	**30**	**12**	**13**	**2**	**1655**	**58**	**5**	**2.10**							
2000-01	**Montreal**	**NHL**	**59**	**20**	**29**	**5**	**3298**	**141**	**2**	**2.57**							
	Quebec Citadelles	AHL	3	3	0	0	180	9	0	3.00							
2001-02	**Montreal**	**NHL**	**67**	**30**	**24**	**10**	**3864**	**136**	**7**	**2.11**	**12**	**6**	**6**	**686**	**35**	**0**	**3.06**
2002-03	**Montreal**	**NHL**	**57**	**20**	**31**	**6**	**3419**	**165**	**2**	**2.90**							
2003-04	**Montreal**	**NHL**	**67**	**33**	**28**	**5**	**3961**	**150**	**6**	**2.27**	**11**	**4**	**7**	**678**	**27**	**1**	**2.39**
2004-05	Djurgarden	Sweden	17				1024	42	0	2.46	12			728	27	0	2.23
2005-06	**Montreal**	**NHL**	**38**	**17**	**15**	**5**	**2114**	**122**	**0**	**3.46**							
	Colorado	**NHL**	**5**	**1**	**3**	**1**	**296**	**15**	**0**	**3.04**	**9**	**4**	**5**	**573**	**29**	**0**	**3.04**
2006-07	**Colorado**	**NHL**	**33**	**13**	**15**	**1**	**1748**	**95**	**0**	**3.26**							

Season	Club	League	GP	W	L	O/T	Mins	GA	SO	Avg	GP	W	L	Mins	GA	SO	Avg
2007-08	Colorado	NHL	53	28	21	3	3028	123	3	2.44	10	4	6	514	27	0	3.15
	Lake Erie Monsters	AHL	1	0	1	0	60	3	0	3.02	....	....	....	....	....	....	....
	NHL Totals		444	183	197	40	25126	1109	26	2.65	47	19	26	2739	126	1	2.76

QMJHL Second All-Star Team (1995, 1996) • NHL Second All-Star Team (2002) • MBNA Roger Crozier Saving Grace Award (2002) • Vezina Trophy (2002) • Hart Memorial Trophy (2002)

Played in NHL All-Star Game (2002, 2004)

• Scored a goal vs. NY Islanders, January 2, 2001. Signed as a free agent by **Djurgarden** (Sweden), December 20, 2004. Traded to **Colorado** by **Montreal** for David Aebischer, March 8, 2006. Signed as a free agent by **Washington**, July 1, 2008.

THIBAULT, Jocelyn (TEE-boh, JAW-seh-lihn)

Goaltender. Catches left. 5'11", 169 lbs. Born, Montreal, Que., January 12, 1975.
(Quebec's 1st choice, 10th overall, in 1993 Entry Draft).

			Regular Season								Playoffs						
Season	Club	League	GP	W	L	O/T	Mins	GA	SO	Avg	GP	W	L	Mins	GA	SO	Avg
1990-91	Laval-Laurentides	QAAA	20	14	5	0	1178	78	1	3.94	5	2	3	300	20	0	4.00
1991-92	Trois-Rivieres	QMJHL	30	14	7	1	1496	77	0	3.09	3	1	1	110	4	0	2.19
1992-93	Sherbrooke	QMJHL	56	34	14	5	3190	159	3	2.99	15	9	6	882	57	0	3.87
1993-94	Quebec	NHL	29	8	13	3	1504	83	0	3.31	....	....	....	....	....	....	....
	Cornwall Aces	AHL	4	4	0	0	240	9	1	2.25	....	....	....	....	....	....	....
1994-95	Sherbrooke	QMJHL	13	6	6	1	776	38	1	2.94	....	....	....	....	....	....	....
	Quebec	NHL	18	12	2	2	898	35	1	2.34	3	1	2	148	8	0	3.24
1995-96	Colorado	NHL	10	3	4	2	558	28	0	3.01	....	....	....	....	....	....	....
	Montreal	NHL	40	23	13	3	2334	110	3	2.83	6	2	4	311	18	0	3.47
1996-97	Montreal	NHL	61	22	24	11	3397	164	1	2.90	3	0	3	179	13	0	4.36
1997-98	Montreal	NHL	47	19	15	8	2652	109	2	2.47	2	0	0	43	4	0	5.58
1998-99	Montreal	NHL	10	3	4	2	529	23	1	2.61	....	....	....	....	....	....	....
	Chicago	NHL	52	21	26	5	3014	136	4	2.71	....	....	....	....	....	....	....
99-2000	Chicago	NHL	60	25	26	7	3438	158	3	2.76	....	....	....	....	....	....	....
2000-01	Chicago	NHL	66	27	32	7	3844	180	6	2.81	....	....	....	....	....	....	....
2001-02	Chicago	NHL	67	33	23	9	3838	159	6	2.49	3	1	2	159	7	0	2.64
2002-03	Chicago	NHL	62	26	28	7	3650	144	8	2.37	....	....	....	....	....	....	....
2003-04	Chicago	NHL	14	5	7	2	821	39	1	2.85	....	....	....	....	....	....	....
2004-05			DID NOT PLAY														
2005-06	Pittsburgh	NHL	16	1	9	3	807	60	0	4.46	....	....	....	....	....	....	....
2006-07	Pittsburgh	NHL	22	7	8	2	1101	52	1	2.83	1	0	0	8	0	0	0.00
2007-08	Buffalo	NHL	12	3	4	2	507	28	2	3.31	....	....	....	....	....	....	....
	NHL Totals		586	238	238	75	32892	1508	39	2.75	18	4	11	848	50	0	3.54

QMJHL All-Rookie Team (1992) • QMJHL First All-Star Team (1993) • QMJHL MVP (1993) • Canadian Major Junior First All-Star Team (1993) • Canadian Major Junior Goaltender of the Year (1993)

Played in NHL All-Star Game (2003)

Transferred to **Colorado** after **Quebec** franchise relocated, June 21, 1995. Traded to **Montreal** by **Colorado** with Andrei Kovalenko and Martin Rucinsky for Patrick Roy and Mike Keane, December 6, 1995. Traded to **Chicago** by **Montreal** with Dave Manson and Brad Brown for Jeff Hackett, Eric Weinrich, Alain Nasreddine and Tampa Bay's 4th round choice (previously acquired, Montreal selected Chris Dyment) in 1999 Entry Draft, November 16, 1998. • Missed majority of 2003-04 season recovering from hip injury suffered in practice, November 9, 2003. Traded to **Pittsburgh** by **Chicago** for Pittsburgh's 4th round choice (Ben Shutrion) in 2006 Entry Draft, August 10, 2005. Signed as a free agent by **Buffalo**, July 5, 2007.

THOMAS, Tim (TAW-mas, TIHM) BOS.

Goaltender. Catches left. 5'11", 208 lbs. Born, Flint, MI, April 15, 1974.
(Quebec's 11th choice, 217th overall, in 1994 Entry Draft).

			Regular Season								Playoffs						
Season	Club	League	GP	W	L	O/T	Mins	GA	SO	Avg	GP	W	L	Mins	GA	SO	Avg
1992-93	Davison High	High-MI	27	....	....	....	1580	87	....	3.30	....	....	....	....	....	....	....
1993-94	U. of Vermont	ECAC	*33	15	12	6	1864	94	0	3.03	....	....	....	....	....	....	....
1994-95	U. of Vermont	ECAC	34	18	13	2	2010	90	*4	*2.69	....	....	....	....	....	....	....
1995-96	U. of Vermont	ECAC	37	*26	7	4	*2254	88	*3	*2.34	....	....	....	....	....	....	....
1996-97	U. of Vermont	ECAC	36	22	11	3	2158	101	2	2.81	....	....	....	....	....	....	....
1997-98	Birmingham Bulls	ECHL	6	4	1	1	360	13	1	2.17	....	....	....	....	....	....	....
	Houston Aeros	IHL	1	0	1	0	59	4	0	4.01	....	....	....	....	....	....	....
	HIFK Helsinki	Finland	18	13	4	1	1034	28	2	1.62	9	9	0	551	14	3	1.52
1998-99	Hamilton Bulldogs	AHL	15	6	8	0	837	45	0	3.23	....	....	....	....	....	....	....
	HIFK Helsinki	Finland	14	8	3	3	833	31	2	2.23	11	7	4	658	25	0	2.28
99-2000	Detroit Vipers	IHL	36	10	21	3	2020	120	1	3.56	....	....	....	....	....	....	....
2000-01	AIK Solna	Sweden	43	....	....	....	2542	105	3	2.48	5	....	....	299	20	0	4.01
2001-02	Karpat Oulu	Finland	32	15	12	5	1937	79	4	2.44	3	1	2	180	12	0	4.00
2002-03	Boston	NHL	4	3	1	0	220	11	0	3.00	....	....	....	....	....	....	....
	Providence Bruins	AHL	35	18	12	5	2049	98	1	2.87	....	....	....	....	....	....	....
2003-04	Providence Bruins	AHL	43	20	16	6	2544	78	9	1.84	2	0	2	84	10	0	7.13
2004-05	Jokerit Helsinki	Finland	54	34	13	7	3266	86	15	1.58	12	8	4	720	22	0	1.83
2005-06	Boston	NHL	38	12	13	10	2187	101	1	2.77	....	....	....	....	....	....	....
	Providence Bruins	AHL	26	15	11	0	1515	57	1	2.26	....	....	....	....	....	....	....
2006-07	Boston	NHL	66	30	29	4	3619	189	3	3.13	....	....	....	....	....	....	....
2007-08	Boston	NHL	57	28	19	6	3342	136	3	2.44	7	3	4	430	19	0	2.65
	NHL Totals		165	73	62	20	9368	437	7	2.80	7	3	4	430	19	0	2.65

ECAC First All-Star Team (1995, 1996) • ECAC Goaltender of the Year (1996) • NCAA East Second All-American Team (1995) • NCAA East First All-American Team (1996)

Played in NHL All-Star Game (2008)

Signed as a free agent by **Edmonton**, June 4, 1998. Signed as a free agent by **Boston**, August 8, 2002. Signed as a free agent by **Jokerit Helsinki** (Finland), May 17, 2004. Signed as a free agent by **Boston**, September 14, 2005.

TOIVONEN, Hannu (TOI-voh-nuhn, HA-noo)

Goaltender. Catches left. 6'2", 200 lbs. Born, Kalvola, Finland, May 18, 1984.
(Boston's 1st choice, 29th overall, in 2002 Entry Draft).

			Regular Season								Playoffs						
Season	Club	League	GP	W	L	O/T	Mins	GA	SO	Avg	GP	W	L	Mins	GA	SO	Avg
2000-01	HPK U18	Fin-U18	....	....	....	....	....	....	....	....	....	....	....	....	....	....	....
2001-02	HPK U18	Fin-U18	5	4	1	0	277	14	0	3.03	....	....	....	....	....	....	....
	HPK Jr.	Fin-Jr.	31	15	12	4	1877	103	2	3.29	7	3	4	440	31	0	4.23
2002-03	HPK Jr.	Fin-Jr.	6	3	3	0	359	20	0	3.34	....	....	....	....	....	....	....
	HPK Hameenlinna	Finland	24	16	2	4	1432	54	2	2.26	2	1	1	117	3	1	1.53
2003-04	Providence Bruins	AHL	36	15	16	4	2162	83	2	2.30	0	0	0	0	0	0	0.00
2004-05	Providence Bruins	AHL	54	29	18	3	3017	103	7	2.05	17	10	7	1038	42	0	2.43
2005-06	Boston	NHL	20	9	5	4	1163	51	1	2.63	....	....	....	....	....	....	....
2006-07	Boston	NHL	18	3	9	1	894	63	0	4.23	....	....	....	....	....	....	....
	Providence Bruins	AHL	27	13	13	1	1618	64	2	2.37	13	6	7	742	36	0	2.91
2007-08	St. Louis	NHL	23	6	10	5	1202	69	0	3.44	....	....	....	....	....	....	....
	Peoria Rivermen	AHL	11	6	4	0	627	33	0	3.16	....	....	....	....	....	....	....
	NHL Totals		61	18	24	10	3259	183	1	3.37	....	....	....	....	....	....	....

Traded to **St. Louis** by **Boston** for Carl Soderberg, July 23, 2007.

TOKARSKI, Dustin (toh-KAHR-skee, DUHS-tihn) T.B.

Goaltender. Catches left. 5'11", 185 lbs. Born, Humboldt, Sask., September 16, 1989.
(Tampa Bay's 3rd choice, 122nd overall, in 2008 Entry Draft).

			Regular Season								Playoffs						
Season	Club	League	GP	W	L	O/T	Mins	GA	SO	Avg	GP	W	L	Mins	GA	SO	Avg
2006-07	Spokane Chiefs	WHL	30	13	11	2	1674	78	2	2.80	6	2	4	364	17	0	2.80
2007-08	Spokane Chiefs	WHL	45	30	10	0	2543	87	6	2.05	*21	*16	5	*1352	31	*3	*1.38

Memorial Cup All-Star Team (2008) • Hap Emms Memorial Trophy (Memorial Cup Tournament - Top Goaltender) (2008) • Stafford Smythe Memorial Trophy (Memorial Cup Tournament - MVP) (2008)

TORDJMAN, Josh (TOHRJ-man, JAWSH) PHX.

Goaltender. Catches left. 6'1", 155 lbs. Born, Montreal, Que., January 11, 1985.

			Regular Season								Playoffs						
Season	Club	League	GP	W	L	O/T	Mins	GA	SO	Avg	GP	W	L	Mins	GA	SO	Avg
2002-03	Valleyfield Braves	QJHL	STATISTICS NOT AVAILABLE														
	Victoriaville Tigres	QMJHL	10	4	3	0	432	24	1	3.33	2	0	1	112	12	0	6.46
2003-04	Victoriaville Tigres	QMJHL	42	10	24	4	2177	143	2	3.94	....	....	....	....	....	....	....
2004-05	Victoriaville Tigres	QMJHL	56	22	28	4	3185	171	5	3.22	7	3	4	435	24	0	3.31
2005-06	Victoriaville Tigres	QMJHL	31	13	17	0	1792	106	2	3.55	....	....	....	....	....	....	....
	Moncton Wildcats	QMJHL	25	18	6	0	1427	55	2	*2.31	21	*15	5	1238	48	*2	2.33
2006-07	San Antonio	AHL	37	15	18	2	2114	91	1	2.58	....	....	....	....	....	....	....
	Phoenix	ECHL	9	4	4	0	480	25	0	3.12	....	....	....	....	....	....	....
2007-08	San Antonio	AHL	43	22	14	4	2466	109	1	2.65	6	3	3	357	11	1	1.85

QMJHL Second All-Star Team (2006)

Signed as a free agent by **Phoenix**, July 2, 2006.

TOSKALA, Vesa (TAWS-kah-lah, VEH-sa) TOR.

Goaltender. Catches left. 5'10", 195 lbs. Born, Tampere, Finland, May 20, 1977.
(San Jose's 4th choice, 90th overall, in 1995 Entry Draft).

			Regular Season								Playoffs						
Season	Club	League	GP	W	L	O/T	Mins	GA	SO	Avg	GP	W	L	Mins	GA	SO	Avg
1994-95	Ilves Tampere Jr.	Fin-Jr.	17	10	5	1	956	36	2	2.26	7	....	....	393	22	....	3.36
1995-96	Ilves Tampere Jr.	Fin-Jr.	3	3	0	0	180	3	0	1.00	....	....	....	....	....	....	....
	KooVee Tampere	Finland-2	2	1	1	0	119	5	1	2.51	....	....	....	....	....	....	....
	Ilves Tampere	Finland	37	14	14	7	2072	109	1	3.16	2	0	2	78	11	0	8.46
1996-97	Ilves Tampere Jr.	Fin-Jr.	3	....	....	....	184	....	....	2.93	....	....	....	....	....	....	....
	Ilves Tampere	Finland	40	22	12	5	2270	108	0	2.85	8	3	5	479	29	0	3.63
1997-98	Ilves Tampere Jr.	Fin-Jr.	2	2	0	0	120	4	0	2.00	....	....	....	....	....	....	....
	Ilves Tampere	Finland	43	26	13	3	2554	118	1	2.77	9	6	3	519	18	1	2.08
1998-99	Ilves Tampere	Finland	33	21	12	0	1966	70	5	2.14	4	1	3	248	14	0	3.39
99-2000	Farjestad	Sweden	44	....	....	....	2652	118	3	2.67	7	....	....	439	19	0	2.59
2000-01	Kentucky	AHL	44	22	13	5	2466	114	2	2.77	3	0	3	197	8	0	2.43
2001-02	San Jose	NHL	1	0	0	0	10	0	0	0.00	....	....	....	....	....	....	....
	Cleveland Barons	AHL	*62	19	33	7	*3574	178	3	2.99	....	....	....	....	....	....	....
2002-03	San Jose	NHL	11	4	3	1	537	21	1	2.35	....	....	....	....	....	....	....
	Cleveland Barons	AHL	49	15	30	2	2824	151	1	3.21	....	....	....	....	....	....	....
2003-04	San Jose	NHL	28	12	8	4	1541	53	1	2.06	....	....	....	....	....	....	....
2004-05	Ilves Tampere	Finland	3	0	1	2	186	8	0	2.58	6	3	3	357	19	0	3.19
2005-06	San Jose	NHL	37	23	7	4	2039	87	2	2.56	11	6	5	686	28	1	2.45
	Cleveland Barons	AHL	1	0	0	1	65	0	1	0.00	....	....	....	....	....	....	....
2006-07	San Jose	NHL	38	26	10	1	2142	84	4	2.35	....	....	....	....	....	....	....
2007-08	Toronto	NHL	66	33	25	6	3837	175	3	2.74	....	....	....	....	....	....	....
	NHL Totals		181	98	53	16	10106	420	11	2.49	11	6	5	686	28	1	2.45

Signed as a free agent by **Ilves Tampere** (Finland), January 31, 2005. Traded to **Toronto** by **San Jose** with Mark Bell for Toronto's 1st (later traded to St. Louis - St. Louis selected Lars Eller) and 2nd (later traded to St. Louis - St. Louis selected Aaron Palushaj) round choices in 2007 Entry Draft and Toronto's 4th round choice in 2009 Entry Draft, June 22, 2007.

TURCO, Marty (TUHR-koh, MAHR-tee) DAL.

Goaltender. Catches left. 5'11", 185 lbs. Born, Sault Ste. Marie, Ont., August 13, 1975.
(Dallas' 4th choice, 124th overall, in 1994 Entry Draft).

			Regular Season								Playoffs						
Season	Club	League	GP	W	L	O/T	Mins	GA	SO	Avg	GP	W	L	Mins	GA	SO	Avg
1993-94	Cambridge	OJHL-B	34	19	10	3	1973	114	0	3.47	....	....	....	....	....	....	....
1994-95	U. of Michigan	CCHA	37	*27	7	1	2063	95	1	2.76	....	....	....	....	....	....	....
1995-96	U. of Michigan	CCHA	*42	*34	7	1	*2335	84	*5	*2.16	....	....	....	....	....	....	....
1996-97	U. of Michigan	CCHA	*41	*33	4	4	*2296	87	*4	*2.27	....	....	....	....	....	....	....
1997-98	U. of Michigan	CCHA	*45	*33	10	1	*2640	95	4	2.16	....	....	....	....	....	....	....
1998-99	Michigan K-Wings	IHL	54	24	17	10	3127	136	1	2.61	5	2	3	300	14	0	2.80
99-2000	Michigan K-Wings	IHL	60	23	27	*7	3399	139	*7	2.45	....	....	....	....	....	....	....
2000-01	Dallas	NHL	26	13	6	1	1266	40	3	*1.90	....	....	....	....	....	....	....
2001-02	Dallas	NHL	31	15	6	2	1519	53	2	2.09	....	....	....	....	....	....	....
2002-03	Dallas	NHL	55	31	10	10	3203	92	7	*1.72	12	6	6	798	25	0	1.88
2003-04	Dallas	NHL	73	37	21	13	4359	144	9	1.98	5	1	4	325	18	0	3.32
2004-05	Djurgarden	Sweden	6	....	....	....	356	12	1	2.02	....	....	....	....	....	....	....
2005-06	Dallas	NHL	68	41	19	5	3910	166	3	2.55	5	1	4	319	18	0	3.39
	Canada	Olympics	DID NOT PLAY – SPARE GOALTENDER														
2006-07	Dallas	NHL	67	38	20	5	3764	140	6	2.23	7	3	4	509	11	3	*1.30
2007-08	Dallas	NHL	62	32	21	6	3629	140	3	2.31	18	10	8	1152	40	1	2.08
	NHL Totals		382	207	103	42	21650	775	33	2.15	47	21	26	3103	112	4	2.17

CCHA Rookie of the Year (1995) • NCAA Championship All-Tournament Team (1996, 1998) • CCHA First All-Star Team (1997) • NCAA West First All-American Team (1997) • CCHA Second All-Star Team (1998) • NCAA Championship Tournament MVP (1998) • Garry F. Longman Memorial Trophy (Rookie of the Year – IHL) (1999) • MBNA Roger Crozier Saving Grace Award (2001, 2003) • NHL Second All-Star Team (2003)

Played in NHL All-Star Game (2003, 2004, 2007)

Signed as a free agent by **Djurgarden** (Sweden), November 13, 2004.

TURPLE, Dan (TUHR-puhl, DAN) ATL.

Goaltender. Catches left. 6'6", 210 lbs. Born, Oakville, Ont., January 1, 1985.
(Atlanta's 6th choice, 186th overall, in 2004 Entry Draft).

			Regular Season								Playoffs						
Season	Club	League	GP	W	L	O/T	Mins	GA	SO	Avg	GP	W	L	Mins	GA	SO	Avg
2002-03	Kingston	OHL	12	2	8	0	449	42	0	5.61	....	....	....	....	....	....	....
2003-04	Kingston	OHL	9	4	4	1	534	29	0	3.26	....	....	....	....	....	....	....
	Oshawa Generals	OHL	35	20	7	3	1843	81	2	2.64	7	3	4	443	19	1	2.57
2004-05	Oshawa Generals	OHL	10	4	4	0	469	29	0	3.71	....	....	....	....	....	....	....
	Kitchener Rangers	OHL	40	17	16	5	2335	92	3	2.36	3	0	2	162	9	0	3.33
2005-06	Kitchener Rangers	OHL	57	40	15	2	3306	124	*7	*2.25	5	1	4	326	20	0	3.68
2006-07	Gwinnett	ECHL	34	18	13	3	2052	129	1	3.77	1	0	1	73	5	0	4.11
2007-08	Grand Rapids	AHL	1	0	0	0	20	1	0	3.00	....	....	....	....	....	....	....
	Gwinnett	ECHL	30	15	12	3	1786	94	0	3.16	1	1	0	60	1	0	1.00

OHL Second All-Star Team (2006)

UNICE, Josh (EW-nihs, JAWSH) CHI.

Goaltender. Catches left. 5'11", 175 lbs. Born, Toledo, OH, June 24, 1989.
(Chicago's 5th choice, 86th overall, in 2007 Entry Draft).

			Regular Season								Playoffs						
Season	Club	League	GP	W	L	O/T	Mins	GA	SO	Avg	GP	W	L	Mins	GA	SO	Avg
2004-05	Det. Victory Honda	MWEHL	48	21	10	0	....	....	....	2.70	....	....	....	....	....	....	....
2005-06	USNTDP	U-17	6	2	3	1	364	23	....	3.79	....	....	....	....	....	....	....
	USNTDP	NAHL	21	11	7	2	1246	62	0	2.99	8	5	3	490	14	2	1.72
2006-07	USNTDP	U-18	27	15	9	2	1582	83	3	3.15	....	....	....	....	....	....	....
	USNTDP	NAHL	6	5	0	1	369	13	1	2.12	....	....	....	....	....	....	....
2007-08	Kitchener Rangers	OHL	42	30	6	3	2376	97	*4	2.45	16	11	4	948	38	1	2.41

VALIQUETTE, Steve (val-ih-KEHT, STEEV) NYR

Goaltender. Catches left. 6'6", 210 lbs. Born, Etobicoke, Ont., August 20, 1977.
(Los Angeles' 8th choice, 190th overall, in 1996 Entry Draft).

			Regular Season								Playoffs						
Season	Club	League	GP	W	L	O/T	Mins	GA	SO	Avg	GP	W	L	Mins	GA	SO	Avg
1993-94	Burlington	OPJHL	30	....	....	....	1663	112	1	4.04	....	....	....	....	....	....	....
1994-95	Rayside-Balfour	NOJHA	2	0	2	0	89	12	0	8.09	....	....	....	....	....	....	....
	Smiths Falls Bears	CJHL	21	10	8	3	1275	75	0	3.53	....	....	....	....	....	....	....
	Sudbury Wolves	OHL	4	2	0	0	138	6	0	2.61	....	....	....	....	....	....	....
1995-96	Sudbury Wolves	OHL	39	13	16	2	1887	123	0	3.91	....	....	....	....	....	....	....
1996-97	Sudbury Wolves	OHL	*61	21	29	7	3311	232	1	4.20	....	....	....	....	....	....	....
	Dayton Bombers	ECHL	3	1	0	0	89	6	0	4.03	2	1	1	118	5	0	2.54
1997-98	Sudbury Wolves	OHL	14	5	7	1	807	50	0	3.72	....	....	....	....	....	....	....
	Erie Otters	OHL	28	16	7	3	1525	65	3	2.56	7	3	4	467	15	1	1.93
1998-99	Lowell	AHL	1	0	1	0	59	3	0	3.05	....	....	....	....	....	....	....
	Hampton Roads	ECHL	31	18	7	3	1713	84	1	2.94	2	0	1	60	7	0	7.00
99-2000	**NY Islanders**	**NHL**	**6**	**2**	**0**	**0**	**193**	**6**	**0**	**1.87**	....	....	....	....	....	....	....
	Lowell	AHL	14	8	5	0	727	36	0	2.97	....	....	....	....	....	....	....
	Providence Bruins	AHL	1	1	0	0	60	3	0	3.00	....	....	....	....	....	....	....
	Trenton Titans	ECHL	12	5	6	1	692	36	1	3.12	....	....	....	....	....	....	....
2000-01	Springfield Falcons	AHL	20	7	10	1	1066	54	0	3.04	....	....	....	....	....	....	....
2001-02	Bridgeport	AHL	20	10	5	1	1071	45	2	2.52	1	0	0	18	1	0	3.30
2002-03	Bridgeport	AHL	34	15	14	3	1962	86	2	2.63	4	3	1	253	9	0	2.13
2003-04	**Edmonton**	**NHL**	**1**	**0**	**0**	**0**	**14**	**2**	**0**	**8.57**	....	....	....	....	....	....	....
	Toronto	AHL	35	14	14	5	2064	89	2	2.59	....	....	....	....	....	....	....
	NY Rangers	**NHL**	**2**	**1**	**1**	**0**	**120**	**6**	**0**	**3.00**	....	....	....	....	....	....	....
	Hartford Wolf Pack	AHL	7	2	4	1	400	15	1	2.25	1	0	0	11	0	0	0.00
2004-05	Hartford Wolf Pack	AHL	35	19	11	1	1900	56	7	*1.77	2	1	1	118	4	0	2.03
2005-06	Yaroslavl	Russia	45	....	....	....	2734	89	4	1.95	8	....	....	458	23	0	3.01
2006-07	**NY Rangers**	**NHL**	**3**	**1**	**2**	**0**	**115**	**6**	**0**	**3.13**	....	....	....	....	....	....	....
	Hartford Wolf Pack	AHL	30	17	12	0	1694	66	2	2.34	....	....	....	....	....	....	....
2007-08	**NY Rangers**	**NHL**	**13**	**5**	**3**	**3**	**686**	**25**	**2**	**2.19**	....	....	....	....	....	....	....
	NHL Totals		**25**	**9**	**6**	**3**	**1128**	**45**	**2**	**2.39**	....	....	....	....	....	....	....

Harry "Hap" Holmes Memorial Trophy (fewest goals against - AHL) (2005) (shared with Jason LaBarbera)

Signed as a free agent by **NY Islanders**, August 18, 1998. Signed as a free agent by **Edmonton**, July 20, 2003. Claimed by **Florida** from **Edmonton** in Waiver Draft, October 3, 2003. Claimed on waivers by **Edmonton** from **Florida**, October 9, 2003. Traded to **NY Rangers** by **Edmonton** with Dwight Helminen and Edmonton's 2nd round compensatory choice (Dane Byers) in 2004 Entry Draft for Petr Nedved and Jussi Markkanen, March 3, 2004. Signed as a free agent by **Yaroslavl** (Russia), April 26, 2005. Signed as a free agent by **NY Rangers**, July 1, 2006.

VARLAMOV, Simeon (vahr-LAH-mawv, sih-MEE-awn) WSH.

Goaltender. Catches left. 6'1", 200 lbs. Born, Kuybyshev, USSR, April 27, 1988.
(Washington's 2nd choice, 23rd overall, in 2006 Entry Draft).

			Regular Season								Playoffs						
Season	Club	League	GP	W	L	O/T	Mins	GA	SO	Avg	GP	W	L	Mins	GA	SO	Avg
2004-05	Yaroslavl 2	Russia-3	8	....	....	....	369	15	1	2.43	....	....	....	....	....	....	....
2005-06	Yaroslavl 2	Russia-3	33	....	....	....	1782	60	8	2.02	....	....	....	....	....	....	....
2006-07	Yaroslavl 2	Russia-3	2	....	....	....	120	3	0	1.50	....	....	....	....	....	....	....
	Yaroslavl	Russia	33	....	....	....	1936	70	3	2.17	6	....	....	368	18	0	2.94
2007-08	Yaroslavl	Russia	44	....	....	....	2592	106	3	2.45	*16	....	....	*924	25	*5	1.62

VOKOUN, Tomas (voh-KOON, TAW-mas) FLA.

Goaltender. Catches right. 6', 195 lbs. Born, Karlovy Vary, Czech., July 2, 1976.
(Montreal's 11th choice, 226th overall, in 1994 Entry Draft).

			Regular Season								Playoffs						
Season	Club	League	GP	W	L	O/T	Mins	GA	SO	Avg	GP	W	L	Mins	GA	SO	Avg
1993-94	HC Kladno	CzRep	1	0	0	0	20	2	0	6.01	....	....	....	....	....	....	....
1994-95	HC Kladno	CzRep	26	....	....	....	1368	70	....	3.07	5	....	....	240	19	....	4.75
1995-96	Wheeling	ECHL	35	20	10	2	1912	117	0	3.67	7	4	3	436	19	0	2.61
	Fredericton	AHL	....	....	....	....	....	....	....	....	1	0	1	59	4	0	4.09
1996-97	**Montreal**	**NHL**	**1**	**0**	**0**	**0**	**20**	**4**	**0**	**12.00**	....	....	....	....	....	....	....
	Fredericton	AHL	47	12	26	7	2645	154	2	3.49	....	....	....	....	....	....	....
1997-98	Fredericton	AHL	31	13	13	2	1735	90	0	3.11	....	....	....	....	....	....	....
1998-99	**Nashville**	**NHL**	**37**	**12**	**18**	**4**	**1954**	**96**	**1**	**2.95**	....	....	....	....	....	....	....
	Milwaukee	IHL	9	3	2	4	539	22	1	2.45	2	0	2	149	8	0	3.22
99-2000	**Nashville**	**NHL**	**33**	**9**	**20**	**1**	**1879**	**87**	**1**	**2.78**	....	....	....	....	....	....	....
	Milwaukee	IHL	7	5	2	0	364	17	0	2.80	....	....	....	....	....	....	....
2000-01	**Nashville**	**NHL**	**37**	**13**	**17**	**5**	**2088**	**85**	**2**	**2.44**	....	....	....	....	....	....	....
2001-02	**Nashville**	**NHL**	**29**	**5**	**14**	**4**	**1471**	**66**	**2**	**2.69**	....	....	....	....	....	....	....
2002-03	**Nashville**	**NHL**	**69**	**25**	**31**	**11**	**3974**	**146**	**3**	**2.20**	....	....	....	....	....	....	....
2003-04	**Nashville**	**NHL**	**73**	**34**	**29**	**10**	**4221**	**178**	**3**	**2.53**	**6**	**2**	**4**	**356**	**12**	**1**	**2.02**
2004-05	Znojmo	CzRep	27	....	....	....	1599	69	3	2.59	....	....	....	....	....	....	....
	HIFK Helsinki	Finland	19	11	4	4	1149	35	2	1.83	4	0	3	205	12	0	3.51
2005-06	**Nashville**	**NHL**	**61**	**36**	**18**	**7**	**3601**	**160**	**4**	**2.67**	....	....	....	....	....	....	....
	Czech Republic	Olympics	7	3	4	0	342	14	1	2.46	....	....	....	....	....	....	....
2006-07	**Nashville**	**NHL**	**44**	**27**	**12**	**4**	**2601**	**104**	**5**	**2.40**	**5**	**1**	**4**	**324**	**16**	**0**	**2.96**
2007-08	**Florida**	**NHL**	**69**	**30**	**29**	**8**	**4031**	**180**	**4**	**2.68**	....	....	....	....	....	....	....
	NHL Totals		**453**	**191**	**188**	**54**	**25840**	**1106**	**25**	**2.57**	**11**	**3**	**8**	**680**	**28**	**1**	**2.47**

Played in NHL All-Star Game (2004, 2008)

Claimed by **Nashville** from **Montreal** in Expansion Draft, June 26, 1998. Signed as a free agent by **Znojmo** (CzRep), September 6, 2004. Signed as a free agent by **HIFK Helsinki** (Finland), December 20, 2004. Traded to **Florida** by **Nashville** for Detroit's 2nd round choice (previously acquired, Nashville selected Nick Spaling) in 2007 Entry Draft and Florida's 1st (later traded to NY Islanders - NY Islanders selected Joshua Bailey) and 2nd (later traded to NY Islanders - NY Islanders selected Aaron Ness) round choices in 2008 Entry Draft, June 22, 2007.

WALL, Michael (WAWL, MIGH-kuhl)

Goaltender. Catches left. 6'2", 209 lbs. Born, Telkwa, B.C., July 25, 1985.

			Regular Season								Playoffs						
Season	Club	League	GP	W	L	O/T	Mins	GA	SO	Avg	GP	W	L	Mins	GA	SO	Avg
2001-02	Prince George	WHL	3	0	1	1	107	7	0	3.92	....	....	....	....	....	....	....
2002-03	Prince George	WHL	13	2	5	1	567	40	0	4.23	....	....	....	....	....	....	....
2003-04	Prince George	WHL	1	1	0	0	60	6	0	6.00	....	....	....	....	....	....	....
	Everett Silvertips	WHL	35	11	13	4	1657	59	2	2.14	3	1	0	104	2	0	2.15
2004-05	Everett Silvertips	WHL	56	24	21	8	3191	102	10	1.92	11	4	7	697	25	1	2.15
2005-06	Portland Pirates	AHL	11	5	5	0	603	34	1	3.38	....	....	....	....	....	....	....
	Augusta Lynx	ECHL	21	8	11	1	1103	70	1	3.81	....	....	....	....	....	....	....
2006-07	**Anaheim**	**NHL**	**4**	**2**	**2**	**0**	**202**	**10**	**0**	**2.97**	....	....	....	....	....	....	....
	Portland Pirates	AHL	19	10	6	1	1014	53	0	3.13	....	....	....	....	....	....	....
	Arizona Sundogs	CHL	9	6	3	0	544	20	1	2.20	14	7	7	795	38	2	2.87
2007-08	Lake Erie Monsters	AHL	33	12	16	4	1946	103	1	3.18	....	....	....	....	....	....	....
	NHL Totals		**4**	**2**	**2**	**0**	**202**	**10**	**0**	**2.97**	....	....	....	....	....	....	....

Signed as a free agent by **Anaheim**, September 29, 2005. Traded to **Colorado** by **Anaheim** for Brad May, February 27, 2007.

WARD, Cam (WOHRD, KAM) CAR.

Goaltender. Catches left. 6'1", 200 lbs. Born, Saskatoon, Sask., February 29, 1984.
(Carolina's 1st choice, 25th overall, in 2002 Entry Draft).

			Regular Season								Playoffs						
Season	Club	League	GP	W	L	O/T	Mins	GA	SO	Avg	GP	W	L	Mins	GA	SO	Avg
1998-99	Sherwood Park	ABHL	24	13	7	4	1403	85	0	3.64	....	....	....	....	....	....	....
99-2000	Sherwood Park	AMHL	20	9	5	1	1194	71	0	3.57	7	4	3	262	22	0	3.57
2000-01	Sherwood Park	AMHL	25	14	6	3	1449	70	0	2.90	....	....	....	....	....	....	....
	Red Deer Rebels	WHL	1	1	0	0	60	0	1	0.00	....	....	....	....	....	....	....
2001-02	Red Deer Rebels	WHL	46	30	11	4	2694	102	1	*2.27	*23	14	9	*1502	53	*2	2.12
2002-03	Red Deer Rebels	WHL	57	*40	13	3	3368	118	5	2.10	*23	14	9	*1407	49	3	2.09
2003-04	Red Deer Rebels	WHL	56	31	16	8	3338	114	4	2.05	19	10	9	1200	37	3	1.85
2004-05	Lowell	AHL	50	27	17	3	2829	94	6	1.99	11	5	6	664	28	2	2.53
2005-06 ♦	**Carolina**	**NHL**	**28**	**14**	**8**	**2**	**1484**	**91**	**0**	**3.68**	***23**	***15**	**8**	***1320**	**47**	**2**	**2.14**
	Lowell	AHL	2	0	2	0	118	5	0	2.54	....	....	....	....	....	....	....
2006-07	**Carolina**	**NHL**	**60**	**30**	**21**	**6**	**3422**	**167**	**2**	**2.93**	....	....	....	....	....	....	....
2007-08	**Carolina**	**NHL**	**69**	**37**	**25**	**5**	**3930**	**180**	**4**	**2.75**	....	....	....	....	....	....	....
	NHL Totals		**157**	**81**	**54**	**13**	**8836**	**438**	**6**	**2.97**	**23**	**15**	**8**	**1320**	**47**	**2**	**2.14**

WHL East First All-Star Team (2002, 2004) • WHL East Second All-Star Team (2003) • WHL Goaltender of the Year (2002, 2004) • WHL Player of the Year (2004) • Canadian Major Junior First All-Star Team (2004) • Canadian Major Junior Goaltender of the Year (2004) • AHL All-Rookie Team (2005) • Conn Smythe Trophy (2006)

WEEKES, Kevin (WEEKS, KEH-vihn) N.J.

Goaltender. Catches left. 6'2", 215 lbs. Born, Toronto, Ont., April 4, 1975.
(Florida's 2nd choice, 41st overall, in 1993 Entry Draft).

			Regular Season								Playoffs						
Season	Club	League	GP	W	L	O/T	Mins	GA	SO	Avg	GP	W	L	Mins	GA	SO	Avg
1990-91	Tor. Red Wings	MTHL					Statistics not available										
	St. Mike's B's	MTJHL	1	0	0	0	41	1	0	1.46	....	....	....	....	....	....	....
1991-92	Tor. Red Wings	MTHL	35	....	....	....	1575	68	4	1.94	....	....	....	....	....	....	....
	St. Mike's B's	MTJHL	2	0	1	1	127	11	0	5.20	4	1	2	214	15	1	4.21
1992-93	Owen Sound	OHL	29	9	12	5	1645	143	0	5.22	1	0	0	26	5	0	11.50
1993-94	Owen Sound	OHL	34	13	19	1	1974	158	0	4.80	....	....	....	....	....	....	....
1994-95	Ottawa 67's	OHL	41	13	23	4	2266	153	1	4.05	....	....	....	....	....	....	....
1995-96	Carolina Panthers	AHL	60	24	25	8	3404	229	2	4.04	....	....	....	....	....	....	....
1996-97	Carolina Monarchs	AHL	51	17	28	4	2899	172	1	3.56	....	....	....	....	....	....	....
1997-98	**Florida**	**NHL**	**11**	**0**	**5**	**1**	**485**	**32**	**0**	**3.96**	....	....	....	....	....	....	....
	Fort Wayne	IHL	12	9	2	1	719	34	1	2.84	....	....	....	....	....	....	....
1998-99	Detroit Vipers	IHL	33	19	5	7	1857	64	*4	*2.07	....	....	....	....	....	....	....
	Vancouver	**NHL**	**11**	**0**	**8**	**1**	**532**	**34**	**0**	**3.83**	....	....	....	....	....	....	....
99-2000	**Vancouver**	**NHL**	**20**	**6**	**7**	**4**	**987**	**47**	**1**	**2.86**	....	....	....	....	....	....	....
	NY Islanders	**NHL**	**36**	**10**	**20**	**4**	**2026**	**115**	**1**	**3.41**	....	....	....	....	....	....	....
2000-01	**Tampa Bay**	**NHL**	**61**	**20**	**33**	**3**	**3378**	**177**	**4**	**3.14**	....	....	....	....	....	....	....
2001-02	**Tampa Bay**	**NHL**	**19**	**3**	**9**	**0**	**830**	**40**	**2**	**2.89**	....	....	....	....	....	....	....
	Carolina	**NHL**	**2**	**2**	**0**	**0**	**120**	**3**	**0**	**1.50**	**8**	**3**	**2**	**408**	**11**	**2**	**1.62**
2002-03	**Carolina**	**NHL**	**51**	**14**	**24**	**9**	**2965**	**126**	**5**	**2.55**	....	....	....	....	....	....	....
2003-04	**Carolina**	**NHL**	**66**	**23**	**30**	**11**	**3765**	**146**	**6**	**2.33**	....	....	....	....	....	....	....
2004-05								Did not play									
2005-06	**NY Rangers**	**NHL**	**32**	**14**	**14**	**3**	**1850**	**91**	**0**	**2.95**	**1**	**0**	**1**	**60**	**4**	**0**	**4.00**
2006-07	**NY Rangers**	**NHL**	**14**	**4**	**6**	**2**	**761**	**43**	**0**	**3.39**	....	....	....	....	....	....	....
2007-08	**New Jersey**	**NHL**	**9**	**2**	**2**	**1**	**343**	**17**	**0**	**2.97**	....	....	....	....	....	....	....
	NHL Totals		**332**	**98**	**158**	**39**	**18042**	**871**	**19**	**2.90**	**9**	**3**	**3**	**468**	**15**	**2**	**1.92**

James Norris Memorial Trophy (fewest goals against – IHL) (1999) (shared with Andrei Trefilov)

Traded to **Vancouver** by **Florida** with Ed Jovanovski, Dave Gagner, Mike Brown and Florida's 1st round choice (Nathan Smith) in 2000 Entry Draft for Pavel Bure, Bret Hedican, Brad Ference and Vancouver's 3rd round choice (Robert Fried) in 2000 Entry Draft, January 17, 1999. Traded to **NY Islanders** by **Vancouver** with Dave Scatchard and Bill Muckalt for Felix Potvin, NY Islanders' 2nd round compensatory choice (later traded to New Jersey – New Jersey selected Teemu Laine) in 2000 Entry Draft and NY Islanders' 3rd round choice (Thatcher Bell) in 2000 Entry Draft, December 19, 1999. Traded to **Tampa Bay** by **NY Islanders** with the rights to Kristian Kudroc and NY Islanders' 2nd round choice (later traded to Phoenix – Phoenix selected Matthew Spiller) in 2001 Entry Draft for Tampa Bay's 1st round choice (Raffi Torres) in 2000 Entry Draft, Calgary's 4th round choice (previously acquired, NY Islanders selected Vladimir Gorbunov) in 2000 Entry Draft and NY Islanders' 7th round choice (previously acquired, NY Islanders selected Ryan Caldwell) in 2000 Entry Draft, June 24, 2000. Traded to **Carolina** by **Tampa Bay** for Shane Willis and Chris Dingman, March 5, 2002. Signed as a free agent by **NY Rangers**, August 26, 2004. Signed as a free agent by **New Jersey**, July 5, 2007.

WEIMAN, Tyler (WIGH-muhn, TIGH-luhr) COL.

Goaltender. Catches left. 5'11", 180 lbs. Born, Saskatoon, Sask., June 5, 1984.
(Colorado's 6th choice, 164th overall, in 2002 Entry Draft).

			Regular Season								Playoffs						
Season	Club	League	GP	W	L	O/T	Mins	GA	SO	Avg	GP	W	L	Mins	GA	SO	Avg
99-2000	Ft. Saskatchewan	AMBHL	21	15	4	2	1239	60	0	2.91	....	....	....	....	....	....	....
2000-01	Tri-City Americans	WHL	44	10	25	4	2464	155	0	3.77	....	....	....	....	....	....	....
2001-02	Tri-City Americans	WHL	47	18	17	5	2492	149	2	3.59	5	1	4	300	14	0	2.80
2002-03	Tri-City Americans	WHL	55	16	34	2	3129	207	1	3.97	....	....	....	....	....	....	....
2003-04	Tri-City Americans	WHL	54	23	21	7	3023	134	1	2.66	5	1	2	234	11	0	2.82
2004-05	Colorado Eagles	CHL	44	*33	6	5	2630	79	*8	*1.80	*13	*8	4	*744	32	1	2.58
2005-06	Lowell	AHL	14	6	6	1	844	36	0	2.56	....	....	....	....	....	....	....
	San Diego Gulls	ECHL	32	14	12	3	1797	84	1	2.81	4	0	4	251	15	0	3.59
2006-07	Albany River Rats	AHL	54	27	22	3	3047	152	2	2.99	5	1	4	294	17	0	3.47
2007-08	**Colorado**	**NHL**	**1**	**0**	**0**	**0**	**16**	**0**	**0**	**0.00**	....	....	....	....	....	....	....
	Lake Erie Monsters	AHL	31	9	19	1	1769	98	2	3.32	....	....	....	....	....	....	....
	NHL Totals		**1**	**0**	**0**	**0**	**16**	**0**	**0**	**0.00**	....	....	....	....	....	....	....

WESLOSKY, Jase (wehs-LAWZ-kee, JAYS) NYI

Goaltender. Catches left. 6'2", 170 lbs. Born, St. Albert, Alta., August 14, 1988.
(NY Islanders' 5th choice, 108th overall, in 2006 Entry Draft).

			Regular Season								Playoffs						
Season	Club	League	GP	W	L	O/T	Mins	GA	SO	Avg	GP	W	L	Mins	GA	SO	Avg
2004-05	St. Albert Blues	EMHA	....	13	3	2	1043	38	....	2.19	....	....	....	....	....	....	....
2005-06	Sherwood Park	AJHL	58	....	....	....	2123	110	2	3.11	....	....	....	....	....	....	....
2006-07	St. Cloud State	WCHA	6	5	1	0	359	16	1	2.67	....	....	....	....	....	....	....
2007-08	St. Cloud State	WCHA	33	16	13	2	1901	67	3	2.11	....	....	....	....	....	....	....

WIIKMAN, Miika (VEEK-man, MEE-kah) NYR

Goaltender. Catches left. 5'11", 187 lbs. Born, Toreboda, Sweden, October 17, 1984.

			Regular Season								Playoffs						
Season	Club	League	GP	W	L	O/T	Mins	GA	SO	Avg	GP	W	L	Mins	GA	SO	Avg
99-2000	HV 71 U18	Swe-U18	4	....	....	....	240	23	0	5.75	....	....	....	....	....	....	....
	HV 71 Jr.	Swe-Jr.	1	....	....	....	20	0	0	0.00	....	....	....	....	....	....	....
2000-01	HV 71 U18	Swe-U18	13	....	....	....	740	45	1	3.65	2	....	....	120	12	0	6.00
	HV 71 Jr.	Swe-Jr.	3	....	....	....	100	6	0	3.60	....	....	....	....	....	....	....
2001-02	HV 71 U18	Swe-U18	7	....	....	....	416	33	0	4.76	....	....	....	....	....	....	....
	HV 71 Jr.	Swe-Jr.	9	....	....	....	501	28	0	3.36	....	....	....	....	....	....	....
2002-03	HV 71 Jr.	Swe-Jr.	27	....	....	....	1569	72	1	2.75	7	....	....	423	28	0	3.97
2003-04	Suomi U20	Finland-2	4	....	....	....	240	9	1	2.25	....	....	....	....	....	....	....
	Hermes Kokkola	Finland-2	31	....	....	....	1845	67	3	2.18	6	....	....	375	15	0	2.40
2004-05	HPK Hameenlinna	Finland	23	9	5	9	1361	54	2	2.38	2	1	1	118	4	0	2.03
2005-06	HPK Hameenlinna	Finland	34	21	5	7	1949	68	3	2.09	11	8	2	607	20	3	1.98
2006-07	HPK Hameenlinna	Finland	18	8	6	4	1066	46	0	2.59	....	....	....	....	....	....	....
2007-08	Hartford Wolf Pack	AHL	34	21	8	3	1907	73	2	2.30	1	0	1	59	3	0	3.07
	Charlotte Checkers	ECHL	4	1	1	2	254	10	0	2.36	....	....	....	....	....	....	....

Signed as a free agent by **NY Rangers**, April 24, 2008.

YORK, Allen (YOHRK, AL-ihn) CBJ

Goaltender. Catches left. 6'4", 185 lbs. Born, Wetaskiwin, Alta., June 17, 1989.
(Columbus' 6th choice, 158th overall, in 2007 Entry Draft).

			Regular Season								Playoffs						
Season	Club	League	GP	W	L	O/T	Mins	GA	SO	Avg	GP	W	L	Mins	GA	SO	Avg
2006-07	Camrose Kodiaks	AJHL	32	23	4	0	1661	60	2	2.17	22	16	6	1391	46	4	1.98
2007-08	Camrose Kodiaks	AJHL	....	24	5	3	2005	75	3	2.24	....	....	....	....	....	....	....

ZABA, Matt (ZA-buh, MAT) NYR

Goaltender. Catches left. 6'1", 185 lbs. Born, Yorkton, Sask., July 14, 1983.
(Los Angeles' 8th choice, 231st overall, in 2003 Entry Draft).

			Regular Season								Playoffs						
Season	Club	League	GP	W	L	O/T	Mins	GA	SO	Avg	GP	W	L	Mins	GA	SO	Avg
2000-01	Yorkton Mallers	SMHL	26	13	10	3	1480	79	0	3.20	....	....	....	....	....	....	....
2001-02	Penticton Panthers	BCHL	33	....	....	....	1980	128	0	3.69	....	....	....	....	....	....	....
2002-03	Vernon Vipers	BCHL	44	34	9	0	2012	96	2	2.21	17	14	3	1006	25	3	1.49
2003-04	Colorado College	WCHA	23	10	10	2	1323	50	1	2.27	....	....	....	....	....	....	....
2004-05	Colorado College	WCHA	18	10	5	2	1050	43	2	2.46	....	....	....	....	....	....	....
2005-06	Colorado College	WCHA	36	20	14	2	2068	87	4	2.52	....	....	....	....	....	....	....
2006-07	Colorado College	WCHA	33	15	13	4	1908	76	3	2.39	....	....	....	....	....	....	....
2007-08	Charlotte Checkers	ECHL	9	3	4	1	496	30	0	3.63	....	....	....	....	....	....	....
	Idaho Steelheads	ECHL	19	12	4	1	1070	39	3	2.19	2	0	1	129	6	0	2.78

WCHA All-Rookie Team (2004)

Signed as a free agent by **NY Rangers** , August 20, 2007.

ZATKOFF, Jeff (ZAT-kawf, JEHF) L.A.

Goaltender. Catches left. 6'1", 180 lbs. Born, Detroit, MI, June 9, 1987.
(Los Angeles' 4th choice, 74th overall, in 2006 Entry Draft).

			Regular Season								Playoffs						
Season	Club	League	GP	W	L	O/T	Mins	GA	SO	Avg	GP	W	L	Mins	GA	SO	Avg
2004-05	Sioux City	USHL	24	13	6	3	1271	54	1	2.55	2	0	0	68	10	0	8.88
2005-06	Miami U.	CCHA	20	14	5	1	1217	41	3	2.02	....	....	....	....	....	....	....
2006-07	Miami U.	CCHA	26	14	8	3	1542	58	1	2.26	....	....	....	....	....	....	....
2007-08	Miami U.	CCHA	36	27	8	1	2161	62	3	*1.72	....	....	....	....	....	....	....

CCHA Second All-Star Team (2008)

Late Additions to Player Register

FREE AGENT SIGNINGS

UOTILA, Juha (ew-OH-tihl-uh, YOO-hah) TOR

Defense. Shoots left. 6', 183 lbs. Born, Espoo, Finland, January 12, 1985.

			Regular Season					Playoffs				
Season	Club	League	GP	G	A	Pts	PIM	GP	G	A	Pts	PIM
2001-02	HIFK U18	Fin-U18	27	4	6	10	8	8	3	1	4	0
2002-03	HIFK U18	Fin-U18	15	3	2	5	8	2	2	0	2	10
2002-03	HIFK Helsinki Jr.	Fin-Jr.	22	0	1	1	16					
2003-04	Suomi U20	Finland-2	4	0	0	0	0					
2003-04	HIFK Helsinki Jr.	Fin-Jr.	41	7	13	20	36	6	0	1	1	2
2004-05	Salamat	Finland-2	6	0	3	3	10					
2004-05	HIFK Helsinki Jr.	Fin-Jr.	28	4	10	14	97	3	1	0	1	0
2005-06	Nebraska-Omaha	CCHA	41	1	14	15	39					
2006-07	Nebraska-Omaha	CCHA	40	5	18	23	51					
2007-08	Nebraska-Omaha	CCHA	22	1	14	15	14					

Signed as a free agent by **Toronto**, August 25, 2008.

RETIRED NUMBERS

BATHGATE, Andy *(Honoured Member – Hockey Hall of Fame)*

His jersey number 9 will be retired by **NY Rangers**, February 22, 2009.

			Regular Season					Playoffs				
First Season	Last Season		GP	G	A	Pts	PIM	GP	G	A	Pts	PIM
1952-53	**1963-64**	**Rangers Totals**	**719**	**272**	**457**	**729**	**444**	**22**	**9**	**7**	**16**	**19**
1952-53	1970-71	NHL Totals	1069	349	624	973	624	54	21	14	35	76

HOWELL, Harry *(Honoured Member – Hockey Hall of Fame)*

His jersey number 3 will be retired by **NY Rangers**, February 22, 2009.

			Regular Season					Playoffs				
First Season	Last Season		GP	G	A	Pts	PIM	GP	G	A	Pts	PIM
1952-53	**1968-69**	**Rangers Totals**	**1160**	**82**	**263**	**345**	**1147**	**34**	**3**	**2**	**5**	**30**
1952-53	1972-73	NHL Totals	1411	94	324	418	1298	38	3	3	6	32

GRAVES, Adam

His jersey number 9 will be retired by **NY Rangers**, February 3, 2009.

			Regular Season					Playoffs				
First Season	Last Season		GP	G	A	Pts	PIM	GP	G	A	Pts	PIM
1991-92	**2000-01**	**Rangers Totals**	**772**	**280**	**227**	**507**	**810**	**68**	**28**	**16**	**44**	**70**
1987-88	2002-03	NHL Totals	1152	329	287	616	1224	125	38	27	65	119

Gerry Abel

Tony Amonte

Tom Anderson

Kent-Erik Andersson

Retired NHL Player Index

Abbreviations: Teams/Cities: – **Ana.** – Anaheim; **Atl.** – Atlanta; **Bos.** – Boston; **Bro.** – Brooklyn; **Buf.** – Buffalo; **Cal.** – California; **Cgy.** – Calgary; **Car.** – Carolina; **Chi.** – Chicago; **Cle.** – Cleveland; **Col.** – Colorado; **CBJ** – Columbus; **Dal.** – Dallas; **Det.** – Detroit; **Edm.** – Edmonton; **Fla.** – Florida; **Ham.** – Hamilton; **Hfd.** – Hartford; **K.C.** – Kansas City; **L.A.** – Los Angeles; **Min.** – Minnesota; **Mtl.** – Montreal; **Mtl.M.** – Montreal Maroons; **Mtl.W.** – Montreal Wanderers; **Nsh.** – Nashville; **N.J.** – New Jersey; **NYA** – NY Americans; **NYI** – NY Islanders; **NYR** – New York Rangers; **Oak.** – Oakland; **Ott.** – Ottawa; **Phi.** – Philadelphia; **Phx.** – Phoenix; **Pit.** – Pittsburgh; **Que.** – Quebec; **St.L.** – St. Louis; **S.J.** – San Jose; **T.B.** – Tampa Bay; **Tor.** – Toronto; **Van.** – Vancouver; **Wpg.** – Winnipeg; **Wsh.** – Washington

A – assists; **G** – goals; **GP** – games played; **PIM** – penalties in minutes; **TP** – total points.
● – deceased. Assists not recorded during 1917-18 season ‡ – Remains active in other leagues.

NHL Seasons – A player or goaltender who does not play in a regular season but who does appear in that year's playoffs is credited with an NHL Season in this Index. Total seasons are rounded off to the nearest full season.

			Regular Schedule					Playoffs							
Name	NHL Teams	NHL Seasons	GP	G	A	TP	PIM	GP	G	A	TP	PIM	NHL Cup Wins	First NHL Season	Last NHL Season
A															
Aalto, Antti	Ana.	4	151	11	17	28	52	4	0	0	0	2	....	1997-98	2000-01
Abbott, Reg	Mtl.	1	3	0	0	0	0	....	....	....	....	....	....	1952-53	1952-53
● Abel, Clarence	NYR, Chi.	8	333	19	18	37	359	38	1	1	2	58	2	1926-27	1933-34
Abel, Gerry	Det.	1	1	0	0	0	0	....	....	....	....	....	....	1966-67	1966-67
● Abel, Sid	Det., Chi.	14	612	189	283	472	376	97	28	30	58	79	3	1938-39	1953-54
Abgrall, Dennis	L.A.	1	13	0	2	2	4	....	....	....	....	....	....	1975-76	1975-76
Abrahamsson, Thommy	Hfd.	1	32	6	11	17	16	....	....	....	....	....	....	1980-81	1980-81
Achtymichuk, Gene	Mtl., Det.	4	32	3	5	8	2	....	....	....	....	....	....	1951-52	1958-59
Acomb, Doug	Tor.	1	2	0	1	1	0	....	....	....	....	....	....	1969-70	1969-70
Acton, Keith	Mtl., Min., Edm., Phi., Wsh., NYI	15	1023	226	358	584	1172	66	12	21	33	88	1	1979-80	1993-94
● Adam, Douglas	NYR	1	4	0	1	1	0	....	....	....	....	....	....	1949-50	1949-50
Adam, Russ	Tor.	1	8	1	2	3	11	....	....	....	....	....	....	1982-83	1982-83
‡ Adams, Bryan	Atl.	2	11	0	1	1	2	....	....	....	....	....	....	1999-00	2000-01
Adams, Greg	Phi., Hfd., Wsh., Edm., Van., Que., Det.	10	545	84	143	227	1173	43	2	11	13	153	....	1980-81	1989-90
Adams, Greg	N.J., Van., Dal., Phx., Fla.	17	1056	355	388	743	326	81	20	22	42	16	....	1984-85	2000-01
● Adams, Jack	Tor., Ott.	7	173	83	32	115	366	10	2	0	2	13	2	1917-18	1926-27
Adams, John	Mtl.	1	42	6	12	18	11	3	0	0	0	0	....	1940-41	1940-41
● Adams, Stew	Chi., Tor.	4	95	9	26	35	60	11	3	3	6	14	....	1929-30	1932-33
Adduono, Rick	Bos., Atl.	2	4	0	0	0	2	....	....	....	....	....	....	1975-76	1979-80
Affleck, Bruce	St.L., Van., NYI	7	280	14	66	80	86	8	0	0	0	0	....	1974-75	1983-84
Agnew, Jim	Van., Hfd.	6	81	0	1	1	257	4	0	0	0	6	....	1986-87	1992-93
Ahern, Fred	Cal., Cle., Col.	4	146	31	30	61	130	2	0	1	1	2	....	1974-75	1977-78
● Ahlin, Rudy	Chi.	1	1	0	0	0	0	....	....	....	....	....	....	1937-38	1937-38
Ahola, Peter	L.A., Pit., S.J., Cgy.	3	123	10	17	27	137	6	0	0	0	2	....	1991-92	1993-94
Ahrens, Chris	Min.	6	52	0	3	3	84	1	0	0	0	0	....	1972-73	1977-78
● Ailsby, Lloyd	NYR	1	3	0	0	0	2	....	....	....	....	....	....	1951-52	1951-52
Aitken, Brad	Pit., Edm.	2	14	1	3	4	25	....	....	....	....	....	....	1987-88	1990-91
‡ Aitken, Johnathan	Bos., Chi.	2	44	0	1	1	70	....	....	....	....	....	....	1999-00	2003-04
Aivazoff, Micah	Det., Edm., NYI	3	92	4	6	10	46	....	....	....	....	....	....	1993-94	1995-96
‡ Alatalo, Mika	Phx.	2	152	17	29	46	58	5	0	0	0	2	....	1999-00	2000-01
Albelin, Tommy	Que., N.J., Cgy.	18	952	44	211	255	417	81	7	15	22	22	2	1987-88	2005-06
● Albright, Clint	NYR	1	59	14	5	19	19	....	....	....	....	....	....	1948-49	1948-49
Aldcorn, Gary	Tor., Det., Bos.	5	226	41	56	97	78	6	1	2	3	4	....	1956-57	1960-61
Aldridge, Keith	Dal.	1	4	0	0	0	0	....	....	....	....	....	....	1999-00	1999-00
Alexander, Claire	Tor., Van.	4	155	18	47	65	36	16	2	4	6	4	....	1974-75	1977-78
● Alexandre, Art	Mtl.	2	11	0	2	2	8	4	0	0	0	0	....	1931-32	1932-33
Allan, Jeff	Cle.	1	4	0	0	0	2	....	....	....	....	....	....	1977-78	1977-78
Allen, Chris	Fla.	2	2	0	0	0	2	....	....	....	....	....	....	1997-98	1998-99
● Allen, George	NYR, Chi., Mtl.	8	339	82	115	197	179	41	9	10	19	32	....	1938-39	1946-47
Allen, Keith	Det.	2	28	0	4	4	8	5	0	0	0	0	1	1953-54	1954-55
Allen, Peter	Pit.	1	8	0	0	0	8	....	....	....	....	....	....	1995-96	1995-96
● Allen, Viv	NYA	1	6	0	1	1	0	....	....	....	....	....	....	1940-41	1940-41
Alley, Steve	Hfd.	2	15	3	3	6	11	3	0	1	1	0	....	1979-80	1980-81
Allison, Dave	Mtl.	1	3	0	0	0	12	....	....	....	....	....	....	1983-84	1983-84
Allison, Jamie	Cgy., Chi., CBJ, Nsh., Fla.	10	372	7	23	30	639	....	....	....	....	....	....	1994-95	2005-06
Allison, Jason	Wsh., Bos., L.A., Tor.	12	552	154	331	485	441	25	7	18	25	14	....	1993-94	2005-06
Allison, Mike	NYR, Tor., L.A.	10	499	102	166	268	630	82	9	17	26	135	....	1980-81	1989-90
Allison, Ray	Hfd., Phi.	7	238	64	93	157	223	12	2	3	5	20	....	1979-80	1986-87
● Allum, Bill	NYR	1	1	0	1	1	0	....	....	....	....	....	....	1940-41	1940-41
● Amadio, Dave	Det., L.A.	3	125	5	11	16	163	16	1	2	3	18	....	1957-58	1968-69
Ambroziak, Peter	Buf.	1	12	0	1	1	0	....	....	....	....	....	....	1994-95	1994-95
Amodeo, Mike	Wpg.	1	19	0	0	0	2	....	....	....	....	....	....	1979-80	1979-80
Amonte, Tony	NYR, Chi., Phx., Phi., Cgy.	16	1174	416	484	900	752	99	22	33	55	56	....	1990-91	2006-07
● Anderson, Bill	Bos.	1	....	....	....	....	....	1	0	0	0	0	....	1942-43	1942-43
Anderson, Dale	Det.	1	13	0	0	0	6	2	0	0	0	0	....	1956-57	1956-57
Anderson, Doug	Mtl.	1	....	....	....	....	....	2	0	0	0	0	....	1952-53	1952-53
Anderson, Earl	Det., Bos.	3	109	19	19	38	22	5	0	1	1	0	....	1974-75	1976-77
Anderson, Glenn	Edm., Tor., NYR, St.L.	16	1129	498	601	1099	1120	225	93	121	214	442	6	1980-81	1995-96
Anderson, Jim	L.A.	1	7	1	2	3	2	....	....	....	....	....	....	1967-68	1967-68
Anderson, John	Tor., Que., Hfd.	12	814	282	349	631	263	37	9	18	27	2	....	1977-78	1988-89
Anderson, Murray	Wsh.	1	40	0	1	1	68	....	....	....	....	....	....	1974-75	1974-75
Anderson, Perry	St.L., N.J., S.J.	10	400	50	59	109	1051	36	2	1	3	161	....	1981-82	1991-92
Anderson, Ron	Det., L.A., St.L., Buf.	5	251	28	30	58	146	5	0	0	0	4	....	1967-68	1971-72
Anderson, Ron	Wsh.	1	28	9	7	16	8	....	....	....	....	....	....	1974-75	1974-75
Anderson, Russ	Pit., Hfd., L.A.	9	519	22	99	121	1086	10	0	3	3	28	....	1976-77	1984-85
Anderson, Shawn	Buf., Que., Wsh., Phi.	8	255	11	51	62	117	19	1	1	2	16	....	1986-87	1994-95
● Anderson, Tom	Det., NYA, Bro.	8	319	62	127	189	180	16	2	7	9	8	....	1934-35	1941-42
Andersson, Erik	Cgy.	1	12	2	1	3	8	....	....	....	....	....	....	1997-98	1997-98
Andersson, Kent-Erik	Min., NYR	7	456	72	103	175	78	50	4	11	15	4	....	1977-78	1983-84
Andersson, Mikael	Buf., Hfd., T.B., Phi., NYI	15	761	95	169	264	134	25	2	7	9	10	....	1985-86	1999-00
‡ Andersson, Niklas	Que., NYI, S.J., Nsh., Cgy.	6	164	29	53	82	85	....	....	....	....	....	....	1992-93	2000-01
Andersson, Peter	Wsh., Que.	3	172	10	41	51	81	7	0	2	2	2	....	1983-84	1985-86
Andersson, Peter	NYR, Fla.	2	47	6	13	19	20	....	....	....	....	....	....	1992-93	1993-94
Andrascik, Steve	NYR	1	....	....	....	....	....	1	0	0	0	0	....	1971-72	1971-72
Andrea, Paul	NYR, Pit., Cal., Buf.	4	150	31	49	80	10	....	....	....	....	....	....	1965-66	1970-71
● Andrews, Lloyd	Tor.	4	53	8	5	13	10	2	0	0	0	0	1	1921-22	1924-25
Andreychuk, Dave	Buf., Tor., N.J., Bos., Col., T.B.	23	1639	640	698	1338	1125	162	43	54	97	162	1	1982-83	2005-06
Andrievski, Alexander	Chi.	1	1	0	0	0	0	....	....	....	....	....	....	1992-93	1992-93
Andruff, Ron	Mtl., Col.	5	153	19	36	55	54	2	0	0	0	0	....	1974-75	1978-79
Andrusak, Greg	Pit., Tor.	5	28	0	6	6	16	15	1	0	1	8	....	1993-94	1999-00
Angelstad, Mel	Wsh.	1	2	0	0	0	2	....	....	....	....	....	....	2003-04	2003-04
Angotti, Lou	NYR, Chi., Phi., Pit., St.L.	10	653	103	186	289	228	65	8	8	16	17	....	1964-65	1973-74
Anholt, Darrel	Chi.	1	1	0	0	0	0	....	....	....	....	....	....	1983-84	1983-84
Anslow, Hub	NYR	1	2	0	0	0	0	....	....	....	....	....	....	1947-48	1947-48
Antonovich, Mike	Min., Hfd., N.J.	5	87	10	15	25	37	....	....	....	....	....	....	1975-76	1983-84
Antoski, Shawn	Van., Phi., Pit., Ana.	8	183	3	5	8	599	36	1	3	4	74	....	1990-91	1997-98
● Apps, Syl	Tor.	10	423	201	231	432	56	69	25	29	54	8	3	1936-37	1947-48
Apps, Syl	NYR, Pit., L.A.	10	727	183	423	606	311	23	5	5	10	23	....	1970-71	1979-80
Arbour, Al	Det., Chi., Tor., St.L.	16	626	12	58	70	617	86	1	8	9	92	4	1953-54	1970-71
● Arbour, Amos	Mtl., Ham., Tor.	6	113	52	20	72	77	....	....	....	....	....	....	1918-19	1923-24
● Arbour, Jack	Det., Tor.	2	47	5	1	6	56	....	....	....	....	....	....	1926-27	1928-29
Arbour, John	Bos., Pit., Van., St.L.	5	106	1	9	10	149	5	0	0	0	0	....	1965-66	1971-72
● Arbour, Ty	Pit., Chi.	5	207	28	28	56	112	11	2	0	2	6	....	1926-27	1930-31
Archambault, Michel	Chi.	1	3	0	0	0	0	....	....	....	....	....	....	1976-77	1976-77
Archibald, Dave	Min., NYR, Ott., NYI	8	323	57	67	124	139	5	0	1	1	0	....	1987-88	1996-97
Archibald, Jim	Min.	3	16	1	2	3	45	....	....	....	....	....	....	1984-85	1986-87
Areshenkoff, Ron	Edm.	1	4	0	0	0	0	....	....	....	....	....	....	1979-80	1979-80
Armstrong, Bill	Phi.	1	1	0	1	1	0	....	....	....	....	....	....	1990-91	1990-91
● Armstrong, Bob	Bos.	12	542	13	86	99	671	42	1	7	8	28	....	1950-51	1961-62
‡ Armstrong, Chris	Min., Ana.	2	7	0	1	1	0	....	....	....	....	....	....	2000-01	2003-04

Name	NHL Teams	NHL Seasons	Regular Schedule					Playoffs					NHL Cup Wins	First NHL Season	Last NHL Season
			GP	G	A	TP	PIM	GP	G	A	TP	PIM			
Armstrong, George	Tor.	21	1187	296	417	713	721	110	26	34	60	52	4	1949-50	1970-71
Armstrong, Murray	Tor., NYA, Bro., Det.	8	270	67	121	188	72	30	4	6	10	2	....	1937-38	1945-46
• Armstrong, Norm	Tor.	1	7	1	1	2	2	....	....	....	....	....	....	1962-63	1962-63
Armstrong, Tim	Tor.	1	11	1	0	1	6	....	....	....	....	....	....	1988-89	1988-89
Arnason, Chuck	Mtl., Atl., Pit., K.C., Col., Cle., Min., Wsh.	8	401	109	90	199	122	9	2	4	6	4	....	1971-72	1978-79
Arniel, Scott	Wpg., Buf., Bos.	12	730	149	189	338	599	34	3	3	6	39	....	1981-82	1991-92
Arthur, Fred	Hfd., Phi.	3	80	1	8	9	49	4	0	0	0	2	....	1980-81	1982-83
• Arundel, John	Tor.	1	3	0	0	0	9	....	....	....	....	....	....	1949-50	1949-50
Arvedson, Magnus	Ott., Van.	7	434	100	125	225	241	52	3	8	11	34	....	1997-98	2003-04
• Ashbee, Barry	Bos., Phi.	5	284	15	70	85	291	17	0	4	4	22	1	1965-66	1973-74
• Ashby, Don	Tor., Col., Edm.	6	188	40	56	96	40	12	1	0	1	4	....	1975-76	1980-81
Ashton, Brent	Van., Col., N.J., Min., Que., Det., Wpg., Bos., Cgy.	14	998	284	345	629	635	85	24	25	49	70	....	1979-80	1992-93
Ashworth, Frank	Chi.	1	18	5	4	9	2	....	....	....	....	....	....	1946-47	1946-47
• Asmundson, Oscar	NYR, Det., St.L., NYA, Mtl.	5	111	11	23	34	30	9	0	2	2	4	1	1932-33	1937-38
Astashenko, Kaspars	T.B.	2	23	1	2	3	8	....	....	....	....	....	....	1999-00	2000-01
‡ Astley, Mark	Buf.	3	75	4	19	23	92	2	0	0	0	0	....	1993-94	1995-96
• Atanas, Walt	NYR	1	49	13	8	21	40	....	....	....	....	....	....	1944-45	1944-45
Atcheynum, Blair	Ott., St.L., Nsh., Chi.	5	196	27	33	60	36	23	1	3	4	8	....	1992-93	2000-01
• Atkinson, Steve	Bos., Buf., Wsh.	6	302	60	51	111	104	1	0	0	0	0	....	1968-69	1974-75
Attwell, Bob	Col.	2	22	1	5	6	0	....	....	....	....	....	....	1979-80	1980-81
Attwell, Ron	St.L., NYR	1	22	1	7	8	8	....	....	....	....	....	....	1967-68	1967-68
Aubin, Norm	Tor.	2	69	18	13	31	30	1	0	0	0	0	....	1981-82	1982-83
‡ Aubin, Serge	Col., CBJ, Atl.	7	374	44	64	108	361	22	0	1	1	10	....	1998-99	2005-06
Aubry, Pierre	Que., Det.	5	202	24	26	50	133	20	1	1	2	32	....	1980-81	1984-85
Aubuchon, Ossie	Bos., NYR	2	50	20	12	32	4	6	1	0	1	0	....	1942-43	1943-44
Audet, Philippe	Det.	1	4	0	0	0	0	....	....	....	....	....	....	1998-99	1998-99
Audette, Donald	Buf., L.A., Atl., Dal., Mtl., Fla.	15	735	260	249	509	584	73	21	27	48	46	....	1989-90	2003-04
• Auge, Les	Col.	1	6	0	3	3	4	....	....	....	....	....	....	1980-81	1980-81
Augusta, Patrik	Tor., Wsh.	2	4	0	0	0	0	....	....	....	....	....	....	1993-94	1998-99
‡ Aulin, Jared	L.A.	1	17	2	2	4	0	....	....	....	....	....	....	2002-03	2002-03
• Aurie, Larry	Det.	12	489	147	129	276	279	24	6	9	15	10	2	1927-28	1938-39
Awrey, Don	Bos., St.L., Mtl., Pit., NYR, Col.	16	979	31	158	189	1065	71	0	18	18	150	2	1963-64	1978-79
• Ayres, Vern	NYA, Mtl.M., St.L., NYR	6	211	6	11	17	350	....	....	....	....	....	....	1930-31	1935-36

B

Name	NHL Teams	NHL Seasons	GP	G	A	TP	PIM	GP	G	A	TP	PIM	NHL Cup Wins	First NHL Season	Last NHL Season
Babando, Pete	Bos., Det., Chi., NYR	6	351	86	73	159	194	17	3	3	6	6	1	1947-48	1952-53
Babcock, Bobby	Wsh.	2	2	0	0	0	2	....	....	....	....	....	....	1990-91	1992-93
Babe, Warren	Min.	3	21	2	5	7	23	2	0	0	0	0	....	1987-88	1990-91
‡ Babenko, Yuri	Col.	1	3	0	0	0	0	....	....	....	....	....	....	2000-01	2000-01
Babin, Mitch	St.L.	1	8	0	0	0	0	....	....	....	....	....	....	1975-76	1975-76
Baby, John	Cle., Min.	2	26	2	8	10	26	....	....	....	....	....	....	1977-78	1978-79
Babych, Dave	Wpg., Hfd., Van., Phi., L.A.	19	1195	142	581	723	970	114	21	41	62	113	....	1980-81	1998-99
Babych, Wayne	St.L., Pit., Que., Hfd.	9	519	192	246	438	498	41	7	9	16	24	....	1978-79	1986-87
Baca, Jergus	Hfd.	2	10	0	2	2	14	....	....	....	....	....	....	1990-91	1991-92
Backman, Mike	NYR	3	18	1	6	7	18	10	2	2	4	2	....	1981-82	1983-84
• Backor, Pete	Tor.	1	36	4	5	9	6	....	....	....	....	....	1	1944-45	1944-45
Backstrom, Ralph	Mtl., L.A., Chi.	17	1032	278	361	639	386	116	27	32	59	68	6	1956-57	1972-73
• Bailey, Ace	Tor.	8	313	111	82	193	472	21	3	4	7	12	1	1926-27	1933-34
• Bailey, Bob	Tor., Det., Chi.	5	150	15	21	36	207	15	0	4	4	22	....	1953-54	1957-58
• Bailey, Garnet	Bos., Det., St.L., Wsh.	10	568	107	171	278	633	15	2	4	6	28	2	1968-69	1977-78
Bailey, Reid	Phi., Tor., Hfd.	4	40	1	3	4	105	16	0	2	2	25	....	1980-81	1983-84
Baillargeon, Joel	Wpg., Que.	3	20	0	2	2	31	....	....	....	....	....	....	1986-87	1988-89
Baird, Ken	Cal.	1	10	0	2	2	15	....	....	....	....	....	....	1971-72	1971-72
Baker, Bill	Mtl., Col., St.L., NYR	3	143	7	25	32	175	6	0	0	0	0	....	1980-81	1982-83
Baker, Jamie	Que., Ott., S.J., Tor.	9	404	71	79	150	271	25	5	4	9	42	....	1989-90	1998-99
Bakovic, Peter	Van.	1	10	2	0	2	48	....	....	....	....	....	....	1987-88	1987-88
‡ Bala, Chris	Ott.	1	6	0	1	1	0	....	....	....	....	....	....	2001-02	2001-02
‡ Balastik, Jaroslav	CBJ	2	74	13	11	24	30	....	....	....	....	....	....	2005-06	2006-07
Balderis, Helmut	Min.	1	26	3	6	9	2	....	....	....	....	....	....	1989-90	1989-90
Baldwin, Doug	Tor., Det., Chi.	3	24	0	1	1	8	....	....	....	....	....	....	1945-46	1947-48
Balfour, Earl	Tor., Chi.	7	288	30	22	52	78	26	0	3	3	4	1	1951-52	1960-61
• Balfour, Murray	Mtl., Chi., Bos.	8	306	67	90	157	393	40	9	10	19	45	1	1956-57	1964-65
Ball, Terry	Phi., Buf.	4	74	7	19	26	26	....	....	....	....	....	....	1967-68	1971-72
Balmochnykh, Maxim	Ana.	1	6	0	1	1	2	....	....	....	....	....	....	1999-00	1999-00
• Balon, Dave	NYR, Mtl., Min., Van.	14	776	192	222	414	607	78	14	21	35	109	2	1959-60	1972-73
Baltimore, Bryon	Edm.	1	2	0	0	0	4	....	....	....	....	....	....	1979-80	1979-80
Baluik, Stan	Bos.	1	7	0	0	0	2	....	....	....	....	....	....	1959-60	1959-60
Bancroft, Steve	Chi., S.J.	2	6	0	1	1	2	....	....	....	....	....	....	1992-93	2001-02
Bandura, Jeff	NYR	1	2	0	1	1	0	....	....	....	....	....	....	1980-81	1980-81
‡ Banham, Frank	Ana., Phx.	4	32	9	2	11	16	....	....	....	....	....	....	1996-97	2002-03
Banks, Darren	Bos.	2	20	2	2	4	73	....	....	....	....	....	....	1992-93	1993-94
‡ Bannister, Drew	T.B., Edm., Ana., NYR	6	164	5	25	30	161	12	0	0	0	30	....	1995-96	2001-02
Barahona, Ralph	Bos.	2	6	2	2	4	0	....	....	....	....	....	....	1990-91	1991-92
• Barbe, Andy	Tor.	1	1	0	0	0	2	....	....	....	....	....	....	1950-51	1950-51
Barber, Bill	Phi.	14	903	420	463	883	623	129	53	55	108	109	2	1972-73	1983-84
Barber, Don	Min., Wpg., Que., S.J.	4	115	25	32	57	64	11	4	4	8	10	....	1988-89	1991-92
• Barilko, Bill	Tor.	5	252	26	36	62	456	47	5	7	12	104	4	1946-47	1950-51
‡ Barinka, Michal	Chi.	2	34	0	2	2	26	....	....	....	....	....	....	2003-04	2005-06
Barkley, Doug	Chi., Det.	6	253	24	80	104	382	30	0	9	9	63	....	1957-58	1965-66
Barlow, Bob	Min.	2	77	16	17	33	10	6	2	2	4	6	....	1969-70	1970-71
Barnaby, Matthew	Buf., Pit., T.B., NYR, Col., Chi., Dal.	14	834	113	187	300	2562	62	7	15	22	170	....	1992-93	2006-07
Barnes, Blair	L.A.	1	1	0	0	0	0	....	....	....	....	....	....	1982-83	1982-83
Barnes, Norm	Phi., Hfd.	5	156	6	38	44	178	12	0	0	0	8	....	1976-77	1981-82
‡ Barnes, Ryan	Det.	1	2	0	0	0	0	....	....	....	....	....	....	2003-04	2003-04
Baron, Murray	Phi., St.L., Mtl., Phx., Van.	15	988	35	94	129	1309	73	2	8	10	78	....	1989-90	2003-04
Baron, Normand	Mtl., St.L.	2	27	2	0	2	51	3	0	0	0	22	....	1983-84	1985-86
Barr, Dave	Bos., NYR, St.L., Hfd., Det., N.J., Dal.	13	614	128	204	332	520	71	12	10	22	70	....	1981-82	1993-94
Barrault, Doug	Min., Fla.	2	4	0	0	0	2	....	....	....	....	....	....	1992-93	1993-94
Barrett, Fred	Min., L.A.	13	745	25	123	148	671	44	0	2	2	60	....	1970-71	1983-84
Barrett, John	Det., Wsh., Min.	8	488	20	77	97	604	16	2	2	4	50	....	1980-81	1987-88
Barrie, Doug	Pit., Buf., L.A.	3	158	10	42	52	268	....	....	....	....	....	....	1968-69	1971-72
Barrie, Len	Phi., Fla., Pit., L.A.	7	184	19	45	64	290	8	1	0	1	8	....	1989-90	2000-01
Barry, Ed	Bos.	1	19	1	3	4	2	....	....	....	....	....	....	1946-47	1946-47
• Barry, Marty	NYA, Bos., Det., Mtl.	12	509	195	192	387	231	43	15	18	33	34	2	1927-28	1939-40
Barry, Ray	Bos.	1	18	1	2	3	6	....	....	....	....	....	....	1951-52	1951-52
‡ Bartecko, Lubos	St.L., Atl.	5	257	46	65	111	107	12	1	1	2	2	....	1998-99	2002-03
Bartel, Robin	Cgy., Van.	2	41	0	1	1	14	6	0	0	0	16	....	1985-86	1986-87
Bartlett, Jim	Mtl., NYR, Bos.	5	191	34	23	57	273	2	0	0	0	0	....	1954-55	1960-61
• Barton, Cliff	Pit., Phi., NYR	3	85	10	9	19	22	....	....	....	....	....	....	1929-30	1939-40
Bartos, Peter	Min.	1	13	4	2	6	6	....	....	....	....	....	....	2000-01	2000-01
‡ Bartovic, Milan	Buf., Chi.	3	50	3	14	17	26	....	....	....	....	....	....	2002-03	2005-06
‡ Bashkirov, Andrei	Mtl.	3	30	0	3	3	0	....	....	....	....	....	....	1998-99	2000-01
Bassen, Bob	NYI, Chi., St.L., Que., Dal., Cgy.	15	765	88	144	232	1004	93	9	15	24	134	....	1985-86	1999-00
Bast, Ryan	Phi.	1	2	0	1	1	0	....	....	....	....	....	....	1998-99	1998-99
Bathe, Frank	Det., Phi.	9	224	3	28	31	542	27	1	3	4	42	....	1974-75	1983-84
Bathgate, Andy	NYR, Tor., Det., Pit.	17	1069	349	624	973	624	54	21	14	35	76	1	1952-53	1970-71
Bathgate, Frank	NYR	1	2	0	0	0	2	....	....	....	....	....	....	1952-53	1952-53
• Batters, Jeff	St.L.	2	16	0	0	0	28	....	....	....	....	....	....	1993-94	1994-95
Batyrshin, Ruslan	L.A.	1	2	0	0	0	6	....	....	....	....	....	....	1995-96	1995-96
• Bauer, Bobby	Bos.	9	327	123	137	260	36	48	11	8	19	6	2	1936-37	1951-52
Baumgartner, Ken	L.A., NYI, Tor., Ana., Bos.	12	696	13	41	54	2244	51	1	2	3	106	....	1987-88	1998-99
Baumgartner, Mike	K.C.	1	17	0	0	0	0	....	....	....	....	....	....	1974-75	1974-75
Baun, Bob	Tor., Oak., Det.	17	964	37	187	224	1493	96	3	12	15	171	4	1956-57	1972-73
Bautin, Sergei	Wpg., Det., S.J.	3	132	5	25	30	176	6	0	0	0	2	....	1992-93	1995-96
Bawa, Robin	Wsh., Van., S.J., Ana.	4	61	6	1	7	60	1	0	0	0	0	....	1989-90	1993-94
Baxter, Paul	Que., Pit., Cgy.	8	472	48	121	169	1564	40	0	5	5	162	....	1979-80	1986-87
Beadle, Sandy	Wpg.	1	6	1	0	1	2	....	....	....	....	....	....	1980-81	1980-81
Beaton, Frank	NYR	2	25	1	1	2	43	....	....	....	....	....	....	1978-79	1979-80
• Beattie, Red	Bos., Det., NYA	9	334	62	85	147	137	24	4	2	6	8	....	1930-31	1938-39
Beaudin, Norm	St.L., Min.	2	25	1	2	3	4	....	....	....	....	....	....	1967-68	1970-71
‡ Beaudoin, Eric	Fla.	3	53	3	8	11	41	....	....	....	....	....	....	2001-02	2003-04

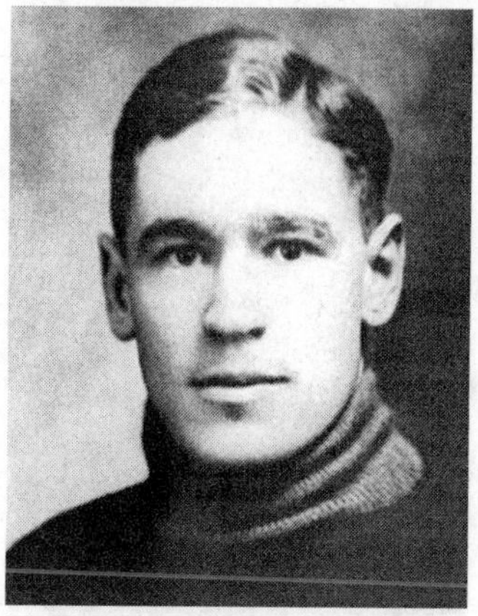
Amos Arbour

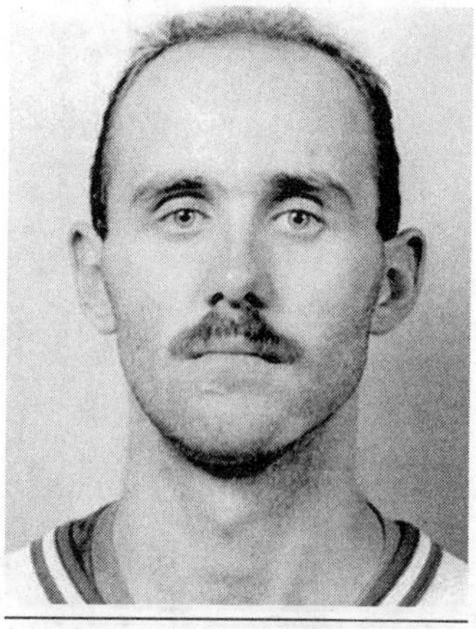
Jergus Baca

Mike Backman

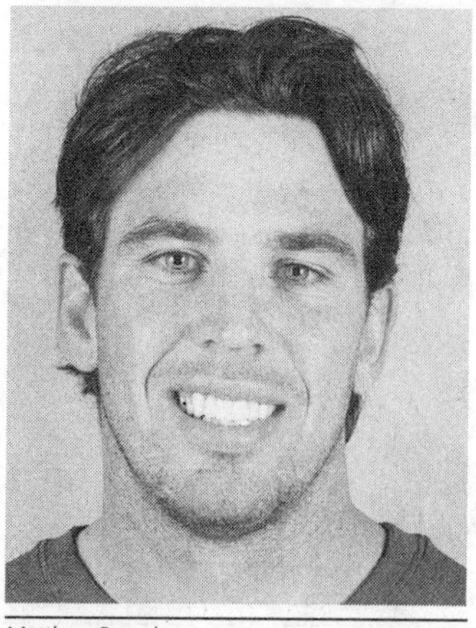
Matthew Barnaby

Alain Belanger

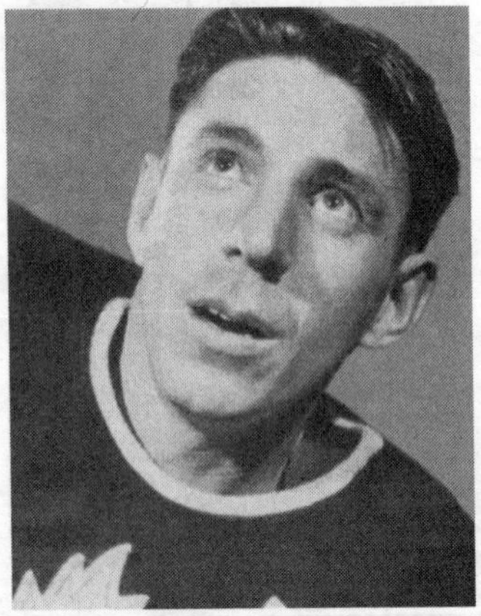

Max Bentley

Doug Berry

Steve Black

Name	NHL Teams	NHL Seasons	Regular Schedule GP	G	A	TP	PIM	Playoffs GP	G	A	TP	PIM	NHL Cup Wins	First NHL Season	Last NHL Season
Beaudoin, Serge	Atl.	1	3	0	0	0	0	....	....	....	....	....	....	1979-80	1979-80
Beaudoin, Yves	Wsh.	3	11	0	0	0	5	....	....	....	....	....	....	1985-86	1987-88
‡ Beaufait, Mark	S.J.	1	5	1	0	1	0	....	....	....	....	....	....	1992-93	1992-93
Beck, Barry	Col., NYR, L.A.	10	615	104	251	355	1016	51	10	23	33	77	....	1977-78	1989-90
Beckett, Bob	Bos.	4	68	7	6	13	18	....	....	....	....	....	....	1956-57	1963-64
Bedard, James	Chi.	2	22	1	1	2	8	....	....	....	....	....	....	1949-50	1950-51
Beddoes, Clayton	Bos.	2	60	2	8	10	57	....	....	....	....	....	....	1995-96	1996-97
‡ Bednar, Jaroslav	L.A., Fla.	3	102	10	25	35	30	3	0	0	0	0	....	2001-02	2003-04
Bednarski, John	NYR, Edm.	4	100	2	18	20	114	1	0	0	0	17	....	1974-75	1979-80
Beers, Bob	Bos., T.B., Edm., NYI	8	258	28	79	107	225	21	1	1	2	22	....	1989-90	1996-97
Beers, Eddy	Cgy., St.L.	5	250	94	116	210	256	41	7	10	17	47	....	1981-82	1985-86
• Behling, Dick	Det.	2	5	1	0	1	2	....	....	....	....	....	....	1940-41	1942-43
• Beisler, Frank	NYA	2	2	0	0	0	0	....	....	....	....	....	....	1936-37	1939-40
‡ Bekar, Derek	St.L., L.A., NYI	3	11	0	0	0	6	....	....	....	....	....	....	1999-00	2003-04
Belanger, Alain	Tor.	1	9	0	1	1	6	....	....	....	....	....	....	1977-78	1977-78
‡ Belanger, Francis	Mtl.	1	10	0	0	0	29	....	....	....	....	....	....	2000-01	2000-01
Belanger, Jesse	Mtl., Fla., Van., Edm., NYI	8	246	59	76	135	56	12	0	3	3	2	1	1991-92	2000-01
Belanger, Ken	Tor., NYI, Bos., L.A.	11	248	11	12	23	695	12	1	0	1	16	....	1994-95	2005-06
Belanger, Roger	Pit.	1	44	3	5	8	32	....	....	....	....	....	....	1984-85	1984-85
Belisle, Danny	NYR	1	4	2	0	2	0	....	....	....	....	....	....	1960-61	1960-61
Beliveau, Jean	Mtl.	20	1125	507	712	1219	1029	162	79	97	176	211	10	1950-51	1970-71
• Bell, Billy	Mtl.W., Mtl., Ott.	6	72	4	2	6	14	5	0	0	0	0	1	1917-18	1923-24
Bell, Bruce	Que., St.L., NYR, Edm.	5	209	12	64	76	113	34	3	5	8	41	....	1984-85	1989-90
Bell, Harry	NYR	1	1	0	1	1	0	....	....	....	....	....	....	1946-47	1946-47
Bell, Joe	NYR	2	62	8	9	17	18	....	....	....	....	....	....	1942-43	1946-47
Belland, Neil	Van., Pit.	6	109	13	32	45	54	21	2	9	11	23	....	1981-82	1986-87
‡ Bellefeuille, Blake	CBJ	2	5	0	1	1	0	....	....	....	....	....	....	2001-02	2002-03
• Bellefeuille, Pete	Tor., Det.	4	92	26	4	30	58	....	....	....	....	....	....	1925-26	1929-30
• Bellemer, Andy	Mtl.M.	1	15	0	0	0	0	....	....	....	....	....	....	1932-33	1932-33
Bellows, Brian	Min., Mtl., T.B., Ana., Wsh.	17	1188	485	537	1022	718	143	51	71	122	143	1	1982-83	1998-99
• Bend, Lin	NYR	1	8	3	1	4	2	....	....	....	....	....	....	1942-43	1942-43
‡ Benda, Jan	Wsh.	1	9	0	3	3	6	....	....	....	....	....	....	1997-98	1997-98
Bennett, Adam	Chi., Edm.	3	69	3	8	11	69	....	....	....	....	....	....	1991-92	1993-94
Bennett, Bill	Bos., Hfd.	2	31	4	7	11	65	....	....	....	....	....	....	1978-79	1979-80
Bennett, Curt	St.L., NYR, Atl.	10	580	152	182	334	347	21	1	1	2	57	....	1970-71	1979-80
Bennett, Frank	Det.	1	7	0	1	1	2	....	....	....	....	....	....	1943-44	1943-44
Bennett, Harvey	Pit., Wsh., Phi., Min., St.L.	5	268	44	46	90	347	4	0	0	0	2	....	1974-75	1978-79
• Bennett, Max	Mtl.	1	1	0	0	0	0	....	....	....	....	....	....	1935-36	1935-36
Bennett, Rick	NYR	3	15	1	1	2	13	....	....	....	....	....	....	1989-90	1991-92
Benning, Brian	St.L., L.A., Phi., Edm., Fla.	11	568	63	233	296	963	48	3	20	23	74	....	1984-85	1994-95
Benning, Jim	Tor., Van.	9	605	52	191	243	461	7	1	1	2	2	....	1981-82	1989-90
• Benoit, Joe	Mtl.	5	185	75	69	144	94	11	6	3	9	11	1	1940-41	1946-47
Benson, Bill	NYA, Bro.	2	67	11	25	36	35	....	....	....	....	....	....	1940-41	1941-42
• Benson, Bobby	Bos.	1	8	0	1	1	4	....	....	....	....	....	....	1924-25	1924-25
• Bentley, Doug	Chi., NYR	13	566	219	324	543	217	23	9	8	17	12	....	1939-40	1953-54
• Bentley, Max	Chi., Tor., NYR	12	646	245	299	544	179	51	18	27	45	14	3	1940-41	1953-54
• Bentley, Reg	Chi.	1	11	1	2	3	2	....	....	....	....	....	....	1942-43	1942-43
‡ Benysek, Ladislav	Edm., Min.	4	161	3	12	15	74	....	....	....	....	....	....	1997-98	2002-03
Beraldo, Paul	Bos.	2	10	0	0	0	4	....	....	....	....	....	....	1987-88	1988-89
‡ Beranek, Josef	Edm., Phi., Van., Pit.	9	531	118	144	262	398	57	5	8	13	24	....	1991-92	2000-01
Berehowsky, Drake	Tor., Pit., Edm., Nsh., Van., Phx.	13	549	37	112	149	848	22	1	3	4	30	....	1990-91	2003-04
Berenson, Red	Mtl., NYR, St.L., Det.	17	987	261	397	658	305	85	23	14	37	49	1	1961-62	1977-78
Berenzweig, Bubba	Nsh.	4	37	3	7	10	14	....	....	....	....	....	....	1999-00	2002-03
Berezan, Perry	Cgy., Min., S.J.	9	378	61	75	136	279	31	4	7	11	34	....	1984-85	1992-93
Berezin, Sergei	Tor., Phx., Mtl., Chi., Wsh.	7	502	160	126	286	54	52	13	17	30	6	....	1996-97	2002-03
‡ Berg, Aki	L.A., Tor.	9	606	15	70	85	374	54	1	7	8	47	....	1995-96	2005-06
Berg, Bill	NYI, Tor., NYR, Ott.	10	546	55	67	122	488	61	3	4	7	34	....	1988-89	1998-99
• Bergdinon, Fred	Bos.	1	2	0	0	0	0	....	....	....	....	....	....	1925-26	1925-26
Bergen, Todd	Phi.	1	14	11	5	16	4	17	4	9	13	8	....	1984-85	1984-85
Berger, Mike	Min.	2	30	3	1	4	67	....	....	....	....	....	....	1987-88	1988-89
Bergeron, Michel	Det., NYI, Wsh.	5	229	80	58	138	165	....	....	....	....	....	....	1974-75	1978-79
Bergeron, Yves	Pit.	2	3	0	0	0	0	....	....	....	....	....	....	1974-75	1976-77
Bergevin, Marc	Chi., NYI, Hfd., T.B., Det., St.L., Pit., Van.	20	1191	36	145	181	1090	79	3	6	9	50	....	1984-85	2003-04
Bergkvist, Stefan	Pit.	2	7	0	0	0	9	4	0	0	0	2	....	1995-96	1996-97
Bergland, Tim	Wsh., T.B.	5	182	17	26	43	75	26	2	2	4	22	....	1989-90	1993-94
Bergloff, Bob	Min.	1	2	0	0	0	5	....	....	....	....	....	....	1982-83	1982-83
Berglund, Bo	Que., Min., Phi.	3	130	28	39	67	40	9	2	0	2	6	....	1983-84	1985-86
‡ Berglund, Christian	N.J., Fla.	3	86	11	16	27	42	3	0	0	0	2	....	2001-02	2003-04
• Bergman, Gary	Det., Min., K.C.	12	838	68	299	367	1249	21	0	5	5	20	....	1964-65	1975-76
Bergman, Thommie	Det.	6	246	21	44	65	243	7	0	2	2	2	....	1972-73	1979-80
Bergqvist, Jonas	Cgy.	1	22	2	5	7	10	....	....	....	....	....	....	1989-90	1989-90
• Berlinquette, Louis	Mtl., Mtl.M., Pit.	8	193	45	33	78	129	11	0	5	5	9	....	1917-18	1925-26
Bernier, Serge	Phi., L.A., Que.	7	302	78	119	197	234	5	1	1	2	0	....	1968-69	1980-81
Berry, Bob	Mtl., L.A.	8	541	159	191	350	344	26	2	6	8	6	....	1968-69	1976-77
Berry, Brad	Wpg., Min., Dal.	8	241	4	28	32	323	13	0	1	1	16	....	1985-86	1993-94
Berry, Doug	Col.	2	121	10	33	43	25	....	....	....	....	....	....	1979-80	1980-81
Berry, Fred	Det.	1	3	0	0	0	0	....	....	....	....	....	....	1976-77	1976-77
Berry, Ken	Edm., Van.	4	55	8	10	18	30	....	....	....	....	....	....	1981-82	1988-89
Bertrand, Eric	N.J., Atl., Mtl.	2	15	0	0	0	4	....	....	....	....	....	....	1999-00	2000-01
Berube, Craig	Phi., Tor., Cgy., Wsh., NYI	17	1054	61	98	159	3149	89	3	1	4	211	....	1986-87	2002-03
• Besler, Phil	Bos., Chi., Det.	2	30	1	4	5	18	....	....	....	....	....	....	1935-36	1938-39
• Bessone, Pete	Det.	1	6	0	1	1	6	....	....	....	....	....	....	1937-38	1937-38
Bethel, John	Wpg.	1	17	0	2	2	4	....	....	....	....	....	....	1979-80	1979-80
Betik, Karel	T.B.	1	3	0	2	2	2	....	....	....	....	....	....	1998-99	1998-99
Bets, Maxim	Ana.	1	3	0	0	0	0	....	....	....	....	....	....	1993-94	1993-94
• Bettio, Sam	Bos.	1	44	9	12	21	32	....	....	....	....	....	....	1949-50	1949-50
Beukeboom, Jeff	Edm., NYR	14	804	30	129	159	1890	99	3	16	19	197	4	1985-86	1998-99
Beverley, Nick	Bos., Pit., NYR, Min., L.A., Col.	11	502	18	94	112	156	7	0	1	1	0	....	1966-67	1979-80
‡ Bezina, Goran	Phx.	1	3	0	0	0	2	....	....	....	....	....	....	2003-04	2003-04
Bialowas, Dwight	Atl., Min.	4	164	11	46	57	46	....	....	....	....	....	....	1973-74	1976-77
Bialowas, Frank	Tor.	1	3	0	0	0	12	....	....	....	....	....	....	1993-94	1993-94
Bianchin, Wayne	Pit., Edm.	7	276	68	41	109	137	3	0	1	1	6	....	1973-74	1979-80
Bicanek, Radim	Ott., Chi., CBJ	7	122	1	11	12	62	7	0	0	0	8	....	1994-95	2001-02
‡ Bicek, Jiri	N.J.	4	62	6	7	13	29	7	0	0	0	0	1	2000-01	2003-04
Bidner, Todd	Wsh.	1	12	2	1	3	7	....	....	....	....	....	....	1981-82	1981-82
Biggs, Don	Min., Phi.	2	12	2	0	2	8	....	....	....	....	....	....	1984-85	1989-90
Bignell, Larry	Pit.	2	20	0	3	3	2	3	0	0	0	2	....	1973-74	1974-75
• Bilodeau, Gilles	Que.	1	9	0	1	1	25	....	....	....	....	....	....	1979-80	1979-80
• Bionda, Jack	Tor., Bos.	4	93	3	9	12	113	11	0	1	1	14	....	1955-56	1958-59
‡ Bishai, Mike	Edm.	1	14	0	2	2	19	....	....	....	....	....	....	2003-04	2003-04
Bissett, Tom	Det.	1	5	0	0	0	0	....	....	....	....	....	....	1990-91	1990-91
Bjugstad, Scott	Min., Pit., L.A.	9	317	76	68	144	144	9	0	1	1	2	....	1983-84	1991-92
Black, James	Hfd., Min., Dal., Buf., Chi., Wsh.	11	352	58	57	115	84	13	2	1	3	4	....	1989-90	2000-01
• Black, Steve	Det., Chi.	2	113	11	20	31	77	13	0	0	0	13	1	1949-50	1950-51
Blackburn, Bob	NYR, Pit.	3	135	8	12	20	105	6	0	0	0	4	....	1968-69	1970-71
Blackburn, Don	Bos., Phi., NYR, NYI, Min.	6	185	23	44	67	87	12	3	0	3	10	....	1962-63	1972-73
• Blade, Hank	Chi.	2	24	2	3	5	2	....	....	....	....	....	....	1946-47	1947-48
Bladon, Tom	Phi., Pit., Edm., Wpg., Det.	9	610	73	197	270	392	86	8	29	37	70	2	1972-73	1980-81
• Blaine, Garry	Mtl.	1	1	0	0	0	0	....	....	....	....	....	....	1954-55	1954-55
• Blair, Andy	Tor., Chi.	9	402	74	86	160	323	38	6	6	12	32	1	1928-29	1936-37
Blair, Chuck	Tor.	1	1	0	0	0	0	....	....	....	....	....	....	1948-49	1948-49
Blair, Dusty	Tor.	1	2	0	0	0	0	....	....	....	....	....	....	1950-51	1950-51
Blaisdell, Mike	Det., NYR, Pit., Tor.	9	343	70	84	154	166	6	1	2	3	10	....	1980-81	1988-89
Blake, Bob	Bos.	1	12	0	0	0	0	....	....	....	....	....	....	1935-36	1935-36
• Blake, Mickey	Mtl.M., St.L., Tor.	3	10	1	1	2	4	....	....	....	....	....	....	1932-33	1935-36
• Blake, Toe	Mtl.M., Mtl.	14	577	235	292	527	272	58	25	37	62	23	3	1934-35	1947-48
‡ Blatny, Zdenek	Atl., Bos.	3	25	3	0	3	8	....	....	....	....	....	....	2002-03	2005-06
• Blight, Rick	Van., L.A.	7	326	96	125	221	170	5	0	5	5	2	....	1975-76	1982-83
• Blinco, Russ	Mtl.M., Chi.	6	268	59	66	125	24	19	3	3	6	4	1	1933-34	1938-39
Block, Ken	Van.	1	1	0	0	0	0	....	....	....	....	....	....	1970-71	1970-71
Bloemberg, Jeff	NYR	4	43	3	6	9	25	7	0	3	3	5	....	1988-89	1991-92
Blomqvist, Timo	Wsh., N.J.	5	243	4	53	57	293	13	0	0	0	24	....	1981-82	1986-87
Blomsten, Arto	Wpg., L.A.	3	25	0	4	4	8	....	....	....	....	....	....	1993-94	1995-96
Bloom, Mike	Wsh., Det.	3	201	30	47	77	215	....	....	....	....	....	....	1974-75	1976-77

			Regular Schedule					Playoffs							
Name	**NHL Teams**	**NHL Seasons**	**GP**	**G**	**A**	**TP**	**PIM**	**GP**	**G**	**A**	**TP**	**PIM**	**NHL Cup Wins**	**First NHL Season**	**Last NHL Season**
Blouin, Sylvain	NYR, Mtl., Min.	6	115	3	4	7	336	....	....	....	....	....	....	1996-97	2002-03
Blum, John	Edm., Bos., Wsh., Det.	8	250	7	34	41	610	20	0	2	2	27	....	1982-83	1989-90
Bodak, Bob	Cgy., Hfd.	2	4	0	0	0	29	....	....	....	....	....	....	1987-88	1989-90
Boddy, Gregg	Van.	5	273	23	44	67	263	3	0	0	0	0	....	1971-72	1975-76
Bodger, Doug	Pit., Buf., S.J., N.J., L.A., Van.	16	1071	106	422	528	1007	47	6	18	24	25	....	1984-85	1999-00
• Bodnar, Gus	Tor., Chi., Bos.	12	667	142	254	396	207	32	4	3	7	10	2	1943-44	1954-55
Boehm, Ron	Oak.	1	16	2	1	3	10	....	....	....	....	....	....	1967-68	1967-68
• Boesch, Garth	Tor.	4	197	9	28	37	205	34	2	5	7	18	3	1946-47	1949-50
Boh, Rick	Min.	1	8	2	1	3	4	....	....	....	....	....	....	1987-88	1987-88
Bohonos, Lonny	Van., Tor.	4	83	19	16	35	22	9	3	6	9	2	....	1995-96	1998-99
Boikov, Alexandre	Nsh.	2	10	0	0	0	15	....	....	....	....	....	....	1999-00	2000-01
• Boileau, Marc	Det.	1	54	5	6	11	8	....	....	....	....	....	....	1961-62	1961-62
‡ Boileau, Patrick	Wsh., Det., Pit.	5	48	5	11	16	26	....	....	....	....	....	....	1996-97	2003-04
• Boileau, Rene	NYA	1	7	0	0	0	0	....	....	....	....	....	....	1925-26	1925-26
Boimistruck, Fred	Tor.	2	83	4	14	18	45	....	....	....	....	....	....	1981-82	1982-83
Boisvert, Serge	Tor., Mtl.	5	46	5	7	12	8	23	3	7	10	4	1	1982-83	1987-88
Boivin, Claude	Phi., Ott.	4	132	12	19	31	364	....	....	....	....	....	....	1991-92	1994-95
Boivin, Leo	Tor., Bos., Det., Pit., Min.	19	1150	72	250	322	1192	54	3	10	13	59	....	1951-52	1969-70
Boland, Mike	K.C., Buf.	2	23	1	2	3	29	3	1	0	1	2	....	1974-75	1978-79
Boland, Mike	Phi.	1	2	0	0	0	0	....	....	....	....	....	....	1974-75	1974-75
Boldirev, Ivan	Bos., Cal., Chi., Atl., Van., Det.	15	1052	361	505	866	507	48	13	20	33	14	1	1969-70	1984-85
Bolduc, Danny	Det., Cgy.	3	102	22	19	41	33	1	0	0	0	0	....	1978-79	1983-84
Bolduc, Michel	Que.	2	10	0	0	0	6	....	....	....	....	....	....	1981-82	1982-83
• Boll, Buzz	Tor., NYA, Bro., Bos.	12	437	133	130	263	148	31	7	3	10	13	....	1932-33	1943-44
Bolonchuk, Larry	Van., Wsh.	4	74	3	9	12	97	....	....	....	....	....	....	1972-73	1977-78
• Bolton, Hugh	Tor.	8	235	10	51	61	221	17	0	5	5	14	1	1949-50	1956-57
Bombardir, Brad	N.J., Min., Nsh.	7	356	8	46	54	127	16	0	1	1	2	1	1997-98	2003-04
Bonar, Dan	L.A.	3	170	25	39	64	208	14	3	4	7	22	....	1980-81	1982-83
Bondra, Peter	Wsh., Ott., Atl., Chi.	16	1081	503	389	892	761	80	30	26	56	60	....	1990-91	2006-07
Bonin, Brian	Pit., Min.	2	12	0	0	0	0	3	0	0	0	0	....	1998-99	2000-01
Bonin, Marcel	Det., Bos., Mtl.	9	454	97	175	272	336	50	11	14	25	51	4	1952-53	1961-62
‡ Bonni, Ryan	Van.	1	3	0	0	0	0	....	....	....	....	....	....	1999-00	1999-00
Bonsignore, Jason	Edm., T.B.	4	79	3	13	16	34	....	....	....	....	....	....	1994-95	1998-99
‡ Bonvie, Dennis	Edm., Chi., Pit., Bos., Ott., Col.	9	92	1	2	3	311	1	0	0	0	0	....	1994-95	2003-04
Boo, Jim	Min.	1	6	0	0	0	22	....	....	....	....	....	....	1977-78	1977-78
• Boone, Buddy	Bos.	2	34	5	3	8	28	22	2	1	3	25	....	1956-57	1957-58
• Boothman, George	Tor.	2	58	17	19	36	18	5	2	1	3	2	....	1942-43	1943-44
Bordeleau, Christian	Mtl., St.L., Chi.	4	205	38	65	103	82	19	4	7	11	17	1	1968-69	1971-72
Bordeleau, J.P.	Chi.	10	519	97	126	223	143	48	3	6	9	12	....	1969-70	1979-80
Bordeleau, Paulin	Van.	3	183	33	56	89	47	5	2	1	3	0	....	1973-74	1975-76
‡ Bordeleau, Sebastien	Mtl., Nsh., Min., Phx.	7	251	37	61	98	118	5	0	0	0	2	....	1995-96	2001-02
Borotsik, Jack	St.L.	1	1	0	0	0	0	....	....	....	....	....	....	1974-75	1974-75
Borsato, Luciano	Wpg.	5	203	35	55	90	113	7	1	0	1	4	....	1990-91	1994-95
Borschevsky, Nikolai	Tor., Cgy., Dal.	4	162	49	73	122	44	31	4	9	13	4	....	1992-93	1995-96
Boschman, Laurie	Tor., Edm., Wpg., N.J., Ott.	14	1009	229	348	577	2265	57	8	13	21	140	....	1979-80	1992-93
Bossy, Mike	NYI	10	752	573	553	1126	210	129	85	75	160	38	4	1977-78	1986-87
• Bostrom, Helge	Chi.	4	96	3	3	6	58	13	0	0	0	16	....	1929-30	1932-33
Botell, Mark	Phi.	1	32	4	10	14	31	....	....	....	....	....	....	1981-82	1981-82
Bothwell, Tim	NYR, St.L., Hfd.	12	502	28	93	121	382	49	0	3	3	56	....	1978-79	1988-89
Botterill, Jason	Dal., Atl., Cgy., Buf.	6	88	5	9	14	89	....	....	....	....	....	....	1997-98	2003-04
Botting, Cam	Atl.	1	2	0	1	1	0	....	....	....	....	....	....	1975-76	1975-76
Boucha, Henry	Det., Min., K.C., Col.	6	247	53	49	102	157	....	....	....	....	....	....	1971-72	1976-77
Bouchard, Butch	Mtl.	15	785	49	144	193	863	113	11	21	32	121	4	1941-42	1955-56
• Bouchard, Dick	NYR	1	1	0	0	0	0	....	....	....	....	....	....	1954-55	1954-55
• Bouchard, Edmond	Mtl., Ham., NYA, Pit.	8	211	19	21	40	117	....	....	....	....	....	....	1921-22	1928-29
Bouchard, Pierre	Mtl., Wsh.	12	595	24	82	106	433	76	3	10	13	56	5	1970-71	1981-82
• Boucher, Billy	Mtl., Bos., NYA	7	213	93	38	131	409	14	3	0	3	17	1	1921-22	1927-28
• Boucher, Bobby	Mtl.	1	11	1	0	1	0	2	0	0	0	0	1	1923-24	1923-24
• Boucher, Clarence	NYA	2	47	2	2	4	133	....	....	....	....	....	....	1926-27	1927-28
• Boucher, Frank	Ott., NYR	14	557	160	263	423	119	55	16	20	36	12	2	1921-22	1943-44
• Boucher, Georges	Ott., Mtl.M., Chi.	15	449	117	87	204	838	28	5	3	8	88	4	1917-18	1931-32
Boudreau, Bruce	Tor., Chi.	8	141	28	42	70	46	9	2	0	2	0	....	1976-77	1985-86
Boudrias, Andre	Mtl., Min., Chi., St.L., Van.	12	662	151	340	491	216	34	6	10	16	12	....	1963-64	1975-76
Boughner, Barry	Oak., Cal.	2	20	0	0	0	11	....	....	....	....	....	....	1969-70	1970-71
Boughner, Bob	Buf., Nsh., Pit., Cgy., Car., Col.	10	630	15	57	72	1382	65	0	12	12	67	....	1995-96	2005-06
Bourbonnais, Dan	Hfd.	2	59	3	25	28	11	....	....	....	....	....	....	1981-82	1983-84
Bourbonnais, Rick	St.L.	3	71	9	15	24	29	4	0	1	1	0	....	1975-76	1977-78
• Bourcier, Conrad	Mtl.	1	6	0	0	0	0	....	....	....	....	....	....	1935-36	1935-36
Bourcier, Jean	Mtl.	1	9	0	1	1	0	....	....	....	....	....	....	1935-36	1935-36
• Bourgeault, Leo	Tor., NYR, Ott., Mtl.	8	307	24	20	44	269	24	1	1	2	18	1	1926-27	1934-35
Bourgeois, Charlie	Cgy., St.L., Hfd.	7	290	16	54	70	788	40	2	3	5	194	....	1981-82	1987-88
Bourne, Bob	NYI, L.A.	14	964	258	324	582	605	139	40	56	96	108	4	1974-75	1987-88
Bourque, Phil	Pit., NYR, Ott.	12	477	88	111	199	516	56	13	12	25	107	2	1983-84	1995-96
Bourque, Raymond	Bos., Col.	22	1612	410	1169	1579	1141	214	41	139	180	171	1	1979-80	2000-01
Boutette, Pat	Tor., Hfd., Pit.	10	756	171	282	453	1354	46	10	14	24	109	....	1975-76	1984-85
Boutilier, Paul	NYI, Bos., Min., NYR, Wpg.	8	288	27	83	110	358	41	1	9	10	45	1	1981-82	1988-89
Bowen, Jason	Phi., Edm.	6	77	2	6	8	109	....	....	....	....	....	....	1992-93	1997-98
Bowler, Bill	CBJ	1	9	0	2	2	8	....	....	....	....	....	....	2000-01	2000-01
Bowman, Kirk	Chi.	3	88	11	17	28	19	7	1	0	1	0	....	1976-77	1978-79
• Bowman, Ralph	Ott., St.L., Det.	7	274	8	17	25	260	22	2	2	4	6	2	1933-34	1939-40
Bownass, Jack	Mtl., NYR	4	80	3	8	11	58	....	....	....	....	....	....	1957-58	1961-62
Bowness, Rick	Atl., Det., St.L., Wpg.	7	173	18	37	55	191	5	0	0	0	2	....	1975-76	1981-82
• Boyd, Bill	NYR, NYA	4	138	15	7	22	72	10	0	0	0	4	1	1926-27	1929-30
• Boyd, Irwin	Bos., Det.	4	96	10	10	20	30	5	0	1	1	4	....	1931-32	1943-44
Boyd, Randy	Pit., Chi., NYI, Van.	8	257	20	67	87	328	13	0	2	2	26	....	1981-82	1988-89
Boyer, Wally	Tor., Chi., Oak., Pit.	7	365	54	105	159	163	15	1	3	4	0	....	1965-66	1971-72
Boyer, Zac	Dal.	2	3	0	0	0	0	2	0	0	0	0	....	1994-95	1995-96
Boyko, Darren	Wpg.	1	1	0	0	0	0	....	....	....	....	....	....	1988-89	1988-89
Bozek, Steve	L.A., Cgy., St.L., Van., S.J.	11	641	164	167	331	309	58	12	11	23	69	....	1981-82	1991-92
Bozon, Philippe	St.L.	4	144	16	25	41	101	19	2	0	2	31	....	1991-92	1994-95
• Brackenborough, John	Bos.	1	7	0	0	0	0	....	....	....	....	....	....	1925-26	1925-26
Brackenbury, Curt	Que., Edm., St.L.	4	141	9	17	26	226	2	0	0	0	0	....	1979-80	1982-83
• Bradley, Bart	Bos.	1	1	0	0	0	0	....	....	....	....	....	....	1949-50	1949-50
Bradley, Brian	Cgy., Van., Tor., T.B.	13	651	182	321	503	528	13	3	7	10	16	....	1985-86	1997-98
Bradley, Lyle	Cal., Cle.	2	6	1	0	1	2	....	....	....	....	....	....	1973-74	1976-77
Brady, Neil	N.J., Ott., Dal.	5	89	9	22	31	95	....	....	....	....	....	....	1989-90	1993-94
Bragnalo, Rick	Wsh.	4	145	15	35	50	46	....	....	....	....	....	....	1975-76	1978-79
‡ Brandner, Christoph	Min.	1	35	4	5	9	8	....	....	....	....	....	....	2003-04	2003-04
• Branigan, Andy	NYA, Bro.	2	27	1	2	3	31	....	....	....	....	....	....	1940-41	1941-42
Brasar, Per-Olov	Min., Van.	5	348	64	142	206	33	13	1	2	3	0	....	1977-78	1981-82
• Brayshaw, Russ	Chi.	1	43	5	9	14	24	....	....	....	....	....	....	1944-45	1944-45
Breault, Francois	L.A.	3	27	2	4	6	42	....	....	....	....	....	....	1990-91	1992-93
Breitenbach, Ken	Buf.	3	68	1	13	14	49	8	0	1	1	4	....	1975-76	1978-79
Bremberg, Fredrik	Edm.	1	8	0	0	0	2	....	....	....	....	....	....	1998-99	1998-99
‡ Brendl, Pavel	Phi., Car., Phx.	4	78	11	11	22	16	2	0	0	0	0	....	2001-02	2005-06
Brennan, Dan	L.A.	2	8	0	1	1	9	....	....	....	....	....	....	1983-84	1985-86
• Brennan, Doug	NYR	3	123	9	7	16	152	16	1	0	1	21	1	1931-32	1933-34
Brennan, Rich	Col., S.J., NYR, L.A., Nsh., Bos.	6	50	2	6	8	33	....	....	....	....	....	....	1996-97	2002-03
• Brennan, Tom	Bos.	2	12	2	2	4	2	....	....	....	....	....	....	1943-44	1944-45
Brenneman, John	Chi., NYR, Tor., Det., Oak.	5	152	21	19	40	46	....	....	....	....	....	1	1964-65	1968-69
• Bretto, Joe	Chi.	1	3	0	0	0	4	....	....	....	....	....	....	1944-45	1944-45
• Brewer, Carl	Tor., Det., St.L.	12	604	25	198	223	1037	72	3	17	20	146	3	1957-58	1979-80
Brickley, Andy	Phi., Pit., N.J., Bos., Wpg.	11	385	82	140	222	81	17	1	4	5	4	....	1982-83	1993-94
• Briden, Archie	Bos., Det., Pit.	2	71	9	5	14	56	....	....	....	....	....	....	1926-27	1929-30
Bridgman, Mel	Phi., Cgy., N.J., Det., Van.	14	977	252	449	701	1625	125	28	39	67	298	....	1975-76	1988-89
• Briere, Michel	Pit.	1	76	12	32	44	20	10	5	3	8	17	....	1969-70	1969-70
‡ Brigley, Travis	Cgy., Col.	3	55	3	6	9	16	....	....	....	....	....	....	1997-98	2003-04
‡ Brimanis, Aris	Phi., NYI, Ana., St.L.	7	113	2	12	14	57	....	....	....	....	....	....	1993-94	2003-04
Brindley, Doug	Tor.	1	3	0	0	0	0	....	....	....	....	....	....	1970-71	1970-71
• Brink, Milt	Chi.	1	5	0	0	0	0	....	....	....	....	....	....	1936-37	1936-37
Brisson, Gerry	Mtl.	1	4	0	2	2	4	....	....	....	....	....	....	1962-63	1962-63
Britz, Greg	Tor., Hfd.	3	8	0	0	0	4	....	....	....	....	....	....	1983-84	1986-87
• Broadbent, Punch	Ott., Mtl.M., NYA	11	303	121	51	172	564	23	4	6	10	60	4	1918-19	1928-29
Brochu, Stephane	NYR	1	1	0	0	0	0	....	....	....	....	....	....	1988-89	1988-89
Broden, Connie	Mtl.	3	6	2	1	3	2	7	0	1	1	0	2	1955-56	1957-58

Dusty Blair

Peter Bondra

Tim Bothwell

Henry Boucha

Brad Brown

Bill Brydge

Marty Burke

George Carey

			Regular Schedule					Playoffs					NHL	First	Last
Name	NHL Teams	NHL Seasons	GP	G	A	TP	PIM	GP	G	A	TP	PIM	Cup Wins	NHL Season	NHL Season
Brooke, Bob	NYR, Min., N.J.	7	447	69	97	166	520	34	9	9	18	59	....	1983-84	1989-90
Brooks, Gord	St.L., Wsh.	3	70	7	18	25	37	....	....	....	....	....	....	1971-72	1974-75
• Brophy, Bernie	Mtl.M., Det.	3	62	4	4	8	25	2	0	0	0	2	1	1925-26	1929-30
Brossart, Willie	Phi., Tor., Wsh.	6	129	1	14	15	88	1	0	0	0	0	....	1970-71	1975-76
Broten, Aaron	Col., N.J., Min., Que., Tor., Wpg.	12	748	186	329	515	441	34	7	18	25	40	....	1980-81	1991-92
Broten, Neal	Min., Dal., N.J., L.A.	17	1099	289	634	923	569	135	35	63	98	77	1	1980-81	1996-97
Broten, Paul	NYR, Dal., St.L.	7	322	46	55	101	264	38	4	6	10	18	....	1989-90	1995-96
Brousseau, Paul	Col., T.B., Fla.	4	26	1	3	4	29	....	....	....	....	....	....	1995-96	2000-01
• Brown, Adam	Det., Chi., Bos.	10	391	104	113	217	378	26	2	4	6	14	1	1941-42	1951-52
Brown, Arnie	Tor., NYR, Det., NYI, Atl.	12	681	44	141	185	738	22	0	6	6	23	....	1961-62	1973-74
‡ Brown, Brad	Mtl., Chi., NYR, Min., Buf.	7	330	2	27	29	747	11	0	0	0	16	....	1996-97	2003-04
Brown, Cam	Van.	1	1	0	0	0	7	....	....	....	....	....	....	1990-91	1990-91
• Brown, Connie	Det.	5	73	15	24	39	12	14	2	3	5	0	1	1938-39	1942-43
Brown, Dave	Phi., Edm., S.J.	14	729	45	52	97	1789	80	2	3	5	209	1	1982-83	1995-96
Brown, Doug	N.J., Pit., Det.	15	854	160	214	374	210	109	23	23	46	26	2	1986-87	2000-01
• Brown, Fred	Mtl.M.	1	19	1	0	1	0	9	0	0	0	0	....	1927-28	1927-28
Brown, George	Mtl.	3	79	6	22	28	34	7	0	0	0	2	....	1936-37	1938-39
• Brown, Gerry	Det.	2	23	4	5	9	2	12	2	1	3	4	....	1941-42	1945-46
Brown, Greg	Buf., Pit., Wpg.	4	94	4	14	18	86	6	0	1	1	4	....	1990-91	1994-95
Brown, Harold	NYR	1	13	2	1	3	2	....	....	....	....	....	....	1945-46	1945-46
Brown, Jeff	Que., St.L., Van., Hfd., Car., Tor., Wsh.	13	747	154	430	584	498	87	20	45	65	59	....	1985-86	1997-98
Brown, Jim	L.A.	1	3	0	1	1	5	....	....	....	....	....	....	1982-83	1982-83
Brown, Keith	Chi., Fla.	16	876	68	274	342	916	103	4	32	36	184	....	1979-80	1994-95
Brown, Kevin	L.A., Hfd., Car., Edm.	6	64	7	9	16	28	1	0	0	0	0	....	1994-95	1999-00
Brown, Larry	NYR, Det., Phi., L.A.	9	455	7	53	60	180	35	0	4	4	10	....	1969-70	1977-78
Brown, Mike	Van., Ana., Chi.	3	34	1	2	3	130	....	....	....	....	....	....	2000-01	2005-06
Brown, Rob	Pit., Hfd., Chi., Dal., L.A.	11	543	190	248	438	599	54	12	14	26	45	....	1987-88	1999-00
‡ Brown, Sean	Edm., Bos., N.J., Van.	9	436	14	43	57	907	9	0	0	0	37	....	1996-97	2005-06
• Brown, Stan	NYR, Det.	2	48	8	2	10	18	2	0	0	0	0	....	1926-27	1927-28
Brown, Wayne	Bos.	1	....	....	....	....	....	4	0	0	0	2	....	1953-54	1953-54
• Browne, Cecil	Chi.	1	13	2	0	2	4	....	....	....	....	....	....	1927-28	1927-28
Brownschidle, Jack	St.L., Hfd.	9	494	39	162	201	151	26	0	5	5	18	....	1977-78	1985-86
• Brownschidle, Jeff	Hfd.	2	7	0	1	1	2	....	....	....	....	....	....	1981-82	1982-83
Brubaker, Jeff	Hfd., Mtl., Cgy., Tor., Edm., NYR, Det.	8	178	16	9	25	512	2	0	0	0	27	....	1979-80	1988-89
Bruce, David	Van., St.L., S.J.	8	234	48	39	87	338	3	0	0	0	2	....	1985-86	1993-94
• Bruce, Gordie	Bos.	3	28	4	9	13	13	7	2	3	5	4	....	1940-41	1945-46
• Bruce, Morley	Ott.	4	71	8	3	11	27	3	0	0	0	2	2	1917-18	1921-22
‡ Brule, Steve	N.J., Col.	2	2	0	0	0	0	1	0	0	0	0	1	1999-00	2002-03
Brumwell, Murray	Min., N.J.	7	128	12	31	43	70	2	0	0	0	2	....	1980-81	1987-88
Brunet, Benoit	Mtl., Dal., Ott.	13	539	101	161	262	229	54	5	20	25	32	1	1988-89	2001-02
• Bruneteau, Eddie	Det.	7	180	40	42	82	35	31	7	6	13	0	....	1940-41	1948-49
• Bruneteau, Mud	Det.	11	411	139	138	277	80	77	23	14	37	22	3	1935-36	1945-46
• Brydge, Bill	Tor., Det., NYA	9	368	26	52	78	506	2	0	0	0	4	....	1926-27	1935-36
Brydges, Paul	Buf.	1	15	2	2	4	6	....	....	....	....	....	....	1986-87	1986-87
• Brydson, Glenn	Mtl.M., St.L., NYR, Chi.	8	299	56	79	135	203	11	0	0	0	8	....	1930-31	1937-38
• Brydson, Gord	Tor.	1	8	2	0	2	8	....	....	....	....	....	....	1929-30	1929-30
Bubla, Jiri	Van.	5	256	17	101	118	202	6	0	0	0	7	....	1981-82	1985-86
• Buchanan, Al	Tor.	2	4	0	1	1	2	....	....	....	....	....	....	1948-49	1949-50
• Buchanan, Bucky	NYR	1	2	0	0	0	0	....	....	....	....	....	....	1948-49	1948-49
Buchanan, Jeff	Col.	1	6	0	0	0	6	....	....	....	....	....	....	1998-99	1998-99
Buchanan, Mike	Chi.	1	1	0	0	0	0	....	....	....	....	....	....	1951-52	1951-52
Buchanan, Ron	Bos., St.L.	2	5	0	0	0	0	....	....	....	....	....	....	1966-67	1969-70
Buchberger, Kelly	Edm., Atl., L.A., Phx., Pit.	18	1182	105	204	309	2297	97	10	15	25	129	2	1986-87	2003-04
Bucyk, John	Det., Bos.	23	1540	556	813	1369	497	124	41	62	103	42	2	1955-56	1977-78
Bucyk, Randy	Mtl., Cgy.	2	19	4	2	6	8	2	0	0	0	0	....	1985-86	1987-88
• Buhr, Doug	K.C.	1	6	0	2	2	4	....	....	....	....	....	....	1974-75	1974-75
Bukovich, Tony	Det.	2	17	7	3	10	6	6	0	1	1	0	....	1943-44	1944-45
Bullard, Mike	Pit., Cgy., St.L., Phi., Tor.	11	727	329	345	674	703	40	11	18	29	44	....	1980-81	1991-92
• Buller, Hy	Det., NYR	5	188	22	58	80	215	....	....	....	....	....	....	1943-44	1953-54
Bulley, Ted	Chi., Wsh., Pit.	8	414	101	113	214	704	29	5	5	10	24	....	1976-77	1983-84
Burakovsky, Robert	Ott.	1	23	2	3	5	6	....	....	....	....	....	....	1993-94	1993-94
• Burch, Billy	Ham., NYA, Bos., Chi.	11	390	137	61	198	255	2	0	0	0	0	....	1922-23	1932-33
• Burchell, Fred	Mtl.	2	4	0	0	0	2	....	....	....	....	....	....	1950-51	1953-54
Burdon, Glen	K.C.	1	11	0	2	2	0	....	....	....	....	....	....	1974-75	1974-75
Bure, Pavel	Van., Fla., NYR	12	702	437	342	779	484	64	35	35	70	74	....	1991-92	2002-03
Bure, Valeri	Mtl., Cgy., Fla., St.L., Dal.	10	621	174	226	400	221	22	0	7	7	16	....	1994-95	2003-04
Bureau, Marc	Cgy., Min., T.B., Mtl., Phi.	11	567	55	83	138	327	50	5	7	12	46	....	1989-90	1999-00
Burega, Bill	Tor.	1	4	0	1	1	4	....	....	....	....	....	....	1955-56	1955-56
• Burke, Eddie	Bos., NYA	4	106	29	20	49	55	....	....	....	....	....	....	1931-32	1934-35
• Burke, Marty	Mtl., Pit., Ott., Chi.	11	494	19	47	66	560	31	2	4	6	44	2	1927-28	1937-38
• Burmister, Roy	NYA	3	67	4	3	7	2	....	....	....	....	....	....	1929-30	1931-32
‡ Burnett, Garrett	Ana.	1	39	1	2	3	184	....	....	....	....	....	....	2003-04	2003-04
Burnett, Kelly	NYR	1	3	1	0	1	0	....	....	....	....	....	....	1952-53	1952-53
• Burns, Bobby	Chi.	3	20	1	0	1	8	....	....	....	....	....	....	1927-28	1929-30
Burns, Charlie	Det., Bos., Oak., Pit., Min.	11	749	106	198	304	252	31	5	4	9	6	....	1958-59	1972-73
Burns, Gary	NYR	2	11	2	2	4	18	5	0	0	0	2	....	1980-81	1981-82
• Burns, Norm	NYR	1	11	0	4	4	2	....	....	....	....	....	....	1941-42	1941-42
Burns, Robin	Pit., K.C.	5	190	31	38	69	139	....	....	....	....	....	....	1970-71	1975-76
Burr, Shawn	Det., T.B., S.J.	16	878	181	259	440	1069	91	16	19	35	95	....	1984-85	1999-00
Burridge, Randy	Bos., Wsh., L.A., Buf.	13	706	199	251	450	458	107	18	34	52	103	....	1985-86	1997-98
Burrows, Dave	Pit., Tor.	10	724	29	135	164	373	29	1	5	6	25	....	1971-72	1980-81
• Burry, Bert	Ott.	1	4	0	0	0	0	....	....	....	....	....	....	1932-33	1932-33
Burt, Adam	Hfd., Car., Phi., Atl.	13	737	37	115	152	961	21	0	1	1	8	....	1988-89	2000-01
Burton, Cummy	Det.	3	43	0	2	2	21	3	0	0	0	0	....	1955-56	1958-59
Burton, Nelson	Wsh.	2	8	1	0	1	21	....	....	....	....	....	....	1977-78	1978-79
• Bush, Eddie	Det.	2	26	4	6	10	40	11	1	6	7	23	....	1938-39	1941-42
Buskas, Rod	Pit., Van., L.A., Chi.	11	556	19	63	82	1294	18	0	3	3	45	....	1982-83	1992-93
Busniuk, Mike	Phi.	2	143	3	23	26	297	25	2	5	7	34	....	1979-80	1980-81
Busniuk, Ron	Buf.	2	6	0	3	3	13	....	....	....	....	....	....	1972-73	1973-74
• Buswell, Walt	Det., Mtl.	8	368	10	40	50	164	24	2	1	3	10	....	1932-33	1939-40
Butcher, Garth	Van., St.L., Que., Tor.	14	897	48	158	206	2302	50	6	5	11	122	....	1981-82	1994-95
‡ Butenschon, Sven	Pit., Edm., NYI, Van.	8	140	2	12	14	86	4	0	0	0	0	....	1997-98	2005-06
Butler, Dick	Chi.	1	7	2	0	2	0	....	....	....	....	....	....	1947-48	1947-48
Butler, Jerry	NYR, St.L., Tor., Van., Wpg.	11	641	99	120	219	515	48	3	3	6	79	....	1972-73	1982-83
Butsayev, Viacheslav	Phi., S.J., Ana., Fla., Ott., T.B.	6	132	17	26	43	133	....	....	....	....	....	....	1992-93	1999-00
‡ Butsayev, Yuri	Det., Atl.	4	99	10	4	14	28	....	....	....	....	....	....	1999-00	2002-03
Butters, Bill	Min.	2	72	1	4	5	77	....	....	....	....	....	....	1977-78	1978-79
Buttrey, Gord	Chi.	1	10	0	0	0	0	....	....	....	....	....	....	1943-44	1943-44
Buynak, Gord	St.L.	1	4	0	0	0	2	....	....	....	....	....	....	1974-75	1974-75
Buzek, Petr	Dal., Atl., Cgy.	6	157	9	22	31	94	....	....	....	....	....	....	1997-98	2002-03
Byakin, Ilja	Edm., S.J.	2	57	8	25	33	44	....	....	....	....	....	....	1993-94	1994-95
Byce, John	Bos.	3	21	2	3	5	6	8	2	0	2	2	....	1989-90	1991-92
• Byers, Gord	Bos.	1	1	0	1	1	0	....	....	....	....	....	....	1949-50	1949-50
• Byers, Jerry	Min., Atl., NYR	4	43	3	4	7	15	....	....	....	....	....	....	1972-73	1977-78
Byers, Lyndon	Bos., S.J.	10	279	28	43	71	1081	37	2	2	4	96	....	1983-84	1992-93
Byers, Mike	Tor., Phi., L.A., Buf.	4	166	42	34	76	39	4	0	1	1	0	....	1967-68	1971-72
‡ Bykov, Dmitri	Det.	1	71	2	10	12	43	4	0	0	0	0	....	2002-03	2002-03
Bylsma, Dan	L.A., Ana.	9	429	19	43	62	184	16	0	1	1	2	....	1995-96	2003-04
Byram, Shawn	NYI, Chi.	2	5	0	0	0	14	....	....	....	....	....	....	1990-91	1991-92
C															
• Caffery, Jack	Tor., Bos.	3	57	3	2	5	22	10	1	0	1	4	....	1954-55	1957-58
Caffery, Terry	Chi., Min.	2	14	0	0	0	0	1	0	0	0	0	....	1969-70	1970-71
• Cahan, Larry	Tor., NYR, Oak., L.A.	13	666	38	92	130	700	29	1	1	2	38	....	1954-55	1970-71
• Cahill, Charles	Bos.	2	32	0	1	1	4	....	....	....	....	....	....	1925-26	1926-27
• Cain, Francis	Mtl.M., Tor.	2	61	4	0	4	35	....	....	....	....	....	....	1924-25	1925-26
• Cain, Herb	Mtl.M., Mtl., Bos.	13	570	206	194	400	178	67	16	13	29	13	2	1933-34	1945-46
Cairns, Don	K.C., Col.	2	9	0	1	1	2	....	....	....	....	....	....	1975-76	1976-77
Cairns, Eric	NYR, NYI, Fla., Pit.	10	457	10	32	42	1182	16	0	0	0	28	....	1996-97	2006-07
Calder, Eric	Wsh.	2	2	0	0	0	0	....	....	....	....	....	....	1981-82	1982-83
• Calladine, Norm	Bos.	3	63	19	29	48	8	....	....	....	....	....	....	1942-43	1944-45
Callander, Drew	Phi., Van.	4	39	6	2	8	7	....	....	....	....	....	....	1976-77	1979-80
Callander, Jock	Pit., T.B.	5	109	22	29	51	116	22	3	8	11	12	1	1987-88	1992-93
Callighen, Brett	Edm.	3	160	56	89	145	132	14	4	6	10	8	....	1979-80	1981-82

Name	NHL Teams	NHL Seasons	Regular Schedule GP	G	A	TP	PIM	Playoffs GP	G	A	TP	PIM	NHL Cup Wins	First NHL Season	Last NHL Season
• Callighen, Patsy	NYR	1	36	0	0	0	32	9	0	0	0	0	1	1927-28	1927-28
‡ Caloun, Jan	S.J., CBJ	3	24	8	6	14	2	....	....	....	....	....	....	1995-96	2000-01
Camazzola, James	Chi.	2	3	0	0	0	0	....	....	....	....	....	....	1983-84	1986-87
Camazzola, Tony	Wsh.	1	3	0	0	0	4	....	....	....	....	....	....	1981-82	1981-82
Cameron, Al	Det., Wpg.	6	282	11	44	55	356	7	0	1	1	2	....	1975-76	1980-81
• Cameron, Billy	Mtl., NYA	2	39	0	0	0	2	2	0	0	0	0	1	1923-24	1925-26
Cameron, Craig	Det., St.L., Min., NYI	9	552	87	65	152	196	27	3	1	4	17	....	1966-67	1975-76
Cameron, Dave	Col., N.J.	3	168	25	28	53	238	....	....	....	....	....	....	1981-82	1983-84
• Cameron, Harry	Tor., Ott., Mtl.	6	128	88	51	139	189	11	5	4	9	16	2	1917-18	1922-23
• Cameron, Scotty	NYR	1	35	8	11	19	0	....	....	....	....	....	....	1942-43	1942-43
Campbell, Bryan	L.A., Chi.	5	260	35	71	106	74	22	3	4	7	2	....	1967-68	1971-72
Campbell, Colin	Pit., Col., Edm., Van., Det.	11	636	25	103	128	1292	45	4	10	14	181	....	1974-75	1984-85
• Campbell, Dave	Mtl.	1	2	0	0	0	0	....	....	....	....	....	....	1920-21	1920-21
Campbell, Don	Chi.	1	17	1	3	4	8	....	....	....	....	....	....	1943-44	1943-44
• Campbell, Earl	Ott., NYA	3	76	6	3	9	14	1	0	0	0	6	....	1923-24	1925-26
‡ Campbell, Jim	Ana., St.L., Mtl., Chi., Fla., T.B.	9	285	61	75	136	268	14	8	3	11	18	....	1995-96	2005-06
Campbell, Scott	Wpg., St.L.	3	80	4	21	25	243	....	....	....	....	....	....	1979-80	1981-82
Campbell, Wade	Wpg., Bos.	6	213	9	27	36	305	10	0	0	0	20	....	1982-83	1987-88
Campeau, Tod	Mtl.	3	42	5	9	14	16	1	0	0	0	0	....	1943-44	1948-49
Campedelli, Dom	Mtl.	1	2	0	0	0	0	....	....	....	....	....	....	1985-86	1985-86
Capuano, Dave	Pit., Van., T.B., S.J.	4	104	17	38	55	56	6	1	1	2	5	....	1989-90	1993-94
Capuano, Jack	Tor., Van., Bos.	3	6	0	0	0	0	....	....	....	....	....	....	1989-90	1991-92
• Carbol, Leo	Chi.	1	6	0	1	1	4	....	....	....	....	....	....	1942-43	1942-43
Carbonneau, Guy	Mtl., St.L., Dal.	19	1318	260	403	663	820	231	38	55	93	161	3	1980-81	1999-00
Cardin, Claude	St.L.	1	1	0	0	0	0	....	....	....	....	....	....	1967-68	1967-68
Cardwell, Steve	Pit.	3	53	9	11	20	35	4	0	0	0	2	....	1970-71	1972-73
• Carey, George	Que., Ham., Tor.	5	72	21	12	33	20	....	....	....	....	....	....	1919-20	1923-24
Carkner, Terry	NYR, Que., Phi., Det., Fla.	13	858	42	188	230	1588	54	1	9	10	48	....	1986-87	1998-99
Carleton, Wayne	Tor., Bos., Cal.	7	278	55	73	128	172	18	2	4	6	14	1	1965-66	1971-72
Carlin, Brian	L.A.	1	5	1	0	1	0	....	....	....	....	....	....	1971-72	1971-72
Carlson, Jack	Min., St.L.	6	236	30	15	45	417	25	1	2	3	72	....	1978-79	1986-87
Carlson, Kent	Mtl., St.L., Wsh.	5	113	7	11	18	148	8	0	0	0	13	....	1983-84	1988-89
Carlson, Steve	L.A.	1	52	9	12	21	23	4	1	1	2	7	....	1979-80	1979-80
Carlsson, Anders	N.J.	3	104	7	26	33	34	3	1	0	1	2	....	1986-87	1988-89
Carlyle, Randy	Tor., Pit., Wpg.	18	1055	148	499	647	1400	69	9	24	33	120	....	1976-77	1992-93
Carnback, Patrik	Mtl., Ana.	4	154	24	38	62	122	....	....	....	....	....	....	1992-93	1995-96
• Caron, Alain	Oak., Mtl.	2	60	9	13	22	18	....	....	....	....	....	....	1967-68	1968-69
Carpenter, Bob	Wsh., NYR, L.A., Bos., N.J.	19	1178	320	408	728	919	140	21	38	59	136	1	1981-82	1998-99
• Carpenter, Ed	Que., Ham.	2	45	10	5	15	41	....	....	....	....	....	....	1919-20	1920-21
Carr, Gene	St.L., NYR, L.A., Pit., Atl.	8	465	79	136	215	365	35	5	8	13	66	....	1971-72	1978-79
• Carr, Lorne	NYR, NYA, Tor.	13	580	204	222	426	132	53	10	9	19	13	2	1933-34	1945-46
Carr, Red	Tor.	1	5	0	1	1	2	....	....	....	....	....	....	1943-44	1943-44
Carriere, Larry	Buf., Atl., Van., L.A., Tor.	7	367	16	74	90	462	27	0	3	3	42	....	1972-73	1979-80
• Carrigan, Gene	NYR, Det., St.L.	3	37	2	1	3	13	4	0	0	0	0	....	1930-31	1934-35
Carroll, Billy	NYI, Edm., Det.	7	322	30	54	84	113	71	6	12	18	18	4	1980-81	1986-87
• Carroll, George	Mtl.M., Bos.	1	16	0	0	0	11	....	....	....	....	....	....	1924-25	1924-25
Carroll, Greg	Wsh., Det., Hfd.	2	131	20	34	54	44	....	....	....	....	....	....	1978-79	1979-80
Carruthers, Dwight	Det., Phi.	2	2	0	0	0	0	....	....	....	....	....	....	1965-66	1967-68
• Carse, Bill	NYR, Chi.	4	124	28	43	71	38	13	3	2	5	0	....	1938-39	1941-42
• Carse, Bob	Chi., Mtl.	5	167	32	55	87	52	10	0	2	2	2	....	1939-40	1947-48
• Carson, Bill	Tor., Bos.	4	159	54	24	78	156	11	3	0	3	14	1	1926-27	1929-30
• Carson, Frank	Mtl.M., NYA, Det.	7	248	42	48	90	166	27	0	2	2	9	1	1925-26	1933-34
• Carson, Gerry	Mtl., NYR, Mtl.M.	6	261	12	11	23	205	22	0	0	0	12	1	1928-29	1936-37
Carson, Jimmy	L.A., Edm., Det., Van., Hfd.	10	626	275	286	561	254	55	17	15	32	22	....	1986-87	1995-96
Carson, Lindsay	Phi., Hfd.	7	373	66	80	146	524	49	4	10	14	56	....	1981-82	1987-88
‡ Carter, Anson	Wsh., Bos., Edm., NYR, L.A., Van., CBJ, Car.	10	674	202	219	421	229	24	8	5	13	4	....	1996-97	2006-07
Carter, Billy	Mtl., Bos.	3	16	0	0	0	6	....	....	....	....	....	....	1957-58	1961-62
Carter, John	Bos., S.J.	8	244	40	50	90	201	31	7	5	12	51	....	1985-86	1992-93
Carter, Ron	Edm.	1	2	0	0	0	0	....	....	....	....	....	....	1979-80	1979-80
• Carveth, Joe	Det., Bos., Mtl.	11	504	150	189	339	81	69	21	16	37	28	2	1940-41	1950-51
Cashman, Wayne	Bos.	17	1027	277	516	793	1041	145	31	57	88	250	2	1964-65	1982-83
Casselman, Mike	Fla.	1	3	0	0	0	0	....	....	....	....	....	....	1995-96	1995-96
Cassels, Andrew	Mtl., Hfd., Cgy., Van., CBJ, Wsh.	16	1015	204	528	732	410	21	4	7	11	8	....	1989-90	2005-06
Cassidy, Bruce	Chi.	7	36	4	13	17	10	1	0	0	0	0	....	1983-84	1989-90
Cassidy, Tom	Pit.	1	26	3	4	7	15	....	....	....	....	....	....	1977-78	1977-78
Cassolato, Tony	Wsh.	3	23	1	6	7	4	....	....	....	....	....	....	1979-80	1981-82
Caufield, Jay	NYR, Min., Pit.	7	208	5	8	13	759	17	0	0	0	42	2	1986-87	1992-93
Cavallini, Gino	Cgy., St.L., Que.	9	593	114	159	273	507	74	14	19	33	66	....	1984-85	1992-93
Cavallini, Paul	Wsh., St.L., Dal.	10	564	56	177	233	750	69	8	27	35	114	....	1986-87	1995-96
Ceresino, Ray	Tor.	1	12	1	1	2	2	....	....	....	....	....	....	1948-49	1948-49
Cernik, Frantisek	Det.	1	49	5	4	9	13	....	....	....	....	....	....	1984-85	1984-85
Chabot, John	Mtl., Pit., Det.	8	508	84	228	312	85	33	6	20	26	2	....	1983-84	1990-91
• Chad, John	Chi.	3	80	15	22	37	29	10	0	1	1	2	....	1939-40	1945-46
• Chalmers, Chick	NYR	1	1	0	0	0	0	....	....	....	....	....	....	1953-54	1953-54
Chalupa, Milan	Det.	1	14	0	5	5	6	....	....	....	....	....	....	1984-85	1984-85
• Chamberlain, Murph	Tor., Mtl., Bro., Bos.	12	510	100	175	275	769	66	14	17	31	96	2	1937-38	1948-49
Chambers, Shawn	Min., Wsh., T.B., N.J., Dal.	13	625	50	185	235	364	94	7	26	33	72	2	1987-88	1999-00
Champagne, Andre	Tor.	1	2	0	0	0	0	....	....	....	....	....	....	1962-63	1962-63
Chapdelaine, Rene	L.A.	3	32	0	2	2	32	....	....	....	....	....	....	1990-91	1992-93
• Chapman, Art	Bos., NYA	10	438	62	176	238	140	26	1	5	6	9	....	1930-31	1939-40
Chapman, Blair	Pit., St.L.	7	402	106	125	231	158	25	4	6	10	15	....	1976-77	1982-83
Chapman, Brian	Hfd.	1	3	0	0	0	29	....	....	....	....	....	....	1990-91	1990-91
Charbonneau, Jose	Mtl., Van.	4	71	9	13	22	67	11	1	0	1	8	....	1987-88	1994-95
Charbonneau, Stephane	Que.	1	2	0	0	0	0	....	....	....	....	....	....	1991-92	1991-92
Charlebois, Bob	Min.	1	7	1	0	1	0	....	....	....	....	....	....	1967-68	1967-68
Charlesworth, Todd	Pit., NYR	6	93	3	9	12	47	....	....	....	....	....	....	1983-84	1989-90
Charron, Eric	Mtl., T.B., Wsh., Cgy.	8	130	2	7	9	127	6	0	0	0	8	....	1992-93	1999-00
Charron, Guy	Mtl., Det., K.C., Wsh.	12	734	221	309	530	146	....	....	....	....	....	....	1969-70	1980-81
Chartier, Dave	Wpg.	1	1	0	0	0	0	....	....	....	....	....	....	1980-81	1980-81
Chartrand, Brad	L.A.	5	215	25	25	50	122	11	1	1	2	8	....	1999-00	2003-04
Chartraw, Rick	Mtl., L.A., NYR, Edm.	10	420	28	64	92	399	75	7	9	16	80	4	1974-75	1983-84
Chase, Kelly	St.L., Hfd., Tor.	11	458	17	36	53	2017	27	1	1	2	100	....	1989-90	1999-00
Chasse, Denis	St.L., Wsh., Wpg., Ott.	4	132	11	14	25	292	7	1	7	8	23	....	1993-94	1996-97
‡ Chebaturkin, Vladimir	NYI, St.L., Chi.	5	62	2	7	9	52	3	0	0	0	2	....	1997-98	2001-02
Check, Lude	Det., Chi.	2	27	6	2	8	4	....	....	....	....	....	....	1943-44	1944-45
Chernoff, Mike	Min.	1	1	0	0	0	0	....	....	....	....	....	....	1968-69	1968-69
Chernomaz, Rich	Col., N.J., Cgy.	7	51	9	7	16	18	....	....	....	....	....	....	1981-82	1991-92
Cherry, Dick	Bos., Phi.	3	145	12	10	22	45	4	1	0	1	4	....	1956-57	1969-70
Cherry, Don	Bos.	1	....	....	....	....	....	1	0	0	0	0	....	1954-55	1954-55
Chervyakov, Denis	Bos.	1	2	0	0	0	2	....	....	....	....	....	....	1992-93	1992-93
• Chevrefils, Real	Bos., Det.	8	387	104	97	201	185	30	5	4	9	20	....	1951-52	1958-59
• Chiasson, Steve	Det., Cgy., Hfd., Car.	13	751	93	305	398	1107	63	16	19	35	119	....	1986-87	1998-99
Chibirev, Igor	Hfd.	2	45	7	12	19	2	....	....	....	....	....	....	1993-94	1994-95
Chicoine, Dan	Cle., Min.	3	31	1	2	3	12	1	0	0	0	0	....	1977-78	1979-80
Chinnick, Rick	Min.	2	4	0	2	2	0	....	....	....	....	....	....	1973-74	1974-75
Chipperfield, Ron	Edm., Que.	2	83	22	24	46	34	....	....	....	....	....	....	1979-80	1980-81
Chisholm, Art	Bos.	1	3	0	0	0	0	....	....	....	....	....	....	1960-61	1960-61
Chisholm, Colin	Min.	1	1	0	0	0	0	....	....	....	....	....	....	1986-87	1986-87
• Chisholm, Lex	Tor.	2	54	10	8	18	19	3	1	0	1	0	....	1939-40	1940-41
‡ Chistov, Stanislav	Ana., Bos.	3	196	19	42	61	116	21	4	2	6	8	....	2002-03	2006-07
Chorney, Marc	Pit., L.A.	4	210	8	27	35	209	7	0	1	1	2	....	1980-81	1983-84
Chorske, Tom	Mtl., N.J., Ott., NYI, Wsh., Cgy., Pit.	11	596	115	122	237	225	50	5	12	17	10	1	1989-90	1999-00
‡ Chouinard, Eric	Mtl., Phi., Min.	4	90	11	11	22	16	....	....	....	....	....	....	2000-01	2005-06
• Chouinard, Gene	Ott.	1	8	0	0	0	0	....	....	....	....	....	....	1927-28	1927-28
Chouinard, Guy	Atl., Cgy., St.L.	10	578	205	370	575	120	46	9	28	37	12	....	1974-75	1983-84
Christian, Dave	Wpg., Wsh., Bos., St.L., Chi.	15	1009	340	433	773	284	102	32	25	57	27	....	1979-80	1993-94
Christian, Jeff	N.J., Pit., Phx.	5	18	2	2	4	17	....	....	....	....	....	....	1991-92	1997-98
Christie, Mike	Cal., Cle., Col., Van.	7	412	15	101	116	550	2	0	0	0	0	....	1974-75	1980-81
Christie, Ryan	Dal., Cgy.	2	7	0	0	0	0	....	....	....	....	....	....	1999-00	2001-02
Christoff, Steve	Min., Cgy., L.A.	5	248	77	64	141	108	35	16	12	28	25	....	1979-80	1983-84
Chrystal, Bob	NYR	2	132	11	14	25	112	....	....	....	....	....	....	1953-54	1954-55
‡ Chubarov, Artem	Van.	5	228	25	33	58	40	27	0	4	4	4	....	1999-00	2003-04
Church, Brad	Wsh.	1	2	0	0	0	0	....	....	....	....	....	....	1997-98	1997-98
• Church, Jack	Tor., Bro., Bos.	5	130	4	19	23	154	25	1	1	2	18	....	1938-39	1945-46

Ed Carpenter

Wayne Cashman

Paul Cavallini

Lex Chisholm

Steve Christoff

Hank Ciesla

Nobby Clark

Charlie Conacher

			Regular Schedule					Playoffs					NHL	First	Last
Name	NHL Teams	NHL Seasons	GP	G	A	TP	PIM	GP	G	A	TP	PIM	Cup Wins	NHL Season	NHL Season
Churla, Shane	Hfd., Cgy., Min., Dal., L.A., NYR	11	488	26	45	71	2301	78	5	7	12	282	....	1986-87	1996-97
Chychrun, Jeff	Phi., L.A., Pit., Edm.	8	262	3	22	25	744	19	0	2	2	65	1	1986-87	1993-94
Chynoweth, Dean	NYI, Bos.	9	241	4	18	22	667	6	0	0	0	26	....	1988-89	1997-98
Chyzowski, Dave	NYI, Chi.	6	126	15	16	31	144	2	0	0	0	0	....	1989-90	1996-97
Ciavaglia, Peter	Buf.	2	5	0	0	0	0	....	....	....	....	....	....	1991-92	1992-93
‡ Cibak, Martin	T.B.	3	154	5	18	23	60	11	0	1	1	0	1	2001-02	2005-06
Ciccarelli, Dino	Min., Wsh., Det., T.B., Fla.	19	1232	608	592	1200	1425	141	73	45	118	211	....	1980-81	1998-99
Ciccone, Enrico	Min., Wsh., T.B., Chi., Car., Van., Mtl.	9	374	10	18	28	1469	13	1	0	1	48	....	1991-92	2000-01
Cichocki, Chris	Det., N.J.	4	68	11	12	23	27	....	....	....	....	....	....	1985-86	1988-89
‡ Ciernik, Ivan	Ott., Wsh.	5	89	12	14	26	32	2	0	1	1	6	....	1997-98	2003-04
Cierny, Jozef	Edm.	1	1	0	0	0	0	....	....	....	....	....	....	1993-94	1993-94
• Ciesla, Hank	Chi., NYR	4	269	26	51	77	87	6	0	2	2	0	....	1955-56	1958-59
Ciger, Zdeno	N.J., Edm., NYR, T.B.	7	352	94	134	228	101	13	2	6	8	4	....	1990-91	2001-02
Cimellaro, Tony	Ott.	1	2	0	0	0	0	....	....	....	....	....	....	1992-93	1992-93
Cimetta, Rob	Bos., Tor.	4	103	16	16	32	66	1	0	0	0	15	....	1988-89	1991-92
Cirella, Joe	Col., N.J., Que., NYR, Fla., Ott.	15	828	64	211	275	1446	38	0	13	13	98	....	1981-82	1995-96
‡ Cirone, Jason	Wpg.	1	3	0	0	0	2	....	....	....	....	....	....	1991-92	1991-92
Cisar, Marian	Nsh.	3	73	13	17	30	57	....	....	....	....	....	....	1999-00	2001-02
Clackson, Kim	Pit., Que.	2	106	0	8	8	370	8	0	0	0	70	....	1979-80	1980-81
• Clancy, King	Ott., Tor.	16	592	136	147	283	914	55	8	8	16	88	3	1921-22	1936-37
Clancy, Terry	Oak., Tor.	4	93	6	6	12	39	....	....	....	....	....	....	1967-68	1972-73
• Clapper, Dit	Bos.	20	833	228	246	474	462	82	13	17	30	50	3	1927-28	1946-47
Clark, Dan	NYR	1	4	0	1	1	6	....	....	....	....	....	....	1978-79	1978-79
Clark, Dean	Edm.	1	1	0	0	0	0	....	....	....	....	....	....	1983-84	1983-84
Clark, Gordie	Bos.	2	8	0	1	1	0	1	0	0	0	0	....	1974-75	1975-76
• Clark, Nobby	Bos.	1	5	0	0	0	0	....	....	....	....	....	....	1927-28	1927-28
Clark, Wendel	Tor., Que., NYI, T.B., Det., Chi.	15	793	330	234	564	1690	95	37	32	69	201	....	1985-86	1999-00
Clarke, Bobby	Phi.	15	1144	358	852	1210	1453	136	42	77	119	152	2	1969-70	1983-84
‡ Clarke, Dale	St.L.	1	3	0	0	0	0	....	....	....	....	....	....	2000-01	2000-01
• Cleghorn, Odie	Mtl., Pit.	10	181	95	34	129	142	12	7	2	9	5	1	1918-19	1927-28
• Cleghorn, Sprague	Ott., Tor., Mtl., Bos.	10	259	83	55	138	538	21	4	3	7	26	2	1918-19	1927-28
Clement, Bill	Phi., Wsh., Atl., Cgy.	11	719	148	208	356	383	50	5	3	8	26	2	1971-72	1981-82
Cline, Bruce	NYR	1	30	2	3	5	10	....	....	....	....	....	....	1956-57	1956-57
Clippingdale, Steve	L.A., Wsh.	2	19	1	2	3	9	1	0	0	0	0	....	1976-77	1979-80
Cloutier, Real	Que., Buf.	6	317	146	198	344	119	25	7	5	12	20	....	1979-80	1984-85
Cloutier, Rejean	Det.	2	5	0	2	2	2	....	....	....	....	....	....	1979-80	1981-82
Cloutier, Roland	Det., Que.	3	34	8	9	17	2	....	....	....	....	....	....	1977-78	1979-80
‡ Cloutier, Sylvain	Chi.	1	7	0	0	0	0	....	....	....	....	....	....	1998-99	1998-99
• Clune, Wally	Mtl.	1	5	0	0	0	6	....	....	....	....	....	....	1955-56	1955-56
Coalter, Gary	Cal., K.C.	2	34	2	4	6	2	....	....	....	....	....	....	1973-74	1974-75
Coates, Steve	Det.	1	5	1	0	1	24	....	....	....	....	....	....	1976-77	1976-77
Cochrane, Glen	Phi., Van., Chi., Edm.	10	411	17	72	89	1556	18	1	1	2	31	....	1978-79	1988-89
Coffey, Paul	Edm., Pit., L.A., Det., Hfd., Phi., Chi., Car., Bos.	21	1409	396	1135	1531	1802	194	59	137	196	264	4	1980-81	2000-01
Coflin, Hugh	Chi.	1	31	0	3	3	33	....	....	....	....	....	....	1950-51	1950-51
Cole, Danton	Wpg., T.B., N.J., NYI, Chi.	7	318	58	60	118	125	1	0	0	0	0	1	1989-90	1995-96
Colley, Kevin	NYI	1	16	0	0	0	52	....	....	....	....	....	....	2005-06	2005-06
Colley, Tom	Min.	1	1	0	0	0	2	....	....	....	....	....	....	1974-75	1974-75
Collings, Norm	Mtl.	1	1	0	1	1	0	....	....	....	....	....	....	1934-35	1934-35
Collins, Bill	Min., Mtl., Det., St.L., NYR, Phi., Wsh.	11	768	157	154	311	415	18	3	5	8	12	....	1967-68	1977-78
Collins, Gary	Tor.	1	....	....	....	....	....	2	0	0	0	0	....	1958-59	1958-59
‡ Collins, Rob	NYI	1	8	1	1	2	0	....	....	....	....	....	....	2005-06	2005-06
Collyard, Bob	St.L.	1	10	1	3	4	4	....	....	....	....	....	....	1973-74	1973-74
• Colman, Michael	S.J.	1	15	0	1	1	32	....	....	....	....	....	....	1991-92	1991-92
• Colville, Mac	NYR	9	353	71	104	175	130	40	9	10	19	14	1	1935-36	1946-47
• Colville, Neil	NYR	12	464	99	166	265	213	46	7	19	26	32	1	1935-36	1948-49
Colwill, Les	NYR	1	69	7	6	13	16	....	....	....	....	....	....	1958-59	1958-59
Comeau, Rey	Mtl., Atl., Col.	9	564	98	141	239	175	9	2	1	3	8	....	1971-72	1979-80
Comrie, Paul	Edm.	1	15	1	2	3	4	....	....	....	....	....	....	1999-00	1999-00
Conacher, Brian	Tor., Det.	5	155	28	28	56	84	12	3	2	5	21	1	1961-62	1971-72
• Conacher, Charlie	Tor., Det., NYA	12	459	225	173	398	523	49	17	18	35	49	1	1929-30	1940-41
Conacher, Jim	Det., Chi., NYR	8	328	85	117	202	91	19	5	2	7	4	....	1945-46	1952-53
• Conacher, Lionel	Pit., NYA, Mtl.M., Chi.	12	498	80	105	185	882	35	2	2	4	34	2	1925-26	1936-37
Conacher, Pat	NYR, Edm., N.J., L.A., Cgy., NYI	13	521	63	76	139	235	66	11	10	21	40	1	1979-80	1995-96
Conacher, Pete	Chi., NYR, Tor.	6	229	47	39	86	57	7	0	0	0	0	....	1951-52	1957-58
• Conacher, Roy	Bos., Det., Chi.	11	490	226	200	426	90	42	15	15	30	14	2	1938-39	1951-52
• Conn, Red	NYA	2	96	9	28	37	22	....	....	....	....	....	....	1933-34	1934-35
Conn, Rob	Chi., Buf.	2	30	2	5	7	20	....	....	....	....	....	....	1991-92	1995-96
• Connelly, Bert	NYR, Chi.	3	87	13	15	28	37	14	1	0	1	0	1	1934-35	1937-38
Connelly, Wayne	Mtl., Bos., Min., Det., St.L., Van.	10	543	133	174	307	156	24	11	7	18	4	....	1960-61	1971-72
Connor, Cam	Mtl., Edm., NYR	5	89	9	22	31	256	20	5	0	5	6	1	1978-79	1982-83
• Connor, Harry	Bos., NYA, Ott.	4	134	16	5	21	149	10	0	0	0	2	....	1927-28	1930-31
• Connors, Bob	NYA, Det.	3	78	17	10	27	110	2	0	0	0	10	....	1926-27	1929-30
Conroy, Al	Phi.	3	114	9	14	23	156	....	....	....	....	....	....	1991-92	1993-94
Contini, Joe	Col., Min.	3	68	17	21	38	34	2	0	0	0	0	....	1977-78	1980-81
Convery, Brandon	Tor., Van., L.A.	4	72	9	19	28	36	5	0	0	0	2	....	1995-96	1998-99
• Convey, Eddie	NYA	3	36	1	1	2	33	....	....	....	....	....	....	1930-31	1932-33
• Cook, Bill	NYR	11	474	229	138	367	386	46	13	11	24	68	2	1926-27	1936-37
• Cook, Bob	Van., Det., NYI, Min.	4	72	13	9	22	22	....	....	....	....	....	....	1970-71	1974-75
• Cook, Bud	Bos., Ott., St.L.	3	50	5	4	9	22	....	....	....	....	....	....	1931-32	1934-35
• Cook, Bun	NYR, Bos.	11	473	158	144	302	444	46	15	3	18	50	2	1926-27	1936-37
• Cook, Lloyd	Bos.	1	4	1	0	1	0	....	....	....	....	....	....	1924-25	1924-25
• Cook, Tom	Chi., Mtl.M.	9	349	77	98	175	184	24	2	4	6	19	1	1929-30	1937-38
• Cooper, Carson	Bos., Mtl., Det.	8	294	110	57	167	111	7	0	0	0	2	....	1924-25	1931-32
Cooper, David	Tor.	3	30	3	7	10	24	....	....	....	....	....	....	1996-97	2000-01
Cooper, Ed	Col.	2	49	8	7	15	46	....	....	....	....	....	....	1980-81	1981-82
• Cooper, Hal	NYR	1	8	0	0	0	2	....	....	....	....	....	....	1944-45	1944-45
• Cooper, Joe	NYR, Chi.	11	420	30	66	96	442	35	3	5	8	58	....	1935-36	1946-47
• Copp, Bobby	Tor.	2	40	3	9	12	26	....	....	....	....	....	....	1942-43	1950-51
• Corbeau, Bert	Mtl., Ham., Tor.	10	258	63	49	112	629	9	2	2	4	38	....	1917-18	1926-27
Corbet, Rene	Que., Col., Cgy., Pit.	8	362	58	74	132	420	53	7	6	13	52	1	1993-94	2000-01
• Corbett, Mike	L.A.	1	....	....	....	....	....	2	0	1	1	2	....	1967-68	1967-68
Corcoran, Norm	Bos., Det., Chi.	4	29	1	3	4	21	4	0	0	0	6	....	1949-50	1955-56
Corkum, Bob	Buf., Ana., Phi., Phx., L.A., N.J., Atl.	12	720	97	103	200	281	62	7	7	14	24	....	1989-90	2001-02
• Cormier, Roger	Mtl.	1	1	0	0	0	0	....	....	....	....	....	....	1925-26	1925-26
Cornforth, Mark	Bos.	1	6	0	0	0	4	....	....	....	....	....	....	1995-96	1995-96
• Corrigan, Chuck	Tor., NYA	2	19	2	2	4	2	....	....	....	....	....	....	1937-38	1940-41
Corrigan, Mike	L.A., Van., Pit.	10	594	152	195	347	698	17	2	3	5	20	....	1967-68	1977-78
Corrinet, Chris	Wsh.	1	8	0	1	1	6	....	....	....	....	....	....	2001-02	2001-02
• Corriveau, Andre	Mtl.	1	3	0	1	1	0	....	....	....	....	....	....	1953-54	1953-54
Corriveau, Yvon	Wsh., Hfd., S.J.	9	280	48	40	88	310	29	5	7	12	50	....	1985-86	1993-94
Corson, Shayne	Mtl., Edm., St.L., Tor., Dal.	19	1156	273	420	693	2357	140	38	49	87	291	....	1985-86	2003-04
Cory, Ross	Wpg.	2	51	2	10	12	41	....	....	....	....	....	....	1979-80	1980-81
Cossette, Jacques	Pit.	3	64	8	6	14	29	3	0	1	1	4	....	1975-76	1978-79
• Costello, Les	Tor.	3	15	2	3	5	11	6	2	2	4	2	1	1947-48	1949-50
Costello, Murray	Chi., Bos., Det.	4	162	13	19	32	54	5	0	0	0	2	....	1953-54	1956-57
Costello, Rich	Tor.	2	12	2	2	4	2	....	....	....	....	....	....	1983-84	1985-86
• Cotch, Charlie	Ham., Tor.	1	12	1	0	1	0	....	....	....	....	....	....	1924-25	1924-25
Cote, Alain	Que.	10	696	103	190	293	383	67	9	15	24	44	....	1979-80	1988-89
Cote, Alain	Bos., Wsh., Mtl., T.B., Que.	9	119	2	18	20	124	11	0	2	2	26	....	1985-86	1993-94
Cote, Patrick	Dal., Nsh., Edm.	6	105	1	2	3	377	....	....	....	....	....	....	1995-96	2000-01
Cote, Ray	Edm.	3	15	0	0	0	4	14	3	2	5	0	....	1982-83	1984-85
Cote, Sylvain	Hfd., Wsh., Tor., Chi., Dal.	19	1171	122	313	435	545	102	11	22	33	62	....	1984-85	2002-03
• Cotton, Baldy	Pit., Tor., NYA	12	503	101	103	204	419	43	4	9	13	46	1	1925-26	1936-37
• Coughlin, Jack	Tor., Que., Mtl., Ham.	3	19	2	0	2	3	....	....	....	....	....	1	1917-18	1920-21
Coulis, Tim	Wsh., Min.	4	47	4	5	9	138	3	1	0	1	2	....	1979-80	1985-86
• Coulson, D'arcy	Phi.	1	28	0	0	0	103	....	....	....	....	....	....	1930-31	1930-31
• Coulter, Art	Chi., NYR	11	465	30	82	112	543	49	4	5	9	61	2	1931-32	1941-42
Coulter, Neal	NYI	3	26	5	5	10	11	....	....	....	....	....	....	1985-86	1987-88
• Coulter, Thomas	Chi.	1	2	0	0	0	0	....	....	....	....	....	....	1933-34	1933-34
Cournoyer, Yvan	Mtl.	16	968	428	435	863	255	147	64	63	127	47	10	1963-64	1978-79
Courteau, Yves	Cgy., Hfd.	3	22	2	5	7	4	1	0	0	0	0	....	1984-85	1986-87
Courtenay, Ed	S.J.	2	44	7	13	20	10	....	....	....	....	....	....	1991-92	1992-93
Courtnall, Geoff	Bos., Edm., Wsh., St.L., Van.	17	1048	367	432	799	1465	156	39	70	109	262	1	1983-84	1999-00
Courtnall, Russ	Tor., Mtl., Min., Dal., Van., NYR, L.A.	16	1029	297	447	744	557	129	39	44	83	83	....	1983-84	1998-99

			Regular Schedule					Playoffs							
Name	NHL Teams	NHL Seasons	GP	G	A	TP	PIM	GP	G	A	TP	PIM	NHL Cup Wins	First NHL Season	Last NHL Season
‡ Courville, Larry	Van.	3	33	1	2	3	16	....	....	....	....	....	....	1995-96	1997-98
• Coutu, Billy	Mtl., Ham., Bos.	10	244	33	21	54	478	19	1	1	2	39	1	1917-18	1926-27
• Couture, Gerry	Det., Mtl., Chi.	10	385	86	70	156	89	45	9	7	16	4	1	1944-45	1953-54
• Couture, Rosie	Chi., Mtl.	8	309	48	56	104	184	23	1	5	6	15	1	1928-29	1935-36
Couturier, Sylvain	L.A.	3	33	4	5	9	4	....	....	....	....	....	....	1988-89	1991-92
Cowick, Bruce	Phi., Wsh., St.L.	3	70	5	6	11	43	8	0	0	0	9	1	1973-74	1975-76
Cowie, Rob	L.A.	2	78	7	12	19	52	....	....	....	....	....	....	1994-95	1995-96
• Cowley, Bill	St.L., Bos.	13	549	195	353	548	143	64	12	34	46	22	2	1934-35	1946-47
• Cox, Danny	Tor., Ott., Det., NYR	8	319	47	49	96	128	10	0	1	1	6	....	1926-27	1933-34
Coxe, Craig	Van., Cgy., St.L., S.J.	8	235	14	31	45	713	5	1	0	1	18	....	1984-85	1991-92
Craig, Mike	Min., Dal., Tor., S.J.	9	423	71	97	168	550	26	2	2	4	49	....	1990-91	2001-02
Craighead, John	Tor.	1	5	0	0	0	10	....	....	....	....	....	....	1996-97	1996-97
Craigwell, Dale	S.J.	3	98	11	18	29	28	....	....	....	....	....	....	1991-92	1993-94
Crashley, Bart	Det., K.C., L.A.	6	140	7	36	43	50	....	....	....	....	....	....	1965-66	1975-76
Craven, Murray	Det., Phi., Hfd., Van., Chi., S.J.	18	1071	266	493	759	524	118	27	43	70	64	....	1982-83	1999-00
Crawford, Bob	St.L., Hfd., NYR, Wsh.	7	246	71	71	142	72	11	0	1	1	8	....	1979-80	1986-87
Crawford, Bobby	Col., Det.	2	16	1	3	4	6	....	....	....	....	....	....	1980-81	1982-83
• Crawford, Jack	Bos.	13	548	38	140	178	202	66	3	13	16	36	2	1937-38	1949-50
Crawford, Lou	Bos.	2	26	2	1	3	29	1	0	0	0	0	....	1989-90	1991-92
Crawford, Marc	Van.	6	176	19	31	50	229	20	1	2	3	44	....	1981-82	1986-87
• Crawford, Rusty	Ott., Tor.	2	38	10	8	18	117	2	2	1	3	9	1	1917-18	1918-19
Creighton, Adam	Buf., Chi., NYI, T.B., St.L.	14	708	187	216	403	1077	61	11	14	25	137	....	1983-84	1996-97
Creighton, Dave	Bos., Tor., Chi., NYR	12	616	140	174	314	223	51	11	13	24	20	....	1948-49	1959-60
• Creighton, Jimmy	Det.	1	11	1	0	1	2	....	....	....	....	....	....	1930-31	1930-31
Cressman, Dave	Min.	2	85	6	8	14	37	....	....	....	....	....	....	1974-75	1975-76
Cressman, Glen	Mtl.	1	4	0	0	0	2	....	....	....	....	....	....	1956-57	1956-57
Crisp, Terry	Bos., St.L., NYI, Phi.	11	536	67	134	201	135	110	15	28	43	40	2	1965-66	1976-77
Cristofoli, Ed	Mtl.	1	9	0	1	1	4	....	....	....	....	....	....	1989-90	1989-90
• Croghan, Maurice	Mtl.M.	1	16	0	0	0	4	....	....	....	....	....	....	1937-38	1937-38
Crombeen, Mike	Cle., St.L., Hfd.	8	475	55	68	123	218	27	6	2	8	32	....	1977-78	1984-85
Cronin, Shawn	Wsh., Wpg., Phi., S.J.	7	292	3	18	21	877	32	1	0	1	38	....	1988-89	1994-95
Cross, Cory	T.B., Tor., NYR, Edm., Pit., Det.	12	659	34	97	131	684	47	2	4	6	62	....	1993-94	2005-06
• Crossett, Stan	Phi.	1	21	0	0	0	10	....	....	....	....	....	....	1930-31	1930-31
Crossman, Doug	Chi., Phi., L.A., NYI, Hfd., Det., T.B., St.L.	14	914	105	359	464	534	97	12	39	51	105	....	1980-81	1993-94
Croteau, Gary	L.A., Det., Cal., K.C., Col.	12	684	144	175	319	143	11	3	2	5	8	....	1968-69	1979-80
Crowder, Bruce	Bos., Pit.	4	243	47	51	98	156	31	8	4	12	41	....	1981-82	1984-85
Crowder, Keith	Bos., L.A.	10	662	223	271	494	1354	85	14	22	36	218	....	1980-81	1989-90
Crowder, Troy	N.J., Det., L.A., Van.	7	150	9	7	16	433	4	0	0	0	22	....	1987-88	1996-97
Crowe, Phil	L.A., Phi., Ott., Nsh.	6	94	4	5	9	173	3	0	0	0	16	....	1993-94	1999-00
Crowley, Mike	Ana.	3	67	5	15	20	44	....	....	....	....	....	....	1997-98	2000-01
Crowley, Ted	Hfd., Col., NYI	2	34	2	4	6	12	....	....	....	....	....	....	1993-94	1998-99
Crozier, Greg	Pit.	1	1	0	0	0	0	....	....	....	....	....	....	2000-01	2000-01
Crozier, Joe	Tor.	1	5	0	3	3	2	....	....	....	....	....	....	1959-60	1959-60
• Crutchfield, Nels	Mtl.	1	41	5	5	10	20	2	0	1	1	22	....	1934-35	1934-35
Culhane, Jim	Hfd.	1	6	0	1	1	4	....	....	....	....	....	....	1989-90	1989-90
Cullen, Barry	Tor., Det.	5	219	32	52	84	111	6	0	0	0	2	....	1955-56	1959-60
Cullen, Brian	Tor., NYR	7	326	56	100	156	92	19	3	0	3	2	....	1954-55	1960-61
‡ Cullen, David	Phx., Min.	2	19	0	0	0	6	....	....	....	....	....	....	2000-01	2001-02
Cullen, John	Pit., Hfd., Tor., T.B.	11	621	187	363	550	898	53	12	22	34	58	....	1988-89	1998-99
Cullen, Ray	NYR, Det., Min., Van.	6	313	92	123	215	120	20	3	10	13	2	....	1965-66	1970-71
Cummins, Barry	Cal.	1	36	1	2	3	39	....	....	....	....	....	....	1973-74	1973-74
Cummins, Jim	Det., Phi., T.B., Chi., Phx., Mtl., Ana., NYI, Col.	12	511	24	36	60	1538	37	1	2	3	43	....	1991-92	2003-04
Cunneyworth, Randy	Buf., Pit., Wpg., Hfd., Chi., Ott.	16	866	189	225	414	1280	45	7	7	14	61	....	1980-81	1998-99
Cunningham, Bob	NYR	2	4	0	1	1	0	....	....	....	....	....	....	1960-61	1961-62
Cunningham, Jim	Phi.	1	1	0	0	0	4	....	....	....	....	....	....	1977-78	1977-78
• Cunningham, Les	NYA, Chi.	2	60	7	19	26	21	1	0	0	0	0	....	1936-37	1939-40
• Cupolo, Bill	Bos.	1	47	11	13	24	10	7	1	2	3	0	....	1944-45	1944-45
Curran, Brian	Bos., NYI, Tor., Buf., Wsh.	10	381	7	33	40	1461	24	0	1	1	122	....	1983-84	1993-94
Currie, Dan	Edm., L.A.	4	22	2	1	3	4	....	....	....	....	....	....	1990-91	1993-94
Currie, Glen	Wsh., L.A.	8	326	39	79	118	100	12	1	3	4	4	....	1979-80	1987-88
Currie, Hugh	Mtl.	1	1	0	0	0	0	....	....	....	....	....	....	1950-51	1950-51
Currie, Tony	St.L., Van., Hfd.	8	290	92	119	211	83	16	4	12	16	14	....	1977-78	1984-85
• Curry, Floyd	Mtl.	11	601	105	99	204	147	91	23	17	40	38	4	1947-48	1957-58
Curtale, Tony	Cgy.	1	2	0	0	0	0	....	....	....	....	....	....	1980-81	1980-81
Curtis, Paul	Mtl., L.A., St.L.	4	185	3	34	37	161	5	0	0	0	2	....	1969-70	1972-73
Cushenan, Ian	Chi., Mtl., NYR, Det.	5	129	3	11	14	134	....	....	....	....	....	1	1956-57	1963-64
Cusson, Jean	Oak.	1	2	0	0	0	0	....	....	....	....	....	....	1967-68	1967-68
‡ Cutta, Jakub	Wsh.	3	8	0	0	0	0	....	....	....	....	....	....	2000-01	2003-04
Cyr, Denis	Cgy., Chi., St.L.	6	193	41	43	84	36	4	0	0	0	0	....	1980-81	1985-86
Cyr, Paul	Buf., NYR, Hfd.	9	470	101	140	241	623	24	4	6	10	31	....	1982-83	1991-92
‡ Czerkawski, Mariusz	Bos., Edm., NYI, Mtl., Tor.	12	745	215	220	435	274	42	8	7	15	18	....	1993-94	2005-06

D

‡ Dackell, Andreas	Ott., Mtl.	8	613	91	159	250	162	44	5	5	10	10	....	1996-97	2003-04
‡ Dagenais, Pierre	N.J., Fla., Mtl.	5	142	35	23	58	58	8	0	1	1	6	....	2000-01	2005-06
Dahl, Kevin	Cgy., Phx., Tor., CBJ	8	188	7	22	29	153	16	0	2	2	12	....	1992-93	2000-01
Dahlen, Ulf	NYR, Min., Dal., S.J., Chi., Wsh.	14	966	301	354	655	230	85	15	25	40	12	....	1987-88	2002-03
Dahlin, Kjell	Mtl.	3	166	57	59	116	10	35	6	11	17	6	1	1985-86	1987-88
‡ Dahlman, Toni	Ott.	2	22	1	1	2	0	....	....	....	....	....	....	2001-02	2002-03
Dahlquist, Chris	Pit., Min., Cgy., Ott.	11	532	19	71	90	488	39	4	7	11	30	....	1985-86	1995-96
• Dahlstrom, Cully	Chi.	8	342	88	118	206	58	29	6	8	14	4	1	1937-38	1944-45
Daigle, Alain	Chi.	6	389	56	50	106	122	17	0	1	1	0	....	1974-75	1979-80
‡ Daigle, Alexandre	Ott., Phi., T.B., NYR, Pit., Min.	10	616	129	198	327	186	12	0	2	2	2	....	1993-94	2005-06
Daigneault, J.J.	Van., Phi., Mtl., St.L., Pit., Ana., NYI, Nsh., Phx., Min.	16	899	53	197	250	687	99	5	26	31	100	1	1984-85	2000-01
Dailey, Bob	Van., Phi.	9	561	94	231	325	814	63	12	34	46	105	....	1973-74	1981-82
• Daley, Frank	Det.	1	5	0	0	0	0	2	0	0	0	0	....	1928-29	1928-29
Daley, Pat	Wpg.	2	12	1	0	1	13	....	....	....	....	....	....	1979-80	1980-81
Dalgarno, Brad	NYI	10	321	49	71	120	332	27	2	4	6	37	....	1985-86	1995-96
Dallman, Marty	Tor.	2	6	0	1	1	0	....	....	....	....	....	....	1987-88	1988-89
Dallman, Rod	NYI, Phi.	4	6	1	0	1	26	1	0	1	1	0	....	1987-88	1991-92
• Dame, Bunny	Mtl.	1	34	2	5	7	4	....	....	....	....	....	....	1941-42	1941-42
• Damore, Hank	NYR	1	4	1	0	1	2	....	....	....	....	....	....	1943-44	1943-44
Damphousse, Vincent	Tor., Edm., Mtl., S.J.	18	1378	432	773	1205	1190	140	41	63	104	144	1	1986-87	2003-04
Daneyko, Ken	N.J.	20	1283	36	142	178	2519	175	5	17	22	296	3	1983-84	2002-03
Daniels, Jeff	Pit., Fla., Hfd., Car., Nsh.	12	425	17	26	43	83	41	3	5	8	2	1	1990-91	2002-03
‡ Daniels, Kimbi	Phi.	2	27	1	2	3	4	....	....	....	....	....	....	1990-91	1991-92
Daniels, Scott	Hfd., Phi., N.J.	6	149	8	12	20	667	1	0	0	0	0	....	1992-93	1998-99
Danton, Mike	N.J., St.L.	3	87	9	5	14	182	5	1	0	1	2	....	2000-01	2003-04
Daoust, Dan	Mtl., Tor.	8	522	87	167	254	544	32	7	5	12	83	....	1982-83	1989-90
‡ Darby, Craig	Mtl., NYI, Phi., N.J.	9	196	21	35	56	32	....	....	....	....	....	....	1994-95	2003-04
Dark, Michael	St.L.	2	43	5	6	11	14	....	....	....	....	....	....	1986-87	1987-88
• Darragh, Harold	Pit., Phi., Bos., Tor.	8	308	68	49	117	50	16	1	3	4	4	1	1925-26	1932-33
• Darragh, Jack	Ott.	6	121	66	46	112	113	11	3	0	3	9	3	1917-18	1923-24
David, Richard	Que.	3	31	4	4	8	10	1	0	0	0	0	....	1979-80	1982-83
• Davidson, Bob	Tor.	12	491	94	160	254	398	79	5	17	22	76	2	1934-35	1945-46
• Davidson, Gord	NYR	2	51	3	6	9	8	....	....	....	....	....	....	1942-43	1943-44
‡ Davidson, Matt	CBJ	3	56	5	7	12	28	....	....	....	....	....	....	2000-01	2002-03
‡ Davidsson, Johan	Ana., NYI	2	83	6	9	15	16	1	0	0	0	0	....	1998-99	1999-00
• Davie, Bob	Bos.	3	41	0	1	1	25	....	....	....	....	....	....	1933-34	1935-36
• Davies, Buck	NYR	1	....	....	....	....	....	1	0	0	0	0	....	1947-48	1947-48
• Davis, Bob	Det.	1	3	0	0	0	0	....	....	....	....	....	....	1932-33	1932-33
Davis, Kim	Pit., Tor.	4	36	5	7	12	51	4	0	0	0	0	....	1977-78	1980-81
• Davis, Lorne	Mtl., Chi., Det., Bos.	6	95	8	12	20	20	18	3	1	4	10	1	1951-52	1959-60
Davis, Mal	Det., Buf.	6	100	31	22	53	34	7	1	0	1	0	....	1978-79	1985-86
• Davison, Murray	Bos.	1	1	0	0	0	0	....	....	....	....	....	....	1965-66	1965-66
Davydov, Evgeny	Wpg., Fla., Ott.	4	155	40	39	79	120	11	2	2	4	2	....	1991-92	1994-95
‡ Daw, Jeff	Col.	1	1	0	1	1	0	....	....	....	....	....	....	2001-02	2001-02
Dawe, Jason	Buf., NYI, Mtl., NYR	8	366	86	90	176	162	22	4	3	7	18	....	1993-94	2001-02
• Dawes, Bob	Tor., Mtl.	4	32	2	7	9	6	10	0	0	0	2	1	1946-47	1950-51
• Day, Hap	Tor., NYA	14	581	86	116	202	601	53	4	7	11	56	1	1924-25	1937-38
Day, Joe	Hfd., NYI	3	72	1	10	11	87	....	....	....	....	....	....	1991-92	1993-94

Keith Crowder

Paul Curtis

Marty Dallman

Nelson Debenedet

Bill Derlago

Chuck Dinsmore

Jordy Douglas

Duke Dukowski

			Regular Schedule					Playoffs					NHL	First	Last
Name	NHL Teams	NHL Seasons	GP	G	A	TP	PIM	GP	G	A	TP	PIM	Cup Wins	NHL Season	NHL Season
Daze, Eric	Chi.	11	601	226	172	398	176	37	5	7	12	8	....	1994-95	2005-06
Dea, Billy	NYR, Det., Chi., Pit.	8	397	67	54	121	44	11	2	1	3	6	....	1953-54	1970-71
• Deacon, Don	Det.	3	30	6	4	10	6	2	2	1	3	0	....	1936-37	1939-40
Deadmarsh, Adam	Que., Col., L.A.	10	567	184	189	373	819	105	26	40	66	100	1	1994-95	2003-04
Deadmarsh, Butch	Buf., Atl., K.C.	5	137	12	5	17	155	4	0	0	0	17	....	1970-71	1974-75
Dean, Barry	Col., Phi.	3	165	25	56	81	146	....	....	....	....	....	....	1976-77	1978-79
Dean, Kevin	N.J., Atl., Dal., Chi.	7	331	7	48	55	138	16	2	2	4	2	1	1994-95	2000-01
Debenedet, Nelson	Det., Pit.	2	46	10	4	14	13	....	....	....	....	....	....	1973-74	1974-75
DeBlois, Lucien	NYR, Col., Wpg., Mtl., Que., Tor.	15	993	249	276	525	814	52	7	6	13	38	1	1977-78	1991-92
Debol, Dave	Hfd.	2	92	26	26	52	4	3	0	0	0	0	....	1979-80	1980-81
DeBrusk, Louie	Edm., T.B., Phx., Chi.	11	401	24	17	41	1161	15	2	0	2	10	....	1991-92	2002-03
DeFauw, Brad	Car.	1	9	3	0	3	2	....	....	....	....	....	....	2002-03	2002-03
Defazio, Dean	Pit.	1	22	0	2	2	28	....	....	....	....	....	....	1983-84	1983-84
DeGray, Dale	Cgy., Tor., L.A., Buf.	5	153	18	47	65	195	13	1	3	4	28	....	1985-86	1989-90
• Delisle, Jonathan	Mtl.	1	1	0	0	0	0	....	....	....	....	....	....	1998-99	1998-99
Delisle, Xavier	T.B., Mtl.	2	16	3	2	5	6	....	....	....	....	....	....	1998-99	2000-01
• Delmonte, Armand	Bos.	1	1	0	0	0	0	....	....	....	....	....	....	1945-46	1945-46
‡ Delmore, Andy	Phi., Nsh., Buf., CBJ	7	283	43	58	101	105	20	6	2	8	16	....	1998-99	2005-06
Delorme, Gilbert	Mtl., St.L., Que., Det., Pit.	9	541	31	92	123	520	56	1	9	10	56	....	1981-82	1989-90
Delorme, Ron	Col., Van.	9	524	83	83	166	667	25	1	2	3	59	....	1976-77	1984-85
Delory, Val	NYR	1	1	0	0	0	0	....	....	....	....	....	....	1948-49	1948-49
Delparte, Guy	Col.	1	48	1	8	9	18	....	....	....	....	....	....	1976-77	1976-77
Delvecchio, Alex	Det.	24	1549	456	825	1281	383	121	35	69	104	29	3	1950-51	1973-74
• DeMarco, Ab	Chi., Tor., Bos., NYR	7	209	72	93	165	53	11	3	0	3	2	....	1938-39	1946-47
DeMarco, Ab	NYR, St.L., Pit., Van., L.A., Bos.	9	344	44	80	124	75	25	1	2	3	17	....	1969-70	1978-79
• Demers, Tony	Mtl., NYR	6	83	20	22	42	23	2	0	0	0	0	....	1937-38	1943-44
‡ Dempsey, Nathan	Tor., Chi., L.A., Bos.	8	260	21	67	88	120	6	0	2	2	0	....	1996-97	2006-07
Denis, Jean-Paul	NYR	2	10	0	2	2	2	....	....	....	....	....	....	1946-47	1949-50
Denis, Lulu	Mtl.	2	3	0	1	1	0	....	....	....	....	....	....	1949-50	1950-51
• Denneny, Corb	Tor., Ham., Chi.	9	176	103	42	145	148	6	1	0	1	7	2	1917-18	1927-28
• Denneny, Cy	Ott., Bos.	12	328	248	85	333	301	25	16	2	18	23	5	1917-18	1928-29
Dennis, Norm	St.L.	4	12	3	0	3	11	5	0	0	0	2	....	1968-69	1971-72
• Denoird, Gerry	Tor.	1	17	0	1	1	0	....	....	....	....	....	....	1922-23	1922-23
DePalma, Larry	Min., S.J., Pit.	7	148	21	20	41	408	3	0	0	0	6	....	1985-86	1993-94
Derlago, Bill	Van., Tor., Bos., Wpg., Que.	9	555	189	227	416	247	13	5	0	5	8	....	1978-79	1986-87
• Desaulniers, Gerard	Mtl.	3	8	0	2	2	4	....	....	....	....	....	....	1950-51	1953-54
Descoteaux, Matthieu	Mtl.	1	5	1	1	2	4	....	....	....	....	....	....	2000-01	2000-01
• Desilets, Joffre	Mtl., Chi.	5	192	37	45	82	57	7	1	0	1	7	....	1935-36	1939-40
Desjardins, Eric	Mtl., Phi.	17	1143	136	439	575	757	168	23	57	80	93	1	1988-89	2005-06
Desjardins, Martin	Mtl.	1	8	0	2	2	2	....	....	....	....	....	....	1989-90	1989-90
• Desjardins, Vic	Chi., NYR	2	87	6	15	21	27	16	0	0	0	0	....	1930-31	1931-32
Deslauriers, Jacques	Mtl.	1	2	0	0	0	0	....	....	....	....	....	....	1955-56	1955-56
Deuling, Jarrett	NYI	2	15	0	1	1	11	....	....	....	....	....	....	1995-96	1996-97
Devine, Kevin	NYI	1	2	0	1	1	8	....	....	....	....	....	....	1982-83	1982-83
• Dewar, Tom	NYR	1	9	0	2	2	4	....	....	....	....	....	....	1943-44	1943-44
• Dewsbury, Al	Det., Chi.	9	347	30	78	108	365	14	1	5	6	16	1	1946-47	1955-56
Deziel, Michel	Buf.	1	....	....	....	....	....	1	0	0	0	0	....	1974-75	1974-75
• Dheere, Marcel	Mtl.	1	11	1	2	3	2	5	0	0	0	6	....	1942-43	1942-43
Diachuk, Edward	Det.	1	12	0	0	0	19	....	....	....	....	....	....	1960-61	1960-61
• Dick, Harry	Chi.	1	12	0	1	1	12	....	....	....	....	....	....	1946-47	1946-47
• Dickens, Ernie	Tor., Chi.	6	278	12	44	56	98	13	0	0	0	4	1	1941-42	1950-51
Dickenson, Herb	NYR	2	48	18	17	35	10	....	....	....	....	....	....	1951-52	1952-53
Diduck, Gerald	NYI, Mtl., Van., Chi., Hfd., Phx., Tor., Dal.	17	932	56	156	212	1612	114	8	16	24	212	....	1984-85	2000-01
Dietrich, Don	Chi., N.J.	2	28	0	7	7	10	....	....	....	....	....	....	1983-84	1985-86
• Dill, Bob	NYR	2	76	15	15	30	135	....	....	....	....	....	....	1943-44	1944-45
• Dillabough, Bob	Det., Bos., Pit., Oak.	9	283	32	54	86	76	17	3	0	3	0	....	1961-62	1969-70
• Dillon, Cecil	NYR, Det.	10	453	167	131	298	105	43	14	9	23	14	1	1930-31	1939-40
Dillon, Gary	Col.	1	13	1	1	2	29	....	....	....	....	....	....	1980-81	1980-81
Dillon, Wayne	NYR, Wpg.	4	229	43	66	109	60	3	0	1	1	0	....	1975-76	1979-80
DiMaio, Rob	NYI, T.B., Phi., Bos., NYR, Car., Dal.	17	894	106	171	277	840	62	7	9	16	40	....	1988-89	2005-06
Dineen, Bill	Det., Chi.	5	323	51	44	95	122	37	1	1	2	18	2	1953-54	1957-58
• Dineen, Gary	Min.	1	4	0	1	1	0	....	....	....	....	....	....	1968-69	1968-69
Dineen, Gord	NYI, Min., Pit., Ott.	13	528	16	90	106	695	40	1	7	8	68	....	1982-83	1994-95
Dineen, Kevin	Hfd., Phi., Car., Ott., CBJ	19	1188	355	405	760	2229	59	23	18	41	127	....	1984-85	2002-03
Dineen, Peter	L.A., Det.	2	13	0	2	2	13	....	....	....	....	....	....	1986-87	1989-90
Dingman, Chris	Cgy., Col., Car., T.B.	8	385	15	19	34	769	52	2	5	7	100	2	1997-98	2005-06
• Dinsmore, Chuck	Mtl.M.	4	100	6	2	8	50	8	1	0	1	2	1	1924-25	1929-30
Dionne, Gilbert	Mtl., Phi., Fla.	6	223	61	79	140	108	39	10	12	22	34	1	1990-91	1995-96
Dionne, Marcel	Det., L.A., NYR	18	1348	731	1040	1771	600	49	21	24	45	17	....	1971-72	1988-89
‡ DiPietro, Paul	Mtl., Tor., L.A.	6	192	31	49	80	96	31	11	10	21	10	1	1991-92	1996-97
Dirk, Robert	St.L., Van., Chi., Ana., Mtl.	9	402	13	29	42	786	39	0	1	1	56	....	1987-88	1995-96
‡ Divisek, Tomas	Phi.	2	5	1	0	1	0	....	....	....	....	....	....	2000-01	2001-02
Djoos, Per	Det., NYR	3	82	2	31	33	58	....	....	....	....	....	....	1990-91	1992-93
Doak, Gary	Det., Bos., Van., NYR	16	789	23	107	130	908	78	2	4	6	121	1	1965-66	1980-81
Dobbin, Brian	Phi., Bos.	5	63	7	8	15	61	2	0	0	0	17	....	1986-87	1991-92
Dobson, Jim	Min., Col., Que.	4	12	0	0	0	6	....	....	....	....	....	....	1979-80	1983-84
• Doherty, Fred	Mtl.	1	1	0	0	0	0	....	....	....	....	....	....	1918-19	1918-19
‡ Doig, Jason	Wpg., Phx., NYR, Wsh.	7	158	6	18	24	285	6	0	1	1	6	....	1995-96	2003-04
Dollas, Bobby	Wpg., Que., Det., Ana., Edm., Pit., Ott., Cgy., S.J.	16	646	42	96	138	467	47	2	1	3	41	....	1983-84	2000-01
‡ Dome, Robert	Pit., Cgy.	3	53	7	7	14	12	....	....	....	....	....	....	1997-98	2002-03
‡ Domenichelli, Hnat	Hfd., Cgy., Atl., Min.	7	267	52	61	113	104	....	....	....	....	....	....	1996-97	2002-03
Domi, Tie	Tor., NYR, Wpg.	16	1020	104	141	245	3515	98	7	12	19	238	....	1989-90	2005-06
Donaldson, Gary	Chi.	1	1	0	0	0	0	....	....	....	....	....	....	1973-74	1973-74
Donatelli, Clark	Min., Bos.	2	35	3	4	7	39	2	0	0	0	0	....	1989-90	1991-92
Donato, Ted	Bos., NYI, Ott., Ana., Dal., St.L., L.A., NYR	13	796	150	197	347	396	58	8	10	18	22	....	1991-92	2003-04
• Donnelly, Babe	Mtl.M.	1	34	0	1	1	14	2	0	0	0	0	....	1926-27	1926-27
Donnelly, Dave	Bos., Chi., Edm.	5	137	15	24	39	150	5	0	0	0	0	....	1983-84	1987-88
Donnelly, Gord	Que., Wpg., Buf., Dal.	12	554	28	41	69	2069	26	0	2	2	61	....	1983-84	1994-95
Donnelly, Mike	NYR, Buf., L.A., Dal., NYI	11	465	114	121	235	255	47	12	12	24	30	....	1986-87	1996-97
‡ Dopita, Jiri	Phi., Edm.	2	73	12	21	33	19	....	....	....	....	....	....	2001-02	2002-03
• Doran, John	NYA, Det., Mtl.	5	98	5	10	15	110	3	0	0	0	0	....	1933-34	1939-40
• Doran, Lloyd	Det.	1	24	3	2	5	10	....	....	....	....	....	....	1946-47	1946-47
• Doraty, Ken	Chi., Tor., Det.	5	103	15	26	41	24	15	7	2	9	2	....	1926-27	1937-38
Dore, Andre	NYR, St.L., Que.	7	257	14	81	95	261	23	1	2	3	32	....	1978-79	1984-85
Dore, Daniel	Que.	2	17	2	3	5	59	....	....	....	....	....	....	1989-90	1990-91
Dorey, Jim	Tor., NYR	4	232	25	74	99	553	11	0	2	2	40	....	1968-69	1971-72
Dorion, Dan	N.J.	2	4	1	1	2	2	....	....	....	....	....	....	1985-86	1987-88
Dornhoefer, Gary	Bos., Phi.	14	787	214	328	542	1291	80	17	19	36	203	2	1963-64	1977-78
Dorohoy, Eddie	Mtl.	1	16	0	0	0	6	....	....	....	....	....	....	1948-49	1948-49
Douglas, Jordy	Hfd., Min., Wpg.	6	268	76	62	138	160	6	0	0	0	4	....	1979-80	1984-85
Douglas, Kent	Tor., Oak., Det.	7	428	33	115	148	631	19	1	3	4	33	3	1962-63	1968-69
• Douglas, Les	Det.	4	52	6	12	18	8	10	3	2	5	2	1	1940-41	1946-47
Doull, Doug	Bos., Wsh.	2	37	0	1	1	151	....	....	....	....	....	....	2003-04	2005-06
Douris, Peter	Wpg., Bos., Ana., Dal.	11	321	54	67	121	80	27	3	5	8	14	....	1985-86	1997-98
• Downie, Dave	Tor.	1	11	0	1	1	2	....	....	....	....	....	....	1932-33	1932-33
Doyon, Mario	Chi., Que.	3	28	3	4	7	16	....	....	....	....	....	....	1988-89	1990-91
• Draper, Bruce	Tor.	1	1	0	0	0	0	....	....	....	....	....	....	1962-63	1962-63
• Drillon, Gordie	Tor., Mtl.	7	311	155	139	294	56	50	26	15	41	10	1	1936-37	1942-43
Driscoll, Peter	Edm.	2	60	3	8	11	97	3	0	0	0	0	....	1979-80	1980-81
Driver, Bruce	N.J., NYR	15	922	96	390	486	670	108	10	40	50	64	1	1983-84	1997-98
Drolet, Rene	Phi., Det.	2	2	0	0	0	0	....	....	....	....	....	....	1971-72	1974-75
‡ Droppa, Ivan	Chi.	2	19	0	1	1	14	....	....	....	....	....	....	1993-94	1995-96
• Drouillard, Clarence	Det.	1	10	0	1	1	0	....	....	....	....	....	....	1937-38	1937-38
Drouin, Jude	Mtl., Min., NYI, Wpg.	12	666	151	305	456	346	72	27	41	68	33	....	1968-69	1980-81
Drouin, P.C.	Bos.	1	3	0	0	0	0	....	....	....	....	....	....	1996-97	1996-97
• Drouin, Polly	Mtl.	7	160	23	50	73	80	5	0	1	1	5	....	1934-35	1940-41
Druce, John	Wsh., Wpg., L.A., Phi.	10	531	113	126	239	347	53	17	6	23	38	....	1988-89	1997-98
Druken, Harold	Van., Car., Tor.	5	146	27	36	63	36	4	0	1	1	0	....	1999-00	2003-04
Drulia, Stan	T.B.	3	126	15	27	42	52	....	....	....	....	....	....	1992-93	2000-01
• Drummond, Jim	NYR	1	2	0	0	0	0	....	....	....	....	....	....	1944-45	1944-45
• Drury, Herb	Pit., Phi.	6	213	24	13	37	203	4	1	1	2	0	....	1925-26	1930-31
‡ Drury, Ted	Cgy., Hfd., Ott., Ana., NYI, CBJ	8	414	41	52	93	367	14	1	0	1	4	....	1993-94	2000-01

			Regular Schedule					Playoffs					NHL	First	Last
Name	NHL Teams	NHL Seasons	GP	G	A	TP	PIM	GP	G	A	TP	PIM	Cup Wins	NHL Season	NHL Season
‡ Dube, Christian	NYR	2	33	1	1	2	4	3	0	0	0	0	....	1996-97	1998-99
Dube, Gilles	Mtl., Det.	2	12	1	2	3	2	2	0	0	0	0	1	1949-50	1953-54
Dube, Norm	K.C.	2	57	8	10	18	54	....	....	....	....	....	....	1974-75	1975-76
Duberman, Justin	Pit.	1	4	0	0	0	0	....	....	....	....	....	....	1993-94	1993-94
Dubinsky, Steve	Chi., Cgy., Nsh., St.L.	10	375	25	45	70	164	10	1	0	1	14	....	1993-94	2002-03
• Duchesne, Gaetan	Wsh., Que., Min., S.J., Fla.	14	1028	179	254	433	617	84	14	13	27	97	....	1981-82	1994-95
Duchesne, Steve	L.A., Phi., Que., St.L., Ott., Det.	16	1113	227	525	752	824	121	16	61	77	96	1	1986-87	2001-02
Dudley, Rick	Buf., Wpg.	6	309	75	99	174	292	25	7	2	9	69	....	1972-73	1980-81
Duerden, Dave	Fla.	1	2	0	0	0	0	....	....	....	....	....	....	1999-00	1999-00
Duff, Dick	Tor., NYR, Mtl., L.A., Buf.	18	1030	283	289	572	743	114	30	49	79	78	6	1954-55	1971-72
Dufour, Luc	Bos., Que., St.L.	3	167	23	21	44	199	18	1	0	1	32	....	1982-83	1984-85
Dufour, Marc	NYR, L.A.	3	14	1	0	1	2	....	....	....	....	....	....	1963-64	1968-69
Dufresne, Donald	Mtl., T.B., L.A., St.L., Edm.	9	268	6	36	42	258	34	1	3	4	47	1	1988-89	1996-97
• Duggan, John	Ott.	1	27	0	0	0	0	2	0	0	0	0	....	1925-26	1925-26
Duggan, Ken	Min.	1	1	0	0	0	0	....	....	....	....	....	....	1987-88	1987-88
Duguay, Ron	NYR, Det., Pit., L.A.	12	864	274	346	620	582	89	31	22	53	118	....	1977-78	1988-89
• Duguid, Lorne	Mtl.M., Det., Bos.	6	135	9	15	24	57	4	1	0	1	6	....	1931-32	1936-37
• Dukowski, Duke	Chi., NYA, NYR	5	200	16	30	46	172	6	0	0	0	6	....	1926-27	1933-34
• Dumart, Woody	Bos.	16	772	211	218	429	99	88	12	15	27	23	2	1935-36	1953-54
Dunbar, Dale	Van., Bos.	2	2	0	0	0	2	....	....	....	....	....	....	1985-86	1988-89
• Duncan, Art	Det., Tor.	5	156	18	16	34	225	5	0	0	0	4	....	1926-27	1930-31
Duncan, Iain	Wpg.	4	127	34	55	89	149	11	0	3	3	6	....	1986-87	1990-91
Duncanson, Craig	L.A., Wpg., NYR	7	38	5	4	9	61	....	....	....	....	....	....	1985-86	1992-93
Dundas, Rocky	Tor.	1	5	0	0	0	14	....	....	....	....	....	....	1989-90	1989-90
• Dunlap, Frank	Tor.	1	15	0	1	1	2	....	....	....	....	....	....	1943-44	1943-44
Dunlop, Blake	Min., Phi., St.L., Det.	11	550	130	274	404	172	40	4	10	14	18	....	1973-74	1983-84
Dunn, Dave	Van., Tor.	3	184	14	41	55	313	10	1	1	2	41	....	1973-74	1975-76
Dunn, Richie	Buf., Cgy., Hfd.	12	483	36	140	176	314	36	3	15	18	24	....	1977-78	1988-89
Dupere, Denis	Tor., Wsh., St.L., K.C., Col.	8	421	80	99	179	66	16	1	0	1	0	....	1970-71	1977-78
Dupont, Andre	NYR, St.L., Phi., Que.	13	800	59	185	244	1986	140	14	18	32	352	2	1970-71	1982-83
Dupont, Jerome	Chi., Tor.	6	214	7	29	36	468	20	0	2	2	56	....	1981-82	1986-87
Dupont, Norm	Mtl., Wpg., Hfd.	5	256	55	85	140	52	13	4	2	6	0	....	1979-80	1983-84
• Dupre, Yanick	Phi.	3	35	2	0	2	16	....	....	....	....	....	....	1991-92	1995-96
• Durbano, Steve	St.L., Pit., K.C., Col.	6	220	13	60	73	1127	5	0	2	2	8	....	1972-73	1978-79
Duris, Vitezslav	Tor.	2	89	3	20	23	62	3	0	1	1	2	....	1980-81	1982-83
Dusablon, Benoit	NYR	1	3	0	0	0	2	....	....	....	....	....	....	2003-04	2003-04
Dussault, Norm	Mtl.	4	206	31	62	93	47	7	3	1	4	0	....	1947-48	1950-51
• Dutton, Red	Mtl.M., NYA	10	449	29	67	96	871	18	1	0	1	33	....	1926-27	1935-36
• Dvorak, Miroslav	Phi.	3	193	11	74	85	51	18	0	2	2	6	....	1982-83	1984-85
Dwyer, Gordie	T.B., NYR, Mtl.	5	108	0	5	5	394	....	....	....	....	....	....	1999-00	2003-04
Dwyer, Mike	Col., Cgy.	4	31	2	6	8	25	1	1	0	1	0	....	1978-79	1981-82
• Dyck, Henry	NYR	1	1	0	0	0	0	....	....	....	....	....	....	1943-44	1943-44
• Dye, Babe	Tor., Ham., Chi., NYA	11	271	201	47	248	221	10	2	0	2	11	1	1919-20	1930-31
Dykhuis, Karl	Chi., Phi., T.B., Mtl.	12	644	42	91	133	495	62	8	10	18	50	....	1991-92	2003-04
Dykstra, Steve	Buf., Edm., Pit., Hfd.	5	217	8	32	40	545	1	0	0	0	2	....	1985-86	1989-90
• Dyte, Jack	Chi.	1	27	1	0	1	31	....	....	....	....	....	....	1943-44	1943-44
Dziedzic, Joe	Pit., Phx.	3	130	14	14	28	131	21	1	3	4	23	....	1995-96	1998-99

E

Eagles, Mike	Que., Chi., Wpg., Wsh.	16	853	74	122	196	928	44	2	6	8	34	....	1982-83	1999-00
Eakin, Bruce	Cgy., Det.	4	13	2	2	4	4	....	....	....	....	....	....	1981-82	1985-86
Eakins, Dallas	Wpg., Fla., St.L., Phx., NYR, Tor., NYI, Cgy.	10	120	0	9	9	208	5	0	0	0	4	....	1992-93	2001-02
Eastwood, Mike	Tor., Wpg., Phx., NYR, St.L., Chi., Pit.	13	783	87	149	236	354	97	8	11	19	64	....	1991-92	2003-04
Eatough, Jeff	Buf.	1	1	0	0	0	0	....	....	....	....	....	....	1981-82	1981-82
Eaves, Mike	Min., Cgy.	8	324	83	143	226	80	43	7	10	17	14	....	1978-79	1985-86
Eaves, Murray	Wpg., Det.	8	57	4	13	17	9	4	0	1	1	2	....	1980-81	1989-90
Ecclestone, Tim	St.L., Det., Tor., Atl.	11	692	126	233	359	344	48	6	11	17	76	....	1967-68	1977-78
Edberg, Rolf	Wsh.	3	184	45	58	103	24	....	....	....	....	....	....	1978-79	1980-81
• Eddolls, Frank	Mtl., NYR	8	317	23	43	66	114	31	0	2	2	10	1	1944-45	1951-52
Edestrand, Darryl	St.L., Phi., Pit., Bos., L.A.	10	455	34	90	124	404	42	3	9	12	57	....	1967-68	1978-79
Edmundson, Garry	Mtl., Tor.	3	43	4	6	10	49	11	0	1	1	8	....	1951-52	1960-61
Edur, Tom	Col., Pit.	2	158	17	70	87	67	....	....	....	....	....	....	1976-77	1977-78
• Egan, Pat	NYA, Bro., Det., Bos., NYR	11	554	77	153	230	776	46	9	4	13	48	....	1939-40	1950-51
Egeland, Allan	T.B.	3	17	0	0	0	16	....	....	....	....	....	....	1995-96	1997-98
Egers, Jack	NYR, St.L., Wsh.	7	284	64	69	133	154	32	5	6	11	32	....	1969-70	1975-76
• Ehman, Gerry	Bos., Det., Tor., Oak., Cal.	9	429	96	118	214	100	41	10	10	20	12	1	1957-58	1970-71
Eisenhut, Neil	Van., Cgy.	2	16	1	3	4	21	....	....	....	....	....	....	1993-94	1994-95
Eklund, Pelle	Phi., Dal.	9	594	120	335	455	109	66	10	36	46	8	....	1985-86	1993-94
Eldebrink, Anders	Van., Que.	2	55	3	11	14	29	14	0	0	0	10	....	1981-82	1982-83
‡ Elich, Matt	T.B.	2	16	1	1	2	0	....	....	....	....	....	....	1999-00	2000-01
Elik, Bo	Det.	1	3	0	0	0	0	....	....	....	....	....	....	1962-63	1962-63
Elik, Todd	L.A., Min., Edm., S.J., St.L., Bos.	8	448	110	219	329	453	52	15	27	42	48	....	1989-90	1996-97
Ellett, Dave	Wpg., Tor., N.J., Bos., St.L.	16	1129	153	415	568	985	116	11	46	57	87	....	1984-85	1999-00
• Elliott, Fred	Ott.	1	43	2	0	2	6	....	....	....	....	....	....	1928-29	1928-29
Ellis, Ron	Tor.	16	1034	332	308	640	207	70	18	8	26	20	1	1963-64	1980-81
Elomo, Miika	Wsh.	1	2	0	1	1	2	....	....	....	....	....	....	1999-00	1999-00
Eloranta, Kari	Cgy., St.L.	5	267	13	103	116	155	26	1	7	8	19	....	1981-82	1986-87
‡ Eloranta, Mikko	Bos., L.A.	4	264	32	44	76	186	7	1	1	2	2	....	1999-00	2002-03
Elynuik, Pat	Wpg., Wsh., T.B., Ott.	9	506	154	188	342	459	20	6	9	15	25	....	1987-88	1995-96
• Emberg, Eddie	Mtl.	1	....	....	....	....	....	2	1	0	1	0	....	1944-45	1944-45
Emerson, Nelson	St.L., Wpg., Hfd., Car., Chi., Ott., Atl., L.A.	12	771	195	293	488	575	40	7	15	22	33	....	1990-91	2001-02
Emma, David	N.J., Bos., Fla.	5	34	5	6	11	2	....	....	....	....	....	....	1992-93	2000-01
Emmons, Gary	S.J.	1	3	1	0	1	0	....	....	....	....	....	....	1993-94	1993-94
Emmons, John	Ott., T.B., Bos.	3	85	2	4	6	64	....	....	....	....	....	....	1999-00	2001-02
• Emms, Hap	Mtl.M., NYA, Det., Bos.	10	320	36	53	89	311	14	0	0	0	12	....	1926-27	1937-38
Endean, Craig	Wpg.	1	2	0	1	1	0	....	....	....	....	....	....	1986-87	1986-87
‡ Endicott, Shane	Pit.	2	45	1	2	3	47	....	....	....	....	....	....	2001-02	2005-06
Engblom, Brian	Mtl., Wsh., L.A., Buf., Cgy.	11	659	29	177	206	599	48	3	9	12	43	2	1976-77	1986-87
Engele, Jerry	Min.	3	100	2	13	15	162	2	0	1	1	0	....	1975-76	1977-78
English, John	L.A.	1	3	1	3	4	4	1	0	0	0	0	....	1987-88	1987-88
Ennis, Jim	Edm.	1	5	1	0	1	10	....	....	....	....	....	....	1987-88	1987-88
Erickson, Aut	Bos., Chi., Tor., Oak.	7	226	7	24	31	182	7	0	0	0	2	1	1959-60	1969-70
Erickson, Bryan	Wsh., L.A., Pit., Wpg.	9	351	80	125	205	141	14	3	4	7	7	....	1983-84	1993-94
Erickson, Grant	Bos., Min.	2	6	1	0	1	0	....	....	....	....	....	....	1968-69	1969-70
Eriksson, Peter	Edm.	1	20	3	3	6	24	....	....	....	....	....	....	1989-90	1989-90
Eriksson, Roland	Min., Van.	3	193	48	95	143	26	2	1	0	1	0	....	1976-77	1978-79
Eriksson, Thomas	Phi.	5	208	22	76	98	107	19	0	3	3	12	....	1980-81	1985-86
Erixon, Jan	NYR	10	556	57	159	216	167	58	7	7	14	16	....	1983-84	1992-93
Errey, Bob	Pit., Buf., S.J., Det., Dal., NYR	15	895	170	212	382	1005	99	13	16	29	109	2	1983-84	1997-98
Esau, Len	Tor., Que., Cgy., Edm.	4	27	0	10	10	24	....	....	....	....	....	....	1991-92	1994-95
Esposito, Phil	Chi., Bos., NYR	18	1282	717	873	1590	910	130	61	76	137	138	2	1963-64	1980-81
• Evans, Chris	Tor., Buf., St.L., Det., K.C.	5	241	19	42	61	143	12	1	1	2	8	....	1969-70	1974-75
Evans, Daryl	L.A., Wsh., Tor.	6	113	22	30	52	25	11	5	8	13	12	....	1981-82	1986-87
Evans, Doug	St.L., Wpg., Phi.	8	355	48	87	135	502	22	3	4	7	38	....	1985-86	1992-93
• Evans, Jack	NYR, Chi.	14	752	19	80	99	989	56	2	2	4	97	1	1948-49	1962-63
Evans, John Paul	Phi.	3	103	14	25	39	34	1	0	0	0	0	....	1978-79	1982-83
Evans, Kevin	Min., S.J.	2	9	0	1	1	44	....	....	....	....	....	....	1990-91	1991-92
Evans, Paul	Tor.	2	11	1	1	2	21	2	0	0	0	0	....	1976-77	1977-78
Evans, Shawn	St.L., NYI	2	9	1	0	1	2	....	....	....	....	....	....	1985-86	1989-90
• Evans, Stewart	Det., Mtl.M., Mtl.	8	367	28	49	77	425	26	0	0	0	20	1	1930-31	1938-39
Evason, Dean	Wsh., Hfd., S.J., Dal., Cgy.	13	803	139	233	372	1002	55	9	20	29	132	....	1983-84	1995-96
Ewen, Todd	St.L., Mtl., Ana., S.J.	11	518	36	40	76	1911	26	0	0	0	87	1	1986-87	1996-97
Ezinicki, Bill	Tor., Bos., NYR	9	368	79	105	184	713	40	5	8	13	87	3	1944-45	1954-55

F

Fahey, Trevor	NYR	1	1	0	0	0	0	....	....	....	....	....	....	1964-65	1964-65
Fairbairn, Bill	NYR, Min., St.L.	11	658	162	261	423	173	54	13	22	35	42	....	1968-69	1978-79
‡ Fairchild, Kelly	Tor., Dal., Col.	4	34	2	3	5	6	....	....	....	....	....	....	1995-96	2001-02
Falkenberg, Bob	Det.	5	54	1	5	6	26	....	....	....	....	....	....	1966-67	1971-72
Falloon, Pat	S.J., Phi., Ott., Edm., Pit.	9	575	143	179	322	141	66	11	7	18	16	....	1991-92	1999-00

Mike Dwyer

Brian Engblom

Bryan Erickson

Bill Fairbairn

Alex Faulkner

Pat Flatley

Bob Frampton

John Gallagher

			Regular Schedule					Playoffs					NHL	First	Last
Name	NHL Teams	NHL Seasons	GP	G	A	TP	PIM	GP	G	A	TP	PIM	Cup Wins	NHL Season	NHL Season
Farkas, Jeff	Tor., Atl.	4	11	0	2	2	6	5	1	0	1	0	....	1999-00	2002-03
• Farrant, Walt	Chi.	1	1	0	0	0	0	....	....	....	....	....	....	1943-44	1943-44
Farrell, Mike	Wsh., Nsh.	3	13	0	0	0	2	....	....	....	....	....	....	2001-02	2003-04
Farrish, Dave	NYR, Que., Tor.	7	430	17	110	127	440	14	0	2	2	24	....	1976-77	1983-84
Fashoway, Gordie	Chi.	1	13	3	2	5	14	....	....	....	....	....	....	1950-51	1950-51
‡ Fast, Brad	Car.	1	1	1	0	1	0	....	....	....	....	....	....	2003-04	2003-04
Faubert, Mario	Pit.	7	231	21	90	111	292	10	2	2	4	6	....	1974-75	1981-82
Faulkner, Alex	Tor., Det.	3	101	15	17	32	15	12	5	0	5	2	....	1961-62	1963-64
Fauss, Ted	Tor.	2	28	0	2	2	15	....	....	....	....	....	....	1986-87	1987-88
Faust, Andre	Phi.	2	47	10	7	17	14	....	....	....	....	....	....	1992-93	1993-94
Feamster, Dave	Chi.	4	169	13	24	37	154	33	3	5	8	61	....	1981-82	1984-85
Featherstone, Glen	St.L., Bos., NYR, Hfd., Cgy.	9	384	19	61	80	939	28	0	2	2	103	....	1988-89	1996-97
Featherstone, Tony	Oak., Cal., Min.	3	130	17	21	38	65	2	0	0	0	0	....	1969-70	1973-74
Federko, Bernie	St.L., Det.	14	1000	369	761	1130	487	91	35	66	101	83	....	1976-77	1989-90
Fedotov, Anatoli	Wpg., Ana.	2	4	0	2	2	0	....	....	....	....	....	....	1992-93	1993-94
Fedyk, Brent	Det., Phi., Dal., NYR	10	470	97	112	209	308	16	3	2	5	12	....	1987-88	1998-99
Felix, Chris	Wsh.	4	35	1	12	13	10	2	0	1	1	0	....	1987-88	1990-91
Felsner, Brian	Chi.	1	12	1	3	4	12	....	....	....	....	....	....	1997-98	1997-98
Felsner, Denny	St.L.	4	18	1	4	5	6	10	2	3	5	2	....	1991-92	1994-95
Feltrin, Tony	Pit., NYR	4	48	3	3	6	65	....	....	....	....	....	....	1980-81	1985-86
Fenton, Paul	Hfd., NYR, L.A., Wpg., Tor., Cgy., S.J.	8	411	100	83	183	198	17	4	1	5	27	....	1984-85	1991-92
Fenyves, David	Buf., Phi.	9	206	3	32	35	119	11	0	0	0	9	....	1982-83	1990-91
Fergus, Tom	Bos., Tor., Van.	12	726	235	346	581	499	65	21	17	38	48	....	1981-82	1992-93
Ferguson, Craig	Mtl., Cgy., Fla.	5	27	1	1	2	6	....	....	....	....	....	....	1993-94	1999-00
Ferguson, George	Tor., Pit., Min.	12	797	160	238	398	431	86	14	23	37	44	....	1972-73	1983-84
• Ferguson, John	Mtl.	8	500	145	158	303	1214	85	20	18	38	260	5	1963-64	1970-71
Ferguson, Lorne	Bos., Det., Chi.	8	422	82	80	162	193	31	6	3	9	24	....	1949-50	1958-59
Ferguson, Norm	Oak., Cal.	4	279	73	66	139	72	10	1	4	5	7	....	1968-69	1971-72
‡ Ferguson, Scott	Edm., Ana., Min.	5	218	7	14	21	310	11	0	0	0	8	....	1997-98	2005-06
Ferner, Mark	Buf., Wsh., Ana., Det.	6	91	3	10	13	51	....	....	....	....	....	....	1986-87	1994-95
‡ Ferraro, Chris	NYR, Pit., Edm., NYI, Wsh.	6	74	7	9	16	57	....	....	....	....	....	....	1995-96	2001-02
‡ Ferraro, Peter	NYR, Pit., Bos., Wsh.	6	92	9	15	24	58	2	0	0	0	0	....	1995-96	2001-02
Ferraro, Ray	Hfd., NYI, NYR, L.A., Atl., St.L.	18	1258	408	490	898	1288	68	21	22	43	54	....	1984-85	2001-02
Fetisov, Viacheslav	N.J., Det.	9	546	36	192	228	656	116	2	26	28	147	2	1989-90	1997-98
‡ Fibiger, Jesse	S.J.	1	16	0	0	0	2	....	....	....	....	....	....	2002-03	2002-03
Fidler, Mike	Cle., Min., Hfd., Chi.	7	271	84	97	181	124	....	....	....	....	....	....	1976-77	1982-83
• Field, Wilf	NYA, Bro., Mtl., Chi.	6	219	17	25	42	151	2	0	0	0	2	....	1936-37	1944-45
Fielder, Guyle	Chi., Det., Bos.	4	9	0	0	0	2	6	0	0	0	2	....	1950-51	1957-58
Filimonov, Dmitri	Ott.	1	30	1	4	5	18	....	....	....	....	....	....	1993-94	1993-94
Fillion, Bob	Mtl.	7	327	42	61	103	84	33	7	4	11	10	2	1943-44	1949-50
• Fillion, Marcel	Bos.	1	1	0	0	0	0	....	....	....	....	....	....	1944-45	1944-45
• Filmore, Tommy	Det., NYA, Bos.	4	117	15	12	27	33	....	....	....	....	....	....	1930-31	1933-34
• Finkbeiner, Lloyd	NYA	1	2	0	0	0	0	....	....	....	....	....	....	1940-41	1940-41
Finley, Jeff	NYI, Phi., Wpg., Phx., NYR, St.L.	15	708	13	70	83	457	52	1	6	7	38	....	1987-88	2003-04
Finn, Steven	Que., T.B., L.A.	12	725	34	78	112	1724	23	0	4	4	39	....	1985-86	1996-97
Finney, Sid	Chi.	3	59	10	7	17	4	7	0	2	2	0	....	1951-52	1953-54
• Finnigan, Ed	St.L., Bos.	2	15	1	1	2	2	....	....	....	....	....	....	1934-35	1935-36
• Finnigan, Frank	Ott., Tor., St.L.	14	553	115	88	203	407	38	6	9	15	22	2	1923-24	1936-37
Fiorentino, Peter	NYR	1	1	0	0	0	0	....	....	....	....	....	....	1991-92	1991-92
Fischer, Jiri	Det.	6	305	11	49	60	295	38	4	3	7	55	1	1999-00	2005-06
‡ Fischer, Patrick	Phx.	1	27	4	6	10	24	....	....	....	....	....	....	2006-07	2006-07
Fischer, Ron	Buf.	2	18	0	7	7	6	....	....	....	....	....	....	1981-82	1982-83
• Fisher, Alvin	Tor.	1	9	1	0	1	4	....	....	....	....	....	....	1924-25	1924-25
Fisher, Craig	Phi., Wpg., Fla.	4	12	0	0	0	2	....	....	....	....	....	....	1989-90	1996-97
Fisher, Dunc	NYR, Bos., Det.	7	275	45	70	115	104	21	4	4	8	14	....	1947-48	1958-59
• Fisher, Joe	Det.	4	65	8	12	20	13	12	2	1	3	6	1	1939-40	1942-43
Fitchner, Bob	Que.	2	78	12	20	32	59	3	0	0	0	10	....	1979-80	1980-81
Fitzgerald, Rusty	Pit.	2	25	2	2	4	12	5	0	0	0	4	....	1994-95	1995-96
Fitzgerald, Tom	NYI, Fla., Col., Nsh., Chi., Tor., Bos.	17	1097	139	190	329	776	78	7	12	19	90	....	1988-89	2005-06
Fitzpatrick, Ross	Phi.	4	20	5	2	7	0	....	....	....	....	....	....	1982-83	1985-86
Fitzpatrick, Sandy	NYR, Min.	2	22	3	6	9	8	12	0	0	0	0	....	1964-65	1967-68
Flaman, Fern	Bos., Tor.	17	910	34	174	208	1370	63	4	8	12	93	1	1944-45	1960-61
Flatley, Pat	NYI, NYR	14	780	170	340	510	686	70	18	15	33	75	....	1983-84	1996-97
Fleming, Gerry	Mtl.	2	11	0	0	0	42	....	....	....	....	....	....	1993-94	1994-95
Fleming, Reggie	Mtl., Chi., Bos., NYR, Phi., Buf.	12	749	108	132	240	1468	50	3	6	9	106	1	1959-60	1970-71
Flesch, John	Min., Pit., Col.	4	124	18	23	41	117	....	....	....	....	....	....	1974-75	1979-80
Fletcher, Steven	Mtl., Wpg.	2	3	0	0	0	5	1	0	0	0	5	....	1987-88	1988-89
• Flett, Bill	L.A., Phi., Tor., Atl., Edm.	11	689	202	215	417	501	52	7	16	23	42	1	1967-68	1979-80
Fleury, Theoren	Cgy., Col., NYR, Chi.	15	1084	455	633	1088	1840	77	34	45	79	116	1	1988-89	2002-03
Flichel, Todd	Wpg.	3	6	0	1	1	4	....	....	....	....	....	....	1987-88	1989-90
Flockhart, Rob	Van., Min.	5	55	2	5	7	14	1	1	0	1	2	....	1976-77	1980-81
Flockhart, Ron	Phi., Pit., Mtl., St.L., Bos.	9	453	145	183	328	208	19	4	6	10	14	....	1980-81	1988-89
Floyd, Larry	N.J.	2	12	2	3	5	9	....	....	....	....	....	....	1982-83	1983-84
‡ Focht, Dan	Phx., Pit.	3	82	2	6	8	145	1	0	1	1	0	....	2001-02	2003-04
• Fogarty, Bryan	Que., Pit., Mtl.	6	156	22	52	74	119	....	....	....	....	....	....	1989-90	1994-95
• Fogolin, Lee	Det., Chi.	9	427	10	48	58	575	28	0	2	2	30	1	1947-48	1955-56
Fogolin Jr., Lee	Buf., Edm.	13	924	44	195	239	1318	108	5	19	24	173	2	1974-75	1986-87
Folco, Peter	Van.	1	2	0	0	0	0	....	....	....	....	....	....	1973-74	1973-74
Foley, Gerry	Tor., NYR, L.A.	4	142	9	14	23	99	9	0	1	1	2	....	1954-55	1968-69
Foley, Rick	Chi., Phi., Det.	3	67	11	26	37	180	4	0	1	1	4	....	1970-71	1973-74
Foligno, Mike	Det., Buf., Tor., Fla.	15	1018	355	372	727	2049	57	15	17	32	185	....	1979-80	1993-94
Folk, Bill	Det.	2	12	0	0	0	4	....	....	....	....	....	....	1951-52	1952-53
Fontaine, Len	Det.	2	46	8	11	19	10	....	....	....	....	....	....	1972-73	1973-74
Fontas, Jon	Min.	2	2	0	0	0	0	....	....	....	....	....	....	1979-80	1980-81
Fonteyne, Val	Det., NYR, Pit.	13	820	75	154	229	26	59	3	10	13	8	....	1959-60	1971-72
Fontinato, Lou	NYR, Mtl.	9	535	26	78	104	1247	21	0	2	2	42	....	1954-55	1962-63
‡ Forbes, Colin	Phi., T.B., Ott., NYR, Wsh.	9	311	33	28	61	213	13	1	0	1	16	....	1996-97	2005-06
Forbes, Dave	Bos., Wsh.	6	363	64	64	128	341	45	1	4	5	13	....	1973-74	1978-79
Forbes, Mike	Bos., Edm.	3	50	1	11	12	41	....	....	....	....	....	....	1977-78	1981-82
Forey, Connie	St.L.	1	4	0	0	0	2	....	....	....	....	....	....	1973-74	1973-74
• Forsey, Jack	Tor.	1	19	7	9	16	10	3	0	1	1	0	....	1942-43	1942-43
• Forslund, Gus	Ott.	1	48	4	9	13	2	....	....	....	....	....	....	1932-33	1932-33
Forslund, Tomas	Cgy.	2	44	5	11	16	12	....	....	....	....	....	....	1991-92	1992-93
Forsyth, Alex	Wsh.	1	1	0	0	0	0	....	....	....	....	....	....	1976-77	1976-77
Fortier, Dave	Tor., NYI, Van.	4	205	8	21	29	335	20	0	2	2	33	....	1972-73	1976-77
Fortier, Marc	Que., Ott., L.A.	6	212	42	60	102	135	....	....	....	....	....	....	1987-88	1992-93
‡ Fortin, Jean-Francois	Wsh.	3	71	1	4	5	42	....	....	....	....	....	....	2001-02	2003-04
Fortin, Ray	St.L.	3	92	2	6	8	33	6	0	0	0	8	....	1967-68	1969-70
Foster, Corey	N.J., Phi., Pit., NYI	4	45	5	6	11	24	3	0	0	0	4	....	1988-89	1996-97
Foster, Dwight	Bos., Col., N.J., Det.	10	541	111	163	274	420	35	5	12	17	4	....	1977-78	1986-87
• Foster, Herb	NYR	2	6	1	0	1	5	....	....	....	....	....	....	1940-41	1947-48
• Foster, Yip	NYR, Bos., Det.	4	83	3	2	5	32	....	....	....	....	....	....	1929-30	1934-35
Fotiu, Nick	NYR, Hfd., Cgy., Phi., Edm.	13	646	60	77	137	1362	38	0	4	4	67	....	1976-77	1988-89
• Fowler, Jimmy	Tor.	3	135	18	29	47	39	18	0	3	3	2	....	1936-37	1938-39
Fowler, Tom	Chi.	1	24	0	1	1	18	....	....	....	....	....	....	1946-47	1946-47
Fox, Greg	Atl., Chi., Pit.	8	494	14	92	106	637	44	1	9	10	67	....	1977-78	1984-85
Fox, Jim	L.A.	9	578	186	293	479	143	22	4	8	12	0	....	1980-81	1989-90
• Foyston, Frank	Det.	2	64	17	7	24	32	....	....	....	....	....	....	1926-27	1927-28
Frampton, Bob	Mtl.	1	2	0	0	0	0	3	0	0	0	0	....	1949-50	1949-50
Franceschetti, Lou	Wsh., Tor., Buf.	10	459	59	81	140	747	44	3	2	5	111	....	1981-82	1991-92
Francis, Bobby	Det.	1	14	2	0	2	0	....	....	....	....	....	....	1982-83	1982-83
Francis, Ron	Hfd., Pit., Car., Tor.	23	1731	549	1249	1798	979	171	46	97	143	95	2	1981-82	2003-04
• Fraser, Archie	NYR	1	3	0	1	1	0	....	....	....	....	....	....	1943-44	1943-44
• Fraser, Charles	Ham.	1	1	0	0	0	0	....	....	....	....	....	....	1923-24	1923-24
Fraser, Curt	Van., Chi., Min.	12	704	193	240	433	1306	65	15	18	33	198	....	1978-79	1989-90
• Fraser, Gord	Chi., Det., Mtl., Pit., Phi.	5	144	24	12	36	224	2	1	0	1	6	....	1926-27	1930-31
• Fraser, Harvey	Chi.	1	21	5	4	9	0	....	....	....	....	....	....	1944-45	1944-45
Fraser, Iain	NYI, Que., Dal., Edm., Wpg., S.J.	5	94	23	23	46	31	4	0	0	0	0	....	1992-93	1996-97
Fraser, Scott	Mtl., Edm., NYR	3	72	16	15	31	24	11	1	1	2	0	....	1995-96	1998-99
Frawley, Dan	Chi., Pit.	6	273	37	40	77	674	1	0	0	0	0	....	1983-84	1988-89
Freadrich, Kyle	T.B.	2	23	0	1	1	75	....	....	....	....	....	....	1999-00	2000-01
• Fredrickson, Frank	Det., Bos., Pit.	5	161	39	34	73	206	10	2	3	5	24	....	1926-27	1930-31
Freer, Mark	Phi., Ott., Cgy.	7	124	16	23	39	61	....	....	....	....	....	....	1986-87	1993-94
• Frew, Irv	Mtl.M., St.L., Mtl.	3	96	2	5	7	146	4	0	0	0	6	....	1933-34	1935-36
Friday, Tim	Det.	1	23	0	3	3	6	....	....	....	....	....	....	1985-86	1985-86

			Regular Schedule					Playoffs							
Name	NHL Teams	NHL Seasons	GP	G	A	TP	PIM	GP	G	A	TP	PIM	NHL Cup Wins	First NHL Season	Last NHL Season
Fridgen, Dan	Hfd.	2	13	2	3	5	2	....	....	....	....	....	....	1981-82	1982-83
Friedman, Doug	Edm., Nsh.	2	18	0	1	1	34	....	....	....	....	....	....	1997-98	1998-99
Friest, Ron	Min.	3	64	7	7	14	191	6	1	0	1	7	....	1980-81	1982-83
Frig, Len	Chi., Cal., Cle., St.L.	7	311	13	51	64	479	14	2	1	3	0	....	1972-73	1979-80
Frost, Harry	Bos.	1	4	0	0	0	0	1	0	0	0	0	1	1938-39	1938-39
Frycer, Miroslav	Que., Tor., Det., Edm.	8	415	147	183	330	486	17	3	8	11	16	....	1981-82	1988-89
Fryday, Bob	Mtl.	2	5	1	0	1	0	....	....	....	....	....	....	1949-50	1951-52
Ftorek, Robbie	Det., Que., NYR	8	334	77	150	227	262	19	9	6	15	28	....	1972-73	1984-85
Fullan, Larry	Wsh.	1	4	1	0	1	0	....	....	....	....	....	....	1974-75	1974-75
Fusco, Mark	Hfd.	2	80	3	12	15	42	....	....	....	....	....	....	1983-84	1984-85
‡ Fussey, Owen	Wsh.	1	4	0	1	1	0	....	....	....	....	....	....	2003-04	2003-04

G

Name	NHL Teams	NHL Seasons	GP	G	A	TP	PIM	GP	G	A	TP	PIM	NHL Cup Wins	First NHL Season	Last NHL Season
Gadsby, Bill	Chi., NYR, Det.	20	1248	130	438	568	1539	67	4	23	27	92	....	1946-47	1965-66
Gaetz, Link	Min., S.J.	3	65	6	8	14	412	....	....	....	....	....	....	1988-89	1991-92
Gage, Jody	Det., Buf.	6	68	14	15	29	26	....	....	....	....	....	....	1980-81	1991-92
• Gagne, Art	Mtl., Bos., Ott., Det.	6	228	67	33	100	257	11	2	1	3	20	....	1926-27	1931-32
Gagne, Paul	Col., N.J., Tor., NYI	8	390	110	101	211	127	....	....	....	....	....	....	1980-81	1989-90
Gagne, Pierre	Bos.	1	2	0	0	0	0	....	....	....	....	....	....	1959-60	1959-60
Gagner, Dave	NYR, Min., Dal., Tor., Cgy., Fla., Van.	15	946	318	401	719	1018	57	22	26	48	64	....	1984-85	1998-99
Gagnon, Germain	Mtl., NYI, Chi., K.C.	5	259	40	101	141	72	19	2	3	5	2	....	1971-72	1975-76
• Gagnon, Johnny	Mtl., Bos., NYA	10	454	120	141	261	295	32	12	12	24	37	1	1930-31	1939-40
Gagnon, Sean	Phx., Ott.	3	12	0	1	1	34	....	....	....	....	....	....	1997-98	2000-01
Gainey, Bob	Mtl.	16	1160	239	262	501	585	182	25	48	73	151	5	1973-74	1988-89
Gainey, Steve	Dal., Phx.	4	33	0	2	2	34	....	....	....	....	....	....	2000-01	2005-06
• Gainor, Dutch	Bos., NYR, Ott., Mtl.M.	7	246	51	56	107	129	22	2	1	3	14	2	1927-28	1934-35
‡ Galanov, Maxim	NYR, Pit., Atl., T.B.	4	122	8	12	20	44	1	0	0	0	0	....	1997-98	2000-01
Galarneau, Michel	Hfd.	3	78	7	10	17	34	....	....	....	....	....	....	1980-81	1982-83
• Galbraith, Percy	Bos., Ott.	8	347	29	31	60	224	31	4	7	11	24	1	1926-27	1933-34
• Gallagher, John	Mtl.M., Det., NYA	7	205	14	19	33	153	24	2	3	5	27	1	1930-31	1938-39
Gallant, Gerard	Det., T.B.	11	615	211	269	480	1674	58	18	21	39	178	....	1984-85	1994-95
Galley, Garry	L.A., Wsh., Bos., Phi., Buf., NYI	17	1149	125	475	600	1218	89	7	23	30	119	....	1984-85	2000-01
Gallimore, Jamie	Min.	1	2	0	0	0	0	....	....	....	....	....	....	1977-78	1977-78
• Gallinger, Don	Bos.	5	222	65	88	153	89	23	5	5	10	19	....	1942-43	1947-48
Gamble, Dick	Mtl., Chi., Tor.	8	195	41	41	82	66	14	1	2	3	4	1	1950-51	1966-67
Gambucci, Gary	Min.	2	51	2	7	9	9	....	....	....	....	....	....	1971-72	1973-74
Ganchar, Perry	St.L., Mtl., Pit.	4	42	3	7	10	36	7	3	1	4	0	....	1983-84	1988-89
Gans, Dave	L.A.	2	6	0	0	0	2	....	....	....	....	....	....	1982-83	1985-86
Gardiner, Bruce	Ott., T.B., CBJ, N.J.	6	312	34	54	88	263	21	1	4	5	8	....	1996-97	2001-02
• Gardiner, Herb	Mtl., Chi.	3	108	10	9	19	52	9	0	1	1	16	....	1926-27	1928-29
Gardner, Bill	Chi., Hfd.	9	380	73	115	188	68	45	3	8	11	17	....	1980-81	1988-89
• Gardner, Cal	NYR, Tor., Chi., Bos.	12	696	154	238	392	517	61	7	10	17	20	2	1945-46	1956-57
Gardner, Dave	Mtl., St.L., Cal., Cle., Phi.	7	350	75	115	190	41	....	....	....	....	....	....	1972-73	1979-80
Gardner, Paul	Col., Tor., Pit., Wsh., Buf.	10	447	201	201	402	207	16	2	6	8	14	....	1976-77	1985-86
Gare, Danny	Buf., Det., Edm.	13	827	354	331	685	1285	64	25	21	46	195	....	1974-75	1986-87
Gariepy, Ray	Bos., Tor.	2	36	1	6	7	43	....	....	....	....	....	....	1953-54	1955-56
• Garland, Scott	Tor., L.A.	3	91	13	24	37	115	7	1	2	3	35	....	1975-76	1978-79
Garner, Rob	Pit.	1	1	0	0	0	0	....	....	....	....	....	....	1982-83	1982-83
Garpenlov, Johan	Det., S.J., Fla., Atl.	10	609	114	197	311	276	44	10	9	19	22	....	1990-91	1999-00
• Garrett, Red	NYR	1	23	1	1	2	18	....	....	....	....	....	....	1942-43	1942-43
Gartner, Mike	Wsh., Min., NYR, Tor., Phx.	19	1432	708	627	1335	1159	122	43	50	93	125	....	1979-80	1997-98
• Gassoff, Bob	St.L.	4	245	11	47	58	866	9	0	1	1	16	....	1973-74	1976-77
Gassoff, Brad	Van.	4	122	19	17	36	163	3	0	0	0	0	....	1975-76	1978-79
Gatzos, Steve	Pit.	4	89	15	20	35	83	1	0	0	0	0	....	1981-82	1984-85
Gaudreau, Rob	S.J., Ott.	4	231	51	54	105	69	14	2	0	2	0	....	1992-93	1995-96
Gaudreault, Armand	Bos.	1	44	15	9	24	27	7	0	2	2	8	....	1944-45	1944-45
• Gaudreault, Leo	Mtl.	3	67	8	4	12	30	....	....	....	....	....	....	1927-28	1932-33
Gaul, Mike	Col., CBJ	2	3	0	0	0	4	....	....	....	....	....	....	1998-99	2000-01
Gaulin, Jean-Marc	Que.	4	26	4	3	7	8	1	0	0	0	0	....	1982-83	1985-86
Gaume, Dallas	Hfd.	1	4	1	1	2	0	....	....	....	....	....	....	1988-89	1988-89
• Gauthier, Art	Mtl.	1	13	0	0	0	0	1	0	0	0	0	....	1926-27	1926-27
Gauthier, Daniel	Chi.	1	5	0	0	0	0	....	....	....	....	....	....	1994-95	1994-95
• Gauthier, Fern	NYR, Mtl., Det.	6	229	46	50	96	35	22	5	1	6	7	....	1943-44	1948-49
Gauthier, Jean	Mtl., Phi., Bos.	10	166	6	29	35	150	14	1	3	4	22	1	1960-61	1969-70
Gauthier, Luc	Mtl.	1	3	0	0	0	2	....	....	....	....	....	....	1990-91	1990-91
Gauvreau, Jocelyn	Mtl.	1	2	0	0	0	0	....	....	....	....	....	....	1983-84	1983-84
Gavey, Aaron	T.B., Cgy., Dal., Min., Tor., Ana.	9	360	41	50	91	272	19	1	2	3	14	....	1995-96	2005-06
Gavin, Stew	Tor., Hfd., Min.	13	768	130	155	285	584	66	14	20	34	75	....	1980-81	1992-93
Geale, Bob	Pit.	1	1	0	0	0	2	....	....	....	....	....	....	1984-85	1984-85
• Gee, George	Chi., Det.	9	551	135	183	318	345	41	6	13	19	32	1	1945-46	1953-54
Geldart, Gary	Min.	1	4	0	0	0	5	....	....	....	....	....	....	1970-71	1970-71
Gendron, Jean-Guy	NYR, Bos., Mtl., Phi.	14	863	182	201	383	701	42	7	4	11	47	....	1955-56	1971-72
Gendron, Martin	Wsh., Chi.	3	30	4	2	6	10	....	....	....	....	....	....	1994-95	1997-98
• Geoffrion, Bernie	Mtl., NYR	16	883	393	429	822	689	132	58	60	118	88	6	1950-51	1967-68
Geoffrion, Danny	Mtl., Wpg.	3	111	20	32	52	99	2	0	0	0	7	....	1979-80	1981-82
• Geran, Gerry	Mtl.W., Bos.	2	37	5	1	6	6	....	....	....	....	....	....	1917-18	1925-26
• Gerard, Eddie	Ott.	6	128	50	48	98	108	11	4	0	4	17	3	1917-18	1922-23
Germain, Eric	L.A.	1	4	0	1	1	13	1	0	0	0	4	....	1987-88	1987-88
Gernander, Ken	NYR	3	12	2	3	5	6	15	0	0	0	0	....	1995-96	2003-04
• Getliffe, Ray	Bos., Mtl.	10	393	136	137	273	250	45	9	10	19	30	2	1935-36	1944-45
Giallonardo, Mario	Col.	2	23	0	3	3	6	....	....	....	....	....	....	1979-80	1980-81
Gibbs, Barry	Bos., Min., Atl., St.L., L.A.	13	797	58	224	282	945	36	4	2	6	67	....	1967-68	1979-80
Gibson, Don	Van.	1	14	0	3	3	20	....	....	....	....	....	....	1990-91	1990-91
Gibson, Doug	Bos., Wsh.	3	63	9	19	28	0	1	0	0	0	0	....	1973-74	1977-78
Gibson, John	L.A., Tor., Wpg.	3	48	0	2	2	120	....	....	....	....	....	....	1980-81	1983-84
• Giesebrecht, Gus	Det.	4	135	27	51	78	13	17	2	3	5	0	....	1938-39	1941-42
Giffin, Lee	Pit.	2	27	1	3	4	9	....	....	....	....	....	....	1986-87	1987-88
Gilbert, Ed	K.C., Pit.	3	166	21	31	52	22	....	....	....	....	....	....	1974-75	1976-77
Gilbert, Greg	NYI, Chi., NYR, St.L.	15	837	150	228	378	576	133	17	33	50	162	3	1981-82	1995-96
Gilbert, Jeannot	Bos.	2	9	0	1	1	4	....	....	....	....	....	....	1962-63	1964-65
Gilbert, Rod	NYR	18	1065	406	615	1021	508	79	34	33	67	43	....	1960-61	1977-78
Gilbertson, Stan	Cal., St.L., Wsh., Pit.	6	428	85	89	174	148	3	1	1	2	2	....	1971-72	1976-77
Gilchrist, Brent	Mtl., Edm., Min., Dal., Det., Nsh.	15	792	135	170	305	400	90	17	14	31	48	1	1988-89	2002-03
Giles, Curt	Min., NYR, St.L.	14	895	43	199	242	733	103	6	16	22	118	....	1979-80	1992-93
Gilhen, Randy	Hfd., Wpg., Pit., L.A., NYR, T.B., Fla.	11	457	55	60	115	314	33	3	2	5	26	1	1982-83	1995-96
Gill, Todd	Tor., S.J., St.L., Det., Phx., Col., Chi.	19	1007	82	272	354	1214	103	7	30	37	193	....	1984-85	2002-03
Gillen, Don	Phi., Hfd.	2	35	2	4	6	22	....	....	....	....	....	....	1979-80	1981-82
• Gillie, Farrand	Det.	1	1	0	0	0	0	....	....	....	....	....	....	1928-29	1928-29
Gillies, Clark	NYI, Buf.	14	958	319	378	697	1023	164	47	47	94	287	4	1974-75	1987-88
Gillis, Jere	Van., NYR, Que., Buf., Phi.	9	386	78	95	173	230	19	4	7	11	9	....	1977-78	1986-87
Gillis, Mike	Col., Bos.	6	246	33	43	76	186	27	2	5	7	10	....	1978-79	1983-84
Gillis, Paul	Que., Chi., Hfd.	11	624	88	154	242	1498	42	3	14	17	156	....	1982-83	1992-93
Gilmour, Doug	St.L., Cgy., Tor., N.J., Chi., Buf., Mtl.	20	1474	450	964	1414	1301	182	60	128	188	235	1	1983-84	2002-03
Gingras, Gaston	Mtl., Tor., St.L.	10	476	61	174	235	161	52	6	18	24	20	1	1979-80	1988-89
Girard, Bob	Cal., Cle., Wsh.	5	305	45	69	114	140	....	....	....	....	....	....	1975-76	1979-80
Girard, Jonathan	Bos.	5	150	10	34	44	46	3	0	1	1	2	....	1998-99	2002-03
Girard, Kenny	Tor.	3	7	0	1	1	2	....	....	....	....	....	....	1956-57	1959-60
• Giroux, Art	Mtl., Bos., Det.	3	54	6	4	10	14	2	0	0	0	0	....	1932-33	1935-36
Giroux, Larry	St.L., K.C., Det., Hfd.	7	274	15	74	89	333	5	0	0	0	4	....	1973-74	1979-80
Giroux, Pierre	L.A.	1	6	1	0	1	17	....	....	....	....	....	....	1982-83	1982-83
‡ Giroux, Raymond	NYI, N.J.	4	38	0	13	13	22	4	0	0	0	0	....	1999-00	2003-04
Gladney, Bob	L.A., Pit.	2	14	1	5	6	4	....	....	....	....	....	....	1982-83	1983-84
Gladu, Jean-Paul	Bos.	1	40	6	14	20	2	7	2	2	4	0	....	1944-45	1944-45
Glennie, Brian	Tor., L.A.	10	572	14	100	114	621	32	0	1	1	66	....	1969-70	1978-79
Glennon, Matt	Bos.	1	3	0	0	0	2	....	....	....	....	....	....	1991-92	1991-92
Gloeckner, Lorry	Det.	1	13	0	2	2	6	....	....	....	....	....	....	1978-79	1978-79
Gloor, Dan	Van.	1	2	0	0	0	0	....	....	....	....	....	....	1973-74	1973-74
• Glover, Fred	Det., Chi.	5	92	13	11	24	62	8	0	0	0	0	1	1948-49	1952-53
Glover, Howie	Chi., Det., NYR, Mtl.	5	144	29	17	46	101	11	1	2	3	2	....	1958-59	1968-69
Glynn, Brian	Cgy., Min., Edm., Ott., Van., Hfd.	10	431	25	79	104	410	57	6	10	16	40	....	1987-88	1996-97
‡ Goc, Sascha	N.J., T.B.	2	22	0	0	0	4	....	....	....	....	....	....	2000-01	2001-02
Godden, Ernie	Tor.	1	5	1	1	2	6	....	....	....	....	....	....	1981-82	1981-82
• Godfrey, Warren	Bos., Det.	16	786	32	125	157	752	52	1	4	5	42	....	1952-53	1967-68

Gerard Gallant

Jean-Guy Gendron

Jere Gillis

Pete Goegan

Hank Goldup

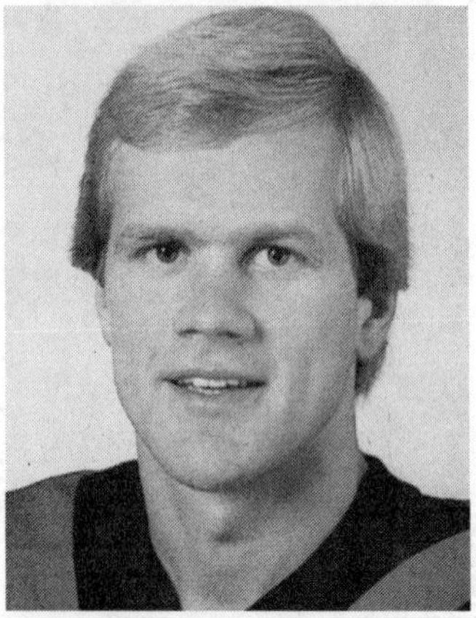

Thomas Gradin

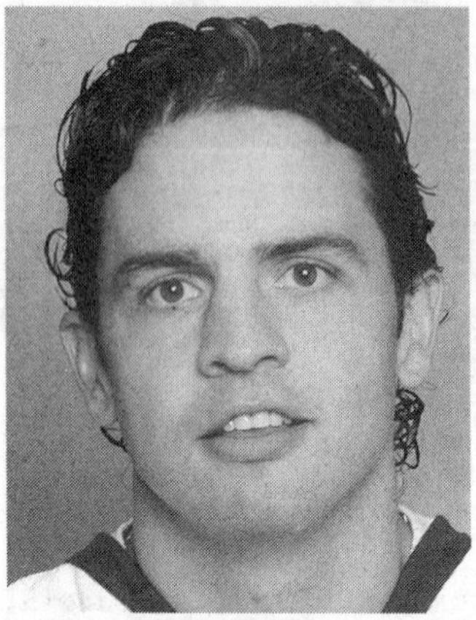

Travis Green

Lloyd Haddon

			Regular Schedule					Playoffs							
Name	NHL Teams	NHL Seasons	GP	G	A	TP	PIM	GP	G	A	TP	PIM	NHL Cup Wins	First NHL Season	Last NHL Season
Godin, Eddy	Wsh.	2	27	3	6	9	12	....	....	....	....	....	....	1977-78	1978-79
• Godin, Sam	Ott., Mtl.	3	83	4	3	7	36	....	....	....	....	....	....	1927-28	1933-34
Godynyuk, Alexander	Tor., Cgy., Fla., Hfd.	7	223	10	39	49	224	....	....	....	....	....	....	1990-91	1996-97
Goegan, Pete	Det., NYR, Min.	11	383	19	67	86	365	33	1	3	4	61	....	1957-58	1967-68
Goertz, Dave	Pit.	1	2	0	0	0	2	....	....	....	....	....	....	1987-88	1987-88
• Goldham, Bob	Tor., Chi., Det.	12	650	28	143	171	400	66	3	14	17	53	5	1941-42	1955-56
‡ Goldmann, Erich	Ott.	1	1	0	0	0	0	....	....	....	....	....	....	1999-00	1999-00
• Goldsworthy, Bill	Bos., Min., NYR	14	771	283	258	541	793	40	18	19	37	30	....	1964-65	1977-78
• Goldsworthy, Leroy	NYR, Det., Chi., Mtl., Bos., NYA	10	336	66	57	123	79	24	1	0	1	4	1	1928-29	1938-39
Goldup, Glenn	Mtl., L.A.	9	291	52	67	119	303	16	4	3	7	22	....	1973-74	1981-82
Goldup, Hank	Tor., NYR	6	202	63	80	143	97	26	5	1	6	6	1	1939-40	1945-46
Golubovsky, Yan	Det., Fla.	4	56	1	7	8	32	....	....	....	....	....	....	1997-98	2000-01
Goneau, Daniel	NYR	3	53	12	3	15	14	....	....	....	....	....	....	1996-97	1999-00
• Gooden, Bill	NYR	2	53	9	11	20	15	....	....	....	....	....	....	1942-43	1943-44
Goodenough, Larry	Phi., Van.	6	242	22	77	99	179	22	3	15	18	10	1	1974-75	1979-80
• Goodfellow, Ebbie	Det.	14	557	134	190	324	511	45	8	8	16	65	3	1929-30	1942-43
Gordiouk, Viktor	Buf.	2	26	3	8	11	0	....	....	....	....	....	....	1992-93	1994-95
• Gordon, Fred	Det., Bos.	2	81	8	7	15	68	2	0	0	0	0	....	1926-27	1927-28
Gordon, Jack	NYR	3	36	3	10	13	0	9	1	1	2	7	....	1948-49	1950-51
Gordon, Robb	Van.	1	4	0	0	0	2	....	....	....	....	....	....	1998-99	1998-99
Gorence, Tom	Phi., Edm.	6	303	58	53	111	89	37	9	6	15	47	....	1978-79	1983-84
Goring, Butch	L.A., NYI, Bos.	16	1107	375	513	888	102	134	38	50	88	32	4	1969-70	1984-85
Gorman, Dave	Atl.	1	3	0	0	0	0	....	....	....	....	....	....	1979-80	1979-80
• Gorman, Ed	Ott., Tor.	4	111	14	6	20	108	8	0	0	0	2	1	1924-25	1927-28
Gosselin, Benoit	NYR	1	7	0	0	0	33	....	....	....	....	....	....	1977-78	1977-78
‡ Gosselin, David	Nsh.	2	13	2	1	3	11	....	....	....	....	....	....	1999-00	2001-02
Gosselin, Guy	Wpg.	1	5	0	0	0	6	....	....	....	....	....	....	1987-88	1987-88
Gotaas, Steve	Pit., Min.	3	49	6	9	15	53	3	0	1	1	5	....	1987-88	1990-91
• Gottselig, Johnny	Chi.	16	589	176	195	371	203	43	13	13	26	18	2	1928-29	1944-45
Gould, Bobby	Atl., Cgy., Wsh., Bos.	11	697	145	159	304	572	78	15	13	28	58	....	1979-80	1989-90
Gould, John	Buf., Van., Atl.	9	504	131	138	269	113	14	3	2	5	4	....	1971-72	1979-80
Gould, Larry	Van.	1	2	0	0	0	0	....	....	....	....	....	....	1973-74	1973-74
Goulet, Michel	Que., Chi.	15	1089	548	604	1152	825	92	39	39	78	110	....	1979-80	1993-94
• Goupille, Red	Mtl.	8	222	12	28	40	256	8	2	0	2	6	....	1935-36	1942-43
Govedaris, Chris	Hfd., Tor.	4	45	4	6	10	24	4	0	0	0	2	....	1989-90	1993-94
Goyer, Gerry	Chi.	1	40	1	2	3	4	3	0	0	0	2	....	1967-68	1967-68
Goyette, Phil	Mtl., NYR, St.L., Buf.	16	941	207	467	674	131	94	17	29	46	26	4	1956-57	1971-72
• Graboski, Tony	Mtl.	3	66	6	10	16	24	3	0	0	0	6	....	1940-41	1942-43
• Gracie, Bob	Tor., Bos., NYA, Mtl.M., Mtl., Chi.	9	379	82	109	191	205	33	4	7	11	4	2	1930-31	1938-39
Gradin, Thomas	Van., Bos.	9	677	209	384	593	298	42	17	25	42	20	....	1978-79	1986-87
Graham, Dirk	Min., Chi.	12	772	219	270	489	917	90	17	27	44	92	....	1983-84	1994-95
• Graham, Leth	Ott., Ham.	6	27	3	0	3	0	1	0	0	0	0	1	1920-21	1925-26
Graham, Pat	Pit., Tor.	3	103	11	17	28	136	4	0	0	0	2	....	1981-82	1983-84
Graham, Rod	Bos.	1	14	2	1	3	7	....	....	....	....	....	....	1974-75	1974-75
• Graham, Ted	Chi., Mtl.M., Det., St.L., Bos., NYA	9	346	14	25	39	300	24	3	1	4	30	....	1927-28	1936-37
Granato, Tony	NYR, L.A., S.J.	14	773	248	244	492	1425	79	16	27	43	141	....	1988-89	2000-01
Grant, Danny	Mtl., Min., Det., L.A.	13	736	263	273	536	239	43	10	14	24	19	1	1965-66	1978-79
‡ Gratton, Benoit	Wsh., Cgy., Mtl.	6	58	6	10	16	58	....	....	....	....	....	....	1997-98	2003-04
Gratton, Dan	L.A.	1	7	1	0	1	5	....	....	....	....	....	....	1987-88	1987-88
Gratton, Norm	NYR, Atl., Buf., Min.	5	201	39	44	83	64	6	0	1	1	2	....	1971-72	1975-76
Gravelle, Leo	Mtl., Det.	5	223	44	34	78	42	17	4	1	5	2	....	1946-47	1950-51
Graves, Adam	Det., Edm., NYR, S.J.	16	1152	329	287	616	1224	125	38	27	65	119	2	1987-88	2002-03
Graves, Hilliard	Cal., Atl., Van., Wpg.	9	556	118	163	281	209	2	0	0	0	0	....	1970-71	1979-80
Graves, Steve	Edm.	3	35	5	4	9	10	....	....	....	....	....	....	1983-84	1987-88
• Gray, Alex	NYR, Tor.	2	50	7	0	7	32	13	1	0	1	0	1	1927-28	1928-29
Gray, Terry	Bos., Mtl., L.A., St.L.	6	147	26	28	54	64	35	5	5	10	22	....	1961-62	1970-71
‡ Green, Mike	Fla., NYR	1	24	1	3	4	4	....	....	....	....	....	....	2003-04	2003-04
• Green, Red	Ham., NYA, Bos., Det.	6	195	59	26	85	290	1	0	0	0	0	1	1923-24	1928-29
Green, Rick	Wsh., Mtl., Det., NYI	15	845	43	220	263	588	100	3	16	19	73	1	1976-77	1991-92
• Green, Shorty	Ham., NYA	4	103	33	20	53	151	....	....	....	....	....	....	1923-24	1926-27
Green, Ted	Bos.	11	620	48	206	254	1029	31	4	8	12	54	1	1960-61	1971-72
‡ Green, Travis	NYI, Ana., Phx., Tor., Bos.	14	970	193	262	455	764	56	10	11	21	60	....	1992-93	2006-07
Greenlaw, Jeff	Wsh., Fla.	6	57	3	6	9	108	2	0	0	0	21	....	1986-87	1993-94
Gregg, Randy	Edm., Van.	10	474	41	152	193	333	137	13	38	51	127	5	1981-82	1991-92
Greig, Bruce	Cal.	2	9	0	1	1	46	....	....	....	....	....	....	1973-74	1974-75
‡ Greig, Mark	Hfd., Tor., Cgy., Phi.	9	125	13	27	40	90	5	0	1	1	0	....	1990-91	2002-03
Grenier, Lucien	Mtl., L.A.	4	151	14	14	28	18	2	0	0	0	0	....	1968-69	1971-72
Grenier, Richard	NYI	1	10	1	1	2	2	....	....	....	....	....	....	1972-73	1972-73
Greschner, Ron	NYR	16	982	179	431	610	1226	84	17	32	49	106	....	1974-75	1989-90
Gretzky, Brent	T.B.	2	13	1	3	4	2	....	....	....	....	....	....	1993-94	1994-95
Gretzky, Wayne	Edm., L.A., St.L., NYR	20	1487	894	1963	2857	577	208	122	260	382	66	4	1979-80	1998-99
Grieve, Brent	NYI, Edm., Chi., L.A.	4	97	20	16	36	87	....	....	....	....	....	....	1993-94	1996-97
• Grigor, George	Chi.	1	2	1	0	1	0	1	0	0	0	0	....	1943-44	1943-44
Grimson, Stu	Cgy., Chi., Ana., Det., Hfd., Car., L.A., Nsh.	14	729	17	22	39	2113	42	1	1	2	120	....	1988-89	2001-02
Grisdale, John	Tor., Van.	6	250	4	39	43	346	10	0	1	1	15	....	1972-73	1978-79
‡ Groleau, Francois	Mtl.	3	8	0	1	1	6	....	....	....	....	....	....	1995-96	1997-98
‡ Gron, Stanislav	N.J.	1	1	0	0	0	0	....	....	....	....	....	....	2000-01	2000-01
Gronman, Tuomas	Chi., Pit.	2	38	1	3	4	38	1	0	0	0	0	....	1996-97	1997-98
• Gronsdahl, Lloyd	Bos.	1	10	1	2	3	0	....	....	....	....	....	....	1941-42	1941-42
Gronstrand, Jari	Min., NYR, Que., NYI	5	185	8	26	34	135	3	0	0	0	4	....	1986-87	1990-91
‡ Grosek, Michal	Wpg., Buf., Chi., NYR, Bos.	11	526	84	137	221	509	45	9	11	20	77	....	1993-94	2003-04
• Gross, Lloyd	Tor., NYA, Bos., Det.	3	62	11	5	16	20	1	0	0	0	0	....	1926-27	1934-35
• Grosso, Don	Det., Chi., Bos.	9	336	87	117	204	90	48	15	14	29	63	1	1938-39	1946-47
• Grosvenor, Len	Ott., NYA, Mtl.	6	149	9	11	20	78	4	0	0	0	2	....	1927-28	1932-33
Groulx, Wayne	Que.	1	1	0	0	0	0	....	....	....	....	....	....	1984-85	1984-85
Gruden, John	Bos., Ott., Wsh.	6	92	1	8	9	46	3	0	1	1	0	....	1993-94	2003-04
Gruen, Danny	Det., Col.	3	49	9	13	22	19	....	....	....	....	....	....	1972-73	1976-77
Gruhl, Scott	L.A., Pit.	3	20	3	3	6	6	....	....	....	....	....	....	1981-82	1987-88
Gryp, Bob	Bos., Wsh.	3	74	11	13	24	33	....	....	....	....	....	....	1973-74	1975-76
Guay, Francois	Buf.	1	1	0	0	0	0	....	....	....	....	....	....	1989-90	1989-90
Guay, Paul	Phi., L.A., Bos., NYI	7	117	11	23	34	92	9	0	1	1	12	....	1983-84	1990-91
Guerard, Daniel	Ott.	1	2	0	0	0	0	....	....	....	....	....	....	1994-95	1994-95
Guerard, Stephane	Que.	2	34	0	0	0	40	....	....	....	....	....	....	1987-88	1989-90
Guevremont, Jocelyn	Van., Buf., NYR	9	571	84	223	307	319	40	4	17	21	18	....	1971-72	1979-80
Guidolin, Aldo	NYR	4	182	9	15	24	117	....	....	....	....	....	....	1952-53	1955-56
Guidolin, Bep	Bos., Det., Chi.	9	519	107	171	278	606	24	5	7	12	35	....	1942-43	1951-52
Guindon, Bobby	Wpg.	1	6	0	1	1	0	....	....	....	....	....	....	1979-80	1979-80
‡ Guolla, Steve	S.J., T.B., Atl., N.J.	6	205	40	46	86	60	....	....	....	....	....	....	1996-97	2002-03
‡ Guren, Miloslav	Mtl.	2	36	1	3	4	16	....	....	....	....	....	....	1998-99	1999-00
Gusarov, Alexei	Que., Col., NYR, St.L.	11	607	39	128	167	313	68	0	14	14	38	1	1990-91	2000-01
Gusev, Sergey	Dal., T.B.	4	89	4	10	14	34	....	....	....	....	....	....	1997-98	2000-01
‡ Gusmanov, Ravil	Wpg.	1	4	0	0	0	0	....	....	....	....	....	....	1995-96	1995-96
Gustafsson, Bengt-Ake	Wsh.	9	629	196	359	555	196	32	9	19	28	16	....	1979-80	1988-89
‡ Gustafsson, Per	Fla., Tor., Ott.	2	89	8	27	35	38	1	0	0	0	0	....	1996-97	1997-98
Gustavsson, Peter	Col.	1	2	0	0	0	0	....	....	....	....	....	....	1981-82	1981-82
Guy, Kevan	Cgy., Van.	6	156	5	20	25	138	5	0	1	1	23	....	1986-87	1991-92

H

‡ Haakana, Kari	Edm.	1	13	0	0	0	4	....	....	....	....	....	....	2002-03	2002-03
Haanpaa, Ari	NYI	3	60	6	11	17	37	6	0	0	0	10	....	1985-86	1987-88
Haas, David	Edm., Cgy.	2	7	2	1	3	7	....	....	....	....	....	....	1990-91	1993-94
Habscheid, Marc	Edm., Min., Det., Cgy.	11	345	72	91	163	171	12	1	3	4	13	....	1981-82	1991-92
Hachborn, Len	Phi., L.A.	3	102	20	39	59	29	7	0	3	3	7	....	1983-84	1985-86
Haddon, Lloyd	Det.	1	8	0	0	0	2	1	0	0	0	0	....	1959-60	1959-60
Hadfield, Vic	NYR, Pit.	16	1002	323	389	712	1154	73	27	21	48	117	....	1961-62	1976-77
• Haggarty, Jim	Mtl.	1	5	1	1	2	0	3	2	1	3	0	....	1941-42	1941-42
Haggerty, Sean	Tor., NYI, Nsh.	4	14	1	2	3	4	....	....	....	....	....	....	1995-96	2000-01
• Hagglund, Roger	Que.	1	3	0	0	0	0	....	....	....	....	....	....	1984-85	1984-85
Hagman, Matti	Bos., Edm.	4	237	56	89	145	36	20	5	2	7	6	....	1976-77	1981-82
‡ Hahl, Riku	Col.	3	92	5	8	13	38	34	2	4	6	4	....	2001-02	2003-04
Haidy, Gord	Det.	1	....	....	....	....	....	1	0	0	0	0	....	1949-50	1949-50
Hajdu, Richard	Buf.	2	5	0	0	0	4	....	....	....	....	....	....	1985-86	1986-87

			Regular Schedule					Playoffs					NHL	First	Last
Name	NHL Teams	NHL Seasons	GP	G	A	TP	PIM	GP	G	A	TP	PIM	Cup Wins	NHL Season	NHL Season
Hajt, Bill	Buf.	14	854	42	202	244	433	80	2	16	18	70	....	1973-74	1986-87
‡ Hajt, Chris	Edm., Wsh.	2	6	0	0	0	2	....	....	....	....	....	....	2000-01	2003-04
Hakansson, Anders	Min., Pit., L.A.	5	330	52	46	98	141	6	0	0	0	2	....	1981-82	1985-86
• Halderson, Harold	Det., Tor.	1	44	3	2	5	65	....	....	....	....	....	....	1926-27	1926-27
Hale, Larry	Phi.	4	196	5	37	42	90	8	0	0	0	12	....	1968-69	1971-72
Haley, Len	Det.	2	30	2	2	4	14	6	1	3	4	6	....	1959-60	1960-61
Halkidis, Bob	Buf., L.A., Tor., Det., T.B., NYI	11	256	8	32	40	825	20	0	1	1	51	....	1984-85	1995-96
Halko, Steven	Car.	6	155	0	15	15	71	4	0	0	0	2	....	1997-98	2002-03
• Hall, Bob	NYA	1	8	0	0	0	0	....	....	....	....	....	....	1925-26	1925-26
Hall, Del	Cal.	3	9	2	0	2	2	....	....	....	....	....	....	1971-72	1973-74
• Hall, Joe	Mtl.	2	38	15	8	23	189	7	0	1	1	38	....	1917-18	1918-19
Hall, Murray	Chi., Det., Min., Van.	9	164	35	48	83	46	6	0	0	0	0	....	1961-62	1971-72
Hall, Taylor	Van., Bos.	5	41	7	9	16	29	....	....	....	....	....	....	1983-84	1987-88
Hall, Wayne	NYR	1	4	0	0	0	0	....	....	....	....	....	....	1960-61	1960-61
Haller, Kevin	Buf., Mtl., Phi., Hfd., Car., Ana., NYI	13	642	41	97	138	907	64	7	16	23	71	1	1989-90	2001-02
• Halliday, Milt	Ott.	3	67	1	0	1	4	6	0	0	0	0	1	1926-27	1928-29
Hallin, Mats	NYI, Min.	5	152	17	14	31	193	15	1	0	1	13	1	1982-83	1986-87
Halverson, Trevor	Wsh.	1	17	0	4	4	28	....	....	....	....	....	....	1998-99	1998-99
Halward, Doug	Bos., L.A., Van., Det., Edm.	14	653	69	224	293	774	47	7	10	17	113	....	1975-76	1988-89
Hamel, Gilles	Buf., Wpg., L.A.	9	519	127	147	274	276	27	4	5	9	10	....	1980-81	1988-89
• Hamel, Herb	Tor.	1	2	0	0	0	4	....	....	....	....	....	....	1930-31	1930-31
Hamel, Jean	St.L., Det., Que., Mtl.	12	699	26	95	121	766	33	0	2	2	44	....	1972-73	1983-84
• Hamill, Red	Bos., Chi.	12	419	128	94	222	160	24	1	2	3	20	1	1937-38	1950-51
Hamilton, Al	NYR, Buf., Edm.	7	257	10	78	88	258	7	0	0	0	2	....	1965-66	1979-80
Hamilton, Chuck	Mtl., St.L.	2	4	0	2	2	2	....	....	....	....	....	....	1961-62	1972-73
• Hamilton, Jack	Tor.	3	102	28	32	60	20	11	2	1	3	0	....	1942-43	1945-46
Hamilton, Jim	Pit.	8	95	14	18	32	28	6	3	0	3	0	....	1977-78	1984-85
• Hamilton, Reg	Tor., Chi.	12	424	21	87	108	412	64	3	8	11	46	2	1935-36	1946-47
Hammarstrom, Inge	Tor., St.L.	6	427	116	123	239	86	13	2	3	5	4	....	1973-74	1978-79
Hammond, Ken	L.A., Edm., NYR, Tor., Bos., S.J., Van., Ott.	8	193	18	29	47	290	15	0	0	0	24	....	1984-85	1992-93
Hampson, Gord	Cgy.	1	4	0	0	0	5	....	....	....	....	....	....	1982-83	1982-83
Hampson, Ted	Tor., NYR, Det., Oak., Cal., Min.	14	676	108	245	353	94	35	7	10	17	2	....	1959-60	1971-72
Hampton, Rick	Cal., Cle., L.A.	6	337	59	113	172	147	2	0	0	0	0	....	1974-75	1979-80
‡ Hamr, Radek	Ott.	2	11	0	0	0	0	....	....	....	....	....	....	1992-93	1993-94
Hamway, Mark	NYI	3	53	5	13	18	9	1	0	0	0	0	....	1984-85	1986-87
Handy, Ron	NYI, St.L.	2	14	0	3	3	0	....	....	....	....	....	....	1984-85	1987-88
Hangsleben, Al	Hfd., Wsh., L.A.	3	185	21	48	69	396	....	....	....	....	....	....	1979-80	1981-82
Hankinson, Ben	N.J., T.B.	3	43	3	3	6	45	2	1	0	1	4	....	1992-93	1994-95
Hankinson, Casey	Chi., Ana.	3	18	0	1	1	13	....	....	....	....	....	....	2000-01	2003-04
• Hanna, John	NYR, Mtl., Phi.	5	198	6	26	32	206	....	....	....	....	....	....	1958-59	1967-68
Hannan, Dave	Pit., Edm., Tor., Buf., Col., Ott.	16	841	114	191	305	942	63	6	7	13	46	2	1981-82	1996-97
• Hannigan, Gord	Tor.	4	161	29	31	60	117	9	2	0	2	8	....	1952-53	1955-56
• Hannigan, Pat	Tor., NYR, Phi.	5	182	30	39	69	116	11	1	2	3	11	....	1959-60	1968-69
Hannigan, Ray	Tor.	1	3	0	0	0	2	....	....	....	....	....	....	1948-49	1948-49
Hansen, Richie	NYI, St.L.	4	20	2	8	10	4	....	....	....	....	....	....	1976-77	1981-82
Hansen, Tavis	Wpg., Phx.	5	34	2	1	3	16	2	0	0	0	0	....	1994-95	2000-01
Hanson, Dave	Det., Min.	2	33	1	1	2	65	....	....	....	....	....	....	1978-79	1979-80
• Hanson, Emil	Det.	1	7	0	0	0	6	....	....	....	....	....	....	1932-33	1932-33
Hanson, Keith	Cgy.	1	25	0	2	2	77	....	....	....	....	....	....	1983-84	1983-84
• Hanson, Oscar	Chi.	1	8	0	0	0	0	....	....	....	....	....	....	1937-38	1937-38
Harbaruk, Nick	Pit., St.L.	5	364	45	75	120	273	14	3	1	4	20	....	1969-70	1973-74
Harding, Jeff	Phi.	2	15	0	0	0	47	....	....	....	....	....	....	1988-89	1989-90
Hardy, Joe	Oak., Cal.	2	63	9	14	23	51	4	0	0	0	0	....	1969-70	1970-71
Hardy, Mark	L.A., NYR, Min.	15	915	62	306	368	1293	67	5	16	21	158	....	1979-80	1993-94
Hargreaves, Jim	Van.	2	66	1	7	8	105	....	....	....	....	....	....	1970-71	1972-73
‡ Harkins, Brett	Bos., Fla., CBJ	4	78	6	30	36	22	....	....	....	....	....	....	1994-95	2001-02
Harkins, Todd	Cgy., Hfd.	3	48	3	3	6	78	....	....	....	....	....	....	1991-92	1993-94
Harlock, David	Tor., Wsh., NYI, Atl.	8	212	2	14	16	188	....	....	....	....	....	....	1993-94	2001-02
Harlow, Scott	St.L.	1	1	0	1	1	0	....	....	....	....	....	....	1987-88	1987-88
• Harmon, Glen	Mtl.	9	452	50	96	146	334	53	5	10	15	37	2	1942-43	1950-51
• Harms, John	Chi.	2	44	5	5	10	21	4	3	0	3	2	....	1943-44	1944-45
• Harnott, Walter	Bos.	1	6	0	0	0	2	....	....	....	....	....	....	1933-34	1933-34
Harper, Terry	Mtl., L.A., Det., St.L., Col.	19	1066	35	221	256	1362	112	4	13	17	140	5	1962-63	1980-81
Harrer, Tim	Cgy.	1	3	0	0	0	2	....	....	....	....	....	....	1982-83	1982-83
• Harrington, Hago	Bos., Mtl.	3	72	9	3	12	15	4	1	0	1	2	....	1925-26	1932-33
• Harris, Billy	Tor., Det., Oak., Pit.	13	769	126	219	345	205	62	8	10	18	30	3	1955-56	1968-69
Harris, Billy	NYI, L.A., Tor.	12	897	231	327	558	394	71	19	19	38	48	....	1972-73	1983-84
Harris, Duke	Min., Tor.	1	26	1	4	5	4	....	....	....	....	....	....	1967-68	1967-68
• Harris, Henry	Bos.	1	32	2	4	6	20	....	....	....	....	....	....	1930-31	1930-31
Harris, Hugh	Buf.	1	60	12	26	38	17	3	0	0	0	0	....	1972-73	1972-73
Harris, Ron	Det., Oak., Atl., NYR	11	476	20	91	111	474	28	4	3	7	33	....	1962-63	1975-76
• Harris, Smokey	Bos.	1	6	3	1	4	8	....	....	....	....	....	....	1924-25	1924-25
Harris, Ted	Mtl., Min., Det., St.L., Phi.	12	788	30	168	198	1000	100	1	22	23	230	5	1963-64	1974-75
Harrison, Ed	Bos., NYR	4	194	27	24	51	53	9	1	0	1	2	....	1947-48	1950-51
Harrison, Jim	Bos., Tor., Chi., Edm.	8	324	67	86	153	435	13	1	1	2	43	....	1968-69	1979-80
Hart, Gerry	Det., NYI, Que., St.L.	15	730	29	150	179	1240	78	3	12	15	175	....	1968-69	1982-83
• Hart, Gizzy	Det., Mtl.	3	104	6	8	14	12	8	0	1	1	0	....	1926-27	1932-33
Hartman, Mike	Buf., Wpg., T.B., NYR	9	397	43	35	78	1388	21	0	0	0	106	1	1986-87	1994-95
Hartsburg, Craig	Min.	10	570	98	315	413	818	61	15	27	42	70	....	1979-80	1988-89
• Harvey, Buster	Min., Atl., K.C., Det.	7	407	90	118	208	131	14	0	2	2	8	....	1970-71	1976-77
• Harvey, Doug	Mtl., NYR, Det., St.L.	20	1113	88	452	540	1216	137	8	64	72	152	6	1947-48	1968-69
Harvey, Hugh	K.C.	2	18	1	1	2	4	....	....	....	....	....	....	1974-75	1975-76
Harvey, Todd	Dal., NYR, S.J., Edm.	11	671	91	132	223	950	68	3	6	9	52	....	1994-95	2005-06
Hassard, Bob	Tor., Chi.	5	126	9	28	37	22	....	....	....	....	....	1	1949-50	1954-55
Hatcher, Kevin	Wsh., Dal., Pit., NYR, Car.	17	1157	227	450	677	1392	118	22	37	59	252	....	1984-85	2000-01
Hatoum, Ed	Det., Van.	3	47	3	6	9	25	....	....	....	....	....	....	1968-69	1970-71
‡ Hauer, Brett	Edm., Nsh.	3	37	4	4	8	38	....	....	....	....	....	....	1995-96	2001-02
Hawerchuk, Dale	Wpg., Buf., St.L., Phi.	16	1188	518	891	1409	730	97	30	69	99	67	....	1981-82	1996-97
Hawgood, Greg	Bos., Edm., Phi., Fla., Pit., S.J., Van., Dal.	12	474	60	164	224	426	42	2	8	10	37	....	1987-88	2001-02
Hawkins, Todd	Van., Tor.	3	10	0	0	0	15	....	....	....	....	....	....	1988-89	1991-92
Haworth, Alan	Buf., Wsh., Que.	8	524	189	211	400	425	42	12	16	28	28	....	1980-81	1987-88
Haworth, Gord	NYR	1	2	0	1	1	0	....	....	....	....	....	....	1952-53	1952-53
Hawryliw, Neil	NYI	1	1	0	0	0	0	....	....	....	....	....	....	1981-82	1981-82
Hay, Bill	Chi.	8	506	113	273	386	244	67	15	21	36	62	1	1959-60	1966-67
‡ Hay, Dwayne	Wsh., Fla., T.B., Cgy.	4	79	2	4	6	22	....	....	....	....	....	....	1997-98	2000-01
• Hay, George	Chi., Det.	7	239	74	60	134	84	8	2	3	5	2	....	1926-27	1933-34
Hay, Jim	Det.	3	75	1	5	6	22	9	1	0	1	2	1	1952-53	1954-55
Hayek, Peter	Min.	1	1	0	0	0	0	....	....	....	....	....	....	1981-82	1981-82
Hayes, Chris	Bos.	1	....	....	....	....	....	1	0	0	0	0	....	1971-72	1971-72
• Haynes, Paul	Mtl.M., Bos., Mtl.	11	391	61	134	195	164	24	2	8	10	13	....	1930-31	1940-41
Hayward, Rick	L.A.	1	4	0	0	0	5	....	....	....	....	....	....	1990-91	1990-91
Hazlett, Steve	Van.	1	1	0	0	0	0	....	....	....	....	....	....	1979-80	1979-80
Head, Galen	Det.	1	1	0	0	0	0	....	....	....	....	....	....	1967-68	1967-68
• Headley, Fern	Bos., Mtl.	1	30	1	3	4	10	1	0	0	0	0	....	1924-25	1924-25
‡ Healey, Paul	Phi., Tor., NYR, Col.	6	77	6	14	20	44	22	0	2	2	4	....	1996-97	2005-06
Healey, Rich	Det.	1	1	0	0	0	2	....	....	....	....	....	....	1960-61	1960-61
Heaphy, Shawn	Cgy.	1	1	0	0	0	0	....	....	....	....	....	....	1992-93	1992-93
Heaslip, Mark	NYR, L.A.	3	117	10	19	29	110	5	0	0	0	2	....	1976-77	1978-79
Heath, Randy	NYR	2	13	2	4	6	15	....	....	....	....	....	....	1984-85	1985-86
Hebenton, Andy	NYR, Bos.	9	630	189	202	391	83	22	6	5	11	8	....	1955-56	1963-64
‡ Hecl, Radoslav	Buf.	1	14	0	0	0	2	....	....	....	....	....	....	2002-03	2002-03
Hedberg, Anders	NYR	7	465	172	225	397	144	58	22	24	46	31	....	1978-79	1984-85
‡ Hedin, Pierre	Tor.	1	3	0	1	1	0	....	....	....	....	....	....	2003-04	2003-04
‡ Hedstrom, Jonathan	Ana.	2	83	13	14	27	48	3	0	1	1	2	....	2002-03	2005-06
‡ Heerema, Jeff	Car., St.L.	2	32	4	2	6	6	....	....	....	....	....	....	2002-03	2003-04
• Heffernan, Frank	Tor.	1	19	0	1	1	10	....	....	....	....	....	....	1919-20	1919-20
• Heffernan, Gerry	Mtl.	3	83	33	35	68	27	11	3	3	6	8	1	1941-42	1943-44
Heidt, Mike	L.A.	1	6	0	1	1	7	....	....	....	....	....	....	1983-84	1983-84
• Heindl, Bill	Min., NYR	3	18	2	1	3	0	....	....	....	....	....	....	1970-71	1972-73
Heinrich, Lionel	Bos.	1	35	1	1	2	33	....	....	....	....	....	....	1955-56	1955-56
‡ Heins, Shawn	S.J., Pit., Atl.	6	125	4	12	16	154	2	0	0	0	0	....	1998-99	2003-04
Heinze, Steve	Bos., CBJ, Buf., L.A.	12	694	178	158	336	379	69	11	15	26	48	....	1991-92	2002-03
Heiskala, Earl	Phi.	3	127	13	11	24	294	....	....	....	....	....	....	1968-69	1970-71

Ted Hampson

Mark Heaslip

Jimmy Herberts

Doug Hicks

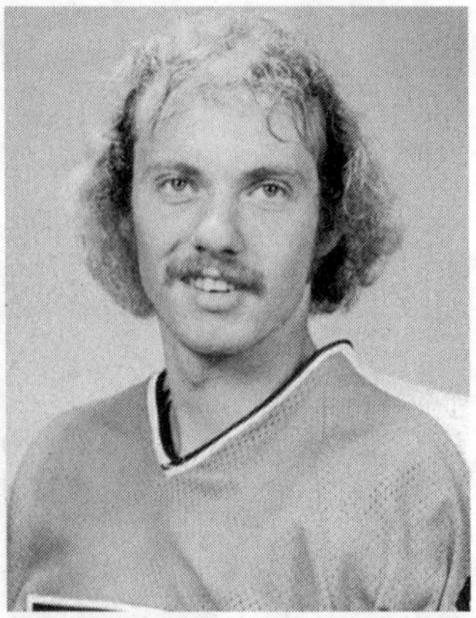
Al Hill

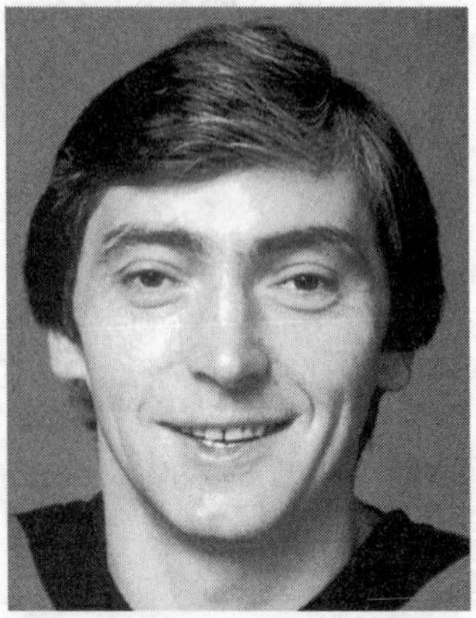
Ivan Hlinka

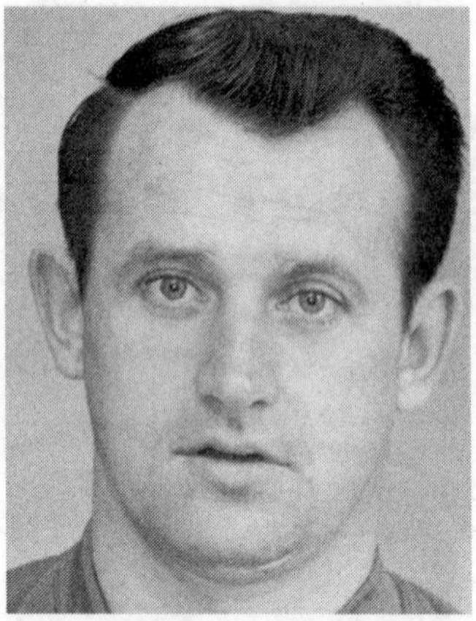
Bronco Horvath

Dave Hunter

Name	NHL Teams	NHL Seasons	Regular Schedule GP	G	A	TP	PIM	Playoffs GP	G	A	TP	PIM	NHL Cup Wins	First NHL Season	Last NHL Season
‡ Heisten, Barrett	NYR	1	10	0	0	0	2	....	....	....	....	....	....	2001-02	2001-02
Helander, Peter	L.A.	1	7	0	1	1	0	....	....	....	....	....	....	1982-83	1982-83
‡ Helbling, Timo	T.B., Wsh.	2	11	0	1	1	8	....	....	....	....	....	....	2005-06	2006-07
‡ Helenius, Sami	Cgy., T.B., Col., Dal., Chi.	6	155	2	4	6	260	1	0	0	0	0	....	1996-97	2002-03
• Heller, Ott	NYR	15	647	55	176	231	465	61	6	8	14	61	2	1931-32	1945-46
Helman, Harry	Ott.	3	44	1	0	1	7	2	0	0	0	0	1	1922-23	1924-25
‡ Helminen, Raimo	NYR, Min., NYI	3	117	13	46	59	16	2	0	0	0	0	....	1985-86	1988-89
‡ Hemingway, Colin	St.L.	1	3	0	0	0	0	....	....	....	....	....	....	2005-06	2005-06
• Hemmerling, Tony	NYA	2	22	3	3	6	4	....	....	....	....	....	....	1935-36	1936-37
Henderson, Archie	Wsh., Min., Hfd.	3	23	3	1	4	92	....	....	....	....	....	....	1980-81	1982-83
‡ Henderson, Jay	Bos.	4	33	1	3	4	37	....	....	....	....	....	....	1998-99	2001-02
Henderson, Matt	Nsh., Chi.	2	6	0	1	1	2	....	....	....	....	....	....	1998-99	2001-02
Henderson, Murray	Bos.	8	405	24	62	86	305	41	2	3	5	23	....	1944-45	1951-52
Henderson, Paul	Det., Tor., Atl.	13	707	236	241	477	304	56	11	14	25	28	....	1962-63	1979-80
Hendrickson, Darby	Tor., NYI, Van., Min., Col.	11	518	65	64	129	370	25	3	3	6	6	....	1993-94	2003-04
Hendrickson, John	Det.	3	5	0	0	0	4	....	....	....	....	....	....	1957-58	1961-62
Henning, Lorne	NYI	9	544	73	111	184	102	81	7	7	14	8	2	1972-73	1980-81
Henry, Burke	Chi.	2	39	2	6	8	33	....	....	....	....	....	....	2002-03	2003-04
• Henry, Camille	NYR, Chi., St.L.	14	727	279	249	528	88	47	6	12	18	7	....	1953-54	1969-70
Henry, Dale	NYI	6	132	13	26	39	263	14	1	0	1	19	....	1984-85	1989-90
‡ Hentunen, Jukka	Cgy., Nsh.	1	38	4	5	9	4	....	....	....	....	....	....	2001-02	2001-02
Hepple, Alan	N.J.	3	3	0	0	0	7	....	....	....	....	....	....	1983-84	1985-86
Herbers, Ian	Edm., T.B., NYI	2	65	0	5	5	79	....	....	....	....	....	....	1993-94	1999-00
• Herberts, Jimmy	Bos., Tor., Det.	6	206	83	31	114	253	9	3	0	3	10	....	1924-25	1929-30
• Herchenratter, Art	Det.	1	10	1	2	3	2	....	....	....	....	....	....	1940-41	1940-41
Hergerts, Fred	NYA	2	20	2	4	6	2	....	....	....	....	....	....	1934-35	1935-36
• Hergesheimer, Phil	Chi., Bos.	4	125	21	41	62	19	6	0	0	0	2	....	1939-40	1942-43
Hergesheimer, Wally	NYR, Chi.	7	351	114	85	199	106	5	1	0	1	0	....	1951-52	1958-59
• Heron, Red	Tor., Bro., Mtl.	4	106	21	19	40	38	21	2	2	4	6	....	1938-39	1941-42
Heroux, Yves	Que.	1	1	0	0	0	0	....	....	....	....	....	....	1986-87	1986-87
‡ Herperger, Chris	Chi., Ott., Atl.	4	169	18	25	43	75	....	....	....	....	....	....	1999-00	2002-03
Herr, Matt	Wsh., Fla., Bos.	4	58	4	5	9	25	....	....	....	....	....	....	1998-99	2002-03
Herter, Jason	NYI	1	1	0	1	1	0	....	....	....	....	....	....	1995-96	1995-96
Hervey, Matt	Wpg., Bos., T.B.	3	35	0	5	5	97	5	0	0	0	6	....	1988-89	1992-93
Hess, Bob	St.L., Buf., Hfd.	8	329	27	95	122	178	4	1	1	2	2	....	1974-75	1983-84
• Heximer, Obs	NYR, Bos., NYA	3	84	13	7	20	16	5	0	0	0	2	....	1929-30	1934-35
• Hextall, Bryan	NYR	11	449	187	175	362	227	37	8	9	17	19	1	1936-37	1947-48
Hextall, Bryan	NYR, Pit., Atl., Det., Min.	8	549	99	161	260	738	18	0	4	4	59	....	1962-63	1975-76
Hextall, Dennis	NYR, L.A., Cal., Min., Det., Wsh.	13	681	153	350	503	1398	22	3	3	6	45	....	1967-68	1979-80
• Heyliger, Vic	Chi.	2	33	2	3	5	2	....	....	....	....	....	....	1937-38	1943-44
• Hicke, Bill	Mtl., NYR, Oak., Cal., Pit.	14	729	168	234	402	395	42	3	10	13	41	2	1958-59	1971-72
Hicke, Ernie	Cal., Atl., NYI, Min., L.A.	8	520	132	140	272	407	2	1	0	1	0	....	1970-71	1977-78
Hickey, Greg	NYR	1	1	0	0	0	0	....	....	....	....	....	....	1977-78	1977-78
Hickey, Pat	NYR, Col., Tor., Que., St.L.	10	646	192	212	404	351	55	5	11	16	37	....	1975-76	1984-85
Hicks, Alex	Ana., Pit., S.J., Fla.	5	258	25	54	79	247	15	0	2	2	8	....	1995-96	1999-00
Hicks, Doug	Min., Chi., Edm., Wsh.	9	561	37	131	168	442	18	2	1	3	15	....	1974-75	1982-83
Hicks, Glenn	Det.	2	108	6	12	18	127	....	....	....	....	....	....	1979-80	1980-81
• Hicks, Henry	Mtl.M., Det.	3	96	7	2	9	72	....	....	....	....	....	....	1928-29	1930-31
Hicks, Wayne	Chi., Bos., Mtl., Phi., Pit.	5	115	13	23	36	22	2	0	1	1	2	1	1959-60	1967-68
Hidi, Andre	Wsh.	2	7	2	1	3	9	2	0	0	0	0	....	1983-84	1984-85
Hiemer, Uli	N.J.	3	143	19	54	73	176	....	....	....	....	....	....	1984-85	1986-87
‡ Higgins, Matt	Mtl.	4	57	1	2	3	6	....	....	....	....	....	....	1997-98	2000-01
Higgins, Paul	Tor.	2	25	0	0	0	152	1	0	0	0	0	....	1981-82	1982-83
Higgins, Tim	Chi., N.J., Det.	11	706	154	198	352	719	65	5	8	13	77	....	1978-79	1988-89
• Hildebrand, Ike	NYR, Chi.	2	41	7	11	18	16	....	....	....	....	....	....	1953-54	1954-55
Hill, Al	Phi.	8	221	40	55	95	227	51	8	11	19	43	....	1976-77	1987-88
Hill, Brian	Hfd.	1	19	1	1	2	4	....	....	....	....	....	....	1979-80	1979-80
• Hill, Mel	Bos., Bro., Tor.	9	324	89	109	198	128	43	12	7	19	18	3	1937-38	1945-46
• Hiller, Dutch	NYR, Det., Bos., Mtl.	9	383	91	113	204	163	48	9	8	17	21	2	1937-38	1945-46
Hiller, Jim	L.A., Det., NYR	2	63	8	12	20	116	2	0	0	0	4	....	1992-93	1993-94
Hillier, Randy	Bos., Pit., NYI, Buf.	11	543	16	110	126	906	28	0	2	2	93	1	1981-82	1991-92
Hillman, Floyd	Bos.	1	6	0	0	0	10	....	....	....	....	....	....	1956-57	1956-57
Hillman, Larry	Det., Bos., Tor., Min., Mtl., Phi., L.A., Buf.	19	790	36	196	232	579	74	2	9	11	30	6	1954-55	1972-73
• Hillman, Wayne	Chi., NYR, Min., Phi.	13	691	18	86	104	534	28	0	3	3	19	1	1960-61	1972-73
Hilworth, John	Det.	3	57	1	1	2	89	....	....	....	....	....	....	1977-78	1979-80
• Himes, Normie	NYA	9	402	106	113	219	127	2	0	0	0	0	....	1926-27	1934-35
Hindmarch, Dave	Cgy.	4	99	21	17	38	25	10	0	0	0	6	....	1980-81	1983-84
Hinse, Andre	Tor.	1	4	0	0	0	0	....	....	....	....	....	....	1967-68	1967-68
Hinton, Dan	Chi.	1	14	0	0	0	16	....	....	....	....	....	....	1976-77	1976-77
Hirsch, Tom	Min.	3	31	1	7	8	30	12	0	0	0	6	....	1983-84	1987-88
• Hirschfeld, Bert	Mtl.	2	33	1	4	5	2	5	1	0	1	0	....	1949-50	1950-51
Hislop, Jamie	Que., Cgy.	5	345	75	103	178	86	28	3	2	5	11	....	1979-80	1983-84
• Hitchman, Lionel	Ott., Bos.	12	417	28	34	62	523	35	2	2	4	73	2	1922-23	1933-34
• Hlinka, Ivan	Van.	2	137	42	81	123	28	16	3	10	13	8	....	1981-82	1982-83
Hlushko, Todd	Phi., Cgy., Pit.	6	79	8	13	21	84	3	0	0	0	2	....	1993-94	1998-99
Hocking, Justin	L.A.	1	1	0	0	0	0	....	....	....	....	....	....	1993-94	1993-94
Hodge, Ken	Chi., Bos., NYR	14	881	328	472	800	779	97	34	47	81	120	2	1964-65	1977-78
Hodge Jr., Ken	Min., Bos., T.B.	4	142	39	48	87	32	15	4	6	10	6	....	1988-89	1992-93
Hodgson, Dan	Tor., Van.	4	114	29	45	74	64	....	....	....	....	....	....	1985-86	1988-89
Hodgson, Rick	Hfd.	1	6	0	0	0	6	1	0	0	0	0	....	1979-80	1979-80
Hodgson, Ted	Bos.	1	4	0	0	0	0	....	....	....	....	....	....	1966-67	1966-67
Hoekstra, Cec	Mtl.	1	4	0	0	0	0	....	....	....	....	....	....	1959-60	1959-60
Hoekstra, Ed	Phi.	1	70	15	21	36	6	7	0	1	1	0	....	1967-68	1967-68
Hoene, Phil	L.A.	3	37	2	4	6	22	....	....	....	....	....	....	1972-73	1974-75
Hoffinger, Val	Chi.	2	28	0	1	1	30	....	....	....	....	....	....	1927-28	1928-29
Hoffman, Mike	Hfd.	3	9	1	3	4	2	....	....	....	....	....	....	1982-83	1985-86
Hoffmeyer, Bob	Chi., Phi., N.J.	6	198	14	52	66	325	3	0	1	1	25	....	1977-78	1984-85
Hofford, Jim	Buf., L.A.	3	18	0	0	0	47	....	....	....	....	....	....	1985-86	1988-89
Hogaboam, Bill	Atl., Det., Min.	8	332	80	109	189	100	2	0	0	0	0	....	1972-73	1979-80
Hoganson, Dale	L.A., Mtl., Que.	7	343	13	77	90	186	11	0	3	3	12	....	1969-70	1981-82
‡ Hoglund, Jonas	Cgy., Mtl., Tor.	7	545	117	145	262	112	59	8	11	19	8	....	1996-97	2002-03
Hogue, Benoit	Buf., NYI, Tor., Dal., T.B., Phx., Bos., Wsh.	15	863	222	321	543	877	92	17	16	33	124	1	1987-88	2001-02
Holan, Milos	Phi., Ana.	3	49	5	11	16	42	....	....	....	....	....	....	1993-94	1995-96
Holbrook, Terry	Min.	2	43	3	6	9	4	6	0	0	0	0	....	1972-73	1973-74
‡ Holden, Josh	Van., Car., Tor.	6	60	5	9	14	16	....	....	....	....	....	....	1998-99	2003-04
‡ Holland, Jason	NYI, Buf., L.A.	7	81	4	5	9	36	1	0	0	0	0	....	1996-97	2003-04
Holland, Jerry	NYR	2	37	8	4	12	6	....	....	....	....	....	....	1974-75	1975-76
• Hollett, Flash	Tor., Ott., Bos., Det.	13	562	132	181	313	358	79	8	26	34	38	2	1933-34	1945-46
Hollinger, Terry	St.L.	2	7	0	0	0	2	....	....	....	....	....	....	1993-94	1994-95
• Hollingworth, Gord	Chi., Det.	4	163	4	14	18	201	3	0	0	0	2	....	1954-55	1957-58
Holloway, Bruce	Van.	1	2	0	0	0	0	....	....	....	....	....	....	1984-85	1984-85
• Holmes, Bill	Mtl., NYA	3	52	6	4	10	35	....	....	....	....	....	....	1925-26	1929-30
Holmes, Chuck	Det.	2	23	1	3	4	10	....	....	....	....	....	....	1958-59	1961-62
Holmes, Lou	Chi.	2	59	1	4	5	6	2	0	0	0	2	....	1931-32	1932-33
Holmes, Warren	L.A.	3	45	8	18	26	7	....	....	....	....	....	....	1981-82	1983-84
Holmgren, Paul	Phi., Min.	10	527	144	179	323	1684	82	19	32	51	195	....	1975-76	1984-85
• Holota, John	Det.	2	15	2	0	2	0	....	....	....	....	....	....	1942-43	1945-46
Holst, Greg	NYR	3	11	0	0	0	0	....	....	....	....	....	....	1975-76	1977-78
Holt, Gary	Cal., Cle., St.L.	5	101	13	11	24	133	....	....	....	....	....	....	1973-74	1977-78
Holt, Randy	Chi., Cle., Van., L.A., Cgy., Wsh., Phi.	10	395	4	37	41	1438	21	2	3	5	83	....	1974-75	1983-84
• Holway, Albert	Tor., Mtl.M., Pit.	5	112	7	2	9	48	6	0	0	0	0	1	1923-24	1928-29
Holzinger, Brian	Buf., T.B., Pit., CBJ	10	547	93	145	238	339	52	11	18	29	61	....	1994-95	2003-04
Homenuke, Ron	Van.	1	1	0	0	0	0	....	....	....	....	....	....	1972-73	1972-73
Hoover, Ron	Bos., St.L.	3	18	4	0	4	31	8	0	0	0	18	....	1989-90	1991-92
Hopkins, Dean	L.A., Edm., Que.	6	223	23	51	74	306	18	1	5	6	29	....	1979-80	1988-89
Hopkins, Larry	Tor., Wpg.	4	60	13	16	29	26	6	0	0	0	2	....	1977-78	1982-83
Horacek, Tony	Phi., Chi.	5	154	10	19	29	316	2	1	0	1	2	....	1989-90	1994-95
Horava, Miloslav	NYR	3	80	5	17	22	38	2	0	1	1	0	....	1988-89	1990-91
Horbul, Doug	K.C.	1	4	1	0	1	2	....	....	....	....	....	....	1974-75	1974-75
Hordy, Mike	NYI	2	11	0	0	0	7	....	....	....	....	....	....	1978-79	1979-80
Horeck, Pete	Chi., Det., Bos.	8	426	106	118	224	340	34	6	8	14	43	....	1944-45	1951-52
• Horne, George	Mtl.M., Tor.	3	54	9	3	12	34	4	0	0	0	4	1	1925-26	1928-29
• Horner, Red	Tor.	12	490	42	110	152	1254	71	7	10	17	170	1	1928-29	1939-40

			Regular Schedule					Playoffs							
Name	NHL Teams	NHL Seasons	GP	G	A	TP	PIM	GP	G	A	TP	PIM	NHL Cup Wins	First NHL Season	Last NHL Season
• Hornung, Larry	St.L.	2	48	2	9	11	10	11	0	2	2	2	....	1970-71	1971-72
• Horton, Tim	Tor., NYR, Pit., Buf.	24	1446	115	403	518	1611	126	11	39	50	183	4	1949-50	1973-74
Horvath, Bronco	NYR, Mtl., Bos., Chi., Tor., Min.	9	434	141	185	326	319	36	12	9	21	18	....	1955-56	1967-68
Hospodar, Ed	NYR, Hfd., Phi., Min., Buf.	9	450	17	51	68	1314	44	4	1	5	208	....	1979-80	1987-88
Hostak, Martin	Phi.	2	55	3	11	14	24	....	....	....	....	....	....	1990-91	1991-92
Hotham, Greg	Tor., Pit.	6	230	15	74	89	139	5	0	3	3	6	....	1979-80	1984-85
Houck, Paul	Min.	3	16	1	2	3	2	....	....	....	....	....	....	1985-86	1987-88
Houda, Doug	Det., Hfd., L.A., Buf., NYI, Ana.	15	561	19	63	82	1104	18	0	3	3	21	....	1985-86	2002-03
Houde, Claude	K.C.	2	59	3	6	9	40	....	....	....	....	....	....	1974-75	1975-76
Houde, Eric	Mtl.	3	30	2	3	5	4	....	....	....	....	....	....	1996-97	1998-99
Hough, Mike	Que., Fla., NYI	13	707	100	156	256	675	42	5	5	10	38	....	1986-87	1998-99
Houlder, Bill	Wsh., Buf., Ana., St.L., T.B., S.J., Nsh.	16	846	59	191	250	412	30	5	6	11	14	....	1987-88	2002-03
Houle, Rejean	Mtl.	11	635	161	247	408	395	90	14	34	48	66	5	1969-70	1982-83
Housley, Phil	Buf., Wpg., St.L., Cgy., N.J., Wsh., Chi., Tor.	21	1495	338	894	1232	822	85	13	43	56	36	....	1982-83	2002-03
Houston, Ken	Atl., Cgy., Wsh., L.A.	9	570	161	167	328	624	35	10	9	19	66	....	1975-76	1983-84
Howard, Jack	Tor.	1	2	0	0	0	0	....	....	....	....	....	....	1936-37	1936-37
Howatt, Garry	NYI, Hfd., N.J.	12	720	112	156	268	1836	87	12	14	26	289	2	1972-73	1983-84
Howe, Gordie	Det., Hfd.	26	1767	801	1049	1850	1685	157	68	92	160	220	4	1946-47	1979-80
Howe, Mark	Hfd., Phi., Det.	16	929	197	545	742	455	101	10	51	61	34	....	1979-80	1994-95
Howe, Marty	Hfd., Bos.	6	197	2	29	31	99	15	1	2	3	9	....	1979-80	1984-85
• Howe, Syd	Ott., Phi., Tor., St.L., Det.	17	698	237	291	528	212	70	17	27	44	10	3	1929-30	1945-46
Howe, Vic	NYR	3	33	3	4	7	10	....	....	....	....	....	....	1950-51	1954-55
Howell, Harry	NYR, Oak., Cal., L.A.	21	1411	94	324	418	1298	38	3	3	6	32	....	1952-53	1972-73
• Howell, Ron	NYR	2	4	0	0	0	0	....	....	....	....	....	....	1954-55	1955-56
Howse, Don	L.A.	1	33	2	5	7	6	2	0	0	0	0	....	1979-80	1979-80
Howson, Scott	NYI	2	18	5	3	8	4	....	....	....	....	....	....	1984-85	1985-86
Hoyda, Dave	Phi., Wpg.	4	132	6	17	23	299	12	0	0	0	17	....	1977-78	1980-81
‡ Hrdina, Jan	Pit., Phx., N.J., CBJ	7	513	101	196	297	341	45	12	14	26	24	....	1998-99	2005-06
Hrdina, Jiri	Cgy., Pit.	5	250	45	85	130	92	46	2	5	7	24	3	1987-88	1991-92
Hrechkosy, Dave	Cal., St.L.	4	140	42	24	66	41	3	1	0	1	2	....	1973-74	1976-77
Hrkac, Tony	St.L., Que., S.J., Chi., Dal., Edm., NYI, Ana., Atl.	13	758	132	239	371	173	41	7	7	14	12	1	1986-87	2002-03
Hrycuik, Jim	Wsh.	1	21	5	5	10	12	....	....	....	....	....	....	1974-75	1974-75
Hrymnak, Steve	Chi., Det.	2	18	2	1	3	4	2	0	0	0	0	....	1951-52	1952-53
Hrynewich, Tim	Pit.	2	55	6	8	14	82	....	....	....	....	....	....	1982-83	1983-84
Huard, Bill	Bos., Ott., Que., Dal., Edm., L.A.	8	223	16	18	34	594	5	0	0	0	2	....	1992-93	1999-00
• Huard, Rolly	Tor.	1	1	1	0	1	0	....	....	....	....	....	....	1930-31	1930-31
‡ Hubacek, Petr	Phi.	1	6	1	0	1	2	....	....	....	....	....	....	2000-01	2000-01
Huber, Willie	Det., NYR, Van., Phi.	10	655	104	217	321	950	33	5	5	10	35	....	1978-79	1987-88
Hubick, Greg	Tor., Van.	2	77	6	9	15	10	....	....	....	....	....	....	1975-76	1979-80
Huck, Fran	Mtl., St.L.	3	94	24	30	54	38	11	3	4	7	2	....	1969-70	1972-73
Hucul, Fred	Chi., St.L.	5	164	11	30	41	113	6	1	0	1	10	....	1950-51	1967-68
Huddy, Charlie	Edm., L.A., Buf., St.L.	17	1017	99	354	453	785	183	19	66	85	135	5	1980-81	1996-97
Hudson, Dave	NYI, K.C., Col.	6	409	59	124	183	89	2	1	1	2	0	....	1972-73	1977-78
Hudson, Lex	Pit.	1	2	0	0	0	0	2	0	0	0	0	....	1978-79	1978-79
Hudson, Mike	Chi., Edm., NYR, Pit., Tor., St.L., Phx.	9	416	49	87	136	414	49	4	10	14	64	1	1988-89	1996-97
Hudson, Ron	Det.	2	33	5	2	7	2	....	....	....	....	....	....	1937-38	1939-40
Huffman, Kerry	Phi., Que., Ott.	10	401	37	108	145	361	11	0	0	0	2	....	1986-87	1995-96
Huggins, Al	Mtl.M.	1	20	1	1	2	2	....	....	....	....	....	....	1930-31	1930-31
• Hughes, Albert	NYA	2	60	6	8	14	22	....	....	....	....	....	....	1930-31	1931-32
Hughes, Brent	L.A., Phi., St.L., Det., K.C.	8	435	15	117	132	440	22	1	3	4	53	....	1967-68	1974-75
Hughes, Brent	Wpg., Bos., Buf., NYI	8	357	41	39	80	831	29	4	1	5	53	....	1988-89	1996-97
Hughes, Frank	Cal.	1	5	0	0	0	0	....	....	....	....	....	....	1971-72	1971-72
Hughes, Howie	L.A.	3	168	25	32	57	30	14	2	0	2	2	....	1967-68	1969-70
Hughes, Jack	Col.	2	46	2	5	7	104	....	....	....	....	....	....	1980-81	1981-82
• Hughes, James	Det.	1	40	0	1	1	48	....	....	....	....	....	....	1929-30	1929-30
Hughes, John	Van., Edm., NYR	2	70	2	14	16	211	7	0	1	1	16	....	1979-80	1980-81
Hughes, Pat	Mtl., Pit., Edm., Buf., St.L., Hfd.	10	573	130	128	258	646	71	8	25	33	77	3	1977-78	1986-87
Hughes, Ryan	Bos.	1	3	0	0	0	0	....	....	....	....	....	....	1995-96	1995-96
Hulbig, Joe	Edm., Bos.	5	55	4	4	8	16	6	0	1	1	2	....	1996-97	2000-01
Hull, Bobby	Chi., Wpg., Hfd.	16	1063	610	560	1170	640	119	62	67	129	102	1	1957-58	1979-80
Hull, Brett	Cgy., St.L., Dal., Det., Phx.	20	1269	741	650	1391	458	202	103	87	190	73	2	1985-86	2005-06
Hull, Dennis	Chi., Det.	14	959	303	351	654	261	104	33	34	67	30	....	1964-65	1977-78
Hull, Jody	Hfd., NYR, Ott., Fla., T.B., Phi.	16	831	124	137	261	156	69	4	5	9	14	....	1988-89	2003-04
Hulse, Cale	N.J., Cgy., Nsh., Phx., CBJ	10	619	16	79	95	1000	1	0	0	0	0	....	1995-96	2005-06
‡ Huml, Ivan	Bos.	3	49	6	12	18	36	....	....	....	....	....	....	2001-02	2003-04
• Hunt, Fred	NYA, NYR	2	59	15	14	29	6	....	....	....	....	....	....	1940-41	1944-45
Hunter, Dale	Que., Wsh., Col.	19	1407	323	697	1020	3565	186	42	76	118	729	....	1980-81	1998-99
Hunter, Dave	Edm., Pit., Wpg.	10	746	133	190	323	918	105	16	24	40	211	3	1979-80	1988-89
Hunter, Mark	Mtl., St.L., Cgy., Hfd., Wsh.	12	628	213	171	384	1426	79	18	20	38	230	1	1981-82	1992-93
Hunter, Tim	Cgy., Que., Van., S.J.	16	815	62	76	138	3146	132	5	7	12	426	1	1981-82	1996-97
Huras, Larry	NYR	1	2	0	0	0	0	....	....	....	....	....	....	1976-77	1976-77
Hurlburt, Bob	Van.	1	1	0	0	0	2	....	....	....	....	....	....	1974-75	1974-75
Hurlbut, Mike	NYR, Que., Buf.	5	29	1	8	9	20	....	....	....	....	....	....	1992-93	1999-00
Hurley, Paul	Bos.	1	1	0	1	1	0	....	....	....	....	....	....	1968-69	1968-69
Hurst, Ron	Tor.	2	64	9	7	16	70	3	0	2	2	4	....	1955-56	1956-57
Huscroft, Jamie	N.J., Bos., Cgy., T.B., Van., Phx., Wsh.	10	352	5	33	38	1065	21	0	1	1	46	....	1988-89	1999-00
Huska, Ryan	Chi.	1	1	0	0	0	0	....	....	....	....	....	....	1997-98	1997-98
Huston, Ron	Cal.	2	79	15	31	46	8	....	....	....	....	....	....	1973-74	1974-75
Hutchinson, Ron	NYR	1	9	0	0	0	0	....	....	....	....	....	....	1960-61	1960-61
Hutchison, Dave	L.A., Tor., Chi., N.J.	10	584	19	97	116	1550	48	2	12	14	149	....	1974-75	1983-84
• Hutton, Bill	Bos., Ott., Phi.	2	64	3	2	5	8	2	0	0	0	0	....	1929-30	1930-31
• Hyland, Harry	Mtl.W., Ott.	1	17	14	2	16	65	....	....	....	....	....	....	1917-18	1917-18
Hynes, Dave	Bos.	2	22	4	0	4	2	....	....	....	....	....	....	1973-74	1974-75
Hynes, Gord	Bos., Phi.	2	52	3	9	12	22	12	1	2	3	6	....	1991-92	1992-93
‡ Hyvonen, Hannes	S.J., CBJ	2	42	4	5	9	22	....	....	....	....	....	....	2001-02	2002-03

I

Iafrate, Al	Tor., Wsh., Bos., S.J.	12	799	152	311	463	1301	71	19	16	35	77	....	1984-85	1997-98
Ignatjev, Victor	Pit.	1	11	0	1	1	6	1	0	0	0	2	....	1998-99	1998-99
Ihnacak, Miroslav	Tor., Det.	3	56	8	9	17	39	1	0	0	0	0	....	1985-86	1988-89
Ihnacak, Peter	Tor.	8	417	102	165	267	175	28	4	10	14	25	....	1982-83	1989-90
Imlach, Brent	Tor.	2	3	0	0	0	0	....	....	....	....	....	....	1965-66	1966-67
Ingarfield, Earl	NYR, Pit., Oak., Cal.	13	746	179	226	405	239	21	9	8	17	10	....	1958-59	1970-71
Ingarfield, Earl	Atl., Cgy., Det.	2	39	4	4	8	22	2	0	1	1	0	....	1979-80	1980-81
Inglis, Billy	L.A., Buf.	3	36	1	3	4	4	11	1	2	3	4	....	1967-68	1970-71
• Ingoldsby, Johnny	Tor.	2	29	5	1	6	15	....	....	....	....	....	....	1942-43	1943-44
• Ingram, Frank	Chi.	3	101	24	16	40	69	11	0	1	1	2	....	1929-30	1931-32
• Ingram, John	Bos.	1	1	0	0	0	0	....	....	....	....	....	....	1924-25	1924-25
Ingram, Ron	Chi., Det., NYR	4	114	5	15	20	81	2	0	0	0	0	....	1956-57	1964-65
Intranuovo, Ralph	Edm., Tor.	3	22	2	4	6	4	....	....	....	....	....	....	1994-95	1996-97
• Irvin, Dick	Chi.	3	94	29	23	52	78	2	2	0	2	4	....	1926-27	1928-29
Irvine, Ted	Bos., L.A., NYR, St.L.	11	724	154	177	331	657	83	16	24	40	115	....	1963-64	1976-77
Irwin, Ivan	Mtl., NYR	5	155	2	27	29	214	5	0	0	0	8	....	1952-53	1957-58
• Isaksson, Ulf	L.A.	1	50	7	15	22	10	....	....	....	....	....	....	1982-83	1982-83
Issel, Kim	Edm.	1	4	0	0	0	0	....	....	....	....	....	....	1988-89	1988-89

J

‡ Jacina, Greg	Fla.	2	14	0	1	1	6	....	....	....	....	....	....	2005-06	2006-07
• Jackson, Art	Tor., Bos., NYA	11	468	123	178	301	144	52	8	12	20	29	2	1934-35	1944-45
• Jackson, Busher	Tor., NYA, Bos.	15	633	241	234	475	437	71	18	12	30	53	1	1929-30	1943-44
Jackson, Dane	Van., Buf., NYI	4	45	12	6	18	58	6	0	0	0	10	....	1993-94	1997-98
Jackson, Don	Min., Edm., NYR	10	311	16	52	68	640	53	4	5	9	147	2	1977-78	1986-87
• Jackson, Harold	Chi., Det.	8	219	17	34	51	208	31	1	2	3	33	2	1936-37	1946-47
Jackson, Jack	Chi.	1	48	2	5	7	38	....	....	....	....	....	....	1946-47	1946-47
Jackson, Jeff	Tor., NYR, Que., Chi.	8	263	38	48	86	313	6	1	1	2	16	....	1984-85	1991-92
Jackson, Jim	Cgy., Buf.	4	112	17	30	47	20	14	3	2	5	6	....	1982-83	1987-88
• Jackson, Lloyd	NYA	1	14	1	1	2	0	....	....	....	....	....	....	1936-37	1936-37
• Jackson, Stan	Tor., Bos., Ott.	5	86	9	6	15	75	....	....	....	....	....	1	1921-22	1926-27
Jackson, Walter	NYA, Bos.	4	84	16	11	27	18	....	....	....	....	....	....	1932-33	1935-36
• Jacobs, Paul	Tor.	1	1	0	0	0	0	....	....	....	....	....	....	1918-19	1918-19

Ron Hurst

Earl Ingarfield, Jr.

Gary Jarrett

Grant Jennings

Bill Johansen

Randy Johnston

Darius Kasparaitis

Ed Kea

			Regular Schedule					Playoffs							
Name	NHL Teams	NHL Seasons	GP	G	A	TP	PIM	GP	G	A	TP	PIM	NHL Cup Wins	First NHL Season	Last NHL Season
Jacobs, Tim	Cal.	1	46	0	10	10	35	....	....	....	....	....	....	1975-76	1975-76
Jakopin, John	Fla., Pit., S.J.	6	113	1	6	7	145	....	....	....	....	....	....	1997-98	2002-03
Jalo, Risto	Edm.	1	3	0	3	3	0	....	....	....	....	....	....	1985-86	1985-86
Jalonen, Kari	Cgy., Edm.	2	37	9	6	15	4	5	1	0	1	0	....	1982-83	1983-84
James, Gerry	Tor.	5	149	14	26	40	257	15	1	0	1	8	....	1954-55	1959-60
James, Val	Buf., Tor.	2	11	0	0	0	30	....	....	....	....	....	....	1981-82	1986-87
Jamieson, Jim	NYR	1	1	0	1	1	0	....	....	....	....	....	....	1943-44	1943-44
Jankowski, Lou	Det., Chi.	4	127	19	18	37	15	1	0	0	0	0	....	1950-51	1954-55
Janney, Craig	Bos., St.L., S.J., Wpg., Phx., T.B., NYI	12	760	188	563	751	170	120	24	86	110	53	....	1987-88	1998-99
Janssens, Mark	NYR, Min., Hfd., Ana., NYI, Phx., Chi.	14	711	40	73	113	1422	27	5	1	6	33	....	1987-88	2000-01
‡ Jantunen, Marko	Cgy.	1	3	0	0	0	0	....	....	....	....	....	....	1996-97	1996-97
‡ Jardine, Ryan	Fla.	1	8	0	2	2	2	....	....	....	....	....	....	2001-02	2001-02
‡ Jarrett, Cole	NYI	1	1	0	0	0	0	....	....	....	....	....	....	2005-06	2005-06
Jarrett, Doug	Chi., NYR	13	775	38	182	220	631	99	7	16	23	82	....	1964-65	1976-77
Jarrett, Gary	Tor., Det., Oak., Cal.	7	341	72	92	164	131	11	3	1	4	9	....	1960-61	1971-72
Jarry, Pierre	NYR, Tor., Det., Min.	7	344	88	117	205	142	5	0	1	1	0	....	1971-72	1977-78
Jarvenpaa, Hannu	Wpg.	3	114	11	26	37	83	....	....	....	....	....	....	1986-87	1988-89
‡ Jarventie, Martti	Mtl.	1	1	0	0	0	0	....	....	....	....	....	....	2001-02	2001-02
Jarvi, Iiro	Que.	2	116	18	43	61	58	....	....	....	....	....	....	1988-89	1989-90
Jarvis, Doug	Mtl., Wsh., Hfd.	13	964	139	264	403	263	105	14	27	41	42	4	1975-76	1987-88
● Jarvis, James	Pit., Phi., Tor.	3	112	17	15	32	62	....	....	....	....	....	....	1929-30	1936-37
Jarvis, Wes	Wsh., Min., L.A., Tor.	9	237	31	55	86	98	2	0	0	0	2	....	1979-80	1987-88
‡ Jaspers, Jason	Phx.	3	9	0	1	1	6	....	....	....	....	....	....	2001-02	2003-04
Javanainen, Arto	Pit.	1	14	4	1	5	2	....	....	....	....	....	....	1984-85	1984-85
Jay, Bob	L.A.	1	3	0	1	1	0	....	....	....	....	....	....	1993-94	1993-94
Jeffrey, Larry	Det., Tor., NYR	8	368	39	62	101	293	38	4	10	14	42	1	1961-62	1968-69
Jelinek, Tomas	Ott.	1	49	7	6	13	52	....	....	....	....	....	....	1992-93	1992-93
Jenkins, Dean	L.A.	1	5	0	0	0	2	....	....	....	....	....	....	1983-84	1983-84
● Jenkins, Roger	Chi., Tor., Mtl., Bos., Mtl.M., NYA	8	325	15	39	54	253	25	1	7	8	12	2	1930-31	1938-39
Jennings, Bill	Det., Bos.	5	108	32	33	65	45	20	4	4	8	6	....	1940-41	1944-45
Jennings, Grant	Wsh., Hfd., Pit., Tor., Buf.	9	389	14	43	57	804	54	2	1	3	68	2	1987-88	1995-96
Jensen, Chris	NYR, Phi.	6	74	9	12	21	27	....	....	....	....	....	....	1985-86	1991-92
Jensen, David	Min.	3	18	0	2	2	11	....	....	....	....	....	....	1983-84	1985-86
Jensen, David	Hfd., Wsh.	4	69	9	13	22	22	11	0	0	0	2	....	1984-85	1987-88
Jensen, Steve	Min., L.A.	7	438	113	107	220	318	12	0	3	3	9	....	1975-76	1981-82
● Jeremiah, Ed	NYA, Bos.	1	15	0	1	1	0	....	....	....	....	....	....	1931-32	1931-32
Jerrard, Paul	Min.	1	5	0	0	0	4	....	....	....	....	....	....	1988-89	1988-89
● Jerwa, Frank	Bos., St.L.	4	81	11	16	27	53	....	....	....	....	....	....	1931-32	1934-35
● Jerwa, Joe	NYR, Bos., NYA	7	234	29	58	87	309	17	2	3	5	16	....	1930-31	1938-39
Jirik, Jaroslav	St.L.	1	3	0	0	0	0	....	....	....	....	....	....	1969-70	1969-70
● Joanette, Rosario	Mtl.	1	2	0	1	1	4	....	....	....	....	....	....	1944-45	1944-45
Jodzio, Rick	Col., Cle.	1	70	2	8	10	71	....	....	....	....	....	....	1977-78	1977-78
Johannesen, Glenn	NYI	1	2	0	0	0	0	....	....	....	....	....	....	1985-86	1985-86
Johannson, John	N.J.	1	5	0	0	0	0	....	....	....	....	....	....	1983-84	1983-84
● Johansen, Bill	Tor.	1	1	0	0	0	0	....	....	....	....	....	....	1949-50	1949-50
Johansen, Trevor	Tor., Col., L.A.	5	286	11	46	57	282	13	0	3	3	21	....	1977-78	1981-82
‡ Johansson, Andreas	NYI, Pit., Ott., T.B., Cgy., NYR, Nsh.	8	377	81	88	169	190	9	0	0	0	0	....	1995-96	2003-04
Johansson, Bjorn	Cle.	2	15	1	1	2	10	....	....	....	....	....	....	1976-77	1977-78
Johansson, Calle	Buf., Wsh., Tor.	17	1109	119	416	535	519	105	12	43	55	44	....	1987-88	2003-04
‡ Johansson, Jonas	Wsh.	1	1	0	0	0	2	....	....	....	....	....	....	2005-06	2005-06
‡ Johansson, Mathias	Cgy., Pit.	1	58	5	10	15	16	....	....	....	....	....	....	2002-03	2002-03
Johansson, Roger	Cgy., Chi.	4	161	9	34	43	163	5	0	1	1	2	....	1989-90	1994-95
Johns, Don	NYR, Mtl., Min.	6	153	2	21	23	76	....	....	....	....	....	....	1960-61	1967-68
Johnson, Allan	Mtl., Det.	4	105	21	28	49	30	11	2	2	4	6	....	1956-57	1962-63
Johnson, Brian	Det.	1	3	0	0	0	5	....	....	....	....	....	....	1983-84	1983-84
● Johnson, Ching	NYR, NYA	12	436	38	48	86	808	61	5	2	7	161	2	1926-27	1937-38
‡ Johnson, Craig	St.L., L.A., Ana., Tor., Wsh.	10	557	75	98	173	260	16	3	2	5	10	....	1994-95	2003-04
● Johnson, Danny	Tor., Van., Det.	3	121	18	19	37	24	....	....	....	....	....	....	1969-70	1971-72
Johnson, Earl	Det.	1	1	0	0	0	0	....	....	....	....	....	1	1953-54	1953-54
Johnson, Greg	Det., Pit., Chi., Nsh.	12	785	145	224	369	345	37	7	6	13	14	....	1993-94	2005-06
Johnson, Jim	NYR, Phi., L.A.	8	302	75	111	186	73	7	0	2	2	2	....	1964-65	1971-72
Johnson, Jim	Pit., Min., Dal., Wsh., Phx.	13	829	29	166	195	1197	51	1	11	12	132	....	1985-86	1997-98
Johnson, Mark	Pit., Min., Hfd., St.L., N.J.	11	669	203	305	508	260	37	16	12	28	10	....	1979-80	1989-90
Johnson, Matt	L.A., Atl., Min.	10	473	23	20	43	1523	16	0	0	0	31	....	1994-95	2003-04
Johnson, Norm	Bos., Chi.	3	61	5	20	25	41	14	4	0	4	6	....	1957-58	1959-60
Johnson, Terry	Que., St.L., Cgy., Tor.	9	285	3	24	27	580	38	0	4	4	118	....	1979-80	1987-88
● Johnson, Tom	Mtl., Bos.	17	978	51	213	264	960	111	8	15	23	109	6	1947-48	1964-65
● Johnson, Virgil	Chi.	3	75	1	11	12	27	19	0	3	3	4	1	1937-38	1944-45
Johnston, Bernie	Hfd.	2	57	12	24	36	16	3	0	1	1	0	....	1979-80	1980-81
● Johnston, George	Chi.	4	58	20	12	32	2	....	....	....	....	....	....	1941-42	1946-47
Johnston, Greg	Bos., Tor.	9	187	26	29	55	124	22	2	1	3	12	....	1983-84	1991-92
Johnston, Jay	Wsh.	2	8	0	0	0	13	....	....	....	....	....	....	1980-81	1981-82
Johnston, Joey	Min., Cal., Chi.	6	331	85	106	191	320	....	....	....	....	....	....	1968-69	1975-76
Johnston, Larry	L.A., Det., K.C., Col.	7	320	9	64	73	580	....	....	....	....	....	....	1967-68	1976-77
Johnston, Marshall	Min., Cal.	7	251	14	52	66	58	6	0	0	0	2	....	1967-68	1973-74
Johnston, Randy	NYI	1	4	0	0	0	4	....	....	....	....	....	....	1979-80	1979-80
Johnstone, Eddie	NYR, Det.	10	426	122	136	258	375	55	13	10	23	83	....	1975-76	1986-87
Johnstone, Ross	Tor.	2	42	5	4	9	14	3	0	0	0	0	1	1943-44	1944-45
‡ Jokela, Mikko	Van.	1	1	0	0	0	0	....	....	....	....	....	....	2002-03	2002-03
● Joliat, Aurel	Mtl.	16	655	270	190	460	771	46	9	13	22	66	3	1922-23	1937-38
● Joliat, Rene	Mtl.	1	1	0	0	0	0	....	....	....	....	....	....	1924-25	1924-25
Joly, Greg	Wsh., Det.	9	365	21	76	97	250	5	0	0	0	8	....	1974-75	1982-83
Joly, Yvan	Mtl.	3	2	0	0	0	0	1	0	0	0	0	....	1979-80	1982-83
Jomphe, Jean-Francois	Ana., Phx., Mtl.	4	111	10	29	39	102	....	....	....	....	....	....	1995-96	1998-99
Jonathan, Stan	Bos., Pit.	8	411	91	110	201	751	63	8	4	12	137	....	1975-76	1982-83
Jones, Bob	NYR	1	2	0	0	0	0	....	....	....	....	....	....	1968-69	1968-69
Jones, Brad	Wpg., L.A., Phi.	6	148	25	31	56	122	9	1	1	2	2	....	1986-87	1991-92
● Jones, Buck	Det., Tor.	4	50	2	2	4	36	12	0	1	1	18	....	1938-39	1942-43
Jones, Jim	Cal.	1	2	0	0	0	0	....	....	....	....	....	....	1971-72	1971-72
Jones, Jimmy	Tor.	3	148	13	18	31	68	19	1	5	6	11	....	1977-78	1979-80
Jones, Keith	Wsh., Col., Phi.	9	491	117	141	258	765	63	12	12	24	120	....	1992-93	2000-01
Jones, Ron	Bos., Pit., Wsh.	5	54	1	4	5	31	....	....	....	....	....	....	1971-72	1975-76
Jones, Ty	Chi., Fla.	2	14	0	0	0	19	....	....	....	....	....	....	1998-99	2003-04
‡ Jonsson, Hans	Pit.	4	242	10	38	48	92	27	0	1	1	14	....	1999-00	2002-03
‡ Jonsson, Jorgen	NYI, Ana.	1	81	12	19	31	16	....	....	....	....	....	....	1999-00	1999-00
‡ Jonsson, Kenny	Tor., NYI	10	686	63	204	267	298	19	1	3	4	6	....	1994-95	2003-04
Jonsson, Tomas	NYI, Edm.	8	552	85	259	344	482	80	11	26	37	97	2	1981-82	1988-89
Joseph, Chris	Pit., Edm., T.B., Van., Phi., Phx., Atl.	14	510	39	112	151	567	31	3	4	7	24	....	1987-88	2000-01
Joseph, Tony	Wpg.	1	2	1	0	1	0	....	....	....	....	....	....	1988-89	1988-89
Joyal, Eddie	Det., Tor., L.A., Phi.	9	466	128	134	262	103	50	11	8	19	18	....	1962-63	1971-72
Joyce, Bob	Bos., Wsh., Wpg.	6	158	34	49	83	90	46	15	9	24	29	....	1987-88	1992-93
Joyce, Duane	Dal.	1	3	0	0	0	0	....	....	....	....	....	....	1993-94	1993-94
● Juckes, Bing	NYR	2	16	2	1	3	6	....	....	....	....	....	....	1947-48	1949-50
‡ Juhlin, Patrik	Phi.	2	56	7	6	13	23	13	1	0	1	2	....	1994-95	1995-96
Julien, Claude	Que.	2	14	0	1	1	25	....	....	....	....	....	....	1984-85	1985-86
Juneau, Joe	Bos., Wsh., Buf., Ott., Phx., Mtl.	13	828	156	416	572	272	112	25	54	79	69	....	1991-92	2003-04
Junker, Steve	NYI	2	5	0	0	0	0	3	0	1	1	0	....	1992-93	1993-94
Jutila, Timo	Buf.	1	10	1	5	6	13	....	....	....	....	....	....	1984-85	1984-85
● Juzda, Bill	NYR, Tor.	9	398	14	54	68	398	42	0	3	3	46	2	1940-41	1951-52

K

			Regular Schedule					Playoffs							
Name	NHL Teams	NHL Seasons	GP	G	A	TP	PIM	GP	G	A	TP	PIM	NHL Cup Wins	First NHL Season	Last NHL Season
Kabel, Bob	NYR	2	48	5	13	18	34	....	....	....	....	....	....	1959-60	1960-61
Kachowski, Mark	Pit.	3	64	6	5	11	209	....	....	....	....	....	....	1987-88	1989-90
Kachur, Ed	Chi.	2	96	10	14	24	35	....	....	....	....	....	....	1956-57	1957-58
Kaese, Trent	Buf.	1	1	0	0	0	0	....	....	....	....	....	....	1988-89	1988-89
Kaiser, Vern	Mtl.	1	50	7	5	12	33	2	0	0	0	0	....	1950-51	1950-51
● Kalbfleisch, Walter	Ott., St.L., NYA, Bos.	4	36	0	4	4	32	5	0	0	0	2	....	1933-34	1936-37
● Kaleta, Alex	Chi., NYR	7	387	92	121	213	190	17	1	6	7	2	....	1941-42	1950-51
‡ Kallio, Tomi	Atl., CBJ, Phi.	3	140	24	31	55	48	....	....	....	....	....	....	2000-01	2002-03
Kallur, Anders	NYI	6	383	101	110	211	149	78	12	23	35	32	4	1979-80	1984-85
Kamensky, Valeri	Que., Col., NYR, Dal., N.J.	11	637	200	301	501	383	66	25	35	60	72	1	1991-92	2001-02
Kaminski, Kevin	Min., Que., Wsh.	7	139	3	10	13	528	8	0	0	0	52	....	1988-89	1996-97
● Kaminsky, Max	Ott., Bos., St.L., Mtl.M.	4	130	22	34	56	38	4	0	0	0	0	....	1933-34	1936-37

			Regular Schedule					Playoffs					NHL	First	Last
Name	NHL Teams	NHL Seasons	GP	G	A	TP	PIM	GP	G	A	TP	PIM	Cup Wins	NHL Season	NHL Season
Kaminsky, Yan	Wpg., NYI	2	26	3	2	5	4	2	0	0	0	4	....	1993-94	1994-95
• Kampman, Bingo	Tor.	5	189	14	30	44	287	47	1	4	5	38	1	1937-38	1941-42
Kane, Francis	Det.	1	2	0	0	0	0	....	....	....	....	....	....	1943-44	1943-44
‡ Kanko, Petr	L.A.	1	10	1	0	1	0	....	....	....	....	....	....	2005-06	2005-06
Kannegiesser, Gord	St.L.	2	23	0	1	1	15	....	....	....	....	....	....	1967-68	1971-72
Kannegiesser, Sheldon	Pit., NYR, L.A., Van.	8	366	14	67	81	292	18	0	2	2	10	....	1970-71	1977-78
Karabin, Ladislav	Pit.	1	9	0	0	0	2	....	....	....	....	....	....	1993-94	1993-94
‡ Karalahti, Jere	L.A., Nsh.	3	149	8	19	27	97	17	0	1	1	20	....	1999-00	2001-02
Karamnov, Vitali	St.L.	3	92	12	20	32	65	2	0	0	0	2	....	1992-93	1994-95
‡ Kariya, Steve	Van.	3	65	9	18	27	32	....	....	....	....	....	....	1999-00	2001-02
Karjalainen, Kyosti	L.A.	1	28	1	8	9	12	3	0	1	1	2	....	1991-92	1991-92
Karlander, Al	Det.	4	212	36	56	92	70	4	0	1	1	0	....	1969-70	1972-73
Karpa, Dave	Que., Ana., Car., NYR	12	557	18	80	98	1374	19	1	1	2	39	....	1991-92	2002-03
Karpov, Valeri	Ana.	3	76	14	15	29	32	....	....	....	....	....	....	1994-95	1996-97
‡ Karpovtsev, Alexander	NYR, Tor., Chi., NYI, Fla.	12	596	34	154	188	430	74	4	14	18	52	1	1993-94	2005-06
Kasatonov, Alexei	N.J., Ana., St.L., Bos.	7	383	38	122	160	326	33	4	7	11	40	....	1989-90	1995-96
‡ Kasparaitis, Darius	NYI, Pit., Col., NYR	14	863	27	136	163	1379	83	2	10	12	107	....	1992-93	2006-07
Kasper, Steve	Bos., L.A., Phi., T.B.	13	821	177	291	468	554	94	20	28	48	82	....	1980-81	1992-93
Kastelic, Ed	Wsh., Hfd.	7	220	11	10	21	719	8	1	0	1	32	....	1985-86	1991-92
Kaszycki, Mike	NYI, Wsh., Tor.	5	226	42	80	122	108	19	2	6	8	10	....	1977-78	1982-83
‡ Kavanagh, Pat	Van., Phi.	4	14	2	0	2	4	3	0	0	0	2	....	2000-01	2005-06
• Kea, Ed	Atl., St.L.	10	583	30	145	175	508	32	2	4	6	39	....	1973-74	1982-83
Keane, Mike	Mtl., Col., NYR, Dal., St.L., Van.	16	1161	168	302	470	881	220	34	40	74	135	3	1988-89	2003-04
Kearns, Dennis	Van.	10	677	31	290	321	386	11	1	2	3	8	....	1971-72	1980-81
• Keating, Jack	Det.	2	11	3	0	3	4	....	....	....	....	....	....	1938-39	1939-40
• Keating, John	NYA	2	35	5	5	10	17	....	....	....	....	....	....	1931-32	1932-33
Keating, Mike	NYR	1	1	0	0	0	0	....	....	....	....	....	....	1977-78	1977-78
• Keats, Duke	Bos., Det., Chi.	3	82	30	19	49	113	....	....	....	....	....	....	1926-27	1928-29
Keczmer, Dan	Min., Hfd., Cgy., Dal., Nsh.	10	235	8	38	46	212	12	0	1	1	8	....	1990-91	1999-00
Keefe, Sheldon	T.B.	3	125	12	12	24	78	....	....	....	....	....	....	2000-01	2002-03
• Keeling, Butch	Tor., NYR	12	525	157	63	220	331	47	11	11	22	34	1	1926-27	1937-38
Keenan, Larry	Tor., St.L., Buf., Phi.	6	233	38	64	102	28	46	15	16	31	12	....	1961-62	1971-72
Kehoe, Rick	Tor., Pit.	14	906	371	396	767	120	39	4	17	21	4	....	1971-72	1984-85
Kekalainen, Jarmo	Bos., Ott.	5	55	5	8	13	28	....	....	....	....	....	....	1989-90	1993-94
Kelleher, Chris	Bos.	1	1	0	0	0	0	....	....	....	....	....	....	2001-02	2001-02
Keller, Ralph	NYR	1	3	1	0	1	6	....	....	....	....	....	....	1962-63	1962-63
Kellgren, Christer	Col.	1	5	0	0	0	0	....	....	....	....	....	....	1981-82	1981-82
Kelly, Bob	Phi., Wsh.	12	837	154	208	362	1454	101	9	14	23	172	2	1970-71	1981-82
Kelly, Bob	St.L., Pit., Chi.	6	425	87	109	196	687	23	6	3	9	40	....	1973-74	1978-79
Kelly, Dave	Det.	1	16	2	0	2	4	....	....	....	....	....	....	1976-77	1976-77
Kelly, John Paul	L.A.	7	400	54	70	124	366	18	1	1	2	41	....	1979-80	1985-86
• Kelly, Pep	Tor., Chi., Bro.	8	288	74	53	127	105	38	7	6	13	10	....	1934-35	1941-42
• Kelly, Pete	St.L., Det., NYA, Bro.	7	177	21	38	59	68	19	3	1	4	2	2	1934-35	1941-42
Kelly, Red	Det., Tor.	20	1316	281	542	823	327	164	33	59	92	51	8	1947-48	1966-67
• Kemp, Kevin	Hfd.	1	3	0	0	0	4	....	....	....	....	....	....	1980-81	1980-81
Kemp, Stan	Tor.	1	1	0	0	0	2	....	....	....	....	....	....	1948-49	1948-49
Kenady, Chris	St.L., NYR	2	7	0	2	2	0	....	....	....	....	....	....	1997-98	1999-00
• Kendall, Bill	Chi., Tor.	5	131	16	10	26	28	6	0	0	0	0	1	1933-34	1937-38
Kennedy, Dean	L.A., NYR, Buf., Wpg., Edm.	12	717	26	108	134	1118	36	1	7	8	59	....	1982-83	1994-95
Kennedy, Forbes	Chi., Det., Bos., Phi., Tor.	11	603	70	108	178	988	12	2	4	6	64	....	1956-57	1968-69
Kennedy, Mike	Dal., Tor., NYI	5	145	16	36	52	112	5	0	0	0	9	....	1994-95	1998-99
Kennedy, Sheldon	Det., Cgy., Bos.	8	310	49	58	107	233	24	6	4	10	20	....	1989-90	1996-97
Kennedy, Ted	Tor.	14	696	231	329	560	432	78	29	31	60	32	5	1942-43	1956-57
• Kenny, Ernest	NYR, Chi.	2	10	0	0	0	18	....	....	....	....	....	....	1930-31	1934-35
Keon, Dave	Tor., Hfd.	18	1296	396	590	986	117	92	32	36	68	6	4	1960-61	1981-82
Kerch, Alexander	Edm.	1	5	0	0	0	2	....	....	....	....	....	....	1993-94	1993-94
Kerr, Alan	NYI, Det., Wpg.	9	391	72	94	166	826	38	5	4	9	70	....	1984-85	1992-93
Kerr, Reg	Cle., Chi., Edm.	6	263	66	94	160	169	7	1	0	1	7	....	1977-78	1983-84
Kerr, Tim	Phi., NYR, Hfd.	13	655	370	304	674	596	81	40	31	71	58	....	1980-81	1992-93
Kesa, Dan	Van., Dal., Pit., T.B.	4	139	8	22	30	66	13	1	0	1	0	....	1993-94	1999-00
Kessell, Rick	Pit., Cal.	5	135	4	24	28	6	....	....	....	....	....	....	1969-70	1973-74
Ketola, Veli-Pekka	Col.	1	44	9	5	14	4	....	....	....	....	....	....	1981-82	1981-82
Ketter, Kerry	Atl.	1	41	0	2	2	58	....	....	....	....	....	....	1972-73	1972-73
Kharin, Sergei	Wpg.	1	7	2	3	5	2	....	....	....	....	....	....	1990-91	1990-91
‡ Kharitonov, Alexander	T.B., NYI	2	71	7	15	22	12	....	....	....	....	....	....	2000-01	2001-02
‡ Khavanov, Alexander	St.L., Tor.	5	348	27	75	102	233	26	5	5	10	18	....	2000-01	2005-06
Khmylev, Yuri	Buf., St.L.	5	263	64	88	152	133	26	8	6	14	24	....	1992-93	1996-97
Khristich, Dmitri	Wsh., L.A., Bos., Tor.	12	811	259	337	596	422	75	15	25	40	41	....	1990-91	2001-02
Kidd, Ian	Van.	2	20	4	7	11	25	....	....	....	....	....	....	1987-88	1988-89
Kiessling, Udo	Min.	1	1	0	0	0	2	....	....	....	....	....	....	1981-82	1981-82
Kilrea, Brian	Det., L.A.	2	26	3	5	8	12	....	....	....	....	....	....	1957-58	1967-68
• Kilrea, Hec	Ott., Det., Tor.	15	633	167	129	296	438	48	8	7	15	18	3	1925-26	1939-40
• Kilrea, Ken	Det.	5	91	16	23	39	8	15	2	2	4	4	....	1938-39	1943-44
• Kilrea, Wally	Ott., Phi., NYA, Mtl.M., Det.	9	329	35	58	93	87	25	2	4	6	6	2	1929-30	1937-38
Kimble, Darin	Que., St.L., Bos., Chi.	7	311	23	20	43	1082	23	0	0	0	52	....	1988-89	1994-95
Kindrachuk, Orest	Phi., Pit., Wsh.	10	508	118	261	379	648	76	20	20	40	53	2	1972-73	1981-82
King, Derek	NYI, Hfd., Tor., St.L.	14	830	261	351	612	417	47	4	17	21	24	....	1986-87	1999-00
King, Frank	Mtl.	1	10	1	0	1	2	....	....	....	....	....	....	1950-51	1950-51
King, Kris	Det., NYR, Wpg., Phx., Tor., Chi.	14	849	66	85	151	2030	67	8	5	13	142	....	1987-88	2000-01
King, Steven	NYR, Ana.	3	67	17	8	25	75	....	....	....	....	....	....	1992-93	1995-96
King, Wayne	Cal.	3	73	5	18	23	34	....	....	....	....	....	....	1973-74	1975-76
Kinnear, Geordie	Atl.	1	4	0	0	0	13	....	....	....	....	....	....	1999-00	1999-00
Kinsella, Brian	Wsh.	2	10	0	1	1	0	....	....	....	....	....	....	1975-76	1976-77
• Kinsella, Ray	Ott.	1	14	0	0	0	0	....	....	....	....	....	....	1930-31	1930-31
‡ Kiprusoff, Marko	Mtl., NYI	2	51	0	10	10	12	....	....	....	....	....	....	1995-96	2001-02
• Kirk, Bobby	NYR	1	39	4	8	12	14	....	....	....	....	....	....	1937-38	1937-38
Kirkpatrick, Bob	NYR	1	49	12	12	24	6	....	....	....	....	....	....	1942-43	1942-43
Kirton, Mark	Tor., Det., Van.	6	266	57	56	113	121	4	1	2	3	7	....	1979-80	1984-85
Kisio, Kelly	Det., NYR, S.J., Cgy.	13	761	229	429	658	768	39	6	15	21	52	....	1982-83	1994-95
Kitchen, Bill	Mtl., Tor.	4	41	1	4	5	40	3	0	1	1	0	....	1981-82	1984-85
• Kitchen, Hobie	Mtl.M., Det.	2	47	5	4	9	58	....	....	....	....	....	1	1925-26	1926-27
Kitchen, Mike	Col., N.J.	8	474	12	62	74	370	2	0	0	0	2	....	1976-77	1983-84
Kjellberg, Patric	Mtl., Nsh., Ana.	6	394	64	96	160	84	10	0	0	0	0	....	1992-93	2002-03
Klassen, Ralph	Cal., Cle., Col., St.L.	9	497	52	93	145	120	26	4	2	6	12	....	1975-76	1983-84
Klatt, Trent	Min., Dal., Phi., Van., L.A.	13	782	143	200	343	307	74	16	9	25	20	....	1991-92	2003-04
• Klein, Lloyd	Bos., NYA	8	164	30	24	54	68	5	0	0	0	2	1	1928-29	1937-38
Kleinendorst, Scot	NYR, Hfd., Wsh.	8	281	12	46	58	452	26	2	7	9	40	....	1982-83	1989-90
Klima, Petr	Det., Edm., T.B., L.A., Pit.	13	786	313	260	573	671	95	28	24	52	83	1	1985-86	1998-99
‡ Klimovich, Sergei	Chi.	1	1	0	0	0	2	....	....	....	....	....	....	1996-97	1996-97
• Klingbeil, Ike	Chi.	1	5	1	2	3	2	....	....	....	....	....	....	1936-37	1936-37
‡ Kloucek, Tomas	NYR, Nsh., Atl.	5	141	2	8	10	250	....	....	....	....	....	....	2000-01	2005-06
• Klukay, Joe	Tor., Bos.	11	566	109	127	236	189	71	13	10	23	23	4	1942-43	1955-56
Kluzak, Gord	Bos.	7	299	25	98	123	543	46	6	13	19	129	....	1982-83	1990-91
• Knibbs, Bill	Bos.	1	53	7	10	17	4	....	....	....	....	....	....	1964-65	1964-65
Knipscheer, Fred	Bos., St.L.	3	28	6	3	9	18	16	2	1	3	6	....	1993-94	1995-96
• Knott, Nick	Bro.	1	14	3	1	4	9	....	....	....	....	....	....	1941-42	1941-42
Knox, Paul	Tor.	1	1	0	0	0	0	....	....	....	....	....	....	1954-55	1954-55
Knutsen, Espen	Ana., CBJ	5	207	30	81	111	105	....	....	....	....	....	....	1997-98	2003-04
Koalska, Matt	NYI	1	3	0	0	0	2	....	....	....	....	....	....	2005-06	2005-06
Kocur, Joe	Det., NYR, Van.	15	820	80	82	162	2519	118	10	12	22	231	3	1984-85	1998-99
‡ Koehler, Greg	Car.	1	1	0	0	0	0	....	....	....	....	....	....	2000-01	2000-01
‡ Kohn, Ladislav	Cgy., Tor., Ana., Atl., Det.	7	186	14	28	42	125	2	0	0	0	5	....	1995-96	2002-03
‡ Koivisto, Tom	St.L.	1	22	2	4	6	10	....	....	....	....	....	....	2002-03	2002-03
‡ Kolarik, Pavel	Bos.	2	23	0	0	0	10	....	....	....	....	....	....	2000-01	2001-02
Kolesar, Mark	Tor.	2	28	2	2	4	14	3	1	0	1	2	....	1995-96	1996-97
Kolstad, Dean	Min., S.J.	3	40	1	7	8	69	....	....	....	....	....	....	1988-89	1992-93
Komadoski, Neil	L.A., St.L.	8	502	16	76	92	632	23	0	2	2	47	....	1972-73	1979-80
Komarniski, Zenith	Van., CBJ	3	21	1	1	2	10	....	....	....	....	....	....	1999-00	2003-04
Konik, George	Pit.	1	52	7	8	15	26	....	....	....	....	....	....	1967-68	1967-68
Konowalchuk, Steve	Wsh., Col.	14	790	171	225	396	703	52	9	12	21	60	....	1991-92	2005-06
Konroyd, Steve	Cgy., NYI, Chi., Hfd., Det., Ott.	15	895	41	195	236	863	97	10	15	25	99	....	1980-81	1994-95
Konstantinov, Vladimir	Det.	6	446	47	128	175	838	82	5	14	19	107	1	1991-92	1996-97
Kontos, Chris	NYR, Pit., L.A., T.B.	8	230	54	69	123	103	20	11	0	11	12	....	1982-83	1992-93
• Kopak, Russ	Bos.	1	24	7	9	16	0	....	....	....	....	....	....	1943-44	1943-44
Korab, Jerry	Chi., Van., Buf., L.A.	15	975	114	341	455	1629	93	8	18	26	201	....	1970-71	1984-85

Tim Kerr

Lloyd Klein

Richard Kromm

Jim Kyte

Claude Laforge

Ted Lanyon

John LeClair

Hec Lepine

Name	NHL Teams	NHL Seasons	Regular Schedule					Playoffs					NHL Cup Wins	First NHL Season	Last NHL Season
			GP	G	A	TP	PIM	GP	G	A	TP	PIM			
Kordic, Dan	Phi.	6	197	4	8	12	584	12	1	0	1	22	....	1991-92	1998-99
● Kordic, John	Mtl., Tor., Wsh., Que.	7	244	17	18	35	997	41	4	3	7	131	1	1985-86	1991-92
Korn, Jim	Det., Tor., Buf., N.J., Cgy.	10	597	66	122	188	1801	16	1	2	3	109	....	1979-80	1989-90
Korney, Mike	Det., NYR	4	77	9	10	19	59	....	....	....	....	....	....	1973-74	1978-79
‡ Korolev, Evgeny	NYI	3	42	1	4	5	20	2	0	0	0	0	....	1999-00	2001-02
‡ Korolev, Igor	St.L., Wpg., Phx., Tor., Chi.	12	795	119	227	346	330	41	0	8	8	6	....	1992-93	2003-04
Koroll, Cliff	Chi.	11	814	208	254	462	376	85	19	29	48	67	....	1969-70	1979-80
‡ Korolyuk, Alexander	S.J.	6	296	62	80	142	140	34	6	8	14	18	....	1997-98	2003-04
Kortko, Roger	NYI	2	79	7	17	24	28	10	0	3	3	17	....	1984-85	1985-86
Kostynski, Doug	Bos.	2	15	3	1	4	4	....	....	....	....	....	....	1983-84	1984-85
Kotanen, Dick	NYR	1	1	0	0	0	0	....	....	....	....	....	....	1950-51	1950-51
Kotsopoulos, Chris	NYR, Hfd., Tor., Det.	10	479	44	109	153	827	31	1	3	4	91	....	1980-81	1989-90
‡ Kovalenko, Andrei	Que., Col., Mtl., Edm., Phi., Car., Bos.	9	620	173	206	379	389	33	5	6	11	20	....	1992-93	2000-01
Kowal, Joe	Buf.	2	22	0	5	5	13	2	0	0	0	0	....	1976-77	1977-78
Kozak, Don	L.A., Van.	7	437	96	86	182	480	29	7	2	9	69	....	1972-73	1978-79
Kozak, Les	Tor.	1	12	1	0	1	2	....	....	....	....	....	....	1961-62	1961-62
‡ Kraft, Milan	Pit.	4	207	41	41	82	52	8	0	0	0	2	....	2000-01	2003-04
‡ Kraft, Ryan	S.J.	1	7	0	1	1	0	....	....	....	....	....	....	2002-03	2002-03
● Kraftcheck, Stephen	Bos., NYR, Tor.	4	157	11	18	29	83	6	0	0	0	7	....	1950-51	1958-59
Krake, Skip	Bos., L.A., Buf.	7	249	23	40	63	182	10	1	0	1	17	....	1963-64	1970-71
Kravchuk, Igor	Chi., Edm., St.L., Ott., Cgy., Fla.	12	699	64	210	274	251	51	6	15	21	18	....	1991-92	2002-03
Kravets, Mikhail	S.J.	2	2	0	0	0	0	....	....	....	....	....	....	1991-92	1992-93
Krentz, Dale	Det.	3	30	5	3	8	9	2	0	0	0	0	....	1986-87	1988-89
‡ Krestanovich, Jordan	Col.	2	22	0	2	2	6	....	....	....	....	....	....	2001-02	2003-04
‡ Kristek, Jaroslav	Buf.	1	6	0	0	0	4	....	....	....	....	....	....	2002-03	2002-03
‡ Krivokrasov, Sergei	Chi., Nsh., Cgy., Min., Ana.	10	450	86	109	195	288	21	2	0	2	14	....	1992-93	2001-02
● Krol, Joe	NYR, Bro.	3	26	10	4	14	8	....	....	....	....	....	....	1936-37	1941-42
Kromm, Richard	Cgy., NYI	9	372	70	103	173	138	36	2	6	8	22	....	1983-84	1992-93
Kron, Robert	Van., Hfd., Car., CBJ	12	771	144	194	338	119	16	3	2	5	2	....	1990-91	2001-02
Krook, Kevin	Col.	1	3	0	0	0	2	....	....	....	....	....	....	1978-79	1978-79
‡ Kroupa, Vlastimil	S.J., N.J.	5	105	4	19	23	66	20	1	2	3	25	....	1993-94	1997-98
Krulicki, Jim	NYR, Det.	1	41	0	3	3	6	....	....	....	....	....	....	1970-71	1970-71
Krupp, Uwe	Buf., NYI, Que., Col., Det., Atl.	15	729	69	212	281	660	81	6	23	29	86	1	1986-87	2002-03
Kruppke, Gord	Det.	3	23	0	0	0	32	....	....	....	....	....	....	1990-91	1993-94
Kruse, Paul	Cgy., NYI, Buf., S.J.	11	423	38	33	71	1074	28	5	2	7	36	....	1990-91	2000-01
Krushelnyski, Mike	Bos., Edm., L.A., Tor., Det.	14	897	241	328	569	699	139	29	43	72	106	3	1981-82	1994-95
Krutov, Vladimir	Van.	1	61	11	23	34	20	....	....	....	....	....	....	1989-90	1989-90
Krygier, Todd	Hfd., Wsh., Ana.	9	543	100	143	243	533	48	10	7	17	40	....	1989-90	1997-98
Kryskow, Dave	Chi., Wsh., Det., Atl.	4	231	33	56	89	174	12	2	0	2	4	....	1972-73	1975-76
● Kryzanowski, Ed	Bos., Chi.	5	237	15	22	37	65	18	0	1	1	4	....	1948-49	1952-53
Kucera, Frantisek	Chi., Hfd., Van., Phi., CBJ, Pit., Wsh.	9	465	24	95	119	251	12	0	1	1	0	....	1990-91	2001-02
‡ Kudashov, Alexei	Tor.	1	25	1	0	1	4	....	....	....	....	....	....	1993-94	1993-94
Kudelski, Bob	L.A., Ott., Fla.	9	442	139	102	241	218	22	4	4	8	4	....	1987-88	1995-96
‡ Kudroc, Kristian	T.B., Fla.	3	26	2	2	4	38	....	....	....	....	....	....	2000-01	2003-04
● Kuhn, Gord	NYA	1	12	1	1	2	4	....	....	....	....	....	....	1932-33	1932-33
Kukulowicz, Aggie	NYR	2	4	1	0	1	0	....	....	....	....	....	....	1952-53	1953-54
Kulak, Stu	Van., Edm., NYR, Que., Wpg.	4	90	8	4	12	130	3	0	0	0	2	....	1982-83	1988-89
Kuleshov, Mikhail	Col.	1	3	0	0	0	0	....	....	....	....	....	....	2003-04	2003-04
● Kullman, Arnie	Bos.	2	13	0	1	1	11	....	....	....	....	....	....	1947-48	1949-50
● Kullman, Eddie	NYR	6	343	56	70	126	298	6	1	0	1	2	....	1947-48	1953-54
‡ Kultanen, Jarno	Bos.	3	102	2	11	13	59	....	....	....	....	....	....	2000-01	2002-03
Kumpel, Mark	Que., Det., Wpg.	6	288	38	46	84	113	39	6	4	10	14	....	1984-85	1990-91
● Kuntz, Alan	NYR	2	45	10	12	22	12	6	1	0	1	2	....	1941-42	1945-46
Kuntz, Murray	St.L.	1	7	1	2	3	0	....	....	....	....	....	....	1974-75	1974-75
‡ Kurka, Tomas	Car.	2	17	3	2	5	2	....	....	....	....	....	....	2002-03	2003-04
Kurri, Jari	Edm., L.A., NYR, Ana., Col.	17	1251	601	797	1398	545	200	106	127	233	123	5	1980-81	1997-98
Kurtenbach, Orland	NYR, Bos., Tor., Van.	13	639	119	213	332	628	19	2	4	6	70	....	1960-61	1973-74
Kurtz, Justin	Van.	1	27	3	5	8	14	....	....	....	....	....	....	2001-02	2001-02
Kurvers, Tom	Mtl., Buf., N.J., Tor., Van., NYI, Ana.	11	659	93	328	421	350	57	8	22	30	68	1	1984-85	1994-95
Kuryluk, Merv	Chi.	1	....	....	....	....	....	2	0	0	0	0	....	1961-62	1961-62
Kushner, Dale	NYI, Phi.	3	84	10	13	23	215	....	....	....	....	....	....	1989-90	1991-92
‡ Kutlak, Zdenek	Bos.	3	16	1	2	3	4	....	....	....	....	....	....	2000-01	2003-04
‡ Kuznetsov, Maxim	Det., L.A.	4	136	2	8	10	137	....	....	....	....	....	....	2000-01	2003-04
Kuznik, Greg	Car.	1	1	0	0	0	0	....	....	....	....	....	....	2000-01	2000-01
Kuzyk, Ken	Cle.	2	41	5	9	14	8	....	....	....	....	....	....	1976-77	1977-78
Kvartalnov, Dmitri	Bos.	2	112	42	49	91	26	4	0	0	0	0	....	1992-93	1993-94
‡ Kvasha, Oleg	Fla., NYI, Phx.	7	493	81	136	217	335	21	1	2	3	8	....	1998-99	2005-06
Kwong, Larry	NYR	1	1	0	0	0	0	....	....	....	....	....	....	1947-48	1947-48
● Kyle, Bill	NYR	2	3	0	3	3	0	....	....	....	....	....	....	1949-50	1950-51
● Kyle, Gus	NYR, Bos.	3	203	6	20	26	362	14	1	2	3	34	....	1949-50	1951-52
Kyllonen, Markku	Wpg.	1	9	0	2	2	2	....	....	....	....	....	....	1988-89	1988-89
Kypreos, Nick	Wsh., Hfd., NYR, Tor.	8	442	46	44	90	1210	34	1	3	4	65	1	1989-90	1996-97
Kyte, Jim	Wpg., Pit., Cgy., Ott., S.J.	13	598	17	49	66	1342	42	0	6	6	94	....	1982-83	1995-96
L															
Labadie, Mike	NYR	1	3	0	0	0	0	....	....	....	....	....	....	1952-53	1952-53
Labatte, Neil	St.L.	2	26	0	2	2	19	....	....	....	....	....	....	1978-79	1981-82
L'Abbe, Moe	Chi.	1	5	0	1	1	0	....	....	....	....	....	....	1972-73	1972-73
Labelle, Marc	Dal.	1	9	0	0	0	46	....	....	....	....	....	....	1996-97	1996-97
● Labine, Leo	Bos., Det.	11	643	128	193	321	730	60	12	11	23	82	....	1951-52	1961-62
Labossiere, Gord	NYR, L.A., Min.	6	215	44	62	106	75	10	2	3	5	28	....	1963-64	1971-72
Labovitch, Max	NYR	1	5	0	0	0	4	....	....	....	....	....	....	1943-44	1943-44
Labraaten, Dan	Det., Cgy.	4	268	71	73	144	47	8	1	0	1	4	....	1978-79	1981-82
Labre, Yvon	Pit., Wsh.	9	371	14	87	101	788	....	....	....	....	....	....	1970-71	1980-81
Labrie, Guy	Bos., NYR	2	42	4	9	13	16	....	....	....	....	....	....	1943-44	1944-45
Lach, Elmer	Mtl.	14	664	215	408	623	478	76	19	45	64	36	3	1940-41	1953-54
Lachance, Michel	Col.	1	21	0	4	4	22	....	....	....	....	....	....	1978-79	1978-79
‡ Lachance, Scott	NYI, Mtl., Van., CBJ	13	819	31	112	143	567	11	1	2	3	6	....	1991-92	2003-04
Lacombe, Francois	Oak., Buf., Que.	4	78	2	17	19	54	3	1	0	1	0	....	1968-69	1979-80
Lacombe, Normand	Buf., Edm., Phi.	7	319	53	62	115	196	26	5	1	6	49	1	1984-85	1990-91
Lacroix, Andre	Phi., Chi., Hfd.	6	325	79	119	198	44	16	2	5	7	0	....	1967-68	1979-80
Lacroix, Daniel	NYR, Bos., Phi., Edm., NYI	7	188	11	7	18	379	16	0	1	1	26	....	1993-94	1999-00
Lacroix, Eric	Tor., L.A., Col., NYR, Ott.	8	472	67	70	137	361	30	1	5	6	25	....	1993-94	2000-01
Lacroix, Pierre	Que., Hfd.	4	274	24	108	132	197	8	0	2	2	10	....	1979-80	1982-83
Ladouceur, Randy	Det., Hfd., Ana.	14	930	30	126	156	1322	40	5	8	13	59	....	1982-83	1995-96
LaFayette, Nathan	St.L., Van., NYR, L.A.	6	187	17	20	37	103	32	2	7	9	8	....	1993-94	1998-99
‡ Laflamme, Christian	Chi., Edm., Mtl., St.L.	8	324	2	45	47	282	9	0	1	1	6	....	1996-97	2003-04
Lafleur, Guy	Mtl., NYR, Que.	17	1126	560	793	1353	399	128	58	76	134	67	5	1971-72	1990-91
● Lafleur, Roland	Mtl.	1	1	0	0	0	0	....	....	....	....	....	....	1924-25	1924-25
LaFontaine, Pat	NYI, Buf., NYR	15	865	468	545	1013	552	69	26	36	62	36	....	1983-84	1997-98
Laforce, Ernie	Mtl.	1	1	0	0	0	0	....	....	....	....	....	....	1942-43	1942-43
LaForest, Bob	L.A.	1	5	1	0	1	2	....	....	....	....	....	....	1983-84	1983-84
Laforge, Claude	Mtl., Det., Phi.	8	193	24	33	57	82	5	1	2	3	15	....	1957-58	1968-69
Laforge, Marc	Hfd., Edm.	2	14	0	0	0	64	....	....	....	....	....	....	1989-90	1993-94
Laframboise, Pete	Cal., Wsh., Pit.	4	227	33	55	88	70	9	1	0	1	0	....	1971-72	1974-75
Lafrance, Adie	Mtl.	1	3	0	0	0	2	2	0	0	0	0	....	1933-34	1933-34
● Lafrance, Leo	Mtl., Chi.	2	33	2	0	2	6	....	....	....	....	....	....	1926-27	1927-28
Lafreniere, Jason	Que., NYR, T.B.	5	146	34	53	87	22	15	1	5	6	19	....	1986-87	1993-94
Lafreniere, Roger	Det., St.L.	2	13	0	0	0	4	....	....	....	....	....	....	1962-63	1972-73
Lagace, Jean-Guy	Pit., Buf., K.C.	6	197	9	39	48	251	....	....	....	....	....	....	1968-69	1975-76
Laidlaw, Tom	NYR, L.A.	10	705	25	139	164	717	69	4	17	21	78	....	1980-81	1989-90
Laird, Robbie	Min.	1	1	0	0	0	0	....	....	....	....	....	....	1979-80	1979-80
Lajeunesse, Serge	Det., Phi.	5	103	1	4	5	103	....	....	....	....	....	....	1970-71	1974-75
Lakovic, Sasha	Cgy., N.J.	3	37	0	4	4	118	....	....	....	....	....	....	1996-97	1998-99
Lalande, Hec	Chi., Det.	4	151	21	39	60	120	....	....	....	....	....	....	1953-54	1957-58
Lalonde, Bobby	Van., Atl., Bos., Cgy.	11	641	124	210	334	298	16	4	2	6	6	....	1971-72	1981-82
● Lalonde, Newsy	Mtl., NYA	6	99	124	41	165	183	7	15	4	19	32	....	1917-18	1926-27
Lalonde, Ron	Pit., Wsh.	7	397	45	78	123	106	....	....	....	....	....	....	1972-73	1978-79
Lalor, Mike	Mtl., St.L., Wsh., Wpg., S.J., Dal.	12	687	17	88	105	677	92	5	10	15	167	1	1985-86	1996-97
● Lamb, Joe	Mtl.M., Ott., NYA, Bos., Mtl., St.L., Det.	11	443	108	101	209	601	18	1	1	2	51	....	1927-28	1937-38
Lamb, Mark	Cgy., Det., Edm., Ott., Phi., Mtl.	11	403	46	100	146	291	70	7	19	26	51	1	1985-86	1995-96
‡ Lambert, Dan	Que.	2	29	6	9	15	22	....	....	....	....	....	....	1990-91	1991-92
Lambert, Denny	Ana., Ott., Nsh., Atl.	8	487	27	66	93	1391	17	0	1	1	28	....	1994-95	2001-02

Name	NHL Teams	NHL Seasons	Regular Schedule GP	G	A	TP	PIM	Playoffs GP	G	A	TP	PIM	NHL Cup Wins	First NHL Season	Last NHL Season
Lambert, Lane	Det., NYR, Que.	6	283	58	66	124	521	17	2	4	6	40	....	1983-84	1988-89
Lambert, Yvon	Mtl., Buf.	10	683	206	273	479	340	90	27	22	49	67	4	1972-73	1981-82
Lamby, Dick	St.L.	3	22	0	5	5	22	....	....	....	....	....	....	1978-79	1980-81
• Lamirande, Jean-Paul	NYR, Mtl.	4	49	5	5	10	26	8	0	0	0	4	....	1946-47	1954-55
Lammens, Hank	Ott.	1	27	1	2	3	22	....	....	....	....	....	....	1993-94	1993-94
• Lamoureux, Leo	Mtl.	6	235	19	79	98	175	28	1	6	7	16	2	1941-42	1946-47
Lamoureux, Mitch	Pit., Phi.	3	73	11	9	20	59	....	....	....	....	....	....	1983-84	1987-88
Lampman, Mike	St.L., Van., Wsh.	4	96	17	20	37	34	....	....	....	....	....	....	1972-73	1976-77
Lancien, Jack	NYR	4	63	1	5	6	35	6	0	1	1	2	....	1946-47	1950-51
Landon, Larry	Mtl., Tor.	2	9	0	0	0	2	....	....	....	....	....	....	1983-84	1984-85
‡ Landry, Eric	Cgy., Mtl.	4	68	5	9	14	47	....	....	....	....	....	....	1997-98	2001-02
Lane, Gord	Wsh., NYI	10	539	19	94	113	1228	75	3	14	17	214	4	1975-76	1984-85
• Lane, Myles	NYR, Bos.	3	71	4	1	5	41	11	0	0	0	0	1	1928-29	1933-34
Langdon, Darren	NYR, Car., Van., Mtl., N.J.	11	521	16	23	39	1251	25	1	0	1	20	....	1994-95	2005-06
Langdon, Steve	Bos.	3	7	0	1	1	2	4	0	0	0	0	....	1974-75	1977-78
Langelle, Pete	Tor.	4	136	22	51	73	11	41	5	9	14	4	1	1938-39	1941-42
Langevin, Chris	Buf.	2	22	3	1	4	22	....	....	....	....	....	....	1983-84	1985-86
Langevin, Dave	NYI, Min., L.A.	8	513	12	107	119	530	87	2	17	19	106	4	1979-80	1986-87
Langlais, Alain	Min.	2	25	4	4	8	10	....	....	....	....	....	....	1973-74	1974-75
Langlois, Albert	Mtl., NYR, Det., Bos.	9	497	21	91	112	488	53	1	5	6	50	3	1957-58	1965-66
• Langlois, Charlie	Ham., NYA, Pit., Mtl.	4	151	22	5	27	189	2	0	0	0	0	....	1924-25	1927-28
Langway, Rod	Mtl., Wsh.	15	994	51	278	329	849	104	5	22	27	97	1	1978-79	1992-93
Lank, Jeff	Phi.	1	2	0	0	0	2	....	....	....	....	....	....	1999-00	1999-00
Lanthier, Jean-Marc	Van.	4	105	16	16	32	29	....	....	....	....	....	....	1983-84	1987-88
• Lanyon, Ted	Pit.	1	5	0	0	0	4	....	....	....	....	....	....	1967-68	1967-68
Lanz, Rick	Van., Tor., Chi.	10	569	65	221	286	448	28	3	8	11	35	....	1980-81	1991-92
Laperriere, Daniel	St.L., Ott.	4	48	2	5	7	27	....	....	....	....	....	....	1992-93	1995-96
Laperriere, Jacques	Mtl.	12	691	40	242	282	674	88	9	22	31	101	6	1962-63	1973-74
Laplante, Darryl	Det.	3	35	0	6	6	10	....	....	....	....	....	....	1997-98	1999-00
Lapointe, Claude	Que., Col., Cgy., NYI, Phi.	14	879	127	178	305	721	34	4	7	11	44	....	1990-91	2003-04
Lapointe, Guy	Mtl., St.L., Bos.	16	884	171	451	622	893	123	26	44	70	138	6	1968-69	1983-84
• Lapointe, Rick	Det., Phi., St.L., Que., L.A.	11	664	44	176	220	831	46	2	7	9	64	....	1975-76	1985-86
Lappin, Peter	Min., S.J.	2	7	0	0	0	2	....	....	....	....	....	....	1989-90	1991-92
Laprade, Edgar	NYR	10	500	108	172	280	42	18	4	9	13	4	....	1945-46	1954-55
• LaPrairie, Benjamin	Chi.	1	7	0	0	0	0	....	....	....	....	....	....	1936-37	1936-37
Larionov, Igor	Van., S.J., Det., Fla., N.J.	14	921	169	475	644	474	150	30	67	97	60	3	1989-90	2003-04
Lariviere, Garry	Que., Edm.	4	219	6	57	63	167	14	0	5	5	8	....	1979-80	1982-83
Larmer, Jeff	Col., N.J., Chi.	5	158	37	51	88	57	5	1	0	1	2	....	1981-82	1985-86
Larmer, Steve	Chi., NYR	15	1006	441	571	1012	532	140	56	75	131	89	1	1980-81	1994-95
• Larochelle, Wildor	Mtl., Chi.	12	474	92	74	166	211	34	6	4	10	24	2	1925-26	1936-37
Larocque, Denis	L.A.	1	8	0	1	1	18	....	....	....	....	....	....	1987-88	1987-88
‡ Larocque, Mario	T.B.	1	5	0	0	0	16	....	....	....	....	....	....	1998-99	1998-99
• Larose, Bonner	Bos.	1	6	0	0	0	0	....	....	....	....	....	....	1925-26	1925-26
Larose, Claude	Mtl., Min., St.L.	16	943	226	257	483	887	97	14	18	32	143	5	1962-63	1977-78
Larose, Claude	NYR	2	25	4	7	11	2	2	0	0	0	0	....	1979-80	1981-82
Larose, Guy	Wpg., Tor., Cgy., Bos.	6	70	10	9	19	63	4	0	0	0	0	....	1988-89	1994-95
Larouche, Pierre	Pit., Mtl., Hfd., NYR	14	812	395	427	822	237	64	20	34	54	16	2	1974-75	1987-88
Larouche, Steve	Ott., NYR, L.A.	2	26	9	9	18	10	....	....	....	....	....	....	1994-95	1995-96
• Larson, Norm	NYA, Bro., NYR	3	89	25	18	43	12	....	....	....	....	....	....	1940-41	1946-47
Larson, Reed	Det., Bos., Edm., NYI, Min., Buf.	14	904	222	463	685	1391	32	4	7	11	63	....	1976-77	1989-90
Larter, Tyler	Wsh.	1	1	0	0	0	0	....	....	....	....	....	....	1989-90	1989-90
Latal, Jiri	Phi.	3	92	12	36	48	24	....	....	....	....	....	....	1989-90	1991-92
Latos, James	NYR	1	1	0	0	0	0	....	....	....	....	....	....	1988-89	1988-89
Latreille, Phil	NYR	1	4	0	0	0	2	....	....	....	....	....	....	1960-61	1960-61
Latta, David	Que.	4	36	4	8	12	4	....	....	....	....	....	....	1985-86	1990-91
Lauder, Martin	Bos.	1	3	0	0	0	2	....	....	....	....	....	....	1927-28	1927-28
Lauen, Mike	Wpg.	1	4	0	1	1	0	....	....	....	....	....	....	1983-84	1983-84
Lauer, Brad	NYI, Chi., Ott., Pit.	9	323	44	67	111	218	34	7	5	12	24	....	1986-87	1995-96
Laughlin, Craig	Mtl., Wsh., L.A., Tor.	8	549	136	205	341	364	33	6	6	12	20	....	1981-82	1988-89
Laughton, Mike	Oak., Cal.	4	189	39	48	87	101	11	2	4	6	0	....	1967-68	1970-71
Laukkanen, Janne	Que., Col., Ott., Pit., T.B.	9	407	22	99	121	335	59	7	9	16	46	....	1994-95	2002-03
Laurence, Don	Atl., St.L.	2	79	15	22	37	14	....	....	....	....	....	....	1978-79	1979-80
Laus, Paul	Fla.	9	530	14	58	72	1702	30	2	7	9	74	....	1993-94	2001-02
LaVallee, Kevin	Cgy., L.A., St.L., Pit.	7	366	110	125	235	85	32	5	8	13	21	....	1980-81	1986-87
LaVarre, Mark	Chi.	3	78	9	16	25	58	1	0	0	0	2	....	1985-86	1987-88
Lavender, Brian	St.L., NYI, Det., Cal.	4	184	16	26	42	174	3	0	0	0	2	....	1971-72	1974-75
Lavigne, Eric	L.A.	1	1	0	0	0	0	....	....	....	....	....	....	1994-95	1994-95
• Laviolette, Jack	Mtl.	1	18	2	1	3	6	2	0	0	0	0	....	1917-18	1917-18
Laviolette, Peter	NYR	1	12	0	0	0	6	....	....	....	....	....	....	1988-89	1988-89
Lavoie, Dominic	St.L., Ott., Bos., L.A.	6	38	5	8	13	32	....	....	....	....	....	....	1988-89	1993-94
‡ Law, Kirby	Phi.	3	9	0	1	1	4	....	....	....	....	....	....	2000-01	2003-04
Lawless, Paul	Hfd., Phi., Van., Tor.	7	239	49	77	126	54	3	0	2	2	2	....	1982-83	1989-90
Lawrence, Mark	Dal., NYI	6	142	18	26	44	115	....	....	....	....	....	....	1994-95	2000-01
Lawson, Danny	Det., Min., Buf.	5	219	28	29	57	61	16	0	1	1	2	....	1967-68	1971-72
Lawton, Brian	Min., NYR, Hfd., Que., Bos., S.J.	9	483	112	154	266	401	11	1	1	2	12	....	1983-84	1992-93
Laxdal, Derek	Tor., NYI	6	67	12	7	19	88	1	0	2	2	2	....	1984-85	1990-91
• Laycoe, Hal	NYR, Mtl., Bos.	11	531	25	77	102	292	40	2	5	7	39	....	1945-46	1955-56
Lazaro, Jeff	Bos., Ott.	3	102	14	23	37	114	28	3	3	6	32	....	1990-91	1992-93
Leach, Jamie	Pit., Hfd., Fla.	5	81	11	9	20	12	....	....	....	....	....	1	1989-90	1993-94
Leach, Larry	Bos.	3	126	13	29	42	91	7	1	1	2	8	....	1958-59	1961-62
Leach, Reggie	Bos., Cal., Phi., Det.	13	934	381	285	666	387	94	47	22	69	22	1	1970-71	1982-83
Leach, Stephen	Wsh., Bos., St.L., Car., Ott., Phx., Pit.	15	702	130	153	283	978	92	15	11	26	87	....	1985-86	1999-00
Leavins, Jim	Det., NYR	2	41	2	12	14	30	....	....	....	....	....	....	1985-86	1986-87
‡ Lebeau, Patrick	Mtl., Cgy., Fla., Pit.	4	15	3	2	5	6	....	....	....	....	....	....	1990-91	1998-99
Lebeau, Stephan	Mtl., Ana.	7	373	118	159	277	105	30	9	7	16	12	1	1988-89	1994-95
LeBlanc, Fern	Det.	3	34	5	6	11	0	....	....	....	....	....	....	1976-77	1978-79
LeBlanc, J.P.	Chi., Det.	5	153	14	30	44	87	2	0	0	0	0	....	1968-69	1978-79
LeBlanc, John	Van., Edm., Wpg.	7	83	26	13	39	28	1	0	0	0	0	....	1986-87	1994-95
LeBoutillier, Peter	Ana.	2	35	2	1	3	176	....	....	....	....	....	....	1996-97	1997-98
LeBrun, Al	NYR	2	6	0	2	2	4	....	....	....	....	....	....	1960-61	1965-66
Lecaine, Bill	Pit.	1	4	0	0	0	0	....	....	....	....	....	....	1968-69	1968-69
Leclair, Jackie	Mtl.	3	160	20	40	60	56	20	6	1	7	6	1	1954-55	1956-57
LeClair, John	Mtl., Phi., Pit.	16	967	406	413	819	501	154	42	47	89	94	1	1990-91	2006-07
Leclerc, Mike	Ana., Phx., Cgy.	9	341	64	94	158	288	26	2	9	11	14	....	1996-97	2005-06
Leclerc, Rene	Det.	2	87	10	11	21	105	....	....	....	....	....	....	1968-69	1970-71
Lecuyer, Doug	Chi., Wpg., Pit.	4	126	11	31	42	178	7	4	0	4	15	....	1978-79	1982-83
Ledingham, Walt	Chi., NYI	3	15	0	2	2	4	....	....	....	....	....	....	1972-73	1976-77
• Leduc, Albert	Mtl., Ott., NYR	10	383	57	35	92	614	28	5	6	11	32	2	1925-26	1934-35
LeDuc, Rich	Bos., Que.	4	130	28	38	66	69	5	0	0	0	9	....	1972-73	1980-81
Ledyard, Grant	NYR, L.A., Wsh., Buf., Dal., Van., Bos., Ott., T.B.	18	1028	90	276	366	766	83	6	12	18	96	....	1984-85	2001-02
• Lee, Bobby	Mtl.	1	1	0	0	0	0	....	....	....	....	....	....	1942-43	1942-43
Lee, Edward	Que.	1	2	0	0	0	5	....	....	....	....	....	....	1984-85	1984-85
Lee, Peter	Pit.	6	431	114	131	245	257	19	0	8	8	4	....	1977-78	1982-83
‡ Leeb, Brad	Van., Tor.	3	5	0	0	0	2	....	....	....	....	....	....	1999-00	2003-04
‡ Leeb, Greg	Dal.	1	2	0	0	0	0	....	....	....	....	....	....	2000-01	2000-01
Leeman, Gary	Tor., Cgy., Mtl., Van., St.L.	14	667	199	267	466	531	36	8	16	24	36	1	1982-83	1996-97
Leetch, Brian	NYR, Tor., Bos.	18	1205	247	781	1028	571	95	28	69	97	36	1	1987-88	2005-06
‡ Lefebvre, Guillaume	Phi., Pit.	3	38	2	4	6	13	....	....	....	....	....	....	2001-02	2005-06
Lefebvre, Patrice	Wsh.	1	3	0	0	0	2	....	....	....	....	....	....	1998-99	1998-99
Lefebvre, Sylvain	Mtl., Tor., Que., Col., NYR	14	945	30	154	184	674	129	4	14	18	101	1	1989-90	2002-03
• Lefley, Bryan	NYI, K.C., Col.	5	228	7	29	36	101	2	0	0	0	0	....	1972-73	1977-78
Lefley, Chuck	Mtl., St.L.	9	407	128	164	292	137	29	5	8	13	10	2	1970-71	1980-81
• Leger, Roger	NYR, Mtl.	5	187	18	53	71	71	20	0	7	7	14	....	1943-44	1949-50
Legge, Barry	Que., Wpg.	3	107	1	11	12	144	....	....	....	....	....	....	1979-80	1981-82
Legge, Randy	NYR	1	12	0	2	2	2	....	....	....	....	....	....	1972-73	1972-73
Lehman, Tommy	Bos., Edm.	3	36	5	5	10	16	....	....	....	....	....	....	1987-88	1989-90
Lehto, Petteri	Pit.	1	6	0	0	0	4	....	....	....	....	....	....	1984-85	1984-85
Lehtonen, Antero	Wsh.	1	65	9	12	21	14	....	....	....	....	....	....	1979-80	1979-80
Lehvonen, Henry	K.C.	1	4	0	0	0	0	....	....	....	....	....	....	1974-75	1974-75
Leier, Edward	Chi.	2	16	2	1	3	2	....	....	....	....	....	....	1949-50	1950-51
Leinonen, Mikko	NYR, Wsh.	4	162	31	78	109	71	20	2	11	13	28	....	1981-82	1984-85
Leiter, Bobby	Bos., Pit., Atl.	10	447	98	126	224	144	8	3	0	3	2	....	1962-63	1975-76
Leiter, Ken	NYI, Min.	5	143	14	36	50	62	15	0	6	6	8	....	1984-85	1989-90

Don Lever

Bob Liddington

Eric Lindros

Jan Ludvig

Chuck Luksa

Jack Lynch

Calum MacKay

Mickey MacKay

Name	NHL Teams	NHL Seasons	Regular Schedule					Playoffs					NHL Cup Wins	First NHL Season	Last NHL Season
			GP	G	A	TP	PIM	GP	G	A	TP	PIM			
Lemaire, Jacques	Mtl.	12	853	366	469	835	217	145	61	78	139	63	8	1967-68	1978-79
Lemay, Moe	Van., Edm., Bos., Wpg.	8	317	72	94	166	442	28	6	3	9	55	1	1981-82	1988-89
Lemelin, Roger	K.C., Col.	4	36	1	2	3	27	....	....	....	....	....	....	1974-75	1977-78
Lemieux, Alain	St.L., Que., Pit.	6	119	28	44	72	38	19	4	6	10	0	....	1981-82	1986-87
Lemieux, Bob	Oak.	1	19	0	1	1	12	....	....	....	....	....	....	1967-68	1967-68
Lemieux, Claude	Mtl., N.J., Col., Phx., Dal.	20	1197	379	406	785	1756	233	80	78	158	529	4	1983-84	2002-03
Lemieux, Jacques	L.A.	3	19	0	4	4	8	1	0	0	0	0	....	1967-68	1969-70
Lemieux, Jean	Atl., Wsh.	5	204	23	63	86	39	3	1	1	2	0	....	1973-74	1977-78
Lemieux, Jocelyn	St.L., Mtl., Chi., Hfd., N.J., Cgy., Phx.	12	598	80	84	164	740	60	5	10	15	88	....	1986-87	1997-98
Lemieux, Mario	Pit.	18	915	690	1033	1723	834	107	76	96	172	87	2	1984-85	2005-06
• Lemieux, Real	Det., L.A., NYR, Buf.	8	456	51	104	155	262	18	2	4	6	10	....	1966-67	1973-74
Lemieux, Rich	Van., K.C., Atl.	5	274	39	82	121	132	2	0	0	0	0	....	1971-72	1975-76
Lenardon, Tim	N.J., Van.	2	15	2	1	3	4	....	....	....	....	....	....	1986-87	1989-90
• Lepine, Hec	Mtl.	1	33	5	2	7	2	....	....	....	....	....	....	1925-26	1925-26
• Lepine, Pit	Mtl.	13	526	143	98	241	392	41	7	5	12	26	2	1925-26	1937-38
Leroux, Francois	Edm., Ott., Pit., Col.	10	249	3	20	23	577	33	1	3	4	34	....	1988-89	1997-98
Leroux, Gaston	Mtl.	1	2	0	0	0	0	....	....	....	....	....	....	1935-36	1935-36
Leroux, Jean-Yves	Chi.	5	220	16	22	38	146	....	....	....	....	....	....	1996-97	2000-01
Leschyshyn, Curtis	Que., Col., Wsh., Hfd., Car., Min., Ott.	16	1033	47	165	212	669	68	2	6	8	34	1	1988-89	2003-04
• Lesieur, Art	Mtl., Chi.	4	100	4	2	6	50	14	0	0	0	4	1	1928-29	1935-36
Lessard, Rick	Cgy., S.J.	3	15	0	4	4	18	....	....	....	....	....	....	1988-89	1991-92
Lesuk, Bill	Bos., Phi., L.A., Wsh., Wpg.	8	388	44	63	107	368	9	1	0	1	12	1	1968-69	1979-80
• Leswick, Jack	Chi.	1	37	1	7	8	16	....	....	....	....	....	1	1933-34	1933-34
• Leswick, Pete	NYA, Bos.	2	3	1	0	1	0	....	....	....	....	....	....	1936-37	1944-45
• Leswick, Tony	NYR, Det., Chi.	12	740	165	159	324	900	59	13	10	23	91	3	1945-46	1957-58
‡ Letang, Alan	Dal., Cgy., NYI	3	14	0	0	0	2	....	....	....	....	....	....	1999-00	2002-03
• Levandoski, Joe	NYR	1	8	1	1	2	0	....	....	....	....	....	....	1946-47	1946-47
Leveille, Normand	Bos.	2	75	17	25	42	49	....	....	....	....	....	....	1981-82	1982-83
• Leveque, Guy	L.A.	2	17	2	2	4	21	....	....	....	....	....	....	1992-93	1993-94
Lever, Don	Van., Atl., Cgy., Col., N.J., Buf.	15	1020	313	367	680	593	30	7	10	17	26	....	1972-73	1986-87
Levie, Craig	Wpg., Min., St.L., Van.	6	183	22	53	75	177	16	2	3	5	32	....	1981-82	1986-87
Levins, Scott	Wpg., Fla., Ott., Phx.	5	124	13	20	33	316	....	....	....	....	....	....	1992-93	1997-98
• Levinsky, Alex	Tor., NYR, Chi.	9	367	19	49	68	307	37	2	1	3	26	2	1930-31	1938-39
Levo, Tapio	Col., N.J.	2	107	16	53	69	36	....	....	....	....	....	....	1981-82	1982-83
Lewicki, Danny	Tor., NYR, Chi.	9	461	105	135	240	177	28	0	4	4	8	1	1950-51	1958-59
Lewis, Dale	NYR	1	8	0	0	0	0	....	....	....	....	....	....	1975-76	1975-76
Lewis, Dave	NYI, L.A., N.J., Det.	15	1008	36	187	223	953	91	1	20	21	143	....	1973-74	1987-88
• Lewis, Doug	Mtl.	1	3	0	0	0	0	....	....	....	....	....	....	1946-47	1946-47
• Lewis, Herbie	Det.	11	483	148	161	309	248	38	13	10	23	6	2	1928-29	1938-39
Ley, Rick	Tor., Hfd.	6	310	12	72	84	528	14	0	2	2	20	....	1968-69	1980-81
Liba, Igor	NYR, L.A.	1	37	7	18	25	36	2	0	0	0	2	....	1988-89	1988-89
Libby, Jeff	NYI	1	1	0	0	0	0	....	....	....	....	....	....	1997-98	1997-98
Libett, Nick	Det., Pit.	14	982	237	268	505	472	16	6	2	8	2	....	1967-68	1980-81
Licari, Tony	Det.	1	9	0	1	1	0	....	....	....	....	....	....	1946-47	1946-47
Liddington, Bob	Tor.	1	11	0	1	1	2	....	....	....	....	....	....	1970-71	1970-71
Lidster, Doug	Van., NYR, St.L., Dal.	16	897	75	268	343	679	80	6	15	21	64	1	1983-84	1998-99
Lilley, John	Ana.	3	23	3	8	11	13	....	....	....	....	....	....	1993-94	1995-96
Lind, Juha	Dal., Mtl.	3	133	9	13	22	20	15	2	2	4	8	....	1997-98	2000-01
Lindberg, Chris	Cgy., Que.	3	116	17	25	42	47	2	0	1	1	2	....	1991-92	1993-94
Lindbom, Johan	NYR	1	38	1	3	4	28	....	....	....	....	....	....	1997-98	1997-98
Linden, Jamie	Fla.	1	4	0	0	0	17	....	....	....	....	....	....	1994-95	1994-95
Lindgren, Lars	Van., Min.	6	394	25	113	138	325	40	5	6	11	20	....	1978-79	1983-84
Lindgren, Mats	Edm., NYI, Van.	8	387	54	74	128	146	24	1	5	6	10	....	1996-97	2003-04
Lindholm, Mikael	L.A.	1	18	2	2	4	2	....	....	....	....	....	....	1989-90	1989-90
Lindros, Brett	NYI	2	51	2	5	7	147	....	....	....	....	....	....	1994-95	1995-96
Lindros, Eric	Phi., NYR, Tor., Dal.	14	760	372	493	865	1398	53	24	33	57	122	....	1992-93	2006-07
‡ Lindsay, Bill	Que., Fla., Cgy., S.J., Mtl., Atl.	13	777	83	141	224	922	42	7	8	15	44	....	1991-92	2003-04
Lindsay, Ted	Det., Chi.	17	1068	379	472	851	1808	133	47	49	96	194	4	1944-45	1964-65
Lindstrom, Willy	Wpg., Edm., Pit.	8	582	161	162	323	200	57	14	18	32	24	2	1979-80	1986-87
Linseman, Ken	Phi., Edm., Bos., Tor.	14	860	256	551	807	1727	113	43	77	120	325	1	1978-79	1991-92
‡ Lintner, Richard	Nsh., NYR, Pit.	3	112	8	12	20	54	....	....	....	....	....	....	1999-00	2002-03
Lipuma, Chris	T.B., S.J.	5	72	0	9	9	146	....	....	....	....	....	....	1992-93	1996-97
• Liscombe, Carl	Det.	9	373	137	140	277	117	59	22	19	41	20	1	1937-38	1945-46
Litzenberger, Ed	Mtl., Chi., Det., Tor.	12	618	178	238	416	283	40	5	13	18	34	4	1952-53	1963-64
Loach, Lonnie	Ott., L.A., Ana.	2	56	10	13	23	29	1	0	0	0	0	....	1992-93	1993-94
• Locas, Jacques	Mtl.	2	59	7	8	15	66	....	....	....	....	....	....	1947-48	1948-49
Lochead, Bill	Det., Col., NYR	6	330	69	62	131	180	7	3	0	3	6	....	1974-75	1979-80
• Locking, Norm	Chi.	2	48	2	6	8	26	....	....	....	....	....	....	1934-35	1935-36
Loewen, Darcy	Buf., Ott.	5	135	4	8	12	211	....	....	....	....	....	....	1989-90	1993-94
Lofthouse, Mark	Wsh., Det.	6	181	42	38	80	73	....	....	....	....	....	....	1977-78	1982-83
Logan, Dave	Chi., Van.	6	218	5	29	34	470	12	0	0	0	10	....	1975-76	1980-81
Logan, Robert	Buf., L.A.	3	42	10	5	15	0	....	....	....	....	....	....	1986-87	1988-89
Loiselle, Claude	Det., N.J., Que., Tor., NYI	13	616	92	117	209	1149	41	4	11	15	58	....	1981-82	1993-94
• Lomakin, Andrei	Phi., Fla.	4	215	42	62	104	92	....	....	....	....	....	....	1991-92	1994-95
Loney, Brian	Van.	1	12	2	3	5	6	....	....	....	....	....	....	1995-96	1995-96
Loney, Troy	Pit., Ana., NYI, NYR	12	624	87	110	197	1091	67	8	14	22	97	2	1983-84	1994-95
Long, Barry	L.A., Det., Wpg.	5	280	11	68	79	250	5	0	1	1	18	....	1972-73	1981-82
• Long, Stan	Mtl.	1	....	....	....	....	....	3	0	0	0	0	....	1951-52	1951-52
Lonsberry, Ross	Bos., L.A., Phi., Pit.	15	968	256	310	566	806	100	21	25	46	87	2	1966-67	1980-81
Loob, Hakan	Cgy.	6	450	193	236	429	189	73	26	28	54	16	1	1983-84	1988-89
Loob, Peter	Que.	1	8	1	2	3	0	....	....	....	....	....	....	1984-85	1984-85
Lorentz, Jim	Bos., St.L., NYR, Buf.	10	659	161	238	399	208	54	12	10	22	30	1	1968-69	1977-78
Lorimer, Bob	NYI, Col., N.J.	10	529	22	90	112	431	49	3	10	13	83	2	1976-77	1985-86
• Lorrain, Rod	Mtl.	6	179	28	39	67	30	11	0	3	3	0	....	1935-36	1941-42
• Loughlin, Clem	Det., Chi.	3	101	8	6	14	77	....	....	....	....	....	....	1926-27	1928-29
• Loughlin, Wilf	Tor.	1	14	0	0	0	2	....	....	....	....	....	....	1923-24	1923-24
Lovsin, Ken	Wsh.	1	1	0	0	0	0	....	....	....	....	....	....	1990-91	1990-91
Low, Reed	St.L., Chi.	5	256	3	16	19	725	....	....	....	....	....	....	2000-01	2006-07
Lowdermilk, Dwayne	Wsh.	1	2	0	1	1	2	....	....	....	....	....	....	1980-81	1980-81
Lowe, Darren	Pit.	1	8	1	2	3	0	....	....	....	....	....	....	1983-84	1983-84
Lowe, Kevin	Edm., NYR	19	1254	84	347	431	1498	214	10	48	58	192	6	1979-80	1997-98
Lowe, Odie	NYR	1	4	1	1	2	0	....	....	....	....	....	....	1949-50	1949-50
• Lowe, Ross	Bos., Mtl.	3	77	6	8	14	82	2	0	0	0	0	....	1949-50	1951-52
• Lowrey, Ed	Ott., Ham.	3	27	2	2	4	6	....	....	....	....	....	....	1917-18	1920-21
• Lowrey, Fred	Mtl.M., Pit.	2	53	1	1	2	10	2	0	0	0	6	....	1924-25	1925-26
• Lowrey, Gerry	Tor., Pit., Phi., Chi., Ott.	6	211	48	48	96	148	2	1	0	1	2	....	1927-28	1932-33
Lowry, Dave	Van., St.L., Fla., S.J., Cgy.	19	1084	164	187	351	1191	111	16	20	36	181	....	1985-86	2003-04
‡ Loyns, Lynn	S.J., Cgy.	3	34	3	2	5	21	....	....	....	....	....	....	2002-03	2005-06
Lucas, Danny	Phi.	1	6	1	0	1	0	....	....	....	....	....	....	1978-79	1978-79
Lucas, Dave	Det.	1	1	0	0	0	0	....	....	....	....	....	....	1962-63	1962-63
Luce, Don	NYR, Det., Buf., L.A., Tor.	13	894	225	329	554	364	71	17	22	39	52	....	1969-70	1981-82
Ludvig, Jan	N.J., Buf.	7	314	54	87	141	418	....	....	....	....	....	....	1982-83	1988-89
Ludwig, Craig	Mtl., NYI, Min., Dal.	17	1256	38	184	222	1437	177	4	25	29	244	2	1982-83	1998-99
Ludzik, Steve	Chi., Buf.	9	424	46	93	139	333	44	4	8	12	70	....	1981-82	1989-90
Luhning, Warren	NYI, Dal.	3	29	0	1	1	21	....	....	....	....	....	....	1997-98	1999-00
Lukowich, Bernie	Pit., St.L.	2	79	13	15	28	34	2	0	0	0	0	....	1973-74	1974-75
Lukowich, Morris	Wpg., Bos., L.A.	8	582	199	219	418	584	11	0	2	2	24	....	1979-80	1986-87
Luksa, Charlie	Hfd.	1	8	0	1	1	4	....	....	....	....	....	....	1979-80	1979-80
Lumley, Dave	Mtl., Edm., Hfd.	9	437	98	160	258	680	61	6	8	14	131	2	1978-79	1986-87
Lumme, Jyrki	Mtl., Van., Phx., Dal., Tor.	15	985	114	354	468	620	105	9	35	44	52	....	1988-89	2002-03
Lund, Pentti	Bos., NYR	7	259	44	55	99	40	19	7	5	12	0	....	1946-47	1952-53
Lundberg, Brian	Pit.	1	1	0	0	0	2	....	....	....	....	....	....	1982-83	1982-83
Lunde, Len	Det., Chi., Min., Van.	8	321	39	83	122	75	20	3	2	5	2	....	1958-59	1970-71
Lundholm, Bengt	Wpg.	5	275	48	95	143	72	14	3	4	7	14	....	1981-82	1985-86
Lundrigan, Joe	Tor., Wsh.	2	52	2	8	10	22	....	....	....	....	....	....	1972-73	1974-75
Lundstrom, Tord	Det.	1	11	1	1	2	0	....	....	....	....	....	....	1973-74	1973-74
• Lundy, Pat	Det., Chi.	5	150	37	32	69	31	16	2	2	4	2	....	1945-46	1950-51
‡ Luoma, Mikko	Edm.	1	3	0	1	1	0	....	....	....	....	....	....	2003-04	2003-04
Luongo, Chris	Det., Ott., NYI	5	218	8	23	31	176	....	....	....	....	....	....	1990-91	1995-96
‡ Lupaschuk, Ross	Pit.	1	3	0	0	0	4	....	....	....	....	....	....	2002-03	2002-03
Lupien, Gilles	Mtl., Pit., Hfd.	5	226	5	25	30	416	25	0	0	0	21	2	1977-78	1981-82
• Lupul, Gary	Van.	7	293	70	75	145	243	25	4	7	11	11	....	1979-80	1985-86
• Lyashenko, Roman	Dal., NYR	4	139	14	9	23	55	17	2	1	3	0	....	1999-00	2002-03
Lyle, George	Det., Hfd.	4	99	24	38	62	51	....	....	....	....	....	....	1979-80	1982-83
‡ Lynch, Doug	Edm.	1	2	0	0	0	0	....	....	....	....	....	....	2003-04	2003-04

Name	NHL Teams	NHL Seasons	Regular Schedule GP	G	A	TP	PIM	Playoffs GP	G	A	TP	PIM	NHL Cup Wins	First NHL Season	Last NHL Season
Lynch, Jack	Pit., Det., Wsh.	7	382	24	106	130	336	....	....	....	....	....	....	1972-73	1978-79
Lynn, Vic	NYR, Det., Mtl., Tor., Bos., Chi.	11	327	49	76	125	274	47	7	10	17	46	3	1942-43	1953-54
Lyon, Steve	Pit.	1	3	0	0	0	2	....	....	....	....	....	....	1976-77	1976-77
• Lyons, Ron	Bos., Phi.	1	36	2	4	6	27	5	0	0	0	0	....	1930-31	1930-31
‡ Lysak, Brett	Car.	1	2	0	0	0	2	....	....	....	....	....	....	2003-04	2003-04
Lysiak, Tom	Atl., Chi.	13	919	292	551	843	567	76	25	38	63	49	....	1973-74	1985-86

M

Name	NHL Teams	NHL Seasons	Regular Schedule GP	G	A	TP	PIM	Playoffs GP	G	A	TP	PIM	NHL Cup Wins	First NHL Season	Last NHL Season
MacAdam, Al	Phi., Cal., Cle., Min., Van.	12	864	240	351	591	509	64	20	24	44	21	....	1973-74	1984-85
MacDermid, Paul	Hfd., Wpg., Wsh., Que.	14	690	116	142	258	1303	43	5	11	16	116	....	1981-82	1994-95
MacDonald, Blair	Edm., Van.	4	219	91	100	191	65	11	0	6	6	2	....	1979-80	1982-83
MacDonald, Brett	Van.	1	1	0	0	0	0	....	....	....	....	....	....	1987-88	1987-88
MacDonald, Doug	Buf.	3	11	1	0	1	2	....	....	....	....	....	....	1992-93	1994-95
MacDonald, Jason	NYR	1	4	0	0	0	19	....	....	....	....	....	....	2003-04	2003-04
MacDonald, Kevin	Ott.	1	1	0	0	0	2	....	....	....	....	....	....	1993-94	1993-94
• MacDonald, Kilby	NYR	4	151	36	34	70	47	15	1	2	3	4	1	1939-40	1944-45
MacDonald, Lowell	Det., L.A., Pit.	13	506	180	210	390	92	30	11	11	22	12	....	1961-62	1977-78
MacDonald, Parker	Tor., NYR, Det., Bos., Min.	14	676	144	179	323	253	75	14	14	28	20	....	1952-53	1968-69
MacDougall, Kim	Min.	1	1	0	0	0	0	....	....	....	....	....	....	1974-75	1974-75
MacEachern, Shane	St.L.	1	1	0	0	0	0	....	....	....	....	....	....	1987-88	1987-88
Macey, Hub	NYR, Mtl.	3	30	6	9	15	0	8	0	0	0	0	....	1941-42	1946-47
MacGregor, Bruce	Det., NYR	14	893	213	257	470	217	107	19	28	47	44	....	1960-61	1973-74
MacGregor, Randy	Hfd.	1	2	1	1	2	2	....	....	....	....	....	....	1981-82	1981-82
MacGuigan, Garth	NYI	2	5	0	1	1	2	....	....	....	....	....	....	1979-80	1983-84
MacInnis, Al	Cgy., St.L.	23	1416	340	934	1274	1511	177	39	121	160	255	1	1981-82	2003-04
MacIntosh, Ian	NYR	1	4	0	0	0	4	....	....	....	....	....	....	1952-53	1952-53
MacIver, Don	Wpg.	1	6	0	0	0	2	....	....	....	....	....	....	1979-80	1979-80
Maciver, Norm	NYR, Hfd., Edm., Ott., Pit., Wpg., Phx.	12	500	55	230	285	350	56	3	11	14	32	....	1986-87	1997-98
MacKasey, Blair	Tor.	1	1	0	0	0	2	....	....	....	....	....	....	1976-77	1976-77
• MacKay, Calum	Det., Mtl.	8	237	50	55	105	214	38	5	13	18	20	1	1946-47	1954-55
MacKay, Dave	Chi.	1	29	3	0	3	26	5	0	1	1	2	....	1940-41	1940-41
• MacKay, Mickey	Chi., Pit., Bos.	4	147	44	19	63	79	11	0	0	0	6	1	1926-27	1929-30
• MacKay, Murdo	Mtl.	4	19	0	3	3	0	15	1	2	3	0	....	1945-46	1948-49
MacKell, Fleming	Tor., Bos.	13	665	149	220	369	562	80	22	41	63	75	2	1947-48	1959-60
• MacKell, Jack	Ott.	2	45	4	2	6	59	2	0	0	0	0	2	1919-20	1920-21
MacKenzie, Barry	Min.	1	6	0	1	1	6	....	....	....	....	....	....	1968-69	1968-69
• MacKenzie, Bill	Chi., Mtl.M., NYR, Mtl.	7	264	15	14	29	145	21	1	1	2	11	1	1932-33	1939-40
Mackey, David	Chi., Min., St.L.	6	126	8	12	20	305	3	0	0	0	2	....	1987-88	1993-94
• Mackey, Reg	NYR	1	34	0	0	0	16	1	0	0	0	0	....	1926-27	1926-27
• Mackie, Howie	Det.	2	20	1	0	1	4	8	0	0	0	0	1	1936-37	1937-38
MacKinnon, Paul	Wsh.	5	147	5	23	28	91	....	....	....	....	....	....	1979-80	1983-84
MacLean, John	N.J., S.J., NYR, Dal.	18	1194	413	429	842	1328	104	35	48	83	152	1	1983-84	2001-02
MacLean, Paul	St.L., Wpg., Det.	11	719	324	349	673	968	53	21	14	35	110	....	1980-81	1990-91
MacLeish, Rick	Phi., Hfd., Pit., Det.	14	846	349	410	759	434	114	54	53	107	38	2	1970-71	1983-84
MacLellan, Brian	L.A., NYR, Min., Cgy., Det.	10	606	172	241	413	551	47	5	9	14	42	1	1982-83	1991-92
MacLeod, Pat	Min., S.J., Dal.	4	53	5	13	18	14	....	....	....	....	....	....	1990-91	1995-96
MacMillan, Billy	Tor., Atl., NYI	7	446	74	77	151	184	53	6	6	12	40	....	1970-71	1976-77
MacMillan, Bob	NYR, St.L., Atl., Cgy., Col., N.J., Chi.	11	753	228	349	577	260	31	8	11	19	16	....	1974-75	1984-85
‡ MacMillan, Jeff	Dal.	1	4	0	0	0	0	....	....	....	....	....	....	2003-04	2003-04
MacMillan, John	Tor., Det.	5	104	5	10	15	32	12	0	1	1	2	2	1960-61	1964-65
MacNeil, Al	Tor., Mtl., Chi., NYR, Pit.	11	524	17	75	92	617	37	0	4	4	67	....	1955-56	1967-68
MacNeil, Bernie	St.L.	1	4	0	0	0	0	....	....	....	....	....	....	1973-74	1973-74
MacNeil, Ian	Phi.	1	2	0	0	0	0	....	....	....	....	....	....	2002-03	2002-03
Macoun, Jamie	Cgy., Tor., Det.	16	1128	76	282	358	1208	159	10	32	42	169	2	1982-83	1998-99
• MacPherson, Bud	Mtl.	7	259	5	33	38	233	29	0	3	3	21	1	1948-49	1956-57
• MacSweyn, Ralph	Phi.	5	47	0	5	5	10	8	0	0	0	6	....	1967-68	1971-72
MacTavish, Craig	Bos., Edm., NYR, Phi., St.L.	17	1093	213	267	480	891	193	20	38	58	218	4	1979-80	1996-97
MacWilliam, Mike	NYI	1	6	0	0	0	14	....	....	....	....	....	....	1995-96	1995-96
Madigan, Connie	St.L.	1	20	0	3	3	25	5	0	0	0	4	....	1972-73	1972-73
Madill, Jeff	N.J.	1	14	4	0	4	46	7	0	2	2	8	....	1990-91	1990-91
Magee, Dean	Min.	1	7	0	0	0	4	....	....	....	....	....	....	1977-78	1977-78
Maggs, Daryl	Chi., Cal., Tor.	3	135	14	19	33	54	4	0	0	0	0	....	1971-72	1979-80
Magnan, Marc	Tor.	1	4	0	1	1	5	....	....	....	....	....	....	1982-83	1982-83
• Magnuson, Keith	Chi.	11	589	14	125	139	1442	68	3	9	12	164	....	1969-70	1979-80
Maguire, Kevin	Tor., Buf., Phi.	6	260	29	30	59	782	11	0	0	0	86	....	1986-87	1991-92
Mahaffy, John	Mtl., NYR	3	37	11	25	36	4	1	0	1	1	0	....	1942-43	1944-45
Mahovlich, Frank	Tor., Det., Mtl.	18	1181	533	570	1103	1056	137	51	67	118	163	6	1956-57	1973-74
Mahovlich, Pete	Det., Mtl., Pit.	16	884	288	485	773	916	88	30	42	72	134	4	1965-66	1980-81
Mailhot, Jacques	Que.	1	5	0	0	0	33	....	....	....	....	....	....	1988-89	1988-89
• Mailley, Frank	Mtl.	1	1	0	0	0	0	....	....	....	....	....	....	1942-43	1942-43
Mair, Jim	Phi., NYI, Van.	5	76	4	15	19	49	3	1	2	3	4	....	1970-71	1974-75
• Majeau, Fern	Mtl.	2	56	22	24	46	43	1	0	0	0	0	1	1943-44	1944-45
‡ Majesky, Ivan	Fla., Atl., Wsh.	3	202	8	23	31	234	....	....	....	....	....	....	2002-03	2005-06
Major, Bruce	Que.	1	4	0	0	0	0	....	....	....	....	....	....	1990-91	1990-91
Major, Mark	Det.	1	2	0	0	0	5	....	....	....	....	....	....	1996-97	1996-97
Makarov, Sergei	Cgy., S.J., Dal.	7	424	134	250	384	317	34	12	11	23	8	....	1989-90	1996-97
Makela, Mikko	NYI, L.A., Buf., Bos.	7	423	118	147	265	139	18	3	8	11	14	....	1985-86	1994-95
Maki, Chico	Chi.	15	841	143	292	435	345	113	17	36	53	43	1	1960-61	1975-76
• Maki, Wayne	Chi., St.L., Van.	6	246	57	79	136	184	2	1	0	1	2	....	1967-68	1972-73
Makkonen, Kari	Edm.	1	9	2	2	4	0	....	....	....	....	....	....	1979-80	1979-80
Malakhov, Vladimir	NYI, Mtl., N.J., NYR, Phi.	13	712	86	260	346	697	75	8	19	27	64	1	1992-93	2005-06
‡ Malec, Tomas	Car., Ott.	4	46	0	2	2	47	....	....	....	....	....	....	2002-03	2006-07
Maley, David	Mtl., N.J., Edm., S.J., NYI	9	466	43	81	124	1043	46	5	5	10	111	1	1985-86	1993-94
Malgunas, Stewart	Phi., Wpg., Wsh., Cgy.	7	129	1	5	6	144	....	....	....	....	....	....	1993-94	1999-00
Malinowski, Merlin	Col., N.J., Hfd.	5	282	54	111	165	121	....	....	....	....	....	....	1978-79	1982-83
Malkoc, Dean	Van., Bos., NYI	4	116	1	3	4	299	....	....	....	....	....	....	1995-96	1998-99
Mallette, Troy	NYR, Edm., N.J., Ott., Bos., T.B.	9	456	51	68	119	1226	15	2	2	4	99	....	1989-90	1997-98
Malone, Cliff	Mtl.	1	3	0	0	0	0	....	....	....	....	....	....	1951-52	1951-52
Malone, Greg	Pit., Hfd., Que.	11	704	191	310	501	661	20	3	5	8	32	....	1976-77	1986-87
• Malone, Joe	Mtl., Que., Ham.	7	126	143	32	175	57	9	6	2	8	6	1	1917-18	1923-24
Maloney, Dan	Chi., L.A., Det., Tor.	11	737	192	259	451	1489	40	4	7	11	35	....	1970-71	1981-82
Maloney, Dave	NYR, Buf.	11	657	71	246	317	1154	49	7	17	24	91	....	1974-75	1984-85
Maloney, Don	NYR, Hfd., NYI	13	765	214	350	564	815	94	22	35	57	101	....	1978-79	1990-91
Maloney, Phil	Bos., Tor., Chi.	5	158	28	43	71	16	6	0	0	0	0	....	1949-50	1959-60
Maltais, Steve	Wsh., Min., T.B., Det., CBJ	6	120	9	18	27	53	1	0	0	0	0	....	1989-90	2000-01
Maluta, Ray	Bos.	2	25	2	3	5	6	2	0	0	0	0	....	1975-76	1976-77
Manastersky, Tom	Mtl.	1	6	0	0	0	11	....	....	....	....	....	....	1950-51	1950-51
• Mancuso, Gus	Mtl., NYR	4	42	7	9	16	17	....	....	....	....	....	....	1937-38	1942-43
‡ Manderville, Kent	Tor., Edm., Hfd., Car., Phi., Pit.	12	646	37	67	104	348	67	3	3	6	44	....	1991-92	2002-03
Mandich, Dan	Min.	4	111	5	11	16	303	7	0	0	0	2	....	1982-83	1985-86
‡ Maneluk, Mike	Phi., Chi., NYR, CBJ	3	85	11	10	21	57	....	....	....	....	....	....	1998-99	2000-01
Manery, Kris	Cle., Min., Van., Wpg.	4	250	63	64	127	91	....	....	....	....	....	....	1977-78	1980-81
Manery, Randy	Det., Atl., L.A.	10	582	50	206	256	415	13	0	2	2	12	....	1970-71	1979-80
‡ Mann, Cameron	Bos., Nsh.	5	93	14	10	24	40	1	0	0	0	0	....	1997-98	2002-03
Mann, Jack	NYR	2	9	3	4	7	0	....	....	....	....	....	....	1943-44	1944-45
Mann, Jimmy	Wpg., Que., Pit.	8	293	10	20	30	895	22	0	0	0	89	....	1979-80	1987-88
Mann, Ken	Det.	1	1	0	0	0	0	....	....	....	....	....	....	1975-76	1975-76
• Mann, Norm	Tor.	3	31	0	3	3	4	2	0	0	0	0	....	1935-36	1940-41
• Manners, Rennison	Pit., Phi.	2	37	3	2	5	14	....	....	....	....	....	....	1929-30	1930-31
‡ Manning, Paul	CBJ	1	8	0	0	0	2	....	....	....	....	....	....	2002-03	2002-03
Manno, Bob	Van., Tor., Det.	8	371	41	131	172	274	17	2	4	6	12	....	1976-77	1984-85
Manson, Dave	Chi., Edm., Wpg., Phx., Mtl., Dal., Tor.	16	1103	102	288	390	2792	112	7	24	31	343	....	1986-87	2001-02
Manson, Ray	Bos., NYR	2	2	0	1	1	0	....	....	....	....	....	....	1947-48	1948-49
• Mantha, Georges	Mtl.	13	488	89	102	191	148	36	6	2	8	24	2	1928-29	1940-41
Mantha, Moe	Wpg., Pit., Edm., Min., Phi.	12	656	81	289	370	501	17	5	10	15	18	....	1980-81	1991-92
• Mantha, Sylvio	Mtl., Bos.	14	542	63	78	141	671	39	5	5	10	64	3	1923-24	1936-37
• Maracle, Bud	NYR	1	11	1	3	4	4	4	0	0	0	0	....	1930-31	1930-31
Marcetta, Milan	Tor., Min.	3	54	7	15	22	10	17	7	7	14	4	1	1966-67	1968-69
• March, Mush	Chi.	17	759	153	230	383	540	45	12	15	27	41	2	1928-29	1944-45
Marchinko, Brian	Tor., NYI	4	47	2	6	8	0	....	....	....	....	....	....	1970-71	1973-74
Marchment, Bryan	Wpg., Chi., Hfd., Edm., T.B., S.J., Col., Tor., Cgy.	17	926	40	142	182	2307	83	4	3	7	102	....	1988-89	2005-06
Marcinyshyn, Dave	N.J., Que., NYR	3	16	0	1	1	49	....	....	....	....	....	....	1990-91	1992-93

Bob MacMillan

Keith Magnuson

Dave Maloney

Joe Matte

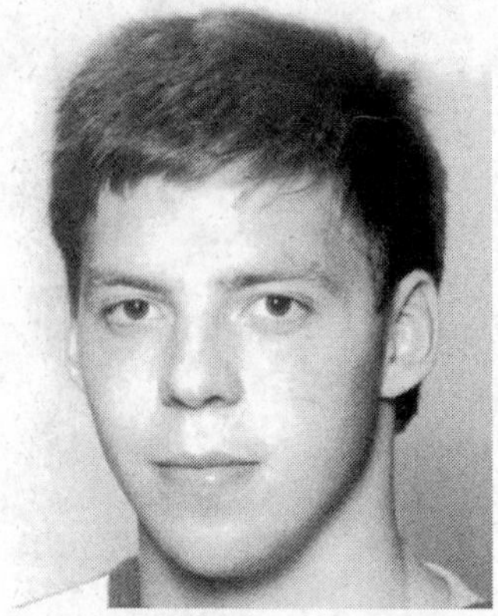

Wayne McBean

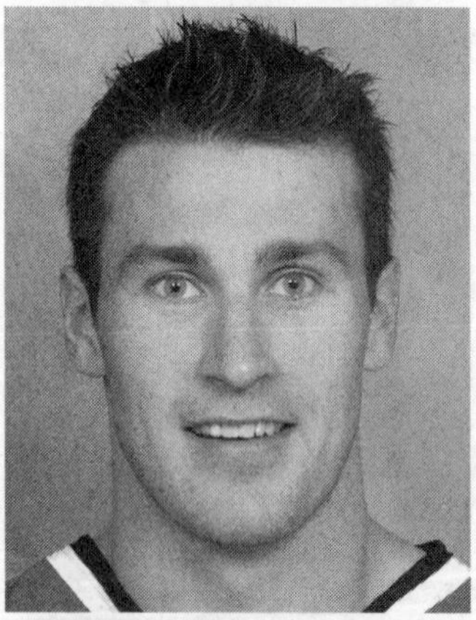

Alyn McCauley

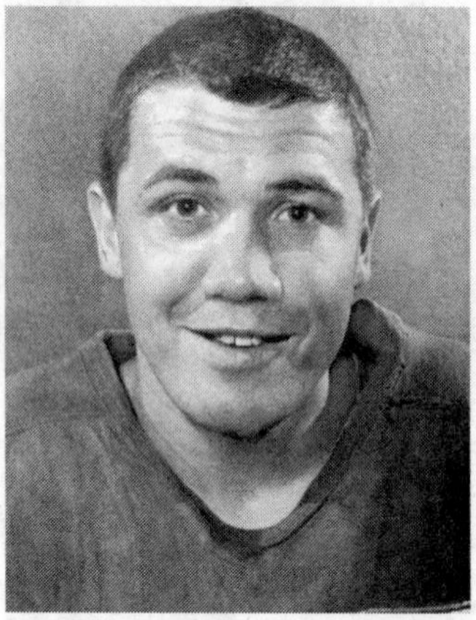

Bob McCord

Sean McKenna

			Regular Schedule					Playoffs					NHL	First	Last
Name	NHL Teams	NHL Seasons	GP	G	A	TP	PIM	GP	G	A	TP	PIM	Cup Wins	NHL Season	NHL Season
Marcon, Lou	Det.	3	60	0	4	4	42	....	....	....	....	....	....	1958-59	1962-63
Marcotte, Don	Bos.	15	868	230	254	484	317	132	34	27	61	81	2	1965-66	1981-82
‡ Marha, Josef	Col., Ana., Chi.	6	159	21	32	53	32	....	....	....	....	....	....	1995-96	2000-01
Marini, Hector	NYI, N.J.	5	154	27	46	73	246	10	3	6	9	14	2	1978-79	1983-84
Marinucci, Chris	NYI, L.A.	2	13	1	4	5	2	....	....	....	....	....	....	1994-95	1996-97
• Mario, Frank	Bos.	2	53	9	19	28	24	....	....	....	....	....	....	1941-42	1944-45
• Mariucci, John	Chi.	5	223	11	34	45	308	12	0	3	3	26	....	1940-41	1947-48
‡ Marjamaki, Masi	NYI	1	1	0	0	0	0	....	....	....	....	....	....	2005-06	2005-06
Mark, Gordon	N.J., Edm.	4	85	3	10	13	187	....	....	....	....	....	....	1986-87	1994-95
Markell, John	Wpg., St.L., Min.	4	55	11	10	21	36	....	....	....	....	....	....	1979-80	1984-85
• Marker, Gus	Det., Mtl.M., Tor., Bro.	10	322	64	69	133	133	46	5	7	12	36	1	1932-33	1941-42
Markham, Ray	NYR	1	14	1	1	2	21	7	1	0	1	24	....	1979-80	1979-80
• Markle, Jack	Tor.	1	8	0	1	1	0	....	....	....	....	....	....	1935-36	1935-36
• Marks, Jack	Mtl.W., Tor., Que.	2	7	0	0	0	4	....	....	....	....	....	1	1917-18	1919-20
Marks, John	Chi.	10	657	112	163	275	330	57	5	9	14	60	....	1972-73	1981-82
Markwart, Nevin	Bos., Cgy.	8	309	41	68	109	794	19	1	0	1	33	....	1983-84	1991-92
Marois, Daniel	Tor., NYI, Bos., Dal.	8	350	117	93	210	419	19	3	3	6	28	....	1987-88	1995-96
Marois, Mario	NYR, Van., Que., Wpg., St.L.	15	955	76	357	433	1746	100	4	34	38	182	....	1977-78	1991-92
• Marotte, Gilles	Bos., Chi., L.A., NYR, St.L.	12	808	56	265	321	919	29	3	3	6	26	....	1965-66	1976-77
Marquess, Mark	Bos.	1	27	5	4	9	6	4	0	0	0	0	....	1946-47	1946-47
Marsh, Brad	Atl., Cgy., Phi., Tor., Det., Ott.	15	1086	23	175	198	1241	97	6	18	24	124	....	1978-79	1992-93
Marsh, Gary	Det., Tor.	2	7	1	3	4	4	....	....	....	....	....	....	1967-68	1968-69
Marsh, Peter	Wpg., Chi.	5	278	48	71	119	224	26	1	5	6	33	....	1979-80	1983-84
Marshall, Bert	Det., Oak., Cal., NYR, NYI	14	868	17	181	198	926	72	4	22	26	99	....	1965-66	1978-79
Marshall, Don	Mtl., NYR, Buf., Tor.	19	1176	265	324	589	127	94	8	15	23	14	5	1951-52	1971-72
Marshall, Jason	St.L., Ana., Wsh., Min., S.J.	12	526	16	51	67	1004	43	2	3	5	55	....	1991-92	2005-06
Marshall, Paul	Pit., Tor., Hfd.	4	95	15	18	33	17	1	0	0	0	0	....	1979-80	1982-83
Marshall, Willie	Tor.	4	33	1	5	6	2	....	....	....	....	....	....	1952-53	1958-59
Marson, Mike	Wsh., L.A.	6	196	24	24	48	233	....	....	....	....	....	....	1974-75	1979-80
‡ Martensson, Tony	Ana.	1	6	1	1	2	0	....	....	....	....	....	....	2003-04	2003-04
• Martin, Clare	Bos., Det., Chi., NYR	6	237	12	28	40	78	27	0	2	2	6	1	1941-42	1951-52
Martin, Craig	Wpg., Fla.	2	21	0	1	1	24	....	....	....	....	....	....	1994-95	1996-97
• Martin, Frank	Bos., Chi.	6	282	11	46	57	122	10	0	2	2	2	....	1952-53	1957-58
Martin, Grant	Van., Wsh.	4	44	0	4	4	55	1	1	0	1	2	....	1983-84	1986-87
Martin, Jack	Tor.	1	1	0	0	0	0	....	....	....	....	....	....	1960-61	1960-61
Martin, Matt	Tor.	4	76	0	5	5	71	....	....	....	....	....	....	1993-94	1996-97
Martin, Pit	Det., Bos., Chi., Van.	17	1101	324	485	809	609	100	27	31	58	56	....	1961-62	1978-79
Martin, Rick	Buf., L.A.	11	685	384	317	701	477	63	24	29	53	74	....	1971-72	1981-82
• Martin, Ron	NYA	2	94	13	16	29	36	....	....	....	....	....	....	1932-33	1933-34
Martin, Terry	Buf., Que., Tor., Edm., Min.	10	479	104	101	205	202	21	4	2	6	26	....	1975-76	1984-85
Martin, Tom	Tor.	1	3	1	0	1	0	....	....	....	....	....	....	1967-68	1967-68
Martin, Tom	Wpg., Hfd., Min.	6	92	12	11	23	249	4	0	0	0	6	....	1984-85	1989-90
• Martineau, Don	Atl., Min., Det.	4	90	6	10	16	63	....	....	....	....	....	....	1973-74	1976-77
Martini, Darcy	Edm.	1	2	0	0	0	0	....	....	....	....	....	....	1993-94	1993-94
Martinson, Steve	Det., Mtl., Min.	4	49	2	1	3	244	1	0	0	0	10	....	1987-88	1991-92
Maruk, Dennis	Cal., Cle., Min., Wsh.	14	888	356	522	878	761	34	14	22	36	26	....	1975-76	1988-89
Masnick, Paul	Mtl., Chi., Tor.	6	232	18	41	59	139	33	4	5	9	27	1	1950-51	1957-58
• Mason, Charley	NYR, NYA, Det., Chi.	4	95	7	18	25	44	4	0	1	1	0	....	1934-35	1938-39
• Massecar, George	NYA	3	100	12	11	23	46	....	....	....	....	....	....	1929-30	1931-32
Masters, Jamie	St.L.	3	33	1	13	14	2	2	0	0	0	0	....	1975-76	1978-79
• Masterton, Bill	Min.	1	38	4	8	12	4	....	....	....	....	....	....	1967-68	1967-68
• Mathers, Frank	Tor.	3	23	1	3	4	4	....	....	....	....	....	....	1948-49	1951-52
Mathiasen, Dwight	Pit.	3	33	1	7	8	18	....	....	....	....	....	....	1985-86	1987-88
Mathieson, Jim	Wsh.	1	2	0	0	0	4	....	....	....	....	....	....	1989-90	1989-90
Mathieu, Marquis	Bos.	3	16	0	2	2	14	....	....	....	....	....	....	1998-99	2000-01
Matte, Christian	Col., Min.	5	25	2	3	5	12	....	....	....	....	....	....	1996-97	2000-01
• Matte, Joe	Tor., Ham., Bos., Mtl.	4	68	17	15	32	54	....	....	....	....	....	....	1919-20	1925-26
• Matte, Joe	Det., Chi.	2	24	0	3	3	8	....	....	....	....	....	....	1929-30	1942-43
Matteau, Stephane	Cgy., Chi., NYR, St.L., S.J., Fla.	13	848	144	172	316	742	109	12	22	34	80	1	1990-91	2002-03
Matteucci, Mike	Min.	2	6	0	0	0	4	....	....	....	....	....	....	2000-01	2001-02
Mattiussi, Dick	Pit., Oak., Cal.	4	200	8	31	39	124	8	0	1	1	6	....	1967-68	1970-71
• Matz, Johnny	Mtl.	1	30	2	3	5	0	1	0	0	0	0	....	1924-25	1924-25
Maxner, Wayne	Bos.	2	62	8	9	17	48	....	....	....	....	....	....	1964-65	1965-66
Maxwell, Brad	Min., Que., Tor., Van., NYR	10	612	98	270	368	1292	79	12	49	61	178	....	1977-78	1986-87
Maxwell, Bryan	Min., St.L., Wpg., Pit.	8	331	18	77	95	745	15	1	1	2	86	....	1977-78	1984-85
Maxwell, Kevin	Min., Col., N.J.	3	66	6	15	21	61	16	3	4	7	24	....	1980-81	1983-84
Maxwell, Wally	Tor.	1	2	0	0	0	0	....	....	....	....	....	....	1952-53	1952-53
May, Alan	Bos., Edm., Wsh., Dal., Cgy.	8	393	31	45	76	1348	40	1	2	3	80	....	1987-88	1994-95
Mayer, Derek	Ott.	1	17	2	2	4	8	....	....	....	....	....	....	1993-94	1993-94
Mayer, Jim	NYR	1	4	0	0	0	0	....	....	....	....	....	....	1979-80	1979-80
Mayer, Pat	Pit.	1	1	0	0	0	4	....	....	....	....	....	....	1987-88	1987-88
• Mayer, Shep	Tor.	1	12	1	2	3	4	....	....	....	....	....	....	1942-43	1942-43
• Mazur, Eddie	Mtl., Chi.	6	107	8	20	28	120	25	4	5	9	22	1	1950-51	1956-57
Mazur, Jay	Van.	4	47	11	7	18	20	6	0	1	1	8	....	1988-89	1991-92
McAdam, Gary	Buf., Pit., Det., Cgy., Wsh., N.J., Tor.	11	534	96	132	228	243	30	6	5	11	16	....	1975-76	1985-86
• McAdam, Sam	NYR	1	5	0	0	0	0	....	....	....	....	....	....	1930-31	1930-31
‡ McAllister, Chris	Van., Tor., Phi., Col., NYR	7	301	4	17	21	634	9	0	1	1	4	....	1997-98	2003-04
McAlpine, Chris	N.J., St.L., T.B., Atl., Chi., L.A.	8	289	6	24	30	245	28	0	1	1	18	1	1994-95	2002-03
• McAndrew, Hazen	Bro.	1	7	0	1	1	6	....	....	....	....	....	....	1941-42	1941-42
McAneeley, Ted	Cal.	3	158	8	35	43	141	....	....	....	....	....	....	1972-73	1974-75
McAtee, Jud	Det.	3	46	15	13	28	6	14	2	1	3	0	....	1942-43	1944-45
McAtee, Norm	Bos.	1	13	0	1	1	0	....	....	....	....	....	....	1946-47	1946-47
• McAvoy, George	Mtl.	1	....	....	....	....	....	4	0	0	0	0	....	1954-55	1954-55
McBain, Andrew	Wpg., Pit., Van., Ott.	11	608	129	172	301	633	24	5	7	12	39	....	1983-84	1993-94
McBain, Jason	Hfd.	2	9	0	0	0	0	....	....	....	....	....	....	1995-96	1996-97
‡ McBain, Mike	T.B.	2	64	0	7	7	22	....	....	....	....	....	....	1997-98	1998-99
McBean, Wayne	L.A., NYI, Wpg.	6	211	10	39	49	168	2	1	1	2	0	....	1987-88	1993-94
McBride, Cliff	Mtl.M., Tor.	2	2	0	0	0	0	....	....	....	....	....	....	1928-29	1929-30
McBurney, Jim	Chi.	1	1	0	1	1	0	....	....	....	....	....	....	1952-53	1952-53
• McCabe, Stan	Det., Mtl.M.	4	78	9	4	13	49	....	....	....	....	....	....	1929-30	1933-34
• McCaffrey, Bert	Tor., Pit., Mtl.	7	260	43	30	73	202	8	2	1	3	10	1	1924-25	1930-31
McCahill, John	Col.	1	1	0	0	0	0	....	....	....	....	....	....	1977-78	1977-78
• McCaig, Doug	Det., Chi.	7	263	8	21	29	255	7	0	1	1	10	....	1941-42	1950-51
• McCallum, Dunc	NYR, Pit.	5	187	14	35	49	230	10	1	2	3	12	....	1965-66	1970-71
• McCalmon, Eddie	Chi., Phi.	2	39	5	0	5	14	....	....	....	....	....	....	1927-28	1930-31
McCann, Rick	Det.	6	43	1	4	5	6	....	....	....	....	....	....	1967-68	1974-75
McCarthy, Dan	NYR	1	5	4	0	4	4	....	....	....	....	....	....	1980-81	1980-81
McCarthy, Kevin	Phi., Van., Pit.	10	537	67	191	258	527	21	2	3	5	20	....	1977-78	1986-87
McCarthy, Sandy	Cgy., T.B., Phi., Car., NYR, Bos.	11	736	72	76	148	1534	23	0	2	2	61	....	1993-94	2003-04
• McCarthy, Thomas	Que., Ham.	2	35	22	7	29	10	....	....	....	....	....	....	1919-20	1920-21
McCarthy, Tom	Det., Bos.	4	60	8	9	17	8	....	....	....	....	....	....	1956-57	1960-61
McCarthy, Tom	Min., Bos.	9	460	178	221	399	330	68	12	26	38	67	....	1979-80	1987-88
• McCartney, Walt	Mtl.	1	2	0	0	0	0	....	....	....	....	....	....	1932-33	1932-33
McCaskill, Ted	Min.	1	4	0	2	2	0	....	....	....	....	....	....	1967-68	1967-68
McCauley, Alyn	Tor., S.J., L.A.	9	488	69	97	166	116	52	7	12	19	18	....	1997-98	2006-07
McClanahan, Rob	Buf., Hfd., NYR	5	224	38	63	101	126	34	4	12	16	31	....	1979-80	1983-84
McCleary, Trent	Ott., Bos., Mtl.	4	192	8	15	23	134	....	....	....	....	....	....	1995-96	1999-00
McClelland, Kevin	Pit., Edm., Det., Tor., Wpg.	12	588	68	112	180	1672	98	11	18	29	281	4	1981-82	1993-94
McCord, Bob	Bos., Det., Min., St.L.	7	316	10	58	68	262	14	2	5	7	10	....	1963-64	1972-73
• McCord, Dennis	Van.	1	3	0	0	0	6	....	....	....	....	....	....	1973-74	1973-74
McCormack, John	Tor., Mtl., Chi.	8	311	25	49	74	35	22	1	1	2	0	2	1947-48	1954-55
McCosh, Shawn	L.A., NYR	2	9	1	0	1	6	....	....	....	....	....	....	1991-92	1994-95
McCourt, Dale	Det., Buf., Tor.	7	532	194	284	478	124	21	9	7	16	6	....	1977-78	1983-84
McCreary, Bill	NYR, Det., Mtl., St.L.	8	309	53	62	115	108	48	6	16	22	14	....	1953-54	1970-71
McCreary, Bill	Tor.	1	12	1	0	1	4	....	....	....	....	....	....	1980-81	1980-81
• McCreary, Keith	Mtl., Pit., Atl.	10	532	131	112	243	294	16	0	4	4	6	....	1961-62	1974-75
• McCreedy, John	Tor.	2	64	17	12	29	25	21	4	3	7	16	2	1941-42	1944-45
McCrimmon, Brad	Bos., Phi., Cgy., Det., Hfd., Phx.	18	1222	81	322	403	1416	116	11	18	29	176	1	1979-80	1996-97
McCrimmon, Jim	St.L.	1	2	0	0	0	0	....	....	....	....	....	....	1974-75	1974-75
• McCulley, Bob	Mtl.	1	1	0	0	0	0	....	....	....	....	....	....	1934-35	1934-35
• McCurry, Duke	Pit.	4	148	21	11	32	119	4	0	2	2	2	....	1925-26	1928-29
McCutcheon, Brian	Det.	3	37	3	1	4	7	....	....	....	....	....	....	1974-75	1976-77
McCutcheon, Darwin	Tor.	1	1	0	0	0	2	....	....	....	....	....	....	1981-82	1981-82
McDill, Jeff	Chi.	1	1	0	0	0	0	....	....	....	....	....	....	1976-77	1976-77
McDonagh, Bill	NYR	1	4	0	0	0	2	....	....	....	....	....	....	1949-50	1949-50

Name	NHL Teams	NHL Seasons	Regular Schedule					Playoffs					NHL Cup Wins	First NHL Season	Last NHL Season
			GP	G	A	TP	PIM	GP	G	A	TP	PIM			
McDonald, Ab	Mtl., Chi., Bos., Det., Pit., St.L.	15	762	182	248	430	200	84	21	29	50	42	4	1957-58	1971-72
McDonald, Brian	Chi., Buf.	2	12	0	0	0	29	8	0	0	0	2	....	1967-68	1970-71
• McDonald, Bucko	Det., Tor., NYR	11	446	35	88	123	206	50	6	1	7	24	3	1934-35	1944-45
• McDonald, Butch	Det., Chi.	2	66	8	20	28	2	5	0	2	2	10	....	1939-40	1944-45
McDonald, Gerry	Hfd.	2	8	0	0	0	4	....	....	....	....	....	....	1981-82	1983-84
• McDonald, Jack	Mtl.W., Mtl., Que., Tor.	5	69	26	14	40	30	7	1	3	4	3	....	1917-18	1921-22
McDonald, Jack	NYR	1	43	10	9	19	6	....	....	....	....	....	....	1943-44	1943-44
McDonald, Lanny	Tor., Col., Cgy.	16	1111	500	506	1006	899	117	44	40	84	120	1	1973-74	1988-89
McDonald, Robert	NYR	1	1	0	0	0	0	....	....	....	....	....	....	1943-44	1943-44
McDonald, Terry	K.C.	1	8	0	1	1	6	....	....	....	....	....	....	1975-76	1975-76
‡ McDonell, Kent	CBJ	2	32	1	2	3	36	....	....	....	....	....	....	2002-03	2003-04
McDonnell, Joe	Van., Pit.	3	50	2	10	12	34	....	....	....	....	....	....	1981-82	1985-86
• McDonnell, Moylan	Ham.	1	22	1	2	3	2	....	....	....	....	....	....	1920-21	1920-21
McDonough, Al	L.A., Pit., Atl., Det.	5	237	73	88	161	73	8	0	1	1	2	....	1970-71	1977-78
McDonough, Hubie	L.A., NYI, S.J.	5	195	40	26	66	67	5	1	0	1	4	....	1988-89	1992-93
McDougal, Mike	NYR, Hfd.	4	61	8	10	18	43	....	....	....	....	....	....	1978-79	1982-83
McDougall, Bill	Det., Edm., T.B.	3	28	5	5	10	12	1	0	0	0	0	....	1990-91	1993-94
McEachern, Shawn	Pit., L.A., Bos., Ott., Atl.	14	911	256	323	579	506	97	12	25	37	62	1	1991-92	2005-06
McElmury, Jim	Min., K.C., Col.	5	180	14	47	61	49	....	....	....	....	....	....	1972-73	1977-78
McEwen, Mike	NYR, Col., NYI, L.A., Wsh., Det., Hfd.	12	716	108	296	404	460	78	12	36	48	48	3	1976-77	1987-88
• McFadden, Jim	Det., Chi.	8	412	100	126	226	89	49	10	9	19	30	1	1946-47	1953-54
• McFadyen, Don	Chi.	4	179	12	33	45	77	11	2	2	4	5	1	1932-33	1935-36
McFall, Dan	Wpg.	2	9	0	1	1	0	....	....	....	....	....	....	1984-85	1985-86
• McFarlane, Gord	Chi.	1	2	0	0	0	0	....	....	....	....	....	....	1926-27	1926-27
McGeough, Jim	Wsh., Pit.	4	57	7	10	17	32	....	....	....	....	....	....	1981-82	1986-87
• McGibbon, Irv	Mtl.	1	1	0	0	0	2	....	....	....	....	....	....	1942-43	1942-43
McGill, Bob	Tor., Chi., S.J., Det., NYI, Hfd.	13	705	17	55	72	1766	49	0	0	0	88	....	1981-82	1993-94
• McGill, Jack	Mtl.	3	134	27	10	37	71	3	2	0	2	0	....	1934-35	1936-37
• McGill, Jack	Bos.	4	97	23	36	59	42	27	7	4	11	17	....	1941-42	1946-47
McGill, Ryan	Chi., Phi., Edm.	4	151	4	15	19	391	....	....	....	....	....	....	1991-92	1994-95
‡ McGillis, Dan	Edm., Phi., S.J., Bos., N.J.	9	634	56	182	238	570	64	8	14	22	76	....	1996-97	2005-06
McGregor, Sandy	NYR	1	2	0	0	0	2	....	....	....	....	....	....	1963-64	1963-64
• McGuire, Mickey	Pit.	2	36	3	0	3	6	....	....	....	....	....	....	1926-27	1927-28
McHugh, Mike	Min., S.J.	4	20	1	0	1	16	....	....	....	....	....	....	1988-89	1991-92
McIlhargey, Jack	Phi., Van., Hfd.	8	393	11	36	47	1102	27	0	3	3	68	....	1974-75	1981-82
• McInenly, Bert	Det., NYA, Ott., Bos.	6	166	19	15	34	144	4	0	0	0	2	....	1930-31	1935-36
McInnis, Marty	NYI, Cgy., Ana., Bos.	12	796	170	250	420	330	22	3	2	5	4	....	1991-92	2002-03
McIntosh, Bruce	Min.	1	2	0	0	0	0	....	....	....	....	....	....	1972-73	1972-73
McIntosh, Paul	Buf.	2	48	0	2	2	66	2	0	0	0	7	....	1974-75	1975-76
• McIntyre, Jack	Bos., Chi., Det.	11	499	109	102	211	173	29	7	6	13	4	....	1949-50	1959-60
McIntyre, John	Tor., L.A., NYR, Van.	6	351	24	54	78	516	44	0	6	6	54	....	1989-90	1994-95
McIntyre, Larry	Tor.	2	41	0	3	3	26	....	....	....	....	....	....	1969-70	1972-73
McKay, Doug	Det.	1	....	....	....	....	....	1	0	0	0	0	1	1949-50	1949-50
McKay, Randy	Det., N.J., Dal., Mtl.	15	932	162	201	363	1731	123	20	23	43	123	2	1988-89	2002-03
McKay, Ray	Chi., Buf., Cal.	6	140	2	16	18	102	....	....	....	....	....	....	1968-69	1973-74
McKay, Scott	Ana.	1	1	0	0	0	0	....	....	....	....	....	....	1993-94	1993-94
McKechnie, Walt	Min., Cal., Bos., Det., Wsh., Cle., Tor., Col.	16	955	214	392	606	469	15	7	5	12	7	....	1967-68	1982-83
McKee, Mike	Que.	1	48	3	12	15	41	....	....	....	....	....	....	1993-94	1993-94
McKegney, Ian	Chi.	1	3	0	0	0	2	....	....	....	....	....	....	1976-77	1976-77
McKegney, Tony	Buf., Que., Min., NYR, St.L., Det., Chi.	13	912	320	319	639	517	79	24	23	47	56	....	1978-79	1990-91
McKendry, Alex	NYI, Cgy.	4	46	3	6	9	21	6	2	2	4	0	1	1977-78	1980-81
McKenna, Sean	Buf., L.A., Tor.	9	414	82	80	162	181	15	1	2	3	2	....	1981-82	1989-90
McKenna, Steve	L.A., Min., Pit., NYR	8	373	18	14	32	824	3	0	1	1	8	....	1996-97	2003-04
McKenney, Don	Bos., NYR, Tor., Det., St.L.	13	798	237	345	582	211	58	18	29	47	10	1	1954-55	1967-68
McKenny, Jim	Tor., Min.	14	604	82	247	329	294	37	7	9	16	10	....	1965-66	1978-79
McKenzie, Brian	Pit.	1	6	1	1	2	4	....	....	....	....	....	....	1971-72	1971-72
McKenzie, Jim	Hfd., Dal., Pit., Wpg., Phx., Ana., Wsh., N.J., Nsh.	15	880	48	52	100	1739	51	0	0	0	38	1	1989-90	2003-04
McKenzie, John	Chi., Det., NYR, Bos.	12	691	206	268	474	917	69	15	32	47	133	2	1958-59	1971-72
McKim, Andrew	Bos., Det.	3	38	1	4	5	6	....	....	....	....	....	....	1992-93	1994-95
• McKinnon, Alex	Ham., NYA, Chi.	5	193	19	11	30	237	....	....	....	....	....	....	1924-25	1928-29
• McKinnon, John	Mtl., Pit., Phi.	6	208	28	11	39	224	2	0	0	0	4	....	1925-26	1930-31
McLaren, Steve	St.L.	1	6	0	0	0	25	....	....	....	....	....	....	2003-04	2003-04
McLean, Don	Wsh.	1	9	0	0	0	6	....	....	....	....	....	....	1975-76	1975-76
• McLean, Fred	Que., Ham.	2	8	0	0	0	2	....	....	....	....	....	....	1919-20	1920-21
• McLean, Jack	Tor.	3	67	14	24	38	76	13	2	2	4	8	1	1942-43	1944-45
• McLean, Jeff	S.J.	1	6	1	0	1	0	....	....	....	....	....	....	1993-94	1993-94
• McLellan, John	Tor.	1	2	0	0	0	0	....	....	....	....	....	....	1951-52	1951-52
McLellan, Scott	Bos.	1	2	0	0	0	0	....	....	....	....	....	....	1982-83	1982-83
McLellan, Todd	NYI	1	5	1	1	2	0	....	....	....	....	....	....	1987-88	1987-88
• McLenahan, Rollie	Det.	1	9	2	1	3	10	2	0	0	0	0	....	1945-46	1945-46
McLeod, Al	Det.	1	26	2	2	4	24	....	....	....	....	....	....	1973-74	1973-74
McLeod, Jackie	NYR	5	106	14	23	37	12	7	0	0	0	0	....	1949-50	1954-55
‡ McLlwain, Dave	Pit., Wpg., Buf., NYI, Tor., Ott.	10	501	100	107	207	292	20	0	2	2	2	....	1987-88	1996-97
• McMahon, Mike	Mtl., Bos.	3	57	7	18	25	102	13	1	2	3	30	1	1942-43	1945-46
McMahon, Mike	NYR, Min., Chi., Det., Pit., Buf.	8	224	15	68	83	171	14	3	7	10	4	....	1963-64	1971-72
McManama, Bob	Pit.	3	99	11	25	36	28	8	0	1	1	6	....	1973-74	1975-76
• McManus, Sammy	Mtl.M., Bos.	2	26	0	1	1	8	1	0	0	0	0	1	1934-35	1936-37
‡ McMorrow, Sean	Buf.	1	1	0	0	0	0	....	....	....	....	....	....	2002-03	2002-03
McMurchy, Tom	Chi., Edm.	4	55	8	4	12	65	....	....	....	....	....	....	1983-84	1987-88
• McNab, Max	Det.	4	128	16	19	35	24	25	1	0	1	4	1	1947-48	1950-51
McNab, Peter	Buf., Bos., Van., N.J.	14	954	363	450	813	179	107	40	42	82	20	....	1973-74	1986-87
• McNabney, Sid	Mtl.	1	....	....	....	....	....	5	0	1	1	2	....	1950-51	1950-51
• McNamara, Howard	Mtl.	1	10	1	0	1	4	....	....	....	....	....	....	1919-20	1919-20
• McNaughton, George	Que.	1	1	0	0	0	0	....	....	....	....	....	....	1919-20	1919-20
McNeill, Billy	Det.	6	257	21	46	67	142	4	1	1	2	4	....	1956-57	1963-64
‡ McNeill, Grant	Fla.	1	3	0	0	0	5	....	....	....	....	....	....	2003-04	2003-04
McNeill, Mike	Chi., Que.	2	63	5	11	16	18	....	....	....	....	....	....	1990-91	1991-92
McNeill, Stu	Det.	3	10	1	1	2	2	....	....	....	....	....	....	1957-58	1959-60
McPhee, George	NYR, N.J.	7	115	24	25	49	257	29	5	3	8	69	....	1982-83	1988-89
McPhee, Mike	Mtl., Min., Dal.	11	744	200	199	399	661	134	28	27	55	193	1	1983-84	1993-94
McRae, Basil	Que., Tor., Det., Min., T.B., St.L., Chi.	16	576	53	83	136	2457	78	8	4	12	349	....	1981-82	1996-97
McRae, Chris	Tor., Det.	3	21	1	0	1	122	....	....	....	....	....	....	1987-88	1989-90
McRae, Ken	Que., Tor.	7	137	14	21	35	364	6	0	0	0	4	....	1987-88	1993-94
• McReavy, Pat	Bos., Det.	4	55	5	10	15	4	22	3	3	6	9	1	1938-39	1941-42
McReynolds, Brian	Wpg., NYR, L.A.	3	30	1	5	6	8	....	....	....	....	....	....	1989-90	1993-94
McSheffrey, Bryan	Van., Buf.	3	90	13	7	20	44	....	....	....	....	....	....	1972-73	1974-75
McSorley, Marty	Pit., Edm., L.A., NYR, S.J., Bos.	17	961	108	251	359	3381	115	10	19	29	374	2	1983-84	1999-00
McSween, Don	Buf., Ana.	5	47	3	10	13	55	....	....	....	....	....	....	1987-88	1995-96
McTaggart, Jim	Wsh.	2	71	3	10	13	205	....	....	....	....	....	....	1980-81	1981-82
‡ McTavish, Dale	Cgy.	1	9	1	2	3	2	....	....	....	....	....	....	1996-97	1996-97
McTavish, Gord	St.L., Wpg.	2	11	1	3	4	2	....	....	....	....	....	....	1978-79	1979-80
• McVeigh, Charley	Chi., NYA	9	397	84	88	172	138	4	0	0	0	2	....	1926-27	1934-35
• McVicar, Jack	Mtl.M.	2	88	2	4	6	63	6	0	0	0	2	....	1930-31	1931-32
Meagher, Rick	Mtl., Hfd., N.J., St.L.	12	691	144	165	309	383	62	8	7	15	41	....	1979-80	1990-91
Meehan, Gerry	Tor., Phi., Buf., Van., Atl., Wsh.	10	670	180	243	423	111	10	0	1	1	0	....	1968-69	1978-79
Meeke, Brent	Cal., Cle.	5	75	9	22	31	8	....	....	....	....	....	....	1972-73	1976-77
Meeker, Howie	Tor.	8	346	83	102	185	329	42	6	9	15	50	4	1946-47	1953-54
Meeker, Mike	Pit.	1	4	0	0	0	5	....	....	....	....	....	....	1978-79	1978-79
• Meeking, Harry	Tor., Det., Bos.	3	64	18	12	30	66	9	3	0	3	6	....	1917-18	1926-27
Meger, Paul	Mtl.	6	212	39	52	91	118	35	3	8	11	16	1	1949-50	1954-55
Meighan, Ron	Min., Pit.	2	48	3	7	10	18	....	....	....	....	....	....	1981-82	1982-83
Meissner, Barrie	Min.	2	6	0	1	1	4	....	....	....	....	....	....	1967-68	1968-69
• Meissner, Dick	Bos., NYR	5	171	11	15	26	37	....	....	....	....	....	....	1959-60	1964-65
Melametsa, Anssi	Wpg.	1	27	0	3	3	2	....	....	....	....	....	....	1985-86	1985-86
‡ Melanson, Dean	Buf., Wsh.	2	9	0	0	0	8	....	....	....	....	....	....	1994-95	2001-02
Melin, Roger	Min.	2	3	0	0	0	0	....	....	....	....	....	....	1980-81	1981-82
Mellanby, Scott	Phi., Edm., Fla., St.L., Atl.	21	1431	364	476	840	2479	136	24	29	53	220	....	1985-86	2006-07
Mellor, Tom	Det.	2	26	2	4	6	25	....	....	....	....	....	....	1973-74	1974-75
• Melnyk, Gerry	Det., Chi., St.L.	6	269	39	77	116	34	53	6	6	12	6	....	1955-56	1967-68
Melnyk, Larry	Bos., Edm., NYR, Van.	10	432	11	63	74	686	66	2	9	11	127	1	1980-81	1989-90
Melrose, Barry	Wpg., Tor., Det.	6	300	10	23	33	728	7	0	2	2	38	....	1979-80	1985-86
Menard, Hillary	Chi.	1	1	0	0	0	0	....	....	....	....	....	....	1953-54	1953-54

Jackie McLeod

Bob McManama

Scott Mellanby

Bill Miller

Lew Morrison

Gus Mortson

Rob Murray

Jim Nahrgang

			Regular Schedule					Playoffs					NHL	First	Last
Name	NHL Teams	NHL Seasons	GP	G	A	TP	PIM	GP	G	A	TP	PIM	Cup Wins	NHL Season	NHL Season
Menard, Howie	Det., L.A., Chi., Oak.	4	151	23	42	65	87	19	3	7	10	36	....	1963-64	1969-70
Mercredi, Vic	Atl.	1	2	0	0	0	0	....	....	....	....	....	....	1974-75	1974-75
Meredith, Greg	Cgy.	2	38	6	4	10	8	5	3	1	4	4	....	1980-81	1982-83
Merkosky, Glenn	Hfd., N.J., Det.	5	66	5	12	17	22	....	....	....	....	....	....	1981-82	1989-90
• Meronek, Bill	Mtl.	2	19	5	8	13	0	1	0	0	0	0	....	1939-40	1942-43
Merrick, Wayne	St.L., Cal., Cle., NYI	12	774	191	265	456	303	102	19	30	49	30	4	1972-73	1983-84
• Merrill, Horace	Ott.	2	8	0	0	0	3	....	....	....	....	....	1	1917-18	1919-20
Mertzig, Jan	NYR	1	23	0	2	2	8	....	....	....	....	....	....	1998-99	1998-99
Messier, Eric	Col., Fla.	8	406	25	50	75	146	72	3	5	8	22	1	1996-97	2003-04
Messier, Joby	NYR	3	25	0	4	4	24	....	....	....	....	....	....	1992-93	1994-95
Messier, Mark	Edm., NYR, Van.	25	1756	694	1193	1887	1910	236	109	186	295	244	6	1979-80	2003-04
Messier, Mitch	Min.	4	20	0	2	2	11	....	....	....	....	....	....	1987-88	1990-91
Messier, Paul	Col.	1	9	0	0	0	4	....	....	....	....	....	....	1978-79	1978-79
Metcalfe, Scott	Edm., Buf.	3	19	1	2	3	18	....	....	....	....	....	....	1987-88	1989-90
• Metz, Don	Tor.	9	172	20	35	55	42	42	7	8	15	12	5	1938-39	1948-49
• Metz, Nick	Tor.	12	518	131	119	250	149	76	19	20	39	31	4	1934-35	1947-48
• Michaluk, Art	Chi.	1	5	0	0	0	0	....	....	....	....	....	....	1947-48	1947-48
Michaluk, John	Chi.	1	1	0	0	0	0	....	....	....	....	....	....	1950-51	1950-51
Michayluk, Dave	Phi., Pit.	3	14	2	6	8	8	7	1	1	2	0	1	1981-82	1991-92
Micheletti, Joe	St.L., Col.	3	158	11	60	71	114	11	1	11	12	10	....	1979-80	1981-82
Micheletti, Pat	Min.	1	12	2	0	2	8	....	....	....	....	....	....	1987-88	1987-88
• Mickey, Larry	Chi., NYR, Tor., Mtl., L.A., Phi., Buf.	11	292	39	53	92	160	9	1	0	1	10	....	1964-65	1974-75
• Mickoski, Nick	NYR, Chi., Det., Bos.	13	703	158	185	343	319	18	1	6	7	6	....	1947-48	1959-60
Middendorf, Max	Que., Edm.	4	13	2	4	6	6	....	....	....	....	....	....	1986-87	1990-91
Middleton, Rick	NYR, Bos.	14	1005	448	540	988	157	114	45	55	100	19	....	1974-75	1987-88
Miehm, Kevin	St.L.	2	22	1	4	5	8	2	0	1	1	0	....	1992-93	1993-94
Migay, Rudy	Tor.	10	418	59	92	151	293	15	1	0	1	20	....	1949-50	1959-60
‡ Mika, Petr	NYI	1	3	0	0	0	0	....	....	....	....	....	....	1999-00	1999-00
Mikita, Stan	Chi.	22	1394	541	926	1467	1270	155	59	91	150	169	1	1958-59	1979-80
Mikkelson, Bill	L.A., NYI, Wsh.	4	147	4	18	22	105	....	....	....	....	....	....	1971-72	1976-77
Mikol, Jim	Tor., NYR	2	34	1	4	5	8	....	....	....	....	....	....	1962-63	1964-65
Mikulchik, Oleg	Wpg., Ana.	3	37	0	3	3	33	....	....	....	....	....	....	1993-94	1995-96
Milbury, Mike	Bos.	12	754	49	189	238	1552	86	4	24	28	219	....	1975-76	1986-87
• Milks, Hib	Pit., Phi., NYR, Ott.	8	317	87	41	128	179	11	0	0	0	2	....	1925-26	1932-33
Millar, Craig	Edm., Nsh., T.B.	5	114	8	14	22	73	....	....	....	....	....	....	1996-97	2000-01
• Millar, Hugh	Det.	1	4	0	0	0	0	1	0	0	0	0	....	1946-47	1946-47
Millar, Mike	Hfd., Wsh., Bos., Tor.	5	78	18	18	36	12	....	....	....	....	....	....	1986-87	1990-91
Millen, Corey	NYR, L.A., N.J., Dal., Cgy.	8	335	90	119	209	236	47	5	7	12	22	....	1989-90	1996-97
• Miller, Bill	Mtl.M., Mtl.	3	95	7	3	10	16	12	0	0	0	0	1	1934-35	1936-37
Miller, Bob	Bos., Col., L.A.	6	404	75	119	194	220	36	4	7	11	27	....	1977-78	1984-85
Miller, Brad	Buf., Ott., Cgy.	6	82	1	5	6	321	....	....	....	....	....	....	1988-89	1993-94
• Miller, Earl	Chi., Tor.	5	109	19	14	33	124	10	1	0	1	6	1	1927-28	1931-32
Miller, Jack	Chi.	2	17	0	0	0	4	....	....	....	....	....	....	1949-50	1950-51
Miller, Jason	N.J.	3	6	0	0	0	0	....	....	....	....	....	....	1990-91	1992-93
Miller, Jay	Bos., L.A.	7	446	40	44	84	1723	48	2	3	5	243	....	1985-86	1991-92
Miller, Kelly	NYR, Wsh.	15	1057	181	282	463	512	119	20	34	54	65	....	1984-85	1998-99
Miller, Kevin	NYR, Det., Wsh., St.L., S.J., Pit., Chi., NYI, Ott.	13	620	150	185	335	429	61	7	10	17	49	....	1988-89	2003-04
Miller, Kip	Que., Min., S.J., NYI, Chi., Pit., Ana., Wsh.	12	449	74	165	239	105	25	6	11	17	23	....	1990-91	2003-04
Miller, Paul	Col.	1	3	0	3	3	0	....	....	....	....	....	....	1981-82	1981-82
Miller, Perry	Det.	4	217	10	51	61	387	....	....	....	....	....	....	1977-78	1980-81
Miller, Tom	Det., NYI	4	118	16	25	41	34	....	....	....	....	....	....	1970-71	1974-75
Miller, Warren	NYR, Hfd.	4	262	40	50	90	137	6	1	0	1	0	....	1979-80	1982-83
Mills, Craig	Wpg., Chi.	3	31	0	5	5	36	1	0	0	0	0	....	1995-96	1998-99
Miner, John	Edm.	1	14	2	3	5	16	....	....	....	....	....	....	1987-88	1987-88
Minor, Gerry	Van.	5	140	11	21	32	173	12	1	3	4	25	....	1979-80	1983-84
Mironov, Boris	Wpg., Edm., Chi., NYR	11	716	76	231	307	891	25	5	11	16	45	....	1993-94	2003-04
Mironov, Dmitri	Tor., Pit., Ana., Det., Wsh.	11	556	54	206	260	568	75	10	26	36	48	1	1991-92	2001-02
Miszuk, John	Det., Chi., Phi., Min.	6	237	7	39	46	232	19	0	3	3	19	....	1963-64	1969-70
Mitchell, Bill	Det.	1	1	0	0	0	0	....	....	....	....	....	....	1963-64	1963-64
• Mitchell, Herb	Bos.	2	44	6	0	6	36	....	....	....	....	....	....	1924-25	1925-26
Mitchell, Jeff	Dal.	1	7	0	0	0	7	....	....	....	....	....	....	1997-98	1997-98
• Mitchell, Red	Chi.	3	83	4	5	9	67	....	....	....	....	....	....	1941-42	1944-45
Mitchell, Roy	Min.	1	3	0	0	0	0	....	....	....	....	....	....	1992-93	1992-93
• Moe, Bill	NYR	5	261	11	42	53	163	1	0	0	0	0	....	1944-45	1948-49
Moffat, Lyle	Tor., Wpg.	3	97	12	16	28	51	....	....	....	....	....	....	1972-73	1979-80
• Moffat, Ron	Det.	3	37	1	1	2	8	7	0	0	0	0	....	1932-33	1934-35
Moger, Sandy	Bos., L.A.	5	236	41	38	79	212	5	2	2	4	12	....	1994-95	1998-99
Mogilny, Alexander	Buf., Van., N.J., Tor.	16	990	473	559	1032	432	124	39	47	86	58	1	1989-90	2005-06
Moher, Mike	N.J.	1	9	0	1	1	28	....	....	....	....	....	....	1982-83	1982-83
Mohns, Doug	Bos., Chi., Min., Atl., Wsh.	22	1390	248	462	710	1250	94	14	36	50	122	....	1953-54	1974-75
Mohns, Lloyd	NYR	1	1	0	0	0	0	....	....	....	....	....	....	1943-44	1943-44
Mokosak, Carl	Cgy., L.A., Phi., Pit., Bos.	6	83	11	15	26	170	1	0	0	0	0	....	1981-82	1988-89
Mokosak, John	Det.	2	41	0	2	2	96	....	....	....	....	....	....	1988-89	1989-90
Molin, Lars	Van.	3	172	33	65	98	37	19	2	9	11	7	....	1981-82	1983-84
Moller, Mike	Buf., Edm.	7	134	15	28	43	41	3	0	1	1	0	....	1980-81	1986-87
Moller, Randy	Que., NYR, Buf., Fla.	14	815	45	180	225	1692	78	6	16	22	197	....	1981-82	1994-95
Molloy, Mitch	Buf.	1	2	0	0	0	10	....	....	....	....	....	....	1989-90	1989-90
• Molyneaux, Larry	NYR	2	45	0	1	1	20	10	0	0	0	8	....	1937-38	1938-39
Momesso, Sergio	Mtl., St.L., Van., Tor., NYR	13	710	152	193	345	1557	119	18	26	44	311	....	1983-84	1996-97
Monahan, Garry	Mtl., Det., L.A., Tor., Van.	12	748	116	169	285	484	22	3	1	4	13	....	1967-68	1978-79
Monahan, Hartland	Cal., NYR, Wsh., Pit., L.A., St.L.	7	334	61	80	141	163	6	0	0	0	4	....	1973-74	1980-81
• Mondou, Armand	Mtl.	12	386	47	71	118	99	32	3	5	8	12	2	1928-29	1939-40
Mondou, Pierre	Mtl.	9	548	194	262	456	179	69	17	28	45	26	3	1976-77	1984-85
Mongeau, Michel	St.L., T.B.	4	54	6	19	25	10	2	0	1	1	0	....	1989-90	1992-93
Mongrain, Bob	Buf., L.A.	6	81	13	14	27	14	11	1	2	3	2	....	1979-80	1985-86
Monteith, Hank	Det.	3	77	5	12	17	6	4	0	0	0	0	....	1968-69	1970-71
Montgomery, Jim	St.L., Mtl., Phi., S.J., Dal.	6	122	9	25	34	80	8	1	0	1	2	....	1993-94	2002-03
Moore, Barrie	Buf., Edm., Wsh.	3	39	2	6	8	18	....	....	....	....	....	....	1995-96	1999-00
Moore, Dickie	Mtl., Tor., St.L.	14	719	261	347	608	652	135	46	64	110	122	6	1951-52	1967-68
Moore, Steve	Col.	3	69	5	7	12	41	....	....	....	....	....	....	2001-02	2003-04
• Moran, Amby	Mtl., Chi.	2	35	1	1	2	24	....	....	....	....	....	....	1926-27	1927-28
Moran, Ian	Pit., Bos., Ana.	12	489	21	50	71	321	66	1	7	8	24	....	1994-95	2006-07
‡ Moravec, David	Buf.	1	1	0	0	0	0	....	....	....	....	....	....	1999-00	1999-00
More, Jay	NYR, Min., S.J., Phx., Chi., Nsh.	10	406	18	54	72	702	31	0	6	6	45	....	1988-89	1998-99
• Morenz, Howie	Mtl., Chi., NYR	14	550	271	201	472	546	39	13	9	22	58	3	1923-24	1936-37
Moretto, Angelo	Cle.	1	5	1	2	3	2	....	....	....	....	....	....	1976-77	1976-77
• Morin, Pete	Mtl.	1	31	10	12	22	7	1	0	0	0	0	....	1941-42	1941-42
• Morin, Stephane	Que., Van.	5	90	16	39	55	52	....	....	....	....	....	....	1989-90	1993-94
Morisset, Dave	Fla.	1	4	0	0	0	5	....	....	....	....	....	....	2001-02	2001-02
Morissette, Dave	Mtl.	2	11	0	0	0	57	....	....	....	....	....	....	1998-99	1999-00
Moro, Marc	Ana., Nsh., Tor.	4	30	0	0	0	77	....	....	....	....	....	....	1997-98	2001-02
‡ Morozov, Aleksey	Pit.	7	451	84	135	219	98	39	4	5	9	8	....	1997-98	2003-04
• Morris, Bernie	Bos.	1	6	1	0	1	0	....	....	....	....	....	....	1924-25	1924-25
Morris, Jon	N.J., S.J., Bos.	6	103	16	33	49	47	11	1	7	8	25	....	1988-89	1993-94
• Morris, Moe	Tor., NYR	4	135	13	29	42	58	18	4	2	6	16	1	1943-44	1948-49
Morrison, Dave	L.A., Van.	4	39	3	3	6	4	....	....	....	....	....	....	1980-81	1984-85
• Morrison, Don	Det., Chi.	3	112	18	28	46	12	3	0	1	1	0	....	1947-48	1950-51
Morrison, Doug	Bos.	4	23	7	3	10	15	....	....	....	....	....	....	1979-80	1984-85
Morrison, Gary	Phi.	3	43	1	15	16	70	5	0	1	1	2	....	1979-80	1981-82
Morrison, George	St.L.	2	115	17	21	38	13	3	0	0	0	0	....	1970-71	1971-72
Morrison, Jim	Bos., Tor., Det., NYR, Pit.	12	704	40	160	200	542	36	0	12	12	38	....	1951-52	1970-71
• Morrison, John	NYA	1	18	0	0	0	0	....	....	....	....	....	....	1925-26	1925-26
Morrison, Kevin	Col.	1	41	4	11	15	23	....	....	....	....	....	....	1979-80	1979-80
Morrison, Lew	Phi., Atl., Wsh., Pit.	9	564	39	52	91	107	17	0	0	0	2	....	1969-70	1977-78
Morrison, Mark	NYR	2	10	1	1	2	0	....	....	....	....	....	....	1981-82	1983-84
• Morrison, Rod	Det.	1	34	8	7	15	4	3	0	0	0	0	....	1947-48	1947-48
Morrow, Ken	NYI	10	550	17	88	105	309	127	11	22	33	97	4	1979-80	1988-89
Morrow, Scott	Cgy.	1	4	0	0	0	0	....	....	....	....	....	....	1994-95	1994-95
Morton, Dean	Det.	1	1	1	0	1	2	....	....	....	....	....	....	1989-90	1989-90
Mortson, Gus	Tor., Chi., Det.	13	797	46	152	198	1380	54	5	8	13	68	4	1946-47	1958-59
• Mosdell, Ken	Bro., Mtl., Chi.	16	693	141	168	309	475	80	16	13	29	48	4	1941-42	1958-59
• Mosienko, Bill	Chi.	14	711	258	282	540	121	22	10	4	14	15	....	1941-42	1954-55
Mott, Morris	Cal.	3	199	18	32	50	49	....	....	....	....	....	....	1972-73	1974-75

Name	NHL Teams	NHL Seasons	Regular Schedule GP	G	A	TP	PIM	Playoffs GP	G	A	TP	PIM	NHL Cup Wins	First NHL Season	Last NHL Season
• Motter, Alex	Bos., Det.	8	255	39	64	103	135	41	3	9	12	41	1	1934-35	1942-43
Moxey, Jim	Cal., Cle., L.A.	3	127	22	27	49	59	....	....	....	....	....	....	1974-75	1976-77
Mrozik, Rick	Cgy.	1	2	0	0	0	0	....	....	....	....	....	....	2002-03	2002-03
Muckalt, Bill	Van., NYI, Ott., Min.	5	256	40	57	97	204	5	0	0	0	0	....	1998-99	2002-03
Mulhern, Richard	Atl., L.A., Tor., Wpg.	6	303	27	93	120	217	7	0	3	3	5	....	1975-76	1980-81
Mulhern, Ryan	Wsh.	1	3	0	0	0	0	....	....	....	....	....	....	1997-98	1997-98
Mullen, Brian	Wpg., NYR, S.J., NYI	11	832	260	362	622	414	62	12	18	30	30	....	1982-83	1992-93
Mullen, Joe	St.L., Cgy., Pit., Bos.	17	1062	502	561	1063	241	143	60	46	106	42	3	1979-80	1996-97
Muller, Kirk	N.J., Mtl., NYI, Tor., Fla., Dal.	19	1349	357	602	959	1223	127	33	36	69	153	1	1984-85	2002-03
Muloin, Wayne	Det., Oak., Cal., Min.	3	147	3	21	24	93	11	0	0	0	2	....	1963-64	1970-71
Mulvenna, Glenn	Pit., Phi.	2	2	0	0	0	4	....	....	....	....	....	....	1991-92	1992-93
Mulvey, Grant	Chi., N.J.	10	586	149	135	284	816	42	10	5	15	70	....	1974-75	1983-84
Mulvey, Paul	Wsh., Pit., L.A.	4	225	30	51	81	613	....	....	....	....	....	....	1978-79	1981-82
• Mummery, Harry	Tor., Que., Mtl., Ham.	6	106	33	19	52	226	2	1	1	2	17	....	1917-18	1922-23
Muni, Craig	Tor., Edm., Chi., Buf., Wpg., Pit., Dal.	16	819	28	119	147	775	113	0	17	17	108	3	1981-82	1997-98
• Munro, Dunc	Mtl.M., Mtl.	8	239	28	18	46	172	21	2	2	4	18	1	1924-25	1931-32
• Munro, Gerry	Mtl.M., Tor.	2	34	1	0	1	37	....	....	....	....	....	....	1924-25	1925-26
Murdoch, Bob	Mtl., L.A., Atl., Cgy.	12	757	60	218	278	764	69	4	18	22	92	2	1970-71	1981-82
Murdoch, Bob	Cal., Cle., St.L.	4	260	72	85	157	127	....	....	....	....	....	....	1975-76	1978-79
Murdoch, Don	NYR, Edm., Det.	6	320	121	117	238	155	24	10	8	18	16	....	1976-77	1981-82
• Murdoch, Murray	NYR	11	508	84	108	192	197	55	9	12	21	28	2	1926-27	1936-37
Murphy, Brian	Det.	1	1	0	0	0	0	....	....	....	....	....	....	1974-75	1974-75
Murphy, Gord	Phi., Bos., Fla., Atl.	14	862	85	238	323	668	53	3	16	19	35	....	1988-89	2001-02
Murphy, Joe	Det., Edm., Chi., St.L., S.J., Bos., Wsh.	15	779	233	295	528	810	120	34	43	77	185	1	1986-87	2000-01
Murphy, Larry	L.A., Wsh., Min., Pit., Tor., Det.	21	1615	287	929	1216	1084	215	37	115	152	201	4	1980-81	2000-01
Murphy, Mike	St.L., NYR, L.A.	12	831	238	318	556	514	66	13	23	36	54	....	1971-72	1982-83
Murphy, Rob	Van., Ott., L.A.	7	125	9	12	21	152	4	0	0	0	2	....	1987-88	1993-94
Murphy, Ron	NYR, Chi., Det., Bos.	18	889	205	274	479	460	53	7	8	15	26	2	1952-53	1969-70
Murray, Allan	NYA	7	271	5	9	14	163	14	0	0	0	10	....	1933-34	1939-40
Murray, Bob	Atl., Van.	4	194	6	16	22	98	10	1	1	2	15	....	1973-74	1976-77
Murray, Bob	Chi.	15	1008	132	382	514	873	112	19	37	56	106	....	1975-76	1989-90
Murray, Chris	Mtl., Hfd., Car., Ott., Chi., Dal.	6	242	16	18	34	550	15	1	0	1	12	....	1994-95	1999-00
Murray, Jim	L.A.	1	30	0	2	2	14	....	....	....	....	....	....	1967-68	1967-68
Murray, Ken	Tor., NYI, Det., K.C.	5	106	1	10	11	135	....	....	....	....	....	....	1969-70	1975-76
• Murray, Leo	Mtl.	1	6	0	0	0	2	....	....	....	....	....	....	1932-33	1932-33
Murray, Mike	Phi.	1	1	0	0	0	0	....	....	....	....	....	....	1987-88	1987-88
Murray, Pat	Phi.	2	25	3	1	4	15	....	....	....	....	....	....	1990-91	1991-92
Murray, Randy	Tor.	1	3	0	0	0	2	....	....	....	....	....	....	1969-70	1969-70
‡ Murray, Rem	Edm., NYR, Nsh.	9	560	94	121	215	161	62	5	12	17	18	....	1996-97	2005-06
Murray, Rob	Wsh., Wpg., Phx.	8	107	4	15	19	111	9	0	0	0	18	....	1989-90	1998-99
Murray, Terry	Cal., Phi., Det., Wsh.	8	302	4	76	80	199	18	2	2	4	10	....	1972-73	1981-82
Murray, Troy	Chi., Wpg., Ott., Pit., Col.	15	915	230	354	584	875	113	17	26	43	145	1	1981-82	1995-96
Murzyn, Dana	Hfd., Cgy., Van.	14	838	52	152	204	1571	82	9	10	19	166	1	1985-86	1998-99
Musil, Frantisek	Min., Cgy., Ott., Edm.	15	797	34	106	140	1241	42	2	4	6	47	....	1986-87	2000-01
Myers, Hap	Buf.	1	13	0	0	0	6	....	....	....	....	....	....	1970-71	1970-71
‡ Myhres, Brantt	T.B., Phi., S.J., Nsh., Wsh., Bos.	7	154	6	2	8	687	....	....	....	....	....	....	1994-95	2002-03
Myles, Vic	NYR	1	45	6	9	15	57	....	....	....	....	....	....	1942-43	1942-43
Myrvold, Anders	Col., Bos., NYI, Det.	4	33	0	5	5	12	....	....	....	....	....	....	1995-96	2003-04

N

Name	NHL Teams	NHL Seasons	Regular Schedule GP	G	A	TP	PIM	Playoffs GP	G	A	TP	PIM	NHL Cup Wins	First NHL Season	Last NHL Season
‡ Nabokov, Dmitri	Chi., NYI	3	55	11	13	24	28	....	....	....	....	....	....	1997-98	1999-00
Nachbaur, Don	Hfd., Edm., Phi.	8	223	23	46	69	465	11	1	1	2	24	....	1980-81	1989-90
Nahrgang, Jim	Det.	3	57	5	12	17	34	....	....	....	....	....	....	1974-75	1976-77
Namestnikov, John	Van., NYI, Nsh.	6	43	0	9	9	24	2	0	0	0	2	....	1993-94	1999-00
Nanne, Lou	Min.	11	635	68	157	225	356	32	4	10	14	8	....	1967-68	1977-78
Nantais, Rich	Min.	3	63	5	4	9	79	....	....	....	....	....	....	1974-75	1976-77
Napier, Mark	Mtl., Min., Edm., Buf.	11	767	235	306	541	157	82	18	24	42	11	2	1978-79	1988-89
‡ Nash, Tyson	St.L., Phx.	7	374	27	37	64	673	23	3	2	5	52	....	1998-99	2005-06
Naslund, Mats	Mtl., Bos.	9	651	251	383	634	111	102	35	57	92	33	1	1982-83	1994-95
Nattrass, Ralph	Chi.	4	223	18	38	56	308	....	....	....	....	....	....	1946-47	1949-50
Nattress, Ric	Mtl., St.L., Cgy., Tor., Phi.	11	536	29	135	164	377	67	5	10	15	60	1	1982-83	1992-93
Natyshak, Mike	Que.	1	4	0	0	0	0	....	....	....	....	....	....	1987-88	1987-88
Nazarov, Andrei	S.J., T.B., Cgy., Ana., Bos., Phx., Min.	12	571	53	71	124	1409	9	0	0	0	11	....	1993-94	2005-06
‡ Ndur, Rumun	Buf., NYR, Atl.	4	69	2	3	5	137	....	....	....	....	....	....	1996-97	1999-00
Neaton, Pat	Pit.	1	9	1	1	2	12	....	....	....	....	....	....	1993-94	1993-94
Nechayev, Viktor	L.A.	1	3	1	0	1	0	....	....	....	....	....	....	1982-83	1982-83
Neckar, Stan	Ott., NYR, Phx., T.B., Nsh.	10	510	12	41	53	316	29	0	3	3	8	1	1994-95	2003-04
Nedomansky, Vaclav	Det., NYR, St.L.	6	421	122	156	278	88	7	3	5	8	0	....	1977-78	1982-83
‡ Nedorost, Andrej	CBJ	3	28	2	3	5	12	....	....	....	....	....	....	2001-02	2003-04
‡ Nedorost, Vaclav	Col., Fla.	3	99	10	10	20	34	....	....	....	....	....	....	2001-02	2003-04
‡ Nedved, Petr	Van., St.L., NYR, Pit., Edm., Phx., Phi.	15	982	310	407	717	708	71	19	23	42	64	....	1990-91	2006-07
Nedved, Zdenek	Tor.	3	31	4	6	10	14	....	....	....	....	....	....	1994-95	1996-97
Needham, Mike	Pit., Dal.	3	86	9	5	14	16	14	2	0	2	4	1	1991-92	1993-94
Neely, Bob	Tor., Col.	5	283	39	59	98	266	26	5	7	12	15	....	1973-74	1977-78
Neely, Cam	Van., Bos.	13	726	395	299	694	1241	93	57	32	89	168	....	1983-84	1995-96
Neilson, Jim	NYR, Cal., Cle.	16	1023	69	299	368	904	65	1	17	18	61	....	1962-63	1977-78
Nelson, Gordie	Tor.	1	3	0	0	0	11	....	....	....	....	....	....	1969-70	1969-70
‡ Nelson, Jeff	Wsh., Nsh.	3	52	3	8	11	20	3	0	0	0	4	....	1994-95	1998-99
Nelson, Todd	Pit., Wsh.	2	3	1	0	1	2	4	0	0	0	0	....	1991-92	1993-94
Nemchinov, Sergei	NYR, Van., NYI, N.J.	11	761	152	193	345	251	105	11	20	31	24	2	1991-92	2001-02
Nemecek, Jan	L.A.	2	7	1	0	1	4	....	....	....	....	....	....	1998-99	1999-00
Nemeth, Steve	NYR	1	12	2	0	2	2	....	....	....	....	....	....	1987-88	1987-88
‡ Nemirovsky, David	Fla.	4	91	16	22	38	42	3	1	0	1	0	....	1995-96	1998-99
Nesterenko, Eric	Tor., Chi.	21	1219	250	324	574	1273	124	13	24	37	127	1	1951-52	1971-72
Nethery, Lance	NYR, Edm.	2	41	11	14	25	14	14	5	3	8	9	....	1980-81	1981-82
Neufeld, Ray	Hfd., Wpg., Bos.	11	595	157	200	357	816	28	8	6	14	55	....	1979-80	1989-90
• Neville, Mike	Tor., NYA	3	65	5	5	10	14	2	0	0	0	0	....	1924-25	1930-31
Nevin, Bob	Tor., NYR, Min., L.A.	18	1128	307	419	726	211	84	16	18	34	24	2	1957-58	1975-76
Newberry, John	Mtl., Hfd.	4	22	0	4	4	6	2	0	0	0	0	....	1982-83	1985-86
Newell, Rick	Det.	2	6	0	0	0	0	....	....	....	....	....	....	1972-73	1973-74
Newman, Dan	NYR, Mtl., Edm.	4	126	17	24	41	63	3	0	0	0	4	....	1976-77	1979-80
• Newman, John	Det.	1	8	1	1	2	0	....	....	....	....	....	....	1930-31	1930-31
Nicholls, Bernie	L.A., NYR, Edm., N.J., Chi., S.J.	18	1127	475	734	1209	1292	118	42	72	114	164	....	1981-82	1998-99
• Nicholson, Al	Bos.	2	19	0	1	1	4	....	....	....	....	....	....	1955-56	1956-57
• Nicholson, Ed	Det.	1	1	0	0	0	0	....	....	....	....	....	....	1947-48	1947-48
• Nicholson, Hickey	Chi.	1	2	1	0	1	0	....	....	....	....	....	....	1937-38	1937-38
Nicholson, Neil	Oak., NYI	4	39	3	1	4	23	2	0	0	0	0	....	1969-70	1977-78
Nicholson, Paul	Wsh.	3	62	4	8	12	18	....	....	....	....	....	....	1974-75	1976-77
‡ Nickulas, Eric	Bos., St.L., Chi.	6	118	15	23	38	82	1	0	0	0	2	....	1998-99	2005-06
Nicolson, Graeme	Bos., Col., NYR	3	52	2	7	9	60	....	....	....	....	....	....	1978-79	1982-83
Nieckar, Barry	Hfd., Cgy., Ana.	4	8	0	0	0	21	....	....	....	....	....	....	1992-93	1997-98
Niekamp, Jim	Det.	2	29	0	2	2	37	....	....	....	....	....	....	1970-71	1971-72
Nielsen, Chris	CBJ	2	52	6	8	14	8	....	....	....	....	....	....	2000-01	2001-02
Nielsen, Jeff	NYR, Ana., Min.	5	252	20	27	47	70	4	0	0	0	2	....	1996-97	2000-01
Nielsen, Kirk	Bos.	1	6	0	0	0	0	....	....	....	....	....	....	1997-98	1997-98
‡ Niemi, Antti-Jussi	Ana.	2	29	1	1	2	22	....	....	....	....	....	....	2000-01	2001-02
Nienhuis, Kraig	Bos.	3	87	20	16	36	39	2	0	0	0	14	....	1985-86	1987-88
Nieuwendyk, Joe	Cgy., Dal., N.J., Tor., Fla.	20	1257	564	562	1126	677	158	66	50	116	91	3	1986-87	2006-07
• Nighbor, Frank	Ott., Tor.	13	349	139	98	237	249	20	4	9	13	13	4	1917-18	1929-30
Nigro, Frank	Tor.	2	68	8	18	26	39	3	0	0	0	2	....	1982-83	1983-84
‡ Niinimaa, Janne	Phi., Edm., NYI, Dal., Mtl.	10	741	54	265	319	733	59	3	21	24	60	....	1996-97	2006-07
‡ Nikolishin, Andrei	Hfd., Wsh., Chi., Col.	10	628	93	187	280	270	43	1	17	18	22	....	1994-95	2003-04
Nikulin, Igor	Ana.	1	....	....	....	....	....	1	0	0	0	0	....	1996-97	1996-97
Nilan, Chris	Mtl., NYR, Bos.	13	688	110	115	225	3043	111	8	9	17	541	1	1979-80	1991-92
Nill, Jim	St.L., Van., Bos., Wpg., Det.	9	524	58	87	145	854	59	10	5	15	203	....	1981-82	1989-90
Nilsson, Kent	Atl., Cgy., Min., Edm.	9	553	264	422	686	116	59	11	41	52	14	1	1979-80	1994-95
Nilsson, Ulf	NYR	4	170	57	112	169	85	25	8	14	22	27	....	1978-79	1982-83
Nistico, Lou	Col.	1	3	0	0	0	0	....	....	....	....	....	....	1977-78	1977-78
• Noble, Reg	Tor., Mtl.M., Det.	16	510	168	106	274	916	18	2	2	4	33	3	1917-18	1932-33
Noel, Claude	Wsh.	1	7	0	0	0	0	....	....	....	....	....	....	1979-80	1979-80
• Nolan, Paddy	Tor.	1	2	0	0	0	0	....	....	....	....	....	....	1921-22	1921-22
Nolan, Ted	Det., Pit.	3	78	6	16	22	105	....	....	....	....	....	....	1981-82	1985-86
Nolet, Simon	Phi., K.C., Pit., Col.	10	562	150	182	332	187	34	6	3	9	8	1	1967-68	1976-77

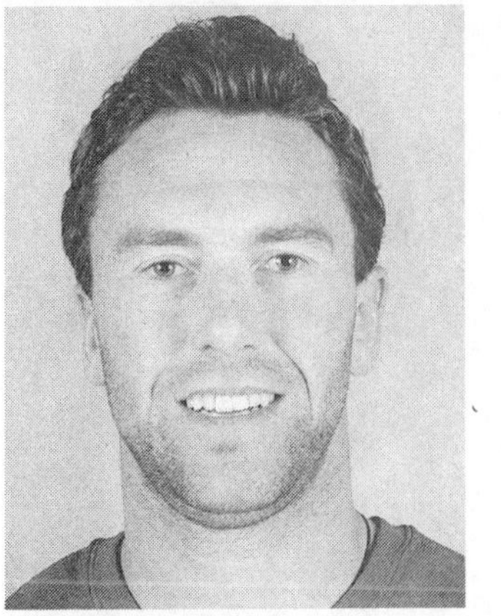

Petr Nedved

Joe Nieuwendyk

Mike OConnell

Gerry OFlaherty

Greg Parks

George Patterson

Barry Pederson

Jimmy Peters, Jr.

Name	NHL Teams	NHL Seasons	Regular Schedule GP	G	A	TP	PIM	Playoffs GP	G	A	TP	PIM	NHL Cup Wins	First NHL Season	Last NHL Season
Noonan, Brian	Chi., NYR, St.L., Van., Phx.	12	629	116	159	275	518	71	17	19	36	77	1	1987-88	1998-99
‡ Nordgren, Niklas	Car., Pit.	1	58	4	2	6	34	....	....	....	....	....	....	2005-06	2005-06
Nordmark, Robert	St.L., Van.	4	236	13	70	83	254	7	3	2	5	8	....	1987-88	1990-91
‡ Nordstrom, Peter	Bos.	1	2	0	0	0	0	....	....	....	....	....	....	1998-99	1998-99
Noris, Joe	Pit., St.L., Buf.	3	55	2	5	7	22	....	....	....	....	....	....	1971-72	1973-74
‡ Norris, Dwayne	Que., Ana.	3	20	2	4	6	8	....	....	....	....	....	....	1993-94	1995-96
Norrish, Rod	Min.	2	21	3	3	6	2	....	....	....	....	....	....	1973-74	1974-75
• Northcott, Baldy	Mtl.M., Chi.	11	446	133	112	245	273	31	8	5	13	14	1	1928-29	1938-39
Norton, Brad	Fla., L.A., Wsh., Ott., Det., S.J.	5	124	3	8	11	287	....	....	....	....	....	....	2001-02	2007-08
Norton, Jeff	NYI, S.J., St.L., Edm., T.B., Fla., Pit., Bos.	15	799	52	332	384	615	65	4	21	25	89	....	1987-88	2001-02
Norwich, Craig	Wpg., St.L., Col.	2	104	17	58	75	60	....	....	....	....	....	....	1979-80	1980-81
Norwood, Lee	Que., Wsh., St.L., Det., N.J., Hfd., Cgy.	12	503	58	153	211	1099	65	6	22	28	171	....	1980-81	1993-94
‡ Novoseltsev, Ivan	Fla., Phx.	5	234	31	44	75	112	....	....	....	....	....	....	1999-00	2003-04
Novy, Milan	Wsh.	1	73	18	30	48	16	2	0	0	0	0	....	1982-83	1982-83
Nowak, Hank	Pit., Det., Bos.	4	180	26	29	55	161	13	1	0	1	8	....	1973-74	1976-77
‡ Nurminen, Kai	L.A., Min.	2	69	17	11	28	24	....	....	....	....	....	....	1996-97	2000-01
Nykoluk, Mike	Tor.	1	32	3	1	4	20	....	....	....	....	....	....	1956-57	1956-57
Nylund, Gary	Tor., Chi., NYI	11	608	32	139	171	1235	24	0	6	6	63	....	1982-83	1992-93
• Nyrop, Bill	Mtl., Min.	4	207	12	51	63	101	35	1	7	8	22	3	1975-76	1981-82
Nystrom, Bob	NYI	14	900	235	278	513	1248	157	39	44	83	236	4	1972-73	1985-86

O

Name	NHL Teams	NHL Seasons	Regular Schedule GP	G	A	TP	PIM	Playoffs GP	G	A	TP	PIM	NHL Cup Wins	First NHL Season	Last NHL Season
Oates, Adam	Det., St.L., Bos., Wsh., Phi., Ana., Edm.	19	1337	341	1079	1420	415	163	42	114	156	66	....	1985-86	2003-04
• Oatman, Russell	Det., Mtl.M., NYR	3	120	20	9	29	100	15	1	0	1	18	....	1926-27	1928-29
O'Brien, Dennis	Min., Col., Cle., Bos.	10	592	31	91	122	1017	34	1	2	3	101	....	1970-71	1979-80
O'Brien, Ellard	Bos.	1	2	0	0	0	0	....	....	....	....	....	....	1955-56	1955-56
‡ Obsut, Jaroslav	St.L., Col.	2	7	0	0	0	2	....	....	....	....	....	....	2000-01	2001-02
O'Callahan, Jack	Chi., N.J.	7	389	27	104	131	541	32	4	11	15	41	....	1982-83	1988-89
O'Connell, Mike	Chi., Bos., Det.	13	860	105	334	439	605	82	8	24	32	64	....	1977-78	1989-90
• O'Connor, Buddy	Mtl., NYR	10	509	140	257	397	34	53	15	21	36	6	2	1941-42	1950-51
O'Connor, Myles	N.J., Ana.	4	43	3	4	7	69	....	....	....	....	....	....	1990-91	1993-94
Oddleifson, Chris	Bos., Van.	9	524	95	191	286	464	14	1	6	7	8	....	1972-73	1980-81
Odelein, Lyle	Mtl., N.J., Phx., CBJ, Chi., Dal., Fla., Pit.	16	1056	50	202	252	2316	86	5	13	18	209	1	1989-90	2005-06
Odelein, Selmar	Edm.	3	18	0	2	2	35	....	....	....	....	....	....	1985-86	1988-89
Odgers, Jeff	S.J., Bos., Col., Atl.	12	821	75	70	145	2364	47	2	1	3	73	....	1991-92	2002-03
Odjick, Gino	Van., NYI, Phi., Mtl.	12	605	64	73	137	2567	44	4	1	5	142	....	1990-91	2001-02
O'Donnell, Fred	Bos.	2	115	15	11	26	98	5	0	1	1	5	....	1972-73	1973-74
O'Donoghue, Don	Oak., Cal.	3	125	18	17	35	35	3	0	0	0	0	....	1969-70	1971-72
Odrowski, Gerry	Det., Oak., St.L.	6	309	12	19	31	111	30	0	1	1	16	....	1960-61	1971-72
O'Dwyer, Bill	L.A., Bos.	5	120	9	13	22	108	10	0	0	0	2	....	1983-84	1989-90
O'Flaherty, Gerry	Tor., Van., Atl.	8	438	99	95	194	168	7	2	2	4	6	....	1971-72	1978-79
• O'Flaherty, Peanuts	NYA, Bro.	2	21	5	1	6	0	....	....	....	....	....	....	1940-41	1941-42
Ogilvie, Brian	Chi., St.L.	6	90	15	21	36	29	....	....	....	....	....	....	1972-73	1978-79
• O'Grady, George	Mtl.W.	1	4	0	0	0	0	....	....	....	....	....	....	1917-18	1917-18
Ogrodnick, John	Det., Que., NYR	14	928	402	425	827	260	41	18	8	26	6	....	1979-80	1992-93
‡ Ojanen, Janne	N.J.	4	98	21	23	44	28	3	0	2	2	0	....	1988-89	1992-93
Okerlund, Todd	NYI	1	4	0	0	0	2	....	....	....	....	....	....	1987-88	1987-88
Oksiuta, Roman	Edm., Van., Ana., Pit.	4	153	46	41	87	100	10	2	3	5	0	....	1993-94	1996-97
‡ Olausson, Fredrik	Wpg., Edm., Ana., Pit., Det.	16	1022	147	434	581	450	71	6	23	29	28	1	1986-87	2002-03
Olczyk, Ed	Chi., Tor., Wpg., NYR, L.A., Pit.	16	1031	342	452	794	874	57	19	15	34	57	1	1984-85	1999-00
Oliver, David	Edm., NYR, Ott., Phx., Dal.	9	233	49	49	98	84	10	0	0	0	2	....	1994-95	2005-06
• Oliver, Harry	Bos., NYA	11	463	127	85	212	147	35	10	6	16	24	1	1926-27	1936-37
Oliver, Murray	Det., Bos., Tor., Min.	17	1127	274	454	728	320	35	9	16	25	10	....	1957-58	1974-75
Oliwa, Krzysztof	N.J., CBJ, Pit., NYR, Bos., Cgy.	9	410	17	28	45	1447	32	2	0	2	47	1	1996-97	2005-06
Olmstead, Bert	Chi., Mtl., Tor.	14	848	181	421	602	884	115	16	43	59	101	5	1948-49	1961-62
Olsen, Darryl	Cgy.	1	1	0	0	0	0	....	....	....	....	....	....	1991-92	1991-92
Olson, Dennis	Det.	1	4	0	0	0	0	....	....	....	....	....	....	1957-58	1957-58
‡ Olson, Josh	Fla.	1	5	1	0	1	0	....	....	....	....	....	....	2003-04	2003-04
Olsson, Christer	St.L., Ott.	2	56	4	12	16	24	3	0	0	0	0	....	1995-96	1996-97
‡ Olvestad, Jimmie	T.B.	2	111	3	14	17	40	....	....	....	....	....	....	2001-02	2002-03
• O'Neil, Jim	Bos., Mtl.	6	156	6	30	36	109	9	1	1	2	13	....	1933-34	1941-42
O'Neil, Paul	Van., Bos.	2	6	0	0	0	0	....	....	....	....	....	....	1973-74	1975-76
• O'Neill, Tom	Tor.	2	66	10	12	22	53	4	0	0	0	6	1	1943-44	1944-45
Orban, Bill	Chi., Min.	3	114	8	15	23	67	3	0	0	0	0	....	1967-68	1969-70
O'Ree, Willie	Bos.	2	45	4	10	14	26	....	....	....	....	....	....	1957-58	1960-61
O'Regan, Tom	Pit.	3	61	5	12	17	10	....	....	....	....	....	....	1983-84	1985-86
O'Reilly, Terry	Bos.	14	891	204	402	606	2095	108	25	42	67	335	....	1971-72	1984-85
Orlando, Gates	Buf.	3	98	18	26	44	51	5	0	4	4	14	....	1984-85	1986-87
• Orlando, Jimmy	Det.	6	199	6	25	31	375	36	0	9	9	105	1	1936-37	1942-43
Orleski, Dave	Mtl.	2	2	0	0	0	0	....	....	....	....	....	....	1980-81	1981-82
Orr, Bobby	Bos., Chi.	12	657	270	645	915	953	74	26	66	92	107	2	1966-67	1978-79
Orszagh, Vladimir	NYI, Nsh., St.L.	7	289	54	65	119	194	6	2	0	2	4	....	1997-98	2005-06
Osborne, Keith	St.L., T.B.	2	16	1	3	4	16	....	....	....	....	....	....	1989-90	1992-93
Osborne, Mark	Det., NYR, Tor., Wpg.	14	919	212	319	531	1152	87	12	16	28	141	....	1981-82	1994-95
Osburn, Randy	Tor., Phi.	2	27	0	2	2	0	....	....	....	....	....	....	1972-73	1974-75
O'Shea, Danny	Min., Chi., St.L.	5	369	64	115	179	265	39	3	7	10	61	....	1968-69	1972-73
O'Shea, Kevin	Buf., St.L.	3	134	13	18	31	85	12	2	1	3	10	....	1970-71	1972-73
Osiecki, Mark	Cgy., Ott., Wpg., Min.	2	93	3	11	14	43	....	....	....	....	....	....	1991-92	1992-93
O'Sullivan, Chris	Cgy., Van., Ana.	5	62	2	17	19	16	....	....	....	....	....	....	1996-97	2002-03
Otevrel, Jaroslav	S.J.	2	16	3	4	7	2	....	....	....	....	....	....	1992-93	1993-94
Otto, Joel	Cgy., Phi.	14	943	195	313	508	1934	122	27	47	74	207	1	1984-85	1997-98
Ouellette, Eddie	Chi.	1	43	3	2	5	11	1	0	0	0	0	....	1935-36	1935-36
Ouellette, Gerry	Bos.	1	34	5	4	9	0	....	....	....	....	....	....	1960-61	1960-61
Owchar, Dennis	Pit., Col.	6	288	30	85	115	200	10	1	1	2	8	....	1974-75	1979-80
• Owen, George	Bos.	5	183	44	33	77	151	21	2	5	7	25	1	1928-29	1932-33

P

Name	NHL Teams	NHL Seasons	Regular Schedule GP	G	A	TP	PIM	Playoffs GP	G	A	TP	PIM	NHL Cup Wins	First NHL Season	Last NHL Season
Pachal, Clayton	Bos., Col.	3	35	2	3	5	95	....	....	....	....	....	....	1976-77	1978-79
Paddock, John	Wsh., Phi., Que.	5	87	8	14	22	86	5	2	0	2	0	....	1975-76	1982-83
Paek, Jim	Pit., L.A., Ott.	5	217	5	29	34	155	27	1	4	5	8	2	1990-91	1994-95
Paiement, Rosaire	Phi., Van.	5	190	48	52	100	343	3	3	0	3	0	....	1967-68	1971-72
Paiement, Wilf	K.C., Col., Tor., Que., NYR, Buf., Pit.	14	946	356	458	814	1757	69	18	17	35	185	....	1974-75	1987-88
• Palangio, Pete	Mtl., Det., Chi.	5	71	13	10	23	28	7	0	0	0	0	1	1926-27	1937-38
• Palazzari, Aldo	Bos., NYR	1	35	8	3	11	4	....	....	....	....	....	....	1943-44	1943-44
Palazzari, Doug	St.L.	4	108	18	20	38	23	2	0	0	0	0	....	1974-75	1978-79
Palffy, Ziggy	NYI, L.A., Pit.	12	684	329	384	713	322	24	9	10	19	8	....	1993-94	2005-06
Palmer, Brad	Min., Bos.	3	168	32	38	70	58	29	9	5	14	16	....	1980-81	1982-83
Palmer, Rob	Chi.	3	16	0	3	3	2	....	....	....	....	....	....	1973-74	1975-76
Palmer, Robert	L.A., N.J.	7	320	9	101	110	115	8	1	2	3	6	....	1977-78	1983-84
• Panagabko, Ed	Bos.	2	29	0	3	3	38	....	....	....	....	....	....	1955-56	1956-57
‡ Pankewicz, Greg	Ott., Cgy.	2	21	0	3	3	22	....	....	....	....	....	....	1993-94	1998-99
‡ Panteleev, Grigori	Bos., NYI	4	54	8	6	14	12	....	....	....	....	....	....	1992-93	1995-96
• Papike, Joe	Chi.	3	20	3	3	6	4	5	0	2	2	0	....	1940-41	1944-45
‡ Papineau, Justin	St.L., NYI	3	81	11	8	19	12	1	0	0	0	0	....	2001-02	2003-04
Pappin, Jim	Tor., Chi., Cal., Cle.	14	767	278	295	573	667	92	33	34	67	101	2	1963-64	1976-77
Paradise, Bob	Min., Atl., Pit., Wsh.	8	368	8	54	62	393	12	0	1	1	19	....	1971-72	1978-79
• Pargeter, George	Mtl.	1	4	0	0	0	0	....	....	....	....	....	....	1946-47	1946-47
Parise, J.P.	Bos., Tor., Min., NYI, Cle.	14	890	238	356	594	706	86	27	31	58	87	....	1965-66	1978-79
Parizeau, Michel	St.L., Phi.	1	58	3	14	17	18	....	....	....	....	....	....	1971-72	1971-72
Park, Brad	NYR, Bos., Det.	17	1113	213	683	896	1429	161	35	90	125	217	....	1968-69	1984-85
Parker, Jeff	Buf., Hfd.	5	141	16	19	35	163	5	0	0	0	26	....	1986-87	1990-91
• Parkes, Ernie	Mtl.M.	1	17	0	0	0	2	....	....	....	....	....	....	1924-25	1924-25
Parks, Greg	NYI	3	23	1	2	3	6	2	0	0	0	0	....	1990-91	1992-93
• Parsons, George	Tor.	3	78	12	13	25	20	7	3	2	5	11	....	1936-37	1938-39
‡ Parssinen, Timo	Ana.	1	17	0	3	3	2	....	....	....	....	....	....	2001-02	2001-02
• Pasek, Dusan	Min.	1	48	4	10	14	30	2	1	0	1	0	....	1988-89	1988-89
Pasin, Dave	Bos., L.A.	2	76	18	19	37	50	3	0	1	1	0	....	1985-86	1988-89
Paslawski, Greg	Mtl., St.L., Wpg., Buf., Que., Phi., Cgy.	11	650	187	185	372	169	60	19	13	32	25	....	1983-84	1993-94
‡ Patera, Pavel	Dal., Min.	2	32	2	7	9	8	....	....	....	....	....	....	1999-00	2000-01
Paterson, Joe	Det., Phi., L.A., NYR	9	291	19	37	56	829	22	3	4	7	77	....	1980-81	1988-89

Name	NHL Teams	NHL Seasons	Regular Schedule GP	G	A	TP	PIM	Playoffs GP	G	A	TP	PIM	NHL Cup Wins	First NHL Season	Last NHL Season
Paterson, Mark	Hfd.	4	29	3	3	6	33	....	....	....	....	....	....	1982-83	1985-86
Paterson, Rick	Chi.	9	430	50	43	93	136	61	7	10	17	51	....	1978-79	1986-87
Patey, Doug	Wsh.	3	45	4	2	6	8	....	....	....	....	....	....	1976-77	1978-79
Patey, Larry	Cal., St.L., NYR	12	717	153	163	316	631	40	8	10	18	57	....	1973-74	1984-85
Patrick, Craig	Cal., St.L., K.C., Wsh.	8	401	72	91	163	61	2	0	1	1	0	....	1971-72	1978-79
Patrick, Glenn	St.L., Cal., Cle.	4	38	2	3	5	72	....	....	....	....	....	....	1973-74	1976-77
Patrick, James	NYR, Hfd., Cgy., Buf.	21	1280	149	490	639	759	117	6	32	38	86	....	1983-84	2003-04
• Patrick, Lester	NYR	1	1	0	0	0	2	....	....	....	....	....	....	1926-27	1926-27
• Patrick, Lynn	NYR	10	455	145	190	335	240	44	10	6	16	22	1	1934-35	1945-46
• Patrick, Muzz	NYR	5	166	5	26	31	133	25	4	0	4	34	1	1937-38	1945-46
Patrick, Steve	Buf., NYR, Que.	6	250	40	68	108	242	12	0	1	1	12	....	1980-81	1985-86
Patterson, Colin	Cgy., Buf.	10	504	96	109	205	239	85	12	17	29	57	1	1983-84	1992-93
Patterson, Dennis	K.C., Phi.	3	138	6	22	28	67	....	....	....	....	....	....	1974-75	1979-80
Patterson, Ed	Pit.	3	68	3	3	6	56	....	....	....	....	....	....	1993-94	1996-97
• Patterson, George	Tor., Mtl., NYA, Bos., Det., St.L.	9	284	51	27	78	218	3	0	0	0	2	....	1926-27	1934-35
• Paul, Butch	Det.	1	3	0	0	0	0	....	....	....	....	....	....	1964-65	1964-65
‡ Paul, Jeff	Col.	1	2	0	0	0	7	....	....	....	....	....	....	2002-03	2002-03
• Paulhus, Rollie	Mtl.	1	33	0	0	0	0	....	....	....	....	....	....	1925-26	1925-26
Pavelich, Mark	NYR, Min., S.J.	7	355	137	192	329	340	23	7	17	24	14	....	1981-82	1991-92
Pavelich, Marty	Det.	10	634	93	159	252	454	91	13	15	28	74	4	1947-48	1956-57
Pavese, Jim	St.L., NYR, Det., Hfd.	8	328	13	44	57	689	34	0	6	6	81	....	1981-82	1988-89
• Payer, Evariste	Mtl.	1	1	0	0	0	0	....	....	....	....	....	....	1917-18	1917-18
Payne, Davis	Bos.	2	22	0	1	1	14	....	....	....	....	....	....	1995-96	1996-97
Payne, Steve	Min.	10	613	228	238	466	435	71	35	35	70	60	....	1978-79	1987-88
Paynter, Kent	Chi., Wsh., Wpg., Ott.	7	37	1	3	4	69	4	0	0	0	10	....	1987-88	1993-94
Peake, Pat	Wsh.	5	134	28	41	69	105	13	2	2	4	20	....	1993-94	1997-98
• Pearson, Mel	NYR, Pit.	5	38	2	6	8	25	....	....	....	....	....	....	1959-60	1967-68
Pearson, Rob	Tor., Wsh., St.L.	6	269	56	54	110	645	33	4	2	6	94	....	1991-92	1996-97
Pearson, Scott	Tor., Que., Edm., Buf., NYI	10	292	56	42	98	615	10	2	0	2	14	....	1988-89	1999-00
Peat, Stephen	Wsh.	4	130	8	2	10	234	....	....	....	....	....	....	2001-02	2005-06
Pedersen, Allen	Bos., Min., Hfd.	8	428	5	36	41	487	64	0	0	0	91	....	1986-87	1993-94
Pederson, Barry	Bos., Van., Pit., Hfd.	12	701	238	416	654	472	34	22	30	52	25	1	1980-81	1991-92
‡ Pederson, Denis	N.J., Van., Phx., Nsh.	8	435	57	71	128	398	27	1	5	6	8	....	1995-96	2002-03
Pederson, Mark	Mtl., Phi., S.J., Det.	5	169	35	50	85	77	2	0	0	0	0	....	1989-90	1993-94
Pederson, Tom	S.J., Tor.	5	240	20	49	69	142	24	1	11	12	10	....	1992-93	1996-97
• Peer, Bert	Det.	1	1	0	0	0	0	....	....	....	....	....	....	1939-40	1939-40
Peirson, Johnny	Bos.	11	545	153	173	326	315	49	10	16	26	26	....	1946-47	1957-58
Pelensky, Perry	Chi.	1	4	0	0	0	5	....	....	....	....	....	....	1983-84	1983-84
Pellerin, Scott	N.J., St.L., Min., Car., Bos., Dal., Phx.	11	536	72	126	198	320	37	1	2	3	26	....	1992-93	2003-04
Pelletier, Roger	Phi.	1	1	0	0	0	0	....	....	....	....	....	....	1967-68	1967-68
Peloffy, Andre	Wsh.	1	9	0	0	0	0	....	....	....	....	....	....	1974-75	1974-75
Peluso, Mike	Chi., Ott., N.J., St.L., Cgy.	9	458	38	52	90	1951	62	3	4	7	107	1	1989-90	1997-98
Peluso, Mike	Chi., Phi.	2	38	4	2	6	19	....	....	....	....	....	....	2001-02	2003-04
Pelyk, Mike	Tor.	9	441	26	88	114	566	40	0	3	3	41	....	1967-68	1977-78
Penney, Chad	Ott.	1	3	0	0	0	2	....	....	....	....	....	....	1993-94	1993-94
Pennington, Cliff	Mtl., Bos.	3	101	17	42	59	6	....	....	....	....	....	....	1960-61	1962-63
Peplinski, Jim	Cgy.	11	711	161	263	424	1467	99	15	31	46	382	1	1980-81	1994-95
Perlini, Fred	Tor.	2	8	2	3	5	0	....	....	....	....	....	....	1981-82	1983-84
Perreault, Fern	NYR	2	3	0	0	0	0	....	....	....	....	....	....	1947-48	1949-50
Perreault, Gilbert	Buf.	17	1191	512	814	1326	500	90	33	70	103	44	....	1970-71	1986-87
Perry, Brian	Oak., Buf.	3	96	16	29	45	24	8	1	1	2	4	....	1968-69	1970-71
Persson, Ricard	N.J., St.L., Ott.	7	229	10	44	54	262	26	1	3	4	59	....	1995-96	2001-02
Persson, Stefan	NYI	9	622	52	317	369	574	102	7	50	57	69	4	1977-78	1985-86
Pesut, George	Cal.	2	92	3	22	25	130	....	....	....	....	....	....	1974-75	1975-76
• Peters, Frank	NYR	1	43	0	0	0	59	4	0	0	0	2	....	1930-31	1930-31
Peters, Garry	Mtl., NYR, Phi., Bos.	8	311	34	34	68	261	9	2	2	4	31	1	1964-65	1971-72
• Peters, Jimmy	Mtl., Bos., Det., Chi.	9	574	125	150	275	186	60	5	9	14	22	3	1945-46	1953-54
Peters, Jimmy	Det., L.A.	9	309	37	36	73	48	11	0	2	2	2	....	1964-65	1974-75
Peters, Steve	Col.	1	2	0	1	1	0	....	....	....	....	....	....	1979-80	1979-80
Peterson, Brent	Det., Buf., Van., Hfd.	11	620	72	141	213	484	31	4	4	8	65	....	1978-79	1988-89
Peterson, Brent	T.B.	3	56	9	1	10	6	....	....	....	....	....	....	1996-97	1998-99
Petit, Michel	Van., NYR, Que., Tor., Cgy., L.A., T.B., Edm., Phi., Phx.	16	827	90	238	328	1839	19	0	2	2	61	....	1982-83	1997-98
Petrenko, Sergei	Buf.	1	14	0	4	4	0	....	....	....	....	....	....	1993-94	1993-94
‡ Petrov, Oleg	Mtl., Nsh.	8	382	72	115	187	101	20	1	6	7	2	....	1992-93	2002-03
‡ Petrovicky, Robert	Hfd., Dal., St.L., T.B., NYI	8	208	27	38	65	118	2	0	0	0	0	....	1992-93	2000-01
Pettersson, Jorgen	St.L., Hfd., Wsh.	6	435	174	192	366	117	44	15	12	27	4	....	1980-81	1985-86
‡ Pettinen, Tomi	NYI	3	24	0	0	0	18	....	....	....	....	....	....	2002-03	2005-06
• Pettinger, Eric	Bos., Tor., Ott.	3	98	7	12	19	83	4	1	0	1	8	....	1928-29	1930-31
• Pettinger, Gord	NYR, Det., Bos.	8	292	42	74	116	77	47	4	5	9	11	4	1932-33	1939-40
Phair, Lyle	L.A.	3	48	6	7	13	12	1	0	0	0	0	....	1985-86	1987-88
Phillipoff, Harold	Atl., Chi.	3	141	26	57	83	267	6	0	2	2	9	....	1977-78	1979-80
• Phillips, Bill	Mtl.M.	1	27	1	1	2	6	4	0	0	0	2	....	1929-30	1929-30
• Phillips, Charlie	Mtl.	1	17	0	0	0	6	....	....	....	....	....	....	1942-43	1942-43
• Phillips, Merlyn	Mtl.M., NYA	8	302	52	31	83	232	24	5	1	6	19	1	1925-26	1932-33
Picard, Michel	Hfd., S.J., Ott., St.L., Edm., Phi.	9	166	28	42	70	103	5	0	0	0	2	....	1990-91	2000-01
Picard, Noel	Mtl., St.L., Atl.	7	335	12	63	75	616	50	2	11	13	167	1	1964-65	1972-73
Picard, Robert	Wsh., Tor., Mtl., Wpg., Que., Det.	13	899	104	319	423	1025	36	5	15	20	39	....	1977-78	1989-90
Picard, Roger	St.L.	1	15	2	2	4	21	....	....	....	....	....	....	1967-68	1967-68
Pichette, Dave	Que., St.L., N.J., NYR	7	322	41	140	181	348	28	3	7	10	54	....	1980-81	1987-88
Picketts, Hal	NYA	1	48	3	1	4	32	....	....	....	....	....	....	1933-34	1933-34
Pidhirny, Harry	Bos.	1	2	0	0	0	0	....	....	....	....	....	....	1957-58	1957-58
Pierce, Randy	Col., N.J., Hfd.	8	277	62	76	138	223	2	0	0	0	0	....	1977-78	1984-85
Pike, Alf	NYR	6	234	42	77	119	145	21	4	2	6	12	1	1939-40	1946-47
Pilon, Rich	NYI, NYR, St.L.	14	631	8	69	77	1745	15	0	0	0	50	....	1988-89	2001-02
Pilote, Pierre	Chi., Tor.	14	890	80	418	498	1251	86	8	53	61	102	1	1955-56	1968-69
Pinder, Gerry	Chi., Cal.	3	223	55	69	124	135	17	0	4	4	6	....	1969-70	1971-72
‡ Pirjeta, Lasse	CBJ, Pit.	3	146	23	27	50	50	....	....	....	....	....	....	2002-03	2005-06
‡ Pirnes, Esa	L.A.	1	57	3	8	11	12	....	....	....	....	....	....	2003-04	2003-04
‡ Piros, Kamil	Atl., Fla.	3	28	4	4	8	10	....	....	....	....	....	....	2001-02	2003-04
Pirus, Alex	Min., Det.	4	159	30	28	58	94	2	0	1	1	2	....	1976-77	1979-80
‡ Pisa, Ales	Edm., NYR	2	53	1	3	4	26	....	....	....	....	....	....	2001-02	2002-03
Pitlick, Lance	Ott., Fla.	8	393	16	33	49	298	24	0	2	2	21	....	1994-95	2001-02
• Pitre, Didier	Mtl.	6	127	64	34	98	84	9	2	4	6	16	....	1917-18	1922-23
‡ Pittis, Domenic	Pit., Buf., Edm., Nsh.	7	86	5	11	16	71	3	0	0	0	2	....	1996-97	2003-04
‡ Pivko, Libor	Nsh.	1	1	0	0	0	0	....	....	....	....	....	....	2003-04	2003-04
Pivonka, Michal	Wsh.	13	825	181	418	599	478	95	19	36	55	86	....	1986-87	1998-99
• Plager, Barclay	St.L.	10	614	44	187	231	1115	68	3	20	23	182	....	1967-68	1976-77
Plager, Bill	Min., St.L., Atl.	9	263	4	34	38	294	31	0	2	2	26	....	1967-68	1975-76
Plager, Bob	NYR, St.L.	14	644	20	126	146	802	74	2	17	19	195	....	1964-65	1977-78
Plamondon, Gerry	Mtl.	5	74	7	13	20	10	11	5	2	7	2	1	1945-46	1950-51
Plante, Cam	Tor.	1	2	0	0	0	0	....	....	....	....	....	....	1984-85	1984-85
Plante, Dan	NYI	4	159	9	14	23	135	1	0	1	1	2	....	1993-94	1997-98
Plante, Derek	Buf., Dal., Chi., Phi.	8	450	96	152	248	138	41	6	10	16	18	1	1993-94	2000-01
Plante, Pierre	Phi., St.L., Chi., NYR, Que.	9	599	125	172	297	599	33	2	6	8	51	....	1971-72	1979-80
Plantery, Mark	Wpg.	1	25	1	5	6	14	....	....	....	....	....	....	1980-81	1980-81
Plavsic, Adrien	St.L., Van., T.B., Ana.	8	214	16	56	72	161	13	1	7	8	4	....	1989-90	1996-97
• Plaxton, Hugh	Mtl.M.	1	15	1	2	3	4	....	....	....	....	....	....	1932-33	1932-33
Playfair, Jim	Edm., Chi.	3	21	2	4	6	51	....	....	....	....	....	....	1983-84	1988-89
Playfair, Larry	Buf., L.A.	12	688	26	94	120	1812	43	0	6	6	111	....	1978-79	1989-90
Pleau, Larry	Mtl.	3	94	9	15	24	27	4	0	0	0	0	....	1969-70	1971-72
‡ Pletka, Vaclav	Phi.	1	1	0	0	0	0	....	....	....	....	....	....	2001-02	2001-02
• Pletsch, Charles	Ham.	1	1	0	0	0	0	....	....	....	....	....	....	1920-21	1920-21
Plett, Willi	Atl., Cgy., Min., Bos.	13	834	222	215	437	2572	83	24	22	46	466	....	1975-76	1987-88
Plumb, Rob	Det.	2	14	3	2	5	2	....	....	....	....	....	....	1977-78	1978-79
Plumb, Ron	Hfd.	1	26	3	4	7	14	....	....	....	....	....	....	1979-80	1979-80
Poapst, Steve	Wsh., Chi., Pit., St.L.	7	307	8	28	36	173	11	0	0	0	0	....	1995-96	2005-06
Pocza, Harvie	Wsh.	2	3	0	0	0	2	....	....	....	....	....	....	1979-80	1981-82
Poddubny, Walt	Edm., Tor., NYR, Que., N.J.	11	468	184	238	422	454	19	7	2	9	12	....	1981-82	1991-92
Podein, Shjon	Edm., Phi., Col., St.L.	11	699	100	106	206	439	127	14	13	27	132	1	1992-93	2002-03
‡ Podkonicky, Andrej	Fla., Wsh.	2	8	1	0	1	2	....	....	....	....	....	....	2000-01	2003-04
Podloski, Ray	Bos.	1	8	0	1	1	17	....	....	....	....	....	....	1988-89	1988-89
Podollan, Jason	Fla., Tor., L.A., NYI	4	41	1	5	6	19	....	....	....	....	....	....	1996-97	2001-02
Podolsky, Nels	Det.	1	1	0	0	0	0	7	0	0	0	4	....	1948-49	1948-49
Poeschek, Rudy	NYR, Wpg., T.B., St.L.	12	364	6	25	31	817	5	0	0	0	18	....	1987-88	1999-00

Merlyn Phillips

Gerry Plamondon

Andre Pronovost

Marcel Pronovost

Marc Reaume

Mark Renaud

Mike Ricci

Vic Ripley

Name	NHL Teams	NHL Seasons	Regular Schedule GP	G	A	TP	PIM	Playoffs GP	G	A	TP	PIM	NHL Cup Wins	First NHL Season	Last NHL Season
• Poeta, Tony	Chi.	1	1	0	0	0	0	....	....	....	....	....	....	1951-52	1951-52
• Poile, Bud	Tor., Chi., Det., NYR, Bos.	7	311	107	122	229	91	23	4	5	9	8	1	1942-43	1949-50
Poile, Don	Det.	2	66	7	9	16	12	4	0	0	0	0	....	1954-55	1957-58
• Poirier, Gordie	Mtl.	1	10	0	0	0	0	....	....	....	....	....	....	1939-40	1939-40
Polanic, Tom	Min.	2	19	0	2	2	53	5	1	1	2	4	....	1969-70	1970-71
• Polich, John	NYR	2	3	0	1	1	0	....	....	....	....	....	....	1939-40	1940-41
Polich, Mike	Mtl., Min.	5	226	24	29	53	57	23	2	1	3	2	1	1976-77	1980-81
Polis, Greg	Pit., St.L., NYR, Wsh.	10	615	174	169	343	391	7	0	2	2	6	....	1970-71	1979-80
Poliziani, Dan	Bos.	1	1	0	0	0	0	3	0	0	0	0	....	1958-59	1958-59
‡ Pollock, Jame	St.L.	1	9	0	0	0	6	....	....	....	....	....	....	2003-04	2003-04
Polonich, Dennis	Det.	8	390	59	82	141	1242	7	1	0	1	19	....	1974-75	1982-83
Pooley, Paul	Wpg.	2	15	0	3	3	0	....	....	....	....	....	....	1984-85	1985-86
Popein, Larry	NYR, Oak.	8	449	80	141	221	162	16	1	4	5	6	....	1954-55	1967-68
Popiel, Poul	Bos., L.A., Det., Van., Edm.	7	224	13	41	54	210	4	1	0	1	4	....	1965-66	1979-80
Popovic, Peter	Mtl., NYR, Pit., Bos.	8	485	10	63	73	291	35	1	4	5	18	....	1993-94	2000-01
• Portland, Jack	Mtl., Bos., Chi.	10	381	15	56	71	323	33	1	3	4	25	1	1933-34	1942-43
Porvari, Jukka	Col., N.J.	2	39	3	9	12	4	....	....	....	....	....	....	1981-82	1982-83
Posa, Victor	Chi.	1	2	0	0	0	2	....	....	....	....	....	....	1985-86	1985-86
Posavad, Mike	St.L.	2	8	0	0	0	0	....	....	....	....	....	....	1985-86	1986-87
Posmyk, Marek	T.B.	2	19	1	2	3	20	....	....	....	....	....	....	1999-00	2000-01
Potomski, Barry	L.A., S.J.	3	68	6	5	11	227	....	....	....	....	....	....	1995-96	1997-98
Potvin, Denis	NYI	15	1060	310	742	1052	1356	185	56	108	164	253	4	1973-74	1987-88
Potvin, Jean	L.A., Phi., NYI, Cle., Min.	11	613	63	224	287	478	39	2	9	11	17	2	1970-71	1980-81
• Potvin, Marc	Det., L.A., Hfd., Bos.	6	121	3	5	8	456	13	0	1	1	50	....	1990-91	1995-96
Poudrier, Daniel	Que.	3	25	1	5	6	10	....	....	....	....	....	....	1985-86	1987-88
Poulin, Daniel	Min.	1	3	1	1	2	2	....	....	....	....	....	....	1981-82	1981-82
Poulin, Dave	Phi., Bos., Wsh.	13	724	205	325	530	482	129	31	42	73	132	....	1982-83	1994-95
Poulin, Patrick	Hfd., Chi., T.B., Mtl.	11	634	101	134	235	299	32	6	2	8	8	....	1991-92	2001-02
Pouzar, Jaroslav	Edm.	4	186	34	48	82	135	29	6	4	10	16	3	1982-83	1986-87
• Powell, Ray	Chi.	1	31	7	15	22	2	....	....	....	....	....	....	1950-51	1950-51
• Powis, Geoff	Chi.	1	2	0	0	0	0	....	....	....	....	....	....	1967-68	1967-68
Powis, Lynn	Chi., K.C.	2	130	19	33	52	25	1	0	0	0	0	....	1973-74	1974-75
Prajsler, Petr	L.A., Bos.	4	46	3	10	13	51	4	0	0	0	0	....	1987-88	1991-92
• Pratt, Babe	NYR, Tor., Bos.	12	517	83	209	292	463	63	12	17	29	90	2	1935-36	1946-47
• Pratt, Jack	Bos.	2	37	2	0	2	42	4	0	0	0	0	....	1930-31	1931-32
Pratt, Kelly	Pit.	1	22	0	6	6	15	....	....	....	....	....	....	1974-75	1974-75
Pratt, Tracy	Oak., Pit., Buf., Van., Col., Tor.	10	580	17	97	114	1026	25	0	1	1	62	....	1967-68	1976-77
Prentice, Dean	NYR, Bos., Det., Pit., Min.	22	1378	391	469	860	484	54	13	17	30	38	....	1952-53	1973-74
• Prentice, Eric	Tor.	1	5	0	0	0	4	....	....	....	....	....	....	1943-44	1943-44
Presley, Wayne	Chi., S.J., Buf., NYR, Tor.	12	684	155	147	302	953	83	26	17	43	142	....	1984-85	1995-96
Preston, Rich	Chi., N.J.	8	580	127	164	291	348	47	4	18	22	56	....	1979-80	1986-87
Preston, Yves	Phi.	2	28	7	3	10	4	....	....	....	....	....	....	1978-79	1980-81
Priakin, Sergei	Cgy.	3	46	3	8	11	2	1	0	0	0	0	....	1988-89	1990-91
Price, Jack	Chi.	3	57	4	6	10	24	4	0	0	0	0	....	1951-52	1953-54
Price, Noel	Tor., NYR, Det., Mtl., Pit., L.A., Atl.	14	499	14	114	128	333	12	0	1	1	8	1	1957-58	1975-76
Price, Pat	NYI, Edm., Pit., Que., NYR, Min.	13	726	43	218	261	1456	74	2	10	12	195	....	1975-76	1987-88
Price, Tom	Cal., Cle., Pit.	5	29	0	2	2	12	....	....	....	....	....	....	1974-75	1978-79
Priestlay, Ken	Buf., Pit.	6	168	27	34	61	63	14	0	0	0	21	1	1986-87	1991-92
• Primeau, Joe	Tor.	9	310	66	177	243	105	38	5	18	23	12	1	1927-28	1935-36
Primeau, Keith	Det., Hfd., Car., Phi.	15	909	266	353	619	1541	128	18	39	57	213	....	1990-91	2005-06
Primeau, Kevin	Van.	1	2	0	0	0	4	....	....	....	....	....	....	1980-81	1980-81
• Pringle, Ellie	NYA	1	6	0	0	0	0	....	....	....	....	....	....	1930-31	1930-31
Probert, Bob	Det., Chi.	16	935	163	221	384	3300	81	16	32	48	274	....	1985-86	2001-02
‡ Prochazka, Martin	Tor., Atl.	2	32	2	5	7	8	....	....	....	....	....	....	1997-98	1999-00
• Prodger, Goldie	Tor., Ham.	6	111	63	29	92	39	....	....	....	....	....	....	1919-20	1924-25
Prokhorov, Vitali	St.L.	3	83	19	11	30	35	4	0	0	0	0	....	1992-93	1994-95
Prokopec, Mike	Chi.	2	15	0	0	0	11	....	....	....	....	....	....	1995-96	1996-97
Pronger, Sean	Ana., Pit., NYR, L.A., Bos., CBJ, Van.	8	260	23	36	59	159	14	0	2	2	8	....	1995-96	2003-04
Pronovost, Andre	Mtl., Bos., Det., Min.	10	556	94	104	198	408	70	11	11	22	58	4	1956-57	1967-68
Pronovost, Jean	Pit., Atl., Wsh.	14	998	391	383	774	413	35	11	9	20	14	....	1968-69	1981-82
Pronovost, Marcel	Det., Tor.	21	1206	88	257	345	851	134	8	23	31	104	5	1949-50	1969-70
Propp, Brian	Phi., Bos., Min., Hfd.	15	1016	425	579	1004	830	160	64	84	148	151	....	1979-80	1993-94
Proulx, Christian	Mtl.	1	7	1	2	3	20	....	....	....	....	....	....	1993-94	1993-94
• Provost, Claude	Mtl.	15	1005	254	335	589	469	126	25	38	63	86	9	1955-56	1969-70
Prpic, Joel	Bos., Col.	3	18	0	3	3	4	....	....	....	....	....	....	1997-98	2000-01
Pryor, Chris	Min., NYI	6	82	1	4	5	122	....	....	....	....	....	....	1984-85	1989-90
Prystai, Metro	Chi., Det.	11	674	151	179	330	231	43	12	14	26	8	2	1947-48	1957-58
• Pudas, Al	Tor.	1	4	0	0	0	0	....	....	....	....	....	....	1926-27	1926-27
Pulford, Bob	Tor., L.A.	16	1079	281	362	643	792	89	25	26	51	126	4	1956-57	1971-72
Pulkkinen, Dave	NYI	1	2	0	0	0	0	....	....	....	....	....	....	1972-73	1972-73
• Purpur, Fido	St.L., Chi., Det.	5	144	25	35	60	46	16	1	2	3	4	....	1934-35	1944-45
Purves, John	Wsh.	1	7	1	0	1	0	....	....	....	....	....	....	1990-91	1990-91
Pushor, Jamie	Det., Ana., Dal., CBJ, Pit., NYR	10	521	14	46	60	648	14	0	1	1	16	1	1995-96	2005-06
• Pusie, Jean	Mtl., NYR, Bos.	5	61	1	4	5	28	7	0	0	0	0	1	1930-31	1935-36
Pyatt, Nelson	Det., Wsh., Col.	7	296	71	63	134	69	....	....	....	....	....	....	1973-74	1979-80

Q

Name	NHL Teams	NHL Seasons	Regular Schedule GP	G	A	TP	PIM	Playoffs GP	G	A	TP	PIM	NHL Cup Wins	First NHL Season	Last NHL Season
• Quackenbush, Bill	Det., Bos.	14	774	62	222	284	95	80	2	19	21	8	....	1942-43	1955-56
Quackenbush, Max	Bos., Chi.	2	61	4	7	11	30	6	0	0	0	4	....	1950-51	1951-52
Quenneville, Joel	Tor., Col., N.J., Hfd., Wsh.	13	803	54	136	190	705	32	0	8	8	22	....	1978-79	1990-91
• Quenneville, Leo	NYR	1	25	0	3	3	10	3	0	0	0	0	....	1929-30	1929-30
• Quilty, John	Mtl., Bos.	4	125	36	34	70	81	13	3	5	8	9	....	1940-41	1947-48
Quinn, Dan	Cgy., Pit., Van., St.L., Phi., Min., Ott., L.A.	14	805	266	419	685	533	65	22	26	48	62	....	1983-84	1996-97
Quinn, Pat	Tor., Van., Atl.	9	606	18	113	131	950	11	0	1	1	21	....	1968-69	1976-77
Quinney, Ken	Que.	3	59	7	13	20	23	....	....	....	....	....	....	1986-87	1990-91
Quintal, Stephane	Bos., St.L., Wpg., Mtl., NYR, Chi.	16	1037	63	180	243	1320	52	2	10	12	51	....	1988-89	2003-04
Quintin, Jean-Francois	S.J.	2	22	5	5	10	4	....	....	....	....	....	....	1991-92	1992-93

R

Name	NHL Teams	NHL Seasons	Regular Schedule GP	G	A	TP	PIM	Playoffs GP	G	A	TP	PIM	NHL Cup Wins	First NHL Season	Last NHL Season
Racine, Yves	Det., Phi., Mtl., S.J., Cgy., T.B.	9	508	37	194	231	439	25	5	4	9	37	....	1989-90	1997-98
• Radley, Yip	NYA, Mtl.M.	2	18	0	1	1	13	....	....	....	....	....	....	1930-31	1936-37
‡ Radulov, Igor	Chi.	2	43	9	7	16	22	....	....	....	....	....	....	2002-03	2003-04
Raglan, Herb	St.L., Que., T.B., Ott.	9	343	33	56	89	775	32	3	6	9	50	....	1985-86	1993-94
• Raglan, Rags	Det., Chi.	3	100	4	9	13	52	3	0	0	0	0	....	1950-51	1952-53
Ragnarsson, Marcus	S.J., Phi.	9	632	37	140	177	482	68	2	13	15	60	....	1995-96	2003-04
Raleigh, Don	NYR	10	535	101	219	320	96	18	6	5	11	6	....	1943-44	1955-56
Ralph, Brad	Phx.	1	1	0	0	0	0	....	....	....	....	....	....	2000-01	2000-01
Ramage, Rob	Col., St.L., Cgy., Tor., Min., T.B., Mtl., Phi.	15	1044	139	425	564	2226	84	8	42	50	218	2	1979-80	1993-94
• Ramsay, Beattie	Tor.	1	43	0	2	2	10	....	....	....	....	....	....	1927-28	1927-28
Ramsay, Craig	Buf.	14	1070	252	420	672	201	89	17	31	48	27	....	1971-72	1984-85
Ramsay, Les	Chi.	1	11	2	2	4	2	....	....	....	....	....	....	1944-45	1944-45
Ramsey, Mike	Buf., Pit., Det.	18	1070	79	266	345	1012	115	8	29	37	176	....	1979-80	1996-97
Ramsey, Wayne	Buf.	1	2	0	0	0	0	....	....	....	....	....	....	1977-78	1977-78
• Randall, Ken	Tor., Ham., NYA	10	218	68	50	118	533	6	2	1	3	27	2	1917-18	1926-27
Ranheim, Paul	Cgy., Hfd., Car., Phi., Phx.	15	1013	161	199	360	288	36	3	8	11	6	....	1988-89	2002-03
Ranieri, George	Bos.	1	2	0	0	0	0	....	....	....	....	....	....	1956-57	1956-57
‡ Ratchuk, Peter	Fla.	2	32	1	1	2	10	....	....	....	....	....	....	1998-99	2000-01
Ratelle, Jean	NYR, Bos.	21	1281	491	776	1267	276	123	32	66	98	24	....	1960-61	1980-81
Rathwell, Jake	Bos.	1	1	0	0	0	0	....	....	....	....	....	....	1974-75	1974-75
Ratushny, Dan	Van.	1	1	0	1	1	2	....	....	....	....	....	....	1992-93	1992-93
Rausse, Errol	Wsh.	3	31	7	3	10	0	....	....	....	....	....	....	1979-80	1981-82
Rautakallio, Pekka	Atl., Cgy.	3	235	33	121	154	122	23	2	5	7	8	....	1979-80	1981-82
Ravlich, Matt	Bos., Chi., Det., L.A.	10	410	12	78	90	364	24	1	5	6	16	....	1962-63	1972-73
Ray, Rob	Buf., Ott.	15	900	41	50	91	3207	55	3	2	5	169	....	1989-90	2003-04
• Raymond, Armand	Mtl.	2	22	0	2	2	10	....	....	....	....	....	....	1937-38	1939-40
• Raymond, Paul	Mtl.	4	76	2	3	5	6	5	0	0	0	2	....	1932-33	1938-39
Read, Mel	NYR	1	1	0	0	0	0	....	....	....	....	....	....	1946-47	1946-47
‡ Ready, Ryan	Phi.	1	7	0	1	1	0	....	....	....	....	....	....	2005-06	2005-06
• Reardon, Ken	Mtl.	7	341	26	96	122	604	31	2	5	7	62	1	1940-41	1949-50
• Reardon, Terry	Bos., Mtl.	7	193	47	53	100	73	30	8	10	18	12	1	1938-39	1946-47

			Regular Schedule					Playoffs							
Name	NHL Teams	NHL Seasons	GP	G	A	TP	PIM	GP	G	A	TP	PIM	NHL Cup Wins	First NHL Season	Last NHL Season
Reaume, Marc	Tor., Det., Mtl., Van.	9	344	8	43	51	273	21	0	2	2	8	....	1954-55	1970-71
• Reay, Billy	Det., Mtl.	10	479	105	162	267	202	63	13	16	29	43	2	1943-44	1952-53
Redahl, Gord	Bos.	1	18	0	1	1	2	....	....	....	....	....	....	1958-59	1958-59
• Redding, George	Bos.	2	55	3	2	5	23	....	....	....	....	....	....	1924-25	1925-26
Redmond, Craig	L.A., Edm.	5	191	16	68	84	134	3	1	0	1	2	....	1984-85	1988-89
Redmond, Dick	Min., Cal., Chi., St.L., Atl., Bos.	13	771	133	312	445	504	66	9	22	31	27	....	1969-70	1981-82
Redmond, Keith	L.A.	1	12	1	0	1	20	....	....	....	....	....	....	1993-94	1993-94
Redmond, Mickey	Mtl., Det.	9	538	233	195	428	219	16	2	3	5	2	2	1967-68	1975-76
Reeds, Mark	St.L., Hfd.	8	365	45	114	159	135	53	8	9	17	23	....	1981-82	1988-89
Reekie, Joe	Buf., NYI, T.B., Wsh., Chi.	17	902	25	139	164	1326	51	3	4	7	63	....	1985-86	2001-02
• Regan, Bill	NYR, NYA	3	67	3	2	5	67	8	0	0	0	2	....	1929-30	1932-33
Regan, Larry	Bos., Tor.	5	280	41	95	136	71	42	7	14	21	18	....	1956-57	1960-61
Regier, Darcy	Cle., NYI	3	26	0	2	2	35	....	....	....	....	....	....	1977-78	1983-84
• Reibel, Dutch	Det., Chi., Bos.	6	409	84	161	245	75	39	6	14	20	4	2	1953-54	1958-59
‡ Reichel, Robert	Cgy., NYI, Phx., Tor.	11	830	252	378	630	388	70	8	23	31	20	....	1990-91	2003-04
Reichert, Craig	Ana.	1	3	0	0	0	0	....	....	....	....	....	....	1996-97	1996-97
• Reid, Dave	Tor.	3	7	0	0	0	0	....	....	....	....	....	....	1952-53	1955-56
Reid, Dave	Bos., Tor., Dal., Col.	18	961	165	204	369	253	118	9	26	35	34	2	1983-84	2000-01
Reid, Gerry	Det.	1	....	....	....	....	....	2	0	0	0	2	....	1948-49	1948-49
Reid, Gord	NYA	1	1	0	0	0	2	....	....	....	....	....	....	1936-37	1936-37
• Reid, Reg	Tor.	2	39	1	0	1	4	2	0	0	0	0	....	1924-25	1925-26
Reid, Tom	Chi., Min.	11	701	17	113	130	654	42	1	13	14	49	....	1967-68	1977-78
Reierson, Dave	Cgy.	1	2	0	0	0	2	....	....	....	....	....	....	1988-89	1988-89
• Reigle, Ed	Bos.	1	17	0	2	2	25	....	....	....	....	....	....	1950-51	1950-51
Reinhart, Paul	Atl., Cgy., Van.	11	648	133	426	559	277	83	23	54	77	42	....	1979-80	1989-90
• Reinikka, Ollie	NYR	1	16	0	0	0	0	....	....	....	....	....	....	1926-27	1926-27
‡ Reirden, Todd	Edm., St.L., Atl., Phx.	5	183	11	35	46	181	5	0	1	1	0	....	1998-99	2003-04
• Reise, Leo	Ham., NYA, NYR	8	223	36	29	65	181	6	0	0	0	16	....	1920-21	1929-30
Reise, Leo	Chi., Det., NYR	9	494	28	81	109	399	52	8	5	13	68	2	1945-46	1953-54
Renaud, Mark	Hfd., Buf.	5	152	6	50	56	86	....	....	....	....	....	....	1979-80	1983-84
‡ Renberg, Mikael	Phi., T.B., Phx., Tor.	10	661	190	274	464	372	67	16	22	38	42	....	1993-94	2003-04
Reynolds, Bobby	Tor.	1	7	1	1	2	0	....	....	....	....	....	....	1989-90	1989-90
Ribble, Pat	Atl., Chi., Tor., Wsh., Cgy.	8	349	19	60	79	365	8	0	1	1	12	....	1975-76	1982-83
Ricci, Mike	Phi., Que., Col., S.J., Phx.	16	1099	243	362	605	974	110	23	43	66	77	1	1990-91	2006-07
Rice, Steven	NYR, Edm., Hfd., Car.	8	329	64	61	125	275	2	2	1	3	6	....	1990-91	1997-98
Richard, Henri	Mtl.	20	1256	358	688	1046	928	180	49	80	129	181	11	1955-56	1974-75
• Richard, Jacques	Atl., Buf., Que.	10	556	160	187	347	307	35	5	5	10	34	....	1972-73	1982-83
Richard, Jean-Marc	Que.	2	5	2	1	3	2	....	....	....	....	....	....	1987-88	1989-90
• Richard, Maurice	Mtl.	18	978	544	421	965	1285	133	82	44	126	188	8	1942-43	1959-60
‡ Richard, Mike	Wsh.	2	7	0	2	2	0	....	....	....	....	....	....	1987-88	1989-90
Richards, Todd	Hfd.	2	8	0	4	4	4	11	0	3	3	6	....	1990-91	1991-92
Richards, Travis	Dal.	2	3	0	0	0	2	....	....	....	....	....	....	1994-95	1995-96
Richardson, Dave	NYR, Chi., Det.	4	45	3	2	5	27	....	....	....	....	....	....	1963-64	1967-68
Richardson, Glen	Van.	1	24	3	6	9	19	....	....	....	....	....	....	1975-76	1975-76
Richardson, Ken	St.L.	3	49	8	13	21	16	....	....	....	....	....	....	1974-75	1978-79
Richer, Bob	Buf.	1	3	0	0	0	0	....	....	....	....	....	....	1972-73	1972-73
Richer, Stephane	Mtl., N.J., T.B., St.L., Pit.	17	1054	421	398	819	614	134	53	45	98	61	2	1984-85	2001-02
Richer, Stephane	T.B., Bos., Fla.	3	27	1	5	6	20	3	0	0	0	0	....	1992-93	1994-95
Richmond, Steve	NYR, Det., N.J., L.A.	5	159	4	23	27	514	4	0	0	0	12	....	1983-84	1988-89
‡ Richter, Barry	NYR, Bos., NYI, Mtl.	5	151	11	34	45	76	....	....	....	....	....	....	1995-96	2000-01
Richter, Dave	Min., Phi., Van., St.L.	9	365	9	40	49	1030	22	1	0	1	80	....	1981-82	1989-90
Ridley, Mike	NYR, Wsh., Tor., Van.	12	866	292	466	758	424	104	28	50	78	70	....	1985-86	1996-97
‡ Riesen, Michel	Edm.	1	12	0	1	1	4	....	....	....	....	....	....	2000-01	2000-01
Riley, Bill	Wsh., Wpg.	5	139	31	30	61	320	....	....	....	....	....	....	1974-75	1979-80
• Riley, Jack	Det., Mtl., Bos.	4	104	10	22	32	8	4	0	3	3	0	....	1932-33	1935-36
• Riley, Jim	Chi., Det.	1	9	0	2	2	14	....	....	....	....	....	....	1926-27	1926-27
Riopelle, Rip	Mtl.	3	169	27	16	43	73	8	1	1	2	2	....	1947-48	1949-50
Rioux, Gerry	Wpg.	1	8	0	0	0	6	....	....	....	....	....	....	1979-80	1979-80
Rioux, Pierre	Cgy.	1	14	1	2	3	4	....	....	....	....	....	....	1982-83	1982-83
• Ripley, Vic	Chi., Bos., NYR, St.L.	7	278	51	49	100	173	20	4	1	5	10	....	1928-29	1934-35
Risebrough, Doug	Mtl., Cgy.	13	740	185	286	471	1542	124	21	37	58	238	4	1974-75	1986-87
Rissling, Gary	Wsh., Pit.	7	221	23	30	53	1008	5	0	1	1	4	....	1978-79	1984-85
Ritchie, Bob	Phi., Det.	2	29	8	4	12	10	....	....	....	....	....	....	1976-77	1977-78
• Ritchie, Dave	Mtl.W., Ott., Tor., Que., Mtl.	6	58	15	6	21	50	1	0	0	0	0	....	1917-18	1925-26
Ritson, Alex	NYR	1	1	0	0	0	0	....	....	....	....	....	....	1944-45	1944-45
Rittinger, Alan	Bos.	1	19	3	7	10	0	....	....	....	....	....	....	1943-44	1943-44
Rivard, Bob	Pit.	1	27	5	12	17	4	....	....	....	....	....	....	1967-68	1967-68
• Rivers, Gus	Mtl.	3	88	4	5	9	12	16	2	0	2	2	2	1929-30	1931-32
Rivers, Shawn	T.B.	1	4	0	2	2	2	....	....	....	....	....	....	1992-93	1992-93
Rivers, Wayne	Det., Bos., St.L., NYR	7	108	15	30	45	94	....	....	....	....	....	....	1961-62	1968-69
Rizzuto, Garth	Van.	1	37	3	4	7	16	....	....	....	....	....	....	1970-71	1970-71
‡ Roach, Andy	St.L.	1	5	1	2	3	10	....	....	....	....	....	....	2005-06	2005-06
• Roach, Mickey	Tor., Ham., NYA	8	211	77	34	111	54	....	....	....	....	....	....	1919-20	1926-27
Roberge, Mario	Mtl.	5	112	7	7	14	314	15	0	0	0	24	1	1990-91	1994-95
Roberge, Serge	Que.	1	9	0	0	0	24	....	....	....	....	....	....	1990-91	1990-91
• Robert, Claude	Mtl.	1	23	1	0	1	9	....	....	....	....	....	....	1950-51	1950-51
Robert, Rene	Tor., Pit., Buf., Col.	12	744	284	418	702	597	50	22	19	41	73	....	1970-71	1981-82
Roberto, Phil	Mtl., St.L., Det., K.C., Col., Cle.	8	385	75	106	181	464	31	9	8	17	69	1	1969-70	1976-77
Roberts, David	St.L., Edm., Van.	5	125	20	33	53	85	9	0	0	0	16	....	1993-94	1997-98
Roberts, Doug	Det., Oak., Cal., Bos.	10	419	43	104	147	342	16	2	3	5	46	....	1965-66	1974-75
Roberts, Gordie	Hfd., Min., Phi., St.L., Pit., Bos.	15	1097	61	359	420	1582	153	10	47	57	273	2	1979-80	1993-94
Roberts, Jim	Min.	3	106	17	23	40	33	2	0	0	0	0	....	1976-77	1978-79
Roberts, Jimmy	Mtl., St.L.	15	1006	126	194	320	621	153	20	16	36	160	5	1963-64	1977-78
• Robertson, Fred	Tor., Det.	2	34	1	0	1	35	7	0	0	0	0	1	1931-32	1933-34
Robertson, Geordie	Buf.	1	5	1	2	3	7	....	....	....	....	....	....	1982-83	1982-83
• Robertson, George	Mtl.	2	31	2	5	7	6	....	....	....	....	....	....	1947-48	1948-49
Robertson, Torrie	Wsh., Hfd., Det.	10	442	49	99	148	1751	22	2	1	3	90	....	1980-81	1989-90
Robertsson, Bert	Van., Edm., NYR	4	123	4	10	14	75	5	0	0	0	0	....	1997-98	2000-01
Robidoux, Florent	Chi.	3	52	7	4	11	75	....	....	....	....	....	....	1980-81	1983-84
Robinson, Doug	Chi., NYR, L.A.	7	239	44	67	111	34	11	4	3	7	0	....	1963-64	1970-71
• Robinson, Earl	Mtl.M., Chi., Mtl.	11	417	83	98	181	133	25	5	4	9	0	1	1928-29	1939-40
Robinson, Larry	Mtl., L.A.	20	1384	208	750	958	793	227	28	116	144	211	6	1972-73	1991-92
Robinson, Moe	Mtl.	1	1	0	0	0	0	....	....	....	....	....	....	1979-80	1979-80
Robinson, Rob	St.L.	1	22	0	1	1	8	....	....	....	....	....	....	1991-92	1991-92
Robinson, Scott	Min.	1	1	0	0	0	2	....	....	....	....	....	....	1989-90	1989-90
Robitaille, Luc	L.A., Pit., NYR, Det.	19	1431	668	726	1394	1177	159	58	69	127	174	1	1986-87	2005-06
Robitaille, Mike	NYR, Det., Buf., Van.	8	382	23	105	128	280	13	0	1	1	4	....	1969-70	1976-77
Roche, Dave	Pit., Cgy., NYI	5	171	15	15	30	334	16	2	7	9	26	....	1995-96	2001-02
• Roche, Des	Mtl.M., Ott., St.L., Mtl., Det.	4	113	20	18	38	44	....	....	....	....	....	....	1930-31	1934-35
• Roche, Earl	Mtl.M., Bos., Ott., St.L., Det.	4	147	25	27	52	48	2	0	0	0	0	....	1930-31	1934-35
Roche, Ernie	Mtl.	1	4	0	0	0	2	....	....	....	....	....	....	1950-51	1950-51
Rochefort, Dave	Det.	1	1	0	0	0	0	....	....	....	....	....	....	1966-67	1966-67
Rochefort, Leon	NYR, Mtl., Phi., L.A., Det., Atl., Van.	15	617	121	147	268	93	39	4	4	8	16	2	1960-61	1975-76
Rochefort, Normand	Que., NYR, T.B.	13	598	39	119	158	570	69	7	5	12	82	....	1980-81	1993-94
• Rockburn, Harvey	Det., Ott.	3	94	4	2	6	254	....	....	....	....	....	....	1929-30	1932-33
• Rodden, Eddie	Chi., Tor., Bos., NYR	4	97	6	14	20	60	2	0	1	1	0	....	1926-27	1930-31
Rodgers, Marc	Det.	1	21	1	1	2	10	....	....	....	....	....	....	1999-00	1999-00
‡ Roest, Stacy	Det., Min.	5	244	28	48	76	54	3	0	0	0	0	....	1998-99	2002-03
Rogers, John	Min.	2	14	2	4	6	0	....	....	....	....	....	....	1973-74	1974-75
Rogers, Mike	Hfd., NYR, Edm.	7	484	202	317	519	184	17	1	13	14	6	....	1979-80	1985-86
Rohlicek, Jeff	Van.	2	9	0	0	0	8	....	....	....	....	....	....	1987-88	1988-89
Rohlin, Leif	Van.	2	96	8	24	32	40	5	0	0	0	0	....	1995-96	1996-97
Rohloff, Jon	Bos.	3	150	7	25	32	129	10	1	2	3	8	....	1994-95	1996-97
Rohloff, Todd	Wsh., CBJ	2	75	0	6	6	40	....	....	....	....	....	....	2001-02	2003-04
Rolfe, Dale	Bos., L.A., Det., NYR	9	509	25	125	150	556	71	5	24	29	89	....	1959-60	1974-75
Romanchych, Larry	Chi., Atl.	6	298	68	97	165	102	7	2	2	4	4	....	1970-71	1976-77
Romaniuk, Russell	Wpg., Phi.	5	102	13	14	27	63	2	0	0	0	0	....	1991-92	1995-96
Rombough, Doug	Buf., NYI, Min.	4	150	24	27	51	80	....	....	....	....	....	....	1972-73	1975-76
Rominski, Dale	T.B.	1	3	0	1	1	2	....	....	....	....	....	....	1999-00	1999-00
• Romnes, Doc	Chi., Tor., NYA	10	360	68	136	204	42	45	7	18	25	4	2	1930-31	1939-40
Ronan, Ed	Mtl., Wpg., Buf.	6	182	13	23	36	101	27	4	3	7	16	1	1991-92	1996-97
• Ronan, Skene	Ott.	1	11	0	0	0	6	....	....	....	....	....	....	1918-19	1918-19
Ronning, Cliff	St.L., Van., Phx., Nsh., L.A., Min., NYI	18	1137	306	563	869	453	126	29	57	86	72	....	1985-86	2003-04
Ronnqvist, Jonas	Ana.	1	38	0	4	4	14	....	....	....	....	....	....	2000-01	2000-01
Ronson, Len	NYR, Oak.	2	18	2	1	3	10	....	....	....	....	....	....	1960-61	1968-69

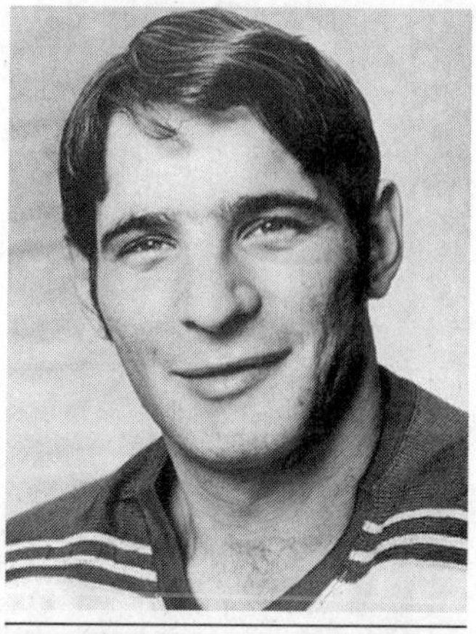
Mike Robitaille

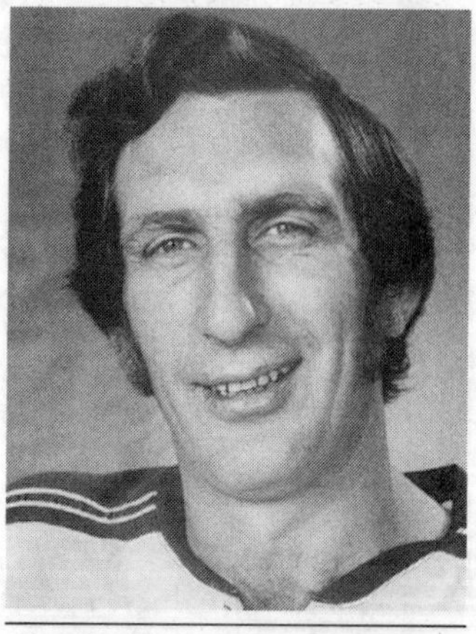
Dale Rolfe

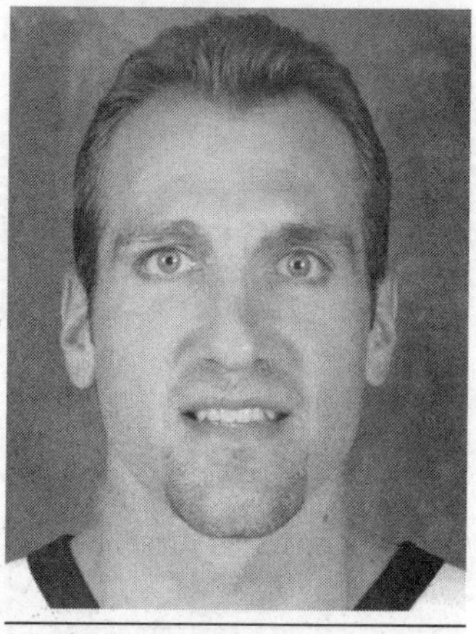
Steve Rucchin

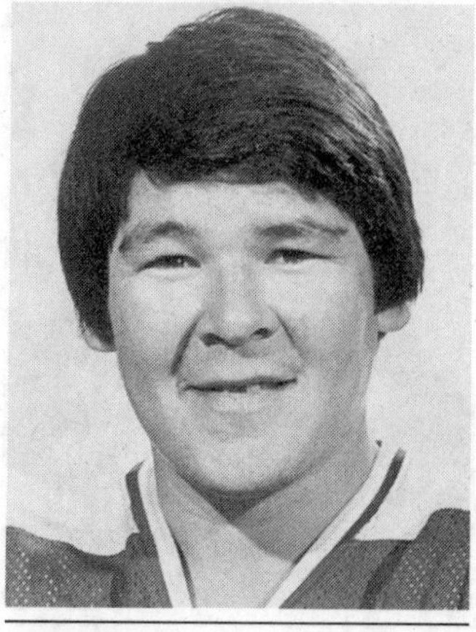
Gary Sargent

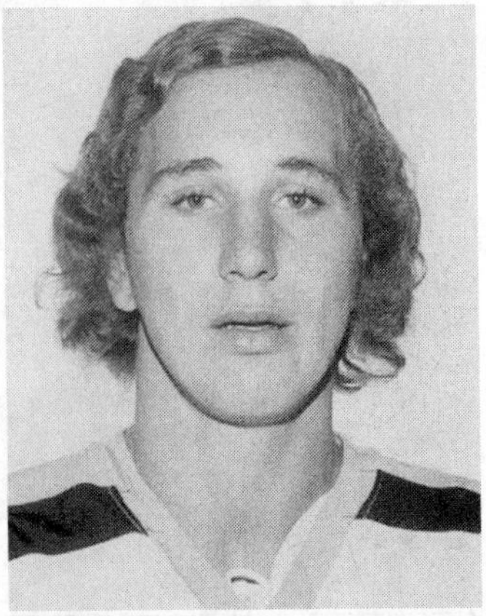

Andre Savard

Milt Schmidt

Glen Sharpley

Johnny Sheppard

Name	NHL Teams	NHL Seasons	Regular Schedule					Playoffs					NHL Cup Wins	First NHL Season	Last NHL Season
			GP	G	A	TP	PIM	GP	G	A	TP	PIM			
Ronty, Paul	Bos., NYR, Mtl.	8	488	101	211	312	103	21	1	7	8	6	....	1947-48	1954-55
Rooney, Steve	Mtl., Wpg., N.J.	5	154	15	13	28	496	25	3	2	5	86	1	1984-85	1988-89
Root, Bill	Mtl., Tor., St.L., Phi.	6	247	11	23	34	180	22	1	2	3	25	....	1982-83	1987-88
‡ Rosa, Pavel	L.A.	4	36	5	13	18	6	....	....	....	....	....	....	1998-99	2003-04
● Ross, Art	Mtl.W.	1	3	1	0	1	12	....	....	....	....	....	....	1917-18	1917-18
Ross, Jim	NYR	2	62	2	11	13	29	....	....	....	....	....	....	1951-52	1952-53
Rossignol, Roly	Det., Mtl.	3	14	3	5	8	6	1	0	0	0	2	....	1943-44	1945-46
Rossiter, Kyle	Fla., Atl.	3	11	0	1	1	9	....	....	....	....	....	....	2001-02	2003-04
Rota, Darcy	Chi., Atl., Van.	11	794	256	239	495	973	60	14	7	21	147	....	1973-74	1983-84
Rota, Randy	Mtl., L.A., K.C., Col.	5	212	38	39	77	60	5	0	1	1	0	....	1972-73	1976-77
● Rothschild, Sam	Mtl.M., Pit., NYA	4	100	8	6	14	25	6	0	0	0	0	1	1924-25	1927-28
● Roulston, Rolly	Det.	3	24	0	6	6	10	....	....	....	....	....	1	1935-36	1937-38
Roulston, Tom	Edm., Pit.	5	195	47	49	96	74	21	2	2	4	2	....	1980-81	1985-86
Roupe, Magnus	Phi.	2	40	3	5	8	42	....	....	....	....	....	....	1987-88	1988-89
Rouse, Bob	Min., Wsh., Tor., Det., S.J.	17	1061	37	181	218	1559	136	7	21	28	198	2	1983-84	1999-00
Rousseau, Bobby	Mtl., Min., NYR	15	942	245	458	703	359	128	27	57	84	69	4	1960-61	1974-75
Rousseau, Guy	Mtl.	2	4	0	1	1	0	....	....	....	....	....	....	1954-55	1956-57
Rousseau, Roland	Mtl.	1	2	0	0	0	0	....	....	....	....	....	....	1952-53	1952-53
Routhier, Jean-Marc	Que.	1	8	0	0	0	9	....	....	....	....	....	....	1989-90	1989-90
● Rowe, Bobby	Bos.	1	4	1	0	1	0	....	....	....	....	....	....	1924-25	1924-25
Rowe, Mike	Pit.	3	11	0	0	0	11	....	....	....	....	....	....	1984-85	1986-87
● Rowe, Ron	NYR	1	5	1	0	1	0	....	....	....	....	....	....	1947-48	1947-48
Rowe, Tom	Wsh., Hfd., Det.	7	357	85	100	185	615	3	2	0	2	0	....	1976-77	1982-83
Roy, Jean-Yves	NYR, Ott., Bos.	4	61	12	16	28	26	....	....	....	....	....	....	1994-95	1997-98
Roy, Stephane	Min.	1	12	1	0	1	0	....	....	....	....	....	....	1987-88	1987-88
Royer, Gaetan	T.B.	1	3	0	0	0	2	....	....	....	....	....	....	2001-02	2001-02
Royer, Remi	Chi.	1	18	0	0	0	67	....	....	....	....	....	....	1998-99	1998-99
● Rozzini, Gino	Bos.	1	31	5	10	15	20	6	1	2	3	6	....	1944-45	1944-45
Rucchin, Steve	Ana., NYR, Atl.	12	735	171	318	489	164	37	9	8	17	12	....	1994-95	2006-07
Rucinski, Mike	Chi.	2	1	0	0	0	0	2	0	0	0	0	....	1987-88	1988-89
Rucinski, Mike	Car.	3	26	0	2	2	10	....	....	....	....	....	....	1997-98	2000-01
● Ruelle, Bernie	Det.	1	2	1	0	1	0	....	....	....	....	....	....	1943-44	1943-44
Ruff, Jason	St.L., T.B.	2	14	3	3	6	10	....	....	....	....	....	....	1992-93	1993-94
Ruff, Lindy	Buf., NYR	12	691	105	195	300	1264	52	11	13	24	193	....	1979-80	1990-91
Ruhnke, Kent	Bos.	1	2	0	1	1	0	....	....	....	....	....	....	1975-76	1975-76
Rumble, Darren	Phi., Ott., St.L., T.B.	8	193	10	26	36	216	....	....	....	....	....	1	1990-91	2003-04
Rundqvist, Thomas	Mtl.	1	2	0	1	1	0	....	....	....	....	....	....	1984-85	1984-85
● Runge, Paul	Bos., Mtl.M., Mtl.	7	140	18	22	40	57	7	0	0	0	6	....	1930-31	1937-38
Ruotsalainen, Reijo	NYR, Edm., N.J.	7	446	107	237	344	180	86	15	32	47	44	2	1981-82	1989-90
Rupp, Duane	NYR, Tor., Min., Pit.	10	374	24	93	117	220	10	2	2	4	8	....	1962-63	1972-73
Ruskowski, Terry	Chi., L.A., Pit., Min.	10	630	113	313	426	1354	21	1	6	7	86	....	1979-80	1988-89
Russell, Cam	Chi., Col.	10	396	9	21	30	872	44	0	5	5	16	....	1989-90	1998-99
● Russell, Church	NYR	3	90	20	16	36	12	....	....	....	....	....	....	1945-46	1947-48
Russell, Phil	Chi., Atl., Cgy., N.J., Buf.	15	1016	99	325	424	2038	73	4	22	26	202	....	1972-73	1986-87
Ruuttu, Christian	Buf., Chi., Van.	9	621	134	298	432	714	42	4	9	13	49	....	1986-87	1994-95
Ruzicka, Vladimir	Edm., Bos., Ott.	5	233	82	85	167	129	30	4	14	18	2	....	1989-90	1993-94
Ryan, Terry	Mtl.	3	8	0	0	0	36	....	....	....	....	....	....	1996-97	1998-99
Rychel, Warren	Chi., L.A., Tor., Col., Ana.	9	406	38	39	77	1422	70	8	13	21	121	1	1988-89	1998-99
Rymsha, Andy	Que.	1	6	0	0	0	23	....	....	....	....	....	....	1991-92	1991-92

S

Saarinen, Simo	NYR	1	8	0	0	0	0	....	....	....	....	....	....	1984-85	1984-85
Sabol, Shaun	Phi.	1	2	0	0	0	0	....	....	....	....	....	....	1989-90	1989-90
Sabourin, Bob	Tor.	1	1	0	0	0	2	....	....	....	....	....	....	1951-52	1951-52
Sabourin, Gary	St.L., Tor., Cal., Cle.	10	627	169	188	357	397	62	19	11	30	58	....	1967-68	1976-77
Sabourin, Ken	Cgy., Wsh.	4	74	2	8	10	201	12	0	0	0	34	....	1988-89	1991-92
Sacco, David	Tor., Ana.	3	35	5	13	18	22	....	....	....	....	....	....	1993-94	1995-96
Sacco, Joe	Tor., Ana., NYI, Wsh., Phi.	13	738	94	119	213	421	26	2	0	2	8	....	1990-91	2002-03
Sacharuk, Larry	NYR, St.L.	5	151	29	33	62	42	2	1	1	2	2	....	1972-73	1976-77
‡ Safronov, Kirill	Phx., Atl.	2	35	2	2	4	16	....	....	....	....	....	....	2001-02	2002-03
Saganiuk, Rocky	Tor., Pit.	6	259	57	65	122	201	6	1	0	1	15	....	1978-79	1983-84
Saleski, Don	Phi., Col.	9	543	128	125	253	629	82	13	17	30	131	2	1971-72	1979-80
Salming, Borje	Tor., Det.	17	1148	150	637	787	1344	81	12	37	49	91	....	1973-74	1989-90
‡ Salomonsson, Andreas	N.J., Wsh.	2	71	5	9	14	36	4	0	1	1	0	....	2001-02	2002-03
Salovaara, Barry	Det.	2	90	2	13	15	70	....	....	....	....	....	....	1974-75	1975-76
Salvian, Dave	NYI	1	....	....	....	....	....	1	0	1	1	2	....	1976-77	1976-77
Samis, Phil	Tor.	2	2	0	0	0	0	5	0	1	1	2	1	1947-48	1949-50
Sampson, Gary	Wsh.	4	105	13	22	35	25	12	1	0	1	0	....	1983-84	1986-87
Samuelsson, Kjell	NYR, Phi., Pit., T.B.	14	813	48	138	186	1225	123	4	20	24	178	1	1985-86	1998-99
Samuelsson, Ulf	Hfd., Pit., NYR, Det., Phi.	16	1080	57	275	332	2453	132	7	27	34	272	2	1984-85	1999-00
Sandelin, Scott	Mtl., Phi., Min.	4	25	0	4	4	2	....	....	....	....	....	....	1986-87	1991-92
Sanderson, Derek	Bos., NYR, St.L., Van., Pit.	13	598	202	250	452	911	56	18	12	30	187	2	1965-66	1977-78
Sandford, Ed	Bos., Det., Chi.	9	502	106	145	251	355	42	13	11	24	27	....	1947-48	1955-56
Sandlak, Jim	Van., Hfd.	11	549	110	119	229	821	33	7	10	17	30	....	1985-86	1995-96
● Sands, Charlie	Tor., Bos., Mtl., NYR	12	427	99	109	208	58	34	6	6	12	4	1	1932-33	1943-44
Sandstrom, Tomas	NYR, L.A., Pit., Det., Ana.	15	983	394	462	856	1193	139	32	49	81	183	1	1984-85	1998-99
Sandwith, Terran	Edm.	1	8	0	0	0	6	....	....	....	....	....	....	1997-98	1997-98
Sanipass, Everett	Chi., Que.	5	164	25	34	59	358	5	2	0	2	4	....	1986-87	1990-91
‡ Sarault, Yves	Mtl., Cgy., Col., Ott., Atl., Nsh.	8	106	10	10	20	51	5	0	0	0	2	....	1994-95	2001-02
Sargent, Gary	L.A., Min.	8	402	61	161	222	273	20	5	7	12	8	....	1975-76	1982-83
Sarner, Craig	Bos.	1	7	0	0	0	0	....	....	....	....	....	....	1974-75	1974-75
‡ Sarno, Peter	Edm., CBJ	2	7	1	0	1	2	....	....	....	....	....	....	2003-04	2005-06
Sarrazin, Dick	Phi.	3	100	20	35	55	22	4	0	0	0	0	....	1968-69	1971-72
Sasakamoose, Fred	Chi.	1	11	0	0	0	6	....	....	....	....	....	....	1953-54	1953-54
Sasser, Grant	Pit.	1	3	0	0	0	0	....	....	....	....	....	....	1983-84	1983-84
Sather, Glen	Bos., Pit., NYR, St.L., Mtl., Min.	10	658	80	113	193	724	72	1	5	6	86	....	1966-67	1975-76
Saunders, Bernie	Que.	2	10	0	1	1	8	....	....	....	....	....	....	1979-80	1980-81
Saunders, David	Van.	1	56	7	13	20	10	....	....	....	....	....	....	1987-88	1987-88
● Saunders, Ted	Ott.	1	18	1	3	4	4	....	....	....	....	....	....	1933-34	1933-34
Sauve, Jean-Francois	Buf., Que.	7	290	65	138	203	114	36	9	12	21	10	....	1980-81	1986-87
Savage, Andre	Bos., Phi.	4	66	10	14	24	14	....	....	....	....	....	....	1998-99	2002-03
Savage, Brian	Mtl., Phx., St.L., Phi.	12	674	192	167	359	321	39	3	8	11	12	....	1993-94	2005-06
Savage, Joel	Buf.	1	3	0	1	1	0	....	....	....	....	....	....	1990-91	1990-91
Savage, Reggie	Wsh., Que.	3	34	5	7	12	28	....	....	....	....	....	....	1990-91	1993-94
● Savage, Tony	Bos., Mtl.	1	49	1	5	6	6	2	0	0	0	0	....	1934-35	1934-35
Savard, Andre	Bos., Buf., Que.	12	790	211	271	482	411	85	13	18	31	77	....	1973-74	1984-85
Savard, Denis	Chi., Mtl., T.B.	17	1196	473	865	1338	1336	169	66	109	175	256	1	1980-81	1996-97
Savard, Jean	Chi., Hfd.	3	43	7	12	19	29	....	....	....	....	....	....	1977-78	1979-80
Savard, Serge	Mtl., Wpg.	17	1040	106	333	439	592	130	19	49	68	88	8	1966-67	1982-83
Savoia, Ryan	Pit.	1	3	0	0	0	0	....	....	....	....	....	....	1998-99	1998-99
Sawyer, Kevin	St.L., Bos., Phx., Ana.	6	110	3	3	6	403	....	....	....	....	....	....	1995-96	2002-03
Scamurra, Peter	Wsh.	4	132	8	25	33	59	....	....	....	....	....	....	1975-76	1979-80
Sceviour, Darin	Chi.	1	1	0	0	0	0	....	....	....	....	....	....	1986-87	1986-87
● Schaeffer, Butch	Chi.	1	5	0	0	0	6	....	....	....	....	....	....	1936-37	1936-37
Schamehorn, Kevin	Det., L.A.	3	10	0	0	0	17	....	....	....	....	....	....	1976-77	1980-81
‡ Schastlivy, Petr	Ott., Ana.	5	129	18	22	40	30	1	0	0	0	0	....	1999-00	2003-04
Schella, John	Van.	2	115	2	18	20	224	....	....	....	....	....	....	1970-71	1971-72
Scherza, Chuck	Bos., NYR	2	36	6	6	12	35	....	....	....	....	....	....	1943-44	1944-45
Schinkel, Ken	NYR, Pit.	12	636	127	198	325	163	19	7	2	9	4	....	1959-60	1972-73
‡ Schlegel, Brad	Wsh., Cgy.	3	48	1	8	9	10	7	0	1	1	2	....	1991-92	1993-94
Schliebener, Andy	Van.	3	84	2	11	13	74	6	0	0	0	0	....	1981-82	1984-85
Schmautz, Bobby	Chi., Van., Bos., Edm., Col.	13	764	271	286	557	988	84	28	33	61	92	....	1967-68	1980-81
● Schmautz, Cliff	Buf., Phi.	1	56	13	19	32	33	....	....	....	....	....	....	1970-71	1970-71
‡ Schmidt, Chris	L.A.	1	10	0	2	2	5	....	....	....	....	....	....	2002-03	2002-03
● Schmidt, Clarence	Bos.	1	7	1	0	1	2	....	....	....	....	....	....	1943-44	1943-44
Schmidt, Jackie	Bos.	1	45	6	7	13	6	5	0	0	0	0	....	1942-43	1942-43
Schmidt, Milt	Bos.	16	776	229	346	575	466	86	24	25	49	60	2	1936-37	1954-55
Schmidt, Norm	Pit.	4	125	23	33	56	73	....	....	....	....	....	....	1983-84	1987-88
Schmidt, Otto	Bos.	1	2	0	0	0	0	....	....	....	....	....	....	1943-44	1943-44
‡ Schnabel, Robert	Nsh.	3	22	0	3	3	34	....	....	....	....	....	....	2001-02	2003-04
● Schnarr, Werner	Bos.	2	26	0	0	0	0	....	....	....	....	....	....	1924-25	1925-26
Schneider, Andy	Ott.	1	10	0	0	0	15	....	....	....	....	....	....	1993-94	1993-94
Schock, Danny	Bos., Phi.	2	20	1	2	3	0	1	0	0	0	0	1	1969-70	1970-71

			Regular Schedule					Playoffs							
Name	NHL Teams	NHL Seasons	GP	G	A	TP	PIM	GP	G	A	TP	PIM	NHL Cup Wins	First NHL Season	Last NHL Season
Schock, Ron	Bos., St.L., Pit., Buf.	15	909	166	351	517	260	55	4	16	20	29	....	1963-64	1977-78
Schoenfeld, Jim	Buf., Det., Bos.	13	719	51	204	255	1132	75	3	13	16	151	....	1972-73	1984-85
Schofield, Dwight	Det., Mtl., St.L., Wsh., Pit., Wpg.	7	211	8	22	30	631	9	0	0	0	55	....	1976-77	1987-88
Schreiber, Wally	Min.	2	41	8	10	18	12	....	....	....	....	....	....	1987-88	1988-89
• Schriner, Sweeney	NYA, Tor.	11	484	201	204	405	148	59	18	11	29	54	2	1934-35	1945-46
Schulte, Paxton	Que., Cgy.	2	2	0	0	0	4	....	....	....	....	....	....	1993-94	1996-97
Schultz, Dave	Phi., L.A., Pit., Buf.	9	535	79	121	200	2294	73	8	12	20	412	2	1971-72	1979-80
Schultz, Ray	NYI	6	45	0	4	4	155	2	0	0	0	2	....	1997-98	2002-03
Schurman, Maynard	Hfd.	1	7	0	0	0	0	....	....	....	....	....	....	1979-80	1979-80
Schutt, Rod	Mtl., Pit., Tor.	8	286	77	92	169	177	22	8	6	14	26	....	1977-78	1985-86
Scissons, Scott	NYI	3	2	0	0	0	0	1	0	0	0	0	....	1990-91	1993-94
Sclisizzi, Enio	Det., Chi.	6	81	12	11	23	26	13	0	0	0	6	1	1946-47	1952-53
• Scott, Ganton	Tor., Ham., Mtl.M.	3	57	1	1	2	0	....	....	....	....	....	....	1922-23	1924-25
• Scott, Laurie	NYA, NYR	2	62	6	3	9	28	....	....	....	....	....	....	1926-27	1927-28
Scott, Richard	NYR	2	10	0	0	0	28	....	....	....	....	....	....	2001-02	2003-04
‡ Scoville, Darrel	Cgy., CBJ	3	16	0	1	1	12	....	....	....	....	....	....	1999-00	2003-04
Scremin, Claudio	S.J.	2	17	0	1	1	29	....	....	....	....	....	....	1991-92	1992-93
Scruton, Howard	L.A.	1	4	0	4	4	9	....	....	....	....	....	....	1982-83	1982-83
Seabrooke, Glen	Phi.	3	19	1	6	7	4	....	....	....	....	....	....	1986-87	1988-89
Secord, Al	Bos., Chi., Tor., Phi.	12	766	273	222	495	2093	102	21	34	55	382	....	1978-79	1989-90
Sedlbauer, Ron	Van., Chi., Tor.	7	430	143	86	229	210	19	1	3	4	27	....	1974-75	1980-81
Seftel, Steve	Wsh.	1	4	0	0	0	2	....	....	....	....	....	....	1990-91	1990-91
Seguin, Dan	Min., Van.	2	37	2	6	8	50	....	....	....	....	....	....	1970-71	1973-74
Seguin, Steve	L.A.	1	5	0	0	0	9	....	....	....	....	....	....	1984-85	1984-85
• Seibert, Earl	NYR, Chi., Det.	15	645	89	187	276	746	66	11	8	19	76	2	1931-32	1945-46
Seiling, Ric	Buf., Det.	10	738	179	208	387	573	62	14	14	28	36	....	1977-78	1986-87
Seiling, Rod	Tor., NYR, Wsh., St.L., Atl.	17	979	62	269	331	601	77	4	8	12	55	....	1962-63	1978-79
Sejba, Jiri	Buf.	1	11	0	2	2	8	....	....	....	....	....	....	1990-91	1990-91
‡ Sejna, Peter	St.L.	4	49	7	4	11	12	....	....	....	....	....	....	2002-03	2006-07
‡ Sekeras, Lubomir	Min., Dal.	4	213	18	53	71	122	15	1	1	2	6	....	2000-01	2003-04
Selby, Brit	Tor., Phi., St.L.	8	350	55	62	117	163	16	1	1	2	8	....	1964-65	1971-72
Self, Steve	Wsh.	1	3	0	0	0	0	....	....	....	....	....	....	1976-77	1976-77
Selivanov, Alex	T.B., Edm., CBJ	7	459	121	114	235	379	13	2	3	5	16	....	1994-95	2000-01
Sellars, Luke	Atl.	1	1	0	0	0	2	....	....	....	....	....	....	2001-02	2001-02
Selmser, Sean	CBJ	1	1	0	0	0	5	....	....	....	....	....	....	2000-01	2000-01
Selwood, Brad	Tor., L.A.	3	163	7	40	47	153	6	0	0	0	4	....	1970-71	1979-80
Semak, Alexander	N.J., T.B., NYI, Van.	6	289	83	91	174	187	8	1	1	2	0	....	1991-92	1996-97
Semchuk, Brandy	L.A.	1	1	0	0	0	2	....	....	....	....	....	....	1992-93	1992-93
Semenko, Dave	Edm., Hfd., Tor.	9	575	65	88	153	1175	73	6	6	12	208	2	1979-80	1987-88
Semenov, Anatoli	Edm., T.B., Van., Ana., Phi., Buf.	8	362	68	126	194	122	49	9	13	22	12	....	1989-90	1996-97
• Senick, George	NYR	1	13	2	3	5	8	....	....	....	....	....	....	1952-53	1952-53
Seppa, Jyrki	Wpg.	1	13	0	2	2	6	....	....	....	....	....	....	1983-84	1983-84
Serafini, Ron	Cal.	1	2	0	0	0	2	....	....	....	....	....	....	1973-74	1973-74
Serowik, Jeff	Tor., Bos., Pit.	4	28	0	6	6	16	....	....	....	....	....	....	1990-91	1999-00
Servinis, George	Min.	1	5	0	0	0	0	....	....	....	....	....	....	1987-88	1987-88
Sevcik, Jaroslav	Que.	1	13	0	2	2	2	....	....	....	....	....	....	1989-90	1989-90
‡ Severson, Cam	Ana., CBJ	3	37	3	0	3	63	1	0	0	0	0	....	2002-03	2005-06
Severyn, Brent	Que., Fla., NYI, Col., Ana., Dal.	7	328	10	30	40	825	8	0	0	0	12	1	1989-90	1998-99
Sevigny, Pierre	Mtl., NYR	4	78	4	5	9	64	3	0	1	1	0	....	1993-94	1997-98
Shack, Eddie	NYR, Tor., Bos., L.A., Buf., Pit.	17	1047	239	226	465	1437	74	6	7	13	151	4	1958-59	1974-75
• Shack, Joe	NYR	2	70	9	27	36	20	....	....	....	....	....	....	1942-43	1944-45
Shafranov, Konstantin	St.L.	1	5	2	1	3	0	....	....	....	....	....	....	1996-97	1996-97
Shakes, Paul	Cal.	1	21	0	4	4	12	....	....	....	....	....	....	1973-74	1973-74
Shaldybin, Yevgeny	Bos.	1	3	1	0	1	0	....	....	....	....	....	....	1996-97	1996-97
Shanahan, Sean	Mtl., Col., Bos.	3	40	1	3	4	47	....	....	....	....	....	....	1975-76	1977-78
Shand, Dave	Atl., Tor., Wsh.	8	421	19	84	103	544	26	1	2	3	83	....	1976-77	1984-85
Shank, Daniel	Det., Hfd.	3	77	13	14	27	175	5	0	0	0	22	....	1989-90	1991-92
Shannon, Chuck	NYA	1	4	0	0	0	2	....	....	....	....	....	....	1939-40	1939-40
Shannon, Darrin	Buf., Wpg., Phx.	10	506	87	163	250	344	45	7	10	17	38	....	1988-89	1997-98
Shannon, Darryl	Tor., Wpg., Buf., Atl., Cgy., Mtl.	13	544	28	111	139	523	29	4	7	11	16	....	1988-89	2000-01
• Shannon, Gerry	Ott., St.L., Bos., Mtl.M.	5	180	23	29	52	80	9	0	1	1	2	....	1933-34	1937-38
‡ Shantz, Jeff	Chi., Cgy., Col.	10	642	72	139	211	341	44	5	8	13	24	....	1993-94	2002-03
Sharifijanov, Vadim	N.J., Van.	3	92	16	21	37	50	4	0	0	0	0	....	1996-97	1999-00
Sharples, Jeff	Det.	3	105	14	35	49	70	7	0	3	3	6	....	1986-87	1988-89
Sharpley, Glen	Min., Chi.	6	389	117	161	278	199	27	7	11	18	24	....	1976-77	1981-82
Shaunessy, Scott	Que.	2	7	0	0	0	23	....	....	....	....	....	....	1986-87	1988-89
Shaw, Brad	Hfd., Ott., Wsh., St.L.	11	377	22	137	159	208	23	4	8	12	6	....	1985-86	1998-99
Shaw, David	Que., NYR, Edm., Min., Bos., T.B.	16	769	41	153	194	906	45	3	9	12	81	....	1982-83	1997-98
• Shay, Norm	Bos., Tor.	2	53	5	3	8	34	....	....	....	....	....	....	1924-25	1925-26
• Shea, Pat	Chi.	1	10	1	0	1	0	....	....	....	....	....	....	1931-32	1931-32
‡ Shearer, Rob	Col.	1	2	0	0	0	0	....	....	....	....	....	....	2000-01	2000-01
Shedden, Doug	Pit., Det., Que., Tor.	8	416	139	186	325	176	....	....	....	....	....	....	1981-82	1990-91
Sheehan, Bobby	Mtl., Cal., Chi., Det., NYR, Col., L.A.	9	310	48	63	111	40	25	4	3	7	8	1	1969-70	1981-82
Sheehy, Neil	Cgy., Hfd., Wsh.	9	379	18	47	65	1311	54	0	3	3	241	....	1983-84	1991-92
Sheehy, Tim	Det., Hfd.	2	27	2	1	3	0	....	....	....	....	....	....	1977-78	1979-80
Shelton, Doug	Chi.	1	5	0	1	1	2	....	....	....	....	....	....	1967-68	1967-68
• Sheppard, Frank	Det.	1	8	1	1	2	0	....	....	....	....	....	....	1927-28	1927-28
Sheppard, Gregg	Bos., Pit.	10	657	205	293	498	243	82	32	40	72	31	....	1972-73	1981-82
• Sheppard, Johnny	Det., NYA, Bos., Chi.	8	308	68	58	126	224	10	0	0	0	0	1	1926-27	1933-34
Sheppard, Ray	Buf., NYR, Det., S.J., Fla., Car.	13	817	357	300	657	212	81	30	20	50	21	....	1987-88	1999-00
• Sherf, John	Det.	5	19	0	0	0	8	8	0	1	1	2	1	1935-36	1943-44
• Shero, Fred	NYR	3	145	6	14	20	137	13	0	2	2	8	....	1947-48	1949-50
• Sherritt, Gordon	Det.	1	8	0	0	0	12	....	....	....	....	....	....	1943-44	1943-44
Sherven, Gord	Edm., Min., Hfd.	5	97	13	22	35	33	3	0	0	0	0	....	1983-84	1987-88
Shevalier, Jeff	L.A., T.B.	3	32	5	9	14	8	....	....	....	....	....	....	1994-95	1999-00
• Shewchuk, Jack	Bos.	6	187	9	19	28	160	20	0	1	1	19	1	1938-39	1944-45
Shibicky, Alex	NYR	8	324	110	91	201	161	39	12	12	24	12	1	1935-36	1945-46
• Shields, Al	Ott., Phi., NYA, Mtl.M., Bos.	11	459	42	46	88	637	17	0	1	1	14	1	1927-28	1937-38
Shill, Bill	Bos.	3	79	21	13	34	18	7	1	2	3	2	....	1942-43	1946-47
• Shill, Jack	Tor., Bos., NYA, Chi.	6	160	15	20	35	70	25	1	6	7	23	1	1933-34	1938-39
Shinske, Rick	Cle., St.L.	3	63	5	16	21	10	....	....	....	....	....	....	1976-77	1978-79
Shires, Jim	Det., St.L., Pit.	3	56	3	6	9	32	....	....	....	....	....	....	1970-71	1972-73
‡ Shishkanov, Timofei	Nsh., St.L.	2	24	3	2	5	6	....	....	....	....	....	....	2003-04	2005-06
• Shmyr, Paul	Chi., Cal., Min., Hfd.	7	343	13	72	85	528	34	3	3	6	44	....	1968-69	1981-82
Shoebottom, Bruce	Bos.	4	35	1	4	5	53	14	1	2	3	77	....	1987-88	1990-91
• Shore, Eddie	Bos., NYA	14	550	105	179	284	1047	55	7	12	19	181	2	1926-27	1939-40
• Shore, Hamby	Ott.	1	18	3	8	11	51	....	....	....	....	....	....	1917-18	1917-18
Short, Steve	L.A., Det.	2	6	0	0	0	2	....	....	....	....	....	....	1977-78	1978-79
Shuchuk, Gary	Det., L.A.	5	142	13	26	39	70	20	2	2	4	12	....	1990-91	1995-96
Shudra, Ron	Edm.	1	10	0	5	5	6	....	....	....	....	....	....	1987-88	1987-88
Shutt, Steve	Mtl., L.A.	13	930	424	393	817	410	99	50	48	98	65	5	1972-73	1984-85
‡ Shvidki, Denis	Fla.	4	76	11	14	25	30	....	....	....	....	....	....	2000-01	2003-04
• Siebert, Babe	Mtl.M., NYR, Bos., Mtl.	14	592	140	156	296	982	49	7	5	12	62	2	1925-26	1938-39
‡ Siklenka, Mike	Phi., NYR	2	2	0	0	0	0	....	....	....	....	....	....	2002-03	2003-04
Silk, Dave	NYR, Bos., Det., Wpg.	7	249	54	59	113	271	13	2	4	6	13	....	1979-80	1985-86
Siltala, Mike	Wsh., NYR	3	7	1	0	1	2	....	....	....	....	....	....	1981-82	1987-88
Siltanen, Risto	Edm., Hfd., Que.	8	562	90	265	355	266	32	6	12	18	30	....	1979-80	1986-87
Sim, Trevor	Edm.	1	3	0	1	1	2	....	....	....	....	....	....	1989-90	1989-90
Simard, Martin	Cgy., T.B.	3	44	1	5	6	183	....	....	....	....	....	....	1990-91	1992-93
‡ Simicek, Roman	Pit., Min.	2	63	7	10	17	59	....	....	....	....	....	....	2000-01	2001-02
Simmer, Charlie	Cal., Cle., L.A., Bos., Pit.	14	712	342	369	711	544	24	9	9	18	32	....	1974-75	1987-88
Simmons, Al	Cal., Bos.	3	11	0	1	1	21	1	0	0	0	0	....	1971-72	1975-76
• Simon, Cully	Det., Chi.	3	130	4	11	15	121	14	1	0	1	6	1	1942-43	1944-45
Simon, Jason	NYI, Phx.	2	5	0	0	0	34	....	....	....	....	....	....	1993-94	1996-97
• Simon, Thain	Det.	1	3	0	0	0	0	....	....	....	....	....	....	1946-47	1946-47
Simon, Todd	Buf.	1	15	0	1	1	0	5	1	0	1	0	....	1993-94	1993-94
Simonetti, Frank	Bos.	4	115	5	8	13	76	12	0	1	1	8	....	1984-85	1987-88
Simpson, Bobby	Atl., St.L., Pit.	5	175	35	29	64	98	6	0	1	1	2	....	1976-77	1982-83
• Simpson, Cliff	Det.	2	6	0	1	1	0	2	0	0	0	2	....	1946-47	1947-48
Simpson, Craig	Pit., Edm., Buf.	10	634	247	250	497	659	67	36	32	68	56	2	1985-86	1994-95
• Simpson, Joe	NYA	6	228	21	19	40	156	2	0	0	0	0	....	1925-26	1930-31
‡ Simpson, Reid	Phi., Min., N.J., Chi., T.B., St.L., Mtl., Nsh., Pit.	12	301	18	18	36	838	10	0	0	0	31	....	1991-92	2003-04
Sims, Al	Bos., Hfd., L.A.	10	475	49	116	165	286	41	0	2	2	14	....	1973-74	1982-83
Sinclair, Reg	NYR, Det.	3	208	49	43	92	139	3	1	0	1	0	....	1950-51	1952-53

Mike Siltala

Glen Skov

John Slaney

Doug Smith

Andre St.Laurent

Pete Stemkowski

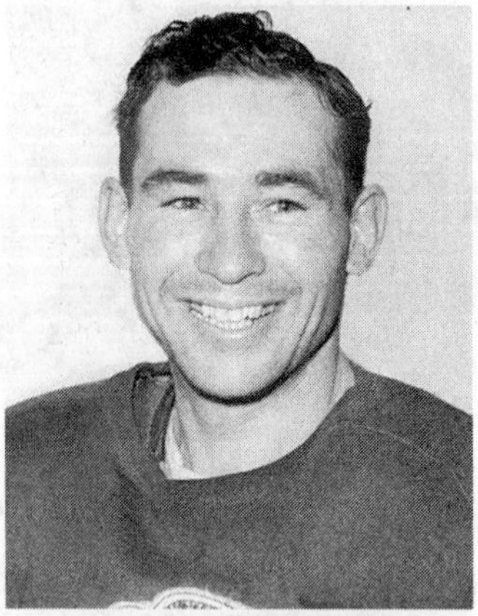

Jack Stewart

Patrik Sundstrom

	Name	NHL Teams	NHL Seasons	Regular Schedule					Playoffs					NHL Cup Wins	First NHL Season	Last NHL Season
				GP	G	A	TP	PIM	GP	G	A	TP	PIM			
•	Singbush, Alex	Mtl.	1	32	0	5	5	15	3	0	0	0	4	....	1940-41	1940-41
	Sinisalo, Ilkka	Phi., Min., L.A.	11	582	204	222	426	208	68	21	11	32	6	....	1981-82	1991-92
	Siren, Ville	Pit., Min.	5	290	14	68	82	276	7	0	0	0	6	....	1985-86	1989-90
	Sirois, Bob	Phi., Wsh.	6	286	92	120	212	42	....	....	....	....	....	....	1974-75	1979-80
	Sittler, Darryl	Tor., Phi., Det.	15	1096	484	637	1121	948	76	29	45	74	137	....	1970-71	1984-85
‡	Sivek, Michal	Pit.	1	38	3	3	6	14	....	....	....	....	....	....	2002-03	2002-03
•	Sjoberg, Lars-Erik	Wpg.	1	79	7	27	34	48	....	....	....	....	....	....	1979-80	1979-80
‡	Sjodin, Tommy	Min., Dal., Que.	2	106	8	40	48	52	....	....	....	....	....	....	1992-93	1993-94
•	Skaare, Bjorn	Det.	1	1	0	0	0	0	....	....	....	....	....	....	1978-79	1978-79
	Skalde, Jarrod	N.J., Ana., Cgy., S.J., Chi., Dal., Atl., Phi.	9	115	13	21	34	62	....	....	....	....	....	....	1990-91	2001-02
	Skarda, Randy	St.L.	2	26	0	5	5	11	....	....	....	....	....	....	1989-90	1991-92
•	Skilton, Raymie	Mtl.W.	1	1	0	0	0	0	....	....	....	....	....	....	1917-18	1917-18
•	Skinner, Alf	Tor., Bos., Mtl.M., Pit.	4	71	26	10	36	87	2	0	1	1	9	1	1917-18	1925-26
	Skinner, Larry	Col.	4	47	10	12	22	8	2	0	0	0	0	....	1976-77	1979-80
‡	Skolney, Wade	Phi.	1	1	0	0	0	2	....	....	....	....	....	....	2005-06	2005-06
‡	Skopintsev, Andrei	T.B., Atl.	3	40	2	4	6	32	....	....	....	....	....	....	1998-99	2000-01
	Skov, Glen	Det., Chi., Mtl.	12	650	106	136	242	413	53	7	7	14	48	3	1949-50	1960-61
‡	Skrbek, Pavel	Pit., Nsh.	3	12	0	0	0	8	....	....	....	....	....	....	1998-99	2001-02
	Skriko, Petri	Van., Bos., Wpg., S.J.	9	541	183	222	405	246	28	5	9	14	4	....	1984-85	1992-93
	Skrlac, Rob	N.J.	1	8	1	0	1	22	....	....	....	....	....	....	2003-04	2003-04
	Skrudland, Brian	Mtl., Cgy., Fla., NYR, Dal.	15	881	124	219	343	1107	164	15	46	61	323	2	1985-86	1999-00
‡	Slaney, John	Wsh., Col., L.A., Phx., Nsh., Pit., Phi.	9	268	22	69	91	99	14	2	1	3	4	....	1993-94	2003-04
•	Sleaver, John	Chi.	2	13	1	0	1	6	....	....	....	....	....	....	1953-54	1956-57
‡	Slegr, Jiri	Van., Edm., Pit., Atl., Det., Bos.	11	622	56	193	249	838	42	4	14	18	39	1	1992-93	2005-06
	Sleigher, Louis	Que., Bos.	6	194	46	53	99	146	17	1	1	2	64	....	1979-80	1985-86
‡	Sloan, Blake	Dal., CBJ, Cgy.	6	290	11	32	43	162	35	0	2	2	20	1	1998-99	2003-04
	Sloan, Tod	Tor., Chi.	13	745	220	262	482	831	47	9	12	21	47	2	1947-48	1960-61
•	Slobodian, Peter	NYA	1	41	3	2	5	54	....	....	....	....	....	....	1940-41	1940-41
•	Slowinski, Ed	NYR	6	291	58	74	132	63	16	2	6	8	6	....	1947-48	1952-53
•	Sly, Darryl	Tor., Min., Van.	4	79	1	2	3	20	....	....	....	....	....	....	1965-66	1970-71
	Smail, Doug	Wpg., Min., Que., Ott.	13	845	210	249	459	602	42	9	2	11	49	....	1980-81	1992-93
	Smart, Alex	Mtl.	1	8	5	2	7	0	....	....	....	....	....	....	1942-43	1942-43
	Smedsmo, Dale	Tor.	1	4	0	0	0	0	....	....	....	....	....	....	1972-73	1972-73
	Smehlik, Richard	Buf., Atl., N.J.	10	644	49	146	195	415	88	1	14	15	40	1	1992-93	2002-03
•	Smillie, Don	Bos.	1	12	2	2	4	4	....	....	....	....	....	....	1933-34	1933-34
‡	Smirnov, Alexei	Ana.	2	52	3	3	6	20	4	0	0	0	2	....	2002-03	2003-04
•	Smith, Alex	Ott., Det., Bos., NYA	11	443	41	50	91	645	19	0	2	2	26	1	1924-25	1934-35
•	Smith, Art	Tor., Ott.	4	144	15	10	25	249	4	1	1	2	8	....	1927-28	1930-31
	Smith, Barry	Bos., Col.	3	114	7	7	14	10	....	....	....	....	....	....	1975-76	1980-81
	Smith, Bobby	Min., Mtl.	15	1077	357	679	1036	917	184	64	96	160	245	1	1978-79	1992-93
	Smith, Brad	Van., Atl., Cgy., Det., Tor.	9	222	28	34	62	591	20	3	3	6	49	....	1978-79	1986-87
‡	Smith, Brandon	Bos., NYI	4	33	3	4	7	10	....	....	....	....	....	....	1998-99	2002-03
	Smith, Brian	Det.	3	61	2	8	10	12	5	0	0	0	0	....	1957-58	1960-61
•	Smith, Brian	L.A., Min.	2	67	10	10	20	33	7	0	0	0	0	....	1967-68	1968-69
•	Smith, Carl	Det.	1	7	1	1	2	2	....	....	....	....	....	....	1943-44	1943-44
	Smith, Clint	NYR, Chi.	11	483	161	236	397	24	42	10	14	24	2	1	1936-37	1946-47
	Smith, D.J.	Tor., Col.	3	45	1	1	2	67	....	....	....	....	....	....	1996-97	2002-03
	Smith, Dallas	Bos., NYR	16	890	55	252	307	959	86	3	29	32	128	2	1959-60	1977-78
	Smith, Dennis	Wsh., L.A.	2	8	0	0	0	4	....	....	....	....	....	....	1989-90	1990-91
	Smith, Derek	Buf., Det.	8	335	78	116	194	60	30	9	14	23	13	....	1975-76	1982-83
	Smith, Derrick	Phi., Min., Dal.	10	537	82	92	174	373	82	14	11	25	79	....	1984-85	1993-94
•	Smith, Des	Mtl.M., Mtl., Chi., Bos.	5	196	22	25	47	236	25	1	4	5	18	1	1937-38	1941-42
•	Smith, Don	Mtl.	1	12	1	0	1	6	....	....	....	....	....	....	1919-20	1919-20
•	Smith, Don	NYR	1	11	1	1	2	0	1	0	0	0	0	....	1949-50	1949-50
	Smith, Doug	L.A., Buf., Edm., Van., Pit.	9	535	115	138	253	624	18	4	2	6	21	....	1981-82	1989-90
	Smith, Floyd	Bos., NYR, Det., Tor., Buf.	13	616	129	178	307	207	48	12	11	23	16	....	1954-55	1971-72
	Smith, Geoff	Edm., Fla., NYR	10	462	18	73	91	282	13	0	1	1	8	1	1989-90	1998-99
	Smith, Glen	Chi.	1	2	0	0	0	0	....	....	....	....	....	....	1950-51	1950-51
•	Smith, Glenn	Tor.	1	9	0	0	0	0	....	....	....	....	....	....	1921-22	1921-22
	Smith, Gord	Wsh., Wpg.	6	299	9	30	39	284	....	....	....	....	....	....	1974-75	1979-80
	Smith, Greg	Cal., Cle., Min., Det., Wsh.	13	829	56	232	288	1110	63	4	7	11	106	....	1975-76	1987-88
•	Smith, Hooley	Ott., Mtl.M., Bos., NYA	17	715	200	225	425	1013	54	11	8	19	109	2	1924-25	1940-41
•	Smith, Ken	Bos.	7	331	78	93	171	49	30	8	13	21	6	....	1944-45	1950-51
•	Smith, Nakina	Det.	1	10	1	2	3	0	....	....	....	....	....	....	1943-44	1943-44
	Smith, Nick	Fla.	1	15	0	0	0	0	....	....	....	....	....	....	2001-02	2001-02
	Smith, Randy	Min.	2	3	0	0	0	0	....	....	....	....	....	....	1985-86	1986-87
	Smith, Rick	Bos., Cal., St.L., Det., Wsh.	11	687	52	167	219	560	78	3	23	26	73	1	1968-69	1980-81
•	Smith, Rodger	Pit., Phi.	6	210	20	4	24	172	4	3	0	3	0	....	1925-26	1930-31
	Smith, Ron	NYI	1	11	1	1	2	14	....	....	....	....	....	....	1972-73	1972-73
•	Smith, Sid	Tor.	12	601	186	183	369	94	44	17	10	27	2	3	1946-47	1957-58
	Smith, Stan	NYR	2	9	2	1	3	0	1	0	0	0	0	1	1939-40	1940-41
	Smith, Steve	Phi., Buf.	6	18	0	1	1	15	....	....	....	....	....	....	1981-82	1988-89
	Smith, Steve	Edm., Chi., Cgy.	16	804	72	303	375	2139	134	11	41	52	288	3	1984-85	2000-01
	Smith, Stu	Mtl.	2	4	2	2	4	2	1	0	0	0	0	....	1940-41	1941-42
	Smith, Stu	Hfd.	4	77	2	10	12	95	....	....	....	....	....	....	1979-80	1982-83
•	Smith, Tommy	Que.	1	10	0	1	1	11	....	....	....	....	....	....	1919-20	1919-20
	Smith, Vern	NYI	1	1	0	0	0	0	....	....	....	....	....	....	1984-85	1984-85
	Smith, Wayne	Chi.	1	2	1	1	2	2	1	0	0	0	0	....	1966-67	1966-67
‡	Smrek, Peter	St.L., NYR	2	28	2	4	6	18	....	....	....	....	....	....	2000-01	2001-02
	Smrke, John	St.L., Que.	3	103	11	17	28	33	....	....	....	....	....	....	1977-78	1979-80
•	Smrke, Stan	Mtl.	2	9	0	3	3	0	....	....	....	....	....	....	1956-57	1957-58
	Smyl, Stan	Van.	13	896	262	411	673	1556	41	16	17	33	64	....	1978-79	1990-91
•	Smylie, Rod	Tor., Ott.	6	74	4	2	6	12	4	0	0	0	2	1	1920-21	1925-26
‡	Smyth, Brad	Fla., L.A., NYR, Nsh., Ott.	6	88	15	13	28	109	....	....	....	....	....	....	1995-96	2002-03
	Smyth, Greg	Phi., Que., Cgy., Fla., Tor., Chi.	10	229	4	16	20	783	12	0	0	0	40	....	1986-87	1996-97
	Smyth, Kevin	Hfd.	3	58	6	8	14	31	....	....	....	....	....	....	1993-94	1995-96
	Snell, Chris	Tor., L.A.	2	34	2	7	9	24	....	....	....	....	....	....	1993-94	1994-95
	Snell, Ron	Pit.	2	7	3	2	5	6	....	....	....	....	....	....	1968-69	1969-70
	Snell, Ted	Pit., K.C., Det.	2	104	7	18	25	22	....	....	....	....	....	....	1973-74	1974-75
	Snepsts, Harold	Van., Min., Det., St.L.	17	1033	38	195	233	2009	93	1	14	15	231	....	1974-75	1990-91
	Snow, Sandy	Det.	1	3	0	0	0	2	....	....	....	....	....	....	1968-69	1968-69
	Snuggerud, Dave	Buf., S.J., Phi.	4	265	30	54	84	127	12	1	3	4	6	....	1989-90	1992-93
•	Snyder, Dan	Atl.	3	49	11	5	16	64	....	....	....	....	....	....	2000-01	2002-03
	Sobchuk, Dennis	Det., Que.	2	35	5	6	11	2	....	....	....	....	....	....	1979-80	1982-83
	Sobchuk, Gene	Van.	1	1	0	0	0	0	....	....	....	....	....	....	1973-74	1973-74
	Solheim, Ken	Chi., Min., Det., Edm.	5	135	19	20	39	34	3	1	1	2	2	....	1980-81	1985-86
	Solinger, Bob	Tor., Det.	5	99	10	11	21	19	....	....	....	....	....	....	1951-52	1959-60
•	Somers, Art	Chi., NYR	6	222	33	56	89	189	30	1	5	6	20	1	1929-30	1934-35
‡	Somik, Radovan	Phi.	2	113	12	20	32	27	15	2	2	4	10	....	2002-03	2003-04
	Sommer, Roy	Edm.	1	3	1	0	1	7	....	....	....	....	....	....	1980-81	1980-81
	Songin, Tom	Bos.	3	43	5	5	10	22	....	....	....	....	....	....	1978-79	1980-81
	Sonmor, Glen	NYR	2	28	2	0	2	21	....	....	....	....	....	....	1953-54	1954-55
‡	Sonnenberg, Martin	Pit., Cgy.	3	63	2	3	5	21	7	0	0	0	0	....	1998-99	2003-04
	Sorochan, Lee	Cgy.	2	3	0	0	0	0	....	....	....	....	....	....	1998-99	1999-00
•	Sorrell, John	Det., NYA	11	490	127	119	246	100	42	12	15	27	10	2	1930-31	1940-41
	Spanhel, Martin	CBJ	2	10	2	0	2	4	....	....	....	....	....	....	2000-01	2001-02
•	Sparrow, Emory	Bos.	1	8	0	0	0	4	....	....	....	....	....	....	1924-25	1924-25
	Speck, Fred	Det., Van.	3	28	1	2	3	2	....	....	....	....	....	....	1968-69	1971-72
•	Speer, Bill	Pit., Bos.	4	130	5	20	25	79	8	1	0	1	4	1	1967-68	1970-71
	Speers, Ted	Det.	1	4	1	1	2	0	....	....	....	....	....	....	1985-86	1985-86
•	Spence, Gordon	Tor.	1	3	0	0	0	0	....	....	....	....	....	....	1925-26	1925-26
•	Spencer, Brian	Tor., NYI, Buf., Pit.	10	553	80	143	223	634	37	1	5	6	29	....	1969-70	1978-79
•	Spencer, Irv	NYR, Bos., Det.	8	230	12	38	50	127	16	0	0	0	8	....	1959-60	1967-68
•	Speyer, Chris	Tor., NYA	3	14	0	0	0	0	....	....	....	....	....	....	1923-24	1933-34
	Spring, Corey	T.B.	2	16	1	1	2	12	....	....	....	....	....	....	1997-98	1998-99
	Spring, Don	Wpg.	4	259	1	54	55	80	6	0	0	0	10	....	1980-81	1983-84
	Spring, Frank	Bos., St.L., Cal., Cle.	5	61	14	20	34	12	....	....	....	....	....	....	1969-70	1976-77
•	Spring, Jesse	Ham., Pit., Tor., NYA	6	133	11	4	15	74	2	0	2	2	2	....	1923-24	1929-30
	Spruce, Andy	Van., Col.	3	172	31	42	73	111	2	0	2	2	0	....	1976-77	1978-79
	Srsen, Tomas	Edm.	1	2	0	0	0	0	....	....	....	....	....	....	1990-91	1990-91
	St. Amour, Martin	Ott.	1	1	0	0	0	2	....	....	....	....	....	....	1992-93	1992-93
	St. Laurent, Andre	NYI, Det., L.A., Pit.	11	644	129	187	316	749	59	8	12	20	48	....	1973-74	1983-84
	St. Laurent, Dollard	Mtl., Chi.	12	652	29	133	162	496	92	2	22	24	87	5	1950-51	1961-62
	St. Marseille, Frank	St.L., L.A.	10	707	140	285	425	242	88	20	25	45	18	....	1967-68	1976-77

Name	NHL Teams	NHL Seasons	Regular Schedule GP	G	A	TP	PIM	Playoffs GP	G	A	TP	PIM	NHL Cup Wins	First NHL Season	Last NHL Season
St. Sauveur, Claude	Atl.	1	79	24	24	48	23	2	0	0	0	0	....	1975-76	1975-76
Stackhouse, Ron	Cal., Det., Pit.	12	889	87	372	459	824	32	5	8	13	38	....	1970-71	1981-82
● Stackhouse, Ted	Tor.	1	13	0	0	0	2	1	0	0	0	0	1	1921-22	1921-22
● Stahan, Butch	Mtl.	1	....	....	....	....	....	3	0	1	1	2	....	1944-45	1944-45
Stajduhar, Nick	Edm.	1	2	0	0	0	4	....	....	....	....	....	....	1995-96	1995-96
Staley, Al	NYR	1	1	0	1	1	0	....	....	....	....	....	....	1948-49	1948-49
Stamler, Lorne	L.A., Tor., Wpg.	4	116	14	11	25	16	....	....	....	....	....	....	1976-77	1979-80
Standing, George	Min.	1	2	0	0	0	0	....	....	....	....	....	....	1967-68	1967-68
Stanfield, Fred	Chi., Bos., Min., Buf.	14	914	211	405	616	134	106	21	35	56	10	2	1964-65	1977-78
Stanfield, Jack	Chi.	1	....	....	....	....	....	1	0	0	0	0	....	1965-66	1965-66
Stanfield, Jim	L.A.	3	7	0	1	1	0	....	....	....	....	....	....	1969-70	1971-72
Stankiewicz, Ed	Det.	2	6	0	0	0	2	....	....	....	....	....	....	1953-54	1955-56
Stankiewicz, Myron	St.L., Phi.	1	35	0	7	7	36	1	0	0	0	0	....	1968-69	1968-69
Stanley, Allan	NYR, Chi., Bos., Tor., Phi.	21	1244	100	333	433	792	109	7	36	43	80	4	1948-49	1968-69
● Stanley, Barney	Chi.	1	1	0	0	0	0	....	....	....	....	....	....	1927-28	1927-28
Stanley, Daryl	Phi., Van.	6	189	8	17	25	408	17	0	0	0	30	....	1983-84	1989-90
Stanowski, Wally	Tor., NYR	10	428	23	88	111	160	60	3	14	17	13	4	1939-40	1950-51
Stanton, Paul	Pit., Bos., NYI	5	295	14	49	63	262	44	2	10	12	66	2	1990-91	1994-95
Stapleton, Brian	Wsh.	1	1	0	0	0	0	....	....	....	....	....	....	1975-76	1975-76
Stapleton, Mike	Chi., Pit., Edm., Wpg., Phx., Atl., NYI, Van.	14	697	71	111	182	342	34	1	0	1	39	....	1986-87	2000-01
Stapleton, Pat	Bos., Chi.	10	635	43	294	337	353	65	10	39	49	38	....	1961-62	1972-73
Starikov, Sergei	N.J.	1	16	0	1	1	8	....	....	....	....	....	....	1989-90	1989-90
● Starr, Harold	Ott., Mtl.M., Mtl., NYR	7	205	6	5	11	186	15	1	0	1	4	....	1929-30	1935-36
● Starr, Wilf	NYA, Det.	4	87	8	6	14	25	7	0	2	2	2	....	1932-33	1935-36
Stasiuk, Vic	Chi., Det., Bos.	14	745	183	254	437	669	69	16	18	34	40	2	1949-50	1962-63
Stastny, Anton	Que.	9	650	252	384	636	150	66	20	32	52	31	....	1980-81	1988-89
Stastny, Marian	Que., Tor.	5	322	121	173	294	110	32	5	17	22	7	....	1981-82	1985-86
Stastny, Peter	Que., N.J., St.L.	15	977	450	789	1239	824	93	33	72	105	123	....	1980-81	1994-95
Staszak, Ray	Det.	1	4	0	1	1	7	....	....	....	....	....	....	1985-86	1985-86
● Steele, Frank	Det.	1	1	0	0	0	0	....	....	....	....	....	....	1930-31	1930-31
Steen, Anders	Wpg.	1	42	5	11	16	22	....	....	....	....	....	....	1980-81	1980-81
Steen, Thomas	Wpg.	14	950	264	553	817	753	56	12	32	44	62	....	1981-82	1994-95
Stefan, Patrik	Atl., Dal.	7	455	64	124	188	158	....	....	....	....	....	....	1999-00	2006-07
Stefaniw, Morris	Atl.	1	13	1	1	2	2	....	....	....	....	....	....	1972-73	1972-73
Stefanski, Bud	NYR	1	1	0	0	0	0	....	....	....	....	....	....	1977-78	1977-78
Stemkowski, Pete	Tor., Det., NYR, L.A.	15	967	206	349	555	866	83	25	29	54	136	1	1963-64	1977-78
Stenlund, Vern	Cle.	1	4	0	0	0	0	....	....	....	....	....	....	1976-77	1976-77
‡ Stephens, Charlie	Col.	2	8	0	2	2	4	....	....	....	....	....	....	2002-03	2003-04
Stephenson, Bob	Hfd., Tor.	1	18	2	3	5	4	....	....	....	....	....	....	1979-80	1979-80
Stern, Ron	Van., Cgy., S.J.	12	638	75	86	161	2077	43	7	7	14	119	....	1987-88	1999-00
Sterner, Ulf	NYR	1	4	0	0	0	0	....	....	....	....	....	....	1964-65	1964-65
Stevens, John	Phi., Hfd.	5	53	0	10	10	48	....	....	....	....	....	....	1986-87	1993-94
Stevens, Kevin	Pit., Bos., L.A., NYR, Phi.	15	874	329	397	726	1470	103	46	60	106	170	2	1987-88	2001-02
Stevens, Mike	Van., Bos., NYI, Tor.	4	23	1	4	5	29	....	....	....	....	....	....	1984-85	1989-90
● Stevens, Phil	Mtl.W., Mtl., Bos.	3	25	1	0	1	3	....	....	....	....	....	....	1917-18	1925-26
Stevens, Scott	Wsh., St.L., N.J.	22	1635	196	712	908	2785	233	26	92	118	402	3	1982-83	2003-04
‡ Stevenson, Jeremy	Ana., Nsh., Min., Dal.	9	207	19	19	38	451	21	0	5	5	20	....	1995-96	2005-06
Stevenson, Shayne	Bos., T.B.	3	27	0	2	2	35	....	....	....	....	....	....	1990-91	1992-93
Stevenson, Turner	Mtl., N.J., Phi.	13	644	75	115	190	969	67	6	12	18	66	1	1992-93	2005-06
Stewart, Allan	N.J., Bos.	6	64	6	4	10	243	....	....	....	....	....	....	1985-86	1991-92
Stewart, Bill	Buf., St.L., Tor., Min.	8	261	7	64	71	424	13	1	3	4	11	....	1977-78	1985-86
Stewart, Blair	Det., Wsh., Que.	7	229	34	44	78	326	....	....	....	....	....	....	1973-74	1979-80
Stewart, Bob	Bos., Cal., Cle., St.L., Pit.	9	575	27	101	128	809	5	1	1	2	2	....	1971-72	1979-80
Stewart, Cam	Bos., Fla., Min.	6	202	16	23	39	120	13	1	3	4	9	....	1993-94	2000-01
Stewart, Gaye	Tor., Chi., Det., NYR, Mtl.	11	502	185	159	344	274	25	2	9	11	16	2	1941-42	1953-54
● Stewart, Jack	Det., Chi.	12	565	31	84	115	765	80	5	14	19	143	2	1938-39	1951-52
Stewart, John	Pit., Atl., Cal.	5	258	58	60	118	158	4	0	0	0	10	....	1970-71	1974-75
Stewart, John	Que.	1	2	0	0	0	0	....	....	....	....	....	....	1979-80	1979-80
Stewart, Ken	Chi.	1	6	1	1	2	2	....	....	....	....	....	....	1941-42	1941-42
● Stewart, Nels	Mtl.M., Bos., NYA	15	650	324	191	515	953	50	9	12	21	47	1	1925-26	1939-40
Stewart, Paul	Que.	1	21	2	0	2	74	....	....	....	....	....	....	1979-80	1979-80
Stewart, Ralph	Van., NYI	7	252	57	73	130	28	19	4	4	8	2	....	1970-71	1977-78
Stewart, Ron	Tor., Bos., St.L., NYR, Van., NYI	21	1353	276	253	529	560	119	14	21	35	60	3	1952-53	1972-73
Stewart, Ryan	Wpg.	1	3	1	0	1	0	....	....	....	....	....	....	1985-86	1985-86
Stienburg, Trevor	Que.	4	71	8	4	12	161	1	0	0	0	0	....	1985-86	1988-89
Stiles, Tony	Cgy.	1	30	2	7	9	20	....	....	....	....	....	....	1983-84	1983-84
Stock, P.J.	NYR, Mtl., Phi., Bos.	7	235	5	21	26	523	8	1	0	1	19	....	1997-98	2003-04
Stoddard, Jack	NYR	2	80	16	15	31	31	....	....	....	....	....	....	1951-52	1952-53
Stojanov, Alek	Van., Pit.	3	107	2	5	7	222	14	0	0	0	21	....	1994-95	1996-97
Stoltz, Roland	Wsh.	1	14	2	2	4	14	....	....	....	....	....	....	1981-82	1981-82
Stone, Steve	Van.	1	2	0	0	0	0	....	....	....	....	....	....	1973-74	1973-74
Storm, Jim	Hfd., Dal.	3	84	7	15	22	44	....	....	....	....	....	....	1993-94	1995-96
Stothers, Mike	Phi., Tor.	4	30	0	2	2	65	5	0	0	0	11	....	1984-85	1987-88
Stoughton, Blaine	Pit., Tor., Hfd., NYR	8	526	258	191	449	204	8	4	2	6	2	....	1973-74	1983-84
Stoyanovich, Steve	Hfd.	1	23	3	5	8	11	....	....	....	....	....	....	1983-84	1983-84
● Strain, Neil	NYR	1	52	11	13	24	12	....	....	....	....	....	....	1952-53	1952-53
Strate, Gord	Det.	3	61	0	0	0	34	....	....	....	....	....	....	1956-57	1958-59
Stratton, Art	NYR, Det., Chi., Pit., Phi.	4	95	18	33	51	24	5	0	0	0	0	....	1959-60	1967-68
‡ Strbak, Martin	L.A., Pit.	1	49	5	11	16	46	....	....	....	....	....	....	2003-04	2003-04
● Strobel, Art	NYR	1	7	0	0	0	0	....	....	....	....	....	....	1943-44	1943-44
Strong, Ken	Tor.	3	15	2	2	4	6	....	....	....	....	....	....	1982-83	1984-85
Stroshein, Garret	Wsh.	1	3	0	0	0	14	....	....	....	....	....	....	2003-04	2003-04
Struch, David	Cgy.	1	4	0	0	0	4	....	....	....	....	....	....	1993-94	1993-94
Strueby, Todd	Edm.	3	5	0	1	1	2	....	....	....	....	....	....	1981-82	1983-84
● Stuart, Billy	Tor., Bos.	7	195	30	20	50	151	12	1	1	2	6	1	1920-21	1926-27
‡ Stuart, Mike	St.L.	2	3	0	0	0	0	....	....	....	....	....	....	2003-04	2005-06
Stumpf, Bob	St.L., Pit.	1	10	1	1	2	20	....	....	....	....	....	....	1974-75	1974-75
Sturgeon, Peter	Col.	2	6	0	1	1	2	....	....	....	....	....	....	1979-80	1980-81
‡ Stutzel, Mike	Phx.	1	9	0	0	0	0	....	....	....	....	....	....	2003-04	2003-04
‡ Suchy, Radoslav	Phx., CBJ	6	451	13	58	71	104	10	1	1	2	0	....	1999-00	2005-06
‡ Suglobov, Alexander	N.J., Tor.	3	18	1	0	1	4	....	....	....	....	....	....	2003-04	2006-07
Suikkanen, Kai	Buf.	2	2	0	0	0	0	....	....	....	....	....	....	1981-82	1982-83
Sulliman, Doug	NYR, Hfd., N.J., Phi.	11	631	160	168	328	175	16	1	3	4	2	....	1979-80	1989-90
● Sullivan, Barry	Det.	1	1	0	0	0	0	....	....	....	....	....	....	1947-48	1947-48
Sullivan, Bob	Hfd.	1	62	18	19	37	18	....	....	....	....	....	....	1982-83	1982-83
Sullivan, Brian	N.J.	1	2	0	1	1	0	....	....	....	....	....	....	1992-93	1992-93
Sullivan, Frank	Tor., Chi.	4	8	0	0	0	2	....	....	....	....	....	....	1949-50	1955-56
Sullivan, Mike	S.J., Cgy., Bos., Phx.	11	709	54	82	136	203	34	4	8	12	14	....	1991-92	2001-02
Sullivan, Peter	Wpg.	2	126	28	54	82	40	....	....	....	....	....	....	1979-80	1980-81
Sullivan, Red	Bos., Chi., NYR	11	557	107	239	346	441	18	1	2	3	6	....	1949-50	1960-61
Summanen, Raimo	Edm., Van.	5	151	36	40	76	35	10	2	5	7	0	....	1983-84	1987-88
● Summerhill, Bill	Mtl., Bro.	4	72	14	17	31	70	3	0	0	0	2	....	1937-38	1941-42
Sundblad, Niklas	Cgy.	1	2	0	0	0	0	....	....	....	....	....	....	1995-96	1995-96
‡ Sundin, Ronnie	NYR	1	1	0	0	0	0	....	....	....	....	....	....	1997-98	1997-98
‡ Sundstrom, Niklas	NYR, S.J., Mtl.	10	750	117	232	349	256	59	6	22	28	22	....	1995-96	2005-06
Sundstrom, Patrik	Van., N.J.	10	679	219	369	588	349	37	9	17	26	25	....	1982-83	1991-92
Sundstrom, Peter	NYR, Wsh., N.J.	6	338	61	83	144	120	23	3	3	6	8	....	1983-84	1989-90
Suomi, Al	Chi.	1	5	0	0	0	0	....	....	....	....	....	....	1936-37	1936-37
‡ Surma, Damian	Car.	2	2	1	1	2	0	....	....	....	....	....	....	2002-03	2003-04
‡ Surovy, Tomas	Pit.	3	126	27	32	59	71	....	....	....	....	....	....	2002-03	2005-06
‡ Sushinsky, Maxim	Min.	1	30	7	4	11	29	....	....	....	....	....	....	2000-01	2000-01
Suter, Gary	Cgy., Chi., S.J.	17	1145	203	641	844	1349	108	17	56	73	120	1	1985-86	2001-02
Sutherland, Bill	Mtl., Phi., Tor., St.L., Det.	6	250	70	58	128	99	14	2	4	6	0	....	1962-63	1971-72
● Sutherland, Max	Bos.	1	2	0	0	0	0	....	....	....	....	....	....	1931-32	1931-32
Sutter, Brent	NYI, Chi.	18	1111	363	466	829	1054	144	30	44	74	164	2	1980-81	1997-98
Sutter, Brian	St.L.	12	779	303	333	636	1786	65	21	21	42	249	....	1976-77	1987-88
Sutter, Darryl	Chi.	8	406	161	118	279	288	51	24	19	43	26	....	1979-80	1986-87
Sutter, Duane	NYI, Chi.	11	731	139	203	342	1333	161	26	32	58	405	4	1979-80	1989-90
Sutter, Rich	Pit., Phi., Van., St.L., Chi., T.B., Tor.	13	874	149	166	315	1411	78	13	5	18	133	....	1982-83	1994-95
Sutter, Ron	Phi., St.L., Que., NYI, Bos., S.J., Cgy.	19	1093	205	329	534	1352	104	8	32	40	193	....	1982-83	2000-01
Sutton, Ken	Buf., Edm., St.L., N.J., S.J., NYI	11	388	23	80	103	338	32	3	4	7	29	1	1990-91	2001-02
Suzor, Mark	Phi., Col.	2	64	4	16	20	60	....	....	....	....	....	....	1976-77	1977-78
‡ Svartvadet, Per	Atl.	4	247	17	34	51	58	....	....	....	....	....	....	1999-00	2002-03
Svehla, Robert	Fla., Tor.	9	655	68	267	335	649	38	1	14	15	42	....	1994-95	2002-03

Peter Sundstrom

Tony Tanti

Mark Taylor

Tim Taylor

Cy Thomas

Fred Thurier

Rocky Trottier

Pierre Turgeon

Name	NHL Teams	NHL Seasons	Regular Schedule GP	G	A	TP	PIM	Playoffs GP	G	A	TP	PIM	NHL Cup Wins	First NHL Season	Last NHL Season
Svejkovsky, Jaroslav	Wsh., T.B.	4	113	23	19	42	56	1	0	0	0	2	....	1996-97	1999-00
Svensson, Leif	Wsh.	2	121	6	40	46	49	....	....	....	....	....	....	1978-79	1979-80
Svensson, Magnus	Fla.	2	46	4	14	18	31	....	....	....	....	....	....	1994-95	1995-96
‡ Svoboda, Jaroslav	Car., Dal.	4	134	12	17	29	62	25	1	4	5	30	....	2001-02	2005-06
Svoboda, Petr	Mtl., Buf., Phi., T.B.	17	1028	58	341	399	1605	127	4	45	49	140	1	1984-85	2000-01
Svoboda, Petr	Tor.	1	18	1	2	3	10	....	....	....	....	....	....	2000-01	2000-01
Swain, Garry	Pit.	1	9	1	1	2	0	....	....	....	....	....	....	1968-69	1968-69
‡ Swanson, Brian	Edm., Atl.	4	70	4	13	17	16	....	....	....	....	....	....	2000-01	2003-04
Swarbrick, George	Oak., Pit., Phi.	4	132	17	25	42	173	....	....	....	....	....	....	1967-68	1970-71
• Sweeney, Bill	NYR	1	4	1	0	1	0	....	....	....	....	....	....	1959-60	1959-60
Sweeney, Bob	Bos., Buf., NYI, Cgy.	10	639	125	163	288	799	103	15	18	33	197	....	1986-87	1995-96
Sweeney, Don	Bos., Dal.	16	1115	52	221	273	681	108	9	10	19	81	....	1988-89	2003-04
Sweeney, Tim	Cgy., Bos., Ana., NYR	8	291	55	83	138	123	4	0	0	0	2	....	1990-91	1997-98
Sykes, Bob	Tor.	1	2	0	0	0	0	....	....	....	....	....	....	1974-75	1974-75
Sykes, Phil	L.A., Wpg.	10	456	79	85	164	519	26	0	3	3	29	....	1982-83	1991-92
Sykora, Michal	S.J., Chi., T.B., Phi.	7	267	15	54	69	185	7	0	1	1	0	....	1993-94	2000-01
‡ Sykora, Petr	Nsh., Wsh.	2	12	2	2	4	6	....	....	....	....	....	....	1998-99	2005-06
Sylvester, Dean	Buf., Atl.	3	96	21	16	37	32	4	0	0	0	0	....	1998-99	2000-01
• Szura, Joe	Oak.	2	90	10	15	25	30	7	2	3	5	2	....	1967-68	1968-69

T

Name	NHL Teams	NHL Seasons	Regular Schedule GP	G	A	TP	PIM	Playoffs GP	G	A	TP	PIM	NHL Cup Wins	First NHL Season	Last NHL Season
Taft, John	Det.	1	15	0	2	2	4	....	....	....	....	....	....	1978-79	1978-79
Taglianetti, Peter	Wpg., Min., Pit., T.B.	11	451	18	74	92	1106	53	2	8	10	103	2	1984-85	1994-95
Talafous, Dean	Atl., Min., NYR	8	497	104	154	258	163	21	4	7	11	11	....	1974-75	1981-82
Talakoski, Ron	NYR	2	9	0	1	1	33	....	....	....	....	....	....	1986-87	1987-88
Talbot, Jean-Guy	Mtl., Min., Det., St.L., Buf.	17	1056	43	242	285	1006	150	4	26	30	142	7	1954-55	1970-71
Tallon, Dale	Van., Chi., Pit.	10	642	98	238	336	568	33	2	10	12	45	....	1970-71	1979-80
Tambellini, Steve	NYI, Col., N.J., Cgy., Van.	10	553	160	150	310	105	2	0	1	1	0	1	1978-79	1987-88
Tamer, Chris	Pit., NYR, Atl.	11	644	21	64	85	1183	37	0	8	8	52	....	1993-94	2003-04
Tancill, Chris	Hfd., Det., Dal., S.J.	8	134	17	32	49	54	11	1	1	2	8	....	1990-91	1997-98
Tanguay, Christian	Que.	1	2	0	0	0	0	....	....	....	....	....	....	1981-82	1981-82
Tannahill, Don	Van.	2	111	30	33	63	25	....	....	....	....	....	....	1972-73	1973-74
Tanti, Tony	Chi., Van., Pit., Buf.	11	697	287	273	560	661	30	3	12	15	27	....	1981-82	1991-92
‡ Tapper, Brad	Atl.	3	71	14	11	25	72	....	....	....	....	....	....	2000-01	2002-03
Tardif, Marc	Mtl., Que.	8	517	194	207	401	443	62	13	15	28	75	2	1969-70	1982-83
Tardif, Patrice	St.L., L.A.	2	65	7	11	18	78	....	....	....	....	....	....	1994-95	1995-96
Tatarinov, Mikhail	Wsh., Que., Bos.	4	161	21	48	69	184	....	....	....	....	....	....	1990-91	1993-94
Tatchell, Spence	NYR	1	1	0	0	0	0	....	....	....	....	....	....	1942-43	1942-43
‡ Taticek, Petr	Fla.	1	3	0	0	0	0	....	....	....	....	....	....	2005-06	2005-06
• Taylor, Billy	Tor., Det., Bos., NYR	7	323	87	180	267	120	33	6	18	24	13	1	1939-40	1947-48
• Taylor, Billy	NYR	1	2	0	0	0	0	....	....	....	....	....	....	1964-65	1964-65
• Taylor, Bob	Bos.	1	8	0	0	0	6	....	....	....	....	....	....	1929-30	1929-30
‡ Taylor, Chris	NYI, Bos., Buf.	8	149	11	21	32	48	2	0	0	0	2	....	1994-95	2003-04
Taylor, Dave	L.A.	17	1111	431	638	1069	1589	92	26	33	59	145	....	1977-78	1993-94
Taylor, Harry	Tor., Chi.	3	66	5	10	15	30	1	0	0	0	0	1	1946-47	1951-52
Taylor, Mark	Phi., Pit., Wsh.	5	209	42	68	110	73	6	0	0	0	0	....	1981-82	1985-86
• Taylor, Ralph	Chi., NYR	3	99	4	1	5	169	4	0	0	0	10	....	1927-28	1929-30
Taylor, Ted	NYR, Det., Min., Van.	6	166	23	35	58	181	....	....	....	....	....	....	1964-65	1971-72
Taylor, Tim	Det., Bos., NYR, T.B.	13	746	73	94	167	433	89	2	12	14	73	2	1993-94	2006-07
Teal, Jeff	Mtl.	1	6	0	1	1	0	....	....	....	....	....	....	1984-85	1984-85
• Teal, Skip	Bos.	1	1	0	0	0	0	....	....	....	....	....	....	1954-55	1954-55
Teal, Vic	NYI	1	1	0	0	0	0	....	....	....	....	....	....	1973-74	1973-74
Tebbutt, Greg	Que., Pit.	2	26	0	3	3	35	....	....	....	....	....	....	1979-80	1983-84
Tepper, Stephen	Chi.	1	1	0	0	0	0	....	....	....	....	....	....	1992-93	1992-93
Terbenche, Paul	Chi., Buf.	5	189	5	26	31	28	12	0	0	0	0	....	1967-68	1973-74
Terrion, Greg	L.A., Tor.	8	561	93	150	243	339	35	2	9	11	41	....	1980-81	1987-88
Terry, Bill	Min.	1	5	0	0	0	0	....	....	....	....	....	....	1987-88	1987-88
• Tertyshny, Dmitri	Phi.	1	62	2	8	10	30	1	0	0	0	0	....	1998-99	1998-99
Tessier, Orval	Mtl., Bos.	3	59	5	7	12	6	....	....	....	....	....	....	1954-55	1960-61
Tetarenko, Joey	Fla., Ott., Car.	4	73	4	1	5	176	....	....	....	....	....	....	2000-01	2003-04
‡ Tezikov, Alexei	Wsh., Van.	3	30	1	1	2	2	....	....	....	....	....	....	1998-99	2001-02
Theberge, Greg	Wsh.	5	153	15	63	78	73	4	0	1	1	0	....	1979-80	1983-84
Thelin, Mats	Bos.	3	163	8	19	27	107	5	0	0	0	6	....	1984-85	1986-87
Thelven, Michael	Bos.	5	207	20	80	100	217	34	4	10	14	34	....	1985-86	1989-90
Therien, Chris	Phi., Dal.	11	764	29	130	159	585	104	4	10	14	68	....	1994-95	2005-06
Therrien, Gaston	Que.	3	22	0	8	8	12	9	0	1	1	4	....	1980-81	1982-83
Thibaudeau, Gilles	Mtl., NYI, Tor.	5	119	25	37	62	40	8	3	3	6	2	....	1986-87	1990-91
Thibeault, Lorrain	Det., Mtl.	2	5	0	2	2	2	....	....	....	....	....	....	1944-45	1945-46
Thiffault, Leo	Min.	1	....	....	....	....	....	5	0	0	0	0	....	1967-68	1967-68
Thomas, Cy	Chi., Tor.	1	14	2	2	4	12	....	....	....	....	....	....	1947-48	1947-48
Thomas, Reg	Que.	1	39	9	7	16	6	....	....	....	....	....	....	1979-80	1979-80
Thomas, Scott	Buf., L.A.	3	63	6	4	10	32	12	1	0	1	4	....	1992-93	2000-01
Thomas, Steve	Tor., Chi., NYI, N.J., Ana., Det.	20	1235	421	512	933	1306	174	54	53	107	187	....	1984-85	2003-04
Thomlinson, Dave	St.L., Bos., L.A.	5	42	1	3	4	50	9	3	1	4	4	....	1989-90	1994-95
Thompson, Brent	L.A., Wpg., Phx.	6	121	1	10	11	352	4	0	0	0	4	....	1991-92	1996-97
• Thompson, Cliff	Bos.	2	13	0	1	1	2	....	....	....	....	....	....	1941-42	1948-49
Thompson, Errol	Tor., Det., Pit.	10	599	208	185	393	184	34	7	5	12	11	....	1970-71	1980-81
• Thompson, Ken	Mtl.W.	1	1	0	0	0	0	....	....	....	....	....	....	1917-18	1917-18
• Thompson, Paul	NYR, Chi.	13	582	153	179	332	336	48	11	11	22	54	3	1926-27	1938-39
Thompson, Rocky	Cgy., Fla.	4	25	0	0	0	117	....	....	....	....	....	....	1997-98	2001-02
• Thoms, Bill	Tor., Chi., Bos.	13	548	135	206	341	154	44	6	10	16	6	....	1932-33	1944-45
• Thomson, Bill	Det.	2	9	2	2	4	0	2	0	0	0	0	....	1938-39	1943-44
Thomson, Floyd	St.L.	8	411	56	97	153	341	10	0	2	2	6	....	1971-72	1979-80
Thomson, Jim	Wsh., Hfd., N.J., L.A., Ott., Ana.	7	115	4	3	7	416	1	0	0	0	0	....	1986-87	1993-94
• Thomson, Jimmy	Tor., Chi.	13	787	19	215	234	920	63	2	13	15	135	4	1945-46	1957-58
• Thomson, Rhys	Mtl., Tor.	2	25	0	2	2	38	....	....	....	....	....	....	1939-40	1942-43
Thornbury, Tom	Pit.	1	14	1	8	9	16	....	....	....	....	....	....	1983-84	1983-84
• Thorsteinson, Joe	NYA	1	4	0	0	0	0	....	....	....	....	....	....	1932-33	1932-33
• Thurier, Fred	NYA, Bro., NYR	3	80	25	27	52	18	....	....	....	....	....	....	1940-41	1944-45
Thurlby, Tom	Oak.	1	20	1	1	2	4	....	....	....	....	....	....	1967-68	1967-68
Thyer, Mario	Min.	1	5	0	0	0	0	1	0	0	0	2	....	1989-90	1989-90
‡ Tibbetts, Billy	Pit., Phi., NYR	3	82	2	8	10	269	....	....	....	....	....	....	2000-01	2002-03
Tichy, Milan	Chi., NYI	3	23	0	5	5	40	....	....	....	....	....	....	1992-93	1995-96
Tidey, Alex	Buf., Edm.	3	9	0	0	0	8	2	0	0	0	0	....	1976-77	1979-80
Tikkanen, Esa	Edm., NYR, St.L., N.J., Van., Fla., Wsh.	15	877	244	386	630	1077	186	72	60	132	275	5	1984-85	1998-99
‡ Tiley, Brad	Phx., Phi.	3	11	0	0	0	0	1	0	0	0	0	....	1997-98	2000-01
Tilley, Tom	St.L.	4	174	4	38	42	89	14	1	3	4	19	....	1988-89	1993-94
‡ Timander, Mattias	Bos., CBJ, NYI, Phi.	8	419	13	57	70	165	23	3	5	8	8	....	1996-97	2003-04
• Timgren, Ray	Tor., Chi.	6	251	14	44	58	70	30	3	9	12	6	2	1948-49	1954-55
Tinordi, Mark	NYR, Min., Dal., Wsh.	12	663	52	148	200	1514	70	7	11	18	165	....	1987-88	1998-99
Tippett, Dave	Hfd., Wsh., Pit., Phi.	12	721	93	169	262	317	62	6	16	22	34	....	1983-84	1993-94
Titanic, Morris	Buf.	2	19	0	0	0	0	....	....	....	....	....	....	1974-75	1975-76
Titov, German	Cgy., Pit., Edm., Ana.	9	624	157	220	377	311	34	11	12	23	18	....	1993-94	2001-02
Tkaczuk, Daniel	Cgy.	1	19	4	7	11	14	....	....	....	....	....	....	2000-01	2000-01
Tkaczuk, Walt	NYR	14	945	227	451	678	556	93	19	32	51	119	....	1967-68	1980-81
Toal, Mike	Edm.	1	3	0	0	0	0	....	....	....	....	....	....	1979-80	1979-80
‡ Tobler, Ryan	T.B.	1	4	0	0	0	5	....	....	....	....	....	....	2001-02	2001-02
Tocchet, Rick	Phi., Pit., L.A., Bos., Wsh., Phx.	18	1144	440	512	952	2972	145	52	60	112	471	1	1984-85	2001-02
Todd, Kevin	N.J., Edm., Chi., L.A., Ana.	9	383	70	133	203	225	12	3	2	5	16	....	1988-89	1997-98
Tomalty, Glenn	Wpg.	1	1	0	0	0	0	....	....	....	....	....	....	1979-80	1979-80
Tomlak, Mike	Hfd.	4	141	15	22	37	103	10	0	1	1	4	....	1989-90	1993-94
Tomlinson, Dave	Tor., Wpg., Fla.	4	42	1	3	4	28	....	....	....	....	....	....	1991-92	1994-95
Tomlinson, Kirk	Min.	1	1	0	0	0	0	....	....	....	....	....	....	1987-88	1987-88
‡ Toms, Jeff	T.B., Wsh., NYI, NYR, Pit., Fla.	8	236	22	33	55	59	1	0	0	0	0	....	1995-96	2002-03
• Tomson, Jack	NYA	3	15	1	1	2	0	2	0	0	0	0	....	1938-39	1940-41
Tonelli, John	NYI, Cgy., L.A., Chi., Que.	14	1028	325	511	836	911	172	40	75	115	200	4	1978-79	1991-92
Tookey, Tim	Wsh., Que., Pit., Phi., L.A.	7	106	22	36	58	71	10	1	3	4	2	....	1980-81	1988-89
Toomey, Sean	Min.	1	1	0	0	0	0	....	....	....	....	....	....	1986-87	1986-87
‡ Toporowski, Shayne	Tor.	1	3	0	0	0	7	....	....	....	....	....	....	1996-97	1996-97
Toppazzini, Jerry	Bos., Chi., Det.	12	783	163	244	407	436	40	13	9	22	13	....	1952-53	1963-64
• Toppazzini, Zellio	Bos., NYR, Chi.	5	123	21	22	43	49	2	0	0	0	0	....	1948-49	1956-57
Torgaev, Pavel	Cgy., T.B.	2	55	6	14	20	20	1	0	0	0	0	....	1995-96	1999-00
Torkki, Jari	Chi.	1	4	1	0	1	0	....	....	....	....	....	....	1988-89	1988-89

Name	NHL Teams	NHL Seasons	Regular Schedule GP	G	A	TP	PIM	Playoffs GP	G	A	TP	PIM	NHL Cup Wins	First NHL Season	Last NHL Season
Tormanen, Antti	Ott.	1	50	7	8	15	28	....	....	....	....	....	....	1995-96	1995-96
• Touhey, Bill	Mtl.M., Ott., Bos.	7	280	65	40	105	107	2	1	0	1	0	....	1927-28	1933-34
• Toupin, Jacques	Chi.	1	8	1	2	3	0	4	0	0	0	0	....	1943-44	1943-44
• Townsend, Art	Chi.	1	5	0	0	0	0	....	....	....	....	....	....	1926-27	1926-27
Townshend, Graeme	Bos., NYI, Ott.	5	45	3	7	10	28	....	....	....	....	....	....	1989-90	1993-94
Trader, Larry	Det., St.L., Mtl.	4	91	5	13	18	74	3	0	0	0	0	....	1982-83	1987-88
• Trainor, Wes	NYR	1	17	1	2	3	6	....	....	....	....	....	....	1948-49	1948-49
• Trapp, Bob	Chi.	2	82	4	4	8	129	2	0	0	0	4	....	1926-27	1927-28
Trapp, Doug	Buf.	1	2	0	0	0	0	....	....	....	....	....	....	1986-87	1986-87
• Traub, Percy	Chi., Det.	3	130	3	3	6	217	4	0	0	0	6	....	1926-27	1928-29
Trebil, Dan	Ana., Pit., St.L.	5	85	4	4	8	32	10	0	1	1	8	....	1996-97	2000-01
Tredway, Brock	L.A.	1	....	....	....	....	....	1	0	0	0	0	....	1981-82	1981-82
Tremblay, Brent	Wsh.	2	10	1	0	1	6	....	....	....	....	....	....	1978-79	1979-80
Tremblay, Gilles	Mtl.	9	509	168	162	330	161	48	9	14	23	4	4	1960-61	1968-69
• Tremblay, J.C.	Mtl.	13	794	57	306	363	204	108	14	51	65	58	5	1959-60	1971-72
• Tremblay, Marcel	Mtl.	1	10	0	2	2	0	....	....	....	....	....	....	1938-39	1938-39
Tremblay, Mario	Mtl.	12	852	258	326	584	1043	101	20	29	49	187	5	1974-75	1985-86
• Tremblay, Nils	Mtl.	2	3	0	1	1	0	2	0	0	0	0	....	1944-45	1945-46
‡ Trepanier, Pascal	Col., Ana., Nsh.	6	229	12	22	34	252	2	0	0	0	0	....	1997-98	2002-03
Trimper, Tim	Chi., Wpg., Min.	6	190	30	36	66	153	2	0	0	0	2	....	1979-80	1984-85
‡ Tripp, John	NYR, L.A.	2	43	2	7	9	35	....	....	....	....	....	....	2002-03	2003-04
‡ Trnka, Pavel	Ana., Fla.	7	411	14	63	77	323	4	0	1	1	2	....	1997-98	2003-04
Trottier, Bryan	NYI, Pit.	18	1279	524	901	1425	912	221	71	113	184	277	6	1975-76	1993-94
• Trottier, Dave	Mtl.M., Det.	11	446	121	113	234	517	31	4	3	7	39	1	1928-29	1938-39
Trottier, Guy	NYR, Tor.	3	115	28	17	45	37	9	1	0	1	16	....	1968-69	1971-72
Trottier, Rocky	N.J.	2	38	6	4	10	2	....	....	....	....	....	....	1983-84	1984-85
• Trudel, Lou	Chi., Mtl.	8	306	49	69	118	122	24	1	3	4	4	2	1933-34	1940-41
• Trudell, Rene	NYR	3	129	24	28	52	72	5	0	0	0	2	....	1945-46	1947-48
‡ Tselios, Nikos	Car.	1	2	0	0	0	6	....	....	....	....	....	....	2001-02	2001-02
‡ Tsulygin, Nikolai	Ana.	1	22	0	1	1	8	....	....	....	....	....	....	1996-97	1996-97
Tsygurov, Denis	Buf., L.A.	3	51	1	5	6	45	....	....	....	....	....	....	1993-94	1995-96
Tsyplakov, Vladimir	L.A., Buf.	6	331	69	101	170	90	18	1	2	3	16	....	1995-96	2000-01
Tucker, John	Buf., Wsh., NYI, T.B.	12	656	177	259	436	285	31	10	18	28	24	....	1983-84	1995-96
• Tudin, Connie	Mtl.	1	4	0	1	1	4	....	....	....	....	....	....	1941-42	1941-42
Tudor, Rob	Van., St.L.	3	28	4	4	8	19	3	0	0	0	0	....	1978-79	1982-83
Tuer, Allan	L.A., Min., Hfd.	4	57	1	1	2	208	....	....	....	....	....	....	1985-86	1989-90
‡ Tuomainen, Marko	Edm., L.A., NYI	4	79	9	9	18	84	1	0	0	0	0	....	1994-95	2001-02
Turcotte, Alfie	Mtl., Wpg., Wsh.	7	112	17	29	46	49	5	0	0	0	0	....	1983-84	1990-91
Turcotte, Darren	NYR, Hfd., Wpg., S.J., St.L., Nsh.	12	635	195	216	411	301	35	6	8	14	12	....	1988-89	1999-00
Turgeon, Pierre	Buf., NYI, Mtl., St.L., Dal., Col.	19	1294	515	812	1327	452	109	35	62	97	36	....	1987-88	2006-07
Turgeon, Sylvain	Hfd., N.J., Mtl., Ott.	12	669	269	226	495	691	36	4	7	11	22	....	1983-84	1994-95
Turlick, Gord	Bos.	1	2	0	0	0	2	....	....	....	....	....	....	1959-60	1959-60
Turnbull, Ian	Tor., L.A., Pit.	10	628	123	317	440	736	55	13	32	45	94	....	1973-74	1982-83
Turnbull, Perry	St.L., Mtl., Wpg.	9	608	188	163	351	1245	34	6	7	13	86	....	1979-80	1987-88
Turnbull, Randy	Cgy.	1	1	0	0	0	2	....	....	....	....	....	....	1981-82	1981-82
Turner, Bob	Mtl., Chi.	8	478	19	51	70	307	68	1	4	5	44	5	1955-56	1962-63
Turner, Brad	NYI	1	3	0	0	0	0	....	....	....	....	....	....	1991-92	1991-92
Turner, Dean	NYR, Col., L.A.	4	35	1	0	1	59	....	....	....	....	....	....	1978-79	1982-83
• Tustin, Norm	NYR	1	18	2	4	6	0	....	....	....	....	....	....	1941-42	1941-42
• Tuten, Aud	Chi.	2	39	4	8	12	48	....	....	....	....	....	....	1941-42	1942-43
Tutt, Brian	Wsh.	1	7	1	0	1	2	....	....	....	....	....	....	1989-90	1989-90
Tuttle, Steve	St.L.	3	144	28	28	56	12	17	1	6	7	2	....	1988-89	1990-91
‡ Tuzzolino, Tony	Ana., NYR, Bos.	3	9	0	0	0	7	....	....	....	....	....	....	1997-98	2001-02
‡ Tverdovsky, Oleg	Ana., Wpg., Phx., N.J., Car., L.A.	11	713	77	240	317	291	45	0	14	14	6	2	1994-95	2006-07
‡ Tvrdon, Roman	Wsh.	1	9	0	1	1	2	....	....	....	....	....	....	2003-04	2003-04
Twist, Tony	St.L., Que.	10	445	10	18	28	1121	18	1	1	2	22	....	1989-90	1998-99

U V

Name	NHL Teams	NHL Seasons	Regular Schedule GP	G	A	TP	PIM	Playoffs GP	G	A	TP	PIM	NHL Cup Wins	First NHL Season	Last NHL Season
Ubriaco, Gene	Pit., Oak., Chi.	3	177	39	35	74	50	11	2	0	2	4	....	1967-68	1969-70
‡ Ulanov, Igor	Wpg., Wsh., Chi., T.B., Mtl., Edm., NYR, Fla.	14	739	27	135	162	1151	39	1	4	5	84	....	1991-92	2005-06
Ullman, Norm	Det., Tor.	20	1410	490	739	1229	712	106	30	53	83	67	....	1955-56	1974-75
‡ Ulmer, Jeff	NYR	1	21	3	0	3	8	....	....	....	....	....	....	2000-01	2000-01
‡ Ulmer, Layne	NYR	1	1	0	0	0	0	....	....	....	....	....	....	2003-04	2003-04
Unger, Garry	Tor., Det., St.L., Atl., L.A., Edm.	16	1105	413	391	804	1075	52	12	18	30	105	....	1967-68	1982-83
‡ Ustorf, Stefan	Wsh.	2	54	7	10	17	16	5	0	0	0	0	....	1995-96	1996-97
Vachon, Nick	NYI	1	1	0	0	0	0	....	....	....	....	....	....	1996-97	1996-97
Vadnais, Carol	Mtl., Oak., Cal., Bos., NYR, N.J.	17	1087	169	418	587	1813	106	10	40	50	185	2	1966-67	1982-83
‡ Vaic, Lubomir	Van.	2	9	1	1	2	2	....	....	....	....	....	....	1997-98	1999-00
Vail, Eric	Atl., Cgy., Det.	9	591	216	260	476	281	20	5	6	11	6	....	1973-74	1981-82
• Vail, Sparky	NYR	2	50	4	1	5	18	10	0	0	0	2	....	1928-29	1929-30
Vaive, Rick	Van., Tor., Chi., Buf.	13	876	441	347	788	1445	54	27	16	43	111	....	1979-80	1991-92
Valentine, Chris	Wsh.	3	105	43	52	95	127	2	0	0	0	4	....	1981-82	1983-84
‡ Valicevic, Rob	Nsh., L.A., Ana., Dal.	6	193	28	20	48	61	....	....	....	....	....	....	1998-99	2003-04
Valiquette, Jack	Tor., Col.	7	350	84	134	218	79	23	3	6	9	4	....	1974-75	1980-81
Valk, Garry	Van., Ana., Pit., Tor., Chi.	13	777	100	156	256	747	61	6	7	13	79	....	1990-91	2002-03
Vallis, Lindsay	Mtl.	1	1	0	0	0	0	....	....	....	....	....	....	1993-94	1993-94
Van Allen, Shaun	Edm., Ana., Ott., Dal., Mtl.	13	794	84	185	269	481	61	1	7	8	45	....	1990-91	2003-04
Van Boxmeer, John	Mtl., Col., Buf., Que.	11	588	84	274	358	465	38	5	15	20	37	....	1973-74	1983-84
Van Dorp, Wayne	Edm., Pit., Chi., Que.	6	125	12	12	24	565	27	0	1	1	42	....	1986-87	1991-92
Van Drunen, David	Ott.	1	1	0	0	0	0	....	....	....	....	....	....	1999-00	1999-00
‡ Van Impe, Darren	Ana., Bos., NYR, Fla., NYI, CBJ	9	411	25	90	115	397	33	3	9	12	28	....	1994-95	2002-03
Van Impe, Ed	Chi., Phi., Pit.	11	700	27	126	153	1025	66	1	12	13	131	2	1966-67	1976-77
VandenBussche, Ryan	NYR, Chi., Pit.	9	310	10	10	20	702	1	0	0	0	0	....	1996-97	2005-06
‡ Varada, Vaclav	Buf., Ott.	10	493	58	125	183	410	87	11	19	30	82	....	1995-96	2005-06
‡ Varis, Petri	Chi.	1	1	0	0	0	0	....	....	....	....	....	....	1997-98	1997-98
‡ Varlamov, Sergei	Cgy., St.L.	4	63	8	7	15	26	1	0	0	0	2	....	1997-98	2002-03
Varvio, Jarkko	Dal.	2	13	3	4	7	4	....	....	....	....	....	....	1993-94	1994-95
Vasilevski, Alexander	St.L.	2	4	0	0	0	2	....	....	....	....	....	....	1995-96	1996-97
Vasiliev, Alexei	NYR	1	1	0	0	0	2	....	....	....	....	....	....	1999-00	1999-00
‡ Vasiljevs, Herbert	Fla., Atl., Van.	4	51	8	7	15	22	....	....	....	....	....	....	1998-99	2001-02
Vasilyev, Andrei	NYI, Phx.	4	16	2	5	7	6	....	....	....	....	....	....	1994-95	1998-99
Vaske, Dennis	NYI, Bos.	9	235	5	41	46	253	22	0	7	7	16	....	1990-91	1998-99
• Vasko, Moose	Chi., Min.	13	786	34	166	200	719	78	2	7	9	73	1	1956-57	1969-70
Vasko, Rick	Det.	3	31	3	7	10	29	....	....	....	....	....	....	1977-78	1980-81
‡ Vauclair, Julien	Ott.	1	1	0	0	0	2	....	....	....	....	....	....	2003-04	2003-04
Vautour, Yvon	NYI, Col., N.J., Que.	6	204	26	33	59	401	....	....	....	....	....	....	1979-80	1984-85
Vaydik, Greg	Chi.	1	5	0	0	0	0	....	....	....	....	....	....	1976-77	1976-77
Veitch, Darren	Wsh., Det., Tor.	10	511	48	209	257	296	33	4	11	15	33	....	1980-81	1990-91
Velischek, Randy	Min., N.J., Que.	10	509	21	76	97	401	44	2	5	7	32	....	1982-83	1991-92
Vellucci, Mike	Hfd.	1	2	0	0	0	11	....	....	....	....	....	....	1987-88	1987-88
Venasky, Vic	L.A.	7	430	61	101	162	66	21	1	5	6	12	....	1972-73	1978-79
Veneruzzo, Gary	St.L.	2	7	1	1	2	0	9	0	2	2	2	....	1967-68	1971-72
Verbeek, Pat	N.J., Hfd., NYR, Dal., Det.	20	1424	522	541	1063	2905	117	26	36	62	225	1	1982-83	2001-02
Vermette, Mark	Que.	4	67	5	13	18	33	....	....	....	....	....	....	1988-89	1991-92
‡ Vernarsky, Kris	Bos.	2	17	1	0	1	2	....	....	....	....	....	....	2002-03	2003-04
‡ Verot, Darcy	Wsh.	1	37	0	2	2	135	....	....	....	....	....	....	2003-04	2003-04
Verret, Claude	Buf.	2	14	2	5	7	2	....	....	....	....	....	....	1983-84	1984-85
Verstraete, Leigh	Tor.	3	8	0	1	1	14	....	....	....	....	....	....	1982-83	1987-88
Ververgaert, Dennis	Van., Phi., Wsh.	8	583	176	216	392	247	8	1	2	3	6	....	1973-74	1980-81
Vesey, Jim	St.L., Bos.	3	15	1	2	3	7	....	....	....	....	....	....	1988-89	1991-92
Veysey, Sid	Van.	1	1	0	0	0	0	....	....	....	....	....	....	1977-78	1977-78
Vial, Dennis	NYR, Det., Ott.	8	242	4	15	19	794	....	....	....	....	....	....	1990-91	1997-98
Vickers, Steve	NYR	10	698	246	340	586	330	68	24	25	49	58	....	1972-73	1981-82
Vigneault, Alain	St.L.	2	42	2	5	7	82	4	0	1	1	26	....	1981-82	1982-83
‡ Viitakoski, Vesa	Cgy.	3	23	2	4	6	8	....	....	....	....	....	....	1993-94	1995-96
Vilgrain, Claude	Van., N.J., Phi.	5	89	21	32	53	78	11	1	1	2	17	....	1987-88	1993-94
Vincelette, Dan	Chi., Que.	6	193	20	22	42	351	12	0	0	0	4	....	1986-87	1991-92
Vipond, Pete	Cal.	1	3	0	0	0	0	....	....	....	....	....	....	1972-73	1972-73
Virta, Hannu	Buf.	5	245	25	101	126	66	17	1	3	4	6	....	1981-82	1985-86
‡ Virta, Tony	Min.	1	8	2	3	5	0	....	....	....	....	....	....	2001-02	2001-02
‡ Virtue, Terry	Bos., NYR	2	5	0	0	0	0	....	....	....	....	....	....	1998-99	1999-00
Visheau, Mark	Wpg., L.A.	2	29	1	3	4	107	....	....	....	....	....	....	1993-94	1998-99
Vitolinsh, Harijs	Wpg.	1	8	0	0	0	4	....	....	....	....	....	....	1993-94	1993-94

Eric Vail

John VanBoxmeer

Claude Vilgrain

Russ Walker

Bill Warwick

Jimmy Watson

Juha Widing

Tom Williams

				Regular Schedule					Playoffs					NHL	First	Last
	Name	NHL Teams	NHL Seasons	GP	G	A	TP	PIM	GP	G	A	TP	PIM	Cup Wins	NHL Season	NHL Season
	Viveiros, Emanuel	Min.	3	29	1	11	12	6	....	....	....	....	....	....	1985-86	1987-88
‡	Vlasak, Tomas	L.A.	1	10	1	3	4	2	....	....	....	....	....	....	2000-01	2000-01
●	Vokes, Ed	Chi.	1	5	0	0	0	0	....	....	....	....	....	....	1930-31	1930-31
	Volcan, Mickey	Hfd., Cgy.	4	162	8	33	41	146	....	....	....	....	....	....	1980-81	1983-84
	Volchkov, Alexandre	Wsh.	1	3	0	0	0	0	....	....	....	....	....	....	1999-00	1999-00
	Volek, David	NYI	6	396	95	154	249	201	15	5	5	10	2	....	1988-89	1993-94
	Volmar, Doug	Det., L.A.	4	62	13	8	21	26	2	1	0	1	0	....	1969-70	1972-73
‡	Von Arx, Reto	Chi.	1	19	3	1	4	4	....	....	....	....	....	....	2000-01	2000-01
	Von Stefenelli, Phil	Bos., Ott.	2	33	0	5	5	23	....	....	....	....	....	....	1995-96	1996-97
	Vopat, Jan	L.A., Nsh.	5	126	11	20	31	70	2	0	1	1	2	....	1995-96	1999-00
‡	Vopat, Roman	St.L., L.A., Chi., Phi.	4	133	6	14	20	253	....	....	....	....	....	....	1995-96	1998-99
	Vorobiev, Vladimir	NYR, Edm.	3	33	9	7	16	14	1	0	0	0	0	....	1996-97	1998-99
●	Voss, Carl	Tor., NYR, Det., Ott., St.L., NYA, Mtl.M., Chi.	8	261	34	70	104	50	24	5	3	8	0	1	1926-27	1937-38
‡	Vujtek, Vladimir	Mtl., Edm., T.B., Atl., Pit.	6	110	7	30	37	38	....	....	....	....	....	....	1991-92	2002-03
	Vukota, Mick	NYI, T.B., Mtl.	11	574	17	29	46	2071	23	0	0	0	73	....	1987-88	1997-98
	Vyazmikin, Igor	Edm.	1	4	1	0	1	0	....	....	....	....	....	....	1990-91	1990-91
‡	Vyshedkevich, Sergei	Atl.	2	30	2	5	7	16	....	....	....	....	....	....	1999-00	2000-01

W

	Waddell, Don	L.A.	1	1	0	0	0	0	....	....	....	....	....	....	1980-81	1980-81
●	Waite, Frank	NYR	1	17	1	3	4	4	....	....	....	....	....	....	1930-31	1930-31
	Walker, Gord	NYR, L.A.	4	31	3	4	7	23	....	....	....	....	....	....	1986-87	1989-90
	Walker, Howard	Wsh., Cgy.	3	83	2	13	15	133	....	....	....	....	....	....	1980-81	1982-83
●	Walker, Jack	Det.	2	80	5	8	13	18	....	....	....	....	....	....	1926-27	1927-28
	Walker, Kurt	Tor.	3	71	4	5	9	142	16	0	0	0	34	....	1975-76	1977-78
	Walker, Russ	L.A.	2	17	1	0	1	41	....	....	....	....	....	....	1976-77	1977-78
	Wall, Bob	Det., L.A., St.L.	8	322	30	55	85	155	22	0	3	3	2	....	1964-65	1971-72
	Wallin, Jesse	Det.	4	49	0	2	2	34	....	....	....	....	....	....	1999-00	2002-03
	Wallin, Peter	NYR	2	52	3	14	17	14	14	2	6	8	6	....	1980-81	1981-82
	Walsh, Jim	Buf.	1	4	0	1	1	4	....	....	....	....	....	....	1981-82	1981-82
	Walsh, Mike	NYI	2	14	2	0	2	4	....	....	....	....	....	....	1987-88	1988-89
	Walter, Ryan	Wsh., Mtl., Van.	15	1003	264	382	646	946	113	16	35	51	62	1	1978-79	1992-93
●	Walton, Bobby	Mtl.	1	4	0	0	0	0	....	....	....	....	....	....	1943-44	1943-44
	Walton, Mike	Tor., Bos., Van., St.L., Chi.	12	588	201	247	448	357	47	14	10	24	45	2	1965-66	1978-79
	Wappel, Gord	Atl., Cgy.	3	20	1	1	2	10	2	0	0	0	4	....	1979-80	1981-82
	Ward, Dixon	Van., L.A., Tor., Buf., Bos., NYR	10	537	95	129	224	431	62	14	20	34	46	....	1992-93	2002-03
●	Ward, Don	Chi., Bos.	2	34	0	1	1	16	....	....	....	....	....	....	1957-58	1959-60
	Ward, Ed	Que., Cgy., Atl., Ana., N.J.	8	278	23	26	49	354	....	....	....	....	....	....	1993-94	2000-01
●	Ward, Jimmy	Mtl.M., Mtl.	12	527	147	127	274	455	36	4	4	8	26	1	1927-28	1938-39
	Ward, Joe	Col.	1	4	0	0	0	2	....	....	....	....	....	....	1980-81	1980-81
‡	Ward, Lance	Fla., Ana.	4	209	4	12	16	391	....	....	....	....	....	....	2000-01	2003-04
	Ward, Ron	Tor., Van.	2	89	2	5	7	6	....	....	....	....	....	....	1969-70	1971-72
	Ware, Jeff	Tor., Fla.	3	21	0	1	1	12	....	....	....	....	....	....	1996-97	1998-99
	Ware, Michael	Edm.	2	5	0	1	1	15	....	....	....	....	....	....	1988-89	1989-90
●	Wares, Eddie	NYR, Det., Chi.	9	321	60	102	162	161	45	5	7	12	34	1	1936-37	1946-47
	Warner, Bob	Tor.	2	10	1	1	2	4	4	0	0	0	0	....	1975-76	1976-77
	Warner, Jim	Hfd.	1	32	0	3	3	10	....	....	....	....	....	....	1979-80	1979-80
	Warriner, Todd	Tor., T.B., Phx., Van., Phi., Nsh.	9	453	65	89	154	249	21	2	1	3	6	....	1994-95	2002-03
●	Warwick, Billy	NYR	2	14	3	3	6	16	....	....	....	....	....	....	1942-43	1943-44
●	Warwick, Grant	NYR, Bos., Mtl.	9	395	147	142	289	220	16	2	4	6	6	....	1941-42	1949-50
	Washburn, Steve	Fla., Van., Phi.	6	93	14	15	29	42	1	0	1	1	0	....	1995-96	2000-01
●	Wasnie, Nick	Chi., Mtl., NYA, Ott., St.L.	7	248	57	34	91	176	20	6	3	9	20	2	1927-28	1934-35
	Watson, Bill	Chi.	4	115	23	36	59	12	6	0	2	2	0	....	1985-86	1988-89
	Watson, Bryan	Mtl., Det., Oak., Pit., St.L., Wsh.	16	878	17	135	152	2212	32	2	0	2	70	1	1963-64	1978-79
	Watson, Dave	Col.	2	18	0	1	1	10	....	....	....	....	....	....	1979-80	1980-81
●	Watson, Harry	Bro., Det., Tor., Chi.	14	809	236	207	443	150	62	16	9	25	27	5	1941-42	1956-57
	Watson, Jim	Det., Buf.	8	221	4	19	23	345	....	....	....	....	....	....	1963-64	1971-72
	Watson, Jimmy	Phi.	10	613	38	148	186	492	101	5	34	39	89	2	1972-73	1981-82
	Watson, Joe	Bos., Phi., Col.	14	835	38	178	216	447	84	3	12	15	82	2	1964-65	1978-79
●	Watson, Phil	NYR, Mtl.	13	590	144	265	409	532	54	10	25	35	67	2	1935-36	1947-48
‡	Watt, Mike	Edm., NYI, Nsh., Car.	5	157	15	26	41	41	....	....	....	....	....	....	1997-98	2002-03
	Watters, Tim	Wpg., L.A.	14	741	26	151	177	1289	82	1	5	6	115	....	1981-82	1994-95
	Watts, Brian	Det.	1	4	0	0	0	0	....	....	....	....	....	....	1975-76	1975-76
	Webb, Steve	NYI, Pit.	8	321	5	13	18	532	14	0	0	0	28	....	1996-97	2003-04
●	Webster, Aubrey	Phi., Mtl.M.	2	5	0	0	0	0	....	....	....	....	....	....	1930-31	1934-35
●	Webster, Don	Tor.	1	27	7	6	13	28	5	0	0	0	12	....	1943-44	1943-44
	Webster, John	NYR	1	14	0	0	0	4	....	....	....	....	....	....	1949-50	1949-50
	Webster, Tom	Bos., Det., Cal.	5	102	33	42	75	61	1	0	0	0	0	....	1968-69	1979-80
●	Weiland, Cooney	Bos., Ott., Det.	11	509	173	160	333	147	45	12	10	22	12	2	1928-29	1938-39
	Weinrich, Eric	N.J., Hfd., Chi., Mtl., Bos., Phi., St.L., Van.	17	1157	70	318	388	825	81	6	23	29	67	....	1988-89	2005-06
	Weir, Stan	Cal., Tor., Edm., Col., Det.	10	642	139	207	346	183	37	6	5	11	4	....	1972-73	1982-83
	Weir, Wally	Que., Hfd., Pit.	6	320	21	45	66	625	23	0	1	1	96	....	1979-80	1984-85
●	Wellington, Alex	Que.	1	1	0	0	0	0	....	....	....	....	....	....	1919-20	1919-20
	Wells, Chris	Pit., Fla.	5	195	9	20	29	193	3	0	0	0	0	....	1995-96	1999-00
	Wells, Jay	L.A., Phi., Buf., NYR, St.L., T.B.	18	1098	47	216	263	2359	114	3	14	17	213	1	1979-80	1996-97
	Wensink, John	St.L., Bos., Que., Col., N.J.	8	403	70	68	138	840	43	2	6	8	86	....	1973-74	1982-83
●	Wentworth, Cy	Chi., Mtl.M., Mtl.	13	575	39	68	107	355	35	5	6	11	20	1	1927-28	1939-40
	Werenka, Brad	Edm., Que., Chi., Pit., Cgy.	7	320	19	61	80	299	19	2	1	3	14	....	1992-93	2000-01
	Wesenberg, Brian	Phi.	1	1	0	0	0	5	....	....	....	....	....	....	1998-99	1998-99
	Wesley, Blake	Phi., Hfd., Que., Tor.	7	298	18	46	64	486	19	2	2	4	30	....	1979-80	1985-86
	Westfall, Ed	Bos., NYI	18	1226	231	394	625	544	95	22	37	59	41	2	1961-62	1978-79
	Westlund, Tommy	Car.	4	203	9	13	22	48	25	1	0	1	17	....	1999-00	2002-03
	Wharram, Kenny	Chi.	14	766	252	281	533	222	80	16	27	43	38	1	1951-52	1968-69
	Wharton, Len	NYR	1	1	0	0	0	0	....	....	....	....	....	....	1944-45	1944-45
	Wheeldon, Simon	NYR, Wpg.	3	15	0	2	2	10	....	....	....	....	....	....	1987-88	1990-91
●	Wheldon, Don	St.L.	1	2	0	0	0	0	....	....	....	....	....	....	1974-75	1974-75
	Whelton, Bill	Wpg.	1	2	0	0	0	0	....	....	....	....	....	....	1980-81	1980-81
	Whistle, Rob	NYR, St.L.	2	51	7	5	12	16	4	0	0	0	2	....	1985-86	1987-88
	White, Bill	L.A., Chi.	9	604	50	215	265	495	91	7	32	39	76	....	1967-68	1975-76
‡	White, Brian	Col.	1	2	0	0	0	0	....	....	....	....	....	....	1998-99	1998-99
	White, Moe	Mtl.	1	4	0	1	1	2	....	....	....	....	....	....	1945-46	1945-46
‡	White, Peter	Edm., Tor., Phi., Chi.	9	220	23	37	60	36	19	0	2	2	0	....	1993-94	2003-04
●	White, Sherman	NYR	2	4	0	2	2	0	....	....	....	....	....	....	1946-47	1949-50
●	White, Tex	Pit., NYA, Phi.	6	203	33	12	45	141	4	0	0	0	4	....	1925-26	1930-31
	White, Tony	Wsh., Min.	5	164	37	28	65	104	....	....	....	....	....	....	1974-75	1979-80
	Whitelaw, Bob	Det.	2	32	0	2	2	2	8	0	0	0	0	....	1940-41	1941-42
	Whitlock, Bob	Min.	1	1	0	0	0	0	....	....	....	....	....	....	1969-70	1969-70
	Whyte, Sean	L.A.	2	21	0	2	2	12	....	....	....	....	....	....	1991-92	1992-93
●	Wickenheiser, Doug	Mtl., St.L., Van., NYR, Wsh.	10	556	111	165	276	286	41	4	7	11	18	....	1980-81	1989-90
●	Widing, Juha	NYR, L.A., Cle.	8	575	144	226	370	208	8	1	2	3	2	....	1969-70	1976-77
	Widmer, Jason	NYI, S.J.	3	7	0	1	1	7	....	....	....	....	....	....	1994-95	1996-97
●	Wiebe, Art	Chi.	11	414	14	27	41	201	31	1	3	4	10	1	1932-33	1943-44
	Wiemer, Jason	T.B., Cgy., Fla., NYI, Min., N.J.	11	726	90	112	202	1420	19	1	0	1	67	....	1994-95	2005-06
	Wiemer, Jim	Buf., NYR, Edm., L.A., Bos.	11	325	29	72	101	378	62	5	8	13	63	....	1982-83	1993-94
●	Wilcox, Archie	Mtl.M., Bos., St.L.	6	208	8	14	22	158	12	1	0	1	8	....	1929-30	1934-35
	Wilcox, Barry	Van.	2	33	3	2	5	15	....	....	....	....	....	....	1972-73	1974-75
●	Wilder, Arch	Det.	1	18	0	2	2	2	....	....	....	....	....	....	1940-41	1940-41
	Wiley, Jim	Pit., Van.	5	63	4	10	14	8	....	....	....	....	....	....	1972-73	1976-77
	Wilkie, Bob	Det., Phi.	2	18	2	5	7	10	....	....	....	....	....	....	1990-91	1993-94
	Wilkie, David	Mtl., T.B., NYR	6	167	10	26	36	165	8	1	2	3	14	....	1994-95	2000-01
	Wilkins, Barry	Bos., Van., Pit.	9	418	27	125	152	663	6	0	1	1	4	....	1966-67	1975-76
●	Wilkinson, John	Bos.	1	9	0	0	0	6	....	....	....	....	....	....	1943-44	1943-44
	Wilkinson, Neil	Min., S.J., Chi., Wpg., Pit.	10	460	16	67	83	813	53	3	6	9	41	....	1989-90	1998-99
	Wilks, Brian	L.A.	4	48	4	8	12	27	....	....	....	....	....	....	1984-85	1988-89
	Willard, Rod	Tor.	1	1	0	0	0	0	....	....	....	....	....	....	1982-83	1982-83
●	Williams, Burr	Det., St.L., Bos.	3	19	0	1	1	28	7	0	0	0	8	....	1933-34	1936-37
	Williams, Butch	St.L., Cal.	3	108	14	35	49	131	....	....	....	....	....	....	1973-74	1975-76
	Williams, Darryl	L.A.	1	2	0	0	0	10	....	....	....	....	....	....	1992-93	1992-93
	Williams, David	S.J., Ana.	4	173	11	53	64	157	....	....	....	....	....	....	1991-92	1994-95
	Williams, Fred	Det.	1	44	2	5	7	10	....	....	....	....	....	....	1976-77	1976-77
	Williams, Gord	Phi.	2	2	0	0	0	2	....	....	....	....	....	....	1981-82	1982-83

Name	NHL Teams	NHL Seasons	Regular Schedule GP	G	A	TP	PIM	Playoffs GP	G	A	TP	PIM	NHL Cup Wins	First NHL Season	Last NHL Season
Williams, Sean	Chi.	1	2	0	0	0	4	....	....	....	....	....	....	1991-92	1991-92
Williams, Tiger	Tor., Van., Det., L.A., Hfd.	14	962	241	272	513	3966	83	12	23	35	455	....	1974-75	1987-88
Williams, Tom	NYR, L.A.	8	397	115	138	253	73	29	8	7	15	4	....	1971-72	1978-79
● Williams, Tommy	Bos., Min., Cal., Wsh.	13	663	161	269	430	177	10	2	5	7	2	....	1961-62	1975-76
‡ Willis, Shane	Car., T.B.	5	174	31	43	74	77	2	0	0	0	0	....	1998-99	2003-04
Willson, Don	Mtl.	2	22	2	7	9	0	3	0	0	0	0	....	1937-38	1938-39
‡ Wilm, Clarke	Cgy., Nsh., Tor.	7	455	37	60	97	336	5	0	1	1	2	....	1998-99	2005-06
Wilson, Behn	Phi., Chi.	9	601	98	260	358	1480	67	12	29	41	190	....	1978-79	1987-88
● Wilson, Bert	NYR, St.L., L.A., Cgy.	8	478	37	44	81	646	21	0	2	2	42	....	1973-74	1980-81
Wilson, Bob	Chi.	1	1	0	0	0	0	....	....	....	....	....	....	1953-54	1953-54
Wilson, Carey	Cgy., Hfd., NYR	10	552	169	258	427	314	52	11	13	24	14	....	1983-84	1992-93
● Wilson, Cully	Tor., Mtl., Ham., Chi.	5	127	59	28	87	243	2	1	0	1	6	....	1919-20	1926-27
Wilson, Doug	Chi., S.J.	16	1024	237	590	827	830	95	19	61	80	88	....	1977-78	1992-93
Wilson, Gord	Bos.	1	....	....	....	....	....	2	0	0	0	0	....	1954-55	1954-55
Wilson, Hub	NYA	1	2	0	0	0	0	....	....	....	....	....	....	1931-32	1931-32
Wilson, Jerry	Mtl.	1	3	0	0	0	2	....	....	....	....	....	....	1956-57	1956-57
Wilson, Johnny	Det., Chi., Tor., NYR	13	688	161	171	332	190	66	14	13	27	11	4	1949-50	1961-62
● Wilson, Larry	Det., Chi.	6	152	21	48	69	75	4	0	0	0	0	1	1949-50	1955-56
Wilson, Mike	Buf., Fla., Pit., NYR	8	336	16	41	57	264	29	0	2	2	15	....	1995-96	2002-03
Wilson, Mitch	N.J., Pit.	2	26	2	3	5	104	....	....	....	....	....	....	1984-85	1986-87
Wilson, Murray	Mtl., L.A.	7	386	94	95	189	162	53	5	14	19	32	4	1972-73	1978-79
Wilson, Rick	Mtl., St.L., Det.	4	239	6	26	32	165	3	0	0	0	0	....	1973-74	1976-77
Wilson, Rik	St.L., Cgy., Chi.	6	251	25	65	90	220	22	0	4	4	23	....	1981-82	1987-88
Wilson, Roger	Chi.	1	7	0	2	2	6	....	....	....	....	....	....	1974-75	1974-75
Wilson, Ron	Tor., Min.	7	177	26	67	93	68	20	4	13	17	8	....	1977-78	1987-88
Wilson, Ron	Wpg., St.L., Mtl.	14	832	110	216	326	415	63	10	12	22	64	....	1979-80	1993-94
● Wilson, Wally	Bos.	1	53	11	8	19	18	1	0	0	0	0	....	1947-48	1947-48
Wing, Murray	Det.	1	1	0	1	1	0	....	....	....	....	....	....	1973-74	1973-74
Winnes, Chris	Bos., Phi.	4	33	1	6	7	6	1	0	0	0	0	....	1990-91	1993-94
Wiseman, Brian	Tor.	1	3	0	0	0	0	....	....	....	....	....	....	1996-97	1996-97
● Wiseman, Eddie	Det., NYA, Bos.	10	456	115	165	280	136	43	10	10	20	16	1	1932-33	1941-42
Wiste, Jim	Chi., Van.	3	52	1	10	11	8	....	....	....	....	....	....	1968-69	1970-71
Witehall, Johan	NYR, Mtl.	3	54	2	5	7	16	....	....	....	....	....	....	1998-99	2000-01
Witherspoon, Jim	L.A.	1	2	0	0	0	2	....	....	....	....	....	....	1975-76	1975-76
Witiuk, Steve	Chi.	1	33	3	8	11	14	....	....	....	....	....	....	1951-52	1951-52
Woit, Benny	Det., Chi.	7	334	7	26	33	170	41	2	6	8	18	3	1950-51	1956-57
Wojciechowski, Steve	Det.	2	54	19	20	39	17	6	0	1	1	0	....	1944-45	1946-47
Wolanin, Craig	N.J., Que., Col., T.B., Tor.	13	695	40	133	173	894	35	4	6	10	67	1	1985-86	1997-98
Wolf, Bennett	Pit.	3	30	0	1	1	133	....	....	....	....	....	....	1980-81	1982-83
Wong, Mike	Det.	1	22	1	1	2	12	....	....	....	....	....	....	1975-76	1975-76
Wood, Dody	S.J.	5	106	8	10	18	471	....	....	....	....	....	....	1992-93	1997-98
Wood, Randy	NYI, Buf., Tor., Dal.	11	741	175	159	334	603	51	8	9	17	40	....	1986-87	1996-97
● Wood, Robert	NYR	1	1	0	0	0	0	....	....	....	....	....	....	1950-51	1950-51
Woodley, Dan	Van.	1	5	2	0	2	17	....	....	....	....	....	....	1987-88	1987-88
Woods, Paul	Det.	7	501	72	124	196	276	7	0	5	5	4	....	1977-78	1983-84
Woolley, Jason	Wsh., Fla., Pit., Buf., Det.	14	718	68	246	314	430	79	11	36	47	44	....	1991-92	2005-06
Worrell, Peter	Fla., Col.	7	391	19	27	46	1554	4	1	0	1	8	....	1997-98	2003-04
Wortman, Kevin	Cgy.	1	5	0	0	0	2	....	....	....	....	....	....	1993-94	1993-94
● Woytowich, Bob	Bos., Min., Pit., L.A.	8	503	32	126	158	352	24	1	3	4	20	....	1964-65	1971-72
Wren, Bob	Ana., Tor.	3	5	0	0	0	0	1	0	0	0	0	....	1997-98	2001-02
‡ Wright, Jamie	Dal., Cgy., Phi.	6	124	12	20	32	54	5	0	0	0	0	....	1997-98	2002-03
Wright, John	Van., St.L., K.C.	3	127	16	36	52	67	....	....	....	....	....	....	1972-73	1974-75
Wright, Keith	Phi.	1	1	0	0	0	0	....	....	....	....	....	....	1967-68	1967-68
Wright, Larry	Phi., Cal., Det.	5	106	4	8	12	19	....	....	....	....	....	....	1971-72	1977-78
Wright, Tyler	Edm., Pit., CBJ, Ana.	13	613	79	70	149	854	30	3	2	5	40	....	1992-93	2005-06
● Wycherley, Ralph	NYA, Bro.	2	28	4	7	11	6	....	....	....	....	....	....	1940-41	1941-42
● Wylie, Bill	NYR	1	1	0	0	0	0	....	....	....	....	....	....	1950-51	1950-51
Wylie, Duane	Chi.	2	14	3	3	6	2	....	....	....	....	....	....	1974-75	1976-77
Wyrozub, Randy	Buf.	4	100	8	10	18	10	....	....	....	....	....	....	1970-71	1973-74

Y Z

Name	NHL Teams	NHL Seasons	Regular Schedule GP	G	A	TP	PIM	Playoffs GP	G	A	TP	PIM	NHL Cup Wins	First NHL Season	Last NHL Season
‡ Yablonski, Jeremy	St.L.	1	1	0	0	0	5	....	....	....	....	....	....	2003-04	2003-04
‡ Yachmenev, Vitali	L.A., Nsh.	8	487	83	133	216	88	....	....	....	....	....	....	1995-96	2002-03
● Yackel, Ken	Bos.	1	6	0	0	0	2	2	0	0	0	2	....	1958-59	1958-59
Yake, Terry	Hfd., Ana., Tor., St.L., Wsh.	11	403	77	120	197	220	32	4	4	8	36	....	1988-89	2000-01
‡ Yakubov, Mikhail	Chi., Fla.	2	53	2	10	12	20	....	....	....	....	....	....	2003-04	2005-06
Yakushin, Dmitri	Tor.	1	2	0	0	0	2	....	....	....	....	....	....	1999-00	1999-00
Yaremchuk, Gary	Tor.	4	34	1	4	5	28	....	....	....	....	....	....	1981-82	1984-85
Yaremchuk, Ken	Chi., Tor.	6	235	36	56	92	106	31	6	8	14	49	....	1983-84	1988-89
Yates, Ross	Hfd.	1	7	1	1	2	4	....	....	....	....	....	....	1983-84	1983-84
Yawney, Trent	Chi., Cgy., St.L.	12	593	27	102	129	783	60	9	17	26	81	....	1987-88	1998-99
● Yegorov, Alexei	S.J.	2	11	3	3	6	2	....	....	....	....	....	....	1995-96	1996-97
Ylonen, Juha	Phx., T.B., Ott.	6	341	26	76	102	90	15	0	7	7	4	....	1996-97	2001-02
York, Harry	St.L., NYR, Pit., Van.	4	244	29	46	75	99	5	0	0	0	2	....	1996-97	1999-00
York, Jason	Det., Ana., Ott., Nsh., Bos.	13	757	42	187	229	621	34	2	7	9	25	....	1992-93	2006-07
● Young, B.J.	Det.	1	1	0	0	0	0	....	....	....	....	....	....	1999-00	1999-00
Young, Brian	Chi.	1	8	0	2	2	6	....	....	....	....	....	....	1980-81	1980-81
Young, C.J.	Cgy., Bos.	1	43	7	7	14	32	....	....	....	....	....	....	1992-93	1992-93
● Young, Doug	Det., Mtl.	10	388	35	45	80	303	28	1	5	6	16	2	1931-32	1940-41
● Young, Howie	Det., Chi., Van.	8	336	12	62	74	851	19	2	4	6	46	....	1960-61	1970-71
Young, Scott	Hfd., Pit., Que., Col., Ana., St.L., Dal.	17	1181	342	415	757	448	141	44	43	87	64	2	1987-88	2005-06
Young, Tim	Min., Wpg., Phi.	10	628	195	341	536	438	36	7	24	31	27	....	1975-76	1984-85
Young, Warren	Min., Pit., Det.	7	236	72	77	149	472	....	....	....	....	....	....	1981-82	1987-88
Younghans, Tom	Min., NYR	6	429	44	41	85	373	24	2	1	3	21	....	1976-77	1981-82
Ysebaert, Paul	N.J., Det., Wpg., Chi., T.B.	11	532	149	187	336	217	30	4	3	7	20	....	1988-89	1998-99
‡ Yushkevich, Dmitry	Phi., Tor., Fla., L.A.	11	786	43	182	225	659	72	4	19	23	52	....	1992-93	2002-03
Yzerman, Steve	Det.	22	1514	692	1063	1755	924	196	70	115	185	84	3	1983-84	2005-06
Zabransky, Libor	St.L.	2	40	1	6	7	50	....	....	....	....	....	....	1996-97	1997-98
Zaharko, Miles	Atl., Chi.	4	129	5	32	37	84	3	0	0	0	0	....	1977-78	1981-82
Zaine, Rod	Pit., Buf.	2	61	10	6	16	25	....	....	....	....	....	....	1970-71	1971-72
Zalapski, Zarley	Pit., Hfd., Cgy., Mtl., Phi.	12	637	99	285	384	684	48	4	23	27	47	....	1987-88	1999-00
‡ Zalesak, Miroslav	S.J.	2	12	1	2	3	0	....	....	....	....	....	....	2002-03	2003-04
Zamuner, Rob	NYR, T.B., Ott., Bos.	13	798	139	172	311	467	34	4	5	9	26	....	1991-92	2003-04
Zanussi, Joe	NYR, Bos., St.L.	3	87	1	13	14	46	4	0	1	1	2	....	1974-75	1976-77
Zanussi, Ron	Min., Tor.	5	299	52	83	135	373	17	0	4	4	17	....	1977-78	1981-82
Zavisha, Brad	Edm.	1	2	0	0	0	0	....	....	....	....	....	....	1993-94	1993-94
Zehr, Jeff	Bos.	1	4	0	0	0	2	....	....	....	....	....	....	1999-00	1999-00
Zeidel, Larry	Det., Chi., Phi.	5	158	3	16	19	198	12	0	1	1	12	1	1951-52	1968-69
Zelepukin, Valeri	N.J., Edm., Phi., Chi.	10	595	117	177	294	527	85	13	13	26	48	1	1991-92	2000-01
Zemlak, Richard	Que., Min., Pit., Cgy.	5	132	2	12	14	587	1	0	0	0	10	....	1986-87	1991-92
● Zeniuk, Ed	Det.	1	2	0	0	0	0	....	....	....	....	....	....	1954-55	1954-55
Zent, Jason	Ott., Phi.	3	27	3	3	6	13	....	....	....	....	....	....	1996-97	1998-99
Zetterstrom, Lars	Van.	1	14	0	1	1	2	....	....	....	....	....	....	1978-79	1978-79
Zettler, Rob	Min., S.J., Phi., Tor., Nsh., Wsh.	14	569	5	65	70	920	14	0	0	0	4	....	1988-89	2001-02
Zezel, Peter	Phi., St.L., Wsh., Tor., Dal., N.J., Van.	15	873	219	389	608	435	131	25	39	64	83	....	1984-85	1998-99
Zhamnov, Alex	Wpg., Chi., Phi., Bos.	13	807	249	470	719	668	35	6	13	19	18	....	1992-93	2005-06
● Zholtok, Sergei	Bos., Ott., Mtl., Edm., Min., Nsh.	10	588	111	147	258	166	45	4	14	18	0	....	1992-93	2003-04
‡ Ziegler, Thomas	T.B.	1	5	0	0	0	0	....	....	....	....	....	....	2000-01	2000-01
Zmolek, Doug	S.J., Dal., L.A., Chi.	8	467	11	53	64	905	14	0	1	1	16	....	1992-93	1999-00
Zoborosky, Marty	Chi.	1	1	0	0	0	2	....	....	....	....	....	....	1944-45	1944-45
Zombo, Rick	Det., St.L., Bos.	12	652	24	130	154	728	60	1	11	12	127	....	1984-85	1995-96
Zuke, Mike	St.L., Hfd.	8	455	86	196	282	220	26	6	6	12	12	....	1978-79	1985-86
● Zunich, Rudy	Det.	1	2	0	0	0	2	....	....	....	....	....	....	1943-44	1943-44

Johnny Wilson

Jim Wiste

Paul Ysebaert

Rudy Zunich

Retired NHL Goaltender Index

Abbreviations: Teams/Cities: – **Ana.** – Anaheim; **Atl.** – Atlanta; **Bos.** – Boston; **Bro.** – Brooklyn; **Buf.** – Buffalo; **Cal.** – California; **Cgy.** – Calgary; **Car.** – Carolina; **Chi.** – Chicago; **Cle.** – Cleveland; **Col.** – Colorado; **CBJ** – Columbus; **Dal.** – Dallas; **Det.** – Detroit; **Edm.** – Edmonton; **Fla.** – Florida; **Ham.** – Hamilton; **Hfd.** – Hartford; **K.C.** – Kansas City; **L.A.** – Los Angeles; **Min.** – Minnesota; **Mtl.** – Montreal; **Mtl.M.** – Montreal Maroons; **Mtl.W.** – Montreal Wanderers; **Nsh.** – Nashville; **N.J.** – New Jersey; **NYA** – NY Americans; **NYI** – NY Islanders; **NYR** – New York Rangers; **Oak.** – Oakland; **Ott.** – Ottawa; **Phi.** – Philadelphia; **Phx.** – Phoenix; **Pit.** – Pittsburgh; **Que.** – Quebec; **St.L.** – St. Louis; **S.J.** – San Jose; **T.B.** – Tampa Bay; **Tor.** – Toronto; **Van.** – Vancouver; **Wpg.** – Winnipeg; **Wsh.** – Washington

Avg. – goals against per 60 minutes played; **GA** – goals agains; **GP** – games played; **Mins** – minutes played; **SO** – shutouts.
• – deceased. § – Forward, defenseman or coach who appeared in goal. For complete career, see Retired Player Index. ‡ – Remains active in other leagues.

NHL Seasons – A player or goaltender who does not play in a regular season but who does appear in that year's playoffs is credited with an NHL Season in this Index. Total seasons are rounded off to the nearest full season.

			Regular Schedule								Playoffs								NHL	First	Last
Name	NHL Teams	NHL Seasons	GP	W	L	T	Mins	GA	SO	Avg	GP	W	L	T	Mins	GA	SO	Avg	Cup Wins	NHL Season	NHL Season
Abbott, George	Bos.	1	1	0	1	0	60	7	0	7.00	....	....	....	....	....	....	....	....		1943-44	1943-44
Adams, John	Bos., Wsh.	2	22	9	10	1	1180	85	1	4.32	....	....	....	....	....	....	....	....	1	1969-70	1974-75
Aiken, Don	Mtl.	1	1	0	1	0	34	6	0	10.59	....	....	....	....	....	....	....	....		1957-58	1957-58
• Aitkenhead, Andy	NYR	3	106	47	43	16	6570	257	11	2.35	10	6	2	2	608	15	3	1.48	1	1932-33	1934-35
• Almas, Red	Det., Chi.	3	3	0	2	1	180	13	0	4.33	5	1	3	....	263	13	0	2.97		1946-47	1952-53
• Anderson, Lorne	NYR	1	3	1	2	0	180	18	0	6.00	....	....	....	....	....	....	....	....		1951-52	1951-52
‡ Askey, Tom	Ana.	2	7	0	1	2	273	12	0	2.64	1	0	1	....	30	2	0	4.00		1997-98	1998-99
Astrom, Hardy	NYR, Col.	3	83	17	44	12	4456	278	0	3.74	....	....	....	....	....	....	....	....		1977-78	1980-81
Bach, Ryan	L.A.	1	3	0	3	0	108	8	0	4.44	....	....	....	....	....	....	....	....		1998-99	1998-99
Bailey, Scott	Bos.	2	19	6	6	2	965	55	0	3.42	....	....	....	....	....	....	....	....		1995-96	1996-97
Baker, Steve	NYR	4	57	20	20	11	3081	190	3	3.70	14	7	7	....	826	55	0	4.00		1979-80	1982-83
Bales, Mike	Bos., Ott.	4	23	2	15	1	1120	77	0	4.13	....	....	....	....	....	....	....	....		1992-93	1996-97
Bannerman, Murray	Van., Chi.	8	289	116	125	33	16470	1051	8	3.83	40	20	18	....	2322	165	0	4.26		1977-78	1986-87
Baron, Marco	Bos., L.A., Edm.	6	86	34	38	9	4822	292	1	3.63	1	0	1	....	20	3	0	9.00		1979-80	1984-85
Barrasso, Tom	Buf., Pit., Ott., Car., Tor., St.L.	19	777	369	277	86	44180	2385	38	3.24	119	61	54	....	6953	349	6	3.01	2	1983-84	2002-03
Bassen, Hank	Chi., Det., Pit.	9	156	46	66	31	8759	434	5	2.97	5	1	3	....	274	11	0	2.41		1954-55	1967-68
• Bastien, Baz	Tor.	1	5	0	4	1	300	20	0	4.00	....	....	....	....	....	....	....	....		1945-46	1945-46
• Bauman, Garry	Mtl., Min.	3	35	5	16	6	1719	102	0	3.56	....	....	....	....	....	....	....	....		1966-67	1968-69
Beaupre, Don	Min., Wsh., Ott., Tor.	17	667	268	277	75	37396	2151	17	3.45	72	33	31	....	3943	220	3	3.35		1980-81	1996-97
Beauregard, Stephane	Wpg., Phi.	5	90	19	39	11	4402	268	2	3.65	4	1	3	....	238	12	0	3.03		1989-90	1993-94
Bedard, Jim	Wsh.	2	73	17	40	13	4232	278	1	3.94	....	....	....	....	....	....	....	....		1977-78	1978-79
Behrend, Marc	Wpg.	3	39	12	19	3	1991	160	1	4.82	7	1	3	....	312	19	0	3.65		1983-84	1985-86
Belanger, Yves	St.L., Atl., Bos.	6	78	29	33	6	4134	259	2	3.76	....	....	....	....	....	....	....	....		1974-75	1979-80
Belhumeur, Michel	Phi., Wsh.	3	65	9	36	7	3306	254	0	4.61	1	0	0	....	10	1	0	6.00		1972-73	1975-76
• Bell, Gordie	Tor., NYR	2	8	3	5	0	480	31	0	3.88	2	1	1	....	120	9	0	4.50		1945-46	1955-56
• Benedict, Clint	Ott., Mtl.M.	13	362	190	143	28	22367	863	57	2.32	28	11	12	5	1707	53	9	1.86	4	1917-18	1929-30
Bennett, Harvey	Bos.	1	25	10	12	2	1470	103	0	4.20	....	....	....	....	....	....	....	....		1944-45	1944-45
Bergeron, Jean-Claude	Mtl., T.B., L.A.	6	72	21	33	7	3772	232	1	3.69	....	....	....	....	....	....	....	....		1990-91	1996-97
Bernhardt, Tim	Cgy., Tor.	4	67	17	36	7	3748	267	0	4.27	....	....	....	....	....	....	....	....		1982-83	1986-87
Berthiaume, Daniel	Wpg., Min., L.A., Bos., Ott.	9	215	81	90	21	11662	714	5	3.67	14	5	9	....	807	50	0	3.72		1985-86	1993-94
Bester, Allan	Tor., Det., Dal.	10	219	73	99	17	11773	786	7	4.01	11	2	6	....	508	37	0	4.37		1983-84	1995-96
• Beveridge, Bill	Det., Ott., St.L., Mtl.M., NYR	9	297	87	166	42	18375	879	18	2.87	5	2	3	....	300	11	0	2.20		1929-30	1942-43
• Bibeault, Paul	Mtl., Tor., Bos., Chi.	7	214	81	107	25	12890	785	10	3.65	20	6	14	....	1237	71	2	3.44		1940-41	1946-47
Bierk, Zac	T.B., Min., Phx.	6	47	9	20	5	2135	113	1	3.18	....	....	....	....	....	....	....	....		1997-98	2003-04
Billington, Craig	N.J., Ott., Bos., Col., Wsh.	15	332	110	149	31	17097	1034	9	3.63	8	0	2	....	213	15	0	4.23		1985-86	2002-03
Binette, Andre	Mtl.	1	1	1	0	0	60	4	0	4.00	....	....	....	....	....	....	....	....		1954-55	1954-55
Binkley, Les	Pit.	5	196	58	94	34	11046	575	11	3.12	7	5	2	....	428	15	0	2.10		1967-68	1971-72
• Bittner, Richard	Bos.	1	1	0	0	1	60	3	0	3.00	....	....	....	....	....	....	....	....		1949-50	1949-50
Blackburn, Dan	NYR	2	63	20	32	4	3499	188	1	3.22	....	....	....	....	....	....	....	....		2001-02	2002-03
Blake, Mike	L.A.	3	40	13	15	5	2117	150	0	4.25	....	....	....	....	....	....	....	....		1981-82	1983-84
Blue, John	Bos., Buf.	3	46	16	18	7	2521	126	1	3.00	2	0	1	....	96	5	0	3.13		1992-93	1995-96
Boisvert, Gilles	Det.	1	3	0	3	0	180	9	0	3.00	....	....	....	....	....	....	....	....		1959-60	1959-60
Bouchard, Dan	Atl., Cgy., Que., Wpg.	14	655	286	232	113	37919	2061	27	3.26	43	13	30	....	2549	147	1	3.46		1972-73	1985-86
• Bourque, Claude	Mtl., Det.	2	62	16	38	8	3830	193	4	3.02	3	1	2	....	188	8	1	2.55		1938-39	1939-40
Boutin, Rollie	Wsh.	3	22	7	10	1	1137	75	0	3.96	....	....	....	....	....	....	....	....		1978-79	1980-81
• Bouvrette, Lionel	NYR	1	1	0	1	0	60	6	0	6.00	....	....	....	....	....	....	....	....		1942-43	1942-43
Bower, Johnny	NYR, Tor.	15	552	250	195	90	32016	1340	37	2.51	74	35	34	....	4378	180	5	2.47	4	1953-54	1969-70
§ • Branigan, Andy	NYA	1	1	0	0	0	7	0	0	0.00	....	....	....	....	....	....	....	....		1940-41	1940-41
‡ Brathwaite, Fred	Edm., Cgy., St.L., CBJ	9	254	81	99	37	13840	629	15	2.73	1	0	0	....	1	0	0	0.00		1993-94	2003-04
• Brimsek, Frank	Bos., Chi.	10	514	252	182	80	31210	1404	40	2.70	68	32	36	....	4395	186	2	2.54	2	1938-39	1949-50
Brochu, Martin	Wsh., Van., Pit.	3	9	0	5	0	369	22	0	3.58	....	....	....	....	....	....	....	....		1998-99	2003-04
• Broda, Turk	Tor.	14	629	302	224	101	38167	1609	62	2.53	101	60	39	....	6389	211	13	1.98	5	1936-37	1951-52
Broderick, Ken	Min., Bos.	3	27	11	12	1	1464	74	1	3.03	....	....	....	....	....	....	....	....		1969-70	1974-75
Broderick, Len	Mtl.	1	1	1	0	0	60	2	0	2.00	....	....	....	....	....	....	....	....		1957-58	1957-58
Brodeur, Richard	NYI, Van., Hfd.	9	385	131	175	62	21968	1410	6	3.85	33	13	20	....	2009	111	1	3.32		1979-80	1987-88
Bromley, Gary	Buf., Van.	6	136	54	44	28	7427	425	7	3.43	7	2	5	....	360	25	0	4.17		1973-74	1980-81
• Brooks, Art	Tor.	1	4	2	2	0	220	23	0	6.27	....	....	....	....	....	....	....	....		1917-18	1917-18
Brooks, Ross	Bos.	3	54	37	7	6	3047	134	4	2.64	1	0	0	....	20	3	0	9.00		1972-73	1974-75
• Brophy, Frank	Que.	1	21	3	18	0	1249	148	0	7.11	....	....	....	....	....	....	....	....		1919-20	1919-20
Brown, Andy	Det., Pit.	3	62	22	26	9	3373	213	1	3.79	....	....	....	....	....	....	....	....		1971-72	1973-74
Brown, Ken	Chi.	1	1	0	0	0	18	1	0	3.33	....	....	....	....	....	....	....	....		1970-71	1970-71
Brunetta, Mario	Que.	3	40	12	17	1	1967	128	0	3.90	....	....	....	....	....	....	....	....		1987-88	1989-90
Bullock, Bruce	Van.	3	16	3	9	3	927	74	0	4.79	....	....	....	....	....	....	....	....		1972-73	1976-77
Burke, Sean	N.J., Hfd., Car., Van., Phi., Fla., Phx., T.B., L.A.	18	820	324	341	110	46442	2290	38	2.96	38	12	23	....	2151	119	1	3.32		1987-88	2006-07
• Buzinski, Steve	NYR	1	9	2	6	1	560	55	0	5.89	....	....	....	....	....	....	....	....		1942-43	1942-43
Caley, Don	St.L.	1	1	0	0	0	30	3	0	6.00	....	....	....	....	....	....	....	....		1967-68	1967-68
Caprice, Frank	Van.	6	102	31	46	11	5589	391	1	4.20	....	....	....	....	....	....	....	....		1982-83	1987-88
Carey, Jim	Wsh., Bos., St.L.	5	172	79	65	16	9668	416	16	2.58	10	2	5	....	455	35	0	4.62		1994-95	1998-99
Caron, Jacques	L.A., St.L., Van.	5	72	24	29	11	3846	211	2	3.29	12	4	7	....	639	34	0	3.19		1967-68	1973-74
Carter, Lyle	Cal.	1	15	4	7	0	721	50	0	4.16	....	....	....	....	....	....	....	....		1971-72	1971-72
Casey, Jon	Min., Bos., St.L.	12	425	170	157	55	23255	1246	16	3.21	66	32	31	....	3743	192	3	3.08		1983-84	1996-97
‡ Cechmanek, Roman	Phi., L.A.	4	212	110	64	28	12085	419	25	2.08	23	9	14	....	1441	56	3	2.33		2000-01	2003-04
‡ Centomo, Sebastien	Tor.	1	1	0	0	0	40	3	0	4.50	....	....	....	....	....	....	....	....		2001-02	2001-02
Chabot, Frederic	Mtl., Phi., L.A.	5	32	4	8	4	1262	62	0	2.95	....	....	....	....	....	....	....	....		1990-91	1998-99
• Chabot, Lorne	NYR, Tor., Mtl., Chi., Mtl.M., NYA	11	412	201	147	62	25411	859	71	2.03	37	13	17	6	2498	64	5	1.54	2	1926-27	1936-37
Chadwick, Ed	Tor., Bos.	6	184	57	92	35	11040	541	14	2.94	....	....	....	....	....	....	....	....		1955-56	1961-62
Champoux, Bob	Det., Cal.	2	17	2	11	3	923	80	0	5.20	1	1	0	....	55	4	0	4.36		1963-64	1973-74
‡ Charpentier, Sebastien	Wsh.	3	26	6	14	1	1350	66	0	2.93	....	....	....	....	....	....	....	....		2001-02	2003-04
Cheevers, Gerry	Tor., Bos.	13	418	230	102	74	24394	1174	26	2.89	88	53	34	....	5396	242	8	2.69	2	1961-62	1979-80
Cheveldae, Tim	Det., Wpg., Bos.	9	340	149	136	37	19172	1116	10	3.49	25	9	15	....	1418	71	2	3.00		1988-89	1996-97
Chevrier, Alain	N.J., Wpg., Chi., Pit., Det.	6	234	91	100	14	12202	845	2	4.16	16	9	7	....	1013	44	0	2.61		1985-86	1990-91
‡ Chiodo, Andy	Pit.	1	8	3	4	1	486	28	0	3.46	....	....	....	....	....	....	....	....		2003-04	2003-04
Chouinard, Mathieu	L.A.	1	1	0	0	0	3	0	0	0.00	....	....	....	....	....	....	....	....		2003-04	2003-04
§ • Clancy, King	Ott., Tor.	2	2	0	0	0	3	1	0	20.00	....	....	....	....	....	....	....	....		1924-25	1931-32
§ • Cleghorn, Odie	Pit.	1	1	1	0	0	60	2	0	2.00	....	....	....	....	....	....	....	....		1925-26	1925-26
§ • Cleghorn, Sprague	Ott., Mtl.	2	2	0	0	0	5	0	0	0.00	....	....	....	....	....	....	....	....		1918-19	1921-22
Clifford, Chris	Chi.	2	2	0	0	0	24	0	0	0.00	....	....	....	....	....	....	....	....		1984-85	1988-89
Cloutier, Jacques	Buf., Chi., Que.	12	255	82	102	24	12826	778	3	3.64	8	1	5	....	413	18	1	2.62		1981-82	1993-94
Colvin, Les	Bos.	1	1	0	1	0	60	4	0	4.00	....	....	....	....	....	....	....	....		1948-49	1948-49
§ • Conacher, Charlie	Tor., Det.	3	4	0	0	0	10	0	0	0.00	....	....	....	....	....	....	....	....		1932-33	1938-39
• Connell, Alec	Ott., Det., NYA, Mtl.M.	12	417	193	156	67	26050	830	81	1.91	21	8	5	8	1309	26	4	1.19	2	1924-25	1936-37
Corsi, Jim	Edm.	1	26	8	14	3	1366	83	0	3.65	....	....	....	....	....	....	....	....		1979-80	1979-80
• Courteau, Maurice	Bos.	1	6	2	4	0	360	33	0	5.50	....	....	....	....	....	....	....	....		1943-44	1943-44

Name	NHL Teams	NHL Seasons	Regular Schedule GP	W	L	T	Mins	GA	SO	Avg	Playoffs GP	W	L	T	Mins	GA	SO	Avg	NHL Cup Wins	First NHL Season	Last NHL Season
Cousineau, Marcel	Tor., NYI, L.A.	4	26	4	10	1	1047	51	1	2.92	....	....	....	....	....	....	....	....		1996-97	1999-00
Cowley, Wayne	Edm.	1	1	0	1	0	57	3	0	3.16	....	....	....	....	....	....	....	....		1993-94	1993-94
• Cox, Abbie	Mtl.M., NYA, Det., Mtl.	3	5	1	1	2	263	11	0	2.51	....	....	....	....	....	....	....	....		1929-30	1935-36
Craig, Jim	Atl., Bos., Min.	3	30	11	10	7	1588	100	0	3.78	....	....	....	....	....	....	....	....		1979-80	1983-84
Crha, Jiri	Tor.	2	69	28	27	11	3942	261	0	3.97	5	0	4	....	186	21	0	6.77		1979-80	1980-81
• Crozier, Roger	Det., Buf., Wsh.	14	518	206	197	70	28567	1446	30	3.04	32	14	16	....	1789	82	1	2.75		1963-64	1976-77
• Cude, Wilf	Phi., Bos., Chi., Mtl., Det.	10	282	100	132	49	17586	798	24	2.72	19	7	11	1	1257	51	1	2.43		1930-31	1940-41
Cutts, Don	Edm.	1	6	1	2	1	269	16	0	3.57	....	....	....	....	....	....	....	....		1979-80	1979-80
• Cyr, Claude	Mtl.	1	1	0	0	0	20	1	0	3.00	....	....	....	....	....	....	....	....		1958-59	1958-59
Dadswell, Doug	Cgy.	2	27	8	8	3	1346	99	0	4.41	....	....	....	....	....	....	....	....		1986-87	1987-88
Dafoe, Byron	Wsh., L.A., Bos., Atl.	12	415	171	170	56	23478	1051	26	2.69	27	10	16	....	1686	65	3	2.31		1992-93	2003-04
D'Alessio, Corrie	Hfd.	1	1	0	0	0	11	0	0	0.00	....	....	....	....	....	....	....	....		1992-93	1992-93
Daley, Joe	Pit., Buf., Det.	4	105	34	44	19	5836	326	3	3.35	....	....	....	....	....	....	....	....		1968-69	1971-72
• Damore, Nick	Bos.	1	1	1	0	0	60	3	0	3.00	....	....	....	....	....	....	....	....		1941-42	1941-42
D'Amour, Marc	Cgy., Phi.	2	16	2	4	2	579	32	0	3.32	....	....	....	....	....	....	....	....		1985-86	1988-89
Damphousse, Jean-Fr.	N.J.	1	6	1	3	0	294	12	0	2.45	....	....	....	....	....	....	....	....		2001-02	2001-02
• Darragh, Jack	Ott.	1	1	0	0	0	2	0	0	0.00	....	....	....	....	....	....	....	....		1919-20	1919-20
Daskalakis, Cleon	Bos.	3	12	3	4	1	506	41	0	4.86	....	....	....	....	....	....	....	....		1984-85	1986-87
Davidson, John	St.L., NYR	10	301	123	124	39	17109	1004	7	3.52	31	16	14	....	1862	77	1	2.48		1973-74	1982-83
Decourcy, Bob	NYR	1	1	0	1	0	29	6	0	12.41	....	....	....	....	....	....	....	....		1947-48	1947-48
Defelice, Norm	Bos.	1	10	3	5	2	600	30	0	3.00	....	....	....	....	....	....	....	....		1956-57	1956-57
DeJordy, Denis	Chi., L.A., Mtl., Det.	12	316	124	128	51	17798	929	15	3.13	18	6	9	....	946	55	0	3.49	1	1960-61	1973-74
DelGuidice, Matt	Bos.	2	11	2	5	1	434	28	0	3.87	....	....	....	....	....	....	....	....		1990-91	1991-92
DeRouville, Philippe	Pit.	2	3	1	2	0	171	9	0	3.16	....	....	....	....	....	....	....	....		1994-95	1996-97
Desjardins, Gerry	L.A., Chi., NYI, Buf.	10	331	122	153	44	19014	1042	12	3.29	35	15	15	....	1874	108	0	3.46		1968-69	1977-78
DesRochers, Patrick	Phx., Car.	2	11	2	6	1	540	33	0	3.67	....	....	....	....	....	....	....	....		2001-02	2002-03
• Dickie, Bill	Chi.	1	1	1	0	0	60	3	0	3.00	....	....	....	....	....	....	....	....		1941-42	1941-42
Dion, Connie	Det.	2	38	23	11	4	2280	119	1	3.13	5	1	4	....	300	17	0	3.40		1943-44	1944-45
Dion, Michel	Que., Wpg., Pit.	6	227	60	118	32	12695	898	2	4.24	5	2	3	....	304	22	0	4.34		1979-80	1984-85
‡ Divis, Reinhard	St.L.	4	28	6	9	3	1212	67	0	3.32	1	0	0	....	18	0	0	0.00		2001-02	2005-06
• Dolson, Dolly	Det.	3	93	35	41	17	5820	192	16	1.98	2	0	2	0	120	7	0	3.50		1928-29	1930-31
Dopson, Rob	Pit.	1	2	0	0	0	45	3	0	4.00	....	....	....	....	....	....	....	....		1993-94	1993-94
Dowie, Bruce	Tor.	1	2	0	1	0	72	4	0	3.33	....	....	....	....	....	....	....	....		1983-84	1983-84
Draper, Tom	Wpg., Buf., NYI	6	53	19	23	5	2807	173	1	3.70	7	3	4	....	433	19	1	2.63		1988-89	1995-96
Dryden, Dave	NYR, Chi., Buf., Edm.	9	203	66	76	31	10424	555	9	3.19	3	0	2	....	133	9	0	4.06		1961-62	1979-80
Dryden, Ken	Mtl.	8	397	258	57	74	23352	870	46	2.24	112	80	32	....	6846	274	10	2.40	6	1970-71	1978-79
Duffus, Parris	Phx.	1	1	0	0	0	29	1	0	2.07	....	....	....	....	....	....	....	....		1996-97	1996-97
Dumas, Michel	Chi.	3	8	2	1	2	362	24	0	3.98	1	0	0	....	19	1	0	3.16		1974-75	1976-77
Dunham, Mike	N.J., Nsh., NYR, Atl., NYI	10	394	141	178	44	21653	989	19	2.74	....	....	....	....	....	....	....	....		1996-97	2006-07
Dupuis, Bob	Edm.	1	1	0	1	0	60	4	0	4.00	....	....	....	....	....	....	....	....		1979-80	1979-80
• Durnan, Bill	Mtl.	7	383	208	112	62	22945	901	34	2.36	45	27	18	....	2871	99	2	2.07	2	1943-44	1949-50
Dyck, Ed	Van.	3	49	8	28	5	2453	178	1	4.35	....	....	....	....	....	....	....	....		1971-72	1973-74
Edwards, Don	Buf., Cgy., Tor.	10	459	208	155	74	26181	1449	16	3.32	42	16	21	....	2302	132	1	3.44		1976-77	1985-86
Edwards, Gary	St.L., L.A., Cle., Min., Edm., Pit.	13	286	88	125	51	16002	973	10	3.65	11	5	4	....	537	34	0	3.80		1968-69	1981-82
Edwards, Marv	Pit., Tor., Cal.	4	61	15	34	7	3467	218	2	3.77	....	....	....	....	....	....	....	....		1968-69	1973-74
• Edwards, Roy	Chi., Det., Pit.	7	236	97	88	38	13109	637	12	2.92	4	0	3	....	206	11	0	3.20	1	1960-61	1973-74
Eklund, Brian	T.B.	1	1	0	1	0	58	3	0	3.10	....	....	....	....	....	....	....	....		2005-06	2005-06
Eliot, Darren	L.A., Det., Buf.	5	89	25	41	12	4931	377	1	4.59	1	0	0	....	40	7	0	10.50		1984-85	1988-89
Ellacott, Ken	Van.	1	12	2	3	4	555	41	0	4.43	....	....	....	....	....	....	....	....		1982-83	1982-83
Erickson, Chad	N.J.	1	2	1	1	0	120	9	0	4.50	....	....	....	....	....	....	....	....		1991-92	1991-92
Esposito, Tony	Mtl., Chi.	16	886	423	306	151	52585	2563	76	2.92	99	45	53	....	6017	308	6	3.07	1	1968-69	1983-84
Essensa, Bob	Wpg., Det., Edm., Phx., Van., Buf.	12	446	173	176	47	24215	1270	18	3.15	16	4	9	....	864	51	0	3.54		1988-89	2001-02
• Evans, Claude	Mtl., Bos.	2	5	1	2	1	260	16	0	3.69	....	....	....	....	....	....	....	....		1954-55	1957-58
Exelby, Randy	Mtl., Edm.	2	2	0	1	0	63	5	0	4.76	....	....	....	....	....	....	....	....		1988-89	1989-90
Fankhouser, Scott	Atl.	2	23	4	12	2	1180	65	0	3.31	....	....	....	....	....	....	....	....		1999-00	2000-01
Farr, Rocky	Buf.	3	19	2	6	3	722	42	0	3.49	....	....	....	....	....	....	....	....		1972-73	1974-75
Favell, Doug	Phi., Tor., Col.	12	373	123	153	69	20771	1096	18	3.17	21	6	15	....	1270	66	1	3.12		1967-68	1978-79
Fichaud, Eric	NYI, Nsh., Car., Mtl.	6	95	22	47	10	4799	251	2	3.14	....	....	....	....	....	....	....	....		1995-96	2000-01
Finley, Brian	Nsh., Bos.	3	4	0	2	0	166	13	0	4.70	....	....	....	....	....	....	....	....		2002-03	2006-07
Fiset, Stephane	Que., Col., L.A., Mtl.	13	390	164	153	44	21785	1114	16	3.07	14	1	7	....	563	37	0	3.94	1	1989-90	2001-02
Fitzpatrick, Mark	L.A., NYI, Fla., T.B., Chi., Car.	12	329	113	136	49	18329	953	8	3.12	9	0	3	....	289	23	0	4.78		1988-89	1999-00
• Forbes, Jake	Tor., Ham., NYA, Phi.	13	210	85	114	11	12922	594	19	2.76	2	0	2	0	120	7	0	3.50		1919-20	1932-33
Ford, Brian	Que., Pit.	2	11	3	7	0	580	61	0	6.31	....	....	....	....	....	....	....	....		1983-84	1984-85
Foster, Norm	Bos., Edm.	2	13	7	4	0	623	34	0	3.27	....	....	....	....	....	....	....	....		1990-91	1991-92
Fountain, Mike	Van., Car., Ott.	4	11	2	6	0	483	28	1	3.48	....	....	....	....	....	....	....	....		1996-97	2000-01
• Fowler, Hec	Bos.	1	7	1	6	0	409	42	0	6.16	....	....	....	....	....	....	....	....		1924-25	1924-25
Francis, Emile	Chi., NYR	6	95	31	52	11	5660	355	1	3.76	....	....	....	....	....	....	....	....		1946-47	1951-52
• Franks, Jimmy	Det., NYR, Bos.	4	42	12	23	7	2520	181	1	4.31	1	0	1	....	30	2	0	4.00	1	1936-37	1943-44
Frederick, Ray	Chi.	1	5	0	4	1	300	22	0	4.40	....	....	....	....	....	....	....	....		1954-55	1954-55
Friesen, Karl	N.J.	1	4	0	2	1	130	16	0	7.38	....	....	....	....	....	....	....	....		1986-87	1986-87
Froese, Bob	Phi., NYR	8	242	128	72	20	13451	694	13	3.10	18	3	9	....	830	55	0	3.98		1982-83	1989-90
Fuhr, Grant	Edm., Tor., Buf., L.A., St.L., Cgy.	19	868	403	295	114	48945	2756	25	3.38	150	92	50	....	8834	430	6	2.92	5	1981-82	1999-00
‡ Gage, Joaquin	Edm.	3	23	4	12	1	1076	67	0	3.74	....	....	....	....	....	....	....	....		1994-95	2000-01
Gagnon, David	Det.	1	2	0	1	0	35	6	0	10.29	....	....	....	....	....	....	....	....		1990-91	1990-91
• Gamble, Bruce	NYR, Bos., Tor., Phi.	10	327	110	150	46	18442	988	22	3.21	5	0	4	....	206	25	0	7.28		1958-59	1971-72
Gamble, Troy	Van.	4	72	22	29	9	3804	229	1	3.61	4	1	3	....	249	16	0	3.86		1986-87	1991-92
• Gardiner, Bert	NYR, Mtl., Chi., Bos.	6	144	49	68	27	8760	554	3	3.79	9	4	5	....	647	20	0	1.85		1935-36	1943-44
• Gardiner, Charlie	Chi.	7	316	112	152	52	19687	664	42	2.02	21	12	6	3	1472	35	5	1.43	1	1927-28	1933-34
• Gardner, George	Det., Van.	5	66	16	30	6	3313	207	0	3.75	....	....	....	....	....	....	....	....		1965-66	1971-72
Garner, Tyrone	Cgy.	1	3	0	2	0	139	12	0	5.18	....	....	....	....	....	....	....	....		1998-99	1998-99
Garrett, John	Hfd., Que., Van.	6	207	68	91	37	11763	837	1	4.27	9	4	3	....	461	33	0	4.30		1979-80	1984-85
Gatherum, Dave	Det.	1	3	2	0	1	180	3	1	1.00	....	....	....	....	....	....	....	....	1	1953-54	1953-54
Gauthier, Paul	Mtl.	1	1	0	0	1	70	2	0	1.71	....	....	....	....	....	....	....	....		1937-38	1937-38
Gauthier, Sean	S.J.	1	1	0	0	0	3	0	0	0.00	....	....	....	....	....	....	....	....		1998-99	1998-99
• Gelineau, Jack	Bos., Chi.	4	143	46	64	33	8580	447	7	3.13	4	1	2	....	260	7	1	1.62		1948-49	1953-54
Giacomin, Ed	NYR, Det.	13	609	289	209	96	35633	1672	54	2.82	65	29	35	....	3838	180	1	2.81		1965-66	1977-78
Gilbert, Gilles	Min., Bos., Det.	14	416	192	143	60	23677	1290	18	3.27	32	17	15	....	1919	97	3	3.03		1969-70	1982-83
Gill, Andre	Bos.	1	5	3	2	0	270	13	1	2.89	....	....	....	....	....	....	....	....		1967-68	1967-68
• Goodman, Paul	Chi.	3	52	23	20	9	3240	117	6	2.17	3	0	3	....	187	10	0	3.21	1	1937-38	1940-41
Gordon, Scott	Que.	2	23	2	16	0	1082	101	0	5.60	....	....	....	....	....	....	....	....		1989-90	1990-91
Gosselin, Mario	Que., L.A., Hfd.	9	241	91	107	14	12857	801	6	3.74	32	16	15	....	1816	99	0	3.27		1983-84	1993-94
Goverde, David	L.A.	3	5	1	4	0	278	29	0	6.26	....	....	....	....	....	....	....	....		1991-92	1993-94
Grahame, Ron	Bos., L.A., Que.	4	114	50	43	15	6472	409	5	3.79	4	2	1	....	202	7	0	2.08		1977-78	1980-81
• Grant, Benny	Tor., NYA, Bos.	6	52	17	27	4	3036	188	4	3.72	....	....	....	....	....	....	....	....		1928-29	1943-44
Grant, Doug	Det., St.L.	7	77	27	34	8	4199	280	2	4.00	....	....	....	....	....	....	....	....		1973-74	1979-80
Gratton, Gilles	St.L., NYR	2	47	13	18	9	2299	154	0	4.02	....	....	....	....	....	....	....	....		1975-76	1976-77
Gray, Gerry	Det., NYI	2	8	1	5	1	440	35	0	4.77	....	....	....	....	....	....	....	....		1970-71	1972-73
Gray, Harrison	Det.	1	1	0	1	0	40	5	0	7.50	....	....	....	....	....	....	....	....		1963-64	1963-64
Greenlay, Mike	Edm.	1	2	0	0	0	20	4	0	12.00	....	....	....	....	....	....	....	....		1989-90	1989-90
Guenette, Steve	Pit., Cgy.	5	35	19	16	0	1958	122	1	3.74	....	....	....	....	....	....	....	....		1986-87	1990-91
‡ Gustafson, Derek	Min.	2	5	1	3	0	265	10	0	2.26	....	....	....	....	....	....	....	....		2000-01	2001-02
Hackett, Jeff	NYI, S.J., Chi., Mtl., Bos., Phi.	15	500	166	244	56	28125	1361	26	2.90	12	3	7	....	610	36	0	3.54		1988-89	2003-04
• Hainsworth, George	Mtl., Tor.	11	465	246	145	74	29087	937	94	1.93	52	22	25	5	3486	112	8	1.93	2	1926-27	1936-37
Hall, Glenn	Det., Chi., St.L.	19	906	407	326	163	53484	2222	84	2.49	115	49	65	....	6899	320	6	2.78	2	1951-52	1970-71
Hamel, Pierre	Tor., Wpg.	4	69	13	41	7	3766	276	0	4.40	....	....	....	....	....	....	....	....		1974-75	1980-81
Hanlon, Glen	Van., St.L., NYR, Det.	15	477	167	202	61	26037	1561	13	3.60	35	11	15	....	1756	92	4	3.14		1977-78	1990-91
Harrison, Paul	Min., Tor., Pit., Buf.	7	109	28	59	9	5806	408	2	4.22	4	0	1	....	157	9	0	3.44		1975-76	1981-82
Hayward, Brian	Wpg., Mtl., Min., S.J.	11	357	143	156	37	20025	1242	8	3.72	37	11	18	....	1803	104	0	3.46		1982-83	1992-93
Head, Don	Bos.	1	38	9	26	3	2280	158	2	4.16	....	....	....	....	....	....	....	....		1961-62	1961-62
Healy, Glenn	L.A., NYI, NYR, Tor.	15	437	166	190	47	24256	1361	13	3.37	37	13	15	....	1930	108	0	3.36	1	1985-86	2000-01

Name	NHL Teams	NHL Seasons	Regular Schedule GP	W	L	T	Mins	GA	SO	Avg	Playoffs GP	W	L	T	Mins	GA	SO	Avg	NHL Cup Wins	First NHL Season	Last NHL Season
Hebert, Guy	St.L., Ana., NYR	10	491	191	222	56	27889	1307	28	2.81	14	4	7	....	744	33	1	2.66		1991-92	2000-01
• Hebert, Sammy	Tor., Ott.	2	4	2	1	0	200	19	0	5.70	....	....	....	....	....	....	....	....	1	1917-18	1923-24
Heinz, Rick	St.L., Van.	5	49	14	19	5	2356	159	2	4.05	1	0	0	....	8	1	0	7.50		1980-81	1984-85
Henderson, John	Bos.	2	46	15	15	15	2688	113	5	2.52	2	0	2	....	120	8	0	4.00		1954-55	1955-56
• Henry, Gord	Bos.	4	3	1	2	0	180	5	1	1.67	5	0	4	....	283	21	0	4.45		1948-49	1952-53
• Henry, Jim	NYR, Chi., Bos.	9	406	161	173	70	24355	1166	28	2.87	29	11	18	....	1741	81	2	2.79		1941-42	1954-55
Herron, Denis	Pit., K.C., Mtl.	14	462	146	203	76	25608	1579	10	3.70	15	5	10	....	901	50	0	3.33		1972-73	1985-86
Hextall, Ron	Phi., Que., NYI	13	608	296	214	69	34750	1723	23	2.97	93	47	43	....	5456	276	2	3.04		1986-87	1998-99
• Highton, Hec	Chi.	1	24	10	14	0	1440	108	0	4.50	....	....	....	....	....	....	....	....		1943-44	1943-44
§ • Himes, Normie	NYA	2	2	0	1	0	79	3	0	2.28	....	....	....	....	....	....	....	....		1927-28	1928-29
Hirsch, Corey	NYR, Van., Wsh., Dal.	7	108	34	45	14	5775	301	4	3.13	6	2	3	....	338	21	0	3.73		1992-93	2002-03
‡ Hnilicka, Milan	NYR, Atl., L.A.	5	121	29	67	13	6509	359	5	3.31	....	....	....	....	....	....	....	....		1999-00	2003-04
Hodge, Charlie	Mtl., Oak., Van.	14	358	150	125	61	20573	925	24	2.70	16	7	8	....	804	32	2	2.39	6	1954-55	1970-71
Hodson, Kevin	Det., T.B.	6	71	17	18	10	2910	134	4	2.76	1	0	0	....	1	0	0	0.00	2	1995-96	2002-03
Hoffort, Bruce	Phi.	2	9	4	0	3	368	22	0	3.59	....	....	....	....	....	....	....	....		1989-90	1990-91
Hoganson, Paul	Pit.	1	2	0	1	0	57	7	0	7.37	....	....	....	....	....	....	....	....		1970-71	1970-71
Hogosta, Goran	NYI, Que.	2	22	5	12	3	1208	83	1	4.12	....	....	....	....	....	....	....	....		1977-78	1979-80
Holden, Mark	Mtl., Wpg.	4	8	2	2	1	372	25	0	4.03	....	....	....	....	....	....	....	....		1981-82	1984-85
Holland, Ken	Hfd., Det.	2	4	0	2	1	206	17	0	4.95	....	....	....	....	....	....	....	....		1980-81	1983-84
Holland, Rob	Pit.	2	44	11	22	9	2513	171	1	4.08	....	....	....	....	....	....	....	....		1979-80	1980-81
• Holmes, Hap	Tor., Det.	4	103	39	54	10	6510	264	17	2.43	2	1	1	0	120	7	0	3.50	1	1917-18	1927-28
§ • Horner, Red	Tor.	1	2	0	0	0	3	1	0	20.00	....	....	....	....	....	....	....	....		1928-29	1931-32
Hrivnak, Jim	Wsh., Wpg., St.L.	5	85	34	30	3	4217	262	0	3.73	....	....	....	....	....	....	....	....		1989-90	1993-94
Hrudey, Kelly	NYI, L.A., S.J.	15	677	271	265	88	38084	2174	17	3.43	85	36	46	....	5163	283	0	3.29		1983-84	1997-98
‡ Hurme, Jani	Ott., Fla.	4	76	29	25	11	4041	176	6	2.61	....	....	....	....	....	....	....	....		1999-00	2002-03
Ing, Peter	Tor., Edm., Det.	4	74	20	37	9	3941	266	1	4.05	....	....	....	....	....	....	....	....		1989-90	1993-94
Inness, Gary	Pit., Phi., Wsh.	7	162	58	61	27	8710	494	2	3.40	9	5	4	....	540	24	0	2.67		1973-74	1980-81
‡ Irbe, Arturs	S.J., Dal., Van., Car.	13	568	218	236	79	32066	1513	33	2.83	51	23	27	....	2981	142	1	2.86		1991-92	2003-04
Ireland, Randy	Buf.	1	2	0	0	0	30	3	0	6.00	....	....	....	....	....	....	....	....		1978-79	1978-79
Irons, Robbie	St.L.	1	1	0	0	0	3	0	0	0.00	....	....	....	....	....	....	....	....		1968-69	1968-69
• Ironstone, Joe	Ott., NYA, Tor.	3	2	0	0	1	110	3	1	1.64	....	....	....	....	....	....	....	....		1924-25	1927-28
Jablonski, Pat	St.L., T.B., Mtl., Phx., Car.	8	128	28	62	18	6634	413	1	3.74	4	0	0	....	139	6	0	2.59		1989-90	1997-98
Jackson, Doug	Chi.	1	6	2	3	1	360	42	0	7.00	....	....	....	....	....	....	....	....		1947-48	1947-48
Jackson, Percy	Bos., NYA, NYR	4	7	1	3	1	392	26	0	3.98	....	....	....	....	....	....	....	....		1931-32	1935-36
Jaks, Pauli	L.A.	1	1	0	0	0	40	2	0	3.00	....	....	....	....	....	....	....	....		1994-95	1994-95
Janaszak, Steve	Min., Col.	2	3	0	1	1	160	15	0	5.63	....	....	....	....	....	....	....	....		1979-80	1981-82
Janecyk, Bob	Chi., L.A.	6	110	43	47	13	6250	432	2	4.15	3	0	3	....	184	10	0	3.26		1983-84	1988-89
§ • Jenkins, Roger	NYA	1	1	0	1	0	30	7	0	14.00	....	....	....	....	....	....	....	....		1938-39	1938-39
Jensen, Al	Det., Wsh., L.A.	7	179	95	53	18	9974	557	8	3.35	12	5	5	....	598	32	0	3.21		1980-81	1986-87
Jensen, Darren	Phi.	2	30	15	10	1	1496	95	2	3.81	....	....	....	....	....	....	....	....		1984-85	1985-86
Johnson, Bob	St.L., Pit.	2	24	9	9	1	1059	66	0	3.74	....	....	....	....	....	....	....	....		1972-73	1974-75
Johnston, Eddie	Bos., Tor., St.L., Chi.	16	592	234	257	80	34216	1852	32	3.25	18	7	10	....	1023	57	1	3.34	2	1962-63	1977-78
Junkin, Joe	Bos.	1	1	0	0	0	8	0	0	0.00	....	....	....	....	....	....	....	....		1968-69	1968-69
Kaarela, Jari	Col.	1	5	2	2	0	220	22	0	6.00	....	....	....	....	....	....	....	....		1980-81	1980-81
Kamppuri, Hannu	N.J.	1	13	1	10	1	645	54	0	5.02	....	....	....	....	....	....	....	....		1984-85	1984-85
• Karakas, Mike	Chi., Mtl.	8	336	114	169	53	20614	1002	28	2.92	23	11	12	0	1434	72	3	3.01	1	1935-36	1945-46
Keans, Doug	L.A., Bos.	9	210	96	64	26	11388	666	4	3.51	9	2	6	....	432	34	0	4.72		1979-80	1987-88
• Keenan, Don	Bos.	1	1	0	1	0	60	4	0	4.00	....	....	....	....	....	....	....	....		1958-59	1958-59
• Kerr, Dave	Mtl.M., NYA, NYR	11	427	203	148	75	26639	954	51	2.15	40	18	19	3	2616	76	8	1.74	1	1930-31	1940-41
Kidd, Trevor	Cgy., Car., Fla., Tor.	12	387	140	162	52	21426	1014	19	2.84	10	3	5	....	550	36	1	3.93		1991-92	2003-04
King, Scott	Det.	2	2	0	0	0	61	3	0	2.95	....	....	....	....	....	....	....	....		1990-91	1991-92
Kleisinger, Terry	NYR	1	4	0	2	0	191	14	0	4.40	....	....	....	....	....	....	....	....		1985-86	1985-86
Klymkiw, Julian	NYR	1	1	0	0	0	19	2	0	6.32	....	....	....	....	....	....	....	....		1958-59	1958-59
Knickle, Rick	L.A.	2	14	7	6	0	706	44	0	3.74	....	....	....	....	....	....	....	....		1992-93	1993-94
Kochan, Dieter	T.B., Min.	4	21	1	11	1	849	56	0	3.96	....	....	....	....	....	....	....	....		1999-00	2002-03
‡ Kolesnik, Vitali	Col.	1	8	3	3	0	370	20	0	3.24	....	....	....	....	....	....	....	....		2005-06	2005-06
Konstantinov, Evgeny	T.B.	2	2	0	0	0	21	1	0	2.86	....	....	....	....	....	....	....	....		2000-01	2002-03
Kuntar, Les	Mtl.	1	6	2	2	0	302	16	0	3.18	....	....	....	....	....	....	....	....		1993-94	1993-94
Kurt, Gary	Cal.	1	16	1	7	5	838	60	0	4.30	....	....	....	....	....	....	....	....		1971-72	1971-72
‡ Labbe, Jean-Francois	NYR, CBJ	3	15	3	6	0	628	36	0	3.44	....	....	....	....	....	....	....	....		1999-00	2002-03
Labrecque, Patrick	Mtl.	1	2	0	1	0	98	7	0	4.29	....	....	....	....	....	....	....	....		1995-96	1995-96
Lacher, Blaine	Bos.	2	47	22	16	4	2636	123	4	2.80	5	1	4	....	283	12	0	2.54		1994-95	1995-96
• Lacroix, Frenchy	Mtl.	2	5	1	4	0	280	16	0	3.43	....	....	....	....	....	....	....	....		1925-26	1926-27
LaFerriere, Rick	Col.	1	1	0	0	0	20	1	0	3.00	....	....	....	....	....	....	....	....		1981-82	1981-82
LaForest, Mark	Det., Phi., Tor., Ott.	6	103	25	54	4	5032	354	2	4.22	2	1	0	....	48	1	0	1.25		1985-86	1993-94
Lajeunesse, Simon	Ott.	1	1	0	0	0	24	0	0	0.00	....	....	....	....	....	....	....	....		2001-02	2001-02
Lamothe, Marc	Chi., Det.	2	4	2	1	1	241	13	0	3.24	....	....	....	....	....	....	....	....		1999-00	2003-04
‡ Langkow, Scott	Wpg., Phx., Atl.	4	20	3	12	1	943	68	0	4.33	....	....	....	....	....	....	....	....		1995-96	1999-00
• Larocque, Michel	Mtl., Tor., Phi., St.L.	11	312	160	89	45	17615	978	17	3.33	14	6	6	....	759	37	1	2.92	4	1973-74	1983-84
Larocque, Michel	Chi.	1	3	0	2	0	152	9	0	3.55	....	....	....	....	....	....	....	....		2000-01	2000-01
‡ Lasak, Jan	Nsh.	2	6	0	4	0	267	18	0	4.04	....	....	....	....	....	....	....	....		2001-02	2002-03
Laskowski, Gary	L.A.	2	59	19	27	5	2942	228	0	4.65	....	....	....	....	....	....	....	....		1982-83	1983-84
Laxton, Gord	Pit.	4	17	4	9	0	800	74	0	5.55	....	....	....	....	....	....	....	....		1975-76	1978-79
LeBlanc, Ray	Chi.	1	1	1	0	0	60	1	0	1.00	....	....	....	....	....	....	....	....		1991-92	1991-92
§ • Leduc, Albert	Mtl.	1	1	0	0	0	2	1	0	30.00	....	....	....	....	....	....	....	....		1931-32	1931-32
Legris, Claude	Det.	2	4	0	1	1	91	4	0	2.64	....	....	....	....	....	....	....	....		1980-81	1981-82
• Lehman, Hugh	Chi.	2	48	20	24	4	3047	136	6	2.68	2	0	1	1	120	10	0	5.00		1926-27	1927-28
Lemelin, Reggie	Atl., Cgy., Bos.	15	507	236	162	63	28006	1613	12	3.46	59	23	25	....	3119	186	2	3.58		1978-79	1992-93
Lenarduzzi, Mike	Hfd.	2	4	1	1	1	189	10	0	3.17	....	....	....	....	....	....	....	....		1992-93	1993-94
Lessard, Mario	L.A.	6	240	92	97	39	13529	843	9	3.74	20	6	12	....	1136	83	0	4.38		1978-79	1983-84
Levasseur, Jean-Louis	Min.	1	1	0	1	0	60	7	0	7.00	....	....	....	....	....	....	....	....		1979-80	1979-80
§ • Levinsky, Alex	Tor.	1	1	0	0	0	1	1	0	60.00	....	....	....	....	....	....	....	....		1931-32	1931-32
• Lindbergh, Pelle	Phi.	5	157	87	49	15	9150	503	7	3.30	23	12	10	....	1214	63	3	3.11		1981-82	1985-86
• Lindsay, Bert	Mtl.W., Tor.	2	20	6	14	0	1238	118	0	5.72	....	....	....	....	....	....	....	....		1917-18	1918-19
Little, Neil	Phi.	2	2	0	2	0	93	6	0	3.87	....	....	....	....	....	....	....	....		2001-02	2003-04
Littman, David	Buf., T.B.	3	3	0	2	0	141	14	0	5.96	....	....	....	....	....	....	....	....		1990-91	1992-93
Liut, Mike	St.L., Hfd., Wsh.	13	664	294	271	74	38215	2221	25	3.49	67	29	32	....	3814	215	2	3.38		1979-80	1991-92
Lockett, Ken	Van.	2	55	13	15	8	2348	131	2	3.35	1	0	1	....	60	6	0	6.00		1974-75	1975-76
• Lockhart, Howard	Tor., Que., Ham., Bos.	5	59	16	41	0	3413	287	1	5.05	....	....	....	....	....	....	....	....		1919-20	1924-25
LoPresti, Pete	Min., Edm.	6	175	43	102	20	9858	668	5	4.07	2	0	2	....	77	6	0	4.68		1974-75	1980-81
• LoPresti, Sam	Chi.	2	74	30	38	6	4530	236	4	3.13	8	3	5	....	530	17	1	1.92		1940-41	1941-42
Lorenz, Danny	NYI	3	8	1	5	0	357	25	0	4.20	....	....	....	....	....	....	....	....		1990-91	1992-93
Loustel, Ron	Wpg.	1	1	0	1	0	60	10	0	10.00	....	....	....	....	....	....	....	....		1980-81	1980-81
Low, Ron	Tor., Wsh., Det., Que., Edm., N.J.	11	382	102	203	38	20502	1463	4	4.28	7	1	6	....	452	29	0	3.85		1972-73	1984-85
Lozinski, Larry	Det.	1	30	6	11	7	1459	105	0	4.32	....	....	....	....	....	....	....	....		1980-81	1980-81
• Lumley, Harry	Det., NYR, Chi., Tor., Bos.	16	803	330	329	142	48044	2206	71	2.75	76	29	47	....	4778	198	7	2.49	1	1943-44	1959-60
MacKenzie, Shawn	N.J.	1	4	0	1	0	130	15	0	6.92	....	....	....	....	....	....	....	....		1982-83	1982-83
Madeley, Darrin	Ott.	3	39	4	23	5	1928	140	0	4.36	....	....	....	....	....	....	....	....		1992-93	1994-95
Malarchuk, Clint	Que., Wsh., Buf.	11	338	141	130	45	19030	1100	12	3.47	15	2	9	....	781	56	0	4.30		1981-82	1991-92
Maneluk, George	NYI	1	4	1	1	0	140	15	0	6.43	....	....	....	....	....	....	....	....		1990-91	1990-91
Maniago, Cesare	Tor., Mtl., NYR, Min., Van.	15	568	190	257	97	32569	1773	30	3.27	36	15	21	....	2245	100	3	2.67		1960-61	1977-78
‡ Maracle, Norm	Det., Atl.	5	66	14	33	8	3430	177	1	3.10	2	0	0	....	58	3	0	3.10		1997-98	2001-02
Marois, Jean	Tor., Chi.	2	3	1	2	0	180	15	0	5.00	....	....	....	....	....	....	....	....		1943-44	1953-54
Martin, Seth	St.L.	1	30	8	10	7	1552	67	1	2.59	2	0	0	....	73	5	0	4.11		1967-68	1967-68
Mason, Bob	Wsh., Chi., Que., Van.	8	145	55	65	16	7988	500	1	3.76	5	2	3	....	369	12	1	1.95		1983-84	1990-91
Mattsson, Markus	Wpg., Min., L.A.	4	92	21	46	14	5007	343	6	4.11	....	....	....	....	....	....	....	....		1979-80	1983-84
May, Darrell	St.L.	2	6	1	5	0	364	31	0	5.11	....	....	....	....	....	....	....	....		1985-86	1987-88
Mayer, Gilles	Tor.	4	9	2	6	1	540	24	0	2.67	....	....	....	....	....	....	....	....		1949-50	1955-56
• McAuley, Ken	NYR	2	96	17	64	15	5740	537	1	5.61	....	....	....	....	....	....	....	....		1943-44	1944-45

Name	NHL Teams	NHL Seasons	Regular Schedule GP	W	L	T	Mins	GA	SO	Avg	Playoffs GP	W	L	T	Mins	GA	SO	Avg	NHL Cup Wins	First NHL Season	Last NHL Season
McCartan, Jack	NYR	2	12	2	7	3	680	42	1	3.71	....	....	....	....	....	....	....	....		1959-60	1960-61
• McCool, Frank	Tor.	2	72	34	31	7	4320	242	4	3.36	13	8	5	....	807	30	4	2.23	1	1944-45	1945-46
McDuffe, Peter	St.L., NYR, K.C., Det.	5	57	11	36	6	3207	218	0	4.08	1	0	1	....	60	7	0	7.00		1971-72	1975-76
McGrattan, Tom	Det.	1	1	0	0	0	8	1	0	7.50	....	....	....	....	....	....	....	....		1947-48	1947-48
McKay, Ross	Hfd.	1	1	0	0	0	35	3	0	5.14	....	....	....	....	....	....	....	....		1990-91	1990-91
McKenzie, Bill	Det., K.C., Col.	6	91	18	49	13	4776	326	2	4.10	....	....	....	....	....	....	....	....		1973-74	1979-80
McKichan, Steve	Van.	1	1	0	0	0	20	2	0	6.00	....	....	....	....	....	....	....	....		1990-91	1990-91
McLachlan, Murray	Tor.	1	2	0	1	0	25	4	0	9.60	....	....	....	....	....	....	....	....		1970-71	1970-71
McLean, Kirk	N.J., Van., Car., Fla., NYR	16	612	245	262	72	35090	1904	22	3.26	68	34	34	....	4189	198	6	2.84		1985-86	2000-01
McLelland, Dave	Van.	1	2	1	1	0	120	10	0	5.00	....	....	....	....	....	....	....	....		1972-73	1972-73
McLennan, Jamie	NYI, St.L., Min., Cgy., NYR, Fla.	11	254	80	109	36	13834	617	13	2.68	5	0	2	....	134	7	0	3.13		1993-94	2006-07
McLeod, Don	Det., Phi.	2	18	3	10	1	879	74	0	5.05	....	....	....	....	....	....	....	....		1970-71	1971-72
McLeod, Jim	St.L.	1	16	6	6	4	880	44	0	3.00	....	....	....	....	....	....	....	....		1971-72	1971-72
McNamara, Gerry	Tor.	2	7	2	2	1	323	14	0	2.60	....	....	....	....	....	....	....	....		1960-61	1969-70
• McNeil, Gerry	Mtl.	8	276	119	105	52	16535	649	28	2.36	35	17	18	....	2284	72	5	1.89	3	1947-48	1957-58
McRae, Gord	Tor.	5	71	30	22	10	3799	221	1	3.49	8	2	5	....	454	22	0	2.91		1972-73	1977-78
‡ McVicar, Rob	Van.	1	1	0	0	0	3	0	0	0.00	....	....	....	....	....	....	....	....		2005-06	2005-06
Melanson, Roland	NYI, Min., L.A., N.J., Mtl.	11	291	129	106	33	16452	995	6	3.63	23	4	9	....	801	59	0	4.42	3	1980-81	1991-92
Meloche, Gilles	Chi., Cal., Cle., Min., Pit.	18	788	270	351	131	45401	2756	20	3.64	45	21	19	....	2464	143	2	3.48		1970-71	1987-88
Micalef, Corrado	Det.	5	113	26	59	15	5794	409	2	4.24	3	0	0	....	49	8	0	9.80		1981-82	1985-86
‡ Michaud, Alfie	Van.	1	2	0	1	0	69	5	0	4.35	....	....	....	....	....	....	....	....		1999-00	1999-00
‡ Michaud, Olivier	Mtl.	1	1	0	0	0	18	0	0	0.00	....	....	....	....	....	....	....	....		2001-02	2001-02
Middlebrook, Lindsay	Wpg., Min., N.J., Edm.	4	37	3	23	6	1845	152	0	4.94	....	....	....	....	....	....	....	....		1979-80	1982-83
• Millar, Al	Bos.	1	6	1	4	1	360	25	0	4.17	....	....	....	....	....	....	....	....		1957-58	1957-58
Millen, Greg	Pit., Hfd., St.L., Que., Chi., Det.	14	604	215	284	89	35377	2281	17	3.87	59	27	29	....	3383	193	0	3.42		1978-79	1991-92
• Miller, Joe	NYA, NYR, Pit., Phi.	4	127	24	87	16	7871	383	16	2.92	3	2	1	0	180	3	1	1.00	1	1927-28	1930-31
Minard, Mike	Edm.	1	1	1	0	0	60	3	0	3.00	....	....	....	....	....	....	....	....		1999-00	1999-00
Mio, Eddie	Edm., NYR, Det.	7	192	64	73	30	10428	705	4	4.06	17	9	7	....	986	63	0	3.83		1979-80	1985-86
• Mitchell, Ivan	Tor.	3	22	10	9	0	1190	88	0	4.44	....	....	....	....	....	....	....	....	1	1919-20	1921-22
Moffat, Mike	Bos.	3	19	7	7	2	979	70	0	4.29	11	6	5	....	663	38	0	3.44		1981-82	1983-84
Moog, Andy	Edm., Bos., Dal., Mtl.	18	713	372	209	88	40151	2097	28	3.13	132	68	57	....	7452	377	4	3.04	3	1980-81	1997-98
• Moore, Alfie	NYA, Chi., Det.	4	21	7	14	0	1290	81	1	3.77	3	1	2	....	180	7	0	2.33	1	1936-37	1939-40
Moore, Robbie	Phi., Wsh.	2	6	3	1	1	257	8	2	1.87	5	3	2	....	268	18	0	4.03		1978-79	1982-83
Morissette, Jean-Guy	Mtl.	1	1	0	1	0	36	4	0	6.67	....	....	....	....	....	....	....	....		1963-64	1963-64
‡ Moss, Tyler	Cgy., Car., Van.	4	30	6	16	1	1496	81	0	3.25	....	....	....	....	....	....	....	....		1997-98	2002-03
• Mowers, Johnny	Det.	4	152	65	61	26	9350	399	15	2.56	32	19	13	....	2000	85	2	2.55	1	1940-41	1946-47
Mrazek, Jerome	Phi.	1	1	0	0	0	6	1	0	10.00	....	....	....	....	....	....	....	....		1975-76	1975-76
• Mummery, Harry	Que., Ham.	2	4	2	1	0	192	20	0	6.25	....	....	....	....	....	....	....	....		1919-20	1921-22
• Munro, Dunc	Mtl.M.	1	1	0	0	0	2	0	0	0.00	....	....	....	....	....	....	....	....		1924-25	1924-25
• Murphy, Hal	Mtl.	1	1	1	0	0	60	4	0	4.00	....	....	....	....	....	....	....	....		1952-53	1952-53
• Murray, Mickey	Mtl.	1	1	0	1	0	60	4	0	4.00	....	....	....	....	....	....	....	....		1929-30	1929-30
‡ Muzzatti, Jason	Cgy., Hfd., NYR, S.J.	5	62	13	25	10	3014	167	1	3.32	....	....	....	....	....	....	....	....		1993-94	1997-98
Myllys, Jarmo	Min., S.J.	4	39	4	27	1	1846	161	0	5.23	....	....	....	....	....	....	....	....		1988-89	1991-92
Mylnikov, Sergei	Que.	1	10	1	7	2	568	47	0	4.96	....	....	....	....	....	....	....	....		1989-90	1989-90
Myre, Phil	Mtl., Atl., St.L., Phi., Col., Buf.	14	439	149	198	76	25220	1482	14	3.53	12	6	5	....	747	41	1	3.29		1969-70	1982-83
‡ Naumenko, Gregg	Ana.	1	2	0	1	0	70	7	0	6.00	....	....	....	....	....	....	....	....		2000-01	2000-01
Newton, Cam	Pit.	2	16	4	7	1	814	51	0	3.76	....	....	....	....	....	....	....	....		1970-71	1972-73
‡ Noronen, Mika	Buf., Van.	5	71	23	32	6	3652	163	3	2.68	....	....	....	....	....	....	....	....		2000-01	2005-06
Norris, Jack	Bos., Chi., L.A.	4	58	20	25	4	3119	202	2	3.89	....	....	....	....	....	....	....	....		1964-65	1970-71
Nurminen, Pasi	Atl.	3	125	48	54	12	7059	338	5	2.87	....	....	....	....	....	....	....	....		2001-02	2003-04
Oleschuk, Bill	K.C., Col.	4	55	7	28	10	2835	188	1	3.98	....	....	....	....	....	....	....	....		1975-76	1979-80
• Olesevich, Dan	NYR	1	1	0	0	1	29	2	0	4.14	....	....	....	....	....	....	....	....		1961-62	1961-62
O'Neill, Mike	Wpg., Ana.	4	21	0	9	2	855	61	0	4.28	....	....	....	....	....	....	....	....		1991-92	1996-97
‡ Ouellet, Maxime	Phi., Wsh., Van.	3	12	2	6	2	663	34	1	3.08	....	....	....	....	....	....	....	....		2000-01	2005-06
Ouimet, Ted	St.L.	1	1	0	1	0	60	2	0	2.00	....	....	....	....	....	....	....	....		1968-69	1968-69
Pageau, Paul	L.A.	1	1	0	1	0	60	8	0	8.00	....	....	....	....	....	....	....	....		1980-81	1980-81
• Paille, Marcel	NYR	7	107	32	52	22	6342	362	2	3.42	....	....	....	....	....	....	....	....		1957-58	1964-65
Palmateer, Mike	Tor., Wsh.	8	356	149	138	52	20131	1183	17	3.53	29	12	17	....	1765	89	2	3.03		1976-77	1983-84
Pang, Darren	Chi.	3	81	27	35	7	4252	287	0	4.05	6	1	3	....	250	18	0	4.32		1984-85	1988-89
Parent, Bernie	Bos., Phi., Tor.	13	608	271	198	121	35136	1493	54	2.55	71	38	33	....	4302	174	6	2.43	2	1965-66	1978-79
Parent, Bob	Tor.	2	3	0	2	0	160	15	0	5.63	....	....	....	....	....	....	....	....		1981-82	1982-83
Parent, Rich	St.L., T.B., Pit.	4	32	7	11	5	1561	82	1	3.15	....	....	....	....	....	....	....	....		1997-98	2000-01
Parro, Dave	Wsh.	4	77	21	36	10	4015	274	2	4.09	....	....	....	....	....	....	....	....		1980-81	1983-84
‡ Passmore, Steve	Edm., Chi., L.A.	6	93	23	44	12	5045	235	2	2.79	3	0	2	....	138	6	0	2.61		1998-99	2003-04
• Patrick, Lester	NYR	1	....	....	....	....	....	....	....	....	1	1	0	0	46	1	0	1.30	1	1927-28	1927-28
Peeters, Pete	Phi., Bos., Wsh.	13	489	246	155	51	27699	1424	21	3.08	71	35	35	....	4200	232	2	3.31		1978-79	1990-91
Pelletier, Marcel	Chi., NYR	2	8	1	6	0	395	32	0	4.86	....	....	....	....	....	....	....	....		1950-51	1962-63
Penney, Steve	Mtl., Wpg.	5	91	35	38	12	5194	313	1	3.62	27	15	12	....	1604	72	4	2.69		1983-84	1987-88
• Perreault, Bob	Mtl., Det., Bos.	3	31	8	16	7	1827	103	3	3.38	....	....	....	....	....	....	....	....		1955-56	1962-63
Pettie, Jim	Bos.	3	21	9	7	2	1157	71	1	3.68	....	....	....	....	....	....	....	....		1976-77	1978-79
Pietrangelo, Frank	Pit., Hfd.	7	141	46	59	6	7141	490	1	4.12	12	7	5	....	713	34	1	2.86	1	1987-88	1993-94
• Plante, Jacques	Mtl., NYR, St.L., Tor., Bos.	18	837	437	246	145	49533	1964	82	2.38	112	71	36	....	6651	237	14	2.14	6	1952-53	1972-73
• Plasse, Michel	St.L., Mtl., K.C., Pit., Col., Que.	11	299	92	136	54	16760	1058	2	3.79	4	1	2	....	195	9	1	2.77	1	1970-71	1981-82
• Plaxton, Hugh	Mtl.M.	1	1	0	1	0	57	5	0	5.26	....	....	....	....	....	....	....	....		1932-33	1932-33
Potvin, Felix	Tor., NYI, Van., L.A., Bos.	13	635	266	260	85	36765	1694	32	2.76	72	35	37	....	4435	195	8	2.64		1991-92	2003-04
Pronovost, Claude	Bos., Mtl.	2	3	1	1	0	120	7	1	3.50	....	....	....	....	....	....	....	....		1955-56	1958-59
‡ Prusek, Martin	Ott., CBJ	4	57	31	12	4	2898	114	3	2.36	1	0	0	....	40	1	0	1.50		2001-02	2005-06
Puppa, Daren	Buf., Tor., T.B.	15	429	179	161	54	23819	1204	19	3.03	16	4	9	....	786	51	0	3.89		1985-86	1999-00
Pusey, Chris	Det.	1	1	0	0	0	40	3	0	4.50	....	....	....	....	....	....	....	....		1985-86	1985-86
Racicot, Andre	Mtl.	5	68	26	23	8	3357	196	2	3.50	4	0	1	....	31	4	0	7.74	1	1989-90	1993-94
Racine, Bruce	St.L.	1	11	0	3	0	230	12	0	3.13	1	0	0	....	1	0	0	0.00		1995-96	1995-96
Ram, Jamie	NYR	1	1	0	0	0	27	0	0	0.00	....	....	....	....	....	....	....	....		1995-96	1995-96
Ranford, Bill	Bos., Edm., Wsh., T.B., Det.	15	647	240	279	76	35936	2042	15	3.41	53	28	25	....	3110	159	4	3.07	2	1985-86	1999-00
Raymond, Alain	Wsh.	1	1	0	1	0	40	2	0	3.00	....	....	....	....	....	....	....	....		1987-88	1987-88
• Rayner, Chuck	NYA, Bro., NYR	10	424	138	208	77	25491	1294	25	3.05	18	9	9	....	1135	46	1	2.43		1940-41	1952-53
Reaugh, Daryl	Edm., Hfd.	3	27	8	9	1	1246	72	1	3.47	....	....	....	....	....	....	....	....		1984-85	1990-91
Reddick, Pokey	Wpg., Edm., Fla.	6	132	46	58	16	7162	443	0	3.71	4	0	2	....	168	10	0	3.57	1	1986-87	1993-94
• Redding, George	Bos.	1	1	0	0	0	11	1	0	5.45	....	....	....	....	....	....	....	....		1924-25	1924-25
Redquest, Greg	Pit.	1	1	0	0	0	13	3	0	13.85	....	....	....	....	....	....	....	....		1977-78	1977-78
Reece, Dave	Bos.	1	14	7	5	2	777	43	2	3.32	....	....	....	....	....	....	....	....		1975-76	1975-76
Reese, Jeff	Tor., Cgy., Hfd., T.B., N.J.	11	174	53	65	17	8667	529	5	3.66	11	3	5	....	515	35	0	4.08		1987-88	1998-99
Resch, Glenn	NYI, Col., N.J., Phi.	14	571	231	224	82	32279	1761	26	3.27	41	17	17	....	2044	85	2	2.50	1	1973-74	1986-87
• Rheaume, Herb	Mtl.	1	31	10	20	1	1889	92	0	2.92	....	....	....	....	....	....	....	....		1925-26	1925-26
Rhodes, Damian	Tor., Ott., Atl.	10	309	99	140	48	17339	820	12	2.84	13	5	7	....	741	27	0	2.19		1990-91	2001-02
Ricci, Nick	Pit.	4	19	7	12	0	1087	79	0	4.36	....	....	....	....	....	....	....	....		1979-80	1982-83
Richardson, Terry	Det., St.L.	5	20	3	11	0	906	85	0	5.63	....	....	....	....	....	....	....	....		1973-74	1978-79
Richter, Mike	NYR	15	666	301	258	73	38183	1840	24	2.89	76	41	33	....	4514	202	9	2.68	1	1988-89	2002-03
Ridley, Curt	NYR, Van., Tor.	6	104	27	47	16	5498	355	1	3.87	2	0	2	....	120	8	0	4.00		1974-75	1980-81
Riendeau, Vincent	Mtl., St.L., Det., Bos.	8	184	85	65	20	10423	573	5	3.30	25	11	12	....	1277	71	1	3.34		1987-88	1994-95
Riggin, Dennis	Det.	2	18	6	10	2	999	52	1	3.12	....	....	....	....	....	....	....	....		1959-60	1962-63
Riggin, Pat	Atl., Cgy., Wsh., Bos., Pit.	9	350	153	120	52	19872	1135	11	3.43	25	8	13	....	1336	72	0	3.23		1979-80	1987-88
Ring, Bob	Bos.	1	1	0	0	0	33	4	0	7.27	....	....	....	....	....	....	....	....		1965-66	1965-66
Rivard, Fern	Min.	4	55	9	27	11	2865	190	2	3.98	....	....	....	....	....	....	....	....		1968-69	1974-75
Roach, John Ross	Tor., NYR, Det.	14	492	219	204	68	30444	1246	58	2.46	29	12	14	3	1901	60	7	1.89	1	1921-22	1934-35
Roberts, Moe	Bos., NYA, Chi.	4	10	3	5	0	501	31	0	3.71	....	....	....	....	....	....	....	....		1925-26	1951-52
Robertson, Earl	Det., NYA, Bro.	6	190	60	95	34	11820	575	16	2.92	15	7	7	....	995	29	2	1.75	1	1936-37	1941-42
Rollins, Al	Tor., Chi., NYR	9	430	141	205	83	25723	1192	28	2.78	13	6	7	....	755	30	0	2.38	1	1949-50	1959-60
Romano, Roberto	Pit., Bos.	6	126	46	63	8	7111	471	4	3.97	....	....	....	....	....	....	....	....		1982-83	1993-94
Rosati, Mike	Wsh.	1	1	1	0	0	28	0	0	0.00	....	....	....	....	....	....	....	....		1998-99	1998-99
Roussel, Dominic	Phi., Wpg., Ana., Edm.	8	205	77	70	23	10665	555	7	3.12	1	0	0	....	23	0	0	0.00		1991-92	2000-01

Name	NHL Teams	NHL Seasons	Regular Schedule GP	W	L	T	Mins	GA	SO	Avg	Playoffs GP	W	L	T	Mins	GA	SO	Avg	NHL Cup Wins	First NHL Season	Last NHL Season
Roy, Patrick	Mtl., Col.	19	1029	551	315	131	60235	2546	66	2.54	247	151	94	....	15209	584	23	2.30	4	1984-85	2002-03
‡ Rudkowsky, Cody	St.L.	1	1	1	0	0	30	0	0	0.00	....	....	....	....	....	....	....	....		2002-03	2002-03
• Rupp, Pat	Det.	1	1	0	1	0	60	4	0	4.00	....	....	....	....	....	....	....	....		1963-64	1963-64
Rutherford, Jim	Det., Pit., Tor., L.A.	13	457	151	227	59	25895	1576	14	3.65	8	2	5	....	440	28	0	3.82		1970-71	1982-83
• Rutledge, Wayne	L.A.	3	82	28	37	9	4325	241	2	3.34	8	2	4	....	378	20	0	3.17		1967-68	1969-70
St. Croix, Rick	Phi., Tor.	8	130	49	54	18	7295	451	2	3.71	11	4	6	....	562	29	1	3.10		1977-78	1984-85
St. Laurent, Sam	N.J., Det.	5	34	7	12	4	1572	92	1	3.51	1	0	0	....	10	1	0	6.00		1985-86	1989-90
‡ Salo, Tommy	NYI, Edm., Col.	10	526	210	225	73	30436	1296	37	2.55	22	5	16	....	1369	58	0	2.54		1994-95	2003-04
§ • Sands, Charlie	Mtl.	1	1	0	0	0	25	5	0	12.00	....	....	....	....	....	....	....	....		1939-40	1939-40
Sands, Mike	Min.	2	6	0	5	0	302	26	0	5.17	....	....	....	....	....	....	....	....		1984-85	1986-87
Sarjeant, Geoff	St.L., S.J.	2	8	1	2	1	291	20	0	4.12	....	....	....	....	....	....	....	....		1994-95	1995-96
Sauve, Bob	Buf., Det., Chi., N.J.	13	420	182	154	54	23711	1377	8	3.48	34	15	16	....	1850	95	4	3.08		1976-77	1988-89
• Sawchuk, Terry	Det., Bos., Tor., L.A., NYR	21	971	447	330	172	57194	2389	103	2.51	106	54	48	....	6290	266	12	2.54	4	1949-50	1969-70
• Schaefer, Joe	NYR	2	2	0	2	0	86	8	0	5.58	....	....	....	....	....	....	....	....		1959-60	1960-61
Schafer, Paxton	Bos.	1	3	0	0	0	77	6	0	4.68	....	....	....	....	....	....	....	....		1996-97	1996-97
Schwab, Corey	N.J., T.B., Van., Tor.	8	147	42	63	13	7476	360	6	2.89	3	0	0	....	40	0	0	0.00	1	1995-96	2003-04
Scott, Ron	NYR, L.A.	5	28	8	13	4	1450	91	0	3.77	1	0	0	....	32	4	0	7.50		1983-84	1989-90
‡ Scott, Travis	L.A.	1	1	0	0	0	25	3	0	7.20	....	....	....	....	....	....	....	....		2000-01	2000-01
Sevigny, Richard	Mtl., Que.	9	176	80	54	20	9485	507	5	3.21	4	0	3	....	208	13	0	3.75	1	1978-79	1986-87
Sharples, Scott	Cgy.	1	1	0	0	1	65	4	0	3.69	....	....	....	....	....	....	....	....		1991-92	1991-92
§ • Shields, Al	NYA	1	2	0	0	0	41	9	0	13.17	....	....	....	....	....	....	....	....		1931-32	1931-32
Shields, Steve	Buf., S.J., Ana., Bos., Fla., Atl.	10	246	80	104	40	13630	606	10	2.67	25	9	16	....	1445	74	1	3.07		1995-96	2005-06
Shtalenkov, Mikhail	Ana., Edm., Phx., Fla.	7	190	62	82	19	9966	480	8	2.89	4	0	3	....	211	10	0	2.84		1993-94	1999-00
Shulmistra, Richard	N.J., Fla.	2	2	1	1	0	122	3	0	1.48	....	....	....	....	....	....	....	....		1997-98	1999-00
Sidorkiewicz, Peter	Hfd., Ott., N.J.	8	246	79	128	27	13884	832	8	3.60	15	5	10	....	912	55	0	3.62		1987-88	1997-98
Simmons, Don	Bos., Tor., NYR	11	249	101	101	41	14555	701	20	2.89	24	13	11	....	1436	62	3	2.59	3	1956-57	1968-69
Simmons, Gary	Cal., Cle., L.A.	4	107	30	57	15	6162	366	5	3.56	1	0	0	....	20	1	0	3.00		1974-75	1977-78
Skidmore, Paul	St.L.	1	2	1	1	0	120	6	0	3.00	....	....	....	....	....	....	....	....		1981-82	1981-82
Skorodenski, Warren	Chi., Edm.	5	35	12	11	4	1732	100	2	3.46	2	0	0	....	33	6	0	10.91		1981-82	1987-88
Skudra, Peter	Pit., Buf., Bos., Van.	6	146	51	47	20	7162	326	6	2.73	3	0	1	....	116	6	0	3.10		1997-98	2002-03
• Smith, Al	Tor., Pit., Det., Buf., Hfd., Col.	10	233	74	99	36	12752	735	10	3.46	6	1	4	....	317	21	0	3.97		1965-66	1980-81
Smith, Billy	L.A., NYI	18	680	305	233	105	38431	2031	22	3.17	132	88	36	....	7645	348	5	2.73	4	1971-72	1988-89
Smith, Gary	Tor., Oak., Cal., Chi., Van., Min., Wsh., Wpg.	14	532	173	261	74	29619	1675	26	3.39	20	5	13	....	1153	62	1	3.23		1965-66	1979-80
• Smith, Normie	Mtl.M., Det.	8	199	81	83	35	12357	479	17	2.33	12	9	2	0	820	18	3	1.32	2	1931-32	1944-45
Sneddon, Bob	Cal.	1	5	0	2	0	225	21	0	5.60	....	....	....	....	....	....	....	....		1970-71	1970-71
Snow, Garth	Que., Phi., Van., Pit., NYI	12	368	135	147	44	19837	925	16	2.80	20	9	8	....	1040	48	1	2.77		1993-94	2005-06
Soderstrom, Tommy	Phi., NYI	5	156	45	69	19	8189	496	10	3.63	....	....	....	....	....	....	....	....		1992-93	1996-97
Soetaert, Doug	NYR, Wpg., Mtl.	12	284	110	104	42	15583	1030	6	3.97	5	1	2	....	180	14	0	4.67	1	1975-76	1986-87
Soucy, Christian	Chi.	1	1	0	0	0	3	0	0	0.00	....	....	....	....	....	....	....	....		1993-94	1993-94
• Spooner, Red	Pit.	1	1	0	1	0	60	6	0	6.00	....	....	....	....	....	....	....	....		1929-30	1929-30
§ • Spring, Jesse	Ham.	1	1	0	0	0	2	0	0	0.00	....	....	....	....	....	....	....	....		1924-25	1924-25
‡ Stana, Rastislav	Wsh.	1	6	1	2	0	211	11	0	3.13	....	....	....	....	....	....	....	....		2003-04	2003-04
Staniowski, Ed	St.L., Wpg., Hfd.	10	219	67	104	21	12075	818	2	4.06	8	1	6	....	428	28	0	3.93		1975-76	1984-85
§ • Starr, Harold	Mtl.M.	1	1	0	0	0	3	0	0	0.00	....	....	....	....	....	....	....	....		1931-32	1931-32
Stauber, Robb	L.A., Buf.	4	62	21	23	9	3295	209	1	3.81	4	3	1	....	240	16	0	4.00		1989-90	1994-95
Stefan, Greg	Det.	9	299	115	127	30	16333	1068	5	3.92	30	12	17	....	1681	99	1	3.53		1981-82	1989-90
• Stein, Phil	Tor.	1	1	0	0	1	70	2	0	1.71	....	....	....	....	....	....	....	....		1939-40	1939-40
Stephenson, Wayne	St.L., Phi., Wsh.	10	328	146	103	49	18343	937	14	3.06	26	11	12	....	1522	79	2	3.11	1	1971-72	1980-81
• Stevenson, Doug	NYR, Chi.	3	8	2	6	0	480	39	0	4.88	....	....	....	....	....	....	....	....		1944-45	1945-46
• Stewart, Charles	Bos.	3	77	30	41	5	4742	194	10	2.45	....	....	....	....	....	....	....	....		1924-25	1926-27
Stewart, Jim	Bos.	1	1	0	1	0	20	5	0	15.00	....	....	....	....	....	....	....	....		1979-80	1979-80
‡ Storr, Jamie	L.A., Car.	10	219	85	86	23	11512	488	16	2.54	5	0	3	....	182	11	0	3.63		1994-95	2003-04
• Stuart, Herb	Det.	1	3	1	2	0	180	5	0	1.67	....	....	....	....	....	....	....	....		1926-27	1926-27
Sylvestri, Don	Bos.	1	3	0	0	2	102	6	0	3.53	....	....	....	....	....	....	....	....		1984-85	1984-85
Tabaracci, Rick	Pit., Wpg., Wsh., Cgy., T.B., Atl., Col.	11	286	93	125	30	15255	760	15	2.99	17	4	12	....	1025	53	0	3.10		1988-89	1999-00
Takko, Kari	Min., Edm.	6	142	37	71	14	7317	475	1	3.90	4	0	1	....	109	7	0	3.85		1985-86	1990-91
Tallas, Robbie	Bos., Chi.	6	99	28	42	10	5069	246	3	2.91	....	....	....	....	....	....	....	....		1995-96	2000-01
Tanner, John	Que.	3	21	2	11	5	1084	65	1	3.60	....	....	....	....	....	....	....	....		1989-90	1991-92
Tataryn, Dave	NYR	1	2	1	1	0	80	10	0	7.50	....	....	....	....	....	....	....	....		1976-77	1976-77
Taylor, Bobby	Phi., Pit.	5	46	15	17	6	2268	155	0	4.10	....	....	....	....	....	....	....	....	1	1971-72	1975-76
• Teno, Harvey	Det.	1	5	2	3	0	300	15	0	3.00	....	....	....	....	....	....	....	....		1938-39	1938-39
Terreri, Chris	N.J., S.J., Chi., NYI	14	406	151	172	43	22369	1143	9	3.07	29	12	12	....	1523	86	0	3.39	2	1986-87	2000-01
Thomas, Wayne	Mtl., Tor., NYR	9	243	103	93	34	13768	766	10	3.34	15	6	8	....	849	50	1	3.53		1972-73	1980-81
• Thompson, Tiny	Bos., Det.	12	553	284	194	75	34175	1183	81	2.08	44	20	24	0	2974	93	7	1.88	1	1928-29	1939-40
§ Toppazzini, Jerry	Bos.	1	1	0	0	0	1	0	0	0.00	....	....	....	....	....	....	....	....		1960-61	1960-61
Torchia, Mike	Dal.	1	6	3	2	1	327	18	0	3.30	....	....	....	....	....	....	....	....		1994-95	1994-95
Trefilov, Andrei	Cgy., Buf., Chi.	7	54	12	25	4	2663	153	2	3.45	1	0	0	....	5	0	0	0.00		1992-93	1998-99
Tremblay, Vincent	Tor., Pit.	5	58	12	26	8	2785	223	1	4.80	....	....	....	....	....	....	....	....		1979-80	1983-84
Tucker, Ted	Cal.	1	5	1	1	1	177	10	0	3.39	....	....	....	....	....	....	....	....		1973-74	1973-74
Tugnutt, Ron	Que., Edm., Ana., Mtl., Ott., Pit., CBJ, Dal.	16	537	186	239	62	29486	1497	26	3.05	25	9	13	....	1482	56	3	2.27		1987-88	2003-04
‡ Turek, Roman	Dal., St.L., Cgy.	8	328	159	115	43	19095	734	27	2.31	22	12	9	....	1342	50	0	2.24	1	1996-97	2003-04
• Turner, Joe	Det.	1	1	0	0	1	70	3	0	2.57	....	....	....	....	....	....	....	....		1941-42	1941-42
Underhill, Matt	Chi.	1	1	0	1	0	61	4	0	3.93	....	....	....	....	....	....	....	....		2003-04	2003-04
Vachon, Rogie	Mtl., L.A., Det., Bos.	16	795	355	291	127	46298	2310	51	2.99	48	23	23	....	2876	133	2	2.77	3	1966-67	1981-82
Vanbiesbrouck, John	NYR, Fla., Phi., NYI, N.J.	20	882	374	346	119	50475	2503	40	2.98	71	28	38	....	3969	177	5	2.68		1981-82	2001-02
Veisor, Mike	Chi., Hfd., Wpg.	10	139	41	62	26	7806	532	5	4.09	4	0	2	....	180	15	0	5.00		1973-74	1983-84
Vernon, Mike	Cgy., Det., S.J., Fla.	19	781	385	273	92	44449	2206	27	2.98	138	77	56	....	8214	367	6	2.68	2	1982-83	2001-02
• Vezina, Georges	Mtl.	9	190	103	81	5	11592	633	13	3.28	13	10	3	0	780	35	2	2.69	1	1917-18	1925-26
Villemure, Gilles	NYR, Chi.	10	205	100	64	29	11581	542	13	2.81	14	5	5	....	656	32	0	2.93		1963-64	1976-77
‡ Waite, Jimmy	Chi., S.J., Phx.	11	106	28	41	12	5253	293	4	3.35	6	0	3	....	211	14	0	3.98		1988-89	1998-99
Wakaluk, Darcy	Buf., Min., Dal., Phx.	8	191	67	75	21	9756	524	9	3.22	8	4	2	....	364	18	0	2.97		1988-89	1996-97
Wakely, Ernie	Mtl., St.L.	5	113	41	42	17	6244	290	8	2.79	10	2	6	....	509	37	1	4.36	2	1962-63	1971-72
• Walsh, Flat	Mtl.M., NYA	7	108	48	43	16	6641	256	12	2.31	8	2	4	2	570	16	2	1.68		1926-27	1932-33
Wamsley, Rick	Mtl., St.L., Cgy., Tor.	13	407	204	131	46	23123	1287	12	3.34	27	7	18	....	1397	81	0	3.48	1	1980-81	1992-93
Watt, Jim	St.L.	1	1	0	0	0	20	2	0	6.00	....	....	....	....	....	....	....	....		1973-74	1973-74
Weeks, Steve	NYR, Hfd., Van., NYI, L.A., Ott.	18	290	111	119	33	15879	989	5	3.74	12	3	5	....	486	27	0	3.33		1980-81	1992-93
Wetzel, Carl	Det., Min.	2	7	1	4	1	301	22	0	4.39	....	....	....	....	....	....	....	....		1964-65	1967-68
Whitmore, Kay	Hfd., Van., Bos., Cgy.	9	155	60	64	16	8596	508	4	3.55	4	0	2	....	174	13	0	4.48		1988-89	2001-02
Wilkinson, Derek	T.B.	4	22	3	12	3	933	57	0	3.67	....	....	....	....	....	....	....	....		1995-96	1998-99
Willis, Jordan	Dal.	1	1	0	1	0	19	1	0	3.16	....	....	....	....	....	....	....	....		1995-96	1995-96
Wilson, Dunc	Phi., Van., Tor., NYR, Pit.	10	287	80	150	33	15851	988	8	3.74	....	....	....	....	....	....	....	....		1969-70	1978-79
• Wilson, Lefty	Det., Tor., Bos.	3	3	0	0	1	81	1	0	0.74	....	....	....	....	....	....	....	....		1953-54	1957-58
• Winkler, Hal	NYR, Bos.	2	75	35	26	14	4739	126	21	1.60	10	2	3	5	640	18	2	1.69		1926-27	1927-28
Wolfe, Bernie	Wsh.	4	120	20	61	21	6104	424	1	4.17	....	....	....	....	....	....	....	....		1975-76	1978-79
• Wood, Alex	NYA	1	1	0	1	0	70	3	0	2.57	....	....	....	....	....	....	....	....		1936-37	1936-37
• Worsley, Gump	NYR, Mtl., Min.	21	861	335	352	150	50183	2407	43	2.88	70	40	26	....	4084	189	5	2.78	4	1952-53	1973-74
• Worters, Roy	Pit., NYA, Mtl.	12	484	171	229	83	30175	1143	67	2.27	11	3	6	2	690	24	3	2.09		1925-26	1936-37
• Worthy, Chris	Oak., Cal.	3	26	5	10	4	1326	98	0	4.43	....	....	....	....	....	....	....	....		1968-69	1970-71
Wregget, Ken	Tor., Phi., Pit., Cgy., Det.	17	575	225	248	53	31663	1917	9	3.63	56	28	25	....	3341	160	3	2.87	1	1983-84	1999-00
‡ Yeats, Matthew	Wsh.	1	5	1	3	0	258	13	0	3.02	....	....	....	....	....	....	....	....		2003-04	2003-04
‡ Yeremeyev, Vitali	NYR	1	4	0	4	0	212	16	0	4.53	....	....	....	....	....	....	....	....		2000-01	2000-01
§ • Young, Doug	Det.	1	1	0	0	0	21	1	0	2.86	....	....	....	....	....	....	....	....		1933-34	1933-34
Young, Wendell	Van., Phi., Pit., T.B.	10	187	59	86	12	9410	618	2	3.94	2	0	1	....	99	6	0	3.64	2	1985-86	1994-95
Zanier, Mike	Edm.	1	3	1	1	1	185	12	0	3.89	....	....	....	....	....	....	....	....		1984-85	1984-85

Daniel Berthiaume

John Garrett

Phil Stein

Bill Durnan

Al Jensen

Bernie Wolfe

Retired Players, Goaltenders and Coaches Research Project

Throughout the Retired Players and Retired Goaltenders sections of this book, you will notice many players with a bullet (•) by their names. These players, according to our records, are deceased. The editors recognize that our information on the death dates of NHLers is incomplete. If you have documented information on the passing of any player not marked with a bullet (•) in this edition, we would like to hear from you. We also welcome information on deceased NHL head coaches. Please send this information to:

Retired Player Research Project
c/o NHL Publishing
194 Dovercourt Road
Toronto, Ontario
M6J 3C8 Canada
Fax: 416/531-3939

Many thanks to the following contributors . . .

Tim Bateman, Corey Bryant, Paul R. Carroll, Jr., Bob Duff, Peter Fillman, Ernie Fitzsimmons, Chris Gory, Gary J. Pearce, Martin Schmid, Al Tario, Drew "Whitey" White.

Hockey Fights Cancer is a joint initiative created by the National Hockey League and the National Hockey League Players' Association that honors those in the hockey community who have struggled, or continue to struggle, with the disease.

The goal of Hockey Fights Cancer is to raise money and visibility for local cancer care or research, as well as to support the American Cancer Society and Canadian Cancer Society national organizations. Founded by the NHL and the NHLPA, Hockey Fights Cancer is supported by NHL member clubs, NHL Alumni, the NHL Officials Association, Professional Hockey Trainers and Equipment Managers, corporate marketing partners, broadcast partners and fans throughout North America.

Join the Fight! If you would like to make a contribution to Hockey Fights Cancer, please forward a check made payable to Hockey Fights Cancer to one of the following addresses:

For Canadian Residents:
Hockey Fights Cancer
P.O. Box 1282, Station B
Montreal, Quebec H3B 3K9

For U.S. Residents:
Hockey Fights Cancer
P.O. Box 5037
New York, NY 10185-5037

Please include your name and current address so that your donation can be acknowledged. All donations are tax-deductible.

For more information, log-on to www.hockeyfightscancer.com or call 1-800-540-6500.

Glenn Anderson

Ed Chynoweth

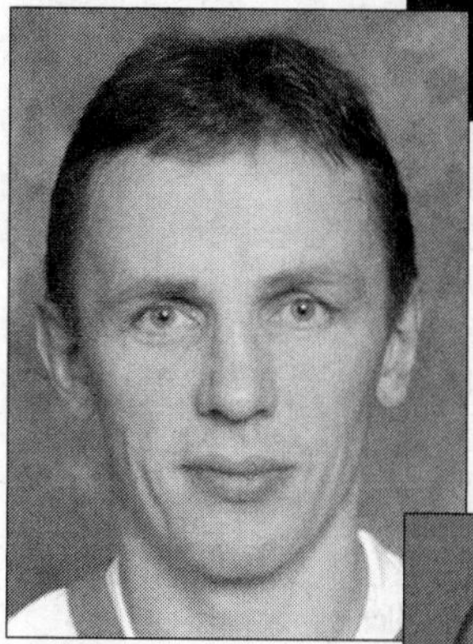

Igor Larionov

Ray Scapinello

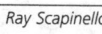

2008
Hockey Hall of Fame Inductees

TWO PLAYERS WITH NHL AND INTERNATIONAL experience are joined by a builder of high-level junior hockey and a respected linesman as inductees to the Hockey Hall of Fame in 2008.

Glenn Anderson scored 30-or-more goals in nine NHL seasons, including a career-high 54 goals in 1983-84 and 1985-86. He was a six-time Stanley Cup winner, winning five with Edmonton and one with the New York Rangers. He ranks fifth in playoff goals (93) and fourth in playoff points (214). He represented Canada at the 1980 Winter Olympics, two Canada Cup tournaments and two IIHF World Championships.

Ed Chynoweth was a founder of the Western Canada Hockey League (now the WHL) and the first president of the Canadian Major Junior Hockey League (now the CHL). Under his leadership, Hockey Canada's Program of Excellence flourished, contributing to Canada's great success at the IIHF World Junior Championships. The WHL's league championship trophy was renamed in his honor in 2007. He passed away April 22, 2008.

Igor Larionov captured eight consecutive Russian league championships with CSKA Moscow from 1982 to 1989. He was a four-time Russian First Team All-Star in the 1980s and won a gold medal at two IIHF World Junior Champioships, four senior World Championships and at the 1984 and 1988 Winter Olympics. He was a member of three Stanley Cup championship teams with Detroit in 1997, 1998 and 2002.

Ray Scapinello officiated his 2,500th and final NHL regular-season game in 2004. As a linesman, he worked in 20 Stanley Cup Finals and 426 playoff games. He never missed a game in 33 years as an official and was one of the first professional hockey officials to work at the 1998 Winter Olympics in Nagano, Japan.

Also honored are Mike Emrick, winner of the Foster Hewitt Memorial Award for excellence in hockey broadcasting and Neil Stevens, winner of the Elmer Ferguson Memorial Award for excellence in hockey journalism.

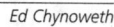

Free Agent Signing Register, 2008

	PLAYER	SIGNED BY	PREVIOUS ORGANIZATION
July 1	– Corey Perry	Anaheim	Anaheim
	– Michael Ryder	Boston	Montreal
	– Blake Wheeler	Boston	Phoenix
	– Patrick Lalime	Buffalo	Chicago
	– Ryan Bayda	Carolina	Carolina
	– Wade Brookbank	Carolina	Carolina
	– Tim Conboy	Carolina	Carolina
	– Brian Campbell	Chicago	San Jose
	– Cristobal Huet	Chicago	Washington
	– Andrew Raycroft	Colorado	Toronto
	– Darcy Tucker	Colorado	Toronto
	– Mike Commodore	Columbus	Ottawa
	– Brad Stuart	Detroit	Detroit
	– Ty Conklin	Detroit	Pittsburgh
	– Cory Stillman	Florida	Ottawa
	– Andrew Brunette	Minnesota	Colorado
	– Craig Weller	Minnesota	Phoenix
	– Andrei Kostitsyn	Montreal	Montreal
	– Drew MacIntyre	Nashville	Vancouver
	– Barry Tallackson	New Jersey	New Jersey
	– David Clarkson	New Jersey	New Jersey
	– Bryce Salvador	New Jersey	New Jersey
	– Jay Pandolfo	New Jersey	New Jersey
	– Bobby Holik	New Jersey	Atlanta
	– Brian Rolston	New Jersey	Minnesota
	– Mark Streit	NY Islanders	Montreal
	– Steve Valiquette	NY Rangers	NY Rangers
	– Michal Rozsival	NY Rangers	NY Rangers
	– Wade Redden	NY Rangers	Ottawa
	– Aaron Voros	NY Rangers	Minnesota
	– Patrick Rissmiller	NY Rangers	San Jose
	– Alex Auld	Ottawa	Boston
	– Glen Metropolit	Philadelphia	Boston
	– Todd Fedoruk	Phoenix	Minnesota
	– Kurt Sauer	Phoenix	Colorado
	– Pascal Dupuis	Pittsburgh	Pittsburgh
	– Mark Eaton	Pittsburgh	Pittsburgh
	– Eric Godard	Pittsburgh	Calgary
	– David Backes	St. Louis	St. Louis
	– Olaf Kolzig	Tampa Bay	Washington
	– Adam Hall	Tampa Bay	Pittsburgh
	– Radim Vrbata	Tampa Bay	Phoenix
	– David Koci	Tampa Bay	Chicago
	– Niklas Hagman	Toronto	Dallas
	– Curtis Joseph	Toronto	Calgary
	– Jeff Finger	Toronto	Colorado
	– Darcy Hordichuk	Vancouver	Nashville
	– Jose Theodore	Washington	Colorado
	– Mike Green	Washington	Washington
July 2	– Ron Hainsey	Atlanta	Columbus
	– Peter Vandermeer	Calgary	Phoenix
	– Curtis Glencross	Calgary	Edmonton
	– Jim Vandermeer	Calgary	Calgary
	– Wojtek Wolski	Colorado	Colorado
	– Kristian Huselius	Columbus	Calgary
	– Sean Avery	Dallas	NY Rangers
	– B.J. Crombeen	Dallas	Dallas
	– Marian Hossa	Detroit	Pittsburgh
	– Kurtis Foster	Minnesota	Minnesota
	– Yann Danis	NY Islanders	Montreal
	– Doug Weight	NY Islanders	Anaheim
	– Jarkko Ruutu	Ottawa	Pittsburgh
	– Shean Donovan	Ottawa	Ottawa
	– Riley Cote	Philadelphia	Philadelphia
	– Randy Jones	Philadelphia	Philadelphia
	– Drew Fata	Phoenix	NY Islanders
	– Brooks Orpik	Pittsburgh	Pittsburgh
	– Ryan Craig	Tampa Bay	Tampa Bay
	– Ryan Johnson	Vancouver	St. Louis
	– Nolan Baumgartner	Vancouver	Dallas
	– Curtis Sanford	Vancouver	Vancouver
July 3	– Chris Beckford-Tseu	Florida	St. Louis
	– Rory Fitzpatrick	Florida	Philadelphia
	– Antti Miettinen	Minnesota	Dallas
	– Georges Laraque	Montreal	Pittsburgh
	– Marc Denis	Montreal	Tampa Bay
	– Alex Henry	Montreal	Nashville
	– Markus Naslund	NY Rangers	Vancouver
	– Dmitri Kalinen	NY Rangers	Buffalo
	– Matt Jones	Phoenix	Phoenix
	– David Hale	Phoenix	Calgary
	– Ruslan Fedotenko	Pittsburgh	NY Islanders
	– Miroslav Satan	Pittsburgh	NY Islanders
	– Rob Blake	San Jose	Los Angeles
	– Yan Stastny	St. Louis	St. Louis
	– Wyatt Smith	Tampa Bay	Colorado
	– Dominic Moore	Toronto	Toronto
	– Keith Aucoin	Washington	Carolina
July 5	– Matt Cooke	Pittsburgh	Washington
July 6	– Owen Nolan	Minnesota	Calgary
July 7	– David LeNeveu	Anaheim	Phoenix
	– Todd Bertuzzi	Calgary	Anaheim
	– Dennis Seidenberg	Carolina	Carolina
	– Matt Walker	Chicago	St. Louis
	– Arron Asham	Philadelphia	New Jersey
	– Matt Stajan	Toronto	Toronto
July 8	– Brendan Morrison	Anaheim	Vancouver
	– Clay Wilson	Columbus	Columbus
	– Jaroslav Halak	Montreal	Montreal
	– Paul Mara	NY Rangers	NY Rangers
	– Jason Smith	Ottawa	Philadelphia
	– Mark Recchi	Tampa Bay	Atlanta
	– Brandon Bochenski	Tampa Bay	Nashville
July 9	– Eric Boulton	Atlanta	Atlanta
	– Junior Lessard	Atlanta	Tampa Bay
	– Chad LaRose	Carolina	Carolina
	– J.F. Jacques	Edmonton	Edmonton
	– Marc Pouliot	Edmonton	Edmonton
	– Anthony Stewart	Florida	Florida
	– Josh Gorges	Montreal	Montreal
	– Brendan Witt	NY Islanders	NY Islanders
	– Christian Ehrhoff	San Jose	San Jose
	– Andrew Hutchinson	Tampa Bay	NY Rangers
	– Brooks Laich	Washington	Washington
July 10	– Jason Strudwick	Edmonton	NY Rangers
	– Mike Weaver	St. Louis	Vancouver

	PLAYER	SIGNED BY	PREVIOUS ORGANIZATION
	– **Zenon Konopka**	Tampa Bay	Columbus
	– **Rob Davison**	Vancouver	NY Islanders
	– **Pavol Demitra**	Vancouver	Minnesota
	– **Eric Fehr**	Washington	Washington
ly 11	– **Steve Montador**	Anaheim	Florida
	– **Michael Peca**	Columbus	Columbus
	– **Brendan Bell**	Ottawa	Phoenix
	– **Marcel Goc**	San Jose	San Jose
	– **Chris Gratton**	Tampa Bay	Tampa Bay
	– **Boyd Gordon**	Washington	Washington
ly 14	– **Jason Williams**	Atlanta	Chicago
	– **Joe Jensen**	Carolina	Carolina
	– **Cody McLeod**	Colorado	Colorado
	– **Nathan Smith**	Colorado	Pittsburgh
	– **Tyler Weiman**	Colorado	Colorado
	– **Craig MacDonald**	Columbus	Tampa Bay
	– **Derek MacKenzie**	Columbus	Columbus
	– **Tom Cavanaugh**	San Jose	San Jose
	– **Matt Foy**	St. Louis	Minnesota
	– **Jay McClement**	St. Louis	St. Louis
	– **Sergei Fedorov**	Washington	Washington
ly 15	– **Aaron Johnson**	Chicago	NY Islanders
	– **Doug Janik**	Chicago	Tampa Bay
	– **Colin Fraser**	Chicago	Chicago
	– **Brian Willsie**	Colorado	Los Angeles
	– **Cody McCormick**	Colorado	Colorado
	– **Zack Stortini**	Edmonton	Edmonton
	– **Bill Thomas**	Pittsburgh	Phoenix
	– **Kris Beech**	Pittsburgh	Pittsburgh
	– **Ryan Stone**	Pittsburgh	Pittsburgh
	– **Alex Foster**	Toronto	Toronto
	– **Ben Ondrus**	Toronto	Toronto
ly 16	– **Kari Lehtonen**	Atlanta	Atlanta
	– **Mark Mancari**	Buffalo	Buffalo
	– **Daniel Paille**	Buffalo	Buffalo
	– **Clarke MacArthur**	Buffalo	Buffalo
	– **Marc Methot**	Columbus	Columbus
	– **Alexandre Picard**	Columbus	Columbus
	– **Steve Kelly**	Columbus	Minnesota
	– **Gabe Gauthier**	Los Angeles	Los Angeles
	– **Matt Moulson**	Los Angeles	Los Angeles
	– **Erik Ersberg**	Los Angeles	Los Angeles
	– **Mike Glumac**	Montreal	St. Louis
	– **Ryan O'Byrne**	Montreal	Montreal
	– **Kevin Klein**	Nashville	Nashville
	– **Jeff Tambellini**	NY Islanders	NY Islanders
	– **Ben Walter**	NY Islanders	NY Islanders
	– **Jeremy Colliton**	NY Islanders	NY Islanders
	– **Sean Bergenheim**	NY Islanders	NY Islanders
	– **Nigel Dawes**	NY Rangers	NY Rangers
	– **Brad Winchester**	St. Louis	Dallas
	– **Jeff Woywitka**	St. Louis	St. Louis
ly 17	– **Brett Sterling**	Atlanta	Atlanta
	– **Marty Reasoner**	Atlanta	Edmonton
	– **Aaron Rome**	Columbus	Columbus
	– **Jay Leach**	New Jersey	Tampa Bay
	– **Andy Wozniewski**	St. Louis	Toronto
ly 18	– **Garth Murray**	Phoenix	Florida

	PLAYER	SIGNED BY	PREVIOUS ORGANIZATION
July 19	– **Stephane Veilleux**	Minnesota	Minnesota
	– **Frans Nielsen**	NY Islanders	NY Islanders
July 21	– **Andre Roy**	Calgary	Tampa Bay
	– **Corey Crawford**	Chicago	Chicago
	– **Jimmy Howard**	Detroit	Detroit
	– **Jonathan Ericsson**	Detroit	Detroit
	– **Peter Harrold**	Los Angeles	Los Angeles
	– **Greg Moore**	NY Rangers	NY Rangers
	– **Jeff Taffe**	Pittsburgh	Pittsburgh
July 22	– **Daniel Carcillo**	Phoenix	Phoenix
July 23	– **Mike Brown**	Vancouver	Vancouver
	– **Nathan McIver**	Vancouver	Vancouver
	– **Ryan Shannon**	Vancouver	Vancouver
	– **Rick Rypien**	Vancouver	Vancouver
July 24	– **Mathieu Darche**	Buffalo	Tampa Bay
July 25	– **Marek Svatos**	Colorado	Colorado
	– **Mike York**	Columbus	Phoenix
	– **Rich Peverley**	Nashville	Nashville
	– **Bruno Gervais**	NY Islanders	NY Islanders
July 26	– **Pierre-Marc Bouchard**	Minnesota	Minnesota
	– **Shaone Morrisonn**	Washington	Washington
July 28	– **Jay Bouwmeester**	Florida	Florida
	– **Fredrik Sjostrom**	NY Rangers	NY Rangers
July 29	– **Josh Hennessy**	Ottawa	Ottawa
July 30	– **Pascal Leclaire**	Columbus	Columbus
	– **Valtteri Filppula**	Detroit	Detroit
July 31	– **Ville Koistinen**	Nashville	Nashville
	– **Antoine Vermette**	Ottawa	Ottawa
Aug. 4	– **Ryane Clowe**	San Jose	San Jose
Aug. 8	– **Teppo Numminen**	Buffalo	Buffalo
Aug. 12	– **Lukas Kaspar**	San Jose	San Jose

Trade Register, 2007-08

September 2007

11– Boston traded C **Ben Walter** and Boston's 2nd-round choice in 2009 to NY Islanders for C/RW **Petteri Nokelainen**.

24– Anaheim traded D **Nathan Saunders** and D **Brett Skinner** to Boston for C Mark **Mowers**.

October 2007

11– Chicago traded RW **Pierre Parenteau** to NY Rangers for future considerations.

November 2007

8– St. Louis traded G **Jason Bacashihua** to Colorado for future considerations.

15– Anaheim traded D **Aaron Rome** and LW **Clay Wilson** to Columbus for C **Geoff Platt**.

19– Dallas traded D **Mario Scalzo** to Tampa Bay for D **Bryce Lampman**.

19– Washington traded C Brian Sutherby to Anaheim for Anaheim's 2nd-round choice in 2009.

December 2007

6– Phoenix traded G **Alex Auld** to Boston for LW **Nate DiCasmirro** and Boston's 5th-round choice in 2009.

10– Philadelphia traded D **Jussi Timonen** to Dallas for a 7th-round choice in 2009.

10– Los Angeles traded C **Evgeny Federov** to Dallas for Dallas' 6th-round choice (later traded to Chicago – Chicago selected D **Braden Birch**) in 2008.

14– Anaheim traded C **Andy McDonald** to St. Louis for C **Doug Weight**, LW **Michal Birner** and St. Louis' 7th-round choice (later traded back to St. Louis – St. Louis selected G **Paul Karpowich**) in 2008.

18– Chicago traded D **Jim Vandermeer** to Philadelphia for LW **Ben Eager**.

January 2008

2– Anaheim traded D **Shane Hnidy** and Anaheim's 6th-round choice (C **Nicholas Tremblay**) in 2008 to Boston for RW **Brandon Bochenski**. In addition, the Ducks relinquished their option to exchange 4th-round choices with the Bruins in 2008.

9– Anaheim traded RW **Matt Keith** to NY Islanders for RW **Darryl Bootland**.

10– Chicago traded D **Magnus Johansson** to Florida for a 7th-round choice in 2009.

15– Dallas traded RW **Junior Lessard** to Tampa Bay for D **Dan Jancevski**.

17– Carolina traded RW **Craig Adams** to Chicago for future considerations.

22– Colorado traded RW **Mark Rycroft** to Columbus for D **Darcy Campbell** and C **Philippe Dupuis**.

29– Columbus traded LW **Jody Shelley** to San Jose for San Jose's 6th-round choice in 2009.

31– Carolina traded C **David Gove** to Pittsburgh for C **Joe Jensen**.

February 2008

1– Columbus traded LW **Curtis Glencross** to Edmonton for D **Dick Tarnstrom**.

7– Carolina traded D **J.D. Forrest** to San Jose for future considerations.

8– Detroit traded RW **Brett Engelhardt** to Montreal for RW **Francis Lemieux**.

11– Carolina traded D **Mike Commodore** and LW **Cory Stillman** to Ottawa for D **Joe Corvo** and RW **Patrick Eaves**.

19– Los Angeles traded D **Jaroslav Modry** to Philadelphia for Philadelphia's 3rd-round choice (LW **Geordie Wudrick**) in 2008.

20– Philadelphia traded D **Jim Vandermeer** to Calgary for Calgary's 3rd-round choice in 2009.

25– Tampa Bay traded LW **Vaclav Prospal** to Philadelphia for D **Alexandre Picard** and Philadelphia's 2nd-round choice in 2009.

26– Anaheim traded RW **Brandon Bochenski** to Nashville for future considerations.

26– Anaheim traded RW **Brandon Segal** and Anaheim's 7th-round choice (D **David Carle**) in 2008 to Tampa Bay for D **Jay Leach**.

26– Atlanta traded RW **Marian Hossa** and RW **Pascal Dupuis** to Pittsburgh for RW **Colby Armstrong**, C **Erik Christensen**, C **Angelo Esposito** and Pittsburgh's 1st-round choice (C **Daultan Leveille**) in 2008.

26– Atlanta traded LW **Alexandre Giroux** to Washington for RW **Joe Motzko**.

26– Buffalo traded D **Brian Campbell** and Buffalo's 7th-round choice (RW **Drew Daniels**) in 2008 to San Jose for RW **Steve Bernier** and San Jose's 1st-round choice (C **Tyler Ennis**) in 2008.

26– Carolina traded LW **Andrew Ladd** to Chicago for C **Tuomo Ruutu**.

26– Chicago traded RW **Martin Lapointe** to Ottawa for Ottawa's 6th-round choice (RW **Ben Smith**) in 2008.

26– Colorado traded D **Karlis Skrastins** and Colorado's 3rd-round choice (D **Adam Comrie**) in 2008 to Florida for D **Ruslan Salei**.

26– Columbus traded C **Sergei Fedorov** to Washington for D **Ted Ruth**.

26– Columbus traded D **Adam Foote** to Colorado for Colorado's 1st-round choice (later traded to Philadelphia – Philadelphia selected D **Luca Sbisa**) in 2008 and a conditional choice in 2009.

26– Dallas traded G **Mike Smith**, C **Jeff Halpern**, LW **Jussi Jokinen** and its 4th-round choice in 2009 to Tampa Bay for C **Brad Richards** and G Johan Holmqvist.

26– Los Angeles traded D **Brad Stuart** to Detroit for Detroit's 2nd-round choice (later traded to Colorado – Colorado selected G **Peter Delmas**) in 2008 and Detroit's 4th-round choice in 2009.

26– Los Angeles traded G **Jean-Sebastien Aubin** to Anaheim for St. Louis' 7th-round choice (previously acquired, later traded back to St. Louis – St. Louis selected G **Paul Karpowich**) in 2008.

26– Montreal traded G **Cristobal Huet** to Washington for Anaheim's 2nd-round choice (previously acquired) in 2009.

26– New Jersey traded RW **Cam Janssen** to St. Louis for D **Bryce Salvador**.

26– NY Islanders traded LW **Chris Simon** to Minnesota for Minnesota's 6th-round choice (C **Justin Dibenedetto**) in 2008.

26– NY Islanders traded D **Marc-Andre Bergeron** to Anaheim for Edmonton's 3rd-round choice (previously acquired, NY Islanders selected RW **Kirill Petrov**) in 2008.

26– NY Rangers traded G **Al Montoya** and LW **Marcel Hossa** to Phoenix for RW **Fredrik Sjostrom**, G **David LeNeveu**, LW **Josh Gratton** and a conditional choice in 2009.

26– St. Louis traded D **Christian Backman** to NY Rangers for NY Rangers' 4th-round choice (later traded back to NY Rangers – NY Rangers selected RW **Dale Weise**) in 2008.

26– San Jose traded D **Rob Davison** to NY Islanders for NY Islanders' 7th-round choice (D **Jason Demers**) in 2008.

26– Tampa Bay traded LW **Jan Hlavac** to Nashville for Nashville's 7th-round choice (later traded to Philadelphia – Philadelphia selected G **Joacim Eriksson**) in 2008.

26– Toronto traded RW **Wade Belak** to Florida for Florida's 5th-round choice (LW **Jerome Flaake**) in 2008.

26– Toronto traded LW **Chad Kilger** to Florida for Florida's 3rd-round choice (later traded to St. Louis – St. Louis selected RW **James Livingston**) in 2008.

26– Toronto traded D **Hal Gill** to Pittsburgh for Pittsburgh's 2nd-round choice (RW **Jimmy Hayes**) in 2008 and Pittsburgh's 5th-round choice (later traded to NY Rangers) in 2009.

26– Vancouver traded LW **Matt Cooke** to Washington for LW **Matt Pettinger**.

May 2008

27– Boston traded D **Jonathan Sigalet** to Columbus for LW **Matt Marquardt**.

June 2008

10– Anaheim traded D **Marc-Andre Bergeron** to Minnesota for Minnesota's 3rd-round choice (C **Brandon McMillan**) in 2008.

19– Nashville traded LW **Darcy Hordichuk** to Carolina for Carolina's 5th-round choice in 2009.

20– Florida traded C **Olli Jokinen** to Phoenix for D **Keith Ballard**, D **Nick Boynton** and Ottawa's 2nd-round choice (previously acquired, later traded to Anaheim – Anaheim selected RW **Jared Staal**) in 2008.

20– Calgary traded Calgary's 1st-round choice (later traded to Anaheim – Anaheim selected D **Jake Gardiner**) in 2008 and Calgary's 2nd-round choice in 2009 to Los Angeles for C **Mike Cammalleri** and Calgary's 2nd-round choice (previously acquired, Calgary selected C **Mitch Wahl**) in 2008.

20– Anaheim traded Edmonton's 1st-round choice (previously acquired, later traded to Buffalo – Buffalo selected D **Tyler Meyers**) in 2008 to Los Angeles for Calgary's 1st-round choice (previously acquired, Anaheim selected D **Jake Gardiner**) in 2008 and Dallas' 1st-round choice (previously acquired, later traded to Phoenix – Phoenix selected W **Viktor Tikhonov**) in 2008.

20– Columbus traded Colorado's 1st-round choice (previously acquired, later traded to Philadelphia – Philadelphia selected D **Luca Sbisa**) in 2008 and Columbus' 3rd-round choice (D **Marc-Andre Bourbon**) in 2008 to Philadelphia for C **R.J. Umberger** and Philadelphia's 4th-round choice (D **Drew Olson**) in 2008.

20– Calgary traded LW **Alex Tanguay** and Calgary's 5th-round choice (F **Maxim Trunev**) in 2008 to Montreal for Montreal's 1st-round choice (C **Greg Nemisz**) in 2008 and Montreal's 2nd-round choice in 2009.

– NY Islanders traded NY Islanders' 1st-round choice (D **Luke Schenn**) in 2008 to Toronto for Toronto's 1st-round choice (later traded to Nashville – Nashville selected C **Colin Wilson**) in 2008, Toronto's 3rd-round choice (later traded to Chicago – Chicago selected D **Shawn Lalonde**) in 2008 and Toronto's 2nd-round choice in 2009.

– NY Islanders traded Toronto's 1st-round choice (previously acquired, Nashville selected C **Colin Wilson**) in 2008 to Nashville for Florida's 1st-round choice (previously acquired, NY Islanders selected C **Joshua Bailey**) in 2008 and Florida's 2nd-round choice (previously acquired, NY Islanders selected D **Aaron Ness**) in 2008.

– Buffalo traded Buffalo's 1st-round choice (D **Colten Teubert**) in 2008 and Buffalo's 3rd-round choice in 2009 to Los Angeles for Edmonton's 1st-round choice (previously acquired, Buffalo selected D **Tyler Meyers**) in 2008.

– Nashville traded Nashville's 1st-round choice (D **Erik Karksson**) in 2008 to Ottawa for Ottawa's 1st-round choice (G **Chet Pickard**) in 2008 and Ottawa's 3rd-round choice in 2009.

– New Jersey traded New Jersey's 1st-round choice (C **Anton Gustafsson**) in 2008 to Washington for Washington's 1st-round choice (later traded to Minnesota – Minnesota selected D **Tyler Cuma**) in 2008 and Washington's 2nd-round choice (C **Patrice Cormier**) in 2008.

– New Jersey traded Washington's 1st-round choice (previously acquired, Minnesota selected D **Tyler Cuma**) in 2008 to Minnesota for Minnesota's 1st-round choice (LW **Mattias Tremblay**) in 2008 and Minnesota's 3rd-round choice in 2009.

– Washington traded D **Steve Eminger** and Washington's 3rd-round choice (G **Jacob Deserres**) in 2008 to Philadelphia for Philadelphia's 1st-round choice (D **John Carlson**) in 2008.

– Anaheim traded Dallas' 1st-round choice (previously acquired, Phoenix selected W **Viktor Tikhonov**) in 2008 to Phoenix for Phoenix's 2nd-round compensatory choice (C Nicolas Deschamps) in 2008 and Phoenix's 2nd-round choice (C **Eric O'Dell**) in 2008.

– Phoenix traded Toronto's 2nd-round choice (previously acquired, Nashville selected D **Roman Josi**) in 2008 to Nashville for Nashville's 2nd-round choice (later traded to Florida – Florida selected D **Colby Robak**) in 2008 and Nashville's 3rd-round choice (D **Mathieu Brodeur**) in 2008.

– Phoenix traded Nashville's 2nd-round choice (previously acquired, Florida selected D **Colby Robak**) in 2008 to Florida for Ottawa's 2nd-round choice (previously acquired, later traded to Anaheim – Anaheim selected RW **Jared Staal**) in 2008 and Florida's 4th-round choice in 2009.

– Tampa Bay traded Tampa Bay's 3rd-round choice (C **Justin Daniels**) in 2008 to San Jose for San Jose's 4th-round (C **James Wright**) and 5th-round (RW **Kyle de Coste**) choices in 2008 and 3rd-round choice in 2009.

– Colorado traded C **Brad Richardson** to Los Angeles for Detroit's 2nd-round choice (previously acquired, Colorado selected G **Peter Delmas**) in 2008.

– NY Islanders traded Toronto's 3rd-round choice (previously acquired, Chicago selected D **Shawn Lalonde**) in 2008 to Chicago for Chicago's 3rd-round (D **Jyri Niemi**) and 4th-round (W **David Ullstrom**) choices in 2008.

– Buffalo traded Buffalo's 3rd-round choice (D **Andrew Campbell**) in 2008 to Los Angeles for the NY Rangers' 3rd-round choice (previously acquired, Buffalo selected D **Corey Fineage**) in 2008 and Vancouver's 4th-round choice (previously acquired, Buffalo selected RW **Justin Jokinen**) in 2008.

– Phoenix traded Pittsburgh's 3rd-round choice (previously acquired, NY Rangers selected D **Tomas Kundratek**) in 2008 to NY Rangers for D **Alex Bourret**.

– Los Angeles traded Tampa Bay's 4th-round choice (previously acquired, San Jose selected D **Samuel Groulx**) in 2008 to San Jose for San Jose's 4th-round choice in 2009 and San Jose's 5th-round choice in 2010.

– Columbus traded Columbus's 4th-round choice (C **Jamie Arniel**) in 2008 to Boston for Boston's 4th-round (D **Steven Delisle**) and 5th-round (D **Brent Regner**) choices in 2008.

– Nashville traded NY Rangers 4th-round choice (previously acquired, NY Rangers selected RW **Dale Weise**) in 2008 to the NY Rangers for NY Rangers' 7th-round choice (C **Jani Lajunen**) in 2008 and NY Rangers' 4th-round choice in 2009.

– Nashville traded Nashville's 4th-round choice (G **Harri Sateri**) in 2008 to San Jose for San Jose's 7th-round choice (G **Anders Lindback**) in 2008 and a 4th-round choice (previously acquired from Toronto) in 2009.

– Los Angeles traded Dallas' 6th-round choice (previously acquired, Chicago selected D **Braden Birch**) in 2008 to Chicago for Chicago's 6th-round choice in 2009.

– Los Angeles traded St. Louis's 7th-round choice (previously acquired, St. Louis selected G **Paul Karpowich**) in 2008 to St. Louis for St. Louis's 7th-round choice in 2009.

21– Philadelphia traded Philadelphia's 7th-round choice (D **Nick Pryor**) in 2008 to Anaheim for Anaheim's 7th-round choice in 2009.

24– Boston traded C **Matt Hendricks** to Colorado for D **Johnny Boychuk**.

24– Nashville traded D **Janne Niskala** to Philadelphia for LW **Triston Grant** and Philadelphia's 7th-round choice in 2009.

26– Ottawa traded RW **Brian McGrattan** to Phoenix for Boston's 5th-round choice (previously acquired) in 2009.

29– Edmonton traded C **Jarret Stoll** and D **Matt Greene** to Los Angeles for D **Lubomir Visnovsky**.

30– Calgary traded D **Tim Ramholt** to Philadelphia for LW **Kyle Greentree**.

30– Philadelphia traded D **Janne Niskala** to Tampa Bay for Tampa Bay's 6th-round choice in 2009.

July 2008

1– Columbus traded C **Gilbert Brule** to Edmonton for LW **Raffi Torres**.

1– Carolina traded LW **Erik Cole** to Edmonton for D **Joni Pitkanen**.

1– Chicago traded LW **Rene Bourque** to Calgary for a future conditional 2nd-round choice.

1– Los Angeles traded D **Patrick Hersley** and LW **Ned Lukacevic** to Philadelphia for D **Denis Gauthier** and Philadelphia's 2nd-round choice in 2010.

1– Minnesota traded LW **Ryan Jones** and Minnesota's 2nd-round choice in 2009 to Nashville for D **Marek Zidlicky**.

2– Columbus traded RW **Nikolai Zherdev** and C **Dan Fritsche** to NY Rangers for D **Fedor Tyutin** and D **Christian Backman**.

3– Montreal traded C **Mikhail Grabovski** to Toronto for D **Greg Pateryn** and Toronto's 2nd-round choice 2010.

4– San Jose traded D Craig Rivet and San Jose's 7th-round choice in 2010 to Buffalo for Buffalo's 2nd-round choices in 2009 and 2010.

4– San Jose traded D **Matt Carle**, D **Ty Wishart**, San Jose's 1st-round choice in 2009 and San Jose's 4th-round choice in 2010 to Tampa Bay for D **Dan Boyle** and D **Brad Lukowich**.

4– Buffalo traded RW **Steve Bernier** to Vancouver for Los Angeles' 3rd-round choice (previously acquired) in 2009 and Vancouver's 2nd-round choice in 2010.

11– Minnesota traded D **Shawn Belle** to Montreal for C **Corey Locke**.

14– NY Rangers traded LW **Ryan Hollweg** to Toronto for Pittsburgh's 5th-round choice (previously acquired) in 2009.

15– Columbus traded LW **Joakim Lindstrom** to Anaheim for a conditional choice in 2010.

17– Chicago traded D **Danny Richmond** to Pittsburgh for C **Tim Brent**.

21– Dallas traded LW **Richard Clune** to Los Angeles for RW **Lauri Tukonen**.

24– Boston traded LW **Pascal Pelletier** to Chicago for C **Martin St. Pierre**.

Trades and free agent signings after August 21, 2008 are listed on page 603.

League Abbreviations

AAHA............Alberta Amateur Hockey Association
AAHL............Alaska Amateur Hockey League
AASHA............Alaska All-Stars Hockey Association
ACHA............American Collegiate Hockey Association
ACHL............Atlantic Coast Hockey League
AFHL............American Frontier Hockey League
AH............Atlantic Hockey
AHL............American Hockey League
AJHL............Alberta Junior Hockey League
Alpenliga........Alpenliga (Austria, Italy, Slovenia 1994-1999)
AMHA............Alberta Minor Hockey Association
AMBHL............Alberta Major Bantam Hockey League
AMHL............Alberta Midget AAA Hockey League
AUAA............Atlantic University Athletic Association
AtJHL............Atlantic Junior Hockey League
AWHL............American West Hockey League
BCAHA............British Columbia Amateur Hockey Association
BCHL............British Columbia (Junior) Hockey League (also BCJHL)
CABHL............Central Alberta Bantam Hockey League
CBHL............Calgary Bantam Hockey League
CCHA............Central Collegiate Hockey Association
CEGEP............Quebec College Prep
CHA............College Hockey America
CHL............Central Hockey League
CIS............Commonwealth of Independent States
CIS............Canadian Interuniversity Sport
CJHL............Central Junior A Hockey League
CMHA............Calgary Minor Hockey Association
ColHL............Colonial Hockey League
CSHL............Central States Hockey League
CSJHL............Central States Junior Hockey League
CWUAA............Canadian Western University Athletic Association
ECAC............Eastern College Athletic Conference
ECACHL............ECAC Hockey League
ECHL............East Coast Hockey League
EEHL............Eastern European Hockey League
EJHL............Eastern Junior Hockey League
EMHA............Edmonton Minor Hockey Association
EmJHL............Empire Junior B Hockey League
EuroHL............European Hockey League
Exhib. ....Exhibition Games, Series or Season
GLHL............Great Lakes Hockey League
GNML............Greater North Midget League
GPAC............Great Plains Athletic Conference
GTHL............Greater Toronto Hockey League
H-East............Hockey East
HJHL............Heritage Junior Hockey League
High-(XX)........High School (state/province)
IEHL............Internationale Eishockey Liga
IHL............International Hockey League
KIJHL............Kootenay International Junior B Hockey League
LCJHL............Little Caesar's Junior Hockey League
MAAC............Metro Atlantic Athletic Conference
MAHA............Manitoba Amateur Hockey Association
MAHL............Mid America Hockey League
MBAHL............Metropolitan Boston Amateur Hockey League
MBHL............Metropolitan Boston Hockey League
MEHL............Midwest Elite Hockey League
Metro-HL........Metro Hockey League
MIAC............Minnesota Intercollegiate Athletic Conference
Minor-(XX)......Minor/Youth hockey (state/province)
MJHL............Manitoba Junior Hockey League
MJrHL............Maritime Junior A Hockey League
MMBHL............Manitoba Major Bantam Hockey League
MMHL............Manitoba Midget AAA Hockey League
MMHL............Michigan Minor Hockey League
MMMHL........Manitoba Minor Midget Hockey League
MNHL............Michigan National Hockey League
MtJHL............Metropolitan Junior Hockey League (New York)
MTJHL............Metropolitan Toronto Junior Hockey League
MTHL............Metro Toronto Hockey League
MWEHL........Midwest Elite Hockey League
NAHL............North American Hockey League (Tier I Junior)
NAJHL............North American Junior Hockey League
Nat-Team........National Team (also Nt.-Team)
NBAHA............New Brunswick Amateur Hockey Association
NBMHL............New Brunswick Midget Hockey League
NBPEI............New Brunswick Prince Edward Island Midget Hockey League
NCAA............National Collegiate Athletic Association
NCHA............Northern Collegiate Hockey Association
NEJHL............New England Junior Hockey League
NFAHA............Newfoundland Amateur Hockey Association
NHL............National Hockey League
NJCAA............National Junior Collegiate Athletic Association
NOBHL............Northern Ontario Bantam Hockey League
NOHA............Northern Ontario Hockey Association
NOJHA............Northern Ontario Junior Hockey Association
NOJHL............Northern Ontario Junior Hockey League
NSBHL............Nova Scotia Bantam Hockey League
NSMHL............Nova Scotia Midget AAA Hockey League
NTHL............North Texas Hockey League
NWJHL............Northwest Junior B Hockey League
NYJHL............New York Junior Hockey League
OCJHL............Ontario Central Junior A Hockey League
OHA............Ontario Hockey Association
OHL............Ontario Hockey League
OJHL-B............Ontario Junior B Hockey Leagues
OMJHL............Ontario Major Junior Hockey League
OPJHL............Ontario Provincial Junior A Hockey League
OUAA............Ontario Universities Athletic Association
PAHA............Pennsylvania Amateur Hockey Association
PCJHL............Pacific Coast Junior Hockey League
PEIHA............Prince Edward Island Hockey Association
PIJHL............Pacific International Junior Hockey League
QAAA............Quebec Amateur Athletic Association
QAHA............Quebec Amateur Hockey Association
QJHL............Quebec Junior Hockey League
QMJHL............Quebec Major Junior Hockey League
QNAHL............(Quebec) North American Hockey League
Q-RHL............(Quebec) Richelieu Elite Hockey League
QSPHL............Quebec Semi-Pro Hockey League
RAMHL............Rural Alberta Midget Hockey League
RMJHL............Rocky Mountain Junior Hockey League
SAHA............Saskatchewan Amateur Hockey Association
SAMHL............Southern Alberta Midget Hockey League
SBHL............Saskatchewan Bantam Hockey League
SCAHA............Southern California Amateur Hockey Association
SIJHL............Superior International Junior Hockey League
SJHL............Saskatchewan Junior Hockey League
SMBHL............Saskatchewan Major Bantam Hockey League
SMHL............Saskatchewan Midget AAA Hockey League
SMMHL............Saskatchewan Minor Midget Hockey League
SPHL............Southern Professional Hockey League
SSJHL............South Saskatchewan Junior B Hockey League
SSMHL............South Saskatchewan Minor Hockey League
SunHL............Sunshine Hockey League
TBAHA............Thunder Bay Amateur Hockey Association
TBJHL............Thunder Bay Junior Hockey League
TBMHL............Thunder Bay Midget Hockey League
U-17............Under 17
U-18............Under 18
UHL............United Hockey League
UMEHL............Upper Midwest Elite Hockey League
UMHSEL........Upper Midwest High School Elite League
USAHA............United States Amateur Hockey Association
USHL............United States (Junior A) Hockey League
VIJHL............Vancouver Island Junior Hockey League
WCHA............Western Collegiate Hockey Association
WCHL............West Coast Hockey League
WHL............Western Hockey League
WNYHA............Western New York Hockey Association
WPHL............Western Professional Hockey League
WSJHL............Western States Junior Hockey League
WMHA............Winnipeg Minor Hockey Association

ntributors

NHL Official Guide & Record Book is produced with the help of many. **cial thanks to:** Chico Adrahtas, George Aivalis, Manny Almela, Tom Annelin, n Ash, A.J. Atchue (AHL), Terri Bain, Bob Borgen, Drey Bradley, Christian gnalo, Greg Brownell, Craig Campbell, Jack Carnefix (ECHL), Elizabeth Casey, n Chaimovitch (AHL), Michael Chraba, Joshua Coholan, Ken Coleman, Tim don, Christina Cooley, Joe Cornacchia, Colleen Corner, Tyler Cragg, Brian Day, is Demers (QMJHL), Robert A. Doerrsam, Éric Dubois, Carey Durant, Rod Evans, Fauchoux, Jamie Fawcett, Pat Ferschweiler, Corey Fienhage, Kelly Findley, John dner, Stephen Gaunce, Michael Gibbons, Curt Giles, Keegan Goodrich, Brian tschalk, Mark Grady, Nolan Graham, Stu Hackel, Andrea Hahn, Hockey Hall of e, Bob Hofman (CenHL), Peter Jagla, Karl Jahnke (QMJHL), Christy Jeffries, Mike son, Timothy Joncas, Adam Kaufman, Edward Krajewski (ECAC), Chad Larsen, s Laurie, James Mancuso, Robert McAfee, Dave McCall, Penny McEwen (SJHL), Moats, Herb Morell (OHL), Dave Morinville, John Moritsugu, Dwight Mullins, A Conference and School Sports Information Departments, NHL Broadcasters' ociation, NHL Central Registry, NHL Officiating, NHL Players' Association, James or, Stephen Ostaszewicz, Nancy Oster, Rod Peltoma, Matthew T. Percival, Chris rs, Fred Pletsch (CCHA), Rod Pipher, Jillian Plewis, Phil Pritchard, Whit Prophet, y Punchard, Pearl Rajwanth, Doug Reynolds, Valentina Riazanova, Allison Rossi, d Rourke (AH), Ken Sachs, Martin Schmid, Scott Sheehan, Ralph Slate, Noah h (Hockey East), SIHR, Peter Souris (Hockey East), Doug Spencer (WCHA), Todd ffer, Andy Stump (IHL), Pete Susens, Brian Sutton, Pete Tobey, Robert Toffoli, n Urick, Rosemary Voulelikas, Thomas Ward, Ray Wareham, Ryan Watters, Jesse s (WHL), Jeff Weiss (CHA), John West, Rick Westra, Drew White, Paul Wilkinson HL) Jack Williams Jorge Woellmer, Brad Young (CHL).

Photo Credits

Hockey Hall of Fame: Various Collections. NHLI/Getty Images: Graig Abel, Scott Audette, Brian and Steve Babineau, Bruce Bennett, Frederick Breedon, Mark Buckner, Andy Devlin, Greg Fiume, Gregg Forwerck, Noah Graham, Norm Hall, Harry How, Glenn James, Mitchell Layton, Terence Leung, Michael Martin, Len Redkoles, Dave Reginek, Andre Ringuette, John Russell, Dave Sandford, Joseph Sargent, Eliot J. Schechter, Gregory Shamus, Bill Smith, Don Smith, Mike Stobe, Gerry Thomas, Tom Turrill, Jeff Vinnick, Bill Wippert. Additional NHL team photographers: Rudy Ayasse, Doug Benc, Andrew D. Bernstein, Scott Cunningham, Bob Fisher, Stan Gilliland, Bruce Kluckhohn, Debora Robinson, Jamie Sabau, Rocky Widner,

Special thanks to Paul Michinard, Getty Images.

Researchers and historians: contact the Society for International Hockey Research www.sihrhockey.org